D0788094

ASCAP
Biographical Dictionary

ASCAP

Biographical Dictionary

Fourth Edition

C. 1

Compiled for the American Society of
Composers, Authors and Publishers by
JAQUES CATTELL PRESS
R. R. BOWKER COMPANY
New York & London, 1980

ALAMEDA FREE LIBRARY

REF
927.8
AMERICAN SOCIETY...
4th ed
1980

Published by the R. R. Bowker Company
1180 Avenue of the Americas, New York, New York 10036
Copyright © 1980 by American Society of Composers, Authors and Publishers,
ASCAP Building, One Lincoln Plaza, New York, New York 10023.

All rights reserved. Reproduction of this work in whole or in part,
without written permission of the copyright owner is prohibited.

International Standard Book Number: 0-8352-1283-1
Library of Congress Catalog Card Number: 80-65351
Printed and bound in the United States of America

The publishers and copyright owner do not assume and hereby disclaim any
liability to any party for any loss or damage caused by errors or omissions in
American Society of Composers, Authors and Publishers Biographical
Dictionary, whether such errors or omissions result from negligence,
accident or any other cause.

CONTENTS

FOREWORD

The *ASCAP Biographical Dictionary* traditionally has been a valuable reference tool for ASCAP writer and publisher members and the music community at large. Now, in response to so many requests, the *ASCAP Biographical Dictionary* is being offered commercially to the public.

I am very pleased by this special demand for the dictionary from the non-music industry community, because it represents to me an increasing interest on the part of the general public in the history of American music, its creators, and particularly in the rich legacy of our ASCAP writers.

If an ASCAP biographical dictionary had been published in 1914, when the Society was founded, the resulting volume would have contained a few scant pages. The book would have consisted of only 200 entries: 8 founding members (Victor Herbert, Louis A. Hirsch, Raymond Hubbell, Silvio Hein, Gustave Kerker, Jay Witmark, George Maxwell and Nathan Burkan) and 170 charter writer members.

Actually, the Society's first biographical dictionary was published in 1948 and contained 1,887 biographies. The present updated fourth edition, 32 years later, has over 8,000 writer member entries, which represent only a portion of the Society's current membership.

Each day songwriters and publishers are joining the ASCAP family, motivated by a strong belief in the organization that has protected their rights as music makers since 1914. ASCAP members reflect all areas of the music community: pop, rock, country, gospel, jazz, rhythm and blues, new wave, theater, film, symphonic and concert, electronic, etc.

ASCAP, therefore, offers a catalogue of music that is diverse and comprehensive in scope — music that has been both a part of our national and international scene.

ASCAP was founded to make it possible for creators of music to be paid for performances of their compositions. Holders of an ASCAP license have the right to use for nondramatic public performance the works of any of our members (plus members of affiliated foreign societies).

This volume represents a conscientious effort to present an accurate picture of the highlights in the careers of the Society's writer members. The directory also includes information on the birth dates and birth places of our members as well as other biographical data.

Not every ASCAP member appears here, nor is every work listed of those members mentioned. In preparing the present edition, we have been guided by the entries in our previous editions and have relied upon our members' responses to a questionnaire from the publisher of the Dictionary. Where there was no response, available source material was consulted. In reporting the works of members, we were primarily governed by the members' own submissions. We encourage our readers to consult the Society for any information not contained here.

We hope this Dictionary will continue to be a useful reference tool to the music industry and a new, exciting discovery for lovers of music everywhere.

Hal David
President of ASCAP

PREFACE

The fourth edition of the *American Society of Composers, Authors and Publishers Biographical Dictionary* is compiled and edited for the Society by Jaques Cattell Press, a subsidiary of R. R. Bowker Company, publishers. 8,200 individual members are profiled in the main section followed by a listing of the over 7,000 publisher members.

Questionnaire forms were sent to qualified ASCAP members, their heirs or representatives during March and April of 1980. Information given in response to these requests has been edited to conform to the entry format approved by ASCAP. In some cases information has been reprinted from the previous edition or taken from other published sources, and submitted to members for verification.

With few exceptions members are listed alphabetically by given name and cross-referenced by professional pseudonym.

A member's musical works are grouped under three main headings: *Songs, Instrumental Works* and *Scores*. These categories can be defined further by subheadings: Music or Lyric for *Songs*, and Opera/Ballet, Broadway Show or Film/TV for *Scores*. When specific information was not available, works appear under the general heading *Songs and Instrumental Works*.

The following sample illustrates the arrangement and content of a typical entry. The names and information are fictional.

[1]MALLORY, DANIELLE [2](DAN LAURY)   [3]ASCAP 1969
    [4]composer, author, singer
[5]b New York, NY, Feb. 28, 41. [6]Educ: Horace Mann High Sch; Syracuse Univ, BA, 62; studied voice with Arnold Marshall, 60-64. [7]In Bway production "The Music Man"; singer, night clubs, TV; recording artist, Columbia Records. [8]Chief Collabr: Michael Dey. [9]*Songs:* Like Now; Long Time No Smile; Floatin'; Music: Mama's Boy; It's OK; Some Other Pleasure. *Instrumental Works:* Nineteen O'Clock.

1. Name (given)	6. Study and Training
2. Professional Name(s)	7. Outline of Career
3. Year Joined ASCAP	8. Chief Collaborators
4. Professional Category	9. Major Published Works
5. Birthplace and Date	

ABBREVIATIONS

A—alto
ABC—American Broadcasting Company
acad—academia, academic, academica, academie, academique, academy
actg—acting
adj—adjunct, adjutant
admin—administration, administrative
adminr—administrator(s)
adv—adviser(s), advisory
advert—advertisement, advertising
AFB—Air Force Base
Ala—Alabama
Alta—Alberta
Am—America, American
app—appoint, appointed
Apr—April
Arg—Argentina, Argentine
Ariz—Arizona
Ark—Arkansas
arr—arranged, arrangement, arranger, arranging
ASCAP—American Society of Composers, Authors & Publishers
asn—association
assoc(s)—associate(s)
asst(s)—assistant(s)
atty—attorney
Aug—August
AUS—Army of the United States
AV—audiovisual

B—bass
b—born
BC—British Columbia
bd—board(s)
Belg—Belgian, Belgium
bk(s)—book(s)
Brit—Britain, British
Bro(s)—Brother(s)
bus—business
Bway—Broadway
BWI—British West Indies

Calif—California
Can—Canada, Canadian
Capt—Captain
Cath—Catholic
CBS—Columbia Broadcasting System
Cent—Central
Cent Am—Central America
cert—certificate(s)
chap—chapter
chmn—chairman
cmndg—commanding
coauth—coauthor
co-dir—co-director
coed—coeditor
Col—Colonel
collab—collaborated
collabr(s)—collaborator(s)
Colo—Colorado
col(s)—college(s), collegiate
Comdr—Commander
comnr—commissioner
comn(s)—commission(s), commissioned
comp—composed, composer, composition
comt(s)—committee(s)
cond—conducted, conductor
Conn—Connecticut

cons—conservatories, conservatory
consult(s)—consult, consultant(s), consultantship(s), consultation, consulting
coordr—coordinator
corp—corporate, corporation(s)
co(s)—companies, company
ctr—center
CZ—Canal Zone
Czech—Czechoslovakia

d—deceased, died
DC—District of Columbia
Dec—December
Del—Delaware
dept—department, departmental
develop—development, developmental
dipl—diploma, diplomate
dir(s)—director(s), directory(ies)
div—division, divisional
DJ—disc jockey
dr—doctor

E—East
ed—edit, edited, editing, edition(s), editor(s), editorial
educ—educate, educated, educating, education, educational
educr—educator(s)
elec—electric, electrical, electricity
elem—elementary
eng—engineering
Eng—England, English
engr(s)—engineer(s)
ens—ensemble
Europ—European
Evangel—Evangelical, Evangelism, Evangelistic
examr(s)—examiner(s)
exec(s)—executive(s)
exp—experiment, experimental

fac—faculty
Feb—February
fedn—federation
fel(s)—fellow(s), fellowship(s)
fest(s)—festival(s)
Fla—Florida
Found—Foundation
Ft—Fort

Ga—Georgia
gen—general
Ger—German, Germanic, Germany
gov—governing, governor(s)
govt—government, governmental
grad—graduate, graduated
Gt Brit—Great Britain

hon(s)—honor(s), honorable, honorary

Ill—Illinois
illus—illustrate, illustrated, illustration
illusr—illustrator
Inc—Incorporated
incl—include, included, includes, including
Ind—Indiana
indust(s)—industrial, industries, industry
Inf—Infantry
instrnl—instructional
instr(s)—instruct, instruction, instructor(s)

inst(s)—institute(s), institution(s)
int—internacional, international, internationale, internazionale
introd—introduction
Ital—Italian

J—Journal
Jan—January
jour—journal, journalism
Jr—Junior

Kans—Kansas
Ky—Kentucky

La—Louisiana
lect—lecture(s)
lectr—lecturer(s)
libr—libraries, library
Lt—Lieutenant
ltd—limited

mag—magazine(s)
Maj—Major
Man—Manitoba
Mar—March
Mass—Massachusetts
MC—master of ceremonies
Md—Maryland
med—medical, medicinal, medicine
Mediter—Mediterranean
mem—member(s), membership(s), memoirs, memorial
metrop—metropolitan
Mex—Mexican, Mexico
mfg—manufacturing
mgr—manager
mgt—management
Mich—Michigan
mil—military
Minn—Minnesota
Miss—Mississippi
Mo—Missouri
Mont—Montana
ms(s)—manuscript(s)
Mt—Mount
munic—municipal, municipalities
mus—museum(s)
musicol—musicological, musicology

N—North
NAm—North America
nat—national
NB—New Brunswick
NBC—National Broadcasting Company
NC—North Carolina
NDak—North Dakota
NEA—National Endowment for the Arts
Nebr—Nebraska
Neth—Netherlands
Nev—Nevada
New Eng—New England
Nfld—Newfoundland
NH—New Hampshire
NJ—New Jersey
NMex—New Mexico
No—Number
Norweg—Norwegian
Nov—November
NS—Nova Scotia

NSF—National Science Foundation
NSW—New South Wales
NY—New York
NZ—New Zealand

Oct—October
off—official
Okla—Oklahoma
Ont—Ontario
orch(s)—orchestra(s)
orchr—orchestrator
Ore—Oregon
orgn—organization(s), organizational

Pa—Pennsylvania
PBS—Public Broadcasting System
PEI—Prince Edward Island
perc—percussion
perf—performance
Philh—Philharmonic
polytech—polytechnic, polytechnical
Port—Portugal, Portuguese
postgrad—postgraduate
PR—Puerto Rico
pract—practice
prep—preparation, preparatory
pres—president
Presby—Presbyterian
prof—professional, professor, professorial
prog(s)—program(s), programmed, programming
Prov—Province, provincial
psychol—psycological, psychology
pub—public
publ—publication(s), publish(ed), publisher, publishing
pvt—private

quart—quarterly
Que—Quebec
rec'd—received
relig—religion, religious

rel(s)—relation(s), relative
rep—represent, representative
Repub—Republic
res—research
rev—review, revised, revision
RI—Rhode Island

S—soprano, South
SAfrica—South Africa
SAm—South America, South American
Sask—Saskatchewan
SC—South Carolina
Scand—Scandinavia, Scandinavian
sch(s)—school(s)
sci—science(s), scientific
SDak—South Dakota
sec—secondary
secy—secretary
sem—seminar, seminary
sen—senator, senatorial
Sept—September
Sgt—Sergeant
soc(s)—societies, society
Span—Spanish
spec—special
sr—senior
St—Saint
sta(s)—station(s)
Ste—Sainte
supt—superintendent
supv—supervising, supervision
supvr—supervisor
supvry—supervisory
Swed—Swedish
Switz—Switzerland
symph—symphony
synd—syndicated
syst(s)—system(s), systematic, systematical

T—tenor
tech—technical
technol—technologic, technological, technology

Tenn—Tennessee
Tex—Texas
theol—theological, theology
transc—transcription(s)
transl—translated, translation(s)
translr—translator(s)
TV—television
twp—township

UK—United Kingdom
UN—United Nations
UNESCO—United Nations Educational, Scientific & Cultural Organization
univ(s)—universities, university
US—United States
USA—United States Army
USAAF—United States Army Air Force
USAF—United States Air Force
USCG—United States Coast Guard
USMC—United States Marine Corps
USN—United States Navy
USNR—United States Naval Reserve
USSR—Union of Soviet Socialist Republics

Va—Virginia
var—various
vchmn—vice chairman
Vet—Veteran(s)
VI—Virgin Islands
vol(s)—volume(s)
vpres—vice president
Vt—Vermont

W—West
Wash—Washington
Wis—Wisconsin
WVa—West Virginia
WW—World War
Wyo—Wyoming

yr(s)—year(s)

MEMBER PROFILES

A

AABERG, PHILIP (EDDY YATES)   ASCAP 1976
composer, keyboardist
b Havre, Mont, Apr 8, 49. Educ: Harvard Col, AB(music), 71; Leonard Bernstein music scholarship; chamber music with Leon Kirchner; musicianship with Luise Vosgerchian. Pianist in improvisational theater "The Proposition." Orchestral soloist; TV network rock shows; recording studio musician; new music chamber groups. Chief Collabr: Elvin Bishop. *Songs:* Music: Struttin' My Stuff; Hey, Hey, Hey. *Instrumental Works:* Gojo Ohashi Bridge.

AARONS, RUTH HUGHES   ASCAP 1956
author
b New York, NY, June 11, 18; d June 6, 80. Lyricist, 40's & 50's; personal mgr. Chief Collabrs: Irving Actman, Albert Hague, Dick Stabile, Albert Selden.

AARONSON, IRVING   ASCAP 1951
composer, author, conductor
b New York, NY, Feb 7, 1895; d Hollywood, Calif, Mar 10, 63. Educ: David Mannes Music Sch; studied with Albert Sendry. Pianist in movie theatres, age 11. Formed musical group, Versatile Sextette; later organized orch, The Commanders. Appeared in vaudeville & nightclubs, US & Europe; also in Bway musical, "Paris"; music supvr, MGM. *Songs:* Boo-Hoo-Hoo; The Song Angels Sing; The Loveliest Night of the Year.

ABBOTT, CHARLIE   ASCAP 1945
composer, author
b Chicago, Ill, Jan 11, 03. Script writer for radio. *Songs:* Five Salted Peanuts; Think of Me Thinking of You; If I Were You; The Guy From the Isle of Capri; As We Walk Into the Sunset.

ABBOTT, EVE
See Niday Canaday, Edna Veronica

ABERNATHY, DAVID MYLES   ASCAP 1933
composer, author
b Connelly Springs, NC, June 27, 33. Educ: High Point Col; Univ Md; Emory Univ; Union Theol Sem, New York; RCA Insts; AB, MDiv, STM, LittD. Chief Collabrs: Paul Jarvis, Gene Carroll. *Songs:* A Man Named Wesley; Music: Saturday Morning; Love in the Morning; Wednesday.

ABESON, MARION   ASCAP 1954
composer, author
b New Haven, Conn, Nov 14, 14. Educ: NY Univ, BA; Sorbonne; Univ Berlin; Columbia Sch Drama. Writer of children's songs & playlets. Assisted production of recordings, Columbia, Decca, Golden, MGM & Young Peoples Records. Collaborated record arr with Henry Brant, Hershey Kay & Charity Bailey. Wrote spec material for performing artists, Martha Schlamme, Jack Gilford & Ellie Stone. Author, "Playtime with Music"; "Willie Woo" (syndicated Sunday musical comic feature). *Songs:* Michie Banjo; Angelico; Singing in the Kitchen; Willie Woo; Do a Little Square Dance; Two by Two; Jolly Doctor Dolliwell; The Monkey and the Elephant; Baby's First Record; Who Wants a Ride?; Let's Play Zoo; Jump Back, Little Toad; Peter and the Wolf (new version); Hansel and Gretel (new version); Lyrics: Queen Esther; Higher Than Heaven. *Albums:* Horatio the Horsie-O; Jolly Dr Dolliwell (Ohio State Award); ABC—A Childs First Record.

ABLER, KEITH DONALD   ASCAP 1975
composer, author, singer
b Plymouth, Wis, Oct 14, 51. Educ: Univ Wis, Oshkosh. Performer & recording artist with var bands, midwestern US & west coast, 68- Appeared, stage play "My Fair Lady," 70. Singer, nightclubs & TV. Chief Collabrs: Michael Dellger, David Steffen.

ABLES, RICHARD LOUIS   ASCAP 1963
composer
b New York, NY, July 30, 11. Educ: Hebrew Tech Inst. Played in Isham Jones, Woody Herman & Charlie Barnet Orchs. Chief Collabrs: Harold (Shorty) Baker; Eddie Thompson. *Songs:* Music: Home Brew; State Occasion; Chile Con Carne; Bread for Ed; Mood for Teachers; Cosmopolitan; Shorty's Dream; Tomorrow; Edge of Love.

ABRAHAM, JOHNNY
See Grothoff, Curtis Eugene II

ABRAHAMS, MAURICE (MAURIE ABRAMS)   ASCAP 1914
composer, author, publisher
b Russia, Mar 18, 1883; d New York, NY, Apr 13, 31. Professional mgr, music publ cos; became publisher, 23. Wrote spec material for vaudeville singers incl Belle Baker (wife). Chief Collabrs: Lewis Muir, Edgar Leslie, Grant Clarke. *Songs:* He'd Have to Get Under; When the Grown Up Ladies Act Like Babies; Pray for Sunshine, But Always Be Prepared for Rain; I'll Always Think I'm in Heaven When I'm Down in Dixie Land; Hitchy Koo; Take Me to That Midnight Cakewalk Ball; Ragtime Cowboy Joe; High, High, High Up in the Hills; Pullman Porters Parade; At the Cotton Pickers' Ball; Everybody Loves My Gal; Is There Still Room for Me?.

ABRAMS, MAURIE
See Abrahams, Maurice

ABRAMS, RITA JANE   ASCAP 1970
composer, author
b Cleveland, Ohio, Aug 30, 43. Educ: Cleveland Heights High Sch; Simmons Col; Univ Mich, AB; Boston Univ, MEd. Music author, Harcourt Brace & Jovanovich, 70- Wrote & recorded with "Miss Abrams & the Strawberry Point Third Grade Class", 70, completed album with group for Warner Bros, 71; wrote & recorded Del Monte Commercial "Nothin's Too Good for Daddy & Me", 74; won Emmy for music, NBC spec "I Want It All Now", 80. Music & lyrics for play "Pink Moon", by Frank Crow, produced in San Francisco. *Songs:* Mill Valley; Wonder; America, Let's Get Started Again; Disco Drag; Where the Rainbow Ends.

ABRAMSON, ROBERT MARVIN
composer, author, teacher
b Philadelphia, Pa, Aug 23, 28. Educ: Inst Jaques-Dalcroze, Geneva, Switz, dipl; Manhattan Sch Music, BM & MM. Comp, pianist & cond. *Songs:* Music: Three Old Songs Resung; Three Elegies From Walt Whitman. *Instrumental Works:* Dance Variations for Piano and Orchestra. *Scores:* Film: Ages of Times; Copper.

ACHESON, MARCUS WILSON, III   ASCAP 1970
composer, author, music critic
b Pittsburgh, Pa, June 4, 05. Educ: Shady Side Acad, 22; Williams Col, grad, Phi Beta Kappa, 26; Cambridge Univ, Queens Col, Eng; Harvard Univ Bus Sch, MBA, 29. Salesman, var businesses, 29-70. Music critic, Southhampton Press newspaper, Long Island, 30 yrs. Writer, var works for 4 part chorus, with solos & orch accompaniment, performed in churches. Secy, Nat Music Critics Asn, 2 yrs; mem, Long Island's South Fork Choral Soc, 25 yrs. *Songs & Instrumental Works:* Twenty-third Psalm (4 part chorus, organ).

ACHRON, ISIDOR   ASCAP 1941
composer, pianist, teacher
b Warsaw, Poland, Nov 24, 1892; d New York, NY, May 12, 48. Came to US after Russian revolution. Educ: Petrograd Cons; studied with Nicolai Doubassoff & Anatol Liadoff. Piano soloist with London Symph & New York Philh. Cond, Miami Symph, Fla, in perf of own works, 39. Teacher music, New York. *Instrumental Works:* Piano Concerto; Valse Dramatique; Valse Intime; Improvisation; Gavotte Grotesque; Minuet Grotesque.

ACKERS, ANDREW ACQUARULO ASCAP 1948
composer, pianist

b New Haven, Conn, Nov 23, 19; d New York, NY, Oct 20, 78. Educ: Yale Univ Sch Music; studied with Bruce Simonds, Tibor Serly. Pianist in dance orchs, 41-48. Cond accompanist for Mindy Carson, Kate Smith, Georgia Gibbs & Jane Morgan. Studio pianist for networks; made many records; wrote commercials. Chief Collabr: Sunny Skylar. *Songs:* If You Were There; A New Shade of Blue; Sundown; Olivia; If You Were Mine. *Songs & Instrumental Works:* The Ten Commandments; Princess Suite.

ACKLEY, ALFRED HENRY ASCAP 1941
composer, author, cellist

b Spring Hill, Pa, Jan 21, 1887; d Whittier, Calif, July 3, 60. Educ: Pa State Univ; Union Theol Sem; Royal Acad of Music, London, studied with Alfred Walker; hon MusD, John Brown Univ; studied with Hans Kronold. Ordained Presby minister, served in DC, Pittsburgh & Escondido, Calif, 18-52. Chief Collabr: Bentley Ackley (brother). *Songs:* Sacred: Only Shadows; He Lives; I Never Walk Alone; It is Morning in My Heart; God's Tomorrow; Dearer Than All; At the End of the Road; When the World Forgets; Take Up Thy Cross; When God Is Near; In the Service of the King; Somebody Knows.

ACKLEY, BENTLEY D ASCAP 1937
composer, author, musician

b Spring Hill, Pa, Sept 27, 1872; d Winona Lake, Ind, Sept 3, 58. Organist, Brooklyn & New York. Secy & pianist, "Billy" Sunday, 8 yrs. Music ed, Rodeheaver Hall-Mack Co. Chief Collabrs: Alfred Ackley (brother), Oswald Smith. *Songs:* Sacred: I Walk With the King; Jesus, I Am Coming Home; Mother's Prayers Have Followed Me; Sunrise; I Would Be Like Jesus; In the Service of the King; Somebody Knows; Jesus; Surrender; God Understands.

ACKMAN, HERMAN ASCAP 1959
composer, author

b Newark, NJ, Mar 27, 04. Educ: High Sch of Commerce, New York. Secy to George M Cohan, 23-42. Comp, music, 24- Licensed real estate & mortgage broker, 26- Chief Collabrs: Leo Wood, Archie Gottler, Lou Davis, Kenneth Casey. *Songs:* Toujours Monte Carlo Toujours; Music: Put Your Arms Where They Belong; Watching and Waiting (for You); Sweet Imagination; Longing for You; At Last.

ACTMAN, IRVING ASCAP 1942
composer, conductor, arranger

b New York, NY, June 2, 07; d. Accompanist to vaudeville singers. Music dir, comp for TV, indust shows & films. Cond, Bway musicals "Guys and Dolls", "Along Fifth Avenue" & "Ballet de Paris." Music coordr, "Producers Showcade," TV; cond, arr for Maurice Chevalier, Mary Martin, Jimmy Durante, Celeste Holm & Milton Berle. Chief Collabrs: Frank Loesser, Lew Brown, Edgar DeLange, Ruth Aarons. *Songs:* A Trip in Tipperary; Bang—the Bell Rang; Wild Trumpets and Crazy Piano; You Took Me Out of This World; Who's Got a Match?; April Can't Do This to Me; La Pintada; The Sky Ran Out of Stars; Cupid's After Me; A Hundred Kisses From Now. *Scores:* Bway Stage: Illustrators' Show; Sleepy Hollow.

ADAIR, FRANCES JEFFORDS
composer, author

b Orangeburg, SC, May 16, 18. Educ: Orangeburg High Sch, grad, 36. Writer of musical & lyrical material, with emphasis on contemporary Christian music, motion picture & TV material for Walt Disney Productions. Chief Collabrs: Tom Adair, Bob Hammack, Buddy Baker, Bob Brunner. *Songs:* Music: How Will I Know My Love?; Bon Jour, Paris; Pat's At Puunulu (Hawaiian); Na Le-O-O-Hawaii (Hawaiian); Lyrics: A Taco and a Burger and Sweet, Sweet Love; A Tower of Strength; River Country (featured at Walt Disney World & TV Spec). *Albums:* What a Wonderful Thing Is Me; A Disney Christmas Carol (nominated for Grammy Award in category of children's records); I Want You.

ADAIR, THOMAS MONTGOMERY ASCAP 1944
author

b Newton, Kans, June 15, 13. Educ: John C Fremont High Sch, Los Angeles, grad, 30; Los Angeles Jr Col, 32-33. Lyricist & TV script writer; lyricist & script writer motion pictures, stage & night clubs. Situation comedy writer, "My 3 Sons", "The Munsters", "My Favorite Martian", etc. Worked different projs for Walt Disney Productions, Disneyland & Disney World. Chief Collabrs: Matt Dennis, Gordon Jenkins, Hal Hopper, Alfonse D'Artega, Buddy Baker, Frances Adair, George Bruns, Bob Bruner, Bob Hamack. *Songs:* Lyrics: Let's Get Away From It All; Everything Happens to Me; In the Blue of Evening; Will You Still Be Mine?; Violets for Your Furs; The Night We Called It a Day; There's No You; Julie; Skyscraper Blues; How Will I Know My Love?; Sleeping Beauty; Sing a Smiling Song.

ADAM, CLAUS
educator, cellist, composer

b Sumatra, Indonesia, Nov 5, 17. Educ: Austria, Ger, Holland, US; orch training with Nat Orch Asn, 35-40; Philh scholarship with Joseph Emonts, 35-38; scholarship with Emanuel Feuermann, 38-43. Came to US, 31, naturalized, 35. Asst first cellist, Minneapolis Symph, 40-43. First cellist, WOR Sta, New York, 46-48. Cellist & organizer, New Music String Quartet, 48-54. Mem, Juilliard String Quartet, 55-74. Mem fac, Juilliard Sch, 55-, Mannes Col Music & Philadelphia Col Performing Arts. Numerous tours, US & abroad, 50- Comp-in-residence, Am Acad, Rome, 76. Rec'd grants & awards: Ford Found; Nat Found Arts; Paderewski Found; Naumberg Found; Guggenheim fel, 75-76. *Instrumental Works:* Piano Sonata; String Trio; Song Cycle; Herbstgesänge; Concerto for Piano and Orchestra; String Quartet; Concerto Variations for Orchestra.

ADAMO, MILO ANGELO (BOBBY ADANO) ASCAP 1975
composer, author, singer

b Brooklyn, NY, Aug 1, 31. Piano player & film writer. Chief Collabrs: Henry Mancini, Victor Feldman, Mike Melvoin. *Songs:* Billy My Love; Day Dream City; Jesus Hammer; Speak of Love; Bayou; Man From Nazareth; Bobby's Thing; 80 Lower Pike; Hard Luck Stories; Goin' Home; Song Rider; Denny; Lady Melinda; Lyrics: Suitcase Full of Dreams; Sometimes Love Songs Make Me Cry; Haunted Ballroom; Wham Bam (Blue Collar Man); I Got No Lites; Feel Good All Over; All That's Love; Secret Thots; I'm Alone; Sons and Daughters of the Los Angeles Sanitation Engineers; Doncha Know; EEE-UU; Fun and Games; When I Think of You; Just for Today; Merry Go Round of Love; Goin' to San Diego; Love Can Be Mine; Relax and Spend the Nite. *Scores:* Film/TV: Murder at Malibu; Jump Street; Lonely Street (Mongos Back in Town).

ADAMS, ANDREW PAUL ASCAP 1977
composer

b Brooklyn, NY, Mar 3, 51. Recording artist, signed with Pyramid Records, Roulette & Dick James Records. *Songs:* Can I Stay?; Pour Tes Beaux Yeux. *Albums:* Egg Cream; One of the Boys.

ADAMS, ANTHONY WALTER ASCAP 1973
composer, author, conductor

b Fort Dodge, Iowa, Nov 12, 48. Educ: San Bernardino Valley Col; studied with Karl L King, C Paul Oxley, Russell Baldwin, Earle Hagen, Joe Reisman, Frederick Fennell & George Tremblay. Arr & comp for Saddleback Concert Chorale; film comp; comp radio & TV commercials. Comp, Civic Light Opera, San Bernardino, Calif. *Songs:* When I Look At You; Girl, You're Something; It Hurts Too Much; Take My Love; You Know How I Feel; Stay Here; I'm Still in Love With You; I Don't Want to Be Hurt Anymore; You're My Country Woman; Music: Sabra's Love; Someday. *Instrumental Works:* Waltz a la King; Nocturne de la Mer; The Crossing; Violin Concerto No 1; The Last Child; Pell-Mell; Something for Ann; After This. *Scores:* Film/TV: The Legend of Jedediah Carver; Little Pioneers; Ransom Money; The Devil's Choice.

ADAMS, AUDRI ASCAP 1955
author

b Clarion, Iowa, July 22, 25. Educ: William Jewell Col, BA. Model; pub relations exec. *Songs:* Love Gone Astray; I Can't Win.

ADAMS, CHRIS (FINGERS) ASCAP 1979
composer, author, producer

b Montevideo, Uruguay, Apr 14, 58. Educ: Self-taught; pvt music study. Solo artist, writer & arr. Performer with own group. Chief Collabrs: Father; Michael Ford. *Songs & Instrumental Works:* Disco Rockin'; On My Way Back Home; Miracles; Friends With Me; Why?

ADAMS, ERNEST HARRY ASCAP 1939
composer, pianist, teacher

b Waltham, Mass, July 16, 1886; d Mass, Dec 25, 59. Educ: Studied with Carrie Gerald Adams (mother), Benjamin Cutter & Henry Dunham. Ed. *Songs:* The Full Tide; Through Miles and Miles of Years; The Lazy Dip of the Oar; Siren Song; Ashes of Memory. *Instrumental Works:* Piano: In the Flower Garden; Concerto Impromptu; Fantasie Polonaise; Tone Fancies After Famous Paintings; At Parting; Parade of the Clowns; The Wind in the Willows; Ice Carnival; Espringale; Dance of the Gnomes; Spooks and Shadows; The King's Jester.

ADAMS, FRANK R ASCAP 1937
author

b Morrison, Ill, July 7, 1883; d Whitehall Lake, Mich, Oct 8, 63. Educ: Univ Chicago, PhB. Reporter, "Chicago Tribune", "Daily News" & Examiner." Screenplays incl "The Cowboy and the Lady" & "Trade Winds." Author, bks, "3,000 Miles Away", "Molly and I", "Five Fridays", "Help Yourself to Happiness", "For Valor", "King's Crew" & "The Secret Attic." Chief Collabrs: Joe Howard, Will Hough, Harold Orlob. *Songs:* I Don't Like Your Family; Blow the Smoke Away; What's the Use of Dreaming?; When You First Kiss the Last Girl You Love; Honeymoon; Be Sweet to Me, Kid; I Wonder Who's Kissing Her Now; Tonight Will Never Come Again; Cross Your Heart. *Scores:* Bway, Chicago stage shows: The Time, the Place and the Girl; The Girl Question; A Stubborn Cinderella; The Goddess of Liberty; The Price of Tonight.

ADAMS, GENE
See Saraceni, Raymond

ADAMS, JACK ASCAP 1971
composer, author, singer
b Hobart, Okla, Mar 27, 30. Singer, nightclubs, radio & TV; recording artist for Golondrina & NBC Records. Chief Collabrs: Freddie Hart, Earl V Phillips, Jerry Chesnut. *Songs:* She Fights That Lovin' Feeling; Mother Nature Made a Believer Out of Me; The Child; Love Took Command; Lifetime in a Week; Geraldine; Can't Be Had; The Devil Is Her Teacher; How Can She Lie Beside Me; The Girl Who Couldn't Say No; You Stand in Loves Way; She Knew How to Love Me; I Still Love Her.

ADAMS, LEE
See Adamski, Leon Stephen

ADAMS, LEE RICHARD ASCAP 1956
author
b Mansfield, Ohio, Aug 14, 24. Educ: Ohio State Univ, BA, 49; Columbia Univ Sch Jour, MScJ, 50. Author Bway shows: "Bye Bye Birdie," Tony Award; "All American"; "Golden Boy"; "Applause," Tony Award; "A Broadway Musical"; "I and Albert."

ADAMS, MARTY
See Bachman, Martha Jeanne

ADAMS, PARK (PEPPER) ASCAP 1978
composer, baritone saxophonist
b Highland Park, Mich, Oct 8, 30. Educ: Wayne State Univ, 48-50. In numerous concert & nightclub appearances, NAm, Europe & Asia. Winner, Down Beat Int Critic's Poll, 79. *Instrumental Works:* Bossa Nouveau; Claudette's Way; Ephemera; I Carry Your Heart. *Albums:* Reflectory (finalist for Grammy Award, 80).

ADAMS, PAUL EUGENE ASCAP 1961
composer, author
b Canton, Ohio, Feb 26, 22. Educ: Ohio State Univ, BS, 46; Univ Calif, Los Angeles. Wrote for records, Calif, 46- *Songs:* Call It Love; Keep That Coffee Hot; I Promise You; Music: The Lack of Love; I Love the Blues.

ADAMS, PEARL G
See Martufi, Pearl Gertrude

ADAMS, RITCHIE
See Ziegler, Richard Adam

ADAMS, STANLEY ASCAP 1934
author
b New York, NY, Aug 14, 07. Educ: NY Univ, Law Sch, LLB. First prof assignment for Connie's Inn Revue. Wrote songs for films & Bway musicals incl "Duel in the Sun", "My Reputation", "The Great Lie", "Road Show", "Everyday's a Holiday", "Viva Villa!", "The Show Is On", "The Lady Says Yes" & "Shoestring Revue." Dir, ASCAP, 44-, pres, 53-56 & 59-80. Hon mem council, Am Guild Authors & Composers, vpres, 43-44; mem adv bd, Musicians Aid Soc; mem exec bd, President's Music Comn (People-to-People Prog); mem adv comt, Nat Cultural Ctr; mem adv bd, Am Fedn Musicians & Nat Music Council, 2nd vpres; mem bd dir, Music for the Blind & Music Comn New York. Pres, Int Confederation of Socs Authors & Composers, 79-80. Participated in Conference for Int Copyright, UN Educ, Sci & Cultural Orgn. Awards: Philadelphia Club Printing House Craftsmen; Henry Hadley Medal, Nat Asn Am Composers & Conductors; Pres Citation, Nat Fedn Music Clubs; Music for the Blind; Bedside Network; Nat Arts Club. Chief Collabrs: Lou Alter, Abel Baer, Hoagy Carmichael, Arthur Gershwin, Maria Grever, Ray Henderson, Victor Herbert, Oscar Levant, George Meyer, Sigmund Romberg, Fred Spielman, Max Steiner, Fats Waller. *Songs:* What a Diff'rence a Day Made; Little Old Lady; There Are Such Things; My Shawl (Xavier Cugat theme); La Cucaracha; Dust on the Moon; Yesterthoughts; Jubilee; Stranger in the Dark; Wacky Dust; Rollin' Down the River; While You're Away; Extra! All About That Gal of Mine; Seein' Is Believin'; Papa Tree Top Tall; My Silent Mood; You Stole My Heart; There Are Rivers to Cross; Open Up That Door; With All My Heart and Soul.

ADAMS, WILLIAM DAVID ASCAP 1969
author
b Chicago, Ill, Oct 10, 20. Educ: Purdue Univ, BS; Univ Chicago; Mass Inst Technol, grad study. Radio & TV writer-producer, Am Broadcasting Co, Grant Advert, Inc, D'Arcy Advert Co, PKG/Cunningham & Walsh Advert Co. Chief Collabr: Robert B Owens, III.

ADAMSKI, LEON STEPHEN (LEE ADAMS) ASCAP 1974
composer
b Perth Amboy, NJ, Apr 12, 39. Educ: Montclair State Col, NJ, BA(music educ), 61; Trenton State Col, NJ, MA(comp), 73. Performing musician; music educator; jr high sch band dir. Comp of over 30 publ band comp for elem & jr high sch bands. Maj instruments: Saxophone, clarinet & flute.

ADAMSON, HAROLD ASCAP 1932
author
b Greenville, NJ, Dec 10, 06. Educ: Univ Kans; Harvard Univ. Wrote Hasty Pudding shows; moved to Hollywood, 33. Chief Collabrs: Lou Alter, Hoagy Carmichael, Peter DeRose, Walter Donaldson, Vernon Duke, Duke Ellington, Burton Lane, Jimmy McHugh, Vincent Youmans, Victor Young, Sammy Fain. *Songs:* Time on My Hands; Sittin' in the Dark; Tony's Wife; Like Me a Little Bit Less (Love Me a Little Bit More); Everything I Have Is Yours; Heigh-Ho, the Gang's All Here; Your Head on My Shoulder; Everything's Been Done Before; It's Been So Long; You; You Never Looked So Beautiful Before; Did I Remember?; There's Something in the Air; With a Banjo on My Knee; Where Are You?; You're a Sweetheart; You're as Pretty as a Picture; It's a Wonderful World; The Thrill of a New Romance; 720 in the Books; We're Having a Baby; The Music Stopped; I Couldn't Sleep a Wink Last Night; A Lovely Way to Spend an Evening; Comin' in on a Wing and a Prayer; How Blue the Night; A Hubba Hubba Hubba; As the Girls Go; I Got Lucky in the Rain; It's a Most Unusual Day; When Love Goes Wrong; You Say the Nicest Things, Baby; My Resistance Is Low; Around the World; An Affair to Remember; Ferryboat Serenade; Too Young to Go Steady. *Scores:* Bway Shows: Smiles; Earl Carroll's Vanities; Banjo Eyes; As the Girls Go; Jones Beach; Around the World in Eighty Days; Films: Dancing Lady; The Great Ziegfeld; Banjo on My Knee; Top of the Town; You're a Sweetheart; That Certain Age; Higher and Higher; Four Jills in a Jeep; Smash-Up; Gentlemen Prefer Blondes; An Affair to Remember; also many other film songs & themes.

ADANO, BOBBY
See Adamo, Milo Angelo

ADDISON, JOHN MERVYN ASCAP 1978
composer
b Chobham, Eng, Mar 16, 20. Educ: Wellington Col, Eng; Royal Col Music, London, ARCM. Joined Performing Right Soc Gt Brit, 49. Prof comp, Royal Col Music, 50-57. Performed in woodwind sextet at Int Soc Contemporary Music, Frankfurt, Ger, 51. Performed orch & chamber works in UK, Ger, France, Can, Australia & US. Wrote music for theatre, incl "Popkiss," 72, revues "Cranks" & "Hamlet." Cond own works in Albert Hall & Fest Hall, London. *Instrumental Works:* Carte Blanche (ballet suite, comn by Royal Ballet, Eng, 53); Concerto (trumpet, strings & perc); Serenade (wind quintet & harp). *Scores:* Bway Show: Cranks; Films: Tom Jones (Oscar & Grammy Awards); Sleuth (Oscar nomination); A Taste of Honey; Torn Curtain; A Bridge Too Far (Brit Film Acad Award); The Seven-Per-Cent Solution; The Entertainer; The Charge of the Light Brigade; TV: Centennial; Pearl.

ADELSON, LEONARD GARY ASCAP 1955
author
b Omaha, Nebr, June 25, 24; d New York, NY, Sept, 72. Educ: Fairfax High Sch; Univ Southern Calif, BA, 48. Writer, special material for TV shows incl "Shower of Stars", "Colgate Comedy Hour" & "Saturday Night Review", movie song titles & lyrics for var artists incl Frank Sinatra, Sammy Davis, Jr & Margaret Whiting. Co-writer, special material & lyrics for Donn Arden & Las Vegas extravaganzas, play "Spectre of the Rose." Coauthor, bk & lyrics, "The Prisoner of Zenda", Los Angeles Civic Light Opera & musical play "Molly." Chief Collabrs: Jerry Livingston, Vernon Duke, Les Baxter, Imogene Carpenter, Ben Hecht, Louis Garfinkle, Fran Loesser. *Songs:* Lyrics: Molly; Any Time Any Where; Don't Change Your Mind About Me; Come Next Spring; A Rebel in Town; Young Guns; Away All Boats; Calla Calla; Born to Sing the Blues; The Living Desert; Indispensable; Animals and Clowns.

ADELSTEIN, MILTON (MILT ROGERS) ASCAP 1958
composer, arranger, pianist
b Brooklyn, NY, Aug 21, 25. Educ: Roosevelt High Sch; Los Angeles City Col, AA, 46; studied comp with Wesley La Violette; studied film scoring with Leith Stevens & Earle Hagen. Pianist-vocalist, night clubs & restaurants; arr-cond for Gale Storm, asst musical dir, Dot Records, 13 1/2 yrs, recording artist, Dot Records & Denon Records (Japan). Chief Collabrs: Billy Vaughn, Jerry Tobias, Vic Corpora. *Songs:* Music: The Jimtown Road; Swiss Retreat; Old Fashioned Christmas; My Cucuzza; Why Did I Let You Go?; Your Love. *Scores:* Film/TV: 600 Days to Cocos Island.

ADES, HAWLEY WARD composer, author, arranger
b Bloomington, Ill, June 25, 08. Educ: Rutgers Univ, LitB, 29; Columbia Teachers Col, MME; studied privately with Tertius Noble & Tibor Serly. Arr, Irving Berlin, Inc, 32-36; arr for Fred Waring, 37- Author textbk, "Choral Arranging."

ADKINSON, HARVEY E (GENE) ASCAP 1956
composer
b Dothan, Ala, Feb 28, 34. Educ: Univ Fla. Formerly with own recording group, Dream Weavers. Served, World War II. Chief Collabr: Wade Buff. *Songs:* It's Almost Tomorrow; You've Got Me Wondering; You're Mine.

ADLAM, BASIL G (BUZZ)   ASCAP 1937
composer, author, conductor

b Chelmsford, Eng; d. Educ: Pub schs, Can; studied with Herman Genss, Albert Coates. Saxophonist, Phil Harris & Ozzie Nelson Orchs. Arr & cond, Horace Heidt Orch. Cond, ABC radio & TV; comp & music dir, TV series, "Ozzie & Harriet." Music dir & producer, US Treasury Savings Bonds series "Guest Star." Chief Collabrs: Nat Burton, Alex Hyde, Art Moore, Al Stillman, Billy Rose. *Songs:* The House Is Haunted; Adventure; My Galveston Gal; Say It; Mr President; A Little Older Than Young; Pin Marin; Poor Robinson Crusoe; With Thee I Swing.

ADLER, JAMES R   ASCAP 1975
composer, concert pianist

b Chicago, Ill, Nov 19, 50. Educ: South Shore High Sch, 69; Curtis Inst Music, BM(piano), 73, MM(comp), 76; pvt study with Rudolph Ganz & Olga Barabini. Recital debut at age 13; appeared as soloist with Chicago Symph Orch at age 16; had further engagements with Chicago Symph & other Am orchs. Appeared in Europe & made London debut at Wigmore Hall, 79. Has broadcast on radio & TV in US. *Instrumental Works:* Passacaglia (piano); Two Concert-Rags (duo-piano, Bicentennial Comn); Classic Rag-Time Suite (orch); A Suite for Strings (string orch); March Grotesque (fantasy for orch); Concerto in G (piano & orch). *Songs & Instrumental Works:* God of All the Nations (SATB choral). *Scores:* Film: The Hat Act (Bronze Hugo Award, Chicago Int Fest); Opera: Treemonisha (by Scott Joplin, orchestration & adaptation).

ADLER, MARVIN S   ASCAP 1968
composer, author, educator

b New York, NY, Feb 25, 38. Educ: Music & Art High Sch, New York; The City Col New York, BA & MA, 60; Columbia Univ Teachers Col, EdD, 70. Teacher of instrumental music, elem, sec & col level. Performing prof musician. Author, "Music and Art in Elementary Education," 76 & "Elementary Teacher's Music Almanack," 78. *Scores:* Opera: Brock's Place.

ADLER, RICHARD   ASCAP 1950
composer, author

b New York, NY, Aug 3, 21. Educ: Univ NC, AB. USN, 42-46; advert dept, Celanese Corp Am, 46-51; composer, lyricist & producer, 46-; produced & staged all shows in & out of White House for Presidents Kennedy & Johnson. Chief Collabr: Jerry Ross. *Songs:* Rags to Riches; Hey There; Hernando's Hideaway; Steam Heat; Whatever Lola Wants; You've Gotta Have Heart; Another Time, Another Place; Lyrics: Everybody Loves a Lover. *Instrumental Works:* Memory of a Childhood; Retrospectrum; Yellowstone. *Scores:* Bway Shows: Pajama Game; Damn Yankees; Kwamina; Film/TV: Little Women; Gift of The Magi; Olympus 7-0000.

ADLER, SAMUEL HANS   ASCAP 1960
composer

b Mannheim, Ger, Mar 4, 28. Educ: Boston Univ, BM; Harvard Univ, MA; Southern Methodist Univ, hon DMus; comp with Piston, Thompson, Copland, Hindemith, Fromm; Tanglewood, 49-50; conducting with Koussevitzky; musicology with Geiringer, Pisk, Davison. Founded Seventh Army Symph Orch, USA, 50-52, awarded Medal of Honor. Music dir, Temple Emanu-El, Dallas, Tex, 53-66 & Dallas Lyric Theater, 54-58. Prof music, NTex State Univ, 57-66; prof comp, Eastman Sch Music, 66-, chmn dept comp, 72- Author, "Choral Conducting" & "Sight-Singing". *Songs & Instrumental Works:* Symphony No 5, We Are the Echoes (mezzo-soprano & orch); Requiescat in Pace (orch); Summer Stock Overture; City by the Lake (orch); The Feast of Lights (orch); Southwestern Sketches (band); A Little Night and Day Music (band); B'shaaray T'filah (choral work for Synagogue); String Quartet No 4; String Quartet No 6; Concertino No 2 (string orch); Music for 11 (6 woodwinds & 5 perc); Seven Epigrams; Sonato No 2 (violin & piano); Concert Piece (brass choir); Three Songs (soprano & voice); Four Songs About Nature; Canto I (trumpet solo); Canto II (trombone solo); Xenia (organ & perc); Four Dialogues (euphonium & marimba); Elegy (string orch); Trio No 1 (violin, cello & piano); Five Vignettes (12 trombones); choral anthems for church & synagogue. *Scores:* Opera/Ballet: The Outcasts of Poker Flat; The Wrestler.

ADRIAN, DIANE   ASCAP 1955
composer, author, singer

b New York, NY. Educ: Columbia Univ. Appeared, Bway musicals "Are You With It?", "Panama Hattie", "The King and I" & "Pal Joey" & in films, radio, TV & nightclubs; actress & dancer. Cond, radio show, "Pop Up," VI. *Songs & Instrumental Works:* Haitian Suite.

AGAY, DENES   ASCAP 1952
composer, author, educator

b Kiskunfelegyhaza, Hungary, June 10, 11. Educ: Liszt Acad Music, Budapest, hon grad, comp & cond; Univ Budapest, PhD. Came to US, 39. Served in USA, 42-46. Cond-orchestrator, radio & TV shows, 46-52. Ed & educ consultant, NY publ firms. Has written many comp for piano, band, orch, chorus & keyboard. Rec'd several Best of Yr citations. Author, "Best Loved Songs of the American People," "Teaching Piano-A Comprehensive Guide" & many mag articles. Chief Collabrs: Walter Hirsch, Nelson Cogane, Fred Wise. *Songs:* How Much Wood Would a Woodchuck Chuck?; When My Ship Comes Sailing Home Again; Music: Old Irish Blessing; The Yankee Pedler; Our Hearts Are Full of

Song; Clarinet Polka (adaptation); We're Making the World a Better World. *Instrumental Works:* Five Dances for Woodwind Quintet; Harlequinade (3 diversions for band); Dance Toccata (band & piano duet); Mosaics (piano solo); Serenata Burlesca (piano solo); Sonatina Hungarica (piano solo); Overture to a Comedy.

AGER, MILTON   ASCAP 1919
composer, publisher, pianist

b Chicago, Ill, Oct 6, 1893; d Los Angeles, Calif, May 6, 79. Educ: McKinley High Sch. Pianist in film-vaudeville theatres; accompanist to vaudeville singers & songpluggers. To New York, 13; arr, Waterson, Berlin & Snyder & Wm Jerome Co. USA morale div, World War I. Co-founder, Ager, Yellen & Bornstein, 22. Chief Collabs: George Meyer, Grant Clarke, Benny Davis, Lester Santly, Joe Young, Jack Yellen, Jean Schwartz, Stanley Adams, Joseph McCarthy. *Songs:* Everything Is Peaches Down in Georgia; I'm Nobody's Baby; A Young Man's Fancy; Lovin' Sam; Who Cares?; Mama Goes Where Papa Goes; I Wonder What's Become of Sally; Big Bad Bill; Ain't She Sweet?; Crazy Words, Crazy Tune; Forgive Me; Hard-Hearted Hannah; Glad Rag Doll; Only a Moment Ago; Happy Feet; A Bench in the Park; Song of the Dawn; Happy Days Are Here Again (FDR campaign song); You Can't Pull the Wool Over My Eyes; Auf Wiedersehn, My Dear; Roll Out of Bed With a Smile; Seein' Is Believing; Ten Pins in the Sky; Trust in Me; Old Mill Wheel. *Scores:* Stage shows: What's in a Name?; Rain or Shine; John Murray Anderson's Almanac; Film: Honky Tonk; King of Jazz; Chasing Rainbows.

AGNOST, FRANK PETER   ASCAP 1971
composer, author, violinist

b Chicago, Ill, June 15, 18. Educ: San Francisco High Sch Commerce; Univ Calif, Berkeley. Choir dir, San Francisco Greek Orthodox Cathedral of the Annunciation; violin soloist & orch leader. Chief Collabrs: Milton Anninos, Herbert Fitch, Carol Agnost. *Songs:* Unless It's Love; Music: Want You Blues; This Is Forever; Let It Rain!; Waiting.

AGUIRRE, JAIME MORAN   ASCAP 1969
composer, author, singer

b Los Mochis, Mex, Apr 26, 31. Educ: Elementary sch, Mex; high schs, US & Mex; Barney Kessel Studio, Hollywood, music studies. Self-taught singer & musician; performing, nightclubs, Mex, 50- Immigrated to US, 60; performer, east & west coasts, especially Calif & Las Vegas; writer & comp of music & lyrics; plays nightclubs. Booking & producing jazz concerts for San Diego Wild Animal Park summer music, 80. Chief Collabrs: Arturo Castro; Paco Moran. *Songs:* A Song for Your Brother (introduced to United Nations, 79); I Found You; Music: Una Mujer Que Me Comprenda; Besos the Arena; Lyrics: A Place Over the Sun (Over the Sun).

AGUIRRE, JUAN GUILLERMO (SANTIAGO)   ASCAP 1975
composer, author, singer

b Santiago, Chile, Dec 22, 50. Educ: Univ Chile, Santiago. Started singing in small clubs with guitar, San Francisco, 73. Recording artist, CBS Records, 80. *Songs:* Dina; Pobre Corazon; Ansias; Immigrante; Lyrics: Amor de Amantes.

AHBEZ, EDEN   ASCAP 1951
composer, author

b Brooklyn, NY, Apr 15, 08. Educ: High sch; studied piano. *Songs:* Nature Boy; Land of Love; The Shepherd; Sacramento; Hey, Jacques; Let Me Hear You Say I Love You; Teenage Love; Runaway Boy; Jalopy Song; Soft-Spoken Stranger; Song of Mating; Oh My Brother; Nature's Symphony; End of Desire.

AHL, FRED ARTHUR (FRED HALL)
composer, author

b New York, NY, Apr 10, 1897; d New York. Vaudeville performer, band leader, recording artist & comp. Chief Collabr: Arthur Fields. *Songs:* Eleven More Months—and Ten More Days; I Got a Code in My Doze; She Only Laughs At Me; Funny Lady; & many others.

AHLBERG, HARRY   ASCAP 1957
composer, arranger, teacher

b Fairfield, Conn, June 4, 12. Educ: Pub schs. Arr, orchs, singers & musicals, 28- Comp, Univ Bridgeport's annual show, 47- Taught guitar & banjo. Chief Collabr: Steve Martin. *Songs & Instrumental Works:* Octave Jump; Fourth R, Religion.

AHLERT, FRED E   ASCAP 1920
composer, arranger

b New York, NY, Sept 19, 1892; d New York, Oct 20, 53. Educ: Townsend Harris Hall; City Col New York; Fordham Univ Law Sch. Arr for Waterson, Berlin & Snyder. Wrote spec material for vaudeville; made first arr for Fred Waring Glee Club. Wrote songs for films incl, "Marianne" & "Free and Easy." Dir, ASCAP, 33-53, pres, 48-50. Chief Collabrs: Roy Turk, Sam Lewis, Joe Young, Harry Richman, Bing Crosby, Edgar Leslie. *Songs:* I'd Love to Fall Asleep and Wake Up in My Mammy's Arms; You Oughta See My Baby; I Gave You Up Before You Threw Me Down; There's a Cradle in Caroline; I'll Get By; Mean to Me; Walkin' My Baby Back Home; Where the Blue of the Night Meets the Gold of the Day (Bing Crosby theme); Love, You Funny Thing; The Moon Was Yellow; Sing an Old-Fashioned Song; Life Is a Song; The Image of You;

I'm Gonna Sit Right Down and Write Myself a Letter; Take My Heart; I Don't Know Why; I Wake Up Smiling. *Scores:* Stage: Riviera Follies (nightclub); It Happens on Ice.

AHLERT, RICHARD   ASCAP 1956
composer, author, publisher

b New York, NY, Sept 4, 21. Educ: Juilliard Sch Music; studied clarinet with Jan Williams, orch & theory with Ferde Grofe, Howard Brockway & Igor Buketoff. After mil serv, played in var bands, New York. Worked for London Records. Free lance writer, later writer, stage musicals. Instr lyric writing, Am Guild Authors & Comp. Chief Collabs: Eddie Snyder, Leon Carr, Marvin Fisher. *Songs:* Music: Never Less Than Yesterday; Lyrics: Rusty Bells; From Atlanta to Goodbye; My Days of Loving You; Runnin' Out of Fools; In Her World; Only the Young; You Don't Need Me for Anything, Anymore; I'd Do it All Again; Someone Is Waiting.

AHLSTROM, DAVID   ASCAP 1979
composer

b Lancaster, NY, Feb 22, 27. Educ: Cincinnati Cons of Music, BM, 52, MM, 53; Univ Rochester Eastman Sch of Music, PhD, 61; studied comp with Alan Hovhaness and Henry Cowell. Cond & comp teacher, Northwestern Univ, Southern Methodist Univ & Eastern Ill Univ. *Songs & Instrumental Works:* Scherzo for Trumpet, Winds and Percussion; Sonata No 4 in Eight Scenes for Clarinet and Piano; Toccatas and Passacaglias for Percussion and Speaking Voices; Sonata Number Eight (bass solo, dance & instruments). *Scores:* Opera: Three Sisters Who Are Not Sisters.

AHMONUEL, ZYAH
See Anthony, Malcolm

AHNELL, EMIL GUSTAVE   ASCAP 1972
composer

b Erie, Pa, Apr 6, 25. Educ: New Eng Cons, BM, 51; Northwestern Univ, MM, 52; Univ Ill, PhD, 57. Teacher of theory & comp at col level; composer numerous works for orch, voice, piano & var ens, vocal & instrumental. *Songs & Instrumental Works:* Nana Songs; Sonatina for Piano; Toccata, Adagio and Allegro (flute & piano); We Praise Thee (a cappella choral); Overture for Band.

AHRENS, THOMAS
See Wilson, Roger Cole

AHROLD, FRANK A   ASCAP 1975
composer, author, teacher

b Long Beach, Calif, Dec 12, 31. Educ: Long Beach Polytech High Sch; Univ Calif, Los Angeles, BA, 53, grad study, 55-56; studied comp with Lukas Foss & John Vincent. Author: "Music Calendar Datebook." Pianist, Oakland Symph Orch. Teacher, accompanist & solo artist. *Instrumental Works:* Second Coming; Star Journey; Four Episodes for Cello and Orchestra; Three Poems of Sylvia Plath. *Scores:* Opera/Ballet: The Tour Guide.

AITKEN, HUGH   ASCAP 1963
composer, teacher

b New York, NY, Sept 7, 24. Educ: Juilliard Sch Music, BS, 49, MS(comp), 50; studied with Vincent Persichetti, Bernard Wagenaar & Robert Ward. Taught theory & literature courses, Juilliard Sch Music, 50-70. Comns: Nat Endowment for Arts; E S Coolidge Found, Library Congress; W W Naumburg Found; Jose Limon Dance Co; Concord String Quartet; NY Fest Orch; White Mountains Fest Orch; NY Chamber Soloists. Prof music, William Paterson Col NJ. *Instrumental Works:* Tromba (quintet, trumpet & string quartet); Piano Fantasy; Partita for String Quartet and Orchestra; unaccompanied works for oboe, clarinet, bassoon, trumpet, trombone, violin, viola, cello & bass. *Songs & Instrumental Works:* Five Solo Cantatas. *Scores:* Chamber Opera: Fables.

AKERS, DORIS
composer, author, singer

b Brookfield, Mo, May 21, 22. Started with children's choir at age 12, Kirksville, Mo. Played piano for church, Colo & Mont. Singer in Calif; country tours. Writer, Manna Music. Recording artist. Awards: Female Gospel Singer of Yr; Most Outstanding Album, RCA Victor; Best Female Vocalist, NEFF & Best Vocal Album, Acad Recording Arts Relig Div. *Songs:* Sweet Jesus; I Cannot Fail the Lord; Lead Me, Guide Me; I Was There When the Spirit Came; Sweet, Sweet Spirit (Song of Yr, Gospel West Award) & many more. *Albums:* Sing Praises Unto the Lord; Forever Faithful; Sweet, Sweet Spirit.

AKERS, HOWARD ESTABROOK (ARCHIE MASTERS)   ASCAP 1955
composer, author, educator

b Laddonia, Mo, July 17, 13. Educ: Curtis Inst Music, Ill; Wesleyan Univ; Murray State Col; Millikin Univ; Berkshire Music Ctr; Chicago Musical Col; BMus, MMus, Hon DMusA; studied with Fritz Reiner, Hugh Ross, Marcel Tabeaten, Russell Harvey, Charles Gerhard, Rudolph Ganz, Hans Rosenwald. Educator, Petersburg Schs, Ill; Los Angeles Sch Syst, Seattle City Schs, Seattle Pacific Univ & Springfield Col Music & Allied Arts, Ill; head music dept Union Col, Ky; prof music, Millikin Univ, Ill. Served in USMC. Ed, Carl Fischer, Inc, NY, 11 yrs; visiting prof at var univs, Wash; lectr, guest cond, clinician & free-lance arr. Mem, Long Beach Municipal Board, Calif. Chief Collab: Al

Wright. *Instrumental Works:* Little Classic Suite; Allegro, Adagio, and Alleluia; March for a Festival; El Alamo; The Showman; In Prospect Park; Berkshire Hills; Normandy; Arrangements: The Whistler and His Dog; Battle Hymn of the Republic; On the Esplanade.

AKIYOSHI, TOSHIKO   ASCAP 1958
composer, author, arranger

b Darien, Manchuria, Dec 12, 29. Educ: Berkelee Sch Music, scholarship, studied Schillinger theory & comp, 56. Began piano training at age 6. Jazz pianist with Latin band, pit orch, string orch & jazz groups throughout Japan; formed own group, 52. Recording artist in US & Japan; also produced albums in Japan. Performed with several Japanese symph orchs, early 60's; also at jazz festivals. Co-leader of Personal Aspect Quartet, Japan's Expo 70. Formed & co-led own big band, 73; band placed first in Talent Deserving Wider Recognition category, Down Beat Critic's Poll, 76; band also voted first in Big Jazz Band category, Down Beat Readers' Poll, 78 & 79. Named one of Mademoiselle's top ten women of yr for comp "A Jazz Suite for String Orchestra"; placed first in arr category, Down Beat Reader's Poll, 78 & 79. *Songs & Instrumental Works:* Tuning Up; Henpecked Old Man; Sumie; Village; Children in the Temple Ground; Opus No Zero; Soliloquy; Lazy Day; Elegy; The First Night; Mobil; Quadrille, Anyone?; American Ballad; I Ain't Gonna Ask No More; Interlude; Kogun; Memory; Notorious Tourist From the East; Strive for Jive; Since Perry/Yet Another Tear; Studio "J"; Tales of a Courtesan; Transcience; Road Time Shuffle; Warning! Success May Be Hazardous to Your Health; Minamata; Yellow Is Mellow; Deracinated Flower; March of the Tadpoles. *Albums:* Long Yellow Road (named Best Jazz Album of Yr, Stereo Review, 76); Insights (voted Jazz Album of Yr in Japan, 76; won Record of Yr, Down Beat Critic's Poll, 78).

AKST, HARRY   ASCAP 1922
composer, pianist, conductor

b New York, NY, Aug 15, 1894; d Hollywood, Calif, Mar, 31, 63. Educ: Pub schs. While in grade sch, gave piano recital at Mendelssohn Hall. Organized orch bureau; accompanist to Nora Bayes, 4 yrs. USA, World War I, Camp Upton, NJ. Assoc with Irving Berlin; led dance band, nightclubs. World War II, toured overseas as accompanist to Al Jolson. Chief Collabrs: Benny Davis, Sam Lewis, Joe Young, Bert Kalmar, Grant Clarke, Al Jolson, Gus Kahn, Richard Whiting, Lew Brown. *Songs:* Laddie Boy; Home Again Blues; You Don't Need Wine to Have a Wonderful Time; A Smile Will Go a Long, Long, Way; Hello, Hello; Dinah; Baby Face; Guilty; Am I Blue?; Birmingham Bertha; There's Nothing Too Good for My Baby; I'm the Medicine Man for the Blues; All My Love; Taking Care of You; Dearest, I Love You; No Sad Songs for Me; The Egg and I; Anema e Core; There's a Little White House; Remember Mother's Day; On With the Dance; Palmy Days; The Kid from Spain; Stand Up and Cheer; The Music Goes Round. *Scores:* Bway shows: Cotton Club Revue; Calling All Stars; Artists and Models of 1927.

AKST, RUTH FREED (PATTY FISHER)   ASCAP 1954
composer, author

b Vancouver, BC. Sister of Arthur, Ralph & Walter Freed. Educ: Univ Wash, first violinist in univ orch. As child gave violin concerts, Seattle, Wash. Mem, Los Angeles Women's Symph Orch. Led singing & instrumental trio on radio & Pasadena Playhouse. Chief Collabrs: David Saxon, Geoff Clarkson, Ernest Gold, Bonnie Lake, Fred Spielman, Walter Jurinan. *Songs:* Graduation Dance; An Old Love Letter; Rendezvous; Perhaps; Does It Show?; Tunnel of Love; Vaya-Vaya; Bull Run; Wall to Wall Heartaches; On and On; Impossible; Apollo; Pretty Patricia; My Heart Is an Island; Make a Circle; Empty Rooms; I'm the Man; Mr Heartbreak; Miss Lonelyheart; Betwixt and Between; The Next Time Around.

ALAGNA, MATTHEW   ASCAP 1955
composer, pianist, trumpeter

b Detroit, Mich, Feb 27, 20; d Chicago, Ill, May 14, 65. Educ: High sch. Trumpeter in dance bands incl Al Trace, Tommy Reed & Buddy Morrow. Arr & pianist for Ralph Marterie orch; later, Mercury Records. *Songs & Instrumental Works:* Carla; Trumpet and a Prayer; Travel At Your Own Risk; Dream Serenade; Nite Cap; Trumpet Soliloquy; Dry Martini With an Olive.

ALAYU, PEDRO SALUSTIANO   ASCAP 1967
composer, author, singer

b Solano, Philippines, Aug 1, 04. Educ: Solano Pub Sch; Provincial High Sch, Bayombong, Philippines; Hyde Park High Sch, grad, 26; Crane Jr Col; studied harmony with Gomer Jones. Singer, Univ Chicago choir & Englewood High Sch, Chicago. Violinist with Beverly Symph. Organized USN Band, Astoria, Ore. With var orchs throughout US. Chief Collabrs: Eddie K Ballantine; Alfred P Jason; Leon Stein; William H Whitaker. *Songs & Instrumental Works:* Carry On to Victory; In God We Trust; One and All Americans; American Colonial Village (minuet); Spanish Colonial Village (jota); Mississippi Valley (waltz); Great Fire 1871; Nena (waltz); Please Give Me Back My Kisses (waltz); Chicago (march).

ALBERS, JOHN KENNETH   ASCAP 1959
composer, singer, arranger

b Woodbury, NJ, Dec 10, 24. Educ: Philadelphia Cons of Music. With USA

Band, World War II. Trumpeter & violist, nightclub orchs; with vocal group The Stuarts. Joined group Four Freshman as trumpeter, bass violist & arr. Chief Collabr: Ross Barbour. *Songs:* Chelsea Bridge; Love Lost; First Affair.

ALBERT, CAROLYN FAYE ASCAP 1979
author, playwright, librettist
b Brooklyn, NY, Nov 11, 37. Educ: James Monroe High Sch; Queens Col, BA, 57; Puerto Rican Travelling Theater Playwrights' Unit with Fred Hudson; Broadcast Music Inc Librettists' Workshop with Lehman Engel; Brooklyn Col, MFA, studied with Jack Gelber. Contributing ed, Songwriter Mag; author of articles for Plays Mag. Playwright; performed at Courtyard Playhouse & Downstage Theater. Co-lyricist of 8 songs, "Learning About Health and Safety." Theater & film reviewer, Lower Manhattan News/Pennysaver, Brooklyn Heights Press & Brooklyn Jour. Charter mem, Am Guild of Authors & Comp Popshop. Chief Collabrs: Alan Greene, Laura Manning, Hy Glaser, Gary William Friedman. *Songs:* Lyrics: Soapy Bubbles; Puppy Dog, Puppy Dog; Stay Out of That Empty Building; Climbing; Milk, Bread, Fruit, Cheese, Greens, Eggs, Meat.

ALBERT, MARTIN
See Milkey, Edward T

ALBERT, STEPHEN JOEL
composer
b New York, NY, Feb 6, 41. Educ: Eastman Sch Music, 58-60; Philadelphia Musical Acad, BM, 62; Univ Pa, fall semester, 63; studied with Elie Siegmeister, 56-58, Darius Milhaud, summer 58, Bernard Rogers, 59-60, Joseph Castaldo, 60-62 & George Rochberg, fall 63. Teacher, Philadelphia Musical Acad, 68-70, Stanford Univ, 70-71 & Smith Col, 74-76. Performer, many orchs, symph & insts. Grants/Prizes: Columbia Bearnes Prize, 62; MacDowell fels, 64; Huntington Hartford fel, 64-65; Martha Baird Rockefeller grants, 65; Rome Prize, 65-67; Ford Found CMP grant, 67-68; Guggenheim Found grants, 67-68 & 78-79; Fromm Found/Berkshire Music Festival Comn joint grant, 74-75; Nat Endowment for Arts grant, 77-78; Martha Baird Rockefeller & Alice Ditson grants for recording, 79; ASCAP Awards. *Songs & Instrumental Works:* Illuminations (brass, pianos, harps & perc); Supernatural Songs (soprano & chamber orch); Imitations (string quartet); Winter Songs (tenor & orch); Wedding Songs (soprano & piano); Bacchae (narrator, chorus & orch); Wolf Time (soprano, chamber orch & amplification, comn by Seattle Players, Univ Wash); Leaves From the Golden Notebook (orch, comn by Chicago Symph); Cathedral Music: Concerto for Four Quartets; Voices Within (orch & pit band, comn by Berkshire Music Festival & Fromm Found); To Wake the Dead (soprano, flute, clarinet, violin, cello & piano); Music From the Stone Harp (seven players).

ALBERT, THOMAS RUSSEL ASCAP 1969
composer, teacher
b Lebanon, Pa, Dec 14, 48. Educ: Atlantic Christian Col, AB, 70, studied comp with William Duckworth; Univ Ill, MMus, 72, DMA, 74, studied comp with Ben Johnston. Teacher theory, Univ Ill, 71-74; assoc prof comp & theory, cond, New Music Ens & chmn, Theory Div, Shenandoah Col & Cons Music, 74- Chief Collabrs: Linde Hayen Herman; Susan Purinton. *Songs & Instrumental Works:* Ancren Chronicles (women's chorus, harp & perc); A Maze (With Grace); . . . And It Comes Out Here; Winter Monarch. *Scores:* Opera: Lizbeth (one act, NEA grant, 76).

ALBERTI, BOB ASCAP 1965
composer, arranger
b Brooklyn, NY, Dec 1, 34. Educ: Fort Hamilton High Sch, Brooklyn, grad, 51; studied piano with Teddy Wilson. Pianist & arr, Charlie Spivak, Louis Prima & Jerry Gray Orchs, 52-55. To Los Angeles, 60; comp & arr for TV. Appeared, "Hollywood Palace," 64-70. Musical dir, var shows incl "Name That Tune," 74-75 & "The Shari Lewis Show," 75-76. Comp, var NBC-TV shows incl "Hizzonner," 79, "Highcliffe Manor," 79 & "The Bob Hope Show," 72-

ALBERTINI, ALBERT NICHOLAS (AL ALBERTS) ASCAP 1953
composer, author, singer
b Philadelphia, Pa, Aug 10, 22. Educ: Drexel Elem Sch; Vare Jr High Sch; South Philadelphia High Sch; Granoff Sch Music; Temple Univ. Organized and sang lead with group, Four Aces. First recording, 51. Appeared on TV and stage, incl London Palladium. Host, TV variety show, "Al Alberts Showcase," WPVI, Philadelphia. *Songs:* Try a Little Love; God's Greatest Gift; Take My Heart; Music: Blue O'Clock in the Morning; Lyrics: Tell Me Why; Philadelphia, My Home Town; I Am a Sick American; Be Still My Heart; Honey in the Horn; Tonight Must Last Forever.

ALBERTS, AL
See Albertini, Albert Nicholas

ALBIN, PETER SCOTT ASCAP 1968
composer, author, electric bassist
b San Francisco, Calif, June 6, 44. Educ: Col of San Mateo; San Francisco State Univ. Folk musician; played bass in Big Brother & Holding Co; recording artist for Mainstream Records, Columbia Records & Vanguard Records; performing

artist on TV, nightclubs & major concert halls. *Songs:* Light Is Faster Than Sound; Caterpillar Song; Roadblock; Blindman.

ALBRECHT, ELMER ASCAP 1942
composer, pianist, organist
b Chicago, Ill, June 21, 01; d Chicago, Ill, Feb 28, 59. Educ: Pub schs; pvt piano study. Organist, pianist, theatres & orchs; led own band. *Songs:* Elmer's Tune; How Can I Live Without You? How Was I to Know?; Sea Shells on the Shore; Take the Whole Darn Farm; You're in It-I'm in It Too; Don't Ever Darken My Door; Elmer Done It Again; Memories of an Old Bouquet.

ALBRIGHT, WILLIAM H ASCAP 1967
composer, organist
b Gary, Ind, Oct 20, 44. Educ: Univ Mich, MM & DMA, 70; studied with George Rochberg, Tanglewood, 66 & Olivier Messiaen, Paris Cons, 68-69. Writer, keyboard, chamber & theater music. Comn numerous works for organ. Performer of early jazz styles for piano. *Instrumental Works:* Five Chromatic Dances; Stipendium Peccati; An Alleluia Super-Round; Father We Thank Thee (hymn); Organ Books I, II, III; Halo; King of Instruments; Doo-Dah; Jericho; Seven Deadly Sins; Chichester Mass; Take That; Danse Macabre; Marginal Worlds; Alliance; The Dream Rags; Sweet Sixteenths; Grand Sonata in Rag; Foils; Caroms; Pneuma; Juba; Pianoagogo; Chorale-Partita. *Scores:* Opera/Ballet: Cross of Gold.

ALDEN, JOHN W ASCAP 1941
composer, teacher
b Pueblo, Colo, Mar 13, 1895; d. Educ: Berlin Hochschule, studied with Anton Wirth, Alexander Fiedelman, Hollander; Univ Wash. Cond, Montrose Cons, Chicago, 15-21. High sch teacher, Wash, 30 yrs; grocer, Yakima, Wash. *Songs:* Moonlight and You; Cloudy Skies; Stars; It Seems Too Good to Be True; La Veeda; If Winter Comes.

ALDEN, JOSEPH REED ASCAP 1943
composer, author
b Grand Rapids, Mich, July 28, 1886; d Grand Rapids, Mich, Sept 18, 51. Educ: Univ Mich, BA; studied music with Francis Mills. Songwriter, vaudeville & stage scores. *Songs:* Sleepy Time Gal; After the Matinee; Girl in Her First Long Gown; Listen in on Lester; Foolish Tears; Sandra; Stick in the Mud; You Leave Me Speechless; Yank on the Strings of My Heart.

ALDEN, TESSIE R
See Tessier, Albert Denis

ALDRICH, DAVID BRENT ASCAP 1978
composer
b Covington, Ky, Aug 30, 51. Educ: Cincinnati Cons Music; Univ Ky. Began playing piano at age 12. Began arr in studios in Midwest at age 21. Played Jazz piano with trio or quartet all over country. Professional comp, orch, jazz orch, theatre, films & var small ens. Chief Collabrs: Stephen Currens, David Richmond, Bob Hall, Edward Gorey. *Scores:* Bway: Gorey Stories; Off Bway: The Passion of Dracula (San Francisco).

ALDRIDGE, DONALD RAY ASCAP 1969
composer, author, singer
b Lancaster, Calif, Apr 24, 47. Educ: High sch; Antelope Valley Jr Col. Began music writing while in high sch. With Johnny Otis, Don Van Vliet & Bill Masters. Solo writer, 67-, incl country & pop music & gospel songs for Kathie Lee Johnson & the Archers, 71. *Songs:* It Wouldn't Be Enough; More (So Much More); With Every Breath I Take; Only His Love.

ALENICK, SUSAN J ASCAP 1978
author
b New York, NY, May 16, 39. Educ: Univ Vt, BA, MA; Exeter Col, Oxford. Lyricist, film "The Angel Has Fallen." Chief Collabrs: Jim Roberge, Herb Oscar Anderson. *Songs:* Lyrics: Silk and Satin; Fire In My Soul; Fallen Angel; Ice on the Mountain; Give Us a Time for Love; Spaces.

ALEXANDER, JEFF ASCAP 1952
composer, author
b Seattle, Wash, July 2, 10. Educ: Becker Inst of Music, Portland Ore; studied with Edmund Ross, Los Angeles, Joseph Schillinger, New York. Comp, arr & choral dir, CBS staff, New York, incl Andre Kostelanetz & Leopold Stokowski; scorewriter & conductor for var motion pictures, var TV series, features, specials & commercials. Chief Collabrs: Larry Orenstein, Jack Brooks, Sammy Cahn. *Songs:* Soothe My Lonely Heart; Lonely Gal, Lonely Guy; Why Can't It Be Christmas; 14 Art Songs; Music: Trouble Man; Ballad for Beatnicks; The Wings of Eagles. *Instrumental Works:* Papa's People..Papa's Places (symph); Two Preludes for Flute and String Quartette; Divertimento for Viola and Piano; The Ground Bass for Piano and String Quartette. *Scores:* Ballet: Partage (comn by Los Angeles Ballet Asn); Grass Roots—A Country Ballet; Films: Escape From Fort Bravo; The Tender Trap; The Sheepman; The George Raft Story; The Rounders; Jailhouse Rock; Why Man Creates (Acad Award, Best Documentary, Cindy Award, Best Score); Support Your Local Sheriff; Dirty Dingus Magee; TV Series: The Lieutenant; Please Don't Eat the Daisies; Julia;

Daughters of Josh McCabe; Kat Bliss and the Ticker Tape Kid; Wild Wild West Revivisted; More Wild Wild West. *Albums:* Color (Frank Sinatra conducting); Music to Be Murdered By (Alfred Hitchcock narrating).

ALEXANDER, JOSEF ASCAP 1952
composer, pianist, conductor
b Boston, Mass, May 15, 10. Educ: New Eng Cons Music, dipl, postgrad artist's degree, spec honors; Harvard Univ, AB(cum laude), AM, John Knowles Paine traveling fel, Europe, Elkan Naumberg fel, studied with Walter Piston, Edward Burlingamc Hill, Hugo Leichtentritt. Concert pianist & cond; concertized in Boston & US; pianist & lectr, Boston Col Summer Inst. Rec'd grants & awards, incl Fulbright fel, Finland, Bernard Ravitch Found Prize, 2 Harvey Gaul (Pittsburgh) Awards, Int Humanities Found in Washington, NEA, Am Music Ctr, grants. Prof music, Brooklyn Col, 42- Author, "Book Reviews," Glanville Press. *Songs & Instrumental Works:* Epitaphs for Orchestra; Williamsburg (suite for orch); Clockwork (Symphony No 1, string orch); Symphony No 2; Symphony No 3; Symphony No 4; Processional (band); Campus Suite (band); Salute to the Whole World (narrator & orch); Concertino for Trumpet and String Orchestra; Duo Concertante for String Orchestra and Percussion; Songs for Eve (song cycle for soprano, English horn, harp, violin & cello); Gitanjali (song cycle for soprano, harpsichord, 5 perc instruments); Three Ludes for Harp; Three Diversion for Timpani(5) and Piano; Aspects of Love (song cycle for soprano, flute or piccolo, clarinet or bass clarinet, violin, cello & piano); Four for Five (brass quintet); Sonata for Trombone and Piano; Trinity (brass & perc); Celebrations (overture, orch); Quiet Music (strings); Divertimento for Three Winds; Andante and Allegro for Violin and Piano; Sonata for Clarinet and Piano; Festivities (five brass & organ); Bagatelles for Piano; Interplay for Four French Horns; Sonata for Horn in F and Piano.

ALEXANDER, LARRY ASCAP 1965
author
b Bronx, NY, July 21, 39. Educ: City Col, New York, BA. Songwriter, off-Bway show "Tour de Four" & nightclub act "Just for Openers." Chief Collabr: Billy Goldenberg. *Songs:* Shouldn't There Be Lightning?; Take You for Granted. *Scores:* Stage show: The Cooperative Way.

ALEXANDER, NICK
See Kokinacis, Alexander

ALEXANDER, ROBIN LYNN ASCAP 1976
composer, author, singer
b New York, NY, June 10, 51. Educ: Studied voice with David Sorin Collyer; Hewlett High Sch; studied solfegio with Maurice Finnel. Lead in summer stock show "Walden Pond," 70; played guitar in clubs, 70-72; sang title song for ABC show "Over F," 74; wrote song & performed in film "Skateboard"; sang Ford & Legend City commercial. Chief Collabrs: David White, Eddie Leonetti. *Songs:* You Know Where My Weakness Lies; Stay Anyway. *Scores:* Film/TV: Point of No Return.

ALEXANDER, VAN ASCAP 1941
composer, author, arranger
b New York, NY, May 2, 15. Educ: George Washington High Sch; Columbia Univ; studied with Otto Cesana, NY & Mario Castelnuovo-Tedesco, Calif. Arr for Chick Webb, Paul Whiteman, Benny Goodman, Les Brown & many others. Formed own orch, 38. Played on radio, theatres & one night stands. Recorded for Bluebird, Victor & Varsity Labels. Scored 22 motion pictures & numerous TV segments. Past pres, Los Angeles Chap of Nat Acad Recording Arts & Sci. Author, "First Chart," a learning method for novice arr. Three time Emmy nominee. Chief arr, Dean Martin Shows; cond-comp, NBC 50th Anniversary Show. Chief Collabrs: Ella Fitzgerald, Ned Washington, Bobby Troup, Charles Tobias. *Songs:* Music: A Tisket a Taskit; Gotta Pebble in My Shoe; I'll Close My Eyes. *Instrumental Works:* The 3 B's for Percussion; Blues in Two's; Tappin' on the Trap. *Scores:* Film/TV: Hazel; I Saw What You Did; Baby Face Nelson; Straight-Jacket; The Big Operator; Andy Hardy Comes Home.

ALFONSO, DON ASCAP 1950
composer
b Italy, May 13, 1899. Educ: Pvt schs, Rio de Janiero; pvt music study. To US, 21, citizen, 24. Formed own orch; introduced samba to US. *Songs:* Batucada; O Carousel; Papa Knows; Dorothea; Brazilian Rhapsody.

ALFORD, DELTON L ASCAP 1978
composer, conductor, arranger
b Lakeland, Fla, Aug 18, 38. Educ: Lee Col, 56-58; Univ Tenn, Chattanooga, BM, 59; Fla State Univ, MME, 60, PhD, 65. Mem music fac, vpres & dean, Lee Col. Cond of Lee Singers, 63-78; made 8 concert tours of Europe. Cond/clinician of choral music for cols & high schs; chorus cond for Chattanooga Symph, 15 yrs. Has written & arr music for TV. Music dir for "Forward in Faith," radio & TV. Producer & arr of relig recordings. Chief Collabr: Myrna McSwain Alford (wife). *Songs:* Worthy Is Our God; Now I'm Free; Winner's Circle; See His Glory (cantata); Lyrics: In the Presence.

ALFRED, ROY ASCAP 1948
composer, author
b New York, NY, May 14, 16. Educ: Univ Mo. Song writer, Jour Sch Musical, Univ Mo. Writer & master of ceremonies for traveling USA show "Sausage Boys", WW II. Writer of spec material for Jackie Gleason, Art Carney, Hildegarde, Paul Winchell, Beatrice Kaye, Janet Blair & David Wayne. Pop song writer. Chief Collabrs: Marvin Fisher, Al Frisch, Paul Vance, Wally Gold. *Songs:* I've Got News for You; Promise Her Anything; Hooray for Santa Claus (theme song); The Garbage Can Goes Clang; Song of the Raccoons; Lyrics: The Huckle Buck; The Rock and Roll Waltz; Congratulations to Someone; Wisdom of a Fool; The Late, Late Show; A Straw Hat and a Cane; The Best Man; Destination Moon; That's It, I Quit; Let's Lock the Door; She Can't Find Her Keys; Kee-Mo Ky-Mo; Fla-Ga-La-Pa; Lean Baby; Then Suddenly Love; Take Me Tonight; The Show Must Go On; Think of the Good Times; What Became of Love.

ALIN, MORRIS (MORRIE ALLEN) ASCAP 1959
author
b Orel, Russia, July 15, 05. Educ: City Col New York, dipl grad accountancy. Wrote for movie industry, 24-33, 37-67; author, 69-79. Chief Collabrs: Leonard Whitcup, Teri Joseforits, Don Baker, Phil Sheer, Newt Oliphant. *Songs:* Lyrics: Rhumba Swing; Sha Sha Sha; Sweet Guy; You Are My Star; John Fitzgerald Kennedy; It Takes Two to Make Love.

ALLAN, ESTHER ASCAP 1971
composer, concert pianist-organist
b Suvalke, Poland, Apr 28, 14. Educ: London Royal Acad Music, music degree piano, 27; Scottish Nat Acad Music, music degree, grad level, 30. Moved to US, 30; grad high sch, 31. Worked for local radio station one yr; songwriter for music co. Played with all girl band; played on local radio program. Comp & recorded two albums with 30 mems of Detroit Symph, 70 & 72. *Instrumental Works:* Piano & Orch: Ocean Rhapsody; Romantic Concerto; Meditation; Norman Concerto; Trailing; Summer Waltz; Enchantment; Interlude; Bethie's Theme; Freddie's Running; Piano: Nancy's Waltz; Karen's Butterflies; Piano & Harp: Autumn Nocturne.

ALLAN, LEWIS (ABEL MEEROPOL) ASCAP 1945
composer, author
b New York, NY. Educ: City Col New York, BA; Harvard Univ, MA. Writer for theatre, radio, TV & films. Instr English & literature. Chief Collabrs: Robert Kurka, Elie Siegmeister. *Songs:* The House I Live In (Acad Award-winning short, 45); Strange Fruit; Apples, Peaches and Cherries. *Scores:* Operas: The Good Soldier Schweik; Darling Corie; Malady of Love; The Soldier; The Town Crier (cantata; Nat 5 Arts Award).

ALLAN, MIKE
See Gaskin, Michael Allan

ALLANBROOK, DOUGLAS PHILLIPS ASCAP 1968
composer
b Melrose, Mass, Apr 1, 21. Educ: Melrose High Sch, 38; Harvard Univ, BA, 48; studied with Nadia Boulanger & Piston. Music writer, incl harpsichord, piano & brass quintet, 33- USA infantry sgt, World War II, 42-45. Taught, St John's Col, 52- Works performed by Nat Symph, Oklahoma City Symph, Munich, Berlin & Baden Baden Orchs. Traveling Fel, Harvard Univ; Fulbright Fel; Ford Found comn. *Instrumental Works:* Four Orchestral Landscapes (Symphony No 3); Forty Changes (piano); Twelve Preludes for All Seasons (piano); Night and Morning Music (brass quintet); Five Studies in Black and White (harpsichord); Symphony for Brass Quintet and Orchestra No 5; Four String Quartets. *Songs & Instrumental Works:* Psalms 130 and 131 (chorus, organ). *Scores:* Opera: Nightmare Abbey; Ethan Frome.

ALLEN, ALLEN DAVID ASCAP 1978
composer, author, producer
b San Francisco, Calif, Aug 26, 36. Lyricist & music writer for musical jingles incl "Don't Cook Tonight, Call Chicken Delight," then popular songs, films & TV scores. *Songs:* Steep Grade Ahead; Danny and the Mermaid (theme song); Christmas Day; Lyrics: Just Married; Music: This Is the Life (main title). *Scores:* Stableboy's Christmas; Miles to Go; The Clones.

ALLEN, BARCLAY ASCAP 1948
composer, conductor, pianist
b Denver, Colo, Sept 27, 18; d. Educ: Pub sch; studied music with mother. Pianist in nightclubs & hotels throughout US, then in Freddy Martin Orch. Music dir for radio. *Songs & Instrumental Works:* Cumana; The New Look; It Began in Havana; Barclay's Boogie; Beginner's Boogie.

ALLEN, CHARLES
See DeVito, Albert Kenneth

ALLEN, DAVID BLISS ASCAP 1966
composer, author
b Moulmien, Burma, Sept 16, 39. Educ: Mt Kisco High Sch, NY; Univ Nebr, Omaha, BGS; La Salle Extension Univ, LLB, 70. Actor, Moral Re-Armament musical productions & dramas, 50-64; song writer, Rajmohan Gandhi's "March

on Wheels," India, 63; writer & producer musical "Up With People," 65-66. USA office, Vietnam, 67-69; var political assignments, Ore, 70-74. Exec, Weyerhaeuser Co, 74-; mgr pub affairs, Portland, 80- Chief Collabrs: Paul Colwell Jr, Herbert Allen. *Songs:* Which Way America?; The Ballad of Joan of Arc; Colorado; Design for Dedication; Sing-out Express; How Do Wars Begin?; The Monkey and the Crow.

ALLEN, DICK
See Markowitz, Richard Allen

ALLEN, HENRY, JR (RED)   ASCAP 1958
composer, conductor, singer
b Algiers, La, Jan 7, 08; d New York, NY, Apr 17, 67. Trumpeter in var orchs incl George Lewis, John Handy, Fate Marable, Fats Pinchon, King Oliver, Luis Russell, Fletcher Henderson & Louis Armstrong. Formed own sextet; mem, house band, Cafe Metropole. New York; made many records & toured Europe with Kid Ory. *Songs & Instrumental Works:* Siesta At the Fiesta; Red Jump; Pleasing Paul; Algiers Stomp; Get the Mop; Ride, Red, Ride.

ALLEN, HERBERT ETHAN   ASCAP 1961
author, musical director
b Seattle, Wash, July 27, 29. Educ: Lincoln High Sch; studied piano with John Hopper, 44-47, cond with Carl Pitzer, 47, oboe with Whitney Tustin, 47, orchestration with William Leonard Reed, Eng & vocal study with G M Fraser, Scotland, 50-56. Studied language, produced 3 musicals, Italy, 50-53. Accompanist, Muriel Smith, contralto. Accompanist & asst cond choral productions, Britain's Fest Hall, 54 & 55. Musical dir, "Up With People," 65. Cond & dir music, "Super Bowl X," also 3 nat TV productions. Produced music, "Super Bowl XIII." Chief Collabrs: Paul Colwell, Ralph Colwell, Ken Ashby. *Songs:* Music: Where the Roads Come Together; We Are Many, We Are One; Till Everyone is Home; There's Gonna Be Another Day; Moon Rider.

ALLEN, JERRY
See Atinsky, Jerry

ALLEN, LANNY   ASCAP 1973
composer, director, vocalist
b Henryetta, Okla, Aug 7, 42. Educ: Duncan High Sch; Okla Baptist Univ, BMus(voice); vocal study with Joe Long, James McKinney, theory & comp with Warren M Angeu, Donald Packard. Chief Collabr: Bob Oldenburg. *Songs:* Calvary's Mountain (cantata); Music: Blessings (cantata); Changes; It Is Well (anthem); Since Jesus Came Into My Heart (anthem). *Instrumental Works:* Bell, Brass, Strings and Things; Ring the Good News (handbell collection).

ALLEN, LAURI
See DelGrosso, Jean Ann

ALLEN, MORRIE
See Alin, Morris

ALLEN, RICHARD GOULD   ASCAP 1959
composer, author, actor
b Kansas City, Mo, Sept 12, 24. Educ: Pasadena City Col, AA; Univ Southern Calif, BA, 53, studied music with Ingolf Dahl. Wrote songs for Rehearsal Club Revue, NY, 54 & two other revues in Hollywood. Radio & TV producer, Young & Rubicam, NY & Hollywood, 18 yrs. Record producer, World Harvest Records. Acted in several movies incl, "Hooper" for Warner Bros. Served in WW II & Korean War. Chief Collabrs: Bob Moline, Geoff Clarkson, Peter Daniels. *Songs:* I Still Believe in You; Love Not Subject to Change; Lyrics: You Are Now; Thank You Father; Touch Me Softly.

ALLEN, ROBERT   ASCAP 1950
composer, author, producer
b Troy, NY, Feb 5, 27. Pianist, arr & cond for Perry Como, Peter Lind Hayes, Arthur Godfrey; also for "Studio One" & "Playhouse 90." Wrote football march for Auburn Col. Created & produced spec material for Jimmy Durante, Jack Benny Ziegfeld Theatre Show, Jane Morgan, Joel Gray & "Carol Burnett and Julie Andrews at Carnegie Hall." *Songs:* Home for the Holidays; You Alone; Chances Are; Moments to Remember; No, Not Much; Sing Along; Happy Anniversary; It's Not for Me to Say; Song for a Summer Night; You Are Never Far Away; A Very Special Love; Come to Me; My One and Only Heart; Who Needs You?; Meantime; Everybody Loves a Lover; I Never Felt More Like Falling in Love; Every Step of the Way; Can You Find It in Your Heart?; Teacher, Teacher; There's Only One of You; To Know You; I Can Do It; Groovin' on the Sunshine; Best Friend; Good Good Morning Day; Music: The Eyes of God; Christmas Spirit. *Scores:* Films: Happy Anniversary; Enchanted Island; Lizzie. *Albums:* 3 Billion Millionaires (UN Comn); Bob McGrath from Sesame Street; Three Ring Circus; An American Christmas Album.

ALLEN, ROBERT E   ASCAP 1960
b Minneapolis, Minn, Feb 1, 20. Educ: Central High Sch; studied comp with Frances Richter, Minneapolis & Kurt George Roger, New York. Coordr of Publ, Carl Fisher, Inc, New York. Ed, Franco Columbo, Inc, New York. *Instrumental Works:* Symphonic Movement; Quartet for Strings; Concerto for Piano and Orchestra; Sonata for Violin and Piano; Introduction and Allegro (cello & piano). *Songs & Instrumental Works:* The Ascension, Cantata (mezzo soprano,

chorus, trumpets, harp, timpani, organ); also numerous choral arrangements. *Scores:* Bway show: Cecily; One More Spring.

ALLEN, ROBERT I   ASCAP 1953
author
b New York, NY, Aug 29, 21. Educ: Col City of New York, BSS; NY Univ Law Sch, LLB, JD. Practiced law; head of electronics co. Writer, documentary "Minority By Choice." Songwriter for var films. Chief Collabrs: Joseph Meyers, Arthur Kent, Phil Springer, Roberto Carlos, Tony Renis, John Benson Brooks, Mark Fredericks. *Songs:* Little Sister; Lyrics: The Greatest Performance of My Life; Tonight I'll Say a Prayer; Son of a Travelin' Man; It Takes Too Long (to Learn to Live Alone); Dancing on My Toes; Love, I Think; When Will the Killing End; New York Scene.

ALLEN, STEVE   ASCAP 1951
composer, author, actor
b New York, NY, Dec 26, 21. Educ: Pub schs; Ariz State Teachers Col. Traveled throughout US with parents, Belle Montrose & Billy Allen, vaudeville team. Radio announcer, Phoenix; radio comedy prog, Hollywood. To NY, 50; with CBS, 4 yrs, then host NBC-TV "Tonight" show, later "The Steve Allen Show" & prog over Westinghouse TV network, also " Meeting of Minds," PBS Network. Has made many records as pianist. Acted in Bway play "The Pink Elephant" & film "The Benny Goodman Story" (title role). Comedian. Author "Bop Fables", "The Funnymen", "Wry on the Rocks", "Fourteen for Tonight", "Not All Your Laughter, Not All Your Tears", "Letter to a Conservative" & "Ripoff." Autobiography "Mark It and Strike It." *Songs:* An Old Piano Plays the Blues; Meet Me Where They Play the Blues; This Could Be the Start of Something; Pretend You Don't See Her; South Rampart Street Parade; Impossible; Oh, What a Night for Love; Tonight; Just Stay a Little While; Playing the Field; Spring in Main; Gravy Waltz; Cutie Pants; Film title songs: Picnic; Houseboat; On the Beach; Sleeping Beauty; Bell, Book and Candle. *Scores:* TV: The Bachelor (Sylvania Award).

ALLEN, WILLIAM CLYDE, JR   ASCAP 1975
composer, author, conductor
b Los Angeles, Calif, Apr 20, 45. Educ: Los Angeles High Sch; Univ Calif, Los Angeles, BA, 66, MA, 67, PhD, 74; studied piano with Gladys Childress, coaching & accompanying with Natalie Limonick, harpsichord with Malcolm Hamilton, harp with Marjorie Call, conducting with Fritz Zweig, comp with Eugene Zador, electronic music with Paul Beaver; studied with Peter Schickele & Carlos Chavez. Cond, Los Angeles Youth Theatre, 64. Music dir, KFAC radio, 71- & Los Angeles Ballet. Producer, High Sch Music Bowl, KFAC. Producer & author, radio specials on Am musical heritage & life of Rudolf Friml. *Instrumental Works:* Orchestration: English Dance (Gigue) (by Tchaikovsky). *Scores:* Ballets: Terpsichore; Discomania.

ALLISON, JOHN A   ASCAP 1959
composer, author
b Des Moines, Iowa, Apr 27, 14. Educ: Occidental Col, Los Angeles, Calif. Second vpres, Occidental Life Insurance Co of Calif. *Songs:* Lilly's Lament; Barefoot Boy; Who's Gonna Walk Me.

ALLMAN, MICHAEL L (LEE)   ASCAP 1952
composer, author, musician
b Cincinnati, Ohio, Oct 9, 11. Educ: Cincinnati Cons Music; Los Angeles Cons Music. Performer & arr for var name bands, incl Jimmy Dorsey, Mitchell Ayres, Freddy Martin, Harry James & Horace Heidt. With USAAF Flying Band, Dayton, Ohio, 42-46. Writer, musical scores for films-TV, themes & incidental songs for motion pictures. Chief Collabrs: Robert M (Bob) Miketta, Lloyd Shaffer, Jaime Mendoza-Nava. *Songs:* I Go Crazy; Pee-Wee (The Christmas Tree); The Price You Pay; Lyrics: Next to the 'X' in Texas; Levee Blues; Goodnight America; Rock, Doc; Bayberry Candles; Fever Heat (title song); This Land; Smoke in the Wind (title song); The Sands of Time.

ALLTON, MINETTE   ASCAP 1951
composer, author
b Oakland, Calif, Apr 13, 16. Educ: Univ Calif. Designer; muralist. Chief Collabrs: Nat King Cole, Isham Jones, Buddy Collette, Herb Ellis, Bob Envoldsen. *Songs:* I Get Sentimental Over Nothing; Pink Shampoo; Melinda; Swan Song; Come to the Party; Emaline; Sweet Dreams.

ALLYN, MARILYN IONE   ASCAP 1977
composer, author, singer
b Bremerton, Wash, Feb 25, 46. Singer with George Jones; traveled on road with var other shows. Chief Collabrs: Joel Sonnier, Glenn Martin, Jr, Judy Ball. *Songs:* Don't Say Love; Never Say Never; Lyrics: Country Blues; First Time; Next Time.

ALMEIDA, EUMIRE DEODATO (EUMIR DEODATO)   ASCAP 1964
composer, author
b Rio de Janeiro, Brazil, June 21, 42. Educ: Self-taught on piano, music reading, writing & arr; Berklee Sch Music, correspondence course arr. Pianist with different groups, Brazil, 58-60, arr, cond & comp, 60-66; to US, 67; arr, cond & comp for many singers, 67-72; recorded & toured, 73-79; producer & recording artist, Warner Bros, 79- Chief Collabrs: Norman Gimbel, A C Jobim,

Ray Gilbert, Roberta Flack, Aretha Franklin, Frank Sinatra, Wes Montgomery. *Instrumental Works:* Rhapsody in Blue (arr). *Songs & Instrumental Works:* Also Sprach Zarathustra (arr); Super Strut; Whistle Bump. *Scores:* Film/TV: Onion Field; Being There.

ALMEIDA, JOHN KAMEAALOHA
composer, author, teacher

b Pauao Valley, Hawaii, Nov 28, 1897. Educ: Blind, self-taught. Songwriter, 18- Chief musician, Matson Navigation Co, on Hawaii-West Coast runs, 24-27. Substituted for Al Kealoha Perry in "Hawaii Calls," 38. Had network show "Island Serenade," for NBC-KGU; owned recording studio & own record label. Played for Prince Kuhio; songwriter, Hawaiian Nat Guard & Selective Services, 40. Toured Japan & mainland cities. Dorothy Kahanaui, Mumi Jones, Randy Oness & Pua Almeida transcribed work for copywriting & Mary Paukui transl songs from Hawaiian into Eng. *Songs:* Jesu Meke Kanaka Wai Wai; Green Rose; Holoholo Kaa; Kiss Me Love; Kuu Ipo Pua Rose; Lei Pua Keni Keni; Noho Pai Pai; Ahulili; Maile Swing; Wear a Lei; Aloha Week; Beautiful Mehealani Moon; Ka Anoi; Lei Loke O Kapunahou; Green Carnation; Aoia; Na Koa Kaulana O Hawaii; Ne'ene'e Mai; Ka Wai Ola Oka Lani.

ALMEIDA, LAURINDO   ASCAP 1951
composer, author, teacher

b Brazil, Sept 2, 17. Educ: Escola Nacional de Musica, Rio de Janeiro, Brazil. To US, 47. Featured jazz guitarist with Kenton Orch, Chicago Opera House & Carnegie Hall, 47-50. Comp, recording artist & in concert. Featured soloist with Modern Jazz Quartet in tours throughout world. Comp, film scores & performer of original works. Recipient, cert of appreciations, Am String Teacher's Asn, cert of hon, Achievement Recognition Inst, var awards from Down Beat & Playboy Mags, 13 nominations & 5 Grammy awards. *Songs:* O Cacador (The Hunter); Choro e Batuque; Caboclo Brasil. *Instrumental Works:* Lament in Tremolo Form (for Rocky); Pavana for Pancho; Brazilliance (Choro); Mystified; Staniana; Three Stories, incl Moon's Story, Story of Longing, Story of Inspiration; Baa-Too-Kee; Amor Flamenco; Serenata; Berimbau Carioca; Bossa Guitarr Folio, incl Autumn in Rio, Assucarado, Poema, Choro Melancolico, Sump'n for Bossa Lovers, Valse Avec Swing; Folio—Popular Brazilian Music; First Concerto for Guitar and Orchestra; Vistas de Los Angeles, incl North Hollywood, Sunset Boulevard, Latin Quarters, San Juan Capistrano, Beverly Hills, Harbor Freeway; Lobiana (guitar, orch); Brazilliance No 1; Discantus; Johnny Peddler; The Naked Sea Suite; Canon Per Quad; Latiniana (aquarelle of Brazillian & Argentinian music); Guitar Tutor (in 3 courses); Standard Guitar Method.

ALMOND, MARSHA RENEE   ASCAP 1978
composer, author

b Coushatta, La, May 25, 59. Sang in church & community functions; appeared 5 times on La Hayride in Shreveport. *Songs:* Memories for Daddy.

ALOMA, HAROLD DAVID   ASCAP 1945
composer, author, musician

b Honolulu, Hawaii, Jan 8, 08. Educ: High sch. Musician in dance orchs, incl Tommy Dorsey, played hotels & restaurants; had own band, 3yrs. Chief Collabrs: John Redmond, Charles King, Eddie White, Mack Wolfson, John Leal. *Songs & Instrumental Works:* Echoes of the South Pacific; Lohelani; Wihi Wihi Mai; Pretty Mauri Girl; Puanani; When It's Luau Time in Hawaii.

ALONI, AMINADAV   ASCAP 1970
composer

b Tel Aviv, Israel, Sept 14, 28. Educ: Haifa Inst Music; Los Angeles City Col; Juilliard; NY Univ. Pianist, concerts, records, movies & TV. Began comp, 66. Has done music for musicals, concerts, stage, choral music, commercials, TV & movies. Classical & pop musician; has 10 comn works.

ALPERSON, EDWARD LEE, JR   ASCAP 1955
composer

b Omaha, Nebr, Apr 3, 25. Educ: Bus sch, Beverly Hills, Calif; Univ Calif, Los Angeles. Worked in motion picture theatres while attending sch in NY & Conn. Started in film production, 45, assoc producer, 10 yrs. Began writing film scores & songs, 55. Started Fairlane Music Co, 59. Chief Collabrs: Jerry Winn, Dick Hughes, Paul Herrick, Raoul Kraushaar, Michael Carr. *Songs:* Music: Magnificent Matador; Love Plays the Strings of My Banjo; Angelita; Never Alone; Black Sunday; Calliope; Passing By; (I'm Gonna) Be By You; Bobbie; Dreamer; The One Finger Symphony; Pistolero; Rollin' River. *Scores:* Film/TV: Mohawk (title song); The Restless Breed (title song); September Storm; Courage of Black Beauty (title song).

ALPERT, DAVID A   ASCAP 1963
songwriter, musician

b Los Angeles, Calif, Mar 2, 29. Educ: Fairfax High Sch, Los Angeles; Los Angeles City Col, AA; Univ Southern Calif. Began with local clubs, 46; worked at Paramount, 20th Century Fox & RKO; free-lanced for several yrs; played with var orchs & TV. *Songs:* Music: Acapulco 1922; Wade in the Water; Bean Bag; For Carlos; Windsong.

ALPERT, HERB
musician

b Los Angeles, Calif, Mar 31, 35. Educ: Univ Southern Calif. Leader, trumpeter & arr music group, Tijuana Brass, 62-; co-owner & pres, A&M Record Co, 62- Named One of Top Artists on Campus, 68. Numerous recordings.

ALPERT, MILTON I (MICKEY)   ASCAP 1951
conductor, personal manager, agent

b Holliston, Mass, Apr 9, 04; d New York, NY, Sept 22, 65.

ALPERT, PAULINE   ASCAP 1953
composer, pianist, arranger

b New York, NY. Educ: Univ Rochester Eastman Sch of Music (scholarship). Jazz pianist, theatres, nightclubs, radio & TV throughout world. Performer, USA camps, World War II. Recording artist. *Songs:* Dream of a Doll; March of the Blues; Perils of Pauline; Ivory Tips; Piano Poker; Night of Romance; The Merry Minnow; Tut Tut; A Happy New Year to Love; Minding the Baby; A Million Stars.

ALTER, LOUIS   ASCAP 1929
composer

b Haverhill, Mass, June 18, 02. Educ: New Eng Cons. Succeeded George Gershwin as accompanist for Nora Bayes. World tour, 22. Song hits, 26-29, then to Hollywood. With film studios incl MGM, "Hollywood Revue", 20th Century-Fox, "Sing Baby Sing" & Paramount, "Trail of the Lonesome Pine"; Bway shows, "Ballyhoo", "Vanities", "Hold Your Horses" & "Sweet and Low." Recipient, Venice Int Film Festival Gold Medal, Outstanding Alumni Award, New Eng Cons, 80 & New Orleans "Hon Citizen" & key to city, 80. Chief Collabrs: Frank Loesser, Sid Mitchell, Oscar Hammerstein, Harold Adamson, Ed Delange. *Songs:* Music: Nina Never Knew; Circus; My Kinda Love; The Sky Fell Down; Stranger in the City. *Instrumental Works:* Manhattan Serenade; Manhattan Suite; Jewels From Cartier (orch suite). *Scores:* Bway shows: I'm One of God's Children; Overnight; Blue Shadows; Film/TV: Do You Know What It Means to Miss New Orleans; Twilight on the Trail; Melody from the Sky (Acad Award nomination); You Turned the Tables on Me; Dolores (Oscar nomination); Rainbow on the River; Come Up and See Me Sometimes; No Wonder I'm Blue; I Was Taken by Storm.

ALTER, PAUL   ASCAP 1966
composer, author

b Chicago, Ill, Mar 11, 22. Educ: NY Univ, BA, 44; Yale Univ, MFA, 49; studied piano with Teddy Wilson, 50. TV producer/dir, CBS, 50-53, Goodson-Todman Productions, 54-, John MacArthur, 67-68 & David Susskind, 68. Chief Collabrs: Carmen Mastren, Steve Allen, Peter Howard, Bob Cobert, Charles Foxx. *Songs:* Music: Go; Say When; Lyrics: Can't We Start Over Like Strangers; To Tell the Truth (theme). *Scores:* Bway Show: Hole in the Head.

ALTERMAN, MICHAEL
composer

Educ: Hofstra Univ, BS(music); Queens Col, grad work in comp, orchestration & conducting; pvt study of piano with Enrique Batiz, Juilliard Sch Music; pvt study of conducting with Emanuel Balaban. Pianist, "Someone New," NBC TV, cond, 3 yrs, comp & scorer, 5 yrs. Pianist, comp & scorer, Woody Herman Band; comp, scorer, cond & producer for Dionne Warwick on Sonday Records. Composing & scoring: Commercials for Ford Pinto, Ford Fairmont, Arid, Rightguard, Chamar Jeans, Ross-Burton Credit Card Dir & Video Variations Logo; original songs for Muzak Corp; original material for NJ Symph, Toronto Symph & Seattle Symph; album recorded in London, Eng; singers on TV, "Merv Griffin", "Tonight" & "Today" shows; Mercer Arts Ctr, "Love Me, Love My Children"; also music dir at Video Variations studio in-house music for commercials, broadcast & cable TV shows. Conducting for: Off Bway show, "Your Own Thing," 1 yr; City Ctr, "Black Expo"; personal cond, Leon Bibb; Elmsford Dinner Theatre, "Pippin"; Arling Park Theater, Chicago, "Dance on a Country Grave." Pianist for: TV shows, "Tonite Show", "Maurice Woodruff Presents", "Dial M for Music"; "Today Show" & "Merv Griffin Show"; Bway, "Johnny Pot"; We Three Trio; Chet Baker Quintet; "Pippin" (all keyboard instruments); Bob Fosse (dance arr). Accompanist for Leon Bibb, Sammy Davis, Jr, Mel Torme, Jerry Vale & Dinah Washington. *Songs:* Come Find Me; Rice and Beans.

ALTMAN, ARTHUR   ASCAP 1934
composer, author

b Brooklyn, NY, Oct 28, 12. Educ: St Johns Col; studied violin with Prof A Karp. Own ens & singer, night clubs & radio. CBS staff librarian & violinist; with E B Marks, Warner Bros & Paramount Famous Music. Themes for TV game shows; themes & songs for motion pictures. Chief Collabrs: Jack Lawrence, Hal David, Don Reid, Billy Meshel, Milton Ager, Irving Taylor, Dick Manning, Al Stillman. *Songs:* American Beauty Rose; Green Years; Music By the Angels; Grand Tour de L'Amour; Cup of Joy; Toy or Treasure; Love Where Are You; Captain Santa Claus; Where Were You When the Moon Came Out?; My World Is You; You're Breaking My Heart All Over Again; Hello Loser; Music: All or Nothing At All; Play Fiddle Play; I Fall in Love With You Every Day; I'll Pray for You; You Can't Hold a Memory in Your Arms; Single Saddle; I Am a Heart; Size 12; Winter Waltz; Loafin' Time; Sudden Fear; Mush-Mush; Ain't

A'hankerin; Protection; Romance a La Mode; Sudden Fear; Alias Jessie James; The Quiet Man; Voice of the City; Princess O'Rourke; What's Cookin; Lyrics: All Alone Am I; I Will Follow Him; Maybe This Summer.

ALTSCHULER, ERNEST   ASCAP 1964
composer, author
b New York, NY, Oct 1, 22; d New York, May 11, 73. Music & Art Sch; RCA Inst, eng degree. With, WNYC Broadcasting Syst; worked with Mayor LaGuardia. Musician & control tower operator, USAAF. With State Dept, "Voice of America." Broadcasting engr, CBS. Dir, popular singles & albums, Columbia Records. Exec producer, RCA, vpres, east & west coast, exec producer. Mgr, popular music & spec projects, Playboy Records. Recipient 9 nominations for records or album of the year, gold awards RIAA certified. Mem, bd of gov, Nat Acad of Recording Arts & Sci, 3 yrs. *Songs:* Tears Keep on Falling; Sunshine Polka; Jing-a-Ling; Seven Days in May; See-Saw; A Summer Place (theme, Grammy award); I Left My Heart in San Francisco (Grammy award).

ALVY, THEODORE BRUCE   ASCAP 1976
author
b Los Angeles, Calif, June 12, 48. Educ: Univ Calif, Los Angeles, BA(theatre arts—film/TV). Began as radio announcer & programmer, Los Angeles FM rock sta, 68-72; operated FM rock sta, Eureka, Calif, 72. Lyricist for two albums. Chief Collabr: William Earl Harkleroad. *Songs:* Lyrics: She's Long and She's Lean; Mama Squeeze; Bigfoot; Texas Weather.

AMALBERT, EMMANUEL JUAN
See Rahim, Emmanuel Khaliq

AMARAL, NESTOR   ASCAP 1956
composer
b Brazil, Sept 16, 13; d Hollywood, Calif, Feb 26, 62. Educ: Pub schs. To US with Carmen Miranda & her group, 40. Singer & comp for motion pictures. Chief Collabrs: Laurindo Almeida, Johnny Mercer, Ray Gilbert. *Songs:* Old Man and the Sea; Sambiana; Sighs.

AMBER, LILI
See Lux, Lillian Sylvia

AMEMIYA, YASUKAZU   ASCAP 1974
composer, percussionist, timpanist
b Tokyo, Japan, July 18, 38. Educ: Tokyo Nat Univ of Fine Arts & Music, BFA; Juilliard Sch, studied with Prof Saul Goodman; Manhattan Sch of Music, studied with Prof Paul Price. Percussionist, Tokyo Symph Orch, 61-62, Yomiuri Nippon Symph Orch, 62- Gewandhaus Chamber Orch, Leipzig, Ger, 77 & Percussion Clinic, Tokyo, 77. Concerts in Japan, US, Can, Europe, Scandinavia, 67-, Repub of China, 79 & 80. Performed at Asian Comp's League, 4th Conference & Fest, 76; perc recitals, Tokyo, 77, NHK Broadcasting, 77; leader, Yasukazu Amemiya Percussive Orch. *Instrumental Works:* Summer Prayer (perc, tape, perc ens); Monochrome Sea (perc, tape). *Scores:* Film/TV: Reason of a Cat.

AMENDOLA, RICHARD   ASCAP 1973
composer, singer, guitarist
b Port Chester, NY, Apr 23, 51. Educ: Rye High Sch, NY, 69; Elon Col, NC, BA(human services), 79. Comp, singer & guitarist for group Breeze, recorded 73-74. Singer, recording artist, nightclubs, TV commercial. *Songs:* For the Love of a Lady; If I Never Saw Your Face; Rosa; Morning at Daybreak.

AMES, MORGAN   ASCAP 1960
composer, author, singer
b Los Angeles, Calif. Educ: Studied with Claire Fischer, Albert Harris, Johnny Carisi, Quincy Jones & Johnny Mandel. Wrote first song age 5. Piano bar singer/player, NY. Worked for Quincy Jones, Los Angeles, 3 yrs. Co-wrote & sang commercials. Assoc producer, producer & writer. Chief Collabrs: Dave Grusin, Johnny Mandel, Clydene Jackson, Tom Scott, Bill Evans, Ian Freebairn-Smith, Mike Melvoir, Bob James, Hugh McCracken, Gene McDaniels. *Songs:* I Am His Lady (She is My Lady); I'd Like to be Baby to You; Far Side of the Hill; Loving Grow Up Slow; Lyrics: Keep Your Eye on the Sparrow (Barretta's theme); But I Love You.

AMFITHEATROF, DANIELE   ASCAP 1948
composer, conductor
b St Petersburg, Russia, Oct 29, 01. Educ: Musical Cons, Petrograd, Russia; studied with Jareslav Kricka, Prague, Czech; Royal Cons of Music, Rome, Italy, grad(with hon), studied under O Respighi; Superior Pontifical Acad of Sacred Music, Rome, studied organ & Gregorian Chant. To US, 37, citizen, 44. Asst cond, Augusteo Symph, Rome. Cond & artistic mgr, radio stations in Italy incl Genoa, Milan, Trieste & Turin. Management exec, Italian Broadcasting network. Guest cond, Lamoureux Orch & Pasdeloup Orch, Paris, Brussels Symph, Vienna Philharmonic, Budapest Symph, Budapest Philh, Boston Symph, Los Angeles Symph & symph orchs in Rome, Naples & Turin. Assoc cond, Minneapolis Symph Orch. Comp of var symph & chamber music works. Mem, Am Guild of Authors & Composers, Composers & Lyricists Guild of Am & former pres, SCAUSA. Recipient, Commander of Order of Star of Solidarity.

Songs & Instrumental Works: American Panorama (symph, awarded Grand Prix du Disque); Requiem (solo voices, choir & orch). *Scores:* Musical drama: The Staring Match; Films: Lassie Come Home; Days of Glory; I'll Be Seeing You; Guest Wife; Song of the South; Cry Havoc; The Beginning Or the End; Angels in the Field; The Damned Don't Cry; A Place in the Sun; The Mountain; Storm Waring; Sand; House of Strangers; Bird of Paradise; The Desert Fox; Salome; Trial; The Naked Jungle; Heller in Pink Tights; Human Desire; Singapore; Ivy; Lost Moment; The Senator Was Indiscreet; Letter From an Unknown Woman; Another Part of the Forest; An Act of Murder; Rogue's Regiment; Fraulein; Major Dundee.

AMMIRATI, JOHN LEWIS (LONESOME JOHN)   ASCAP 1978
composer, author
b Sacramento, Calif, Nov 10, 44. Educ: Univ Calif, Davis, BA, 69; NY Univ Sch of Arts, MFA, 71; spec study of electronic music with Morton Subotnick. Instr, Univ Calif, Santa Cruz, 72-74. Musician & writer, Hot Dada Band, 72-73, Intergalactic Threat, 76-78; musician, Rama Lama Band, 72-74. Chief Collabrs: Rama Lama, Lol Halsey, Mary Nygren. *Songs:* DOA in San Jose; Lyrics: Urban Homicide; Paper Shuffle; One Way Ticket; The Red Rocket Roll; The Tamari Belongs to Me; Eva Evil Eva; Foodstamps.

AMOROSE, ANTHONY ALFRED   ASCAP 1978
composer, author, singer
b New Alexandria, Pa, May 21, 18. Educ: Elem sch, Sharon, Pa; high sch, Salina, Pa. Involved in broadcasting with radio sta WHJB, Greensburg, Pa & WJPA, Washington, Pa. Entertainer, spec services, USAF. Entertained & played music in var local nightclubs, 42 yrs. Chief Collabrs: Thomas Mossburg, William DePaoli. *Songs:* Mandolins of Love; Believe Me; Santa's Letter; Santa's on His Way; Soft Winds.

AMSBERRY, ROBERT WAYNE   ASCAP 1956
actor, songwriter
b Boring, Ore, June 2, 28; d Portland, Ore, Nov 23, 57. Educ: Univ Ore. DJ, KGW, Ore; In "Uncle Bob's Squirrel Cage," KEX, Ore, 52-55; with Walt Disney, Mickey Mouse Club. Chief Collabrs: Walt Disney, Muzzy Marceliano. *Songs:* Lyrics: Clippety Clap; Dry Gulch Cowboy; I'm a British Grenadier; Laughing Song; Smile and Face the Music; Who Do You Call a Friend; Who Writes the Music.

AMSTERDAM, CHET   ASCAP 1958
composer, musician
b New York, NY, Aug 20, 26. Educ: Manhattan Sch of Music. Musician with bands & small groups; recording artist. Appeared on TV. *Songs:* Kiki.

AMSTERDAM, MOREY   ASCAP 1945
composer, author
b Chicago, Ill, Dec 14, 14. Educ: Univ Calif, Berkeley. Musician, author, composer, comedian & comedy writer. Nightclub & restaurant owner. Performer vaudeville, nightclubs, Bway shows, fairs, concerts, radio, TV & motion pictures. Best known on TV as co-star of "Dick Van Dyke Show." *Songs:* Rum and Coca Cola; Why Oh Why Did I Ever Leave Wyoming; Just for You; True Mon True; Plain Old Me; Nothing; Yuk a Puk; Cathy Darlin'; Can't Get Offa My Horse; My Kind of Woman; Without Your Love; You're Priceless; Caliope Pete; Oh My Achin' Back; My Wife Does the Cutest Things; Cheese and Crackers; Your Baby Has Gone Down the Drainpipe; Let's Eat.

ANDALINA, MICHAEL J   ASCAP 1961
composer, saxophonist
b Chicago, Ill, June 28, 25. Educ: High sch; pvt music study. Saxophonist, dance groups. Served, USCG, World War II. Co-owner, EveRecords. *Songs:* Looking for a Love; Your Love Is Just for Me; Can't You See; Waiting for You; You Can Say That Again.

ANDERS, JOHN FRANK (ANDY) (JON DERSAN,   ASCAP 1966
BENNIE FRANCIS)
composer, author, singer
b Upward, NC, Apr 24, 07. Educ: Univ NC; Columbia Univ; Washington & Lee Univ. Vocalist, saxophonist & clarinetist with several big bands, late 20's to mid-30's. Organized vocal & instrumental group The Swingsters, live radio prog, Knoxville, Tenn. Guest vocalist numerous bands & groups at clubs, lounges & ballrooms. Sears retail store mgr; Maj USAF, WWII; USN Civil Service, retired, 72- Chief Collabrs: Miguel de la Vega, Edsel M Johns, Lottie A Lederer, Alana Rogers, Jack Wintrode, Pat Holmes, Patricia Nobles. *Songs:* Julie; Florida; Well, Well, Well; Miss Jacksonville; Jalinda; I'm So Glad; It's All Because of You; It's So Hard to Pretend; Music: Lonesome for You; Dear God, Bless Old Georgia.

ANDERSEN, ARTHUR OLAF   ASCAP 1940
composer, educator
b Newport, RI, Jan 30, 1880; d Tucson, Ariz, Jan 11, 58. Educ: Am Cons, Chicago, hon MusD; studied with d'Indy, Guilmant, Durra & Sgambati. Taught theory, Berlin, 05-08. Mem fac, Am Cons, 08-33 & Chicago Musical Col, 33-35. Dean Col Fine Arts & head theory & comp depts, Univ Ariz, 34. Author bks on harmony, counterpoint & orchestration. Former pres, Ariz Music Teachers. Wrote incidental music for play, "Jade Bracelet." *Instrumental Works:* Suite for

Strings; Arizona Sketches No 1 and 2; 3 string quartets; 3 string trios; Piano and String Trio; 2 woodwind quartets; Quartet for Flute, Strings; Symphony in F. *Scores:* Ballet: A Chinese Ballet; Operetta: Arizona Hi-Ho.

ANDERSEN, MICHAEL   ASCAP 1959
composer, author, conductor

b Los Angeles, Calif, Jan 26, 38. Educ: Univ Southern Calif, BMus, 61, DMA, 78; USA Command & General Staff Col, 75; studied comp with Halsey Stevens, Ingolf Dahl & Miklos Rozsa. Performances of concert music, 57-; comp, cond, & orchr for motion pictures & TV, 59- Comp, concert & commercial media; cond, symph & recording orchs, in US & Europe; pianist & organist. Recalled to USA, combat arms officer, service in SE Asia, 68, awarded 4 Bronze Star Medals & Air Medal. Fac, Calif Lutheran Col. Chief Collabs: Sidney Shrager, Alexander Chorney, Linda Matthews Andersen, Leo Shuken. *Songs:* Bahama Beguine; No Hideaway Here; Music: Three Song Cycles (texts by A E Housman). *Instrumental Works:* Twelve to the Moon; Wings of Chance; Boy on the Run; The Builders; The Doomed; The Runaway; Tower of London; Terrified; Tell Me in the Sunlight; Symphony in A, Commemorating Carl Sandburg; Symphony No 2: Variations on a Hymn Tune, & No 3; Chamber Symphony; Concerto for Trumpet and Orchestra; Concerto for Alto Saxophone and Orchestra; Concertino a Due (two keyboards); String Quartet; String Quintet; Seven Viola Duos; Missa Solemnis (chorus, orch); Te Deum Laudamus (chorus, orch); Trio for 2 Violins and Viola; Five Piano Sonatas; plus 40 other chamber, orchestral, dramatic & choral works. *Scores:* Opera: Proxy Fight (3 acts).

ANDERSON, CARL E   ASCAP 1963
author

b Omaha, Nebr, Jan 4, 1892; d. Educ: High sch. Chief Collabr: Lee Hudson. *Songs:* Arizona Polka; Our Space Ship; Each Moment I Live; Where You Belong; You Ran Into My Heart; Sundown Valley.

ANDERSON, CAROL GRACE   ASCAP 1973
composer, author, singer

b Flint, Mich, Oct 7, 45. Educ: Orange County Community Col, NY, AAS; Bloomfield Col, BA(psychol), 69; NY Univ, MA(counseling, guidance), 73. Taught third grade, New York, 69-70, Eng & basic psychol, Rehabilitation Ctr for Drug Addicts, Mid-Hudson, NY, 70-74. Formed all-girl country & western band, Ladysmith, 74. To Nashville, staff writer for Chappell Music; Ladysmith became a background vocal group, 74-; free-lance songwriter working with var publishers. Chief Collabs: Mary Beth Anderson, Rory Bourke, Rob Parsons. *Songs:* Your Place or Mine; Million Dollar Memories; Once or Twice; You Know My Heart; Heartbreak Hall of Fame.

ANDERSON, EDMUND   ASCAP 1950
composer, author, producer

b New York, NY, Sept 19, 12. Educ: Franklin Sch; St John's Col, Annapolis. Dir & writer for var TV & radio network progs; advert exec for major agencies. Pres, Edmund Anderson Productions, Inc. Co-produced Bway plays "The Beauty Part" & "Close Quarter." Chief Collabs: Ted Grouya, Alec Wilder, Robert Stolz, Rex Stewart, Billy Stray Horn, David Broekman, Billy Taylor, Teo Macero. *Songs:* Please Say Yes (March of Dimes song); Is It Raining in New York?; Lyrics: Flamingo; The Olive Tree; Thank You for Everything (Lotus Blossom); Swamp Mist; Frost on the Moon; Walkin the Right Way on the Wrong Side of the Street; Jade Green. *Instrumental Works:* Tropicale. *Scores:* Film/TV: Someday When Tomorrow Comes Along.

ANDERSON, FRANK H, JR   ASCAP 1925
composer, author, conductor

b Minneapolis, Minn, Apr 9, 1895; d Oakland, Calif, Jan 4, 52. Educ: Armstrong Col. Pianist & singer on own radio prog, 8 yrs. Organized own orch, 21, played nightclubs & dance halls. Served in USA, WW II. Chief Collabs: Larry Yoell, Robert Spencer. *Songs:* I Wish I Knew; Funny Waltz; Love Me, Love Me, Love Me; I'm All Alone.

ANDERSON, GARLAND LEE   ASCAP 1977
composer, pianist

b Union City, Ohio, June 10, 33. Educ: Univ Edinburgh, studied comp with Hans Gal, 54-55; Ind Univ, studied comp with Roy Harris, 59-60; Earlham Col, BA, 75; Ball State Univ, studied piano with Michel Bourgeot, 75-76. First orchestral pieces played at ages 16 & 17. Has given concerts of own works at Radford Col, Earlham Col, Oakland City Col, Miami Univ & Ball State Univ. Rec'd fel from NEA, 75. Chief Collabs: John Holzer; librettist, Jamie Cooper. *Songs:* Music: Three Songs on Poems by Rilke; We, the Dreamers (oratorio). *Instrumental Works:* Sonata for Tenor Saxophone and Piano; Sonata for Baritone Saxophone and Piano; Sonata for Alto Saxophone and Piano; Concertino for Piano and Orchestra; Sonata for Violin and Piano; Three Preludes for Piano. *Scores:* Soyazhe (opera in one act, ASCAP Award, 80).

ANDERSON, JOHN MAXWELL   ASCAP 1969
composer

b Lincoln, Nebr, Aug 11, 48. Educ: Beverly Hills High Sch; Aspen Sch Music, Univ Southern Calif, full scholarship, BA, 70; studied with Darius Milhaud. Comp of symph music, chamber works, concerti, piano pieces, tone poems, symph & others; music performed by Los Angeles Philh; comp of TV pilot

themes, co logos & others. Chief Collabr: Caryl Ledner. *Songs:* Music: Every Evening At Six. *Instrumental Works:* Symphony No 1; Concerto for Organ and Orchestra; The Red Laugh; Concerto No 3 (piano & orch); Sonatas No 1 and No 2 (piano forte); Canterbury Tales (bassoon & orch). *Songs & Instrumental Works:* Psalm 70 (chorus & organ). *Scores:* Bway Show: Questions; Film/TV: Hang Ups! (main title); The Secret Mirror; TAT Communications Co Logo; PITS Logo.

ANDERSON, JOHN MURRAY   ASCAP 1950
author, director, producer

b St John's, Nfld, Sept 20, 1886; d New York, NY, Jan 30, 54. Educ: Edinburgh Acad, Scotland; Lausanne Univ, Switz; studied drama with Herbert Beerbohm Tree. WW I, with Am Bureau of Information. Dir: "Greenwich Village Follies" (5 ed); "Jack and Jill"; "What's in a Name?" (also librettist, producer); "The League of Notions" (London); "Music Box Revue of 1924"; "Dearest Enemy"; "John Murray Anderson's Almanac" (29, also produced, 53); "Bow Bells" (London); "Fanfare" (London); "Ziegfeld Follies" (34, 36 & 43); "Life Begins at 8:40"; "Thumbs Up!"; "Jumbo"; "One for the Money"; "Two for the Show"; "Laffing Room Only"; "Three to Make Ready"; "New Faces of 1952"; "Two's Company." Film dir, "The King of Jazz." Dir, Radio City Music Hall, 33, Great Lakes Expos, Cleveland, 37 & Billy Rose's Diamond Horseshoe, 38-50 & Ringling Bros Circus, 42-51. Autobiography: "Out Without My Rubbers." Chief Collabrs: A Baldwin Sloane, Carey Morgan. *Songs:* Eileen Avourneen; The Girl in the Moon; That Reminiscent Melody; The Valley of Dreams; The Last Waltz; Come to Vienna; Some Day When Dreams Come True; A Young Man's Fancy; At the Krazy Kat's Ball; Annabell Lee. *Scores:* Bway stage: Greenwich Village Follies; Jack and Jill.

ANDERSON, LEROY   ASCAP 1947
composer, conductor

b Cambridge, Mass, June 29, 08; d Woodbury, Conn, May 18, 75. Educ: New Eng Cons, studied piano at age 11; Harvard Univ, BA & MA. Church choirmaster & organist, 29-35. Mem fac, Div Music, Radcliffe Col, 30-32. Played double bass & cond orchs, Boston. Dir, Harvard Univ Band, 31-35. Guest cond, Boston Pops Orch & other symph orchs. Mem, NY Nat Guard, 37-39. Capt, Mil Intelligence, USA, Washington, DC, 44-46 & Ft Bragg, NC, 51-52. Made many records. Chief Collabs: Mitchell Parish, Walter & Jean Kerr, Joan Ford. *Songs & Instrumental Works:* Irish Suite; Christmas Festival; Horse and Buggy; Fiddle Faddle; Sleigh Ride; Jazz Legato; Jazz Pizzicato; Blue Tango; The Syncopated Clock; The Penny Whistle Song; Belle of the Ball; The Girl in Satin; Forgotten Dreams; A Trumpeter's Lullaby; Sandpaper Ballet; The Bugler's Holiday; Serenata; The Typewriter; Plink, Plank, Plunk; Promenade; The Phantom Regiment; The Pussy Foot; Who's Been Sitting in My Chair?; I Never Know When to Say When; Saraband; Harvard Festival; Suite of Carols; Lady in Waiting; Alma Mater; Ticonderoga (band); Chicken Reel; The Waltzing Cat; China Doll; Song of Jupiter; Song of the Bells; Summer Skies; The First Day of Spring; The Bluebells of Scotland; Arietta; Balladette; The Golden Years; Clarinet Candy; The Captains and the Kings; Home Stretch; Waltz Around the Scale; Birthday Party; Lullaby of the Drums; Save a Kiss; Shall I Take My Heart and Go; Lazy Moon; Heart of Stone (pyramid dance). *Scores:* Bway stage: Goldilocks.

ANDERSON, MARY BETH   ASCAP 1978
composer, author, singer

b Nyack, NY, July 26, 54. Educ: Univ Bridgeport; Ramapo Col, NJ. Staff writer for Chappell Music; free-lance writer with Blendingwell Music, ATV Music & Chappell Music. Copartner with Carol Anderson (sister) in Sweet Street Music. Has sung backup vocals for Roy Clark, David Allan Coe, Alex Harvey & others. Chief Collabs: Carol Anderson, Jeannie Bare, Sharon Ruhlman, Jerry Gillespie, Bob Johnson, Rory Bourke. *Songs:* Your Place or Mine; You Know My Heart; I Gotta Know; I Can't Be Your Backdoor Anytime.

ANDERSON, MAXWELL   ASCAP 1939
author

b Atlantic, Pa, Dec 15, 1888; d Stamford, Conn, Feb 28, 59. Educ: Univ NDak, BA; Stanford Univ, MA. Taught sch, NDak & Calif. Reporter, Grand Forks "Herald", NDak, San Francisco "Chronicle" & "Bulletin," 14-18. Ed writer, "New Republic", "Evening Globe" & "Morning World," 18-24. Playwright incl "What Price Glory?", "Saturday's Children", "Elizabeth the Queen", "Both Your Houses", "Mary of Scotland", "Valley Forge", "Winterset", "The Wingless Victory", "High Tor" (also TV score), "Key Largo", "The Bad Seed." Chief Collabs: Kurt Weill, Arthur Schwartz. *Songs:* September Song; There's Nowhere to Go But Up; It Never Was You; Stay Well; Lost in the Stars; Trouble Man; Thousands of Miles; Cry, the Beloved Country; When You're in Love. *Scores:* Bway shows: Knickerbocker Holiday; Lost in the Stars.

ANDERSON, ROBERT ALEXANDER   ASCAP 1939
composer, author

b Honolulu, Hawaii, June 6, 1894. Educ: Cornell Univ, 16; studied voice, orch & choir. Piano studies during grade sch; active in dramatics in high sch, comp sch song. Joined Honolulu Glee Men Chorus; sang part of KoKo in Opera Mikado. Mem, Am Guild Authors & Composers. Honolulu Symph Salute/Prog of Anderson songs, 75. Chief Collabs: Jack Owens, Leonie Weeks, Milton Beamer, Carter Nott, Charles Bud Dant, Richard P Crew. *Songs:* Christmas in Hawaii; Reach Up and Pick a Star; Remember I Gave My Aloha; Santa's Hula;

Merriest Hawaiian Christmas; The Sea the Sky and the Mountains; There Are Two Eyes in Hawaii; Two Shadows on the Sand; That's Patriotic; Haole Hula; I'll Weave a Lei of Stars for You; I Will Remember You; Lovely Hula Hands; Malihini Mele; Mele Kalikimaka; Narcissus Queen; On a Coconut Island; Red Opu; Cockeyed Mayor of Kaunakakai; White Ginger Blossoms; They Couldn't Take Niihau No How; Music: Soft Green Seas; Lyrics: Blue Lei.

ANDERSON, WILLIAM (CAT)   ASCAP 1958
composer
b Greenville, SC, Sept 12, 16. Trumpeter in orchs incl Lucky Millinder, Erskine Hawkins, Lionel Hampton, Duke Ellington. Led own band, 3 yrs, then rejoined Ellington, 50-59. *Songs & Instrumental Works:* Night Walk; El Gato; Teardrops in the Rain; How 'Bout That Mess; Bluejean Beguine.

ANDRE, DEAN
See Wallschlaeger, Dean Andre

ANDRE, FABIAN   ASCAP 1941
composer, conductor, arranger
b La Crosse, Wis, Jan 8, 10; d Mexico City, Mex, Mar 30, 60. Educ: St Joseph's Col; Marquette Univ; studied music with Joseph Schillinger & Carl Eppert. Arr for dance orchs, NBC, Chicago. Specialist in Latin Am music. Led own orch & made many records. Served in USA, WW II. Author, "Rhythms of Latin-America." *Songs & Instrumental Works:* Dream a Little Dream of Me; From Me to You; When They Played the Polka; Antonio; A Windy Day on the Outer Drive; Pedigree on Pomander Walk; The Maid With the Slight Swiss Accent; The Man Who Came to Rhumba; Lullaby for Latins.

ANDRE, WAYNE J   ASCAP 1973
composer
b Manchester, Conn, Nov 17, 31. Educ: Manhattan Sch Music, BA; studied with Miss Ulehla. Trombonist with name bands, incl Benny Goodman, Woody Herman, Zavter Finnegan, Thad Jones, Clark Tenny & Gerry Mulligan; free-lance studio musician, 58- *Songs & Instrumental Works:* AYO; Nutcracker.

ANDREWS, CURCY H, JR (BUD)   ASCAP 1970
composer, author, musician
b Lubbock, Tex, July 5, 40. Educ: Tex Tech Univ, studied mass communications. Started as musician on elec bass for Nicky Sullivan of Buddy Holly & The Crickets, 58-59; music dir for KSEL radio, Lubbock; music & prog dir for KFYO, Lubbock, currently. Has done comedy material, Country Comedy Artists by Jerry Clower; was producer & co-writer for comedy album by Jerry Jordan on MCA records. *Songs:* Coonhunt; A Phone Call From God.

ANDREWS, JAMES WILLIAM   ASCAP 1977
composer, band director, flute teacher
b Clearwater, Fla, Aug 12, 45. Educ: Vega High Sch, Tex; WTex State Univ, BME, 68, MA, 75; studied flute with Gary Garner, comp with Houston Bright & Norman Nelson. Music dir, Bovina, Tex schs, 68-70; asst band dir, Friona, Tex schs, 70-75; staff comp/arr, Alice Independent Sch District, 75- Winner of Col Band Dirs Nat Asn Comp Award, 75. Clinician & adjudicator. *Instrumental Works:* Sinfonietta for Winds and Percussion; Overture: Disones; Threnos; Illusions.

ANDREWS, MARK   ASCAP 1937
composer, organist, conductor
b Gainsborough, England, Mar 21, 1875; d Dec 10, 39. Educ: Studied music with John Thomas Ruck, Westminster Abbey. Organist & choirmaster churches, Montclair, NJ. Mem exam comn, Am Guild of Organists. *Songs & Instrumental Works:* Rock of Ages; String Quartet; two organ sonatas; Cantatas: Galilee; The Highwayman.

ANDROZZO, A BAZEL
See Thompson, Alma I

ANELLO, ANN MARIE   ASCAP 1977
composer, author, singer
b Brooklyn, NY, Sept 13, 54. Educ: Studied with Ralph Lewando, Carlo Menotti, Sue Seton, Warren Robertson, Herert Berghoff, Henry Le Tang, Phil Black. Actress & dancer, Bway shows, films & TV. In concert throughout world; recording artist. Chief Collabrs: Mitch Kerper, Martin Dunayer, Russ Anello. *Songs:* My Little Man; Lyrics: Magic in My Life; My Sweet Life; Get Back to the One You Love; My Sweet Love.

ANGELL, WARREN MATHEWSON   ASCAP 1960
composer, educator
b Brooklyn, NY, May 13, 07. Educ: Syracuse Univ, BMus, MMus; Univ Rochester Eastman Sch Mus, grad studies; Columbia Univ, EdD; studied with Kirk Ridge, George Mulfinger, Abram Chasins, Fred Waring, Robert Shaw, Harry Robert Wilson, Arthur Gerry, William Berwald, piano with Severin Eisenberger. Dean fine arts, Okla Baptist Univ, 36-73. Professional singer, Fred Waring & The Pennsylvanians, 42-44. Serious arr & composing, 50- Comns: many church anthems, incl Southern Baptist Church Musicians Conference, 80. Cond clinics & workshops for church choirs. Author, bks: "Look Up You Singers" & "Piano Improvisations." Chief Collabrs: Geoffrey O'Hara, Daniel Twohig, George Graff, Rosemarie Cooper, Walter Ehret, Evalyn Angell. *Songs:*

Music: This Is the Day; How Excellent Is Thy Name; What Tongue Can Tell; Great Is the Lord; Hallelujah! I Love Him; O Jesus, My Saviour; Our God Is One God; There Will Your Heart Be; The Rod of God; I Will Extol Thee; Glorious Is Thy Church; Go Ye Into All the World; Arise Proclaim the Word; All That I Am or Have; God Is My Refuge; Be Thou Exalted; Great Is the Glory of the Lord; Sing God's Praise; O Thou My God; Voice of Triumph; Let God Be Magnified; Children of America; Cantata; This Is the Gospel; This Is the Good News.

ANKROM, THELMA EILEEN   ASCAP 1962
author
b Wick, WVa, Jan 28, 31. Educ: High sch. Hotel worker; nurse. Chief Collabrs: Ted Fiorito, Jack Curry. *Songs:* I Never Dreamed; Safe Harbor Baby; When in That Moonlight Mood; My Little Baby.

ANNARINO, JOHN JOSEPH   ASCAP 1961
author
b Punxsutawney, Pa, Feb 15, 29. Educ: St Bonaventure Univ, BA(jour); Univ Calif, Los Angeles, songwriting class taught by Hal Levy. Writer: Hallmark Cards, Capitol Records & Doyle Dane Bernbach Advert. Chief Collabrs: Mavis Rivers, Sid Woloshin, Karl Brix. *Songs:* Lyrics: Now I Know; Things to Do Today; Take Life a Little Easier.

ANSON, BILL   ASCAP 1950
composer, author
b Chicago, Ill, Nov 15, 07. *Songs:* When I Write My Song; The Loveliness of You; Some Things Will Never Change; How Could We Ever Have Been Strangers?; I Got a Frame Without a Picture.

ANSON, GEORGE   ASCAP 1962
composer, author, educator
b Middletown, Ill, July 3, 04. Educ: Ill Wesleyan Univ, BM, hon LHD; Univ Ariz, MM; studied piano with Rudolph Ganz, comp with Arthur Olaf Andersen. Taught piano, Ill Wesleyan Univ, Univ Okla & Tex Wesleyan Col; prof emeritus of piano. Piano workshops, throughout US; numerous concert & recital appearances, incl City Symph & Ft Worth Symph. New piano music dept ed of Clavier. *Instrumental Works:* Anson Introduces (series); New Directions; Thirty Pieces in Thirty Keys (2 vols); The Spinning Top; Two Chinese Sketches; Kid Koncerto; Whirling Dervish (2 piano); When the Sun Goes Down (2 piano); Small Suite for Organ; Pedal Pushers—Pedal Patterns; & other ed collections & piano solo teaching pieces.

ANTHEIL, GEORGE   ASCAP 1945
composer, pianist
b Trenton, NJ, July 8, 1900; d New York, NY, Feb 12, 59. Educ: Curtis Music Settlement Sch; studied with Constantin von Sternberg, Ernest Bloch & Clark Smith; Guggenheim fel. Gave piano concerts, Europe, 21-26. Wrote incidental music to play, "Oedipus." Autobiography, "Bad Boy of Music." *Songs & Instrumental Works:* Piano Concerto; Violin Concerto; Concerto for Flute, Bassoon, Piano; Chamber Concerto for 8 Instruments (League of Composers Comn); Crucifixion (string orch); Decatur at Algiers; McKonkey's Ferry Overture; 2 Odes of Keats; Songs of Experience; Tom Sawyer; 8 Fragments from Shelley; Valentine Waltzes; Serenade for Strings; 6 symphonies; 3 string quartets; 2 violin sonatas; 2 sonatas for violin, piano; 4 piano sonatas. *Scores:* Film background: Once in a Blue Moon; Angels Over Broadway; The Plainsman; The Buccaneer; Spectre of the Rose; We Were Strangers; In a Lonely Place; Ballets: Ballet Mecanique; The Capital of the World; Operas: Helen Retires; Transatlantic; Volpone; The Brother; The Wish (Louisville Orch Comn).

ANTHONY, MALCOLM (ZYAL AHMONUEL)   ASCAP 1977
composer, author
b Birmingham, Ala, May 24, 50. Educ: Self-taught. Played piano in var night clubs, Birmingham, age 15. Chief Collabr: Wayne Bell (brother). *Songs:* I Gotta Keep Dancing (Keep Smiling); You Are Number One; (Olivia) Lost and Turned Out; I Fell in Love Las Night (at the Disco); Tick Tock; You'll Never Get Away; If I Don't Get Your Love; But My Heart Says No; Depths of My Soul; Tender; Leave It All Up to Love; Cindy, Cindy.

ANTHONY, RICHARD
See Little, Richard Anthony

ANTHONY, VINCE
See D'antuono, Vincent Joseph

ANTLE, GARY WAYNE   ASCAP 1976
composer, author, singer
b Chelsea, Mass, Feb 10, 54. Has taught drum corps. Guitarist & vocalist in nightclubs. Author of bk, "Better Band Business," 78. *Songs:* The End; Heaven Knows (Where You Are).

ANTON, BARBARA (BJ)   ASCAP 1976
composer, author, singer
b Pocono Pines, Pa, Apr 3, 36. Educ: Columbia Univ, Sch of Drama-Actors Studio, studied with Louise Gifford, Bill Lovejoy & John Cassavetes. Toured

with cos & clubs for musicals on & off Bway. *Songs:* Jolly Cholly; The Candles of Saint Lucia; Hot Dog! I'm American; Little Girl's Dream of Love; Did Jesus Ever Kick a Dog?; No One Should Be Lonely on New Year's Eve.

ANTONINI, ALFREDO   ASCAP 1946
composer, conductor
b Alessandria, Italy, May 31, 01. Educ: Cons of Milan, Italy, grad organ & comp. Organist & pianist, La Scala Orch under Toscanini. Dean music, St John's Univ, Brooklyn. Cond, CBS, New York, 41-74; guest cond with major symph orchs in US, Europe, SAm & NZ. *Instrumental Works:* Great City; United States of America; Sarabande; Saltarello; Twentieth Century Doll (woodwind quintet); Roman Holiday.

APOLINAR, DANIEL GEORGE   ASCAP 1967
composer, author, singer
b Brooklyn, NY, Mar 15, 34. Educ: Pvt musical and dance training. Performer, Danny Apolinar Trio, supper clubs & toured US major cities. Singer, Atlantic Reocrds, Stereoddities & RCA. Appeared in "Your Own Thing," New York, Los Angeles, London, Monte Carlo. Chief Collabrs: Hal Hester, Addy Fieger. *Songs:* The Middle Years; Don't Leave Me; The Flowers; What Do I Know?; Lyrics: Happy New Year; Merry Christmas to Me; All of a Sudden It's Spring; Running Out of Time. *Scores:* Off Bway: Your Own Thing; Changes.

APPELL, DAVE   ASCAP 1955
composer
b Philadelphia, Pa, Mar 24, 22. Educ: Northeast High Sch, Philadelphia, Pa. Wrote arr for big bands early in career; orch cond, Ernie Kovacs Show, Philadelphia, 58. A&R staff, Cameo-Parkway Records. Own band, Applejacks, recording for Cameo-Parkway. Chief Collabs: Kal Mann, Fran Robins, Mark Connor, Sandy Linzer, Bernie Lowe, Max Freedman, Vince Taft. *Songs:* Morning Beautiful; My Love Has No Pride; Thats the Way a Wallflower Grows; Pick It Up; House of Strangers; Fancy Meeting You Baby; Dance Rosie Dance; Sacrifices; You Can Bet; Sweet Sensational Love; Hello Hello; Little Heads in Bunkbeds; Growin' on Me; Sweet Summer Days of My Life; Ukulele Man; You Say the Sweetest Things; Music: Smarter; Tiny Hands; Sweet Patootie Pie; The Cha Cha Cha; Dancing Party; Don't Hang Up; Gravy; Hully Gully Baby; Popeye (The Hitchhiker); Wa Wa Watusi; Let's Limbo Some More; South Street; Butterfly; Do the Bird; Loddy Lo; Swingin School; Wild One; Good Time Baby; Wildwood Days; Hey Bobba Needle; Let's Twist Again; Bristol Stomp; Slow Twistin; Twist It Up; Crossfire; Straight Ahead; Have I Done Something Wrong; Beyond the Hurt; Joy Girl.

APPERT, DONALD LAWRENCE   ASCAP 1978
composer, author, trombonist
b Moses Lake, Wash, Jan 2, 53. Educ: New Eng Cons, BM, 75, MM, 77; studied trombone with John Coffey & Ronald Barron. Col teacher; cond. Trombonist & comp/arr, 700 Club Orch, Christian Broadcasting Network, 77-78. Songwriter, Christian Broadcast Music, 77-78. Instr of music, Hampton Inst; also dir, Jazz Ens & Brass Ens, 78- Trombonist with Va Opera Orch, 78-, principal trombonist, Va Philh, 79- Co-founder & secy, Tidewater Comp Guild, 79- Author "A Progressive Study of Multiphonics on the Trombone." Mem: Int Trombone Asn; Am Fedn Musicians & Am Symph League. *Songs:* Three Songs of Praise. *Instrumental Works:* This Man Jesus; Come Bless the Lord; A Vision; Lay It Down; Elegy (unaccompanied cello); Query (unaccompanied trombone); Who Shall Know (brass choir); Three Pieces for Piano; Lament (brass trio); Jazz Fantasia on Emmanuel (brass trio); Jazz Ens: Odyssey, Boogs, Bossa Profunda, Ichabod.

APPLEBAUM, STANLEY   ASCAP 1954
composer, conductor, author
b Newark, NJ, Mar 1, 22. Studied music with Stefan Wolpe, Wallingford Riegger, George Halprin, Vladimir Drozdoff, Irma Wolpe & Leon Barzin. Arr for dance orchs incl Benny Goodman, Tommy Dorsey, Harry James, Raymond Scott, also for E H Morris Co. Cond & arr for records, industrial & Bway musicals. Eastern A&R dir, Warner Bros, 62-63. Own publ cos. Author, "How to Improvise" & series of 6 bks on natural sci. *Instrumental Works:* Karin's Theme; Brainwave; Piano books: Introduction to Dissonance; Musical Miniature for 4 Hands; Folk Music, Bach Style; Soundworld; Bach Music, Simple Style; Double Play; Frenzy; Four Hand Toccata; Summer Cloud; Symph band: Theme for the Lost Hour; Spring Magic; Danza Boleriana; Jamaican Jamboree; Maraakech Bazaar (4 movement suite); Toboggan Ride; Cimarron; Irish Suite (3 movements); Choral: The Irish Suite; An American's Heritage.

APPLEMAN, SIDNEY HERBERT   ASCAP 1975
composer, author, pianist
b Chicago, Ill, Apr 10, 27. Educ: Von Steuben Sr High Sch; Am Cons Music, Chicago, studied piano with Crawford Keigwin & Heniot Levy; Univ Ariz, BMus, 53, MMus, 72, studied with Arthur Olaf Anderson, Andrew Buchhauser, comp & theory with Robert McBride; Univ Calif, Los Angeles, postgrad studies, 54; studied piano with Madame Elenire Altman & Julia Rebeu, bass with Rudolph Fahsbender. String bassist with Clyde McCoy band, var jazz & dance bands, Chicago. Played with own band during col in clubs, on radio & TV, Tucson; also comp, arr & started teaching. To Los Angeles, 60. Joined Red Nichols for 3 yrs. Played piano with Freddy Martin, 9 yrs. Led own dance & show band for TV, hotels & clubs. Taught piano & theory. Has performed with

& arr for var singers & acts. Directed music on Sitmar ships Fairsea & Fairwind for productions of "My Fair Lady", "South Pacific", "Annie Get Your Gun," a Bway revue & variety of cabaret acts. Orchestrated TV under-score for Nelson Riddle & Gil Grau. Rec'd gold medal in piano competition, Am Cons Music. *Songs & Instrumental Works:* Choreographics (symph band); Serenade (woodwind quintet); Jabberwocky (voice, clarinet & piano); The New Colossus (voice & piano); Will She Love Me?; Brich Aus in Lauten Klagen (voice & piano); Young and Old (voice & piano).

APPLETON, JON HOWARD   ASCAP 1969
composer
b Los Angeles, Calif, Jan 4, 39. Educ: Reed Col, BA, 61; Univ Ore, MA, 65; Columbia-Princeton Electronic Music Ctr, 65-66. Comp, instrumental & electronic music; Guggenheim & Fulbright Fels. Prof music, Dartmouth Col, 67- Dir, Bregman Electronic Music Studio, 67- Co-inventor & performer, Synclavier (digital synthesizer); recordings on var labels. Author bks & articles on electronic music. *Songs:* Sonaria for Synclavier and Choir. *Instrumental Works:* Chef d'Oeuvre; Times Square Times Ten; 'Otahiti; Georganna's Farewell; In Deserto; In Medias Res; String Quartet; Prelude for Synclavier; Kapingamrangi for Synclavier; Nukuoro for Synclavier; Vava'u for Synclavier.

AQUINO, FRANK JOSEPH (BERNIE KANE)   ASCAP 1956
composer, author, singer
b Buffalo, NY, Dec 3, 06. Educ: Studied solfeggio at age 7; played xylophone sch orch & studied perc; Hutchinson High Sch, Buffalo, dipl; Buffalo Sch Music. Toured Midwest with Harold Austin Orch; played with Jimmie Green Orch, 26. Cond own band as Bernie Kane; played Congress Hotel, Los Angeles; Mickey Mouse TV Show, Disney Studios & Golden Horseshoe, Disneyland. Retired 71. Chief Collabrs: Jimmie Green; Frank Loesser. *Songs:* Till the Shadows Retire; More and More; Music: Come a Little Closer (radio show theme); I Kinder Dream; My Mothers Wedding Gown.

ARAKELIAN, MELVIN SAM   ASCAP 1974
composer, singer, musician
b Los Angeles, Calif, Apr 19, 46. Educ: Washington Elem Sch; Montebello Jr High Sch; Montebello High Sch; La State Col; pvt vocal instr, age 5 yrs to age 19 yrs; studied keyboards, since age 9, guitar, age 14 yrs. Prof singer, from 8 yrs old; toured world with Mitchell Boys Choir, age 12 yrs. Performer with TV, motion pictures, live concerts, clubs & commercials; arr; songwriter, MGM Records. Chief Collabr: Ed Beram. *Songs:* Sunshine and Love.

ARANT, JACK
composer, author
b Deeth, Nev, July 4, 17. Educ: Humboldt County High Sch; Cath Univ Am; Loras Col; Washington Col Law. *Songs:* Pretty Firefly; I Wish I Were a Gypsy; Saints Or Sinners; Music: Hail Mary.

ARBUCKLE, DOROTHY M FRY   ASCAP 1960
composer, author
b Eldred, Ill, Jan 23, 10. Northwestern Univ; Univ Ill; State of Ind Libr, librarian cert. Teacher; radio journalist; librarian; author; comp; bus exec; free lance writer. *Songs:* The Tall Cathedral Windows; Jerusalem; I Never Knew; By the Kankakee River; The Hour Will Come; Seed Time and Harvest; This Day. *Instrumental Works:* Nocturne of Summer; Elegy to Grief. *Scores:* Opera/Ballet: Hear the Bells; Film/TV: The Church Wherein I Worship.

ARBUCKLE, RONNIE
See Fierstein, Ronald K

ARCHER, STEPHEN MARK   ASCAP 1977
composer, singer
b Mojave, Calif, Jan 5, 53. Toured, family band, The Archers, US, Europe, SAfrica & Can. Performed special concert for President Carter, White House, 79. Recording artist & on TV incl Dr Schuller's "Hour of Power." Chief Collabrs: Tim Archer, Phil Kristianson. *Songs:* Stand Up; Sanctified Life; Sunshine on a Cloudy Day; Lyrics: Water Into Wine; Waitin', Anticipatin'.

ARCHER, TIM JAMES   ASCAP 1976
composer, author, singer
b Lancaster, Calif, July 29, 49. Educ: Southern Calif Col, Costa Mesa; Antelope Valley Jr Col, Calif. Started singing in church, 65. Organized group, The Archers, 71, traveling to US, Can, SAfrica & Europe. Singer radio commercials & backup singer records; producer. Chief Collabrs: Steve Archer, Janice Archer, Bill Cole, Bill Maxwell, Larry Muhoberac, John Guess, Bobby Sisco, Ralph Carmichael, Gary Archer, Lee Ritenour, Jay Graydon, Chris Christian, Andrae Crouch. *Songs:* Happy Are the People; Water Into Wine; Pickin' Up the Pieces (Of My Life); Waitin' Anticipatin'.

ARELLANO, GEORGE ISIDRO (GEORGE ARNO)   ASCAP 1961
composer, teacher, singer
b San Francisco, Calif, Feb 22, 23. Educ: Arrilliaga Musical Col; San Francisco Cons of Music. Arr & pianist, nightclub dance bands, San Francisco. Dir of music, choral groups, Los Angeles, 56-71. Writer & arr, jingles, Los Angeles; singer, TV show "Playhouse 90." Music dir, Ste Catherine's Mil Acad. Chief Collabr: James Day, Bobby Troup, Walter O'Keefe. *Songs:* Music: Billy Goat

Hill; Anything Will Do; Georgie; The Everroad Brothers; No One Who Waits; A Light Shall Shine; The Nations Shall Revere Your Name; Suddenly There Came a Sound; The Eyes of All Look Hopefully to You, O Lord.

ARGENTINA, SARENO S   ASCAP 1963
composer, author
b Philadelphia, Pa, Feb 7, 17. Educ: Univ Pa. Taught bugle, Boy Scout troop, 32-40. IBM supvr, Philadelphia Dept of Finance, 40- *Songs:* Just a Dream; Back of the Room.

ARGENTO, DOMINICK   ASCAP 1958
composer
b York, Pa, Oct 27, 27. Educ: Fulbright fel, 51-52; Peabody Cons, BM & MM, 53; Eastman Sch Music, PhD, 57; studied comp with Nicholas Nabokov, Hugo Weisgall, Henry Cowell, Luigi Dallapiccola, Bernard Rogers, Howard Hanson & Alan Hovahness. Guggenheim grants, 57-58, 64-65. Pulitzer Prize in Music, 75. Mem, Am Acad & Inst Arts & Letters. Regents' prof music, Univ Minn. Chief Collabrs: Librettists: John Olon-Serymgeour, Charles Nolte, John Donahue. *Songs:* Music: Six Elizabethan Songs; From the Diary of Virginia Woolf. *Scores:* Opera/Ballet: Postcard From Morocco; The Voyage of Edgar Allan Poe; The Masque of Angels.

ARGESE, LEONARD   ASCAP 1970
composer, author, guitarist
b Brooklyn, NY, Oct 6, 42. Educ: Cent High Sch, Paterson, NJ; Manhattan Sch Music; spec studies with Louis Meccia & Edward Vitale. Arr & studio musician. Has done TV commercials & movie music. Chief Collabr: Louis Argese. *Songs:* Star Dreams; In My World; Plastic People; Days of the Night; Garbage; Everyone.

ARGIR, FREDERICK EMMETT   ASCAP 1968
composer, author, performer
b Hibbing, Minn, Sept 4, 43. Educ: Mary Hardin-Baylor Col, 67-68; Univ Tex, Austin, 69-70. Toured the New York based Col Coffeehouse Circuit, 70-73, Minneapolis, 3 yrs & San Francisco, 1 yr; mem, The Fred Argir Trio, Austin, Tex, 77-; recording artist, singer & guitarist. *Songs:* Sugarcane; Tonight's the Night; Save the Island; Last Time Around; Survivors; Mother Country. *Albums:* Thistledew.

ARGIRO, JAMES ANTHONY   ASCAP 1971
composer, conductor, pianist
b Springfield, Mass, July 11, 39. Educ: Hartford Cons Music, Conn; studied with Ray Cassorino & Robert Brawley. Performer & bandleader, rythmn & blues & jazz, on the east coast, 50's & 60's. Assoc cond & arr for Ice Capades, 67-68. Cond for King Family, Joan Rivers, Leslie Uggams, Carol Lawrence, Florence Henderson, Marlena Show & Susan Anton, 69- Top arr & accompanist in Hollywood for many stars. Music Coordr & orchr for TV shows incl Sonny & Cher, Tony Orlando, Donny & Marie, King Family, Emmy Awards & others. Chief Collabr: W Earl Brown. *Instrumental Works:* Dance.

ARICK, RON
See Frederick, Donald R

ARIDAS, CHRIS WILLIAM JOHN   ASCAP 1979
composer, author, singer
b New York, NY, Nov 12, 47. Began to comp & publ liturgical music, mid 70's. Record producer for Aslan Records, Inc. *Songs:* Answer Me; The Canticle; Out of the Darkness; Someday; Jesus Meets the Blind Man; Song of Mary; Psalm 57; The Lord Has Come; One More Time; Suffering Servant Song; I Lifted My Eyes; Hear Me, Lord; Fear Not; Song of Moses.

ARKIN, ALAN   ASCAP 1963
composer, author, actor
b New York, NY, Mar 26, 34. Educ: Los Angeles City Col; Los Angeles State Col. Sang with folk group The Tarries. Joined Compass Theatre, St Louis & Second City, Chicago; to NY with Second City troupe, 61; appeared on TV; acted in Bway plays "Enter Laughing" & "Luv." *Songs:* Cuddle Bug; That's Me; Best Time of the Year.

ARKIN, DAVID F   ASCAP 1961
author
b New York, NY, Dec 19, 06. Educ: NY Univ, BA; Nat Acad Design. Author of children's books, "Twenty Children of Johann Sebastian Bach" & "Tricky Dick and His Pals." Painter & designer. Chief Collabrs: Earl Robinson, George Smith, Dave Koonse. *Songs:* Lyrics: Black and White; The Klan; The Lion and the Lamb; The Dove; The Maybe Song; New Shoes; The Gold Fish Bowl; The Pony Track.

ARKIN, ROBERT B   ASCAP 1961
composer, author
b New York, NY, Aug 1, 23. Educ: NY Univ; Colgate Univ, NY. Sales mgr, Decca & Columbia Records. Pres, Eagle, Rori & Trojan Record Cos. *Songs:* The Untouchables.

ARLEN, HAROLD   ASCAP 1930
composer, author
b Buffalo, NY, Feb 15, 05. Educ: Pub schs; pvt music study with Arnold Cornelissen & Simon Bucharoff. At age 7, sang in choir of synagogue where father was cantor. Professional pianist at age 15, nightclubs, on lake steamers. Organized group The Snappy Trio, which became The Southbound Shufflers. To NY, singer, pianist & arr with dance bands; in Arnold Johnson's pit orch, Bway revue "George White's Scandals of 1928." Appeared in Palace Theatre, NY, toured Loew's vaudeville circuit. Wrote songs for Bway musicals "9:15 Revue", "Earl Carroll Vanities (1930, 1932)", "Americana", "George White's Music Hall Varieties" & "The Show Is On." Biography: Harold Arlen: Happy With the Blues, by Edward Jablonski. Chief Collabrs: Ted Koehler, E Y Harburg, Johnny Mercer, Ira Gershwin, Lew Brown, Leo Robin, Ralph Blane, Dorothy Fields, Truman Capote, Dory Previn, Jack Yellen. *Songs:* Get Happy; Hittin' the Bottle; You Said It; Sweet and Hot; Between the Devil and the Deep Blue Sea; Kickin' the Gong Around; I Love a Parade; I Gotta Right to Sing the Blues; Satan's Li'l Lamb; I've Got the World on a String; Minnie the Moocher's Wedding Day; It's Only a Paper Moon; Happy As the Day Is Long; Stormy Weather; Let's Fall in Love; This Is Only the Beginning; As Long As I Live; Ill Wind; Shoein' the Mare; You're a Builder Upper; Fun to Be Fooled; What Can You Say in a Love Song?; Let's Take a Walk Around the Block; Last Night When We Were Young; You're the Cure for What Ails Me; In Your Own Quiet Way; Fancy Meeting You; Song of the Woodman; God's Country; I've Gone Romantic on You; Moanin' in the Mornin'; Down With Love; In the Shade of the New Apple Tree; Buds Won't Bud; Over the Rainbow (Acad Award, 39); We're Off to See the Wizard; Ding-Dong the Witch Is Dead; If I Only Had a Brain; Two Blind Loves; Lydia the Tattooed Lady; When the Sun Comes Out; Blues in the Night; This Time the Dream's on Me; Says Who? Says You, Says I!; The Moment I Laid Eyes on You; That Old Black Magic; Hit the Road to Dreamland; Happiness Is a Thing Called Joe; Life's Full of Consequences; My Shining Hour; One for My Baby; Now I Know; Tess's Torch Song; When the Boys Come Home; Evelina; The Eagle and Me; Right As the Rain; T'morra T'morra; Sunday in Cicero Falls; I Got a Song; I Promise You; Let's Take the Long Way Home; Ac-Cen-Tchu-Ate the Positive; Out of This World; June Comes Around Every Year; Any Place I Hang My Hat Is Home; Legalize My Name; Cakewalk Your Lady; Come Rain Or Come Shine; I Wonder What's Become of Me; I Had Myself a True Love; Ridin' on the Moon; It Was Written in the Stars; For Every Man There's a Woman; Hooray for Love; What's Good About Goodbye?; Fancy Free; Andiamo; Today I Love Ev'rybody; The Man That Got Away; It's a New World; Here's What I'm Here For; The Search Is Through; A Sleepin' Bee; I Never Has Seen Snow; Two Ladies in de Shade of de Banana Tree; House of Flowers; Pretty to Walk With; Push de Button; Cocoanut Sweet; Pity de Sunset; Take It Slow, Joe; A Game of Poker; Goose Never Be a Peacock; The Man in My Life; Little Drops of Rain; The Morning After; I Could Go on Singing; So Long, Big Time; Silent Spring. *Instrumental Works:* Americanegro Suite; Mood in Six Minutes; American Minuet. *Scores:* Bway Stage: You Said It; Cotton Club Parade (4 ed); Life Begins At 8:40; Hooray for What; Bloomer Girl; St Louis Woman; House of Flowers; Jamaica; Saratoga; Free and Easy (blues opera); Films: Let's Fall in Love; Strike Me Pink; The Singing Kid; Stage Struck; Gold Diggers of 1937; The Wizard of Oz; At the Circus; Blues in the Night; Rio Rita; Star Spangled Rhythm; Cabin in the Sky; The Sky's the Limit; Up in Arms; Kismet; Here Come the Waves; Out of This World; Casbah; My Blue Heaven; The Petty Girl; Down Among the Sheltering Palms; Mr Imperium; The Farmer Takes a Wife; A Star Is Born; The Country Girl; Gay Purr-ee.

ARLUCK, ELLIOT   ASCAP 1979
composer, author
b New York, NY, June 23, 15. Educ: Abraham Lincoln High Sch; New Sch of Soc Research Dramatic Workshop. Saxophonist in var clubs. USA, 43-45, wrote musical for Army. Wrote bk, lyrics & music for "Things Are No Different Here," London; also wrote play with music, "Wolf Are You Ready?" & opera, "The Audition," rec'd Nat Award, Ohio State Univ contest. Wrote Am version, "Meet Peter Grant." Chief Collabrs: Ted Harris, Alfred Grant Goodman. *Songs & Instrumental Works:* Susan and the Merry-Go-Round; Bumpo the Ballerina.

ARMBRUSTER, ROBERT   ASCAP 1955
composer, conductor, pianist
b Philadelphia, Pa. Educ: West Philadelphia High Sch; studied with Constantin von Sternberg. Former pianist, then cond & comp for radio, TV & films. *Songs & Instrumental Works:* Cuddle Up; High Barbaree; Western Ballet; Variations in Miniature on Chopsticks; We the People (SATB); Acapulco (concert band).

ARMEN, KAY   ASCAP 1953
composer, singer
b Chicago, Ill. Singer, theatres, films, nightclubs & TV; recording artist. *Songs:* My Love and I; Be Good to Yourself; It's a Sin to Cry Over You.

ARMENTROUT, LEE   ASCAP 1954
composer, author, trombonist
b Mattoon, Ill, Apr 30, 09. Educ: High sch. Arr, var orchs incl Ben Bernie, Alec Templeton & NBC & CBS. Chief Collabr: Bobby Christian. *Songs:* Crickets on Parade; Stretch Stock for Santa.

ARMOCIDA, WILLIAM FRANCIS   ASCAP 1960
composer, author
b Cleveland, Ohio, Mar 29, 22. Educ: Carnegie Inst Technol, BFA, 48;
Duquesne Univ, MEduc, 64; Univ Pittsburgh, sociology & psychol, 65-67.
Served, WW II, Eng, France, Belg & Ger. Teacher, 1 yr; admin technician, Pa
Army Nat Guard, 51-68; active duty, SAC, USAF, Omaha, Nebr, 68- *Songs:*
Definition of Love.

ARMSTRONG, HARRY   ASCAP 1929
composer, singer
b Somerville, Mass, July 22, 1879; d New York, NY, Feb 28, 51. Educ: Pub schs.
Was prize fighter, pianist, booking agent & producer. During WW I, entertained
in hosps & other places. Then entertainer in radio, TV & nightclubs. *Songs:*
Sweet Adeline; Goodbye Eyes of Blue; The Frisco Rag; I Love My Wife, But
Oh You Kid; Follow the Crowd on a Sunday; Can't You See I'm Lonely?; Baby
Doll; Nellie Dear.

ARMSTRONG, LILLIAN HARDIN   ASCAP 1957
composer, pianist
b Memphis, Tenn, Feb 3, 02; d Chicago, Ill, Aug 27, 71. Educ: Col, teacher's
cert. Pianist in New Orleans Creole Jazz Band, King Oliver & Louis Armstrong
bands. Many records made; toured Europe, 52-56. *Songs:* Just for a Thrill;
Brown Gal; Struttin' With Some Barbecue; Perdido Street Blues.

ARMSTRONG, LOUIS   ASCAP 1939
composer, author, trumpeter
b New Orleans, La, July 4, 1900; d 1971. Brought up in Waifs' Home, New
Orleans, where he learned to play cornet. Began career as trumpeter with Kid
Ory Band; joined King Oliver & Fletcher Henderson Orchs. Mem symphonic
jazz orch of Erskine Tate, Chicago, 26; also played in Carroll Dickerson Orch.
Appeared with band in Bway revue "Hot Chocolates"; actor in "Swingin' the
Dream." Appeared at Palladium, London, 32. Film appearances: "Pennies From
Heaven"; "Auf Wiedersehen"; "A Girl, A Guitar and a Trumpet"; "Goin'
Places"; "Every Day's a Holiday"; "Artists and Models"; "Pillar to Post"; "The
Strip"; "Glory Alley"; "A Song Is Born"; "The Glenn Miller Story"; "The Five
Pennies"; "High Society"; "Jazz on a Summer's Day." First jazz concert at
Metrop Opera House, NY, 44; appeared in jazz fest, Nice, France, 48; made
Europ tours, 49-52, Japanese tour, 54, Ghana, 56 & British WI, 57. Author,
"Swing That Music." Awards: Esquire; Down Beat Int Critics' Poll; Down Beat
Hall of Fame; Grammy. Made many records. *Songs & Instrumental Works:*
Hear Me Talkin' to Ya'; Satchel Mouth Swing; Sugar Foot Stomp; Wild Man
Blues; Struttin' With Some Barbecue; Ol' Man Mose; Hobo, You Can't Ride
That Train; No Variety Blues; Joseph 'n' His Brudders; Someday.

ARMSTRONG, SINCLAIR (BOB)   ASCAP 1964
composer, author, arranger
b Buffalo, NY, Feb 12, 12. Educ: Pvt music study. Cellist, Buffalo Symph. Music
dir, WBEN; cond, NBC radio shows, 10 yrs; cond & arr for records; arr, "Jack
Paar Show," TV. *Songs:* Where There's Love.

ARNABOLDI, JOSEPH P   ASCAP 1963
composer, author
b Union City, NJ, Dec 2, 20. Educ: Cornell Univ, DVM. *Instrumental Works:*
Could It Be; I'm Sorry.

ARNATT, RONALD   ASCAP 1962
composer, conductor, organist
b London, Eng, Jan 16, 30. Educ: Westminster Abbey Choir Sch, 38-40; Kings
Col Choir Sch, Cambridge, 41-44; Trent Col, 45-47; Trinity Col Music, London,
51; fel Am Guild Organists, 52; Durham Univ, Eng, BMus, 54; Westminster
Choir Col, Princeton, NJ, DMus, 70. Organist & choir dir, several churches &
temples, Washington, DC, 47-54. Founder & cond, Washington Cantata
Chorus, 50-54 & St Louis Chamber Orch & Chorus, Mo, 56-78. Instr organ &
piano & lectr theory, Am Univ, DC. Became US citizen, 53. Dir music, Mary
Inst, St Louis, 54-68. Dir music & organist, Christ Church Cathedral, St Louis,
54-80. Cond & music dir, Kirkwood Symph Orch, Mo, 64-68 & Bach Soc St
Louis, 74-80. Prof music, Univ Mo, St Louis, 68-80. Organist & dir music,
Trinity Church, Boston, Mass, 80- *Instrumental Works:* Introduction and
Rondo for Organ, Brass and Timpani; Fanfare for Organ; Fantasia, Aria and
Fugue for Organ; Three Plainsong Preludes for Organ; Procession for Organ;
Variations on a Theme by Leo Sowerby. *Songs & Instrumental Works:* Chorus:
Blessed Are the Poor in Spirit (choir & organ); Festival Psalm (choir & organ);
Easter Triumph (choir & organ); Lord, Thou Hast Been Our Dwelling Place
(tenor solo, choir & organ); I Waited Patiently for the Lord (boys' or women's
voices & organ); Blessed City, Heavenly Salem (choir); A Coventry Anthem for
3 Trumpets, Two Choirs & Organ; Praise to God (choir & organ); The Lamb
(choir); The Angel Gabriel (choir); Now Begin on Christmas Day (choir); Gloria
and Sanctus/Benedictus for Congregation, Choir and Organ; Communion
Service for the People for Brass Quartet, Congregation, Choir & Organ; Prayer
at Christmas (choir).

ARNDT, FELIX   ASCAP 1914
composer, pianist, organist
b New York, NY, May 20, 1889; d Harmon-on-Hudson, NY, Oct 16, 18. Educ:
New York Cons; Trinity Sch. ASCAP charter mem. Organist, Trinity Church;
pianist for music publ; orch cond. Made over 3000 piano roll recordings;
husband of Nola Arndt. *Songs & Instrumental Works:* Nola; Marionette; Soup
to Nuts; Toots; Clover Club; Love in June; Kakuda; Lovelette; Desecration Rag
Humoresque; Operatic Nightmare.

ARNDT, NOLA   ASCAP 1951
composer, singer, teacher
b DeQueen, Ark, July 11, 1889; d New York, NY, July 19, 77. Educ: Maddux
Sem; Wash Univ; Beethoven Cons; Juilliard Sch; Sorbonne. Gave many recitals,
US & Europe. Soloist, toured with St Louis Symph. Teacher, Cape Cod Inst of
Music; organized music dept, DeQueen High Sch. Wife of Felix Arndt.

ARNHEIM, GUS   ASCAP 1925
composer, conductor
b Philadelphia, Pa, Sept 11, 1897; d Los Angeles, Calif, Jan 19, 55. Cond of own
orch, toured US & Europe; appeared in theatres, nightclubs & ballrooms. Chief
Collabrs: Arthur Freed, Jules Lemare, Abe Lyman, Harry Tobias. *Songs:* Sweet
and Lovely; I Cried for You; I'm Gonna Get You; It Must Be True; After All
Is Said and Done; It Might Have Been You; One Kiss.

ARNO, GEORGE
See Arellano, George Isidro

ARNOLD, BERNARD (BUDDY)   ASCAP 1951
composer, author
b New York, NY, Aug 11, 15. Educ: City Col New York. Writer spec material
for Milton Berle, Red Buttons, Ray Bolger, Andy Williams, also for "Your Hit
Parade," "Ed Sullivan Show," Staff writer, ABC-TV for "The Jimmy Dean
Show." Chief Collabrs: Milton Berle, Victor Young, Woody King, Jay Burton,
Larry Gelbart, Jack Gould. *Songs:* Lucky Lucky Lucky Me; It Only Takes a
Moment; Summer Love; Wall Flowers; If I Knew You Were There.

ARNOLD, DAVID H   ASCAP 1965
composer
b Buffalo, NY, Oct 9, 33. Educ: Hiram Col, Ohio, BA, 55; Western Reserve
Univ, MA, 60. TV dir & producer, Cleveland, Ohio, 60-65; film producer & ed,
Los Angeles, Calif, 66- Comp two full-length musicals, 66 & 68, perf community
theater, "The Three-a-Day" & "Dancing Dan's Christmas." Chief Collabrs:
Dave Bell, Gene Cavanaugh.

ARNOLD, FRANK ARTHUR   ASCAP 1976
composer, author
b Brooklyn, NY, Jan 12, 44. *Songs:* It Happens Everyday; How About a Kiss
for Me Baby?.

ARNOLD, HUGH
See Richter, Ada A

ARNONE, DOMINICK L (DON)   ASCAP 1966
composer, teacher, guitarist
b Elizabeth, NJ, Dec 2, 20. Worked with jazz combos, NJ; to New York, 46;
began career as TV & studio guitarist, incl TV shows with Fred Waring, Ken
Murray, Jack Benny, Arthur Godfrey, Ed Sullivan, Mitch Miller, Dick Van
Dyke, Merv Griffin, Garry Moore and others. Worked with TV commericals &
top vocalist & arr for Percy Faith, Kostelanetz, Neal Hefti, Don Costa, Pat
Williams, Peter Matz and others; teaching. Chief Collabr: Al Calola.
Instrumental Works: Pablo; Country Barn Dance; Vibrations; Chinese Guitar;
Poinsetta.

AROMANDO, JOSEPH S   ASCAP 1959
composer, author
b Belleville, NJ, Jan 19, 12; d. Educ: Newark Sch of Fine & Indust Arts.
Commercial artist; adv mgr & dir for drug co. Chief Collabr: Nick Di Nardo.
Songs: Garden State Rhapsody; Rockin' Calypso.

ARQUETTE, CLIFF   ASCAP 1959
composer, author, pianist
b Toledo, Ohio, Dec 28, 05; d. Was pianist in nightclubs; joined Henry Halstead
Orch, 23. Appeared on radio & TV; created character of Charlie Weaver on
"Jack Paar Show," TV. Chief Collabr: Charles Bud Dant. *Songs:* Fight for
Sub-Normal U; Who'll Sign the Pardon for Wallace Swine?; It's Xmas in Mt Idy;
Just Got a Letter From Mama; On the Boardwalk at Snider's Swamp; Don't
Give the Chair to Buster.

ARRELL, GREG F   ASCAP 1979
composer, singer
b Shahopee, Minn, Jan 15, 50. Educ: Univ Ore, philosophy major. Started
singing in Portland, Ore at age 18; worked in clubs; signed with Al Ross, then
with MCA, 80- *Songs:* Be My Lady Tonight; Do It All Again; Lullabye;
Everything I Need.

ARTHUR, BOBB
See Shaftel, Arthur

ARTHUR, ROBERT ASCAP 1953
composer, author, conductor
b Flushing, NY. Educ: Colgate Univ, BA; cond with Tibor Serly; piano with Joseph Prostikoff. Songwriter, musicals at Bayside High Sch, Colgate Univ & US Army. Music supvr, "Ed Sullivan Show," CBS-TV. Bway, song in "Mademoiselle Colombe" starring Julie Harris; songs in Julius Monk's "Plaza 5" revues; score for Theatre Guild's "Idiots Delight" (unproduced). Writer/producer TV, "TV Annual", "Natalie Cole Special", "David Soul Special", "ABC Silver Anniversary Celebration", "25th Anniversary of American Bandstand", "Ringling Bros Circus Specials", "American Music Awards" & "The Sullivan Years." *Songs:* Small Town; All About Love; I Walked Alone Last Night; Bouncy Bouncy Bally; Granny Claus; The Leaves; A Chance to Live in Camelot; TV Theme Songs: The Way We Are; It's American Music; Circus Super Heroes; The Greatest Show on Earth; Lyrics: It's Been a Long Time.

ARTMAN, RUTH ELEANOR ASCAP 1977
composer, choral director, clinician
b Hamilton, Ind, Sept 19, 19. Educ: Cornell Col; Westminster Col, Pa, BME; St Francis Col, Ind, MA; postgrad work, Ill State Univ, Ill Wesleyan Univ, Butler Univ & Univ Ky. Teacher in Ind & Ill pub schs, 22 yrs; has had experience on all levels from kindergarten through high sch; also has taught short courses in var cols & univs at grad level. Music dir in numerous churches; has had experience with preschoolers through adult choirs. Traveled widely to direct reading sessions, clinics, fests, workshops & make professional appearances. *Songs:* Song of the Littlest Angel; Scatter the Joy; In the Still of the Morning; Sounds of Hope; Little Lamb; Come, Walk With Me; Kids Are Music; I Have Only One Life to Live; Back-a-Rock!; Music: The Night Before Christmas (arr); Five Foot Two, Eyes of Blue (arr).

ARVEY, VERNA (MRS WILLIAM GRANT STILL) ASCAP 1943
author
b Los Angeles, Calif, Feb 16, 10. Educ: Los Angeles pub schs; studied piano with Margeurite d'Aleria, Rose Cooper Vinetz, Alexander Kosloff & Ann Eachus. In concert, US & Latin Am. Soloist in "Kaintuck'" with Los Angeles Philh Orch. Author, var articles on dance & music; bk: "Choreographic Music." Chief Collabr: William Grant Still. *Songs:* Lyrics: The Path of Glory; The Little Song That Wanted to Be a Symphony; Rhapsody; Mississippi; Song for the Valiant; Song for the Lonely; Up There; Lament; Wailing Woman; Those Who Wait; A Psalm for the Living; All That I Am; From the Hearts of Women. *Songs & Instrumental Works:* Lenox Avenue; Miss Sally's Party; A Bayou Legend; Highway 1, USA (A Southern Interlude); Costaso; Mota; The Pillar; Minette Fontaine.

ARVON, BOBBY
See Arvonio, Robert Anthony

ARVONIO, ANGELO CARMEN, JR ASCAP 1971
composer, lyricist, singer
b Scranton, Pa, June 4, 48. Educ: Cent High Sch, Bridgeport, Conn; Housiatnoic Community Col; Calif State Univ, Northridge, 69-71. Keyboardist & drummer; performed & toured with Sergio Mendez, Brazil 66. Singer with own band, 3 yrs. Joined band, Wynchester. Drummer for Phil Everly (Everly Bros). *Songs:* The Desert; Goodbye Bluesome Lady; The Days of You and Me; My Fantasy; If Only I'da Known It; Celebration; Welcome. *Albums:* Angelo; Angelo Midnight Prowl.

ARVONIO, ROBERT ANTHONY (BOBBY ARVON) ASCAP 1969
composer, author, singer
b Scranton, Pa, Sept 13, 41. Educ: Voice training with Helen Teddi Hall, 59-60. Former singer with Les & Larry Elgart & Harry James. Solo act, nightclubs & TV. Pianist; recording artist, Metro-Goldwyn-Mayer, MTA & First Artists Jingle's. *Songs:* Until Now; From Now On; Rock and Roll Music Man; Can You Hear Me Lord?; You're a Part of Me.

ASCHAFFENBURG, WALTER EUGENE ASCAP 1969
composer, educator
b Essen, Ger, May 20, 27. Educ: Hartford Sch Music, dipl, 45; Oberlin Col Cons Music, BA, 51; Univ Rochester Eastman Sch Music, MA, 52; studied comp with Herbert Elwell, Bernard Rogers, Luigi Dallapiccola. Prof comp & theory, Oberlin Col Cons Music, 52- Recipient, Fromm Music Found award, 53, Nat Inst of Arts & Letters award, 66, Cleveland Arts Prize, 80, Guggenheim Fels, 55-56 & 73-74. Chief Collabr: Jay Leyda. *Songs:* Music: The 23rd Psalm, Anthem for Mixed Chorus, Tenor and Oboe. *Instrumental Works:* Three Dances for Orchestra; Libertatem Appellant for Tenor, Baritone and Orchestra; Poem for Brass and Percussion; Conversations, Six Pieces for Piano; Quintet for Winds; Ozymandias, Symphonic Reflections for Orchestra. *Scores:* Opera: Bartleby (prologue, two acts).

ASCHER, EMIL ASCAP 1936
composer, conductor, pianist
b Hamburg, Germany, Apr 12, 1859; d New York, NY, Oct 22, 22. Educ: Studied with Niels Gade & Cornelius Gurlitt; Royal Cons, Leipzig, with Liszt & Wagner. Founded publ firm, Hamburg. To US, 1889. Cond & organist churches, NY; cond band concerts, Old Madison Square Garden; organized 75

woman orch, Atlantic Garden, NY. *Instrumental Works:* Maximillan Overture; Royal Overture; La Rose Intermezzo; Our Heroes March; Pilgrims Love Song; Our Students March; Olympia Overture.

ASCHER, EVERETT (FRANK MORTON, RICHARD HOFFMAN, ED ASTER) ASCAP 1959
composer
b New York, NY, Apr 3, 36. Educ: New York High Sch; Univ Rochester, BA, 57. Wrote background music & titles for TV shows. Mem trustees coun, Univ Rochester, mem vis comt, Eastman Sch of Music.

ASCHER, KENNETH LEE ASCAP 1968
composer
b Washington, DC, Oct 26, 44. Educ: Columbia Univ, AB(musical comp), AM(musical comp) & DMA(musical comp); studied with Otto Luening, Jack Beeson & Vladimir Ussochevsky; studied piano with William Beller. Studied piano since age 5; started study of arr & comp at age 16; began songwriting in 73. Chief Collabrs: Paul Williams, Carol Bayer Sager. *Songs:* Music: You and Me Against the World (nominated for Grammy Award, 74); The Rainbow Connection (nominated for Oscar Award, 80); With One More Look At You; Loneliness; With You; Movin' Right Along; Never Before, Never Again; You Know Me. *Scores:* Films: A Star Is Born (Golden Globe Award, Hollywood Foreign Press, 76, nominated for Grammy Award, 77); The Muppet Movie (nominated for Oscar Award, 80, nominated for Grammy Award, 80).

ASH, GAIL ASCAP 1953
composer, author
b New York, NY. Educ: Jamaica Training Sch Teachers, grad. *Songs:* Am I the One; Lyrics: Miss Me.

ASH, PAUL ASCAP 1955
composer, author, conductor
b Saxony, Ger, Feb 11, 1891; d New York NY, July 13, 58. To US, 1892. Educ: Milwaukee pub schs; studied piano with Charles Hambitzer. USMC, World War I. Toured US with own orch; presented band shows, San Francisco, Chicago at the Oriental Theatre, New York, Brooklyn at Paramount Theatres. Cond, Roxy Theatre, New York. *Songs:* I'm Knee Deep in Daisies; I'd Love to Call You My Sweetheart; Hoosier Sweetheart; Gonna Get a Girl; It's a Happy Old World After All; When Night Time Comes; Rosa Lee; Just Once Again; That's Why I Love You; Thinking of You; Pesticatin' Mama; You're Wonderful.

ASHERMAN, ALICE CORNETT ASCAP 1946
composer, singer, teacher
b Plant City, Fla, July 21, 11. Educ: Fla State Col for Women. Featured singer, "Coca Cola Song Shop," 39 weeks, 37; vocalist with Xavier Cugat Orch, 39; own radio prog, NBC, 5 times weekly, 42-45, also singer on "Garry Moore Show." Chief Collabr: Ed Asherman. *Songs:* Music: All That Glitters Is Not Gold; Slap'er Down Agin', Paw; With This Ring I Thee Wed; Cool Blue Waters; Thanksgiving At Home; There's a Tear in My Beer Tonite; Mm Mm, It's Time to Say Hello; All Day Singing and Dinner on the Ground; Who Said There's No Santa Claus.

ASHERMAN, EDWARD M ASCAP 1946
composer, guitarist, singer
b New York, NY, Jan 19, 13. Educ: City Col New York. Guitarist & vocalist with Xavier Cugat Orch, 37-42; free-lance guitarist on major networks & recording cos; Bloomer Girl Show; David Broekman Orch; Campbell Soup Prog; Texaco Prog. Treasury Star Parade Transc with Bing Crosby, Frank Sinatra & others. Chief Collabr: Alice Cornett. *Songs:* Music: All That Glitters Is Not Gold; Slap 'Er Down Agin', Paw; With This Ring I Thee Wed; The Cat Serenade; Cuba Libra; Cool Blue Waters; Thanksgiving At Home; Theres A Tear In My Beer Tonite; All Day Singing and Dinner on the Ground; Who Said There's No Santa Claus.

ASHERMAN, NAT ASCAP 1958
composer, pianist
b New York, NY, Aug 12, 09. Educ: Columbia Univ, PhD; Juilliard. Pianist with dance orchs incl, Leo Reisman, Meyer Davis & Lester Lanin. *Songs:* Music: Spring Has Sprung; Just Like a Bumble Bee (Looking for a Honey Like You). *Instrumental Works:* Subway Rush; Boiling Point; Don't Lose It.

ASHFORD, NICKOLAS
composer, lyricist, singer
b Fairfield, SC, May 4, 42. Recorded with Glover, Sceptor & Motown Records. Songwriter & performer with Valerie Simpson. Chief Collabr: Valerie Simpson. *Songs:* Ain't No Mountain High Enough; Reach Out and Touch; Ain't Nothing Like the Real Thing; Gimme Something Real; Let's Go Get Stoned; Found A Cure; The Boss; Remember Me; It Seems to Hang On; Stuff Like That; I'm Every Woman. *Albums:* Gimme Something Real; I Wanna Be Selfish; Come; So, So Satisfied; Send It; Is It Still Good To Ya; Stay Free.

ASHMAN, HOWARD ELLIOTT ASCAP 1979
composer, author
b Baltimore, Md, May 17, 50. Educ: Goddard Col, Vt, 71; Ind Univ, MA(theater), 74. Author bk for musical, "Dream Stuff," 76 & play,

"Conformation," 77; author bk & lyrics (revision), "The Vagabond King," 79; author bk & lyrics, "God Bless You Mr Rosewater," 79, also prod off-Bway play; artistic dir, WPA Theater, New York, 76-80; dir musical version, "Nine." Chief Collabrs: Allen Menken, Maury Yeston.

ASHTON, BOB BRUCE   ASCAP 1964
composer, author, educator
b Omaha, Nebr, Jan 2, 21. Educ: Peru State Col; Omaha Univ; Univ Colo; Denver Univ; Southwest Mo State Univ; BA, MA; studied voice with Arthur Westbrook, choral with Paul Christensen. Instr music, Omaha & Denver Pub Schs. Pres, Stylist Records & Ashton Publ Co. Many publ & recorded works. Teaching creative writing, Drury Col, Mo. *Songs:* A Summer's Love; It's Cozy and Warm Inside; Christmas Shopping; It's a Good Land; Of Course; It Took Awhile; His Lonesome Way; Hand in Hand; A Country Christmas; Wonderful Love (cantata); The Prodigal (cantata); Would You Mind; The Greatest Gift; Under Colorado Skies; Autumn Farewell; More Than Likely; He's My Saviour; True Words of Wisdom; Let's Pray Together; Magic in the Moon; I'll Spend Christmas Without You. *Instrumental Works:* Colorama.

ASHTON, JOHN HOWARD   ASCAP 1977
composer, conductor, trumpeter
b Pittsburgh, Pa, July 11, 38. Educ: Carnegie-Mellon Univ, BFA, 60, MFA, 61; Cath Univ Am, 62-65; WVa Univ, 72-74; studied with Nikolai Lopatnikoff & Thomas Canning. Trumpeter with US Naval Acad Band, Savannah Symph Orch, RTE Symph Orch & New Orleans Philh. Asst prof music, Univ Nebr. Asst prof music, Fairmont State Col, founder & dir, Fairmont Col Community Symph Orch & Fairmont Brass Quintet. *Songs & Instrumental Works:* Theme and Five Variations (piano solo); Quintet for Clarinet and Strings; Songs from The Unknown Eros; Dialogues, Discourses (saxophone quartet); Music for a Community Orchestra; Sonata for Trumpet and Piano; Lyric Piece for Brass Quintet; Jeremiah 20: 7-13 (chorus, brass).

ASHWANDER, DONALD JOHN   ASCAP 1962
composer
b Birmingham, Ala, July 17, 29. Educ: Manhattan Sch Music. Comp of six shows for Paper Bag Players, America's foremost children's theater; performed & recorded by comp on electric harpsichord. Had ragtime comp in repertory, The Royal Ballet. Comp of many concert songs, ballet music, documentary film music & much else. Rec'd ASCAP award, 76-80 & Guide Found award. *Albums:* Ragtime, the New View; Turnips; Sunshine and Shadow.

ASKEW, DENNIS LEE   ASCAP 1977
composer, author, performer
b Las Vegas, Nev, Apr 19, 53. Has own group, Universe. Played in local & regional clubs. Recording artist, singer, guitarist & synthesist. Chief Collabr: Gary Paul Van. *Songs:* Rock in the Sky; Oceans; Touchdown; Remember the Stars; Star Child. *Albums:* Universe.

ASPER, FRANK W   ASCAP 1957
composer, conductor, organist
b Logan, Utah, Feb 9, 1892; d Salt Lake City, Utah, Nov 8, 73. Educ: New Eng Cons of Music; Boston Univ; Univ Utah; hon MusD, Bates Col. Taught piano, harmony & counterpoint, New Eng Cons of Music & McCune Sch of Music & Art. Organist, Salt Lake Tabernacle Choir & for broadcasts. Gave concerts in US, Europe, Can & Mex. Recording artist. Author, bk "The Organ in Church." Fel, Am Guild of Organists. *Instrumental Works:* Devotional Duets. *Albums:* Devotional Organ Album; Recreational Organ Album.

ASRO, GENE
See Rossana, Augustine

ASSANTE, ALLISON
composer, author
b Lafayette, Ind, Mar 6, 23. Educ: Stevens Finishing Sch, grad, voice & music tutoring by Purdue Univ instrs; studied voice with Carlo Menotti, Carnegie Hall. First hit song at age 13. Chief Collabrs: Duke Ellington, Don George. *Songs:* Goodbye, My Love; Broken Butterfly; Baby, Baby, Run From Me; I Don't Want You-Anymore; Kiss, Kiss, Kiss; Lonely River; Lyrics: Moon Lady; What Is It Like-Where She Has Gone?.

ASTAIRE, FRED   ASCAP 1942
composer, dancer, actor
b Omaha, Nebr, May 10, 1899. Professional debut as dancer at age 5, Paterson, NJ. In vaudeville with sister, Adele, until 16. Appeared with sister in Bway musicals "Over the Top", "Passing Show of 1918", "Apple Blossoms", "Lady, Be Good!", "Funny Face", "Smiles" & "The Band Wagon," 16-32, then in "Gay Divorce"; appeared in films, "Dancing Lady", "Flying Down to Rio", "The Gay Divorcee", "Roberta", "Top Hat", "Follow the Fleet", "Swing Time", "Shall We Dance", "A Damsel in Distress", "Carefree", "The Story of Vernon and Irene Castle", "Broadway Melody of 1940", "Second Chorus", "You'll Never Get Rich", "Holiday Inn", "You Were Never Lovelier", "The Sky's the Limit", "Ziegfeld Follies", "Yolanda and the Thief", "Blue Skies", "Easter Parade", "The Barkleys of Broadway", "Three Little Words", "Let's Dance", "Royal Wedding", "The Belle of New York", "The Band Wagon", "Daddy Long Legs", "Funny Face", "Silk Stockings", "Towering Inferno" & "On the Beach."

Featured on TV specials, also TV series; founded Ava Records. Autobiography: "Steps in Time." Chief Collabrs: Johnny Mercer, Gladys Shelley. *Songs:* Blue Without You; I'm Building Up to an Awful Let-Down; I'll Never Let You Go; Just One More Dance, Madame; Just Like Taking Candy From a Baby; If Swing Goes, I Go Too; Sweet Sorrow; Oh, My Achin' Back; The Afterbeat; I Love Everybody But You; Life Is Beautiful; City of the Angels.

ASTER, ED
See Ascher, Everett

ATCHLEY, SAMUEL LEE   ASCAP 1979
composer, author
b Waxahachie, Tex, June 26, 45. Owned & operated 2 recording studios, Tex; owner, 2 publ cos; songwriter. Chief Collabrs: James Sandy Pinkard, Dian Johnston, Mac Curtis, Michael Tate, Tom Wayne. *Songs:* Coca Cola Cowboy; Lookin At You; Ole Piano Bench Song; Heart of Stone; I Can't Get to Where I Don't Want You.

ATENCIO, F XAVIER   ASCAP 1969
author
b Trinidad, Colo, Sept 4, 19. Educ: Chouinard Art Inst. Employed by Walt Disney Productions, 38-, cartoon animator for first 27 yrs, writer/designer for W E D Enterprises, a subsidiary of Walt Disney Productions, creating show concepts, dialogue & narration scripts & songs for Disneyland, Walt Disney World & Epcot Pavilions. Chief Collabrs: Buddy Baker, George Bruns. *Songs:* Lyrics: Yo Ho (A Pirate's Life for Me); Grim Grinning Ghosts; The Bear Band Serenade; If You Had Wings; Here's to the Future.

ATINSKY, JERRY (JERRY ALLEN)   ASCAP 1970
composer, author, guitar teacher
b Milwaukee, Wis, Oct 9, 17. Educ: Los Angeles Inst Music, Calif, 46-48. Folk singer; community based performer. Wrote topical songs for meetings, parties, fund raisers, 30 yrs. Chief Collabr: William Wolff. *Songs:* The Liberty Bell Went Ding Dong Ding (songbook of 10 children's songs); Golden Years; Mazeltov; Senor Allende; Peace March Song.

ATKERSON, PAUL   ASCAP 1960
composer, author, pianist
b Phoenix, Ariz, July 2, 21. Educ: Los Angeles Cons, BME. Served, USAAF, World War II. Pianist & radio announcer; writer for films. Chief Collabrs: Hal Levy, Bill Okie, Pete Peterson. *Songs:* Nobody Home But the Blues; The Velvet Hammer; Lady Lonely; The Wrong Door; You Taught Me How to Cry.

ATKINSON, CONDIT ROBERT   ASCAP 1969
composer, author, professor
b New Brunswick, NJ, July 4, 28. Educ: Southeastern La Univ, BME; La State Univ; Rutgers Univ; Trenton State Col, MA. Prof club date musician, 44-; played with Baton Rouge Symph, La, 46-50; bassist & arr, US Mil Acad Band, West Point, NY, 51-55. Teacher instrumental music, Highland Park Pub Schs, NJ, 55-69; prof music, Middlesex County Col, 69- *Songs:* The Monster Song (vocal novelty); Music: The House By the Side of the Road (gospel). *Instrumental Works:* Going Baroque and All That Jazz (16 jazz-baroque numbers); A Taste of Licorice (clarinet solo with band accompaniment); It Still Takes Two (piano duet book).

ATTANASIO, DONALD JOSEPH (DON CHRISTOPHER) ASCAP 1967
composer, author
b Newark, NJ, Mar 15, 38. Carnegie-Mellon Univ, Pa, BFA, 60; Montclair State Col, grad studies, 72-75. Songwriter of many recorded songs; prof mgr for United Artists Music Corp, Notable Music Corp & ABC Music Publ Co. Owner, Caterpillar Music, 80- Chief Collabrs: Joseph Fanelli, Stanley J Gelber, Mario Lombardo. *Songs:* God Is Alive; You Are Not Alone; Love and Let Love; Lyrics: The Ol' Race Track.

ATTAWAY, WILLIAM A   ASCAP 1956
composer, arranger
b Greenville, Miss, Nov 19, 15. Educ: Univ Ill, BA. TV writer "Comedy Hour" & "Wide, Wide World." Author "Let Me Breathe Thunder" & "Blood on the Forge." Arr in folk field. *Songs:* Noah; Jump Down, Spin Around.

ATTERIDGE, (RICHARD) HAROLD   ASCAP 1914
author
b Lake Forest, Ill, July 9, 1886; d Lynnbrook, NY, Jan 15, 38. Educ: Univ Chicago, PhB. Staff writer for Shuberts. Librettist: "The Midnight Rounders"; "Big Boy"; "Artists and Models"; "Gay Paree"; "A Night in Paris"; "A Night in Spain"; "Ziegfeld Follies of 1927"; "Greenwich Village Follies of 1928"; "Everybody's Welcome." Charter mem, ASCAP. Chief Collabrs: Harry Carroll, Louis Hirsch, Al Jolson, Otto Motzan, Sigmund Romberg, Jean Schwartz, Al Goodman. *Songs:* My Yellow Jacket Girl; By the Beautiful Sea; Omar Khayyam; My Lady of the Telephone; Sister Susie Started Syncopation; The Ragtime of Pan; Fascination; Lotus Flower; Galli Curci Rag; Broadway Butterfly; Jazza-Da-Doo; Doing My Bit. *Scores:* Bway stage: The Whirl of Society; Honeymoon Express; The Peasant Girl; also librettist: Vera Violetta; The Passing Show (12 ed); The Whirl of the World; Dancing Around; Maid in America; A World of Pleasure; Robinson Crusoe, Jr; The Show of Wonders;

Doing Our Bit; Sinbad; Monte Cristo, Jr; The Last Waltz; Bombo; The Rose of Stamboul; The Dancing Girl; Topics of 1923; Innocent Eyes; Pleasure Bound.

ATWELL, ROY ASCAP 1957
composer, comedian
b Syracuse, NY, May 2, 1878; d New York, NY, Feb 6, 62. Educ: Sargent Sch Acting. Bway stage appearances incl "The Little Missus", "The Mimic World", "The Firefly" & "How's Your Health?" Mem, Fortune Gallo Opera Co. *Songs:* Some Little Bug Is Going to Find You.

AUDEN, WYSTAN HUGH (W H AUDEN) ASCAP 1958
author
b York, Eng, Feb 21, 07. US citizen, 46. Educ: Oxford Univ. Coauthor of verse plays "The Dog Beneath the Skin", "The Ascent of F6", "On the Frontier," vols of poetry incl "Double Man", "The Shield of Achilles" (Nat Bk Award), "For the Time Being", "Collected Shorter Poems" & "The Age of Anxiety" (Pulitzer Prize, 48). Author "Spain." Coauthor "Education, Today and Tomorrow"; co-ed "Poet's Tongue." Awards: Bollingen; Alexander Droutsky; Guinness. Chief Collabr: Igor Stravinsky. *Instrumental Works:* On This Island (poems set to music). *Scores:* Opera: The Rakes Progress.

AUER, LEOPOLD ASCAP 1924
composer, violinist, educator
b Veszprem, Hungary, June 7, 1845; d Loschwitz, Ger, July 15, 30. Educ: Vienna Cons, with Jakob Dont; also studied with Ridley Kohnel & Joseph Joachim. Concertmaster, Dusseldorf Orch, 1863-65; also Hamburg Orch. Prof violin, St Petersburg Cons, 1868-1917. Cond symph concerts, Imperial Musical Asn, 3 yrs; violin soloist in courts of Czars Alexander II, Alexander III & Nicholas II; also with ballet of Russian Imperial Opera. Founded string quartet in St Petersburg. Moved to US, 18, citizen, 26. Taught at Juilliard Sch Music & Curtis Inst; also gave violin recitals. Pupils incl Elman, Heifetz, Zimbalist, Seidel, Achron, Piastro & Milstein. Author: "Violin Playing As I Teach It"; "My Long Life in Music"; "Violin Masterworks and Their Interpretation." *Instrumental Works:* Transc of works by Tschaikovsky, Beethoven, Schumann, Wagner.

AUGUSTINE, DANIEL SCHUYLER ASCAP 1974
composer, teacher, arranger
b Washington, Pa, July 3, 42. Educ: Univ Nev, Reno, BS(mathematics), 64, MA(music theory), 67; Univ Tex, Austin, PhD(music theory), 79; studied with Gilbert Chase, Kent Kennan & Karl Korte. Tubist, Univ Nev Community Symph, 61-66, 523rd USAF Band at March AFB, Riverside, Calif, 67-68, Reno Philh Symph Orch, 69-73. Free-lance musician in Reno, 69-73. Teaching asst in music theory, Univ Tex, Austin, 74-79. *Instrumental Works:* Arr: Duets and Trios for Tubas (Bach); Canzon Trigesimaquinta (brass ens, Massaino).

AULD, GEORGIE ASCAP 1955
composer, conductor, saxophonist
b Toronto, Ont, May 19, 19. Saxophonist with var orchs incl Bunny Berigan, Artie Shaw, Jan Savitt, Benny Goodman. Served, World War II. Leader, orch, 44-46 & var small groups. Saxophonist, TV orch; recording artist. *Songs:* Take Care; The Back to Back.

AUSTIN, BILLY ASCAP 1955
composer, author
b Denver, Colo, Mar 6, 1896; d Hollywood, Calif, July 24, 64. Educ: New York Pub Schs. Sailor, lumberjack & construction worker. *Songs:* Is You Is Or Is You Ain't My Baby?; Can't Be Bothered; Don't Let Your Eyes Go Shopping for Your Heart.

AUSTIN, FRANCES
See Catts, Frances Austin

AUSTIN, GENE ASCAP 1925
composer, author, singer
b Gainesville, Tex, June 24, 1900; d. Educ: Baltimore Univ. Served in US Army with Mexican Punitive Exped, 16; also WW I. Singer in vaudeville, 23; also in theatres, radio, films & TV; made many records. Chief Collabrs: Roy Bergere, Jimmy McHugh, Nat Shilkret. *Songs:* Whippoorwill, Go Tell My Honey That I Love Her; The Lonesome Road; Please Come Back to Me; How Come You Do Me Like You Do?; When My Sugar Walks Down the Street; Ridin' Around in the Rain; Take Your Shoes Off Baby.

AUSTIN, PATRICIA ASCAP 1974
composer, author, singer
b New York, NY, Aug 10, 50. Educ: High sch grad. Began career at age 4. Music writer & recording artist, 74- Chief Collabrs: David Grusin, Quincy Jones. *Songs:* End of the Rainbow; Havana Candy; That's Enough for Me; I've Got the Melody; You Don't Have to Say You're Sorry; Love I Never Had It So Good.

AUSTIN, RAY ASCAP 1957
composer, arranger, conductor
b New York, NY, May 26, 15. Educ: Studied Schillinger Syst of comp with Franklyn Marks & conducting with Leanard Walker. Comp & arr for most big bands of the Big Band Era incl the Casa Loma Band, Russ Morgan Orch &

Freddy Martin Orch. Comp & arr for many radio shows incl Philip Morris, Lady Esther & others. Arr recording backgrounds for many singers incl Connie Boswell. Chief Collabrs: Lyricists, Bobby Worth, Paul Herrick, Irving Taylor. *Songs:* Music: Tonight We Love; Where in the World; I Look At Heaven; He'll Be There; Carmen Carmela. *Instrumental Works:* Morning Walk; Fiesta Time; Adaptations: Concerto in B flat minor (Tschaikovsky); Concerto in A minor (Grieg); Nutcracker Suite (Tschaikovsky); Serenade in C for Strings (Tschaikovsky); Clair De Lune (Debussy).

AUSTIN, TONY ASCAP 1972
composer, author, publisher
b Jackson, Tenn, Oct 29, 38. Educ: J B Young High Sch, Bemis, Tenn. Started with Johnny Burnett, 56-57. Musician, Grand Ol' Opry. Nightclub owner, Somewhere Else Club, Jackson. Has own publ co, Full Swing Music Co. Full Swing Band, 72- Awards: Eight Chart-Buster Awards; Four Ten Week Awards. Chief Collabrs: Johnny Wilson, Gene Dabbins, Curly Putman. *Songs:* Smile, Somebody Loves You; Blue Eyes and Waltzes; Gather Me to You; Living Here and Loving There and Lying in Between.

AUTRY, ORVON GENE ASCAP 1940
author, singer
b Tioga, Tex, Sept 29, 07. Educ: Ravia High Sch, Okla. Worked as telegrapher, Frisco Railroad. First appeared on radio, Tulsa, Okla; had own radio show, "Melody Ranch Show," CBS. Flight officer, ATC, USAAF, WW II. Top Western box office attraction. Actor & producer, films & TV; Singing Cowboy in 95 feature films & 12 part serial, "Phantom Empire." Recording artist, Columbia Records; nine gold records, incl "Rudolph, the Rednosed Reindeer", "Peter Cottontail", "Here Comes Santa Claus", "Tumbling Tumbleweeds", "Silver Haired Daddy of Mine", "Back in the Saddle Again", "You Are My Sunshine", "South of the Border" & "Mexicali Rose." Won Nat Parents-Teachers Film Award. Owner, Gene Autry Records, Inc. Publ, four music publ cos. Chief Collabrs: Fred Rose, Johnny Marvin. *Songs & Instrumental Works:* Back in the Saddle Again; Be Honest With Me; Here Comes Santa Claus; Tears on My Pillow; Tweedle O Twill; Blue Canadian Rockies; I Thought I Heard You Call My Name; Just Walking in the Rain; Shuckin' the Corn; You're the Only Good Thing That's Happened to Me; I Will; Slow Poke; You Belong to Me.

AVELLINO, ALFRED ASCAP 1954
composer, author, arranger
b Brooklyn, NY, Feb 10, 13. Educ: High sch; pvt music study. Arr for Irving Fields & for records. Chief Collabr: Charles O'Flynn. *Songs:* Dancing Castanets.

AVOLA, ALEXANDER ALBERT ASCAP 1951
composer, author, teacher
b Boston, Mass, Jan 27, 14. Educ: Violin studies with Scandoni; Allandale Art Studio; Suffolk Univ, LLB; guitar, self-taught; comp with Morris Mamorski & Paul Creston; conducting with Victor Bay; Calif State Univ, Los Angeles, teaching credential. Violin prodigy at 6 yrs; Jr Symph Boston at 13 yrs. Mass atty. Guitarist, arr with dance bands incl, Artie Shaw, T Dorsey, Tony Pastor, Frankie Carle, Raymond Scott, CBS; arr & cond for RCA. Teacher, Los Angeles City Schs. Chief Collabrs: Tony Pastor, Marty Symes, Al Hoffman, Artie Shaw, Frankie Carle, Mort Greene. *Songs:* Music: Song and a Star; Never Introduce Your Sweetheart; Love, You Belong to Me; Don't Ever Say Goodby. *Instrumental Works:* Blossoms; Fee Fi Fo Fum; Carle Boogie; Flag Waiver; Wigwam Stomp; Amerhumba; March of the Marines; Sunrise Boogie; Plam Trees and Surf; Copley Square; Piano Polka; SOS; Syncopated Doll; Sunrise in Napoli; Doodle, Do Ya Love Me. *Scores:* Films: Riverboat Rhythm; Marylou; Sweetheart of Sigma Chi.

AXLEROD, DAVID ASCAP 1962
author
b Buffalo, NY, Jan 13, 37. Educ: Univ Syracuse. Writer for TV shows, incl "Captain Kangaroo." Chief Collabrs: Sam Pottle, Tom Whedon. *Songs:* Who Wants to Work. *Scores:* Off-Bway Show: Money; TV: America, Be Seated.

AXT, WILLIAM ASCAP 1924
composer, conductor
b New York, NY, Apr 19, 1888; d Ukiah, Calif, Feb 12, 59. Educ: DeWitt Clinton High Sch; pvt music study, Berlin. Asst cond, Hammerstein Grand Opera Co, New York; cond, Emma Trentini, 14-18. Music dir, Capitol Theatre, New York, 19. Head music dept, MGM. *Scores:* Film: Grand Hotel; Parnell; The Garden Murder Case; Reunion in Vienna; The Thin Man; Rendevous; O'Shaughnessy's Boy; Penthouse; The Big Parade; Ben-Hur; The Merry Widow; La Boheme; Don Juan; Pygmalion; Flesh and the Devil; Love; Greed; He Who Gets Slapped; The Big House; Libeled Lady; Northwest Passage; Boomtown; Grand Hotel; Red Dust; Passion; Four Horsemen of the Apocalypse; Birth of a Nation; Barrets of Wimpole Street; Operator 13; In Little Old New York; Queen Christina; Bardelys the Magnificent; Eskimo; Nanook of the North; Mare Nostrum; The Torrent; Tarzan and His Mate; Gabriel Over the White House; White Shadows in the South Seas; The Prisoner of Zenda; Richard the Lion Hearted; Mark of Zorro; Woman of Affairs; Scaramouche; San Francisco; Trail of '98; The Navigator; Jimmy Valentine; Dinner at Eight; The Champ; Madame Curie; and many others.

AYALA, ROBERT STEVEN — ASCAP 1978
composer, singer

b Los Angeles, Calif, Mar 9, 51. Began performing contemporary Christian music, 69. Released first album, 77. Toured nationally as well as Can. Chief Collabr: Buddy King. *Songs:* Joy By Suprise; To the Ancient of Day; Wood Between the Worlds; I Need Love; Stephanie, With Love; Born on Easter Morning; Empty Cup; Nicodemus.

AYERS, ROY — ASCAP 1969
vibraharpist, vocalist

b Los Angeles, Calif, 1940. Educ: Los Angeles City Col, studied music. Led own group, 70- Toured Nigeria, with Fela Anikulapo Kuti, 79. Was in Kool Jazz Fest, Atlantic City, 80. Produced 80's Ladies-Uno Melodic Records.

AYNES, EDITH ANNETTE (PAT) — ASCAP 1969
composer, author

b Atwood, Kans, Apr 2, 09. Educ: Univ Calif, Berkeley, BS; Kean Col NJ, MA; Famous Writer's Sch. Played with high sch orch & five piece dance band; coordr information for Army Nurse Corps; entertainer, Army Service & Officer Clubs. Chief Collabr: Mildred Powell. *Songs:* Nurses Prayer; We'll See the World Grow Better; We're Going to Have a Sweet Week; I Want to Spend Christmas in Dallas; Lyrics: Army Medics; Music: Let Me Grow Lovely Growing Old.

AYRES, MITCHELL — ASCAP 1955
composer, author, conductor

b Milwaukee, Wis, Dec 24, 10; d. Educ: Columbia Univ. Music dir, TV prog, "Perry Como Show" & records. *Songs:* I'm a Slave to You; He's a Wolf; Scratchin' the Surface; Madeira; arr: Eli Eli; Kol Nidre.

AYRES, WARREN JOYCE — ASCAP 1944
composer, author

b Omaha, Nebr, Feb 6, 08. Educ: Univ Nebr-Lincoln, AB & cert jour; studied trumpet with Jaraslav Cimarra. Publicity writer, Omaha Chamber of Commerce; dir news & feature service, Univ Nebr; dir pub rels & advert for 2 midwestern utility cos. USN, WW II, 44 months. With Ayres & Assocs, Lincoln & Omaha, 46-78; now consult communications rels. Advert Man of Yr, 75. Past dir, Nat Advert Agency Network, New York; past pres, Rotary Club. Chief Collabr: Wilbur R Chenoweth (deceased). *Songs:* Fighting Amphibians (off song, USN Amphibious Forces); Lincoln Centennial Song; Lyrics: Hail Varsity (Univ Nebr Fight Song); One Rose; Love Everlasting; Ridin' Back to Arizona; Welcome to Nebraska; Holiday in Hawaii.

AYSCUE, BRIAN THOMAS — ASCAP 1972
composer, saxophonist, clarinetist

b Camden, NJ, Apr 25, 48. Educ: Haddon Heights High Sch, dipl, 66; Glassboro State Col, BA, 70; studied clarinet & saxophone with Anthony Ciccarelli, 64-69; studied saxophone with Sigurd Rascher, 68 & comp with Joel Thome, 68-70. Clarinetist & bass clarinetist with var local orchs; saxophone soloist in var recitals. Performer with Rascher Saxophone Ens, 69. Contributor of reviews, Saxophone Symposium. *Instrumental Works:* Three Pieces for Alto Saxophone Solo; The Plane of Peace; Permutations I; First Butterfly for Flute.

AZPIAZU, RAUL — ASCAP 1963
composer, singer, musician

b Havana, Cuba, Sept 23, 24. Educ: Studied solfege & theory with father, Cuba; clarinet, Modesto Bravo; tenor saxophone, Al De Joseph, US; voice, Lalo Elozequi, Cuba. Played with own orch, Roseland Ballroom; singer & musician, Argueso's Orch, Roseland Ballroom, Rainbow Room, also in hotels, NY, Atlantic City & others. ABC-TV, 41-47. Did Span records with MGM, Decca, RCA, Fania, Fifi & others. Concert, Carnegie Hall; on radio, CBS. *Songs:* Mambo Habanero; Doin' the Cha Cha Cha; Porque; Dame Guaracha; Tu Partida; Le Canto a Borinquen; Inexplicable; Shake Baby Shake; Clasico Cha Cha Cha; No, No, Otra Vez; Coralita; Vacilando; Ki Ku Ki Kan; Paqueton; Cha Cha Cha in Boogie; Puchunga Pachanga; Sabrosa; Cuando Tu Me Digas Que Si; Music: Por Tus Ojos Negros.

AZZARA, BENNIE ANTHONY (BENNIE MARTINI) — ASCAP 1948
composer, author, singer

b Newark, NJ, Nov 2, 10. Educ: Self-taught piano, 3 to 11 yrs of age, studied with Rafael Saumell. Orch leader for var clubs, incl Club 51, Club 66 & Greenwich Village Inn, New York, 29-39. Pianist for Jackie Gleason, 8 yrs. Pianist-entertainer, nightclubs, vaudeville, radio & TV, incl Dumont, CBS & a piano team with Joseph Lilley, CBS. Assoc of Carlo Menotti (voice). Piano bar entertainer, Bills Gay 90's, 60-80. Musical cond for Bway show "Love in a Changing World" & accompanist & arr for Dolly Dawn. Chief Collabrs: Saul Joel Tepper, Bert Douglas, Fred Meadows, Milt Kellem. Panel Award ASCAP, 77. *Songs:* Music: Don't Cry, Cry Baby; You Are Everything That's Beautiful; Please Say Hello for Me; Why?; Poor Little Partygirl; Crosswinds; Lyrics: Incident'ly; The 4 Seasons; Ting Me a Tong.

B

BAASCH, MERLE DOROTHY — ASCAP 1969
composer, author

b Hamilton, Md. Educ: Syracuse Univ; Suffolk Community Col, Long Island, NY. Nat artist, Smithsonian Archives, DC. Ed-in-chief, The Crows Nest, Odenbach Shipbuilding Corp, Rochester, NY. Chief Collabr: Dave Mathes. *Songs:* Rag Doll for Christmas; I Am America; When Nobody Cares; I'm in Love Again. *Scores:* TV show: Hard Hats.

BABCOCK, EDWARD CHESTER (JAMES VAN HEUSEN) — ASCAP 1938
composer, publisher, pianist

b Syracuse, NY, Jan 26, 13. Educ: Cazenovia Sem, Distinguished Alumnus Award, 61; Syracuse Univ, studied music with Colburn, Howard Lyman; hon doctor of letters, Gonzaga Univ. Announcer, Radio Sta WSYR, age 16. Own radio prog, WFBI, featuring original works. To New York, 33; songwriter at Harlem's Cotton Club. Pianist with Tin Pan Alley publ houses; under contract to Remick Music. To Hollywood, 40; under contract to Paramount Studios, writer of film scores. Joined Lockheed Aircraft Corp as test pilot, 42-44. Formed partnership with Johnny Burke, 44, under contract to Crosby, Century-Fox, MGM, Columbia & Universal Int. Formed music publ co, Burvan at Famous Music. Partners with Sammy Cahn, 55-69; writers for nightclub stars, singers, film producers & TV stars & progs incl "Hazel", "Joey Bishop Talk Show" & "The Frank Sinatra Show," (winner of Sylvania TV Award). Recipient var awards incl Christopher, Cash Box, Emmy & Acad. Mem, Composers & Lyricists Guild, Am Guild of Authors & Composers & Authors League. Chief Collabrs: Johnny Mercer, Johnny Burke, Eddie DeLange, Sammy Cahn. *Songs:* It's the Dreamer in Me; So Help Me; Deep in a Dream; Heaven Can Wait; Oh, You Crazy Moon; Blue Rain; I Thought About You; All This and Heaven, Too; Darn That Dream; Imagination; Dearest, Darest I?; Isn't That Just Like Love?; It's Always You; Birds of a Feather; Constantly; Road to Morocco; Ain't Got a Dime to My Name; Moonlight Becomes You; Sunday, Monday or Always; If You Please; Suddenly, It's Spring; A Friend of Yours; Polka Dots and Moonbeams; Going My Way; Swinging on a Star (Acad Award, 44); The Day After Forever; It Could Happen to You; And His Rocking Horse Ran Away; Like Someone in Love; Sleigh Ride in July; Yah-Ta-Ta Yah-Ta-Ta; Put It There, Pal; Welcome to My Dream; It's Anybody's Spring; Personality; Nancy; Just My Luck; Aren't You Glad You're You?; My Heart Is a Hobo; Country Style; Smile Right Back At the Sun; Apalachicola, Florida; But Beautiful; You Don't Have to Know the Language; If You Stub Your Toe on the Moon; Once and For Always; You're in Love With Someone; Someplace on Anywhere Road; Sunshine Cake; High on the List; And You'll Be Home; Life Is So Peculiar; Early American; Here's That Rainy Day; Ring the Bell; The Magic Window; Moonflowers; To See You; The 86th! The 86th! (off song, USA 86th Inf Reg); Love and Marriage (Emmy, Christopher Awards, 55); The Impatient Years; Look to Your Heart; All the Way (Acad Award, 57); Come Fly With Me; Only the Lonely; To Love and Be Loved; High Hopes (Acad Award, 59; Pres Kennedy campaign song, 60); The Second Time Around; Call Me Irresponsible (Acad Award, 63); September of My Years; My Kind of Town; I Like to Lead When I Dance; Love Is a Bore; Everybody Has a Right to Be Wrong; I'll Only Miss Her When I Think of Her; Film title songs: The Tender Trap; Indiscreet; Pocketful of Miracles; Come Blow Your Horn; Where Love Has Gone. *Scores:* Stage shows: Cotton Club Parade; Billy Rose's New Acquacade (New York World's Fair, 40); Marionette show: Les Poupees de Paris; Bway shows: Swingin' the Dream; Nellie Bly; Carnival in Flanders; Skyscraper; Walking Happy. Films: Love Thy Neighbor; Playmates; Road to Zanzibar; Road to Morocco; Dixie; Going My Way; And the Angels Sing; Belle of the Yukon; Road to Utopia; Welcome Stranger; Road to Rio; A Connecticut Yankee in King Arthur's Court; Top o' the Morning; Riding High; Mister Music; Road to Bali; Say One for Me; Let's Make Love; Road to Hong Kong; Robin and the 7 Hoods.

BABCOCK, THERON CHARLES — ASCAP 1958
composer, author, organist

b Seattle, Wash, Dec 30, 25. Educ: Bellevue High Sch, 43; Practical Bible Training Sch, 50, ordained minister, 50. Joined Hal Webb Evangelistic Team, assoc, songwriter & organist, 56- *Songs:* Lord, I Believe; God Never Promised; Can't Wait!; The Best of Five Thousand (songbk); Music: Oh The Mountain Is High.

BABER, JOSEPH W — ASCAP 1971
composer, performer

b Richmond, Va, Sept 11, 37. Educ: Mich State Univ, BM, 62; Eastman Sch Music, MM, 65. Perf with Tokyo Philh, Japan, 3 yrs. Instr, Southern Ill Univ. Comp-in-residence, Univ Ky. Has string quartet that has recorded. Songwriter from Shakespeare texts. Chief Collabr: John Gardner. *Songs:* Songs From the Plays of Shakespeare. *Instrumental Works:* Symphony in E. *Scores:* Frankenstein; Rumpelstiltskin; Samson.

BABICH, HERMAN BERNARD (HI BABIT) — ASCAP 1970
composer, arranger

b Brooklyn, NY, Nov 9, 17. Educ: Erasmus Hall High Sch, Brooklyn, grad; New York Col Nusic, teacher's cert, 54; studied orchestration with Sigfried Landau. Started playing in band, 31. Rehearsed Bway shows, 30's. Served in Army, 5 yrs. Traveled with USO hospital shows. Arr & played for radio & TV spots. Joined

ORS Music Rolls as arr, 63; also arr for Aeolian & Melodee Music Rolls. *Songs:* Dear Mister Santa Claus; Away From You; Lyrics: Chopsticks. *Instrumental Works:* Tarantella (4 hands, 2 pianos).

BABIN, VICTOR   ASCAP 1945
composer, pianist

b Moscow, Russia, Dec 12, 08; d Cleveland, Ohio, Mar 1, 72. Educ: Riga State Cons, studied with Wihtol, Dumbrovsky, Dauge, Berliner; Hochschule für Musik, studied with Schnabel, Schreker; hon DFA. Concert pianist, toured Europe; formed 2-piano team with wife, Vitya Vronksy, 33. Am debut, Town Hall, New York, 37, toured until 43. USA, World War II. Resumed 2-piano concert career with orchs, in radio, TV, films & recordings, 45. Dir, Cleveland Inst of Music, 61. *Songs:* Beloved Stranger (song cycle); Ritual (low voice); I Wake From Dreams (low voice); Life's Midway; The Night Wanderer; Sun Shafts; 10 Songs for Tenor and Six instruments. *Instrumental Works:* Concerto Piece for Violin, Orchestra; Two Concerti for Two Pianos and Orchestra; Sonata-Fantasia (cello, piano); Variations on Theme by Purcell (cello, piano); 6 Etudes (2 pianos); 3 Fantasies on Old Themes; String Quartet; Capriccio for Orchestra; Trio for Violin, Cello, Piano; Hillandale Waltzes; Fantasia on Themes by Telemann; 3 March Rhythms; Piano solos: Deux Mouvements Dansants; Fantasia Aria and Cafriccio; Variations on a Theme by Beethoven; 1 Piano, 4 Hands: David and Goliath (11 pieces); 2 Pianos, 4 Hands: Adagio and Fugue in C Minor; Solo Clarinet: Divertissement Asfeneis.

BABIT, HI
See Babich, Herman Bernard

BACAL, DAVE   ASCAP 1966
composer, organist, pianist

b New York, NY, Aug 7, 08. Educ: Studied piano with Lucien Phillips, Philadelphia, organ with Sigmund Krumgold, New York. Musician, silent pictures, 24; chief organist, Wilmer Vincent Theatres, Pa, 26. Pianist with the Leo Zollo Orch, Pa, 30; radio stations in Philadelphia, 30 & Chicago, 34; var radio progs, 34-37. Staff organist, CBS radio, 39. US Army Air Corp, World War II. Entertainer, bars & radio, Calif, 46-; TV shows, incl Jack La Lanne, Truth or Consequences, 58-74. *Songs & Instrumental Works:* Weaving a Dream; Tales From the Great Book; Themes: Jack La Lanne Show; Truth or Consequences.

BACAL, HARVEY   ASCAP 1952
composer, author, arranger

b Quebec, Can, May 24, 15. Educ: Philadelphia Col of Performing Arts. Comp, music dir, arr for radio; comp, musicologist, arr for TV; musicologist for "Name That Tune", "Stop the Music" & "Yours for a Song", TV Progs; author, "Fun With Music", "ABC of Modern Arranging" & "Key to Modern Dance Band Arranging." Musicologist for music publ, record cos & advert agencies, specializing in plagiarism & infringement cases. Chief Collabs: Irving Caesar, Leonard Whitcup. *Songs:* Music: I'm Afraid to Remember; I Cry Your Name; A La Parisienne; Pianino; Shadow Tango; Good Humor. *Instrumental Works:* 5 Pieces for Children; (orch suite).

BACH, JAN MORRIS   ASCAP 1975
composer

b Forrest, Ill, Dec 11, 37. Educ: Univ Ill, Urbana, BM(comp), 59, MM(comp), 61, DMA(comp), 71; additional comp study with Robert Kelly, Kenneth Gaburo, Robert Gerhard, Aaron Copland, Donald Martino, Thea Musgrave. With US Army Band, Washington, DC, 62-65. Instr music, Univ Tampa, 65-66; from instr to assoc prof music, Northern Ill Univ, 66-79, prof music, 79- Harvey Gaul Comp Award, 72; Mannes Opera Prize, 73; SAI Choral Comp Award, 74; Pulitzer Prize Nomination, 74; Int Brass Quintet Competition First Prize, 74; Nat Endowment for Arts grant, 75; Brown Univ Choral Comp Prize, 78; Nebr Sinfonia First Prize, 79; comns, Tubists Universal Brotherhood Asn, Orpheus Trio, Orch of Ill, Int Trumpet Guild, Int Brass Congress, Richard Fredrickson, and others. *Songs:* Music: My Wilderness (choral cycle). *Instrumental Works:* Woodwork (perc quartet); Skizzen (woodwind quintet); Laudes (brass quintet); Eisteddfod (flute, harp, viola trio); Four Two-Bit Contraptions (flute, horn); The Happy Prince (chamber orch & narrator); Dionysia (symphonic band); The Eve of St Agnes (antiphonal wind ensemble); Fanfare and Fugue (trumpet quintet); Quintet for Tuba and Strings; Concert Variations (euphonium & piano); My Very First Solo (alto saxaphone & elec piano); Gala Fanfare (orch). *Scores:* One-Act Operas: The System; The Student From Salamanca.

BACH, P D Q
See Schickele, Peter

BACHARACH, BURT F   ASCAP 1955
composer, conductor, arranger

b Kansas City, Mo, May 12, 28. Educ: McGill Univ, 3 yrs; New Sch for Social Res, NY; Mannes Sch Music; Music Acad West, Santa Barbara, Calif, scholarship; studied with Darius Milhaud, Bohuslav Martinu & Henry Cowell. Army service, 50-52. Began as comp & arr, Steve Lawrence, Vic Damone, Ames Bros & Marlene Dietrich; worked with rhythm & blues figures, incl Dione Warwick, Chuck Jackson, Tommy Hunt, Gene Pitney. Wrote scores for films; wrote Bway musical "Promises, Promises." Chief Collabs: Hal David, Mack David, Paul Anka, Bob Hilliard, Jack Wolf. *Songs:* Keep Me in Mind; It's Great to Be Young; Any Day Now; Tower of Strength; You're Following Me; Baby,

It's You; The Man Who Shot Liberty Valance; Magic Moments; Don't Make Me Over; Make It Easy on Yourself; Only Love Can Break a Heart; The Story of My Life; Blue on Blue; True Love Never Runs Smooth; 24 Hours From Tulsa; Who's Been Sleeping in My Bed?; Anyone Who Had a Heart; Wishin' and Hopin'; Walk on By; Any Old Time of the Day; Reach Out for Me; I Wake Up Cryin'; Don't Envy Me; (There's) Always Something There to Remind Me; Magic Potion; This Empty Place; You'll Never Get to Heaven; To Wait for Love; Trains and Boats and Planes; A Lifetime of Loneliness; Don't You Believe It; What the World Needs Now Is Love; Alfie; I'll Never Fall in Love Again; Message to Michael; The April Fools; The Look of Love; Raindrops Keep Falling on My Head; Do You Know the Way to San Jose; Close to You; One Less Bell to Answer; Film title songs: Wives and Lovers; A House Is Not a Home; What's New Pussycat?; Promise Her Anything; Send Me No Flowers.

BACHMAN, MARTHA JEANNE (MARTY ADAMS, MARTHA J NAMETH)
composer, author

b Rochester, Pa, Oct 6, 24. *Songs:* Let's Make Believe; Lover's Prayer; Stop Blowing Horn; I'm Just the Co-Pilot.

BACKER, WILLIAM MONTAGUE   ASCAP 1972
composer, author

b New Rochelle, NY, June 9, 26. Educ: Episcopal High Sch; Yale Univ. From advert copywriter to pres own agency, Backer & Spielvogel, Inc, 52-79. Composer many commercials. Chief Collabs: Billy Davis, Roger Cook, Roger Greenway. *Songs:* I'd Like to Teach the World to Sing; Hello Summertime; Here's to Good Friends.

BACON, ERNST L   ASCAP 1959
composer, pianist, conductor

b Chicago, Ill, May 26, 1898. Educ: Northwestern Univ, Ill; Univ Calif, Berkeley, MA; studied piano with G D Guna, Alexander Raab, Franz Schmidt, Vienna, theory with P C Lutkin, Karl Weigl, Thomas Otterstroem, Ernest Bloch, conducting with Eugene Goosens. Opera coach & asst cond, Rochester Opera; cond, San Francisco Fed Orch; founder, Carmel Bach Fest; supvr, San Francisco & Los Angeles WPA. Fac, San Francisco Cons Music; prof, Hamilton Col; dean, Converse Col Sch Music; dir, Syracuse Univ Sch Music; visiting prof, Stanford Univ, Denver Univ, Wyo Univ. Author bks, "Words on Music", "Notes on Piano", "Elaborations of Rare Folio Music." Pulitzer Prize, 33. Guggenheim fels; Nat Inst Arts & Letters & Bispham Awards. Chief Collabs: Paul Horgan, John Edmunds, Raish Stoll, Phil Mathias. *Songs:* Songbks: Quiet Airs; Five Songs; Six Songs; Fifty Songs; Tributaries; The Hootnanny; Sassafras; Music Along Unpaved Roads; From Emily's Diary; (cantata); Nature; Spirits and Places; The Animals' Christmas Oratorio (cantata, narrator). *Instrumental Works:* From These States (symph orch); Airs From Many Sources; Sonata for Cello and Piano; Symphonies II and III; Great River (symph, narrator); The Last Invocation; Concerto I, II (piano, orch); Trio; Quintet; Oratorios: Ecclesiastes; By Blue Ontario; Usania. *Scores:* Play: A Tree on the Plains.

BACON, W GARWOOD, JR (WAYNE ROGERS)   ASCAP 1955
composer, author, singer

b Camden, NJ, June 26, 20. Educ: Temple Univ, 41; New Sch Music, 45; studied violin, guitar, voice. Began comp music & lyrics, 41; prof, 55- Singer, guitarist, recording artist, 55- Performed nat TV, Dick Clark's Bandstand; regional TV, var cities. Chief Collabs: Leroy Lovett, Jimmy DeKnight, Woody Bacon. *Songs:* Mary Jane; I Miss You; Hush Our Secret; My Dearest Darling; In the Good Old USA; The Creator; Amore Mio; The Quiet Boy; The Wiggle; Drag Foot; Too Young to Die; Chains of Love; Baby Blue Eyes; Where Do the Years Go (So Soon); Teenage Dream; Beatin' Around; Round House Boogie.

BADALAMENTI, ANGELO DANIEL (ANDY BADALE)   ASCAP 1965
composer

b Brooklyn, NY, Mar 22, 37. Educ: Lafayette High Sch; Eastman Sch Music, 54-56; Manhattan Sch Music, BM, 58, MA, 59. Comp of film scores, TV, radio & TV commercials; record producer; music publ; recording instrumental & vocal artist; comp for theatre. Chief Collabs: Frank Stanton, Barbara Fried, Al Elias, Sammy Cahn, Francine Trevens. *Songs:* Music: Face It Girl, It's Over. *Instrumental Works:* Nashville Beer Garden; Visa to the Stars. *Scores:* Bway shows: The Boy Who Made Magic; Earle Beaver's Jamboree; D'Archangelo; Film/TV: Across the Great Divide; Law and Disorder; It's a Brand New World.

BADALE, ANDY
See Badalamenti, Angelo Daniel

BAER, ABEL   ASCAP 1924
composer, author, pianist

b Baltimore, Md, Mar 16, 1893; d New York, NY, Oct 5, 76. Educ: Col Physicians & Surgeons. 2nd Lt, USAAF, WW I. Gave up dentistry to join staff, New York music publ co, 20. Accompanist to Nora Bayes. Moved to Hollywood, 29; wrote songs for films incl, "Paramount on Parade", "True to the Navy" & "Frozen Justice." Mem, Appeals Bd, ASCAP, 12 yrs. Treas, Songwriters Am, 19 yrs. In 55, mgr, show sponsored by ASCAP & United Serv Orgn touring Ger for Armed Forces. Pres, Am Guild Authors & Comp, 55-57, then chmn council. Arr. Chief Collabs: L Wolfe Gilbert, Stanley Adams, Cliff Friend, Sam Lewis, Mabel Wayne. *Songs:* June Night; There Are Such Things;

My Mother's Eyes; Gee, But You're Swell; I Miss My Swiss; Don't Wait 'Til the Night Before Christmas; Lucky Lindy; It's the Girl; Am I to Blame?; Mama Loves Papa; Blue Hoosier Blues; Garden in Granada; When the One You Love, Loves You; Don't Wake Me Up, Let Me Dream; The Night When Love Was Born; Chapel of the Roses; Harriet; I'm Sitting Pretty. *Scores:* Bway Stage: Lady Do.

BAER, CHARLES E　　　　　　　　　　　　　ASCAP 1941
composer, author
b Fairview, Pa, Nov 17, 1870; d Ambler, Pa, Feb 5, 62. Educ: Spring Garden Inst. Worked for Baldwin Locomotive Works; Foley Dog Show Co. Publ poems in newspapers & mags. *Songs:* Pictures From Life's Other Side; A Harp With Broken Strings; Things in the Bottom Drawer; Dreams of the Old Love; Wait for the Rainbow Dearie; Swinging (On the Grape Vine Swing); Keep It Up for Old Times Sake; Music: The Song I Heard in Heaven; When the Robin Redbreast Sings His Home Sweet Home; A Miner's Home Sweet Home; Let the Love Light Linger Longer Lady Lou; Lyrics: After All the Old Love's Best; A Flower From Home Sweet Home; Look for Me in Cherry Time; Though Your Hair Is Turning Silver (You've a Heart of Gold); Ev'ry Ship Will Find a Harbor; In the Valley of Contentment; While I Dream of You; The Vale of Dreams; The Moonlight, the Rose and You; A Song of Old Kilkenny; Tahmineh; The Sea Shell; Adieu, Beloved, Adieu; The Song of the Open Sea; Where We Listened to the Mocking Bird; Say Pal Find My Gal; When You Were in Your Teens; Just a Little Loving When You're Lonely; Way Down Yonder; At the Gate of the Palace of Dreams; Love Is a Rose; For Somebody's Sake; Then Say Good-Bye; Once in a Thousand Years; When You Were Queen of the May; also Gospel Songs of Sunshine (hymn bk).

BAEZ, JOAN CHAWDOS
composer, author, singer
b Staten Island, NY, Jan 9, 41. Educ: Boston Univ; DHumL, Antioch Univ, 79 & Rutgers Univ, 80. Recorded 29 albums, 8 gold records & 1 gold single. Author, "Daybreak," co-author, "Coming Out." Comp & illus, "Joan Baez Song Book" & "And Then I Wrote." Chief Collab: Ennio Morricone. *Songs:* Honest Lullaby; Diamonds and Rust; Love Song to a Stranger; Song for David; Altar Boy and the Thief. *Scores:* Sallo and Vanzetti.

BAGDASARIAN, ROSS (DAVID SEVILLE)　　　ASCAP 1951
composer, author, actor
b Fresno, Calif, Jan 27, 19; d Beverly Hills, Calif, Jan 16, 72. Educ: Col. Writer & producer, "The Alvin Show," CBS-TV; did chipmunk & other voices. Had made records. *Songs:* Come On-a My House; Chipmunk Song; Armen's Theme; Witch Doctor; Hey, Brother, Pour the Wine; Alvin's Harmonica; Alvin's Orchestra.

BAILEY, CHARITY ALBERTA
composer, arranger, teacher
b Providence, RI, Sept 7, 04; d Providence, Sept 15, 78. Educ: RI Col Educ, 27, hon MEd, 58; Juilliard Sch Music, advanced piano, 30's; Dalcroze Sch Music, studied with P Boepple, H Schuster, dirs. Music educr; pioneer in teaching music to young children through folk music/dance; taught Henry St Settlement, New York, NY; music dir, Little Red Sch House, 10 yrs; music teacher, Heathcote Pub Sch, Scarsdale, NY, 12 yrs; teachers workshops, Bank St Col, New York; taught presch, Harlem Sch Arts; wrote prof publ; cond workshops, demonstrations & other classes nationwide; produced records & bks; wrote & performed in two children's TV music prog, "Sing a Song," WMCA, New York & "Here's Charity," WNET-TV, New York. Author, "Sing A Song." Chief Collab: Eunice Holsaert. *Albums:* Sing a Song With Charity Bailey (vols I & II); Follow the Sunset; Music Time With Charity Bailey.

BAILEY, HARRY P　　　　　　　　　　　　　ASCAP 1955
composer, author, arranger
b Indianapolis, Ind, Aug 2, 12. Educ: DePauw Univ, AB, Law Sch. Arr & pianist, dance bands incl Herbie Kay, Ben Bernie. Comedy writer for radio & TV shows incl "Fred Allen." Founder, own service agency. *Songs:* The Hottentot; Start Dancin' With a Smile.

BAILEY, LYNN　　　　　　　　　　　　　　ASCAP 1977
composer, lyricist, singer
b Indianapolis, Ind, Apr 18, 42. Educ: Univ Colo Col Music, Boulder, 60-62; studied comp with Rudolph Schram, 62-63 & voice with Myron (Pappy) Earnhard, 63-64. Recording artist on Fraternity Records, 75-78; then with Wartrace Records. Mem of Donna Fargo Road Show. Lead vocalist on several Midwest regional radio & TV commercials. *Songs:* Messin' With My Mind."

BAILEY, PEARL　　　　　　　　　　　　　　ASCAP 1958
composer, singer
b Newport News, Va, Mar 29, 18. Dancer & singer, New York, early 40's. Toured with Cootie Williams Band; featured singer in nightclubs, theatres & TV. Appeared in "Arms and the Girl", "St Louis Woman", "House of Flowers"; films incl "Carmen Jones", "That Certain Feeling", "St Louis Blues", "Porgy and Bess." Recording artist. *Songs:* Jingle Bells Cha Cha Cha; I'm Gonna Keep on Doin'; Don't Be Afraid to Love; A Five Pound Box of Money.

BAILIN, HARRIETT　　　　　　　　　　　　ASCAP 1957
composer, author
b Bridgeport, Conn, Nov 1, 23. Educ: Univ Conn; Juilliard Sch; pvt music study. Writer, musicals for community theatre groups & non-profit institutions. Chief Collabrs: Fay Tishman, Elisse Boyd.

BAKER, CASSIETTA (CASSIETTA GEORGE)　ASCAP 1979
composer, singer, recording artist
b Memphis, Tenn, Jan 23, 29. Educ: Douglas Jr High Sch, Memphis; Booker T Washington High Sch, Memphis; McKinley High Sch, Canton, Ohio. Started writing in early 50's while traveling & singing with Famous Caravan's of Chicago. Performed in var auditoriums all over US, incl Madison Square Garden, Carnegie Hall & Van Wezel Performing Arts Hall, Sarasota, Fla. Chief Collabs: Madelon Baker, Isiah Jones, Bernard R Smith. *Songs & Instrumental Works:* You Just Don't Trust God Enough; There's a War Going On; Trust in the Lord; Come On Children Let's Sing; Walk Aroun' Heaven.

BAKER, DAVID KEITH　　　　　　　　　　ASCAP 1955
composer, teacher
b Portland, Maine, June 6, 26. Educ: Juilliard Sch Music; studied piano with Joseph Battista. Pianist, dance comp & comp for Bway musicals, 48-; musical dir, Agnes de Mille Heritage Dance Theatre, Am Dance Machine; teacher theatre singing, Am Univ, DC & Young Men's Hebrew Asn, New York. Chief Collabrs: Will Holt; lyricists, David Craig, Sheldon Harnick, Ira Wallach. *Instrumental Works:* On a Small Scale (etudes for piano). *Scores:* Bway Musical Shows: Phoenix '55; Copper and Brass; Come Summer; Smiling, the Boy Fell Dead; Shoestring Revues (contributor); Vintage '60 (contributor); Ballet: Texas Fourth (music); Logger's Clog (music); Matrix (music).

BAKER, DON　　　　　　　　　　　　　　　ASCAP 1947
composer, organist
b St Thomas, Ont, Feb 26, 03. Educ: Mt Royal Col; Toronto Cons, ATCM. Pianist, film theatre bands, 23. Organist, Rivoli & Rialto Theatres, New York, 26-28, Sidney Bernstein Theatres, London, 33-34. Staff mem, WOR, 34-35. Organist, New York Paramount, 35-48. Toured country for Rodgers Organs, 60-61, Conn Organ Corp. Recording artist. Chief Collab: Edward Lane. *Songs:* You're the Only Pebble on the Beach; Bless You for Being an Angel; Snowtime Serenade.

BAKER, HAROLD (SHORTY)　　　　　　　ASCAP 1960
composer, author, trumpeter
b St Louis, Mo, May 26, 14; d. Organized own band with brother. Trumpeter, var orchs incl Don Redman, Teddy Wilson, Andy Kirk, Mary Lou Williams & Duke Ellington. European tour with Ellington. Formed own quartet; taught trumpet. *Instrumental Works:* Shorty's Blues.

BAKER, HERBERT　　　　　　　　　　　　ASCAP 1955
composer, author
b New York, NY, Dec 25, 20. Educ: Yale Univ, BA. Wrote morale & training films, WW II; wrote spec material for Danny Kaye, Lena Horne, Ethel Merman, Beatrice Lillie & Belle Baker; writer for films & TV. Two-time Emmy & Peabody award winner. Chief Collabr: Erich Wolfgang Korngold. *Songs:* I Love to Love; Turn on Love; All Grown Up; Lyrics: The Ambushers. *Scores:* Bway: Helen Goes to Troy.

BAKER, LARRY　　　　　　　　　　　　　　ASCAP 1975
composer
b Ft Smith, Ark, Sept 7, 48. Educ: Univ Okla, BMusEd & BM(comp), 71, studied comp with Spencer Norton; Cleveland Inst Music, MMus(comp), 73, studied comp with Donald Erb. Mem fac, Cleveland Inst Music, 73- Cond of recording "Margins." Rec'd NEA grants, 76 & 79 & Ohio Arts Council grants, 79 & 80. *Instrumental Works:* Trimophony; Before Assemblage III; Flute; Childness. *Scores:* Opera: Chairs.

BAKER, NORMAN D (BUDDY)　　　　　　　ASCAP 1953
composer, conductor
b Springfield, Mo, Jan 4, 18. Educ: Central High Sch; Southwest Mo Baptist Col. Film comp for Walt Disney Productions, 26 yrs. Comp, arr & cond, original "Mickey Mouse Club." Scored & cond feature films, TV shows & park attractions. Music dir, Disney World's "EPCOT" Project & Disney Park to be built in Tokyo, Japan; also scoring animated feature film, "The Fox and the Hound." Has rec'd 2 Grammy Awards & one Oscar nomination.

BAKER, PHIL　　　　　　　　　　　　　　　ASCAP 1929
composer, author, accordionist
b Philadelphia, Pa, Aug 24, 1896; d Copenhagen, Denmark, Nov 30, 63. Educ: Boston Schs. First stage appearance in Boston amateur show. Teamed in violin-accordion act with Ed Janis, later with Ben Bernie. Served in USN, WW I. In vaudeville & films. Featured on radio, "Take It Or Leave It." Appeared in Bway musicals: "Music Box Revue"; "Crazy Quilt"; "Artists and Models"; "Greenwich Village Follies"; "A Night in Spain"; "Calling All Stars." Comedian. *Songs:* Look At Those Eyes; Park Avenue Strut; Just Suppose; Antoinette; Strange Interlude; Humming a Love Song; Rainy Day Pal; Pretty Little Baby; Did You Mean It?; My Heaven on Earth; Invitation to a Broken Heart.

BAKER, RICHARD E (TWO TON) ASCAP 1950
composer, author, pianist
b Chicago, Ill, May 2, 16; d. Educ: Morton Sch; Fenger Sch. Pianist in orchs, vaudeville & nightclubs. Writer, actor, radio & TV commercials; also announcer, singer & pianist on radio & TV. *Songs:* The Tree in the Wood; I Like You, You're Silly; Sentimental Sleepy Head; The Tem-per-aye-chure Song; A Little Pansy in a Flower Pot.

BAKER, ROBERT HART ASCAP 1978
composer, conductor
b Bronxville, NY, Mar 19, 54. Educ: Acad Int d'Ete, Nice, France, dipl, 70; Mozarteum Cons, Salzburg, Austria, dipl, 71, studied with Herbert von Karajan; Horace Mann High Sch, New York, dipl, 71; Harvard Col, AB(cum laude), 74, studied with Leonard Bernstein & Leon Kirchner; Yale Sch Music, MM, 76, MMA, 78, studied with Frank Lewin, Otto-Werner Mueller & Arthur Weisberg. Ed & arr for Vanguard Records, London, 70-78. Guest cond with var orchs. Music dir & cond: Bach Soc Orch, Cambridge, Mass, 72-74; Youth Symph Orch of New York, 77-81; Danbury Little Symph, Conn, 78-81; Putnam Symph Orch, Brewster, NY, 79-81; Conn Philh Orch, 74- Arr & comp for Macy's New York Thanksgiving & Christmas parades, 79, 80. Rec'd Conn Comn on Arts Comp Comn, 78. *Songs:* Tombling Day Songs. *Instrumental Works:* Nocturne from String Quartet No 2; Sinfonietta. *Scores:* Opera/Ballet: Comus, Part 3; Film/TV: Sculpture.

BAKER, TWO TON
See Baker, Richard E

BAKER, WILLIAM CLAUDE ASCAP 1974
composer, teacher
b Lenoir, NC, Apr 12, 48. Educ: ECarolina Univ, BM, 70, studied theory-comp with Gregory Kosteck; Eastman Sch Music, MM(comp), 73, DMA, 75, studied comp with Samuel Adler & Warren Benson. Honors: ASCAP Award; NY Coun on the Arts Grant; Yaddo & MacDowell Colony Fels. Music publ by Southern Music Co & Carl Fischer, Inc. Asst prof theory & comp, Univ Louisville. *Instrumental Works:* Speculum Musicae (string quartet, woodwind quartet, brass trio, perc & piano); Capriccio (wind ens); Four Songs on Poems by Kenneth Patchen (soprano & orch); Three Songs on Poems by Kenneth Patchen (soprano & chamber ens); Canzonet (unaccompanied tuba).

BAKER, WILLIAM STANFORD ASCAP 1957
composer, author, pianist
b La Crosse, Wis, Aug 6, 25. Educ: Logan High Sch, La Crosse; studied orchestration with Mario Castelnuovo-Tedesco; studied piano with Joseph Levine & Harry Fields. Professional pianist in Hollywood for 30 yrs. Worked with Doris Day, Jack Jones, Gene Krupa Orch, Johnny Carson and others. Chief Collabrs: Buddy Feyne, Jimmy LaSane, Susanne Quickel, Dok Stanford. *Songs:* Hey, Bartender; Look What We Found; Music: Too Much; Movin' on Man; Beautiful People; Mad. *Scores:* Film/TV: Diary of a Stewardess.

BAKSA, ROBERT FRANK ASCAP 1962
composer
b New York, NY, Feb 7, 38. Educ: Univ Ariz, BA, 59; Tanglewood, scholarship, 59. Began composing at age 13; has composed more than 300 works in all categories incl film scores, more than 40 publ. Opera "Aria Da Capo" premiered 69 by Lake George Opera. *Songs:* Music: Songs of Late Summer For Women's Chorus (SSA); Madrigals to Poems of Shakespeare (SATB); 14 Songs to Poems of Emily Dickinson. *Instrumental Works:* Quintet for Oboe and Strings. *Scores:* One-Act Opera: Red Carnations (comn by Lincoln Ctr for Metrop Opera Studio, now in repertory of Children's Free Opera of New York).

BAL, ADRIAN (P) ASCAP 1965
composer, piano teacher, singer
b Riverside, NJ, Jan 24, 25. Educ: Riverside High Sch; Kans Wesleyan, Salina, BA, 49; Wichita State Univ, Kans, MEd, 52; Univ Pa; Univ Calif, Los Angeles & Berkeley; Univ Southern Calif. Played saxophone & clarinet, high sch dance band; performed many high sch productions. Served in USN 3 yrs. Teacher physiology & biology, Beverly Hills High Sch, Calif, 50- Opened Bal & Bal Music Publ Co, 65 & Bal Records, 71. Chief Collabr: Berdella M Freeman Bal (wife). *Songs:* Music: Christmas Is Coming; Yuletime; Speak Softly; I'm in a Melancholy Mood; Whisper My Name; Love, Love, Love; I Wish You Knew.

BAL, BERDELLA M (BERDELLA FREEMAN) ASCAP 1965
author
b Boone, Iowa, Aug 10, 28. Educ: Salina High Sch, Kans, 45; Marymount Col, Salina, BS, 48; Univ Calif, Los Angeles. Played clarinet & sang with vocal groups in sec sch. Opened Bal & Bal Music Publ Co, 65 & Bal Records, 71. Teacher mathematics, La Canada, Calif, 67- Chief Collabr: Adrian P Bal (husband). *Songs:* Lyrics: Christmas is Coming; Yuletide; I'm in a Melancholy Mood; Love, Love, Love; I Wish You Knew.

BALADA, LEONARD
composer, educator
b Barcelona, Spain, Sept 22, 33. Educ: Cons of Barcelona, Profesorado de Teoria, 53, Profesorado de Music, 54; Juilliard Sch Music, dipl comp, 60; Mannes Col Music, postgrad, 61-62. Past instr, Institucion Cultural, Barcelona.

Instr, Walden Sch, New York, 62-63. Head dept music, UN Int Sch, New York, 63-70. Comp-in-residence, Aspen Inst, Colo, 70. Prof comp, Carnegie-Mellon Univ, 70- Guest comp, Univ Tel Aviv, Israel, 75. Comp of several ballets, songs & works for many soloists. Music recorded by Serenus Records. Awards: B Martinu Prize in Comp, Mannes Col Music, 62; Int Comp Prize, Cuidad de Zaragoza, 74; Foundacion March fel. Mem: Am Music Ctr; Hispanic Soc Am. *Songs & Instrumental Works:* Guernica; Sinfonia en Negro-Homenaje a Martin Luther King (comn by Span Radio TV Symph Orch); Maria Sabina (oratorio); Cumbres; Sinfonia Concertante for Guitar and Orchestra (comn by Narciso Yepes); Steel Symphony; Auroris (comn by Nat Orch Spain, Madrid); Ponce de Leon (narrator, orch); No-Res; Concerto for Piano, Winds and Percussion (comn by Carnegie-Mellon Univ Alumni Asn); Homage to Casals and Homage to Sarasate (City of Barcelona Comp Prize, 76); Analogias (guitar solo); Elementalis (organ solo; comn by D G Bellas Artes, Spain); Chamber Works: Voces (mixed chorus a capella); Tresis (guitar, flute, cello; comn by Comp Theatre, Inc); Apuntes (guitar quartet).

BALAY, JOAN ROSE ASCAP 1975
composer, author, singer
b Wichita, Kans, July 3, 32. Educ: North Wichita High Sch, grad, 50; Wichita State Univ, 70-78; studied orchestral cond & arr with Gene Hammers. Singer, writer & dir, original musical variety progs; comp choral works for children's choirs, youth & col choirs; arr. Chief Collabrs: Milt Rogers, Betty Fidler. *Songs:* One of the Ones; Let Go and Listen; The Lemon Song.

BALENT, ANDREW ASCAP 1970
composer, educator
b Washington, Pa, July 23, 34. Educ: Washington High Sch; Syracuse Univ; Univ Mich, BMus, 56, MMus, 60; studied comp with William Russo. Band dir pub schs, New Haven, Utica & Warren, Mich. Comp & arr of band literature for many publishers. *Instrumental Works:* Chorale and Festival March; Summation; Spartans of Tomorrow; Century Celebration; Spirit A' Plenty; Two Seascapes for Band; Rocspagnol.

BALES, RICHARD HORNER ASCAP 1957
composer, conductor, educator
b Alexandria, Va, Feb 3, 15. Educ: Univ Rochester, Eastman Sch Music, BMus, 36; Juilliard Berkshire Music Ctr, 40; Juilliard Sch, grad studies, dipl in cond, 41; studied with Albert Stoessel, Olga Samaroff-Stakowski, Abram Chasins, Bernard Wagenaar, Bernard Rogers, Frederick Jacobi, Burrill Phillips, cond with Serge Koussevitzky. Cond, Va-NC Symph, 36-38; music dir, Nat Gallery Art & cond TV concerts, 43-; music dir, Nat Symph, summer 47. Guest cond for many US orchs; taught cond, Univ Rochester Eastman Sch Music, summers 65, 66 & 67. Lectr & broadcaster. *Songs:* Music: Ozymandias; Mary's Gift; Gate of the Year (chorus, orch); Come Away, Death (a cappella chorus). *Instrumental Works:* Music of the American Revolution (2 string suites); Stony Brook, Suite for Strings; Blue and Gray Quadrille (orch); The Black Forest Clock (pizzicato polka); String Quartet in D; Music for Strings (string orch); Theme and Variations (string orch); Checkmate on the Hudson; Gate to World Weather; Conflagration; The Great American Fishing Industry (4 parts); A Fragile Place; Cantatas: The Republic; The Confederacy; The Union.

BALKCOM, MARION HUYETT ASCAP 1960
composer
b Reading, Pa, Dec 23, 02. Educ: Reading High Sch, 20; Curtis Inst, Philadelphia, 23; Philadelphia Col Art, 60; studied piano with Walter Heaton, 16-22 & organ, 20-22. Comp three pieces for children, Baystate Music Publ, 16; accompanied several artists; comp music & lyrics for local performances. Chief Collabrs: Roy Reder, George Peace. *Songs & Instrumental Works:* Holiday From Love; Turn Back the Dawn.

BALKIN, ALFRED (ALAN BLAKE) ASCAP 1963
composer, author, lyricist
b Boston, Mass, Aug 12, 31. Educ: Ind Univ, BA, 52, MA, 53; Columbia Univ, EdD, 68; Manhattan Sch Music; Boston Univ; studied piano with Leon Kushner & acting with Claudia Frank. Prof educ, Western Mich Univ; prof music, var cols & univs. Singer & pianist in nightclubs, radio, TV & recordings. Comp, "Captain Kangaroo Show" & specializing in music for children. Author of textbooks & other music educ materials. *Songs:* We Live in the City (song cycle, 21 songs for children); City Scene (song cycle, 17 songs for children); America's About... (song cycle with narrative); Dr B's TV Tunes (18 songs for TV); The Musicians of Bremen (full length musical bk); I Can Hear the Drums; Reaching and Teaching Through Music.

BALL, ERNEST R ASCAP 1914
composer, pianist
b Cleveland, Ohio, July 22, 1878; d Santa Ana, Calif, May 3, 27. Educ: Cleveland Cons. Staff comp, music publ co, 07-27. Pianist, vaudeville throughout US. Charter mem, ASCAP. Chief Collabrs: Chauncey Olcott, George Graff, Darl MacBoyle, J Kiern Brennan, James J Walker, Arthur Penn, Annelu Burns, David Reed. *Songs:* Will You Love Me in December as You Do in May?; Love Me and the World Is Mine; Saloon; Mother Machree; Till the Sands of the Desert Grow Cold; Dear Little Boy of Mine; I'll Forget You; A Little Bit of Heaven; Let the Rest of the World Go By; In the Garden of My Heart; My Dear; Who Knows?; Goodbye, Good Luck, God Bless You; Turn

Back the Universe; I Love the Name of Mary; To the End of the World With You; When Irish Eyes Are Smiling; West of the Great Divide; Ireland Is Ireland to Me; She's the Daughter of Mother Machree; To Have, to Hold, to Love; Mother of Pearl; For the Sake of Auld Lang Syne; You Planted a Rose. *Scores:* Chauncey Olcott Bway musicals incl: The Heart of Paddy Whack; Macushla.

BALL, MEL
See Franchini, Anthony Joseph

BALLANTINE, EDWARD D ASCAP 1948
composer, conductor, arranger
b Chicago, Ill, Jan 26, 07. Educ: Northwestern Univ, BM, 43; pvt lessons theory & comp with Albert Noelte, 11 yrs. With NBC Staff Orch, 32-42; cond, ABC Breakfast Club Orch, 44-68. Active in advert commercial spots, making phonograph records, arr stock arrangements for publ & composing. Chief Collabs: Johnny Lange, Lewis Green, Jack Fulton, Redd Evans. *Songs:* They Planted Old Glory on a Mountain; It's the NFC (off song of Nat Football Conference); The AFC's for You and Me (off song of Am Football Conference); Music: A Silent Prayer; Blue Dreams; America for Me.

BALLARD, CLINT C, JR (B L PORTER) ASCAP 1959
composer, author, producer
b El Paso, Tex. Educ: El Paso High Sch; NTex State Univ, BA; Iowa State Univ. Lead fraternity choir & dance band in col. Songwriter, in nightclub acts, motion pictures, commericals & musicals, both Bway & regional. Chief Collabs: Conn Fleming, Bob Hilliard, Fred Tobias. *Songs:* You're No Good; The Game of Love; I'm Alive; The Ladder of Love; Hey Little Baby; Go Greyhound (commercial); Music: Good Timin'; Gingerbread; One of Us (Will Weep Tonight). *Scores:* Bway shows: The Ballad of Johnny Pot; The Red Blue Grass Western Flyer Show; Come Back Little Sheba; Film/TV: Come Out Dancin'.

BALLARD, FRANCIS DRAKE (PAT) ASCAP 1932
composer, author
b Troy, Pa, June 19, 1899; d New York, NY, Oct 26, 60. Educ: Univ Pa. Wrote 2 mask & wig shows. Music ed, College Humor. Sgt, USA, WW I. Wrote radio scripts & mag articles. Chief Collabs: Charles Henderson, Tom Waring, Larry Clinton, Abel Green. *Songs:* So Beats My Heart for You; Please Handle With Care; Variety Is the Spice of Life; You're Precious to Me; In the Quiet of the Autumn; Here Is My Heart; So Weary; Say That You're Sorry; Let Me Talk to Your Heart; Where'll I Be Tomorrow Night?; Just a Faded Rose; Love Is Mine; Mr Santa (Christmas version); Oh Baby Mine. *Songs & Instrumental Works:* The Princess of Virginia (operetta).

BALLARD, LOUIS WAYNE (JOE MIAMI) ASCAP 1966
composer, author, conductor
b Miami, Okla, July 8, 31. Educ: Bacone Col, Okla, cert, 49; Okla Univ & Northeast Okla A&M, AA, 51; Univ Tulsa, BA(music theory), BMusEd, 54, MMus(comp), 62; pvt study with Darius Milhaud, 63, Mario Castelnuovo-Tedesco, 66-67, Carlos Surinach, 67 & Felix Labunski, 68-69; hon DMus, Col Santa Fe, 73. Singer, Tulsa Univ Radio Choir, 51-54. Music dir, Marquette High Sch, Tulsa, 54 & Nelagoney Consolidated Schs, Okla, 54-56. Choral music dir, Webster Sr High Sch, Tulsa, 56-58. Relig music dir, Mem Baptist Church, Tulsa, 54, Madalene Cath Church, Tulsa, 55-56 & First Presby Church, Pawhuska, Okla, 54-56. Pvt piano teacher, Tulsa, 58-59. Tympanist with Santa Fe Symph, NMex, 62-64. Music dir, Inst Am Indian Arts, Santa Fe, 62-68. Nat music curriculum specialist, Bur Indian Affairs, Washington, DC, 68-79. Consult on Indian music, Silver-Burdett Publ, Holt, Rinehart & Winston Publ & Arete Encyclopedia, 70's. Lectr, singer, journalist, painter. Annual ASCAP Awards, 66-80; comp assistance grants, 67-76; Ford Found grant, 70; cert spec achievement, Dept Interior, 74. Chief Collab: Ruth Dore Ballard. *Songs:* Portrait of Will Rogers (choral cantata, narrator, orch); Thus Spake Abraham (choral cantata, piano); Espiritu De Santiago (song, piano); The American Indian Sings, No 1 and No 2 (songbook); American Indian Music for the Classroom (teaching kit); Oklahoma Indian Chants for the Classroom (teaching kit); Music: The Gods Will Hear (choral cantata, orch). *Instrumental Works:* Why the Duck Has a Short Tail (symph orch, narrator); Scenes From Indian Life (symph orch, concert band); Devil's Promenade (symph orch); Incident at Wounded Knee (chamber orch); Ritmo Indio (woodwind quartet); Desert Trilogy (wind, perc, string octet); Kacina Dances (cello, piano); Rio Grande Sonata (violin, piano); String Trio No I; Rhapsody for Four Bassoons (quartet); Nighthawk Keetowah (concert band); Ocotillo Festival Overture (concert band); Wamus-77 (half-time band show); Pan-Indian Rhythms (graded perc studies); Siouxiana (woodwind choir); Mid-Winter Fires (trio); Cacega Ayuwipi (perc ens); Fantasy Aborigine (No 1, symph orch, No 2, string choir, No 3, symph orch). *Scores:* Ballet: Ji-Jo-Gweh, The Witch Water Gull; Koshare; The Four Moons; Film: The Sacred Ground.

BALLARD, ROBERT HUDSON ASCAP 1956
composer, orchestrator, arranger
b Nyack, NY, Sept 23, 13. Educ: Occidental Col, BA(music), 34; studied violin, Zoellner Cons; studied comp, arr & orchestration with Edmund Ross & Lyle Murphy. Arr, Gus Arnheim Orch, Freddy Martin Orch, Phil Harris Orch, CBS Radio Orch & Ray Conniff, also recording dir. Arr, orchestrator, choral dir & musical adv, The Lawrence Welk Show. Arr, The New Ore Singers. *Songs:* Music: It's Time for Love; I Knew What I Wanted; Once Upon a Rhumba;

Brazilian Boogie. *Instrumental Works:* Oh Henry!; Toy Piano Boogie; We Live for Love Tonight; Once Upon a Samba; Beginner's Boogie; Oboe, Oh Boy!.

BALLENGER, LARRY DESMOND ASCAP 1973
composer, author, conductor
b Los Angeles, Calif, June 7, 37. Educ: Westmont Col, Santa Barbara, Calif, BA(music), 59; Calif State Univ, Fresno, MA(music history & literature), 67. With relig youth group, Youth for Christ, 59-74; in Presby ministry, 74- Dir, trumpeter, singer & arr with var groups. Chief Collabr: Ralph Carmichael. *Songs:* When You're Young; Dimensions.

BALOGH, ERNO ASCAP 1937
composer, pianist
b Budapest, Hungary, Apr 4, 1897. To US, 24; citizen, 29. Educ: At age 7 entered Royal Acad Music, Budapest; studied with Bela Bartok & Zoltan Kodaly; grad with hon, prof music; studied with Kreutzer, Berlin. WW I service. Cond, operas & operettas. Concert debut, Berlin, 20. Accompanist to Fritz Kreisler in Europe. Concertized US & Can, 24-57; soloist with many symph orchs. Liszt Prize; Nat Asn Am Comp & Cond Award, 44. *Songs:* Do Not Chide Me; Night Is Coming. *Instrumental Works:* For Orch: Divertimento; Portrait of a City; For Piano: Peasant Dance; Magyar Dance; Dirge of the North; Caprice Antique; Dance Infernale.

BALOO, SAM (SPUNKY)
See Beaulieu, Donald George

BALSAM, ARTUR ASCAP 1970
composer, pianist, educator
b Warsaw, Poland, Feb 11, 06. Educ: Lodz, Poland; Berlin, Ger. Pianist; accompanist; musician for chamber music; comp of songs & cadenzas; recording artist, incl piano works of Haydn, Mozart & others. Winner, 2 first prizes for pianists, Berlin, 30 & 31. *Songs & Instrumental Works:* Cadenza for Paganini Concerto No 2; Cadenza for Beethoven Concerto No 2; Cadenza for Fifteen Mozart Concertos; Five Songs.

BALTOR, HAROLD ASCAP 1959
composer, author
b Oakland, Calif, Sept 2, 15. Educ: High sch; pvt music study. Has been publ, realtor & photographer. *Songs:* How Lucky Am I (Freedom Found Award).

BAMBERGER, BERNICE MARIAN ASCAP 1965
author
b New York, NY, Mar 26, 19. Educ: High sch grad; NY Univ (journalism). Film writer; wrote special material for var artists; song-writer of 200 publ works; author & script writer, 80- Chief Collabrs: Addy Fieger, Lor Crane, Rod McBrian, Wes Farrell, Marian McPartland. *Songs:* Lyrics: White on White; Funny Little Butterflies; A Girl Is a Girl; Lonely Little In-Between; I'll Make All Your Dreams Come True; Somewhere There's Love; Ribbons and Roses; Wedding Cake; Bora Bora Bambino; Dream Big; Echoes of Yesterday; Here to Stay; Say Something Funny; Shake Hands With a Fool. *Albums:* Destiny's Child; Something to Believe In; Today I Saw the Sunrise; What a We Gotta Lose; The Happening People; The Sunshine Seekers; The Airways of Imagination.

BAMBRIDGE, JOHN ASCAP 1971
composer, instrumentalist
b St Louis, Mo, Feb 1, 31. Educ: Juilliard, 50. Performer & writer of arr or comp, USAF Band & Orch, 51-54, Les Elgart Band, 56-58, Si Zentner Band; David Rose Orch, 65-70; Los Angeles Civic Light Opera, 60-70 & Tonight Show Orch, 71-80. *Songs & Instrumental Works:* Do-It; If I Only Had the Time; Hard Luck Your Lordship; WFO; Bottom Line; Martha; Plain Ol' Good Ol'; Discaloo; No Doubt About It; Stop—You're Giving Me the Blues; Write-On; Hickory-Dickory; Rock Island; RIP.

BAMERT, MATTHIAS ASCAP 1971
composer
b Ersigen, Switz, July 5, 42. Educ: Bern Cons & Univ; Paris Cons, 1st & 2nd Prizes; Darmstadt-Ferienkürse für Neue Musik. Principal oboist, Mozarteum Orch, Salzburg, 65-69; cond fel, Cleveland Orch, 69-70; asst cond, Am Symph Orch, 70-71; asst cond, Cleveland Orch, 71-76, resident cond, 76-78; music dir, Swiss Radio Orch, Basel, 77- *Instrumental Works:* Five Aphorisms for Flute and Harp; Septuria Lunaris; Mantrajana; Cortege for Five Percussionists; Inkblot for Band; Organisms for Organ; Introduction and Tarantella; Woodwind Quintet; Circus Parade; Once Upon an Orchestra; Concertino for English Horn, Strings and Piano; Rheology; Ol-Okun; Brass Quintet; Incon-Sequenza for Solo Tuba; Keepsake.

BANDINI, ALBERT JACOVINO ASCAP 1954
composer, author, conductor
b New York, NY, Feb 6, 16; d. Educ: High sch. Band leader, 34; made many records. Publ, 47. Chief Collabrs: Al Hoffman, Bennie Benjamin, George David Weiss, Sol Marcus. *Songs:* A Girl! A Girl!; Bermuda; Do What You Want; Gabriel Found His Horn; King of Kings.

BANDLER, RICHARD M ASCAP 1972
composer, author, musician
b New York, NY, Apr 24, 24. Educ: West High, Minneapolis, Minn; Univ Tex; Duval Inst. Teacher, singer. Appeared with Tu-Tones, Three Guys and a Doll, Don Wolf Show & Bob Cummins Show. Chief Collab: Bob Anderson. *Songs:* Sybil; The Rich Get Rich and the Poor Get Poorer; My Wife's a Topless Dancer; *Music:* If It Feels Good, Do It.

BANKS, CARY CRAIG ASCAP 1976
composer, author, musician
b Big Spring, Tex, Jan 24, 50. Educ: Began guitar study, 65; Coahoma High Sch, John Philip Sousa Band Award, 68; col musical training, Lubbock Christian Col, 69. Joined high sch band, 66; played with var bands; taught guitar, 67-75; began songwriting, 68, first song recorded, 76; quarter finalist winner, Am Song Festival, 76, 77 & 78. Permanent mem, KLLL WTex Saturday Nite Opry. Performing musician, songwriter & publisher. Chief Collabrs: Jack W Tyson, Willie Redden. *Songs:* I Can't Sing a Love Song; Fools Like Me; Love Is a Gamble; Aint No Body Lonely; Sing a Song for Jesus.

BANKS, CHARLES O ASCAP 1942
composer, organist, conductor
b Wilkes-Barre, Pa, Aug 10, 1899; d Brooklyn, NY, July 12, 44. Educ: Studied organ with R Huntington Woodman; New York Col Music, MusD. Organist & choir dir, Episcopal Church of St Luke & St Matthew, Brooklyn, 20 yrs. Organist, Apollo Club; dir, Polytech Inst Glee Club; dir, Brooklyn Dime Savings Bank chorus. Organist, Church of the Incarnation. Fel, Am Guild of Organists. *Songs: Sacred Songs:* God That Madest Heaven and Earth; The Ninety and Nine; Communion Service in A.

BARAB, SEYMOUR ASCAP 1950
composer, author, cellist
b Chicago, Ill, Jan 9, 21. Educ: Studied with Lou Harrison, Edgard Varese, Stefan Volpe. With, Indianapolis, Cleveland, All-American Youth, San Francisco, Philadelphia, ABC, CBS & Brooklyn Symph Orchs. Performer with New York Trio, Galimir String Quartet, Composers String Quartet & New York Pro Musica. Fac, Black Mountain Col, Rutgers Univ & New Eng Cons of Music. *Instrumental Works:* Gage. *Scores:* Opera/Ballet: Little Red Riding Hood; The Toy Shop; Chanticleer; A Game of Chance; Phillip Marshall.

BARBE, JOHN ASCAP 1965
composer
b New York, NY, Jan 6, 27. Educ: Juilliard, 50. Composer of songs, film scores & commercials; self-employed commercial & sound track producer. Chief Collabrs: Jane Barbe, Grace Hawthorne.

BARBER, BENJAMIN REYNOLDS ASCAP 1978
author
b New York, NY, Aug 2, 39. Educ: Harvard Univ, PhD, 66. Playwright, lyricist, novelist, editor & author. Chief Collabrs: John Duffy, Martin Best. *Songs: Lyrics:* Fightsong; Journeys; Knight on the Road; American Dream; Close Up the Gate; City Is a Woman; Weary Man.

BARBER, JOHN ASCAP 1959
composer, author, singer
b Columbus, Ohio, Jan 12, 32. Educ: Ohio State Univ, 2 yrs; Juilliard Sch Music. Actor, singer & stage mgr, Music Circus Corp Am, 49-51. Free-lance vocal contractor & choral dir, Choral, MGM & RCA Victor Record Cos, New York, 51-54. Choral dir & production singer, Sahara Hotel, Las Vegas, 53-55. With Paul Gregory Productions, Los Angeles, 55-56. Independent producer of radio & TV commercials, 56-58. With "Dinah Shore Show," 58-60. Toured with Liza Kirk, 60. Radio & TV commercial producer, 61-65. With Commercial Sound Recorders, Los Angeles, 65-70. With Newjack Sound Recorders, Los Angeles, 70-75. Free-lance, 75- *Songs:* Autumn Weather; Pretty Miss; Incredible.

BARBER, SAMUEL ASCAP 1939
composer
b West Chester, Pa, Mar 9, 10. Educ: Hon MusD, Curtis Inst, studied with Isabelle Vengerova, Emilio de Gogorza, Rosario Scalero & Fritz Reiner; hon MusD, Harvard Univ. Sgt, USAF, WW II. Cond & recorded own comp with orchs, US & Europe. Mem, Nat Inst Arts & Letters & Am Acad Arts & Letters. Awards: Am Prix de Rome, 35; Pulitzer Awards, 35 & 36; Guggenheim Fellowship. Chief Collab: Gian Carlo Menotti. *Instrumental Works:* Serenade for String Quartet; Cello Sonata; Overture to "The School for Scandal" (Bearns Prize); Music for a Scene From Shelley; String Quartet No 1; Adagio for Strings; 2 Essays for Orch; Three Reincarnations; A Stopwatch and an Ordnance Map; Violin Concerto; Commando March; Capricorn Concerto; 4 Excursions for Piano; Cello Concerto (NY Music Critics Award, 46); Nuvoletta; Knoxville; Summer of 1915; Piano Sonata; Prayers of Kierkegaard (cantata); Hermit Songs; Summer Music for Woodwind Quintet; A Hand of Bridge; Toccata Festiva; Nocturne; Adromache's Farewell; Piano Concerto No 1 (Pulitzer Prize, 63; NY Critics Award, 64). *Scores:* Operas: Vanessa (Pulitzer Prize, 58); Anthony and Cleopatra (Metrop Opera, Ford Found, comn); Ballets: Medea; Souveniers.

BARBIERO, MICHAEL F ASCAP 1978
composer, author, producer
b New York, NY, June 25, 49. Educ: Choir Sch St Thomas' Church; The Hill Sch; Univ NC, studied electronic comp with Roger Hannay. Asst engr, Mediasound Studios, 71-72; sr engr, 74- Assoc dir A&R, Paramount Records, 72-74; producer of Grammy Award nominee soundtrack LP, "Serpico," 73. Chief Collabrs: Jimmy Maelen, Steve Love, Lonnie Groves, Louis St Louis. *Songs:* If It Wasn't for You; Squeeze Play; Two Good Reasons.

BARBOUR, DAVID ASCAP 1947
composer, conductor, arranger
b Flushing, NY, May 28, 12; d Hollywood, Calif, Dec 11, 65. Educ: Flushing High Sch; pvt music study. Guitarist in small bands incl Wingy Manone & Red Norvo; joined Artie Shaw, Benny Goodman orchs. Appeared in films, "Stage Door Canteen", "The Powers Girl" & "Mr Music." Cond & arr for record cos. Chief Collabrs: Peggy Lee, Henry Beau. *Songs:* Manana; It's a Good Day; You Was Right, Baby; What More Can a Woman Do?; I Don't Know Enough About You; If I Had a Chance With You; Forever Paganini; Forever Nicki; Just an Old Love of Mine.

BARBOUR, KEITH ASCAP 1975
composer, actor, singer
b New York, NY, Jan 21, 41. Educ: Univ Calif, Los Angeles, BA(music, English), 64. Sang with New Christy Minstrels, 67; recording artist, Echo Park, 69- Opened Barbour Music, 78. Actor, radio & TV commercials. Chief Collabr: Jim Stein. *Songs:* Dance Any Way That Feels Good. *Albums:* Pan; Echo Park.

BARBOUR, ROSS ASCAP 1959
composer, author, singer
b Columbus, Ind, Dec 31, 28. Educ: Arthur Jordan Cons. Mem vocal group, Four Freshmen. Made many records. Chief Collabr: Ken Albers. *Songs:* Love Lost; First Affair.

BARCLIFT, NELSON ASCAP 1956
composer, author, actor
b Hopewell, Va, Sept 14, 17. Educ: Bennington Col; William & Mary Col. Actor & dancer in Bway musicals. Dance dir, "This Is the Army", "Around the World", "I Love Lydia" & "Marie Antoinette in Pennsylvania." Actor in films; lyric writer for films, TV show, "Shower of Stars." *Songs:* You Forgot (To Tell Me That You Love Me); Little Babe; Country Serenade; Dictation; It's Cold Outside; Navy's Coming Home.

BARER, MARSHALL LOUIS ASCAP 1956
composer, author, director
b Long Island City, NY, Feb 19, 23. Educ: Palm Beach High Sch; Cavanagh Sch Art; Camp Tamiment, Pa. Advert designer & illusr, Esquire Mag, McCall's & Seventeen, also Container Corp & others. Wrote spec material, then children's records, pop songs & musical theatre in all its forms. Chief Collabrs: Dean Fuller, Mary Rodgers, Alec Wilder, Duke Ellington, Hugh Martin, Michel Legrand, David Ross, William Roy, Jacques Offenbach. *Songs:* Promise Me No Promises; *Lyrics:* I'm Just a Country Boy (ASCAP Award, 78); Summer Is A'Comin' In; Lost in Wonderland. *Scores:* Bway stage: Once Upon a Mattress; New Faces of 1956; Ziegfeld Follies of 1957; Pousse Cafe; The Mad Show; La Belle (based on "La Belle Helene" of Offenbach).

BARI, GWEN ASCAP 1959
composer, author, pianist
b Philadelphia, Pa, Dec 22, 27. Educ: Temple Univ; Juilliard Sch Music. Started career as singer & pianist, New Yorker Hotel, NY. Appeared in nightclubs throughout world. Formed own trio, Los Angeles; appeared in films, TV & radio; made records.

BARKER, DALE WILLARD ASCAP 1962
composer, choral arranger
b Wakonda, SDak, Feb 4, 20. Educ: Univ SDak, BFA; Univ Colo; Lewis & Clark Col, Portland, Ore; studied with L Stanley Glarum. Served during WW II, 4 yrs. Teacher music, pub schs, 46-54. Clerical work music stores, 54-68; music store owner, 68-

BARKER, DANIEL ASCAP 1954
composer, author, guitarist
b New Orleans, La, Jan 13, 09. Educ: Studied clarinet with Barney Bigard, drum with Paul Barbarin (uncle) & guitar with Bernard Addison. Prof guitarist, 26-; played with var bands incl Fess Willaims, Dave Nelson, Orville Browne, Harry White, James P Johnson, Jimmy Jones, Lucky Millinder, Benny Carter, Cab Calloway & many others. Songwriter & recording artist for King Zulu Records & D B Publ Co. Leader, combo accompanying blues singer Blue Lu Barker (wife), 46 & 49. With Conrad Jams & free-lance work, 50- Appeared in TV spec "World of Jazz," 60. Fronted own all-banjo band, New York World's Fair, 64. Asst to curator, New Orleans Jazz Museum. Taught jazz history, Xavier Col, 2 yrs. Dir, Fairview Baptist Church Christian Marching Brass Band, 71- Chief Collabr: Blue Lu Barker (wife). *Songs:* Save the Bones for Henry Jones; Don't You Make Me High; Don't You Feel My Legs; Hot Dogs That Made Him Mad; So Long, Good-bye Joe; Conchita—Cares Nothing Bout Love; You Gotta Get

Yourself a Job Girl; I Had to Stoop to Conquer You; Silly Old Moon; Buy Me Some Juice; There Was a Lil Mouse Lived on a Hill; You Gotta Show It to Me Baby; Nix on Those Lush Heads.

BARKER, JACK ASCAP 1959
composer, author
b Alexandria, Minn, Apr 16, 22. Educ: Pvt piano study. Pianist in nightclubs; writer of spec material. *Songs:* A Five Pound Box of Money.

BARKER, LOUISA DUPONT ASCAP 1976
composer, lyricist, singer
b New Orleans, La, Nov 13, 13. Singer since age 7. With Danny Barker's Jazz Hounds, 39. Recording artist. Chief Collabr: Danny Barker. *Songs:* Don't You Feel My Legs; I Feel Like Laying in Another Woman's Husband's Arms; Lou's Blues.

BARLOW, HAROLD ASCAP 1947
composer, author, music plagiarism consultant
b Boston, Mass, May 15, 15. Educ: Boston Univ Col Music, MusB, 37; Army Music Sch, 43. Armed Forces, World War II, 41-46; Warrant Officer, bandleader, 43-46. Music plagiarism consult for publ, writers, performers, radio & TV stations, recording cos, advert agencies, 50- Author, bks: "A Dictionary of Musical Themes" (selected one of best Am bks on music, Music Libr Asn, 48) & "A Dictionary of Opera and Song Themes." Awarded violin prize in New Eng contest under Fabien Sevitzky at age 18. *Songs:* I've Got Tears in My Ears (From Lyin' On My Back in My Bed While I Cry Over You); Why Should I Love You?; In My Own Quiet Way; As Young As We Are; Lyrics: The Things I Love; Mama; Oh, Marie.

BARLOW, JOHN PERRY ASCAP 1972
author
b Jackson, Wyo, Oct 3, 47. Educ: Fountain Valley Sch, Colorado Springs, Colo; Wesleyan Univ, BA. Rancher; pres, Bar Cross Land & Livestock Co, Cora, Wyo. Songwriter for group, Grateful Dead. Chief Collabr: Bob Weir. *Songs:* Lyrics: Cassady; Mexicali Blues; Black Wind; Looks Like Rain; The Music Never Stopped; Money, Money; Heaven Help the Fool; Wrong Way Feelin'; Lazy Lightnin'; Salt Lake City; Lost Sailor; Saint of Circumstance; You Don't Know How Easy It Is.

BARLOW, WAYNE BREWSTER ASCAP 1954
composer, teacher, author
b Elyria, Ohio, Sept 6, 12. Educ: Pub schs, Rochester, NY; Univ Rochester Eastman Sch of Music, BM, 34, MM, 35, PhD, 37; studied comp with Bernard Rogers, Howard Hanson, Arnold Schoenberg. Mem, theory & comp depts, Univ Rochester Eastman Sch of Music, 37-, incl grad dean, chmn, comp dept, dir, electronic music studio, project dir, Exxon Educ Found grant for teaching tapes in acoustics. Lectr throughout US & Can. Church organist & choir dir. Emeritus prof, 78. Author, bk, "Foundations of Music," encyclopedia articles on acoustics & church music (as coauthor & periodical articles. Recipient, 2 Fulbright appointments in teaching & res, Musician of Year, Mu Phi Epsilon, Rochester Chapter, hon Phi Beta Kappa. *Songs & Instrumental Works:* The Winter's Passed (oboe, strings); Night Song (orch); Lyrical Piece for Clarinet and Strings (or piano); Hymn Voluntaries for Organ; Missa Sancti Thomae (chorus, organ); Intrada, Fugue and Postlude (brass ens); Overture, Hampton Beach (orch); Trio for Oboe, Viola and Piano; Dynamisms (2 pianos); Voices of Faith (chorus, orch, bicentennial comn).

BARMAK, IRA ASCAP 1969
composer, author
h New York, NY, Jan 2, 36. Educ: Cornell Univ, AB, 56, MD, 60; studied piano with Lotte Landau & Maria DeVries Smith. *Songs:* Terry; Marry Me Soon; Foggy; Our House; Ode to Simon and Garfunkel.

BARNES, BOSBY
See Cavanaugh, Robert Barnes

BARNES, CLIFFORD P ASCAP 1941
composer, author, conductor
b Cleveland, Ohio, July 3, 1897; d. Educ: Studied with Karl Grossman, C V Rychlik, Carl Groenwald, James Rogers, Johann Beck, Herbert Clarke, Gustave Heim, Ed Llewellyn. Coronetist, trumpeter in bands, symph & opera orchs. Arr of music for symph orchs at high sch level; also comp instrumental teaching pieces. Cond, opera, ballet, concert bands & orchs. Author, "The Barnes Better Method" (for pre-band flutes). *Instrumental Works:* Gypsy Holiday (overture); Shadow Mountain (overture); Fiddle Folly; Fiddlosophy; Persian Carnival; Hawaiian Holiday; Alpine Holiday; Gypsy Life; Marcia Con Brio; 3 Gaybriellos; Birds of a Feather (flute caprice for band).

BARNES, EDWARD MARTIN ASCAP 1977
composer
b Gettysburg, Pa, Dec 16, 57. Educ: Peabody Cons Music, studied with Robert Hall Lewis, 73-75; Juilliard Sch, BM, MM, studied with Vincent Persichetti, 75-80; Dartington Hall Sch Music, Devon, Eng, studied with Peter Maxwell Davies, summers only, 76-78. Comp music, theater/opera, film scores & instrumental works. Comns: Aspen Music Fest, Juilliard Am Opera Ctr & Am

Brass Quintet. Comp-in-residence, Aspen Music Fest, 78. Awards: Lado Prize in Comp, Percussive Arts Soc Prize in Comp & Henry Mancini Fel. Chief Collabr: Maurice Valency. *Instrumental Works:* The Ballad of Bill Doolin. *Scores:* Opera/Ballet: Feathertop; In the Garden; The Frog Who Became a Prince; Film/TV: The Writers.

BARNES, EDWARD SHIPPEN ASCAP 1950
composer, organist, choirmaster
b Seabright, NJ, Sept 14, 1887; d Idyllwild, Calif, Feb 14, 58. Educ: Lawrenceville Sch; Yale Univ, BA; studied with David Smith, Horatio Parker, Harry Jepson, Louis Vierne, Abel Decaux & Vincent d'Indy. Church organist & choirmaster, Rutgers Presby, New York, 11 yrs; St Stephen's Episcopal, Philadelphia, 13 yrs; First Presby, Santa Monica, Calif, 40-58. Fel, Am Guild Organists. Author: "School of Organ Playing"; "Modulation in Theory and Practice and Interludes for the Church Organist"; "Bach for Beginners in Organ Playing." *Songs:* Father Whate'er of Earthly Bliss; Kneel Before the King; He Who Would Valiant Be; Benedictus es Domine; Abide With Me; Chanson; Shining Shore. *Instrumental Works:* Two symphonies.

BARNES, HELLEN ASCAP 1957
composer, author
b Xmas Creek, Tex, Nov 23, 08; d. Educ: Tex State Col; Peabody Cons. *Songs:* White Winterland; Will It Make Any Difference?; My Second Date; Waiting; Will You Be Mine; Sunrise in Seville.

BARNES, HOWARD LEE ASCAP 1963
author
b Andover, Ohio, Jan 29, 18. Song-writer for var artist, incl John Wayne & Elvis Presley, 48-; joined folk songs publ firm, 50; contract writer for Hill & Range Songs, Inc, 53- Chief Collabrs: Hal Blair, John Mitchum, Harold Hensley, Don Robertson, Billy Liebert, Eddie Dean, William Peppers. *Songs:* Lyrics: I Really Don't Want to Know; So Much to Remember; One More Time Around; How Many; The Good Things; The People; American Boy Grows Up; The Hyphen; I'll Slip Around and Do It in My Dreams Tonight; Hog Wild; Stop Me; Phonograph Record; I Couldn't Be So Happy If I Hadn't Been So Blue.

BARNES, JAMES CHARLES ASCAP 1975
composer, arranger
b Hobart, Okla, Sept 9, 49. Educ: Univ Kans, BMus, 74, MMus, 75. Staff arr & asst to dir of bands, Univ Kans, 75- Clinician & cond of sch bands in midwest & southeast; arranger for Warner Brothers Publ. *Instrumental Works:* Golden Brass (concert march); Hunter Park, Tone Poem for Symphonic Band; Rapscallion, Overture-Scherzo for Symphonic Band; Brookshire Suite (younger band); Lyric Interlude (younger band); Symphony, Opus 35 (ABA-Ostwald Competition Winner, 78); Visions Macabre, Opus 40 (band); Invocation and Toccata, Opus 43 (band).

BARNES, JESSIE
See Sigman, Carl

BARNES, WADE ASCAP 1963
composer, author, announcer
b Alliance, Ohio, May 15, 17. Educ: Mt Union Col; Philadelphia Music Sch; Kingsborough Community Col; studied piano with Herman Grüss & Jan Gorbati. Pianist with dance bands; announcer-pianist at WHBC, Canton, Ohio; announcer-writer, NBC, Cleveland & WCAU, Philadelphia; sales mgr, RCA Recorded Prog Services, 43-50; supvr advert & pub rels for Howard Hughes with Foot Cone & Belding; sales mgr, Gen Teleradio Film Div; vpres, Bonded TV Film Services; partner, Barnes Assocs Pub Rels, pub rels consult to "Ringling Bros Circus"; exec dir, Int Radio & TV Soc, 65; actor in movies, "Cold River" & "Hair." Chief Collabr: Ralph Blane. *Songs:* How Many Stars?; I Believe in Something; No Such Word As Can't; Nothing Is the Hardest Thing to Do; The Most Watchable Girl (official Girl Watchers Soc song); Kiss Me Goodbye; You Ache in My Bones; I Don't Know Who I Really Am; The Helmsley Walk; You're Gonna Break My Heart Again; In Spring the Roses; Tall People Never Have Any Fun; The Prettiest Girl in Town; I Love Art. *Instrumental Works:* First Suite for Piano. *Scores:* Film/TV: Quillow and the Giant; Lefgook (dance & theme music); Bway Show: Lefgook; Background: Nat Sci Found Exhibit at New York World's Fair, 64.

BARNES, WILLIAM ASCAP 1957
composer, author
b Los Angeles, Calif, Jan 27, 27. Educ: Univ Calif, Los Angeles. Writer of spec material for nightclubs, TV & revues. *Songs:* Something Cool; Too Long At the Fair; Mental Blocks; Does Anybody Here Love Me?; Speak Up America; Make a Little Magic. *Scores:* Stage: Billy Barnes Revue; The Billy Barnes People; Billy Barnes' LA; TV: Pinocchio.

BARNETT, ALICE ASCAP 1924
composer, teacher
b Lewiston, Ill, May 26, 1886; d. Educ: First study with father, Orrin Barnett; Chicago Musical Col; Am Cons, Chicago; studied with Borowsky, Weidig, Middelschulte, Ganz & Kaun. Taught music theory, history & harmony, San Diego High Sch, 17-26. Music chmn, San Diego Symph, 14 yrs. *Instrumental*

Works: Musical Settings of Poems: Serenade; In a Gondola; Chanson of the Bells of Oseney; A Caravan From China Comes; In May; Harbor Lights.

BARNETT, BERYL   ASCAP 1958
author
b Seattle, Wash, July 31, 14. Educ: Occidental Col, BA(jour), 36. Free-lance writer for var mags. Chief Collabrs: Lee Fielding, Ray McMillan, Lewis Elliot. *Songs:* Lyrics: Trampoline; I'm So Busy, Lord; Richard the Third; Bayou Baby; Dust the Stars; Jamaica Girl; Apres L' Amour L' Amitie.

BARNETT, BEVERLY HELENE   ASCAP 1975
composer, author, singer
b New York, NY, Feb 16, 37. Educ: City Col New York, grad; Brooklyn Law Sch; Ga State Univ, studied songwriting with Lincoln Chase, 78; Music Bus Inst, studied songwriting, 79. Began singing career with a pvt teacher, Cantor Benjamin Siegel; then staff mem, Stuyvesant Opera Co, New York; later began free lance writing. Chief Collabr: Tamarra Bliss. *Songs:* When the Kissing Ends; Lyrics: If the Stars Could Speak; Then There's Blanche Louise.

BARNETT, JACKIE   ASCAP 1949
composer, author
b New York, NY. Educ: NY Univ. Wrote musical spec material for Jimmy Durante, Bob Hope, Al Jolson, Eddie Cantor, Jack Albertson, Don Rickles & others. Produced & wrote record albums. *Songs & Instrumental Works:* Good Night, Good Night, Good Night; A Real Piano Player; I Love You, I Do; I Just Want to Be Friends; Bandido; Mustapha; Visit Me Tonight.

BARNETT, LAUREL J   ASCAP 1973
composer, author, actress
b Los Angeles, Calif. Educ: Univ Calif Los Angeles. Pianist & violinist as child. Accompanist & soloist in jr symph orchs; comp, background tracks; professional actress & singer, stage & films, 73- Chief Collabr: Scott Seely. *Instrumental Works:* Sassolaise; Persuasions (Persuasiones); Touch and Go; Coyote Woman.

BARNETT, MARK ANDREW   ASCAP 1971
composer, author, teacher
b Jersey City, NJ, Apr 18, 50. Educ: Drew Univ; Bard Col; Univ Colo; The Last Recording Sch; studied with Phil Elwood & Elie Yarden. Played with var bands across US as musician & writer; built own recording studio, Boulder, Colo, 78. Now works out of studio as teacher, producer & recording artist. Chief Collabrs: James Pritchard Turner, Ben Carnes. *Songs:* Amanita Muscaria; Nevada Gamble; Silver Heels.

BARNHILL, JOE BOB (BILLY JOE ROBERTS)
composer, author, guitarist
b Turkey, Tex. Educ: West Tex State Univ, BS, 54. Played with The Pharoahs & JB's Nashville Sound Co. Artist, publ, producer & nightclub performer. *Songs:* Party Dolls and Wine; JB's Boogie; Wine, Women and Music; Nevada's Theme; Salty Dog From Texas; Arr: Chattanooga Choo Choo; In the Mood.

BARON, HERMAN ALEXANDER   ASCAP 1973
composer, author
b New York, NY, Jan 23, 20. Educ: Kingston Col, Jamaica, social sci dipl; NY Univ, BS(sociology); Union Theol Sem, New York, scholarship. Admin, supv & prog develop, 15 yrs; community organ, 7 yrs; sales mgt & personnel supv, 6 yrs. Ministry, United Church of Christ, 20 yrs; assoc minister, Christ Congregational Church, Bronx. Exec dir, Corona-East Elmhurst Community Corp; dir, prog & parent activity, United Neighborhood Houses; acting dir, McDonough St Community Ctr. Interim chaplain, Brooklyn House of Detention. Writer, music for World's Fair Follies, 39. Comp, special material for Vincent Lopez; with WOR Mutual Broadcasting, "Howard Clothes Show of the Week," 40-43; staff comp, NBC, 43-48. Chief Collabrs: Hughie Woolford, Bernie Stein, Bob Saffer. *Songs:* Black Tempo; Slick Little Chick; What Will the Neighbors Say; No Exception to the Rule; Teasin; Chico; You Never Miss the Water; When Tomorrow Comes; Pots and Pans; God Make Us Free; Music: Brown Women in White; Dance of the Creation; Seven Buttons; Safari; Gun Shy GI; The Gal Behind the Guy Behind the Gun. *Instrumental Works:* Swinging on the Chandelier; Scaling the Fence; Falling Off a Cleft. *Scores:* Play: One Wheel Chariot.

BARON, MARION WEISS   ASCAP 1961
composer, author, singer
b Jersey City, NJ, June 9, 23. Educ: Lincoln High Sch, Jersey City; Jersey City State Col. Sang with pop orchs. After years of writing for charitable orgn, became prof songwriter, 61. Became independent record producer. *Songs:* I Wish That We Were Married. *Songs & Instrumental Works:* Twistin' and Kissin'; Slow Dance; Send My Love-Special Delivery.

BARON, MAURICE   ASCAP 1926
composer, conductor, arranger
b Lille, France, Jan 1, 1889; d Oyster Bay, NY, Sept 5, 64. Educ: Lille Cons; studied with A W Lilienthal. Asst cond, Boston Opera Co. Violinist, Seattle Symph; violist, San Francisco Symph. Gen music dir, Roxy Theatre, New York; staff comp & cond, Radio City Music Hall, 32-49; cond of var symph orchs for radio. Founded own publ firm, 37; founder & pres, Soc for French-Am Symph

Music Abroad & affiliate, Asn Musicale Franco-Am. Received title of Officier d'Acad from French govt. *Songs & Instrumental Works:* The Wedding Festival (tone poem); Kissamiss; I Must Be Going to the Dogs; Ode to Democracy (setting to Lincoln's Gettysburg Address); Fosteriana; Indian Wedding Festival; The Conqueror; American Gothic (clarinet, orch). *Scores:* Film: Four Sons; The Big Parade; Ben Hur; The Merry Widow; What Price Glory; The River; Sunrise; The Lover; The Better 'Ole; Opera: Villon; The Enchanted Forest; Ballet: Susan at the Zoo.

BARON, VIC
See Baroni, Vasco

BARONE, MARK F   ASCAP 1979
composer, producer, keyboard player
b Rockville Centre, NY, Jan 24, 52. Educ: Hauppauge High Sch; Hartt Col Music, BMus(comp), 75; studied comp with Arnold Francetti & Norman Dinerstein. Performer, clubs, concerts & TV shows; composer, cond & recording artist, independent producer for Vanguard Records. Chief Collabrs: Allen Brandt, Wendell Morrison, Arthur Federico. *Songs:* The Ring; Savage Lover; Insurgentes Sur; Hollywood; Jump!; Jazz Made Me; Music: It's the Only Way; Your Love. *Instrumental Works:* Deathbed (chamber suite & voice); Brief Feelings (perc); Pictures of Women (guitar & soprano); Suite No 1 (orch). *Scores:* Ballet: Rhoecus; Film: You're My Hero; TV: Be Be Mello.

BARONE, MICHAEL JOSEPH   ASCAP 1968
composer, arranger, trombonist
b Detroit, Mich, Dec 27, 36. Educ: Pvt & self-taught. Studio trombonist, Los Angeles, 60- Liberty Recording artist. Arr for Quincy Jones, Paul Anka, Della Reese, Al Hirt, Chuck Barris TV shows & others. Wrote original comps for Doc Severinsen & "Johnny Carson Tonight Show," incl closing themes. Staff arr & comp, Jenson Publ. *Instrumental Works:* Peachy; Superslick; Half Unison; Wishbone; Maiden Switzerland; Chalet-Co-Win; The Outside John; Gums; Old Shiphead; Henry; Hoam Groan; I Wanna Be With My Love; Just Another Melody; Just Waltzing; Lightly; Love Handles; Love Tool; Legs and Thighs; Lucy and Lulu; Miss Matazz; Ms Dusty; Note Resistant; Riffer Madness.

BARONI, VASCO (VIC BARON)   ASCAP 1961
composer, accordionist, arranger
b Vicopisano, Italy, Dec 16, 10. To US 1914. Arr for Louis Prima, Dean Martin, Jerry Lewis, Luba Malina. Founded Music Reproduction Service, Hollywood. *Songs:* At Our Fireplace; I'll Never Cry; I'll Never Say Goodbye to Baby; Louisa; Make Me Your Slave; Algiers; As Though You Don't Know; Lanikai.

BAROVICK, FRED   ASCAP 1953
composer, arranger
b New York, NY. Educ: Curtis Inst; Univ Pa, PhD. Arr for orchs, incl Hal Kemp, Kay Kyser, Mal Hallet, Vincent Lopez, Tommy Dorsey & Jimmy Dorsey; also for Bway musicals, recordings, TV & educ field. *Songs:* Chant Indigo; The Fat Fat Man; I Wanna; Rock Around the Christmas Tree; The Whistler's Serenade. *Instrumental Works:* Symphony for Strings; Trombone Quartet With Symphony Orchestra; Modern Trombone Solo With Brass Choir; The Lost Horizons.

BARR, ALBERT EARL   ASCAP 1962
composer
b Preakness, NJ, Nov 23, 31. Educ: Self-taught, with piano training as a child; studied comp with Ernest Lubin. Pianist, arr, teacher & comp, 25 yrs. Chief Collabr: Martin Barr (brother). *Instrumental Works:* Nine Pieces for Kids Who Take Piano Lessons and Hate It; Suite for a Sunday Afternoon. *Scores:* Opera: The Coat of Many Colors; Ballet: I Buffoni; Film: Who Will Love My Child. *Albums:* The Red Balloon (adaptation of Acad Award winning French film).

BARR, RAPHAEL (RAY)   ASCAP 1962
composer, arranger, pianist
b New York, NY, July 16, 12. Educ: NY Univ Sch Fine Arts, BA, 32, studied with Otto Cesano. Pianist with Russ Morgan Orch, Harry Reiser Chiquot Club Eskimos & Kay Kayser Orch, also var radio commercials. Pianist & ballet background music for Martha Raye & Imogene Coca TV. Arr, cond & pianist, Patti Page, Judy Garland & Frankie Laine. Chief Collabrs: Paul Francis Webster, Frankie Laine. *Songs:* Music: Teach Me to Pray; Deuces Wild. *Instrumental Works:* Variations in E Flat (piano & symph orch); Sweet Country Suite (4 movements, symph orch); Tranquility (tone poem & symph orch). *Scores:* Ballet: Call Me Mr.

BARRACLOUGH, HENRY   ASCAP 1975
composer, author
b Windhill, Eng, Dec 14, 1891. Educ: Studied piano & organ privately. Scholarship, studied at Bradford Grammar Sch, Windhill, grad, 07; Bloomfield Col & Sem, NJ, LLD, 46. Insurance adjuster, Bradford, Eng, 07-11. Secy, Sir George Scott Robertson, 11-13. Pianist, Chapman-Alexander Evangel Team, Scotland, Eng & US, 13-17. Regimental Sgt Maj, 78 Div, AEF, 17-19. Serv with United Presby Church, US, 19-61. Emer assoc stated clerk. *Songs:* Ivory Palaces (gospel hymn).

BARRANCO, JOHN, JR   ASCAP 1970
composer, author, singer
b Jackson, Miss, June 26, 51. Played with Barry Manilow, Stephen Stills, Richie Haven, James Taylor, The Allman Bros. Had band, The Barranco Bros. Writer, arr & producer. *Songs:* Lonesome Love Song; A Second Part of Me; Take a Little Heartache.

BARRERE, PAUL
composer, author, singer
b Burbank, Calif, July 3, 48. Educ: Hollywood High Sch; North Hollywood High Sch; Los Angeles City Col. Guitar sideman for Hank Schifter, 68; guitarist, vocalist & writer for var groups, 69-80. Chief Collabrs: Bill Payne, Lowell George, Tom Snow. *Songs:* All That You Dream; Keeping up With the Jones'; Old Folks Boogie; Skin It Back; Time Loves a Hero; Missin' You; One Love Stand; Feets Don't Fail Me Now; Walkin' All Night; High Roller; Romance Dance; Perfect Imperfection; Love Sweet Love; Over the Edge; Sweet Coquette; Long Road; Who Knows for Sure; Music: Day At the Dog Races.

BARRETT, JOANNE LENHERT   ASCAP 1977
composer, author, singer
b Abilene, Kans, Mar 29, 36. Educ: Messiah Acad; Case-Western Reserve Univ, BA. Singer of church music; children's music for church. Chief Collabr: Ron E Long. *Songs:* Everyone Calls Him "Sir" (children's musical).

BARRIE, GEORGE   ASCAP 1971
composer
b Brooklyn, NY, Feb 9, 12. Educ: De Witt Clinton High Sch, grad; NY Univ, 2 yrs. Self-taught to read music, play guitar, banjo, piano, clarinet & saxophone; joined Benny Meroff's Dance Orch, playing in New York & on road. Chmn, pres & chief exec officer, Faberge, Inc; pres, Brut Pictures, Inc & Brut Productions, Inc. Chief Collabr: Sammy Cahn. *Songs & Instrumental Works:* Who Can Tell Us Why; Thieves; Rome is a Song; Nudge Me Every Morning; Now That We're in Love; Now Is Forever; The Night Has Many Eyes; I Just Need a Lover; The Ballad of Billy; Baby, You're Mine; A Touch of Class; Amor Mio; All That Love Went to Waste; Once and Only Once.

BARRIS, CHARLES H
producer
b Philadelphia, Pa, June 2, 29. Educ: Drexel Inst, grad, 53. Mgt trainee, NBC; dir, West Coast daytime TV progs ABC-TV, 59-65; creator & producer TV shows "The Dating Game", "The Newlywed Game", "Dream Girl", "How's Your Mother-in-Law?", "The Family Game", "Operation Entertainment", "The Parent Game" & "The New Treasure Hunt"; exec producer & host "The Gong Show" & "Chuck Barris Rah-Rah Show." Author, "You and Me, Babe."

BARRIS, HARRY   ASCAP 1931
composer, author, pianist
b New York, NY, Nov 24, 05; d Burbank, Calif, Dec 13, 62. Educ: Denver pub schs. At 14, prof pianist; later led own orch on tour of Orient. Mem, Paul Whiteman Rhythm Boys with Bing Crosby, Al Rinker. First Am entertainer in CBI Theatre of War, 43-44. Singer. Chief Collabrs: Bing Crosby, Clifford Gordon, Mort Greene, Gus Arnheim, Ralph Freed, James Cavanaugh, Ted Koehler, Bill Moll. *Songs:* Mississippi Mud; I Surrender, Dear; Little Dutch Mill; Let's Spend an Evening at Home; That's Grandma; From Monday On; It Was So Beautiful; It Must Be True; Wrap Your Troubles in Dreams; At Your Command; Beyond Compare; I'm Satisfied; Lies.

BARRON, TED   ASCAP 1923
composer, pianist, publisher
b Flushing, NY, Dec 14, 1879; d Flushing, Nov 28, 43. Educ: NY Univ, eng. Pianist, mgr & publ. *Songs:* Georgia Moon; If Time Was Money I'd Be a Millionaire.

BARROWS, WALT
See Whippo, Walter Barrows

BARRY, AL   ASCAP 1956
composer, author
b New York, NY, Nov 14, 03; d. Educ: Trade sch. Poet & short story writer. *Songs:* Rainbow 'Round the World.

BARRY, GERRY   ASCAP 1959
composer, author, actor
b Limerick City, Ireland, Feb 2, 13; d. Educ: Marino Col, Dublin; Prof Ray's Acad, Limerick. Actor, production mgr of shows touring Europe. Publicity dir, United Artists; co mgr, General Artists. Columnist, Irish-Am weekly newspaper, New York. *Songs:* In the Heart of Donegal.

BARRY, KEVIN MICHAEL   ASCAP 1957
composer, author
b Cincinnati, Ohio, Nov 1, 31. Working lounge musician, world wide, incl US, Mex, Can. Chief Collabrs: Norman Kaye, Joe Maize. *Songs:* Spring Never Comes; Believe in Me; Hawaii Calls; Lotus.

BARRY, STEVE
See Lipkin, Stephen Barry

BARRY, WILLIAM   ASCAP 1954
composer, author
b Los Angeles, Calif, June 4, 11. Educ: Col. Entertainer in nightclubs & vaudeville. Nat sales mgr, Bloomfield Molding Co. Chief Collabrs: Lew Pollack, Herman Pincus, Jean Herbert. *Songs:* Poor Little Doll; Little Sweetheart of the Mountains; Partner, It's the Parting of the Way; In the Hills of Old Montana; Heart to Heart; Is That All I Mean to You.

BARRYMORE, LIONEL   ASCAP 1944
composer, actor, director
b Philadelphia, Pa, Apr 28, 1878; d Van Nuys, Calif, Nov 15, 54. Son of Maurice Barrymore; bro of Ethel & John Barrymore. Stage debut, "The Rivals," 1893. Appeared in plays incl "Peter Ibbetson", "The Copperhead", "The Jest", "Macbeth" & "Laugh, Clown, Laugh"; films incl "The New York Hat", "Mata Hari", "A Free Soul" (Acad award, 31), "Rasputin and the Empress", "Grand Hotel", "Dinner At Eight", "David Copperfield", "Ah, Wilderness!", "You Can't Take It With You" & "Dr Kildare" series. Author, "Mr Cartonwine: A Moral Tale" (novel); autobiography, "We Barrymores." Biography, "The Barrymores" by Hollis Alpert. *Instrumental Works:* Russian Dances; Partita; Ballet Viennois; The Woodman and the Elves; Behind the Horizon; Fugue Fantasia; In Memorium; Hallowe'en; Preludium and Fugue; Elegie for Oboe, Orchestra; Farewell Symphony (1-act opera); Elegie (piano pieces); Rondo for Piano; Scherzo Grotesque.

BARSKI, ROSALIE ANNE   ASCAP 1978
composer, author
b San Jose, Calif, Sept 20, 49. Educ: Pacific Christian Col; Ozark Bible Col; Azusa Pacific Col. Toured with Christian group through Europe & Mex; performed as single artist in church concerts & others, 2 yrs; also some TV appearances; gave personal concert for John Wayne in his home, 77. *Songs:* Smile; He's the One Who Loves Me; Skydove; Love One Another.

BARSKY, PHILIP   ASCAP 1956
composer, author
b Philadelphia, Pa, Sept 12, 14. Chief Collabr: George Sherzer. *Songs:* Juke Box Joe; By and By; I'm Goin'; For the Rest of My Life; No More Love.

BARSTOW, RICHARD HATTON
choreographer, producer, director
b Ashtabula, Ohio, Apr 1, 08. Educ: Studied with pvt tutors. Began show bus career, 16. Danced & appeared in stock cos on tour, Mont, Okla & Tex, 18-21; appeared Midnight Frolic, Chicago, 24-25 & The Palace, New York; also on tour. US. Featured musical comedies, Australia, then movie houses, US, London & on tour in Europe, 28-30; appeared with sister, The Palace, 30-39; single dancing act, Radio City Music Hall, New York & Palmer House, Chicago, 39; choreographer motion pictures, "Buck Benny Rides Again", "Love Thy Neighbor" & "Swing Fever"; also road co musical, "Helzapoppin." Producer, Olsen & Johnson Show, Carnival Night Club, 46; choreographer & producer shows incl, "Barefoot Boy With Cheek", "Tonight at 8:30", "New Faces of 1952," revival of "Sally" & others; choreographer, Munic Opera, St Louis, 48; dir & writer, First Symph of Fashion, St Louis, 48-49; choreographer, Greatest Show on Earth, Ringling Bros Barnum & Bailey Circus, 49-51, dir, stager & choreographer, 52-78; dir three summer tent theatres simultaneously, 57; spec writer, choreographer & stager, "Colgate Comedy Hour" & numerous other TV shows; producer, choreographer & dir revues, "Shooting High", "What's My Act", "Toast of the Town"; motion pictures incl, "Girl Next Door", "New Faces", "Greatest Show on Earth" & "A Star Is Born." Staged, produced, dir & choreographed with sister, "Champagne on Ice," London Hippodrome, 53; produced, wrote, dir & staged with sister, Motorama Shows, Gen Motors, New York & on tour, also Powerama, Chicago, 55; dir music tent show, Theatre-in-the-Round, Westbury, Long Island, summers 56 & 57; author, producer & dir, March of Dimes Show, Waldorf Astoria, New York, 58; dir & choreographer, appearances of Judy Garland, New York, Chicago & San Francisco, 59; staged & dir, "Song of Norway," New York, 59 & "Annie Get Your Gun," Jones Beach, Long Island, 77-78; staged shows for Ray Price & Brenda Lee; dir summer theatres; songwriter; owner, Richbar Publ Co, Nashville. Rec'd Circus Oscar. Originated toe skate, with sister tap toe dancing on a staircase; acclaimed World's Greatest Toe Dancer. *Songs:* May All Your Days Be Circus Days (Ringling Bros Circus sign off theme); The Circus Was Made for Me; The Happiness Train; Let the Bells Ring Out; It's Still the Big Parade; The Animal Walk; I Know Who You Are; What Do You Do?; Time for Love.

BART, JAN   ASCAP 1964
composer, author, singer
b Poland, Jan 26, 19; d. Educ: Warsaw Acad of Music; Berlin Cons. To US, 30. Began career as cantor. Traveled with Maj Bowes Unit, 7 yrs. Had own radio show. Author "I Lost a Thousand Pounds." *Songs:* Book of Yinglish Songs (Yiddish songs with original English lyrics).

BART, TEDDY   ASCAP 1960
composer, author
b Johnstown, Pa, Feb 7, 36. Singer/songwriter, until 70; now host of radio & TV shows on WSM, Nashville. Chief Collabr: Beasley Smith. *Songs:* Music: Taste of Tears; New Orleans My Home Town; Day Dreamer; To Be in Love.

BARTELS, JEAN TANN   ASCAP 1979
author
b Blytheville, Ark, Sept 23, 19. Educ: DeKalb High Sch, Miss, gen dipl; Miss State Col for Women, BA(Latin & Eng); Univ Nev. Taught Latin & Eng in Miss, Mo, Fla & Nev. *Songs:* Lyrics: Hold Out Your Arms to Me; My Heart Found You.

BARTELSTONE, IRA (IRA STONE)   ASCAP 1973
composer, author
b Kew Gardens, NY, Apr 10, 48. Educ: W T Clarke High Sch; Hofstra Univ, BFA. Musician & songwriter; played guitar with Music Explosion at Woodstock Festival, 69. Chief Collabrs: Maxine Stone, Leslie West, Mick Jagger. *Songs:* When Will the Rain Come; Music; High Roller; So Much Better.

BARTELSTONE, MAXINE (MAXINE STONE)   ASCAP 1973
composer, author
b Qew Gardens, NY, May 15, 50. Educ: Lawrence HS; New Col of Hofstra, BA. Musician & songwriter; involved with Woodstock Fest, 69. Chief Collabrs: Ira Stone (husband), Leslie West, Mick Jagger, Bert Sommer. *Songs:* High Roller; Lyrics: So Much Better; Music: Rush Hour.

BARTH, HANS   ASCAP 1949
composer, pianist
b Leipzig, Ger, June 25, 1897; d Jacksonville, Fla, Dec 8, 56. Came to US, 03, became citizen, 12. Educ: Leipzig Cons (scholarship); MacDowell Col (fel), 3 yrs. Inventor of portable one-quarter tone piano. Concertized throughout US & Europe. Pianist with Philadelphia, Cincinnati & Havana Philh; also Austin (Tex) & Springfield (Mass) Symph Orchs. Dean of judges, Nat Guild Piano Teachers. *Songs:* Fair Ones With Golden Locks; Save Me the Waltz. *Instrumental Works:* Concerto for Orchestra, Quarter-Tone Piano; Peace Symphony; Miragia; Piano Concerto; 9 Etudes for Piano, Orchestra; 2 piano sonatas.

BARTHELSON, JOYCE
See Holloway, Helen Joyce

BARTHOLOMEW, MARSHALL MOORE   ASCAP 1924
composer, author, conductor
b Belleville, Ill, Mar 3, 1885; d. Educ: Yale Univ, BS, hon MA; Univ of Pa, BM; Berliner Hochschule fur Musik. Dir, Nat War Work Coun, USA, 17-19. Dir, Yale Glee Club, 21-53. Exec dir, then pres, Inter Collegiate Music Coun, 27-53. Pres, Int Student Musical Coun, 31-39. Prof, Yale Sch of Music, 39-53. WW II, mem Army-Navy Comn Welfare & Recreation. Mem, US State Dept Comn on Cultural Relations, Inter-Am Affairs, 40-43. Author "Music for Everybody", "Mountain Songs of North Carolina", "70 Songs for School and High School Singers", "Yale Glee Club Series" & "Yale Song Book."

BARTLES, ALFRED HOWELL (GENE MAC HOWELL)   ASCAP 1964
author, cellist, pianist
b Nashville, Tenn, Nov 10, 30. Educ: Univ Miss, BA, 53; Ohio Univ, MFA(comp). Free-lance comp, cellist & jazz pianist, New York, 54-69. Fac, Schiller Col, Heidelberg, Ger, 70-73, Tenn Technol Univ, 73-77 & Eurythmeum, Stuttgart, Ger, 77-80. Chief Collabrs: Bryan Lindsay, Basil Payne. *Songs & Instrumental Works:* Ballad for Flügel Horn and Jazz Ensemble; Music for Symphony Orchestra and Jazz Ensemble; Quartet for Piano, Violin, Clarinet and 'Cello; Tone Sculpture for Orchestra; And Well I Shall Be There (chorus, SATB, string orch).

BARTOK, BELA   ASCAP 1946
composer, pianist
b Nagyszentmiklos, Hungary, Mar 25, 1881; d New York, NY, Sept 26, 45. Educ: Franz Liszt Cons, Budapest. First appearance as pianist at 9. Prof music, Royal Acad, 07-40. Moved to US, 40. Toured Europe & US as concert pianist of own works & in other progs. Began collaboration with Zoltan Kodaly in collecting Hungarian folk music, 05; made collection of traditional melodies of Hungary, Roumania, Slovakia, Turkey, Serbia, Ruthenia & Arabia; also wrote articles on res in folklore, folk songs. Biography, "The Life and Music of Bela Bartok," by Halsey Stevens. *Songs:* Hungarian Folk Songs; Rumanian Folk Songs; Slovak Folk Songs; Szekely Songs; From Olden Times; Music: Songs, Opus 15 and 16 (voice, piano). *Instrumental Works:* Kossuth Symphony; Elegies; Easy Pieces; Sketches; Burlesques; Dirges; Allegro Barbaro; Hungarian Folk Tunes; Suite; Rondos; Studies; Little Pieces for Piano; Four Orchestra Pieces, Opus 12; two rhapsodies for violin & piano; Rhapsody for Piano; two suites for orch; Portraits for Orchestra; Bagatelles; two violin concertos for children; six string quartets; Roumanian Dances; Deux Images for Orchestra; Bluebeard's Castle; The Wooden Prince; Christmas Carols; Roumanian Folk Dances; Piano Sonatina; 27 a cappella choruses; The Miraculous Mandarin; Improvisations; Two Sonatas for Violin, Piano; Dance Suite; Out of Doors; Piano Sonata; Village Scenes; Three Piano Concertos; Hungarian Sketches; Rhapsody No 1 for Cello, Piano; two rhapsodies for violin, orch; Cantata

Profana; Duos for Violins; Hungarian Peasant Songs; Mikrokosmos; Mikrokosmos Suite, Music for Strings, Percussion, Celeste; Sonata for Two Pianos, Percussion; Contrasts for Violin, Clarinet, Piano; Divertimento for String Orchestra; Concerto for Orchestra; Violin Sonata; Viola Concerto.

BARTON, BEN (GARY BRUCE)   ASCAP 1953
composer
b Minsk, Russia, Apr 4, 00. Arrived in US when 3 yrs old. Studied violin since age of 8. Started in vaudeville when 15 yrs old playing violin & had own band; when vaudeville died worked for Jack Robbins plugging songs. Started own publ co; founder & pres, Barton Music Corp, in partnership with Frank Sinatra publ songs. Now operating, Greenbar Music Corp & Dunaway Music Corp. Mem, Musicians Union Local 802, New York. Chief Collabrs: Sammy Cahn, Buddy Kaye, Al Hoffman, Sam Ward, James Van Heusen, Ken Hecht, Andy Razaf, Leon Carr. *Songs:* My Thrill; Since You Went Away; It's Illegal, It's Immoral; Music: There's No Place Like Home (Especially Christmas Eve); Forgetting You; It Won't Be Easy; Don't Speak of Love; Lyrics: Out With Somebody Else.

BARTON, JAMES DEREK   ASCAP 1977
composer, author, singer
b Chicago, Ill, June 7, 49. Educ: Prospect High Sch, Mt Prospect, Ill, 67; Univ Ill, Urbana, grad BA(Eng, theatre), 71. Songwriter, 70- Fronted The James Barton Ensemble, 71-73; joined The Ship, 73, writer & singer, 73-77; now writing songs & performing in commercials as voice-over, on-camera & singing talent. Chief Collabrs: Thom Bishop, Scott Nelson. *Songs:* Your Backyard; Minnesota Dawn; Mile After Mile; Lost Weekend Farewell; Tornado; Looking Back At Midnight; If You Really Want Me to Leave; What a Difference a Dream Makes; Collect; Baby's Coming Home; Music: Main Drag.

BARTOSIEWSKI, EDWIN CHARLES   ASCAP 1976
composer, author
b San Francisco, Calif, Dec 20, 48. Educ: Lincoln High Sch; Long Beach State Col, BS. Performed in bands as guitarist & singer. *Songs:* Barren Prairie; Image of Just One Man; No Boundaries.

BARTOW, NEVETT   ASCAP 1960
composer, pianist, conductor
b New York, NY, Nov 7, 34; d Philadelphia, Pa, Nov 22, 73. Educ: Blair Acad; studied piano & comp with Andrew Salama, 5 yrs; Manhattan Sch of Music, New York, MA, 57, studied piano with Goldsand, comp with Vittorio Gianini. Taught music, comp-in-residence & chmn of music dept, Blaire Acad, 61-73. *Songs & Instrumental Works:* Variations and Fugue for Piano; Six Character Pieces for Students (piano); Toccata for Piano; Toccata, Chorale and Fugue (solo organ); Passacaglia, Andante and Scherzo (solo organ); Three Early American Hymn Tunes (service sonata for organ); Sonata for Flute and Piano; Divertimento for Woodwind Quintet; Summershadow (Elegy for Orchestra); Three Characteristic Dances for Solo Accordion; Choral works for mixed chorus: The King of Love My Shepherd Is; Adam Lay Y-Bounden; A Christmas Canticle (chorus, harp, piano or organ); A Thanksgiving Exultation; Scene on Easter Morning (dramatic anthem, organ, optional Bibilical narration); Tower of Babel (cantata, piano, perc).

BARTY, BILLY JOHN   ASCAP 1957
composer, author, entertainer
b Millsboro, Pa, Oct 25, 24. Began in movies, age 3 yrs; toured in vaudeville, 9 yrs; with Spike Jones, 8 yrs & James Melton Show, 1 1/2 yrs; own children's show on ABC, New York, KTTU, Los Angeles, performed in many movies incl, "Foul Play", "Skatetown USA" & "True Confessions." Featured in Busby Berkley Musicals, "Goldiggers," 33 & "Footlight Parade." With Donald O'Conner & London Palladium. Chief Collabr: Eddie Brandt. *Songs:* Christmas Cheer.

BASIE, WILLIAM (COUNT)   ASCAP 1943
composer, pianist
b Red Bank, NJ, Aug 21, 06. Educ: First music study with mother; later with Fats Waller. Accompanist to vaudeville acts. Joined Bennie Moten Orch, Kansas City; later organized own orch & appeared on radio. To NY, 36; appeared in hotels, theatres, nightclubs, jazz fests; toured US & Europe, 54. Elected to Down Beat, Hall of Fame, 58. Has made many records. Chief Collabrs: Mack David, Eddie Durham, Jerry Livingston, Andy Gibson, James Rushing, Lester Young. *Songs & Instrumental Works:* One O'Clock Jump; Every Tub; Good Morning Blues; John's Idea; Jumpin' At the Woodside; Basie Boogie; Blue and Sentimental; Gone With the Wind; Two O'Clock Jump; Swingin' the Blues; I Ain't Mad At You; Futile Frustration; Good Bait; Don't You Miss Your Baby?; Miss Thing; Riff Interlude; Panassie Stomp; Shorty George; Out the Window; Hollywood Jump; Nobody Knows; Swinging At the Daisy Chain; I Left My Baby.

BASILE, JOE   ASCAP 1953
composer, author, cornetist
b Newark, NJ, Sept 13, 1889; d Bloomfield, NJ, June 22, 61. Educ: Nat Cons, New York. Led Elks', Shriner's & Eagles' bands; 17 seasons at Madison Square Garden; at state fairs & circuses, 20 yrs. Known as "The Brass Band King," winner of 63 cups at nat conventions. *Songs:* One in a Million Fools; Curtain

Time; Excelsior; Morochita; Wild Horse Galop; Big Time March; Big Top; Whisp'ring Waters.

BASKERVILLE, DAVID ASCAP 1958
composer, author, conductor
b Freehold, NJ, Aug 15, 18. Educ: Univ Calif, Los Angeles, MA(comp), 55, PhD(historical musicol, first PhD awarded for jazz res), 65, pvt study orchestration with Mario Castelnuovo-Tedesco. Trombonist with Seattle Symph Orch & Los Angeles Philh, staff comp & cond for NBC, Hollywood, 47-59; orchn-arr with Paramount Pictures & 20th Century Fox; TV producer, BBC, London, 61; pres, Sherwood Recording Studios, Los Angeles, 64-67; exec vpres, Ad-Staff (radio-TV productions), Hollywood. Prof music, Univ Colo, Denver, 69- ASCAP Deems Taylor Award, 80 as author, "Music Business Handbook and Career Guide." *Instrumental Works:* Night Song; Grand Entry Swing March; Ventura Venture; Moonride; Hollywood Swing March; Monograph for Orchestra (premiered by Denver Symph Orch).

BASKETTE, BILLY ASCAP 1923
composer, pianist, bassist
b Henderson, Ky, Oct 20, 1884; d Culver City, Calif, Nov 8, 49. Educ: Col. Bassist in circus band; dancer & pianist in stock cos & vaudeville. Early radio entertainer. Staff comp, music publ firms, NY & Chicago. Chief Collabrs: Benny Davis, Art Berman, George Little, Charles Riesner, Ed Rose, Lew Pollack, Jesse Crawford. *Songs:* Dream Train; Waitin' for the Evenin' Mail; Hawaiian Butterfly; Goodbye Broadway, Hello France; Everybody Wants a Key to My Cellar; Talking to the Moon; Whistlin' Joe From Kokomo; For Ever and Ever and Ever; That's When I Learned to Love You; Roses in the Rain; Same Old Moon; Land Where Poppies Bloom; Keep the Lovelight Burning.

BASNEY, ELDON EUGENE ASCAP 1971
composer, violinist, conductor
b Port Huron, Mich, June 14, 13. Educ: Peabody Cons of Music, Baltimore, Md, studied comp with Gustave Strube, violin with Frank Gittleson, J C van Hulsteyn, Stanislaw Schapir, Detroit. Violinist, started playing at age 22 months, on stage, Liberty Bond Drives, age 3 yrs. Played concerts, US, Can, Australia & Honolulu. Cond for var orchs incl Baltimore String Symph, Kankakee Civic Orch & Chorus, Kankakee, Ill; guest cond, Chicago Women's Symph Strings & Buffalo Philh. Taught music theory & applied music, var cols, 46-78; retired. Recipient, MacDowell Colony Fel, Thomas Prize & Composer's Forum, New York, 68. *Instrumental Works:* Essay for Strings; Ninau—Poem for Orchestra; Seventh String Quartet; Fall River. *Scores:* Ballet: Marriage of the Rivers (comn).

BASS, JULES ASCAP 1963
author
b Philadelphia, Pa, Sept 16, 35. Educ: Forest Hills High Sch; NY Univ. Lyricist, TV & motion picture films. Also lyricist & co-producer off-Bway musical "Month of Sundays," Theatre DeLys, 67. Partner, film production co of Rankin/Bass Productions. Chief Collabr: Maury Laws. *Scores:* Film/TV: The Last Dinosaur; The Bermuda Depths; The Daydreamer; Mad Monster Party; The Return of the King; The Hobbit; TV Spec: The Enchanted World of Danny Kaye; Cricket on the Hearth; Year Without a Santa Claus; The First Easter Rabbit; The Easter Bunny Is Comin' to Town.

BASS, ROGER ASCAP 1961
composer, pianist, producer
b New York, NY, Sept 20, 25. Educ: Juilliard Sch Music; NY Univ Sch of Commerce; Univ Miami; studied with Leonard Bernstein, Herman Wasserman, David Saperton, Otto Cesana, Ernst Toch & Schillinger System with Rudolf Schramm. Instr comp, NY Univ. Pres, Bass Films, Inc. *Songs:* The Golf Widow.

BASS, SIDNEY ASCAP 1951
composer, conductor, pianist
b New York, NY, Jan 22, 13. Educ: NY Univ, music ed. Accompanist & arr for singers, dancers & nightclub acts; cond & arr of many top ten recordings; cond, arr & comp for Muzak; several solo albums on RCA Victor as featured cond & arr. Chief Collabrs: Roy Jordan, Mann Curtis. *Songs:* Music: Soft Shoe Song; One Man Woman; Greatest Feeling in The World; More of Everything; The Story of Man. *Instrumental Works:* The Bells are Swinging; Blue Bells; Funny Bone.

BASS, WARNER S ASCAP 1965
composer
b Brandenburg, Ger, Oct 6, 15. Educ: Berlin Univ, MA Equivalency; Berlin State Acad Music, MM Equivalency; NY Col Music, MusB; NY Univ, MA. Cond, State Opera, Kassel & Kulturbund Theatre, Berlin, Ger; assoc cond, Am Symph Orch, 62-64. Assoc prof, NY Univ, 67-69; assoc prof, City Univ New York, Kingsborough, 69-72, prof, 72- *Instrumental Works:* Song of Hope (overture & fugue for large orch); Suite for String Orchestra; Taps (adagio for string orch with trumpet & drums); Larghetto for Oboe and String Orchestra; Serenata Concertante for Viola and String Orchestra; Psalm 96 (solo-tenor, women's chorus & organ); Sonata for Viola and Piano; Sonatinetta for Trumpet and Piano.

BASSETT, KAROLYN WELLS ASCAP 1924
composer, pianist
b Derby, Conn, Aug 2, 1892; d Briarcliff Manor, NY, June 2, 31. Educ: In Europe; Felton Sch, NY; studied with Van York, Carl & Reinhold Faelton & Treharne. Gave first piano recital at age 6. Mem, Authors League Am & Nat League Am Pen Women. *Songs:* Little Brown Baby; Yellow Butterfly; Optimism; A Child's Night Song; The Moon of Roses; Take Joy Home.

BASSMAN, GEORGE ASCAP 1946
composer
b New York, NY, Feb 7, 14. Educ: Boston Cons, studied orchestration & comp with Ernst Toch, cond with Leon Barzin & Hugo Strelitzer. Arr for Fletcher Henderson, Chick Webb & Duke Ellington, 30-32 & Andre Kostelanetz, 34-35. Comp & arr of 60 films, MGM, 34-50. Arr music Bway shows, "Guys and Dolls" & "Alive and Kicking." Comp & cond, many TV shows, incl "Producers' Showcase", "Omnibus" & others, 52-60. Comp films, MGM, 60- Chief Collabr: Ned Washington. *Songs:* I'm Getting Sentimental Over You; Dangerous; Ride the High Country (MGM film theme song); Mail Order Bride (MGM film theme song). *Scores:* Meet the People (also arr); Best House in Naples; Films: Babes in Arms; The Big Store; Cabin in the Sky; Canterville Ghost; The Clock; A Day at the Races; For Me and My Gal; Go West; Postman Always Rings Twice; Ride the High Country; Romance of Rosy Ridge; That's Entertainment, Parts 1 and 2; Wizard of Oz; Bonnie and Clyde; Jo Louis Story; Marty; Middle of the Night and others.

BAT'ADA, JUDITH
See Reisman, Judith

BATCHELOR, RUTH ASCAP 1964
composer, author, singer
b New York, NY, Feb 12, 34. Songwriter for var artists & shows; lyricist for TV shows & records; transl Eng versions of "Stay" for Charles Azavanour & "Where Did It Go?" for Louis Bonfa from the Mania De Carnaval. Author of bk & lyricist, off-Bway show "A Quarter for the Ladies Room." To London, journalist for The Sunday Times, Punch & Time Out. To Los Angeles, critic for Los Angeles Free Press & Globe Newspapers; founded Los Angeles Film Critics Asn, pres, 3 yrs. Produced critics award show, 2 yrs. Chief Collabrs: Sherman Edwards, Bob Roberts, Mort Shuman, Jerry Goldsmith, Brian Wells, Charles Azavanour, Louis Bonfa, Arthur Seigel, Kenny Rankin. *Songs:* Test Tube Baby; You Got It All; Lyrics: King of the Whole Wide World; He's Moving On; Haven't We Met?; Because of Love; Stay (Reste); The Clock; I Will Follow (theme from Stagecoach); and other publ songs. *Scores:* Film/TV: Tom Jones; Who's Afraid of Mother Goose; William Tell; Theater: Dorian Grey.

BATES, CHARLES L ASCAP
composer, pianist
b Villisca, Iowa, Sept 17, 1897; d New York, NY, Aug 5, 37. Educ: Drake Univ. Accompanist in vaudeville & radio prior to 1923; organized & accompanied The Rhythm Girls with the Paul Whitman Band; worked as pianist & song demonstrator with the Feist Music Co. *Songs:* Hard Hearted Hannah; Music: On the Nodaway Road.

BATES, KATHLEEN DOYLE (BOBO) ASCAP 1970
composer, author, singer
b Memphis, Tenn, June 28, 48. Educ: Southern Methodist Univ, Tex, BFA, 69. Wrote & performed song for "Taking Off", 70. Off-Bway debut in "Vanities", 76; "Straight Time" & "Loveboat." Bway debut in "Goodbye Fidel", 80. Mem, Lion Theatre Co. *Songs:* And Even the Horses Had Wings.

BATSFORD, J TUCKER
See Kapp, Paul

BATSON, JONATHON KINGSLEY ASCAP 1979
composer, author
b Washington, DC, Dec 10, 44. Singer, nightclubs & coffeehouses. Author, "Snow White" for Los Angeles Schs, musicals "Hollywood Arcade", "Jonathan Who Revue" & "A Special Step to Hollywood"; music for TV show "Off Hollywood." Chief Collabrs: Jerry Powell, Morris McClellan. *Songs:* A Special Step to Hollywood; Take Me Back; My Fav'rite Girl.

BATTEAU, DWIGHT WAYNE, JR (ROBIN) ASCAP 1969
composer, singer
b New York, NY, Jan 12, 48. Educ: Longy Sch of Music; Kinhaven Music Sch; Phillips Acad, Andover; Harvard Univ; studied violin with Bales, Schneider & Schell, writing with Kurt Vonnegut. Chief Collabrs: David Buskin, Janelle Cohen, Carl D'Errico. *Songs:* Take This Heart; The Boy With the Violin; Hot Summer Night; California; If Only He Would Make Love to Me; Single Wing; Eye of the Day. *Albums:* Appaloosa; Compton and Batteau in California; Batteaux; Pierce Arrow; Pierce Arrow: Pity the Rich.

BATTLE, EDGAR WILLIAM ASCAP 1941
composer, trumpeter, arranger
b Atlanta, Ga, Oct 3, 07; d. Educ: Ga Cons; also pvt study. Asst bandmaster; led own orch; trumpeter & arr with orchs. Music dir, USO, War Dept, Overseas. *Songs & Instrumental Works:* Puddin' Head Serenade; Sliphorn Jive; Texas

Shuffle; Doggin' Around; Blues in the Groove; One Is Never Too Old to Swing; Strictly Instrumental; Crescendo in Drums; You Mean So Much to Me; Uncle Tom's Cabin Suite; Be Happy; Jazzphony No 5; Bluesphony. *Albums:* Ballads Beautiful; Harlem House Hop.

BAUDUC, RAYMOND   ASCAP 1953
composer, drummer
b New Orleans, La, June 18, 06. Educ: Studied with father & under Paul DeTroit, Vic Burton & Earl Hatch. Drummer in silent movie houses, age 13; joined jazz bands, Billy Lustig's Scranton Sirens & Jimmy & Tommy Dorsey's Wild Canaries, 26; drummer in orchs incl Joe Venuti, Freddie Rich, Ben Pollack & Bob Crosby. Drummer, 211 Coast Artillery, WW II. With Jimmy Dorsey, 47-50 & Jack Teagarden, 50-55. Co-leader with Nappy Lamare Riverboat Dandies, 56-60. Own group, TV, movies, concerts & recording. Ed & research consult for jazz bk. Chief Collab: Bob Haggart. *Songs:* Music: Louise, Louise. *Instrumental Works:* South Rampart Street Parade; Big Noise from Winnetka; March of the Bobcats; Air Mail Stomp; Smokey Mary; Big Crash from China; I Hear You Talkin'; Big Tom; Mardis Gras Parade.

BAUER, WALTER KAYE   ASCAP 1977
composer, arranger, conductor
b Hartford, Conn, May 21, 1899. Educ: Hartford Sem Found; studied guitar with William Foden, mandolin with Samuel Siegel, banjo with Frederick J Bacon, viola with Herman Beacheman & piano with Lesser. *Instrumental Works:* Maestro (The); X-N-Trick Rag; Kow Tow; Method for the Tenor Banjo; Fingerboard Harmony for Tenor Banjo; Familiar Music for the Classic Guitar; More Music for the Classic Guitar; Graded Anthology for the Classic Guitar; Familiar Music for the Five String Banjo; Jigs and Reels for the Five String Banjo; Method for the Classical Five String Banjo.

BAUER, WILLIAM HENRY   ASCAP 1959
composer, author, guitar teacher
b New York, NY, Nov 14, 15. Educ: NY Univ (comp); studied with Stefin Wolfe. Guitarist for var artists, incl Woody Herman, Benny Goodman & Lennie Tristano. Down Beat, 49-50; Bway show "How Now Dow Jones"; NBC staff, 50-58; staff guitarist, Ice Capades, 5 yrs; publ with William H Bauer, Inc, 58- Author, "Basic Guitar Studies Text I, II." *Instrumental Works:* Marionette; Pam; Night Cruise-Lincoln Tunnel; Blue Misty; Ballet School; Purple Haze; Skyscraper.

BAUM, BERNIE   ASCAP 1950
composer, author
b New York, NY, Oct 13, 29. Educ: Music & Art High Sch, New York, grad; child prodigy-violin, studied with Herman Silverman. Concertmaster, All-City Orch. Awarded Serge Koussevitzky & Rohman Award. USA, 48. Staff writer, Hill & Range Songs, 62-69. Comp, network radio show theme for "Monitor"; comp, theme songs TV network shows, "It Takes Two", "Kimba, the White Lion", and others; jingles for TV & radio commercials; recorder, manager & producer for recording artists, The Crystals, The Chantels, Lou Johnson, & others; wrote songs for Elvis Presley Films. Chief Collabrs: Florence Kaye, Bill Giant. *Songs:* Music Music Music (Put Another Nickel In); You're the Devil in Disguise; That's Old Fashioned (That's the Way Love Should Be); Paradise Hawaiian Style (Hawaii, USA); A Time to Love, a Time to Cry; Ask Me; Edge of Reality; Poof!; Young and in Love; On the Outside Looking In; Walking in the Shadow of Love; Unsatisfied; It's No Good for Me; Watch What You Do With My Baby; Lonely Sunday.

BAUM, CLAUDE   ASCAP 1953
author
b Berlin, Ger, Mar 28, 28. Educ: Hollywood High Sch; Univ Calif, Los Angeles, BA, 55; Pepperdine Col, MBA, 75. *Songs:* Lyrics: If I Had Three Wishes; On My Word of Honor; Just Close Your Eyes; This Above All.

BAVICCHI, JOHN ALEXANDER   ASCAP 1961
composer, conductor
b Boston, Mass, Apr 25, 22. Educ: Mass Inst Technol; Newark Col Eng; Cornell Univ; New Eng Cons Music, BM; Harvard Univ, studied with Walter Piston. Am Symph Orch League recording grant; Nat Inst Arts & Letters Award, 59. Mem fac, Dept Comp, Berklee Col Music, 64- Cond, Arlington Philh Orch & Chorus, 68- *Songs:* Music: Psalm 98; Five Short Poems; Six Korean Folk Songs in a Contemporary Setting; Fly Hence Shadows. *Instrumental Works:* Mont Blanc (overture); Band of the Year; Violin Sonata No 1; A Duet Dozen; Saxophone Quartet No 2; Music for Mallets and Percussion; Corley's March; Sonata for Two Pianos; A Clarinet Handbook; Unaccompanied Clarinet Sonata No 2; Sonatina for Oboe and Piano; Six Duets for Flute and Clarinet; Toccata for Piano; Brass Quartet No 1; Three Preludes for Unaccompanied Trombone; Unaccompanied Clarinet Sonata No 1; Fantasy for Harp and Chamber Orchestra; Concert for Clarinet and String Orchestra; Suite for Orchestra; Five Dialogues for Two Clarinets; Festival Symphony for Band. *Songs & Instrumental Works:* Three American Choruses.

BAXTER, JAMES   ASCAP 1957
composer, author
b Thorpe Springs, Tex, May 15, 13; d Yucalpa, Calif, Dec 11, 64. Educ: Wayne Univ. Author: "The Circle on the Plain" (novel); "Next Case" (play); also short

stories, radio & TV scripts. Wrote songs for films & records. Chief Collabrs: Les Baxter (bro), Karl Suessdorf. *Songs:* Shooting Star; Calypso Boogie; A Gun Is My True Love; Black Sheep; Destination Honeymoon; Memories of Maine.

BAXTER, LARRY
See Setaro, Peter D

BAXTER, LESLIE   ASCAP 1954
composer, author
b Mexia, Tex, Mar 14, 22. Educ: Washington High Sch; Detroit Cons Music; Pepperdine Col, LLD. Tenor sax/arr, Freddie Slack, Tommy Dorsey & Bob Crosby Bands; arr/cond radio shows, Bob Hope, Abbott and Costello & Ronald Coleman. Comp, arr & cond series albums, Capitol Records. Comp/cond numerous motion picture scores, concert works, musicals & TV series & specials. *Instrumental Works:* Quiet Village; Exotica Suite; The Movies: A Satirical Essay for Orchestra; Metamorphosis; Suites: Que Mango; Ports of Pleasure; Tamboo; The Voice of Xtabay; Jewels of the Sea; Jungle Jazz; African Jazz; La Femme; Love Is a Fabulous Thing; Le Sacre Du Sauvage; The Passions; The Primitive and the Passionate; The Sacred Idol; Soul of the Drums; Space Escapade. *Scores:* Film/TV: Born Again; Master of the World; Lassie TV Series; A Woman's Devotion; Monika; Goliath and the Barbarians; Fall of the House of Usher; The Pit and the Pendulum; Tales of Terror; The Raven; The Dunwich Horror; Cry of the Banshee; The Man With the X-Ray Eyes; Hell's Belles; A Boy Ten Feet Tall; Frogs; Hot Blood; Beach Party; Beach Blanket Bingo; How to Stuff a Wild Bikini; Muscle Beach Party; Fireball 500; Sargeant Deadhead; Wild in the Streets; Panic in the Year Zero; Bop Girl Goes Calypso; I Escaped From Devil's Island; Savage Sisters; The Tycoon TV Series; The Cliffhangers TV Series; The Buck Rogers TV Series.

BAXTER, PHIL   ASCAP 1931
composer, author, conductor
b Navarro County, Tex, Sept 5, 1896; d Dallas, Tex, Nov 21, 72. Educ: Daniel Baker Col. Mem, Mare Island Navy Yard orch, World War I. Organized own band called Texas Tommies. Chief Collabrs: Billy Rose, Gus Kahn, Joseph Young, Cliff Friend. *Songs:* Piccolo Pete; Going, Going Gone; I'm a Ding Dong Daddy from Dumas; The One Man Band; 'Leven Miles From Leavenworth; Have a Little Dream on Me; Smile for Me; A Faded Summer Love; Let's Have a Party; Harmonica Harry; Five Piece Band; You're the Sweetest Girl.

BAYES, NORA
See Goldberg, Doris

BAYHA, CHARLES A   ASCAP 1920
composer, author
b New York, NY, May 12, 1891; d New York, NY, Feb 28, 57. Writer, Camp Dix show, World War I. Chief Collabrs: James Kendis, Charles McCarron. *Songs:* Come Out of the Kitchen, Mary Ann; Uncle Tom's Cabin Door; She Lives Down in Our Alley; Bessie Couldn't Help It; And Tommy Goes Too; Have a Nice Weekend; You Can Always Tell an Irish Girl; Eve Cost Adam Just One Bone; On Biscayne Bay; When the Moon Shines in Coral Gables; I'd Rather Be in Miami.

BAZELON, IRWIN ALLEN   ASCAP 1955
composer, author
b Evanston, Ill, June 4, 22. Educ: De Paul Univ, BA, 44, MA, 45; studied with Leon Stein, Mills Col, studied comp with Darium Milhaud, Univ Calif, studied analysis with E Bloch. Comp, Am Shakespeare Fest Theater, 58-59; var TV progs, 59-77. Comp-in-residence, Wolftrap, 74; Univ Akron, 79. Cond, Nat Symp, Detroit Symph & Kansas City Philh. Author, "Knowing the Score on Film Music." Comns: Nat Endowment Arts; Empire Brass Quintet, Mass; New Orleans Symph. *Instrumental Works:* Suite for Young People (piano); Sonatine for Piano; Five Pieces for Piano; Five Pieces for Cello and Piano; Short Symphony (Testament to a Big City); Brass Quintet; Symphony No 5; A Quiet Piece for a Violent Time; Propulsions (Percussion Concerto); Double Crossings (trumpet, perc); Churchill Downs Concerto (chamber ens); Imprints on Ivory and Strings (piano); Duo for Viola and Piano; De-Tonations (brass, quintet & orch); Theme: NBC TV News Signature Theme. *Scores:* Film: Wilma.

BEACH, ALBERT ASKEW (LEE WILSON)   ASCAP 1955
composer, author
b Bartow, Fla, July 22, 24. Educ: Fla Southern Col, Lakeland. Vpres, Leeds Music Corp, 53-57. Chief Collabrs: Willard Robison, Sidney Lippman, Guy Wood. *Songs:* The Wedding; Lyrics: The Heel; I Wish You Love; Stairway to the Sea; Through the Eyes of Love.

BEACH, MRS H H A   ASCAP 1924
composer, pianist
b Henniker, NH, Sept 5, 1867; d New York, NY, Dec 27, 44. Educ: Studied with mother, Perabo, Baermann, Junius Hill. Pianist, debut, Boston, 1883; soloist, appeared with many orchs. In concert, Europe, 10. *Songs:* Sacred: Let This Mind Be In You; Benedictus es Domine; Lord of the World Is Above; Benedicite Omnia Opera; Canticle of the Sun. *Instrumental Works:* Mass in E; Gaelic Symphony; Piano Concerto in C; Festival Jubilate; Song of Welcome; Panama Hymn; Piano Quintet; String Quartet; Suite for Two Pianos; Variations on Balkan Themes (piano).

BEADELL, ROBERT MORTON   ASCAP 1966
author, teacher

b Chicago, Ill, June 18, 25. Educ: High sch, Blue Island, Ill, 41; Northwestern Univ, BM, 49, MM, 50; studied with Leo Sowerby, 51 & Darius Milhaud, 62. Dance band sideman, 41; bandsman in USMC, 42-45; col & prof musician, 46-50; Ray Anthony Band, 47. Teacher theory & comp, Cent Col, Fayette, Mo, 50-54 & Univ Nebr, 54- Chief Collabrs: Stanley Peters, Dean Tschetter, William Wallis, Virginia Faulkner; libretto, Bruce Nicoll. *Songs & Instrumental Works:* Blow, Prairie Wind (choral; introd & allegro); Symphony No 1; Mirage Flats: Homage to Sandoz (orch, choral); Improvisation and Dance (orch, jazz ensemble). *Scores:* Opera: Napoleon; The Number of Fools.

BEAL, JOSEPH CARLETON   ASCAP 1955
composer, author, publisher

b Braintree, Mass, June 25, 1900; d. Educ: Boston Sch of Radio, TV. Pub relations dir, City Col New York Sch of Bus & Bus Ctr. Mem, Cancer Ctr Fund & Assoc Hosp Plan, NJ. Prod mgr, WDSU-TV, New Orleans & WRUL, New York. Author, "Romances of Matilda." Own pub relations firm & lectured in high schs & cols; also publisher & record co exec. Chief Collabrs: Jim Boothe, Joe Shank, Bob Singer, Russ Taylor. *Songs:* Jingle Bell Rock; Unsuspecting Heart; Welcome Conventioneer (off Atlantic City song); Take the Time; Always Look Up; The Heavens Cried; Winter Champagne.

BEALL, JOHN OLIVER   ASCAP 1974
composer

b Belton, Tex, June 12, 42. Educ: Baylor Univ, BMus(comp), 64, MMus(comp), 66, studied with Richard Willis; Univ Rochester Eastman Sch Music, PhD(comp), 73, studied with Samuel Adler. Comp-in-residence, WVa Univ; comp, teacher & cond of New Music Ens. Two NEA grants, plus ASCAP awards. Works performed by Dallas Symph, Rochester Philh & Pittsburgh Symph. *Instrumental Works:* Lament for Those Lost in the War; Concerto for Piano and Wind Orchestra; Concerto for Brass Quintet and Wind Orchestra; Sextet for Piano and Woodwind Quintet; Sonata for Violin and Piano No 3; Black Raindrops (piano solo).

BEARD, LESLIE LOIS (LESLIE CHAIN)   ASCAP 1977
composer, author, singer

b Warren, Ohio, June 21, 50. Educ: Juilliard Sch Music, 76-79; Columbia Univ, 79; Dana Sch Music, 79-, full-time student working towards BA; studied voice with Carlo Menotti, New York; studied piano with Marcellene Hawk. Performer in stock, off Bway, one film, "The Private Worlds of Sophie and Bernie Schwartz" & tours; comp songs; pianist. Chief Collabrs: Jeff Ray, Ron Austalosh. *Songs:* Knowing You; The Love Song; My Mama, She's A Lady; I'm Gonna Love Ya the Best I Can; Seedtime and Harvest (based on Genesis 8:22).

BEARDSLEY, THEODORE S, JR   ASCAP 1974
author

b East St Louis, Ill, Aug 26, 30. Educ: Southern Ill Univ, BS, 52; Wash Univ, MA, 54; Univ Pa, PhD, 61. Prof Span, Rider Col, 57-61, Southern Ill Univ, 61-62 & Univ Wis, 62-65. Dir, Hispanic Soc Am, 65- Adj prof, NY Univ, 66-69 & Columbia Univ, 69. Librettist, "Maria Sabina Suite" (Eng version), 72 & "Ponce de Leon" (Eng & Span), 73. Fulbright Lectr, Ecuador, 74. Weekly radio series, WBGO-FM, "Caribbean Music in the US," 79 & "Cugat!," 80.

BEARSE, RICHARD STUART   ASCAP 1963
composer, author

b Hyannis, Mass, Aug 18, 39. Educ: Pub sch. Chief Collabr: Julia Copeland. *Songs:* God Gave Me You.

BEATTY, HAROLD T   ASCAP 1974
composer, producer

b Lexington, Ky, Dec 26, 46. Educ: Jamaica High Sch, New York, 69, studied with Peter J Wilhouski. Wrote first chart record, "Almost" by Deon Jackson, Atlantic Recording Co, New York, 69; did five chart records, by Jackson Five, Donnie & Marie & Supremes. Currently writing & producing, Holland, Dozier & Holland Publ Co, 80-; producing, Atlantic Recording Co. Chief Collabrs: Edward & Brian Holland. *Songs:* I'm Gonna Let My Heart Do the Walking; Moving Violation; Winning Combination; Dance, Baby Dance.

BEATTY, NORMAN PAUL   ASCAP 1956
composer, trumpeter

b Farrell, Pa, Oct 8, 24. Educ: High sch, Coshocton, Ohio; Juilliard Sch Music, dipl, 50; began study of trumpet & piano minor with Edward Treutel at age 6. Played & arr in army bands during WW II. Mem of the Radio City Music Hall Orch, 50. Chief Collabrs: Gene Bianco, Jac Hein. *Songs:* Music: Midnight Breeze; Cairo After Dark; Angelique. *Instrumental Works:* Aruba Samba; Chicago Swinger; Cincinnati Ratamatiti; Exotique (bk of 17 piano pieces).

BEAU, HENRY JOHN (HEINIE)   ASCAP 1954
composer, arranger, musician

b Calvary, Wis, Mar 8, 11. Educ: High Sch, Fond du Lac, Wis. Played & arr, Wally Beau Orch, Red Nichols, Tommy Dorsey, Benny Goodman, Alvino Rey Orchs & Hollywood Studios. Chief Collabrs: Dave Barbour, Peggy Lee, Axel Stordahl, Ziggy Elman, Red Nichols. *Instrumental Works:* Blue Iris; Delta Roll;

Guitar Mambo; Harlem Mambo; Jasmine and Jade; Moonset Boulevard; Samba With Zig; Man With the Golden Embouchure.

BEAULIEU, CAMILLE   ASCAP 1972
composer, author

b St Michaels, Que, May 8, 21. *Songs:* Desiring Others; Honeymoon Promise; You Must Take Time; Let Them Talk; Disco Jogging.

BEAULIEU, DONALD GEORGE (SAM (SPUNKY)   ASCAP 1978
BALOO)
composer, author, performer

b Stafford Springs, Conn, Oct 14, 39. Educ: Emerson Col, Mass, BS & MS; Tufts Univ. Univ prof, 63-68. Comp & author, Muppet Show, "Sesame Street", 78. Theme, "George Plimpton Special." Performing original material, Los Angeles, 80. Chief Collabr: Dewey Bergman. *Songs:* Dynamite; Buyer Beware; Music: Three Fingers; Morganetta; Ripple.

BEAULIEU, TONI
See DePaolis, Leone F

BEAUMONT, JAMES LAWRENCE   ASCAP 1959
composer, singer

b Pittsburgh, Pa, Oct 21, 40. Lead singer with The Skyliners, 59-; play nightclubs, concerts & TV shows, incl Dick Clark, Midnight Special & Am Bandstand. Chief Collabr: Joseph Vincent Rock. *Songs:* Music: Since I Don't Have You; This I Swear; It Happened Today; Lonely Way; How Much; Tell Me.

BEAUMONT, VIVIAN
See Hoff, Vivian Beaumont

BEBERUS, VIRGINIA   ASCAP 1959
composer, author

b Mercer, Maine, June 30, 1893; d Glen Mills, Pa, Oct 3, 64. Educ: Col; studied piano & violin. Wrote newspaper column. Cond radio prog. Many poems set to music. *Songs:* Thanksgiving (Medal of Honor, George Washington Found).

BECK, JOHN NESS   ASCAP 1965
composer, author, publisher

b Warren, Ohio, Nov 11, 30. Educ: Ohio State Univ, BA, BScEd, BMus & MA. Fac mem, Ohio State Univ Sch of Music. Owner retail sheet music store. Founder, owner & pres, Beckenhorst Press, Inc. *Songs:* Choral: Speak to Me, Lord; Lullaby; Music: Canticle of Praise; Upon This Rock; Song of Exaltation; Every Valley; Assurance; I Need Thee Every Hour.

BECK, MARTHA   ASCAP 1959
composer, pianist, educator

b Sodaville, Ore. Educ: Univ Chicago; Columbia Sch Music; Oberlin Cons, BM; Am Cons, BM; Juilliard Sch Music, scholarship; also studied in Berlin. Fac mem, Am Cons, NCentral Col & Emma Willard Sch; pvt teacher, Troy, NY. Author, "The Martha Beck Rhythm Rule Method." Winner comp prizes, Mu Phi Epsilon.

BECKER, WILLIAM
See Schickele, Peter

BECKET
See Cyrus, Alston Becket

BECKETT, WHEELER   ASCAP 1944
composer

b San Francisco, Calif, Mar 7, 1898. Educ: Columbia Univ; Univ Calif, MA; studied with Camille Decruse, Cornelius Rybner, Walter Henry Hull, Daniel Gregory Mason & Felix Weingartner. Organist & choirmaster, Grace Cathedral, San Francisco. Cond & founder, Youth Concerts, Boston, NY, San Francisco & Richmond, Va. Guest cond, Berlin Philh; Vienna Philh; Vienna Symph; Straram Orch, Paris; Boston Pops Orch; Watergate Concerts & Nat Symph; cond, Richmond Symph. Head music consult, War Prod Bd, Wash, 44. App by Dept State to conduct & found new orchs in southeast Asia, 59-61. Gave first music appreciation prog, Manila Symph, 60. Author "Music in Industry." *Songs:* Shall I Compare Thee. *Instrumental Works:* Cinderella Fantasy; Symphony in C; The Sea At Point Lobos; The Open Road (march); Reverie for Strings; Dedication to Indonesia (orch, chorus); Mystic Trumpeter; The Complete Orch. *Scores:* Stage: Rajvara; Asses Ears; Opera: Snow White and the 7 Dwarfs.

BECKLENBERG, IRMA ELSIE (IRMA GLEN)   ASCAP 1954
composer, author

b Chicago, Ill, Aug 3, 02. Educ: Sherwood Music Sch; Am Cons Music, MusM; Univ Southern Calif, studied with Nicholas Rosza; Golden State Univ, BMus & MusD; Church of Relig Sci, RScD. Orch leader, Teatro Empire, Buenos Aires, Arg; featured organist, Ascher Bros Theatres, Chicago; staff organist & comp, NBC, Chicago, 12 yrs. Christian Sci Church organist, 46; moved to Hollywood continued NBC feature work free-lance. TV & radio with Dr Ernest Holmes; compiled, ed & contrib 23 songs to "The Religious Science Hymnal";

author "Religious Science Junior Church Song Book." Chief Collabrs: Dr Ernest Holmes, Don Blanding. *Songs:* Lovable Music; This I Know; When I'm Alone I Pray. *Instrumental Works:* Meditation to Saint Cecelia; Quiet Waters.

BECKMEIER, STEPHEN DEVINNEY
ASCAP 1971
composer, author, guitarist
b Atlantic City, NJ, Oct 11, 48. Writer, music for off-Bway play "Stop You're Killing Me," 69, songs for var artists, 71- Recording session guitarist, 74- Recording artist with Fred Beckmeier (brother), 79. Chief Collabrs: Fred Beckmeier, Al McKay, Phillip Bailey, Gregg Allman, August Johnson, Steve Berlin. *Songs:* Rock and Roll Dancing (platinum record); Crying Shame; There She Goes Again; See the Monkey Run; Move Me; Over My Head; Music: I'll Write a Song for You (platinum record). *Albums:* Beckmeier Brothers.

BECVAR, BRIAN FRANCIS
ASCAP 1979
composer, author
b Louisville, Ky, Dec 20, 54. Educ: St Xavier High Sch, Louisville, dipl, 72; Duke Univ, BA(psychol), 75, semester study in Vienna, Austria, 74; Ind Univ Sch Music, spec study with David Baker & Jerry Coker, 76-77. Played piano concerto on brief concert tour with Duke Univ Wind Symph, Austria, Italy, Hungary, 74; comp music for & performed several jazz concerts, Ind Univ, 76; recorded & toured with John Cougar Band, Eng & Europe, 77-78; recorded with var groups, 78-79. Chief Collabrs: John Cougar, Bob Parissi, Cheryl Lynn, Foxy, Bobby Caldwell. *Songs:* Feel It; I Feel the Flame; Tomorrow; Give It All; Live the Song You Sing; Let It Come From the Heart; Music: Pray for Me.

BEDELL, ALBERT CHARLES
ASCAP 1964
author
b Brooklyn, NY, Apr 18, 31. Educ: Studied guitar with Ralph Collichio, trumpet with Harry Berkin. Music mgr, Linn Music & Records. Music warehouse mgr, Mills Music. Spec projects mgr, Music Production, Robbins Music. Staff, Reference Dept, Walter Kane Music Jobbing. Chief Collabrs: Paul E Giasson, Robert Allen. *Songs:* Lyrics: Holiday Time of Year; Ciao for Now; Cafe Di Roma; Mi Amore Italiano; America Is; He Paints Me a Rainbow; Wedding Promise; My Album of Memories; Christmas in Manhattan; Dear Mr Snowman; Help Me Lord; You Are the Theme; Winter Comes Early; Loneliness of Autumn; The Most Important Thing; Walk With the Lord; The Music of Love; How Sweet the Wine; Gypsy Heart; To Those in Love; Strangers a Moment Ago; A Time and a Place for Everything; The Sunday Monday Blues; The Voice of the Lord; To Be Worthy of You; Living Together.

BEDELL, LEW (LOU BIDEU, B J HUNTER)
ASCAP 1961
composer, author, comedian
b El Paso, Tex, Mar 21, 19. Educ: Santa Barbara State Col, 4 yrs. Entertainer comedy, nightclubs & TV. Had "Lew Bedell Show", WOR, NY, 54. Recording bus, 55. Publ firm, Meadowlark Music Inc. Chief Collabr: Ernie Freeman. *Songs & Instrumental Works:* Percolator.

BEDELL, STEPHEN L
ASCAP 1974
composer, author
b New York, NY, Sept 7, 39. Educ: Midwood High Sch, Brooklyn, NY, dipl; NY Univ, BS; City Col New York, MA. Joined Wes Farrell Orgn, 68, head of publ operation & created jingle div, 70, became pres music group, wrote & produced new material for "Captain Kangaroo" TV show, 74. Vpres publ, Casablanca, 77-80. Started own co, Music Concepts, Int, 80. Chief Collabrs: Charlie Calello, Adam Miller. *Songs:* The Ones You Love; A Party Day; Music: A Friend; Goin' Around In Circles; Bring Back Those Good Old Days; I'm a Happy Man.

BEE, JOSEPH THOMAS
ASCAP 1971
composer, author, singer
b Gallup, NMex, Nov 8, 47. Educ: Univ NMex, cert jour. Former leader, writer & co-producer of Motown Am Indian Musical Group XIT. Has written for Smokey Robinson & Jackson 5. *Songs:* Blue Skies (We've Got); Joyful Jukebox Music; Red Hot; Lyrics: Reservation of Education; Roxanne (You Sure Got a Fine Design).

BEE, LAURIE
See Bobrow, Laura J

BEECHER, CLARE RODMAN (CLARE KUMMER)
ASCAP 1934
composer, author
b Brooklyn, NY, Jan 9, 1888; d Carmel, Calif, Apr 21, 58. Educ: Packer Inst; pvt music study. Playwright: "Good Gracious Annabelle"; "A Successful Calamity"; "Rollo's Wild Oats"; "Pomeroy's Past"; "Her Master's Voice." Chief Collabrs: Jerome Kern, Sigmund Romberg. *Songs:* Dearie; Egypt; Other Eyes; Blushing June Roses; Somebody's Eyes; Thro' All the World; Only With You; The Bluebird; Garden of Dreams; Sunset; The Road to Yesterday; Today; Lover of Mine. *Scores:* Bway stage (librettos): 90 in the Shade; One Kiss; Annie Dear; Madame Pompadour; The Three Waltzes.

BEECHER, WILLIAM GORDON, JR
ASCAP 1944
composer, author
b Baltimore, Md, Jan 19, 04; d Arlington, Va, Dec 7, 73. Educ: USN Acad, BS; Nat War Col. Served in USN, 34 yrs, incl dir, USNA musical clubs, 33-35,

Comdr, destroyer squadron, World War II, fought at Pearl Harbor, Iwo Jima, Okinawa & awarded Legion of Merit, chief of Naval Information, 54-55, Comdr, Middle East Force, 54, retired as Vice Admiral, 55. Tech adv, film "Shipmates Forever." Chief Collabr: Johnny Noble. *Songs:* A Song of Old Hawaii; The Ramparts We Watch (from film "March of Time"); Sing an American Song; Counting on You; All Pau Now; Just a Happy Kamaaina; Nimitz, Halsey and Me; Up and At 'Em, Navee! (USNA football song).

BEELBY, MALCOLM
ASCAP 1950
composer, conductor
b Grand Rapids, Mich, Nov 11, 07. Educ: High sch; pvt music study. Pianist in dance bands; organist in film theatres. Pianist & music adv, film cos; music dir, Royal Hawaiian Hotel, Honolulu, 39-40 & Buster Crabbe's Aqua Parade, 48-49. Has been asst head of music dept, Paramount Pictures, music advisor & music exec, 9 yrs; head of music dept, CBS, Hollywood; music advisor & music exec, Warner Bros Pictures, 16 yrs; music advisor, 20th Century Fox, MGM, RKO, Columbia & Universal Pictures; wrote music included in motion pictures for Warner Bros & Paramount Pictures. Chief Collabr: Gerda. *Songs:* My Song, My Love.

BEESLEY, RUSH
ASCAP 1973
composer, producer
b Tulsa, Okla, Oct 28, 47. Educ: Southern Methodist Univ, BA. Head TV & radio production, Tracy-Locke Advert, produced & recorded many nat music spots, 69-71; started Sundance Productions, Inc, 71, then added video & post-production facilities, 75. Chief Collabr: Euel Box. *Songs:* Disco-U.

BEESON, JACK HAMILTON
ASCAP 1959
composer, teacher, author
b Muncie, Ind, July 15, 21. Educ: Univ Toronto, cert, 38; Eastman Sch Music, BM, 42, MM, 43; pvt study with Bela Bartok, 44-45; Columbia Univ, grad work & conducting, 45-48. Pvt teaching piano & elem theory, Muncie, Ind, 37-39. Teaching fel theory, Eastman Sch Music, 42-44; asst music, Columbia Univ, 45-46, assoc, 46-47, instr, 47-48 & 50-52, from asst prof to prof, 52-67, MacDowell prof, 67-, actg chmn dept music, spring 64 & 76, chmn, 68-72, actg chmn div music, Sch Arts, 3 terms. Coach, asst cond & assoc cond, Columbia Univ Opera Workshop & opera productions of Columbia Theatre Assocs, 45-48 & 50-52. Lectr, Juilliard Sch Music, 61-63. Comp-in-residence, Am Acad Rome, 65-66. Mem & officer in charge, Am Musical Assocs, 60-76; mem bd, Comp Recording Ins, 67-80, vpres, 67-75, co-actg pres, 75-76, hon trustee, 80-; mem bd & vpres-secy, Int Contemporary Music Exchange, 73-80; mem adv bd, Am Landmark Fest, 77-; mem, pres, Comn on Priorities in the Arts & Sci, 78-80; adv panel to O'Neill Comp/Librettist Comp, Eugene O'Neill Theater Ctr, 79-; mem comp policy panel, Nat Endowment for Arts, 79- Mem: Int Soc Contemporary Music (NY Sect, Forum Group, 44-47, bd, League Comp, 69-72); Am Comp Alliance (bd governors, 54-65); Comp Forum (mem bd, 50-75, vchmn, 59-62 & 68-75, chmn, 62-68, adv bd, 75-); fel Am Acad Rome (pres, 63-64, bd trustees, 75-); Am Acad Inst Arts & Letters (treas, 80-). Fels & Awards: Seidl fel, Columbia Univ, 44-45; Rome Prize, Am Acad Rome, 48-50; Fulbright fel, Italy, 49-50; Guggenheim fel, 58-59; Annual ASCAP Award, 65-; Marc Blitzstein Award, Nat Inst Arts & Letters, 68; Gold Medal for Music, Nat Arts Club, 76. Chief Collabrs: Sheldon Harnick, William Saroyan, Kenward Elmslie, Paul Goodman. *Instrumental Works:* Symphony No 1 in A; Transformations; Sonata for Viola and Piano; Fifth Sonata for Piano; Two Diversions for Piano; Round and Round (piano 4 hands); Sonata Canonica (two alto recorders); numerous vocal & choral works. *Scores:* Hello Out There; The Sweet Bye and Bye; Lizzie Borden (comn by Ford Found); My Heart's in the Highlands (comn by Nat Educ TV); Captain Jinks of the Horse Marines (comn by Nat Endowment for Arts); Dr Heidegger's Fountain of Youth (comn by Nat Arts Club).

BEGLARIAN, GRANT
ASCAP 1961
composer
b Tbilisi, USSR, Dec 1, 27. Educ: Univ Mich, 47-52, BM & MM in comp, 55-57, DMA in comp; comp teachers incl Ross Lee Finney & Aaron Copland. Teaching asst, Univ Mich, 50-52. US Army, Europe, 52-54, comp, arr, teacher & violist with 7th Army Symph. Regents fel, Univ Mich, 54-57. Owner & pres, Music-Book Assocs, 57-65. Ford Found composer, Cleveland Heights, 59-60. Ed, Prentice-Hall, 60-61. From field rep to dir, Ford Found Contemporary Music Proj, 61-68. Dean, Sch Performing Arts, Univ Southern Calif, 69- *Instrumental Works:* To Manitou (soprano & chamber orch); Fables, Foibles and Fancies (cellist & actor); Sinfonia (strings); Ellegy (cellist); Divertimento (orch; Gershwin Prize, 59).

BEHRENS, JACK
ASCAP 1963
composer, educator
b Lancaster, Pa, Mar 25, 35. Educ: Juilliard Sch Music, BS & MS, studied with William Bergsma, Peter Mennin, Vincent Persichetti; Edward Benjamin Prize; also studied with Darius Milhaud (Copley Found Grant). Teaching fel, Juilliard Sch Music, 2 yrs; fac mem, Bronx House Music Sch, Berkley Summer Music Sch & Emma Willard Sch, Troy, NY. Asst prof music & head theory dept, Univ Sask Cons, 62. Mem, Nat Asn for Am Composers & Conductors. *Instrumental Works:* Trombone Concerto (Davis Shuman Comn); Transfigured Season (Am Dance Fest Comn); Encounters (Sask House Summer Fest Comn); Declaration

(Regina Orch Soc Comn); Incidental Music: A Midsummer Night's Dream (Sask House Summer Fest Comn); A Pocket Size Sonata (Adele Marcus Comn); In a Manger (choral). *Scores:* Film background: The Old Order Amish.

BEHUNIN, LESLIE MERRILL, JR (BUDDY MERRILL) ASCAP 1965
composer, guitarist
b Torrey, Utah, July 16, 36. Worked var bands, 49-55; with Lawrence Welk TV Show, 55-74; arr for USA at West Point Acad, 59-61. Recorded many albums, 65-; produced commercials & albums for other artists. Chief Collabrs: Scott Seely & Joe Rizzo. *Instrumental Works:* Los Guitarras; The Worm; Echoette; Melody Lane; Roadrunner; *Scores:* Film/TV: Living Sea.

BEILENSON, GERDA MALINE
author
b Aitken, Minn, June 11, 03. Chief Collabrs: Harpo Marx, Malcolm Beelby, Alvin Kaleolani (Isaacs). *Songs:* Lyrics: Guardian Angels; My Song, My Love; Nalani; Dance the Hula in the Sea; My Sweet Pikake Lei.

BELAFONTE, HAROLD GEORGE, JR ASCAP 1956
composer, author, producer
b New York, NY, Mar 1, 27. Educ: NY Dramatic Workshop. Grew up in Jamaica, BWI. Folk singer in TV, nightclubs, theatre, films & on records. Debut, Village Vanguard, NY. Appeared in Bway revues "John Murray Anderson's Almanac", "Three for Tonight," also in films "The Bright Road", "Carmen Jones", "Island in the Sun"; producer of "Odds Against Tomorrow", "The World, the Flesh and the Devil" & "Buck and the Preacher." Owner, music publ firm & film co. Awards: Tony Award, 53, Donaldson Award, 53-54, Show Bus Award, 54, Diners' Club Award, 55-56 & Emmy Award for "Tonight With Belafonte." Has made many records. *Songs:* Shake That Little Foot; Turn Around; Glory Manger.

BELASCO, KEYSTONE
See Wiemer, Robert Ernest

BELEFAN, SAM
See Robinson, Edward Alfred

BELFER, HAROLD BRUCE ASCAP 1972
composer, author, producer
b Los Angeles, Calif, Feb 16, 27. Educ: Univ Southern Calif; Univ Calif, Los Angeles. Music & comedy performer, Fanchon & Marcos Revues. Asst to LeRoy Prinz. Appeared in var films incl "Yankee Doodle Dandy," Acad award winner. Head, dance dept, Universal & 20th Century Fox Studios. Dir & producer of entertainment, Rivera Hotel & Flamingo Hotel, Las Vegas. Producer, dir & choreographer, Premore Productions, 69-80. Chief Collabrs: Mike Dolinsky, LeRoy Prinz, Louis Bellson. *Songs:* Nouns Are At Least Human; Woodshop Number; A Giant Step; Jow Cow; Belfer Blues; Jefferson Dropouts; Music: You're Bringing Me Down.

BELL, C CLARK ASCAP 1975
composer, author, singer
b Connersville, Ind, Dec 7, 30. Educ: Univ Fla, 49-51; Univ Miami, Coral Gables, BMusic, 58; Fla State Univ, MMusEd, 63. Musician, USAF, 51-55; music educr, 59- Church soloist; taught pub sch music, 59-63, teacher col level, 64-, Pres, Fla Elem Music Educr Asn. Trumpet player, clinician & adjudicator. Chief Collabrs: Bill Prince, Jo Ann Cavanagh. *Songs:* Special Kind of Magic; Love Is; Coco; Chris; Hey Little Girl; Stop, Look and Listen; This Tune; Weekend TV Blues; Presidential Count; Birthday Drum; Intro-Song; Gratitude; Spirit of Christmas With Keys to the Kingdom; Circle Song; Music: Reaching Out.

BELL, GERTRUDE WILLIS ASCAP 1973
composer, musician
b Sunderland, Vt, Dec 21, 15. Educ: Arlington Schs; self-taught on piano, accordion & guitar. In early yrs, played in small band; had benefits for orgn; comp bicentennial area music. *Songs & Instrumental Works:* This Is Your Country, This Is My Country; Have You; Songs of Faith, Love and Country (bk). *Albums:* Songs of Faith, Love and Country.

BELL, LOUISE
See Belline, Mary L

BELL, LUCILE ANDERSON ASCAP 1962
composer, author, teacher
b St Louis, Mo. Educ: Visitation Convent, St Louis, grad(piano, counterpoint); studied with Aleyander Raab, comp with Paul Creston at Chicago Musical Col; studied with Felix Guenther at NY Univ & Philip Dettra at Pa State Univ. Piano soloist, WNYC, New York; recitals; teacher with own studio at Carnegie Hall, New York; teacher, DuBois, Pa, also concerts at Pa State Univ campus. *Songs:* Lead Us On (Thomas Paine); Lullaby (George Ward); Black Eagle (song cycle, Elizabeth Browning). *Instrumental Works:* Three Moods (flute & piano).

BELL, PETER
See Birch, Peter

BELL, SAMUEL AARON ASCAP 1956
composer, author, educator
b Muskogee, Okla, Apr 24, 34. Educ: Xavier Univ, BA; NY Univ, MA; Columbia Univ, MEd & PhD(comp). Began study of music at age 5; played piano, trumpet & tuba in high sch; made first concert band arr at age 13; began comp at age 14; played trumpet, flute, string bass & piano in col. Performed as bassist with Duke Ellington, 6 yrs. Mem staff at NBC. Now chmn dept music, Essex County Col, NJ. Chief Collabrs: Ed Bullins, Karl Friedman, Carla Huston. *Songs:* Way in the Middle of the Night; Take a Chance; Music: Black Terror. *Songs & Instrumental Works:* Bi-Centennial Symphony; Watergate Piano Sonata; Rondo-Schizo (piano & clarinet); Fugue at 3:00 AM (trumpet, tenor, trombone). *Scores:* Bway Show: Home Boy; Short Bullins (trilogy); Jazz Ballet: Facets.

BELLAK, RHODA ASCAP 1963
author
b New York, NY, July 21, 23. Educ: Walden High Sch; NY Univ, BA(Eng lit); workshop studies with Lehman Engel. Poet; author, children's poems, songs & operas incl "Ashmedai" & "Jewish Heritage," musical theater, "A Modern Dame", "April's Fool" & "Mrs Godolphin Says No." Chief Collabrs: Doris Schwerin, Ira Wallach. *Songs:* Lyrics: Discover America; Love Me Goodbye. *Albums:* From Morning Till Night; A Bagful of Poems.

BELLAMY, DAVID MILTON ASCAP 1974
composer, author, singer
b Darby, Fla, Sept 16, 50. Played in nightclub groups as teen; started writing at age 15. Recording artist with group, Bellamy Bros; has written & recorded country music & several albums. Chief Collabr: Jim Stafford. *Songs:* Spiders and Snakes; If I Said You Have a Beautiful Body (Would You Hold It Against Me?); You Ain't Just Whistlin' Dixie; Sugar Daddy; Dancin' Cowboys; Miss Misunderstood; Livin' in the West; You Can Get Crazy With Me; Nothin' Heavy; Hiway 2-18.

BELLAND, BRUCE G ASCAP 1962
author
b Chicago, Ill, Oct 26, 36. Started recording with Four Preps for Capitol Records & had first hit, 57; has had seven gold records & two gold albums; has written title songs for five feature films & has had three Emmy nominations for TV show songs. Had Number One hit in Eng & Australia, "Kahmal." Writer of Bway play, "The Patriot." *Songs:* Lyrics: Twenty-Six Miles (Santa Catalina); Big Man; Down By the Station; More Money for You and Me; Got a Girl; What Would I Do Without My Music?; The Troublemaker.

BELLE, BARBARA
See Newman, Barbara Belle

BELLER, ALEX ASCAP 1955
composer, author
b Chicago, Ill, June 11, 05. Educ: High sch; studied violin & music with Victor Young. Violinist with Ben Pollack, Artie Shaw, Tommy Dorsey & Nelson Riddle Orchs; also on records, films & TV shows. Chief Collabrs: Jack Meskill, Fred Norman, Bob Josephson. *Songs:* Two Voices in the Night; Adios My Madonna; Once in a Blue Moon; Love Me Or I'll Die; My Summer Baby; Heaven Help Us, We're in Love; Make Love, Make Love, Make Love; Ma Chanson D'Amour; Dreams for Sale; A Love Without End; Fernando, Manuel and Jose; Forever More; In All the World and Texas; I'm Knee Deep in Dreams; In Nineteen Hundred Ninety Nine; Say With Your Lips; There's a New Look in Your Eyes; There's Nothing Like Love; The Diff'rence in Me Is You; Music: You Drive Me to Dream. *Instrumental Works:* Knock It Down.

BELLER, JACKIE ASCAP 1963
composer, author
b New York, NY, Aug 3, 16. Educ: St Johns Univ, BA, LLB. Singer on radio, in nightclubs (US & Europe) & films; also wrote for films. Chief Collabrs: Henry Tobias, Harry Tobias, Bob Emmerich, Moe Jaffe, Clay Boland, Dave Oppenheim, Abner Silver, Bill Borrelli, Billy Hayes, Irving Carroll, Ben Benjamin. *Songs:* Little Red Riding Hood; Lovable; Don't Kiss and Tell; Let Me Love You; Ooh What a Little Love Will Do; I Had a Dream.

BELLI, REMO
See Bellson, Louis Paul

BELLIN, LEWIS PAUL ASCAP 1942
composer, author
b London, England, Sept 11, 05. Educ: Holy City Univ, Rome. US citizen, 35. Concert pianist at age 12; recitals at Carnegie Hall. Radio & nightclub entertainer. Chief Collabrs: Redd Evans, Ted Koehler, Abner Silver, Milton Ager, Lee Pearl, Danny DiMinno, Milton Berle, Lucky Millinder, Ray Evans, Jay Livingston, Teddy Powell, Mitchell Parish. *Songs:* This Is the Night; Take Me Back to Little Rock and Rock Me; You Should Have Told Me; Love Is a Beautiful Thing; When; The Mountaineer and the Jabberwock; Play Me Hearts

and Flowers; Say It With Love; Out of the Shadows and Into the Light; Hit of the Season; Mad Love; Not Now John, Not Now.

BELLINE, MARY L (LOUISE BELL) ASCAP 1958
composer, author
b Washington, Pa, Nov 15, 20. Chief Collabr: Jimmy Lytell. *Songs:* Keep God in the Home; Giro, Giro; This is Real; Don't Forget; All I Want; The Warning Voice. *Instrumental Works:* La Nuit.

BELLINO, VITO ASCAP 1963
composer, author
b Irvington, NJ, Dec 25, 22. Educ: Self-taught. Lyricist. Chief Collabr: Russ Morgan. *Songs:* Lyrics: Someday Soon.

BELLIS, RICHARD R ASCAP 1975
film composer
b Pasadena, Calif, Apr 3, 46. Educ: John Muir High Sch, Pasadena; pvt study. Child actor until age 13. Started cond for Johnny Mathis, 64; cond var artists, incl Connie Stevens, Abbe Lane, Leslie Uggams, 10 yrs. Scored films; arr. *Songs:* Breakin' Up Is Hard to Do (source music). *Scores:* Film/TV: Black Market Baby; A Shining Season.

BELLOC, DAN ASCAP 1954
composer, conductor
b Chicago, Ill, Nov 26, 24. Educ: De Paul Univ, BA. USN, WW II; did series "Teentown, USA" for Navy Dept, 52. Music dir, Fraternity Records; dir, Billy May Orch. Chief Collabrs: Lew Douglas, Frank Levere. *Songs:* Pretend.

BELLOW, ALEXANDER ASCAP 1959
composer, author, conductor
b Moscow, Russia, Mar 22, 12; d. Educ: MA, PhD(music). Cond, symph orch, Europe; teacher, Cons of Music, Gottingen, Ger. Teacher, classical guitar, NY. *Instrumental Works:* Prelude e Rondo; 5 Diversions; Suite Miniature.

BELLSON, LOUIS PAUL (REMO BELLI) ASCAP 1955
composer, author
b Rock Falls, Ill, July 6, 24. *Songs & Instrumental Works:* Skin Deep; The Hawk Talks.

BELSON, HORTENSE GOLD (HORTENSE ZWIBELSON) ASCAP 1953
composer, author
b Baltimore, Md, June 21, 15. Educ: Wadleigh High Sch, NY; Hunter Col; Peabody Cons of Md. Lyrics for "Little Brown Jug", fall 80. Wrote commentaries for charity shows. Poetry publ in Am Baby Mag & Port Chester Daily Newspaper. Chief Collabr: Frances Ziffer. *Songs:* Don'cha Know; I'd Rather Be in Love; Clothes Make the Man; I'll Take a Raincheck; Lyrics: Say When. *Scores:* Off-Bway Shows: Dakota; Surprise Package; Make Him Magnificent; The Virgin King; Three on a Bed.

BELT, JAMES PRESTON, JR ASCAP 1970
composer
b Ridgeview, WVa, Sept 11, 40. Chief Collabrs: Roger Bowling, Neal Hefti, Martha Eddins. *Songs:* Coal River; Fragment of My Time; Half My Life Is Gone; Who Is the Man.

BEMIS, BIG BEN
See Dellger, Michael Lawrence

BENATZKY, RALPH ASCAP 1945
composer, author
b Moravske Budejovice (Moravia), Austria, June 5, 1894; d Zurich, Switz, Oct 17, 57. Came to US, 38. Comp for films & theatre in Europe. Honors: Austria Cross for Arts & Sci; Chevalier of French Foreign Legion. Chief Collabr: Irving Caesar. *Songs:* White Horse Inn; I Cannot Live Without Your Love; Always in My Heart. *Scores:* Stage: White Horse Inn (Berlin, NY); Meet My Sister (NY); The Apaches Cocktail; Casanova.

BENCRISCUTTO, FRANK PETER ANTHONY ASCAP 1970
composer, conductor, performer
b Racine, Wis, Sept 21, 28. Educ: Univ Wis, BMus, 51, MMus, 57; Northwestern Univ; Univ Rochester Eastman Sch Music, DMusA, 60; studied comp with Howard Hanson & Bernard Rogers. Head arr & saxophone soloist, Fifth Army Band, 51-54. Prof music & dir bands, Univ Minn, Minneapolis, 60- Univ Minn Concert Band 7-week tour, USSR, 69. Honored guest, Tschaikovsky Competition, 70. Guest cond, adjudicator & jazz saxophone soloist. *Instrumental Works:* Symphonic Jazz Suite (jazz quintet with concert band); Sing a New Song (mixed choir & concert band; Neil A Kjos Int Comp Contest Award, 77); Concerto Grosso (saxophone quartet & concert band); Concertino (tuba & concert band); Serenade (alto saxophone & band); The President's Trio (trumpet trio & band); Lamp of Liberty (concert band with optional narrator); Lyric Dance (concert band); Dialogue (clarinet & concert band or clarinet & piano); Let the Light Shine (concert band); Latina (concert band); Jazz March (concert band); Escapade for Trombones (trombone quartet & concert band); Spirit of Our Land (concert band); Festina (concert band); Six Concert Fanfares (brass & perc); Elegy (clarinet & piano); Valse Rondo (clarinet & piano);

Metamorphosis (concert band); Concerto for Trumpet (concert band). *Scores:* Film/TV: To Fly (prologue).

BENDER, JOAN ASCAP 1958
author
b Elizabeth, NJ. Writer for TV, documentaries & singers incl Julie Wilson, Ilene Woods. Chief Collabr: Donald Kahn. *Songs:* It's Late; Find the Lady a Man.

BENDER, LUCY
See Sokole, Lucy Bender

BENFANTE, IGNAZIO ASCAP 1961
author
b New York, NY, Jan 30, 14. Educ: New Utrecht High Sch; Brooklyn Col, BA, 36; City Col New York, MA, 37. Language teacher, New York City Syst. Adj prof, C W Post Col, Bronx Community Col & Queensborough Community Col. Chief Collabrs: Frank Dale, David Ormont, Carmine Coppola. *Songs:* Lyrics: Why Do You Break My Heart; Until We Kiss Again; You're Dangerous; Good Luck to You; Talking Through My Heart; Fishin' Beats Wishin'.

BENJAMIN, BENNIE ASCAP 1941
composer, author
b St Croix, VI, Nov 4, 07. Educ: Hy Smith Music Sch, studied banjo. Played with bands. Toured with vaudeville team, Olson & Johnson. Appeared at the Cotton Club (Copacabana). Served USAF, WW II, 3 yrs. Formed own publ firm, 68. Chief Collabr: Sol Marcus. *Songs:* I Don't Want to Set the World on Fire (Top Writers Award, 41); Confess; Strictly Instrumental; When the Lights Go on Again; Oh, What It Seemed to Be (Top Writers Award, 46); Surrender (Top Writers Award, 46); I Want to Thank Your Folks; I May Hate Myself in the Morning; These Things I Offer You; Jet; Rumors Are Flying (Top Writers Award, 46); I Don't See Me in Your Eyes Anymore; I'll Never Be Free; Don't Let Me Be Misunderstood; To Think You've Chosen Me; The Fabulous Character; I Ran All the Way Home; You're All I Want for Christmas; Are You Certain; Thanks to the Fool; Lonely Man; Anyone Can Fall in Love; Fine and Fancy Free; Melody Time; Can Anyone Explain; How Important Can It Be; Cross Over the Bridge; Wheel of Fortune.

BENJAMIN, THOMAS EDWARD ASCAP 1972
composer
b Bennington, Vt, Feb 17, 40. Educ: Bard Col, BA; Harvard, MA; Brandeis, MFA; Eastman, PhD; studied comp with Carlos Surinach, Ernst Krenek, Arthur Berger, Bernard Rogers. Taught comp & theory at Sch Music, Univ Houston. 68- Teacher (summers) at Nat Music Camp, Interlochen. Chief Collabr: Cynthia Macdonald (opera librettos). *Instrumental Works:* That Old Second Viennese School Rag; The Fruit of Love; Articulations. *Scores:* Opera/Ballet: The Rehearsal; Te Deum; Three Vocalises.

BENNARD, GEORGE ASCAP 1938
composer, author
b Youngstown, Ohio, Feb 4, 1873; d Reed City, Mich, Oct 10, 5. Educ: Pub schs. Salvation Army officer, 1892-1907; evangelist in US & Can, 07-58. Author, "The Story of the Old Rugged Cross." *Songs:* Sacred Songs: God Bless Our Boys; The Old Rugged Cross; also: Heart and Life Songs; Sweet Songs of Salvation; Divine Praise; Bennard's Melodies; Full Redemption Songs; Revival Classic; Old Rugged Cross Song Specials.

BENNER, LORA MERLE
composer, author, teacher
b Milwaukee, Wis, Sept 23, 07. Educ: Univ Ga, jour; Univ Wis, music; NY Univ, accounting; spec work at Carre' Musical Col, St Louis Inst Music & Juilliard Sch Music with Leland Thompson & Rosina Lhevinne. Began study of piano at age 3; first publ perf, age 5; taught piano & theory in Calif, Tex, Wis & NY; educ adv for piano teachers in Tex; lectr piano pedagogy, cols, univs & teachers' asns; piano & piano pedagogy teacher. Author: "Benner Theory for Piano Students" (5 bks); "Benner Teachers' Reference for the Theory Books" (1 bk); "Benner Make Your Own Scales and Arpeggios" (1 bk); "Benner Handbook for Piano Teaching" (1 bk). *Instrumental Works:* Benner Exercises and Etudes-Mostly Majors (1 bk); Benner Exercises and Etudes-Mostly Minors (1 bk).

BENNETT, BERNARD ASCAP 1956
composer, author
b Boston, Mass, Nov 8, 15. Educ: Col. Wrote film background scores. *Songs:* Apres Moi; Moth and a Flame.

BENNETT, DAVID D ASCAP 1944
composer, author
b Ida Grove, Iowa, Sept 3, 1892. Educ: Chicago Col Music, studied harmony, counterpoint & theory, arr with var teachers. Played clarinet in Municipal Band, Sioux City, Iowa, 10. Also played piano & clarinet in theatre pit orchs. Studied saxophone, flute & arr, Chicago, 19. Arr for leading name bands in US. Chief arr for var coast to coast radio shows; orch leader radio studios. Started concert band arr, 37; under contract to Carl Fischer Publ, New York. *Songs:* Music: Bye Bye Blues. *Instrumental Works:* Blues and Badinage (clarinet solo); Clarinet Royale (clarinet solo); Flute Royale (flute solo); Latinata (E flat alto saxophone solo); Moderne (E flat alto saxophone solo); Saxophone Royale (E flat alto

saxophone solo); El Matador (trumpet solo); Four Hornsmen (French horn quartet); Trombone Troubadors (trombone quartet); Tournament of Trumpets (trumpet quartet); Repartee (piano solo); Clarinet Carousel (clarinet duet); La Rougette (harp solo); Concert Bands: Scenes From The Sierras (fantasy); Caribbean Carnival; Majesty of America; Band Day; From Africa to Harlem (descriptive); Rhapsody in Rhumba (Latin); Broadcast From Brazil (Samba Latin); Lilt of the Latin (Samba Latin); Citadel (overture); Chalet (overture); Cajun Country (descriptive); Azalea Trail (descriptive).

BENNETT, ELSIE MARGARET　　　　　　ASCAP 1963
composer, author, arranger
b Detroit, Mich, Mar 30, 19. Educ: Ganapal Sch Music, Detroit, teachers & performers cert, 41; Wayne Univ, BMus, 45; Columbia Univ, MMus, 46; Manhattan Sch Music; piano studies with Ethel Mendelson, Mrs Ganapal, Mischa Kottler, George Cailatto, Rudy Molinaro & Joe Biviano; comp studies with Bernard Heiden & Otto Luening. Ed, Accordion World Mag, 45; owner music sch, 46; music teacher, Robotti Accordion Acad & Parkway Music Sch; teacher pub & parochial schs; dir, Bennett Music Studios & Schiff Sch. Chmn comp commissioning comt, Am Accordionists Asn, 52-, pres, 73-74. Mem: Brooklyn Music Teachers Guild; Accordion Teachers Guild; NY State Accordion Asn; Long Island Music Teachers Asn. *Songs & Instrumental Works:* American Home Album; Accordion Music in the Home; Folk Melodies for Accordion; First Steps in Scaleland; First Steps in Chordland, bks 1 & 2; Bass Chord Pattern; Bass Solo Primer; Hebrew and Jewish Songs and Dances for Accordion, bks 1 & 2; Hebrew and Jewish Songs and Dances for Piano; Hanon for Accordion; Italian Folk Songs; Easy Solos for Accordion; Single Arr: Sway; Mambo Jambo; Besame Mucho; April Showers; March from Concertstuk; Prayer of Thanksgiving; William Tell Overture; Sleeping Beauty Waltz; Bei Mir Bist Du Schoen; Yossel, Yossel; Vos Du Vilst; Mein Shtalele Belz; Les Preludes; Viva La Compagne; Waltz of the Flowers; Ukranian Dances; Waltz from Coppelia; Ode to Joy; Dus Tolessel; Der Neier Yid, Eisches Chail; Shene vi de Levonne; My Hero; March of Marionettes; In My Merry Oldsmobile; Smiles.

BENNETT, GEORGE J　　　　　　　　　ASCAP 1922
composer
b New York, NY, Oct 3, 1897; d. Wrote songs for "Greenwich Village Follies." *Songs:* Shadows on the Wall; Two Violins; Spring Is Here; Someone Cares.

BENNETT, JOYCE W　　　　　　　　　ASCAP 1959
composer, author, pianist
b Trenton, NJ, July 28, 23. Educ: Eastman Sch Music, BM; Montclair State Col. Taught music, Montclair. Assisted husband (Phil Bennett) in managing dance orch. Chief Collabr: Phil Bennett. *Songs:* Honeymoon Mambo; It Isn't Surprising.

BENNETT, MAX R　　　　　　　　　　composer, musician
b Des Moines, Iowa, May 24, 28. Educ: Univ Iowa, 2 yrs. Worked with jazz groups until late 50's. Cond for Peggy Lee. Worked with Ella Fitzgerald & others. Became studio musician in early 60's. Composed instrumentals & vocal comp for L A Express musical group, & others, 60's & 70's. Chief Collabrs: John Guein, Joni Mitchell. *Songs:* Simple Life; Sweet Loveliness; O Lavinia; Lyrics: Just Couldn't Help Myself; Come With Me. *Instrumental Works:* Rock Island Rocket; Suavemente; Midnight Flite; Keep on Doin' It; Tom Cat; L A Expression; Velvet Lady; TCB in E; Cry of the Eagle; Nunya; Vertigo.

BENNETT, NORMAN　　　　　　　　　singer
b Melbourne, Australia, Dec 16, 02. Educ: Pub schs; London Extension bus col; studied singing with Ivor Boostead. Solo tenor, St Pauls Cathedral, Melbourne. Appeared with Dame Nellie Melba in first concert, first nat hookup in Australia. Toured with contralto Phylis Lett, Australia & NZ, 27. Broadcasted & in concert, Japan, 28. To US, 28. Joined Rounders Quintet, broadcast over KNX-radio, 28. Winner, Pasadena Artists Found scholarship to Univ Rochester Eastman Sch of Music, 29. Singer, var studios, Hollywood, 5 yrs. With RKO Studios music dept, 32-58. Ed film music, incl "Lucy Show", 5 yrs. Mgr, Bing Crosby music dept, 60-62. Music ed for Paramount, CBS, Columbia, Orson Welles & Republic, 62. Retired, 68. Chief Collabr: Max Steiner. *Songs:* Alice From Dallas; Calypso (Fishing Song); Lyrics: Golden Moon; O Lord We Pray; Lonely Song; My Very Very Own; Gentle Star.

BENNETT, PHIL　　　　　　　　　　ASCAP 1959
composer, author, conductor
b New York, NY, Sept 4, 13. Educ: Oberlin Cons, BM; Montclair State Col. Taught voice, 5 yrs. Service, WW II. Own orch, played charity balls. Appeared on radio, TV & in concerts. Chief Collabr: Joyce Bennett (wife). *Songs:* Honeymoon Mambo; It Isn't Surprising; You Never Can Tell; Happy Birthday Song; The International Waltz.

BENNETT, ROBERT JOSEPH　　　　　　ASCAP 1977
composer, author, singer
b Downey, Calif, Mar 21, 55. Educ: Warren High Sch; Cerritos Col. Recording artist; solo performer, vocals & acoustic guitar in concerts, TV & radio. Chief Collabrs: Michael Aguilar. *Songs:* You're Welcome Here; The Night Shift; Carpenter Gone Bad?; Whistling in the Dark; Forgive and Forget; The Garden

Song; Healings; Children of the Lord; Spiritual Equation; Come and See; Music: My Redeemer Lives (adaptation).

BENNETT, ROBERT RUSSELL　　　　　ASCAP 1935
composer, arranger, musician
b Kansas City, Mo, June 15, 1894. Educ: High sch; studied piano with mother & other instruments with father; studied comp, harmony & counterpoint with Carl Busch, 4 yrs; studied comp & theory with Nadia Boulanger, 4 yrs; hon DHL, Franklin & Marshall Col. Began cond at age 11; played violin, piano & trombone, 06-16. Organist, Kansas City theatre; violinist & violist in string ens Arr, copyist & ed, 16- Cond, USA bands, theaters, films & recordings, 17- Arr for Bway musicals & TV. Scored films, incl "Oklahoma!" (Acad Award, 56). Former pres, Nat Asn for Am Comp & Cond. *Songs & Instrumental Works:* Suite of Old American Dances (band); Down to the Sea in Ships (band); Hexapoda (violin & piano); A Song Sonata (violin & piano); Abraham Lincoln Symphony (orch); Sights and Sounds (orch, RCA Victor awards); Symphonic Songs for Band; Four Preludes for Band; Autobiography for Band; Symphony; Violin Concerto; Hollywood (League of Comp comn); 8 Etudes for Symphony Orch (CBS comn); Charleston Rhapsody; Concerto Grosso; Stephen Foster; Armed Forces Suite; Organ Sonata; 4 Freedoms Symphony; Celebration; Symphonic Story of Jerome Kern; He Is Risen (Emmy award); Suite for Band Track Meet; Commemoration Symphony. *Scores:* Opera: Maria Malibran; The Enchanted Kiss; An Hour of Delusion.

BENNETT, ROY C　　　　　　　　　　ASCAP 1947
composer, author, singer
b Brooklyn, NY, Aug 12, 18. Educ: Thomas Jefferson High Sch; City Col New York, BA, 65; Schillinger Syst studies with Prof Rudolph Schramm, 4 yrs; studied choral cond with George V Rose. With 14th USAAF, China-Burma-India Theatre, WW II. Songwriter & publ, 45. Staff writer, Mills Music, Aberbach Group. Record producer & recording artist, Big Top Records. Writer for pop artists, night club acts & motion pictures. Author, "The Choral Singer's Handbook." Adj lectr, Queens Col, NY; pres, Great Neck Choral Soc. Chief Collabrs: Sid Tepper, Arthur Kent. *Songs:* Red Roses for a Blue Lady; Naughty Lady of Shady Lane; Nuttin' for Christmas; Travelin' Light; Summer Sounds; My Bonnie Lassie; Stairway of Love; Stop and Think It Over; Kewpie Doll; Say Something Sweet to Your Sweetheart; Baciagaloop; Twenty Tiny Fingers; Busybody; One for the Wonder; Outsider; When the Girl in Your Arms; I'll Step Down; Wonderful World of the Young; Suzy Snowflake; Eggbert the Easter Egg; All That I Am; Am I Ready; Angel; Little Train Who Said Ah-Choo; Jennie Kissed Me; New Orleans; Christmas Child; Cap and Gown; If I Had a Girl; The Woodchuck Song; I've Got a Crush on New York Town; You're Next; Shoppin' Around; Stay; Glad All Over; Have Heart, Will Love; Don't Say Goodbye; Don't Be Mad At Me; D in Love; I Found a Rose; Walkin' the Blues; Softly, My Love; Little White Donkey; Mr Words and Music; Beginner's Luck; Petunia, the Gardener's Daughter; Cane and a High Starched Collar; I Know Only One Girl; Beach Boy Blues; Five Sleepyheads; Island of Love; Hawaiian Sunset; Slicin' Sand; A Boy Like Me, a Girl Like You; Earth Boy; Walls Have Ears; It's a Wonderful World; Take Me to the Fair; Song of the Shrimp; Vino, Dinero, y Amor; Ito Eats; The Lady Loves Me; Bullfighter Was a Lady; Wheels on My Heels; Drums of the Islands; Kismet; Once Is Enough; Mexico; House That Has Everything; Fort Lauderdale Chamber of Commerce; Movie Title Songs: GI Blues; The Young Ones; Stay Away, Joe.

BENNO, ALEC MARC　　　　　　　　ASCAP 1969
composer, author, singer
b Dallas, Tex, July 1, 47. Educ: NTex State Univ, 65. Singer, nightclubs throughout Calif & Tex. Recording artist, 70-80; wrote, produced & recorded 2 albums with Leon Russell. Has written for var artists. Guitarist. Chief Collabrs: Leon Russell, Rita Coolidge, Mike Utley. *Songs:* Good Times; Nice Feelin'; Tryin' to Stay Live; Speak Your Mind; Music: Rollin' On. *Instrumental Works:* Jive Fade Jive.

BENSON, ARTHUR H　　　　　　　　ASCAP 1956
composer, publicist, publisher
b Spokane, Wash, Mar 25, 19. Educ: Lincoln High Sch. Publicity dir, Trianon Ballroom, Seattle, 41-44; owner-mgr, Aragon Ballroom, 45-46. Ed music mag, Platter Chatter, 46. Mgr, Jan Garber Orch, 47. Featured on "Hi-Jinks," KTVW, Seattle. Publ & owner of record co. Has led own dance band. Publicity dir, Hollywood Int Talents; also record distributor, personal mgr. Has written spec material for singers & comedians. Pres, Celestial Records Releasing Corp, Grosvenor House Music, Star Tunes Music, Arbette Corp, Artrex Corp, Creative Minds, Inc & Art Benson Creative Development Enterprises, Inc. Secy-treasurer, Robert Stigman Productions & United Gen Investment & Mortgage Corp of Nevada. Chief Collabrs: William Seaman, Donald Dinges (Scott Meade), Robert Alan Henry, Don Borzage, Chris Smith. *Songs:* By the River; I Guess I'll Have to Go to Sleep Again; The Last Day; Nobody Else But You; The Thrill Is Gone From Yesterday's Kiss; The Most Wonderful Things Happen; Have a Heart and Help a Heart (off song Riverside County, Palm Springs Heart Asn); How Beautiful (off song, Beautiful People, Inc); Ava Care, Ava Care, Ava Care (off song, Ava Care, Inc Health Products); Country Dreaming; A Fool in Love; I'll Sing the Blues; A Touch of Love; I Have a Dream; It Don't Hurt Me Anymore; Am I the Latest One?; I'll Never Walk the Line Again; He Couldn't Love You; I'll Never Break Another Heart; I Don't

Want to Be Alone Again; Westward Ho! (oratorio on conquest of West, 12 themes). *Scores:* A Touch of Paris (Las Vegas revue); And the Angel Swings (motion picture); Young and ATTR (stage).

BENSON, ELLSWORTH HARLOW   ASCAP 1954
composer
b Duluth, Minn, June 18, 10; d Queens, NY, Feb 21, 64. Educ: Newtown High Sch, Elmhurst, NY. Musician, Waldorf Astoria, Riviera, Latin Quarter & El Morroco; with Shep Fields Band; arr, Art Waner Band. Chief Collabrs: Eduardo Roy, Carlos Varela. *Songs:* Dance the Mambo This Way.

BENSON, JOHN T, JR   ASCAP 1952
composer, publisher
b Nashville, Tenn, Apr 30, 04. Started in publ bus, 35; pres, John T Benson Publ Co, retired, 69; pres, Heartwarming Music Co. Holds about 2,000 copyrights. Involved in church & Sunday sch music. Pres, Sunday Sch of Music Publ Asn, 2 yrs; charter mem & former mem bd, Gospel Music Asn. *Songs:* Music: Love Lifted Me.

BENSON, WARREN FRANK   ASCAP 1954
composer, teacher, conductor
b Detroit, Mich, Jan 26, 24. Educ: Univ Mich, BMus, 49, MMus, 51. Timpanist, Detroit Symph, 45. Fulbright teacher, Anatolia Col, Salonika, Greece, 50-52. Composer-in-residence, Ithaca Col, 53-67. Prof comp, Eastman Sch Music, 67-Founder-cond, Ithaca Perc Ens & Anatolia Col Chorale. Lectr-cond at leading US Univ Fests & in Can, Latin Am & Europe. *Instrumental Works:* Concertino for Alto Saxophone and Wind Ensemble; Helix (tuba & wind ens); The Leaves Are Falling (wind ens); The Solitary Dancer (wind ens); Symphony for Drums and Wind Orchestra; The Passing Bell (wind ens); Shadow Wood (soprano & wind ens); Trio for Percussion; Streams (perc ens); The Dream Net (saxophone & string quartet); Five Lyrics of Louise Bogan (mezzo soprano & flute); Concerto for Horn and Orchestra; Farewell (alto saxophone & piano). *Songs & Instrumental Works:* Choral: Love Is (antiphonal choruses); Songs of O (chorus, brass quintet & marimba); Earth, Sky, Sea (chorus, flute, trombone, marimba).

BENTER, CHARLES   ASCAP 1937
composer, conductor, arranger
b New York, NY, Apr 29, 1887; d Washington, DC, Dec 2, 64. Educ: Pub schs; hon MusD, Columbia Univ. Apprentice Boy Musician, USN, 05, then bandmaster. Organized Navy Band, DC, 19, leader until retirement, 42. Commissioned Lt, USN, act of Congress, 25; first to attain officer's rank in music branch of Navy. WW I service, Cuba & Vera Cruz. Awarded Order of St Sava, 4th class, Yugoslavia. Mem, Am Bandmaster's Asn. Founder & officer in charge, USN Sch Music. Leader, Metrop Police Dept Band, DC; retired, 62. Ed & publ "Lt Charles Benter's Book of National Airs." *Instrumental Works:* Fantasia; A Day Aboard an American Man of War; Marches: Irresistible; Lure of Alaska; Major Denby; Washington Times; Light Cruisers; Our Navy; Class of '91; USNA; Shenandoah National Park; All Hands; A Great American; The Submarine Force.

BENTON, DANIEL JOSEPH   ASCAP 1973
composer
b Newport, RI, Apr 10, 45. Educ: Univ Iowa, AB(piano), MA(theory), MFA(comp), PhD(comp); pvt piano & harmony study with David Saperton, New York, NY, 64-65. Comp var chamber works, piano pieces & songs. *Songs & Instrumental Works:* Nocturne (piano); Studies on Yeats' "A Crazed Girl" (piano); Preceptory (tape/piano); Dirge: In Memoriam Igor Stravinsky (soprano & 11 instruments).

BENTZ, CECIL WILLIAM   ASCAP 1975
composer, organist
b Platte Center, Nebr, Sept 17, 15. Educ: Kearney State Teachers Col; Pius X Sch Liturgical Music; Am Theatre Wing. Organist, Radio City Music Hall, 59-79. Chief Collabr: Jerry Grant. *Songs:* Music: Old Habits Are Hard to Break; I've Forgotten More About You; Two Short Poems of Robert Frost; The Rose Family; All This Night My Heart Rejoices. *Instrumental Works:* String Quartet; Piano Sonata. *Scores:* Opera/Ballet: Window Game.

BEREZOWSKY, NICOLAI T   ASCAP 1945
composer, conductor, violinist
b St Petersburg, Russia, May 17, 1900; d New York, NY, Aug 26, 53. Educ: Imperial Capella Sch, studied with Klimov; Juilliard Sch, studied with Rubin Goldmark, Paul Kochanski. Concertmaster, Nat Opera, Saratoff; mem, Bolshoi Theatre. To US, 21. Violinist, New York Philh, 23-28. Cond, Atwater Kent radio concerts, 24-26; asst cond, CBS, 30; guest cond, Dresden Symph, 30 Bremen Fest, 31 & symph orchs throughout US. Mem, Coolidge String Quartet, 35-40. Recipient, Juilliard Sch Comp award, Am Acad Arts & Letters award & Guggenheim fel. *Instrumental Works:* Theme and Variations; Hebrew Suite; Four Symphonies; Three String Quartets; Brass Suite; Sextet Concerto; Suite for Woodwinds; Duo for Clarinet and Viola; Two Wind Quintets; Quartet Concerto; Fantasie for Two Pianos and Orchestra; Violin Concerto; Sinfonietta (NBC prize); Hymn to St Cecilia; Toccata Variations; Finale for String Quartet (Elizabeth Sprague Coolidge comn); Music for Seven Brass Instruments (League of Composers comn); String Sextet (Libr of Congress comn); Soldier on the Town (League of Composers comn); Christmas Festival Overture (Howard

Barlow comn); Harp Concerto (Philadelphia Orch comn). Opera: Prince Batrak; Babar, the Elephant (children's, Little Orch Soc comn).

BERG, DAVID   ASCAP 1921
author, publisher
b Brooklyn, NY, Nov 20, 1892; d New York, NY, Feb 18, 44. Educ: Pub schs. Became music publ. Served in Am Expeditionary Force, WW I. *Songs:* There's a Quaker Down in Quaker Town; When You've Nothing Else to Do; Someone Is Longing for Home Sweet Home.

BERG, HAROLD C   ASCAP 1926
composer, author
b Saginaw, Mich, May 3, 1900; d Southfield, Mich, July 24, 73. Educ: High sch. Staff lyricist, Warner Brothers, early 30's, then pub rels counsel, Detroit. Chief Collabrs: M K Jerome, Jesse Greer, Jack Meskill, Alfred Bryan, Buddy Field, Sam Coslow, Maurice Spitalny, Russ Morgan. *Songs:* Freshie; Holding Hands; Parting Kiss; You Left Me Nothing But Mem'ries; This Is the Last Time.

BERG, JEAN HORTON LUTZ   ASCAP 1964
composer, author, teacher
b Clairton, Pa, May 30, 13. Educ: Friends' Cent High Sch; Univ Pa, BS in Ed, 35, AM in Latin, 37. High sch teacher English & Latin. Author of 48 bks for children (pre-sch-elem); lectr writing for children.

BERG, RICHARD   ASCAP 1972
composer, author, singer
b Springfield, Ohio, Sept 28, 49. Educ: Music & Art High Sch; Long Island Univ; New York City Col of Music; studied clarinet with Jack Kreislman. Formed var rock groups, 60's. Writer, incidental music for movie, "Chaffed Elbows." Writer, commercials incl Kool-Aid, Canada Dry, Morton's Bake Shop & Nat Highway Safety. Assoc music dir, Gray Advert. Singer, commercials & back-up on recordings & live concerts for Johnny Cash, Olivia Newton-John, Dottie West, Maynard Ferguson & others. Songwriter for Tony Orlando. Writer, music for indust films, incl ITT, Coca-Cola & others. Chief Collabrs: Neil Sheppard, Enid Futterman, Robert Gollrick, David Spinozza. *Songs:* When Keeping Up Gets You Down; Pullin' Together; She Always Knew; City Lights.

BERGANTINE, BORNEY   ASCAP 1948
composer, conductor, trumpeter
b Kansas City, Mo, Oct 5, 09; d North Kansas City, July 4, 54. Educ: Bus Col. Organized own orch, Happiness Boys, 29. Chief Collabr: Betty Peterson. *Songs:* My Happiness; Forever With You; Watch Your Step; This Is the Fourth Time You've Broken My Heart.

BERGDAHL, EDITH
See Gillette, Leland James

BERGEN, NORMAN I   ASCAP 1975
composer, author, record producer
b Brooklyn, NY, May 17, 45. Educ: Wingate High Sch, Brooklyn, NY, grad, 62; Manhattan Sch Music, New York, BM(theory), 66 & MME, 67. Received two gold records for musical arr "Candida" & "Knock Three Times," 70. Music direction "Oh Calcutta!," original NY production, 69-72 & current Bway production, 77- Received two nominations Best Song Category, Billboard Mag Disco Forum IV Awards, 78. Comp, produced & arr music for film "Nocturna," 79. Chief Collabrs: Reid Whitelaw, Shelly Coburn, Mark Barkan. *Songs:* Extra, Extra (Read All About It); Helplessly; Nighttime Fantasy; Love Is Just a Heartbeat Away; Only a Fool Breaks His Own Heart; Desperately; Little Bird; Colors of Love; Chained to Your Love; You Got Me Hummin'; Loving You Is Killing Me.

BERGENDORFF, FREDERICK L   ASCAP 1972
composer, author
b Bremerton, Wash, Feb 7, 44. Educ: San Diego State Univ, BA, 65; San Diego State Univ & Univ Southern Calif, grad work. Dir, advert & promotion, CBS Radio, Los Angeles. Fifteen yr broadcast vet. Winner, 36 maj regional & nat awards for excellence in advert, incl Clio Award, 79 & Am Advert Fedn Award, 80. Created jingle packages, radio & TV stas. Coauth col textbk on broadcast advert & promotion. *Instrumental Works:* Rain Song.

BERGER, ARTHUR VICTOR
educator, composer, critic
b New York, NY, May 15, 12. Educ: NY Univ, BS(music), 34; Harvard Univ, MA, 36; Longy Sch Music, Cambridge. Ed, Musical Mercury, 34-37; music reviewer, Boston Transcript, 34-37. Instr, Mills Col, 39-41, NTex State Col, 41 & Brooklyn Col, 42-43. Music reviewer, New York Sun, 43-46; assoc music critic, New York Herald Tribune, 46-53. Mem fac, Brandeis Univ, 53-, Naumburg prof music, 62-, Irving G Fine prof music, 69-80, prof emeritus, 80- Comp-in-residence, Juilliard Sch, 46 & Berkshire Music Ctr, 64. Mem fac, New Eng Cons, 80- Rec'd comns from CBS, 44, Dimitri Mitropoulos, 52, Louisville Orch, 55, Fromm Music Found, 59 & League Composers. Awards: Am Coun Learned Soc Grant; Nat Inst Arts & Letters Award; Fulbright Res Grants; Naumburg Recording Award; New York Music Critics Circle; St Botolph Club Arts Award. Mem: Fel Am Acad Arts & Sci; Am Composers Alliance (bd gov, 57-59 & 63-); Nat Inst Arts & Letters. Author "Aaron Copland," 53; also

articles & reviews. Co-founder & ed, Perspectives of New Music, 62-63, ed bd, 62- *Instrumental Works:* Serenade Concertante (orch); Ideas of Order (orch); Polyphony (orch); also 3 pieces for strings; chamber concerto; woodwind quartet; string quartet; chamber music for 13 players; duos for violin & piano, piano & clarinet, cello & piano, oboe & clarinet & for 2 pianos; trio for violin, cello & piano; trio for guitar, violin & piano; also numerous solo piano works.

BERGER, JEAN ASCAP 1952
composer
b Hamm, Ger, Sept 27, 09. Educ: Univ Heidelberg, PhD (musicol); pvt comp studies with Louis Aubert in Paris, 34-38. Pianist & choral dir, Paris, 33-39. Fac, Cons Brasileiro Musica, Rio de Janeiro, Brazil, 39-40; fac, Middlebury Col, Vt, Univ Ill, Univ Colo, 48-68. Frequent lectr & cond at var univ & col in US & abroad. *Songs & Instrumental Works:* Brazilian Psalm (mixed chorus); Skelton Poems (mixed chorus; baritone, piano); The Eyes of All Wait Upon Thee (mixed chorus); Four Songs (voice & piano); Short Overture for Strings.

BERGERE, ROY ASCAP 1942
composer, author
b Baltimore, Md, Feb 3, 1899; d. Educ: McDonogh Sch. WW I, Army band leader. In B F Keith, Keith-Albee vaudeville circuits; also musical comedies, 19-29. MC, Publix Theatres. Chief Collabrs: Gene Austin, Edward Claypoole, Billy Frisch, Harry Link. *Songs:* Georgia Moon; Meet Me Where the Swanee River Flows; Tell Me If You Want Somebody Else; Me, Myself and I; Everything Is Spanish Now; Cincinnati; Trying; How Come You Do Me Like You Do?.

BERGERSEN, (LOUIS) BALDWIN ASCAP 1948
composer, pianist
b Vienna, Austria, Feb 20, 14. Educ: Trinity Sch, NY. US citizen. Comp dance music for "Ziegfeld Follies of 1943" & "Early to Bed." Comp music for concert revue, "Musical Americana." Accompanist to Jane Froman, Imogene Coca & Milton Berle. Wrote for "Show of Shows," NBC-TV. Chief Collabrs: June Carroll, Irvin Graham, George Marion, Jr, Bob Russell. *Songs:* Love and I; Where Can I Go From You?; April in Harrisburg; That's Good Enough for Me; Sleep Baby, Don't Cry; Woman Is a Rascal; Nobody Told Me; Saturday's Child; Where's the Boy?. *Instrumental Works:* Far Harbour (lyric drama; Lincoln Kirstein Comn). *Scores:* Bway stage: All in Fun; Allah Be Praised; Carib Song; Small Wonder; Off-Bway (London): The Crystal Heart.

BERGH, ARTHUR ASCAP 1919
composer, conductor, violinist
b St Paul, Minn, Mar 24, 1882; d Los Angeles, Calif, Feb 11, 62. First violinist, New York Symph & Metrop Opera House Orch, 03-08. Cond, munic concerts, New York, 11-14. Dir recording for phonograph cos, 15-30. Radio music dir for advert agencies, 31-38. Music librarian, film co, 41. Wrote incidental music to play, "Rhapsody." *Songs & Instrumental Works:* Ave Maria; The Imprisoned Soul; Destiny; Come With Arms Outstretched; Pack, Clouds Away; Together; The Congo (song cycle); Festival March; Honor and Glory; The Raven (melodrama with orch); The Pied Piper of Hamelin (melodramas with orch); Piano: Jollity; 4 Tone Pastels; Orientale; Legend.

BERGH, HAAKON PEDER ASCAP 1965
composer, flutist, teacher
b Gregory, SDak, June 22, 13; d Los Angeles, Calif, July 8, 59. Educ: Los Angeles High Sch; Univ Calif, Los Angeles; studied flute with Jules Furman, comp with Ernest Toch, classical forms with Walter Kelsey. Comp as youth. Prof flutist, studios & radio, age 21. Flutist, Los Angeles Symph. Bandleader, 378 ASF Band, writer & cond, USA shows, World War II. Returned to Hollywood, 49; under contract to RKO, 5 yrs. Comp, chamber music, ballets, childrens' plays & records. Taught flute, doubling musicians on vibrato; authority on Schillinger Syst. Chief Collabrs: Joe Edward Grenzeback, Josephine Fetter Royle. *Songs:* Song of Rejoicing. *Instrumental Works:* Caprice No 4 (flute, piano); Praeludeum (bass clarinet solo); Suite I, II (chamber music). *Scores:* Ballet: Pecos Bill; Sleeping Beauty; Childrens' plays: Sing Ho for a Prince (prize winner); Old King Cole (prize winner).

BERGMAN, ALAN ASCAP 1955
composer, author
b Brooklyn, NY. Educ: Ethical Culture Sch; Univ NC, BA; Univ Calif Grad Sch, Los Angeles. Wrote & dir, Spec Serv shows, WW II. TV dir, CBS, Philadelphia, 49-53. Wrote TV prod numbers for "Shower of Stars." Wrote theme songs for "Nat King Cole Show", "Maude", "Alice" & "Good Times." Has written songs for revues, night clubs & films. Won 2 Grammy Awards & 2 Golden Globe Awards. Inducted into Songwriters Hall of Fame, 80. Chief Collabrs: Marilyn Bergman (wife), Lew Spence, Norman Luboff, Paul Weston, Sammy Fain, Alex North, Johnny Mandell, John Williams, Quincy Jones, Dave Grusin, Michel Legrand, Marvin Hamlisch, Billy Goldenberg, Henry Mancini, David Shire, Neil Diamond. *Songs:* Lyrics: Yellow Bird; Nice 'n' Easy; I've Never Left Your Arms; What Matters Most; Sleep Warm; That Face; The Windmills of Your Mind (Acad Award, 68); What Are You Doing the Rest of Your Life?; Little Boy Lost; All His Children; The Summer Knows; Marmelade, Molasses and Honey; Summer Me, Winter Me; In the Heat of the Night; Make Me Rainbows; Like a Lover; Pretty World; Sweet Gingerbread Man; The Way We Were (Acad Award, 73); I Believe in Love; I Love to Dance; You Don't Bring Me Flowers; The Last Time I Felt Like This; I'll Never Say Goodbye. *Scores:* Stage: That's

Life (Los Angeles); Bway stage: Ice Capades 1957; Something More; Ballroom; Film/TV: Queen of the Stardust Ballroom (Emmy Award); Sybil (Emmy Award).

BERGMAN, DEWEY (DON OSBORNE) ASCAP 1943
composer, author, arranger
b Buffalo, NY, Oct 4, 02. Educ: Eastman Sch Music. Organized, played piano & arranged for Jean Gold Kette & Ted Weems. Arranged for Guy Lombardo, Gene Krupa, etc. A&R dir, King, Decca & RCA Records. Vocal coach, Guy Mitchell, Steve Lawrence, Janice Harper & Eddie Fisher. Scored movies for MGM. Co-produced, Lombardo New Years Eve Shows, 25 yrs. Chief Collabrs: Jack Segal, Benny Davis, Billy Hill, Fred Wise. *Songs & Instrumental Works:* Years and Years Ago; Lonesome; Bright Lights of Brussels; Cat Walk; Narcissus; Horoscope in Music (suite); Arr: Humoresque.

BERGMAN, LLOYD MICHEL ASCAP 1974
composer, publisher
b New York, NY, Aug 11, 43. Educ: Studied trumpet at age 5; Far Rockaway Pub Schs, 56. At age 13 was lead trumpeter with Charlie Johnson's 17-piece big band. At age 18 played lead for Maynard Ferguson; has played lead for Stevie Wonder, Jose Feliciano, Frank Sinatra, Judy Garland, The Supremes, Gladys Knight, Peggy Lee, Tony Bennett, Sergio Franchi & others. Founder, musical writer, arr, producer, recording engr & backer of band Mistura. Formed own record & publ co. Was on Bway "Jesus Christ, Superstar", "Rosenblum" & "Hearts Club Band on the Road." In concert, Michel Legrand, New York, Englebert Humperdink, Sara Vaughn, Wolf Trap, Burt Bacharach, Pine Knob; Newport Jazz Fest & with Sammy Davis. Recorded more than 250 albums & jingles; was on TV "The Dick Cavett Show", "David Frost Show", "Black Journal." Now touring high schs & cols performing as soloist & with Mistura in clinics & in concert, NY Brass Conference for Scholarships & Annual Jazz Workshop, Indian Hills, NJ. *Songs & Instrumental Works:* Life Is a Song; The Flasher; Let the Dance Go On; A Certain Kind of Music.

BERGMAN, MARILYN KEITH ASCAP 1953
author
b Brooklyn, NY. Educ: High Sch Music & Arts; NY Univ. Wrote songs for revues, night clubs, TV, stage & films. Won 2 Golden Globe Awards & Two Grammy Awards. Wrote TV themes for "Maude", "Good Times" & "Alice." Chief Collabrs: Alan Bergman (husband), Lew Spence, Norman Luboff, Paul Weston, Alex North, Sammy Fain, John Williams, Quincy Jones, Dave Grusin, Henry Mancini, Michel Legrand, Marvin Hamlisch, Billy Goldenberg, David Shire, Neil Diamond. *Songs:* Lyrics: Yellow Bird; Nice 'n' Easy; What Matters Most; In The Heat of the Night; The Windmills of Your Mind (Acad Award, 68); What Are You Doing the Rest of Your Life?; Little Boy Lost; All His Children; Marmelade, Molasses and Honey; The Summer Knows; Summer Me, Winter Me; Make Me Rainbows; Like a Lover; Pretty World; You Must Believe in Spring; Sweet Gingerbread Man; The Way We Were; I Believe in Love; I Love to Dance; You Don't Bring Me Flowers; The Last Time I Felt Like This; I'll Never Say Goodbye. *Scores:* Stage: That's Life (Los Angeles); Bway stage: Ice Capades 1957; Something More; Ballroom; Film/TV: Queen of the Stardust Ballroom (Emmy Award); Sybil (Emmy Award).

BERGMAN, NANCY ASCAP 1966
composer, arranger, singer
b Washington, DC, Oct 2, 27. Educ: Grinnell Col, Iowa; Tulsa Univ. Specialist in four-part vocal harmony, barbershop style. Exec dir, Sweet Adelines, Inc, 57-68. Mem, Int Champion Quartet. Arranger, coach & choral dir. *Songs:* Harmonize the World; Opening Night on Broadway; World, Here I Am!; Georgie; Dixie Sunshine.

BERGSMA, WILLIAM LAURENCE ASCAP 1945
composer
b Oakland, Calif, Apr 1, 21. Educ: Stanford Univ; Eastman Sch Music, BA & MM; studied with Howard Hanson. Mem comp fac, chmn & assoc dean, Juilliard Sch Music, 46-63; prof & dir, Sch Music, Univ Wash, Seattle, 63- Rec'd Guggenheim & NEA fels; comns from Koussevitzky, Coolidge, Juilliard Foundations, Louisville & Seattle Symphonies & Chamber Music Soc of Lincoln Center. Mem, Am Acad & Inst Arts & Letters. Chief Collabr: Janet Lewis. *Instrumental Works:* Two Symphonies; Two Concerti; Four String Quartets; much choral, orchestral & chamber music. *Scores:* Opera/Ballet: The Wife of Martin Guerre; The Murder of Comrade Sharik.

BERK, LEW ASCAP 1950
composer, author
b Russia, Feb 10, 1888; d. Educ: High sch. *Songs:* Hello Little Girl of My Dreams; Since You Went Away; I Met You Dear in Dreamland; I've Got the Blues.

BERK, MORTY ASCAP 1942
composer
b Philadelphia, Pa, Mar 8, 00; d Philadelphia, Sept 4, 55. Chief Collabrs: Louis Herscher, Harry James, Billy Hays, Max Freedman. *Songs:* Down Home Blues; No One to Love; Sweet Virginia Rose; Lazy Silvery Moon; From the Bottom of My Heart; Every Day of My Life; A Thrill to Remember; Dreamy Old New England Moon; Heartbreaker; Blue Sapphire; Starlight Serenade.

BERKOWITZ, SOL

ASCAP 1960

composer, author, arranger

b Warren, Ohio, Apr 27, 22. Educ: Queens Col, NY, BA; Columbia Univ, MA; studied with Otto Luening, Karol Rathavs, Abby Whiteside. Comp, works for concert hall, chamber music & opera. Staff comp, Tamiment Playhouse, 53-57, Garry Moore TV Show, 63, Carol Burnett TV Show, 64 & other TV & film scores. Comp Bway musicals, "Nowhere To Go But Up" & "Miss Emily Adams." Author, bks, "A New Approach to Sight Singing" & "Improvisation Through Keyboard Harmony." Ford Found grant, 56. Chief Collabs: James Lipton, Eliot Feld, Herb Hartig. *Songs:* Music: Game of Dance. *Instrumental Works:* Introduction and Scherzo (viola, piano); Dialogue (cello, piano); Suite of Minatures (concert band); Suite for Wind; Two Letters from Lincoln (chorus); Two Letters from Jefferson (chorus); Dance Suite for String Orchestra; Jazzettes (piano); also 75 publ instrumental, choral and symphonic works. *Scores:* Opera/Ballet: Papillon; A Footstep of Air; The Real McCoy; Fat Tuesday; Bway show: Unsinkable Molly Brown.

BERLE, MILTON

See Berlinger, Milton

BERLIN, DAVID

ASCAP 1974

composer, teacher

b Pittsburgh, Pa, Jan 23, 43. Educ: Carnegie Inst Technol, BFA Mus, 65, BFA MusEd, 65; Carnegie Mellon Univ, MFA MusEd, 69, MFA MusComp, 72; WVa Univ. Mem, Am Soc Univ Composers. Mem exec bd, Pittsburgh Alliance Composers. Music performed at, Int Music Fest, Menorca, Spain & Los Alamos Wind/String Chamber Music Award Fest. *Songs:* Articulations for Soprano and Tape; Exclamations for Mixed Chorus; Music: Museum Piece (baritone voice & piano). *Instrumental Works:* Synchronization for Band and Tape; Octet for Chamber Ensemble; Variants for Orchestra; Three Mixtures for Four Bassoons and Tape; Interactions for Flute and Tape; Music for Brass and Percussion; Quadraphonics for Brass Quintet; Fragments for Percussion Ensemble; Essences for Viola and Tape; Quintet for Bassoon and Strings; Structures for Chamber Orchestra; Patterns for Saxophone Quartet; Caricature for Wind Band; Fluctuations for Flute Choir; Synergism No 1; Trio for Flute Oboe and Guitar; Trio for Flute Oboe and Clarinet; Quintet for Woodwinds; In Two (cello duet); Menagerie (chamber ens); Quintet for Wind Instruments; Three Miniatures for Guitar; Metamorphism (orch).

BERLIN, IRVING

ASCAP 1914

composer, author, publisher

b Temun, Russia, May 11, 1888. To US at age 5. Educ: NY pub schs, 2 yrs; earliest musical educ from father, cantor; hon degrees: Bucknell Univ, Temple Univ & Fordham Univ. Began career as song plugger for publ Harry Von Tilzer & as singing waiter in Chinatown. Hired as staff lyricist by Ted Snyder Co, 09; partner in firm 4 yrs later. Began vaudeville appearances in US & abroad, 10, also appeared with Snyder in Bway musical, "Up and Down Broadway." WW I, Sgt, USA Inf, Camp Upton, NY. After war, established own publ firm. Built Music Box Theatre with Sam Harris, 21. Wrote songs for musicals, incl "Ziegfeld Follies" (1911, 1919, 1920), also for films, incl "Puttin on the Ritz", "Hallelujah", "Reaching for the Moon" & "Sayonara." Mem, French Legion of Honor. Charter mem, ASCAP, 14, on first Bd of Dirs, 14-18. Rec'd Medal of Freedom from President Ford. Biographies: "The Story of Irving Berlin" by Alexander Woollcott; "The Story of Irving Berlin" by David Ewen. *Songs:* Marie From Sunny Italy; Sadie Salome, Go Home; My Wife's Gone to the Country, Hurrah! Hurrah!; Alexander's Ragtime Band; Everybody's Doin' It; The Ragtime Violin; That Society Bear; That Mysterious Rag; Call Me Up Some Rainy Afternoon; When I Lost You; When the Midnight Choo-Choo Leaves for Alabam'; Snookey Ookums; That International Rag; I Want to Go Back to Michigan; Play a Simple Melody; This Is the Life; The Girl on the Magazine Cover; I Love a Piano; Oh, How I Hate to Get Up in the Morning; Mandy; I've Got My Captain Working for Me Now; A Pretty Girl Is Like a Melody; You'd Be Surprised; Tell Me, Little Gypsy; All By Myself; Everybody Step; Say It With Music; Crinoline Days; Lady of the Evening; Pack Up Your Sins and Go to the Devil; An Orange Grove in California; Some Sunny Day; All Alone; Lazy; What'll I Do?; Always; How Many Times?; Remember; Blue Skies; It All Belongs to Me; Russian Lullaby; Shakin' the Blues Away; The Song Is Ended; Coquette; How About Me?; Let Me Sing and I'm Happy; Marie; Puttin' on the Ritz; Reaching for the Moon; Soft Lights and Sweet Music; How Deep Is the Ocean?; I'm Playing With Fire; Let's Have Another Cup o' Coffee; Say It Isn't So; Easter Parade; Heat Wave; Supper Time; Not for All the Rice in China; How's Chances?; Maybe It's Because I Love You Too Much; I Never Had a Chance; Cheek to Cheek; Isn't This a Lovely Day?; The Piccolino; Top Hat, White Tie and Tails; I'm Putting All My Eggs in One Basket; Get Thee Behind Me, Satan; Let Yourself Go; Let's Face the Music and Dance; The Girl on the Police Gazette; I've Got My Love to Keep Me Warm; Slumming on Park Avenue; You're Laughing at Me; This Year's Kisses; Now It Can Be Told; Change Partners; I Used to Be Color Blind; God Bless America (Congressional Medal of Honor; proceeds to God Bless America Fund); I'm Sorry for Myself; I Poured My Heart Into a Song; It's a Lovely Day Tomorrow; When Winter Comes; Fools Fall in Love; It'll Come to You; Latins Know How; You Can't Brush Me Off; You're Lonely and I'm Lonely; Angels of Mercy; Any Bonds Today; Be Careful, It's My Heart; Happy Holiday; Plenty to Be Thankful For; White Christmas (Acad Award, 42); I Left My Heart at the Stage Door Canteen; This Is the Army, Mr Jones; You Keep Coming Back Like a Song; Anything You Can Do; Doin' What Comes Natur'lly; The Girl That I Marry; I Got the Sun in the Morning; There's No Business Like Show Business; They Say It's Wonderful; You Can't Get a Man With a Gun; Better Luck Next Time; A Couple of Swells; A Fella With an Umbrella; It Only Happens When I Dance With You; Steppin' Out With My Baby; Let's Take an Old Fashioned Walk; Give Me Your Tired, Your Poor (proceeds to God Bless America Fund); Homework; Just One Way to Say I Love You; You Can Have Him; The Best Thing for You; The Hostess With the Mostes' on the Ball; It's a Lovely Day Today; Marrying for Love; They Like Ike; You're Just in Love; Count Your Blessings Instead of Sheep; For the Very First Time; Sisters; Sayonara; This Is a Great Country (proceeds to God Bless America Fund); Don't Be Afraid of Romance; Laugh It Up; Pigtails and Freckles; An Old-Fashioned Wedding. *Scores:* Bway Stage: Watch Your Step; Stop! Look! Listen!; The Century Girl; The Cohan Revue of 1918; Yip, Yip Yaphank (all-soldier show written at Camp Upton); Music Box Revue (1921, 1922, 1923, 1924); The Cocoanuts; Ziegfeld Follies of 1927; Face the Music; As Thousands Cheer; Louisiana Purchase; This Is the Army (all-soldier show; awarded Medal for Merit; toured US, Europe, South Pacific battle zones; proceeds assigned to Army Emergency Relief and other service agencies); Annie Get Your Gun; Miss Liberty; Call Me Madam; Mr President; Film: Top Hat; Follow the Fleet; On the Avenue; Alexander's Ragtime Band; Carefree; Second Fiddle; Holiday Inn: Blue Skies; Easter Parade; White Christmas; There's No Business Like Show Business.

BERLINE, BYRON DOUGLAS

ASCAP 1970

composer, entertainer, fiddler

b Caldwell, Kans, July 6, 44. Educ: Univ Okla, BS(educ). Mem, Bill Monroe & the Bluegrass Boys, 67. Spec serv, USA, 67-69. Mem, Dillard & Clark Expedition, 69-71. With Country Gazette, 72-75 & Sundance, 75- Chief Collabr: John Hickman. *Instrumental Works:* Huckleberry Hornpipe; Storm Over Oklahoma; Birmingham Fling; Coming Home; Byron's Barn.

BERLINGER, MILTON (MILTON BERLE)

ASCAP 1942

composer, author, comedian

b New York, NY, July 12, 08. Educ: NY Professional Children's Sch. Began performing at 5. Child actor in films. First stage appearance, "Florodora," Atlantic City. Appeared at Palace Theatre, NY, then nightclubs, theatres. Appeared in Bway musicals: "Saluta"; "See My Lawyer"; "Ziegfeld Follies of 1943." Debut on TV, closed-circuit, Chicago, 29; on radio, 34. TV shows: "Texaco Star Theatre"; "Buick Show," 48-56; "Kraft Music Hall," 58-59; 3 Milton Berle specials, 59; "Jackpot Bowling," 60-61. Made film appearances, incl "Tall, Dark and Handsome," "Always Leave 'Em Laughing," "Margin for Error." Chief Collabs: Jerry Livingston, Ervin Drake, Buddy Arnold, Sammy Cahn, Abner Silver. *Songs:* ; I'd Give a Million Tomorrows; Stars Never Cry; Lucky Lucky Lucky Me; Foolishly; Sam, You Made the Pants Too Long; Always Leave 'Em Laughing; Li'l Abner; Save Me a Dream; The Song of Long Ago; It Only Takes a Moment to Fall in Love; Gotta Darn Good Reason Now; Moon Magic; What's Gonna Be (With You and Me); Here Comes the Girl; I'm So Happy I Could Cry; I Wuv a Wabbit; If I Knew You Were There; Summer Love; Leave the Dishes in the Sink, Ma; It Must Have Been Two Other People; I've Got a Heart Full of Sunshine; Ink Dries Quicker Than Tears. *Scores:* Film: Always Leave 'Em Laughing.

BERLINSKI, HERMAN

ASCAP 1964

composer, organist

b Leipzig, Ger, Aug 18, 10. Educ: State Cons, Leipzig; Ecole Normale de Musique, Paris; Jewish Theol Sem, NY. Instr music, Hebrew Union Col; vis prof, Cath Univ of Am. Organist, Temple Emanu-El, NY; organist & dir music emer, Washington Hebrew Cong, DC; music dir, Nat Jewish Musical Art Found; music critic, The Jewish Week, Washington. *Songs & Instrumental Works:* The Burning Bush (organ); Symphonic Visions for Orchestra; Avodat Shabbat; Sinfonia No 2 (organ); Sinfonia No 3 (organ solo); Sinfonia No 8 (Eliyahu); Oratorio: Job; Sinfonia No 9: The GlasBead Game; Sinfonia No 10 (cello & organ); High Holyday Cycle: The Days of Awe; Festival Cantata: Sing to the Lord a New Song.

BERMAN, ART HARRY

ASCAP 1945

composer, whistler

b Stanislau, Austria, Apr 7, 02; d Flushing, NY, Sept 14, 59. Educ: New York & Cleveland pub schs. Prof athlete in baseball & basketball; also whistler. Chief Collabs: Leo Pearl, Billy Baskette, Bernard Bierman, Jack Manus, Jimmy Dale, Morrey Davidson, Buddy Fields. *Songs:* Blue Moments Without You Dear; Whistlin' Joe From Kokomo; Don't Say You're Sorry Again; With the Help of the Lord; A Whistle and a Prayer; Midnight Masquerade; Symphony of Spring; The Scissors Grinder's Serenade; More Than Anything Else in the World; Suzanne; It'll Take a Little Time.

BERMAN, EDWARD

ASCAP 1952

composer, author, publisher

b Philadelphia, Pa, Apr 20, 11. Educ: Charles Morris Price Sch Jour. Guest prof marketing & business admin, La Salle Col, Philadelphia. Newspaper reporter, advert exec, film reviewer, music critic; later bus exec for nat firms. Aerial, motion picture & combat photographer, USN, WW II. Consult & pub rel writer. Lectr, mag & newsletter writer. Photography has appeared in Holiday Mag & bk "Toots," newspapers, mag & others. Chief Collabs: Fred Hall, Carol Loveday, Pasquale DiIrio. *Songs:* Main Street, USA; Slantawallaga (Here's to

Your Health); Little Leaguers of America; What Are We Gonna Name the Baby?; Come and Live in My Heart; Everyday Is Tomorrow; Blue Cowboy; Don't Shaka Da Pinball (Shesa Tilt); Lyrics: Did I Do Wrong (When I Did Right By You).

BERMAN, NORMAN L   ASCAP 1977
composer
b Detroit, Mich, Mar 19, 49. Educ: NY Univ, Pace Col. Composer-in-residence, Circle Repertory, 72-, comp 13 scores incl premiere of "Battle of Angels", "Him" & "Hamlet." Incidental music scores incl productions at New York Shakespeare Fest, Arena Stage, etc. Co-comp, orchr & cond Bway musical "Strider." Musical consult, "By Bernstein," Chelsea Theater Ctr. Chief Collabr: Steve Brown. *Songs:* Music: Live Long Enough.

BERMONT, GEORGE J   ASCAP 1961
composer, teacher
b New York, NY. DeWitt Clinton High Sch; Columbia Univ; Philadelphia Cons; David Mannes Music Sch; studied piano with Kate Chittenden & Constantine Von Sternberg, harmony & theory with Joseph Gahm & Julius Vogler, improvization with Frederick Schlieder (organist), counterpoint & comp with Rosario Scalero. Dir music, Bronx Community Ctr. Ed, Musicord Publ, 53-74. Writer of many piano collections & educ piano pieces. *Instrumental Works:* Anyone Can Play Piano; Play Popular-Be Popular; Joy to the World; Make Mine Music (6 bks); Play That Tune (4 bks); Spell It With Music.

BERNARD, AL   ASCAP 1935
composer, author, actor
b New Orleans, La, Nov 23, 1888; d New York, NY, Mar 9, 49. Educ: Cath Schs. Appeared on radio, 23; wrote minstrel shows; made one of first sound film shorts. Writer & dir in early TV. Chief Collabr: J Russel Robinson. *Songs:* Let Me Be the First to Kiss You Good Morning; Sugar; Shake, Rattle and Roll; Read 'Em and Weep; Blue-Eyed Sally; Birmingham Papa; Twenty-Five Years From Now; I Got Horses and Got Numbers On My Mind; Pick That Bass; When Dixie Stars Are Playing Peek-a-Boo.

BERNARD, FELIX   ASCAP 1934
composer, conductor, pianist
b Brooklyn, NY, Apr 28, 1897; d Hollywood, Calif, Oct 20, 44. Educ: Rensselaer Polytech Inst, CE; early music educ with father. Professional pianist from childhood. Toured US, Orpheum Keith Vaudeville Circuits, also abroad. Pianist for music publ & in dance orchs; then formed own band. Wrote & produced 1 act musical comedies for vaudeville. Wrote special material for Sophie Tucker, Nora Bayes, Marilyn Miller, Al Jolson, Eddie Cantor. Music supvr, film co. Wrote, produced & acted in own radio show. Chief Collabrs: Johnny Black, Richard Smith, L Wolfe Gilbert, Sam Coslow. *Songs:* Winter Wonderland; Dardanella; The Whistlin' Cowboy; You Opened My Eyes; Cutest Kid in Town; Jane; Tom Thumb and Tiny Teena; What Am I Goin' to Do For Lovin'?; The Mailman's Got My Letter; Painter in the Sky; Twenty One Dollars a Day Once a Month; I'd Rather Be Me; Wanderers.

BERNDT, JULIA HELEN (BONNIE B KING)   ASCAP 1963
composer, author
b Union City, NJ, July 14, 05. Educ: Primary study. Vocalist with husband's band, 20's. Lyric writer, 15 yrs. Chief Collabr: L Leslie Loth. *Songs & Instrumental Works:* Love Just Laughed at Me Again; Gracie, Gracie; I'm So in Love With You; Sleigh Bells; The Sky! (mixed voices); Heavenly Father I Thank Thee (choral arr); Woman of Destiny; Chee Chee-Fairy Tale With Music; It's Just a Crazy Dream.

BERNEY, BERYL   ASCAP 1963
composer, author, actor
b New York, NY. Educ: Pa State Univ; Columbia Univ. Packager, writer & performer, "All Join Hands," TV. Made many children's records. *Songs:* All Join Hands.

BERNHARD, FRANK JAMES, (JR)   ASCAP 1979
author
b Beaumont, Tex, Oct 20, 37. Educ: Lamar High Sch, Houston, Tex, dipl, 55; Rice Inst, BA in hist, summa cum laude, 59; Univ Birmingham, Eng, MA in Eng literature, 61. Actor, 59-; asst city ed & drama critic, Houston Press, 61-62; asst prof Eng, Muhlenberg Col, Pa, 62-64; drama critic, Tex Cath Herald, 64-66; asst mgr, Commercial Letter Serv, 64-68; playwright & lyricist, 69-; gen mgr, Soc Performing Arts, Houston, 70-78; arts management consult, 78- Mem: Phi Beta Kappa; Int Soc Performing Arts Adminr (pres, 68); Actors Equity Asn. Chief Collabrs: Ned Battista, Mark Holden. *Scores:* Bway Shows: Scrooge; Sir Jack!

BERNHART, MARTHA ANN (MARTIE HUBBLE)   ASCAP 1958
composer, author
b Pomona, Calif, Sept 28, 22. Educ: Studied voice with Ralph Thomas, 37-39; Pomona Col, BA(music), 43, studied voice with Ralph Lyman; studied voice with Richard Cummings, 44-46. Proofread radio scripts, programmed records & cleared music for legal purposes, CBS, Hollywood, 43-44. Managed music clearance dept for all Hollywood-originated radio & TV progs, Blue Network/ABC, 44-56. Secy to Walter Schumann, 56-58. Sang in girls' quartets & mixed choruses. Vocal arr, songwriter & pianist. Chief Collabr: Milton

William Raskin. *Songs:* I'll Be There; Lift Up Your Voice, America! (chorus & narrator).

BERNIE, BEN   ASCAP 1934
composer, author, violinist
b New York, NY, May 30, 1891; d Beverly Hills, Calif, Oct 20, 43. Educ: New York Col Music; City Col New York; Columbia Sch of Mines. Organized own orch, 22. Featured with Maurice Chevalier. Featured on radio, 20 yrs. Chief Collabrs: Kenneth Casey, Al Goering, Walter Hirsch, Maceo Pinkard. *Songs:* Who's Your Little Whoosis?; I Can't Believe It's True; Holding My Honey's Hand; A Bowl of Chop Suey and Youey; After the Dance Was Over; Was Last Night the Last Night?; Ain't That Marvelous (My Baby Loves Me); I Can't Forget That You Forgot About Me; Strange Interlude; Sweet Georgia Brown.

BERNIER, BUDDY   ASCAP 1938
composer
b Watertown, NY, Apr 21, 10. *Songs:* Lyrics: Poinciana; Our Love; The Night Has a Thousand Eyes; The Big Apple; Hurry Home; This Time It's Real; Bamboo; Tomorrow for Sure; And So Goodbye.

BERNIKOFF, MORRIS (BERNARD MORRIS)   ASCAP 1973
author, teacher
b New York, NY, Oct 5, 20. Educ: Boys High Sch; Brooklyn Acad; Pace Univ, BBA, 50; US Sch Music, studied drumming; studied music theory, pvt & pub schs, incl WPA Sch, 30-38. Asst cond to Luis Ceccanti, Viennese Ens. Actor, "Death Takes a Holiday", Willet Stock Co. Music teacher, Sterling Island, Solomon Islands, WW II. Playwright, "Echoes of Freedom." Wrote lyrics, "Speak of the Devil." Collab on show & pop tunes. Author self-teaching music manuals: "Morrie Method of Elementary Music Theory"; "Morrie Method of Linear Solfege"; "Morrie Method of Triad Solfege." Chief Collabrs: J Gordon Danel, Van King, Emmanuel Caldwell, Paul Nichols. *Songs:* Lyrics: Love Is Like a Little Child; Honey, I Don't Know. Do You?; Where Is She?; A Yellow Moon Sailing By; How Do You Feel When You're Lonely?.

BERNS, LARRY   ASCAP 1962
composer, author
b Philadelphia, Pa, June 25, 08; d. Educ: Univ of Pa, BS.

BERNSTEIN, ALAN K
author
b New York, NY, Oct 26, 37; d New York, May 1, 78. Chief Collabr: Richie Adams. *Songs:* Lyrics: After the Lovin'; This Moment in Time; Yellow Days.

BERNSTEIN, CHARLES HARRY   ASCAP 1969
composer, author
b Minneapolis, Minn, Feb 28, 43. Educ: Los Angeles City Col, AA, cum laude, 63; Juilliard Sch Music, 63-64; Univ Calif Los Angeles, BA, 66, Woodrow Wilson Nat Fel & Chancellor's Teaching Fel; studied with Roy Harris, 66-69. Began career in musical theater, Los Angeles & NY. Scored feature films & movies for TV incl many songs as lyricist, composer & producer. *Songs:* These Moments; Foolin' Around; Fly by Night; Dancin' Through the Night. *Scores:* Films: Foolin' Around; Love at First Bite; Gator; Outlaw Blues; Mr Majestyk; White Lightning; TV Films: Scruples; Bogie; The House on Garibaldi Street; The Women at West Point; The Winds of Kitty Hawk; Look What's Happened to Rosemary's Baby; Documentary Films: Czechoslovakia 1968 (Acad Award); Sautine (First Place, Venice Film Fest).

BERNSTEIN, ELMER   ASCAP 1954
composer, conductor
b New York, NY, Apr 4, 22. Educ: Walden Sch; NY Univ; Juilliard Sch Music; studied with Roger Sessions. In USAF, WW II. *Songs:* Walk on the Wild Side; Love With the Proper Stranger; To Kill a Mockingbird; The Sons of Katie Elder; Baby, the Rain Must Fall. *Instrumental Works:* Serenade for Solo Violin, String Orchestra, Harp and Percussion. *Scores:* Film Background: The Man With the Golden Arm; The Ten Commandments; Sweet Smell of Success; Desire Under the Elms; God's Little Acre; Kings Go Forth; Some Came Running; From the Terrace; The Magnificent Seven; Summer and Smoke; To Kill a Mockingbird; Walk on the Wild Side; Hud; Love With the Proper Stranger; The Great Escape; The Carpetbaggers; Four Days in November; Baby, The Rain Must Fall; The Caretakers; The Sons of Katie Elder; The Hallelujah Trail; 7 Women; The Silencers; Cast a Giant Shadow; Hawaii; TV Backgound: The Making of the President (Emmy Award, 64).

BERNSTEIN, LEONARD   ASCAP 1944
conductor, pianist, composer
b Lawrence, Mass, Aug 25, 18. Educ: Harvard Univ, AB(cum laude), 39; Curtis Inst Music, grad, 41; studied conducting with Fritz Reiner & Serge Koussevitzky; studied piano with Helen Coates, Heinrich Gebhard & Isabella Vengerova; numerous hon degrees from var cols & univs. Asst to Serge Koussevitzky, Berkshire Music Ctr, 42, mem fac, 48-55, head conducting dept, 51-55; prof music, Brandeis Univ, 51-56; Charles Elliot Norton prof poetry, Harvard Univ, 72-73. Asst cond, NY Philh, 43-44, co-cond with Dimitri Mitropoulas, 57-58, music dir, 58-69, app Laureate Cond, 69- Cond, New York Symph, 45-48; frequent cond, Israel Philh Orch, 47-, music adv, 48-49; cond major orchs of US on Europ Tours, 46-; cond, Metrop Opera, La Scala, Milan,

Metrop Opera, New York & Vienna State Opera; shared transcontinental tour in US with Serge Koussevitzky & Israel Philh, 51; toured Europe with Vienna Philh Orch, 70; Gala Bicentennial Tour of Am & Europe with NY Philh, 76; Leonard Bernstein's 60th Birthday Celebration Concert, given by Nat Symph Orch at Wolf Trap Farm Park for Performing Arts, Vienna, Va, 78; at invitation of President Carter, led Orquesta Filarmonica de la Ciudad de Mex, 79. Recipient Emmy Awards for Young People's Concerts, 60 & for Outstanding classical music prog, "Leonard Bernstein and the New York Philharmonic," 76; Handel Medallion, 77. Author: "The Joy of Music," 59 (Christopher Award); "Leonard Bernstein's Young People's Concerts for Reading and Listening," 62, rev ed, 70; "The Infinite Variety of Music," 66; "The Unanswered Question: Six Talks at Harvard," 76. *Songs & Instrumental Works:* Clarinet Sonata; Seven Anniversaries for Piano; I Hate Music (song cycle); Four Anniversaries for Piano; La Bonne Cuisine (song cycle); Symphony No 2, The Age of Anxiety (piano & orch); Trouble in Tahiti (one act opera; also wrote libretto); Symphony No 3, Kaddish; Chichester Psalms (mixed chorus, boys' choir, orch); Serenade (violin & string orch with perc); Five Anniversaries for Piano; Mass (theatre piece for singers, players & dancers); Dybbuk Variations, Suites No 1 & 2 (from ballet by Jerome Robbins); Songfest (song cycle); Slava! (overture for orch); Three Meditations From Mass (cello & orch); Songs: Afterthought; Silhouette; Two Love Songs. *Scores:* Ballet: Fancy Free; Facsimile; Dybbuk; Musical Show: On the Town; Bway Musicals: Wonderful Town; Candide; West Side Story; Incidental Music: Peter Pan; The Lark; Film: On the Waterfront.

BERNSTEIN, MORRIS (MOREY)   ASCAP 1958
composer, author
b Capuline, Colo, Feb 29, 16. Began writing music & lyrics, 32. Owner, Finer Arts Records & Transworld Records. Wrote & recorded many songs. Writer, musical, "Israel Oh Israel." *Songs:* The Miracle of Life; Who Do We Turn To?; I Know When It's Raining; My People; Blow The Shofar Blow; Ho-Ree-Dee; I Hurt So Bad; Kol Yisrael; Mama Lights a Candle; Time Will Make My Hurt Go Away; Miracles and Dreams; Come Home; Shalom Shalom; A Handful of Dust; Lust for Gold; Shabbus Night; Debra; Free Life of a Whore; Once Was Enough for Me; The Soft Touch of You; Zelda; A Time in History; Stop; Beware My Love.

BERNSTEIN, SEYMOUR ABRAHAM   ASCAP 1975
composer, author, teacher
b Newark, NJ, Apr 24, 27. Educ: Mannes Col, 48; Juilliard, 49; Premier Prix de Piano, Fontainebleau, France, 53; studied with Alexander Brailowsky, Nadia Boulanger, Georges Enesco, Clifford Curzon. NY debut, 54. Tours, Southeast Asia, Far East, Europe, North & South Am. Mem of Philomusica Ens & Alsop-Bernstein Trio. Debut with Chicago Symph, 69. Grants & Awards: Nat Fedn Music Clubs Award; Beebe Found grant; 2 Martha Baird Rockefeller grants; ASCAP Award, 79; 4 State Dept grants. *Instrumental Works:* Birds (bks 1 & 2); Concerto for Our Time; Insects (bks 1 & 2); Raccoons (bks 1 & 2); Earth Music Series (bks 1-5); New Pictures at an Exhibition; Toccata Francaise.

BERNSTEIN, SYLVIA   ASCAP 1958
composer, author
b Milwaukee, Wis, Apr 5, 24. Educ: High sch. Short story writer & newspaper ed. Chief Collabr: Seymour Lefco. *Songs:* My Kindergarten Hero.

BERQUIST, BERNARD H (WHITEY)   ASCAP 1945
composer, author
b Wasco, Ill, Mar 19, 03; d Hollywood, Fla, Jan 13, 62. Educ: Studied with Leo Sowerby. Joined NBC staff, Chicago, 28. *Songs:* Blue Interlude; Your Caress; It Won't Be Long; Memory Time; On the Bridge of Marco Polo; If You Only Knew; Musicana; Cozy; Gypsy Nights.

BERRY, FRANK JOSEPH   ASCAP 1979
composer, arranger, teacher
b Teaneck, NJ, May 27, 53. Educ: San Diego State Univ, 71-72; Calif State Univ, Fullerton, 72-75; studied with Roger Bobo & Jeffrey Reynolds, Los Angeles & with Edward Kleinhammer & Arnold Jacobs, Chicago. Performed with: Bellflower Symph Orch, 72-73; Los Angeles Debut Orch, 74-77; Los Angeles Philh Chamber Orch, 77; Lakewood Philh, 76-79; Disneyland musician, 76-80. Gong Show winner, 77, casted in "The Gong Show Movie," 80. Taught: Elem & jr high sch in Anaheim, Calif; clinics, sectionals & rehearsals at Arcadia, Loara, Los Altos, El Dorado & Sunny Hills high schs. *Instrumental Works:* Fugue in G minor (J S Bach, arr); Tublues; Bagatelle (Beethoven, arr); Barnum & Bailey's Favorite (King, arr) Commedian's Gallop (Kabelevsky, arr).

BERRY, HESTER ELIZABETH (BETTY)   ASCAP 1973
composer, singer, teacher
b Denver, Colo, May 15, 29. Educ: Col Music of Cincinnati; Univ Cincinnati, BS; Columbia Univ. With WCPO TV & Duke Ellington Sacred Concerts. Chief Collabr: Jane Jarvis. *Songs:* Music: Worry Woods.

BERRY, WALLACE   ASCAP 1968
composer, author, educator
b La Crosse, Wis, Jan 10, 28. Educ: Univ Southern Calif, PhD, 56, studied comp with Halsey Stevens; Nat Cons of Paris, studied with Nadia Boulanger, 53-54. Theorist & pianist. Author, "Form in Music" & "Structural Functions in Music"; contributor, Musical Quart & Jour of Music Theory; contributor & mem of Ed Bd, Perspectives of New Music. Founding officer, Soc for Music Theory. Cited by Am Acad-Inst of Arts & Letters for award in comp, 78. *Instrumental Works:* Duo for Violin and Piano; Five Pieces for Small Orchestra;

Concerto for Piano and Orchestra; String Quartet No 2; Canto Lirico for Viola and Piano; Fantasy in Five Statements for Clarinet and Piano; Duo for Flute and Piano; Fantasy for Organ on Von Himmel Hoch; Trio for Piano, Violin and Cello; Sonata for Piano; Intonation (Victimis hominum inhumanitatis, in memoriam, for orch); Acadian Images; Two Movements for Orchestra; Of the Changeless Night and the Stark Ranges of Nothing (mezzo-soprano, piano & cello; on text by Earle Birney).

BERRY, WILLIAM RICHARD   ASCAP 1968
composer, trumpeter, arranger
b Benton Harbor, Mich, Sept 14, 30. Educ: Col Music of Cincinnati; Berklee Sch Music, Boston. With Woody Herman, Maynard Ferguson & Duke Ellington Orchs; staff, NBC & CBS. Records with most important jazz artists. *Songs:* Music: Sho; Betty; Bloose; The Bink/And How; Chained.

BERTONCINI, GENE   ASCAP 1967
guitarist, teacher
b New York, NY, Apr 6, 37. Univ Notre Dame, BArch; studied with Johnny Smith, Chuck Wayne, Albert Valdez Blaine, Leonide Bolotine & Helen Hobbs Jordan. Performer, cols & clubs. Staff musician, "Tonight Show", NBC & "Merv Griffin." Played with Michael Legrand, Gerry Mulligan & Buddy Rich. Teacher, Eastman Sch Music & New Eng Cons. *Songs:* Music: You Are a Story. *Instrumental Works:* Preachmenship.

BERTRAM, ROBERT FLETCHER   ASCAP 1959
composer, author, publisher
b Sharon, Mass, Apr 30, 16. Educ: Col jour; Anglo-Am Inst Drugless Therapy, naturopathic physician. Commercial art studio, 32; painted portrait of Franklin Delano Roosevelt for the White House. AUS press cameraman & aerial photographer in 5th Air Force. Newspaper ed. Recording artist, Ode Records. Record producer, Int, Dot, Liberty & Polynesian. Performed on stage, radio & TV. Musician; writer & producer radio commercials; author several bks incl "How Loud Can I Scream!"; health lectr; runs mail order business. *Songs:* My Girl; Song of America; Billy; Honey Coated Lips; A Christmas Aloha for You; Mr Imagination; Welcome Home Elvis; Poppa's Gone; Give the Reins to the Lord; Hula Rock 'N Roll; Silver Coin; The One They Call Fradelle; My Pride Got in the Way; Marine's Rock. *Scores:* Film/TV: Pete's Pad.

BERWALD, WILLIAM   ASCAP 1941
composer, conductor
b Schwerin, Mecklenberg, Ger, Dec 26, 1864; d Loma Linda, Calif, May 8, 48. Educ: Studied with Joseph Rheinberger, Immanuel Faisst; Syracuse Univ, MM, MusD. Dir, Philh Soc, Librau, Russia, 1888-92. Head of music theory dept, Syracuse Univ, 1892-1945. Cond, Syracuse Symph, 21-24. Winner organ & orch comp contest, Nat Asn Organists, 28. *Songs & Instrumental Works:* Quintet for Piano, Strings (Philadelphia MS Soc prize); Utopia (musical drama); Dramatic Overture; Walthari; Symphonic Legend; Eros and Psyche; Prelude and Fugue; Scherzo Fantastique; Violin Sonata; Choral: The Way of the Cross; Seven Last Words of Christ; Crucifixion and Resurrection; From Old Japan; The Voice of Fate; Fair California.

BESSE, ROBERT JOHN   ASCAP 1961
composer, author
b Butternut, Wis, Dec 19, 20. *Songs:* Eventide; Look to the Mountain; Just Passing Thru.

BESSIRE, ANTONY GLENN   ASCAP 1978
composer, singer
b Garden City, Kans, Mar 24, 49. Educ: Ft Hays Kans State Col, BS. Songwriter & singer in Nashville. Chief Collabrs: Jake Brooks, Chip Hardy.

BESTOR, DON   ASCAP 1941
composer, conductor, pianist
b Langford, SDak, Sept 23, 1889; d Metamora, Ill, Jan 13, 70. Pianist in vaudeville; organized own orch playing hotels, nightclubs, ballrooms, theatres, radio. Music dir, Jack Benny radio prog, then WHN, New York. Chief Collabrs: Art Kassel, Gus Kahn, Roy Turk. *Songs:* Doodle Doo Doo; Down by the Winegar Woiks; Teach Me to Smile; The Whole World is Dreaming of Love; Gee But I Hate to Say Goodnight; Contented; You're a Darling; I'm Not Forgetting; It's Always Raining on Me; Babe and Me; J-E-L-L-O (commercial); Music: Night in Spain. *Instrumental Works:* Crow in a Cornfield; First Love.

BETZNER, JOHN FRED   ASCAP 1942
composer, author, conductor
b Newark, NJ, Mar 16, 08. Educ: Madison High; music self-taught; piano studies, 2 yrs. Pianist saloons & hotels; led own orch hotels & supper clubs; retired, 71. Chief Collabrs: Charlie O'Flynn, Bob Godfrey, Dick Sanford, Lou Perry, Joe Davis. *Songs & Instrumental Works:* Gypsy Violin; Ophelia; Gambler in Hearts; I'll Meet You at Sundown; Little Americans; Ho-Ho-Hokus Polka; Back in Dad and Mother's Day; There's Something I Like About B'way; We Kinda Miss Those Good Ol' Songs; Barbershop Strut; I Wonder What Happened (To That Old Quartette of Mine); Lil.

BEVEL, CHARLES WILLIAM (MISSISSIPPI)   ASCAP 1973
    composer, author, singer
b Swifton, Miss, Dec 7, 38. Educ: San Diego Evening High Sch; San Diego City Col. Singer, clubs, concerts, TV; recording artist, A & M Records. Chief Collabr: Chic Streetman. *Songs:* Overheard; You've Got the Power; Keep on Stepping; Making a Decision; Sally B White.

BEVERIDGE, THOMAS GATTRELL   ASCAP 1960
    composer
b New York, NY, Apr 6, 38. Educ: Harvard Col, BA, 59, Longy Sch Music, soloist dipl, 61; Fontainebleau Cons, comp study with Walter Piston & Nadia Boulanger. Prof singer. Comp songs, symph, many chamber works for solo instruments & piano. Choral music extensively performed. Coolidge Found Comn. *Songs & Instrumental Works:* Once: In Memory Martin Luther King (cantata); Odysseus; Leaves of Grass (20 songs); Symphony No 2 (To the Masters; chamber orch); Symphony of Peace (chorus & orch). *Scores:* Ballet: Krishna and the Gopi Maidens: the Dance of Celestial Love.

BEVERSDORF, SAMUEL THOMAS   ASCAP 1965
    composer, librettist
b Yoakum, Tex, Aug 8, 24. Educ: Univ Tex, Hoblitzel fel, BMus(cum laude), 45; Eastman Sch Music, Univ Rochester, MMus, 46; Danforth fel, DMA, 59. First trombonist, Houston Symph Orch, 46-48, resident comp, 46-48. Instr music comp, Univ Houston, 46-48. Bass Trombonist, Pittsburgh Symph Orch, 48-49. Mem fac, Ind Univ Sch Music, Bloomington, 51-, prof music comp, 64- Comp-in-residence, Bucknell Univ, Lewisburg, Pa, 70-71. Guest cond, Indianapolis Symph Orch, 51, Houston Symph, 53 & Eastman-Rochester Summer Symph Orch, 57. Chief Collabr: John Wheatcroft. *Instrumental Works:* Christmas (sonata; horn & piano); Suite on Baroque Themes for Clarinet, Violincello, Piano; Cathedral Music for Brass Quartet and Organ; Quartet No 1 (strings); Symphony No 3 for Winds and Percussion; Three Epitaphs (in memory of Eric DeLamarter; brass quartet); Three Songs (poems of E E Cummings; soprano & piano); Sonata for Tuba and Piano; A Pretty Maid (theme & variations; piano); Sonata for Trumpet and Piano; Sonata for Violin and Piano; Sonata for Flute and Piano; Sonata for Violoncello and Piano; Divertimento Da Camera (flute, piccolo, oboe, Eng horn, double bass & harpsichord); 3 fold Amen, 4 fold Amen for Chorus; Mini Motel (SATB; soprano solo, baritone solo, organ); Vision of Christ, a 20th Century Mystery Play; Seven Short Piano Pieces; Concerto for Tuba and Orchestral Winds; La Petite Exposition (solo violin or solo clarinet and eleven strings); Sonata for Violin and Harp; Hymns of Praise and Thanksgiving (3 anthems; chorus); Cathedral Music (brass choir); Quartet No 2 (strings); Symphony No 4 (orch); Corelliana Variations (trio for flutes & violoncello or violins & violoncello); Concerto for Two Pianos and Orchestra.

BEY, MICKEY
    See Gray Bey, Michael Ashley

BEYER, HOWARD GEORGE   ASCAP 1929
    composer, performer, singer
b Chicago, Ill, Mar 25, 29. Educ: Am Cons Music, Chicago, BA(piano), MA(comp). Pianist for Carol Lawrence, Johnny Desmond, Four Lads, Jimmy Durante & Harmonicats Shows & var touring & local dance orchs. Also orchestrator. *Songs & Instrumental Works:* Romance on the Road.

BIALOSKY, MARSHALL H   ASCAP 1974
    composer, teacher
b Cleveland, Ohio, Oct 30, 23. Educ: Converse Col, SC, 42-43, 46; Syracuse Univ, BMus, cum laude, 49; Northwestern Univ, MMus, 50; Tanglewood, summer 52; comp studies with Lionel Nowak, Luigi Dallapiccola, Roy Harris, Ernst Bacon & Robert Delaney. Asst prof music, Milton Col, Wis, 50-54, asst cond, Milton Col Band, one yr; asst prof humanities & music, Univ Chicago, 56-61; assoc prof music & humanities & cond univ chorale, State Univ NY, Stony Brook, 61-64; prof & chmn dept fine arts, Calif State Univ, Dominguez Hills, 64-77, chmn dept music, 77-78, prof dept music, 78- *Songs & Instrumental Works:* Two Movements for Brass Trio; There Is a Wisdom That is Woe (choral); A Song of Degrees (choral); A Spring Song (piano); An Old Picture (vocal); Five Western Scenes (piano); Of Music and Musicians (choral); Be Music, Night (choral); Suite for Flute, Oboe and Clarinet; Fantasy Scherzo for Saxophone and Piano; Two Voices in a Meadow (voice & viola); Little Ghost Things (choral); Six Riddles from Symphosius (voice & instruments); Sonatina for Oboe and Piano; Three Canzonets (choral); Two Movements for String Quartet and Piano; Sonata for Solo Violin; Fantasy for Solo Cello; The Engagement (choral); Seven Academic Graffiti (choral); Starting Over (solo flute); Variations on An Elizabethan Lute Theme (3 recorders); Pastoral (with dark edges, solo viola); At Last (choral); A Spell Before Winter (choral); Guitarondo (solo guitar); Three Movements for Piano; Suite for Unaccompanied Cello; Constantly Bending (solo recorder or oboe); A Fanfare for DH (brass instruments & perc); A Christmas Hymn (voice & instruments); The Tree, The Bird (choral); Three Mysteries of Emily Dickinson (voice & Eng horn); Two Songs to Poems of Richard Wilbur (voice & Eng horn); American Poets Suite (choral); Two Songs to American Indian Poems (choral).

BIANCO, ROBERT   ASCAP 1959
    composer, author, guitarist
b Mt Vernon, NY, Oct 7, 34. Educ: Pvt schs. Singer & guitarist in jazz bands; also teacher of comp & arr.

BIBO, IRVING   ASCAP 1920
    composer, author, publisher
b San Francisco, Calif, Aug 22, 1889; d West Los Angeles, Calif, May 2, 62. Founded own publ firm. Wrote songs for Bway musicals & films; also USO acts for Marlene Dietrich, Billy Gilbert, Jim Burke & Ann Sheridan. Mem, Am Guild Authors & Composers; dir, ASCAP, 24-27. Chief Collabrs: Al Piantadosi, Leo Woods, Don R George. *Songs:* Good Night Waltz; Sweet Little You; My Man; Cherie; Am I Wasting My Time on You?; Forever and a Day; My Annapolis and You; Where Are You, Girl of My Dreams?; Do You Believe in Dreams?; Huggable Kissable You; Old Man Atom; All Things Are Passing; Ain't Nature Grand?; Sousa's March of the Blues; The Stanford Scalp Song; Sing UCLA; Fight on for Michigan State; March on America (Freedoms Found Award).

BICKELHAUPT, WILLIAM EDWARD   ASCAP 1975
    composer, producer, arranger
b St Louis, Mo, Feb 11, 52. Educ: Horton Watkins High Sch, 70; Webster Col, BMus(piano), 74; piano master class with Jules Gentil, Ecole Normale, Paris. Pianist & arr (predominantly recording), St Louis, 68-75 & Los Angeles, 75- Musical dir recording group, The Montclairs, 71-73; independent contractor for var recording labels; did extensive arr & co-production work with: High Inergy; Major Lance; Helen Sexton. *Songs:* Think (About the Love We Had); (I) Didn't Wanna Tell You; Last Precious Moments; Once Again; Lovelight.

BIDEU, LOU
    See Bedell, Lew

BIELAWA, HERBERT WALTER   ASCAP 1974
    author
b Chicago, Ill, Feb 3, 30. Educ: Univ Ill, BM, MM, BA, studies with Gordon Binkerd & Burrill Phillips; Univ Southern Cal, DMA, studies with Ingolf Dahl & Halsey Stevens; Aspen, studies with Milhaud, Carter, Sessions & Foss. Ingram-Merrill Prize in comp, 58. Composer-in-residence, Spring Branch Sch Dist, Houston, 64-66 & San Francisco Summer Music Workshop, 76. Fac mem, San Francisco State Univ, 66-, founder & dir, Electronic Music Studio & Pro Musica Nova. Regular appearances as pianist performing contemporary music. Chief Collabrs: Warren Kliewer, Ruth Langridge. *Songs:* Music: An Emily Dickinson Album (choir, piano, tape & guitar); Eight Antiphons. *Instrumental Works:* Spectrum (band & tape); Quodlibet SF 42569 (organ & tape); Concerto (organ, strings & timpani); Warp (piano & flute). *Scores:* A Bird in the Bush (chamber opera in one act).

BIERBOWER, ELSIE (ELSIE JANIS)   ASCAP 1914
    author, actress
b Columbus, Ohio, Mar 16, 1889; d Los Angeles, Calif, Feb 26, 1956. Charter mem, ASCAP. Appeared in vaudeville as Little Elsie as child. Actress, Bway musicals incl "The Vanderbilt Cup", "The Hoyden", "The Fair Co-ed", "The Slim Princess" & "The Lady of the Slipper." London debut, 14; first Am to entertain Am Expeditionary Force, World War I. Co-author & producer, musical "Elsie Janis and Her Gang." Paris debut, 21; in concert throughout US, 23-25. Writer, producer & supvr, films incl "Close Harmony." Author, "Love Letters of an Actress", "A Star for a Night", "The Big Show" & autobiography "So Far So Good." Chief Collabrs: Jerome Kern, Edmund Goulding. *Songs:* Love, Your Magic Spell Is Everywhere; Any Time's the Time to Fall in Love; I'm True to the Navy Now; Live and Love Today; Molly-O-Mine; From the Valley; Your Eyes; Some Sort of Somebody; Oh, Give Me Time for Tenderness; A Little Love.

BIERMAN, BERNARD   ASCAP 1947
    composer, author
b New York, NY, Aug 26, 08. Educ: NY Univ; Brooklyn Law Sch, LLB. Practiced law, 32-42. US Army, WW II. Staff writer, Shapiro-Bernstein. Painting contractor. Chief Collabr: Jack Manus. *Songs:* Midnight Masquerade; My Cousin Louella; Vanity; Unless It Can Happen With You; This Is the Inside Story; Forgiving You; The Hills of Colorado; Too Many Kisses; Puppet on a String. *Instrumental Works:* The Love of Two Cabbages (operetta).

BIGARD, ALBANY LEON (BARNEY)   ASCAP 1958
    composer, clarinettist
b New Orleans, La, Mar 3, 06. Educ: Studied with Lorenzo Tio, New Orleans. With King Oliver, Chicago, 25-27, Duke Ellington Orch, 24-42, Freddie Slack, 42-44, Louis Armstrong All Stars, 47-61; had own combo, 44. Semi-retirement, 61; concert appearances, radio, TV & motion picture recordings, col lect & seminars with Leonard Feather, guest star appearances at jazz fests worldwide, 70's; col concert tour, Stars of Jazz, 72. Recipient, Esquire Mag Silver Esky award, 44-46. Elected to the Nat Acad Recording Arts & Sci Hall of Fame for comp, "Mood Indigo," this record by Duke Ellington won a Grammy Award. Chief Collabrs: Duke Ellington, Eddie Condon, Art Hodes, Wild Bill Davison. *Songs:* Music: Mood Indigo; Rockin in Rhythm; Steps Steps Up-Step Steps

Down; Clouds in My Heart; Minuet in Blues; Barney's Bounce; also many others.

BIGELOW, ROBERT WILCOX   ASCAP 1955
composer, pianist
b New Britain, Conn, Apr 17, 1890; d New Rochelle, NY, May 2, 65. Mem piano act, Bigelow & Campbell, in vaudeville 14 yrs. Pianist with Larry Lee in nightclubs, 23; with Texas Guinan, 3 yrs & Stork Club, 2 yrs. Wrote spec material. *Songs:* Hard-Hearted Hannah; Sob Sister Sadie; Take Your Sunkist Oranges.

BIGGERS, W WATTS   ASCAP 1963
composer, author
b Atlanta, Ga. Educ: Emory Univ. Advert account exec, Dancer, Fitzgerald & Sample, New York. Partner, Total TV Productions, Inc, New York; produced & created TV cartoons; in advert & promotion for NBC, 78- Associated with Harwichport Music Co, New York. Chief Collabrs: Tread Covington, Joe Harris, Chet Stover. *Songs:* Tennessee Tuxedo and His Tales; Underdog; The Beagles. *Scores:* TV Cartoon Series: King Leonardo and His Short Subjects.

BIGGS, JAMES THERAN   ASCAP 1972
author
b Richwood, Ohio, Aug 3, 06. Educ: Cent High Sch, Columbus, Ohio; Univ Md. Radio & telegraph operator, WVZ radio sta, USA; Master Sergeant, USAF, retired after 21 yrs; WW II Vet; Fed Civil Service, retired after 24 yrs. Author, "Soldier's Creed" on bronze plaques & publ in Congressional Record, 52; author & publ, "My Scrapbook of Poems and Lyrics." Chief Collab: George Liberace. *Songs:* Playing Peek-A-Boo (With You and the Moon); The Owl Serenade; Lyrics: Starvin' for Love; Passport to Heaven; Pontiac for Two.

BIGGS, JOHN JOSEPH   ASCAP 1967
composer
b Los Angeles, Calif, Oct 18, 32. Educ: Univ Calif Los Angeles; Univ Southern Calif; Royal Flemish Acad, Belg; studies with Roy Harris, Lukas Foss, Flor Peeters & Halsey Stevens. Violin Scholarship, age 7; piano studies, ages 10-15; bassoon studies in col. Founder/dir, John Biggs Consortium. Composer-in-residence, Kans State Teachers Col, 67-70. Music for instruments, voice, choir, orch, dancers & films. *Songs:* Train; Auction Cries. *Instrumental Works:* Variations on a Theme of Shostakovich; Concerto (viola, woodwinds & perc); Invention (viola & tape).

BIGGS, RICHARD KEYS   ASCAP 1953
composer, organist, conductor
b Glendale, Ohio, Sept 16, 1886; d Hollywood, Calif, Dec 17, 62. Educ: Cincinnati Col Music; Univ Mich; hon MusD, Loyola Univ. Instr, Univ Mich. Made first commercial organ recording for Victor, 15. Solo organist, San Diego Exposition, also San Francisco World's Fair, 15. Cond boys' choir, Madison Ave Synagogue & St Luke's Episcopal Church, New York. World War I, US Naval Hosp Unit. Established boys' choir, Queen of All Saints Church, Brooklyn, then St Patrick's, Montreal. Became music dir, Blessed Sacrament Church, Hollywood & St Paul's Church, Los Angeles, 28. Cond 4 boy choirs & high sch choral groups. Taught at Mt St Mary & Immaculate Heart Cols. Recorded for Columbia & Capitol. Honored by Pope with medal, Pro Ecclesia et Pontifice. *Instrumental Works:* Sunset Meditation; Queen of All Saints; Saint Ambrose; In Te Speravi; Out Lady of Lourdes; St Joseph the Worker; also 16 masses, 5 hymns, 11 motets, 7 organ pieces.

BIG TINY LITTLE
See Little, Dudley Richard

BILBY, HELEN OWEN   ASCAP 1960
composer
b Miami, Fla, July 22, 28. Educ: Col. Has written songs for Hildegarde; scores for children's musicals.

BILCHICK, RUTH COLEMAN   ASCAP 1972
composer, author, educator
b New York, NY, May 16, 04. Educ: Mannes Sch, studied theory & ear training with Angela Diller, piano with Elizabeth Quaile; Diller-Quaile Sch, 16-23. Columbia Univ, studied orch & advanced comp with Seth Bingham, 22-26, Teachers Col, grad courses in music educ; Barnard Col, BA, 26; Juilliard, studied advanced comp with Howard Brockway, orch with Adolph Schmidt; Comp Fel, Ernst Toch, 34-35. Mem music fac & publicity dir, High Sch Music & Art, New York. Singer & pianist on radio. Compiled & revised, "Barnard College Song Book." Chief Collabr: Sigmund Spaeth. *Songs & Instrumental Works:* Moods (symphonic band); American Holiday (symphonic band); Fifth Avenue Suite (symph orch); Shepherds Were Watching (Old Bohemian Carol; SSA with piano or organ); A Garden of Verses (SSA); Elizabethan Lyric (SATB); Little Trio (violin, cello, piano); Bourree (string quartet); Dreaming (flute solo); Little Romanza (piano); Caprice (piano); Letter to a Police Car Siren; Hope and Fear; Song of Songs (Biblical text); Orpheus and Eurydice; Crabbed Age and Youth; Song Cycle for the Young; Bed in Summer.

BILDER, ROBERT M   ASCAP 1952
composer, author
b Newark, NJ, Mar 14, 11; d Mountainside, NJ, June 9, 61. Educ: Choate Sch; Williams Col; Harvard Law Sch. WW II, Lt Comdr, USN. To Hollywood, 47; contract songwriter to film studio; later free-lance. Wrote songs for films incl "Rogues of Sherwood Forest"; "Shamrock Hill"; "There's a Girl In My Heart"; "Sweetheart of the Blues"; "Smoky Mountain Melody." Partner in law firm, 50. *Songs:* Take Me Down to the Sea; Keep Your Chin Up, Baby; Come, Sweet Lass; Party Time on the Prairie.

BILIK, JERRY H (WILLIAM GERRARD)   ASCAP 1959
composer, conductor, lecturer
b New Rochelle, NY, Oct 7, 33. Educ: Nat Music Camp, Interlochen, Mich; Univ Mich Sch of Music, BMus, 55, MMus, 60; studied with Tibor Serly. Arr, US Mil Band, West Point, then free-lance arr in New York. Prof music, Univ Mich & Wayne State Univ; music dir & cond, Jackson Symph Orch, Mich; free-lance comp, cond & arr, Los Angeles & guest lectr, cond throughout US. *Instrumental Works:* American Civil War Fantasy; Block M March; Symphony for Band; Concertino for Alto Saxophone; They Walked in Darkness.

BILLINGSLEY, DERRELL L (D S TODD)   ASCAP 1973
composer, author
b Prattville, Ala, Jan 23, 40. Educ: Troy State Col, BS; Southern Baptist Theol Sem, MCM; studied with J Phillip Landgrave. Minister of music, Fla, Miss & Tenn, 68-77; ed, The Music Leader, Music Time & Preschool Music Resource Kit, 77-; preschool music & literary design ed, Baptist Sunday Sch Bd, Broadman Press, Nashville, Tenn. Chief Collabrs: Veteria Billingsley, Betty Bedsole. *Songs:* Music: I Will Arise (SATB, anthem); Short Musical Dramas for Children; More Short Musical Dramas for Children; Stepping Stones to Matching Tones.

BILOTTI, ANTON   ASCAP 1936
composer, pianist
b New York, NY, Jan 17, 06; d New York, NY, Nov 10, 63. Educ: Royal Cons Naples, scholarship; DeRosay & MacJennet Schs, Paris; studied with Busoni, Vladimir de Pachmann, Leopold Godowsky, Maurice Ravel. Made piano debut, NY, 21; toured US & Europe. *Songs:* Lord I Call on Thee. *Instrumental Works:* Spanish Dance; two piano concertos; Tango Triste; Firefly; Violin Concerto; Saxophone Concerto; Suite for Band; Quintette for Piano, Strings; Suite for String Quartet; Suite for Flute, String Orchestra; Roman Suite.

BINDER, ABRAHAM WOLFE   ASCAP 1939
composer, conductor, educator
b New York, NY, Jan 13, 1895; d New York, Oct 9, 66. Educ: Columbia Univ, Mosenthal fel & BM; hon DHL; hon Mus Dir music, 92nd St YM & YWHA, cond of Choral Soc. Instr Jewish Lit Music, Hebrew Union Col-Jewish Inst Relig. Town Hall concert, 29. Guest cond, Manhattan Symph, Palestine Symph Ens. Vis prof, Union Theol Sem Sch of Sacred Music. Dir, Stephen Wise Free Synagogue; chmn, Jewish Music Forum, 39-43. Chmn comt sacred music, Nat Fedn Music Clubs. Founder Jewish Liturgical Music Soc Am, 63. Won Frank L Weil Award. Ed, New Palestine Folk Songs; Palestine in Song; Pioneer Songs of Palestine; Jewish section of Army and Navy Hymnal. Music ed, Union Hymnal (3rd ed). *Instrumental Works:* Concertino and Night Music for String Orch; Ha-Chalutzim Overture; Holy Land Impressions; Concertante; Israeli Suite; Poem of Freedom; Rhapsody (piano, orch); Lament (in memory of the defenders of the Warsaw Ghetto); Hibbath Shabbath; Evening Service for the New Year; Kabbalath Shabbath; Amos on Times Square; Israel Reborn (choral poem); Requiem Yiskor (oratorio); City of the Ages; The Time is Now.

BINDER, DAVE   ASCAP 1973
composer, author, musician
b London, Eng, Sept 13, 03. Educ: Trenton High Sch, NJ; Drexel Inst, Philadelphia, Pa. Reed instrumentalist; musical dir vaudeville & stage shows; comp score & produced "Village Vanities," 72, 73 & 74; cond dance orchs, NY & NJ; formed Jingle Jem Co to produce radio jingles for NY & NJ advert agencies. Chief Collabr: Carroll W Lucas. *Songs:* Count Your Blessings Every Day; Light a Candle in the Chapel; It's a Great Life; Whatcha Gonna Dream About Tonight?; Come Out o' That Dream; I Wanna Be Loved; Beyond Compare; Wherever You May Be Tonight; Music:There's No Feelin' Like That Old Feelin!; Darlin'; Singing Hosanas As I Fly; Whispering Wind.

BINER, FRANK   ASCAP 1976
composer, author, vocalist
b Milwaukee, Wis, June 26, 50. Educ: Self-taught. Began career with The Little Boy Blues, Chicago, 67; moved to San Francisco, 71 and worked with Mike Bloomfield & var other bands. Guitarist. Chief Collabrs: Steve Kupka, Emilio Castillo, Alicia & Danny Daniels. *Songs:* You're So Wonderful, So Marvelous; Just Enough and Too Much; If I Play My Cards Right, It's So Nice (Like Paradise); Because I Think the World of You. *Songs & Instrumental Works:* Just As Long As We Have Each Other; My Lady Is My Music.

BINGHAM, SETH   ASCAP 1952
composer, author, conductor
b Bloomfield, NJ, Apr 16, 1882; d New York, NY, June 21, 72. Educ: Yale Univ, BA & BM; studied with Widor. Cond, first New York performances, Bach's St

John Passion, 18 & Faure's Requiem, 26. Assoc music prof, Columbia Univ. Instr, Sch Sacred Music Union Theol Sem. Organist-music dir, Madison Ave Presby Church, New York. Lectr on organ music. *Songs & Instrumental Works:* Wilderness Stone (chorus, orch, narr); Canticle of the Sun (chorus, orch); Baroques (organ); Roulade (organ); Concerto for Brass, Organ; Utqueant Laxis Opus 61 (organ); Perfect Through Suffering (SATB); Harmonies of Florence (organ); Credo (SATB); Te Deum (SATB).

BINGHAM, WILLIAM L, JR (BING)　　　　　ASCAP 1972
composer, author, singer
b New York, NY, Sept 13, 45. Educ: Williams Col, Mass, BA, 73; studied voice with J A Fracht, 79. Recording artist with Epic & RCA; singer concerts, night clubs, nat TV & on-camera commercials. Appeared in "Elvis, the Legend Lives"; co-star of ABC-TV's "Alex 'n Annie" show. *Songs:* Hockey Player; Barn Stormer; Goodbye Hollywood; Harmony; Music: Come to Ireland (Clio Award, 75).

BINKERD, GORDON WARE　　　　　ASCAP 1966
composer
b Lynch, Nebr, May 22, 16. Educ: Wesleyan Univ, BM, Gail Kubik; Eastman Sch Music, MM, Bernard Rogers; Harvard Univ, MA, Walter Piston. Teacher, Jr Col, Garden City, Kans, 37-38, Franklin Col, Ind, 38-40, Harvard Univ, 45-49 & Univ Ill, 49-71. US Naval Reserve, 42-45. *Songs & Instrumental Works:* Sonata for Piano; Noble Numbers for Wind Ensemble; The Battle (brass, perc); The Ebb and Flow (mixed voices); Christmas Day (mixed voices); Sung Under the Silver Umbrella (treble voices, piano); A Scotch Mist (men's voices); Dum Medium Silentium (men's voices); Garden (mixed voices); Symphony No 1 (orch); On the King's Highway (children's chorus, chamber orch); String Quartet No 1; Trio for 3 Strings; Sonata for Cello and Piano.

BINKLEY, THURMAN G, JR (BOOKIE)　　　　　ASCAP 1969
composer, author
b Winston-Salem, NC, May 15, 44. Educ: Guilford Col. Wrote music for groups, Head West & Blue Beard. Chief Collabr: Bobby Welch. *Songs:* Fly Willie; Baby I Need You; Too Many People; Country Man; Butter Queen; Desire; La Puntnion (title song).

BIONDO, ROSE LEONORE VICTORIA (VIKKI DALE)　　ASCAP 1959
composer, author, singer
b New York, NY, Aug 19, 31. Educ: Rhodes Sch; Queens Col, NY. Prof dancer, toured with Polynesian troupes, 47-60. Comp, 54-; singer, nightclubs, 62- Jazz lyricist, Creative World of Stan Kenton. Publ with Junonia Corp, 75; recording artist, 80. Nominated, poet laureate, Fla, 80. Chief Collabrs: Willie Maiden, Jeannine Clesi, George R Davis, Jr. *Songs:* The Way to Go; The Time Is Now; Variation on a Theme; Lyrics: Like in Love; Hymn to Her; Children Beautiful; Close Enuff for Jazz; In Five-Four; A Love Song to Jesus; Woman Aglow; Fringe Benefit; Minor Booze; Samba Siete; The Little Man in the Boat; A Walk Into the Wild; On a Quiet Night; The ABC of It; Burnt Toast; Like Yesterday; I Had Time; Little Bar; My Hymn to Him; Con Cuidado; There Is One Face; April Fool. *Albums:* In My Own Little World.

BIRCH, PETER (PETER BELL, JOHNNY LYNN)　　　ASCAP 1970
composer, author, singer
b Bridgeport, Conn, May 21, 40. Educ: Danbury High Sch; Berklee Sch Music, Boston. Singer, United Artists Records with var groups incl The Sultans, Jay and the Americans, 60's & the group NAIF; producer. Chief Collabrs: George Morgio, Noel Thatcher, Jerry Pezzella, Artie Schroeck. *Songs:* Music: Black on White; In the USA.

BIRCH, PETER HUDSON
author, dancer, director
b Bronx, NY, Dec 11, 22. Educ: DeWitt Clinton High Sch; studied dance with Fokine, Dolin, Caton, Carlos, Haper, Nemchineva, Veola & Schwetzoff. Soloist with Fokine Ballet. Appeared in nightclubs. Lead dancer, Bway shows incl "One Touch of Venus", "Dream With Music", "Carousel", "Oklahoma" & "Gentlemen Prefer Blondes." Choreographer, Roxy Theatre, Papermill Play House & musical variety shows at ABC, NBC & CBS incl "Stop the Music", "Voice of Firestone", "Ezio Pinza Show", "Jimmy Durante Show", "Saturday Night Review Show", "Jane Froman Show" & var indust shows. Dir, var CBS shows incl "Jack Paar Show", "Morning Show", "Vic Damone Show", "Garry Moore Show" & "Captain Kangaroo," 25 yrs. Chief Collabr: Jose Melis. *Songs:* Lyrics: A Day At the Beach; Sailboats Are Sleeping; Sing Little Bird; A Little Drop of Rain.

BIRCH, ROBERT FAIRFAX　　　　　ASCAP 1963
composer
b Chevy Chase, Md. Educ: High sch; pvt music study. Concert mgr, DC & NY; mgr, Patelson Music House, NY. *Songs & Instrumental Works:* Repose; Snowfall; I Want to Be Married; The Owl and the Pussy Cat; I Will Worship the Lord; Prayer to Jesus; Haiku (song cycle).

BIRCSAK, THUSNELDA A　　　　　ASCAP 1962
composer, author, teacher
b Chicago, Ill. Educ: Kansas City artist teachers, Sir Carl Busch, Sol Alberti & Mrs Busch; studied with Leipzig, 6 yrs; studied theory with Carreno, 7 yrs; Kansas City Cons, 1 yr; studied with Lubwasky, 1/2 yr; Acad Vienna, Austria;

studied organ with Soreng Wright, Los Angeles. Organist & choir dir, piano & organ studio, Kansas City; organist & dir, Kansas City, Mo & San Diego, Calif, 20 yrs; own studio, San Diego. Has won several nat & state competition prizes in comp. *Songs & Instrumental Works:* Clouds (SSAA); Brook in the Forest (SSAA); Viennese Dance (piano; 2nd Presser Prize, 40); Lullaby of Christ Child (SSA); Desert Nostalgia (SSA); Fields of Grain (SSA); The Lord Is Nigh (SATB).

BIRD, GEORGE T　　　　　ASCAP 1961
composer, author
b Fayette, Ohio, Dec 19, 1900; d Cincinnati, Ohio, 78. Educ: Ohio State Univ; Univ Cincinnati, BS, PSM. Was student dir of marching band while at Ohio State Univ. Trumpeter & arr, studio orch, WLW, Cincinnati; trumpeter in bands incl Joe Venuti, Jimmy & Tommy Dorsey, Gene Goldkette & Jan Garber. Dir, Xavier Univ Band, Cincinnati; supvr of music & band dir, high schs, Trotwood, Dayton & Massilon, Ohio; teacher & band dir, Univ Pa, 50-51; later Whitoak Schs, Mowrystown, Ohio. Entertainment dir, football team, Cleveland Browns, 46, organizer & dir, musical majorettes, 67; entertainment dir, professional football team, Cincinnati Bengals, 68-74, adv to entertainment dir, 74-78. *Songs:* Hi O Hi O for Cleveland; Cleveland Browns for Cleveland; The Bengal Growl; Carry On. *Instrumental Works:* Bengal Boot; Dig, Dig, Dig; Fanfare; No Use Pretending.

BIRD, JAMES EDWARD　　　　　ASCAP 1979
composer, author, singer
b Plymouth, Pa, Aug 27, 50. Educ: Kings Col, Pa, BA(Eng), 72. Singing career began in church choirs, then to barrooms & night clubs, traveling extensively. *Songs:* Philadelphia Kid; Goodbye (Doesn't Have to be Forever); Whiskey (What You Done to Me).

BIRDT, ROBERT　　　　　ASCAP 1963
composer, author
b New York, NY, July 30, 35. Educ: City Col New York. Chief Collabr: Bill Harrington. *Songs:* Pray for Peace.

BIRKENHEAD, SUSAN　　　　　ASCAP 1974
composer, author
b New York, NY, Aug 14, 35. Educ: High Sch Music & Art; Brooklyn Col, BA, 57. Songwriter for "Captain Kangaroo," CBS, 74- One of the writers of Bway, "Working." Lyricist, "A Long Way to Boston," for Goodspeed Opera House, 79 & under option for Bway. Comp-lyricist, "Roaring Donuts," United Children's TV; lyricist, "Alex and the Wonderful Lamp" & "Unicorn Tales," NBC. Chief Collabrs: Donald Siegal, Mary Rogers, Jule Styne. *Songs:* Film/TV songs: The Starfish; I'm Always in the Mood for Food; I Want to Be an Acrobat; Grandma and Me; Big and Small; Beverly Square and Barnaby Box; Workin Together; Together Time (lyrics); Bway Song lyrics: Nobody Tells Me How; Lookin Out for Mama; What About Me; I'd Do It Again.

BISHOP, ELVIN
musician
b Tulsa, Okla. Joined Paul Butterfield; formed group, Butterfield Blues Band, early 60's, lead guitar, then second guitar, then lead guitar. Formed own band, 68, then signed with Fillmore Records & later San Francisco Records (both Bill Graham affiliations). Distributed by CBS Records; signed with Epic Records, 71 & with Capricorn Records, 73. *Albums:* Elvin Bishop; Feel It; Rock My Soul; Crabshaw Rising—The Best of Elvin Bishop; Let It Flow; Juke Joint Jump; Struttin' My Stuff; Hometown Boy Makes Good; Raisin' Hell; Hog Heaven.

BISHOP, JOE　　　　　ASCAP 1939
composer, tuba & flugelhorn player, arranger
b Monticello, Ark, Nov 27, 07; d Houston, Tex, May 12, 76. Educ: Hendrix Col. Played tuba in bands incl, Al Katz & Isham Jones. Helped form Woody Herman Orch, 36. Had been arr & comp for dance bands & publ. Chief Collabrs: Gordon Jenkins, Gene Gifford, Leo Corday. *Songs:* Blue Prelude; Jealousy; Out of Space; At the Woodchopper's Ball; Blue Evening; Blue Lament; Blue Flame; New Orleans Twist; The Cobra and the Flute; Is Love That Way?; Blues Upstairs and Downstairs; Gotta Get to St Joe; Be Not Discouraged; Ain't It Just Too Bad; Indian Boogie Woogie.

BISHOP, WALTER F, JR
composer, pianist, teacher
b New York, NY, Oct 4, 27. Educ: Ida Elkan Sch, 67; Rudolph Schramm, 68; Juilliard Sch, 69; studies with A Overton & Lyle Murphy. Pianist with, Art Blakey, M Davis & Charles Parker, 51-55; Europ tours, 61-63; perf incl, Light House, Shelley's & Donte's, Los Angeles, 69-74; NY clubs incl, Village Gate, Vanguard, Sweet Basil's, Tin Palace & Jazzmania, 75-80. Chief Collabr: Mitch Farber. *Songs:* Valley Land; Music: Coral Keys; Soul Turnaround; Soul Village; Cubicle. *Songs & Instrumental Works:* Valerie; Those Who Chant; Sweet Rosa; Our November.

BISHOP, WALTER FRANCIS, SR　　　　　ASCAP 1936
composer, author, musician
b Kingston, BWI, Jan 9, 05. To US in 23. Educ: Pub sch, Jamaica; studied music under Fed Music Proj, NY; NY Univ, musical comp with Vic Mizzy & Rudy Schram (Schillinger Syst); NY Sch Social Res, course in writing for musical

theatre with Aaron Frankel & Kenny Jacobson. WW II serv. Vpres, Am Guild Comp & Authors for several yrs. Chief Collabrs: Willie Smith, Clarence Williams, Alan Courtney, Emma P La Freniere, Bob Hilliard, Dizzy Gillespie, Charlie Parker, Jule Styne, Roger Ramirez, Ray Rivers, Buzz Adlam, William Kaufman, Addison Amor. *Songs:* The Devil Sat Down and Cried; Surprise Party; Shh' It's a Military Secret; What More Could I Ask of Love; There's Only One In Love; Love Not Subject to Change; Any Resemblance to Love (Is Purely Co-Incidental); The Old Stamping Ground; Doghouse Polka; Penthouse In the Basement; Kickin Up a Storm; Rainbow At Midnight; Everything That's Made of Wood Was Once a Tree; Sex Is a Misdemeanor (The More You Miss de Meaner You Get); Alas Poor Yorick (I Didn't Know Him Well); Touch Me With Your Eyes; Music: The Quicker I Gets to Where I'm Goin' (The Sooner You'll Be Seein Me); Lyrics: Anthropology; Bop Goes My Heart; We Can't Go on This Way; Swing Brother Swing; Goin' Back to Memphis; Mad About You; Black Pearl; I Just Refuse to Sing the Blues; Guijara Blues. *Instrumental Works:* Skyline.

BISKAR, JOHN L ASCAP 1960
composer, author, violinist
b Lovington, Ill, June 21, 18. Educ: High sch; Chicago Musical Col, BM, studied violin with Max Fischel & Leon Sametini, comp with Max Wald & Louis Gruenberg; NY Univ, studied Schillinger System of music comp with Rudolph Schramm, pvt study with Richard Benda. Taught violin, Chicago. Violinist with Univ City Symph & Gateway Fest Orch, St Louis; played with dance & stage show orchs. Chief Collabr: Herbert B Greenhouse. *Songs:* Jo-Ann Polka; Music: St Louis Polka; Forever Near You; You Started Something; A Thousand Times Yes.

BITGOOD, ROBERTA ASCAP 1958
composer, organist, choral director
b New London, Conn, Jan 15, 08. Educ: Conn Col Women, 28; Guilmant Organ Sch, NY, 30; Columbia Univ Teachers Col, MA, 32; Sch Sacred Music, Union Theol Sem, MSM, 35 & SMD, 45; FAGO, 30, ChM, 42; studied organ with J Lawrence Erb, 24-28, Dr William C Carl, 28-32, Dr Clarence Dickinson, 33-35, 43-45 & Dr David M Williams, 37-41; comp studies with Edwin Stringham, 33-35, T Tertius Noble, 43-45 & Wayne Bohrnsted, 57-60. Church musician, First Moravian Church, NY, 29-32; asst organist, First Presby Church, 29-32; church musician, Westminster Presby Church, Bloomfield, NJ, 32-47; dir music, Bloomfield Col & Sem, 35-47; church musician, Holy Trinity Lutheran Church, Buffalo, 45-52, Calvary Presby Church, Riverside, Calif, 52-60, Redford Presby Church, Detroit, Mich, 60-63, First Presby Church, Bay City, Mich, 63-69, First Congregational Church, Battle Creek, 69-76 & St Marks Episcopal Church, Mystic, Conn, 77-; mem nat coun, Am Guild of Organists, nat pres, 75- Violist var symph. *Songs:* Music: The Greatest of These Is Love (solo, SATB & duet); Hosanna (arr from Moravian Liturgy; jr & adult choir); Give Me a Faith (SATB, solo, duet); Christ Went Up Into the Hills (SA & SAB); Job (cantata; SATB with STB solos); A Good Thing It Is to Give Thanks (SATB); How Excellent Thy Name (SA); Prayer Is the Soul's Sincere Desire (SSATBB); Lord, May We Follow (SATB). *Instrumental Works:* Choral prelude on Jewels (organ solo); choral prelude on God Himself Is With Us; choral prelude on Covenanters Tune; On An Ancient Alleluia; meditation on Kingsfold; Rejoice, Give Thanks (organ & brass).

BIVENS, BURKE ASCAP 1948
composer, author, arranger
b Kirbyville, Tex, Aug 15, 03; d Los Angeles, Calif, Nov 6, 67. Educ: Pub schs. First saxophonist in Wayne King Orch, 29 yrs; also arr. WWII, USA. Has been soloist on radio, TV. Chief Collabrs: Gus Kahn, Wayne King, Mitchell Parish, Jerome Brainin, Sammy Gallop. *Songs:* Josephine; Annabelle; Swamp Blues; Don't Let Julia Fool-Ya; Pretty Penny With the Million Dollar Smile; Pigeons in the Park; Frankie; The Swamp Ghost.

BIVONA, S RICHARD ASCAP 1959
composer, author
b New York, NY, Feb 14, 11; d New York, Aug 29, 64. Educ: Fordham Univ. Worked in construction bus; then became realtor. *Songs:* He Is Always There.

BLACK, BEN ASCAP 1926
composer, author, producer
b Dudley, Eng, Dec 11, 1889; d San Francisco, Calif, Dec 26, 50. Music dir, Paramount Theatres, New York, San Francisco & Los Angeles; Saenger Theatre, New Orleans; also others in San Francisco. Produced shows in NY & Calif. Chief Collabrs: Edwin Lemare, Neil Moret. *Songs:* Moonlight and Roses; Hold Me; Tears; You and I; Don't Sing Aloha When I Go.

BLACK, BUDDY ASCAP 1954
composer, author
b Huntingdon, Pa, July 22, 18. Educ: Kansas City Univ & Cons; Chicago State Univ, BA(commun); LittD, Mallinckrodt Col, Ill. Radio & TV announcer, musician & MC. Owns, operates radio sta, WEBH, Chicago; pres, Cummings Communications Corp; licensee & owner, KSEE Radio, Santa Maria, Calif. *Songs:* A Christmas Song in Summertime; Time Will Tell; I Fell in Love With a Pony Tail; Auctioneer.

BLACK, CHARLES ASCAP 1962
composer
b Augusta, Maine, Nov 24, 03. Educ: Eastman Sch Music, BM; Union Theol Sem, Sch Sacred Music, MSacredMus. USAF, WW II. Minister music, churches in NJ, NY & Calif. *Songs:* Sacred: To Calvary's Summit; Christmas—Tide (processional service); Hymn to Resurrection; Mary Had a Baby; The Lord Is My Shepherd; Jacob's Ladder.

BLACK, DAVID MICHAEL ASCAP 1969
composer, pianist
b Oklahoma City, Okla, May 26, 41. Educ: Oklahoma City Univ, BMus, 64, studied with Ray Luke; Univ Southern Calif, grad study, 64-66, studied with Ellis Kohs & Harold Owens. Pianist-dance arr for TV shows & nightclub acts: Carol Burnett, 3 yrs, Dean Martin, Bob Hope, Diana Ross, John Denver, John Davidson, Shirley MacLaine & others. Accompanist, Danny Kaye Summer Tour. Cond-music dir, Florence Henderson, 3 1/2 yrs, Jim Nabors, Los Angeles Civic Light Opera Production "Bells Are Ringing" revival; other TV spec: The Carpenters, 2 yrs, Oscars, Emmys, "Tonite Show," Merv Griffin, Dick Cavett, David Frost, Jack Parr, Pinocchio, Sonny & Cher, Bernadette Peters & others. Chief Collabrs: Artie Malvin, Harry Shannon. *Songs:* Music: She Cared for Me; M' Lover.

BLACK, GLORIA (ROSEBUD) ASCAP 1969
composer, author, singer
b New York, NY, May 18, 44. Educ: New York Schs Music, 65-70; Essex County Col, 77-78. Songwriter. Recording artist for Jody Records. Appeared in nightclubs, cols, radio & TV. *Songs:* Double Dealin' Dude; Recipe for Love; God Smile on Me; Double Dealin' Daddy; The Rain Is Fallin'.

BLACK, JENNIE PRINCE ASCAP 1942
composer
b New York, NY, Oct 10, 1868; d New York, Sept 20, 45. Charter mem, Hudson River Music Sch. Mgr, Tarrytown & Dobbs Ferry Hospitals, 30 yrs. Founder & chmn, fund-raising comt, Washington Irving Mem, New York; founder, Robin's Nest (home for crippled children). Autobiography, "I Remember." *Songs:* Autumn Leaves; Lord's Prayer; When Arbutus Blooms; Old Dutch Nursery Rhyme; It Is Night.

BLACK, KAREN ASCAP 1972
composer, actress
b Park Ridge, Ill. Educ: Northwestern Univ. Primarily known as an actress; wrote some of music for movie, "Nashville." *Songs:* Music: Nashville; I'd Like to Go to Memphis; Rolling Stone; I Don't Know If I Found It.

BLACKBURN, JOHN M ASCAP 1953
composer, author, actor
b Massilon, Ohio, Oct 19, 13. Educ: Western Reserve Univ. Dir, Cleveland Playhouse. Teaching fel, Drama Dept, Bennington Col, 2 yrs. Actor & dir, Pasadena Playhouse, 3 yrs. Former film agent, recording distributing mgr & song plugger; former owner, record co. Retired, Rockwell Space Div, 76. Chief Collabrs: Lew Porter, Karl Suessdorf, Bert Carroll. *Songs:* Moonlight in Vermont; Need You; I Don't Want to Waltz With Anyone But You.

BLACKMAN, MICHAEL BRUCE (KARL MARION) ASCAP 1967
author
b Pine Bluff, Ark, July 30, 46. Educ: Miss State Univ; Delta State Col. Singer, concerts & TV. Recording artist with United Artists. Producer, Starbuck, Pvt Stock & United Artists, Korona, United Artists & Choice, Polydor. *Songs:* Moonlight Feels Right; Everybody Be Dancin'; Let Me Be; Little Bird; Mrs Bluebird; Lucky Man; I Got to Know; Searchin' for a Thrill; Rock and Roll Rocket.

BLACKMON, FREDERICK MOSLEY ASCAP 1979
composer, author, singer
b Meridian, Miss, Oct 8, 47. Educ: Studied piano with Clara Thompson, 8 yrs; Harris High Sch, dipl, 64; Stillman Col, BS(music), 71; Fisk Univ; Delta State Univ; Jackson State Univ. Started musical training at age 7; during col yrs, performed with & wrote music for popular regional singing group, The Jaedes; presently, writing & producing original material; teacher. Chief Collabrs: Richard Powell, Joe Wilson. *Songs:* Uh, Uh, What Did I Do; Diblin and Dablin; I Can't Feel the Cold; Money Can't Buy You Love; This Town's Too Small for Both of Us; You Got to Live; There's Only 24 Hours a Day; Let's Do It.

BLACKMORE, CARL ASCAP 1955
composer, educator
b Grand Rapids, Mich, Nov 26, 04; d St Petersburg, Fla, Dec 2, 65. Educ: London, Paris, Leipzig, BM, MM, MusD. Dir & dean grad sch, St Louis Inst Music. Founded own music sch, St Petersburg, Fla.

BLACKTON, JAY S ASCAP 1958
composer, conductor, pianist
b New York, NY, Mar 25, 09. Educ: Juilliard; also studied in Berlin. Gave piano concert, Brooklyn Acad Music at age 12. Cond, New York Opera Comique, Fed Grand Opera Proj, Fed Gilbert & Sullivan Proj, St Louis Munic Opera & Del Philh. Music dir Bway productions incl "Oklahoma!", "Annie Get Your Gun",

"Inside USA", "Miss Liberty", "Call Me Madam", "Wish You Were Here", "New Faces of 1956", "Happy Hunting", "Oh Captain!", "Redhead", "Mr President" & "The Girl Who Came to Supper." Also cond films, radio & TV.

BLACKWOOD, EASLEY RUTLAND
composer, pianist

b Indianapolis, Ind, Apr 21, 33. Educ: Pvt piano study; Berkshire Music Ctr, 48-50, studied comp with Messiaen; Ind Univ, studied with Bernard Heiden; Yale Univ, PhD, 54, studied with Hindemith; also study with Nadia Boulanger, Paris, 54-56. Appeared as soloist with Indianapolis Symph at age 14; appointed to fac, Univ Chicago, 58. *Instrumental Works:* Symphony No 1 (Koussevitzky Music Found Prize); Symphony No 2 (comn for centenary of music firm G Schirmer); Symphony No 3 (small orch); Symphony No 4; Chamber Symphony for 14 Wind Instruments; Clarinet Concerto; Symphonic Fantasy; Concerto for Oboe and String Orchestra; Violin Concerto; Concerto for Flute and String Orchestra; Piano Concerto; Viola Sonata; Concertino for 5 Instruments; Fantasy for Cello and Piano; Pastorale and Variations (wind quintet); Fantasy for Flute, Clarinet, Violin and Piano; Symphonic Movement (organ); Un Voyage d Cythere (soprano & 10 players); Piano Trio; 2 string quartets; 2 violin sonatas & 3 short fantasies for piano.

BLACKWOOD, WILLIAM LE (BILLY)   ASCAP 1971
composer, author, singer

b Memphis, Tenn, Apr 7, 53. Educ: Avon Elem Sch; White Station High Sch; pvt voice & piano with var instrs for several yrs. Played drums, Stamps Quartet, 62-69; comp, 69- Drums & vocals, Blackwood Brothers, 69-73, Elvis Presley Show, 73-75; drums, vocals & guitar, Sunrise, 75-78; drums, guitar, piano & vocals, Harmony, 79; drums, Andrus, Blackwood & Co, 79; TV, RCA Victor recording artist. *Songs:* Can't Hold on to Nothin'; Goin' Back to Memphis; (Dying for Love) Too Many Reasons.

BLADES, RUBEN   ASCAP 1977
composer, author, singer

b Panama, Panama, July 16, 48. Educ: Elementary & high sch, Panama, 55-67; National Univ, Panama, law degree, 68-74. Singer, age 16 & songwriter, age 18. To New York, 74; mail clerk, Fanta Records Inc; legal adv, Panamanian Fanta Co. Recording artist, 74-; joined Fanta All Stars; working with Willie Colon, 77- Chief Collabr: Louie Ramirez. *Songs:* Pablo Pueblo; Pedro Navaja; Plastico; El Calanguero; Numero 6; Amor Pa Que?; Cipriano Armenteros; Lyrics: Juan Pachanga; Sin TV Carino.

BLAGMAN, NORMAN
composer, author

b New York, NY, Aug 18, 26. Educ: Christopher Columbus High Sch; studied clarinet, guitar, piano & arr. Served in USNR. Melody writer for var artists incl Polly Bergen, Toni James, Elvis Presley, Ral Donner & Tiny Tim. Developed contemporary comedy song specialty, wrote material for Dick Schawn & produced 2 albums & specials for inserts for Mad Magazine. Movies incl "Tickle Me" & "The Producers"; producer of jazz music. Chief Collabrs: Fred Wise, Sam Bobrick, Joni Bross, Nick Meglin, Edna Lewis, Joe Sauter. *Songs:* Music: Nose Job; Its a Gas; To Love Someone; Give Me the Right; Put the Blame on Me; Jazz Is His Old Lady and My Old Man; Love Power; Elegant Butterfly; It'll Never Be Over for Me; The Viper; The Second Noel; Letter of Love; Hello Son; The American Pioneer; Snow Bunny; You Were There; Loves Short Day.

BLAHNIK, JOEL ARTHUR   ASCAP 1972
composer, teacher, conductor

b Fish Creek, Wis, June 7, 38. Educ: Lawrence Cons of Music, BM; studied comp & conducting with Vaclav Nelhybel. Guest cond, cols, univs & summer camps. Clinician; teach state adjudication & comprehensive musicianship through perf workshops; clinics & workshops at state music conventions. Band perf incl Mid-West Nat Band Clinic, 3 times & 3 Green Bay Packer football games. Recipient, numerous comns & state & nat awards for teaching excellence. *Songs:* Easter Fanfare. *Instrumental Works:* Invention No 1; Battalia; Prague Trombones; Concertino for Percussionist and Wind Ensemble.

BLAINE, CHIP
See Chipolone, Nunzio

BLAIR, HAL KELLER   ASCAP 1959
composer, author, singer

b Kansas City, Mo, Nov 26, 15. Educ: High sch grad; Kansas City Inst Music, voice, 33-34; Denver Inst Music, voice with Bernice Humphries, 36-37. Joined Follies "Midnight in Paris Review"; joined Jazz String Quartet, played stage, hotels, clubs until 49; joined Rhythm Rangers Western Band. Signal Corps, Armed Forces, 44-45. Resumed writing & picture work, 46. Toured US as singer & guitarist until 48, made motion pictures & wrote music for "Stars Over Texas" & "Scatter Brain." Wrote for Elvis Presley pictures, 61-67. Chief Collabrs: Dean Kay, Jimmy Haskel, Buddy Baker, Cristof Comida, Eddie Dean, Don Robertson, Elvis Presley. *Songs:* Lyrics: One Has My Name (The Other Has My Heart); Please Help Me I'm Falling; Ringo; Ninety Miles an Hour (Down a Dead End Street); I Was the One; I Think I'm Gonna Like It Here; No More; I'm Yours; Valerie; Moment In Time; Waco; Brotherly Love; Wild Geese Calling; What Now-What Next-Where To; I Met Her Today; Not One Minute More; All But the Remembering; Autumn on the Trail; My Lips Are Sealed; So

Much to Remember; You Don't Need Me Anymore; Go Back You Fool!; I Let Her Go; Margretta; What Have I Done for Her Lately.

BLAKE, ALAN
See Balkin, Alfred

BLAKE, BEBE   ASCAP 1954
composer, author, publisher

b Los Angeles, Calif, May 7, 25. Educ: Univ Southern Calif. Discovered by Gus Edwards, wrote songs for his shows. Film contract actress. Writer for films, radio & TV. Artist's mgr & music publ. Chief Collabrs: Victor Young, Walter Scharf, Jimmy McHugh, Sammy Fain, Daniele Amfitheatrof. *Songs:* Christmas in Jail (Nat Safety Song); I Thank God (Freedom Found Award); Cowboys Never Cry; Dreamy Eyes; Hidden in My Heart.

BLAKE, EUBIE   ASCAP 1922
composer, arranger

b Baltimore, Md, Feb 7, 1883. Educ: NY Univ, studied Schillinger Syst; studied with Margaret Marshall & Llewellyn Wilson. Pianist & organist in cafes, vaudeville & theatres. Mem, vaudeville team with Noble Sissle, formed, 15. Asst cond to Jim Europe, Clef Club, 17. Toured in musical show organized by Europe from musicians of US 369th Inf, WW II, toured 5 yrs, USO. Chief Collabrs: Noble Sissle, Andy Razaf. *Songs:* I'm Just Wild About Harry; Love Will Find a Way; You Were Meant for Me; Shuffle Along; Bandana Days; Gypsy Blues; Goodnight, Angeline; Slave of Love; Lowdown Blues; Memories of You; You're Lucky to Me; Lindy Hop; Lovin' You the Way I Do; Green Pastures; My Handy Man; I'm Cravin' for That Kind of Love; Music: We Are Americans Too; Weary; Boogie Woogie Beguine. *Instrumental Works:* Classical Rag; Blue Rag in 12 Keys; Rhapsody in Ragtime; Capricious Harlem; Valse Marion; Boston Pops March; Charleston Rag. *Scores:* Bway Stage: Shuffle Along; Chocolate Dandies; Blackbirds of 1930; Swing It; Eubie.

BLAKE, GEORGE   ASCAP 1950
author, director, producer

b New York, NY, July 14, 17; d New Rochelle, NY, Oct 7, 55. Educ: Townsend Harris Hall; NY Univ, BA. Film writer, dir & producer, also TV dir. *Songs:* Come Dance With Me; With All My Heart; Place of My Own; Topsy-Turvy Time; Let's Stay Home; I Could Go For You; You Look Like Someone.

BLAKE, GEORGE M (JOHN TROUTMAN)   ASCAP 1961
composer, organist

b Nutley, NJ, July 8, 12. Educ: Studied organ with Lew White, organ & piano with Frank Kasschau, choir with Darlington Richards. Organist & choir master, Episcopal churches, 45 yrs. Comp, sacred anthems & organ music. *Instrumental Works:* Arr: 17 Pieces for Organ.

BLAKE, JAMES W   ASCAP 1933
author

b New York, NY, Sept 23, 1862; d New York, May 24, 35. Educ: Pub schs. Hat salesman, then songwriter. Chief Collabr: Charles Lawlor. *Songs:* The Sidewalks of New York; The Best in the House Is None Too Good for Reilly; I Did My Drinking When the Drinking Was Good; Pretty Jennie Slattery; Forgive Her as Your Heart Tells You to Do; McFadden's Row of Flats.

BLAKE, LOWELL
See Schoenfeld, William C

BLAKE, MYRTLE ANN   ASCAP 1963
composer, author

b Washington Co, Maine, Jan 23, 06. Educ: High sch. *Songs:* So Blue; Sweet Mary Lee; Wonderful Pal; God Will Help You.

BLAKELY, BILL W   ASCAP 1972
composer, singer, pianist

b Stapp, Okla, May 19, 26. Educ: Todds Sch Music, Portland, Ore; studied piano with Gene Confer & Sam Sax, voice with Gene Byram. Singer & pianist in nightclubs. *Songs & Instrumental Works:* Along Came You; To Hold You Again; You; I'm Falling for You.

BLAKER, CHARLES RANDOLPH   ASCAP 1967
composer, arranger, author

b Chicago, Ill, June 30, 43. Educ: John Burroughs High Sch, Calif; Los Angeles City Col, 61-63; Univ Southern Calif, BM, 66; studied film scoring with David Raksin & Nathan Scott. Composed, produced & supervised music for animated NBC series "I am the greatest: The Adventures of Muhammad Ali"; orchr for TV show "Lassie"; arrangements for Chad Everett, Joe Frazier & Richard Harris. Performed, Edinburgh Fringe Fest, in own show "Coney Island of the Mind." Played nightclubs, TV & military clubs in US, Orient & Pacific. Scored several films, jingles & Sesame Street cartoons. Chief Collabrs: Rita Graham, Robert V Greene, Jan Harrington. *Songs:* When Last I Saw My Love; Music: Can I Go With You; Ardeena Moore. *Instrumental Works:* Sonata for Flute and Piano; String Quartet. *Scores:* Film: Warlock Moon.

BLAKLEY, RONEE
composer
b Idaho. Educ: Stanford Univ, grad; Juilliard Sch Music, degree. Began studying piano at age 8. Comp film score & gave Moog synthesizer recital at Carnegie Hall. Began playing clubs in Los Angeles area, 71. Played part of Barbara Jean in movie, "Nashville," rec'd Acad Award nomination. Was one of stars of Bob Dylan's Rolling Thunder tour, 75. *Albums:* Ronee Blakley; Welcome.

BLANC, MEL J ASCAP 1955
composer, author, actor
b San Francisco, Calif, May 30, 08. Educ: High sch; studied violin. Played in dance, radio orchs. Cond, Orpheum Theatre, Portland, Ore; recorded own works. Does voices in animated cartoons. *Songs:* Big Bear Lake; Ugga Ugga Boo; Tia Juana; OKMNX; Wheezy Whoosy Whatamobile.

BLANCH, JEWEL EVELYN ASCAP 1971
composer, author
b Australia. With singing group The Blanches, Australia. Recorded for var cos, with group & as solo, 69- *Songs:* The Sweetest Song; Will I Ever Learn; How Long Must It Be.

BLANCHARD, MICHAEL KELLY
composer, author, performer
b Hartford, Conn, Oct 23, 48. Educ: Trinity Col; Berklee Col of Music, assoc degree(comp), 75. *Songs:* Then the Quail Came; Be Ye Glad; Claire; Give It Up.

BLANCHARD, RICHARD ASCAP 1969
composer, author
b Chungking, China, Mar 14, 25. Educ: Davidson Col; Mercer Univ; Candler Sch Theol, Emory Univ. Minister, United Methodist Church, 48-, mem, Fla Conf, 50; served pastorates in Ga, 48-50; served as sr pastor for several churches in Fla. Chief Collabr: Lee Turner. *Songs:* Fill My Cup, Lord; The Gospel According to You; Treasures in Heaven; God Can!; Revelation; Thy Will Be Done; Lyric: Who Moved?

BLANE, RALPH
See Hunsecker, Ralph Blane

BLANKMAN, HOWARD MILFORD ASCAP 1956
composer, author, producer
b Lancaster, Pa, June 23, 25. Educ: Franklin & Marshall Col; West Chester State Teachers Col; studied with Thomas Timothy & Kathryn Grube. Cond & arr of own band. Assoc producer, "Who Do You Trust?," ABC TV. Writer of spec material, commercials & industrials. *Songs:* It Takes Time. *Scores:* Stage: Sugar 'n Spice; Wonderful Good; By Hex; Treasure Island (children's musical).

BLASCO, MRS LOUIS
See Peterson, Betty J

BLASDELL, RAYMOND LYNN ASCAP 1972
composer
b Los Angeles, Calif, Oct 12, 32. Chief Collabr: Helen Dell. *Songs:* Lyrics: Coffee Cake; Show Time; My Girl; Up.

BLAUFUSS, WALTER ASCAP 1921
composer, conductor, pianist
b Milwaukee, Wis, July 26, 1883; d Chicago, Ill, Aug 23, 45. Educ: Chicago Musical Col; Sherwood Music Sch. Accompanist to Mary Garden, Fritzi Scheff, Emma Calve. Cond, Chicago Orch Hall, also theatres. Cond radio shows, incl "Breakfast Club"; "Farm and Home Hour"; "Viennese String Ensemble." Chief Collabrs: Gus Kahn, Egbert Van Alstyne. *Songs:* Your Eyes Have Told Me So; My Isle of Golden Dreams; My Cathedral; Sometimes When Lights Are Low; Daisy Days.

BLEES, ROBERT ASCAP
author, writer, producer
b Lathrop, Mo, June 9, 22. Educ: Dartmouth Col. Photographer/writer, Life mag, London & US. Motion picture writer, "Magnificent Obsession", "Autumn Leaves", "Phobia" & others. TV writer & producer, "Columbo", "Harry O", "Quincy", "Kraft Theater", "Bonanza", "Cannon", "Barnaby Jones" & others. Mem exec bd, Writers Guild of Am, Producers Guild of Am, Acad Motion Picture Arts & Sci. Chief Collabrs: John Williams, David Rose, Lionel Newman, Joe Greene. *Songs:* Lyrics: The Stripper; I Need You Here With Me; Love Is Something Else; The Name of the Game.

BLEIWEISS, PETER RICHARD (P RICHARD BLYTHE) ASCAP 1964
composer, author
b Newark, NJ, July 6, 44. Educ: Great Neck N High Sch, 62; NY Univ, BA, 67, MA, 72; Hunter Col. Bassist in rock groups; TV performer; artists mgr; record co exec; film ed; media consultant. Chief Collabrs: Gary Toms, Bill Stahl. *Songs:* She's Coming Home; Suite Disco (Movement 2); Feeling Good Again; Stand Up and Shout.

BLESSINGS, LYNN ROBERTS ASCAP 1974
composer
b Cicero, Ind, Dec 4, 38. Educ: Studied with Terry Biggs & Earl Hatch. Played vibraphone with Martin Denny, Tim Wiesburg, Al Joure & John Klemer. Chief Collabr: Tim Wiesburg. *Instrumental Works:* Sunshine in Her Hair; Moonchild; Tibetan Silver; For Those Who Never Dream.

BLEVINS, SCOTTY LEE ASCAP 1973
composer, musician, singer
b Austell, Ga, Jan 18, 54. Educ: Brewton-Parker Col, Ga, music scholarship. Professional musician & entertainer, touring 310 different towns a yr; recording artist, Katona, Concord-Con-Brio, Request & Folkway's Records. Chief Collabr: Tommy Lee Scott. *Songs:* Exorcism; You Ain't Worth It; Stacy; Hitchhiker; Harmonica Man; Why Don't Somebody Write Me a Love Song; Lying Lips and Crying Eyes; You Bought the Ticket; Music: Come on Home; Nightmare at 17; Medicine Man; Lyrics: Ode to John.

BLISH, NATHANIEL PIERCE, JR ASCAP 1957
composer, arranger, pianist
b Somerville, Mass, July 16, 25. Educ: New Eng Cons, Boston, 43-44. Played piano, Boston area, 40's; organized own orch, 48-50; joined Woody Herman Orch, 51; arr & comp for Count Basie & Woody Herman, 51-55; free-lance arr for Ella Fitzgerald, Jimmy Rushing, CBS TV & others, recorded for Capital, RCA Victor, Coral, Columbia & Savoy, 55-61; rejoined Woody Herman Orch, 61; returned to free-lancing, 66, with Carmen McRae & Harry James, recorded for Concord Jazz, 71; now co-leader, The Capp-Pierce Juggernaut Orch. Chief Collabrs: Count Basie, Woody Herman, Norton Cooper, Louis Bellson. *Instrumental Works:* Buck Dance; New Basie Blues; One for Johnny; Stingray; Basie's Deep Fry; Capp This; Do It in Blue; Lightly and Politely; Pee Wee's Blues; Society Jumps; Dicty; Pomp and Circumstance Stomp; Well Alright Then; New York Shuffle; Open All Night. *Scores:* Off Bway: The Ballad of Jazz Street.

BLITZSTEIN, MARC ASCAP 1939
composer, author, pianist
b Philadelphia, Pa, Mar 2, 05; d Martinique, WI, Jan 22, 64. Educ: Univ Pa; Curtis Inst; Acad der Kuenste, Berlin; studied with Alexander Siloti, Rosario Scalero, Nadia Boulanger, Arnold Schoenberg. Piano soloist with Philadelphia Orch at age 15. WW II, USAAF. Founder & vpres, Arrow Music. Grants: Guggenheim (2); Acad Arts & Letters; Ford Found. Awards: Newspaper Guild "Page One" & Am Aeronautical Inst. Chief Collabr: Kurt Weill. *Songs:* Nickel Under the Foot; The Cradle Will Rock; Art for Art's Sake; Francey; Mack the Knife; Pirate Jenny; Barbara's Song; Army Song; The Liffey Waltz; One Kind Word; I Wish It So; How I Met My New Grandfather; With a Woman To Be. *Instrumental Works:* Piano Sonata; Serenade (string quartet); The Airborne Symphony; Freedom Morning (symph poem); Piano Concerto; This is the Garden (Cantata); 6 Elizabethan Songs; From Marion's Book. Ballets: The Guests; Cain. Operas: Regina (Koussevitzky Found comn); 1 act: I've Got the Tune (radio); Triple Sec; Harpies (League of Comp comn). *Scores:* Film Background: Hands; Surf and Seaweed; Valley Town; Native Land; Night Shift; The True Glory; Spanish Earth. Bway stage: The Cradle Will Rock; Juno. Off-Bway stage: No For an Answer. Opera: Sacco and Vanzetti (comn by Metrop Opera Co, New York); Idiots First. Incidental music to plays: Julius Caesar; Danton; Androcles and the Lion; Another Part of the Forest; King Lear; A Midsummer Night's Dream; A Winter's Tale; Toys in the Attic. Translr & adaptor: The Threepenny Opera; Mother Courage; Rise and Fall of Mahngony City.

BLOCH, ERNEST ASCAP 1929
composer, educator
b Geneva, Switz, July 24, 1880; d Portland, Ore, July 15, 59. US citizen, 24. Educ: Studied with Jaques-Dalcroze, Ysaye, Rasse, Ivan Knorr. First publ work, 03. Cond symph concerts, Lausanne & Neuchatel, 09. Lectr, Geneva Cons, 11-15; then to US as cond of orch for dancer Maud Allan, on Am tour. Taught at Mannes Sch, NY, 17. Dir, Cleveland Inst Music, 20-25; head, San Francisco Cons, 25-30; then lived in Switz & France. Cond works in Amsterdam, Italy, London & Paris. Returned to US, 38. Prof music, Univ Calif, 40-59. Awards: Hon mem, Accademia di Santa Cecilia, Rome; hon DHL; Am Acad Arts & Letters (first comp honored). *Instrumental Works:* Macbeth (opera); Symphony No 1 in C; 3 Jewish Poems for Orch; Israel Symphony; Schelomo (Rhapsody for Cello); Viola, Piano Suite (Coolidge prize); 2 violin sonatas; Baal Shem; Nigun from Baal Shem Suite; 2 concerti grossi; 2 piano quintets; America Symphony (Musical Am prize); Sacred Service; Piano Sonata; Violin Concerto; 5 string quartets; Concerto Symphonique for Piano; Sinfonia Breve; 5 Sketches in Sepia; Poems of the Sea; Meditation and Processional for Viola, Organ; Abodah for Violin, Piano; Prelude and 3 Psalms; Proclamation for Trumpet, Orchestra; Scherzo Fantasque for Piano, Orchestra; Helvetia Symphony; Symphony in E Flat Major; Suite Modale (flute & piano); Symphony for Trombone and Orchestra; 2 suites for unaccompanied violin; 3 suites for unaccompanied cello; 2 Last Poems for Flute and Orchestra; Meditation Hebraique (cello & piano); Enfantines for Piano; also Historiettes au Crepuscule (voice & piano); Winter-Spring (orch); Poems of Autumn (mezzo-soprano & piano).

BLOCH, RAYMOND   ASCAP 1939
composer, author, conductor
b Alsace-Lorraine, France, Aug 3, 02. Educ: DeWitt Clinton High Sch, New York. Pianist in New York ballrooms; organized orch & toured US in vaudeville; pianist, music dir & arr on radio & TV network shows incl Ed Sullivan, Jackie Gleason, Philip Morris & others. Recording artist; cond for var works incl themes, mood & background music. *Songs:* Au Revoir; When Love Has Gone; You're Everything That's Lovely; In the Same Old Way; The Wide Open Spaces; Sam the Vegetable Man; Let's Make Up a Little Party; If You Were Mine; Music: You're My Love; In My Little Red Book.

BLOOD, ESTA DAMESEK   ASCAP 1970
composer, teacher
b New York, NY, Mar 25, 33. Educ: Manhattan Sch Music; Washington Irving High Sch; Bennington Col, comp workshops, summers, 77-78; studied with Vivian Fine, Louis Calabro & Henry Brant. Taught piano at age 17, later began comp. Comp many pieces, mostly chamber works & solo instrument pieces, also some vocal works. Performer, NY, Mass, Vt, Ind, Va & NMex. Winner, Int Wind & String Chamber Music Competition, 79. *Instrumental Works:* Balkan Suite (solo piano); 3 Variations for 2 Pianos, 8 Hands; Five-Legged Spider (solo piano piece for students).

BLOOM, A LEON
See Lewis, Leon

BLOOM, ERIC   ASCAP 1972
composer, author, vocalist
b New York, NY, Dec 1, 44. Educ: Cheshire Acad, 62; Hobart Col, NY, BA (modern languages), 67. In early yrs played bars & clubs, fraternity parties, etc; original founding mem of BOC, 71; lead vocalist & comp/arr, Blue Oyster Cult. Recording artist, Columbia Records (9 albums, 3 gold, 1 platinum). Chief Collabrs: Ian Hunter, John Trivers & Michael Moorcock. *Instrumental Works:* Goin' Thru the Motions; The Great Sun Jester; Black Blade; The Subhuman; Me-262; The Red and the Black; Harvester of Eyes.

BLOOM, LARRY   ASCAP 1955
composer, author, conductor
b New York, NY, July 14, 14. Educ: High sch. Cond orch in hotels, incl Waldorf-Astoria. *Songs:* Mambocila; Mambo Mambero; I Found a New Love.

BLOOM, RUBE   ASCAP 1929
composer, pianist, arranger
b New York, NY, Apr 24, 02; d New York, Mar 30, 76. Educ: Pub schs. Accompanist to vaudeville singers. Made recordings of piano solos and with own orch; also with Bix Beiderbecke, Miff Mole, Frank Trumbauer & Dorsey Bros. Cond own jazz recording orchs. Wrote bks on piano method. Arr for music publ. Toured with US Govt-sponsored ASCAP group, entertaining overseas, 55. Chief Collabrs: Johnny Mercer, Harry Ruby, Ted Koehler, Sammy Gallop, Harry Woods, Mitchell Parish. *Songs & Instrumental Works:* Don't Worry 'Bout Me; Truckin'; Out in the Cold Again; Big Man From the South; Fools Rush In; Day In—Day Out; Take Me; Give Me the Simple Life; Maybe You'll Be There; Stay on the Right Side, Sister; Here's to My Lady; I Can't Face the Music; Good for Nothin' Joe; Song of the Bayou (Victor Phone Co award); Suite of Moods; Soliloquy; Spring Fever; Sapphire; Serenata; Silhouette; On the Green; Penthouse Serenade; Floogie Walk; Got No Time; The Ghost of Smokey Joe; Fifth Avenue Bus; Jumping Jack; Lady on a Late Evening; Love Is a Merry-Go-Round; What Goes Up Must Come Down; Savage in My Soul; I Wish I Could Tell You; Feelin' High and Happy.

BLOOM, VERA   ASCAP 1942
author
b Chicago, Ill, May 17, 1898; d Washington, DC, Jan 10, 59. Daughter of Rep Sol Bloom. Educ: Horace Mann Sch. Lyricist, "East Is West." Author, "There's No Place Like Washington" & "The Entertaining Lady." Chief Collabr: Jacob Gade. *Songs:* Jalousie; My Message in the Stars; Souvenir Waltz; Just Keep Loving Me; Ecstasy; I Wish I Could Write a Love Song; When You Come Back to Me; The Only Thing That Matters; Laredo; Yet I Know You're Here.

BLOSSOM, HENRY   ASCAP 1914
author
b St Louis, Mo, May 6, 1866; d New York, NY, Mar 23, 19. Educ: Stoddard Sch. Was in insurance business. Charter mem, ASCAP, dir, 17-19. Author, "The Documents in Evidence"; "Checkers"; "A Hard Luck Story"; "The Brother of Chuck McCann." Chief Collabrs: Victor Herbert, Alfred Robyn. *Songs:* Kiss Me Again; I Want What I Want When I Want It; The Mascot of the Troop; When You're Pretty and the World Is Fair; The Isle of Our Dreams; Every Day Is Ladies Day With Me; The Streets of New York; Because You're You; I'll Be Married to the Music of a Military Band; Neapolitan Love Song; Moonbeams; Thine Alone; The Irish Have a Great Day Tonight; Free Trade and a Misty Moon; Eileen Alanna Asthore; When Shall I Again See Ireland?; When You're Away. *Scores:* Bway Stage: The Rose Maid; The Century Girl; The Velvet Lady; also librettist: The Yankee Counsel; Mlle Modiste; The Red Mill; The Prima Donna; The Slim Princess; All for the Ladies; The Only Girl; The Princess Pat; Eileen.

BLUEFIELD, DAVID
See Pearlstein, David Bluefield

BLUM, HARRY   ASCAP 1959
composer, author
b New York, NY, Apr 15, 26; d. Educ: NY Univ, BA. Writer of special material for nightclubs & TV. *Songs:* Out in the Middle of the Night; Old Fashioned Ways.

BLUMBERG, MARK EUGENE   ASCAP 1974
composer, arranger, trumpetist
b Detroit, Mich, Nov 15, 47. Educ: Catholic High Sch; Memphis State Univ, BM, 70, studied arr & orchestration with Rayburn Wright, Manny Albam, 69, 71 & 72, Hank Levy, 71-72. Writer, numerous radio & TV commericals, AV presentations & industrial film scores. Recording musician; instrumentalist, nightclubs. Chief Collabrs: Jack Hale, Sr, Ron Nelson, Bill McMath. *Songs:* She; New Beginnings; No Time for Tears. *Instrumental Works:* Disco Duck (Pt II).

BLUME, DAVID NASON (T S KING)   ASCAP 1965
composer, author, pianist
b Boston, Mass, June 26, 31. Educ: Northeastern Univ, Mass, BA. Chief Collabrs: Jerry Keller, Carolyn Hester, Phil O'Kelsey. *Songs:* The Shakiest Gun in the West; Music: Turn-Down Day; What's So Bad About Feeling Good?; Angel In My Pocket.

BLUMENFELD, HAROLD   ASCAP 1968
composer, author, opera specialist
b Seattle, Wash, Oct 15, 23. Educ: Eastman Sch Music, comp with Bernard Rogers, 41-43; Yale Sch Music, comp with Paul Hindemith, 46-49, BM, 48, MM, 49; Zurich Konservatorium, fall of 78; Tanglewood, conducting with Robert Shaw & Leonard Bernstein, opera direction with Boris Goldovsky, 48-52. Comp, opera specialist, writer-critic, translr, lectr. Prof music, Wash Univ, 50- Artistic dir, St Louis Opera Theatre, 62-66. Co-founder, New Music Circle St Louis. Comp Award, Am Acad Nat Inst Arts & Letters, 77. Maj grant for opera "Opposites Attract," Nat Endowment Arts, 79. Comp of wide & varied body of choral & vocal chamber music; contribr to var mags & newspapers. Chief Collabr: Librettist, Charles Kondek. *Songs & Instrumental Works:* Miniature Overture; Transformations (piano); Expansions (woodwind quintet); War Lament (mixed chorus with guitar); Eroscapes (mezzo-soprano & 8 instruments); Song of Innocence (choruses, orch, solo tenor, mezzo-soprano); Rilke (voice, guitar); Circle of the Eye (high voice, piano); Starfires (cantata in 3 parts; mezzo, tenor, orch); La Vie Anterieure (spatial cantata in 3 parts; baritone with tenor, mezzo, low strings, guitar, piano, 5 percussionists; tape); Voyages (baritone, viola, guitar, 2 percussionists); Fritzi (opera-bagatelle); Essence (original Russian & Eng version; medium voice, piano); La Voix Reconnue (cantata; tenor, soprano, chamber ens); Symphony Amphitryon 4; in prep: Ilbrahim, Amen! (opera in 1 act).

BLY, ALBERT E   ASCAP 1963
composer, author
b Ill, Nov 22, 1892; d. Educ: High sch. Toured, tent shows in Pantages vaudeville circuit. *Songs:* In the Land of Uncle Sam; Why Don't Somebody Care?; I Picked Some Oranges in California; Diddy Wah Doo!; Today in Omaha.

BLYTHE, P RICHARD
See Bleiweiss, Peter Richard

BOARDMAN, EARLE M   ASCAP 1966
composer, teacher
b New Haven Township, Ohio, Jan 26, 22. Educ: Oberlin Col Cons, BM, 50; Univ Mich, MM, 59; studied cello with Ivor James, Royal Col of Music, John Fraser, Oliver Edel & Robert Swenson, comp with Herbert Elwell & Normand Lockwood. Taught, string instruments in pub schs in Colo, Mich & Nebr, Western Ky Univ & Univ Wis, Platteville. Cellist, Nashville Symph, Int Symph & String Quartet & Nashville recording studios. Soloist with var community orchs; string clinician & involved with Suzuki workshops. Piano technician with restoration shop for old keyboard instruments. *Songs:* Music: Praise Ye the Lord (fest chorus).

BOATNER, EDWARD H   ASCAP 1954
composer, conductor, singer
b New Orleans, La, Nov 13, 1898. Educ: Chicago Col Music; studied with Louis Saar, Felix Deyo, Effie Grant, Otley Cranston, Charles Cease, Arthur Wilson & Arthur Frank. Concert singer, 26-30. Cond choirs throughout US. Music dir, Nat Baptist Conv, 25-33. Dean of music, Wiley Col & Houston Col. Teacher of voice & theory, New York. *Instrumental Works:* Arr: On My Journey; O What a Beautiful City; Trampin'; I Want Jesus to Walk With Me.

BOATWRIGHT, HOWARD L   ASCAP 1961
composer, violinist
b Newport News, Va, Mar 16, 18. Educ: Yale Univ, MusB, 47, MMus, 48; studied with Paul Hindemith. Concert violinist, New York debut, Town Hall, 42. Assoc prof violin, Univ Tex, 43-45; asst prof music theory, Yale Univ, 48-56, assoc prof, 56-64; dean, Sch Music, Syracuse Univ, 64-71, prof music, 72- *Songs:*

Music: The Passion According to Saint Matthew; Canticle of the Sun; Star in the East; Hear My Cry, O God; Lament of Mary Stuart; Six Prayers of Kierkegaard. *Instrumental Works:* Quartet for Clarinet and Strings; Serenade for Two Strings and Two Winds; Variations for Small Orchestra; String Quartet No 3; Symphony; Twelve Pieces for Violin Alone. *Songs & Instrumental Works:* But Black Is The Colour (voice & violin); One Morning in May (voice & violin).

BOBRICK, SAM   ASCAP 1962
  composer, author
b Chicago, Ill, July 24, 32. Educ: Univ Ill, BS. TV writer, shows incl "Andy Griffith Show", "Flintstones", "Get Smart", "Smothers Brothers" & "Kraft Music Hall." Coauthor of Bway shows incl "Norman Is That You", "No Hard Feelings", "Murder At the Howard Johnsons" & "Wally's Cafe." Chief Collabrs: Norman Blagman, Ron Clark. *Songs:* Girl of My Best Friend; It'll Never Be Over for Me; Did You Ever Love Someone? *Albums:* Mad Twists Rock 'n' Roll; Sing Along With Mad; Folk Songs of Madison Avenue.

BOBROW, LAURA J (LAURIE BEE)   ASCAP 1962
  composer, author, singer
b Mt Vernon, NY, Dec 25, 28. Educ: A B Davis High Sch; Tufts Univ, BS(educ). Folksinger; children's author & comp. Chief Collabr: Joseph Roff. *Songs:* Sing With Me, Laurie Bee.

BOCK, FRED (JASON ROBERTS)   ASCAP 1959
  composer
b Jamaica, NY, Mar 30, 39. Educ: Ithaca Col, BS(music educ), 60; Univ Southern Calif, MM(church music), 62, studies for DMA(church music). Pianist & organist, movies, TV, commercials & recordings. Comp, specifically in church music related areas; dir music, Bel Air Presbyterian Church, Los Angeles, 14 yrs. Ed, hymnal "Hymns for the Family of God"; writer for churchs, schs, choirs, orchs, organ & piano. Owner, music publ firm, Fred Bock Music and Gentry Publ. *Songs:* Music: One Solitary Life; I Sing the Greatness of Our God; Praise His Holy Names; Song of Triumph (cantata); Praise God; Praise Hymn; Praise Him With Joyful Song; God Is At Work Within You. *Instrumental Works:* Grand Recessional (organ solo); Three Moods for Piano.

BODNER, MARK L   ASCAP 1969
  composer, pianist
b New York, NY, Feb 27, 56; Educ: Juilliard Sch Music; Haverford Col, BA, 78; Benjamin N Cardozo Sch Law. Cond, collegiate choral groups. Comp & arr, stage band & jazz ens. Chief Collabr: Neal Bodner. *Instrumental Works:* Jumpin' Jack; Double Date; Sunday.

BODNER, NEAL   ASCAP 1969
  composer, musician
b New York, NY, July 2, 58. Educ: Haverford Col, BA, 80; Mt Sinai Med Sch. Bassist, jazz, rock & fusion groups. Comp & arr, col stage band & jazz ens. Chief Collabr: Mark Bodner. *Instrumental Works:* Cinnamon Bay; In a Dream World; Double Date; Sunday.

BODNER, PHILIP L   ASCAP 1960
  composer, instrumentalist, arranger
b Waterbury, Conn, June 13, 21. Educ: NY Univ, pvt study of clarinet, flute & oboe, study comp & orchestration with Tibor Serly. Saxophonist, dance bands incl Benny Goodman & Tommy Dorsey. Multi-woodwind instrumentalist, soloist, arr & cond, network, film, jingle & recording studio orchs. Creator & producer albums, The Brass Ring instrumental group. Recording artist, RCA, RCA Camden, Dunhill & ABC record cos. Chief Collabrs: Al Stillman, Sunny Skylar, Mort Goode. *Songs:* Music: Like a Breath of Spring; Amanha; Moon Mist; Hanky Panky. *Instrumental Works:* Bahama Shuffle; The Dating Game; Bossa Nove One A.M.; The Soul of Brazil; Sandy; Bongolino; Sprinkles; The Now Sound; Gazpacho; Plymouth Rock; Oh So Good; I'm Goin' Home; Mud-Turtle Blues.

BOEHNLEIN, FRANK CLIFFORD   ASCAP 1970
  composer, author
b Bedford, Ohio, Feb 2, 45. Educ: Rollins Col, BM(comp), 67; Case Western Reserve Univ & Cleveland Inst Music, DMA, 71, studied comp with Donald Erb & Marcel Dick. Rec'd grants & awards from NEA, Presser Found & Ford Found. Asst prof, Dodge City, Kans & Denton, Tex. Supvr of assembly at NEC Am, Ltd, Irving, Tex. Author of texts, "Essays and Analysis" & "Comprehensive Musicianship in the Contemporary Classroom." *Instrumental Works:* Piano Sonata; Music for Moon Children (piano). *Scores:* Film/TV: To Teach Yourself.

BOGGESS, GARY THOMAS   ASCAP 1976
  composer, author, keyboardist
b Orlando, Fla, June 17, 52. Educ: Dana Sch Music, comp maj; Youngstown State Univ. Band mem, I Don't Care, 72-76; formed Musico Technilab, an electronic music recording studio, work full time on recording music, film soundtracks, commercials; comp music for synthesizer & scores for theatrical plays. *Songs & Instrumental Works:* Call It What? (jazz); Find Your Garden (rock). *Scores:* Theater plays: Eye and the Mind of God (electronic music); Equus (synthesizer music); The Tempest (electronic music); Rhinoceros (electronic music); Alice in Wonderland (electronic music); Film/TV: Gandy Hopper.

BOHANNON, HAMILTON F
  composer, author, publisher
b Newnan, Ga, Mar 7, 42. Educ: Central High Sch, Newnan, 60; Clark Col, Atlanta, Ga, BA, studied theory & band with Wayman Carver. Drummer for Stevie Wonder, 65; band leader, Motown Records, 67; played for Smoky Robinson & Miracles, Stevie Wonder, Temptations, Four Tops, Diana Ross & Supremes, also other Motown artists; with Brunswick Records, 72, Mercury Records, 77 & own record co, Phase II Record Ltd, 80- *Songs:* South African Man; Footstomping Music; Let's Start the Dance; Disco Stomp.

BOHME, DAVID M (DAVID ROMAINE)   ASCAP 1954
  composer, author
b Poland, Mar 24, 16. To US 28. Educ: Chicago Col Music; Am Cons; Paris Cons. Violinist, Chicago Philh, 3 yrs; on staff, WLS, WGN, radio, mutual network, 4 yrs. Made records. Music dir, Sherman House, Chicago, 61- Chief Collabr: Al Trace. *Songs & Instrumental Works:* Padre; A Broken Promise; Nightingale; Rumba Flamenco; Gypsy Louis; The Last Waltz; Cascade; Romaine Salad; Magic Flower; Tango Tzigana.

BOHN, WALTER (BUDDY) MORROW (MORO)   ASCAP 1972
  composer, author, singer
b Evanston, Ill, Aug 21, 39. Educ: Los Gatos Union High Sch; Principia Col, Ill, BA(drama, journalism). Troubador & concert guitarist, worldwide tours incl royal courts in 43 nations. Classical & flamenco guitarist; comp & writer of film scores; recording artist; featured on TV & radio specials. *Songs:* Rain, Sun and Moon; Hummingbow. *Instrumental Works:* Sonata in D Major (Mountainbird Sonata); Moonset; Vermouth Rondo; Hosanna Blue.

BOHRNSTEDT, WAYNE   ASCAP 1969
  composer
b Onalaska, Wis, Jan 19, 23. Educ: Univ Wis, Univ Mich; Northwestern Univ, BM, MM; Eastman Sch Music, Univ Rochester, PhD, studied with Howard Hanson. Instr, Northwestern Univ, 46-47. From asst prof to assoc prof, Bowling Green State Univ, 47-53. From assoc prof to prof, Univ Redlands, dir, Sch Music, 68-, dean, Div Fine Arts, 72-79. *Instrumental Works:* Symphony No 1; Concerto for Trumpet; Festival Overture; Concertino for Timpani, Xylophone and Orchestra; Concertino for Trombone and Strings.

BOLAND, CLAY A   ASCAP 1936
  composer, author, publisher
b Olyphant, Pa, Oct 25, 03; d Queens, NY, July 23, 63. Educ: Univ Scranton; Univ Pa, DDS; postgrad, Bryn Mawr & Pa Hosps. Wrote Mask & Wig shows, Univ Pa, 34-49. Comdr, USN, WW II; Capt, Korean War. Dentist. Chief Collabrs: Moe Jaffe, Bickley Reichner, Edgar De Lange. *Songs:* Too Good to Be True; The Gypsy in My Soul; I Live the Life I Love; Stop Beatin' 'Round the Mulberry Bush; When I Go a-Dreaming; Stop, It's Wonderful; Midnight on the Trail; An Apple a Day; Havana; Ya Got Me; I Like It Here; Holiday; Not So Long Ago; I've Got My Eye on You; The Morning After; Christmas Eve; Something Has Happened to Me. *Instrumental Works:* Cinderella of Rittenhouse Square (suite). *Scores:* Stage: Cotton Club Revue, 1958.

BOLAND, CLAY A, JR   ASCAP 1958
  composer, author
b Philadelphia, Pa, Dec 6, 31. Son of Clay A Boland. Educ: Univ Pa; Juilliard; Am Theatre Wing. Wrote Mask & Wig Shows, Univ Pa, 50-53. Music dir, "Boy With a Cart" (off-Bway). *Songs:* Any Distance Between Us; Our Home; Spinning a Dream; A Night in December; Nineteen-Nineteen. *Scores:* Stage (summer stock): Clarence; New Bridge a-Comin'; Tossed Salad; Two By Two; Children's musicals: Christopher Fish; Jack and the Beanstalk; Pinocchio.

BOLIN, NICOLAI   ASCAP 1952
  composer, author, arranger
b Belgorod, Ukraine, Oct 6, 1898. Educ: High sch, Kiev, Ukraine; Univ Calif, Berkeley, BS(mechanical eng); studied cond with Modest Altshuler & Albert Coates. Pianist in vaudeville & silent films. Choir dir, United Artists & other motion picture studios. Winner, Hollywood Bowl Gershwin Mem Award. Publ, Bet Songs. Producer, Hollymovie Shorts & Nu-Art Video Records. Music chmn, Acad Sci Fiction, Fantasy & Horror Films, 75. Founder, Nick Bolin Balalaika Gypsy Band & Nick & Laura Duo, 75. Chief Collabr: Baron Keyes. *Songs:* California Valse; I Gave My Heart to You; Pony Express; Eyes of Blue; My Secret; I'll Put a Star on the Christmas; Leapo (The Bounding Kangaroo) (narration); Black Frankenstein Calypso; Dracuela Waltz; Count Dracula Suite (12 songs); Mandrake Revue (6 songs); Welcome to Hawaii (suite of 4 songs); On the Rock Pile (orch background); Would You Like to Be Alone With Me?; Just for You Alone. *Instrumental Works:* Majorette (piano solo); Toy Symphony (orch with narration); Transylvanian Rhapsody (violin, piano); Sirto Greek Dance (violin, piano); Three Indian Legends (orch with narration); Big Town Concerto (piano, orch; 3 movements); California Sketches (symph suite in 4 parts); Symphonic Tzigane (3 movements). *Scores:* Opera: Tale of Tsar Saltan (adaptation & Eng lyrics of Rimsky-Korsakov's Grand Opera); Ballet: Silent Night (narration).

BOLIN, THOMAS RICHARD　　　　　　ASCAP 1968
composer, author, singer

b Sioux City, Iowa, Aug 1, 51; d Miami, Fla, Dec 5, 76. Recording artist, solo and with var groups. Appeared on TV shows incl "American Bandstand", "Rock Concert" & "Midnight Special." Guitarist. Chief Collabrs: Jeff Cook, John Tesar, Glenn Hughes, Roy Kennel, David Coverdale. *Songs:* Show Bizzy; See My People Come Together; Standing in the Rain; Summer Breezes; Red Skies; The Devil Is Singing Our Song; Alexis; Ride the Wind; Got No Time for Trouble; Miami Two Step; From Another Time (Rather Be Alone With You); Mystery; People, People; Post Toastee; Bustin Out for Rosie; Music: Cross the River; Hard Chargin Women; Sail On; Suns A'Risin; Somebody Listen; Hunabuna; Keep Me; Back to Colorado; I'll Be Right Here; Crusin Down the Highway; Do It; Wilfire; Sleepwalker; Spanish Lover; Head Above the Water; Must Be Love; You Told Me That You Love Me; The Grind; Savannah Women; Wild Dogs; Lotus; Sweet Burgundy; Shake the Devil; Gypsy Soul; Hello Again; Some Day We'll Bring Our Love Home; Comin Home; Lady Luck; Gettin Tighter; Dealer; I Need Love; Drifter; Love Child; This Time Around; You Keep Me Moving; Faded Satin Lady. *Instrumental Works:* Homeward Strut; Marching Powder; Owed to "G." *Albums:* Bang; Miami; Teaser; Private Eyes; Come Taste the Band; Remade in Japan.

BOLLARD, ROBERT GORDON　　　　　ASCAP 1951
composer, author

b Buffalo, NY, Jan 8, 20; d Stamford, Conn, Nov 2, 64. Educ: Buffalo State Col, BA, 40; Juilliard Sch Music, grad studies, 48-52; studied piano, Olga Samaroff, New York & Leonard Trick, Buffalo. Special services, USA, 44-46. Coordr, radio stas services; pianist in concerts. Producer of children's records, 46-50; music dir, Neighborhood Playhouse Sch of Theatre, 46-55; record producer, RCA Victor, 58-61; music dir/recording producer, Harry Belafonte, 61-64. *Songs:* Night Must Fall.

BOLLON, JOSEPH　　　　　　　　ASCAP 1968
composer, author

b Bronx, NY, July 12, 15. Educ: DeWitt Clinton High Sch, majored in music; Moller Col, studied cosmetichology; Jhirmack Sch, studied hair waving, coloring & business mgt. Played in high sch band. Led orch during big band era. Produced big band shows, 70's. Chief Collabrs: Phil Medley, Hal David, Johnny Tucker, Billy Ward, Paul Francis, Danny DiMinno, Al Volpe. *Songs:* Give My Broken Heart a Break; Old Fashioned Baby; Say You Love Me; I'm a Big Girl Now; Is It True?; Music: Down the Milky Way; The Joke's on Me; It Always Rains, But Always; Wond'ring; I'll Come Home; I Lost Out on Love.

BOLTE, CARL EUGENE, JR　　　　　　ASCAP 1962
composer, author, playwright

b Kansas City, Mo, Feb 4, 29. Educ: Univ Mo, BS(bus admin), 51, AB(economics), 55, Law Sch, 58-60; Naval War Col, Newport, RI, grad, 79. Col Band leader. Playwright, 24 plays including: "Give 'Em Hell, Harry!" Author, "Successful Songwriting"; designer/producer, "Songwriters Creative Matrix." Instr popular songwriting, Cons Music, Univ Mo, Kansas City. Musicologist & appraiser of music & lyrics. Designer of music appraisal form. Chief Collabrs: Harold McKemy, Lee Reeder. *Songs:* The Most; I'm Goin'; Oh So Charming; Time and Time Again; I Like Being I; April Fool; My Last Fling; Snowbound; Rather Be Me With You; Share It With You; A Bunny Hug; Happy Easter; Have a Nice Day; I Like Four-Letter Words; Tiny Tim; Elvin the Little Black Elf; Christmas Eve By the Golden Gate; A Royal Welcome; Fight on, Griffons!; Lyric: Chopsticks.

BOLTZ, VIOLET MARIE　　　　　　ASCAP 1965
author

b Stevens Point, Wis, May 29, 20. Housewife. Has run postal station for 10 yrs. Service station work & seasonal factory work. Buys, redresses & sells dolls. *Songs:* Lyrics: The Rain Keeps Falling, Falling Down; Whippoor-Will, Whippoor-Will; Yodel Me to Sleep; Snowed Under By Heartaches; My Poor Heart and I.

BOLZ, HARRIETT HALLOCK　　　　　ASCAP 1967
composer, author

b Cleveland, Ohio. Educ: Pvt study voice & piano, Cleveland Inst Music; Case Western Reserve Univ, BA(music); Ohio State Univ, MA(comp); pvt study with Leo Sowerby & Paul Creston. Composer, pvt teacher piano & comp, choir dir & music consult, pub schs. Music ed nat magazine, Winner comp awards, Nat Fedn Music Clubs, Phi Beta Prof Fraternity Music & Speech & Nat League Am Pen Women (10 awards since 70). Performer, US major cities, incl Lincoln Ctr, New York, Columbia Univ & others. *Instrumental Works:* Episode for Organ; Narrative Impromptu for Harp; Two Profiles for Piano; Floret (a mood caprice for piano); Capitol Pageant (piano, 4 hands).

BONACIO, BENNIE　　　　　　　ASCAP 1950
composer, saxophonist, clarinetist

b Mineo, Italy, Sept 4, 03; d Clearwater, Fla, Jan 10, 74. Educ: Cons, Italy; Juilliard Sch Music. Moved to US, 20; saxophonist in dance orchs incl Paul Whiteman, Vincent Lopez, Rudy Vallee, Percy Faith, Morton Gould & Andre Kostelanetz; also with network staff orchs, theatre orchs & New York Philh. Had own publ firm. Publ. Chief Collabrs: Eugene West, Henry Jerome, Walter

Bishop, Jimmie La Marge, Helen McKiernan. *Songs & Instrumental Works:* Te Amo; The Wishing Well; My Search for You Is Ended; My Love for You; Even You; One Glance; Dad; Dance of the Pelicans; Chiquita From Chi-Wah-Wah; Flying Home.

BONAGURA, MICHAEL JOHN, JR (MICHAEL　　ASCAP 1975
MARTIAL)
composer, author, singer

b Newark, NJ, Mar 26, 53. Educ: Univ Del, BS. Musician, singer & songwriter of var jingles; has done backup vocals for different performers & records. Leader of vocal group, Bitter Sweet. Chief Collabr: Kathie Baillie. *Songs:* Please Don't Tell Me Goodnight; I Must Have Been Blind; I'm Crazy About You; Didn't We Love; Lyrics: Loved You So Long.

BONANO, JOSEPH (SHARKEY)　　　　　ASCAP 1959
composer, conductor, trumpeter

b Milneburg, La, Apr 9, 04; d. Trumpeter, dance bands, early 20's. Leader, small group in New Orleans, performances throughout US. Recording artist. *Songs:* I'm Satisfied With My Gal.

BONBREST, JOSEPH B　　　　　　ASCAP 1958
composer, author, conductor

b Washington, DC, Feb 3, 1895. *Songs:* (I Don't Bother Work) And Work Don't Bother Me; Where the Trade Winds Blow; Night Shades; Crazy to Be Crazy About You; Love Is Just a Dream.

BOND, SHELLY　　　　　　　　ASCAP 1959
composer, author, dancer

b Bossburg, Wash, July 13, 10. Educ: High sch; studied piano, ballet; also Schillinger Syst. Has been prof dancer. Had wig & manikin bus. Chief Collabrs: Vin Sandry, Jeanne McComb, Herb Weiner. *Songs:* Hail the United World.

BONDS, MARGARET　　　　　　ASCAP 1952
composer, author, conductor

b Chicago, Ill, Mar 3, 13; d. Educ: Northwestern Univ, BM, MM; Juilliard Sch Music; studied with Roy Harris, Emerson Harper & Robert Starer. Toured as pianist. Taught at Am Theatre Wing. Music dir, Stage for Youth, 52 Asn, East Side Settlement House & White Barn Theatre. Chmn, Afro-Am Music for Eastern Region & Nat Asn Negro Musicians. Scholarships: Nat Asn Negro Musicians, Alpha Kappa Alpha, Julius Rosenwald & Roy Harris. Won Rodman Wanamaker Award. Chief Collabrs: Langston Hughes, Countee Cullen. *Songs:* Empty Interlude; Peachtree Street; Spring Will Be So Sad; Fields of Wonder; Arr: Dry Bones; Lord I Just Can't Keep From Crying; I'll Reach to Heaven; Sit Down Servant; Ezekiel Saw the Wheel. *Instrumental Works:* The Negro Speaks of Rivers; 3 Dream Portraits; Peter and the Bells; Mass in D; Troubled Island. *Scores:* Stage Background: Shakespeare in Harlem; USA.

BONE, GENE　　　　　　　　　ASCAP 1948
composer, author, singer

b Newman, Calif. Educ: Col of the Pac; Stanford Univ; San Francisco Cons; Juilliard; studied with Benjamin Moore, Blanche Young, Edith Griffing, Harry Jompulsky & Warren Allen. Singer with Fred Waring's Pennsylvanians & Robert Shaw Chorale. Appeared in Bway musical, "Laffing Room Only." Toured in concerts & supper clubs. Has written for films, TV & records. Chief Collabrs: Howard Fenton, Langston Hughes. *Songs & Instrumental Works:* Strange and Sweet; White Magnolias; I Live to Love; Say Yes to Life; My Magic Island; Nickelodeon Holiday; Orchids of Aloha; Friendship Tree; Gee, Dad, It's a Wurlitzer; Everything That I Can Spy; Green Fields; Pray for Peace; Prayer for a Waiting World; Wind in the Treetops; Marine Corps Reserve Marching Song (off song, USMCR). Also Music to Cook By (album-bk). Sacred: The First Psalm; Thy Word Is a Lamp; also Birthday in Bethlehem (cantata).

BONELLI, MONA MODINI　　　　　ASCAP 1940
author

b Los Angeles, Calif, Jan 18, 03. Educ: Bishop's Sch; Mills Col, BA. Had poems publ in mags. Chief Collabrs: Charles Wakefield Cadman, Elinor Remick Warren, Ernest Charles, Kenneth Walton, Solon Alberti. *Songs:* My Lady Walks in Loveliness; White Swan; Four Sonnets From California Hills; My Lady Lo-Fu; Gifts.

BONFA, LUIZ FLORIANO
composer, singer, guitarist

b Rio de Janeiro, Brazil, 1922. Studied guitar at age 12 under father; made debut, 46. Wrote music for Brazilian film, "Black Orpheus," incl "Manha de Carnival" & "Samba de Orfeu." Came to New York, 58 & played with Stan Getz. Toured Ger & Italy, 62. *Albums:* The Brazilian Scene.

BONHAM, JOHN　　　　　　　　ASCAP 1969
composer, author

b Redditch, Eng, May 31, 48. Was in a group known as the Band of Joy. Known throughout Eng as one of rock's premier drummers. Now in rhythm section of super-group Led Zeppelin. Chief Collabrs: Jimmy Page, Robert Plant. *Songs:* Good Times Bad Times; Communication Breakdown; Whole Lotta Love; Heartbreaker; Rock and Roll; D'yer Mak'er; Kashmir.

BONIME, JOSEF   ASCAP 1950
composer, conductor, pianist
b Vilna, Poland, Feb 26, 1891; d Westport, Conn, Nov 8, 59. To US as a child. Educ: City Col New York; Juilliard. Toured as accompanist to Mischa Elman, Eugene Ysaye. Recorded for early Vitaphone talkies; arr for film shorts. Cond, radio, 25-, incl CBS Symph & Columbia Sch of the Air. Was in radio dept, McCann Erickson & on fac, Juilliard. *Instrumental Works:* The City of Light (Con Ed exhibit, New York World's Fair, 39).

BONNER, RONNIE   ASCAP 1953
composer, author, arranger
b Philadelphia, Pa, July 1, 20. Educ: High sch. S/Sgt, First Cavalry Div, WW II. Wrote songs for "Uncle Wip" (children's radio prog). Top winner of Radio Guide Nat Song Search. Writer spec material for charitable orgn. Chief Collabr: Edward A Khoury. *Songs:* Hook, Line and Sinker; Ya Gotta Give Love a Try; Daddy's Day; Cowpuncher's Polka; The Mountain of Heartaches; Give, So More Will Live (off theme song, Heart Asn); Be a Big Brother (off theme song, Big Bros of Am); *Music:* Pray for Peace; Headin' for a Heartache; Philadelphia; Pennsylvania.

BONX, NATHAN J   ASCAP 1942
composer, author
b Philadelphia, Pa, May 1, 1900; d Washington, DC, Oct 23, 50. Educ: Univ Pa Law Sch. Lawyer. Chief Collabrs: Lew Brown, Moe Jaffe, Jack Fulton. *Songs:* Collegiate; I Love the College Girls; If You Are But a Dream; You Bring Me Music.

BOONE, CHARLES EUGENE (PAT)   ASCAP 1961
author, singer
b Jacksonville, Fla, June 1, 34. Educ: David Lipscomb High Sch, Nashville, Tenn; David Lipscomb Col; N Tex State Col; Columbia Univ, BS(magna cum laude), 58. Rec'd honors on Ted Mack Amateur Hour & Arthur Godfrey Talent Scout Show. Recording artist, Dot Records, 54. Starred in 15 motion pictures incl "Bernadine", "April Love", "All Hands On Deck", "Mardi Gras", "Yellow Canary" & "Journey to the Center of the Earth," 20th Century Fox. TV series, ABC, 57-60. Author, "Twixt, Twelve and Twenty", "Between You, Me and the Gatepost", "The Real Christmas", "A New Song", "A Miracle a Day Keeps the Devil Away", "Joy" & "My Brother's Keeper"; coauth, "The Honeymoon Is Over," 77. Rec'd Israel Cultural Award, 79. Nat Entertainment Chmn, Cancer Found & March of Dimes. *Songs:* Little Green Tree (Christmas song); *Lyrics:* Exodus Song; Hostage Prayer.

BOONE, CHARLES N   ASCAP 1967
composer
b Cleveland, Ohio, June 21, 39. Educ: Univ Southern Calif, BM; San Francisco State Col, MA; Academy of Music, Vienna, studied with Karl Schiske, Ernst Krenek, Adolf Weiss. Chmn, San Francisco Comp Forum, 64-66. Coordr, Mills Col Performing Group & Tape Music Ctr, 66-68. Music writer for San Francisco Examiner, 65 & Oakland Tribune, 70. Founder of BYOP Concerts. Comp-in-residence for City of Berlin, Ger Acad Exchange Serv, 75-76. *Songs: Music:* Raspberries; Shunt; First Landscape; Second Landscape; Vocalise; A Cool Glow of Radiation; Linea Meridiana; San Zeno/Verona; Streaming; Chinese Texts; String Piece; Oblique Formation; Not Now; Quartet.

BOONE, CHERRY
See O'Neill, Cheryl Lynn

BOONE, LEONARD COLEMAN, 2ND   ASCAP 1977
composer, author, singer
b Trenton, NJ, Nov 8, 51. Educ: Rutgers Univ, BA(history), 74. Intern writer with the Wes Farrell Orgn, 72-73; staff, Chrysolis Music, with var hit songs, 73- *Songs:* You Made Me Believe in Magic; Love Won't Be Denied; You're the One; You Got to Me; (You Are) The Music in Me.

BOONE, PAT
See Boone, Charles Eugene

BOOTHE, JAMES R   ASCAP 1958
composer, author
b Sweetwater, Tex, May 14, 17; d New York, NY, Dec 30, 76. Educ: Univ Southern Calif, MA. Newspaper reporter, advert copywriter. Wrote scores for col & army shows. WW II, USA. Chief Collabr: Joe Beal. *Songs:* Jingle-Bell Rock; The Heavens Cried; I Reached For a Star.

BORETZ, ALVIN   ASCAP 1962
author
b New York, NY, June 15, 19. Educ: Brooklyn Col, BA. Served USAAF, WW II. Radio, TV & film writer. Chief Collabr: Richard Uhl.

BORGE, VICTOR   ASCAP 1961
composer, comedian, actor
b Copenhagen, Denmark, Jan 3, 09. Educ: Borgerdydskolen; Cons of Copenhagen; studied with Egon Petri, Frederic Lammond. Concert pianist, 22. In musical revue, 34; films 37. To US, 40. US radio debut "Bing Crosby Show." Featured in "Comedy in Music" (one-man show). Has given concerts

throughout US & Europe; made TV appearances & records. *Instrumental Works:* Blue Serenade.

BORISOFF, ALEXANDER   ASCAP 1936
composer, author
b Odessa, Russia, Dec 20, 02. Educ: Cons of Odessa, grad doctor's degree; studied comp with F Malishevsky, cello with Joseff Press. Concert cello soloist, toured Europe; principal cellist, Los Angeles Philh. Cello & music master class, Los Angeles & Honolulu. Writer, motion picture scores, Hollywood, cello solos, duets for violin, cello, flute with cello & clarinet with cello. Comns incl tone poem "America," for NBC & played by Los Angeles Philh & others & opera "Liliu," based on the life of Queen Lilioukalani. Author, bk, "How to Write a Melody." Chief Collabr: Samuel Crowningburg Amalu. *Instrumental Works:* Variations on a Theme of Paganini (string quartette); Concerto for Bassoon; Impressions of Hawaii (symph, soloists, chorus); Symphonic Poem Ancien; Cello Concerto; Two String Quartettes.

BORK, J S
See Langdon, Verne Loring

BORNE, HAL   ASCAP 1938
composer, author, musical director
b Chicago, Ill, Dec 25, 11. Educ: Univ Ill, music; Northwestern Univ, Chicago, jour, music. RKO Studios, Hollywood, 32-39. Arr-comp-pianist, Fred Astaire & Ginger Rogers. Comp music for Marx Bros movie, "The Big Store," 40; collab with Duke Ellington musical show, "Jump for Joy," Los Angeles, 40. Mus dir, NBC radio, "A Date With Judy," 47-49, Tony Martin, 49-57 & Ginger Rogers, 76- Produced & wrote musical show, "Point of View," Hollywood, 61. Chief Collabrs: Paul Francis Webster, Sammy Cahn, Gus Kahn, Johnny Mercer, Frank Loesser, Ray Gilbert, Sid Kuller, Mort Greene, Jerry Seelen, Buddy Kaye, Fred Astaire. *Songs:* For the Right Guy; When You're Near; Part Time Lover; Promise Her Anything; Give Me a Guy; Universal Language of Love; Flight of the Lost Balloon; Wait for Me; *Music:* Tenement Symphony; Alive and Kickin; When You're Playing With Fire; If You Catch a Little Cold; I'm Building Up to an Awful Let Down; The Brown Danube; I Ain't Hep to That Step But I'll Dig It; Put Your Heart in to Your Feet and Dance; Sing While You Sell.

BORNET, FRED   ASCAP 1963
composer, author, singer
b Scheveningen, Netherlands, Feb 25, 15. To US, 39. Educ: Lycee D'Anvers; Athenee D'Anvers; studied with Jimmy Rich, voice with Stefan Kosakewicz & Coe Glade, direction with Lee Strasberg. Wrote plays in Europe. Wrote & performed numerous French ballads. USA, WW II, 41-45, wrote most of music & lyrics for Army show, "Bottlenecks 1941," Fort Monmouth; combat cameraman overseas. Now filmmaker & singer. Chief Collabr: Arr, Arthur DeCenzo. *Songs:* I'm Wasting My Time (Theatre Wing Prize); The Little Curl. *Scores:* Film/TV: In the Rivers of Streets; The Paris of Francois.

BORNSCHEIN, FRANZ   ASCAP 1928
composer, conductor, choirmaster
b Baltimore, Md, Feb 10, 1879; d Baltimore, June 8, 48. Educ: Peabody Cons; studied with Van Husteyn, Hammerick, Kahmer & Boise. Cond, Baltimore Music Sch Orch; choirmaster, First Unitarian Church; cond, Baltimore Music Club Chorus. Fac mem & cond of orch, Peabody Cons. Teacher. *Instrumental Works:* String Quartet; Leif Ericson; Southern Night; The Mission Road; The Earth Sings; Ode to the Brave; Moon Over Taos; Phantom Canoe Suite; 3 Persian Poems; Lament; A Cry to Arms; Theirs Be the Glory; Sea Cycle; *Choral:* The Sea God's Daughter; Onawa (cantata); The Vision of Sir Launfal; Arethusa; Tuscan Cypress; Day; The Conqueror Worm; Joy (Nat Fedn Music Clubs Award). *Scores:* Operetta: The Willow Plate.

BORODKIN, ABRAM E   ASCAP 1959
composer, conductor, cellist
b Russia, 06; d New York, NY, Aug 25, 78. Educ: Studied with Maurice Baron, Rubin Goldmark. Cellist, NBC & CBS Networks. Cond, radio, TV & concerts. *Instrumental Works:* Istanbul; At Saint Basil's; String Fever; Harlem Hop.

BOROWSKI, FELIX   ASCAP 1940
composer, author, educator
b Burton, Eng, Mar 10, 1872; d Chicago, Ill, July 6, 56. Educ: Cologne Cons; also pvt study. Moved to US, 1897. Dir comp dept, Chicago Musical Col, 1897-1916, pres, 16-25. Supt, Civic Music Asn, Chicago, 26-32. Prof musicol, Northwestern Univ, 32-42. Wrote prog notes for Chicago Symph. Music critic & ed, Chicago Sun-Times. Coauth: "Standard Concert Guide" & "The Standard Operas." *Instrumental Works:* Elegie Symphonique; 3 symphonies; Peintures; Le Printemps; Passionne; Fantasie-Overture; Youth (tone poem); Semiramis; Piano Concerto; Ecce Homo (tone poem); Requiem for a Child; 3 string quartets.

BORZAGE, DONALD DAN   ASCAP 1967
composer, teacher
b Salt Lake City, Utah, Jan 3, 25. Educ: Los Angeles Cons, studied concert piano, comp, theory & writing. Songwriter; prof singer & pianist in nightclubs. Writer, film "Teenage Millionaire." Taught piano & singing. Chief Collabrs: Ned Washington, Johnny Mercer, Sammy Cahn, Paul Webster, Bob Edwards,

Josie Stalcup, Nat Cole, Jr, Andy Razaf, Carter Wright, Susanne Quickel, Steve Swartz. *Songs:* Longing; Tonight May Have to Last Me All My Life; Glad to Be Me; Everything I Touch Turns to Tears; In a Garden By a Chapel; A Miracle; I Never Knew a Love That Was So Lonely; Don't Call It Love; Bank of Memories; To Think You Choose Me.

BOSSONE, FRANK   ASCAP 1964
composer, author, singer
b Philadelphia, Pa, Jan 3, 17. Educ: Lower Merion Sr High Sch, Ardmore, Pa, grad, majored in art, photography, set design make-up; Philadelphia Col Arts, degree, 61, majored in fashion & color design; Hedgerow Theatre, studied acting under Jasper Deeter, 42-43. Rec'd Most Outstanding Athlete Award, 36; suburban & state record holder for 2 1/2 mile cross country run, Lower Merion Sr High Sch; winner of mile run, state & city area, Pa. One of winners in search for talent contest conducted nationwide by Movie Fan Mag, 45. State dir & dean of judges, Miss NJ & Miss Pa Universe Beauty Pageant, 59-61 & Miss Pa World Beauty Pageant, 60-77. Set designer for Miss Hemisphere Nat Beauty Pageant, Walt Disney World, Fla, 77. Dir-producer of Soc Models Guild, Philadelphia. Free-lance photographer & teacher of body control movement. Mem: AGAV, 37-44, Philadelphia, New York; Nat Amateur Athletic Union; Main Line Art League, 47-61; Songwriters Hall of Fame, 67; Philadelphia Mummers Asn. Awards: Best Dressed Costume, Fancy Div, Philadelphia Mummers Asn, 61; Pa Bicentennial, Red, White & Blue theme, 76; Best Dress, Rittenhous Square Easter Parade, Philadelphia; Best Interior Design, eastern seaboard area, for Cafe Int nightclub, Philadelphia, 77. Dancer, artist, dir, producer & actor. Chief Collabr: Charles Johnson. *Songs:* My Heart Is Yours; Alone; Santo Amore (Sacred Love); Little French Cafe; My Heart Surrenders; I'll Try Again; September Moon; Melodie; A Good Sign.

BOSTICK, MARIE ROBINSON   ASCAP 1978
composer, author
b Farmersville, Tex, May 20, 21. Mem: Nat Writers Asn; NMex State Poetry Soc Inc. Began writing lyrics in 40's with Five Star Music Masters & in 60's with West Coast Music Inc; later with Preview Records of Calif, Nashville Productions, Hollywood Music Productions & Medallion Records of Calif. *Songs:* Oh Jamie Girl; Rock a Billy Santa; Our Remember Whens; Until Dawn; In My Dreams.

BOSWELL, CONNEE (CONSTANCE FOORE'BOSWELL) ASCAP 1953
composer, cellist, arranger
b Kansas City, Mo, Dec 3, 07; d New York, NY, Oct 11, 76. Educ: Pub sch & pvt sch; studied music & cello with Prof Fincke, New Orleans, La. Formed Boswell Sisters Trio with two sisters, Martha & Vet; trio disolved, 36; then soloist, 40 yrs; voted No 1 Vocalist, 41 & 42; appeared in films, TV shows & with radio, Kraft Music Hall, 2 yrs; appeared in Bway & touring shows, "Star Time" & "Curtain Time." Gave benefits for armed forces & for all causes, especially for all handicapped hospitals & mil. Musician, singer, painter & recording artist. *Songs & Instrumental Works:* Heebie Jeebies; It's Too Late Now; When Xmas Is Gone; Smile in the Sunshine; Whispers in the Dark (nominated for Acad Award); Puttin It On; I Don't Mind; You Ain't Got Nothin'; Mommy, Martha (adaption); Home on the Range (adaption); In Universal Short; Never Took a Lesson in My Life; I'm Away From It All; Saving All I Can; Lummir Zingin; It's Too Late Now to Say I'm Sorry; You Burned Your Name in My Memory.

BOTKIN, PERRY   ASCAP 1950
composer, guitarist, accompanist
b Richmond, Ind, July 22, 07; d. Guitarist, music supvr, Bing Crosby, 17 yrs; assoc with Al Jolson & Eddie Cantor in radio, recording, 20 yrs. Guitarist in orchs incl Paul Whiteman, John Scott Trotter, Victor Young & Johnny Green. Soloist in films, TV & concerts. Chief Collab: Preston Foster. *Songs & Instrumental Works:* Two Shillelagh O'Sullivan; Duke of the Uke; Ukey-Ukulele; Pick-A-Lili; Executioner Theme; Waltz of the Hunter. *Scores:* Film Background: Murder By Contract; Seventy Times Seven.

BOTSFORD, GEORGE   ASCAP 1914
composer, conductor
b Sioux Falls, SDak,, Feb 24, 1874; d New York, NY, Feb 11, 49. Music dir for stage. Charter mem, ASCAP. *Songs:* The Grizzly Bear; Sailing Down the Chesapeake Bay; Black and White Rag; Pride of the Prairie; Honeymoon Bells; Sahara Butterfly; Back to Dixie Land; Silvery Bells; Traveling (Iowa Corn Song); When Big Profundo Sang Low C.

BOTSFORD, TALITHA   ASCAP 1960
composer, author, poet
b Millport, NY, Sept 21, 01. Educ: Elmira Acad; Ithaca Cons Music (violin scholarship). Violinist in symphs. Violinist & pianist, concert, lyceum, resort hotels, theatres, vaudeville, summer stock, TV & radio, US & Can. Newspaper artist & verse columnist. Original watercolors on a set of 25 postcards. Many one-man art exhibits, some exclusively musical subjects. Many original musical comps, watercolors & drawings acquired by Cornell Univ. Elmira Art Club Award, 50; Mark Twain Hotel Art Award, 52. *Songs:* Hymn to the Flag; Bicentennial Celebration. *Instrumental Works:* Piano: Frolic; Carnival Capers; Danse de Ballet; Whimsical Dance; Jolly Dance; Tribute to Teal Park Bandstand.

BOUCHARD, JOSEPH J   ASCAP 1971
composer, author
b Watertown, NY, Nov 9, 48. Educ: Clayton High Sch; Ithaca Col Sch Music, BM(piano), 70. Bass player & vocalist for Blue Oyster Cult; recorded 9 albums for Columbia Records, incl 3 gold & 1 platinum album. Chief Collabs: H Wheels, S Pearlman, R Binder, R Meltzer. *Songs:* Hot Rails to Hell; Morning Final; Music: Astronomy; Nosferatu; Dr Music.

BOUCHER, ROBERT   ASCAP 1960
composer, conductor
b Kent, Ohio, Jan 16, 19. Educ: Eastman Sch Music, BM; Univ Rochester, BA. WO (Glenn Miller Band), WW II. Music dir, Roxy Theatre, New York, 15 yrs & TV series, "Music on Ice." Chief Collab: Perry Burgett. *Instrumental Works:* Waltz of the Wind; Music on Ice; Curtain Call; Upbeat.

BOUCHER, VIVIAN E   ASCAP 1964
composer, author
b Lemberg, Sask, Aug 17, 15. Educ: Dakota Wesleyan Univ, BA, 37; Univ Wyo; NMex State Univ. Taught, Dakota secondary schs, 7 yrs. Librarian, Vet Admin Hospital, Sheridan, Wyo, 60-65; tech librarian, Holloman AF Base, NMex, 65-66, White Sands Missile Range, NMex, 66-79; retired. *Songs:* In the Shadow of the Big Horn Mountains; Cowtown Jubilee.

BOUDREAU, JOHN T   ASCAP 1955
composer, conductor, arranger
b Bathhurst, Que, Sept 26, 01; d Inglewood, Calif, Nov 22, 76. Educ: Univ Southern Calif. Bandmaster, USN, 19-24, Calif Nat Guard & Trojan Band, Univ Southern Calif, 27-34. Dir Olympic Bands, 32. Music dir & producer of entertainment for Los Angeles Rams, Dodgers. Organized Loyola Univ Band. Comp, cond, arr & musician for films & TV. Bandmaster, USAAF Band, WW II. Music dir, Nat Democratic Comt. Organized Honolulu Music Fest. *Songs & Instrumental Works:* Rock and Sock; Big Brass Band Parade; Roll On, Loyola; Fight On, Loyola; Sometime; Hit That Line; Rainbow Serenade; Go, Dallas Cowboys; Roll, 49ers; Suzette; The Football Rock 'n' Roll; Desert Romance; Touchdown Music; President Kennedy March; Rams Marching Song; Ride Dallas Cowboys; We Had the Best Band There; Hail Hail Mr Touchdown.

BOULANGER, ROBERT FRANCIS (VAN TREVOR)   ASCAP 1962
composer, author, singer
b Lewiston, Maine, Nov 12, 40. Educ: High sch. Sang on radio at age 7. Led own band, Saturday Knights. Has been record producer, publ. Chief Collabs: Dick Heard, Eddie Rabbitt. *Songs:* Abigail Beecher; Christmas in Washington Square; Sunday Morning; You've Been So Good to Me.

BOURDON, ROSARIO   ASCAP 1938
composer, conductor, cellist
b Montreal, Que, Mar 8, 1889; d New York, NY, Apr 24, 61. Educ: Acad de Musique de Quebec (won first prize); Ghent Royal Cons; studied with Joseph Jacob, Albert Beyer, Oscar Roels, Adolph Bogeart, Alphonse d'Hulst, Paul Lebrun; hon MusD, Univ Montreal. Concertized in Europe, 3 yrs; toured throughout Quebec. Soloist, Quebec Symph, 03. Cellist, Cincinnati Symph, Philadelphia Orch & St Paul Orch, also asst cond. Organized St Paul String Quartet. Music dir & cellist for Victor Records, 11-31. Cond, Montreal Symph, 35-43. *Instrumental Works:* Ginger Snaps; Dance Bagatelle; Chinese Lament; Through the Line; Love's Lullaby; March Automatic; Blue Grass; Nina.

BOURGEOIS, MARY ALICE   ASCAP 1979
composer, author, organist
b Baldwyn, Miss, May 8, 43. Educ: Studied organ with John Hutton, New Orleans, La. Church organist & pianist since age 14; played for church choirs & spec groups for many yrs; presently, staff organist, PTL TV Network; comp; did some studio work making records, teacher. Chief Collabr: Milton V Bourgeois (husband). *Songs:* That I May Know Him; Abide in Me; Lyrics: Come, Return Unto the Lord.

BOURGEOIS, MILTON VERNON   ASCAP 1979
composer, author, arranger
b New Orleans, La, May 13, 37. Educ: La State Univ; Univ New Orleans. Was involved in music from grade sch to col; played string bass in jazz groups & singer & instrumentalist for var other groups, 11 yrs; had been a minister music in churches; had several own gospel groups; now, a staff arr, PTL TV Network, Charlotte, NC, musician, singer & comp; teacher. Chief Collab: Mary Alice Bourgeois (wife). *Songs:* Rise and Be Healed; Love Beyond Compare; That I May Know Him; Come, Return Unto the Lord; Wonder of Wonders; God's Not Finished With Me Yet; Bought With a Precious Price; I Am Not What I Used to Be.

BOURKE, RORY MICHAEL   ASCAP 1971
composer, author
b Cleveland, Ohio, July 14, 42. Educ: High sch; Gilmour Acad; Mt St Mary's Col, Emmittsburg, Md, BS. Product mgr, Smash Records, 67-69; with Nat Sales & Promotion of Country & Western Music, Mercury Records, 69-71; writer, Chappell & Co, 72- ASCAP Country Writer of the Yr, 76 & 79. Chief Collabs: Charlie Black, Gene Dobbins, Johnny Wilson. *Songs:* Shadows in the

Moonlight; I Know a Heartache When I See One; Easy As Pie; I Promised Her a Rainbow; Sweet Magnolia Blossom; Honky Tonk Memories; Neon Rose; Lyrics: Most Beautiful Girl; Lucky Me; I Just Can't Stay Married to You.

BOUTELJE, PHIL   ASCAP 1930
composer, author, conductor
b Philadelphia, Pa, Aug 6, 1895; d Los Angles, Calif, July 29, 79. Educ: Philadelphia Music Acad. Pianist, arr, Paul Whiteman Orch. Bandmaster, WW I. Music dir, Paramount & United Artist Studios; also comp for films. Chief Collabrs: Dick Winfree, Ned Washington, Rubey Cowan, Foster Carling, Harry Tobias, Al Dubin. *Songs:* China Boy; Lonesome; Little Doll; The Man With the Big Sombrero; Teton Mountain Stomp; Star of Hope; Blue Dawn; I Loved You Too Little; I Love You, Believe Me I Love You; Hippy Happy Henny; Monna Vanna.

BOUTNIKOFF, IVAN   ASCAP 1959
composer, author, conductor
b Koupiansk, Russia, Dec 13, 1893; d. Educ: Imperial Cons of Music, Charkoff, Russia, studied with Sergei Tanejeff, Arthur Nikisch. Prof & cond, Poltawa symph, Russia; symph orch & opera, Royal Cons of Music, Athens. Cond, var orchs incl Lamoureux Symph, Symph de Paris, Bruxelles Philh, Berlin Philh, London Symph & Vienna Philh. Guest cond, Hollywood Bowl, Chicago Symph, Cincinnati Symph, Denver Symph & Dallas Symph. Music dir & arr, Ballet Russe de Monte Carlo; arr, Int Ballet of Marquis de Cuevas, Paris. *Instrumental Works:* En Galicie (orch suite); Orch transc: works by Bach, Brahms, Chopin, Scriabin, Moussorgsky. *Scores:* Opera: Aelitta; Ballet: The Spring Recital.

BOVA, BASIL A   ASCAP 1960
composer, author
b Boston, Mass, July 12, 19. Past pres, 20th Century-Fox Record Corp. Pres & owner, Kennebek Music. Producer & pres, World-over Communications, producing records, TV & motion pictures. Writer, 3 publ bks. *Songs:* The Greatest Story Ever Told.

BOWDEN, CHRISTINA MARY   ASCAP 1950
composer, author, teacher
b Bedford, Ind, Aug 17, 08. Educ: Jordan Cons Music; DePauw Univ Sch Music; studied piano, organ theory & music essentials. Chief Collabrs: Tade & Frances Dolen. *Songs:* Indianapolis (Off song of city); My Crescent Girl; Dance of the Shmoos; Music: The Cannibal's Menu; Why Oh Why; Pigtails on Parade. *Albums:* Listen and Do (3 records); Once Upon a Time; Dandy Dog in Storyland; Fun With a Purpose (5 records).

BOWDEN, RICHARD GEORGE   ASCAP 1972
composer
b Sydney, Australia, Sept 23, 44. Educ: Primarily self-taught; NSW Cons, pvt comp studies with Raymond Hanson, 66-69 & with Russell Garcia, 67. Career incl TV/film comp & arr many LP records, Sydney. Occasional comp-arr-cond, Disney Studios. Orchr movie scores for Maurice Jarre. Chief Collabrs: Tom West, Anne Del, Pat Hardin, Tom Russell. *Songs:* Music: 12 O'Clock Flight to San Francisco. *Instrumental Works:* Concert Overture (orch); Quietly Blows the Don; Bunyip Waltz; The Dealer; Whimsey (woodwind quintet). *Scores:* Film/TV: Happy 50th Birthday Mickey Mouse; The North Avenue Irregulars; Halloween Hall of Fame; The Whiz Kids and the Carnival Caper; Disneyland's 25th Anniversary; The Last Flight of Noah's Ark; The Sweet Creek County War; The Black Marble; The Preparatory (1976 Acad Award Student Film); A Christmas Carol; Heidi; The Christmas Star; A Connecticut Yankee in KA's Court; Tales of Washington Irving; Marco Polo; The Prince and the Pauper; The Swiss Family Robinson; Robinson Crusoe; Oliver Twist and the Artful Dodger; Wait 'Til Your Father Gets Home.

BOWEN, JOHN G   ASCAP 1960
author
b San Antonio, Tex, Mar 6, 1896. Educ: St Mary's Col; Georgetown Univ, MA, LLB, LLM, PhD. Exec secy to pres, Georgetown Univ, 29-38. Ed, Alert Cath Men, 38- *Songs:* I Know What God Is.

BOWER, MAURICE (BUGS)   ASCAP 1960
composer, conductor, publisher
b Atlantic City, NJ, July 16, 22. Educ: High sch; studied with Tom Timothy, Maury Deutsch & Wallingford Riegger. Trumpeter with Ice Capades & Billy Rose Aquacade. In charge of dance bands, US, European Theater of Operations, WW II. Author "Chords and Progressions" & "Rhythms." Pres, Nancy Music. Chief Collabrs: Jack Wolf; Earl Shuman. *Songs:* Caterina; The Closing Credits; Las Vegas.

BOWERS, BRYAN BENSON   ASCAP 1977
composer, author, autoharpist
b Yorktown, Va, Aug 18, 40. Street singer turned fest (folk & bluegrass) player. *Songs:* Berkely Woman; The View From Home; Lone Lone Mountain. *Instrumental Works:* Arr: Battle Hymn of the Republic.

BOWERS, FREDERICK V   ASCAP 1923
composer, singer
b Boston, Mass, June 11, 1874; d Los Angeles, Calif, Apr 29, 61. Educ: New Eng Cons. Mem vaudeville team with Charles Horwitz, 1894. Appeared in Dockstaders and Primrose & West Minstrels; on Bway in "His Bridal Night", "Kiss Me Again" & "Too Many Wives." Entertained Armed Forces, Spanish-Am War, WW I & II. *Songs:* Lucky Jim; Because (I Love You); Wait; When I Think of You; The Pig Got Up and Slowly Walked Away.

BOWERS, ROBERT HOOD   ASCAP 1914
composer, conductor
b Chambersburg, Pa, May 24, 1877; d New York, NY, Dec 29, 41. Educ: Franklin & Marshall Col; studied music with Thomas Surette, Frederic Gleason & Constantin von Sternberg; Chicago Auditorium Cons. Cond record cos, 16-32 & radio stas, NY, 28-34. Music dir, Sch of Radio Tech, 35-41. Cond, Open Air Theatre, Memphis, Tenn. Chief Collabrs: Raymond Peck, Henry Blossom, Harry B Smith, Robert B Smith. *Songs:* Chinese Lullaby; Give Me Someone; Let's Pretend; Day Dreams. *Scores:* Bway stage: The Vanderbilt Cup; The Hoyden; The Silver Star; A Lonely Romeo; The Red Rose; Temptations; Oh Ernest!.

BOWERS, WILLIAM
composer, author
b Las Cruces, NMex, Jan 17, 16. Educ: Univ Mo, studied jour. Wrote Bway play, "Where Do We Go From Here?" 37. Contract writer for RKO Pictures, 38. Has written over 60 feature films. Has owned 2 record cos. Screenwriter, producer, TV, radio & stage. Rec'd 2 Acad Award nominations & 5 Writers Guild Award nominations. *Songs:* Oh Love Has Thou Forsaken Me?; Solid Gold Cadillac; Lyrics: You Meet the Nicest People Every Year Around Christmas Time.

BOWES, THOMAS J   ASCAP 1972
composer, author
b New York, NY, Oct 5, 48. Educ: NY Univ. Songwriter of about 20 songs. Chief Collabr: Jane Jarvis. *Songs:* Lyrics: Antique; How Does It Play in Peoria?; And I March On; Da Da.

BOWLES, PAUL   ASCAP 1945
composer, author
b New York, NY, Dec 30, 10. Educ: Univ Va; studied with Aaron Copland & Virgil Thomson. Grants: Guggenheim & Rockefeller. Res folk music, Spain, NAfrica, Antiles, South & Cent Am. Author of novels: "The Sheltering Sky"; "The Delicate Prey"; "Let It Come Down"; "The Hours After Noon." Wrote incidental music to plays: "Dr Faustus"; "My Heart's in the Highlands"; "Love's Old Sweet Song"; "Twelfth Night"; "Watch on the Rhine"; "Liberty Jones"; "Jacobowsky and the Colonel"; "The Glass Menagerie." *Songs & Instrumental Works:* Picnic Cantata; Music for a Farce; Scenes d'Anabase; Suite for Small Orchestra; Preludes for Piano; Blue Mountain Ballads. *Scores:* Film background: Roots in the Soil (US Dept Agriculture); Congo (Belgian Govt); Opera: The Wind Remains; Denmark Vesey; Ballets: Yankee Clipper; Pastorales; Sentimental Colloquy.

BOWLES, RICHARD WILLIAM   ASCAP 1961
composer, author
b Rogers, Ark, June 30, 18. Educ: Ind Univ, BPSM, 40, comp study with Robert Sanders; Univ Wis, MS, 50, comp study with Cecil Burleigh. Prof trombonist, 37-39. Band dir, Culver Pub Schs, Ind, 40-42. WOJG bandleader, 715th USAAF Band, 42-46. Dir music, Heights Christian Church, Houston, Tex, 46-47. Band dir, Culver, Ind, 47-49, 50-53; band & orch dir, Lafayette, Ind, 53-58. Dir bands, Univ Fla, 58-73, prof music, 73- Mem: Am Bandmasters Asn; Outdoor Writers Asn Am; Fla Outdoor Writers Asn. Chief Collabr: Philip Maxwell. *Instrumental Works:* Away We Go, Concert Carnival; Armida (overture); Concert March: Burst of Flame; Heat Lightning; Sword and Shield; Back Talk; The Invisible Boundary; Field of Color; Swing March: Marching the Blues; The Saints; East Street Blues.

BOWMAN, BROOKS   ASCAP 1936
composer, author
b Cleveland, Ohio, Oct 21, 13; d Garrison, NY, Oct 17, 37. Educ: Stanford Univ & Princeton Univ; pvt music study. *Songs:* Fiesta; Give Me a Gibson Girl; East of the Sun; Love on a Dime; Stupid Cupid; Gone With the Wind; Will Love Find a Way?.

BOWMAN, EUDAY L   ASCAP 1946
composer, author, arranger
b Ft Worth, Tex, Nov 9, 1887; d New York, NY, May 26, 49. Educ: Pub schs. Arr for dance orchs. *Songs & Instrumental Works:* 12th Street Rag; Colorado Blues; Kansas City Blues; Fort Worth Blues; Petticoat Lane; Tipperary Blues; Shamrock Rag; 11th Street Rag; Water Lily Dreams; Old Glory On Its Way.

BOX, EUEL   ASCAP 1974
composer, conductor, producer
b Georgetown, Tex, Dec 31, 28. Educ: NTex State Univ; USM Corps Band. Music prod, maj radio markets, US, London, Luxembourg & Australia. Comp, film music for Braniff Int, Dr Pepper, Buick, USN, Haggar Slacks, Zales, Tex Instruments, LTV Aerospace & Bell Helicopter. Songwriter, film incl "Benji",

"For the Love of Benji", "Double McGuffin", "Hawmps" & "Oh Heavenly Dog." Recorded, cond & contracted for var artists incl Stevie Wonder, Boz Scaggs, Glen Campbell, Lou Rawls, Charlie Rich & Chet Atkins. Recording artist with 2 albums. Recipient, Golden Globe Award, Hollywood Foreign Press & Acad Award nomination. Chief Collabrs: Betty Box, Joe Camp. *Songs:* I Feel Love; Sunshine Smiles; Multiplicity; Live for Today; Somebody Who Really Cares.

BOYADJIAN, HAYG   ASCAP 1978
composer
b Paris, France, May 15, 38. Educ: Elem schs in Paris & in Valentin Alsina, Arg; high sch equivalency dipl in Mass, 61; Liszt Cons, studied piano & comp, 58; Arg, studied with Bestriz Balzi; Northeastern Univ, Boston, BA, 67; Brandeis Univ, 69, studied with Seymour Shiffrin. Free lance comp chamber music; assoc with contemporary chamber ensemble, The Annex Players of Boston, 72-76; had works performed in Mass, Maine, Calif, Spain, Scotland, Brazil & Arg; also on radio & TV in Boston, Detroit & Madrid. *Songs:* Music: Noche; Scythe Song; Song Cycle on Poems of William Blake. *Instrumental Works:* Movement No 1 (piano); Movement No 4 (piano); Sonata for Violin Solo; Triaco; Contours; Suite for Brass Quintet; Nocturnes for Cello Solo; Episodes for Sextet.

BOYD, JACK ARTHUR   ASCAP 1966
composer, author, choral conductor
b Indianapolis, Ind, Feb 9, 32. Educ: Abilene Christian Univ, BMusEd, 55; North Tex State Univ, MMusComp, 59; Univ Iowa, PhD(choral literature), 71. Minister of music, Irving, Tex, 55-57; choral dir, Paducah Tilghman High Sch, Ky, 57-63, Univ Dubuque, Iowa, 64-67, Abilene Christian Univ, 68-79. Prof musicology, Abilene Christian Univ, 79- Author bks, "Rehearsal Guide for the Choral Director", "Teaching Choral Sight Reading" & "The Lord's Singing"; also choral arr, scholarly ed & original choral compositions publ.

BOYD, MULLEN
See Kapp, Paul

BOYD, WYNN LEO   ASCAP 1960
composer, author, teacher
b Gaithersburg, Md, July 28, 02. Educ: Ithaca Piano Sch. Operated own piano studio, 30-45. Had piano tuning studio for blind vets. Founded own firm, rebuilding pianos. *Songs:* Make a Joyful Noise Unto God (anthem); also American Art Songs (poems by Paul Lawrence Dunbar); 23rd Psalm.

BOYELL, RICHARD S   ASCAP 1966
b Chicago, Ill, Sept 21, 23. Educ: Northwestern Univ, MS(comp), 49. Pianist & arr in Chicago until late 60's. Owner of production & publ co, Nuance Productions, commercials & indust films; arr for Honeytree & Ken Medena, Word Records; arr for numerous albums. *Songs:* Music to Think By. *Instrumental Works:* Theme for Piano and French Horn. *Albums:* Animated Film: What's Up Is Down.

BOYER, CHARLES SCOTT   ASCAP 1969
composer, author, guitarist
b Binghamton, NY, Oct 17, 47. Educ: Englewood High Sch, Jacksonville, Fla; Fla State Univ Music Sch, viola major, 65-66. Started recording, 67; with group Cowboy, 70-71 & 74-76; did studio work on guitar with Wet Willie, Bonnie Bramlett, Kitty Wells, Gregg Allman, Billy Joe Shaver & Cher, 70-78. Violist & singer. *Songs:* Please Be With Me; All My Friends; It's Time; Pat's Song; Takin' It All the Way; Southern Kids.

BOYLE, BOBBI
See Young, Barbara Marie

BOYLE, GEORGE F   ASCAP 1944
composer, pianist, teacher
b Sydney, Australia, June 29, 1886; d Philadelphia, Pa, June 20, 48. Educ: Studied with Busoni. Toured as pianist & cond, Australia, Ger, Holland & Great Brit. Moved to US, 10; taught piano at Peabody Cons, Curtis Inst & Juilliard Sch Music; had own piano studios, Philadelphia. *Songs & Instrumental Works:* Piano Concerto; Piano Concertino; Cello Concerto; Symphonic Fantasie; Holiday Overture; Piano Sonata; Sonata for Violin, Piano; Sonata for Viola, Piano; Sonata for Cello, Piano; Ballade Elegiaque (piano, violin, cello); Pied Piper of Hamelin (cantata); The Black Rose (operetta).

BRABEC, JEFFREY JOSEPH   ASCAP 1968
composer, author
b Long Beach, Calif, Dec 30, 43. Educ: Loyola Sch; Boston Col; NY Univ Sch Law. Recording artist, Audio Fidelity Records. Atty, Community Legal Counsel, 68-70. With ASCAP Membership & Distribution Depts, 70-72. Pvt pract, 73-78. Dir bus affairs, Interworld Music Group, Inc, 78- *Songs:* People Getting Younger; Good Morning Sunshine.

BRACKMAN, GEORGE   ASCAP 1959
composer, author, arranger
b Brooklyn, NY, Jan 5, 22. Educ: Abraham Lincoln High Sch, Brooklyn; Juilliard Sch Music, BS & MS, 48; studied comp & arr with Wallingford Riegger, Bernard Wagenaar, Vittorio Giannini & Adolph Schmidt. Army bandmaster, 433rd ASF Band, WW II, Brussels, Belg; arr, comp, music supvr & producer for

TV shows, "Colgate Comedy Hour", "Two For the Money", "Treasure Hunt", "Macy's Thanksgiving Day Parade", "CMA Country Music Awards Show", "Orange Bowl Parade", "The Tonight Show", "America's Junior Miss Pageant," plus others; commercials, General Motors, Esso, Dupont, plus others; feature films, "Only One New York", "Gulliver Travels Beyond the Moon," plus others; records, Columbia, RCA, Atlantic, plus others. Cond & music & recording producer. Chief Collabrs: Milton Delugg, Sally Eaton. *Songs:* Music: I Don't Want to Love You Anymore; Beads; The Young Set. *Instrumental Works:* New Music for the Sabbath Worship (Musical setting for the Reform Jewish Sabbath serv; for solo voices, choir & orch or organ); The Ninety-Eighth Psalm (for choir, orch or organ); Jangle Bangle.

BRACKMAN, JACOB   ASCAP 1970
author, lyricist
b New York, NY, Sept 22, 43. Educ: Buxton High Sch; Harvard Univ, BA, 65. Songwriter. Lyricist, Bway play "King of Hearts," 78 & for var musicals. Author of screenplay for film "Times Square." Chief Collabrs: Michael Polnaeff, Carley Simon, James Taylor, Dr John, Jerry Ragaudy, Lamont Docier. *Songs:* Lyrics: That's the Way I've Always Heard It Should Be; Haven't Got Time for the Pain; Attitude Dancing; It Was So Easy.

BRADEN, JOHN STUART   ASCAP 1969
composer, author, singer
b Ashboro, NC, Jan 17, 46. Educ: Southwest High Sch, Miami, Fla. Resident comp, La Mama Exp Theatre Club; recording artist. Chief Collabrs: Jeff Tamborino, Barry Arnold. *Scores:* Bway shows: Downriver; The Derby; Silver Queen Saloon; The Writers Opera; La Justice; Gullivers Travels; A Book of Etiquette; Horse Opera.

BRADFORD, GLENN DALE   ASCAP 1975
composer, author, singer
b West Plains, Mo, June 18, 32. Singer/songwriter, cameo TV, recordings, shows & nightclub entertaining. Recording artist, Nashville Cats Productions. Chief Collabr: Doyle Turner. *Songs:* Ode to Trooper Ron; It's Not the Same Anymore; My Heart Belongs to You.

BRADFORD, JOHN MILTON (JOHN M   ASCAP 1953
LEVINSON)
composer, author, singer
b Long Branch, NJ, July 2, 19. Educ: Univ Southern Calif, studied with Frank Baxter; Univ Santa Clara, studied with J Fenton McKenna; San Francisco State Univ, BA, 47. Singer, RCA Victor, 47-51; TV performer, NBC, 48-51; TV writer, 56- Recipient, Nat Acad of TV Arts & Sci Emmy award, 75 & 2 Christopher awards. Chief Collabrs: Michel Legrand, Dean Elliott, Robert Wells, Hoyt Curtin, Frank Perkins, William Friml, Tony Romano, Dimitri Tiomkin, Russ Black. *Songs:* Lyrics: Fandango. *Scores:* Film/TV: Michel's Mixed Up Musical Bird; Battle of San Pietro; Magical Mystery Trip Through Little Red's Head; Purple Heart Diary; Robber's Roost.

BRADFORD, ROARK   ASCAP 1951
author
b Lauderdale Co, Tenn, Aug 21, 1896; d New Orleans, La, Nov 13, 48. Newspaperman in Atlanta & New Orleans. Author: "Ol' Man Adam and His Chillun"; "This Side of Jordan"; "Ol' King David and the Philistine Boys"; "John Henry" (also play with music); "Kingdom Coming." Chief Collabr: Jacques Wolfe. *Songs:* Careless Love; Sundown In My Soul; The Crawfish Song; No Bottom.

BRADFORD, SYLVESTER HENRY (ANN THOMPSON) ASCAP 1958
composer, author
b Brooklyn, NY, Jan 7, 42. Educ: NY Inst for Educ of Blind; City Col New York, BA; NY Univ, MA; NY Lighthouse Music Sch; studies with Charles Beets. Played music to get through col; wrote popular songs while working as vocational counselor for the blind; mem rock & roll groups; toured Canada as pianist. Chief Collabrs: Antwon Fats Domino, Al Lewis. *Songs:* Tears on My Pillow; I'm Ready; Spanish Twist; Wishful Thinking; Uh-Mm-Huh; Right Now; I Found Love on a Disco Floor; I Want a Boy for My Birthday; I Like Girls. *Instrumental Works:* Vodka.

BRADFORD, WILLIAM
See Walker, William Stearns

BRADLEY, LEO HERMAN   ASCAP 1979
composer, author, singer
b Waltz, Ky, Oct 21, 38. Educ: Morehead State Univ, AB; Xavier Univ, MEd; Univ Cincinnati, EdD. Writer & recorder, country songs. Chief Collabr: Shad O'Shea. *Songs:* The Place; What Are We Doing Here; Matinees at Melbas; Common Man; Southern Ohio.

BRADLEY, MILUS L   ASCAP 1969
composer, teacher, singer
b Lake Charles, La, Jan 21, 27. Educ: Southwestern Bible Inst, studied voice with Harold Miles, piano with Bonnie Burke; Univ Tex, studied piano with Verna Harder; Tex Wesleyan Col, BS(cum laude), 62. Minister. Pianist,

accordion soloist & singer, revival meetings, live radio progs & TV progs. Chief Collabrs: Olive Bradley Ford, Charles Hamilton. *Songs:* Dallas Is the City for Me; There Is a Need to Pray.

BRADSHAW, LESLIE GLEN   ASCAP 1974
composer, author, singer
b Wayne, WVa, Aug 14, 34. Educ: Gilkerson Grade Sch; Wayne High Sch; Marshall Univ. BA. Wrote first song, 58. Recording artist & publ, WVa Ramblers Label. Pres, WVa Band. Work for Chessie Syst. Mem, USA Reserve. *Songs:* West Virginia Blues; Lord I Can't Make It Without You; Our Only Hope; Take Me Back to the West Virginia Hills; Going Down to Nashville.

BRADSHAW, MERRILL KAY   ASCAP 1976
composer, educator
b Lyman, Wyo, June 18, 29. Educ: Brigham Young Univ, AB, 54, MA, 55, studies with Leon Dallin & Crawford Gates; Univ Ill, MMus, 56, DMusA, 62, studies with Robert Palmer, Robert Kelly, Gordon Binkerd & Burrill Phillips. Prof music, Brigham Young Univ, 57-, composer-in-residence, 68- *Songs:* The Restoration (oratorio); Music: Three Psalms (choir); Title of Liberty (musical); Conversation Piece (musical); Brass Quintet; Kingdom Psalmes (choir). *Instrumental Works:* Four Mountain Sketches (orch); Peace Memorial (orch); Nocturnes and Revels (string orch); Homages: A Concerto (viola & small orch); Mosaics: 20 Pieces for Piano; Five Symphonies (orch); Music for Worship; Miniature Preludes; Lovers and Liars (orch). *Scores:* Zion (pageant music).

BRADSHAW, MYRON CARLTON (TINY)   ASCAP 1941
composer, author, singer
b Youngstown, Ohio, Sept 23, 08; d Cincinnati, Ohio, Nov 26, 58. Educ: South High & Chaney High Schs, Youngstown; Oberlin Sch of Music (Cons). Started playing drums at age 10; performed professionally as drummer & vocalist; drummer with Jump Johnson Band, Buffalo, NY; joined Louis Russell Band, New York. Formed his own band & performed & recorded, 35 yrs. Chief Collabrs: Jean Bradshaw Redd (daughter) & Red Prysock. *Songs:* The Jersey Bounce; Train Kept a Rollin'; San Fernando Valley. *Instrumental Works:* Soft.

BRAGGIOTTI, MARIO   ASCAP 1952
composer, author, pianist
b Florence, Italy, Nov 29, 09. Educ: New Eng Cons, studied with Adamowsky & Converse; Fountainebleu & Paris Cons, studied with Nadia Boulanger, Caussade & Cortot. Debut, duo piano team with Jacques Fray, Salle Pleyel, Paris. US debut, Carnegie Hall. With Fray, had own weekly radio series, 6 yrs. Cond, arr & soloist, radio. Toured in concert progs, "From Bach to Boogie Woogie." Radio prog dir, US occupational army, Africa & Italy, WW II. Piano soloist with symph orchs in Gershwin fest tour, 2 seasons; also toured Europe. *Songs & Instrumental Works:* Variations on Yankee Doodle; Lincolns' Gettysburg Address. *Scores:* Ballet: The Princess.

BRAININ, JEROME   ASCAP 1941
composer, pianist, teacher
b New York, NY, Sept 3, 16. Educ: Piano scholarship under Tobias Westlin of Cons Sweden; studied piano harmony & theory with Max Friedman of Berlin Cons. Pianist & vocal arr popular orchs. Wrote score for "Gay New Orleans" (NY World's Fair, 40); contributed to Bway production "Star and Garter"; TV theme "Cavalcade of Bands." Served in US Signal Corps, Okinawa & Korea, World War II. Chief Collabrs: Allen Roberts, Buddy Bernier & Buddy Kaye. *Songs:* Music: Teacher's Pet; Don't Let Julia Fool Ya; Ain't Ya Got No Romance; I Can't Change My Heart. *Scores:* Film/TV: The Night Has a Thousand Eyes; Chatterbox; Bway show: It Wouldn't Be Love; I Touched a Star.

BRANCH, CHARLIE (SONGSTRESS)   ASCAP 1971
author, publisher, lyricist
Educ: Studied bel canto vocal technique with Walter Taussig, Metrop Opera Asn. Lyric soprano, Mozart specialist & singer of lyric operas, operettas, musicals & popular ballads. Established Charlie Branch Music Co, St Louis, Mo. *Songs:* Lyrics: Roses for My Love.

BRANDEWINE-MONTGOMERY, KANDEDA RACHEL   ASCAP 1969
composer, author, instrumentalist
b Macomb, Ill, July 5, 40. Educ: Carthage Col, studied art with James Melchert, 57-59; Brigham Young Univ, 58; Univ Ill, 59-62; San Francisco Art Inst, studied art with Manuel Neri, Graff & William Geis, 65-66; Univ Calif, Berkeley, BA, 68, studied art with James Melchert & Pete Folkous; Northern Ariz Univ; Humboldt State Univ. Free-lance rock & roll performer, 55-60; free-lance folk music performer, 60- Univ & free-lance lectr, 69- Teacher of all subjects, 70-; col instr, 78- Scholar of Indo-Europ myths as found in ballads, 75- *Songs & Instrumental Works:* Where Have You Been Today, James Rector?

BRANDON, SEYMOUR (SY)   ASCAP 1976
composer
b New York, NY, June 24, 45. Educ: Ithaca Col, NY, BS in MusEd, 66, MS in MusEd, 68; Univ Ariz, AmusD(comp), 72. Studied comp with Warren Benson, Elie Siegmeister & Robert McBride, 73-74; visiting comp-in-residence, Boise State Univ; assoc prof theory-comp, Millersville State Col, Pa, presently. Comns: Boise Philh & Music Teachers Projects Assistance Prog, Pa. Awards: Martha Baird Rockefeller Comp Assistance Prog. Maj perf: Boise Philh, York

Symph Orch & Harrisburg Symph Orch. *Instrumental Works:* Concert Overture for Saxophone Quartet; Trio for Brass.

BRANDT, EDWARD AUGUST   ASCAP 1957
composer, author
b Chicago, Ill, Aug 5, 24. Educ: Northwestern Univ Sch of Music. Writer of spec material for Spike Jones, stage, screen, radio & TV, 45-65. Wrote for Joan Davis, Eddie Cantor, Vaughan Monroe & Spade Cooley, 46-58. Wrote animated TV series, "Beany and Cecil," also for Hanna-Barbara TV animated series, 60-71. Chief Collabrs: Freddy Morgan, Spike Jones, Paul Frees, George Motola. *Songs:* There's No Place Like Hawaii; Rock and Roll Wedding; The Late, Late Movies; I Was a Teenage Brain Surgeon; Shortnin' Bread Rock; I'm Having a Breaking Up Party; I'm Drowning My Sorrows; The Tears in Your Eyes; I Don't Want to Ever Be a Princess; Flying Saucers; When I Grow Up I Wanna Be a Cowboy; Sideburns and Sympathy.

BRANDT, PAMELA ROBIN   ASCAP 1975
composer, author, singer
b Brooklyn, NY, Feb 6, 47. Educ: Montclair High Sch, NJ; Mt Holyoke Col, BA(art); vocal studies with Amri Galli-Campi, 75-76, stand-up bass with Doc Goldberg. Recording artist, Spirit & RCA (Phantom) Records. Performing artist on TV shows, incl "Sesame Street", "A M America", "Dinah Shore Show", "Barbara Walters Special", "Of Women and Men" & others, concert clubs & halls, incl Other End & Bottom Line, New York & Boarding House, San Francisco, toured with Billy Joel, 76 & in bands, incl The Moppets, Ariel & The Deadly Nightshade. Free lance songwriter for Children's TV Workshop. Accepted into womens' hist collection, Smithsonian Inst, 79. Chief Collabr: Helen Hooke. *Songs:* Dance, Mr Big, Dance; Ain't I a Woman?; Everybody's Song; High Flyin' Woman; Lyrics: Mary Hartman, Mary Hartman (disco theme).

BRANEN, JEFF T   ASCAP 1943
author, publisher
b Sycamore, Ill, Dec 9, 1872; d Butte, Mont, Jan 19, 27. Educ: Pub schs. Taught country sch; studied law in Chicago. Active in minstrel field. *Songs:* I'm Looking for a Nice Young Fellow; In the Valley of the Moon; Just a Little Bit of Green; You May Be the World to a World of Friends; I Wouldn't Be Lonely If I Had You.

BRANNON, BOB
See Maschek, Adrian Mathew

BRANNUM, HUGH ROBERTS (MR GREEN JEANS,   ASCAP 1950
UNCLE LUMPY)
composer, author, singer
b Sandwich, Ill, Jan 5, 10. Educ: Redlands High Sch, Calif; Univ Redlands; studied with pvt teachers. Musician & entertainer; mem, Calif Collegians & Fred Waring's Pennsylvanians. Chief Collabrs: Paul Kapp, Tom Howell, Frank Stanton. *Albums:* Many children's stories and song albums, incl "Littly Orly" series.

BRANO, ROSCOE
See Culbertson, Roy Frederich

BRANSCOMBE, GENA (MRS JOHN   ASCAP 1932
FERGUSON TENNEY)
composer, author, conductor
b Picton, Ont, Nov 4, 1881; d New York, NY, July 26, 77. Educ: Chicago Musical Col, BM; hon MA, Whitman Col; studied with Felix Borowski, Engelbert Humperdinck, Rudolph Ganz, Wilhelm Klatte, Frank Damrosch & Albert Stoessel. Toured in recitals of own works. Head piano dept, Whitman Col Cons, 07-09. Cond, Branscombe Choral, State Chorus of NJ; Contemporary Club Choral, Newark & MacDowell Chorale, NJ. Nat chmn, Am Music & Folksong, Gen Fedn Women's Clubs, 30-35; chmn, Choral Music, NY Fedn Music Clubs, 49; 1st vpres & bd mem, Nat Asn for Am Comp & Cond. Awards: Nat League Am Pen Women; Daughters Am Revolution; Am Mothers Comm Golden Rule Found. *Songs & Instrumental Works:* Quebec (suite); Pacific Sketches (Am suite; for horn); Sonata (violin); Choral: Youth of the World; Prayer for Song; Into the Light; Pilgrims of Destiny; Arms That Have Shelter'd Us (Navy hymn); Coventry's Choir; Sun and the Warm Brown Earth; Our Canada from Sea to Sea; Prayer for Song; The Lord Is Our Fortress; Hail Ye Tyme of Holie Dayes; Songs: The Morning Wind; I Bring You Heartsease; A Lute of Jade; The Best Is Yet to Be; Blow Softly, Maple Leaves; Happiness; Songs of the Unafraid; Two Indian Love Songs; Three Unimproving Songs for Enthusiastic Children; Spirit of Motherhood; many choral arr with original texts & transl.

BRANT, HENRY
composer
b Montreal, Que, Sept 15, 13. Educ: Juilliard Sch, 34. Comp & cond, documentary films for US Govt Office of War Info, 40-47, var radio network prog series for NBC, CBS & ABC, 42-46. Fac, Juilliard Sch, 47-55, dept music, Columbia Univ, 43-53, Bennington Col, Vt, 57- Pioneer in develop spatial-antiphonal music. Recipient, Prix Italia, 55, Alice M Ditson awards, 62 & 64, Guggenheim fel, 46 & 55, Inst Arts & Letters grant, 55, Copley grant, 60,

Huber grant, 60, Dollard grant, 66, Thorne fel, 72, NY State Council for Arts grant, 74, NEA grant, 76. *Songs & Instrumental Works:* Angels and Devils; Signs and Alarms; Antiphony 1; Millenium 2; Encephalograms 2; Ceremony; Galaxy 2; December; Hieroglyphics; The Children's Hour; Mythical Beasts; Atlantis; Concerto With Lights; Barricades; Headhunt; Voyage 4 (total antiphony in 83 parts); Odyssey—Why Not?; Kingdom Come; Crossroads; Immortal Combat; American Requiem; Prevailing Winds; Solomon's Gardens; Homage to Ives; A Plan of the Air; Spatial Piano Concerto. *Scores:* Spatial opera: Grand Universal Circus.

BRANT, IRA ASCAP 1953
composer, pianist, teacher
b New York, NY, Feb 28, 21. Educ: Columbia Univ; Juilliard Sch Music; studied with Wallingford Riegger. Concert pianist during 30's; cond, pianist in hotels, nightclubs. Music teacher. Chief Collabr: Hal David. *Songs:* Cling to Me.

BRASHEAR, JANICE MARIE ASCAP 1978
composer, author
b Vilonia, Ark, Oct 1, 41. Educ: Piano study, 48-52 & 57; high sch, North Little Rock, Ark; Capital City Bus Col. Secy; then pianist for Brashear Family, church & evangelistic work, 72-80. Chief Collabr: Jerrel Brashear. *Songs:* I Was Nothing; He Didn't Quit on Me; One Moment of Time; Come on and Sing; Who Will Reach Them? (TV theme song).

BRATMAN, CARROLL CHARLES (GARY CAROL) ASCAP 1969
composer
b Baltimore, Md, June 27, 06. Educ: Baltimore City Col, grad; Peabody Inst Music, studies with Gustav Strube & Howard Thatcher; Curtis Inst Music. Mem, Nat Symph Orch, 31 & NY Philh Orch, 57; instr perc dept, Peabody Inst, 36; staff percussionist, Stokowski All-Am Youth Orch, 41-42 & CBS Radio, 42; formed Carroll Musical Instr Serv, 46; originator of creative sound effects for radio networks, etc, 41. Mem: Percussive Arts Soc; Am Fedn Musicians; Nat Acad TV Arts & Sci. Composer music, Electronic Musical Instruments, 68- Chief Collabrs: Harry Breuer, Jean Jacques Perrey. *Instrumental Works:* Electronic Music Recordings: An Elephant Never Forgets; Flight of the Bumble Bee; In a Happy Mood; In a Latin Mood; Saturn Ski Jump; Space Express; Gypsy in Rio; Perpetual Gossip; Space Express; Short Circuit; Paris 2079; Histoires San Paroles; Blast off Country Style; March of the Martians; Des Autos Et Des Hommes; Bruit D Abeilles; Krazy Kat Rag.

BRATTON, JOHN W ASCAP 1914
composer, author, actor
b Wilmington, Del, Jan 21, 1867; d Brooklyn, NY, Feb 7, 47. Educ: Harkness Acad; Philadelphia Col Music. Baritone soloist, St Andrew's Church, Wilmington. Actor, cond, mgr & producer in theatre. Chief Collabrs: Harry B Smith, Paul West, A Seymour Brown. *Songs:* The Sunshine of Paradise Alley; Henrietta, Have You Met Her?; Sweetheart, Let's Grow Old Together; I Talked to God Last Night; The Teddy Bears' Picnic; The Rose's Honeymoon; Wooden Soldier; In a Pagoda; One World. *Instrumental Works:* An American Abroad (overture). *Scores:* Bway stage: Hodge Podge and Co; The Liberty Belles; The Pearl and the Pumpkin; Buster Brown; The Newlyweds and Their Baby.

BRATU, ALEXANDRU ASCAP 1978
author, professor, economist
b Sipote-Iasi, Romania, Apr 14, 18. Educ: C C Negruzzi High Sch, Iassy, Romania, BA, 36; Iassy Univ Col Law, bachelor's degree, 40; Iassy Univ Law Sch, PhD(law, economics), 42. Asst prof, Iassy Univ Col Law, 40-43. Lawyer, Bucharest Bar Asn, 44-68. Playwright, 59- Economist, US, 65-74, accountant, 77. Chief Collabr: Emma-Emilia Bratu. *Scores:* Blossoms of Lime, Blossoms of Acacia; Rivers' Cycle (four librettos for ballet); Librettos: Cosinzeana (opera); Sinziana (ballet); The Ten Commandments (opera); The Golden Calf (ballet); The Fall of Sarmisegetosa; Cecilia.

BRATU, EMMA ASCAP 1978
composer, teacher, pianist
b Ohaba-Bistra, Romania, Oct 11, 10. Educ: Timisoara Cons Music, BA(piano, comp); Franz Liszt Music Acad, Budapest, studied piano & harmony; pvt studies orch & harmony, Sabin Dragoi & Matyas Csany. Comp & pianist, Oradea & Bucuresti, 38-52. Teacher piano & comp, Bucuresti, 68-76. Comp & piano teacher, New York, 77- Chief Collabrs: Alexandru Bratu, Petru Vaida. *Songs:* Music: Romanian Brothers; Blossoms of Lime, Blossoms of Acacia. *Instrumental Works:* Rivers' Cycle (4 concert waltzes); Symphony of Patria No 1 in F Major; Symphony No 2 in C Major (Eileen's Dream). *Scores:* Operas: Ten Commandments; Cosinzeana.

BRAU, ALEXIS R ASCAP 1955
composer, author
b San Juan, PR, Dec 9, 21. Educ: Univ Va. *Songs & Instrumental Works:* Que Fue De Ti; Llevate Mis Recuerdos; Llamandote; Primer Amor; Rosa Dormida; Buscandote; Nuestro Regimiento; Vendaval; Que Bonita Iba; Nunca; Muy Tarde; Pobrecita; Las Almas Que Se Aman.

BRAUN, ALEXANDER (SHONY) ASCAP 1967
composer, author, teacher
b Romania, July 14, 30. Educ: High sch, Hungary & Ger; univ in Ger; Mozarteum, Salzburg, Austria; Western Reserve Univ; studied with Ede

Zaturecky, Vasa Prihoda & Josef Gingold. Concerts in Europe & US; recording artist, Impromptu Label; TV & motion picture appearances; command performance for royalties. Chief Collabr: Gregory Stone. *Songs:* Gypsy in Blue; Don't Say Goodby; That Summer Night; Music: Serenada Romantic; Sha'rika. *Instrumental Works:* Mexican Danse; Andaluzia; La-Mento (Returning Memories); Spanish Romance; Hope Faith and Courage; Walse Tzigany (Gypsy Walse); Touch of Love; Hej, Hej, Hej; Aili; Memories of You; Forever My Love; Cansone de La More (A Song of Love); To Dinah; Midnight in Paris; Lovers Walse; Melody in E; Hebrew Fantasy; Confused Gypsy; Caprice Oryantal; Strippers Blues.

BRAUN, ARTHUR DAVID ASCAP 1971
composer, author, singer
b New York, NY, Nov 5, 52. Educ: Bayside High Sch; Queens Col. Songwriter and/or professional mgr, George Pincus & Sons, Buddah Music & Midsong Music. Has done extensive work as producer & arr. Dir of A&R/professional mgr, Spice Productions, Inc. Gen mgr, Dick James Music, Inc, 74- Recording artist & music publ. Chief Collabrs: Scott English, James O'Loughlin, Dale Frasheur. *Songs:* Reborn Friend; Alice, I Love You; Music: Rescue Man; Isabela; Inside an Outside Chance.

BRAUN, RICHARD WILLIAM ASCAP 1965
composer, teacher, performer
b Hanford, Calif, May 28, 26. Educ: Hanford High Sch, grad; Univ Southern Calif, BM, 50, MM, 52. USN, 44-46. Band & orch instr, Fresno, Calif County Schs, 50-52 & San Diego City Schs, 52-72. Mem fac, San Diego State Univ, 72-77, Grossmont Community Col, 72-78 & Univ San Diego, 74-78. Cond of children's concerts, arr & bassoonist, San Diego Symph, 52-76. Cond, San Diego Symphonic Band, 52-78. Has played clarinet, saxophone, trumpet, trombone, piano, flute & bassoon for var symphonies, operas & groups. Has own 15 piece big band. Arr & cond, 45 piece Pacific Pops Orch. Has music publ firm, Ybarra Music & record co, Harlequin Records. Has done chamber music, jazz, band & orch comp & arr. Comp, Bway type musical, "A Far Off Sound." Mem: San Diego Comp Group; Music Educr Nat Conference; Nat Asn Jazz Educr; Phi Mu Alpha (life). *Albums:* A Clarinet on the Trail of a Wounded Bassoon.

BRAUNSTEIN, ALAN R ASCAP 1971
composer, author, singer
b Brooklyn, NY, Apr 30, 47. Educ: Lafayette High Sch. Began writing at age 19. Wrote several jingles for radio & TV; indust shows, music for children's theatre & music for recording artists & films. Chief Collabrs: Joe Parnello, Peppy Castro. *Songs:* Lyrics: A Man Can't Have Everything; Jamie.

BRAVERMAN, ROY M ASCAP 1976
composer, author, singer
b Philadelphia, Pa, Apr 28, 54. Educ: Boston Univ, 71-73. Recorded for RCA, Fantasy & Crunch/Paramount Records. Playing keyboards, 59-, prof, 68-; studio musician, 73-; recording engr, 77-; producing, 79- Chief Collabrs: Michael Caruso, Walt Barr. *Songs:* Music: Scarlet; Nightfire; Every Road I See; Colorado Summer; Your Love's Got a Hold on Me; Take to the Woods (The Ballad of Joey Small); Say It; Lyrics: I Fell in Love on the Hollywood Freeway. *Instrumental Works:* Moonlight.

BRAVIN, STEVEN KIRK ASCAP 1977
composer, author, recording engineer
b New York, NY, July 16, 54. Educ: High Sch Performing Arts, New York, studied guitar; pvt guitar studies with Jose Franco & Huey Long. Studied music & record eng in New York. Moved to Hawaii. Worked as staff writer, engr/producer music, Polynesia, Inc. Joined commercial recording, Hawaii, staff recording engr, Ochoa Recording Studios, San Juan PR. Chief Collabr: Jack DeMello. *Songs:* We Both Waited Too Long; Song for Honolulu; Sweet Molokai.

BRAWNER, KENNETH ROY ASCAP 1978
composer, author, singer
b Augusta, Ga, Aug 9, 44. Educ: Immaculate Conception High Sch; Howard Univ, BA, 66; Manhattan Sch Music, 73-74, voice study with Eugene Brice; piano study with Lance Hayward & Nat Jones; acting study with Paul Mann. In Bway production, "Censored Scenes from King Kong" & in movie, "Hair." Singer & keyboardist night clubs, concerts & TV; TV commercials as actor, musician & singer. Recording artist, United Artists. *Songs:* Take Your Time; Why is it On Me.

BREAU, LOUIS (LEW) ASCAP 1923
composer, conductor, publisher
b Chicago, Ill, Apr 6, 1893; d New York, NY, Sept 28, 28. Educ: High sch. Cond orchs, Chicago. Staff writer, music publ co, NY; became publisher. USAAF, WW I. Took part in exp radio broadcasts. Wrote film music. *Songs:* Humming; Underneath the Mulberry Tree; Keep It Under Your Hat; There's a Bend at the End of Swanee; In the Old Arm Chair; Cheritza; Lolita; I Want My Mammy.

BRECK, CARRIE ELLIS (MRS FRANK A BRECK) ASCAP 1948
composer, author
b Walden, Vt, Jan 22, 1855; d Portland, Ore, Mar 27, 34. Educ: Pub schs.

Author, "To Comfort Thee" (poems). *Songs:* Face to Face; When Love Shines In; Nailed to the Cross; Shall I Crucify My Saviour; If He Abide With Me; Help Somebody Today.

BREDT, JAMES
See Pagenstecher, Bernard

BREEN, MAY SINGHI　　　　　　　　　　　　ASCAP 1949
composer, author, player
b New York, NY; d. In radio with husband, Peter DeRose, as "Sweethearts of the Air," 16 yrs. Made many records & appeared on TV. Taught ukulele, known as "The Ukulele Lady"; originated use of ukulele arr on sheet music. *Songs:* Back in the Old Sunday School; Somebody Sweet; Blow the Man Down; Even the Best of Friends Must Part; Copper Colored Moon in Old Montana; Heaven in Hawaii; Someday I'll Have You; Because You're True; Hawaiian Kisses; I Told You I'd Never Forget You; No One But You Knows How to Love; Music: Brokenhearted Sue; Rudy Your Love Songs Reach My Heart; I Wish You Knew; New Ukulele Method; May Singhi Breen (The Ukulele Lady); May Singhi Breen's Ukulele Songs and Method; May Singhi Breen's Kiddy-Ukes; Lyrics: Way Back Home; I Looked At Norah and She Looked At Me; Bird of Paradise; Forever and Ever; Cross My Heart, I Love You; Desert Eyes; It's a Wonderful World We're In (Give Thanks); I'll See You So' More in Samoa; Marvelous; On the Rainbow Trail; Mother's Quilting Party; Texas Star; AWVS; Song of the OCD; Little Red Feather; Over the Valley; Fast Falls the Evening; My Heart Keeps on Throbbing; All Night Long; Ukulele Blues; Melody Moon of Hawaii; Sudanby; Sweet Kalula Lou; Honolulu Chimes; When You're Gone I Know I'll Miss You; It's Time to Say Aloha; My Hawaiian Love; Malia; Ev'ryone Knows; Give Thanks; Still in Love; The Hala Niu Tree.

BREES, BUD　　　　　　　　　　　　　　　　ASCAP 1954
composer, author, singer
b New York, NY, June 19, 21. Educ: High sch. Vocalist with dance orchs incl Bob Chester, Irving Aaronson & Art Mooney; also in theatres, radio & TV. DJ, WPEN, Philadelphia, 50-62. Made many records. Chief Collab: Mildred Phillips. *Songs:* Monte Carlo; If You're Not Completely Satisfied; Memory Lane.

BREESKIN, BARNEE　　　　　　　　　　　　ASCAP 1950
composer, conductor, publicist
b Washington, DC, Aug 17, 10. Educ: George Washington Univ. Led dance band, Shoreham Hotel, Washington, DC, 30-57; then pub relations consult. Chief Collabr: Corrine Griffith. *Songs:* Hail to the Redskins (Wash Redskins song).

BREHM, ALVIN　　　　　　　　　　　　　　ASCAP 1960
teacher, composer, conductor
b New York, NY, Feb 8, 25. Educ: Juilliard Grad Sch, dipl (fellowship), 43; Columbia Univ, BS, 46, MA, 50; string bass studies with Fred Zimmerman, 38-43; orchestration with Vittorio Giannini, 42-43; comp with Wallingford Riegger, 48-51. Teacher, State Univ NY, Plattsburgh, 51-53, artist in residence, Stonybrook, 68-75 & Purchase, 72-80, prof, 80-; teacher, Mannes Sch, 68-70, Manhattan Sch, 69-75 & Queens Col, 72-75; in comp sem & cond concerts, Ind Univ, NC Sch of Fine Arts, Swarthmore Col, Bennington Col, Columbia Col & others. Personnel mgr, RCA Victor Records, 58-63, Robert Shaw Chorale, 59-65, Masterworks Chorus, 60-68 & Vanguard Records, 65-72. Assoc presiding officer, all arts fac, State Univ NY, Purchase. Mem bd dirs, Am Music Ctr. Elected to NY State Coun for the Arts, Music Panel, 80. Guest artist with Budapest Quartet, Lenox Quartet, Comp Quartet, NY Woodwind Quintet, The White House, Lincoln Center Chamber Music Soc (regular guest, 70-), Speculum Musicae, NY Philh & all major record cos. Cond, Music in Our Time, 65-68, Comp Theatre Orch (founder), 70-, State Univ NY, Purchase, 74-, Int Soc for Contemporary Music, 74 & 77, Speculum, 75, The Music Project, 77, also in many cols & univs, 65- Mem: Casals Fests, 57-73, Mostly Mozart Fest, 66-74, Group for Contemporary Music, 67-72, Philomusica Chamber Music Soc, 69- & Contemporary Chamber Ens, 69-73. Awards & Grants: NY State Coun, Ford Found, Recording Proj, 72, ASCAP Awards, 74-77 & 78, Nat Endowment of the Arts grants, 76 & 80 & Naumburg Found, 77. *Instrumental Works:* Metamorphy (to Thomas Fuller; solo piano); A Pointe At His Pleasure (chamber piece for Renaissance instruments; comn by Walter W Naumburg Found); Divertimento for Brass Trio; Concertino for Violin and Strings; Sonata for Cello and Piano; Sextet for String Quartet and Piano (comn by Philomusica); Colloquy and Chorale (4 bassoons); Dialogues for Bassoon and Percussion; Cycle of Songs for Soprano and 10 Instruments (set to poems; Variations for Piano; Consort and Dialogues for Flute, Trumpet, Cello, Piano, Percussion; Quintet for Brass (comn by Am Brass Quintet); Quartet for Brass; Trio for 3 Double Basses; Trio for Trumpet, Horn, Trombone; Suite for Orchestra; Hephaestus (orch overture; comn by Nat Orch Asn); Divertimento for Woodwind Quintet; Duo for Viola and Piano; Variations for Cello Alone; 2 piano sonatas; 2 string quartet; 32 songs & 21 pieces for elem sch orch.

BRENNAN, J KEIRN　　　　　　　　　　　　ASCAP 1914
author, singer
b San Francisco, Calif, Nov 24, 1873; d Hollywood, Calif, Feb 4, 48. Educ: Pub schs. Sang in vaudeville; worked in Chicago publ house. Wrote songs for Bway revue, "Artists and Models of 1927." Charter mem, ASCAP. Chief Collabrs:

Ernest Ball, Rudolf Friml, Billy Hill, Karl Hajos, Harry Akst, Walter Donaldson, Werner Janssen, Maurie Rubens. *Songs:* Dear Little Boy of Mine; Let the Rest of the World Go By; Goodbye, Good Luck, God Bless You; A Little Bit of Heaven; Empty Saddles; Turn Back the Universe; When My Boy Comes Home; A Little Bit of Love; My Bird of Paradise; I'll Follow the Trail; You Hold My Heart; Ireland Is Ireland to Me. *Scores:* Bway stage: White Lilacs; The Red Robe; Boom-Boom; Music in May; A Night in Venice; Luana.

BRENNAN, JAMES ALEXANDER　　　　　　ASCAP 1922
composer, pianist, artist
b Boston, Mass, Nov 18, 1885; d Middleboro, Mass, Aug 24, 56. Educ: Normal Art Sch. Was artist, then pianist for Maurice, ballroom dancer. Camoufleur, USN, WW I & II. Worked in radio with Jones & Hare. *Songs:* Rose of No Man's Land; In the Little Red School House; When Will I Know?; Down at the Old Swimming Hole; Poor Little Rich Girl; Barefoot Days.

BRENNER, MARY LOUISE E　　　　　　　ASCAP 1978
author, singer
b Newport, RI, Apr 25, 48. Author, children's lyrics for TV. Chief Collabrs: Bill Thomas. *Songs:* Lyrics: Hands; Sign Talk; Puddle Pirate; Book of My Own; Growing Pains.

BRENNER, RAYMOND　　　　　　　　　　　ASCAP 1958
composer, author
b Calif, Oct 21, 27. Educ: Col. Writer of spec material for radio, TV & nightclubs. *Songs:* Sorta Blues; A Love to Call My Own.

BRENNER, SELMA HAUTZIK　　　　　　　ASCAP 1958
author
b New York, NY, Mar 9, 12. Educ: Cornell Univ; NY Univ; Columbia Sch Jour. Reporter, New York Herald Tribune, 30-32; Pulitzer traveling scholar, 32-33; writer for films; also short stories & novels. Chief Collabrs: Hugo Reisenfeld, Harry Puck, Ovady Julber. *Songs:* Lullaby; Flower Song.

BRENNER, WALTER　　　　　　　　　　　　ASCAP 1958
composer
b Wynberg, Union of SAfrica, Jan 21, 06; d Hollywood, Calif, Dec 19, 69. Educ: Studied music in Europe; also with Dominco Brescia, San Francisco. Became US citizen. *Songs & Instrumental Works:* Piano Concerto; Quintet for Flute, Strings; Sextet for Strings; Capriccio; May the Words (mixed voices, organ); Organ: Sabbath Joy; Processional; Sabbath Meditation; Glory to God; Contemplation Hassidique; Hassidic Soliliquy; Day of Rest; Silent Prayer; Sabbath Peace; Hassidic Interlude; Silent Devotion; Accordion: Impromptu; Ole Torero; Wanderlust; Choral: Memorial Prayer; Psalm 121; Hashkivenu; God Is Love; Kol Nidre; Symph poems: Home They Brought Her Warrior Dead; The Birth of Venus; Adoration; Prophecy; Valse Symphonique.

BRENT, EARL KARL　　　　　　　　　　　　ASCAP 1946
composer, author
b St Louis, Mo, June 27, 14; d Brentwood, Calif, July 8, 77. *Songs:* How Strange; Around the Corner; Say That We're Sweethearts Again; Waltz Serenade; His; To the End of the World; You, So It's You; Serenade; Time and Time Again; Love Is Where You Find It; Lyrics: Angel Eyes; The Holiday Song.

BRESLER, JEROME (JERRY)　　　　　　　ASCAP 1950
composer, author, conductor
b Chicago, Ill, May 29, 14. Educ: Chicago Musical Col; DePaul Univ, theory, comp, cond & orchestration studies with Dr Samuel Lieberson; NY Univ, Schillinger method with Rudolf Schramm. Played piano, age 2; pianist, cond & arr for Robert Goulet, Kate Smith, Gordon MacRae, Jan Peerce, Marguerite Piazza & Arthur Godfrey & Ed Sullivan Shows. Comp, Jackie Gleason "Honeymooners" TV shows, 60-70. Commercials & indust shows. Chief Collabrs: Lyn Duddy, Larry Wynn. *Songs:* Without You; I'm All for You; The Clock Song. *Instrumental Works:* Waltz Viennese. *Scores:* Bway Show: Spotlight.

BRESNICK, MARTIN I　　　　　　　　　　　ASCAP 1970
composer, educator
b New York, NY, Nov 13, 46. Educ: High Sch Music & Art, dipl, 63; Mannes Col Music, NY State Regents grant & pvt comp study with William Sydeman; Univ Hartford Hartt Col Music, BA, 67, studied with Arnold Franchetti & Edward Miller; Stanford Univ, MA, 68, DMA, 72, grad fel & studied computer music with John Chowning & comp with Leland Smith, also studied with Gyorgy Ligeti; Academie fuer Musik, Vienna, Fulbright fel, 69-70, studied comp with Gottfried von Einem & electronic music with Friedrich Cerha. Taught at San Francisco Cons Music, Stanford Univ, 71-75, directed Alea II, Stanford New Music Ens; asst prof music theory & comp, Yale Univ, 76-, founder & dir of Sheep's Clothing, Yale Col Ens Contemporary Music. NEA comp grants, 75 & 79; Rome Prize, 75-76; MacDowell Colony fel, 77. Numerous perf in Europe & US, 70- *Instrumental Works:* Trio for Two Trumpets and Percussion; Ocean of Storms (orch); Three Intermezzi (violoncello solo); B's Garlands (8 cello); Wir Weben, Wir Weben (string orch or string sextet); Conspiracies (solo flute & 4 other flutes); Introit (16 wind instruments); Musica (9 instruments). *Songs & Instrumental Works:* Ants (5 actors, 4 singers, chamber orch).

BREUDER, W EDWARD   ASCAP 1940
composer, author, conductor
b Hoboken, NJ, Nov 23, 11. Educ: NY Univ; pvt music study. Led own orch in hotels & nightclubs. On CBS music staff, 35-, dir, CBS Radio Network Div music library. Pianist, Essex Hotel, Spring Lake, NJ, 79 & Kings Grant Inn, Point Pleasant, NJ, 80. Also arr. Chief Collabrs: Paul Rusincky, Collins Driggs, Ray Bloch, Gladys Shelley, Jack Segal. *Songs:* As You Sow So Shall Ye Reap; Daybreak Serenade; I Travel Alone; Moondust Rhapsody; When You Have a Dream to Share; The Day That I Was Seventeen; I Can't Pretend; If You Were Mine; Fantasy; Blue and Melancholy Mood; Out of the Night; Midnight Moon; Sam the Vegetable Man; Jersey Jungle; Wonderful Napoli; Moon Is Back in Business; Young Fella You're Ready for Love; Pepito and His Violin; You Can't Do That to Me; Gee But You're Cute; Call Me Young; Waltzin' With the Blues; Barefoot Native By the Sea; Beautiful Days I Remember; Ring Ring the Bells; The Oceana; Old Wooden Bridge; When You Have a Dream to Share; Festival Night in Santa Barbara; America We're on Our Way; Fatima's Drummer Boy.

BREUER, ERNEST H   ASCAP 1914
composer, pianist
b Augsburg, Ger, Dec 26, 1886. Came to US in early youth. Charter mem, ASCAP. Pianist in vaudeville. Interpreter, Gen Pershing's staff & entertainment dir, Army of Occupation, Coblenz, Ger, WW I. Entertainer, Army hospitals, WW II. Chief Collabrs: Raymond Leveen, George Whiting, Billy Rose, Bert Douglas, Olson & Johnston, Billy Hueston. *Songs & Instrumental Works:* Oh Gee, Oh Gosh, Oh Golly I'm in Love; Passionetta; Continental Nights; Kid You've Got Some Eyes; The Chewing Gum Song; The Cat Came Back; In a Shelter From a Shower; When The Boys From Dixie Eat the Melon on the Rhine.

BREUER, HARRY   ASCAP 1962
composer, xylophone soloist, studio musician
b Brooklyn, NY, Oct 24, 01. Educ: Bushwick High Sch, Brooklyn; pvt tutors, music & harmony, Paul Yartin, Erno Rapee. Studied violin & xylophone. Made debut as soloist, New York Acad Music, 18. Soloist, Brooklyn Strand Theatre, & movie palaces, 20's. Joined Roxy's Gang, New York Roxy Theatre, 27 & later Radio City Music Hall. Staff percussionist & soloist, NBC studios, New York, 40 yrs. Chief Collabr: Jean Jacques Perrey. *Instrumental Works:* Country Rock Polka; Kiyouli Le Clown; Paris 2079; Fusee Dans Le Ciel; Xylophone Solos: Bit O' Rhythm; Minor Movement. *Albums:* The Happy Moog; Mallet Magic.

BREWER, TERESA   ASCAP 1956
composer, author
b Toledo, Ohio, May 7, 32. Educ: Holy Rosary & Birmingham Grade Schs, Toledo, Ohio; Waite High Sch, Toledo. Started singing local radio sta, Toledo, age 2; appeared on Maj Bowes Amateur Hour, 38; worked professionally in movies, radio, records, TV, nite clubs & concerts, US, England & Europe. Chief Collabrs: Bob Thiele, Glenn Osser, George David Weiss, Ruth Roberts, Bill Katz. *Songs:* Gonna Telephone Jesus; I Love Mickey; We Love You Fats; Take a Message to Jesus; There's Nothin' as Lonesome as a Saturday Night; The Imp; What Is a Grandmother.

BRICCETTI, THOMAS B   ASCAP 1961
composer, conductor
b Mt Kisco, NY, Jan 14, 36. Educ: Studied with Dr Jean Dansereau; Univ Rochester Eastman Sch of Music, 53-55; studied with Samuel Barber. Music dir, St Petersburg Symph, Sun Coast Opera, 62-68, Indianapolis Symph & assoc cond, 68-72, Ft Wayne Philh, 70-78, Cleveland Inst of Music, 73-76, Omaha Symph Orch & Nebr Sinfonia, 75- Pianist, comp & cond. Recipient, Prix de Rome, Italian govt, 58-59, Ford Found fel & residency, 60-61, NEA Comn, violin concerto, 69. *Instrumental Works:* Three Songs, Opus 2 (voice, piano); Three Songs, Opus 2 (voice, chamber orch); Trio, From Roman Sketches (violin, viola, cello); Partita for Reeds, Opus 9; Sonata for Flute and Piano, Opus 14; Fountain of Youth (overture); Five Love Poems (mixed chorus, orch); Millaydy's Madrigals (a cappella chorus); Violin Concerto; Symphony No 1; Turkey Creek March; Festival March.

BRICKMAN, JOEL IRA   ASCAP 1973
composer, educator, annotator
b New York, NY, Feb 6, 46. Educ: Manhattan Sch Music, BMus, 68, MMus, 70; studied with Nicolas Flagello, Ludmila Ulehla & David Diamond. Comp of orchestral, choral, chamber & solo works. Performer, US, Can, SAm & Europe. Mem theory & comp fac, Marymount Col & Manhattan Sch Music. Educator instrumental & gen music, pub schs, Ridgewood, NJ. *Songs & Instrumental Works:* Suite for Woodwind Quintet; Of Wonder (mixed choir; a cappella); Prelude and Caprice (solo accordion); Dialogue for Oboe and Wind Ensemble; Three Songs for Voice and Orchestra.

BRIDGES, ETHEL   ASCAP 1920
composer
b San Francisco, Calif, Nov 10, 1897. Educ: Miss Hamlin's Finishing Sch. Winner songwriting contest as a child, Portola Fest. Staff writer, publ co, NY; later lived in Panama & Hawaii. *Songs:* Hawaiian Lullaby; Just Like the Rose; Ching a Ling's Jazz Bazaar; Here You Are; Whispering (Hawaiian Love Song).

BRIDGES, OTIS CORNELIUS   ASCAP 1963
composer, author, teacher
b Muskogee, Okla, May 5, 16. Studied music with father & Boston Russell; Morgan State Col, studied with Dr Stryder; Mozarteum, Salzberg, Austria, studied with Lisolotte Brandl. Businessman; columnist & music reviewer, Kansas City Philh. Pres, Kansas City Jazz Theatre. Nat mem, AFI & Smithsonian Assocs. Served in USA. Taught music, Munich, Ger. Mem, GEMA. Chief Collabrs: Evelyn Cook, Erich Hartl. *Songs:* Do You Know I Love You?; Glodene; How I Miss You; If You Only Knew; Music: Can't You See I Care?. *Instrumental Works:* Elvira Beguine; I Can't Forget; Do You Remember?; Say You're Mine.

BRIDGEWATER, CECIL VERNON   ASCAP 1971
composer, arranger, trumpeter
b Urbana, Ill, Oct 10, 42. Educ: Univ Ill, Urbana-Champaign, music educ major, 60-64. Co-owner, Bridgewater Bros Band, 69- Worked with Horace Silver Quintet, New York, 70-71, Thad Jones-Mel Lewis Orch, 70-76 & Max Roach Quartet, 71- Owner, Bridgewater Publ Co, 71- Chief Collabr: Ronald Bridgewater. *Songs:* Music: Lightening and Thunder; Love and Harmony; Wefe; Criss Cross; Louisiana Street; Scott Free; Magic; What's Gonna Be Is Gonna Be; Gemini's Lullabye; Samba Para Ustedes Dos; Your Ballad.

BRIEGEL, GEORGE F   ASCAP 1946
composer, conductor, musician
b Scranton, Pa, June 5, 1890; d. Educ: US Mil Acad, studied with George Essigke. Trombonist & violin soloist, West Point Band. Arr, music publ co, New York, 10. Bandmaster, 22nd Regiment Band, to Pelham Bay Naval Training Station, World War I, then returned to 22nd Regiment. Formed own publ firm. Bandmaster, New York Fire Dept; hon deputy chief. Writer, theme music for radio. *Instrumental Works:* Overture Victorious; Cathedral Echoes; Soloette; God's Temple.

BRIGGS, GEORGE WRIGHT, JR   ASCAP 1960
composer, teacher, conductor
b Taunton, Mass, Oct 17, 10. Educ: Taunton High Sch; Harvard Col, AB(French, Spanish; cum laude), 31; Harvard Bus Sch; Harvard Grad Sch Arts & Sci, AM(music), 35; studied with Walter Piston, W R Spalding, C Heilmann, E B Hill, Edward Balantyne, A Davison & Aaron Copland; piano with Grace Dean & William McCormack; organ with Carl McKinley; clarinet & saxophone with Robert Park. Dance orch work with Ranny Weeks, Ruby Newman, Jack Marshand & Al Donahue. Staff pianist, organist & arr, WBZ radio & TV, 35-63. Duo pianist with Phil Saltman, radio & concerts, 20 yrs. Teacher, New Eng Cons, 42-55, dept chmn, 48-55. Dir, Harvard Univ Band, 53-60. Radio & TV dir, 55-68. Teacher, Berklee Col Music, 68-70. Music head, Beaver Country Day Sch, 70-72. Wrote several arr for Arthur Fiedler; guest pianist & cond, Boston Pops. *Songs:* Music: Sunset at Sea. *Instrumental Works:* Concord and Lexington March; Boston Globe March; 20th Century Gavotte (piano, symph orch); Ballet of the Teddy Bear (full orch); Commemoration March (band, orch; comn by Harvard Bus Sch Student's Asn, 56); USA-200 (Am nat tunes; band, orch).

BRIGHT, HOUSTON   ASCAP 1960
composer, educator
b Midland, Tex, Jan 21, 16; d. Educ: West Tex State Col, BS, MA; Univ Southern Calif, PhD, studied with Halsey Stevens, Ernest Kanitz & Charles Hirt. WW II serv. Prof, Dept of Music, West Tex State Col, also choir dir & composer in residence. Author "Elementary Counterpoint in Two Parts" (text bk). *Songs:* Benedictus and Hosanna; Come to Me, Gentle Sleep; Joyous Christmas Carol; Never Tell Thy Love; Rainsong; Now Sing We All His Praise. *Instrumental Works:* Marche de Concert; 4 for Piano; Prelude and Fugue in F (band); 3 Short Dances (woodwind quintet); 2 Short Pieces for Brass Quartet.

BRIGHT, RONNELL LOVELACE   ASCAP 1956
composer, author, teacher
b Chicago, Ill, July 3, 30. Educ: Calif State Univ, Northridge, BA(music); Univ Southern Calif, MMus; Juilliard Sch, music scholarship; Roosevelt Univ, Chicago; Univ Ill; Navy Sch of Music, DC. Studied with Jeanne Fletcher Mallette & Saul Dorfman, Chicago, Gerald Tracy, New York, Prof Jane C Watt, Champaign, Dr Frank McGinnis, Northridge, Lillian Steuber, Los Angeles, comp & orchestration with Dr Albert Harris & Lyle Speed Murphy, Los Angeles. Accompanist & musical dir, Sarah Vaughan, 3 1/2 yrs, Nancy Wilson, 3 yrs; accompanist, Lena Horne's "9 O'Clock Review Show," on tours, Peggy Lee, Carmen McCrae, Abby Lincoln, Gloria Lynn, Lorez Alexandria, Chris Conners, Teddi King, Marian McCall, Helen Merrill, Lou Rawls, Joe Williams, Al Hibbler, Sammy Davis Jr, Sarah Vaughan & Count Basie. Recorded with var artists; with Dizzy Gillispie Orch, Max Roach Jazz Group, Terry Gibbs Quartet, Dexter Gordon, Jackie Paris, Les Brown, Georgie Auld, Joe Williams & Anthony Newley; arr & pianist, Ray Anthony Orch. Performer on var TV shows; pianist, "Flip Wilson Show," 70-73; vocal arr, "Carol Burnett Show," 74-75; pianist & actor, "Don Adams TV Show"; arr & bandleader, TV show "Good Times," 78; with var TV shows, incl "Bob Hope Show", "Danny Kaye Show", "Jack Paar Show" & "Nancy Wilson Show." Pianist, actor & comp of soundtrack, film "Love Has Many Faces." Performer, 12 Europ & 3 SAm countries, supper clubs incl Fountainbleu, Caribe Hilton, Americana Hotel & many others & with own group on Bob Hope's Christmas Party. Musical dir,

play "Purlie," Aquarius Theatre, Hollywood. Taught, Calif State Univ; lectr, Univ Calif, Los Angeles. Entertainer & pianist, Dunkan's Wilshire West (Bat Rack), Los Angeles, currently. Mem, Am Fedn of Musicians, Song Writers Guild of Am & Juilliard Alumni Asn. Recipient, Nat Piano Playing Tournament Superior Rating, Nat Guild of Piano Teachers. Chief Collabrs: Johnny Mercer, Paul Francis Webster, Horace Silver. *Songs:* Be a Sweet Pumpkin; Funnier Than Funny; Alone With My Thoughts of You; And Satisfy; Music: Tender Loving Care; Ages Ago; You Ain't Had the Blues. *Instrumental Works:* Cherry Blossom. *Albums:* Super-Sax Plays Bird (Grammy award).

BRIGHT, SOL KEKIPI ASCAP 1959
composer, performer, director
b Honolulu, Hawaii, Nov 9, 09. Educ: St Louis Col, Honolulu. Produced, dir & performed in night club, hotel & steamship shows. USMS, WW II. Produced, dir & performed in "Hawaiian Revue" (62), "Treasure of Hawaii" (64). Appeared on radio, TV & films. *Songs:* Hawaiian Cowboy; Sophisticated Hula; Lovely Sapphire of the Tropics; Duke Kahanamoku; Polynesian Love Song.

BRIGNOLE, ROSA (ROSE IVANOFF) ASCAP 1962
composer, author
b Berlin, Ger, Oct 15, 08. Educ: Studied music in Italy, Ger & US. *Songs:* Secret; Shadows; If My Love Has Eyes of Blue; Into the Lonely Night; Ave Maria.

BRIMHALL, JOHN ASCAP 1962
composer, publisher, teacher
b Huntington Park, Calif, Nov 22, 28. Educ: Loyola Univ, BM; San Francisco State Col, MA; Stanford Univ. Music supvr, Corcoran, Calif Schs, 53-56; instr, Porterville Col & Orange Coast Col, 56-62. Arr, production mgr, Hansen Publ, Miami Beach, Fla. Chief Collabrs: Bill Hansen, Mel Leven. *Songs:* Doin' the Twist; Beatle Boogie; Lonely; Wonder Why.

BRINE, MARK VINCENT (JACK FROST) ASCAP 1977
composer, author, singer
b Cambridge, Mass, Nov 28, 48. Educ: Agassiz Grammar Sch; Rindge Tech Sch. Recording artist, Door Knob Records. Appeared on TV & radio, nat & int. Nightclub entertainer, concerts. *Songs:* The Christmas Carol No One Listens For; May It Be You; Coming Home to Love; Lyrics: Daddy's Girl. *Instrumental Works:* The Christmas Carol (No One Listens For) Rag.

BRINGS, ALLEN STEPHEN ASCAP 1973
composer, pianist, educator
b New York, NY, Feb 24, 34. Educ: Queens Col, NY, BA, 55; Columbia Univ, MA, 57, studied with Otto Luening; Boston Univ, MusAD, 64, studied with Gardner Read; Princeton Univ, studied with Roger Sessions; Berkshire Music Ctr, studied with Irving Fine; Third St Music Sch Settlement, studied piano with Sylvia Lopez & comp with Robert Ward. Asst cond & cond, Armed Forces regimental band, 58-59. Instr music, Bard Col, 59-60; teacher, co-dir, Weston Music Ctr, Conn, 60-; teaching fel, Boston Univ, 60-62; Naumburg fel, Princeton Univ, 62-63; lectr, from instr to prof of music, Queens Col, NY, 63- Pianist, extensive performances in US & Europe & with Genevieve Chinn in progs for 4-hand piano music; also recorded with Genevieve Chinn. *Songs:* Music: Sound Pieces for Voices and Noises; Tre Sonetti di Michelangelo Buonarroti (soprano & small chamber ens); Tre Madrigali Concertati (soprano, harpsichord & cello). *Instrumental Works:* Passacaglia, Interlude and Fugue for Piano (4-hands); Three Pieces for Violin and Piano; Essay for Band; Sonata for Violin Alone; Concerto da Camera No 1 (piano & chamber orch), No 2 (violin & perc), No 3 (flute & strings); Three Fantasies (saxophone quartet).

BRINSON, ROSEMARY GREENE ASCAP 1956
composer, author, conductor
b East St Louis, Ill, Sept 8, 17. Educ: Univ Ill, BS; Northwestern Univ, MA; Indiana Univ; St Louis Univ. Instr, Univ Ill; choral dir, St Louis Univ. Writer, producer & music dir, CBS, NBC-TV, St Louis & NY. Assoc producer & cond "Make Mine Missouri." *Songs:* Am I the Guy?; My First Love.

BRISMAN, HESKEL (BURT HASKELL, BEN BRITT) ASCAP 1973
composer
b New York, NY, May 12, 23. Educ: Juilliard; Yale Sch Music; Columbia, studied electronic music; Tanglewood, studied with Ernst Toch; studied with Luigi Dallapiccola, Italy. Scored for films, Italy. Dir, Joseph Achron Cons, Israel. Teacher, theory & chamber music. Writer, incidental music for plays, "Troilus and Cressida", "Liliom", "The Wall" & others. Comns & grants: NJ Arts Council; NEA; Martha Baird Rockefeller Found. Chief Collabr: Jerome Greenfield. *Songs & Instrumental Works:* Sinfonia Breve; Concerted Music for Piano and Percussion Ensemble; Concerto for Piano and Strings; Don't Listen to the Wind (cantata). *Scores:* Opera/Ballet: Whirligig.

BRISTOL, MARGARET ASCAP 1943
composer, author, conductor
b Seattle, Wash. Educ: Northwestern Univ, BA, summa cum laude; pvt voice study. Singer with concert group, Army & Navy Hosps, 16 yrs. Dir, radio, TV & church choirs. Own voice studio. Mem, NYSTA. Chief Collabrs: Walter Golde, Carl Deis, Leo Kempinski, Jacques Wolfe, Giuseppe Bamboschek, Idabelle Firestone, Solon Alberti. *Songs:* Mile After Mile; Friar Jacques; They Live Forever; On Freedom's Wings; Prayer of the Slavic Children; Give Peace, O Lord; God of the Mountain Top; Thoughts of Love; Do You Recall.

BRITAIN, RADIE ASCAP 1940
composer
b Silverton, Tex, Mar 17, 08. Educ: Am Cons, Chicago, BMus; Univ Chicago, DMus; Musical Arts Cons; studied with Albert Noelte, Leopold Godowsky & Pietro Yon-Marcel DuPre. Comp debut, Munich, Ger. Comns: Marygrove Col; St Mary's Col, Nebr. Comps performed at the White House. Nat music chmn, Nat League Am Pen Women. Awards: Nat Band Asn; Mary Carr Moore Club; Westwood Symph Orch; Juilliard Publ Award; Award of Merit, Nat League Am Pen Women; MacDowell Colony (2 seasons). Teacher comp, Chicago Cons. *Songs & Instrumental Works:* Prelude to a Drama (orch); Heroic Poem (orch); Light (orch); Southern Symphony (orch); Pastorale (orch); Saturnale (orch); Suite for Strings; Prison (lament; small orch); Phantasy for Oboe and Orchestra; Cactus Rhapsody (orch); Cowboy Rhapsody (orch); Cosmic Mist Symphony (orch); Epic Poem for String Quartet; Prison (string quartet); In the Beginning for 4 Horns; Prayer (SATB); Noontide (SATB); Lasso of Time (TTBB); The Star and the Child (SATB); Brothers of the Clouds (TTBB); Epiphgllm (piano); Radiation (piano); Sonata Opus 17 (piano); Anima Divina for Harp. *Scores:* Operetta: Happyland; Opera: Carillon (3 acts); Kuthara (3 acts).

BRITT, ADDY ASCAP 1934
author
b New York, NY, May 27, 1891; d May 14, 38. Educ: City Col New York. Staff mem, music publ. *Songs:* Aggravatin' Papa; Ting-a-Ling; Waltz of the Bells; Was It a Dream?; Where's My Sweetie Hiding?; Hello, Swanee, Hello; Do You Believe in Dreams?; Normandy; May the Sun Shine Brighter; I'm Gonna Let the Bumble Bee Be; My Sugar.

BRITT, BEN
See Brisman, Heskel

BRITT, ELTON ASCAP 1946
composer, author, singer
b Marshall, Ark, June 27, 13; d. *Songs:* When a Cowboy Is Happy; Over the Trail; Chime Bells; Tall Cedars; Weep No More My Darling; Dusty Old Trunk in the Attic; I'll Be Crying Over You.

BRITT, PATRICK EUGENE ASCAP 1975
composer, musician, producer
b Pittsburgh, Pa, Jan 18, 40. Educ: Col San Mateo, music maj, 59-61; San Francisco Cons Music, pvt studies, 62. Leader of jazz group, Pat Britt Quintet; started Catalyst Label in 76. *Albums:* Jazz From San Francisco; Jazzman; Starrsong.

BRITTON, RONNIE ASCAP 1972
composer, author
b Buffalo, NY. Prof dancer & actor prior to joining ASCAP. *Songs & Instrumental Works:* Off Bway Shows: Twanger!; Gift of the Magi; Greenwich Village Follies; Bway Show: Toulouse.

BROADBENT, ALAN ASCAP 1970
composer, pianist, arranger
b Auckland, NZ, Apr 23, 47. Educ: Royal Trinity Col Music, NZ, 54-63; Berklee Col Music, Boston, 66-69; pvt piano study & improvisation with Lennie Tristano, 66-69. Joined Woody Herman Orch, 69; comp, arr & pianist, 69-72; moved to Los Angeles, 72; studio musician, comp & arr; comp performed by Symph Orch & Woody Herman Orch, 74. Comn to do composition for The Orchestra, currently. *Instrumental Works:* Children of Lima (Grammy Award Nomination, 75); Aja (Grammy Award Nomination, 78); Palette; Dream Your Dream.

BROADHURST, CECIL ARTHUR ASCAP 1952
composer, author
b Winnipeg, Man, May 8, 08. Violinist, studied art, 20's. Painter with own studio; singer on Canadian radio; part in play "Outward Bound," 30's. Writer, songs & plays, & "Jotham Valley," New York, 52; actor for Moral Re-Armament productions, worldwide, 40's-60's; full-time artist, 80- Chief Collabrs: Richard M Hadden, Frances Hadden, Paul Misraki, George M Fraser. *Songs:* Cowboy Carol.

BROCK, BLANCHE KERR ASCAP 1950
composer, pianist, singer
b Greenfork, Ind, Feb 3, 1888; d Winona Lake, Ind, Jan 3, 58. Educ: Indianapolis Cons; Am Cons, studied with Carleton Hackett. Accompanist, church choir; pianist & soloist with evangelists. Chief Collabr: Virgil Brock (husband). *Songs:* Sacred: Beyond the Sunset; He's a Wonderful Savior to Me; Sing and Smile and Pray; Keep Looking Up; We Should See Jesus; O Wonderful Day; Some Happy Morning; Men of God Awake, Arise; Music: Resting in His Love.

BROCK, VIRGIL P ASCAP 1950
composer, author
b Mercer County, Ohio, Jan 6, 1887; d. Educ: Fairmount Friends Acad; Earlham Col, BA. Comp writer, Rodeheaver Co. Chief Collabr: Blanche Brock (wife). *Songs:* Sacred: Beyond the Sunset; He's a Wonderful Saviour to Me; Sing and Smile and Pray; Men of God Awake, Arise; The Glory Road to Heaven.

BROCKMAN, JAMES ASCAP 1921
composer, author, comedian
b Dec 8, 1886; d Los Angeles, Calif, May 22, 67. Educ: Cleveland Cons; also pvt study. Comedian in vaudeville & musicals. Staff mem music publ co. To Hollywood; song writer for films. Chief Collabrs: James Kendis, Abe Olman. *Songs:* Strumbery, Pich, Hample Pies; I'm Forever Blowing Bubbles; Golden Gate; Feather Your Nest; I Faw Down and Go Boom; I Know What It Means to Be Lonesome; Down Among the Sheltering Palms; As Long As the Shamrock Grows Green; Let's Grow Old Together.

BROCKWAY, JENNIE M
See Owen, Mary Jane

BRODAX, ALBERT P ASCAP 1967
author, lyricist, producer
b New York, NY, Feb 14, 26. Educ: Univ Wis-Madison, BA, 48, studied creative writing with Prof Glicksman & Am literature with Prof Quintana. Writer for TV in New York, early 50's. Producer-writer of 500 animations on TV & feature film "Yellow Submarine." Animation supvr, "Animals, Animals, Animals," ABC-TV; also working on Elton John feature animation, "Captain Fantastic." Chief Collabrs: Bernard Green, Jerry Abbott, Diane Gess. *Songs:* Lyrics: Cool McCool (title song & theme music, TV series, NBC). *Scores:* TV: Sunshine Porcupine (Easter TV special).

BRODERICK, JOHNNY ASCAP 1953
composer, author, entertainer
b Sharon, Pa, Nov 30, 01; d Port Charlotte, Fla, Apr 14, 77. Educ: St Scholastica Cons. Mem team, Arren & Broderick, appearing in theatres & night clubs. Chief Collabr: Barbara Ruth. *Songs:* A Star Stood Still; Do You Mind If I Dream About You?; And So It Ends; Way Up the Hill; When U and I Are One; Old Glory (Bi-Centennial Song of SFla); Charlotte County Is Calling YOU. *Instrumental Works:* Mod-Mannerism's (piano solo); Patricia Ballet (piano solo).

BRODY, DAVID S (TUNICA DARTOS) ASCAP 1975
composer, author
b New York, NY, Sept 4, 55. Educ: Boston Sch Electronic Music; Berklee Col Music; NY Inst Technol, BFA, magna cum laude, comp & cond studies with William Strickland. Film score & jingle composer, Real Time Productions, Inc, 74-77; recording engr, Master Sound Productions, 77-; composer/producer, Starsong, 78-; composer/author, Am Nocturne Proj, Inc, 79- Chief Collabr: William Strickland. *Songs:* National Pastime; Hot Tin Roof; We the Living; Cindy's Space Case; Dark Land; The Time and All; Listen to Her Silence; A Portrait of the Portrait Painter; Crown of Thorns; Sedan. *Instrumental Works:* Full Circle; An Electric Fanfare; Ondine; Onward and Outward (fanfare & march for space shuttle); Quaternion Ballet Suite; Daddy-O's Dance; The Pony Poem.

BRODY, MURRAY LEE ASCAP 1959
composer, author
b New York, NY, Dec 27, 09. Educ: Pub schs. Wrote book, music & lyrics for several musical productions produced on Long Island, NY. Wrote lyrics & scripts, Bonny Maid TV Show, 51-52. Producer radio show, KOH, Reno, Nev, 45-48. Sales exec, transportation indust. Dir choral group, The Cresthaven Minstrels, West Palm Beach, Fla. Chief Collabrs: Dave Ringle, James Selva. *Songs:* We'll Never Disagree; The Toy Maker's Song; I Wonder Where My Doggie Is?; Don't Be Sad, Little Ballerina; I'm Mommy's Little Helper.

BRODY, SELMA RUTH (SELMA RICH) ASCAP 1968
composer, author
b New York, NY, June 1, 26. Educ: Evander Childs High Sch, 42; Hunter Col, BA, 46. TV writer & performer, var shows incl "Captain Kangaroo", "Wonderama" & "Merry Mailman." A&R dir, PeterPan Records. Writer & producer, Pickwick Records; record publ relations. Pres, Miller-Brody Productions, Inc. Nat trustee & mem, bd of gov, NY Chapter, Nat Acad of Recording Arts & Sci. *Songs:* All About Days Months and Seasons of the Year; All About Numbers and Counting; All About the Alphabet; All About Time; All About Habits and Manners; All About Money; Be a Train.

BROEKMAN, DAVID HENDRINES ASCAP 1947
composer, conductor
b Leiden, Holland, May 13, 1899; d New York, NY, Apr 1, 58. Educ: Royal Cons, The Hague, studied with Van Anrooy, Hofmeester. In youth, cond Residentie Orch, The Hague; also orchs, French and Royal Opera houses. Moved to US, 24, citizen, 29. Wrote for films; comp dir, radio. Violinist, New York Philh Orch under Mengelberg & Toscanini, 24-26; musical adv, ERPI, also associated with Warner Bros, New York, 26-29. Musical dir: Universal Pictures, Hollywood, Calif, 29-31; Columbia Pictures, 31-34; CBS (KHJ), 34-41; US Treas Dept, War Bond Progs & Recordings, 41-45; Texaco Star Theatre, 45. Comp-cond, Peabody Awards Shows on Am Broadcasting Network, 48-49; guest cond, Carnegie Pops Concerts, 46-47; comp-cond, Ken Murray TV Show, 50-52; comp-cond, "Ford Festival", NBC-TV, 51 & "Wide Wide World", NBC-TV, 55-57; originator & cond, "Music in the Making", a contemporary concert series at Cooper Union for the Advancement of Sci & Art, 52-57. Author autobiographical novel, "Shoestring Symphony", 48; music critic &

contribr for periodicals. Music ed, Electrical Research Products. *Songs:* Through an Old Cathedral Window; Little Boy Blue on Broadway; This-Our Land; The Birds Will Sing No More; Dialogue for Lovers; Samba for Orchids; Intermezzo for a Day in May; I Will Bring You Music; Fanfare. *Instrumental Works:* Manhattan Fairy Tale Suite; Jericho; Barbara Allen (opera); The Stranger (opera); The Toledo War (opera); First and Second Symphonies; Violin Concerto; String Quartet; Piano Concerto; Concerto for Piano, Percussion and Orchestra; Piano Sonatas and Etudes; also Music of David Broekman Series. *Scores:* Film background: All Quiet on the Western Front; Phantom of the Opera.

BROHN, WILLIAM DAVID ASCAP 1975
composer, author
b Flint, Mich, Mar 30, 33. Educ: Mich State Univ, AB(mus), 55; studied cond with Boyd Neel, Royal Cons, Toronto, Ont, 55; New Eng Cons, MMus(comp), 58; Tanglewood Berkshire Music Ctr; Mozarteum, Salzburg, 57-60; cond master class with Leopold Stokowski, 63; studied contrabass with Georges Moleux, principal, Boston Symph. Perf with Boston Pops; Am Ballet Theatre; Joffrey Ballet; Royal Ballet; Stuttgart Ballet; Moiseyev & Bolshoi Ballets, Hurok concerts, New York & tours playing contrabass. Cond, Robert Joffrey Ballet, 61-62, Am Ballet Theatre, 63-64; Am Guest Cond, Royal Ballet, 66-67; music dir & cond 2nd nat tour "Oliver!"; tour with Franz Allers, "Showboat," Lincoln Ctr, 66; music dir, "Knickerbocker Holiday," Town Hall, 77. Arr for Bway shows, "Rodgers & Hart", "Sergeant Peppers", "Cyrano", "Rockabye Hamlet", "King of Hearts", "Timbuktu!"; arr TV & films & for Victor Borge. Comp incidental music for two Theatre in Am Productions, PBS & Chelsea Theatre; review songs, New York & Washington, DC. Chief Collabrs: Bill Maher, Bob Cessna, George Guilbault. *Songs:* Spectrum of Music (seven rock songs). *Instrumental Works:* Trip for Strings; Shenandoah (adaptation for Cleveland Orch & Chorus); Symphony in D; Metamorphoses (masque for narrator, dancers & orch); The Scene (dance score). *Scores:* Musicals: Boston Boston; Werewulff.

BROMA, CARLETON
See Dorn, Veeder Van

BROMBERG, DAVID ASCAP 1973
composer, musician
b Philadelphia, Pa, Sept 19, 45. Educ: Columbia Univ. Guitarist, Greenwich Village, New York, while in col. Writer, music. Sideman for var recording artists, incl Bob Dylan, Ringo Starr, Phoebe Snow & Chubby Checker & group The Eagles. Musician & recording artist for var record cos, 70- Formed David Bromberg Band; disbanded, 80.

BRONSON, MENZO FRANK ASCAP 1976
composer, singer
b Hancock, Wis, Feb 4, 28. Educ: Cent High Sch, studied music; also studied with Rick Miller. Musician & singer, nightclubs, TV & recordings. Chief Collabr: Charlie Fields. *Songs:* She Likes It; Your Eyes Light the Path to My Heart; I Would Like To; I Love You, Darling.

BROOK, BARRY S ASCAP 1963
composer, arranger, educator
b New York, NY, Nov 1, 18. Educ: City Col New York, BSS; Columbia Univ, MA; Sorbonne, Docteur d l'Universite. Grants: Ford Found; Fulbright; Guggenheim Found; French Govt. Assoc prof, Queens Col; vis prof, Hunter Col & NY Univ. Col music ed, Holt, Rinehart & Winston Publ. Author, "La Symphonie francaise dans la seconde moitie du XVIII siecle" (3 vols). *Instrumental Works:* Arr: Symphony in G (Martin); Symphony in D (Gossec); Symphonie-Concertante in G for 2 Violins (St George); Symphony in E Flat (Simon Le Duc).

BROOKS, DUDLEY ALONZO ASCAP 1953
composer, pianist, singer
b Los Angeles, Calif, Dec 22, 13. Educ: Jefferson High Sch; Univ Calif Los Angeles; piano with Prof Koplanoff. Pianist arr for Benny Goodman, 40 & Count Basie, 41. Pianist arr for Nick Castle, 40-68. Choreographer, Paramount Pictures, MGM, 20th Century Fox, Columbia, Universal, RKO & Republic. Great Lakes Naval Sta, 42-45. Chief Collabrs: Ellis Walsh, Charles O'Curran, F E Miller, Henry Nemo, Wally Holmes, Sammy Cahn & Harvey O Brooks. *Songs:* Teddy Bear; Big Fat Butterfly; You Gotta Show Me; Tell Me How Long the Trains Been Gone; The Gal Looks Good; Mama; We'll Be Together; I Found Someone; Nothin' But Jazz; Paying the Price; Mister Beebe.

BROOKS, FRED
See Hellerman, Fred

BROOKS, HARRY ASCAP 1930
composer, pianist
b Homestead, Pa, Sept 20, 1895; d Teaneck, NJ, June 22, 70. Educ: High sch; studied with Walter Spriggs. Pianist in dance orchs & staff comp publ co. Chief Collabrs: Andy Razaf, Fats Waller. *Songs & Instrumental Works:* Ain't Misbehavin'; Rockin' in a Rockin' Chair; Swing, Mr Charlie; Black and Blue; Saturday; Low Tide; When the Sun Sets South; In the Meantime; Strictly From

Dixie; On the Loose. *Scores:* Bway stage: Snapshots of 1921; Connie's Hot Chocolates.

BROOKS, HARVEY
See Goldstein, Harvey

BROOKS, HARVEY OLIVER   ASCAP 1942
composer
b Philadelphia, Pa, Feb 17, 1899; d. Wrote songs for films incl, "Going to Town." *Songs:* I Want You, I Need You; That Dallas Man; I Found a New Way to Go to Town; They Call Me Sister Honky Tonk; I'm No Angel; La Martinique; It's a Mighty Pretty Night for Love; A Little Bird Told Me; That's When I Long for You.

BROOKS, JACK   ASCAP 1946
composer, author
b Liverpool, England, Feb 14, 12; d. To US 1916. Wrote spec material for Bing Crosby, Fred Allen & Phil Harris; also "Command Performance," AFRS. Under contract to film studios; wrote songs for revue, "Meet the People." Chief Collabrs: Walter Scharf, Walter Schumann, Hoagy Carmichael, Harry Warren, Serge Walter. *Songs:* I Can't Get You Out of My Mind; Ole Buttermilk Sky; Once Upon a Dream; It's Dreamtime; Song of Scheherazade; You Wonderful You; Look At Me; Saturday Date; Just for Awhile; Is It Yes, Or Is It No?; Who Can Tell; Lonesome Gal; Am I in Love; That's Amore; also English lyrics to four Rimsky-Korsakov songs. *Instrumental Works:* The Dybbuk (libretto). *Scores:* Film background: The Killers; Song of Scheherazade; The Chase; The Black Angel; This Love of Ours; Abroad With Two Yanks; Summer Stock; Harvey; Yes, Sir, That's My Baby; The Countess of Monte Cristo.

BROOKS, JOHN BENSON   ASCAP 1943
composer, arranger, pianist
b Houlton, Maine, Feb 23, 17. Educ: New Eng Cons; studied with Mrs Wallace Ross, Josef Schillinger, John Cage. Pianist in nightclubs, dance halls, hotels & on radio, Boston, 37. Arr for Eddie DeLange, Les Brown, Tommy Dorsey, Boyd Raeburn & Randy Brooks Orchs, New York, 40. Vocal coach, Witmark Publ, 43. Leader, own jazz group, 50- Chief Collabrs: Eddie DeLange, Joseph McCarthy, Bob Russell, Mack Discant, Robert Graves. *Songs:* Music: You Came a Long Way From St Louis; Where Flamingos Fly; Over the Weekend; A Boy From Texas; Season's Greetings; 99 Years; A Door Will Open. *Instrumental Works:* Holiday Forever. *Albums:* Folk Jazz USA; Alabama Concerto (chamber group); Avant Slant.

BROOKS, JOSEPH   ASCAP 1965
composer, author
b New York, NY, Mar 11, 38. Top advert comp, 15 yrs. Wrote, produced, dir & scored, "You Light Up My Life." *Scores:* Films: Marjoe; Jeremy; Garden of the Finzi Continis; Lords of Flatbush.

BROOKS, RICHARD ALLMAN   ASCAP 1972
composer, author, producer
b Chattanooga, Tenn, May 13, 40. Educ: Washburne Trade Sch; self-taught. Singer, original group, Impressions & Jerry Butler. *Songs:* For Your Precious Love; The Gift of Love; I Need Your Love; Sinner, Have You Been There; Smoke Screen; Did I Scare You; Something Is Wrong With Your Mind.

BROOKS, SHELTON   ASCAP 1929
composer, author, pianist
b Amesburg, Ont, May 4, 1886; d Los Angeles, Calif, Sept 6, 75. Professional pianist in cafes, Detroit; vaudeville entertainer, US & Can, 45 yrs. With Lew Leslie's "Blackbirds", Europe, 23; command perf for King George & Queen Mary. Wrote songs for Nora Bayes, Al Jolson & Sophie Tucker. Appeared in Ken Murray's "Blackouts", 2 yrs. *Songs:* Some of These Days; The Darktown Strutters' Ball; All Night Long; Jean; Walkin' the Dog; You Ain't Talkin' to Me; Honey Gal; If I Were a Bee and You Were a Red, Red Rose.

BROOKS, VALERIE
See Schaff, Sylvia

BROONES, MARTIN   ASCAP 1950
composer
b New York, NY, June 10, 03; d Beverly Hills, Calif, Aug 10, 71. Educ: City Col New York; Columbia Univ; studied with John Ireland. Writer for Bway musicals, films. Chief Collabrs: Paul Francis Webster, William Luce. *Songs:* I Can't Get Over a Girl Like You; Golden Girl; Bring Back Those Minstrel Days; I Don't Want Your Kisses If I Can't Have Your Love; Moon Melody; One Last Love Song; The Prodigal Son; Let No Walls Divide; Be Still and Know; Be a Child At Christmastime.

BROUGHTON, PHILIP F   ASCAP 1953
composer, author
b Boston, Mass, July 1, 1893; d. Educ: Morristown Sch, NJ. Wrote songs for Bway musical "9:15 Revue." Insurance broker. Author "The Adventures of Pandy." Chief Collabrs: Marcia Neil, Will Johnstone. *Songs:* She's a Pretty Little Thing; Your Way Is My Way; Funny (Not Much); Here's to Our Lovely Models (theme song). *Scores:* Stage: Society of Illustrators (revue).

BROWN, A SEYMOUR   ASCAP 1914
author
b Philadelphia, Pa, May 28, 1885; d Philadelphia, Dec 22, 47. Educ: Pub schs. Appeared in vaudeville, 11-14. On prof staff, music publs, 14-26. Wrote songs for "Ziegfeld Follies of 1909." Actor. Charter mem, ASCAP. Chief Collabrs: John Bratton, Silvio Hein, Albert Von Tilzer, Nat Ayer. *Songs:* Oh, You Beautiful Doll; Can't You See I Love You?; Great Big Blue-Eyed Baby; Rebecca of Sunnybrook Farm; If You Talk in Your Sleep, Don't Mention My Name; Moving Day in Jungle Town; Chin Chin. *Scores:* Bway stage: The Newlyweds and Their Baby; The Matinee Idol; Adrienne (also librettist).

BROWN, AL W   ASCAP 1923
composer, pianist
b Cleveland, Ohio, Jan 3, 1884; d New York, NY, Nov 27, 24. Educ: Chicago Pub Schs. Prof pianist at early age. Wrote Winter Garden shows; also spec material for vaudeville acts. *Songs:* You're in Style When You're Wearing a Smile; Georgia Sunset; You're the Same Sweet Girl; Ragtime Whistlin' Cowboy Joe; Hello, Hello, Hello; Liberty Bell, Ring On; There's a Service Flag Flying At Our House; Go Over the Top With Reilly.

BROWN, ATHALEEN ELIZABETH   ASCAP 1963
composer, author, pianist
b Macomb, Ill, Mar 13, 08. Educ: Drake Univ, teaching cert, 27; Univ Colo, 35. Music teacher in primary grades. Chief Collabrs: Athena Hosey, Hal Gordon. *Songs:* You Can't Hear a Heart That Breaks; Walk Along With the Angels; My Competition; Night Without End; Engagement Waltz.

BROWN, BARNETTA   ASCAP 1937
author
b New York, NY, Jan 7, 1859; d New York, Dec 5, 38. Educ: Miss Bean's Boarding Sch, New York. Taught sch in Brooklyn, NY. Chief Collabr: William Stickles. *Songs:* Cradle Song; Anthology of Classics (trans, original lyrics); also Ride of the Cossacks.

BROWN, BERNARD LIONEL   ASCAP 1976
composer, author, singer
b Cape Town, SAfrica, Feb 10, 46. Educ: Teacher's Col, Cape Town; Univ Cape Town, BA(Eng lit); Ger, Ital, French, Span, Portuguese & Dutch Language Schs. Formed group at age 18; went solo at age 22. Left SAfrica at age 25. Sang across Africa, Europe & US, 71- Toured Ger. *Songs:* Waiting for the Sunrise; I Just Want to Be With You; Sunshine Man. *Scores:* Film/TV: Noon Show; Ray Stevens Show; Soul of the City; Telefantasy.

BROWN, BERTRAND   ASCAP 1925
composer, publisher, teacher
b Norborne, Mo, July 13, 1888; d New York, NY, June 3, 64. Educ: Oberlin Cons, BA; Columbia Univ, MA. Asst instr Eng, Oberlin Col, 11-12; teacher & adminr, pub schs, Minn, 12-14. Asst in social res, NY Sch Social Work, 15-16; res asst, Am Asn Labor Legislation, 15. Ed, NY Dept Pub Welfare, 16-17. Asst dept dir, AEF Univ, Beaune, France, 17-18; publ, Musique Picturesque Series. Pub relations counselor, New York, 18-64. Publicist. *Songs:* All for You; On Life's Highway; Baby; Winter Memories; Little White Moon of My Heart; Little Red Wagon; Maybe; I Never Knew; Lonesome-Like; The Vagabond.

BROWN, BRADLEY SCOTT   ASCAP 1978
composer
b Bedford, Ind, Aug 15, 55. Started playing at age 12. With Jazz, Rock, Fusion Band. Free-lance drummer, Ind. *Songs:* Music: For Me.

BROWN, BUSTER B
See Rye, Sven

BROWN, EUNICE F   ASCAP 1975
composer, author
b Providence, RI, Jan 5, 17. Educ: Hope High Sch; Pembroke Col, Brown Univ, 38; Vesper George Art Sch. Sold creative ideas for var cos. Wrote music for sch productions. Chief Collabr: Dr Benjamin Suchoff. *Songs:* Bicentennial Waltz; Wedding Waltz; Hi Sweetie Pie; Song of Peace; Lyrics: Sands of Time.

BROWN, FORMAN   ASCAP 1959
composer, author
b Otsego, Mich, Jan 8, 01. Educ: Univ Mich, BA, 22, AM, 23. Instr Eng, Univ Mich, 23-24; asst prof Eng, NCCW, 25-26. Co-founder, Yale Puppeteers, 27. Operated Teatro Torito, Los Angeles, 2 yrs. Wrote for CBS Radio, NY. Wrote material for Turnabout Theater, Los Angeles, 41-56. New lyrics for 12 productions, Los Angeles & San Francisco Light Opera Asns. Author bks, "Spider Kin" (verse), "The Pie-Eyed Piper" & "Punch's Progress." Chief Collabrs: Raymond Scott, Mitch Leigh, Erich Korngold & Rudolf Friml. *Songs:* Lyrics: The Red Mill. *Albums:* Songs From a Shuttered Parlor; Songs from a Smoke-Filled Room; The Merry Widow; The Great Waltz.

BROWN, GENE   ASCAP 1953
composer, author
b Borger, Tex, Feb 7, 28. Educ: High sch. *Songs:* A Letter Instead of a Rose; I Thought the World of You.

BROWN, GEORGE MURRAY　　　　　　　　ASCAP 1938
author
b Yarmouth, NS, Aug 4, 1880; d Belmont, Mass, Apr 10, 60. Moved to US, 1885, citizen, 1902. Educ: Univ Mass, BS. Chief Collabr: Charles Wakefield Cadman. *Songs & Instrumental Works:* No Song Is Beautiful Enough; Guide Thou Me; The Through Freight; Manana; Love Is a Gypsy Bird; Naranoka (song cycle). *Scores:* Operettas: Lelawala; The Golden Trail; Belle of Havana; Hollywood Extra; Meet Arizona; Thunder Waters.

BROWN, GEORGE R　　　　　　　　　　　ASCAP 1942
author, composer, publisher
b New York, NY, Nov 7, 10. Educ: NY Univ, 28; Univ NC, BA, 33. Wrote songs for films incl "House Across the Bay", "Slightly Honorable", "Thousands Cheer", "Melody and Moonlight" & "Hit Parade." Wrote songs for Hollywood & Bway Revues incl "Calling All Stars", "Hollywood Sweater Girl Revue", "Fun for the Money", "Big Show", "Palm Island Revue", "Ziegfeld Follies" & "Passing Show." Wrote musical acts for stage stars, Lillian Roth, Don Ameche, Joe E Louis, Milton Berle & Ritz Bros. Special Service Officer, chmn Armed Forces Entertainment Comt, WW II. Wrote official songs of Eglin Field, Keesler Field, The Air Force Training Command & other marching songs. Chief Collabrs: Jule Styne, Lew Brown, Al Von Tilzer, Irving Actman, Henry Vars & George Tibbles. *Songs:* You Took Me Out of This World; A Hundred Kisses From Now; I Never Loved Anyone; We Knew It All the Time; Fiddle-A-Delphia; If You Don't Want My Love; Sleep My Child; Good Will; Hallelujah Brother; The Sword and a Rose; Who Am I; Have a Heart and Lend a Hand; Songs of Good Behavior.

BROWN, GLENN J　　　　　　　　　　　ASCAP 1945
composer, pianist, organist
b Lehi, Utah, June 7, 1900; d Salt Lake City, Utah, June 18, 60. Taught piano. Organized first dance band, Salt Lake City; pianist in bands & nightclubs. *Songs:* When Mother Nature Sings Her Lullaby; Sleepy Head; When the Wild Wild Roses Bloom; When I Look to the West; Tennessee Moon.

BROWN, JACK MARTIN　　　　　　　　　ASCAP 1977
composer, author, singer
b Brooklyn, NY, Apr 19, 46. Educ: Ridgewood High Sch, 64; Knox Col, BA, 68; studied voice with R Decker, 72, G Mariani, 77 & acting with William Alderson & G Zittel, 78-80. Chief Collabr: Henry Krieger. *Songs:* I'm a Job; Strangers Again; Before I Go; Acrobat; Gambler's Daughter.

BROWN, JAMES B
composer, musician, singer
b Savannah, Ga, Mar 16, 45. Educ: Savannah State Col. Singer; plays trumpet, flute, fluegelhorn, trombone & saxophone with group Brick, currently. Chief Collabrs: Reginald J Hargis, Edward Irons, Jr, Raymond L Ransom, Jr. *Songs:* Dazz; Dusic; Ain't Gonna Hurt Nobody.

BROWN, JERRY LEONARD　　　　　　　　ASCAP 1968
composer, author, singer
b New Brighton, Pa, Sept 30, 44. Educ: Beaver Area High Sch; Los Angeles Valley Col. Drummer & writer with "The Griffin," 67-69, "The Match," 70-71 & "Main Street," 71-72. Moved to Colorado Springs; guest singer, Air Force Acad Falconaires Band; free lance jingle writing; prof actor & producer; entertainer, Four Seasons Motor Inn, 72- *Songs:* In My Other Life; Lady; Whose Hands Are These?.

BROWN, JONATHAN BRUCE　　　　　　　ASCAP 1975
composer, teacher
b Highland, Ill, June 18, 52. Educ: Cent Mich Univ, BA, 74; Univ Hawaii, MM, 76; NTex State Univ, doctoral candidate, studies with Martin Mailman & Merrill Ellis. Asst prof music, Pikeville Col, Ky, 76-79; dir, Symphonic Wind Ens. Music premiered by Honolulu Symph Orch & Concordium Hawaii, 76. *Instrumental Works:* Laminations: Five Pieces for Brass Quintet; Strata: Five Pieces for Tuba and Percussion Quintet; Lyric Variations for Tuba and String Orchestra; Warmth of Distant Suns (orch, three pieces); Galaxy Visions (orch, six pieces).

BROWN, KEITH CROSBY　　　　　　　　ASCAP 1936
composer, educator
b Port Maitland, NS, Sept 1, 1885; d Newton Center, Mass, Sept 8, 48. Educ: New Eng Cons; Harvard Univ; Liceo Musicale, Rome. To US 1886, Citizen. Head music dept, Mt Ida Jr Col, Mass. *Songs:* Night on the Lagoon; Sonnet to the Moon; The Pirate's Daughter. *Instrumental Works:* Bostonia Suite; On the Esplanade; Latin American Suite; Who Discovered America? (operetta).

BROWN, LESTER RAYMOND
composer, author, conductor
b Reinerton, Pa, Mar 14, 12. Educ: Ithaca Cons Music, NY, 26-29; NY Mil Acad, 29-32; Duke Univ, 32-36. Toured with own group, Duke Blue Devils, 36-37; free-lance arr, New York, 37-38. Organized Band of Renown, perf, 38- Cond, Bob Hope Show, 47-, Steve Allen Show, 58-60, Hollywood Palace TV Show, 62 & Dean Martin Show, 63-73. Chief Collabrs: Ben Homer, Bud Green, Sonny Burke, Lee Hale, Edna Osser. *Songs:* We Wish You the Merriest; Papoose; Perishere Shuffle; Trylon Stomp; Music: Sentimental Journey; It's the

Time to Be Jolly; My Number One Dream Came True; Are You Still in Love With Me?; Comes the Sandman.

BROWN, LEW　　　　　　　　　　　　ASCAP 1921
producer
b Odessa, Russia, Dec 10, 1893; d New York, NY, Feb 5, 58. To US 1898. Educ: DeWitt Clinton High Sch, NY. Joined B G DeSylva & Ray Henderson as song writing team & music publ, 25. Sold publ firm, 29; to Hollywood under contract to Fox. Other Collabrs: Albert Von Tilzer, Con Conrad, Moe Jaffe, Sidney Clare, Harry Warren, Cliff Friend, Harry Akst, Jay Gorney, Louis Alter, Harold Arlen, Sammy Fain, Sammy Stept, Charles Tobias. *Songs:* Give Me the Moonlight, Give Me the Girl; Oh, By Jingo!; I Used to Love You But It's All Over Now; Dapper Dan; Wait Until You See My Madeline; I'd Climb the Highest Mountain; Last Night on the Back Porch; Shine; Don't Bring Lulu; Then I'll Be Happy; Collegiate; Lucky Day; Birth of the Blues; Black Bottom; It All Depends on You; Manhattan Mary; The Best Things in Life Are Free; Good News; The Varsity Drag; Just Imagine; Lucky in Love; Broken Hearted; Just a Memory; So Blue; I'm on the Crest of a Wave; You're the Cream in My Coffee; Button Up Your Overcoat; You Wouldn't Fool Me; My Lucky Star; Sonny Boy; Together; My Sin; I'm a Dreamer, Aren't We All?; Sunny Side Up; If I Had a Talking Picture of You; Little Pal; Without Love; Thank Your Father; Red Hot Chicago; You Try Somebody Else; My Song; The Thrill Is Gone; Life Is Just a Bowl of Cherries; This Is the Missus; Strike Me Pink; I've Got to Pass Your House; Baby, Take a Bow; If Love Makes Me Give Up Steak and Potatoes; The Lady Dances; Love Is Never Out of Season; That Old Feeling; Down Home Rag; Comes Love; Beer Barrel Polka; Don't Sit Under the Apple Tree With Anyone Else But Me; I Came Here to Talk for Joe; I Dug a Ditch in Wichita; The Beer That I Left on the Bar; Oh, Ma-Ma; Madam, I Love Your Crepe Suzette. *Scores:* Bway Stage: George White's Scandals (1925, 1926, 1928, 1931); Manhattan Mary; Good News; Hold Everything; Three Cheers; Follow Through; co-librettist: Flying High; Hot-Cha; Strike Me Pink; Yokel Boy (also produced & dir). Films: Sunny Side Up; The Singing Fool; Just Imagine; Stand Up and Cheer; New Faces of 1937.

BROWN, LOUIS (YULE)　　　　　　　　ASCAP 1956
composer, conductor, arranger
b Brooklyn, NY, May 4, 12. Educ: NY Univ, BS(educ); self-taught in music. Pianist, society bands, incl Vincent Lopez Orch, Dick Stabile Orch, Gene Krupa Orch, New York. Pianist with Martin & Lewis, 50, stayed with Jerry Lewis as cond, to present. Scored var motion pictures. Chief Collabrs: Lil Mattis, Bill Richmond, Jerry Lewis, Sammy Cahn, Alan Handley. *Songs:* Music: We've Got a World That Swings; A Now and a Later Love; That's My Way; The Time is Now; Life's Not That Simple; Make the World a Better Place; Until You Fall in Love. *Scores:* Nutty Professor; Three On a Couch; The Errand Boy; Which Way to the Front.

BROWN, MARGARET WISE　　　　　　　ASCAP 1952
author
b New York, NY, May 23, 10; d Nice, France, Nov 13, 52. Educ: Hollins Col, BA. Ed & author about 100 children's bks incl "The Noisy Books"; "The Little Island"; "Goodnight Moon". *Songs:* I Like People; Where Have You Been?; Bks with records: The Golden Egg; Five Little Firemen; Little Brass Band; Little Fat Policeman.

BROWN, MARSHALL RICHARD　　　　　ASCAP 1951
composer, jazz musician, music educator
b Framingham, Mass, Dec 21, 20. Educ: NY Univ, BSc(cum laude, music), 49; Columbia Univ, MS, 53. Musician, USA, WW II. Band dir, East Rockaway High Sch, NY, 49-51 & Farmingdale High Sch, 51-57. Pioneered the teaching of jazz in pub schs, initiated the stage band movement; organized the Int Band, 58 & The Newport Youth Band, 58-61. Toured & recorded with Pee Wee Russell, Ruby Braff, Lee Konitz & Johnny Dankworth, 60-70. Arr & cond for Louis Armstrong & Bobby Hacket. Pvt instr, jazz improvisation. Chief Collabrs: Alden Shuman, Earl Shuman. *Songs & Instrumental Works:* Seven Lonely Days; The Banjo's Back in Town; Cinnamon Kisses; Copley Square; Rock Bottom; Cha Cha Cha for Judy; Dateline Newport; Solid Blue.

BROWN, MAURICE　　　　　　　　　　ASCAP 1944
composer, conductor, cellist
b Brooklyn, NY, Aug 4, 05. Educ: Columbia Col, BA; Columbia Law Sch, LLB; studied with William Ebann. *Songs:* When a Gypsy Falls in Love; Sunshine Back Home; Baby's Bedtime Prayer; This Land We Love; Sweet Dreams. *Instrumental Works:* English Village Scenes (Suites I, II); Valse Precieuse; Valse Charmante.

BROWN, NACIO HERB　　　　　　　　ASCAP 1927
composer, publisher
b Deming, NMex, Feb 22, 1896; d San Francisco, Calif, Sept 28, 64. Educ: Musical Arts High Sch, Los Angeles. Had tailoring bus, then became realtor before becoming comp. Moved to Hollywood, 28, under contract to MGM. Songs for films incl, "Hollywood Revue", "A Night At the Opera", "San Francisco" & "Babes in Arms." Chief Collabrs: Arthur Freed, B G DeSylva, Gus Kahn, Leo Robin, Gordon Clifford. *Songs:* The Woman in the Shoe; Avalon Town; Love Songs of the Nile; Rag Doll; Do You Remember; Our Big Love Scene; Bundle of Old Love Letters; When Buddha Smiles, Coral Sea; The

Wedding of the Painted Doll; Broadway Melody; Singin' in the Rain; You Were Meant for Me; Chant of the Jungle; Pagan Love Song; Should I?; The Moon Is Low; Paradise; You're an Old Smoothie; Eadie Was a Lady; We'll Make Hay While the Sun Shines; Our Big Love Scene; After Sundown; Temptation; Beautiful Girl; All I Do Is Dream of You; A New Moon Is Over My Shoulder; You Are My Lucky Star; Sing Before Breakfast; I've Got a Feelin' You're Foolin'; Broadway Rhythm; Alone; Would You?; Smoke Dreams; I'm Feelin' Like a Million; Your Broadway and My Broadway; Yours and Mine; Good Morning; You Stepped Out of a Dream; If I Steal a Kiss; Love Is Where You Find It; Make 'Em Laugh. *Instrumental Works:* Doll Dance; American Bolero; Dance of Fury; You, So It's You; One Heavenly Night; Situation Wanted. *Scores:* Stage: Hollywood Music Box Revue (Los Angeles); Take a Chance (Bway); Film: Broadway Melody (29, 36, 37 & 38); Going Hollywood; Sadie McKee; Student Tour; Greenwich Village; The Kissing Bandit; Singin' in the Rain; On an Island With You; Ziegfeld Girl; My Wonderful One, Let's Dance.

BROWN, NACIO HERB, JR   ASCAP 1957
composer, author, publisher
b Los Angeles, Calif, Feb 27, 21. Educ: Univ Southern Calif. Prof mgr, Freddy Martin Music Publ & Mark Warnow Music Publ Firms; mgr music catalogs for Hoagy Carmichael, Richard Whiting, Al Dubin, Arthur Freed, Walter Donaldson, Sammy Fain & many others. Pres, NHB Music Enterprises, Inc. Songwriter. Chief Collabrs: Carolyn Leigh, Buddy Feyne, Eddy de Lange. *Songs:* Who Put That Dream in Your Eyes; Goodbye for Just a Little While; I Laughed to Keep From Crying; Just Because You're You; You Gotta Talk Me Into It, Baby; I Thought I'd Seen Everything, Then I Saw You; Let Us Eat Lettuce.

BROWN, NATHANIEL S   ASCAP 1979
composer, author
b Baltimore, Md, Oct 25, 21. Educ: Suffolk Univ; Boston Univ; Harvard Univ; Univ Mich; City Univ New York; Third Street Settlement Music Sch, New York; Brooklyn Cons Music; studied with Rudolph Schramm & Schillinger Syst with Richard Benda. Wrote & produced off-Bway play, "Dance Darling Dance," 79, won ASCAP Award, 79. Mem, New York Dramatist Guild. Chief Collabr: Walter Murray. *Songs:* Dance Darling Dance; Love Is My Everything; No Other Love Can Be So Sweet As Loving You; Happy Feet; Today Is the First Day of My Life; I Guess I Better Change My Style; I Cried So Hard; Lord Give to Me Thy Daily Bread; Love and Flowers—A Wedding Song; Music: How to Make a House a Home.

BROWN, PAUL D (PAUL PAGE)   ASCAP 1957
composer, author, singer
b North Vernon, Ind, May 9, 20. Educ: Studied piano with two pvt piano teachers as a child. Youngest US commercial newspaper ed at 18; formed own band at 19 in Juneau, Alaska. Staff mem, NBC radio, Chicago & Hollywood, 40-50; appeared in RCM Hawaiian movie shorts & a few Universal Films in Hollywood. DJ nightly Polynesian radio show, "Ports o' Call," Los Angeles, until 66. Went to Hawaii, 68. Artist, cartoonist, publ, band leader & pianist. Mem: Hawaiian Prof Songwriters Soc; Am Guild Authors & Comp. Pres, Hawaiian Music Awards Acad (Annual "Nani" Awards in recording indust). Life mem, Los Angeles local, Am Fedn Musicians. Chief Collabrs: Don R George, Bernie Kaai Lewis, Bob Merrill. *Songs & Instrumental Works:* Big Luau in the Sky; Chapel at Kahaluu (Best Song of the Year, "Nani" Awards, Honolulu, 79); Music: Gloria's Got a Glow; Nani (theme of Annual Honolulu Nani Awards show); Passport to Paradise.

BROWN, RAYMOND HARRY   ASCAP 1973
composer, teacher, musician
b Oceanside, NY, Nov 7, 46. Educ: Freeport High Sch, NY; Ithaca Col, BMus; C W Post Col, Long Island Univ, MS; arr lessons from Willie Maiden, Manny Albam, Roy Wright, Henry K Levy & Glenn Brown. Arr, comp & played jazz trumpet with Studio Band of USA Field Band, 70-71 & Stan Kenton Band, 71-72; performed jazz improvisation clinics. Arr & played with Bill Watrous Big Band, 73-74. Played with New York Orch, Thad Jones, Joe Newman, Ray Brown, Leroy Vineger, Mundell Lowe, Bill Berry Big Band, until 79 & Frankie Capp-Nat Pierce Big Band, 80. NEA comp grant, 73, improvisation grant, 80. Recorded album, 80. *Instrumental Works:* Is There Anything Still There?; Neverbird; The Opener; My Man Willie; Afterthoughts; Toma's Gato; Mi Burrito; Arthur Author; Two Rare T-Bones.

BROWN, RAYMOND SHANNON, II   ASCAP 1976
composer, author, singer
b Okmulgee, Okla, May 30, 52. Educ: Henryetta High Sch; Okla Baptist Univ; Univ Okla. Mem, Christian Arts Ctr, Little Rock, Ark, 71. Appeared in prof productions of "Amahl and the Night Visitors", "Godspell", "A Funny Thing Happened on the Way to the Forum", "Mountain Light" & "The Lady's Not for Burning." Honored as 1 of the 5 outstanding choral composers, Southern Baptist Convention, 76. Chief Collabrs: Ragan Courtney, John Hadley. *Songs:* In Obedience (cantata); The Light in His Eyes; Singer's Lullaby; Music: In the Name of the Lord (cantata); Softly and Tenderly; I Heard About a Man; Sometimes a Light Surprises; How Tedious and Tasteless the Hours; The Tabernacle of God; Blessed Quietness; Buchanan Street; Eternity's Children (octavo); All of Us Like Sheep (octavo); The Gates of Righteousness (octavo); They That Wait (octavo). *Instrumental Works:* Suite From the Lady's Not for Burning. *Scores:* Musical: Lottie D; Revelations; Mountain Light.

BROWN, RAYNER   ASCAP 1964
composer
b Des Moines, Iowa, Feb 23, 12. Educ: Univ Southern Calif, BMus, 38, MMus, 47. Organist, Wilshire Presby Church, Los Angeles, 41-77. Prof music, Biola Col, Calif, 48-77, emer prof, 77- *Instrumental Works:* Concerto (two pianos, brass & perc); Concertino (piano & band); Symphony (clarinet, choir); Concerto (clarinet & wind orch); Concerto (flute & wind orch); Concerto (organ & wind orch); Concerto (harp & brass ens); Sinfonietta (trombone, choir); Sonata (clarinet & organ); Sonata (flute & organ); Sonata (bassoon & organ); Sonata (viola & organ); Sonata (four trumpets & organ); Sonata Breve (piano); Sonata (cello & organ); Chaconne (violin & organ); Prelude and Fugue (violin & organ); Passacaglia (harpsichord & organ); five pieces for organ, harp, brass & percussion; 35 sonatinas for organ; three symphonies for orchestra.

BROWN, ROGER WILLIAM   ASCAP 1970
composer, author, singer
b New Brunswick, NJ, Jan 10, 36. Educ: New Brunswick High Sch, 53; Middlesex County Col, AA, 70; Rutgers Univ, BA(psychol), 73; Fordham Univ, 73-74; Calif Lutheran Col, MS(educ), 80; Calif State Univ, Northridge, MA candidate, 80- Singer, nightclubs, radio & TV. Recording artist, Chestnut Records. Leader, Roger Brown and The Kountry Kings. *Songs:* Kathy; One Nighters and Other Sweet Things; She's My Woman, She's My Soul; What's Gonna Happen With the Boy?; You Step Aside.

BROWN, SAMUEL FRANKLIN, III   ASCAP 1971
composer, producer, arranger
b Tacoma, Wash, July 28, 47. Educ: USN Sch of Music; Columbia Univ; Chicago Cons of Music; studied comp with Stella Roberts, film scoring with Earle Hagen. Songwriter with Jerry Butler Workshop, 71. Staff writer & producer, Motown Records, 73. Music dir for Jacksons & Lola Folana, 75-77. Producer for Al Wilson & Luther Rabb, 78. Formed Git Down Brown Productions, 78-80. Chief Collabrs: Jerry Butler, Renee Armand, Christine Yarian, Leslie Ruchala, Judy Wieder, Ron Brown. *Songs:* You Really Turn Me On; This Time It's Right; Music: One Day in Your Life; I Think That She's in Love; You're So Good for Me; All My Life.

BROWN, TED ALLAN (THEO)   ASCAP 1970
composer, singer, drummer
b Ft Wayne, Ind, Oct 2, 45. Educ: Ind Univ, studied with George Gaber. Worked with Counts V & in var nightclubs; had own band, late 60's. Developed writing & gained studio experience, Nashville, Tenn. Songwriter. Drummer & singer front man in Nashville area. Writer for Mary Reevs Davis. Chief Collabrs: Ron Helliard, Butch Davies. *Songs:* Sunday Afternoon Boatride in the Park on the Lake; Want Want Gimme Gimme; Waltzing Through the Years With You; Screamin' in Harmony; Boogie for the Lord; On and On. *Scores:* Film: How Hot You Can Get.

BROWN, THOMAS ALFRED   ASCAP 1965
composer, author, clinician
b Schenectady, NY, June 27, 32. Educ: Hartwick Col, BS, 57; State Univ NY Col, Potsdam, MS, 61. Comp, arr & performing artist, WRGB TV, Schenectady. Staff, Stan Kenton Clinics; staff, asst dir & dir, Nat Stage Band Camp; NY State Music Camp; founder & dir, Eastern US Music Camp, Bard Col. Clinician & solo artist, Ludwig Industries, Chicago; recording artist, Crest Records, Inc; cond, clinician & soloist throughout US. *Songs & Instrumental Works:* Rock Velvet; Percussion Particles; Percussionata; Happy to Be; Symphonic Celebration; Once Upon a Time; Winter Wishes.

BROWN, WALTER EARL   ASCAP 1958
composer, author, singer
b Salt Lake City, Utah, Dec 25, 28. Educ: High sch; pvt music study. Singer & arr with Skylarks, 10 yrs & other groups. Has written spec musical material, songs and/or scripts for numerous top stars. Wrote vocal arr for Liza Minnelli & cast in film, "New York, New York" & in Bway show, "The Act." Has rec'd five Emmy nominations for songs on TV. Chief Collabrs: Ticker Freeman, Billy Barnes, Billy Goldenberg, Heinz Kiessling, Michel Legrand, Ian Freebairn-Smith. *Songs:* Gotta Love You; Chimney Sweeps; Just a Brief Encounter; Wanna Belong to You; Balloons; Don't Call Me Mama Anymore; I Came Here to Sing a Torch Song; If I Can Dream; She Was a Vamp; Time; My Life; Your World; Waltz 'Round the Christmas Tree; Lyrics: Dreams of Glass; Power Flowers; In the Shadow of the Moon. *Scores:* Film: Young Ladies of Rochefort.

BROWN, WILLIAM F   ASCAP 1963
author
b Jersey City, NJ, Apr 16, 28. Educ: Montclair Acad; Princeton Univ, AB. Mag staff writer; literary agent; TV producer with advert agency; free-lance writer. Writer, special material for TV & industrial shows. Playwright, "The Girl in the Freudian Slip", "A Single Thing in Common." Chief Collabrs: William Roy, Ted Simons, Albert Hague, Clay Warnick. *Songs:* Dime a Dozen; Four in Hand; Theme: That Was the Week That Was. *Scores:* Librettos: The Wiz; A Broadway Musical; Song; How to Steal an Election.

BROWNE, BRADFORD ASCAP 1952
composer, author, singer
b North Adams, Mass; d. Educ: Georgetown Univ, LLB. In govt serv, DC. WW I, overseas. Joined Al Llewelyn as singing team on radio, 25. Became singer, pianist, writer, announcer & dir, CBS. Developed network prog "Nit Wit Hour." Produced shows. *Songs:* The Girl in the Little Green Hat; Maurice, the Gendarme.

BROWNE, DIANE GAIL (DAISY) ASCAP 1975
composer, author, singer
b Detroit, Mich, June 5, 54. Educ: U S Grant High Sch; Calif State Univ, Fullerton. Singer & entertainer, nightclubs. Studio background vocalist, RCA records, A&M Records, Michael MacDonald & Wilson Pickett. Chief Collabr: Tony Peluso. *Songs:* That's the Way Our Story Goes; Since I've Found You; Listen to the Rain; Lyrics: Happy.

BROWNE, JACKSON
singer, songwriter
b Heidelberg, Ger, Oct 9, 48. Coproducer, "Warren Zevon and Excitable Boy" for Asylum artist, Warren Zevon. *Songs:* Doctor My Eyes; Song for Adam; These Days; Fountain of Sorrow; The Pretender; Here Come Those Tears; Rock Me on the Water; Take It Easy; Boulevard. *Albums:* Jackson Browne; For Everyman; Late for the Sky; The Pretender; Running on Empty; Hold Out.

BROWNE, JOHN LEWIS ASCAP 1924
composer, conductor, choirmaster
b London, Eng, May 18, 1866; d Chicago, Ill, Oct 23, 33. Moved to US, 1872. Educ: Studied organ with father; then with S P Warren & F Archer; NY Univ. Organist, Holy Name Cathedral, Chicago, 1888; San Francisco, 1892-98, also cond concerts; Sacred Heart Church, Atlanta, Ga, 1899-1907. Music dir, John Wanamaker's, Philadelphia, 08-10. Church organist & choirmaster, St Patrick's & Our Lady of Sorrows, Chicago, many yrs. Designed organ, Medinah Temple, Chicago. Gave concerts throughout US. *Instrumental Works:* The Granite Walls Rise Fair; Ecce Sacerdos Magnus; Missa Solemnis. *Scores:* Opera: La Corsicana.

BROWNE, PHILIP ASCAP 1968
composer, educator
b Norman, Okla, July 27, 33. Educ: Aspen Music Sch, 55; Ariz State Univ, BA, 56; Univ Rochester Eastman Sch Music, MM(comp), 60; Univ Calif, Los Angeles, PhD, 68; studied comp with Bernard Rogers, Wayne Barlow, Darius Milhaud, Roy Harris. Professional arr & woodwind performer in dance & jazz bands, Phoenix pub schs, while at univ. Cond, USA, 424th Army Band, Ft Bliss, 56-58. Commercial arr, Mercury Records, Chicago, 58. Worked with TV firm in Ont & Eastman Wind Ens while at Univ Rochester. Taught pub schs, Phoenix, 59-60, high sch, Calif, 60-63. Fac, Calif State Polytech Univ, 63, chmn music dept, 10 yrs, prof music & dir bands. Comp & author, publ works for sch bands & orchs; cond & adjudicator. *Instrumental Works:* Sonoro and Brioso (band); Ballad for Trumpet and Band; Suite No 2 (band, Col Band Dir Nat Asn award, 73); Windroc Overture (band); Concerto for Strings; Carousel (band); Serenade for Orchestra (Nat Sch Orch Asn comp award, 75); Skyride (band); Symphony No 1 and No 2; Concerto for Clarinet and Orchestra; Ballad for Horn and Band; Three Lyric Variants (band); Inaugural Procession (band, comn by Calif Polytech Univ).

BROWNE, RAYMOND A ASCAP 1939
composer, author, publisher
b New York, NY, Dec 17, 1871; d Wakefield, RI, May 9, 22. Educ: Cooper Union. Reporter, New York Sun. Wrote spec material for vaudeville. *Songs:* Take Back Your Gold; Down on the Farm; Lass from the County Mayo; Just Because I Love You So; I'm Looking for a Sweetheart.

BROWNE, RICHMOND ASCAP 1975
composer
b Flint, Mich, Aug 8, 34. Educ: Mich State Univ, BMus(theory, comp), 55; studied comp with H Owen Reed; Yale Univ, BMus, 57, comp), 58, studied comp with Richard Donovan, Quincy Porter. Fulbright fel, Akademie für Musik, Vienna & Mozarteum, Salzburg, Austria. Taught theory & comp, Yale Univ, 60-68, prof of music theory, Univ Mich, 68- Mem, exec committee & nat council, Am Soc of Univ Composers; founding mem & nat secy, Soc for Music Theory. Recipient, Yale Univ Morse Grant, France, 65. *Songs & Instrumental Works:* Chortos I (speech chorus); Reri Velocitatem (trio for any 3 instruments); Triphthong (instrumental trio).

BROWNE, SYLVIA THERESA ASCAP 1973
composer, author, singer
b Los Angeles, Calif, Dec 11, 43. Educ: Eubanks Cons Music, studied voice & piano; Los Angeles City Col, AA(music), 78; Calif State Univ, Dominguez Hills, studied music; studied voice with Marvin Jenkins. Dir, church choirs. Pianist, children's choir, Sunday sch & sr choir. Singer, concerts & pianist, recitals. Comp words & music. Guest singer & co-emcee for talent show, Los Angeles City Col. *Songs:* Call on the Lord.

BROWNEE, ZING
See Brownstein, Samuel Hyman

BROWNELL, WILLIAM EDWARD ASCAP 1972
composer, author, trumpeter
b Grand Rapids, Mich. Educ: Northwestern High Sch; Wayne State Univ, BA. Plays on CBS-TV, NBC-TV & ABC Radio. Wrote stories for Sat Eve Post, Collier's, Argosy & Cosmopolitan. In advert, Young & Rubican Int, DFS, N W Ayer & Ted Bates. Chief Collabs: William Edwin Lesquereaux Young, Richard Klaus. *Songs:* The Ice Cream Song; I'm Just an Ordinary Guy; The Door is Wide Open; Light Up and Relax; She Don't Know Nothin But No; The Savings Song; The Fine Cigar.

BROWNING, MORTIMER ASCAP 1934
composer, organist, choirmaster
b Baltimore, Md, Nov 16, 1891; d Milford, Del, June 24, 53. Educ: Peabody Cons; Chicago Musical Col; David Mannes Sch (all scholarships); studied with Harold Phillips, George Boyle, Hans Weisse, Adolf Schmid & Percy Grainger. Head, Organ Dept, Greensboro Col & Theory Dept, Sch of Musicianship, New York. Teacher of spec courses, Juilliard Sch Music; Westchester Cons. Organist & choirmaster, Baltimore churches; also St Andrew's Church, New York; Seventh Church of Christ, Scientist, New York. Fac mem, Greenwich House Music Sch; Chapin Sch, New York. Documentary film background scores incl "Basic Dance"; also for films at Libr of Modern Art, New York. *Songs:* Little Old Foolish Man; The Night Is But a Mirror; The Philanderer; O Let Me Dream; O Perfect and Eternal One; For I Am Persuaded. *Instrumental Works:* Concerto for Theramin; Trio for Violin, Cello, Piano; Piano Suite in D; Scherzo Rondo (violin, orch); Caprice Burlesque (violin); Moods and Characters (piano suite).

BROWNSTEIN, SAMUEL HYMAN (ZING BROWNEE) ASCAP 1969
composer, author
b Roman, Romania, Sept 8, 05. Educ: Pub sch, Brooklyn; Boys' High Sch, Brooklyn; New York Col Pharmacy. Began songwriting after becoming registered pharmacist. Wrote screenplays, "Hey, Ninnie!" & "Schnozzola (The Tragedy of a Clown)," 35. Owner of Samuel H Brownstein Enterprises, ASCAP music publ. Chief Collabs: M Russel Goudey, Eddie Brown. *Songs & Instrumental Works:* American Pledge; US: Our Freedom Song; The United Nations (The Hope of the World Today); 13 Banana; The Banana Vendor (Wha' Hoppen to De Thirteen Floor); You're My Love; 555-1212, I'm Calling Information.

BROZA, ELLIOT LAWRENCE
See Lawrence, Elliot

BROZEN, MICHAEL ASCAP 1968
composer
b New York, NY, Aug 5, 34. Educ: Bard Col, studied with Paul Nordoff, 50-52; Berkshire Music Ctr, studied with Lukas Foss, 52; Juilliard Sch Music, BS & MS, studied with Vincent Persichetti, 52-57. Rec'd Howard Hanson Comn, 68. Rec'd ASCAP Annual Award, 68-73; Nat Inst-Am Acad Arts & Letters grant & recording award, 69; Ingram Merrill Found Award, 69-70; Guggenheim fel, 71; spec citation Koussevitzky Int Recording AAward, 71; Wurlitzer Found Residence Grant, 75. *Songs & Instrumental Works:* Canto (orch); Dark Night, Gentle Night (soprano, tenor & orch); Piano Fantasy; In Memoriam (soprano & string orch); The Bugle Moon (baritone & nine instruments); instruments). *Scores:* Musical play: Caliban.

BRUCE, GARY
See Barton, Ben

BRUNELLI, LOUIS JEAN ASCAP 1958
composer
b New York, NY, June 24, 25. Educ: Guildhall Sch Music, London, cert; NY Univ, BA; Manhattan Sch Music, MM, 50; studied comp with Marion Bauer, Vittorio Giannini, piano with Harold Bauer, Myra Hess, cond with Adrian Boult. Arr & asst cond, Longines Symphonette, 49-54. Dir, theatrical & symph libr, Chappell & Co, 54-71. Theory fac, Manhattan Sch Music, 70, extension div dir, 72, dir for perf, 72-77. Adminr, Juilliard Col, 77-, asst dean, 78- Guest cond, NH Philh, Wellesley Symph, Am Fest Orch, Univ Wis, Ohio State Univ. ASCAP Found for Young Comp Judge, 79 & 80. Am Symph League, Recording Repertoire award, 60; comn from Strategic Air Command Band, 70. Mem, Nat Asn for Am Composers & Conductors. *Instrumental Works:* Chronicles for Concert Band; Essay for Cyrano (concert band, orch versions); In Memoriam (concert band); Arlechino for Concert Band; Preludium and Fugue (concert band).

BRUNNER, BARBARA JEANNE ASCAP 1973
author, pianist, singer
b Mesa, Ariz, Nov 22, 14. Educ: High sch, Venice, Calif; studied piano with Lillian Liknaitz, vocal with David Reese. Alto singer, sch & church choral groups. Pianist, classical & combos. Chief Collabs: John Thomas Reese, Rosa Raile Reese, Francis R Brunner, Robert F Brunner. *Songs:* Music: Here He Comes (Santa Claus).

BRUNNER, FRANCIS RUDOLF   ASCAP 1973
author
b Santa Monica, Calif, Dec 17, 1899. Educ: Pomona Col; Univ Mich, Ann
Arbor, BA. Ed, Student Publ. Makeup ed, Los Angeles Examiner. Mem, Santa
Monica Rotary Club. Retiree, Hughes Aircraft Co. Publ, Fun Guide, Los
Angeles & vicinity. Chief Collabrs: Barbara Jeanne Brunner, Robert F Brunner.
Songs: Lyrics: Here He Comes (Santa Claus).

BRUNNER, ROBERT F   ASCAP 1964
composer, conductor, arranger
b Pasadena, Calif, Jan 9, 38. Educ: Univ Calif, Los Angeles; studied with Helen
Dixon, Lionel Taylor & Alfred Sendrey. Rec'd Young Musicians Found
scholarship & Bank of Am Achievement Award; twice winner, Univ Redlands
Symph of Am Comp. Capt & cmndg officer, 562nd Air Force Band (Calif Air
Nat Guard). Cond own dance orch. Staff comp/cond, Walt Disney Studios, 17
yrs; comp over 125 motion picture & TV scores; comp music & songs for
"Invitation to Paradise" (nighttime show at Polynesian Cult Ctr, Laie, Hawaii);
comp 6 musicals for Mormon Church; pres, Brunner Music Publ Co & BMC
Records. Chief Collabrs: Bruce Belland, Tom Adair, Roy E Disney, L Clair
Likes. *Songs:* You're Really Terrific (Emmy Award nomination); Music:
Encircle the Child; Suddenly You're Older; A Taco and a Burger; I Wanna Talk
Hawaiian; Hands Across the Water; Remember All Your Dreams; Stars Over
Laie; Aloha; Someone Is There; Families Have a Way of Growing Up; Language
of Love; Seek After These Things; Sleep Warm; Come Take a Little Hand; Keep
Your Eye Upon the Doughnut. *Instrumental Works:* Symphonietta; Scherzo.
Scores: TV Background: Wonderful World of Color (series); Bway show: Within
These Walls; Film/TV: That Darn Cat; Blackbeard's Ghost; Snowball Express;
The Computer Wore Tennis Shoes; The Barefoot Executive; The Castaway
Cowboy; Mustang!; The North Avenue Irregulars; Chandar, the Black Leopard
of Ceylon; Animated Featurettes (winner of Film Adv Bd Awards); Banjo, the
Woodpile Cat; The Small One.

BRUNS, GEORGE E   ASCAP 1963
composer, musician, orchestrator
b Sandy, Ore, July 3, 14. Arr & played in dance bands, 36-50; comp for motion
pictures, 51-74. Chief Collabr: Tom Adair. *Songs & Instrumental Works:* Davy
Crockett; Farewell to the Mountain; Zorro. *Scores:* Films: Sleeping Beauty; 101
Dalmations; Sword in the Stone; Jungle Book; Aristocats; Robin Hood; Absent
Minded Professor; Love Bug; TV Shows: Wonderful World of Disney.

BRUSH, RUTH DAMARIS   ASCAP 1961
composer, author, organist
b Fairfax, Okla. Educ: Cons Music, Kansas City, Mo, BM, grad study in summer
sessions, studied with Wiktor Labunski, David van Vactor & Gardner Read.
Studio pianist, radio sta WHB, Kansas City. Head of piano dept, Frank Phillips
Col, Borger, Tex, 3 yrs. Concert piano under Stahler Booking Agency. Lect
recitals of own comp for music teachers conventions, music clubs & other
organizations; also lect recitals of Am music, contemporary music & standard
classics. Chief Collabrs: poets, Elinor Wiley, Sara Teasdale, Lorene Chinn.
Songs: Bartlesville, Our Town; O Those Hills of Oklahoma (vocal solo); Music:
The Lord Is My Shepherd (SATB); This Same Jesus (SATB); Give Me the Sea
(vocal solo); Goddess of the Sun (vocal solo); Twilight (vocal solo). *Instrumental
Works:* Valse Joyeuse (violin & piano); Two Expressive Pieces for Organ;
Pastorale for Organ; Playtime Piano Pieces; River Moons (orch); Suite for
Strings; Romance Sans Paroles (violin & piano); Osage Hills Suite (piano).

BRYAN, ALFRED   ASCAP 1914
author
b Brantford, Ont, Sept 15, 1871; d Gladstone, NJ, Apr 1, 58. Educ: Parochial
schs. On staff, New York publ firms. Wrote songs for films & for Warner Bros,
Calif. Chief Collabrs: Fred Fisher, George Meyer, Larry Stock, Alfred Gumble,
Al Piantadosi, Joe McCarthy, John Klenner. *Songs:* I Want to Be Good But My
Eyes Won't Let Me; Peg o' My Heart; I Didn't Raise My Boy to Be a Soldier;
I'm on My Way to Mandalay; Who Paid the Rent for Mrs Rip Van Winkle?;
The High Cost of Loving; Joan of Arc; Lorraine; Oui, Oui, Marie; Come
Josephine in My Flying Machine; Puddin' Head Jones; Down in the Old Cherry
Orchard; Brown Eyes, Why Are You Blue?; The Irish Were Egyptians Long
Ago; Hooray for Baffins Bay; Daddy, You've Been a Mother to Me; Madelon;
Blue River; My Mother's Eyes; Red Lips, Kiss My Blues Away; Winter; I Want
You to Want Me to Want You; Dream Serenade; Rainbow; Beautiful Annabelle
Lee; Wear a Hat With a Silver Lining; Cleopatra; When the Bees Are in the
Hive; Are You Sincere?; When the Harbor Lights Are Burning; Green Fields
and Bluebirds; Japansy; I Was So Young; Be Sweet to Me, Cherie; In a Little
Dutch Kindergarten; Down the Colorado Trail; A Cradle in Bethlehem; When
You Add Religion to Love; To the Last Beat of the Drum. *Scores:* Bway stage:
The Shubert Gaieties of 1919; The Midnight Rounders (20, 21); The Century
Revue; A Night in Spain; Paris.

BRYAN, CHARLES FAULKNER   ASCAP 1955
composer, educator
b McMinnville, Tenn, July 26, 11; d Helena, Ala, July 7, 55. Educ: Nashville
Cons, BM; Tenn Poly Inst, BS; George Peabody Col, MS; Yale Univ, MA,
studied with Paul Hindemith; Guggenheim fel. Head music dept, Tenn Poly
Inst, 36; state supvr, Fed Music Project, Tenn, 40, later head project for
Southern area; regional consult, Civilian Defense, WW II. Fac mem, George

Peabody Col, 47; music master, Indian Springs Sch Boys, Helena, 52; lectr on
Am folk music; gave many concerts. *Songs & Instrumental Works:* White
Spiritual Symphony; Cumberland Interlude: 1790; Birmingham Suite; Ballad of
the Harp Weaver; American Folk Music for High Schools (25 arr); Singin' Billy
(opera); The Bell Witch (cantata); From the Textbooks (choral suite); Music:
Folk Fun for Four Hands; Choral Music: Charlottetown; Amazing Grace; Look
to the Past; Skip to M'Lou; Ev'rybody's Welcome.

BRYANT, ANNE MARIE   ASCAP 1974
composer, author
b Toronto, Ont, Mar 2, 37. Educ: Royal Cons Music, Toronto, Ont; Guildhall
Sch Music, London, Eng. Chief Collabrs: Ardie Bryant, David P Bryant. *Songs:*
American Dream; Lyrics: America.

BRYANT, ARDIE   ASCAP 1974
composer, author
b Dallas, Tex, Mar 20, 29. As musician, arr & performer worked with Louis
Armstrong, Cab Calloway, Lionel Hampton, Billy May, Nat King Cole, Duke
Ellington & Count Basie. Chief Collabr: Anne Bryant. *Songs:* Music: America;
I Need You; What's It Really All About; Now's the Time to Do It.

BRYANT, CLIFFORD LISLE   ASCAP 1975
composer, teacher, arranger
b Needham, Mass, Apr 22, 33. Educ: High sch, Manchester, Conn; Hartt Col
Music, BM, 55. Professional pianist in Los Angeles. Worked on Ann-Margret,
Petula Clark & Lola Falana musical TV specials. Road work with Si Zentner,
Louie Nye, Rod McKuen & others. Also worked on TV shows, "Taxi" &
"Laverne and Shirley." Chief Collabr: Mark Fleming. *Songs:* Music: Don't It
Feel Good?; Whatcha Do to Me; Here We Go Again; Melissa; Dancin' (Movin'
to the Rhythm).

BRYANT, WILLIAM STEVEN   ASCAP 1960
composer, conductor, singer
b New Orleans, La, Aug 30, 08; d Hollywood, Calif, Feb 9, 64. Led dance band,
33-39 & 46-48. Became DJ, nightclub MC. *Songs:* It's Over Because We're
Through; Blues Around the Clock; Do You Wanna Jump Children?

BRYDON, WILSON P   ASCAP 1959
composer, author
b Ashtabula, Ohio, June 1, 18. Educ: WVa Wesleyan Col, BA; Univ Pa, MA;
Univ SC. WW II service, Korean War service to 63. *Songs:* Making Believe It's
Christmas Eve.

BRYMN, J TIM   ASCAP 1933
composer, conductor, arranger
b Kinston, NC, Oct 5, 1881; d New York, NY, Oct 3, 46. Educ: Christian Inst;
Shaw Univ; Nat Cons, New York. Music dir, Clef Club. Led orchs in
Reisenweber's, Jardin de Dance & Ziegfeld Roof. Led musical unit, 350th Field
Artillery, AEF, WW I; also WW II service. Chief Collabrs: Chris Smith,
Clarence Williams. *Songs:* Please Go 'Way and Let Me Sleep; La Rumba; Shout,
Sister, Shout; Josephine My Joe; Camel Walk; Look Into Your Baby's Face and
Say Goo-Goo; My Pillow and Me.

BUBALO, RUDOLPH DANIEL   ASCAP 1969
composer
b Duluth, Minn, Oct 21, 27. Educ: Univ Minn, 45-46; Chicago Musical Col,
BM, 54; Univ Ill; Roosevelt Univ, MM, 56; Western Reserve Univ, 57; Kent
State Univ, 65; comp with Ernst Krenek, Vittorio Rieti & John Becker; cond &
piano with Rudolph Ganz; musicology with Hans Tischler; Grishwold Tech
Inst, electronic technol. Began musical career as jazz pianist & arr. Prof of comp
& dir, Electronic Music Studio, Cleveland State Univ. Past pres, Cleveland
Comp Guild; bd mem, Nat Asn of Comp. Awards: Music Award, Cleveland
Arts Prize, 70, 8 ASCAP Comp Awards. Grants: Nat Endowment for the Arts,
Bascom Little Fund, Ohio Arts Coun & Rockefeller Found. *Instrumental
Works:* Spacescape (orch, tape); Trajectories (tape, orch); Soundposts (violin,
clarinet, piano); Strands (orch); Valence II (clarinet, bassoon, tape); Concerto
for Alto Saxophone, Orchestra and Tape; Three Pieces for Brass Quintet; Five
Pieces for Brass Quintet and Percussion; Conicality (saxophone quartet);
Organic Concretion (alto saxophone, perc, organ, tape); Albert's System
(clarinet, tape); The Gay Bassoon (bassoon, tape); Electrum (alto saxophone,
tape); Modules (large jazz ens, tape).

BUCHTEL, FORREST LAWRENCE (LAWRENCE   ASCAP 1963
BUCK, VICTOR LAURENCE)
composer, teacher
b St Edward, Nebr, Dec 9, 1899. Educ: Coin High Sch, Iowa, 17; Simpson Col,
Iowa, AB, 21; Northwestern Univ, MS Ed, 31; VanderCook Col Music,
BMusEd, 32, MMusEd, 33; Univ Chicago; Columbia Univ; Chicago Musical
Col; pvt study with Louis Victor Saar, H A VanderCook & G E Holmes.
Teacher, South High Sch, Grand Rapids, Mich, 21-25, Emporia Kans State,
25-30, Lane Tech, Chicago, 30-34 & Amundsen High Sch, Chicago, 34-54;
part-time teacher, VanderCook Col Music, 31-54, full-time teacher, 54-
teaching career incl band, orch & choral groups. Publ incl 30 sets band bks &
about 800 solos & ens for sch band musicians; plus separate publ for sch bands.
Instrumental Works: Overtures: Crusaders; Traveller; Horatius; Young Prince;

Crimson Dawn; Mavourneen; Magic Wand; Tampico; Christmas Scenes; Joyous Christmas; Bagdad; Lochinvar; Mystic Gardens; Evangeline; Magic Isle; Bolaton; Mandalay; Narrator; Mirage Hongroise; Beau Geste; Melody Fun (tonette & song flute); Renaissance Method (recorder; String Quartet Arr: The Entertainer; Strenuous Life.

BUCK, CARLTON C ASCAP 1954
composer, author, teacher
b Salina, Kans, Aug 31, 07. Educ: Poly High Sch, Santa Ana, Calif; Bible Inst of Los Angeles, Biola Col, dipl, 30; Chapman Col, cert church music, 31; Whittier Col, 43, 48; Bible Theol Sem, BSacredMus, 46; San Gabriel Col, MA, 50, DD, 55; Utah Sch Alcohol Studies, studied with S J Mustol, Herbert Tovey, John B Trowbridge, 68. Dir of music at First Christian Church, Bell, Calif, 29-34. Taught music at Sch of Christian Training, Los Angeles Cons Music, Maywood branch & Biola Col. Ordained to ministry of Christian Church, 34. Served churches & as choir dir in Calif, Ore, Idaho, Mont & Tenn. Served on Gov Comt for Alcohol & Drug Studies, Ore. Wrote theme songs & dir music at rallies & conventions. Also author of several books. Chief Collabrs: John W Peterson, S Clarence Trued, Noble Cain, Henry Slaughter, Frank A Simpkins, Howard L Brown, B D Ackley. Songs: Today Is Ours; Make Us One; Picture Divine; The Hour Divine; Lyrics: I Believe Miracles; When God Speaks; A Fellowship Sweet; The Sweetest Hallelujah; Come Now to His Table; I'll Walk the Way That Jesus Walked; In Royal Splendor Rides the King; O Lord, May Church and Home Combine.

BUCK, CHARLES STARY ASCAP 1963
composer, author, singer
b Rochester, Minn, May 10, 28. Educ: Pvt vocal, piano & drumming instr, 40's; studied fundamentals in songwriting, 48; USA Band Sch, 51. Recording artist; works recorded by var artists. Drummer & singer, USA bands, Korean War, & on stage, radio & TV. Writer, works premiered at NY Univ's Town Hall & NBC-TV "Today Show." Columnist, music mag The Songsmith, 50's. Chief Collabrs: Ray Rivera, Dick Hyman, Al Moquin. Songs: Cool Lover; Keen Baby; With Your Love; We Can't Miss This Christmas; Forever Young; Music: If the Moon Could Tell; I Wish I Were a Christmas Tree; Lyrics: You're Wonderful. Instrumental Works: Fourteenth of September; Sweet Side of You; Soul Child; Green Sauce. Albums: The Two Sides of Charlie Buck.

BUCK, GENE (EDWARD EUGENE) ASCAP 1914
author, artist, director
b Detroit, Mich, Aug 8, 1885; d Great Neck, Long Island, NY, Feb 25, 57. Educ: Univ Detroit; Detroit Art Sch. Early designer of sheet music covers. Moved to New York, 07; designed, dir act for Lillian Russell. Chief writer & asst to producer, Florenz Ziegfeld, 12-26. Bway stage sketches: "Ziegfeld Follies" (13 ed); "Ziegfeld Midnight Frolics" (11 ed; also originator, dir); "Ziegfeld's 9 O'Clock Revue" (2 ed); "No Foolin'"; "Zig-Zag" (London). Producer musicals: "Yours Truly"; "Take the Air" (also score). Producer drama, "Ringside." Pres, Cath Actors Guild. Won Nat Asn for Am Comp & Cond award. Charter mem, ASCAP, dir, 20-57, pres, 24-41. Chief Collabrs: David Stamper, Rudolf Friml, Jerome Kern, Mischa Elman, Fritz Kreisler, Augustus Thomas, Werner Janssen, James Hanley, Ray Hubbell, Victor Herbert, Louis Hirsch. Songs: Daddy Has a Sweetheart (and Mother Is Her Name); Hello, Frisco; Have a Heart; In the Cool of Evening; Hello, My Dearie; Tulip Time; Sally, Won't You Come Back?; Sweet Sixteen; Sunshine and Shadows; The Love Boat; My Rambler Rose; 'Neath the South Sea Moon; Lovely Little Melody; No Foolin'; Florida, the Moon and You; Some Boy; Garden of My Dreams. Scores: Bway stage: Ziegfeld Follies (13 ed); Ziegfeld Midnight Frolics (11 ed; also originator, dir); Ziegfeld's 9 O'Clock Revue (2 ed); No Foolin'; Zig-Zag (London).

BUCK, LAWRENCE
See Buchtel, Forrest Lawrence

BUCK, RICHARD HENRY ASCAP 1938
author
b Philadelphia, Pa, July 11, 1870; d Manhasset, NY, Sept 10, 56. Educ: Pub schs. Chief Collabrs: Adam Geibel, Theodore Morse. Songs: Kentucky Babe; Dear Old Girl; Where the Southern Roses Grow; Little Cotton Dolly; Diaper Kid; I Never Thought I'd Miss You As I Do; Dream on, Dear Heart, Dream On; My Kingdom of Heart's Desire; I Live for You Alone, Dear.

BUCKLEY, TIMOTHY CHARLES, III
composer, author
b Washington, DC, Feb 14, 47; d Santa Monica, Calif, June 29, 75. Recording artist with Elektra Records at age 18, then with Warner Bros. Chief Collabr: Larry Beckett. Songs: Once I Was; Morning Glory; Look At the Fool; Ain't It Peculiar; Stone in Love; Because of You; Understand Your Man; Blue Melody; Bring It on Up; Driftin'; Pleasant Street; Song of the Siren; Sweet Surrender; Happy Time; Helpless.

BUDKA, HARRY H ASCAP 1961
composer, pianist, arranger
b Chicago, Ill, Jan 13, 13. Educ: Fenger High Sch. Arr for orchs incl Hal Kemp, Earl Burtnett, Ted Weems; WGN, Chicago. Weights estimator, Chicago Bridge & Iron Works. Pianist in local dance bands. Songs: Night Clouds; Four Winds; Silent Snow. Instrumental Works: Arr: De Camptown Races.

BUDKA, MILDRED LIVESAY ASCAP 1961
author
b Chicago, Ill, July 7, 12. Educ: Fenger High Sch. Secy, Ferro Alloys, Chicago. Songs: To a Wild Rose (new lyrics).

BUERKLE, RUSSELL C ASCAP 1964
composer, author, musician
b Pittsburgh, Pa, May 2, 15. Educ: St Vincent Col, BA. Songs: The Bells of Aspen; The Colorado River; Denver, Queen of the Mountains and Plains.

BUFFANO, JULES ASCAP 1950
composer, author, director
b St Louis, Mo, Nov 18, 1897; d Santa Monica, Calif, Sept 12, 60. Educ: Special instruction with prominent instrs, New York, St Louis, Chicago & Europe. Began professional career with Ziegfeld Follies, then dir with Ziegfeld Follies Orch. Accompanist to Sophie Tucker on European tour, 2 yrs. First music cond for talking pictures, MGM Studios, also musical dir for the first "Broadway Melody." While at MGM, wrote original scores for Fred Astaire & Gene Kelly, arr & accompanied Judy Garland on production numbers. Comp & cond all original stage productions for Fanchon & Marco Presentations. With Jules Buffano Dance Band traveled throughout US. Musical dir, pianist & comp, Jimmy Durante. Comp & arr musical numbers. Chief Collabrs: Jimmy Durante, Jack Barnett. Songs: Thanks for the Buggy Ride; Ambitious With Wishes; She's My Private Property; I Wonder What's Become of Tomorrow. Instrumental Works: Cafeteria Jangle.

BUFFINGTON, DON ASCAP 1959
composer, author, arranger
b Cleveland, Ohio, Feb 26, 07. Educ: Univ Chattanooga. Has appeared in films, vaudeville, radio & TV. Songs: Penny Teardrops; Riches; Yellow Moon; Please Dear Lord; Browsin'.

BUGATCH, SAMUEL ASCAP 1958
composer, conductor, teacher
b Rogochov, Russia, June 20, 1898. To US 1911. Educ: Peabody Cons (Teacher's Cert); Johns Hopkins Univ. Comp, cond & arr of synagogue, theatre music. Cond, choruses throughout US; toured Israel with chorus, participating in Fest of Choruses, 56. Dir music, Temple Adath Israel, Bronx, NY, 46- Music teacher in Hebrew schs. Instrumental Works: Israel (cantata); The Holy Ark; Zog Maran; 15 Compositions for Solo, Chorus. For Friday eve serv: Manginot Shabat; Shirei Shabat Kodes.

BUGOS, KEITH RICHARD ASCAP 1977
composer, author, singer
b Columbus, Ohio, Oct 21, 48. Educ: Ohio State Univ, BS. Performed with local bands & started writing during col yrs. Road mgr & tour coordr with Kenny Rogers, 7 yrs. Chief Collabrs: Kenny Rogers, Dann Rogers. Songs: Heaven Is a Hard Act to Follow; You're So Far Away; I Have Loved You Now.

BUHRMAN, ALBERT JOHN, JR ASCAP 1961
composer, organist
b Springfield, Mo, Apr 19, 15. Educ: Univ Kans, grad, 36; studied with Glen Stambach, Charles S Skilton & Laurel Everett Anderson. Began as radio & TV organist & comp, Kansas City, Mo, 32, New York, 40-63. Army Spec Services, 43-45. Organ recitals & comp, Sch of The Ozarks, 63-, retired. Chief Collabr: Karl Bratton. Songs: Galaxies; Music: Songs of the Ozarks; Glory to God in the Highest. Scores: The Bald Knobbers (Ozark Folk opera).

BUKETOFF, IGOR ASCAP 1969
symphony conductor
b Hartford, Conn, May 29, 15. Educ: Univ Kans, 31-32; Juilliard Inst Musical Art, BS(music educ), 35, MS(comp), 41, Juilliard Grad Sch, fel cond, 39-42; Los Angeles Cons Music & Art, hon MusD, 49. Mem fac, Juilliard, 35-45, Chautauqua Sch Music, summers 41-47, Columbia Univ, 43-47; assoc prof music, Butler Univ, 53-63; vis prof, Univ Houston, 77-79. Choral cond, Russian Orthodox Church, New York, 30-35; head choral dept, Juilliard, 38-46; dir, Adelphi Col Chorus, Garden City, NY, 40-44, Barnard Col Chorus, Columbia Univ, 43-47 & Ft Wayne Philh Chorus, 48-66. Orch cond, Juilliard, 40-46, Columbia Univ Orch, 46-48, Butler Univ Symph Orch, 53-63 & Univ Houston Symph Orch, 77-79; guest cond var orchs in US, SAm & Europe. Co-dir, Chautauqua Opera Asn, 45-47; music dir, Bway production, Gian-Carlo Menotti's twin operas, "The Medium" & "The Telephone," on Am tour & in London & Paris; cond var operatic presentations with Ft Wayne Philh, also with NBC Opera, 60-66; music dir, St Paul Opera Asn, incl world premiere, "Summer & Smoke," Am premiere, "Maskarade" & "Betrothal in San Domingo," 68-75; dir, "Rape of Lucretia," Univ Houston, 79. Music dir: New York Philh Young Peoples Concerts, 48-53, Ft Wayne Philh Orch, 48-66, Ft Wayne Philh, 48-66, Iceland Symph Orch, 63-66, NBC Nationwide Children's TV Prog (Peabody Award), 65 & Piedmont Chamber Orch (Rockefeller Found Proj), 69-71. Ballet cond, Butler Univ Ballet Co, 54-64, First Chamber Dance Quartet, 66 & St Paul Opera Asn, 71. Mem bd dirs, Am Symph Orch League, 59-62; State Dept cultural exchange grantee to USSR; dir, Int Contemporary Music Exchange, 73-; mem adv bd, Van Cliburn Competition, Ft Worth, 75- Rec'd First Alice M Ditson Award for Am Cond, 41; Rockefeller Found Grant for establishment of World Music Bank, 59; Alice M Ditson Award for cond

who has done most on behalf of Am music, 67; Alice M Ditson grants, 70, 72 & 75 & Ford Found grant, 73 for develop of Int Contemporary Music Exchange. Contribr chap, Russian Music, In: Music in the Middle Ages. *Songs & Instrumental Works:* 1812 Overture (Tchaikovsky; transcribed for chorus & orch).

BULKIN, KELLY LYNN
composer, musician, singer
b Hollywood, Calif, June 29, 57. Educ: Providence High Sch; Pierce Jr Col. Recording artist. Background vocalist, Marc Joseph. Background vocalist & comp, England Dan & John Ford Coley. Singer, motion picture "Last Detail." Chief Collabrs; John Ford Coley, Bob Gundry. *Songs:* Love Has Got to Start With Us; Without You; Lyrics: Running After You.

BULKIN, LESLIE ANN
composer, musician, singer
b Hollywood, Calif, Aug 8, 59. Educ: Providence High Sch. Recording artist. Background vocalist, Marc Joseph. Background vocalist & comp, England Dan & John Ford Coley. Singer, motion picture "The Last Detail." Chief Collabrs: John Ford Coley, Bob Gundry. *Songs:* Love Has Got to Start With Us; Without You; Lyrics: Running After You.

BULLINGTON, JAMES WILEY (JIMMY EDWARDS)   ASCAP 1977
composer, author
b Senath, Mo, Feb 9, 33. Educ: High sch; Univ Ark. Singer, Mercury Records, 57 & RCA, dir by Chet Atkins. *Songs:* Music: A Place for the Lonesome; Comin' Down With Love; Love Bug Crawl; Honey Lovin'; My Honey.

BULLOCK, WALTER   ASCAP 1936
author
b Shelburn, Ind, May 6, 07; d Los Angeles, Calif, Aug 19, 53. Educ: DePauw Univ, BA. Chief Collabrs: Harold Spina, Alfred Newman, Richard Whiting, Abraham Ellstein. *Songs:* I Still Love to Kiss You Goodnight; I'd Like to See Samoa of Samoa; This Is Where I Came In; This Is a Happy Little Ditty; Someday You'll Find Your Bluebird; I Love to Walk in the Rain; Song of the Musketeers; The You and Me That Used to Be; When Did You Leave Heaven? *Scores:* Bway stage: Great to Be Alive; Film: 52nd Street; Sally, Irene and Mary; Just Around the Corner; Little Miss Broadway; The Bluebird.

BUNCH, BOYD   ASCAP 1936
composer, author, arranger
b Chamois, Mo, Feb 24, 1889; d. Educ: High sch, Reno, Nev. Pianist in stock cos. WW II serv. Pianist & arr with dance orchs incl Guy Lombardo, 30-42; also for Balaban & Katz Theatres. Became fruit grower, Calif, then entered Ministry of the Gospel, ordained, 55. Chief Collabrs: Cliff Friend, Charles Tobias, Jerry Livingston, Al Neiburg, Dave Fleischer, Vee Lawnhurst, Tot Seymour. *Songs:* The Broken Record; The Day I Let You Get Away; There Goes My Attraction; Did Anyone Call for Me?; Oh! Oh! Marie; Baby; Frankie and Johnnie (new lyrics).

BUNCH, JOHN LUTHER, JR   ASCAP 1976
composer, pianist
b Tipton, Ind, Dec 1, 21. Educ: Ind Univ, BA(speech), 50. Jazz pianist, played & recorded with Maynard Ferguson, Benny Goodman, Woody Herman, Buddy Rich, Tony Bennett, Gene Krupa. *Songs:* Music: Why You; Feathers; Fatha' Time; John's Bunch; Cecilly; I'll Take New York; The Bunch; Don't Remember Me; Floating Down Broadway; Is This Really New; Just to See Your Face Again; It's Love in the Spring; Mish Mash.

BUNCIE, JOSEPH MICHAEL   ASCAP 1974
composer, teacher
b Whitney, Pa, Sept 12, 34. Educ: St Vincent Col, 4 yrs; Syracuse Univ, grad; State Univ NY Col Potsdam, grad; Pa State Univ, grad, studied trombone with M Shiner & E Shiner; Duquesne Univ, BS(music educ), grad studies. Adjudicator & mem, NY State & Pa State Judging Asn; mem, NYSSMA, 10 yrs, PMEA, 13 yrs, PSEA, 13 yrs & NEA, 23 yrs. Guest cond on numerous occasions. *Instrumental Works:* Bandido.

BUNDY, EVE M   ASCAP 1962
author
b Seattle, Wash, Sept 12, 10. Educ: Univ Wash. Chief Collabr: Rudolf Friml. *Songs:* Po Ling, Ming Toy.

BUNDY, RUDY H   ASCAP 1965
composer
b Quaker City, Ohio, Apr 28, 07. Educ: Am Cons of Music, Chicago; studied clarinet with Gus Langunus. With George Olson, Benny Meroff & Frank & Milt Britton in Good News. Had own dance bands, 32-54. Vpres & treasurer, Ringling Brothers Barnum & Bailey Circus, retired, 70; back in music bus. Chief Collabrs: E Ray Goetz, Bud Green. *Songs:* Weary Nights; When I'm All Alone; Falling Apart Together; My Goodbye; Flying High; Thrill.

BUNTON, MARGARET RACHEL   ASCAP 1976
composer
b Hunt City, Ill, Sept 28, 05. Educ: Jr high sch. Housewife; lyric writer. *Songs:* I Like Your Style.

BURDETTE, EUGENE (GENE)   ASCAP 1960
composer, author, pianist
b Chicago, Ill, Aug 27, 1900; d Honolulu, Hawaii, Oct 3, 68. Educ: Col. Appeared in vaudeville, radio, films & night clubs. Wrote & dir films incl "Pirate Party on Catalina Isle"; also wrote commercials & parodies for Groucho Marx. *Songs:* Lolita; Mama's Mumu; Tower of Love; Sunset in Hawaii; Elisa.

BURDGE, GORDON   ASCAP 1949
composer, author, record executive
b New York, NY, Mar 20, 06; d Los Angeles, Calif, Feb 7, 75. Educ: In South & abroad. Prof jour grad schs. Newspaper & mag ed. Pres, Trend Records. Prod writer cartoon features: "Buzzards Bait and Blithe Spirits"; "Enchanged World of Mother Goose". Chief Collabrs: J Russel Robinson, Galen Denning. *Songs:* Portrait of Jennie; Anniversary Toast; Old Cowboy Church; Israeli Lullaby; Yemenite Love Song; Single and Sentimental.

BURGDORF, JAMES ALAN (ALAN JAMES)   ASCAP 1978
composer, author, singer
b Evansville, Ind, Oct 30, 53. Educ: F J Reitz HS; Southeastern Col. Touring as singer & musician. Recording artist, Impact Records & Housetop Records. *Songs:* Turn the Moments Into Hours; Let it Dawn on You; Now is the Time; Lyrics: You Gave Me Life.

BURGER, DAVID MARK (DAVID MASTERS)   ASCAP 1970
composer, author, singer
b New York, NY, Jan 8, 50. Educ: Queens Col, City Univ New York, BA(music & classical languages), 70, MA(musicol & music theory), 73; studied theory & analysis with Felix Salzer, Jacques-Louis Monod & Henry Weinberg. Songwriter for Richie Havens & Theodore Bikel; comp choral & orchestral works; had maj perf in Carnegie Hall, Alice Tully Hall & Mann Auditorium in Tel Aviv. Won the Alter Machlis Award in music; comn by Northeastern Univ; comp-in-residence for Zamir Chorale of New York, 74- Recording artist & arr. Chief Collabr: Mati Lazar, arr. *Songs & Instrumental Works:* Windblown; Child of Light; Travels; Hot Sun/Cold Moon; Chiefest Joy; Chorus & Orch: T'Filah; Hatikvah; Shalom Rav; When I Am Dead, My Dearest; Songs to Jerusalem.

BURGER, JACK   ASCAP 1959
composer, author, teacher
b New York, NY, Nov 2, 25. Educ: Southern Calif Sch Music & Art; Univ Southern Calif; Univ Calif, Los Angeles; Calif State Univ, Northridge; Los Angeles City Col; BA(anthropology). Musician; worked with Jan Savitt & Joe Reichman road bands, radio, "Gene Autry Show," motion pictures & TV. Recording artist with var cos. Personal accompanist to Fred Astaire, Debbie Reynolds & Jane Powell. Wrote spec music material. Pres, Boco Publ & Phonic Records. Teacher; has written 3 method bks. WW II, instr, Army band training unit. Directed workshops at Claremont Cols. Served on panel at Idylwilde, music extension. Chief Collabrs: Jimmy Haskell, Leon Pober. *Songs & Instrumental Works:* Tonkabushi Rock and Roll; The Three Handed Drummer; Pulsation; Maid in Japan; Black Satin.

BURGESS, DANIEL LAWRENCE   ASCAP 1976
composer, author
b Buffalo, NY, Dec 26, 46. Educ: Kenmore East HS; Bob Jones Univ; Houghton Col; Buffalo Bible Inst. Dir, Continental Singers & New Hope Singers. Recording artist, Light Records. *Songs:* Thank You, Lord; By His Grace; Fill My Life; I'm a Miracle Lord; Victorious Lord; The Father Knows; The Disciples Song; Joy in the Mornin'; When We See Him; Founded in Christ; Surely You've Cared For Me; Don't Miss The Glory; It's Time for Jesus; All Sufficient; God Will Provide; Let Your Spirit Fall on Me; Higher; Praise Song; The Love of the Lord; Jesus Is the Solid Rock; Share the Word of the Lord; We Will Claim Victory; Lord We Lift Our Praise; A Holy Nation; The Mercy of God; The Joy of the Lord Is My Strength.

BURGESS, LORD
See Burgie, Irving L

BURGH, STEVEN LAWRENCE   ASCAP 1976
composer, author, musician
b Trenton, NJ, Dec 17, 50. Educ: Studied piano at ages 9 to 11; self-taught guitar at age 12. To New York, 68, guitarist for rock band Jacobs Creek; played bass with David Bromberg, 69-72. Played guitar, produced & comp with Steve Goodman, 72-75; music dir with Phoebe Snow, 74-78, record producer, Steve Forbert, 78, Carolyne Mas, 79 & 80, Suzanne Fellini, 79 & Mike Cross, 80. Chief Collabrs: Steve Goodman, Lisa Garber. *Songs:* Banana Republics; Between the Lines; Music: Old Fashioned Girl. *Instrumental Works:* Chubby Thighs.

BURGHOFF, GARY
actor
b Bristol, Conn. Educ: Music & Dramatic Theater Acad, New York. Regular on TV series "MASH," 72-; film appearances incl "MASH," 70, "PS, I Love

You," 71; appeared on stage in "You're a Good Man, Charlie Brown"; TV appearances incl "Love Boat", "Donny and Marie", "Fantasy Island", "Kraft Special", "Name of the Game" & "Don Knotts Show"; nightclub performer. Recipient Emmy Award as best supporting actor in series, 77.

BURGIE, IRVING L (LORD BURGESS)　　ASCAP 1956
composer, author
b Brooklyn, NY, July 28, 24. Educ: Juilliard Sch Music, 46-48; Univ Ariz, 48-49; Univ Southern Calif, 49-50. Singer in nightclubs, radio & TV; wrote songs for film, "Island in the Sun." Folksinger, guitarist, lyricist & comp. *Songs:* Island in the Sun; I Do Adore Her; Jamaica Farewell; The Wanderer; Day O; El Matador; Dolly Dawn; The Seine; Jackass Bray; Silver Earring; Come Back, Liza; Yesterday Was Such a Lovely Day; Land of the Sea and Sun; Cocoanut Woman; Angelina. *Scores:* Off Bway Musical: Ballad for Bimshire.

BURGIO, FRANCES (FRAN ZIFFER)　　ASCAP 1954
composer, singer, pianist
b Baltimore, Md, June 5, 17. Educ: Peabody Inst, Baltimore, full scholarships; studied with D Saperton. Singer & pianist on radio, "Girl With a Million Melodies." Entertainer, Hilton, Sheraton & Shelburne, Atlantic City, also for Gov Clinton, nightclubs & TV. Chief Collabrs: Hardy Wieder, Horty Belson, Martin Kalminoff. *Songs:* Music: Faith Alone; Reward, Reward; Which Way. *Instrumental Works:* One Foot to Sea; Street Car Named Desire; Gordon Reilly. *Scores:* Maestro; Sam Grey; Little Brown Jug; Off-Bway Shows: Dakota; Surprise Package; Make Him Magnificent.

BURGOYNE, ROBERT H
author
b Montpelier, Idaho, Nov 22, 20. Educ: Utah State Univ, BS(physics), 42; Cornell Univ Med Col, MD, 50; Univ Southern Calif, residency in psychiatry, 59-62. Physicist, Mass Inst Technol, 42-45. Family dr, Idaho, 51-59. Psychiatrist, Salt Lake City, Utah, 62- *Songs:* Lyrics: Encircle the Child.

BURGSTAHLER, ELTON E　　ASCAP 1972
composer, teacher
b Orland, Calif, Sept 16, 24. Educ: Univ Pacific, AB & BMus; Millikin Univ, MMus; Fla State Univ, PhD. Worked way through high sch & col as church organist & pvt piano studio. Music teacher, high schs, Calif, 2 yrs. Grad assistantship music theory & comp. Mem fac, Millikin Univ, 7 yrs & Southwest Mo State Univ, 24 yrs. *Songs & Instrumental Works:* Sonata for Flute and Piano; Three Fragments for Clarinet and Piano; Three Shades of Blue (flute ens); The Truth About Christmas (cantata); The Wind Bloweth (choral); Four Clarinet Solos (clarinet & piano); 13 Saxophone Quartets; Let's Play Quartets (clarinet).

BURKE, JOHNNY　　ASCAP 1932
composer, author, publisher
b Antioch, Calif, Oct 3, 08; d New York, NY, Feb 25, 64. Educ: Crane Col; Univ Wis. Staff mem music publ cos, Chicago & New York. Under contract to Paramount, Hollywood. Formed publ co with James Van Heusen. Chief Collabrs: James Van Heusen, James Monaco, Arthur Johnston, Victor Schertzinger, Harold Spina, Bob Haggart, Erroll Garner. *Songs:* Annie Doesn't Live Here Any More; The Beat of My Heart; Pennies From Heaven; One, Two, Button Your Shoe; Let's Call a Heart a Heart; So Do I; It's the Natural Thing to Do; All You Want to Do Is Dance; The Moon Got in My Eyes; My Heart Is Taking Lessons; This Is My Night to Dream; On the Sentimental Side; I've Got a Pocketful of Dreams; Laugh and Call It Love; Don't Let the Moon Get Away; Go Fly a Kite; An Apple for the Teacher; A Man and His Dream; East Side of Heaven; That Sly Old Gentleman; Sing a Song of Sunbeams; Hang Your Heart on a Hickory Limb; Scatterbrain; Sweet Potato Piper; Too Romantic; April Played the Fiddle; Meet the Sun Half Way; Only Forever; Ain't It a Shame About Mame?; I Don't Want to Cry Any More, Oh, You Crazy Moon; Imagination; Dearest, Darest I?; Isn't That Just Like Love?; It's Always You; Birds of a Feather; Constantly; Road to Morocco; Ain't Got a Dime to My Name; Moonlight Becomes You; Sunday, Monday or Always; If You Please; Suddenly, It's Spring; A Friend of Yours; Polka Dots and Moonbeams; Going My Way; Swinging on a Star (Acad Award); The Day After Forever; It Could Happen to You; And His Rocking Horse Ran Away; Like Someone in Love; Sleigh Ride in July; Yah-Ta-Ta Yah-Ta-Ta; Put It There, Pal; Welcome to My Dream; It's Anybody's Spring; Personality; Just My Luck; Aren't You Glad You're You?; My Heart Is a Hobo; Country Style; Smile Right Back At the Sun; Apalachicola, Florida; But Beautiful; You Don't Have to Know the Language; If You Stub Your Toe on the Moon; Once and for Always; You're in Love With Someone; Someplace on Anywhere Road; Sunshine Cake; High on the List; And You'll Be Home; Life Is So Peculiar; Early American; Here's That Rainy Day; Ring the Bell; The Magic Window; Moonflowers; To See You; Misty; If Love Ain't There; He Makes Me Feel I'm Lovely; What's New?; Fauntleroy; Worry Not a Whit, Not I; God Bless You All the Day; If the Girl's Got Charm; I'm Myself; It's the Company; I Wish You Needed Me; Refer Them to Me; A Fancy, Dancy Day; I'm Collecting You; Music: I Hate Little Boys. *Scores:* Films: Pennies From Heaven; Double or Nothing; Doctor Rhythm; Sing, You Sinners; East Side of Heaven; The Star Maker; Road to Singapore; If I Had My Way; Rhythm on the River; Love Thy Neighbor; Playmates; Road to Zanzibar; Road to Morocco; Dixie; Going My Way; And the Angels Sing; Belle of the Yukon; Road to Utopia; Welcome Stranger; Road to Rio; A Connecticut Yankee in King Arthur's Court; Top o' the Morning; Riding High; Mister Music; Road to Bali; Bway: Nellie Bly; Carnival in Flanders; Donnybrook.

BURKE, JOSEPH A　　ASCAP 1920
composer, pianist
b Philadelphia, Pa, Mar 18, 1884; d Upper Darby, Pa, June 9, 50. Educ: Univ Pa. On staff, publ firm, New York. To Hollywood, 29. Chief Collabrs: Al Dubin, Edgar Leslie, Benny Davis, Mark Fisher, Marty Symes, Charles Tobias. *Songs:* Baby Your Mother; Tip Toe Through the Tulips; For You; Moon Over Miami; Carolina Moon; Dancing With Tears in My Eyes; Yearning; Oh How I Miss You Tonight; A Little Bit Independent; On Treasure Island; In a Little Gypsy Tearoom; It Looks Like Rain in Cherry Blossom Lane; In the Valley of the Moon; Painting the Clouds With Sunshine; At a Perfume Counter; Rambling Rose; Who Wouldn't Love You; By the River of the Roses; The Kiss Waltz; She Was Just a Sailor's Sweetheart; Robins and Roses; Cling to Me; We Must Be Vigilant (American Patrol); Midnight Blue; Villanova Alma Mater; Getting Some Fun Out of Life. *Scores:* Film: Gold Diggers of Broadway; Hold Everything.

BURKE, JOSEPH FRANCIS (SONNY)　　ASCAP 1942
conductor, arranger, executive
b Scranton, Pa, Mar 22, 14; d May 31, 50. Educ: Univ Detroit; Duke Univ, BA(English). Arr for dance orchs; musical dir & cond. Arr, Dinah Shore, 46; A&R dir, Decca, 49-63 & Reprise Records, 63-66. Music dir & vpres, Music Div, Warner Bros, 53-70. Free-lance, A&R producer & comp; began own record label, Daybreak, 70-73; sound track album recordings, var MCA feature films, 74. Produced Frank Sinatra's album "Trilogy." Chief Collabrs: Peggy Lee, Johnny Mercer, Paul Francis Webster. *Songs:* Midnight Sun; Somebody Bigger Than You and I; Music: Hennesy (TV theme); Follow the Sun (TV theme); How It Lies, How It Lies, How It Lies. *Scores:* Film: Lady and the Tramp.

BURKE, LEE
See Sigman, Carl

BURKHARD, LEONARD A　　ASCAP 1959
composer, publisher, record exec
b Akron, Ohio, Nov 9, 11. Educ: High sch. Pianist in dance bands; also radio during 30's. Pres, Burkhard Enterprises, Inc; also owns Wes Mar Music Publ Co, Wes Mar & Criteria Records. *Songs:* High Heeled Shoes With Pointed Toes; Time That We Wasted; When Your Heart Belongs to Someone.

BURLEIGH, CECIL　　ASCAP 1941
composer, violinist, educator
b Wyoming, NY, Apr 17, 1885. Educ: Klindworth-Scharwenka Cons, Berlin, Ger, 03-05; Chicago Musical Col, 06-08; studied with Leopold Auer, New York, 19-21. Hon Doctorate, Am Cons Music, Chicago, 38. Instr, Denver Inst Music & Dramatic Art, Colo, 09-11 & Morningside Col, Univ Mont, Missoula, 11-14. Concert artist, New York, 19-21. Prof, Sch Music, Univ Wis-Madison, 22-55, emer prof, 55- *Songs:* Music: Break, Break, Break; The Lighthouse; Wings; Sunrise; Song of the Brook; The Sea Hath its Pearls. *Instrumental Works:* First Violin Concerto; Third Violin Concerto; St Paul Sonata (violin); Ascension Sonata (violin); Ballad of Early New England (piano); Indian Concerto (scored for full orch).

BURLEIGH, HARRY T　　ASCAP 1914
composer, singer
b Erie, Pa, Dec 2, 1886; d Stamford, Conn, Sept 12, 49. Educ: Nat Cons (scholarship); studied with Christian Fritsch, Rubin Goldmark, John White & Max Spicker; Atlanta Univ, hon MA; Howard Univ, MusD; won Spingarn Medal. Baritone soloist, St George's Episcopal Church, New York, 1894-1946; Temple Emanu-El, New York, 1900-25. Had many concert tours, US & Europe. Charter mem, ASCAP *Songs:* Jean; Deep River; Little Mother of Mine; Just You; Everytime I Feel de Spirit; The Grey Wolf; The Young Warrior; The Soldier; Ethiopia Saluting the Colors; also settings to The Five Songs of Laurence Hope.

BURNETT, ERNIE　　ASCAP 1921
composer, pianist, publisher
b Cincinnati, Ohio, Dec 19, 1884; d Saranac Lake, NY, Sept 11, 59. Educ: Music studies in Italy & Austria; Charlottenburg Cons. Returned to US, 01; became vaudeville pianist & entertainer. 89th Div, AEF, WW I. Led dance orchs. Active in music, Panama Canal Zone, 3 yrs. Founded own publ co. Chief Collabrs: George Norton, Paul Cunningham. *Songs:* My Melancholy Baby; Steamboat Rag; My Kathleen; Please Take a Letter, Miss Brown; Romance Rides the Range Tonight; Georgia Moonlight; There's a New Moon in the Sky Tonight; There'll Be a Jubilation Bye and Bye; Only Ashes Remain.

BURNHAM, CARDON VERN　　ASCAP 1972
composer, teacher
b Kewanee, Ill, Feb 25, 27. Educ: Bradley Univ, BME, 49; Univ Ill, MM, 50; Eastman Sch Music, AMusD, 60. Instr, East Peoria HS, Ill, 47-49, Alliance Col, Pa, 50-52, Tulane Univ, 52-58 & Bowling Green State Univ, Ohio, 58-61; chmn dept, Carroll Col, Wis, 61-74 & Ind State Univ, 74-76. Assoc cond, Florentine Opera Co, Milwaukee, Wis, 76-78. Chmn dept fine arts, Hampden-Sydney Col, Va, 78- *Instrumental Works:* Symphony I (Bharata). *Songs & Instrumental*

Works: Festival Chorale (organ & brass); Cantata of Peace (solo, chorus & orch). *Scores:* Opera: Nitecap (chamber opera in 1 act); Ceremony of Strangers (sacred opera in 1 act).

BURNS, ANNELU ASCAP 1925
author, teacher
b Selma, Ala, Nov 12, 1889; d Mt Kisco, NY, July 12, 42. Educ: Judson Col; Boston Cons; Brenau Col; Leopold Auer Sch. Taught privately & in pub schs, Pleasantville, NY, 32-42. Chief Collabr: Ernest Ball. *Songs:* I'll Forget You; For the Sake of Auld Lang Syne; Little Brown Shoes; Little Spanish Villa By the Sea; Shadows on My Heart.

BURNS, JAMES F ASCAP 1950
composer, author, publisher
b Buffalo, NY, May 10, 1898; d Buffalo, June 25, 60. Educ: Canisius Col. 102nd Trench Mortar Battery, 27th Div, WW I. Arr music publ firms; formed own co. *Songs:* There's Happiness Ahead; Locked Up in Prison; There's Still a Few of Us Left; I'll Keep the Stars and Stripes Together; Nola.

BURNS, JOSEPH W
composer, author
b New York, NY, June 5, 08. Educ: Columbia Col, AB, 29; Columbia Law Sch, LLB, 32. Chief Collabr: Dave Oppenheim. *Songs:* The Church Bells Are Ringing on Easter Morn; Music: Easter Bunny Day; Beside the Blue Pacific Shore; Investigatin' Papa.

BURNS, RALPH ASCAP 1947
composer, conductor, arranger
b Newton, Mass, June 29, 22. Educ: New Eng Cons; studied piano with Marion Deviney. Pianist, arr with Charlie Barnet Orch; later with Woody Herman, 7 yrs. Arr, Bway musicals incl "No Strings", "Little Me", "Funny Girl" & "Golden Boy." Chief Collabrs: Woody Herman, Johnny Mercer. *Songs & Instrumental Works:* Early Autumn; Bijou; Summer Sequence; Lady McGowan's Dream; Rhapsody in Wood; Northwest Passage; Keen and Peachy; Panacea.

BURNS, STEPHEN JOHNSON ASCAP 1977
composer, author, singer
b Hartford, Conn, Sept 16, 54. Educ: Memphis State Univ, BA(communications, cum laude). Assoc with Ardent Studios, Memphis, Tenn & Power Play Records, Memphis. Assoc with group, The Scruffs. *Songs:* Break the Ice; Teen-age Girls; Edge of Disaster; My Mind; Bedtime Stories. *Albums:* Wanna Meet the Scruffs?

BURNSIDE, R H ASCAP 1914
author, director, producer
b Glasgow, Scotland, Aug 13, 1870; d Metuchen, NJ, Sept 14, 52. Educ: Great Yarmouth Acad. Came to US as dir of Lillian Russell productions. Dir many Hippodrome spectacles. Dir Bway stage shows: "The Tourists"; "Fascinating Flora" (also producer); "Jack O' Lantern"; "Happy Days"; "Good Times"; "Tip Top"; "Better Times"; also Librettist: "A Trip to Japan" (also producer); "The International Cup"; "Chin Chin"; "Hip Hip Hooray!"; "The Big Show"; "Cheer Up"; "Everything"; "Stepping Stones"; "Three Cheers." Dir, "Criss Cross." Charter mem, ASCAP. Chief Collabrs: Raymond Hubbell, Gustave Kerker. *Songs:* Ladder of Roses; Nice to Have a Sweetheart; Annabelle Jerome; You Can't Beat the Luck of the Irish. *Scores:* Bway stage (librettos): The Tourists; Fascinating Flora; Jack O' Lantern; Happy Days; Good Times; Tip Top; Better Times; A Trip to Japan; The International Cup; Chin Chin; Hip Hip Hooray!; The Big Show; Cheer Up; Everything; Stepping Stones; Three Cheers.

BURR, WILLIAM ORNDOFF ASCAP 1975
author
b Vaughn, NMex, Aug 11, 32. Chief Collabrs: Ted Rosen, Clarence Freed. *Songs:* Lyrics: Who, What and Where Is God?; Walkin' Out the Door; In His Own Way; Tom, Uncle Sam's Son.

BURRELL, BOZ ASCAP 1979
composer, author
b Spalding, Eng, Aug 1, 46. Started playing in 65; singer of the blues in sch, Lincolnshire, Eng. Prof career started as bass player with King Crimson; played & toured with Alexis Korner's band Snake, 73; with Bad Company, 74- Chief Collabr: Simon Kirke. *Songs:* Gone, Gone, Gone; Rhythm Machine.

BURRELL, KENNY ASCAP 1959
composer, conductor, guitarist
b Detroit, Mich, July 31, 31. Educ: Wayne Univ, BM. Guitarist in orchs, incl Dizzy Gillespie & Benny Goodman; formed own group. Appeared at Newport Jazz Fest. *Instrumental Works:* Sugar Hill; Kenny's Blues.

BURROUGHS, BOB LLOYD (ROBERT DAVIDSON) ASCAP 1963
composer, teacher
b Tazewell, Va, Mar 10, 37. Educ: Mars Hill Col; Okla Baptist Univ; Southwestern Baptist Theol Sem Sch Church Music; pvt comp study with T W Dean & Warren M Angell. First comp publ, 62. Served as minister of music for several local churches. Comp-in-residence, Samford Univ, 9 yrs. Chief Collabrs:

Esther Burroughs, Ed Seabough. *Songs:* Music: Now Hear It Again!; A Chosen People; Love; Walk in Love; The Trial; Treasures in Heaven; Jesus My Lord, My Life, My All.

BURROUGHS, EARL S (JACK HAMMER)
composer, author, singer
b New Orleans, La, Sept 18, 40. Singer, tap dancer, impressionist, comedian, actor, author, film writer & painter. Internationally known cabaret artist. Has made worldwide appearances. Chief Collabr: Otis Blackwell. *Songs:* Great Balls of Fire; Fujiyama Mama; Plain Gold Ring; Peek a Boo; Ballad of James Dean; Kissin' Twist; Don't Take Pretty to the City; Live It Up (One Time); Touch the Sky; Shalom Aleichum; Obviously, I Love You; We Also Ran; Kiss Me You Fool; The Wiggle; Absurd Bird; Autobahn Baby; O D; Boogie Woogie Twist; Sweet Thing; Blue Zero; Cupid's Inspiration; Colour Combination; Lyrics: Do I Like It; Hawaiian Rock. *Albums:* Electric God; Brave New World; Rebellion.

BURROWS, ABE ASCAP 1953
composer, author, librettist
b New York, NY, Dec 18, 10. Educ: City Col, New York; NY Univ. Writer for radio, Duffy's Tavern, Rudy Vallee, John Barrymore, Abe Burrows Show & TV panel shows. Nightclub performer. Bway theatre librettist in "Guys and Dolls", "Can-Can" & other shows. Pulitzer Prize for "How to Succeed in Business Without Really Trying," 61. Author of "Honest Abe," autobiography. Chief Collabr: Frank Loesser. *Songs:* The Girl With the Three Blue Eyes, also other songs in Abe Burrows Song Book; Lyrics: Leave Us Face It.

BURSTEIN, JOHN (SLIM GOODBODY) ASCAP 1978
composer, educator
b Mineola, NY, Dec 25, 49. Educ: Colgate Univ; ballet study with Maurice Byart, Brussels; Hofstra Univ, BA(dramatic literature). Singer/performer at age 12. Child health educator, 74- Appeared in shows & concerts throughout US, also in "Captain Kangaroo Show." Author of many bks. Chief Collabr: Christian Stoudt. *Songs:* Lubba-Dubba; The Large and Lovely Liver; Down, Down, Down.

BURSTEIN, LILLIAN
See Lux, Lillian Sylvia

BURT, BENJAMIN HAPGOOD ASCAP 1914
composer, author
b Rutland, Vt, June 27, 1882; d Amityville, NY, Sept 17, 50. Educ: Trinity Chapel Sch, New York. Actor with Weber & Fields Co, 1900-01; also appeared in "Mistress Nell", "As You Like It" & "Silver Slipper." Charter mem, ASCAP. Chief Collabr: Karl Hoschna. *Songs:* Well, I Swan; The Pig Got Up and Slowly Walked Away; Whoa, Josephine; My Gal Irene; I'd Rather Two-Step Than Waltz; I Used to Be Afraid to Go Home in the Dark; Hang Out the Front Door Key; Some Little Bug Is Going to Find You; Here Comes the Groom; There's No One With Endurance Like the Man Who Sells Insurance. *Scores:* Stage: The Wall Street Girl; A Modern Eve.

BURTNETT, EARL ASCAP 1924
composer, author, arranger
b Harrisburg, Pa, Feb 7, 1896; d Chicago, Ill, Jan 2, 36. Educ: Pa State Col. Pianist & arr for Art Hickman orch, at Hickman's death, became leader of band. Played in hotels & ballrooms throughout country. Chief Collabr: Adam Geibel. *Songs:* Leave Me With a Smile; Mandalay; Have You Forgotten?; Down Honolulu Way; Where There's a Will, There's a Way; Never Before, Never Again; This Time Is the Last Time; When I Hear an Irishman Sing; After Every Party; Canadian Capers; Sleep.

BURTON, EDWARD J (TIP) ASCAP 1966
composer
b Boston, Mass, Jan 31, 26. Educ: Framingham State Col. Wrote bk & lyrics for two musical comedies: "James Micheal Curley" & "Red Riding Hood." Chief Collabr: John Domunad (music). *Songs:* Lyrics: The Circus is on Parade; Bozo the Happy Clown; Montreal.

BURTON, (THOMAS) ELDIN ASCAP 1956
composer
b Fitzgerald, Ga, Oct 26, 13. Educ: Atlanta Cons of Music, degree in piano & comp; studied with Dr Georg Liebling; Juilliard Grad Sch, 3 fels in comp, 43-46. Pianist, concerts & broadcasts, Atlanta, 36-43. Dir, Ga Cons & Music Ctr, 40-41. Pianist, debut, Carnegie Recital Hall, 49; perf of own compositions, New York, Philadelphia, Newark & Yonkers. *Instrumental Works:* Sonatina for Flute and Piano (New York Flute Club award, 48); Sonatina for Violin and Piano; Sonata for Viola and Piano; Quintet for Piano and String Quartet; Concerto for Piano with Orchestra; Concerto for Flute with Orchestra.

BURTON, JOSEPH R ASCAP 1962
composer, author, conductor
b Chicago, Ill, July 6, 28. Educ: Eastman Sch Music; Chicago Cons Music; Westlake Col; Loyola Univ, New Orleans, La; McGill Univ, Montreal, Que. Pianist with Hal McIntyre Band at age 14. Substitute pianist for var bands, incl Harry James, Artie Shaw, Benny Goodman, Charlie Ventura & var soc bands, incl Benny Strong & Henry Bussy. Accompanist, Anita O'Day & Jane Russell.

Had own clubs in New Orleans, 17 yrs. Had own TV show, WWL, New Orleans, 12 yrs. Worked in Las Vegas hotels cutting & cond shows. World travel with USO shows. Made many records. Own TV show, "The Joe Burton Show," KTSF, San Francisco. Mem: Am Fedn TV & Radio Artists; Screen Actors Guild; Screen Extra Guild; Am Fedn Musicians. Co-owner with wife, Jeani Lason Burton, JOG Music Publ & Jeani Records. Chief Collabrs: Jeani Lason Burton, Sal Campagna, James Sagorac, Bob Joyce. *Songs:* Piano Joe; Jeani; Summer's Gone; Music of Life; Waitin' for a Fool; The Gift; Fool's Gold; Wind, Sand and Stars; Guess I Believe in You; Bags Wigs Out; Wag-ner; Just Walking; Table Talk; Ice Tea; Quajiro (Cuban Country Boy); Scintillating; Soft Touch; Pretty, Your Mother; Call Me on the Phone; If You Cared; Collette; Theme for Joe; Wisemen; Smile Joe; Fatter All the Time.

BURTON, NAT　　　　ASCAP 1934
author
b New York, NY, Nov 20, 01; d Hollywood, Calif, Mar 21, 45. Educ: Pub schs. Wrote spec material for vaudeville. Chief Collabrs: J C Johnson, George Whiting, Arthur Altman, Walter Kent, David Rose. *Songs:* The White Cliffs of Dover; Somebody Loses, Somebody Wins; Believe It Beloved; The Secret of My Success; Rhythm and Romance; My Dream of Tomorrow; Our Waltz; When the Roses Bloom Again; Say It; Two Seats in the Balcony; That's How Rhythm Was Born; You're the Dream, I'm the Dreamer.

BURTON, STEPHEN DOUGLAS　　　　ASCAP 1976
composer, author, conductor
b Whittier, Calif, Feb 24, 43. Educ: Oberlin Cons, 60-62; comp with Hans Werner Henze, Mozarteum Acad, Salzburg, Austria, 62-65; Peabody Inst, 73-74. Comns & perf, Berlin Philh Orch, Chicago Symph, Nat Orch of Paris (ORTF), Israel Philh, Nat Symph, Pittsburgh Symph, Wolf Trap, Am Dance Fest, Artpark, et al. Recordings, Louisville Masterworks & Peter's Int. Music dir, Munich Kammerspiele, 63. Guggenheim fel, 69, Nat Opera Inst grant, 75, Nat Endowment for the Arts grants, 75 & 77. ASCAP awards. Mem, Am Coun Ger, Paul Chamber Music Awards Panel & Va Arts Comn Adv Panel. Chief Collabr: Christopher Keene. *Songs:* Music: Requiescat (SATB). *Instrumental Works:* Ode to a Nightingale (soprano, flute, harp & strings); Symphony No 1; Dithyramb (orch); Stravinskiana (flute & orch); Symphony No 2 Ariel (on poems of Sylvia Plath); Songs of the Tulpehocken (tenor & orch). *Scores:* Finisterre (ballet); The Duchess of Malfi (opera in three acts).

BURTON, VALENTINE　　　　ASCAP 1929
composer, author, producer
b London, Eng, Feb 22, 1900. Educ: Oundle Sch, Northamptonshire, Eng; London Acad Music & Dramatic Art; Northern Polytech London, Eng. Began musical career during World War I with Royal Air Force concert "The Stunters." Wrote musical revues for C B Chochrane Productions. Active in Hollywood as producer-writer & comp. Two Acad Awards for musical shorts. Scenarios include "Lord Jeff", "Henry Aldrich" series, "Glamour Boy", "Bright Victory", "Bedtime for Bonzo", "Passport to Destiny", "True to the Army", "Hulla Baloo", "Two Years Before the Mast", "Time of Their Lives." Chief Collabrs: Carleton Kelsey, Max Steiner, Will Jason, Edmund Roth & Edward Kilenyi. *Songs:* Singing a Vagabond Song; Penthouse Serenade; The Day I Met You; Isn't This a Night for Love; The Big Bad Wolf is Dead; I'd Like to Dilly Dally; Lady of the Morning; Waiting for the Springtime; You Alone; If It Isn't Love; Josephine; Some Day Soon; Mon Pappa; Buy a Kiss; The Tiny Little Finger on Your Hand. *Scores:* Film/TV: Igloo; Hotel Continental; Carnival.

BURWELL, CLIFFORD R　　　　ASCAP 1944
composer, pianist, arranger
b New Haven, Conn, Oct 6, 1898; d West Haven, Conn, Oct 9, 76. Educ: Hillhouse High Sch. Pianist in dance orchs incl Barney Rapp; toured with Paul Whiteman. Pianist & arr with Rudy Vallee Orch, 28-43, appeared in films with Vallee. Chief Collabr: Mitchell Parish. *Songs & Instrumental Works:* Swing Express to Harlem; Going Wacky; Why; Sweet Lorraine.

BUSBY, GERALD
composer, pianist, teacher
b Abilene, Tex, Dec 16, 35. Educ: Pub schs, Tyler, Tex; Yale Music Sch, Yale Col, BA, 60, studied piano with Oscar Ziegler & comp with Quincy Porter. Made debut as pianist & comp at Town Hall, New York, 66. Actor. Chief Collabrs: Paul Taylor, Robert Altman, Carl Laanes, Albert Crabtree. *Instrumental Works:* Runes (dance suite for solo piano, comn by Paul Taylor, 75, NEA Award, 76); Nocturne for Organ; Noumena (suite for solo flute). *Songs & Instrumental Works:* An American Magnificat (chorus, trumpet, organ). *Scores:* Three Women (Robert Altman film).

BUSH, LOUIS F (JOE FINGERS CARR)　　　　ASCAP 1951
composer, author, conductor
b Louisville, Ky, July 18, 10; d Los Angeles, Calif, Sept 19, 79. Educ: High sch; pvt music study. Had own orch at age 12. Pianist & arr with orchs incl Henry Busse, Clyde McCoy, Vincent Lopez, George Olsen & Hal Kemp. Served USAAF, WW II. A&R exec, Capitol Records, Los Angeles; made many records. Recorded with Lincoln Mayorga, The Brinkerhoff Piano Co. Chief Collabrs: Allan Sherman, Leon Pober. *Songs:* Music: Hello Muddah, Hello Fadduh; My Birthday Comes on Christmas. *Instrumental Works:* Roller Coaster; Ivory Rag; Sabre Dance Boogie; Portofino; Waltz in Ragtime; Tango Afrique; The Anti-Establishment Rag.

BUSHKIN, JOSEPH　　　　ASCAP 1946
composer, pianist, conductor
b New York, NY, Nov 6, 16. Educ: High sch; pvt music study. Pianist in orchs incl Louis Prima, Bunny Berigan, Joe Marsala, Muggsy Spanier & Tommy Dorsey. WW II, trumpeter in Army Band. Pianist in Benny Goodman Orch, 46. Acted in Bway play, "The Rat Race." Formed own quartet, appeared at the Embers, NY. Joined Louis Armstrong band, 53; later reorganized own group. Has given concerts & made many records. *Songs:* Oh, Look At Me Now; Whatcha Doin' After the War?; There'll Be a Hot Time in the Old Town Tonight; Every Day Is Christmas; If I Knew You Were There; Portrait of Tallulah; Lucky Me; Love Is Everything; Lovely Weather We're Having; Something Wonderful Happens in the Summer. *Instrumental Works:* Serenade in Thirds.

BUSKIN, DAVID　　　　ASCAP 1970
author, singer, pianist
b New York, NY, Dec 13, 43. Educ: Brown Univ, BA(Am lit); Berklee Col Music. Wrote songs and was accompanist for Mary Travers & Tom Rush. Has recordings on Epic & Columbia labels; songs have been recorded by Peter, Paul & Mary, Shirley Bassie, Tony Orlando, Tracy Nelson & Kiss; currently recording an album with Robin Batteau. Chief Collabrs: Robin Batteau, David Wolfert. *Songs:* When I Need You Most of All; He Used to Treat Her; Warm; Another Time, Another Place. *Albums:* David Buskin; He Used to Treat Her; Pierce-Arrow; Pity the Rich.

BUSS, HOWARD J　　　　ASCAP 1979
composer, teacher, trombonist
b Allentown, Pa, Jan 6, 51. Educ: West Chester State Col, BA, 72, studied comp with Larry Nelson; Mich State Univ, MM(applied music, trombone), 74, MM(music comp), 75, studied comp with H Owen Reed; Univ Ill, DMA(music comp), 77, studied comp with Thomas Fredrickson & Sal Martirano. Trombonist, comp & arr with group, Tijuana Brats, 60's. Comp in col & has incorporated theatrics in his works. Mem fac, Fla Southern Col, Lakeland. *Songs:* Night Watch. *Instrumental Works:* Camel Music for Solo Trombone; Flourishes for 2 Brass Quintets; Eclipse; Nocturne for Solo Clarinet; Currents for Percussion Ensemble; Coexistence for Clarinet and Percussion Ensemble; Trigon for Wind Ensemble; Exodus for Orchestra; Grand Lake Morning.

BUSSE, HENRY　　　　ASCAP 1941
composer, conductor, trumpeter
b Magdeburg, Germany, May 19, 1894; d Memphis, Tenn, Apr 23, 55. Trumpeter in Paul Whiteman Orch, 18-28; formed own orch, appearing in nightclubs, radio & dance halls. Made records, concert tours, US & Europe. Chief Collabrs: Lou Davis, Henry Lange. *Songs & Instrumental Works:* Hot Lips; Wang Wang Blues; Horn Tootin' Blues; Fiesta; Haunting Blues.

BUTCHER, DWIGHT　　　　ASCAP 1953
composer, author, actor
b Oakdale, Tenn, Aug 6, 11; d Covina, Calif, Nov 11, 78. Stage actor. Chief Collabrs: Louis Herscher, Jimmie Rodgers. *Songs:* Old Love Letter; When Jimmie Rodgers Said Goodbye; A Tribute—Jimmie Rodgers in Retrospect; Jimmie Rodgers, A Legendary Performer (mem folio); Songs by Dwight Butcher, 1932-1972; Kill Her With Kindness.

BUTLER, A L (PETE)　　　　ASCAP 1971
composer, author
b Noble, Okla, June 29, 33. Educ: Capitol Hill High Sch; Okla Baptist Univ, BM, 55; Southern Baptist Theol Sem, MSM, 57. Minister of music, First Baptist Church, Madill, Okla, 57-60 & Ada, Okla, 60-, choral & church music admin clinician. Chief Collabr: Bobby Altmiller. *Songs:* Samuel Was a Friend of God; Praise the Lord! I've Been Redeemed; Music: Something Wonderful (cantata); Redeemed; Stir Thy Church, God Who Touchest Earth With Beauty; I Think When I Read That Sweet Story; Hallelujah! What a Saviour; When We All Get to Heaven.

BUTLER, CHARLES FRANCIS　　　　ASCAP 1973
composer, author, singer
b Lynwood, Calif, Oct 29, 46. Educ: Downey Sr High Sch; Cerritos Jr Col. Singer, concerts & TV. Recording artist, soloist & lead vocalist with group, Parable; toured US, Can & Europe. Chief Collabr: Fred Field. *Songs:* Song for the Church; Maybe; The Promise; All Alone; Ladder Song; Peter, James and John; I Know What It's Like; Friends; Sweet, Sweet Song; Let the Old Man Die; Lyrics: Two Hands; The Plain Truth.

BUTLER, EUGENE SANDERS　　　　ASCAP 1972
composer, educator
b Durant, Okla, Jan 13, 35. Educ: Okla Univ, BMusEd, 57; Union Theol Sem, MSMus, 60; Univ Mo, Kansas City, DMA, 74. Dir of music, First Methodist Church, Wichita, Kans, 60-70. Dir of choirs, Rockhurst Col, Kansas City, 71-73. Dir of choral activities & music theory, Johnson County Community Col, Kans, 73- *Songs:* Music: How Excellent is Thy Name; Go Ye Into All the World; O Thou to Whose All Searching Sight; Notes From Paul; Music When Soft Voices Die; Immortal Love, Forever Full; Don't Let the Music Stop; And Thou, America. *Instrumental Works:* Paean of Praise (brass sextet). *Scores:* Opera/Ballet: Samuel; The Promise.

BUTLER, HENRY W (BILL)   ASCAP 1967
author
b Eureka, Kans, May 3, 19. Stage dir, Metrop Opera, New York City Opera, Santa Fe Opera, San Francisco Opera, Miami Opera & Bway show "Desert Song." Chief Collabrs: Marvin David Levy, Richard Cumming, Dickson Hughes. *Scores:* Libretto: Mourning Becomes Electra; The Picnic; Terrace.

BUTLER, JACK   ASCAP 1964
composer, teacher
b Augusta, Ga, June 18, 24. Educ: Erskine Col; Univ SC. Piano teacher, 18 yrs; taught in public schs, also church music dir. *Songs & Instrumental Works:* Piano: Lonely As a Star; The Weary Plowman; Daydreaming; The Gettysburg Address (chorus, orch).

BUTLER, JERRY   ASCAP 1969
composer, singer, publisher
b Sunflower County, Miss, Dec 8, 39. Educ: Jenner & Sexton Grade Schs, Chicago, Ill; Washburne Vocational High Sch, Chicago, music course; Roosevelt Univ, Chicago, spec studies with Phil Moore, Sr. Started recording career with The Impressions; recording artist, 58- Produced albums; operated songwriters workshop. Producer. Chief Collabrs: Huff Gamble, Curtis Mayfield, Billy Butler, Otis Redding, Homer Talbert, Samuel F Brown, III. *Songs & Instrumental Works:* Glad to be Back; When I Find You, Love; Was That All It Was?; Would You Mind; I'm So Lonely Tonight; That's the Way It Is; Stop Steppin on My Dreams; Butterfly; If I Could Remember; He'll Break Your Heart; I Wanna Do It to You; I Stand Accused; For Your Precious Love; Brand New Me; Suite for a Single Girl; Never Gonna Give You Up; Only the Strong Survive; Western Union Man; Coolin Out; Dream World; Nothing Says I Love You Like I Love You.

BUTTERWORTH, WILLIAM JESSE, JR   ASCAP 1971
composer
b Abington, Pa, July 5, 52. Educ: William Tennent High Sch; Fla Bible Col, BA; Dallas Theol Sem, MA; Fla Atlantic Univ, EdD. *Songs:* He That Believeth; The Lord Makes Me Happy; What If Someone Had Not Shared?; Make It Clear; Heaven Help the Home.

BUTTIGIEG, RAYMOND FRANCIS   ASCAP 1977
composer, author
b Qala, Malta Repub, May 1, 55. Educ: Tech Inst, Victoria, Malta Repub; theory & practical electronics, self-taught. Musician, artist, writer, producer, engr, comp & performer. Poet of 3 publ books & 8 anthologies. *Songs:* Maltese Summer; Gone With the Wind; Citizens of Earth. *Instrumental Works:* Planet Earth.

BUTTOLPH, (JAMES) DAVID   ASCAP 1944
composer, conductor, arranger
b New York, NY, Aug 3, 02. Educ: Juilliard; Acad für Musik, Vienna. Played in nightclubs, Vienna & Munich, 23-26. Opera coach, Munich, 26-27. Cond, NBC, 27. Music dir, WGY, 32-33. To Hollywood, 33. *Scores:* Film Background: This Gun for Hire; Wale Island; My Favorite Blonde; Guadalcanal Diary; Chad Hanna; The Horse Soldiers; Crash Dive; TV: Maverick.

BUTTOLPH, DAVID LYMAN   ASCAP 1965
composer, conductor
Educ: Yale Univ, BA, 44, studied with Paul Hindemith; Juilliard Sch Music, BS(piano), 49, MS(conducting), 59; studied with Nadia Boulanger, Paris, 49-51; with Pierre Monteux, Maine, 51. Timpanist, New Orleans Philh, 52-54; dir musical activities & chmn dept, Dillard Univ, 54-58; mem conducting staff, Manhattan Sch Music, 58-65; free-lance cond & arr, New York Metrop Area, 58-65; dir choral activities, State Univ NY Binghamton, 65- Chief Collabr: Stanley Baum. *Songs & Instrumental Works:* Sweet Sound of Your Own Horn; Looking Backward; Program Signature for New Orleans Police Department Series; He Is Born the Beloved Child; The Beatitudes; Bye an' Bye (arr of black spiritual); He's Gone Away (folk song arr); Johny Has Gone for a Soldier (folk song arr).

BUTTONS, RED   ASCAP 1963
composer, author, actor
b New York, NY, Feb 5, 19. Has been comedian in nightclubs, TV & theatre. Acted in films, incl "Sayonara," Acad Award, 57. *Songs:* Strange Things Are Happening; The Ho-Ho Song.

BUTTS, CARROL MAXTON
composer, author, teacher
b Shenandoah, Iowa, Apr 15, 24; d Feb 26, 80. Educ: Pub schs, Scottsbluff, Nebr; Univ Colo, BME & MME; Northern Colo State Univ; Utah State Univ; Univ Wyo. Teacher instrumental music, pub schs, 29 yrs. Judge, music fests. Staff arr, Northern Colo Univ, 9 yrs. Author of 10 bks, many concert band arr, ens & solos. Comns: Univ Wyo; Chadron State Col; San Diego Univ. *Instrumental Works:* Heritage West (concert band); Contemporary Overture (concert band); Warsaw 1939 (6 drums); Contrasts for Three—Tuba Trio (tuba, piano, clarinet).

BUTTS, R(OBERT) DALE   ASCAP 1946
composer, author, pianist
b Lamasco, Ky, Mar 12, 10. Educ: Louisville pub schs; Louisville Cons of Music. Began in vaudeville at age 16. Pianist with Clyde McCoy, Roger Pryor & Jan Garber; arr for Vincent Lopez, Ted Weems, Henry Busse, Anson Weeks, Freddy Martin, Mitch Ayers, Ray Noble, Carl Hoff & Victor Young; vocal arr for Lena Horne, Dinah Shore, King Sisters, Dick Haymes & Perry Como. Staff arr, NBC, Chicago, 4 yrs. Comp & cond, Republic, Fox & United Artists for var motion pictures, Hollywood, 41- Acad nomination for "Flame of the Barbary Coast," 45. Radio shows, Edgar Bergen, Gracie Fields, Jack Carson, Lux Radio, Carnation Hour; TV shows, "Wagon Train", "Laramie", "Riverboat", "Dragnet", "Virginian", "Whispering Smith." Chief Collabrs: Jack Elliott, Bert Kalmar, Dale Evans. *Songs:* Please Take Me Home This Very Moment; There's Only One You; Welcome to My Heart; I'm Gonna Call It a Day; Music: I Get to Feeling Like This; Lilacs in the Spring; Will You Marry Me Mister Larramie; I'm in Love With a Guy; Phrenology.

BUZZELL, EDWARD   ASCAP 1961
author, actor, producer
b Brooklyn, NY, Nov 13, 1900. Educ: High sch. Boy actor with Gus Edwards Co. Appeared in Bway musicals: "The Gingham Girl", "The Desert Song" & "Lady Fingers." Film actor, wrote & dir films incl "Best Foot Forward"; "Ship Ahoy"; "Neptune's Daughter." Wrote & produced TV films. *Songs:* Mary Had a Little; Find 'Em, Feed 'Em, Fool 'Em and Forget 'Em.

BUZZI-PECCIA, ARTURO   ASCAP 1925
composer, conductor, teacher
b Milan, Italy, Oct 13, 1854; d New York, NY, Aug 29, 43. Educ: Royal Cons of Milan; studied with father, Antonio Buzzi, also Massenet, Saint-Saens. Taught at Chicago Cons. Cond music studio, New York. Author, "How to Succeed in Singing and Italian Diction." *Songs:* Torna Amore; Ave Maria; Conscientious Deacon; Under the Greenwood Tree; Little Birdies; Serenata Gelata; Mal d'Amore; also musical settings to poems of Fiona McLeod & Tagore. *Instrumental Works:* Forza d'Amore (opera); Gloria (liturgical work); Saturnale Romano; Voyage des Noces (piano suite).

BYERS, JOY
See Johnston, Joy

BYRD, CHARLIE
See Thomason, Alexander

BYRNE, DAVID   ASCAP 1977
composer, author, singer
b Dumbarton, Scotland, May 14, 52. Educ: RI Sch Design; Md Inst Col Art. Guitarist, singer & principal comp/author with rock band, Talking Heads, 75-76; with string orch, 80. Chief Collabrs: Brian Eno, Peter Gordon, Robert Fripp. *Songs:* Psycho Killer; Life During Wartime; The Big Country; Cities; Music: I Zimbra; My Life in the Bush of Ghosts. *Scores:* Film/TV: Into the Spirit World.

BYRON, AL   ASCAP 1960
composer, author, teacher
b Brooklyn, NY, Sept 16, 32. Educ: Brooklyn Col, BA; Hunter Col, MA(theatre), 72; NY Univ, PhD candidate, theatre. Teacher, New York City Board of Educ. Shubert fel for playwriting, 72. Author of non-musical play, "I Can't Go on Without You, Minna Maudelbaum," produced off off-Bway. Chief Collabrs: Jack Reardon, Paul Evans, Guy Wood, Woody Harris, Bobby Darin. *Songs:* Some of My Best Friends Are the Blues; Music: Only Memories; Lyrics: Roses Are Red (My Love); Happy-Go-Lucky Me; Something Blue; The Zebra; Forget Me Not (ASCAP Country Music Award); Chairman of the Board; Round About Midnight.

BYRON, RICHARD   ASCAP 1936
composer, author
b New York, NY, Jan 9, 08; d North Hollywood, Calif, Dec 31, 69. Educ: Cornell Univ, BA; Univ Southern Calif, MM. Radio comedy writer, 39-42 & 45-51. US Army, WW II. High sch teacher, 51-61. Asst prof, Calif State Col, 61- Chief Collabrs: Jerome Jerome, Walter Kent. *Songs:* So Red the Rose; I Wanna Know All About You; Country Boy; Love Is Like a Cigarette; Moonlight Masquerade; Mama I Wanna Make Rhythm; A Portrait of a Lady; Over a Bowl of Suki-Yaki; The Harlem Waltz; I Saw a Ship A-Sailing; also, "A Lincoln Song Book for Young America".

C

CAARON
See Huston, Carla A

CACAVAS, JOHN
ASCAP 1954

composer, author, conductor

b Aberdeen, SDak, Aug 13, 30. Educ: Northwestern Univ, BM, 52. Arr, USA Band, 52-56; free-lance comp & arr, New York; dir of publ, Chappell & Co Inc, 65-69. To London, scored motion pictures & guest cond Europ orchs, 70-73. Scored TV shows & movies, Hollywood, 73- Over 1500 publ works for band, orch, chorus & chamber; songs recorded by Andre Kostelanetz, Lotte Lenya, Les Brown, Roger Williams, Telly Savalas, Guy Lombardo & Nancy Wilson. Author, textbk "Music Arranging and Orchestration." Elected gov, Motion Picture Acad, 78; pres, Comp & Lyricists Guild of Am, 80. Freedoms Found Music Award, 66. Chief Collabrs: Charles Osgood, Bonnie Becker, Don Black, James McAdams. *Songs:* Music: Black Is Beautiful; Gallant Men; Sand in My Shoes (choral). *Instrumental Works:* Days of Glory (concert band); Fanfare and Scenario (concert band); American Sea Rhapsody (concert band); The Day the Orchestra Played (symph orch); Burnished Brass (concert band); Danse Pavane (concert band). *Scores:* Films: Airport 1975; Blade; Pancho Villa; Airport 1977; Redneck; Valentine; Horror Express; TV Films: Human Feelings; She Cried Murder; Friendly Persuasion; Elevator; Time Machine; Superdome; Linda; Hellinger's Law; Amy Prentiss; Kate McShane; TV Series: Mrs Columbo; NBC Mystery Movie; Eischied; Eddie Capra Mysteries; Quincy; Bionic Woman.

CADDIGAN, JACK J
ASCAP 1923

composer, author

b Boston, Mass, Sept 21, 1879; d Corning, NY, Jan 1, 52. Educ: Pub schs. Asst vpres, Boston Edison Co; businessman. *Songs:* Rose of No Man's Land; We're All Going Calling on the Kaiser; Caroline Is Calling; Dreams of Mother; Little French Mother, Goodbye.

CADMAN, CHARLES WAKEFIELD
ASCAP 1924

composer, author, pianist

b Johnstown, Pa, Dec 24, 1881; d Los Angeles, Calif, Dec 31, 46. Educ: Studied music with Leo Oehmler, Emil Paur, W K Steiver & Luigi von Kunits; Univ Southern Calif, MusD; Univ Denver, hon PhD. Music critic, Pittsburgh Dispatch. Researched Indian music & customs; lectr, 09-23. Mem, Nat Inst Arts & Letters. Chief Collabr: Nelle Richmond Eberhart. *Songs & Instrumental Works:* Piano Sonata in A; Sonata in G for Violin, Piano; Quintet for Strings, Piano; Trio in D; American Suite; Thunderbird Suite; Pennsylvania (tone poem); Father of Waters (cantata); House of Joy (cantata); Aurora Borealis; A Mad Empress Remembers; Dark Dancers of the Mardi Gras; Trail Pictures; Huckleberry Finn Goes Fishing; Oriental Rhapsody; Hollywood Suite; Indian Love Charm (children's choir); The Vision of Sir Launfal (chorus); Songs: I Hear a Thrush at Eve; From the Land of the Sky Blue Water; At Dawning; The Far Horizon; Song Cycles: Four American Indian Songs; Sayonara; Three Songs to Odysseus; White Enchantment; The Morning of the Year. *Scores:* Operas: Shanewis (The Robin Woman); A Witch of Salem; The Sunset Trail; The Garden of Mystery; The Willow Tree (radio); Sch Operettas: Lelawala!; Hollywood Extra; The Ghost of Lollypop Bay; The Golden Trail; The Belle of Havana; The Bells of Capistrano; Meet Arizona; South in Sonora.

CAESAR, IRVING
ASCAP 1920

composer, author, publisher

b New York, NY, July 4, 1895. Educ: NY Pub Sch; Chappaqua Mountain Inst; City Col New York. Bway theatre scores, Greenwich Village Follies, George White's Scandals & Shubert & Zeigfeld Musicals; comp lyrics "No, No, Nanette." Occasional West Coast employment & stage appearances abroad. Producer, author & comp Bway musical "My Dear Public." ASCAP bd dirs, 40 yrs; past pres, Song Writers Protective Asn. Chief Collabrs: George Gershwin, Vincent Youmans, Rudolph Friml, Sigmund Romberg. *Songs & Instrumental Works:* Swanee; Tea for Two; I Want to Be Happy; Sometimes I'm Happy; If I Forget You; Animal Crackers in My Soup; Is It True What They Say About Dixie; Nashville Nightingale; Yankee Doodle Blues; I Was So Young, You Were So Beautiful; The Pilgrim Suite (symph orch); several volumes of children's songs incl The Sing a Song of Safety Series.

CAESAR, SID
ASCAP 1955

composer, comedian, saxophonist

b Yonkers, NY, Sept 8, 22. Educ: Juilliard Sch. Saxophonist, var dance bands incl Charlie Spivack, Shep Fields & Claude Thornhill. Served, USCG, World War II; appeared in service show, "Tars and Spars" & in film version. Appeared, TV shows incl "Your Show of Shows" & "Caesar's Hour," in Bway shows "Make Mine Manhattan" & "Little Me," in films incl "It's a Mad, Mad, Mad, Mad World." *Songs:* I Wrote This Song for Your Birthday; Was That You?

CAESAR, VIC
See Cesario, Victor Louis

CAFFEY, HOWARD DAVID
ASCAP 1977

composer, educator

b Austin, Tex, June 2, 50. Educ: Univ Tex, Austin, BM(music theory), 72, MM(music theory), 74, studied comp with G R Goodwin; Calif State Univ, Northridge. Asst prof music, Southern Ore State Col, 74-76. Dir jazz studies, Sam Houston State Univ, 76-79 & Lamont Sch Music, Univ Denver, 79- *Instrumental Works:* Carnival Night in Vera Cruz; Heather's Song; Chanson; Keeping Up With the Jones; Samba de Linda; You've Got What?!; Snow Princess; Grape Masher; Woodwind Quartet; Dialogues for Trombone and Piano, Tangents for Brass Choir.

CAGE, JOHN
ASCAP 1955

composer

b Los Angeles, Calif, Sept 5, 12. Educ: Pomona Col; studied with Fannie Dillon, Richard Buhlig, Lazare-Levy, Henry Cowell, Adolph Weiss & Arnold Schoenberg. Author, "Silence", "A Year from Monday", "M" & "Empty Words." Invented prepared piano. *Songs & Instrumental Works:* Amores (prepared piano & perc); The Seasons (ballet); Aria with Fontana Mix; Cartridge Music; Sonatas and Interludes (prepared piano); Renga with Apartment House 1776 (orch, four quartets & eight soloists).

CAGGIANO, ROSEMARY
ASCAP 1975

author, lyricist

b New York, NY, Feb 2, 38. Psychotherapist. Comp of many children's albums; made albums with Tony Randall as narrator & singer. *Albums:* Children Are People; The Power Is You.

CAHN, SAMMY
ASCAP 1936

author

b New York, NY, June 18, 13. Educ: Seward Park High Sch. Violinist in vaudeville orch. Organized dance band with Saul Chaplin. Went to Hollywood, 40. Wrote songs for "She's Working Her Way Through College", "Serenade", "Anything Goes", "The Joker Is Wild" & "The Pleasure Seekers"; also many title and theme songs. Became music publ, 55. Starred in show "Words and Music," Golden Theater, 74, leading to new career as performer. Wrote special material for Frank Sinatra, Paul Anka, Dean Martin, Bob Hope, Barbra Streisand, Vic Damone, Perry Como & others. Starred in 2 TV specials featuring his songs. Elected to ASCAP Bd of Dirs; elected pres, Songwriters Hall of Fame. Chief Collabrs: Saul Chaplin, Jule Styne, James Van Heusen, George Barrie. *Songs:* If I Had Rhythm in My Nursery Rhymes; Rhythm Is Our Business; Shoe Shine Boy; Until the Real Thing Comes Along; Dedicated to You; If It's the Last Thing I Do; Bei Mir Bist Du Schon; Posin'; Please Be Kind; Joseph, Joseph; I've Heard That Song Before; Victory Polka; I'll Walk Alone; Saturday Night Is the Loneliest Night in the Week; Poor Little Rhode Island (off state song); The Charm of You; I Fall in Love Too Easily; What Makes the Sunset; Guess I'll Hang My Tears Out to Dry; It's Been a Long, Long Time; Day By Day; Let It Snow, Let It Snow, Let It Snow; I Should Care; I'm Glad I Waited for You; The Things We Did Last Summer; Five Minutes More; Time After Time; Papa, Won't You Dance With Me?; You're My Girl; I Still Get Jealous; It's Magic; Be My Love; Because You're Mine; Teach Me Tonight; The 86th! The 86th! (off song USA 86th Inf Reg); Love and Marriage (Emmy, Christopher Awards, 55); The Impatient Years; Look to Your Heart; I'll Never Stop Loving You; Hey, Jealous Lover; All the Way (Acad Award, 57); Come Fly With Me; Only the Lonely; To Love and Be Loved; High Hopes (Acad Award, 59; Pres Kennedy campaign song, 60); The Second Time Around; Call Me Irresponsible (Acad Award, 63); September of My Years; My Kind of Town; I Like to Lead When I Dance; Love Is a Bore; Everybody Has a Right to Be Wrong; I'll Only Miss Her When I Think of Her; Film title songs: Three Coins in the Fountain (Acad Award, 54); It's a Woman's World; The Tender Trap; The Long Hot Summer; Indiscreet; Pocketful of Miracles; Come Blow Your Horn; The Best of Everything; Where Love Has Gone; Thoroughly Modern Millie; Touch of Class; Now That We're in Love. *Scores:* Nightclub: Connie's Hot Chocolates of 1936; New Grand Terrace Revue; Cotton Club Parade (39); Films: Anchors Aweigh; Tonight and Every Night; Tars and Spars; The Kid From Brooklyn; Romance on the High Seas; Two Guys From Texas; It's a Great Feeling; The Toast of New Orleans; The West Point Story; Rich, Young and Pretty; April in Paris; Peter Pan; Three Sailors and a Girl; You're Never Too Young; The Court Jester; Meet Me in Las Vegas; The Opposite Sex; Ten Thousand Bedrooms; Say One for Me; Let's Make Love; Road to Hong Kong; Robin and the 7 Hoods; Bway stage: High Button Shoes; Two's Company; Skyscraper; Walking Happy; Look to the Lillies; also Les Poupees de Paris (marionette show).

CAILLIET, LUCIEN
ASCAP 1946

composer

b Chalon Sur Marne, France, May 22, 1891. Educ: French Nat Cons, 1st prize, clarinet, studied harmony & counterpoint with Paul Fauchet & Georges Caussades, fugue with Andre Gedage, orchestration & arr with Gabriel Pares, comp with Vincent d'Indy; Philadelphia Musical Acad & Carthage Col, DMus. Clarinettist, saxophonist & arr under Stokowski & Ormandy, Philadelphia Orch. Taught, Curtis Inst; prof, Univ Southern Calif & Trenton State Col. Cond, Ballet Russe de Monte Carlo. Comp & cond, motion pictures studio; music & educ dir, G Leblanc Corp. Guest cond & clinician, var state & fest bands & orchs. Recipient, Officier of Order of Arts & Letters, Officier d'Academie, Kappi Kappi Psi & Distinguished Service Medal. *Instrumental Works:* Pop Goes the Weasel; Romantic Tone Poem; Voice of Freedom; Selections of Victor Herbert;

Love Song; Our United States; Jesu Joy of Man's Desiring; Rhapsody for Violin and Orchestra; Clarinet Poem; Spirit of Christmas; Overture-Fanfare; A Birthday Fantasy; Parisian Festival; Fantasy for Clarinet and Orchestra; Memories of Stephen Foster; Elsa's Processional to the Cathedral; Homage to US Navy; I Am Music; Arrangements: Fugue in G minor (Bach); Phedre Overture (Massenet); Les Sylphides (Chopin); Le Roi d'ys Overture (Lalo); Waltzes From Der Rosen Kavalier (Strauss); The Pearl Fishers Overture (Bizet); Prelude, Cannon and Fugue (Bach); E Major Prelude (Bach); Orchestration films & TV shows: She Wore a Yellow Ribbon; Three Godfather's; Fugitive; Cheyenne; Fort Apache; Quiet Man; Ten Commandments. *Scores:* Film/TV: Crosswinds; Hong Kong; Sangree; Fun on a Weekend; The Last Outpost; Blazing Forest; Night Holds Terror; Harpoon; Tripoli; Angel on My Shoulder.

CAIN, JOE JACK   ASCAP 1962
composer, arranger, producer
b Philadelphia, Pa, Jan 31, 29. Educ: Theodore Roosevelt High Sch, Bronx, NY, music major; studied harmony, theory with Hugo Montenegro. Mem Am Fedn Musicians, 30 yrs. Musician for NBC, CBS, & ABC TV, Bway musicals, bands, Stamford Symph, movie sound tracks, radio & TV commercials, 54-66. Independent producer, arr & comp for Joseph Cain Assocs, 59-71. Gen mgr, producer & arr for Tico-Alegre (Roulette), 71-75, Caytronic-Salsoul, 75-80. *Songs:* Papa Bajo. *Instrumental Works:* El Blues Latino; The Cat From Cadiz; Rum and Mumbles; Italianissima; Beautiful; Money Man; Ghana Spice. *Scores:* Off-Bway: The Olathe Response; TV: It's a Mad-Mad-Mad-Mad Mambo (part 1 & 2).

CAIN, NOBLE   ASCAP 1939
composer, conductor, organist
b Aurora, Ind, Sept 25, 1896; d North Hollywood, Calif, Aug 28, 77. Educ: Univ Chicago, MA; Am Cons, BM; Friends Univ, BA, hon MusD; Lawrence Col, hon MusD. Founded Senn High Sch Chorus, Chicago & Chicago A Cappella Choir. Choral dir & producer, NBC, 32-39. Guest cond music fests; cond schs, cols & clinics. Author, "Choral Music and Its Practice". *Songs & Instrumental Works:* Choral: Christ in the World (oratorio); Evangeline; The King and the Star; Paul Revere's Ride; Ode to America; Anthems: Holy Lord God; Our Father Who Art in Heaven; The Twenty-Third Psalm; Ye Servants of God; Thanks Be to God (arr); Noel Noel; Psalm 103; Music: Homeland; The Years At the Spring; settings of Seven Famous Hymn Texts; also arr of Negro spirituals & folk songs.

CAIOLA, AL   ASCAP 1959
composer, musician
b Jersey City, NJ, Sept 7, 20. Educ: NJ Music Col. Has made many records. Chief Collabr: George Romanis. *Songs & Instrumental Works:* Big Guitar; Tuff Guitar; Wheels West.

CALABRO, JOHN A (JOHN CALE)   ASCAP 1950
composer, author, musician
b Providence, RI, Oct 16, 09. Educ: Elem sch; high sch; col, BSEE. Elec engr, Fleetwings Aircraft, Dept of Army, Gen Elec Co, Automated Technol Corp. Positions held, chief of prog & evaluation Div, USA Procurement Div & Civilian Area Supv, Eng Div, Dept of Defense, mgr, quality assurance, Gen Elec Co & vpres, Automated Technol Corp; inventor of 2 patents for electronic systs. Chief Collabr: T Bennet, Ernie Burnett, Larry Stock, George D Weiss, D Broderick, Hal David, Bob Miller, Jim Robertson, Tod Navarre. *Songs:* The Voice of Love; Eskimo Kiss Polka; Carmellina; They Don't Say; The Wedding Waltz; There's Lots-a Room; Santa's Little Sleigh Bells; Gondola Rock; Hey Marie, Rock With Me; Filalulu Birdie; My Ma She Told Me So; Love's A-Poppin in My Heart; In Swaddling Clothes; and others.

CALABRO, LOUIS   ASCAP 1954
composer
b Brooklyn, NY, Nov 1, 26. Educ: Juilliard, dipl & postgrad dipl, 48-53, all comp work with Vincent Persichetti. Fac mem, Bennington Col, 55- Guggenheim fels, 54-55, 59; Vt Council grants, 71, 77; Nat Endowment for Arts grants, 73, 76; many other comns, awards & grants. Chief Collabrs: John Gardner, Nicholas Delbanco. *Instrumental Works:* Symphony No 3; Five for a Nickel Pie; 10 short pieces for strings; Cantilena; Voyage (oratorio); Piano Variations; Diversities (piano); Young People's Sonatine (piano); several choral works.

CALDWELL, GLORIA   ASCAP 1964
composer, arranger, writer
b St Matthews, SC, Apr 15, 33. Educ: SC State Col, BA(music); pvt instr in piano. Arr band music in high sch & col. Arr for var artists, 60-, radio & TV commercials incl Avon, Alka Seltzer & Ajax, movies & Bway shows. Working with group Village People, 80. Started production co, The Son of Julius; founder of publ co, Well-Made Music, Inc. Free-lance arr. Chief Collabrs: Bernie Benjamin, Sol Marcus, Francia Luban, Rafael Benitez, Jack Wolf. *Songs:* Don't Let Me Be Misunderstood; The Dove (La Paloma); It Ain't What'Cha Got.

CALDWELL, MARY ELIZABETH   ASCAP 1958
composer, author, organist
b Tacoma, Wash, Aug 1, 09. Educ: Univ Calif, Berkeley, AB(music); studied comp with Richard G Schrey, Munich Cons & Bernard Wagenaar, Juilliard Col, piano & organ with Benjamin Moore, San Francisco. Organist & dir, First Reformed Church, NY, 9 yrs; organist, First Baptist Church, Pasadena, 3 yrs, State St Presbyterian Church, NY, 3 yrs, San Marino Community Church, 48-

Dir, children's choir, Calif, 15 yrs; composer, first publ work, 49. Writer of texts & librettos for anthems, cantatas & 4 operas. *Songs:* Tell Us Shepherd Maids (carol arr); The Noel Carol (SATB); Up and Wake Thee, Peter Lad (SATB); Polish Easter Carol (SA, SATB); Song of Praise (SAB); God's Open Road (youth, unison); The Garden (youth); Gloria, Gloria (SATB); The Freedom Song (cantata, SA, SATB); A Song Is a Gift to God; Calm and Lovely (arr from Schubert); The Yodler's Carol; Carol of the Christmas Chimes (SATB, hand bells); Of Time and Eternity (cantata, SATB, brass, perc); Let Us Follow Him (cantata, youth, adult solos); The Road to Bethlehem (youth, adult solos); A Christmas Triptych (medium voice, flute); A Lute Caroll (SAB, SATB, solo, flute); Music: Carol of the Little King (SA, SSA, SATB, solo with descant). *Scores:* Opera: Pepetos's Golden Flower; The Night of the Star; A Gift of Song.

CALE, JOHN
See Calabro, John A

CALEO, MICHAEL ANGELO (MICKEY)   ASCAP 1954
composer, author
b Utica, NY, July 12, 02; d Utica, Nov 12, 68. Educ: Assumption Acad, 21; studied clarinet & saxophone with A Anunziato, 09-17. Mem, prof staff of Jack Mills, Inc, New York, 23-25. Leader, dance band, Utica, NY, toured Eastern seaboard & Fla. Author, comp & librettist, musical play "Art and Beer." Chief Collabrs: Will Osborne, Jack Miles. *Songs:* Moon; Tell Me That It's True; Christmas Story.

CALISCH, EDITH LINDEMAN (EDITH LINDEMAN)   ASCAP 1954
author
b Pittsburgh, Pa, Mar 21, 1898. Educ: Barnard Col, 2 yrs. Wrote children's bks & promotional brochures; movie & drama critic, entertainment ed, Richmond Times-Dispatch, Va, 33-64. Chief Collabr: Carl Stutz. *Songs:* Lyrics: Little Things Mean A Lot; I Know; The Red-Headed Stranger; Blackberry Winter; Cling to Me; Jamestown Suite; The Kissing Tree; Don't Ask Me Why; Good Night, Sweet Dreams, Mary Lou.

CALKER, DARRELL W   ASCAP 1953
composer, conductor, arranger
b Washington, DC, Feb 18, 05; d Malibu, Calif, Feb 20, 64. Educ: Md Univ, BS; Curtis Inst, studied with David Pell & Edgar Priest. Scores for ballet cos incl Ballet Russe de Monte Carlo, Ballet Russe, Sadlers Wells. *Instrumental Works:* Penguin Island; Golden Land. *Scores:* Film: Adventure Island; Bachelor's Daughters; El Paso; Albuquerque; Geronimo; Savage Drums. Ballets: Royal Coachman; Quiet Week; Decameron.

CALL, AUDREY   ASCAP 1938
composer, violinist
b Alton, Ill, Apr 12, 05. Educ: Sherwood Music Sch, Chicago, Ill, BMus, 23, MMus, 26; studied with Maurice Hayot, L'Ecole Normale, Paris, 27; Paris Cons, studied with Edouard Nadaud, Firmin Touche & Vincent D'Indy, 27-29. Began musical educ at age three; appeared as prodigy at age eight. Won two maj violin competitions, Am Fest Music, New York & Soc Am Musicians, Chicago, 26. Her perf of Paganini Concerto won a place in the Paris Cons, 27, became a laureate there, 29. Concertized extensively as violinist. *Songs:* Indiana Lullaby; I Just Telephone Upstairs. *Instrumental Works:* Serenade to a Cornstalk Fiddle; The Witch of Harlem; Streamline; Canterbury Tales; To a Lady From Baltimore; The Bishop Checkmates; The Duke Takes the Train.

CALLAHAN, J WILL   ASCAP 1924
author
b Columbus, Ind, Mar 17, 1874; d New Smyrna Beach, Fla, Nov 15, 46. Educ: High sch. Accountant; then 4 yrs as singer of illustrated songs. Chief Collabr: Max Kortlander. *Songs:* Tell Me; Patches; When I Came Home to You; The Story of Old Glory, the Flag We Love; God Put a Rose in My Garden; You Planted a Rose; Smiles.

CALLAHAN, MARIE JOAN   ASCAP 1960
composer, author
b Chicago, Ill, May 21, 06. Educ: Providence Acad; Juilliard. Asst dir, then dir, producer & creator, radio & TV. Exec vpres, writer, creator & producer, radio & TV musical jingles, Pam Advert Agency. Pres, Creative Enterprises, Inc. *Songs & Instrumental Works:* Suddenly the Music Stopped; House on Main Street; Driftwood; I'm Gonna Take Love Easy; Twilight Interlude.

CALLENDER, CHARLES R   ASCAP 1956
composer, author, arranger
b Phrae, Thailand, Oct 27, 11. Educ: Berkeley Pub Schs, Calif; studied piano with Kathleen Armitage, voice with Wheeler Beckett; Univ Sci & Philosophy, Va. Played & sang on radio; worked with musical groups & orchs; music copyist & rehearsal pianist with motion picture studios. USCG Band, WW II, 11th Naval District, Long Beach, Calif. Voice coach & piano teacher, San Fernando Valley, Los Angeles, Calif. Chief Collabrs: June Baldwin, Jimmie Grier. *Songs:* Snowbound; Remember, I Knew You When; It's Funny How It Happened; Big Chief Albuquerque; Time's A-Wastin'; Cornered; Twilight Moon; Don't Worry; Chirothesian Prayer; Music: My Old Chum; Dixie Jamboree; There'll Always Be a Christmas; Stupid Little Cupid; Coast Guard Hymn; Put Your Trust in the

Moon. *Instrumental Works:* Concerto for Piano and Orchestra; Sierra Suite (piano); American Idyls (piano).

CALLENDER, GEORGE SYLVESTER (RED)   ASCAP 1957
composer, author, teacher
b Richmond, Va, Mar 6, 18. Educ: Studied harmony, comp, bass & tuba with Prof Alexander Valentine, Bordentown, NJ, age 12. At age 17 joined a road-show as band leader. Appeared on many TV shows. Chief Collabrs: Wayne Shanklin & Mary Lou Callender. *Songs:* Skyline; All For You; You're Part of Me; Be Happy Pappy; Music Walking on Air; On Again; Greenery; October Blue; Dancers; Bihari. *Instrumental Works:* Pastel; Sleigh Ride; Primrose Lane. *Albums:* Swinging Suite; Callender Speaks Low.

CALLINICOS, CONSTANTINE   ASCAP 1953
composer, conductor, lecturer
b New York, NY, June 12, 13. Educ: Conservatories in Greece; La Forge Berumen Studios, NY, scholarship; Juilliard, scholarship; studied with Josef Lhevinne, Ernst Hutcheson, Egon Petri, Bernard Wagenaar, Dimitri Mitropoulous & Albert Stossel. WW II, USA. Debut as cond, NY Philh, Carnegie Hall, 46. Made concert tours as cond & pianist, 46-51. Gen dir & cond, Highland Park Symph, Calif, 52-56; Pacific Opera Co, 54-57. Cond, New York Opera Co, 57-60; guest cond, symph orchs, 57- Author, "The Mario Lanza Story." Chief Collab: Paul Francis Webster. *Songs & Instrumental Works:* You Are My Love; Two Greek Dances; Nani-Nani; Memories of Athens.

CALLISON, JO ANN (JENNIE SMITH)   ASCAP 1963
composer, singer
b Burnwell, WVa, Nov 13, 38. Educ: Charleston High Sch, WVa, grad, 56. Singer, nightclubs, radio & TV. Recording artist for var cos. Chief Collab: Steve Allen. *Songs:* Music: After Awhile; After You.

CALLOWAY, CAB   ASCAP 1942
composer, author, conductor
b Rochester, NY, Dec 25, 07. Educ: Crane Col. While law student, sang with band, The Alabamians; took over group, 28. Led orch, The Missourians; then organized own orch. Played hotels, theatres & nightclubs throughout US; made many records. Made film appearances, incl "The Singing Kid", "Big Broadcast of 1933", "Stormy Weather" & "Sensations of 1945." Acted in stage musical, "Porgy and Bess," on tour throughout US & Europe, 52-54. Formed own quartet, 54. Chief Collabrs: Jack Palmer, Andy Gibson, Buck Ram, Clarence Gaskill, Irving Mills, Paul Mills. *Songs:* Minnie the Moocher; Lady With the Fan; Zaz Zuh Zaz; Chinese Rhythm; Are You in Love With Me Again?; That Man's Here Again; Peck-a-Doodle Doo; I Like Music; Rustle of Swing; Three Swings and Out; The Jumpin' Jive; Are You Hep to That Jive?; Boog It; Come on With the Come-on; Silly Old Moon; Sunset; Rhapsody in Rhumba; Are You All Reet?; Hi-De-Ho Man; Levee Lullaby; Let's Go, Joe; Geechy Joe; Hot Air.

CAMARATA, SALVADOR (TUTTI)   ASCAP 1948
composer, author, arranger
b Glen Ridge, NJ, May 11, 13. Educ: Juilliard; Damrosch Grad Sch, studied orch & comp with Bernard Wagenaar; Columbia Univ, studied orch & comp with Howard Murphy; cond with Cesare Sudero & Jan Myerwitz. Lead trumpeter in Big Bands. Arr for Jimmy Dorsey Orch. Musical dir, ABC, NY & Decca Records. Co-founder, London Records, Eng. Co-founder & producer, Disneyland Records. Recording artist for Decca, Ltd. *Songs:* Lyrics: No More; The Breeze and I. *Instrumental Works:* Trumpeter's Prayer; Trumpet Soliloquy Louis; Rumbalero; Operatic Transcriptions; Bach Transcriptions. *Scores:* Portrait of Jesus.

CAMBERN, MAY HOGAN (MICHAEL)   ASCAP 1962
author, harpist
b Ft Worth, Tex. Educ: Studied harp with Alfred Kastner. Harpist, Los Angeles Philh & Hollywood Bowl Orch, 12 yrs, first harpist, 45. Soloist with var film studios. On radio & TV; recording artist. Chief Collab: Robert Armbruster. *Songs:* Lord God of Our Fathers; We the People.

CAMERO, CANDIDO   ASCAP 1974
composer, author, drummer
b Havana, Cuba, Apr 22, 21. Began on bass & guitar, then switched to bongos & conga drums. With CMQ Radio & Tropicana Club, Havana, 6 yrs. Came to US in 52. Worked clubs in Miami & New York, then with Stan Kenton in 54. Free-lanced & did a series of Carnegie Hall concerts, also recordings & TV shows. Now a recording artist. *Albums:* Candido 1,000 Finger Man; Candido Latin Fire; Candido Drum Fever; Candido in Indigo; Candido Beautiful; Candido Comparsa; Candido Conga Soul; Candido Calypso Dance Party; Candido; Candido the Volcanic; Candido Brujerias and McGoofa Dust; Dancin' and Prancin'.

CAMERON, ALAN   ASCAP 1957
composer, author, director
b Anderson, Ind, Nov 22, 1900; d Tiburon, Calif, Mar 28, 72. Educ: DePauw Univ. Emcee, KDKA, Pittsburgh, 21; had radio show, WCX. Pianist, accompanist & singer with B F Keith, Keith Orpheum, Loew's Circuits. Writer, dir & producer for advertisers on radio & TV. Account exec, Lennon & Newell,

San Francisco. Chief Collabs: Milton Ager, Ted Weems. *Songs:* The Martins and the Coys; Sweet Muchacha; It's a Girl.

CAMERON, BARBARA MARIE   ASCAP 1964
composer, author, singer
b Dayton, Ohio, Feb 14, 28. Educ: Roosevelt High Sch, Dayton; Cincinnati Col of Music, piano. Singer & vocal staff, for shows incl "Moon River" & "Midwestern Hayride." Featured in music show "Dave & Barbara," WKRC-radio & TV. Actress, WCPO-TV in "Girl Alone." Writer, singing commercials & voice-over for many commercials incl "Tide." To New York, free-lance singer with Satisfiers, Ray Charles Singers & Andy William Show; recording artist. *Songs:* The Cisco Kid; The Road Runner (TV cartoon theme); Porky Pig (TV cartoon theme); Lyrics: Bach Minuet Song (200 Miles). *Albums:* Invitation to Love.

CAMP, HAMID HAMILTON
composer, singer, guitarist
b London, Eng, Oct 30, 34. Educ: Old Town Sch Folk Music. Became partner of Bob Gibson, 60 & collab & performed in folk clubs. Formed own band The Skymonters, 70, performed in clubs in US & Can. Chief Collabrs: Bob Gibson, Shell Silverstien, Lauren Pickford, Lewis Ross. *Songs:* Prize of Man; Here's to You; Time; Well Well Well. *Scores:* Bway Show: Story Theatre; More From Story Theatre.

CAMPANILE, PETER BENJAMIN   ASCAP 1969
composer, author, teacher
b Orange, NJ, Apr 24, 28. Educ: Seton Hall, NJ, studied with Maestro Lombardi & Tony Villanova; studied voice with Robert Gerber; Orange High Sch. Interior decorator, designer & musician in NJ, NY, Pa, Fla & Nebr. Chief Collabrs: Tony Villanova, Walter Rooney, Robert Gerber, Irwin & Charlotte Horwitz. *Songs:* Remember Me; Colleen; Donna; Lyrics: Tropic Christmas; Buona Natale.

CAMPBELL, ALAN
See Montgomery, Merle

CAMPBELL, HENRY C   ASCAP 1958
composer, teacher
b Osceola, Nebr, Nov 13, 26. Educ: Univ Rochester Eastman Sch of Music, MM; Univ Wash. With music dept, Mont State Col, 49- *Songs & Instrumental Works:* Jump Tune; A Song or Two; Then Silence (collection); Folk Song Suite (choral); Waltz—Then March (piano).

CAMPBELL, MICHAEL RECTOR   ASCAP 1975
composer, author, singer
b Hollywood, Calif, Feb 21, 44. Educ: Ulysses S Grant High Sch; Los Angeles Valley Col; studied voice with Sally & Lee Sweetland, counterpoint & comp with Abbey Fraser, piano with Fletcher Peck & arr with Jack Smalley. With Doodletown Pipers, 66-69; on summer TV show, CBS "Our Place." Recording artist. Formed own group & worked around the country. Began demo, background work & commercials in Los Angeles. Writer & musician. Chief Collabrs: Moacir Santos, John Heard. *Songs:* Lyrics: Quiet Carnival; Tomorrow Is Mine.

CAMPBELL, PAUL
See Hellerman, Fred

CAMPBELL, ROBERT MYRON   ASCAP 1979
composer
b Edgewood, Md, June 23, 44. Educ: NTex State Univ, BA(jour). Music journalist, writer & publ. Nashville ed, Cashbox Magazine, 77-79 & Country Music Magazine, 80- Owner, South Street Music Publ Co. Chief Collabr: Winston Henry (Hank) Riddle. *Songs:* Pilgrim's Progress.

CAMPLIN, WILLIAM MICHAEL   ASCAP 1975
composer, author, musician
b Pewaukee, Wis, May 20, 47. Educ: Studied & sang under Margaret Hawkins, 5 yrs. Former machinist, foundry worker & landscape laborer. Performer of own comp & other selected songs, 6 yrs. Performed with Milwaukee Symph Orch; wrote & performed with William Rielly's Mid-West Dance Theatre. Singer & producer. Chief Collab: Roger Ruggeri. *Songs:* Weary Eyes; Questions and Lies; January/Guitar; Somebody Tried; Take Me to the Woods.

CAMPO, FRANK PHILIP   ASCAP 1966
composer, teacher
b New York, NY, Feb 4, 27. Educ: Univ Southern Calif, BM, MM & DMus, studied with Ingolf Dahl & Leon Kirchner; Ecole Normal de Musique, Paris, studied with Arthur Honegger; Fulbright scholarship, Rome, studied with Goffredo Petrassi. Began as instrumentalist, clarinet & saxophone, age 13. Comp, arr, orchestrater & instrumentalist, Los Angeles, 51-67. Mem fac, Univ Southern Calif & Calif State Univ, Fullerton; prof comp & chmn dept comp-theory, Calif State Univ, Northridge, 67- Occasionally performs as clarinetist in concerts of new music. *Instrumental Works:* Divertimento (violin, clarinet & guitar); Alba for 15 players; Viaggi (flute, oboe, clarinet, horn, bassoon & perc); Variations (orch); Commedie II (trumpet, pianoforte & tape); Preludes (flute, clarinet & guitar); Duet for Equal Trumpets; Capriccio

(symphonic wind orch); Dualidad (bass clarinet & perc); Commedie (trombone & perc); Times (solo trumpet); Madrigals (brass quintet); Tres Cubito (flute, viola & perc); Music for Agamemnon (band); Concertino (3 clarinets & piano); Suite (7 brass); Five Pieces (5 winds); Alpine Holiday (overture for orch); Kisesis (clarinet & piano).

CANADA, RICHARD   ASCAP 1969
composer, author
b Bridgeport, Conn, Apr 2, 42. Educ: El Camino Col, Calif, BA; Harbor Col, Calif; Univ Southern Calif, studied theory with Robert Haigg. Musician for clubs in Southern Calif, 62-66. Writer for motion picture & TV, such as "Fat Albert," "Treasure Island" & "Oliver Twist." Chief Collabr: Sherry Fournier. *Songs:* Fat Albert Theme.

CANADAY, VERONICA
See Niday Canaday, Edna Veronica

CANDIDO
See Camero, Candido

CANDLYN, T FREDERICK H   ASCAP 1954
composer, organist, educator
b Eng, Dec 17, 1892; d Point Lookout, NY, Dec 16, 1964. Asst church organist, Doncaster, Eng; organist & choirmaster, St Paul's, Albany, NY. Served, USA, World War I. Head, music dept, State Univ NY, 19-43; organist & choirmaster, St Thomas Church, New York, 43-54. *Songs:* Sacred: Thee We Adore; Christ, Whose Glory; Divinum Mysterium.

CANDY, MARY
See Ryder, Mary E

CANNAN, GERALD FRANK   ASCAP 1977
composer, author
b Sanger, Calif, Mar 2, 22. Educ: Chanute Sr High Sch, Kans. Began writing in jr high sch; played trumpet in band & French horn in orch in sr high sch; first recording, 50. *Songs:* China Doll; Shifting Sand; My Proudest Possession.

CANNON, FREDDY
See Picariello, Frederick Anthony

CANNON, MURRAY FRANKLIN (BUDDY)   ASCAP 1973
composer
b Lexington, Tenn, Apr 20, 47. Educ: Lexington High Sch, Tenn. Back-up musician for several country music stars including Bob Luman & Mel Tillis. Chief Collabrs: Gene Dunlap, Kenny Starr, Jimmy Darrell & Frank Dycus. *Songs:* I Believe In You; Naked In The Rain; Woman, You Should Be In Movies; Whiskey Chasin'.

CANO, EDWARD, JR   ASCAP 1955
composer, pianist, conductor
b Los Angeles, Calif, June 6, 27. Educ: Los Angeles Cons. Pianist, var orchs incl Miguelito Valdes, Herb Jeffries, Bobby Ramos & Tony Martinez. Leader, own group; recording artist. *Songs & Instrumental Works:* Cotton Candy; Bacao; Cal's Pals; Panchita.

CANOSA, MICHAEL RAYMOND   ASCAP 1960
composer, author, singer
b New Haven, Conn, May 25, 20. Educ: High sch. Singer & harmonica player, dance orchs & nightclubs. Chief Collabr: Buddy De Franco. *Songs:* I Was Such a Fool to Fall in Love With You; Kiss 'n' Twist.

CANTON, DONALD   ASCAP 1953
composer, author, poet
b Syracuse, NY, Apr 24, 15. Lyric writing, 45-70. Author bks "The Intelligent Atom", "Let Me Do The Words." Chief Collabrs: John Nagy, Milton Lance, Ira Kosloff, Bert Mann, George Goehring. *Songs:* Lyrics: There's Something About (A Home Town Band); Five Hundred Guys; Say No More; Two Faced Heart. *Albums:* Connie Francis Sings (Fun Songs for Children).

CANTOR, EDDIE   ASCAP 1951
author, comedian
b New York, NY, Jan 31, 1892; d Hollywood, Calif, Oct 10, 64. Educ: Pub schs. First appearance in vaudeville, Clinton Music Hall, NY, 07. Mem, Gus Edwards Gang. Toured vaudeville with Lila Lee as team Cantor & Lee. Bway stage appearances in "Canary Cottage", "Ziegfeld Follies", 17-19 & 27, "Broadway Brevities of 1920", "Make It Snappy", "Kid Boots", "Whoopee" & "Banjo Eyes." Film appearances incl "Palmy Days", "The Kid from Spain", "Roman Scandals", "Kid Millions", "Strike Me Pink", "Ali Baba Goes to Town" & "Thank Your Lucky Stars." Made var records, incl own one man show "Eddie Cantor at Carnegie Hall." Had own radio show, "The Eddie Cantor Chase and Sanborn Hour" for many yrs in 30's. Appeared on TV on "The Colgate Comedy Hour" & won awards on "Playhouse 90" for dramatic perf in "Seidman & Son." Author, autobiographies "My Life Is in Your Hands" & "Take My Life", bks "Ziegfeld, the Great Glorifier" & "As I Remember Them." *Songs:*

Get a Little Fun Out of Life; Merrily We Roll Along; It's Great to Be Alive; The Old Stage Door.

CANTRELL, BYRON   ASCAP 1972
composer, author, musicologist
b Brooklyn, NY, Nov 14, 19. Educ: Third Street Settlement, grad, 35; Nat Orch Asn, New York, 37-38; NY Univ, BA(music), 39; Berkshire Music Sch, Tanglewood, 41; studied with Paul Emerich, 42-44; Univ Calif, Los Angeles, MA(comp), 55, PhD(musicol), 57; spec studies with Marion Bauer, Philip James, Leon Barzin, Serge Koussevitzky & Emerson Buckley. Teacher, piano, opera repertoire, comp & cond, 39-; cond, Hampton Roads Civic Orch, Los Virtuosos de Los Angeles, Young Peoples' Opera Asn & New York Little Symph; prog annotator, Ambassador Int Cultural Found, ABC Westminster Records, MCA Records & Capitol Records; music reviewer, New York Post, Newport News Daily Press, Hicks-Deal Newspapers, Los Angeles Times & Los Angeles Herald-Examiner; music ed, Summit Publ Co & Western Periodicals Co; teacher, Emerich Music Sch, Univ Calif, Los Angeles, Tahoe Paradise Col, Calif State Univ, Fullerton, El Camino Col & Int Col. Young Artists Competition Award, Los Angeles Philh, 44. Chief Collabrs: Bernard Hanighen, Donn E Hart. *Songs & Instrumental Works:* Sechs Sprüche; A Tooth for Paul Revere (opera); Songs; What Child Is This?; The Land of Heart's Desire (opera); Jubilee Overture; Variations on "Dunya"; Piano Pieces; The Eagle That Is Forgotten (choral); Sacred Service (choral); Arr: Four Elizabethan Pieces; Choral Preludes. *Scores:* Bway Show: Raisins and Almonds; Film/TV: Documentaries. *Albums:* A Mark Twain Album.

CAPANNA, ROBERT   ASCAP 1975
composer
b Camden, NJ, July 7, 52. Educ: New Sch of Music; Philadelphia Col Performing Arts, BM, 73, summa cum laude, MM, 75; comp study with Joseph Castaldo, Theodore Antoniou & Jacob Druckman; Berkshire Music Ctr, Bruno Maderna fel, 74. Koussevitzky Prize, 74; MTNA/Koss Prize, 76. Grad asst, Philadelphia Col Performing Arts, 73-75, dir admissions, 75-76; asst exec dir, Settlement Music Sch, 78-, dir, Kardon-Northeast Br, 76- Perf by Milwaukee Symph, Berkshire Music Ctr Orch, Philadelphia New Music Group, WUHY-FM, Philadelphia & Dallas Civic Orch. *Instrumental Works:* Phorminx for Solo Harp; Rota for Percussion Quartet; Concerto for Chamber Orchestra.

CAPANO, FRANK X   ASCAP 1936
author, singer
b Philadelphia, Pa, June 16, 1899; d Philadelphia, Feb 10, 56. Educ: La Salle Col. Singer & prog dir, radio. Chief Collabrs: Morty Berk, Max Freedman, Tony Starr, Johnny Fortis, Josef Myrow, John Farrow, Herman Parris. *Songs:* You Wanted Someone to Play With; Tears; Who'll Take Your Place When You're Gone?; Don't Say We're Through; Illusions; Mother; Daddy o'Mine; Shangri-La; Heartbreaker; Tea Leaves; Dreamy Old New England Moon; My ABC Song; Lyrics: I Stole You From Somebody Else; Are You Lonesome and Blue; How Could I Know; Marionette.

CAPELLAN, RICHARD VICTOR (RICK MARTIN)   ASCAP 1973
composer, author, singer
b Santo Domingo, Dominican Repub, Jan 29, 43. Educ: Weehawken High Sch, NJ, 60; Fairleigh Dickinson Univ, Rutherford, NJ, 64. Mem of group with Charo & Xavier Cugat Orch doing TV & nightclub shows. Singer, guitarist with Joey Dee & the Starlighters, Rick Martin & the Showmen, & Society's Children. Record productions on Decca, United Artists & Atlantic. Also a disc jockey, nightclub mgr, musical dir, secretary & newsletter ed for the Conference of Personal Managers, E. *Songs:* Images of You; And Then Suddenly (it's Spring); Haydee; Phoney People; Brand New Feeling; Get on a Happy Kick; The Game.

CAPITANELLI, ARNOLD JOSEPH, JR (ARNOLD JAY)   ASCAP 1968
composer, author, singer
b East Paterson, NJ, Jan 26, 32. Began writing professionally in 67. Wrote and produced for CBS, RCA, Mercury, WEA Polydor. Recording with Big Tree, 74. Chief Collabr: Robert O'Connor. *Songs:* I Can't Live a Dream; Mommy and Me; A Banquet for the World; Hollywood Man; Lyrics: Move in a Little Closer Baby; Father O'Conner.

CAPORALE, FRED   ASCAP 1979
composer, teacher
b New York, NY, June 30, 53. Educ: Manhattan Sch Music, BM, MMEd, trumpet, piano & theory. Played professionally at age 12; also played on Maybellion commercials, Riverhead Saving Bank commercials & others. Music teacher, Massapequa, NY. *Songs & Instrumental Works:* It's All Up to You.

CAPOTE, TRUMAN   ASCAP 1954
author
b New Orleans, La, Sept 30, 24. Educ: Trinity Sch; St John's Acad. Author: "Other Voices, Other Rooms"; "Tree of Night"; "Local Color"; "The Grass Harp"; "Breakfast at Tiffany's," also film; "The Muses Are Heard"; "In Cold Blood." Screenplay, "Beat the Devil." Awards: O Henry Mem, Nat Inst Arts & Letters. Chief Collabr: Harold Arlen. *Songs:* A Sleepin' Bee; I Never Has Seen Snow; Two Ladies in de Shade of de Banana Tree; House of Flowers. *Scores:* Bway Stage: House of Flowers.

CAPPELLI, AMY SPENCER   ASCAP 1959
author, teacher
b Providence, RI, Feb 6, 04. Educ: Brown Univ, BA. Taught, Cranston High Sch & St Dunstan's Choir Sch. Writer, poetry for newspapers & mags. Chief Collabr: Paul Kapp. *Songs:* A Letter to Teacher.

CAPPELLINI, PHILLIP THOMAS   ASCAP 1967
author
b Jessup, Pa, June 3, 30. Educ: Scranton High Sch, Pa. Writer for TV. Chief Collabr: Tommy Vig. *Songs:* Lyrics: Oriental Bossa Nova.

CARABETTA, FRANK LOUIS   ASCAP 1964
composer, musician
b Staten Island, NY, July 6, 44. Educ: New Dorp High Sch; Brooklyn Cons Music. Saxophonist, small groups, nightclubs & TV. Recording artist, MGM Records & Dot Records. *Instrumental Works:* Teenage Blues; Monkey Work Out.

CARANDA, MICHAEL J   ASCAP 1959
composer, author, pianist
b Alliance, Ohio, May 6, 18. Educ: High sch. Pianist, arr & mgr, Russ Carlyle Orch. Chief Collabr: Russ Carlyle. *Songs:* Studola-Pumpa; Stashu Pandowski.

CARASTATHIS, NICHOLAS SAM (NICHOLAS CARRAS) ASCAP 1961
composer, conductor
b Donora, Pa, Jan 31, 22. Educ: Hollywood High Sch; Los Angeles City Col, 40-42; Washington & Lee Univ, USA Special Service, 44; Los Angeles Cons of Music, studied violin, comp & conducting, 46-50; apprenticeship study, arr & orchestration with David Rose, Hollywood, 51-54. Began as asst comp & orchestrator for David Rose & George Antheil. Comp & cond, title themes & production songs for var films & TV series incl "New Loretta Young Show", "The FBI", "Cannon", "Barnaby Jones" & "Circus of the Stars." Comp of incidental music for theatre shows & revues; head orchestrator & music supvr, Bway show "Happy Town." Chief Collabrs: Ric Marlow, Buddy Kaye, Carl Eugster, Maria E Cellino. *Instrumental Works:* Loretta's Theme; Willy; Song for Sabrina; Touching and Sharing; Illusions. *Scores:* Film/TV: Untouchables; The Fugitive.

CARAZO, CASTRO   ASCAP 1940
composer, conductor, teacher
b San Jose, Costa Rica, June 18, 1895. Santa Cecilia Sch Music; Munic Sch Music; Liceo Cons, Barcelona, Spain; studied piano with Enrique Granados, violin with Bordas Comas & comp with Sanchez Gavanach. Cond, New Orleans Fed Symph; dir, mil bands, Costa Rica; dir, La State Univ Cadet Band. Had own music studio. Comp of songs & semi-classics for concert band & var instruments & for symph orch. *Songs:* Your Lips and Eyes; Tu Sonrisa; Music: Bonita; Darling of LSU; Every Man a King; Fight for LSU; Louisiana, My Home Sweet Home (off state march-song); Touchdown for LSU. *Instrumental Works:* Castanets; Celajes; Dance of the Silhouettes; The March of Progress; National Guard March (off march); Spanish Moment; Tango of Memories; Torch of Liberty; Overture to an Imaginary Play (symp orch).

CARBONARA, GERARD   ASCAP 1946
composer, conductor, violinist
b New York, NY, Dec 8, 1886; d Sherman Oaks, Calif, Jan 11, 59. Educ: Nat Cons, New York, scholarship; Naples Cons; studied with Martucci Dworzak. Opera coach, Milan, 10. Concert violinist & opera cond, Europe & US. Music dir & comp for film studios. *Songs:* Calm; Song to Pierrot; Waiting; Dusk of Roses. *Instrumental Works:* Armand (opera); Ode to Nature; Concerto Orientale; Scherzetto Fantasia; Violin & Piano: Aria; Serenata Gotica; Alla Tarantella; Dusk; Piano: Danse Fantastique; Rhapsodie; Hollywood Boulevard; An American Tone Sketch; Minuet; Petite Valse. *Scores:* Film background: Stagecoach; The Kansan; The Promised Land.

CARDER, RICHARD CAMERON   ASCAP 1973
composer, author
b Pittsfield, Mass, Dec 12, 17. Educ: Guitar lessons. Comp, 39-; sang & played guitar with musical groups & as a single. Linotype operator & compositor, 40- Chief Collabrs: Joseph Neff, Frankie Adams. *Songs:* Too Late; I Don't Want Everything.

CARDINI, GEORGE   ASCAP 1959
composer, author, violinist
b La Spezia, Italy, Sept 24, 13. Educ: Cons Music, Bologna, Italy; La Reggia Acad Filarmonica, Di Bologna, grad, 32. Orch mem, Monteverdi Opera House, Italy. Second Prize winner, Nat Tournament, 34. Appeared as soloist, New York Town Hall & Carnegie Hall. Hotel engagement led to permanent career playing int favorite popular classics & semiclassic music; pop music, gypsy & show pieces currently. Chief Collabr: Danny Di Minno. *Songs:* From the Bottom of My Heart; Love My Love; Roma Di Notte; Return to Rome; One More Blessing; Vieni; Arrivederci Forestiera; Tu Sei Cosi Amabile. *Instrumental Works:* Serenity; Cool Sea Gull; A Home In Our Heritage; Integrated Circuits.

CAREY, DAVID AARON   ASCAP 1960
composer, author, musician
b Pittsburgh, Pa, Feb 14, 26. Educ: Pittsburgh Musical Inst; Manhattan Sch Music; studied with Leon Kushner, Eddie Sauter & Lennie Tristano. Pianist, percussionist, arr & cond on TV shows, recordings & films. Chief Collabrs: Paul Alter, Searcy Lee Johnson. *Songs & Instrumental Works:* Excitement Now; Love's a Way of Life; Song for Home Viewers; Suite for Xylophone and Orchestra; Eight Pieces for Two Percussionists; Encounters for Horn and Percussion.

CAREY, JOSIE
See Vicari, Josephine M

CAREY, LEW
See Conetta, Lewis D

CAREY, WILLIAM D   ASCAP 1946
composer, author, actor
b Hollister, Calif, May 20, 16. Educ: High Sch Commerce, San Francisco. Singer with Ted Fiorito & Ben Bernie, 30's. Actor, singer for motion pictures, radio & nightclubs. Songwriter, 33- USA, 41-45. Writer for motion pictures. Chief Collabrs: Carl Fischer, Gene Howard, Don Kahn, Hank Mancini. *Songs:* Lyrics: Who Wouldn't Love You; You've Changed; It Started All Over Again; The Day Isn't Long Enough; Weep They Will; How Cute Can You Be; Could 'Ja; To Know You is to Love You; What's it Gonna Be; Summer Love; Promise; When You Trim Your Xmas Tree; Sun Forgot to Shine This Morning; Tootles the Cross Country Choo-Choo; You're Just the Kind; Where is Our Love; The Honey Moon is Over; If Spring Never Comes; I Love You For That; Heaven Only Knows; You Came Along (Golden Glover Story); Fool Am I.

CARILLO, FRANK   ASCAP 1972
composer, singer, musician
b Brooklyn, NY, July 14, 50. Educ: Publ sch 133; publ sch 172, jr high sch; Martin Van Buren High Sch; Nassau Community Col, 1 1/2 yrs; Sch Visual Arts, 1 1/2 yrs; studied guitar with Dom Minas. Began playing guitar, 58-, writing music, 63- & recording, 73- Played on first 2 Peter Frampton albums. Chief Collabr: Luke Spagnuolo. *Songs:* Music: What'd You Light the Fire With; It Carries On; She Takes the Night; Pure Sin; Under the Gun.

CARL, JOSEPH MICHAEL   ASCAP 1977
composer, author, teacher
b Detroit, Mich, June 20, 55. Univ Mich, BMus & MMus, 73-78; studied with H Robert Reynolds, Abe Torchnsky & William D Revelli. Band dir, South Haven Pub Schs, Mich, 78- Arr & comp for band; choir dir. Chief Collabr: Albert Ahronheim. *Instrumental Works:* Let's Go Blue (marching band).

CARLE, FRANKIE
See Carlone, Francis Nunzio

CARLETON, ROBERT LOUIS   ASCAP 1942
composer
b St Louis, Mo, Nov 8, 1896; d Burbank, Calif, July 12, 56. Educ: Pub schs. Wrote musicals, Great Lakes Naval Training Sta, WW I. *Songs:* Ja Da; Teasin'; I've Spent the Evening in Heaven; I've Got to Break Myself of You; Where the Blues Were Born in New Orleans.

CARLEVARO, ABEL JULIO   ASCAP 1975
author, guitarist
b Montevideo, Uraguay, Dec 16, 18. Educ: Univ Nacional Sch of Agriculture; Nat Cons of Music; studied with Andres Segovia, P Komlos, H Tossar, G Santorsola. Guitarist, int recital & concert tours. Creator, sch of instrumental techniques. Comp; recording artist. Educr; conducts seminars & master classes; juries int music competitions. *Instrumental Works:* Preludios Americanos, incl Campo, Scherzino, Evocacion, Ronda, Tamboriles); Homenaje a Villalobos (estudios para guitarra); Cronomias (sonata); Concierto Del Plata (guitar & orch); Suite de Antiguas Danzas Espanolas; Cuadernos Didacticos; Fantasia para las Seis Cuerdas; Cuarteto (para guitarra, violin, viola & cello).

CARLO, JOHNNY
See Selvaggio, John Ralph

CARLO, MONTE   ASCAP 1923
composer, author
b Gravenstein, Denmark, July 14, 1883; d. Educ: Univ Denmark; pre-med training, Chicago. To US, 06. Chief Collabr: Alma Sanders (wife). *Songs:* Hong Kong; That Tumble-Down Shack in Athlone; Little Town in the Ould County Down; My Home in the County Mayo; Two Blue Eyes; The Hills of Connemara; Dreaming of Louise; I Love Too Much, But Oh He Cares So Little; I've Got a Hole in the Sole of My Shoe; How Strange Is Love; No One to Care; Your Lips Are Getting Stranger Ev'ry Day; Singing's Good for the Soul; Ten Baby Fingers; Tangerine. *Scores:* Bway shows: Tangerine; Elsie; The Chiffon Girl; The Houseboat on the Styx; Film: Ireland Today.

CARLONE, FRANCIS NUNZIO (FRANKIE CARLE)　　ASCAP 1940
composer, pianist, band leader
b Providence, RI, Mar 25, 03. Educ: Pvt instr with Nicholas Colangelo. Played in vaudeville, 20. Joined New Eng band, Mal Hallet, 30, Horace Heidt, 39. Had own local band in New Eng, 35-38. Wrote first comp, 30. Played in ballrooms & theatres in US, 40 yrs. Did 9 movies with own band. Recorded for Decca, Columbia, Dot & RCA record cos. Had own radio shows, "The Old Gold", "Electric Hour" & "The Chesterfield." Also had TV show, 56. *Songs:* Music: Oh What it Seemed to Be; Carleboogie; Falling Leaves; Lover's Lullaby; Georgianna. *Instrumental Works:* Sunrise Serenade (song of the yr, 38).

CARLSON, HARRY A　　ASCAP 1952
composer, author
b Funk, Nebr, Dec 28, 04. Educ: Univ Nebr Cons of Music. Played & dir dance bands. Founded Fraternity Records, 54; publ firm, 55. Chief Collabr: Erwin King. *Songs:* I Thought-I-Was Dreaming; What Can I Do?; Cincinnati Ding Dong; No One Ever Lost Love; Dream Girl of Pi Kappa Alpha; When I'm Alone; Turn on the Bright Lights; Cattle Drive; Up the Chimney in Smoke; I Want to See You One More Time; You're the Sweetest Thing; Goodbye My Love.

CARLTON, JACK　　ASCAP 1970
composer, author, singer
b Philadelphia, Pa, Mar 25, 10. Educ: Central High Sch, Philadelphia; Drexel Inst Technol. Soloist in church choir, Philadelphia; sang silent movie theme songs on stage; became radio singer, 22; staff singer, actor & announcer, WCAU (CBS), 25; was singer on many network progs; with Jack Denny Orch, French Casino, New York, 35; organized & part of singing group for Jan Savitt Tophatters, Philadelphia, toured East Coast playing nightclubs & theatres; singer with Tony Pastor Orch, 41; songplugger, Chicago, 42; West Coast mgr, Peer-Southern publ group, Los Angeles, 46-65. Formed own publ co, 65. Chief Collabrs: Russ Morgan, George Howe, Betty Carlton. *Songs:* Christmas in Hawaii; The Biggest Hurt of All; Lyrics: Beyond the Coral Sea; Black Orchids; Island Love; Soft Is the Wind; Tell Me; Whispering Breeze; Paris in Spring. *Instrumental Works:* El Regimiento.

CARLTON, LARRY EUGENE　　ASCAP 1969
composer
b Torrance, Calif, Mar 2, 48. Educ: Studied guitar with Slim Edwards, 54-60; Harbor Jr Col, Calif, 66-68; Calif State Univ, Long Beach, 68-69. Began studying guitar at age 6; joined Musicians Union at age 12. Mem, Crusaders, 5 yrs. Voted most valuable studio guitarist, Naras, 73, 74 & 75; voted best studio guitarist, Guitar Player Mag, 79. Recording artist, Warner Bros, currently. *Instrumental Works:* Mellow Out; Room 335; Rio Samba.

CARLYLE, AILEEN　　ASCAP 1964
author
b San Francisco, Calif. Chief Collabrs: Arthur Bergh, Robert Ecton, Radie Britain. *Songs:* A Christmas Song; Marching Song; Where Freedom Walks; Lullaby of the Bells.

CARLYLE, RUSS　　ASCAP 1950
composer, singer, conductor
b Cleveland, Ohio, Dec 3, 14. Educ: High sch. Singer, Blue Barron Orch. Served, USA, World War II. Leader, own orch, 46. Appeared on TV; recording artist. Chief Collabr: Michael Caranda. *Songs:* If I Never Love Again; Stashu Pandowski; Studola Pumpa.

CARMICHAEL, HOWARD HOAGLAND (HOAGY)　　ASCAP 1931
composer, author, entertainer
b Bloomington, Ind, Nov 22, 1899. Educ: Bloomington High Sch, Ind, grad; Ind Univ, Bloomington, LLB, 26, DMus, 72. Practiced law, West Palm Beach, Fla; law clerk, New York City Bank. Draftsman, WW I, Chillicothe, Ohio, one yr. Own orch while attending col & in Indianapolis. Roles in motion pictures incl "To Have and to Have Not", "Johnny Angel", "Canyon Passage", "Night Song" & "Best Years of Our Lives." TV show, "At Home With Hoagy Carmichael"; TV & personal appearance tours; retired. Chief Collabrs: Johnny Mercer, Mitchell Parish, Frank Loesser, Stuart Gorrell, Stanley Adams, Paul Francis Webster, Sammy Lerner, Ned Washington, Jack Brooks, Jo Trent, Connie Dane, Harold Adamson, Dick Voynow, Irving Mills. *Songs:* Mediterranean Love; Rogue River Valley; Blue Orchids; Rockin' Chair; Hong Kong Blues; Ivy; I Get Along Without You Very Well; Music: Small Fry; The Lamplighter's Serenade; Can't Get Indiana Off My Mind; My Resistance Is Low; Winter Moon; Who Killed 'Er (Who Killed the Black Widder?); There Goes Another Pal of Mine; Just for Tonight; A Perfect Paris Night; A Woman Likes to Be Told; When Love Goes Wrong (Nothing Goes Right); My Christmas Song for You; Music, Always Music; From Nikki's Garden; Hawaii, Pearls of the Sea; New Orleans; Old Man Harlem; Watermelon Weather; I Walk With Music; Moon Country is Home to Me; Serenade to Gabriel; The White World of Winter; Washboard Blues; Riverboat Shuffle; Stardust; Little Old Lady; Lazy Bones; Georgia On My Mind; One Morning in May; Up the Lazy River; Two Sleepy People; Heart and Soul; Skylark; The Nearness of You; In the Cool Cool Cool of the Evening (Acad Award, 51); Ole Buttermilk Sky; Memphis in June; Thanksgivin'; Doctor Lawyer Indian Chief; How Little We Know; Baltimore Oriole; I Should Have Known You Years Ago; Judy.

CARMICHAEL, RALPH R　　ASCAP 1954
composer, arranger
b Quincy, Ill, May 27, 27. Educ: Abraham Lincoln High Sch. Host, arr & cond for TV prog "The Campus Christian Hour," 49. Arr & comp of last series of original TV prog "I Love Lucy Show," 54. Arr & cond, Nat King Cole, 56-65, Roger Williams, incl gold record "Born Free," 60-70. Music dir of 20 Billy Graham films incl "Mr Texas" & "Joni," 79. Chief Collabr: Kurt Kaiser. *Songs:* He's Everything to Me; The Savior Is Waiting; Tell It Like It Is.

CARMINES, ALVIN ALLISON　　ASCAP 1964
composer, author, singer
b Hampton, Va, July 25, 36. Educ: Swarthmore Col, BA, 58; Union Theol Sem, BD, 61, STD, 63. Chief Collabrs: Irene Formen, David Epstein, Rosalyn Dresler, Joel Oppenheimer, Gertrude Stien, Paul Goodmen, H M Koutowkas, Helen Adam, Lawrence Kornfeld. *Songs:* Joan; Christmas Rappings; Music: In Circles; Promenade; Peace; Pome Grenada.

CARNEY, RICHARD E　　ASCAP 1954
composer, author, publisher
b Fond du Lac, Wis, June 8, 23. Educ: Univ Wis, BS; Univ Chicago. WW II, 1st Lt, USAF. Mgr, Richard Maltby Orch. Has own publ co. Chief Collabrs: David Martin, Bill Stegmeyer, Richard Maltby, John Gluck, Jr. *Songs:* Faraway Star; Who Put the Devil in Evelyn's Eye?; Midnight Mood; The Jazz Man Blues.

CAROL, GARY
See Bratman, Carroll Charles

CAROL, MARTY
See Meehan, Martha

CAROLIN, MARTHA
See Meehan, Martha

CAROLL, EVELYN　　ASCAP 1958
author
b Detroit, Mich. Educ: Wayne Univ, BA. Writer & illustrator of children's books. Cartoonist for King Features. Chief Collabr: Anita Leonard. *Songs:* Graduation Ring; Jingle-Dingle; Letters Tied in Blue; Walking With Joe; The Ever So Many Adventures of Johnny; Animal Supermarket.

CARPENTER, ALICIA (ALICIA SMITH)　　ASCAP 1964
author, singer
b Miami, Fla, Aug 13, 30. Educ: Miami High Sch; Univ Calif, Los Angeles, BA, 51, hon alumni in Phi Beta Kappa; Cornell Univ. Chorister & soloist with the Roger Wagner Chorale; prof chorister & soloist & artistic dir, The Gregg Smith Singers; recording artist; translator/lyricist for G Schirmer, Shawnee Press, Lawson-Gould, Walton Music & Elkan-Vogel. Comn by Tex Boys Choir. Recipient of ASCAP standard awards. Painter. Chief Collabrs: Gregg Smith, Norman Luboff, Roy Ringwald, Jean Berger. *Songs:* Lyrics: The Story of the Other Wise Man (opera); The Fable of Chicken Little (Madrigal Opera); Das Lieben Bringt Gross Freud (choral); Heilig (choral); European Madrigals (mixed & equal voices); Four to Sing; Concord Chorales; Here and Now; Gypsy Song (Ziguenerleben); Walkin'; Invocation; Knock on Wood; Bible Songs (young voices).

CARPENTER, CARLETON　　ASCAP 1956
composer, author, actor
b Bennington, Vt, July 10, 26. Educ: Bennington High Sch; summer scholarship, Northwestern Univ, Ill. Appeared in many Bway shows incl "Bright Boy" (1944) to "Spinechiller" (1980); films: "Lost Boundaries" (1949) to "Simon" (1980); over 5,000 TV shows; radio; recordings. Author six publ mysteries, "Games Murderers Play", "Deadhead", plus others. Chief Collabrs: David Baker, G Wood, Michael Barr, Dion McGregor. *Songs:* Christmas Eve; Cabin in the Woods; Nice Thing About Music; Lyrics: Come Away. *Scores:* Opera/Ballet: Twofer; SRO; Film/TV: Ev'ry Other Day; I Wouldn't Mind; A Little Love.

CARPENTER, CHARLES E　　ASCAP 1941
author, manager
b Chicago, Ill, Aug 22, 12; d. Educ: Hyde Park High Sch. Wrote special material for nightclub shows. Road mgr, Fletcher Henderson Orch; personal mgr, Earl Hines Orch, 41-42 & George Kirby. WW II, USAF; wrote & produced radio & stage shows. Co mgr, road show concerts for Nat King Cole, Duke Ellington, Ella Fitzgerald, Chubby Checker & Connie Francis. *Songs:* Bolero At the Savoy; You Taught Me to Love Again; Blue Because of You; Now You Know; When I Dream of You; Sweet Jenny Lou.

CARPENTER, ELLIOT J　　ASCAP 1955
composer, author, conductor
b Philadelphia, Pa, Dec 28, 1894. Educ: Temple Sch of Music; French Cons, studied with Fouchet, Decroux; Tadlewski Inst, Nice, France. Pianist, Jim Europe Orch, New York Syncopated Orch. Soloist, nightclubs & theatres, New York, London & Paris. Author, "Syncopation." Chief Collabr: Clarence Muse. *Songs:* No More Sleepy Time; The Little Things You Do; The Hills Are Mine.

CARPENTER, IMOGEN (JANE) ASCAP 1954
composer, pianist, singer
b Hot Springs, Ark, Feb 2, 18. Educ: Chicago Musical Col, studied with Moicsaye & Lillian Boguslawski; Guildhall Sch of Music, London; Pierce Col, studied with John Clark, Lois Caillet, Mary Jo Farr. Scholarship at Chicago Musical Col. Appeared in Bway shows incl, "Ziegfeld Follies" & "Mexican Hayride," & in many hotels & clubs, incl Essex House, Pierre Hotel & Savoy Plaza. Singer, pianist & lectr on Gershwin's music in mini "Gershwin Concerts." Chief Collabrs: Kim Gannon, Lenny Adelson, Billie Weber. *Songs:* If Winter Comes; Say So; Anytime Anywhere; Animals and Clowns; Young Guns.

CARPENTER, JOHN ALDEN ASCAP 1929
composer
b Park Ridge, Ill, Feb 28, 1876; d Chicago, Ill, Apr 27, 51. Educ: Hon MA, Harvard Univ; studied with John Knowles Paine. Amy Fay, Edward Elgar, Berhard Ziehn; hon MusD, Wis Univ & Northwestern Univ. Businessman, Chicago, to 36. Mem, Nat Inst Arts & Letters; award for distinguished services. *Songs:* Jazz Boys; Player Queen; The Home Road; Gitanjali (song cycle); Chinese Water Colours; Berceuse de Queue; Improving Songs for Anxious Children. When Little Boys Sing. *Instrumental Works:* Adventures in a Perambulator; Song of Faith (chorus, orch); Song of Freedom (chorus, orch); Two Symphonies; Violin Sonata; Violin Concerto; Concertino for Piano and Orchestra; String Quartet; Piano Quintet; Carmel Concerto; Seven Ages (suite); Patterns; Sea Drift (symph poem). *Scores:* Ballet: Krazy Kat; Skyscraper; The Birthday of the Infanta.

CARPENTER, JUANITA ROBINS (BEVERLY STYLES) ASCAP 1975
composer, author
b Richmond, Va, June 6, 23. Educ: Highland Springs High Sch, studied music & gymnastics; studied violin & viola with Henry Leisco & Frank Wendt; piano basics, chord structure & music writing with Ike Carpenter; NY Sch Modern Photography, photography, modeling, design; Am Nat Theatre & Acad, speech, projection, acting & stage presence; Master Plan Inst, dipl personal mgt, leadership & communications. Independent contractor, 47- Professional model, actress, photographer & advertiser, 6 yrs, also singer, dancer, 17 yrs & entertaining musician, 7 yrs; played violin, viola, piano & drums; vocalist, led own all-girl trio, 3 yrs, then solo. Was on radio, theater, nightclubs, dinner houses, yacht clubs & motel lounges incl Sheridan Inns, Holiday Inns & Hilton circuit. *Songs:* Joshua Tree; Music: I'm Thankful; The Perpetual Styles of Beverly; Lyrics: A Special Plan to Think Upon; The Truth, As Seen By a Composer. *Albums:* The Primitive Styles of Beverly.

CARPENTER, RICHARD LYNN ASCAP 1971
composer, arranger, singer
b New Haven, Conn, Oct 15, 46. Educ: Wilbur Cross High Sch, New Haven; Downey High Sch, Calif; Univ Calif, Long Beach; Yale Univ, music, Seymour Fink; Univ Southern Calif, music, Ronald Tarr. Piano player, Coke Corners, Disneyland; sweepstakes winner, Battle of the Bands, Hollywood Bowl; finalist winner, All Am Col Show, TV; two Whitehouse appearances, honorable mention in Congressional Record, 11 Grammy nominations, 3 awards, 66 Gold records, 8 platinum & 2 silver. Five TV specials & numerous guest appearances. Chief Collabr: John Bettis. *Songs:* All of My Life; Music: Someday; One Love; Top of the World; Goodbye to Love; Yesterday Once More; Only Yesterday; I Need to Be in Love; Merry Christmas Darling. *Instrumental Works:* Flat Baroque.

CARPENTER, STEPHEN LISBY ASCAP 1964
composer, singer
b Philadelphia, Pa, Jan 13, 43. Educ: West Catholic High Sch, dipl; studied guitar with Don Reed, 8 yrs. Singer, original material for var record cos. Songwriter for var artists. Chief Collabrs: Mildred Phillips, Ralph Gary Brauner, Vince Montana. *Songs:* Cookie Jar; Disco Fever; Am I Lost; It's Always Jill; No Way.

CARR, JOE (FINGERS)
See Bush, Louis F

CARR, LEON ASCAP 1945
composer, arranger, pianist
b Allentown, Pa, June 12, 10; d New York, NY, Mar 27, 76. Educ: Pa State Univ; NY Univ, studied Schillinger System. Wrote musicals at col; led own dance orch. To New York, 35; writer, special material for nightclubs & TV commercials incl "See the USA in your Chevrolet." Chief Collabrs: Earl Shuman, Leo Corday, Paul Vance. *Songs:* There's No Tomorrow; Your Socks Don't Match; Bell Bottom Blues; A Man Could Be a Wonderful Thing; Goblins in the Steeple; Gina; Big Name Button; If You Smile at the Sun; Skiddle-Diddle-Dee; Should I Wait?; Hey There, Lonely Boy; Our Everlasting Love; Another Cup of Coffee; Most People Get Married; Hotel Happiness; Clinging Vine; Marriage If for Old Folks; The Secret Life; Confidence; Film title songs: The Disorderly Orderly; Robinson Crusoe on Mars.

CARR, ROBERTA
See Feldner, Roberta Emily

CARR, SANDRA BEATRICE ASCAP 1973
composer, author
b St Louis, Mo. Educ: Calif State Univ, BA(government), 69; piano study, St Louis & pvt study, Buddy Harper, Southern Calif, 10 yrs. Background in classical piano. Had TV roles; dir choral groups. Has written 2 poetry bks. *Songs:* Baby, We Ought to Be Together; The Best of Me; Sketches of Home; Can't Deal With Nothing Else ('Cept Loving You); You Want to Dance This Number (Or Sit It Out)?.

CARRADINE, KEITH IAN
actor, singer
b San Mateo, Calif, Aug 8, 49. Educ: Colo State Univ, studied drama, 67. Appeared on Bway "Hair," Biltmore Theatre, 69-70; appeared in films "A Gunfight", "McCabe and Mrs Miller", "Emperor of the North", "Thieves Like Us", "Nashville", "The Duellists", "An Almost Perfect Affair", "Pretty Baby", "Welcome to Los Angeles" & "Old Boyfriends." Recording artist. Mem: Acad Motion Picture Arts & Sci & Green Peace Found. *Songs:* I'm Easy (Acad Award for Best Song of a Motion Picture, 75; Hollywood Foreign Press Asn Golden Globe Award for Best Song, 75).

CARRAS, NICHOLAS
See Carrastathis, Nicholas Sam

CARREAU, MARGARET ASCAP 1950
composer, organist, pianist
b Bedford, Pa, Jan 23, 1899. Educ: Pub schs; studied with Oliver Denton, Kate Chittenden. Rehearsal pianist for Irving Berlin, Hassard Short & Sam Harris; accompanist to John Charles Thomas. Chief Collabr: Frederick Martens. *Songs & Instrumental Works:* Thy Heart and the Sea; Comparison; Eventide; Query; Rapture; Sea Nocturne; Pastures of the Soul; You and I Together.

CARRELL, RUTH
See Dodd, Ruth Carrell

CARRETTA, JERRY ASCAP 1953
composer, pianist
b New York, NY. Educ: Studied with Tom Timothy & Richard Benda. Pianist & arr, Sammy Kaye Orch; pianist, Janis Paige; pianist-arr cond, Don Cornell; arr, Miss USA & Miss Universe. Recording artist, Coral, Decca. Pianist, Condominium Circuit, SE Fla, currently. Chief Collabrs: Carolyn Leigh, Larry Fotine, Al Neiburg, Carl Sigman. *Songs:* Music: Let's Have an Old Fashioned Christmas. *Instrumental Works:* Caprice; Music Box Clock; Piccadilly Pizzicato.

CARRISON, CLIFFORD THOMAS ASCAP 1971
composer, drummer, pianist
b Chicago, Ill, Sept 29, 46. Educ: High sch bands; Univ Ill. With var bands in Chicago area. Recording artist for var record cos incl London cos. Toured Europe, 8 yrs. Guitarist. *Songs:* Music: Gettin' High Again; Rusty Door; Nightshift; Where Have All Your Clothes Gone; Greenwich Meantime; Martin Flew In; Rockin', Rollin', Fallin' Down.

CARROLL, BARBARA
See Coppersmith, Barbara C

CARROLL, BOB
See Jones, Robert Carroll

CARROLL, CARROLL ASCAP 1950
author, columnist, critic
b New York, NY, Apr 11, 02. Educ: Hyde Park High Sch, Chicago. Humorist, Life, Judge, Saturday Evening Post & New Yorker. Bway revues, journalist, columnist for New York Sunday World. Advert, J Walter Thompson, Ward Wheelock Co. Radio writer for Burns & Allen, Paul Whiteman, Bing Crosby, Al Jolson. Columnist in Variety, "And Now a Word From...", 67- Ghost writer for Bob Hope, Ed McMahan, Liberace, Henny Youngman. Chief Collabrs: Dick Manning, Sy Miller, John Scott Trotter, Jerry Gray. *Songs:* Lyrics: You Are the One; Moonlight on a White Picket Fence; Baby Me; You Say the Nicest Things; Christmas is for Children; Learn to Pray Everyday; Why Woncha; Never Ask a Man if He's From Texas; Mish Mash Polka; Time Has Come to Bid You Adieu; I Met My Baby in Macy's; Keep Your Eye on the Doughnut; Tell Ya Momma.

CARROLL, EARL ASCAP 1914
composer, producer, director
b Pittsburgh, Pa, Sept 16, 1893; d Mt Carmel, Pa, June 17, 48. Staff writer, New York publ co, 12-17. Served in USAAF, WW I. Producer & dir Bway musicals, "Earl Carroll Vanities" (11 ed); "Earl Carroll Sketch Book" (2 ed); "Fioretta" (also librettist); "Murder at the Vanities" (also co-librettist). Built two Earl Carroll Threatres, New York, 23 & 31; also Earl Carroll Restaurant, Hollywood, 39. Produced films. Charter mem, ASCAP. *Songs:* Isle d'Amour; So Long, Letty; One Look At You; Dreams of Long Ago; Give Me All of You; While We Dance; Just the Way You Are; I Never Knew; Dreaming. *Scores:* Bway stage: So Long, Letty; Canary Cottage; The Love Mill (also librettist); Earl Carroll Vanities (23, 24).

CARROLL, HARRY ASCAP 1914
composer, pianist
b Atlantic City, NJ, Nov 28, 1892; d Santa Barbara, Calif, Dec 26, 62. Charter mem, ASCAP, dir, 14-17. Pianist, film theatres, cafes & vaudeville; arr for music publishers. Contract writer, Winter Garden productions; songwriter for "Ziefgeld Follies," 20 & 21 & "Greenwich Village Follies." Chief Collabs: Joseph McCarthy, Ballard Macdonald, Harold Atteridge, Al Bryan. *Songs:* I'm Always Chasing Rainbows; Trail of the Lonesome Pine; By the Beautiful Sea; I Take a Little Rain With the Sunshine; There's a Girl in the Heart of Maryland; The Land of My Best Girl; Tip Top Tipperary Mary; Smother Me With Kisses and Kill Me With Love; Down in Bom-Bom Bay; She Is the Sunshine of Virginia; On the Mississippi; Our Home Town; Wherever There's Music and Beautiful Girls; A Kiss for Cinderella; Roll on River Missouri. *Scores:* Bway shows: The Passing Show of 1914; Dancing Around; Maid in America; Oh, Look!; The Little Blue Devil.

CARROLL, JIMMY ASCAP 1957
composer, conductor, arranger
b New York, NY, Dec 13, 13; d Hollywood, Calif, Mar 18, 72. Educ: Univ Rochester Eastman Sch of Music, BM. Arr for var records cos, orchs incl Mitch Miller, Harry James, Vaughn Monroe & for Frankie Laine & Rosemary Clooney. USA Special Servies, World War II. Chief Collabs: Marshall Barer, Paul Parnes. *Songs:* Helen Polka; Set Sail; Happy Flying; Daddy's New Car; Speed the Parting Guest.

CARROLL, JUNE BETTY (JUNE SILLMAN) ASCAP 1952
composer, author, singer
b Detroit, Mich. Educ: Hollywood Sch for Girls. Wrote lyrics for "New Faces" revues, 34, 36, 40, 52, 56 & 69; also appeared as singer & comedienne in 52 version & motion picture. Sang on Jack Paar Tonight show; singer in Soho at the Ballroom, 78. Chief Collabs: Arthur Siegel, Kurt Weill, Baldwin Bergeson, Sanford Greene. *Songs:* Lyrics: Love Is a Simple Thing; Penny Candy; He Takes Me Off His Income Tax; Monotonous; I Want You to Be the First One to Know; Where Is Me? *Scores:* Movie: An Angel Comes to Brooklyn.

CARROLL, RICHARD
See McGowen, Frank S

CARSON, KEN ASCAP 1951
composer, author, singer
b Coalgate, Okla, Nov 14, 14. Educ: Primary grades, Coalgate, Okla; high sch, Los Angeles, Calif. Began radio broadcasting career in Hollywood & Chicago. Joined group, The Ranch Boys; TV show, 41. Joined The Sons of the Pioneers & Roy Rogers at Republic Pictures, 42; singer, Breakfast in Hollywood, 46; singing commercials, 46-50. Appeared in "It Happened One Night." Joined Garry Moore TV Show as featured singer, 50. Chief Collabs: Johnny Lange, Buddy Feyne, Tim Spencer, Bob Nolan, Henry Russell. *Songs:* The Wondrous Word of the Lord; I Can't Stop Loving You; I'm Gonna Throw Away All of My Yesterdays; How Can I Pretend (I'm Only a Friend); Believe Me When I Tell You; Teardrops On The Roses; My San Fernando Rose; The Great Oklahoma Land Rush (of 1889); May Heaven Forgive You; She's Gone, She's Gone; I'll Never Be Alone; If You Need Me; Two Tickets to Nashville; I'll Never Forget You; It's Never Too Late; If Jesus Came Today; I Want to Hear it From You; (I'm Livin' In) Dullsville, USA; Here You Come With Love; Everybody Loves Me (Everybody But You); Sweet and Tender; Fasten Your Seat Belts.

CARTER, BEN ASCAP 1968
composer, arranger, pianist
b Montclair, NJ, Feb 18, 37. Educ: Self-taught. Musical dir of var off-Bway shows, incl "Music Magic", "The Believers" & "Transcendental Blues." Vocal arr & recording artist. *Songs:* Rock Me Baby; Disco Man. *Scores:* Off Bway Shows: Bitter Trails; Spiritual Rock Incident; This Piece of Land; Malcomb; Journey Into Blackness; The Exodus; Ballad of Two People. *Albums:* The Believers; Roots; Scriptures of God; Scratch My Back; You Ain't No Friend of Mine.

CARTER, BENNETT LESTER (BENNY) ASCAP 1942
composer, conductor, saxophonist
b New York, NY, Aug 8, 07. Educ: Wilberforce Univ, studied theology. Saxophonist in Horace Henderson's Wilberforce Collegians; then played in orchs, incl Fletcher Henderson & Chick Webb. To Paris, 35, joined Willie Lewis orch. Staff arr, BBC, Eng. Formed own band in NY & Hollywood. Wrote for films; has made many records. Appeared in films, "The View From Pompey's Head" & "The Snows of Kilimanjaro." *Songs & Instrumental Works:* Blues in My Heart; Hot Toddy; Shoot the Works; Dream Lullaby; Everybody Shuffle; Take My Word; Blue Interlude; Because of You; When Lights Are Low; Night Falls; Devil's Holiday; Deep South Mood; Harlem Mood; Manhattan Mood; Cow Cow Boogie; Poor Fool; Kansas City Suite. *Scores:* TV Background: M Squad; Film Background: A Man Called Adam.

CARTER, CHARLES EDWARD
composer, arranger, teacher
b Ponca City, Okla, July 10, 26. Educ: Ohio State Univ, BM; Eastman Sch Music, MM, studied with Bernard Rogers & Wayne Barlow. Arr for marching band & taught lower brass, Ohio State Univ; arr for numerous univ marching bands; staff arr, Florida State Univ, 53- *Instrumental Works:* Bold City Overture; Chorale and Variations; Overture for Winds; Rhapsodic Episode; Sonata for Winds; Symphonic Overture.

CARTER, EVERETT ASCAP 1943
composer, author
b New York, NY, Apr 28, 19. Educ: Univ Calif, Los Angeles, BA, MA, PhD. Lyric writer, Universal Pictures, 41-49; writer of lyrics, scores & special material for short subjects, westerns & musicals. Chief Collabr: Milton Rosen. *Songs:* A Dream Ago; So Good Night; Just a Step Away From Heaven; I'm Old Enough to Dream; Nice to Know You.

CARTER, HAYWARD HAYES ASCAP 1975
composer, author, singer
b Hahira, Ga, Oct 11, 47. Educ: Colonial High Sch; Miss State Univ, indust eng; Midland Technol Col, indust mgt; Ctr for Degree Studies Elec Eng Technol, personnel mgt cert & drafting cert. On TV, nightclubs & "Jerry Lewis Telethon for Truck Stops of America"; recording artist, Scorpion Records & White Oak Records. Chief Collabr: Lathan Hudson. *Songs:* Are You Leading Me On; A Helping Hand; The Old Man in the Rain; Who Started the Loving; That's Not a Cowboy's Way.

CARTER, JAN- BROBERG ASCAP 1977
composer, author, teacher
b Provo, Utah, Dec 23, 51. Educ: Study abroad, 14 countries, 73; studied with Merrill Bradshaw, 70 & with Newell B Weight, 6 months; Dartmouth Col, cert; Univ Utah, BA, 79. Professional musician, 67- Began with Norman Kame's Young Ambassador's as vocalist, soloist, Las Vegas, 67. With Symph Vocal Ens, 71-77 & Sunset Mag, Los Angeles, 75. Singer, Mormon Tabernacle choir, 72-73; vocal coach, Betty J Chipman, 72-74. Film critic & journalist, Utah Daily Chronicle, Great Salt Lake Newspaper, The Dartmouth & The Entertainer, 74- Pub, "101 Ideas for the Bicentennial," with Joyce Evans, Utah, 76. Commercial writer, TV & radio, Los Angeles, 77-78. Chief Collabs: Oleg Lopatin, Norman Kaye, Joyce Evans, Marie Myer. *Songs:* Song for Arbie (secular); Just for You (secular); Alleluia! (sacred); Yesterdays and Yesteryears (secular); Music: For the Children (vocal, instrumental); Calif Adv Council (milk commercial). *Songs & Instrumental Works:* I'm a Yankee Doodle Dandy (arr); Fugue in D Minor (classical); Christ Was Born in a Lowly Stable (instrumental arr; vocal SSAATTBB; sacred).

CARTER, JOHN ASCAP 1972
author, actor, film director
b Center Ridge, Ark, Nov 26, 27. Educ: Univ Mo, BA; Lehman Engels Musical Writing Workshop. Actor in Bway productions, "No Strings", "110 in the Shade", "The Lovers" & "Tamburlaine"; co-star in TV series "Barnaby Jones"; guest star on numerous TV shows, incl "Roots, Part II"; dir, episodic TV & Los Angeles area stage productions. Chief Collabs: Kerry Chater, Jack Keller. *Songs:* Lyrics: Good Morning, Love; Here Comes the Rain.

CARTER, JOHN WALLACE ASCAP 1969
composer, woodwinds performer
b Ft Worth, Tex, Sept 24, 29. Educ: Lincoln Univ, BA; Univ Colo, MA; grad study, Univ Tex, Denton & Calif State Univ, Los Angeles. High sch band dir, Ft Worth, 50-61; instrumental music instr, Los Angeles City Schs, 61- Gave extensive performances, US; recording artist in US & Europe; toured throughout Europe, incl most maj jazz fests. Chief Collabs: Bobby Bradford, James Newton. *Albums:* Seeking; Flight for Four; Self Determination Music; Echoes From Rudolph's; Variations.

CARTER, RAY (MAURICE KRUMBEIN) ASCAP 1946
composer, author, conductor
b Chicago, Ill, Nov 24, 08. Educ: DePaul Univ; Chicago Musical Col; studied with Maurice Rosenthal & Leon Benditsky. Cond, arr, pianist & writer for radio, TV & children's records. Chief Collabs: Lucile Johnson (wife), Paul Tripp. *Songs:* I'm in a Lazy Mood; Troubadour's Serenade; The Song I Sing; Woodland Reverie; Freedom Road; Dance of the Bobby Sox Doll; Calling Winds; Sagebrush Serenade; Cara Cara, Bella Bella; All Right, Louis, Drop the Gun; Little Mr Big; Billy on a Bike; The Cuckoo Who Lived in a Clock; Merry-Go-Round; Little Switch Engine. *Albums:* Songs From Birthday House.

CARTER, WILLIAM R ASCAP 1954
composer, author
b Philadelphia, Pa, May 2, 08; d Philadelphia, Mar 14, 76. Educ: Temple Univ Sch Music. Organist in silent film theatres; pianist in small bands; soloist in nightclubs, radio & TV. Made many records. *Songs:* Wanderin' Road; Lady in the Rain; Crystal Polka; Come Back to Me; Savannah Beauty; Lost Lady; Lucie Waltz; Fly Away Polka; John Three Sixteen.

CARUSO, ANTHONY
composer, teacher
b Italy, Dec 22, 1889; d Chester, Pa, July 29, 73. To US, 05. Played as a solo clarinetist with The Royal Italian Band. Founded the Caruso Music Store, 21. Had own dance band, 30's & 40's. Performed many broadcasts, WCAU & WIP, Philadelphia. Chief Collabr: Al Alberts. *Songs:* Music: Be Still My Heart. *Instrumental Works:* United States March.

CARVALHO, URBAN FARRINGTON ASCAP 1973
composer
b Hilo, Hawaii, July 26, 39. Educ: Hilo High Sch; USN Sch Music; St Leo Col. Joined Navy, 57; served as musician in Navy Bands, Kodiak, Alaska & Pearl Harbor, Hawaii. Played clarinet & saxophone, head arr, USN Band, Washington, DC. Instr, Armed Forces Sch Music. Master chief musician, USN, 72- Now at Naval Educ & Training Prog Develop Ctr, Pensacola, Fla. *Instrumental Works:* Song and Dance (alto saxophone solo); Fanfare and Festival (band); Banuelos (concert march, band); Three Pictures (band).

CARVER, GILMAN MARSTON ASCAP 1975
composer, singer, musician
b Los Angeles, Calif, Apr 5, 52. Educ: Newport Harbor High Sch; studied music, Univ Calif, Irvine, 3 yrs. With Dick Dale & The Deltones, Las Vegas & Lake Tahoe, 3 yrs; as solo & with groups. *Songs:* Get Back the Feelin'.

CASALS, PABLO ASCAP 1962
composer, conductor, cellist
b Vendrell, Spain, Dec 29, 1876; d 1973. Educ: Studied music with father, also with Jose Garcia & Jose Rodoreda; Barcelona Municipal Sch of Music, studied with Tomas Breton & Jesus de Monasterio. Cellist, Madrid, also with Paris Opera, 1895. Taught at Paris Cons, 1897; led string quartet. Gave concerts throughout western Europe & London, 1898, throughout US, 01-04 & 14-17, SAm, 03. Cond, Orquestra Pau Casals, Barcelona, 19. Mem, Cortot-Thibaud-Casals Trio. Dir, Prades Music Fest, France, 50-53; also Perpignan. Dir, San Juan Music Fest, PR; performer-in-residence, Marlboro Music Fest, NH. Biographies: "Pablo Casals" by L Littlehales & "Conversations with Casals" by J M Corredor. *Instrumental Works:* La Sardana (cello); La Vision de Fray Martin (choral); El Pessebre (oratorio); Poems of the Manger; transc of Bach unaccompanied suites for cello.

CASANOVA, FELIPE ASCAP 1944
composer, author, publisher
b Mayaguez, PR, Mar 9, 1898. Educ: Studied music with father. Music publ, PR. *Songs:* Volveras Otra Vez; Te Quise y Te Quiero; Me Dijiste; Ilusiones.

CASCARINO, ROMEO ASCAP 1958
composer
b Philadelphia, Pa, Sept 28, 22. Educ: Philadelphia Cons of Music, BMus, studied with Paul Nordoff; hon DMus, Combs Col of Music, 60. Orchestration & chief arr, Armed Forces Special Services Orch, NBC & CBS, World War II. Commercial arr, 47-63. Cond & music dir, co-opera co, 50-57; recording artist. Recipient, Guggenheim fels in comp, 48 & 49 & Benjamin award for tranquil music, 60. *Songs:* Music: Eight Songs. *Instrumental Works:* Sonata for Bassoon and Piano; Acadian Land. *Scores:* Ballet: Pygmalion; Opera: William Penn.

CASE, JUSTIN
See Hammett, Paul Dean

CASE, RUSSELL D ASCAP 1957
composer, conductor, arranger
b Hamburg, Iowa, Mar 19, 12; d Miami, Fla, Oct 10, 64. Educ: High sch. Free-lance arr & trumpeter, 27-45. Cond, arr for radio, TV & recordings, 45-64. *Instrumental Works:* Midnight Oil; Sliphorn Sam; La Valse; Frantic Fiddles; Gambler's Ballet; Little Genius Ballet; Gabriel's Heater. *Scores:* TV Background: Pulitzer Prize Playhouse.

CASEY, CLAUDE ASCAP 1951
composer, author, singer
b Enoree, SC, Sept 13, 12. Educ: Pub schs, SC & Va. In radio for 42 yrs. Started at WMTM, Danville, Va, 38. First big break Maj Bowes Amateur Hour, toured with units. On WBT & CBS Radio, Charlotte, NC for 12 yrs. Singer & entertainer night clubs & TV; recording artist on Victor & MGM. Appeared in 11 movies, latest being "Buster and Billie." With WGAC Radio, Augusta, Ga, 51; with WFBC Radio & TV, Greenville, SC, 53, plus guest appearances on WSM Grand Ole Opry. Pres, WJES Radio, Johnston, SC, presently. Chief Collabr: Mel Foree. *Songs:* Long Lonesome Road; Look in the Looking Glass (At You); Hillbilly Gal; Journey's End; Days are Long, Nights are Lonely; Carolina Waltz; Yodeling Blues; Juke Box Gal; Down with Gin.

CASEY, KENNETH, SR ASCAP 1939
composer, conductor, publisher
b New York, NY, Jan 10, 1899; d Newburgh, NY, Aug 10, 65. Educ: Marquand Prep; NY Univ; studied piano with Vincent Lopez. Child actor in silent films; organized own band; cond on radio & records; pres publ & theatrical production cos. USN Commendation for work on radio show, "Winnie the Wave." Wrote stage scores & spec material. Chief Collabrs: Kenneth Sisson, Ben Bernie, Maceo Pinkard, George Briegel. *Songs:* Wide Open Spaces; Sweet Georgia Brown; Sincerely Yours; Craving; Gotta Hit That Texas Trail; You'll Find a Bit of Gay Paree in Dear Old Montreal; I Won't Be Ridin' No More; Tall Cedars Are Calling Me; Two Gun Gertie; The President Eisenhower March; Wings in Flight (for Stewart AFB); Give, Give, Give (for Community Chest Drive).

CASEY, WARREN ASCAP 1972
composer, author
b New York, NY, Apr 20, 35. Educ: Syracuse Univ, BFA, 57. Chief Collabr: Jim Jacobs. *Scores:* Bway show: Grease.

CASEY, WESLEY EUGENE ASCAP 1961
composer, conductor, arranger
b Ft Sill, Okla, Jan 16, 33. Educ: NTex State Col, BM. Writer, revues & nightclub acts. Music dir, summer stock & off-Bway shows. *Songs:* The Night Was Made for Lovers. *Scores:* Stage show: The Magic Weave.

CASHMAN, TERRY
See Minogue, Dennis Michael

CASON, JAMES E (BUZZ) ASCAP 1970
composer
b Nashville, Tenn, Nov 27, 39. Began career in Brenda Lee's backup band, The Casuals; later sang solo under name, Gary Miles, with hit, "Look for a Star." Then began writing songs; moved to Los Angeles; co-producer & hit for The Crickets; then returned to Nashville; songwriter. Formed a publ co with Bobby Russell; built a recording studio, Creative Workshop; then formed Angel Wing Music Publ Co. Chief Collabrs: Mac Gayden, Freddy Weller, Dan Penn, Bobby Russell, Leon Russell, Bucky Wilkin. *Songs:* Popsicle; La Bamba; Sandy; Ann, Don't Go Runnin'; Emmylou; Fantasy Island; Another Woman; Lost in Austin; Million Old Goodbyes; Go for the Night; Everlasting Love.

CASSEL, IRWIN M ASCAP 1934
author
b New York, NY, Oct 14, 1886; d Miami Beach, Fla, July 22, 71. Chief Collabr: Mana-Zucca (wife). *Songs:* I Love Life; In Loveland; Peace At Last; Romany Gypsy; There's a Joy in My Heart; Fluttering Birds; also In Bibleland (12 songs).

CASSEL, MARWIN S
composer
b New York, NY, July 4, 25. Educ: Univ Fla, JD.

CASSETT, BOYD ASCAP 1969
composer, author
b Rochester, Minn, Feb 15, 11. Educ: Mankato High Sch, Minn; Cincinnati Bible Sem; Int Correspondence Schs. Writer poetry & song lyrics, 29-; writer words & music for hymns & gospel songs, 63- Secy, Christian men's groups, Ohio, Ind & Ky, 60's. Writer off theme songs, Nat Missionary Conventions of the Churches of Christ & Christian Churches, 68-72 & Eastern Christian Convention, 73. Awards: Best Poem of the Month, Minneapolis Sunday Journal, Aug, 31 & Sept, 32; 1st Place in lyric-writing contest, Minn-Iowa-Dak Christian Conference, 33; hon mention for melody, Song of the Yr Contest, Songwriters Review Magazine, 77. Chief Collabrs: Cora (Vawter) Cassett, Carl Dobkins, Sr, Clarence D Hawkins, David J London, David T London, Prue O Mason, Ken Read, Leonard G Reid, Thurman H Smith, Charles Spargur, Florence E Trento, Stephen A Winch. *Songs:* Little Barb'ra Faye; The Fold; Somewhere Beyond; Train to Glory; Chapel in the Sky; Prince of the Kingdom; You Died That We Might Live; Amen; I Broke Bread With Christ; Saving Power; Guardian Angel; Christian; A Little Child; Nothing Is Too Hard; Commissioned and Committed; His Mission—Our Mission; Fill the Earth; Your Will Be Done; Church of Christ; Translated; Preach the Word; Unmerited Favor; The Bible; Music: Get Down Upon Your Knees; Send a Pair of Angels; I'd Rather Be.

CASSEUS, FRANTZ GABRIEL ASCAP 1957
composer, author, arranger
b Port-Au-Prince, Haiti, Dec 14, 21. Educ: Self-taught. To New York, 56; concertized in Town Hall, Carnegie Hall, Cooper Union, plus others; on TV as classical guitarist & accompanist for Harry Belafonte; arr, wrote songs & perf as guitarist on Belafonte Albums; did 2 Folkway Albums of original material; arr & compiled 7 vols of classical guitar music. *Songs:* Ballet, Haitian suite: Petro; Yanvalloux; Mascavon; Coumkite; Haitianesques: Such a Lovely Morning; Girl In the Woods; Assoto (congo); Danse of the Hounsies (congo).

CASSEY, CHARLES R ASCAP 1961
composer, conductor, arranger
b Chicago, Ill, July 22, 33. Educ: Univ Ill, BS, MS. Asst cond, USA Chorus, 55-57. Arr & singer, "Hit Parade." Vocal dir, comp & arr, "Garry Moore Show," 58-59, "Holiday on Ice," 60; also film & TV background scores.

CASSIDY, DAVID BRUCE ASCAP 1970
composer, author, singer
b New York, NY, Apr 12, 50. Actor & singer, Bway show "Fig Leaves." Comp of special material, singer & actor, TV series "Partridge Family," 70. Recording artist with solo albums. Co-comp, theme song for TV series "David Cassidy-Man Undercover," 79. Chief Collabrs: Kim Carnes, Dave Ellingson, Gerry Beckley, Richie Furay. *Songs:* Cruise to Harlem; Hard Times; Gettin' It in the Street. *Albums:* Two Time Loser; Can't Go Home Again.

CASSIDY, DONALD RAYMOND   ASCAP 1978
composer
b South Hero, Vt, Oct 9, 34. Educ: Studied voice & comp with Mrs Swenson; took singing lessons. Writer of lyrics. Chief Collabrs: Lindsey McPhail, Gene Mattoon, Archie Swindell. *Songs:* Lyrics: My Party Doll; Beautiful Love; The Girl That I Love; All I Want From This Old World; O Holy Spirit; My Guiding Angel; Saint Michael.

CASSIDY, SHAUN
singer, actor
b Beverly Hills, Calif, Sept 27, 58. Recording artist, 75-; appeared in starring role, TV series, "The Hardy Boys' Mysteries," 76-78. TV movies incl "Like Normal People," 79; recordings incl three gold & platinum records & three gold singles. Mem: Screen Actors Guild; Am Fedn of TV & Radio Artists; Am Fedn Musicians.

CASSIN, JAMES JOSEPH, JR   ASCAP 1976
composer
b St Louis, Mo, Nov 2, 26. Educ: Normandy High Sch, Mo; studied Cathedral Latin-Gregorian chant. Songwriter, 50- *Songs:* Goodbye Papa; Down in the Tavern; Santa's on His Way; The Peeler; If You Love Me Let Me Know Today. *Scores:* TV: Makin' Little Ones Out of Big Ones.

CASSINARI, JOHN   ASCAP 1963
composer, musician
b New York, NY, Aug 14, 20. Educ: Pvt music study. Musician, radio, TV & nightclubs. Chief Collabrs: Joe Maize, Milton Gabler. *Songs:* Catamaran.

CASSONE, MICHAEL, JR (MIKE MICHAELS)   ASCAP 1967
composer, singer
b Brooklyn, NY, Sept 22, 38. Educ: Kingsboro Col, Brooklyn, NY. Songwriter, 67-; work recorded by var artists. Singer, country & western music at clubs & Coney Island Hospital. Coproducer, film "The Good Old Days"; writer, biography of Mike Cassone, Sr. Chief Collabrs: Don Cornell, Louie Prima. *Songs:* In Time; Angela; I Must Be Dreaming; Should You Forsake Me; Don't Say Goodbye; The Wise Man; Bravo; Forever in Your Heart; Lady Blue; Here 'till the End of Time; What's to Become of Me.

CASSTEVENS, MARK   ASCAP 1976
composer
b Ft Worth, Tex, Aug 9, 49. Educ: Univ Tex, Austin, BA. Studio musician, Nashville.

CASTALDO, JOSEPH F   ASCAP 1963
composer, educator, lecturer
b New York, NY, Dec 23, 27. Educ: Philadelphia Cons, MB, MM. Taught at Art Ctr, jr high sch, Phiadelphia Cons & adult sch. Chmn, comp & theory dept, Philadelphia Musical Acad. Also chmn, Philadelphia Composer's Forum; Eastern div, Am Music for Music Teachers Nat Asn. *Songs & Instrumental Works:* Sonatina for Piano; Toccata for Piano; At Her Feet (chorus).

CASTELLUCCI, LOUIS STANISLAUS
composer, trombonist, teacher
b Italy, Oct 26, 1897. Educ: Band training with bandmasters, Italy. Mem, John Philip Sousa Band; toured with Chatauqua Circuit; played in score first talkie movie, "Jazz Singer"; played in movie scores for Dimitri Tiomkin, Alfred Newman, Max Steiner, Victor Young & Miklos Roscza. Played radio & TV broadcasts "Dragnet" series. Cond, Los Angeles County Band; cond band albums, Capitol Records. Chief Collabrs: Wolfe E Gilbert, Robert MacKimsey. *Songs:* Music: Goia Mia. *Instrumental Works:* Minute Marches for Band; Control Booth March; US and You March; Stand By March; Television March; Canta Surriento. *Albums:* Here Comes the Band; A Festival of Symphonic Band Music.

CASTELLUCCI, STELLA   ASCAP 1960
composer, author, harpist
b Los Angeles, Calif, Oct 14, 30. Educ: Manual Arts High Sch, Los Angeles; St Cecilia Acad of Music, Rome, MA; studied harp with Alfred Kastner, Vienna. Harpist on radio; with jazz quintet backing Peggy Lee in var nightclubs throughout US, 8 yrs. Arr standard & contemporary songs & ballads; scores var movies. Recording artist for Motown, A&M, Capitol, RCA, Columbia & Warner Brothers Records. Co-authored textbk, "Rhythm for Harp." Chief Collabr: Peggy Lee. *Songs:* Music: Christmas Riddle. *Songs & Instrumental Works:* Arr for harp solo: Evergreen; If; As Time Goes By; Yesterdays; Watch What Happens; But Not For Me; Someone to Watch Over Me; The Look of Love.

CASTELNUOVO-TEDESCO, MARIO   ASCAP 1940
composer, teacher
b Florence, Italy, Apr 3, 1895; d Beverly Hills, Calif, Mar 16, 68. Educ: Cherubini Royal Inst of Music, studied with Ildebrando Pizzetti, Edgardo del Valle de Paz. To US, 39, citizen, 46. Taught many composers. *Instrumental Works:* The Lark (violin, piano); The Prophets; Poem (violin, orch); An American Rhapsody; Variazioni sinfoniche (violin, orch); Liverty, Mother of Exiles; Coplas (voice, orch); Le Danze del Re David (piano); Cipressi (piano);

Concertos: Concerto Italiano (violin); Concerto for Piano; Symphonic Variations (violin); The Prophets (violin); Concerto in D (guitar); Third Concerto for Violin; Capriccio Diabolico (guitar); Concerto da Camera (oboe, strings); Concerto for Two Guitars and Orchestra; Concertino for Harp and Chamber Orchestra; Sonatas: Sonata for Cello and Harp; Sonata for Violin and Viola; Sonata for Clarinet and Piano; Sonata for Bassoon and Piano; Sonata for Viola and Cello; String Trio for Violin , Viola and Cello; Sonata for Violin and Cello; Guitar: 24 Capricios de Goya; Les Guitares bien temperees (24 preludes & fugues for 2 guitars); Platero and I; Quintet for Guitar Strings; Homage to Boccherini (sonata); Piano: Alghe; Two Piano Concertos; Alt Wien; Oratorios: Ruth; Jonah; Overtures: The Taming of the Shrew; Twelfth Night; The Merchant of Venice; Julius Caesar; A Midsummer Night's Dream; Coriolanus; Much Ado About Nothing. *Scores:* Operas: La Mandragola (Nat prize, Venice); Il Bacco in Toscana; Savonarola; I Giganti del Montagna; Aucassin et Nicolette; Il Mercante di Venezia; The Importance of Being Ernest; Ballets: The Birthday of the Infanta; The Octoroon Ball.

CASTILLO, EMILIO   ASCAP 1970
composer, singer, musician
b Detroit, Mich, Sept 24, 50. Educ: Pvt teachers. Band leader, Tower of Power, 12 yrs; record producer. Chief Collabr: Stephan Kupka. *Songs:* You're Still a Young Man; Sparkling in the Sand; This Time It's Real; Down to the Nite Club; What Is Hip; So Very Hard to Go; You Ought to Be Having Fun; Below Us All the City Lights.

CASTILLO, MARVIN P(AUL)
composer, singer
b Breckenridge, Mich, July 27, 36. Educ: Emery High Sch; Peralta Jr Col; Chabot Col. Singer, nightclubs. *Songs:* Love Me No More; Sing Me a Love Song; Still a Fool.

CASTLE, IRENE
See Murrell, Irene Janet

CASTLE, NICHOLAS (NICK)   ASCAP 1951
composer, author, choreographer
b Brooklyn, NY, Mar 21, 10; d. Educ: Pub sch. In vaudeville, 27. Choreographer for film studios, & nightclub acts; staged TV shows. Chief Collabrs: Sidney Clare, Jule Styne, Dudley Brooks, Eddie Beal. *Songs:* Limpy Dimp; Candy Store Blues; Chula Chihuahua; Relax; Ginger!.

CASTRO, ARMANDO   ASCAP 1948
composer, conductor
b Naguabo, PR, Apr 13, 04; d New York, NY, Oct 6, 61. Educ: Univ of PR. Orch leader; made many records. *Songs:* Cu-Tu-Gu-Ru (Jack, Jack, Jack); Mary Ann; Cose, Cose, Cose; El Papylon; Take Me, Take Me; Escambao.

CASWELL, OSCAR CHARLES   ASCAP 1953
composer, author, conductor
b Austria, Apr 3, 13. Educ: BA(philosophy); MA(economics). Comp, ABC & var films. Instr economics, Univ Southern Calif; asst prof economics, music lectr, Los Angeles State Col.

CATCHAPAW, DOROTHY DEANE JOHNSON   ASCAP 1965
composer, author
b Richmond, Vt, Mar 31, 12. Educ: Richmond High Sch, grad, 31; self-taught piano & comp; Univ Extension Cons, lessons in Normal piano & harmony. Started writing lyrics, 43 & comp, 47. Songs recorded on records & albums. Sings in choir. Teaches basic piano. Chief Collabrs: Ruth Camp, Frank J Albright, Dorothy Hossington, Hubert M Faurear, Jimmy Johnson, Will Goldberg, Willie Ashbury, Mar L Miller, Harley Fletcher, Janice Dunster, Samuel J Keller, Walter Edward Burnham, Ernest LaCour, Ester Day, Iva Moriall, Bill Kearney. *Songs:* I Have a Song; My Dear Green Mountain Home; What I Want for Christmas; Closing Hours; Give Us Lord the Faith of Daniel; My Dear Green Mountain Sweetheart; Mother's Violin; Duxbury Days of Yore; Frisky the Frisky Calf; That Silly Song of a Silly Cat; Diamonds in the Snow; Music: Blood on His Bible; Cancel All My Dreams; On Second Thought; With Open Arms of Mercy; When I Grow Up; Stockings in the Bathroom.

CATES, GEORGE   ASCAP 1951
composer, arranger, conductor
b New York, NY, Oct 19, 11. Educ: NY Univ, Joseph Schillinger. Arr & asst cond, Olsen & Johnson, "Hellzapoppin"; arr & saxophonist, Dick Stabile Orch, Henry Busse Orch & Russ Morgan Orch; west coast A&R, Coral Records; arr, Bing Crosby, Danny Kaye, Andrew Sisters, Teresa Brewer & others. Musical dir, "Lawrence Welk TV Show," 25 yrs. Chief Collabrs: Paul Francis Webster, Mort Greene, Irving Taylor, Mack David, Jack Elliot. *Songs:* Music: Fantastic That's You; My North Dakota Home; Champagne Time; Adios, Au Revoir, Auf Wiedersehen.

CATIZONE, JOSEPH   ASCAP 1961
composer, trumpeter, teacher
b Italy, Aug 18, 02; d Pittsburgh, Pa, Jan 20, 73. Educ: High sch. Trumpeter in theatres, radio, TV, ice shows & opera. Music teacher; taught trumpet, trombone, tuba, flute, clarinet & drums in sch bands. *Songs:* Green Acres.

Instrumental Works: Valvette for Trumpet and Piano (also trumpet trio, piano); Alcala (full band score); Bazaar Polka (accordian); Stamp Your Feet Polka (accordian); Trumpet & Piano: Jemez; Trumpeters Three; Alverado; Valse Sardo; Rod and Reel March; Wow-Wow Polka; Laddie McClure; Fun for Pepi; Forest Pines; Waltzing Cadet; Piano: Moon Crater Rock; Easter Time; Let's Fly to the Moon; Ridin' Along Mandeville Trail; Zippy; Talking Grace Notes; Crystal; Little Admiral; Just a Hummin; Polar Bear Polka; March of the Drums; Tune for Two Hands.

CATLETT, JOSEPH THOMAS, JR   ASCAP 1976
composer
b Philadelphia, Pa, Jan 11, 53. Educ: Neupauer Cons Sch Music, dipl, studied with Jacob Neupauer & William Schimmel. Musician, TV & nightclubs, also behind Harold Melvin, The Blue Notes, Delphonics, Teddy Pendergrass & William De Vaughn. Comp, background music for radio show "KMAX FM," Los Angeles, also for groups Ebb Tide, Philadelphia & Xmas Belles, Calif, has written spirituals for The Chapel Recording Co, Wollaston, Mass. Cert Award, Recording Inst Am, New York; Mem Award, Audio Eng Soc New York; Lyrics Award, Chapel Recording Co, 76. *Songs:* The Love Light; The Spirit for Joy; Oh Lord You've Heard Me; Bittersweetness; The Wonderer; Remnance; Tapestry; Just for a Moment; Blue Velvet; Music: Spirit II; Lyrics: Sweet Joy in the Rain; The Love of a Dream; The World Inside; The Freedom Express.

CATRON, JOHN H   ASCAP 1963
composer, author
b Henryetta, Okla, Sept 24, 16. Educ: Okla Col Music. Big band leader, 39- Own show, KFI-NBC, Los Angeles; had off band for Los Angeles County Fair, 7 yrs. Had house band Glendora, Timbers Ballroom, Glendora, Calif, 63- Toured country several times. Made records for Nortac Records. *Songs:* Valarie; There's a Time and a Place for Everything; Love Day; A Little Affection; This Old Place; I'll Take Los Angeles; Somewhere West of Laramie; What Can I Do With a Broken Heart?; How Can She Tell Him?; Simplicity; Why Did I Let Christmas Get Away From Me?.

CATSOS, NICHOLAS A (GARY ROMERO)   ASCAP 1954
composer, author
b New York, NY, Aug 14, 12. Educ: Studied Schillinger Syst. Record producer, vocal coach, prof mgr music firms & talent mgr. Chief Collabrs: Paula Frances, Lee Russell, Joseph D D'Agostino, Nat King Cole, Joseph Meyer, Ray Rivera, Dickson Hall & A P Carter. *Songs:* My True Carrie, Love; I Will Pray; Christmas Roses; You Ain't Got Faith (Till You Got Religion); Healing Hands; Lulubelle; Buzzie, The Bumble-Bee; Keep on the Sunny Side; Lonesome World; Blue Nocturne; You Are the Love for Me; Fifty Miles from Hartford Town; The Little Big Horn; On the Texas Side (Of the Rio Grande); Lyrics: Wildflower; Living in the Shadow of the Past; The Best of Men Lose Sometime. *Albums:* Healing Hands; Folk Songs and Legends of Great American Rivers; Songs and Stories of The Gold Rush; Abe, The Rail Splitter.

CATTS, FRANCES AUSTIN   ASCAP 1964
composer, author, pianist
b Atlanta, Ga, May 2, 14. Educ: Washington Sem High Sch, studied creative writing with J N Haddock, piano with Valeska Fuente, comp with Dr John Corina. Feature writer, Atlanta Journal Mag & woman's dept, The Atlanta Constitution. Comp, piano music; author, song lyrics. *Songs:* The Moon and I; Quilting Bee; Musical Adventure (A Story in Piano Music and Songs); Indian Warrior (piano). *Instrumental Works:* Hot Dogs and Chili.

CAULFIELD, SANDRA LEE   ASCAP 1978
composer
b Bismarck, NDak, Oct 18, 54. Educ: Lawrence Cent High Sch, music & art; Ind Univ, Bloomington, music degree (voice), jazz with David Baker & voice with Eileen Farrel. Started as professional singer at age 16, in local clubs, Indianapolis & throughout col. At age 19 performed first commercial, then continued in jingles such as United Airlines, Schlitz Malt Liquor, Nationwide Insurance & Juicy Fruit Gum. Has been in var bands; now touring US with Tantrum band as co-writer & singer. Chief Collabrs: Ray Sapko, Pam Bradley, Barb Erber, Bill Syniar, Phil Balsano, Vern Wennerstrom. *Songs:* Lyrics: How Long; Runnin'; Applaud the Winner; Night on Main Street; Listen; You Came to Me.

CAVALIERE, FELIX A   ASCAP 1968
composer, singer, producer
b New York, NY, Nov 29, 42. Educ: Allaire Sch of Music; Pelham High Sch; Syracuse Univ; studied with Hall Overton, New York. With Joey Dee & Starliters, 63-65, Rascals, 65-70. Soloist & producer, 70-80. Chief Collabr: Edward Brigati Jr. *Songs:* Music: Groovin; People Got to Be Free; How Can I Be Sure; A Beautiful Morning; A Girl Like You.

CAVALLARO, CARMEN   ASCAP 1957
composer, pianist
b New York, NY, May 6, 13. Pianist with var dance orchs incl Rudy Vallee; formed own orch. Soloist in films, TV & nightclubs. Pianist for film, "The Eddy Duchin Story." Recording artist. *Songs & Instrumental Works:* While the Nightwind Sings; Masquerade Waltz.

CAVALLI, TONY
composer, author
b Ripi, Italy, Dec 4, 37. Educ: Nunzio Sch Music. Mem, Talent Workshop Inc; Town Hall recital; perf, local clubs & TV. Chief Collabrs: Teresa Tart, Joe Pennypacker. *Songs:* On the Beach of Portofino; On Via Veneto; Tropical Splendor; Lyrics: Motorcycle Man; Until the Honeymoon; House of Light.

CAVANAUGH, JAMES   ASCAP 1933
author
b New York, NY; d New York, Aug 18, 67. Educ: Pub schs. Wrote own vaudeville material. Chief Collabrs: John Redmond, Nat Simon, Frank Weldon, Vincent Rose, Larry Stock, Dick Robertson, Harry Barris. *Songs:* Mississippi Mud; I Like Mountain Music; You're in My Power; The Horse With the Lavender Eyes; The Umbrella Man; The Gaucho Serenade; Crosstown; Whistling in the Wildwood; The Man With the Mandolin; You're Breaking My Heart All Over Again; I Came, I Saw, I Conga'd; A Little on the Lonely Side; I'd Do It All Over Again; You're Nobody 'til Somebody Loves You; On a Simmery Summery Day; Dearest Darling; Christmas in Killarney.

CAVANAUGH, PAGE   ASCAP 1959
composer, singer, pianist
b Cherokee, Kans, Jan 26, 22. Educ: West Mineral High Sch. Pianist with Bobby Sherwood Orch, 42. WW II, USA. Formed & led own trio, 43-60. Signed with RCA Victor, 46. Has done movies & made many recordings. Chief Collabrs: Jack Smalley, Michael E Cavanaugh, Dan Ferrone. *Songs:* Music: Here I Am; Lazy Lover; Special Date; I'm Hip Daddy-Bird. *Songs & Instrumental Works:* Slim Jim; Swingin' Saints; Downtown Cherokee 1929; Shy Guy; Whatever Became of Me; Don't I Wish; Merry Merry Christmas Baby; The Christmas Tree.

CAVANAUGH, ROBERT BARNES (BOSBY BARNES)   ASCAP 1948
composer, author, teacher
b New York, NY, Oct 3, 02. Educ: Pub schs. Banjoist, vaudeville, 22, then guitarist & pianist. With popular orch, played hotels & toured vaudeville. Entertained with USO, World War II. Chief Collabrs: Redd Evans, Lewis Bellin, Ben Martini, Jim Morehead, Arthur Richardson, Harry Stride, Rusty Ferguson, Bert Douglas. *Songs:* You Should Have Told Me; Seven So Is My Love for You; I'm BA OO BA; Midnight Waltz; Long As the One I Love Still Loves Me; Sentimental Gypsy; Greens and Grits; One Night in County Clare; Any Old Town; Who Told You; If You Care for Me; Back Stage Door; Bass Slappin' Pappa; Toy Piano Polka; Meet Me In Hawaii; When You Gotta Go You Gotta Go; I'm Just a Fool; You Are My Love.

CAVANAUGH, THOMAS MARTIN   ASCAP 1975
composer
b Pittsburgh, Pa, June 20, 46. Educ: High sch; IBM Sch. On radio WYMO & WYEP, Pittsburgh. Author & poet. *Songs:* In the Spring of Time; Today; Look for Tomorrow; I Have Loved Too Little; The Silence of Night; Distant As the Wind; I Will Remember; Our Lord the King; When Today Is Gone; The Leaves of Summer.

CAVETT, MORGAN A   ASCAP 1971
composer, author, producer
b Los Angeles, Calif, Apr 26, 44. Educ: Hollywood High Sch; Los Angeles City Col; Univ Calif, Los Angeles; pvt piano study with Dave Robertson. Staff writer & producer, Johnny Mercer, 68-76; writer for group Steppenwolf, Yellow Payges, Power & East Side Kids; produced "Captain & Tennille", "Blues Image", "Vaughn Meader" & "Tret Fure." Chief Collabrs: John Kay, Mars Bonfire, Bernie Swartz, Loren Newkirk. *Songs:* Take a Look in the Mirror; Children Ask (If He Is Dead); She Is the Color Of; Lyrics: A Girl I Knew; The Nightimes for You; The Mood I'm In; Sleeping Minds; Time to Fly.

CAWLEY, ROBERT MASON
composer, author, pianist
b Columbus, Ohio, Jan 24, 25. Educ: Capital Col Music, studied with Frank Robert Mier; Greenbrier Col, BA; Ohio State Univ, BA(mass communication). Child actor in early motion pictures. Winner, Nat Piano Classical Championship, Chicago World's Fair, age 9. Worked maj hotels & clubs with own orch, then trio. Later formed show group, played maj hotels in Nev & toured maj cities, US. Featured pianist/singer, "Kate Smith Hour." Had own TV show. Musical dir, "Kathy Godfrey Show." Producer, maj TV specials, series & motion pictures. *Songs:* Tayopa (motion picture theme); Witchcraft of Love; They Won't Believe; Raindrops on My Window, Teardrops in My Heart; Yellow Roses; Reina—Reina—Reina.

CAWTHRON, JANIE M   ASCAP 1959
composer, author
b Mt Carmel, SC, Nov 27, 1888; d Chicago, Ill, May 21, 75. Educ: Harbison Col; Teacher's Normal. Supt Sunday Sch, 27 yrs; evangelist, Apostolic Church. *Songs:* Live for Him; You Can't Make It Alone; Oh Lord What's Next; The Song of the Savior; Praise Him Wherever You Go; Marvel Not; I Need Him All the Time; Just Before Sunset; There'll Be Sunshine After Rain; Dry Bones in the Valley; My Soul Wants Something New; More Wonderful All the Time; The Heavenly Jet; My Jesus Is Listening; His Hand Is Outstretched Still; God Is

Blessing You Right Now; He Chose Me; Why Stand Ye Idle; Sacred Songs: In That Beautiful Home Above; I See Him; Won't You Come and See the Man?; Somebody He Can Use; Call Him Anytime.

CAYTON, WILLIAM D'ARCY   ASCAP 1970
composer, author, producer
b Chevy Chase. Md, June 6, 18. Educ: Univ Md, BS(chemical eng), 37 & MM(Eng/advert), 38. Chemical engr, E I Dupont, Wilmington, 38-40. Pres, Cayton Asbestos & Eng Co, 40-43. Copywriter, Newell-Emmett Advert Agency, 43-44. Pres, Cayton, Inc/Advert Agency, 45-80; also Radio & TV Packagers, Inc, Greatest Fights of Century, Inc, Big Fights, Inc, Sports of Century, Inc, Reel Sports, Inc, Cayton Chemical Co Inc & Turn of Century Fights, Inc. Mem Nat Roster of Scientific & Specialized Personnel. *Scores:* Film/TV: Greatest Fights of the Century (now Big Fights of the Decades), 400 subjects; Knockout, 400 subjects; Jungle, 59 subjects; When Funnies Were Funny, 40 subjects; The Heavyweight Championship; Sugar Ray Robinson/Pound for Pound; Animatoons, 30 Featurettes, incl Mario and the Marvelous Gift, The Lost Sun, Alexander and the Sleep People, Goldilocks and the Three Bears & The Shepherd's Hat; Cartoon Classics, 26 Features & Featurettes, incl The Space Explorers, The Frog Princess, The Magic Antelope, The Fisherman and the Fish & New Adventures of the Space Explorers.

CERBUS, PAUL   ASCAP 1966
composer, author, singer
b Butler, Pa, June 11, 19. Educ: Sharon High Sch, 37; Univ Houston, mem of Phi Theta Kappa, 47, BS, 49; Case Western Reserve Univ, studied with Dr Evans; Kent State Univ, MEd, 67. Dance band musician with Benny Jones & Dick Rogers Orchs, 38; taught pub sch in Tex, 3 yrs; taught pub schs in Pa, 16 yrs. App to staff, Kent State Univ, 66, prof emeritus. Cond church choirs & community choirs, 50-78; performed as singer & pianist in ballrooms & nightclubs, 38- *Songs:* Be It So; *Music:* How Lovely Is Thy Dwelling Place; Eternal Spring; Let the People Praise Thee. *Instrumental Works:* Enigma; "C" Syndrome.

CERE, EDVIGE C (ADDIE)   ASCAP 1964
composer, teacher
b Turin, Italy. Educ: Giuseppe Verdi Cons, Turin; studied piano, theory & harmony with Prof Rolando & accordion with Mindie Cere. Comp, teacher & performer; appeared on radio, TV & concert stage; an adjudicator in nat & int music competitions. Mem, Am Accordionists' Asn, past vpres & past secy. Chief Collabr: Mindie Cere (husband). *Instrumental Works:* Accordionizin' on the Swanee; Mira Mira Cha Cha; Mucho Gusto Cha Cha; Beat 'n Boogie; Accordion Jump; Musette Dance Rhythms; Music Italian Style; Hello Madrid; Chico Hustle; Hustle Americano; Viva Toro; Gay Fiesta; El Dorado; Arriba (Merengue); Cha Cha Serenade; Speedway; Sea Breeze; La Corrida; On the Beat; TV Polka; Skipper Polka; Rockin' Time Waltz; Twinkling Waltz; Morita Merengue; Latina Merengue. *Albums:* Rockfest; Disc-o-Set.

CERE, MINDIE A   ASCAP 1960
composer, accordionist, teacher
b Roselle Park, NJ, Mar 11, 10; d New York, NY, Dec 29, 68. Accordionist in vaudeville & on records; teacher, Pietro Deiro Accordion Acad; gave concerts with Deiro throughout US; opened own accordion sch. Chief Collabrs: Pietro Deiro, Addie Cere. *Instrumental Works:* Sparkling; Mantillas; Celeste Tango; Cha Cha Doll; Dixieland Rag; Accordion Jump; Beat'n Boogie; Jamboree; Riviera Samba; Samba Nova; Touchdown Polka; Gleaming; Valse Unique; Crystal Waltz; Picadilly Polka; Chic Chic Boogie; Latina Merengue; Morita Merengue.

CERNEY, TODD DAVID   ASCAP 1979
composer, author
b Detroit, Mich, Aug 8, 53. Educ: Zanesville High Sch; Earlham Col, BS(biol/fine arts); Great Lakes Cols Asn Arts Prog, New York. Learned to play guitar at 14; started singing & writing songs in col; produced first record, 73; apprentice with Buzz Cason & Brent Maher, Creative Workshop, recording engr, 5 yrs; songwriter, Southern Writers Group. Background singer, Nashville, 2 yrs; still writing. Chief Collabrs: Bill Martin, John Goin, Austin Roberts, Marc Chapman, Max Merritt. *Songs:* Don't Play That Song Again; Blue House of Broken Hearts; Sleepless Nights; I'll Fall in Love Again; Full Moon Fool.

CEROLI, NICK   ASCAP 1965
composer
b Warren, Ohio, Dec 22, 39. Cincinnati Cons Music. Prof drummer, 60- Played with major big bands. Joined Herb Alpert, wrote songs, played drums, mid 60's. Doing Merv Griffin Show & free-lancing, Los Angeles. Chief Collabrs: Herb Alpert, John Pisano. *Songs:* For Carlos; Wind Song.

CESANA, OTTO   ASCAP 1942
composer, author, arranger
b Brescia, Italy, July 7, 1899. Educ: San Francisco schs; studied comp & arr with Julius Gold. Arr, Hollywood studios & Radio City Music Hall; author of comp, harmony & arr bks; comp, arr & cond of 12 albums. *Songs & Instrumental Works:* Ecstasy; Devotion; Enchantment.

CESANA, RENZO   ASCAP 1953
composer, author, actor
b Rome, Italy, Oct 30, 17; d. Educ: Jesuit Acad, Italy. Playwright, actor in Rome. Film contract writer & actor, MGM & RKO. Created radio progs "Art Linkletter's Party", "Stop That Villain", "Radio Hall of Fame." Appeared in road production "Time of the Cuckoo." Had own TV series, "The Continental." *Songs:* Buy a Bond for a Soldier for Christmas (off song, 6th War Bond Drive); Roses and Champagne; Don't Be Afraid, My Darling; Halfway to the Stars.

CESARIO, VICTOR LOUIS (VIC CAESAR)   ASCAP 1970
composer, author, musician
b Chicago, Ill, May 27, 31. Educ: St Ignatius High Sch; Art Inst of Chicago. Played piano at early age; drummer; singer & entertainer. Appeared in Las Vegas, Reno, Lake Tahoe & as singer in New York, Chicago & Los Angeles. Owner niteclub, Caesar's Forum, Phoenix, Ariz. Scored 24 films. Producer for Motown Records, 79 & show for Playboy Int, 80. Chief Collabr: Shel Silverstein (lyrics). *Songs:* Nixon's the One; Reach Out for Love; Laser World; The Playmate Song; Gosh (Alice B Good Body); State Street Samba; Comin' to Getcha; *Music:* Little Girls and Ladies; Ride in a Pink Car; Bare Knuckles. *Instrumental Works:* Olympiad '84.

CHACHKES, MAURICE (CECIL MAURICE)   ASCAP 1950
composer
b Yonkers, NY, Mar 13, 07; d Yonkers, Dec 31, 64. Educ: Yonkers High Sch; NY Univ; St John's Law Sch, Brooklyn, NY. Attorney. In furniture business; comp music. Chief Collabr: Pinky Herman. *Songs:* Lucky; Havin' a Wonderful Time; Second Honeymoon; My Blessing; Over and Over; La Belle Mamselle.

CHADABE, JOEL   ASCAP 1968
composer, teacher
b New York, NY, Dec 12, 38. Educ: Univ NC, Chapel Hill, BA, 59; Yale Univ Sch Music, MM, 62; studied comp with Elliott Carter, 61-64. Dir, Electronic Music Studio, State Univ NY, Albany; performer & comp electronic music. *Songs & Instrumental Works:* Works for Electronics and Instruments: Street Scene; Echoes; Flowers; Rhythms; Works for Computer: Solo; Play Things; Scenes from Stevens.

CHAIKIN, JULES   ASCAP 1968
composer, conductor, producer
b Brooklyn, NY, Oct 10, 34. Educ: Roosevelt High Sch, Los Angeles; Los Angeles City Col, jazz band instr Robert McDonald; trumpet studies with James Stamp. Played trumpet with, Stan Kenton, Gerald Wilson, Jerry Gray & Ray Anthony. Trumpet player & contractor motion picture & recording studios. Motion pictures music supvr, "Invasion of the Body Snatchers", "On The Nickel", "Bugsy Malone", "Lifeguard", "Executive Action", "Uptown Saturday Night" & "A Different Story." Chief Collabrs: Gary Coleman, Max Hardy, Emil Richards, Ellen Sander, Ron Anthony, Bob Thiele. *Instrumental Works:* Have a Little Bit More; Harmonica Boogaloo; Lanoola Goes Limp; Banks at Barclay; Blues for Big Jimi; Blues for We; Chicago Charva Chapter; Cynthia's Blues; Diane's Blue Plate Special; Joint Venture; Plaster Caster; Pray Tell Brian; Seven Foot Drummer Boy from Fleetwood Mac; Welcome Hampton's Outstanding; You Didn't Try to Ball Me; Slalom; South Central Avenue Municipal Blues Band; Maharimba; I Am Yellow; Hadani.

CHAIN, LESLIE
See Beard, Leslie Lois

CHAITKIN, DAVID   ASCAP 1976
composer, teacher
b New York, NY, May 16, 38. Educ: Pomona Col, BA, 59, principal studies with Karl Kohn; Univ Calif, Berkeley, MA, 65, comp studies with Seymour Shifrin, Luigi Dallapiccola & Andrew Imbrie; pvt comp study with Max Deutsch, Paris, 65-66. Followed early experience as jazz musician with studies in composition. Awarded the Honnold Fel, 59 & Ladd Prix de Paris, 64-66. Comns from Philadelphia Comp Forum, NH Music Fest & others. Awards incl Am Acad & Inst of Arts & Letters, Goddard Lieberson Fel, 80, Martha Baird Rockefeller recording grant, 75, Am Music Ctr. Taught at Reed Col, NY Univ, Brooklyn Col, City Univ New York & privately. *Songs:* Music: Seasons Such As These (mixed chorus a cappella). *Instrumental Works:* Light Breaks Where No Sun Shines (symph); Serenade (seven players); Scattering Dark and Bright (duo for piano & perc); Etudes for Piano; Music in Five Parts. *Scores:* Film: The Game.

CHAJES, JULIUS T   ASCAP 1953
composer, teacher, pianist
b Lwow, Poland, Dec 21, 10. Educ: Studied piano with Richard Robert, Angelo Kessissoglu, Julius Isserlis, Hedwig & Moritz Rosenthal; Vienna Univ, studied comp with Hugo Kauder. First piano recital & first comp at age nine. Hon Prize Winner, First Int Piano Competition, Vienna, Austria, 33. Head piano dept, Music Col, Tel Aviv, Israel, 34-36. To US, 37. Music dir, Jewish Community Ctr, Detroit, Mich, 40-; prof, Wayne State Univ, 50- *Songs:* Music: Song of Galilee; Adarim; Old Jerusalem; By the Rivers of Babylon; Eros (symph poem); Cantatas: The 142 Psalm; Zion, Rise and Shine; The Promised Land. *Instrumental Works:* Piano Concerto in E; Cello Concerto in A Minor; Piano Sonata in A Minor; Hebrew Suite; Eros (symph poem). *Scores:* Opera: Out of the Desert.

CHALK, SARAH SLAY   ASCAP 1973
composer, author
b Dallas, Tex, Sept 26, 35. Educ: Tex Christian Univ, BA(Eng); Univ Tex, Austin, MA(Eng). Taught Eng for several yrs. *Songs:* It's Gonna Be a Blue New Year.

CHAMBERLAIN, DAVID WAYNE   ASCAP 1976
composer, author, singer
b Ft Worth, Tex, Dec 23, 44. Nightclub entertainer. Chief Collabr: Jim Vest. *Songs:* I'm Not Easy; It Just Won't Feel Like Cheating; Cotton to Satin; Warm Up the Night With You; Chunky People; Land of Cotton.

CHAMBERLAIN, ROY S   ASCAP 1956
composer, conductor, arranger
b New York, NY, Aug 28, 07. Educ: Wesleyan Univ; St John's Col, Annapolis; Univ SC. Arr, orchs incl Harry Reser, Meredith Willson, Carmen Dragon, Merry Macs & King Sisters. Officer, USN, World War II. Cond & arr, CBS radio, 53. Realtor, 61. *Songs:* If You Cared.

CHAMBERS, ERNEST A   ASCAP 1963
author
b Philadelphia, Pa, Dec 28, 28. Educ: Columbia Univ, BA. Writer of spec material for revues & TV. On staff, "Danny Kaye Show," TV.

CHAMPLIN, WILLIAM BRADFORD   ASCAP 1969
composer, author, singer
b Oakland, Calif, May 21, 47. Educ: High sch; Col of Marin, Kentfield, Calif. Leader & singer for group, Sons of Champlin, 65-77. Recording artist, arr, guitarist & keyboard player. Chief Collabrs: David Foster, Jay Graydon, Pat Craig. *Songs:* Here Is Where Your Love Belongs; We Both Tried; Freedom; Music: Hold On; Lyrics: I Don't Want You Anymore; Morning Glory; After the Love Is Gone (Grammy Award).

CHANCE, DAVID
See Schantz, David Mathew

CHANCE, JOHN BARNES   ASCAP 1970
composer, teacher
b Beaumont, Tex, Nov 20, 32; d Lexington, Ky, Aug 16, 72. Educ: Univ Tex, masters, 56, studied comp, Clifton Williams & Kent Kennan. Prof theory, Univ Ky, 66-72. Ford Found Grant, 60-61. *Instrumental Works:* Blue Lake; Incantation and Dance; Symphony No 2 (winds, perc); Variations on a Korean Folk Song (Oswald Award, 65); Elegy; Credo (trumpet, piano); Introduction and Capriccio and 24 Winds.

CHANCE, NANCY LAIRD   ASCAP 1975
composer
b Cincinnati, Ohio, Mar 19, 31. Educ: Foxcroft Sch, 49; Bryn Mawr Col, 49-50; Columbia Univ, 59-67, studies with Vladimir Ussachevsk & Otto Luening; C W Post Col, 71-75. Performances incl, Philadelphia Orch, Museum of Modern Art, Paul Price Perc Ens, The New Music Consort, Contemporary Music Forum, DC, Int Soc Contemporary Music League & Opus I Showcase. *Songs:* Three Rilke Songs (soprano, Eng horn, flute, cello); Edensong (soprano, flute, clarinet, cello, harp, 3 perc); Darksong (harp, guitar, piano, 5 perc, 2 flutes, 2 clarinet, 2 horns); Duos I (flute & soprano); Lyrics: Motey (double chorus a cappella). *Instrumental Works:* Daysongs (alto flute & 2 perc); Ritual Sounds (brass quintet, 3 perc); Ceremonial (perc quartet); Declamation and Song (piano, vibes, violin, cello); Liturgy (orch); Duos II (oboe, Eng horn); Duos III (violin, cello).

CHANDLER, JEFF (IRA GROSSEL)   ASCAP 1954
author, actor
b Brooklyn, NY, Dec 15, 18; d Hollywood, Calif, June 17, 61. Began actg career in stock cos. Appeared in films incl, "Johnny O'Clock", "Broken Arrow", "Away All Boats", "Jeanne Eagels" & "Raw Wind in Eden." *Songs:* Six Bridges to Cross; One Desire; The Moon Won't Let You Tell a Lie.

CHANDLER, PAT   ASCAP 1962
composer, stage manager
b Baltimore, Md, Jan 15, 22. Educ: Univ Baltimore. Stage mgr, Bway plays; toured Europe in "The Fourposter" & "Angel Street" & with Josephine Baker Co & Johann Strauss Operetta Co. Production mgr, TV network shows. *Songs:* New Shoes.

CHAPIN, HARRY FORSTER
singer, songwriter
b New York, NY, Dec 7, 42. Educ: US Air Force Acad; Cornell Univ, 60-64; LittD (hon), Adelphi Univ, 78, Dowling Col, 79. Filmmaker, 65-71; singer & songwriter, 71- Comp bk & lyrics for plays "Night That Made America Famous" & "Zinger." Author, "Looking...Seeing," 75. Comp for "Make a Wish," Emmy Award winning TV series for children, 74. Pres, Story Songs Inc. Hon chmn, Suffolk County Hunger Hearings. Mem bd trustees, Performing Arts Found of Long Island, NY. Founding trustee, World Hunger Yr. Mem, President's Comn on Int, Domestic & World Hunger. Bd dirs, Eglevsky Ballet, 79-, Long Island Bus Asn, 79- Acad Award nominee for best feature documentary "Legendary Champions," won first prizes in NY & Atlanta film

fests, 69; Grammy nominee for best new artist, 72, for best male vocal performance, for "Cats in the Cradle," 75. Awards: Rock Music Award for pub serv, 76 & 77; Humanitarian Award B'nai B'rith, 77; Long Island Advertisers Man of Yr Award, 77; Lone Eagle Award, Long Island Pub Relations Soc, 78; named One of Ten Outstanding Young Men, US Jaycees, 77. Mem: Screen Guild; Am Fedn Musicians & Actors Equity. *Albums:* Head and Tails; Sniper and Other Love Songs; Short Stories; Verities and Balderdash; Portrait Gallery; Greatest Stories Live; Road to Kingdom Come; Dance Band on the Titanic; Living Room Suite; Legends of the Lost and Found; Sequel.

CHAPLIN, MARIAN WOOD
See Wood, Marian Louise

CHAPLIN, SAUL   ASCAP 1936
composer, author, arranger
b Brooklyn, NY, Feb 19, 12. Educ: Self-taught pianist & arranger; NY Univ Sch Commerce. With Sammy Cahn Band. Wrote material for Vaudeville Acts, 35-40. Night club scores for, "Connie's Hot Chocolates, 1936", "Grand Terrace, 1939" & "Cotton Club, 1939." Wrote scores, Columbia Pictures, 40-41, arr, songwriter, or musical dir, 41-49; films incl, "Cover Girl", "The Jolson Story", "Jolson Sings Again", plus many others. With MGM, 49-58, films incl, "On the Town", "Summer Stock", "Kiss Me Kate", "High Society", "An American in Paris" (Acad Award), "7 Brides for 7 Brothers" (Acad Award). Free lance, 59-; assoc producer, "West Side Story" (Acad Award), "Can Can", "The Sound of Music"; producer, "Star" & "That's Entertainment, Part 2." Chief Collabrs: Sammy Cahn, Johnny Mercer. *Songs:* Music: Rhythm is Our Business; Rhythm in My Nursery Rhymes; Shoe Shine Boy; Until the Real Thing Comes Along; It It's the Last Thing I Do; Posin'; Dedicated to You; Savin' Myself for You; I Could Make You Care; Lyrics: Bei Mir Bist Du Schoen; Joseph, Joseph; Anniversary Song; You Wonderful You. *Scores:* Film/TV: Merry Andrew; Bonanza Bound.

CHAPMAN, WALTER LYNN   ASCAP 1961
composer, musician
b Hoosick Falls, NY, Jan 12, 13. Educ: Music Cons. With Bob Crosby's service band, 46-48.

CHARIG, PHIL   ASCAP 1927
composer
b New York, NY, Aug 31, 02; d New York, July 21, 60. Educ: Commerce High Sch. Songwriter, var Bway revues incl "Allez-Oop", "Americana" & "Shoot the Works," films & for Milton Berle & Jackie Gleason, TV. Chief Collabrs: Ira Gershwin, Irving Caesar, Leo Robin, Dan Shapiro, Milton Pasca. *Songs:* For Days and Days; Six O'Clock; Happy Melody; One-Two-Three; Where Are You?; Let Yourself Go; Sunny Disposish; Sweet So-and-So; Fancy Our Meeting; The One I'm Looking For; It's Not You; Take It Or Leave It; There's Always Tomorrow; I Wanna Get Married; Twelve O'Clock and All Is Well. *Scores:* Bway shows: Yes, Yes, Yvette; Just Fancy; Follow the Girls; London shows: That's a Good Girl; Stand Up and Sing.

CHARITY
See Bailey, Charity

CHARKOVSKY, WILLIS   ASCAP 1959
composer, performer
b Chicago, Ill, Mar 1, 18. Educ: Morton High Sch; DePaul Univ, BM, 50; Northwestern Univ, MM, 56. Concert pianist; prof, Univ Ill & Northeastern Ill State Univ; pianist, Grant Park Symph Orch, Chicago, Ill. *Instrumental Works:* Penatonic Clock; Tour for Two.

CHARLAP, MORRIS (MOOSE)   ASCAP 1954
composer
b Philadelphia, Pa, Dec 19, 28; d. Educ: Univ Pa (writer, Mask & Wig shows); Univ Wis; Philadelphia Cons, studied with Tibor Serly. Chief Collabrs: Carolyn Leigh, Bob Hilliard. *Songs:* You, Only You; Mademoiselle; Great Day in the Morning; I'm Flying; I Gotta Crow; I Won't Grow Up; Wrong Joe; Soft in the Heart; Young Ideas; When the Tall Man Talks; Love Eyes. *Scores:* Bway shows: Peter Pan; Whoop-Up; The Conquering Hero; TV: The King and Mrs Candle; Ballet: So This Is New York.

CHARLES, DICK
See Krieg, Richard Charles

CHARLES, ERNEST   ASCAP 1936
composer, author, singer
b Minneapolis, Minn, Nov 21, 1895. Educ: Pvt instr after high sch; Univ Southern Calif, harmony; studied voice with Modini Wood, Los Angeles. Singer, "George White's Scandals", 29 & "My Maryland", also nightclubs, NY & recitals. Dir Romany Chorus, Palm Beach, 35. Produced "Great Moments of Music", radio, 43-44. Nat patron, Delta Omicron, Phi Mu Alpha. Hom mem Apollo Club, Minneapolis. Fel, Am Inst Fine Arts. *Songs:* Let My Song Fill Your Heart; The House on the Hill; When I Have Sung My Songs; Music: Clouds; My Lady Walks in Loveliness; Love is of God; Oh Lovely World; The Sussex Sailor.

CHARLES, NORMAN   ASCAP 1969
composer, author, singer
b Baltimore, Md, Jan 11, 35. Educ: Clark Col, Ga, AB; Oberlin Col, Ohio, MDiv. Began writing music, age 10; formed a cappella choral group, Baltimore, age 16; group appeared on local TV shows. Featured appearance, "To Tell the Truth", 77. *Songs:* Follow the Way; I Need Ya; Now is the Time.

CHARLES, RAY   ASCAP 1954
composer, lyricist, arranger
b Chicago, Ill, Sept 13, 18. Arr & cond, The Ray Charles Singers. Has made many records. Works primarily in TV, incl "Perry Como Show", "Your Hit Parade", "Hollywood Palace", "Glen Campbell Show", "Sha-Na-Na", "The Muppet Show", "Academy Award Show", "Grammy Shows"; also specials with John Denver, Bob Hope, Bing Crosby, Sandy Duncan, Carpenters, Mac Davis. Winner of 2 Emmy Awards, 69-70 & 70-71. *Songs:* Letters, We Get Letters; Sing to Me, Mister C; Dear Perry; 50 Nifty United States; I Can Almost Read Your Mind; Lyrics: Christ Is Born; That Ragtime Piano Man.

CHARLESWORTH, FLORENCE M   ASCAP 1955
composer, author
b New York, NY, Jan 26, 1885; d. Writer of poetry for newspapers. *Songs:* I'm Drifting Back to Dreamland.

CHARLTON, (FREDERICK) ANDREW   ASCAP 1975
composer, author, teacher
b South Pasadena, Calif, May 16, 28. Educ: Los Angeles State Col, MA, 55; Univ Southern Calif, doctoral work; studied with Ingolf Dahl, Mario Castelnuovo-Tedesco, Halsey Stevens & David Raksin. Univ prof musicol & comp, 65- Free lance instrumentalist, comp, arr & orchestrator. Author of three-vol text in arr. *Instrumental Works:* Concerto da Camera for Alto Recorder and String Orchestra; Prelude for Saxophone Quartet; Idyllwild Suite; Three Movements for Four Recorders; Ayre Conditioned; Harlequin for Flute Duo; Theme and Variations for Trumpet Duo; Cha Cha Dolce; Chaccone for Saxophone Quartet.

CHARNIN, MARTIN   ASCAP 1961
composer, author, director
b New York, NY, Nov 24, 34. Educ: High sch; studied music & art; Cooper Union, BFA. Actor, "West Side Story", 57-60. Lyricist, 60-; dir, producer, 64- Dir of "Annie", "Bar Mitzvah Boy" (London), "Music, Music", "Nash at 9." Chief Collabrs: Richard Rodgers, Charles Strouse, Vernon Duke, Harold Arlen, Edward Thomas, Mary Rodgers, Eliot Lawrence. *Songs:* Arianne; The Best Thing You've Ever Done; Lyrics: Maman; A Fine Kind of Freedom; numerous TV songs. *Scores:* Bway shows: Annie; Mata Hari; I Remember Mama; Two by Two; Hot Spot; Zenda; Softly.

CHASE, J NEWELL   ASCAP 1931
composer, conductor, organist
b West Roxbury, Mass, Feb 3, 04; d New York, NY, Jan 26, 55. Educ: Roxbury Latin Sch; Huntington Sch; Boston Univ; Harvard Univ; New Eng Cons of Music; studied with Whelpley, Goodrich, Converse, Tibor Serly. Church organist & pianist; cond, dance orchs. Asst cond, Capitol Theatre, New York, 24; solo pianist for "Roxy Gang." To Hollywood, comp & music adv, 28; scored silent films; writer for radio. 2nd Lt, USA, World War II. Chief Collabrs: Leo Robin, Richard Whiting. *Songs:* My Ideal; Music in the Moonlight; It's a Great Life If You Don't Weaken; Weather Man; Sweet Like You; As Long As You Believe in Me; Never Say Die; Just a Kiss in the Moonlight; I'll Take Care of You; Kitchimikoko Isle. *Songs & Instrumental Works:* Concerto for Louise; Midnight in Mayfair; Tanglewood Pool; Trickette; Idawanna; Classical Satire; Tiddlywinks; Bachette; In Chiffon.

CHASINS, ABRAM   ASCAP 1931
composer, author, pianist
b New York, NY, Aug 17, 03. Educ: Ethical Culture Sch, Columbia Univ; Juilliard Sch; Curtis Inst; studied piano with Ernest Hutcheson & Leopold Godowsky, comp with Donald Francis Tovey & Rubin Goldmark; pupil & protege of Josef Hofmann. Mem fac, Curtis Inst, Berkshire Ctr at Tanglewood & Univ Southern Calif. Debut as soloist with Philadelphia Orch under Gabrilowitsch, 28 & soloist under Stokowski, 33. Composer of over 100 published works, performed & recorded by leading artists. First contemporary Am composer performed by Toscanini, 31. Appeared in recitals & as soloist with primary orchs, Am & Europe; also recorded extensively. Music dir, WQXR Radio Sta, New York, 40-65 & KUSC Radio Sta, Univ Southern Calif, Los Angeles, 72-77. Author bks, "Speaking of Pianists", "The Van Cliburn Legend", "Music at the Crossroads", "Leopold Stokowski" & "The Appreciation of Music" among others. Served as consult to foreign govts on music educ; also served on juries of leading competitions of US, Israel & Can. Winner of Peabody Award, Music Teachers' Award & Distinguished Serv Award. *Instrumental Works:* The Blue Danube Waltzes, Fledermaus, Artists Life (Free Fantasies on J Strauss for two-pianos); A Shanghai Tragedy, Flirtation in a Chinese Garden, Rush Hour in Hongkong (three Chinese pieces for piano); Two Piano Concertos, Parade, Period Suite (orch); Twenty-four Preludes for Piano; Fairy Tale, Carmen Fantasy (two-piano transc works, Bach, Gluck, Rimsky-Korsakov); Offering to Eros (six songs to poems by Elissa Landi); Tricky Trumpet (piano);

Banjo Boy (piano); Nocturne, Humoresque (cello, piano); Three Preludes (violin, piano); Keyboard Karikatures (piano).

CHASTAIN, TILFER EARL   ASCAP 1962
composer, author, arranger
b Borden, Ind, Jan 11, 23. Singer; var radio shows incl Far East Armed Services network, Japan. Stage performer, incl piano bar. MC for var shows. *Songs:* Shoes of a Beggar; Born to Walk Alone; Who Am I; House of Blues; Cry Baby Cry Baby.

CHATTAWAY, JAY A 1974
composer
b Monongahela, Pa, July 8, 46. Educ: WVa Univ; Univ Rochester Eastman Sch of Music. Comp-in-residence, USN Band, DC, 7 yrs. Mem, A&R staff, Columbia Records. Independent record producer, arr & comp. Music writer for films. *Instrumental Works:* Parade of the Tall Ships; Introduction and Dance; Prelude and Celebration; Rock Encounter; Odyssey; Northwest Overture; Jazz works: Conquistador; Afro-Cuban Fantasy; Mr Mellow; Good Morning; Andromeda. *Scores:* Film: Maniac.

CHATTAWAY, THURLAND   ASCAP 1929
composer, author
b Springfield, Mass, Apr 18, 1872; d Milford, Conn, Nov 12, 47. Educ: Pub schs. Moved to New York, 1896; wrote for music mag ed by Theodore Dreiser. *Songs:* Mandy Lee; Red Wing; Can't You Take It Back and Change It; Kerry Mills Barn Dance.

CHAUDET, MARY   ASCAP 1958
composer, author, singer
b Hartford, Conn, Oct 7, 20. Educ: High sch. Appeared in vaudeville & with husband Bill Chaudet in nightclubs, hotels & TV. Toured, with USO in "Sons O'Fun," & with Blackstone the Magician. With singing group, Flanagan Sisters. Chief Collabrs: Hal Johnson, Jack Elliott, Joyce Wellington.

CHAVEZ, CARLOS   ASCAP 1948
composer, conductor, lecturer
b Mexico City, Mex, June 13, 1899; d Mexico City, Aug 2, 78. Educ: Studied with Manuel Ponce, Pedro Luis Ogazon, Asuncion Parra, Juan Fuentes; hon Doctorate Arts, Columbia Col, Chicago, 78. First concert of own works, Mex, 21. Organized & cond, Conciertos de Musica Nueva, Mexico City, 23-25. Founded, Orquesta Sinfonica de Mex, 28, cond, 28-48 & of Nat Cons, 28-33. Founder & dir, Coro de Conservatorio, 29 & chief of fine arts, 33-34, Nat Inst Fine Arts, Orquesta Sinfonica Nacional, 47-52. Founding mem, Acad of Arts, Mexico City; life mem, El Colegio Nacional, 43, with conferences held annually. Pres, Jury of the Cassadeseus Piano Competition, Cleveland. Artistic cond, Cabrillo Music Fest, Aptos, Calif, 4 yrs. Guest cond of major symph orchs, US, SAm, Paris, Cuba & Mex. Cond, 20th Anniversary of the Inter-Am Music Fest, John F Kennedy Ctr, DC, 78. Lectr, concerts & seminars, Univ Buffalo & Harvard Univ. Taught comp, Nat Cons, Mex, 60-61; lectr, El Colegio Nacional. Adv, Pres Jose Lopez Portillo, Mex. Comns: Mex Minister Educ, Guggenheim, Nelson Rockefeller, Museum of Modern Art, New York, Libr Congress, Murray Kirkwood, Louisville Orch, Clare Booth Luce, Koussevitzky Found, Lincoln Kirstein, New York Ctr of Music & Drama, New York Philh, Pan Am Union. Author, bks "Toward a New Music" & "Musical Thought." Hon mem, Am Acad Arts & Sci, Am Acad & Nat Inst of Arts & Letters, Costarricense Musical Union, San Jose, Costa Rica; hon pres, Int Conference About Music & Communication in Mex. Awards: Chevalier Legion of Honor, Comdr Order of the Crown, Belg, Comdr Order of the Polar Star, Sweden, Officer, Legion of Honor, France, Cross Star of the Italian Solidarity, Italy, Caro de Boesi, Caracas, Premio Nacional de Artes y Ciencias, Mex, Prize of the House of Las Americas, Acapulco, Golden Medal of Artistic Merit, Univ Chicuahua, Mex, Band of Honor of the Order of Andres Bello, govt of Venezuela, Order of Francisco de Miranda, first class, from Pres Carlos Andres Perz, Venezuela. *Instrumental Works:* Six Symphonies; Three Piano Sonatas; Tierra Mojada; Llamadas; Concerto for Four Horns; Piano Concerto No 1; Soli No 1 (wind quartet) No 2 (wind quintet) No 3 (bassoon, trumpet, timpani, orch) No 4 (brass trio); Chaconne in E; Invention (piano); Seven Pieces for Piano; Horse Power Suite; Toccata for Percussion; Obertura Republicana; Corrido de el Sol; Danza a Centeotl; Xochipilli Macuilxochitl; Invention Two (trio for violin, viola, cello); Resonances (orch); Tambuco (6 perc); VI Sonata (piano); Left Hand Inversions of Five Chopin Etudes (piano); Etude IV (piano); Three Etudes (piano); Concerto (violin, orch); Sarabande (strings); Suite for Double Quartet; Ten Preludes (piano); Three Spirals (violin, piano); Chapultepec (3 Mex pieces, orch); Unity (piano); Sonata (4 horns); Sonatina (piano); Sonatina (violin, piano); Sonatina (cello, piano); Poligons (piano); Three Pieces (guitar); Energia (9 instruments); Solo (piano); Blues (piano); Fox (piano). *Songs & Instrumental Works:* La Casada Infiel (voice, piano); Paloma azul (chorus); North Carolina Blues (mezzo-soprano, baritone, piano); Three Poems (voice, piano); All (mezzo sporano, baritone, piano); Wet Earth (chorus, SATB, a cappella); Tree of Sorrow (chorus, a cappella); Full chorus, mixed voices: A Freedom; A Woman Is a Worthy Thing; The Wanning Moon; Rarely; A Pastoral; Epistle; Nonantzin. *Scores:* Ballets: El Fuego Nuevo, (Vasconcelos comn); Four Suns; Opera: Love Propitiated; The Visitors.

CHAYEFSKY, PADDY — ASCAP 1955
author, producer

b Bronx, NY, Jan 29, 23. Educ: City Col New York, BS. Served, USA, World War II, received Purple Heart. Writer, TV plays incl "Marty" (Acad award, 55), "The Catered Affair", "The Bachelor Party," plays incl "Middle of the Night" (film, also), "The Tenth Man", "Gideon," screenplays incl "The Goddess" & "The Americanization of Emily." Chief Collabrs: George Bassman, Harry Warren. *Songs:* Marty; Middle of the Night.

CHECK, JOHN FELIX
composer, teacher, musician

b Rosholt, Wis, Aug 22, 21. Educ: Univ Wis, BA, MAdmin & PhD(psychol). Musician & leader from age 14 to present. Weekly TV show for 11 yrs. *Instrumental Works:* Two Eddies Polka; Salt and Pepper Polka; Wisconsin Dutchmen Waltz; Algoma Schottische; Harv's Schottische; Little Girl Waltz; Haupt Polka; WLUK Polka; Wisconsin Dutchmen Theme; John David's Polka; Wisconsin Schottische; Flint Polka; German-Bohemian Waltz; Fox Valley Polka; Murphy Polka; Prof's Polka; Bunkleman Waltz; WAGO Polka.

CHEESEMAN, JAMES RUSSELL (RUSTY DAVIS) — ASCAP 1978
composer

b North East, Pa, Oct 5, 37. Educ: North East High Sch; Orange Coast Col; Univ East Carolina. In legit theatre; singer, nightclubs. Recording artist, Ducal Records. Chief Collabrs: Ralph P McCabe, Paige M Cheeseman. *Songs:* House on the Hilltop; You Don't Believe Me; Look At the New Friends (I Have Found); Getting Back on the Family Plan; Lyrics: It's Christmas Time Again.

CHEETHAM, JOHN EVERETT — ASCAP 1979
composer

b Taos, NMex, Jan 13, 39. Educ: Univ NMex, BFA, MM; Univ Wash, DMA(comp). Assoc prof theory & comp, Univ Mo, Columbia, 69- *Instrumental Works:* Scherzo (brass quintet); Quintet for Woodwinds; Concoctions for Unaccompanied Trumpet; Consortium for Euphoniums and Tubas; Concert Dialogue for Two Trumpets.

CHENETTE, EDWARD STEPHEN — ASCAP 1941
composer, conductor, educator

b London, Ky, Aug 17, 1885; d Bartow, Fla, Sept 10, 63. Educ: High Park Cons, Des Moines, MA; Bush Tempe Cons; Soc Acad, Paris. Cond with Chautauquas until 16, entire band enlisted in 211th Battalion, Can Expeditionary Forces. Dir music, Iowa State Col, Chicago Reg Band, Ill State Legion Band. Fac, Fla Southern Col. Author, bks, "Building the Band", "Advanced Technique." Recipient of 1st prize, twice, Chicagoland Music Fest. *Instrumental Works:* Four World Suite; Parade of the Republic; Gala Night; Aces of the Air; Blaze of Glory; National Band Book; Up Front Band Book.

CHENETTE, MAUDE JOHNSON HOWE — ASCAP 1957
composer, author

b Bartow, Fla, Apr 9, 1887. Educ: Summerlin Inst, Bartow, Fla; Fla Sem, Sutherland; studied music with Miss Stilwell, 03-04. Musician & comp. Mem: Fla Comp League; Nat League Am Pen Women. Chief Collabrs: Edward S Chenette (late husband). *Songs:* Daughters of the UDC; Watch Your Step; Flag of Liberty; Your Shrine; My Valentine; Wanting You; Come Back to Me; Three Cheers for Old USA.

CHENOWETH, WILBUR — ASCAP 1932
composer, conductor, pianist

b Tecumseh, Nebr, June 5, 1899. Educ: Lincoln Musical Col, (scholarship), studied with May Pershing, Aloys Kremer; Univ Nebr, BM(scholarship), studied with Sidney Silber; studied with Sigismund Stojowski, Alexander Lambert, Pietro Yon. Prof of piano & organ & comp, Univ Nebr. Organist & choirmaster, First Plymouth Congregational Church, Lincoln, Nebr, 28-38, Neighborhood Church, Pasadena, Calif, 38-62. Head, piano dept, Occidental Col, 39-44. Piano soloist, symph orchs. Own music studio, Calif. Chief Collabr: Joyce Ayres. *Songs & Instrumental Works:* Welcome to Nebraska (comn, Native Sons & Daughters of Nebr); The Arrow and the Song; Love, I Come to You; Concert Waltz; Hidden Waterfall; Waltz Caprice; Harvest Festival; La Pampita; March Triumphant; Cortege; Arabesque; Fiesta (piano, orch); Of the Father's Love Begotten (choral); Vocalise; Hear Our Prayer; The Brotherhood of Man; Noel, Noel, Bells Are Ringing.

CHERDAK, JEANNE SYLVIA — ASCAP 1952
author, lyricist

b Newark, NJ, Dec 2, 15. Educ: Kean Col; Summit Art Ctr; Writer's Digest Sch, certified Braillist. Wrote poetry column daily for large newspaper. Conducted weekly cable TV segment "Rhyme Time." Editor & writer, Red Cross Publ, "Red, White and You." Published poetry in mag. Chief Collabrs: Richard Loring, Guy Wood, Jack Manus, Sylvia Schaff, Thomas Parente. *Songs:* Lyrics: Jump Through the Ring; Do Me a Favor; I'll Leave the Door Open; Say Hello for Me; Little White Mark; No Money Can Buy; Maid of Honor; The Old Heartaches; Bashairt; Whatever I Touched; The Sawdust on the Floor; Changing Trains.

CHERKOSE, EDDIE
See Maxwell, Eddie

CHERNEY, BORIS E — ASCAP 1962
author

b Los Angeles, Calif, July 5, 21. Educ: Lawrence Col; Northwestern Univ, BS & BA, 45; Harvard Grad Sch Bus, MBA, 47. Served in USN, 42-64, retired Comdr, Supply Corps. Dir bus & communications, Am Psychol Asn, 64-65 & 70-78. Controller, Am Chemical Soc, 66-69; consult to associations mainly Am Soc Asn Exccs, chicfly cngagcd in cxcc scarchcs, 78- Chief Collabr: Leonard McCall. *Songs:* Lyrics: Forgive Me; It's All Over; Dancing Silhouettes; Just a Puppet.

CHERNIAVSKY, JOSEF — ASCAP 1944
composer, conductor

b Russia, Mar 31, 1895; d New York, NY, Nov 3, 59. To US, 19. Educ: Imperial Cons, St Petersburg (Gold Medal); studied with Alexander Glazounov, Rimsky-Korsakov, also with Julius Klengel, Leipzig. Toured US as cond in concert & theatres. Created & cond "Musical Camera," NBC, radio, NY. Music dir, WLW, Cincinnati. Scored film "Show Boat," 29. *Instrumental Works:* The Dybbuk (musical drama). *Scores:* Operetta: Barnum.

CHERNIS, (SIR) JAY — ASCAP 1948
composer, author, conductor

b Norwich, Conn, Nov 21, 06. Educ: Townsend Harris Hall; Juilliard; studied with Goetschius, Schoenberg, L Ulehla. Comp, arr, cond, vocal coach, Hollywood. Films, "Sign of the Cross", "Song of the Flame", "Flirtation" & others. Cond 24 musicals, incl "Gentlemen Prefer Blonds", "Plain and Fancy." Gen music dir, Wash Music Fest. *Songs:* I Look at You; In Your Cucamonga; Knights of Malta Anthem; Music: Crying. *Instrumental Works:* April Concerto. *Scores:* Bway shows: It's About Time; Film/TV: Sign of the Cross; Central Park; Wide Open Faces; Flirtation; Song of the Flame.

CHESLOCK, LOUIS — ASCAP 1975
composer, author, teacher

b London, Eng, Sept 25, 1898. Educ: Baltimore City Col; Peabody Cons Music, Baltimore, teacher's cert violin, 17, teacher's cert dipl comp & theory, 21, Dr Musical Arts (hon causa), 64. Teacher violin, theory & comp, Peabody Cons Music, 16-76; violinist, Baltimore Symph Orch, 16-37, asst concertmaster, 32-37, guest cond several times of own works; tributes upon retirement from Peabody Inst, Baltimore Symph & City of Baltimore through mayor, 76. Maj symphonic works performed in NAm, SAm, Europe & Orient. *Instrumental Works:* Descant (solo clarinet); Concertos for Violin, French Horn; Symphony in D major; also variety of other chamber, symph, instrumental & vocal works. *Scores:* Opera: The Jewel Merchants; Ballet: Cinderella.

CHESSLER, SHIRLEY (DEBORAH) — ASCAP 1953
composer, author

b Baltimore, Md, Feb 24, 23. Educ: Forest Park High Sch, Baltimore, Md. Mgr singing group Orioles. Chief Collabr: Fanny Wolfe. *Songs:* It's Too Soon to Know; Tell Me So; Forgive and Forget; Lyrics: Tear Drops on My Pillow; Before It's Too Late.

CHESTER, ROBERT T — ASCAP 1962
composer, conductor

b Detroit, Mich, Mar 20, 08. Educ: Col. Orch leader, theatres, hotels & cols, 39-52. *Songs & Instrumental Works:* Sunburst (theme); Octave Jump; You're the One Love.

CHEYETTE, IRVING — ASCAP 1974
composer, author, educator

b New York, NY, Aug 1, 04. Educ: High Sch Commerce; Inst Musical Art, 25-26; Columbia Univ Teachers Col, BS, 29, MA, 30, EdD, 36. Instr music educ, Horace Mann & Lincoln Schs, Columbia, 28-35; pub sch dir instrumental music, 30-38; dir music educ, State Teachers Col, Indiana, Pa, 38-48; prof music educ, Syracuse Univ, 48-54; Fulbright prof music educ, Tokyo Univ Fine Arts, Japan, 54-55; dir/prof music educ, State Univ NY Buffalo, 55-72, emer prof, 72-; adj prof art, Fordham Univ, 74-77. Author textbook "Teaching Music Creatively." Chief Collabrs: Charles J Roberts, Edwin Salzman, Joseph Paulson, Herbert Cheyette. *Songs & Instrumental Works:* Developing Instrumental Musicianship; Beginning String Musicianship; 3-Way Band Method; Fourtone Folios (3 vols); Songs to Sing with Recreational Instruments; Bridging the Gap Band Series (3 vols); Fundamentals of Band and Orchestra Playing; Master Woodwind Ensembles (13 transc); Basic Piano for Music Educators; Basic Theory-Harmony for School Musicians; Tune Ups for Choral Groups; Spirit of Valley Forge March; Pageantry Processional March; Band Marches: Yankee Clipper; Football Parade; 98th Infantry Division; The Whistler; High Flyer; Band Overtures: Sage Brush Saga; Cape Cod Capers; 49er Fantasy.

CHIANCO, BERNARD V (BERNIE SEA) — ASCAP 1968
composer

b Philadelphia, Pa, May 10, 32. Educ: Studied bass, arr & theory with Denis Sandoli. Played professional bass on road, 3 yrs. Has done A&R work for Chestnut Records & Atlantic Records; has had songs recorded by Decca

Records & Chestnut Records. Now active in music & writing, nightclubs, TV, A&R work. Chief Collabr: Vern Godown. *Songs:* Lily; My Conscience; What Kind of Magic; Sticks and Stones; Two Wrongs; There Goes My Life; Music: Stop, Look, Surrender; I Wanna Be.

CHIASSON, WARREN ASCAP 1962
composer, vibraphonist, percussionist
b Cheticamp, NS, Apr 17, 34. Educ: St Francis Xavier Univ, 52-54; Maritime Cons of Music, 55-57; pvt study with Lenny Tristano & George Russell, 59-60. With George Shearing Quintet, 59-61 & 72-74. Toured with Roberta Flack, 75; with Chet Baker & Tal Farlow, 74-77. Studio musician, New York, 60's. Percussionist, Bway shows "Foxy", "Hair" & "Brainchild." Solo career as vibraphonist; tours, own group, 75- Leader on var albums incl, "Quartescence" & "Good Vibes for Kurt Weill." Chief Collabrs: Jimm Garrison, Chuck Wayne. *Instrumental Works:* Bedouin; My Own; Para Siempre; Bossa Nova Scotia; Ultramarine.

CHICHESTER, GEORGE FORREST (CHET FORREST) ASCAP 1937
composer, author, producer
b Brooklyn, NY, July 31, 15. Educ: Palm Beach High Sch, Fla, grad. Pianist, dance orchs, clubs & nightclubs, 28-35. Contract comp & lyricist, MGM for var films incl "Maytime", "Sweethearts", "The Firefly" & "Balalaidka," 36-47. Writer & dir, 11 revues, Camp Tamiment, 8 revues, Copacabana, New York; writer, US Treasury Star Parade, World Broadcasting. Dir, Bway shows, musicals in London, Los Angeles, San Francisco & SAfrica, & TV spectaculars & films. Chief Collabrs: Robert Wright, Walter Donaldson, Herbert Stothart, Edward Ward, Erich Korngold, Heitor Villa-Lobos, P G Wodehouse, Guy Bolton, Jerome Chodorov, Edwin Lester, Milton Lazarus, Charles Lederer, Luther Davis, Peter Stone, George Abbott, Jose Ferrer, Andrew L Stone. *Songs:* It's a Blue World; Stranger in Paradise; Baubles, Bangles and Beads; And This Is My Beloved; Sands of Time; Night of My Nights; Bored; He's In Love; The Olive Tree; Strange Music; Three Loves. *Scores:* Bway shows: Song of Norway; Kismet; Kean; Anya; Magdalena; Timbuktu!; The Great Waltz; The Love Doctor; Film/TV: Song of Norway; The Great Waltz; The Firefly; Sweethearts; Balalaika; Music in My Heart; Fiesta.

CHICKERING, JOSEPH COOPER ASCAP 1965
composer, author
b Louisville, Ky, May 5, 17. Was part-owner, Magnet Records, Hollywood, Calif, 64-67; cond several recording sessions with Empala Records, Hollywood. *Songs:* Hollywood; It's Heavenly; Bad and Beautiful.

CHIDESTER, LAWRENCE WILLIAM ASCAP 1951
composer, author, arranger
b St Paul, Minn, July 9, 06. Educ: Hamline Univ, AB, 27; Tufts Univ, AM, 29, EdM, 36; studied with Nadia Boulanger, 38-39; Univ Iowa, PhD, 43. Instr music, Tufts Univ, 27-39; asst prof music, Western Reserve Univ, 39-43; assoc prof music, NTex State Univ, 43-45; prof music & head music dept, Tex A&I Univ, 45-55; prof music, Del Mar Col, 55-73, dean fine arts, 69- *Instrumental Works:* Brahms's Variations on a Theme of Haydn (arr, band); Bands & Orchs: Chorale Time; Baroque Chorales and Preludes; solo works arr from Telemann; numerous works arr for band by Bach, Rimsky-Korsakow, Delibes, Borodin & Pares.

CHIHARA, PAUL SEIKO
composer, educator
b Seattle, Wash, Sept 9, 38. Educ: Univ Wash, BA, 60; Cornell Univ, MA, 61, DMA, 65, studied with Robert Palmer; studied with Nadia Boulanger, Paris, Ernst Pepping, Ger & Gunther Schuller, Tanglewood. Appeared in concerts as performer, cond & comp, US, Japan & Mex. Assoc prof music, Univ Calif, Los Angeles, 66- Awards: Lili Boulanger Award, 63; Fulbright Fel, Berlin, 65 & Tanglewood Fels, 66-68. *Songs & Instrumental Works:* Forest Music (orch); Wind Song (cello, orch); Grass (amplified double bass, orch); Ceremony IV; Suite From Shinju; Chamber Music: Tree Music (3 violas, 3 trombones); Branches (2 bassoons, perc); Redwood (viola, perc); Willow, Willow (amplified bass flute, tuba, perc); Logs (one or more string basses); Logs XVI (amplified bass, electronic tape); Driftwood (string quartet); Ceremony (oboe, 2 celli, bass, perc); Chorus: The 90th Psalm; Magnificat (treble voices); Three Dream Choruses; Nocturne (24 solo voices); The 101st Psalm; also string quartet in one movement.

CHILDRESS, LILLIAN HANNAH ASCAP 1967
composer, author, teacher
b Nebraska City, Nebr, Apr 5, 1893. Educ: Peter's Accordion Sch Music, Bryan, Tex; Lillian Beaumont's Pvt Sch Music, piano & accordion. At 9, took pvt piano lessons; at 11, played piano for Sunday sch & church & play parties; at 45, advertised for Texo Feed Co, Ft Worth & at Bryan; played accordion in rodeo arenas, street parades & other places. Regional chmn, Tex Press Women, 47-48. Mem, Poetry Soc Tex. Accordion & piano teacher; taxidermy teacher; pvt nurse; clay sculptor & painter. *Songs:* When It's Autumn Time in Texas; Padri Island; Port Lavaca; I'm So Lonesome; Log Cabin Rendezvous.

CHIPOLONE, NUNZIO (CHIP BLAINE) ASCAP 1975
composer, author, singer
b Clifton, NJ, July 24, 22. Educ: Clifton High Sch, NJ, 2 yrs. Singer, nightclubs; recording artist. *Songs & Instrumental Works:* It's a Boy.

CHIPRUT, ELLIOT ASCAP 1968
composer, author
b Brooklyn, NY, Mar 14, 44. Educ: Brooklyn Col. Songwriter, 68- Writer & producer of film "Wit's End," 69. Producer & score writer, TV spec "Popeye Meets the Man Who Hates Laughter." *Songs:* Simon Says; May I Take a Giant Step; Little Bit of Soul; Last Day of the War. *Albums:* Roly-Poly.

CHOBANIAN, LORIS OHANNES ASCAP 1970
composer, musician
b Mosul, Iraq, Apr 17, 33. US citizen. Educ: La State Univ, MM; Mich State Univ, PhD. Has been prof comp & guitar, Baldwin-Wallace Col; prof of lute, Oberlin Col Cons. Chmn, Guitar Div, Am String Teachers Asn, 74-76. Has performed as guitarist in concerts & on TV. Comns by Int Guitar Fest of Toronto, Ohio Chamber Orch, Cleveland Ballet, The Rocky River Chamber Music Soc, Am String Teachers Asn & The Elysian Trio. *Instrumental Works:* Soliloquy—Testament of a Madman; Sonics (4 guitars; Cleveland Area Arts Coun Grant); The Gift; Christmas Ballet; The Id (symph wind ens); Caprico (piano, symph wind ens); Chamber Music: Lieutenant Kosmusov's Dream (piano trio); Brass Ensemble (music for brass & timpani); Armenian Dances (symphonic wind ens); also five pieces for guitar.

CHONG, THOMAS
comedian, writer, musician
b Edmonton, Alta, May 24, 38. Educ: Pub schs. Co-founder rhythm & blues band, The Shades; mem group, Bobby Taylor & the Vancouvers. Founder of improvisational theater troupe, City Works. Formed comedy duo with Cheech Marin called Cheech & Chong; appeared in nightclubs, Can & Los Angeles. Co-writer & co-star of film "Up in Smoke," 78. Recipient with Cheech, Grammy Award for Best Comedy Recording, 73. *Albums:* Cheech and Chong; Big Bambu; Los Cochinos; The Wedding Album; Sleeping Beauty.

CHOSET, CHARLES ASCAP 1978
composer, author, publisher
b Brooklyn, NY, Sept 8, 40. Educ: Hunter Col, NY, BA(ancient Greek), 65. Movie/theater critic; translator; lyricist for Sesame Street; novelist; playwright; composer; music publ, Popliteal Music Co, Inc. Chief Collabrs: Sam Pottle, Rosalyn Drexler, Alan Sues. *Songs:* Lyrics: Como Estas? *Scores:* Bway shows: Star Struck; The Meehans (lyrics); The Writer's Opera (music).

CHRISTENSEN, JAMES HARLAN ASCAP 1965
composer, conductor, arranger
b Madison, Wis, Aug 27, 35. Educ: Univ Wis, BM, 57 & MM. Arr, West Point Band, 58-61. Prof music, Univ Wis, 61-68. Music dir, Disneyland & Walt Disney World, 68-80, also Los Angeles Rams Football Club. Now cond, Pacific Pops Orch. Comp of educ music. *Songs:* Sing Praise to Him Our Lord. *Instrumental Works:* Holiday on Ice; Seasons' Greetings; Snow Chase; Overture Americana; Trombone Country; Trumpets in Stereo; Dreaming Winds; Piccolo Espagnol; Contrasts; Variations on an Original Theme; Christmas Shopping; Hey Ride!; Clarinet Party; Folk Fling; Paris at Rest; Slidin' Saints; Three to Get Ready; Pomp and Pageantry Overture; Impressions of the New West; Meditation; Five for the Fun of It; Comedy for Trombones; Beguine for Trombones; Trumpet Takeover; Champions in Every Way.

CHRISTIAN, BOBBY ASCAP 1953
composer, conductor, pianist
b Chicago, Ill, Oct 20, 11. Educ: McKinley High Sch; studied music with Fred Huffer, Alfred Walthall & Roy Shield. Toured in dance bands during 30's. Worked in radio, then percussionist & arr, NBC staff, Chicago. To NY, cond & arr, ABC staff. Cond & scored TV shows, incl "Tales of Tomorrow" & "Adventure." With NY Philh; toured Orient with NBC Symph of the Air under Toscanini. Returned to Chicago, 56, formed own dance band & played concerts. Has made many records. *Songs & Instrumental Works:* Moonlight Reflection; Reach Me; Crickets on Parade; Tuba Square Dance; Song of Lotus Lee; Space Suit; Scotch Mist; Krazy Kwilt; Orinoco; Wanderin' Fifer; Bomba.

CHRISTIAN, DAVID
See Egli, David Christian

CHRISTOPHER, BERRIE
See Gerak, Berrie Lee

CHRISTOPHER, DENNIS
See Ferrante, Dennis Christopher

CHRISTOPHER, DON
See Attanasio, Donald Joseph

CHUBBY CHECKER
See Evans, Ernest

CHURCHILL, FRANK E   ASCAP 1938
composer, pianist
b Rumford, Maine, Oct 20, 01; d Castaic, Calif, May 14, 42. Educ: Univ Calif. Pianist, film theatres. Under contract to Walt Disney Studios, Hollywood. Chief Collabrs: Ann Ronell, Larry Morey. *Songs:* Who's Afraid of the Big Bad Wolf?; Spring Is in the Air; Ain't Nature Grand?; The Golden Youth; Slow But Sure; Some Day My Prince Will Come, With a Smile and a Song; I'm Wishing; Heigh-Ho; Happy As a Lark; The Sunny Side of Things; One Song; Whistle While You Work; Baby Mine; I Bring You a Song; Love Is a Song. *Scores:* Films: Three Little Pigs; Dumbo (Acad award, 41); Snow White and the 7 Dwarfs; Bambi.

CIANI, SUZANNE ELIZABETH   ASCAP 1977
composer
b Indiana, June 4, 46. Educ: Thayer Acad, 60-64; Wellesley Col, BA(music), 68; Univ Calif, Berkeley, MA(music comp), 70; Stanford Univ, spec studies computer music, 68-70. Pioneer in electronic music synthesis & perf; songwriter & comp for commercials & films. First artist comn to create a digital comp for pinball machine, Bally's "Xexon." Formed music production co, Ciani Music Inc, New York, 77. Awards: NEA Comp Grant; Ford Found; Mills Col Tape Music Ctr; Hertz Memorial Fel; Creative Artists Pub Service Grant; Clio, Golden Globe. *Songs:* Have a Coke and a Smile. *Instrumental Works:* Koddesh-Kodeshim; New York, New York; New Waves (orchestral electronic works); also musical electronics for Meco Star Wars. *Instrumental Works:* Electronic: Help, Help, the Globolinks; The Stepford Wives; The Incredible Shrinking Woman.

CIARCIA, JOHN   ASCAP 1960
composer, author, pianist
b Brooklyn, NY, May 24, 40. Educ: High sch. *Songs:* Choo Choo to Heaven; Double Dutch Twist.

CICALELLO, JOSEPH   ASCAP 1958
composer, author, publisher
b Philadelphia, Pa, Dec 16, 09.

CICATELLO, FRANK DOMENICK (FRANK JACEY)   ASCAP 1972
composer, author
b Staten Island, NY, Oct 2, 11. Educ: Curtis High Sch, grad; self-improvement courses. Local showings, "Music Man", "South Pacific" & "My Fair Lady"; asst cond, St Ann's Choir; chorus cond, Am Asn Retired Persons; bass, Barbershop Quartet; play piano, Eger Nursing Home. Chief Collabrs: Howard F Stocksdale, John J Lynch. *Songs:* The Santa Claus Parade; Until Now; Many Faces; Minnie in Her Mini; Music: The Twenty-Third Psalm.

CIMA, ALEX   ASCAP 1976
composer, author, synthesist
b Havana, Cuba, Jan 11, 46. Educ: Calif State Univ, Northridge, BA(psychol), 71, grad work psychobiol & music; studied piano with Margarita Nogueras, Cesar Perez Sentenat, Adrian Ruiz & Sergei Tarnowski; studied film scoring with E Manson; studied comp with Aurelio de La Vega. Performer, producer & songwriter; recording artist; producer, Final Alley Ltd; electronic music comp & teacher; consult synthesizers & musical applications of signal processors. Engr. Author: "The Synthesizer Book." *Songs:* Anna; Scat Cat Kitty. *Instrumental Works:* Transformations; Briarcliff Improvisation; Primera; Deception.

CINA, ALBERT I   ASCAP 1964
composer, teacher
b Italy, Nov 1, 1896; d. Educ: Studied in Italy. Taught high sch bands.

CINES, EUGENE   ASCAP 1955
author
b New York, NY. Educ: Juilliard Sch Music; Eastman Sch Music; spec study with Paul Creston, Hall Overton & Rayburn Wright. Mgr, CBS Music Libr. Composer of many TV dramatic shows. *Songs:* Trust in the Lord (cantor solo & orch). *Instrumental Works:* Allegheny Morning; Teton Range Sketches; Abbreviations (solo piano); Cantilena.

CIOROIU, ALEXANDRU SORIN (SORIN MOGA)   ASCAP 1977
composer
b Bucharest, Romania, July 10, 41. Educ: High sch, Bucharest; Cons Music, Bucharest, MA, 65; studied comp with Martian Negrea, Alfred Mendelsohn & Tiberiu Olah, counterpoint with Zeno Vancea, forms with Tudor Ciortea. Teacher harmony, theory & piano, Sch Music No 1, Bucharest, 65-76. Part-time musical supvr, TV variety shows, 71-74. Came to US, 76. Analyst/programmer, Irving Trust Co & Am Express Int Banking Corp. Mem, Romanian Composers Asn, 67. Chief Collabrs: Petre Ghelmez, Victor Tulbure. *Songs:* Music: The Motherland; Vacation, the Trumpet of Happiness; The Clock.

CIRONE, ANTHONY J   ASCAP 1970
composer, professor, performer
b Jersey City, NJ, Nov 8, 41. Educ: Juilliard Sch Music, BS & MS. App percussionist with San Francisco Symph, 65; joined fac, San Jose State Univ, 65. Chief Collabrs: Saul Goodman & Vincent Persichetti. *Instrumental Works:* Symphony No 1 (perc); Symphony No 2 (perc); Triptych (perc quartet); 5 items for soprano & perc; a sacred mass for chorus & perc; Cairo Suite (concerto for Middle Eastern instruments & perc); Sonata No 1 (timpani & piano); Sonata No 2 (trumpet & perc); Sonata No 3 (clarinet & perc); Sonata No 4 (violin, piano & perc); Double Concerto (two perc & orch); Japanese Impressions (perc quintet); Overture in Percussion (perc quintet); 4/4 for Four (perc quartet).

CLAMPETT, BOB   ASCAP 1961
composer, author
b San Diego, Calif. Educ: Otis Inst of Arts. Leader of band, Inst Exposition. Creator of cartoon characters Tweetie Pie, Porky Pig, Beany, Cecil the Sea Sick Serpent & others. Author, cartoons "Looney Tunes" & "Merrie Melodies," Warner Brothers. Authored & comp, own "Time for Beany" TV puppet show, "Beany & Cecil" network cartoon show & "Bugs Bunny Superstar," feature film. Chief Collabrs: Carl W Stalling, Michael Sasanoff, Warren Foster, Sody Clampett, Eddie Brandt, Freddie Morgan, Ian Whitcomb. *Songs:* I Tot I Taw a Putty-tat; There's Food Around the Corner; Termite Terrace (Rah Rah Rah); The Huffenpuff Song; Snorky, Snorky; Lyrics: Nothing Could Be Feena (Daffy Duck scat song); Beany Theme Song; Cecil's Ragmop; Bugs Bunny Superstar (theme).

CLAMPETT, SODY   ASCAP 1961
composer
b Buffalo, Wyo, Apr 4, 31. Educ: Heimann Col, Wyo. Assoc with live TV shows incl, "Time for Beany", "Thunderbolt the Wonder Colt", "Buffalo Billy" & "Willy the Wolf," cartoon show "Beany & Cecil" & film "Bugs Bunny Superstar." Chief Collabrs: Bob Clampett, Eddie Brandt. *Songs:* Music: Beany and Cecil Theme.

CLAPP, CHARLES (SUNNY)   ASCAP 1939.
composer, author, conductor
b Battle Creek, Mich, Feb 5, 1899; d San Fernando, Calif, Dec 9, 62. Educ: Danus Cons; Univ Mich. Served, World War I & II. Trombone soloist, Pryor's Band. Cond own orch, 27-35, & made many records. Chief Collabrs: Carmen Lombardo, Hoagy Carmichael. *Songs:* Girl of My Dreams; When Shadows Fall; Don't Say She's a Bad Little Girl; In My Dreams; A Bundle of Southern Sunshine; I'll Wait Forever For You; Hail to the Wings of the Navy; Congratulations to You; Come Easy-Go Easy Love; You; Loafing On a Lazy River; There Goes My Dream; Old Southern Moon; A Place Called Paradise.

CLAPP, DEBORAH GAIL   ASCAP 1978
composer, author, teacher
b Philadelphia, Pa, Sept 21, 54. Educ: Pvt study, organ, 16 yrs, vocals with Robert Edwin, 2 yrs. Performing singer & organist, age 8, professionally, age 13. Toured with var rock, show & jazz bands; original works performed. Taught, 7 yrs. Won hon mention, Am Lyric Competition, 78. Chief Collabr: Felix Cavaliere. *Songs:* Music: A Mellow Progression for Paul C; Lyrics: Jubilation; Love Me Tonight; My Lady Once Told Me; Have a Good Time On Me; Winterfire; Words to Sing.

CLAR, ARDEN   ASCAP 1959
composer, conductor, pianist
b Baltimore, Md, Dec 28, 15. Educ: Wilson Teachers Col; Catholic Univ, BM, MM. Pianist & violinist, Shoreham Hotel; with 4-piano team, Miami, Fla. Music dir for Harry Richman. Cond, own orch; pianist, Town House, Greenwich, Conn. Chief Collabr: Richard Hayman. *Songs & Instrumental Works:* Similau; Port of Spain; Jade; Voodoo Album.

CLARE, SIDNEY   ASCAP 1922
author
b New York, NY, Aug 15, 1892; d Los Angeles, Calif, Aug 29, 72. Educ: High sch of Commerce. Dancer, comedian & special materials writer, vaudeville. To Hollywood, 33, writer for films. Chief Collabrs: Con Conrad, Cliff Friend, Lew Pollack, Sam Stept, Lew Brown, Richard Whiting, Jay Gorney, Harry Warren, Vincent Youmans, Oscar Levant, James Monaco, B G DeSylva. *Songs:* What Do You Mean By Loving Somebody Else?; Ma, He's Making Eyes at Me; I'm Missin' Mammy's Kissin'; Weep No More My Mammy; Oo-oo Ernest; A New Kind of Man; Big Butter and Egg Man; Me and the Boy Friend; We're Back Together Again; I'd Climb the Highest Mountain; Then I'll Be Happy; Miss Annabelle Lee; One Sweet Letter From You; Lovable and Sweet; My Dream Memory; Keeping Myself for You; You're My Thrill; I've Got You on Top of My List; Please Don't Talk About Me When I'm Gone; It Was a Night in June; On the Good Ship Lollipop; Polly Wolly Doodle; It Was Sweet of You; Hit the Deck; Jimmy and Sally; Bright Eyes; The Littlest Rebel. *Scores:* Films: Street Girl; Tanned Legs; Transatlantic Merry-Go-Round; Sing and Be Happy.

CLARE, THOMAS TRUITT   ASCAP 1962
composer, author
b Holcomb, Kans, Aug 23, 24. Comp & author for dance hall & nightclubs, 10 yrs. With gas co, 50-

CLARIDA, ORVILLE CLIFTON   ASCAP 1957
composer, author, singer
b Loving, Tex, Feb 21, 10. Played on radio stas throughout Tex; played prominent dance & show spots along with own Rhythm Valley Boys, 30 yrs; made first record, 50. Country songwriter; recording artist; band leader. *Songs & Instrumental Works:* Along the Rio Grande; Mother's Understanding Heart; Shake Hands With Trouble; The Smile on Your Face; Divided; Someday I Will Forget; I've Not Forgotten; You Got the Wrong Party; Our Love Fell Victim; It's So Wonderful; Have a Little Sympathy for Me.

CLARK, ALLAN (ALEX MORRISON)   ASCAP 1963
composer, author, pianist
b Los Angeles, Calif, Oct 20, 07. Educ: Univ Ore, BA(music); pvt study with Ferde Grofe, Paul Yartin (New York) & Paul Held (Chicago). Arr for orchs incl Jimmie Grier, 29-30; staff arr, Freed & Powers Publ, 30-31; short subjects, RKO; arr for Phil Harris, 32-35; pianist & arr, George "Spike" Hamilton Orch, 35-36; music dir, WKY Radio & WKY-TV, 36-72; arr, mgr, cond & vocal coach for Anita Bryant, 48-60. Chief Collabrs: Neil Moret, Harry Tobias, Ben Oakland, Frank Skinner, Al Skinner, Mark Houston, Pat Clark, Chris Thompson. *Songs & Instrumental Works:* I'll See You in Oklahoma (Semi-Centennial theme for Okla, 57); I'm Dreaming of My Old Kentucky Home; I Got Shook; Ol' Virginny; The Answer Man.

CLARK, AMY ASHMORE   ASCAP 1924
composer, author, publisher
b Toronto, Ont, May 6, 1882; d New York, NY, Jan 9, 54. Toured in vaudeville, incl "Crepe Paper Girl"; gen mgr, William Von Tilzer's Art Music Co, 2 yrs. Advert dir, Jr League Mag, 10 yrs. Chief Collabrs: Ernest Ball, Frederick Vanderpool, William Polla, Edward Laska. *Songs:* My Rosary For You; In a Little Town Nearby; The Heart of You; If Thoughts Be Prayers; With Love He Cleanses Every Sin; I Am Lost Without the Lovelight in Your Eyes; And So Your Soul Was Born.

CLARK, CHARLIE A   ASCAP 1974
author, singer
b Sylvester, Ga, Oct 31, 48. Educ: Webster Sch Music. Record producer for local talent; singer & arr. *Songs:* Make It Right; If You Just Come Back Home; We Tried It, We Made It; Dancin Is Good for You; Girls Was Made to Be Loved.

CLARK, EDWARD   ASCAP 1940
composer, author, actor
b Russia, May 6, 1878; d Los Angeles, Calif, Nov 18, 54. To US, 1891. Comedian, vaudeville. Playwright, "Coat Tails" & "The Blushing Bride"; playwright & actor, "Relations." Contract film writer. Own drama sch, Hollywood, 17 yrs. Chief Collabrs: Rudolf Friml, Otto Harbach, Albert Von Tilzer. *Songs:* Say Sis, Give Us a Kiss; My Old Man Is Baseball Mad; Ring a Ding Dong; On Hawaiian Shores; Take a Look At Me Now; Heart of My Heart; You're in Love; I'm Only Dreaming; Just One Good Time. *Scores:* Stage scores & librettos: Little Miss Charity; You're in Love (also dir); Oh, What a Girl (also dir); Honey Girl; Paradise Alley.

CLARK, GLEN ARLEN   ASCAP 1975
composer, singer
b Ft Worth, Tex, Apr 21, 48. Educ: N Tex State Univ. Began playing in clubs, late 60's. Started recording, 71; recorded as part of duo act named Delbert & Glen, Clean Records. Now playing keyboards & singing background vocals with Kris Kristofferson. Chief Collabrs: Daniel Moore, Billy Swan, Delbert McClinton, Mike Utley, Stephen Bruton. *Songs & Instrumental Works:* I Feel the Burden; Sugar Daddy; Old Standby; I Don't Want to Hear It Anymore.

CLARK, GUY CHARLES
composer
b Tex, 41. Art dir on local TV sta, Houston, 60's. Played coffee house circuits, Houston, Dallas & Austin. Worked with Dopyera Bros factory constructing dobros, Los Angeles. Moved to Nashville, 71. *Songs:* Desperadoes Waiting for a Train; LA Freeway; Texas 1947; The Last Gunfighter Ballad. *Albums:* Old No 1; Texas Cooking.

CLARK, KENNETH S   ASCAP 1943
composer, author, conductor
b Pittsburgh, Pa, May 25, 1882; d Princeton, NJ, Jan 22, 43. Educ: Shadyside Acad; Princeton Univ. WW I, YMCA secy, song leader 79th Div, AEF. Active in community music; exec in publ cos. Ed: "Municipal Aid for Music in America"; "Music in Industry"; "Bottoms Up" (anthology). Exec ed, 25th issue, "Carmina Princetonia." Editor. *Songs & Instrumental Works:* The Princeton Jungle Song; Going Back to Nassau Hall; Princeton, That's All; Princeton Forward March; Our Glorious America; An Indian Cradle Song; Kissing Games; A Moonlight Buggy Ride; Vesper Bells.

CLARK, LESTER LEROY   ASCAP 1955
author
b Robinson, Kans, Nov 4, 05; d London, Eng, 59. Was the Bugle Boy in the Andrews Sisters', "The Bugle Boy of Company 'B'." Played a part in Elvis Presley movie, "Loving You." Worked with Bing Crosby & Bob Hope; was a

dancer & writer of song lyrics. Chief Collabr: Matt Dennis. *Songs:* Lyrics: Show Me the Way to Get Out of This World; Ain't It a Beautiful Day.

CLARK, ROBERT KEYS   ASCAP 1962
composer
b Cambridge, Md, Nov 18, 25. Educ: Philadelphia Cons Music, MusB(comp), 49; Juilliard Sch Music, MSc(comp), 53; studied with Vincent Persichetti. Teacher in var schs & cols; had several comp-in-residences; lectr, founder & cond, Conn Fest Orch. First Prize: The Roth Nat Orchestral Award, 70. Chief Collabr: Leland McCoy, poet. *Songs & Instrumental Works:* Monument (Guillaume de Machaut, fantasia for orch); Iam Moriturus (cantata, soprano, chorus, orch); Patterns for Percussion; Brevities for Band; Clarinet Concerto; Third Symphony; Lamentation for String Orchestra.

CLARK, TERRELL LEE (TERRY)   ASCAP 1979
composer, singer
b Fort Worth, Tex, Sept 22, 46. Leader of group Children of Faith, Tex, 72-75. With group Liberation Suite, UK & Europe, 75-76. With Chuck Girard Band, int tour, 76-79. Solo artist for var record cos, 78- *Songs:* Ugadano Thawanu Maija; Let's Have a Good Time; Make a Noise; Welcome; Your Love for Me; Living Loving Eyes; Melodies; River; There's the Light; Father of Light; Jesus Is At the Wheel; Following. *Albums:* Welcome; Melodies.

CLARKE, GRANT   ASCAP 1914
author, publisher
b Akron, Ohio, May 14, 1891; d Calif, May 16, 31. Educ: Akron High Sch. Actor in stock cos; wrote plays. New York music publ. Then became publ. Wrote spec material for Bert Williams, Fanny Brice, Eva Tanguay, Nora Bayes & Al Jolson. Wrote songs for films incl, "The Jazz Singer", "Weary River", "On With the Show" & "Is Everybody Happy?" Charter mem, ASCAP. Chief Collabrs: George Meyer, Harry Akst, James Monaco, Fred Fisher, Harry Warren, Al Piantadosi, Milton Ager, Archie Gottler, Arthur Johnston, James Hanley, Lewis Muir. *Songs:* Dat's Harmony; Ragtime Cowboy Joe; He'd Have to Get Under; When You're in Love With Someone; Beatrice Fairfax; There's a Little Bit of Bad in Every Good Little Girl; You Can't Get Along With 'Em Or Without 'Em; In the Land of Beginning Again; Everything Is Peaches Down in Georgia; I Hate to Lose You; Second Hand Rose; Oogie Oogie Wa Wa; Dirty Hands, Dirty Face; Home in Pasadena; Mandy, Make Up Your Mind; Dixie Dreams; I'm a Little Blackbird Looking for a Bluebird; Am I Blue?; Birmingham Bertha; I'm the Medicine Man for the Blues; Weary River.

CLARKE, HERBERT LINCOLN   ASCAP 1938
composer, author, conductor
b Woburn, Mass, Sept 12, 1867; d Long Beach, Calif, Jan 31, 45. Educ: Pub schs; hon DMus, Phillips Univ, Okla, 34. Cornet soloist with var bands, Ontario Beach. Instr, violin, viola & all brass instruments, Toronto Cons. With Patrick Gilmore's New York Band, F N Innes' Band, 7th Reg Band (under Victor Herbert). Cornet soloist & asst cond on 4 Europ tours with John Philips Sousa. Dir, Anglo-Can Concert Band, Huntesville, Ont, 18-23; Municipal Band, Long Beach, Calif, 23-43. Author, instr bks, "Elementary Studies for the Cornet, 1st Series", "Technical Studies for the Cornet, 2nd Series" & "Characteristic Studies for the Cornet, 3rd Series." *Instrumental Works:* King of the Deep; Youth Dauntless; Sounds From the Deep; Post Glad Hours (waltz); Fraternity Overture; Tiberius Overture; Marches: New England's Finest; Naval Brigade; Culver Alumni; Pacific Southwest; Exposition; and others; Cornet solos: Bride of the Waves; Birth of Dawn; Caprice Brilliant; Sounds From the Hudson; Southern Cross; Stars in a Velvety Sky; La Veta; Twilight Dreams; Showers of Gold; and others; Duets: Side Partners; Flirations; and other trios & saxophone solos.

CLARKSON, GEOFFREY   ASCAP 1938
composer, pianist, conductor
b Yonkers, NY, Sept 21, 14. Educ: Inst of Musical Art, NY. Pianist, Les Brown, Ray Anthony & Bobby Hackett Orchs. Pianist-cond for Bob Hope, Margaret Whiting & Doris Day. Pianist, Dean Martin TV Show, 65-74. Chief Collabrs: Harry Clarkson (father), Lee Hale & Van Alexander. *Songs:* Music: Home (When Shadows Fall); I Can Spell Banana (But I Never Know When to Stop); An A-Flat Cricket and a B-Flat Frog; 'Way Ahead of the World; A Night at the Movies.

CLARKSON, HARRY F   ASCAP 1938
author, pianist, arranger
b London, Eng, Nov 29, 1882; d Hempstead, NY, Oct 7, 59. Educ: St Matthew's Parochial Sch. Chorister, St Margaret's Church, London. Pianist & arr with dance orchs. Chief Collabr: Geoffrey Clarkson (son). *Songs:* Home (When Shadows Fall); I Struck a Match in the Rain; No Sun; The Organ, the Monkey and Me; Goodbye to Love; Sitting on a Rainbow.

CLARY, SALONE THEODORE   ASCAP 1968
composer, educator
b Portsmouth, Va, Feb 8, 39. Educ: Norfolk State Univ, BS MusEd; Va State Univ, MS MusEd; Cath Univ. Studied with Noah Ryder, Reginald Parker, Dr Georgia A Ryder, Buckney Gamby, Dr Nathaniel Gatlin, Dr Carl Harris & Dr Howard Jones. Asst band dir, Cardozo High Sch, Washington, DC, presently; minister of music, Sargent Mem Presby Church, presently. Chief Collabrs: Dr

Jester Hairston, Hall Johnson, Dr Eugene Simpson & Edward Boatner. *Songs:* I Want to Live with God (SATB); Where Shall I Go; When You Hear Those Bells; The Blind Man Stood on the Road and Cried.

CLAUSEN, ALF H   ASCAP 1970
composer, arranger, conductor
b Minneapolis, Minn, Mar 28, 41. Educ: NDak State Univ, BA(music theory), 63; Univ Wis, grad studies (music theory), 64; Berklee Col Music, prof dipl(music comp & arr), 66; studied film scoring with Earle Hagen & musical theater with Lehman Engel. Musical dir for TV variety series incl, "Donny & Marie", "Mary", "Mary Tyler Moore Comedy Hour" & "Paul Lynde Comedy Hour." Comp & arr for TV variety spec: Dorothy Hamill, Goldie Hawn, Fred Travelena, Emmy Awards, Bea Arthur, Tony Orlando & others; comp & arr TV dramatic shows: "Charlie's Angels", "The FBI", "Jigsaw" & others; also var TV & radio commercials; comp & arr musical theater: "Mother Earth" & "Happy Side of the 30's"; comp & arr big bands: Thad Jones, Mel Lewis, Ray Charles, Stan Kenton, Buddy Rich, Woody Herman & others; comp & arr entertainment personalities: Buddy Greco, Lisa Donovan, Hal Linden, Captain & Tennille, Trini Lopez, The Osmonds & Dionne Warwick; comp & arr recordings. Producer, performer & teacher. Twice recipient of NEA Comp Fel Grant. Chief Collabr: Tommy Wolf. *Songs & Instrumental Works:* Music: Something in the Wind; To Build, to Plant; In Thee Will I Trust; Sing a New Song; Deliverance; Comfort Me; He's Asleep; Jeremiah's Song; A Blues of Glory; We Are the Privileged; Why Does the Way of the Wicked Prosper?; Let Me Lay Down in Peace & Sleep; Isn't Anybody Ever Gonna Learn?; Blessed Is He Who Has Crowned Us Kings; Rejoice! Hosanna! Glory Hallelujah! Amen!; Quintet No 1 for Brass; Won't Somebody Please Sound an 'A'?; Oh, Where Am I Going?-Goodbye Joan; Lou'siana Baby; What's a Nice Girl Like You Doing in a Place Like This?; We Love to Play the Game; The Sweet Sixteen; The Super Bowl; From There to Here; Trollin' for Thadpoles; Captain Perfect; Jack Acid's Revenge; 'S That You, Wilt?; A Pair of Threes; Walking Ovation Blues; For Her; One for Russ; Blues for a Graying Walrus; Evening Over the River; Mains Street, USA; Just Feelin' So Blue; Radar Approach; Brief Encounter; Ballad for Gary; A Final Farewell; Three Sounds for Jazz Orchestra; Finale for Jazz Orchestra; Ode to an East Boston Ferry; Samba de Elencia; The Soul Collector; The Legacy; The Midnight Salute; (She's Lost) The Love of Her Life; Dawn & Lizz; Brooming Blues.

CLAUSI, ANTHONY (JOHN)   ASCAP 1971
composer, arranger, guitarist
b Jamaica, NY, Dec 11, 48. Played in var bands; accompanist for var artists; now studio musician. Chief Collabrs: Steve Wittmack, lyricist Sherry Paige. *Songs & Instrumental Works:* I Want to Be a Cowboy; Cowboy (Come Love Me Tonight); Instrument: Flyin' High; Care Free.

CLAUSON, WILLIAM   ASCAP 1964
composer, lyricist, recording artist
b Ashtabula, Ohio, May 2, 30. Educ: Los Angeles High Sch; studied voice with Victor Fuchs & guitar with Jose Barroso. Five world tours as singer & guitarist in concert halls. Recorded 55 LP's on major labels. Composed over 200 songs. Eighteen songs publ for use in English Sch System, by Oxford Univ Press. Author guitar instruction bks used in Scandinavia. Began performing at Santa's Village as The Rainbow Man, 79. Publ, Rainbow Man Music, 80- & Rainbow Man Records, 80- Mem, Songwriters Hall of Fame. Chief Collabr: Basil Swift. *Songs:* The Worm Song; Circle of Love; Little Guy in Blue Jeans; All the World Is Waiting (Calif Asn Educ Young Children comn, conv theme song, 81).

CLAXTON, ERIE   ASCAP 1970
composer, author
b Indiana. Author, poetry bk "Memphis Memories." *Songs:* This I Pray; Heavenly Father Thanks; Darling Mother I Miss You So; They Have Torn Down Beale Street and Hauled It Away.

CLAY, CARL B   ASCAP 1973
composer, author
b New York, NY, Dec 5, 51. Educ: Pace Univ, MS(drama, educ); Brooklyn Col Grad Sch, grad work in TV & theatre dir; Third World Cinema. Chief Collabrs: Richard Clay, Wayne Garfield, Roy Ayers, Lonnie Beckhan. *Songs:* Coffy Is the Color; Virgo Red; King George; Shining Symbol; Love From the Sun; Sensitize; I Am Your Mind; 2000 Black (Think About Your Future); Yin and Yang; Fruit; Take Nothing But the Best. *Scores:* Film: Coffy (ASCAP Popular Music Work Motion Picture Soundtrack Panel Award, 74); Babies Making Babies (Award Winning Film); TV: Turkey Treasure (1st Place Award, Annual Media Woman's Fest, 76 & Action for Children's TV, Harvard Univ, 76).

CLAYPOOLE, EDWARD B   ASCAP 1929
composer, author, pianist
b Baltimore, Md, Dec 20, 1883; d Baltimore, Jan 16, 52. Educ: Pub schs. Pianist, World's Fair, St Louis & on radio, Baltimore & DC. Songwriter, minstrel shows, Paint & Powder Club, Baltimore, films & Bway musicals incl "Nearly a Hero" & "The Echo." *Songs & Instrumental Works:* Ragging the Scale; My Sahara Belle; I Don't Want to Marry You; My Guiding Star; Little Echo; Why Don't You Get Yourself a Man Like Me?; I Wonder; Trying; Cake Walk Lindy; Bouncing on the Keys.

CLAYTON, STEVE
See Tedesco, Pat Louis

CLAYTON, WILBUR DORSEY (BUCK)   ASCAP 1957
composer, teacher
b Parsons, Kans, Nov 12, 11. Educ: High sch, Parsons, Kans. Joined Count Basie Band, 36. With mil forces, 43. Jazz at the Philh, 46. Extensive travels to Europe. Teacher, Hunter Col, NY, currently. *Songs:* Music: Red Bank Boogie; Love Jumped Out; Avenue C; Swing Shift; Blues Blase; Clayton Place; Casa Bar; Candy's Tune; Boss Blues; Case Closed; Easy Blue; Play Boy; Kansas City Woman; The One for Me; Pamela; Even Steven; Steevos; Candyville; Clarinet Lemonade; Outer Drive; Swingin' at the Copper Rail; Swinging Along on Broadway; How Hi the Fi; Birdland Betty; Dallas Delight; A Swinging Doll.

CLEARY, MICHAEL H   ASCAP 1929
composer
b Weymouth, Mass, Apr 17, 02; d New York, NY, June 15, 54. Educ: US Mil Acad, West Point. Organist, Catholic Chapel & wrote shows, US Mil Acad. Left USA, 26; newspaper reporter, Boston. Writer, Bway stage scores, songs for films & revues incl "Earl Carroll's Vanities", 31, "Shoot the Works" & "Third Little Show"; writer of special material, nightclubs & Kate Parson's "Show Boat Revue." Reentered USA as Capt, World War II, retired as Maj. Chief Collabrs: Nat Lief, Max Lief, Herbert Magidson, Maurice Sigler, Arthur Swanstrom, Ned Washington. *Songs:* Is There Anything Wrong in That?; Singin' in the Bathtub; H'lo Baby; Here It Is Monday, and I've Still Got a Dollar; Deep in the Blue; When a Lady Meets a Gentleman Down South; It's in the Stars; My Impression of You; Ten O'Clock Town; Faith of the Army Air Force; Spirit of the Technical Training Command; Music: Myrtle the Turtle and Flip the Frog.

CLEARY, RUTH (RUTH CLEARY PATTERSON)   ASCAP 1942
composer, author, pianist
b Brooklyn, NY. Educ: St Brendan's Acad; Brooklyn Music Sch; studied piano with Berge, Pulgar & organ with Beebe. Piano soloist in radio, TV & hotels; led all women's orch; wrote musical commercials. Honored by Lambs. Chief Collabrs: Floria Vestoff, Fred Heider, Rube Goldberg, Gladys Shelley, Don Raye, Margaret Wise Brown. *Songs:* Music: The Wedding of the Wooden Soldier and the Painted Doll; Down in Toyland Village; A Merry American Christmas; Willie the Whistling Giraffe; The Noise Song; Just a Real Old-Fashioned Sunday; You're Out of My Arms But Still in My Mind; Taffy O'Toole; My First Love; I Like People (The Friendly Song); Rolito; Little Patriots (26 songs); The Land of Lost Buttons; Francois. *Scores:* The Wedding of the Wooden Soldier and the Painted Doll (children's operetta); Stage: Illustrators Shows (12 editions); Russell Patterson's Sketch Book.

CLEBANOFF, HERMAN   ASCAP 1960
composer, conductor, violinist
b Chicago, Ill, May 2, 17. Educ: High sch; studied violin. Violinist, Chicago Civic Orch, became concertmaster; violinist, Chicago Symph & WPA Ill Symph. Staff musician, NBC Chicago, 41, concertmaster later. With New Orleans Symph, 2 yrs. Organized Roosevelt Univ string quartet. Mem, Pro Musica Trio. Cond, Clebanoff Strings. Recordings for Mercury, Decca & Victor of Japan. Extensive concert tours of US & Can. Active as violinist in Hollywood motion picture & TV studios. Comp & arr of orch & string orch works.

CLEMENT, DORIS
composer, author
b Memphis, Tenn. Songwriter. *Songs:* Does My Ring Hurt Your Finger?

CLEMENTS, OTIS   ASCAP 1958
composer, pianist
b Baltimore, Md, July 5, 26. Educ: Peabody Inst, studied comp & orchestration with Nicholas Nabokov, teacher's cert theory & harmony, 47; Juilliard Grad Sch, New York, studied comp with Bernard Wagenaar, 47-49. Rehearsal pianist for John Murray Anderson's Almanac, 53; house pianist, original Blue Angel, NY. Wrote songs & material for Dorothy Loudon, Johnny Mathis, Mabel Mercer & Bobby Short. Comp new songs for Bway revival 73. Performed in twin piano team of Colston & Clements, 65-69 & Bway revival "No, No, Nanette," 71. Chief Collabrs: Charles Gaynor, Sid Shaw, David Rogers, Rod McKuen & Frank Gehrecke. *Songs:* Lonely Little Boy; Music: Once; No Sun in San Francisco. *Scores:* Bway show: An Irish Girl; The Great Lover Tango; Film/TV: Change for the Better; School Play (entry Cannes Fest, 70).

CLEMENTS, PAUL D   ASCAP 1976
composer, author, singer
b Independence, Mo, Jan 11, 47. Educ: William Chrisman High Sch; Univ Mo, Kansas City. Singer & rhythm guitarist with show group, The North Door, 70-73; group worked with Charley Pride, Las Vegas, 71-72. Advert writer & producer, Kansas City, 73-78. Has had work recorded by Columbia Records. Now songwriter & session vocalist, Nashville. *Songs:* Road Song; Feel Good (campaign theme, Heart of America United Way).

CLEVELAND, ROBERT R ASCAP 1966
composer, conductor, teacher
b Batavia, NY, Oct 18, 21. Educ: Univ Rochester Eastman Sch of Music; Univ Buffalo; State Univ NY Fredonia, BS(music educ); Hofstra Univ, MS(educ admin); Univ Mich, choral workshop with Fred Waring. Dir, music educ & performing arts, Amityville pub schs & community band, high sch band, chorus & orch, 49-56, West Islip pub schs, 56-76, Bayport-Bluepoint pub schs, 78- Dir, band, choral activities & Bway shows, Republic Aviation Corp, 53-64. Music & entertainment dir, New York Jets football club, 66-, New York Cosmos, 76-78. Chief Collabs: Michael Stoner, Joan Cleveland. *Instrumental Works:* Jets, Jets, Jets, Jets; Inn Zone; Here Come the Jets; Jet Set Swing; Big Shea; Pep Music Medley; Very Interesting Jets; Go Jets Go.

CLIFF, CHARLES JOSEPH ASCAP 1963
composer, teacher, conductor
b Asheville, NC, Apr 4, 12. Educ: Lee Edwards High Sch; Cath Univ Am, BM, 50, MA, 51, PhD, 53. Performing musician, comp, cond & teacher. Has played in, comp, arr or cond all types orchs, bands & combos, Dixieland, Theatre & Symph. Leader orch, NBC, CBS & MBS Radio, Washington, DC. Comp & cond radio plays & TV shows. Played in many Bway type shows, ballet, operas, concert halls, theatres, etc. Teacher, USN Sch Music, Univ Laval & privately. *Songs:* Music: Victorious; Burgundy and Gold; Passing Along; Time Out; Lucy. *Instrumental Works:* Symph Orch: Overture Pentatomic; Orangoutang Harangue; George Washington's River; Passacaglia (also for organ); Organ: Wedding March (processional); Wedding March (recessional); Piano: Triumvirate. *Songs & Instrumental Works:* Missa Sanctae Joannae de Chantal (mass for male voices with organ & string orch).

CLIFFORD, DOUG R (COSMO) ASCAP 1972
composer, author, singer
b Palo Alto, Calif, Apr 24, 45. Drummer with Creedence Clearwater Revival, 67-72; record producer, 72-78; songwriter, 72- Chief Collabs: Bobby Whitlock, David Vega, Randy Oda & Stu Cook. *Songs:* Need Someone to Hold; What Are You Gonna Do; Tearin up the Country with a Song.

CLIFFORD, GORDON ASCAP 1932
author, actor
b Providence, RI, Mar 28, 02; d Clark, Nev, June 11, 68. Educ: Pawtucket High Sch; studied violin. Actor & songwriter in films, & for Rhythm Boys (Bing Crosby, Harry Barris, Al Rinker). Chief Collabrs: Harry Barris, Nacio Herb Brown. *Songs:* I Surrender Dear; It Must Be True; Paradise; Was It Wrong; Who Am I; Somebody's Birthday; Sahara Nights; The Golden Years.

CLIFFORD, JOHN WILLIAM ASCAP 1968
author
b Springfield, Ill, Oct 19, 18. Educ: Univ Emporia, BS, 52. Vpres writing services, Centron Films; novelist; screenwriter. Chief Collab: Andy Badale. *Songs:* Lyrics: Another Spring; I Hold No Grudge; I Had to Know My Way Around. *Scores:* Opera: Malooley and the Fear Monster (libretto).

CLIFTON, JOHN
See Kestner, John Nelson

CLINT, H O'REILLY ASCAP 1947
composer, author, organist
b Smith Falls, Ont, Sept 20, 1900; d Detroit, Mich, Sept 30, 61. Educ: SFCI; Toronto Cons. Writer, col musical. To US, 20, citizen, 26. Accompanist, with group Wolverine Four, 20-31. Writer & dir for radio shows. Music dir, Knights of Columbus, Mich, 4 yrs. Organist, BPOE, Detroit Lodge, 45-60, St Mary's Church, Detroit. *Songs:* My Michigan (off state song); When It's Night Time in Nevada; I Like to Go Back in the Evening; Step By Step (Am Legion song); Shoulder to Shoulder (off Mich VFW song); When I Dream of the Sweethearts I've Had; We're the Knights of the KofC.

CLINTON, LARRY ASCAP 1937
composer, author
b Brooklyn, NY, Aug 17, 09. Jazz trumpet player; became arr for Dorsey Bros Orch, Glen Gray, Isham Jones, Louis Armstrong & Bunny Berigan, had own orch, 38-50, recorded on RCA Victor & Decca Records. Air Force pilot, 42-46. Studio recording dir, stage & TV appearances, writer of short stories & sci fiction. *Songs:* The Dipsy Doodle; Satan Takes a Holiday; My Reverie; Martha; Molasses, Molasses; An Empty Ballroom; Dreamy Melody; Calypso Melody; Bolero in Blue; Pass the Jam, Sam; Whoa Babe; Lyrics: Our Love. *Instrumental Works:* A Study in Brown; Midnight in a Madhouse; Strictly for the Persians; Tap Dancers Nightmare; Study in Blue; Study in Green; Study in Surrealism; Zig Zag; Shades of Hades; Dodging the Dean; Waddlin' at the Waldorf; Dusk in Upper Sandusky. *Scores:* Film/TV: The Devil With the Devil.

CLOKEY, JOSEPH WADDEL ASCAP 1940
composer, organist, educator
b New Albany, Ind, Aug 28, 1890; d San Dimas, Calif, Sept 14, 1960. Educ: Miami Univ, Ohio, BA, LHD; Cincinnatti Cons. Taught, Western Col for Women, 19-21, Miami Univ, 15-26; prof of organ, Pomona Col; organist, Claremont Col, 26-39; dean, sch of fine arts, Miami Univ, 39-46. Author, "In Every Corner Sing" & "Outline of Church Music." *Songs & Instrumental*

Works: Dorian Symphony; Canterbury Symphony (choral); Violin Sonata; Cello Sonata; Symphonic Fantasy on "St Patrick's Breastplate" (organ); Concert Prelude; Cathedral (prelude); Ballade in D; Symphonic Piece for Organ, Piano; Partita for Organ Piano; South American Nocturnes; The Temple (choral); Missa Festiva; A Canticle of Peace; Christ Conquereth; Nights; The Marshes of Glyn; Te Deum; Steadfast in Faith (cantata: prayer for peace); A Rose From Syria (music drama).

CLOUSER, LIONEL RANDOLPH (LIONEL RAND)
composer, conductor, arranger
b Shamokin, Pa, Feb 19, 10; d New York, NY, Oct 17, 42. Educ: Shamokin High Sch, grad; studied piano with Helen Weysser. Accompanist for Hudnut Sisters in vaudeville; arr, Hildegarde & David Rose; cond & dir orch, Int Casino & Paradise Club, New York; pianist with Milt Herth Trio; worked with Bing Crosby one summer on radio show. Chief Collabrs: Ian Grant, Bob Musel, Gypsy Rose Lee. *Songs & Instrumental Works:* Gone But Not Forgotten; Music: Let There Be Love; Jo-Jo the Hobo; Just Quote Me; Star and Garter.

CLOUTIER, MAURICE E ASCAP 1964
composer, author
b Manchester, NH, June 28, 33. Educ: High sch; USAF Tech Schs; Univ Md. DJ on AFRS-KSRW, Rapid City, SDak; did remote broadcasts for KOTA, Rapid City. Chief Collabr: Raymond E Cloutier. *Songs:* A Memory; Every Star; I'll Try; Music: I Want Your Love; Te Amore; When Spring Is Here.

COAN, NONEE EDWARD ASCAP 1961
author
b Portsmouth, Va, Nov 2, 10. Educ: Southern Bus Univ; Univ Va. Writer for cartoonists & syndicated feature "Small Fry Diary." *Songs:* Boom-A-Dip-Dip; Punkanilla; The Interview; Teen Age Treat; Call, Baby Call.

COATES, CARROLL (ASHTON LLOYD) ASCAP 1968
composer, lyricist, producer
b Old Bridge, Eng, Sept 23, 29. Educ: Oxford Univ; Cambridge Univ. Began as pianist & lyricist comp, musical reviews & stage. Came to US, 52. Wrote spec material for opening stage production, Dunes Hotel, Las Vegas. Entertainment dir, White House Jazz, Laguna Beach. Producer, Jazz Forum Series & Friends of Jazz Fest, Irvine Bowl, Laguna Beach. Extended own jazz label, Jazzworks, 80. Writer lyrics for Peter Nero & Lionel Newman. Worked on summer jazz fest, "Where Did the Summer Go?" *Songs:* No One Ever Tells You; Soft Sand; Kiss Them for Me; A Kiss Before Dying.

COATS, R ROY ASCAP 1954
composer, author, conductor
b Adair, Ill, Jan 3, 1898. Educ: Univ Miss, BA. Clarinetist & saxophonist, bands, pit orch, 16-23. Leader, Shriner Saxophone Band, Univ Miss Band, Brownsville Band, Tenn, R Roy Coats' Sax Band. Organized Memphis Youth Concert Band, 48. Dir, Al Chymia Shrine Band, 51- Author, text for clarinet, "Flying Fingers"; pres, Shrine Bandmasters of NAm, 52-53. *Songs & Instrumental Works:* Keep Your Head Up, America; America Forever, March On; Judge Cliff Davis Blues; Down Where the Sweet Magnolia Blooms; Under the Big Top; The Commercial Appeal March; Golden Nuggets (bk of sacred songs).

COBB, GEORGE L ASCAP 1942
composer, author, arranger
b Mexico, NY, Aug 31, 1886; d Brookline, Mass, Dec 25, 42. Educ: Syracuse Univ. Staff mem, Boston publ. Chief Collabr: Jack Yellen. *Songs & Instrumental Works:* Are You From Dixie; All Aboard for Dixieland; See Dixie First; Alabama Jubilee; Listen to That Dixie Band; Just for Tonight; Mississippi Volunteers; Peter Gink; Power and Glory March.

COBB, TYRONE JENNINGS ASCAP 1970
author
b Salina, Kans, Oct 22, 24. Educ: New Frankfort Grade Sch, Mo; Gonzaga High Sch, Spokane, Wash; Maren Elwood Col, BA. Author, radio scripts incl "Richard Diamond, Private Detective," TV scripts, 50-70, motion pictures incl "Bearheart" & "The Mustangers" & bk, "For You." *Albums:* For You.

COBB, WILL D ASCAP 1927
author
b Philadelphia, Pa, July 6, 1876; d New York, NY, Jan 20, 30. Educ: Girard Col. Dept store salesman before becoming songwriter. Collabr: Gus Edwards. *Songs:* Waltz Me Around Again Willie; Yip-I-Addy-I-Ay; The Little Red School House; School Days; Sunbonnet Sue; I Can't Tell Why I Love You But I Do; Goodbye Little Girl, Goodbye; I Just Can't Make My Eyes Behave; Goodbye Dolly Gray; I'll Be With You When the Roses Bloom Again; Way Down Yonder in the Cornfield; In Zanzibar; If a Girl Like You Loved a Boy Like Me; Laddie Boy.

COBEN, CY ASCAP 1947
composer, author
b Jersey City, NJ. Started career as a trumpeter, became composer in late 40's, wrote country & popular songs until 51. Went to Europe, wrote songs for many prominent singers, 61. *Songs:* The Old Piano Roll Blues; Sweet Violets; A Good Woman's Love; Nobody's Child; Burning a Hole in My Mind; Lonely Little

Robin; The Game of Triangle; Chet's Tune; Eddy's Song; The Great El Tigre; Souvenirs, Souvenirs; The Name of the Game Was Love; You're a Real Good Friend; There's Been a Change in Me; I Wanna Play House With You; Would You Mind?; I'm a Walkin' Advertisement for the Blues; Punky Punkin; Greasy Kid Stuff; Johnny's Cash and Charlie's Pride; Every Body Wants to Go to Heaven; How Come There's No Dog Day?; Lyrics: If You're Irish Come Into the Parlor; How Do Y'a Do and Shake Hands.

COBEY, LOUIS ASCAP 1944
composer, pianist
b Poughkeepsie, NY, Oct 4, 1897; d Nutley, NJ, Nov 9, 72. Educ: Studied piano with Harry Bock, Carl Roeder & Jacques Friedberger. Pianist in orchs, radio & for player piano rolls. USAAF, WW II. *Songs:* Out of a Million; A Picture of You; Cinderella's Wedding Day; Red Roses; So Is My Love for You; Silhouettes; Love Is Just a Gamble; plus many others.

COBURN, RICHARD ASCAP 1921
author, singer
b Ipswich, Mass, June 8, 1886; d Phelan, Calif, Oct 27, 52. Songwriter for revue "Fancies." Chief Collabrs: John Schonberger, Vincent De Rose, Richard Winfree. *Songs:* Whispering; Tell Me Why; Oriental; Mummy; Nightingale; Behind a Silken Veil; I'll Keep Loving You; Day by Day; Patsy; Day Dreaming.

COBURN, WILLIAM JAMES ASCAP 1973
composer, author, teacher
b Allegan, Mich, Feb 25, 13. Educ: Mich State Univ, BA(music, piano), studied comp under Arthur Farwell & Llewellyn Gomer, piano under Lewis Richards; Eastman Sch Music, MA, studied comp under Bernard Rogers. Music dir, World Radio Univ & New York Song Spinners; concert pianist; music dir & performed sacred works, Hollywood Congregational Church; performed sacred works in Hollywood Bowl & Forest Lawn. *Songs:* Bright 'n' Shiny; Music: The Master Is Coming.

COCHRANE, TALIE
See Wright, Lilian Cochrane

CODIAN, MICHAEL (MICKEY) ASCAP 1957
composer, author, conductor
b Akron, Ohio, July 7, 15. Educ: Col. Trumpeter, var orchs incl Jerry Wald, Art Mooney. Cond, New York Symph, 3 yrs. Has own band, Calif. *Songs:* Thanks for Christmas; I Can't Believe It; Johnnies in the Pantry; Snow Country.

CODY, PHILIP
composer, author
b Westchester, NY, June 6, 45. Educ: Valhalla High Sch. Songwriter. Chief Collabr: Neil Sedaka. *Songs:* Laughter in the Rain; Bad Blood; Love in the Shadows; Solitaire; The Immigrant; Should Have Never Let You Go. *Albums:* Sedakas Back (gold album); The Hungry Years (gold album).

CODY, WILLIAM FREDERICK ASCAP 1959
composer, author, singer
b New York, NY, June 6, 13. Educ: Los Angeles City Col; Univ Calif, Los Angeles; Don Martin Radio Broadcasting Sch, grad, studied voice with Albert Ruff; Am Operatic Acad. With Los Angeles Catholic Theatre Guild. Sgt, Army Airways Communications, India, World War II. Singer, radio, nightclubs, TV & with Los Angeles Opera Co. Writer, special material & featured songs for revue "Les Hollywood", Statler Hotel, Los Angeles. Winner, Andy Award cert for Coca-Cola commercial, 68 & Am Song Fest lyric contest, 78. Chief Collabrs: Karen O'Hara, Denny McReynolds, Phil Methot. *Songs:* Lyrics: Petite Chanson; Suddenly I'm Sad; Fire on the Mountain; Over My Shoulder; Mambo Shmambo; Hollywood and Vine; This Is Show Biz; My Young Heart; Remember Your First Love.

COELHO, TERRYE LYNN (TERRYE STROM)
composer, author, singer
b Camp Roberts, Calif, Aug 6, 52. Educ: Ariz State Univ. Began writing Christian music in 71; sang in group called, Lamb, 72; songwriter; sang on 2 albums. *Songs:* Father, I Adore You; Matthew 16:24. *Albums:* The Praise; The Joy.

COGANE, NELSON ASCAP 1940
composer, author
b Dayton, Ohio, Dec 25, 02. Educ: Pub schs. Sports writer, Dayton Journal. Bus mgr, Mike Riley Orch. Columnist, Music Business mag. ASCAP Writers Adv Comt, chmn, Clef Award, Carnegie Hall, 45. Chief Collabrs: Sigmund Romberg, Charles Tobias, James P Johnson, Frank Weldon, Sammy Mysels, Sammy Fain, J Russel Robinson, Jerry Livingston, Mike Riley, Denes Agay, Lee David, James F Hanley, Jimmie Davis. *Songs:* Oh How He Can Salute; Talk to the Boss in the Sky; Michigan Bankroll; Hey, Hey; Number Twenty in the Books; Eight Little Notes; Is There Somebody Else?; We Three (My Echo, My Shadow and Me); Yesterday's Gardenias; There's a Chill on the Hill; The Spelling Bee; Old Songs Bring Memories; Off the Shores of Somewhere; Emancipation; What Does the Lord Look Like?; (We're Making the World) A Better World; Our Hearts Are Full of Song; (Now Is the Time to) Thank the Lord.

COGGIN, C ELWOOD ASCAP 1965
composer, author
b Hamlet, NC, Nov 13, 14. Educ: Campbell Col, NC, AA; Univ NC, Chapel Hill; Southern Baptist Theol Sem, Louisville, BSM. Minister music, assoc pastor in Southern Baptist Churches, Ky, SC, NC, 25 yrs. Dir of Pastoral Care, PTL TV Network, Int Counseling Ctr. Adjunct teacher comp, arr, Heritage Sch Evangel. *Songs:* Thy Love Brings Joy; Thou Art Jesus, Savior and Lord; Alleluia, Praise God; Music: Resurrection Fanfare; Ye Are the Light of the World; From the Rising of the Sun; Sing Praise to God, O My Soul; Here is Joy for Every Age, In the Cross of Christ I Glory; Brother, Clasps the Hand of Brother; It is a Thing Most Wonderful; Lord Jesus Christ, All Praise to Thee; What Grace, O Lord, and Beauty Shone; O God, Let People Praise Thee; Thy Hand, O God, Has Guided; Blessed is the Nation; Glorious is the Lord Almighty; O Come, Let Us Worship; Christian, Rise; Be Glad and Rejoice; Thou Wilt Keep Him in Perfect Peace; Sing, O Sing This Blessed Morn; The Lord of Glory Came to Earth; O God's Love Freely Given; Hosanna in the Highest; Jesus is the Name We Treasure.

COHAN, GEORGE MICHAEL ASCAP 1914
composer, author, producer
b Providence, RI, July 3, 1878; d New York, NY, Nov 5, 42. At 9, joined parents vaudeville act incl sister, Josephine; act then known as "The Four Cohans." Wrote songs, sketches for own act, also others. In producing, mgt partnership with Sam Harris, 04-20. Bway stage actor: "The Governor's Son"; "Broadway Jones"; "A Prince There Was"; "The Song-and-Dance Man"; "American Born"; "Gambling"; "Dear Old Darling"; "The Return of the Vagabond." Bway stage dir: "Forty-Five Minutes From Broadway." Bway stage actor, co-producer & dir: "Little Johnny Jones"; "George Washington, Jr"; "The Honeymooners"; "The Yankee Prince"; "The Little Millionaire"; "Hello, Broadway." Bway stage Co-producer & dir: "The Talk of New York"; "Fifty Miles From Boston"; "The American Idea"; "The Man Who Owns Broadway"; "The Cohan Revue" (16, 18); "The Royal Vagabond." Bway stage actor, producer & dir: "The Merry Malones." Bway stage producer & dir: "Little Nellie Kelly"; "The Rise of Rosie O'Reilly"; "The Tavern"; "Elmer the Great." Playwright, co-producer & dir: "Get-Rich-Quick Wallingford"; "Seven Keys to Baldpate"; "The Miracle Man"; "Hit-the-Trail Haliday." Producer, "The O'Brien Girl." Other Bway appearances: "Ah, Wilderness!"; "I'd Rather Be Right." Awarded Congressional Medal of Honor for patriotic songs. Autobiography, "Twenty Years on Broadway." Biography, "George M Cohan - Prince of the American Theatre", by Ward Morehouse. Film biography, "Yankee Doodle Dandy." Charter mem, ASCAP. Dir. *Songs:* Venus, My Shining Love; I Guess I'll Have to Telegraph My Baby; The Yankee Doodle Boy; My Musical Comedy Maid; Revolutionary Rag; Give My Regards to Broadway; You Remind Me of My Mother; Life's a Funny Proposition After All; Mary's a Grand Old Name; So Long, Mary; Forty-Five Minutes From Broadway; I Was Born in Virginia; Harrigan; Over There; You're a Grand Old Flag; In a Kingdom of Our Own; Nellie Kelly, I Love You; When June Comes Along With a Song; Molly Malone; Where Were You, Where Was I?; Billie. *Scores:* Bway Stage, librettos: The Governor's Son; Forty-Five Minutes From Broadway; Little Johnny Jones; George Washington, Jr; The Honeymooners; The Yankee Prince; The Little Millionaire; Hello, Broadway; The Talk of New York; Fifty Miles From Boston; The American Idea; The Man Who Owns Broadway; The Cohan Revue (16, 18); The Royal Vagabond; The Merry Malones; Little Nellie Kelly; The Rise of Rosie O'Reilly.

COHEN, AV SHALOM ASCAP 1962
composer, author
b Tel Aviv, Israel, May 13, 28. Educ: Teacher's Inst. *Songs:* Agala Ve-Sussa; Hasabta Banegev; Mechol Hakerem.

COHEN, CHARLES
See Kingsford, Charles

COHEN, DANIEL (CASEY KELLY) ASCAP 1970
composer, author, arranger
b Baton Rouge, La, Educ: La State Univ, Baton Rouge. Pianist; lead singer & guitarist for bands; recorded for var artists; producer, recording artist. Chief Collabrs: Julie Didier, Lewis Anderson. Other Collabrs: Bitsy Didier, Boomer Castleman, Paul Harrison, Marlin Greene, Jerry Barlow, Kenny Loggins, Paul Craft, Mark James, Dennis Parnell, Jeff Silbar, Phil Everly. *Songs:* Anyone Who Isn't Me Tonight; Beautiful to Handle; For Love's Own Sake; God, Does She Look Good; I'd Do Anything for You; I Loved You All the Way; May You Find Yourself in Heaven; Let Me Sing for You; Love to Burn; Nashville Connection; Pretty Lies; She's Gonna Do Somebody Right; To Get Back At Me; Where You Been; You Still Know the Way to My Heart; Do It in the Name of Love; Crossfires of Desire; Best Friends Make the Worst Enemies; Your Love Baby; Only Game in Town; Princess Lala; Take What You Find; Lassiez Les Bon Temps Rouler (Let the Good Times Roll); A Good Love Is Like a Good Song; Poor Boy; You Set a Fire in My Soul; Polly (The Newspaper Dolly).

COHEN, EDWIN GREINES ASCAP 1958
composer, author
b Ft Worth, Tex, Feb 1, 34. Educ: Tulane Univ; Tex Christian Univ, BA, MA. Owner, Greines Furniture Co; vpres & dir, Cash Mgt Consulting, Inc. *Songs:*

Mr Success; Compromise; A Million to One; Hurt Me; Someone Someone; Dark.

COHEN, JEROME D ASCAP 1966
composer, conductor, arranger
b Spokane, Wash, Feb 6, 36. Educ: Eastern Wash State Col, 54-56; New Eng Cons Music, BMus (with hons), 59, MMus, 63, studied comp with F Judd Cooke, cond with Richard Burgin; Tanglewood. Cond experience incl Boston Pops, RI Philh, NJ Symph & var community orchs; music asst to Boston Pops Cond, John Williams, currently. *Instrumental Works:* Old Folks Quadrille; Lullaby of Birdland (arr for symph orch); Concert Overture No 1.

COHEN, JOSEPH (JOE COWEN) ASCAP 1956
composer, author, musician
b New York, NY, Aug 16, 18. Educ: Studied violin privately; piano, comp & harmony self-taught. Started composing at age 9. Wrote classical (modern) type music, country western, blues, ballads, Latin melodies & instrumentals. Chief Collabrs: Buddy Kaye, Don Canton, Lee Kauderer, George Mysels, Harry Gitter, Harry Fenster & Redd Evans. *Songs:* Quack-a-Doodle, Deedle; A Promise Made a Fool of Me; My Gay Paree Waltz; Music: Santa Claus March; Mountain Gold.

COHEN, JOSEPH M ASCAP 1958
composer, author, arranger
b New York, NY, Aug 3, 17. Educ: Tex Christian Univ, BM, MM; Univ Rochester Eastman Sch of Music. Pianist & arr, dance bands & singers. *Songs:* Mother's Little Soldier Boy; Keeper of Dreams; The World Stands Still; Anyone at All; Is It Too Late?. *Instrumental Works:* Rondo; Theme and Variations; Allegro; Adagio Assa. *Scores:* Ballet: Rhapsody for Three.

COHEN, LANE NATHAN ASCAP 1978
composer, author
b Hamilton, Ohio, Jan 2, 51. Educ: Univ Cincinnati, BA(political sci), Cons Music, musical theatre minor. Singer, nightclubs; stage performer, "West Side Story." In local TV prog. Chief Collabr: Mitch Cohen (brother). *Songs:* Back in My Arms Again; Eyes of a Stranger; Lyrics: All the Sad Young Girls.

COHEN, SHELDON ASCAP 1959
composer, author
b Brooklyn, NY, Nov 8, 33. Educ: Brooklyn Col; Juilliard Sch Music; Hartnett Sch Music. Music librarian, NBC; played violin & clarinet as a prof musician; arr & comp, choral cond, St Mels Church, 8 yrs; asst musical cond, "The Tonight Show," 62-; recording artist, NAm Liturgy Resources & The Franciscan Communication Ctr. Has written many comp, both popular & classical. Chief Collabrs: Don K Epstein & Joseph Mazza. *Songs:* Yosemite Suite; The Life of Christ; Celestial Echoes; Rejoice in the Lord; Rejoice and be Glad; It's a Brand New Day; Brother Love Brother; Go in Peace; My Friend Jesus; Hear His Holy Word; Lullaby of the Angels; One Little Babe; He is Here; Seascape; The Song of Roland; Beauty and the Beast; Magnificat; Requiem.

COHEN, SOL B (ANDRE VANEUF) ASCAP 1944
composer, conductor, violinist
b Urbana, Ill, Jan 11, 1891. Educ: Chicago Musical Col; Ecole Normal de Musique, Paris; studied with Emile Sauret, Hugo Heermann, Jeno Hubay, Ottokar Sevcik, Max d'Ollone. Debut as violinist, Chicago, 11; recitals throughout midwest & west coast of US. First violinist, Cincinnati Symph, 12-13, Los Angeles Philh, 22-23. Comp & arr, films, 21-24. Cond, Ruth St Denis & Ted Shawn Ballet, 29-30, Peoria Symph, 42-43, Champaign-Urbana Community-Arts Orch, 51-52. Fac, Nat Music Camp, Interlochen, 36. Music dir, Springdale Sch, Canton, NC, 44-49, Asheville Sch for Boys, 55-59, Roosevelt Sch, Stamford, Conn, 59-62. Mem, MacDowell Colony. *Songs:* The White Swan; Gethsemane; *Instrumental Works:* Alabama Sketches (4 clarinets); Colonial Sketches (4 flutes); Ballad of Olympus (symph); Contrapuntal Capers (string orch).

COHN, AL ASCAP 1955
composer, saxophonist
b Brooklyn, NY, Nov 24, 25. Educ: Pvt music study. Saxophonist in orchs, incl Joe Marsala, Alvino Rey, Buddy Rich & Woody Herman. On "Hit Parade," radio. Wrote for Andy Williams, Pat Boone & Steve Allen TV shows. Arr & saxophonist, RCA Victor, 55-56. Formed quintet, 57 & appeared in nightclubs, jazz fests. Has made many records.

COHN, ARTHUR ASCAP 1958
composer
b Philadelphia, Pa, Nov 6, 10. Educ: Combs Cons; Juilliard Sch Music, fellowship. Curator, dir, Edwin A Fleisher Music Col, 34-52; head of music dept, Free Libr Philadelphia, 46-52. Exec dir, Settlement Music Sch, Philadelphia, 52-56. Head of symph, Foreign Music Dept, NY publ co, 56- Cond, Symph Club Orch, Philadelphia, 23 yrs & Haddonfield Symph Soc, NJ, 59- Guest cond many orchs. Dir of serious music, Carl Fischer, Inc, 73- Author "The Collectors 20th Century Music in Western Hemisphere", "20th Century Music in Western Europe" & "Musical Quizzical." Recorded classical music. *Instrumental Works:* Quotations in Percussion; Kaddish for Orchestra; Bassoon: Declamation and Toccata; Hebraic Study.

COHN, GREGORY PHIL (WALTER LANE) ASCAP 1957
composer, author, organist
b St Louis, Mo, Apr 20, 19. Educ: Strassberger Cons Music, 33-37, studied with Carl Wilhelm Kern. Organist, TV; recording artist; dir; teacher. Chief Collabr: Norman Kaye. *Songs:* Strange; Don't You Wanna Be in St Louis?; Music: Regretfully. *Instrumental Works:* Fire Dancer; Imitationettes (vols I, II); Forest Solitude.

COHN, JAMES MYRON ASCAP 1960
composer, musicologist
b Newark, NJ, Feb 12, 28. Educ: Pre-col pvt instr with Hans Weisse, Rudolph Gruen, William Berwald, Wayne Barlow, Roy Harris, Bernard Wagenaar; Juilliard, studied musicol with Robert Tangeman; Juilliard Grad Sch, scholarship, 45-49, BS(comp), 49; Juilliard Sch Music, MS, 50; Hunter Col Electronic Music Studio, studied with Ruth Anderson, 73. Var jobs in New York, 50-52. Joined ASCAP staff, program dept, New York, 52, transferred to symph & concert div, became musicologist, 53- Comp works incl 8 symphonies, 3 string quartets, 3 piano sonatas, chamber & choral music. *Instrumental Works:* Symphony No 2 (Queen Elisabeth Belg Prize, 53); Symphony No 3; Variations on The Wayfaring Stranger (for orch); The Little Circus (orchestral suite); Baroque Suite (for flute alone); Sonata for Flute and Piano; Variations on John Henry (concert band or orch); A Song of the Waters (Variations on Shenandoah). *Scores:* Opera: The Fall of the City.

COHN, STEPHEN ASCAP 1965
composer, author, producer
b Hollywood, Calif. Educ: Whitman Col, Wash; Calif State Col, Northridge, BS(music), 63; Univ Calif Sch Music, Los Angeles, grad. Gave classical guitar recital in col. Joined group, Pleasure Faire; recorded with MCA Records. Staff writer, Koppleman-Rubin Co & Jobette Music. Writer, artist & producer (3 yrs.), 2 albums & over 50 recorded & released songs, Motown Records. Writer of numerous TV title themes. Wrote songs for films, "Free-Wheelin'" & "Hang on to a Star." Wrote commercials for Hang Ten Leisure Clothing. Teacher, Oval Music Eng Sch, Univ Sound Arts, Sherwood Oaks Exp Col & Hollywood Sch Recording Arts, 78- Has own co with Raffaello Mazza, Oval Productions, 79- *Scores:* TV: Carleton, Your Doorman (Emmy Nomination); Heaven on Earth. *Albums:* Stephen Cohn.

COHN, STEWART ASCAP 1960
author
b Crestwood, Ky, July 18, 21. Educ: Ind Univ, BS. Writer, musical commericals & radio & TV scripts. *Songs:* Too Soon.

COHON, BARUCH JOSEPH (BARRY) ASCAP 1962
composer, author, singer
b Chicago, Ill, Apr 28, 26. Educ: Hughes High Sch; Univ Cincinnati; Univ Calif, Los Angeles, BA; cantorial studies with A Z Idelsohn, Jacob Beimel; rabbinical ordination by Dr Henoch Singer, Los Angeles, 69. Served, USN, World War II. Pianist, dance bands, 46-50. Writer & production mgr, TV films, 52-62. Cantor & music dir, var congregations, 43- Instr, Jewish music, Hebrew Union Col & Univ of Judaism, Los Angeles, 72- Music ed, "The Jewish Song Book", by A Z Idelsohn. *Songs & Instrumental Works:* Let There Be Light (cantata with chorus & orch); Avodas Simchoh—Service of Joy (collection of original liturgical compositions).

COLAIACO, ALFRED JAMES ASCAP 1971
composer, arranger, trombonist
b Rome, Italy, Nov 22, 13. Educ: Pvt study of violin, guitar & banjo with Walter Selnick, harmony & comp with Otto Cesana, & trombone. Arr, var dance orchs, incl Bunny Berigan. Free-lance arr, var artist incl Roberta Peters, Robert Merrill, Maurice Chevalier, Hildegard, Elaine Malbin, Dorothy Sarnoff, Kaye Ballard, Diahann Carrol & Jimmy Dean. Staff arr, CBS-TV progs incl "American Musical Theater" & WOR-radio, "Mutual Melody Hour." Trombonist & arr, Jack Teagarden Orch. Writer, NBC & CBS for var TV shows incl "Ed Sullivan Show", "Perry Como Show", "Jack Paar" & "Johnny Carson." Chief Collabr: Thomas Hood. *Songs:* I Remember, I Remember. *Instrumental Works:* Dusk (string orch, tone poem); Prelude in E flat (piano); Etude in E flat (piano); Prelude in B flat (piano).

COLAMOSCA, FRANK O (FRANK COLE) ASCAP 1960
composer, author, pianist
b Philadelphia, Pa, May 30, 10. Educ: Studied piano & comp with Joseph Messina, 5 yrs. Played many yrs with small combos & solo, local Philadelphia & NJ taverns & nightclubs. Worked for Merck, Sharp & Dohme, 27 yrs. *Songs:* Sunbeams; My Saturday Date.

COLANZI, RICHARD P ASCAP 1961
composer, author
b Philadelphia, Pa, Feb 26, 29. Educ: High sch. Promotion mgr for Elvis Presley; professional mgr, Myers Music. *Songs:* Little Girl.

COLBERT, WARREN ERNEST (DANE WARREN) ASCAP 1973
composer, author
b Baltimore, Md, Feb 24, 29. Educ: Grammer & high schs, Glen Burnie, Md; Cons Music, Paris, France; Baltimore Col Commerce, accounting; studied piano

with Edmund Hammerbacher, Jack Sylvester & Marcel Ciampi. Pianist & arr, Joe Hoffman's Top Hatters, 40's; staff pianist, The Cheshire Inn, Ellicott City, Md, 11 yrs; author, "Who in the Hell Is J Fred Coots?" *Songs:* A Mother's Day Card in a Song; Fifty Bucks Down South (Alimony Blues); The Swing Years; Those Good Old-Fashioned Ice Cream Parlor Days. *Instrumental Works:* Corrida de Toros.

COLBY, MICHAEL ELIHU   ASCAP 1976
author
b New York, NY, Oct 29, 51. Educ: Syracuse Univ, Sch Press Inst, degree in jour, 68; Northwestern Univ, BA, 73; NY Univ, MA, 74. Contributed lyrics and/or librettos to Bway Musicals, "Olmsted", "North Atlantic" & "Another Time." Wrote Christmas opera, "Ludlow Ladd"; wrote lyrics for children's shows "Androcles and the Lion" & "Harlequin and Company." Best Production of the Year Award, 77. Chief Collabrs: Jerry Markoe, Jack Urbont & Jim Fradrich.

COLBY, ROBERT   ASCAP 1954
composer, author, publisher
b Rolling Fork, Miss. Educ: Univ Miss; Juilliard Sch; Am Theatre Wing; studied with Otto Cesana. Lt(sg), USN, WW II. Writer, Tommy & Jimmy Dorsey Orch, Ella Fitzgerald, Red Buttons, Vaughn Monroe, Teresa Brewer, Howard Keel, Barbra Streisand, Jack Jones, Nancy Wilson, Maurice Chevalier, Steve Lawrence & Eydie Gorme; produced stage shows, "The Male of the Species", "Kennedy's Children" & "The Red Devil Battery Sign" (Tennessee Williams). *Songs:* Jilted; My Friend the Ghost; How Lovely, How Lovely; Warm Heart-Cold Feet; The Day the West Was Swung; To the Movies We Go; That Ol' Christmas Spirit; Hey! Go a Little Slow; Baby; Too Bad; Women Are Here to Stay; Wintertime; When Ev'rything Was Green; Where Do I Go From Here?; Free Again; The Male of the Species; Grandparents (Ev'ry Baby's Best Friend); Companionship; To the Movies We Go; Marry Me! Marry Me!; Last Summer. *Scores:* Off-Bway Show: Half-Past Wednesday.

COLDER, BEN
See Wooley, Sheb

COLE, FRANK
See Colamosca, Frank O

COLE, GEORGE BURT   ASCAP 1959
composer, arranger, teacher
b South Portland, Maine, Mar 25, 05. Educ: Providence High Sch, RI; Brown Univ, BA; Columbia Univ; NY Univ; Fairleigh Dickinson Univ; studied with Mme Herscher-Clement, Paris, France, Dr Jacques Spaanderman, France & Dr Wesley LaViolette, Los Angeles, Calif. Studied piano at age 5 1/2; professional when in high sch. Worked in Europe, 27-32; arr-pianist for Enoch Light until 38. Free lance arr for music publ until 41; arr for CBS, 41-56; arr, Hollywood, 57; house arr for Peer-Southern, E B Marks, Allied Artists & Warner Bros. Chosen as rep contemporary composer, Univ Wyo Library Contemporary Music. Mem: Composers & Lyricists Guild of Am; Am Soc Music Arrangers. Chief Collabrs: James Cole, Evelyn Cole, Peter Johnstone, Donald J Hayes & Hank Sylvern. *Songs:* Music: Pop Eye's Zoo; Mini-Mass (choral); A Child's Day in Song. *Instrumental Works:* Seven Impressions (3 trombones & baritone/tuba); Six Character Impressions of Friends (piano); Hands at a Spanish Gate; Tango del Alma; Rippling Tango; Tango de Amor; Tango Pampero; Timbales Mambo; The Hawaiian Waltz; The Alaskan Waltz; The Ingenue Mambo; The Panther Mambo; Top Hat Mambo; The Arabian Nights.

COLE, NATHANIEL ADAMS (NAT KING)   ASCAP 1948
composer, author, pianist
b Montgomery, Ala, Mar 17, 19; d Santa Monica, Calif, Feb 15, 65. Educ: Pub schs; pvt piano study. Formed own band & toured vaudeville with revue, "Shuffle Along." Pianist in nightclubs; formed own trio, 39, appeared in nightclubs, theatres & concerts. Radio series with jazz group, 48-49; solo TV series, 56-57. Singer, US & var foreign countries; recording artist with many records. Appeared in motion pictures incl "The Blue Gardenia", "The Nat King Cole Story", "St Louis Blues" & "China Gate." *Songs:* I'm a Shy Guy; Straighten Up and Fly Right; That Ain't Right; It's Better to Be By Yourself; Just for Old Time's Sake; Calypso Blues; With You on My Mind; To Whom It May Concern.

COLE, OLENA J   ASCAP 1979
composer, author
b Magdalena, N Mex, Aug 7, 26. Chief Collabr: Bobbie Jenkerson. *Songs:* Lyrics: Honky Tonk Tears.

COLE, ROBERT L (ROBERTO)   ASCAP 1947
composer, author
b Mayagüez, PR, Sept 7, 15. Educ: Studied with Maestro Jose A Gaudier, harmony & counterpoint with Alfredo Romero. Guitarist & Puertorican cuatro (4 string guitar) player, early yrs. Comp, popular tunes. String bassist with Gay Collegians Orch; To San Juan, PR, bassist & arr, Rafael Munoz Orch. In govt service, chief photographer, 36 yrs, now retired; comp & arr, currently. *Songs:* Olvidame; Romance del Campesino; Cancion de la Serrania; Lirio Blanco; Sigue tu Camino; Le-Lo-Lah; Querida Mia; Penumbra; Que Bonita; Mensajes; A Mayagüez; Lamento del Campesino; Timida; Me Gustas Mucho; Terrible Duda;

No Importa; Mi Loca Fantasia; Sera Mejor; Tu Olvido; En Luna Llena; Enigma; Imagen (waltz-song); Siempre Linda; Para Ti; Una Aventura. *Instrumental Works:* Gisela (dance, prize winner, Puertorican Culture Inst, 78).

COLE, ULRIC   ASCAP 1941
composer, pianist, teacher
b New York, NY, Sept 9, 05. Educ: Pvt piano instr from mother, then with Homer Grunn, Los Angeles, until 23; Inst Musical Art, studied advanced counterpoint with Percy Goetschius & piano with George Boyle; awarded piano fel with Josef Lhevinne & comp fel with Rubin Goldmark, Juilliard Grad Sch, 24; studied with Nadia Boulanger, Paris, 27-28. Appeared as pianist; at 18, Chautauqua Tour of Midwest; guest artist, Cincinnati Symph; performed own works with NBC String Symph, Juilliard Orch, Gordon String Quartet, Conn String Quartet & others; piano & comp teacher. *Instrumental Works:* Quintet for Piano and String Quartet; Sonata for Violin and Piano (Soc Publ Am Music Awards); Divertimento for String Orchestra and Piano; Three Vignettes (piano); Three Metropolitones (piano); Man-About-Town (two pianos); Two Pieces for String Orchestra; Sunlight Channel (orch); Nevada (orch); String Quartet No 1; Concerto for Piano and Orchestra No 2; Piano Concerto.

COLEMAN, CY   ASCAP 1953
composer, pianist
b New York, NY, June 14, 29. Educ: High Sch of Music & Art; New York Col of Music; studied with Rudolph Gruen (scholarship), Adele Marcus. First piano recitals at age 6, Carnegie Hall, Steinway Hall & Town Hall, New York. Led own trio; soloist in nightclubs, hotels & TV; songwriter, "John Murray Anderson's Almanac"; music writer for industrials; writer TV spec, "If They Could See Me Now" (two Emmy Awards); co-author & co-producer, "Gypsy in My Soul" (Emmy Award); artist, producer & arr for major labels; honored with six Grammy nominations, five Tony nominations, a Drama Desk Award & Cue's Golden Apple. Pres, Notable Music Co, Inc, mem bd dirs, The Dramatists Guild Coun & ASCAP. Chief Collabrs: Carolyn Leigh, Joseph Allen McCarthy, Bob Hilliard, Peggy Lee, Dorothy Fields, Michael Stewart; Betty Comden, Adolph Green. *Songs:* Paris Is My Old Kentucky Home; Why Try to Change Me Now; I'm Gonna Laugh You Right Out of My Life; The Riviera; Isn't He Adorable?; Early Morning Blues; Playboy Theme; I Walk a Little Faster; Firefly; Witchcraft; You Fascinate Me So; On Second Thought; Hey, Look Me Over; Tall Hopes; El Sombrero; One Day We Dance; The Best Is Yet to Come; The Other Side of the Tracks; I've Got Your Number; Real Live Girl; Here's to Us; It Amazes Me; That's My Style; A Doodlin' Song; When in Rome; Pass Me By; Pussycat; Then Was Then, Now Is Now; Big Spender; There's Gotta Be Something Better Than This; Where Am I Going?; If My Friends Could See Me Now; Pass Me By; Music: Theme From the Heartbreak Kid; Seesaw; It's Not Where You Start It's Where You Finish; Nobody Does It Like Me; I Love My Wife; Hey There Good Times; On the Twentieth Century; Never; Our Private World; The Colors of My Life; There Is a Sucker Born Every Minute; Come Follow the Band. *Scores:* Bway Musicals: Seesaw; I Love My Wife; On the Twentieth Century (Tony Award); Barnum; Bway Stage: Wildcat; Little Me; Sweet Charity; Films: The Troublemaker; Father Goose; The Art of Love; Sweet Charity (Oscar nominee); The Heartbreak Kid; Background Music: Compulsion.

COLEMAN, HERBERT   ASCAP 1963
composer, author
b New York, NY, Oct 2, 27. Educ: City Col New York. Chief Collabrs: Bobby Scott, Phil Davis, Vin Roddie, Joe Fanelli, Fred Norman. *Songs:* Lyrics: Four Square Melody; Whispering My Name; How Long; High Iron Man; Grand Finale. *Scores:* Bway show: Bo; Film/TV: Festival Time; Kokomo; Travel Is Love.

COLEMAN, JACK LAMBERT   ASCAP 1971
composer, author, conductor
b Denver, Colo, Jan 23, 20. Educ: Univ Southern Calif, BS & MEd, 58; studied comp with Joseph Wagner. Songwriter, 60- Singer in Hollywood TV & radio. Mem, Country Church of Hollywood Quartet, 12 yrs. Music supvr, city schs, Santa Ana, Calif. Music coordr, Orange County schs. Educ dir, Walt Disney Music Co, Burbank, Calif & Hansen Publ, Miami Beach, Fla. Coordr, Geneva Youth Musicale, Switz, 72-75. *Songs:* A City of the King; The Centurion; The Boy Who Caught the Fish; Zack Junior; Journey From Bethlehem. *Albums:* Centurion (Emmy Nomination, 72); Zack Junior.

COLEMAN, ORNETTE   ASCAP 1963
composer, saxophonist
b Ft Worth, Tex, Mar 29, 30. Educ: Sch of Jazz, Lenox, Mass. Saxophonist with many bands. Worked in Ft Worth carnival; toured with var groups. Involved with progressive jazz; appeared in jazz concerts; recording artist with many records; trumpeter & violinist. Retired, 2 yrs to study, resumed prof career, 65. *Instrumental Works:* Lonely Woman; Sadness; Ramblin'; Turnaround.

COLEMAN, PATRICIA   ASCAP 1972
composer, author
b Philadelphia, Pa, Mar 17, 30. Songwriter, 18 yrs. *Songs:* Stop the Traffic; His Unspeakable Gift; The Eyes of a Child; Conversing With a Fool; Locked in Love.

COLEMAN, RICHARD E   ASCAP 1959
composer, author, singer
b Anniston, Ala, Dec 17, 33. Educ: Col. Writer of musical commercials. Chief Collabrs: Jerry Keller, George Goehring, Marc Fredericks. *Songs:* Workin' Hands; Some Summer; The Slosh.

COLEMAN, RUTH
See Bilchick, Ruth Coleman

COLGRASS, MICHAEL
composer
b Chicago, Ill, Apr 22, 32. Educ: Univ Ill, MusB, 56; Tanglewood (scholar), Mass, 52 & 54, Aspen, Colo, 53; studied with Paul Price, Eugene Weigle, Darius Milhaud, Lukas Foss, Wallingford Riegger & Ben Weber. Served in AUS, 54-56. Free-lance solo percussionist, maj New York music orgns, 56- Soloist, Danish Radio Orch, 65. Author & poet of own theatre works, 66- Narrator, Boston Symph, 69 & Philadelphia Orch, 70. Dir, "Virgil's Dream," Brighton Fest. Dir opera, "Nightingale, Inc," Univ Ill Contemporary Music Fest, 75. Grants & Awards: Guggenheim Fels, 64-65 & 68-69; Fromm Award, 66; Rockefeller Grantee, 67-69; Chem Bank Award, 71. Works comn by New York Philh, CBC, Boston Symph, Lincoln Ctr Chamber Music Soc, Fromm Found, Corp Pub Broadcasting, Ford Found, Spokane, Detroit, Springfield, Minn Symph Orchs, Musica Aeterna Orch New York, Young Concert Artists, New York & Nat Arts Centre Orch of Can. *Songs & Instrumental Works:* Divertimento; Fantasy Variations; Wind Quintet; Light Spirit; Rhapsody; Rhapsodic Fantasy; Sea Shadow; As Quiet As; Virgil's Dream; Three Brothers; Percussion Music; Chamber Music for Four Drums and String Quintet; Chamber Music for Percussion Quintet; Variations for Four Drums and Viola; The Earth's a Baked Apple; New People (mezzosoprano, viola, piano); Auras for Harp and Orch; Image of Man; Concertmaster (3 violins, orch); Best Wishes USA (black & white choruses, folk instruments, jazz band, orch); Theatre of the Universe (soloists, chorus, orch); Mystery Flowers of Spring (soprano, piano); Wolf (solo cello); Letter From Mozart (orch); Deja Vu (Pulitzer Prize, 78); The Tower (a musical play for children's theatre); Flashbacks (a musical play for five brass); Night of the Raccoon (5 songs for soprano & 4 players); Delta (violin, clarinet, perc, orch). *Scores:* Comic Jazz Opera: Nightingale, Inc.

COLICCHIO, RALPH   ASCAP 1964
composer, guitarist
b Brooklyn, NY, Mar 27, 1896; d. Educ: High sch; studied with August Schmidt, Carl Diton, Schillinger Syst. Became asst to Schmidt. Guitarist in hotel orchs, NY, also on radio. On staff, record cos; also in pit orchs of Bway musicals. Author "Modern Graded Studies," "Master Chord Studies," "Nu Art Technical Exercises for All Instruments." *Songs & Instrumental Works:* Ticklin' the Strings; Go! Go!; Arthur King Guitar Solos (series).

COLLAZO, BOBBY   ASCAP 1952
composer, author, pianist
b Havana, Cuba, Nov 22, 15. Educ: Havana Munic Acad Music. Pianist in theatres, nightclubs, on radio & TV, Latin Am & US; arr & entertainer. *Songs:* Nostalgia Habanera; Que te Has Creido; Esto es Felicidad; Serenata Mulata; Lindo Puerto Rico; Raro Hechizo; Mi Desgracia; Nostalgia Guajira; Ultima Noche; Vivir de los Recuerdos; Tenia Que Ser Asi; Tan Lejos; Rumba Matumba. *Scores:* Stage: La Jibara.

COLLETTE, WILLIAM M (BUDDY)   ASCAP 1961
composer, author, conductor
b Los Angeles, Calif, Aug 6, 21. Led own quintet, Los Angeles; with "Groucho Marx TV Show," 10 yrs; recording artist with many records. Chief Collabr: Joe Greene. *Songs:* Blue Sands; Santa Monica; Soft Touch; Room With Skies. *Scores:* Films: The George Washington Carver Story; Trauma; A Comedy Tale of Fanny Hill.

COLLIER, THOMAS W   ASCAP 1977
composer, vibraphonist, drummer
b Puyallup, Wash, June 30, 48. Educ: Univ Wash, BA, BM, 71; studied comp with William O Smith & perc with John Bergamo. To Los Angeles, 71, percussionist for many top names in music incl Johnny Mathis, Barbra Streisand, Sammy Davis Jr, Olivia Newton-John, Ry Cooder & many others. Performed with Ry Cooder, Carnegie Hall, NY, 78; formed jazz quintet, Los Angeles, wrote many comp for same group & others. To Seattle, 78, formed vibes-bass duo with Dan Dean. Rockefeller Fellowship, 20th Century music performance, 67-71. Chief Collabr: Dan Dean. *Songs:* Music: Turning to Spring; Hopscotch; San Juan. *Instrumental Works:* Piece for Electric Bass, Vibraphone and Orchestra; Xenolith (jazz quintet, string quartet).

COLLINS, AARON   ASCAP 1969
composer
b Kress City, Ark, Sept 3, 30. Singer church choir from age 15-19 & var quartets to age 23. Mem rock & roll groups, The Jacks, The Cadets & The Flairs. *Songs:* Eddie My Love; Foot Stomping; Every Saturday Nite.

COLLINS, CARRIE B H   ASCAP 1974
composer, author, publisher
b Meridian, Miss, Nov 14, 30. Educ: T J Harris High Sch; Tenn State Col, BS, 50; Tenn State Univ, MS, 57; Univ Denver, MA(librarianship), 77. Music educator, Meridian Pub Schs, 50-57, Jones County Schs, 59-61, Littleton Pub Schs, 65- & Univ Northern Colo, 73-75; pvt piano teacher. Minister of music, var churches; lectr, clinician. Dir, Littleton Elem Vocal Music Fest; duo-piano recital, TV & radio. Served on Colo Educ Accreditation Team. Coordinated music prog, Univ Northern Colo, Colo Women's Col & Univ Denver. *Songs:* Love for Mankind; Look to Jesus; Two Hundred Years Ago; Mother-Dear; Lyrics: Black Folks Music.

COLLINS, GAIL
See Pappalardi, Gail Collins

COLLINS, JOYCE LOUISE   ASCAP 1973
composer, pianist, singer
b Battle Mountain, Nev, May 5, 30. Educ: San Francisco State Univ, BA(music); studied classical piano with Victor Aller, Shirley Howard & Phil Cohen, arr with Dick Grove. Moved to Los Angeles, 56; recorded album with original jazz comp, 61; free lance musician & teacher; recording artist; arr, played piano & sang with Bill Henderson on an album, 79. *Songs:* Music: Spring Rain. *Albums:* Street of Dreams.

COLLINS, JUDY MARJORIE   ASCAP 1967
singer
b Seattle, Wash, May 1, 39. Educ: Pvt piano study, 53-56. Made debut as professional folk singer, Boulder, Colo, 59; has appeared in numerous clubs in US & Can. Performer in concerts incl Newport Folk Fest, Orch Hall, Chicago, Carnegie Hall, New York, also appeared on radio & TV. Has made tours in Europe. Producer & co-dir of documentary film, "Antonia: A Portrait of the Woman," nominated for Acad Award, rec'd Silver Medal Atlanta Film Fest, Blue Ribbon Award Am Film Fest & Christopher Award. Recording artist with Elektra. Recipient 6 gold LP's, hit singles. Author of "Judy Collins Songbook." *Songs:* Since You've Asked; Secret Gardens; Houses; My Father; Open the Door (Song for Judith). *Albums:* A Maid of Constant Sorrow; Golden Apples of the Sun; Judy Collins 3 and 5; The Judy Collins Concert; In My Life; Wildflowers; Who Knows Where the Time Goes; Recollections; Whales and Nightingales; Living; Colors of the Day; True Stories and Other Dreams; Judith; Bread and Roses; So Early in the Spring/The First Fifteen Years; Hard Times for Lovers; Running for My Life.

COLLINS, LARRY
singer, guitarist, songwriter
b Tulsa, Okla, 1944. Was a team with sister Lorrie, they made their debut on the "Town Hall Party Show," Compton, Calif, 53. *Songs:* In My Teens; My First Love; Go 'Way Don't Bother Me; Hop, Skip and Jump; Young Heart; Heart Beat; Whistle Bait; Mercy; Sweet Talk. *Albums:* Country Spectacular; Town Hall Party.

COLLINS, SUSAN
composer, author, singer
b Brooklyn, NY, July 7, 50. Singer, background vocals with Electric Light Orch, Kiki Dee, New Riders of the Purple Sage, Richie Haven, Brian Wilson, Odyssey & Rex Smith. Satire voice overs on commercials, TV show "Saturday Night Live." Chief Collabrs: Paul Davis, Jeff Kent, David Buskin, Ron Dante, Howard Greenfield, Phil Cody, Robin Batteau. *Songs:* Sweet Life; I Want You to Know; The Rest of My Years; Stay By My Side; Don't Cheat on My Heart.

COLLINS, WILL   ASCAP 1924
composer, singer
b New York, NY, Oct 22, 1893; d Ann Arbor, Mich, May 14, 68. Educ: Pub schs. Publ midwest rep, 17-68, with Chappell, 32-68. Pioneer radio entertainer, WCK, Detroit; introduced & known as "Whispering Will Collins" on weekly radio show & on "In Shadowland" for many yrs. Chief Collabrs: Gerald Marks, Sammy Stept, Buddy Fields, Jimmy McHugh, Walter Hirsch, Francis Craig. *Songs:* Falling; After Midnight; Little Heart O'Mine; Night Shall Be Filled With Music; Until Sunrise.

COLLOM, STEVE DONALD   ASCAP 1973
composer, author, guitarist
b National City, Calif, Sept 9, 44. Guitarist, Detroit, 62; to Nashville, 72. Guitarist for var artists, incl Ronnie Milsap & Dolly Parton. Arr; writer, MilEne Music, 75. *Songs:* Get Back to Loving Me; The Ninth of September; Gone Away; Show Me a Brick Wall; Music: Stoney Mountain Rag.

COLOMBO, ALBERT CARL   ASCAP 1952
composer, author, arranger
b New York, NY, Nov 27, 1888; d Los Angeles, Calif, Mar 24, 54. Educ: Studied music incl violin & cello, New York. Cellist, Manhattan Opera House Orch; orch mgr under Oscar Hammerstein; arr for Paul Whiteman; musical dir for RKO, New York & RKO Studio, Hollywood; gen musical dir, Repub Pictures & MGM Studio. *Scores:* Film/TV: Annie Oakley; The Three Musketeers; They Were Expendable; Go for Broke; Romance in Manhattan; The Lone Ranger.

COLONNA, JERRY   ASCAP 1956
composer, author, comedian
b Boston, Mass, Sept 17, 04. Educ: High sch. Began career as trombonist; played with Columbia Symph, 31-36. Mem, Bob Hope radio prog; ringmaster, TV show "Super Circus." Has appeared in many films. *Songs:* At Dusk; Life of a Sailor; Sleighbells in the Sky; Take Your Time; I Came to Say Goodbye; One Day.

COLTRANE, CHI   ASCAP 1972
composer, author, singer
b Racine, Wis. Educ: Vocal study with Key Howard, 2 yrs; Salter Sch of Music, Los Angeles, Calif, 2 yrs. Began piano at age 7; first pub perf, piano solo, age 12. Prof singer, clubs in Ill, age 17. To Los Angeles; toured with var bands & orchs, Los Vegas, Bahamas & Chicago. Formed own bands; signed with CBS Columbia Records, 71, then with TK Records. Appeared as guest artist at Brazilian Music Fest, Rio de Janeiro. Performed with Johnny Carson, Merv Griffin, Mike Douglas, Virginia Graham & on var TV specials incl "Midnight Special." *Songs:* Thunder and Lightning; Go Like Elijah; The Tree; Turn Me Around; Oh Baby; It's a Spell (What's Happening to Me); Whoever Told You.

COLUM, PADRAIC   ASCAP 1950
author
b Longford, Ireland, Dec 8, 1881; d. Educ: Pub schs; hon LittD, Columbia Univ & Trinity Col (Dublin). Author of poems "Wild Earth", "The Story of Lowry Maen" & "Creatures," also plays: "The King of Ireland's Son", "The Adventures of Odysseus", "Tale of Troy" & "Balloon" & essays: "A Half-Day's Ride," autobiography "Vive Moi." Mem: Acad of Irish Letters; Nat Inst Arts & Letters; Am Acad Arts & Letters. Awards: Acad of Am Poets; Gregory Medal, Acad of Irish Letters; Regina Medal, Cath Lib Asn & Boston Arts Fest. *Songs:* Poems set to Music: O Men From the Field; An Old Woman of the Roads; Songs From Connacht; Wild Earth; Creatures; Old Pastures.

COLWELL, RALPH JOHNSON   ASCAP 1965
composer, author
b Detroit, Mich, July 2, 37. Touring, performing, comp & dir, "Up With People," 68- Chief Collabr: Paul Colwell. *Songs & Instrumental Works:* Up With People; Moon Rider; We Are Many, We Are One.

COMBERIATE, JOSEPHINE BERTOLINI   ASCAP 1968
composer, author, pianist
b Washington, DC, Mar 14, 17. Educ: Eastern Sch, valedictorian, acad studies; Strayer Col (secy, accountant); Cath Univ; Univ Md (creative writing, poetry & prose), studied with Gustav G Weckel & Ralph B Turek; Dept Agriculture Grad Sch; Comptometer Sch. Secy, comptometer operator, statistical clerk, draftsman & economic asst, 11 yrs. Taught piano; MC & pianist, Washingtonians Dance Band; pianist & organist, stage recitals & on radio. Poet; publ of own works incl poetry, picture collages & songs; commercial recordings. Author songbks, "Love, Life and Liberty", "Star of Splendor", "A Baby's Love", "Forever Yours" & "It's Christmas Time." *Songs:* Live a Little and Love a Lot; Music Says It All; I Will Always Remember You; Let Freedom Ring; Lovely Lady; Lovely Lady Love; My Dad; My Favorite Friend, My Friends, My Girl, My Hopes and Dreams; My Son; My Song for You; Our President; Romance, My Love; Say It With a Prayer; Sad River; Somehow; Start the Day Off Singing; Somewhere, Love's Calling; Sweetheart Without a Heart; Take Time to Live; The Glory Road; The Heart of Me; Tonight; We'll Always Be Together; Where Is My Little Boy (Girl) Tonight?; Your Most Wonderful Wedding Day; Catherine Mary; Early in the Morning; Everyday; Forever Yours; How Wonderful!. *Albums:* Loving and Living.

COMDEN, BETTY   ASCAP 1944
author, performer
b Brooklyn, NY, May 3, 19. Educ: Brooklyn Ethical Culture Sch; Erasmus Hall High Sch; NY Univ, BS. Wrote material & performed with group The Revuers, 39-43 (incl Judy Holliday & Adolph Green). Coauthor, book & lyrics, "On the Town," 44; author, "Applause." Author screenplays incl, "On the Town", "Good News", "The Barkleys of Broadway", "Singin' in the Rain", "The Band Wagon", "Auntie Mame", "Bells Are Ringing" & "What a Way to Go." Appeared with Adolph Green on stage in "A Party" & on TV. Chief Collabrs: Adolph Green, Leonard Bernstein, Jule Styne, Andre Previn, Morton Gould, Cy Coleman, Roger Edens. *Songs:* New York, New York; I Get Carried Away; I Can Cook, Too; Some Other Time; Lonely Town; Lucky to Be Me; Bad Timing; Ohio; A Little Bit in Love; It's Love; A Quiet Girl; The French Lesson; If You Hadn't But You Did; Give a Little, Get a Little; There Never Was a Baby Like My Baby; The Party's Over; Long Before I Knew You; Just in Time; Never-Never Land; Something's Always Happening on the River; Dance Only With Me; Adventure; Make Someone Happy; Fireworks; Ride Through the Night; Comes Once in a Lifetime; I'm Just Taking My Time; Now; Fade Out—Fade In; The Wrong Note Rag; I Like Myself; Our Private World; If. *Scores:* Bway Shows: Wonderful Town (New York Drama Critics & Tony Awards, 53); Peter Pan; Do Re Mi; On the Town (also co-librettist); Billion Dollar Baby; Two in the Aisle; Bells Are Ringing; Say, Darling; Subways Are for Sleeping; Fade Out—Fade In; On the 20th Century; Films: It's Always Fair Weather (also screenplay); On the 20th Century; Good News; Barkleys of Broadway; On the Town; Take Me Out to the Ball Game; Singin' in the Rain; The Band Wagon; Auntie Mame; What a Way to Go.

COMER, CAROLYN JANE   ASCAP
composer, author, pianist
b Tulsa, Okla, Sept 30, 37. Educ: Kans State Teachers Col, 2 yrs. Pvt teacher vocal jazz/theory, 68-; co-owner, Palaco Music, Inc, 67-; co-founder, Women's Jazz Fest, Inc, 77, exec dir; leader/pianist/vocalist, Calico, 79-; ed, Nat Directory of Female Jazz Performers, 79, 80. Mem: Am Fedn Musicians; Am Fedn TV & Radio Artists; assoc Nat Asn Jazz Educrs. *Songs:* I See the Rainbow Now; Pretty Things Come in Twos; Nobody for Me; Lyrics: I've Learned the Way to Sing the Blues.

COMMANDER, MAURICE DAVID (MATAVANI)   ASCAP 1975
composer, author, arranger
b Chicago, Ill, Apr 11, 48. Educ: Self-taught pianist; protege of arr Riley Hampton; Roosevelt Univ Chicago, studied orchestration & band arr; Chicago Cons Music, currently. Started professional career at age 19 as lead vocalist for Chicago Soul Seven. Mem A&R staff, Curtom Record Co, 71, worked with Curtis Mayfield, Donny Hathaway & Leroy Hutson. Co-owner publ cos & GEC Record Co, Chicago, currently. Chief Collabr: Jerline Shelton. *Songs:* Ballad of Matheia; One More Time; You're the One; Sweat; Rock You Tonight; Music: When You Smile; I'm Just Fooling Myself; I Can't Seem to Forget You; Spank your Blank Blank; Spank Your Thang; Never Stop Dancin'; Hot Spot; Goddess of Love; Slip and Dip; Can You Get to This; March Across This Land; Up With It (People of the World).

COMPTON, HARRY J   ASCAP 1966
composer, author
b Bonne Terre, Mo, Apr 13, 47. Singer; guitarist; recording artist. Started writing, 64; sang with bros, 7 yrs. *Songs:* How Much More Can She Stand (And Still Stand By Me); The Long Arm of Love.

COMPTON, LACY WILFORD   ASCAP 1976
composer, author
b Linton, Ky, July 7, 16. Educ: High sch, Cadiz, Ky; Radio & Electronic TV Sch, Detroit, Mich; Callahan Music Sch, Ferndale, Mich. Recording artist. Chief Collabr: Donn Petrak. *Songs:* That Great Book; The Flag of the Free; It's So Easy to Say Yes; Never Haft to Go.

COMSTOCK, FRANK G   ASCAP 1955
composer, conductor, arranger
b San Diego, Calif, Sept 20, 22. Educ: San Diego High Sch, 39. Arr dance bands incl Benny Carter, 42-43 & Les Brown, 43-62, arr/comp, Bob Hope shows, 46-62, arr/orchr, many Hollywood musicals & dramatic pictures, cond/arr, many recordings, comp/cond many TV series & movies, also background scoring. *Scores:* Film/TV: Rocky and His Friends; Ensign O'Toole; Temple Houston; Adam-12; The D A.

COMSTOCK, WILLIAM COLLINS (BILL)   ASCAP 1960
composer, author, singer
b Rockbridge, Ohio, Feb 1, 24. Educ: Ohio Wesleyan Univ. Performed & wrote for groups in New York, Los Angeles, Nev & Europe. Mem group, Four Freshmen, 13 yrs. Arr & original material avocationally. Chief Collabrs: Gene DiNovi & Ken Albers. *Songs:* Tout Va Bien; Wail for the Bread; Spring Isn't Spring (Without You); Come Live Your Life With Me; Lyrics: Summer has Gone; Lonely for My Love; Nashville Blues; Give Me Time; Oh Lonely Winter; I've Had One Too Many. *Instrumental Works:* Bella Melodia.

CONDON, ALBERT EDWIN (EDDIE)   ASCAP 1958
composer, conductor, guitarist
b Goodland, Ind, Nov 16, 04; d. Guitarist in jazz groups at 15. Came to NY, 28, played in Bobby Hackett & Artie Shaw Orchs. Producer jazz concerts, incl Town Hall, NY, 46; had own TV series, 48; played at Newport Jazz Fest; toured Gt Brit, 57. Autobiography, "We Called It Music." Honored at "Salute to Eddie Condon," Carnegie Hall, 64. Made many records. *Songs & Instrumental Works:* We Called It Music; Home Cooking; That's a Serious Thing.

CONELY, JAMES HANNON, JR   ASCAP 1969
composer, organist, teacher
b New Smyrna Beach, Fla, July 9, 38. Educ: Univ Fla, BAE, pvt study under Russell Danburg, 60, MEd, pvt study under Willis Bodine, 61; Columbia Univ Teachers Col, EdD, pvt study under Thomas Richner, 68. Contest judge for organ & piano in Tex & Colo; harpsichordist, Colorado Springs Symph, 70-71; played numerous organ concerts across the country; interim cond, Montgomery Ala Symph Orch, 79. Instr Eng & assoc prof fine arts (music), USAF Acad, 7 yrs, now chief, Prof Relations Div, Community Col Air Force, Maxwell AFB, Ala. Chief Collabr: Barton Clapp. *Songs & Instrumental Works:* Moses! Moses!; 18 Short Pieces and Modulations for Organ; A Guide to Improvisation for Church Organists.

CONETTA, LEWIS D (LEW CAREY)   ASCAP 1958
composer, author, producer
b Stamford, Conn, Jan 20, 27. Educ: Juilliard Sch; Univ Conn; studied with John Quilian. Singer, big bands. Own TV musical show, WOR-TV; own radio show, ABC. Producer, A&R & records. Recording artist. Chief Collabr: Al Bandini.

CONFREY, EDWARD E (ZEZ) ASCAP 1922
composer, author, pianist
b Peru, Ill, Apr 3, 1895; d Lakewood, NJ, Nov 22, 71. Educ: Chicago Musical Col. Pianist for many piano rolls. USN, World War I. Led own orch, in vaudeville, nightclubs, theatres & radio. *Instrumental Works:* Concert Etude; Oriental Fantasy; Piano studies: Four Candy Pieces; Four Easy Pieces; Musical Alphabet Rhymes. *Songs & Instrumental Works:* Kitten on the Keys; Stumbling; Dizzy Fingers; Valse Mirage; Three Little Oddities; Buffoon; Grandfather's Clock; Sittin' on a Log. *Scores:* Minature opera: Thanksgiving.

CONGA, STU
See Dorn, Veeder Van

CONLEY, EARL THOMAS ASCAP 1973
composer, author, singer
b Portsmouth, Ohio, Oct 17, 41. First three top twenty country chart songs written for Billy Larkin while working in honky-tonks & bars in Huntsville, Ala; wrote songs for Mel Street, Conway Twitty & Bobby G Rice; after signing with GRT Records, three singles released on Warner Bros; recording artist with Sun Bird Records. Chief Collabrs: Dick Heard, Nelson Larkin. *Songs:* Smoky Mountain Memories; This Time I've Hurt Her More Than She Loves Me; Sure Thing; Lust Affair; Stranded on a Dead End Street.

CONLEY, LARRY ASCAP 1927
composer, author, trombonist
b Keithsburg, Ill, Nov 29, 1895; d Lindenhurst, NY, Feb 29, 60. Trombonist in dance orchs. Chief Collabrs: Willard Robison, Johnny Marks. *Songs:* A Cottage for Sale; Summer Holiday; Easy Melody; My Sweetheart; I Guess There's an End to Everything; My Love for You; Dim the Harbor Lights; Cryin' for the Moon; Tia Juana; Let's Have an Old Fashioned Christmas.

CONLEY, LLOYD EDGAR ASCAP 1971
composer
b Rogers City, Mich, Mar 8, 24. Educ: Cent Mich Univ, BMus, 49; Mich State Univ, MMus, 50. Played prof during high sch, 38-42. Served with 740th USAAF Band, WW II. Teacher, 50-79. Ed, Kendor Music, Inc, 63-64. Writer educ oriented msuic, 55- *Instrumental Works:* Kansa (suite for band; Winner, Kans Centennial Comp Competition, 61); Symphonic Invention; Diversion No 1 (saxophone quartet); Diversion No II (woodwind quintet); Diversion No 3 (concert band); Tawas Suite (concert band); Portrait of a Mariner (concert band).

CONN, CHESTER ASCAP 1924
composer, publisher
b San Francisco, Calif, Apr 14, 1896; d. Educ: Univ Calif. Mgr music publ co; prof mgr, Leo Feist Inc. Co-founder, Bregman, Vocco & Conn, 38, pres, 60. *Songs:* Why Should I Cry Over You; Outside of Heaven; Night Lights; Forgive My Heart; The Right Thing to Say; Make Her Mine; Sunday; Don't Mind the Rain; I'll Never Know Why; That's You; Crying for You; You Don't Like It, Not Much; Sicilian Tarantella; Will o' the Wisp Romance.

CONN, IRVING ASCAP 1946
composer, author, conductor
b London, Eng, Feb 21, 1898; d Ft Lee, NJ, July 12, 61. Educ: Juilliard Sch. Served, USA, World War I. Cond with own orch, New York hotels. Chief Collabr: Frank Silver. *Songs:* Yes, We Have No Bananas; Sweet Butter; F'rinstance; Thank You for Love.

CONN, MERVIN ASCAP 1965
composer, author, singer
b Washington, DC, Feb 19, 20. Educ: Benjamin Franklin Univ, accounting degree; studied piano & accordion with Sylvia Kaplowitz. Performed for President Truman at White House. Music man for baseball team, Washington Senators, 64-69. Music dir for Miss Universe Contest & Miss Teen All American Contest. *Songs & Instrumental Works:* The Washington Senators; Jitter Bug Rock; Bugle Rock Parade; Melinda; Benjamin Franklin University Alumni March; Miss Teen All American.

CONNELL, HOWARD ASCAP 1957
author
b New York, NY, Feb 29, 12. Educ: Ohio Univ, BA; Columbia Univ, MA. Vpres, Foote, Cone & Belding & Ogilvy Benson & Mather; creative dir, Biow Co, then vpres & chmn, Plans & Review Comn, Warwick & Legler. Chief Collabr: James Van Heusen. *Songs:* There You Are.

CONNER, DAVID ALLEN ASCAP 1975
composer, author
b Hume, NY, June 2, 36. Educ: Lima High Sch, 54; State Univ NY, Potsdam, BS, 58; New Eng Cons Music, MM(orch cond), 71; pvt studies with Louis Greenwald, Leon Bakzin & Fred Zimmermann. Music teacher, 58-69; principal string bass, Hudson Valley Philh, 59; music dir, 30 Summer Stock Productions, Melody Tent, Hyannis, Mass; head music theatre dept, Boston Cons, 69-72; joined children's TV workshop staff, 72; music dir, "The Electric Company" & "Sesame Street." Chief Collabrs: Tom Whedon, Jim Thurman, John Boni, Sammy Cahn. *Scores:* Film/TV: Tampa Blues; Jennifer's Journey; Our Story.

CONNOR, JOSEPH P (PIERRE NORMAN CONNOR) ASCAP 1925
composer
b Kingston, Pa, Nov 16, 1895; d Teaneck, NJ, Mar 31, 52. Educ: Wyoming Cons; studied with Ergildo Martinelli; St Bonaventure Col, BA, MA & MusD. Pastor, St John's Church, Cliffside, NJ; chaplain, NJ State Police & NJ State Guard. Chief Collabrs: Sammy Fain, Irving Kahal. *Songs:* Lord's Prayer; Our Father; Ave Maria; The Golden Dawn; Lillies of Lorraine; The Far Green Hills of Home; Little Black Dog; I Shall Return; Miracle of the Bells; When I Take My Sugar to Tea; You Brought a New Kind of Love to Me. *Instrumental Works:* Gregorian Mass in Honor of Our Lady of Victory. *Scores:* Film themes: The Big Pond; Young Man from Manhattan; Perfect Fool; Laughter; Stars on Ice; I Shall Return; Blood and Sand; With Byrd at the South Pole; Back Door to Heaven; Footlights on Parade.

CONQUET, JOHN HENRY ASCAP 1959
composer, author, singer
b Brooklyn, NY, July 17, 27. Led own orch, playing piano & singing nite clubs, hotels & TV. Recording artist, RCA Victor. Arr for Latin Bands, NY, 49-64. Working as single singing & playing piano. Chief Collabrs: Cecilo Benitez, Ruben Rios & Tito Rodriguez. *Songs:* Ciegamente Enamorado; Music: Guajiro Boricua; Nitza. *Instrumental Works:* Piano Merengue; Ecstasy.

CONRAD, CON
See Dober, Conrad K

CONRAD, HUGH
See Schoenfeld, William C

CONRAD, WILLIAM
actor, producer, director
b Louisville, Ky, Sept 27, 20. Educ: Fullerton Jr Col. Radio announcer, KMPC, Los Angeles. Served in USAAF, 43-45. Starred in radio series, "Gunsmoke," 49-60. Made film debut in "The Killers," 46; other film appearances incl "30," 59, "Body and Soul," "Sorry, Wrong Number," "East Side, West Side," "The Naked Jungle" & "Moonshine County Express," 77. Produced films "Two on a Guillotine," 65, "Brainstorm," 65, "An American Dream," 66, "A Covenant With Death," 67, "First to Fight," 67, "The Cool Ones," 67 & "The Assignment." TV credits incl "This Man Dawson," "Night Cries," 78, "The Brotherhood of the Bell" & "Conspiracy to Kill." Producer & dir, "Klondike"; producer, "77 Sunset Strip"; dir 35 episodes of "True." Star of TV series "The DA," 71-72, "O'Hara, US Treasury," 71-72 & "Cannon," 71-76.

CONSTANTEN, THOMAS CHARLES ASCAP 1969
composer
b Long Branch, NJ, Mar 19, 44. Educ: Krauichsteiner Musikinstitut, Darmstadt, Ger; studied comp with Luciano Berio, Henri Pousseur, Pierre Boulez & Karlheinz Stockhauser, 62-63. Presented as comp by Univ Nev Orch, Las Vegas, 61-67; keyboard player, the Grateful Dead, 68-70; comp & music dir, off-Bway play, "Tarot," 70-71; prof music, State Univ NY Buffalo, 74-75; comp & pianist, 74-, toured US, Austria & Yugoslavia. Comp music for film, "Maya," 80. Chief Collabrs: Jerry Garcia, Lejaren A Hiller. *Instrumental Works:* Dejavalse (multiple pianos); We Leave the Castle (electronic interlude); Tarot. *Scores:* Film: Love Song of Charles Faberman.

CONSTANTINIDES, DINOS DEMETRIOS ASCAP 1974
composer, violinist, educator
b Ioannina, Greece, May 10, 29. Educ: Greek Cons, Athens, Greece, violin dipl, 45-50, theory dipl, 56-57; Juilliard Sch Music, violin dipl, 58-60, studied with Ivan Galamian; Ind Univ, MM, 63-65, studied with Josef Gingold; Mich State Univ, PhD(comp), 65-68, studied with Owen Reed. Citizen of US; had works presented in US, Can & Europe; had orchestral works performed by the New Orleans Symph, Baton Rouge Symph, State Orch of Athens, Symph Salonica & Athens Radio Symph. At present, prof violin & comp, La State Univ; dir, New Times, orgn for promotion of new music; chmn, La State Univ Fest Contemporary Music; concertmaster, Baton Rouge Symph. Rec'd many grants, comns & awards from US & Greece; rec'd four ASCAP Standard Awards for Comp. Chief Collabr: David Madden. *Songs & Instrumental Works:* Theme and Variations for Piano; Woodwind Quartet; Sonata for Viola or Cello and Piano; Trio No 1 for Violin, Cello and Piano; Symphony No 1; Concerto for Violin, Cello, Piano and Orchestra; Kaleidoscope for Chamber Ensemble; Dedications for Orchestra; Impressions for Clarinet and Piano; Fugue for Two Voices (one-act opera); Rhapsody for Oboe or Flute and Harp; Rhapsody for Oboe or Flute and Piano; Designs for Strings; Percussion Quartet; Antitheses for Chamber Orchestra; Evangeline for Soprano and String Quartet; Dedications for Woodwind Quintet; Composition for Flute, Harp and Percussion; Four Songs on Poems by Sappho; Sonata No 1 for Solo Violin; String Quartet No 1; Lament of Antigone; Sonata for Solo Guitar; Exploding Parallels for Speaker and Ensemble; Improvisation for Trombone and Piano.

CONSTANTINO, JOSEPH GEORGE ASCAP 1970
composer, teacher, pianist
b New York, NY, Sept 1, 31. Educ: NY Univ, studied Schillinger Syst musical comp with Rudolf Schramm; Manhattan Sch Music, BM & MM, studied orchestration with Vittorio Giannini. Adj fac mem, Dowling Col, Long Island; comp, arr & music literature teacher; music dir, Connetquat Sch Dist, Long

Island; arr in jazz idiom & comp primarily educ materials. *Songs:* Music: All This Time This Song Is Best; The Oxen. *Instrumental Works:* Warwick; The Buccaneers; Passacaglia.

CONTI, DICK
See Cuchetti, Richard Frank

CONVERSE, FREDERICK SHEPHERD   ASCAP 1940
composer, educator
b Newton, Mass, Jan 5, 1871, d Westwood, Mass, June 8, 40. Educ: Harvard Univ, studied with Paine, Chadwick, Rheinberger; Royal Acad, Munich; Boston Univ, hon MusD. Fac mem, New Eng Cons, 1899-01; taught comp, Harvard Univ, 01-04, asst prof, 04-07; prof theory & comp & dean fac, New Eng Cons, 31-38. Mem: Nat Inst Arts & Letters; Am Acad Arts & Letters. *Instrumental Works:* Youth (overture); The Pipe of Desire; The Sacrifice (David Bispham Medal); Festival of Pan; Endymion's Narrative; The Mystic Trumpeter; Job (oratorio); Ave Atque vale; Prophecy; California; Flivver Ten Million; incidental music for Jeanne d'Arc; The Scarecrow; American Sketches (suite); 3 string quartets; 2 piano concertinos; 3 symphonies.

COOK, IRA LEIGH   ASCAP 1957
composer, author
b Duluth, Minn, Aug 17, 16. Educ: Stanford Univ, BMS. Entered radio field, 38; DJ specialized in music records, sports & spec events; cond, "Ira Cook Show", radio sta, KMPC, Los Angeles, 25 yrs. Chief Collabrs: Ray Gilbert, Mort Greene, Bobby Worth, Pete King, Bobby Hammack, Les Baxter, Stan Worth. *Songs:* Pony Tail; Music: Hawaii, Hawaii; Have a Happy Day; Lyrics: Sunday Barbecue.

COOK, RICHARD LEONARD, JR   ASCAP 1975
composer, producer, arranger
b Franklin, NJ. Minister of music, several churches; minister of music & producer, Melodyland Musicals; songwriter for Benson Publ Co, Nashville; songwriter & arr, Manna Music, Burbank, Calif; performer with Rich Cook Trio; recording artist. Chief Collabr: Allene Bledsoe. *Songs:* I Live; Living Witnesses; Worthy Is the Lamb; He's Here Right Now; There's Life in Jesus Name; In Everything I Do; Lord, You Do All Things Well; Lyrics: Before the Rocks Cry Out.

COOK, SHORTY
See Hinderer, Everett Roland

COOK, W MERCER   ASCAP 1932
composer, author, educator
b Washington, DC, Mar 30, 03. Educ: Amherst Col, BA; Brown Univ, MA, PhD; Univ of Paris; Univ of Havana. Prof romance languages, Howard Univ; visiting lectr in Haiti for US State Dept, 50. Taught languages, Atlanta Univ & Univ Haiti. Decorated by Haitian govt. Fellowships: Amherst Col; Brown Univ; Rosenwald & General Educ Bd. Author: "Education in Haiti"; "Haitian American Anthology"; "5 French Negro Authors"; "Portraits Americains." Appointed US ambassador to Niger Rep, 61, later ambassador to Senegal. Chief Collabr: Will Marion Cook (father). *Songs:* Stop the Sun, Stop the Moon; Is I in Love, I Is; Roamin' for Romance; Hold Up Your Hands; Georgia Lee and Me; How Can I Hi-De-Hi When I Feel So Low-De-Low?; In Between; Troubled in Mind; A Little Bit of Heaven Called Home.

COOK, WILL MARION   ASCAP 1924
composer, author, conductor
b Washington, DC, Jan 27, 1869; d New York, NY, July 19, 44. Educ: Oberlin Col, studied music with Joachim; Nat Cons, studied with Dvorak. Cond, musicals featuring Williams & Walker. Organized Am Syncopated Orch, toured US & Europe. Vocal coach for Bway musical "Great Day!." Chief Collabrs: Donald Heywood, Joe Jordan, W Mercer Cook (son). *Songs:* I'm Comin' Virginia; Exhortation; On Emancipation Day; That's How the Cakewalk's Done; The Rain Song; Swing Along Children; I May Be Crazy But I Ain't No Fool; Happy Jim; Darktown Is Out Tonight; Mandy Lou; Down the Lover's Lane; Bon Bon Buddy; Red Red Rose; Mammy; Lovey Joe; A Little Bit of Heaven Called Home. *Scores:* Stage shows: In Dahomey; Abyssinia; Bandana Land.

COOKE, CHARLES L   ASCAP 1940
composer, arranger
b Louisville, Ky, Sept 3, 1891; d Wurtsboro, NY, Dec 25, 58. Educ: Chicago Musical Col, BA, MM & MusD, studies with Felix Borowski, Louis Victor Saar. Staff comp publ firms, Detroit. Led own orch, Chicago. Held exec posts with RKO. Staff comp & arr, Radio City Music Hall. Arr, Bway Musicals, incl "Hot Mikado"; "Cabin in the Sky", "Sons o'Fun", "Banjo Eyes", "Sadie Thompson", "Follow the Girls." *Songs:* I Wonder Where My Loving Man Is Gone; Blame It on the Blues; Messin' Around; Sing Song Swing; Drummer's Say; Lovin' You the Way I Do; Girl of the Golden West; Goodbye Pretty Butterflies.

COOKE, JACK KENT
publisher, business executive
b Hamilton, Ont, Oct 25, 12. Educ: Malvern Collegiate. Joined Northern Broadcasting & Publ Ltd, Can, 37; partner, Thomson Cooke Newspapers, 37-52;

pres, Radio Sta CKEY, Toronto, Ont, 44-61; pres, Liberty of Can Ltd, 47-61; pres, Toronto Maple Leaf Baseball Club Ltd, 51-64; chmn bd & pres, Consolidated Press Ltd, 52-61; pres, Consolidated Frybrook Industries Ltd, 52-61; pres, Precision Die Casting Ltd, Toronto, 55-60; pres, Robinson Indust Crafts Ltd, London, Ont, 57-63; first vpres, Pro-Football Inc, Washington, DC, 60-79, chmn bd, chief exec officer & chief operating officer, 79-; pres, Aubyn Investments Ltd, 61-68; pres, Jack Kent Cooke Inc, 64-68, chmn bd, chief exec officer & chief operating officer, 79-; pres, Continental Cablevision Inc, 65-68; chmn bd, Transam Microwave, Inc, 65-69; chmn bd & pres, Calif Sports Inc, 65-79; pres, Forum of Inglewood Inc, 66-79; dir & chmn exec comt, H&B Am Corp, 69-70; dir, Teleprompter Corp, New York, 70-73, chmn bd & chief exec officer, 73-; pres, Forum Boxing Inc, 72-79; chmn bd, chief exec officer & chief operating officer, JKC Realty Inc, New York, 79-

COOKE, JAMES FRANCIS   ASCAP 1934
composer, author
b Bay City, Mich, Nov 14, 1875; d Philadelphia, Pa, Mar 3, 60. Educ: State Univ NY Grand Cons, MusD; hon degrees: LLD, LHD, LittD, MusD, EdD & DFA. Taught piano & voice, New York & Brooklyn. Asst dir, Brooklyn Inst of Arts & Sci. Ed, Etude, 07-50, ed emeritus. Pres, Presser Found, 18-60, Chestnut St Bus Men's Asn, Philadelphia, 39-60. Awarded Cross of Chevalier, Legion of Honor by French govt. Author, works on music instruction. *Songs & Instrumental Works:* Sea Gardens; White Orchids; Roses at Dawn; O Car'lina; Laughing Roses; Nile Night; Italian Lakes Suite; Chateaux Francais; Ballet Mignon; Fire Dance.

COOKE, JAMES PATRICK   ASCAP 1970
composer, author, performer
b Wausau, Wis, Nov 12, 44. Educ: Wausau Sr High, 63. Original mem, Steve Miller Band; instrumentalist & vocalist, Abeskhy Band, MGM Records. Formed own group Curly Cooke's Hurdy Gurdy Band. Worked on approx 25 maj labels with other people. Producer of records. Chief Collabrs: Les Doodek, Ben Sidran. *Songs:* Sacrifice; Hey, Hey, Baby; Baby Blues. *Instrumental Works:* The Cuban Connection; Fat Jam; Gazebo; Jubitz Mudflaps.

COOL, HAROLD   ASCAP 1920
author
b New York, NY, Nov 13, 1890; d New York, Sept 8, 49. Educ: Pub schs. Succeeded father as owner of music store. *Songs:* Just Like the Rose; Under Southern Skies; Cotton Pickin' Time in Alabam'.

COOLIDGE, PEGGY STUART   ASCAP 1958
composer
b Boston, Mass, July 19, 13. Educ: Studied comp with Heinrich Gebhard, Raymond Robinson, Quincy Porter. Works performed extensively throughout the world. Medal of Soviet House of Workers in art, 70. Performed with Boston Pops under Fiedler. Wrote "The Blue Planet", comn by World Wildlife Fund, theme for orgn, also "American Mosaic", comn by Am Wind Symph Orch of Western Pa. Chief Collabr: J R Coolidge. *Instrumental Works:* Pioneer Dances; New England Autumn; Spirituals in Sunshine and Shadow; Rhapsody for Harp and Orchestra. *Scores:* Opera/Ballet: An Evening in New Orleans.

COOMBS, CHARLES WHITNEY   ASCAP 1924
composer, organist
b Bucksport, Maine, Dec 25, 1859; d Orange, NJ, Jan 24, 40. Educ: studied with Speidel, Seifritz, Draeseke, Herman John, P Janssen & Lamperti; hon MusD, Syracuse Univ. Organist, Am Church, Dresden, 1887-1891; church music dir, Holy Communion Church, New York & St Luke's Church, 08-28. *Songs & Instrumental Works:* Cantatas: The Vision of St John; Hymn of Peace; The First Christmas; The Ancient Days; The Sorrows of Death.

COOMES, THOMAS WILLIAM
composer, author, singer
b Long Beach, Calif, May 19, 46. Educ: Paramount Schs, Calif; Long Beach State Col. Started on trumpet in fourth grade; began guitar, bass & piano in col. With big bands, stage bands & rock bands. Recording in gospel field as artist/writer, 70-; producer LP's, 72-; instrumentalist. Chief Collabrs: Chuck Girard, Chuck Butler, Tom Stipe & Bob Bennett. *Songs:* Front Seat, Back Seat; Two Hands; Praise the Lord; The Cossack Song; Book of Life; Light Our Way; The Sweetest Name of All.

COOPER, DAVID   ASCAP 1979
composer, author, singer
b Redwood City, Calif, Feb 2, 52. Educ: San Carlos High Sch; Univ Calif, Davis, BA, 74. Began playing, 72, writing, 73. Played in clubs, San Francisco, 74-79; in Oslo, Norway, 75-76, toured Europe as singer/performer, 76; played on TV & radio specials, both US & overseas. Guitarist & arr. Chief Collabrs: Harvey Rich, Kai Eide. *Songs:* Headstones; Who Do You Think You Are?; What Price, the Sky?; Lyrics: Mile After Mile; You May Be the Fool; Love Is a Wheel.

COOPER, EDWARD   ASCAP 1958
composer, author, pianist
b New York, NY, May 28, 25. Arr. *Songs:* Just for Laughs; The Frustrated Clown; The Turtle Song; I'm Lost for Words.

COOPER, EVELYNE LOVE ASCAP 1955
composer, author
b Chicago, Ill; d. Educ: NY Univ. Producer, writer & dir for radio & TV. Writer, speical material for Pearl Bailey, Dorothy Shay, Monica Lewis & Sophie Tucker. *Songs:* He's Gone; Call Me Again When You're in Town; From Mouton to Muskrat to Mink; Goodbye Song; I'd Do It All Over Again.

COOPER, JOHN CRAIG ASCAP 1961
composer, conductor
b Kansas City, Mo, May 14, 25. Educ: Kansas City Cons; Univ Mo, BA, MA; Mills Col; Am Cons, Fontainebleau; Wentworth Mil Acad; Aspen Inst, scholarship with Darius Milhaud; New Sch; studied with Charles Jones, Robert Sheldon, Solomon Rosowsky, Ben Weber, Nadia Boulanger & Hans Neumann. Founded Mo Comp Concerts, 51, Three Arts Theatre, 56 & concert series, Donnell Libr, NY, 58-59. Lectured at Stephens Col; dir music, Bearnstow Camp, 56; teacher piano, King's Col, Briarcliff Manor. Awards: Paulina Creative Arts, Univ Mo, 3 MacDowell Fellowships & Alice Ditson grants. *Songs:* Free Me From the Bonds; Do Not Go My Love; Where Are You Going to, My Pretty Maid?; Child of a Day; Ah, Sunflower (chorus).

COOPER, KENT ASCAP 1955
composer, author
b Columbus, Ind, Mar 22, 1880; d West Palm Beach, Fla, Jan 31, 65. Hon LLD, Ind Univ, Drake Univ, Clark Univ, Northwestern Univ, Univ Western Ont & St Lawrence Univ; hon LittD, NY Univ. Violinist theatre orchs. Founded Assoc Press, SAm, Gt Brit, Ger & other countries. Established Assoc Press Syst of Wirephoto. Gen mgr in charge of news service & personnel, Assoc Press & subsidiaries, 25-51; mem adv bd, Pulitzer Sch Jour, Columbia Univ, 25-56. Author, "Barriers Down", "Anna Zenger", "It's News to You", "The Right to Know." *Songs & Instrumental Works:* Dixie Girl; About the Girl; Indiana Forever; 48 States March; Spirit of Freedom; What Is Time; There Came the Day; Sunset; America Needs You; The Magic of the Violin; I'll Not Forget.

COOPER, LESTER
writer, producer
b New York, NY. Educ: Columbia Univ; NY Univ. Began career as film writer, Warner Bros Studios, Hollywood, 37. In USA, wrote first joint British-Am film, 41-46. Writer of feature films for J Arthur Rank & British Nat Productions, Eng. Returned to US & started own film production co, 49. Chief copywriter, Esquire mag; also wrote free-lance mag pieces. Writer, CBS News, "Eye on New York", "A Day Called X" & "FYI," 53-56. Writer, NBC News "Today" show; left NBC to become head-writer & supervising producer of "PM", then free-lance, produced a series of shows with Dave Garroway "Exploring the Universe" (Emmy Award). Staff producer, ABC News, 64, exec producer, ABC News Documentary Unit, 67, exec producer & writer of children's series "Make a Wish" (Peabody & Emmy Awards), 71. Exec producer, ABC News series "Summer Focus" & "View From the White House"; writer & producer, "ABC Scope." Created the ABC News children's series "Animals Animals Animals" (Peabody, Emmy, Ohio State, Action for Children's TV Awards & Award of Excellence), 76. Producer, writer & exec producer of 2 "National Polling Day" specials, also "Hemingway's Spain: A Love Affair", "The Right to Love", "Can You Hear Me?", "Heart Attack" & "This Land Is Mine."

COOPER, LOUIS BUDD ASCAP 1925
composer, author
b New York, NY, Apr 17, 1899. Played the Keith Orpheum Circuit, Cavanagh & Cooper, vaudeville, 10 yrs. Chief Collabrs: Herman Ruby, Harry Warren, Young & Lewis. *Songs:* You; Red Hot Mama; The Minute I Laid My Eyes on You; I Meet the Nicest People in My Dreams; Feelin' Kind of Blue; Hot Tamale Molly; My Sunday Girl.

COOPER, PAUL
musician
b Victoria, Ill, May 19, 26. Educ: Univ Southern Calif, BA, 50, MA, 53, DMusArts, 56; Nat Cons Paris & Sorbonne, Fulbright fel, 53. Performer, 53-; music critic, Los Angeles Mirror, 52-55 & Ann Arbor News, 59-65; minister music, St Matthew's Lutheran Church, North Hollywood, Calif, 54-55. Fac mem, Univ Mich, Ann Arbor, 55-68; prof music, 65-68; chmn theory dept, 66-68; prof music, comp-in-residence & head acad div, Univ Cincinnati, 69-74; prof music, comp-in-residence & chmn scholar fac, Shepherd Sch Music, Rice Univ, 74- State Dept cult rep, Int Exhibition, Zagreb, Yugoslavia, 65; comp & recorder, 67-; guest lectr cols & univs, 68- Author, "Workbooks for Perspectives in Music," 73-75, "Perspectives in Music Theory," 73 & "Music for Sight Singing," 80. Mem: Music Teachers Nat Asn (vpres, 75-77, exec bd, 77-). Grants & Awards: Horace H Rackham res grant, 60 & 68; Ford Found res grant, 67; Rockefeller Found perf grant, 67; Nat Endowment for Arts grant, 73 & 79; Guggenheim Found fels, 65 & 72; Am Acad & Inst Arts & Letters Award, 77 & Martha Baird Rockefeller grant, 79. Rec'd Annual Standard Award, ASCAP, 68-

COOPER, ROBERT WILLIAM ASCAP 1959
composer, saxophonist, woodwind specialist
b Pittsburgh, Pa, Dec 6, 25. Educ: Pvt studies with Harry Baker, Henri de Busscher & Mario Castelnuovo-Tedesco. Joined Stan Kenton Orch, 45. Joined Light House All Stars. Toured Europe & SAfrica, 59 & 60. TV, recording &

motion pictures, Los Angeles. *Songs:* Music: Gone for the Day; Bossa Nova. *Instrumental Works:* Solo for Orchestra; Witch Doctor; Jubilation; A Building is Many Buildings; Yo Yo.

COOPER, ROSE MARIE ASCAP 1960
composer
b Cairo, Ill, Feb 21, 37. Educ: Okla Baptist Univ, BM, 59; Teachers Col, Columbia Univ, MA(music & music educ), 60; Univ NC, Greensboro, PhD, 75; studied comp with Henry Cowell. Chief Collabr: Warren Angell. *Songs & Instrumental Works:* Songs to Share (accompaniments); Oh, Penelope (musical); Cantatas: Lord Most Holy; Morning Star; Collections: Melodies With Descants; Plainsongs and Carols; Sing With Me; Octavo: 5 spirituals; Crown of Thorns; Psalm 150; Settings of Five Haiku; This Is The Hand That I Love.

COOPER, SANDRA RANEE ASCAP 1977
composer, author
b New York, NY, Nov 4, 52. Educ: Bronx Community Col, 70-72. Started as dancer, age 7. Active in promotion & pub relations, 70's. Songwriting, 77- Chief Collabr: Patrick Adams. *Songs:* Push Push in the Bush; Love Massage; You Made Me Love; Where Do We Go From Here; Speak Out Loud; My Man; I Want to Give Love.

COOPER, SIDNEY ASCAP 1958
composer, arranger, teacher
b Montreal, Nov 2, 18. Saxophonist at 12 years. Arr for Henry Jerome, Tommy Dorsey, Jimmy Dorsey, Sy Oliver & Ziggy Elmer Orchs. Staff mem, NBC "Tonight Show," 62-74. Arr & studio musician, Decca, Columbia, RCA & MGM. *Instrumental Works:* Drumology; Clarinet Cascades; Night Is Gone; Good Mornin'; Piccolo Polka (Caribbean Polka); Flower People; Dum Dum; Trumpets Ole; Saxology; Croupier of Monte Carlo.

COOPER, ZACK (ZACKIE)
See Florio, Zackie Cooper

COOPERSMITH, JACOB MAURICE ASCAP 1943
composer, conductor
b New York, NY, Nov 20, 03; Educ: NY Univ, BS; Columbia Univ, MA; Harvard Univ, PhD; studied organ with Samuel Baldwin, A Richardson. Honored by Dominican Rep, Order of Juan Pablo, for survey of native music. With recording co, 19-29; radio exec, Mutual Broadcasting Syst, 34-46. Guest prof musicology, Univ of Tex, 47-48; prof of music & cond of Symph Orch, Univ of Okla, 48-49. Senior music cataloguer & reviser, Descriptive Cataloguing Div, Libr of Congress, 49. Compiled thematic index of complete works of Handel. Grants: Schepp Found, Harvard, John Paine, Charles Ditson & Juilliard Found. *Songs:* A Navajo Lullaby; I Always Knew; Tropical Serenade.

COOTS, JOHN FREDERICK ASCAP 1922
composer, author
b Brooklyn, NY, May 2, 1897. Educ: Brooklyn Pub Sch 118. Pianist, song-plugger, vaudeville performer, songwriter, 15- Chief Collabrs: Benny Davis, Sam M Lewis, Dorothy Fields, Haven Gillespie. *Songs:* Music: Santa Claus Is Coming to Town; For All We Know; Love Letters in the Sand; You Go to My Head; also songs for film: Shopworn Angel; also many popular songs & Bway shows. *Songs & Instrumental Works:* I Still Get a Thrill. *Scores:* Bway Show: Sons O' Guns; Bway Show, Film/TV: Sally, Irene and Mary.

COPANI, PETER
composer, author
b Syracuse, NY, Sept 2, 42. Educ: Eastwood High Sch. Founder & exec dir, People's Performing Co, Inc. Creator, Washington Square Outdoor Art Exhibit. Playwright, Dramatist Guild Am. Awarded New York Cert of Appreciation. Chief Collabrs: Bob Tuthill, Christian Staudt, David McHugh. *Songs:* Street Jesus; The Blind Junkie; Fire of Flowers; New York City Street Show; Choices.

COPE, DAVID HOWELL ASCAP 1969
composer
b San Francisco, Calif, May 17, 41. Educ: Ariz State Univ, BMus; Univ Southern Calif, MMus. Performer cello, piano, bass & perc. Author bks "New Directions in Music", "New Music Composition" & "New Music Notation"; 17 articles on new music; 16 works on records; 70 publ works; 3000 performances world-wide in all maj fests & halls. Chief Collabr: Philip Jose Farmer. *Instrumental Works:* Variations for Piano and Wind Orchestra; Streams (orch); Threshold and Visions (orch); Concerto (saxophone & orch); Concerto (piano & orch); Re-Birth (concert band); Margins (chamber ens); Vectors; 4 piano sonatas; Arena (cello & tape); Parallax (solo piano); Triplum (flute & piano); Rituals (cello); Tyger, Tyger (choir); Requiem for Bosque Redondo (brass & choir).

COPELAND, ALAN R ASCAP 1954
composer, author, arranger
b Los Angeles, Calif, Oct 6, 26. Began singing & writing with Modernaires; writer for Count Basie, Horace Silver, Sarah Vaughan, Ella Fitzgerald & others. Has done own albums; wrote spec musical material for Red Skelton Hour, CBS TV, 5 yrs. Formed own group, Alan Copeland Singers; wrote for TV; comp &

scored commercials & variety shows; comp jazz. Cond & singer. Chief Collabr: Jack Lloyd. *Songs:* Make Love to Me; Mission Impossible/Norwegian Wood (Grammy Award).

COPENHAGEN, A
See Glaser, Victoria Merrylees

COPLAND, AARON   ASCAP 1946
composer, author, conductor
b Brooklyn, NY, Nov 14, 1900. Educ: Brooklyn pub schs; Boys High Sch, grad, 18; studied piano with his sister, continued studies with Leopold Wolfson, Victor Wittgenstein & Clarence Adler; studied theory with Rubin Goldmark, 17-21; Fountainebleau Sch Music, France, comp, summer 21; studied with Nadia Boulanger in Paris, 3 yrs; to US, 24; first comp to win Guggenheim Fel, 25, renewed, 26; hon degrees: Oberlin Col, Princeton, Harvard, Brandeis, Hartford, Temple, Ill Wesleyan, Syracuse, Mich & RI Univs, since 56. Lectr, New Sch Social Res, New York, 27-37; taught comp, chmn fac & head dept, Harvard Univ & Berkshire Music Ctr. With Roger Sessions, organized Copland-Sessions concerts for young Am comp; dir, Am Fest Contemporary Music at Yaddo for its first 2 yrs. Cond, US & abroad; toured Latin Am, appearing as pianist, cond & lectr in concerts of Am music, 41-47; guest cond, Boston Symph, toured with Charles Munch throughout Far East, 60; guest cond, New York Philh, 60— Co-chmn, League of Comp-Int Soc Contemporary Music; vpres, Edward MacDowell Asn; dir, Walter M Naumburg Music Found & Am Music Ctr; pres, Am Comp Alliance, 8 yrs. Author of bks: "What to Listen for in Music", "Our New Music", "Music and Imagination" & "Copland on Music." Mem, Nat Inst Arts & Letters. Awards: Creative Arts Medal, Brandeis Univ, 60; Edward MacDowell Medal, 61; Henry Hadley Medal, Nat Asn Am Comp & Cond, 64; Pres Medal Freedom, President of US, 64; Kennedy Ctr Honor Lifetime Achievement Perf Arts, 79. *Songs & Instrumental Works:* El Salon Mexico; Concerto for Clarinet and String Orchestra; Fanfare for the Common Man; Lincoln Portrait; Music for the Theatre; Our Town; An Outdoor Overture; Symphony No 3; Quiet City; Old American Songs Set I & II; Piano Variations; Connotations for Orchestra; Music for a Great City; Orchestral Variations; Short Symphony; Symphonic Ode; Symphony for Organ and Orchestra; Nonet for Strings; Eight Poems of Emily Dickinson. *Scores:* Films (background): Of Mice and Men; North Star; The Red Pony; Our Town; The Heiress (Acad award, 49); Ballet: Appalachian Spring; Billy the Kid; Rodeo; Operas: The Second Hurricane; The Tender Land.

COPPERSMITH, BARBARA C (BARBARA CARROLL)   ASCAP 1953
composer
b Worcester, Mass, Jan 25, 28. Educ: Studied classical piano, Worcester; New Eng Cons Music. Played with small groups at all major music rooms incl, Embers & Roundtable, Boston & NY. Appeared, major music rooms & concerts throughout US, Europe, Australia & others. Featured at Newport Jazz Fest; TV appearances incl "Today Show" & "Tonight Show." Recording artist, RCA, Verve & United Artists. *Instrumental Works:* Barbara's Carol; From the Beginning; In Some Other World; A Little Warm; Blues for Artie; What Time Is It.

CORB, MORTY G   ASCAP 1958
composer, musician, bass player
b San Antonio, Tex, Apr 10, 17. Educ: Calif Acad Music; studied arr with Walter Kelsey, cond, Leo Damiani. Played bass with big bands, 40's, movie studios & recording cos, Los Angeles. Played for Benny Goodman, Bob Crosby, Louis Armstrong, Jack Teagarden, Billy May, Dave Rose, Nelson Riddle, Mitch Ayres, Liberace, TV shows. Chief Collabrs: Alan Copeland, Mort Greene, Nappy Lamare, Jack Lloyd, Hal Dickenson. *Songs:* Music: Goodbye My Love; Romantique; Every Body Happy; Zombie. *Instrumental Works:* Guitars Incorporated; Oasis; Bayou Blues; Sugar Cane Strut; Savanah Shakedown; Ramble In.

CORBETT, DUANE   ASCAP 1969
composer, band director
b Steubenville, Ohio, Nov 17, 24. Educ: Follansbee High Sch; West Liberty State Col, WVa, BA, 49; Univ Mich, MMus, 51. Band dir, Bellevue High Sch, Ohio, 51-56 & Sexton High Sch, Lansing, Mich, 56- (concert band, marching band, dance band-ens). *Instrumental Works:* Waves of Glory (march for band); War Dance Entrance March (band); War Dance Exit March (band); Marching Band Arrangements: Dance Band Arrangements.

CORBETTA, JERRY ANTHINY   ASCAP 1969
composer, author
b Denver, Colo, Sept 23, 47. Educ: Metropolitan State Col, Colo. Studied music privately from age 6; studied accordion & piano, 12 yrs. Started playing drums, age 4 & Rock & Roll, age 13. Formed pop group, Sugarloaf, 69, lead singer & keyboard player; joined pop group, Frankie Valli and the Four Seasons, 80. Producer, Far Out Productions, Los Angeles. Chief Collabrs: Bob Crewe, Frankie Valli, Bob Gaudio, Molly Ann Leikin, Frank C Slay, Jr, Jerry Goldstein, D C LaRue, John Carter, J C Phillips, David Riordan. *Songs:* Green Eyed Lady; Don't Call Us, We'll Call You; Passion From Paris; On Your Knees; Mother Nature's Wine; I Wish That I Was Makin' Love (To You Tonight); If It Really Wasn't Love.

CORDA, MIKE   ASCAP 1953
composer
b New York, NY, July 8, 21. Educ: New York Col Music. Songwriter, entertainer, prof musician, bassist; jazz oriented. Played with Cole Porter's "Kiss Me Kate" original co; with Sands Hotel, 5 yrs; now leader music, Landmark Hotel, Las Vegas. Recorded theme for the sound track of film, "Psychic Killer." Chief Collabrs: Paul Francis Webster, Jacques Wilson, Johnny Mercer, Johnny Burke. *Songs:* Music: The Green Years of Love; Let's Make the Most of a Beautiful Thing; Lover of the Simple Things; Bittersweet; Here She Is; The Gifts of God; Piano Bar (musical show).

CORDASCO, GERALD MICHAEL   ASCAP 1978
composer, author, drummer
b Newark, NJ, Jan 27, 52. Educ: Seton Hall Univ; pvt study with Jim Chapin & Norman Grossman. Instrumentalist & writer, recording act "Stanky Brown," Sire/Warner Bros. Recorded 3 LP's; toured extensively, now free-lance; drum teacher. *Songs:* Took a Chance on Love; Right This Time.

CORDAY, LEO   ASCAP 1943
author
b New York, NY, Jan 31, 02. Educ: NY Univ, LLB. Admitted to bar, 27. Writer spec material for vaudeville, nightclubs, radio & TV. WW II, wrote radio shows for War Manpower Comn. Chief Collabrs: Jack Edwards, Leon Carr, Bert Mann, Louis Singer, Joe Bishop, Paul Mann, Stephan Weiss, Al Hoffman. *Songs:* There's No Tomorrow; If You Smile at the Sun; A Man Could Be a Wonderful Thing; He Like It—She Like It; How Many Stars Have to Shine?; I Have No Heart; Your Socks Don't Match; Leap Frog; Blue Flame; Big Boat Whistle; Three Little Rings; The Turtle Song; A Guy Named Joe; Gotta Get to St Joe; Night of Nights; Be Not Discouraged; See the USA in Your Chevrolet (commercial).

CORDERO, ERNESTO   ASCAP 1976
composer
b New York, NY, Aug 9, 46. Educ: Grad as Prof of Guitar, Royal Cons Music, Madrid, Spain; studied comp, Chigiana Acad, Siena, Italy & with Julian Orbon, New York. Guitar concerts, US, Spain, Italy, Greece & Puerto Rico; concert appointments, Festival Casals, Carnegie Recital Hall, 77. Radio & TV artist; recording, Inst Cultura Puertorriquena & Sociedad Puertorriquena de Musica Contemporanea. Prof comp & guitar, Univ Puerto Rico. *Instrumental Works:* Mapeye (guitar solo); Cinco Preludios Para Guitarra.

COREA, ARMANDO ANTHONY (CHICK)
composer, author
b Chelsea, Mass, June 12, 41. Educ: Columbia Univ; Juilliard Sch Music. Began classical piano study at age 4. Pianist with father, dinner & dance music, country clubs, Boston & Cape Cod. Played with Billy May & Warren Covington Orchs, Mongo Santamaria, Willie Bobo, Stan Getz, Blue Mitchell. Comp & recording artist, 66- Pianist for Sarah Vaughn; joined Miles Davis, Baltimore, Md. Own group, Circle; duet with Gary Burton. Formed own band, Return to Forever, recorded albums. Two world tours; White House Jazz Fest. Chief Collabrs: Neville Potter, Gayle Moran. *Songs:* Music: Five Hundred Miles High. *Instrumental Works:* Spain; La Fiesta; Crystal Silence; Central Park; Windows; Tones for Joan's Bones. *Albums:* Inner Space (Tones for Joan's Bones); Files de Kilimanjaro; In a Silent Way; Bitches' Brew; Return to Forever; Light As a Feather; Hymn of the Seventh Galaxy; Where Have I Known You Before; No Mystery; Romantic Warrior; The Leprechaun (Grammy Award, Best Instrumental Arr & Best Jazz Perf, Group); My Spanish Heart; Musicmagic (Grammy nomination); The Mad Hatter; Duet (Grammy Award, Best Jazz Instrumental Perf); Secret Agent; Delphi I; Tap Step.

CORIGLIANO, JOHN   ASCAP 1963
composer
b New York, NY, Feb 16, 38. Educ: Columbia Col, BA; studied comp with Otto Luening & Vittorio Giannini. Music dir, WBAI Radio, CBS-TV "Young People's Concerts." Now teacher, Lehmann Col & Manhattan Sch Music. Chief Collabrs: Davis Hess, William Hoffman. *Instrumental Works:* Clarinet Concerto; Oboe Concerto; Piano Concerto; A Dylan Thomas Trilogy (choral symph for chorus, soloists & orch). *Scores:* Film: Altered States.

CORINA, JOHN H   ASCAP 1969
composer, professor, oboist
b Cleveland, Ohio, Apr 21, 28. Educ: Western Reserve Univ, BS, 51, MA, 56; Fla State Univ, DM, 65. Instr, Emerson Jr High, Lakewood, Ohio, 51-57; instr orch, North Miami Beach Jr High, 57-60; instr theory, band & orch, Dade County Jr Col, Fla, 60-66; prof theory, comp & oboe, Univ Ga, 66-; principal oboist, Augusta Symph, Ga, 68-; organist choirmaster, Emmanuel Episcopal Church, Athens, Ga. *Songs & Instrumental Works:* The Last Supper (womens chorus, piano & perc); Woodwind Quintet; Peter Quince at the Clavier (soprano, tenor, horn, violin, cello, harpsichord & perc); Partita (solo oboe & perc); Sonet (solo oboe & strings); Cantata: A Prophecy of Peace (soprano, chorus & orch).

CORNELL, CHARLES SYDNEY   ASCAP 1977
composer
b Budapest, Hungary, Aug 7, 02. Educ: Cons Music, Budapest, piano; studied organ with C A J Parmenier, US. Was under contract to Judson Music B; opened

CBS in NY; played under most prominent conductors incl Ormandy, Mendoza, Barlow, Artzt, Rich & others. Had piano team, Schut & Cornell. Recording artist under own name. Played on 37 radio progs a week; wrote music for "Boston Blackie" & "Date With Judy" on radio shows; had own radio prog on CBS during war yrs. Chief Collabrs: Al Bayan, Wolfe Gilbert, Mitchell Parish, Abner Silver, Nick Lenny, Dianne Carroll, Adlene Busick, Dale Wimbrow, Harriet Pressman, Jack Hope, Aldon Nash. *Songs:* Music: I Hate Myself; Where; Accordion Joe; Gypsy Sweetheart; Laughing At Life; Nani; also musicals: Cosette; Not So Fast.

CORNER, PHILIP L   ASCAP 1977
composer, author
b New York, NY, Apr 10, 33. Educ: High Sch Music & Art, New York, 48-51; City Col New York, BA, 55; Paris Cons, with Olivier Messaien, 55-57; Columbia Univ, MA, 59; piano with Dorothy Taubman, 61-76. Pvt piano teacher, 61-68; teacher, New Lincoln High Sch, 66-72, New Sch Social Res, 68-71 & Livingston Col, Rutgers Univ, 72- Comp-performer of new music, US & Europe. Recording artist; publ articles & numerous periodicals. Chief Collabrs: Malcolm Goldstein, James Tenney, Alison Knowles, Peter Garland, Dick Higgins, Charlie Morrow, Julie Portman, Julie Winter, James Fulkerson, Dan Goode, Barbara Benary, Carlos Santos, Tom Johnson. *Instrumental Works:* Metal Meditations; Sprouting; 7 Joyous Flashes (piano); Stücke (flute); Worded Music; Breath: Rubbing Rock; Uhmm-After a Deep and Tibetan Image; Certain Distilling Processes; Chopin Prelude; Chord; Attempting Whitenesses; Big Trombone; Etincelles (Sparks); Ritual Pieces; One Note Once; Elementals; Inner Ear; Outer Ear: Birds in Tree; Passionate Espanse of the Law; Lovely Music; Collections: OM; Gamelan; Gong!; Flux and Form; Pieces for String Instruments; Peace, Be Still; Rounds.

CORNETT, ALICE
See Asherman, Alice Cornett

CORNETT, EWEL   ASCAP 1970
composer, theatre producer, director
b Louisville, Ky, Jan 10, 37. Educ: Univ Sch Music, Univ Ill, BM, 59. Founder, Actors Theatre Louisville, produced & directed two seasons; exec dir, WVa Arts & Humanities Council, 71-74; producer, Theatre Arts WVa, Inc, 6 seasons. Actor & singer, TV, "Labyrinth," NBC & "Oedipus Rex," NY Philh; dir CBS-TV shows, "The Boor" & "A Village Christmas." Actor, toured "Unsinkable Molly Brown", "Camelot", "South Pacific" & "Most Happy Fella." Stock actor & dir, "Stephen Foster Story" & "Wilderness Road," Iroquois Amphitheatre, 3 seasons; Papermill Playhouse, NJ & Mineola Playhouse, NY. Actor, "Little Mary Sunshine" & "Three Penny Opera"; actor & dir, "Meet Peter Grant" & "Trip to Chinatown." Chief Collabr: Billy Edd Wheeler. *Instrumental Works:* Hatfields and McCoys Orchestral Suite. *Scores:* Musical Dramas: Hatfields and McCoys; Honey in the Rock; John Brown; Barbry and Willie.

CORPORA, VICTOR GARI   ASCAP 1957
composer, author, percussionist
b Cleveland, Ohio, Feb 9, 19. Educ: John Adams & John Hay Senior High Schs, Cleveland; Los Angeles Fine Arts Cons Music. Drummer, dance bands. Served in 140th Inf, South Pacific; Ohio Nat Guard, 40. To Los Angeles, 47, continued with dance bands. Worked for North Am Aviation & Rockwell Int, 50-80. Chief Collabrs: Al Lerner, Milt Rogers, Perry Hettel. *Songs:* My Cucuzza; You Can't Hide the Truth; Water Under the Bridge; Lyrics: So Until I See You; Annabel Lee; Old Fashioned Christmas; Such Is My Love; I'm Tired of the Rain; Show Me a Man; Strange the Wind.

CORRELL, STEPHEN MUNGIA   ASCAP 1972
composer
b Los Angeles, Calif, Feb 15, 49. Educ: Notre Dame High Sch; Valley Col, AA, 70; Calif State Univ, Northridge, studied comp; studied piano with Daniel Pollack, 70-71. With Peppered Snowfall Co, worked local nightclubs, Los Angeles area; also studio work, player & arr. *Instrumental Works:* The Corner; Celestial Infinity. *Albums:* Symposium.

CORTESE, DOMINIC   ASCAP 1975
accordion player
b Nizza Monferrato, Italy, Oct 16, 21. Educ: Pvt study in US. Accordion player, for jingles, Bway shows, major orchs & TV shows incl "Sing Along With Mitch Miller", "Jack Paar Show" & "Johnny Carson." Recording artist with var performers. *Songs:* Music: Good Bye Ringo Paul et al; Pebbles (Bossa Nova); Sensible Shoes.

CORWIN, NORMAN   ASCAP 1944
composer, author
b Boston, Mass, May 3, 10. Writer-dir-producer, CBS; chief spec proj, UN Radio; wrote, directed, hosted Westinghouse Group W TV Series "Norman Corwin Presents"; wrote libretto of one-act operas "Esther" & "The People, Yes" broadcast over CBS; wrote, directed, produced radio series "An American in England"; wrote, directed "The Odyssey of Runyon Jones" both for theatrical production in Los Angeles, 72 & TV version, Can, 73. *Scores:* Film/TV: Lust for Life; Norman Corwin Presents; Bway Show: The Rivalry; The World of Carl Sandburg; Libretto: The Warrior (one-act opera).

CORWIN, ROBERT ALFRED
composer, pianist
b New York, NY, Oct 2, 33. Educ: Andrew Jackson High Sch; Manhattan Sch Music; Hunter Col. Jazz pianist with var groups; accompanist for var singers. Pianist & entertainment dir, Playboy Club, Hollywood. Musical stenographer & accompanist for Johnny Mercer. Chief Collabrs: Phil Zeller, Johnny Mercer. *Songs & Instrumental Works:* Montevideo; Take Care My Heart.

CORY, GEORGE C, JR   ASCAP 1955
composer, pianist, conductor
b Syracuse, NY, Aug 3, 20; d. Educ: Univ Calif. WW II, USA. Music dir, Gilbert & Sullivan Rep Co, San Francisco. Asst to Gian-Carlo Menotti, 46-50; arr & cond recordings. Pianist in nightclubs & hotels throughout US. Chief Collabr: Douglass Cross. *Songs:* I'll Look Around; Deep Song; I Left My Heart in San Francisco (Grammy Award, 63); You Will Wear Velvet; Carry Me Back to Old Manhattan; It Happens All Over the World; Ivory Tower; Whenever Winds Blow; Sonnet; Tenderness; Warm Tonight; Peace of Mind.

COSBY, HENRY, SR   ASCAP 1969
composer, author
b Detroit, Mich, May 12, 38. Educ: Northern High Sch, Detroit; Wayne State Univ; Teal Studio of Musicians, studied saxophone. Songwriter, producer, arr & A&R dir, Motown Records, 10 yrs. Producer & artist coordr, CBS. A&R dir, Fantasy Records. Producer, recordings incl "Fingertips", "Love Child", "Living in Shame", "No Matter What Sign You Are" & instrumental album. Recipient, 5 gold records; 3 ASCAP gold records. Chief Collabrs: Stevie Wonder, Smokey Robinson, Frank Wilson, Barry Gordy, Jr, Marvin Gaye, Sylvia Moy, Ron Miller. *Songs:* My Cherie Amore; Tears of a Clown; Uptight; With a Child's Heart; I Was Made to Love Her; Shoo-Be-Doo-Be; Never Had a Dream Come True; Sylvia; Nothin's Too Good for My Baby; That'll Be the Day; I Want to Make Her Love Me; I'm Wondering; Angie Girl; We Could Make It Last Forever; Everytime I See You (I Go Wild); Somebody Knows, Somebody Cares; You Can't Judge a Book By It's Cover; High Place; I'd Be a Fool Right Now; Love Look's Good on You; Home Cookin'; I'm More Than Happy (I'm Satisfied); Work Out Stevie, Work Out; That Girl. *Instrumental Works:* More Than a Dream.

COSCIA, SILVIO (SYLVIUS C)   ASCAP 1960
composer, author, conductor
b Milan, Italy, Nov 27, 1899. Educ: Verdi Cons. At age 8, cantor at St Ambrogio Cathedral, Milan. Mem, wind ens, Milan Cons; mem & arr Goldman Band. Pianist, Soloist's Night Concerts; mem, Metrop Opera Orch, NY. Performed in Toscanini concerts. Co-dir, Am YMCA concerts for Armed Forces (Milan Branch). Hon vpres, Creatore Band & Orch Soc. Voice teacher for opera singers. Author "Yesterday and Today Bel Canto." *Instrumental Works:* Visione Eroica (symph poem); Begli Occhi Lucenti; I Come Tomorrow (voice, piano); Modern French Horn Player (5 studies); 20 Original Duets for Trumpet.

COSLOW, SAM   ASCAP 1923
composer, author, producer
b New York, NY. Owned & organized music co with Larry Spier, sold to Paramount in 29; first Bway songwriter, Paramount, Hollywood, 29-38, did scores for Bing Crosby's starring musicals, also did complete scores for many film musicals. Produced best short "Heavenly Music," MGM, Acad Award, 43, also produced feature musicals incl "Copacabana", "Out of This World" & "Dreaming Out Loud." Elected to Songwriters Hall of Fame, 74. Recording artist, RCA Victor, Decca & Columbia Records. Chief Collabrs: Arthur Johnston, Hoagy Carmichael, Richard Whiting, Leo Robin, Larry Spier, Sigmund Romberg, J Fred Coots, Fred Hollander, Will Grosz. *Songs:* Cocktails for Two; My Old Flame; Was It a Dream; This Little Piggie; In the Middle of a Kiss; Thanks; Learn to Croon; The Day You Came Along; Mister Paganini (You'll Have to Swing It); Hello, Swanee, Hello; Bebe, Be Mine; Little White Gardenia; Moonstruck; Je Vous Aime; It's Love Again; Music: Make-Believe Island; True Blue Lou; Lyrics: Sing You Sinners; Moon Song; Just One More Chance; Kitten on the Keys; The Old Ox Road; If I Were King; True Confession; Have You Forgotten So Soon?; Tomorrow Night; Texas Ranger Song. *Instrumental Works:* Good Morning.

COSTA, JOHN   ASCAP 1955
composer, pianist, teacher
b Arnold, Pa, Jan 17, 22. Educ: Arnold High Sch, dipl; Carnegie Inst Technol, BA(music comp) & BA(pub music educ), studied with Martin Meisller & Nicolai Lopotnikoff. Musical dir, KDKA-TV, Pittsburgh, Pa, 51-65, also for "Mister Rogers Neighborhood," 65- & Mike Douglas, 3 months. Played, The Embers, NY, 55-63. Recorded, Coral, Dot, J Arthur Rank Eng & Music Voice Labels. Appeared on "Tonight Show." Now with Mister Rogers Productions along with concert tours, night clubs with own group. Chief Collabrs: Fred M Rogers, Josie Carey, Bob McCully. *Songs & Instrumental Works:* I'm a Man Who Manufactures; Live on Tape; Neighborhood Trolley Song; Piney the Christmas Tree; The Battle of the Wind; The McFeely Picnic Rag (piano solo); Lady Elaine's Mirror Dance (piano solo); Prepare for the Spring Time; Yes It's Very Strange; A Groovy Cow; Unfrozen Wail; Philip Photographer; Oh No! No More Snow; Laundry Work Song; Potato Train Song.

COSTA, WILLIAM F ASCAP 1960
composer, conductor, producer
b Atlas, Pa, Oct 18, 20. Producer commercials, Maxon, Inc; arr. Chief Collabr: Chet Amsterdam. *Instrumental Works:* New York Waltz; Valse Charmante.

COSTANTAKOS, CHRIS ANASTASIOS ASCAP 1964
(CHARLES DUKE)
composer, author, violinist
b Durham, NC, Apr 27, 24. Educ: Central High Sch, Pa; Brooklyn Cons of Music, prof dipl; Juilliard Sch; Mannes Col; Manhattan Sch of Music; St Francis Col, BA; Pace Univ, MS; NY Univ, PhD; studied violin with D C Dounis, 47-54, chamber music with William Kroll & Paul Doktor, 59-61, comp with Felix Deyo & Angelo Musolino, Byzantine music with Christos Vrionides & Simon Karas. Violinist, var symphonies under Oscar Straus, David Mendoza, Bob Stanley, Walter Hendl, George Sebastian, Freder Weissman & Christos Vrionide. Choir dir; music dir & comp, plays & film "Elodia," 63. Organized & dir Int Music Trio, concerts & radio, 49-55. Teacher & registrar, Brooklyn Cons of Music, 52-62; cond. Taught & composed pvtly, Brooklyn Studio. Chief Collabrs: Alex Caldiero, Jack Ennis, Lew Shaw, Germaine Mamalaki. *Songs:* Kyrie Eleison (SATB); Christmas Bell (SATB); Music: Soufrir; Tis Theos Megas (One Great God) (SATB); Sailor's Song. *Instrumental Works:* Anixis (Spring); Memories; Anatoli (Orient); Syrtos Dance; Festive Dance; Sailor-Butcher Dance No 1, No 2; Mediterranean Serenade No 1, No 2; Spartan Dance; Dance of Piraeus; Syrtos; Mediterranean Dance No 1, No 2; Greek Sailor Dance No 1, No 2. *Scores:* Play: Oedipus Rex.

COSTANZO, JACK J (MR BONGO) ASCAP 1958
composer
b b Chicago, Ill, Sept 24, 24. Introduced bongos to jazz with Stan Kenton Band, 47-48. With Nat King Cole, 5 yrs, then with Peggy Lee, 1 yr; worked on TV shows incl "Judy Garland", "Dinah Shore Show", "Perry Como" & "Ed Sullivan." Recorded 16 albums; did many TV & movie sound tracks; many movie appearances incl, "Satan Bug My Song", "Harum Scarum" & "Bongo Blues." Chief Collabrs: Jay Corre, Paul Lopez, Eddie Cano, Mike Pagone. *Instrumental Works:* El Diablito; Equinot; Sax Con Ritmo; G and J Blues; Get It On; Quire; Conga Boogie; Atu; Mambo Costanzo; Mr Bongo; Bongo Festeris; Hornicopia; Bongo Fever; Latin Fever; Bongo Blues; La Loca; Go Bongo; Guantanamera.

COSTELLO, BARTLEY C ASCAP 1940
author
b Rutland, Vt, Jan 21, 1871; d Germantown, Pa, Jan 14, 41. Assoc with publ cos, NY. Wrote background music for silent films. *Songs:* Ace in the Hole; Just an Old Banjo; If You Had All the World and Its Gold; Hot Coffee; Lyrics: El Rancho Grande.

COSTELLO, DONALD JAMES, JR ASCAP 1965
composer
b Cleveland, Ohio, May 23, 33. Educ: Self-taught on piano, organ & guitar. *Instrumental Works:* Eighty-Eight Keys; I Need You.

COSTER, WAYNE JOSEPH ASCAP 1971
composer, arranger
b Los Angeles, Calif, Jan 3, 53. Educ: Univ Calif, Los Angeles, studied comp with Paul Glass, 71-73 & Henri Lazarof, 74-75, orchestration with Hugo Friedhofer, 73-74 & BA(summa cum laude), 76. Began comp for the Universal Studio TV Show "Ironside." Comp & arr songs & scores for TV series & movies. *Songs:* Wedding Song. *Instrumental Works:* Sonatina (guitar, oboe, clarinet, bassoon); String Trio. *Songs & Instrumental Works:* I Stepped on a Flower.

COTEL, MORRIS MOSHE ASCAP 1973
composer, pianist
b Baltimore, Md, Feb 20, 43. Educ: Peabody Cons; Juilliard Sch Music, BM, 64, MS, 65; studied with Vincent Persichetti, 62-64 & Roger Sessions, 64-66. Comp symph at age 13. Am Rome Prize at age 23; 2nd prize, Int Schoenberg Piano Competition, 75; US winner, Int Competition, "Holocaust and Rebirth." Pianist, conductor, teacher. Chief Collabrs: Richard Dreyfuss, Eli Wallach, Sergiu Comissiona. *Instrumental Works:* August 12, 1952; Harmony of the World; The Fire and the Mountains; Humanoid Ritual Dances; My Shalom, My Peace.

COTTON, NORMAN PAUL
composer, singer, guitarist
b Camp Rucker, Ala, Feb 26, 45. Educ: Studied mellowphone, 4 yrs; high sch, studied French horn, 3 yrs & with James Bostwick; studied with Chicago Symph Orch; studied on electric guitar at age 13. With group, Illinois Speed Press, Chicago, 69-70; joined Poco, 70. *Songs:* Bad Weather; Indian Summer; Heart of the Night (Gold Album); Under the Gun; Midnight Rain.

COUGAR, JOHN
See Mellencamp, John J

COUNTRY KOJAC
See Riggs, John Frederick

COURTNEY, ALAN ASCAP 1941
composer
b New York, NY, Nov 29, 12; d Miami, Fla, Sept 16, 78. Educ: Pub sch. In radio; DJ on WOR, WNEW & WMCA; commentator; creator of open phone forum, WINZ, WGBS, WQAM & WIOD, Miami. Chief Collabrs: Lanny Grey, John Loeb, Walter Bishop. *Songs:* Joltin' Joe DiMaggio; Smile for Me; Sh-h It's a Military Secret; Hereafter.

COURTNEY, DEL ASCAP 1963
composer, conductor, pianist
b Oakland, Calif, Sept 21, 10. Educ: St Mary's Col, Moraga, Calif; Univ Pac, Stockton; Univ Calif, Berkeley, Teacher's degree (music) & MMus. Band leader, radio & TV, 45 yrs. Recording artist & actor, motion pictures & stage. *Songs:* Oakland Raiders Fight Song; Black and White Jazz; Oakland Oddessy; Raiders March; Del's Danse.

COURTS, EDDY
See Kurc, Adolf

COUSINS, M THOMAS ASCAP 1955
composer, conductor, arranger
b Wilson, NC, Oct 9, 14; d Charlotte, NC, Oct 22, 72. Educ: Juilliard; also pvt study. Trumpeter & arr, Nat Symph, CBS, Washington, DC, 39-42 & 42-46. Bandleader, 251st Army Band, WW II. Dir music city schs, Morganton, NC; arr, NC Symph, 48-58; cond, Asheville Symph & Greensboro Symph. Head music dept, Brevard Col, 58-63; lectr, Univ NC; ed publ, Brodt Music Co, Charlotte, 70-72. *Songs:* Anthems: Glorious Everlasting; O Clap Your Hands; Praise the Lord! Ye Heavens Adore Him; Rejoice in the Lord Alway; And the Word Was Made Flesh; Holy Father, Pure and Gracious. *Instrumental Works:* Academic March; Moses (choral symph).

COVAIS, JACK
See Fontini, James

COVINGTON, TREADWELL D ASCAP 1963
composer, director
b Coral Gables, Fla. Educ: Univ NC, AB(Eng); studied musical comp. Advert account exec, Ayer & Gillett Advert, Charlotte, NC, Grant Advert, Miami, Fla, Gaynor & Ducas, New York & Dickie, Raymond, New York. Partner, Total TV Productions, Inc, New York; associated with Harwichport Music Co, New York; group account supvr, currently. Chief Collabrs: Joe Harris, Chet Stover, Watts Biggers. *Songs:* Tennessee Tuxedo and His Tales; Underdog; The Beagles. *Scores:* TV Cartoon Series: King Leonardo and His Short Subjects.

COVINGTON, WARREN LEWIS ASCAP 1956
composer, singer, arranger
b Philadelphia, Pa, Aug 7, 21. Educ: High sch, Philadelphia; NY Univ, comp studies with Danny Hurd; voice studies with Dr Stetson Humphrey, Hollywood. Trombonist & vocalist, Horace Heidt Band, 41, USCG Tars & Spars Show, 43, Les Brown & Gene Krupa, 46. CBS Staff Orch, 46-56. Led own dance bands. Led, Tommy Dorsey Orch, 58-62. With, The Pied Pipers, 73- *Instrumental Works:* Toy Trombone; Sic 'em Tiger; The Mood is Right; Runnin' from Satan; All About Me; Trombonitis; Wall Street Cha Cha; Trombone Boogie; High Fever; Shortnin' Bread Twist.

COWAN, CATHY (CATHY 'KITTY' FURNISS) ASCAP 1968
composer, author, singer
b Kansas City, Mo, Oct 12, 29. Educ: John Marshall High Sch; Univ Calif, Berkeley; studied vocal with Leo Wolf, Los Angeles & Bill Hayes, San Francisco; Hollywood Prof Sch. Vocalist since age 10. Bit player & singer in many hollywood films incl "Hollywood Hotel", "Pennies From Heaven" & "Curley Top." Performer, nightclubs, TV & radio, San Francisco; also stage & motion pictures. Singer voice-overs, commercials. Handle publicity for singers, music publ & record cos. Chief Collabrs: Chuck Sagle, Ken R Browne. *Songs:* Music: What Ever Became of the Two-A-Day?; Lyrics: The Super Skunk (Train song).

COWAN, LYNN F ASCAP 1942
composer, actor, director
b Iowa Falls, Iowa, June 8, 1888; d. Educ: Iowa State Col, BCivil Eng. Mem, Vaudeville team with Bill Bailey. Appeared in films; wrote background score for early sound film, also songs for "Ladies Must Love." WW II, Corps of Engrs, Lt Col; received Legion of Merit. Mgr, Castle Terrace Club, Okinawa. Retired to Kauai, Hawaii, 63. Chief Collabr: Alex Sullivan. *Songs:* Kisses; Dream House; Just Give Me a Week in Paris; Secret; I'm in Love With You. *Scores:* Film Background: The Great Gabbo.

COWAN, MICHAEL ASCAP 1962
composer
b Cleveland, Ohio, Mar 8, 44. Educ: Univ Miami. Chief Collabr: Max Freedman. *Songs:* The Float; A Pretzel Ain't Nothing But a Twist; The Yoo Hoo Spin; Something Else.

COWAN, RUBEY   ASCAP 1923
composer, author, pianist
b Brooklyn, NY, Feb 27, 1891; d Beverly Hills, Calif, July 28, 57. Pianist, film theatres at age 13. With var publ cos; co-founder own publ firm, 26. Pres, 1st Music Men's Asn, The Knights of Harmony, 13-14. Writer, first show, Paramount Theatre, New York; asst producer of stage shows. Head, radio talent dept, NBC, New York, 32. To Hollywood, 37, head, radio dept, Paramount. Chief Collabrs: Phil Boutelje, Charles Tobias, George Bennett, Stanley Cowan (son). *Songs:* You Can't Expect Kisses From Me; I Love You, Believe Me, I Love You; Lonesome Little Doll; I Had to Change the Words; You Never Can Be Too Sure About the Girls; If I Had My Way; Mine, All Mine.

COWAN, STANLEY EARL   ASCAP 1943
composer, author, director
b New York, NY, Feb 3, 18. Educ: High sch. To Hollywood, 37; asst film dir; writer, special material for orchs, musicals & films incl "Hopalong Cassidy." Produced show for USAF, World War II. In radio & TV productions, 48. Publicist, 49, with Rogers & Cowan, 60- Chief Collabrs: Rubey Cowan (father), Bobby Worth, Sidney Miller. *Songs:* Do I Worry; Be Young Again; I Give You a Smile for a Smile; Taps 'Til Reveille; Who Are You?; What's This; Listen to Me Sing; I Realize Now; A Cowgirl Dreams On.

COWELL, SHIRLEY IONE   ASCAP 1959
composer, author
b Tulsa, Okla, Jan 14, 23. Educ: Miss Harris' Fla Sch; Ogontz Sch; Jr Col, Rydal, Pa, drama maj, grad with hons, 42; studied voice with Estelle Liebling & Sid Franklin, 46-48. Appeared in Hugh Martin Co Production, "Best Foot Forward," 49; radio singer/entertainer, "The Shirley Cowell Show," WGBS, Miami, 53; writer spec material for nightclub acts, recordings & TV, 55- Chief Collabr: George Abbott. *Songs:* I'm Just a Boy in Love; Save Your Love; I'm So Lost; A Game for Two; Stay With Me; Here; Have Heart Will Travel; Born to Be Loved; I Won't Do It; Grab It; State of Mind; I'm in Love; Good Lord Handles Everything; I Dream of You; Whenever a Soft Rain Falls; Music: Day Follows Day.

COWEN, JOE
See Cohen, Joseph

COWGER, ROGER RAY   ASCAP 1964
composer, teacher, singer
b Palo Alto, Calif, Nov 22, 38. Educ: San Jose City Col; San Francisco State Col. Creator of musical group, Saturday's Children; recording artist; entertainer, TV & radio; songwriter; supper club entertainer in San Francisco Bay area; pianist. Chief Collabr: William Munday. *Songs:* No One; Cry Wind; Music: Cotton Pickers Song.

COWLES, CECIL   ASCAP 1941
composer, author, pianist
b San Francisco, Calif; d Sewanee, Tenn, Nov 20, 66. Educ: Schs in San Francisco & New York; studied with mother, then Hugo Mansfeldt, Otto Bendix, Sigismund Stojowski, Wallingford Reigger, William McCoy, Carl Engle, Carl Deis. Piano debut, age 9; recitals in US, Europe & Near East. Own radio progs. Chief Collabrs: Elfrida Norden, Lorraine Finley, Florence Tarr, Lily Strickland. *Songs:* The Fragrance of a Song; White Birches; A Little Chinese Fly; Grasshopper; I Love Thee; Till the Tale Is Told; Hey Nonney No; Star Gleam; Flight Over Ireland; Persian Dawn. *Instrumental Works:* Jesu Bambino (mass); Shanghai Bund; Oriental Sketches; Country Club Waltz; Cubanita; Carmelita; Nocturne in G; Nocturne in A flat; Pictures on a Chinese Panel (for children).

COX, JIMMY   ASCAP 1975
composer, author
b July 28, 1882; d Washington, DC. Writer, songs, lyrics & music. Trained daughter, Baby Cox. *Songs:* Nobody Knows You When You're Down and Out; Last Go Round Blues.

COX, LAWRENCE L   ASCAP 1963
composer
b Vernon, Tex, Jan 29, 42. Educ: Tex Tech; West Tex State Univ. *Songs:* Come on Over; A Little Affection; The Memory of a Girl.

COX, RALPH   ASCAP 1926
composer, organist, choirmaster
b Galion, Ohio, Aug 29, 1884; d New York, NY, June 10, 41. Educ: Oberlin Cons; Guilmant Organ Sch; Wooster Univ; studied with d'Aubigne, Braggiotti, Sawaga & Dufft. Organist & choirmaster, Greenwich Presby Church, New York & First Presby Church, Orange, NJ. *Songs:* To a Hilltop; The Road to Spring; In a Southern Garden.

COX, WALLACE MAYNARD (WALLY)
composer, author, actor
b Detroit, Mich, Dec 6, 24; d Bell, Calif, Feb 15, 73. Comedian, nightclubs incl Blue Angel, The Village Vanguard & Mocombo, Hollywood. Actor, Bway show "Dance Me a Song," TV shows incl "Mr Peepers," 52-55 & "Hiram Holiday," 56-57 & var motion pictures. Voice, cartoon character "Under Dog," 65-68;

spoke 7 languages incl Swahili, Mongolian & Swedish. Author, "My Life As a Small Boy", "Rhalph Makes Good" & coauthor juvenile bk "The 10th Life of Osiris Oakes." *Songs:* Margery; Well—I'm Available; Larado.

COYLE, JOSEPH ANTHONY   ASCAP 1969
composer, musician
b Philadelphia, Pa, Dec 7, 46. Educ: Msgr Bonner High Sch, dipl; studied guitar & music theory with William C La Pata, 10 yrs. Worked as back-up & studio musician for Keith at Mercury, RCA & Discreet Record Cos. Taught music & theory, 76-79. Presently formed own publ & talent agency in Philadelphia. Chief Collabr: James Barry Keefer (Keith). *Songs:* Melody; To Opa Locka and You; When Sunshine Was; Because of You; Let Yourself Unwind; Love's Not What It Seems; Music: Trixons Election; The Problem.

COYLE, PAUL RAYMOND   ASCAP 1976
composer, performer
b Norwich, Conn, Oct 29, 44. Educ: Studied saxophone with Bob Koper, Quincy Col, 63-66; Parsons Col, 66-67; Berklee Col Music, BA, saxophone with Joe Viola. Worked with many rock groups, also in shows. Played warm-up or back-up for Chubby Checker, Flash, The Supremes, Dion, The Olympics, The Four Seasons, Chuck Berry & others. Had own Fusion Jazz Rock group, 70- Played at The Plaza, New York, also at Northeastern Univ. *Songs:* I'm Your Salvation. *Instrumental Works:* On Saint John's Eve (suite; 3 movements); Quincy Nights; Lad From Lombard; The Morning After.

CRABTREE, WILLIAM NELSON   ASCAP 1979
composer, author
b Wardell, Mo, Feb 14, 55. Educ: North Pemiscot High Sch, dipl, studied trombone, electric bass guitar & cello; Univ Mo, studied violin, acoustic bass; Univ Tenn, BS, 77. Bass guitarist in rock groups, 69- Teacher, beginning guitar, 73-76. Jazz bass guitarist, high sch & col, comp-author, 75. TV, radio, works in recording sessions. Electric bass guitarist, Univ Mo production, "Celebration." Chief Collabrs: Kenneth Moss, Jeff Roehn, Theresa Crabtree. *Songs:* Goodnight Evening Star; Music: Beyond Imagination; Let the Child Come Out of You; Let Love In; Why the Sun Still Shines.

CRAFT, GARLAND   ASCAP 1975
composer, author
b Wilson, NC, Jan 5, 49. Worked with Keystone Singers & Oak Ridge Boys, 70- Chief Collabr: Aaron Brown. *Songs:* That's Just Like Jesus; I Wanna Be Ready; One More Day.

CRAFT, LOIS ADELE   ASCAP 1963
composer, author, harpist
b Chicago, Ill. Educ: Kansas City Cons; Boulder Univ; harp study & coaching with Alberto Salvi. Soloist & first harp with Kansas City Philh. Harpist, 20th Century Fox Motion Picture Co, Las Vegas entertainment world & world premiere of William Grant Stills' harp concerto, "Ennanga." Recording artist. *Songs & Instrumental Works:* Contemporary Mary (harp solo); Faralones (harp solo); So Obvious (musical reading with harp accompaniment).

CRAIG, BRADFORD JOSEPH   ASCAP 1965
composer, author, director
b New Bedford, Mass, May 3, 37. Acted in films, "Music Man", "Bye Bye Birdie" & "Hello Dolly." Staged major star acts. Golden Globe nomination, 72. Chief Collabrs: Quincy Jones, Pat Williams, H B Barnum. *Songs:* Sign of the Dove; The Doberman Gang; Lyrics: Where Are They Now; What You See Is What You Get. *Scores:* Film/TV: The Doberman Gang; Amateur Night At the Dixie Bar and Grill.

CRAIG, DONALD MICHAEL   ASCAP 1953
composer
b San Francisco, Calif, Dec 7, 25. Educ: San Jose State Col; Southern Calif Cons Music, BFA, 80. Started as staff songwriter for major music publ house in early 50's. Now in TV news, mostly with NBC. Comp, 74- *Instrumental Works:* Nightly News; Theme for Tomorrow.

CRAIG, FRANCIS   ASCAP 1947
composer, author, pianist
b Dickson, Tenn, Sept 10, 1900; d Sewanee, Tenn, Nov 20, 66. Educ: Vanderbilt Univ. USA, WW I. Led own orch, Hermitage Hotel, Nashville, 42; cond own radio show, WSM, 53. Chief Collabrs: Kermit Goell, Beasley Smith. *Songs:* Red Rose; Near You; Beg Your Pardon; Tennessee Tango; A Broken Heart Must Cry; When Vandy Starts to Fight—Dynamite (official Vanderbilt Univ fight song).

CRAIG, JIMMY
See Kellem, Milton

CRAM, JAMES D   ASCAP 1959
composer, conductor, arranger
b Heavener, Okla, May 10, 31; d. Educ: Okla Baptist Univ, BM, MM. Dir, Wayland Col Int Choir, 60, then asst prof of music. *Songs:* Come, Thou Fount; When Jesus Left His Father's Throne; I'm Gonna Sing; I Love Thee, My Lord.

CRANE, JIMMIE
See Fraieli, Loreto

CRANE, PHILIP MILLER   ASCAP 1957
author
b Chicago, Ill, Oct 3, 30. Educ: DePauw Univ, 48-50; Hillsdale Col, BA(psychology, history), 52; Univ Mich & Univ Vienna, postgrad work, 52-54; Ind Univ, MA(history), 61, PhD(history), 62. USA, 54-56. Taught history, Ind Univ, 3 yrs; asst prof history, Bradley Univ, 63-67; dir schs, Westminister Acad, Northbrook, Ill, 67-68. US Rep, Ill, 69-, ranking Republican, Ways & Means Comt, ranking minority mem, Health Subcomt, serves on Pub Assistance & Unemployment Compensation Subcomt, was founding mem & acts as vchmn, Republican Study Comt, serves on Republican Policy Comt Task Force on Health. Trustee, Hillsdale Col, dir, Intercollegiate Studies Prog; mem adv bd, Young Americans for Freedom. Mem: Am Historical Asn; Orgn Am Historians; Am Political Service Acad; US Capitol Historical Soc. Honors & Awards: Vet Foreign Wars; B'nai B'rith; Nat Taxpayers Union; Freedoms Found at Valley Forge; Nat Fedn Independent Businessmen; Statesman Father of Yr, 79. *Songs:* Lyrics: Little Sandy Sleighfoot.

CRAWFORD, DAVID B   ASCAP 1969
author, producer, composer
b Jacksonville, Fla, Oct 24, 43. Educ: Fla A&M Univ, Tallahassee, DJ, WOL, Wash, WAOK, Atlanta & WPDQ, Jacksonville, 62-73; staff producer, Atlantic Records, 69; producer, ABC Records, 72; also produced for Warner Bros Records; independent with Los Angeles Records, Tapes & Films. *Songs & Instrumental Works:* Young Hearts Run Free; Victim; Mighty High; To Know You Is to Love You; Precious—Precious; Don't Knock My Love; Here Am I; Electric Skyway; Where Has All the Love Gone.

CRAWFORD, JESSE   ASCAP 1954
composer, pianist, organist
b Woodland, Calif, Dec 2, 1895; d Sherman Oaks, Calif, May 27, 62. Educ: Pub schs; studied comp & arr with Joseph Schillinger. Pianist & organist in variety shows & film theatres; first organ soloist, Grauman's Theatre, Los Angeles, 18; featured organ soloist, Chicago Theatre, New York Paramount & others; comp & cond of music for radio dramas, NBC & CBS; recording artist. Author: "The Jesse Crawford Organ Courses in the Popular Style of Organ Playing on the Hammond Organ," (elem, intermediate & advanced courses). *Songs & Instrumental Works:* Starlight Rendezvous; Louisiana Nocturne; Harlem Holiday; Mood Tragic; Vienna Violins; March of the Matadors; The Swiss Doll; Hawaiian Honeymoon; Lonely Hour; Forgotten Melody; Pal O' My Heart; Thank You; Old Virginia Moon; What's the Good of Dreams (That Never Come True)?; Blue Bell; Love Lit Hollow; Roses in the Rain; Birdie; Gazing at the Stars.

CRAWFORD, JOHN CHARLTON   ASCAP 1969
composer, professor
b Philadelphia, Pa, Jan 19, 31. Educ: Yale Sch Music, BMus, 50, studied with Paul Hindemith, MMus, 53; Fulbright Grant, studied with Nadia Boulanger & Arthur Honegger, Paris, 50-51; Harvard Univ, PhD, 63; studied with Walter Piston & Randall Thompson. John Knowles Paine Travelling Fel, Harvard Univ, 59. Instr music, Amherst Col, 61-63. Asst prof music, Wellesley Col, 63-70. Assoc prof music, Univ Calif, Riverside, 70-75, prof, 75- Pianist, Lieder & chamber music recitals with wife, Dorothy Crawford. Cond chorus & prof symph orch oratorio, "Ash Wednesday"; cond prof cast & chamber orch opera, "Don Cristobal and Rosita." *Songs & Instrumental Works:* Magnificat (mixed chorus, string orch); Ash Wednesday (oratorio for mixed chorus, narrator, soloists, symph orch); String Quartet No 2; Metracollage (symph orch); Calvaries of Love (Emily Dickinson; song cycle for soprano, clarinet, vocal & piano).

CRAWFORD, ROBERT M   ASCAP 1941
composer, author, conductor
b Dawson, Yukon Terr, July 27, 1899; d New York, NY, Mar 12, 61. Educ: Princeton Univ; Fontainebleau Cons, France (scholarship); Juilliard (scholarship); studied with Francis Rogers. Dir, Princeton Glee Club, cond of orch. Taught at Juilliard. Soloist, St Thomas Church, New York, 10 yrs. Dir, Music Found, Newark, NJ & Bach Cantata Club, 31. Cond, Contemporary Choral, Maplewood, NJ & Aeolian Choir, Trenton. Summer cond, Newark Symph. Soloist, Chautauqua Opera, Rochester & Worcester Fests, Oratorio Soc of New York & Bach Choir, Bethlehem, Pa. Maj, ATC, WW II. Became assoc prof, Univ Miami, 47. *Songs & Instrumental Works:* Les Etoiles (symph suite); Tiger (prelude & fugue); Orientale (choral); Romany Rye (choral); Songs: Pagan Prayer; To Everyman; Behold What Manner of Love; The US Air Force (The Army Air Corps); Mechs of the Air Corps; Cadets of the Air Corps; Born to the Sky (off ATC song).

CRAWLEY, JAMES ELVIN   ASCAP 1975
composer, author, musician
b Winterpock, Va, Mar 27, 31. Educ: Rutuger Sch Music & Voice. Started singing in churches; preacher & singer, churches, nursing homes & hospitals. Singer, Protherson Chapel Serv, USMC. Singer at Carnegie Hall, New York. *Songs:* What Is Your Life Without God?; Working Man; There's Been a Change; Time Don't Wait; Babe Jesus; New Born King.

CRAY, KEVIN EARL   ASCAP 1977
author, pianist
b Erie, Pa, June 20, 22. Educ: Cath Univ Am; State Univ NY; Univ Wis; Fredonia Chautauqua Inst; St John's Univ, Collegeville, Minn, BMus, MMus. Roman Cath priest. Fac, Gregorian Inst Am & Am Col Musicians. Music critic, Erie Morning News; district pres, Pa Music Teachers Asn. Pvt teacher piano & comp; music therapist. *Songs & Instrumental Works:* Mass: Savior of the World (voices, organ); Mass of the Psalms (voices, organ); Mass of St Peter (unison choir, organ); Sonatine (piano solo); Images (piano solo).

CREAMER, HENRY   ASCAP 1924
composer, author, singer
b Richmond, Va, June 21, 1879; d New York, NY, Oct 14, 30. Educ: New York pub schs. Co-founder, Clef Club. With Gotham-Attucks Music Co. Appeared in vaudeville, US & Europe, with collabr, Turner Layton. *Songs:* After You've Gone; Dear Old Southland; Way Down Yonder in New Orleans; Sweet Emmalina My Gal; Goodbye, Alexander, My Honey; Down by the River; If I Could Be With You One Hour Tonight; My Little Bluebird Was Caught in the Rain. *Scores:* Bway stage: Three Showers; Strut, Miss Lizzie.

CREATORE, LUIGI   ASCAP 1953
author, publisher, producer
b New York, NY, Dec 21, 20. Formed writing, arr & producing unit with Hugo Peretti for records & musical commercials. With Roulette & RCA Victor Records. *Songs:* Bimbombey; Can't Help Falling in Love With You; The Lion Sleeps Tonight; Wild in the Country; Oh, Oh, I'm Falling in Love Again; Secretly; A Walkin' Miracle; And Now; Carnival.

CREEDEN, TERRY L   ASCAP 1972
composer, author, singer
b Cincinnati, Ohio, Dec 27, 49. Singer, with show band in nightclubs. *Songs:* Hey Girl.

CRESTON, PAUL   ASCAP 1945
composer, author, conductor
b New York, NY, Oct 10, 06. Educ: Studied piano with Carlo Stea, G Aldo Randegger & Gaston Dethier, organ with Pietro Yon; Guggenheim fel in comp, 38 & 39. Organist, St Malachy's Church, New York, 34-67; music dir, radio network progs, composer, radio & TV music scores; made concert tour as pianist & accompanist, 36; music dir, "The Hour of Faith" prog, NBC, 44-50. Bd Gov, The Bohemians, 50-68; mem, Nat Asn Am Comp & Cond, received Citation of Merit, 41-43, pres, 56-60; exec comt, Nat Music Council, 56-68; State Dept grant, Am Specialist in Israel & Turkey, 60; life fel, Int Inst Arts & Letters, 62. Prof music, NY Col Music & Cent Wash Univ, 68-75. Author of "Creative Harmony", "Principles of Rhythm" & "Rational Metric Notation." Christopher Award, "Revolt in Hungary"; Music Award, Nat Inst Arts & Letters; Alice M Ditson Award, "Poem" (harp, orch); also Gold Medal, Nat Arts Club. *Instrumental Works:* Toccata for Orchestra (Comn by George Szell); Concerto for Accordion and Orchestra (Comn by Am Accordionists Asn); Janus for Orchestra (Comn by Asn Women's Comt for Symph Orchs); Concerto No 2 for Violin and Orchestra (Comn by Ford Found); Corinthians: XIII for Orchestra (Comn by Phoenix Symph Orch); Choreografic Suite for Orchestra (Comn by Harkness Ballet); Pavane Variations for Orchestra (Comn by La Jolla Musical Arts Soc); Chthonic Ode (orch; comn by Detroit Symph Orch); The Psalmist for Contralto and Orchestra (Comn by Jackson Symph Orch); Anatolia (Turkish Rhapsody; comn by Eastern Ill Univ); Kalevala (symph band; comn by Ohio Music Educ Asn); Jubilee (symph band; comn by USA Band); Rapsodie (saxophone, organ, piano; comn by Jean-Marie Londeix); Suite (saxophone quartet; comn by Swiss Saxophone Quartet, 79); Trio (piano, violin, violoncello; comn by Mirecourt Trio, 80); Symphony No 2 (Fedn Music Clubs Award); Symphony No 3 (Comn by Worcester Fest); Symphony No 4 (Comn by Viola Malkin); Symphony No 5 (Comn by Nat Symph Orch); Partita for Flute, Violin and String Orchestra; Two Choric Dances, Opus 17 (orch); Suite for Violin and Piano; Sonata for Saxophone and Piano (comn by Cecil Leeson); Symphony No 1 (NY Music Critics Circle Award; Paris Referendum Award); Concertino for Marimba and Orchestra (Comn by Frederique Petrides); Concerto for Saxophone and Orchestra (Comn by Cecil Leeson) A Rumor for Orchestra (Comn by CBS); Chant of 1942 for Orchestra; Frontiers by Andre Kostelanetz); Psalm XXIII (voice, piano, orch); Fantasy for Trombone and Orchestra (Comn by Alfred Wallenstein); Piano Concerto (Comn by Viola Malkin); Concerto for Two Pianos (Comn by Yarbrough & Cowan); Walt Whitman (orch; comn by Thor Johnson); Suite for Flute, Viola and Piano (Comn by Coleman Chamber Music Group); Invocation and Dance (Comn by Louisville Orch); Celebration Overture (symph band; comn by Edwin Franco Goldman); Dance Overture (Comn by Nat Fedn of Music Clubs); Concerto No 1 for Violin and Orchestra (Comn by Zlatko Balokovic); Suite for Violoncello and Piano (Comn by Elizabeth Sprague Coolidge Found). *Scores:* Films: Tears of the Moon; Brought to Action (USN); TV documentaries: Strangled (Air Power series, CBS); The Twentieth Century (14 episodes, CBS); In the American Grain (CBS; Emmy Citation).

CRETECOS, JAMES NICHOLAS   ASCAP 1971
composer, author
b Lynn, Mass, Aug 14, 48. Produced Bruce Springsteen's "Greetings From Asbury Park, NJ" & "The Wild, the Innocent and the E Street Shuffle." Chief

Collabrs: Mike Appel, Wes Farrell, Jeff Barry. *Songs:* Lay a Little Lovin' on Me; Doesn't Somebody Want to Be Wanted; I Can Feel Your Heart Beat; Rainmaker; When Michael Calls.

CREW, RICHARD PAGE ASCAP 1972
composer, author
b Roanoke Rapids, NC, Mar 12, 41. Educ: Woodrow Wilson High Sch; Leeward Community Col. Trumpet player in mil bands. Chief Collabrs: R Alex Anderson, Albert C Johnston, Jr, Ernie Washington, Martin Denny. *Songs:* What Am I This Thing Called Man?; It's My Life; I Just Bought the House We Lived In; Only You Can Kill the Pain; Lyrics: I Don't Wanna Be Your Part Time Girl.

CRIBARI, DONNA MARIE ASCAP 1972
composer, teacher, singer
b Mt Vernon, NY, Apr 30, 39. Educ: Duquesne Univ, MMEd; Marymount Col, Tarrytown, NY, BA(music), conducting & repertoire with Edwin McArthur. Teacher music for 15 yrs; began comp in 70 with songs for Cath liturgy. Became free lance cond/musical dir regional & off off Bway, 72-; had publisher's contract with Labrador Music, 72-74, free lance, 74- Comp for regional theatre & off Bway. Chief Collabr: Camille Linen. *Songs & Instrumental Works:* Pop; Thomas J a Musical Portrait (comn by Bicentennial Comt, 76); songs cycle: Prayers from the Ark; You Found Me; Indian Heart Prayer (mixed chorus)

CRIBARI, JOE ASCAP 1959
composer, pianist, arranger
b Providence, RI, July 15, 20; d. Educ: High sch; pvt music study. Pianist in touring bands, 37-40. WW II, on Adm Nimitz staff; mem, CINPAC Band. Pianist in orchs incl Tommy Reynolds, Dick Rogers, Victor Lombardo, Sammy Kaye, Ray McKinley, Sauter-Finegan & Glenn Miller. *Songs:* Candlelight Serenade.

CRIDER, CLARENCE W ASCAP 1969
composer, musician
b Summersville, Mo, Apr 30, 34. Educ: Mo Sch for Blind, High Sch. Prof musician, spent several yrs in radio broadcasting, as well as some TV appearances. First song publ in 69. Chief Collabr: Urel Albert. *Songs:* Saturday Night in Nashville; I'm an Imitator; The American Dream; Your Love Keeps Me Alive; Tribute to Country Music; Going Back to Nashville; Home; Jesus Is His Name; Everything But Love; I'll Be True.

CRISCUOLO, JAMES MICHAEL (JAMES SAVOY) ASCAP 1970
composer, author, singer
b New York, NY, Apr 15, 30. Educ: Pub schs: Lincoln Hall; Bronx Vocational High. Recording artist, Ram Records. Has done work in TV; inventor. *Songs:* Song of Love; A-1-Girl; Hell Breaks Loose; Air Pollution; Lyrics: Sunshine Day.

CRIST, BAINBRIDGE ASCAP 1925
composer, author, teacher
b Lawrenceburg, Ind, Feb 13, 1883; d Hyannis, Mass, Feb 7, 69. Educ: Washington Univ, LLB; studied with Theodore Hahn, George Enesco, Paul Juon, Claude Landi, William Shakespeare, Charles Clark, Franz Emerich. Practiced law, Boston, 6 yrs. Cond own works, US & Europe. Singing teacher, Boston, Wash & Europe. Author, "The Art of Setting Words to Music." *Songs & Instrumental Works:* In a Swiss Toy Shop; Fantasie in D; The Sorceress; La Pied de La Momie; Pregiwa's Marriage; Festival Overture; Hindu Rhapsody; Souvenir of Ballet (suite); Egyptian Impressions (suite); Japanese Nocturne; Intermezzo; Abhisarika (violin, orch); St Francis Prayer (chorus); To a Water Fowl (chorus); Song Cycles: Chinese Mother Goose Rhymes; Drolleries; Colored Stars; Remember; The Way That Lovers Use; Noontime; Evening; By a Silent Shore; Into a Ship Dreaming.

CROCE, INGRID ASCAP 1968
composer, author
b Philadelphia, Pa, Apr 27, 47. Educ: Rhode Island Sch of Design; Moore Col of Art; Mexican Fine Arts Fellowship, 67. Began singing & writing with husband, Jim Croce, 63-71. Now writer, comp & singer. Mem bd dirs, Women's Bank of San Diego, 77-79. Vice consul of Costa Rica, San Diego, 77- Chief Collabrs: Jim Croce, Maury Muehleisen, Jimmy Horowitz, Eric Bikales. *Songs:* Hey Tomorrow; Age.

CROCE, JAMES JOSEPH ASCAP 1968
composer, author, teacher
b Philadelphia, Pa, Jan 10, 43; d. Educ: Villanova Univ, studied psychol & foreign language. Played accordion at age 6; guitarist in small bars & coffee houses at age 18. Singer in duo with wife, Ingrid, 62-71. Recorded first album, 65; signed with ABC Dunhill, 71. Chief Collabrs: Ingrid Croce, Maury Muehleisen. *Songs:* Bad, Bad Leroy Brown; Time in a Bottle; I'll Have to Say I Love You in a Song; You Don't Mess Around With Jim.

CROCKETT, DAVID
See Sutton, David C, Sr

CROMARTY, GEORGE MICHAEL ASCAP 1973
composer, author, singer
b Los Angeles, Calif, Sept 15, 41. Educ: Univ Calif, Santa Cruz, BA(hist). Began performing folk music professionally, West Coast nightclub circuit & col

concerts, 60. Did 3 LP's, 62-74; guitarist & poet. *Songs:* I Want to Keep You As My Friend; We All Need a Good Home; One of These Days; What You Need; Sunshine, Come Down; All Last Night; Bees Make Honey; The Zebra; Change, Change; Many Hands; Captain Owl; Valley Land. *Instrumental Works:* Flight; Harpsichord; Symmetry; Renaissance Faire; Topinambour; Rose and Briar; Buena Vista; Poppyfield; Rainsong; Star Ark; Wingshiner; Wild Rice; Southern Sunday; Arboretum. *Songs & Instrumental Works:* Here They Are: The Gold Coast Singers!; Grassroots Guitar; The Only One: Music for People Who Are Still Growing.

CROMWELL, LINK
See Kaye, Leonard Jay

CRONIN, KEVIN P, JR ASCAP 1979
composer, publisher
b Chicago, Ill, Oct 6, 51. Educ: Loyola Univ. Songwriter, 65- *Songs:* Roll With the Changes; Time for Me to Fly; Keep Pushing; Keep on Loving You.

CROOKER, EARLE T ASCAP 1942
author, director, educator
b Boston, Mass, Aug 11, 1899. Educ: Univ Pa, PhD. Wrote special material for Beatrice Lillie, 26-41; wrote songs for Bway revues "Thumbs Up!" & "Walk a Little Faster." Combat service, USS Bataan, WW II. Dir dramatics & prof English Drexel Tech, 52- Chief Collabrs: Henry Sullivan, Frank Gray, Frederick Loewe. *Songs:* Lorelei; Through the Night; Keeping on the Sunny Side of You; Mad Over You; Happy; Falling in Love; Flamenco; Lilly Belle May June; A Waltz Was Born in Vienna; Somehow; Salute to Spring; April Day; One Robin; I'm a Camp Fire Girl. *Scores:* Stage, librettos: Salute to Spring; Great Lady.

CROSBY, BOB
See Crosby, George Robert

CROSBY, DAVID VAN CORTLANDT
composer, author, singer
b Los Angeles, Calif, Aug 14, 41. Started playing/singing profesionally in coffee houses, 60. Formed the Byrds with McGuinn, Clark & Hillman, 64; helped form Crosby, Stills & Nash, 67, later became Crosby, Stills, Nash & Young. Was instrumental at Woodstock & 2 Monterey Pop Fests. Chief Collabrs: R McGuinn, G Clark, S Stills, N Young, G Nash, P Kantner, C Doerge. *Songs & Instrumental Works:* Guinevere; Long Time Gone; Eight Miles High; Deja Vu; Almost Cut My Hair; Wooden Ships; Carry Me; Critical Mass.

CROSBY, GEORGE ROBERT (BOB) ASCAP 1936
composer, author
b Spokane, Wash, Aug 25, 23. Educ: N Cent High Sch, Spokane, Wash; Gonzaga Univ. Began career singing with Anson Weeks' Orch; later became first male vocalist in Dorsey Bros Orch; formed own band, Bob Crosby and the Bobcats, 36, Downbeat Mag voted it Best All-Am Jazz Band, 38. Made many recordings, appeared in numerous motion pictures & radio & TV progs. Still working as bandleader. Chief Collabrs: Del Sharbutt, Carroll Carroll, Jack Fulton, Bob Haggart, Ray Bauduc, Eddie Miller, Matty Matlock. *Songs:* Lyrics: Until; Silver and Gold; Learn to Pray Every Day; Time Has Come to Bid You Adieu. *Instrumental Works:* Big Noise From Winnetka; March of the Bob Cats; Smokey Mary.

CROSBY, HARRY LILLIS (BING) ASCAP 1932
composer, singer, actor
b Tacoma, Wash, May 2, 04; d Madrid, Spain, Oct 14, 77. Educ: Gonzaga Univ, hon PhD. Singer in vaudeville with Al Rinker; formed Rhythm Boys Trio with Rinker & Harry Barris, 26. Toured with Paul Whiteman Orch, 3 yrs. Film appearances incl, "King of Jazz", "The Big Broadcast", "College Humor", "Too Much Harmony", "We're Not Dressing", "She Loves Me Not", "Mississippi", "Pennies From Heaven", "Anything Goes", "Rhythm on the Range", "Double or Nothing", "Waikiki Wedding", "Dr Rhythm", "Sing You Sinners", "The Star Maker", "East Side of Heaven", "If I Had My Way", "Road to Singapore", "Road to Zanzibar", "Birth of the Blues", "Holiday Inn", "Road to Morocco", "Going My Way" (Acad Award), "The Bells of St Mary's", "Road to Utopia", "Ridin' High", "Road to Bali", "The Country Girl", "White Christmas", "High Society", "Stagecoach." Had own TV series. Autobiography, "Call Me Lucky." Chief Collabrs: Al Rinker, Harry Barris, Roy Turk, Fred Ahlert, Ned Washington, Victor Young. *Songs:* Where Are You (Girl of My Dreams)?; Love Me Tonight; At Your Command; That's Grandma; From Monday On; I Don't Stand a Ghost of a Chance With You; Where the Blue of the Night Meets the Gold of the Day (theme).

CROSS, DOUGLASS ASCAP 1954
composer, author, producer
b Englewood Cliffs, NJ, May 4, 20; d. Educ: Oakland High Sch, Calif. Baritone with San Francisco Opera. WW II, USA; OWI. Was record producer; sta mgr & prog dir, WBAI, NY. Music ed, Hi Fi Music mag. Chief Collabr: George Cory. *Songs:* I'll Look Around; Deep Song; I Left My Heart in San Francisco (Grammy Award, 63); You Will Wear Velvet; Carry Me Back to Old Manhattan; It Happens All Over the World; Ivory Tower; Whenever Winds Blow; Sonnet; Tenderness; Warm Tonight; Peace of Mind.

CROSS, FRANK LEROY (JAMES VELMONT)   ASCAP 1960
author
b Lamont, Okla, Jan 2, 1904. Educ: Waukomis Okla High Sch; Oklahoma City Univ. Worked on railroad, farms, selling clothes & as a minister. Became literary ed of Lorenz Publ Co, 10 yrs; retired. Chief Collabrs: Ellen Jane Lorenz-Porter, Roger Wilson, Rob Roy Peery, Robert Hughes, John Rasley, Jack Rasley. *Songs:* Lyrics: There'll Always Be a Christmas; I Saw the Lord; King Forever; Man and His World (used at Exposition 67, Can); For All Mankind; many cantatas and single anthems.

CROSS, JIMMIE   ASCAP 1963
composer, author, musician
b Geneva County, Ala; d Los Angeles, Calif, Oct 8, 78. Educ: High sch; Univ Calif, Los Angeles film sch. Producer & singer; recording artist. *Songs:* Portant Tu M'aimes (I Still Love Him).

CROSS, VERNON
See Reardon, Frank C

CROSWELL, ANNE PEARSON   ASCAP 1957
author, playwright
b Tuscaloosa, Ala. Educ: Randolph-Macon Woman's Col, BA(art); Sch of ·Radio/TV Technique, studied with Gilbert Seldes. Author of advert jingles, pop songs, TV musicals, Bway & off-Bway shows & repertory theater. Songs in revues, "Pieces of Eight," London & "Wet Paint," New York. Production asst on "Howdy Doody," "Arthur Godfrey-TV" & "Kate Smith-TV." Author bk, "Some of My Best Friends Are Runners." Writer of newspaper & mag features & current commercials for The Conservatory Restaurant in the Mayflower Hotel, New York. Chief Collabrs: Lee Pockriss, Ernest Gold, Jerry Blatt, Burt Bacharach, Ed Thomas, John Duffy, Clint Ballard, Jr & Ed Scott. *Songs:* Lyrics: Believe in Stevenson (campaign song for Adlai Stevenson); I Know the Feeling; A Wicked Man; The Only One; You Can't Make Love; The Bells of Christmas. *Scores:* Ernest in Love (off-Bway); Tovarich (Bway musical); I'm Solomon (Bway musical); Chips 'n' Ale (musical); TV: Who's Earnest?; Huck Finn; Washington Square; also concerts of works at Carnegie Hall & Philh Hall. *Albums:* Cast: Ernest in Love; Tovarich.

CROTHERS, BENJAMIN SHERMAN (SCATMAN)   ASCAP 1959
composer, author, singer
b Terre Haute, Ind, May 23, 10. Educ: Wiley High Sch. Drummer, tenor guitarist, actor & comedian. Has appeared in nightclubs, hotels, films & on TV, incl series "Chico and the Man," 4 yrs. Has made many records. Chief Collabrs: E E Miller, Riff Charles. *Songs:* I Was There; Dearest One; The Gal Looks Good; Nobody Knows Why; A Man's Gotta Eat; When, Oh When. *Songs & Instrumental Works:* Mean Dog Blues; Waitin' for My Baby; Wondering; Talkin' 'Bout a Man; Stanley (Does It All); Everything Will Be OK; Bowery Blues; Elaine Elaine.

CROTHERS, BERT   ASCAP 1976
composer, singer
b Jackson, Ohio, Mar 3, 37. Folk musician. Chief Collabr: Shirley Crothers (wife). *Songs:* I'm Called Loneliness.

CROTHERS, SHIRLEY EVANS   ASCAP 1976
composer, author, teacher
b Rio Grande, Ohio. Ohio State Univ, BS(music educ); Ohio Univ, MFA; Cincinnati Cons, studied voice; studied voice with Jane Shepherd, WVa, arr with Alice Parker. Teacher music, pub schs, now Shawnee State Col. Prof singer & musician; also comp. Chief Collabr: Bert Crothers, husband. *Songs:* Who Are You; I'm Called Loneliness; Sing a Little Song of Love.

CROUCH, ANDRAE E   ASCAP 1969
composer, author
b Los Angeles, Calif, July 1, 42. Has recorded albums for Light Records; toured throughout US, Can, Eng, Ireland, Europe, SAfrica, Australia & The Far East. Grammy Award, 75, 78 & 79. *Songs:* My Tribute (To God Be the Glory); It Won't Be Long; Bless His Holy Name; Jesus Is the Answer; Soon and Very Soon; I've Got Confidence; If Heaven Never Was Promised to Me; Take Me Back; Quiet Times; I'll Be Thinking of You.

CROW BAIT, OPHELIA MAE
See Smith, C U

CROZIER, JAMES ALVIN   ASCAP 1971
composer, author, bassist
b Dayton, Ohio, Mar 15, 51. Educ: Indiana Univ Pa, 69-73; Fla State Univ, Sch Music, BM(comp), cert perf-double bass, 79; studied with John Boda. Musical dir, Plowright Playhouse, Warren, Pa, 68-70; co-comp, arr & music dir, off-Bway show, 70-71; drove a taxi, New York, NY, 73-76; performed with many bands, Tallahassee, Fla; performed for film, "Gal Young'un." Jazz musician & publ, The Tennessee Street Rag, arts & entertainment weekly, Tallahassee; teacher. Chief Collabrs: Kenn Long, John R Zapor. *Instrumental Works:* String Quartet No 1; Luna (bass quartet); Pair of Deuces (String Quartet No 2). *Scores:* Off-Bway show: Touch; Film/TV: Shell Ladies.

CRUMIT, FRANK   ASCAP 1923
composer, author, singer
b Jackson, Ohio, Sept 26, 1889; d Springfield, Mass, Sept 7, 43. Educ: Culver Mil Acad; Univ Ohio. Singer & ukulele player in vaudeville; made many records. Stage appearances incl "Tangerine", "Moonlight", "Ziegfeld Follies of 1923", "No, No, Nanette", "Queen High" & "Oh, Kay!." Had own radio series with wife, Julia Sanderson, both appearing on stage. Shepherd of Lambs Club, 4 yrs. *Songs:* The Buckeye Battle Cry (Ohio State Univ football song); Sweet Lady; Gay Caballero; Tale of the Ticker; Song of the Prune; King of Borneo; A Parlor is a Pleasant Place to Sit In, Abdul Abulbul Amir; There Is No One With Endurance Like the Man Who Sells Insurance; Donald the Dub.

CRUTCHER, JAY LEROY   ASCAP 1977
composer, singer
b Houston, Tex, June 13, 51. Educ: Tex Christian Univ; Southern Methodist Univ, BA(broadcast, film); studied saxophone with Hal Tennyson. Nightclub work, 7 yrs; session work, Los Angeles.

CRUTCHFIELD, KEVIN   ASCAP 1978
composer
b Mt Vernon, NY, Apr 23, 53. Singer in studios incl Media Sound, Electric Lady Studios, Master Sound, Vangard Studios, also nightclubs, Westchester, NY. *Songs:* Special Love.

CUCHETTI, RICHARD FRANK (DICK CONTI)   ASCAP 1970
composer, author, producer
b Detroit, Mich, Sept 6, 37. Educ: Boys Cath Cent High Sch, Detroit; Wayne State Univ, BA; pvt trumpet study with James Tamburini. Musician; played lead trumpet with big bands & big stars. Teacher; coach; promotion for St Jude Children's Res Hosp. Mem, Phi Mu Alpha; Mich Educ Asn (scholarship); Am Fedn Teachers; Am Fedn Musicians. Chief Collabr: Don Dominguez. *Songs:* Jesus My Sweet Jesus; You Got Love.

CUCINOTTA, ROBERT EDWARD   ASCAP 1976
composer, teacher, guitarist
b Brooklyn, NY, Apr 13, 49. Educ: Brooklyn Tech High Sch; Brooklyn Col, City Univ New York, BA; studied comp with Jacob Druckman, Robert Suderburg & Robert Starer, guitar with Patrick O'Brien, electronic music with Jacob Druckman. Comp performances in NY, Tex, Tenn and others; perc pieces & guitar chamber music. Mem music fac, City Univ New York; pvt teacher, guitar, theory & comp. Performs in New York, appeared on WBAI radio & CBS-TV. Chief Collabrs: Karen Mullin, Richard Wilbur. *Songs & Instrumental Works:* The Sky Is Waiting (solo drum); Triangulation (timpani, electronic tape); Beasts (vocal, baritone, guitar, 2 percussionists); Serenade (viola, guitar); Fantasy (solo vibraphone).

CULBERTSON, ROY FREDERICH (ROSCOE BRANO, ROY EFF)   ASCAP 1975
composer, author, singer
b East St Louis, Ill, Sept 4, 46. Educ: Southern Ill Univ, Edwardsville, BS(math, psychol). Performed in clubs, St Louis, Boston & New York. Joined The New Christy Minstrels, 72-73 & Opryland, 73-74; played guitar, bass & sang. Wrote "Fallen Rock", 74. Chief Collabrs: Larry Keith, Rafe Van Hoy, Connie Culbertson (wife). *Songs:* Do It Again; Goodbye 'Ole Mighty Friend; Make Me Love; A Motel in Virginia; Lyrics: We Got Love (ASCAP Award, 78).

CULL, ROBERT M   ASCAP 1971
composer, arranger
b Los Angeles, Calif, May 24, 49. Educ: Southern Calif Col, Costa Mesa, 67-70. Free-lance arr, 3 yrs; comp & arr, Maranatha Music Co, 6 yrs; producer & arr, Chalce Music Co, 2 yrs. Toured around world in 30 countries. *Songs:* Sail Away; Open Our Eyes; Welcome to the Family; Remember.

CULPEPPER, EDWARD J (JACK)   ASCAP 1960
composer, author, entertainer
b Palestine, Tex, June 14, 03; d Los Angeles, Calif, Apr 1, 79. Educ: High sch. Appeared in vaudeville, nightclubs & theatres; mem team, Salt & Pepper. *Songs:* I'm Building a Bungalow for Baby; Did You Mean It; Grand Old Acquaintance of Mine; Sorry 'Bout the Whole Darned Thing.

CULVERWELL, ANDREW ROBERT   ASCAP 1974
composer, singer
b Somerset, Eng, Dec 19, 44. Educ: Self-taught. Comp & singer; gospel concerts in NZ, Australia, Jamaica, Can, Gt Brit, Ger & Finland. *Songs:* Born Again (Dove award); Come on Ring Those Bells; May This Be the Place; This Is the Song; Every Day; Follow Me; The Winner's Song; Open Your Heart Now.

CUMMING, RICHARD   ASCAP 1956
composer, writer, pianist
b Shanghai, China, June 9, 1928. Educ: San Francisco Cons Music; Aspen Inst Music; Music Acad West; pvt study with Ernest Bloch, Arnold Schoenberg & Roger Sessions. Concert pianist/accompanist; recorded, DESTO, Duke Univ Press & Music Heritage; comp-in-residence, Milwaukee Repertory Theatre & Trinity Square Rep Co, RI. Co-author music & lyrics "Life Among the Lowly" & "Feasting With Panthers." Awards: Fedn Music Clubs; Ford Found; Nat

Endowment Arts; RI State Council Arts & Wurlitzer Found. *Songs:* Music: We Happy Few (cycle of 10 songs); Go, Lovely Rose; As Dew in April; The Little Black Boy. *Instrumental Works:* Twenty-Four Preludes for Piano. *Scores:* Opera: The Picnic (two-act opera).

CUMMINGS, E(DWARD) E(STLIN)
author
b Cambridge, Mass, Oct 14, 1894; d North Conway, NH, Sept 3, 62. Poet lyricist.

CUMMINGS, PATRICIA HAGER   ASCAP 1959
author
b Springfield, Ill, Nov 1, 24. Educ: Northwestern Univ, BA with hons. Had songs recorded by Columbia Records; free lance writer & ed. *Songs:* Lyrics: Crocodile Chile; Law Ma'am.

CUNDICK, ROBERT MILTON   ASCAP 1967
composer, organist, arranger
b Salt Lake City, Utah, Nov 26, 26. Educ: Univ Utah, PhD(comp), 55; studied comp with Leroy Robertson & organ with Alexander Schreiner. Teaching asst, Univ Utah, 50-57; prof theory, Brigham Young Univ, 57-79. Organist, comp & arr with Tabernacle Choir, Salt Lake City, 65- *Songs & Instrumental Works:* Our God Is a God of Love; The West Wind; Thou Whose Unmeasured Temple Stands; Organ Concerto; Overture to Celebration; A Full House; Sonatina (organ); An Oratorio: The Redeemer (chorus & orch); Song of Nephi (chorus & orch); Sonata for Violin & Piano; Sonata for Viola & Piano; Turnabouts (oboe & piano); To Utah (a cappella chorus). *Scores:* Ballet: Epsom Esquire; Pioneer Woman.

CUNKLE, FRANK   ASCAP 1946
composer, author, teacher
b Ft Smith, Ark, June 17, 05. Educ: Grade & high schs, Ft Smith, Ark; Eastman Sch Music, Univ Rochester, BMus & MMus; Teachers Col, Columbia Univ. Asst prof, Univ Kans; assoc prof, Univ Nebr. Script writer, arr, Fred Waring Show, NBC, 45-51; ed, Diapason Mag, 56-70. Chief Collab: Harry Simeone. *Songs:* A Musical Christmas Card; Lyrics: Grandma's Thanksgiving; Roumanian Rhapsody; Nutcracker Suite.

CUNLIFFE, RICHARD R   ASCAP 1949
composer, author, arranger
b McKeesport, Pa, Aug 8, 06; d Galena, Ill, Dec 12, 68. Educ: Am Cons; studied with Robert Lindeman, Leighton Wells, Clarence Warmelin, Theodore Yshke. Musician & arr, Ted Weems Orch, 12 yrs. Joined CBS Staff Orch, Chicago, 37. *Songs:* Quien Sabe; Who's Got a Tent for Rent?; O'Leary Is Leery; I Met a Miss in Texas; In My Heart; Are You Still My Valentine?; The Three Bears and Goldilocks.

CUNNINGHAM, ARTHUR   ASCAP 1962
composer, author, conductor
b Nyack, NY, Nov 11, 28. Educ: Metrop Music Sch, New York, studied with Wallingford Riegger, Johnny Mehegan, Teddy Wilson; Fisk Univ, BA, studied with John W Work; Juilliard Sch, studied with Peter Wilhousky, Peter Mennin, Norman Lloyd, Henry Brant, Margaret Hillis; Columbia Teachers Col, MA, studied with Murphy Church. Served, USA, Special Services. Bassist, Suburban Symph & Rockland Co. Writer, special material for TV show "Play Your Hunch." Music dir, summer theaters & adv, Rockland Co Playhouse, 64. *Songs & Instrumental Works:* Everywhere I Go; This Love Is True Love; Song of Songs (Wilfred Owen poem); Turning of the Babies in the Bed (Paul Dunbar poem); Adagio for Strings, Oboe; Lights Across the Hudson (tone poem). *Scores:* Stage plays: The Beauty Part; Violetta (adaptation, Le Mal Coeur).

CUNNINGHAM, JOHN COLLINS   ASCAP 1970
composer
b Brownsville, Tenn, Nov 13, 50. Educ: Byrd High Sch; San Antonio Col. In movie "Day of the Wolves"; singer, TV; recording artist, Capitol Records. *Songs:* Norma Jean Wants to Be a Movie Star; All the Kings Horses; Takin' What I Can Get; Wrap Your Love All Around Your Man; Sweet Talkin' Man.

CUNNINGHAM, MICHAEL GERALD   ASCAP 1969
composer, professor
b Warren, Mich, Aug 5, 37. Educ: Wayne State Univ, BMus, 59, comp with Ruth S Wylie; Univ Mich, MMus, 61, comp with Ross Lee Finney & Leslie Bassett; Ind Univ, DMus, 73, comp with Bernhard Heiden. Prof jazz pianist, Detroit, 59-69. USA, 62-63. Music dir & pianist, Wayne State Univ Dance Workshop & classes, 61 & 64-67, instr theory, Music Dept, 67-69; teacher theory, Kans Univ, 72 & Univ of the Pac, 73; prof theory & comp, Univ Wisc, Eau Claire, 73- Chief Collabr: Playwright, Wil Denson. *Instrumental Works:* Trigon (tenor saxophone, piano); Polyphonies (perc ensemble); Counter Currents (string orch); Triple Sonata (flute, clarinet, piano); Gnosis (SSA); Symphonie Arias (soloist, chorus, orch). *Scores:* Opera/Ballet: Aladdin Mc Faddin (children's musical); Catherine Sloper.

CUNNINGHAM, PAUL   ASCAP 1921
author, singer
b New York, NY, Jan 25, 1890; d New York, Aug 14, 60. Educ: Manhattan Col, BA. Mem, music publ co, then singer & staff writer. Sang in vaudeville as mem of team, Cunningham & Bennett (Mrs Cunningham). Dir, ASCAP, 45-60, secy, 51-53, pres, 56-59. Chief Collabs: Abel Baer, Leonard Whitcup, Ernie Burnett. *Songs:* I Am an American; Please Take a Letter, Miss Brown; Have a Smile for Everyone You Meet; Coronation Waltz; All Over Nothing at All; The Shores of Tripoli; That's How I Believe in You; You Can't Make a Fool Out of Me; Piggy Wiggy Woo; Hats Off to MacArthur; Four Buddies; Dakota; From the Vine Came the Grapes.

CUNNINGHAM, MRS RUDOLPH   ASCAP 1961
composer
b Johnson City, Tenn, Mar 1, 07; d. Nurse. *Songs:* He Guides My Way; Standing in the Moonlight.

CUPPETT, CHARLES HAROLD   ASCAP 1942
composer, arranger
b Coquismo, Chile, June 25, 1894. Educ: Ohio Wesleyan Univ, BSChem(summa cum laude), 16, Phi Beta Kappa; studied organ & piano with Edward Young Mason, Ohio Wesleyan Univ Cons. Wrote Alma Mater prize song for Ohio Wesleyan Univ. Army, France, WWI; real estate. Comp orch works, 29-; wrote grand opera. Vocal arr for Norsemen Quartet, other music productions. Comp & cond music for indust films. Joined NY Ordnance District, 42; introduced process eng after WW II. Retired, 68. Chief Collabs: Peter DeRose, Gerald Griffin, Tom Waring, Fred Fisher. *Songs:* Inspiration; Night Fall; Music in the Air; I'll Sing My Song to You; Where Is Love?; Paint in the Sky. *Instrumental Works:* Piano Concerto in C minor.

CURBELO, FAUSTO   ASCAP 1954
composer, author, musician
b Cuba, Feb 15, 11. Educ: High sch. Played in Xavier Cugat Orch, then formed own orch; conductor. Chief Collab: Harold Adamson. *Songs:* The Thrill of a New Romance; Le Espero; The Girl With the Spanish Draw.

CURLETTO, GIORGIO FRANCESCO   ASCAP 1971
composer, author, singer
b Genova, Italy, July 15, 37. Educ: Col & sch music, Italy; studied accordion with Prospero Drago, harmony & comp with Mario Barbieri of Liceo Musicale Paganini, Genova & Luigi Ferrari Trecate, Parma, Italy; Berklee Col Music, Boston, Mass, studied modern harmony, improvisation, arr & orchestration. Toured with big & small bands, trios, Europe, Middle East, Far East, South Pacific, Caribbean Islands, Greek Islands & North Cape; also as soloist & leader on several ocean liners & cruiser ships; performing in Washington, DC, 70-; music writing & publ, 70- Accordion virtuoso. *Songs:* Let Me Reach You; Spinning Mind; Tender As a Flower; Space Dreams (Way Out Dreams); The Brand New Other Side of Me. *Instrumental Works:* Impressions of New York; Gliding; Tricks; Gulf Stream; Kaleidoscope; Green Meadows; Calm-Rough (Sea).

CURNOW, JAMES EDWARD (JIM)   ASCAP 1974
composer, teacher
b Port Huron, Mich, Apr 17, 43. Educ: Wayne State Univ, BS; Mich State Univ, MM, studied with Dr Jere Hutchinson & Paul Harder. Taught pub sch music, 66-69; taught col level instrumental music, comp, low brass, 69-; writer, 74- Chief Collabr: Choral: Cyril Kingston (England). *Songs & Instrumental Works:* Symphonic Triptych for Band (Volkwein Award, 77); Collage for Band (Volkwein Award, 79); Variations in Memoriam (ASCAP Standard Award, 79); Mutanza (symphonic variations for band, Am Bandmasters Asn Ostwald Award, 80); Hymn and Allelujah; Psalm 37 (chorus SATB, brass & organ); The Good Shepherd (choral); Psalm 100 (brass band); Rhapsody for Euphonium and Band; Concertino for Tuba and Band; Capriccio for Trombone and Band; Lord, Teach Us How to Pray (choral); Christ's Part (choral).

CURNUTT, JOHN PAUL   ASCAP 1975
composer, author, singer
b Victoria, BC, May 27, 39. Educ: Garibaldi Grade Sch, Ore; Columbia Acad, Wash; Walla Walla Col, BA(Eng), 64; Univ Ore, MSc(spec educ); studied songwriting, Bob Gibson & guitar with Ray Tate. Recording artist. Chief Collabrs: Bert Wells, Vick Knight. *Songs:* Powder River; The Circus Is Ending Soon; Comfort One Another; Precious Jesus.

CURRAN, PEARL GILDERSLEEVE   ASCAP 1925
composer
b Denver, Colo, June 25, 1875; d New Rochelle, NY, Apr 16, 41. Educ: Denver Univ; studied with Otto Pfeffercorn, Flora Hunsicker, M Miner Richards & Stella Alexander. Mem, Westchester Co Music Fest Asn. *Songs:* Two Magicians; A Picture; Contentment; Gratitude; Holiday; To the Sun; The Best Is Yet to Be; Blessing; Dawn; Ho! Mr Piper.

CURRIS, IRWIN   ASCAP 1960
author
b New York, NY; d Los Angeles, Calif, Feb 23, 72. Educ: NY Univ. Field correspondent, Yank Mag, WW II. Pub acct & corp controller. Chief Collabrs:

Elaine Caress, Carter Wright, Paul Atkerson, Edward Cuomo. *Songs:* A World of Law and Peace (Women Lawyers Am Prize); You Taught Me How to Cry; Run Like the Wind.

CURRY, JACK A ASCAP 1961
composer, author
b Columbus, Ga, Oct 19, 02. Educ: Pub schs; business schs. Has been salesman, accountant, orch leader, teacher & publ. *Songs:* You're the Answer to My Dreams; I'll Never Leave Miami; Singing in the Sunshine in Florida.

CURRY, W LAWRENCE ASCAP 1959
composer, conductor, educator
b Parnassus, Pa, Mar 19, 06; d Pa, Feb 25, 66. Educ: Univ Pa, BA; Union Theol Sem, MSM, SMD. Lectured, Univ Pa, 31-38; piano instr, Beaver Col, 29-35, cond, glee club, 35-59, chmn, music dept, many yrs. Former Minister of Music, First Methodist Church, Philadelphia. Cond, Matinee Musical Chorus, 47-55; Fortnightly Male Chorus, 51-59. Ed, Westminister Press. Music consult, Bd Christian Educ, Presby Church (US). Mem, Phi Beta Kappa. *Songs:* Psalm of Gratitude; God Is Our Refuge; Sing Ye! Sing the Savior's Birth; Lincoln Speaks; In Christ There Is No East Or West; Once for Us a Child Was Born; also Sacred Works: Songs for Early Childhood; Hymns for Primary Worship; Hymnal for Youth; For Jr Choir; For Youth Choir; For Sabbath Choir; For Mixed Choir; For Adult Choir; Music for Communion; Service for Adult Choir.

CURSIO, JAN
See Giancursio, Joseph

CURTIS, BILLY ASCAP 1924
author
b Lowell, Mass, Sept 9, 1885; d Fairhaven, Mass, Apr 28, 54. Educ: High sch. Vaudeville entertainer. Writer, radio scripts & on staff for music publ firms. Chief Collabr: Frank Crumit. *Songs:* Little Wooden Whistle; The Way He Loves Is Just Too Bad; South Bound; The Ghost of the St Louis Blues; The Return of Abdul Abulbul Amir.

CURTIS, EDDIE (TEX) ASCAP 1959
composer, author, singer
b Galveston, Tex, July 17, 27. Educ: Boston Cons of Music; Schillinger House; Univ Calif, Los Angeles; Pepperdine Univ. Led own band, age 14; played nightclubs; arr. USA, World War II. *Songs:* You're Gonna Miss Me; Starlight, Starbright; Jolly Polly; I'll Do the Same Thing for You; Mama and Papa Twist; Deep Down Love; Drop It Joe.

CURTIS, LOYAL ASCAP 1925
composer, author, cellist
b Fowlerville, Mich, Apr 8, 1877; d New York, NY, Feb 21, 47. Educ: Pub schs; pvt music study. Cellist, Toledo Symph; also in bands; organized & dir string ens, vocal quartets; publisher. *Songs:* Bo-Peep; Heartaches and Dreams; Just One More Dance; Roses or Remembrance; Arcady; In Springtime; Mary Jane; Rose o' the Morn; What Is Love?; Drifting and Dreaming.

CURTIS, MANN
See Kurtz, Emanuel

CURTIS, RICHARD OLIN ASCAP 1973
composer, author, singer
b Washington, DC, June 18, 47. Educ: Boston Univ. Wrote & performed with bands, Thundergrin & Jesse's First Carnival, 67-70; worked with Barbara Keith, Jeff & Maria Muldaur & Jeff Gutcheon, 70-72; producer & artist, Intermedia Productions, Boston, 72-73; worked with Rory Block, 73-77. *Songs:* Mama Can't You Hear Me Calling; Summer Is Gone; Easy Credit; Junie.

CURZON, CLARA-JEAN ASCAP 1970
composer
b Hemet, Calif, Aug 29, 24. Educ: Univ Redlands, BM, 46, MM, 47, studied with Halsey Stevens, Paul Pisk & Rowland Leach; Univ Southern Calif, studied with John Crown; Univ Wash, studied with George Frederick McKay. Teacher, Va Intermont Col; teacher, Univ Calif, Santa Barbara, also wrote scores for documentary film & radio at same time; teacher, Western Wash State Univ; pvt teacher, 50-; comp piano teaching material & sacred music; as recitalist toured with prog, "Keyboard Kaleidoscope!," western states. Author harmony text: "Discovering Music Through Theory." Chief Collabr: B J Rosco. *Instrumental Works:* Saturn's Rings; March of the Astronauts; Fireflies; Humbug Wizard.

CUSENZA, FRANK JEROME ASCAP 1950
composer, author, publisher
b San Vito, Italy, Dec 25, 1899. Educ: Royal Cons, Palermo, Italy; Great Lakes Col, MA. To US, 20. On fac, Detroit Cons, 22-34, Univ Detroit & Detroit Inst Musical Art, 35- Author "Thorough Master Pianist" (5 vols), "Nature's Musical Method for Piano" (2 vols) & "Encyclopedia of Modern Chords and Harmony for Guitar." *Instrumental Works:* Symphony in 4 Movements; Captivity (oratorio); Vivo Per Te (soprano, tenor). *Scores:* Opera: Creation.

CUSHING, CATHERINE C ASCAP 1935
composer, author
b Mt Perry, Ohio, Apr 15, 1874; d Mt Perry, Oct 19, 52. Educ: Girls' schs. Playwright: "Miss Ananias"; "The Real Thing"; "Widow-By-Proxy"; "Kitty McKay"; "Jerry"; "Pollyanna"; "Edgar Allan Poe"; "Master of the Inn." Librettist: "Marjolaine"; "Topsy and Eva." Chief Collabrs: Rudolf Friml, Hugo Felix. *Songs:* L'Amour, Toujours L'Amour; Chianti; John and Priscilla; When Brown Eyes Looked in Eyes of Blue; Dilly-Dally-O; Read Between the Lines. *Scores:* Bway stage (librettos): Glorianna; Lassie.

CUSTER, CALVIN ASCAP 1976
composer, conductor
b Atlantic City, NJ, July 15, 39. Educ: Carnegie-Mellon Univ, BFA(performance), BFA(comp); Syracuse Univ, MA(fine arts). With Syracuse Symph Orch, 17 yrs, resident cond, 7 yrs. Arr; guest cond, Atlanta Symph, summers 77-78, Artpark, 80 & Buffalo Philh. *Songs & Instrumental Works:* Horn Concerto; Elegy for Yesterday and Tomorrow; Central Coach Special (rock ballad); Variations on a Theme of William Byrd & others.

CUSTER, RUDOLF PRESBER ASCAP 1964
composer, author
b Madison, Wis, July 16, 12. Educ: Univ Wis, BA, 35. *Instrumental Works:* Windy City; Midway March.

CUTLER, FOREST A ASCAP 1974
author
b Arcadia, Mich, July 23, 14. Chief Collabr: John W Stephenson. *Songs:* Lyrics: Lady Is My Mother; My Saddled Heart; Forgive Me; Housemaid Knees and Dishpan Hands; My Sweet Lovely Marie; It Hurt Me When I Hurt You.

CUTLER, JESSE
See Gibaldi, Louis Milo

CUTLER, MAX ASCAP 1979
author, music publisher
b Hartford, Conn, July 24, 07. Educ: Hartford High Sch; Univ Calif, Los Angeles, bus admin & real estate. Motion picture actor, 28-68; real estate broker, 45-65; music publ & lyricist, 78- Chief Collabr: Victoria-Diane Cutler. *Songs:* Lyrics: In Harmony; Only Music; A Heart of Gold; Tears; Why.

CUTLER, VICTORIA-DIANE ASCAP 1979
composer, singer, teacher
b Los Angeles, Calif, June 12, 53. Educ: Calif State Univ, Northridge, BA(voice perf), 75, MA(voice perf), 76. Professional classical artist; did motion picture & TV dubbings; recording artist; appeared in var opera co performances; voice instr, Los Angeles Pierce Col. Chief Collabr: Max Cutler. *Songs:* Music: Only Music; In Harmony; Heart of Gold; Tears; Why?.

CUTNER, SIDNEY BENJAMIN ASCAP 1952
composer, arranger, orchestrator
b Mariupol, Russia, Apr 16, 03; d Los Angeles, Calif, Sept 20, 71. Educ: Vienna Cons, studied piano, orchestration & comp; studied with Robert Klein, Vienna. Moved to Hollywood, 33; staff comp, Columbia Pictures, 38-42; orchestrator of motion pictures & TV films incl "When Worlds Collide", "Around the World in 80 Days", "Shane", "Three Coins in the Fountain", "April in Paris", "Best Years of Our Lives" & many others; scored many segments of TV series such as "The FBI", "Wagon Train", "The Invaders", "The Virginian" & others; comp several ballets for Lester Horton Dance Group; had works performed by Univ Calif Los Angeles Chamber Orch & by other community symph orchs. Rec'd the Nat Asn Am Comp & Cond Award for one symph work. Mem of Comp & Lyricists Guild. Chief Collabr: Leo Shuken. *Songs:* Mink Shmink. *Scores:* Film: Pepe; The Big Circus; Green Mansions; The Lost World; Gunsmoke At Tucson; Hold Back Tomorrow; Three Sisters From Seattle; This Is Cinerama; Too Young to Kiss; Mystery Street; The Best Years, MGM Anniversary; Paleface; Sailor Takes a Wife; Cafe Hostess; Here Comes Mr Jordan; TV: The Paper Curtain.

CUTTER, MURRAY ASCAP 1946
composer
b Nice, France, Mar 15, 02. Writer, special material for films. *Instrumental Works:* Interlude Carnavalesque. *Scores:* Ballet: Snow Queen.

CYRILLE, ANDREW CHARLES ASCAP 1968
author, percussionist, teacher
b Brooklyn, NY, Nov 10, 39. Educ: Juilliard Sch Music; Hartnett Sch Music; pvt comp study with George Robinson. Has recorded LP records as sideman & leader, 61- Percussionist with Cecil Taylor Unit, 64-75; joined clinician/endorsee staff, Ludwig Indust Educ Dept, 67. Began teaching drums, 71; fac, Antioch Col, Yellow Springs, Ohio, 71-73. Founded creative music band, Maono, 75; co-founded, Inst Percussive Studies, 78. Chief Collabrs: Milford Graves, Verna Gillis, Ted Daniel, David S Ware, Nick DiGeronimo, Jeanne Lee, Jimmy Lyons, Cecil Taylor, Joe Rigby, Walt Dickerson. *Songs & Instrumental Works:* Dialogue of the Drums; Junction; Metamusicians' Stomp; Nuba; The Loop.

CYRUS, ALSTON BECKET (BECKET) ASCAP 1976
composer, author, singer
b Layou, West Indies, Aug 1, 49. Educ: Intermediate High Sch; Anacostia Sr High Sch; DC Teachers Col. Prof appearances as calypso-rock performer in US & abroad, 76- Chief Collabr: Frankie McIntosh. *Songs:* Coming High; Hula-Soul; Disco Jam; Dig Me Calypso; Oppression; St Vincent, I Love You; Carnival History; Wine Down Kingstown; Human Rights; Miss Must Duck. *Scores:* Film: Calypso Disco. *Albums:* Raw Calypso; Disco Calypso; Coming Higher.

CZARNECKI, HARRY EDWARD ASCAP 1960
composer
b Wyandotte, Mich, Sept 11, 05. Educ: Self-taught. Played trumpet, 60 yrs; had own band, 30 yrs. *Songs:* One More Time I Must Go; When I Hear Your Voice; Have Somebody; I Love You; Trumpet Harry's Cha Cha.

CZERWONKY, RICHARD RUDOLPH ASCAP 1938
composer, conductor, violinist
b Birnbaum, Ger, May 23, 1886; d Chicago, Ill, Apr 16, 49. Educ: Studied violin with Joseph Joachim, Florian Zajic, Andreas Moser; Klindworth-Scharwenka Cons; Royal Sch of Music. Debut with Berlin Philh, 06. Asst concertmaster, Boston Symph, 07-08. Concertmaster, asst cond & soloist, Minn Symph, 09-18. US citizen, 15. Head, violin dept, Bush Cons, Chicago, 18-32; founder & cond, Bush Cons Symph. Guest cond & violin soloist, Berlin Symph. Vpres, Chicago Cons, 32-35. Head, violin & orch dept, De Paul Univ Sch of Music; cond, De Paul Univ Symph, 35, Kenosha Symph, 40-49. *Instrumental Works:* Violin Concerto; Carnival of Life; Weltschmerz (symph poem); Episode.

D

DABNEY, FORD T ASCAP 1937
composer, conductor, pianist
b Washington, DC, Mar 15, 1883; d New York, NY, June 21, 58. Educ: Armstrong Manual Training Sch; studied music with father, also with Charles Donch, William Waldecker, Samuel Fabian. Official court musician for pres of Haiti, 04. Returned to US, 07; led own quartet. Owner-operator, film & vaudeville theatre, DC. Organized Tempo Club, Negro Talent Bur, NY, 13. Created original dance numbers for Mr & Mrs Vernon Castle. Cond, Ziegfeld Midnight Frolics Orch, 8 yrs. Chief Collabrs: Joe Trent, Cecil Mack, Lew Brown. *Songs & Instrumental Works:* That Minor Strain; Oh You Devil; Puerto Rico; Shine. *Scores:* Bway Stage: Rang Tang.

DA COSTA, NOEL GEORGE ASCAP 1965
composer, educator
b Lagos, Nigeria, Dec 27, 29. Educ: Queens Col, BA(music), 52; Columbia Univ, MA(theory, comp), 56; comp (Fulbright Fellowship), studied with Luigi Dallapiccola, Florence, Italy, 61. Teacher, Hampton Inst, Va, Queens & Hunter Cols, 63-66. Violinist & cond, choral groups & contemporary music ens. Prof of music, Rutgers Univ, 70- *Songs & Instrumental Works:* 5 Verses With Vamps for Cello and Piano; Spiritual Set for Organ; Ceremony of Spirituals (soprano, saxophonist, chorus, symph orch); also instrumental, vocal, choral comp & theatre pieces for children.

D'AGOSTINO, JOSEPH D ASCAP 1959
composer, author, arranger
b Garfield, NJ, May 30, 29. Educ: Juilliard Sch Music. Saxophonist in dance bands; has produced records.

DAHDAH, ROBERT SARKIS ASCAP 1968
composer, author, director
b San Juan, PR, Mar 8, 26. Educ: Hartnett Music Sch, degree in music. Dir, original production of "Dames at Sea"; producer, dir & co-auth, "Curley McDimple", "Up in the Air, Boys", "Those Darn Kids", "Now Is Forever" & "The Insect Musical." Chief Collabrs: Mary Boylan, Walter Kotrba. *Songs:* Selections & vocal score, "Curley McDimple."

DAHL, INGOLF ASCAP 1956
composer, conductor, pianist
b Hamburg, Ger, June 9, 12; d Frutigen, Switz, Aug 7, 70. Educ: Cologne Music Acad, studied with Philip Jarnach, H Abendroth; Zurich Cons, studied with V Andreae, W Frey; Univ Zurich, studied with Cherbuliez, Woelfflin, Stadler; also with Nadia Boulanger. To US, 39. Grants: Guggenheim (2); Hartford (2). Awards: Nat Inst Arts & Letters; Soc for Publ Am Music; ASCAP-Stravinsky; Alice Ditson Found. Cond & coach, Municipal Opera House, Zurich. Arr films & radio. Fac mem, Univ Southern Calif, cond, Collegium Musicum, 45-70. Concertized as cond & pianist through western US. On fac, Middlebury Comp Conf, 49. Founder & leader, Tanglewood Study Group, 52-56. On tour, State Dept, Munich & Nuremberg, WBerlin, 61-62. Cond, Ojai Fest, 64-66. *Instrumental Works:* Saxophone Concerto (Sigurd Rascher Comn); Symphony Concertante (2 clarinets, orch; Benny Goodman comn); Tower of St Barbara (Louisville Orch comn); Piano Quartet (Fromm Found, Univ Ill comn); Piano

Trio (Koussevitzky Found, Libr Cong comn); Allegro and Arioso; Music for Brass Instruments; Concerto a tre; Duo for Cello, Piano; Divertimento (viola, piano); Sonata Seria (piano); Fanfares; Variations on a Swedish Folk Tune; Aria Sinfonica (orch); Sinfonietta (concert band); Elegy Concerto (violin & small orch); Variations on a Theme by Bach (string orch); Four Intervals (string orch); Quodlibet on American Folk Tunes (orch) & (2 pianos, 8 hands); Sonata Pastorale (piano); Serenade for Four Flutes; A Noiseless Patient Spider (womens chorus & piano); Sonata da Camera (clarinet & piano); Five Duets for Clarinets.

DAHLANDER, NILS-BERTIL (BERT DALE)
composer, teacher, drummer
b Gothenburg, Sweden, May 13, 28. Educ: Schs in Sweden; studied violin, piano; Juilliard. Worked with Thore Ehrling radio band & with own quartet; emigrated to US in 54; played for house band at Beehive, Chicago, then with Terry Gibbs combo. Toured with Chet Baker, Europe, 56. In US again, 57, rejoined Gibbs, then mem of Teddy Wilson Trio, 57-60. Had own TV show, Sweden, 65, worked with Earl Hines; worked with Ralph Sulton, Aspen, Colo, 66. Chief Collabrs: Walt Smith, Staffan Nilson. *Songs:* Music: How Do You Do; A Very Special Day; Latin Joy; Jamaican Love; Sometimes the Days Go Faster (It Seems); Just Easy; Keep on Truckin'; Answer Me; Let's Begin; Aspen Festival; Little Bit; Bert's Waltz; Good Old Swingtime; With the Help of the Lord; Winter Waltz; After a Busy Day; Keep on Marching; Around 8 at Night.

DAHLSTROM, PATRICIA CORNELIA (PATTI) ASCAP 1971
composer, singer
b Houston, Tex, Mar 24, 47. Educ: Univ Tex, Austin, 65-67; studied voice intermittently with Warren Barigian, 71-80. Staff writer, Jobete Music Co, 70-72; recording artist, Uni, 71-72 & 20th Century Records, 73-77. Own Publ Co, Patti Dahlstrom Music. Chief Collabrs: Tom Snow, Severin Browne, Artie Wayne, Al Staehely. *Songs:* What If; And I Never Did; Wait Like a Lady; Lyrics: Emotion; Dialogue; He Did Me Wrong, But He Did It Right; Without Love.

DAHROUGE, RAYMOND ANTHONY ASCAP 1975
composer, author, singer
b Newark, NJ, July 9, 42. Educ: Neptune High Sch, NJ, grad, 61; Murray State Univ, BS(educ), 66. Recording artist, Bell Records, 73-74; exclusive writer for Blending Well Music, 74-79; recording artist, Polydor Records, 79; now writing exclusively for Charles Calello. *Songs:* Never Get Enough of Your Love; Any Kind of Love At All; Lifetime Guarantee of Love; You're My One Weakness, Girl.

DALE, BERT
See Dahlander, Nils-Bertil

DALE, FRANK Q ASCAP 1959
composer, author, playwright
b Foggia, Italy, Oct 17, 11. Educ: Pvt study; high sch grad; col, 2 yrs; St Felix Cons Music, studied violin, comp, theory & teaching. Has taught violin & other string instruments. Played violin with many orchs; leader of own orch, Frank Dale & Radio Rhythm Ramblers Orch. Played on Mutual Network for several yrs, also Village Barn Nightclub, New York, several hotels, one-night stands & important functions. Chief Collabrs: Henry Tobias, Bill Gale, Tommy Dorsey, David Ormont, Iggy Benfante, Max Smith, Ben Ross, Lewis Dale, Jean Lewis, Joe Shapiro, Syd Jacobson, Pat Noto. *Songs:* Take My Heart; Giannina; Oh, How I Love You; Sunday Stroll; Take Me to Your Heart; Lost in Your Arms; Last Night's Dream; I Can't Explain But I Love You; Why Do You Break My Heart?; My Jealous One; You're My Angel of Love; Poetry of Love; I Wanna Be Your Lifetime Sweetheart; Magic Love; Lonely; Is This the Last Goodbye My Love?; Back Scratch (disco); The Chains That Bind Me; Caress Me; You Hurt My Pride; I'll Always Be Faithful; Someday I'll Make You Mine; You Can Lie to Anyone, But You Can't Lie to Your Heart; Today Is Your Wedding Day; Don't Let Our Love Be an Ember; Spanish Mood; Heart Breaker; You Are My Life; Baby, Baby, Baby; You're Dangerous to Me; Music: My Whole World Is You; Until We Kiss Again; Oceans Apart; Make Me a King or Make Me a Slave; Fortune Teller; Your Heart and My Heart; Don't Give Up Hope; Typhoon; The Wishbone Song; Take Me As I Am; If Tears Were Gold; Melodie; So Long Darling; Paper Kisses; Near or Far; Monkey See-Monkey Do; Poco Loco in the Coco; Forever More; Guilty of Loving You; Forgive and Forget; Lyrics: Echoes of Love.

DALE, JIMMIE ASCAP 1954
composer, singer, musician
b Newark, NJ, July 13, 17. Educ: High sch. Musician in radio & TV, 12 yrs; played Carnegie Hall & nightclubs; appeared on radio show, "Grand Ole Opry." Recording artist. Chief Collabrs: Roger Genger, Irving Weiser. *Songs:* The Rabbit With the Two Buck Teeth; Intoxicated Rat; Skinny Little Christmas Tree.

DALE, JIMMY ASCAP 1942
composer, arranger
b Bronx, NY, June 18, 01. Educ: Stuyvesan High Sch; Columbia Univ. Pianist-arr, music publ & popular dance band leaders, incl Tommy Dorsey, Benny Goodman, Frankie Carle & Red Nichols, also picture cos. Played piano

with The Original Alabama Five. Taught theory, comp, harmony, arr & orchestration, Essex Cons. Chief Collabrs: Lee Pearl, Eugene West, Art Berman, Roy Alfred, Jack Val, Murray Semos, Martin Kalmanoff. *Songs:* Music: Just Say I Love Her; Sentimental Afternoon; Hackensack Jump; Blue Silhouette; You Better Get With It; The Whistling Walker; Sudan; Blue Dream; The Navy Bounce; Rumpus in Columbus; Military Swing; Dinner for the Duchess; Sandy; Kentucky Lullabye; Smile From the Heart; Invest in Me; Lazy, Lazy Summer; I Saw Her Face Last Night; Rhythm; Cuban Jive Session; Serenade to a Wild Cat; Jumpy Nerves; I've Got a Cookie in Kansas; I Hate to See the Evening Sun Go Down; Suzanne; Call on Me; Goo-Ga; Must I Forget; At A Georgia Camp Meeting; The Smugglers Nightmare; The Russian Dressin'; If I'm Lucky; Don't Have A Minute to Myself; Tarantella Jump.

DALE, VIKKI
See Biondo, Rose Leonore Victoria

DALLAS, MITZI   ASCAP 1952
composer, author
b Evanston, Ill, Nov 22, 28. Educ: Wellesley Col, BA. Writer, WGN, 50-52 & Leo Burnett Co, Chicago, 53. Has worked for record cos. Chief Collabr: Dave Lambert. *Songs:* Humanity's Insanity; I Walk and Sing; Hang the Mistletoe.

DALLIN, LEON   ASCAP 1962
composer, author, professor
b Silver City, Utah, Mar 26, 18. Educ: Eastman Sch Music (scholarship), BM & MM; Univ of Southern Calif, PhD; studied comp with Howard Hanson, Bernard Rogers & Milos Rozsa, cond with Paul White & violin with Samuel Belov. Served in WW II. Prof, Colo State Univ, Brigham Young Univ & Calif State Univ, Long Beach. Author: "Techniques of 20th Century Comp"; "Listeners Guide to Musical Understanding"; Found in Music Theory"; "Introduction to Music Reading"; "Basic Music Skills"; Coauthor: "Music Skills for Classroom Teachers"; "Heritage Songster"; "Folk Songster"; "Christmas Caroler"; Comp: educ solos & ens. *Songs:* Songs of Praise (alto & tenor solo, mixed chorus, orch or band). *Instrumental Works:* Sierra Overture for Band; Interlude for Organ (in 25 pieces for small organ); Symphony in D; String Quartet in F; Divertimento; Concerto for Clarinet.

DALTON, LARRY RANDALL   ASCAP 1974
composer, pianist
b Big Stone Gap, Va, Apr 24, 46. Educ: Oral Roberts Univ, BA(music), 69; studied piano with Val Goff Norton & Andrej Wazowski, cond with Franco Autori. Collaborated & comp outdoor musical version of "Trail of the Lonesome Pine," 64. Founder of worldwide music evangel ministry, Living Sound, Int, 69. Music dir, Oral Roberts TV Shows, 73-75. Recording artist, Light Records; comp & arr, Lexicon Music Co. Studio keyboardist, concert pianist & choral-instrumental clinician. Chief Collabr: Don Moen. *Songs:* The Genesis Song; The Great Praise Meeting (contemporary Christian musical). *Instrumental Works:* Brass, Strings and Ivory; Abundant Life Mural. *Scores:* TV: Spring Event.

DALY, JOSEPH   ASCAP 1938
composer, conductor
b Boston, Mass, Feb 7, 1891; d. Educ: Pub schs; studied music with Percy Goetschius, Felix Fox. Organized first all-girl band in vaudeville, Joe Daly & His Co-eds; later had act, Joe Daly & His RKO Discoveries. Joined production dept, NBC, 43. *Songs:* Chicken Reel; In the Heart of the City That Has No Heart; Scented Roses; Turkey Trot; I'm All Dressed Up and No Place to Go; It's a Great Life If You Don't Weaken.

DALY, M E
See Hayman, Richard Warren Joseph

DALYA, JACQUELINE
See Hilliard, Jacqueline Dalya

DAMERON, TADLEY   ASCAP 1954
composer, author, conductor
b Cleveland, Ohio, Feb 21, 17; d New York, NY, Mar 8, 65. Educ: Col. Comp & arr for bands, incl his own. Co-leader with Miles Davis, Paris Jazz Fest, 49. Comp & arr, Ted Heath Orch. Made many records. Chief Collabr: Bernard Hanighen. *Songs & Instrumental Works:* Good Bait; If You Could See Me Now; Hot House; Cool Breeze; The Squirrel; Our Delight; Stay on It; Fontainbleau; Casbah; Dial B for Beauty; Lady Bird. *Scores:* Film background: Bird of Paradise.

DAMICO, FRANK JAMES (FRANK DENNING, FRANK TALLEY)
ASCAP 1960
composer, arranger, pianist
b Jersey City, NJ, Mar 25, 09. Educ: High sch; pvt study of music, arr & comp. Pianist in dance bands, 29-35, arr, dance bands, radio & TV, 35-, staff arr, NBC, 37-, comp, dramatic background music for TV, 59-, radio & TV shows incl "Wide Wide World", "Ford Star Theater", "Ken Murray Show", "Texaco Radio", "Treasury Star Parade", "Treasury Song Parade", "Evening in Paris" & "Celanese."

D'AMICO, LESLEE ANN   ASCAP 1970
composer, author, singer
b Cleveland, Ohio, Apr 26, 48. Comp, performer, incl flutist & guitarist, Los Angeles & Santa Barbara, 67-; teacher.

DAMROSCH, WALTER   ASCAP 1936
composer, author, conductor
b Breslau, Prussia, Jan 30, 1862; d New York, NY, Dec 22, 50. Came to US, 1871. Educ: New York pub schs; studied music with Leopold Damrosch (father), Rischbieter, Urspruch & Von Bulow. Hon degrees: NY Univ, Princeton Univ, Columbia Univ, Univ Pa, Brown Univ, NY State Univ, Washington & Jefferson Col. Accompanist to August Wlhelmj on US tour. Permanent cond, Newark Harmonic Soc, 1881. Succeeded father as Wagnerian dir, Metrop Opera, 1885-1891, staff cond, 1900. Cond, NY Symph, NY Oratorio Soc Prod & series of Wagner operas, Carnegie Hall, 1893-1894. Organized Damrosch Grand Opera Co, 1895. Reorganized NY Symph, 03, dir until 27. Founded sch for bandmasters, Fontainebleau, France, WW I. Music counsel, NBC, 27, cond, series of broadcasts. Pres, Nat Inst Arts & Letters, 27-29 & Am Acad Arts & Letters, 40-48. *Songs & Instrumental Works:* Choral: Death and General Putnam; Danny Deever; The Looking Glass; Dunkirk; An Abraham Lincoln Song. *Scores:* Operas: The Scarlet Letter; The Dove of Peace; Cyrano; The Man Without a Country; The Opera Cloak; Congress and the Two Elephants.

DANA, BILL   ASCAP 1951
composer, author
b Quincy, Mass, Oct 5, 24. Educ: Emerson Col, AB & MA. Writer, producer & performer of musical material in TV, 51-; head writer, "Steve Allen Show"; guest performer, "Ed Sullivan Show", "Hollywood Palace" & "Dean Martin Show"; star of own TV show, "Bill Dana Show," NBC, 63-65; producer, "Milton Berle Show," 68; creative consultant, "Speak Up America," NBC, 80. Chief Collabr: Robert Arthur. *Songs:* I'm Going to Maui Tomorrow; The Anniversary Hula; When You're Caught, You're Caught; Aloha Means Love; Lyrics: All About Love.

DANCY, EDWARD L   ASCAP 1977
author, singer, arranger
b St Louis, Mo, Oct 15, 46. Educ: East St Louis Sr High Sch, 60-64, studied theory & voice; Los Angeles City Col, 75-76, studied voice & theory. Vocalist with vocal group: The Mustangs, St Louis, 66-69; The Gifts, St Louis, 69-76; The Gifted Four, Los Angeles, Calif, 76; recording artist, 77- Engr. Chief Collabrs: Rene Francois, Erwin Jefferson. *Songs:* Lyrics: Fallen Star; Warm and Tender Love; Maybe When I'm Gone; Some Kind of Web; When a Good Love Goes Bad.

DANDREA, ANTHONY AUGUSTINE   ASCAP 1975
composer, author, singer
b Elmira, NY, Sept 7, 11. Educ: Col Elmira. Learned to read music at age 10. Lead trumpeter, USA Bands, 30-37. Trumpeter & pianist, local orchs, 37-45. Pianist, nightclubs, 46-72. *Songs:* This Heavenly Day; Crime Doesn't Pay.

DANEL, J GORDON
See Gold, Joe D

DANIELS, CHARLES NEIL   ASCAP 1925
composer, music publisher
b Leavenworth, Kans, Apr 12, 1878; d Los Angeles, Calif, Jan 23, 43. Educ: Pub schs, St Joseph & Kansas City, Mo; studied piano from early age; studied musical comp & arr with Carl Preyer, Kansas City. Comp & music publ, 50 yrs; comp first hit at 18; managed Detroit office, Jerome H Remick Co, 04-12; established publ firm, Daniels & Wilson, San Francisco, 14· pres, Villa Moret, Inc, San Francisco, 24-31; then was free-lance song comp, Los Angeles. Chief Collabrs: Earle C Jones, James O'Dea, Harry Williams, Weston Wilson, Ben Black, Gus Arnheim, Richard Whiting, Gus Kahn, Harry Tobias. *Songs & Instrumental Works:* Song of the Wanderer (Where Shall I Go?); Music: Hiawatha; On Mobile Bay; You Tell Me Your Dream, I'll Tell You Mine; Moonlight; Mickey; Chloe; Moonlight and Roses; I've Got a Woman Crazy for Me, She's Funny That Way; Don't Sing Aloha When I Go; Call of the Rockies; Good Night My Love; Sweet and Lovely; Yearning; Ready for the River; Dark Eyes; Wild Honey; Margery; Cavalcade of Marches; Democracy Forever (March).

DANIELS, DON
See Borzage, Donald Dan

DANIELS, DONALD O'NEAL   ASCAP 1974
composer, author, teacher
b Little Rock, Ark, July 28, 49. Educ: Los Angeles City Col, 68-70; Calif State Univ, Long Beach, 73-77; studied theory with Dr Daniel. Pianist with group Jackson Five, 73-74; on tour, 74. Recording artist. Joined group Love & Kisses for film "Thank God It's Friday." Performed on TV progs incl "Merv Griffin Show", "American Bandstand" & "Midnight Special." Toured eastern US. Billed with group Village People & Donna Summer. Songwriter, film "Mohogany." Songwriter for var artists. Writer & independent producer of Donna Washington album, 80. Chief Collabrs: John Springer, Jermaine Jackson,

Kathy Wakefield, Michael Smith, Terri McFadden. *Songs:* Let's Be Young Tonight; She's the Ideal Girl; For the Sake of Love; Music: I Only Meant to Wet My Feet; Down to Love Town; Erucu; First Things First.

DANIELS, M L ASCAP 1964
composer, teacher
b Cleburne, Tex, Jan 11, 31. Educ: Abilene Christian Univ, BS, 55, MEd, 56; NTex State Univ, EdD, 64, studied comp with Samuel Adler & William Latham. Symph work, trumpet. Won comp contests, Nat Sch Orch Asn. Teacher music, Abilene Christian Univ; judge music, guest cond, staff arr. *Songs:* Music: Seasons of Time (choral). *Instrumental Works:* Festique (orch); Reflections (band); Pendleton Suite (strings); Sunfest (orch).

DANIELS, MABEL WHEELER ASCAP 1937
composer
b Swampscott, Mass, Nov 27, 1879; d. Educ: Girls Latin Sch; Radcliffe Col, BA(magna cum laude); studied music with George Chadwick & Ludwig Thuille; hon degrees, Tufts Col, Boston Univ, Wheaton Col & New Eng Cons. Dir, Glee Club, Bradford Acad, 11-13; music dir, Simmons Col, 13-18. Author "An American Girl in Munich." Dir, Beneficent Soc, New Eng Cons, Nat Acad Am Comp & Cond & Friends of Music. Mem, Adv Comt on Music, Boston Pub Schs, MacDowell Col & Music Comt, Wheaton Col; hon mem, Radcliffe Club, Musical Guild of Boston. Trustee: Radcliffe Col, 45-51 & New Eng Cons. Awards: Nat League Am Pen Women, Nat Fedn Music Clubs & Nat Acad Am Comp & Conds. *Instrumental Works:* The Story of Jael (cantata); Exultate Deo (for Radcliffe Col 50th anniv); Deep Forest; 3 Observations for 3 Woodwinds; The Wild Ride (Nat League Am Pen Women Prize); A Psalm of Praise; Canticle of Wisdom.

DANIELS, PETER H B ASCAP 1966
composer, author, conductor
b London, Eng, Aug 9, 23. Educ: Royal Col Music, LRCM, comp, Benjamin Frankel; Juilliard Sch Music, comp, Del Piecola. Assoc mus dir "Funny Girl," mus dir, Barbra Streisand, Lainie Kazan, Ed Ames & Eddie Fisher. Recorded, MGM & Columbia Records, cond many TV shows, United Kingdom & US. Pianist, teacher. Chief Collabrs: Sammy Cahn, Sydnee Macall, Carrol Coates, Woody Harris. *Songs:* We'll Meet in the Spring; Music: You Must Have Faith; You Can't Go Home Again; Is This the Way It Ends. *Instrumental Works:* Magic Time.

DANOFF, MARY CATHERINE (TAFFY NIVERT) ASCAP 1970
composer, singer
b Washington, DC, Oct 25, 44. Educ: Col Steubenville, Ohio, two yrs. Became performer, 68; started in five voice group, became duo with Bill Danoff, Fat City, 69. Sang background vocals with John Denver, 70; duo Fat City became Bill & Taffy. Recorded four albums. Joined Starland Vocal Band, 74. Chief Collabrs: Bill Danoff, Jon Carroll, John Denver, Margot Kunkel. *Songs:* Take Me Home, Country Roads; I Guess He'd Rather Be in Colorado; Friends With You; Loving You With My Eyes.

DANOFF, SIDNEY ASCAP 1958
composer, author, singer
b Baltimore, Md, June 27, 20. Educ: Hunter Col, BA, 59; Univ Miami, MEd, 65. Actor, off Bway & TV incl "Everglades", "Follow That Man", also Schlitz Playhouse & community theatre. Singer-performer, Catskill Mountains, Palace, NY, nightclubs & TV; recording artist, Hanover Records. Writer-performer-teacher, TV educ series "Mighty Mouth." Chief Collabrs: Johnny Marks, Eddie White, Mack Wolfson. *Songs:* Dance Everyone Dance; Mashuga; I'll Be a Little Angel; The Devil Jumped Out; It's Your World Lover; The Last Big Joke; Lyrics: Flyin' Soldiers.

DANOFF, WILLIAM THOMAS ASCAP 1970
composer, author, singer
b Springfield, Mass, May 7, 46. Educ: Inst Languages & Linguistics, Georgetown Univ, BS(Chinese language). Amateur songwriter & performer since age 13. Formed group Fat City, 69, became Bill & Taffy, 73. Formed Starland Vocal Band, recorded four albums since 76. "Starland Vocal Band Show," CBS-TV, 77. Chief Collabrs: Taffy Danoff, John Denver, Jon Carroll. *Songs:* Take Me Home, Country Roads; Afternoon Delight; Friends With You; I Guess He'd Rather Be in Colorado; Late Nite Radio.

DANOWSKI, CONRAD JOHN (CONRAD TAYLOR) ASCAP 1979
composer, author, singer
b Greenport, NY, Dec 6, 50. Educ: Southold High Sch, 68; self-taught on guitar; started keyboard lessons at age 7 & guitar at age 13. Toured with Genya Ravan in nightclubs, 78; toured with Carolyne Mas in nightclubs, 80; recording artist; guitarist, pianist & arr. Chief Collabrs: Genya Ravan, Carolyne Mas. *Songs:* Music: Messin' Around; Steve; I'm Wired, Wired, Wired; Roto Root Her.

DANOWSKI, HELEN K ASCAP 1976
composer, author, librettist
b Cutchogue, NY, Jan 27, 32. Educ: Eastman Sch Music, Univ Rochester, 50-54; pvt study with Joseph Castaldo, 60-62; Combs Col Music, studied comp & orchestration with Romeo Cascarino, 63-66. Soprano mem, Vox Humana Choral, 62- Comn to write piano accompaniments for ancient Chinese folk

songs, publ in Taiwan, China, 68 & performed in Univ Peking. Rec'd Arion Nat Found Music Award, 50. Narrator for Chinese New Year Prog. Chief Collabr: Y H Ku (translr). *Songs & Instrumental Works:* Ten Songs (collection of ancient Chinese folk songs for voice & piano); The Frost-King (children's chorus, chamber orch); He Writes His Mystic Name (children's chorus, chamber orch); Legend of the Lotus (ballet, orch); April (children's chorus, chamber orch, part I); A Shepherd Is Born (tenor, chamber orch).

DANSER, JOHN ASCAP 1973
composer, arranger, musician
b London, Eng, June 5, 34. Educ: Brooklyn Col, BA; Manhattan Sch Music, MM; studied arr with Herbert Bourne & comp with Tibor Serly. Comp, arr & produced albums: Danser's Inferno; Suite for Brass; Musical Christmas. Musical dir, Copacabana; has been musical dir, Pines Hotel in South Fallsburg & Laurels CC in Sackett Lake. Awards: Am Music Ctr; Ascap Panels Awards, 79-80. *Instrumental Works:* Concertino for Band and Violin; The G flat String Quartet; Suite for Brass Quintet; The Crystal Variations (woodwind quintet). *Scores:* Bway shows: The Big Band Show; The Mark of Cain.

DANT, CHARLES (BUD) GUSTAVE (J KIEFER)
composer, author
b Washington, Ind, June 21, 07. Educ: Ind Univ Sch Music, BM(pub sch music & comp), 32. Played jazz cornet in vaudeville, 25-26. Started col dance band, Bud Dant's Collegians, went on road with band after grad, MCA signed band, 33. Joined Ted Weems, 37. Mus dir, comp & arr, NBC Red & Blue Radio Networks, Hollywood, 39-46. Musical dir for commercial radio & TV shows. Comp & record producer, Decca/Coral Records, 55; chief production, West Coast, Decca Records, 65. Active in independent record production & comp, 71- Composing & orchestrating an Hawaiian dance suite for symph orch & dance co. Chief Collabrs: J A Stebbins (June Dant), Leon Pober, Beverly Lange. *Songs:* Honolulu, Blue and Green; The Music of Hawaii; Nobody's Song; Magic Garden; Take My Hand; Licorice Stick Rag; Beautiful, Beautiful Hawaii; My Hawaiian Country; Country Girl; My Heart's in Hawaii; Make Believe Days; Happy Hawaiian Anniversary; (Komo Mai) Come Together; I Never Miss the Sunshine; Red Eye Gravy and Poi; The Merriest Hawaiian Christmas; Aloha, My Promised Land (Big Island Anthem); Music: New Orleans, Tennessee; Misty Rainbow; I Love You, Hawaii; The Magic Island Suite (symphonic); Lyrics: Walk Through Paradise;

DANT, JUNE ANNE (J A STEBBINS)
composer, author
b Lincoln, Nebr, June 11, 18. Educ: Univ Nebr Premed Sch, grad, 36. Exec secy, radio, 40 & later TV, Hollywood. Writer & amateur pianist. Chief Collabrs: Charles Bud Dant (husband), M Grass. *Songs:* Take My Hand; My Hawaiian Country; Country Girl; The Music of Hawaii; Together; Aloha, My Promised Land (Big Island Anthem); Music: Blues in a Mist; Hanohano Molokai; I Love You Hawaii.

DANTES, PERRY
See Nowakowski, Perry Casey

D'ANTUONO, VINCENT JOSEPH (VINCE ANTHONY) ASCAP 1978
composer
b Brooklyn, NY, Oct 1, 40. Recording artist; has own record co, Sounds & Rhythm, Ltd. Has had works publ by April-Blackwood Music & CBS. *Songs:* A Christmas Glow; Country Christmas Eve; Christmas Children; Everyday You Grow a Little Bit Younger; Blessed Be God; Guiding Light; A Love That Glows; This Is My Love Song; Snowflakes and Heartaches.

DANZIG, DOROTHY
See Hull, Dorothy Spafard

DANZIGER, HOWARD ASCAP 1969
composer, author, lyricist
b Bronx, NY, Oct 20, 38. Educ: Manhattan Sch Music, MM, 60; studied orchestration with Nicholas Flagello. Has written nightclub acts & spec material for Engelbert Humperdinck, Alexis Smith & Gloria Gaynor; comedy writer for Johnny Yune, Gabriel Kaplan & Freddie Prinze; writer for "Merv Griffin Show" & var radio & TV commercials. *Scores:* Film: The Delta Factor.

DA'OUD, GARY
See David, Gary

DAPEER, HARRY ELLIS (HARRY DUPREE) ASCAP 1955
composer, author, publisher
b Newport, RI, Nov 26, 11. Educ: Columbia Univ. With Maj Bowes Capitol Family, 8 yrs; on CBS Radio with The Dalton Boys, nightclubs & theaters. Chief Collabrs: Sid Silvers, R D Farrell (Rusty Draper), Lou Hirscher. *Songs:* Gamblin' Gal; Yours, My Love; Como Se Viene, Se Va; Mister Cowboy; Music: Your Love; Lyrics: Lisbon Antigua.

DARBY, KENNETH LORIN ASCAP 1946
composer, author, conductor
b Hebron, Nebr, May 13, 09. Educ: Piano studies at age 5; trumpet lessons at age 9; Santa Monica Sch, Calif, studied sight singing, harmony, counterpoint & comp with Mae Nightingale & Doris Moon; later studied with Tibor Serly & Ernest Toch; Santa Monica High Sch: Chapman Col. Played pipe organ, Forum Theatre, 28 & for films, 29, organist, Uplifter's Club. Formed The King's Men Quartet, also sang, made arr & played, 29, appeared on Fibber McGee & Molly Radio Broadcasts, 40-56. Joined Paul Whiteman Orgn, 34-37, choral arr-dir for musical films, MGM. Invented the Munchkin voices via subspeed recording with film "The Wizard of Oz"; staff, Walt Disney Studios, 40-47, choral dir "Westinghouse Prog" with John Charles Thomas & Victor Young's Orch. With 20th Century-Fox, 48-59, became musical assoc of Alfred Newman on many films. Nominated by Acad Motion Pictures Arts & Sci for "The King and I" (won 1 Oscar), "Porgy and Bess" (won 1 Oscar), "Camelot" (won 1 Oscar), "South Pacific" & "Flower Drum Song." Chief Collabrs: Alfred Newman, Lionel Newman. *Songs:* Love Song of Kalua (From Bird of Paradise); The Magic Islands; Legend of Chuckaluck (Rancho Notorious); Endless Prairie; Bus Stop Song; Tall Men; Legend of Jesse James; This Is Canada; Boar's Tooth Ceremony; Merry Christmas, Neighbor; Get Away, Young Man (Dietrich); Rock Around the Island; Saga of the Ponderosa; God Bless Your Life; Music: I Wish They Didn't Mean Goodbye; 'Twas the Night Before Christmas; Lyrics: Backstreet; Song From Desiree; Come Share My Life; I'm Gonna File My Claim; Ports of Paradise; Madonna of the Flowers; Whispering Wind; Legend of the Rain; Hana Maui; New York; Once You Kiss a Stranger; Down in the Meadow; Make Mine Music; Casey at the Bat; No Goodbye; One Silver Dollar; Soldier of Fortune; Old Father Briny; Look At Me; Springtime in New York. *Instrumental Works:* Man of Nazareth (orch-choral cantata). *Scores:* Film/TV: River of No Return; How the West Was Won; Love Me Tender; Daniel Boone Was a Man; Wyatt Earp Scoring Cues; Jim Bowie, Adventurin' Man.

DARBY, RAY ASCAP 1957
author
b Edmonton, Can, Mar 9, 12. Educ: High sch. Radio script writer for Canadian & US networks incl series "Once Upon a Tune." Wrote musicals: "Rip Van Winkle", "In Murphy Park" & "The Trial of Joshua Tripp." With Walt Disney studio, 2 yrs; writer of children's bks & TV scripts, also documentary films for Naval Missile Ctr, Point Mugu, Calif. Chief Collabr: Gregory Stone. *Songs:* My Chapel; Boys of the Western Sea; Love Will Come Again; Buy My Violets.

DARCH, ROBERT RUSSELL
composer, author, singer
b Detroit, Mich, Mar 31, 20. Educ: St Clements Grammar Sch, Center Line, Mich; De La Salle Col, Detroit; Paris Univ. Parachute engr army officer, 40-53; ragtime piano player, 53- Played ragtime concerts with var symph orchs & in nightclubs & univs; toured US & Europe; recording artist; appeared on TV in US & Can. Chief Collabrs: Haven Gillespie, Burl Ives, Joseph F Lamb, Eubie Blake, Joe J Jordan. *Songs & Instrumental Works:* I'm Certainly Goin' Back to New Orleans; Flicker Red Rag; Opera House Rag; The Carson City Rag; Billy Goat Strut; Sedalia Rag. *Albums:* Ragtime Piano; Golden Reunion in Ragtime; Gold Rush Daze.

DARCY, THOMAS F, JR ASCAP 1948
composer, conductor, cornetist
b Vancouver, Wash, May 7, 1895; d Somerset, Pa, May 19, 68. Educ: Juilliard; Army Bandmaster's Sch. Led 18th Inf Band, First Div AEF, WW I. Assoc leader & cornet soloist, US Army Band, 24; leader of band, 53; cond, US Army Band & dean of Army Bandmaster's Sch, WW II. Awarded many medals. Cond int expositions, Philadelphia, 26, Barcelona & Seville, Spain, 29, Cleveland, 37 & New York, 39-40. *Instrumental Works:* The US Army March; March of the Free Peoples; An American Overture; Trio for Trumpets; Romance.

DARENSBOURG, JOSEPH WILMER ASCAP 1979
composer, musician
b Baton Rouge, La, July 9, 06. Educ: Grade sch & high sch. Played clarinet since age 10; played for circus, riverboats & ocean liners; played with Jack Teagarden, Bob Scobey, Kid Ory & Louis Armstrong's All Stars, 4 yrs; recording artist; had hit record, "Yellow Dog Blues," with own band; played in Carnegie Hall, "Ed Sullivan TV Show", "Mike Douglas Show" & "Dinah Shore Show." Appeared in several movies & TV shows. *Songs:* Lou-Easy-An-I-A; Sacramento Jubilee.

DARIAN, FRED ASCAP 1957
composer, singer
b Detroit, Mich, June 16, 27. Educ: New York Opera Inst; Los Angeles City Col. Vocalist, RCA Records & Decca Records; entertainer-vocalist in nightclub. Artist, arranger & record producer. Chief Collabrs: Van Winkle, de Lory. *Songs:* Mr Custer; Out on the Floor; Calypso Joe; Lyrics: Here Is Happiness. *Scores:* Film/TV: Out of Sight.

DARING, KEVIN MASON ASCAP 1976
composer, author
b Ithica, NY, Sept 26, 49. Educ: Amherst Col, BA, 71, independent scholar; Suffolk Univ, JD, 76. Recording & performing artist, comp of popular songs, writer of scores & film adaptations, 71- Record producer, 77- Chief Collabr:

Beatrice (Jeanie) Stahl. *Songs:* Marblehead Morning; Paint the Town Blue; The Years That Come to Pass. *Scores:* Film: Return of the Secaucus Seven.

DARION, JOSEPH ASCAP 1951
author
b New York, NY, Jan 30, 17. Educ: City Col New York. Worked as lyricist, popular song, musical theatre, opera, cantata, children's works & others. Awards: Antoinette Perry (Tony) Award; Drama Critics Circle Award; Outer Critics Circle Award, Int Broadcasting Award, gold records; awards with Ezra Laderman: The Gabriel Award, The Ohio State Award, TV Arts & Sci Award. Chief Collabrs: Ezra Laderman, Mitch Leigh, George Kleinsinger, Guy Wood, John Benson Brooks, Hermann Krasnow. *Songs:* Ricochet Romance; The Ho Ho Song; Lyrics: Changing Partners; Midnight Train; The Lollipop Tree; Christmas Is a Feeling in Your Heart; The Impossible Dream. *Scores:* Opera Librettos: Galileo; And David Wept; The Tree That Found Christmas; Cantata Librettos: The Questions of Abraham; A Handful of Souls; Mass: A Mass for Cain (libretto); Bway Shows: Archy and Mehitabel (Shinbone Alley); Man of La Mancha; Illya Darling.

DARLING, DENVER ASCAP 1945
composer, author, musician
b Cumberland County, Ill, Apr 6, 09. Country music artist for radio, TV & films, Decca & MGM Records. Chief Collabrs: Fred Rose, Vaughn Horton, Michael Stoner. *Songs:* Silver Stars Purple Sage; Choo Choo Ch-Boogie; Address Unknown; I Didn't Have the Heart; Heart Break Trail; Don't Bring Your Blues; Don't Hang Around Me Anymore; The Old Family Bible; Ding Dong Polka; I Just Fell Out of Love; My Dreamboat Sailed Without Me; Think of Home; Spring Rain; I've Just Got to Be a Cowboy; I Kiss Your Hand; The Gentle Touch; I'm Gonna Sue, Sioux City Sue; Don't Turn Green.

DARMANIN, JOSEPH (JOE LONDON) ASCAP 1964
composer, pianist, arranger
b New York, NY, Oct 18, 27. Educ: Saint John Baptist Della Salle, Malta; Royal Col Music, London, Eng; studied with comp-cond Joseph Casa Pinta. Played piano & arr local radio sta, Malta, 3 yrs; weekly jazz show, Brit Broadcasting Corp, 2 yrs. Returned to US; joined Johnny Long's Orch, 2 yrs. Comp popular songs; now comp score for Bway show, "In Search of a Sinner." Chief Collabrs: Eddie Deane, Pat Noto, William Bairn. *Songs:* Music: Another Broken Heart; Only a Fool; The Colors Seem to Change; Just Follow Me; Come on and Take Me. *Instrumental Works:* Malta; Streets of Madrid; Two Way Street. *Scores:* Bway Shows: Color Her Beautiful; Yes, I've Been Here Before; Film/TV: Mr Lincoln's Pad; The Crawl; Till Dawn.

D'ARROW, PHILIP ASCAP 1979
composer, author, singer
b Dallas, Tex, Dec 18, 45. Educ: Pelham High Sch; Univ Kans; Mo Univ. TV & film actor; recording artist; guitarist. Chief Collabr: Jacques Levy. *Songs:* Burn the Disco Down. *Scores:* Film/TV: Battle of the Bands. *Albums:* Philip D'Arrow; Sub Zero.

DARST, WILLIAM GLEN ASCAP 1963
composer, organ teacher
b Shelby County, Ill, Apr 21, 1896. Educ: Studied piano, Am Cons Music, Chicago, Ill; studied organ, harmony & counterpoint with pvt teachers. Served in WW I. Organist & choirmaster, St Andrew's Episcopal Church & St John's Episcopal Church, Ft Worth, Tex, 45-58. *Songs:* Over 100 songs, incl A Lenten Carol (Lent, with descant); O God of Youth; Psalm of Praise (SS); Stand Up and Bless the Lord; Ride On! Ride On in Majesty (Palm Sunday, SAB); Come, Faithful People (Palm Sunday); Christ Is Born Today (Christmas); In Quiet Confidence; Joyful We Adore Thee; Let Us Rejoice (Easter); Search, Prove My Heart; A Mighty Fortress (variants with descant & optional trumpets); Christ Is Our Cornerstone; Christ, the New-Born King (Christmas); Hosanna, Loud Hosanna (Palm Sunday); Draw Nigh to Thy Jerusalem (Palm Sunday); Spirit of God; Lead On, O King Eternal; Praise to God, Immortal Praise (SAB); Honor Him, Our King (Palm Sunday, SAB); Christ the Lord Is Risen Again (Easter); Jesus, the Very Thought of Thee; Let Us Walk in the Light (a capella); Hosanna to the Son of David (Palm Sunday); Walk Humbly With Thy God; To God All Praise and Glory; Come, Thou Redeemer of the Earth (Christmas); Lift Up Your Hearts, Ye People (Easter); Jesus, Thou Joy of Loving Hearts.

D'ARTEGA, ALFONSO ASCAP 1946
composer, conductor, arranger
b Silao, Mex, June 5, 07. To US, 18. Educ: Strassberger Cons; studied with Boris Levenson. Cond of orchs for radio networks incl Radio-TV Italia in Milan & Rome, theatre, records, films, concerts & throughout US incl Buffalo Philh, Stadium Symph, Miami Symph, Symph of the Air, St Louis Symph & New London Symph. Comp, cond & arr for TV, incl NBC Chimes Theme. Portrayed Tchaikowksy in film "Carnegie Hall." Originated Pops Concerts, Carnegie Hall. Recipient of Medaille d'Or. *Songs:* In the Blue of Evening; Ask Your Heart; Fiesta en Granada. *Instrumental Works:* American Panorama (tone poem); Niagara Falls; Romanesque Suite. *Scores:* Ballet: Fire and Ice Ballet.

DARTOS, TUNICA
See Brody, David S

DARYLL, TED
See Meister, Theodore Henry

DASH, JULIAN ASCAP 1952
composer, author, saxophonist
b Charleston, SC, Apr 9, 16; d New York, NY, Feb 25, 74. Educ: Ala State Teachers Col. Saxophonist, Erskine Hawkins Orch, over 20 yrs. Chief Collabrs: Erskine Hawkins, William Johnson. *Songs & Instrumental Works:* Tuxedo Junction; Nobody Met the Train; House Party; Double Shot; Zig-Zag; Goin' Along; So Let It Be.

DASHOW, JAMES ASCAP 1975
composer
b Chicago, Ill, Nov 7, 44. Educ: Princeton Univ, BA(comp), 66; Brandeis Univ, MFA(comp), 69; Acad Nazionale di Santa Cecilia, Rome, dipl, 71; studied with G Petrassi. Fulbright fel, Rome, 69; organized & directed group for new music, Forum Players, Rome, 71-75, tours to Greece, Turkey, Spain, Yugoslavia, Scotland, Ireland. Founder & dir, Studio di Musica Elettronica Sciadoni, Rome, 74- Computer music progs, Univ Padova, 75, mem council dirs, Centro Sonologia Computazionale; helped organize Padova Computer Music Group. Biennale comn new computer comp, "Conditional Assemblies," Venice, 80; founding mem, Int Computer Music Asn. Travel widely presenting electronic works, especially computer pieces & techniques, Europe & US. Chief Collabrs: John Ashbery & John Berryman. *Instrumental Works:* Effetti Collaterali (clarinet in A & computer-generated electronic accompaniment); Whispers Out of Time (First Prize, Bourges electronic music competition, 77); A Way of Staying (soprano & computer-generated electronic accompaniment); Partial Distances (electronic music); Mappings (cello & electronic accompaniment); Timespace Extensions (flute, piano & 2 perc); Ashbery Setting (soprano, flute, piano); Some Dream Songs (soprano, violin, piano); Punti di Vista (piano); Second Voyage (tenor & computer-generated electronic accompaniment, NEA Grant).

DAUGHERTY, PATRICK DALE (DIRTY)
composer, author, singer
b Jonesboro, Ark, Nov 11, 47. Appeared on TV. Co-writer; has recorded many albums with Know Body Else Band, 69 & Black Oak Arkansas Band, 70-77; 3 gold LP's; bass guitarist. *Songs & Instrumental Works:* Hot and Nasty; Lord Have Mercy; When Electricity Came to Arkansas; Hot Rod; Highway Pirate; We Can Make That Scene; Fightin' Cock; Jim Dandy to the Rescue; Up; Uncle Lijiah.

DAUNCH, VIRGINIA OBENCHAIN ASCAP 1964
composer, author, teacher
b Ohio, Apr 26, 19. Educ: St Louis Inst of Music; also pvt music study. Pres, Ohio Music Teachers Asn. *Songs & Instrumental Works:* Peppermint Candy; Organ Originals. *Scores:* Operetta: Uncle Billy's Candy Shop.

DAVENPORT, CHARLES (COW COW) ASCAP 1946
composer, author, pianist
b Anniston, Ala, Apr 26, 1895; d Cleveland, Ohio, Dec 2, 55. Educ: Selma Univ. Singer, pianist in carnivals & vaudeville, 14-30; teamed with singer Dora Carr. Began writing songs, with wife Peggy Davenport, 36, later played the Gus Son Vaudeville circuit with the Lowestime & the Keith Familytime, also the Pantagetime. To Cleveland, 37; worked for WPA. Made many records. *Songs:* Old Fashion One Woman Man; Mommies Angel Child; Last Go Round; My Eugene; Back Where I Started From; Love My Man Better Than I Love Myself; Jump Little Jitterbug; Say I Do; I'll Be Glad When You're Dead, You Rascal You; Do You Call That Religion?; Mama Don't Allow It. *Instrumental Works:* Cow Cow Blues; State Street Jive; Hobson City Stomp.

DAVENPORT, DAVID N ASCAP 1961
composer, author, teacher
b Richmond, Ind, Sept 27, 25. Educ: Ind Univ, BA, MA. High sch choral dir; cond fests, Ind, Ill & Ohio. Guest cond, Hollywood Bowl; publisher. Chief Collabrs: Walter Ehret, Les Taylor. *Songs:* Choral: Little David; Sea Scenes; The Everliving God; Reach Down Dat Hand.

DAVENPORT, PEMBROKE MORTIMER ASCAP 1954
composer, author, musical director
b Dallas, Tex, July 3, 11. Educ: Southern Methodist Univ Sch Music, 31-32; pvt study comp with Tibor Serly, cond with George Szelle. Comp, Radio City Music Hall. Solo pianist & arr, Fred Waring's Pennsylvanians. Music dir & cond, Bway musicals, incl "Kiss Me Kate", "Out of This World", "Can-Can" & "Fanny." Music dir & cond, New York Ctr Light Opera & Los Angeles Civic Light Opera Asn. Chief Collabrs: Joe Linz, Edward Eager. *Songs:* You Should Be Set to Music; What's Gonna Happen to Me?; Jacqueline; Lyrics: Tonight in Vienna; Nonchalant; Stars in a Southern Sky; Sinful Senorita; My Restless Lover. *Scores:* Film: Sweet Devil; Bway stage: Dr Willy Nilly; Incidental music: The Long Dream.

DAVID, DAVID
See Powell, David

DAVID, GARY (GARY DA'OUD) ASCAP 1969
composer
b Sacramento, Calif, Oct 27, 35. Educ: Sacramento State Univ, BA; Union Grad Sch, Yellow Springs, Ohio, PhD. Comp & arr for The Sound of Feeling, albums for Verve & Mercury, 64-73; publ, Feeling Music, 72-73; singer & pianist, nightclubs; did commercials, Ford Motors; did film music, US Information Agency. *Songs & Instrumental Works:* Who Knows What Love Is; The Time Has Come for Silence; Waltz Without Words; Spleen; Hex; Up Into the Silence; Mixolmdian Mode.

DAVID, HAL ASCAP 1943
author
b New York, NY, May 25, 21. Educ: Journalism, NY Univ. Pres, ASCAP, 80- Songwriter for TV & film, stage & records; produced LP's for leading recording artists. Brother of Mack David. Chief Collabrs: Burt Bacharach, Sherman Edwards, Lee Pockriss, Henry Mancini, Joe Raposo & John Barry. *Songs:* Lyrics: Walk on By; Reach Out for Me; Always Something There to Remind Me; You'll Never Get to Heaven; What the World Needs Now Is Love; Raindrops Keep Falling on My Head (Academy Award Winner, 69); Alfie (Academy Award nominee); The Look of Love (Academy Award nominee); Wives and Lovers (Grammy nominee); I'll Never Fall in Love Again (Grammy nominee); It Was Almost Like a Song (Grammy nominee); This Guy's in Love With You (Grammy nominee); Wishin' and Hopin'; The Windows of the World; One Less Bell to Answer; I Say a Little Prayer; Do You Know the Way to San Jose?; A House Is Not a Home; Close to You; April Fools; Trains and Boats and Planes; Promises, Promises (Grammy Winner); After the Fox; The Man Who Shot Liberty Valance; Oklahoma Crude; Two Gals and a Guy; Promise Her Anything; Don't Make Me Over; Make It Easy on Yourself; Only Love Can Break a Heart; The Story of My Life; Blue on Blue; Anyone Who Had a Heart. *Scores:* Film/TV Lyrics: Casino Royale (Grammy nominee); Lost Horizon; What's New Pussycat? (Academy Award nominee); Butch Cassidy and the Sundance Kid; Moonraker.

DAVID, JAMES ASCAP 1966
author
b New York, NY, Apr 10, 51. First song publ, 66. Mem, WCoast Publ Adv Comt, ASCAP. Chief Collabr: Steve Dorff. *Songs:* Lyrics: Room Enough for Two; Do I Have to Cry; Maybe It's Time to Start Calling It Love.

DAVID, LEE ASCAP 1923
composer, author
b New York, NY, Dec 13, 1891; d Brooklyn, NY, Aug 31, 78. Educ: City Col New York; Columbia Univ Teachers Col. Wrote songs for "Greenwich Village Follies", "Padlocks of 1927", "Cotton Club Revues" & "Ziegfeld Follies." Chief Collabrs: John Redmond, Billy Rose, J Keirn Brennan, Benjamin David (brother), Charles O'Flynn, Pete Wendling, Benny Davis. *Songs:* Tonight You Belong to Me; Big Apple; Just a Year Ago Tonight; Sorority Waltz; Sipping Cider Thru a Straw; They're Burning Down the House I Was Brung Up In; Junior Miss; Janie (film title song); Where Is the Sun; Headin' for Heaven; Old Plantation; Down South; Seeing You Again Did Me No Good; Wand'ring Romance Waltz; The Fool; Just a Bit of Heaven in Your Smile; Honey Bunny Boo; Moon River Waltz. *Scores:* Bway stage: A Night in Venice; Broadway Nights.

DAVID, MACK ASCAP 1934
composer, author
b New York, NY. Educ: Cornell Univ; St John's Univ Law Sch. Started in Tin Pan Alley; to Hollywood in 48, wrote for motion pictures, received 8 Acad Awards nominations. Elected to Songwriters Hall of Fame. Chief Collabrs: Jerry Livingston, Duke Ellington, John Green, Elmer Bernstein, Frank DeVol, Jimmy Van Heusen, Al Hoffman, Alex Kramer, Joan Whitney, Count Basie, Ernest Gold, Franz Waxman, Louiguy. *Songs:* La Vie en Rose; Cherry Pink and Apple Blossom White; My Own True Love (Tara's theme); It Must Be Him; I Don't Care If the Sun Don't Shine; Candy; Bibbidi Bobbidi Boo; A Dream Is a Wish Your Heart Makes; Moon Love; Lili Marlene; Hush, Hush Sweet Charlotte; Baby, It's You; Walk on the Wild Side; It Only Hurts for a Little While; It Was a Good Time; Sunflower; I'm Just a Lucky So-and-So; Chi-Baba Chi-Baba; A Sinner Kissed an Angel; Sweet Eloise; On the Isle of May; The Hanging Tree; It's a Mad, Mad, Mad, Mad World; The Ballad of Cat Ballou; Spellbound; It's Love, Love, Love; Take Me; 77 Sunset Strip (TV theme); Hawaiian Eye (TV theme); Bimbombey; Don't You Know I Care; The Unbirthday Song; The Singing Hills; Blue and Sentimental; Young Emotions; Wednesday's Child; Sixty Seconds Got Together; Just a Kid Named Joe; Rain, Rain, Go Away; Baby, Baby, Baby; Falling Leaves; Trick or Treat; Casper the Friendly Ghost (TV theme); The Call of the Far Away Hills; In a Persian Market; The Lesson; Films: Cinderella; Alice in Wonderland; The Hanging Tree; Walk on the Wild Side; Bird Man of Alcatraz; Tara's Bulba; It's a Mad, Mad, Mad, Mad World; Hush, Hush Sweet Charlotte; Cat Ballou; Hawaii; among others. *Scores:* Bway Musical: Molly.

DAVID, NATHAN
See Risser, Bryce Nathan

DAVID, WILL
See Powell, David

DAVIDSON, CHARLES STUART   ASCAP 1966
composer, cantor
b Pittsburgh, Pa, Sept 8, 29. Educ: Univ Pittsburgh, BMus; Col Jewish Music, Jewish Theol Sem Am, MSacredMus; Cantors Inst, Jewish Theol Sem, Degree of Hazzan; Eastman Sch Music; C W Post Col. Cantor-clergyman, Wantagh, NY & Elkins Park, Pa. Fac, Jewish Theol Sem, Cantors Inst. Ed, New Union Hymnal, Cantor's Voice & Jewish Music Journal. Chief Collabrs: Samuel Rosenbaum, Ray Smolover. *Songs:* Music: I Never Saw Another Butterfly; Chassidic Service; Blues Service; Hush of Midnight; Baroque Suite; Trial of Anatoly Shcharansky; A Singing of Angels; Sephardic Service; He's Got the Whole World in His Hand; Take Care; Gimpel the Fool (opera); 5 children's holiday musicals.

DAVIDSON, DOUGLASS ALBERT   ASCAP 1975
composer, tuba player
b Springfield, Mo, June 18, 26. Educ: Southwest High Sch, St Louis, 43; Eastman Sch Music, BM, 49, MM, 55. Tuba player, Indianapolis Symph & Denver Symph; first tuba, Detroit Concert Band. Brass instr, clinician & soloist, Troy State Univ; lectr, U of M Sch of Music. Free-lance tuba player, New York. *Instrumental Works:* Southwind March (concert band); Scaramouche (quintet for brass); Fantasy on a Theme of Scarlatti (bass tuba or trombone & band).

DAVIDSON, DUANE ANDREW   ASCAP 1962
composer
b Marion, Va, Apr 15, 34; d Washington, DC, Dec 17, 64. Educ: Emory & Henry Col, BA, studied music with Ludwig Sikorski; Yale Univ, MMus, studied with Quincy Porter; also studied in Paris & Tanglewood, Mass. Won Block Award; awarded First Prize, Queen Elizabeth Int Contest, Wind Music Soc, London, 60. With Va Symph Orch. Comps have been presented to Yale Univ, establishing the Duane Davidson Archives, Sch Music. *Songs & Instrumental Works:* Full orch: Stravaganza No 1; Jazz Implications; French Suite; Petite Piece for Orchestra; Chorus & orch: Psalm 23; Psalm 100; Cantata No 1 (Melora's Song), No 2 (Journey of Paradoxes), No 3 (The Execution) & No 4 (The Queen's Marie); Choral: Psalm 150 (SATB); Madrigal (Judith Glaser), SATB); Summer Day (piano, voice); 3 Songs for Gabrielle (piano, voice); Pretense (piano, voice); Piano: Sonata No 1; Le 14 Juillet; Fugue in F Minor; Danse Rituelle (2 hands); Chamber works: String Quartet No 1 (2 violins, viola, cello); Divertissement in F (oboe, horn, bassoon); Fugue in F Minor (flute, oboe, clarinet, bassoon); Two Part Inventions (clarinet, bassoon); Five Short Pieces (woodwind or string quartet); Instrumental solo works: Introduction, Berceuse and Rondino (french horn, piano); Sonata for Horn and Piano (in E); Sonatina for Horn and Piano (in F); Introduction, Song and Parody (bassoon, harp); Introduction and Song (cello, harp); Sonatina for Oboe and Piano. *Scores:* Joanna (opera in three acts).

DAVIDSON, HARLEY
See York, Harley C

DAVIDSON, MORRIS (MORREY)   ASCAP 1934
composer, author, singer
b New York, NY, Mar 6, 1899. Educ: High Sch, 2 yrs. Former vpres, Int Artists Corp, as chief booking agent & talent scout, traveled extensively throughout US. Former prog, continuity & publicity dir, Cleveland Radio Sta WJAY. At age 75 produced & sang own album. Chief Collabrs: J Fred Coots, Fats Waller, Benny Davis, Lew Brown. *Songs:* Guess Who?; I Can't Stop Crying; Let's Toast the Bartender; Get 'M in a Rumble Seat; Love Lit Hollow; In New Orleans; Baby Mine; Who Loved You Best; The Sweetest Girl in All the World; If You Ever Learn to Love; Mississippi Holiday; Music: Red Nose; Lyrics: Thrill Me; Just an Ivy Covered Shack.

DAVIDSON, ROBERT
See Burroughs, Bob Lloyd

DAVIDSON, RUSSELL EDWARD (RUSTY DAY)   ASCAP 1970
composer, author, singer
b Detroit, Mich, Feb 1, 46. Educ: Garden City High Sch, band & theory. Started playing drums & singing at age 9. Played in nightclubs in Mich & Calif. Recorded single I Gotta Move. Did TV in Can & Mich. Lead singer for Detroit Wheels, 67, Amboy Dukes, 68, formed Cactus, 69-71. Writer in Fla, 76- Chief Collabrs: James McCarty, Carmine Appice. *Songs:* Lady From South of Detroit; Oleo; Lyrics: Guiltless Glider; 1 Way Or Another; Restrictions.

DAVIES, LEWIS A (LEW)   ASCAP 1958
composer, arranger
b Ashland, Ky, Sept 25, 11; d. Educ: Cincinnati Cons, studied with Tibor Serly. Arr, dance bands, 28-43, also for radio. Chief arr, Command Records. Chief Collabr: Enoch Light. *Songs & Instrumental Works:* Song of Daniel Boone; The Look of Love; Lemon Meringue; Once Over Lightly; Paper Back Ballet Suite; Via Veneto.

DAVIES, WILLIAM HENRY (WILL HENRY)   ASCAP 1955
composer, author, piano teacher
b Philadelphia, Pa, Sept 9, 11. Educ: Temple Univ, BS(educ). Piano & arr, radio stas in Philadelphia & with Jan Savitt & Bobby Byrne. Leader of own dixieland orch. *Songs:* Knock-Knock Who's There? *Instrumental Works:* Barnyard Cakewalk.

DAVIS, ALLAN GERALD   ASCAP 1963
composer, professor
b Watertown, NY, Aug 29, 22. Educ: Syracuse Univ Sch Music, BM, 44, MM, 45; Eastman Sch Music, grad study. Dir, Third Street Music Sch Settlement, 2 yrs. Teacher, Syracuse Univ, Cincinnati Cons Music, New Paltz State Teachers Col, Queens Col, Brooklyn Col & Hunter Col. Mem music fac, Herbert H Lehman Col. Writer, music magazines. Radio lectr, WNYC, New York. *Songs & Instrumental Works:* Razorback Reel for Piano; Festival Concerto for B Flat Clarinet and Small Orchestra; Italian Festival Suite for Brass Choir and Percussion; Psalm of Praise for Chorus, Brass Choir and Percussion; A Song for Daniel for Chorus, Piano, Brass Choir and Percussion; Hometown Suite for Band; Divertimento: Music for an Imaginary Movie of the Thirties for Orchestra; Five Nursery Miniatures for Piano; Sonata Veneziana for Piano; The Married Years for A Cappella Chorus (cycle); Three Songs on Poems by Robert Frost (soprano). *Scores:* Opera/Ballet: The Sailing of the Nancy Belle (comn by Syracuse Univ); The Ordeal of Osbert (comn by NShore Sch Music & Art); The Departure; Death Takes a Holiday (comn by Youngstown State Univ).

DAVIS, BENNY   ASCAP 1921
composer, author
b New York, NY, Aug 21, 1895; d. Educ: Pub schs. Appeared in vaudeville, age 14; toured country with Benny Fields as accompanist to Blossom Seeley. Chief Collabrs: Milton Ager, Harry Akst, Con Conrad, J Fred Coots, Nathaniel Shilkret, Billy Baskette, Arthur Swanstrom, Ted Murry, J Russel Robinson. *Songs:* Goodbye Broadway, Hello France; Margie; Baby Face; There Goes My Heart; Oh How I Miss You Tonight; Yearning; Carolina Moon; Sleepyhead; I Still Get a Thrill; Why; Cross Your Fingers; It's You I Love; Lonesome and Sorry; I'm Nobody's Baby; Chasing Shadows; Sweetheart; With These Hands; Make Believe; Angel Child; Lost a Wonderful Girl; A Smile Will Go a Long Long Way; Copper-Colored Gal; You Started Me Dreaming; To You; When Will the Sun Shine for Me; Patricia; Baby's First Christmas; Don't Break the Heart That Loves You; Say It While Dancing; The Old Mill Wheel; Follow the Boys; This Is My Happiest Moment; There's No Other Girl. *Scores:* Bway stage: Artists and Models of 1927; Sons o' Guns; also Cotton Club revues (3 editions).

DAVIS, BOB   ASCAP 1950
composer, author
b Charleston, Miss, Aug 8, 09; d. Educ: Charleston High Sch. Singer, Beale Street Boys in theatres, films, radio & TV. *Songs:* I Guess I'll Have to Get Along Without You; Ain't Gonna Worry 'Bout a Soul; Could It Be Love?; My Last Rainy Day; You Can Quote Me; Please Take Me; Brother, Treat Your Other Brother Right.

DAVIS, BUSTER   ASCAP 1963
composer, lyricist
b Johnstown, Pa, July 4, 18. Educ: Princeton Univ, BA. Cond/vocal arr for Bway musicals. Adapted Cole Porter songs for Bway musical "Happy New Year." Did special material & underscored many TV shows, incl "Bell Telephone Hour," 5 yrs. Emmy Award, Art Carney Special, 60. Co-comp score for "Movie Movie," 79. *Songs:* Everybody Leaves You; Anywhere the Wind Blows; Love Is. *Songs & Instrumental Works:* But the People Were Nice!; Lions in the Stable. *Scores:* Bway Show: Doctor Jazz.

DAVIS, DAVID H   ASCAP 1957
composer, conductor, orchestrator
b New Orleans, La, Dec 19, 30. Educ: George Peabody Col, Nashville, Tenn, BMus(theory & comp), 54, studied comp with Roy Harris & Philip Slates; Harvard Univ, MA(music), 58, studied comp with Walter Piston & Randall Thompson. Assoc prof music, Univ Va, 56-66, dir, Univ Glee Club, 57-62, chmn, Dept Music, 62-66. Free-lance comp, orchr & cond, film & TV productions, Los Angeles, Calif, 66- Guest lectr in film music techniques, var cols & cities across US. Chief Collabr: Michael B Stillman. *Songs:* Cycles and Changes (soprano & 10 instruments); Music: Seven Poems of Basho (voice & piano); Summer Songs (men's voices & piano); Broken Glass (men's voices & piano). *Instrumental Works:* Quotation (trumpet & piano); String Quartet; Sonata for Trumpet; Three Canzone (mixed quartet); Dialogue (viola, bassoon & chamber orch); Passacaglia and Fugue (brass quintet). *Scores:* Thrillseekers (TV series); Films: Double-Stop; The Real Thing; H O T S.

DAVIS, DON
See Fisher, Marvin

DAVIS, DONALD   ASCAP 1976
composer, author
b Detroit, Mich, Oct 25, 38. *Songs:* Disco Lady; I Believe in You (You Believe in Me); I Came Here to Party; Don't Make Me a Story Teller; I Have Learned to Do Without You; I'm Just a Shoulder to Cry On; It Ain't What You Do (It's

How You Do It); Lyrics: I Like Making You So Happy; It's Party Time; Ocean of Thoughts and Dreams.

DAVIS, EARL B (BILL) ASCAP 1964
composer, author
b DuQuoin, Ill, Jan 29, 30. Educ: DuQuoin High Sch, Ill; studied clarinet & saxophone, Col. Co-produced records; managed talent; composed music. Chief Collabr: Peggy Adams. *Songs:* That's How I Am Without You; Doggone It; Hypnotized; It's Been All Pretense; Another Lonely Night.

DAVIS, FRANK ASCAP 1950
author, singer
b Brooklyn, NY, June 30, 1894; d New York, NY, Oct 9, 70. Educ: Pub schs. Worked for music publ firms. Singer radio, WGY, Schenectady, 6 yrs. Chief Collabrs: Billy Glason, Ed Nelson, Harry Pease, William Tracy, Bix Reichner, Eddie Deane, Robert Godfrey. *Songs:* Lullaby Land; Swanee River Rose; I Wish I Had a Sweetheart; Why Do They Always Say No?; Mama Get the Hammer; If I Had My Life to Live Over.

DAVIS, FREDERICK ASCAP 1961
composer, conductor
b Friendly Islands, South Pacific, Jan 15, 09. Educ: Auckland Univ, New Zealand. To US, 34. Music dir, Salt Lake City Civic Opera Asn, 36. Cond, Mormon Choir of South Calif, Ellis-Orpheus Club & Women's Lyric Club. Guest cond, Hollywood Bowl. Mem, Nat Asn Singing Teachers & Nat Asn Am Comp & Cond. On bd, Calif Fedn Music Clubs. *Songs:* Hear Our Prayer; Choral Arr: To Music; The Fishermaiden; Come, Come, Ye Saints; Contentment.

DAVIS, GENEVIEVE ASCAP 1949
composer, singer, pianist
b Falconer, NY, Dec 11, 1889; d Plainfield, NJ, Dec 3, 50. Educ: Syracuse Univ, studied with Adolph Frey; also studied with Franklin Cannon, Ruth Burham, Arthur Stahlschmidt & Edwin Swain. Soloist, First Presby Church, Irvington-on-Hudson, NY. *Songs:* I Am Joy; Eventide; Love At Dusk; Children of Light; Caprice; The River in Spring; A Maid and the Moon. *Instrumental Works:* The Shepherd and the Echo (piano).

DAVIS, GEORGE COLLIN ASCAP 1943
composer, author
b Chicago, Ill, Aug 22, 1867; d Montclair, NJ, Apr 23, 29. Educ: Pub schs. *Songs:* Yama Yama Man; Feather Your Nest; Worried.

DAVIS, HOUSTON ASCAP 1965
composer, author
b Tahlequah, Okla, Dec 15, 14. Educ: Northeastern Okla State Univ, studied music. Played drums with traveling name bands during Swing Eras of late 30's & 40's. Taught high sch music & band. Wrote campaign songs for Gov Barnett & Gov Paul Johnson, Miss. Elected Justice Court judge, 72. Writer, fiction for nat mag. *Songs:* Go Mississippi (off state song adopted by state legislature, 62); I'm Broke (country); Girls Don't Wear Dresses Anymore (country); Crop Duster (country).

DAVIS, JEAN REYNOLDS ASCAP 1960
composer, author, teacher
b Cumberland, Md, Nov 1, 27. Educ: Upper Darby High Sch; Univ Pa, Sch Fine Arts, BMus; studied comp & orchestration, Robert Elmore, comp, William R Smith & orchestral analysis, Constant Vauclain. Recited & taught, Greater Philadelphia; served as ed consult, Music Publ Holding Corp, New York; publ piano & choral materials, sacred & secular, wrote & publ bks, many articles & poems, texts & stories. Lectr for numerous groups & conventions, Pa, also TV & radio talk shows; verse interpretations of major symph works. Served as judge for poetry & comp competitions, Nat Fedn Music Club. Thornton Medal; Benjamin Franklin Medal; Philadelphia Acad Music Award of Merit; grad cum laude with major in piano performance & comp. Chief Collabr: Cameron McGraw. *Songs:* Music: Wayfaring Stranger (choral arr); Lyrics: Basque Choral Works (Pablo Sorozabal, 16 English texts adapted from original Basque); Carnival of the Animals (Saint Saens, metrically correlated texts); The Comedians (Kabalevsky's, metrically correlated texts); Tunes for Dessert (easy piano); Pet Silhouettes (easy piano). *Instrumental Works:* Doors Into Music (10 vol piano teaching series); Slick Tricks (works for the intermediate pianist); Yankee Doodle Doodles (piano variations); 2nd Movement Gershwin Concert in F (arr for piano) *Scores:* Opera/Ballet: Sleeping Beauty (Tschaikowsky, Six Fairy Variations); Shenandoah Holiday.

DAVIS, JOHN CARLYLE ASCAP 1925
composer, author, choirmaster
b Cincinnati, Ohio, Mar 31, 1878; d Wymoming, Ohio, July 17, 48. Educ: Cincinnati Col of Music (awarded Springer Gold Medal); Harvard Univ. Reporter, Cincinnati Post. Founder & dir, Wyoming Inst of Musical Art. Church organist & choirmaster, Hartwell Presby Church, 04-08, Wyoming Presby Church, 08-15, Avondale Methodist Church, 15-17. Music lectr; inventor, improvements on piano & electric pipe organ. *Songs:* Heart of Nature; Pippa Passes; Hymn to Spring; Through the Leaves; Where Willows Droop; For a Rainy Day. *Instrumental Works:* Violin Concerto; Prairie Song; Sonata in D;

About the World Suite; Three Dances (orch, piano); Zira Dances; Valse Vieux Carre.

DAVIS, JOHN EDWARD, JR ASCAP 1965
composer, author, singer
b Philadelphia, Pa, Aug 31, 52. Educ: Philadelphia Pub Schs; Philadelphia Musical Acad, BMus; pvt study with Joe Stefano & Settlement Music Sch. Began playing clarinet at age 9, then saxophone & other woodwinds. After high sch served in US Naval Acad Band. After col worked in Philadelphia until 74, then produced & arr "Be Thankful for What You Got." Now artist at CBS Records, John Davis/Monster Orch. *Songs:* Ain't That Enough for You; Love Magic; I'm a Superstar. *Instrumental Works:* Bachamania. *Scores:* Bway show: Gottu Go Disco.

DAVIS, JOSEPH M ASCAP 1946
composer, author, publisher
b New York, NY, Oct 6, 1896; d Louisville, Ky, Sept 3, 78. Chief Collabrs: Fats Waller, Andy Razaf, Paul Denniker, John Marks. *Songs:* Nighty Night; I Learned a Lesson I'll Never Forget; The Meetin's Called to Order; Queen Isabella; Riding on the Old Ferris Wheel; Nero; Am I Dreaming?; Miles Apart; Alligator Crawl; Indiana Moonlight; Neglected; Julia; I Was a Fool to Let You Go; Peach Tree Street; Cu Tu Gu Ru; Perhaps, Perhaps, Perhaps; Sunset Serenade; Milkmen's Matinee; Save It, Pretty Mama; A Porter's Love Song; Make Believe Ballroom; S'posin'; Dallas Blues; The Joint is Jumpin'; Little Green Valley; My Blue Ridge Mountain Home; Bend Down Sister; Dream Serenade; Daddy's Little Boy; Manhattan Merry-Go-Round; Casa Loma Stomp; Blue, Turning Grey Over You; Truthfully; Find Out What They Like and How They Like It; Daddy's Little Girl; Basin Street Blues; After You've Gone; Sweethearts on Parade; You Call It Madness; A Good Man Is Hard to Find; Christopher Columbus; Keepin' Out of Mischief Now; In the Hush of the Night; Rosetta; I Would Do Anything for You; Yesterday; I'm Drifting Back to Dreamland; Sweet Hawaiian Moonlight.

DAVIS, KARL ASCAP 1964
composer, singer
b Mt Vernon, Ky, Dec 17, 05; d May 30, 79. Partner in duo of Karl & Harty; with Cumberland Ridgerunners. With radio station WLS, Chicago, 45 yrs; appeared on WLS-radio "National Barn Dance." Singer, WJJD-radio prog, "Supper Time Frolic," Chicago. First country music musician to receive gold mem card from musicians' union. *Songs:* Kentucky (rec'd hon Ky Colonel rank for song by Ky Gov); Country Hall of Fame (ASCAP plaque); Jeanie.

DAVIS, KATHERINE K ASCAP 1941
composer, author, teacher
b St Joseph, Mo, June 25, 1892; d Apr 20, 80. Educ: Wellesley Col; studied with Stuart Mason, Nadia Boulanger. Taught at Wellesley Col & pvt schs in Philadelphia & Concord. Free-lance ed & arr. *Songs & Instrumental Works:* The Burial of a Queen (symph poem); This Is Noel (cantata); Green Hill Book (choral); Carol of the Drum; Sing Gloria; Our God Is a Rock.

DAVIS, LEMUEL A ASCAP 1962
composer, saxophonist, clarinetist
b Tampa, Fla, June 22, 14; d. Educ: Col. Saxophonist, clarinetist in bands incl Eddy Heywood, John Kirby, Buck Clayton & Coleman Hawkins. Chief Collabrs: Jack Palmer, Beatrice Knight, Joe Williams. *Songs:* 'Tain't Me; Some a Dis 'n Some a Dat; Come Spring; Give Jazz, Jazz, Jazz; Let Me Sing My Song.

DAVIS, LOTTIE MCNEILL ASCAP 1969
composer, author
b Dublin, Tex, July 29, 20. Educ: High sch. Songwriter since very young; also has written & publ poetry; won several poetry awards; has been a notary pub & operates rural post office, also country store owner for 16 yrs plus. Chief Collabrs: Charles McNeil, Chaw Mank, Lance Hill. *Songs:* I'll Remember; Lyrics: Playing Hide and Seek With Love; Just Drifting Thru; An Old Flame; Winsome Ways.

DAVIS, LOU ASCAP 1923
author
b New York, NY, May 14, 1881; d New York, Oct 18, 61. Educ: Pub schs. Businessman, wholesale meat bus. Chief Collabrs: Abel Baer, Harold Arlen, Henry Busse, Henry Lange, J Fred Coots. *Songs:* Hot Lips; I'm Sitting Pretty in a Pretty Little City; While We Danced Till Dawn; Put Your Arms Where They Belong; Love Tale of Alsace Lorraine; A Precious Little Thing Called Love; Once Upon a Time; When the World Is At Rest; Moonlight Madness; My Little Dream Boat; Where Are You?

DAVIS, MACK ASCAP 1939
author
b New York, NY, Dec 7, 1898; d New York, Mar 27, 47. Educ: DeWitt Clinton High Sch. Cond own orch. On exec staff, CBS Artist Bureau, MCA. Chief Collabrs: Sammy Stept, Mack David, Don George, Walter Kent. *Songs:* Moon Love; I Never Mention Your Name (Oh No); There's Honey on the Moon Tonight; What Is Love?; An Evening in Paris; Just a Moon Ago; Yesterday's Love; My Songs; Pretty Little Hindu; For Your Love; Nothing Ever Happens to Me; Serenade to Love.

DAVIS, NORMAN
See Lucas, Christopher Norman

DAVIS, PHILIP LINCOLN   ASCAP 1956
composer, author
b Uniontown, Pa, Feb 12, 11. Educ: Uniontown High Sch; Pitt Jr Col, Uniontown; Univ Pa, AB, 32; Columbia Sch Jour, BS, 35. Reporter, Pittsburgh Post-Gazette, 36; continuity ed, WCAE radio, Pittsburgh, 36-55. USA, 42-46. Promotion mgr, WWSW radio, Pittsburgh, 55-73; reporter/columnist, By Line Pittsburgh, 74; staff writer, "Sporting Life" mag, 75; now free lance writer for advert agencies & radio sta. Created slogan for Lawrence Welk's "Champagne Music" while writing announcers' scripts for Welk's broadcasts from Pittsburgh's William Penn Hotel, 38. His cartoon gags have appeared in numerous publ; also created slogan for "A Rhythmic New Deal by Dick Stabile." Chief Collabrs: Joe Lescsak, Anna Lescsak, Bob Merrill, Hank Fort, Lenny Martin, Dick Stutz, Marie Moss Mansfield, Sam Spada, Al Dero, Baron Elliott. *Songs:* No One Could Love You (The Way That I Do); Lyrics: You Did, You Did; I Want Bushels and Bushels of Kisses (But I Just Get a Peck from You); As Long As You're Mine; The New Pittsburgh Polka; Henry's Polka; The Hurdy Gurdy Polka; Polka Pete; Polka Lilly; The Okle Dokle Polka; Make Yourself at Home at My Home; A Pebble in a Pool; Forbidden Fruit; I Didn't Know You Cared; Nothing's the Same Without You.

DAVIS, RAY DEAN   ASCAP 1979
composer, author, singer
b Mountain Home, Ark, Apr 29, 49. Educ: Cotter High Sch. Worked in nightclubs; played live music on radio broadcasts; drummer & singer on several tours in US; worked as drummer for recording artists; solo singer & guitarist. *Songs:* On My Own; Back to Texas; 'Til You Smile; I Won't Need You Then; Ol' Man Blues.

DAVIS, RICHARD   ASCAP 1969
composer, author, teacher
b Chicago, Ill, Apr 15, 30. Educ: DuSable High Sch; VanderCook Col Music, Ill; pvt instr with Rudolf Fahsbender, 10 yrs; Chicago Civic Orch, 4 yrs. USSR tour with Thad Jones/Mel Lewis Band, 72. Played under batons of Igor Stravinsky, Leonard Bernstein & Gunther Schuler. Performed with most maj New York TV studio orchs. Author, "Walking on Chords for String Bass and Tuba." *Albums:* Dealin'; Epistrophy and Now's the Time; With Understanding; Astral Weeks.

DAVIS, ROQUEL (BILLY)   ASCAP 1969
composer, author, producer
b Detroit, Mich, July 11, 42. Educ: Northern High Sch, Detroit, Mich; Wayne Univ; Maurice King Sch Music, Detroit. Mem of Four Tops group, 60; A&R dir, Chess Records, 61; wrote & produced with Barry Gordy of Motown; music dir, McCann Erickson Advert, 68, sr vpres & dir, Sound Waves Dept, 80- Chief Collabrs: Roger Cook, Roger Greenaway, Robert Gordy. *Songs:* Lonely Teardrops; Rescue Me; You've Got What It Takes.

DAVIS, RUSTY
See Cheeseman, James Russell

DAVIS, SHARON
See Schmidt, Sharon Yvonne Davis

DAVIS, SHEILA   ASCAP 1959
composer, author, lyric writing instructor
b New York, NY, Aug 6, 27. Educ: Dominican Acad, New York; Marymount Col, jr col dipl; Dalcroze Music Sch. Chief Collabrs: Laurindo Almeida, Roberto Carlos, Michael Leonard. *Songs:* Changing, Changing; Let Love Come Slowly; Time to Let Me Go; What Do I Need?; Who'll Sing My Song?; Have a Good Day; Lyrics: Who Will Answer?; I'm Not There; Living Together; Going to Bethel; Never Let Go of Your Dream; Try a Little Music; Last Summer; A Walk in the Spring Rain; 80-90-100 Miles an Hour; Keep Cool; Don't Love Me (Unless It's Forevermore). *Instrumental Works:* Cool Cats Keep Coats On.

DAVIS, THOMAS L   ASCAP 1965
composer, author, educator
b Casper, Wyo, Apr 21, 31. Educ: Northwestern Univ, Evanston, BME, 57, MM, 58; studied perc with Edward Metzinger. Auxiliary mem, Chicago Symph Orch; mem, Dick Schory's Perc Pops Orch. Free-lance perc & studio percussionist. Col teacher of jazz & perc. Perc/jazz clinician, Ludwig & Slingerland Drum Cos. Chief Collabrs: Dick Schory, Bobby Christian. *Instrumental Works:* Oriental Mambo; Two-for-Six; Snares, Traps and Other Hunting Devices; Bossanovacaine; Waltz for Swingers; Flat Baroque; Mau-Mau Suite; Practical Analysis of Independence (method bk); Recital for Vibraharp (method bk); Improvise Vibe-wise! (method bk); Cloud Nine; Fughetta Rock; Parallels for Brass and Percussion; Requiem and Ritual for Brass and Percussion; El Races De La Campground; Greensleeves; A Taste of Brahms: Panda Pause; Fancy That!.

DAVISON, LESLEY
See Perrin, Lesley Davison

DAVISON, LITA (SERENA SHAW, SERENA DE SAXE)   ASCAP 1958
composer, author, singer
b New York, NY, Apr 17, 27. Educ: Theodore Roosevelt High Sch, Los Angeles, Calif; Los Angeles City Col, maj in theatre & music; Univ Calif, Los Angeles; Hunter Col, NY, BA cum laude, MA(educ); studied voice with Nina Koshetz, Hollywood & Hugo Strelitzer, Los Angeles. Appeared prof as singer & recording artist; worked in film studios, choral groups, dubbing & Roger Wagner Chorale; appeared in nightclubs & concerts in Los Angeles & San Francisco & western states; appeared in New York exclusive supper clubs. Chief Collabrs: Rudy de Saxe, William Fox, Mamoru Takahara, David Martin. *Songs:* Music: Hey, Jack Daniel; Let Me Fly in Your Arms; Lyrics: Standing Together; Angela; What's Love; Kiss Me; Solitary Blues; You're No Good For Me.

DAVISON, SID I (DAVE DIAMOND)   ASCAP 1963
composer, author, singer
b Howard, SDak, Aug 7, 41. Educ: Univ Southern Miss, BS(jour), 62; Univ Calif, Los Angeles, MFA(Eng), 68. Broadcast & wrote; performed on KHJ, KFWB & KFI radio, Los Angeles, also KFRC, San Francisco, WIL, St Louis & MBTR, Denver. Did short stories "Street Scenes" & "Panic Blues." Own Black Hills Music, 67- Co-publ "Incense and Peppermints" also "Acapulco Gold"; records for Claridge Records. *Songs:* Heat of a Kansas Night; Diesel Drivin' Daddy; Hobo John; I Play Country Music; The Club Bayou; Life's Like a Canvas; The Great Depression.

DAWSON, ELI
See Marks, Elias J

DAWSON, HAROLD ALLEN   ASCAP 1978
composer, author
b Lima, Ohio, Sept 20, 50. Performer in nightclubs, radio & TV, Honolulu, Hawaii, 71-73 & Columbus, Ohio, 73- Recording artist; co-owner & mgr, Boxer Studios, Columbus, 78- Chief Collabrs: Richard Deitch, Aggie Kessel. *Songs:* Run From Love; Imagination; Love Surreal.

DAY, JAMES K   ASCAP 1961
author, publisher, producer
b Columbus, Ind, May 17, 17. Educ: Univ Ky; Univ Calif, Los Angeles. Lyricist, publ, record producer & artist mgr. Chief Collabrs: George Arellano, Hal Perrin, Terry Gordon, Zedric Turnbaugh, Scarlett Gray. *Songs:* Lyrics: Billy Goat Hill; Everroad Brothers; Georgie; Anything Will Do; Del Rio; Eldorado; Touch of the Blues; Ride With the Devil; Like It Stands; Our Stairway to the Stars; As Long As You Care; Ola Linda Chi Chi; Sensations; Winter in Your Arms; A Whisper in the Wind.

DAY, RALPH WILLIAM   ASCAP 1961
composer, author, violinist
b Waitsberg, Wash, Sept 28, 1895. Educ: Studied voice with mother; Twin Falls Cons Music, Idaho, studied violin with Pauline Alphonte. Served in WW I, 2 yrs. Sang between acts in Ed Redmond Stage Shows; had own orch, southern Idaho, 09-17. Started bean & grain elevator bus, 22. Violinist until 35, had prog on KTFI radio sta, 28; comp & song writer, 57- Chief Collabr: Ted Silva (deceased). *Songs:* The Things I've Left Undone; We Need Thee Now; Let God Tune Your Heart Strings; When Jesus Walks With Me; I Think of Home Beyond the Sunset.

DAY, RUSTY
See Davidson, Russell Edward

DAY, STANLEY A   ASCAP 1950
composer, conductor, organist
b Melbourne, Australia, Dec 20, 1894; d Point Pleasant, NJ, Sept 10, 75. Educ: Trinity Col, London; NY Col of Music; Columbia Univ; studied with Seth Bingham, Douglas Moore & Tertius Noble. Church organist & dir, Presby Labor Temple, NY, 20-35, First Methodist, Mt Vernon, 32-58, Elmsford Reformed, NY, 60-75. Dir music, Professional Children's Sch, NY, 34-50.

DAYTON, CRAIG   ASCAP 1977
composer, author, arranger
b Myrtle Point, Ore. Educ: Pvt instr in writing with Fred Kepner, USAF. Chief comp & arr, Bill Dayton's big band; comp & arr, Sammy Kaye Orch; free lance comp & arr for several bands & nightclub entertainers, also for music bus & jingle producers; copyist. *Songs:* Killer Bee; When I Offer You My Hand; Guess It Looks Like Spring, Again; I Remember. *Instrumental Works:* Soft Voices; Joy.

DEACON, MARY CONNER   ASCAP 1954
composer, teacher
b Johnson City, Tenn, Feb 22, 07. Educ: Studied piano with Ella Matthews, 10 yrs; Va Intermont Col, studied with Samual Schroetter; ETenn State Univ, studied harmony & theory; accompanying with Frank Laforge & Stuart Ross, New York, song comp with Carl Deis, New York. Teacher piano & pub sch music, high schs, Tenn, 27-29. Prof accompanist, concerts for singers & radio stas WOR & NBC, New York, 29-36. Affil, Royal Cons Music Toronto, Ont;

teacher piano, Belleville, Ont, 36. Wrote songs & choral works, 43. Chief Collabrs: Lyrics, Elfrida Norden, Carl Deis, Marcel G Frank. *Songs:* I Will Lift Up Mine Eyes; Besides Still Waters; Your Cross; Whistle While You Whittle; Little Holy Jesus; The Call of the Sea; Ocean Lore; Follow the Road; Hear My Prayer; Awake Men; You; A Child Asleep; A New Day; Behold! Spring; Eternal Life.

DEAN, DEAREST
See Glosup, Lorene St Clare

DEAN, LORENE
See Glosup, Lorene St Clare

DEAN, PETER   ASCAP 1977
composer, author, singer
b Philadelphia, Pa, Feb 9, 11. Educ: George Washington High Sch; Savage Sch Physical Educ; NY Univ. In professional baseball, 2 yrs; personal mgr, Paul Whiteman & Johnny Nash; worked with Dinah Shore & Peggy Lee; formed Peter Dean Assocs with Budd Weed; singer & comp, 72- Chief Collabr: Cherry Robins. *Songs:* Baby, Baby, Baby; Help That Man; Music: Only Time Will Tell; Lyrics: Fun City Blues.

DEAN, ROBERT G, JR
composer, author, musician
b Marion, NC, Nov 22, 39. Educ: Played music since early childhood; Mannheim Music Cons, Ger. Producer, performer, singer. USA Spec Serv Music, 57-59, mem of Spec Serv Reserve, 59-63. Performed in Beirut, Lebanon, 58, also with Wagner Music Fest, Bayreuth, Ger & Bayreuth Symph, 59. Pvt music instr, Atlanta, Ga, 60-65. Cond music clins in several southeastern univs & cols. Recorded for numerous TV commercials, Miami, Fla & Atlanta, 65-67; toured the US with numerous appearances in Las Vegas & Los Angeles. Asst band dir, Pace Mil Acad, Atlanta & Emory Univ; pioneered prog in music therapy for spastic children at Emory Univ. Mem: Nashville Songwriters Asn; Int Songwriters Asn; Nat Acad Recording Arts & Sci (nat electoral bd); Country Music Asn; Am Fedn Musicians; SESAC; Am Rifle Asn; Jewish Relief Fund; Pete Fountain's Half Fast Walking Club (8 yr participant at Mardi Gras, New Orleans). Recipient of 12 comp awards, ASCAP; Expert Rifleman Award, USA, 59. *Songs:* I Want to Hold You in My Dreams Tonight; It's not Funny Anymore; Paper Planes; Adious Amegio Goodbye; Truck Driving Mother; When the Fire Went Out Last Night; Ode to Olivia; You Kiss the Fire Out of Me; Don't Do It Again; You've Crossed My Mind.

DEANE, DOROTHY
See Catchapaw, Dorothy Deane Johnson

DEANE, EDDIE V   ASCAP 1956
composer, author, singer
b New York, NY, Feb 14, 29. Educ: Music Sch Settlement. Singer, actor & writer TV & radio; niteclub comedian. Gen mgr, United Artists, Big Three & RCA Music Publ Cos. Produced Stephanie Mills first album. Taught popular songwriting classes, Am Guild of Authors & Composers, served on var comts. Founded own publ firm, 58. Wrote lyrics for movie "The Wild Eye." Chief Collabrs: Sunny Skylar, Woody Harris, Ben Weisman, Gloria Shayne. *Songs:* Rockabilly; Princess; Hootenanny; A Little Dog Cried; Ne Ne Na Na Na Na Nu Nu; Flip Top Box; Third Finger Left Hand; Small Sad Sam; Lyrics: When Two Lovers Come Together; When You Look in Her Eyes; The Men in My Little Girls Life; Hungry Eyes.

DEANGELIS, PETER   ASCAP 1953
composer, author
b Philadelphia, Pa, June 18, 29. Producer, ABC-Paramount Records, 65- Chief Collabrs: Jean Sawyer, Bob Marcucci. *Songs:* Painted, Tainted Rose; With All My Heart; You You You; I Believe in You; Why; Music: Just Yesterday; Living a Lie; I'm Living My Heaven With You; My Cherie; Got to Live It Up to Live You Down; You No One But You; Always Together; Two People; Christmas Isn't Christmas Without You; Let Me Into Your Life. *Instrumental Works:* Alpha Centuri. *Scores:* Film/TV: Elbo Elf (musical).

DEASON, WILLIAM DAVID   ASCAP 1977
composer, teacher
b Sioux Falls, SDak, May 24, 45. Educ: Began piano study with mother; Fla State Univ, 67, MMus, 68; pvt conducting study with Richard Burgin, pvt comp study with Lester Trimble. Teacher, Caldwell Col, NJ. Awards: 2 ASCAP Standard Awards; Meet-the-Composer Grant. *Instrumental Works:* Wind Tunnels (brass trio); Doubletake (alto saxophone, trumpet); Six Inventions (woodwind quintet); Paper Webs (voice, clarinet, piano); Entropy (woodwind trio); Concert Piece (organ).

DEBENEDICTIS, RICHARD
composer
b New Milford, NJ, Jan 23, 37. Educ: Ithaca Col, BFA; Manhattan Sch Music. Rehearsal pianist for TV Carol Burnett specials; dance music for TV "Barry Moore Show", "Bell Telephone Hour", "Ed Sullivan Show" & "Kraft Music Hall", also many others; dance music for Bway, "Fade Out, Fade In", "Do I Hear a Waltz", "Showboat" & "Annie Get Your Gun"; music dir for TV, Bing Crosby, Liza Minelli & Lily Tomlin specials; asst music dir, Barbra Streisand special; special music material for "Carol Burnett Show", John Denver, Diana Ross & Mitzi Gaynor specials. Comp, "Columbo", "McCoy", "McCloud", "Quincy", "Born Free", "Hawaii Five-O", "Murder By Natural Causes", "The Greatest Gift", "Barbra Streisand and Other Musical Instruments" (Emmy Citation, 73), Emmy nominations for "Police Story," 77, "Ziegfeld the Man and His Women," 78 & "Dear Detective," 79. Chief Collabrs: Bill Dyer, Herb Martin, Woody Kling, David Rogers.

DE BRANT, CYR
See Higginson, Joseph Vincent

DE CIMBER, JOSEPH VALENTINO   ASCAP 1956
composer, author, pianist
b Clinton, Iowa, Oct 5, 1898. Educ: Pvt music study; high sch & col. Pianist on radio, own band & vocal quartet. Chief Collabrs: Ted Lewis, Ted Fiorito, Jack Eigen, Al Trace, Enrico Caruso Jr, Frank Magine, Charley Straight, John R Meyer, Freddie S Fischer, Capt Stannard, Dave Pritchard, Lester Melrose, Chuck Foster, Bill Curril. *Songs:* Was You Ever in Cincinnati (polka); Music: Spirit of 98 (off United Spanish War Vet); Gold Star Mother Hymn; Fly to Tokyo (All Expenses Paid); Props and Wings; Toast to Marquette; Yes Dear; Schatzie; Wailin' Blues; Haven of Peace; Good Feelin' Blues; National High School March; God Keep America (hymn); Between You and Me and the Lamp Post; Senorito Polka; How Can My Heart Forget You; I Wish I Was Back in Milwaukee; Jingling Tunes; Send Me a Bit of Home for Christmas; Herman, Take Me Home; Love Came Down From Heaven; Open Country (western pastoral).

DE COLA, FELIX   ASCAP 1957
composer, author, entertainer
b Cape Town, SAfrica, Dec 17, 06. Educ: Studied piano as a child in Ger, Eng & SAfrica. Began career as song plugger in SAfrican music stores; established piano sch & mail order piano lessons in SAfrica & later in US. Performed in nightclubs, mainly as duo-piano team; gave piano lessons to many Hollywood celebrities incl Shirley Temple, Harpo Marx, Jimmy McHugh & others. Invented music syst for blind, "Easy Chord" a mechanical chord player; made many "Romantic Piano" albums; radio host, KLAC late night shows; performed on music assembly tours. Musical dir on SS Rotterdam Round the World Cruise & other cruise ships; formed non-profit Audio/Visual Music Found; wrote, produced & hosted 16 musical shows for Los Angeles Bd Educ; also creator of musical TV shows. *Songs & Instrumental Works:* Romance in Vienna; bk of duets for piano and organ; Collections of SAfrican Folk Songs.

DE COLLIBUS, NICHOLAS (DON NICHOLAS)   ASCAP 1955
composer, conductor, violinist
b Philadelphia, Pa, Apr 10, 13. Educ: Philadelphia Musical Acad, studied with Leopold Auer, Otto Meyer; Curtis Inst, studied with Albert Meiff; Univ Pa, studied with Harl McDonald, Emil Fogelmann. Taught, pub schs. Cond, ballet, musicals, radio & TV. Violinist, hotels in US & Europe; in concert. Music dir, Meyer Davis Music. Chief Collabrs: Peter De Angelis, Bob Marcucci. *Songs:* All I Ask of You; Guitar Mambo; I'll Smile.

DE CORMIER, ROBERT   ASCAP 1958
composer, conductor, arranger
b Pinelawn, NY, Jan 1, 22. Educ: Juilliard Sch. Taught, Little Red Schoolhouse, 6 yrs. Cond & arr with Harry Belafonte; founder, Robert De Cormier Singers; made many records. Arr, Bway musicals incl "The Happiest Girl in the World" & "110 in the Shade." *Songs & Instrumental Works:* Walking Together Children; The Jolly Beggars (cantata).

DE COSMO, EMILE   ASCAP 1966
composer, author, performer
b Foggia, Italy, Nov 27, 24. Educ: Brooklyn Cons Music, perf degree, 50; Jersey City State Col, BA(music educ), 74, MA(music educ), 77. Music dept fac mem, Jersey City State Col & also Ft Lee High Sch; musician, teacher, clinician, adjudicator & publ. Cond jazz workshops at var cols throughout US. Prof musician doing recordings, club dates, TV commercials & movie soundtracks. Author & publ: "The Polytonal Rhythm Series," 19 bks incl "The Cycle of Fifths", "The 11-7th V-7th Progression", "The Blues Scales", "The Diatonic Cycle" & "The Polytonal Guitar."

DECOSTA, HARRY   ASCAP 1925
composer, author, pianist
b New York, NY, June 25, 1885; d Hollywood, Calif, June 23, 64. Pianist for music publishers; accompanist to Jones & Hare; also wrote spec material for vaudeville; radio script writer & comp. *Songs:* Tiger Rag; Little Gray Mother; Ragamuffin Romeo; That Soothing Serenade; Slappin' the Bass; Mary Dear; Love Me a Little Little; My Mammy Knows; Love Made a Gypsy Out of Me.

DECOU, HAROLD H   ASCAP 1979
composer, author, arranger
b Philadelphia, Pa, Oct 7, 32. Educ: Collingswood High Sch, NY; Temple Univ. Comp & arr for sacred music publ, 55- Organist & pianist in sacred music concerts. *Songs & Instrumental Works:* A Night to Remember (Christmas musical for choir & orch); Spread the News! (choral compilation); Harold DeCou Organ Solos; Harold DeCou Piano Solos.

DECOU, PATRICIA R
composer, author, singer

b Aurora, Nebr, July 23, 45. Educ: Pembroke Col, Brown Univ, AB; Boston Univ Sch Law, 1 1/2 yrs. Began songwriting, 75, publ, 77. album of original material, Rainbow Snake Records, 79. Performer at major anti-nuclear rallies, Seabrook, 76-79, Shoreham, NY, 79 & Washington, DC, 79-80. Singer with duo, Pat and Tex & folk-band, Bright Morning Star. Has written songs for film, "The Last Resort" & TV documentary, "Seabrook, 1977." Chief Collab: Tex LaMountain. *Songs:* Seabrook Song; Karen Silkwood; Mama; Cowboys and Indians; Vermont Landscape; Crossroads; Lyrics: No Nukes (Hangin' Tree); Ten Below Zero.

DECRESCENZO, VINCENZO   ASCAP 1914
composer, conductor, pianist

b Naples, Italy, Feb 18, 1875; d New York, NY, Oct 13, 64. Educ: Music Cons, Naples, Palermo & Sicily; studied with Zuelli, Benjamin Cesi. To US 03. Accompanist to Caruso, Gigli, Schipa, De Luca, Galli Curci & Albanese. Cond concert orchs. *Songs:* Guardanno a Luna; Uocchie Celeste!; Tarantella Sincera; Quanno 'a Femmena Vo; Rondine Al Nido; Triste Maggio; Notte d'Amore; Canto di Primavera; Ce Steva'na Vota; Candon le Foglie.

DE DENISE, FRED   ASCAP 1967
composer, singer, drummer

b New York, NY, Apr 18, 12. Educ: Lafayette High Sch, Brooklyn, NY; studied voice with John Martinelli; music & drum lessons with Ernesto Marrero. Drummer with Xavier Cugat & His Orch. Sang for USO Camp Shows, Armed Forces of US in Southwest Pacific, 44 & 45. Mem, Local 802 AM of Greater New York, Am Fedn Musicians. Orch leader. Chief Collabrs: Russell Dunn, Pat C Strangis. *Songs & Instrumental Works:* These Are the Things We Share; I'm Yours Forever; My Life Has Overflowed With Sorrow; Cha Cha Fiesta; Slow and Easy Tra-La-La (band arr).

DEE, SYLVIA (JOSEPHINE PROFFITT FAISON)   ASCAP 1943
author, lyricist

b Little Rock, Ark, Oct 22, 14; d New York, NY, June 12, 67. Educ: Univ Mich. Advert copywriter, newspaper, Rochester, NY. Author, "And Never Been Kissed" & "Dear Guest and Ghost", also short stories. Chief Collabrs: Sidney Lippman, Arthur Kent, Elizabeth Evelyn Moore (mother), George Goehring, Al Frisch, Guy Wood. *Songs:* Chickery Chick; It Couldn't Be True; Stardreams; I'm Thrilled; Have You Changed; My Sugar Is So Refined; After Graduation Day; Laroo Laroo Lili Bolero; Angel Lips, Angel Eyes; Pushcart Serenade; Too Young (Michael TV Radio Award); A House With Love in It; Moonlight Swim; That's the Chance You Take; Somebody Nobody Wants; The End of the World; Please Don't Talk to the Lifeguard. *Scores:* Bway Stage: Barefoot Boy With Cheek.

DE FILIPPI, AMEDEO   ASCAP 1952
composer, pianist, conductor

b Ariano, Italy, Feb 20, 00. Educ: New York Pub Schs, 06-13; Juilliard Grad Sch Music, 26-29; studied violin with Arthur Lichenstein, piano with Stanley Haschek, comp with Rubin Goldmark. Has been comp, arr & orchestrator, Pathe Films, Judson Radio Program Co, Victor Phonograph Co & var theatres & publ. Mem staff, CBS, 30- Has orchestrated ballets for Ballet Russe & Ballet Theatre. *Songs & Instrumental Works:* Concerto for Orchestra; Twelfth Night Overture; Medieval Court Dances; Five Arabian Songs (voice & orch); Diversions; Serenade; Music for Recreation; Provencal Airs; String Quartet; Piano Quintet; Sonata for Viola and Piano (award, Contemporary Am Music Fest, Princeton, 36); Suite for Brass Quartet; Piano Sonata; Six Sonatinas for Piano; Prelude, Passacaglia and Toccata; Partita for Piano; Two Sonnets (voice & orch); Five Medieval Norman Songs (voice & orch); Three Poems (Thoreau, a cappella); Three Poems (Whitman, men's voices & brass instruments); Children of Adam (cantata); Orchestrations: Les Sylphides (Chopin); Carnaval (Schumann); Jardins aux Lilas (Chausson); Trans: Prelude and Fugue in A Minor (Bach); La Campanella (Paganini-Liszt); Suite From the Harpsichord Works (Rameau); Four Pieces (Scarlatti); Wachet Auf (chorale prelude, Bach); Concerto for Flute (Pergolesi); Reverie (Debussy); The Nursery (song cycle, Moussorgsky); The Musician's Peep Show (Moussorgsky); Sunless (song cycle, Moussorgsky).

DEFOOR, JOHN W   ASCAP 1959
composer, arranger

b Huntington, WVa, Oct 10, 29. Educ: Westlake Sch Music, Hollywood, Calif; Cincinnati Cons. Trumpeter in USAF dance bands, New Rochelle, NY & DC, 48-52. Toured in dance bands; became arr, 57. *Songs:* Meet Rey.

DE FOREST, CHARLES   ASCAP 1959
composer, author, singer

b Genoa, NY, Apr 4, 28. Educ: Business Col. Newspaper writer. Singer-pianist, nightclubs, TV, records. Sang on film track for "City By Dawn." Sang on Benny Goodman Jazz Tours, USA. *Songs:* What's Happened to Spring?; Yesterday's Child; You Look Like Someone; If There's Someone Who'll Love You More Than I Do; When Do the Bells Ring for Me?; If You Think I'm a Lover, You're a Loser; Look At Me; He's Coming Home; Don't Wait Up for Me; Heart of Winter; It Was Love, Wasn't It?; Wait for Me; End of the Line; Is There Anyone Here?; Where Do You Go From Love? *Scores:* Film: City By Dawn.

DE FRANCESCO, LOUIS E   ASCAP 1930
composer, conductor

b Atessa, Italy, Dec 26, 1888; d Northridge, Calif, Oct 5, 74. Educ: Cons of Naples, dipl of Maestro. Toured US as cond of light operas. Music dir for film studio; comp & arr. Comp & cond, "March of Time", "Magic Carpets" & "Movie-Tone." *Songs:* Cavalcade; Ah, Love, But a Day; The White Parade; Should She Forget Me Not; Heart, My Heart; The Sun Shines Brighter; Daddy. *Scores:* Films: Cavalcade; George White's Scandals; Six Hours to Live; The Power and the Glory; Berkeley Square; State Fair.

DE FRANCO, BONIFACE (BUDDY FERDINAND)
composer, musician, clarinetist

b Camden, NJ, Feb 17, 23. Educ: Pvt clarinet & saxophone lessons; harmony & theory at Mastbaum Sch, Philadelphia, Pa. Began playing clarinet at age 9; won Tommy Dorsey Swing Contest at age 14; began road career at age 15. Numerous concerts & recording appearances; also appeared on "Steve Allen Show", "The Mike Douglas Show" & "Johnny Carson's Tonight Show." Has done countless clinics: Tri-State Fest, Stan Kenton Clinics, NTex State Teachers Col; clinician & soloist, NORAD Band & Air Men of Note. Clinics & concerts, Oral Roberts Univ. Featured soloist with jazz orch on 5 week tour, also featured soloist on "The Stars of Jazz" TV show. Joined Gene Krupa, 41, Ted FioRito & Charlie Barnet, 42-43, Tommy Dorsey, 44-45 & 47-48, Boyd Raeburn, 46 & Count Basie Septet, 50. Recorded for Capital & MGM. Concerts appearances incl: Carnegie Hall, Hollywood Bowl, Europ tours, Far East, Australia, New Zealand & Miller Orch, 66-74. Resumed jazz career, 74- *Songs:* Burut Water; If You Cared; Strings Have Sprung; Really Swell; Renfrew's Caper; Warm Evening; Danse Du Mitchell; Playing It Cool; Bus Driver in the Sky; The Monkey; Clarinet Studies; Lunar Lunacy; Blues Rag; Charlie Cat; I Love You; Easy; Our Street; Blue Poly; Count Downing; Sweet Baby; Double Trouble; Otono; Young Man of Osaka; Threat of Freedom (suite for jazz group); Ten jazz Etudes for Clarinet and Guitar; Playa Del Sol; Melancholy Stockholm; Exaggeration.

DEGASTYNE, SERGE   ASCAP 1957
composer, author

b Paris, France, July 27, 30. Educ: Univ Portland, BA; Eastman Sch Music, studies with Howard Hanson; Univ Md, MM & DMA. Composer-in-residence, USAF Symph & Band, 53-72; prof music, Northern Va Community Col, 72-; author & publ, The DeGastyne Papers, 80- *Songs:* Music: The Sleeper of the Valley; May My Heart; The Last Words; Tres Morillas; 110 songs in Eng, French, Swed, Russian, Latin, Japanese & Span. *Instrumental Works:* Symphony No 2 (L'Ile Lumiere); Symphony No 4 (band); Symphony No 5 (orch); Symphony No 6 (orch); Three Elegies to Hungary (voice & orch; Am-Hungarian Fedn Prize); String Quartet; Partita Americana (organ).

DE GRAFF, ROBERT   ASCAP 1964
author

b Stettler, Alta, Aug 15, 09. Educ: Pub sch. Hotel bellhop. Chief Collabrs: Richard Bearse, J W Stephenson.

DEGRAFFENREID, GEORGE MERL   ASCAP 1979
composer, author, conductor

b Salina, Kans, June 23, 46. Educ: George Washington High Sch, Denver, Colo; Univ Colo, BMEd, 72; studied arr & theory with Cecil Effinger & Wayne Scott; studied film comp with Pat Williams. Band dir, Jefferson County Schs, 6 yrs; now music dir, Faith Bible Chapel, Arvada, Colo; founder, dir & arr, International Singers; performer & arr, concerts, records, TV & radio commercials. Singer & instrumentalist. *Songs:* Soldier's Lament; Bright Promise; Music: The Wailing Wall.

DEGRAW, JIMMY DWAINE (JIMMY LAWTON)   ASCAP 1972
composer, author, singer

b Taloga, Okla, June 10, 36. Educ: Dickens High Sch, Tex; Pierce Jr Col, Wynettka, Calif; studied comp, theory & harmony with var teachers for 3 yrs. Singer/bandleader, Las Vegas' Golden Nugget & Riviera Hotel, nightclubs & TV; now recording artist & producer, Polydor Records, Hilversum, Holland. Chief Collabrs: Simon T Stokes, Bobbejaan Schoepen, Jack De Nijs. *Songs:* Oklahoma Square; Fire and Blisters; I'm Country; Lonely Blue Boy.

DEITZ, GERALD (JERRY)   ASCAP 1967
author, singer

b Rochester, NY, Dec 26, 03. Educ: Pub schs, Hornell & Alden, NY; Benjamin Franklin High Sch, Rochester. Lyricist-spec material writer. Insurance agent, John Hancock Mutual Life Insurance, 41-69. Salesman, Sundry Merchandise. Social dir, Catskill Mountains. Wrote for Ben Yost Groups, Mac Perrin, Phil Baker & others; jingles for clothiers-furniture stores in 30's; articles for Comedy World-Trade Mag; wrote for Bway, Beckman & Pransky's, Bagels & Yocks & Bert Ross, 52. Chief Collabrs: Stanley Applebaum, Mischa & Wesley Portnoff, Lillian Anne Miller, Marshall Moss, Stan Frits, Murray Rumsey, Hayward Morris. *Songs:* Lyrics: I Take Thee; Two Wonderful Hands; An American's Heritage; A Bouquet of Lillies and Tears; The George Washington Carver Cantata.

DE JESUS, LOUIS A (LUCHI)
composer, arranger

b New York, NY, Aug 19, 23. Educ: Dalcroze Sch Music; Am Theatre Wing; High Sch of Music & Art. Performed as instrumentalist, arr-cond with own act throughout Europe & Middle East, 3 yrs; A&R dir, Mercury Records, 3 1/2 yrs. Comp, TV & films; also accompanist. Cond symph orch. Record producer & arr. Chief Collabrs: Paul France Webster, Arthur Hamilton, Rich Marlo. *Scores:* TV: Gunsmoke; Ironside; That Girl; McMillan and Wife; Six Million Dollar Man; Bionic Woman; Mannix; Chase.

DE JONG, CONRAD JOHN
ASCAP 1969
composer

b Hull, Iowa, Jan 13, 34. Educ: North Tex State Univ, BM(with honors), 54; Ind Univ, MM, 59, with Bernhard Heiden; with Ton de Leeuw, Amsterdam Cons, 69. Prof of music, Univ Wis, 59- Participating comp, Bennington Comp Conference, Vt, 65. Summer studies, Univ of Mich & Univ of Denver, 68, also studies in Montreux, Switz, 74. Guest rehearsal cond, Civic Orch of Minneapolis, 71; guest comp, Fine Arts Ctr, Univ of Minn, 75. Mem: Am Soc Univ Comp; League of Comp, Int Soc for Contemporary Music; Col Music Soc; Nat Asn of Col Wind & Perc Instrs (state chmn, 69-72); Phi Mu Alpha Sinfonia, Nat Music Fraternity; Pi Kappa Lambda, Nat Hon Music Fraternity; Wis Contemporary Music Forum; Nat Asn of Comp; Minn Comp Forum. Awards: 6 ASCAP Awards, 70-75. *Songs & Instrumental Works:* Chamber Music: Three Studies (brass septet); Music for Two Tubas; Suite of Wisconsin Folk Music (brass trio); String Trio (First prize, Wis Comp Contest); Fun and Games (woodwind, brass, string instruments, piano); Little Suite (piano solo); Three Pieces for 3 Trumpets and Piano; Aanraking (Contact; solo trombone); Hist Whist (voice, flute, viola, perc); Grab Bag (tuba ens, Comn by Tenn Technol Univ); Etenraku (The Upper Cloud Music; carillon, piano); Four Songs (voice, piano); Resound (Comn by Adele Zeitlin & Jeffrey Van; flute, guitar, perc, tape delay syst, 35 mm slide); Song and Light (voice, multiple tuned perc); Heliotrope (Pop Song; instruments or voices, keyboard, electric bass, perc); Elm Street Dance Company Capers (tape, dance); Quarter Break Bit (an activity); Kaleidoscopic Vision (With Flashbacks; tape, synchronized swimmers); Andante and Allegro (trumpet, piano); Three Studies for Piano; Prelude and Fugue for Brass Trio (trumpet, horn, trombone); Jabberwocky (SATB; chorus unaccompanied); Unicycle (harpsichord or piano); Three Studies for Brass Septet (3 trumpets, 3 trombones, tuba); Essay for Brass Quintet; String Trio (violin, viola, cello); Thou, Trumpet (Shakespeare; baritone voice, trumpet, piano); Looking Forward (voice, piano); A Kingdom of Bells (voice, piano); Diary Before a Concert; Strange Formations (voice, piano); Spoon (voice, piano); 6 Bits for Horns and Trombones; The Silence of the Sky in My Eyes (Versions 1 & 2; 1/2 track stereo tape, large group of musicians, light, optional dance, audience particiapation); TV Time Capsule (1/2 track stereo tape); Ring! My Chimes (chimes, 1/2 track stereo tape, slides); Piano Piece for William Abbott (2 performers); December, 1962 (mixed chorus, performer); Soprano and Piano: Infant Innocence; Morning At the Window; A Minor Bird; Risque Reflections; News Item. Transc: Mit Fried Und Freud Ich Fahr Dahin (Bach Chorales No 325 & No 49; brass quintet); From the Diary of a Fly (Bartok-Microcosmos No 142); Trumpet Quartet; Three Josquin Pieces for Brass Trio (trumpet, horn, trombone); Canzona Bergamasca (brass quintet). Chorus: Four Choruses After Langston Hughes (women's voices); Peace Maker (a capella); Peace on Earth (unison chorus, organ); A Prayer (chorus, piano, brass, wind chimes, audience).

DE KNIGHT, JIMMY
See Myers, James E

DE KOVEN, (HENRY LOUIS) REGINALD
ASCAP 1929
composer, author

b Middletown, Conn, Apr 3, 1859; d Chicago, Ill, Jan 16, 20. Educ: St John's Col, Oxford, Eng; studied with Lebert, Pruckner, Vannucini, von Suppe, Genee, Delibes; hon MusD, Racine Col. First worked in brokerage firm, also owned dry-goods bus, 1882. Music critic, Chicago Evening Post, 1889; Harper's Weekly, 1895-97; New York World, 1898-1900, 1907-12. Organized, cond, Washington Symph, DC, 02-04. Mem, Nat Inst Arts & Letters. Chief Collabr: Harry B Smith. *Songs:* Oh, Promise Me; Brown October Ale; Sweetheart, My Own Sweetheart; The Spinning Song; Little Boy Blue; My Home Is Where the Heather Blooms; Come, Lads of the Highlands; Dearest Heart of My Heart; Do You Remember Love?; Moonlight Song; Gypsy Song; Hammock Love Song. *Scores:* Bway Stage: The Begum; Robin Hood; The Knickerbockers; The Algerian; The Fencing Master; Rob Roy; The Highwayman; Papa's Wife; The Little Duchess; Maid Marian; Red Feather; Happyland; The Beauty Spot; Operas: Canterbury Pilgrims; Rip Van Winkle.

DE LADOMERSZKY, THOMAS L
ASCAP 1964
composer

b Püspöklele, Hungary, Mar 24, 23. Educ: Univ of Economics & Bus, Budapest, Hungary, BA, MA, PhD; studied classical music & comp with Erich Schneider, Vienna, Hungarian folksongs & gypsy music for piano with Eleanor Szekely, Budapest. Comp of popular & classical songs for orch. Chief Collabrs: Dick Manning, Al Hoffman. *Songs:* Music: Gypsy Nostalgia (orch); Spring in Budapest (violin, piano); Music Box Etude No 3 (piano); Where Did We Meet? *Instrumental Works:* Theme for a Lost Love (orch, piano solo).

DE LAMARTER, ERIC
ASCAP 1939
composer, author, conductor

b Lansing, Mich, Feb 18, 1880; d Orlando, Fla, May 17, 53. Educ: Studied with G H Fairclough, Wilhelm Middleschulte, Guilmant, Widor. On fac, Olivet Col, 04-05. Music critic, Chicago Record Herald, 08-09, Tribune, 09-10, Inter-Ocean, 10-14. Organist, First Church of Christ Scientist, Chicago, 12. Cond, Chicago Symph & Chicago Civic Orch. Organist, Fourth Presby Church, Chicago, 14-36. On fac, Chicago Musical Col. Mem, Nat Inst Arts & Letters. *Songs & Instrumental Works:* The Black Orchid (ballet); 4 symphonies; The Giddy Puritan (overture on 2 New Eng hymns); The Fable of the Hapless Folktune; Dialogue for Viola (orch); The 144th Psalm (choral, Eastman Sch Publ Award).

DELANEY, CHARLES OLIVER
ASCAP 1956
composer, teacher, performer

b Winston-Salem, NC, May 21, 25. Educ: Davidson Col, BS, 47; Cons Lausanne, Switz, Virtuosity Degree, 49; Univ Colo, MMComp, 51; study with Cecil Effinger, Lamar Stringfield & Hans Haug. Instr, Earlham Col, 50-52; prof music, Univ Ill, 52-76; prof music, Fla State Univ, 76-, instr summer music camps, 76- Teacher-performer, Brevard Music Ctr, 46-62; instrumental music dir, NC Gov Sch, 62-69; instr, Ill Summer Youth Music Camps, 69-76. Cond, Univ Ill Symph Orch, Albany Georgia Symph & All-State & Fest Orchs in Ill, Tex, Fla & Ga.

DELANEY, FRANCIS EDWARD (ANTHONY DE PADUA) ASCAP 1967
composer, author, singer

b Chicago, Ill, Oct 20, 36. Educ: Mt Carmel High Sch; Boston Col Music, 71. Owner: Icka-Delick-Music & Records Corp & Blinky Records. Recording artist. Chief Collabrs: Maureen T Murray, Al Dero, Alice L Olson, Yvonne L Olson. *Songs:* Real Live Toys; Blinky, the Blue Nosed Snowdeer; The Chill Is Off The Flower; Lyrics: Country in My Heart (The Bluegrass Is Sweet); Ruffian.

DELANEY, SEAN
ASCAP 1977
composer, author, producer

b Tempe, Ariz, Jan 8, 45. Educ: Self-taught keyboardist & guitarist; studied bassoon with Jacob Bos. Musician; played in numerous clubs & Palladium. Produced four albums. Choreographed for "Saturday Night Live" & "The Kiss Show." Produced Gene Simmons' solo album, "Gene Simmons." Arr, producer & co-writer album, "Toby Beau," RCA Records. Producer & arr for group, Piper. Wrote Grace Slick's album, "Dreams." Co-producer & mem group, Skatt Bros, Casablanca Records. *Songs:* I Want You; Making Love; Take Me; The All American Boy; Ready to Rock; I Can't Stop the Rain; Dreams. *Albums:* Sean Delaney Highway (solo album); Can't Wait.

DELANGE, EDGAR
ASCAP 1934
composer, author, conductor

b Long Island City, NY, Jan 12, 04; d Los Angeles, Calif, July 13, 49. Educ: Univ Pa. Organized orch with Will Hudson, 34. Chief Collabrs: Will Hudson, Louis Alter, Duke Ellington, Josef Myrow, Joseph Meyer, Sammy Stept, James Van Heusen, John Benson Brooks. *Songs:* Moonglow; Solitude; Haunting Me; I Wish That I Were Twins; So Help Me; Good for Nothing But Love; Deep in a Dream; Heaven Can Wait; This Is Worth Fighting For; A String of Pearls; Just As Though You Were Here; Who Threw the Whiskey in the Well; Isn't It Strange What Music Can Do; Along the Navajo Trail; Velvet Moon; Man With a Horn; Darn That Dream; One More Tomorrow; If I'm Lucky; Shake Down the Stars; Endie; It Ain't Right to Say Ain't; Soft and Warm; Holiday Forever; What Are Little Girls Made Of?; All This and Heaven, Too. *Scores:* Bway stage: Swinging the Dream; Films: New Orleans; If I'm Lucky.

DELANO, JACK
composer

b Kiev, USSR, Aug 1, 14. Educ: Comp & viola, Settlement Music Sch (scholarship), Philadelphia, Pa; Pa Acad Fine Arts, Philadelphia. Started studying violin with father in Russia at age 6. Came to US, 23; played professionally in string quartet. Studied painting & drawing; became photographer, 39. Moved to PR, 46. Dir, producer & score writer for documentary films; comp chamber music, songs & ballets. Gen mgr, TV & radio stas, Govt PR, until 69. *Songs:* Music: Tres Cancioncitas del Mar (Three Songs of the Sea); Four Songs of the Earth (Cuatro Sones de la Tierra); Six Songs for Laura. *Instrumental Works:* Sonatina for Flute and Piano; Concerto for Trumpet and Orchestra; La Reina Tembandumba (overture-fantasy); Musical Offering (solo viola, horn & strings); Prelude for Guitar. *Scores:* Children's Ballet: El Sabio Dr Mambro (2 trumpets, 2 trombones & drums).

DELEATH, VAUGHN
ASCAP 1923
composer, author, pianist

b Mt Pulaski, Ill, Sept 26, 1896; d Buffalo, NY, May 28, 43. Educ: Mills Col. Concert singer, early teen yrs. First woman to broadcast on radio. Mgr, dir & singer, WDT, New York. Singer, vaudeville; appeared on TV, 39. Actress, Bway play "Laugh, Clown, Laugh." Recording artist. *Songs:* Drive Safely; Hi Yo Silver; Blue Bonnets Underneath the Texas Skies; Little Bit of Sunshine; At Eventide; Bye Lo; Ducklings on Parade; I Wasn't Lying When I Said I Love You; If It Hadn't Been For You; My Lover Comes A-Riding; Rosemary for Remembrance; The Gingerbread Brigade; Madonna's Lullaby.

DE LEON, ROBERT   ASCAP 1941
author
b Laredo, Tex, Nov 17, 04; d San Francisco, Calif, July 18, 1961. Educ: Stephen Austin Sch. In USN, 19-24. Mem, Am Guild Authors & Comp. Chief Collabr: Hoagy Carmichael. *Songs:* Can't Get Indiana Off My Mind; The Miracle of Santa Anne; Dear Son; Will I Ever Learn?; Coast to Coast.

DELEONE, CARMON, JR   ASCAP 1972
composer, author, instrumentalist
b Ravenna, Ohio, Mar 23, 42. Educ: Univ Cincinnati Col Cons Music, BM, 64, BS, 65, MM, 67, DMA, 70, studied horn & piano; cond studies with Max Rudolf, Dobbs Franks, Erich Kunzel, Thomas Schippers & Erich Leinsdorf. Cond, Cincinnati Symph Orch; music dir, Cincinnati Ballet Co. Fac, Univ Cincinnati, Northern Ky State Univ & Miami Univ. Tours with Juliet Prowse, Allan Sherman, Henry Mancini & State Theatre of Lincoln Ctr. Musicals & operas with Univ Cincinnati Mummers Guild, Theatre & Opera Depts. Jazz/rock drummer; French horn soloist, studio band leader & arranger. Chief Collabr: David Matthews. *Songs:* Black Christmas; Go Home and Tell Your Friends About It. *Instrumental Works:* The Poot Town Musicians (narrative); Harper Sets No 1, No 2, No 3 & No 4 (with visuals); Overture to an Intermission; Amissio Nostro; TSK (In Memory of the Maestro). *Scores:* Ballets: Guernica; Samba De Jixie (Frevo); Variegations.

DE LEONE, FRANCESCO BARTOLOMEO   ASCAP 1934
composer, conductor, pianist
b Ravenna, Ohio, July 28, 1887; d Akron, Ohio, Dec 10, 48. Educ: Dana Musical Inst, MusD; Royal Cons of Naples; studied with Ernest Bloch. Educator. Debut as cond, Naples, 10. Founded music dept, Univ Akron. Cond, Cleveland Opera Guild, 27-29, Akron Symph, Akron Civic Opera League, 30-31, Akron Light Opera, 33. Gen dir, Goodyear Light Opera, 34-35. Head piano dept, De Leone Sch Music, 39-48. *Instrumental Works:* Symphony in D; 6 Italian Dances; Italian Rhapsody; Gibraltar Suite; Amalfi Suite; Portage Trail Suite; In Sunny Sicily Suite; Death Ray (musical drama); The Spinner (musical fantasy). *Scores:* Operas: Algala (David Bispham Mem Medal); New York; Operettas: Princess Ting-Ah-Ling; A Millionaire's Caprice; Cave Man Stuff.

DELGROSSO, JEAN ANN (LAURI ALLEN)   ASCAP 1976
composer
b New Kensington, Pa, Nov 28, 38. Educ: Univ Calif, Los Angeles, BA. Summer stock, Valley Music Theater; stage & TV singer; performer with "Kids Next Door." Soloist, Las Vegas & US tour; toured Australia with Jean Leccia. Began writing music, 60; studio singing & prof music copying. Mem, Am Fedn Musicians. Chief Collabr: Lyrics, Eileene Winters. *Songs:* Music: Hold On; Opening Night; Allelujah Pasadena. *Scores:* Film/TV: Gone With the West (cues-music).

DELISA, VICTOR V   ASCAP 1968
composer, author
b Hartford, Conn, Oct 31, 24. Educ: Waurberton Chapel, Hartford, piano lessons, 31-35; studied piano accordion, Florence Rogers at Conn Music Inc & Benny-Berandino Studio, Hartford, 36-38; studied piano with Henry Bonander, West Hartford, 39-41; Julius Hartt Sch Music, maj in piano; Los Angeles Cons Music & Arts, studied comp with White Krueger & conducting with Thomas Usigli, 46-47; Hartford Sch Music, studied comp with Robert Doelner & conducting with George Heck, 48-51; Hartt Col Music, dipl comp, 52; studied comp with Isadore Freed & conducting with Vytantas Marizoscis, 52-53; Teacher's Col, Columbia Univ, BSMA, 58. Rec'd Int Piano Teachers Asn Award; hon mem, Keyboard Music Teachers Asn. Mem: Musicians Union, Local 398, Ossining, NY; Westchester County Sch Music Educr Asn, Peekskill, NY; Nat Acad Popular Music Hall Fame, NY; Int Aspiring Comp, NY (pres); Songwriters Hall Fame, NY; Comp, Authors & Artists Am. Author: "Little Keyboard for Piano" (vol I & II); "Vacation Time—Progressive Guitar Pieces" (vol I); "20 Simple Tunes for Soprano Recorder" (vol I). *Songs & Instrumental Works:* The Hudson River.

DELL, TOMMY
See Fagan, Thomas O

DELLA GALA, MICHAEL D   ASCAP 1977
composer, author, singer
b Utica, NY, Nov 17, 50. Educ: Thomas R Proctor High Sch; Mohawk Valley Community Col; self-taught on electric bass. Played nightclubs in Northeastern US, 68- Recording artist; presently writing songs in Southern Calif. Chief Collabr: Duane L Walker. *Songs:* Steppin' Out on Saturday Night.

DELLARIO, MICHAEL RICHARD   ASCAP 1979
composer, author
b Schenectady, NY, Aug 5, 49. Educ: Georgetown Univ, BA, 71; George Washington Univ, MMus, 73; Princeton Univ, MFA, 77; studied comp with Guffredo Petrassi, Rome & Franco Donatoni, Siene. Guitarist in folk clubs & studio work; teacher comp & electronic music; arr & cond. *Songs:* Problems. *Instrumental Works:* Acquaforte. *Scores:* Opera/Ballet: Maud; Film/TV: Run Wild With the Wind.

DELLA RIPA, DOMINIC J   ASCAP 1957
composer, author, singer
b East Hartford, Conn, Jan 23, 21. Educ: Studied with Frank Caruso. Writer music & lyrics, in Eng & Italian. *Songs & Instrumental Works:* I Know You Don't Love Me Any More (Eng & Italian); I'll Always Want You (Eng & Italian); It's Xmas Time Again; I Wiped a Tear Drop From My Eye; You're All I Need.

DELLGER, MICHAEL LAWRENCE (BIG BEN BEMIS)   ASCAP 1976
author, musician, drummer
b Plymouth, Wis, May 4, 5C. Educ: Univ Wis-Oshkosh, BS(speech-radio, TV, film & Eng), 74. Began playing drums, 65. Wrote lyrics for albums, Pilgrim, 74 & Observer, 75; wrote lyrics & played drums on album, Above and Beyond, 78. Chief Collabrs: Keith Abler, David Steffen, Richard Colbath, Jr. *Songs:* Lyrics: Jamaican Holiday; Someone Like You; The Girl I Can't Forget; Sunshine Love.

DEL MONTE, LOUIS J   ASCAP 1960
composer, teacher
b Jersey City, NJ, May 29, 12. Educ: Juilliard Sch Music. Dir, Del Monte Accordion Sch. Accordionist in concert, radio, TV & on recordings.

DELMORE, LIONEL ALTON   ASCAP 1970
composer, author, teacher
b Birmingham, Ala, Mar 19, 40. Educ: Univ Tulsa; studied with father, Alton Delmore. Began writing prof in 59. Singer, nightclub entertainer, songwriter, publ & guitarist. Recorded on Simco Records, radio & stage; teacher. Chief Collabr: John Anderson. *Songs:* Naked and Crying; Ways of a Country Girl; Hitchin' Rides to Memories in My Mind; Girl At the End of the Bar; Low Down Blues; Havin' Hard Times; Wantin' My Woman Again; Mountain High, Valley Low; I Wish I Could Write You a Song; It Looks Like the Party Is Over; Diesel Devil; I Don't Have to Come This Far to See It Rain; Lonesome Time in Memphis Town Tonight; Everytime; Girl for You.

DELO, KENNETH EDWARD   ASCAP 1969
composer, author, singer
b Detroit, Mich. Educ: Our Lady of Lourdes High Sch. Singer, legitimate stage, night clubs, TV & concert stage. Produced & starred in Australian TV series. Eleventh yr on "Lawrence Welk TV Show." *Songs:* The Best There Is; Santa Claus; Mom; I Wanna Sing Country But I Got No Twang; Oh, To Be a Child Again.

DELORIEA, MARYBELLE C(RUGER) (MAMIE ODELL)   ASCAP 1973
composer, author
b Albany, Ga, Nov 16, 17. Educ: Atlanta Cons Music; Agnes Scott Col, BA(minor in music); studied piano with C W Dieckmann; studied voice with Lula Clark King & John Hoffman; studied voice & cello with Enrico Leide, Atlanta. Singer & pianist: Beefed up bassoon section with tenor saxophone in original Atlanta Phil; dance band in high sch & col days & Atlanta Young Ladies' Orch. Staff pianist with Emzelle' Trio, WAGA radio, Atlanta, 38-39; worked for Diversey Corp, 40-44, then for Calhoun Co Audio Visual Service, 45-68. Began lead sheet making & simple arr for songwriters, 68. Chief Collabrs: Ralph M Smith, Barbara Chance, George DeLeva. *Songs:* I Need You Ev'ry Day, I Need You Ev'ry Way, Baby; Zoom Loppa Fiddle Faddle Zing!; Music: Walking With My Lord; This Dozen Roses; A Tiny Baby.

DEL TREDICI, DAVID
composer
b Cloverdale, Calif, Mar 16, 37. Educ: Piano student of Bernhard Abramowitsch & Robert Helps; Univ Calif, Berkeley, BA, 59; Princeton Univ, MFA, 64. Recital & symph pianist, incl appearances with San Francisco Symph Orch. Fac mem, Harvard Univ, 68-72, Buffalo Univ, 73 & Boston Univ, 73-; comp-in-residence, Tanglewood Music Fest, 64-65, Marlboro Music Fest 66-67 & Aspen Music Fest, 75. Mem bd of dirs, Yaddo & MacDowell Colony. Awards: Hertz; Nat Coun Arts & Letters; Creative Arts, Brandeis Univ; Naumberg Recording Award; Phi Beta Kappa, Woodrow Wilson Fel; Guggenheim Fel & Pulitzer Prize, 80. Numerous comns for comp. *Instrumental Works:* String Trio; Piano: Soliloquy; Fantasy Pieces; Scherzo (4 hands); Chorus and Orch: The Last Gospel; Pop-Pourri; Settings of James Joyce for Soprano and Var Chamber Instruments: I Hear an Army; Four Songs on Poems of James Joyce; Night Conjure-Verse; Syzygy; Settings of Lewis Carroll for Soprano and Orch: Pop-Pourri; The Lobster Quadrille (orch alone); In Wonderland; Illustrated Alice; An Alice Symphony; Vintage Alice; Adventures Underground; Final Alice; In Memory of a Summer Day; Happy Voices; All in the Golden Afternoon.

DE LUCIA, RALPH LAWRENCE   ASCAP 1969
composer, author
b New Haven, Conn, Aug 10, 20. Educ: Univ Conn, BS; Univ Erlangen, Ger. *Songs:* Love in Rome; Only Sometimes; It Never Was Love; He Walks Like You; The Leaves Came Tumbling Down; My Lifetime; Are We The Same Two People?

DELUGG, ANNE RENFER ASCAP 1956
composer, author
b Wenatchee, Wash, Apr 22, 23. Educ: Santa Ana High Sch; Santa Ana Col, majored in music. Rehearsal pianist & dance instr, Meglin Kiddie Dance Studios, during high sch & col; moved to New York, 50; wrote music & lyrics for childrens' films & numerous Golden Records & Golden Bks; wrote lyrics for main titles, Walter Reade Films, incl full length animation "Gulliver's Travels", themes for Jr Miss Pageant, Country Music Hit Parade & openings for Macy's Thanksgiving & Orange Bowl Parades. Chief Collabrs: Milton Delugg, Bob Hilliard. *Songs:* Honolulu; Gulliver's Travels; Gypsy Girl; *Music:* Little White Horse; The Big Beat; *Lyrics:* Junior Miss Theme.

DELUGG, MILTON ASCAP 1949
author, conductor, arranger
b Los Angeles, Calif, Dec 2, 21. Educ: John Marshall High Sch; Los Angeles City Col; pvt study harmony, piano & accordion, Los Angeles; study with Tibor Serly, New York, 5 yrs. During sch yrs, soloist on maj radio progs & all motion picture studios. Joined Matty Malneck Orch, 38. Appeared as actor-soloist in musical "Very Warm for May." Enlisted in Air Force, 42, assigned to radio production unit. Worked for Frank Loesser in many picture assignments, 46. Arr-cond-comp for Al Jolson, Abe Burrows, Herb Shriner, Morey Amsterdam, Fred Allen & many other radio & TV series, incl Country Music Specials, Daytime Emmys, Jr Miss Pageant, etc. Music dir, Chuck Barris Productions, Los Angeles, 76- Composed symphonic works performed by San Francisco Symph & CBS Symph. Chief Collabrs: Frank Loesser, Bob Hilliard, Sammy Gallop, Anne Delugg, Willy Stein, Herb Hartig, Matty Malneck. *Songs: Music:* Hoop Dee Doo; Orange Colored Sky; Be My Life's Companion; Shanghai; Just Another Polka; My Lady Loves to Dance; A Poor Man's Roses; Be-Bop Spoken Here; Send My Baby Back to Me; Junior Miss Pageant Theme; Honolulu. *Instrumental Works:* Roller Coaster; The Big Beat; Little White Horse; Barnaby Jones; Center Ring. *Scores: Film/TV:* Gulliver's Travels; Only One New York; Pinocchio.

DELVICARIO, SILVIO PATRICK (DEL VICAR) ASCAP 1963
composer
b Brooklyn, NY, Mar 18, 21. Educ: Textile High Sch. New York city policeman; comp music. Chief Collabr: Tony Vicar. *Songs:* Have Faith; Don't Ever Leave Me; Lift Your Eyes to Heaven; A Kiss and a Promise; Rockaway Your Blues Down Rockaway.

DE MADINA, FRANCISCO ASCAP 1961
composer, author
b Onate, Spain, Jan 29, 07; d Onate, June 30, 72. Educ: Canon Regular of Lateran. Ordained in Burgos, Spain, 29; priest with Religious Order of Canons Regular of Lateran. To US, 58. *Songs & Instrumental Works:* Basque Sonata (harp); Basque Songs (male chorus, a cappella); Piezas Infantiles (piano); Flor de Durazno (opera); La Cadena de Oro (cantata); Endecha-Zortziko; Our Father (motet); Ecumenical Psalm (choral); Christmas Carols; Danza Rapsodica (4 guitars); Onati (Basque rhapsody for chorus & orch); Illeta (elegie for soloists, chorus & orch); Arantzazu (poem for soloists, chorus & orch); Concierto Vasco (4 guitars & orch); Concierto Andaluz (guitar & orch); Orreaga (orch).

DEMAIO, JAMES PAUL (JIMMY PAUL) ASCAP 1967
composer, author
b Cedar Grove, NJ, Aug 5, 13. Educ: Rutgers Univ, studied journ; Pa State Univ. Free lance writer, newspaper & magazine articles. Worked at Frank Dailey's Meadowbrook, music publ. Wrote spec material for shows, USA, WW II. Chief Collabrs: Harold Potter, Dick Charles, Matt Matlin, Ted Black. *Songs:* Travelin' Blues; Just Another Blues; *Lyrics:* Drifting Along; Nita; When Winter Comes; We Can't Go on This Way; Goodbye Ole Paint.

DEMARCO, ROSALINDA JILL
See Johns, Rosalinda Jill

DE MASI, JOSEPH ASCAP 1952
composer, author, trumpet soloist
b Orange, NJ, Nov 1, 04. Educ: Pvt instruction. Professional musician, 50 yrs; played at Madison Square Garden, 10 yrs, CBS-TV, 7 yrs, state & county fairs, 30 yrs, dance bands, 40 yrs & Ital fiestas, 10 yrs. Cond concert bands for Local 802, NY, 5 yrs, amusement parks, 30 yrs & Sallam Temple, Livingston, NJ, 35 yrs. Chief Collabrs: Charles O'Flynn, Alfred Longo. *Songs: Music:* Take Me to the Circus; Circus Ballet; Rodeo; Lovin' You; Viva Vaqero; At the Funny Paper Ball; Someday You'll Know Dear; Dancing Clown; Marrachita. *Instrumental Works:* The Big Time March; Rough and Ready; The Jet; Brass Hat; Dreams; wish I Had a Record of You.

DE MASI, JOSEPH ANTHONY ASCAP 1956
composer, teacher
b Orange, NJ, Dec 5, 35. Studied with father, Joseph De Masi, with whom he owns music store & sch, West Orange. *Songs:* Don't Let Me Down; Band Master.

DEMBO, GERALD ASCAP 1969
composer, singer
b New York, NY, June 18, 22. Educ: Evander Childs High Sch; NY Univ; studied voice with Matty Levine. Singer in nightclubs; recording artist, Finer Arts Records. Chief Collabr: Morey Bernstein. *Songs:* I Felt My Life Begin; Much More Than Time Will Allow; *Music:* Kol 'Israel; Time Will Make My Hurt Go Away; What Went Wrong Since Yesterday.

DE METRUIS, CLAUDE composer, author, pianist
b Bath, Maine, Aug 3, 17. Educ: Columbia Univ, music study, 1 yr. *Songs:* Mean Women Blues; Mop Mop; Hard Headed Women; Please Stop Playing Those Blues Boys; Take Me Back Baby.

DEMMING, LANSON F ASCAP 1962
composer, author, conductor
b Buffalo, NY, Oct 25, 02. Educ: Eastman Sch Music, BM; Univ Ill, MM. Prof music, Univ Ill, 30-45; prof, Univ Houston, 46-62. Dir, Extension Chorus, Dept Agriculture, 33-40, Women's Glee Club, 37-43 & sta WILL, 37-45. Minister of music, St Paul's Methodist Church, Houston, 45-; organist, Temple Beth Yeshurun, Houston, 53- *Songs:* Oh, Crown Him; Our Song of Thanks; The Eternal Gate; An Easter Song; Seasonal Introits and Responses; O Come, Let Us Adore Him; Festival Processional; A Wedding Song; A Christmas Song.

DEMPSEY, JAMES E (POWELL I FORD, PAUL GRAYSON) ASCAP 1953
composer, author, singer
b Philadelphia, Pa, Oct 29, 1876; d Philadelphia, Oct 9, 18. Educ: High sch. Singer with Dumont Minstrels. Staff writer for music publ firms. *Songs:* She Sleeps Tonight Among the Alleghenies; Under the Big September Moon; Though Your Lips Belong to Others Your Heart Belongs to Me; A Soldier Who Wears No Uniform; Just a Dream of Home Sweet Home; Starshine.

DEMUTH, THEODORE LOUIS ASCAP 1965
composer, educator, conductor
b New Orleans, La, Aug 5, 24. Educ: Tulane Univ, BA & MAT, 47-58. Professional trombonist, 40-; band master, USMC, 47-51; cond numerous shows, 50-; instr, Tulane Univ, 51-58, asst dir, 58-68, dir bands, 68- Vpres, Am Fedn Musicians Local, 63- *Instrumental Works:* Super; Kicks; Points.

DENAUT, GEORGE MATTHEWS (JUD) ASCAP 1960
conductor, bassist, arranger
b Walkerton, Ind, Jan 28, 15. In vaudeville with Bobby & Gale Sherwood, 29. Bassist in dance bands incl Artie Shaw, Ray Noble, Richard Himber, Ozzie Nelson, Kay Kyser, Woody Herman, Paul Whiteman & Bobby Sherwood. US Army, WW II. Played in radio orchs. Own group, Disneyland Hotel.

DENBOW, STEFANIA BJÖRNSON ASCAP 1974
composer
b Minneota, Minn, Dec 28, 16. Educ: Univ Minn, BA, 37, MA, 39; studied organ with Arthur Poister; Ohio Univ, grad study in music theory with James Stewart, 72. Organist in churches in Ohio & Md. *Songs & Instrumental Works:* Exaltatio (organ solo); Trio Islandia (piano, violin, cello); Christ Is Risen, Alleluia (cantata, based on "Christ ist Erstanden," instrument accompaniment, chorus & solos); All Glory for This Blessed Morn (cantata, organ, chorus & solos); Magnificat (chamber orch, solo mezzo-soprano & chorus).

DE NEERGAARD, VIRGINIA ASCAP 1960
composer, conductor, pianist
b New York, NY. Educ: Holy Child Acad; Granberry Piano Sch, scholarship, studied with Nicholas Elsenheimer; Columbia Univ; Juilliard Sch Music; studied with Claire Cocci. Gave recitals, 13-18; supvr music, NY Pub Schs, 22-55; organist & choir dir, St Mary's Church, City Island, NY; choral dir, New Rochelle Women's Club, 59-60. *Songs:* Sleep Precious Babe; A Happy Day; U and the UN.

DENNI, GWYNNE ASCAP 1942
author, actress, director
b Green Island, NY, May 24, 1882; d San Pedro, Calif, Dec 14, 49. Educ: Holy Cross Sch, Troy, NY; voice with J Ireland Tucker; piano, Signor Pietro Gonzales; Emma Willard Sem, Troy; New Eng Cons of Music, Boston; voice with C A White & Signor Rotili; piano, J Albert Jeffrey & Carl Faelten; theory, Louis Elson; harmony, George Chadwick; dramatics, Samuel R Kelly; drama, Sargent Sch, Carnegie Hall, New York. Appeared in Bway musicals "Chaperones", "Happyland", "Filibuster" & "The Only Girl." Wrote special material & sketches for vaudeville & radio. Staged & produced musical comedies. Producer. *Songs:* Suppose the Rose Were You; Mystery of Night; Memory's Garden; I Gave a Rose to You; Forgotten Perfume; In a Beautiful Song; You're Just a Flower From an Old Bouquet. *Scores: Stage:* Happy Go Lucky.

DENNI, LUCIEN ASCAP 1935
composer, conductor
b Nancy, France, Dec 23, 1886; d Hermosa Beach, Calif, Aug 20, 47. Educ: New York Pub Schs; piano with Philip Breivogel, Leipzig, Ger; harmony, theory &

music with Andrew Brown, Columbia Col, NY. Vaudeville pianist & musical dir. Featured with orch in nightclubs; guest cond, Kansas City Symph Orch. Comp & dir, "Molly Bawn", "Don't Tell My Wife" & "Oh, Judge." Musical dir, New Amsterdam Theater; composed scores for motion pictures & cartoons. Chief Collabrs: Gwynne Denni, Roger Lewis. *Songs:* The Nation's Awakening; The Oceana Roll; Memory's Garden; The Mystery of Night; You're Just a Flower From an Old Bouquet; Forgotten Perfumes; I Gave a Rose to You. *Scores:* Stage: Happy Go Lucky.

DENNIKER, PAUL　　　　　ASCAP 1930
composer, author, pianist
b London, Eng, May 30, 1897; d. Came to US, 19. Educ: Dower House Sch, Wallington, Eng; studied with Samuel Coleridge-Taylor. WW I, Brit Army; wrote shows, ed mag. In US, led own band in vaudeville, nightclubs; pianist & arr with Will Osborne Orch; revues at Grand Terrace, Chicago, Apollo Theatre, NY. Writer of spec material, radio commercials. Conducted Songwriter's Service; music teacher. Chief Collabr: Andy Razaf. *Songs:* S'posin'; Milkmen's Matinee; Beside an Open Fireplace (Will Osborne theme); Make Believe Ballroom; Save It, Pretty Mama; Jamadoodle. *Scores:* Stage: Hot Chocolates of 1935.

DENNING, FRANK
See Damico, Frank James

DENNING, WADE FULTON, JR　　　　　ASCAP 1950
composer, arranger, author
b Albemarle, NC, June 21, 22. Educ: Univ NC; US Merchant Marine Acad; Gene von Hallberg & Tibor Serly. Trumpeter with bands; Bway shows, 41-50; arr TV shows, "Ted Mack Amateur Hour", "Herb Shriner & Fred Allen Shows", 50-70; NBC staff. Comp numerous commercials & advert jingles incl: Maxwell House Coffee Pot, Muriel Cigars, Old Gold Dancing Cigarette Packs & "US Steel Hour"; also comp many children's bks & records. A&R dir for Pickwick Int; free lance record producer; cond. Chief Collabrs: Lloyd Marx, Kay Lande, Elaine Gold. *Songs:* Halloween; Fun in Fall; Fun in Spring; Sounds of Terror; Sounds of '76; Famous Ghost Stories (adaptations); Music: Rain for a Dusty Summer; 1:30 Polka; Let's Go on With the Show (Ted Mack Amateur Hour Theme). *Instrumental Works:* Theme for Regional Emmy Awards TV Show. *Scores:* Film/TV: Guns of the Revolution.

DENNIS, GINNY MAXEY　　　　　ASCAP 1964
composer, singer, actress
b Indianapolis, Ind, Sept 4, 23. Educ: Pub schs. Singer with orchs incl Charlie Barnet, Tony Pastor, Ziggy Elman; also with Modernaires & on records. Appeared in nightclubs & TV. Chief Collabr: Matt Dennis (husband). *Songs:* Lyrics: Spring Isn't Spring Anymore; Little Sweetheart, Little Darlin'; Scott Joplin (a dedication); We've Reached the Point of No Return; Snuggle Up, Baby; You Can Believe Me.

DENNIS, MATT L　　　　　ASCAP 1951
composer, singer, pianist
b Seattle, Wash, Feb 11, 14. Educ: San Rafael High Sch, Calif. Comp, Tommy Dorsey, wrote songs & vocal arr, Frank Sinatra, Jo Stafford, Connie Haines & Pied Pipers. WW II, USAAF, with Radio Production Unit & Glenn Miller AF Orch. Singer/pianist, nightclubs, had own NBC-TV series & films, recorded, RCA & others. Has own publ firm, comp piano bks, has publ own method for piano. Teach piano; arr music, had own concert of original songs by request of Smithsonian Inst, recorded for Libr of Congress. Performs with singer-spouse, Ginny Maxey Dennis. Chief Collabrs: Tom Adair, Earl K Brent, Jerry Gladstone, Sammy Cahn, Bob Russell, Ginny Maxey Dennis. *Songs:* Relax; Music: Let's Get Away From It All; Will You Still Be Mine?; Everything Happens to Me; Violets for Your Furs; The Night We Called It a Day; Angel Eyes; Show Me the Way to Get Out of This World; Love Turns Winter to Spring; Little Man With a Candy Cigar; The Spirit of Christmas (Off song, Nat Tuberculosis, Christmas Seal Campaign, 54); Blues for Breakfast; Who's Yehoodi?; Junior and Julie; We Belong Together. *Instrumental Works:* Matt Dennis Popular Piano Method.

DENNIS, ROBERT　　　　　ASCAP 1968
composer
b St Louis, Mo, May 5. 33. Educ: Juilliard Sch Music, New York, 51-56, studied comp with Vincent Persichetti, 53-56; Conservatoire Paris, Fulbright fel, 56-57. Started playing piano at age 8, oboe at age 12. Comp of music for theatre, dance & films, 68- Comp of orchestral chamber music. Worked with group, Open Window, 68-71. Chief Collabrs: David Rosenak, Bob Randall. *Songs:* Music: Peter Quince At the Clavier. *Instrumental Works:* Pennsylvania Station (orch); Introduction and Variations (cello & piano). *Scores:* Written six scores for Pilobolus Dance Theatre, which incl Untitled; Monkshood's Farewell.

DENNISON, GWENDOLYN ELAINE　　　　　ASCAP 1976
composer, author, singer
b Philadelphia, Pa, Oct 20, 54. Educ: John Bartram High Sch; Philadelphia Music Acad; studied voice with Edward Boatner & Benjamin Matthews. In Bway production, "Porgy and Bess." In nat cos, "The Wiz" & "South Pacific" (Audeico Award). In "Simply Heavenly" & "Broadway in Black," Europe Ctr, West Berlin, Ger. Singer, nightclubs, TV & films; recording artist, Toledo Records, West Berlin, Ger. Chief Collabrs: Arthur Manning, John Simmons,

Jürgen Rudolf Schulz, Robert Butler, Marcus Nowak, Sylvia Branchcomb. *Songs:* Ain't It Time You Went Home; Be There; Going Down Town to See Jesus; Wake Up Children; Ahead of Your Time.

DENNY, MARTIN　　　　　ASCAP 1959
composer, author
b New York, NY, Apr 10, 11. Educ: Los Angeles Cons; pvt study with Wesley La Violette & Arthur Lange. Originated the "Exotic Sounds of Martin Denny" in Hawaii. Recorded for Liberty Records, 57-69. Toured with group throughout US appearing at major hotels, nightclubs, cols & concerts; also appeared in SAm, Europe & Japan. Introduced a sound device used in recording field. Chief Collabrs: Harold V Johnson, Mack David. *Songs:* Lyrics: Island of Dreams. *Songs & Instrumental Works:* Burma Train; Exotica; Hawaiian Rhapsody; Forbidden Island.

DENOFF, SAMUEL　　　　　ASCAP 1957
composer, author
b New York, NY, July 1, 28. Educ: James Madison High Sch; Great Neck Hunt Sch, 46; Adelphi Col, (Eng, music), 51. Writer, songs in col, jingle & comedy, WNEW, New York, until 61. To Calif, producer & writer, TV shows incl theme music & original material for "Dick Van Dyke Show", "That Girl" & "Steve Allen Show." Chief Collabrs: Jim Haines, Gene Klavan. *Songs:* Music: You Know Too Much; Lyrics: Let's Keep the Dodgers in Brooklyn; That Girl (theme).

DENSMORE, JOHN H　　　　　ASCAP 1941
composer
b Somerville, Mass, Aug 7, 1880; d Boston, Mass, Sept 21, 43. Educ: Harvard Univ, BA, 04. Worked as comp. While at Harvard Univ wrote 2 Hasty Pudding Club Productions, one of them was: "Boodle and Company." Chief Collabr: Lyrics, Mary Gardenia. *Songs:* Music: Veritas (Harvard Univ football song); I Must Go Down to the Seas Again; Cigarette (tango); Dardanella.

DENSMORE, JOHN PAUL　　　　　ASCAP 1967
composer, musician
b Santa Monica, Calif, Dec 1, 44. Educ: Santa Monica City Col; San Fernando Valley State Col, studied with Fred Katz. Founder & mem, musical group The Doors, recorded eight gold albums, toured US, Europe & Can, played in Carnegie Hall, Olympia Hall, Paris & others. Chief Collabrs: Jim Morrison, Ray Manzarels, Robly Krieger. *Songs:* Light My Fire; The End; Riders on the Storm; Hello, I Love You; Touch Me.

DENTON, JAMES
See Hughes, Robert James

DENVER, JOHN
See Deutschendorf, Henry John, Jr

DEODATO, EUMIR
See Almeida, Eumire Deodato

DEPACKH, MAURICE　　　　　ASCAP 1946
composer, conductor, arranger
b New York, NY, Nov 21, 1896; d Beverly Hills, Calif, May 24, 60. Educ: Pub schs; studied music with Maurice Gold, Jeanne Franco & Frank Saddler. Cond, DePackh Ens, 28-31. Arr, Bway musicals, incl "The Girl Friend" & "Manhattan Mary." Wrote songs for "Glory." Went to Hollywood, 33; scored films. *Songs:* Just for You; Evening Song; Glory. *Instrumental Works:* Suite.

DE PADUA, ANTHONY
See Delaney, Francis Edward

DEPAOLIS, LEONE F (TONI BEAULIEU)　　　　　ASCAP 1974
composer, author, violinist
b Highmore, SDak. Educ: Huron Col; MacPhail Sch of Music, Minneapolis, Minn; Univ Rochester Eastman Sch of Music, MM(piano), PhD(violin). Radio work, stations WCCO, WHAM, WHEC & owner of Artistic Record Co, 46-49. Piano soloist, Minn Symph. Taught, MacPhail Sch of Music. Established Toni Beaulieu Music Publ, 74. Mem, Am Guild of Authors & Composers, Musician's Union Local 47. Chief Collabrs: Jack Allen, Ray Gilbert, Gordon Clifford, Jerry Gladstone, Marla Shelton, Hertha Peck. *Songs:* Caribbean Moon. *Instrumental Works:* Jungle Rhumba; Moonlight on the Riviera; Caribbean Rhapsody; Autumn Rhapsody; Granada Rhapsody; New Horizons.

DE PATIE, DAVID HUDSON
business executive
b Los Angeles, Calif, Dec 24, 30. Educ: Univ of South, 47-48; Univ Calif, Berkeley, AB, 51. Motion picture exec; with Warner Bros Pictures, Inc, 51-63, vpres/gen mgr, Commercial & Cartoons Div, 63. Pres, DePatie-Freleng Enterprises, Inc, Van Nuys, Calif, 63-80; pres, Marvel Productions, Ltd, 80- Producer theatrical cartoon series, "Pink Panther and Inspector"; producer TV series: "The Super 6"; "Super President"; "The Roadrunner"; "Here Comes the Grump"; "Pink Panther and 1/2 Hour and 1/2"; "The Ant and the Aardvark"; "The Texas Toads"; "The Houndcats and the Barkleys"; also Merry Melodies & Looney Tunes cartoon series: "Return to the Planet of the Apes"; "The

Oddball Couple"; "Mister Jaw-Supershark"; "The New Mr Magoo." Producer TV specials: "Flip Wilson in the Miracle of PS 14"; "Clerow Wilson Great Escape"; "Fantastic Four"; "Spider Woman"; Christmas TV specials: "The Bear Who Slept Through Christmas"; "The Tiny Tree"; "The Pink Panther Christmas Special"; "The Bugs Bunny Christmas Special" & others. Producer TV live-action & animation specials: "Goldilocks"; "Dr Doolittle" (series); Dr Seuss TV specials: "The Cat in the Hat"; "The Lorax" (First Award, Zagreb Int Film Fest, 72: nominated for Emmy Award, 74-75); "Dr Seuss on the Loose"; "The Hoober Bloob Highway"; "Halloween Is Grinch Night" (Emmy Award); "Dr Seuss' Pontoffel Pock, Where Are You?" (nominated for Emmy Award, 80); "The Pink Panther in Olym-Pinks" (nominated for Emmy Award, 80); ABC After Sch Special: "My Mom's Having a Baby" (Emmy Award). Mem, Acad Motion Picture Arts & Sci (Oscar Award for Pink Panther, 64) & Soc Motion Picture Editors.

DE PAUL, GENE   ASCAP 1941
composer, pianist, arranger
b New York, NY, June 17, 19. Educ: Benjamin Franklin High Sch; pvt piano study. Pianist in dance orchs. Toured theaters as singer, also pianist & arr for vocal groups. Under contract to film studios. WW II, USA. Wrote film scores for Abbott & Costello & Andrew Sisters. Chief Collabrs: Don Raye, Johnny Mercer, Sammy Cahn. *Songs:* Music: Teach Me Tonight; You Can't Run Away From It; Music for Sesame Street: You Are Your Own Best Friend; Imaginings; A Singy Kind of Song; Hello. *Scores:* Bway shows: Li'l Abner; Love in a Home; If I Had My Druthers; The Country's in the Very Best of Hands; Namely You; Jubilation T Cornpone; Film/TV: Seven Brides for Seven Brothers (Acad Award for best musical score); I'll Remember April; Mister Five By Five; He's My Guy; Milkman, Keep Those Bottles Quiet; Cow Cow Boogie; Love Me; Star Eyes; You Don't Know What Love Is; Irresistible You; When You're in Love; Lonesome Polecat; Sobbin' Women; Your Red Wagon; A Song Was Born; Pigfoot Pete (Acad Nomination).

DE PAUR, LEONARD   ASCAP 1958
composer, conductor
b Summit, NJ. Cond, Orch of America. *Songs:* Glory Manger.

DEPIERRO, THOMAS   ASCAP 1977
author
b New York, NY, May 24, 50. Asst mgr, Sam Goody, 70-72. Asst vpres: Painted Smiles Records, New York, 72-73; Composers Recordings Inc, New York, 73-75; Motown Records, 75-79. Pres & owner, Blue Standard Music/Airwave Records, 78- Chief Collabr: Wayne Duncan. *Songs:* Lyrics: Is It Still Warm; Sunrise; If You're Leavin.

DEPUE, WALLACE EARL   ASCAP 1963
composer, author, educator
b Columbus, Ohio, Oct 1, 32. Educ: Capital Univ, BM & BME(comp-voice), 55; Ohio State Univ, Columbus, MA(music theory), 56; Mich State Univ, PhD(music comp), 65, studied with H Owen Reed. Mem, Columbus Boys Choir Sch, 44-47. Pianist on "Horace Heidt Show," 50. Pub sch music teacher, 2 yrs. Music curator, Toledo Museum of Art, 64-66. Prof music comp-history, Bowling Green State Univ, 66- Has rec'd state & nat comp awards. *Instrumental Works:* Sonata Primitif; Concerto for Percussion and Orchestra; Sonata Lycanthrope. *Scores:* Opera: Dr Jekyll and Mr Hyde; Something Special (barbershop chorus & quartets); The Three Little Pigs.

DE RIENZO, SILVIO   ASCAP 1960
composer, pianist, arranger
b New York, NY, Oct 6, 09; d. Educ: NY Col of Music; Cons of Musical Art. Arr for Glenn Miller Orch. Pianist in concerts, also in Meyer Davis Orch. *Instrumental Works:* Holiday in Naples (Tarantella); White Waters; Kautious Kittens.

DERO, AL
See Di Robbio, Armando

DE ROSA, CARMELLA MILLIE   ASCAP 1959
composer, author, singer
b Paterson, NJ, July 26, 14. Educ: High sch. Singer; mgr; also writer of musical commercials for films & TV. *Songs:* Get With It.

DE ROSA, CLEM R   ASCAP 1965
composer, music educator, conductor
b Brooklyn, NY, May 20, 25. Educ: Juilliard Sch Music; Manhattan Sch Music, MM. Played with Big Bands of the 40's; recording artist & performer. Teacher, Teachers Col, Columbia Univ, Ind Univ & Univ Vt. Percussionist. Chief Collabrs: Dick Hyman, Phil Woods, Urbie Green. *Instrumental Works:* Bye, Bye Blues; Gone With the Wind; method bks for piano, bass, drums, saxophone, trumpet & trombone.

DE ROSA, PAT A   ASCAP 1966
composer
b Brooklyn, NY, Dec 6, 21. Educ: South Huntington High Sch; Manhattan Sch Music, BMus, MMusEduc; studied with Claude Minteaux. Staff sgt, USAAF Band, World War II, 43-46. Musician with var bands incl Boyd Raeburn, Percy Faith, Tommy Tucker, Ted Straeter & movie & TV stars incl Jerry Lewis, Dean Martin, Jackie Gleason & Bob Hope; song-writer. Began teaching, 54, music

dept chmn, 66-78. Chief Collabr: Frank Como. *Songs:* Music: Totem Pole; Drum Fiesta; Mantilla Lace; Rockin' Horse.

DE ROSE, PETER   ASCAP 1922
composer, author, pianist
b New York, NY, Mar 10, 1900; d New York, Apr 23, 53. Educ: DeWitt Clinton High Sch; first music study with sister. On staff, G Ricordi Co. Early performer in radio with wife, May Singhi Breen; featured on NBC network as "Sweethearts of the Air," 23-39. Wrote songs for Bway musicals "Yes Yes Yvette", "Earl Carroll's Vanities of 1928" & "Ziegfeld Follies of 1934," for films "Song of Love" & "The Fighting Seabees." Chief Collabrs: May Singhi Breen, Jo Trent, Harry Richman, Charles Tobias, Billy Hill, Mitchell Parish, Bert Shefter, Benny Davis, Al Stillman, Sammy Gallop, Sam Lewis, Stanley Adams, Carl Sigman. *Songs:* Music: When You're Gone I Won't Forget; Muddy Water; I Just Roll Along Havin' My Ups and Downs; When Your Hair Has Turned to Silver I Will Love You Just the Same; One More Kiss Then Goodnight; Wagon Wheels; Somebody Loves You; Have You Ever Been Lonely?; There's a Home in Wyoming; Rain; Just Say Aloha; That's Life I Guess; In a Mission By the Sea; Royal Blue; Maytime in Vienna; Starlit Hour; Deep Purple; The Lamp Is Low; Lilacs in the Rain; On a Little Street in Singapore; All I Need Is You; Moonlight Mood; Evening Star; American Waltz; Autumn Serenade; That's Where I Came In; As Years Go By; In the Market Place in Old Monterey; Who Do You Know in Heaven?; Twenty-Four Hours of Sunshine; God of Battles; I Hear America Singing; I Hear a Forest Praying; God Is Ever Beside Me; A Marshmallow World; Buena Sera; Love Ya.

DEROSIER, MICHAEL JOSEPH   ASCAP 1978
composer
b Seattle, Wash, Aug 24, 51. Educ: Woodbury High Sch, Edmonds, Wash, grad, 69; North Seattle Community Col, 70-71. Drum lessons in sixth grade; played perc in concert & marching bands in jr & sr high sch; played in numerous Seattle bands; percussionist in group, Heart, 75- Chief Collabrs: Ann & Nancy Wilson. *Songs:* Barracuda; Little Queen.

DERR, ZAN
See McGonigal, Alexander Andrew

DERRICK, FRANK JOHN, JR   ASCAP 1973
composer, author, instrumentalist
b Maywood, Ill, Jan 15, 13. Educ: From age 6 to 13 studied voice at Chicago Music Col with Ray Huntington, Max Fischel & Leon Samentini (also harmony-theory); Provisco High Sch; Crane Jr Col & Cent YMCA Col, 2 1/2 yrs pre-med course. Played in first string sect, concert orch, Proviso High Sch; mem, Al Kilian band, Detroit, 36; mem, Bill Wright band, toured Chicago, Buffalo & Toronto, 37; had own band, toured Chicago, Cleveland, Detroit & Buffalo, 5 yrs; leader, Hellcat Jazz Band, USN, Barber's Point, Oahu, Hawaii; played with Walter Dyett, Lonnie Simmons & Marl Young Orchs & recorded with Erskine Hawkins Orch & Earl Hines All-Stars, 46-49. Mem, Fletcher Butler Soc Orch & took short road trip with Duke Ellington, 50-57; mem, Red Saunders Regal Theater Band, 57-64; mem staff orch, WBBM (CBS), 64-66; played with Dom Geraci, Les Waverly & Franz Bentler Orchs, 67-70; stage band teacher at high sch & col levels, 66-68; arr & lead alto in big band led by son, 70-75. Currently free lance instrumentalist, arr for jazz bands & Bway shows. Chief Collabrs: Prentice McCarey, Ocie Johnson, Frank Derrick III. *Songs & Instrumental Works:* Those Little Moments; Sloopy's Blues; The Message (stage band); A Latin Rock Shop (stage band).

DERSAN, JON
See Anders, John Frank

DESANTIS, EMIDIO   ASCAP 1963
composer, clarinetist, publisher
b Introdacqua, Italy, May 18, 1893. Educ: Pvt music study. Became US citizen, 21. Clarinetist, Providence Symph Orch, 50 yrs. Pres, DeSantis Music Publ & Records Co. Rec'd title, Maestro Commendatore di Merito & Gold Cross, by Supremo Scaligero Nobiliare e Militare Ordine dei Cavalieri della Concordia, Rome, Italy. Chief Collabr: Olivio Di Domenico. *Songs & Instrumental Works:* American National Grand Symphony March; Empire State Military March; Rhode Island Military March; Leesona Characteristic March; and 275 other compositions.

DESANTIS, ERNEST   ASCAP 1965
composer
b Catanzaro, Italy, Aug 12, 1892. Educ: Studied music & harmony with father, Pasquale Desantis. Retired as Chief Petty Officer, Musician Branch, USN. Chief Collabr: Charles Adam Zimmerman. *Songs & Instrumental Works:* Learning to Live; Montebello Sue; Poppies; Dawn; Song Without Words; I Foll-ow-God (hymn).

DE SAXE, SERENA
See Davison, Lita

DE SAXE (SAVORIAN), RUDOLPH (AMAURY)   ASCAP 1957
composer, author

b Cairo, Egypt, Feb 28, 05; d New York, NY, Dec 27, 58. Educ: Col des Freres, Helouan, Egypt; Liceo Musicale, Bologna, Italy; studied comp with Ottorino Respighi, Rome. Comp, arr, pianist & vocal coach; started to comp & orchestrate for motion pictures in Hollywood, 43; became a citizen of US, 45; was ed, Score, a bulletin of Am Soc Music Arr. Musical ed films, Hollywood Review. Comp & arr for numerous singers, incl singer, Serena Shaw, wife; arr & recorded at Esoteric & Counterpoint Record cos; recorded for Rama & Jubilee Records; established Serena Music Publ House; was mem, Am Fedn Musicians, Local 47; life mem, Am Soc Musical Arr, treas, 7 yrs. Mem: Screen Actors Guild; Am Comp & Lyricists Guild; Nat Asn Am Comp & Cond. Chief Collab: Serena Shaw. Songs: Kiss Me; Solitary Blues; Music: You're No Good for Me; Let Me Fly Into Your Arms. Instrumental Works: Parodiette (pianoforte); Hail My Native Land (march); Orch: La Belle Morena; Amor Gitano; Prayer for a Soldier; Symphonic Poem: Aurora; Paumanok (based on Walt Whitman's "Sea Drift"). Scores: Film/TV: Bells of San Fernando; Beyond One's Self; Mystery Range; Calamity Jane and the Texan; Outlaw Marshall.

DES GRANGES, LOUIS ANTHONY (LOU GRANGER)   ASCAP 1970
composer

b Providence, RI, Apr 22, 35. Educ: High sch; studied piano with Al Antonelli & Salvator Fransosi; studied saxophone. Songwriter, lyricist, arr & Navy musician; also has done work with var record cos. Songs: My Son; Love Alone; My Heart Will Break; Busy Bee; Snow; Songwriter; I'll See You Dear; Cleo, With the Yellow Tail; Would You Mind?; Lyrics: Skiers Prayer.

DE SHANNON, JACKIE   ASCAP 1970
composer, author, singer

b Hazel, Ky. Educ: Self taught. Started singing at age 6 yrs; began writing at age 13; toured with the Beatles in their first Am tour, 64-65, also toured with Neil Diamond; writer, 80- Chief Collabr: Randy Myers. Songs: Music: Come and Stay With Me; When You Walk in the Room; Put a Little Love in Your Heart; What the World Needs Now.

DESYLVA, B G (BUDDY)
See DeSylva, George Gard

DESYLVA, GEORGE GARD (BUDDY, B G DESYLVA)   ASCAP 1920
composer, author, publisher

b New York, NY, Jan 27, 1895; d Los Angeles, Calif, July 11, 50. Educ: Univ Southern Calif. To NY with Al Jolson. Wrote songs for Bway musicals incl "Ziegfeld Follies (1918, 1921)", "Sinbad", "Sally", "The Perfect Fool" & "The French Doll." Dir, ASCAP, 22-30. Joined Lew Brown & Ray Henderson as song writing team & music publ, 25. Sold publ firm, 29; to Hollywood under contract to Fox. Produced films incl "The Little Colonel", "The Littlest Rebel", "Captain January", "Poor Little Rich Girl" & "Stowaway." Producer & co-librettist, Bway musicals "Du-Barry Was a Lady" & "Panama Hattie"; produced "Louisiana Purchase." Exec producer, Paramount, 41-44. Film biography, "The Best Things in Life Are Free." Chief Collabrs: Gus Kahn, Al Jolson, George Gershwin, Jerome Kern, Vincent Rose, Louis Silvers, Joseph Meyer, Victor Herbert, Emmerich Kalman, Ira Gershwin, Ballard Macdonald, Lewis Gensler, James Hanley, Nacio Herb Brown, Richard Whiting, Vincent Youmans. Songs: 'N' Everything; I'll Say She Does; You Ain't Heard Nothin' Yet; Yoo-Hoo; Memory Lane; Why Do I Love You?; Whip-poor-will; Look for the Silver Lining; Avalon; April Showers; In Arcady; California, Here I Come; A Kiss In the Dark; I'll Build a Stairway to Paradise; Do It Again; I Won't Say I Will But I Won't Say I Won't; Somebody Loves Me; Keep Smiling At Trouble; Hello, 'Tucky; If You Knew Susie; Just a Cottage Small By a Waterfall; Tell Me More; Alabamy Bound; Kickin' the Clouds Away; My Fair Lady; When Day Is Done; Lucky Day; Birth of the Blues; Black Bottom; It All Depends on You; The Best Things in Life Are Free; Good News; The Varsity Drag; Just Imagine; Lucky in Love; Broken Hearted; Just a Memory; So Blue; I'm on the Crest of a Wave; You're the Cream in My Coffee; Button Up Your Overcoat; You Wouldn't Fool Me, Would You?; Sonny Boy; Together; My Sin; I'm a Dreamer, Aren't We All?; Sunny Side Up; If I Had a Talking Picture of You; Little Pal; Without Love; Thank Your Father; Red Hot Chicago; You Try Somebody Else; Eadie Was a Lady; My Lover; I Want to Be With You; Oh, How I Long to Belong to You; Rise 'n Shine; You're an Old Smoothie; Should I Be Sweet?; Gather Lip Rouge While You May; Polly Wolly Doodle; Wishing. Scores: Bway Stage: La La Lucille; Bombo; Orange Blossoms; The Yankee Princess; George White's Scandals (1922, 1923, 1924, 1925, 1926, 1928); Big Boy; Sweet Little Devil; Tell Me More; Captain Jinks; Manhattan Mary; co-librettist: Good News; Hold Everything; Three Cheers; Follow Through; Flying High; Take a Chance (also co-produced); Films: Sunny Side Up; The Singing Fool; Just Imagine.

DE TEDLA, AL
See Tessier, Albert Denis

DETT, ROBERT NATHANIEL   ASCAP 1925
composer, author, teacher

b Drummondsville, Ont, Oct 11, 1882; d Battle Creek, Mich, Oct 2, 43. Educ: Oliver Willis Halstead Cons, Lockport, NY; Oberlin Cons, Ohio, BMA; Harvard Cons Music, Master degree; Oberlin Cons, PhD; Eastman Cons,

Rochester, NY, MM, postgrad study. Music teacher, Lane Col, 08; dir music, Hampton Inst, Va, 17-33; free lance, Rochester, 33-37; dir music, Bennett Col, 37-42; comn by US Govt to do USO Tours, 42-43. Mem, AMORC (Rosicrucian Soc). Songs & Instrumental Works: Dett Collection of Spirituals (arr for choruses); Ordering of Moses (oratorio); Song of Seven (poem, literary); In the Bottoms (suite for piano); Magnolia Suite (piano); Ramah Violin Solo; Enchantment Suite (piano); Tropic Winter Suite (piano); Cinnamon Grove Suite (piano); American Sampler (symph); No Auction Block (symph); Marche Negre (organ); Choral: Listen to the Lambs; Ascapezza.

DEUTSCH, ADOLPH   ASCAP 1940
composer, conductor, arranger

b London, England, Oct 20, 1897; d. Educ: London Polytech; Royal Acad Music. To US, 1910, citizen, 1920. Led own orch; comp, arr & asst cond dance bands. Music dir & arr, Bway musicals. Three seasons with Paul Whiteman's Music Hall. Under contract with film studios, Hollywood. Founder, Screen Composer's Asn, pres, 43-53. Chief Collabr: Vincent Lopez. Songs & Instrumental Works: The Scottish Suite; March of the United Nations; Margot; Lonely Room; Clarabelle; Three Sisters; Piano Echoes; Skyride; Stairways; March Eccentrique. Scores: Film background: They Won't Forget; The Maltese Falcon; Action in the North Atlantic; High Sierra; They Drive By Night; The Mask of Dimitrios; Father of the Bride; The Stratton Story; Some Like It Hot; The Apartment; Films scored: Annie Get Your Gun (Acad Award, 50); Seven Brides for Seven Brothers (Acad Award, 54); Oklahoma! (Acad Award, 55); Show Boat; The Band Wagon.

DEUTSCH, ELIZABETH VERONICA WELLS   ASCAP 1968
composer, author

b Richmond Hill, NY, Jan 25, 15. Educ: Richmond Hill High Sch; Russell Sage Col, BS; NY Univ, MA. Children's songwriter; co-founded Sing 'n Do Co, Inc. Author & comp of 11 record albums of illus dramatic-action song stories & complete musical progs for grades Pre-K through 6 and spec educ; all albums publ by Sing 'n Do Co, Inc, NJ & produced for the sch market. Albums: Christmas Windows; Musical Participation Stories; Rain or Shine With Sing 'n Do; Clap Hands With Sing 'n Do; In the Toy Shop.

DEUTSCH, EMERY   ASCAP 1937
composer, conductor, violinist

b Budapest, Hungary, Sept 10, 07. Educ: Fordham Univ; Juilliard; Royal Cons, Budapest; studied with Percy Goetschius. Husband of Marjorie Goetschius, father of Gregory Paul Deutsch. Music dir, CBS, 12 yrs. Led own dance orch, appearing in theatres, hotels throughout US. Lt(jg), USN, WW II. Made many records & radio appearances. Chief Collabrs: Jack Lawrence, Jimmy Rogan, Bud Green, Paul Francis Webster. Songs: Play Fiddle Play; My Gypsy Rhapsody; When a Gypsy Makes His Violin Cry; Moon of Desire; Stars and Soft Guitars; Stardust on the Moon; You Started Something; Halgato; Heart and Soul; Moonlight Mood.

DEUTSCH, HELEN   ASCAP 1953
author

b New York, NY, Mar 21, 06. Educ: Barnard Col, BA, 27. Screenwriter, motion pictures: "Lili", "National Velvet", "Golden Earrings", "I'll Cry Tomorrow", "The Glass Slipper", "The Unsinkable Molly Brown", "Valley of the Dolls" & "King Solomon's Mines"; TV: "Hallmark Christmas Show", "Jack and the Beanstalk" & "General Motors Fiftieth Anniversary Show." Author of short stories, newspaper features & plays. Chief Collabr: Bronislau Kaper. Songs: Lyrics: Hi-Lili-Hi-Lo; The Ill-Assorted Guards; The Ballad of Jack; Take My Love; I'll Go Along With You; Looka Me; He Never Looks My Way; Twelve Feet Tall; Sweet World.

DEUTSCH, HERBERT ARNOLD
composer, author

b Baldwin, NY, Feb 9, 32. Educ: Hofstra Univ, BS(educ), 56; Manhattan Sch Music, BMusic, 60, MMusic, 61; NY Univ, doctoral study, 74-77. Joined fac, Hofstra Univ, 63, asst prof, 67, dir electronic music studio, 69, assoc prof & dept chmn, 73- Dir, Hofstra Inst of Arts. Comp, jingles, commercials & film scores. Author, "Synthesis-An Introduction to Electronic Music." Developed prog in music merchandising for Hofstra Univ. Consultant, Multivox Music, 75-76, Norlin Music Inc, 76-79. Marketing dir, Moog Music Inc, 80. Songs: Mutima, An African Tale of the Creation (chorus). Instrumental Works: Moon Ride; Sonorities for Orchestra and Electronic Tape; Fantasia I (wind ens & electronic tape). Scores: Film/TV: The Man You Loved to Hate.

DEUTSCHENDORF, HENRY JOHN, JR (JOHN DENVER)
singer, songwriter

b Roswell, NMex, Dec 31, 43. Educ: Tex Tech Univ. With Mitchell Trio, 65-68. Solo recording & concert artist, 68- Appeared on TV variety specials, 73-; appeared in film, "Oh, God!"; writer of numerous songs. Rec'd Golden Apple Prize, Hollywood Women's Press Club, 77. Songs: Leaving on a Jet Plane; Rocky Mountain High; Take Me Home, Country Roads. Albums: Rhymes and Reasons; Take Me to Tomorrow; Whose Garden Was This?; Poems, Prayers and Promises; Rocky Mountain High; Aerie; Farewell Andromeda; Back Home Again.

DEVENPORT, FRANK PERRY
composer, author, teacher
b Texarkana, Tex, Sept 30, 20. Educ: Los Angeles State Col, BA; cert sec teacher, Los Angeles City Sch District; studied piano with Wesley Coonley, Los Angeles, 41-44, comp & orchestration with Arnold Schoenberg, Los Angeles, 49-50. Studied piano & harmony from mother, a prof teacher, age 6-16. Wrote arrangments & original compositions for Lionel Hampton, Freddie Slack, Barney Biggard, Jimmy Lunceford, Harry James & many local bands, 49-52. Played piano with Barney Biggard, Bob Chester & local bands. Had own quartet featuring Herbie Stewart. *Songs:* Forgotten; Elegy for the Brave; Transformed Man; Loose Wig; Furlough Fling; Stay With Me; The Lady is Moody; The People's Choice; A Tree Grows in Burbank; New York Blues; Madona in the Starlight; When Winter Comes; Please Believe Me; Going on the Wagon; In a Mist; Nine O'clock Beer; Penthouse Serenade; Sweet and Lovely; Ahmur; Music: Only Yesterday; Chinero.

DEVEREAUX, RICHMOND
See Heard, Richard Martin

DEVINNY, DAREY GRANT   ASCAP 1968
composer, author, singer
b Montrose, Colo, May 27, 43. Educ: Montrose County High Sch; Pasadena Playhouse, BA, 69; Calif State Univ, Los Angeles; Calif teaching credential, 70; studied acting with Jeff Corey, 66-67; studied tae-kwon do karate under Master Young Park, 77-79, achieved Purple Belt. Appeared in many plays at Pasadena Playhouse & some TV shows. Won writing awards at Pasadena Playhouse. Artist, teacher & actor. Chief Collabrs: Tommy Leonetti, Dean Kay, Ron Harris, Ben DiTosti, Rod Burke. *Songs:* Song for My Son; Lyrics: The Deepest Part of Me; You're Someone Very New; Who in the World Can You Tell?; Whatever Happened to You?

DE VITO, ALBERT KENNETH (KENNETH   ASCAP 1954
ROGERS, KENNETH LISBON, CHARLES ALLEN)
composer, author, educator
b Hartford, Conn, Jan 17, 19. Educ: Hartford Federal Col, 39-40; NY Univ Sch Educ, BS, 48, MA, 50; Teachers Col, Columbia Univ; Midwestern Univ, PhD, 75; hon MusD, Eastern Nebr Christian Col, 74. Pres, The Piano Teachers Cong of New York, Inc. Comp/author of over 100 works. Teacher, writer, publ, ed, arr, music consult & lectr. Pianist & organist in concerts, theatres & radio. Mgr, G Schirmer. Teacher in pub schs & adult educ classes. Pianist in Armed Forces, WW II. Author, "Chord Dictionary", "Chord Encyclopedia", "Fake It", "Chord Charts", "Chord Approach to Pop Organ Playing", "Modern Organ Course" & "Chord Approach to Pop Piano Playing." Chief Collabrs: Ricardo Weeks, Harold Affros. *Songs & Instrumental Works:* Barn Dance; Big Bass Tuba; Caribbean Adventure; He Plays It Crazy; Listen to the Sleighbells; Long Ago in Bethlehem; Sea Fever; Piano Sonata No 1; Seven Novelletes for Piano; Three Conversational Pieces; In a Canon Style; Dance Suite; Fiddlers Tune; Contrasts for Two Pianos; Petite Moderne; Music: I Can't Believe; Collections: Pedro Dances; Toys.

DEVOE, DALE   ASCAP 1973
trombonist, arranger
b Abington, Pa, Feb 14, 51. Educ: Philadelphia Musical Acad, BM, 72; Ga State Univ, grad studies, 76; studied trombone with Roy Stevens, Glenn Dodson & Donald Reinhardt. Has done touring of NAm & Europe with name bands, incl Stan Kenton, Glenn Miller, Jimmy Dorsey & Stanley Clarke. Performed with top name entertainers, incl Tony Bennett, Burt Bacharach, Lou Rawls & Nancy Wilson. Arr for Stan Kenton, Stanley Clarke & Dave Stahl. *Instrumental Works:* Roy's Blues; 2002-Zarathustrevisited.

DE VOL, FRANK   ASCAP 1964
composer, conductor, arranger
b Moundsville, WVa, Sept 20, 11. Educ: Miami Univ. Violinist with Father's orch; with George Olsen, Horace Heidt & Alvino Rey. Cond & arr for records. Radio shows, "Rudy Vallee", "Ginny Sims", "Jack Carson" & "Jack Smith-Dinah Shore." TV shows, "Rosemary Clooney", "George Gobel", "Colgate Comedy Hour", "Betty White", "Tennessee Ernie Ford", "College of Musical Knowledge", "Dinah Shore" & "Danny Thomas." Academy nominations, "Pillow Talk", "Cat Ballou", "Hush, Hush, Sweet Charlotte" (song & score) & "Guess Who's Coming to Dinner." TV series, "My Three Sons", "Family Affair", "Brady Bunch", "Love Boat", "McCloud" plus others. Motion pictures, "The Frisco Kid", "Hustle", "The Longest Yard", "McClintock", "Dirty Dozen" plus others. Actor, "Fernwood Tonite" & "America To-Nite." Many guest shots on TV. Chief Collabr: Mack David. *Songs:* Hush, Hush, Sweet Charlotte; I Never Loved; Look At Me; I Found a New Friend; Music: A Man and a Train. *Scores:* Film: Herby Goes to Monte Carlo; Herby Goes Bananas; My Three Sons; Family Affair; Brady Bunch.

DE VOLL, CALVIN JOSEPH   ASCAP 1921
composer, author, violinist
b Omaha, Nebr, Sept 19, 1886; d Ft Worth, Tex, July 14, 70. Educ: Chicago Musical Col. Violinist symph orchs incl, Chicago & Dallas; made concert tours; taught violin. Chief Collabrs: Jack Yellen, Maurice Baron, Maceo Pinkard, Abe Olman, Clinton Keithley, Ernie Erdman. *Songs:* Alabama Lullaby; How Do You Do Everybody; Rose of Araby; Whippoorwill; Cabin in the Hills; Daddy's

Lullaby; Tie a Little String Around Your Finger; Land Beyond the Sun; Kiss-a-Miss; How's Your Folks and My Folks; Are You Tired of Me.

DE VRIES JOHN   ASCAP 1944
author
b Wayne, Pa, Dec 2, 15. Chief Collabr: Joe Bushkin. *Songs:* There'll Be a Hot Time in Berlin; How Do You Do Without Me?; You Can Never Shake Love; Wherever There's Love; The Things I Know About You; Slow Burn; Oh, Look At Me Now; Lovely Weather We're Having; Something Wonderful Happens in Summer.

DEWAR, ALLISON
See Turnbull, Graham Morrison

DEWAR, TED ROYAL   ASCAP 1958
orchestrator, musician
b Skedee, Okla, Sept 6, 04. Educ: Studied harmony & theory with Joseph Schillinger & Aldrich Kidd. Worked with numerous bands in Midwest. Orchr for Wayne King & Ted Weems, Chicago; also Paul Whiteman, Ben Burnie & Emil Coleman. Saxophonist & clarinetist, Chicago Theatre & Oriental Theatre, Balaban & Katz. Orchr for Rockette routines & overtures, Radio City Music Hall, 43-53; also Bway shows, 25 yrs. Arr Bway musicals: "Brigadoon"; "Guys and Dolls"; "Pal Joey"; "Mister Wonderful"; "Paint Your Wagon"; "Annie Get Your Gun"; "New Faces of 1952." Chief Collabrs: Russell Bennett, Hans Spialek, Don Walker.

DEWEY, RAY F   ASCAP 1968
composer, author, arranger
b Cleveland, Ohio, Mar 5, 33. Educ: North Olmsted High Sch; Glendale Col, AA; studied keyboard with Victor Feldman & orchestration with Albert Harris. With radio series "Piano Portraits", age 16; musical dir & spec serv pianist, AFRS; pianist in clubs, motion pictures & recording field, Los Angeles; comp & arr recording field with The Temptations, Jimmy Ruffin, Johnny Bristol, The Jackson Sisters, Switch & Walter Jackson; comp & arr for Doc Severinson in the "Tonight Show." Chief Collabrs: Clay McMurray, Jimmy Georgantones, Bruce Fisher, Ernie Watts. *Songs:* Give It Up; Magic Man. *Instrumental Works:* Sky High; Git Down; Funky Peacock.

DEY, LARRY
See Deybrook, L M

DEYBROOK, L M (LARRY DEY)   ASCAP 1959
composer, author
b New York, NY, Aug 8, 10; d Long Beach, Calif, June 18, 76. Educ: Univ Calif, Los Angeles. Sang & acted in vaudeville, nightclubs, radio & films. Wrote & dir revues. Chief Collabrs: George Liberace, Thomas Powers. *Songs:* Dream Faces; Gold Diggers' Blues; Hit and Run Lover; Dingle Dangle; Is It Love or Fascination?.

DE YOUNG, DENNIS   ASCAP 1971
composer, author
b Chicago, Ill. Singer & keyboardist. Chief Collabrs: Tommy Shaw, James Young. *Songs:* Babe; Lady; Lorelei; Grand Illusion; Come Sail Away.

DHARMA, BUCK
See Roeser, Donald

DIA, DICK   ASCAP 1959
composer, guitarist, mandolinist
b New York, NY, Feb 21, 17. Educ: High sch. Musician in nightclubs, New York. Music dir, 15 yrs. Made many records. *Instrumental Works:* Ciuo; Tarantelle Chopinesque; Valse Giorgiano.

DIAMOND, CLIFF
See Mann, Stephen Follett

DIAMOND, DAVE
See Davison, Sid I

DIAMOND, DAVID LEO   ASCAP 1943
composer, author, educator
b Rochester, NY, July 9, 15. Educ: Univ Rochester Eastman Sch Music; Cleveland Inst Music; New Music Sch & Dalcroze Inst, New York; studied with Nadia Boulanger, Paris, Hermann Scherchen, Neuchatel, Roger Sessions, New York. First orchestral works heard in New York, 33. Lectr, 42-; cond New York Philh, Fiftieth Birthday concert. Awards: Guggenheim Fel, Prix de Rome, 38 & 42; Juilliard Publ Award for Psalm for Orchestra; Music Critics Circle Awards. Chief Collabrs: E E Cummings; Glenway Wescott. *Songs:* David Mourns for Absalom; Brigid's Song; We Two (song cycle); Hebrew Melodies (song cycle). *Instrumental Works:* Rounds for String Orchestra; Fourth Symphony; Music for Shakespeare's Romeo and Juliet; Overture to The Tempest; Elegy in Memory of Ravel; String Quartet No 3, No 4, & No 10; Sonata for Piano No 1; Eight Piano Pieces for Children; Sonata for Violin and Piano; Symphony No 5 & No 7; Quintet (clarinet, two violas, two cellos); Concertino for Piano and Small Orchestra; Preludes and Fugues for Piano.

DIAMOND, DOROTHY FLORENCE (ROBERTS)　　ASCAP 1965
author
b Jersey City, NJ, Apr 14, 10. Educ: High sch; Rice Inst, maj Eng & jour. Dancer for Earl Carroll; ballerina in Europe, 5 yrs; songwriter. Chief Collabs: Art Todd, Dotty Todd, Dorothy Daniels. *Songs:* Lyrics: Black Velvet Eyes; Special Kind of Love; Really in Love With the Guy; Secrets; Time Will Tell.

DIAMOND, ISIDORE (A L)　　ASCAP 1959
author
b Ungheni, Romania, June 27, 20. Educ: Columbia Univ, BA, 41. Author, Columbia Varsity Show. Sketches & Lyrics: "Leonard Sillman's 8:30 Revue", "Alive and Kicking", "Catch a Star" & "Joy Ride." Screenwriter: "Love in the Afternoon", "Some Like It Hot", "The Apartment", "Irma La Douce" & "Cactus Flower." Acad Award; NY Film Critic's Award; Writers Guild Laurel Award. Chief Collabrs: Lee Wainer, Matty Malneck, Andre Previn. *Songs:* Lyrics: Some Like It Hot.

DIAMOND, JOEL　　ASCAP 1970
producer, publisher
b Passaic, NJ. Educ: Rider Col. Producer for Engelbert Humperdinck, 6 yrs. Owner, Silver Blue Productions. *Instrumental Works:* Like a Sunday Morning; Song for Lovers; Look on the Good Side.

DIAMOND, JOSEPH E　　ASCAP 1971
composer
b Cheyenne, Wyo, Mar 15, 44. Educ: Univ Calif Los Angeles, BA; Calif State Univ, Northridge, MA. Nat & int tours, Roger Wagner Chorale; motion picture promotional tours, Walt Disney Productions. Casual orch leader. Instrumentalist (accordion, piano, clarinet) & vocalist. Creator of gourmet/variety TV show "Tableside" & "The Telephone Game." *Songs:* You Won't Believe It; So Long Escanaba; Music is the Life I Sing; My Trip Up to the Moon. *Instrumental Works:* Juvenile Jury (TV theme).

DIAMOND, LEO　　ASCAP 1954
composer, author, arranger
b New York, NY, June 29, 15; d Los Angeles, Calif, Sept 15, 66. Educ: Pub schs. Arr & lead harmonicaist, Borrah Minevitch Harmonica Rascals, 30-46; performed in films & on records. *Songs & Instrumental Works:* Mediterranean Suite; Off Shore; Skin Diver's Suite; Mr X; Hold on to Your Dreams; Tijuana Border Patrol; Shtiggy Boom; Nashville Nights; Mirimar; Rainy Season; Misty Night.

DIAMOND, LEO　　ASCAP 1960
composer, author, conductor
b New York, NY, Oct 8, 07. Educ: Pub schs. Led own band; columnist, The Metronome. Saxophonist. Chief Collabs: Mann Curtis, Lou Haber, Tommy Mac Williams, Max Rich. *Songs & Instrumental Works:* Let Roses Be For-Get-Me-Nots; Save a Little Love for a Rainy Day; Ich Hob Dir Lieb; Candles in the Wind; Peter Platypus; Mission of the Moon; In a Roundabout Way; Love So Long; Trinidad Daddy; There Is a Santa Claus.

DIAMOND, NEIL　　ASCAP 1970
composer, author, singer
b Brooklyn, NY, Jan 24, 41. Educ: Pvt guitar study. Songwriter for var publ cos; free-lance comp, New York, 7 yrs. Comp, musician & singer, signed to Bang Record Co & released 3 hit songs, signed to Uni Records (later MCA Records) & produced var albums, 67-72, signed to Columbia Records & wrote score for film "Jonathan Livingston Seagull"; in concert throughout US. Presented in concert by Shubert Orgn, Winter Garden Theatre, New York, 72. Sabbatical from concerts, 3 yrs. In concert, Australia, Europe & NAm & composing, 76- Recorded 14 platinum & gold albums. *Songs:* Cherry, Cherry; Kentucky Woman; Cracklin' Rosie; Song Sung Blue; You Don't Bring Me Flowers; September Morn; Jonathan Livingston Seagull; Sweet Caroline. *Albums:* You Don't Bring Me Flowers; I'm Glad You're Here With Me Tonight; Beautiful Noise; Hot August Night.

DIASIO, DANIEL JOSEPH (DAN D LYONS)　　ASCAP 1970
composer, author, manager
b Bridgeport, Conn, Sept 7, 41. Educ: Stratford High Sch, Conn; New York Inst, studied photography, 60; studied music with Tony Esposito, 63-68. Lyricist for off-Bway musical, "The Laughing Feather" & movie, "The White Rat." Personal mgr, Eddie Delmar, singer. Staff lyricist, Little Darlin Records. Author: "In Between Marriages." Columnist of single parent, In Our Own Backyard. Chief Collabs: Anthony (Tony) Esposito, Richard Diasio. *Songs:* Littlest Nightmare; I Will Find a Way; My First Laugh; I Feel Funny; Organ Grinder Man; Got Lotsa Time Now; Miracles; Lyrics: What Kind of World Would It Be?; Terrible Land of the Gruffs; Old Man and a Young Boy; Chief Gruff—The Meanest Man; Animal Sleep; Laughing Feather; Remember; Take My Heart With You; As a Boy Becomes a Man; So I'll End Up Cryin My Heart Out; Marie—With You; As You Go By; Just a Simple Melody; A Face in a Crowd; Hey—Look At Us. *Instrumental Works:* Mystic Love.

DI BONAVENTURA, SAM　　ASCAP 1960
composer, teacher
b Follansbee, WVa, Nov 17, 23. Educ: Juilliard Sch Music, BS; Yale Univ, BM & MM; Harvard Univ, MA; Peabody Cons, DMA; studied with Paul Hindemith, Walter Piston, Vincent Persichetti. Taught at Yale Sch of Music, Miss Southern Col, Harvard Univ, Wellesley Col, Peabody Cons, Neighborhood Music Sch, New Haven & Dartmouth Col; taught at New Eng Cons, head theory dept, 61-63. *Songs:* I Hope Tomorrow Never Comes; No Compree.

DICENZO, PANFILO ANTHONY　　ASCAP 1975
composer, author, singer
b McKees Rocks, Pa, Sept 30, 49. Educ: Duquesne Univ, BM(perf, educ), MEduc. Singer & woodwind player beginning at age 13, for opera & supper clubs; actor. *Songs:* I Love You So; Without You; Theme: The Majorettes.

DICK, DOROTHY
See Link, Dorothy

DICK, MARCEL　　ASCAP 1960
composer, violinist, educator
b Miskolc, Hungary, Aug 28, 1898. Educ: Royal Acad of Music, Budapest, music degree. Asst prof, Royal Acad, 16-17. First violinist, Budapest Opera, Philh, 19-21; first violist, Vienna Symph, 23-24; violist & co-founder, Kolisch Quartet, 24-27; violist, Rose Quartet, 33-34, Detroit Symph, 34-35, Stradivarius Quartet, 35-42 & Cleveland Orch, 43-49. Head grad theory & comp dept, Cleveland Inst of Music. *Instrumental Works:* Four Elegies and an Epiloque (cello); Symphony; Capriccio; Adagio and Rondo.

DICKERSON, ROGER DONALD　　ASCAP 1965
composer, lecturer, teacher
b New Orleans, La, Aug 24, 34. Educ: Dillard Univ, BA(music educ; cum laude), 55; Indiana Univ, MM(musical comp), 57; Akademie Musik Darstellende Kunst, Vienna, Austria, Fulbright Fellow, special studies of musical comp, 59-62. Composer of musical comp, New Orleans, 62-; played as jazz pianist in the French Quarter & traveled with var groups. Fellowships incl: 2 Fulbright Fellowships, John Hay Whitney Fellowship & Nat Endowment of the Arts Award, also numerous comn. Was honored at Kennedy Ctr, 80. Lyceum guest at var univs. With Southern Music Publ Co Inc, NY; educ consult. Documentary film entitled "New Orleans Concerto" made of premiere performance & life & work of the composer, PBS special, 78. *Instrumental Works:* Sonatina (solo piano); A Musical Service for Louis (requiem for Louis Armstrong; comn & premiered by New Orleans Philh Symph Orch, 72); Orpheus an' His Slide Trombone (narrator, orch); Ten Concert Pieces for Beginning String Players (Comn by Rockefeller Found); New Orleans Concerto (piano, orch; comn by New Orleans Bicentennial Comn).

DICKEY, DAN BENJAMIN　　ASCAP 1978
composer, author, singer
b Houston, Tex, June 22, 49. Educ: Tex Mil Inst, San Antonio; Univ Plano, Tex, 66-68. Began performing professionally in small nightclubs & road houses, 77. Songwriter, publ & recording artist, 78- Chief Collabr: Donald Riis. *Songs:* Hot Mama; Close the Door; Bye Bye Baby; Country Sky; Foolish Heart.

DICKEY, RICHARD SCOTT (RICHARD ESTES)　　ASCAP 1979
composer, author, arranger
b Los Angeles, Calif, Aug 19, 56. Educ: San Clemente High Sch; San Diego State Univ; studied twelve tone with George Knight; studied arr with Herb Allen, 75-79. Lead trumpeter, "Up With People Show," band leader & music mgr; contributing arr for 79-80 "Up With People Show," album & TV; instrumentalist on vibes & trumpet. *Songs:* Sailor Pete.

DICKINSON, CLARENCE　　ASCAP 1941
composer, author, organist
b Lafayette, Ind, May 7, 1873; d. Educ: Hon MusD, Northwestern Univ, Gustavus Adolphus Col & Ohio Wesleyan Univ; LittD, Miami Univ; studied with Harrison Wild, Adolf Weiding, Heinrich Reimann, Otto Singer, Alexander Guilmant & Louis Vierne. Cond orchs & choral groups; gave recitals, US & Europe; cond fests of own works. Organist & choirmaster, St James Cathedral, Chicago, Brick Presby Church, NY, 09-59 & Temple Bethel, NY, 20 yrs. Founder, Am Guild of Organists. With wife, Helen, founded Sch of Sacred Music, Union Theol Sem. Coed, "Presbyterian Hymnal" & "Reformed Evangelical Hymnal." Coauth, "Excursions in Musical History", "Troubadour Songs", "The Choir Loft and Pulpit" & "Technique and Art of Organ Playing." Chief Collabr: Helen Dickinson. *Songs & Instrumental Works:* For Organ: Storm King Symphony; Joy of the Redeemed; Berceuse. Oratorio: The Redeemer; Anthems: In Joseph's Lovely Garden; Beneath the Shadow of the Great Protection; Great and Glorious.

DICKINSON, HAROLD H, JR (HAL)　　ASCAP 1956
composer, author, singer
b Buffalo, NY, Dec 12, 13; d. Educ: High sch. Organized Modernaires, vocal group; sang with dance orchs incl Paul Whiteman, Fred Waring, Charlie Barnet, Glenn Miller & Bob Crosby, also in films, TV & nightclubs. Pres, Compass Productions. Chief Collabrs: Allan Copeland, Jack Lloyd, Sid Lippman, Jack

Elliott. *Songs:* These Things You Left Me; Everytime I See You; Jingle Bell Polka; Romantique; Birds and Puppies and Tropical Fish; Tabby the Cat; Too Young to Know.

DICKINSON, HELEN A
ASCAP 1943
author, educator
b Port Elmsley, Ont, Dec 5, 1875; d Tucson, Ariz, Sept 25, 57. Educ: Queens Univ, Can, MA; Heidelberg Univ, Ger, PhD. Lectr art, Union Theol Sem, NY. Wrote texts & translated foreign texts for sacred works set to music by husband, Clarence Dickinson. Author: "German Masters of Art", "The Philosophy of Henry Thoreau", "A Treasury of Worship." Co-author: "Troubadour Songs", "The Choir Loft and Pulpit" & "Technique and Art of Organ Playing." Co-ed: "Presbyterian Hymnal" & "Reformed Evangelical Hymnal." Chief Collabr: Clarence Dickinson. *Songs:* In Joseph's Lovely Garden (anthem).

DICKINSON, JUNE MCWADE
ASCAP 1964
composer
b Rochester, NY, June 26, 24. Chief Collabr: Ed Dickinson *Songs & Instrumental Works:* Glass Balls on a Christmas Tree; High School Memories (march).

DICKSON, LARUE
ASCAP 1960
composer, conductor, violinist
b Grove City, Pa, Mar 13, 01. Educ: Pub schs. Organized orchs, Grove City; played in orch, Cleveland; dir youth orch & church choirs. Mem, Indust Relations Dept, GM. *Songs:* There Is No One on Earth Like Your Mother; Supplication.

DIEKEMA, WILLIS ALCOTT
ASCAP 1947
composer, author
b Holland, Mich, Oct 5, 1892. Educ: Hope Col Preparatory; Univ Mich, BA, 14. While in sch, wrote music for 2 student operas. Pilot, air service, awarded Distinguished Service Cross, World War I. Pres, De Pree Pharmaceutical Mfg Co. *Songs:* Keep America Singing.

DIEMENTE, EDWARD PHILIP
ASCAP 1971
composer, author, teacher
b Cranston, RI, Feb 27, 23. Educ: Boston Univ, 41-43; Hartt Sch Music, 46-48; Eastman Sch Music, BM, 49. Teacher, Hartt Sch Music, Univ Hartford, 49-. Comp concert music for instruments & chamber ens, for voices & large ens. Performed in Eng, Scotland, Sweden, Norway, Poland, France, Ger & USSR. *Songs & Instrumental Works:* Celebration (wind ensemble); Mirrors III (taped electronic sounds); Murmurs (orch); You Can Go Home Again (soprano, clarinet, cello & piano); Caritas (double bass & organ); The Eagles Gather (organ, perc & tape); It Is If You Say It Is; Quartet (66 & 67); Development (double bass & wind ensemble); Dairy II (2 saxophones & tape); Forms of Flight and Fancy (soprano & brass quintet); Shadows (wind quintet & perc); Sound Scenes (film & tape); Mirrors VII (cello & piano); The Epiphany Clock (flute & tape); Things Heard (trombone & tape); Wheels (chamber orch); Orbits (trombone & horn); Orenda (organ); Love Song for Autumn (14 brass); Trio (69); Dimensions IV (wind ensemble & tape); Mirrors VI (saxophone & piano); Harmonies (3 trombones & tape); Songs for Winter (SATB chorus).

DIEMER, EMMA LOU
ASCAP 1961
composer, teacher, organist
b Kansas City, Mo, Nov 24, 27. Educ: Yale Univ Sch Music, BM, 49, MM, 50, studied with Paul Hindemith, Richard Donovan; Brussels Cons, Fulbright scholar, 52-53; Berkshire Music Ctr, 54 & 55, studied with Ernst Toch, Roger Sessions; Eastman Sch Music, PhD, 60, studied with Howard Hanson, Bernard Rogers, David Craighead. Ford Found comp-in-residence, Arlington Schs, Va, 59-61; prof theory & comp, Univ Md, 65-70; prof theory & comp, Univ Calif, Santa Barbara, 71- Organist in var churches, 40-; pianist. Awards: ASCAP, Nat Fedn Music Clubs, Louisville Orch, Univ Md, Univ Calif, plus others. Comns: Kindler Found, Wayne State Univ, Lutheran Church in Am, Armstrong Flute Ensemble, plus others. *Songs:* Music: Four Chinese Love-Poems (soprano & harp or piano); Four Poems (by Alice Meynell for soprano & chamber ensemble or piano); Three Madrigals (SATB & piano); O Come, Let Us Sing Unto the Lord (SATB & piano); Dance, Dance, My Heart (SATB, perc & piano); The Shepherd to His Love (SA or TB & piano with flute); Fragments From the Mass (SSA); Alleluia (SSA); Three Poems of Ogden Nash (TTB & piano); Two Madrigals (2-part & piano). *Instrumental Works:* Youth Overture; Symphonie Antique; Concerto for Flute; Sonata for Flute and Piano or Harpsichord; Quartet for Piano, Violin, Viola and Cello; Toccata for Flute Chorus; Music for Woodwind Quartet; Trio for Flute, Oboe, Harpsichord and Tape; Movement for Flute, Oboe and Organ; Fantasy on O Sacred Head for Organ; Celebration, Seven Hymn Settings for Organ; Toccata for Organ; Toccata for Marimba; Seven Etudes for Piano; Patchworks (electronic tape); Scherzo (electronic tape).

DIENI, JOHN
ASCAP 1961
author
b Philadelphia, Pa, May 18, 24. Educ: Pub schs. Chief Collabrs: Joseph Dieni, William Armocida. *Songs:* Lovebound; Definition of Love; Only in My Dreams; The One You Love.

DIENI, JOSEPH
ASCAP 1961
composer
b Philadelphia, Pa, Mar 8, 23. Chief Collabrs: John Dieni, William Armocida. *Songs:* Lovebound; Definition of Love; Only in My Dreams; The One You Love.

DIERCKS, JOHN HENRY
ASCAP 1964
composer
b Montclair, NJ, Apr 19, 27. Educ: Oberlin Col Mus, BM, 49; Univ Rochester, Eastman Sch Music, MM, 50, PhD, 60; studied comp with Herbert Elwell, Bernard Rogers, Howard Hanson, Alan Hovhaness. Chmn, music dept, Hollins Col, Va. *Songs:* He Is Risen, Alleluia!; Music: Clap Your Hands! *Instrumental Works:* Mirror of Brass (septet); Sonata for Oboe and Piano; Diversions for Recorder and Harpsichord.

DIETERLE, TIL
ASCAP 1959
composer, author, pianist
b Feldkirch, Austria; d. Educ: Univ Calif, Los Angeles, BA. Accompanist for Rodgers & Hammerstein, Calif. Pianist, singer in supper clubs, hotels throughout US, Europe, Can & Caribbean. Formed own group; made many records. Chief Collabrs: Jim Goodfriend, Jan Harland, Philip Raye. *Songs:* Vegas Blues; Trudel; Impressions of London Bridge.

DIETZ, HOWARD (DICK HOWARD)
ASCAP 1929
author, lyricist, librettist
b New York, NY, Sept 8, 1896. Educ: Townsend Harris Hall; Columbia Univ Sch of Journalism; var hon degrees. Dir, ASCAP, 59-66. Served, USN, World War I. While in col, worked as newspaper stringer & contributing columnist, won slogan contest & began career as agency copywriter. Dir of advert & promotion, Samuel Goldwyn, then MGM, 24; created Leo the Lion. With MGM, 30 yrs, former vpres. Mem of bd, Loew's Inc, 25- Lyricist, librettist & author for Bway & radio shows & films. Top songs featured at Museum of City of New York, exhibition, "The Career of Howard Dietz," 72; Lyric & Lyricist Howard Dietz evening, 90th Street YMHA, 74; TV special "Song By Song By Howard Dietz," 80. Recipient, 50 yr honors, Columbia Univ; elected to Songwriter's Hall of Fame, 70. Author, autobiography "Dancing in the Dark, Words By Howard Dietz," (ASCAP award, 74). Chief Collabrs: Arthur Schwartz, Vernon Duke, Jerome Kern, Jimmy McHugh, Ralph Rainger, Sammy Fain, George Gershwin, Rouben Mamoulian, George S Kaufman. *Songs:* Gypsy Caravan; If You Think It's Love—You're Right; All Lanes Must Reach a Turning; I Want to Be There; Weeping Willow Tree; Why Did I Leave Wisconsin? Kenosha Wisconsin; Heaven On Earth; Oh Kay; Sentimental Billy; New York Town; Hogan's Alley; I've Got a Yes Girl; That Old Quartette on the Corner; That Melody of Love; In a Little Hideaway; What Makes My Baby Blue; When I Am Housekeeping for You; High and Low; I'm Like a Sailor Home From the Sea; I've Made a Habit of You; I Guess I'll Have to Change My Plan; Moanin' Low; Caught in the Rain; Red Hair and Freckles; I Can't Forget; I Need You So; Seems to Me; Got a Man on My Mind Worryin' Away; Dancing Town; Out in the Open Air; Forget All Your Books; All the King's Horses; Right At the Start of It; The Moment I Saw You; Something to Remember You By; Practising Up on You; Lucky Seven; I Like Your Face; You're the Sunrise; What a Case I've Got On You; Miserable With You; Hoops; Sweet Music; Confession; New Sun in the Sky; I Love Louisa; Dancing in the Dark; High and Low I've Been Looking for You; Is It All a Dream; Alone Together; A Shine on Your Shoes; Smokin' Reefers; Louisiana Hayride; A Rainy Day; Two Faced Woman; Fatal Fascination; Love Lost; Jungle Fever; Feelin' High; Born to Be Kissed; What About Me; How High Can a Little Bird Fly; Hi-de-Home Sweet Home; Under Your Spell; Absentminded; Cowboy Where Are You Riding O; Liza Lou; The Hurdy Gurdy Man; Square Dance; I'll Make You Happy; If There Is Someone Lovelier Than You; When You Love Only One; You and the Night and the Music; Maria; Wand'ring Heart; That Fellow Manuelo; That's Not Cricket; Thief in the Night; Farewell My Lovely; What a Wonderful World; O Leo; Love Is a Dancing Thing; Got a Bran' New Suit; The Hottentot Potentate; Sleigh Bells; Amigo; My Little Mule Wagon; By Myself; You Have Everything; I See Your Face Before Me; Why Did You Do It; I Believe in You; Don't Go Away Monsieur; How Can We Be Wrong; Two in a Taxi; On the Old Park Bench; 'Til You Return; Tondelayo; Keep the Light Burning Bright; Irresistible You; Dancing in the Streets; Indefinable Charm; Got a Bran' New Daddy; I Have Grown to Love New York; Sugarfoot; There Are Yanks From the Banks of the Wabash; What Happened; I've Got a One Track Mind; Silver Shield; Arm in Arm; Palm Beach; Civilian; Apprentice Seaman; Farewell for a While; If You Can't Get the Love You Want; Love I Long For; Poor As a Churchmouse; Sailing At Midnight; When You Live on an Island; Life's a Funny Present; Alone With You; The Dickey-Bird Song; Rhode Island Is Famous for You; Blue Grass; My Gal Is Mine Once More; First Prize At the Fair; Haunted Heart; That Element of Doubt; That's Entertainment; Triplets; I'm Part of You; Wish. *Scores:* Bway shows: Dear Sir; Oh Kay; Merry-Go-Round; The Battle of Paris; Here Comes the Bride; The Little Show; Three's a Crowd; Second Little Show; The Band Wagon; Flying Colors; Revenge With Music; At Home Abroad; Under Your Spell; Between the Devil; Keep Off the Grass; Dancing in the Streets; Jackpot; Tars and Spars (USCG revue, World War II); Sadie Thompson; Inside USA; A Bell for Adano; Films: The Band Wagon; That's Entertainment; That's Entertainment II; Operas: Fledermaus; La Boheme; Radio: The Gibson Family.

DIFRANCESCO, BURNADETTE ASCAP 1975
composer, author
b New York, NY, July 27, 44. Writer & producer of children's songs & records; with Sounds of 76 Co & Rainbow TV productions for children. Chief Collabr: Joey DiFrancesco. *Songs:* Have a Good Day; Smile—Ability; Can Do Person; Success; Good News; The Alley.

DIFRANCESCO, JOSEPH ASCAP 1965
composer, author
b New York, NY, Oct 6, 42. Writer, S & J Music, New York, 2 yrs. Writer & producer, MCA Music Co, New York, 5 yrs. Wrote music for Jello commercial. Independent writer & producer. Dir, Sounds of 76 Co, New York, 2 yrs. Pres, Rainbow TV Productions for Children, Inc, Orlando, Fla, 3 yrs. Chief Collabrs: Alan Dishell, Lou Zerato, Bernadette DiFrancesco. *Songs:* Beg, Borrow and Steal; Girl You Captivate Me; Just Another Face. *Scores:* TV: The Alexander Goodbuddy Show.

DIGGLE, ROLAND ASCAP 1932
composer, author
b London, Eng, Jan 1, 1887; d Los Angeles, Calif, Jan 13, 54. Educ: London, Oxford. To US 04. Church organist & choirmaster, St John's Episcopal, Wichita, Kans, 07-11, St John's Cathedral, Quincy, Ill, 11-14 & St John's, Los Angeles, 14-54. *Songs & Instrumental Works:* Concert Overture; Fairy Suite; Legend; Trio (piano, violin, cello); Cello Sonata (Baldwin prize); Trio (organ, violin, harp); Violin Sonata; Sonata Gothique; California Suite; Passacaglia and Fugue; American Fantasy; Vesper Prayer; 2 string quartets.

DIGIOVANNI, ROCCO (ROCK JOHNSON) ASCAP 1967
composer, author, voice teacher
b New York, NY, May 20, 24. Educ: Brooklyn Cons Music, professional degree, studied comp with Wallingford Riegger; Benedetto Marcello Cons, Venice, studied with Franco Ferrara. Has had compositions performed throughout Europe; studied Bel Canto singing technique, 55-64. *Songs:* Have You Heard (It's All Over). *Instrumental Works:* Zephyr; Direction (soprano & orch); Sonatina for Piano. *Scores:* Opera: Medea.

DI GIUSEPPE, SEVERINO (JAC D'JOSEPH) ASCAP 1954
composer, author
b Brooklyn, NY, July 10, 19. Educ: Amityville High Sch, Long Island; Whitmans Sch Interior Design & Decoration, New York. Songwriter; wrote spec material; publ poetry. Chief Collabrs: Vin Roddie, Marty Greene, Frank Signorelli, Jacob Jacobs, Alvin Lucier. *Songs:* Ask Yourself; Summer in Manhattan; Lyrics: And Then; Don't Play With Fire; Don't Be Afraid.

DI JULIO, MAX JOSEPH ASCAP 1963
composer, author, teacher
b Philadelphia, Pa, Oct 10, 19. Educ: Univ Denver, BM & MM; Univ Colo. Trumpet player in clubs, radio & symph, Philadelphia. WW II, Glenn Miller Band, Atlantic City. Arr, NBC Radio, Denver & for var media incl Denver Symph, cond & music dir, The Denver Post Operas, 21 yrs, guest cond, Denver Symph, Omaha Symph, Sioux City Symph & others; music arr-cond, "The Pearle Rae Show," cond many symph pops concerts. *Songs:* A Sacred Service (choir, electric guitar). *Instrumental Works:* Celebration (A Festive Overture); Concerto in One Movement for Electric Guitar and Orchestra; Reflections on the City (overture); Ski Run (string orch). *Scores:* Opera: Portrait of Baby Doe; Bway show: Boom Town; Film/TV: The Artist; Jerry; Little Children, Listen.

DILL, WILLIAM LESLIE ASCAP 1962
composer, author
b Chiselhurst, NJ, Oct 27, 13. Educ: Pub & parochial schs, Philadelphia. Became youngest mem of Philadelphia Transportation Co band at age 15; played dance-theatre & club dates. Teacher of band, perc & vibracussion instruments. Cond, E L James Memorial Band & Philadelphia Civic Concert Band. Clerk & prog planner, leading music publ firms, Philadelphia, 56- Mem, Am Fedn of Musicians. *Songs & Instrumental Works:* Rhythmology; Band: Champions of Democracy; Synocracy; Modeerf.

DILLARD, DOUGLAS FLINT ASCAP 1963
composer, author, musician
b East St Louis, Ill, Mar 6, 37. Mem music group The Dillards; banjo player & singer on TV "Andy Griffith Show" & "Judy Garland Show." Recording artist, Elektra, Capitol, Together, A&M, Warner Bros, Twentieth Century Fox Records & Flying Fish Records. Appeared on "Dean Martin Show," also in Twentieth Century Fox film "The Rose" & "Popeye," Paramount. Wrote bk "The Bluegrass Banjo Style of Douglas Dillard." Chief Collabrs: Rodney Dillard, Dean Webb, Mitch Jayne, Gene Clark, Bernie Leadon, Bill Knoph, Kathryn Dillard, John Hartford, Byron Berline. *Songs & Instrumental Works:* Doug's Tune; Hickory Holler; Runaway Country; Sinkin' Creek; My Grass Is Blue; Don't Come Rollin'.

DILLON, FANNIE CHARLES ASCAP 1939
composer, pianist
b Denver, Colo, Mar 16, 1881; d Sierra Madre, Calif, Feb 21, 47. Educ: Pomona Col. Debut as pianist, 08. Taught at Pomona Col, 10-31 & Los Angeles High Sch, 18-47. Gave concert of own works, NY, 18. *Instrumental Works:*

Celebration of Victory; The Cloud; A Letter From the Southland; Mission Garden; The Alps; Chinese Symphonic Suite; Western Saga; For Piano: Birds At Dawn; Melodic Poems of the Mountains; Fantasy Sonata & many more.

DILLON, WILLIAM A ASCAP 1914
composer, author, actor
b Cortland, NY, Nov 6, 1877; d Ithaca, NY, Feb 10, 66. Educ: Cortland Normal Sch. Appeared in medicine shows, minstrel shows & vaudeville; acted in many plays. Toured US & London with Harry Lauder unit. Retired, 12. Became bldg constructor, theatre owner & head of finance co. Charter mem, ASCAP. Autobiography: "Life Doubles in Brass." Chief Collabrs: Harry Von Tilzer, Albert Von Tilzer, Henry Tobias, Harry Tobias. *Songs:* I Want a Girl Just Like the Girl That Married Dear Old Dad; My Little Girl; All Alone; Don't Take My Darling Boy Away; Keep Right on Until the End of the Road.

DILORENZO, RANDY PAUL (RANDY LOREN) ASCAP 1978
composer, author, singer
b Schenectady, NY, Feb 28, 52. Educ: Pvt lessons in voice, guitar, piano, organ, accordian & dance. Prof singer & entertainer, 70- Chief Collabr: Robert Zepf. *Songs:* Love Is New; Music: My Only Need Is Loving You; I Think I'm Gonna Cry; I Feel the Spirit.

DILSNER, LAURENCE ASCAP 1961
composer, organist, teacher
b New York, NY. Educ: Guilmant Organ Sch, scholarship; Cons, Fontainebleau, France, dipl organ pedagogy; NY Univ, MA; Philadelphia Musical Acad, MusD; studied with Charles Courboin, Nadia Boulanger. Bd mem, NJ Dept Music; fac mem, Monmouth Col & stage cols in Paterson & Montclair, NJ. Guest consult, Music Educ Workshop, NY Univ. Second vpres, NJ Chap Music Teachers Nat Asn; dir music, Long Branch. Princeton Award for Distinguished Teaching in NJ. *Instrumental Works:* O Mistress Mine; Lord Make Me an Instrument of Thy Peace; We Praise Thee; Carol of the Friendly Beasts; From a Paris Organ Loft.

DI MINNO, DANIEL GAETANO ASCAP 1951
composer, author
b New York, NY, June 20, 11. Educ: Jr High Sch. Song & dance man on free lance circuit. Has written for movies, theatre & pop market. Chief Collabrs: Carmen Lombardo, Larry Conley, Al Stillman, Ted Koehler, Morty Neff, Jimmy Crane, Skinny Skylar, Athena Hosey, George Cardini, Johnny Tucker, Guy Wood. *Songs:* Return to Me; I Can't Get You Out of My Heart; From the Bottom of My Heart; Napoli; I Don't Wanna Go Home; If You Believe; Mama's Moo-Len-Yanna; Walk Among the Roses; La Santa Venuta; The Voice in the Choir-Sang Ava Maria; If I Can't Have You All to Myself; Dance On; Pardon; Wanderlust Blues; Blame It on Yourself; Foolish Me; Music: That One Last Leaf on the Tree; Once in Love and Nevermore; Till the World Knows Your Mine; Bouna Fortuna. *Instrumental Works:* Danny's Theme. *Songs & Instrumental Works:* Pass the Wine. *Scores:* Bway Show: A Very Honorable Guy.

DIMUCCI, DION FRANCIS
composer, singer
b New York, NY, July 18, 39. Recorded as Dion & The Belmonts, Laurie, 57-60, as Dion, Columbia, 61-64, ABC, 66-67, Laurie, 68, Warner Bros, 69-77 & Lifesong, 77-79. Chief Collabrs: Ernie Maressca, Tony Fasce, Bill Tuohy, Dan Beck. *Songs:* Runaround Sue; Midtown American Main Street Gang; Donna the Primadonna; Little Diane; Lost for Sure; Love Came to Me; Lovers Who Wander; Born to Cry; Sandy; (I Used to Be a) Brooklyn Dodger; Queen of 59; Josie; Guitar Queen; Pattern of My Lifeline; Power of Love Within; You've Awakened Something in Me; So Long Friend; Lonely World; He'll Only Hurt You; Sit Down Old Friend; He Looks Alot Like Me; Your Own Backyard; New York City Song; More to You (Than Meets the Eye); Lover Boy Supreme.

DINAPOLI, MARIO JOHN (MIKE) ASCAP 1953
composer, author, pianist
b Roxbury, Mass, Oct 8, 14. Educ: Piano, New Eng Cons Music. Pianist & arr, Frank Petty Trio, 16 yrs; recording artist. Soloist & arr TV show, "Swan Boat," WBZ, Boston, Mass, 54-56; TV shows for Narragansett Beer, Boston & Chevrolet, Providence, RI. Chief Collabrs: June Burnett, Joe Paulini, Lee Morris & Sherm Feller. *Songs:* She Was Five and He Was Ten; She's Got to Be a Saint; Music: Frolic on Fifth Avenue; Mister Pogo; Viennese Lantern Waltz; Everybody's Got a Girl But Me.

DI NARDO, NICHOLAS E ASCAP 1959
composer, violinist, conductor
b Palazzo S Gervasio, Italy, Feb 22, 06. Educ: Grad of Newark Schs, NJ; Ithaca Col, MusB, 29; Columbia Univ, 29-30; Rutgers Univ, MEd, 49; studied comp with Wallingford Liegger, violin with Otto K Schill, W G Egbert, Stefan Sopkin & Adolf Pick, conducting with Pat Conway & Wladimir Bakapeinikoff. Band & orch dir, E S High Sch, Newark; taught in Harford Schs, Pa & Ramsey High Sch, NJ; counselor at Interlochen, Mich, Summer Music Camp; cond, Newark Park Concerts & NJ State Orch, Atlantic City; violinist, Binghamton Symph Orch, NJ Symph Orch, NJ State Opera Orch, Garden State Arts Center Orch, NJ Ballet Co & Bolshoi Ballet Co. Chief Collabrs: Marc Fredericks, Bernie Hailperin, Joe Aromando, Joe Pallitto, Annette Marcheggianno, Dino Palermo. *Songs & Instrumental Works:* An Oscar to Santa; If My Heart Could Only Talk,

Dear; Our Song of Love; I've Been Thinking of You; In Losing You; But Never Forget; If I Should Ever Fall in Love Again; Prayerfully; Love Is Blind to Lovers; Road to Romance; Please Give Me Your Lips; Go-Go-Cha Cha; Come Dance With Me; Rockin Chalypso; Garden State Rhapsody.

DINERSTEIN, NORMAN M   ASCAP 1969
composer
b Springfield, Mass, Sept 18, 37. Educ: Boston Univ, BM; Hartt Col, MM; Princeton Univ, MFA & PhD; Tanglewood; Sch Music, Berlin; Darmstadt Ferienkurse; student of Gardner Read, Arnold Franchetti, R Session, M Babbitt, G Schuller & W Lutoslawsli. Sagalyn Award, Tanglewood, 62, Koussevitzky Prize, 63; Fulbright grant, Ger, 63; Ford-Music Educ Nat Conference comp-in-residence, Pasadena, 66-68; Univ RI Creative Award, 68; Inter-Am Music Award, Buenos Aires, 70; Nat Endowment for Arts Bicentennial Comn, 75; Leps Award, Brown Univ, 76; Ohio Arts Coun fels, 78 & 79; Zalmen selected for inclusion in Int Soc Contemporary Music World Music Days, Israel, 80; Comns, WGUC-FM, Cincinnati, 80, Stanford Univ, St Lawrence Col, Col of Sequoias & Hartt Col; Bertram Turetzky-contrabass; Alumnus of Yr, Hartt Col, 80. *Songs:* Music: Cinque Laude (acappela chorus); Four Settings on Texts of Emily Dickinson (soprano & string quartet); When David Heard (acappela chorus); Our Father (2 part treble choir); Frogs (acappela chorus); Songs of Remembrance (soprano & string orch); Pound (soprano & piano); Poema Ultrasonico (acappela chorus); Herrickanna (acappela chorus). *Instrumental Works:* Refrains (large orch); Zalmen (solo violin); The Answered Question (wind ensemble).

DININO, LOUIS LEE (LOYE LEE)   ASCAP 1970
composer, musician, instructor
b Coalton, WVa, Aug 6, 28. Educ: Ambridge High Sch, Pa; studied guitar under George Sharon; grad of radio & TV arts, Pittsburgh. Instrumentalist, nightclubs, radio & TV; recording artist. Chief Collabrs: Wayne Duncan, James Duncan, Betty DiNino, Carolyn DiNino. *Songs:* One Year Ago Today. *Songs & Instrumental Works:* Simple Theme; Dummy Dum Dum.

DININO, VINCENT RAIRDEN   ASCAP 1969
composer, author, educator
b Manhattan, Kans, Oct 24, 18. Educ: Univ Minn, BS; NDak State Univ, MS; Univ Tex Claremont Col, doctoral work. Dir bands & prof music, Univ Tex, Austin; dir, Univ Tex Longhorn Bands. Cond, clinician, adjudicator for Internation Fests Inc. Comp/arr. Author bk, "Marching Bands Through the Eyes of Texas." Chief Collabr: Jane Dahlgren DiNino. *Instrumental Works:* Texas Fight Song; Texas Victory March; Texas Alma Mater.

DINO, RALPH
See Palladino, Ralph Francis

DINOVI, EUGENE SALVATORE   ASCAP 1962
composer, pianist, conductor
b Brooklyn, NY, May 26, 28. Educ: Studied orchestration & counterpoint with Mario Castelnuovo-Tedesco, cond & comp with Mario di Bonaventura, piano with Jacob Gimpel. Started as jazz pianist, New York, 44. Cond, pianist & arr for Lena Horne, Peggy Lee, Tony Bennett, Dinah Shore & Mitzi Gaynor, 50's; pianist & arr, Benny Goodman, Artie Shaw & Buddy Rich Orchs. Songwriter, 60's; comp, arr & pianist, Desi-Lu, Spencer Hagen TV, 61-69. Cond & orch films, "Big North" & "Puss 'n' Boots"; musical dir, four TV specials, "Changing Scene," ABC, 70-71. Comp & cond music for over 30 Molson Export Ale commercials, Softball Award, Canadian Commercials Fest, 73 & Rash Award, Graphica, Montreal, Que, 76; "Of All People," "All About Toronto" & "The Gene and Jodie Show," CBC-TV, Toronto, Ont. Became performer, singing, playing & telling of the lives & times of Am Popular Composers. Chief Collabrs: Johnnie Mercer, Tony Velona, Spence Maxwell, Bill Comstock & Mary Ann Maurer. *Songs:* Music: I Can Hear the Music; Brand New Morning; Walk an Autumn Day With Me; Tout Va Bien; Summer Has Gone; Have a Heart; Songs of Inner Dialogue. *Instrumental Works:* Scandinavian Suite No 1; Toronto the Good. *Scores:* TV: And Then Mr Jones. *Albums:* The Scandinavian Suite No 1.

DINU, ROBERT A   ASCAP 1960
composer, author
b Brooklyn, NY, June 23, 28. Educ: Col.

DION
See Dimucci, Dion Francis

DI PIRANI, EUGENIO   ASCAP 1924
composer, pianist, educator
b Ferrara, Italy, Sept 8, 1852; d Berlin, Ger, Jan 12, 39. Came to US, 04. Educ: Lyceum Galvani & Rossini Cons, Bologna. Prof, Acad Music, Berlin, 1873-83. Won Gold Medal for concerts, Florence Acad. Mem, Royal Acad of Florence, Bologna & Rome. Honored by Emperors Frederick, William II & King Humbert of Italy. Toured Europe, US with Alma Webster Powell, 5 yrs. Dir, Powell-di Pirani Musical Inst, NY. Author, "Secrets of the Success of Great Musicians." Officer, Order of Imperial Ger Crown; Comdr of Order of Royal Ital Crown. *Songs & Instrumental Works:* Scene Veneziane; Fete au Chateau; Choral: Ocean; The Bells. *Scores:* Operas: Witch's Song; Black Blood.

DIRKSEN, RICHARD WAYNE   ASCAP 1975
composer, organist, choirmaster
b Freeport, Ill, Feb 8, 21. Educ: Peabody Cons of Music, COC, 42; studied organ with Virgil Fox, 40-42; hon DFA, George Washington Univ, 80. Assoc organist & choirmaster, Washington Nat Cathedral, 46-64, dir of prog, 64-77, dir of worship & music, 77- Dir of Cathedral Schs music, 50-69. Active in theatrical music direction, Arena Stage, Olney Theatre, 55-76. Harpsichord, piano & organ recitalist. *Songs:* Anthems-Hymns: A Child My Choice; Chanticleer; Christ Our Passover; Welcome All Wonders; Rejoice Ye Pure in Heart.

DI ROBBIO, ARMANDO (AL DERO)   ASCAP 1963
composer
b Providence, RI, Aug 7, 15. Educ: High sch; Army Air Force Sch Music. Drummer, AF Band, 43-46. Worked with P W Hunt, Bobby Hackett, Joe Lilly & others. Chief Collabrs: Johnny Mercer, Billy Strayhorn, Frances E Delaney, Frances Stelzer, Norman Kelly, Dolly-O & Jack Curran, Alice Hammerstein, Bruce Kingery, Paul Vandervoort II, George Wagner, Celeta Felby. *Songs:* Catch the Alley Cat; Country in My Heart; It's Heavenly to Feel Young Again; Spinning in the Right Direction; Will I Know; Take Me to Hear the Concert; Leroy Was a Spider Man; Summer on the Cape; You've Cast a Spell Over Me; Lights Burning.

DISCANT, MACK   ASCAP 1954
author
b New York, NY, Mar 2, 16; d New York, Sept 17, 61. Chief Collabr: Max Steiner. *Songs:* In the Kingdom of My Heart; Theme from A Summer Place; Hold Me Forever; Seasons Greetings.

DISDIER, RAMIRO E(DMUNDO)   ASCAP 1980
composer, author, singer
b Patillas, PR, May 2, 27. Educ: Vila Mayo High Sch; Univ PR; Antonio Paoli Acad, voice studies with Joaquin Oliver; Ramon Fonseca Acad, voice studies with Ramon Fonseca. With Univ PR Chorus & Los Universitarios Quartet; singer nightclubs, TV, radio & theaters; recording artist, University, Cafamo & Disdier Records; guitar player. *Songs & Instrumental Works:* En Primavera; Entre Las Sombras; Beso Loco; Mascara; Sin Tu Amor; Tu Secreto; Dejame Hablarte; Tarde Triste; Miedo; Amor Tropical; Hoy; Error de Juventud; Lo Imposible; Puerto Rico; Triguena; Borinquen; Por Las Calles de San Juan; Tus Labios; Quisiera Reir; Conozco la Verdad; Ya No Eres Tu; Promesas de Amor; Ingenuo Corazon; Asi es Mi Navidad; Testigo la Luna; Si Tu Quisiera; Roja Flor; Hermosos Recuerdos; Mi Bella Borinquen; Mirando Al Cielo; Recuerdos de Ayer; Lo Que Tu Ignoras; En Cada Noche; Amor Sonado, Cuando?; Besame Mas; Momento Intimo; Mi Campo; Con Mi Guitarra; Mi Sueno de Amor; Piensa; Hablemos de Los Dos; Mi Preocupacion; Juegas Con Mi Amor; Nostalgia Jibara; Carino Viejo; A Solas Pensando; Estos Celos; Todavia; Ni Tu Ni Yo; En la Distancia; Cuando Me Miras; Ansias Locas; Sublime Creacion; Mi Bella Mujer; Cuando Tu Me Quieras; Locuras Del Destino; Tu Voz; Una Ilusion Loca; Irrealidad; Mientras Cae la Noche; Canto Al Amor; Al Compas Del Vals.

DITMARS, IVAN DALE   ASCAP 1968
composer, conductor, pianist
b Olympia, Wash, Apr 12, 07. Educ: Grad: Univ Wash & New Eng Cons, Boston. Pianist & organist with Victor Young, Lud Gluskin, Wilbur Hatch, Bernard Herrmann, Andre Kostelanetz; leader with Jack Paar, John Nelson, Ralph Edwards, Monty Hall, Arthur Godfrey, Bert Parks. Written var TV & radio commercials. Mem: Am Fedn of Musicians, Composers & Lyricists Guild & Pacific Broadcast Pioneers. Chief Collabrs: Glen Spencer, Wendell Niles, Jerry Bowne. *Songs:* Little White Cross; Themes: Stars Over Hollywood; All American College Show. *Instrumental Works:* Pseudo Brahms Esquire (Star Trek); Hawaii Isn't Heaven Anymore; Luau Lou; Northern Lights; Klondike Kate.

DIX, ROBERT KNIGHT   ASCAP 1978
composer
b Gallatin, Mo, June 10, 17. Educ: Iowa State Univ, BS(chem eng); Mass Inst Technol, ScD(chem eng); studied comp with Stanley Wolfe of Juilliard, 71-76. With Exxon Corp, 43-77, became pres, Exxon's US Chemical Co & sr vpres, Exxon's worldwide chemical interests. Involved with music since childhood; commenced serious comp, 70; had works for full symph orch & var chamber ensembles performed. Full time comp, 77-

DIXON, DAVID GEORGE   ASCAP 1967
composer, author, broadcaster
b Detroit, Mich, Sept 20, 38. Radio & TV performer, late 60's. Co-comp & co-author for Peter, Paul & Mary. Prog dir, WABX radio station, Detroit, 68-73. Host of TV show "All Night Show," Fort Lauderdale-Miami, 80- Chief Collabrs: Jim Mason, Noel Paul Stookey, Peter Yarrow, Mary Travers, Dick Kniss. *Songs:* Whatshername?; The Song Is Love; Lyrics: I Dig Rock and Roll Music.

DIXON, FLORENCE ROSE   ASCAP 1977
composer, author, singer
b Owen, Wis, Dec 24, 44. Educ: Reedsburg Elem, Wis; Webb High Sch, Reedsburg. Recording artist; singer in nightclubs, 78. *Songs:* Two Separate Worlds; The Waiting's All Over.

DIXON, MORT   ASCAP 1924
author
b New York, NY, Mar 20, 1892; d Bronxville, NY, Mar 23, 56. Educ: DeWitt Clinton High Sch. Vaudeville actor. Served, World War I; dir, USA show "Whiz Bang," toured France after war. Songwriter, Bway shows incl "Sweet and Low" & "Crazy Quilt" & var films. Chief Collabrs: Billy Rose, Ray Henderson, Harry Warren, Harry Woods, Allie Wrubel. *Songs:* That Old Gang of Mine; Bam Bam Bamy Shore; If I Had a Girl Like You; Just Like a Bufftterfly That's Caught in the Rain; Bye, Bye Blackbird; River, Stay 'Way From My Door; Marching Along Together; My Old Man; Nagasaki; You're My Everything; I'm Looking Over a Four Leaf Clover; Would You Like to Take a Walk?; Ooh, That Kiss; I Found a Million Dollar Baby in a Five and Ten Cent Store; Pop Goes Your Heart; Happiness Ahead; Mr and Mrs Is the Name; Flirtation Walk; Fare Thee Well, Annabell; I See Two Lovers; The Lady in Red. *Scores:* Bway show: The Laugh Parade; Films: Happiness Ahead; Flirtation Walk; Sweet Music.

D'JOSEPH, JAC
See Di Giuseppe, Severino

D'LOWER, DEL   ASCAP 1960
composer, author
b Warsaw, Poland, Sept 21, 12. Educ: Stuyvesant High Sch; City Col New York; Tulsa Univ; New Sch, New York. Musician & drummer, Divers Creative Enterprises. *Songs:* High Cheek Bones; It's You, It's You, It's You; The Bumpy Bumpy Trail; Such Fun; If I'm Sad; Ginny the Pretty White Doe.

DOANE, DOROTHY   ASCAP 1950
composer, author, teacher
b Leesburg, Ind, Aug 2, 17. Educ: Manchester Col; Sherwood Music Sch; Univ Wis. Jr high sch music teacher; also participated in writing & publ children's musical plays. *Songs:* Indiana Style; The Enterprise March; Laughing Just to Keep From Crying; The Peppermint Stick Parade; Because Somebody Cares.

DOBBINS, EUGENE DAVID (GENE)   ASCAP 1970
composer, author
b Memphis, Tenn, Mar 19, 34. Educ: Memphis State Univ, biology major, 2 yrs. Played guitar & drums in bands, Memphis & west Tenn, 10 yrs. Started writing songs, 64. Writer for var publ; worked for RCA, 3 yrs; with Two Rivers Music, 71-74 & Chappell Music Co, 74- Chief Collabrs: Rory Bourke, Johnny Wilson, Rayburn Anthony, Tony Austin, Skippy Barrett, Tim Daniels, Ed Penny. *Songs:* Easy As Pie; Roses for Mama; Sing Me a Love Song to Baby; Rock on Baby; Honky Tonk Memories; Red Skies Over Georgia; He's Everywhere; It's Too Late; No Relief in Sight; Only Tomorrow Knows; Gather Me to You; I'm Gonna Keep on Loving You.

DOBER, CONRAD K (CON CONRAD)   ASCAP 1920
composer, pianist, publisher
b New York, NY, June 18, 1891; d Van Nuys, Calif, Sept 28, 38. Educ: Mil acad. Pianist in film theatre, then vaudeville entertainer, US & Europe. Became music publ. Went to Hollywood, 29. Wrote songs for films, incl "Palmy Days", "The Gay Divorcee" & "Here's to Romance." Chief Collabrs: Joe Young, Sidney Clare, Billy Rose, B G DeSylva, Benny Davis, Leo Robin, Herb Magidson, J Russel Robinson, Vincent Rose, Archie Gottler, Sidney Mitchell, William Friedlander. *Songs:* Oh, Frenchy; Margie; Palesteena; Ma, He's Making Eyes at Me; Barney Google; Come On, Spark Plug; You've Got to See Mama Every Night; Memory Lane; Big City Blues; Walking With Susie; Lonesome and Sorry; Sing a Little Love Song; Mercenary Mary; Prisoner of Love; You Call It Madness But I Call It Love; Bend Down, Sister; My Baby Said Yes Yes; The Continental (Acad Award, 34); Looking for a Needle in a Haystack; Midnight in Paris; Here's to Romance; Champagne Waltz; Singin' the Blues. *Scores:* Bway stage: Moonlight; Mercenary Mary; Kitty's Kisses, Americana; Films: Fox Movietone Follies.

DOBRIN, GEORGE WILLIAM   ASCAP 1972
composer, author, musician
b Brooklyn, NY, Jan 20, 36. Educ: Fla Int Univ, BA, studied French Horn with Gunther Schuller. Started studying piano & accordion at age 4. Winner, Arthur Godfrey Talent Scouts, age 15. Toured US & Europe as musical act. Produced children's albums. Has been on children's show staff as writer; performer on "Arthur & Co" WPLG, Miami for past 8 yrs. Pres, The Learning Party, Inc, Stars Unlimited, Inc. Chief Collab: Lucille Dobrin. *Songs:* Be Happy Smile; Show Me How; Go to the Zoo; Arthurs Party; Follow the Leader.

DOBRIN, LUCILLE REBECCA (LUCILLE STRACHAN)   ASCAP 1972
composer, author, teacher
b Homestead, Fla, Aug 18, 35. Educ: Knoxville Col, BA(music, Span), with Dr Newell C Fitzpatrick. Taught music, Gretna, Va, 7 yrs; taught pre-sch for Headstart Prog, Miami, 9 yrs. Has written scripts & music & performs on "Arthur & Co" on WPLG, Miami, for last 8 yrs. Has produced short children's films for TV syndication; directed radio shows in Span for Lutheran Radio; produced children's albums. Vpres, The Learning Party, Inc, Stars Unlimited, Inc. Chief Collab: George Dobrin. *Songs:* Follow the Leader; Be Happy Smile; I've Got the Blues, Greens; Show Me How; Arthurs Party.

DR SEUSS
See Geisel, Theodore Seuss

DODD, J D (JAY LARRIN)   ASCAP 1975
composer, author, singer
b Jackson, Tenn, Apr 9, 44. Educ: Parson Elementary Sch; Parsons High Sch; Harrison Chilhowee Baptist Acad, Tenn; Univ Tenn, Nashville, BA; Univ Hawaii, teachers cert; studied with Guy Bockman, Ambrose Holford. Soloist with Univ Tenn Singers, 63-66. Pianist-singer at var hotels, Honolulu, Hawaii, 67-80; entertainer, Sheraton Surfrider Hotel, 76- Awards: Radio KCCN Bicentennial Search for Songs, 76; Na Kohu Hano Hano Awards, twice for male vocalist of the yr & producer of the yr, 79. Chief Collabs: Eddie Kamae, Myrna Kamae, Brian Robert Shaw. *Songs:* The Snows of Mauna Kea; The Koolaus Are Sleeping Now; Moloka'i Lullaby; I Wish You Forever Hawaii; Between the Laughter and the Tears; The Windows of Amsterdam; Little Lei Lady; Annie and Jessie. *Albums:* Jay Larrin.

DODD, JIMMIE   ASCAP 1946
composer, author, actor
b Cincinnati, Ohio, Mar 28, 10; d Honolulu, Hawaii, Nov 10, 64. Educ: Univ Cincinnati; Cincinnati Cons; Vanderbilt Univ. Singer & guitarist in radio, 33. Played in Louis Prima orch, Hollywood, 37. Appeared in films, incl series "The Three Mesquiteers." WW II, toured Aleutians, China, Burma & India for USO with wife, Ruth Carrell Dodd. Made TV appearances, 52-54; MC, "Mickey Mouse Club", TV, 55-59. Toured Australia, 59-60. Led own dance group. Chief Collabs: Ruth Carrell Dodd, George Wyle, John Jacob Loeb, Will Fowler, Sonny Burke, Gil George, Mack David, Al Hoffman, Jerry Livingston, Roy Williams, Tom Adair, Charles Shows, Cubby O'Brien. *Songs:* He Was There; Mickey Mouse March; Lonely Guitar; I Love Girls; Rosemary; Nashville Blues; Mamie; Be a Good Guest; Amarillo; Hi to You; I'm No Fool; Proverbs; Washington (off song DC); Meet Me in Monterey (for Monterey Centennial); Encyclopedia; A Bluebird Is Singing the Blues; Annette; The Shoe Song; The Pencil Song; Disco Mouse; Pussycat Polka; The Merry Mouseketeers; Anything Can Happen Day; Today Is Tuesday; You; What Happened to Yesterday?; I'm a Guitar; Hey, Cubby Boy; Mickey Mouse Mambo; Ask! Seek! Knock!; The Nature of Things; Here Comes the Circus; Mousekartoon Time; Simple Simon; The Book Song; Friendly Elephant; The Mousekedance; A New Word A Day; Tiny Little TV Girl; Do Something for Someone; The Telephone Song; Animal Alphabet; Quack, Quack, Quack, Donald Duck; The Little Cow; Music: Hi Hiawatha; Bob-O the Clown; Painting Aunt Polly's Fence; Get Busy; Lyrics: The Jungle; Aloha Club; It's So Much Better That Way; Fun With Music; Anyone For Exploring?; When I Grow Up; Drums; Date Night.

DODD, RUTH CARRELL   ASCAP 1956
composer, author, singer
b Cincinnati, Ohio. Educ: Univ Cincinnati; Univ Calif Los Angeles. Sang on own radio prog, WCKY, Covington, Ky. Featured on radio & TV shows, Hollywood. Dubbed singing voice for motion picture films. Toured Aleutian Islands & China-Burma-India with husband, USO, WW II. Toured Australia, 59-60. Sang with husband's dance group. Wrote music & appeared on Disney's "Mickey Mouse Club TV Program" & own children's TV show (KGMB). Wrote & produced memorial prog for Jimmie Dodd, Calif State Univ, Northridge, 5/25/80. Chief Collabs: Jimmie Dodd, Bob Amsberry. *Songs:* Amarillo; Do What the Good Book Says; Share the Blessings; Rose Festival Time; Music: God's Valley; The Lord's Prayer; Darlene; Be a Good Guest; Date Night; It's So Much Better That Way; Aloha Club; The Jungle.

DODGEN, GARY NORMAN   ASCAP 1978
composer, author
b Charlotte, NC, Feb 13, 54. Educ: Duke Univ, BA(anthropology), 76; Columbia Univ, MBA(marketing & finance), 81. Singer & guitarist at nightclubs, New York. Chief Collabr: Roy Eaton. *Songs:* Negative Numbers Song.

DODSON, MILTON ALLEN   ASCAP 1971
composer, author, teacher
b Deming, NMex, Apr 10, 14. Educ: Los Angeles Theol Sem; Pasadena Col; Univ Southern Calif; Pioneer Sem; Long Beach State Col; degrees conferred: AB, MA, PhD & ThD. Ministry, 45 yrs. Taught in Calif state col syst, 15 yrs. *Songs:* I Want to Stroll Over Heaven With You; Something More; I'll Keep Smiling Through My Tears; Christ Will Make It Right Some Day; On the Middle Cross, on Calv'r'y's Hill; also many gospel songs & hymns.

DOERFEL, HERBERT   ASCAP 1963
author, conductor
b Zwota, Austria, July 16, 24. Educ: Musik Schule Klingenthal, Ger; Music Hochschule West Berlin, DrMusic; Univ Tenn, Dr Culture; World Univ, Ariz, DD; studied conducting with Furt Waengler; studied 12 tone & serial comp with Georg Tremblay. Studied violin & performed as soloist with Radio Symph Orch Leipzig, Graz, Austria; employed by 15 film cos as mgr for 45 films in Europe, Ger & Eng. Film screen credit for music, "Operation-Eichman." Arr for "Daktari", CBS TV show. Commn for Symphonic Poem by Int Evangel Crusades in honor of first three astronauts on moon; dir symph orch with Onde-Marienod. Dean of Music Dept, Int Evangel Crusades, World Univ. Chief Collabrs: Heinz Friedel Hedden Hausen, Warner Knoepp, Betty Schweitzer.

DOLAN, ALIDA MARY   ASCAP 1960
composer, author
b Vancouver, BC, July 2, 12. Educ: Wilson Bus Col, Seattle, Wash; studied piano, Stockton, Calif. Admin secy to Lewis Milestone, Lawrence Welk, Louis Prima, Keely Smith & Jack Chertok; secy to A&R, Dot Records, Hollywood, Calif. Wrote songs 7 yrs. Chief Collabs: Hope Rider, Paul Weirick, Mary Lacey, Maxine Bamford. *Songs:* Break It to Me Gently; Ocean of Tears; One Wild Oat; Waiting for Joe; Come Back to Me; You Ain't Gonna Get It; Jiggedy Wiggedy Wolly; Popcorn Polka; Seven Silver Dollars; Go On About Your Business.

DOLAN, JOHN   ASCAP 1961
composer, author, publisher
b Milwaukee, Wis, Apr 23, 29. Educ: Univ Wis, BA; Univ Chicago, PhD; Yale Sch Drama. Copywriter & account exec, advert agency, Milwaukee, 54-61. Formed music publ firm & record co, 60. *Songs:* God, Country and My Baby.

DOLAN, ROBERT EMMETT   ASCAP 1946
composer, conductor
b Hartford, Conn, Aug 3, 06; d. Educ: Loyola Col, scholarship; studied piano with mother, then with Letonal, Mortimer Wilson, Joseph Schillinger & Ernst Toch. Comp & cond, radio. Music dir, MGM, 41, also for Bway productions "Good News", "Follow Through", "Flying Colors", "Strike Me Pink", "Hot-Cha", "May Wine", "Horray for What", "La Rose De France," Paris, "Leave It to Me", "Very Warm for May" & "Louisiana Purchase." Chief Collabs: Johnny Mercer, Walter O'Keefe. *Songs:* At Last I'm in Love; Little By Little; Hullabaloo; Song of the Highwayman; You; Out of the Past; I Love You; And So to Bed; Glamour Waltz; Your Heart Will Tell You So; Big Movie Show in the Sky; A Month of Sundays; The Yodel Blues; A Home in the Meadow; Talk to Me, Baby. *Scores:* Bway Stage: Texas, Li'l Darling; Foxy.

DOLIN, LYNN MARIE (LYNN MANN)   ASCAP 1974
composer, author, singer
b Burbank, Calif, Oct 22, 48. Educ: Grant High Sch; classical guitar study with Guy Horn, sightreading instr with Lillian Mann, pvt dance study. Started as singer, Doodletown Pipers at age 16; then Inner-Dialogue. Joined Johnny Mann Singers, 70; toured US. Appeared on TV series, "Stand Up and Cheer," 3 yrs. Made many recordings. Group singer for commercials & films, also sacred recordings & back up. Recorded own album, Light Records, 76. Concertize with husband, Johnny Mann, US & TV appearances. Chief Collabs: Johnny Mann, Sharalee Lucas. *Songs:* Oh God I Hurt Inside; My Praise Song; God's Quiet Love; Sing a Song of Love; You Make Me Feel Like a Woman.

DOLPH, JOHN M   ASCAP 1943
author
b Portland, Ore, Aug 11, 1895; d San Diego, Calif, Oct 2, 62. Educ: Univ Ore. Served, World War I. Novelist; writer for advert, films & radio. On sales staff, CBS, west coast. Agency producer & writer, with Fred Waring, 43-62. Chief Collabs: Fred & Tom Waring, Harry Simeone, Livingston Gearhart. *Songs:* Army Hymn; The Men of the Merchant Marine; They Too Shall Rise; When Angels Sang of Peace; I Hear Music; Where in the World; Jesus Had a Mother Like Mine; A Place in the Sun.

DOLPH, NORMAN EDWARD   ASCAP 1979
author
b Tulsa, Okla, May 11, 39. Educ: Yale Univ. With Columbia Records, 60-67; independent, 67- Formed Stoy, Inc, music publ firm; writer, 72- Council mem of Am Guild of Authors & Composers. *Songs:* Lyrics: Stay the Night; Life Is a Rock (But the Radio Rolled Me); I Changed My Mind; Whip; Butterfly.

DOMURAD, JOHN J   ASCAP 1968
composer, author, pianist
b Boston, Mass, Sept 27, 31. Formed local groups in neighborhood; played in downtown nightclubs, society bands & resort hotels. Keyboardist & arr, Boston & Nashville studios; demo producer, Nashville. Now pianist at Ritz Carlton Hotel, Boston. Chief Collabs: Ed Penney Jr, Ed J Burton. *Songs:* Music: Where Do You Go?; Let Me Be the One; Montreal. *Instrumental Works:* Boston Suite.

DONAHUE, ROBERT L   ASCAP 1971
composer, educator
b Chicago, Ill, Mar 8, 31. Educ: Univ Wis, BM, 54; Univ Ill, MM, 59, studied with Benjamin Johnston; Cornell Univ, DMA, 64, studied with Robert Palmer & Karel Husa. Taught at Wis State Univ, Oshkosh, 64-67 & Spelman Col, 67- *Songs & Instrumental Works:* The Lord's Prayer (SAB); April (SATB); The Hour Glass (mixed chorus & piano); Chromatic Sketches for Piano; Through the Night (two part chorus & piano); Sonatine No 2 for Flute and Piano; Sonata for Alto Saxophone and Piano; Sonata No 3 for Piano (Delius Fest Award, 78); Sonata for Tenor Saxophone and Piano.

DONALDSON, HERBERT FRANKLIN
composer, concert pianist, teacher
b Yankton, SDak, Aug 13, 18. Educ: Yankton High Sch; Chicago Cons Col, MMus; studied with Moritz Rosenthal, Glenn Dillard Gunn & Rosina Chevinne; Fel, Am Inst Fine Arts. Substantial contributor educ recordings, Bowmar Records. Concert pianist, recitals for youth in schs, West Coast.

Instrumental Works: Concerto Ecclessia (piano & orch); Fun With Music; Once Upon a Time Suite. *Scores:* Ballet: Emperor's Nightingale; Dorian Grey.

DONALDSON, WALTER   ASCAP 1921
composer, author, pianist
b Brooklyn, NY, Feb 15, 1893; d Santa Monica, Calif, July 15, 47. Educ: Pub schs. Worked for Wall Street brokerage firm. Pianist for music publ co. Entertainer, Camp Upton, NY, WW I. Mem staff, Irving Berlin Music Co. Co-founder, Donaldson, Douglas & Gumble, 28. Went to Hollywood, 29. Chief Collabs: Sam Lewis, Joe Young, Gus Kahn, Edgar Leslie, Harold Adamson, Johnny Mercer. *Songs:* Back Home in Tennessee; We'll Have a Jubilee in My Old Kentucky Home; The Daughter of Rosie O'Grady; Don't Cry, Frenchy, Don't Cry; On the Gin Gin Ginny Shore; How Ya Gonna Keep 'Em Down on the Farm?; You're a Million Miles From Nowhere; My Mammy; My Buddy; Carolina in the Morning; Beside a Babbling Brook; That Certain Party; Yes, Sir, That's My Baby; I Wonder Where My Baby Is Tonight; After I Say I'm Sorry; At Sundown; My Blue Heaven; Sam, the Old Accordion Man; Just Like a Melody Out of the Sky; I'm Bringing a Red Red Rose; Makin' Whoopee; Love Me or Leave Me; Kansas City Kitty; Changes; My Baby Just Cares for Me; 'Tain't No Sin; Little White Lies; You're Driving Me Crazy; Lazy Lou'siana Moon; Hello, Beautiful; My Mom; An Earful of Music; Did I Remember?; Could Be; It's Been So Long; You; You Never Looked So Beautiful Before; Cuckoo in the Clock; Mister Meadowlark; Without Your Love; Molly O'Malley; Sweet Indiana Home; What Are We Waiting for Mary; Cynthia; My Papa Don't Two-Time No Time; Where'd You Get Those Eyes; Sweet Jennie Lee; Music: Romance; Nevada; Mexico City; In the Middle of the Night; Because My Baby Don't Mean Maybe Now; A Thousand Goodnights; My Sweetie Turned Me Down; Sleepy Head; Tender is the Night; (Oh My) Sweet Hortense; Oh! Baby, Don't Say No Say Maybe; Nice Going; Fit to be Tied; Beside a Babbling Brook; Let's Talk About My Sweetie; My Ohio Home; Until You Get Somebody Else; You've Got Everything. *Scores:* Bway stage: Sweetheart Time; Whoopee; Films: Glorifying the American Girl; Kid Millions; The Great Ziegfeld; songs for Suzi; Two Girls on Broadway; Panama Hattie; Follow the Boys.

DONALDSON, WILL   ASCAP 1923
composer, pianist, vocal coach
b Brooklyn, NY, Apr 21, 1891; d Hollywood, Calif, Dec 16, 54. Educ: Pratt Inst; Art Students League. Vaudeville accompanist to Elizabeth Brice, Adele Rowland & Elsie Janis. Voice coach for radio performers; had own studio in Hollywood. *Songs:* Step on the Blues; The Dark Madonna; Spellbound; Oh How She Lied to Me; Time Will Tell; Doo Wacka Doo; Love Ain't Blind; Why Can't We Be Sweethearts All Over Again; I Can't Resist You; We're on Our Way; Come to the Barn; Life Is Sweet Again.

DONATO, ANTHONY   ASCAP 1949
composer, author, educator
b Prague, Nebr, Mar 8, 09. Educ: Univ Nebr, 26-27; Eastman Sch Music, BMus, 37, PhD, 47; violin, Gustave Tinlot, comp, E Royce, Howard Hanson & B Rogers, cond, Eugene Goosens. Head violin dept & cond, Univ Orch, Drake Univ, 31-37; head violin dept, Iowa State Teachers Col, 37-39 & Univ Tex, 39-47; cond, Northwestern Univ Chamber Orch, 47-58, prof theory-comp, Northwestern Univ, 47-76, emeritus prof, 76- *Songs & Instrumental Works:* Orch: 2 Symphonies; 2 Sinfoniettas; Divertimento; Serenade; The Plains and Prairie Schooner; Centennial Ode; Improvisations Improvisation; Elegy for Strings; Suite for Strings; Band: Concert Overture; The Hidden Fortress; Cowboy Reverie; Choral: Prelude and Choral Fantasy (men's voices, brass, organ, timpani); Blessed Is the Man (SATB, organ, brass); Make a Joyful Noise (children's voices, organ, brass); March of the Hungry Mountains (SATB, small orch); The Congo (chorus, orch); Chamber Music: 4 String Quartets; Wind Quintet; Three Poems From Shelley (voice, string quartet); Sonatina for Three Trumpets; 2 Sonatas for Violin and Piano; Sonata for Horn and Piano; Piano Sonata; 2 pastels for organ; solos for violin & piano, flute & piano, saxophone & piano; also songs for voice & piano. *Scores:* Opera: The Walker Through Walls.

DONENFELD, JAMES   ASCAP 1963
composer, author, teacher
b Brooklyn, NY, Aug 10, 17. Educ: Brooklyn Col; NY Univ; studied Schillinger Syst with Rudolf Schramm. Music dir summer camps; teaches privately. *Songs:* God's Pattern; En Keloheynu (hymn). *Instrumental Works:* Children's Musicals: New York Town; The Magic Ring.

DONNELLY, ANDREW   ASCAP 1929
composer, author
b Haverstraw, NY, Oct 13, 1893; d New York, NY, July 7, 55. Educ: High sch. *Songs:* Baby Your Mother; I Tore Up Your Picture; You're Too Good for Good for Nothing Me; Little Red Riding Hood's Christmas Tree.

DONNELLY, DOROTHY   ASCAP 1923
author, actress
b New York, NY, Jan 28, 1880; d New York, Jan 3, 1928. Educ: Convent. With Henry Donnelly Stock Co. Created role of Candida in US. Appeared in "Madam X." Chief Collabs: Sigmund Romberg, Stephen Jones. *Songs:* Three Little Maids; Tell Me Daisy; My Springtime Thou Art; Song of Love; Golden Days;

Drinking Song; Deep in My Heart, Dear; Serenade; Just We Two; Your Land and My Land; Silver Moon; Mother; Boys in Gray. *Scores:* Bway scores & librettos: Blossom Time; The Student Prince in Heidelberg; My Maryland; Poppy.

DONNELLY, RUTH   ASCAP 1971
author
b Trenton, NJ, May 17, 1896. Educ: Calwalader Sch, Trenton, grammar sch grad. Stage & screen featured comedienne, 65 yrs; lyric writer. Chief Collabr: Marvin Lewis. *Songs:* Wake-Up! Everybody! (peace, patriotic march song). *Albums:* Souvenirs.

DONNET, JACQUES   ASCAP 1963
composer, conductor, arranger
b New York, NY, Aug 26, 17; d. Educ: Juilliard Sch; Univ Miami, BM. Cond & arr, CBS. Cond, Carillon Hotel & Carillon Symphonette, Miami Beach, Miss Universe Pageant. Mem, exec bd, Univ Miami Symph. *Songs & Instrumental Works:* Little Miss Universe; International March. *Scores:* Film: Once Upon a Coffee House.

DONOVAN, WALTER   ASCAP 1942
composer, pianist
b East Cambridge, Mass, Dec 19, 1888; d North Hollywood, Calif, Jan 10, 64. Educ: Pub schs. Mem of vaudeville piano & singing act. Professional mgr, music publ firms. Wrote songs for films. Chief Collabrs: Don Bestor, Roger Lewis, Dick Jergens, Country Washburne. *Songs:* One Dozen Roses; Aba Daba Honeymoon; Down By the Winegar Woiks; Gila Galah Galoo; Deeply in Love; Sad; Somebody Sweet Is Sweet on Me; Arizona Mary; Then You'll Come Back to Me; Perfume of Roses; Angel; I Thank You; Say With Your Lips.

DONSON, DON
See Scarpa, Salvatore

DOOLEY, EDNA MOHR   ASCAP 1960
composer, author, educator
b Brooklyn, NY, Aug 11, 07. Educ: Columbia Univ, BS; Teacher's Col; Wyo Univ, MA. Teacher pub schs, New York, 29-50 & Ivenson Hall Sch & pub schs, Newcastle & Casper, Wyo, 50-58; also Morris Plains & Millburn, NJ. Chief Collabrs: Dave Ringle, James Selva, Francis Gnass. *Songs:* My Garden State (Song of NJ); Two Little Pink Ballet Slippers; Graduation Day; Go in Peace; In the Twinkling of an Eye; *Music:* It's All Up to You Sweetheart; I'll Never Never Never Leave Nevada.

DOOLEY, PHIL S
composer, author
b Aurora, Ill, Feb 22, 1898; d Milwaukee, Wis, Nov 16, 67. Began playing at age 13. Trumpet & drums player, leader. *Songs:* Purple Shades; Junk Man Blues; Get Cannabal; Can't Do Without Love; Yes Habit; also many others.

DORAN, ELSA   ASCAP 1956
author
b Chicago, Ill, Feb 11, 15. Educ: High sch; bus sch. Chief Collabr: Sol Lake. *Songs:* Roly Poly; Blond Hair, Blue Eyes and Ruby Lips; Free and Easy; Love Was Born; Falling Star; Crawfish.

DORAN, MATT HIGGINS   ASCAP 1967
composer, opera librettist
b Covington, Ky, Sept 1, 21. Educ: Los Angeles City Col, AA, 41; Univ Southern Calif, BMus, 46, MM & DMA, 54; studied comp with Ernst Toch & Hanns Eisler, orch with Played flute, Corpus Christi Symph, Tex & Muncie Symph, Ind, 53-58. Comp operas, symphs, concerti, chamber & choral music, piano pieces & songs. Chief Collabrs: Sonya Brown; Suzanne Serbin. *Instrumental Works:* Sonata for Clarinet and Piano; Sonatina for Flute and 'Cello; Concerto for Piano and Orchestra; Concerto for 'Cello and Orchestra; Poem for Flute and Piano; Pastorale for Organ; Sonatina for Two Flutes; Quartet for Oboe, Clarinet, Bassoon and Piano; Two Movements for Alto Saxophone and Piano; Four Solo Pieces for Flute; Seven Solo Pieces for Clarinet; Suite for Flute and Guitar; Double Concerto for Flute and Guitar and String Orchestra. *Scores:* Comic Operas: The Committee; Sign Here.

DORFF, DANIEL JAY   ASCAP 1977
composer
b New Rochelle, NY, Mar 7, 56. Educ: Cornell Univ, BA, 78, studied saxophone with Sigurd Rascher, clarinet with Ronald Reuben; Univ Pa, MA, 80; studied with George Crumb, George Rochberg, Elie Siegmeisler, Karel Husa. *Songs & Instrumental Works:* Fantasy, Scherzo and Nocturne for Saxophone Quartet (first prize, Aspen Music Fest competition, 74); Concertino Molto Grosso for Twelve Soloists and Wind Ensemble; Kuruntokai (tenor, piano); 5 Songs From the Goliards (countertenor & medieval consort).

DORFMAN, HELEN HORN (PRETTY PENNY)   ASCAP 1967
composer, author, teacher
b Troy, NY, Apr 26, 13; d 1968. Educ: Teachers Col, Conn, BA; Hillyer Col, MA. Teacher music, New Britian Pub Schs, 41-45; journalist, wrote advert column in New Britian Herald, 49-60; was teacher kindergarten, New Britian Pub Schs. *Songs:* Children Sing Around the Year; Rhythm Is the First R.

DORN, VEEDER VAN (CARLETON BROMA, STU   ASCAP 1968
CONGA, STEVE ROPER)
composer, author
b Ilion, NY, Sept 7, 46. Educ: Univ Colo, MBA, 77; Radio Res Inst NS, 78. Songwriter; artist, producer & songwriter for rock bands; was original mem of performing group, The Moonrakers & group, Sugarloaf. Teacher & producer. Chief Collabrs: Jerry Corbetta, J C Phillips, Randy Walrath, Bob Webber. *Songs:* Things Gonna Change Some; Pot Starts to Boil; Planet of Love; Out of Notion; *Music:* Love Train. *Instrumental Works:* Slider's Glider.

DORO, GRACE (LORA LEE)   ASCAP 1963
composer, author
b St Louis, Mo, Sept 20, 12. Educ: High sch, Kansas City, Mo. Went in vaudeville at age 16; did single piano act at age 18; played the Palace, also London, Paris, Ger & Rio de Janeiro. *Songs:* Pettin' and Pokin'; Captured; Waste No Tears Over Me; Put Your Lips to Mine; Legend of the Desert; Dude Ranch; Jump for Joy; Flip Me Baby; Too Lazy to Love; The Ocean's Face; Race of the Huskies.

DORRIS, GAYLON DOYLE   ASCAP 1975
author, singer
b Rector, Ark, Nov 10, 45. Started in music bus locally, 64; worked road gigs with Marvel Felts, 69-70; worked with Clyde Beavers Show from Nashville, 71-72; organized own group, 73. *Songs:* I Saw an Angel (Heaven Lee); *Music:* Claudette English.

DORSEY, BILL BALLANTINE   ASCAP 1967
composer, author
b Washington, DC, Apr 30, 32. Educ: Studied with Mickey Baker. Writer for Screen Gems; has written for TV, films & records. Chief Collabr: Michael Murphey. *Songs:* Find Peace in Your Soul; Seldovia (Where the Seagulls Go); The Other Side; *Lyrics:* Greyhound Goin' Somewhere.

DORSEY, DONALD MERRILL   ASCAP 1976
composer, author, arranger
b Orange, Calif, Oct 5, 53. Educ: Calif State Univ, Fullerton, 71-78; Exten, Univ Calif, Los Angeles, 79-80. Comp, arr, electronic music specialist & independent producer. Arr music & comp selections for Disney's "Main Street Electrical Parade", "Electrical Water Pageant" & other productions; also did albums, jingles & live shows. *Instrumental Works:* '76 Medley (Sing Out, America); Fanfare of Lights; Music for Thursday.

DORSEY, JIMMY   ASCAP 1941
composer, conductor, saxophonist
b Shenandoah, Pa, Feb 29, 04; d New York, NY, June 12, 57. Educ: Pub schs; studied cornet with father. Saxophonist in orchs, incl Calif Ramblers, Paul Whiteman & Red Nichols, 20's. Formed orch with brother, Tommy Dorsey, 33-35; then led own orch. Joined Tommy's orch, 53; took over band at brother's death. Made many records. Film biography, "The Fabulous Dorseys." Chief Collabrs: Larry Clinton, Paul Mertz, James Van Heusen. *Songs & Instrumental Works:* Beebe; Dusk in Upper Sandusky; Waddlin' at the Waldorf; It's the Dreamer in Me; I'm Glad There Is You; Two Again; Contrasts; Oodles of Noodles; John Silver.

DORSEY, TOMMY, JR   ASCAP 1965
conductor, trombonist
b Mahanoy City, Pa, Nov 19, 05; d Greenwich, Conn, Nov 26, 56. Educ: Pub schs. Started playing the trombone, age 5; learned from his father Thomas F Dorsey, Sr, a noted music teacher. At age 15, he was playing professionally with his brother Jimmy Dorsey. Played in orchs incl Paul Whiteman & Red Nichols. Had own band, Wild Canaries. Formed an orch with his brother Jimmy, 33-35. Wrote trombonology & made many recordings incl "Boogie Woogie." Made numerous films incl "The Fabulous Dorsey's", "Thrill of a Life Time", "Babes in Arms" & "A Star Is Born." Owned two music publ firms, Dorsey Brothers Music Inc & Embassy Music Corp.

DOUGHERTY, ANNE HELENA   ASCAP 1962
composer, author, pianist
b Wilmington, Del, Mar 24, 08. Educ: Ursuline Acad, Wilmington, Del, studied piano; Mt St Joseph Acad, Chestnut Hill, Pa; Nat Park Sem, Forest Glen, Md, studied organ & piano. Secy to pres, Wilmington Sunday Star; social service worker, State of Del; dir communications, FMC Corp, Philadelphia, Pa. Chief Collabrs: Charles F Dougherty (bro), Alice Elizabeth Dougherty (sister), Norman W Morris. *Songs:* Old Fashioned Christmas; Castle of Dreams; Who's Who; Keep Your Fingers Crossed; *Music:* Don't Take the Love Out of Tennis, It Won't Be Cricket, If You Do; He's Just the Breadman But He's Got the Dough; What's the Use. *Songs & Instrumental Works:* Let's Make Love in a Jenny Lind (horse & buggy); Let's Not Say Goodbye; So Nice to Be With You Again; Everyday's a Holiday on Broadway; Lady of Ole Seville.

DOUGHERTY, CELIUS H   ASCAP 1948
composer
b Glenwood, Minn, May 27, 02. Educ: Univ Minn, BA, magna cum laude; Juilliard Found Scholarships; studied comp with Rubin Goldmark & piano with Josef & Rosina Lhevinne. While undergrad, played my own piano concerto with orch. Schubert Prize for piano, 24. *Songs:* Music: Five Sea-Chanties; Love in the Dictionary; Declaration of Independence; Children's Letter to the United Nations; Primavera; Loveliest of Trees; A Minor Bird; The K'e; Hush'd Be the Camps Today (memories of President Lincoln); Song of the Jasmin (Arabian Nights); Seven Songs; Whispers of Heavenly Death (song cycle for baritone & piano). *Instrumental Works:* Music From Seas and Ships (sonata for two-pianos). *Songs & Instrumental Works:* Five American Folk-Song Duets (comn by Evelyn Lear & Tom Stewart); Eglantine and Ivy (comn for Phyllis Curtin); Ballad of William Sycamore (comn by James King). *Scores:* Many Moons (one-act opera, comn for Young Audiences Inc).

DOUGHERTY, DAN   ASCAP 1927
composer
b Philadelphia, Pa, July 17, 1897; d New York, NY, June 13, 55. Wrote spec material for Sophie Tucker; songs for films. Dir, Pathe Lot & asst to Bakalinofkop on Columbia Lot. Chief Collabrs: Jack Yellen, Nick Kenny, Rudy Vallee, Sam S Freedman. *Songs:* It Certainly Must Be Love; Glad Rag Doll; Mollie; Alone in the Rain; Moaning for You; I'm Dreaming; Sittin' on a Rainbow; You're Still in My Heart; One Cigarette for Two; Let's Get Behind the President; Mr Segal, Make It Legal; This Is It; If I Said I Don't Love You I'd Be Lying; Music: I Met God.

DOUGHERTY, JOSEPH RYMER   ASCAP 1967
composer, author
b Knoxville, Tenn, Oct 5, 49. Educ: Univ Ala, Birmingham, BS(biol), 72. Moved to Nashville after grad. Songwriter. Chief Collabrs: David Gillon, Linda Hargrove, Don Goodman, Steve Davis, Milton Blackford. *Songs:* That's the Way Love Should Be (ASCAP Chartbuster's Award); Lonesome City Blues; Take Off Them Shoes; You Don't Have to Change the World; Chattanooga Night; Nobody Touches My Baby; Going to the Cordon Bleu; Dixie Darlin'; The Holding on Is Over.

DOUGLAS, BERT   ASCAP 1942
composer, author, singer
b Buffalo, NY, May 10, 1900; d New York, NY, Feb 19, 58. Chief Collabr: Bennie Martini. *Songs:* When Your Old Wedding Ring Was New; Got Myself in Love; So Nice of You; Fooled; I'm Afraid to Love You; Why?; I Guess I'll Have to Find Another Sweetheart; How Could You?

DOUGLAS, CHARLES (CHARLES LAPLANTE)   ASCAP 1979
composer, singer, musician
b Glen Cove, NY, Apr 1, 56. Educ: Oral Roberts Univ. Nightclub performer; has done TV work; recording artist; has own label, Passion Records; plays guitar, piano & drums; also lead singer. *Songs:* Dear Wendy; Summer Days in Boston; I've Been Wrong Before; Before Your Eyes; Shadows.

DOUGLAS, DARRELL RAMON   ASCAP 1968
composer, educator
b St Paul, Minn, June 28, 30. Educ: Univ Minn, BS(music educ); Ariz State Univ, MA(music educ); Univ Southern Calif, DMusA(music educ). Taught pub schs, 54-64; col instr, Calif State Univ, Fullerton, Univ Wis, Parkside & Elizabethtown Col, 64- *Songs:* Music: Simple Gifts (SATB).

DOUGLAS, LAERTEAS LARRY   ASCAP 1953
composer, author
b Detroit, Mich, Mar 28, 17. Educ: Univ Mich, Ann Arbor. Comp, music & lyrics. Movie actor, appearing in many French productions. Compositions performed with int revues of "Holiday on Ice." *Songs:* Seabreeze; Laugh (Tho' You Feel You Want to Cry); Snoopy; Love and Understanding.

DOUGLAS, RON
See Lowden, Ronald Douglas, Jr

DOUGLASS, HARRY MONROE   ASCAP 1970
composer, singer
b Bridgeville, Del, May 6, 16. Educ: Phyllis Wheatley Grade Sch, Bridgeville, Del; high sch; Del State Col; Hampton Inst, 34-36, special studies with Prof Ed Boatner. Leader, Deep River Boys, 36; personal appearances in theaters & concerts throughout North Am, CBS Radio Broadcasting, 37; appeared in musical production, "Midsummer Nights Dream," Center Theater, Radio City, New York, 38; personal appearances for Nat Broadcasting Co, 40. Served in Spec Serv, USA, 43-46. Reorganized Deep River Boys, 46; toured Europe, London Palladium, 49, Royal Command Perf before Queen Elizabeth & the Royal Family, 52; personal appearance, The White House for Pres Dwight D Eisenhower, 55; int tours, 56-57; goodwill tour of six African countries sponsored by US State Dept, 70; with CBS TV spec, "The Song Has Soul," "Lamp Unto My Feet Series," 72; actor, TV series, "Infinity Factory Number 2," fall 77; visited Australia, 78. Chief Collabr: Ed Kirkeby. *Songs:* Juba. *Instrumental Works:* Arr: Nobody Knows the Trouble I've Seen; Little David, Play on Your Harp; Listen to the Lambs; Who'll Be a Witness; Deep River;

Sometimes I Feel Like a Motherless Child; When the Saints Go Marchin' In; Go Tell It on the Mountain; Swing Low, Sweet Chariot; Study War No More (Down By the Riverside); Ezekial Saw De Wheel; Whole World in His Hand; Go Down Moses; Honey, Honey, Honey (Little Lize I Love You); Live Humble; Old Ark's a-Moving; Wait Till I Put on My Robe; Show Me the Way; Git on Board Little Children; Good News the Chariot's Comn'; I'm Troubled in Mind; Let Us Break Bread Together; Look Away Into Heaven; My Brothers Don't Get Weary; Oh Freedom; They Look Like Men of War; We Are Walking in the Light; My Castle on the River Nile; Why Adam Sinned.

DOUGLASS, JANE
See White, Jane Douglass

DOVE, LEWIS U, JR   ASCAP 1959
composer, pianist, arranger
b Lightstreet, Pa, July 31, 25; d Aug 6, 65. Educ: Susquehanna Univ, BS. Served, USAAF, World War II. Taught music, Pa Pub Schs, 10 yrs, pvt teacher. Pianist & arr with dance bands. *Songs:* Can This Be Love?; Traffic Jam.

DOWELL, HORACE KIRBY (SAXIE)   ASCAP 1941
composer, conductor, saxophonist
b Raleigh, NC, May 29, 04; d Scottsdale, Ariz, July 22, 74. Educ: Univ NC. Saxophonist in Hal Kemp orch, 15 yrs; then formed own band. WW II, USN; bandmaster, USS Franklin, until sunk in S Pacific, 45. After war, reorganized band. DJ, sta WGN, Chicago. *Songs:* Three Little Fishies; I Don't Care; Tonight I'm Thinking of You; Tell Her; Playmates; V for Victory; Rugged But Right; She Told Him Emphatically No; All I've Got Is Me; Oo-Goo the Little Worm; Canasta Song; Turnabout Is Fair Play; Our Favorite Waltz; I Don't Know If I'm Comin' or Goin'.

DOWNEY, FAIRFAX DAVIS   ASCAP 1941
author
b Salt Lake City, Utah, Nov 28, 1893. Educ: Hill Sch, Pa, 12; Yale Univ, BA, 16. Staff, Kansas City Star, NY Tribune, Herald Tribune, Sun, 18-27. Capt, Field Artillery, Am Expeditionary Force, WW I; Silver Star. Author, "A Comic History of Yale", "When We Were Rather Older", "Portrait of an Era as Drawn By C D Gibson", "Famous Horses of the Civil War", "Clash of Cavalry", "Storming of the Gateway", "Richard Harding Davis", "Sound of the Guns", "The Guns at Gettysburg", "Chattanooga 1863." Chief Collabrs: Channing Lefebvre, Arthur E Hall, Morris W Hamilton, Sigmund Spaeth, Marshall Bartholomew. *Songs:* Lyrics: Forever Free; Two Swedish Melodies; Battle Chant of the Janissaries; True Blue Elihu; Battle of the Books.

DOWNEY, JOHN WILHAM   ASCAP 1970
composer, author, pianist
b Chicago, Ill, Oct 5, 27. Educ: De Paul Univ, BM, 49; Chicago Musical Col, MM, 51; Prix de Comp, Cons Nat Musique, 56; Univ of Pairs, PhD, 56. Went to Paris on a Fulbright Scholarship in comp for 2 yrs, followed by grants from the French & Ger Govts. Was mem, Soc Advancement Continuing Educ for Ministry, 54-70. Returned to US. Prof theory-comp & composer-in-residence, Univ Wis-Milwaukee, 64- Founder & chmn, Wis Contemporary Music Forum. Has been a Fellow at MacDowell Colony on several times. Received additional res grants from the French Govt, Univ Wis, Ford Found & NEA. Chevalier, l'Ordre des Arts et Lettres, 80. Chief Collabr: Irusha Downey (wife). *Songs:* A Dolphin (high voice, viola, alto flute, piano, perc); What If? (full choir, brass, perc); Gaudeamus Igitur; The Lake Isle of Innisfree (voice, piano); Come Away Death (voice, piano); Hey, Ho, The Wind and the Rain (voice, piano). *Instrumental Works:* Sonata for Cello and Piano; Eastlake Terrace (piano solo); Tabu for Tuba (tuba, piano); Agort (woodwind quintet); Jingalodeon (large orch); Symphonic Modules Five (large orch); String Quartet No 2; Pyramids (piano solo); Octet for Winds; Fantasy for Bassoon and Orchestra; Almost Twelve (flute, oboe, clarinet, bassoon, horn, violin, viola, violoncello, contrabassoon, perc); Lydian Suite (solo violoncello); Adagio Lyrico (two pianos); Chant to Michelangelo (orch); Silhouette (solo double bass).

DOWNEY, MORTON   ASCAP 1949
composer, singer, pianist
b Wallingford, Conn, Nov 14, 01. Educ: Lyman Hall. Began singing career in movie theatre, Greenwich Village. Vocalist with Paul Whiteman Orch aboard SS Leviathan; toured Europe, 27. Opened own nightclub, The Delmonico, NY, 30; also sang over radio. Mem bd dirs, Coca-Cola & other corporations. Chief Collabrs: Dave Dreyer, Paul Cunningham, James Rule, Dick Sanford. *Songs:* California Skies; Wabash Moon; All I Need Is Someone Like You; In the Valley of the Roses; That's How I Spell Ireland; Sweeten Up Your Smile; There's Nothing New; Now You're in My Arms.

DOWNEY, RAYMOND J (ROY WELLS)   ASCAP 1953
composer, author
b Wallingford, Conn, Oct 4, 12. Educ: St Thomas Sem. Came to NY, 35, pianist, singer in hotels & on radio. *Songs:* In the Stillness of My Heart; Helpless; Lonely Wine; You Listen So Nice; She Looked Down From Her Window.

DOWNEY, SEAN MORTON, JR (CALVIN FINCH)   ASCAP 1959
composer, author, singer
b New York, NY, Dec 9, 33. Educ: NY Univ, BS, 55; LaSalle Univ, LLB, 62. Co-founder, Am Basketball Asn. Nightclub & recording artist. Political activist officer, Democratic Nat Comt. Vatican Medal for humanitarian work in Africa. Chief lobbyist, Nat Right to Life, Washington, DC; chmn, Life Amendment Political Action Comt Inc; political consult, Nat Campaigns & US Dept Justice. Chief Collabrs: James A Ware, Lloyd Schoonmaker, Don Great. *Songs:* Please Don't Mention My Name; Treasure of Love; Ballad of Billy Brown; I Believe America; Last Day on Earth; Teach Me How to Pray; Colorado Rain; Ten Years of Hard Labor; Gotta Right to Live; Sounds of Yesterday; Because We're Young; Franklin Delano Roosevelt; Harry S Truman; American History; Red Neck American Hero's; John Fitzgerald Kennedy; Roaring 20's; Those Were the 50's; Music: You Cheated; Lyrics: Little Rose. *Instrumental Works:* South Swell; You Alone.

DOWNS, M CLIFFORD, III   ASCAP 1976
composer, author
b Birmingham, Ala, Nov 27, 53. Educ: Univ Ala, BA(communications), 75. Wrote TV & radio spots in col. Songwriter & guitarist in nightclubs & sessions. Chief Collabr: Joe Chambers. *Songs:* Lonesome Is a Cowboy; April Fool; The Last Goodbye; This Is the Night.

DOYLE, ROBERT JOSEPH   ASCAP 1965
composer, pianist, arranger
b Toledo, Ohio, June 9, 1925. Educ: Syracuse Univ, studied piano & comp, 48-50, music educ, 70. Pianist & arr, WSYR Radio & TV Channel 3, Syracuse, 60-70. Jazz pianist, Syracuse, 48- Chief Collabrs: Bill Coons, Frankie Laine. *Songs:* Silver Kisses and Golden Love; Jessie Slocum; Music: Scarlet Tree; Cryin' Need. *Instrumental Works:* Rhapsody for Piano and Concert Band; Poem for Piano (piano & concert band); Barcelona (guitar solo with concert band).

DOYLE, WALTER   ASCAP 1941
composer, author
b Scranton, Pa, July 8, 1899; d Millville, NJ, Mar 30, Educ: Grade sch; self-taught piano. 45. WW I, USMC. *Songs:* Sweet Dixie Lady; Whenever I Think of You; Collegiate Love; No One; Mysterious Mouse; To the Steins; Egyptian Ella.

DRACHMAN, TED   ASCAP 1979
composer, author
b New York, NY, June 21, 45. Educ: Harvard Col, BA, 67; San Francisco State Univ, grad study Eng & creative writing, 68. Actor & writer with The Proposition, improvisational revue, Cambridge, Mass, 68-69; radio & stage actor, Boston, 69-71; freelance writer & ed, New York, 72-; co-writer book, music & lyrics for "Work and Win!" (off off-Bway), 79. Chief Collabrs: Mary Chaffee, John Forster, Alan Bellink, John Alper. *Songs:* If My Heart Was a Willow; Bein' There; Lyrics: Anelica; Good-bye Yesterday; Higher Than Heaven.

DRAGER, BRIAN MICHAEL   ASCAP 1976
composer, author, singer
b Portland, Ore, Mar 9, 43. Educ: Grades 1-12, choral training & 6 yrs classical piano; Portland State Col, 2 yrs pre-music. Nightclub entertainer, 64-; duo "Blue Kangaroo" with Jay Cook, 64-; worked 12 yrs music & comedy. Recorded 3 albums of original material.

DRAGON, CARMEN   ASCAP 1950
composer, conductor, arranger
b Antioch, Calif, July 28, 14. Educ: San Jose State Col, MA. Cond, Hollywood Bowl Symph, 10 yrs, Capitol Symph, Royal Philh, BBC Symph, var TV series, symph orchs throughout US & for many records. Comp, cond & arr, TV & radio. Music dir, Stand Sch Broadcast, 49. *Instrumental Works:* Sante Fe Suite. *Scores:* Film: Cover Girl (Acad award, 44).

DRAKE, EDWIN DALE   ASCAP 1977
composer, author
b Grand Rapids, Mich, Mar 4, 44. Educ: Grand Valley State Col, BA; Roosevelt Univ, studied studio arr with Rich Manners. Songwriter, 65- Comp & producer of prog theme for "Back to God Hour," 78. Writer & recording artist. *Songs:* Others; Wish I Would Have Known.

DRAKE, ERVIN   ASCAP 1948
composer, author
b New York, NY, Apr 3, 19. Educ: Townsend Harris Hall; City Col New York, BSS; Juilliard Sch Music, studied orchestration with Jacob Druckman; theory, comp & orchestration with Tibor Serly; piano with Bernard Spencer. First publ songs in early 40's; combined songwriting with related work in TV, writing, comp & producing some 700 prime time network progs, 48-62; TV Series: "Sing It Again", "Songs for Sale", "Jane Froman Show", "Frankie Laine Show", "Mel Torme/Teresa Brewer Show" & "Merv Griffin/Betty Ann Grove Show." Producer, "Timex Comedy Hour." Writer & producer of some 40 spec starring Ethel Merman, Gower Champion, Mike Nichols, Elaine May, Julie Andrews, Ginger Rogers, Margaret Truman, Eddie Cantor, Nat Cole, Johnny Mathis, Paul Anka, Yves Montand, Polly Bergen, Gene Autry, Jayne Mansfield, Tony

Bennett, Perry Como, Arthur Godfrey, Gene Kelly & others. Won Sylvania Award for music, lyrics & coproducing bk musical "The Bachelor," NBC-TV, 57; Emmy nominee as writer & coproducer of "Yves Montand on Broadway." Wrote script & original song for birthday tribute to Mamie Eisenhower TV simulcast by CBS & NBC called "To Our First Lady With Music," 56. Writer & coproducer of "Accent on Love", "Seasons of Youth", "Ethel Merman Special" & others. Pres, Am Guild Authors & Comp, 73-80, led successful writers' campaign in Congress for passage of US Copyright Law of 1976; dir, Nat Acad Popular Music, 78-; sponsor, Nat Music Theatre; mem, Authors League, Dramatists Guild & Writers Guild of Am, E; dir, Social Services Bd of Cancer Care, Inc, 79- Chief Collabrs: Jimmy Shirl, Juan Tizol, Johnny Hodges, Ernesto Lecuona, Zequinha Abreu, Max Steiner, Irene Higginbotham, Paul Misraki, Robert Stolz, A Donida, Tony Renis. *Songs:* I Believe; It Was a Very Good Year; A Room Without Windows; Beloved Be Faithful; Father of Girls; My Friend; The Rickety Rickshaw Man; Across the Wide Missouri; After All; I Wuv a Wabbit; The Friendliest Thing; My Hometown; Something to Live For; Some Days Everything Goes Wrong; You're No Good; Just for Today; In Vino Veritas; I Fell in With Evil Companions; One God; Easter Sunday Morning; A Heart Full of Christmas; The Big Record (TV theme); Texas, Brooklyn and Heaven; Weather Pains; Music: Theme From Sherlock Holmes (TV series); Lyrics: Good Morning Heartache; Al Di La; Tico Tico; Perdido; Come to the Mardi Gras; Sonata; Castle Rock; Made for Each Other; Quando, Quando, Quando; Can You Guess?; Yo Te Amo Mucho; Meet Mister Callaghan; Wendy (TV theme); Intrigue (TV series theme); Our Crazy Affair; Let's Keep It That Way; The Right to Love; Long After Tonight. *Scores:* Libretto: Her First Roman.

DRAKE, JIM   ASCAP 1958
composer, arranger, singer
b Pittsburgh, Pa, Dec 8, 35. Educ: Duquesne Univ. Mem vocal group, The Tempos; made records & appeared on TV. Music teacher pub sch, Sewickley, Pa. Chief Collabr: Gene Schacter. *Songs:* Tornado.

DRAKE, JOSEPHINE ELEANOR   ASCAP 70
composer, author
b Yellow Frame, NJ, July 20, 31. Educ: Dalcroze Connection; studied music & movement with Frances Aronoff, NY Univ, 80. Singer & entertainer. *Songs:* Help Me God; Trusted; Blessings; Why?; Gone.

DRAKE, MILTON   ASCAP 1932
composer, author, performer
b Brooklyn, NY. Educ: NY Univ; Baruch Sch Bus Admin, BA & MBA. Radio performer/announcer, NBC & mutual networks; Bway theater production songs & film songs, Hollywood. Retired from popular songwriting, 59; joined McGraw-Hill as marketing dir, later formed independent marketing firm specializing in International Electronics Market Res. Chief Collabrs: Al Hoffman, Jerry Livingston, Ben Oakland, Con Conrad, Oscar Levant, Artie Shaw, Vic Mizzy, David Mann, Walter Kent, Abner Silver, Milton Berle, Louis Alter, Larry Stock. *Songs:* Kiss Me Sweet; Fuzzy Wuzzy; I Don't Care; Lyrics: Champagne Waltz; Mairzy Doats; I'm a Big Girl Now; Java Jive; Nina Never Knew; Pu-Leeze! Mr Hemingway!; Bless Your Heart; Instant Love; If Wishes Were Kisses; Felicia No Capicia; The Man With the Weird Beard. *Scores:* Bway shows: I Loved You Wednesday; Folies Berger; Folies Fantastique; Film/TV: Li'l Abner; The Big Store; My Little Chickadee; For Whom the Bell Tolls; The Awful Truth.

DRAKE, RONALD B   ASCAP 1976
composer, author, singer
b Robertson County, Tenn, Oct 9, 37. Educ: Belmont Col, BA. Back-up singer, Sound 70 Singers. Toured US with Phillip Morris Country Music Show, 59. Teacher of music, Maplewood High Sch, 63-69. Became exec dir, Calvary Records, 77. Music dir, Union Hills Baptist Church. Did background work for several country-western singers. *Songs:* Keep Her Waving; Freedom Is a Five Letter Word.

DRAWBAUGH, JACOB W (BILL ST ONGE,   ASCAP 1958
JIM RUNNINGBROOK)
composer, author
b Baltimore, Md, Jan 12, 28. Educ: Forest Park High Sch; Johns Hopkins Univ. *Songs:* A Little Bit of Kindness.

DRAYTON, CLARENCE R, JR   ASCAP 1973
author, producer, arranger
b Jacksonville, Fla, Aug 4, 47. Educ: Newark Sch Fine & Indust Arts, 65-67; Fuller Theol Sem, 80- Played guitar & bass in bands since age 14. Bass player, recording & writer, Motown Records. Arr & cond touring. Wrote for Jackson Five, High Energy, Lenny Williams, Diana Ross, Bette Midler, plus others. Producer for groups, Onyx, Osborne & Robinson, The Monroe Brothers, Jacksons. Minister, Mt Zion Missionary Baptist Church, Los Angeles. Independent writer & gospel songwriter. Chief Collabrs: Judy Weider, Tamy Smith, Jonah Ellis, Pam Sawyer, Hal Davis, Jermaine Jackson. *Songs:* Life of the Party; Though We Loved Once; Love Is All You Need; Fire; Rhythm Child; Window Shopping; I Can't Stop Dancing; Love Hangover; Do It Now; What Does It Take?; I Know That I'm Born Again; Somebody; Steal Away; I Want to Be What You Want Me to Be; Going Home Now; You Got Me Running.

DREHER, THEODORE　　　　　　　　ASCAP 1964
composer, orchestrator, arranger
b Calgary, Alta, Jan 5, 12. Educ: Kansas City Jr Col, Mo, 2 yrs; self-taught music. Pianist; nite clubs & road bands, 30's; theaters & clubs, 40's. Pres, Musicians Local No 34, Kansas City, Mo, 51-69; active as writer & arr. Asst to pres, Am Fedn Musicians, New York, 69- Chief Collabrs: Barnett Shaw & Ralph Rose, Jr. *Songs:* Music: It Was Music.

DREIBRODT, IRVING D　　　　　　　　ASCAP 1969
composer, educator
b San Antonio, Tex, Oct 12, 20. Educ: Baylor Univ, BM; Tex Univ, MM; Southern Col Fine Arts, DMus. Dir of Bands: Corpus Christi, Brackenridge High Sch, Trinity Univ, Southern Methodist Univ; prof musician: San Antonio Symph, Waco Symph, Corpus Christi Symph, Ice Capades, Dallas; adjudicator & clinician throughtout US. *Songs:* Music: Southern Methodist University Loyalty Song; Pony Battle Cry; Peuna.

DRESSER, LEE M　　　　　　　　ASCAP 1969
composer, author, singer
b Washington, DC, May 22, 41. Educ: Moberly High Sch, Mo, grad, 59; Moberly Jr Col, grad, 61; Univ Mo, 61-64. Founded rock & roll band, Krazy Kats, 57; played in Midwest, 57-65. Served in Army, 65-68. Performer, TV shows & clubs, Los Angeles area; sang sound track of motion picture "The Wilderness Family," 75; signed with Capitol Records, 77; has had songs recorded by many country & pop artists; nominated for Best New Male Vocalist, Acad of Country Music, 78. *Songs:* You're All the Woman I'll Ever Need; A Beautiful Song (For a Beautiful Lady); Redneck Disco; El Camino Real; Poor Old Billy.

DRESSER, PAUL　　　　　　　　ASCAP 1939
composer, author, singer
b Terre Haute, Ind, Apr 21, 1857; d New York, NY, Jan 30, 06. Bro to novelist Theodore Dreiser. Educ: St Meinrad's, Switz City, Ind, trained for priesthood. Joined medicine show at 16, then toured in vaudeville as singer & monologist; end man, Billy Rice Minstrels, 1885; mem, publ firm, Howley, Haviland & Dresser; later formed own firm; actor, publ & producer. Film Biography, "My Gal Sal." *Songs:* Wide Wings; The Letter That Never Came; My Gal Sal; On the Banks of the Wabash (off Ind State song); The Blue and the Gray; Just Tell Them That You Saw Me; Once Ev'ry Year; The Curse of the Dreamer; The Pardon Came Too Late; Don't Tell Her That You Love Her; Your Mother Wants You Home, Boy; Bethlehem; The Outcast Unknown; Mr Volunteer; I Was Looking for My Boy, She Said; The People Are Marching By; Come Tell Me What's Your Answer; The Hudson.

DRETKE, LEORA NYLEE
See Klotz, Leora

DREW, JAMES M　　　　　　　　ASCAP 1973
composer
b St Paul, Minn, Feb 9, 29. Educ: New York Sch Music; Tulane Univ, MA; studied comp with Wallingford Riegger, Edgard Varese. Comp for concert hall, theater, dance & film, 56- Fac mem, Northwestern Univ, 65-67; Yale Univ, 67-73; La State Univ, 73-75. Fromm Music Found Comp, Tanglewood, 73; visiting comp, Calif State Univ, Fullerton, 76-77; Univ Calif Los Angeles, 77-78; free-lance comp, 79- Active as pianist, cond, Decca Recording artist & publ for The Theodore Presser Co. Dir, Am Music Theater, 77- Awards: Guggenheim Fel, 72-73; Panamericana Prize, 74. *Songs:* Orangethorpe Aria; Songs of Death and Bluelight Dancing; Five O'Clock Ladies; Whispers. *Instrumental Works:* String Quartet No 1 (Lux Incognitus); Symphony No 2; Metal Concert; West Indian Lights; Trio for the Firery Messengers; Omens; Circle Sonata; St Dennis Variations; All Saints' Chorales; In Memoriam: Edward Kennedy Ellington; Crucifixus Domini Christi; In Memoriam: Mark Rothko; St Mark Concerto.

DREW, KENNY SIDNEY　　　　　　　　ASCAP 1971
composer, author, pianist
b New York, NY, Aug 28, 28. Educ: Classical piano lessons at age 5; High Sch Music & Art, New York, grad; studied arr & orchestration privately. Toured with Pearl Primus Dance Group, 46-47; began jazz career, 48-; first recording, 49; first piano trio recording, 53. Recorded & performed with var jazz artists incl Charlie Parker, Miles Davis, Coleman Hawkins, Ben Webster, John Coltrane, Dizzy Gillespie, Carmen McRae, Dinah Washington, Sonny Rollins. Formed publ firm, Copenhagen, 72; co-owner, Matrix Records, 78-; production co, 80- *Instrumental Works:* Undercurrent; Serenity; Suite for Jazz Orchestra; Lite-Flite; Some Minor Changes.

DREWERY, ISIAH (OZZIE)
composer, author, singer
b Jasper, Fla, Aug 16, 42. Educ: Stanton Vocational High Sch, Fla; Bronx Community Col, NY. Acted, off-Bway play & show for Red Cross at Waldorf-Astoria; built own record co. Chief Collabr: Eddie Jones. *Songs:* The Picture Became Quite Clear.

DREYER, DAVE　　　　　　　　ASCAP 1925
composer, author, pianist
b Brooklyn, NY, Sept 22, 1894; d. Pianist, music publ co; vaudeville accompanist to Al Jolson, Sophie Tucker, Belle Baker & Frank Fay. Staff pianist, Irving Berlin Music Co, 23; mgr, 41. Wrote film scores, 29-40; head of music dept, RKO Radio. Founded own publ co, 47. Chief Collabrs: Billy Rose, Ballard Macdonald, Herman Ruby. *Songs:* Me and My Shadow; There's a Rainbow 'Round My Shoulder; Back in Your Own Back Yard; Cecilia; Four Walls; Golden Gate; In a Little Second Hand Store; Wabash Moon; I'm Following You; I Wanna Sing About You; I'm Keeping Company; You Can't Be True, Dear; The Wall; Next Stop Paradise; Hold My Hand; What Am I Supposed to Do?; Honey Babe.

DRIGGS, COLLINS H　　　　　　　　ASCAP 1950
composer, author, organist
b Manchester, Conn, June 27, 11; d Cape Coral, Fla, Aug 29, 66. Educ: Pub schs; studied with Harry Heald. Organist, known as World's Youngest Featured Organist, Paramount Theatres, 26. Staff organist, CBS, 4 yrs; led New World Ens, Ford Motor Co, NY World's Fair, 39. Consult in develop of Hammond organ, assoc with firm over 20 yrs. Author "The Spinet Drawbars", "Tone Patterns", "Left Hand Styles", "Vowel Tones", "Here's How You Can Get More Out of Your Hammond Spinet" & "Special Christmas Effects for Hammond Spinet Organ." Chief Collabr: W Edward Breuder. *Songs:* The Templed Hills; All This I Pray; I Alone Shall Never Be; Sleep Happy; You're Sweeter Than Any Bouquet; It's a Law-aw-aw-aw Way Back Home; The Day That I Was 17; Fantasy; In Memoriam; Benediction; Tie a Little Love on Your Christmas Tree (This Year); John, John, John; Let's Make a Date for Sunday Morning; I Can't Put My Arms Around a Memory; No Farther Than From Me to You; Music: The Lord Is My Shepherd; The Lords Prayer.

DRUCKMAN, JACOB RAPHAEL
composer
b Philadelphia, Pa, June 26, 28. Educ: Juilliard Sch Music, BS, 54, MS, 56; Ecole Normale de Musique, Paris, 54-55; studied comp with Aaron Copland, Louis Gessensway, Peter Mennin, Vincent Persichetti & Bernard Wagenaar. Mem fac, Juilliard Sch Music, 56-72 & Bard Col, 61-67. Assoc, Columbia-Princeton Electronic Music Ctr, 66- Dir, Electronic Music Studio, Yale Univ Sch Music, 71-72, chmn, Comp Dept, 76- Dir, Electronic Music Studio, Brooklyn Col, 72-76. Comp music for Joffrey City Ctr Ballet Co's "Animus", "Valentine" & "Jackpot." Mem bd dirs, Koussevitzky Found, 72-, pres, 80; past mem bd dirs, ASCAP. Mem music adv panel, NY State Council Arts, 75-77; co-chmn, NEA Comp & Librettist Panel, 80. Grants & Awards: Fulbright Grant, 54; Guggenheim Grants, 57 & 68; Soc Publ Am Music Award, 67; Am Acad/Nat Inst Arts & Letters Award, 69; Pulitzer Prize, 72; citation in music, Brandeis Univ. Juilliard String Quartet Comn through LADO, 66; Libr Cong, Koussevitzky Found Comn, 69; Bicentennial NEA Comn, St Louis & Cleveland Orchs, 76; Creative Arts Comn, 75. Mem, Am Acad & Inst Arts & Letters.

DRUMM, GEORGE　　　　　　　　ASCAP 1932
composer, conductor, violinist
b Rhenish, Ger, Sept 28, 1874; d Dobbs Ferry, NY, Dec 16, 59. To US, 04. Citizen, 11. Solo violinist with orchs; mem, Dublin Orch Soc. Music dir in Ireland. Cond, Ireland's Own Band, La Purchase Expos, 04. Guest cond, Army & Navy Bands. *Instrumental Works:* Irish Patrol; Mediation; Springtime; Rookies March; Hail America; Reverie; Janina; Irelandia.

DRUMMOND, DEAN J　　　　　　　　ASCAP 1971
composer
b Santa Monica, Calif, Jan 22, 49. Educ: Univ Southern Calif, BM, 71; Calif Inst Arts, BFA, 73. Musician & asst for Harry Partch in concerts & recordings. Co-dir & cond, Calif New Music Ens. Inventor of zoomoozophone, a 31 tones-per-octave mallet perc instrument. Comp, microtonal music. Now directs band. *Instrumental Works:* Columbus (flute & 3 zoomoozophonists); Copegoro (zoomoozophone/perc solo); Dirty Ferdie (perc quartet); Cloud Garden I (chamber ens); Zurrjir (chamber ens).

DRURY, CHARLES　　　　　　　　ASCAP 1950
composer, conductor
b Randolph, Mass, Oct 27, 1890. Educ: Pvt music study. Cond, Bway musicals. *Songs:* Blue Bonnet Lane; Skippy and Me; Hey Grampap, Take Off That Hat.

DRUTMAN, IRVING　　　　　　　　ASCAP 1946
composer, author, editor
b New York, NY, July 28, 10; d New York, NY, Sept 20, 78. Educ: City Col New York. Free lance writer for newspapers & mag. Author of bk, "Good Company-A Memoir Mostly Theatrical." Edited bks, "Paris Was Yesterday", "London Was Yesterday" & "Janet Flanner's World." *Songs:* Twilight Song; Mama Never Told Me; Bel Ami; Pigeon Talk; My Imaginary Love.

DUANE, EDDY
See Hansen, Edward Duane

DUBENSKY, ARCADY   ASCAP 1937
    composer, conductor, violinist
b Viatka, Russia, Oct 3, 1890; d. Came to US, 21. Educ: Moscow Cons, studied with Grjimali, Ilyinsky. First violinist, Moscow Imperial Opera Theatre Orch, 10-19; NY Symph; NY Philh. *Songs & Instrumental Works:* On the Highway (opera); Fugue for 18 Violins; Tom Sawyer Overture; The Raven; Suite Anno 1600; Variations on Stephen Foster Themes; Gossips; From Old Russia; Andante Russe; Prelude and Fugue for 4 Bassoons; Intermezzo and Compliment; Tartar Song and Dance; Old Russian Soldier's Song.

DUBENSKY, LEO ARCADY   ASCAP 1959
    composer
b Moscow, Russia, Dec 10, 14. Educ: Began violin study with father at age 4. Immigrated to US, 22; studied with Franz Kneisel on scholarship, Inst Musical Art, 4 yrs; later won scholarship at Juilliard Grad Sch with Paul Kochansky, then went to Paris to study orchestration with Alexandre Glazunof; continued violin studies with Mishel Piastro. Moved to Constantinople after the Bolshevik Revolution & appeared as child prodigy, also with Constantinople Philh. After immigrating to the US, joined New York Philh through audition for Maestro Arturo Toscanini, 31; resigned to compose, 48. Played with Los Angeles Philh & New Orleans Philh. Appeared as violin soloist with New York Philh under Sir John Barbirolli. *Songs:* Hymn of Joy (choir). *Instrumental Works:* Violin Concerto in D Minor; Scherzo for Violin and Piano/Orchestra; Impromptu for Piano Solo; Theme and Variations for Clarinet and Piano/Strings; Theme and Variations for Full Orchestra; Prelude and Allegro for Full Orchestra; Prelude, Nocturne, Waltz for Piano Solo; Sinbad the Sailor (violin, piano); Blue Heron of Chincoteague.

DUBEY, MATT   ASCAP 1954
    composer, author
b Philadelphia, Pa, Jan 20, 28. Educ: Milford Prep; Univ Miami, BBA. Writer, col shows, special material for Lena Horne, Dolores Gray, nightclubs (incl score for "After Hours"), hotel revues & TV. Songwriter for "New Faces of 1956." Chief Collabrs: Harold Karr, Dean Fuller. *Songs:* Just Another Girl; The Game of Love; The Greatest Invention; How You Say It?; I'd Do Anything; Where Did He Go?; Here Today and Gone Tomorrow Love; The Song of the SeWer; Lyrics: Mutual Admiration Society; A New-Fangled Tango; If'n; This Is What I Call Love; She's Just Another Girl; Gee, But It's Good to Be Here; How Does the Wine Taste?; The Gentle Rain; A Wedded Man; Non-Stop to Brazil; A House Is Not a Home; Spooks. *Scores:* Bway shows: Happy Hunting; Smith.

DUBIN, AL   ASCAP 1921
    author
b Zurich, Switz, June 10, 1891; d New York, NY, Feb 11, 45. To US 1893. Educ: Perkiomen Sem, Pa. Staff mem, New York music publ cos. WW I, 77th Div. Under contract to Warner Bros, Hollywood. Chief Collabrs: Harry Warren, Joe Burke, J Fred Coots, Jimmy McHugh, Sammy Fain, Victor Herbert, Jimmy Monaco, Mabel Wayne, Joseph Meyer, J Russel Robinson, Burton Lane. *Songs:* 'Twas Only an Irishman's Dream; Just a Girl That Men Forget; A Cup of Coffee, a Sandwich and You; My Dream of the Big Parade; Tiptoe Through the Tulips; Painting the Clouds With Sunshine; The Kiss Waltz; Dancing With Tears in My Eyes; For You; 42nd Street; Shuffle Off to Buffalo; You're Getting to Be a Habit With Me; Young and Healthy; Shadow Waltz; We're in the Money; Pettin' in the Park; Remember My Forgotten Man; I've Got to Sing a Torch Song; Keep Young and Beautiful; Honeymoon Hotel; Shanghai Lil; Boulevard of Broken Dreams; Fair and Warmer; I'll String Along With You; Why Do I Dream Those Dreams?; I Only Have Eyes for You; Sweet Music; Lullaby of Broadway (Acad Award, 35); The Words Are in My Heart; I'm Going Shopping With You; About a Quarter to Nine; She's a Latin From Manhattan; Go Into Your Dance; The Little Things You Used to Do; Lulu's Back in Town; The Rose in Her Hair; Where Am I?; Don't Give Up the Ship; I'd Love to Take Orders From You; Page Miss Glory; I'll Sing You a Thousand Love Songs; With Plenty of Money and You; All's Fair in Love and War; Summer Night; September in the Rain; Remember Me; Am I in Love?; 'Cause My Baby Says It's So; I Know Now; You Can't Run Away from Love Tonight; Song of the Marines; The Latin Quarter; Day Dreaming; Garden of the Moon; Love Is Where You Find It; The Girl Friend of the Whirling Dervish; Feudin' and Fightin'; Indian Summer; Anniversary Waltz. *Scores:* Film: Gold Diggers of Broadway; 42nd Street; Gold Diggers (33, 35 & 37); Roman Scandals; Footlight Parade; 20 Million Sweethearts; Wonder Bar; Dames; Go Into Your Dance; Broadway Gondolier; Shipmates Forever; Mr Dodd Takes the Air; The Singing Marine; Garden of the Moon; Bway Shows: The Streets of Paris; Keep Off the Grass.

DUCHESNE, RAFAEL
    composer, author, singer
b San Juan, PR, Oct 24, 1900; d 1958. With orch in Paris. Formed own orch, traveled throughout world, 30 yrs. To US, music writer & teacher. *Songs:* Rayo de Luz; El Raton; Uugue Alor Vido; No Soy Culpable; Mujer Borico; Linda Mujer; La Copa.

DUCHIN, PETER OELRICHS
    musician
b New York, NY, July 28, 37. Educ: Hotchkiss Sch, grad, 54; Yale Univ, BA, 58; student political science & music cons, Paris, 57. Served with USA, 58-60. Pres, Peter Duchin Orchs, 63- Mem bd of dirs, Greater NY Coun Boy Scouts Am, Boys Harbor, Dance Theater Harlem, Young Audiences & Am Coun of the Arts. Mem of coun, Yale Univ, 74-79 & NY State Council on Arts, 76-

DUCKWORTH, WILLIAM ERVIN   ASCAP 1968
    composer, author, teacher
b Morganton, NC, Jan 13, 43. Educ: East Carolina Univ, BM, studied comp with Martin Mailman; Univ Ill, MS, EdD, studied comp with Ben Johnston. Assoc prof music, Atlantic Christian Col, 66-73 & Bucknell Univ, 73- Pres, Media Press, Champaign, Ill, 69-72; founder & dir, Asn Independent Comps & Performers, 69-72. Pa Comp Project Award, 74; NEA Comp Fel, 77-78. Coauth book, "Theoretical Foundations of Music," 78. Chief Collabr: Edward Brown. *Songs:* A Mass for These Forgotten Times; A Summer Madrigal. *Instrumental Works:* The Time Curve Preludes; A Book of Hours; Seven Shades of Blue; Pitch City; A Ballad in Time and Space; Non-Ticking Tenuous Tintinnabule Time; Gambit; Music in Seven Regions; Year; Binary Images; Pitt County Excursions; A Summer Madrigal.

DUCKWORTH, WILLIE LEE   ASCAP 1951
    author
b Sandersville, Ga, Jan 8, 24. Educ: High sch. Army service, 43-57. Operator pulpwood business. *Songs:* Sound Off.

DUCLOUX, WALTER ERNEST   ASCAP 1962
    author, conductor, stage director
b Lucerne, Switz, Apr 17, 13. Educ: Univ Munich, PhD(philosophy), 35; Vienna State Acad, dipl conducting, 37; teachers Felix Weingartner & Josef Krips. Asst to Toscanini, Switz, 38-39. Came to US, 39. USA, 43-46, translr on staff, Gen George S Patton, Jr; 5 Battle Stars; Bronze Star; Europ Campaign. Guest cond, Europe, 46-48. Musical dir, Voice of Am, 49-53. Dir opera & symph, Univ Southern Calif, 53-68; dir opera & symph, Univ Tex, 68-, Ashbel Smith prof music, 80- Translr of operas. *Scores:* Operas (Eng transl): Aida (Verdi); Falstaff (Verdi); Otello (Verdi); MacBeth (Verdi); Don Carlos (Verdi); Orpheus and Euridice (Gluck); Samson and Delilah (Saint-Saens); Manon Lescaut (Puccini); La Gioconda (Ponchielli); Love for Three Oranges (Prokofiev); Rusalka (Dvorak); Mathis D Maler (Hindemith); Harmony of World (Hindemith, comn by Nat Endowment); Die Liebe Der Danae (R Strauss); Friedenstag (R Strauss); La Pietra Del Paragone (Rossini); Abu Hassan (Weber); Simon Boccanegra (Verdi); Das Rheingold (Wagner).

DUDDY, JOHN H   ASCAP 1949
    composer, author, organist
b Norristown, Pa, Dec 19, 04. Educ: Temple Univ, MusB & MA; Univ Chicago, MusB; Philadelphia Musical Acad; Christian Choral Sch; Westminster Choir Col; Princeton Univ; studied with Harry Sykes, Ralph Kinder, Julius Leefson & H A Matthews. Church organist, Pa; head music dept, Albright Col; taught in pvt sch & Roger Greaves Sch Blind; head vocal dept, Lutheran Theol Sem, Philadelphia. Mem: Nat Asn of Teachers of Singing; Nat Guild Piano Teachers; Am Musicol Soc. *Songs & Instrumental Works:* Evensong; Carillon du Soir; Idyll; A Twilight Lullaby; The Peanut Man; In Normandy; Bless the Lord O My Soul.

DUDDY, LYN   ASCAP 1951
    composer, author, producer
b New York, NY. Educ: Bryant High Sch. Cond, Lyn Duddy Singers on CBS & NBC network shows. Did Copacabana & Sands Hotels production numbers, 51-56, also "Arthur Godfrey TV Calendar Show." Formed partnership with Jerry Bresler & wrote many musical commercials incl "Ford Specials", "Kent Cigarettes", "Lux", "Chesterfield", "Pillsbury" & many others, 56, also wrote/produced concert, nightclub & original material for Robert Goulet, Gordon & Sheila MacRae, Steve Lawrence & Eydie Gorme, Kate Smith, Bing Crosby, Joey Heatherton, Sophie Tucker, Jane Morgan, Van Johnson, Arlene Dahl, also for shows incl "Jaye P Morgan Show", "Merv Griffin Show" (Radio-TV Daily Award, 58) & "Ed Sullivan Show." Chief Collabrs: Joan Edwards, Lee Pockriss, Jerry Bresler. *Songs & Instrumental Works:* Darn It Baby, That's Love; Johnny Angel; You Can't Take It With You When You Go; Anytime; Television's Tough on Love; Without You. *Scores:* Bway Stage: Tickets Please.

DUDEK, LES   ASCAP 1975
    composer, author, singer
Recording artist, RCA Records. Joined band, Dudek, Finnigan & Krueger. Chief Collabrs: Finnigan, Krueger, Cher. *Songs:* City Magic; Old Judge Jones; Get It Right; Don't Stop Now; Baby, Sweet Baby. *Albums:* Black Rose.

DUDLEY, WALTER BRONSON (BIDE)   ASCAP 1942
    author
b Minneapolis, Minn, Sept 8, 1877; d New York, NY, Jan 5, 44. Reporter, St Joseph News, Mo, 03. Drama critic, Kansas City Star, Denver Post, NY Morning Telegraph & Evening World. Playwright: "Oh, Henry" & "Borrowed Love." Chief Collabrs: James Byrnes, Rudolf Friml, Otto Harbach, Frank Grey.

Songs: Give Me an Old-Fashioned Girlie; Where Did You Get Those Irish Eyes?; You'll Dream and I'll Dream; 'Round the Corner; Oh, What a Little Whopper; Lover's Lane With You. *Scores:* Stage: Odds and Ends of 1917; The Little Whopper; Sue Dear (co-librettist); The Matinee Girl; Co-Librettist: Bye, Bye Bonnie.

DUEY, PHILIP A   ASCAP 1963
composer, author, arranger
b Macy, Ind, June 22, 01. Educ: Indiana Univ, BA & MM; Columbia Univ, MA & PhD; Juilliard Sch Music, fel. Singer in Bway musicals, "Good News" & "Lady Do"; soloist on radio shows incl "Philip Morris" & "Lucky Strike." Head music dept, Butler Univ; prof voice & dir glee club, Univ Mich. *Songs & Instrumental Works:* Spirituals: My Good Ol' Man; Clementine; Ain't Got Time to Die; plus arr Bach, Handel.

DUFFY, JAMES J, JR   ASCAP 1963
composer, bandleader, arranger
b New York, NY, June 11, 25. Played with Tommy & Jimmy Dorsey, New York; also arr for big bands incl Russ Morgan. Writer of show material for var acts, Las Vegas. Player & writer of lounge acts; also production shows for MGM Hotel & Stardust Hotel. *Songs:* Love Me a Little Bit; Crazy Heart; Don't Ever Leave Me; I Love to Hear That Dixie Land Band.

DUFFY, JOHN   ASCAP 1966
composer
b New York, NY, June 23, 28. Educ: New Sch for Social Research; Tanglewood; Lenox Sch of Jazz; studied with Aaron Copland, Luigi Dallapiccola & Salomon Rosowsky. Music dir & comp, Am Shakespeare Fest, Stratford, Conn, 65-69; comp, Tyrone Guthrie Theatre, Long Wharf Theatre, Vivian Beaumont, Bway, off-Bway, NBC, ABC-TV & Univ Mich Theatre, 70-73. Berkshire Bicentennial Award; ASCAP Awards; Outstanding Composer in Theatre Award; Emmy Award, 80; Laurel Leaf Award, 80. *Instrumental Works:* Antiquity of Freedom (orch); Concerto for Stan Getz and Concert Band (band). *Scores:* Theatre: Everyman Absurd; MacBird; Horseman Pass By; also incidental music for Hamlet, King Lear, Romeo and Juliet & Macbeth.

DUFFY, TIMOTHY E   ASCAP 1978
composer, author, singer
b North Kingstown, RI, Dec 1, 48. Educ: RI Sch Design, BFA, 70. Founder & dir, NAm invocation orch, Orch of Clouds, 74- Recording artist, 78- Chief Collabrs: Terry James, Charles Lloyd. *Songs & Instrumental Works-* In the Evenin'; Real Eyes; Initiation Suite; Witness; Village of Origin.

DUGAS, EMMA L N   ASCAP 1959
composer, author
b New Orleans, La. Educ: High sch. *Songs:* Let Hearts Rule.

DUKE, BETTY
See Walls, Betty Duke

DUKE, CHARLES
See Costantakos, Chris Anastasios

DUKE, GEORGE MAC (DAWILLIE GONGA)   ASCAP 1969
composer, teacher, singer
b San Rafael, Calif, Jan 12, 46. Educ: San Francisco Cons, BM(comp), studied piano with Mario Wemian & Jules Imbrie, comp with Andrew Imbrie; San Francisco State Col, MA(comp), studied comp with Henry Onderdonk. Began piano studies at age 7. With var bands incl Latin band, 60, jazz co-op band, 61 & own group George Duke Band, 63-67. Half-Note Club with Al Jarreau, 68-69; with Don Ellis Band, George Duke Trio, 69. Keyboardist with Frank Zappa & Mothers of Invention, 70; sideman with Cannonball Adderley Quintet, 71-73 & Frank Zappa & Mothers of Invention, 73-76. Billy Cohan & George Duke Band, 76-77; George Duke Band, world tour, 77-80. Chief Collabrs: Jean Luc-Ponty, Frank Zappa, Quinery Jones, Cannonball Adderley, Flora Purina, Airto, Stanley Clark, Bill Cohan, Al Jarreau. *Songs:* Reach for It; Sweet Lucy; Someday; Say That You Will; Dukey's Stick; Brazillian Love Affair; I Want You for Myself; Love Reborn; excerpts from opera "Tzina." *Albums:* Reach for It (gold album); Don't Let Go (gold album).

DUKE, JOHN WOODS   ASCAP 1947
composer, teacher, pianist
b Cumberland, Md, July 30, 1899. Educ: Peabody Cons, 15-18; piano studies with Harold Randolph & Franklin Cannon; comp studies with Gustave Strube & Bernard Wagenaar; studies with Nadia Boulanger & Artur Schnabel, Paris & Berlin. Debut, Aeolian Hall, 21. Soloist with New York Philh, 21. Joined music fac as teacher of piano, Smith Col, 23, prof, 38-60, Henry Dike Sleeper Chair Music, 60-67, emer prof, 67- Prog chmn, Yaddo Concerts of New Music, 37. Written 220 songs, in addition to many chamber & orchestral works. Chief Collab: Dorothy Duke *Songs:* Music: A Piper; I Can't Be Talkin' of Love; The Bird; Loveliest of Trees; Bells in the Rain; In the Fields; Just-Spring; Luke Havergal; Miniver Cheevy; Richard Cory; Morning in Paris; Acquainted With the Night; Three Gothic Ballads; When I Set Out for Lyonnesse; Viennese Waltz; Velvet Shoes; six songs on poems by Emily Bronte; six songs on poems by Emily Dickinson. *Scores:* Captain Lovelock (chamber opera in one act).

DUKE, VERNON
See Dukelsy, Vladimir

DUKELSY, VLADIMIR (VERNON DUKE)   ASCAP 1934
composer, author, pianist
b Parafianovo, Russia, Oct 10, 03; d. Educ: Studied music with Reinhold Gliere & Marian Dombrovsky; Kiev Cons (entered at age 13). Fled Russia after revolution. Comp ballets for Diaghilev's Ballet Russe. To NY, 29. Songs for Bway revues: "Garrick Gaieties" (1930), "Thumbs Up!" & "The Show Is On." Completed score for "Goldwyn Follies." WW II, Lt Comdr, USCG; wrote score for "Tars and Spars." Founder & pres, Society for Forgotten Music. Author: "Passport to Paris" (autobiography) & "Listen Here!"; vols of poetry written in Russian. Chief Collabrs: E Y Harburg, Ira Gershwin, Ogden Nash, Howard Dietz, John Latouche. *Songs:* I Am Only Human After All; Too Too Divine; That's Life; April in Paris; Speaking of Love; So Nonchalant; Water Under the Bridge; I Like the Likes of You; Suddenly; What Is There to Say?; Autumn in New York; I Can't Get Started; Island in the West Indies; Words Without Music; Now; Taking a Chance on Love; Do What You Wanna Do; Love Turned the Light Out; Honey in the Honeycomb; Cabin in the Sky; We're Having a Baby; Not a Care in the World; Summer Is A-Comin' In; The Love I Long For; The Sea-Gull and the Ea-Gull; Spring Again; Roundabout; Out of the Clear Blue Sky; Just Like a Man; That's What Makes Paris Paree; London in July; Goood Little Girls; You're Far From Wonderful; Madly in Love. *Instrumental Works:* Violin Concerto; Cello Concerto; Sonata in D for Violin, Piano; Parisian Suite; String Quartet in C; Surrealist Suite; 6 Songs From A Shropshire Lad; Souvenirs de Monte Carlo; Ode to the Milky Way: also 3 symph & 2 piano sonatas. *Scores:* Ballets: Zephyr and Flora; Lady Blue. Bway Stage: Walk a Little Faster; Ziegfeld Follies (34-36); Cabin in the Sky; Banjo Eyes; Sadie Thompson; Two's Company; It Happens on Ice; Zenda; Bway Stage Background: Time Remembered; Off-Bway: The Littlest Revue; London Stage: Yvonne; The Yellow Mask. Films: April in Paris; She's Working Her Way Through College.

D'UMBERTO, ANGELO
See Herrera, Humberto Angel

DUNBAR, ROBERT LEON   ASCAP 1978
composer, musician, singer
b Oak Harbour, Wash, Dec 14, 51. Educ: Recording Inst Am, Course I & II; high sch. Performer touring East Coast from Maine to Ga, 70- Recording artist. Chief Collabrs: Dave Dunbar (bro), Melinda Root, Rem Cussen. *Songs:* Circus Love; Studio Dreams; I Want to Go Back Again; Chiccy, Chiccy; Good, Good Guys; One Side Ways; Just a Little Bit Longer; Rock n' Roller At Heart. *Albums:* Rock n' Roller At Heart.

DUNCAN, JIMMY   ASCAP 1956
composer, author, arranger
b Houston, Tex, June 25, 35. Educ: Houston Univ. Comp & arr for var singers & performers. Singer; owns record co; producer. *Songs:* I Asked the Lord; Goodbye to Love; Pauline; Pretty Little Mama; Someone Else, Not Me; Spin the Wheel; Unloved.

DUNCAN, LARRY WAYNE   ASCAP 1971
composer, author, producer
b Chicago, Ill, Dec 22, 45. Educ: Hollywood High Sch, piano theory; Art Van Dam Music Sch, Mt Prospect, Ill, guitar theory; studied voice with Jack Segal, theory with Bill Euchers & Jack Keller; pvt training production with Barry Gordy. Live perf on TV & radio spots & groups. Sang jingles "KTTV, That's Entertainment," 71-76. Produced Academy Award song "All That Love Went to Waste." Charts written for Nelson Riddle (Golden Globes live, 74). Chief Collabrs: Charlene Duncan, Kathy Wakefield, Dennis Provisor. *Songs:* Give It One More Try; You Can't Have Your Cake and Eat It Too; Temptations (Gold Single); Music: The Prophet; Lyrics: Glass House.

DUNCAN, ROSETTA   ASCAP 1942
composer, author, entertainer
b Los Angeles, Calif, Nov 23, 1900; d Chicago, Ill, Dec 4, 59. One of Duncan Sisters; played Topsy & songwriter for Bway musical "Topsy and Eva." Appeared in vaudeville & Bway shows incl "Doing Our Bit", "She's a Good Fellow", "Tip Top." *Songs:* Rememb'ring; I Never Had a Mammy; Do Re Mi; The Moon Am Shinin'; Someday Soon.

DUNCAN, VIVIAN   ASCAP 1942
composer, author, entertainer
b Los Angeles, Calif, June 17, 02. One of Duncan Sisters. Songwriter & appeared as Eva in Bway musical "Topsy and Eva." Appeared with sister in "Doing Our Bit", "She's a Good Fellow" & "Tip Top"; vaudeville entertainer. *Songs:* Rememb'ring; I Never Had a Mammy; Do Re Mi; The Moon Am Shinin'; Someday Soon; Los Angeles; Hollywood Belongs to the World; United We Stand.

DUNCAN, WAYNE O   ASCAP 1967
composer, author, singer
b Pine Bluff, Ark, June 20, 49. Educ: Pine Bluff Cons Music; Univ Ark. Chief Collabrs: Christin Shadrach, Tom DePierro, Dennis Hardy, James Duncan.

Songs: Star Dancing; Slippin Into Something New; Is It Still Warm; Can You See Me Now; Music: Be Gentle With Me.

DUNCAN, WILLIAM CARY   ASCAP 1922
author

b North Brookfield, Mass, Feb 6, 1874; d North Brookfield, Mass, Nov 21, 45. Educ: Amherst Col, BA. Teacher, Brooklyn Polytech Sch, 1897-17. Author, "The Amazing Madame Jumel" & "Golden Hoofs." Ed, "American Kennel Gazette" & "Outdoor Life." Chief Collabrs: Karl Hoschna, William Frederick Peters, William Schroeder, Jean Schwartz, Clifford Grey, Rudolf Friml. *Songs:* Katy Did; When the Cherry Blossoms Fall; Love of Mine; I Love the Love That's New; The Heart of a Crimson Rose; The Best I Ever Get Is the Worst of It; A Twelve O'Clock Girl in a Nine O'Clock Town; No One Else But You; Lyrics: Titina. *Scores:* Bway stage, librettos: His Little Widows; Fiddlers Three; The Royal Vagabond; The Rose Girl; The Blue Kitten; Sunny Days; Co-librettist: Molly Darling; Yes, Yes, Yvette; Great Day!

DUNGAN, OLIVE
See Pullen, Olive Dungan

DUNHAM, KAYE LAWRENCE   ASCAP 1973
composer, lyricist

b Philadelphia, Pa, Sept 27, 33. Foxhole Sch, Dartington Hall, Devonshire, Eng; City Col San Francisco, AA, 63; San Francisco State Univ; San Francisco Col Music & Fine Arts, 64-65; pvt study with Hall Johnson. Writer & accompanist to folk singer; writer-performer, Ctr Theatre Group, Los Angeles, Calif. Musician, "The Dream on Monkey Mountain," world premiere, New York production & overseas. Chief Collabrs: Richard Markowitz, Johnny Mandel, Michael Masser, Bob Gundry, Walter Heath. *Songs:* One Step; Black Betty; I Never Knew My Daddy (Jangle); Lyrics: Piano Man; Golden Pony; I Thought You Might Like to Know; You Did It for Me; Don't Look Back; Good Ole' Country Livin'; Nothin' Ever Stays the Same; Africa (She's My Lady); Don't You Be Worried; From Day One; Baby, That's You.

DUNHAM, WILLIAM D (BY)   ASCAP 1947
author

b New York, NY, May 2, 10. Writer, scripts & special material. *Songs:* With You in My Arms; Dream Street; Where Does It Get You in the End; Possum Song; Ah, But It Happens; If You're Ever Down in Texas; Any Way the Wind Blows; Flipper; Cotton Candy; Twinkle and Shine; Love in the Country.

DUNING, GEORGE WILLIAM   ASCAP 1949
composer, conductor

b Richmond, Ind. Educ: Cincinnati Cons Music; Univ Cincinnati, comp study with Mario Castelnuovo-Tedesco. Jazz & symphonic trumpet player. Arr for var bands & orchs. Music dir for "Kay Kyser Radio Show" & "College of Musical Knowledge" NBC. Contract comp & cond, Columbia Pictures, 17 yrs. TV series, movies of the week for NBC, ABC, CBS, OPT. Feature pictures for Warner Bros, United Artists, Paramount, MGM, Mel Simon Productions, 20th Century Fox. Mem bd dirs, ASCAP. Chief Collabrs: Ned Washington, Stanley Styne, Richard Quine, Steve Allen. *Scores:* Film background: Picnic; The World of Susie Wong; Toys in the Attic; Cowboy; The Big Valley; Bell Book and Candle; 1001 Arabian Nights; Star Trek, episodes; The Partridge Family; Houseboat.

DUNLAP, PAUL   ASCAP 1952
composer

b Springfield, Ohio, July 19, 19. Educ: Univ Calif, Los Angeles; studied with Ernst Toch. Comp of over 200 film & TV scores, also more recently an opera, Electra XI. Owner publ house, Anthion Music, 61- *Instrumental Works:* Concerto for Piano and Jazz Bands; Ballet-Sonata for Piano; Celebration (choral). *Scores:* Film/TV: I Was a Teenage Werewolf; Black Tuesday; Stranger on Horseback.

DUNN, BONNIE   ASCAP 1958
composer, singer

b New York, NY, June 9, 20. Educ: Convent. Vocalist, Al Donahue, Paul Baron & Carl Ravazza Orchs. Chief Collabr: Michael Dunn (husband). *Songs:* Only the Mocking Bird Heard; Dearest Santa; There's No Happiness for Me; Hazel Eyes; That's How It Feels to Love.

DUNN, EDWARD THOMAS   ASCAP 1960
composer, author, singer

b Miami, Ariz, Mar 12, 25. Educ: Odessa High Sch, Tex, 42; studied woodwinds & voice; NTex State Univ; Univ Southern Calif, BA, 51, MA, 54; Loma Linda Univ, MD. Gospel singer, KXLA & KFSG radio, also on TV, 46-68. Comp & author, 47- With music dept, NBC-Radio & TV, 48-50. Evangelist singer, 53-59; medical practice, 61- Chief Collabr: E Thomas Dunn, Jr (son). *Songs:* The Tree of Life; You Can't Worship God When You're Fishin'; Hey Texas; The Slowest Gun in Texas; God Is Everywhere; Senorita; I Love You; I'll See You in Heaven; Humble; Wings of the Wind; For You.

DUNN, JAMES PHILIP   ASCAP 1924
composer, organist

b New York, NY, Jan 10, 1884; d Jersey City, NJ, July 24, 36. Educ: City Col New York, BA; Columbia Univ; studied with MacDowell, Rybner. Church

organist, NY, Jersey City & Bayonne, NJ. *Songs:* The Bitterness of Love; Serenade; Come Unto Him; A Fairy Song; Heart to Heart; Under the Greenwood Tree; A White Rose; Weary; Annabel Lee. *Instrumental Works:* Piano Quintet; Violin Sonata; We (tone poem); The Phantom Drum (cantata); Overture on Negro Themes; Mass in C; two string quartets. *Scores:* Opera: The Galleon.

DUNN, MICHAEL   ASCAP 1958
composer, conductor, singer

b New York, NY, June 15, 18. Educ: Brooklyn Cons; pvt study. Singer, radio shows incl "This Is Fort Dix," 42-46. Actor, films; has own orch. Chief Collabr: Bonnie Dunn (wife). *Songs:* Dearest Santa; Hazel Eyes; There's No Happiness for Me; That's How It Feels to Love.

DUNN, MONTE   ASCAP 1967
composer, author, guitarist

b Brooklyn, NY, June 20, 46. Educ: Univ Buffalo, informal work with musicologist Bill Talmadge; Emerson Col, Boston; Longy Sch Music, Boston. Went on the road with Ian & Sylvia, 63; did sessions with Ian & Sylvia, Sonny & Cher, Tim Hardin, Richie Havens, Peter, Paul & Mary, Kui Lee, Cher, David Blue, Peter Walker, Fred Neil and others, 63-73. Recorded as soloist, Columbia, 66 & as part of a duo for Cyclone, 70. Writer, Hill & Range, 67. Music therapist, 72-; also soloist & avant-garde composer. Mem & union official, Am Fedn Musicians. Chief Collabrs: Kui Lee, Walter Raim, Stu Scharf, S T Coleridge, Karen Cruz. *Songs:* Order to Things; Loving You; Self Satisfaction; Music: All I Want To Do; No Other Song.

DUNN, REBECCA WELTY   ASCAP 1960
composer, author, pianist

b Guthrie, Okla, Sept 23, 1890. Educ: Washburn Col, BA; Kans State Univ; Wichita Univ; Southwestern Col. Founder, service revising song poems & music. Former pres, Kans Federated Music Clubs; mem, Nat League of Am Pen Women. *Songs:* Sunflower Song; As Channels of Thy Grace; Tick Tock. *Scores:* Operettas: Sunny (children); Purple on the Moon.

DUNN, RUSSELL   ASCAP 1968
composer, author, arranger

b Grafton, NDak, June 1, 10. Professional musician for fifty yrs. Chief Collabrs: Glenn A Williams; Fred De Denise; Pat C Strangis. *Instrumental Works:* Peridokt.

DUNNE, HERBERT PEYTON (KIRBY)   ASCAP 1969
composer, organist

b Morris Park, NY, Oct 19, 09. Educ: Baldwin High Sch; studied notation, theory & comp with Jesse Crawford & Arthur Gutow. Chief Collabr: Jefferson Bailey. *Songs:* Who's Fooling Who; Fathoms Deep.

DUNSTEDTER, EDDIE   ASCAP 1956
composer, organist

b Edwardsville, Ill, Aug 2, 1897; d Reseda, Calif, July 30, 74. Educ: Wash Univ, studied with Charles Galloway. Directed dance bands. Head of Radio Production Unit, WW II, West Coast Band. Later with film orch, TV, "Playhouse 90," Sam Spade & Johnny Dollar. *Songs:* San Francisco Beat; Hello, Mom; Pi Ka Ke; Music: Open Your Eyes; Flight of the Bumble Bee; Just a Few Thrills Ago. *Scores:* Film: Donavan's Brain; Rebecca.

DUPAGE, FLORENCE ELIZABETH   ASCAP 1961
composer, organist

b Vandergrift, Pa, Sept 20, 10. Educ: Studied piano with Ignace Hilsberg, comp with Tibor Serly, harmony with Rubin Goldmark, orchestration with Richard DuPage, counterpoint with Aurelio Giorni & organ with Thomas Richner. Music dir, Advent Tuller Sch, Westbury, NY, 54-66; choral dir, Cathedral Sch of St Mary, Garden City, NY, 66-69. Chief Collabr: Sister Jean Thompson. *Instrumental Works:* Two Sketches for String Orchestra; Alice in Wonderland Ballet Suite for Symphony Orchestra; The Pond for Symphony Orchestra; Concerto for Piano and Strings; Contemporary Mass (chorus, trumpet, perc, organ). *Scores:* Opera: Lost Valley (symph); New World for Nellie (ballad opera for tenor, baritone, chorus & standard orch); Trial Universelle (chamber opera); Operetta for Children-Alice in Wonderland (piano); Whither (music drama, chamber orch).

DUPAGE, RICHARD PORTER, II   ASCAP 1946
composer

b Kansas City, Mo, Aug 10, 08. Educ: Washington & Lee Univ; Vanderbilt Univ Law Sch; studied with Rubin Goldmark, John Warren Erb, Aurelio Giorni, Tibor Serly. Arr for Andre Kostelanetz, Alfred Wallenstein, Sylvan Levin, Emerson Buckley, Lloyd Shaffer, Raymond Paige, Ray Bloch, dance orchs, radio shows, Bway musicals, 32- Orchr numerous theatrical productions; comp & cond commercial films; cond & arr, Sperry (Gyroscope) Symph. Staff comp & arr, WOR-Mutual, New York, 46-53. Mem, Am Soc Music Arr, Sons of Am Revolution. *Instrumental Works:* Suite for Small Orchestra; The Woodwind Suite; Missouri Suite; Polyrhythmic Overture (Saratoga Spa Music Fest comn); Variations on an Irish Theme; Prelude for Harp and Orchestra; Prelude and Blues for Symphony Orchestra; Symphonic Song; Central Park Suite; In the Valley of Morpheus; Afghanistan.

DUPRE, JIMMY R　　　　　　　　　　　ASCAP 1945
composer, author
b New Orleans, La, Nov 8, 1906; d. Educ: Loyola Univ. On staff, music publ firm. Wrote special material for radio & films. Chief Collabr: Jack Palmer. *Songs:* Love Doesn't Grow on Trees; Dreams for Sale; He's a Curbstone Cutie; Red Roses for My Blue Lady; Don't You Dare Call Me Darling; Wasting My Time; Sweet and Pretty Mama; Jelly Bean.

DUPREE, HARRY
See Dapeer, Harry Ellis

DURAND, WADE HAMPTON　　　　　　ASCAP 1945
composer, conductor, pianist
b Bloomington, Ind, Dec 3, 1887; d New York, NY, Feb 29, 64. Educ: Notre Dame Univ. Pianist with Howley, Haviland & Dresser Co, also other publ, Chicago. Wrote stage scores. *Songs:* My Alabama Sue; Stingy; Grand Baby, or Baby Grand; Coney Island Washboard.

DURANG, CHRISTOPHER　　　　　　　ASCAP 1978
author
b Montclair, NJ, Jan 2, 49. Educ: Grad work, Yale Univ Sch Drama. Wrote book & lyrics for Bway Play, "A History of the American Film" (Tony Nomination for Best Book); coauthored musical & performed in, "Das Lusitania Songspiel"; played in and wrote the lyrics for "Idiots of Karamanov."

DURANTE, JIMMY　　　　　　　　　　ASCAP 1941
composer, author, comedian
b New York, NY, Feb 10, 1893. Educ: Pub schs. Began career as pianist at Coney Island. Organized 5-piece band, 16. Opened Club Durant with Eddie Jackson & Lou Clayton with whom he later formed comedy team in vaudeville. Appeared in Bway musicals: "Show Girl"; "The New Yorkers"; "Strike Me Pink"; "Jumbo"; "Red Hot and Blue"; "Stars in Your Eyes." Films incl: "Get-Rich Quick Wallingford"; "Her Cardboard Lover"; "George White's Scandals"; "Sally, Irene and Mary"; "Jumbo." Appeared at Palladium, London, 36. Own radio & TV shows; featured in nightclubs. Biography, "Schnozzola" by Gene Fowler. Chief Collabrs: Jackie Barnett, Ben Ryan. *Songs:* Inka Dinka Doo; I'm Jimmy That Well-Dressed Man; I Know Darn Well I Can Do Without Broadway; I Ups to Him and He Ups to Me; Daddy Your Mamma Is Lonesome for You; Umbriago; Any State in the Forty-Eight; Chidabee Chidabee Chidabee; I'm Jimmy's Girl.

DURHAM, EDDIE　　　　　　　　　　ASCAP 1942
composer, guitarist, trombonist
b St Marcus, Tex, Aug 19, 09. Trombonist & guitarist in var bands incl Bennie Moten, Jimmie Lunceford & Count Basie. Arr & cond for orchs; formed own orch, made many records. Chief Collabrs: James Rushing, Count Basie. *Songs & Instrumental Works:* John's Idea; Out the Window; Every Tub; Time Out; Topsy; Blues in the Groove; Glen Island Special; Wham (Re Bob Boom Bam); Four Letters; Sent for You Yesterday, and Here You Come Today; Swinging the Blues; Don't You Miss Your Baby?.

DURKIN, BETSY
See Matthes, Betsy Durkin

DURSO, MICHAEL ALFRED　　　　　　ASCAP 1956
composer, trombonist, orchestra leader
b Brooklyn, NY, Feb 13, 05; d Bolton Landing, NY, Dec 25, 75. Educ: Studied & played for St Lucy Church Band, Brooklyn. Left grade sch in early teens to play in bands; trombonist in theaters: Chicago Oriental & New York Paramount; also on radio shows: Eddie Cantor Show, Kate Smith Show, Jan Pierce Show & Rudy Vallee Show; trombonist for shows, Billy Rose's Aquacade & Mike Todd's Gay New Orleans at New York Worlds Fairs, 39 & 40; petty officer & musical dir in mil service, 4 yrs; musical dir, New York Copacabana, 15 yrs. *Songs:* Music: Petticoats of Portugal.

DURST, JAMES RODNEY　　　　　　　ASCAP 1973
composer, author, singer
b Pasadena, Calif, Nov 6, 45. Educ: Magnolia High Sch, Anaheim, Calif; Fullerton Col; Calif State Univ, Long Beach, BA, 69. In Munich production of "Hair," Mermaid Theater, Copenhagen. Singer, songwriter & guitarist for concerts, cols, clubs, fests, TV, radio. Concert-toured 25 countries in Europe, Scandinavia, Middle East, Southeast Asia. Recording artist for PhoeniXongs Records. Author of 4 songbooks. Producer-host for folkmusic radio series, "Peregryn," WBEZ-FM, Chicago. Chief Collabr: Pham Duy. *Songs:* Credo: Get Behind Yourself and Push!; A Whaling Trilogy; Cyprus; Next to You; Lyrics: Little Child, Catch a Cricket!.

DVORINE, SHURA　　　　　　　　　　ASCAP 1959
composer, pianist, teacher
b Baltimore, Md, June 22, 23. Educ: Baltimore City Col; Peabody Cons Music. Piano concerts throughout US, incl Town Hall, Carnegie Hall & Brooklyn Acad Music. Mem piano fac, Peabody Inst, Johns Hopkins Univ. *Songs:* I Danced With an Angel; What Do I Keep. *Instrumental Works:* Viva Viva; Miray; The Lovers (ballet concerto).

DYER, JANICE WILLIAMS　　　　　　ASCAP 1975
composer, author
b Jasper, Tex, Oct 9, 46. Educ: French High Sch; Durham Bus Col, studied shorthand; Lamar Univ, studied real estate. Admin asst, Hall-Clement Publ, Nashville, 72. Admin asst songwriting, United Artists Music, 74. Free-lance writer, 76- Chief Collabrs: Ron Peterson, Jeff Tweel, Milton Blackford, Richard Mainegra. *Songs:* Everytime Two Fools Collide (Grammy nomination); We've Been Lyin' Here Too Long; Let's Dance to the Music.

DYER, WILLIAM DEWITT　　　　　　ASCAP 1973
author
b San Diego, Calif, Mar 21, 34. Educ: Helix High Sch; San Diego State Col. Writer of TV specials; producer of Bway show "The Suicide," 80. Three Emmy nominations. Chief Collabrs: Billy Goldenberg, Dick DeBenedictis, Bob Prince. *Songs:* Lyrics: May I?; Until the Music Ends; Look How Far We've Come; I Can Remember.

DYESS, TONY R Q　　　　　　　　　　ASCAP 1958
composer, author
b Thalia, Tex, Apr 10, 10. Educ: Emory & Henry Col; Emory Univ. Appeared in vaudeville & concert singing group. Methodist minister. *Songs:* The Old Circuit Rider; A Heart and a Ring; Lonesome Teenagers Don't Cry; Wilhemina.

DYLAN, ROBERT　　　　　　　　　　ASCAP 1963
composer, author, singer
b Duluth, Minn, Apr 24, 41. Educ: Princeton Univ, DMus(hon), 70. Began as folk/protest singer in early 60's, was among the first that incorporated serious poetry with pop music, introduced the musical concept of folk-rock in the mid 60's; musician. *Songs:* Blowin' in the Wind; The Times They Are A-Changin'; I Shall Be Released; Lay, Lady, Lay; Just Like a Woman; Like a Rolling Stone; Knockin' on Heaven's Door; All Along the Watchtower; Forever Young; Mr Tambourine Man; Gotta Serve Somebody.

DYSON, HAL　　　　　　　　　　　　ASCAP 1924
composer, author, conductor
b Sydney, Australia, Oct 5, 1884; d. Educ: High sch. Cond, Wellington Opera House, New Zealand, 04 & Nat Theatre, Sydney, 05-07. Wrote songs for Bway musicals incl "Sky High" & "June Days"; stage scores in Toronto, Australia & London. Wrote shows for Columbia Circuit, NY; cond, Shubert Theatre, NY. Charter Mem, Am Guild of Authors & Comp. Chief Collabrs: Billy Wells, James Kendis. *Songs:* Let It Rain; All I Want Is Love; Waltz of Love; Lonely Melody; Harmonica Song; You're Too Good for Good for Nothin' Me; Hop, Skip and Jump; Honolulu Mary; I'm Coming Back to You.

E

EAGER, EDWARD　　　　　　　　　　ASCAP 1946
author
b Toledo, Ohio, June 20, 11; d Stamford, Conn, Oct 23, 64. Educ: Tome Sch; Harvard Univ. Wrote songs for "Sing Out" & "Sweet Land." Author of children's bks, incl "Half Magic", "Magic or Not", "The Well-Wishers", "Knights Castle" & "Seven Day Magic." Chief Collabrs: Elie Siegmeister, Clay Warnick, David Broekman, Jerome Moross, John Mundy, Alec Wilder. *Songs:* Goodbye, John; I'm Afraid I'm in Love; Where?; As I Was Going Along; More Than These; Love at Second Sight; Farewell, My Lovely; The Girl on the Front Porch Swing; Beyond the Sunset; Is It You?. *Scores:* Operas: Pieces of Eight; The Stranger; Barbara Allen; The Toledo War; Miranda and the Dark Young Man; Gentlemen, Be Seated; Bway Stage: Dream With Music; The Liar; Dr Willy Nilly; Stage Adaptations: The Gambler; Rugantino; TV: Marco Polo; TV Adaptations: Mozart's Cosi fan tutti; The Marriage of Figaro.

EAGER, MARY (MOLLY) ANN　　　　　ASCAP 1954
composer, author
b Drumshambo, Ireland. Educ: Nat Sch; Washington Irving High Sch; studied violin. Girl Scout leader, 15 yrs; Lt Civilian Defence; Red Cross; entertained servicemen, Camp Kilmer, Vet Hospitals, Kessler Inst; Am Legion Cath & Jewish War Vets. Original mem Talent Time; founder, Thomas Moore Soc, Dublin, Ireland. Mem, Int Platform Asn. Chief Collabrs: Robert Harry Wilson, Hugo Frey, Dan Savino, Hugo Rubins, George Gartland, Cecil Cowles, Elfrida Warden, Morton Dawney, Walter Freed, Marcel Frank, Sue Eager, George Thorn, Tony Mascari. *Songs:* God's Will Be Done; Glory Train; Way of the Cross; Painting Piano Pleasures (teaching book); Rejoicing in the Risen Lord; It's Christmas Time Again; Oh Glorious Christmas Morn; Hitch a Ride With the Lord; Blue Eyed Kathleen from Killarney; Roughish Roseleen; Mind If I Do; Never Let Your Shadow Shade a Sunbeam; When the World Smiles Again; Don't Walk in Snow With Velvet Slippers; Check the Yellow Pages; It's Hard Trying Hard to Forget; Where is There a Love Like Ours; Lyrics: Sliding on a Sunbeam; Flame of Hope; My Fair Land; Bid Me Enter In; Let's Worship Together; Oh Mary the Mother of Man; Ode to Thomas Moore; The Light of God; Thank God for the Newborn Day.

EARHART, WILL   ASCAP 1939
composer, author, conductor
b Franklin, Ohio, Apr 1, 1871; d Portland, Ore, Apr 23, 60. Educ: High sch; pvt music study; hon MusD, Univ Pittsburgh. Choral cond & arr. Sch supvr, Ohio & Ind, 1900-12; dir of music, Pittsburgh Pub Schs, 12; music lectr, 13-18. Prof, Sch of Educ, Pittsburgh, 18-21; lectr, Carnegie Tech, 21-40. Author, "The Eloquent Baton" & "Music to the Listening Ear." *Songs & Instrumental Works:* Arr: Here Amid Thy Shady Woods; Cradle Song; Golden Sun Streaming; Vouchsafe, O Lord; Blessed Redeemer; Ring, Ring de Banjo.

EARL, BILLY
See En Earl, William Allan

EARL, MARY
See King, Robert A

EARLY, DELLOREESE PATRICIA (DELLA REESE)
singer
b Detroit, Mich, July 6, 31. Educ: Wayne State Univ. Singer in choirs, 38-; summers with Mahalia Jackson troupe, 45-49. Organized gospel group while in col. Club appearances, Detroit, later joined Erskine Hawkins, New York. Solo artist, 57-, appeared on radio shows with Robert Q Lewis & on TV with Jackie Gleason, Ed Sullivan, "McCloud", "Twice in a Lifetime", "Police Woman", "Petrocelli" & "Sanford and Son." Role in motion picture, "Let's Rock," 58. Hostess TV variety show, "Della," 69-70. Substitute hostess, "Tonight Show." Appeared in TV series, "Chico and the Man," 76-78 & others. Appeared in theatre, "The Last Minstrel Show," 78. Recordings for Jubilee, RCA Victor Records & ABC Paramount Records. Voted Most Promising Singer of Yr, 57.

EARLY, ROBERT BRUCE   ASCAP 1971
composer, pianist, educator
b Seattle, Wash, Apr 13, 40. Educ: Albion Col, AB, 62; Mich State Univ, MM, 63, PhD, 78. Pianist, US & Switz; musical dir, pageants & showboats; cond, award winning groups; chmn, Music Dept, Aquinas Col. *Songs:* Music: Sigma Chi Prayer. *Instrumental Works:* Alice New Sound; Never Can Pay the Price; Samba de Serta; That Old Bossa in C; Ditty-More; Up and Atom; Prelude; Variations on a Theme.

EAST, ED   ASCAP 1942
composer, author, producer
b Bloomington, Ind, Apr 4, 1894; d New York, NY, Jan 18, 52. Educ: Col. Pianist in dance orch; produced, wrote & acted in own radio network series, "Ed East and Polly." *Songs:* The Swing Waltz; What Is Love?; Twilight in Granada; Pig Latin Song; Nettie, Nitwit of the Network; What a Beautiful Morning; Good Evening.

EASTES, HELEN M   ASCAP 1961
composer, author, teacher
b Galesburg, Ill, Apr 21, 1892. Educ: Knox Col Cons of Music, BM. Taught piano, pub schs. Mem, Nat League Am Pen Women. Chief Collabr: J Fred Coots. *Songs:* April Came Across the Hill; Can You Sing a Song?; Thou Lovely Spring; God Grant Us Peace; The Little Lamb That Followed; Dreams Were Made for Lovers.

EASTON, JACK   ASCAP 1966
composer, author, pianist
b New York, NY, July 10, 18. Educ: Erasmus Hall High Sch, 36; Yale Univ, BA, 40, also cert in music; studied comp with Ernst Toch, cond with Pierre Monteux. Writer & producer of radio & TV commercials incl: Arnold Bread, Avon, Beechnut Coffee, Buick, Betty Crocker, Dentyne Chewing Gum, El Producto, Filtertip Tereyton, General Motors, Ipana Toothpaste, Johnson & Johnson, Liberty Mutual, NY Times, du Pont, Reynolds Wrap, Texaco, US Steel, The Yellow Pages (partial list). Comp and/or arr, musical dir of indust shows & films incl: AFM, Bell Telephone, Buick, Burlington Mills, Campbell's Soups, Chrysler-Plymouth, Dow Chemical, Esso, General Electric, General Motors, Kodak, Mc Kesson & Robbins, Milliken Breakfast Show, Nabisco, S & H Green Stamps, US Army Reserve, Wamsutta Mills. Pianist, cond or arr-orchr in Bway, Off-Bway & summer stock theater incl: Bway: "Applause", "Mame", "New Faces of 1968", "Plain and Fancy"; Off-Bway: "The Big Winner", "Come of Age", "Fly Blackbird", "Livin' the Life", "Smiling, the Boy Fell Dead"; stock: "Fiddler on the Roof", "A Funny Thing Happened on the Way to the Forum." On var radio & TV prog incl: "Assignment Manhunt", "Bell Telephone Hour", "Chamber Music Society of Lower Basin Street", "The Doctors", "The Ford Show" & documentaries: "Time" & "Life." Special material for club acts, revues & var individual artists incl, Eddie Albert and Margo, Maxene Andrews, Kaye Ballard, Betty Garrett, Georgia Gibbs, Ella Logan, Zero Mostel, Janis Paige Felicia Sanders. Chief Collabrs: David Greggory, Lionell Hampton. *Songs:* Kissing Cousin; Prouder Than a Peacock (extended version of NBC Peacock Theme); Music: Anywhere; I See the Moon at Noon; It's Not the Same; Lantern on the Levee; That's What a Dream Can Do. *Instrumental Works:* NBC Peacock Theme; King David Suite (symph orch, jazz quartet, solo vibes). *Scores:* Bway show: It Happens on Ice (2nd ed); Film/TV: Baby Boogie (UPA cartoons).

EASTON, SIDNEY   ASCAP 1955
composer, author, actor
b Savannah, Ga, Oct 2, 1886; d Flushing, NY, Dec 24, 71. Educ: Pub schs. Appeared in carnivals, minstrel shows, burlesque, vaudeville & films. Writer of spec material. *Songs:* Go Back Where You Stayed Last Night; Tell 'Em About Me When You Reach Tennessee; Cast Away on an Island of Love.

EASTWOOD, JANIS YVONNE   ASCAP 1970
composer, singer, guitarist
b Poughkeepsie, NY, Nov 19, 50. Singer, radio, nightclubs, benefits; TV perf. *Songs:* Race With the Wind.

EATON, MALCOLM   ASCAP 1954
composer, author, singer
b New York, NY, Oct 26, 14. Educ: Brooklyn Cons Music; NY Univ. Singer & MC, theatres, radio, hotels. USN, WW II; cond shows, radio progs; cantor Jewish services & soloist & choir cond Cath & Protestant services. Sang with Gus Edwards, Paul Whiteman, Don Baker, Hal Kemp & Gene Krupa Orchs. Chief Collabrs: Albert Gamse, Harold Lambert. *Songs:* The Rumba-Cardi; Do the Dubonnet; Marianna Mia; Santa Claus Express; Out of My Heart.

EATON, ROY FELIX   ASCAP 1978
composer, author, pianist
b New York, NY, May 14, 30. Educ: Music & Art High Sch, 46; Manhattan Sch Music, BM, 50, MM, 52; City Col New York, BSS(magna cum laude); Yale Univ; Univ Zurich, Switz; studied piano with Helen Scoville, Harold Bauer & Edwin Fisher. Concertized internationally, 49-53; Kosckuszko Foundation Chopin Award, 50. Radio broadcast specialist, USA, 53-55. Copywriter & comp, Young & Rubicam, 55-59. Assoc creative dir, Music Makers, Inc, 59; music dir, Benton & Bowles Advert, 59-, vpres, 67; music dir, Infinity Factory II, 78. Mem comp fac, Manhattan Sch Music, 80- *Songs:* Infinity Factory (theme). *Instrumental Works:* Bop Blues.

EBBINS, MILTON KEITH   ASCAP 1942
composer
b Springfield, Mass, Feb 20, 14. Educ: Amherst Col, studied with Chester Griffin. Formed own orch, 36. Music dir with CBS. To New York, 38, joined radio dept advert agency. Road mgr, Jack Jenny Orch, & personal mgr, Count Basie Orch. Assoc producer, TV series "Dear Phoebe" & film "Johnny Cool." Exec vpres, Chrislaw Productions. Chief Collabrs: Count Basie, Bob Russell, Henry Nemo. *Songs:* Hip Hip Hooray; Coming Out Party; Tune Town Shuffle; Song of the Casbah; Dance of the Gremlins; Yale Blues; Basie Boogie.

EBERHART, NELLE RICHMOND   ASCAP 1927
author
b Detroit, Mich, Aug 28, 1871; d Kansas City, Mo, Nov 15, 44. Taught sch in Nebr. Chief Collabr: Charles Wakefield Cadman. *Songs:* At Dawning; From Wigwam to Tepee; From the Land of the Sky-Blue Water; I Hear a Thrush at Eve; 4 American Indian Songs; Morning of the Year (song cycle). *Scores:* Operas: Shanewis; A Witch of Salem; Garden of Mystery; The Willow Tree (radio).

EBSEN, CHRISTIAN, JR (BUDDY)   ASCAP 1954
composer, author, actor
b Belleville, Ill, Apr 2, 08. Educ: Rollins Col, Orlando, Fla; Univ Fla. Dancer, Bway musicals, vaudeville & with sister, Vilma. Served, USCG, World War II. Appeared in films "Broadway Melody of 1936 and 1938", "Davy Crockett", "Breakfast at Tiffany's", TV series "Davy Crockett", "The Beverly Hillbillies" & "Barnaby Jones." *Songs:* Wild Card; Behave Yourself; Be Sure You're Right; Angelica; Handsome Stranger; Howdy; Back Home USA; Audience; Rendezvous; Baby Blues.

ECHITO, MARTIE   ASCAP 1969
composer, musician
b Upland, Calif, Sept 3, 51. Educ: Chino High Sch, chorus; La Verne Col, music maj, 3 yrs, studied with Ralph Travis, Tom Schultz; Dick Grove Music Workshop, orchestration. Classical piano, 8 yrs. Local bands, 7 yrs. Road work, Top Forty Club Band, 3 yrs. Studio musician, 75- Staff writer-co-publ, April/Blackwood Music CBS. Musical dir & keyboard-guitar-flute, on tour with Cecilio & Kapono from Hawaii. *Songs:* Moonlight Sympathy; In the Back of Your Mind; Kathy's Song; Wish I Had a Music Box; It's Not Easy to Live Together.

ECKER, JUDITH K (JUDITH KOCH)   ASCAP 1957
author, teacher
b Louisville, Ky, Dec 27, 33. Educ: Western Ky State Col, BS; Iowa State Univ, MA. Instr mass media, Western Ky State Col. Chief Collabr: Thomas Ecker (husband). *Songs:* Who Is He?; Full Moon Above; Beware; Crocodile Hop.

ECKER, TOM   ASCAP 1957
composer, author
b Waverly, Iowa, Feb 6, 35. Educ: Univ Iowa, BA, 57; Western Ky Univ, MA, 63. Writer & arr, group "The Hawkeyes"; mgr, rock group "Gangster" now touring & recording in Sweden. *Songs:* Someone, Someday; I've Been Lonely; Waiting in the Dark; Music: Who Is He?; Beware; Crocodile Hop.

ECKSTEIN, MAXWELL　　　　　　　　ASCAP 1952
composer, pianist, arranger
b New York, NY, Feb 6, 05; d Yonkers, NY, May 16, 74. Educ: Pub & pvt schs; studied comp with Lazare Saminsky & Frederick Jacobi; hon MusD, Chicago Cons. Ed & consult, Piano Music Div, Carl Fischer Inc, 46-74. Was lectr throughout US. *Instrumental Works:* Let Us Have Music (series); Eckstein Piano Course; Concerto for Young Americans; By a Blue Lagoon (piano); Stratford Sonata (piano); Piano Graphics (piano).

ECTON, ROBERT MAX　　　　　　　　ASCAP 1954
composer, vocal teacher, coach
b LaJunta Colo, May 24, 15. Educ: Univ Ariz, BS; studied voice & method with Florence Russell. Pianist & singer, nightclubs, US; cond, var singers; teacher & coach, prof singers, Hollywood, New York. Chief Collabrs: Frances Kane, Kay Smith, Robert Altman. *Songs:* Music: Road to Nowhere; Where Freedom Walks; Star Seven (children's operetta); Wind Bells. *Scores:* Film/TV: Thick and Thin-Picture Health.

EDDLEMAN, DAVID　　　　　　　　　ASCAP 1971
composer
b Winston-Salem, NC, Aug 20, 36. Educ: R J Reynolds High Sch, 54; Appalachian State Univ, BS, 58; Va Commonwealth Univ, MM, 63; Boston Univ, DMA, 71; studied comp with Gardner Read. Teacher pub schs, Savannah, Ga & Morristown, NJ; teacher, Boston Univ, Mass & Col St Elizabeth, Convent Station, NJ. Cond, Third Army Band; music ed, Silver Burdett Co. *Songs:* The Innkeeper's Carol; I'm Gonna Walk; Listen to the Music; Little Tiny Baby; Listen to the Singing; Sing, Hallelujah!; Sing, Hosanna; Lord of All; Thanksgiving Calypso; You Shall Know the Truth; Calypso Carol; Light the Candle; Winter is Here; Love is All Around; Marching to Bethlehem; Holiday Hoedown; Traveling Home; Music: Sing, O Sing; Clap Your Hands; Hodie Christus Natus Est; The King of Love; Benediction; Sing to the Lord; Rejoice in the Lord; The Friendly Beasts; Peace I Leave With You.

EDDY, DAVID MANTON　　　　　　　ASCAP 1960
author
b Hartford, Conn, July 1, 28. Educ: Princeton Univ. Former art agent. *Songs:* Another Summer Gone; Dreamers Before the Dawn.

EDDY, TED
See Simonetti, Ted Eddy

EDDY, WALTER
See Edelstein, Walter

EDELHEIT, HARRY　　　　　　　　　ASCAP 1925
author
b Vienna, Austria, May 3, 1891; d New York, NY, Oct 28, 55. To US 1893. Singer & writer of spec material for vaudeville. Chief Collab: Al Piantadosi. *Songs:* Ten Baby Fingers; Whistlin' Joe From Kokomo; Princess and the Clown; Christmas Comes But Once a Year; If You Had All the World and Its Gold.

EDELSON, EDWARD　　　　　　　　ASCAP 1963
composer, teacher
b New York, NY, Jan 30, 29. Educ: Juilliard Sch Music, comp, 47-49; Manhattan Sch Music, 49-53, studied with Vittorio Giannini & Wallingford Riegger. Served with USA, 51-53. High sch music teacher; comp educ music; author, articles on music educ & book "The Secondary School Music Program From Classroom to Concert Hall." *Instrumental Works:* The Negev (band); Israeli Folk Suite (orch); Night Song (flute solo with piano accompaniment); The Chase Trumpet Trio; Sunrise at Riverview (trumpet solo with piano accompaniment).

EDELSTEIN, WALTER (WALTER EDDY)　　ASCAP 1971
composer, violinist, teacher
b New York, NY, Feb 20, 03. Educ: Juilliard Sch Music, dipl in violin & teaching, studied violin with Franz Kneisel, theory with Percy Goethius; Fontainebleau Cons, France, dipl, studied theory with Nadia Boulanger. Rec'd Calif State teaching credential in music. Had debut, Aeolian Hall, New York; joined CBS staff as soloist & orch player; joined Hartman String Quartet, had tours in US; soloist debut, Salle Pleyel & Orch Poulet, Paris, 30; joined NBC staff orch, Los Angeles, 41; also played, movie studios & recording studios; concert master for Victor Young, Walter Scharf & Gordon Jenkins. Concert & recording violinist. Chief Collabrs: Johnny Mercer, Sid Kuller. *Songs & Instrumental Works:* Chant Oriental (theme & variations for piano & violin); I Belong to You; I Came, I Saw, You Conquered.

EDENS, ROGER　　　　　　　　　　ASCAP 1941
composer, author, arranger
b Hillsboro, Tex, Nov 9, 05; d. Pianist, pit orch for "Girl Crazy." Accompanist & vocal arr for Ethel Merman. Associated with MGM for many yrs. Produced films incl "Deep in My Heart" & "Funny Face," assoc producer of var other films. Songwriter for films incl "Broadway Melody of 1938", "Babes in Arms", "Little Nellie Kelly", "Ziegfeld Girl", "Good News", "Ziegfeld Follies", "Deep in My Heart", "Funny Face" & "Jumbo." Chief Collabrs: Hugh Martin, Ralph Freed, Betty Comden, Adolph Green, Jimmy Monaco, Sigmund Romberg.

Songs: It's a Great Day for the Irish; Our Love Affair; Pass the Peace Pipe; In-Between; The Right Girl for Me; The French Lesson; Think Pink; Bonjour, Paris; Figaro; A Pretty Girl Milking Her Cow; Minnie From Trinidad; Dear Mr Gable (You Made Me Love You); Sawdust, Spangles and Dreams. *Scores:* Films: Strike Up the Band; Take Me Out to the Ball Game; Easter Parade (Acad award, 48); On the Town (Acad award, 49); Annie Get Your Gun (Acad award, 50).

EDISON, HARRY (SWEETS)　　　　　ASCAP 1959
composer, trumpeter
b Columbus, Ohio, Oct 10, 15. Trumpeter, Count Basie Band, 37-50, Buddy Rich. Toured with Josephine Baker. Appeared in "Jazz At the Philharmonic," films & TV; made many records. *Instrumental Works:* Jive at Five; Beaver Junction; Center Piece; Shorty George; Pound Cake; Sweets; Evil Blues; Free Eats; Mutton Leg; Every Tub.

EDMONDS, SHEPARD N　　　　　　　ASCAP 1923
composer, author, publisher
b Memphis, Tenn, Sept 25, 1876; d Columbus, Ohio, Nov 21, 57. Educ: Ohio State Univ. Appeared in minstrel shows, musical comedy & vaudeville; operated first Negro Detective Bureau, New York, retired, 25; in 08, founded first Negro music publ house; actor. *Songs:* I'm Goin' to Live Anyhow Until I Die; You Can't Fool All the People All the Time; Business Is Business; I'm Living in Hopes of Tomorrow; Just What Did I Do?

EDMONDSON, JOHN BALDWIN　　　　ASCAP 1965
composer, author, arranger
b Toledo, Ohio, Feb 3, 33. Educ: Univ Fla, BA, 55; Univ Ky, MMus, 59. Taught instrumental music in central Ky area pub schs, 60-70. Chief arr, Univ Ky Wildcat Marching Band & others, 63-70. Educ ed with Charles Hansen, 70-79. Dir of Concert Band Publ, Jenson, 79-80. Free-lance comp, arr & ed, 80- Chief Collabrs: Cynthia Medley, Paul Yoder. *Songs:* Miss Kentucky; Let's Fly; Another Time Another Day; Music: The End of the Line; The Trees Are Bare. *Instrumental Works:* Mini Fun-Way Band Book; Fun-Way Band Method; First Fun-Way Concert Band Book; John Edmondson's Young Band Book; Works for Young Bands: Fun-Way Bandsman; Song for Winds; Winchester March; Fantasy on a Fanfare; Norland March; Flute Fever; Space Race; Big Band Dixieland; Big Band Bossa Nova; Big Band Bugaloo; Big Band Rock; Scandinavian Folk Fantasy; Two Sketches for Band; Concert band works: Three Pieces for Winds; Monody in Blue for Trumpet and Band; To the Colors; Pageantry Overture.

EDMUNDS, JOHN FRANCIS　　　　　ASCAP 1965
composer, educator, arranger
b Cheraw, SC, Dec 12, 28. Educ: Univ Fla, BA, 51; US Naval Sch Music, dipl, 52; Fla State Univ, MME, 56. Taught instrumental music in pub schs, Greenwood, SC & Orlando, Fla, 56-64. Asst dir bands, Univ Tex, Austin, 64-67. Prof music theory & staff arr La State Univ Bands, La State Univ, Baton Rouge, 67-; acting dir bands, 80- *Instrumental Works:* Britannia—an English Folk Rhapsody; Latin and Lace; Embarcadero; March of the Centurions; Commemorative March; March of the Longhorns; Lullaby in Latin.

EDMUNDSON, GARTH　　　　　　　ASCAP 1943
composer, organist
b Pittsburgh, Pa, Apr 11, 00; d. Educ: Leipzig Cons, studied with Harvey Gaul, Lynwood Farnam, Joseph Bonnet, Isidor Phillipp; hon MusD, Westminster Col. Organist, dir & teacher, churches & schs in western Pa. Organist, First Presby Church, Newcastle, Pa. *Instrumental Works:* Concert Variations; In Modum Antiquum (organ suite); Music for Episcopal Service; Symphony No 1, 2; 56 Organ Choral-Preludes; Elfin Dance (organ).

EDWARD, JIMMY
See Vickers, James Edward

EDWARD, PAUL
See Yalen, Paul Edward

EDWARDS, CLARA (BERNARD HAIG)　　ASCAP 1925
composer, author, singer
b Mankato, Minn; d. Educ: Mankato State Normal Col; Cosmopolitan Sch of Music, Chicago; studied in Europe. Singer, churches & concerts, US & abroad. Writer, music for Tony Sarg's Marionettes & animated films. Chief Collabr: Jack Lawrence. *Songs:* By the Bend of the River; With the Wind and the Rain in Your Hair; Into the Night; The Fisher's Widow; A Love Song; Ol' Jim; The Snow; Gypsy Life; Sacred works: 27th Psalm; When Jesus Walked on Galilee; Dedication.

EDWARDS, EDWIN B　　　　　　　　ASCAP 1953
composer, violinist, trombonist
b New Orleans, La, May 22, 1891; d New York, NY, Apr 9, 63. Violinist, theatre & film orch. Trombonist with parade bands. To Chicago, 16, with Johnny Stein's Dixie Jazz Band, Nick La Rocca, Larry Shields, Henry Ragas & Tony Sbarbaro. Founder, Original Dixieland Jazz Band, made first jazz recording ever, 17. Served, USA, World War I. Organized band, Silver Slipper, NY; played with society orchs, 30's & 40's. Reorganized Dixieland Jazz Band,

43, toured with Katherine Dunham. Formed jazz sextet. *Songs & Instrumental Works:* Tiger Rag; Livery Stable Blues; Clarinet Marmalade; Fidgety Feet; Sensation; Lazy Daddy; Barnyard Blues; At the Jazz Band Ball; Bluin' the Blues; Ostrich Walk; Satanic Blues; Skeleton Jungle; I'll Never Forget I Love You; Take That.

EDWARDS, GUS　　　　ASCAP 1914
composer, producer
b Hohensaliza, Ger, Aug 18, 1879; d Los Angeles, Calif, Nov 7, 45. Bro of Leo Edwards, uncle of Joan & Jack Edwards. Educ: pub schs. Vaudeville singer & later had own co vaudeville. Discovered Elsie Janis, Eddie Cantor, Walter Winchell, George Jessel, Georgie Price, Lila Lee, Eleanor Powell, Ray Bolger, Duncan Sisters, Sally Rand, Jack Pearl, Lane Sisters, Paul Haakon, Ina Ray Hutton. Founded Gus Edwards Music Hall, New York; also own publ co. Produced spec subjects for films. Returned to vaudeville, 30-37; retired, 39. Film biography "The Star Maker." Charter mem, ASCAP. Chief Collabs: Edward Madden, Will Cobb, Robert B Smith. *Songs:* Meet Me Under the Wisteria; School Days; Sunbonnet Sue; Tammy; By the Light of the Silvery Moon; I Can't Tell Why I Love You But I Do; Goodbye Little Girl, Goodbye; I Just Can't Make My Eyes Behave; In My Merry Oldsmobile; I'll Be With You When the Roses Bloom Again; He's My Pal; Way Down Yonder in the Cornfield; In Zanzibar; If a Girl Like You Loved a Boy Like Me; Jimmy Valentine; If I Were a Millionaire; Laddie Boy. *Scores:* Bway Stage: When We Were Forty-One; Hip Hip Hooray; The Merry-Go-Round; School Days; Ziegfeld Follies of 1910; Sunbonnet Sue; Show Window.

EDWARDS, JACK　　　　ASCAP 1944
composer, author
b New York, NY, Apr 9, 24. Educ: NY Univ, grad, broadcasting & music. Wrote music for TV show "Sealtest Big Top," CBS, 51-56. Author of songs for own music publ firm, Commercial Music Co. Chief Collabs: Willie Lion Smith, Irving Fields, Leo Corday. *Songs:* And So it Ended; Go West Young Man, Go West; The Laugh's on Me; You Turned My Love to Hate; Sly Mongoose; Mrs Santa Claus; Partners in Paradise; Music: How Many Stars Have to Shine; America, Sweet America; Big Boat Whistle; In Spite of Everything You Do; Takin' the Trains Out; Lyrics: Take Her to Jamaica; Mop Mop; You Can't Be True, Dear; A New Kind of Song; If I Could Steal You From Somebody Else; Here Comes the Band; The Zig Zag.

EDWARDS, JIMMY
See Bullington, James Wiley

EDWARDS, JOAN　　　　ASCAP 1950
composer, author, singer
b New York, NY, Feb 13, 20. Niece of Gus & Leo Edwards, sister of Jack Edwards. Educ: Hunter Col; studied piano with Raphael Samuel. Singer & pianist, Paul Whiteman Orch, 38-40. Featured singer on radio, "Hit Parade," 42-47. Has appeared in hotels, nightclubs, films incl "Hit Parade of 1947." Wrote songs for Copacabana revues, New York. Chief Collabs: Lyn Duddy, Jack Edwards. *Songs:* Darn It Baby, That's Love; Anytime; You Can't Take It With You When You Go; And So It Ended; Do You Still Feel the Same?; Television's Tough on Love; I Love Bosco (commercial). *Scores:* Bway stage: Tickets, Please. *Albums:* Arthur Godfrey TV Calendar Show.

EDWARDS, JULIE ANDREWS
actress, singer
b Walton-on-Thames, England, Oct 1, 35. Educ: Studied with pvt tutors, also with Mme Stiles-Allen. Debut as singer, Hippodrome, London, 47; appeared in pantomime, Cinderella, London, 53; appeared in Bway production, "The Boy Friend", "My Fair Lady" & "Camelot"; films incl "Mary Poppins" (Acad Award), "The Americanization of Emily", "Torn Curtain", "The Sound of Music", "Hawaii", "Thoroughly Modern Millie", "Star!", "Darling Lili", "The Tamarind Seed" & "10." Star TV series, "The Julie Andrews Hour." Rec'd NY Drama Critics Award, Golden Globe Award & named World Film Favorite. Author, "Mandy" & "The Last of the Really Great Whangdoodles."

EDWARDS, LEO　　　　ASCAP 1914
composer, author, producer
b Ger, Feb 22, 1886; d New York, NY, July 12, 78. To US as child. Bro of Gus Edwards, uncle of Joan & Jack Edwards. Educ: Pub schs. Appeared in vaudeville. Staff writer, music publ firms. Produced cabaret shows, New York. Wrote songs for Bway musicals, "Maid in America" & "The Blue Paradise." Charter mem, ASCAP. Chief Collabs: Blanche Merrill, Earl Carroll, Herbert Reynolds. *Songs:* Sweetheart, Let's Grow Old Together; Isle d'Amour; My Fantasy; Here's to You, My Sparkling Wine; I'm an Indian; Inspiration; Pierrot and Pierrette; We Take Our Hats Off to You, Mr Wilson; Just for Me and Mary; Wings Over America; Then, Now, Forever; That's Where the West Begins; Tomorrow's America (off Boy Scout song); The Beer That I Left on the Bar.

EDWARDS, MICHAEL (MICHAEL SLOWITZKY)　　ASCAP 1941
composer, conductor, violinist
b Hazleton, Pa, Sept 29, 1893; d Malverne, NY, Sept 26, 62. Educ: Studied violin with father & Eugene Ysaye. Violinist, Kaier Grand Opera Orch. WW I, USA Med Div. Violinist, Cincinnati Symph. Cond & organist in Pa theatres. Ed & arr, New York publ firms. Chief Collabs: Bud Green, Gladys Shelley. *Songs:*

Once in a While; I Whisper Good Night; Love Isn't Love; Tell Me Why; Music in the Zoo (12 songs). *Instrumental Works:* Band: American Seamen; National Unity; My America (also for chorus); Aladdin and the Princess; March Modernistic; Piano: Nimble Fingers (Concerto Minature); Sword Dance.

EDWARDS, OLEN　　　　ASCAP 1965
composer, author
b Okemah, Okla, July 15, 23. Educ: Pvt lessons for guitar & music theory. Worked in dance bands. Gospel soloist & quartet mem. Chief Collab: Sonny Dawson Stephens. *Songs & Instrumental Works:* When I'm Led By the Master's Great Hand; Searching; Thy Image; Thy Word.

EDWARDS, SHERMAN　　　　ASCAP 1953
composer, author, arranger
b New York, NY, Apr 3, 19. Educ: NY Univ, BA(history); Schillinger Syst Music Comp, Rudolph Schramm. Actor, "Pins and Needles" & "My Sister Eileen." USAF, 42-46. Pianist with Roy Eldridge, May Kaminsky, Wingy Manone, Joe Marsala, Sol Yageo. Accompanist, arr for Mindy Carson. Chief Collabs: Ingrid Edwards, Sid Wayne, Hal David, Ben Raleigh, Leon Carr. *Songs:* Music: See You in September; Dungaree Doll; Broken Hearted Melody; Wonderful Wonderful!; Johnny Get Angry. *Scores:* Bway show: 1776; Film/TV: Who's Afraid of Mother Goose; Flaming Star; GI Blues; Kid Galahad.

EDWARDS, THOMAS JAY (TEX)　　　　ASCAP 1979
composer, author, singer
b Dallas, Tex, Nov 14, 54. Educ: Thomas Jefferson High Sch, Dallas; Richland Col. Founder pioneer Tex punk group, The Idiots! Founder-mem band, The Nervebreakers; also vocalist for rockabilly band, Tex and the Saddle Tramps. Chief Collabs: Michael D Haskins, Barry Kooda. *Songs:* Hijack the Radio; Why Am I So Flipped?; Politics; My Life Is Ruined; Let's Fall Apart; Beyond the Borderline; I've Got a Problem; I Don't Believe in Anything; I Love Your Neurosis; Everything Right to Me Is Wrong; Just Yawn; Wake Me Up; Breaking Down; Formerly Street Queen; Girls Girls Girls; What's Left of Me; Wild Wild Wild; Hey Daddy-o.

EDWARDS, THOMAS MORGAN
composer, harmonica player
b Los Angeles, Calif, Dec 4, 32. Educ: Univ Calif, Los Angeles, BS(accounting), 54, MA(comp), 61. Scores commercials; studio player; TV & motion pictures. *Scores:* TV: Gunsmoke; Twilight Zone; Have Gun Will Travel.

EDWARDS, WEBLEY ELGIN (JOHN KALAPANA)
composer, author
b Corvallis, Ore, Nov 11, 02; d Honolulu, Hawaii, Oct 5, 77. Educ: Ore State Univ, BA. Originator & producer of radio show, "Hawaii Calls," 37 yrs; recording artist for Capitol Records; producer of "Hawaii Calls" series albums.

EDWIN, ROBERT
See Steinfort, Robert Edwin

EFF, ROY
See Culbertson, Roy Frederich

EFFINGER, CECIL STANLEY　　　　ASCAP 1954
composer, educator, inventor
b Colorado Springs, Colo, July 22, 14. Educ: Colorado Springs High Sch, 31; Colo Col, BA(math), 35, DM(honoris causa), 59; Am Cons, Fontainbleau, France, 39, studied comp with Nadia Boulanger. Instr math, Colorado Springs High Sch, 36; prof music, Colo Col, 36-41 & 46-48; First oboe, Denver Symph, Colo, 38-41; commanding officer, 506th Army Band, 42-45. Fac, Biarritz Am Univ, France, 45-46; music ed, Denver Post, 46-48; pres, Music Print Corp, Boulder, 55- Inventor, Musicwriter typewriter for music, 55; designer, Tempowatch for musicians, 69. Chief Collabs: Thomas Hornsby Ferril. *Instrumental Works:* The Invisible Fire, Opus 61 (oratorio for choir, orch, SATB soloists); Four Pastorales for Chorus and Oboe, Opus 68; Little Symphony No 1, Opus 31 (chamber orch); Fifth Symphony, Opus 62 (full orch); Paul of Tarsus, Opus 79 (chorus, organ, strings & baritone solo); Prelude and Fugue, Opus 14 (organ); Fifth Quartet, Opus 70; Tone Poem on the Square Dance, Opus 58 (full orch); Concerto for Violin and Chamber Orch, Opus 82. *Scores:* Opera: Cyrano, Opus 72.

EFFROS, ROBERT　　　　ASCAP 1958
composer, trumpeter
b London, Eng, Dec 6, 1900. To US as youth. Educ: High sch. Trumpeter with Vincent Lopez Orch; radio shows incl "Hit Parade," 12 yrs. Recording artist. Chief Collabs: J Russell Robinson, Al Sherman, Phil Wall. *Songs:* Tin Ear; Why Don't You Get Lost?; Jazz Frappe Rag; Southern Comfort; Creole Rag; Love Wears a Mask; Tonight Tonette.

EGAN, JOHN C　　　　ASCAP 1925
composer, pianist
b New York, NY, Oct 2, 1892; d New York, NY, Sept 28, 40. Educ: Fordham Univ, BA. Pianist for music publ. WW I service in Inf, France. Wrote songs for Bway musicals, "Ziegfeld Follies of 1917" & "Poppy." Chief Collabs: Al Harriman, Allan Flynn, Lew Brown, Rachel Crothers, Dorothy Donnelly.

Songs: That's the Kind of a Baby for Me; Be Still My Heart; Express Yourself; Over on the Sunny Side; Stars Over Devon; Top o' the Morning; A Picnic Party With You; Moonspun Dreams; Seven Million People.

EGAN, RAYMOND B   ASCAP 1917
author

b Windsor, Ont, Nov 14, 1890; d Westport, Conn, Oct 13, 52. Came to US, 1892. Educ: Univ Mich. Bank clerk, then staff writer, Grinnells Music Co, Detroit. Wrote songs for Bway musicals: "Robinson Crusoe, Jr"; "Silks and Satins"; "Holka Polka"; "Earl Carroll's Sketch Book" (35) & for films: "Paramount on Parade"; "Red Headed Woman"; "The Prizefighter and the Lady." Chief Collabrs: Walter Donaldson, Ted Fiorito, Harry Tierney, Richard Whiting, Gus Kahn. *Songs:* They Called It Dixieland; Mammy's Little Coal Black Rose; Till We Meet Again; Where the Morning Glories Grow; Ain't We Got Fun?; Japanese Sandman; In a Little While; Tea Leaves; Sleepy Time Gal; You're Still an Old Sweetheart of Mine; Some Sunday Morning; Three on a Match; Somebody's Wrong; Tell Me Why You Smile, Mona Lisa; Dear Old Gal, Who's Your Pal Tonight?; There Ain't No Maybe in My Baby's Eyes; I Never Knew I Could Love Anybody; Downstream Drifter; Red Headed Woman.

EGAN, WALTER LINDSAY   ASCAP 1977
composer, author, guitarist

b Jamaica, NY, July 12, 48. Educ: Georgetown Univ, BA(fine arts), 70. Made many records. *Songs:* Magnet and Steel; Hot Summer Nights; Only the Lucky; Hearts on Fire; You're the One; Tuesday Weld; Tunnel o' Love; Blonde in the Blue T-Bird. *Albums:* Fundamental Roll; Not Shy; The Last Stroll; Hifi.

EGGERS, ROBERT WAYNE   ASCAP 1977
composer, author, guitarist

b Jefferson City, Mo, May 5, 39. Educ: Blair Sch Music, Nashville, Tenn, instr classical guitar, John Knowels. Road musician as guitarist with, Marty Robbins, Jim Ed Brown, Charlie Louvin, Dottie West & var other artists of the "Grand Ole Opry" in Nashville, Tenn, also, The Four Guys; staff musician, "Opryland USA," Nashville, 2 yrs; studio recording musician, Nashville, 10 yrs; with Jingle Production, 77- *Songs:* Cripple Creek (arr). *Instrumental Works:* The 18th Century Rosewood Clock.

EGLI, DAVID CHRISTIAN (DAVID VAZ DIAS)   ASCAP 1975
author

b Richmond, Eng, June 3, 37. Educ: London Sch Economics; Univ Geneva, Switz; Grad Inst Int Studies, MA(political sci). Chief Collabr: Anita Kerr. *Songs:* Lyrics: Does He Ever; Walk His Way.

EGNATZIK, JOSEPH (SANDY NELSON)   ASCAP 1964
composer, author, bassist

b New York, NY, Apr 24, 20. Educ: Boonton High Sch, NJ; Juilliard Sch Music, studied string bass with Frederick Zimmerman. Bassist with symph orchs & popular music groups in dances & shows. Was piano & vocal entertainer for 15 yrs. Played with John Martin as a piano-banjo team, 73-, also recorded for Duet Records; completed a musical comedy with Ted German. Chief Collabrs: William E (Ted) German, Aarold Mott, Lynn Greiner, Ray Rivera. *Songs:* A Very, Very Merry Christmas (From Our House to Your House); In No Time At All; Please Think It Over; Pamela; Fun Galore in Seventy Four (Shriners' show); Music: Ev'ryone's a Part of America; Another Summer Love Affair; Forty Dollars; Leanin' Over the Ole Back Fence; Lyrics: You're Puttin' Me On; You Surprised Me.

EGNER, PHILIP   ASCAP 1936
composer, author, conductor

b New York, NY, Apr 17, 1870; d Seaside Park, NJ, Feb 3, 56. Educ: Pub schs. Led orch at age 16. Cellist in orchs, incl Theodore Thomas, Walter Damrosch, Opera House & New York Philh, 1888-1898. Bandmaster, 17th US Inf Band, serv in Philippines, 1898-1901. Taught music, 01-09 & US Mil Acad, 09-17. Cond bands, New York. Officer, USA, WW I. Led West Point Band & Orch, 25 yrs. Author: "The Emergency Band Book"; "Military and Civil Band Book." *Songs & Instrumental Works:* Sound Off; West Point March; Luck O'Blarney; West Point From Dawn to Midnight; A Moorish and Spanish Episode; At the Fair; On Brave Old Army Team; On to Victory; It's the Army; Down in Maryland; Army Team.

EGYUD, ANNA JUDITH   ASCAP 1975
author

b Budapest, Hungary, Dec 15, 27. Educ: Franz Liszt Acad Music, Budapest, BA(piano), 49; Univ Letter & Sci, Budapest, BA(humanities), 49; studied communication & liberal studies, Univ Calif, Los Angeles; professional writing, Univ Southern Calif, 79. Libbrettist, playwright essayist; numerous publ & productions incl "Yehu", "Portrait of a Soldier", "The Legend of Saint Elizabeth" & essays on art, literature & music. Author essay "Surrealism in Music, Art and Literature." Chief Collabr: Music, Eugene Zador. *Songs:* Lyrics: The Song of the Nymph Called Echo (soprano, women's chorus with piano); Lulluby (soprano voice, piano); Lulluby to Peter (piano); Song of Hope (soprano voice, piano); Christmas Te Deum to Commemorate George Washington's Victory At Trenton (baritone, chorus, orch).

EHLE, ROBERT CANNON   ASCAP 1978
composer, author, teacher

b Lancaster, Pa, Nov 7, 39. Educ: Eastman Sch Music, BM(theory), 61; studied with William Russo, New York, NY, 62; NTex State Univ, MM(comp), 65, PhD(comp), 70. Author of essays on music theory, comp & electronic music, 67- Teacher computer technol, Denver Inst Technol, 70-71; prof music, Univ Northern Colo, 71-, asst dir, Sch Music, 78- Had works performed by Eastman Rochester Symph, Dallas Symph Orch, Jazz Lab Band of Univ Northern Colo, USAF String Orch, Washington, DC & Univ Northern Colo Chamber Orch & others. *Songs & Instrumental Works:* A Space Symphony (Op 5, orch); Soundpiece (Op 16, orch); Folk Song Suite (Op 14, string orch); A Whole Earth Symphony (seven tone poems, winds & perc, Op 56); Bay Psalmes (1640, Op 31 for choir & orch, four movements); Five Pieces for Instruments with Prepared Electronics (Op 27); Algorythms (soprano, electronic piano, clarinet, bass, Op 29); Soundscapes (electronic symph, prepared tape, Op 45); Lunar Landscape; Hypothetical Orbits for Trumpet and Tape; Second Suite for Jazz Orchestra; A Jazz Symphony.

EHRET, WALTER CHARLES
composer, author, teacher

b New York, NY, Apr 12, 18. Educ: Juilliard Sch, BS(music), studied violin with Samuel Gardner, comp with George Wedge; Teachers Col, Columbia Univ, MA. Taught in NY & NJ, 35 yrs. District coordr of music, Scarsdale Pub Schs, NY. Clinician & lectr, state & county fests. Arr & ed, choral works. Author, textbooks "Functional Lessons in Singing" & "Choral Conductors Handbook."

EHRLICH, SAM   ASCAP 1921
author

b New Orleans, La, Apr 18, 1872; d New York, NY, June 14, 27. Educ: Toule Col Mil Sch; Columbia Univ, BA. Writer, special material for Lillian Russell, Marie Dressler, Charlie Chaplin, Lon Chaney, Pearl White & Mabel Normand. *Songs:* Out in the New Mown Hay; Short and Sweet; Dixie Ain't What Dixie Used to Be; I Leave It All to You; Oh Frenchy.

EHRY, ALFRED F   ASCAP 1963
author

b Atlanta, Ga, Dec 3, 36. Educ: Brown Univ, BA; studied songwriting with Frank Loesser. Lyric writer for Bway show, "Here's Where I Belong." TV shows for 3 major networks, "Hootenanny", "That Was the Week That Was", "Carol Burnett Show" & "Sing Along With Mitch." Wrote lyrics for "The Robber Bridegroom," it received a Tony Nomination & 2 drama disc's; did Stewart Ostrow musical, "Fling." Did adaptation of George M Cohen musical, "Little Johnny Jones", Goodspeed Opera House; also musical adaptation of "The Italian Straw Hat," the new version is "Chapeau." Chief Collabr: Robert Waldman.

EICHHORN, HERMENE WARLICK   ASCAP 1954
composer, author, conductor

b Hickory, NC, Apr 3, 06. Educ: Univ NC, BSM; pvt music study. Organist, Holy Trinity Episcopal Church, Greensboro, NC, 26-, choirmaster, 32- Writer, music column, Daily News, Greensboro, 28-51. Dir, Greensboro Civic Music Asn, 32-, mem, exec comt, 59-; mem of bd, Greensboro Chamber Music Soc, 45- Mem, Comt on Church Music of Diocese of NC & chmn, Greensboro district, 53-, Hymn Soc of Am, Am Guild of Organists. *Songs & Instrumental Works:* Cantatas: Mary Magdalene; Song of the Highest; First Corinthians.

EICHLER, JULIAN   ASCAP 1963
composer, author

b New York, NY, Dec 6, 10. Educ: Columbia Col of Pharmacy; David Berend Sch of Music; pvt music study. Songwriter, Muzak & music publs. Writer, musical commercials, Parkson Advert Co. *Songs:* I'm Allergic to Love; Something Wonderful Happens; I'm Glad I Made You Cry.

EILERS, JOY   ASCAP 1967
composer, author, singer

b Hollywood, Calif, Feb 13, 34. Educ: San Fernando High Sch; Univ Calif, Los Angeles, 1 yr; Westminster Choir Col, Princeton, NJ, BMus, studied voice with Janice Harsanyi & Lorene Hodapp, 4 yrs, also studied piano with Robert Woodside. Actress, pianist, guitarist, publ & arr, Hollywood music comedies; toured in many Hollywood Overseas Comts USO, incl Vietnam, 64-72. World entertainer, performer of original stage production (solo), "Abraham Lincoln Concert," 74-, Freedoms Found Award, 74 & Religion in Media Award, 78. Also incidental background music, special material & some TV scoring. *Songs:* What Color Is Love?; Peter, Peter. *Songs & Instrumental Works:* Live.

EISENBERG, MICHAEL ALLEN   ASCAP 1978
composer, author

b New York, NY, Mar 30, 56. Educ: Bentley High Sch; Columbia Col, BA, 78. Writer of bk, lyrics & music "At War With Artificial Men" (sci fiction musical); co-wrote "The Great Columbia Riot of 1978," Columbia's Varsity Show, 78.

EISENBERG, SYLVIA WHITE (SIL SEDORES)   ASCAP 1956
composer, author

b New York, NY. Educ: High sch; music courses; studied theory & organ with Hal Shutz. Free-lance publicist for music publ & artists; record promotion;

pianist in music dept & buyer of pop music in music store until 60, also sales in sheet music dept. Chief Collabrs: Sherm Ellis; Robert Robbins; Lewis Allan. *Songs:* Min Skol, Din Skol; Ring the Bell, Beat the Drum; Siman Tov; Traded Off; Touch Me; Put Your Arm Around Me; Music: California, the Golden State; Oh, Lord, Make Me an Instrument of Thy Peace; Lyrics: China Nights (Shina No Yoru).

EISENHAUER, WILLIAM G — ASCAP 1958
composer, author, musician

b Newark, NJ, Mar 13, 25. Educ: Juilliard Sch, BS; Teachers Col, Columbia Univ, MA; USN Sch of Music; Inst of Music. Dir & arr, Navy Dance Band. Chief Collabrs: Horace Linsley, Pat Noto. *Songs:* Never Go Away; Blind Date; Let's Put Our Hearts Together; Too Young to Cry; The Way the World Would Be.

EISENSTADT, EVELYN — ASCAP 1966
composer, author, publisher

b New York, NY. Educ: City Col New York; NY Univ Law Ctr; Practicing Law Inst, New York; Katherine Dunham Sch Dance, NY, music & dance. Chief, Rights Clearance Div, US Information Agency, Voice Am, Washington, DC, 41-72. Distinguished Serv Awards, 57 & 62. US delegate, Diplomatic Conference, Neighboring Rights Convention, UNESCO, 10/61. Singer. *Songs:* A Thousand Kisses; Won't You Come Back; Burn, Baby, Burn; Going Home for Christmas; You Don't Have to Know How to Read a Note to Enjoy a Melody; Two in Love Are One; Promises, Promises, Promises; Some Tomorrow, You'll Call Back Yesterday; I Live Each Day; Com-Sit Comsat; Me Without You; You're the Only One. *Instrumental Works:* Moonmist.

EISENSTEIN, ALFRED — ASCAP 1951
composer, author

b Brody, Poland, Nov 14, 1899. Educ: Pvt tutors, Family Estates, Strupkow, Poland; Gymnasium Tech Univ, Vienna, civil eng degree, dipl in Berlin; prof eng lics, NY & Fla; music studies with Anton Trost, Vienna. Structural eng, Berlin; structural designer, builder & pvt proj, New York, NY. Mgr, Family Estates. Retired & arr benefit concerts for Var Children's Hosp & Archbishop Curley High Sch, participated as pianist. *Songs:* Life Was Beautiful; Two Castanets; If You Were Mine; Love's Grief; Elegy; Barcarole, O! Stay Signorina; Romance for Piano; Memento for Piano; Music: Der Fischer (The Fisherman); Wenn Ich In Deine Augen Seh' (When I Look Into Your Eyes). *Instrumental Works:* Adagio Lamentoso (symphonic tone poem); Impromptu (symphonic tone poem); Movements (string, orch, quartet); Melodic Reflections (cello, orch, piano); Romance (violin, orch, piano); Souvenir (violin, orch, piano); Tango of Love (orch, piano). *Scores:* Opera/Ballet: Petite Suite, Ballet Suite (4 movements).

EISLER, LAWRENCE (EDDIE LAWRENCE) — ASCAP 1964
author, actor, playwright

b New York, NY, Mar 2, 19. Educ: Brooklyn Col, BA; Atelier Mont-Marte, Paris; Atelier De La Grande Chaumiere, Paris; Atelier Leger, Paris. Wrote comedy. Wrote & appeared in Roxy Theatre shows, promoted to production staff. Wrote & directed original music shows after transfer from Med Corps to Army Exchange Service Stations, WW II, featuring Bogart, Bruce Cabot, Annabella, Arthur Treacher, Leo Durocher, John Marley & others. Did nightly comedy show with Marley, NBC. Wrote & performed on own TV shows, Victor Borge & Kay Kyser shows & others. Did featured roles in theatre shows, incl "Bells Are Ringing", "3 Penny Opera", "Sherry." Wrote several plays "The Natives Were Restless", "A Nose for a Nose", "Animals", "Kelly", books & lyrics, "The Expressionist", musical about Gaugin, book & lyrics. Appeared in several films; wrote "The Ladies and Men." Created & recorded 7 albums featuring own character, The Old Philosopher. Wrote magazine articles for Esquire & Mad. Chief Collabrs: Moose Charlap, Bernie Wayne. *Songs:* Lyrics: The Old Philosopher; Old Old Vienna. *Scores:* Bway shows: I'll Never Go There Anymore; Oh You Great Big Bridge; Film/TV: Abner the Baseball.

ELDER, ERIC YALE — ASCAP 1979
composer, author, singer

b Wichita, Kans, Jan 3, 50. Educ: Univ Kans, BA(Eng), 74. Singer & picker, country-rock circuit; mem, Treefrog, dance band; recording artist. Chief Collabrs: Jim Fey, Dave Flamming. *Songs:* Just a Simple Song; One More Second Time Around; Over the Falls; Baby Come Out of the Rain; Annie, Do You Love Me?; Paradise Run.

ELDRIDGE, DAVID ROY
composer, trumpeter

b Pittsburgh, Pa, Jan 30, 11. Started own group, 26. Joined carnival, Rock Dinah & Co. Played with many bands, incl with bro, Eldridge Bros Rhythm King, Oliver Muldoon's Band, Fletcher Henderson's Stompers, Zack White, Steve Webb's Orch, Johnny Neal's Midnight Ramblers, Cecil Scott Orch, Elmer Snowdon, Charlie Johnson's Orch, Teddy Hill, Connie's Hot Chocolates, McKinney's Cottonpickers, Three Deuces, Billy Holiday, Gene Cooper Band, Paul Baron, Artie Shaw's Orch & others. Toured with Jazz at the Philh; touring, bands & single performances. *Songs:* I Remember Harlem; Une Petite Laitue; Drum Boogie. *Instrumental Works:* The Heat Is On; That Drummer's Band; The Gasser; Ball of Fire; Heckler's Hop; Wabash Stomp.

ELIAS, ALBERT SAHLEY — ASCAP 1977
composer, author, singer

b Charleston, WVa, Jan 13, 29. Educ: Charleston High Sch; Philadelphia Cons Music; voice studies with Clarence Reinert, scholarship, 49; Univ Calif, Los Angeles, extension courses. Opera singer; switched to commercial while in AF. Toured Far E as singer; sang on W Coast, 53. Returned to Philadelphia, resumed studies with Reinert. Recorded for RCA Records, Steve Shoals, 61-63. Writer for Paul Anka, Jan Pence, Sarah Vaughn, George Mehavir, Anthony Newly, Roberta Flack & others. Chief Collab: Andy Badale. *Songs:* Love Me As I Love You; Faith; Music: And the Heavens Cried. *Scores:* Film/TV: It's a Brand New World; Law and Disorder; Gordon's War.

ELIAS, MICHAEL — ASCAP 1954
composer, author

b Jeannette, Pa, Mar 15, 18; d Greensburg, Pa, Oct 15, 74. Educ: High sch. *Songs:* I Cried.

ELIE, JUSTIN — ASCAP 1926
composer, conductor, pianist

b Port-au-Prince, Haiti, Sept 1, 1883; d New York, NY, Dec 2, 31. Educ: Paris Cons, studied with de Beriot, Marmontel, Vital, Pessard. Toured NAm & SAm as concert pianist; then to NY. Mem, 2-piano concert team with daughter, Lily. *Instrumental Works:* Les Chants de la Montagne; Voudou (ballet); Legende Creole; Piano Concerto; Quisqueye (symph suite); Aphrodite; Cleopatra.

ELIFRITZ, EILEEN DENTON — ASCAP 1976
composer, author, singer

b Vera, Ill, Jan 27, 18. Owner, Elifritz Publ. *Songs:* What Is Happiness; When the Trumpet Sounds; I Wasn't There; Music: My Dream of Heaven; Oh, Won't That Be Wonderful.

ELISCU, EDWARD — ASCAP 1930
author

b New York, NY. Educ: City Col New York, BSS. Actor, dir, author, producer. Acted in "The Racket", "Quarantine" & "The Dybbuke." Co-produced Bway show, "Meet the People." Ed & sketch writer for Bway show, "The Third Little Show." Author of screenplays, "The Jones Family", "Letter to Three Husbands", "Sis Hopkins", "Out of the Blue." Also co-author & co-producer of Hollywood & New York production "The Banker's Daughter." Performed own works, Lyrics & Lyricists Series at YMCA, "Rewind and Play," W Conn State Col & "Rimes & Times", Westport White Barn Theatre. Mem exec bd, Songwriters Hall of Fame, ASCAP Writers Adv Bd, pres, Am Guild of Authors & Comp, 63-68. Chief Collabrs: Vincent Youmans, Billy Rose, Jay Gorney, Henry Myers, Gus Kahn, Ned Lehac, Vernon Duke, Billy Hill, Harry Akst. *Songs:* Lyrics: Without a Song; Great Day!; More Than You Know; Carioca; Orchids in the Moonlight; Flying Down to Rio; Happy Because I'm in Love; You Forgot Your Gloves; Music Makes Me; A Fellow and a Girl; Damn the Torpedoes!; They Cut Down the Old Pine Tree; It's No Fun Eating Alone; Ankle Up the Altar With Me; It's the Same Old South; Heavenly Night; A Kiss to Remind You; The Four Rivers; You're Perfect!; Why Did You Kiss My Heart Awake?; When the Clock is Striking Twelve; Whoopee; Bird of Paradise. *Scores:* Bway shows: Lady Fingers; The Street Singer; A Little Racketeer; Frederika (also librettist); Meet the People; The Banker's Daughter.

ELIZALDE, JOHN SANTIAGO — ASCAP 1968
composer

b Manila, Philippines, May 23, 25. Educ: Bellarmine & Loyola High Sch; Menlo Jr Col; USAAF Pilot Training Prog, grad, 45; piano with Emma Evans, Homer Samuels, US, also piano with Leopoldo Queron, Madrid, Yves Nat, Paris, orchestration with Albert Harris & comp, George Tremblay. Music ed, MGM, CBS, Daystor & QM Productions, 53-65; dir music, QM, 65- Chief Collabrs: Herman Groves, Monica Riordan. *Scores:* Film/TV: The FBI incl: The Dynasty, The Quarry, The Savage Wilderness, Break Through, The Challenge, The Last Job; Barnaby Jones incl: The Killing Defense, Secret of the Dunes, Foul Play, Time to Kill, The Alpha Bravo War, The Damocles Gun, Yesterday's Terror, Final Judgement, Blind Jeopardy, Stages of Fear, Fatal Overture; The Streets of San Francisco incl: The Bullet, Most Feared in the Jungle, The 24 Karat Plague, Target: Red, Poisoned Show, The Break Up; Cannon incl: The Hit Man, The Exchange; Dan August, Nickle Bag; Caribe, Lady Killer; Operation Runaway, Too Young to Love.

ELKUS, ALBERT
composer, pianist, educator

b Sacramento, Calif, Apr 30, 1884; d Oakland, Calif, Feb 19, 62. Educ: Univ Calif, BA, MA; studied music with Hugo Mansfeldt, Harold Bauer, Josef Lhevinne, Oscar Weil & Carl Prohaska. Head, Music Theory Dept, San Francisco Cons, 23, dir, 51-57. Lectr & piano instr, Dominican Col, 24-31 & Mills Col, 29-40. Head, Music Dept, Univ Calif, 35-51. *Songs & Instrumental Works:* Impressions From a Greek Tragedy (Juilliard Award); On a Merry Folk Tune; Concertino on Lezione of Ariosti (cello, string orch); 8 Pieces for Pianoforte; Serenade (string quartet); Violin Sonata; Choral: I Am the Reaper; Sir Patrick Spens.

ELKUS, JONATHAN   ASCAP 1962
composer, author, teacher

b San Francisco, Calif, Aug 8, 31. Educ: Univ Calif, Berkeley, BA; Stanford Univ, MA; studied comp with Charles Cushing, Leonard Ratner, Ernst Bacon & Darius Milhaud. Dir instrumental music, Lehigh Univ, 57-73, prof music, 65-73. Vis lectr & guest cond, Yale Univ, Univ Calif, Davis, NCarolina Sch Arts & others, 73-; ed & consult to var music publ. Chief Collabrs: Robert Gene Bander, Richard Franko Goldman. *Songs:* Music: The Dorados (men's chorus, piano). *Instrumental Works:* 5 Sketches (two clarinets, bassoon); 3 Medieval Pieces (organ); Concert Band: Camino Real; Serenade; CC Rag; The Apocalypse; Chiaroscuro. *Scores:* Operas: Tom Sawyer; The Outcasts of Poker Flat; Treasure Island; Medea; The Mandarin; Helen in Egypt; A Little Princess.

ELLINGTON, EDWARD KENNEDY (DUKE)   ASCAP 1953
composer, conductor, pianist

b Washington, DC, Apr 29, 1899; d 74. Educ: studied piano with Henry Grant; Wilberforce Univ, hon MusD; Milton Col, LHD. Led own orch, 18; to New York, 23; appeared at Cotton Club, New York, 27-32; first European tour, 33; annual concerts, Carnegie Hall, 43-50; Middle East tour (auspices, State Dept) incl appearance at Int Fair, Damascus, 63. Recording artist. Chief Collabrs: Billy Strayhorn, Irving Mills, Mitchell Parish, Mann Curtis, Barney Bigard, Henry Nemo, Mercer Ellington (son), Bob Russell, Don George, Lee Gaines, Paul Francis Webster, Eddie De Lange, Johnny Hodges, Cootie Williams, Juan Tizol, Carl Sigman. *Songs & Instrumental Works:* Black, Brown and Beige; Deep South Suite; New World A-Comin'; Sepia Panorama; A Drum Is a Woman; Harlem (NBC comn); Suite Thursday; Liberian Suite (Liberian govt comn); Such Sweet Thunder; Shakespearean Suite; My People (Century Negro Progress Exchange, Chicago, 63); Night Creatures; Non-Violent Integration; Far Eastern Suite; Blind Man's Bluff; Sophisticated Lady; Mood Indigo; Creole Love Call; Black and Tan Fantasy; Solitude; I Let a Song Go Out of My Heart; Rockin' in Rhythm; Caravan; Pyramid; Creole Rhapsody; In a Mellotone; Don't Get Around Much Anymore; I Got It Bad and That Ain't Good; I'm Beginning to See the Light; In a Sentimental Mood; East St Louis Toodleoo; Birmingham Breakdown; Black Beauty; Awful Sad; The Duke Steps Out; Saturday Night Function; Old Man Blues; Ring Dem Bells; It Don't Mean a Thing If It Ain't Got That Swing; Drop Me Off in Harlem; Daybreak Express; Delta Serenade; Reminiscing in Tempo; In a Jam; Clarinet Lament; Echoes of Harlem; Blue Reverie; I've Got to Be a Rug Cutter; Please Forgive Me; Chatterbox; Harmony in Harlem; Dusk on the Desert; Lost in Meditation; If You Were in My Place; Skronch; Braggin' in Brass; Blue Light; Buffet Flat; That Gal From Joe's; Subtle Lament; Old King Dooji; Boy Meets Horn; Stevedore's Serenade; You Gave Me the Gate and I'm Swinging; Grievin'; The Sergeant Was Shy; Tootin' Through the Roof; Rumpus in Richmond; Jack the Bear; Me and You; Flaming Sword; Harlem Air Shaft; Bojangles; Portrait of Bert Williams; Do Nothin' Till You Hear From Me (Concerto for Cootie); Kind of Moody (Serenade to Sweden); Morning Glory; Blue Goose; Cotton Tail; Conga Brava; Chocolate Shake; Rocks in My Bed; San Juan Hill; Crescendo in Blue; Diminuendo in Blue; Dusk; C Jam Blues; Main Stem; I Didn't Know About You; Just a-Sittin' and a-Rockin'; Jazz Convulsions; I'm Just a Lucky So and So; The Blues; Come Sunday; Magenta Haze; Just Squeeze Me; Merry-Go-Lucky Local; Take Love Easy; Tomorrow Mountain; Satin Doll; I'm Gonna Go Fishin; Money Jungle; Prelude to a Kiss; Jump for Joy; I'm Checking Out, Goom-bye; The Mooche; Warm Valley; Blue Serge; I Wish I Was Back in My Baby's Arms; Lament for a Lost Love; It Shouldn't Happen to a Dream; Afro-Bosso; In the Beginning, God; Christmas Surprise. *Scores:* Stage: Jump for Joy; Beggars Holiday (Bway); Stage Background: Timon of Athens; Film Background: Anatomy of a Murder; Paris Blues.

ELLINGTON, MERCER   ASCAP 1957
composer, conductor, trumpeter

b Washington, DC, Mar 11, 19. Educ: Columbia Univ; Juilliard; NY Univ. Leader, Mercer Ellington Orch, 39-49. Exec, Tempo Music Inc, 50-54. Road mgr & trumpeter, Cootie Williams Orch, 54 & Duke Ellington Orch, 50-59. Radio commentator, WLIB, New York, 61-63. Cond, Duke Ellington Orch, 74-78. Chief Collabr: Duke Ellington. *Songs & Instrumental Works:* Things Ain't What They Used to Be; Blue Serge; Moon Mist; The Girl in My Dreams; John Hardy's Wife; Jumpin' Punkins; Les Trois Noir; Harlem; A New World A'comin; Happy Go Lucky Local; Squeeze Me; Love You Madly; Satin Doll; Librarian Suite; Continuim; Freshup; Black and Tan Fantasy.

ELLIOTT, ALONZO (ZO)   ASCAP 1940
composer, author

b Manchester, NH, May 25, 1891; d Wallingford, Conn, June 24, 64. Educ: St Paul's Sch; Philip's Acad; Yale Univ, BA; Trinity Col, Cambridge, Eng; Columbia Univ Law Sch; Am Cons, Fontainebleau, France; studied with Nadia Boulanger, Leonard Bernstein, Robert Zeller, Willy de Sadler & Harry Wittemore. Wrote musicals at Yale Univ. Chief Collabr: Stoddard King. *Songs & Instrumental Works:* There's a Long, Long Trail a'Winding (Joseph Vernon Prize); Tulips; British Eighth; Captain of the Crew; Wait for Me; There's a Wee Cottage on a Hillside; The World Was Made for You and Me; In the Heart of Paradise; Enchanted River; Bluebird; Oh! Oh, Abdullah; El Chivato (opera).

ELLIOTT, BRAXTON
See Floyd, Stafford Marquette

ELLIOTT, DAVID
See Stingle, David Ellot

ELLIOTT, JOHN B (JACK MOON)   ASCAP 1953
composer, author

b Ark, June 18, 07; d. Educ: Univ Tex, BA; Juilliard Sch. Appeared in tab shows, burlesque, carnivals, circus, nightclubs, stock cos & films. With radio station KXYZ, Houston, Tex. Served, World War II. Founder, own record co. *Songs:* Danglin'; Cherry Red; Foggy Mist; Ha Ha Ha and a Ho Ho Ho; High Sierra Moon; Hey Mister Moonbeam; Jolly Santa Claus.

ELLIOTT, JOHN M (JACK)   ASCAP 1945
composer, author, singer

b Gowanda, NY, May 7, 14; d Los Angeles, Calif, Jan 3, 72. Educ: High sch. Singer in vaudeville, nightclubs, theatres & radio; wrote spec material for own acts & others. Reporter, Chicago "Variety," 39. Wrote songs for films; has had songs recorded by var artists. Creative dir, advert agency, 5 yrs; wrote & produced commercials, some of which won awards. Created syndicated series "If These Walls Could Speak." Chief Collabrs: Lew Quadling, Harold Spina, Victor Young. *Songs:* It's So Nice to Have a Man Around the House; Sam's Song; Do You Care?; Ivory Rag; Be Mine; The Pansy; In the Wee Small Hours of the Morning; Sugar Coated Lies; I Don't Wanna Be Kissed; Our Very Own; A Weaver of Dreams; Toot Whistle Plunk and Boom. *Scores:* Film: Toot Whistle Plunk and Boom (Acad Award, 53).

ELLIOTT, MARJORIE REEVE (SINCLAIR FAY,   ASCAP 1970
FOX REEVE)
composer, author, choir director

b Syracuse, NY, Aug 7, 1890. Educ: Syracuse Univ, MusB; Colo State Christian Col, DM. Poet, educr, singer. Vpres, high sch grad class. Author poetry book "Patterns of Life", 77 & "Guide Lines for School Music." Served, Ill Fedn Music Clubs; served Women's Clubs, Nat Bd Fedn Music Clubs, 10 yrs; mem, Zonta Int, Music Educ Conference & Music Leaders Am. Awards: George Arents Award, Syracuse Univ, 73; Centennial Award, City Syracuse, 48; Distinguished Service Award, Nat League Am Pen Women, 80. *Songs:* Three Little Maids; Let There Be Music; Give Me a Song to Sing; Our Exultant Song; Where Willows Bend; A Joyful Song; Life Is a Song; Spring Gossip; An Understanding Heart; Christmas Alleluia; Somewhere, A Child Is Praying; April Music; Shortcake Social; Hurdy Gurdy Man; It's State Fair Time; Easter Bunny; The Man in the Moon; Navajo Trail. *Scores:* Operetta: The Happy Scarecrow; Opera: Gypsy Moon.

ELLIOTT, RONALD CHARLES
composer, author

b Healdsburg, Calif, Oct 21, 44. Educ: San Francisco State Univ, music study, 63 & 64. With the Beau Brummels, 64-68; recording guitar player, Los Angeles, 69-80, occasional recording artist, Pan, Columbia & Giants, Casablanca; songwriter. Chief Collabrs: Bob Durand, Butch Engle. *Songs:* Laugh Laugh; You Tell Me Why; Music: Just a Little; Don't Talk to Strangers.

ELLIOTT, WALTER ULRIC   ASCAP 1969
composer, author, organist

b Berlin, Ger, Sept 17, 13. Educ: Los Angeles City Col & Santa Monica City Col, AA; studied music theory & comp with pvt tutor, Ger, studied organ with Frank Brownstead, Charles Shaffer & Thomas Foster, Los Angeles. Music ed, Universal Studios, 57- Mem, Am Guild of Organists & Southern Calif Guild of Temple Musicians. Chief Collabr: Billy Goldenberg. *Songs & Instrumental Works:* TV Series: Night Gallery (lyrics); Alias Smith and Jones (piano pieces).

ELLIS, GREGORY A   ASCAP 1978
composer, singer

b Bloomington, Ill, Oct 28, 55. Educ: Self-taught in music. Singer in nightclubs, concerts & on TV; recording artist. Chief Collabrs: Dan Young, Tim McEnary, Mark J Spink. *Songs:* A House in the Country; Show Me Love; Reflections; Crazy; Music: Stay Awhile.

ELLIS, JACK   ASCAP 1942
author

b New York, NY, Mar 28, 08; d. Educ: NY Univ. Exec, film co for many yrs. Chief Collabrs: Charles Tobias, Henry Tobias. *Songs:* I Can Get It for You Wholesale; If I Can't Have Anna in Cuba; I'll Never Let You Go; Blue Underneath a Yellow Moon; Who Pushed the Button.

ELLIS, MERRILL   ASCAP 1966
composer, performer, researcher

b Cleburne, Tex, Dec 9, 1916. Educ: Univ Okla, BA & MM; Univ Mo, grad study; pvt study with Roy Harris, Spencer Norton, Charles Garland. Prof comp & dir, Electronic Music Ctr, Sch Music, N Tex State Univ. Appeared throughout central & southwestern US in numerous performances of electronic & intermedia comp; lectr at cols & univs. Interested in advancement of new music, carries out research in new compositional techniques, development of new instruments & exploration of new notation techniques for scoring &

performing new music. ASCAP Award, 79. *Instrumental Works:* Kaleidoscope (mezzo soprano, electronic synthesizer & orch); A Dream Fantasy (tape, clarinet, perc, 16 mm film & slides); Nostalgia (orch, film & theatrical events); Mutations (brass choir, film tape & slides); Scintillation (solo piano); Celebration (flute, oboe, clarinet, bassoon, perc, tape, lasers & visual events, comn by Baylor Univ, Richard Shanley & Soc for Commissioning New Music); Dream of the Rode (tape & 16 mm film). *Scores:* Opera: The Sorcerer (solo baritone, tape, film, slides & chorus); Film/TV: The Choice Is Ours (intermedia work for 2 films, slides, tape & audience participation).

ELLIS, SEGER PILLOT — ASCAP 1942
composer, author, pianist

b Houston, Tex, July 4, 04. Educ: Univ Va. Pianist, singer in vaudeville, night clubs; made many records, 20's & 30's. Cond own band, Choir of Brass; first band with 8 brass & 1 reed. Featured on WLW radio sta, Cincinnati & KFWB, Hollywood. Discovered The Mills Bros & Sammy Cahn; 1 hour documentary, "The Time & Tunes of Seger Ellis," Pub Broadcasting Syst, 76. Chief Collabs: Al Stillman, Mitchell Parish, Glen Moore, Harry James, Don George. *Songs:* O What a Night for Love; My Beloved Is Rugged; After You; Christmas Will Be Here; You Don't Have to Be a Santa Claus; If I Can't Wear the Pants; No, Baby, Nobody But You; Unless You're Free; Goin' Steady Anniversary; I Wish I Had My Old Time Sweetheart Back Again; I'm Never the Lover; You Be You; If You've Got Someplace to Go; Oilers (off song Houston Oilers); I Left Myself Wide Open; December; Two Lonesome People; A Little More Mature; I May Be Sorry Tomorrow; I Want Gold in My Pockets When There's Silver in My Hair; So Many Songs Were Wrong About Us; Let's Drive Out to Joe's Drive Inn; Before You Know It Christmas Will Be Here; Daddy's Little Ranger; The Old Time Fiddler; Music: Little Jack Frost, Get Lost; Eleven Sixty PM; What You Don't Know Won't Hurt You; You're All I Want for Christmas; It Hurts Me More Than It Hurts You; I Need You Like I Need a Hole in the Head; Too Lazy for Love; Butterfly Kisses and Fly By Night Love. *Instrumental Works:* Prairie Blues; Sentimental Blues.

ELLSASSER, RICHARD — ASCAP 1958
composer, conductor, organist

b Cleveland, Ohio, Sept 14, 26; d. Educ: Oberlin Col; Baldwin-Wallace Col, BM; NY Univ; Boston Univ Sch of Theol; USC Sch of Religion, MTh; studied organ with Winslow Cheny, Albert Riemenschneider. Organist with symph orchs, toured Eastern states, age 7. New York debut, 37. Founder & dir, Bach Circle of Boston. Minister of Music, Wiltshire Methodist Church, Los Angeles; creator & dir, series of music films. Appeared in var films incl "The Lost Chord", "Of Men and Music", "The Miracle of Our Lady of Fatima" & "So This Is Love." Featured on TV show "Nightfall." Minister of recitals, First Cond Church, Los Angeles; recording artist. Life fel, Int Inst of Arts & Letters, Switz. *Instrumental Works:* Scherzo on Mendelssohnian Themes; Only the Valiant (comn, Methodist Church); Toward Evening; March Fantastique; The Decalogue (10 anthems); Organ Concerto. *Scores:* Ballet: Greenwich Village (Henry Levitt award).

ELLSTEIN, ABRAHAM — ASCAP 1958
composer, author, conductor

b New York, NY, July 9, 07; d New York, NY, Mar 22, 63. Educ: Third Street Settlement; Manhattan Sch Music; Juilliard, scholarship; studied with Frederic Jacobi, Rubin Goldmark & Albert Stoessel. Mem, Metrop Opera's Children's Chorus, 16-20; sang in John Barrymore production "Richard III." World tour as accompanist to Cantor Joseph Rosenblatt. Comp operettas for Yiddish Theatre. Music dir, WMGM, New York; had own program, WEVD, New York, 51-63. Music dir, Advert Broadcasting Co. Chief Collabs: Walter Bullock, Molly Picon, Jacob Jacobs, Samuel Rosenbaum. *Songs:* The Wedding Samba. *Instrumental Works:* Negev (orchestra (piano); Friday Evening Traditional Service (Metrop Synagogue comn); Haftorah (violin & piano); Shabbat Menuchah; A Passover Service. *Songs & Instrumental Works:* Ode to the King of Kings (cantata, 10th anniversary of Israel); Redemption (oratorio); Ima (cantata). *Scores:* Bway Stage: Great to Be Alive; Film: Yid'l Mit'n Fid'l (Warsaw); Opera: The Thief and the Hangman (Ohio Univ prize); The Golem (Ford Found comn).

ELLSWORTH, ROBERT H — ASCAP 1942
composer, author, publisher

b Boston, Mass, Dec 27, 1895; d. Educ: Boston Cons. Served, World War I. Writer, special material for radio. Mgr, New Eng offices, 2 New York music publ; publ. Hon citizen, Wheeling, WVa. *Songs:* We Will Meet At the End of the Trail; I Want Them All to Know; Did I Make a Mistake in You?; Carmelita; Where I First Whispered Sweetheart to You; Saying Adieu; It Won't Be Long Till You Belong to Me; Somebody Else Is Taking My Place; Keep Lookin' Around for the Sunshine; Old New Hampshire Moon; Back to Wheeling, West Virginia; Blue Eyes; The Beantown Polka.

ELMAN, HARRY (ZIGGY) — ASCAP 1961
composer, trumpeter, conductor

b Philadelphia, Pa, May 26, 14; d. Trumpeter in Benny Goodman & Tommy Dorsey Orchs, 36-43. WW II, USAAF. Rejoined Dorsey, 45-47. Formed own orch; appeared in films, made many records. Chief Collab: Johnny Mercer. *Songs:* And the Angels Sing; Zaggin With Zig; Forgive My Heart.

ELMAN, IRVING — ASCAP 1962
author, producer

b Paterson, NJ, June 28, 22. Educ: City Col New York, BS. Playwright & producer, "Uncle Willie", "The Brass Ring" & "The First Million." Writer, films & TV. TV show producer incl "Ben Casey" & "The Eleventh Hour." Chief Collabrs: Harry Sukman, Norman Luboff. *Instrumental Works:* The Eleventh Hour Theme.

ELMAN, MISCHA — ASCAP 1924
composer, violinist

b Stalnoje, Russia, Jan 21, 1891; d. Educ: Royal Music Sch, Odessa, studied with Fiedelman; Petrograd Univ, studied with Leopold Auer; hon MusD, Chicago Musical Col. Berlin debut, 04; London debut, 05; New York debut with Russian Symph, 08. Violin soloist with symph orchs throughout world; performer, concert tours & records. *Instrumental Works:* Violin works: Romance; In a Gondola; Transc: works of Schubert, Rachmaninoff & Beethoven.

ELMER, CEDRIC NAGEL — ASCAP 1964
composer, author, teacher

b Reading, Pa, Jan 15, 39. Educ: Reading High Sch; Combs Col Music, MusB, 61, MusM, 63; Philadelphia Musical Acad, MusBEd, 66; comp study with Romeo Cascarino, piano with Allison R Drake & Julia Shanaman Elmer. Mem fac piano, theory & comp, Community Sch Music & the Arts, 63-, dir, 64- Asst dir, Reading Philh Orch. Instrumental music instr, Reading Sch Dist, 66- Author: "Musical Remembrances." Past pres, Music Club of Reading. Adjudicator piano, Am Col Musicians; comp, Berks County Arts Council. Mem, Phi Mu Alpha Sinfonia. *Songs & Instrumental Works:* Petite Pavane (piano or chamber orch); A Bit Mischievous (piano); Sarabande (piano; also arr for woodwind ens; bass flute, harp; chamber orch); Liliputian Suite (chamber orch; also arr for piano); Psalm Five (SATB); Psalm 21 (SATB); Caprice (woodwind ens).

ELMORE, ROBERT HALL — ASCAP 1943
composer, organist, educator

b Ramaputnam, India, Jan 2, 13. Educ: Studied with Harl McDonald, organ with Pietro A Yon, 26-33; Royal Acad Music, London, ARCO & LRAM, 33; Univ Pa, MB, 37. Debut as concert organist, Carnegie Hall, NY, 36; concertized throughout US & Europe. Organist, music dir, Holy Trinity Church, Philadelphia, 38-55. Prof piano & organ, Clark Cons; organ instr, Philadelphia Col Performing Arts. Organist, choirmaster, Cent Moravian Church, Bethlehem, Pa, 55-68; dir music, Tenth Presby Church, Philadelphia, 69- Cond, Choral Club of Musical Art Soc, Camden, NJ. Awards: Nitsche, Univ Pa, 3 yrs; Thornton Oakley Medal, also two hon doctorates for outstanding contributions to church music in US, LHD, Moravian Col, Bethlehem, 58 & LLD, Alderson, Broaddus Col, WVirginia, 58. Mem, Am Guild of Organists. *Songs:* Cantatas: The Incarnate Word; The Cross; Shepherd of Israel; Psalm of Redemption; Three Psalms; Wondrous Child Divine; Psalm of a Pilgrim People; Reconciliation; The Prodigal Son; Anthems: All Ye Servants; Lord Jesus Think on Me; Three Exhortations; God of Ages; Come to Calvary's Holy Mountain; We in One Covenant Are Joined; Glory to God (Gregor, arr). *Instrumental Works:* 3 Colors (string orch); Valley Forge 1777 (tone poem); Legend of Sleepy Hollow (suite); Narrative (horn, orch); Prelude to Unrest (tone poem); Two String Quartets; Swing Rhapsody—Two Pianos; Organ: Rhythmic Suite; Rhumba; Concerto for Organ, Brass and Percussion; Festival Toccata; Fanfare for Easter; Three Meditative Moments on Moravian Hymns; Three Miniatures; Contemporary Chorale Preludes; Sonata; Holiday; Triad; Donkey Dance. Opera: It Began At Breakfast (1 act opera; first Am opera on TV).

ELMSLIE, KENWARD G — ASCAP 1959
author

b New York, NY, Apr 27, 29. Educ: Harvard Col, BA, 50. Wrote bk, "The Grass Harp", musical play produced on Bway in 72. Musical theatre works have been produced by New York City Opera, Houston Grand Opera, Mich Opera Theatre, Seattle Opera, Kansas City Lyric Theatre, Atlanta Civic Opera & Wash Opera at Kennedy Ctr. Chief Collabrs: Jack Beeson, Ned Rorem, Thomas Pasatieri. *Songs:* Lyric: Love-Wise. *Scores:* Librettos: Lizzie Borden; The Seagull; Washington Square; Miss Julie; The Sweet Bye and Bye; Bway show: The Grass Harp.

ELOW, LAWRENCE — ASCAP 1955
composer, conductor, author

b New York, NY, June 4, 27. Educ: NY Univ, BA; studied arr & orchestration with Tom Timothy. Songwriter, films; wrote theme music for TV serial "As the World Turns." Music dir, Allied Artists. Chief Collabrs: Mark Rydell, Raymond Scott. *Songs & Instrumental Works:* Not As a Stranger; Penny; Tropical Merengue; Never Love a Stranger; Everytime I Dance With You; Billie Boy.

ELSMO, RALPH NORMAN (ROLF NORMAN) — ASCAP 1963
composer, author

b Racine, Wis, Aug 27, 19. Educ: Pub schs; Univ Wis. Began plugging music with Sverre (brother) at age 8, as teenager hit midwest Big Bands with Elsmo Bros Music. Wrote & produced many radio & TV shows, Md, also wrote music for political campaigns & many jingles. Chief Collabrs: Sverre S Elsmo, I Robert Goodman. *Songs & Instrumental Works:* Go You Fighting Colts; The Preakness

Song; Christmas At Home; Merry Christmas and a Happy New Year; My Maryland.

ELSMO, SVERRE S   ASCAP 1958
composer, author, teacher
b Christiania, Norway, Sept 28, 10; d Racine, Wis, Dec 16, 68. Teacher of piano & organ. Chief Collabr: Ralph Elsmo (brother).

ELTON, FRED (FRED ELTON SEIGLE)   ASCAP 1953
composer, pianist, conductor
b NY, Dec 25, 31; d NJ, Apr 26, 60. Played, cond & wrote spec material for Jaye P Morgan, Robert Q Lewis, Eydie Gorme, Steve Lawrence, Joel Grey & many others. *Songs:* You, You Romeo; Whatever Happened to the Old Songs; I Love the Plunk, Plunk, Plunk of a Banjo.

ELTON, JOHN M (JACK)   ASCAP 1971
pianist, conductor, vocal arranger
b Cleveland, Ohio, May 5, 23. Educ: Baldwin-Wallace Col, BA(music); Am Cons Music, Fontainebleau, France; Univ Geneva Cons Music, Switz. Vocal arr & comp of spec material, "Carol Burnett Show," 7 seasons. Vocal arr & cond for George Chakiris, Rosemary Clooney, Monte Hall, Shari Lewis, Jane Powell, Shirley Jones & Jack Cassidy. Music dir for Rodgers & Hart, "Dames At Sea", "Grease", "Showboat" & "I Do, I Do." Rec'd 2 Emmy Awards. Chief Collabr: Artie Malvin.

ELWELL, HERBERT   ASCAP 1950
composer, educator, music critic
b Minneapolis, Minn, May 10, 1898; d. Educ: Univ Minn; studied with Ernest Bloch, Nadia Boulanger; fel, Am Acad Rome, 24-27. Head comp dept, Cleveland Inst of Music, 28-45; teacher comp, Oberlin Cons, 45-53 & Univ Rochester Eastman Sch of Music, summers for many yrs. Music critic, Cleveland Plain Dealer, 31-64. *Instrumental Works:* The Happy Hypocrite (suite, overture for band); Piano Sonata; Piano Pieces; Ode for Orchestra; Songs.

EMBREE, CHARLES B (RIFF), JR   ASCAP 1964
composer, author, publisher
b Moberly, Mo, Dec 8, 19. Educ: Scholarship at KC Art Inst; Univ Iowa, BA & MFA. Artist, USN, WW II. Publ, Esquire mag, 47-55. Writer of special material for Eddie "Rochester" Anderson, 49-52, also others. Formed publ & recording co, 64. *Songs:* Dead Man's Blues; The Thing; Room at the Bottom.

EMERSON, HARRIETT ANNE   ASCAP 1967
composer, performer, violinist
b Corsicana, Tex. Educ: Univ Tex, BMusEd, 45, MMus, 47; studied with Louis Persinger at Juilliard; studied chamber music with William Kroll, New York, Emanuel Ondricek, Boston, New York, Prague & Michelangelo Abbado/Baroque chamber music, Milano. Concert debut, New York, 49, debuts, Gardiner Museum, Boston, Baltimore & Nat Gallery of Art, Washington, DC; began US tours, 52; began int tours, Europe, 57; toured as a young Am artist under the auspices of Dept of Defense & Dept of State, 7 yrs; concertized in Italy for the Minister of Cultural Affairs, also, Turkey, Finland & Ger, also Korea, Taiwan, Vietnam & Japan, all sponsored by local govts. Played concerts in 38 countries for the US govt. Chief Collabr: Remus Harris.

EMERY, ELLEN CHYANN   ASCAP 1977
composer, singer
b Brooklyn, NY, Feb 15, 51. Educ: Babylon High Sch, dipl; Adelphi Univ; Dowling Col, BA(music, drama); vocal training with Marty Larwence, New York. Prof singer, age 15. Model; actress, TV commercials incl Alan Carpet & Clairol. Singer, radio commercials, Long Island radio & Scholastics Mag, New York. Recording artist. Chief Collabr: Victor Milrose, Rock Ludden. *Songs:* Jimmy; Oh Sweet Colorado. *Albums:* Windsong.

EMIG, LOIS IRENE (MYERS)
composer
b Roseville, Ohio, Oct 12, 25. Educ: Roseville High Sch; Ohio State Univ, BS(educ; with distinction), grad work, studied comp with Kent Kennan; Queen's Col. Pub sch music, 10 yrs. Began writing after col, first publ date, 54. Many publ for choral work; also 2 piano bks & 2 children's songs educ magazines. Author of lyrics & comp music. *Songs & Instrumental Works:* Round for Christmas (SATB; SSA; SAB; SA acc); Pin a Star on a Twinkling Tree (SAB; SA; SSA acc); Christmas Festival (4 pt canon acc); Soft Is the Night (SSA acc); Candles, Candles (SA, flutes, acc); Let Everything Praise the Lord (4 pt canon, trumpet, perc, acc); Beautiful Savior (SATB acc cantata, Easter); Song of Bethlehem (SA acc cantata, Christmas); Shepherds, I Can See You (2 pt acc).

EMMERICH, ROBERT D   ASCAP 1936
composer, author, pianist
b New York, NY, July 26, 04. Educ: Horace Mann High Sch; Business Sch. Pianist in vaudeville, nightclubs & radio; newspaper columnist & advert dir. Chief Collabrs: Buddy Bernier, Joseph Meyer. *Songs:* If I Were You; I'd Love to Make Love to You; If Yesterday Could Only Be Tomorrow; The American Way; Way Up in New Hampshire; Music: Our Love; Hurry Home; This Time It's Real; The Big Apple; Darling; You Went to My Head; Gandy Dancer; Believing; So Lovely; I Haven't Got a Hat; Woe Is Me; No Wonder; Hear My

Song Violetta; Lost in the Shuffle. *Instrumental Works:* Notes to You; Riding the Kilocycles.

EMURIAN, ERNEST KRIKOR   ASCAP 1963
composer, author
b Philadelphia, Pa, Feb 20, 12. Educ: Davidson Col, NC, BA, 31; Union Theol Sem, Va, BD, 34; Westminster Choir Col, Princeton, NJ, 34-35; Princeton Theol Sem, ThM, 35; hon DD, Randolph Macon Col, Va, 71. Jr preacher, Park Place Methodist Church, Norfolk, Va, 35-36; Methodist minister, Va Conference, 36-; minister, Fox Hall & Denby Methodist churches, Norfolk, 36-39; chaplain & prof, Ferrum Col, Va, 39-41; minister, Madison Heights Methodist Church, Va, 41-47, Elm Ave Methodist Church, Portsmouth, Va, 41-62 & Cherrydale United Methodist Church, Arlington, Va, 62- Playwright, transl Hispanic hymns to Eng. Author books, "Dramatized Stories of Hymns and Hymn Writers", "More Dramatized Stories of Hymns and Hymn Writers", "Plays and Pageants for Many Occasions", "More Plays and Pageants for Many Occasions", "Living Stories of Famous Hymns", "Famous Stories of Inspiring Hymns", "Forty Stories of Famous Gospel Songs", "Stories of Civil War Songs", "Stories of Christmas Carols", "Stories of Songs About Heaven", "Living Stories of Favorite Songs", "Stories of Yuletide", "Hymn Stories for Programs", "The Sweetheart of the Civil War", "Renewed Saints", "Great Hymns of Testimony", "Popular Programs Based on Hymn Stories", "Ten New Plays for Church and School", "Twentieth Century Hymns" (54 original hymns). Auth play, "The Living Dramatization of Da Vinci's The Last Supper." *Songs:* Three Songs by Ernest K Emurian; Christmas Songs (book 12 original songs); Shouting Songs for Children; Five Ballads; Virginia Is for Lovers; Jonah and the Whale; You Can Do Anything (With the Lord by Your Side); The Pledge of Allegiance; Arlington; Washington; Let Us Go to Dothan; Reaching Out; When They Play That Great Tape in the Sky; Flop to the Top.

ENDERS, HARVEY   ASCAP 1934
composer, author, singer
b St Louis, Mo, Oct 13, 1892; d New York, NY, Jan 12, 47. Educ: Wash Univ, scholarship; studied with Charles Galloway, Richard Keitel, Muenchen-Gladbach, Cesare Sodero & David Bispham. To New York, 14. Soloist in churches; also investment banker. Pres, Mendelssohn Glee Club; first pres, Asn Male Choruses of Greater New York. *Songs:* Hangman, Hangman; Trav'lin'; I Sing My Songs For You; Daniel; On the Road to Mandalay (arr); Vienna Will Sing Again (text). *Instrumental Works:* To the Great Pyramid; Death in Harlem; Russian Picnic.

EN EARL, WILLIAM ALLAN (BILLY EARL)   ASCAP 1975
composer, author, singer
b San Francisco, Calif, Sept 18, 46. Educ: Las Lomas High Sch, Calif; studied voice with Duane Studio, Oakland, Calif & Jack Sparrow, San Francisco, Calif. Singer, ventriloquist & musician with comedy musical act, int tours. Appears with singer Bonnie Earl (wife) in "Bonnie & Clyde Show." Writer, special material for other acts & shows. Plays clubs, fairs & TV. Recording artist. Owner, Tommy Gun Music. *Songs:* Walk With Me; Lovin' You Is on My Mind; A Lonesome Song; One Way Ticket; Dirty Dan; Magic; Circus Day; My Moment of Truth. *Instrumental Works:* Cat Walk.

ENGBLOM, VERNE A   ASCAP 1964
composer, author, teacher
b Chicago, Ill, Oct 13, 24. Educ: High sch; pvt music study. Served, USAF. Owner, Chordcraft Music Publ Co, recording studio & record label; publ several song bks & sheet music, also several music teaching aids such as chord charts for keyboard, guitar, banjo, mandolin & chordcraft transposition guide. Author, song bks "8 New Songs in the Old Style" & "19 Original Songs Mostly Country." *Songs:* I'm the Only Girl; If I Should Forget; My Neighbor; I Was a Fool; The Cutest Tune; Bring Back That Old Quartet; Our Dusty Old Organ; The Saga of Charlie Brown Christmas; Save a Soul Band; Crazy Heart; Live By the Good Book; This Great Big World; Step Aside; The Corner Cafe; Tavern for Heartache and Tears; Love My Love; Nothing But Teardrops; There Goes My Tender Heart; Wonderful, Wonderful You; Bright Lights; Those Good Old Melodies.

ENGEL, CARL   ASCAP 1935
composer, editor, publisher
b Paris, France, July 21, 1883; d New York, NY, May 6, 44. To US, 05, citizen. Educ: Univ Strasbourg; Univ Munich, studied with Ludwig Thuille; Oberlin Col, MusD. Ed, Boston Music Co, 09-21. Pres, G Schirmer, 29-32, 34-44. Ed, "Musical Quarterly", 29-44. Fel, Am Acad Arts & Sciences; mem, Musical Asn London; hon mem, Harvard Musical Asn; pres, Am Musicol Asn, 37-38. Chevalier, Legion of Honor. Chief mus div, Library of Congress, 32-34. Author, "Alla Breve", "From Bach to Debussy" & "Discords Mingled." *Songs:* Sea Shell. *Instrumental Works:* Triptych (violin & piano).

ENGEL, GARY ALAN
composer, author
b Los Angeles, Calif, Aug 10, 48. Educ: Univ Calif, Los Angeles, AB, 70, MS, 72. Writer, arr, record producer, record co pres. Chief Collabrs: Jeff Oxman, Ron Walton. *Songs:* Soul Disco; Always Be the One; You Turned the Fire On; Electrifying.

ENGLES, GEORGE   ASCAP 1966
composer, teacher
b New York, NY, Apr 6, 16. Educ: New Rochelle High Sch, NY; Cornell Univ, BA(music); Am Theatre Wing, studied musical comp with Richard Bends; Julliard, comp; Hunter Col, postgrad music courses. Nightclub pianist, Le Ruban Bleu, Rainbow Grill & Club 21, New York; pianist, Cape Cod-Coonamessett Inn, Falmouth, Mass; teacher elem vocal music, Pub Sch 116, New York; teacher vocal music, Intermediate Sch, Falmouth, Mass; teacher piano & theory, Cape Cod Cons, Falmouth & Barnstable, Mass. Chief Collabs: Robert Colby, Jane Livingston, Paul Rosner, James T Murphy. *Songs:* Music: Heavenly (You Are So); If You Need Me.

ENGLISH, GRANVILLE   ASCAP 1926
composer, pianist, teacher
b Louisville, Ky, Jan 27, 00; d. Educ: Chicago Musical Col, BM, studied with Felix Borowski, Rudolph Reuter, Glenn Dillard Gunn; also with Tibor Serly, Wallingford Riegger, Nadia Boulanger; Ford Found grant. Comp-in-residence, Baylor Univ, 61. Chief Collab: Langston Hughes. *Songs & Instrumental Works:* An Island Festival (ballet suite); Robin in the Rain (3-part chorus); Tropicana; Scherzo in C; Law West of the Pecos (4-part chorus, male voices; Mendelssohn Glee Club Prize); Wide Wide River (1-act folk opera); Sea Drift (ballet); Moon Tropicale (concert band); Colonial Portraits (suite for strings); Evening By the Sea (tone poem); The Ugly Duckling (cantata); If I Gave You a Rose; Ceasing to Care.

ENGLISH, TINA
See Roach, Christine English

ENNIS, SUSAN LEE   ASCAP 1978
composer
b Peoria, Ill, May 5, 50. Educ: Willamette Univ, BA(English), BA(Ger); Univ Calif, Berkeley, MA(Ger literature). Teaching asst of Ger, Univ Calif, Berkeley, 74-78. Song-writer & producer for var albums, 78- Chief Collabs: Ann Wilson & Nancy Wilson. *Songs:* Straight On; Dog and Butterfly; Even It Up; Bebe Le Strange; Mistral Wind; Down on Me; Nada One; Lighter Touch; Pilot.

EPHROS, GERSHON   ASCAP 1950
composer, author, teacher
b Serotzk, Poland, Jan 15, 1890; d. Educ: Prof A Z Idelsohn's Inst of Jewish Music, Jerusalem (choir dir); studied with stepfather, a cantor & Herman Spielter, Joseph Achron. Instr, Jewish music, New York Bureau of Jewish Educ, Hebrew Union Col Sch of Sacred Music, 48-58. Cantor, Beth Elohim, 19-27, Beth Mordecai, Perth Amboy, NJ, 27-57. Pres, Jewish Music Forum; mem, exec bd, Nat Jewish Music Council, Nat Jewish Welfare Bd, Nat Asn for Am Composers & Conductors, Cantors Assembly of Am. TV biography, "Song of My People." *Songs & Instrumental Works:* Cantorial Anthology (5 vols); Album of Jewish Folk Songs; Priestly Benediction, I, II; A Junion Sacred Service; Children's Suite (musical setting, poems of Bialik); Biblical Suite (chorus, solo, orch); Midnight Penitential Service (chorus, solo, orch); String Quartet; Friday Evening Service; L'Yom Hashabbat.

EPPERT, CARL   ASCAP 1941
composer, conductor, teacher
b Carbon, Ind, Nov 5, 1882; d Milwaukee, Wis, Oct 1, 61. Studied in Ger with Hugo Kaun, Nikisch, Kunwald. Founder cond, Terre Haute Symph, 03-07. Guest cond, Waldenberg & Goerlitz, Ger, 13. Founder cond, Milwaukee Civic Orch, 21-25; cond, Milwaukee Symph, 26. Head theory, comp depts, Wis Cons, Wis Col Music, Milwaukee Inst Music, 22-28. *Songs & Instrumental Works:* Symphony of the City (Traffic (1st prize, NBC Contest), City Shadows, Speed, City Lights); Symphony of the Land; Escapade; 2 Symphonic Impressions (1st prize, Chicago Symph Golden Jubilee, Juilliard Award); A Little Symphony; Concerto Grosso; Symphony No 4 in F; Symphony No 6 in G; Image of America; Ballet of the Vitamins; Escort to Glory; Argonauts of '49; Kaintuckee (opera); Choral: The Fog Bell; The Road of the Bander-Log; The Candle; A Ballad of Beowulf; Ah's Gwine to Heb'n.

EPSTEIN, DAVID M   ASCAP 1963
composer, conductor, professor
b New York, NY, Oct 3, 30. Educ: Antioch Col, AB; New Eng Cons Music, MM; Brandeis Univ, MFA; Princeton Univ, PhD; studied comp with Roger Sessions, Darius Milhaud & Irving Fine. Music critic, Musical Am, 56-57; music dir, Educ Broadcasting Corp, New York, 62-64. Guest cond, Royal Philh, Cleveland Orch, Vienna Tonkuenstler, Czech Radio Orch & others. Recordings for Vox & DGG; arr, Everest, CRI & EMI. Asst prof, Antioch Col, 57-62; assoc prof, Mass Inst Technol, 65-69, prof, 69- *Songs:* Music: The Seasons; Fancies; Five Scenes for Chorus; The Concord Psalter; also four songs for soprano, solo horn, and string orch. *Instrumental Works:* Night Voices; String Trio; String Quartet 1971; Fantasy Variations for Solo Viola or Violin; Sonority-Variations; Vent-ures.

EPSTEIN, DONALD K   ASCAP 1962
author
b Chicago, Ill, May 4, 33. Educ: Northwestern Univ, Evanston, Ill, BS(speech), 54. TV producer & writer of major musical & event specials for all 3 networks & syndications. Producer & writer of indust shows & films.

ERDMAN, ERNIE   ASCAP 1920
composer
b Pittsburgh, Pa, Oct 23, 1879; d Rockford, Ill, Nov 1, 46. Pianist in Original New Orleans Jazz Band. Professional staff, Chicago music publ. Chief Collabs: Gus Kahn, Ted Fiorito, Robert King, Elmer Schoebel, Billy Meyers. *Songs:* Toot Toot, Tootsie, Goodbye; Nobody's Sweetheart; Jean; Underneath Hawaiian Skies; Ireland and Someone I Love; No No Nora; The Waltz That Made You Mine; Sail on, Silv'ry Moon; I'm Going Back, Back, Back to Carolina; The Little Red School.

ERDMAN, THEODORE JOHN   ASCAP 1959
composer
b Horicon, Wis, Mar 26, 30. *Songs:* Hear My Silent Prayers.

ERDODY, LEO   ASCAP 1942
composer, author, conductor
b Chicago, Ill, Dec 17, 1888; d Los Angeles, Calif, Apr 5, 49. Educ: Studied violin with Joachim & Wirth; Royal High Sch Music, Berlin, studied with Max Bruch. Comp & cond for films; violinist. *Songs & Instrumental Works:* Random Thoughts; Only a Song; Never to Know; Come Along; A Little Song; Senorita Chula. *Scores:* Opera: Peasants Love; The Terrible Meek.

ERICKSON, FRANK WILLIAM   ASCAP 1953
composer
b Spokane, Wash, Sept 1, 23. Educ: Studied comp with Mario Castelnuovo-Tedesco, 47-48; Univ Southern Calif, MM, 51. Comp, concert band music. Lectr in orchestration, Univ Calif, Los Angeles, 58. Prof comp & theory, San Jose State Univ, 59-61. Over 100 publ original works for concert band. *Instrumental Works:* Taccata for Band; Air for Band; Fantasy for Band; Balladair; Deep River Suite; Little Suite for Band; Symphonette for Band; Sonatina for Band; Rhythm of the Winds; Blue Ridge Overture; Overture Jubiloso; First Symphony for Band; Second Symphony for Band; Double Concerto for Trumpet, Trombone and Band; Concerto for Saxophone and Band.

ERIKSSON, WALTER ALGOT   ASCAP 1973
composer, teacher, musician
b Brooklyn, NY, May 30, 26. Educ: High Sch Music & Art, studied accordion with Eric Olzen. Specialized in Scandinavian Music, arr folios on Scandinavian Music, TV & radio work; toured Scandinavian countries. Knighted by King of Sweden, Carl XVI Gustaf. Now teacher, comp, accordionist. Chief Collabr: Andrew Walter. *Instrumental Works:* Amerikanska Jularbo Vals; Hemlangtan; Farfars Schottis; Per Eriks Vals; Finska Polkan.

ERNSBERGER, JAMES E   ASCAP 1974
author
b La Grange, Ind, Aug 13, 38. Educ: Ind Univ. Chief Collabs: Dean Kay, Roger Perry, Craig Bartock. *Songs:* Lyrics: Do Apples Look Like Oranges; Whatcha Doin' With Your Love Tonight.

ERRANTE, BELISARIO ANTHONY   ASCAP 1972
composer, author, arranger
b New York, NY, Jan 12, 20. Educ: NY Univ, BS(music educ), MA(music educ), 50, studied violin with Wesley Sontag & piano with Roger Boardman. Master Sgt, USA, 41-46. Music teacher strings, Ellenville Pub Schs, 51-54; chmn, Music Dept, orch dir & dir, Summer Music Prog, 54-; adjudicator, solo festivals & guest cond for country & other festivals. Mem, NYSSMA, Music Educ Nat Conf, Am String Teachers Asn & Sinfonia Fraternity. *Instrumental Works:* Tardecita (orch); Three Trio Etudes for Flutes; Schizzo Moderno (woodwind quintet); Terzetto in G Minor (clarinet trio); Suite Chinois (orch), plus others.

ERRICO, GREGORY VINCE   ASCAP 1975
composer, drummer, producer
b San Francisco, Calif, Sept 1, 48. Educ: Jefferson High Sch; studied basic fundamental music, Univ Calif, Los Angeles; self taught drummer. Drummer Drumer at age 14, also with The Family Stone, 67-71. As drummer toured with Weather Report, Peter Frampton, David Bowie, Santana, Electra & others, Japan, Europe & US. Record producer for Lee Oskar, Ike White, Betty Davis, Giants (MCA). Chief Collabr: Lee Oskar. *Songs:* Music: I Remember Home (a peasant symph); B L T; Feelin' Happy; San Francisco Bay.

ERWIN, GEORGE (PEE WEE)   ASCAP 1946
composer, trumpeter
b Falls City, Nebr, May 30, 13. Educ: High Sch, Kansas City, Mo; studied with Joseph Schillinger & Michael Feviesky. Jazz trumpeter, dance bands incl: Joe Haymes, Isham Jones, Freddie Martin, Ray Noble, Benny Goodman, Glenn Miller & Tommy Dorsey, 31. Own albums on United Artists, Cadence, Brunswich, Urania. Staff musician, radio, TV, recording cos. Jazz soloist, festivals & concerts, US, Europe, Far East & Africa, on tour. Chief Collabs: Willard Robison, Spencer Williams, Ralph Douglas, Robert Effros. *Songs:* Music: Music Southern Style; Crazy Over You; Stay on the Train. *Instrumental Works:* Creole Rag; Jazz Frappe.

ERWIN, LEE ORVILLE ASCAP 1948
composer, organist
b Huntsville, Ala, July 15, 08. Educ: Huntsville High Sch; Huntsville Jr Col; Cincinnati Cons Music, BM, 37; comp study with Nadia Boulanger & organ with Andre Marchal, Paris, France. Distinguished Alumnus, Col Cons Music, Cincinnati, 79. Organist, First Methodist Church, Birmingham, Ala, Alabama Theatre & Loews Temple Theatre, Birmingham. Staff musician, radio sta WLW, Cincinnati, Ohio, 11 yrs & CBS, NY, 22 yrs. Theatre organist & comp music scores for numerous silent films, also popular songs & church organ music. Chief Collabrs: Mel Howard, Ted Creech. *Songs:* Music: There Ought to Be a Society; Dance Me Loose; Hello Sunshine; Mighty Navy Wings. *Scores:* Films: The General; College; Go West; Sherlock, Jr; The Navigator; Seven Chances; Three Ages; The Sap Head; Steamboat Bill, Jr; Battling Butler; Queen Kelly; Langdon Films: The Strong Man: Tramp, Tramp, Tramp; The Chaser; Three's a Crowd.

ESCOSA, JOHN BRISCOE, SR ASCAP 1976
composer, author, harpist
b Ft Wayne, Ind, Oct 25, 28. Educ: Arthur Jordan Cons; Juilliard Sch Music, studied with Carlos Salzedo, Richard Ellsasser, Gardner Read & Fabian Sevitzky. Musical dir, Ft Wayne Ballet, Civic Theatre & Arena Dinner Theatre. Organist choirmaster, UCC, 22 yrs; teacher jazz harp, summers, Univ Calif, Santa Barbara. Tours US & Can, Columbia Artists Mgt, Inc, New York, 64- *Instrumental Works:* Trompe L'Oeil; Three Dances for Two Harps.

ESKOVITZ, BRUCE LOUIS ASCAP 1976
composer, musician
b Los Angeles, Calif, Feb 2, 55. Educ: University High Sch; Calif State Univ, Northridge; studied woodwinds with Don Menza, 68-72 & Vic Morosco, 76-80; studied improvisation, Warne Marsh, 75-78. Saxophonist, nightclubs, TV & radio commercials, also in theatre orch, "Beatlemania" & "Timbuktu." Comp, Merv Griffin Orch. *Instrumental Works:* Nova Tique; Down the Line; Damien's Dance; Fantasy Nights; No Name for Now.

ESROM, D A
See Morse, Theodora

ESSER, CARL ASCAP 1969
composer, author
b Mobile, Ala, July 1, 35. Educ: Univ Hawaii, Phi Kappa Phi; Univ Calif, Los Angeles, BA(theatre arts, cum laude), 57. Actor in movies "South Pacific", "F I S T" & Bway show "Half a Sixpence"; author & comp, "Neighbors," a rock musical produced in New York, DC & Los Angeles; song writer for films "People Who Care", "Carnal Haven" & "Day of the Balloons"; star of TV series, "Campus Canteen." Best supporting actor, 55; best actor, 57. Mem, Acad TV Arts & Sci Workshop, 62- Marshall Award for best new musical, "East River Anthology," 79. *Songs:* Seven Lumps of Sugar; My Lady; Midnight Woman; People Who Care.

ESTELLE, VICKI
See Harrington, Vicki

ESTES, RICHARD
See Dickey, Richard Scott

ESTRELLA, JOSEPH C ASCAP 1963
composer, author, musician
b Philippines, Aug 14, 08; d. Educ: High sch. Teacher. *Songs:* Malayan Rose; Beautiful Eyes.

ETTORE, EUGENE ASCAP 1958
composer, author, horn player
b New Bedford, Mass, June 2, 21. Educ: Studied theory, counterpoint, comp form, orchestration with Gene Von Hallberg & Edwin Bave. Ed & arr for Pietro Deiro Publ; arr solo, duets & band works for piano, recorder, melodica & accordion. Author, bks: "Ettore Course", 6 bks for accordion; "Nine Supplementary Study Books for Accordion"; "Course for French Horn." Chief Collabr: Richard C Moore. *Instrumental Works:* Five O'Clock Rush; Manhattan Concerto; Pioneer Concerto; Spanish Holiday; Conflict Over (band).

EUGSTER, (DONALD) CARL ASCAP 1957
composer, author
b Hollywood, Calif, Apr 14, 25. Educ: Univ Southern Calif, studied with Ernst Toch; Univ Calif, Los Angeles; Los Angeles State Col, BA, music comp. Free-lance comp, author of musicals. Spec material & arrangements for Frankie Laine, Monique Van Vooren. Chief Collabrs: Harry Haldane; picture songs & recordings with Michel Legrand, Peter Matz, Nicholas Carras & others. *Songs:* Midnight on a Rainy Monday; A Kiss Can Change the World; Do Something; Feel it Deep, Say it Simple; It Takes a While; You're My Four Seasons; Love Doesn't Hurt a Bit; Don't Wear Your French Perfume; When a Bashful Young Lady; Who Knows What Love Is?; The Call of Love; Let's Try It!; Nightcap; The Flashing Blade. *Scores:* Opera/Ballet: Cantabile 1976 (for symph orch); Bway shows: Love for Love; H C Andersen; TV/Film: The Djinn of Winn.

EVANS, DALE
See Rogers, Frances Octavia

EVANS, ERNEST (CHUBBY CHECKER) ASCAP 1964
composer, author, singer
b Philadelphia, Pa, Oct 3, 41. Popularized var dances incl the Twist. Appeared on TV, in theatres & films; recording artist. *Songs:* Spread Joy; She Said.

EVANS, JAMES RODERICK ASCAP 1970
composer, author, teacher
b Willard, Ohio, July 13, 30. Educ: New York Col Music; Ashland Col, MusB; comp studies with Eric Katz & Noble Cain. Music teacher, pub jr high & high schs, 60-; dir, Mansfield Master Singers male chorus; founder & dir, Lexington Community Choral Soc & Scioto Musicke Consort, a Renaissance group. Singer & instrumentalist. *Songs:* Unto the Lord, O Sing Ye (SATB); A Joyful Song to God (SATB); Gladness Is Ours, Halleluja; Glorious Thy Work, O Lord of Hosts (SATB); Festival Alleluia (SATB).

EVANS, JEAN MARIE
See Palumbo, Camille Marie

EVANS, LEE ASCAP 1960
composer, author, pianist
b Bronx, NY, Jan 7, 33. Educ: High Sch of Music & Art, New York, 51; NY Univ, BA, MA, 57; Columbia Univ, MA, 58, EdD, 78. Musical contractor for var artists incl Tom Jones & Engelbert Humperdinck, Emerson, Lake & Palmer, 70-. Music dir, Americana Hotel, New York, 64-70; concert tour for Columbia Artists mgt, 65-75; recording artist with 7 albums for var recording cos. *Songs:* Tongue Twister; 1950's Rock 'n Roll; Music: Crystal Heart. *Instrumental Works:* Keyboard Techniques in Jazz; The Elements of Jazz; Beginning Jazz Improvisation; Learning to Improvise Jazz Accompaniments; Teachers' Blues; Theme of Love; Ladybird; Funky Night.

EVANS, MARION ASCAP 1958
composer, conductor
b Goodwater, Ala, May 1, 26. *Songs:* The Day the West Was Swung; Music: Make Me Laugh; To the Movies We Go; Three; Sorta Nice.

EVANS, PAUL ASCAP 1957
composer, author, singer
b New York, NY, Mar 5, 38. Educ: Andrew Jackson High Sch, Queens, NY; Columbia Univ, 1 yr. Singer 59-60, now writer & pop jingle singer, New York. Chief Collabrs: Al Byron, Paul Parnes, Reardon, Fred Tobias. *Songs:* When; Happy-Go-Lucky Me; Roses Are Red, My Love (No 1 on Billboard Charts); Happiness Is; Think Summer; Feelin'; Followed Closely By My Teardrops; There's a Fool Born Every Minute; Forget Me Not; Hello, This Is Joannie (The Telephone Answering Machine Song (No 32 on Billboard's Country Charts & No 4 in the English Pop Charts); Seven Little Girls; Midnite Special. *Scores:* Bway Show: Loot; Film/TV: Live Young.

EVANS, RAYMOND BERNARD ASCAP 1945
author
b Salamanca, NY, Feb 4, 15. Educ: Salamanca High Sch, 31. Wharton Sch; Univ Pa, BS(economics), 36. Began career in New York, then Livingston & Evans became proteges of famous stage, screen & vaudeville team of Olsen & Johnson. To Calif, contract writer, Paramount Studios, 45-55, free-lance at all Hollywood studios; did spec material & acts for Betty Hutton, Mitzi Gaynor, Joel Grey, Cyd Charisse & Polly Bergen. Mem, Songwriters' Hall of Fame. Chief Collabrs: Jay Livingston, Victor Young, Henry Mancini, Percy Faith, Max Steiner, Neal Hefti. *Songs:* Lyrics: G'Bye Now; To Each His Own; Buttons and Bows; Golden Earrings; I'll Always Love You; Silver Bells; Never Let Me Go; Mona Lisa; A Thousand Violins; The Ruby and the Pearl; Que Sera Sera; Tammy; All the Time; His Own Little Island Island; Dreamsville; Mr Lucky; Dear Heart; In the Arms of Love; Wish Me a Rainbow; Maybe September; As I Love You; Almost in Your Arms; Through Children's Eyes; Home Cookin'; My Love Loves Me; Stuff Like That There; Lyrics theme songs for TV shows: Bonanza; Mr Ed; To Rome With Love. *Scores:* Bway Shows: Oh Captain!; Let It Ride; Sugar Babies.

EVANS, REDD (LOUIS) ASCAP 1943
composer, author, publisher
b Meridian, Miss, July 6, 12; d Scarsdale, NY, Aug 29, 72. Educ: Univ Ariz; Kent Col. Singer & ocarina soloist, then saxophonist & clarinetist in dance orchs incl Teddy Wilson & Horace Heidt. Founded own music publ, record firms. Chief Collabr: David Mann. *Songs:* Pushin' Along; The Major and the Minor; Rosie the Riveter; He's 1-A in the Army; Are You Livin', Old Man?; There I've Said It Again; Unconditional Surrender; This Is the Night; Made Up My Mind; American Beauty Rose; No Moon at All; Let Me Off Uptown; The Frim Fram Sauce; Don't Go to Strangers; Gobs of Love (for USN); Birmingham Jailhouse; Walking Down to Washington (new lyric); If Love Is Good to Me.

EVANS, RHYS STERLING ASCAP 1967
composer, author, singer
b St Paul, Minn, July 26, 23. Educ: Univ Minn, BA & BS. Began songwriting, 30's. Radio show, Los Angeles, late 40's; staff vocalist, radio, Minneapolis & St Paul, 50; singer several appearances, TV, 50's. Piano & vocals entertainer, night

clubs, hotels & others, 62- Songs publ & recorded, 67- Recording artist, Turtle Records & Reva Records. *Songs:* Jeannie in Her Bikini; A Feather Fell From a Sparrow; I Remember St Paul; The Devil Train; Ev'ning.

EVANS, RICHARD
See Kunitz, Richard E

EVANS, WILLIAM ROBERT, III (BUTCH)   ASCAP 1976
composer, arranger, reed player
b Camden, NJ, May 13, 40. St Petersburg Sr High Sch, Fla, 59; Berklee Col Music, Boston, Mass (Downbeat Scholarship Award, 64); Univ SFla, Tampa, BA(anthropology), 69; studied with Herb Pomeroy, John LaPorta, Joe Viola. Woodwind player & arr staff, US Third Army Band, 61-63; saxophone player, arr & comp, var road bands. Taught at Berklee Col Music, 70. Now staff arr, Walt Disney World, Orlando, Fla, 72-; recordings, radio, TV, commercials for Disneyworld & Disneyland; comp & arr, Doc Severinsen's "Tonight Show" Band, NBC-TV, 76- *Instrumental Works:* Moon Monkey; Dear John; Main Street Strut.

EVENS, CLIFFORD ROBERT   ASCAP 1978
composer
b Riverside, Calif, Apr 25, 52. Played guitar & piano since age 12; played in clubs & small concerts; recorded songs, Hollywood, 75. Chief Collabrs: Mike Sherlock, James Brewer, Art Fisher. *Songs & Instrumental Works:* Stop; Take Your Life; I Do Believe; A Child in This World.

EVERETT, HORACE
See Johns, Erik

EVERITT, RICHARD M   ASCAP 1962
author
b Atlanta, Ga, Oct 28, 35. Educ: Ithaca Col, BS. Chief Collabr: Laurence Stith. *Songs:* More Than I Should; One Summer Love; Every Time Is the First Time; It's Just a Matter of Time; Maybe Soon.

EVERLY, (ISAAC) DONALD   ASCAP 1970
composer, author, singer
b Brownie, Ky, Feb 1, 37. Educ: West High Sch, Knoxville. Singer, recording artist, Cadence, 57-60, Warner Bros, 60-70, RCA, 71-72, ODE, 70 & 74 & Hickory Records, 76. Mem, The Grand Ole Opry. On radio "The Everly Family Show," 45-55 & "The Everly Brothers," 57-72, now comp, author & singer. *Songs:* I'm Tired of Singing My Song in Las Vegas; Evelyn Swing; Green River; Turn the Memories Loose Again.

EWELL, DONALD TYSON   ASCAP 1964
composer, pianist
b Baltimore, Md, Nov 14, 16. Educ: Peabody Cons, Baltimore, Md, comp scholarship. Devoted career to Am Jazz; played with Bunk Johnson, Kid Ory, Sidney Bichet, Jack Teagarden, Muggsy Spanier, Eddie Cordon, Bobby Hackett & others. Toured Europe, Asia & Australia several times. Plays only selected concerts, fests & tours. *Instrumental Works:* Delmar Drag; Parlor Social; Frisco Rider; Walleritis; Migrant Worker Blues.

EYERMANN, ALBERT TIMOTHY   ASCAP 1977
composer
b Philadelphia, Pa, July 20, 46. Educ: Duquesne Univ, BA(music) & BS(music); Peabody Cons, Baltimore, Md, masters studies. With Airmen of Note Air Force Jazz Ens, 4 yrs. Player with Mike Douglas, Nancy Wilson, Donald Byrd & Jack McDuff. Scored three films; many jingle & record dates, New York, Philadelphia & Washington, DC. Outstanding jazz soloist, Williamsport Jazz festival, Nat Asn Jazz Educ Award. *Instrumental Works:* Catherine; The Skipper; Soft Touch; Bogatau. *Albums:* Unity; Gorilla; Alo Ha-Ha.

EYMANN, DALE WEBER   ASCAP 1967
composer, conductor, teacher
b Graymont, Ill, Apr 5, 16. Educ: Pontiac High Sch; Ill Wesleyan Univ, BMus & MMusEd; Univ Mich; Univ Southern Calif, Gen Admin Credential. Music teacher pub schs, Mich & Calif; dir, Los Angeles Symph Band, 15 yrs; dir, South Gate City Youth Band, 30 yrs. Comp & arr of many instrumental works. *Instrumental Works:* Beguine for Band; Poco Acapulco; Castle Mountain Overture; Ballad and Bounce; Great Gate of Kiev (Moussorgsky-Eymann); Process of the Sardar (Ippolitv-Ivanov-Eymann).

EZELL, HELEN INGLE   ASCAP 1958
composer, pianist, teacher
b Marshall, Okla, May 18, 03. Educ: Juilliard Sch; Columbia Univ; Univ Okla, BFA; studied with Faye Trumball, Clarence Bing, Jacques Abram, Digby Bell, Lyle Dowling, Otto Luening, Henry Cowell, Spencer Norton, Violet Archer. Author, music bks for beginners, "We Two" & "Small Fry." *Instrumental Works:* Oklahoma Windmill; Louisiana Levee; A Lovely Day; Pollyanna; River Boat; Ghost Town; Square Dance; Two Pigeons.

F

FABER, WILLIAM E   ASCAP 1942
author
b New York, NY, Oct 5, 02; d Yorktown Heights, NY, Apr 7, 67. Educ: NY Univ. WW I, 102nd Engrs. Chief Collabrs: Ernie Burnett, Larry Royal, Fred Meadows, Larry Fotine, John Kamano, Andy Iona Long, Bert Mann. *Songs:* You Were Only Fooling; I'm a Lonely Little Petunia in an Onion Patch; If I Live to Be a Hundred; No Hard Feelings; Too Long, Too Long; Why Do Peanuts Whistle?; Caught in a Dream; Dream Another Dream; Waltz With Me.

FAGAN, SCOTT WILLIAM   ASCAP 1968
composer, author, actor
b New York, NY, Aug 26, 45. Educ: Charlotte Amalie High Sch, St Thomas, VI. Recording artist, Columbia, Atco, Epic & RCA. Writer, Hill & Range, 66, Touchstone, 67-69, Metromedia, 69-70, Screen Gems, 70-71, E B Marks, 71-72 & S&S Fagan, 72- Bway rock opera "Soon," 71 & Mark Tabor Forum, Los Angeles, 72. Chief Collabrs: Joe Kookoolis, Mort Shumman. *Songs:* Soon; Roll Out the Morning; Please Be Well; Surrender to the Sun; Everybody Loves a Winner; Mademoiselle; What Are You Doing After the War; Crystal Ball; Ghetto Fighter; Tutsie/LaBeign Carousel; Sure Has Been Good.

FAGAN, THOMAS O (TOMMY DELL)   ASCAP 1960
composer, singer
b Augusta, Ga, Feb 10, 36. Exclusive writer for 2 yrs with Claridge Music & Milean Music. Recording artist, Swann Records, Philadelphia, Pa & Hickory Records, Nashville, Tenn. Chief Collabr: Robert E Fagan (bro). *Songs & Instrumental Works:* The Beggar; This Little World; That's It; Fabulous Night; Jail Break; Mr James; Just Two Young People; God's Duet; Tiger Tamer.

FAGAS, JAMES JIMMIE (DIMITMOS PHAGAS)   ASCAP 1958
composer, conductor, arranger
b New York, NY, July 19, 24. Educ: NY Sch Indust Art; studied guitar with Hy White; Greenwich House Music Sch. With US troops, Italian Campaign, 3 yrs. Wrote music. Asst to D'Artega on TV "Startime," then with David Broekman, NBC's "Wide, Wide World," also comp, arr & cond the show; formed own production co. Chief Collabrs: Ed Reveaux, Gordon Auchincloss, Jerome Alpen, Ken Darby. *Songs:* Something Strange; Music: Talk, Talk, Talk (Bell Tel Exhibit, Expo '61). *Instrumental Works:* Futurama Suite (At GM Exhibit, world's fair). *Scores:* Film/TV: Never Kiss a Stranger; Pumpkin People; Connie's Song.

FAIN, SAMMY   ASCAP 1926
composer, singer, pianist
b New York, NY, June 17, 02. Educ: Pub sch; high sch; self-taught piano & music. On staff with music publ; performed & sang on radio, stage & made records, also TV. Wrote songs & scores for motion pictures & Bway shows, NY & Hollywood. Under contract to Warner Bros, MGM, 20th Century Fox & Paramount. Bd dir, ASCAP. Elected to Songwriters Hall of Fame. Awards: 10 Acad Award Nominations; 2 Oscars; 2 Laurel Awards; Int Dipl Di Benemeranza; Hall of Artists, Nice, France; The Agosto Messinese Gold Award, Italy & Nashville Country Music Award. Chief Collabrs: Irving Kahal, Paul Francis Webster, E Y Harburg, Lew Brown, Jack Yellen, Bob Hilliard, Sammy Cahn, Harold Adamson, Howard Dietz, Alan & Marilyn Bergman, Dan Shapiro, Mitchell Parish. *Songs:* Katie; Music: The Springtime Cometh; I Left My Sugar Standing in the Rain; Here's to Your Illusions; Please Don't Say No, Say Maybe; The Gift of Love; Let a Smile Be Your Umbrella; Wedding Bells Are Breaking Up That Old Gang of Mine; When I Take My Sugar to Tea; You Brought a New Kind of Love to Me; Was That the Human Thing to Do; By a Waterfall; That Old Feeling; I Can Dream, Can't I; I'll Be Seeing You; Are You Having Any Fun; Something I Dreamed Last Night; Love Is a Random Thing; Dear Hearts and Gentle People; I'm Late; The World Is Your Balloon; April Love (Acad nomination); A Certain Smile (Acad nomination); A Very Precious Love (Acad nomination); Tender Is the Night (Acad nomination); Secret Love (Acad Award, 53); Love Is a Many Splendored Thing (Acad Award, 55); Someone's Waiting for You (Acad nomination); A World That Never Was (Acad nomination); Strange Are the Ways of Love (Acad nomination); The Dickey Bird Song; Ev'ry Day; Happy in Love. *Instrumental Works:* March of the Cards. *Scores:* Bway Shows: Helzapoppin; Sons o' Fun; George White's Scandals; Around the World in Eighty Days; Christine; Flahooley; Ankles Aweigh; Film/TV: Alice in Wonderland; Peter Pan; Mardi Gras; April Love; Calamity Jane; Lucky Me; Three Sailors and a Girl; A Diamond for Carla; The Milkman; The Jazz Singer.

FAIR, CHARLES B   ASCAP 1957
author
b Ranger, Tex, Jan 16, 21. Educ: Tex Tech, BS. Chief Collabrs: Anita Leonard, John Cacavas, Don Rodney. *Songs:* Over and Over; Tell Me, Tell Me; The Colors of Christmas; Christmas Time, Merry Time.

FAIR, MELVIN ANTHONY   ASCAP 1958
composer, author
b New York, NY, Sept 19, 39. Son of Cat Anderson; singer, 50's & 60's, then started playing guitar, 70's. Worked at the Apollo Theater & the Howard, DC. Now touring with Wilson Picket & others. *Songs:* I Wonder Why.

FAIRCHILD, CRAIG E   ASCAP 1972
composer, author, singer
b Milwaukee, Wis, May 21, 49. Educ: Wauwatosa East High Sch; Univ Wis, Milwaukee, BA. Rock musician, keyboards & vocals. Recording artist, A&M Records; studio work, Los Angeles. Chief Collabr: Tony Dancy. *Songs:* Never Gonna Leave My Rock 'n' Roll; In No Hurry; Sing Song; Being With You; Everything I Do.

FAIRCHILD, EDGAR   ASCAP 1942
composer, pianist, conductor
b New York, NY, June 1, 1898; d Los Angeles, Calif, Feb 20, 75. Educ: Juilliard (scholarship); studied with Percy Goetschius. Led own trio, also two piano teams. Cond orch on radio network progs. Featured pianist in Bway musicals. Dir, Aeolian Recording Dept; made many recordings. Collabrs: Jack Brooks, Milton Pascal, Vic Knight. *Songs:* Gotta Go to Work Again; I Made Arrangements With the Moon; Gee! It Was a Beautiful Song; Lady Precious Stream; These 'n' That 'n' Those; Moon In the Parlor; Recipe for Love; Are You Listenin' Joe?; I Can't Get You Out of My Mind. *Scores: Films:* Here Come the Co-Eds (also dir); She Wrote the Book (also dir).

FAIRCLOUGH, THOMAS H   ASCAP 1957
composer, organist
b Morris, Ill, Dec 31, 05; d. Educ: Bus col. Organist at own roller skating rink. Chief Collabr: Eddie Ballantine. *Songs:* (You're Happy When You) Dance; Merry Christmas to Michael; Whistlin' Bar.

FAIRLIE, KENNETH MACLEOD   ASCAP 1972
composer, author
b Montreal, Que, June 14, 38. Educ: Sir George Williams Univ, Montreal, BA; Whittier Col, Calif, MA. Chief Collabr: Scott Seely. *Songs: Lyrics:* I'm the Man.

FAIRMAN, GEORGE   ASCAP 1924
composer, author
b Front Royal, Va, Dec 3, 1881; d Miami, Fla, Oct 16, 62. Educ: Pub schs. Trumpeter in minstrel shows & circuses. Pianist in cafes & vaudeville. *Songs:* The Preacher and the Bear; Way Down South; Hello America, Hello; Forever and Forever; Not in a Thousand Years; I Don't Know Where I'm Going.

FAISON, JOSEPHINE PROFFITT
See Dee, Sylvia

FAITH, PERCY   ASCAP 1949
composer, conductor, pianist
b Toronto, Can, Apr 7, 08; d Encino, Calif, Feb 9, 76. Educ: Toronto Cons, studied with Louis Waizman & Frank Wellsman. Pianist in film theatres, later in dance bands. Cond own orch in radio, 31. Became staff arr-cond, Canadian Broadcasting Corp. To US in 40. Played on radio shows incl "The Carnation Hour", "The Woolworth Hour" & "The Coca Cola Hour", 40-50, then to TV. Chief Collabr: Carl Sigman. *Songs & Instrumental Works:* Music Through the Night; Cheerio; March of the Junior Scouts; Buy a Bond for Victory; The Snow Goose; Aphrodite; Noche Caribe; Perpetual Notion; Nervous Gavotte; Contrasts; Brazilian Sleighbells; My Heart Cries for You; The Love Goddess; Carefree; The Virginian Theme.

FAITH, RICHARD BRUCE   ASCAP 1967
composer, pianist, teacher
b Evansville, Ind, Mar 20, 26. Educ: Chicago Musical Col, BM & MM, 52, studied with Rudolph Ganz; Ind Univ, 54-56; St Cecelia Cons, Rome, Italy, Fulbright scholar, 60-61. Appeared as pianist in recital, Orch Hall & as soloist, Chicago Symph, 49. Prof piano, Morningside Col, Sioux City, Iowa, 56-60; prof music, Univ Ariz, 61- Pianist & comp, recitals in Italy, 60-61; premiere of opera "Sleeping Beauty," Tucson; tour of Eng with cantata "The Waters of Babylon," 76. Chief Collabr: Michel Ard. *Instrumental Works:* Fingerpaintings for Piano; Three Sonatinas for Piano; Night Songs for Piano; Sonata for Piano; Five Preludes and a Nocturne for Piano; Concerto for Two Pianos; Movements for Horn and Piano; Elegy for Symphony Orchestra.

FAITH, RUSSELL H   ASCAP 1954
composer, author, pianist
b Horsham, Pa, Jan 28, 29. Educ: Studied Schillenger Syst with Clarence Cox, Hamilton Cons. Teacher, arr, record exec & vocal coach. Played with small groups in nightclubs, on radio & TV. A&R dir, Chancellor Records, 61-64. Singing coach, Andrea McArdle. Wrote string arr for "Yes I'm Ready" (no 3 nat), also arr "Party Lights" (no 5 nat). Chief Collabrs: Clarence Kehner, Robert Marcucci, Peter Deangelis, Richard Rome, Palmer Rakes. *Songs:* Somewhere in Your Heart; Bobbysox to Stockings; Live It Up; Togetherness; That's When the Lyin' Stops (ASCAP Award); Hello Memory; Theme for Jacqueline; Snowbound; Mother Music; Voyage to the Bottom of the Sea; If I Ever Come

Back (ASCAP Award); Classical Love; How; Our Never Ending Love. *Songs & Instrumental Works:* Blood Is Thicker Than Water.

FALANA, LOLA
singer, dancer, actress
Lead dancer, Bway Musical "Golden Boy"; regular summer series, NBC-TV, 75; specials entitled "Lola!," ABC-TV, 75-76; appeared in Bway show, "Doctor Jazz" (Tony nomination); performer nightclubs. Rec'd Theatre World Award, 75.

FANIDI, THEO
See Theofanidis, Iraklis B

FARAGO, MARCEL   ASCAP 1969
composer, teacher, cellist
b Timisoara, Roumania, Apr 17, 24. Educ: Cons Timisoara; Royal Acad Bucharest; Acad Chigiana Siena; Cons Paris; studied with Cassado, Fournier, Bazelaire, Frazzi, Lavagnino & Mizhaud. Mem: Bucharest Symph; Budapest Munic Orch; Cape Town Munic Orch. Principal cellist, Symph Orch, Porto Alegre, Brazil; cellist doubling at the keyboard of the Philadelphia Orch, 55- *Songs & Instrumental Works:* Prayer (cello, piano); Duets (2 celli); Rhythm and Color (perc group); Children's March Orch; Scherzo (3 flutes & orch); Children's Suite (orch); Mazel & Schlimazel, Children's Opera; 6 string quartets; Sonata (2 celli & timpani); One Symphony; Violin Concerto; Cello Concerto; The Fire and the Mountain (cantata); other chamber music works; works for cello.

FARBER, BURTON ALBERT   ASCAP 1959
composer, pianist, conductor
b Brooklyn, NY, June 2, 13. Educ: Erasmus Hall High Sch, Brooklyn, NY; Washington & Lee Univ, Lexington, Va. WLW-Radio & WLW-TV, Cincinnati, Ohio, 34-52. Free-lance cond, pianist & arr, New York, 53-72 & Chicago, 73-; orch leader, Hotel Plaza, New York, 65-72. Chief Collabr: Peter Lind Hayes. *Songs:* Music: Come Down to Winter Haven. *Instrumental Works:* Fountain Square.

FARBER, NATHANIEL C   ASCAP 1958
composer, pianist, arranger
b Chicago, Ill, Jan 20, 18; d Los Angeles, Calif, Sept 14, 75. Educ: Chicago Musical Col; Los Angeles Cons; studied with Ernst Toch, Mario Castelnuovo-Tedesco. Pianist, arr, comp, TV shows featuring Dinah Shore, 8 yrs, Carol Burnett, CBS-TV, 8 yrs, Roy Rogers, Andy Williams & Danny Kaye, also Columbia, RKO & Walt Disney Studios. Chief Collabr: Paul Weston.

FARBERMAN, HAROLD
composer, conductor
b New York, NY, Nov 2, 29. Educ: Seward Park High Sch, NY, 43-47; Juilliard Sch Music, dipl perc, 51, studied timpani & perc with Saul Goodman; New Eng Cons, BS(comp), 54, MS(comp), 56. Mem, Boston Symph Orch, 51-63; cond, New Arts Orch, 57-63, Colorado Springs Symph, 66-71 & Oakland Symph Orch, 71-79. Guest cond: London Symph Orch, BBC, Royal Philh Orch, New Philh Orch, Hessischer Rundfunk, Danish Radio & others. Comns: Denver Symph, Colorado Springs Symph, Oakland Symph, Nat Endowment for Arts & others. Chief Collabr: Barbara Fried. *Songs & Instrumental Works:* Evolution (7 perc, soprano & French horn); Greek Scene (solo mezzo-soprano & orch or mezzo, piano & perc); Elegy, Fanfare and March (orch); New York Times, August 30, 1964 (mezzo, piano, perc); Trio (violin, piano, perc); Concerto (alto saxophone & string orch); If Music Be (jazz singer, rock group, films, symph orch); Great American Cowboy Suite; Progressions (solo flute & perc); Impressions (solo oboe, strings, perc); Mud Rodeo. *Scores:* Operas: Medea; The Losers.

FARGO, MILFORD H   ASCAP 1975
composer, author, teacher
b Alexander, NY, Feb 11, 28. Educ: Attica High Sch; State Univ NY, Col Fredonia, BS, 50, MS(music educ), 54; grad study, Eastman Sch of Music; studied voice with Herbert Beattie, Arthur Kraft, Anna Kaskas; coached with Ralph Vaughn Williams & Josef Krips. Prof of music educ, Eastman Sch of Music, 30 yrs. Singer, opera & oratorio with Buffalo Philh, Rochester Philh & Chautauqua Opera Co; cond of world premieres "Children's Plea for Peace" & "The Truth About Windmills"; guest cond, NY Choral Soc Summer Sing & Rochester Philh in own work "Sing to America" & "Porgy and Bess." Historical researcher early phonograph recordings of Am popular music. Mem, Assoc for Recorded Sound Collections. Chief Collabrs: Dane Gordon, David Romig. *Songs:* The Animals of Christmas; Music: A Family Christ Mass (oratorio); Church Bells and Fishermen. *Scores:* Opera: Away He Run; TV: The Journey.

FARINA, MIMI M
composer, author
b Palo Alto, Calif, Apr 30, 45. Recorded with Vanguard Records, performed with husband, Richard Farina, 64-66. Actress with San Francisco Comt, improvisational review, 68-69. Recorded album with Tom Jans, 72. Exec dir & founder of Bread & Roses, a non-profit social change orgn to bring free live entertainment into insts such as prisons & hospitals, 74. Asst producer, Bread

& Roses Fest, 77-80. Toured clubs & concert halls in US & Europe, 72-80. *Songs:* In the Quiet Morning; Music: Bread and Roses.

FARLEY, EDWARD J ASCAP 1941
composer, author
b Newark, NJ, July 16, 04. Educ: Sacred Heart & St Benedict Prep Sch, Newark. Musician in dance orchs; organized own orch, 35, had own prog, NBC network, also toured US. *Songs:* Music Goes Round and Round; I'm Gonna Clap My Hands; Something in the Wind; You Are the Lyric (To a Love Song in My Heart); Looking for Love; Ophelia; Wrestlers Song.

FARNUM, CHARLES EDWARD ASCAP 1972
composer, singer
b Maquoketa, Iowa, July 28, 51. Educ: Simpson Col, 69-71; Univ Northern Iowa, 74-76; Univ Calif, Los Angeles, songwriter course with Al Kasha. Drummer, singer & writer, The Guys in the Band, 65-71, Happening '69, ABC-TV Battle of Bands, Paul Revere & Raiders Show & ABC-TV Mail Room, 72. Singer, Minn Chorale, Minneapolis, 76-78. PBR announcer, KUNI-FM radio, 76; trio, Midday Show, WCCO-TV, 79. Songwriter, choral, solo & popular songs; some recording. *Songs:* Nightmare 1980; First Comes Love; Growth; Beautiful Children (choral); Thanks for Listenin'.

FARRAR, GERALDINE ASCAP 1936
author, singer
b Melrose, Mass, Feb 28, 1882; d. Educ: Pub schs; studied with Mrs J H Long, Trabadello, Emma Thursby, Lilli Lehmann, Graziani. Operatic debut as Marguerite in "Faust," Royal Opera House, Berlin, 01. With Metrop Opera, New York, 06-22. Appeared in var films incl "Carmen." With Red Cross & Am Women's Voluntary Services, World War II. Lect tours; two autobiographies. *Songs:* Rachmaninoff Music: Ecstasy of Spring; Here Beauty Dwells; The Tryst; The Alder Tree; The Mirage; Oh, Thou Field of Waving Corn; Morning; The Fountain; The Dream; Fritz Kreisler music: Love Comes and Goes; The Whole World Knows; Dear Homeland; Fair Rosemarin; Moussorgsky Music: Tears.

FARRAR, SIDNEY BOB ASCAP 1968
composer, author
b Dallas, Tex, June 16, 28. Educ: North Tex State Univ; Northwestern Univ; Southern Methodist Univ, BA(music comp, jour); comp study with Jack Kilpatrick. Asst dir music, Liberty Broadcasting; prog mgr, KENS-TV; asst creative dir, Commercial Recording Corp, creative dir, PAMS Productions. Formed Farrar Music Productions, 72; independent producer of original music for films, radio-TV advert & promotion. *Scores:* Film/TV: The Athletes (film series); Jot (animated cartoon series); Human Dimension (documentary series).

FARRAR, WALTON T ASCAP 1948
author
b Oakland, Calif, Mar 5, 18; d Los Angeles, Calif, Mar 14, 76. Chief Collab: Walter Kent. *Songs:* Movie Tonight; Uptown Saturday Night; Two Things to Worry About; Just a Friendly Feeling; I Cross My Fingers; The Last Mile Home; Baby I Need You; Sad Cowboy; So Easy to Please; The Beat Generation; Blast Off; Something Called Love; Children's Picnic Song; From the Earth to the Moon; Falling Star; Nothing in the World; Not Mine; A Song and a Prayer; Don't You Care.

FARRELL, KENNETH L ASCAP 1963
composer
b Woodward, Okla, Nov 10, 20. Educ: Northwestern State Univ, BA; Univ Mich, MA; spec studies conducting with Eli Farney; comp & arr, Eric Leidzen, Boris Kremenliev & Frank McCartor. Sec schs instrumental music, 35 yrs. Prof musician; mem, Am Fedn Musicians. *Instrumental Works:* Concert Band: Two Impressions; Escapade; Chica Bum; Latin Reverie; Sons of the Golden West.

FARRER, CARL EDVERT ASCAP 1978
composer
b Austin, Tex, Nov 30, 26. Educ: Govalle Grade Sch, Metz Sch, Allan Jr High, Austin High, Austin; Life Bible Col, Los Angeles. Played guitar & piano by ear at an early age. Was church pianist for many yrs. Traveled as pianist with evangelists all over US. Had own radio prog while at Life Bible Col; was accompanist for many singers. Chief Collab: Audrey Mieir. *Songs:* Holy Hands; His Love; Touch Me, Savior; Adoration; What Was He Looking For.

FARROW, JOHNNY ASCAP 1947
composer
b Philadelphia, Pa, Feb 11, 12. Educ: Zwecker-Hahn Cons, Philadelphia, also studied in Vienna. With vocal group, Tony Pastor Orch, 38-41. On professional staff, Chicago music publ. Owns publ firm. *Songs:* I Have But One Heart; Tara Talara Tala; Formal Night in Harlem; Swinging in a Swing; Catch On; A New Shade of Blues; If You Were There; Memories of Sorrento; If Your Heart Doesn't Dance (It Isn't Love); The Vision of Bernadette (Lady of Lourdes); Monkey See, Monkey Do; Music: Life Begins When You're in Love; Show Me, Show Me; I'm Sorry I Answered the Phone.

FARWELL, ARTHUR ASCAP 1942;
composer, educator
b St Paul, Minn, Apr 23, 1872; d New York, NY, Jan 20, 52. Educ: Baldwin Sem, MIT. Founded Wa-Wan Press, Newton Ctr, Mass, 01. Lectr on Am music, 04-09, staff, Musical Am, 09-15; supvr, Munic Concerts, NY, 10-13. Dir, Music Sch Settlement, NY, 15-18, acting head music dept, Univ Calif, 18-19, head of theory, Music Dept, Mich State Col, 27-39. Composers fel, Pasadena Music & Arts Asn, 21-25. *Songs & Instrumental Works:* Domaine on Hurakan; A Ruined Garden; Pageant Scene; March! March!; Prelude to a Spiritual Drama; Mountain Song Opus 90 (orch in 5 movements with occ chorus); Caliban; Violin Sonata; Piano Quintet; Sonata for Solo Violin; Cello Sonata; Dawn Opus 12 (orch); American Indian Melodies Opus 27 (piano); Navajo War Dance Opus 28 (piano); Mountain Vision (Symbolistic Study No 6; pianos, orch); The Gods of the Mountain Opus 52 (A Suite for Orch); Rudolph Gott Symphony Opus 95; The Hound of Heaven Opus 100 (baritone, orch); Quintet in E Minor Opus 103 (piano, strings); Polytonal Studies Opus 109 (piano solo); The Heroic Breed Opus 115 (orch; dedicated to Gen George S Patton); Spanish Songs of Old California Opus 59; and many others.

FASCINATO, JACK ASCAP 1955
composer
b Bevier, Mo, Sept 11, 15. Culver-Stockton Col, BA; studied harmony with Adolph Weidig, piano, Louise Robyn & comp, Mario Castelnuovo-Tedesco. Music supvr, Hannibal, Mo High Sch. Worked in Chicago dance bands. Arr & conductor for Curt Massey, Dinning Sisters, Kukla, Fran & Ollie, Tennessee Ernie Ford. Have 135 nat products jingle credits. Arr of "Sixteen Tons" for Ernie Ford. Chief Collabs: Ernie Ford, Arthur Hamilton, Harold Spina. *Songs:* Music: Sissy; These Years; God Lives; more than 250 hymn adaptations.

FASMAN, BARRY ALAN ASCAP 1971
composer, arranger, producer
b Chicago, Ill, Oct 9, 46. Educ: Univ Ill, BA. Performed as singer, songwriter & keyboardist with One Eyed Jacks, 66-69; staff producer, RCA/Wooden Nickel Records, 71-74; arr & cond recordings for var singers & singing groups, 73-; music dir-cond for Jose Feliciano, 75-78; cond, Los Angeles Philh, 78. Chief Collabs: Richard Reicheg, Gail Heideman, David Batteau. *Songs:* Blackmail.

FASS, BERNIE (BERNIE TAYLOR, DAVID HALSMAN) ASCAP 1968
composer, author
b New York, NY, Aug 30, 32. Educ: James Monroe High Sch, NY; Hunter Col, NY; theory & comp studies with Morris Fass. Composer, author & record producer. Extensive background in music publishing. Dir production with major record label. Composed & produced childrens songs & record albums for use within the educ syst, US & Can. Chief Collabs: Mack Wolfson, Rosemary Caggiano. *Songs:* Tomorrow is Another Day; Invitation to Love; Come to Where the Love Is; Music: Children are People; The Power Is You.

FAST, LAWRENCE ROGER ASCAP 1975
composer, electronic music producer
b Newark, NJ, Dec 10, 51. Educ: Livingston High Sch, NJ, 69; Lafayette Col, Pa, BA, 73. Free lance electronic musical instrument design, 68-; Synergy all-electronic comp proj recordings, Passport Records, 75-; synthesizer session work, NY & London, 76- *Instrumental Works:* Electronic Realizations for Rock Orchestra; Sequencer; Cords; Games.

FATOR, FINIS EWING ASCAP 1968
composer, singer
b San Antonio, Tex, Dec 23, 47. Educ: Chicago Cons Col, degree in music; studied classical guitar & voice. Singer & comp, Youth for Christ Teen Team, 67 & Up with People 68; mem, The New World Singers, 69-71 & Finis and Marcia, 72-75. Chief Collab: Bob Henley. *Songs:* Lord of My Life; Jesus, I Love You; I Love You; Music: A New Dimension; Loving Is Forever.

FAULKNER, JACK ASCAP 1955
composer, author, musician
b Elmore, Ohio, Jan 20, 18. Educ: Tri-State Univ. Writer of early radio & TV musical commercials; originated singing station breaks. *Songs:* Wherever You Go There's a Radio; Recovery; Sometimes a Dream Comes True; You're No More Than a Minute From Music; Guy With a Dream; Can't Believe a Word You Say; U R the 1 4 Me; What'll We Dream Tonight.

FAUST, RANDALL EDWARD ASCAP 1978
composer, teacher, hornist
b Vermillion, SDak, July 3, 47. Educ: Interlochen Arts Acad; Eastern Mich Univ, BS summa cum laude; Mankato State Univ, MM(comp); Univ Iowa, doctoral study; studied comp with Peter Tod Lewis, Donald Jenni, Rolf Scheurer, Anthony Iannaccone & Warren Benson; studied horn with Paul Anderson, Orrin Olson, Marvin C Howe & Donald Haddad. Fac mem, Shenandoah Col & Con Music, Winchester, Va, 73- Had works performed by or in: Eastern Trombone Workshop, 76; Nat Gallery Art, Washington, DC, 76 & 77; Int Trombone Workshop, Nashville, Tenn, 79; Electronic Music Plus Fest, 79. *Instrumental Works:* Chapel Music for Brass Quintet and Organ; Horn Call for Horn and Electronic Media; Soliloquies: Double Concerto for Solo Tenor Trombone, Solo Bass Trombone and Trombone Octet; Sonata for Bass Trombone; Prelude for Horn (alone); Celebration for Horn and Organ; Concerto

for Brass Quintet, Percussion and Strings (comn by Nat Gallery Orch, 77); Rhapsody for Alto Saxophone, Vibraphone and Electronic Media (comn by Paul Baird, 76-79); Canzona for String Orchestra (Instrumental Div Winner, Minn Fedn Music Clubs, 73); Gallery Music for Brass Quintet.

FAY, SINCLAIR
See Elliott, Marjorie Reeve

FAY, VINCENT MICHAEL   ASCAP 1979
composer, teacher, musician
b Philadelphia, Pa, Feb 29, 52. Educ: Cardinal Dougherty High Sch, studied with Albert Stauffer & Napoleon Cerminara. Began playing bass in grade sch, started writing in high sch; working musician, incl, road tours with Tommy Dorsey & Bernard Pfeiffer, plus theater work; recording artist incl, jingles, records & background; writer for John Davis Productions. Chief Collabr: John E Davis. *Songs:* Music: Holler; Power of Love; Please Don't Break My Heart; Do You Wanna Dance; Baby I Got It; That's What I Get.

FAZIO, SUZANNE M   ASCAP 1979
composer, singer, guitarist
b Bronx, NY, Oct 30, 51. Educ: State Univ NY, New Paltz, BA; Sorbonne, Le Col de France; Vassar Col, BA(philosophy); studied guitar with Beverly Maher; studied voice with Barbara Conrad, Katherine Hager & Arlene Slater-Stone. Played in many clubs incl, Reno Sweenys, The Guitar & Folk City, 74. Original material performed. Singer in many regional commercials & national spots. *Songs:* You Are Not Alone; Sometimes, Someone; Without the Pain of You; The scale model song for The Electric Co TV Show.

FAZIOLI, BERNARDO   ASCAP 1942
composer, author
b Italy, June 21, 1897; d Boston, Mass, Nov 29, 42. Educ: Tufts Med Sch; New Eng Cons. Had own radio prog. Author, "How to Lead an Orchestra." *Songs:* Just Call on Me; Caressing You; You Can Count on Me; Does a Duck Like Water?; Parade of the Little White Mice; The Lonely Little Music Box.

FAZIOLI, BILLY   ASCAP 1923
composer, pianist, arranger
b Frosolone, Italy, Oct 27, 1898; d New York, NY, May 4, 24. Moved to US, 04. Educ: Pub sch; Tufts Col. Entertained in nightclubs; mem, Ray Millers Orch & the Black & White Melodie Boys. *Songs:* Rose of Spain; Music: Rose of Brazil; Who'll Take My Place; Am I to Blame; Little Boy; Underneath the Dixie Moon; Blue Eyed Blues; Some Early Morning; Gimme Blues; Who Cared for Me. *Instrumental Works:* Piano Mania.

FEATHER, LEONARD GEOFFREY   ASCAP 1943
composer, author, lecturer
b London, Eng, Sept 13, 14. Educ: Univ Col Sch, London; St Paul's, London. Comp, musician, critic & concert producer, London, 30's, New York, 40-50 & Los Angeles, 60- Gave first jazz lect series, New Sch, New York, 41-42; many univ lect incl, Harvard Univ, Princeton Univ, Univ Calif, Loyola-Marymount Univ & Calif State Univ, Northridge. Own radio series incl, award winning prog for KUSC, Los Angeles, 77- Grammy Award for album liner Notes, 64; nominated for Emmy Award as producer of Jazz TV Series, 71. Chief Collabrs: Langston Hughes, Andy Razaf, Steve Allen, Dick Hyman. *Songs:* Evil Gal Blues; Salty Papa Blues; Blowtop Blues; Where Were You?; Born on a Friday (Unlucky Woman); How Blue Can You Get?; Counting My Tears; You Could Have Had Me Baby; Lyrics: You Can't Go Home Again; Natural Affection; In Time; Music: Meet Me Halfway; Sounds of Spring; Dedication; Long, Long Journey. *Instrumental Works:* I Remember Bird; Signing Off; Mighty Like the Blues; Twelve Tone Blues; Winter Sequence (suite); I Remember Duke (A Portrait of Duke); Romeo; Bass Reflex (Blues in 5/4); Hi Fi Suite; Smack!; Snafu.

FEDERLEIN, GOTTFRIED HARRISON   ASCAP 1924
composer, organist
b New York, NY, Dec 31, 1883; d Flushing, NY, Feb 26, 52. Educ: Sachs Inst; Trinity Sch. Gave organ recitals; made many records. Organist, Soc for Ethical Culture, 11-21 & Temple Emanu-El, 15-45. Fel, Am Guild Organists. *Scores:* Operetta: Christina of Greenland.

FEESE, FRANCIS L   ASCAP 1963
composer
b La Junta, Colo, Sept 11, 26. Educ: Univ Denver, BME, 50; Univ Northern Colo, 53. Teacher, professional musician, composer & publisher. *Instrumental Works:* Colorado Suite; Jazz Waltz for Strings; Contrasts in E Minor; Young World of Strings; Strings on Stage; Performing Strings.

FEIBEL, FREDERICK   ASCAP 1956
composer, organist, teacher
b Union City, NJ, July 11, 06; d. Educ: High sch. Organist, film theatres incl Paramount, New York, 7 yrs, CBS, 22 yrs, other networks & First Presby Church, Vero Beach, Fla. Author, "Master Course in Organ Playing in the Popular Music Style," 2 vols. *Instrumental Works:* Organ works: Toccata in Blue; The Pixie Patrol; Elegy to a Deserted Homestead; Eastern Postlude; Modern Etudes, Bks I, II, III.

FEIN, MICHAEL S   ASCAP 1976
composer, lyricist
b Bronx, NY, May 11, 51. Educ: Studied piano with A Oliver, New York, 61-69; studied with D Saturn, Farleigh Dickinson Univ, 69-73. Wrote novelty music, 76-78. Lyricist/composer, Calif, 79- *Songs:* Something to Write About; Souvenirs; Lifetime of Love; When I Thought I Was Losin' You. *Instrumental Works:* Where Are All the Years. *Scores:* 9 tunes for Boys Will Be Boys.

FEIN, PEARL   ASCAP 1942
composer, author, dance teacher
b Chicago, Ill, Oct 22, 1900. Educ: Murray F Tuley High Sch, grad; Northwestern Univ, 2 yrs, studied harmony. Advert secretary. Dancing teacher for Arthur Murray Studio, Chicago; trained teachers at Dale Dance Studio, Chicago. Chief Collabrs: Al Dubin, George W Meyer, Murray Bloom. *Songs:* Why Can't I Kiss You; Yankee Doodle Ain't a Doodlin' Now; Lonely Street; Sing a Song of Funnies (bk of 16 songs); Lyrics: Can't You Read Between the Lines; God's Christmas. *Scores:* Musical Drama: Yesterday Ended Last Night.

FEINSMITH, MARVIN PAUL   ASCAP 1977
composer, bassoon player
b New York, NY, Dec 4, 32. Educ: Juilliard Sch Music, dipl, studied bassoon with Simon Kovar & comp with Henry Brant; Mozarteum of Salzburg, dipl; Manhattan Sch Music, BM, 64, MM, 67; NY Univ, grad study for DMA. Played first bassoon, Indianapolis Symph Orch, 56-59; played bassoon, Symphony of the Air, 59-63, Little Orch Soc, 59-68 & 70-72. Was co-principal bassoon player, Israel Philh Orch, 68-70; was solo bassoon player, "Mass," 72; asst principal bassoon player, Denver Symph Orch, 72- Played bassoon in Bway productions: "A Funny Thing Happened on the Way to the Forum"; "Superman"; "Baker Street"; "Cabaret"; "Anya"; "The Rothschilds." *Songs & Instrumental Works:* Sky Sailing; Molly Brown Wouldn't Recognize It Anymore; Peerkay A'Vot—Ethics of the Fathers (symph); Two Hebraic Studies, Isaiah, Yizkor for Bassoon Alone (music for wind instruments); Isaiah (symph for bass/baritone voice, augmented symph orch with sound-sculpture).

FEKARIS, DINO GEORGE   ASCAP 1972
composer, author, producer
b Pittsburgh, Pa, Jan 24, 45. Educ: MacKenzie High Sch, Detroit, Mich; Wayne State Univ, PhB, 68, studied music with Harry Langsford. Began as a vocalist & developed into a songwriter/record producer, Detroit; writer/producer, Motown, 7 yrs, formed, Fekaris-Perren Team, 78. Awards: Grammy Award for Disco Record of the Yr, 80; Platinum & Gold Awards, Recording Indust Asn Am; ASCAP Awards for top ten records & for exceptional songwriting skills & inspiring young songwriters. Chief Collabrs: Freddie Perren; Nick Zesses; Tom Baird. *Songs:* I Will Survive (Grammy nominations for song of the yr, Record of the yr & disco record of the yr, 80); Reunited (Grammy nominations for best song of the yr & best rhythm & blues song, 80); I Just Want to Celebrate; Shake Your Groove Thing; Makin' It; Hey Big Brother; I Pledge My Love.

FELBY, CELETA
See Hart, Cynthia Mary Kathleen

FELCIANO, RICHARD   ASCAP 1967
composer
b Santa Rosa, Calif, Dec 7, 30. Educ: Santa Rosa Jr Col, AA, 50; San Francisco State Col, BA, 52; Mills Col, MA, 55; Paris Cons, 2 dipl; studied with Darius Milhaud at Mills Col & in Paris; Univ Iowa, PhD, 59; studied with Luigi Dallapiccola in Florence, 58-59. Four gen areas of interest, concert music, exp video, environments & liturgical music. Was one of Am pioneers of electronic sound. Wrote "Linearity," first musical work using TV syst as compositional element. Created environments, indoor for Boston City Hall, outdoor for Ft Worth Art Museum. Prof music, Univ Calif, Berkeley. *Songs:* Four Poems From the Japanese (harps, voices). *Instrumental Works:* Crasis (7 players, electronic sounds); Galactic Rounds (orch); The Angels of Turtle Island (4 performers, live electronics); Lumen (soprano, organ); Evolutions (clarinet, piano); Spectra (flute, cymbals); In Celebration of Golden Rain (Indonesian gamelan, organ); Glossolalia (baritone, perc, organ, electronic sounds); Gravities (piano, 4 hands); Mutations (orch); Pentecost Sunday (voices, organ, electronic sounds); Noösphere II (electronic sound).

FELDER, DAVID C   ASCAP 1977
composer, author, electronic synthesist
b Cleveland, Ohio, Nov 27, 53. Educ: Miami Univ, BM(theory/comp), MM, studied with David Cope & W Cummings; Cleveland Inst Music, spec study with Donald Erb, 77-78; Univ Calif, San Diego, studied comp with Roger Reynolds, Barnard Rands, Robert Erickson & computer music with F Richard Moore, 79- Comp & cond of current music; choral cond; performed as synthesist in own works & other electronic music; recording engr; teacher/clinician at prominent cols & univs. *Instrumental Works:* Nexus; Rondage; Continuum; Rocket Summer; Vertices.

FELDER, DONALD WILLIAM
musician
b Gainesville, Fla, Sept 21, 47. Educ: Cent Fla Jr Col, 66-67; Boston Univ, 70. With Continentals Band, 61-64, The Maundy Quintet Band, 64-67, The Flow Band, 67-71 & Crosby-Nash Band, 72-73. Teacher, Hillis Sch Music,

Gainesville, 66-67. Lead guitar & songwriter, The Eagles, 73- Vpres, Eagles Ltd. Rec'd Grammy Awards, Golden Reel Award, Platinum & Gold Records & var rock music awards. Mem, Am Fedn TV & Radio Artists. *Songs:* Visions; Too Many Hands; Hotel California; Victim of Love; Disco Strangler.

FELDER, MICHAEL EARL   ASCAP 1969
composer, author, singer
b New York, NY, Nov 5, 46. Educ: Benjamin Franklin High Sch; Manhattan Community Col. Self taught. Began guitar age 9; formed vocal group & jazz quintet, jr high sch; played in band, Benjamin Franklin High Sch. USA, 64; sang with Romeo Four, Romeo Co, Ft Dix, NJ; toured with Armed Forces acts, Europe. Producer & writer var record labels, incl own Moving Up Productions, 74- Chief Collabr: William Daniels. *Songs:* Somebody's Gotta Go (Sho Ain't Me); Where Do I Stand; Mama (He Treats Your Daughter Good). *Scores:* Films: The Long Night; Death Promise.

FELDMAN, IMOGEN CARPENTER
See Carpenter, Imogen (Jane)

FELDMAN, VICTOR (STANLEY)   ASCAP 1971
composer, arranger, vibraphonist
b London, Eng, Apr 7, 34. Educ: London Col Music; studied film scoring with Leith Stevens & Earl Hagan. At age 6 played drums on conert stage, Eng; appeared on BBC, also with Glenn Miller. Featured in motion pictures & on stage. Toured US with Woody Herman as percussionist; became one of the original Lighthouse All Stars, toured with Cannonball Adderley Quintet as pianist. Has made many records; concerts with Seals & Croft, Los Angeles Express; records with Steely Dan Group. Multi-instrumentalist; drummer. Chief Collabrs: Miles Davis, Tommy Wolfe. *Instrumental Works:* Seven Steps to Heaven; Skippin'; Your Smile; Dance the Night Away.

FELDNER, ROBERTA EMILY (ROBERTA CARR,   ASCAP 1970
ROBERTA STUART)
author, singer, actress
b Brooklyn, NY, June 6, 39. Educ: Westwood High Sch, NJ; Am Acad Dramatic Arts; acting studies with Milton Katselas & John Lehne, voice with Herb Buchanan; Univ Calif, Los Angeles, 76. Acted in stock & off-Bway, 59-62. Mem singing team, Bobbie & Lynn, 62-64. Recorded for Epic Label; played nightclubs. Acted in TV commercials, 66- Appeared in series, "Family," 77 & 79 & film, "Blinded By the Light." Writer musical, bk & lyrics, "Movin' West." Chief Collabrs: Greg Evigan, Herb Buchanan, Pete Dino. *Songs:* Lyrics: Tomorrow; And I'll Never Leave; And You Know I Want You; She's Goin' Home; Time to Let Go.

FELDSTEIN, SAUL (SANDY)   ASCAP 1964
composer, author
b Brooklyn, NY, Sept 7, 40. Educ: State Univ Col, Potsdam, NY, BS(music educ); Columbia Univ, MA(music), DMusEd(comp). Professional performer, comp, cond & clinician. Prof music, State Univ Col, Potsdam, 64-70. Educ dir/exec vpres, Alfred Publ Co, Inc, 70- Author of orch instr bks incl "Alfred's Basic Band Method", "Orchestral Suite for Old St Nick" & "Bartok Rock Bahirava." *Instrumental Works:* Concert Band Comp & Arr incl: Fanfare and March; Bach in Rock; Christmas Variations; Celebration Concert March; Choral Comp & Arr incl: Wind of Life; Hope for the Future; I Want a Harmonica for Hanukah; also perc works. *Songs & Instrumental Works:* Jazz Band Comp & Arr incl: Blowin' the Blues; Suburban Soul; Scarborough Fair.

FELICIANO, JOSE
composer, author, singer
b Lares, PR, Sept 8, 45. Started music at age 3, first pub performance at age 9, became guitarist & performed from Greenwich Village coffeehouses to London Palladium, Greek Theater. Toured Japan, Hawaiian Islands & Europe. Acting debut on "McMillan and Wife," also appeared on "Lucas Tanner," then guest-starred on "Kung Fu"; comedic acting debut on "Chico and the Man"; has appeared on "The Mike Douglas Show", "The Tonight Show", "The Today Show", "Dinah", "Good Morning America" & others. Has been with symph orchs, DC, Cincinnati, Dallas & Denver, headlined at major showrooms incl the Fairmont Hotel, San Francisco & Las Vegas Showrooms, also host of col concerts; has earned 32 Gold Records. Worked with John Lennon & with Joni Mitchell played lead guitar on "Free Man in Paris." Now entertainer, guitarist, singer & comp. Was nominated in four categories & was awarded two Grammy Awards, Nat Acad Recording Arts & Sci, 69. *Songs:* Chico and the Man (theme song, NBC-TV show; Emmy nomination); Feliz Navidad; Essence of Your Love; Destiny; Rain; Music: Aaron Loves Angela. *Instrumental Works:* Affirmation; Disco Flam. *Songs & Instrumental Works:* Light My Fire (Grammy Award); California Dreamin'.

FELL, ARTHUR MARSHALL   ASCAP 1978
composer, pianist
b Bloomington, Ind, Dec 19, 35. Educ: Ind Univ Sch Music, studied piano with Ernst Hoffzimmer, 45-49, Univ, BS, 57, Sch Law, JD, 66. Led jazz group, 52-57;

comp music for Jordan River Rev, 56. *Songs:* Music: Teri's Theme. *Scores:* Musical show: Springtime and Stephanie.

FELL, TOM
See Knight, Vick Ralph, Sr

FELLER, SHERMAN   ASCAP 1951
composer, author
b Brockton, Mass, July 29, 18. Educ: Roxbury Mcm High Sch; Suffolk Univ Law Sch, 40; Emerson Col of Oratory. In radio, 41-; WEEI first talk show in Am, 41. With WROL, Boston. Chief Collabrs: Carl Signan, Mike Dinapoli, Bill Leavitt. *Songs:* Francesca; This Is Heaven; Take Another Chance on Me; Music: Snow! Snow! Beautiful Snow!; Lyrics: Summertime! Summertime!; My Baby's Comin Home; Latin Lady. *Songs & Instrumental Works:* It Doesn't Take Very Long; Why Don't You Go Home for X-mas!; I'm in Love With the Mother of the Girl I Love.

FELLOWS, FLOYD GEORGE (GEORGE FRANK)   ASCAP 1978
composer, author, musician
b Gloversville, NY, May 27, 07. Educ: Rensselaer Polytech Inst, grad engr. Musician & writer/comp, 20- Chief Collabrs: Art Korb, Josh Garrett, Lillian Rottman, Mary Sarlow. *Songs:* If Only You'd Believe; Half a Half a Dollar; A Single Kiss; So Exclusively; Vivienne; Dear Little Girl; Put Your Love Around Me; Music: Where There's a Will; They Say It's Spring.

FENADY, ANDREW JOHN   ASCAP 1959
author
b Toledo, Ohio, Oct 4, 28. Educ: Univ Toledo. Writer-producer, motion pictures & TV series: "The Rebel"; "Branded"; "Hondo"; Movies: "Black Noon"; "The Woman Hunter"; "The Stranger"; "The Hanged Man"; "Sky Heist"; "Mayday 40,000 Feet"; "The Hostage Heart"; Features: "Stakeout on Dope Street"; "The Young Captives"; "Ride Beyond Vengeance"; "Chisum"; "Terror in the Wax Museum"; "Arnold"; "The Man With Bogart's Face." Chief Collabrs: Richard Markowitz, Dominick Frontiere, George Duning. *Songs:* Lyrics: Johnny Yuma Was a Rebel; You Can't Ever Go Home Again; Chisum (Ballad of); Arnold; Looking At You; The Man With Bogart's Face.

FENDELL, MURIEL ROBERTS   ASCAP 1966
composer, pianist, singer
b Bayonne, NJ, Dec 16, 36. Educ: Piano instr, Alexander Lipsky; NY Univ, grad; New York Sch Interior Design, grad. Concert pianist; jazz pianist, major clubs & hotels throughout US & metrop New York; recording artist with Dot-Scepter; mem, Am Acad Music. *Songs:* Music: Ain't Gonna Sing No More Blues. *Instrumental Works:* Advent of Autumn; Winter Waltz (Moon Music); That's Where It's At; Muriel's Theme.

FENDLER, EDVARD   ASCAP 1956
composer, conductor
b Leipzig, Ger. Educ: Stern Cons, Berlin, BA(humanities). Toured as asst cond; in concert, Berlin; formed own chamber orch. Cond, Paris Cons Orch. To US, 41. Founder & dir, Nat Cons, Dominican Repub, 42-44. Guest cond with var orchs incl New York Philh, CBS Symph, Nat Symph of Guatemala. Music dir, Nat Symph of Costa Rica, 48-49, Mobile Symph, 52-57, Beaumont Symph, 57- Ed, unpublished works of Purcell, Haydn & Mozart. Recipient, Grand Prix du Disque.

FENNER, BEATRICE   ASCAP 1940
composer, author, publisher
b Los Angeles, Calif, Apr 15, 04. Educ: Juilliard; Master Inst of United Arts; comp studies with Reubin Goldmark; piano studies with Harold Triggs. Foster mother for handicapped infants. *Songs & Instrumental Works:* Spring Dropped a Song into My Heart; Garden Wind; I Wonder; When Children Pray; Weep Little Mary; The Dew Man; Little Boat of Sleep; Suite for a Little Girl (piano).

FENNER, BURT L   ASCAP 1973
composer
b New York, NY, Aug 12, 29. Educ: Mannes Col Music, BS(comp); Columbia Univ, MA(comp). Teaching positions at Turtle Bay Music Sch, New York, The Young Men's Hebrew Asn Sch Music, New York, Mannes Col Music, New York, Pa State Univ. *Instrumental Works:* Variations for String Quartet and Orchestra; Symphony No 2; Symphony No 3; Prelude for Brass and Tape; I Like a Look of Agony (11 songs with chamber ens & tape).

FENNIMORE, JOSEPH WILLIAM
composer, pianist
b New York, NY, Apr 16, 40. Educ: Univ Rochester Eastman Sch of Music, BM, 62; Juilliard Sch, MS, 65; studied piano with Rosina Lhevinne, comp with Virgil Thomson. Pianist, var concerts; toured Orient, Europe & US. Comp, full-time, 70- Founder, concerts devoted to Am music "Hear America First," 72, dir of recording proj for Spectrum Records. Recipient, awards from var int

competitions, Fulbright & Rockefeller grants, 65-70. *Songs:* Berlitz: Introduction to French. *Instrumental Works:* Concerto Piccolo (piano, small orch); Quartet (after Von Tesil).

FENNO, DICK　　　　　　　ASCAP 1963
　　composer, arranger
b Fitchburg, Mass, Jan 17, 27; d. Educ: Berklee Sch of Music; Westlake Col of Music, BA. Dir, Westlake Col of Music, Hollywood. Mem, Disneyland Band. Chief arr, Heritage Square Music. *Songs & Instrumental Works:* I Remember Basie; Montage; Festival for Trumpets.

FENSTER, HARRY (TEX)　　　　　ASCAP 1959
　　composer, author, singer
b Lwow, Poland, Dec 21, 19. Educ: James Monroe High Sch, grad, 38; City Col New York; Columbia Univ. Began songwriting, 49. Appeared on var TV shows, incl "Don Imus", "Imus Plus", "The Stanley Siegel Show", "Midday Live", "Cinevision TV", Vienna, Austria; now producing & starring in "Tex Fenster, Super-Star." Chief Collabrs: Paul Insetta, Sammy Mysels, George Mysels, Roy Benowitz, Sy Gottlieb, Joe Cohen, Sammy Baron, Sid Prosen, Billy Hayes, Robert Mellin. *Songs:* You Knew Me When You Were Lonely; Blueberry Kisses From My Strawberry Blonde; My Heart Is Yours; The Only Break You Gave Me Was a Broken Heart; Stay in My Arms; Lyrics: It's All Over But the Crying; You Knew Me When.

FENSTOCK, BELLE　　　　　　ASCAP 1939
　　composer, pianist, artist
b New York, NY. Educ: Studied music with Joseph Schillinger; Art Students League. Staff comp, publ cos. Guest comp, Nat Opera Club of Am, Nat Asn Am Composers & Conductors, South Shore Music Club, Women's City Club & Stage Door Canteen, Washington, DC. Camoufleur, WW II. Muralist for hotels. Chief Collabrs: Stanley Adams, Otto Harbach, Billy Rose, Irving Caesar. *Songs & Instrumental Works:* American Rhapsody; Safari; Assorted Ladies; Simonetta; Stranger in the Dark; Song of the Refugee; Cafe Society; Mexican Fiesta; Holiday in Venice; Calypso Man.

FENTON, HOWARD　　　　　　ASCAP 1948
　　composer, author, actor
b New York, NY. Educ: Wilson Sch of Music; NY Univ; Neighborhood Playhouse; Henry Street Settlement; Feagin Sch of Dramatic Arts; studied with Mme Farrington Smith, Alberto Jeanotte, Mildred Fainstein. Singer, writer, announcer & DJ on radio. Actor, summer stock & Bway plays. Personal representative for performers in music & drama. Writer, special material for Hildegarde, Ilona Massey. Mem, Am Guild of Authors & Composers. Chief Collabrs: Gene Bone, Langston Hughes. *Songs & Instrumental Works:* Strange and Sweet; White Magnolias; I Love to Love; Say Yes to Life; My Magic Island; Nickelodeon Holiday; Orchids of Aloha; Friendship Tree; Gee, Dad, It's a Wurlitzer; Everything That I Can Spy; Green Fields; Pray for Peace; Prayer of a Waiting World; Wind in the Treetops; Marine Corps Reserve Marching Song (off song, USMCR); Sacred works: The First Psalm; Thy Word Is a Lamp; Cantata: Birthday in Bethlehem. *Albums:* Music to Cook By (album-book).

FERDINAND, BUDDY
　　See De Franco, Boniface

FERGUSON, EDWIN EARLE　　　　ASCAP 1970
　　composer, author, accompanist
b Brocket, NDak, Aug 4, 10. Educ: Drake Univ, BS & LLB; Yale Univ, JSD; Drake Cons, comp with Franz Kuschan; comp with Meyer Kupferman. Prof pianist & arr, Des Moines, Iowa, 28-35; accompanist, coach, choral cond & comp, Washington, DC, 38- Dir music, Chevy Chase United Methodist Church, Md, 60-; lectr church music. ASCAP Standard Awards, 76- *Songs:* Easter Fanfare; Resurrection Tidings; Two Spanish Songs; Music: Two Shaker Songs; Ye Followers of the Lamb; A Woman Unashamed. *Instrumental Works:* Three Idiomatic Exercises (violin, clarinet & piano). *Scores:* Films: Volcanos; Glaciers; Oratorios: The Betrayal; The Confrontations of Judas; Cantata: The St Luke Christmas Canticles.

FERGUSON, JAMES MIKEL　　　　ASCAP 1977
　　composer, singer
b Colbin, Tex, Jan 30, 42. Educ: Trawick Sch, West Covina, Calif; West Covina High Sch. Singer in nightclubs; recording artist; band leader. *Songs:* Muddy Road's; Slow Down the Pace; Gettin the Blame; The More I Try; Cold Woman.

FERRANTE, ARTHUR　　　　　　ASCAP 1956
　　composer, pianist, arranger
b New York, NY, Sept 7, 21. Educ: Juilliard, studied with Carl Friedbert. Teacher, Juilliard, 44-47. Mem 2-piano team, Ferrante & Teicher. Has given concerts throughout US & Can; also on radio & TV. Made many records. Chief Collabr: Louis Teicher. *Songs & Instrumental Works:* You're Too Much; What More Can I Say?; American Fantasy; Dream of Love; Possessed; A Rage to Live (film theme). *Scores:* Film background: Undersea Conquest.

FERRANTE, DENNIS CHRISTOPHER　　　ASCAP 1968
　　singer, engineer, producer
b Hoboken, NJ, Dec 25, 46. Educ: Cliffside Park Sr High Sch, 64; RCA Inst, electronics, 65-67; Inst Audio Res, studio operation, 71- Singer, nightclubs & commercials; recording artist, Epic Records; engineer, Record Plant Studios Ltd & RCA Records; producer, Hit Factory Studios.

FERRARA, FRANK W　　　　　　ASCAP 1975
　　composer
b North Bergen, NJ, July 28, 09. Educ: Polytech High Sch, Los Angeles, Calif; Sch for the Blind, Berkeley, Calif; studied piano with Otto Fleissner, San Francisco. Entertainer, progs, service clubs, masonic lodges & nightclubs. *Songs:* Bankrupt Millionaires.

FERRARIS, RICHARD　　　　　　ASCAP 1959
　　composer, accordionist
b San Francisco, Calif, Dec 14, 22. Educ: San Francisco Cons. With groups The Vagabonds & Hurtado Marimba Band. Served, USAAF, World War II. *Songs:* Let's Love; I'm in Love; Hear My Love.

FERRARO, RALPH ALBERT　　　　ASCAP 1968
　　composer
b Waterbury, Conn, July 3, 29. Educ: Manhattan Sch of Music, MM(comp). Comp, Chrysler Theatre, Los Angeles, 68; TV shows incl "The Virginians", "Men From Shiloh", "It Takes a Thief", "Mannix", "Marcus Welby, MD" & "The Name of the Game." Comp, pilots for Carroll O'Connor's co incl "Bender's Force", "Riding for the Pony Express" & "Our Place." *Scores:* Films: After the Fox (Europ version); The King's Pirate; Antonio.

FERRAZANO, ANTHONY JOSEPH (ANTHONY ZANO) ASCAP 1966
　　composer, author, pianist
b Worcester, Mass, June 4, 37. Educ: New Eng Cons, 54-56; Boston Cons, 56-57; Boston Univ, 58-63; Forest Cons, DM; Sussex Univ, Eng, 63; studied comp with Hugo Norden, Walter Piston, Rouben Gregorian, Margaret Mason, Wei-ning Lee. Taught, pub schs, 56-57. Cond of own orch, NY & New Eng, 57-Fac, New York Sch of Music, 59, Worcester Polytech Inst, 61, Schenectady Cons, 66-67. Music arr, Boston & New York, 60- Studio work, RCA Studios, 75-78. Pianist with Hal McKusick, Toots Thielemans, Jim Chapin, Ted Brown, Lee Konitz, Larry Elgart & Ray McKinley. Author, "Mechanics of Modern Music." Chief Collabr: Richard Goicz. *Songs:* Music: Why Must This Be Love; Goodbye My Darling; When You're On Stage; Till You Came By. *Instrumental Works:* The Gathering Place; To a Certain Miss; Ballad for Dee; Loss; Restless; OK?; Walk for Happy; Waltz; Concert works: Concert in the Round Overture; Atonement; Mass; String Quartet No 2; Hale Recollections; Vita Brevis, Ars Longa; The Soul's Season (chorus); Symphonic Portrait. *Albums:* The Gathering Place; Everything Swings.

FERRE, CLIFFORD F　　　　　　ASCAP 1950
　　composer, author, singer
b Waitsfield, Vt, June 18, 20. Educ: Deerfield Acad. Singer & dancer, Billy Rose's "Aquacade" & Bway musicals. Served, USA, World War II & in "This Is the Army." With group, The Dunhills, nightclubs & TV, 45-49. Originator & MC of TV show "Make Mine Music," New York. Host, "Good Morning Show" & "Just for Fun"; appeared in films. Staff TV announcer, Miami, 57-62; prog dir, WKBN, Youngstown, Ohio. Chief Collabr: Mark McIntyre. *Songs:* The Money Tree.

FERREIRA, DJALMA　　　　　　ASCAP 1964
　　composer
b Rio de Janeiro, Brazil, May 5, 13. Educ: High sch. To US, 63. Musician on radio & at Casino da Urca. Opened two nightclubs in Brazil; founder, Drink Records (SA Industria Comercio). Chief Collabrs: Leonard Feather & Iza Ferreira. *Songs & Instrumental Works:* Funny Fellow; You Can't Go Home Again; Samba Que Eu Quero Ver; Carnaval; Destinos; Retorno; Sambadin; Nosso Samba; My Place; Devaneio (Day Dream); I'm Happy Now; Lamento; Murmurio; Samba Do Perroguet; Lady from Leblon; Peace of Mind; Recado (The Gift); Taste of Sadness; Izabella.

FERRELL, BEN PAYNE　　　　　ASCAP 1975
　　composer, author
b Prestonsburg, Ky, June 18, 53. Educ: Univ Ky; Oral Roberts Univ, BS. Gospel performer at age 16-21; Nat album at age 21, Caravelle Records; songwriter with spoone music at age 23-25. Producer & publisher, Morning Star Productions. Performed & recorded with group Everitt & Ferrell. Chief Collabr: Eddie Everitt. *Songs:* I've Been Redeemed; My Eyes Are on You, Lord; Rollin' On; Talkin' Bout Kentucky; The Total Team (Silk N Steel, King N Kong); Glory Train.

FERRIS, DON A　　　　　　　ASCAP 1949
　　composer, pianist
b Boonton, NJ, May 22, 19. Educ: Liner Acad Music, Boston. Pianist for Horace Heidt's Orch, 3 yrs, Henry Busse, Louis Prima & David Rose Orch, 26 yrs. Pianist & arr, Ozzie Nelson Orch. Cond & arr, personal appearances of Red Skelton & Carroll O'Connor. *Songs:* For My Love; Santa Is Checking on You; Father Knows Best (Waiting); Captain Midnight (theme).

FERTEK, MACK BENJAMEN ASCAP 1971
composer, author
b Pittsfield, Mass, Mar 15, 17. Educ: US Sch Music, 4 yrs (cert award guitar, 69; cert award accordion, 75). Songwriting, 12 yrs. *Songs:* You Took My Heart Away; I Remember You; A Heart in Tears; My Pretty Pretty Little Girl.

FETLER, PAUL ASCAP 1957
composer, educator, lecturer
b Philadelphia, Pa, Feb 17, 20. Educ: Pvt study, Sweden & Switz; Northwestern Univ, BM, 43, studied with David Van Vactor; Yale Univ, MM, 48, studied with Quincy Porter & Paul Hindemith; Berlin Acad Music, 54, studied with Boris Blacher; Univ Minn, PhD, 56. From instr to prof music theory & comp, Univ Minn, 58-; lectr & cond own works at numerous cols, univs & churches. Composed over 100 works for orch, chorus, songs, chamber music, film scores & music for theatre & dance. *Songs:* Music: Songs of the Night; Lamentations (chorus, flute, perc & narrator); A Contemporary Psalm (chorus, organ, perc, soloists); Te Deum (chorus); Jubilate Deo (chorus & brass); Easter Fanfare (voices & brass); Sing Unto God (chorus); Wild Swans (chorus); Snow Toward Evening (chorus); Madman's Song (chorus); All Day I Hear (chorus). *Instrumental Works:* Contrasts for Orchestra; Whitman Poems (orch & narrator); Violin Concerto; Three Impressions (guitar & orch); Dialogue (flute & guitar); Celebration (orch); Cycles (perc & piano); Pastoran Suite (violin, cello & piano); Six Pastoral Sketches (guitar); Four Movements (guitar); Five Pieces (guitar); Three Venetian Scenes (guitar); Six Songs of Autumn (guitar); Five Piano Games; Three Pieces for Violin and Piano.

FETTER, DAVID (J) ASCAP 1976
composer, arranger, trombonist
b Washington, DC, Nov 24, 38. Educ: Eastman Sch Music, BM, 60; Am Univ, MA(musicol), 69; studied trombone with Emory Remington & Lewis Van Haney. Trombonist with the San Antonio Symph & the Cleveland Orch under George Szell; with, Baltimore Symph; cond, Baltimore Trombone Choir; comp, ed, arr & transcriber music for brass. *Instrumental Works:* Impossible Joke; Bicentennial Brass Music; Rockola; Six Sonatas (ed).

FETTER, TED ASCAP 1939
author
b Ithaca, NY, June 10, 06. Educ: Swarthmore Col, BA, 28. Actor, New York, 28-41; lyricist, 29-41; with Army, 41-46; TV dir, producer & exec, 46-74; curator theatre collection, Museum City of New York, 74-79. Chief Collabrs: Vernon Duke & Richard Lewine. *Songs:* Lyrics: Taking a Chance on Love; Now; Yours for a Song; Doin' The Waltz; It's a Lovely Night on the Hudson River; The Nose on Your Face; I Cling to You; Tired of Love.

FEYNE, BUDDY ASCAP 1940
composer, author, singer
b New York, NY, June 9, 12. Educ: Am Acad TV, Los Angeles. Singer, dancer, vocalist with orchs. Radio spot on WNEW, New York. Wrote & co-produced segment of network radio show "Rhythm School of the Air." 77th Inf Div, S Pacific, World War II, Bronze Star for combat duty. Produced & emceed shows for servicemen. Writer for Am Forces Radio Service, "Preview Theatre," KFWB, Calif. Writer & producer, spec material, "Bill Harrington Show," TV. Songwriters Hall of Fame, 78. Chief Collabrs: Erskine Hawkins, Bill Harrington, Harry Revel, Raymond Scott, Milton Berle, Peter Tinturin, Al Sherman. *Songs:* Everybody Wants to Be Loved By Someone; I'll Remember the Good Things; Jumpin' With Symphony Sid; Lyrics: Tuxedo Junction; Jersey Bounce; After Hours; Oh to Be Young Again; Why; Blue Velvet Waltz; Radar Blues; Dolimite; Willow in the Wind; The Shadow Knows; Love Had a Preview Last Night; I'm So Happy I Could Cry; Let My Heart Alone; Joe's Notion; Harlem Stomp; My Treasure; The World is Filled With Beautiful People; Fasten Your Seat Belt. *Scores:* Film: Diary of a Stewardess. *Albums:* Time for Fun (children, educ).

FICHTHORN, CLAUDE L ASCAP 1948
composer, organist, choirmaster
b Reading, Pa, June 7, 1885; d Marshall, Mo, Aug 26, 72. Educ: Mo Valley Col, BA; hon MusD & MA, Columbia Univ; studied voice with Louis Dubigny. Soloist, asst organist & choirmaster, Reading Episcopal Church. Church organist & choirmaster, Zion Reformed, 4 yrs, First Presby, 5 yrs, Westport Presby, Kansas City, 20-35 & Marshall Methodist, 20 yrs. Prof music, Mo Valley Col, 12, dean, Sch Music, 14-48, chmn music dept, 47. Founded Marshall Little Symph. Teacher history, Naval unit, WW II. Mem, Nat Asn Am Comp & Cond. *Songs:* Cantatas: In Judea's Hills; The Everlasting Light; Sacred: Behold What Manner of Love; Trusting in Thee; Behold the Angel of the Lord. *Instrumental Works:* Chanson d'Ete (organ); O Saving Victim (a capella).

FIEDEL, BRAD ASCAP 1976
composer, author, singer
b New York, NY, Mar 10, 51. Educ: Barlow Sch; State Univ NY Col Old Westbury; studied keyboard harmony with Sanford Gold; studied voice with Arthur Joseph. Played keyboards for RCA recording artists, Daryl Hall & John Oates; played & sang original songs in clubs & cols around the country; scored award winning educ films, including theme song, words & music; comp & cond scores for feature films & TV films. *Songs:* I Don't Want to Be Your Fool Anymore; The Love That I Gave You. *Scores:* Film/TV: Mayflower: The Pilgrims Adventure (CBS Thanksgiving Spec); Hardhat and Legs (CBS TV

film); Seven Wishes of a Rich Kid (ABC After Sch Spec); A Movie Star's Daughter (ABC after sch spec); Deadly Hero (feature film, CBS).

FIEDEL, IVAN
composer, teacher, lyricist
b New York, NY, Jan 20, 27. Educ: Juilliard Sch Music; New Sch Social Res; NY Col Music, prof dipl; studied with Saul Goodman, Henry Cowell & Erich Katz. Pres & founder, Fiedel Sch, Glen Cove & Bayville, Long Island. Nat Model Site, NCAH of John Kennedy Ctr, Washington, DC; site coordr, AIS prog, NEA. Adj full prof educ, C W Post Ctr, Long Island Univ. Comns for major theatre works & ballets. *Songs:* Lyrics: Rumania Rumania (Eng transl). *Instrumental Works:* Suite for Piano. *Scores:* Ballet: Volcano; Ixtlan.

FIEDEL, SAM S ASCAP 1952
composer, string bassist, tuba player
b New York, NY, Oct 6, 16. Educ: NY Univ, BS(music); studied comp with Tibor Serly, Zoltan Kodaly. Bassist & tuba player with top bands. With music staff, CBS, 39-58. Served, World War II, 42-44. Mgr, record & publ cos. Performing with theatre pit orchs. *Songs & Instrumental Works:* Beyond the Milky Way; Elf on a Pogo Stick; Pirouette; Playground in the Highlands; Electronic Music From Outer Space.

FIEGER, ADELINE OPPENHEIMER ASCAP 1959
composer, pianist
b New York, NY. Educ: Calhoon High Sch; studied piano with Michael Fields; workshops with Jay Gorney & Lehman Engel; Juilliard, Arnold Arnstein. Wrote & performed WNEW 20th Anniversary song, Madison Sq Garden, 65. Wrote campaign song for Governor Rockefeller, 66. Distinguished Woman Award by Northwood Inst, 77. Chief Collabrs: Caryl Young, Danny Apolinar, Carl Ulrich Blecher. *Songs:* I Love Rudy Ruderman; Music: Danke Fur Die Blumen; I Kneel At Your Throne; Bella, Bella Bambina; Love Is Best of All; Shake Hands With a Fool; Runnin' Out of Time; Natchez Parade; Sad Eyes; Merry Christmas to Me; All of a Sudden It's Spring. *Scores:* Off Bway: Changes; Bway Show: Dear Oscar; TV: Puncinello.

FIELD, EUGENE ASCAP 1940
author
b St Louis, Mo, Sept 3, 1850; d Kenilworth, Ill, Nov 4, 1895. Educ: Williams Col; Knox Col; Univ Mo. Began newspaper work, St Joseph, Mo, then St Louis, Kansas City, Denver & Chicago, 1883-95. Early newspaper columnist, "Sharps and Flats," Chicago, Morning News. Wrote poems for his columns; known as "The Children's Poet." *Songs:* Poems set to music: Little Boy Blue; Wynken, Blynken and Nod.

FIELD, LORRAINE F (LORRAINE WICH) ASCAP 1962
composer, author, entertainer
b New Haven, Conn, Feb 22, 21. Performer & writer, 35- Chief Collabr: Vin Roddie.

FIELDING, JERRY ASCAP 1957
composer, conductor, arranger
b Pittsburgh, Pa, June 17, 22; d Feb 17, 80. Educ: Carnegie Tech. Cond, arr for films & TV. Film background score, "Advise and Consent"; TV incl Betty Hutton series & "Hogan's Heroes." *Instrumental Works:* City of Brass; Polynesian Peace Chant; The Essence of Calculated Calm; Paris Magicque.

FIELDING, LEE ASCAP 1960
composer, author, pianist
b Ida Grove, Iowa, Apr 4, 1888; d Santa Maria, Calif, May 16, 63. Educ: High sch. Singer; teacher. Chmn music res, Ind Fedn Music Clubs, 41-43. Music dir churches & clubs. Coed, "The World's Great Madonnas." *Songs:* Down San Bernardino Way; Counterfeit Kisses; Trampoline; Winkey Doll; Are You Sure?

FIELDING, MICHAEL
See Sciapiro, Michel

FIELDS, ARTHUR ASCAP 1937
composer, author, actor
b Philadelphia, Pa, Aug 6, 1888; d Largo, Fla, Mar 29, 53. Appeared in minstrel shows, vaudeville & radio; publ, made many records. Chief Collabrs: Walter Donovan, Theodore Morse, Fred Hall, George Graff. *Songs:* On the Mississippi; Aba Daba Honeymoon; Auntie Skinner's Chicken Dinner; There's a Blue Sky Way Out Yonder; Eleven More Months and Ten More Days; I Got a Code Id By Dose; Our Hometown Mountain Band; And the Angels Sing; Who Else But God; There Shall Be No More Tears; also 48 Hymns of Happiness.

FIELDS, ARTHUR B (BUDDY) ASCAP 1925
composer, author, agent
b Vienna, Austria, US parents, Sept 24, 1889; d Detroit, Mich, Oct 4, 65. Educ: Pub schs, Chicago. 133rd Machine Gun Btn, 36th Div, WW I. Appeared in vaudeville & cafes; then theatrical agent. Chief Collabrs: Al Sherman, Al Lewis, Gerald Marks, Art Berman. *Songs:* You Gotta Be a Football Hero; Falling; You're the One, You Beautiful Son-of-a-Gun; The Night Shall Be Filled With Music; With You on My Mind I Can't Write the Words; By the Sign of the Rose;

Chinnin' and Chattin' With May; The Pump Song; Remember; Indoor Outdoor Girl; By a Camp Fire; If It Wasn't for You; How Can I Be Anything But Blue; I'll Get Along Somehow.

FIELDS, CHARLES WILLIAM
ASCAP 1971

composer

b Glynn's Creek, Ky, Sept 9, 24. Educ: Henry Clay High Sch, Lexington, Ky. Musician with big bands, 40's, 50's. Worked with country bands, radio, TV, nightclubs. Own independent record co, Charta Records, Nashville. Writer & producer for several artists. Chief Collabrs: Bobby G Rice, Donald Riis. *Songs:* You Lay So Easy on My Mind; Sunshine Lady; The Whole World's Making Love Again Tonight; Sweet Country Music; Can't Shake You Off My Mind.

FIELDS, DOROTHY
ASCAP 1929

lyricist, author

b Allenhurst, NJ, July 15, 05; d New York, NY, Mar 28, 74. Educ: Benjamin Sch for Girls. Daughter of comedian Lew Fields. Chief Collabrs: Jimmy McHugh, Jerome Kern, Arthur Schwartz, Fritz Kreisler, Sigmund Romberg, Morton Gould, Harold Arlen, Harry Warren, Burton Lane, Albert Hague, Cy Coleman. *Songs:* I Can't Give You Anything But Love, Baby; Diga Diga Doo; Doin' the New Low Down; Porgy; I Must Have That Man; Blues Again; Exactly Like You; On the Sunny Side of the Street; Cuban Love Song; Hey Young Fella; Don't Blame Me; Dinner at Eight; Thank You For a Lovely Evening; I Dream Too Much; Jockey on the Carrousel; I Won't Dance; Lovely to Look At; I Feel a Song Coming On; I'm in the Mood for Love; Stars in My Eyes; The Way You Look Tonight (Acad Award, 36); Pick Yourself Up; Bojangles of Harlem; Never Gonna Dance; A Fine Romance; Just Let Me Look at You; You Couldn't Be Cuter; This Is It; It's All Yours; I'll Pay the Check; Terribly Attractive; A Lady Needs a Change; Remind Me; April Snow; Close As Pages in a Book; The Big Back Yard; When You Walk in the Room; Today I Love Ev'rybody; Andiamo; Nothin' for Nothin'; There Must Be Something Better Than Love; Look Who's Dancin'; I'm Like a New Broom; Love Is the Reason; Make the Man Love Me; I'll Buy You a Star; More Love Than Your Love; Alone Too Long; Merely Marvelous; Look Who's in Love; Big Spender; There's Gotta Be Something Better Than This; Where Am I Going?; Lyrics: It's Not Where You Start, It's Where You Finish; Welcome to Holiday Inn; Poor Ev'rybody Else. *Scores:* Bway Shows: Blackbirds of 1928; Hello, Daddy; International Revue; Stars in Your Eyes; Up in Central Park; A Tree Grows in Brooklyn; Arms and the Girl; Sweet Charity; By the Beautiful Sea; Seesaw; Redhead (Tony, Grammy Awards, 59); Let's Face It; Something for the Boys; Mexican Hayride; Annie Get Your Gun; Film: I Dream Too Much; The King Steps Out; Swing Time; Joy of Living; Excuse My Dust; My Imperium; The Farmer Takes a Wife; TV: Junior Miss.

FIELDS, EDDIE

See Waganfeald, Edward James, III

FIELDS, HARRY
ASCAP 1969

composer, author, pianist

b Portland, Ore, Jan 20, 13. Educ: Ethel B Wilson Sch, Portland; Dent Mowery Sch, Portland; Juilliard Sch Music; studied with Carl Friedberg, comp with George Wedge & jazz with Art Tatum. Nightclub pianist, concert pianist, recording artist; music sch, WHollywood, 35 yrs. Auth two piano method books, "Modern Approach to Popular Piano Playing" & "Key to Learning Popular Piano." Chief Collabrs: Sylvia Wilson, Cheryl Christensen, Bobby Troup. *Songs:* Music: My Rhapsody Is You; Springtime of Love. *Instrumental Works:* Jazz Sonata. *Scores:* Film/TV: You're a Woman; Tania.

FIELDS, IRVING
ASCAP 1952

composer, author, teacher

b New York, NY, Aug 4, 15. Educ: Eastman Sch Music, Masters Inst, Manhattan. Has led own trio in hotels & night clubs worldwide. Concerts, Symph Hall, Boston & Carnegie Hall, NY. Recording artist, singer, pianist, arr & entertainer for past 30 yrs. Chief Collabrs: Albert Gamse, Benny Davis. *Songs & Instrumental Works:* Managua, Nicaragua; Miami Beach Rhumba; Chantez Chantez; Take Her to Jamaica.

FIEN, LUPIN
ASCAP 1942

composer, author

b Philadelphia, Pa, June 15, 08. Educ: Temple Univ, BS; Philadelphia Cons; studied with Gustav Leubert & William Craig Schwartz. Has written special material & musical commercials; advert exec. Chief Collabrs: Al Siegel, Irving Mills, Josef Myrow, Ella Fitzgerald. *Songs:* Don't Know If I'm Comin' Or Goin'; Wee Willie Winkie; We Had to Give Godfrey the Gate; Why Didn't William Tell; Reflection; Just One of Those Nights; So You Wanna Fall in Love; While the Music Plays On; Miss Johnson Phoned Again Today; Slow Freight.

FIERSTEIN, RONALD K (RONNIE ARBUCKLE)
ASCAP 1971

composer, singer, musician

b Brooklyn, NY, Dec 4, 50. Educ: State Univ NY Stony Brook, BS, 71; Brooklyn Law Sch, JD, 78. Lead singer, pianist & guitarist with recording group, Arbuckle, 71-76. Chief Collabrs: Jan Flato, Steve Addabbo, Bobby Flax, Rolf "Hank B" Berntsen, Elliott Zeuser. *Songs:* Wondering Why; Try Again; Quake; To You I'll Run; Living on Love.

FIG, ANTON MICHAEL
ASCAP 1978

composer, author, drummer

b Cape Town, SAfrica, Aug 8, 52. Educ: New Eng Cons, BMus with hons; studied perc with Vic Firth; studied jazz theory with George Russel & Jaki Byard. Played drums since age 5 in var rock bands; performed with George Russell big band, Carnegie Hall; as drummer recorded albums with Ace Frehely of KISS, Garland Jefferies, Joan Armatrading, Link Wray. Presently has own band, Spider & recorded debut ablum with band. Percussionist. Chief Collabrs: Holly Knight, Amanda Blue. *Songs:* Wiped Out; Walk Away From Love; She's No Good; New Romance; What's Going On.

FILAS, THOMAS J
ASCAP 1949

composer, author, musician

b Chicago, Ill, Mar 5, 08. Educ: Armour Tech, Am Cons, Chicago, BA, MA. Oboist, clarinetist, saxophonist in dance orchs. In radio, Chicago, 41- WW II service. *Instrumental Works:* Concerto for Reed Doubles (Paul Whiteman Award); Freedom Bell; Hushabye Lullaby; Lost River, Velocity; Campaign March.

FILIP, PAUL FRANCIS (FRANCIS GRADE)
ASCAP 1974

composer, author

b Plymouth, Mass, June 21, 17. Educ: Jamaica High Sch, New York, 36; Columbia Univ, New York, 40. Joined hotel bus, 36, now sr asst mgr, NY Hilton Hotel. Chief Collabr: Fred Barovick. *Songs:* When I Hold You in My Arms; Unlock Your Heart; My Only Love; You'll Always Be a Dream to Me; I'm Tired of Fooling Around.

FILLER, HARRY
ASCAP 1951

composer, author, arranger

b Odessa, USSR, Jan 15, 08. Began career as writer, singer with Lyn Murray, radio. Wrote background music for WPA Federal Theatre productions of Eugene O'Neil's earliest plays. Wrote local productions of reviews & first Am marionette musical show. Wrote & arr words & music for many vaudeville acts, radio orchs & bands. *Songs:* Christmas Bells; Happy New Year to You; We Just Hate to Say Goodbye; Folio of Hymns; The Jukebox Bill (Jukebox Blues).

FILLMORE, HENRY
ASCAP 1937

composer, author, publisher

b Cincinnati, Ohio, Dec 2, 1881; d Miami, Fla, Dec 7, 56. Educ: Jr col; Miami Inst. Bandmaster from 16. Mem, Am Bandmasters Asn. *Instrumental Works:* Marches: Footlifter; Men of Florida; Miss Trombone; Americans We; Military Escort; Men of Ohio; His Honor; Miami; Overtures: Gypsy Festival; Determination.

FINA, JACK
ASCAP 1948

composer, pianist, conductor

b Passaic, NJ, Aug 13, 13; d Sherman Oaks, Calif, May 14, 70. Educ: NY Col Music, studied with August Fraemcke & Elsa Nicilini. Pianist in dance orchs; then led own orch. *Instrumental Works:* Dream Sonata; Bumble Boogie; Samba Caramba; Rhumbanera; Chango; Piano Portraits.

FINCH, CALVIN

See Downey, Sean Morton, Jr

FINCH, DICK
ASCAP 1940

composer, author

b New York, NY, Nov 22, 1898; d Hudson, NY, Oct 28, 55. *Songs:* You (and Only You); Where's My Sweetie Hiding?; Jealous; You'll Never Know; Rocky Road to Dublin.

FINCH, RUTH GODDARD
ASCAP 1961

author

b Boston, Mass, Sept 27. 06. Educ: Pub Schs. *Songs:* Knockin' on the Door to Heaven; Bound; Sing Me a Song; I Found You in Another's Arms; I Found the Key; Riding Along With You.

FINCKEL, EDWIN A
ASCAP 1959

composer

b Washington, DC, Dec 23, 17. Educ: Columbia Univ, study with Otto Luening; comp with George Antheil; choral techniques with/for Jones, Bethlehem Bach Fests; comp conf study groups, Bennington Col. Staff arr, Boyd Raeburn, Gene Krupa & Buddy Rich & original scores, Gerry Mulligan, Ted Heath & others; comp music, Ann Arbor Drama Fest. Recording artist, Victor, Columbia, Decca, Golden, Crest & Vox. Founder & dir, Young Artists Chamber Orch of NJ; dir music, Far Brook Sch, Short Hills, NJ, 51- *Songs:* Music: Where is the One; Ready to Go Steady; Pennsylvania. *Instrumental Works:* Gypsy Mood; Leave Us Leap; Dateless Brown; Star Burst; Calling Dr Gillespie; Boyd Meets Stravinsky; Boyd Meets the Duke; Two Spoos in an Igloo; Up and Atom; Brief Encounter (4 cellos, strings, woodwind quintet & string quartet); Cello Concerto (solo cello & orch); Cello Suite (cello & piano); Flamenco Fantasy (concert band, woodwind quintet & string quartet); Clarinet Concerto (clarinet & orch); Caprice (piano, violin, cello). *Scores:* Ballet: Of Human Kindness; Bway Show: Red Roses for Me; Film/TV: George White's Scandals.

FINE, IRVING
composer
ASCAP 1949

b Boston, Mass, Dec 3, 14; d Boston, Mass, Aug 23, 62. Educ: Harvard Univ, BA & MA, studied with Walter Piston & Edward Burlingame Hill; also studied with Archibald Davison, Nadia Boulanger & Serge Koussevitzky. Grants: 2 Guggenheim; Fulbright; MacDowell Asn & Wyman Found. Awards: Nat Inst Arts & Letters & Soc Publ Am Music. Asst prof music, Harvard Univ, 39, asst cond, Harvard Glee Club, dir, Basic Piano Prog; on fac, Berkshire Music Ctr, 46-57; co-dir, Music Sem, Salzburg Sem for Am Studies, 50; prof music & chmn, Sch of Creative Arts, Brandeis Univ, 50-62. Comn: Ford Found; Univ Ill; Louisville Orch; Libr of Congress; Koussevitzky Found; Juilliard Sch Music; League of Comp. *Songs & Instrumental Works:* Notturno (strings, harp; Chamber Music Prize); Partita for Wind Quintet; Fantasia for String Trio; A Serious Song - A Lament for String Orch; Mutability (song cycle); String Quartet; The Hour Glass (choral cycle); Sonata for Violin and Piano; Children's Fable for Grown-Ups; Alice in Wonderland (choral settings & suite); Diversions for Orch; Music for Piano (suite); Toccata Concertante for Orch; Romanza for Winds; Symphony - 1962; The Choral New Yorker.

FINE, JACK WOLF
composer, author
ASCAP 1954

b Boston, Mass, Jan 25, 22; d. Educ: Wayne Univ. Gen professional mgr, Irving Caesar Music Co, 9 yrs. Nat sales & promotion dir, Dimension, Amy-Mala Records. Nat promotion dir, Atlanta Records & ABC Paramount Records. Chief Collabrs: Mack Wolfson, Eddie White, Belle Fenstock, Eddie Lisbona, Will Collins. *Songs:* Until Sunrise; Mary Contrary; Be Fair; With Cindy; Texas and Pacific; Tonite He's Out to Break Another Heart; Loretta; Kicking Up Dust in the Nursery; My Arms, My Heart, My Love.

FINE, SYLVIA
composer, author
ASCAP 1948

b New York, NY. Educ: Brooklyn Col. Writer of spec material for Danny Kaye (husband). Wrote songs for "Up in Arms." Chief Collabr: Max Liebman. *Songs:* Molly O; Delilah Jones; Happy Times; Eileen; Lullaby in Ragtime; Five Pennies Saints; Life Could Not Better Be; Bali Bogie; Happy Ending; Spec songs: Lobby Number; Stanislavsky Vonschtickfitz Monahan; Anatole of Paris; Pavlova; Melody in 4 F; Songs in motion pictures, incl: Up in Arms; Wonder Man; Kid From Brooklyn; Five Pennies; On the Double; The Moon Is Blue (title song); The Man With the Golden Arm (main theme). *Scores:* Bway show: Straw Hat Revue; Let's Face It; Film/TV: The Secret Life of Walter Mitty; On the Riviera; Inspector General; Knock on Wood; Court Jester.

FINE, VIVIAN
composer, pianist, teacher
ASCAP 1967

b Chicago, Ill, Sept 28, 13. Educ: Piano study with Djane Lavoie-Herz & Abby Whiteside; comp with Ruth Crawford-Seeger & Roger Sessions. Comp ballets for modern dance incl Martha Graham & Jose Limon. Nat Endowment Arts grants, 74 & 76; mem, Acad & Inst Arts & Letters, 80; Guggenheim Fellowship, 80. *Instrumental Works:* Alcestis (orch); Paean (brass ens, narrator, chorus); Quartet for Brass; Concertante for Piano and Orchestra; Teisho (small chorus, string quartet); Concerto for Piano, Strings and Percussion (one performer); Missa Brevis (cellos, taped voice); String Quartet; Lieder for Viola and Piano; Music for Flute, Oboe and Cello. *Scores:* Opera: The Woman in the Garden (chamber).

FINEGAN, WILLIAM J
composer, conductor, arranger
ASCAP 1952

b Newark, NJ, Apr 3, 17. Educ: Studied with Rudolph Wintrop, Elizabeth Connolly, Stefan Wolpe & Valerie Soudere; Paris Cons. Arr, Glenn Miller Orch, 38-42 & Tommy Dorsey Orch, 42-52. Co-leader with Eddie Sauter, Sauter-Finegan Orch, 52-57; made many records. Has written spec material for TV & radio. *Songs:* Church Mouse. *Scores:* Films: Sun Valley Serenade; Orchestra Wives; Fabulous Dorseys.

FINK, HENRY
composer, author
ASCAP 1941

b Milwaukee, Wis, Mar 8, 1893; d Mexico City, Mex, Dec 23, 63. Educ: Foster Sch; Goodrich Sch, Chicago. Comedian in vaudeville, then in musical comedies. Became restaurateur, then returned to stage. To Mexico, where he owned & operated Cuernavaca tourist hotel. Wrote songs for nightclub revues. Chief Collabrs: Al Piantadosi, Abner Silver. *Songs:* The Curse of an Aching Heart; My Spanish Rose; There Must Be a Reason; Skate With Me; When the Rains Come in Samoa; Till the End of Time; Cuernavaca Sunset; One Moment, Please Go Slowly; Tomorrow and Tomorrow; You're More Than Heaven to Me.

FINK, MICHAEL ARMAND
composer, professor, guitarist
ASCAP 1964

b Long Beach, Calif, Mar 15, 39. Educ: Univ Southern Calif, BM, 60, PhD, 77; Tanglewood, Berkshire, 61; New Eng Cons Music, MM, 62. Teacher, Univ Tex, San Antonio & Calif State Univ, Fullerton; choir cond, USAF. Comns for choral or guitar works; comp & arr, Hollywood. *Songs:* Music: Jubilate Deo (choir, brass); Te Deum (soloist, choir, piano); O Come, Emmanuel (choir, guitar); What Sweeter Music (choir, guitar); What Lips My Lips Have Kissed (voice, piano); Rain Comes Down (voice, piano); Ever 'Gainst That Season (choir, guitar); Full Fadom Five (choir); This Is the Day (choir, organ). *Instrumental*

Works: Wedding March (organ); Sonata da Camera (flute solo); Caprices for Clarinet and Piano.

FINKE, JOHN, JR
composer, conductor, arranger
ASCAP 1947

b Naugatuck, Conn, Sept 16, 1898; d Los Angeles, Calif, Feb 14, 65. Educ: Juilliard Sch. Leader, dance band, hotels & nightclubs. Assoc cond, "Rose Marie." Staff cond & arr, WRGB, Schenectady, 7 yrs. *Songs & Instrumental Works:* Cynthia; Lucinda; All This I Pray; I Alone Shall Never Be; All Ears; The Risen Lord (anthem).

FINLAYSON, WALTER ALAN
composer, teacher, artist
ASCAP 1964

b Burlington, Vt, Mar 2, 19. Educ: Katonah High Sch; Ithaca Col, BS MusEd, 41; Columbia Univ, MA Mus, 57, studied comp with Norman Lockwood; Juilliard Sch Music, NY. Professional artist; composer-arranger; free lance artist. Music educr & chmn dept music, Katonah-Lewisboro Sch, retired 74. Many publ musical comp & arr for piano, symphonic & mil bands. Guest cond, West Point Mil Band, All-State High Sch Band Fest, Middletown, NY, 61. Illustrated many children's piano pieces for Boosey & Hawkes Publ Co. Piano Quart Review Awards, 57 & 61. Mem, Phi Mu Alpha. *Songs:* I Had a Premonition. *Instrumental Works:* Storm King (march; listed in Instrumental Mag as one of 100 most popular marches publ); Thunder Song (march); Piano Pictures; Sketches for Piano; Bright Eyes (trumpet trio with band or piano); Little Prelude (band); Early English Suite (band); Three Pieces for Band; Flash of Crimson (march).

FINLEY, GUY LARRY
composer, author, singer
ASCAP 1969

b Los Angeles, Calif, Feb 22, 49. Educ: Beverly Hills High Sch; Univ Calif Los Angeles; Univ Southern Calif, AA. Recording artist, 68-76 & 79-80; live perf & singer TV shows, 68- Chief Collabrs: Billy Preston, Michelle Rubini, Bob Gaudio, Dick Halligan. *Songs:* All the World Needs is You; Payin' for It With My Heart; No One's Ever Touched Me That Way; Lyrics: I Come to Rest in You; When I Look at You (My Love); Where Do We Go From Here?

FINLEY, LORRAINE NOEL
composer, author
ASCAP 1936

b Montreal, Que, Dec 24, 1899; d. Educ: Schs in Can, Switz & Ger; Wellesley Col; Juilliard Sch; Columbia Univ; studied with J J Goulet, Ada Richardson, Louise Heritte-Viardot, Frank La Forge, Percy Goetschius, Rubin Goldmark. Appeared in recitals with Theodore Fitch (husband), as Mr and Mrs Composer. Was bd mem: Beethoven Asn, New York; Oratorio Soc, New York; New York Fedn of Music Clubs. Mem, Nat League of Am Pen Women, New York branch, incl vpres, 54-62, nat chmn of music, 62-64, nat music bd, 64, won 4 awards, Drama League, vpres, 55-62, Nat Asn for Am Composers & Conductors. *Songs & Instrumental Works:* Symphony in D; Three Theatre Portraits; Brave Horse of Mine (male chorus); Violin Sonata No 1, 2; Clarinet Sonata; Voices of Freedom (27 songs); Birth of Beauty (cantata); 25 Sandoval's 25 Favorite Latin-American Songs; Concert Arias (Mozart); La Pauvre Matelot (Milhaud); Eng transl of National Anthems of the United Nations and Associated Powers; Dreaming, Hoping, Dreaming; The Devil's Tail; Cat-Astrophes; When I Love You Best; Herons; Question; Bondage; Recompense; Within the Haven; Where Are the Years; Not For These Things; Grey Veils. *Scores:* Ballet: Persian Miniature.

FINN, WILLIAM J
composer, organist, choirmaster
ASCAP 1938

b Boston, Mass, Sept 7, 1881; d Bronxville, NY, Mar 20, 61. Educ: St Charles Col; Catholic Univ; ordained Catholic priest, 06; Notre Dame, LLD, 14. Choirmaster, Mission Church, Boston, 02-04, St Paul's Church, DC, 04. Organized Paulist Choristers, Old St Mary's Church, Chicago, 04-18, concert tours. Transferred with Choristers to Church of St Paul the Apostle, New York, 18-46, returned to Old St Mary's Church, 47. Author, "Epitome of Choral Technique" & "Art of the Choral Conductor." *Songs & Instrumental Works:* Sixty Christmas Carols; Quintette of Carols; A Rhythmic Trilogy for Easter; Easter Sermon of the Birds; Brother Ass and St Francis; Paschal Suite.

FINNERTY, DAVID EDMUND
composer, singer, guitarist
ASCAP 1975

b Brighton, Mass, Dec 30, 50. Started songwriting, 65. Mem high sch bands, The Peppars, 65-66, Tangl, 67-68, The Apteryx Bird Band, 68-69. Mem, first professional band, Finnerty, Morse & Richmond, 71; first performance at Jack's, Cambridge. Band became The Road Apples, 72; played in New Eng clubs, 72-78. Chief Collabr: Peter C Johnson. *Songs & Instrumental Works:* Let's Live Together; Holding On; For Love; Don't Turn Out the Light; Nine O'Clock.

FINNEY, ROSS LEE
composer, teacher
ASCAP 1953

b Wells, Minn, Dec 23, 06. Educ: Carleton Col, BA; Harvard Univ, 28-29; studies with Nadia Boulanger, 27-28, Alban Berg, 31-32 & Roger Sessions, 35-36. Teacher, Smith Col, 29-49; comp-in-residence, Univ Mich, 48-74 & Am Acad in Rome, 60. Pulitzer Scholarship, 37; Guggenheim Grants, 37 & 47; Rockefeller Grant, 55; Boston Symph Award & Nat Inst of Arts & Letters Award, 56; Fulbright Fel, France, 64; UNESCO Rostrum, 64; Brandeis Gold

Medal, 67. Hon Degrees, LHD, Carleton Col, 57 & DMus, New Eng Cons, 67. Elected to Nat Inst Arts & Letters, 62 & Am Acad Arts & Sci, 69. *Songs:* Choral Music: Sperical Madrigals; Still Are New Worlds; Earthrise. *Instrumental Works:* Fantasy in Two Movements (solo violin); Symphony No 2; Fourth String Quartet; Concerto for Alto Saxophone; 20 Piano Games; Summer in Valley City; Landscapes Remembered.

FINSTON, LEWIS NORMAN ASCAP 1959
composer, author, teacher
b New York, NY, June 11, 1894; d Los Angeles, Calif, Dec 20, 74. Educ: Columbia Univ. Orch contractor, MGM Studios, 42-47; owner, Studio & Artists Recorders, Hollywood, 42-72. Officer, Musician's Union, New York Local. Pianist & recording engineer.

FINSTON, NAT W ASCAP 1950
composer, author, violinist
b New York, NY. Educ: City Col New York. Violinist & later concertmaster, Russian Symph. Asst concertmaster, Boston Opera Orch, New York Symph & New York Philh, 07-17. Cond, Rialto & Capitol Theatres, New York & Tivoli & Uptown Theatres, Chicago, 17-25. Gen music dir, Paramount & MGM, Calif, 28-45. Guest cond, Los Angeles Philh & Hollywood Bowl. Chmn, Acad Motion Picture Arts & Sci, 38-44, mem bd, 41-44. Mem adv bd, US State Dept Latin-Am Relations (cultural & musical), 2 yrs. Chief Collabr: Gus Kahn. *Songs & Instrumental Works:* Satin Fan; Little Coquette; If You Should Die; Sleepy Eyes; Valse Silhouette. *Scores:* Film background: Song of My Heart; New Orleans; Abilene; Here Lies Love; Strange Holiday.

FIORINO, VINCENT C ASCAP 1953
composer, author, musician
b Sicily, June 20, 1899; d. Educ: Studied in Italy. Musician with dance orchs, ballrooms, theatres & hotels. With CBS, 16 yrs. Recording artist with own group. Owned record & publ firms; conductor. Mem, Miami Symph, Ft Lauderdale Symph, Hollywood Philh & Miami Civic Symph Band. *Songs:* Blue Canary; Red Canary; Skinnie Minnie; Ricky Tick.

FIORITO, ERNEST ASCAP 1955
composer
b New York, NY, Sept 10, 07; d New York, Aug 22, 60. *Songs:* The Last Mile; Swing Fugue; 20th Century Limited; Emotional Episode; Strategic Unit; Rambling Along; Frolicsome.

FIORITO, TED ASCAP 1921
composer, conductor
b Newark, NJ, Dec 20, 1900; d. Educ: Barringer High Sch. Pianist, NY music publ co. Organized dance orch, St Louis & Chicago; toured throughout US during 30's; made many records; appeared in films. Owner, membership club, Scottsdale, Ariz. Chief Collabrs: Gus Kahn, Ernie Erdman, Robert King, Sam Lewis, Joe Young, Cecil Mack. *Songs:* Toot Toot Tootsie, Good-bye; No, No, Nora; Charley My Boy; When Lights Are Low; Sometime; I Never Knew; Drifting Apart; Laugh, Clown, Laugh; King for a Day; Then You've Never Been Blue; Now That You're Gone; Three on a Match; Kalua Lullaby; Roll Along, Prairie Moon; Alone At a Table for Two; Yours Truly; Lily of Laguna; Soft Green Seas.

FIRESTONE, IDABELLE (MRS HARVEY S FIRESTONE) ASCAP 1948
composer
b Minnesota City, Minn, Nov 10, 1874; d Akron, Ohio, July 7, 54. Educ: Alma Col, Ont. *Songs:* In My Garden and If I Could Tell You (theme songs radio & TV prog, "Voice of Firestone"); You Are the Song in My Heart; Do You Recall?; Melody of Love; Bluebirds.

FIRTH, EVERETT JOSEPH (VIC) ASCAP 1965
composer, performer
b Winchester, Mass, June 2, 30. Educ: New Eng Cons Music, BM. Dept head, New Eng Cons Music, 50-; solo timpanist, Boston Symph Orch, 52-; fac head, Berkshire Music Ctr, 56- *Instrumental Works:* Perc: Advanced Etudes; Solo Impression for Two Timpani; Solo Impression for Three Timpani; Solo Impression for Four Timpani; Snare Drum Method; Advanced Etudes and Duets; Marching Drums; Percussion Symposium; Mallet Technique; Six Little Indians; Roll-Off Rhumba; Encore in Jazz; Sitting Bull; Red Cloud; Lone Wolf; Geronimo; Little Crow; Crazy Horse; Changing Moods; The Eighth Wonder; Nine to Go.

FISCHER, CARL THEODORE ASCAP 1946
composer, arranger conductor
b Los Angeles, Calif, Apr 9, 12; d Sherman Oaks, Calif, Mar 28, 54. Educ: Pvt music study. Pianist in film studios, Hollywood. Asst orch leader, WW II. USNR, USMS. Cond-accompanist-arr for Frankie Laine, 46-54. *Songs:* Promise; Could Ja; Give Me a Kiss for Tomorrow; Black Lace; Baby, Just for Me; We'll Be Together Again; Music: Who Wouldn't Love You; You've Changed; It Started All Over Again. *Instrumental Works:* Reflections of an Indian Boy.

FISCHER, EDNA ASCAP 1955
composer, author
b San Jose, Calif. Educ: High sch. Worked for music publ; played vaudeville circuits; in radio, 27-40. Pianist in Meredith Wilson Orch, 30-40, also on TV. Teacher of music. *Songs:* Someday Soon; My Great Great Great Great Grandfather; The Dream in My Heart; Driftwood.

FISCHER, EDWARD ARNOLD (PHAST EDDIE) ASCAP 1971
composer, author, musician
b Cleveland, Ohio, Mar 19, 50. Educ: Cleveland Inst of Music, 59-60; Nova High Sch, Ft Lauderdale, Fla, 69. Singer, guitarist & rock performer nightclubs & cols, 62-68; singer/songwriter, solo performer, 68-70; ABC-Dunhill recording musician/songwriter, 70-72; singer/songwriter/musician, 72-79; producer, writer & performer, Ever Ready Eddy Band, 79- Chief Collabrs: Linda Woodward, Denny (Dennis) Doherty, Nancy Abbott Young, Kane & Deedee Phelps, David Bean. *Songs:* Twenty Years a Cowboy (Never Rode a Horse); ECCS (A Love Story); Music: The Drummer Song; New Book; Chinatown; Modern Music.

FISCHER, JOHN W ASCAP 1969
composer, singer
b Pasadena, Calif, May 17, 47. Educ: Wheaton Col, BA(social sci). Pioneer in contemporary Christian music; songwriter/singer, FEL Publ Label, 1st album, 69. Later signed with Light Records, has publ albums of original songs. Author, bible-teacher within gospel music indust. *Songs:* The All Day Song.

FISCHER, ROBERT WARREN ASCAP 1963
composer, author, singer
b Wilton, Iowa, Aug 5, 35. Educ: Studied piano with pvt instr for 3 1/2 yrs. Has own traveling bands; songwriter; publ; gen mgr of several publ cos, pres, publ co. Produced many recording sessions. Nat promoter for several cos. Chief Collabrs: Sonny Throckmorton, Don Wayne, Dave Kirby. *Songs:* Temporarily Yours; What in Her World Did I Do; One of a Kind; The Great Chicago Fire; I Don't Know How to Tell Her; Love Isn't Love.

FISCHER, WILLIAM SAMUEL ASCAP 1964
composer, author, teacher
b Shelby, Miss, Mar 5, 35. Educ: Xavier Univ, La, BS in MusEd, 56, studied with Clifford Richter & Istvan Nadas; Colo Col, MA(theory & comp), 62, studied with Albert Seay; Acad Musik & darstellende Kunst, Vienna, Austria, studied with Gottfried von Einem, 65-66. Began piano at age 7; studied reeds at age 14 with Kermit Holly, Sr & band with William Davis, Jackson. Began writing & performing professional keyboards & saxophones at age 16. Toured with Smiley Lewis, Joe Turner, Ivory Joe Hunter & others. Recorded Ray Charles first New Orleans hits, 53. Played flute & piccolo, Marine Corps Band, Miami, 56-57. Rec'd grants & awards, incl Fulbright to Austria, 65, Deutsches Akademischer Austausdienst to WGer, Rockefeller Orch grant & New Orleans Philh Nat Endowment. Music arr & dir for many albums. Has written for stage, TV, feature films & ballet. Producer & cond. Chief Collabrs: Joe Zawinul, David Newman, Herbie Mann, Cannonball Adderley, Gene Ammons. *Songs:* Elected Silence, Sing to Me (SATB). *Instrumental Works:* A Quiet Movement (orch & perc solo); St M (jazz quintet & orch); Experience in E (jazz quintet & orch); Concerto Grosso in D Blues (jazz quintet & orch). *Scores:* Opera: Jesse; Ballet: Gazelle.

FISCHOFF, GEORGE ALLAN ASCAP 1972
composer, author, pianist
b South Bend, Ind, Aug 3, 38. Educ: Juilliard Sch Music, BS, 60; studied piano with Rudolf Serkin, Beveridge Webster & Rudolph Ganz. Piano recording artist, Columbia & United Artists Records. Composer, artist piano instrumentals, Billboard Charts, 74-80. Performed col piano concerts, 76-80. Bway musical in prep for 81, "Sayonara." Chief Collabrs: Carole Bayer Sager, Tony Powers, Hy Gilbert. *Songs:* That Great Old Song; When; Forever; My Little Girl; Music: Lazy Day; 98.6; Ain't Gonna Lie; Run to My Lovin' Arms. *Instrumental Works:* Georgia Porcupine; The Piano Picker; Love Fantasy; Piano Dancing; King Kingston.

FISHER, BRUCE C ASCAP 1971
composer, author
b Washington, DC, Jan 8, 51. Educ: Evanston Township High Sch, 68. Writer for Billy Preston; recording artist, United Artist & Mercury. Chief Collabrs: Billy Preston, Quincy Jones, Roy Ayres. *Songs:* Lyrics: Will It Go Round in Circles; You Are So Beautiful; Nothing From Nothing; Body Heat.

FISHER, DAN ASCAP 1953
author, publisher
b Mt Vernon, NY. Educ: George Washington High Sch. Son of Fred Fisher, brother of Doris & Marvin Fisher. Pres, Fisher Music Corp; wrote special material for Billie Holiday, Mabel Mercer, Mildred Bailey & Hope Emerson. Produced "A Lady in Danger", "Springtime for Henry", "A Second String", road cos, "You Can't Take It With You" & "The Three Sisters." Chief Collabrs: Irene Higgenbotham, Sammy Galup, Ervin Drake. *Songs:* Goodmorning Heartache; No Pad to Be Had; I'm Reading Old Letters; Fritzie; No Good Man; Mama, Put That Skillet On; My Love May End; Changing My Tune.

FISHER, DORIS　　　　　　　　　　ASCAP 1941
composer, author, singer
b New NY. Educ: Daughter of Fred Fisher, sister of Marvin & Dan Fisher. Educ: Juilliard; pvt music study. Singer with Eddie Duchin. Own show, CBS. Recorded with own group, Columbia Records. Contract with Columbia pictures, 45. Spec material for Henny Youngman, Pearl Bailey, Mary Meade. Chief Collabr: Allan Roberts. *Songs:* You Always Hurt the One You Love; Into Each Life Some Rain Must Fall; Invitation to the Blues; Tampico; Whispering Grass; Good Good Good; Tired; That Ole Devil Called Love; Angelina-The Waitress at the Pizzeria; I Wish; Amado Mia; Put the Blame on Mame; Either it's Love or it Isn't; You Can't See the Sun When You're Cryin'; Gee, it's Good to Hold You; They Can't Convince Me; Fifteen Years; That's Good Enough for Me; Tutti Frutti. *Scores:* Film: Gilda; Down to Earth; Thrill of Brazil; Lady From Shanghai; Corpse Came COD; 1946 Judy Canova Musicals.

FISHER, FRED　　　　　　　　　　ASCAP 1921
composer, author, publisher
b Cologne, Ger, Sept 30, 1875 (Am parents); d New York, NY, Jan 14, 42. Father of Doris, Dan & Marvin Fisher. Educ: In Germany. Serv in Ger Navy; French Foreign Legion. To US 1900. Began songwriting career in Chicago, then to NY; mgr, Harms & Co & Leo Feist & Co. Founded own publ firm, Fisher Music Corp, 18. Wrote background scores for silent films, songs for talkies & spec material for vaudeville & nightclubs. Chief Collabrs: Joseph McCarthy, Billy Rose, Alfred Bryan, Grant Clarke, Doris Fisher, Howard Johnson. *Songs:* Peg O' My Heart; Dardanella; Chicago; Daddy, You've Been a Mother to Me; Come Josephine in My Flying Machine; Ireland Must Be Heaven; Every Little Bit Helps; My Brudda Sylvest; That Red Head Gal; In the Land of Yama Yama; I Want to Go to Tokyo; That Little German Band; Norway, the Land of the Midnight Sun; She Wore a Little Jacket of Blue; Sing Me a Song of Araby; If the Man in the Moon Were a Loon; Make Me Love You Like I Never Loved Before; Don't Want Your Kisses If I Can't Have Your Love; I'm All Dressed Up With a Broken Heart; They Go Wild, Simply Wild, Over Me; There's a Little Bit of Bad in Every Good Little Girl; Oui, Oui, Marie; There's a Broken Heart for Every Light on Broadway; Gee, But It's Great to Meet a Friend From Your Home Town; Lorraine, My Beautiful Alsace Lorraine; Fifty Million Frenchmen Can't Be Wrong; Happy Days and Lonely Nights; Blue Is the Night; Your Feet's Too Big; Whispering Grass; You Can't Get Along With 'Em or Without 'Em; I Found a Rose in the Devil's Garden; And the Band Played On; There Ain't No Sweet Man That's Worth the Salt of My Tears; I Want You to Want Me to Want You; Who Paid the Rent for Mrs Rip Van Winkle?; When I Get You Alone Tonight; Any Little Girl That's a Nice Little Girl; There's a Little Spark of Love Still Burning; I'm on My Way to Mandalay; Siam; Music: That's When Your Heartaches Begin; Beautiful Face Have a Heart; I'd Rather Be Blue. *Scores:* Film: Oh You Beautiful Doll (biography).

FISHER, JESSIE SEVIL NEUSMAN　　　　ASCAP 1959
composer, author, teacher
b Brielle, NJ, July 16, 09. Educ: Philadelphia Cons, studied violin with Koutzen; Trenton State Col, BS, studied comp with Frank Campbell-Watson. Music supvr, schs in NJ & NY. Established community choral & symph groups. Violinist, concerts; first chair violinist under Benjamin Britten during Am tour. Taught pvt violin, piano & voice. Comp, choral music & piano solos; singer. *Instrumental Works:* The Mysterious Forest. *Songs & Instrumental Works:* Choral works: Of Any Land or Sea; Shades of Song; Ho! Mr Snowman; Have You Ever Seen a Star?; The County Countryside Fair; Nocturne; Hail! The Prince of Peace; Joyous Tidings; The Shepherd's Story; Dance of the Wooden Shoes; The Devil Dancer of Kandy; Zell am Ziller; Light, Light the Candle; Me, Myself and I; Little Two-Deer and the Bear. I Want to Play the Glockenspiel; The Penguin Parade.

FISHER, MARJORIE WILLIAMS　　　　　ASCAP 1958
composer, author
b Graceville, Fla, Oct 27, 16. Educ: Col. Wrote songs for col productions. *Songs:* Op; Letters From You.

FISHER, MARK　　　　　　　　　　ASCAP 1926
composer, conductor
b Philadelphia, Pa, Mar 24, 1895; d Long Lake, Ingleside, Ill, Jan 2, 48. Led own orch in dance halls & hotels. Chief Collabr: Joe Burke. *Songs:* Who Wants a Bad Little Boy; Don't Forget to Remember; Dear One; Oh How I Miss You Tonight; When You're Smiling; Everywhere You Go; You're Too Much; Heart-Breaker; Take Me Back to the Garden of Roses.

FISHER, MARVE A　　　　　　　　　ASCAP 1955
composer, author
b Ill, June 21, 07; d Pacific Palisades, Calif, Sept 1, 57. Educ: High sch. Writer for Jack Oakie, Bob Hope, Phil Harris & Jack Carson. Chief Collabrs: Gus Levene, David Gussin, Matt Dennis, Jean Plummer. *Songs:* Ring Those Christmas Bells; Just an Old Fashioned Girl; Hat I Got for Chreesmas Ess Too Beeg; It Must Be Charlie; Old Uncle Fud; Why Shore.

FISHER, MARVIN (DON DAVIS)　　　　ASCAP 1947
composer, pianist, arranger
b New York, NY, Sept 26, 16. Educ: Juilliard Sch Music; pvt study. Arr for many dancebands; pianist, Justin Stone Orch; song plugger pianist, BVC &

Bourne. West coast rep, Fisher Music, later headed firm; founder, co-owner Marvin Music, NY. Chief Collabrs: Jack Segal, Roy Alfred, Richard Ahlert, John Latouche, Bart Howard, Kenward Elmslie. *Songs:* Music: Captain Kidd; Cloudy Morning; Don't Do Something to Someone Else; My First and Last Love; Destination Moon; Strange; Nothing Ever Changes; When Sunny Gets Blue; Love-Wise; I Keep Goin' Back to Joe's; When She Makes Music; She's Warm, Willing, Wonderfull; Can't Help It; Run to Love; May I Come In; A Good Thing; She Doesn't Know; Trouble Comes; The Geek; Impatient Lover; Sentimental Thing to Do; Kicks; Never Like This; Open Up the Doghouse; When Rock and Roll Come to Trinidad; A Woman Always Understands; Calico Pie; I Cry By Night; Something Happens to Me; Refuse It; For Once in Your Life; Unspoken; Love Is a Necessary Evil; Words and Music; With Feeling; Quiet Girl; Lovers Caravan; Chicken in the Car; A New Style of Life; Lonely Waltz; For Want of a Smile. *Instrumental Works:* Piano Jazz Three Deep; Hanky-Panky.

FISHER, NANCY LOU　　　　　　　ASCAP 1979
composer, lyricist
b Everett, Wash. Educ: Lake Stevens High Sch; Everett Community Col, art class. Songwriter. Chief Collabrs: Archie Swindell, Ruth Knight, John Means, Buren Leach. *Songs:* I'm Going Home; Just Call Me Lonesome; I Know; When I Get the Time; Lyrics: Lily Rose.

FISHER, NICHOLAS E　　　　　　　ASCAP 1951
composer, author, musician
b Concord, NH, Dec 3, 1894; d New York, NY, Feb 8, 61. Educ: Boston Sch Music. WW I service, played in 303rd Regiment Field Artillery band. Moved to New York, 23, played in Willard Robison & Jolly Coburn orchs; became music teacher. *Songs:* Music of the Night Wind; Muchachas, Muchachas; Let's Divide Our Kisses; (Let's Have) A Rendezvous At the Zoo.

FISHER, PATTY
See Akst, Ruth Freed

FISHER, REUBEN (RUBY)　　　　　ASCAP 1960
composer, author
b Long Island, NY, Aug 20, 23. Educ: De Witt Clinton High Sch; City Univ New York; Manhattan Sch of Music. Writer for films, TV & commercials. TV, film credits: CBS "Climax," ABC "General Hospital" & WB "Baby Doll." Record production incl jazz, country & pop. Chief Collabrs: Otis Blackwell, Hal David, Norman Gimbel, Kenyon Hopkins, Buddy Kaye, Al Neiburg, Bobby Scott, Al Stillman, Ben Weisman. *Songs:* The Ingenue; Jazzland; Lonely Lights; Music: Last Bicycle to Brussels; Twilight in the City.

FISHER, WILLIAM ARMS　　　　　ASCAP 1926
composer, author, editor
b San Francisco, Calif, Apr 27, 1861; d Brookline, Mass, Dec 18, 48. Educ: Studied with John Morgan & Horatio Parker; Nat Cons, NY, studied with Dvorak. Teacher, Nat Cons until 1895. Ed & publ mgr of music publ co, 1897-1937, vpres, 26-37. Ed: "The Musician's Library"; "Music Students' Library"; "Music Students' Piano Course." Author: "Notes on Music in Old Boston"; "Music That Washington Knew"; "50 Years of Music Publishing." Ed & arr: "70 Negro Spirituals"; "Ye Olde New England Psalm-Tunes"; "60 Irish Songs." *Songs:* Goin' Home (based on Dvorak's New World Symphony).

FISHMAN, JAY DAVID　　　　　　ASCAP 1969
composer, author
b Brooklyn, NY, Nov 27, 27. Educ: Sch Indust Art; studied music with Paul Knopf, learned theory & harmony. Began writing lyrics. Contract writer, Joy Music, Bright Tunes, Robert Lissauer & for Artie Kernfeld at Roulette Records. Produced recordings for Glory Records, Columbia, Ribben Records & own label, Up Records. Has several publ cos. Chief Collabrs: Don Gohman, Wilbur Meshel, Kenny Young. *Songs:* Today Has Been Canceled; Reaching Out on All Sides; Busdriver; Lyrics: The World of Horses; Raise the Level of Your Conscious Mind; This Spot.

FISKE, HOMER　　　　　　　　　ASCAP 1961
composer, author, publisher
b Hayden, Colo, Feb 4, 14. Educ: State Teachers Col. Organized dance bands; became teacher, 39. Wrote & dir musicals for local theatres & organizations. Pres, Fiske Music Co & F&F Records. Chief Collabrs: Laura Owen, Karleen Carley. *Songs:* Please Believe; Anyhow; Sundown Valley; Just Passing Through; The Road to the Right; Could It Be; Be My Guest.

FITZGERALD, ELLA　　　　　　　ASCAP 1940
composer, singer
b Newport News, Va, Apr 25, 18. Joined Chick Webb Orch, as singer, 35; after his death, led band 1 yr. Singer, nightclubs, theatres & concerts incl Hollywood Bowl & Carnegie Hall; also throughout Europe & Japan. Actress in film, "Pete Kelly's Blues." Made many TV appearances & over 125 albums. Now with Pablo Records. Chief Collabrs: Van Alexander, Chick Webb, Lupin Fien, Josef Myrow. *Songs:* A-Tisket, A-Tasket; You Showed Me the Way; Spinnin' the Web; I Found My Yellow Basket; Chew, Chew, Chew; Please Tell the Truth; Oh! But I Do; Just One of Those Nights.

FITZGERALD, ROBERT BERNARD ASCAP 1963
composer, author, educator
b Martinsville, Ill, Apr 26, 11. Educ: Oberlin Cons Music, BMus, 32; Jordan Cons, MMus, 35. Head wind instrument dept, Jordan Cons, 33-36; dir instrumental dept, Kans State Teachers Col, Emporia, 36-37; prof music, Hendrix Col, Ark, 37-38; dir bands, Univ Idaho, Moscow, 38-40; prof music educ & cond symphonic band, Univ Tex, Austin, 40-56; prof music & dir bands, Univ Ky, 56-63, head music dept, 57-63; dir contemporary music proj, Music Educr Nat Conf, Washington, DC, 63-65; prof music, Univ Ky, 65-76, emer prof, 76- Mem ed bd, Music Educr J; bd dirs, Music Educr Nat Conf; pres, Col Band Dirs Nat Asn, 50; mem, Am Bandmasters Asn, 51-; mem, Phi Mu Alpha, Pi Kappa Lambda & Kappa Kappa Psi. *Instrumental Works:* Concerto in A Flat Minor (trumpet & orch); Modern Suite (trumpet & piano); Four Gaelic Miniatures (flute & piano); Soliloquy (band); Trilogy (band); Concertino (trumpet & band); Ode to America (chorus & band); Arr: Sonata VII (Corelli; trumpet & piano); Aria con Variazioni (Handel; trumpet & piano).

FITZPATRICK, SEAN KEVIN ASCAP 1973
author
b Atlanta, Ga, Sept 28, 41. Educ: Hamilton Col, BA. Sr vpres, Dancer Fitzgerald Sample Advert; creative dir, Columbia Pictures, Bing Crosby Productions-Motion Pictures & J Walter Thompsen Co.

FLACK, MICHAEL JOHN ASCAP 1971
composer, singer
b Davenport, Iowa, Jan 14, 52. Educ: High sch grad. Amateur since age 3; professional since age 10. Appeared on stage, radio & TV many times. *Songs:* Someone Remembered; Little Forget Me Nots; Sugar Bottom; Take My Hand; Son of a Jack of All Trades.

FLAGELLO, NICOLAS ORESTE ASCAP 1960
composer, conductor
b New York, NY, Mar 15, 28. Educ: Manhattan Sch Music, New York, BM, MM; doctorate, Accademia di St Cecilia, Rome; DrPsychol, Univ Rome, studied with Vittorio Giannini, Ilde Brando Pizzetti, Dmitri Mitroupolous. Performed in US, Europe, SAm; cond & founder of Fest of Salerno, Fest Costa del Sol, Spain. Prof comp, Manhattan Sch Music & Curtis Inst. Founder, Am Artists Astra Found. Cond, Orch da Camara di Roma; many recordings as comp & cond. *Songs:* Music: La Bella Aurora; The Land. *Instrumental Works:* Symphony No 2 (Symphony of the Winds; orch); Electra (piano solo, perc orch); Divertimento (piano solo, perc orch); Concertino for Piano and Brass; Capriccio for Cello and Orchestra; Serenade for Orchestra; Burlesca for Flute and Guitar; Piano Sonata; Sonata for Violin and Piano. *Scores:* Operas: The Judgement of St Francis; The Piper of Hamelin; Ballets: Passion of Martin Luther King (bass, chorus, orch); Lautrec Suite (orch).

FLANAGAN, RALPH ASCAP 1950
composer, conductor
b Lorain, Ohio, Apr 7, 19. Arr for Sammy Kaye, Hal McIntyre, Charlie Barnet & Alvino Rey. Toured with own band, 50. Made many records. *Instrumental Works:* Flanagan's Boogie.

FLANIGAN, ROBERT LEE ASCAP 1959
composer, author, singer
b Greencastle, Ind, Aug 22, 26. Educ: Jordan Cons. Army of Occupation, Ger, 45. Joined singing group, Four Freshmen, 48. Trombonist & bassist.

FLASTER, KARL ASCAP 1940
author
b New York, NY, Feb 8, 05; d Atlantic City, NJ, Jan 26, 65. Educ: Pub schs. Newspaper feature writer, reporter. Chief Collabrs: Vittorio Gianini, Julia Smith. *Songs:* Tell Me, Oh Blue, Blue Sky; It Is a Spring Night; Heart Cry; Far Above the Purple Hills; Waiting; Sea Dream; Moonlight; Song of the Albatross; If I Had Known; I Shall Think of You; Triptych. *Scores:* Operas: Lucedia; The Harvest.

FLATO, LUDWIG ASCAP 1955
composer, pianist, conductor
b Warsaw, Poland, Dec 25, 11. Educ: Educ in Europe; Julliard, studied with Lonny Epstein, Leopold Mitmann & Hall Overton. Came to US in 27. Joined staff, CBS, 45; pianist for Arthur Godfrey Radio, TV shows, 18 yrs; also wrote special material, later with Jackie Gleason; accompanist, Jeanne Mitchell & Florian Zabach; music dir, Frank Parker, Andrews Sisters & Buffalo Bills. Cond & pianist Bway Musicals: "Half a Sixpence"; "Henry, Sweet Henry"; "Cabaret"; "Zorba"; "1776"; "Man of La Mancha." Revised & ed the complete vocal score with piano accompaniment of the musical play "Man of La Mancha." Chief Collabr: Moe Jaffe. *Songs:* Music: Let Me Love You; My Lady Won't Be Here Tonight; Blue Ridge Blues; One More Tomorrow; I Wish You the Top of the Mornin'; Time; Shalom, Shalom; A Cafe in Montmartre. *Instrumental Works:* Divertimento; Folio Arr for Piano: A Song to Remember; I've Always Loved You; Trans for Piano: Symphony in D Minor (Cesar Franck); Symphony No 1 (Dmitry Shostakovich); Gayne Ballet (Aram Khachaturian).

FLATOW, LEON ASCAP 1922
composer
b New York, NY, Nov 21, 1889; d New York, Feb 3, 44. Educ: City Col New York. Pianist in Loew's first film theatre, also in vaudeville. Among first composers of theme music for silent films. Staff mem, NY Music Publ Co. *Songs:* A New Kind of Man; I Must Go to Moscow; Everybody Loves a Jazz Band; Popeye the Sailor Man; It's a Long Way to Berlin, But We'll Get There; Broken Toy; also music for many other songs.

FLAUM, HARLEY
composer, author
b Miami Beach, Fla, 1945. Educ: Syracuse Univ, BA; Temple Univ, MA. Newscaster/investigative reporter with Metromedia. Founder, Radio Band of Am, 71. Winner of 18 Clios. Musical commercials incl: Kodak, Kraft, Greyhound, Sara Lee, Gillette Right Guard, Air Jamaica, Bubblicious, Spalding, Certs, Chiquita, Tame, RCA, Hertz, Haagen Dazs, Dunlop, Canon, Maybelline, Schwepps. Chief Collabr: Tom Sellers.

FLEAGLE, JACOB ROGER (BRICK) ASCAP 1938
composer, author, arranger
b Hanover, Pa, Aug 22, 06. Educ: Hanover High Sch; Peabody Inst. Had own orch. With var bands & progs, 23-35. A&R comp-arr for Hot Record Soc, 40's. Arr & comp for Jimmie Lunceford, Red Norvo, Duke Ellington, Fletcher Henderson, New York Philh & others. Chief Collabrs: Rex Stewart, Luther Henderson. *Songs & Instrumental Works:* So I'll Come Back for More; I'm True to You; A Little Goose; Double Doghouse; Safari-Sagudi; Solid Rock (Smorgasborg & Schnapps); A Pixie From Dixie; San Juan Hill; You Ain't in Harlem Now; Tea and Trumpets; Big Eight (Gate) Blues; After Hours on Dream Street; Simple Simon; Carnival (Zulu Strut); Mrs Mississippi; Background for a Parade; Subtone; The Fried Piper; When the Mice Are Away; Same Old Sheaves (SOS); Dreamer Blues; The Subway Song; Ciao (Chow). *Scores:* Ballet: The Barrel-House Ballet; As I Like It; Open Letter.

FLECK, CHARLES S ASCAP 1955
composer, author, conductor
b Philadelphia, Pa, Dec 25, 16. Educ: Am Tech Inst; Belvoir Eng Sch. Entertained troops & cond own orch, AFRS, WW II, 2 yrs. Gave concerts in Philadelphia, Rio de Janeiro, Calcutta, Bombay & Burma. Own radio show, WIP, Philadelphia. Curator, Theatre Organists Hall of Fame. Chief Collabrs: Dave Franklin, Thomas Gindhart. *Songs:* I'm Riding a Rainbow; Forgotten; Who Am I to Dream?; Music: A Garden in the Moonlight; Merrily Love Rolls Along.

FLEESON, NEVILLE ASCAP 1921
author, pianist
b Tarentum, Pa, June 8, 1887; d Glen Ellyn, Ill, Sept 13, 45. Educ: Studied music with Mrs Henry Hadley & Harry Archer. Wrote vaudeville sketches, NY. Served in USA, WW I. Mem cast, "Yip, Yip, Yaphank." Mem staff, music publ co. Wrote songs for films. Chief Collabrs: Albert Von Tilzer, Mabel Wayne, Alec Templeton. *Songs:* When Is the Moment of Falling in Love; Mendelssohn Mows 'Em Down; His Majesty the Baby; I'll Be With You in Apple Blossom Time; Say It With Flowers; You'll Be Sorry You Made Me Cry; Waters of Venice; Dear Old Daddy Long Legs. *Scores:* Bway stage: The Gingham Girl; Bye, Bye, Bonnie.

FLEISCHER, DAVE ASCAP 1959
composer, author, director
b New York, NY; d Los Angeles, Calif, June 25, 79. Educ: Cooper Union Art Sch. Producer film cartoons incl "Popeye the Sailor", "Superman", "Betty Boop" & "Gulliver's Travels." *Songs:* Did Anyone Call?; Try Imagination; Raggedy Ann; Calico Millionaire.

FLEISCHER, ROBERT
composer
b Vienna, Austria, Feb 13, 02. Educ: Violin studies with Carl Prill, Julius Stwertka, Paul Fischer; comp studies with Maria L Balling & Prof Loesser-Schloesinger. Concertized in Vienna, Austria; performed in Carnegie Recital Hall, etc. *Instrumental Works:* Concerto No 2; Mazurka No 1; Serenade No 2; Spanish Dance; Serenade No 1 (violin & harp or piano).

FLEISCHHACKER, DAVID ASCAP 1956
composer, author
b New York, NY, June 10, 33. Educ: High Sch of Music & Art; Long Island Univ; City Col New York. Taught English in high sch, 5 yrs. Writer of advert copy & commercials, 60- Chief Collabr: Ulpio Minucci. *Songs:* On a Lonely Walk; What's Wrong?.

FLEISCHMAN, DAVID ASCAP 1958
composer, conductor
b Toronto, Can, Feb 20, 12. Educ: Toronto Cons. Music dir & pianist for Frances Langford, Lillian Roth, Carl Brisson, Dorothy Sarnoff & Belle Baker; toured with musical productions. *Songs:* Take a Walk in the Sun; What Will Tomorrow Bring; I Swear; Peekaboo.

FLEITMAN, ALEXANDER OSCAR (AL FOSTER) ASCAP 1956
composer, author, singer
b New York, NY, May 26, 24. Educ: High Sch of Music & Art, New York; Curtis Inst Music, Philadelphia, Pa; studied with Joseph Hoffman & Isabelle Vengerova, New York; NY Univ Sch Educ. Pianist & music dir, Theatre Showcase Group, New York, 40-41. AF Band & special serv, WW II. Pianist cond, Copa Cabana, Beach Comber, Martha Rayes 5 O'Clock Club & Vagabond Club. Wrote musicals for Miami Univ & was TV music dir, New York, 50-52; music dir for NY Copacabana & was music coordr for CBS-TV, 68-72. *Songs:* How Very Wonderful.

FLEMING, BILLY CONN
author, playwright
b Huntington, WVa, June 6, 41. Educ: Va Commonwealth Univ, BFA(theatre). Began writing as playwright, 70. Wrote bk & lyrics for "The Red Blue-Grass Western Flyer Show"; wrote bk for "Swing." Plays have been produced off-Bway, regional & univ theatres. Chief Collabrs: Clint Ballard, Jr, Robert Waldman, Alfred Uhry.

FLETCHER, ARCHIE ASCAP 1937
author, singer, publisher
b Philadelphia, Pa, Apr 24, 1890; d. Educ: Pub schs. Singer, cafes & theatres. Staff mem, music publ cos, Philadelphia, Atlantic City & New York; publ, 38. Chief Collabrs: Al Sherman, Joseph Burke, Edgar Leslie. *Songs:* When Tony Goes Over the Top; Down Linger Longer Lane; On a Little Bamboo Bridge; I'm Lonesome for You Caroline; In the Sweet Long Ago; Little Church Around the Corner.

FLETCHER, H GRANT ASCAP 1953
composer, author, conductor
b Hartsburg, Ill, Oct 25, 13. Educ: Ill Wesleyan Univ, BMus 32; Univ Mich, MMus, 39; Tanglewood, comp with Healy Willan, Howard Hanson, Ernst Krenek & conducting with George Szell; Eastman Sch Music fel, PhD, 51. Prof theory & comp, Winthrop Col, SC & Ariz State Univ; prof emeritus, Ariz State Univ, 78- Author of 4 bks & numerous articles. Cond, Akron Symph; Chicago Music Col Symph; Chicago Symphonietta; Am Opera Co; 2 Europ Citations, Rome & Nice. Comp Awards: Paul Le May; Ohio Music Teachers Asn; State Wash Bicentennial; Int Festliche Musiktage, Switz, 74-77; Delius Fest, US, 79. Mem: Phi Mu Alpha, Kappa Kappa Psi, Sigma Alpha Iota; Am Fedn Musicians; bd mem, Int Soc Contemporary Music; Nat Fedn Music Clubs. Chief Collabrs: Opera, John Jacob Niles; opera, John Myers; Lawrence Margolies. *Songs:* Sacred Cantata No 1 (Childe Swete); Carol, Chorale and Finale; A Noel; Sumare-wintare; Music: At the Cry of the First Bird; Rise Up My Love; By the Waters of Babylon; The Crisis; Two Mexican Songs; Searching for Lambs. *Instrumental Works:* An American Overture; A Rhapsody of Dances; Little Suite; Seven Cities of Cibola; Song of Honor; Concerto for Winds III; Diaphony; Symphony No 1; Carrion Crow Overture; Symphonic Suite; Glyphs; String Quartet; Diversion for Strings III. *Scores:* Opera: Cinco de Mayo; The Sack of Calabasas; The Carrion Crow.

FLETCHER, TEX ASCAP 1950
composer, author
b Harrison, NY, Mar 8, 10. Educ: High sch. Was cowboy in Mont, Wyo & SDak; rode in Sells Floto Circus & many rodeos; was SDakota's official Singing Cowboy. Appeard in western films & Bway play "Howdy Stranger." Singing cowboy, WOR, NY, 15 yrs; also on TV. Singer, MC, in nightclub, NY. Chief Collabrs: Leonard Whitcup, Richard Kuhn, George Henkel. *Songs:* Lyin' Lips; Holdin' Hands; Wild Bill Hickok; Pearls and Wine; Butterfingers; The Wall You Built; also Tex Fletcher Song Folio.

FLOREN, MYRON ASCAP 1950
composer, accordionist, singer
b Webster, SDak, Nov 5, 19. Educ: Augustana Col. With USO camp shows, WW II; rec'd citation for front-line entertaining, War Dept. In radio, St Louis, 46-50. Head, Accordion Dept, St Louis Col Music, 49-50. Soloist with dance orchs. *Instrumental Works:* Skating Waltz in Swing; Swingin' in Vienna; Kavallo's Kapers; Windy River; Dakota Polka; Long Long Ago in Swing; Minute Waltz in Swing.

FLORENCE, GORDON LOUIS ASCAP 1968
composer, author, pianist
b Manchester, NH, Apr 21, 15. Educ: Mil schs; Tootorsky's Music Acad; piano studies with John Padavano; songwriting course cert. Composed songs for Nat Songwriters Guild, De Land, Fla, 20 yrs. Author poetry bks, "The Priest and the Youth" & "The Story of a Song." *Songs:* Music: Don't Count Me Out; Make Your Mind Up; Lyrics: Oh, Little Child.

FLORES, IGNACIO F ASCAP 1961
composer, author
b El Centro, Calif, Feb 25, 34. Educ: High sch. Served in USN. Drill press operator. *Songs:* Trying to Forget.

FLORIO, ANDREA NICOLA (RAVEN GREY EAGLE) ASCAP 1973
composer, author, teacher
b St Marys, Pa, May 25, 27. Educ: Self-taught. Began prof drumming-musical career at age 10; joined Am Fedn Musicians Union at age 10; performed with older brother's orch & many name bands & shows; leader of own groups; musician, bandleader, composer, author & arr; prof musician-drummer, 43 yrs; actor, 26 yrs, appearing in many motion pictures & TV shows & features. Chief Collabr: Mrs Zackie Cooper Florio (wife). *Instrumental Works:* Brides for Wakando (perc ens, drums, bells & rattles); Sundial Killing (perc ens); Knobb Hill-Bad Ass Blues (perc-harmony ens); Critical Point-Blues (steel drums & flutes ens); Ho-De-No-Sani-Chant (perc ens).

FLORIO, ZACKIE COOPER ASCAP 1971
composer, author, musician
b Lee's Summit, Mo, Aug 3, 12. Educ: Paseo High Sch; Santa Monica Community Col, spec training in music. Jazz musician, clarinet, vocals & later piano comp, 50 yrs. Mem, jazz clubs, Kansas City, Mo, 29-38, Ina Ray Hutton Girl Band, 38 & Ada Leonard Girl Band, 50; also small groups. Appeared TV, "Jack Benny Show" & "Jeffersons," Los Angeles & movies incl "My Fair Lady", "Nickelodeon", "Paradise Alley" & "Counterpoint." Featured instrumentalist & singer, Andy Florio Band, jazz concerts. Author, teaching aid chord chart educ, "Zack's Zip Chords." Chief Collabr: Andy Florio, husband. *Songs:* I Love You But Now I'll Say Goodbye.

FLOURNOY, ROBERTA JEAN (DODIE RANDLE) ASCAP 1955
composer, author
b Royal Oak, Mich, July 25, 27. Recording artist, Decca, 56; TV singer; record producer. Chief Collabrs: Tom Randall, Janet Pace Perez. *Songs:* How Do You Learn to Love; Man Hunt; I Cried All the Way to the Altar; Lyrics: Soft Explosion.

FLOYD, CALVIN JAMES ASCAP 1962
composer, author
b Stockholm, Sweden, Nov 15, 31. Educ: Univ Calif, Los Angeles, BA. Jazz pianist & singer. Film writer & producer "Time of the Heathen", "Faust" & "The Platform." Pres, Kalmar, Inc. *Songs:* Back With Me.

FLOYD, CARLISLE ASCAP 1957
composer, author, teacher
b Latta, SC, June 11, 26. Educ: Converse Col (scholarship), studied music with Ernst Bacon; Syracuse Univ, BM & MM; also studied with Sidney Foster & Rudolph Firkusny. Mem fac, Fla State Univ Sch Music; has taught piano & opera comp, 47- Guggenheim Fel. *Songs & Instrumental Works:* Piano Sonata; Pilgrimage (5 Biblical songs); Mystery (5 Songs of Motherhood; comn by Ford Found); Death Came Knocking (male chorus; comn by Brown Univ). *Scores:* Operas: Slow Dusk; Fugitives; Susannah (New York Music Critics Award, 56); Wuthering Heights (comn by Santa Fe Opera); The Sojourner and Mollie Sinclair; The Passion of Jonathan Wade (comn by Ford Found for New York Opera).

FLOYD, STAFFORD MARQUETTE (BRAXTON ELLIOTT) ASCAP 1976
composer, author
b Las Vegas, Nev, Dec 12, 51. Educ: Amityville Memorial High Sch; Wilberforce Univ, 69-71; studied songwriting & production techniques with Holland-Dozier-Holland, 76-79. Was in Off-Bway production "Marjorie"; instrumentalist, nightclubs & TV; recording artist, CBS Records, Invictus Records & VAP Records, producer. Chief Collabrs: Brian Holland, Edward Holland, Reginald Brown. *Songs:* I Don't Want to Work; No Limit; Every Night I Dance; Music: You're My Driving Wheel; Happy Song.

FLOYD, WILLIAM J
See Wilson, John Floyd

FLYNN, ALLAN ASCAP 1935
composer, author
b New York, NY, Apr 13, 1894; d New York, Sept 10, 65. Educ: Fordham Univ. Worked in Biograph Studios, Bronx. Went to Eng, 35, became writer for films & revues. Chief Collabrs: John Egan, Frank Madden. *Songs:* Moonspun Dreams; Rags; Maybe; Be Still, My Heart; Somewhere Beyond the Sunset; They Called Him 'Johnny Appleseed'.

FLYNN, FRANK ASCAP 1956
composer, author
b New York, NY, Sept 1, 1900; d Fords, NJ, Jan 25, 64. Educ: High sch. Drummer in orchs incl Rudy Vallee, Freddy Martin, Tommy & Jimmy Dorsey. Became liquor salesman, 41. *Songs:* Outside; She's a Very Good Friend, of a Friend, of a Friend, of a Very Good Friend of Mine.

FLYNN, GEORGE WILLIAM ASCAP 1973
composer, pianist
b Miles City, Mont, Jan 21, 37. Columbia Univ, BS, 64, MA, 66, DMA, 72; studied comp with Otto Luening, Jack Beeson, Chou Wen-Chung & Vladimir Ussachevsky. Teacher, Columbia Univ, City Univ New York, DePaul Univ, Chicago. Pianist, Tone-Roads concerts, New York; founder, Music by Concerts,

New York; founder/dir, Chicago Soundings Concerts. Recording artist, Turnabout, Atlantic, Finnadar Records. Chief Collabr: Jan Akkerman. *Instrumental Works:* Lammy; Javeh; Wound; Four Pieces; American Rest.

FODY, ILONA (HELEN JACOB)   ASCAP 1960
composer, author, teacher
b Elizabeth, NJ, July 13, 20. Educ: Woodrow Wilson No 12 Sch; Passaic High Sch; St Mary's Convent, piano degree. Author poems, Passaic Citizen Weekly; author songs for Joe Franklin's TV Prog & WABC Radio "Memory Lane." Chief Collabrs: Frank F Oliva, Texas Jim Robertson. *Songs:* A Woman; Till Eternity; Green Is the Color; Angel Face. *Scores:* Film/TV; Legend of the Cowboy Saint; You Are My Love; Ask For Me; Ring of Virgin Gold.

FOGARTY, J PAUL   ASCAP 1952
composer, author
b Michigan City, Ind, Nov 8, 1893; d Delray Beach, Fla, Mar 24, 76. Educ: Notre Dame Univ. WW I, USA, Capt Inf. Instr, Culver Mil Acad, 20-23. Entertainment dir, Edgewater Beach Hotel, Chicago. Had own radio & TV shows, WGN for 20 yrs. Author "Your Figure, Ladies," also record producer. Chief Collabrs: Ted Fiorito, Guy Lombardo, Arnold Johnson, Jule Styne. *Songs:* Betty Co-Ed; Joe College; You Are the Girl I Can't Forget; Tonight; She Loves Me Just the Same; In a Canoe; When I Wrote a Song; Charlie Cadet; Saturday Afternoon.

FOGELBERG, DANIEL GRAYLING
composer, musician
b Peoria, Ill, Aug 13, 51. Educ: Univ Ill. Founder, Hickory Grove Music. Founder & vpres, Full Moon Productions. Free-lance record producer; studio musician. Mem, Am Fedn of TV & Radio Artists & Telstar. *Songs:* Souvenirs; Captured Angel. *Albums:* Homefree; Souvenirs; Captured Angel; Netherlands; Twin Sons of Different Mothers.

FOGERTY, JOHN CAMERON   ASCAP 1971
composer, author, singer
b Berkeley, Calif, May 28, 45. Wrote, recorded & performed with Creedence Clearwater Revival, 68-72, recorded as the Blue Ridge Rangers in 73, also has recorded as a self-contained unit, 74- *Songs:* Proud Mary; Have You Ever Seen the Rain; Who'll Stop the Rain; Bad Moon Rising; Lodi; Fortunate Son; Travelin' Band; Lookin' Out My Back Door; Down on the Corner; Green River; Up Around the Bend; Run Through the Jungle; Keep on Chooglin'; It Came Out of the Sky; Hey Tonight; Don't Look Now; Born on the Bayou; Commotion; Rockin' All Over the World.

FOLEY, SYD   ASCAP 1954
composer, author
b New York, NY, May 6, 09; d. Educ: High sch; TV Workshop; studied radar techniques, operation with USAF. WW II, USAF; Flying Tigers Squadron. Personal mgr, 3 yrs. Publicity writer, music publ. *Songs:* Anytime Is Lovin' Time; Fire Island; Amazing What a Cigarette Can Do; Ev'rything Is Chlorophyl Today; That Christmas'y Feelin'; If You Know How to Love.

FOLLAS, RONALD W   ASCAP 1976
composer
b Toledo, Ohio, July 10, 46. Educ: Bowling Green State Univ, BMus, 68, studied comp with Donald Wilson; Univ NC, Greensboro, MFA, 75, studied comp with Jack Jarrett & Arthur Hunkins. Bassoonist & contrabassoonist, Toledo Orch & Greensboro Symph Orch. Instr theory, Drake Univ, 75-77; now dir electronic music, Weaver Educ Ctr, Greensboro. *Instrumental Works:* Oceta (4 instruments); Infrared (piccolo trumpet, amplified piano); Breakstone (band); Shadows and Reflections (orch, electronic tape).

FOMEEN, BASIL   ASCAP 1957
composer, author, accordionist
b Kharkoff, Russia, Jan 10, 02. Educ: Mil Acad, Russia; studied with Andrew Sobolski, Paul Ouglitzki, Constantine Schwedow & Alexander Gretchaninoff. To US, 22. Choirmaster, Russian nightclub, NY. Arr for record cos. Led all-accordion band in vaudeville & film theatres. Invented Basichimes, vibraphone & harpsichord. *Instrumental Works:* Piano: Prelude in D Flat; Valse in A; Valse Impromptue. *Songs & Instrumental Works:* Let's Dream My Love; Sing to Me; All Is Just a Misty Haze; Manhattan Gypsy; What Is All This For; Song of Life; Drinking Song; It's Hard Going Up the Hill.

FONTANA, DON GIFFORD   ASCAP 1977
composer, author, conductor
b Santa Ana, Calif, Feb 18, 31. Educ: Univ Southern Calif, BMusEd, 53, MM(church music), 63; cond study with Dr Charles C Hirt & Dr Howard S Swan; organ study with Dr Irene Robertson & Clarence Mader. Recording & radio organist, The Laymen's Hour, 52-; teacher, Sec Schs, High Sch & Jr Col, 56-74; cond & music dir, Robert Schuller & The Hour of Power, 74- *Songs:* Enjoy Jesus; Lord, Make My Life a Window; In the Stillness of This Moment; Seeking, Trusting, Lord I Come to You; I Can Do All Things Through Christ.

FORBERT, SAMUEL STEPHEN (STEVE)   ASCAP 1978
composer, singer
b Meridian, Miss, Dec 13, 54. Educ: Meridian pub schs. Started playing guitar, age 11; worked var day jobs & sang in the streets & at several clubs. Recording artist, Nemperor Records. Toured with & without band. *Songs & Instrumental Works:* Romeo's Tune; The Sweet Love That You Give; I'm in Love With You; Goin' Down to Laurel; Grand Central Station March 18, 1977; Thinkin'; What Kinda Guy?; You Cannot Win if You Do Not Play; It Isn't Gonna' Be That Way; Tonight I Feel So Far Away From Home; Big City Cat; Steve Forbert's Midsummer Night's Toast; Baby; Complications; Make It All So Real; Sadly Sorta Like a Soap Opera; January 23-30, 1978; You're Darn Right; Song for the South; House of Cards; Steve Forbert's Moon River; Wait; Say Goodbye to Little Jo; Settle Down.

FORBES, LOU   ASCAP 1951
composer, conductor
b St Louis, Mo, Aug 12, 02. Educ: Studied music with Edward Kilenyi & Max Steiner. To Hollywood; scored films; under contract to David Selznick, 7 yrs; music dir "Intermezzo", "Gone With the Wind" & "This Is Cinerama"; also mus dir, Goldwyn Productions, 3 yrs & with RKO. *Songs:* Passion Tango; The Bat; Hong Kong Affair; What Would I Do Without You; What's the Use of Crying; Heart of Gold; From the Earth to the Moon; Appointment in Honduras; The River's Edge.

FORD, CARL   ASCAP 1958
composer, author
b Albany, NY, June 5, 20. Educ: High sch. Harmonica player, mem, Borrah Minevitch Harmonica Rascals, 38-47. Formed own harmonica act, Madcaps. Chief Collabr: Lori Ford (wife). *Songs:* Choo Choo Cha Cha.

FORD, DELVIN ALLEN   ASCAP 1971
composer, singer
b Lebanon, Ore, May 26, 48. Educ: Eugene Bible Col, grad; Northwest Christian Col, BS; Mt Hood Community Col, Sch Music. Traveled with group, The Fury Three, 67-68; singer gospel concerts, 70-; under contract, Ralph Carmichael, Light Records, 71. *Songs:* The Love of God; Love Songs for Believers (10 weddings songs).

FORD, ERNEST BEVIL   ASCAP 1952
author
b D'lo, Miss, Feb 23, 16. Educ: Mineola High Sch; Stephen F Austin Univ, BA; Univ Tex, cert pub health admin; Tex A&M Univ, cert personnel admin. Began writing lyrics in col. Author, 2 novels. Advert account exec, Houston Chronicle, 47- Chief Collabrs: Eubie Blake, Harry Tobias, Jose Melis, Richard 'Two-Ton' Baker, Larry Stock, Geoffrey O'Hara, Billy Baskette, Gene Lynn, Frank Signorelli. *Songs:* Lyrics: Sweet Lips (Kiss My Blues Away); I'm Shuffling a New Pack of Dreams; You Can't Get Texas Outta Me; Pray; Give Me a Rod, a Reel, a Boat and a Creel; Sweet and Lovely Forever; Daddy Brings Home the Bacon (But Mama's Gotta Fry It); Sweet Talk; Baby, Be Smart; Time Drags Along; There's No One Around (To Say Goodbye To).

FORD, ERNEST JENNINGS (TENNESSEE ERNIE)   ASCAP 1958
composer, author, singer
b Bristol, Tenn, Feb 13, 19. Educ: Cincinnati Cons. Had own TV show; guest on many others. Appeared at London Palladium. Owns cattle ranch, Calif. Has made many records. *Songs:* Hogtied Over You; Kiss Me Big; Softly and Tenderly.

FORD, HERBERT EUGENE   ASCAP 1973
composer, author, percussionist
b Brooklyn, NY, Sept 13, 50. Educ: James Madison High Sch; Brooklyn Sch Music; Hunter Col; studied perc with Richard Cook, music theory & harmony with Tippy Larkin. Recording artist, Roadshow, Shotgun, Delite, Mercury & Genuine Records. TV & nightclub concerts; understudy for Old Calcutta; record producer, writer & arr. Chief Collabrs: William S Armour (Wee Willie), Tinker Barfield. *Songs & Instrumental Works:* Get Some; Plan for the Man; Wipe Your Feet and Dance; Hey You; Get on Up and Do It; Dance Line; It's Better to Give Than to Receive; Teenage Love Affair; Dedicated to Mom and Dad; I Found the Funky Man; I Don't Know What You've Got, But I Know What You Need; Boys Are Boys, Girls Are Girls.

FORD, JOAN   ASCAP 1959
author
b Denver, Colo, Dec 12, 21. Educ: Loretta Heights Col, BA; Cath Univ, MA. Chief Collabrs: Jean Kerr, Walter Kerr. *Songs:* The Pussy Foot; Who's Been Sitting in My Chair?; Give the Little Lady a Great Big Hand. *Scores:* Bway stage: Goldilocks.

FORD, LORI   ASCAP 1958
composer, author, singer
b Chicago, Ill, Feb 11, 28. Educ: High sch. Mem, vocal trio. Chief Collabr: Carl Ford (husband). *Songs:* Choo Choo Cha Cha.

FORD, OLIVE ELIZABETH   ASCAP 1971
composer, author, pianist
b Big Spring, Tex, Sept 2, 18. Educ: Lake Charles High Sch, La, 36; Vincent's Bus Col, 42; Life Bible Col, Los Angeles, 49; scholarships under Stella Champagne & Kathleen Blair Foster; continued study piano on West Coast. Arr for choral groups; taught piano; singer; church musician principally; traveled with husband in worldwide evangelism & music ministry; recorded album with Dayspring Publ; now writer of children's songs. *Songs:* The Gospel According to Mother Goose; Blow Gentle Breeze; Waters Are Flowing From Shiloh; More Than a Bridge; His Majesty, Jesus; The Theme of My Song (cantata); I Didn't Know; Because of Calvary; My Yesteryears; Oh, Praise the Lord; One Look That Day; Thanks Be to God (cantata); Through the Heat of Summer; For God and Country; He Silently Plans for Me; In the Meantime.

FORD, POWELL I
See Dempsey, James E

FORD, SHERMAN, JR   ASCAP 1957
composer, author
b Va, Mar 30, 29. Educ: Occidental Col, NY Univ. Served in Korea, 51-53. Newspaper reporter, Conn, NY & NJ; ed, Visitor. Author "The McCarthy Menace." Pres, Ford Record Co. *Songs:* Green River Waltz; Take Away Your Rosy Lips.

FORD, TENNESSEE ERNIE
See Ford, Ernest Jennings

FORD, TOM
See O'Keefe, Lester

FOREE, JAMES MELDIN (MEL)   ASCAP 1969
composer, author
b Athens, Tenn, July 25, 17. Educ: Sweetwater High Sch, Tenn, grad. Started writing songs after serving in US Navy during WW II. With publ firm, Acuff-Rose, 46-, nat promotion dir, currently. Chief Collabs: Cliff Carlisle, Bill Carlisle, Fred Rose & Cy Coben. *Songs:* All the World is Lonely Now; Lyrics: Heartbreak Avenue; I Know I Shouldn't Worry (But I Do); No One Will Ever Know; Music: Nobody's Child.

FORMAN, DAVID JESSE   ASCAP 1975
composer, author, singer
b Brooklyn, NY, Mar 31, 49. Educ: Forest Hills High Sch; Hunter Col, Musicianship with Helen Hobbs Jordan & voice with David Sorin Collyer. Pianist, guitarist; songwriter, 65- With Bell Records, 74 & Arista Records, 75. Has written several TV commercial jingles, 80. Comp music for, "Gymnast" & "Cafe Pittoresque." Chief Collabs: David M Levine, Gerry Goffin, Jack N Weber, David M Horowitz, Ben Susswein, H M Koutoukas. *Songs:* Dream of a Child; If It Take All Night; Rosalie; Treachery; I Wanna Be Your John; My Girl JoJo; Music: Smokey China Tea; A Train Lady; Sleeping on Her Doorstep; Lay Down Your Arms; Endless Waters; Persia; Lyric: What Did I Do (To Lose You). *Scores:* Opera/Ballet: The Butterfly Encounter.

FORNES, MARIA IRENE   ASCAP 1970
playwright, director
b Havana, Cuba, May 14, 30. Educ: Havana pub schs. Came to US, 45, naturalized, 51. Writer plays: "Tango Palace", "The Successful Life of 3", "Promenade", "The Office", "A Vietnamese Wedding", "The Annunciation", "Dr Kheal", "The Red Burning Light", "Molly's Dream", "The Curse of the Langston House", "Aurora", "Cap-a-Pie", "Lolita in the Garden", "Fefu and Her Friends", "Eyes on the Harem" & "Evelyn Brown (A diary)." Pres, New York Theatre Strategy, 73- John Hay Whitney Found grant, 61; Centro Mexicano de Escritores grant, 62; Cintas Found grant, 67; Creative Artists Pub Service Prog grants, 72 & 75; Yale/ABC fel, 67; Yale/Levine Found fel, 68; Rockefeller Found fel, 71; Guggenheim Found fel, 72; NEA, 74. Obie Awards: "Promenade" & "The Successful Life of 3," 65; "Fefu and Her Friends," 77; "Eyes on the Harem," 79.

FORNUTO, DONATO DOMINIC   ASCAP 1970
composer, teacher
b New York, NY, Sept 12, 31. Educ: City Col New York, BA; Hunter Col, MA; Columbia Univ Teachers Col, EdD; comp studies with Mark Brunswick & Josef Schmid. Pub sch teacher, New York & NJ, 53-66; part-time instr, Columbia Univ, 65-75; prof music, William Paterson Col, 67-; free-lance pianist & arr. Pedagogical works publ: "Tricks With Triads" (sets 1-3); "The Block Chord Style" & "Improvising the Blues." *Songs:* Music: Songs of Innocence and Experience (mezzo soprano & piano); Choral settings on poems of William Blake: The Lamb; The Tiger. *Instrumental Works:* Three Pieces for Clarinet and Piano; Suite for Alto Saxophone and Piano; Concerto for Piano and Concert Band.

FORRELL, GENE
composer, conductor, teacher
b Pittsburgh, Pa, May 5, 15. Educ: Duquesne Univ; Dalcroze Sch Music, NY, grad; comp & cond studies with Tibor Serly; piano studies with Erno Balogh; theory studies with Paul Emerich & Wallingford Riegger. Teacher & cond,

Creston Sch Music, NY; comp creative dance, Mettler Studios; comp over 200 film documentaries, US Off War Information, Dept Agr & Navy Dept; music dir, Int Film Found. Independent comp for TV films, signatures & commercials. Asst prof, Mills Col, Calif. Cond, Master Virtuosi, NY, 65-72, Ibiza Int Fest, Spain, Haifa Symph Orch, Israel, London Philh Orch, Vienna Symph, Vienna Philh Orch, Alexandra Choral Soc, Eng, Enfield Grand Opera Soc, Eng, CBC Orch, Vancouver, San Francisco & Syracuse Symphonies, English Nat Orch & English Sinfonia. *Songs:* Music: God is My Partner. *Scores:* Minstrels (ballet); The Trouble with King Twillus (children's opera); Film/TV: To Be Alive (Acad Award); Boundary Lines (Brussels Int Film Award); Picture in Your Mind (Brussels Int & Edinburgh Film Awards); Lincoln Speaks at Gettysburg; The Hereford Heritage; Corn's Hidden Enemies; Signature (TV Reader's Digest); Signature (Ford Playhouse).

FORREST, CHET
See Chichester, George Forrest

FORREST, GEORGE
See Chichester, George Forrest

FORRESTER, HUGH
See Waldman, Robert H

FORST, RUDOLF
composer, performer
b New York, NY, 1900; d Hartsdale, NY, 73. Educ: Music studies at age 8; Columbia Univ, Daniel Gregory Mason; self-taught comp. Violin instr, NY Col Music. Musical dir, radio sta WLWL; violinist & comp. Music consult in charge of sound, Radio City Music Hall & Music Hall of the Arts. Chief Collabr: George McKreig. *Instrumental Works:* Symphonia Brevis; Symphonietta for Strings; Sonata da Camera; Trio for Flute, Viola & Harp; Quartet for Strings (NBC Music Guild Award, 36); Fragment Partique; Symphonic Rhapsody on Ozark Folk Melodies; Music for Ten Instruments; Divertimento & numerous others.

FORSTER, JOHN MARSHALL   ASCAP 1975
composer, author, arranger
b Philadelphia, Pa, Apr 1, 48. Educ: Harvard Univ, BA(music), 69. Wrote a Hasty Pudding Show & co-founded, "The Proposition." Wrote revue material, one-act operas, pop tunes & music, NY. Arr & musical dir theatre & clubs. Chief Collabrs: Ted Drachman & Thomas Tierney. *Instrumental Works:* Love, Natalie. *Scores:* Grownups; Off-Bway & TV: Pretzels; Stage & TV: Clever Jack; Opera: Frio's Progress; The Dream Song.

FORSYTH, CECIL   ASCAP 1929
composer, author, violist
b London, Eng, Nov 30, 1870; d New York, NY, Dec 7, 41. Came to US, 14. Educ: Edinburgh Univ; Royal Col Music. Exec, NY music publ co, until 41. Author: "Music and Nationalism"; "A Treatise on Orchestration"; "A History of Music." *Instrumental Works:* Chant Celtique (viola, orch); Viola Concerto; Orch: Studies After Les Miserables; Ode to a Nightingale. *Scores:* Operas: Westward Ho!; Cinderella.

FORT, ELEANOR H (HANK)   ASCAP 1949
composer, author, teacher
b Nashville, Tenn, June 19, 14; d. Educ: Peabody Demonstration Sch. Has acted in summer stock & sung in nightclubs, on TV & radio. Has written scripts & musical commercials. Taught dancing. *Songs:* Save Your Confederate Money, Boys, the South Shall Rise Again; Protocol; Put Your Shoes on, Lucy; I Didn't Know the Gun Was Loaded; Pic-a-Nic-In the Park; Lady Bird; Cherry Blossom Spring; The Boardwalk; Southern Cookin'; My One Track Heart; I Love Connecticut; Tall Tales of Texas; Ah-Nah-Palip-Pah-La Day, Can't Wait; My Favorite Friend; The Written Guarantee.

FORTE, NICHOLAS A (APOLLO)   ASCAP 1973
composer, author, entertainer
b Waterbury, Conn, June 14, 38. Educ: Pvt instr music; high sch. Radio, TV & stage entertainer; produced albums. Pres, Versatility Music & Fan Records. Int entertainer; musician. *Songs:* The Scungilli Song (The Italian Delight); Can I Depend on You; Powdery Stuff the Skiers Song; Mr Music; I Love Ya Country (Tho I'm a City Slikin Guy); Beans and Sardines; Why Go It Alone; And Penny Marie; Sticks and Stones (Will Never Fall).

FORTGANG, JEFFREY   ASCAP 1973
composer, author, singer
b Brooklyn, NY, June 3, 49. Educ: Yale Univ, BA, 71; Adelphi Univ, Inst Advan Psychol Studies, MA, 76, doctoral candidate, 80. Arr, comp & performer on campus, leader, Yale Whiffenpoofs. Full-time music career, 71-74; wrote & recorded musical pub service radio spots. Clinical psychologist; composer & performer. *Songs:* Some Guys Have All the Luck.

FORTINI, JAMES (PETE JAMES, JIMMY WALKER, JACK COVAIS)   ASCAP 1956
composer, author, singer
b Ashville, Pa, Apr 8, 26. Educ: Univ Cent Fla, BA(admin/personnel mgt);

Jones Col, Jacksonville, Fla, business admin; Univ Pittsburgh, music major. Nightclub owner & entertainer. Publ, NuView Publ Co. Writer & independent recording producer, Fortini Records. With Federal Serv, 30 yrs. Chief Collabrs: Bob Quimby, James Timothy Fortini (son). *Songs & Instrumental Works:* This Is Me; Our Red, White and Blue; I Had a Dream; Lonely Star; Heavenly Treasure; Night Lover; In the School Yard.

FORTINI, JAMES TIMOTHY PETER (SPIDER)   ASCAP 1973
(PETE JAMES JR)
composer, author, teacher
b Eleuthera, BWI, Oct 28, 58. Educ: Los Angeles Cent High Sch; Orvidio Music Sch; Pvt Music Sch, Vallejo, Calif. Music writer for Nu View Publ Co; recording artist; formed new musical group Night Lovers. Chief Collabrs: James Fortini, Bob Quimby. *Songs:* Bashful Country Kid; Music: Night Lover; Devil in Me; In the School Yard; Heavenly Treasure.

FORTIS, JOHNNY   ASCAP 1946
composer, arranger
b Philadelphia, Pa, Mar 25, 13; d. Educ: Pa Acad of Fine Arts, scholarship. Writer, special material for "Icetime." *Songs & Instrumental Works:* Barnyard Band; The Blue Serge Suit With the Belt in the Back; Cowboy in Khaki; Get in Touch With Me; You Oughta Learn to Dance.

FORTNER, CLARKE   ASCAP 1975
composer, author
b Bethany, Ill, Aug 9, 04. Educ: Bush Cons Music, Chicago, 20; studied violin, Richard Czerwonky; comp, Kenneth M Bradley; harmony & analysis, Ernest A Leo. Cond, theatre orchs, St Louis & Chicago, 20-28. Mem fac, Nat Music Camp, Interlochen, Mich, 38. *Songs:* You Always Seem to Be With Me; Day By Day; Music: Ridin'. *Instrumental Works:* Blue Waters (piano & string ens); Ten Easy Tunes (accordion & organ).

FORTUNATE, LOU M   ASCAP 1965
composer, author
b Detroit, Mich, June 20, 38. Educ: Univ Detroit High Sch; Wayne State Univ, BMusic; Pius X Sch, Manhattanville Col. Past pres, Detroit Cath Guild of Organists & Choir Dirs; mem, Music Comn, Archdiocese of New York. Comp & producer, LP's of relig music. Creative dir, Parish Productions, Inc. *Songs:* Hurray for God; Alive in Christ; Do This in Remembrance of Me; The Spirit of Jesus; I Want to Learn More About You; Come to Me; The Christmas Story; People; Helping Hands; The Snow Storm; New Friends; We All Need One Another; The Moon; A Sign of His Love; Lyrics: New Life. *Scores:* Bway Show: The Man From Broadway.

FORTUNE, JOE
See Hastings, Ross Ray

FOSTER, AL
See Fleitman, Alexander Oscar

FOSTER, CHARLES W   ASCAP 1978
composer, author
b Long Beach, Calif, June 22, 48. Played in var Southern Calif bands incl Ethyl Mertz, The Slugs, Crotalus, Mr Lizard & Oasis. Writer of lyrics for The Bouncers Band. Chief Collabrs: Rex Bailey, Dave Travis, John Larson. *Songs:* Cargo Cult; Lyrics: Sinsemilla Shake; I'll Treat You Nice (And Beat You Twice a Day); Comin' on In.

FOSTER, FRANK BENJAMIN   ASCAP 1960
composer, author, educator
b Cincinnati, Ohio, Sept 23, 28. Educ: Walnut Hills High Sch; Wilberforce Univ. Saxophonist, comp & arr, Count Basie Orch, 53-64; bandleader, Non-Electric Company Sextet, Living Color (12 shades of black) & Loud Minority Big Bang, 64-; free-lance musician, arr & comp, appearing as leader & guest soloist, var int jazz festivals & New York jazz clubs; jazz educr, lectr & clinician, cols & univs throughout US. *Instrumental Works:* Shiny Stockings; Hip Shakin'; Simone; Cecilia Is Love; Blues in Hoss' Flat; Square Knights of the Round Table; Manhattan Fever; Chiquito Loco; Janie Huk; Someone's Rocking My Jazzboat.

FOSTER, JERRY GAYLON   ASCAP 1969
composer, singer
b Tallapoosa, Mo, Nov 19, 35. Received 10 ASCAP Awards, 72, 11 ASCAP Awards, 77; as Foster & Rice team rec'd ASCAP record for most awards in 1 yr, also holders of ASCAP Award Record for a Country & Western writing team in the history of the soc. Chief Collabr: Bill Rice. *Songs:* Lyrics: The Easy Part's Over; Heaven Everyday; Someone to Give My Love To; When You Say Love; For a Minute There; Would You Take Another Chance on Me; Think About It Darlin'; Let's Put It Back Together Again; She's Pulling Me Back Again; Gotta Quit Lookin' at You Baby; Take Time to Love Her; Here Comes the Hurt Again; Just Long Enough to Say Goodbye; Is It Any Wonder That I Love You; Somebody Loves Me; I Hate Goodbyes; When Your Good Love Was Mine; Rising Above It All; Loving You Has Changed My Life; Hey There Girl; There's Something About You I Love; Song and Dance Man; All I Want to Do Is Say I Love You; Love Survived; Ain't She Somethin' Else; I'll Think of Something.

FOSTER, LAWRENCE JEROME   ASCAP 1964
composer, author, musician
b Chicago, Ill, June 1, 09. Educ: San Diego State Univ, BA & MA; US Int Univ, PhD; perc & harmony studies with Roy Knapp, Chicago. Drummer & vocalist, Carl Sands, Ted Fiorito, Jack Fina, Freddie Martin, Husk O'Hare, Maurie Sherman & Don Pedro Orchs, plus many other bands of the 30's & 40's. Co-author educ bk, "Secret of Reading." Chief Collabr: Polly Foster. *Songs:* Music: Singing Sounds (38 educ songs for children).

FOSTER, PAULA HARTFORD (CHAPIN HARTFORD)   ASCAP 1977
composer, author, singer
b Boston, Mass, May 15, 44. Educ: Colby Col, Waterville, Maine. Back-up harmony singer, 9 yrs; writer, 12 yrs; artist-writer, Pic Records, 77-78 & LS Records, 78-80. Co-owner, Albino Buzzard Music & Electric Mule Music. Now writer, singer back-up harmony, studio & local shows, Nashville. Chief Collabrs: Jim Foster; Don Graham. *Songs:* Rainsong; I Knew the Mason; Borrowing; Rio Grande; Puttin' the Lady Back Together.

FOSTER, PRESTON S   ASCAP 1953
composer, author, guitarist
b Ocean City, NJ, Aug 24, 1900; d San Diego, Calif, July 14, 70. Singer in radio; Grand Opera Co. Bway actor, 28-32, then film actor appearing in many motion pictures incl "Last Mile", "Informer", "Last Days of Pompeii", "Annie Oakley", "Plough and the Stars", "Outcasts of Poker Flats", "Submarine Patrol", "Northwest Mounted Police", "Unfinished Business", "Thunderbirds", "My Friend Flicka", "Thunderhead, Son of Flicka", "Harvey Girls", "I Shot Jesse James", "Tomahawk", "Kansas City Confidential" & many others, 32-52, also starring in TV series incl "Waterfront", "Gunslinger", "Chubasco" & many others, 54-65. Toured US as guitarist-singer with wife & daughter. Exec producer, El Camino Playhouse, Calif. Chief Collabr: Perry Botkin. *Songs:* Good Ship Lalapaloo; Two Shillelagh O' Sullivan.

FOSTER, ROBERT ESTILL   ASCAP 1971
composer, author, conductor
b Raymondville, Tex, Jan 21, 39. Educ: Univ Tex, Austin, BMus, 62; Univ Houston, MEd, 64. Taught in pub schs, Tex, 61-64. Teacher & asst dir bands & trumpet, Univ Fla, 64-71; dir bands, Univ Kans, 71- Author of bk, "Multiple-Option Marching Techniques." Chief Collabr: Sandy (Saul) Feldstein. *Instrumental Works:* Marching Band: The Screamer; The Pony Express; Patriotic Finale; The Dude.

FOSTER, WARREN   ASCAP 1956
actor
b Brooklyn, NY, Oct 24, 04; d. Educ: Brooklyn Tech; Pratt Inst. Writer & cartoonist, Paramount & Warner Bros, TV incl "Flintstones" & "Yogi Bear." Co-script writer for film "Hey, There-It's Yogi Bear." Chief Collabr: Alan Livingston. *Songs:* I Taut I Taw a Puddy Tat.

FOTE, RICHARD JOSEPH   ASCAP 1970
composer
b Olean, NY, Aug 13, 32. Educ: State Univ NY Col, Fredonia, BS, 57; Univ Rochester Eastman Sch Music, MA, 62; studied with E Remington. Music teacher pub schs & at col level, 10 yrs. Worked for music publ, 8 yrs. Freelance trombonist & writer, Fla, 78-

FOTI, JACQUES   ASCAP 1961
composer, author, pianist
b Hungary, June 23, 24. Educ: Commercial Acad, Budapest. WW II, worked with Hungarian underground; escaped to US, 47. Singer in nightclubs & hotels; had own TV show. *Songs:* Intimately Yours; I'd Like It.

FOTIN, LARRY
See Fotinakis, Lawrence Constantine

FOTINAKIS, DOROTHY OWENS (DOROTHY FOTINE) ASCAP 1971
composer, author, teacher
b Philadelphia, Pa, Jan 6, 12. Educ: Collingswood High Sch, NJ; Brower Cons Music, studied piano, harmony & theory. Chief Collabrs: Larry Fotine, Charles 'Bud' Dant. *Songs:* Go Back to the Bible; A World of Prayer (Is a World of Peace); Show Me the Way.

FOTINAKIS, LAWRENCE CONSTANTINE   ASCAP 1947
(LARRY FOTIN, LARRY FOTINE)
composer, author
b Camden, NJ, Apr 27, 11. Educ: Self-taught in piano & orchestration; Univ Calif, Los Angeles, had advanced courses & pvt teachers in twelve tone studies & writing for motion pictures. Had own orch in Middle Atlantic states, 30's. Arr & orchestrator, Sammy Kaye Orch, 40-45, Blue Barron Orch, 45-48. Started own orch, 48 & toured US & Can; recorded with orch on Decca, Coral & King. Arr, Lawrence Welk Orch, 58-60. Has made recordings with own orch on Balboa under name Constantine & his Orch, 60- Author: "Theory and Techniques of Twelve Tone Composition"; "Musicians and Other Noisemakers"; "The Contemporary Musician's Handbook." Chief Collabrs: Frank Stanton, Gladys Shelley, Tommie Connor, Jerry Gladstone. *Songs:* Music: You Were Only Fooling; Windmill in Motion; Blue Guitar; Kitty Kat

Parade; Orange Blos'm Serenade; If Tears Were Roses; I Ain't Got Nothin' But the Blues; If We All Said a Prayer; On Rotten Row; It's a Lovely Day in Paree; Spring in Montmartre; Mon Souvenir; I Give Myself to You. *Songs & Instrumental Works:* The Big Bird; Midnight Ride; Steamboat Rag; Nevada.

FOTINE, DOROTHY
See Fotinakis, Dorothy Owens

FOUTS, TOM C ASCAP 1959
composer, author
b Carroll Co, Ind, Nov 24, 18. Educ: Col. Appeared on WLW, Cincinnati. USN Fleet Entertainment Div, WW II. With WLS "National Barn Dance," Chicago, 10 yrs & "Polka Go Round," ABC-TV, 3 yrs. On music staff, WBKB-TV; DJ, WLS, Chicago. Chief Collabr: Jerry Richards. *Songs:* Peter Piper Pickle Pepper Polka.

FOWLER, REX MARCH ASCAP 1972
composer, performer, guitarist
b Kansas City, Mo, Sept 16, 47. Educ: Aroostook State Col, 2 1/2 yrs. Left col to pursue music career as singer & songwriter. Recorded with Elektra, RCA & Waterhouse. Chief Collabrs: Con Fullam, Billy Mernit. *Songs & Instrumental Works:* Aztec Two Step; Second Step; Two's Company; Adjoining Suites; Times of Our Lives; also many other songs.

FOWLER, WILLIAM RANDOLPH ASCAP 1959
composer, author
b Jamaica, NY, Aug 29, 22. Educ: Studies with Roger Auber, Lucien Moroweck, Ferde Grofe & Joseph J Lilley. Mem & student cond band & orch, Beverly Hills High Sch, winner nat championship at San Francisco World's Fair. Taught piano, comp & orchestration privately. Author bk "Young Man from Denver." Newspaper background reporter & writer. Head writer for "Red Skelton TV Show," 52-53. Chief Collabrs: Jimmie Dodd, Joseph J Lilley. *Songs:* Sleep, Sleep, Sleep; Beverly; Music: Morning in Manhattan; He's So Married; A Letter to Ray Turner; Lyrics: The Oregon Trail; Robin, Robin; Lonely Road.

FOX, BAYNARD LAYNE ASCAP 1972
composer, author, director
b Louisville, Ky, Sept 21, 32. Educ: Georgetown Col; Southern Baptist Sem Sch Church Music; Univ Louisville Sch Music, BMusEd. Pvt teacher vocal instrumental, 20 yrs; pub sch music teacher, 2 yrs. Minister music/church choir dir, 20 yrs; founder/dir, Atlanta Christian Chorus Inc, 74- Comp church music, 30 yrs. *Songs:* I'll Tell the World That I'm a Christian; Amazing Grace, How Can It Be?

FOX, FREDERICK ALFRED ASCAP 1970
composer
b Detroit, Mich, Jan 17, 31. Educ: Wayne State Univ, BMus, 53; Univ Mich, 53-54; Ind Univ, MMus, 57, DMus(comp), 59. Composer-in-residence, Minneapolis Pub Sch, The Young Composers Proj, 62-63. Prof comp & dir new music ens, Ind Univ, 74- NEA grants, 76 & 79. *Instrumental Works:* A Stone, a Leaf, an Unfound Door (soprano, clarinet, perc, small chorus); BEC-1 (winds & perc); BEC-10 (chamber orch); The Descent (chorus, piano, perc); Variations (violin, cello, piano); Ternion (oboe & orch); Variables-1 (violin & piano); Variables-3 (flute, clarinet, horn, violin, cello, piano); Variables-5 (orch); Variables-6 (flute, clarinet, violin, cello, 1 perc); Time Excursions (soprano, speaker, flute, clarinet, violin, viola, cello, piano, 2 perc); Beyond Winterlock (orch); Ambient Shadows (flute, clarinet, trombone, violin, viola, cello, piano, 1 perc); Night Ceremonies (orch); SAX (solo alto saxophone & saxophone quartet); Inside Out (dancers, flute, clarinet, bassoon, horn, trumpet, trombone, 2 violins, viola, cello, doublebass, piano, 2 perc).

FOX, J BERTRAM ASCAP 1925
composer, singer, teacher
b Stamford, Conn, Aug 8, 1881; d New York, NY, Jan 24, 46. Studied music with Victor Maurel, Max Spicker. Singer in concerts & Bway musicals, incl "The Enchantress." Choral dir, Victor Herbert Concerts. Accompanist, St Cecilia Club of N Y. *Songs:* Two Cranes; Evening; Strings in the Earth; One Lovely Name; The Bugle; The Horn.

FOX, JULES LEE ASCAP 1952
composer, author
b Covington, Ky, Dec 27, 16. Educ: Woodward High Sch, Cincinnati, Ohio, 38; Hollywood High Sch, nights, 38-39. Press relations for Ella Fitzgerald, Sarah Vaughan, George Shearing, Jack Teagarden, Billy Eckstein, Lionel Hampton, Sammy Davis, Jr, Miyoshi Umeki & Dinah Washington. Author commercials for Ford, Rit Dye, US Agriculture Dept, Squirt & Tecate, spec material for singers in nightclub acts; mgr, Ann Weldon, Damito Jo & Barbara Randolph. Chief Collabrs: Sam Friedman, Darrel Calker, Louis Palange. *Songs:* Carrier Pigeon; Love Ya Like Mad; The Iggidy Song; Who Cares; Blues Aint News to Me; Flim Flam; Til You Return; Kissin' Bug; Treat Me Nice; Soft Spot; Walk Back Through Mem'ries; We Need Each Other.

FOX, OSCAR J ASCAP 1927
composer, conductor, teacher
b Burnet County, Tex, Oct 11, 1879; d Charlottesville, Va, July 29, 61. Educ: Munic Col Music, Switzerland, studied with Lothar Kempter, Carl Attenhofer; also with Percy Goetschius. Organist, choir dir, churches, glee clubs & Univ Choral Soc, Univ Tex. Gave recitals, appear'd on radio. Mem, Comp & Authors Guild & Nat Asn Am Comp & Cond; hon mem, Tex Music Teachers Asn. *Songs:* The Hills of Home; My Heart Is a Silent Violin; Rounded Up in Glory; O Perfect Love; White in the Moon the Long Road Lies; They Did Not Tell Me; In the High Hills; Rain and the River.

FOX, RAY ERROL ASCAP 1969
author
b Philadelphia, Pa. Educ: Central High Sch, Philadelphia; Boston Univ, 57-60; Temple Univ Law Sch, 60-61. Staff writer; theatre lyricist; theatre & dance critic. Author "Angela Ambrosia"; contributor to newspapers & mag. Chief Collabrs: Albert Hague, Jim Steinman, Gary William Friedman, Neil Sheppard. *Songs:* Lyrics: Here's to Love; The Face on the Cutting-Room Floor; The Clowns (film title song); Seeing You Like This. Scores: Bway Show: The Sign in Sidney Brustein's Window; Children's Show: Young Ben Franklin.

FOX, WALTER KENT composer, author
b Lexington, Ky, Oct 16, 47. Recording artist with own recording studio & production company. Chief Collabrs: Robert E Walker; Norm Null, Bob Santos. *Songs:* New York Callin' Miami; Midnight in the Morning (The All Night DJ); Ben Franklin Said It; Married to the Girl I Love; G'rage Sale.

FRACKENPOHL, ARTHUR ROLAND ASCAP 1964
composer, teacher
b Irvington, NJ, Apr 23, 24. Educ: Millburn High Sch, NJ, grad, 41; Eastman Sch Music, Univ Rochester, BA, 47, MA, 49; McGill Univ, MusDoc, 57; studied with Darius Milhaud at Tanglewood, summer 48; studied with Nadia Boulanger at Fontainebleau, summer 50, awarded 1st Prize Comp. Mem, USA, 43-46. Instr, Crane Sch Music, State Univ NY Col Potsdam, 49-54, asst prof, 54-57, assoc prof, 57-61, prof music & coordr, Keyboard Courses, 61- Grants: Fac res fel to write keyboard harmony text, State Univ NY Res Found, 59, fac res fel comp, 63, 67, 71 & 73; Ford Found Grant to serve as comp-in-residence for Hempstead Pub Schs, NY, 59-60. Annual Awards, ASCAP, 64-; many comns to write choral & instrumental comp. Mem: NY Sch Music Asn; Music Educr Nat Conference; Nat Asn Jazz Educr; Phi Mu Alpha Sinfonia. *Songs:* Music: Annie Laurie (arr chorus); Londonderry Air (arr chorus). *Instrumental Works:* String Quartet; Breviates for Brasses; Variations on a March of Shostakovitch (trombone & piano); Concertino (tuba & strings); Variations for Tuba and Winds; Brass Trio; Brass Quartet; Brass Quintet No 1; Brass Quintet No 2; Trombone Quartet; American Folle Song Suite (band); Short Overture (orch); Pop Suite for Euphonium (tuba quartet); Pop Suite (brass quintet); Sonatina for Clarinet and Piano; Toccata for Woodwind Quartet; Three Short Pieces for String Quartet. *Songs & Instrumental Works:* Domestic Relations (chamber opera); Gloria (chorus, soloists & orch); Winter Celebrations (chorus, narrator & band); Three Shakespearean Songs (chorus); The Natural Superiority of Men (treble chorus & orch); Three Limericks in Canon Form (var choral groups); Lovers Love the Spring (var choral groups); A Child This Day (soloists, chorus, narrator, brasses & organ); Make a Joyful Noise (chorus, brasses & organ).

FRADKIN, LESLIE MARTIN ASCAP 1970
composer, author, singer
b New York, NY, Jan 15, 51. Educ: Barnard Sch for Boys; Kenyon Col, studied voice with David Sarin Collyer, 77. Recording artist, MGM/Sunflower, 70; producer writer, Laurie Records, 73 & 76. On tour with TFU, 74-75; original cast mem, "Beatlemania," 76-79, on Bway tour, 80. Formed new group, The Allies. Chief Collabr: Diana Haig. *Songs:* Song of a Thousand Voices; God Bless California; You Can Cry If You Want To; Christopher's Sorrow; You Program Me; I Can Never Say Goodbye.

FRAIELI, LORETO (JIMMIE CRANE) ASCAP 1953
composer, author
b Providence, RI, Aug 1, 10. Educ: High sch. Jewelry manufacturer. Chief Collabr: Al Jacobs. *Songs:* Lonely People; Somewhere Elvis Is Smiling; Music: If I Give My Heart to You; I Need You Now; Hurt; Every Day of My Life; I Can't Get You Out of My Heart.

FRAMER, WALTER H ASCAP 1954
author, producer
b Pittsburgh, Pa, Apr 7, 08. Educ: Univ Pittsburgh. Mgr, Warner Bros theatres. Organized Pittsburgh Playhouse. Radio announcer, commentator & DJ; created & produced radio & TV shows, incl "The Big Payoff", "Break the Bank" & "For Love or Money." Am prog consult, ABC-TV, Eng, 59-61.

FRAMPTON, PETER KENNETH ASCAP 1976
composer, singer, guitarist
b Beckenham, Eng, Apr 22, 50. Former mem of group The Herd. Soloist with rock group Humble Pie, 68-71. Founder of group Frampton's Camel, 71, with group until 74. Soloist, 74- Recording artist, 68- Appeared in film "Sergeant

Peppers Lonely Heart's Club Band." *Songs:* Show Me the Way; I'm in You; Do You Feel Like We Do. *Albums:* As Safe As Yesterday; Humble Pie; Rock On; Performance Rockin' At the Fillmore; Frampton's Camel; Wind of Change; Somethin's Happening; Frampton; Frampton Comes Alive; I'm in You, Where I Should Be.

FRANCES, PAULA
See Timpano. Paola Francesca (Ianello)

FRANCESCHINI, ROMULUS   ASCAP 1967
composer
b Brooklyn, NY, Jan 5, 29. Educ: Comp with Vincent Persichetti, Stefan Wolpe & Morton Feldman. Dir, EMP Electronic Music Productions, Morristown, NJ, 69-71; secy, Philadelphia Comp Forum Inc, 69-75; comp & music dir, Solaris Dance Co, New York, 75-76. Staff, Edwin A Fleisher Music Collection, Free Libr Philadelphia, 60- Music adv, Relache New Music Ens, Philadelphia, 77- *Songs:* Music: High Rise (song cycle for voice); White Spirituals (soprano, 12 instruments). *Instrumental Works:* Prelude and Celebration for Band; Omaggio a Kurt Weill (accordion); Polar (2 pianos); 5 Pieces for Orchestra; Omaggio a Satie (piano); Synastry (alto flute, English horn, clarinet).

FRANCHINI, ANTHONY JOSEPH (MEL BALL,   ASCAP 1956
TONY ZACHARY)
composer, author, music teacher
b Naples, Italy, Aug 2, 1898. Educ: Pvt tutor; Washington Heights High Sch, New York; Houston Univ, 45; studied harmony with Busoni & music theory with Denardis, Zangarelli, Tenaroli & Schroeder; studied violin with Fiumara & Ralf del Sordo, 16 yrs. Child prodigy at age 8. Mem of duo with Frank Ferrera, 20-27. Music teacher, 32-47. Arr for music publ, 18 yrs, J J Shubert, Rodgers & Hammerstein, Mantovani, 3 yrs & Charles Gould Satin Strings, 62- Cond; played violin, guitar & mandolin; mem of var symphonies; with Reno & Las Vegas casino orchs, 18 yrs. Chief Collabrs: Jimmy Dorsey, J Fred Coots, Sam Perry. *Songs:* Talkin' to My Heart; Violinola; Fiddlinette; Pretending; Just an Old Bouquet; My Sweet Hawaiian Baby; Lorraine; Moana (Of the South Sea Isle); Sweet Lei Lehua; Koni Au I Ka Wai; Royal Hawaiian Hotel; Hame Pila; Tomi Tomi; Lei E; Wahiikaahuula; Maui Girl; Ua Like No a Like; Mauna Kea; Mai Poina Oe Ia'u; My Hawaiian Maid; Aloha Oe; One, Two, Three, Four; Hawaii Ponoi; Sweet Kalua Lady; Dreams of Aloha; Hawaiian Ripples; Moana Chimes.

FRANCIS, ANNETTE   ASCAP 1956
composer, author, pianist
b Waco, Tex, Dec 12, 28. Educ: Waco High Sch, valedictorian; Sophie Newcomb Col; Col of Music of Cincinnati, studied piano with Marcian Thalberg. Pianist, radio & TV; author, med bks for laymen. *Songs:* Wishing Well; My Heart's Desire.

FRANCIS, ART
See Otto, Joseph Francis

FRANCIS, BENNIE
See Anders, John Frank

FRANCIS, CONNIE
See Franconero, Constance

FRANCIS, LEE
See Sukman, Frances Paley

FRANCIS, MICHAEL FRANK   ASCAP 1974
composer, producer, arranger
b Salt Lake City, Utah, Sept 8, 50. Educ: Blackford High Sch, San Jose, Calif; Univ Southern Calif, Los Angeles; Calif State Univ, Los Angeles, BA(comp), studied comp with Ted Nichols, 67-72, Byong-Kong Kim, 70-73, Roy Harris, 71, Earle Hagen, 73. Started as woodwind musician with Stan Kenton Orch, 66-67, Hanna Barbera Cartoons, 69-72; comp for schs & jazz fests, 68-74, cond own orch, Mike Francis & the Megalocephalic Machine, 70-78; formed publ co, Mike Francis Music, 73. Producing records, 74-; comp for "Merv Griffin Show," 74-75, free-lance studio arr-comp, 70- Chief Collabrs: Rik Cutler, Dean Babcock, Peter Sevalay, Antonio Spagnola, Darrell Briske. *Songs:* My Love, My Life; Music: My Woman, My Lady. *Instrumental Works:* Dreams of a Psychopath; A New Kind of Blues; Marche; Megalocephalic Machine; Along My Way.

FRANCIS, PAUL P   ASCAP 1961
composer, author, producer
b Woburn, Mass, Sept 2, 11. Educ: Boston Cons Music. Dir in vaudeville ballrooms, throughout US. Owner, Frank Paul Enterprises. *Songs:* Happy Birthday, Baby; My Congratulations, Baby; Crying Roses; Rose in a Garden; I Do; Ring Around the Rosie.

FRANCIS, SESEEN   ASCAP 1961
composer, author
b Mannington, WVa, Feb 14, 37. Music & lyrics for pop songs & comp of bk,

music & lyrics for musicals incl, "When a Bell Rings." Chief Collabr: Elmer Willett. *Songs:* Whole Lotta Lovin'; Now You Know What It Feels Like.

FRANCISCO, MANUEL
See Terr Mischa, (Michael) Richard

FRANCONERO, CONSTANCE (CONNIE FRANCIS)   ASCAP 1959
composer, singer, publisher
b Newark, NJ. Educ: Arts High Sch; early music study with father. Appeared as singer & accordionist on "Arthur Godfrey Show" at age 11. Toured US, Australia, New Zealand, SAfrica & Europe. Singer, nightclubs, films & concerts. Had own TV show. Owns publ cos. Made many records. Author: "For Every Young Heart." *Songs:* Italian Lullaby; Senza Mama.

FRANCOUR, CHARLES HARVEY   ASCAP 1972
composer, singer
b South Bend, Ind, May 28, 47. Educ: Ind Univ Sch of Music; classical training, 10 yrs. Prof musician, 8 yrs. Recording artist, as instrumentalist & for incidental music, var record cos. Singer & songwriter, under contract to EMI-America. Chief Collabrs: Carlos Garcia, Arturo Casado, Victor Angulo, Carl Driggs. *Songs:* Because of You (the Sun Don't Set); Over the Line. *Instrumental Works:* Under the Boulevard Lights.

FRANGKISER, CARL   ASCAP 1953
composer, author, conductor
b Loudonville, Ohio, Sept 18, 1894; d. Educ: Capito Col of Music & Oratory, BM, MM, MusD; US Band Sch, France. Cond, 308th Engrs Band, World War I. Cornetist, Buffalo Bill, Sells-Floto & Barnum & Bailey Circuses, theatres & touring shows. Music dir & ed, Unity Sch of Christianity for many yrs. Cond, park concerts, Kansas City area, 38 yrs. Taught, Kansas City Cons. Cond, radio prog, Lee's Summit, Mo. *Songs:* God Bless You Everyone. *Instrumental Works:* Symph band overtures: Transcendence; Dedication; Stratosphere; Mightier Than Circumstance; Rendezvous With Destiny; The Victorious; Three Gates of Gold; Hickory Hill.

FRANK, CAMILLA MAYS   ASCAP 1958
author
b Blacksburg, SC, Apr 22, 1899. Educ: Cent High Sch, Memphis, Tenn, grad, 17; Presby Hosp Sch Nursing, Memphis, 20. Produced & broadcast, "Shut-in Shelter," New Orleans, La, 40-42; from pvt to Capt, WAAC & WAC, WW II, 42-46; with spec serv sch, Washington & Lee Univ, 43; active in Int Outdoor Poetry Show, New Orleans, 53-72; Poet Laureate, State Soc, Colonial Dames XVII Century, 63-80. Chief Collabr: Jane Douglass White. *Songs:* Lyrics: Song of the Women's Army Corps (official song); Come Unto Me; I Am Not Worthy; Sun Comin' Up in the Morning.

FRANK, DAVID MICHAEL   ASCAP 1977
composer
b Baltimore, Md, Dec 21, 48. Educ: Peabody Cons Music; Paris Am Acad Music; Northwestern Univ, BM, studied piano with Gui Mombaerts. Musical dir & arr, Jane Olivor; cond/pianist, 6 Bway shows "Grease", "Pippin", "The Me Nobody Knows", "Tricks", "Sextet" & "Pretty Belle." Comp music for off-Bway bicentennial musical "I Paid My Dues." Mem, Nat Acad Recording Arts & Sci, Nat Acad TV Arts & Sci & Am Soc Music Arr. *Scores:* Film/TV: A Different Story; Bad News Bears; Here's Boomer; The Kid From Left Field.

FRANK, GEORGE
See Fellows, Floyd George

FRANK, MARCEL GUSTAVE   ASCAP 1951
composer, arranger
b Vienna, Austria, Dec 3, 06. Educ: Univ Vienna State Acad Music & Art. Cond opera in Vienna, Munich & San Francisco; comp & arr in New York. *Songs & Instrumental Works:* A Ceremonial Prelude; Gypsy Fantasy; Chaconne with Variations; Symphonic Prelude; Pas de Deux; Lyric Poem; Mardigras Masquerade; Concertino; Dance Humoresque; Centurion Theme; 20 Flute Solos; Evening Reverie; Golden Gate Concerto; Canon and Fugue; Classical Improvisation; Prayer for Young People; recorded music for film, radio & TV; dramatic & soap opera themes; mood & background music.

FRANK, RENE   ASCAP 1958
composer, pianist, teacher
b Mulhouse, Alsace-Lorraine, Feb 16, 10; d Ft Wayne, Ind, Mar 21, 65. Educ: Oberrealschule, Pforzheim, Ger; studied with Nicolai Lopatnikoff, Hermann Reutter, Wolfgang Fortner & Rudolf Fetsh; Ind Univ, MM & MusD. Taught music, USA Sch Kyoto, Japan, 46-47. To US in 47. Fac, Pikeville Col, 48-51; chmn music dept, Ft Wayne Bible Col, 51-65; instr, Ind Univ Ctr, 56-64. Mem, Nat Church Mus. Music Fellowship; Int Soc Contemporary Music, Chicago & Univ Comp Exchange. *Songs & Instrumental Works:* 5 Psalms (voice, orch); The Spite of Michal (cantata; Ernest Bloch Award); Passion Symphony; The Prodigal Son (cantata); Little Suite; Piano Sonatina; Sonata for Violin, Piano; String Quartet; And God Came (Christmas oratorio); Triptych of Heavenly Love (song cycle). *Scores:* Opera: Call of Gideon.

FRANK, RUTH VERD (RUTH UHL) ASCAP 1955
composer, author, teacher
b Bristol, Ind, Aug 28, 1899; d Ft Lauderdale, Fla, Mar 6, 77. Educ: Moyer Music Sch, Freeburg, Pa. Staff organist, WCFL, Chicago, 42. Pianist, music publ. Coach & writer of spec material for radio & TV. Chief Collabr: Eddie Ballantine. *Songs:* Alone in a Fog; Down Hoosier Way (ABC network theme); Above the Sun; Allegheny March; Skyway March; My Indiana; Stay Away; Sing a Long (children's songs).

FRANKENFIELD, PARKE T ASCAP 1961
composer, conductor
b Allentown, Pa, July 6, 29. Educ: High sch. Musician in dance bands. Music teacher in elementary schs, Pa. Led own jazz band. Chief Collabr: Joseph Mascari. *Songs:* I'm From New Jersey; Seek, Seek, Seek; Lucky Day; Like Someone in Love; Infatuation.

FRANKIE, LOU
See Graziano, Caesar Frankie

FRANKLIN, DAVE ASCAP 1934
composer, author, pianist
b New York, NY; d Los Angeles, Calif, Feb 3, 70. Pianist, music publ firms, then in vaudeville & nightclubs, US & Europe. Wrote spec material for Ben Bernie, also for Connie's Inn, Paradise Restaurant, NY; wrote songs for films. Chief Collabrs: Cliff Friend, Al Dubin, Irving Taylor, Isham Jones. *Songs:* I Ain't Lazy, I'm Just Dreaming; When My Dreamboat Comes Home; Anniversary Waltz; I Must See Annie Tonight; You Can't Stop Me From Dreaming; The Merry-Go-Round Broke Down; The Concert in the Park; Breakin' in a Pair of Shoes; Everything You Said Came True; Dreamer's Holiday; If I Had a Magic Carpet; One-zy Two-zy; Cincinnati Rag; A Man Wrote a Song; Voice in My Heart.

FRANKLIN, HENRY CARL ASCAP 1971
composer, author
b Los Angeles, Calif, Oct 1, 40. Recording artist for Black Jazz Records & Catalyst Records. *Songs & Instrumental Works:* Plastic Creek Stomp; Outbreak; Little Miss Laurie; Beauty and the Electric Tub; For Penny. *Albums:* The Skipper; The Skipper at Home; Tribal Dance.

FRANKLIN, JOHN ASCAP 1968
lyricist
b Detorit, Mich, Apr 11, 37. Educ: Northwestern Univ, BS(speech). Writer, Bway play "Miss Kerry B Phillips." In advert, Ford Motor Co & Express Mail. Chief Collabr: Stan Carner. *Songs:* Lyrics: The Warm of Him; Until You.

FRANKLIN, MALVIN MAURICE (WILKIE WHITE, GEORGIS GIRALDI) ASCAP 1914
composer, author, pianist
b Atlanta, Ga, Aug 24, 1889. Educ: Studied piano with Edna Gochel; Ziegfeld Col of Music, Chicago, 02; studied trumpet with Jules Levy, St Louis, 03; Nat Cons Music, New York, scholarship, studied with Edna Thurber & Raphael Josephy, 04; studied harmony, theory, counterpoint & arr with Frank Sadler. Pioneer in piano-roll & recording field. Pianist, cond & writer of spec material, vaudeville & show performers. Staff comp for Lew Fields & Shubert Bros, 13-27. First publ folios for piano, orch & silent films; scored films, MGM. Author: "Practical Songwriting" (2 vols); "Automatik Komposer"; "Secrets of Songwriting"; "Motion Picture Folios" (2 ed); "Modern Dances" (2 ed); "Magic Melody Charts" (automatic songwriter). Charter mem, ASCAP. Chief Collabrs: Harry B Smith, Robert B Smith, Edgar Smith, Addison Burkhardt, Tommy Grey, Edgar Leslie, Al Bryan, Alex Gerber, Billy Jerome, Wolfe Gilbert, Anatole Friedland, Edgar Allen Wolfe, Doyle Williams, E Ray Goetz. *Songs:* Jingle, Jingle, Jingle; I Was Born in Michigan; La La Melody; A Lonely Romeo; Good Old Days; Lilac Domino; Down at Mammy Ginny's Cabin Door; Let's Get Behind the Man Behind the Gun; The Baby Song; Music: Love Is Just the Same Old Game; Underneath a Big Umbrella; Will O' Wisp; Oui Oui Marie; Shades of Night; When the Animals Are Gone; Goodfellows Polka (The Little Brown Jug); Every Girlie Wants to Be a Sally. *Songs & Instrumental Works:* Hot Chocolate Rag; Magpie Rag; Elephant Rag; The Miserable Rag. *Scores:* Musical Shows: Belle of the Boulevard; The Wife Hunters; A Lonely Romeo; All Aboard; Dearie; Snapshots of 1922; His Little Widows; Sweetest Girl in Paris; Louisiana Lou; The Lilac Domino.

FRANKLIN, RICHARD
See Widman, Franklin Darryl

FRANKLYN, BLANCHE ASCAP 1922
composer, author
b Los Angeles, Calif, Jan 27, 1895; d Los Angeles, Calif, July 23, 73. Educ: Pub schs. Wrote special material for Al Jolson, Sophie Tucker, Frank Crumit, Bert Williams & Eddie Cantor. Chief Collabr: Nat Vincent. *Songs:* Pucker Up and Whistle; Pretty Little Cinderella; Oh You Can't Fool an Old Hoss Fly; Mississippi Missy; China Toy; I'm Tired of Building Castles; I Want a Kiss for Christmas.

FRANKLYN, MILT J ASCAP 1954
composer, conductor, arranger
b New York, NY, Sept 16, 1897; d Los Angeles, Calif, Apr 24, 62. Educ: Univ Utah; Univ Calif; Univ Pa. MC for Fanchon & Marco, 27-30 & for Paramount Publix, Loews, 31-33. Cond & comp, Warner Bros Cartoons, 35.

FRANTZ, DOROTHY ASCAP 1972
composer, author, lyricist
b Iola, Kans, Dec 1, 18. Educ: Iola High Sch, 35; Allen County Community Col, degree & dipl, 37; Pittsburg State Univ, 66. Started writing music at age 50. Amateur singer with Billy Hew Len Orch, Moana Banyan Court, Honolulu, Hawaii. Chief Collabrs: Charles Frantz, Pua Almeida, Norman Lee, Hil Radtke. *Songs:* Aloha, Hawaiian Dolly; Without Your Love; The Sweetest Lei; Let's Go to Hawaii (Let's Not Put It Off!); Hawaii Is a Feeling; Destination Hawaii; Grind the Coffee (Bump the Apple).

FRANZ, WILLIAM FREDERIC ASCAP 1969
composer, drummer, teacher
b Milford, Conn, Apr 9, 47. Educ: Stratford High Sch; Berklee Sch Music. Performer, road & nightclubs, 66-80. Studio work, RCA, Capitol, Mounted & Metro Media Records, New York & A&M Records, Los Angeles. Writer & player jazz works for trio, Conn. Chief Collabrs: Tom Everett, Ray Erroll Fox. *Songs & Instrumental Works:* Someday Boy; Rewake the Coolness of the Wind.

FRASER, IAN ASCAP 1973
composer, arranger, conductor
b Hove, Eng, Aug 23, 33. Educ: Eastbourne Col, Eng. Arr & cond original production "Stop the World, I Wanna Get Off," 62; adaptation & cond "Scrooge." Emmy Awards for music dir, 77 & 78. Chief Collabrs: Anthony Newley, Judith Morton Fraser. *Songs:* Music: There's No Such Thing As Love; To Know You.

FRASURE, JACK ASCAP 1976
composer
b Garret, Ky, Aug 21, 35. Educ: High sch; studied English, Purdue Univ, North Central Campus, Westville, Ind. Composer, 25 yrs. Chief Collabr: Bob Frasure (brother). *Songs:* Reasons; I'm Letting You Go; Lyrics: Haven't Had a Good Night (Since She's Gone).

FRAZIER, EDDIE
producer
b Meriden, Conn, 1898; d 1972. Began in silent films. With Columbia & Paramount, then Universal, 56-64. Songwriter, TV review, 60. Life mem, Local No 47.

FRAZZINI, AL ASCAP 1938
composer, author
b Boston, Mass, June 27, 1890; d Boston, Sept 4, 63. Educ: Pvt music study. Church organist & choir dir, 5 yrs. Radio performer; songplugger, Boston. *Songs:* The Yanks Are Comin' Again; My Cabin of Dreams; If You See Margie; Sunset at Sea; If I Live to Be a Hundred; Carolina Sweetheart; Dream Valley Home; When Banana Skins Are Falling (I'll Come Sliding Back to You); I'm Just Like An Old Umbrella (Forgotten Til a Rainy Day); Brazilian Eyes; Silv'ry Moon; They'll Forget About You; Violet; Leapin' Lena.

FREBERG, STAN ASCAP 1959
composer, author, comedian
b Los Angeles, Calif, Aug 7, 26. Educ: High sch. Served in Med Corps, Spec Serv, WW II. Developed puppet series for KTLA TV, "Time for Beany," 49-54. Did voices for UPA cartoon characters & Walt Disney films; had own radio show; writer of commercials, incl Butternut Coffee commercial, perf by Omaha Symph, 59. Mem, Nat Soc Art Dirs. Pres, Freberg, Ltd, adv firm, Hollywood. Gold Medal, New York Art Dirs Club; Grand Prize, Venice Film Festival. *Songs & Instrumental Works:* John and Marsha; St George and the Dragonet; Little Blue Riding Hood; Omaha; Incident at Los Voraces (Writer's Guild of Am Award, Comedy Radio Script, 57-58); Green Christmas; The United States of America (revue).

FREDERICK, DONALD R (RON ARICK) ASCAP 1964
composer, teacher, conductor
b Nappanee, Ind, Jan 13, 17. Educ: Nappanee High Sch; Manchester Col, BS(music); Bethany Sem, BD; Northwestern Univ, MM; advanced studies music, Ohio State Univ, Wichita State Univ & Univ Kans. Music teacher, Brookville, Ohio, 39-43. Prof music, McPherson Col, 46-70. Minister music, McPherson Church of the Brethren, 46-79. Music ed-comp & piano technician, 71-74. Cond, McPherson Community Symph, 74-76. Asst bus mgr, McPherson Col, 75- *Songs & Instrumental Works:* O Church of Christ, Count Well Your Charge (SATB, organ); Built on the Rock (SATB, organ); Prayer of Dedication (SATB, organ or orch); Meeting at Night (SATB, piano); Praise and Prayer (anthems, hymns & responses, SATB); Four Pieces for Eight Brasses; Five Moods for Brass Choir and Percussion; To Heal the Broken; As Channels of Thy Healing Grace.

FREDERICKS, MARC ASCAP 1957
composer, author
b Philadelphia, Pa, Jan 26, 27. Educ: Univ Pa, BA; Rutgers Univ, MA. Has been writer, cond, pianist & arr for record cos. Owner of publ firm. *Songs:* Blue Jean Rhapsody; Isle of Romance; Bashful Debutante; Eclipse; Mirage in the Night; The Workshop; Tina's Theme.

FREDRICKS, WILLIAM ARTHUR ASCAP 1960
composer, author, singer
b Jersey City, NJ, Mar 18, 24. Educ: New York Col Music; Am Theatre Wing; Juilliard Sch Music. Joined Am Fedn Musicians, 45, Am Fedn TV & Radio Artists, 59 & Screen Actors Guild, 59. Established, Woodwyn Music Co, 71. Chief Collabrs: Hal Moore, Bill Linn, David De Noon. *Songs:* Wendy; You Can Trust Your Car to the Man Who Wears the Star; Was There Ever Such a Christmas?; How Times Have Changed; Just for Laughs; Whirlwind; Trust is a Must; Apples Are; How Well I Know; On the Ferris Wheel; Coaly Bay; The Wonderful World of WCBS; That's The Way; Trust is Everything; White, White Whiskers; The Star March; Wait for the Message; Music: Must Be Santa. *Instrumental Works:* Who Will?

FREDRICKSON, L(AWRENCE) THOMAS ASCAP 1963
composer
b Kane, Pa, Sept 5, 28. Educ: Ohio Wesleyan Univ, BM, 50; Univ Ill, MM, 52, DMA, 60, studied with Tildon Wells, Burrill Phillips, Hubert Kessler. Prof comp & theory, Univ Ill, Urbana-Champaign, 52-, dir, Sch Music, 70-74. Performer double bass in symph orchs, contemporary music ens & jazz groups. *Instrumental Works:* Allegro for Cello and Piano; Music for the Double Bass Alone; Brass Quintet; Four for Two (cello, bass); Hefti-Bag (jazz band); Triptych (oboe, viola, trumpet, trombone); Five Pieces for Percussion Quartet; Images (youth orch); Sinfonia II (orch); Trio for Flute, Vibraphone, Double Bass. *Songs & Instrumental Works:* Impressions (mixed chorus).

FREED, ARNOLD ASCAP 1961
composer, writer
b New York, NY, Sept 29, 26. Educ: Third Street Music Sch, piano with Sylvia Lopez & comp with James Bleecker; City Col New York, BA(music), Philip James; Juilliard Sch of Music, BA(comp), scholarship with Vittorio Giannini; cond with Hugh Ross & Dean Dixon; NY Univ, MA(musicology), Gustave Reese; Tanglewood with Luigi Dallapiccola, Fulbright scholarship, Florence, Italy, 2 yrs, also piano with Pietro Scarpini & later with Paul Wittgenstein, New York. Writer of orch, choral & vocal comp. Chief music ed, Boosey & Hawkes Publ; ed consult & dir of choral activities, Hansen Publ. Wrote scores for TV, documentaries & films. *Instrumental Works:* Alleluia (orch); Win, Place Or Show (overture for orch). *Songs & Instrumental Works:* Three Elizabethan Songs (soprano, piano); Choral: Dance Alleluia (SATB); The Willow Tree (SATB); Who Is That Man? (SATB); How Much Farther Must We Go? (SATB); Gloria (SATB, brass, timpani); Toccata for Piano. *Scores:* Opera/Ballet: The Zodiac (masque for orch, chorus, dance, narration).

FREED, ARTHUR ASCAP 1924
author, producer
b Charleston, SC, Sept 9, 1894; d Apr 12, 73. Educ: Phillips Exeter Acad. Assoc with Gus Edwards musical acts. In vaudeville with Louis Silvers, with whom he wrote revues for NY restaurants. Staged mil shows, WW I. Theatre mgr; then produced own musical shows. Under contract to MGM. Songs for films incl "Hollywood Revue", "A Night At the Opera", "San Francisco", "Babes in Arms" & "Ziegfeld Follies." Produced films: "The Wizard of Oz"; "For Me and My Gal"; "Girl Crazy"; "Meet Me in St Louis"; "The Harvey Girls"; "Till the Clouds Roll By"; "Good News"; "The Pirate"; "Easter Parade"; "Words and Music"; "Barkleys of Broadway"; "On the Town"; "Annie Get Your Gun"; "Royal Wedding"; "Show Boat"; "An American in Paris" (Acad Award, 51); "The Band Wagon"; "Brigadoon"; "It's Always Fair Weather"; "Silk Stockings"; "Gigi" (Acad Award, 58); "Bells Are Ringing." Winner, Acad Motion Picture Arts & Sci Irving Thalberg Awards, pres Acad, 64. Chief Collabrs: Nacio Herb Brown, Gus Arnheim, Al Hoffman, Harry Warren. *Songs:* I Cried for You; When Buddha Smiles; The Wedding of the Painted Doll; Broadway Melody; Singin' in the Rain; You Were Meant for Me; Chant of the Jungle; Pagan Love Song; Should I Reveal?; The Moon Is Low; Fit As a Fiddle; We'll Make Hay While the Sun Shines; Our Big Love Scene; After Sundown; Temptation; Beautiful Girl; All I Do Is Dream of You; A New Moon Is Over My Shoulder; You Are My Lucky Star; Sing Before Breakfast; I've Got a Feelin' You're Fallin'; Broadway Rhythm; Alone; Would You?; Smoke Dreams; I'm Feelin' Like a Million; Your Broadway and My Broadway; Yours and Mine; Good Morning; This Heart of Mine; Make 'Em Laugh. *Scores:* Films: Broadway Melody; Going Hollywood; Sadie McKee; Student Tour; Yolanda and the Thief; Pagan Love Song; Singin' in the Rain.

FREED, ISADORE ASCAP 1938
composer, organist, choirmaster
b Russia, Mar 26, 1900; d Oceanside, NY, Nov 10, 60. Educ: Univ Pa, BM; Philadelphia Cons (Gold Medal); NY Col Music, MusD; studied with Ernest Bloch, d'Indy, Maitland & Boyle; Schola Cantorum, Paris. Cond, Concerts Spirituels, Paris, 30-33. Founder, Comp Lab, Philadelphia. Teacher, Curtis Inst, Temple Univ Fine Arts Sch. Organist & choirmaster, Temple Keneseth Israel, Philadelphia. Visiting prof comp, Julius Hartt Found, Hartford, Conn. *Songs &*

Instrumental Works: 3 string quartets; Rhapsody for Viola, Orchestra; Rhapsody for Clarinet, Strings, Piano; Piano Sonata; Violin Sonata; Suite for Viola; Suite for Harp; Sacred Service for the Synagogue; Jeux de Timbres; Pastorales; Music for Strings; Vibrations (ballet suite); Violin Concerto; Triptych (violin, viola, cello, piano; SPAM Award); Postscripts (Eurydice Choral Prize). *Scores:* Operas: Homo Sum; Princess and the Vagabond.

FREED, RALPH ASCAP 1931
composer, author, producer
b Vancouver, BC, May 1, 07; d Los Angeles, Calif, Feb 13, 73. Educ: Hollywood High Sch. Brother of Arthur, Ruth & Walter Freed. Contract writer, Paramount, Universal & MGM. Wrote songs for films incl "Babes on Broadway", "Du Barry Was a Lady", "Two Girls and a Sailor", "Two Sisters From Boston", "Anchors Aweigh", "Thrill of a Romance", "No Leave, No Love, This Time for Keeps." Produced TV shows & films, 54. Chief Collabrs: Sammy Fain, Burton Lane, Harry Barris. *Songs:* Little Dutch Mill; Who Walks in When I Walk Out?; Hawaiian War Chant; How About You?; Mama Don't Allow It; You Leave Me Breathless; Lovelight in the Starlight; Please Don't Say No, Say Maybe; I Never Felt More Like Falling in Love; Adios Amigo; I Thought of You Last Night; Just the Way You Are; All the Time; The Young Man With a Horn; In a Moment of Madness; Madam, I Love Your Crepe Suzettes.

FREED, RUTH
See Akst, Ruth Freed

FREED, WALTER ASCAP 1946
composer, author
b Spokane, Wash, June 17, 03. Educ: Pvt piano study; Col of Music, Univ Southern Calif, scholarship; studied with Edmund Ross. Brother of Arthur, Ralph & Ruth Freed. Theatre organist, 10 yrs; also taught piano for 10 yrs. USA, World War II. Organist, Fraunces Tavern, NY, 10 yrs. Author of 5 bks on teaching organ. *Songs:* High in the Hills of God; Last Night; Ev'ning Reveries; I Find Solace; I Heard a Prayer; Dawn of a New Day. *Instrumental Works:* Fiesta (Won Nat Contest Modern Am music sponsored by Paul Whiteman); The What-Not Shelf (ballet suite); Concerto in Miniature (piano concerto).

FREEDMAN, GERALD ASCAP 1966
author
b Lorain, Ohio, June 25, 27. Educ: Northwestern Univ, BS, MA, studied voice, Hermanus Baer & Emmy Joseph. Cocktail pianist, concert singer, cantorial soloist, stage dir, also TV & film. Lyricist & bk writer "Dick Button Ice Extravaganza", "Take One Step," children's musical & "A Time for Singing," Bway musical. Chief Collabr: John Morris. *Songs:* Lyrics: How Green Was My Valley; Let Me Love You; There Is Beautiful.

FREEDMAN, M CLAIRE
See Sunshine, Madeline

FREEDMAN, MAX C ASCAP 1942
composer, author
b Philadelphia, Pa, Jan 8, 1893; d Philadelphia, Oct 8, 62. Educ: Pub schs. On staff, music publ co. Radio entertainer, announcer & writer. Chief Collabrs: Dick Thomas, Jimmy DeKnight, Morty Berk. *Songs:* Sioux City Sue; Rock Around the Clock; Dreamy Old New England Moon; Tea Leaves; In the Heart of a Fool; If I Had Another Chance; Lyrics: Merry Widow Waltz; Song of India; Liebestraum; Blue Danube Waltz; Dark Eyes.

FREEDMAN, MELVIN HOWARD ASCAP 1978
author, playwright
b Malden, Mass, Feb 25, 20. Educ: Harvard Univ, AB, 41. Author bks, "How to Enjoy This Moment" & "We're Still Killing Indians"; co-author musical, "Reunion"; author play, "Oh, Soho!" Chief Collabr: Ron Roullier. *Songs:* Lyrics: Reunion; A World I'll Make For Me; That Moment is Now; Give Me Love; If It's Really Love; Wild Strawberries; How to Enjoy This Moment; Time, You Thief; New York is the Capital of the World; The South American Wedding Tango Waltz.

FREEDMAN, ROBERT MORRIS ASCAP 1958
composer, author, conductor
b Mt Vernon, NY, Jan 23, 34. Educ: Cranston High Sch, RI. Taught at Berklee Col Mus, Boston, Mass. Pianist, Johnny Long Orch; saxophonist, Woody Herman Orch. Comp, arr & played for Herb Pomeroy Orch; comp-arr-mus dir, Harry Belafonte & Lena Horne; comp & arr music for indust films, radio, TV commercials & spec. Orchr Bway shows; orchr-arr, Feature Films; arr, phonograph albums such as "52nd Street." Instrumentalist. *Songs:* Thank You, Love; Beautiful Music; Turn the World Around; Music: And We Listened. *Songs & Instrumental Works:* Concerto for Trumpet and Orchestra (comn by Carol Dawn Reinhart); Trois M'emoires (solo pour la harpe).

FREEMAN, BERDELLA
See Bal, Berdella M

FREEMAN, BUD   ASCAP 1957
author, record executive
b Chicago, Ill, Oct 31, 15. Co mgr & press agent, Johnny Mack Brown, Tex
Ritter & others. Pub dir, Capitol Records, 2 yrs, A&R dir, 2 yrs. Co-owner,
Commentary Records. Chief Collabr: Leon Pober. *Scores:* Bway stage: Beg,
Borrow or Steal. *Albums:* Songs of Couch and Consultation.

FREEMAN, ERNEST AARON, JR   ASCAP 1960
composer, arranger, pianist
b Cleveland, Ohio, Aug 16, 22. Educ: Cent High Sch, Cleveland, 40; Cleveland
Inst Music, BA, violin major; Univ Southern Calif, MM, comp with Kanitz. Asst
bandmaster, USN Band, Bunker Hill, Ind, 42-45. Arr/cond many gold records;
recording artist, Imperial Records, 56-61, musical dir "Leslie Uggams TV
Show," 69. Did commercials for Bank of Calif, Buick & Richfield Oil. Arr/cond,
Vicki Carr, Frank Sinatra, Connie Francis, Desi Arnaz, Carol Kinsley, Bobby
Vee, Barry Young, Dean Martin, Sammy Davis Jr & many others; arr nightclub
acts for Edie Adams, Joi Lansing, Sammy Davis Jr, Marguerite Piazza, Tony
Martin, Earl Grant & Gary Puckett. Received Cash Box Award for best Small
Combo. Now arranger, composer & pianist. Chief Collabrs: Thomas Garrett,
Jim Bowen, Joe Saraceno, Frances Kirk. *Songs:* Music: Beautiful Obsession;
Lost Dreams; Do the Funky Hula; Yellow Moon; Ninety Nine Point Eight;
Sweet Cherry Wine; Valerie. *Instrumental Works:* Jivin' Around; Funny Face.
Songs & Instrumental Works: Spring Fever; Raunchy; Stranger in the Night
(Grammy Award); Bridge Over Troubled Water (Grammy Award). *Scores:*
Film/TV: Duffy; To Catch a Thief; Jolly Pink Jungle. *Albums:* Truth of Truths.

FREEMAN, GEORGE D   ASCAP 1964
composer, author
b Ala, Apr 20, 37. Educ: High sch. *Songs:* You Guessed It; You're Guilty; Down
and Out.

FREEMAN, LAWRENCE (BUD)   ASCAP 1955
composer, conductor, saxophonist
b Chicago, Ill, Apr 13, 06. Educ: High sch; pvt music study. Saxophonist in
dance bands, 15 yrs. Soloist with Paul Whiteman, Tommy Dorsey & Benny
Goodman. Formed own group. Served USA, WW II. Toured Brazil with trio,
47, Chile & Peru, 52-53. Leader of jazz quartet in TV, concerts & nightclubs.
Made many records. Chief Collabr: Bob Haggart. *Instrumental Works:* The Eel;
The Sailfish; The Octopus; Crazeology; Inside on the Southside; The Eel's
Nephew; The Atomic Era; Dr Peyser's Dilemma.

FREEMAN, NED   ASCAP 1954
composer, arranger
b Hallowell, Maine, Dec 27, 1895. Educ: Pub schs; studied music with John
Orth, Stuart Mason & Phillip Clapp. Served, WW I. Pianist & arr, theatre orchs,
19-27. Arr, dance orchs & publ, 28-37. Comp & arr for radio, 38-50 & films,
51-60. Chief Collabr: Don Raye. *Songs & Instrumental Works:* Gallery (12
sketches for orch); I Know What God Is.

FREEMAN, ROY ROBERT   ASCAP 1959
author
b Derby, Conn, Feb 10, 26. Educ: New York High Schs. Writer of songs &
stories for children: author "10th Avenue Pig." Motion picture & TV script
writer. Chief Collabrs: Warren Vincent, Stanley Applebaum, Ed King, Frank
Slay. *Songs:* Lyrics: Barefoot in Baltimore; Sit With the Guru; Square Dances
for Children; The Skin Song (children's special); Highway 101. *Scores:* Off
Bway: Vegas.

FREEMAN, RUSSELL DONALD   ASCAP 1955
composer, pianist, arranger
b Chicago, Ill, May 28, 26. Educ: Manual Arts High Sch. Pianist & comp of jazz
comp for Chet Baker, Shelly Manne, Art Pepper, Lighthouse All-Stars, Dexter
Gordon, Wardell Gray, Howard McGhee, Shorty Rogers, Charlie Barnett &
Benny Goodman; cond; recording artist for Pac Jazz Records & Contemporary
Records; performed many songs on radio, TV & nightclubs. Chief Collabrs:
Dory Previn, Joel Reisner, Tommy Wolf, Jerry Gladstone, Fran Landesman.
Songs: Music: The Wind; Run, Run, Run; Summer Sketch; Band-Aid; Bea's Flat;
Two Peas in a Pod; Russ Job; Woody's Dot; Funky Old You; An Afternoon At
Home; Amblin'; A Slight Minority; Brushes; Bones for Zoot; Bock's Tops;
Backfield in Motion; Batter Up; Fan-Tan; Happy Little Sunbeam; Hugo
Hurwhey; Laugh, Cry; Maid in Mexico; No Ties; Say When; Speakeasy; You
Name It.

FREEMAN, SCOTT
See McNulty, Frank Fremont

FREEMAN, STAN   ASCAP 1955
composer, author
b Waterbury, Conn. Educ: Hartt Sch Music. Piano soloist symph orchs,
Cincinnati, Buffalo, DC & Symph of the Air; pianist night clubs, US & London.
Conductor, Marlene Dietrich & Ethel Merman. Musical material writer shows,
Carol Burnett, 78, Mary Tyler Moore, 79, Tim Conway, 80 & CBS 50th
Anniversary Special. Emmy Award, 78. Chief Collabrs: Jack Lawrence, Frank
Underwood, Arthur Mawin. *Scores:* Bway Shows: I Had a Ball; The Other Half
of Me; Almost; Lovely Ladies, Kind Gentlemen; Call Me Back.

FREEMAN, TICKER   ASCAP 1946
composer
b Paterson, NJ, Oct 13, 11. Pianist for Irene Bordoni, 35-36. Song plugger for
Chappell, Miller & Feist, 37-42. Pianist for Dinah Shore, 42-62. Chief Collabrs:
Sonny Skylar, Mack David, Irving Taylor. *Songs:* Music: So Dear to My Heart;
You'll Always Be the One I Love; Star of Bethlehem; Ready Set Go; You Take
My Word for It Baby; Baby Don't Be Mad at Me; That's All I Want to Know.

FREESOIL, MASON
See Stull, Donald Earl

FREEZE, GEORGE RICHARD   ASCAP 1972
composer, author, singer
b Farley, Iowa, Oct 6, 48. Educ: Western Dubuque County Community High
Sch; Kirkwood Community Col; Univ Northern Iowa; Boddicker Sch Music.
Singer, nightclubs. Appeared on TV spec, "Someday—Oneday." Recording
artist & producer, Frekyl Records & Corrugated Records. Chief Collabrs: Paul
Blue, Nancy Hoffman, Dan Healy. *Songs:* Mary Nell Blair; Go Get 'Em, George
Handy; Why Is It Bad to Know You; Levaleika; Something Tells You Knew;
On My Own; Every Love's a Season; Another Lonely Night; When You
Hurt—I Bleed; Highway Hotel.

FREITAG, DOROTHEA HACKETT   ASCAP 1969
composer
b Baltimore, Md. Educ: Curtis Inst, grad; Ecole Normale, Paris, France, studied
with Nadia Boulanger; Peabody Cons, grad. Writer of dance music for
Baryshnikov, ballet for Alvin. Works performed throughout US. Recipient, 5
Emmy awards & Peabody award. *Instrumental Works:* Zorba; King of Hearts;
Golden Boy; Dear World; Courtin' Time. *Scores:* Ballet: Storyville.

FREITAS, RICHARD   ASCAP 1953
composer, author, educator
b Portugal, Oct 1, 15. Educ: Columbia Univ, BA, MA. Comp, arr & cond for
var record cos & off-Bway show "Difficult Woman." Head, instrumental music
dept, elem schs, Lawrence, NY. Chief Collabr: Morty Neff. *Songs &
Instrumental Works:* Fiddlesticks; Balerico; Querida; Zip; Shoemaker's Tune;
The Bull's Eye.

FRELENG, ISADORE (FRIZ)
producer, director
b Kansas City, Mo, Aug 21, 06. Educ: Horner Art Sch, Kansas City. Animator,
United Film Advancement Services, Kansas City, 24-27, Walt Disney Studios,
27-28 & Mintz Studio, New York, 28-29. Animator & producer, Warner Bros
Studios, 30-63, innovator, Merrie Melodies-Looney Tunes, 30-31. Dir, Acad
awards, 47, 56, 57, 63 & 66. Co-owner & producer, DePatie-Freleng Studio, Van
Nuys, Calif, 63- Recipient, Animation Soc Int Film Artists award, 76, Emmy
awards, 77, 78 & others. Mem, Motion Picture Acad of Arts & Sci, bd gov, TV
Acad.

FREMONT, FRANK
See McNulty, Frank Fremont

FRENCH, EARL   ASCAP 1978
composer, author
b Baltimore, Md, Jan 23, 44. Educ: Valley Col, AA(theatre arts). Singer &
songwriter, clubs & concerts, overseas tour, Japan & Guam & film "Clay."
Songs: Outlaw Cowboy; Come Up to Love; The Chance to Love You More;
Golden Horse Saloon. *Scores:* Play: Heldorado.

FRENCH, EDMUND
See Reynolds, George French

FREUDENTHAL, JOSEF   ASCAP 1937
composer, author, publisher
b Geisa, Ger, Mar 1, 03; d New York, NY, May 5, 64. Educ: Studied in
Frankfort & Munich. Lived in Palestine in early 30's. Came to US in 36.
Founded Transcontinental Music Corp. *Songs:* Smile, Cherie; Katherine;
Sacred: The Last Words of David; Precepts of Micah; Let Us Sing Unto the
Lord; A Lamp Unto My Feet; The Earth is the Lords.

FREUND, DARRAL J   ASCAP 1971
composer
b New York, NY, Sept 6, 19. Educ: Accordion training, New York, 29-37. Pilot
& engr as primary profession, 40-80, music as avocation. Performer at local
levels. Interested in tech aspects of musical instruments; invented an electronic
musical instrument. Pres, Electronic Music, Inc, Md. *Songs:* Music: Christmas
Peace.

FREUNDLICH, RALPH B (RAY FRIENDLY)   ASCAP 1965
composer, flutist, guitarist
b New York, NY, Oct 10, 12. Educ: George Washington High Sch; Columbia
Col; City Col New York, BS(music), 36; Juilliard, studied flute with Georges
Barrere, 39; Nat Orchestral Asn, studied with Leon Barzin, 38-40; Columbia
Univ Teacher's Col, MA(music educ), 47; Tanglewood Music Ctr, 50. With
New Friends of Music Chamber Orch, 40; USAAF, 42-46. Teacher orch music,

19 yrs. Chamber concerts & radio, 53- Free lance musician, 58-68 & 75- Asst flutist to Luis Bonfa recording, "Amor," 58. Accompanist to Elly Stone & Angus Godwin, Columbia Artists, 60's. Solo tours, summer camps, cols, inns, 60-68. Off-Bway comp-performer, 63. *Instrumental Works:* Four Old Dances (two flutes); Two Pieces (two flutes); Theme and Eight Variations (flute); Five Little Melodies (flute & guitar).

FREY, GLENN L
songwriter, vocalist, guitarist

b Detroit, Mich, Nov 6, 48. Performer with Bo Diddely & Linda Ronstadt. Founder, groups, Longbranch Penny whistle & the Eagles. *Songs:* Take It Easy; Lyin' Eyes (Grammy award, 75); New Kid in Town (Grammy award, 77). *Albums:* Eagles; Desperado; On the Border; One of These Nights; Hotel California (Grammy award, album of yr, 77); The Long Run.

FREY, HUGO
ASCAP 1914
composer, violist, pianist

b Chicago, Ill, Aug 26, 1873; d New York, NY, Feb 13, 52. Educ: Chicago Cons; studied with Luigi van Kunits. Violist, Listemann String Quartet, 1896-1898. Pianist, Red Path Grand Concert Co, 1898-1899. Cond & arr, dance orchs; also for music productions. Cond & arr, Victor Phonograph Co, 16-24. On staff, music publ co, NY. Scored many films. Charter mem, ASCAP. *Songs:* Havanola; Rockin' the Boat; Yodel Dodel Doh; Sarah From Sahara; When You Come Back; American's Creed; On the Home Front. *Scores:* Stage: The Elopers (Chicago).

FREY, MAURICE
See Friedman, Maurice Herman

FREY, SIDNEY
ASCAP 1960
composer, author

b New York, NY, Oct 20, 20; d. Educ: City Col, New York (eng). Served USMS, World War II. Founder, Audio Fidelity records, 53. Producer, first stereophonic record, 56.

FRIBERG, CARL
ASCAP 1967
composer, producer, artist

b Chicago, Ill, Oct 16, 39. Educ: Northwestern Univ Schs of Speech & Music, Evanston, BA(radio, TV, film). Has done many commercials & records. Wrote theme & incidental music for theatre play, "Sea Marks." Comp & musical dir, "Goodbye Tomorrow" & "Mr Gynt Inc." Comp, "New Faces of '68," original musical rev presented at Booth Theatre on Bway. Copywriter, Compton Advert, Inc, 64-67, Ted Bates Advert, 67-69. Artist, performing original songs; guest piano soloist with DePaul Symph Orch; percussionist & keyboards with Chicago Civic Orch, Chicago Youth Orch & 566th Air Force Reserve Band; numerous personal & TV appearances. Chief Collabrs: Hal Hackady, Sue Brock, Richard Falcone, Ira Gasman. *Songs:* Music: I Climbed the Mountain; Prisms; Philosophy; Close Up Smile (jingle); Puppy Chow for a Full Year (jingle).

FRIED, BARBARA RUTH
ASCAP 1969
author

b Providence, RI, May 28, 24. Educ: Univ RI, BS; NY Univ, MA(musicol). Ed bk publ for 15 yrs; writer, 5 non-fiction bks incl: "The Middle-Age Crisis & 1 novel. Wrote bk & lyrics for two children's musicals, libretto for a two-act opera performed at Juilliard, lyrics for shows. Chief Collabrs: Cy Coleman, Albert Hague, John Morris, Andy Badale, Milton Shafer, opera, Harold Farberman. *Songs:* Lyrics: The No-Color Time of the Day; Suddenly I Can Tell You; The Way I See It; Sing Out Sweet Land. *Scores:* Libretto: The Loser.

FRIED, GERALD
ASCAP 1957
composer, author

b New York, NY, Feb 13, 28. Educ: High Sch of Music & Art; Juilliard, BS, 48. First oboist, Dallas Symph, New York Little Orch Soc, 48-55. Comp & cond, movies & TV, 55- Mem, Bd of Governors, Comp & Lyricists Guild Am & Acad TV Arts & Sciences; mem, Exec Comt, Acad Motion Picture Arts & Sciences. *Songs:* Music: Theme From Roots. *Scores:* Opera/Ballet: Les the Least Straightens the Lord; Film/TV: Roots (Emmy Award, 76); One Potato, Two Potato; Killing of Sister George; Birds Do It, Bees Do It (Oscar nomination, 75); Paths of Glory; Gauguin in Tahiti (Emmy nomination, 68).

FRIED, MARTIN
ASCAP 1923
composer, arranger

b New York, NY. Accompanist & arr for Al Jolson & many Jolson musicals. *Songs:* Broadway Rose; Honeymoon Bay; Strawberries; Hindoo Moon; Dolly; Nobody's Rose; Days; Who and Where; In Our House.

FRIED, SUELLEN
ASCAP 1967
author, dance therapist

b St Louis, Mo, Sept 18, 32. Educ: University City Senior High Sch, 50; Wash Univ, St Louis, 50-52; Park Col, Kansas City, Mo, BA, 75; Registered dance therapist, 77. Dancer, St Louis Munic Opera, 49-51; on TV, Kansas City, 55-59; dance therapist, 61- Chief Collabr: Henry Tobias. *Songs:* Lyrics: A Man Needs to Know.

FRIEDBERG, PATRICIA ANN
ASCAP 1973
composer, author

b London, Eng, May 4, 34. Educ: London Sch Journ, 50-52; Marquette Univ, 69-71. TV writer, theatre productions, Rhodesia, SAfrica & US. Moderator/producer, WTMJ, NBC affil, Milwaukee. Chief Collabrs: Sylvia Bernstein, Goldie Kossow. *Scores:* Opera/Ballet: The Return; Bway stage: Simcha 73; 21 Aldgate; Plays: Is Today Tomorrow; Masquerade.

FRIEDELL, HAROLD WILLIAM
composer, organist, choirmaster

b Jamaica, NY, May 5, 05; d Hastings on Hudson, NY, Feb 17, 58. Educ: Pvt study, David McK Williams; organ & theory, Clement B Gale; theory & comp, Bernard Wagenaar, Gen Theol Sem, NY; comp, Juilliard Sch of Music; hon MusD, Mo Valley Col, 57. Organist & choirmaster, St John's Church, Jersey City, NJ, 30-39, Calvary Episcopal Church, New York, 39-46 & St Bartholomew's Church, New York, 46-58; organist, Downtown Glee Club, Golden Hill Chorus, 30-40. Teacher theory, comp & organ, Union Theol Sem, 43-58, theory & comp, Juilliard Sch of Music, 45-46. Comp of choral & instrumental music. Chief Collabrs: Lee H Bristol, Jr, Leonard Young. *Instrumental Works:* Feast of the Star (pageant); Elegie (harp, violin, organ); Verses for the None Dimittis (organ); Communion Service in A Flat (unison); SATB: Draw Us in the Spirit's Tether; Jesus So Lowly; King of Glory, King of Peace; Song of Mary.

FRIEDENBERG, RICHARD C
ASCAP 1963
composer

b Brooklyn, NY, Oct 23, 33. Educ: Schillinger Inst; Queens Col, NY; Manhattan Sch of Music. Writer, popular music, 8 yrs. With Columbia Records, mail order div.

FRIEDLAND, ANATOLE
ASCAP 1923
composer, author, pianist

b St Petersburg, Russia, Mar 21, 1881; d Atlantic City, NJ, July 24, 38. Educ: Moscow Cons; Columbia Univ, studied architecture. Wrote spec material for "Passing Show" revues. Pianist in vaudeville. Had own nightclub, Club Anatole. Chief Collabrs: L Wolfe Gilbert, Harold Atteridge. *Songs:* My Little Persian Rose; My Little Dream Girl; Lily of the Valley; Are You From Heaven?; My Sweet Adair; I Love You That's One Thing I Know; Riga Rose; Shades of Night; My Own Iona; Singapore.

FRIEDLANDER, WILLIAM BARR
ASCAP 1947
composer, author, librettist

b Chicago, Ill, Jan 12, 1884; d New York, NY, Jan 1, 68. Educ: West Bend High Sch, Wis; studied piano. Professional mgr at age 19, Will Rossiter. Wrote music, bk & lyrics for weekly stock musical comedies; dir all shows at Standard Theatre, Ft Worth, Tex, 2 yrs. Produced & wrote music for several shows, Western vaudeville circuit. With Keith & Orpheum circuits, co-authored bks, wrote music & lyrics for several large feature vaudeville acts, New York. Produced various musical comedies & Bway dramas. Dir & mgr; operated summer stock cos, Great Neck, NY, NJ & Mass. Chief Collabrs: Con Conrad, L Lawrence Weber, Harry Archer, Harlan Thompson, W M Hough, Nan Halperin, Isabelle Leighton. *Songs:* I Love You; Little Jessie James; Honey, I'm in Love With You; The Naughty Princess; Nikki; The Cuddle-Uddle; The Peacock Alley; That Is Love; On a Moonlight Night; The Farmerettes; Adam and Eve; Araby; In Barcelone; Military Marches; Send for Me; You Can Never Tell; Bagdad on the Subway; Since You Came Into My Life; I Saved a Waltz for You; The Wedding Blues; Meet Your True Love Half Way; Hold Me; How Do I Know He Loves Me?; I Can't Live Without Love; Old Man in the Moon; Honeymoon Blues; On Such a Night; Forever; Tell Me Am I Shooting At the Moon?; Say It Again; The Daffy-Dill; In a Bungalow; Charleston Mad; Waiting; Over a Garden Wall; Just You and I and the Baby; They Still Look Good to Me; Come on Along; Tomorrow; Beautiful Baby; I've Got to Be a Chaste Woman; Get Your Woman Cherchez La Femme; Everything's Gonna Be Alright; That's When a Fella Needs a Friend; I Want Somebody; Tonight Or Never; Love Is a Will O' the Wisp; Junior Miss; Travelin' Man; They Can't Ration My Love; The Youngest in the Family; Kiss Me; I'm Going to Kill You With Love; Oh, You Wonderful Girls; Play Me Wedding March in Ragtime; Fresh Out of Kisses; Here Comes Spring; Holka Polka; I Make Believe That It's You; Remember Gay Vienna; Mama Mia; The Ghost Got Up and Danced; Uncle Samba; When You Appear; You Can't Walk Back From an Airplane Ride; Manhattan; The Iron Curtain; Indian Movie Star; Sweet to Me; United Nations; Pogo Stock; Something on the Ball; Cry If You Want to Get Rich; Canada; Cry, Baby, Cry; Don't Go Yet; Rowdy-Dow Drag; I've Got to Have You; Medals on My Chest; My Gal Sue; Never Say Yes; Nobody, But Nobody; Party of the First Part; Unpredictable Falling in Love; Have You Found Heaven?; Hymns: Only a Prayer Away; If You Believe; When the Church Bells Ring; Calvary; This Is My Hymn; There's a Place Up in Heaven for You; A King Was Born. *Scores:* Bway Shows: Pitter Patter; Moonlight; Jonica; The Time, the Place and the Girl; Morocco Bound; Frivolities of 1919 and 1920; Nice Women; High Tide; Divided Honors; The Sea Woman; Separate Rooms; Crosstown; Cobra (drama); The Dagger; The Shelf; The Roman Servant; We Never Learn; She Lived Next Door to the Firehouse; Right Next to Broadway.

FRIEDMAN, CHARLES   ASCAP 1954
author, producer, director
b Russia, Sept 20, 02. Educ: High sch. Film producer & dir; assoc producer with Samuel Goldwyn, Arthur Freed & Darryl Zanuck. Dir, Bway musicals incl "Pins and Needles", "Sing Out the News", "Carmen Jones", "Street Scene" & "My Darlin' Aida" (also librettist). Creator, TV show "Colgate Comedy Hour" & producer & dir of var shows incl "Ruggles of Red Gap" & "Sgt Bilko." Mem, Dramatists Guild, Authors League. Co-author of play, "The Education of H Y M A N K A P L A N " *Songs:* King Cotton; Me and Lee; Why Ain't We Free?; My Darlin' Aida.

FRIEDMAN, DAVID A   ASCAP 1979
composer, author, vibraphonist
b New York, NY, Mar 10, 44. Educ: Juilliard Sch, MA. With New York Philh Orch, Metrop Symph Orch & Luciano Berio Contemporary Chamber Orch. Toured Europe & recorded with London Symph & others. Jazz player with Wayne Shorter, Horace Silver, Hubert Laws & others, 78. Author, method bk "Vibraphone Techniques, Dampering and Peddling." *Albums:* Winter Love—April Joy; Futures Passed; Double Image.

FRIEDMAN, HENRY   ASCAP 1966
composer
b Philadelphia, Pa, June 25, 1897. Educ: Univ Pa, Wharton Sch. Song plugger, Waterson, Berlin & Snyder, Philadelphia, 14-25. Chief Collabs: Louis Herscher, Billy Higgins, Benton W Overstreet, Joseph A McCarthy, Jr. *Songs & Instrumental Works:* Mr Honky Tonk; Say Yes To-Night; Love Me Forever; There's Nobody But You; After To-Night; They'll Be Some Changes Made; It Was an April Fools Day in June; What Will I Do Without That Someone Like You; You Are the Music in My Heart.

FRIEDMAN, IRVING   ASCAP 1955
composer
b Ind, Dec 25, 03. Educ: High sch. Musician in Isham Jones & Paul Whiteman Orchs; asst head of music dept, Warner Bros, 32-43, MGM, 43-45 & Eagle-Lion, 46-49. Founded Primrose Co (music & sound effects). Film exec; did background music for Gene Autry series. *Songs & Instrumental Works:* Waiting (theme).

FRIEDMAN, JAMES M   ASCAP 1963
composer, author, producer
b New York, NY, Apr 3, 27. Educ: Cornell Univ, BA, 48; Juilliard Sch Music, 50; Manhattan Sch Music, 54-55; pvt study with Stefan Wolpe, Johnny Mehegan, Vittorio Giannini, Wallingford Riegger & Hall Overton. Comp producer radio commercials, 57-62; comp-music dir several folk groups, 60's; producer "Chrysalis," MGM Records; cond "Lovin' Spoonful"; music dir industrial shows incl: "Goodyear." Originated ASKAPRO Prog for Am Guild Authors & Comp, 77; starred "Songwright," off-Bway production consisting of 22 own songs, 80. Chief Collabs: Shel Silverstein, Larry Holofcener, Billy Edd Wheeler, William J Lubinsky, Judge White. *Songs:* The Girls in Their Summer Dresses; Harry Was A One-Man Band; Music: In the Hills of Shiloh; Hey Nelly Nelly; The Mermaid.

FRIEDMAN, LEO   ASCAP 1939
composer
b Elgin, Ill, July 16, 1869; d Chicago, Ill, Mar 7, 27. Educ: Studied with Emil Liebling, Chicago & Berlin Cons with Yetlitzki. Chief Collab: Beth Slater Whitson. *Songs:* Let Me Call You Sweetheart; Meet Me Tonight in Dreamland; When I Dream of Old Erin; If I Should; In His Steps; Baby Mine; In Poppyland; Wigwam Dance; Indian Sun Dance; The Trailing Arbutus.

FRIEDMAN, MAURICE HERMAN (MURRAY)   ASCAP 1973
(MAURICE FREY)
composer, author, musician
b New York, NY, Aug 25, 05. Educ: Clinton High Sch; Juilliard. Had own orch, Great Neck, Long Island, 34-42. Played for Jan Peerce, Livingston Manor. Worked for Max Werner & Harry Levant, later publ music bus, Notogravure. Chief Collabr: Robert Rhodes. *Songs:* You Gotta Have Nuts; Music: What Time Is It?; I'll Write a Song for You.

FRIEDMAN, RICHARD H   ASCAP 1954
composer, author
b New York, NY, Oct 23, 24; d New York, Feb 5, 54. Educ: Col. WW II service. Chief Collabr: Arnold Peckjian. *Songs:* Why Go On; Life Was Made for Living.

FRIEDMAN, RON   ASCAP 1964
composer, author
b Pittsburgh, Pa, Aug 1, 32. Educ: Taylor Allderdise High BA(arch), Pittsburgh; Carnegie Inst Technol, 55. Became writer for TV & theatre, New York, 61 & for "Danny Kaye Show," Los Angeles, 63. Wrote original music and/or lyrics in addition to scripts for TV shows incl "The Odd Couple", "Chico and the Man", "Fantasy Island", "Starsky and Hutch" & others.

FRIEDMAN, SOL   ASCAP 1954
composer, pianist, teacher
b New York, NY, Mar 15, 20. Educ: Brooklyn Col, BA; Henry Street Settlement Music Sch; Hunter Col; Queens Col. Taught piano, theory & harmony. Pianist in dance orchs. Chief Collabr: Roy Alfred. *Songs:* If You Could Only Read My Mind.

FRIEDMAN, STANLEIGH P   ASCAP 1940
composer
b Albany, NY, Aug 12, 1884; d New York, NY, Sept 30, 60. Educ: Yale Univ, BA, Music Sch with Horatio Parker; Harvard Law Sch, LLB. Cond, Yale Orch. Played in New Haven Symph, also sang with New Haven Oratorio Soc. Pres, Schola Cantorum, NY. Practiced law, NY. *Songs:* Academy Cadet; Under the Elms; Down the Field; Whoop It Up; Glory for Yale; Academy Centennial March (A Thousand Feet Are Marching the Old Familiar Way); Albany Charter March (Albany 250th anniversary commercial); Cheer Pennsylvania. *Songs & Instrumental Works:* All Ye That Cleave Unto the Lord (cantata); God is My Trust (anthem).

FRIEDMAN, THEODORE LEOPOLD (TED LEWIS)   ASCAP 1957
author, conductor, clarinetist
b Circleville, Ohio, June 6, 1892; d New York, NY, Aug, 71. Bandleader in vaudeville, nightclubs & films. Made many records. Chief Collabs: Billy Munro, Andrew Sterling, Harry Von Tilzer. *Songs:* When My Baby Smiles At Me; Is Everybody Happy Now?; While We Danced Till Dawn; Sing a Little Love Song for Your Baby.

FRIEND, CLIFF   ASCAP 1922
composer, author, pianist
b Cincinnati, Ohio, Oct 1, 1893; d Las Vegas, Nev, June 27, 74. Educ: Cincinnati Col & Cons. Test pilot, Wright Field. Accompanist to Harry Richman in vaudeville, 3 yrs. Featured in Eng music halls, also throughout the world. Wrote for films. Chief Collabrs: Lew Brown, Sidney Clare, Billy Rose, Irving Caesar, Dave Franklin, Abel Baer, Charles Tobias. *Songs:* Oo-oo Ernest; You Tell Her, I Stutter; Lovesick Blues; Blue Hoosier Blues; June Night; Mama Loves Papa; There's Yes Yes in Your Eyes; Big Butter and Egg Man; Then I'll Be Happy; Where the Lazy Daisies Grow; Tamiami Trail; Hello, Bluebird; Give Me a Night in June; When the Pussywillow Whispers to the Catnip; My Blackbirds Are Bluebirds; Bigger and Better Than Ever; Bottoms Up; Freddie the Freshman; When My Dreamboat Comes Home; The Broken Record; Wah-hoo; The Merry-Go-Round Broke Down; You Can't Stop Me From Dreaming; I Must See Annie Tonight; Trade Winds; We Did It Before and We Can Do It Again; Don't Sweetheart Me; You Missed the Boat; Time Waits for No One; Old Man Time. *Scores:* Bombo; The Passing Show of 1921; Bway stage: Piggy; George White's Scandals of 1929.

FRIENDLY, RAY
See Freundlich, Ralph B

FRIGO, JOHN VIRGIL   ASCAP 1965
composer
b Chicago, Ill, Dec 27, 16. Educ: Started violin lessons at age 8; Scanlon Grade Sch; Curtis Jr High; Fenger High Sch, self taught bass-violin. Played & sang in bands on radio, middle 30's. Joined Chicago Marx Orch, theatre tour, 41, piano, violin comedy routine. Played, Coast Guard Orch, Ellis Island & Curtis Bay, Md, during war, 43-45. Jazz, violin, Jimmy Dorsey Orch. Formed Soft Winds Trio, 47-52. Returned to Chicago, studio player. Bass player on many commercials. Chief Collabrs: Louis Carter, Herb Ellis. *Songs:* Detour Ahead; I Told Ya' I Love Ya' Now Get Out; Hey, Hey, Holy Mackerel (off Chicago Cubs song); Some Night, Some Where.

FRIML, RUDOLF   ASCAP 1914
composer
b Prague, Czech, Dec 7, 1879; d Los Angeles, Calif, Nov 12, 72. Educ: Prague Cons, studied with Dvorak & Jiranek. Concert pianist; toured Europe with violinist, Jan Kubelik; Am tours, 01 & 06. Chief Collabrs: Otto Harbach, PG Wodehouse, Rida Johnson Young, Oscar Hammerstein 2nd, Brian Hooker, Clifford Grey, Harold Atteridge, Dailey Paskman. *Songs:* Giannina Mia; Love Is Like a Firefly; When a Maid Comes Knocking At Your Door; Sympathy; Something Seems a Tingle-ing-eling; Love's Own Kiss; Katinka; Not Now But Later; 'Tis the End, So Farewell; Allah's Holiday; Rackety Coo; L'Amour, Toujours, l'Amour; On the Blue Lagoon; In Love With Love; Somewhere in My Heart; You're in Love; Cutie; The Door of Her Dreams; Rose-Marie; The Mounties; Indian Love Call; Pretty Things; Totem Tom-Tom; Song of the Vagabonds; Some Day; Tomorrow; Only a Rose; Huguette Waltz; Love Me Tonight; Nocturne; Wild Rose; One Golden Hour; Give Me One Hour; March of the Musketeers; Ma Belle; Your Eyes; Donkey Serenade (adapted); I Have the Love; Raindrops on a Drum; One More Mile to Go; Nearer and Dearer; Now Is the Time; Love and Kisses; The Right Place for a Girl; Free to Be Free; I Have the Love; Comparisons; Bonjour; This Same Heart; Vive La You; Loveliest of the Lovely; Cackling Chickens; Puppets on Parade; also a ballad Jacqueline. *Instrumental Works:* Workout for Strings; Hong Kong; Faster and Faster; Scherzo Tarantella; Romantic Mood; Czech Rhapsody; Matterhorn (tone poem); Scenes of My Youth; Spirit of America; Classical Mood; Round the World Symphony; Miami Beach Theme. *Scores:* Bway musical: The Firefly;

Bway stage: High Jinks; The Peasant Girl; Katinka; You're in Love; Sometime; Glorianna; Tumble In; The Little Whopper; June Love; The Blue Kitten; Rose-Marie; The Vagabond King; No Foolin'; The Wild Rose; The Three Musketeers; Film: Northwest Outpost; Lottery Bride; Music for Madame.

FRIML, WILLIAM ASCAP 1953
composer, author
b New York, NY, Mar 20, 21; d Loma Linda, Calif, Mar 1, 73. Educ: Schs in Europe; Staunton Mil Acad; Univ Southern Calif; studied music with Rudolf Friml (father) & Ernst Toch. Carnegie Hall recital, age 9. Wrote scores for ice shows, Hollywood & Las Vegas; wrote spec material for Dinah Shore, Ray Bolger, Gene Nelson, Zsa Zsa Gabor, Billy Eckstine, Crosby Boys & Bob Hope; also for nightclub acts. Chief Collabrs: John Bradford, E Y Harburg, John Latouche. *Songs:* Stack of Blues; Mr A-merican.

FRINK, GEORGE MALANCTHAN DAME ASCAP 1973
composer, author, minister of music
b Ft Pierce, Fla, Sept 16, 31. Educ: Ft Pierce High Sch; Univ Fla, BS(bus admin), 57; Southwestern Baptist Theol Sem, BCM(voice), 65 & MM(music theory), 77. In bus with father, 57-62. Minister of music in Southern Baptist churches, Tex, Ga, SC & Va, 62- *Songs:* I Want to Thank You; In Love He Came; Sweet, Sweet Child; Speak, Still Voice; Sing Jesus; Music: Come, Ye Sinners; To Sing That God Is Love.

FRISCH, ALBERT T ASCAP 1944
composer, pianist, saxophonist
b New York, NY, Mar 27, 16; d New York, Apr 11, 76. Educ: High sch. Saxophonist in nightclubs, on ocean liners & summer resorts; also entertainer, pianist & singer. Writer weekly column, Music in Print, Billboard Magazine. Mem, Am Guild Authors & Composers & Dramatists Guild. USA, WW II (5 Battle Stars). Wrote words & music, songs, instrumentals, albums, shows & TV spec material. Chief Collabrs: Roy Alfred, Buddy Bernier, Johnny Burke, Sylvia Dee, Buddy Kaye, Larry Kusick, Julian More, Allan Roberts, Al Neiburg, Bernard Spiro, Charles Tobias, Sid Wayne, Fred Wise. *Songs & Instrumental Works:* This Is No Laughing Matter; Two Different Worlds; I Won't Cry Anymore; Roses in the Rain; All Over the World; That's What They Meant By the Good Old Summertime; Monte Carlo Melody; Congratulations to Someone; Flowers Mean Forgiveness; The Show Must Go On; Winner Take All; Broadway at Basin Street; What Lies Over the Hill; The Language of Love; Just Married Today; Sipping Cider By the Zuyder Zee; Let It Rain; The Best President We Ever Had (Pancho Maximillian Hernandez); The Cool School; The Wonderful World of Christmas; Come On, Come In; Late in December; Starry-Eyed and Breathless; Little Miss Irish; My Mother's Lullaby; She Never Left the Table; April and You; Something for Nothing; Let's Harmonize; Go You Where You Go; Tears to Burn; The Same Old Moon; Here Comes That Heartache Again; The Melancholy Minstrel; Now; Palermo; Lovin' Up a Storm; The Moment of Truth; You Have to Believe in Someone; Weep for the Boy; Winter in Miami; Music From Out of Space; If I'm Elected; Gregory's Chant; It Must Be Emily; Come Back to Rome; Idle Conversation; Always Love Me; I've Got Some Cryin' to Do; All I Get From You Are Heartaches; A Chocolate Sundae on a Saturday Night; In Time; Not So Long Ago; My Need for You; He Came on a Long Long Journey; Wherefore Art Thou Romeo; Sweet Brown-Eyed Baby; What More Is There to Say; Give Me the Right; Unafraid; Four Walls, Two Windows, and One Broken Heart; He Cha Cha'd In; After the Fall; No Hard Feelings; Really O, Truly O; Mama, Teach Me to Do the Charleston; Io Canto; You Pass This Way Only Once; People, Places and Things; Fiddle Rock; The Hornet's Nest; Tunes for Muzak; My Love Song to You; Song of the Raccoons; Bordello; A Place Like This; Yourself; A Country Bride; Morality; Business Tango; Simple Pleasures; Art Should Be Art; Family Life; If You Should Leave Me; Madame Misia; All the Time in the World; I Love Me; The Way I See It; The Girl in Cabin 54; What Does It Take; Can-Can Ballet; Hallucination Ballet; When the Penny Poets Sing; A Somewhere Rainbow; Where's My Rainbow; To Please the Woman in Me; Grain of the Salt of the Earth; Until the Likes of You; Come Out Wherever You Are; Picture Me; The Morning After; It's a Lonesome Thing; All's Fair in Love and War; Great Company; With One Fell Swoop; Beach Ballet; The Heart's a Wonder; Down the Hatch; Gallant Little Swearers; Be a Hero.

FRISCH, BILLY ASCAP 1923
composer, author
b Philadelphia, Pa, Mar 16, 1882; d Jamaica, NY, Apr 25, 68. Educ: Drexel Inst. "Illus Slide" singer in film theatres. Mem, Dumont Minstrels, Philadelphia, 10-15. Featured in vaudeville; one of originators of act, "A Trip to Hitland." Chief Collabrs: Roy Bergere, Irving Caesar, Harry Ling, Otto Motzan, George Whiting. *Songs:* I'd Like to See the Kaiser With a Lily in His Hand; When Tony Goes Over the Top; Nobody Knows But My Pillow and Me; Me, Myself and I; Sweet Nellie Brown; Strolling Through the Park One Day; Minnie, Shimmie for Me; Smile and the World Smiles With You; Why Do They Call Them Wild Women?; Where Are You Dream Girl?

FRISHBERG, DAVID LEE ASCAP 1963
composer, author, performer
b St Paul, Minn, Mar 23, 33. Educ: Univ Minn, BA(jour), 55. Jazz pianist & singer bands, clubs, concerts, TV & recordings. Lyrics & music for TV, incl "The Funny Side" series, "Scholastic Rock" series & "Mary Tyler Moore" special.

Albums on Concord Jazz label. Chief Collabrs: Johnny Mandel, Al Cohn, Bob Dorough. *Songs:* Peel Me a Grape; Van Lingle Mungo; The Wheelers and Dealers; I'm Just a Bill; Dodger Blue; Lyrics: I'm Hip; You Are There; The Underdog.

FRITSCHEL, JAMES ERWIN ASCAP 1977
composer, choral conductor
b Greeley, Colo, May 13, 29. Educ: Wartburg Col, Iowa, BME, 51; Colo State Col, MA, 54; Univ Iowa, PhD, 60. Pub sch teacher, 54-58; prof music & dir choir, Wartburg Col, 59- *Songs:* Music (SATB): O Come Little Children; In Peace and Joy; Be Still; Be Not Silent; Away in a Manger; Song of the Skyloom; Poor Li'l Jesus; Make Haste; Four About Life and Death; A Great Light; Kling, Glöckchen; Search Me, O God; King of My Soul; My Heart Dances. *Instrumental Works:* Everyone Suddenly Sang (brass, organ, chorus); Psalm 19 (band, chorus); The Light of the World (soprano, chorus); Canticle: A Song of David (double choir, women's voices).

FRITTER, GENEVIEVE DAVISSON ASCAP 1974
composer, violinist
b Clarksburg, WVa, Dec 13, 15. Col, BM, 37; Juilliard Sch Music, studied violin with Reber Johnson & Harry Glickman, 37 & 38; Birmingham Cons, violin with Otto Kar Cadek, 39-40; Cincinnati Cons, violin with Mihail Stolarevsky & comp with Esther Williamson Ballou, 41-43. Concertmaster, Nat Ballet Orch, 5 1/2 yrs; mem Kennedy Ctr Orch, DC & Filene Ctr Orch, Wolf Trap Farm Park; music dir & comp-in-residence, Montgomery Ballet Co, Silver Spring, Md, 19 yrs. Comp Awards incl: Nat Fedn Music Clubs, Mu Phi Epsilon Nat Comp Contest & several others. *Songs:* Music: Monotone; Judean Hills Are Holy (anthem). *Instrumental Works:* Theme and Variations for String Orchestra; Sinfonietta No 1 (chamber orch); Poem for Flute With Orchestral Accompaniment; Suite for Flute and Piano; Lament (flute, piano). *Scores:* Opera/Ballet: Hansel and Gretel (ballet for children).

FRITZ, RICHARD ERNEST ASCAP 1970
composer, orchestrator, arranger
b Lawrence, Kans, Dec 19, 32. Educ: Univ Kans, BME; Westlake Col Music, studied with Roger Segura & Ferde Grofe. Staff musician, CBS TV & KTLA TV, Los Angeles. Free-lance arr, TV, motion picture, records, acts. Teacher. *Instrumental Works:* Hot Mud; House of the Rising Funk; Drum of Nothingness; Momma Jive; Zambezi; Maug Maws 'N Greens; Steal the Feel; Dueling Guitars; Hot Doggin'; Get It; Boogalooin'; Reelin' With the Feelin'; Slow Burn; Afro-Disiac; Bella Donna; Chanson De Nuit; Odds On; Lime Twig; Hot Sause; Shout; Slop Jar.

FROCK, GEORGE A ASCAP 1967
composer, educator
b Danville, Ill, July 16, 38. Educ: Univ Ill, 56-60, perc studied with Jack McKenzie; Univ Kans, 60-63, comp studies with John Pozdro. Teacher, Univ Kans, 60-63, Memphis State Univ, 63-66 & Univ Tex, 66- Timpanist, Memphis Symph & Austin Symph Orch; performer, Corpus Christi & San Antonio Symph Orchs. Mem, Educ Bd Consult for Premier Perc, Div of Selmer Band Instruments. Chief Collabr: Johnnie Warrington. *Instrumental Works:* Drums of America; Concertino for Marimba; Variations for Flute and Percussion; Three Asiatic Dances (perc ens); Fanfare for Double Trio (perc ens).

FROEBER, RICHARD REINHOLD ASCAP 1963
composer, author, singer
b Saginaw, Mich, Aug 29, 29. Educ: Mich State Univ, BMus. Under contract, Buzza-Cordozo musical greeting cards. Pres, Double F Enterprises, incl Double F Records. Writer, music for Las Vegas revue "Around the World in Sexty Minutes," music for TV series "Hawaii Calls" & documentary "Wild and Free." Entertainer, Alaska-Sitmar cruises. Chief Collabrs: Jack Hoffman, Helen Farries, George Madill, Lucile Palmer, Irene Holt, Gene Emmet Clark, Ernest Holmes. *Songs:* Palm Springs (dedicated to Bob Hope); Music: I Thot of You and Said a Little Prayer; Welcome to Hawaii; Look Into My Heart; Hula Hands I Love You; Wild and Free; Magic of Love; Just to Be Sure; Sonnet in the Silence; If You Have a Gift, Bring It; Good Morning, Lord; Say a Little Prayer for Someone; There's Someone Who Loves Us; If You Just Believe and Pray; I Know There's a God; Think How Lucky You Are.

FROMHOLZ, STEVEN JOHN ASCAP 1969
composer, author, singer
b Temple, Tex, June 8, 45. Began writing while attending NTex State Univ, 63. Played & wrote on West Coast, late 60's. Appeared in film, "Outlaw Blues," 76. *Songs:* Yellow Cat; I'd Have To Be Crazy; Texas Trilogy.

FROMM, HERBERT ASCAP 1965
composer, author, organist
b Kitzingen, Ger, Feb 23, 05. Educ: State Acad Music, Munich, MA, 30; pvt studies with Paul Hindemith, 40-41. Conductor, Civic Operas, Bielefeld, Ger, 30-31 & Würzburg, 31-33. Music dir & organist, Temple Beth Zion, Buffalo, NY, 37-40 & Temple Israel, Boston, Mass, 40-72. Ernest Bloch Award, 45. Hon Degree: DHL, Lesley Col, Mass. Literary works: "The Key of See" (travel journals), "Seven Pockets" (writings) & "On Jewish Music" (a composer's view). *Songs:* Musical works: Choral cycles, song cycles, chamber music,

cantatas, organ works, piano music, a large body of liturgical works; Sacred song: Grant us Peace; Choral work: Psalm 23.

FROSINI, PIETRO　　　　　　　　　　　ASCAP 1942
composer, accordionist
b Mascalucia, Italy, Aug 9, 1885; d Woodside, NY, Sept 29, 51. To US, 05. Educ: Municipal Cons of Fine Arts, Catania, Italy; studied with Francesco Frontini; Milan Cons. Cornetist, British Navy, Malta, 2 1/2 yrs. Vaudeville accordionist. *Instrumental Works:* Accordion: The Sunkissed Waltz; The Accordion World March; Overture in C; Swedish Steel Mazurka; Silver Moon Waltz; Sicilian Shore; Northern Skies; The Jolly Caballero.

FROST, HAROLD G (JACK)　　　　　　　ASCAP 1943
composer, author
b Boston, Mass, Nov 25, 1893; d North Hollywood, Calif, Oct 21, 59. Educ: High sch. Contract writer with music co, Chicago. 2nd Lt, Inf, WW I. Went to NY, assoc with Fred Fisher & other music publ. Wrote spec material for Eva Tanguay & Trixie Fraganza. Worked in newspaper, radio & TV magazine advert. In vaudeville, 4 yrs. *Songs:* Sweet Hawaiian Moonlight; Floatin' Down to Cotton Town; When You and I Were Young Maggie Blues; Mysterious Blues; The Annie Laurie Blues; The Girl at the End of the Bar. *Scores:* Bway stage: Keep Kool.

FRY, GARY D　　　　　　　　　　　　　ASCAP 1977
author, performer
b Keswick, Iowa, Nov 29, 55. Educ: Univ Miami, BM, 76. Arr/comp for publ, live acts & commercial recordings. Teacher, pub schs & Univ Miami. *Songs:* Reach for the Stars; If You Believe in Music.

FRY, TOMMY JOE
composer, teacher
b Sweetwater, Tex, Oct 23, 33. Educ: McMurry Col; Sul Ross State Univ. Band dir, pub schs of Tex, 6 yrs. Mgr music co & music buyer for five store chain, 17 yrs. Dir of bands & asst prof music, McMurry Col, 2 yrs. *Instrumental Works:* Triptych for Band; Triptych for Orchestra; Blasenfest (band).

FRYBERG, MART　　　　　　　　　　　ASCAP 1943
composer
b Poznan, Poland, Jan 18, 1890; d New York, NY, Oct 23, 52. Educ: High sch, Poland. Went to Czech, 34-45, Italy, 36, then US, 39. Chief Collabrs: Bert Reisfeld, Dorothy Dick. *Songs:* Call Me Darling; What Will My Mammie Say Now?; Waltzing on the Kalamazoo; Small World; Home Town.

FUCHS, LEO
See Springer, A L

FUCHS, PETER PAUL　　　　　　　　　ASCAP 1967
composer, author, conductor
b Vienna, Austria, Oct 30, 16. Educ: Acad Music, Vienna, cond dipl with hons; studies with Weingartner, Krips, Karl Weigl, Eugene Zador & Leone Gombrich. With Europ Theatres, 2 yrs; mem music staff, Metrop Opera, 40-50; Army serv, 43-45; Tanglewood fac, 46; with San Francisco Opera, 46, 50 & 54; fac mem & dir opera, La State Univ, 50-76; mus dir & cond, Baton Rouge Symph, 60-76; artistic dir, Beaumont Civic Opera, 63-75; guest cond, New Orleans Philh, New Orleans Opera & in 6 Europ Countries; mus dir & cond, Greensboro Symph, NC, 76- Ed bk, "The Music Theater of Walter Felsenstein." *Instrumental Works:* Fantasy for English Horn and Strings. *Scores:* Comic opera: Serenade at Noon; Transl: Un bello in Meschere (Verdi).

FUGATE, RICHARD DELL　　　　　　　ASCAP 1977
composer, author
b Louisville, Ky, Nov 27, 54. Educ: Self-taught. Played clarinet in grade sch. Played guitar & bass in var nightclubs & studio work. Chief Collabr: Ernie Tungate. *Songs:* West Virginia.

FULEIHAN, ANIS　　　　　　　　　　　ASCAP 1943
composer, pianist
b Cyprus, Apr 2, 1900; d. Educ: Schs in Near East; studied piano with Alberto Jonas; Guggenheim fel. To US, 15. Concert pianist debut, Aeolian Hall, New York, 19; toured Near East, 3 yrs. Comp, cond & pianist on radio. Staff mem, publ co, 32-39. *Instrumental Works:* Mediterranean; Preface to a Child's Story Book; Symphony No 1; Piano Concerto No 1, 2; Concerto for Two Pianos; Fantasy for Viola and Orchestra; Symphonie Concertante; Invocation to Isis; Epithalamium (piano, strings); Fiesta (piano); Cypriana Suite; Air and Fugue on White Keys.

FULLER, DEAN　　　　　　　　　　　　ASCAP 1956
composer, conductor, arranger
b Woodbury, NH, Dec 12, 22. Educ: Yale Univ, BA. Accompanist & writer for Mary McCarty. Dir, summer stock musicals, 6 yrs. Arr & cond for Tallulah Bankhead, Las Vegas. Staff comp, Tamiment Playhouse, 3 yrs. Vocal coach, arr & ballet comp for touring co A Tree Grows in Brooklyn. Songwriter for "New Faces of 1956" & "Ziegfeld Follies," 57. Comp, background music for "Grand Tour", "Ring Around the Moon", "Lilliom" & "She Stoops to Conquer." Co-author, "Once Upon a Mattress" (& TV adaptations). Chief Collabrs:

Marshall Barer, Matt Dubey. *Songs:* One Perfect Moment; Isn't She Lovely; Scratch My Back; Roller Coaster Blues; Intoxication; Warm Winter; What'll I Do With All the Love I Was Savin' for You?; La Ronde (This Is Quite a Perfect Night).

FULLER, LORENZO DOW　　　　　　　ASCAP 1953
composer, author, teacher
b Stockton, Kans, Mar 22, 19. Educ: Univ Kans, BME; Univ Chicago, MM; Columbia Univ, DM(music); Juilliard Sch Music, comp under Vittorio Giannini & voice with Belle Soudant. Singer, pianist & harpist; soloist with Ky Symph Orch; spec material writer & music dir, WNBC-TV; asst dir to Hall Johnson, Hall Johnson Choir; TV show, "Man About Music"; Bway shows: "Cabin in the Sky", "Blues Holiday", "St Louis Woman", "Finian's Rainbow", "Kiss Me Kate" & "Sporting Life" in the int "Porgy & Bess" co. Has cond orchs in US & abroad. Radio disc jockey for WLIB. Chief Collabrs: Karley Mills, Lila Levant, Haya Murray, Bernard K Kay, Phillip Bourneuf. *Songs:* Encore Heartache; Come Spring; Who Wants to Remember?; Music: Playing the Game; Take a Stand; Sailor Man, Sailor Man; Draw to an Inside Straight.

FULTON, JOHN COLLINS　　　　　　　ASCAP 1943
composer, author, musician
b Philipsburg, Pa, June 13, 03. Began career with small bands, Pa; spent short time with George Olsen Band; with Paul Whiteman Orch, 26-34; musical dir, Chicago Theater, retired; WBBM-CBS Chicago, 20 yrs. Chief Collabrs: Moe Jaffie, Lois Steele. *Songs:* Until; My Greatest Mistake; Say A Prayer Every Day; Sweetie Pie; Wanting You; Lets Return to God; Moody; Music: Wanted; Ivory Tower; Silence Is Golden; Mrs Santa Claus; Theme of Love; Lyrics: If You are But a Dream; Make America Proud of You; Keep Your Promise Willie Thomas.

FULTON, REG　　　　　　　　　　　　　ASCAP 1959
composer, author, singer
b San Francisco, Calif, Dec 24, 24. Vocal coach; writer of special material; singer. *Songs:* Trees of Paris; Paris in the Rain; Your Special Christmas Angel.

FULTON, ROSSWELL HENRY, SR (LUCKY)
composer, author
b Plymouth, Mich, Dec 23, 29. Started writing at an early age; singer, sch dance, VFW, fairs, homecomings & gospel concerts. *Songs:* Gooski's Riders; Tomorrow Never Comes; Better One Than You (Waiting At Home); Praise the Lord; Going Thru the Motions; Number One Winner; Gospel Jamboree; The Golden Hymns.

FUOCO, JOSEPH G　　　　　　　　　　ASCAP 1979
composer, author, teacher
b New York, NY, Nov 23, 54. Educ: Christ the King High Sch Cons; music study, Queens Col; studied guitar with Billy Bauer. Lead guitarist, singer, band leader & nightclub performer; free-lance. Proprietor, music sch & retail music business. Chief Collabr: Jeanette Piccininni. *Songs:* I Am Here; Summer Fields; Bringing a Song to You; One-Way Street; Sunset.

FURAY, PAUL RICHARD　　　　　　　ASCAP 1966
composer, author, singer
Mem groups, Buffalo Springfield, Poco, Southern Hillman Furay Band. *Songs:* Kind Woman; Crazy Eyes; A Good Feeling to Know; Any Way Bye Bye; Fallin' in Love; Pickin' Up the Pieces.

FUREDI, JUDITH SUSAN　　　　　　　ASCAP 1970
author
b Nyiregyhaza, Hungary, Sept 4, 49. Educ: High Sch of Music & Art; State Univ NY, Stony Brook; City Col, City Univ New York, BA, 73. Winner of David Mankovitz Award in Poetry, 73; ed & contributor, "Promethian"; publ & ed, "Who's Who in Poetry in American Colleges and Universities," 74-76. Writer poetry, fiction & screenplay; part-owner poster production co, 76- Chief Collabr: Paul Reif. *Songs:* Lyrics: Duo for Three.

FURMAN, SAMUEL HERBERT　　　　　ASCAP 1955
composer, author
b Hollywood, Calif, Sept 3, 18; d Los Angeles, Calif, Dec 12, 70. Educ: Los Angeles City Col; pvt music study. Sam Furman and His Orch, 37. Pianist, Skinny Ennis Orch, 40 & Ray Noble Orch, 41. Staff pianist, NBC Blue Network Orch, 43 & CBS Orch, 16 yrs. Arr, Frankie Lane, Frank Sinatra & Bing Crosby, later had own group; with Night Blooming Jazzmen & Orren Tucker Orch. Chief Collabr: Warn Johnson. *Songs & Instrumental Works:* Pray, Pray, Pray; Lazy Susan; Cashmere.

FURNISS, CATHY (KITTY)
See Cowan, Cathy

FURTADO, THOMAS A　　　　　　　　ASCAP 1957
composer, singer
b West Warwick, RI, Nov 20, 28. Educ: Berklee Sch of Music; Fordham Univ Sch of Educ. With USN Band, World War II. Soloist, radio, nightclubs & on records. *Songs:* Isabella; Walk Like a Man.

FUTCH, EDWARD GARVIN (EDDY RAVEN) ASCAP 1972
composer, author, singer
b LaFayette, La, Aug 19, 44. Sang in Jimmie Davis Band, La; recording artist, Acuff-Rose Milene Music, 70- Mem, Southern Writers Adv Bd, ASCAP; bd dirs, Nashville Songwriters Asn & bd dirs, Am Fedn TV & Radio Artists, Nashville. Chief Collabrs: Whitey Shafer, Dave Powelson. *Songs:* Touch the Morning; Back in the Country; I Don't Wanna Talk It Over; Sometimes I Talk in My Sleep; Sweet Mother Texas; Dealin' With the Devil; Free to Be; You've Got Those Eyes.

FUTTERMAN, ENID SUSAN ASCAP 1975
author
b Brooklyn, NY, Oct 28, 43. Educ: Abraham Lincoln High Sch, 57-60; Douglass Col, Rutgers Univ, BA, 64. Copywriter & lyricist for Grey Advert, 64-77; lyricist for a PBS children's show, 78; lyricist for an album & musical theatre projects, "Portrait of Jennie" & "Cousin, Cousin," 80. Chief Collabrs: Michael Cohen, Howard Marken, John Duffy, Jeff Waxman, Suzanne Fellini. *Songs:* Lyrics: Permanent Damage; Give Me the Light; Crazy.

G

GAAL, CHARLES J ASCAP 1958
composer, author, musician
b New York, NY, May 14, 1893. Educ: Indust Traffic Col; pvt music study. Golf pro & instr. Musician in dance bands. Author, "Your Golf." *Songs:* God's Gift; It's Wonderful; Knee Deep in Stardust; Till the End of the World; Old Swimming Hole.

GABLER, MILTON ASCAP 1947
author, record producer, discographer
b New York, NY, May 20, 11. Educ: Stuyvesant High Sch; City Col New York, 2 yrs. Founded Commodore Music Shop while in high sch, 26. Specialized in jazz recordings, reissued jazz masters from major cos, 34. Founder of United Hot Clubs of Am. Started first independent jazz record label Commodore, 38. On A&R staff, Decca Records, 41, vpres, mid 50's; with Decca Records until retirement, 71. Recorded every category of music & produced records. Responsible for introduction of many great standards in popular Am music. In span of career produced over 36 million seller hits, many prior to Gold Record Awards, Record Indust Asn Am. Founding father of Nat Acad of Recording Arts & Sciences. Chief Collabrs: Bert Kaempfert, Herbert Rehbein, Vaughn Horton, Jimmie Crane, Duke Ellington, Billy Haley. *Songs:* Tell Me Why; Sing Until the Cows Come Home; You Had Better Change Your Ways; Skinny Minnie; Lyrics: Danke Schoen; L-O-V-E; If I Give My Heart to You; Choo, Choo, Ch'Boogie; In a Mellow Tone; Weiderseh'n; Sweet Maria; Don't Talk To Me.

GABRIEL, CHARLES H, JR ASCAP 1959
composer, author, pianist
b San Francisco, Calif, Mar 2, 1892; d Los Angeles, Calif, Nov 13, 34. Educ: Chicago Musical Col. Served in WW I. Mem staff, Chicago Tribune. Ed, Popular Mechanics. Prog mgr, WGN, Chicago, KLX, Oakland, Calif, NBC, San Francisco & KNX, Hollywood. *Instrumental Works:* Piano Concerto.

GABRIEL, CHARLES H, SR ASCAP 1940
composer, author, conductor
b Wilton, Iowa, Aug 18, 1856; d Los Angeles, Calif, Sept 14, 32. Educ: Pub schs. Cond, church choir, San Francisco. Compiled hymnals for pub cos. *Songs:* Sacred: Awakening Chorus; All Hail Immanuel; He Is So Precious to Me; Brighten the Corner Where You Are; Since Jesus Came Into My Heart; Way of the Cross Leads Home.

GABRIL, MERCDES
See Jacobs, Al T

GABURO, KENNETH LOUIS ASCAP 1960
composer, educator, conductor
b Somerville, NJ, July 5, 26. Educ: Eastman Sch Music, BM, MM; Cons di Santa Cecilia, Rome; Univ Ill, MusD; studied with Goffredo Petrassi, Bernard Rogers, Burrill Phillips, Hubert Kessler & Herbert Elwell. Rec'd George Eastman hon fel, Univ Rochester, grants from Univ Ill & Fulbright fel. Taught at Kent State Univ & McNeese Col; prof music, Univ Ill, 56-68, assoc fel, Inst Advanced Study; prof music, Univ Calif, San Diego, 68-75, in-residence, Ctr Music Experiment, 72-75. Rec'd United Nations Educ, Scientific & Cultural Orgn Creative Artist Award; ASCAP Serious Music Awards; Thorne Found Award; Nat Endowment for the Arts Award; Guggenheim Fel; Comns: Fromm & Koussevitzky Foundations & Magnavox Corp. Founder/dir, New Musical Choral Ens I-IV. Publ, Lingua Press. *Songs & Instrumental Works:* 2 Shorts and a Long (piano); 3 String Interludes (both Phi Mu Alpha Award); On a Quiet Theme (Gershwin Mem Award); Music for 5 Instruments (Victor Allesandro comn); Elegy (Sagalyn Orch Award); Line Studies; Two; Viola Concerto (Walter Trampler comn); Hydrogen Jukebox Music (Univ Ill Fest comn); Ideas

and Transformations No 1; Choral: The Night Is Still (Sigma Alpha Iota Award); 3 Dedications to Lorca (Eastman Alumni Asn Choral Award); Mass for Tenors, Basses (World Library Sacred Music Award); Ad Te Domine (Christo-Centric Fest, Univ Ill comn); Antiphony II & III (chorus & electronics), IV (instruments & tape, electronics), VI (string xtet, slides & electronics); Cantilena III & IV; Music Theater: Lingua One: Poems & Other Theaters; Lingua II; Maledetto; Lingua III: In the Can; Collaboration One; My, My, My, What a Wonderful Fall; Subito; 20 Sensing (Instruction) Compositions. *Scores:* Opera: The Snow Queen; The Widow (Fest Contemporary Arts, NY); Stage: Tiger Rag (Univ Ill Fest Contemporary Arts Award).

GAGLIARDI, GEORGE ANTHONY ASCAP 1969
composer, author
b Paris, Tex, June 1, 47. Educ: Paris Jr Col; Wayland Baptist Col, studied with Dr James Cram; NTex State Univ. Began writing songs in high sch; first choral piece publ, 69; travelled with New Hope, 70-71. Music was selected as one of the top ten gospel songs for 79-80. *Songs:* A Brand New Song; Words and Music; Ye Who Are Lonely; Ain't It The Gospel Truth; You Have Been My Finest Hour; His Music; All I Can Give is Myself; You Have Loved Me Through It All.

GAILLARD, BULEE (SLIM) ASCAP 1949
composer, author, pianist
b Detroit, Mich, Jan 4, 16. Appeared with Slam Stewart as team, Slim & Slam; later formed own group. Acted in films, incl "Hellzapoppin'," "Go, Man, Go" & "Star Spangled Rhythm." Singer. Chief Collabrs: Slam Stewart, Bud Green, Harry Squires. *Songs:* Flat Foot Floogie; Cement Mixer; Vol Vist du Gaily Star; Tutti Frutti; Chicken Rhythm.

GAINES, ADRIAN DONNA (DONNA SUMMER) ASCAP 1980
composer, author, vocalist
b Boston, Mass, Dec 31, 48. Educ: Jeremiah E Burke High Sch, Boston. Starred in "Thank God It's Friday" & ABC-TV "The Donna Summer Special," 80. Made many records. Acad Award for Best Song. Chief Collabrs: Bruce Sudano, Giorgio Moroder, Pete Bellotte, Bruce Roberts. *Songs:* On the Radio; Love to Love You Baby; Heaven Knows; Bad Girls; Dim All the Lights; Startin' Over Again; Try Me, I Know We Can Make It; I Feel Love. *Albums:* On the Radio; Bad Girls; Live and More; Once Upon a Time; Four Seasons of Love; A Love Trilogy; I Remember Yesterday; Love to Love You Baby; Thank God It's Friday.

GAINES, (OTHO) LEE ASCAP 1951
composer, author, singer
b Houston, Miss, Apr 26, 14. Educ: High sch, Tupelo, Miss; Dillard Univ; studied with Frederik Hall. Sang with Delta Rhythm Boys; appeared on radio & TV, actor in Bway musicals: "Sing Out the News", "Hot Mikado", "Hellzapoppin", also films incl "Crazy House", "Weekend Pass" & "Follow the Boys." Chief Collabrs: Duke Ellington, Count Basie, Jimmie Mundy. *Songs & Instrumental Works:* One O'Clock Jump; 9:20 Special; Take the A Train; Just Squeeze Me; Just a-Sittin' and a-Rockin'; Hello, Goodbye, Forget It; Finlandia; Just a Game; Memories; Kultani (Please Come Back).

GAINES, SAMUEL RICHARDS ASCAP 1924
composer, conductor, organist
b Saginaw, Mich, Apr 23, 1869; d Boston, Mass, Oct 9, 45. Educ: Am Cons, NY; studied with Rommaldo Sapio, Antonin Dvorak, George Chadwick & Percy Goetschius. Solo tenor, St Thomas Church, NY; organist, Orthodox Synagogue. Voice teacher, Detroit, 1895. Organist, Jefferson Ave Presby Church. Cond, Elgar Choral Soc. Organist & choir dir, Shawmut Cong Church, Boston. Founder & dir, Musical Art Soc. Teacher, Columbia Univ. Guest cond, var music fests, New Eng & NY. *Songs & Instrumental Works:* The Vision (oratorio); The Village Blacksmith (cantata); Fantasy on a Russian Folk Song (orch, chorus); Salutation (choral); Yonder, Yonder. *Scores:* Opera: Daniel Boone.

GAITHER, GLORIA LEE ASCAP 1973
composer, author, singer
b Battle Creek, Mich, Mar 4, 42. Educ: Anderson Col, BA, 63. Songwriter, lyricist, author & recording artist. Chief Collabr: William J Gaither. *Songs:* Lyrics: Because He Lives; There's Something About That Name; Let's Just Praise the Lord; Something Beautiful; The Church Triumphant; The King Is Coming; I Am Loved; Alleluia-A Praise Gathering for Believers (Gold Album, Recording Industry Asn Am; musical cantata.)

GAITHER, WILLIAM JAMES ASCAP 1973
b Alexandria, Ind, Mar 28, 36. Educ: Anderson Col, BA, 59; Ball State Univ, MA, 61. Songwriter, mgr, The Bill Gaither Trio; recording artist, publ. Chief Collabr: Gloria Gaither. *Songs:* He Touched Me; Alleluia-A Praise for Believers (Gold Album, Recording Industry Asn Am; musical cantata.); Music: Because He Lives; Something Beautiful; The King Is Coming; Let's Just Praise the Lord; The Church Triumphant; I Am Loved.

GALBRAITH, GORDON (GORDON YOUNG) ASCAP 1964
composer, author, singer
b Philadelphia, Pa, July 23, 30. Educ: John Bartram High Sch; Purdue Univ; studied voice with Carlo Menoti, 64-65. Recording artist, Chancellor Records, ABC Paramount & 20th Century Fox. Chief Collabrs: Peter DeAngelis, Ricci Mareno. *Songs:* I Got You (ASCAP Award); I Love the Way That You've Been Loving Me (ASCAP Award); Pardon Me; Puppet on a String (Party Girl); Painted Tainted Rose; Living a Lie; I'm Living My Heaven With You; Always Together; My Cherie; How Do You Keep From Crying?

GALBRAITH, VICTORIA GARRETT ASCAP 1979
composer, author
b Chicago, Ill, Aug 6, 48. Educ: Col Wooster, BA(music, religion), 70; Manhattan Sch Music, MM(voice), 72; voice study with Ellen Faull, 70-; pvt comp study with Daniel Ricigliano, 72-; Univ Ill, Urbana, 77-78. Writing songs for worship, 72- Singer, guitarist & recording artist; with New York City Opera, regular & assoc chorus, 73-75 & 79-80. Chief Collabr: Ronald Kauffmann. *Songs:* Praise the Lord!; Good People; God Be With You.

GALDSTON, PHILIP EDWARD ASCAP 1968
composer, author, pianist
b New York, NY, Sept 28, 50. Educ: Union Col, BA(Am studies), studied with Edgar Curtis. Record producer, arr; vocalist, comp & author for Epic Records, 65-69; leader, vocalist, keyboardist, comp, author & arr, Freeway, 69-72; partner with Peter Thom, 73-, comp & authored many songs. Grand Prize winners, Am Song Festival, 75; recording artists for Warner Bros, 76-77. Formed Far Cry, Columbia recording artists, 79-; produced three Grammy nominated albums. Chief Collabr: Peter Thom. *Songs:* Why Don't We Live Together; No One Gave Me Love; Savannah Sunny Sunday; Everybody's Goin' Hollywood; Some Things Will Never Change; Eldorado Escape; Suddenly Strings; American Gypsies.

GALE, EDDIE
See Stevens, Edward Gale

GALE, STEPHEN
See Krasnow, Hermann (Hecky)

GALLAGHER, EDWARD A ASCAP 1961
composer, author
b Philadelphia, Pa, Nov 7, 28. Educ: High sch. Works in advert. Author, bk on songwriting. *Songs:* The Perfect Couple; Somebody Else; Time to Go Again; Baby Till You Say You Love Me; De Limbo Dance; Turn to Him.

GALLAGHER, JAMES RICHARD ASCAP 1963
composer
b Chicago, Ill, June 21, 43. Drummer & comp with rock & roll group, The Astronauts. Recording artist, RCA. Popular in Japan, 63-65. Had own bus, then retired. Chief Collabrs: Dennis L M Lindsey, John Storm Patterson, Robert G Demmon, Richard Otis Fifield. *Songs:* 456 Gears. *Scores:* Film/TV: Wild, Wild Winter.

GALLA-RINI, ANTHONY ASCAP 1965
composer, concert accordionist, teacher
b Manchester, Conn, Jan 18, 04. Educ: Studied traditional harmony & counterpoint with Van Broekhoven, New York; San Francisco Cons Mus, harmony, counterpoint & conducting with Gastone Usigli. At age 7 began playing accordion & toured Am & Can on Chauteuqua & Vaudeville, 11-32. Taught accordion, San Francisco, 32. First to conduct master classes for accordionists, teachers & students & to give formal accordion recitals, Philh Auditorium, Los Angeles, Town Hall, New York, Civic Opera House & Temple Sholom, Chicago & others, US & Can, 40- Concertized in Eng, Scotland, Norway, Sweden, France & Italy. First accordion concerto with Detroit & Denver Symph & with other orchs. Was made Cavalier of the Order of the Star of Solidarity by Italian Government, 74. *Instrumental Works:* Concerto for Accordion and Orchestra in G Minor; Concerto No 2 in E Minor (accordion & orch).

GALLEGOS, CHARLES B ASCAP 1962
composer, author, conductor
b Alamoso, Colo. Educ: High sch. Cond of group, Fabulous Cyclones. *Songs:* Little Bossa Nova; I've Found the Girl I Love; I Love You So; And Now You Know.

GALLICO, GRACE (LANE) THORPE ASCAP 1954
composer, author
b Fairfield, Conn, July 6, 21. Educ: Rodger Ludlowe High Sch. Sang with sisters on radio & with dance bands incl: McFarland Twins, Carl Hoff, Tony Pastor & Vaughn Monroe. Chief Collabrs: Tom Glazer, Earl Shuman, Leon Carr, George Weiss, Steve Davis, Morty Garson. *Songs:* Clinging Vine; Pass the Plate of Happiness Around; Hall of Famous Losers; Bla, Bla, Cha Cha Cha; Believe in Me; Darling You Make It So; Music: Twilight Waltz; Margarita; Fontainebleu; Lyrics: Penny; Birmingham Rag; Love Insurance.

GALLINA, JILL C ASCAP 1979
composer
b Bronx, NY, Nov 5, 46. Educ: Clifton High Sch; Trenton State Col, BA, 68. Teacher music, elem sch. Writer, educ, children's & choral fields. *Songs:* Christmas Lullaby of Joy; Santa and the Snowmobile (children's musical play). *Albums:* For Children: Alphabet in Action; Sing a Song of Sounds; Rockin' Rhythm Band.

GALLOP, SAMMY ASCAP 1942
composer, author
b Duluth, Minn, Mar 16, 15; d Encino, Calif, Feb 24, 71. Wrote revues, Latin Quarter, NY, also songs for Bway musicals, "Star and Garter", "John Murray Anderson's Almanac" & "All for Love." Chief Collabrs: Peter DeRose, David Rose, Guy Wood, Jerry Livingston, David Saxon, Elmer Albrecht, Rube Bloom, Howard Steiner, Steve Allen, Chester Conn, Milton Delugg, James Van Heusen. *Songs:* Autumn Serenade; Holiday for Strings; Shoofly Pie and Apple Pan Dowdy; There Must Be a Way; Elmer's Tune; Count Every Star; Outside of Heaven; Somewhere Along the Way; My Lady Loves to Dance; Make Her Mine; Forgive My Heart; Wake the Town and Tell the People; Half as Lovely; No Good Man; Maybe You'll Be There; Caribbean Clipper; Vagabond Shoes; Bluebird Singing in My Heart; Night Lights; The Right Thing to Say; Meet Me Where They Play the Blues; Lyrics: The Tricks of the Trade; I Guess I Expected Too Much; I'll Never Know Why; It Happens to Be Me; Azuza; A Thousand Thoughts of You; That's The Moon My Son.

GALLOWAY, TOD B ASCAP 1933
composer, singer
b Columbus, Ohio, Oct 13, 1863; d Columbus, Dec 12, 35. Educ: Amherst Col, BA, MA. Was probate judge, then secy to governor of Ohio. WWI, YMCA entertainer in France. *Songs:* O Heart of Mine: The Gypsy Trail; When Spring Comes Laughing; Where the Highway Steps Along; Little Boy Blue; My Laddie; Pickaninny Lullaby; Along Upon the House Tops to the North; The Whiffenpoof Song.

GANDY, CAROLYN (CONNIE) VIRGINIA
composer, singer
b Florence, Ala, Nov 20, 41. Educ: Lewis County High Sch; Univ Tenn, Nashville, studied accounting for 1 yr. Sang in churches. *Songs:* The Sun's Gonna Shine; God's Little Extras'; In God We Trust; Sacred Words; He Changed a Beggar Into a Millionaire.

GANNON, JAMES KIMBALL (KIM) ASCAP 1940
author
b Brooklyn, NY, Nov 18, 1900; d Delray Beach, Fla, Apr 29, 74. Educ: St Lawrence Univ, BS; Albany Law Sch, LLB. Admitted to NY Bar, 34. Wrote for films. Chief Collabrs: J Fred Coots, Max Steiner, Mabel Wayne, Walter Kent, Josef Myrow. *Songs:* Five O'Clock Whistle; I Understand; Always in My Heart; Moonlight Cocktail; I'll Be Home for Christmas; A Dreamer's Holiday; It Can't Be Wrong; I Want to Be Wanted; Autumn Nocturne; Under Paris Skies; also Johnny Appleseed (complete Disney Production). *Scores:* Bway stage: Seventeen.

GANZ, AARON
See Gonzalez, Aaron Ruben

GANZ, RUDOLPH ASCAP 1940
composer, conductor, pianist
b Zurich, Switz, Feb 24, 1877; d Chicago, Ill, Aug 2, 72. Educ: Studied music in Lausanne, Strasbourg, Berlin; DePaul Univ, MusD(hon); Cincinnati Cons; Grinnell Col; Univ Rochester; Roosevelt Univ, LHD. Pianist with Lausanne Munic Orch. Debut as pianist with Berlin Philh, 1899. Made Europ concert tour. Head, Piano Dept, Chicago Musical Col, 01, artistic dir, 28, pres, 33, emer pres, 54. Cond, St Louis Symph, 21-27. Guest cond symph orchs, US, Havana, London & Paris. Cond, Young People's Concerts, NY Philh & San Francisco Symph, 38-40, also Children's Concerts, Chicago. Officer, French Legion of Honor; Chevalier de l'Ordre des Arts et des Lettres, Lincoln Acad III, former pres, MacDowell Asn. Gave joint recitals with wife, Esther La Berge. Edited 14 early Webern songs. Updated & revised book with Ernest Hutcheson, "The Literature of the Piano." *Instrumental Works:* Symphony in E; Animal Pictures (symph suite); Laughter-Yet Love; Sunday Morning in the Mountains; Scherzino in B; Piano Concerto; Piano Variations on Themes by Brahms.

GAONA, RALPH RAYMOND, SR ASCAP 1963
author
b St Louis, Mo, Aug 13, 22. Educ: High sch. Served USN, WW II. Worked for UP Railroad, retired, 70; later Sheraton-St Louis Hotel. *Songs:* Lyrics: Valley of Lost Men; Just a Little Sweetheart; Drifting Snow of Jealousy; Give Me This Woman; A Thousand Tears Ago; I Want to Ride With Santa Claus.

GARCIA, FELIX ASCAP 1958
composer, author, singer
b Guayama, PR, May 26, 06. Educ: Enid Bus Col; Southern Calif Col Bus. Played theatres & night clubs, 30 yrs; with Universal Studios, 60; played sound music to production "This Earth is Mine." *Instrumental Works:* Chili Beans; The Beach-Comber; Stars Will Cry; Spanish Spy.

GARCIA, JEROME JOHN
composer, guitarist
b San Francisco, Calif, Aug 1, 42. Guitarist & banjo player, folk music duo with Sarah Garcia. Musician with var groups, 59-65. Founding mem, rock group The Warlock, 65; with The Grateful Dead, 66- Co-author, "Garcia: Signpost to a New Age." *Songs:* St Stephen; Uncle John's Band; Sugaree; Truckin'; Casey Jones; China Cat Sunflower. *Albums:* The Grateful Dead; Anthem of the Sun; Aoxomoxoa; From the Mars Hotel; Live Dead; Wake of the Flood; Shakedown Street.

GARCIA, RUSSELL E
composer, author, conductor
b Oakland, Calif, Apr 12, 16. Educ: Oakland Tech High Sch; San Francisco State Col; pvt study with Ernst Toch, Edmund Ross, Castelnuovo-Tedesco, Ernst Krenek & Albert Coats. Recorded with Ella Fitzgerald, Louis Armstrong, Mel Torme, Sarah Vaughan, Oscar Peters, Stan Kenton, Stan Getz & others. Staff comp-arr, NBC, Hollywood for many yrs; author text bks "The Professional Arranger Composer" Bks I & II. Feature films & TV series at Universal & MGM Studios, 20 yrs; symph, tone poems, ballet & chamber works performed in US, Vienna, Munich, Hamburg, Stuttgart & New Zealand; comn to write a symph & "Four Pieces for Orchestra" by Am Found for New Music, 80. Taught privately, also at Westlake Sch Music, Kenton Clinics, Pori Jazz Fest, Finland, 80. *Instrumental Works:* Variations on a Five Note Theme; Adventure in Emotions; New Era Symphony; New Zealand Panorama; Concerto for Brass Section; Charmed Life; Music City; When I Go, I Go All the Way; Variations for Flugel Horn, String Quartet, Bass and Drums. *Scores:* Film/TV: Time Machine; Atlantis, Lost Continent; The Pad; Laredo. *Albums:* A new jazz album of 10 comp.

GARDANO, ALLESANDRO
See Gardner, Maurice

GARDNER, ADELAIDE
See Halpern, Adelaide Gardner

GARDNER, CHARLES VANESS
ASCAP 1969
composer, pianist
b Waterloo, Iowa, Nov 29, 35. Educ: East Waterloo High Sch; Univ Northern Iowa, 53-54; studied comp with Henry Mancini, 62; St Phillips Col, AAS, 80. With USAF Acad Band, produced recording for Band; leader, Falconaires Show Band. Pianist, nightclubs & TV. Recording artist with var performers; performed with Vic Damone, Bob Hope & Mel Torme. *Songs:* As One; You Were There With Me; Only Time Will Tell. *Instrumental Works:* Falcon's Away; Little Prune.

GARDNER, DAVE
See Weingarten, David

GARDNER, DONALD YETTER
ASCAP 1949
composer, author
b Portland, Pa, Aug 20, 13. Educ: West Chester State Col, Pa, BS(music educ); NY Univ, MMusEd. Taught music educ pub sch, Smithtown, NY, 36-46; cond var choral groups. Consult music dept, Ginn & Co, New York, 47-57; head music dept, Ginn & Co, Boston, Mass, 57-72. *Songs:* All I Want for Christmas Is My Two Front Teeth; Weather Or Not; also numerous childrens songs for music textbks; Music: A Christmas Folk Song; Man Shall Not Live By Bread Alone; O Give Thanks Unto the Lord.

GARDNER, JOAN
See Janis, Joan Gardner

GARDNER, KOSSI
ASCAP 1965
composer
b Nashville, Tenn, Feb 25, 41. Educ: Fisk Univ, Nashville, BA(bus admin); Univ Southern Calif. Songwriter, 70- *Songs:* Funny Bones; Dance With You; Hit; Lovely Lady; Southern Star; Pretty Lady; Girl. *Albums:* I Love You.

GARDNER, MAURICE (ALLESANDRO GARDANO, ROBERT NORMAN, GERALD TOLMAGE, MARTIN POLLOCK)
ASCAP 1955
composer, author
b New York, NY, Feb 16, 09. Educ: Juilliard Sch Music; spec studies comp with Mark Andrews, Howard Murphy & Leopold Mannes; violin & viola studies with Edgar Stowell. Composer, arranger & conductor radio, TV & motion pictures. Film & background scores for dramatic productions. Founder & conductor, Great Neck Symph, NY. Over 800 publ works for strings, orch, symphonic band & chorus. Educ dir, Staff Music Publ Co, Inc. Numerous prizes & awards. *Songs:* Choral: The Story of Music; Little Rock Mass; Clap Your Hands. *Instrumental Works:* Tricinium (sonata for solo viola); Variations on the King's Hunting Jigg (solo viola & violin); Rhapsody for Viola and Orchestra (comn by William Primrose Libr, Brigham Young Univ); Concerto (violin, viola or cello & orch); The Orchestrator's Handbook; October Mountain (symphonic band); The Great Wall of China (symphonic band); Fanfare and Chorale (symphonic band); Prelude for Strings. *Scores:* Film/TV: This Is America.

GARDNER, SAMUEL
ASCAP 1937
composer
b Elizabethgrad, Russia, Aug 25, 1891. To US as a child. Educ: Studied violin with Franz Kneisel, Juilliard Sch Music; violin study with Charles M Loeffler & Felix Winternitz, Boston, Mass; musical comp with Percy Goetschius. Concertized as violin soloist, 13-40; mem, Kneisel String Quartet. Teacher violin & string ens, Juilliard Sch Music, free-lance teaching & radio work, 41-74; author "School of Violin, Based on Harmonic Thinking," bks 1 & 2. *Instrumental Works:* Violin Solos: From the Canebrake; Coquetterie; Troubadour; Vaqueros; From the Rockies; Whimsical Whistler; Two Birds; Slovaak; also 6 Preludes; Essays for Solo Violin (advanced technique & rhythms); Manifestations (for the virtuoso solo violinist); Hebraic Fantasie (violins, piano); String Quartet No 1 (Pulitzer Scholarship Prize, Columbia Univ, 18); String Quartet No 2; Broadway, 24 (orch); Piano Quintet in F Minor; Violin Concerto in E Minor (orch).

GARDNER, WILLIAM HENRY
ASCAP 1920
author
b Boston, Mass, Oct 28, 1865; d Newton, Mass, Mar 12, 32. Educ: Roxbury High Sch; pvt music study. Head of mfg firm. Mem, Author's Club, London & Boston City Club. *Songs:* Thy Beaming Eyes; Can't You Heah Me Callin' Caroline; Grateful O Lord Am I; Thy Will Be Done; The Crown of Life; also Sacred Songs for Little Singers; Merry Songs for Little Folks. *Scores:* Operettas: Christmas With the Old Woman Who Lived in a Shoe; The Moon Queen.

GARELLICK, JACK L
ASCAP 1966
composer, musician
b Atlantic City, NJ, Aug 18, 18; d Montpelier, Vt, Sept 12, 75. Educ: Atlantic City High Sch; Berklee Col Music; hon dipl in arts & letters, Athens, Greece. Mem, Flying Dutchman's Army/Airforce Band, European Theatre, WW II. Began comp with wife Arwin F B Garellick Sexauer, 62, then founded Music Mission, Inc, 63; together were known as the "words & music" team. Featured in Conn Album of Music Stars. Played on Steel Pier, Atlantic City for events such as Miss America Pageants & Ice Capades; played with bands & orchs incl Lawrence Welk Orch & Myer Davis Soc Band. Had own Garellick Combo, 60's & 70's. Teacher of wind instruments; radio announcer. Mem, Atlantic City Musicians Local 661, Am Fedn Musicians, life mem, Disabled Am Veterans, hon mem, Am Jewish Comt. Awards: Nat Disabled Am Veteran's Commander Award of Merit; George Washington Honor Medal, 63; Freedoms Found Hon Cert; Community Leaders & Noteworthy Am Who's Who Award Plaque, 75; Gold Star Cert of Merit, Nat Fedn Music Clubs; People-to-People Music Award; 9 Popular Panel ASCAP Awards for music & many others. Chief Collabr: Arwin F B Garellick Sexauer. *Songs:* Music: Forward Together (Vt State Bicentennial comn); Patterns for Peace; Men of Apollo; Pray for Peace; A Better World; God Is Not Dead; Universal Friendship Hymn; My Brother's Hand in Mine; I'm the Flag of All the People-Stand Up America (George Washington Honor Medal); One Last Coin for Brotherhood (commendation, Minister of Cultural Affairs, Cairo, Egypt, 77; selected for Brotherhood Week); For Some the War Will Never End (State Song of Dept of Vt Disabled Am Veterans & Auxiliary); For Connecticut; If I Had But One Day to Live (tribute to Robert Kennedy); The People's President; Song of the Shofar (commendation of late Prime Minister, Golda Meir); One World-Under God; The Golden Scale; also music for many mission songs.

GARF, GENE
ASCAP 1955
composer, pianist, arranger
b New York, NY, Dec 16, 18. Educ: Boys High Sch, Brooklyn; Brooklyn Col; Univ Southern Calif. Pianist, NY, 41; composed & arranged music for "Stars and Gripes." Pianist, Monogram Studios; musical dir, Ad-Staff. Composed, arranged & conducted over 1000 commercials. Arranger, David Rose, for Bob Hope Show. Musical dir, Ray Bolger, 18 yrs. *Instrumental Works:* Etude for Orchestra; California Sketchbook; 2nd Etude for Orchestra. *Scores:* Film/TV: Hollywood Stuntman; King Dinosaur; several segments of "My Three Sons."

GARFIELD, DAVID LENEORD
ASCAP 1975
composer
b Evanston, Ill, Sept 27, 56. Educ: Interlochen Summer Music Prog; pvt study piano with Terry Trotter, Los Angeles, 78; pvt study comp with Albert Harris, Los Angeles, 79. Played jazz & rock piano in St Louis area, 73-74; prof arr, 73-74; moved to Los Angeles, 74; played with Peggy DeCastro & Willie Bobo; formed own group, Karizma. Traveled with Freddie Hubbard & Tom Scott; recorded with Freddie Hubbard & Willie Bobo. Chief Collabrs: Mike Landau, Larry Klimas, Pat Murphy, John Valenti. *Instrumental Works:* Rainy Day Song; From Behind. *Scores:* Film/TV: Big Blue Marble (cues).

GARI, BRIAN
ASCAP 1968
composer, author, singer
b New York, NY, Feb 18, 52. Educ: Lincoln Square Acad. Singer, night clubs & TV; recording artist, Vanguard Records. Written for Kaye Ballard, Don Ciccone, Andrea Marcovicci & Leslie Gore. *Songs:* Late Nite Comic; Better Than Average; I Hope I'm Getting Close; Bicycle Ride; She Doesn't Live Anywhere; Am I So Easy to Replace?

GARLAND, DONALD
See MacInnis, Donald

GARLAND, JOSEPH C ASCAP 1941
composer
b Norfolk, Va, Aug 15, 03; d. Educ: Shaw Univ; Aeolian Cons; NY Sch of Portraiture & Comml Photography; NY Inst of Photography. Mem, Cosmopolitan Brass Band, Baltimore, 20-22 & Excelsior Mil Band, Norfolk, 22-29. Saxophonist & arr, Louis Armstrong; appeared with small groups. Chief Collabrs: Robert Bruce, Gilbert Mills. *Instrumental Works:* In the Mood; The Stuff Is Here; Harlem After Midnight; Jazz Martini; Congo Caravan; Brown Sugar Mine; Once in Ev'ry Heart; Keep the Rhythm Going; Serenade to a Savage; Leap Frog; Easy Go; What's Your Hurry?.

GARLOCK, THOMAS MARTIN ASCAP 1962
composer, author
b New York, NY, Jan 21, 29. Educ: Fieldston High Sch; Col of Wooster, NY Univ, 49. Started writing after discharge from Army, 53. Wrote spec material for club acts & stage. Bway musical credit "Vintage Sixty." Chief Collabrs: Alan Jeffreys, Bob Winter, Michael Colicehio, Al Cohn. *Songs:* Here Comes Trouble Again; Lyrics: Sooner Or Later; What Ever Happened to You?; Echoes of You; Make It the Blues; One Step At a Time.

GARMO, JOHN CHARLES (SKIP) ASCAP 1976
composer, author, singer
b Oak Park, Ill, June 9, 47. Educ: Bell High Sch, Calif; Moody Bible Inst, Ill, dipl; Biola Col, BMus; Calif State Univ, Los Angeles, MA(comp); psychomusicol study, Univ Wash. Music educator, pub sch & pvt col. Leader, church music, 70- Guest cond; sem lectr. *Songs:* Praise God!; Fruitfulness; Fruit of the Spirit.

GARNER, ADAM ASCAP 1964
composer, pianist, arranger
b Warsaw, Poland, Sept 30, 1898; d. Educ: Warsaw Cons; Royal Prussian Acad, Berlin; studied with Michalowski, Scharwenka. In concert throughout Europe. Founder, First Piano Quartet, US, 41. *Instrumental Works:* The Wrong Note Polka; var arr for 4 pianos.

GARNER, ERROLL ASCAP 1955
composer, pianist
b Pittsburgh, Pa, June 15, 23; d. Educ: High sch. Brother of Linton Garner. Prof pianist, age 7, KDKA radio, Pittsburgh, later nightclubs & theatres, New York & Calif. Featured with Slam Stewart Trio. Formed own trio, appeared at Paris Jazz Fest, 48. First jazz artist to be presented by S Hurok, to give concerts in outdoor circuit & to present a concert-in-the-round in summer tents. Performer, Europ tours, concert & TV incl Seattle World's Fair. Chief Collabrs: Edward Heyman, Johnny Burke. *Songs & Instrumental Works:* Misty; Dreamy; Solitaire; Blues Garni; Trio; Turquoise; Other Voices; No More Shadows; Passing Through; Dreamstreet; A New Kind of Love (theme); Paris Mist; Play, Play, Play (Prix du Disque, France); Erroll's Bounce. *Scores:* Films: A New Kind of Love.

GARNER, LINTON S ASCAP 1960
composer, pianist
b Thomasville, NC, Mar 25, 15. Brother of Erroll Garner. Pianist with Fletcher Henderson Orch. Served, World War II. Pianist & arr with Billy Eckstine Orch; arr with Dizzy Gillespie. Pianist with small groups, 47-

GAROFALO, CARLO GIORGIO ASCAP 1970
composer
b Rome, Italy, Aug 5, 1886; d Rome, Apr 6, 62. Educ: St Cecilia Acad & Cons, studied comp, organ & piano. To US, 10. Music dir, Immaculate Conception of Boston. Returned to Rome, was teacher & rep of Boston Music Co. Chief Collabrs: Max Zach, Tullio Serafin, Marziano Perosi, Adolfo Bossi. *Instrumental Works:* Romantic Symphony of St Louis; Symphonic Caprice; Second Symphony; Vesper (meditation); Violin Concerto; Tone Poems: Ireland; Anima (Soul); Masses: Immaculate Conception; Trinity; Missa in Honorem Patris Pii; Missa in Honorem Sancti Ludovici (St Louis Mass); Missa in Honorem Sanctae Ritae; Tu Es Petrus; Requiem Mass. *Scores:* Opera: The Juggler.

GARRETT, JARRELL JACKSON, JR (JACKIE) ASCAP 1977
composer, author, singer
b Lafayette, Ala, Apr 28, 55. Educ: Handley High Sch; Southern Union State Jr Col, music studies. Started playing & singing at age 5, keyboards at age 9. Played in small bands throughout sch, also traveled. Worked with Vassar Clements. Recording artist. Chief Collabrs: Jim Prater, Skip Mginn, Vassar & Millie Clements, Jerry Farmer, Chips Momon, Bobby Emmons. *Songs:* Don't Mess With My Funk; Love Me Like There's No Tomorrow.

GARRETT, PATSY ASCAP 1965
composer, author, singer
b Atlantic City, NJ, May 4, 21. Educ: John Marshall High Sch, Richmond, Va; Univ Richmond Westhampton Col; Elinor Fry Sch of Dance. Featured singer with Fred Waring's Pennsylvanians; recurring roles in TV's "Nanny and the Professor" & "Room 222"; featured in over 50 TV commercials. Starred in the "Benji" movies & "Benji Christmas Special," ABC-TV. Teacher summer season, Fred Waring Music Workshop. Chief Collabr: Nick Alexander (husband). *Songs:* Listen to Lacy. *Albums:* A Walk With Mr Peeps; Benji Story Book.

GARRETT, VICKY
See Galbraith, Victoria Garrett

GARRISON, ROBERT C ASCAP 1977
author
b Monroe, La, Aug 16, 34. Educ: Univ Miss, BA; Univ Pavia, Italy, grad study. Taught French in Miss; taught Eng, exhibited woodcuts & other prints & worked as translator, France, 60-67; asst dir, Bodley Gallery, New York, 67-72; free-lance proofreader & copy ed for NY publ houses, 72- Chief Collabrs: G P Plano, R Gorobetz, P Giasson. *Songs & Instrumental Works:* Flying Home for Christmas; That's What a Dance Floor is For; I Will Be With You (on Christmas Day); Moving Day.

GARROW, WILLIAM ASCAP 1963
composer, author
b New York, NY, Dec 25, 1893. Educ: Grade sch. Vaudeville entertainer; produced Tab Shows. Chief Collabrs: Ben Forest, Richard Thurston, Gene Lucus. *Songs & Instrumental Works:* Bend Your Knee; Children of the World; Letter to the Lord; A Million Canaries; Mr Ragtime Back in Town; Lift My Little Pinkey High; This Cockeyed World; What Made America Great.

GARSON, MORT ASCAP 1956
composer
b St John, NB, July 20, 24. Educ: Juilliard Sch Music; NY Univ. Special Services, WW II. Pianist & arr with dance orchs, also comp, cond & accompanist to Doris Day, Patti Page & Arthur Prysock. Chief Collabrs: Bob Hilliard, Earl Shuman. *Songs:* Our Day Will Come; Left Right Out of Your Heart; My Summer Love; Young Wings Can Fly; The World of Lonely People; Baby Come Home; Theme for a Dream; Starry-Eyed; Au Revoir; Film title song: Dondi. *Scores:* Film/TV: Son of Blob; Gambit; Mad House 90; 2,000 Year Old Man; Untamed World; National Geographic-Zoos of the World; Moon Journey; Do Not Disturb; Black Eye; Killers of the Wild; Kentucky Fried Movie. *Albums:* The Little Prince (Grammy Award); This Is My Beloved.

GART, JOHN (JOHN MARION) ASCAP 1953
composer, conductor, arranger
b Russia, June 6, 05. Educ: Moscow Imperial Konservatory Music, studied with Gliere; studied with Tibor Serly, Boris Levenson & Dr Clarence Dickinson, US. Comp/cond, "Robert Montgomery Presents", "Who Do You Trust", "Paul Winchell Show" plus numerous nat commercials. Organ recordings, Kapp Records. *Instrumental Works:* Dansant Caprice; Perspectives; Accordion Solo's: Scherzo; Vivo; Prelude. Superman, Batman & Aquaman themes & background music comp & arr for 30 piece orch. *Scores:* Film/TV: Superman; Batman; Aquaman.

GARTH, LESTER ALAN ASCAP 1971
composer, author, teacher
b Merced, Calif, Dec 16, 44. Educ: Ukiah High Sch, Calif; Univ Calif, Berkeley, BA(music), 67; studied violin with John Coppin; studied clarinet with Maurice Fath. Instrumentalist, singer, arr & comp, Loggins & Messina, 70-76; instrumentalist, singer & arr, Poco, 77; instrumentalist, singer, arr & comp, Dirt Band, 78-80; vocal & instrumental recording artist for var labels. Chief Collabrs: Jim Messina, Merel Bregante, Jeff Hanna, John McEuen. *Songs:* Holiday Hotel; Listen to a Country Song; Happy Feet. *Instrumental Works:* Mullen's Farewell to America; Jas'Moon.

GARTLAN, GEORGE H ASCAP 1955
composer, author, teacher
b New York, NY, July 19, 1882; d New York, May 11, 63. Educ: City Col New York, BA; Columbia Univ; Juilliard. Teacher music, 04. Asst dir music, Bd Educ, 11, dir, 19-52. *Songs:* The Lilac Tree; April Fool; The Top of the Morning; also School Music Series.

GARWOOD, MARGARET ASCAP 1973
composer, author
b Haddonfield, NJ, Mar 22, 27. Educ: Settlement Music Sch, Philadelphia; Philadelphia Col of Performing Arts, MM(comp); studied with Miriam Gideon & Joseph Prostakoff. Began career as pianist, coach & accompanist with considerable experience in solo piano & vocal repertoire. Composer, 63- *Songs:* Music: The Cliff's Edge; Spring Songs. *Scores:* Opera/Ballet: The Trojan Women; The Nightingale and the Rose; Rappaccini's Daughter.

GARY, JOHN ASCAP 1960
composer, singer
b Watertown, NY, Nov 29, 32. Singer, Don McNeill's radio prog, "Breakfast Club," 2 yrs. Salvage diver; singer, radio, New Orleans. Featured in nightclubs & on records. *Songs:* Life of My Life; Forget It; Where Did You Go Last Night?; Possom Song.

GASKILL, CLARENCE   ASCAP 1921
composer, author, pianist
b Philadelphia, Pa, Feb 2, 1892; d Ft Hill, NY, Apr 29, 47. Educ: St John's Sch, Friends Sch, Philadelphia; studied music with mother & pvt teachers. Pianist in Philadelphia theatre at age 16. Owned music publ firm at age 21. Machine gunner, WW I (Purple Heart). Toured in vaudeville as Melody Monarch. Author: "Memories of Vichy." Chief Collabrs: Jimmy McHugh, Cab Calloway, Irving Mills, Leo Robin, Duke Ellington. *Songs:* I Can't Believe That You're in Love With Me; Another Perfect Day Has Passed Away; Minnie the Moocher; Prisoner of Love; Doo-Wacka-Doo; Swanee River Rhapsody; Strange Interlude; Still I Love Her.

GASKIN, MICHAEL ALLAN   ASCAP 1978
composer
b Bronx, NY, Jan 21, 45. Educ: James Monroe High Sch; Hunter Col, BA; City Col New York, MA; pvt studies with Alan Combs. Pianist, Catskill Mountains, Concord, Browns & Raleigh Hotels; co-dir music for movie "That Man From Africa." *Songs:* Hustle-Bustle; Love Gone Away; Sil Vous Plait.

GASMAN, IRA   ASCAP 1964
composer, author, lyricist
b New York, NY, May 29, 42. Educ: NY Univ, BA(jour); New Sch Musical Theatre Workshop, studies with Aaron Frankel. Work has been performed from the Palace Theatre to Lincoln Ctr, from London to Hollywood, to Australia & Africa. Wrote lyrics, "The Front." Vpres & creative supvr, Dancer-Fitzgerald & Sample Advert, 12 yrs. Chief Collabrs: Larry Grossman, Gary Friedman, Jule Styne, Galb MacDermot, Cary Hoffman, Jonathan Tunick, George Fischoff, Steve Lawrence, Don Pippin, Jack Urbant, Larry Hurwit, Joe Baque, Carl Friberg, Ian Frazier, Jorge Santana, Michel Columbier. *Songs:* Lyrics: I Climbed the Mountain; Poor New York; Special Occasions; No One Makes Love Anymore. *Songs & Instrumental Works:* At This Point in Rhyme. *Scores:* Off-Bway: What's a Nice Country Like You Doing in a State Like This; Genesis Revisited; Dick Deferred; Marty.

GASSO, BERNARD   ASCAP 1958
composer, author
b New York, NY, Feb 27, 26; d. Educ: NC State Col. Wrote songs for film, "Big Beat"; Latin Quarter revue; worked as salesman. Chief Collabrs: Irving Fields, Henry Tobias. *Songs:* Call Me; Lazy Love; Engagement Waltz.

GASTON, LYLE R   ASCAP 1958
composer, author, musician
b Woodward, Okla, Dec 24, 29. Educ: High sch; US Sch of Music. Guitarist, pianist, bass violinist & arr for orch, 18 yrs. Began working on radio & TV, 47. Chief Collabrs: Hank Thompson, Larry Fotine. *Songs:* Blackboard of My Heart; How Do You Hold a Memory?

GATES, B CECIL   ASCAP 1947
composer, publisher
b Hawaii, Aug 7, 1877; d Salt Lake City, Utah, Aug 31, 41. Educ: Boston Cons; Berlin Cons; studied with Scharwenka, Heffley, Denee & Robitchek. Head, Music Dept, Latter Day Saints Univ, 13-22. Organized Latter Day Saints Sch Music, now McCune Sch, 19. Head, Music Dept, Agricultural Col, Logan, 24-29. Organized Choir Publ Co, Salt Lake City. Asst cond, Tabernacle Choir, 37. Dir, Lucy Gates (sister) Grand Opera Co & Salt Lake Oratorio Soc. *Songs:* I Met My Love O'er Hill and Dale; The Lord's Prayer; My Redeemer Lives. *Instrumental Works:* Gates Story Music; Brighton Sketches; Cornfield Melodies No 1; Gates' Anthems: Festival Overture; Resurrection Morning (cantata); The Restoration; Eternal Life.

GATES, CRAWFORD MARION   ASCAP 1963
composer
b San Francisco, Calif, Dec 29, 21. Educ: Col of Pacific; San Jose State Col, BA(with great distinction); Columbia Univ; Brigham Young Univ, MA; Univ Rochester Eastman Sch Music, PhD. Lt(jg), USNR World War II Pacific Theatre Amphibious Forces, 43-46. Orchr, KSL Orch, 46-48. Grad asst theory fac, Eastman Sch Music, 48-50. Brigham Young Univ, music fac, 50-60, chmn music dept, 60-66, cond symph & opera, 64-66. Artist-in-residence & prof music, Beloit Col, 66- Music dir, San Jose Light Opera Asn, 42-43, Beloit Symph, 66-, Quincy Symph, 69-70 & Rockford Symph, 70- Comn by State of Utah as comp Centennial Musical Play "Promised Valley," 47. Chief Collabrs: Arnold Sundgaard, Don Oscarson, Keith Engar, Carol Lynn Pearson, C S Lewis, Jon Beck Shank. *Songs & Instrumental Works:* Promised Valley; Symphony No 2 (chorus, orch); Wisconsin Profiles (orch); Beloved Mormon Hymns (arr for orch); O My Father (chorus, orch); O My Luve's Like a Red Red Rose; Man's Search for Happiness (orch); Perelandra, Symphony No 5 (chorus, orch); Ballad of the Prairie State (orch); Three Songs for the Young Heart (voice, piano); Sonata for Horn and Piano; Sonata for Percussion Trio; Sails, Winds and Echoes (flute choir); Suite for Tuba (celesta, harp, perc, piano); Trumpet Concertino (trumpet, chamber orch); Symphony No 4 A New Morning (chorus, orch); An Overture to Spring (orch); Symphony No 3 (orch); The Wind Is a Lion; Valley Home; Love Is My Song; Eternally.

GATES, DAVID A
songwriter
b Tulsa, Okla, Dec 11, 40. Arr, Hollywood. Founder of group Bread. Recording artist, with group & solo. *Albums:* David Gates; Never Let Her Go.

GATES, GEORGE E   ASCAP 1971
composer
b Kankakee, Ill, May 21, 20. Educ: Kankakee High Sch; Hardin Simmons Univ; Vandercook, Chicago. Band dir, Tex. Perc instr, Southern Methodist Univ. With Dallas Symph Orch; Dallas Summer Musicals. Retail music stores, La & Tex. *Instrumental Works:* Concert band: Sol y Sombra (concert march); Mosaico de Mexico (suite); La Contessa (concert march); Two Russian Songs; Two Mexican Songs of Chiapas.

GATES, VIRGIL WILLIAM (PETER)   ASCAP 1956
composer, author, teacher
b Dallas, Tex, Nov 23, 14. Educ: Denton High Sch; NTex State Univ, BS, 41; Westlake Col Music, grad, 51; studied with Madam Chantal, Alfred Sendrey & Russ Garcia. Pianist & arr dance band; comp & author of songs for films, Hollywood, 46-56; musician. Chief Collabrs: Isham Jones, Babe Russin, Walter Greene, Rudy Shrager. *Songs:* Tradewind Island; Get in Tune With the Lord; Annette; Song of the Little Red Hen; One-Way Street; Saddle With a Golden Horn; Rosanne of San Jose; West of the Pecos; In the Shadow of the Mission; Punchinello; Cathy; Right Kind of Love; Ain't no Gal Gotta Brand on Me; God's Little Lanterns.

GATSBY, PACO
See Porter, Robert Morris

GAUL, HARVEY BARTLETT   ASCAP 1927
composer, author, conductor
b New York, NY, Apr 11, 1881; d Pittsburgh, Pa, Dec 1, 45. Educ: Studied music with George Lejeune & Alfred Gaul; Schola Cantorum; Paris Cons, studied with Guilmant, Widor, d'Indy & Decaux; Univ Pittsburgh, MusD(hon). Assoc organist, St John's Chapel, NY, 1899. Church organist & choirmaster, Emmanuel, Cleveland, 01-09 & Calvary, Pittsburgh, 10-45. Choral dir, Univ Pittsburgh, Carnegie Tech & Washington & Jefferson Col. First music dir, radio sta KDKA. Founder & cond, Pittsburgh Savoyards, Civic String Orch. Mem fac, Fillion Studios. Music critic, Pittsburgh Post-Gazette. Mem, Am Guild of Organists; founder & mem, Musicians Club of Pittsburgh; hon mem, Pa Fedn of Music Clubs, which established Harvey Gaul scholarship. *Instrumental Works:* A Spring Ditty (Chicago Madrigal Club prize); Water Lillies (Tuesday Musical Club prize); For the Numberless Unknown Heroes (Mendelssohn Club prize); Thou Art the Night Wind; Cry of Micah (Pittsburgh Art Soc prize); Babe of Bethlehem (Mendelssohn Club prize); The Carol of the White Russian Children; Spring Rapture; Johnny Appleseed; Tubal Cain; Strong Son of God; I Hear America Singing; The Song of Man; Thanksgiving; Suite Ecclesiasticus; April; Chanson Du Soir; Easter Morning at Mt Rubidoux; Yasnaya Polyana; Operettas: Pinocchio; Storyland; Alice in Wonderland.

GAUTIER, DICK   ASCAP 1959
composer, author, comedian
b Los Angeles, Calif, Oct 30, 31. Comedian in nightclubs. Singer with dance bands. Served USN, WW II. Appeared on TV & in Bway musical, "Bye Bye Birdie." *Songs:* Like Our Love; Lonely River; Quiet Place.

GAY, BYRON   ASCAP 1922
composer, author, musician
b Chicago, Ill, Aug 28, 1886; d Los Angeles, Calif, Dec 23, 45. Educ: US Naval Acad, 07-09. On Byrd expedition, 33. Chief Collabrs: Richard Whiting, Zez Confrey, Haven Gillespie, Rudy Vallee, Marian Gillespie. *Songs:* Little Ford Rambled Right Alone; Sand Dunes; The Vamp; Fate; Horses; Just a Little Drunk; Sitting on a Log Petting My Dog; Song of the Navy; Navy of the Air; A Buddie's Prayer; The Soul of a Rose. *Scores:* Stage: Navigator's Holiday (Naval Air Base, Pensacola, Fla).

GAYLE, ROZELLE I, JR   ASCAP 1977
composer, author
b Chicago, Ill. Educ: Wilson Col, BA(vocal scholarship); Chicago Univ; Am Cons of Music, studied voice, comp & piano. Singer & pianist, local bands, Chicago, 38, Roy Eldridge, New York, 43. Performer, nightclubs, Chicago, 44 & clubs in Los Angeles, San Diego, San Francisco & Fresno, 48. Actor, singer & musician, films & TV shows incl "The Jeffersons", "Sanford and Son", "Barreta", "Barnaby Jones" & "Dan August." *Songs:* Dreaming By the Fire; Like Be My Guest; Take It All.

GAYNOR, CHARLES   ASCAP 1952
composer, author
b Boston, Mass, Apr 3, 09; d Washington, DC, Dec 18, 75. Educ: Dartmouth Col; studied music in Vienna with Edmund Eysler & Franz Lehar. Wrote & produced musicals for civic & summer theatres. Wrote songs for "Sweeter and Lower," London. Writer of spec material for nightclub singers, also for industrial shows & TV. Wrote col songs with Fred Waring. *Songs:* After Hours; Molly O'Reilly; Neurotic You and Psychopathic Me; When Someone You Love Loves You; I'm on the Lookout; Who Hit Me?; Moonlight and VPI; The Girl in the

Show; My Kind of Love; You Haven't Lived Until You've Played the Palace; Somewhere There's a Little Bluebird; Mother, Angel Darling; also The Gladiola Girl; Lyrics: The Great Lover Tango; An Irish Girl. *Scores:* Bway stage: Lend an Ear; Show Girl.

GEALLIS, PAUL JAMES ASCAP 1957
composer, author

b Chicago, Ill, Sept 28, 23. Educ: Bobby Christian Sch Music; studied with Frank Rullo, Bob Christian & Tommy Thomas. Played professionally, 45-62. Had own recording label, 57-62. Worked for Coral Records. Free-lance promotion, 64- Rec'd over 5 Billboard Awards. Has own band. Chief Collabrs: Frank (Porky) Panico, Joe Rumoro. *Songs:* Green Lite; Lyrics: Just Leave Me Alone.

GEARHART, LIVINGSTON ASCAP 1959
composer, pianist, arranger

b Buffalo, NY, Dec 31, 16. Educ: Grace Church Choir Sch; Curtis Inst; studied with Nadia Boulanger, Darius Milhaud. Pianist, nightclubs & hotels. Annual concert tours with wife. Arr & pianist, radio show "Fred Waring," 43-54. Music fac, Univ Buffalo. *Instrumental Works:* Rhapsody (2 pianos); American Sketch; Devil's Dream; Dynamo; Suite for Woodwinds; Baby Boogie; The Hot Music Box.

GEARHISER, LA VERNE ASCAP 1960
compsoer, author

b Big Sandy, Tenn, Sept 23, 06. Educ: Big Sandy High Sch; Lambuth Col; LaSalle Univ, correspondence. Writer, 59- *Songs:* Waiting for Me; Without Your Love; The Waltz of the Stars; Tonight Is Mine to Dream Alone; Why Did We Meet?

GEARINGER, LEMUEL CYRUS (MARK HALE) ASCAP 1976
composer, author

b Petersburg, Pa, July 24, 1894. Educ: Allegheny Vocational Sch, Pittsburgh, 20-22; Carnegie Inst Tech, Pittsburgh, music, 22-25. Violin teacher. Chief Collabr: Mercy Ray. *Songs:* Music: On Our Wyoming Range; also ballads, country, western, sacred & classical words & music & rumbas, waltzes.

GEBEST, CHARLES J ASCAP 1956
composer, conductor, violinist

b Ill, Dec 8, 1872; d New York, NY, Jan 11, 37. Made violin concert tour, 1879. Comp, music dir & arr with George M Cohan, 30 yrs. *Songs:* Never Mind Singing, Just Dance My Dear; I Love Love; Longing, My Dearie, for You. *Scores:* Bway Stage: The Red Widow; The Beauty Shop.

GEE, MATTHEW, JR
composer, author, teacher

b Houston, Tex, Nov 25, 21; d Brooklyn, NY, July 18, 79. Educ: Jack Yates High Sch, Tex; Ala State Teachers Col; Wayne Univ; Juilliard Sch of Music. Began professional music career while in col with the Bama State Collegians. Was featured trombone soloist with orchs incl Erskin Hawkins, Count Basie, Lionel Hampton, Jimmie Lunceford, Dizzie Gillespie, Illinois Jacquet, Sonny Stitt, Lou Donaldson, Gene Ammons & Duke Ellington. Participated in jazz workshops, Nat Endowment for the Arts. In nightclubs & TV; recording artist. *Songs & Instrumental Works:* Bed Room Eyes; Oh, Gee; The Swingers Get the Blues; Slowly With Expression.

GEIBEL, ADAM ASCAP 1939
composer, organist, conductor

b near Frankfort-on-Main, Ger, Sept 15, 1855; d Philadelphia, Pa, Aug 3, 33. Came to US, 1862. Educ: Pa Inst for Blind, Philadelphia; studied with David Wood; hon MusD, Temple Univ. Instr piano, violin, harmony & comp, Pa Inst for Blind, 17 yrs. Organist, John Stetson Mission Sunday Sch, 1885-1925. Founded publ firm. Chief Collabrs: Richard Buck, Earl Burtnett. *Songs:* Evening Bells; Kentucky Babe; The Nativity; The Incarnation; Light Out of Darkness; Stand Up, Stand Up for Jesus; Some Day He'll Make It Plain; Let the Gospel Light Shine Out; Sleep.

GEIGER, GEORGE ASCAP 1960
composer, conductor, organist

b Troy, NY, Dec 12, 05. Educ: Troy Cons. Taught piano & organ, 7 yrs. Organist & choir dir, 31-; organist in film theatres. Cond of own band. Chief Collabr: Alma Hatton. *Songs:* Violino; Our Wedding Prayer.

GEISEL, THEODORE SEUSS (DR SEUSS) ASCAP 1953
author, artist

b Springfield, Mass, Mar 2, 04. Educ: Dartmouth Col, BA; Lincoln Col, Oxford, Eng. Maj, USA, WW II. Wrote & produced information films. Liaison Officer, ETO; Legion of Merit. Writer & illusr of children's books incl "The 500 Hats of Bartholomew Cubbins", "Horton Hatches the Egg", "Yertle the Turtle", "The Cat in the Hat", "One Fish Two Fish" & "The Grinch Who Stole Christmas." Author of film cartoons, "Gerald McBoing-Boing" & "Dungeon Schlim-Schlam." *Songs:* Victory Processions; Dress Me; The Kid's Song; Dream Stuff; Get-Together Weather. *Scores:* Films: 5000 Fingers of Dr T.

GELBART, LARRY ASCAP 1957
composer, author

b Chicago, Ill, Feb 25, 28. TV comedy writer. *Songs:* Wallflower; Let's Go Steady. *Scores:* Bway musical: A Funny Thing Happened on the Way to the Forum (co-librettist).

GELBER, STANLEY JAY ASCAP 1964
composer, author, pianist

b Brooklyn, NY, June 2, 36. Educ: Ohio State Univ, BA, 57; Brooklyn Law Sch, LLB, 60; studied comp with Buster Bromley & Chester Jackson. Staff writer & asst prof mgr, United Artists Music, 66-71; staff writer, Metromedia Music; with New York Times Music, Music Publ Holding Corp & Albert Grossman Mgt, Inc. Chief Collabr: Bernard Hoffer. *Songs:* My Desert Serenade; Brush a Little Sunshine; I Can See It Now; On a Snowy Christmas Night; House of Laughter; Infinidad; I Didn't Mean to Care; Too Busy Being Me; Rapido; Tears and Kisses; Another Monday; Walk Among the Roses; The Ol' Race Track; Lyrics: Now I Know; Lingering On; Love's the Only Answer; Blame It on Me; All the Loves of My Life; Time; Wonder; Wait a While; No Way to Go; We Had it All. *Scores:* Off-Bway: Love and Let Love (musical version of Shakespeare's Twelfth Night).

GELD, GARY ASCAP 1961
composer

b Paterson, NJ, Oct 18, 35. Educ: NY Univ, BS, 57; classical piano studies with Arthur Newstead & Clarence Adler; Juilliard Sch Music, comp studies. Comp Bway musicals, "Purlie," 70, "Shenandoah," 75 & "Angel," 78. Began writing songs in 59; wrote, produced & publ songs & records in pop/rock field, 59-68. Became independent record producer, 60; formed own publ co, 61. ASCAP Country & Western Award, 64. Chief Collabr: Peter Udell. *Songs:* Music: I Got Love; Walk Him Up the Stairs; Next to Lovin' (I Like Fightin'); Freedom; We Make a Beautiful Pair; Sealed With a Kiss (gold record); Save Your Heart for Me; Ginny Come Lately; Let Me Belong to You; Hurting Each Other (gold record); He Says the Same Things to Me; The Tear of the Year. *Scores:* It Takes a Lot of Love (CBS-TV Spec).

GELLERT, LAWRENCE ASCAP 1960
composer, author

b Budapest, Hungary, Sept 14, 1898. Author, bks & articles on folk music. Recipient, Rockefeller grant.

GELMAN, HAROLD S ASCAP 1959
composer, musicologist, pianist

b Portland, Ore, Apr 21, 12. Educ: Univ Mich, BMus, 33; Juilliard Grad Sch Music, New York, piano student of Alexander Siloti. Music supvr & head music librarian, Metro-Goldwyn-Mayer Studios; music supvr & asst to head music dept, Columbia Pictures; fac mem, Marlborough Sch for Girls, Los Angeles, Calif; fac mem, Music Dept, Col of the Desert, Calif. Lectures for Los Angeles Philh Orch & San Francisco Opera Asn. Contributed compositions to music scores of var Metro-Goldwyn-Mayer pictures, Columbia pictures, theatrical features & Columbia Pictures TV shows.

GENGER, ROGER ASCAP 1954
composer

b Staten Island, NY. Educ: Pub sch. Chief Collabrs: Jimmie Dale, Ralph Stein. *Songs & Instrumental Works:* You'd Better Believe It; More Than You Realize; Love Eyes; If I Could Change My Heart; Just Cancel My Dream; Last Night in a Dream; Sentimental Me and Heartless You; Wishee Washee; But Good; Up Till Now; Teasin Heart; Spin the Bottle Polka; Congratulations; For a While for a While; Santa is My Cousin; Monitor and the Merrimac; No Money Down; Tex the Cowboy Santa Claus; My Love for You; My Tears Will Not Fall Tonight; The Waltz That Broke My Heart; Crazy With the Blues; I'm in Between Two Loves; April; I'm a Nothing; Devil's Brooms (The Mender of Broken Guitars).

GENSLER, LEWIS E ASCAP 1923
composer, author, producer

b New York, NY, Dec 4, 1896; d New York, Jan 10, 78. Educ: High Sch; studied music with Louis Oesterle. Went to Hollywood, became producer & wrote Paramount films incl "The Big Broadcast of 1937" & "Artists and Models": songs for films incl "Here Is My Heart." Chief Collabrs: Oscar Hammerstein II, Ira Gershwin, B G DeSylva, Robert Simon, E Y Harburg, Leo Robin, Johnny Mercer, Harlan Thompson. *Songs:* Keep Smiling at Trouble; Fond of You; Love is Just Around the Corner; Me Without You; Fatal Fascination; It's a Great Life; When You Are in My Arms; Boys Will Be Boys; Old Man Rhythm; I Never Saw A Better Night; Cross Your Heart; Thrill Me; Falling Off the Wagon; Riddle Me This; Ups-a-Daisy; Will You Remember?; You Need Someone. *Scores:* Bway stage: Queen o' Hearts; Be Yourself; Captain Jinks; Queen High; Ups-a-Daisy; Ballyhoo of 1932.

GENTRY, BOBBIE
singer, songwriter, instrumentalist

b Chickasaw County, Miss, July 27, 44. Educ: Los Angeles Cons of Music; Univ Calif, Los Angeles. Secy. Nightclub entertainer; organizer, dance & vocal group, Las Vegas, Nev. Co-founder & pres, production & publ co, Gentry Ltd, Los Angeles. Performer, San Remo Music Fest, Italy, 67; TV shows incl spec series, BBC, London, progs in Italy & var musicals & specials, US. Recipient, Best Female Performer, Best New Artist, Best Contemporary Female Vocal

Performer, Nat Asn of Recording Arts & Sci, 67, Achievement Award, Mademoiselle Mag, 67, Most Promising New Vocalist of Yr, Sixteen Mag & 3 Grammy awards, 67. *Songs:* Ode to Billy Joe; Chickasaw County Child; Mississippi Delta.

GEORGANTONES, JIMMY P (JIMMY GEORGE)   ASCAP 1970
composer, musician, producer

b Amarillo, Tex, Feb 27, 40. Educ: North Tex State Univ, grad. Recording artist, Mercury Records, 60-69, Viva Records, 69; recording studio musician for records, commercials & movies, 60- Staff comp, United Artists, 65-70; staff writer & producer, Motown Records, 70-75; played var nightclubs & TV; singer. Toured with var artists incl Beach Boys, Shaun Cassidy, Dobie Gray & Leif Garrett. Chief Collabs: Ray Dewey, Lydia Triantos, Dobie Gray. *Songs:* Magic Man; In Hollywood; Is This the Thanks I Get; Give It Up; Walk With Love; Fine Young Girl; Monkey Jerk; Tend to Business; Better Believe Me.

GEORGE, CASSIETTA
See Baker, Cassietta

GEORGE, DON   ASCAP 1942
composer, author

b New York, NY, Aug 27, 09. Educ: Pub schs. Song writer for var films & music dir for "Holiday in Brussels". Spec material written for Nat King Cole, Patti Page, Ida Lupino, Pointer Sisters. Wrote stage score for "Wet Paint" & biography of Duke Ellington "Sweet Man." Has had one man art shows. Chief Collabs: Duke Ellington, Steve Allen, Acquaviva, Robert Maxwell, Lionel Newman, Nat King Cole, Bee Walker, Peter De Rose, Harry James. *Songs:* The Yellow Rose of Texas; Lyrics: I'm Beginning to See the Light; I Never Mention Your Name; Calypso Blues; To Know You Is to Love You; I Ain't Got Nothin' But the Blues; The Wonder of You; Two Thirds of the Tennessee River; The Beautiful Blonde From Bashful Bend; Eleven Sixty PM; I Was Telling Her About You; Cuban Nightingale; Coal Dust on the Fiddle; Slowly with Feeling; Smoking My Sad Cigarette; A Touch of the Blues; The Magic Fountain; That's Life, I Guess; Tulip Or Turnip; How Bitter, My Sweet; I Fell and Broke My Heart; The Right Kind; It Shouldn't Happen to a Dream; Guess I Had Too Much to Dream Last Night; When Will I Forget You; Holiday in Brussels.

GEORGE, DON R   ASCAP 1945
composer, conductor, organist

b San Francisco, Calif, Mar 25, 03; d Los Angeles, Calif, Mar 22, 78. Educ: Am Cons; studied organ with Edward Lemare. Asst dir Bway revue, "Passing Show of 1918." Organist & cond, theatre circuits, later producer. Went to Honolulu, 32. Became theatre mgr, also organized USO camp shows. Pres, Honolulu Musician's Union, 9 yrs & Labor Comn for Territory, 2 terms. Chmn, Nat Music Week, Hawaii, 3 yrs. Theatre mgr, 7 yrs. Had own radio prog, 9 yrs. Became music counselor to film studio, 43, then exec head, Music Dept. Chief Collabs: Irving Bibo, Al Piantadosi, Jack Meskill. *Songs & Instrumental Works:* Prelude to a Ballet; The Ascension; Merrily We Sing; Walkin' Away With My Heart; Walk a Little, Talk a Little; Do You Believe in Dreams?; You Love Me, You Love Me Not; Tropic Trade Winds; The Day You Said Goodbye to Old Hawaii; Fight for Old Hawaii (Univ Hawaii song); Mainstreet Rhapsody; Piano teaching pieces: Gay Ballerina; Lilac Time.

GEORGE, DONA LYN   ASCAP 1974
composer, author

Educ: Univ Wis, voice with Seila Hakms. Chief Collabs: Kenny Loggins, Marilyn Messina Tucker. *Songs:* Love Song; Brighter Days; Time to Space; All Alone Tonite.

GEORGE, EARL ROBERT   ASCAP 1955
composer, critic, conductor

b Milwaukee, Wis, May 1, 24. Educ: Univ Rochester Eastman Sch Music, BM, 46, MM, 47, PhD, 58, studied comp with Howard Hanson & Bernard Rogers; Berkshire Music Ctr, Tanglewood, studied comp with Bohuslav Martinu. Orchestral works performed by Charles Muench, Leonard Bernstein, Antal Dorati, Fritz Mahler, Fabian Sevitzky, Dean Dixon, Howard Hanson. George Gershwin Mem prize, 47; Koussevitzky Music Found comn, 47; James Millikin Univ Choral prize, 47; Nat Fedn Music Clubs prize, 50; Boosey & Hawkes, Univ Ill Publ Award, 53; US Educ Found grant, Fulbright Lectureship, 55; Guggenheim fel, 57. *Instrumental Works:* Concerto for Piano and Orchestra; Concerto for Violin and Orchestra; A Thanksgiving Overture; Introduction and Allegro; String Quartet. *Songs & Instrumental Works:* Opera: Pursuing Happiness; Genevieve.

GEORGE, GIL
See Gilman, Hazel Inez

GEORGE, JIMMY
See Georgantones, Jimmy P

GEORGE, THOM RITTER   ASCAP 1965
composer, conductor

b Detroit, Mich, June 23, 42. Educ: Redford High Sch, Mich, 60; Univ Rochester Eastman Sch Music, BM, 64, MM, 68; Catholic Univ Am, DC, DMA, 70. Comp & arr, US Navy Band, DC, 66-70; music dir & cond, Quincy

Symph Orch, Ill, 70-; guest cond of orchs & bands. *Instrumental Works:* Proclamations (band); Western Overture (band); Hymn and Toccata (band); Two Piano Concerti; Concerto for Bass Trombone and Orchestra; Concerto for Flute; The People, Yes (cantata); Three Brass Quintets; Woodwind Quintet No 3; Aria and Dance (trombone ens); Flute sonata; Clarinet Sonata; Trombone Sonata. *Scores:* Ballet: Four Games.

GERAK, BERRIE LEE (BERRIE CHRISTOPHER)   ASCAP 1968
composer, author

b Denver, Colo, Sept 22, 42. Staff songwriter, ABC-Paramount & Columbia Screen Gems, late 60's. Eng lyricist, specializing in studio supv of French artists recording in Eng language, Paris, 71-74. Worked as exclusive Eng lyricist for French star Patrick Juvet; also wrote lyrics for Nicole Croisille & Joel Dayde. Chief Collabrs: Hubert Giraud, Andre Popp, Pierre Cour, Patrick Juvet, Michel Renard, Andre Salvet, Jose Bartel, Jack Keller, Guy Woods, Joe Renzetti, Gil Slavin. *Songs:* Lyrics: Do It Now (Midem Theme, France, 72); I Will Be in Los Angeles (Le Lundi Au Soleil); Everybody Sing My Song (La Chanson Parlait D'Amour).

GERARD, RICHARD H   ASCAP 1927
composer

b New York, NY, June 8, 1876; d New York, July 2, 48. Educ: Eclectic Med Col; NY Col Dental & Oral Surgery. With Am Red Cross overseas; rec'd French, Southern Serbia & Polish comns. *Songs:* I've Got My Eyes on You; Sweet Summer Time; Follow the Crowd on a Sunday; You're My Heart's Desire, I Love You; Sweetest Girl of All; Sweet Adeline.

GERARD, WILL
See Jacobs, William B

GERARDI, JESS LOUIS, JR   ASCAP 1969
composer, teacher, conductor

b Trinidad, Colo, May 25, 38. Educ: Holy Trinity High Sch, Trinidad; Regis Col, Colo; US Naval Acad, Annapolis; Univ Northern Colo, Greeley, BA, 60; Univ Calif Los Angeles, MA, 61; Univ Colo, Boulder, PhD, 73. Professional musician. Dir bands, Englewood High Sch, Colo, 67-; dir entertainment, Denver Broncos, 68-, dir band; dir, Rocky Mountain Flag Camps, Inc. *Instrumental Works:* Trumpeter's Nightmare; Pirate Belles; Hail to King Karl Fanfare; Ice Cream Man.

GERARDI, ROBERT   ASCAP 1972
composer, author, singer

b Brooklyn, NY, Jan 11, 37. Educ: Brooklyn Tech High Sch; Queens Col; Am Acad Dramatic Arts, 69; Manhattan Sch Music; studied jazz, comp & piano with Hall Overton, John Solo, Don Friedman & Gabby Budd, voice with Richard Field, studied the Schillinger Syst with Richard Benda. Singer, pianist & band leader in nightclubs, hotels, cocktail lounges, radio & TV. Recording artist, Recorte Records & Starkay Records. Had small acting roles in films & commercials. Formed rock n' roll group, late 50's; had two hit records. *Songs:* Find Me a Lover; Smile; The Arizona; Memories of Love.

GERBER, ALEX   ASCAP 1921
author

b New York, NY, June 2, 1895; d Mt Vernon, NY, Apr 10, 69. Educ: Stuyvesant High Sch. Served in WW I. Wrote spec material for musical comedies, vaudeville (also producer), films & radio. Chief Collabrs: Abner Silver, Sigmund Romberg. *Songs:* My Home Town Is a One-Horse Town; Stepping Into Society; Stumbling; There Is a Typical Tipperary Over Here; At the Fountain of Youth; Cecelia. *Scores:* Bway stage: Poor Little Ritz Girl.

GERBER, MIKLOS TEGHZE   ASCAP 1965
composer, author, teacher

b Zsolna, Hungary, June 11, 06; d Dearborn, Mich, Sept 5, 69. Educ: Royal Hungarian Agr Acad, 29; Hungarian Liszt Ferenc Music Acad, Budapest, music degree (comp). Composer, age 7; at age 19, first song won hon award; Silver Wreath award. Concerts: Liszt Ferenc Music Acad, also in Vienna, Breslau, Italy, Amsterdam, Munich, Philadelphia & NY. Dean, Royal Hungarian Music Acad, 33; dir, State Music Acad, Budapest; bd dirs, Hungarian Soc Composers, Budapest; dir music, Trenton Music Sch, Mich. Owner, Globe Record Co, 50-53; organist var churches, 53-69. Composed ballads, orchestrations for symph, film music & operettas. Hungarians celebrated his 40th Anniversary as composer, 66. *Songs & Instrumental Works:* Waltz Caprice (violin solo & piano); Dance of the Huns; Hungarian Dance; Sorrowful Hungarian Prayer (hymn); Farewell Sacuntala (ballad).

GERICH, VALENTINE (VAL)   ASCAP 1959
composer, author, accordionist

b Great Falls, Mont, Jan 10, 1898; d. Educ: High sch; studied accordion. Had own ballroom; formed orch, 27. *Songs:* Stay on This Side of the Ocean (in Congressional Record); Progress March; I Wanna Play Post Office; I'm Going Back to Hawaii; Rainbow Valley.

GERKE, WELLMAN E   ASCAP 1971
composer, author, organist
b San Angelo, Tex, Dec 25, 07. Educ: Main Avenue High Sch, San Antonio, Tex; night schs; Newspaper Inst Am, cert in writing; Lewis Hotel/Motel correspondence course, grad. Served US Govt, 20 yrs. With railroads, 12 yrs. Did institutional & church work. Writer, religious articles. Author: "Music Man of the West" & "Just for Fun." Bd chmn & treas, orgns. Traveled US, Can & Mex. Writer, mail order reports.

GERMINARO, RICHARD   ASCAP 1977
composer, lyricist
b Pittsburgh, Pa, Sept 28, 45. Educ: Self-taught. Started writing with Evie Sands, 72 & with Ben Weisman, 74. Has written lyrics for TV show, "Captain Kangaroo." Chief Collabrs: Evie Sands, Ben Weisman. *Songs:* Love in the Afternoon; I Love Making Love to You; You Can Do It; As We Fall in Love Once More; Lady of the Night; Get Up.

GERMINO, MARK RAYMOND   ASCAP 1977
composer, author
b Durham, NC, Aug 12, 50. Educ: PSSOHK, Nashville, Tenn, 75; Writers Night Music, Nashville, Tenn, 77-78. Listening Club singer; song writer with four piece band; with Peer Southern Music, 80- *Songs:* Lean on Jesus (Before He Leans on You); Tobacco Leaf Breakdown; Love for a Rose; Too Late for Leaving Me Tonight; I Set It All on Fire; Once in Every Life Time; Don't Give Yourself to the Salvation Army.

GERONIMO
See Tolbert, Gregory Jerome

GERRARD, WILLIAM
See Bilik, Jerry H

GERSHENSON, JOSEPH
director, producer
b Kishinev, Russia, Jan 12, 04. Educ: Pvt study & training; studied comp with Edward Kelenyi. Violinist. Asst to music dir, RKO Theatres, New York. Producer, musical shorts, New York. Producer, films, Universal Studios, Hollywood, 39, exec producer of pictures, music cond & head of music dept, 50-69; retired, 69. Supvr & cond of music for over 100 motion pictures. Chief Collabr: Henry Mancini.

GERSHWIN, ARTHUR   ASCAP 1945
composer
b New York, NY, Mar 14, 1900. Brother of George & Ira Gershwin. Chief Collabrs: Stanley Adams, Fred Spielman, Doris Fisher. *Songs:* Invitation to the Blues; Slowly But Surely; After All These Years; Blue Underneath a Yellow Moon; No Love Blues; You're More Than a Name and Address. *Scores:* Stage show: A Lady Says Yes.

GERSHWIN, GEORGE   ASCAP 1920
composer
b Brooklyn, NY, Sept 26, 1898; d Beverly Hills, Calif, July 11, 37. Educ: Pub schs; studied music with Charles Hambitzer, Edward Kilenyi, Rubin Goldmark & Joseph Schillinger. Pianist for Remick Music Co at age 15, later accompanist to Louise Dresser & Nora Bayes. Hired by Max Dreyfus as staff comp for T B Harms. Biographies: "Gershwin" by Isaac Goldberg; "A Journey to Greatness" by David Ewen; "The Gershwin Years" by Edward Jablonski & Lawrence Stewart; "George Gershwin" by Robert Payne; "The Gershwins" by Robert Kimball & Alfred Simon. Film biography: "Rhapsody in Blue." Chief Collabrs: Ira Gershwin (brother), Irving Caesar, B G De Sylva, Oscar Hammerstein, 2nd, Otto Harbach, Gus Kahn. *Songs:* Swanee; The Real American Folk Song; I Was So Young; Drifting Along With the Tide; Do It Again; I'll Build a Stairway to Paradise; So Am I; I Won't Say I Will; Blue Monday Blues; Somebody Loves Me; Fascinating Rhythm; Oh, Lady Be Good; The Half of It Dearie Blues; Little Jazz Bird; The Man I Love; Kickin' the Clouds Away; Looking for a Boy; These Charming People; That Certain Feeling; Sweet and Low-Down; Song of the Flame; Dear Little Girl; Maybe; Clap Yo' Hands; Do Do Do; Someone to Watch Over Me; Strike Up the Band; Let's Kiss and Make Up; Funny Face; 'S Wonderful; He Loves and She Loves; My One and Only; The Babbitt and the Bromide; How Long Has This Been Going On?; I've Got a Crush on You; Oh, So Nice; Where's the Boy, Here's the Girl; Liza; Soon; Bidin' My Time; Could You Use Me?; Embraceable You; Sam and Delilah; I Got Rhythm; But Not for Me; Boy! What Love Has Done to Me!; Blah-Blah-Blah; Wintergreen for President; Love Is Sweeping the Country; Of Thee I Sing (Baby); Who Cares?; Hello, Good Morning; Lorelei; Isn't It a Pity; My Cousin in Milwaukee; Mine; Summertime; A Woman Is a Sometime Thing; My Man's Gone Now; I Got Plenty of Nuttin'; Bess, You Is My Woman Now; It Ain't Necessarily So; I Loves You, Porgy; There's a Boat dat's Leavin' Soon for New York; By Strauss; Beginner's Luck; Let's Call the Whole Thing Off; Shall We Dance?; They All Laughed; They Can't Take That Away From Me; A Foggy Day; Nice Work If You Can Get It; I Was Doing All Right; Love Is Here to Stay; Love Walked In; Aren't You Kind of Glad We Did?; Changing My Tune; For You, For Me, For Evermore. *Instrumental Works:* Rialto Ripples; Blue Monday (chamber opera); Waltz I & II (piano); Rhapsody in Blue; Piano Concerto in F; Preludes for Piano; An American In Paris; Second Piano Rhapsody; Cuban Overture; I

Got Rhythm Variations. *Scores:* Opera: Porgy and Bess; Bway stage: La, La, Lucile; George White's Scandals (20-24); Sweet Little Devil; Lady, Be Good; Tell Me More; Tip-Toes; Song of the Flame; Oh, Kay; Funny Face; Rosalie; Treasure Girl; Show Girl; Strike Up the Band; Girl Crazy; Of Thee I Sing (Pulitzer Prize, 32); Let 'Em Eat Cake; Films: Delicious; Shall We Dance; A Damsel in Distress; The Goldwyn Follies; The Shocking Miss Pilgrim.

GERSHWIN, HENRY
See Mazlen, Henry Gershwin

GERSHWIN, IRA (ARTHUR FRANCIS)   ASCAP 1920
author
b New York, NY, Dec 6, 1896. Educ: Student Townsend Harris Hall, 10-13; Col City of New York, 14-16; Columbia Univ Extension, 18; hon DFA, Univ Md, 66. Began as contributor to newspapers. Worked for touring carnival. Writer of songs & scores for Bway shows & films. Author, "Lyrics on Several Occasions." Recipient, Pulitzer Prize, 32 (first lyricist awarded); Townsend Harris Medal, City Col, New York, 52. Chief Collabrs: George Gershwin, Harold Arlen, Aaron Copland, Vernon Duke, Jerome Kern, Burton Lane, Arthur Schwartz, Vincent Youmans, Harry Warren, Kurt Weill. *Songs:* Lyrics: Oh, Me! Oh, My!; I'll Build a Stairway to Paradise; Fascinating Rhythm; Oh, Lady Be Good; The Half of It Dearie Blues; Little Jazz Bird; The Man I Love; Looking for a Boy; These Charming People; That Certain Feeling; Sweet and Low Down; Sunny Disposish; Maybe; Clap Yo' Hands; Do, Do, Do; Someone to Watch Over Me; Strike Up the Band; Let's Kiss and Make Up; Funny Face; 'S Wonderful; My One and Only; He Loves and She Loves; The Babbitt and the Bromide; How Long Has This Been Going On?; I've Got a Crush on You; Oh, So Nice; Liza; Do What You Do; Soon; Bidin' My Time; Could You Use Me?; Embraceable You; Sam and Delilah; I Got Rhythm; But Not for Me; Cheerful Little Earful; Blah, Blah, Blah; Wintergreen for President; Love Is Sweeping the Country; Of Thee I Sing (Baby); Who Cares?; Lorelei; Isn't It a Pity?; My Cousin in Milwaukee; Mine; You're a Builder Upper; Fun to Be Fooled; Let's Take a Walk Around the Block; I Got Plenty of Nuttin'; Bess, You Is My Woman Now; It Ain't Necessarily So; I Loves You, Porgy; There's a Boat Dat's Leavin' Soon for New York; I Can't Get Started; That Moment of Moments; By Strauss; Beginner's Luck; Let's Call the Whole Thing Off; Shall We Dance?; They All Laughed; They Can't Take That Away From Me; A Foggy Day (In London Town); Nice Work If You Can Get It; Love Is Here to Stay; Love Walked In; Spring Again; One Life to Live; Girl of the Moment; This Is New; Tschaikowsky; The Saga of Jenny; My Ship; The Princess of Pure Delight; Long Ago (And Far Away); Sure Thing; The Nina, the Pinta, the Santa Maria; Sing Me Not a Ballad; Don't Be a Woman If You Can; Aren't You Kind of Glad We Did?; Changing My Tune; For You, for Me, for Evermore; My One and Only Highland Fling; You'd Be Hard to Replace; It Happens Every Time; In Our United State; The Man That Got Away; Here's What I'm Here For; Someone At Last; It's a New World; The Search Is Through (You've Got What It Takes); Dissertation on the State of Bliss; All the Livelong Day. *Scores:* Bway shows: A Dangerous Maid; Two Little Girls in Blue (written under pseudonym Arthur Francis); Lady Be Good; Tell Me More; Tip Toes; Oh, Kay; Funny Face; Rosalie; Treasure Girl; Strike Up the Band; Show Girl; Girl Crazy; Of Thee I Sing; Pardon My English; Let 'Em Eat Cake; Life Begins At 8:40; Porgy and Bess; Ziegfeld Follies; Lady in the Dark; The Firebrand of Florence; Park Avenue; Films: Delicious; Shall We Dance?; A Damsel In Distress; Goldwyn Follies; Cover Girl; The Shocking Miss Pilgrim; The Barkleys of Broadway; An American in Paris; A Star Is Born; The Country Girl; Kiss Me Stupid; Opera: Porgy and Bess.

GERTZ, IRVING   ASCAP 1952
composer, director
b Providence, RI, May 19, 15. Educ: Hope Street High Sch, Providence, 32; Providence Col Music, 33-36, studied with Wassili Leps, Providence & Walter Piston, Boston, Mass; Ernst Toch & Mario Castelnuovo-Tedesco, Los Angeles, Calif, 46-49. With Columbia Pictures, Hollywood, 38. Maj, USA Signal Corps, Mil Serv, WW II, 41-46. Back with Columbia Pictures as comp, 46; comp, NBC Radio, 48 & Universal Studios, 50; comp/musical dir, Twentieth Century Fox, 60 & for films & TV, United Artist, RKO & others. *Songs:* Music: The First Traveling Saleslady; A Corset Can Do a Lot for a Lady. *Scores:* Nobody's Perfect; Fluffy; To Hell and Back; It Came From Outer Space; Francis in the Navy; Francis Joins the WACS; Raw Edge; East of Sumatra; A Day of Fury; Istanbul; Posse From Hell; Congo Crossing; Hell Bent for Leather; Seven Ways From Sundown; The Incredible Shrinking Man; The Creature Walks Among Us; Gun for a Coward; Cult of the Cobra; The Deadly Mantis; Monolith Monsters; Marines Let's Go; The Fiercest Heart; The Wizard of Baghdad; Plunder Road; Thundering Jets; The Alligator People; Daniel Boone; Hong Kong; Follow the Sun; The Legend of Jesse James; Custer; Voyage to the Bottom of the Sea; America; Golden Voyage; Across the Seven Seas; The Fearmakers; Tombstone Express; Top Gun; Gun Belt; Overland Pacific; Khyber Patrol; Brushfire; The Traveling Saleslady. *Albums:* Leaves of Grass (Walt Whitman; mixed voices, organ, trumpets, perc; commemoration of the Centennial Yrs).

GESENSWAY, LOUIS   ASCAP 1956
composer, violinist
b Latvia, Feb 19, 06; d Philadelphia, Pa, Mar 13, 76. Educ: Toronto Cons, studied violin with Luigi von Kunits; Curtis Inst Music, studied comp; Budapest Acad, with Zoltan Kodaly. Toured Can in recitals as violin prodigy, 16-18.

Joined Philadelphia Orch, 26. Developed syst of music, Color Harmony, demonstrated in Philadelphia, 44. *Instrumental Works:* 2 string quartets; Duo for Violin, Viola; Fantasy for Organ; Quartet for English Horn, Flute, Violin, Cello; 3 Movements for Strings; Percussion (Hartman Kuhn Award); Concerto for 13 Brass Instruments; Flute Concerto (comn by Dimitri Mitropoulos for William Kincaid); Sonata for Bassoon; Suite on Jewish Folk Themes (orch, var chamber ens); Double Portrait (orch); Quartet for Violin, Oboe, Viola, Bassoon; Duo for Flute, Clarinet; The 4 Squares of Philadelphia (symphonic tone poem); Let the Night Be Dark for All of Me (tone poem); Ode to Peace (tone poem); 8 Rounds for 4 Percussion Players; 8 Miniatures for Flute, Timpani, Percussion; Quartet for Violin, Cello, Timpani, Percussion; 5 Russian Pieces (orch, var chamber ens); Commemoration Symphony; A Pennsylvania Overture (orch); Cello Concerto; Duo for Violin, Flute; Duo for Violin, Cello; Duo for 2 Celli; Two Silhouettes for Flute, Piano (also for flute, harp, timpani, string orch); Quartet for Clarinet, Violin, Viola, Cello; March (orch); Duo for Oboe, Guitar; Duo for Viola, Bassoon; Suite for Harp; Divertimento for Woodwind Quintet; Divertimento for Flute, 2 Violins, 2 Viola; Trans: Chaconne (Bach).

GESNER, CLARK (JOHN GORDON) ASCAP 1962
composer, author

b Augusta, Maine, Mar 27, 38. Educ: Princeton Univ, BA. Spec services, USA, 61-63; staff writer for "Captain Kangaroo," CBS-TV, 63-66; free lance TV, records, theater & bks, 66-; contributing writer, comp & filmmaker for "Sesame Street" & "Electric Company," PBS-TV, 68- *Scores:* Bway show: You're a Good Man, Charlie Brown; The Utter Glory of Morrissey Hall.

GESOFF, HILDA IDA ASCAP 1960
composer, author, performer

b Allentown, Pa. Educ: Pvt study piano, dance & drama. Lectr poetry reading in elem, high sch & col levels; performances of own music; writer comedy material, stories, etc. Mem, Nat Acad Popular Music. *Songs:* I Wanna; The Spinsters Three; A Little Gold Locket; Sorry; All America City March; Thanks to You It's Working (United Fund); Land of Hope, Land of Dreams (United Jewish Appeal); Player Pie-Ana; Come Spring; Music (jazz themes): Polished Brass; Sixth Dimension; Frantic Guitar; Bleecker Street Stomp. *Instrumental Works:* Hildi's Tune.

GETZOV, RAMON M ASCAP 1954
composer

b Brooklyn, NY, Feb 19, 25. Educ: Lafayette Col, BA. Partner in mfg co, Springfield, Mass. *Songs:* Our Song.

GHENT, EMMANUEL ROBERT
composer

b Montreal, Que, May 15, 25. Educ: McGill Univ, BS, 46, MD, 50; studied piano with Samuel Blumenthal, bassoon with R de H Tupper, comp with Ralph Shapey; McGill Cons. Comp-in-residence, Bell Laboratories, 69- Recipient of numerous comns, Nat Endowment for the Arts grants; Guggenheim Fellowship. Chief Collabrs: Film, Ken Knowlton, dance, Mimi Garrard & James Seawright. *Instrumental Works:* Entelechy (viola, piano); Divertimento (electronic violin and computer brass); Helices (violin, piano, tape); Hex (an ellipsis for trumpet, chamber ens, tape, special equipment); Dithyrambos (brass quintet, special equipment); Lustrum (a concerto grosso for electronic string quintet, brass quintet and tape); A Little Hammerpiece (2 mallet players). Computer Generated Tape: Phosphones; Brazen; Five Brass Voices; Innerness. Computer Music & Computer Graphics Film: Baobab.

GHEZZO, DINU DUMITRU ASCAP 1975
composer, conductor

b Tuzla, Romania, July 2, 40. Educ: Cons of Music, Bucharest, Romania, BA & MA; Univ Calif Los Angeles, PhD(comp), 73. Prof music, Sch of Music, Constantza, Romania, 64-69; asst prof, Cons Music, Bucharest, 69; asst prof, Univ Calif Los Angeles, 72-74, Queens Col, 74-77 & NY Univ, 76- Dir, NY Univ Symph Orch & Washington Square Chamber Orch, 77-; co-dir & founder, New Repertory Ens of NY Inc & NY Univ Contemporary Players. Comp Awards: Georges Enesco, Gus Kahn Award, Creative Artists Pub Serv & ASCAP. *Instrumental Works:* Ritualen; Music for Flutes and Tapes; Kanones; Pontica II; Cantos Nuevos; Seven Short Pieces; Aphorisms (clarinet & piano); Structures for Cello and Piano; Nonetto.

GIACOBBE, NELLO (NINO ROSSANO)
composer, author, singer

b Ribera, Italy, Apr 15, 40. Educ: Schs in Italy; studied voice with Carlo Menotti, New York. Chief Collabr: Carlo Menotti. *Songs:* Lyrics: Sei Bella; Au Revoir My Love.

GIANCURSIO, JOSEPH (JAN CURSIO) ASCAP 1968
composer, teacher, instrumentalist

b Rochester, NY, June 21, 21. Educ: Jefferson High Sch, Rochester, grad; Eastman Sch of Music, studied clarinet with Richard Joiner & comp with Rayburn Wright. Played in Jefferson High Sch Band; leader of own 10-piece band. Played solo clarinet in 14th Div Army Band. Leader of own group, playing locally. *Songs & Instrumental Works:* Mr Santa's on His Way; Christmas Time; There Are Songs to Sing; Now; Oodles of Poodles.

GIANGRECO, THOMAS (TOMMY GRECO) ASCAP 1978
composer, author

b Racalmuto, Italy, Nov 8, 11. Educ: Studied music in Italy; harmony lessons from Donald Nelligan. Played trumpet & trombone in local symphonic band, Sicily. To US, 29. Played with Buffalo Philh & some dance bands, incl Vincent Lopez, Sammy Kaye & Harry James. Played some at maj movie cos, incl 20th Century Fox, Universal Studios & Columbia. Composed some marches for the Rams Football Team Band. Chief Collabr: Donald Nelligan. *Instrumental Works:* Charge, Team; Meet the Drummer; Touch Down Or Kicking It Through; When Our Team Comes Running In; Spec Arr: America-Freedom.

GIANNINI, VITTORIO ASCAP 1927
composer, educator

b Philadelphia, Pa, Oct 19, 03; d Nov 25, 66. Educ: Milan Cons (scholarship); Am Acad, Rome; studied with Martini, Trucco & Hans Letz; Juilliard, studied with Rubin Goldmark. Awards: Juilliard; Am Acad, Rome; Publ Am Music. Mem fac, Curtis Inst Music, Juilliard & Manhattan Sch Music, NY Col Music. First dir, All-State High Sch, Col Performing Arts, Winston-Salem, NC. Chief Collabr: Karl Flaster. *Songs:* Tell Me, Oh, Blue, Blue Sky; It Is a Spring Night; Heart Cry. *Instrumental Works:* Prelude & Fugue; Triptych: Concerto Grosso; Divertimento No 2; three symphonies. *Songs & Instrumental Works:* Choral: Stabat Mater; Madrigal; Primavera (cantata); Requiem; Lament for Adonis (cantata); Canticle of the Martyrs (500th anniversary Moravian Church, Winston-Salem comn). *Scores:* Operas: Lucedia; Flora; The Scarlet Letter; Beauty and the Beast; Blennerhasset; The Taming of the Shrew.

GIARRATANO, TONY ASCAP 1963
composer

b Kansas City, Mo, Nov 28, 07. Educ: High sch. Singer in cabarets, nightclubs & radio. Owned & operated, Italian Specialties Restaurant; also real estate broker. *Songs:* Mine Is the Broken Heart; Mariuch; Empty Arms and Lonely Nights; I Can't Fool My Heart; Aimless Love.

GIASSON, PAUL EMILE (GUY PAULSON) ASCAP 1960
composer, author, publisher

b New Bedford, Mass, Mar 6, 21. Educ: New Bedford High Sch; Boston Univ; comp studies with Keith Crosby Brown & with Eldin Burton & Charles Mills in 50's. Played solo piano & with small groups in Boston; taught history of popular music in sch of modern music until 48; pursued bus & comp careers in New York; worked for an aromatic chemical co, then for an eng firm; now with Red Seal Div, RCA Records. Off Bway shows: "Baker's Dozen", "What's Up" & "All Our Love." Has written & publ dozens of piano solos, piano duets & sacred choral, organ & vocal solo works. Chief Collabrs: Fred Ebb, David Herzbrun, Bette Sykes, Al Bedell, Gerald Plano, R C Garrison, Freeman Cohn. *Songs:* Little Christmas Tree Waltz; God is Just a Prayer Away; A Merry Christmas Wish; Music: Where Was I?; I Knew Him When; Softly, Softly; The Voice of the Lord; Christmas in Manhattan; If You've Forgotten Me; I Will Be With You (on Christmas Day); Walk With the Lord. *Instrumental Works:* Starlight; Theme for Young Lovers; Rain Forest; Prelude to Dawn; Canadian Childhood (piano suite); Preludes for Piano (piano suite); Indian Summer (piano suite); Portrait of a City (piano solo); Vienna-on-the-Hudson (piano solo); A Waltz for Cinderella (piano solo); Summer Soliloquy (piano solo); A Waltz Rhapsody (piano solo); The Snows of Yesteryear (piano solo). *Songs & Instrumental Works:* Sing Alleluia Now! (Christmas cantata, piano suite).

GIBALDI, LOUIS MILO (JESSE CUTLER) ASCAP 1972
composer, author, singer

b Brooklyn, NY, Aug 28, 51. Educ: Highland High Sch; Hofstra Univ; NY Univ, BA. Mem, group The Young Executives, age 12; mem original cast Bway prod of "Godspell," 72; co-arr score for original cast "Godspell" album; recording artist for Brut Records, 73; appeared on TV film "The Buddy Holly Story." *Songs:* Can You Remember; Richman's Son; Mirror Mirror; Look At Them Laugh At Me; Give the Little Girl a Chance.

GIBB, ROBERT W ASCAP 1937
composer, arranger

b Dedham, Mass, May 2, 1893; d Dedham, May 15, 64. Educ: New Eng Cons, studied with Frederick Converse; Boston Univ; Harvard Univ. Co-author: "Glee Music for Girls" & "Glee Music for Boys." Past pres, Mass Music Educ Asn. *Songs & Instrumental Works:* Oriental (suite); Three Waltzes; Nobody Knows the Trouble I See; Steal Away to Jesus; Song of the Buccaneers (TTBB); The Challenge of Youth (SAB); Gather Roun' Children; Song of Faith; Song of Hope; The Rain Drop; Exaltation; Autumn Clouds (SSATBB); America, Forever Free!; I'm Proud to Be an American!; The Cheerful Arn (TTBB); Gettysburg Address (TTBB & SATB); Matins (SSA); Summer Dawn (SSA); Overtures: Youth Triumphant; Carnival; Festival.

GIBB, STANLEY GARTH ASCAP 1970
composer

b Chicago, Ill, June 22, 40. Educ: San Francisco State Univ, BMus & MMus; NTex State Univ, DMA; studied comp with Herbert Bielawa, Merrill Ellis, Merrill Bradshaw. Worked in electronic, computer & exp music, NTex State Univ. Prof music theory, comp & perc, Calif State Polytech Univ, 74- Comp works for orch, choir, woodwind, brass & perc ens. *Songs & Instrumental Works:*

Lokalization (12 trombones); Parity (trombone, electronic tape); Sound Action (perc, electronic tape); An Easter Cantata (choir, piano); Documentus (choir, orch).

GIBB, STEPHEN M   ASCAP 1974
composer
b Onancock, Va, Nov 20, 45. Educ: Peabody Cons, Baltimore, Md, BA, MA & BM. Started with Buzz Cason, Angel Wing Publ Co, Nashville, Tenn, 74; producer & composer, 80- *Songs:* She Believes in Me; If I Ever Had to Say Goodbye to You; Look What You've Done; Now He's Comin' Home.

GIBBS, ARTHUR H   ASCAP 1937
composer, conductor, pianist
b Savannah, Ga, Dec 25, 1895; d New York, NY, Mar 17, 56. Educ: High sch, Atlantic City, NJ. Went to NY, 13. Pianist in dance orch. AEF, WW I. Led own orch, 23; toured Europe, 29-30. Mem, 2-piano team in nightclubs. *Songs:* Runnin' Wild; Rocky Road; How Can You Tell; You Bet; I Got the Fever.

GIBBS, TERRY
See Gubenko, Julius

GIBSON, ALBERT ANDREW   ASCAP 1949
composer, musician, arranger
b Zanesville, Ohio, Nov 6, 13; d Cincinnati, Ohio, Feb 11, 61. Educ: Pub schs. Played in dance bands; then arr for orchs, incl Duke Ellington, Charlie Barnet, Harry James, Billy Hays, Morty Berk, Roy Alfred, Count Basie, James Rushing & Cab Calloway. *Songs & Instrumental Works:* The Great Lie; The Huckle Buck; Geechy Joe; I Left My Baby; From the Bottom of My Heart; Shorty George.

GIBSON, ROXIE E (CAWOOD)   ASCAP 1974
author
b Spring City, Tenn, Jan 24, 34. Educ: Spring City High Sch, grad, 52. Secretary, Oak Hill Sch, Tenn. Author, bks, "Hey, God, Where Are You?", "Hey, God, Listen!" (also a musical), "Hey, God, Hurry!" (also a musical), "Hey, God, What Is Christmas?" (also a musical), "Two Little Fishes and Five Loaves of Bread" & "Just Me, Lord." Chief Collabr: Ken Krause.

GIERLACH, CHESTER MITCHELL   ASCAP 1951
composer
b New Castle, Pa, Mar 31, 19. Educ: Transylvania Col; Univ Ky, music scholarships; studied with Adolf Schmid, Fritz Mahler, Tibor Serly. Radio producer & dir for New York Philh, Boston Pops & the Woody Herman Show; TV dir for commercials & writer & producer for musical commercials. Pres, MusicMusicMusicInc. Chief Collabrs: Leonard Whitcup, Johnny Olsen. *Songs:* Music: Heaven Knows; Pee Wee, the Kiwi Bird; Happy Birthday, Dear Christ Child; People to People; Book of 70 Hymns; The Sunshine of Love; Themes: Mona, The Little Red Goose; The Loving Heart. *Instrumental Works:* Village Festival Dances.

GIFFORD, H EUGENE   ASCAP 1934
composer, guitarist, arranger
b Americus, Ga, May 31, 08; d Memphis, Tenn, Nov 12, 70. Educ: Univ; pvt music study. Teacher of theory, solfeggio & advanced counterpoint. Arr, radio orchs; also for Glen Gray Orch, 6 yrs & free lance. Mem staff, record cos & CBS. *Songs & Instrumental Works:* Out of Space; White Jazz; Ode to a Kiss; Smoke Rings; Casa Loma Stomp; Paramour; Maniac's Ball; Dance of the Lame Duck; Black Jazz; Blue Jazz; Buji; Bye, Bye Bonnie; Ain't It Just Too Bad; Cobra and the Flute; Dizzy Glide; Everything Is Just the Same; Dream in Blue; Georgia Camp Meeting; The Goblin Band; Going Back to Memphis; In the Valley of Yesterday; Mr Rhythm Man; Moonlight and Cotton; Moth and the Flame; New Orleans Twist; Nothin' But the Blues; The Moment I Looked in Your Eyes.

GIL, ROBERT VELAZQUEZ
composer, author
b El Paso, Tex, Dec 26, 23. Educ: Los Angeles City Col; Los Angeles Cons; Westlake Col of Music, studied piano with Dr Wagner, comp & arr with Russell Garcia & Dave Robertson; harmony with Leonard Stein. Worked in nightclubs; recorded extensively, 48-50. Did TV & stage production work. Comp & orch many types of music incl Latin music. One of the originators of Latin Am Symph Orch. *Songs:* Sin Amor; Music: Sparkling Meringue; Mambo; Stop When Swinging; Magitos; Hop Skip and Jump; Round Robin; Gil's Dilemma; Bobby's Fables; Cruising; 99 Clunk.

GILBERT, HERSCHEL BURKE   ASCAP 1952
composer, conductor, producer
b Milwaukee, Wis, Apr 20, 18. Educ: Milwaukee State Teachers Col; Juilliard Sch; cond fel with Albert Stoessel; studied with Aaron Copland, Bernstein, comp with Bernard Wagenaar. Comp, films & TV progs incl "The Rifleman", "Robert Taylor's Detectives", "Dick Powell Theatre" & "Rawhide." Music dir, 4 Star TV, 5 yrs. Exec music dir, CBS-TV, 1 yr. Exec music producer, var albums. Pres, Screen Composers of Am. Recipient, Western Heritage award. *Songs:* Music: The Moon Is Blue (Acad award nomination). *Scores:* The Thief (Acad award nomination); Carmen Jones (Acad award nomination, best music dir).

GILBERT, L WOLFE   ASCAP 1924
author, publisher
b Odessa, Russia, Aug 31, 1886; d July 12, 70. Educ: Pub schs. Began career singing in amateur nights, then vaudeville as cafe entertainer. Toured with John L Sullivan. Went to Hollywood, 29, wrote for films & Eddie Cantor radio show. Many appearances on radio & TV. Had own publ firm, Calif. Autobiography, "Without Rhyme or Reason." Dir, ASCAP, 41-44. Chief Collabrs: Lewis Muir, Mabel Wayne, Abel Baer, Ben Oakland, Jay Gorney, Nat Shilkret, Richard Fall, Anatole Friedland. *Songs:* Waiting for the Robert E Lee; Hitchy Koo; Lucky Lindy; Mama Don't Want No Peas an Rice and Cocoanut Oil; My Sweet Adair; My Little Dream Girl; Jeannine, I Dream of Lilac Time; Mama Inez; Oh Katharina; I Miss My Swiss; Marta; By Heck; Green Eyes; The Peanut Vendor; Hopalong Cassidy March; My Mother's Eyes; Down Yonder; Maria My Own (Maria La O); Lily of the Valley; African Lament (Lamento Africano); Chiquita.

GILBERT, LELA (LELA KEENE)   ASCAP 1976
author, lyricist
b San Diego, Calif, Sept 22, 46. Educ: Bonita High Sch, La Verne, Calif, grad, 63; Biola Col, 65-68. Model & fashion coordr, 70- Started writing professionally, 74; writer of lyrics. Author bk "Just Five Days Till Friday." Chief Collabrs: Ron Harris, Tom Keene, Paul Johnson. *Songs:* Lord, Send That Morning; Anticipation; Isn't That Just Like Jesus; Touch My Friend, Lord Jesus; Didn't I Tell You; Older and Wiser; Follow the Children; No Time for Crying.

GILBERT, RAY   ASCAP 1946
composer, author
b Hartford, Conn, Sept 15, 12; d Los Angeles, Calif, Mar 3, 76. Educ: Pub schs. Wrote spec material for Sophie Tucker, Harry Richman, Buddy Rogers & Carmen Miranda. Went to Hollywood, 39. Wrote for Earl Carroll, then under contract to Walt Disney, 3 1/2 yrs. Played major nightclubs with Sidney Miller, US. Chief Collabrs: Hoagy Carmichael, Ted Fiorito, Allie Wrubel, Eddie Suater, Paul Nero, Antonio Carlos Jobim, Marcos Valle, Bob Russel, Doug Goodwin, Ben Oakland, Donald Kahn, Sidney Miller, Lou Busch, Kid Ory, Buddy Greco. *Songs:* The Three Caballeros; You Belong to My Heart; That's a-Plenty; Zip-a-Dee-Doo-Dah (Acad Award, 47); Sooner or Later; My Fickle Eye; All the Cats Join In; The Hot Canary; Everybody Has a Laughing Place: Bahia; Cuanto le Gusto; Muskrat Ramble; Johnny Fedora and Alice Blue Bonnet; I Want a Zoot Suit; Whistle Your Way Back Home; Ashcan Parade; Vene, Veno, Vena; And Roses and Roses; Cherry; Casey at the Bat; Bonita; She's a Carioca; If You Went Away; Lyrics: Once I Loved; Dindi; Berimbau; The Face I Love; If You Never Come to Me; Crickets Sing for Anna Maria; A Little Tear; Somewhere in the Hills; The Day It Rained; Voce; Without You; Adios Mariquita Linda; I Live to Love You; Two Silhouettes; The Merrily Song; Lora Belle Lee; Mickey and the Beanstalk; Tell Me Pretty Star; I Wonder; Let's Get Busy Too; Safely in Your Arms; It's Time to Sing; 99 Lollipops; Chup Chup I Got Away. *Scores:* Films: The Three Caballeros; Make Mine Music; Song of the South; A Date With Judy; Nancy Goes to Rio; Hey There, It's Yogi Bear; The Answer Tree. *Albums:* The Nina, the Pinta, the Santa Maria (We Think the World is Round).

GILBERT, RICHARD E   ASCAP 1962
composer, author
b New York, NY, Sept 12, 19. Educ: NY Univ. *Songs:* A Tear, A Kiss, A Smile; A Million Moons Ago; Can This Be You?

GILBERT, TIMOTHY PROUT   ASCAP 1966
composer, author
b New York, NY, Jan 6, 42. Chief Collabr: John Carter. *Songs:* Music: Incense and Peppermints; That Acapulco Gold.

GILBERT, WILLIAM   ASCAP 1971
author
b Cleveland, Ohio, Feb 24, 16. Educ: Glenville High School, Cleveland Ohio, 34; Ohio State Univ, BS(educ), 38. Performer "Micromaniacs" comedy trio vaudeville theatres & clubs, 40-41. USA Signal Corps, Special Services Pacific Theatre, 42-46. TV script writer, 49- Co-author bks "How to Succeed In Business, Etc", 61-65 & "Hot Spot," 63; co-author play "Catch Me If You Can," 65. Chief Collabrs: Jack Weinstock, R Nicholson. *Songs:* Lyrics: Right on Through; I Love a Riddle; I Love to Hear the Children Laugh; The Brand New Peanut Band; The Cheer-Up Song; Pickin' and Strummin'; Liza Belle; Without My Music; Nowhere Can Be Somewhere; Summer Day; Hominy Grits.

GILBERTO, ASTRUD   ASCAP 1972
composer, author
b Salvador, Brazil, Mar 30, 40. Educ: Var schs in Brazil, 57. Launched singing career with a hit single "The Girl From Ipanema"; comp, 72- Chief Collabrs: Eumir Deodato, Hal Shaper. *Songs:* Zigy, Zigy, Za; Gingele; Where Have You Been?; All I've Got; We'll Make Today Last Night Again; Music: Make Love to Me; Far Away; Lyrics: Black Magic.

GILBERTSON, VIRGINIA MABRY   ASCAP 1963
composer, author, pianist
b Memphis, Tenn, Dec 2, 14. Educ: De Shazo Col Music, BM; Memphis State Univ; Winthrop Col; studied with Edwin Hughes, 44-64. Assoc teacher, De Shazo Col Music, Memphis, 36-41; pvt teacher, Memphis, Wilmington, NC, Charlotte, NC, Fremont, Ohio, New Canaan, Conn, Smoke Rise, Kinelon, NJ

& Tarboro, NC. Dir music, Charlotte NC County Day Sch, 2 yrs; accompanist, Silvermine Opera Guild; wrote special material for Westport, Norwalk, New Canaan & Smoke Rise. Chief Collabr: Edward Eager. *Songs:* One Bronze Feather (NJ Tercentennial); If I Had Three Wishes; Blueberry Moon; Next to Heaven; Music: Johnny, Come Kiss Me; The Loneliest Boy About Town; Change Here for Heaven.

GILES, JOHNNY
See Mellenbruch, Giles Edward

GILKINSON, DONALD MITCHEL   ASCAP 1975
composer

b Far Rockaway, NY, Apr 20, 50. Educ: Sullivan County Community Col, AS(bus admin, hon) & AA(liberal arts, hon), 78; New York Inst Technol. Singer, nightclubs, TV & radio; radio announcer, WDLA, Walton, NY. Recording artist, Caprice Records, Nashville, Tenn & KDB Records, Walton. *Songs:* One More Memory; Open the Door to Paradise.

GILL, CAROLYN   ASCAP 1959
composer, author, singer

b Royalton, Minn, Dec 24, 18. Educ: High sch. Singer, radio show "National Barn Dance"; soloist, "Sonja Henie Ice Revue." On staff, WSM, Nashville, Tenn. With group The Cackle Sisters on "Eddy Arnold Show"; appeared on Grand Ol' Opry. Joined ABC staff, 54; appeared on TV. Chief Collabr: Ralph Gill (husband); *Songs:* Swiss Kiss Polka; Dancing the Polka; Windmill Waltz; Yumpin' Yiminy Yodel; Sweetheart Waltz; A Happy Serenade; Polka Go Round (theme).

GILL, RALPH (RUSTY)   ASCAP 1959
composer, author, singer

b St Louis, Mo, June 10, 19. Educ: High sch. Singer, radio progs, 37-47 & on network TV. Chief Collabr: Carolyn Gill (wife). *Songs:* Prettiest Girl Waltz; Windmill Waltz; Yumpin' Yiminy Yodel; Sweetheart Waltz; Whirling Skirts; Polka Go Round (theme).

GILLAM, DAVID S   ASCAP 1954
composer, author

b Huntingdon, Pa, Jan 1, 15; d. Educ: Pasadena Jr Col. Writer for revues, films & TV. Chief Collabr: Matt Dennis. *Songs:* A Teenager's Romance; Don't Look My Way; It Wasn't the Stars That Thrilled Me; Beach Time.

GILLES, ELOISE
See Moore, Eloise Irene

GILLESPIE, HAVEN   ASCAP 1925
author, composer

b Covington, Ky, Feb 6, 1888; d Las Vegas, Nev, Mar 14, 75. Left high sch to enter printing trade, became journeyman. Worked on New York Times & other newspapers. Wrote songs for films, theatre & radio. Chief Collabrs: J Fred Coots, Beasley Smith, Henry Marshall, Henry Tobias, Harry Tobias, Neil Moret, Peter DeRose, Egbert Van Alstyne, Victor Young, Jack Little, Charles Tobias, Richard Whiting, Peter Wendling, Seymour Simons, Byron Gay, Rudy Vallee, Lee David, Larry Shay. *Songs:* That Lucky Old Sun; Santa Claus is Coming to Town; Breezin' Along With the Breeze; You're in Kentucky Sure As You're Born; You Go to My Head; The Old Master Painter; Drifting and Dreaming; Honey; The Sleepy Town Express; Whose Honey Are You?; Our Old Home Team; Don't Forget; God's Country (Freedom Found Award); You Happened to Me; Tin Pan Parade; The Wedding of Jack and Jill; Right or Wrong; By the Sycamore Tree; Beautiful Love; Until Tomorrow; Come Home; There's Honey on the Moon Tonight; Song of the Navy; Seeing You Again Did Me No Good; Our Silver Anniversary; This Holy Love.

GILLESPIE, JOHN BIRKS (DIZZY)   ASCAP 1957
composer, conductor, trumpeter

b Cheraw, SC, Oct 21, 17. Educ: Laurinburg Inst; hon degrees: DMus, Tuft Univ & Rutgers Univ, DHL & DMus, Univ SC. Comp at age 15. Jazz trumpet player, 30-; toured with Teddy Hill Band, 37-39, with Earl Hines, Billy Eckstine, Mercer Ellington, Cab Calloway, Ella Fitzgerald, Benny Carter, Charlie Barnet & Les Hite. Leader, own band, 46-50, toured Scandinavia, 48, combo, 50-56. Rep of US Dept of State on culture tour of Middle East & Latin Am, 56-58; toured Argentina, 61. Appeared at Jazz Workshop, San Francisco, Monterey Jazz Fest, Juan-les-Pins Fest, France, 62. With Giants of Jazz, toured US, Europe & Japan, 71-72; in Musical Life of Charlie Parker, 74, toured Europe, 74. Appeared in concert "Tribute to Dizzy Gillespie," Avery Fisher Hall, New York, 75. Appeared in var tours, fests, nightclubs & on TV. Recording artist. Recipient, first prize for sound track Berlin Film Fest, 62, Downbeat Critics Poll award, 71-75, Handel Medallion, 72, Grammy award, 75, Nat Music award, 76; named Musician of Yr by Inst of High Fidelity, 75, hon by SC Legislature, 76. Author, "To Be Or Not to Bop." Chief Collabrs: Bob Russell, John Hendricks. *Songs & Instrumental Works:* A Night in Tunisia; Woody'n You; Ow; Groovin' High; Tour de Force; Con Alma; Fais Gaffe; This Is the Way; Manteca; Lorraine; Anthropology; Cool World; Double Six of Paris; Something Old, Something New; Swing Low Sweet Cadillac. *Albums:* Jazz for a Sunday Afternoon; Dizzy Gillespie Reunion Band; Trumpet Kings at Montreaux; Trumpet Kings Meet Joe Turner; Giants of Jazz; Party; Bahiana; At Village

Vanguard; My Way; Greatest Jazz Concert Ever; Oscar Peterson and Dizzy Gillespie; Carter; Gillespie, Inc; Havin' a Good Time in Paris.

GILLESPIE, MARIAN   ASCAP 1920
composer, author, pianist

b Muncie, Ind, Jan 26, 1889; d New York, NY, Dec 26, 46. Educ: Columbia Univ; studied with Clarence Carson, Georgia Galvin; St Louis Cons, with Kathryn Lively. Early radio prog dir, actress. Cond educ prog for schs, WNYC, NY. *Songs:* When You Look in the Heart of a Rose; The Want of You; Japanese Garden; Twilight Lullaby; Doubts; Ashes of Dreams; Bring Back the Golden Days; Assurance; Soul of a Rose.

GILLETTE, LELAND JAMES (JIMMY LEE, EDITH   ASCAP 1954
BERGDAHL, LEE JAMES, KIRK PATRICK)
composer, author

b Indianapolis, Ind, Oct 30, 12. Educ: Hyde Park High Sch, Chicago, Ill. Musician, singer, radio announcer, prog dir & musical dir, Chicago, WAAF, WBBM, WJJD, WIND, CBS, NBC, 33-44; phonograph record producer, Capitol Records, Hollywood, Calif, 44-65; independent producer, records & TV, Hollywood, 66-73; A & R producer for Tex Ritter, Nat King Cole, Dean Martin, Kay Starr, Guy Lombardo, Stan Kenton, Alvino Rey, King Sisters, Four Freshmen, Nelson Riddle, Ray Anthony, Freddy Martin, Jan Garber, Margaret Whiting, Jimmy Wakely & Tex Williams. Chief Collabrs: Robert MacGimsey, Lou Busch, Tex Ritter, Nat Cole, Oakley Haldeman, Nelson Riddle, Ray Anthony. *Songs:* Carbon the Copy Cat; Lyrics: That's What I Like About the West; Tom's Tune; Brush Those Tears From Your Eyes; Your Love. *Instrumental Works:* Foghorn Boogie; Dream Girl; Dancing Over the Waves; Easter Isle; Love Tides.

GILLIS, DON   ASCAP 1946
composer, author, conductor

b Cameron, Mo, June 17, 12; d Columbia, SC, Jan 10, 78. Educ: Tex Christian Univ, student cond, trombone scholarship, BA, BM & hon MusD; NTex Teachers Col, MM. Band dir & music fac, Tex Christian Univ, 7 yrs. Staff trombonist, comp & music dir, Ft Worth, Tex. Guest cond, bands & orchs throughout US; also Orch de Camera, Rome. Producer, NBC Symph Concerts cond by Toscanini. Vpres, Nat Music Camp, Interlochen, 45-62. Chmn dept arts, Dallas Baptist Col, Tex, 68-73; comp-in-residence & dir, Ctr for Media Arts Studies, Univ SC, Columbia, 73-78. *Songs:* The Alamo; The Raven; Thomas Wolfe, American. *Instrumental Works:* Symphony No 5-1/2; Portrait of a Frontier Town; The Man Who Invented Music; Tulsa—A Symphonic Poem in Oil; This Is Our America; A Symphony for Fun; Short Overture to an Unwritten Opera; January, February, March; The Dance Symphony; Land of Wheat; A Ceremony of Allegiance; Alice in Orchestralia; Four Scenes From Yesterday; The Coming of the Kings; Symphony X; Stage Works: Gift of the Magi; The Nazarene; Behold the Man.

GILLIS, RICHARD W   ASCAP 1968
composer, author

b Hollywood, Calif, Dec 15, 38. Singer, guitarist & songwriter, 65- *Songs:* Moon Song; Butterfly Mornings; CB Santa Claus; Themes: The Ballad of Cable Hogue; The Bees; Macabra.

GILLIS, SYLVESTER   ASCAP 1954
composer, author, musician

b Brooklyn, NY, Dec 29, 1899. Educ: High sch. Played prof baseball, 4 yrs. Toured with dance bands, US & Can. *Songs:* My Hometown; Every Christmas Morning; & New York Giants football team off song.

GILLMAN, CAROLYN ANNETTE   ASCAP 1972
composer, singer

b Plant City, Fla, Apr 18, 38. Educ: Plant City Sch; studied with Jacque Abram; specialized in music & studied voice with Everett Anderson, Univ San Francisco. Publ with Paragon, 77; recorded on Greentree Label of Benson Co; writer, arr & singer with group Revelation of All Three; TV, studio musician, concerts. *Songs:* Stand Up Together; The Lord Will Go Before You; This Generation Shall Not Pass; Resurrection Power; And He's Ever Interceding.

GILMAN, HAZEL INEZ (GIL GEORGE)   ASCAP 1958
author

b Bisbee, Ariz, Feb 21, 04. Educ: Los Angeles County Sch Nursing, RN, 24; Univ Calif, Los Angeles, AF (Eng literature), 28. Nurse at Disney Studios; writer for TV shows incl the original "Mickey Mouse Club", "From All of Us", "Chip & Dale" & "The Simple Things." Chief Collabrs: Paul Smith, George Bruns, Oliver Wallace, Joseph Dubin, Frank Marks, Jimmy Dodd. *Songs:* Pioneer's Prayer; Light in the Forest; Tonka; Together Time.

GILMORE, CHARLOTTE POLITTE   ASCAP 1973
composer, author, keyboardist

b Somerville, Mass, Dec 5, 35. Educ: Culver Stockton Col; Pacific Christian Col; Harbor Col; Cleveland Chiropractic Col. Prof dancer, 51-53; music, 54- Chief Collabr: John Rowin Jr. *Songs:* Raw Sugar; Don't Mess With Me; Funky Business; I'm Your Shadow; I'm Your Woman; Lyrics: Rambler; It's Your Love; Music: 5/4; Sauda; Music Is My Conversation; Vulcan Dreams.

GILROY, JOHN   ASCAP 1958
composer
b New York, NY, Feb 5, 1872; d New York, NY, May 8, 37. Appeared in vaudeville & musicals with wife. *Songs:* Don't Go in the Lion's Cage Tonight.

GINASTERA, ALBERTO   ASCAP 1963
lecturer
b Buenos Aires, Arg, Apr 11, 16. Educ: Nat Cons, Buenos Aires. Dean & prof in univs & cons, Arg; dir, Latin Am Ctr for High Musical Studies, Rockefeller Found/Di Tella Found, 61-70. Prof emeritus, Arg Cath Univ, 66. Dr HC, Yale Univ, 75. Received many comns by opera houses, major orchs, found, solo performers, fests & others, also many nat & int distinctions incl the decoration of the Officier de l'Ordre des Arts et Lettres du Gouvernement de France. Guggenheim Fellowship, 45-47; Deutscher Akedemischer Austanschdienst & Ford Found, 65. Hon mem, Univ Chile, 50; Academia Nacional de Bellas Artes, Arg, 57; Academia Brasileira de Musica, 58; Am Acad Arts & Sci, 65; Am Acad Arts & Letters, 68; Inst France, 70; Royal Swedish Acad Music, 75; Int Music Coun of the UNESCO, 80. *Instrumental Works:* Chorus and Orchs: Psalm 150; Turbae ad Passionem Gregorianam; Concertos: Piano Concerto No 1 and 2; Cello Concerto No 1 and 2; Harp Concerto; Violin Concerto; Voice & Orch: Cantata Bomarzo; Cantata Para America Magica; Milena; Orch: Variaciones Concertantes; Pampeana No 3; Estudios Sinfonicos; Glosses Sobre Temes de Pau Casals; Concerto per Corde; also others; Chamber Music: Serenata on the Love Poems of Neruda; String Quartets No 1, 2 and 3; Piano Quartet; Instrumental and Vocal: Many works for piano, voice, organ, guitar, cello & others.

GINSBERG, SOL (VIOLINSKY)   ASCAP 1920
composer, pianist, violinist
b Kiev, Russia, July 4, 1885; d Binghamton, NY, May 5, 63. Came to US, 01. Music dir, Williams Bros, Pittsburgh. Vaudeville entertainer, US & abroad. Gag-writer for early TV, incl Milton Berle. Wrote music for films. Chief Collabrs: Ben Ryan, Billy Rose, William Raskin. *Songs:* When Francis Dances With Me; Honolulu Eyes; Dancing to the Rhythm of My Heart; You Left Me Out in the Rain; Tum Tum Tumbling in Love; When We Get Together in the Moonlight; Remember Mother's Day.

GINSBURG, GERALD M   ASCAP 1975
composer, educator, pianist
b Lincoln, Nebr, July 7, 32. Educ: Oberlin Col Cons Music, BMus; Manhattan Sch Music, MMus. Studied comp with Roy Harris, piano with Rudolph Ganz. Debut recital, Carnegie Hall, 74. Performed: Bi-Centennial Parade of Am Music at Kennedy Ctr, 76, Alice Tully Hall, 77, Nat Arts Club, Liederkranz Club, Willa Cather Pioneer Memorial & NY Singing Teachers' Asn.

GIOE, JOSEPH GUISEPPE   ASCAP 1963
composer, teacher, conductor
b Caltanisetta, Italy, Sept 4, 1890; d New York, NY, Oct 8, 57. Educ: Studied music with Ricotta, Orlando & De Santis, Caltanisetta, 00-06; studied with Leotti, Mondrone & Gilda Rutta, US, 06-09. Comp first opera, "Il Dottore del Villagio," 09 & wrote 11 other operas; songwriter; had many songs recorded on piano rolls & discs, early 20's; orch leader: Glen Island Casino, 14; Pathe Film Co, 19; Piccadily Theater; Old Hippodrome. Had own radio prog, "Gioe Music Hour," WCAD, 28; arr; taught at Metrop Opera House Studio until 57. Chief Collabrs: R Cordiferro, P L Esposito. *Songs:* Music: I' M'arricordo 'e Napule; Occhi Appassionati; Fascino Infranto; Ammore e' Core; Ammore Sincero; Ben Turnata Primavera; Caruso Mmieza 'll' angeli; Francesca; Lettera a Momma; Morena Mia; Non Ti Conosco Piu; Pavero Core Mio; Scurdatavene; Surriento Bello Mio; Tarantella Traduta; Torna Sul Mar; Visione. *Instrumental Works:* Piano Concerto; Violin Rhapsody; 2 overtures; orchestral suite; Adriana; Cuore Sincero; Fior Gentile; Flavia; Fra Diavlo; Gli Aspiranti Bandisti; La Rondinella; Siciliana Mazurka; Tutti in Fiesta.

GIOVANNINI, CAESAR   ASCAP 1956
composer
b Chicago, Ill, Feb 26, 25. Educ: Chicago Cons Music, BM(piano), MM(comp). Began music studies at age 5; enrolled, Chicago Cons Music at age 8; pianist, US Navy Band, Washington, DC, 45-46. Joined NBC Chicago Staff Orch, 49. Pianist & comp music for bands at educ level. *Instrumental Works:* Concert Band: Overture in B-Flat; Chorale and Capriccio; Alla Barocco; Jubilance; Symphony in One Movement.

GIRALDI, GEORGIS
See Franklin, Malvin Maurice

GIRARD, ADELE
See Marsala, Adele Girard

GIRVIN, SHARON   ASCAP 1978
composer
b Chicago, Ill, Aug 10, 31. Educ: Chicago Sch Syst; Wright Jr Col; studied privately with Dick Girvin. Comp of film & TV background music. *Songs & Instrumental Works:* Wild Kingdom.

GLADSTONE, JERRY   ASCAP 1956
author, educator
b New York, NY, May 6, 23. Educ: High sch; studied with Walter Bishop, Buddy Kaye. 300 commercials written & aired incl; Arrowhead Drinking Waters, Treesweet Frozen Orange Juice, Nesbitt's Soft Drinks, Kelvinator Kitchen Appliances & others. 490 songs under contract, publ & recorded. Former lyric ed & staff writer for Mills Music. Owns & conducts lyric sch. Mem, Nat Acad Popular Music; Am Guild Authors & Comp. Chief Collabrs: Matt Dennis, Josef Myrow, Lew Spence, Lyn Murray, Terry Gibbs, Gene De Paul, Al De Lory, Jimmie Haskell, Bob Friedman, Larry Fotine, Juan Tizol, Ken Lane. *Songs:* Lyrics: One Step From Nowhere; There I Was in Love; There's a Song in the Heart of Paree; It's a Man's World; The Way of a Wanderer; All in My Mind; You Know All the Answers; Nina; In Days Gone By; Coco, The Corduroy Cocker Spaniel; The Entertainer; Blues for Breakfast; White Roses (From a Blue Valentine); The Lorelei; Me and My Big Ideas; The River and I; The Wind; Q'est-Ce C'est L'Mour; Thanks for Nothing; Via Veneto; Nobody Cares; Nena; Fast Movin' Mama; What Fools We Mortals Be; Too Young for Love.

GLARUM, L STANLEY   ASCAP 1955
composer, conductor, educator
b Portland, Ore, Apr 19, d Seaside, Ore, Dec 24, 76. d. Educ: Olaf Col, BM; Univ Wash, MA, Danforth scholarship. High sch teacher & supvr, 5 yrs. Accompanist & arr, radio & concert, 10 yrs. Chaplain's asst, WW II. Church organist & choirmaster, 34. Music fac, Lewis & Clark Col, 47, chmn music dept, 59. *Songs:* Be Merciful Unto Me; Offer Unto God Thanksgiving; They That Know Thy Name; Bow Down Thine Ear; Be Still and Know; Create in Me a Clean Heart, O God; I Will Lift Mine Eyes; What Is Man; Consider My Meditation; O Clap Your Hands; O Come Let Us Sing; Praise Ye the Lord; Blessed Are They; Blessed Be the Lord; Alleluia! Alleluia!; Dearest Jesus Draw Thou Near Me; Let Them Shout for Joy; Search Me, O God; Blessed Is He; In Thee, O Lord; Trust in the Lord; All Things Work Together for Good; Seek Ye First the Kingdom; I Sought the Lord; Praise to Him, Alleluia!; Our Father Who Art in Heaven; Praise Ye Forever; My Soul Doth Wait; A Choral Prayer; Fanfare for Thanksgiving; Lord Hosanna in the Highest; Exalt Ye; Thy Word Is a Lamp; Sing Aloud Unto God; Blessed Is the Man; Unto Thee Will I Sing; Rejoice in the Lord; The Stars; When One Knows Thee; The Bells Do Ring; Ask and It Shall Be Given You; Alleluia! Sing Hosanna; Hast Thou Forsaken Me; Make Joyful Noise Unto God; A Babe Is Born; Easter Carol; Worship Him With Song; Great Is the Lord; Peace I Leave With You; Six Introit Responses; Be Glad in the Lord; Bless the Lord O My Soul; The Lord Liveth; My Soul Doth Magnify the Lord; Music: God of All Nations (arr); The Bells At Speyer; Brumbasken I Bumba; I Saw a Stranger Yestreen; Wisdom; The Choir Invisible; To Sail Beyond the Sunset; Sing Praises; The Beatitudes; Oh Be Joyful. Come Unto Me; He That Dwelleth; Remember Now Thy Creator; I Will Extol Thee, O Lord.

GLASER, DONALD HOWARD   ASCAP 1976
composer, singer
b San Diego, Calif, Dec 5, 41. Educ: Stanford Univ, AB(political sci), 63; Univ Calif, Los Angeles, LLB, 66; studied classical piano with var jazz artists. Practicing lawyer, San Diego, 70- Comp (music & lyrics), singer, jazz pianist & drummer; performs with own jazz trio in nightclubs; producer of var albums. *Songs:* San Diego; Love; Baby I'm All I've Got; Strawberry Jam. *Instrumental Works:* Caral.

GLASER, HY   ASCAP 1960
composer, author
b New York, NY, Sept 4, 23. Educ: Columbia Univ. Began as short story writer, changed to lyric writing; have written many publ songs & jingles for radio & TV. Gave lyric writing seminars at Hofstra Univ. Author of bk "How to Write Lyrics That Make Sense...& Dollars." Partner with wife Lynn in Ultrasound Records Co, deals with educ materials sold to schs & libraries. Chief Collabrs: Jamie Glaser, Lynn Glaser, Randy Glaser, Jerry Solomon, Sam Glaser, Sy Muskin, Sy Mann, Pim Thomas. *Songs:* Lyrics: A Rag a Bone and a Hank of Hair; I Am Curious; Here Am I Without My Valentine; The Lonely Hours; The City Is a Jungle.

GLASER, LYNN   ASCAP 1973
author
b New York, NY, Nov 12, 34. Educ: NY Univ, BS(educ). Writer of lyrics for children's educ records. Co-owner Ultrasound Record Co. Chief Collabrs: Hy Glaser, Jamie Glaser. *Songs:* Lyrics: All About Colors; There's Nobody Just Like Me; Don't Be Afraid to Be Afraid; I Like Me; Looking for a Friend.

GLASER, SAM   ASCAP 1959
author
b New York, NY, Dec 3, 12. Educ: High sch. Pianist. Had own band at age 13; now a salesman in the wine & liquor indust. Chief Collabrs: Hy Glaser, Jerry Solomon, Sy Mann, Sy Muskin, Jamie Glaser. *Songs:* Lyrics: Warm, Sweet, Tender and Dreamy; A Rag, a Bone and a Hank of Hair; The Minimum Wage; The Other Guy; If I Ever Love Again.

GLASER, SIOMA   ASCAP 1963
composer, author, producer
b Odessa, Russia, Aug 5, 19. Educ: Israel & Paris; NY Univ; Ambassador Col, Calif. US citizen, 42. Actor films, Israel. War correspondent, Brit Palestinian Press Bureau; journalist, Czech & Israel; US Army war correspondent, Am Europ Publ, 36-42, US Army attached services, 42-45. Taught merchandising & salesmanship, Manhattan Bus Inst. Dir, Bway Artists, NY; dir & producer, Israel Motion Pictures & Int Newsreel Co. Dir concerts, Carnegie Hall & Universal Theatre Ballet, NY. Producer & dir TV opera; dir & voice coach, Opera-tunity Workshop; music & drama critic, Phenix Features, NY, 45-54. Taught at Yeshivah, Mesifta Arugath Habosem, Brooklyn, NY, 55. Dir & producer records, 3-D. Music & drama critic, "Jewish World"; ed & revised musical bks. Mem, Nat Acad of TV Arts & Sci, Am Fedn Musicians & Int Platform Asn. *Songs:* When Christmas Comes; Caro Amor; An American in Napoli; The Gondolier's Love Call. *Scores:* Stage: The Song of the American Jew; My Born Enemy.

GLASER, VICTORIA MERRYLEES (A COPENAHGEN)   ASCAP 1956
composer, author, teacher
b Amherst, Mass, Sept 11, 18. Educ: Harvard Univ, AB(cum laude), 40, MA, 43; theory Walter Piston & Nadia Boulanger, flute Georges Laurent, piano Frederick Tillotson, later voice with Bernard Barbeau, New Eng Cons; choirmaster cert AGO, 61. Sang Belinda in Purcell's "Dido & Aeneas," Harvard Univ, 39. Instr music, Wellesley Col, 43-46; chmn theory dept, Dana Hall Sch, 45-59; teacher theory, New Eng Cons, 57- & Longy Sch Music, 73- Hon mention, Gedok Competition, Ger, 62. "Birthday Fugue" performed Boston Symph Youth Concerts, 60 & Boston Symph Pops, 65 & 67; "Two Pieces for Orchestra," New Eng Cons Youth Orch, 71; "Three Carols," dedication to Boston Pub Libr Wing, 73; "Music for Piano C Three Performers," New Eng Cons, 78. Author bk "Training Musicianship," 76. *Songs:* Third Concord Anthem Book; Choral arrangements incl: Twelve Days of Christmas; Biibidi-Bobbidi-Bo. *Instrumental Works:* Telemann Airs (arr trumpet, organ).

GLASON, BILLY   ASCAP 1950
author, teacher, comedy writer
b Boston, Mass, Sept 10, 04. Educ: Phillips Grammar Sch; English & Roxbury High Schs, Boston. Singer for local music publ, Boston, later became a comedian; headlined all vaudeville circuits. Author: "How to Master the Ceremonies"; "Fun-Master Gag Files"; "Fun-Master Book of Parodies"; "Giant Encyclopedia of Classified Gags" (20 vols); also The Comedian, monthly service for comedians. Creator, Am Guild of Variety Artists. Mem, Am Acad of Humor, Hollywood Comedy Club & The Authors Guild. Chief Collabrs: J Fred Coots, Howard Johnson, Lou Pollack, Frank Davis, M K Jerome, Abner Silver, Milton Ager. *Songs:* Why Do They Always Say No?; Sing a Song; Croon a Tune; He'll Always Be One of Those Guys; Hugo; There Are Two Sides to Every Story; Tell Them They're Beautiful; Thievin' Colleen; I Don't Want a Doctor; Suppose; I Hadda Walk in to Find You Out; I'd Give a Lot to Know Just What My Sweet Sweet Mama's Got; That's Me Without You.

GLASS, PAUL   ASCAP 1967
author, educator
b Lithuania, Mar 1, 10. Educ: Columbia Univ, BS & MA; Inst Musical Art, studied violin with Naoum Blinder & Paul Kochanski; comp with Bernard Wagenaar. Prof violinist for yrs. Prof music, City Univ New York, 47-75, emer prof, 75- Did many arr, author bks & articles in music jour. Deems Taylor Award, ASCAP 72. State Dept Inst lect Am Music at var univs & cols. Chief Collabrs: Louis C Singer, Norval Church. *Songs:* Books with Music: Singing Soldiers (A History of the Civil War in Song); Songs of the Sea; Song of the West; Songs of the Forests and Rivers; Songs of the Mountain Folk; Songs of the Towns and Cities. *Instrumental Works:* String Orch Transc: masterworks for string orch, incl Organ Concerto (Bach); Concerto (Scarlatti); Suite from the Fairy Queen (Purcell); Concerto for String Orchestra (Avison).

GLASS, PAUL EUGENE   ASCAP 1961
author
b Los Angeles, Calif, Nov 19, 34. Educ: Univ Southern Calif, BM, studied with Ingolf Dahl; Tanglewood, studied with Boris Blacher; studied with Geoffredo Petrassi, Rome; Princeton Univ, studied with Roger Sessions; studied with Witold Lutostawski, Warsaw. Began comp at early age. Rec'd many awards, incl Fulbright, Franklin Murphy, Jr, Alfred Hertz Memorial, Minister of Culture, Warsaw & Reine Marie-Jose, Geneva. Has written film & TV music, 57- Now prof theory & comp, Acad Ars et Musica, Curio, Switz; comp vocal, chamber & symph music. *Songs & Instrumental Works:* Rondo for Violin and Piano; Quintet for Clarinet and String Quartet; Trio for Flute, Violoncello and Piano; Music for Brass and Percussion; Eschatos (ballet, chamber orch); Tre pezzi per Violino e Pianoforte; Sinfonia 1959 (large orch); Concerto for Violoncello and Orchestra (Geneva Prize); Symphonic Suite (large orch); Trio for Flute, Clarinet and Bassoon; E Changes for 16 Players; String Quintet (Suite pour Soeur et Frere); Woodwind Quintet No 2; Quartet for Flute, Clarinet, Viola, Violoncello; Cinq Chansons pour une Princesse Errante; Sahassavagga (children's choir); Wie ein Naturlant (chamber ens); Quartet for Oboe and String Trio; Saxophone Quartet (comn by Swiss Saxophone Quartet, Bale, Switz). *Scores:* Film: Abductors; Interregnum (Venice Prize); Fear No More; Narcissus; Lady in a Cage; Nightmare in the Sun; Bunny Lake Is Missing; Test of Violence (Moscow, Cork, Venice, Edinburgh & Berlin Prizes); Catch My Soul; Overlord (Berlin

Film Prize); To the Devil a Daughter; TV: Sole Survivor; Five Desperate Women; Sandcastles; TV series: Jacques Cousteau; Night Gallery; Sarge.

GLASS, PHILIP
composer, musician
b Baltimore, Md, Jan 31, 37. Educ: Univ Chicago, AB, 56; Juilliard Sch, MS(comp), 64; studied with Nadia Boulanger, Paris, 64-66. Comp-in-residence, Pittsburgh Pub Schs, 62-64. Founder, Philip Glass Ens, 68, performer on var US & Europ concert tours, 68- Founder, record co, Chatham Square Productions, New York, 72. Co-comp, opera "Einstein on the Beach." Recipient, Broadcast Music Indust award, 60, Lado Prize, 61, Benjamin award, 61 & 62, Young Composer's award Ford Found, 64-66, Fulbright grant, comp, 66-67, Found for Contemporary Perf Arts, 70-71, Changes, Inc, 71-72, NEA, 74 & 75 & Menil Found, 74. *Albums:* Music With Changing Parts; Music in Similar Motion; Music in Fifths; Music in Contrary Motion; Music in Twelve Parts; North Star.

GLASSER, ALBERT   ASCAP 1950
composer, orchestrator, conductor
b Chicago, Ill, Jan 25, 16. Educ: Univ Southern Calif, Alchin Chair Found scholarship; studied with Arne Oldberg. Music comp for Frank Capra Spec Services Dept, Off War Info Radio Shows for overseas broadcasts; comp & cond, "Hopalong Cassidy Radio Shows", "Tarzan Radio Shows" & "Clyde Beatty Radio Shows." Orchestrated, MGM Studios, 43-48; musical dir & comp, Lippert Productions, 47-53. Winner of Variety 10 Most Prominant Orchr, 46. Cond, Hollywood Bowl Gershwin Night, 47. *Songs:* I Remember Your Love; Some Day; Shirley-Shirley; Who Knows; Happy Birthday Dr Horwitz; Give Me One More Tomorrow. *Instrumental Works:* Concert Works: Concert for Violin and Orchestra; 2 Preludes (orch); Pied Piper of Hamlin (orch); Sextete for Flute, Piano and String Quartet; Concerto for String Bass and Symphony Orchestra; Sonata (viola & piano); The Raven (tone poem); Interludes for Flute and Piano; Orchestrations: New York World's Fair Suite (Grofe); The Matterhorn (Friml); Exodus from Hong Kong (Friml); Faster and Faster (Friml); Champaigne Waltz (Grofe). *Scores:* TV Background: The Cisco Kid; Big Town; Heart of the City; Dr Jekyll and Mr Hyde in Harlam (Am folk opera); Motion Pictures: Huk; The Boss; The Cisco Kid series; Flight to Hong Kong; Grand Canyon; Paris Model; Return of Wildfire; Tokyo File 212; Valerie; The Amazing Colossal Man; Fantastic Puppet People; War of the Colossal Beast; The Boy and the Pirates; Top of the World; Invasion USA; Geisha Girl; Best Generation; Air Patrol; Beginning of the End; The Big Caper; John Smith and Pocahontas; The Cyclops; Destination 60,000; The Gay Amigo; Girl in the Woods; The High Powered Rifle; Unmei; When Hell Broke Loose; High School Confidential; Cop Hater; Motorcycle Gang; The Mugger; Prehistoric World; The Spider; Bandit Queen; 3 Desperate Men; Apache Chief; Hollywood Varieties; The Indestructable Man; I Shot Billy the Kid; I Shot Jesse James; The Last of the Wild Horses; Lecoque; Man of Conflict; Murder Will Out; Neanderthal Man; Domo, Dumo-The Shark God; Satan's Cradle; Street of Sinners; Tormented; Tough Assignment; Treasure of Monte Cristo; 20,000 Eyes; The Unbelievable; Urubu; Western Pacific Agent; Four Boys and a Gun; Buckskin Lady; Please Murder Me; Viking Women.

GLAZER, MELVIN JACOB   ASCAP 1960
author
b Jersey City, NJ, Feb 25, 31. Educ: Rutgers Univ, Col Pharmacy, BS. Lyricist. Chief Collabrs: Sammy Fain, Stephan Weiss, Aaron Schroeder, Sol Marcus, Bennie Benjamin, Arthur Segal, Jack Perricone, Steve Schlaks. *Songs:* Lyrics: Speedway; Guess Again; Bobby, Bobby, Bobby; Your Ma Said You Cried in Your Sleep Last Night; The Touchables; The Touchables in Brooklyn (sequel); If at First You Don't Succeed (Try-Try Again).

GLAZER, THOMAS ZACHARIAH   ASCAP 1949
composer, author, singer
b Philadelphia, Pa, Sept 2, 14. Educ: High sch, Philadelphia, 3 yrs; music sch, 6 months; City Col New York. Played tuba/bass sch jazz bands, symph & brass bands, high sch. Sang in church choirs professionally, Corpus Christi & St Ignatius Loyola. Worked at Libr of Cong, DC, 41-43. Active in church choirs, folksinging, songwriting & author numerous bks & musical. *Songs:* A Worried Man; Old Soldiers Never Die; Lyrics: Melody of Love; Skokiaan; On Top of Spaghetti. *Scores:* Film/TV: A Face in the Crowd.

GLEASON, JACKIE   ASCAP 1953
composer, conductor, actor
b Brooklyn, NY, Feb 26, 16. Educ: Pub schs. Emcee, carnival barker, daredevil driver & DJ in amateur shows. Comedian in nightclubs. Featured on TV show, "The Life of Riley" & own show, "The Jackie Gleason Show" & "Jackie Gleason's American Scene Magazine." Cond orch for records. Appeared in Bway musicals: "Follow the Girls"; "Along Fifth Avenue"; "Take Me Along" & in films: "Navy Blues"; "The Hustler"; "Requiem for a Heavyweight"; "Gigot"; "Papa's Delicate Condition." *Instrumental Works:* Melancholy Serenade; Lover's Rhapsody; Glamour; To a Sleeping Beauty; On the Beach. *Scores:* Film background: Gigot.

GLENN, FAREIL (FAREIL SANDERS)   ASCAP 1975
composer, author
b New York, NY, Feb 20, 49. Educ: Cooper Jr High 109; Washington Irving, steno, switchboard & bus machines; special sch of counseling; Manhattan

Community Col, bus admin; Richmond Col, AA(English). Studies music; writer songs, poetry & short stories; counselor. Chief Collabrs: Zachory Sanders, Roberta Flack. *Songs:* Lyrics: Rock Me Arms.

GLENN, TONY
See Bessire, Antony Glenn

GLENN, (EVANS) TYREE   ASCAP 1956
composer, conductor, vibraphonist
b Corsicana, Tex, Nov 23, 12; d Englewood, NJ, May 18, 74. Joined Tommy Mills orch, Washington, DC, 34. Went to NY, 36. Played in orchs, incl Eddie Barefield, Eddie Mallory, Benny Carter & Cab Calloway. Toured Europe with Don Redman, 46 & with Duke Ellington orch, 5 yrs. Staff musician & actor, WPIX, NY & staff musician, CBS Radio, NY. Cond own quartet, nightclubs. Led groups on TV, 52-65. Toured with Louis Armstrong group, 65-71. *Songs & Instrumental Works:* Waycross Walk; Sterling Steel; After the Rain; Roulette; How Could You Do a Thing Like That to Me; Sultry Serenade.

GLESS, ELEANOR MATTIE   ASCAP 1963
composer, author
b Willoughby, Ohio, Feb 7, 08. Educ: Ravenna High Sch; Port Charlotte Univ, Fla, (nursing); Newspaper Inst Am, New York, (journalism training, specialized course in TV, radio & dramatic writing); Hon BA, Univ Md. Poetry, sonnet & story writer; poem "Whity Lawson" recorded for radio WEFG for The Personal Poetry Prog of Quality Readings. Chief Collabrs: Harry Stride, Tresa Tate, Roger Mathews, Sandy Stanton, Hugh Disher & Ray Rivera. *Songs:* Twistin on the Moon; Flower Girl's Dream; Lyrics: Build Your Home in Heaven; Snow Bows; Sun and Fun Time; Same Old Moon; Dancing and Romancing With You; The Purple Heart; Open Skies; I Wish I Were a Christmas Tree; Lean on His Shoulder; Derby Downs; Square Dance Polka; Derby Feavor; Taxation Blues; Precious Silver Crown; Red Shoes; Doodlyn Dan; Ravenna Rock (Ohio Rock Boogie); Home Run Polka. *Instrumental Works:* Scouts Honor March; Blue Rainbows. *Albums:* Memory Book of Dreams.

GLICK, JESSE G M   ASCAP 1925
author, publisher
b Ansonia, Ohio, Jan 1, 1874; d San Francisco, Calif, Nov 21, 38. Educ: Pub schs. Mem, Kansas City Glee Club. Mgr of own music publ co. Owner of vaudeville theatre, Topeka, Kans. *Songs:* Pale Moon; My Love of the Sunset Sea; Sarita; My Waikiki Ukulele Girl; Guess I'm Falling in Love; Fair Dove. *Scores:* Operettas: Rose of the Antilles; Nananlam.

GLICKMAN, FRED   ASCAP 1949
composer, author, violinist
b Chicago, Ill, Sept 22, 03. Educ: Columbia Sch Music; Chicago Musical Col; studied violin with Harry Diamond, Ludwig Becker, Richard Czerwonky & Victor Young. Violinist in dance bands & symph orchs. Mem staff, NBC. Played in Bway musicals & as soloist. Cond own orch. Writer of spec material. First violinist, film studios, 20 yrs. Had own recording & publ cos. Chief Collabrs: Hy Heath, Johnny Lange, Charles Newman. *Songs:* Mule Train; Little Old Band of Gold; Two Brothers; Angel of Mine.

GLICKMAN, MORT H
composer, arranger
b Chicago, Ill, Dec 6, 1898; d Los Angeles, Calif, 1952. Educ: Pub schs in Chicago. Moved to Calif & began motion picture producing, 39; worked for Republic Studios; produced motion pictures, serials & early TV serials incl, "G-man Versus the Black Dragon", "Dare Devil of the West", "Spy Smasher", "The Perils of Nyoka", "King of the Mounties", "Jessie James Rides Again", "Thundering Trails", "The Black Widow", "G-men Never Forget", "The Secret-Service in Darkest Africa" & "Danger of the Canadian Mounties."

GLICKMAN, SUSAN RAE   ASCAP 1978
lyricist, author
b Los Angeles, Calif, Jan 23, 45. Educ: Buddy Kaye, Univ Calif, Los Angeles; Annette Tucker & Arthur Hamilton, ASCAP West Workshop. Chief Collabrs: Fred Werner, Sheila Styron. *Songs:* Lyrics: Flo's Yellow Rose (TV theme).

GLINES, JOHN   ASCAP 1965
composer, author
b Santa Maria, Calif, Oct 11, 33. Educ: Piedmont High Sch; Yale Univ, BA, 55. Began as actor-performer playing off-Bway & touring in clubs; wrote "Captain Kangaroo," 65-71; songwriter for numerous children's progs. Co-founder, non-profit arts orgn, The Glines, 76; scriptwriter "Sesame Street," 80- *Songs:* Off-Bway: God Bless Coney; Gulp!

GLOGAU, JACK   ASCAP 1914
composer, author, pianist
b New York, NY, Dec 31, 1886; d New York, Oct 30, 53. Joined staff of music publ, 10. Wrote spec material. Scored early film musicals. Pioneer in modern music printing practices. Charter mem, ASCAP. Chief Collabrs: Al Piantadosi, Robert King, Herbert Magidson, Will Rossiter. *Songs & Instrumental Works:* On the Shores of Italy; Fashionette; Lucky Day; King Sol.

GLOSUP, EDGAR D (EDDIE DEAN)   ASCAP 1965
composer, singer, entertainer
b Posey, Tex, July 9, 07. Educ: High sch, Sulphur Springs, Tex; studied voice. Appeared on radio shows, Chicago & Midwest, 33-39 & also appeared in own western picture series, 46-48; singer night clubs & TV. Pioneer Award, Acad Country Music, 78; recording artist, Shasta Records. Chief Collabrs: Dearest Dean, Hal Blair, Hal Sothern, Glen Strange, Freddie Hart. *Songs:* One Has My Name; Hank Williams Guitar; Didn't Know What Lonesome Was; The Lonely Hours; There's a Time; Courtin' Time; Tumbleweed Trail; Black Hills; Stars Over Texas; Sunny San Juan; Wild Prairie Rose; Boogie-Woogie Cowboy, West to Glory; 1501 Miles of Heaven; Home Beyond the Blue; Song of the Range; Give Me Love; Country Blues; Substitutes and Imitations; I'm Back in the Game; Another Time-Another Place; Write Him Off as Just a Friend; Cotton Pickin' Machine; One More Time Around; Save a Little-Spend a Little; Music: I Dreamed of a Hillbilly Heaven.

GLOSUP, LORENE ST CLARE (DEAREST DEAN,   ASCAP 1975
LORENE DEAN)
composer
b Yankton, SDak, Oct 4, 11. Educ: Yankton High Sch. Pvt secy. Served on bd of dir, Acad Country Music, 60. Chief Collabr: Eddie Dean (husband). *Songs:* Lyrics: One Has My Name; The Lonely Hours; Write Him Off as Just a Friend; Didn't Know What Lonesome Was; 1501 Miles of Heaven; A Heart Will Not Be Silent Long; From the Crib to the Cross; Walk Beside Me.

GLOVER, CHARLES JOSEPH (JUSTIN STRANGE)   ASCAP 1978
composer, author, singer
b Detroit, Mich, Sept 26, 51. Educ: Macon Jr Col. Started first band, nightclubs, 70; concert promotion, Ezrah Pike & Frankenstein, 72 & Last American Heroes, 76. Producer; formed Dream Seven Music & became songwriter for Peer Southern Music, 78; formed Heaven Sent Records, 80. *Songs:* Gone Wild; Pretty Poison; The Kid Next Door; Hold on to My Love; Starseekeers; Dream Control; Glimpse of Heaven.

GLOVER, DAVID CARR, JR   ASCAP 1959
composer, arranger, editor
b Portsmouth, Va, Apr 7, 25. Educ: Bristow Hardin Sch Music; studies with Guy Maier. Composer & ed, Schroeder & Gunther, 49-54 & Hansen Publ, 55-61. Over 700 bks & 500 solo sheets publ. Given over 600 music teachers' workshops, US, Australia & Japan. *Instrumental Works:* Piano Library; Contemporary Organ Library; Sacred Music Library; Entertainment Series; Studio One (piano libr); Studio Two (organ libr).

GLOVER, JOE   ASCAP 1959
composer, author, conductor
b Westhampton Beach, NY, Feb 6, 03; d. Educ: Univ Pa; studied with Pietro Floridia, Joseph Schillinger, Ernst Toch. Arr, orchs incl Fletcher Henderson & Andre Kostelanetz. With film studios, 7 yrs. Arr, Bway musicals. Life mem & former pres, Am Soc Music Arrangers. *Songs & Instrumental Works:* Over the Top; Melon Street Stomp; Hurricane Rag; Celestial Rag; A Sunday Tune.

GLUCK, JOHN R   ASCAP 1954
composer, author, producer
b Cleveland, Ohio, Aug 7, 25. Educ: Pvt tutoring in music since age 7; Shaker Heights High Sch, Ohio; Case Western Reserve Univ, BA(English). Popular songwriting, 48-70; personal mgr of recording groups, 70-76; theatre comp & producer, 76- Chief Collabrs: Enoch Anderson, Diane Lampert, Herb Wiener, Ben Raleigh, Neval Nader. *Songs:* It's My Party; Up Jumped a Rabbit; Music: Mecca; Trouble Is My Middle Name. *Scores:* Bway show: Why Doesn't Father Come Home?

GLUCKMAN, BERNARD LOUIS   ASCAP 1950
composer, teacher
b Hoboken, NJ, Oct 26, 09. Educ: Univ Mich, BA; Yale Univ Law Sch; Teachers Col, Columbia Univ, MA(music educ). Staff musician, NBC, New York, also in Bway musical. Teacher music, High Sch Music & Art, NY & Manhattan Sch Music & Woodwinds. *Songs:* I'm the Girl Who Married the Man on the Flying Trapeze; A Prayer Is a Wonderful Thing; Kathy; I Love Your Love.

GNAZZO, ANTHONY JOSEPH   ASCAP 1969
composer, author
b New Britain, Conn, Apr 21, 36. Educ: Hartt Col of Music, BMus, 57; Univ Hartford, BA, 63; Brandeis Univ, MFA, 65. Primarily known as composer of electronic music & designer of electronic music instruments/systems. Taught at Simon Fraser Univ, BC, Mills Col, Calif, York Univ, Ont & Univ Calif, Davis. Chief Collabrs: James Cuno, Roger Pritchard. *Songs:* Peace Piece (soprano & piano). *Instrumental Works:* Three Movements for String Quartet; Music for Piano I; Music for Cello and Tape, No 1; Music for Piano III; Profile (vibraphone & tape). Electronic Tape: Variations on a Name by Alden Jenks; Stereo Radio 5: about talking; Certain Aspects of Mechanized Music; Begin Again; Asparagus: (Everybody likes it); Fusion. *Scores:* Compound Skill Fracture (actor, electronic tape & slide projections); Waiting for J B.

GODDARD, GLENDON BOYCE ASCAP 1963
composer
b Albany, Vt, June 29, 1899. Educ: Craftsbury Acad, Vt; Univ Vt, Burlington, Col Med, 28; piano study with Leonard Meretta, 4 yrs. Player clarinet & saxophone in dance bands, Boston area. Became mem, Boston Musician's Union, 23. Gen med pract & anesthesiology, 48 yrs; retired, 76. Comp & arr study, 4 yrs; arr, own music. *Instrumental Works:* Sheffield March; Our Space Frontier March; March—Our Nation's Colors; Moods for Saxophone (solo alto, piano); Music for Choir and Organ for 23rd Psalm.

GODDARD, LEROY A (LEE PENNY)
composer, author
b Venice, Ill, Nov 23, 15. Educ: McKinley High & Crane Tech, Chicago; Gregg Business Col; pvt music study. Wrote comedy songs for "Tom, Dick & Harry", NBC, specialty songs for shows & acts "Lum & Abner", "Ted Lewis", "Mr Kitzel", "The Leo Carillo Show", TV, children's shows "Sheriff John", Los Angeles, "Deputy Dave & Fireman Frank", San Francisco, "Sheriff Tex", Seattle, "Sheriff Scotty", Denver & others for Imperial Records. A&R, Mercury, Imperial & others. *Songs:* Birthday Cake Polka (Put Another Candle on My Birthday Cake); My Adobe Hacienda; Shine on My Boots; A New Ten Gallon Hat; also many more.

GODFREY, ARTHUR ASCAP 1957
composer, author, entertainer
b New York, NY, Aug 31, 03. Educ: Naval Radio Sch, Great Lakes, Ill; Green Lakes Material Sch, Bellevue, DC. Served USN. On radio as Warbling Banjoist, 29, also radio announcer & entertainer with own progs, CBS radio; TV performer with own progs. *Songs:* Magic of Hawaii; Fifty-Second and Madison.

GODFREY, KENNETH ASCAP 1966
composer, author, teacher
b New York, NY, Sept 14, 06. Educ: Canterbury Col, NZ, cert in comp, 4 yrs; Princeton Univ, pvt comp study; flute study with Georges Barrere, 2 yrs & John Amans, 6 yrs. With Nat Orchestral Asn, NY, 3 yrs. Extra flutist, New York Philh Symph, 10 yrs. 1st flutist, El Paso Symph Orch, 3 yrs & Radio City Music Hall, 1 yr. With 266th AGF Band, USA, Ft Bliss, Tex, 3 yrs. Free lance work, var orchs, chamber music groups. Pvt teacher, lectr music. *Instrumental Works:* The Happy Flutist; Double Play (two flutes); Fugue in G Major (three flutes); Two Fugues (two flutes); Petite Serenade (flute solo, piano).

GODFREY, ROBERT H ASCAP 1953
composer, author
b Newbury, Vt, July 31, 05. Educ: High sch. *Songs:* Thirty-five Years Ago; Every Christmas Morning; If All These Things Have Meaning; Who Told You?; Aloha Nui Loa; At the Funny Paper Ball.

GODIOS, JOSEPH THOMAS ASCAP 1973
composer, author, teacher
b Buffalo, NY, Aug 24, 29. Educ: Erie Community Col, Buffalo, NY, 47-48; USN Sch Music, Washington, DC, grad degree, 49; pvt study with Joe Allard, New York, 51-52. Musician, USN, 4 yrs; pvt teaching of saxophone, clarinet, flute & piccolo, 20 yrs; played & cond with travelling bands, 10 yrs; entertainment dir for Buffalo Bill's Football Club (half time shows), 16 yrs; substitute performer with Buffalo Philh Orch; played, Melody Fair & art park shows, Western NY area. Chief Collab: John Baudreau. *Songs:* Music: Bills Battle Cry; Kick off Bills; Fight Bills Fight; Bills Fight Song; Let's Go Bills; Touch Down Bills; Bills Marching Song.

GODOWSKY, LEOPOLD ASCAP 1932
composer, pianist
b Vilna, Russia, Feb 13, 1870; d New York, NY, Nov 21, 38. Educ: Berlin Hochschule; studied with Saint-Säens, Paris; Hon MusD, Curtis Inst. First concert at age 9; toured Russia, Poland & Ger. Toured US, 1884-1885. Taught in Philadelphia & at Chicago Cons. Berlin debut, 1900; performed throughout Europe. Dir, Klaviermeisterschule, Vienna. Settled in NY, 12. *Songs & Instrumental Works:* Renaissance (23 pieces); Walzermasken (24 pieces); Piano Sonata; 3 Symphonic Metamorphoses; Triakontameron (incl Alt Wien); Passacaglia; Prelude and Fugue (for left hand); Phonoramus (Java cycle, 12 pieces); Suite; also 53 pieces on Chopin Etudes; piano transc: Bach sonatas and suites for violin, cello; 12 Schubert songs.

GODWIN, HARRY EASTON ASCAP 1963
author, historian, lecturer
b Washington, DC, Aug 22, 06. Educ: Washington & Lee Univ, BA, 29. Mfr rep automotive parts, 35 yrs. Pres, Jazzette Records, Memphis; bd dirs, Memphis Develop Found & Beale St Develop Corp; vpres, Memphis Cotton Carnival Asn; producer, Jazz Blues Perf, Memphis Mid-South Fair. Chief Collabrs: Narvin Kimball, Alton Purnell, Don Ewell. *Songs:* My Memphis Baby; New Orleans; Lyrics: Jazzman's Blues; Let's All Join Hands; Long Ago.

GOEBERT, ROBERT JACOB ASCAP 1972
composer, educator, trumpeter
b Johnstown, Pa, Mar 24, 20. Educ: Ohio Univ, 4 yrs; Col Music, Cincinnati, Ohio, BMus; Cons of Music, Cincinnati, MMus; Tex Tech Univ; Univ of Tex, Austin; NTex State Univ; comp with Felix Lubunski, Donald Mayor, Leo Sowerby, Merrill Ellis & William Latham; studied trumpet with Aloish Ruby & Herbert Tiemeyer. Trumpet & arr comp while in high sch & col; wrote for bands, 36-41. In WW II. Arr with band, 2 1/2 yrs; lead trumpet in large dance bands, also with 7-piece dance band. Instr, Oklahoma State Univ, 49-50, Univ Kansas City & Odessa State Univ, 50-51 & Tex Col, 51-67; assoc prof of music, Tarrant County Jr Col, 67- *Instrumental Works:* Rhapsody for Four Trumpets; Exulticus Fanfarius; Oom, Goo, Ba; Theme for June; Gabe's Bugle.

GOEHRING, GEORGE ANDREW ASCAP 1957
composer, author, singer
b Philadelphia, Pa, July 16, 33. Educ: Studied piano with Edmond Vichnin & Dorothea Persichetti, comp with Vincent Persichetti, Philadelphia Cons Music. Concert & pop pianist, TV, radio & nightclubs. Recording artist, songwriter under contract with Joy Music, 10 yrs. Chief Collabrs: Dennis O'Brien, Ed Marshall, Aaron Schroeder. *Songs:* Half Heaven-Half Heartache; Hootenanny; You Get Better Looking Every Day; Music: Lipstick on Your Collar; Please Don't Talk to the Lifeguard; Adonis. *Songs & Instrumental Works:* Lady Audley's Secret (17 songs; Bway show).

GOELL, KERMIT ASCAP 1942
composer, author
b New York, NY, Jan 28, 15. Educ: Erasmus Hall High Sch, Brooklyn; Cornell Univ Col Agriculture, BS(agriculture); Frank Lee Forge Studio, vocal study. Studied singing in high sch & wrote songs in col. Farmer, Albany, NY; worked in construction. Songwriter, 40- Served as Flight Instr & Flight Test Engr, WW II. Wrote songs for shows, pictures & recordings. Author, "Pocahontas" & other children's books; ed, "The Sea Grammar, (1627)." Chief Collabrs: Fritz Spielman, Walter Donaldson, Oscar Strauss, Arthur Kent, Mabel Wayne. *Songs:* Clopin Clopint; Luna Rossa; How Wonderful to Know; This Must Be Wrong; America the Beautiful, 1976; Cajun Bow; Keepin' Me Warm for You; The Love That Never Failed; Lyrics: Near You; Wonder When My Baby's Coming Home; Rose Anne of Charing Cross; The Right Kind of Love; Huggin' and Chalkin'; Slowly; Snap Your Fingers; The One Finger Melody; You Won't Forget Me; Where's My Heart?; Que Bueno; Tonight; Since You Went Away; When Our Hearts Were Young and Gay; I Don't Care; An Orchid and a Kiss; Shepherd Serenade; Ever True Evermore; Johnny With the Gentle Hands; Close Your Pretty Eyes; My Love Serenade; Ein Zwei Drei; I Thought It Was Over; Leave It to Your Heart; I Can't Get the You Out of Me. *Scores:* London Shows: Old King Cole; Bolero; Pocahontas; Latin Quarter.

GOEMANNE, NOEL ASCAP 1972
composer, choral director, organist
b Poperinge, Belg, Dec 10, 26. Educ: Lemmens Inst, Mechelen, Belg, grad dipl Laureate; Cons Royal de Liege, Belg, post grad study; studied with Flor Peeters, Staf Nees, Marinus Dejong; Jules Van Nuffel. Regular piano recitals, station NAMUR, Belg Nat Radio Broadcast, 50-51. Became US citizen, 59. Appeared as organist, choral cond, lectr of own works in NAm, Europe & Philippines. Choral cond, organist & teacher. Awards: Manila Inst Sacred Music, 74; Pro Ecclesia award & medal, Vatican, 77, several ASCAP awards. Chief Collabr: Sharon Benge. *Instrumental Works:* Missa Internationalis; Hosanna; Ode to St Cecilia; Fanfare for Festivals; Ode to Love; also over 100 anthems, motets, piano & organ works. *Songs & Instrumental Works:* The Walk.

GOERING, AL ASCAP 1934
composer
b Chicago, Ill, Dec 20, 1898; d Chicago, Apr 16, 63. Educ: High sch. Chief Collabrs: Ben Bernie, Walter Hirsch, Jack Fulton, Caesar Petrillo, Raymond Klages. *Songs:* Who's Your Little Whosis?; One of Us Was Wrong; Holding My Honey's Hand; Paradise Isle; Face to Face; Looks Like a Cold Cold Winter; Heads You Do (and Tails You Don't).

GOES, DERRYL F ASCAP 1975
teacher, musician
b La Crosse, Kans, Sept 9, 29. Educ: Ft Hays State Univ, BA; Colo State Univ, MA. Mem, Stan Kenton & Ralph Marterie Orchs, Johnny Smith & Art Va Damne Quintets. *Instrumental Works:* Bronco Buster (off Denver Bronco Song).

GOETSCHIUS, MARJORIE ASCAP 1946
composer, author, pianist
b Raymond, NH, Sept 23, 15. Educ: Georgian Court Col; Juilliard Sch, studied with James Friskin, Percy Goetschius (grandfather), Bernard Wagenaar, Joseph Schillinger, Maria Stefany (grandmother). Solo pianist & cellist in orch. Pianist & singer on radio; performer in own dramatic shows, 2 yrs. Writer, background music & scripts for network progs. Chief Collabrs: Edna Osser, Jascha Heifetz. *Songs & Instrumental Works:* I Dream of You (More Than You Dream I Do); I'll Always Be With You; The Last Time I Saw You; When You Make Love to Me; The Hora Swingcato; So Much in Love; You're Different; Can I Canoe You Up the River?; Green Grass and Peaceful Pastures; Piano works: Sonata in B; Theme and Variations; Scherzo in Thirds; Rondo; Berceuse; Poetique; Rhapsody in G; Violin works: Lament; Tango del Ensueno; Valse Burlesque; Nebuleuses; Choral: Reminiscence.

GOETZ, E RAY   ASCAP 1914
composer, author, producer
b Buffalo, NY, June 12, 1886; d Greenwich, Conn, June 12, 54. Producer Bway musicals: "As You Were"; "The French Doll"; "Little Miss Bluebeard"; "Paris"; "Fifty Million Frenchmen"; "The New Yorkers." Charter mem, ASCAP, dir, 14-17. Chief Collabrs: A Baldwin Sloane, Silvio Hein, Raymond Hubbell, George Meyer, Jean Schwartz, Pete Wendling, George Gershwin, Edgar Leslie. *Songs:* For Me and My Gal; Who'll Buy My Violets?; Argentina; Let's Be Lonesome Together; So This Is Love; Don't Go in the Lion's Cage Tonight; If You Could Care; Yaaka Hula Hickey Dula; The Life of a Rose; Meet Me in the Shadows; The Land of Going to Be; Boom.

GOETZL, THOMAS MAXWELL   ASCAP 1964
composer, author
b Chicago, Ill, May 31, 43. Educ: Univ Calif, Berkeley, BA(psychol), 65, JD, 69. Songwriter, singer & guitarist, rock & roll band, 64-66. Atty, pvt pract, 70-72. Professor law, 72- Frequent speaker on art law & copyright law. Participant, Arts Task Force, Nat Conference of State Legislatures. *Songs:* Girl, I Want; Dark Is Near.

GOGA, JACK ALAN   ASCAP 1974
composer, author
b Detroit, Mich, Jan 2, 44. Educ: Wayne State Univ, BA. Producer, Motown Record Co & writer, Jobete Music Co, 6 yrs; comp for numerous commercials; worked on many short films, incl "Last Detail." Chief Collabrs: Ivy Hunter, Pam Sawyer, Chris Forde, Richard Segall, Bobbi Goga, Joseph Nazzaro, Pats, Rae Baughn, Kaye Dunham, Jim David, Johnny Bristol, Janie Bradford. *Songs:* Music: You; Farewell Is a Lonely Sound; Yesterday's Dreams; The Best Years of My Life; Can't You See It's Me; No One There; Crossfire. *Scores:* Film: The Last Detail; The Photographer.

GOHMAN, DONALD   ASCAP 1956
composer
b Cincinnati, Ohio, Jan 8, 27; d. Educ: Miami Univ; Univ Cincinnati; Juilliard Sch; Am Theatre Wing. Writer, films incl short subjects. *Songs:* Never My Love; Every Woman; Once Before. *Scores:* Ballet: I Laughed At Spring; Stage show: The Ambassadors.

GOINS, PAUL DOUGLAS   ASCAP 1975
composer, author, singer
b Indianapolis, Ind, Sept 8, 44. Educ: Roosevelt High Sch, Wash, 62; Whitworth Col, BA, 66; Fuller Theological Sem, Calif, MA, 78. Singer, nightclubs & gospel concerts; recording artist & record producer, Discovery Records; music publ, Makarios & Lexicon Music Cos. Chief Collabrs: Clark Gassman, Si Simonson. *Songs:* New Life; Love One Another; Do I Care Enough; Hard to Believe; Lyrics: We're His Church; Peace Maker.

GOITEIN, GEORGE (GEORGE GORODY)   ASCAP 1959
composer, teacher
b Budapest, Hungary, Jan 12, 14. Educ: High sch; Univ Szeged Law Sch, DPolSci; studied music, Bela Bartok Col Music; piano & comp, Cons Music Budapest; motion picture scoring with Miklos Rozsa, Univ Southern Calif. Teacher piano, Fodor Sch Music, Budapest. Played piano prof in clubs, Budapest; US, 56- Now teacher music adult students. Chief Collabrs: Lawrence Welk, Mort Greene, Mary Lacey. *Songs:* Music: All of a Sudden; India; Lullaby. *Instrumental Works:* Happy Yodeler Polka; Penguin Polka. *Songs & Instrumental Works:* California Concerto for Accordion and Symphony Orchestra.

GOLAND, ARNOLD   ASCAP 1965
composer, arranger
b Brooklyn, NY, Apr 26, 28. Educ: High Sch Music & Art; Cornell Univ; Juilliard Sch Music. Arr music for major recording artists & Bway productions. Chief Collabrs: Jack Gold, Don Walker. *Songs:* Music: It Hurts to Say Goodbye; No Chemise, Please; The Best Days of My Life; That Special Time of Year; The Best Thing We Can Do Is Say Goodbye. *Scores:* Film/TV: Mistress of the Inn; Say When.

GOLD, ANITA   ASCAP 1960
composer, author
b Chicago, Ill, Dec 25, 32. Educ: High sch; art sch. Has been artist, actress & dancer. Author of plays & short stories. *Songs:* Another Heart Ache; Zoom Bali Oh.

GOLD, BERT JOSEPH   ASCAP 1946
composer, author
b New York, NY, Aug 18, 17. Educ: Cooper Union. TV producer, dir & station consult for var stations, incl 650 local shows; TV production artist, 53- Producer of film "The Painting," 62. Chief Collabr: Ken Hart. *Songs:* Dogface Soldier; Mariannina.

GOLD, ERNEST   ASCAP 1957
composer, conductor
b Vienna, Austria, July 13, 21. Educ: State Acad Music, Vienna, 37-38; comp studies with Otto Cesana, cond with Leon Barzin, 40-44; comp studies with

George Antheil, 48-50. Song writer, New York, 39-43; film comp, 45-; guest cond, 58- Chief Collabrs: Robert Sour, Don McCray, Anne Croswell, Jeanette Keller. *Songs:* Music: Practice Makes Perfect; Songs of Love and Parting. *Instrumental Works:* Symphony for Five Instruments; String Quartet (Soc for Publ Am Music Award); Piano Sonata (Steinway Award). *Scores:* I'm Solomon (musical); Film/TV: Exodus (Acad Award); On the Beach; It's a Mad, Mad, Mad, Mad World; The Secret of Santa Vittoria; Ship of Fools.

GOLD, HAL
See Goldberg, Harry

GOLD, JACOB   ASCAP 1947
composer, author
b Chelsea, Mass, Feb 13, 21. Educ: Tufts Univ, BA; Harvard Bus Sch, IA, MBA. Taught economics at Tufts Univ & Boston Univ. Started songwriting, Boston, 44. To New York, 51; publ, wrote & formed record label, 53-61. Head of United Artists Records, 62-66. Exec producer, A&R chief, Columbia Records, nat vpres, 68-73, exec producer, Los Angeles, 73- Chief Collabr: Arnold Goland. *Songs:* Lillette; Give Me Your Love for Christmas; Just in Case You Change Your Mind; Love Me Again; Never Leave Your Sugar Standing Out in the Rain; Lyrics: My Favorite Song; Anytime At All; Midnight Cowboy; It Hurts to Say Goodbye; The Best Days of My Life; The Best Thing We Can Do Is Say Goodbye; Sing Along Song; The Lights of Rio; Lilacs; Wish Me Good Luck As You Wish Me Goodbye; Rainbow Gal; If I Could Steal You; No One But the One You Love.

GOLD, JOE   ASCAP 1925
composer, publisher, pianist
b New York, NY, Nov 20, 1894; d. Educ: Pub schs. Pianist for Mae West, Sophie Tucker & var dance orchs. Staff, music publ cos; formed own firm. *Songs:* Grieving for You; Somebody's Lonely; Slow Poke; Everybody Shimmies Now; Fuzzy-Wuzzy.

GOLD, JOE D (J GORDON DANEL)   ASCAP 1973
composer
b Brooklyn, NY, Sept 18, 22. Educ: Studied elem music theory with Bernard Morris, advanced music theory & music comp with Vernon Martin, advanced music comp with Dr Katz, New York Col Music, piano with Richard Shadroui. Wrote popular & semi-classical music comps. Chief Collabrs: Bernard Morris, Gary Sanders. *Songs:* Danel's March of the Clowns; Music: Love Is Like a Little Child; Honey, I Don't Know Do You?; Where Is She?; This Sunday Afternoon.

GOLD, MANNY   ASCAP 1969
composer, author
b Brooklyn, NY, July 23, 20. Educ: Lincoln High Sch, Brooklyn; Juilliard Inst Musical Art. Owned publ co. Chief Collabr: Charles Jay Gold. *Songs:* Sad and Lonely; Sacred Day; Thanksgiving Prayer; Nuclear Power. *Instrumental Works:* Nocturne (piano).

GOLD, MARTY   ASCAP 1950
composer, teacher
b New York, NY, Dec 26, 15. Educ: City Col New York; studied the Schillinger Syst with Tom Timothy. Self-study & practical application in recording studios. Pianist, arr with bands incl Charlie Barnet, Phil Napoleon & others. Pianist, arr & cond in recording studios, New York, 50's. Joined RCA as artist, made many orch albums instrumentally as Marty Gold & Orch. Producer, arr & cond for many artists incl Sergio Freuchi, Ed Ames, Sarah Vaughn, Peter Hers, 4 Aces, Roger Williams & others. Chief Collabrs: Sammy Gallop, Tom Glazer, Charles Green, Al Alberts. *Songs:* Music: Tell Me Why; It's Dawn Again; Give Me the Right; Ready, Willing and Able. *Instrumental Works:* Rush Hour; Feelin' Funky (TV signature theme); Story of My Love. *Scores:* Film background: Face in the Crowd; TV background: Water World (series).

GOLD, WALTER   ASCAP 1959
composer, author
b Brooklyn, NY, May 15, 28. Educ: Stuyvesant High Sch, 45; Boston Univ, BS(jour), 51. Studied comp with Hall Overton, New York. Began musical career playing saxophone in high sch, played summers in Catskills. Organized group The Four Esquires, sang bass, incl "Hideaway" & "Love Me Forever," 51. Began writing, 59. Staff artist & repertory at CBS Records, 68-70. Produced & publ works of var artists & groups. Joined Don Kirshner, 71. Chief Collabr: Aaron Schroeder. *Songs:* It's My Party; Look Homeward, Angel; Lyrics: It's Now Or Never; Because They're Young; Music: Good Luck Charm; Time and the River.

GOLDBERG, BERNARD Z   ASCAP 1978
teacher, editor, flutist
b Belleville, Ill, Jan 27, 23. Educ: Juilliard Sch Music, dipl, 43, studied with Georges Barrere; spec study with Diran Alexanian & Pablo Casals; flute study with Lucien Lavaillotte, Paris. Flutist, Cleveland Orch, 43-46, principal flutist at age 21. Free lance, WOR, Little Orch Soc, New York. Principal flutist, Pittsburgh Symph, 47- Flutist & soloist, Casals Fest, Prades, France & PR. Principal & flute soloist, Mostly Mozart, Lincoln Ctr. Teacher & orch cond, Duquesne Univ, founder-cond, Three Rivers Training Orch, Pittsburgh.

Instrumental Works: Editor: Sonatas for Flute and Keyboard (J S Bach); Etudes (H Soussmann; flute); Duets (H Soussmann; 2 flutes); Airs de Ballet (C Saint-Saëns; flute, piano).

GOLDBERG, DORIS (NORA BAYES)
composer, author, singer

b Joliet, Ill, 1880; d New York, NY, Mar 17, 28. In teens, was with chorus, Chicago Opera House; later starred in, "Little Miss Fix It"; starred in "Ziegfeld Follies of 1908" & "Cohan Revue," 1918; in vaudeville with Jack Norworth. Solo command perf before queens, kings & others; also played Paladium Theatre, London. Chief Collabrs: Jack Norworth, George Cohan, Lou Alter. *Songs:* Shine on Harvest Moon; Mr Moon Turn Off the Light; How Can They Tell Them I'm Irish; Take Me Out to the Ballgame; Over There.

GOLDBERG, HARRY (HAL GORDON)   ASCAP 1952
composer, author

b New York, NY, May 1, 10. Educ: Col, 2 yrs; art sch, 2 yrs. Started writing as a hobby, became involved in Off-Bway shows, then to pop music. Chief Collabrs: Guy Wood, John Benson Brooks, Steve Nelson, Phil Medley, Athena Hosey, Ruth Kardon, Ed Nelson, Sr, Horace Linsley. *Songs:* Someone Else's Boy; Date With the Blues; What Kind of An Animal Are You; Blinky The Traffic Light; I Need You; Tell Me Now; His Arms are Open to Everyone; Who'll Be My Judge; Last Bus Home; Book of Happiness; Partners for Life; Teenage Heart; Saturday Dance; Makin' Time; Lonely Road; Peter The Parking Meter; High Flyin' Baby; Guess Who I Am; What Have I Done (To Deserve This Day); In the Kingdom of My Heart; Fools Hall of Fame; The Glide; Angel of Love.

GOLDBERG, HARRY (HAL GOLD)   ASCAP 1954
composer, drummer, teacher

b New York, NY, May 24, 12. Educ: NY Univ, BS, MA. Drummer in dance orchs incl Ted Lewis & Abe Lyman. Taught music in schs, also privately. *Songs:* It's the Little Things; Who Put the Law in Mother-in-Law; Hello Mr Snow Man.

GOLDBERG, MARK LEON   ASCAP 1965
composer

b Chicago, Ill, Mar 15, 27. Educ: Univ Ill, BS; Northwestern Univ, grad studies, 50-51; studied piano with Alan Swain, 60-64. Pres, Polo Food Products, Inc until 69 & Mesa Electronics Sales, Ltd, 75- Mem bd dirs, Fulton Market Cold Storage Co. Dir, Young Men's Jewish Council. Chief Collabrs: Thomas Peat, Lysle Wilson. *Songs:* Music: La Mi Fa Mi La You (Love Me for Me Loves You); When the Candlelight Is Low.

GOLDBERG, NEIL BRIAN (GANDHARVA)
author, teacher, composer

b Philadelphia, Pa, Aug 20, 43. Educ: Temple Univ, BA; studied music theory & producing with Joe Renzetti, music theory & music bus with Bernie Lowe. Started out with small hit in Philadelphia, "What About the Music", at 15 yrs of age; with Jamie/Guyden Records & Cameo/Parkway Records, 60; songwriter & producer, New York, 65; produced & performed A&M Records, Mercury Records, RCA Records & Epic Records; staff writer; did several chart records, recorded by Dusty Springfield, Tom Jones, Bill Medley, Candy Staton, Bobby Sherman, Robin MacNamara, Bobby Bloom, The Monkees, The Archies & Perry Como. Currently writing & performing with wife under the name of Flamming Pioneers, at concerts and on live radio. Chief Collabrs: Leon Huff, Kenny Gamble, Dave Appel, Joe Renzetti, Jeff Barry, Jerry Ross, Howard Boggess, Bobby Bloom, Robin MacNamara. *Songs:* Mr Factory; We're One Big Family; Got to Believe in Love; We're All Going Home; Do It in the Name of Love; Love in LaLa; It's Up to the Women; Land of the Free; Brother, Sister. *Albums:* Energy; The Money Box.

GOLDBERG, REUBEN L (RUBE)   ASCAP 1950
author, cartoonist

b San Francisco, Calif, July 4, 1883; d New York, NY, Dec 7, 70. Educ: Univ Calif, BS. Cartoonist, San Francisco Chronicle, 04-05, San Francisco Bulletin, 05-07 & New York Evening Mail, 07-21. Cartoons syndicated, 21. Dir cartoon course, Inst Commercial Art. Pulitzer Prize, 48, for editorial cartoon. Author: "Foolish Questions"; "Chasing the Blues"; "Boobs Abroad"; "Is There a Doctor in the House?"; "Post-War World"; "Soup to Nuts" (film). Chief Collabrs: Bert Grant, Irving Caesar, Ruth Patterson. *Songs:* You're Everywhere; I'm the Guy; Willie the Whistling Giraffe.

GOLDE, WALTER H   ASCAP 1940
composer, conductor, pianist

b Brooklyn, NY, Jan 4, 1887; d Chapel Hill, NC, Sept 4, 63. Educ: Columbia Univ; Dartmouth Col, BA; Imperial Cons, Vienna; studied voice with William Vilonat. Wrote score for Dartmouth Prom Show. Accompanist to Pablo Casals, Mischa Elman, Mary Garden, Elizabeth Rethberg & Lauritz Melchior. Cond, DeFeo Grand Opera Co. Head, Voice Dept, Columbia Univ, 44-48. Head, Inst of Opera, Univ NC, 53. Gave recitals incl Town Hall, New York. Mem, Am Guild Musical Artists & New York Singing Teachers Asn (pres, 44-46). Chief Collabr: Margaret Bristol. *Songs:* O Beauty, Passing Beauty; Among Shadows; Awakening; Prayer of the Slavic Children; To an Invalid; Mile After Mile; The US Army Engineers; musical setting, Psalm XXIII.

GOLDEN, JOHN   ASCAP 1914
composer, author, producer

b New York, NY, June 27, 1874; d New York, June 17, 55. Educ: NY Univ. Was actor, reporter, playwright & producer. Producer Bway plays: "Turn to the Right"; "Three Wise Fools"; "Lightnin'"; "The First Year"; "Seventh Heaven"; "Counselor-at-Law"; "Susan and God"; "When Ladies Meet"; "As Husbands Go"; "Let Us Be Gay"; "Claudia"; "Skylark." Founder, Stage Relief Fund & Stage Door Canteen. Autobiography: "Stagestruck." Charter mem, ASCAP, dir, 14-15, first treas. Chief Collabr: Raymond Hubbell. *Songs:* Poor Butterfly; Goodbye Girls, I'm Through; Willie Off the Yacht; I'm Growing Fond of You; Your Heart Looked Into Mine; I Can Dance With Everybody But My Wife; You Can't Play Every Instrument in the Band. *Scores:* Bway stage: The Candy Shop; Over the River; Hip, Hip, Hooray!; The Big Show; Cheer Up; Everything.

GOLDEN, SYLVIA   ASCAP 1934
composer, author

b New York, NY, Mar 27, 04. Educ: Hunter Col. Author of bk "Neighbors Needn't Know." Exec dir of League in Aid of Crippled Children; ed theatre mag. Writing lyrics & bk. Chief Collabrs: Mana Zucca, Daniel Wolff, Erno Balogh, Dr Weinberger, Lotta Lehmann, Giuseppe Bombashek. *Songs & Instrumental Works:* Head Over Heels (songbk); 3 Dramatic Songs; Do Not Chide Me, My Beloved; Your Love Is a Song; La Caramita; If I Could Turn Back the Pages; Three Encore Songs, the First Concert; Wot's So Awful Good About Spinach; Om Got a Co'd In By Head.

GOLDENBERG, MORRIS OSCAR   ASCAP 1962
composer, teacher, performer

b Holyoke, Mass, July 28, 11; d New York, NY, Aug 17, 69. Educ: Juilliard Sch Music, grad, 32. Was mem WOR staff & NBC staff; taught at Manhattan Sch Music; head perc dept, Juilliard Sch Music, teacher, 25 yrs. *Instrumental Works:* Classical Overtures for Timpani (excerpt bk); Modern School for Xylophone; Modern School for Snare Drum (method bk); Snare Drum for Beginners; Studies for Solo Percussion (excerpt bk); Romantic Symphonies (excerpt bk); Lucy's Riff (ensemble); Snare Drum Solos: 5/8 Romp; 5/8 Etude; Graduation Etude; Left Light March; March for Two Drums; No Roll Etude; Ramble Rumble; 7/8 Romp; Simple Simon March; Simple Minuet.

GOLDHAHN, RICHARD THOMAS   ASCAP 1946
composer, author, singer

b Philadelphia, Pa, Sept 4, 15. Educ: West Philadelphia High Sch; studied violin under Joseph Herman, 2 yrs, accordion under Arnold Crowe. Played first violin, High Sch Symph Orch, 4 yrs. Entered radio playing guitar & singing, night clubs & theatres, 34-36. Singing cowboy, clubs, radio & movies, Hollywood, 41. Performer, TV, hotel & restaurant lounges, Philadelphia, 55- Recording vocalist, National, Decca & Jubilee Records. Chief Collabr: Max C Freedman. *Songs:* Esmereldy; Weary Nights and Broken Dreams; Give Me Back My Heart; Music: Forgetful; I've Got a Gal in Laramie; Sioux City Sue; Pancho; The Sister of Sioux City Sue; The Beaut From Butte.

GOLDMAN, EDWARD MERRILL   ASCAP 1965
composer, author, teacher

b Manchester, Conn, July 2, 17. Educ: Boston Latin Sch; Longy Sch Music, Cambridge, Mass, grad; Juilliard Sch Music, studies with Beveridge Webster & Robert Mann; comp studies with Nadia Boulanger; Univ Grenoble. Pianist, composer, conductor & teacher. *Songs:* Some Day, Lord; Hymn for Peace; Happy Birthday, America. *Instrumental Works:* Hebrew Rhapsody; Hebrew Suite.

GOLDMAN, EDWIN FRANKO
composer, author

b Louisville, Ky, Jan 1, 1878; d New York, NY, Feb 21, 56. Educ: NY Nat Cons; studied with Antonin Dvorak, Jules Levy & Carl Sobst. Joined Metrop Opera Orch at age 17. Played under uncle Nahan Franko, Toscanini, Mahler, Mancinelli & others. Started Goldman Band, 11. Cond first radio performance broadcast, Cities Serv Prog. Received many hon degrees & decorations from foreign countries. Author of text bks "The Foundation to Cornet Playing" & "Band Betterment." *Instrumental Works:* Marches: On the Mall; The Pride of America; Cherokee; Stepping Along; Cheerio; The Chimes of Liberty; University & others; Cornet Solos: Echo Waltz; Scherzo; The Bugler; Sans Souci; My Heaven of Love; American Caprice & others.

GOLDMAN, MAURICE   ASCAP 1958
composer, author, educator

b Philadelphia, Pa, Apr 20, 10. Educ: Cleveland Inst Music, grad(musical studies), 35; Western Reserve Univ, Ohio, BS(educ), 35. Choral dir, Western Reserve Univ; opera & choral dir, Cleveland Inst Music & Cleveland Music Sch Settlement; opera cond, Akron Civic Opera, Los Angeles Opera Co, Am Opera Co, Calif. Film comp, 46-50. Larger choral works composed for synagogues throughout US. *Songs:* Choral arr: Hava Nageelah; Zum Gali; Music: Jerusalem (cantata); By the Waters of Babylon (chorus & orch); Song of Ruth (solo, chorus, chamber orch); Sabbath Eve Service (cantor, choir, organ).

GOLDMAN, ROBERT   ASCAP 1959
author
b New York, NY, Sept 10, 32. Educ: Phillips Exeter Acad; Princeton Univ. Wrote Triangle shows. Producer's asst, "Hazel Flagg." Wrote scripts for TV shows; producer, "Seven Lively Arts," TV series. Chief Collab: Glenn Paxton. *Songs:* I Feel Sorry for the Girl; Love Will Find Out the Way; This Really Isn't Me; I Suddenly Find It Agreeable. *Scores:* Bway stage: First Impressions.

GOLDMARK, ANDREW G   ASCAP 1977
composer, author, singer
b Stamford, Conn, Oct 8, 51. Educ: New Canaan County Day Sch; Pomfret Sch, 69; Yale Univ, 69-71; Juilliard Sch, Extension Div, 73-74. Staff writer, Blackwood Music, 69-70, Warner Brothers Music, 73-76. Solo recording artist & with own group, Wondergap. Co-publ with Irving/Almo Music Co & Waller Music. Chief Collabrs: Bruce Roberts, Beth Duskell, Jim Ryan. *Songs:* After You; Light in the Window; Back Seat of Heaven; If Ya Ever Believed; Isn't It Crazy.

GOLDSEN, MICHAEL H (STEVE GRAHAM,   ASCAP 1950
VERNON LEE)
composer, author
b New York, NY, Sept 5, 12. Educ: George Washington High Sch, grad, 30. Started in the music bus with Song Lyrics Mag, 34. Joined Irving Mills' Exclusive Publ, 37 & Leeds Music, 39-43. Joined Buddy De Sylva, Johnny Mercer & Glenn Wallichs, heading Capitol Songs, Inc, 43, acquired co & renamed it Criterion Music Corp, 50. Became interested in Polynesian music early 50's. Music consult for island songs on "From Here to Eternity", "Mr Roberts", produced native music for "Mutiny on the Bounty." Chief Collabs: Jack Pitman, Leon Pober & Danny Stewart. *Songs:* Silhouette Hula; You'll Never Go Home; The Lights of Home; Ori Ori E; Lyrics: Off Shore; Save the Bones for Henry Jones; I Got Hooked At a Hukilau; Intermission Riff.

GOLDSMITH, LEE   ASCAP 1970
lyricist
b New York, NY, Jan 4, 23. Educ: George Washington High Sch, New York, grad, 40. Started writing as lyricist, 68. First production on Bway, New York, 74. *Scores:* Sextet; Sheba (musical version of play "Come Back Little Sheba"); Gold Diggers of 1633 (musical version of Moliere's play, "School for Wives"); Shine (based on works of Horatio Alger).

GOLDSTEIN, ARNOLD H   ASCAP 1978
composer, author
b New York, NY, Dec 6, 34. Educ: Morris High Sch; City Col of City Univ New York, BA, 63; Wagner Col, MBA, 68. Musician, 52-63; asst adminr, Montefiore-Morrisania Affiliation, 63-65, adminr, 65-68; dep asst comnr & dep dir, Bellevue Hosp, 68-71; dep dir, Long Island Jewish-Hillside Med Ctr, 71-80; assoc prof, State Univ NY at Stony Brook, 71- Chief Collab: Timmi Goldstein. *Songs:* I'd Be Tellin' a Lie; Might Turn Out to Be Forever; Music: The Apple Don't Fall Far From the Tree; A Woman Knows; Love Is Muddy Water; You've Become a Lonely Feelin'.

GOLDSTEIN, BENJAMIN   ASCAP 1969
lyricist, songwriter
b Bronx, NY, Nov 11, 44. Made var musical films for "Sesame Street." Writer, 4 childrens' plays for first all-childrens' theatre, The Meri-Mini Players. Recording artist. *Songs:* Music: Looice-Been There; The Adventures of Guess Again; Winter, Spring, Summer and Fall; One Family. *Scores:* Rock Ballet: Caviar.

GOLDSTEIN, BOB   ASCAP 1962
composer, author
b Philadelphia, Pa. Educ: Temple Univ; Los Angeles Pierce Col, San Fernando Valley; Naropa Inst, Boulder. Child radio actor; teenage comedy writer with Woody Allen, Tamiment Playhouse in Poconos. Wrote & dir intimate revues, New York. Introduced to popular music first hyphenated arr, Folk-Dixie Sound of Washington Square, 63. Designed & displayed first generation of disco lighting equipment & coined terms Lightworks, Multimedia & Tower of Power, 65. Wrote & produced first big-budget soundtrack recording for underground film, Andy Warhol's "Lonesome Cowboys", 69. Devisor of novel ways to visualize music. Chief Collabrs: David Shire, Kenny Laguna, Elmo Glick. *Songs:* Washington Square; Lyrics: San Fernando Valley Valerie.

GOLDSTEIN, HARVEY (HARVEY BROOKS)   ASCAP 1967
composer, bassist
b Manhattan, NY, July 4, 44. Played with Bob Dylan, Doors, Miles Davis, Seals & Crofts. Mem, Electric Flag, Fabulous Rhinestones & Harvey Brooks Band. *Songs:* What a Wonderful Thing We Have; Love on My Mind; Free. *Instrumental Works:* Harvey's Tune.

GOLDSTEIN, MARK DAVID   ASCAP 1978
author
b Baltimore, Md, Sept 24, 47. Educ: Northwestern Univ, Medill Sch Jour, BSJ, 69, MSJ, 70. Copywriter, Gerson Howe & Johnson, Chicago, 70; copy supvr, Leo Burnett Co, Chicago, 71-75; advert exec; exec vpres & creative dir, Earle Palmer Brown & Assoc, DC, 75- Awards: Wash Advert Club, best original song,

76 & 77; Clio Award, best original song for TV & radio, 79. Chief Collabrs: Al Gorgoni, Dick Behrke. *Songs & Instrumental Works:* Themes: We Fly the World; Turn Us On.

GOLDSTEIN, WILLIAM S   ASCAP 1959
composer, author, teacher
b Baltimore, Md, June 11, 26. Educ: Temple Univ. Pianist in orchs; music dir, summer resorts. Co-owner, Norgold Record Co. Owner & mgr, Livingstone Sch Music, Cheltenham, Pa; also piano teacher. Chief Collabr: Harold Nussbaum.

GOLDSTICK, ROBERT J   ASCAP 1977
composer
b Philadelphia, Pa, Jan 14, 43. Pianist, small groups, 5 yrs; appeared in show, Hollywood, 77. Writer songs, country music & jazz, also commercials. Chief Collab: Mary Margaret Goldstick. *Songs:* Shrink.

GOLDSWORTHY, WILLIAM ARTHUR   ASCAP 1934
composer, conductor, organist
b Cornwall, Eng, Feb 8, 1878; d. Educ: Pub schs; studied with S P Warren, Charles Jolley. To US 1887; organist, Bd Educ, New York, 17-27 & Waldorf Astoria Hotel, 31-34; church organist & dir, St Ann's, St Andrews & St Marks-In-the-Bouwerie, 26-42; also wrote music for services; ed, series of Bach "Cantatas." Mem, Am Guild Organists. *Songs & Instrumental Works:* Majesty; Scherzo (organ); Te Deum; The Prophet (oratorio); The Return of the Star (music drama). *Scores:* Opera: The Queen of Sheba.

GOLLAHON, GLADYS   ASCAP 1951
composer
b Cincinnati, Ohio, Apr 8, 08. Educ: Parochial schs. *Songs:* Our Lady of Fatima.

GOMEZ, RICHARD   ASCAP 1969
composer, author
b Bayonne, NJ, June 1, 50. Educ: Bayonne High Sch; studied voice with Bea Dobelle, Boston Cons Music. In Bway production, "Beatlemania." Singer & guitarist, nightclubs & TV. Rec'd gold record for perf on "Indian Giver," 69. Mem, 1910 Fruitgum Co. Chief Collabrs: Louis Gomez, Jon Davis, Merry Roth. *Songs:* Welcome to My Dreams; All These Things; Riding Home From Kansas; Music: Just Go 'Round; Lyrics: Creations of Simon.

GOMEZ, URBANO (URBANO GOMEZ MONTIEL)   ASCAP 1975
author
b Havana, Cuba, Jan 16, 26. Educ: High sch, Havana; Escuela Taller de Diseno H C, studied commercial art; Havana Cons Music, studied music & guitar, 5 yrs. Founder Latin-Am musical movement, Feeling, 48. Mem, SACEM, France, 66. *Songs:* Canta Lo Sentimental (Best Song, Cuba, 62); Cancion Enamorada (first mention of honor, Varadero Fest Songs, Cuba, 66); Cantar (first prize, Cuban Folkloric Fest, 67); Tengo Ganas De Gritar Que Te Quiero; Amada Sombra; Gran Paris; Cha Cha Cha Del Amor; Esta Fiebre; Mi Nuevo Mundo; Cancion Gris; Wampo; Jose Luis Pata Vira; Mi Amor Sera De Ti; Lejos De Tu Amor; Alba De Amor; Melodia En Abril; Esta Dulce Verdad; El Arpa Del Tiempo; Mi Cha Cha Cha Si Es Sabro; Canto Al Destino; Pensar Que Sus Manos Van Sin Mi; Mi Corazon Es Una Pandereta; Triste Cancion.

GOMEZ, VICENTE   ASCAP 1946
composer, guitarist, teacher
b Madrid, Spain, July 8, 11. Educ: Real Cons Madrid, grad music; studied classical guitar with Quintin Esquembre. First concert, Madrid, age 13; toured throughout Europe, Russia, SAm & US; US debut, 38. Weekly prog, NBC Network, 38-41. Guest soloist with Wis & Rochester Symph Orchs; guest artist TV progs. Decca recording artist, 38-; teacher, writer & recorder, Acad Spanish Arts, currently. Film appearances include: "Blood and Sand", "The Snows of Kilimanjaro", "The Sun also Rises", "The Fighter", "The Captain from Castille", "Crisis", etc. Bway Shows include: "Nice Going", "For Your Pleasure", "Mexicana", etc. *Songs:* Romance de Amor; Verde Luna (Green Moon); Chi-Qui-Chi. *Instrumental Works:* El Albaicin (guitar & orch); Concerto Flamenco (guitar & orch); Toros Suite (2 guitars); Guitar: Goya Suite; The Fighter; Blood Wedding Suite; Rio Flamenco Suite; Sonata in F Major; Torero; Triste Santuario; Granada Arabe; Pepe Romero Suite; Danza Gitana; Cantina; La Farruca; Alegrias; El Girasol; Solea; Flamenco No 2; Studio Caprichoso; Studio Sentimental; Tricolor. *Scores:* Film/TV: Blood and Sand.

GONGA, DAWILLIE
See Duke, George Mac

GONSKY, LARRY E   ASCAP 1972
composer
b Paterson, NJ, Oct 20, 49. Educ: Rutgers Univ. Co-founder & keyboard player for pop group, Looking Glass. Chief Collabrs: Elliot Lurie, Pieter Sweval. *Songs:* Wooly Eyes; Who's Gonna Sing My Rock 'n' Roll Song; Music: Just Another Music Man.

GONZALEZ, AARON RUBEN (AARON GANZ)   ASCAP 1952
composer, author, pianist
b El Paso, Tex, Jan 25, 08. Educ: Univ Southern Calif, Col Music & Sch Eng; West Coast Univ; Univ Calif. Organized own orch, 20. Orch leader, Beverly

Hills Hotel, 15 yrs & Beverly Wilshire Hotel, 2 yrs, plus others. Pianist-arr-comp motion picture studios; Span transl coach. Chief Collabrs: Mitchell Parish; Alfredo Palacios; Leo Rojo; Jack Elliott. *Songs & Instrumental Works:* Tropicana; Palomita Mia; Zapeateado; Timbalero; Muchachita; Bolero; Guarachita; Samba Movida; Cuban Slave; Si Quires Que Te Quiera; Two Shadows in the Moonlight; Vida Mia; Tu Carino; Ayer, Hoy y Manana; Luna Salvaje; Estrella de Oracion; Perdoname; El Marranito; San Clemente del Tuyu (tango); Isla San Andres (bolero); These Things I Ask; Jesus Loves You and So Do I.

GONZALEZ, LILY (LYDIA)   ASCAP 1977
composer, singer
b Cayey, PR, Sept 29, 24. Educ: Pvt piano & guitar study. Recording & radio artist, 40's & 50's; entertainer, nightclubs & resort hotels, 60's. *Songs:* A Bailar La Salsa; Mi Precioso San Juan; No Se Va Poder; Amor Ajeno.

GOODBODY, SLIM
See Burstein, John

GOODHART, AL   ASCAP 1932
composer, pianist
b New York, NY, Jan 26, 05; d New York, Nov 30, 55. Educ: DeWitt Clinton High Sch. Radio announcer, vaudeville pianist & spec material writer. Mem, 2-piano team, radio. Owner, theatrical agency. Went to Eng, 34-37. Chief Collabrs: Al Hoffman, Mann Curtis, Maurice Sigler, Sammy Lerner, Ed Nelson, Kay Twomey, Allan Roberts. *Songs:* I Apologize; Auf Wiedersehn, My Dear; Fit As a Fiddle; Black-Eyed Susan Brown; Jimmy Had a Nickel; Who Walks in When I Walk Out?; I Saw Stars; Why Don't You Practice What You Preach?; Roll Up the Carpet; I'm in a Dancing Mood; Without Rhythm; There Isn't Any Limit to My Love; Everything Stops for Tea; From One Minute to Another; I Can Wiggle My Ears; Say the Word; Everything's in Rhythm With My Heart; Let's Put Some People to Work; Gangway; Lord and Lady Whoozis; She Shall Have Music; Romance Runs in the Family; I Must Have One More Kiss Kiss Kiss; I Ups to Her and She Ups to Me; Johnny Doughboy Found a Rose in Ireland; Serenade of the Bells. *Scores:* London stage: This'll Make You Whistle; Going Greek; Hide and Seek; Brit films: Come Out of the Pantry; First a Girl; When Knights Were Bold; She Shall Have Music; Gangway.

GOODIS, JAY   ASCAP 1956
composer, author, pianist
b Philadelphia, Pa, Jan 1, 31. Educ: Olney High Sch; pvt music study. Accordionist & pianist in dance bands, hotels & nightclubs. Piano & accordion teacher. Chief Collabr: George Sherzer. *Songs:* Goodbye Fifties—Hello Sixties; Hey Roly Poly; I Surrender; I Cannot Live Without You; That Never Never Land of Love; Well I Do Declare.

GOODMAN, AILENE SYBIL (AILENE PRESSMAN)   ASCAP 1960
composer, author, performer
b Malden, Mass, Oct 15, 29. Educ: Malden High Sch; Cushing Acad; Radcliff Col, BA(cum laude), 51; Univ Pittsburgh Grad Sch of Speech Therapy, 55-57; Naganuma Sch of Japanese Language, Tokyo, 70; Univ Vienna, Austria, 74-78. With "Mister Rogers," WOED-TV, Pittsburgh. Recording artist, media writer & producer. Res assoc to Marcel Prawy, chef dramaturg of Vienna State Opera, Austria. Scriptwriter, "No Man Is an Island," United Nations Fest of Arts, DC. Singer & guitrist, with Nat Symph, Lincoln Ctr, Constitution Hall & Kennedy Ctr. First person to perform in Ford's theatre since Lincoln's assasination. Author, children's bks & albums incl "I Heard It With My Own Two Ears" a 12 hour tape for progs on Spoken Arts, & monograph on Athanasius Kircher, scientist & musician. Recipient, 3 ASCAP awards for White House spec assignments, Japan & Ohio prizes for educ radio. Chief Collabrs: Pamela Brooke, Barbara Nuchims. *Albums:* Animals, Funny Folk, and Wee People; I'll Tell You What I'm Thinking I'll Do; Abe Lincoln in Song and Story; Pittsburgh, Songs of a City.

GOODMAN, ALFRED   ASCAP 1922
composer, conductor, pianist
b Nikopol, Russia, Aug 12, 1890; d New York, NY, Jan 10, 72. Educ: Peabody Cons (scholarship). Pianist in film theatres. Chorus dir, then music dir, Aborne Opera House. Cond & arr for Al Jolson, Earl Carroll Vanities & "Life of Riley". Cond Bway musicals, "Blossom Time", "My Dream Girl", "Good News", "The Band Wagon", "The New Moon", "Ziegfeld Follies" & "George White's Scandals." Cond first part-sound film, "The Jazz Singer". Became radio cond, 32, TV cond, 49, also records. Head cond, Shuberts, 15-20 yrs. Cond for Abbot & Costello, Donald O'Connor, Fred Allen "The Hit Parade" & "The Family Hour." Arr, DeMarco Sisters. A&R man, Kasin Industs. Chief Collabrs: Edgar Smith, Cyrus Wood, Clifford Grey. *Songs:* When Hearts Are Young; Love Has Found My Heart; I Came, I Saw, I Fell; Call of Love; Twilight; The Lady in Ermine; Who Knows Why. *Scores:* Bway stage: Linger Longer Lettie; Cinderella on Broadway; The Whirl of New York; The Passing Show of 1922; The Lady in Ermine; Dew Drop Inn; Artists and Models of 1925; Gay Paree.

GOODMAN, BENNY   ASCAP 1945
composer, conductor, clarinetist
b Chicago, Ill, May 30, 09. Educ: Lewis Inst, Chicago; studied with Schoepp & Schillinger; LLD, Ill Inst Technol, 68. Clarinetist in bands incl Bix Beiderbecke, Jules Herbuveaux, Arnold Johnson & Ben Pollack. Played in Bway theatre orchs. Led own band, Billy Rose Music Hall, 34. Cond orch on weekly radio show, "Let's Dance," 34-35. Radio progs incl "Camel Caravan," 37-40, "Old Gold," 41 & "Victor Borge-Benny Goodman Show," 46-47; appeared in motion pictures "Big Broadcast of 1937", "Hollywood Hotel", "The Powers Girl", "Stage Door Canteen", "Sweet and Lowdown", "Make Mine Music" & "A Song Is Born"; commentator on serious music WNEW; recorded for Columbia, Capitol, Chess, Command, Decca, Philips & RCA Victor Records. Life story filmed, "The Benny Goodman Story," 56. Organized new band, 1958 Brussels World's Fair, toured Europe, 59; appeared with London Philh, 61; State Dept Cult Exchange Prog tour of Russia, 62. Winner Int Jazz Critics Poll; Apollo Award, 56; named to Playboy Hall of Fame & Downbeat Hall of Fame. Played hotels, cols, theatres. Has appeared in chamber music concerts. Toured throughout US, Europe, Far East, SAm & USSR. Made many records. Autobiography: "The Kingdom of Swing" (with Irving Kolodin). Chief Collabrs: Count Basie, Harry James, Mitchell Parish, Andy Razaf, Edgar Sampson, Chick Webb, Teddy Wilson. *Songs & Instrumental Works:* Stompin' at the Savoy; Lullaby in Rhythm; Don't Be That Way; Flying Home; Two O'Clock Jump; Seven Come Eleven; Air Mail Special; Dizzy Spells; Four Once More; If Dreams Come True; Georgia Jubilee; The Kingdom of Swing.

GOODMAN, JOSEPH MAGNUS   ASCAP 1965
composer, professor
b New York, NY, Nov 28, 18. Educ: Johns Hopkins Univ, BA, 38; Harvard Univ, MA, 48. Studied with Paul Hindemith at Yale Univ, Walter Piston at Harvard Univ. Taught Span at Yale Univ & Harvard Univ to continue grad studies. Taught music theory, Brooklyn Col, then Queens Col, 52- Lect music history & theory at Univ Veracruz, Mex, summers 46 & 47. Began to comp, 47; choral works, then chamber music & works for organ, orch. Head of comp dept, Sch Sacred Music, Union Theol Sem, New York, 58-73. Performed works in US, SAm, Europe & Japan. Comns: Nat Council of Churches, organ works; Presbyterian Church & Gen Sem of New York, anthems & service music; Harvard Univ, Hymnal; Thor Johnson & Soni Ventorum Wind Quintet, var pieces; and others. *Songs:* Music: Three Responsories (mixed chorus a cappella); *Instrumental Works:* Quintet for Wind Instruments; Three Preludes On Gregorian Melodies for Organ; Fantasia on Panis Angelicus for Organ; Seven Bagatelles for Organ; Two Dialogues for Organ and Electronic Tape; Five Bagatelles for Flute, Clarinet and Bassoon.

GOODMAN, LILLIAN ROSEDALE   ASCAP 1928
composer, author, pianist
b Mitchell, SDak, May 30, 1887; d. Educ: Columbia Univ; Juilliard Sch; studied with Alexander Lambert, Percy Gretchin, Julius Gold, Buzzi-Peccia, Mme Jandenzi, Emil Fuchs; hon MusD, Boguslawski Col. Singer, vaudeville, operettas, radio, theatres & concerts. Head, vocal dept, Boguslawski Col. Staff mem, Federal Theatre Project. Organized own musical booking agency, Chicago. Vocal coach, Desilu Workshop, Hollywood, 58; taught privately. Mem, Nat Asn for Am Composers & Conductors, Calif Music Teachers Asn. Chief Collabrs: Anton Bilotti, Mark Goodman (husband). *Songs:* Cherie, I Love You; If I Could Look Into Your Eyes; Just a Bit of Dreaming; The Sun Goes Down; You Have My Heart; My Shepherd Is the Lord; Let There Be Peace; I Found You; Ecstasy; Our Prayer; I Say You Can Sing (recorded vocal exercises).

GOODMAN, MAURICE, JR   ASCAP 1956
author
b New York, NY, Feb 26, 21. Educ: Yale Univ; Am Theatre Wing. Lt, USN, WW II, rec'd Distinguished Flying Cross & Air Medal & Star. Businessman; worked in sales promotion & advert. Pres, Antro Abrasives, Inc. Chief Collabrs: George Wallington, Billie Wallington. *Songs:* Way Out There; My April Heart; The Middle of Love.

GOODMAN, RICHARD JOHN (RICHARD SUPA)   ASCAP 1974
composer, singer
b Brooklyn, NY, Apr 9, 44. Started playing in high sch; singer & lead guitarist in several prominent local bands, New York & Long Island, 10 yrs. Recorded several albums on Paramount & CBS. Played with The Young Rascals. Lead role in Bway show "Hair," 70. Joined Screen Gems as staff writer, 74. *Songs:* Somethin' 'Bout You Baby I Like; At Every End There's a Beginning; Could It Be Love I Found Tonight; Papa's Knee; Lovers Knot.

GOODMAN, SAUL   ASCAP 1957
composer, author, teacher
b Brooklyn, NY, July 16, 06. Educ: Pvt timpani studies with Alfred Friese, theory with Arthur Waldeck. Principal timpanist, NY Philh, 46 yrs, played more than 6,163 concerts. Chmn dept perc, Juilliard Sch Music, last 40 yrs. *Songs & Instrumental Works:* Modern Method for Timpani; Theme and Variations; Timpiana; Introduction and Allegro; Ballad for the Dance; Proliferation Suite.

GOODMAN, STEVE
songwriter
b Chicago, Ill, July 25, 48. Educ: Univ Ill. Performer, folk fests. Writer, advert jingles. Recording artist with var record cos, 71- *Songs:* City of New Orleans. *Albums:* Steve Goodman; Somebody Else's Troubles; Jessie's Jig and Other Favourites; Words We Can Dance To; The Essential Steve Goodman.

GOODWIN, CHARLES DOUGLAS   ASCAP 1957
composer, author, arranger
b Pittsburgh, Pa, Apr 21, 29. Educ: Trinity Cathedral Boys & Mens Choir, Pittsburgh, 10 yrs. Pvt piano lessons from grade thru high sch, Pittsburgh; trombonist band & orch high sch, 47. Played trombone & piano in bands, Spec Services, Korea, 51. Worked in furniture & construction bus. Worked as music copyist, 66. Wrote underscore for weekly animated TV series, "Super President," 67. Writer TV, movies, records & theater shows. Chief Collabrs: Ray Gilbert, Johnny Bradford, John McCarthy. *Songs:* He Leads Me; You Are Mine; Got to Find a Way; The Whole World Is Watching; Don't Go Home; Show Me the Way to Love You; Twelve Red Devils; When the Sky is Clear, When the Waters Clean; When You Wear a Happy Smile; Dog Gone Dog; On a Train Goin' West; A Friend in Need; Back on the Track; A Dollar and a Dime; You Can Really Fly; You've Got an Allergy; You Can Do It; The Tiger Moo; Silver Seals; Saint Lawrence Seaway; One Sure Way; Mouth Full of Bubblegum; Magic Show; Heavy Date; It's the Happenin' Thing; Good Friends Come in All Sizes; Everything's Gonna Be Fine; Every Hundred Years; Because We're We; Ann Adell Is Here; The L E Phant Stomp. *Scores:* Motion Pictures: Hey There, It's Yogi Bear; The Man Called Flintstone; Santa and the Three Bears; My Boys Are Good Boys; The Ant and the Aardvark; Roland and Rattfink; The Tijuana Toads; The Blue Racer; TV: The Pink Panther Show; Here Comes the Grump; The Oddball Couple; The Bear Who Slept Through Christmas; The Bugs Bunny Easter Special; A Pink Christmas (Pink Panther Christmas Spec); The Bugs Bunny Looney Christmas Tales; Where Do Teenagers Come From?; Musical Bk Shows: The Sandman.

GOODWIN, JOE   ASCAP 1914
author
b Worcester, Mass, June 6, 1889; d Bronx, NY, July 31, 43. Educ: Pub schs. Wrote shows for 81st Wildcats, WW I. Monologist in vaudeville. Prof mgr, music publ. Wrote songs for films incl "Hollywood Revue," also for London revues. Chief Collabrs: Nat Ayer, Louis Alter, Gus Edwards, George Meyer, Al Piantadosi, Mark Fisher, Larry Shay. *Songs:* That's How I Need You; Billy; When I Get You Alone Tonight; When You Play in the Game of Love; Baby Shoes; Liberty Bell It's Time to Ring Again; Gee, But I Hate to Go Home Alone; I'm Knee Deep in Daisies; When You're Smiling; They're Wearing 'Em Higher in Hawaii; Everywhere You Go; Breeze.

GOODWIN, WALTER   ASCAP 1942
composer, author, pianist
b Brooklyn, NY, Aug 31, 1889; d. Performer, vaudeville incl Keith & Orpheum circuits, 25 yrs. Pianist, nightclubs. Chief Collabr: Clyde Hager. *Songs:* That Wonderful Mother of Mine; Just a Little Sympathy; Who Are You Fooling Tonight?; Pal of My Heart; Back o' the Yards; Back in the Old Neighborhood; Just for No Reason At All; When State Street Was Just a Lane; We're Coming Home.

GOOLD, SAM   ASCAP 1924
composer, author, pianist
b Philadelphia, Pa, Jan 29, 1893; d Philadelphia, Pa, Jan 14, 31. Pianist in film theatres; later on staff, music publ co. *Songs:* To Know You Care; Angel Eyes; I'm With You; Song of the South; Broken-Hearted Rose; Curly Head.

GORDON, ARTHUR ARNOLD   ASCAP 1959
composer
b Cleveland, Ohio, Dec 9, 28. Educ: Oberlin Cons of Music, grad. Prof musician, many yrs. Recording artist for radio & TV. *Instrumental Works:* Mediterranean; Irridescence. *Scores:* Off-Bway show: Hooray! It's a Glorious Day and All That.

GORDON, BEN (FRED MEADOWS)   ASCAP 1934
composer, author, singer
b New York, NY, June 19, 12. Educ: Studied voice with William Houston & drama with Robert Barrat; coached by Emil Pollack. Vocalist, cafes, New York Paramount Theatre, Leo Reisman, Vincent Lopez, Red Nichols & other bands. Concertized with wife, Belle. Vocalist in "Bouncing Ball" cartoons. Chief Collabrs: Lee David, Larry Stock, David Guion, Pete Wendling, Larry Fotine, James Hanley, Charles McCarthy, Geoff O'Hara, James Cavanagh. *Songs:* Honey, Dontcha Love Me Any More?; I'm All Thats Left of That Old Quartet; Honey Mine; The Song's the Thing; When They Changed My Name to a Number; Who's Calling You Sweetheart Tonight?; Lyrics: You Were Only Fooling; Blue Echoes (Eng lyrics, Mex song); Howdy Do, Mis Springtime; Still, You're in My Arms.

GORDON, BOB
See Bollard, Robert Gordon

GORDON, DANE R   ASCAP 1976
author
b London, Eng, June 15, 25. Educ: Univ Cambridge, Eng, BA, 51, MA, 58; Univ London, BD, 56; Univ Rochester, MA, 60. Actor in West End Productions: "Jeannie"; "Housemaster"; "Dear Octopus" & others. Actor movies: "Those Kids From Town"; "Goodbye, Mr Chips"; "Major Barbara" & others. Repertory in Birmingham & Hereford; touring cos. Served Royal Navy, 43-47. Bookseller, Hatchards, Piccadilly, London, 47-48. Ordained Presby minister, US, 58. Prof philosophy & assoc dean, Col Gen Studies, Rochester Inst Technol.

Author plays: "The Polling Booth"; "Palm Sunday Bandwagon"; "Down Will Come Baby"; "Too Little for Milo." Chief Collabr: Milford Fargo. *Songs:* Lyrics: A Family Christ Mass; Away He Run; The Violence Tree; Sing to America; The Boy Who Stayed in Bed; Forsooth; Pilgrim.

GORDON, DAVID MARVIN   ASCAP 1970
composer
b Winnipeg, Man, May 19, 08. Worked for music publ, Irving Berlin Inc & Shapiro, Bernstein & Co, Inc; piano accompanist for var vaudeville performers & nightclubs, also ASCAP music publ, Gordon Music Co, Inc. *Songs & Instrumental Works:* Lassie; Leave It to Beaver.

GORDON, FRANK (FRANCIS) JOHN   ASCAP 1970
composer, author
b Brooklyn, NY, May 20, 45. Educ: Los Angeles Pierce Col, AA; Calif State Univ, Northridge, BA(speech/drama). Singing, playing & writing since childhood in all types of shows, plays & contests. Chief Collabrs: Robert Butler, Freddie Cannon, Aron Charmatz, Sue Hutchinson, Dennis Penna, Gary Kochacki. *Songs:* I'm Leaving; Music: Always; My Child.

GORDON, HAL
See Goldberg, Harry

GORDON, IRVING   ASCAP 1939
composer, author
b New York, NY, Feb 14, 15. Chief Collabrs: Duke Ellington, Allan Roberts, Al Kaufman, Jack Lawrence. *Songs:* Me, Myself and I; What Will I Tell My Heart?; Moments in the Moonlight; The Band Played On and On; Stevedore's Serenade; Gypsy Without a Song; Pyramid; Prelude to a Kiss; When?; Nine Little Broken Hearts; All Dressed Up to Smile; Save a Little Sunbeam; Mama From the Train; Unforgettable; Be Anything (But Be Mine); Mister and Mississippi; Delaware; Two Brothers; The Kentuckian Song.

GORDON, JOHN
See Gesner, Clark

GORDON, KELLY L   ASCAP 1967
composer, author, singer
b Frankfort, Ky, Nov 19, 32. Educ: Los Angeles City Col; pvt instr. Toured with band, 58. Writer & producer, 4 Star TV, 62. Producer, Capitol Records, 67. Independent writer & producer, 71- Chief Collabrs: Dave Grusin, Patrick Moody Williams, Shorty Rogers, Bobbie Gentry. *Songs:* That's Life. *Scores:* Film/TV: Don't Drink the Water; Where Were You When the Lights Went Out; Gidget Grows Up; Partridge Family.

GORDON, MACK   ASCAP 1933
composer, author
b Warsaw, Poland, June 21, 04; d New York, NY, Mar 1, 59. Came to US at early age. Educ: Pub schs. Boy soprano in minstrel show, then vaudeville comedian & singer. Wrote song for "Smiles." Went to Hollywood under contract to Paramount. Chief Collabrs: Harry Revel, Harry Warren, Josef Myrow, Ray Henderson, James Van Heusen, Vincent Youmans, James Monaco, Edmund Goulding. *Songs:* Time on My Hands; Help Yourself to Happiness; Listen to the German Band; Underneath the Harlem Moon; I Played Fiddle for the Czar; An Orchid to You; A Tree Was a Tree; It Was a Night in June; Did You Ever See a Dream Walking?; Doin' the Uptown Lowdown; She Reminds Me of You; Once in a Blue Moon; May I?; Love Thy Neighbor; With My Eyes Wide Open I'm Dreaming; Stay As Sweet As You Are; College Rhythm; Take a Number From One to Ten; Straight From the Shoulder; My Heart Is an Open Book; Lookie, Lookie, Lookie, Here Comes Cookie; Paris in the Spring; Without a Word of Warning; Takes Two to Make a Bargain; From the Top of Your Head to the Tip of Your Toes; I Feel Like a Feather in the Breeze; You Hit the Spot; A Star Fell Out of Heaven; Goodnight, My Love; In Old Chicago; But Definitely; Oh My Goodness; When I'm With You; It's Swell of You; Never in a Million Years; Wake Up and Live; There's a Lull in My Life; Afraid to Dream; Danger, Love At Work; You Can't Have Everything; May I Have the Next Romance With You?; Sweet Someone; An Old Straw Hat; In Any Language; Meet the Beat of My Heart; Thanks for Everything; You Say the Sweetest Things, Baby; Two Dreams Met; Down Argentine Way; It Happened in Sun Valley; I Know Why; Cattanooga Choo-Choo; I Yi Yi Yi Yi I Like You Very Much; Chica Chica Boom Chic; There Will Never Be Another You; I Had the Craziest Dream; People Like You and Me; I've Got a Gal in Kalamazoo; At Last; Serenade in Blue; My Heart Tells Me; You'll Never Know (Acad Award, 43); The More I See You; Once Too Often; I Can't Begin to Tell You; On the Boardwalk at Atlantic City; You Make Me Feel So Young; Somewhere in the Night; Kokomo, Indiana; You Do; Everytime I Meet You; What Did I Do; It Happens Every Spring; If You Feel Like Singing, Sing; Mam'selle; A Lady Loves; Baby, Won't You Say You Love Me; Wilhelmina; Nowhere Guy; All About Love; Through a Long and Sleepless Night; Somebody Soon. *Scores:* Bway stage: Meet My Sister; Ziegfeld Follies of 1931; Films: Sitting Pretty; Broadway Through a Keyhole; We're Not Dressing; She Loves Me Not; Shoot the Works; College Rhythm; Love in Bloom; Paris in the Spring; Two for Tonight; Collegiate; Stowaway; Poor Little Rich Girl; AliBaba Goes to Town; Wake Up and Live; You Can't Have Everything; Head Over Heels; Love and Kisses; Love Finds Andy Hardy; Down Argentine Way; Sun

Valley Serenade; Weekend in Havana; Song of the Islands; Iceland; That Night in Rio; Springtime in the Rockies; Orchestra Wives; Diamond Horseshoe; Pin-Up Girl; Three Little Girls in Blue; Mother Wore Tights; Wabash Avenue; Summer Stock; I Love Melvin; The Girl Next Door; Bundle of Joy.

GORDON, ODETTA HOLMES FELIOUS
composer, singer, teacher

b Birmingham, Ala, Dec 31, 30. Educ: Studied classical voice; hon LHD, Johnson C Smith Univ. Singer, coffeehouses, clubs, supper clubs, TV & var fests with Kaye Ballard, Harry Belafonte, Johnny Cash, Della Reese, Mike Douglas & Joey Bishop. In concert, Europe, USSR, Japan, Africa, Brazil, Australia & Can. Singer, with symph orch at Carnegie Hall & with Pittsburgh Symph Orch. Participated in reopening of Ford's Theatre, DC. Can debut, play "The Crucible," Shakespeare Theatre, Ont; actress in "The Effects of Gamma Rays on Man-in-the-Moon Marigolds." Appeared in film "Sanctuary." Recording artist for var cos. Fellow with Duke Ellington Fel, Yale Univ. *Songs:* Music: Give Me Your Hand; Got to Be Me.

GORDON, PHILIP   ASCAP 1959
composer, author, conductor

b Newark, NJ, Dec 14, 1894. Educ: Columbia Univ, AB, AM & PhD; Teachers: Daniel Gregory Mason & Cornelius Rubner. Arr; prof, Chicago Musical Col, Seton Hall Univ & Westminster Choir Col. Cond: Newark Civic Symph & Bach Cantata Soc. Comp-in-residence, Am String Teachers Asn Summer String Conference, Douglass Col, New Brunswick, NJ, 65- *Instrumental Works:* Sonatina (clarinet & piano); Meditations on an Ancient Air (comn by Nat Am String Teachers Asn Orch); Capriccio (clarinet choir); Invocation and Ritual Dance (band); Three Preludes for String Orchestra; Rhapsody (band); Concertino (violin & piano); Midsummer Idyl (orch); Two Nativity Cards (band); Prelude and Rondo (string, bass & piano); Soliloquy (violin solo); Intrada, Scene and Finale (viola solo); The Declaration of Independence (orch & reader); Exotic Dance (string orch); New England Chronicle (band); Sonata (clarinet & piano); A Miniature String Quartet; Anniversary Overture (orch); Suite for Woodwind Quintet; Fantasia on Westron Wynde (orch); Three Miniatures for Violin and Viola. *Songs & Instrumental Works:* An Elizabethan Garland (soprano, clarinet & string orch or piano); The Pasture (mixed voices); Sweet Was the Song the Virgin Sang (mixed voices); Card for a Wassel Bowl (mixed voices); Cradle Song (mixed voices). *Scores:* Opera: A Tale From Chaucer (one act opera); The Shoe of Little Noby (Christmas opera, two acts).

GORDON, ROBERT CAMERON   ASCAP 1964
composer, conductor, clarinetist

b Hartford, Conn, June 29, 41. Educ: Berklee Sch Music; Lenox Sch Jazz; Univ Calif, studies with Joe Marsala. Clarinetist, Muggsy Spanier, Bill Davidson, Bobby Hackett & Eddie Condon. Formed own group; toured US & Europe. Winner, Down-Beat Mag Poll. *Songs:* How Long Blues; I'm Praying For You; It's Only You; Playing Hooky; My Heart Belongs With You; Music: Malta; Bobby's Blues; Blues For B Flat Clarinet.

GORDON, ROBERT J   ASCAP 1962
composer, author, arranger

b Vienna, Austria, Apr 30, 11. Educ: Pvt music study. Arr for radio, Europe; also for Franz Lehar. Wrote & produced musicals, Chicago.

GORDON, RUTH L (RUTH LAYNE)   ASCAP 1969
composer

b Chicago, Ill, Apr 1, 13. Performer, vaudeville, nightclubs, radio, appeared with Abe Lyman Band, Clayton, Jackson & Durant & others.

GORDON, WILLIAM MARVIN (FLASH)   ASCAP 1975
composer, author, singer

b Miami, Fla, Mar 16, 47. Educ: Miami Dade Jr Col. First band, Vietnam, 69. Club work, Miami, 69-72; musician, Nashville & on the road. Writer, 71- Chief Collabrs: Freda Parton, Mark Anderson, Ted Barton, Buzz Rabin, Jim Vest, David Chambellain, Don Coggins. *Songs:* All You Ever Have to Do Is Touch Me.

GORDY, BERRY
director, producer

Exec with record & motion picture cos. Founder, Motown Record Corp; chmn, Entertainment Complex, Motown Industs; exec producer, var films incl "Mahagony." Exec producer, var films incl "Lady Sings the Blues", "Bingo Long Traveling All-Stars and Motor Kings." Mem, Dirs Guild of Am. Recipient, Bus achievement award, Interracial Council for Bus Opportunity, 67; 2nd Annual Am Music award, 75; named one of five leading entrepreneurs of Nation, Babson Col, 78.

GORIN, IGOR   ASCAP 1941
composer, singer

b Ukraine, Russia, Oct 26, 08. Educ: Vienna Cons, (scholarship) studied with Victor Fuchs. Debut as singer, Czech State Opera. Moved to US, 33, citizen, 39. US debut, Hollywood Bowl, 39. Actor. Has sung in films & on radio. *Songs:* Lament; Caucasian Song; Safe By de Lawd; Lullaby; Within My Dreams.

GORMAN, FREDERICK C   ASCAP 1967
composer, singer, producer

b Detroit, Mich, Apr 11, 39. Educ: Glendale Community Col, Calif. Started producing with Motown, 72; independent, 77-80. Chief Collabs: Bryan Holland, Lamont Dozier, Janie Bradford, Lee Harrington, Bob Hamilton. *Songs:* Tears of Love; I Wanna Guy; We Should Be Closer Together; Rose; You Put a Crush on Me; Lyrics: Forever; Please Mr Postman; Just Like Romeo and Juliet; I Like Your Style; Strange I Know.

GORMAN, PATRICK E   ASCAP 1958
composer, author

b Louisville, Ky, Nov 27, 1892. Educ: Univ Louisville, LLB. Mem bd dirs, Louis Braille Music Inst Am, Inc. Labor leader; vpres, Amalgamated Meat Cutters & Butchers Workmen of NAm, 44-; int secy-treas, 41- Awards: Nat Jewish Labor Comn Man of the Year, 61; Nat Brotherhood Week, 62; St Edwards Univ Coronet Medal; Clarence Darrow. Biography, "Picket and the Pen," by Hilton Hanna & Joseph Belsky. Chief Collabrs: Nick Kenny, William Taylor. *Songs:* A Girl As Sweet As You; Shamrock; A Cow in Switzerland; I'm Goin' Home; Golden Years Waltz. *Instrumental Works:* Pawn Shop Suite (symphonic poem).

GORMAN, ROBERT LEE   ASCAP 1976
composer, singer, vocal coach

b Peoria, Ill, Dec 30, 28. Educ: Wesleyan Univ, BMus; Teacher's Col, Columbia Univ, MMusicEd. Singer, actor & dancer, eight Bway musicals. Writer, spec musical material, "Carol Burnett Show," 76-78. Chief Collabr: Arthur Malvin.

GORME, EYDIE
singer

b New York, NY. Entertainer, var nightclubs. With "Steve Allen's TV Troupe Tonight Show," 54. Bway debut with Steve Lawrence (husband), in "Golden Rainbow," 67. Appeared in var theatres throughout US. Recipient, Emmy awards for TV specials honoring Gershwin, Porter & Berlin; Grammy award as best female vocalist, 67.

GORNEY, JAY (DANIEL JASON)   ASCAP 1925
composer, author, producer

b Bialystok, Russia, Dec 12, 1896. Educ: Univ Mich, BA, LLB, JD; studied music with Earl Moore. Comp 5 Mich Union musicals. USN Bandmaster, World War I. Songwriter for var productions incl: "Greenwich Village Follies", 24, "Artists & Models", 24, "The Ritz Revue", 24, "Earl Carroll Vanities-3rd Edition", 25, "Miss Happiness", 26, "Americana", 31, "The Battle of Paris & "Applause", 29-30, "Stand Up and Cheer", "Jimmy and Sally", "Moonlight and Pretzels", "Marie Galante", "Redheads on Parade." Producer of stage shows incl "Merry-Go-Round", 27, "First Nighter", "Meet the People", "They Can't Get You Down", 41. Comp & musical adv, Paramount Studios, New York, 29-30, mem ed boards as adv on musical motion pictures, 33. Writer, Fox Films, Hollywood, of screen plays & stories for films incl "College Holiday" & "Troubador in Trouble." Exec producer of musicals, Columbia Pictures, 42-43, incl "The Gay Senorita" & "Hey Rookie." Chmn, musical play dept, Dramatic Workshop New Sch, New York, 48-51, co-producer of 5 student musicals. Comp, dir & producer of CBS TV, 51-52; co-authored, TV series "Holiday Hotel" & "Mama." Fac, Am Theatre Wing prof training prog, 52-65. Lectr on musical theatre. Am Theatre Wing "Tony" award for teaching, 62; Yale Drama Sch Citation salute for 40 yrs creativity, 65; Songwriters Hall of Fame outstanding song award, 76. Board mem, Am Guild Authors & Comp & ASCAP. Chief Collabrs: E Y Harburg, Henry Myers, Edward Eliscu, Lew Brown, Sidney Clare, Howard Dietz, Walter & Jean Kerr. *Songs:* Music: Brother, Can You Spare a Dime?; You're My Thrill; Baby, Take a Bow; A Girl in Your Arms; What Wouldn't I Do for That Man?; Ah, But Is It Love?; What Makes My Baby Blue?; When I'm Housekeeping for You; Meet the People; The Bill of Rights; A Fellow and a Girl; In Chi-Chi-Castenango; The Stars Remain; Let's Steal a Tune From Offenbach; Love in a Changing World; The Four Rivers; There Goes That Guitar; You and Your Broken Heart; You Are So Near (And Yet So Far); It Will Be All Right (In a Hundred Years); This Had Better Be Love; Wish Me Luck. *Scores:* Bway: Top Hole; Vogues of 1924; Merry-Go-Round; Sketch Book; Earl Carroll's Vanities; Meet the People; Heaven on Earth; Touch and Go; The Happiest Girl in the World; Film: They Can't Get You Down; Mona and Lisa; Kris Kringle Rides Again.

GORODY, GEORGE
See Goitein, George

GOROVETS, EMIL   ASCAP 1975
composer, singer

b Gaisin, USSR, June 10, 26. Educ: Moscow Theatrical Sch; Gnessin's Musical Inst, Moscow. Actor on stage, Moscow, 50's. Singer, Jewish & Russian popular songs. Singer, performer & comp. Immigrated West, 73. Many recordings & TV shows, Russia. Toured Europe, US & Israel. *Songs:* Yiddish; Balalaika; Russland; Music: Romans; I Am a Jew.

GORRIE, ALAN E   ASCAP 1974
composer, singer, musician

b Perth, Scotland, July 19, 46. Educ: Dundee Col of Art, Dundee, Scotland. Mem of group The Average White Band. Chief Collabrs: Hanish Stuart, Roger

Ball, Robbie MacIntosh. *Songs:* Let's Go Round Again; Pick Up the Pieces; Cut the Cake; Person to Person; Soul Searching; Atlantic Avenue. *Albums:* AWB.

GOSH, BOBBY   ASCAP 1966
  composer, author, singer
b Stouchsburg, Pa, May 31, 36. Educ: Albright Col, BS, 58; Juilliard Sch Music, 63, studied orchestrating with Jacob Druckman. Singer/song writer/recording artist, RCA, Capitol, Paramount & Polydor Labels. Chief Collab: Sammy Cahn. *Songs:* A Little Bit More; You Made a Believer Out of Me; Love Ballet; Two for a Dollar; Music: A Song for Erik.

GOSHORN, LAWRENCE JAY   ASCAP 1976
  composer, author, singer
b Dayton, Ky, Oct 2, 47. Educ: Withrow High Sch; Cincinnati Art Acad. Guitarist. With Sacred Mushroom, 3 yrs, Mushroom Jones, 2 yrs & Pure Prairie League, 5 yrs. *Songs:* Two Lane Highway; Kentucky Moonshine.

GOTTFRIED, JONAS   ASCAP 1959
  composer, author, singer
b Buffalo, NY, Nov 7, 29. Educ: Univ Buffalo, BA; City Col New York, MEd. Armed Forces vocalist, 55. Recording artist, Gone Records. Producer & personal mgr, Ernestine Anderson, Teresa Brewer, Mark Richardson, Les Emmerson, Rick Springfield, J P Morgan & others. Officer, Conference of Personal Mgrs. Owner recording studio, Sound City, Inc, Los Angeles, Calif. Music with Ed Scott, "Pieces of Eight," 60. Chief Collabs: Ed Scott, George Stalter, Herb Eldemiller Buchanan. *Songs:* Lover Mine; Three Time Looser; Lyrics: The Power of Love; I'll Go on Loving You.

GOTTLER, ARCHIE   ASCAP 1917
  composer
b New York, NY, May 14, 1896; d Calif, June 24, 59. Educ: City Col New York; Long Island Bus Col. Wrote songs for "Ziegfeld Follies" & Winter Garden revues; also for musicals & films in Eng. Early comp & dir for sound films. Consult to spec serv, Signal Corps Training Film Prog, WW II. Chief Collabs: Sidney Mitchell, Edgar Leslie, Con Conrad, Johnny Lange, George Meyer, Jerome Gottler (son). *Songs:* America, I Love You; Would You Rather Be a Colonel With an Eagle on Your Shoulder or a Private With a Chicken on Your Knee?; Baby Me; What Do You Mean By Loving Somebody Else; Easter Sunday on the Prairie; Santa Claus Is Riding the Trail; Kiss Me Good Night; In the Gold Fields of Nevada; I Hate to Lose You; To Whom It May Concern; Love Me or Leave Me Alone; Walking With Susie; Big City Blues; Oogie Oogie Wa Wa; Sing a Little Love Song; Hittin' the Ceiling; Wine, Women and Song; All American; Yes, There Ain't No Moonlight So What; Bye Bye Mr Dream Man; Girl on the Isle of Man; How's About It? *Scores:* Bway stage: Broadway Brevities.

GOTTLER, JEROME SHELDON   ASCAP 1940
  composer, author, teacher
b New York, NY, Dec 2, 15. Educ: DeWitt Clinton, Fairfax & Beverly Hills High Schs; Comnock Sch, Los Angeles; piano study with Walter Freed. Child actor & singer for amateur shows; then radio & band singer. Wrote first song for Phil Harris & first script for Three Stooges. Served in Signal Corps, WW II, 4 yrs; wrote over 50 films. Wrote first TV show for NBC. Lectr, City Col New York. Wrote songs for radio, TV & films, incl "Duffy's Tavern"; "High Society"; "Spy Chasers"; "The Addams Family"; "How to Marry a Millionaire"; "Bewitched" & others. Chief Collabs: Archie Gottler, Mort Greene. *Songs:* Yes, There Ain't No Moonlight; Music: How's About It; He Took Her for a Sleighride; Two Hearts in Danger; Swell.

GOTTLIEB, ALEX   ASCAP 1966
  author
b Zhitomir, Russia, Dec 21, 06. Educ: Hutchinson High Sch, Kans; Univ Wis, BA. Reporter & ed, Brooklyn Daily Eagle. Publicity dir, Paramount Theatre, New York. Advert mgr, United Artists & Columbia Pictures. Producer & writer, motion picture cos incl Universal Pictures, Warner Bros & United Artists, & 7 TV series & many shows on major TV networks. Writer, var artists incl Bob Hope, Al Jolson, Eddie Cantor, Edgar Bergen, Sammy Davis Jr; var Bway shows, incl 5 produced plays & 3 under contract. Author of "Best Short Plays of 1969" & "Best Short Plays of 1975." *Songs:* Lyrics: Frankie and Johnny.

GOTTLIEB, JACK S   ASCAP 1962
  composer, author, publisher
b New Rochelle, NY, Oct 12, 30. Educ: Queens Col, BA (cum laude), 53, study with Karol Rathaus; Brandeis Univ, MFA, 55, study with Irving Fine; Univ Ill, residency, 55-58, DMA, 64, study with Burrill Phillips, Robert Palmer; Berkshire Music Ctr, 54 & 55; study with Aaron Copland & Boris Blacher. Asst to Leonard Bernstein, New York Philh, 58-66; music dir, Temple Israel, St Louis, Mo, 70-73; prof music, Hebrew Union Col/Jewish Inst Relig, New York, 73-77; publ dir, Amberson Enterprises, Inc, currently. Awards: ASCAP, Brown Univ, Ohio Univ, Nat Fedn Music Clubs & Nat Endowment for the Arts. *Songs:* Kids' Calls (quodlibet for chorus & piano); Downtown Blues for Uptown Halls (voice, clarinet & piano); Sharing the Prophets; Music: Articles of Faith (orch & voices); Haiku Souvenirs; Shout for Joy (choir, flutes, drums & piano); Verses from Psalm 118 (choir & organ); Four Affirmations (choir & brass sextet); The Song of Songs, Which Is Solomon's (operatorio); Psalmistry (four singers &

eleven players). *Songs & Instrumental Works:* Songs of Loneliness (cycle for baritone & piano); New Year's Service for Young People; From Shtetl to Stage Door. *Scores:* Tea Party (one-act opera); In Memory Of...(cantata on poems; choir, solo, organ).

GOTTUSO, TONY   ASCAP 1959
  composer, musician
b Bronx, NY, Feb 2, 16. Educ: High sch; studied violin, banjo & guitar. Had own band at 16; later joined act playing theatre circuits. Played in dance bands incl Artie Shaw, Paul Whiteman & Andre Kostelanetz. Accompanist to Frank Sinatra, Bing Crosby, Tony Bennett, Dinah Shore, Bobby Darin & Ella Fitzgerald. Performed on radio & TV; has made many records. Chief Collabrs: Lee David, Herb Waters. *Songs:* I Wonder If You Care; I Ain't Confessin' My Troubles to Nobody.

GOULD, DANNY   ASCAP 1953
  composer, author, conductor
b Brooklyn, NY, Apr 28, 21. Educ: NY Univ, BA; Univ Calif, Los Angeles, studied film scoring with Leith Stevens. Arr; comp, cond & arr, NY Univ Varsity Show; cond & instrumentalist in own band, The Rajahs of Rhythm; staff arr, ERA Records; music coordr & adminr, Paramount Pictures & now for Warner Bros; comp songs for var TV episodes for Warner Bros. Chief Collabrs: William L Hendricks, Harry Tobias, George Howe, Roger Davenport, David Taxe, Bob Josephson. *Songs:* Love, Love; The Alumnus; Waterford, Waterford (Grand Prize, Waterford, Ireland Music Fest); Pals Forever (YMCA Indian Guides Prog theme); Music: Shama, Shama; On With the Show; The Dream Girl Song; Cakewalk Rag; So Exciting; Count Your Blessings; In His Name; Mazel Tov. *Instrumental Works:* Belly Laughs; Lesgloriado; Tiptoe Tango; Back Street; Lonely People Waltz.

GOULD, EDWARD E   ASCAP 1960
  composer, author, producer
b New York, NY, Dec 9, 11. Educ: San Francisco State Col; Columbia Univ. Magazine writer; also record producer. *Songs:* New Kind of Gold; I Take Your Hand; Where I Come From; Americans, We're All Americans!; Rockin' the Tease. *Instrumental Works:* Concerto in C Minor (piano concerto).

GOULD, ELIZABETH DAVIES   ASCAP 1954
  composer, piano teacher
b Toledo, Ohio, Mar 8, 04. Educ: Toledo Univ, BA; Oberlin Col Cons Music, BMus; Univ Mich, Artist's Dipl; piano teachers, Guy Maier & Artur Schnabel. Two-piano recitals, solo & with orch. Private teacher of piano. Started composing, incl sonatas for violin, viola, cello & piano, string quartets, orch, vocal, chorus & other, 50- Most works deposited at Am Music Ctr, Fleisher Collection.

GOULD, JACK   ASCAP 1952
  composer, author
b New York, NY, May 20, 17. Educ: City Col New York, BA. Served in USAAF, NAfrica, WW II. Language teacher, New York pub schs. Chief Collabrs: Dave Gardner, Martin Haynes, Joe Leahy, Jack Jason, Buddy Arnold, Betty Barton, Vic Mizzy & Irving Taylor. *Songs:* Put a Penny in the Slot; Are You Kidding?; On the Sunnyside of the Moon; The Moon Is Upside Down; It Happens Every Day; No, Mama, No; What D'Ya Hear From Your Heart?; Comfort Me With Apples.

GOULD, MORTON   ASCAP 1936
  composer, conductor, arranger
b Richmond Hill, NY, Dec 10, 13. Educ: Richmond Hill High Sch; piano studies with Abby Whiteside & comp with Dr Vincent Jones. Child prodigy; radio recordings; guest cond concerts, US, Europe, Australia, Japan, SAm & Mex. Chief Collabrs: Betty Comden, Adolph Green, Dorothy Fields. *Instrumental Works:* Pavanne; American Salute; Spirituals for Orchestra; Latin American Symphonette; Interplay; Jekyll and Hyde Variations; Vivaldi Gallery Jericho; Santa Fe Saga; West Point Symphony; American Ballads. *Scores:* Fall River Legend (ballet); Film/TV: Holocaust; World War I Documentary Series; Windjammer.

GOULDING, EDMUND   ASCAP 1947
  composer, author, director
b Feltham, Eng, Mar 20, 1891; d Los Angeles, Calif, Dec 24, 59. Came to US, 19. Dir films, "The Trespasser", "Grand Hotel", "Dark Victory", "The Old Maid", "The Constant Nymph", "Down Among the Sheltering Palms" & "The Razor's Edge." Chief Collabrs: Elsie Janis, Mack Gordon. *Songs:* Love, Your Magic Spell Is Everywhere; You Are a Song; Alone in the Rain; Oh, Give Me Time for Tenderness; Mam'selle; To Rest in the Glory; Fury of the Sea; The Lovely Song My Heart is Singing; Sweetest Moment.

GOVSKY, JOHN M (JACK SKY)   ASCAP 1961
  composer
b Philadelphia, Pa, July 18, 21. Educ: Classical violin study, 10 yrs, organ, 2 yrs; Drexel Univ, studied eng, 39-41. Motion picture mixing, 27 yrs. Has own studio, Jack Sky Productions. Electronic engr, sound & computer background. Chief Collabrs: Nicholas Catucci, Leon Rhodes. *Songs:* Ballad of Diver Dan (theme for children's show series).

GOWER, ALBERT E, JR   ASCAP 1967
composer
b Weed, Calif, June 4, 35. Educ: Calif State Univ, Sacramento, AB; Univ Ore, MM; NTex State Univ, PhD; studied comp with George McKay & Samuel Adler. Instrumental music teacher, North Sacramento Pub Schs, 57-66. Prof, Univ Southern Miss, 66- *Instrumental Works:* Three Short Pieces for Baritone Horn; Sonata for Tuba; Excursion for Symphonic Band; Improvisations for Brass Trio; Symphony No 1.

GRACE, BESS DAVIS   ASCAP 1976
author, teacher
b Foxburg, Pa, June 16, 1892. Educ: Piano lessons, 07; Los Angeles High Sch; State Normal Sch. Teacher, elem sch, 15-57, then retired. Chief Collabr: Frank Devaney Grace. *Songs:* Lyrics: I'd Be Nothing Without You; I'm Glad I Belong to You.

GRACE, FRANK DEVANEY   ASCAP 1964
composer, author
b North Little Rock, Ark, Dec 24, 1891. Educ: North Little Rock & San Diego High Schs; Blackstone Col of Law, LLB; Baars Music Sch, Little Rock; studied lyric writing, Univ Calif, Los Angeles. Railway clerk, Mo Pacific Railway, North Little Rock; in publicity dept, Pacific Electric Railway. Asst supt constabulary, Los Angeles County, 24-48, retired. Sgt, Army Div Criminal Invest, WW I; Marine Corps Paymaster Dept, WW II. Chief Collabrs: Anna G Howard, Lindsay McPhail, V Raymond Grobholz. *Songs:* I Live on Doolittle Avenue; Git 'Er With Glitter; You're the Only Angel (That I Ever Knew); I'm Gonna Be a Lady (In Spite o' Hell); Music: M'm, M'm, That's Good.

GRADE, FRANCIS
See Filip, Paul Francis

GRAFF, GEORGE   ASCAP 1914
author, business executive
b New York, NY, Aug 5, 1886; d Stroudsburg, Pa, Jan 24, 73. Educ: De Witt Clinton High Sch. Charter Mem, ASCAP. Chief Collabrs: Ernest Ball, Chauncey Olcott, Jesse Deppen, Caro Roma, Annelu Burns, Arthur Penn. *Songs:* As Long As the World Rolls On; When Irish Eyes Are Smiling; To the End of the World With You; In the Garden of Tomorrow; I Love the Name of Mary; Till the Sands of the Desert Grow Cold; Teach Me to Pray; I Come to Thee; Mother of Pearl; Little Man; Who Else But God; For the Sake of Auld Lang Syne; also Hymns of Happiness.

GRAFF, JONNY ELIAS   ASCAP 1958
composer, author, dance band leader
b Atlantic City, NJ, Dec 2, 11. Educ: Atlantic City High Sch; Univ Pa, 2 yrs. Orch leader & musician with Meyer Davis, Howard Lanin, Ted Straetter, etc, 28-42; radio writer, 42-47; TV sta prog dir, WBKB Chicago; TV sta mgr, KGGM-TV Albuquerque & WNTA-TV NY; Vpres for TV, Nat Telefilms Assoc, 9 yrs & Embassy Pictures, 13 yrs. Chief Collabr: Lenny Whitcup. *Songs:* Dodo the Kid From Outer Space; The Barefoot Mailman; Lyrics: Pippi Longstocking; Unofficial Ambassador; It's the Beat Not the Boodle; Dust in a Penthouse.

GRAHAM, HAROLD LEROY   ASCAP 1962
composer, author, voice teacher
b Portland, Ore, Mar 31, 1897. Educ: Degree in music; studied in New York. Singing evangelist; soloist in "Quiet Hour Program." Has led many choirs. *Songs:* He's Only a Prayer Away; Far Beyond the Sun; There Are No Yesterdays in God's Tomorrow; Justified; The Hill of the Cross; Singing River; Have Faith in God; Beyond Tomorrow; Won't You Be There?; In the Borders of America; Liberty Bell; Music: That's When I Know He's There.

GRAHAM, IRVIN (ROBERT)   ASCAP 1951
composer, author
b Philadelphia, Pa, Sept 18, 09. Educ: West Philadelphia High Sch; Hunter Col, studied with composer Donald Lybbert. Wrote first publ song at 15; began in local radio in Philadelphia, singing & playing. Writer radio shows, Fred Waring & Jimmy Durante; TV, Show of Shows, Colgate Comedy Hour, Jane Froman Show, Specials for Ford, Guy Mitchell Show, Garry Moore Show. Wrote special material for Imogene Coca, Constance Bennett, Patrice Munsel, Eddie Albert. Co-authored supper club musical "All About Love"; wrote score & lyrics "New Faces 1936" & other revues. Chief Collabrs: Ervin Drake, Alex North, Elmer Bernstein, Moose Charlap, Al Stillman, Bickley Reichner. *Songs:* With a Twist of the Wrist; You Should Be Set to Music; I'm in Love With a Married Man; I Believe; Music: You Better Go Now.

GRAHAM, JOHNNY   ASCAP 1953
composer, author, conductor
b New York, NY, Jan 6, 11; d Fla, Mar 7, 78. Educ: City Col New York; Juilliard Sch Music. Violinist in dance orchs; also led own orch; salesman. *Songs:* Shame on You; Let's Leave It That Way; I Never Was the One.

GRAHAM, L LEE (YAKIMA LEE)   ASCAP 1968
composer, author, singer
b Seattle, Wash, Feb 15, 45. Educ: Cent Wash State Col; San Francisco State Col; Univ Wash; studied voice with Leon Lischner. Musician since age 5. Recorded album with Crome Syrcus, ABC Command. Chief Collabrs: Stephen Sullivan, Theodore W Shreffler, Dick Powell. *Songs:* Heroe's Lament; Thinkin Man Blues; You Made a Change in Me. *Scores:* Ballet: Astarte.

GRAHAM, ROBERT (VIRGIL)   ASCAP 1963
composer, teacher, organist
b El Dorado, Kans, Sept 5, 12. Educ: Univ Rochester Eastman Sch Music, BMus, 50, studied with Howard Hanson, Edward Royce, Bernard Rogers, Herbert Elwell, Wayne Barlow; Redlands Univ, Calif, MMus, 51, studied with Paul Pisk. Concert artist, teacher in NY, Calif, Japan, Hawaii; music therapist. Free-lance comp of 500 publ; Hawaiian language hymnal music ed, 72. Hubert Award, ASCAP Awards. Fac, Am Col Musicians; Pi Kappa Lambda. Chief Collabr: Jeana Graham. *Songs:* Music: Drop, Drop Slow Tears (SATB); Dawn of Redeeming Grace (cantata); Lo, a Star (cantata); Golgotha (cantata); Jonah's Tale of a Whale; David's Hotshot Slingshot; We Beseech Thee, O Lord (SATB); Shout In Joy Unto the Lord (SAB); Gethsemane (SATB); In the Bamboo Wood (SSA, SAB, SATB); Barefoot School (cantata); Have You Seen Three Kings? (SA); Robert Graham Organ Meditations; Green the Weeping Willow Tree (SA, flute); Sing Praise! (unison). *Instrumental Works:* Concerto for Piano II (orch); Suite for Harpsichord (orch); Obookiah (oratorio); Come Lord Jesus (Barnes Award, oratorio). *Scores:* Opera: Paul in Chains.

GRAHAM, ROGER   ASCAP 1958
composer, author, publisher
b Providence, RI, June 12, 1885; d Providence, RI, Oct 25, 38. Educ: Dental col. Came to NY: music salesman, then prof mgr music cos. Founded own publ co. Chief Collabrs: May Hill, Spencer Williams, Maceo Pinkard. *Songs:* Peggy From Panama; I Believe in You; You'll Want Me Back Some Day; I Ain't Got Nobody; I'm a Real Kind Mama.

GRAHAM, RONNY   ASCAP 1952
author, composer, comedian
b Philadelphia, Pa, Aug 26, 19. Comedian in nightclubs throughout US. Wrote songs for Bway revues, "New Faces" (52, 56 & 62; appeared in 52 ed) & for Julius Monk nightclub revues; appeared in "Take Five." Has appeared on TV. Wrote for Phil Silvers & George Gobel shows, also "Colgate Comedy Hour." Acted in Bway play, "The Tender Trap." Chief Collabr: Milton Schafer. *Songs:* It's a Wonderful Day to Be Seventeen; Lucky Pierre; Take Off the Mask; I'm in Love With Miss Logan; Harry the Hipster; Steady, Steady; Ah, Camminare!; I'm All I've Got. *Scores:* Bway stage: Bravo, Giovanni!

GRAHAM, STEVE
See Goldsen, Michael H

GRAHM, ROBERT DAVID   ASCAP 1972
composer, author
b Los Angeles, Calif, Dec 27, 54. Educ: Los Angeles City Col; Immaculate Heart Col; studied guitar with Dave Morgan. Lead guitarist with Shaun Cassidy & in rock group, Longfellow. Concert appearance, Aquarius Theatre, Hollywood. Producer, arr & studio engr on several albums. Chief Collabrs: Shaun Cassidy, Ruth Grahm, Randall Paige. *Songs:* Music: Robin Hood; I'm Sittin' Pretty; Through the Storm; Goodbye to You; The Gang Rides Again.

GRAHM, RUTH HERSCHER   ASCAP 1952
composer, author
b Philadelphia, Pa, Apr 4, 24. Educ: Univ Calif; NY Univ. Acted in films. Secy to Red Barber. Asst, Sports Dept & New Prog Ideas Dept, CBS, New York. Chief Collabrs: Louis Herscher (father), Ron Morris, John Debney, Doug Talbert. *Songs:* Orange Blossoms; Where Were You?; Mama Never Said a Word About Love; Fifty Games of Solitaire; In the Park; I Didn't Believe I'd Fall in Love; Elmer the Knock-Kneed Cowboy; The Best Years in Our Lives; Baby, I'm the Greatest; Break the Chain; Lyrics: You Sure Know How to Hurt a Guy; Stay With Me Tonight; I Found a Friend; Turn to Me; These Lonely Days; These Are the Jokes; Slip My Heart Under the Door; With Every Step You Take; It Aint Easy; Cocoon; Baby, I'm a Fool for You; He Saw You First; Let's Go Back to Yesterday; Save Me; Give Me Good Loving.

GRAINGER, PERCY ALDRIDGE   ASCAP 1924
composer, pianist
b Brighton, Melbourne, Australia, July 8, 1882; d White Plains, NY, Feb 20, 61. US citizen, 18. Studied piano with Louis Pabst, James Kwast. Made concert appearances from 01. Protege of Grieg. Am debut, NY, 15. WW I, USA; in band; then instr, Army Music Sch. Experimented with "Free Music." *Songs & Instrumental Works:* Molly on the Shore; Shepherd's Hey; Irish Tune From County Derry; Clog Dance (Handel in the Strand); Marching Song of Democracy; Kipling "Jungle Book" Cycle (mixed chorus, chamber orch); The Warriors (3 pianofortes, orch); In a Nutshell (suite, piano, orch); Lincolnshire Posy (wind band); The Christian Heart and the Power of Rome (wind band, string orch, organ); Hill Songs No I, II (22 solo instruments); Children's March; Lads of Lamphray; Colonial Song; Danish Folk Music Suite; Youthful Suite; Spoon River; To a Nordic Princess; Country Gardens.

GRAND, MURRAY
ASCAP 1953

composer, author, performer

b Philadelphia, Pa, Aug 27, 19. Educ: High sch; Philadelphia Sch Textile & Design, 40; Juilliard Sch Music, 46-50. Started playing nightclubs at Fireside Inn, 49; also Spivy's Roof, Manhattan, NY; Bricktop's, Rome, Italy; Spivy's, Paris, France. Wrote for several revues incl "New Faces of 1952-56." Wrote var bk shows incl "The Dancing Heiress", "Triple Galop" & "Good Good Friends." *Songs:* Guess Who I Saw Today; April In Fairbanks; Thursdays Child; Come By Sunday; Too Old to Die Young; Love At An Auction.

GRANDE, VINCENT

composer, trombonist, trombone teacher

b New York, NY, Nov 13, 02; d New York, Nov 18, 70. Educ: Pub sch. Played for Paul Whiteman Orch, Paramount Theater; played for Glenn Miller Orch. Bus agent, Local 802, Am Fedn Musicians. *Songs:* Blues Serenade.

GRANDJANY, MARCEL
ASCAP 1947

composer, harpist, educator

b Paris, France, Sept 3, 1891; d New York, NY, Feb 24, 75. Educ: Cons Nat Musique; studied with Paul Vidal & Roger-Ducasse; scholarship with Henriette Renie. Premier Prix for harp at age 13. Concert debut, Paris, 08. Served in French Army, WW I. Appeared with Maurice Ravel. Organist & choirmaster, Basilique du Sacre-Coeur. London debut, 22; NY debut, 24. Recitals throughout US, Europe, Can & Cuba. Harp soloist with symph orchs. Head of harp dept, Fontainebleau, 21-36. To US, 36. Citizen, 45. Head of harp dept, Juilliard Sch Music, 38 & Manhattan Sch Music, 56; founded harp dept, Cons de Musique, Que, 43-63. Taught summer sch, Mills Col, 38-40. Jury mem, 1st Int Harp Contest, Israel, 59; founded Am Harp Soc, 62. Made many records. *Songs:* Le Vanneur; Parmi les Marroniers; Berceuse; also many transcriptions. *Instrumental Works:* For Harp: Rhapsodie; Children's Hour (suite); Divertisement; Deux Chansons Populaires Francaises; Poeme (harp, French horn, orch); Aria in Classic Style (harp, strings); Fantaisie on Theme From Haydn; The Colorado Trail; The Erie Canal; Cadenzas for Mozart's Concerto for Flute and Harp.

GRANGER, LOU

See Des Granges, Louis Anthony

GRANT, ALFRED J
ASCAP 1958

composer, arranger, accordionist

b Yonkers, NY, May 10, 14. Educ: Columbia Univ. Comp & arr, music publ cos; music dir, Major Music. *Instrumental Works:* Western Star (scored concert); Arr for accordion: Sonata IX (Mozart); Concerto No IV (Vieuxtemps); La Folia (Corelli); Rondo Brilliant (Weber); Fuga (Bach).

GRANT, ALLAN
ASCAP 1939

composer, pianist

b Newcastle-on-Tyne, Eng, July 2, 1892; d. To US, 1897. Educ: Balatka Music Col; Juilliard Sch, scholarship; studied with Sigismund Stojowski, Percy Goetschius, Franklin Robinson. Concert pianist. *Instrumental Works:* Gramercy Square; Candid Camera Sketches; Piano Concerto in E; Symphony in D; 15 Piano Suites for Educational Purposes.

GRANT, AMY LEE
ASCAP 1977

composer, author

b Augusta, Ga, Nov 25, 60. Educ: Harpeth Hall Sch for Girls, 78; Vanderbilt Univ. Appeared with Bill Gaither Trio in concert & Billy Graham televised crusades. Tour as solo act for approximately 50 concerts per yr. Chief Collabrs: Brown Bannister, Chris Christian, Gary Chapman. *Songs:* Brand New Start; Grape, Grape Joy; He Gave Me a New Song; On and On; I Know Better Now; Father; Faith Walkin' People; Always the Winner; All I Need Is You; Fair Tale; Giggle; There Will Never Be Another; Keep It on Going; Lyrics: Never Give You Up.

GRANT, BERT
ASCAP 1914

composer, pianist

b New York, NY, July 12, 1878; d New York, May 10, 51. Pianist in vaudeville; played in first musical broadcast, Roselle Park, NJ. Charter mem, ASCAP. Chief Collabrs: Joe Young, Sam Lewis, Harry Williams. *Songs:* In the Light of the Same Old Moon; I'm the Guy; Don't Blame It All on Broadway; If I Knock the 'L' Out of Kelly; Let Bygones Be Bygones; When the Angelus Is Ringing; Arrah Go on, I'm Gonna Go Back to Oregon; The Broadway Glide; Along the Rocky Road to Dublin.

GRANT, CHARLES N
ASCAP 1914

composer, arranger

b Jersey City, NJ, Feb 7, 1887; d Los Angeles, Calif, Nov 9, 37. Educ: Cooper Union; Stevens Tech, studied eng; studied music with Rubin Goldmark & Clifton Chalmers. Arr for music publ, 21 yrs. Chief arr, broadcasting co, 28-35; also vocal arr for films. Charter mem, ASCAP. *Songs & Instrumental Works:* Girls, If You Ever Get Married; Pickin' 'Em Up and Layin' 'Em Down; Where's the Little Boy for Me?; You're the Girl That Sets Me Stuttering; King of Hearts; Oriental Nights; A Shy Coquette.

GRANT, FRANK K
ASCAP 1972

composer, author

b Baltimore, Md, Jan 25, 42. Educ: Johns Hopkins Univ, BA, 64. With Westinghouse Broadcasting Co, Compton Advert, Young & Rubicam Advert; jingle writer, copywriter & songwriter. Chief Collabr: J Billy Verplanck. *Songs:* When You Can Laugh (Candid Camera theme song); The Pleasures of Love; Lyrics: Red and Yellow Flowers and Me; Why Don't the Good Girls Ever Know?; Knife in the Drain.

GRANT, GERALD FREDERICK
ASCAP 1959

author

b Seattle, Wash, Apr 11, 23. Educ: Textile High Sch; Pratt Inst, art maj. Commercial artist, photo illusr & photo technician. Writes lyrics in spare time. Chief Collabrs: Arthur Kent, Bee Walker, George Goehring, Guy Wood, Cecil Bentz. *Songs:* Lyrics: Ring a Ling a Lario; Too Little Too Late; Mystery of You; Someone Must Have Hurt You a Lot; Old Habits Are Hard to Break; Tryin' to Catch the Wind; The Power of Love; I Wish You Were Waiting For Me; I've Forgotten More About You Than He'll Ever Know; Time and the Tide; My Heart Can't Remember to Forget; Let's Drop Out of Sight; Lost in a Trance; You'll Get Over It; Wandrin' Eyes.

GRANT, MARSHALL
ASCAP 1958

composer, conductor

b Hartford, Conn, Aug 29, 26. Educ: Univ Conn. *Songs:* Bahamian Merengue.

GRASSI, FRANCO PIO
ASCAP 1971

composer, author

b Taranto, Italy, Dec 12, 30. Educ: Marinarmi Mil Sch, Taranto Arsenal, professional study, 4 yrs; radio announcing course, New York. Nightclub singer, 51-60. Owner, actor, dir & producer, Starlight Dinner Theatre, 57-63. Owner & operator, New Start Recording Studio, Hazlet, NJ, 65-76. Producer & DJ radio prog, "Dreams of Italy," WRLB, NJ, 70-77. Emcee variety show, 76-77 & several beauty contests. Writer & producer of several movie scripts; also interior decorator. *Songs:* Addio; Bring Back the Boogie Woogie; What Is Love; Don't Hang My Heart; How Can I Go to Dance.

GRASSO, RALPH
ASCAP 1964

composer, conductor, guitarist

b Newark, NJ, Mar 5, 34. Educ: High sch. Guitar soloist on radio, TV & in films; has made many records. Music dir & accompanist, "Jimmie Rodgers Show," TV, Los Angeles. Chief Collabr: Randy Sparks. *Songs:* Wagoners Song (Land of the Sacramento).

GRAVES, RALPH SEAMAN, JR
ASCAP 1961

composer, author, publisher

b Los Angeles, Calif, Mar 8, 23. Educ: Univ Fla. Wrote col musicals. Served in USAAF, WW II; wrote musical, "About Face." Has had own mgt, publicity, recording & publ bus. Chief Collabr: Sheldon Smith. *Songs:* Why Don't You Marry the Girl?

GRAVES, WILLIAM
ASCAP 1960

composer, author, educator

b Aspen, Colo, Sept 11, 16. Educ: Colo State Col, BA; Eastman Sch Music, BM; Colo Col, MA; Philadelphia Cons, MusD; Ecole des Artes Americaines, Fountainebleau, France; summer resident, MacDowell Colony; studied with Gardner Read, Roy Harris, Nadia Boulanger, Vincent Persichetti. Bandleader, USAAF, WW II. Prof music, Cath Univ, 50-60; Univ WVa. Author, "Twentieth Century Fugue." *Songs:* God's Grandeur. *Instrumental Works:* Offertories: Lux Perpetua; Jubilate Deo. *Scores:* Opera: The Juggler (Nat Coun Cath Men comn).

GRAY, CHAUNCEY EUGENE
ASCAP 1942

author, conductor, pianist

b Rock City Falls, NY, Jan 5, 04. Educ: High sch; spec study with Prof Gene Somers. Piano soloist & band leader, ballrooms, vaudeville & nightclubs. Chief Collabrs: Fred Hamm, Dave Bennett, Bert Lown, Harry Link, Dorothy Dick, Sy Taylor, Charles Reade. *Songs:* Music: Bye Bye Blues; You're the One I Care For; By My Side; No More Rain; I Had Too Much to Dream Last Night.

GRAY, JERRY
ASCAP 1942

composer, conductor, arranger

b East Boston, Mass, July 3, 15; d Dallas, Tex, Aug 10, 76. Educ: High sch; studied music with Ondricek. Solo violinist, Boston Jr Symph, age 13. Formed own jazz band; played in night clubs. First violinist & arr, Artie Shaw Orch, 36; later arr for Andre Kostelanetz & Glenn Miller. USAAF, WW II. Arr, asst cond & later cond, Glenn Miller Band. Own radio shows, 46-52. Led dance orch; made many records. Joined Warner Bros, 62. Chief Collabrs: Robert Bruce, Leonard Ware, John Benson Brooks, Jerome Lawrence. *Songs & Instrumental Works:* String of Pearls; Crew Cut; Sun Valley Jump; Pennsylvania 6-5000; Keep 'Em Flying; I Dreamt I Dwelt in Harlem; The Man in the Moon.

GRAY, JOHN BAKER (TIMOTHY)
ASCAP 1960

composer, author, singer

b Chicago, Ill. Educ: Kelvyn Park High Sch, Ill; studied drama with Maurice Tei Dunn, voice with Keith David & piano with Hedy Spielter, all of New York. Writer of music, lyrics & bks for musicals incl "High Spirits", "Love from Judy",

"Welcome Darlings", "September Song", "The Musical World of Kurt Weill", "Taboo Revue" & "From Here and There." Performer in var shows incl "Heaven on Earth", "As the Girls Go", "Gentlemen Prefer Blondes", "Salute to Cole Porter", "Airs on a Shoe String" & "Scapa", London. Dir & producer, "Penny Plain" & Bway show, "Johnny Johnson"; TV performer, 4 yrs. Chief Collabrs: Hugh Martin, Jerry De Bond, Dolores Claman, Claus Ogerman, Dennis Buck. *Songs:* You'd Better Love Me; Forever and a Day; Was She Prettier Than I?; *Lyrics:* Darling Joe; Meet Me in St Louis, Louis.

GRAY, THOMAS J ASCAP 1914
author

b New York, NY, Mar 22, 1888; d New York, Nov 30, 24. Educ: Holy Cross Sch. WW I, overseas. Wrote songs for Bway & London revues. Spec material for Frank Tinney, Bert Williams, Blossom Seeley, Savoy & Brennan, Trixie Friganza, Mae West. Columnist for Variety & Dramatic Mirror. Wrote film screenplays. Chief Collabrs: Fred Fisher, Ray Walker. *Songs:* Any Little Girl That's a Nice Little Girl Is the Right Little Girl for Me; Think It Over, Mary; Take Me With You, Cutey; That's How You Can Tell They're Irish; Not Me; Your Mother's Gone Away to Join the Army.

GRAY BEY, MICHAEL ASHLEY (MICKEY BEY) ASCAP 1972
composer, author

b Detroit, Mich, Jan 9, 47. Educ: Pvt trumpet study with Carlos Riveria, 4 yrs; Mumford High Sch. Played at var service clubs while in the Army. Recording artist, Curtom Records, 69; on the road, played with Bobby Franklin's Insanity until 71, also recorded. Retired from writing & playing, 72. Mgr, Music Publ Co, Inc, Detroit, 73-75. Has own publ co Bey-El Music; adv, Carlis Munroe Proj through Mechan Productions. Chief Collabrs: Bobby Franklin, Charles Ted Johnson, Pat Meehan, De Nesia Bey. *Songs:* Grass Ain't Greener; I'll Always Love You; That Old Circle; Live Life for the Good (song fest); *Music:* I Wish I Knew; We Made It; *Lyrics:* Disco Love; You Got to Be My Woman. *Instrumental Works:* 1-2-3; Our Theme.

GRAYSON, ALAN ASCAP 1959
composer

b London, Eng, Sept 11, 30. Educ: Pvt music study. Moved to US, 52; served in USA, Korea. *Instrumental Works:* Tambalino; Autumn in Retrospect (concert band).

GRAYSON, PAUL
See Dempsey, James E

GRAZIANO, CAESAR FRANKIE (LOU FRANKIE) ASCAP 1963
composer, author, teacher

b Asti, Italy, Nov 10, 04. Educ: High sch; studied instrumentation, harmony, comp, arr & many instruments; studied with Paris Federici & John P Bariellas. Started music study at age 6. 1st clarinet, Chicago Opera Co; 1st trumpet, John P Sousa's Band, age 9. Player at dances, vaudeville, bands & nightclubs, age 15. Asst to Guido Deiro, toured US & Can. Has Standard Designated Teaching Cert in instrumental music, State of Calif. Comp, arr & player of jazz, latin, country & continental dance music for own bands, Dance Combo & 25 Piece Dance Band.

GREAN, CHARLES RANDOLPH ASCAP 1978
composer, author, conductor

b New York, NY, Oct 1, 13. Educ: Wesleyan Univ, 2 yrs. Began as bass player, 32-44. Copyist, free-lance & Glenn Miller Orch, 39-42. USCG, 42-45. Recording dir, RCA, DOT & free-lance; wrote var works; now doing films & soap opera backgrounds. Chief Collabr: Cy Coben. *Songs:* The Thing; Sweet Violets; Never Been Kissed; Eddy's Song; You're a Real Good Friend.

GREAN, ROBIN T ASCAP 1969
composer, author, singer

b New York, NY, Oct 2, 50. Educ: Ithaca Col; NY Univ, voice with David Collyer. In Bway "Jesus Christ Superstar", "Clams on the 1/2 Shell", "Platinum." Singer, recordings, jingles & TV; tours for var artists incl Midler, Manilow; artist on Ranwood Records. Chief Collabrs: Dennis Cooley, Paul Parnes. *Songs:* Call Me Down to Chelsea; The Best Thing We've Got Is Love. *Instrumental Works:* The Masterpiece.

GRECO, ANTHONY BATTISTA ASCAP 1977
composer, author, actor

b Los Angeles, Calif, May 27, 48. Educ: High Sch, St Anthony's Sem; Loyola High Sch; studied playwrighting with Arnold Weinstein. Has comp for TV "Sally Struthers Show" & records, Bo Diddley. Singer, musician, dir. Chief Collabr: Librettist, Arnold Weinstein *Scores:* Bway Shows: Metamorphoses; Ormer Locklear; The American Revolution; Lady Liberty's Ice Cream Cone; Gypsy New York; American More or Less.

GRECO, ARMANDO (BUDDY) ASCAP 1957
composer, pianist, singer

b Philadelphia, Pa, Aug 14, 26. Cond own trio, 44-49. Pianist, singer & arr, Benny Goodman Orch, 49-52. Singer, theatres & nightclubs; also made many records. *Songs:* Make Up Your Mind; El Greco; Just Walk Away; Stay Warm.

GREELEY, GEORGE HENRY ASCAP 1957
composer, conductor, pianist

b Westerly, RI, July 23, 17. Educ: Westerly High Sch; Juilliard Sch Music, 35-39; Columbia Univ; Univ Southern Calif; pvt study with Ernst Toch; studied piano with Gaston Dethier. Staff, Columbia Pictures, 10 yrs. Composer & music dir for series: "My Favorite Martian", "The Ghost and Mrs Muir", "Nanny and the Professor" & "My Living Doll." Pianist, arr & cond, WB Records. Music dir & arr for Gordon MacRae, Jane Powell, Jane Froman, & others. Soloist with Chicago, Montreal, Atlanta, Buenos Aires & Phoenix Symphonies. Chief Collabrs: Carl Sigman, Leon Pober. *Songs: Music:* Lonely Holiday. *Instrumental Works:* Tristan and Isolde (adaptation).

GREEN, ABEL ASCAP 1952
author, editor

b New York, NY, June 3, 1900; d New York, May 10, 73. Theatrical trade reporter, writer & editor; organizer theatrical news coverage of Europ, NAfrican & SAm Capitols for Variety, 29-30, also ed, coauthor & producer, "Philco-Variety Radio Hall of Fame". Author, "Tin Pan Alley", "Outward Bound and Gagged" & co-author, "Show Biz (From Vaudeville to Video)"; ed, "The Spice of Variety." Chief Collabrs: Jesse Greer, Pat Ballard, Al Stillman, Fletcher Henderson. *Songs:* Variety Stomp; Variety Is the Spice of Life; Blue Baby; Florida; Who's Who Are You?; Encore; Humming Waters.

GREEN, ADOLPH ASCAP 1945
author, actor

b New York, NY, Dec 2, 15. Mem nightclub act, The Revuers, with Betty Comden & Judy Holliday; appeared with Betty Comden on stage in "A Party" (Obie Award) & on TV. Coauthor, "Applause" (Tony Award) & "On the 20th Century" (Tony Award). Co-librettist & co-lyricist, "On the Town"; "Billion Dollar Baby"; "Two on the Aisle"; "Bells Are Ringing"; "Subways Are for Sleeping"; "Fade Out—Fade In"; "On the 20th Century"; lyricist, "Wonderful Town" (Drama Critics & Tony Awards); "Hallelujah Baby" (Tony Award); "Do Re Mi"; "Peter Pan." Film score, screenplay, "It's Always Fair Weather" (Academy Award nominee). Screenplays: "On the Town" (Screen Writer's Guild Award); "Good News"; "The Barkleys of Broadway"; "Singin' in the Rain" (Screen Writer's Guild Award); "The Band Wagon" (Academy Award nominee); "Auntie Mame"; "Bells Are Ringing"; "What a Way to Go"; "Hallelujah, Baby"; "My Own Morning"; "Being Good Isn't Good Enough"; "Talking to Myself"; "On the 20th Century"; "Our Private World"; "To-Gether." Chief Collabrs: lyrics, libretto & screenplay, Betty Comden, comp, Leonard Bernstein, Jule Styne, Andre Previn, Morton Gould, Cy Coleman. *Songs:* New York, New York; I Get Carried Away; I Can Cook, Too; Some Other Time; Lonely Town; Lucky to Be Me; Bad Timing; Ohio; A Little Bit in Love; It's Love; A Quiet Girl; The French Lesson; If You Hadn't But You Did; Give a Little, Get a Little; There Never Was a Baby Like My Baby; The Party's Over; Long Before I Knew You; Just in Time; Never-Never Land; Something's Always Happening on the River; Dance Only With Me; Adventure; Make Someone Happy; Fireworks; Ride Through the Night; Comes Once in a Lifetime; I'm Just Taking My Time; Now; Fade Out—Fade In; Get Acquainted.

GREEN, ALFRED MARTIN ASCAP 1976
composer, author, producer

b Hollywood, Calif, July 20, 52. Educ: William Taft High Sch, Woodland Hills, Calif; Pierce Col; comp study with Joseph Weiss. Pianist, 66- Writer for groups & promoter. Joined Shoestring Records, 76. Promoter & producer of records. Comedy musician, with Zack Hoffman, 77- Chief Collabrs: Zack Hoffman, Jeff Platts, Jay Dennis. *Songs:* Don't Let Skylab Fall on Me. *Instrumental Works:* Vagabond Rag.

GREEN, BERNARD ASCAP 1955
composer, conductor

b New York, NY, Sept 14, 08; d Westport, Conn, Aug 8, 75. Comp & cond, films, TV & records; records incl "Futura", "Musically Mad" & "Tony Randall." Chief Collabr: Helen Deutsch. *Instrumental Works:* Symphony; Waltz Etudes; The White Magnolia Tree; Parisian Street Dance; Idyll. *Scores:* Film background: 30 Years of Fun; MGM Big Parade of Comedy; All the Way Home; TV: Cool McCool; Caesar's Hour; Mr Peepers; Garry Moore Show; Miss USA & Miss Universe Pageants (67-75); Film/TV: Zotz.

GREEN, BRUCE H ASCAP 1966
composer, author

b Harrogate, Tenn, Nov 17, 43. Educ: Long Island Univ, BS. *Songs:* Dawn to Dusk; Here With Me; Somethin' Else.

GREEN, BUD ASCAP 1921
composer, author

b Austria, Nov 19, 1897. Educ: New York pub schs; Sch Archit, Educ Alliance, New York. Wrote spec material for vaudeville. Wrote Bway stage scores & songs in musicals for Cecil Lean, Cleo Mayfield, Winnie Lightner & Sophie Tucker. Staff writer for music publ, 20-28; formed own firm. Author bk, "Writing Songs for Fame and Fortune." ASCAP Citation, Fiftieth Yr Membership. Elected to Songwriters Hall of Fame, 75. Chief Collabrs: Les Brown, B G De Sylva, Al Dubin, Ella Fitzgerald, Slim Gaillard, Ray Henderson, Ben Homer, Raymond Scott, Sam Stept, Harry Warren. *Songs: Lyrics:* Alabamy Bound; That's My

Weakness Now; I Love My Baby; Oh Boy, What a Girl; In My Gondola; Away Down South in Heaven; I'll Always Be in Love With You; Do Something; Congratulations; Good Little, Bad Little You; My Mother's Evening Prayer; Simple and Sweet; Dream Sweetheart; Moonlight on the River; Swingy Little Thingy; Blue Fedora; More Than Ever; You Showed Me the Way; Tia Juana; Once in a While; The Man Who Comes Around; Flat Foot Floogie; Sentimental Journey; My Number One Dream Came True; On Accounta I Love You. *Albums:* Two Shades of Green.

GREEN, DAVID LEWIS   ASCAP 1979
composer, author, musician

b Port Chester, NY, Oct 22, 51. Educ: Rye High Sch; Yankton Col, classical study; Berklee Col Music, instr & comp cert. Performer & recorder with group, Breeze & Just Sunshine Records. Writer & recorder with own group, Green's Friends. Chief Collabrs: Raymond Bardani, Mike Colina, Randy Adler. *Songs:* Feelin' Kinda Good (Song Fest Winner); Girls! Girls! Girls! (Song Fest Winner); Take Time; Dedication to Muhammad Ali (Medley incl The Story, The Greatest, The Double Shuffle).

GREEN, FRANK T   ASCAP 1977
composer, author

b Talledega, Ala, Nov 29, 51. Educ: Nebr Wesleyan Univ. Writer, producer & music eng.

GREEN, GARY M   ASCAP 1979
composer, author, singer

b Hamlet, NC, Feb 1, 54. Educ: Univ Tenn & NC Comn Arts & Sci Spirit Square Proj, studied Am topical music. Teacher Am topical music, Univ Tenn & NC Comn Arts & Sci Spirit Square Proj. Recording artist, Folkways Records. Founder of topical music proj, I Hear America Singing. *Songs:* I Wore His Gun; There Ain't No Easy Way; Annie and Her Violin; The Hammer. *Scores:* Film/TV: The Siege of Fort Apache.

GREEN, H LELAND   ASCAP 1954
composer

b Anaheim, Calif, Aug 1, 07. Educ: Occidental Col; Univ Southern Calif. Teacher, sec schs, 52- Coordr music educ, Pasadena City Schs. *Songs:* If You Come to Jesus; Jesus Is Coming; Victory.

GREEN, HAROLD   ASCAP 1951
composer, author

b Pauline, Kans, Sept 20, 13. Educ: Washburn High Sch; Kans Univ, studied with Donald Swarthout. Pianist & organist in hotels, cabarets, restaurants, New York, 34- Chief Collabr: Michael Stoner. *Songs:* It's Make Believe Balloon Time; I Guess I'll Have to Dream the Rest; Faithful to You; What Did You Do Last Night; Oh, What a Sad, Sad Day; It's Sad, But True.

GREEN, JOHN   ASCAP 1931
composer, conductor, pianist

b New York, NY, Oct 10, 08. Educ: Horace Mann Sch, New York; Harvard Univ, BA, 28; music theory studies with Clifton J Furness, Walter Raymond Spalding & Clair Leonard, orchestration with Adolph Deutsch, cond with Frank Tours & piano with Herman Wasserman & Ignace Hilsberg. Arr, Lombardo Royal Canadians, 27, Victor Young Atwater Kent Hour, 31 & Paul Whiteman, 32. Comp, music dir, arr, theatre cond & emcee, Paramount Studios & Paramount-Publix Theatres, 30-33. Leader, Johnny Green, 33-40. CBS in-house music dir, 33-40. With commercial radio, 34-37. Music dir & cond, Rodgers & Hart's "By Jupiter," 42. Staff comp & cond, MGM Studios, 42-46, gen music dir & exec-in-charge music, 49-58. Guest cond maj symph orchs, 49- Five times Acad Award winner. Chief Collabrs: Edward Heyman, E Y Harburg, Johnny Mercer, Paul Francis Webster, Billy Rose, Ira Gershwin, Robert Sour. *Songs:* Music: Coquette; I'm Yours; Out of Nowhere; I Cover the Waterfront; I Wanna Be Loved; The Song of Raintree County; You're Mine, You, Body and Soul. *Instrumental Works:* Night Club (six impressions for three pianos & orch); Music for Elizabeth (fantasia for piano & orch); Mine Eyes Have Seen (symph parallels & contradictions for orch; Bicentennial comn, Denver Symph Orch); Materia Media (three impressions for solo piano); Serenade for a New Baby; Raintree County (three themes for symph orch). *Scores:* Bway shows: Here Goes the Bride; Beat the Band; Mr Whittington; Raintree County (film score); Empire (TV series); Miami Undercover (TV series).

GREEN, LEWIS G   ASCAP 1955
composer, author, musician

b Omaha, Nebr, Oct 25, 09. Educ: NY Univ; Racine Col; Wilson Cons. Musician in dance bands, also arr. Mem recording group, Green Bros. Asst production mgr, Ferde Grofe radio show. Writer of musical commercials. Producer, Don McNeill's "Breakfast Club," ABC; also industrials. Has own production agency. Chief Collabr: Edward Ballantine. *Songs:* Silent Prayer; Blue Dreams; Banjo Blues; Mandolino Serenade; My Home Is O-Hi-O; I Dreamt About a Dixieland Band; They Planted Old Glory on a Mountain.

GREEN, LILLIAN PEARL   ASCAP 1978
composer, author, singer

b Renfrew, Ont, Sept 13, 51. Educ: Spring Arbor Col, Mich, 2 yrs. Recording artist, Destiny & Myrrh Records. *Songs:* Misty Morning; Crucify Him; God, a Woman and a Man.

GREEN, MAXIE
See Greenberg, Susan M

GREEN, MORTON JOSEPH   ASCAP 1962
composer, author, producer

b Brooklyn, NY, Dec 19, 19. Writer, producer, dir & creator of radio & TV shows, 44-, shows incl "The Big Show" (Tallulah Bankhead), "Easy Aces", "Berle-Buick Show", "Perry Como Show", "Andy Williams Show", "Garrison's Gorillas", "Vaudeville Specials", "Mitzi and 100 Guys", "Yes, Virginia, There is a Santa Claus", "Make Me Laugh" & others. Awards: Emmy, George Foster Peabody, Sylvania, Christopher Medal & others. Chief Collabr: George Wyle. *Songs:* Lyrics: May Each Day.

GREEN, NORMA
See Helms, Norma Hale

GREEN, PAUL ELIOT   ASCAP 1938
composer, author

b Lillington, NC, Mar 17, 1894. Educ: Buie's Creek Acad, NC; Univ NC, 21; Cornell Univ, 21-22. Guggenheim fels, 28-30. Pres, Nat Folk Fest, 34-44 & Nat Theatre Conf, 40-42. From assoc prof philosophy to prof dramatic art, Univ NC, 35-45. From pvt to 2nd Lt, Engrs, AEF, WW I. Mem, Nat Inst Arts & Letters. Author plays, motion picture scripts, short stories, novels & several volumes of critical essays. Author plays: "In Abraham's Bosom" (Pulitzer Prize); "The Field God"; "The Honeycomb"; "The House of Connelly"; "Tread the Green Grass"; "Roll Sweet Chariot"; "Johnny Johnson"; "Native Son"; "The Lost Colony"; "The Highland Call"; "The Common Glory"; "Faith of Our Fathers"; "The 17th Star"; "Wilderness Road"; "The Founders"; "The Confederacy"; "The Stephen Foster Story"; "Cross and Sword"; "Texas"; "Trumpet in the Land"; "Drumbeats in Georgia"; "Louisiana Cavalier"; "The Lone Star"; "We the People"; "Palo Duro" (drama). *Songs & Instrumental Works:* A Christmas Prayer; Song in the Wilderness (two cantatas for piano, chorus & orch).

GREEN, SANFORD   ASCAP 1953
composer, pianist, conductor

b Hartford, Conn. Contract writer, M Witmark & Sons. Writer songs, Warner Bros. Musical coordr, TV shows incl "Kate Smith Hour", "Caesar's Hour", "Arthur Murray Show", "Garry Moore Show", "Philco Playhouse" & NBC specials. Vpres, Sherwin Music Publ Corp. Chief Collabrs: Irving Kahal, Mack David, Mann Curtis. *Songs:* Music: Play Me Hearts and Flowers; Bermuda Buggyride; Brokenhearted Troubador.

GREEN, URBAN CLIFFORD   ASCAP 1963
composer, trombonist, conductor

b Mobile, Ala, Aug 8, 26. Trombonist in orchs incl Tommy Reynolds, Bob Strong, Jan Savitt, Frankie Carle, Gene Krupa, Woody Herman & Benny Goodman. Has led own band; has made many records. *Instrumental Works:* Sentimental Blues; The Poor Soul.

GREEN, WILLIAM   ASCAP 1952
composer, conductor, pianist

b New York, NY, Dec 3, 13. Educ: Boston Latin Sch; Harvard Univ. Pianist, Olympic Ice Skating Champions, Lake Placid; also in Ruby Newman Orch; joined radio sta WHDH, 48; cond, WHDH TV Orch, 55. *Songs:* The Happy Waltz; I Wants to Marry 'Arry; Whozits From Massachusetts.

GREENBERG, ABNER   ASCAP 1938
composer, author, publisher

b Philadelphia, Pa, June 2, 1889; d New York, NY, Jan 4, 59. Educ: Townsend Harris Hall; City Col New York; NY Univ Law Sch. Lawyer, legislator. Elected to NY State Assembly, 16. Became music publ. *Songs:* Two Hearts on a Window Pane; Ghost Town; Thank God; C'est Vous.

GREENBERG, HENRY F   ASCAP 1959
author

b Malden, Mass, Feb 28, 12. Educ: Harvard Univ, BA, MA. Writer for films & TV; also teacher.

GREENBERG, NORMAN (NORMAN GREENE)   ASCAP 1953
composer, recording artist

b Brooklyn, NY, Jan 16, 30. Educ: Formal training at age 10 with piano & instr in clarinet, bassoon, oboe & saxophone. Mem Local Am Fedn Musicians, 48. Arr, cond & comp with MGM Records, age 21. Recorded for Decca Records & orchestrated background music for pop singers, 53. Chief Collabrs: Richard Hayman, Nelson Gimbel, Burt Bacharach, Helena Paris. *Songs:* Suspicion.

GREENBERG, SUSAN M (MAXIE GREEN)   ASCAP 1976
composer, author, singer

b Brooklyn, NY, Aug 1, 44. Educ: Pratt Inst, fine arts degree. Worked as singer in top 40 show groups across the country; some single work playing piano & singing. Wrote & recorded commercials for national accounts. Own five piece group working SE area & Caribbean Islands. Chief Collabr: Norman Dolph. *Songs:* Stay the Night; I Changed My Mind; I'm a Dreamer.

GREENE, ALAN ASCAP 1956
composer, author, singer
b New York, NY, May 23, 21. Educ: Studied piano, harmony & theory, 35-36; high sch, 39. Played harmonica & sang with vaudeville act, 40-45. Began vocal teaching, 45. Comp, arr & cond var Harry Belafonte albums & singles. Composed theme music for "The World, the Flesh and the Devil." Composed one-act jazz opera "The Corner," 59. Author of bk on vocal technique, "The New Voice," 76. Chief Collabrs: Lewis Allan, Edwin Haldman, Laura Manning. *Songs:* Music: Fifteen (16-18); Turn Around; Lean on Me. *Songs & Instrumental Works:* Antiques; The Corner. *Albums:* Music: Know Your Body From Head to Toe; What Can the Difference Be (children's albums).

GREENE, HARRY WELLINGTON ASCAP 1961
composer, author, singer
b Castalia, NB, Nov 22, 28. Chief Collabr: Lewis Elliott. *Songs & Instrumental Works:* Country Music; You Were So Sure; House Full of Love; Except for an Old Guitar; Ten Years; Five Hundred Dollars.

GREENE, JOHN L ASCAP 1964
author
b Buffalo, NY, Nov 10, 12. Educ: Duke Univ; Ohio State Univ; State Univ Iowa, BA. Radio & TV writer; created "My Favorite Martian," TV series. Chief Collabr: Bonnie Lake. *Songs:* St Francis of Assisi.

GREENE, JOSEPH PERKINS ASCAP 1946
composer, author, conductor
b Spokane, Wash, Apr 19, 15. Educ: High sch; studied comp & arr, 2 yrs. Singer, KFRC, San Francisco. Produced records, RCA Victor, Liberty & Vee Jay. Comp scores for 6 motion pictures. Mem, Am Fedn Musicians, Acad Motion Picture Arts & Sciences, Writer's Guild Am West. Rec'd Urban League Achievement Award. Chief Collabrs: Stan Kenton, Charles Lawrence, Eddie Beal, Nelson Riddle. *Songs:* Across the Alley From the Alamo; Don't Let the Sun Catch You Cryin'; All About Ronnie; Chicken Road; Make Me a Present of You; Soothe Me; Dusky January; Be Easy, Be Tender; Lyrics: And Her Tears Flow'd Like Wine; Annabelle; Softly.

GREENE, MILTON L ASCAP 1958
composer, conductor, arranger
b New York, NY. Educ: Long Island Univ, pre-med; NY Univ Sch Educ, BS & MA. Music dir, "Bert Parks Show," 50. Staff cond, CBS, 52. Cond, Bway musicals incl "Fiorello!" & "Fiddler on the Roof." Chief Collabr: William Margaretten. *Songs & Instrumental Works:* Fugue for Thought; Fallin'; Like This; Going Steady With the Moon.

GREENE, MORT ASCAP 1941
author, producer
b Cleveland, Ohio, Oct 3, 12. Educ: Univ Pa Wharton Sch Finance; Univ Akron. Contract writer for films, then assoc producer, 20th Century-Fox. Producer, TV shows incl Bob Cummings, Herb Shriner. Writer for var artists & shows incl Bob Crosby, Red Skelton, Johnny Carson, "Laugh-in" & many TV specials. Producer, writer & dir of nightclub acts. Songwriter for var films incl "The Big Street", "Call Out the Marines", "Beyond the Blue Horizon", "Seven Days Ashore", "Stations West", "Tulsa", "Mayor of 44th Street", "Stage Door", "Honeymoon", "Five Jacks and a Jill" & "The Velvet Touch." Chief Collabrs: Walter Donaldson, Harry Revel, Allie Wrubel, Leigh Harline, Lew Pollack, Harry Barris, George Cates. *Songs:* High Society; Sleepy Serenade; Thrilled; When There's a Breeze on Lake Louise; Stars in Your Eyes; Nevada; Heavenly, Isn't It?; A Full Moon and an Empty Heart; Sing Your Worries Away; Sioux City Sue; My Grandfather's Clock; Fantastic, That's You; He Took Her for a Sleighride; The Circus is Coming to Town; Teen Age Waltz; Merry Christmas From Our House to Your House; Helena Polka; Nocturne; Weary Blues; I Want You; From This Day Forward; I've Got My Fingers Crossed; Boogie Woogie Conga; Wherever You Are; Ven Aqui; Sunday Barbecue; Bombay; Who Knows. *Songs & Instrumental Works:* TV theme songs: Leave It to Beaver; Restless Gun; Tales of Wells Fargo; Buckskin; Lawrence Welk Champagne Time.

GREENE, NORMAN
See Greenberg, Norman

GREENE, ROBERT VICTOR (CORKY) ASCAP 1973
composer, author, singer
b New York, NY, Aug 23, 41. Educ: Calif State Univ, Northridge, BA(speech & educ), 63, MA(admin, supv), 66. Teaching & admin credential for grades 1-12 & col. Started as band leader & singer musician in high sch & col. Featured on & did music for game show "Hold That Pose." Co-producer, comp & sound effects for NBC cartoon show "Adventures of Muhammad Ali." Numerous stage appearances in US. Co-star & music dir, KNBC TV show, "Whitney and the Robot". Writer & producer of var commercials. Mem: Am Fedn Musicians, Am Fedn TV & Radio Artists, Screen Actors Guild. Chief Collabrs: Charles Blaker, Erich Bulling. *Songs:* I Start My Diet Monday; Lyrics: It's Saturday; Themes: Hold That Pose; Whitney and the Robot; Adventures of Muhammad Ali.

GREENE, SCHUYLER ASCAP 1914
author
b Newport, RI, Dec 23, 1880; d Saranac Lake, NY, Aug 13, 27. Mem staff, music publ co. Charter mem, ASCAP. Chief Collabrs: Jerome Kern, Vincent Youmans, Otto Harbach, Charles Grant. *Songs:* Babes in the Wood; Some Sort of Someone; The Boy Next Door; He's Such a Wonderful Boy; Fascination; You Know and I Know; Girls, If You Ever Get Married. *Scores:* Bway: Nobody Home; Very Good Eddie.

GREENE, WALTER WESLEY ASCAP 1952
composer, conductor, orchestrator
b Tarkio, Mo, Jan 10, 10. Educ: High sch, Tarkio, 27; Horners Cons, Kansas City, Mo, 30; Tarkio Col, BA, 33, LHD, 78. Arr, Orville Knapp, 2 yrs, Freddy Martin, 3 yrs, Horace Heidt, 1 yr & MGM, 4 yrs. Comp, cond & orchr for film at following motion picture studios: PRC-Eagle Lion, Warner Bros, Walter Lantz, De-Pattie-Freling & Filmation, plus many TV films, incl over 200 for Gene Autry, var full length motion pictures & TV films for independent producers & dozens of TV commercials. Nominated for Acad Award for PRC picture, "Why Girls Leave Home." Recorded some music in Ger, Eng & Mex. Wrote cues for, "Ann Sothern Show", "Bozo the Clown", "The Pink Panther" (cartoon), "The Inspector" & "Journey to the Center of the Earth", scores for, "Dick Tracy Series" (partial) & "Woody Woodpecker" (partial for series), background music for, "The New Three Stooges" & incidental music for Jody. *Songs:* That's Our Love Song; The Call; Wackity Woody; Poesy; Music: We're Leaving; That's All; Time Ran Out; The Smokin' General; Atlanta Has a Certain Way; Autumn in Georgia; Stars Over America; Georgia Is My Home; Flim Flam Fountain (Vacation Time); The Hippie Song (Woody's Magic Touch); Where's the Dragon (Woody's Magic Touch); Oh Give Me a Horse; Jolly Ole England; Don't Eat Turkey. *Scores:* Film: Frontier Woman; Natchez Train; Gunfight at Tombstone; Ringo; Naked Gun; Teenage Monster; Brains From Planet Argus; War of the Satellites; Teenage Doll; Teenage Thunder; Carnival Rock.

GREENHILL, MITCH ASCAP 1964
composer, author, singer
b Brooklyn, NY, Mar 20, 44. Educ: South End Sch Music; Boston Latin Sch; Harvard Col, BA, 65; Berklee Col Music, Boston, Mass; Sonoma State Col, Calif; studied arr with Walt Oster, guitar with Russ Di Fillipis, Rolf Cahn, Wayne Clifton. Recording artist on several albums. Produced var albums for other artists; comp & produced music for TV commercials for Toyota, Mattel, Bell Telephone, Calif Raisin Growers. Singing & acting role in film "The Long Riders," 80. Chief Collabrs: Mayne Smith, Fred Gardner. *Songs:* Ain't No Instant Replay (In the Football Game of Life); Foggy Tuesday; Won't You Tell Me (Tell Me Mama); Joshua; Music: People Change. *Albums:* Pickin' the City Blues; Shepherd of the Highways; Storm Coming.

GREENLUND, ALYS GERTRUDE ASCAP 1957
composer, teacher, organist
b Tacoma, Wash, Mar 14, 02. Educ: Studied comp with Louis Victor Sauer, organ with Albert Hay MaLotte. Picked out tunes at age 3; started piano study at age 6. Studied organ during high sch. Played for silent films, theatres, 10 yrs. Played theatre organ, Fox. Worked at Loews State, Los Angeles. Daily radio show, KTM. Chief Collabr: Teresa Smith. *Songs & Instrumental Works:* Trinidad Transfer; Jig of the Elves (piano solo); The Leaky Fawcett (piano solo); Bethlehem Road (vocal solo & SATB arr).

GREENWALD, JOEL ASCAP 1960
composer, conductor, trumpeter
b New York, NY, Sept 7, 38. Educ: City Col New York, BA; Teachers Col, Columbia Univ. Trumpeter & vocal arr; has toured with dance orchs.

GREENWOOD, MICHAEL VERNON ASCAP 1972
composer, author, singer
b London, Eng, Feb 13, 51. Educ: Halifax High Sch, Pa; Dickinson Col; Exeter Col Art; Univ Exeter. Singer, guitarist & pianist night clubs, concert halls, int tours, TV & radio. Recording artist, MCA & Warner Bros Records. *Songs:* Living Game; Taxi; After the First World War; To the Sea; Nobody Knows Me; Share the Load; Spooked; Mother Earth; Diana Demons; Lady Midnight; Knock, Knock, Knocking; Shine a Light. *Scores:* Film: Space Place. *Albums:* Living Game; To Friends; Mick Greenwood's Midnight Dreamer.

GREER, JESSE ASCAP 1923
composer, pianist
b New York, NY, Aug 26, 1896; d. Educ: High Sch of Commerce. Relief pianist in film theatre. Served in WW I. Pianist for music publ. Chief Collabrs: George Jessel, Walter Hirsch, Raymond Klages, Harry Rose, Stanley Adams, Harold Adamson, Bert Mann. *Songs:* Kitty From Kansas City; Baby Blue Eyes; Climbing Up the Ladder of Love; Sleepy Head; Once in a Lifetime; Just You, Just Me; Spellbound; You Fit Into the Picture; Did You Mean It?; On the Beach With You; I Fell and Broke My Heart; Old Mill Wheel; Sittin' in the Dark; Flapperette; Freshie; What Do I Care; The Hills of My Connecticut; You Can't Tell a Lie to Your Heart; Two Broken Hearts; Wrong; Two Timer; Extra! All About That Gal of Mine.

GREER, MICHAEL BARRY   ASCAP 1968
composer, singer, actor
b Durham, NC, Dec 16, 38. Educ: Cornell Univ, BA, 59; Harvard Univ, MA, 61; City Univ New York, PhD, 75. Actor, Off-off, Off & On-Bway, dinner theatres, regional, summer stock & TV commercials. Composer-lyricist; poet; essayist; short-story writer; free lance journalist. *Songs:* Corporate Lady; All Behind Me Now; Lyrics: After the Circus. *Instrumental Works:* Better Than You Know. *Scores:* Lyrics: The Way It Is (Off-Bway).

GREGG, MARY LOUISE   ASCAP 1958
composer, pianist, organist
b Pike County, Ohio, May 30, 21. Educ: Bus col; BM in music. Church organist & pianist. *Songs:* Forget Me Not Polka.

GREGORY, BOBBY   ASCAP 1940
composer, author, singer
b Staunton, Va, Apr 24, 1900; d Nashville, Tenn. Been cowboy, lumberjack, sailor, circus & rodeo musician. Accordionist & leader band, Cactus Cowboys. Made many records. *Songs:* Little Darlin'; Am I Dreaming?; Sunny Side of the Mountain; Riding on the Old Ferris Wheel; She's Only a Moonshiner's Daughter; I'd Love to Be a Cowboy, but I'm Afraid of Cows; Ramblin' Hobo; Will the Circle Be Unbroken; Old Rattler.

GREGORY, CATHERINE ELIZEBETH
composer, author, singer
b Chicago, Ill, Feb 1, 13. Chief Collabrs: Bobby Gregory, Jack Bowers. *Songs:* Who Stole Grandpa's Wooden Leg; Maggie Get the Hammer There's a Fly on Baby's Head; The Circus Caliope; I Stepped on a Banana Peel; My Red Head Gal; In Our Little Rock Home in the Rockies; Cross Eyed Susie From Buffalo Gap; There's Cobwebs on the Old Ranch Door; My Old Tar Papered Shack in the West; There's a Home on the Range; She's Somebody's Darling Once More; Since Papa Cut His Toe Nails; In a Little Bar and Grill; A Nickel Makes the Music Play; There's a Heart That's Carved in the Old Pine Tree; The Little Wooden Whistle Wouldn't Whistle; Down At the Old Barn Dance; That Mother and Daddy of Mine; I'm Try'na Go Straight on a Cross Eyed Mule; Since Abie Turned Hillbilly.

GREGORY, DAVID L   ASCAP 1969
author
b Bridgeport, Conn, Apr 27, 44. Educ: Milford High Sch, 62; Boston Univ, BFA, 66. Disc jockey, WILI, 66; light designer or stage mgr, 67-70. Chief Collabr: Craig Carnellia. *Songs:* Lyrics: When I See You.

GREGORY, LINDA O'HARA
See O'Hara, Linda

GREINER, ALVIN G   ASCAP 1957
composer, teacher, musician
b Staplehurst, Nebr, June 20, 11. Educ: Univ Nebr. Organist & pianist on radio & TV. Vocal coach, New York. Chief Collabr: Gordon Rod Parker. *Songs:* Christmas Song; Donde Esta Santa Claus.

GRENET, ELISEO   ASCAP 1937
composer, author
b Havana, Cuba, June 12, 1893; d Havana, Nov 4, 50. Educ: Cons Nacional de Musica, Havana. Cond theatrical group, toured Mex & Cent Am, 20, then founded own troup & presented own works. Awarded Gold Medal for folklore compositions, Seville Expos. Scored films in France, Mex & Cuba. Chief Collabrs: Al Stillman, Bickley Reichner, Marion Sunshine, Nat Burton, Walter Kent. *Songs:* Mama Inez; Lamento Esclavo; Facundo; Habanera; Rica Pulpa; Spic and Spanish; True and Sincere Love; I'll Always Remember; Cuba de mi Vida; The Lady Likes to Love; Congo Conga; Viena la Conga. *Scores:* Stage: La Virgen Morena; Nina Rita; La Camagueyana.

GRENNARD, ELLIOTT   ASCAP 1941
composer, author
b New York, NY, Dec 20, 07; d New York, July 23, 68. Ed, The Billboard. Writer of spec material for musicals & nightclubs. O'Henry Short Story Award for "Sparrows Last Jump," 47. *Songs:* I Didn't Dream It Was Love; To Be or Not fo Be (in Love); I Understand; Time Will Tell; Will o' the Wisp; Monday in Manhattan.

GRESHAM, HUBERT E   ASCAP 1977
composer, author, teacher
b Marietta, Ga, Jan 2, 16. Educ: Marietta High Sch; Watch Tower Col Gilead; studied piano & voice. Writer for several artists & groups. Chief Collabr: Duke Anderson. *Songs:* Sleep On; Long Dark Night; Tonight I'm Longing for You; Hope; Want to Be With You; Lyrics: So Great; Never Peace of Mind; I Do Believe; Fine Fine Daddy.

GREVER, MARIA   ASCAP 1935
composer, singer, pianist
b Mexico City, Mex, Aug 15, 1894; d New York, NY, Dec 15, 51. Educ: Pvt music study. Scored many films. Wrote spec material for film performers & concert singers. Made concert tours, chiefly in Latin Am. Chief Collabrs:

Stanley Adams, Irving Caesar, Raymond Leveen. *Songs:* What a Difference a Day Made; Ti-Pi-Tin; Jurame; Lamento Gitano; Lero, Lero From Brazil; Magic Is the Moonlight; Make Love With a Guitar; My First, My Last, My Only.

GREY, CLIFFORD   ASCAP 1925
author
b Birmingham, Eng, Jan 5, 1887; d Ipswich, Eng, Sept 25, 41. Educ: King Edward VI Sch; also Cambridge. Began career as actor. Olympic Gold Medals, 28 & 32. Chief Collabrs: J Freed Coots, Jay Gorney, Jerome Kern, Sigmund Romberg, Rudolf Friml, Lewis Gensler, John Green, Oscar Levant, Leo Robin, Richard Myers, Victor Schertzinger, Herbert Stothart, Vincent Youmans, Werner Janssen, Al Goodman, Maurie Rubens, William Cary Duncan, Jean Schwartz. *Songs:* If You Were the Only Girl in the World; Wild Rose; Sally; Whip-Poor-Will; The Lorelei; The Church 'Round the Corner; Valencia; Hallelujah; Why, Oh Why; My Love Parade; The Rogue Song; Dream Lover; Ma Belle; March of the Musketeers; Got a Date With an Angel. *Scores:* Bway stage: Sally; Vogues of 1924; Artists and Models; Annie Dear; June Days; Gay Paree; A Night in Paris; Great Temptations; The Merry World; Hit the Deck; The Madcap; The Three Musketeers; also librettist: Lady Butterfly; Marjorie; Mayflowers; Sunny Days; Ups-a-Daisy.

GREY, FRANK H   ASCAP 1921
composer, conductor, publisher
b Philadelphia, Pa, Nov 15, 1883; d Beverly Hills, Calif, Oct 3, 51. Educ: Harvard Univ; New Eng Cons, studied with Charles Dennee; studied with G B Nevin & R Huntington Woodman. Cond musicals & light operas, 09-26. Cond & producer in hotel ballrooms, "Celebrity Supper Dances." Became publ, 39. Chief Collabrs: Bide Dudley, Earle Crooker, McElbert Moore, Daniel Twohig. *Songs & Instrumental Works:* Sunny Sicily; Dream of Summer (violin, piano); Valse Fascination; Men of Harvard; Think of Me; Give Me One Rose to Remember; Mother of My Heart; Ce Soir, Ce Soir, Cherie; In the Dusk; Last Year's Roses; Love's Magic. *Scores:* Stage: Sue Dear; Happy.

GREY, GANDALF T
See Wilson, Chris Richard

GREY, GINGER
See Stewart, Joan Beatrice

GREY, JOSEPH W   ASCAP 1939
author, singer
b Salt Lake City, Utah, Oct 5, 1879; d New York, NY, Jan 9, 56. Educ: La Salle Univ. Advert salesman & stage mgr, Eng, Europe. Actor, London, 15. Sang in trio, nightclubs, 14 yrs. *Songs:* Runnin' Wild; The Call of the Red, White and Blue; Come on and Follow Me; I Got the Fever; Pickin' the Blues Away; Rocky Road; How Can You Tell?

GREY, LANNY   ASCAP 1941
composer, singer, pianist
b Elkins, WVa, Jan 2, 09. Educ: Wharton Sch, Univ Pa. On staff, New York music publ. With wife, mem of singing team, Ginger & Lanny; had own radio show. Founded production firm, Ginger & Lanny Grey Productions, musical commercials; also Little Grey Fixit Shop & Grey Industs. Producer. Chief Collabrs: Mitchell Parish, Bing Crosby. *Songs:* I Would If I Could But I Can't; He Holds the Lantern While His Mother Chops the Wood; I Never Harmed an Onion So Why Should They Make Me Cry?; Sayonara-Goodbye; My Flame Went Out Last Night With Somebody Else; also commercials: I Go for a Man Who Wears an Adams Hat; Baby, Bring Me Barricini.

GRIEB, HERBERT C   ASCAP 1960
composer, author
b Syracuse, NY, Sept 17, 1898; d Birmingham, Ala, Aug 23, 73. Educ: Syracuse Univ. Staff organist, Radio Sta WAPI, 30-34; music dir, WBRC, 44-50; dir music, Episcopal Church of the Advent & Temple Emanu-El, Birmingham, Ala. *Songs & Instrumental Works:* Choral: A Carol Service for Children; An Easter Carol Service; Magnificat; Hail the Day.

GRIER, GENE   ASCAP 1979
composer, author, teacher
b Camden, NJ, Aug 5, 42. Educ: Glassboro State Col, BA, 68, MA, 70; studied voice with Roy Hoffmeister, 60-64 & Clarance Miller, 65-68. Church soloist, nightclub singer, summer stock, Winged Victory Singers, Norman Luboff Choir, TV, radio recording artist, concert tours, teacher, adjudicator, workshop clinician & businessman. Chief Collabr: Lowell Everson. *Songs:* The Happiest Time of the Year; Celebration; Dancing With George M; American Folk Collage; Choo-Choo Mama; Life Is a Dream.

GRIER, JAMES W   ASCAP 1937
composer, author, arranger
b Pittsburgh, Pa, Mar 17, 02; d Calif, June 4, 59. Educ: Los Angeles Polytech High Sch. Musician in dance orchs; led own orch playing nightclubs & dance halls, 31-33. Led 11th Naval Dist CG Band, USCG, WW II. Scored films. Chief Collabr: Pinky Tomlin. *Songs:* The Object of My Affection; Music in the Moonlight; Bon Voyage; Remember Cherie; Hollywood at Vine; Silver River; Anitra's Boogie; What's the Reason?; Ivy-Covered Arbor.

GRIFF, JOHN RAY
composer, author, recording artist

b Vancouver, Can, Apr 22, 42. Songwriter & recording artist; started in Can, then moved to Nashville. *Songs & Instrumental Works:* Where Love Begins; You Ring My Bell; I Love the Way That You Love Me; The Last of the Winfield Amateurs; Raymond's Place; Show Me Where; The Morning After Baby Let Me Down; If I Let Her Come In; A Passing Thing; Her Body Couldn't Keep You Off My Mind; Soft Touch; Even; Chances; I May Be Married; You Draw the Line; Darlin'; A Cold Day in July; After the Laughter; Baby; Baby's Gettin' Around.

GRIFFES, CHARLES TOMLINSON   ASCAP 1945
composer, educator

b Elmira, NY, Sept 17, 1884; d New York, NY, Apr 8, 20. Educ: Elmira Acad, studied piano with Mary Broughton; also Jedliczka, Galston, Rufer, Humperdinck, Klatte & Loewengard, Berlin. Appeared occasionally as piano soloist & accompanist, Berlin; also gave piano & harmony lessons. Came to US, 07. Dir music, Hackley Sch for Boys, Tarrytown, NY, until death. *Songs:* By a Lonely Forest Pathway; Three Poems by Fiona MacLeod (incl "The Lament of Ian the Proud"; "Try Dark Eyes to Mine"; "The Rose of the Night"); Symphony in Yellow; An Old Song Re-Sung; The Sorrow of Mydath; Five Poems of Ancient China and Japan; Four Impressions. *Instrumental Works:* The Pleasure Dome of Kubla Khan (symph poem); Bacchanale (orch); Poem for Flute, Orchestra; 2 Sketches Based on Indian Themes (string quartet); The Kairn of Koridwen; Shojo (pantomime drama); Piano works: Fantasy Pieces; Roman Sketches (incl "The White Peacock"; "Nightfall"; "The Fountains of the Acqua Paolo"; "Clouds"); 3 Tone Pictures (incl "The Lake at Evening"); Piano Sonata; Three Preludes; De Profundis (piano).

GRIFFIN, CLAUD N, JR   ASCAP 1979
composer, author, singer

b Cabool, Mo, Feb 2, 40. Educ: Cabool High Sch; Mo Auctioneering Col. Songwriter, Singer, trumpeter & organist. Ordained Pentecostal Minister. *Songs & Instrumental Works:* Poplar Bluff, Missouri Is a Big Disco City; Pomona, Little Town on the Move; Cabool, Missouri Country Yodel; I Love Cabool, My Old Country Home; You Got to Get the Holy Ghost; West Plains, Missouri Country Music Showtown; Revival of Holiness and of Joy; On This Starry Sky of Heaven; Mountain View, Missouri Country Blue Grass Polka; Where Could I Go; Mother's Not Dead, She's Only a-Sleeping; I'm in Love With You; Sheryl Is My Whirly Girl; Twisting Auctioneer; Glenpa, Missouri Yodel; Missouri Hillybilly Twist; I've Got That CB Yodel in the Sky; Oh, She's My Judy.

GRIFFIN, GERALD   ASCAP 1937
composer, author, singer

b Chicago, Ill, May 19, 1891; d Rhinebeck, NY, Jan 11, 62. Educ: St Michael's Parochial Sch; Wheaton Col; studied with DeMarius & H Plunkett Greene. Appeared in & wrote songs for "The Heir of Garry Castle." Toured Eng, Ireland, Australia, New Zealand & US in Irish plays; also appeared in musicals, opera & vaudeville. Soloist, 7th Regional Nat Guard Band. Entertainer, WW I; spent 4 yrs with his Shamrock Revue, USO Camp Shows, WW II. Nat pres, Cath Actors Guild Am, 30-36. Pres, Songwriters Guild Am, 36-41. Nat exec secy, Am Guild Variety Artists, 40-42. *Songs:* Mother in Ireland; I Talked With God; It's Only a Step From Killarney to Heaven; Sunset in Bermuda; Lift Up Your Voice in Praise of God; The Christlike Way.

GRIFFIN, KENNETH WILSON   ASCAP 1947
composer, organist

b Boone County, Mo, Dec 28, 09; d Chicago, Ill, Mar 11, 56. Theater organist, Colo, 30-36. With new portable organ traveled in & around Chicago, 36-42. Played in chapels, Spec Services, US Army, Tex. Solo organist; recorded for several labels incl Columbia. TV, radio & theater appearances followed. Chief Collabrs: Jerry Wayne, Johnny Hill, Johnny Knapp, Marion Spelman, Andy Nelson. *Songs & Instrumental Works:* You Can't Be True, Dear; Lonesome; Louisiana Waltz; Kringle's Jingle; Symphony in 3/4 Time; Jukebox Polka; Oh, Ma Kodi Polka; Polka Pops; Bumble Bee on a Bender; Tears Never Lie; You're My Love Song.

GRIFFIN, ROBERT A, JR   ASCAP 1972
composer, author, singer

b Long Beach, Calif, Nov 1, 49. Educ: Self-taught; Oitis Art Inst. Mem recording groups, Side Effect, Boppers & Popkorn. Recording artist, Fantasy Records, ABC, A&B Records & Oak Tree Records; percussionist. Chief Collabrs: Forest Hamilton, Augie Johnson, Wayne Henderson. *Songs:* In the Meantime; Money's Funny Change Is Strange; Music: Life Is What You Make It; Kicking the Habit; Boppin.

GRIFFIN, WALLY   ASCAP 1957
composer, author

b Detroit, Mich. Educ: Mass Col Pharmacy, BS. Actor & comedian; appeared in hotels, nightclubs; Bway musicals, "Show Girl" & "Sound of Music"; also NBC-TV. *Songs:* You're Fooling Someone; It's Illegal, It's Immoral.

GRIFFITH, JAMES J   ASCAP 1958
composer, conductor, arranger

b Los Angeles, Calif, Feb 13, 16. Educ: Santa Monica Jr Col. Arr & cond, USMC, 34-47. Film & TV actor, 48- *Songs:* Bullwhip.

GRILLO, FRANK R (MACHITO)   ASCAP 1976
composer, author, singer

b Tampa, Fla, Feb 16, 12. Bandleader & vocalist, US, 40 yrs. Singer in nightclubs; recording artist with var record cos. Chief Collabrs: Ray Santos, Millet, Lito Pena, Mario Bauza, Chico O'Farril, Walter Fuller, Rene Hernandez, Modera. *Songs:* Sopa de Pichon; Paella; Mambo a la Savoy; Pineiro Tenia Razon; Amalianos; Bailan Chacha y Guaguanco; Ha y Que Mate; Mambo a la Concord; Salsero; Despierta Boricua; Yerbero; Cada Loco con Su Tema; Congo Mulense; Chevere Que Chevere.

GRIMES, LLOYD (TINY)   ASCAP 1960
composer, author, guitarist

b Newport News, Va, July 7, 16. Educ: Self-taught. Began playing drums; prof pianist & tap dancer. Four-string guitar master. Mem group, The Cats and Fiddle. Joined Art Tatum Trio. Played with Billy Holliday. Chief Collabr: Lenore Avin Grimes. *Songs:* Romance Without Finance; Frankie and Johnnie Boogie; Tiny's Tempo; Tiny's Exercise.

GRISELLE, THOMAS ELWOOD   ASCAP 1933
composer

b Upper Sandusky, Ohio, Jan 28, 1893; d Hollywood, Calif, Dec 27, 55. Educ: Piano, Albino Gorno; theory, Louis Victor Saar, Col Music Cincinnati, 11; comp, Nadia Boulanger, France & Arnold Schenberg. Toured as accompanist and solo pianist with Nora Bayes, Clarence Whitehill & Alice Nielsen. Taught piano & harmony, Muskingum Col. Cond & arr for phonograph & radio. Springer Gold Medal, Col Music Cincinnati. *Songs:* The Cuckoo Clock. *Songs & Instrumental Works:* Two American Sketches (Nocturne, march; first prize, Victor Talking Machine Co); Cubist; A Keyboard Symphony (6 pianos); also piano pieces, chamber music & orch numbers.

GROB, ANITA JEAN (ANITA KERR)   ASCAP 1965
composer, author, arranger

b Memphis, Tenn, Oct 13, 27. Educ: St Thomas & Cath High Schs, Memphis. Arr many Nashville sound records. Founder & lead singer, Anita Kerr Singers. Composer, San Sebastian Strings LPs. Conducted & composed film, Universal. Conducted, Royal Philh. Four Gold Records (one platinum & three Grammies). Chief Collabrs: Rod McKuen, Jan Baker. *Songs:* Happy Cat. *Albums:* The Sea; The Earth; The Sky.

GROCE, LARRY THOMAS   ASCAP 1971
composer, author, singer

b Dallas, Tex, Apr 22, 48. Educ: Principia Col, BA. Professional singer/songwriter, 10 yrs. Writer & singer variety of material incl pop, folk, country, hymns & children's songs. Worked extensively with Walt Disney Records. Recorded 11 albums, Warners & RCA Labels. *Songs:* Junk Food Junkie; Winnie-the-Pooh for President; We've Been Malled; The Ballad of Billy Don Rice.

GROFE, FERDE   ASCAP 1923
composer, conductor, pianist

b New York, NY, Mar 27, 1892; d. Educ: Studied with mother; also with Pietro Floridia & Ricardo Dallera; St Vincent's Col; Hon MusD: Wesleyan Univ & Western State Col of Colo. Violist, Los Angeles Symph, 10 yrs. Arr, var dance bands & pianist with Paul Whiteman Orch, 23. Taught orchestrations, Juilliard Sch. Formed own ens & appeared, concerts & radio. Guest cond, var symph orchs. Performer with wife in 2 piano concerts. Recipient, Griffith Found award, Golden Eaglet from Hollywood Bowl & Sinfonia Nat Hon award. *Songs:* Daybreak; Wonderful One. *Instrumental Works:* Mississippi Suite; Grand Canyon Suite; Death Valley Suite; Piano Concerto in D; Hollywood Suite; Wheels Suite; Symphony in Steel; World's Fair Suite (New York World's Fair official suite, 64); Three Shades of Blue; Knute Rockne; Killarney; Valley of Enchantment; New England Suite; Atlantic Crossing; A Day At the Farm. *Scores:* Films: King of Jazz; Time Out of Mind; The Return of Jesse James; Minstrel Man.

GROGAN, PHIL   ASCAP 1950
composer, author

b Oklahoma City, Okla, July 21, 09; d Southold, NY, July 20, 70. Educ: Univ Okla. Worked on midwest newspaper & radio sta; became mgr & publicist for dance orch. News correspondent, NAfrica, WW II; later wrote revue for War Bond Drive. Pub rels dir for record manufacturer; managing ed music trade publ; TV writer. *Songs:* Especially for You; How Can You Pretend?; Spring in My Heart; Peachy Pie; On the Rebound.

GROH, B J
See Roscoe (Bumpus), B Jeanie

GROSS, BETHUEL
ASCAP 1960
composer, author, conductor

b Leavenworth, Kans, Mar 7, 05. Educ: Washburn Col, BA, BM; Northwestern Univ, BM, BME, MM, PhD; Univ Chicago; Loyola Univ. Head music dept, Univ Akron, 41-45; grad div, Ill Wesleyan Univ, 45-46; dean, Shurtleff Col, 46-48; dir, Tests & Measurements, De Paul Univ, 48-50; dir choral & orch dept, Chicago Cons, 50-61. Dir, Baker Sch Fine Arts, 55-, also, Northwest Sch Fine Arts; lectr, Loyola Univ, 61- Organist & dir, Chicago churches, 40- Assoc ed, Musical Leader, 41- Exec secy, Northtown Ind Mgt Club, Chicago; dir, Ind Relations, Chicago Met YMCA. Organized Personalysis Measurements Counsel. Author, "Blueprints for Living." *Songs & Instrumental Works:* Five Modal Carols; Six Modernistic Carols; Father Sent a Child Again; 3 Christmas Moods; The Lost Star; Reflections on Christmas (oratorio); 6 organ symphonies; 2 symphonic poems; art songs.

GROSS, CHARLES H
ASCAP 1962
author

b Cambridge, Mass, May 13, 34. Educ: Harvard Col, AB, 55; New Eng Cons Music, 55-56, student of Judd Cooke; Mills Col, 56-57, student of Darius Milhaud & Leon Kirchner. Army draftee, served as arr for USMA Band, West Point, 57-60. *Instrumental Works:* Band: Three From the Hills; Childsplay; Songs of the Sea; Alle Psallite; Irish Suite; Three American Folks Songs. *Scores:* Bway show: Richard III; Do You Turn Somersaults; The Great White Hope (Tony Award); The Eccentricities of a Nightingale; The Blacks (Obie Award); Semmelweiss (Kennedy Ctr); The Condemned of Altona (Lincoln Ctr); King Lear (NY Shakespeare Fest); Theatres & Stage: The Plough and the Stars; The Door Park; The Firebugs; Galilee; He Who Gets Slapped; St Joan; MacBeth; Skin of Our Teeth; Lonesome Train/Hard Travelin'; Film/TV: N.Y.P.D.; Heartland; Blue Sunshine; The Group; Robert Frost, a Lovers Quarrel With the World (Acad Award); Post No Bills; Across the River; No Other Love; You Can't Go Home Again; The Dain Curse; The Gardeners Son; Teachers Teacher (Emmy Award); The Tenth Level; Twenty Shades of Pink; Bicentennial Minutes (Spec Emmy); The Trojan Women; Good Day; On the Yard; Football, 100 Years Old...; The Ceremony of Innocense; The Dark Side; The Jolly Corner; Rodeo Rod and the Runaway (Emmy Award); King Lear; The Gold Bug; My Hands Are the Tools of My Soul.

GROSS, WALTER
ASCAP 1943
composer, author, conductor

b New York, NY, July 14, 09; d Los Angeles, Calif, Nov 27, 67. Educ: High sch; pvt music study. Gave piano recital, age 10; pianist in concert, radio & with Paul Whiteman, Andre Kostelanetz & Tommy Dorsey Orchs. Cond radio progs, ATC, US Army, WW II. Music dir, CBS & Musicraft Records, also for Gordon MacRae, Sarah Vaughan, Mel Torme, Frank Sinatra & Buddy Clark. Pres, Interlude Music. Chief Collabrs: Jack Lawrence, Carl Sigman, Ned Washington, Raymond Klages, Bobby Troup. *Songs & Instrumental Works:* Tenderly; Your Love; To Be Worthy of You; I'm in a Fog About You; Just a Moon Ago; Improvisation in Several Keys; Creepy Weepy; A Slight Case of Ivory; Please Remember; How Will I Remember You; Mexican Moon.

GROSSEL, IRA
See Chandler, Jeff

GROSSMAN, BERNARD
ASCAP 1922
author

b Baltimore, Md, Aug 21, 1885; d Hollywood, Calif, Oct 2, 51. Educ: Pub schs. Wrote spec material for films. Chief Collabr: Al Goodman. *Songs:* How I Love You, Mother Mine; Little Grey Mother; Too Beautiful for Words; Thank You, America; Wonder If She's Lonely, Too; We're Going Over; Buddy; You Didn't Want Me When You Had Me.

GROSVENOR, RALPH L
ASCAP 1934
composer, author, organist

b Grosvenor's Corners, NY, Dec 5, 1893. Educ: Brooklyn Poly Country Day Sch; studied music with R Huntington Woodman, Dijon, Moissenet, Poillot, Gunzman, Pasquale Amato, A Y Cornell & Ernest Bloch. Organist & choirmaster, St Bartholomew's Parish House, New York. Accompanist to singers & violinists; sang with Little Theatre Opera Co, New York. Singer, choral dir, pianist & organist in radio, 10 yrs. Cond, New York Singers Club; Assoc Glee Clubs Am; Jr League Glee Club. Dir music, pub schs, Westchester, NY, 15 yrs; organist & choirmaster in churches. Voice, organ & piano teacher. *Songs:* I Carry You in My Pocket; One Golden Day; What Good Does a Long Face Do?; Far Away in Bethlehem; Sea Gulls and Sails; *Scores:* Calls to Worship for Minister and Choir.

GROSZ, WILHELM (HUGH WILLIAMS)
composer, concert pianist

b Vienna, Austria, Aug 11, 1894; d New York, NY, Dec 10, 39. Educ: Wiener Staatsakadamie for Music, grad with hons & acad dipl, 19; studied under Richard Robert & Franz Schrecker; Univ Vienna, DMus, 20, studied under Guido Adler. Began career as pianist at age 18 in Vienna; later was cond, Operahouse in Mannheim, Ger. Free comp & pianist, Vienna, 22-26; concert toured Austria, Ger, Yugoslavia, Holland & other countries; performed own works; played under Bruno Walter, Furtwangler, Mengelberg, Richard Strauss & others; musical dir, Ultraphone Gramophone Co, Berlin, 27-33; musical dir,

Kammerspiele, Vienna, 33-34; moved to Eng, 34. Chief Collabr: Jimmy Kennedy. *Songs & Instrumental Works:* Piano Concerto; Kleine Melodie (first radio opera); Isle of Capri; Red Sails in the Sunset; Harbour Lights; Poor Little Angeline; Santa Fe Trail; Tomorrow Night; In an Old Dutch Garden; Bird on the Wing; Tina. *Scores:* Opera: Sganarell; Der Arme Reinhold; Ballet: Baby in der Bar.

GROTHOFF, CURTIS EUGENE, II (JOHNNY ABRAHAM)
composer, author, singer

b Mt Vernon, Ill, Nov 4, 38. Educ: Understudy with Marilyn Sellars, Jerry Clower, George Morgan & Billy Grammer. Writer & singer locally since age 10. Performed spec progs for Grand Old Opry, Nashville, Tenn. Numerous patriotic progs throughout Midwest & South. Worked with many popular groups. Chief Collabrs: John Riis, Tommy Williams, Charley Fields. *Songs:* I'll Forget Our Yesterday; Muddy Rivers Child; Thunder and Flash; The Old Country Church (Down the Road); Lyrics: The Talking Flag; The Tired Old Flag.

GROUYA, THEODORE (TED) J
ASCAP 1943
composer, author, pianist

b Bucharest, Roumania July 31, 10. Educ: Cath Sch; high sch; Sorbonne, Paris, DL; Ecole Normale de Musique, Paris, studied piano with Alfred Cortot, harmony with & Nadia Boulanger. Songwriter, pianist, pub relations; was head of Robbins-Feist & Miller Subsidiary of MGM. Chief Collabrs: Sammy Cahn, Ira Gershwin, Fran Loesser, Johnny Mercer, Eddy Heyman, Eddie de Lange, Nat Burton, Paul Francis Webster, Ned Washington, Ed Anderson, Dan George. *Songs & Instrumental Works:* Flamingo; In My Arms; When Am I Gonna Kiss You Good Morning?; Ballade New Yorkaise; I Heard You Cried Last Night; Don't Ever Change; Two Heavens; Since You Went Away; Will You Remember Me?; The Road I Didn't Take; Just Friends.

GROVE, RICHARD D
ASCAP 1958
composer, author, pianist

b Lakeville, Ind, Dec 18, 27. Educ: Denver Univ; pvt study Schillinger Syst with Earl Brown. Teacher, Westlake Col Modern Music, 55-59. Formed jazz concert orch, 60. Pianist & arr for groups & singers. Wrote songs for Mavis Rivers, Fran Jeffries, King Sisters, Terry Gibbs, Paul Horn & Pete Jolly. Chief Collabrs: Pete Jolly, Tommy Wolf, Jack Smalley. *Songs:* Something in the Air; Little Bird; also Little Bird Suite.

GROVER, ARTHUR BUDDY
ASCAP 1956
composer, teacher

b Brooklyn, NY, Sept 25, 18. Educ: Brooklyn Acad, studied piano, harmony, theory & comp with Ralph Wolf. Pianist, Buddy Grover Trio; played hotels & clubs, NY, Beverly Hills Country Club, Ky, Desert Inn Hotel, Las Vegas, 8 yrs, Flamingo Hotel, Hacienda Hotel & Tropicana Hotel. Chief Collabrs: Lanny Shore, Max Solis, Lee Allman. *Songs:* Music: Immortal Love; To Say You're Mine; Faded Gardenia; You Wonderful You; Who Cares; Some Day Come Summer Time.

GRUELLE, JOHNNY
ASCAP 1956
composer, author, artist

b Arcola, Ill, Dec 24, 1880; d Miami Beach, Fla, Dec 9, 38. Educ: High sch. Illus "Raggedy Ann" bks & "Mr Tweedeele" for NY Herald. *Songs:* Raggedy Ann Song Books.

GRUENBERG, LOUIS
ASCAP 1934
composer, pianist

b Brest-Litovsk, Russia, Aug 3, 1884; d Beverly Hills, Calif, June 9, 64. Educ: Vienna Cons, Master Class with Ferruccio Busoni, studied with F E Koch. To US, 1885. Debut as pianist, Philh Orch, Berlin, 12; gave concert tours, Europe & US, 12-19. Chmn comp dept, Chicago Musical Col, 34-37. Co-founder, League of Comp; past pres, Int Soc Contemporary Music; mem, Nat Inst Arts & Letters. *Songs & Instrumental Works:* Jazzberries; Polychromatics; Jazz Masks; Daniel Jazz; Creation; A Song of Faith (oratorio); The Hill of Dreams (Flagler Prize); The Enchanted Isle; Vagabondia; Jazz Suite; Violin Concerto (Heifetz Comn); Americana (suite); Indiscretions (string quartet); Piano Quintet (Lake Placid Club Prize); Diversions (string quartet); II String Quartet (Coolidge Medal); 3 violin sonatas; 5 symphonies. *Scores:* Film: The Fight for Life; So Ends Our Night; The Commandos Strike at Dawn; Operas: Volpone; Emperor Jones (David Bispham Medal); The Man Who Married a Dumb Wife; Jack and the Beanstalk; Antony and Cleopatra; Green Mansions (radio opera).

GRUENWALD, ALFRED
ASCAP 1942
author

b Vienna, Austria, Feb 16, 1886; d Forest Hills, NY, Feb 24, 51. To US, 40. Citizen, 48. Educ: Gymnasium, Vienna. Newspaper drama critic. Co-librettist & lyricist of scores of Viennese operettas produced on Bway: "Die Rose von Stambul (Rose of Stamboul)", "Der Letzte Walzer (The Last Waltz)", "Die Bajadere (The Yankee Princess)", "Graefin Mariza (Countess Maritza)" & "Die Zirkusprinzessin (The Circus Princess)"; others: "Hoheit Tanzt Walzer", "Die Goldene Meisterin", "Die Herzogin von Chicago", "Viktoria und ihr Hussar", "Bozena" & "Arizona Lady." Translated Am songs into Ger for OWI, during WW II. Chief Collabrs: Emmerich Kalman, Oscar Straus, Edmund Eysler, Paul Abraham, Leo Fall, Fritz Loehner-Beda, Julius Brammer. *Songs:* O Rose von

Stambul; Oo-La-La; Der letzte Walzer; Komm Zigan, komm Zigan, spiel mir was Vor (Play Gypsies, Dance Gypsies); Zwei Maerchenaugen (Dear Eyes That Haunt Me).

GRUNDMAN, CLARE EWING   ASCAP 1950
composer, orchestrator

b Cleveland, Ohio, May 11, 13. Educ: Shaw High Sch, East Cleveland, Ohio; Ohio State Univ, BS(educ), 34, MA, 39; studied comp with Paul Hindemith, 41. Taught instrumental music at Univ High Sch, Columbus, Ohio, 34-35 & at Lexington Pub Schs, Ky, 35-37. Instr woodwinds, bands & orchestration, Ohio State Univ, 37-41. Chief musician, USCG, World War II, 42-45. Comp & arr, radio & TV, films, theater, records, publ; arr & cond Bway musical "Lend an Ear." Associated with Boosey & Hawks, 47- *Instrumental Works:* American Folk Rhapsody, No 1, 2, 3, 4; Fantasy On American Sailing Songs; Two Sketches for Orchestra; Kentucky 1800; Two Moods; The Blue-Tail Fly; Three Songs for Christmas; Music for a Carnival; The Blue and the Gray; Hebrides Suite; The Spirit of '76; Burlesque for Band; English Suite; Three Noels; Western Dance; Three Sketches for Winds; Welsh Rhapsody; Festive Piece; Japanese Rhapsody; Irish Rhapsody; Zoo Illogical; Concertante for Saxophone; A Colonial Legend; Nocturne for Harp; Norwegian Rhapsody; Tuba Rhapsody.

GRUNN, HOMER   ASCAP 1927
composer, pianist, educator

b West Salem, Wis, May 5, 1880; d Los Angeles, Calif, June 6, 44. Educ: Stern's Cons, Berlin, studied with Emil Liebling, A Brune & E Jedlicka. Debut as concert pianist, Chicago, 1900. Teacher piano, Chicago Music Col, 03-07. Dir, Piano Dept, Ariz Sch Music, 07. Founder, Brahms Quintet. Piano soloist, Los Angeles Symph. *Songs:* Peyote Drinking Song. *Instrumental Works:* March Heroique (piano, orch); Hopi Indian Dance; Zuni Indian Suite; The Shadow World (Symph poem); Humoresque Negre; 'Tis Raining (piano). *Scores:* Ballets: Xochitl; The Flower Goddess; Operettas: The Mars Diamond; The Golden Pheasant; The Isle of Cuckoo; In a Woman's Reign.

GRUPP, MARTIN   ASCAP 1973
composer

b Brooklyn, NY, Aug 15, 25. Educ: Juilliard Grad Sch. Percussionist, NBC Symph, radio & TV shows; music contractor, Bway, Mitch Leigh, David Frost & Merv Griffin Shows.

GRZANNA, DONALD E   ASCAP 1964
composer, accordionist, teacher

b Milwaukee, Wis, Aug 22, 31. Educ: Rizzo Sch Music, BM; Roosevelt Univ; Loyola Univ; Univ Wis. Taught accordion at Rizzo Sch Music & Arnold's Music Sch; then at Alverno Col & Cascio Sch Music. Gave concert performances, New York, Chicago & Milwaukee. *Instrumental Works:* 3 Pictorial Sketches; Enchanted Villa; Holiday for Accordion; Parisienne Waltz; Cotton Candy Twist; Prelude and Toccata.

GUARDINO, LOUIS JOSEPH (LOU GARDNER)   ASCAP 1968
composer, author, singer

b New York, NY, Nov 28, 23; d Los Angeles, Calif, Jan 18, 68. Violinist, Bob Chester Orch, 40's & 50's. Recorded, Bell Records; screen writer. Chief Collabrs: Phil Gilbert, Tony Ferina. *Songs:* Lyrics: I Know How It Feels to Be Lonely.

GUARE, JOHN
composer, author

b New York, NY, Feb 5, 38. Educ: Georgetown Univ, grad; Yale Univ Sch of Drama, MFA. Co-adapter & lyricist, "Two Gentlemen of Verona", "Marco Polo Sings a Solo", "Rich and Famous" & "Landscape of the Body." Lectr, NY Univ. Playwright-in-residence, New York Shakespeare Fest, 76-77. Co-author, screenplay "Taking Off." Author, plays "Muzeeka", "Cop-out" & "House of Blue Leaves." Recipient, Obie awards, 68 & 71, most promising playwright, 68-69, best Am play, 71 & best musical, 72 from New York Drama Critics, Outer Critics Circle prize, 71, Tony award, best musical, 72, best libretto, 72, Jefferson award, 77. Mem, Dramatist Guild Council & Authors League.

GUARNIERI, JOHN ALBERT   ASCAP 1953
composer, author, pianist

b New York, NY, Mar 23, 17. Educ: Studied piano & violin with father (Ferdinand). Played piano for George Hall, Benny Goodman, Jimmy & Tommy Dorsey, plus harpsichord with Arte Shaw's Gramercy 5. Staff pianist, CBS & NBC, 43-62. Musical cond for Army recruiting shows, 50-57. Comp original music for over 1500 progs. Recorded more than 6000 titles during career. Chief Collabrs: Harold Orlob, Gordon Clifford, Frank Defelitta, Art Small, Cal Harris. *Songs:* Music: Dream Waltz; I Would, Would You; Lonely Gondolier; Blue Mood; Why Did You Tell Me Those Lies?; The Curtain's Going Up, My Dear; Looky Here, Here's Me!; Isn't It Marvelous; A Waltz for Jeannie; Tiddledy Winks. *Instrumental Works:* Piano Concerto in D; Violin Concerto in A; Gliss Me Again; So Proudly We Hail; Tom Swift in Birdland; Five Quarters for Pearl; Beethoven's Dream; Orinoco; Silent Movie Days; Johnny's Blues; Amigo Simpatico; Great Fred Harding Circus Shout; Major Holley Caper; Call J C Heard; Taking Chopin in Stride; Sacramento; Piano Paganini; Walla-Walla.

GUBENKO, JULIUS (TERRY GIBBS)   ASCAP 1958
composer, conductor, vibraphonist

b Brooklyn, NY, Oct 13, 24. Won Maj Bowes Contest, age 12. Vibraphonist in orchs incl Chubby Jackson, Buddy Rich, Woody Herman & Benny Goodman. Led own band, appeared on TV; made many records. Music dir & comp, "Regis Philbin Show"; musical dir, "Steve Allen Show" & ABC TV show "Operation Entertainment"; over 35 long playing albums on Mercury, Verve, Impulse, Roost & Dot labels. *Songs & Instrumental Works:* S & S; Shaine Une Zees; Peaches; Terry's Tune; Regis Philbin Show (TV theme); Operation Entertainment (TV theme); The Fat Man; Town House 3; Those Eyes, Those Lips, That Nose, That Face, That Girl; PBS Blues; Samba Wazzoo; Smoke Em Up; Blues for Brady; Nina; That Austin Mood; The Beautiful People; Chant of Love; No Name Theme; Four AM; 8 Lbs 10 Oz.

GUCKENHEIMER, FRITZ
See Gump, Richard

GUERIN, JOHN P   ASCAP 1965
composer, author, drummer

b Honolulu, Hawaii, Oct 31, 39. Musician with group as teenager. Joined Buddy Defranco, 59. To Los Angeles, 63; joined George Shearing, 65; worked with Thelonius Monk, Victor Feldman, Donald Byrd & Frank Zappa & others, 68- Formed L A Express Band, 74; recording artist. Producer, albums for var artists. Author, drum instruction bk, "Jazz Plus Rock Equals John Guerin." *Songs:* Pretending; Music: Just Couldn't Help Myself; Don't Be Blue. *Instrumental Works:* Mr and Mrs America and All the Ships At Sea; Down the Middle.

GUERTIN, ROBERT HARVEY
composer, clarinetist, conductor

b Cedar Rapids, Iowa, Sept 16, 21; d San Diego, Calif, June 13, 74. Educ: Lewis Clark High Sch, grad, 38; Univ Wash; Gonzaga Law Sch, 45-48. Served in USAF, 41-45, asst dir, USAF Band. First clarinetist, Spokane Symph. Nat sales mgr, Scherl & Roth & Reynolds Musical Instrument Cos; sales rep for musical instruments. Educ dir, C F Martin Guitar Co. Chief Collabr: Rudy Foglia. *Instrumental Works:* The Graphic Guitar Book (vols 1-3, workbk).

GUEST, CHRISTOPHER HADEN   ASCAP 1971
composer, author

b New York, NY, Feb 5, 48. Educ: High Sch Music & Art; Stockbridge Sch; Bard Col; Sch Arts, NY Univ. Co-wrote & co-comp National Lampoon's Lemmings, nominated for Obie Award; co-wrote & comp music for five Lampoon Albums, receiving two Grammy nominations. Comp music for Lily Tomlin Show, TV Show, Chevy Chase Show. Playing with rock group Spinal Tap. Chief Collabrs: Sean Kelly, Tom Leopold, Michael McKean. *Songs:* Kung Fu Christmas; Music: Deteriorata; Colorado; Positively Wall Street.

GUETTEL, MARY RODGERS (MARY RODGERS)   ASCAP 1954
composer, author

b New York, NY, Jan 11, 31. Educ: Brearley High Sch; Mannes Music Sch; Wellesley Col, 48-51. Comp of musicals, 59- Chief Collabrs: Stephen Sondheim; lyricist, Marshall Barer, Martin Charnin, Sheldon Hernick. *Songs:* Some of My Best Friends are Children; Music: The Boy From. *Scores:* Bway Shows: Davy Jones Locker; Once Upon a Mattress; Hot Spot; The Wed Show; Pinocchio. *Albums:* Free to Be You and Me.

GUEVARA, RUBEN   ASCAP 1972
composer, singer

b Los Angeles, Calif, Oct 17, 42. Educ: North Hollywood High Sch, 60; Los Angeles City Col (music comp), 71. Singer in movie "Coogan's Bluff," 68. Avant garde comp for clarinet, bassoon, harpsichord & piano. Writer & dir, rock cantata "Who Are the People," 71. Staged rock theatre band, Ruben and the Jets, 72. Recorded spoof on nat anthem, 76. Appeared in 2 Cheech & Chong movies, 79. Recipient, Los Angeles City Col Hugo Davise award for comp, 71. Chief Collabrs: Frank Zappa, Cheech & Chong. *Songs:* Ma Man Flash; Spiderwoman; Santa Kari.

GUILMARTIN, KENNETH KELLS   ASCAP 1978
composer, author, teacher of performance and musicianship

b New York, NY, May 28, 46. Educ: Swarthmore Col, Pa, BA, 68; Manhattan Sch Music, comp & theory, 73-76; studied comp with Ludmilla Ulehla & Elias Tannenbaum; studied Dalcroze eurhythmics & musicianship pedagogy with Robert M Abramson; studied voice & kinetic awareness with Ray Evans Harrell. Comp & performed progressive blues & rock, esp with Sidetrack, Montreal, Can, 65-70. Comp, arr & orchr, off-Bway, NY Shakespeare Fest & Chelsea Theatre Ctr, 70's. Exploration of new forms of opera & vocal perf. *Songs:* Congratulations; Music: The Old Lizard (poem by F Garcia Lorca). *Instrumental Works:* 2314-B; Cadenza for Four Saxophones. *Scores:* Opera: The Marriage of Heaven and Hell (poetry of William Blake); The Caucasian Chalk Circle (Brecht).

GUINN, NEDRA   ASCAP 1969
composer, author, teacher

b Jena, La, Sept 26, 14. Educ: South Park High Sch, Beaumont, Tex, grad, 45; pvt piano lessons; Freeman's Guitar Sch, dipl, 50; Lamar Univ, 60-62; US Sch Music, dipl, 68. Appeared regularly on "Bob Freeman Show." Steel guitarist in var bands; later organized own band, The Wheels, performer, mgr & dir, 2 yrs. Opened music studio & taught guitar, steel guitar, piano & drums, Beaumont, 5 yrs & Chattanooga, Tenn, 5 yrs. Formed publ co, Solar Beam Music & record label, Solar Beam Records. Chief Collabr: John Irick. *Songs:* Picture, Voice and Letters; Heartaches in the Mail; Tell Her I Love Her; *Music:* Our Love Will Always Abound; Solid and Sound.

GUION, DAVID WENDELL ASCAP 1927
composer
b Ballinger, Tex, Dec 15, 1892. Educ: Whipple Acad, Jackson, Ill; Polytech Col, Ft Worth, Tex; Royal Cons, Vienna, Austria, 11-14, studied with Leopold Godowsky; hon DM, Howard Payne Col, Brownwood, Tex, 50. Taught piano, Southern Methodist Univ, Dallas, Tex & Chicago Musical Col, Ill. Radio show & all-Guion revue at Roxy Theatre. Wrote music for Tex Centennial Celebration, 36. Chief Collabrs: Marie Lussi, Grace Noll Crowell, John Bratton, Daniel Twohig. *Songs: Music:* Home on the Range; At the Cry of the First Bird; Prayer; Mary Alone; I Talked to God Last Night; The Cross Bearer; Wild Geese; Mamselle Marie; Lonesome Song of the Plains; Ride, Cowboy, Ride; All Day on the Prairie. *Instrumental Works: Piano:* The Arkansas Traveler (transc); Turkey in the Straw (transc); Two Country Jigs; Jazz Scherzo; Sheep and Goat; The Mother Goose Concert Suite; The Harmonica Player; The Lonesome Whistler; The Scissors Grinder; Valse Arabesque; *Orch:* The Texas Suite; The Prairie Suite. *Scores: Ballet:* Shingandi (African); A Western Ballet.

GUISINGER, EARL C (GUY SINGER) ASCAP 1956
composer
b Columbus, Ohio, Dec 7, 04. Educ: Ohio State Univ, BSc(ceramic eng), 27. Ceramic engr, combustion engr & consult engr; sr liaison engr, Northrop Aircraft, proj engr, Corporal Missile. Col, Ordnance Dept, USA, WW II. *Songs:* Whither Thou Goest; Bless My Soul; COD (My Broken Heart); The Old Village Choir; Young, Young Love.

GUIU, JOSE MELIS ASCAP 1946
b Havana, Cuba, Feb 27, 20. Came to US, 37, became citizen, 44. Educ: Entered Havana Cons at age 6, teacher at age 10; scholarship from Cuban govt to study in Paris; studied with Alfred Cortot & Erwin Bodky; scholarship, Juilliard, studied with Josef & Rosina Lhevinne. Piano soloist, Havana Symph & concerts in Havana. Music dir, USO shows, USA, WW II. Appeared in nightclubs & theatres, New York; music dir, Jack Paar's TV show, "Tonight Show"; cond & soloist with orchs incl, Boston Pops, St Louis Symph, Rochester Symph, Fla Symph; comp for films; recording artist. *Songs & Instrumental Works:* Amor Tropical; Night Fall; Fantasia Cubana; Modern Piece; El Vendedor; El Pregon de Santiago; Rhumba Instrumental; Timba-Timba; Quita Quita; Cancion de Illusion; The Stars Are Mine; Once in a Lifetime; A Prayer Was Born; The Story of Christmas; I-M-4-U (Jack Paar theme); Nocturne; Latin Fantasy.

GULLICKSON, GRANT ORVIS ASCAP 1978
composer, author, singer
b Jamestown, NDak, July 31, 44. Educ: NDak State Univ, 62-64; Univ NDak, BA, 66; Univ Minn Sch Law, JD, 69. Rock vocalist, night clubs, concerts & TV; recording artist, Playboy, A&M & RCA Records. Chief Collabrs: Lance Gullickson, Brian Whitcomb & Roger Kellaway. *Songs: Lyrics:* Take Me Away; Sunrise; Gypsy Girl; Road to Louveciennes; Morning Song.

GULLIKSEN, KENNETH ASCAP 1979
composer, author, singer
b New York, NY, June 28, 45. Educ: Southern Calif Col, BA. Writer & performer on var albums. Pastor, West Los Angeles & Beverly Hills. *Songs:* Charity. *Albums:* Charity.

GULLIVER, ANDREW
See Stein, Herman

GUMBLE, ALBERT ASCAP 1914
composer, pianist
b North Vernon, Ind, Sept 10, 1883; d New York, NY, Nov 30, 46. Educ: Auditorium Sch of Music, with Herman Froehlich; also studied with Clarence Adler. Pianist, Remick Co; on staff, Donaldson, Douglas & Gumble. Wrote spec material for McIntyre & Heath. Entertained at debarkation ctr, WW I. Chief Collabrs: Jack Yellen, B G De Sylva, Al Bryan. *Songs:* Are You Sincere?; Winter; Rebecca of Sunnybrook Farm; How's Every Little Thing in Dixie?; You'll Do the Same Thing Over Again; Somebody's Waiting for You.

GUMP, RICHARD (FRITZ GUCKENHEIMER) ASCAP 1961
composer, author, clarinetist
b San Francisco, Calif, Jan 22, 06. Educ: Stanford Univ; Calif Sch Fine Arts, Music & Arts Inst, with Irwin Brusletten; studied with Domenico Brescia. Businessman; joined Gump's Retail Store, 25, pres, 47- Organized Guckenheimer Sauer Kraut Band, 48. Lectr. Author: "Good Taste Costs No More" & "Jade, Stone of Heaven." Award, Star of Italian Solidarity. *Songs & Instrumental Works:* Seven Variations on an American Theme; Polynesian Impression; Clarinet Quintet; Violin, Piano Sonata; Cambodian Impression (string quartet); Sonata for Oboe, Piano; Fantasia for Four Hands (2 pianos); Gift of December (cantata); My Tane.

GUNSKY, MAURICE J ASCAP 1934
author, singer
b Petaluma, Calif, Aug 10, 1888; d San Francisco, Calif, Mar 3, 45. Educ: Pub schs. Active in radio, WCoast, 25. Appeared in vaudeville, 26-29. *Songs:* Honolulu Blues; That Haunting Waltz; Consolation; Why Do I Always Remember?; Linger Longer in My Arms; Because I Care So Much.

GUNTER, EDWARD CHARLES ASCAP 1956
composer
b Baltimore, Md, Apr 23, 17. Educ: Capitol Radio Inst; Life Underwriter Training Coun. Chief Collabrs: Fred Thompson, Cliff Friend. *Songs:* Love Burns High; Seconded Love; Make Out; More Than Ever; Holy Ghost; Remember; *Music:* Do You Really Care; I Wanna Be Loved; Forever; Pray America Pray; Dolphin Rolling Song.

GUNTHER, WILLIAM
See Sprecher, Gunther William

GURYAN, MARGO ASCAP 1958
composer, author, producer
b Far Rockaway, NY, Sept 20, 37. Educ: Boston Univ, MusB, 59, studied comp with Hugo Norder & Gardner Read, classical piano with Margaret Chaloff, jazz piano with Jaki Byard; Lenox Sch Jazz, 59-60, studied comp with Gunther Schuller. Writer for var recording artists, 58- Signed to MJQ Music, 68, then to Blackwood Music, Inc. Recorded as writer & singer, Bell Records, 68. Co-producing & publ for Bicycle Music Co. Chief Collabrs: Ornette Coleman, John Lewis, Gary McFarland, Ran Blake, Bob Brookmeyer, Richard Bennett. *Songs:* Sunday Mornin'; Think of Rain; *Lyrics:* Lonely Woman.

GUSENOFF, STEVEN IRA ASCAP 1970
composer, author
b Boston, Mass, June 4, 46. Educ: Boston Univ, BS. Creative advert, marketing develop; wrote jingles for clients. Wrote themes for Grossman's Homes, Grossman's Retail stores & radio prog, "My Son the Announcer."

GUSMAN, MEYER ASCAP 1930
composer
b Russia, Sept 1, 1894; d Miami Beach, Fla, Jan 4, 60. US citizen, 19. Educ: Pub schs, Russia & US; PharD. *Songs:* In the Dark of the Night; Where You Are There I Want to Be; What a Fool I Was; On a Night Like This; Underneath the Russian Moon. *Scores: Opera:* Ishmael.

GUSSIN, DAVID ASCAP 1956
composer, conductor, pianist
b Russia, July 3, 1899; d. Educ: High sch. Cond, staff orch, CJRC-radio, Can & in var hotels & nightclubs. Comp, accompanist & cond for Eleanor Powell. Chief Collabrs: George Howe, Marve Fisher. *Songs:* Envy; My Little One; Rockin' Horse Rock; Shameless.

GUSTAFSON, HOWARD JOSEPH (BART HOWARD) ASCAP 1952
composer, author
b Burlington, Iowa, June 1, 15. Educ: Bus sch; Juilliard Sch Music, piano, theory & harmony studies, 5 yrs; pvt study comp with Howard Brockway. US Army, WW II. Accompanist, Mabel Mercer, 4 yrs. Emcee & musical dir, Blue Angel Cabaret Cradle, 8 yrs. *Songs:* Fly Me to the Moon (In Other Words); Let Me Love You; My Love Is a Wanderer; It Was Worth It! (That's What I'll Say); The Man in the Looking Glass; Year After Year; Welcome Home, Angelina; Perfect Stranger; *Lyrics:* Don't Dream of Anybody But Me.

GUTCHEON, JEFFREY ASCAP 1969
composer, author, pianist
b New York, NY, Jan 3, 41. Educ: Stuyvesant High Sch, 58; Amherst Col, BA, 62; Mass Inst Technol, BArch, 66. Band leader & recording artist, 68-72; studio keyboardist. Author of "Improvising Rock Piano" & "Teach Yourself Rock Piano." TV, movie & musical comedy writer, 75-80. Chief Collabrs: Beth Gutcheon, Eugene Pistilli. *Songs:* Off-Time; Lookin' Good; Fat and Greasy; Your Feets Too Big; Sweet Potatoes; Listen to Your Heart; theme from Car. *Instrumental Works:* Gimblelock. *Scores: Film/TV:* The Learning Path.

GUTHRIE, ARLO ASCAP 1970
composer, author
b New York, NY, July 14, 47. Performer in coffee folk clubs, 64-65; author, 66. Appeared in United Artist film "Alice's Restaurant," 68; appeared in concerts, US & Europe; recording artist, Warner Bros Records. *Songs:* Alice's Restaurant; The Motorcycle Song; Coming in to Los Angeles; Oh, in the Morning; Washington County; Massachusetts.

GUY, ROSE MARIE ASCAP 1956
composer, performer, singer
b New York, NY, Aug 15, 25. Educ: Professional Children's Sch; Epiphany Acad. Began as singer at age 3, known as "Baby Rose Marie," NBC; own radio show on NBC at age 6. Made movies "International House" with W C Fields & Rudy Vallee. Toured vaudeville & played in Bway show "Spring in Brazil." Played in TV shows: Phil Silvers, Jackie Gleason Comedy Hour, Bob Cummings, Dick Van Dyke, Doris Day Show, Hollywood Squares. Currently

touring US with "4 Girls 4." Chief Collabrs: Ruth Bivova, Gene Di Nova. *Songs:* Chena' Luna; Start Talking Pappy; *Music:* One Misty Morning; Yellow Pages; It's Just a Dream; I Wish I Could Sing Like Durante.

GUYER, LAWRENCE MCILROY   ASCAP 1975
composer, author
b Brookings, SD, Mar 9, 07. Educ: Louisville Male High Sch, Ky; US Mil Acad, West Point, NY. Author of publ fiction, poetry & lyrics, 26- Chief Collabr: Don Swan. *Songs:* Lyrics: Sweet Cinderella.

GWIRTZ, IRVIN R   ASCAP 1954
composer, author
b Philadelphia, Pa, Feb 3, 03; d New York, NY, Dec 4, 57. *Songs:* Everlovin'; I Love Lucy; I Want a Girl; Just Wishing.

H

HAACK, BRUCE C   ASCAP 1958
composer, author, publisher
b Alberta, Can, May 4, 32. Educ: Univ Alberta, BA. Writer spec material; radio musical commercials; background music, Bway play, "How to Make a Man." Founded publ firm, Dimension 5. *Instrumental Works:* Windsong (comn by New York Orpheum Symph); Suite Adeline; Dance, Sing and Listen (children's series); Mass for Solo Piano. *Scores:* Ballet: The Constant She (comn by New York Ballet Club); Les Etapes; Bway stage: The Kumquat in the Persimmon Tree.

HAAS, PETER   ASCAP 1968
author, folksinger
b New York, NY, Feb 2, 29. Educ: City Col, City Univ New York, BA. Featured singer & co-star, "Once Upon a Day," WNET, New York, 62-63. Script & lyric writer for recordings, Pickwick Records, Til Records, Peter Pan Records & Casablanca Records, 65- Folksinger & banjoist, Pickwick Records & Til Records; TV personality. Chief Collabr: Maurice (Bugs) Bower. *Songs:* Lyrics: The Singles Scene; Great Day in the Morning; Nice Time for a Party; A Little Book; For a Friend; A Musical Recipe; Fundamentals (pieces for musical educ).

HACKETT, BUDDY   ASCAP 1936
composer, author
b Brooklyn, NY, Aug 11, 24. Educ: New Utrecht High Sch. Comedian in nightclubs, hotels & TV; featured in TV series, "Stanley." Appeared in Bway productions: "Lunatics and Lovers"; "I Had a Ball"; films incl "The Music Man"; "It's a Mad Mad Mad Mad World." *Songs:* Chinese Rock and Egg Roll.

HADDAD, DONALD WAYNE   ASCAP 1966
composer
b Marietta, Ohio, Jan 11, 35. Educ: Univ Ohio, BFA, MFA; Univ Colo, doctoral studies; Aspen Fest, Chautauqua Inst; studied comp with Ernst Von Dohnanyi. Taught, high schs, jr cols & Western Tex State Univ, Interlochen Arts Acad, Univ Ky, Univ Colo & Midland Col, Nebr. Performed on NBC show "Today"; appeared on Towne Hall recital, New York. Over 200 works for band, orch, chamber music, solo, chorus & piano. Comns from Ill State Univ, Northern Col & Interlochen Arts Acad. *Instrumental Works:* Adagio and Allegro (horn & band); Air and Adagio (woodwind quintet & band); Allegro Giocoso (horn & piano); Andante and Allergro (clarinet); Encore 1812 (woodwind quintet); Fugue in D Minor (brass choir); Grand Processional (band); Jazz Etude (brass quintet); Mini-Suite No 1 (band); Quartet for Brass; for Horn and Piano; Suite for Tuba and Piano; T-Bone Party (trombone quintet); Two Impressions (horn quartet); Blues Au Vent (woodwind quintet); Knoxville, 1974 (tuba octet); Suite for Tuba and Band; Suite for Baritone and Piano; and Allegro for E flat Alto Saxophone; Sonata 1984 (horn & perc); Four Sketches (horn & piano); Contrapunctus (quartal piece, 4 horns); Dance band: Ars Nova Blues; Buffalo Stomp; Knit 1, Purl 2.

HADDEN, FRANCES ROOTS   ASCAP 1951
composer, author, concert pianist
b Kuling, China, Aug 24, 10. Educ: Kuling Am Sch, 22-26; St Mary's Sch, Concord, NJ, 26-28; Mt Holyoke Col, BA, 32, Phi Beta Kappa, Otto Kahn Music Scholarships; Univ Mich, MMus, 67; studied piano with E Robert Schmitz. Concert debut tours, teaching music & art history, Yangtze River Ports, central China, 32-34. Concert pianist & comp for musicals, stage-plays & films, US, Europe & Far East, 34-65. Duo-pianist with Richard Hadden; dramatico-musical cultural missions to critical world areas. Prof music, Mackinac Col, 67-70. Nation-wide concert tours, 71- World Premiere perf Lu Shan Suite, Peking, 72; command perf, White House, 73. Perf TV & pub radio. Chief Collabrs: Cecil Broadhurst, Richard Hadden, George Fraser. *Songs:* A Chinese Christmas Cradle Song (Shiao Bao-Bao); Arch Rock; The Message Is the Medium; Carol of the Empty Hand; Mister Grumpbug; A New Thing is Born (chorus & orch, G Gabrieli); The One and Only; *Music:* Sweet Potato Pie; A New Year Carol; I'm the Luckiest Girl Alive; Look to the Mountains; Change in a Home on the Range; Twicklehampton School for Girls; We're All the Same

Underneath; Irish Blessing; Song for Canadians (chorus); *Lyrics:* Jersey Isle of Destiny. *Instrumental Works:* Two Pianos: Arch Rock-A Rock Excursion; Lu Shan-Suite for Two Pianos; Two Hundred Years-A Celebration Suite; Transc for Two Pianos: Orb and Sceptre Coronation March (William Walton); Now Thank We All (traditional processional; Karg Elert); This Is Mackinac (non-traditional processional; medley); The Bells Must Ring (for two; R Hadden). *Scores:* Bway show: The Good Road; A Statesman's Dream; Pickle Hill; Turning of the Tide (Asian musical); Take It to the World (airline musical); The Tiger (Japanese musical); Bway show & Film: Jotham Valley; The Crowning Experience; Voice of the Hurricane; The Forgotten Factor. *Albums:* The Crowning Experience (soundtrack).

HADDEN, RICHARD MOULTON   ASCAP 1951
composer, author, concert pianist
b East Orange, NJ, Nov 20, 10. Educ: Perth Amboy High Sch, 28; Rutgers Univ, BA, 32; Princeton Theol Sem, ThB, MDiv, 35; Univ Mich, MMus, 67; studied piano with Paul Hanff, George Vause, Maxwell MacMichael; studied duo-piano with Eugene Bossart & Karen Keys; studied conducting with John Finley Williamson & William Revelli. Produced musicals & documentaries, Britain, Europe, Asia & US, 39-65. Volunteer war service, musical theatre, Can & US, 41-45; dramatico-musical cultural missions to critical world areas, 47-48, 52-53 & 62-64; cond, US-India tour. Music consult & co-dir music dept, Mackinac Col, 65-70. Duo-pianist with Frances Hadden, 71-; command perf, White House, 73; nat TV & radio perf. Dir, Richard Hadden Mgt, 75- Mem: Am Fedn Musicians; SMP/TVE; Music Educr Nat Conf; Music Ed Asn; IPA; Nat Acad Popular Music, Int Soc Picture Prof; Sons Am Revolution; Phi Gamma Delta. Chief Collabrs: Cecil Broadhurst, Frances Roots Hadden. *Songs:* Roll Away That Stone; Dawning of a New Tomorrow; December; I Wish I Could Say What I Feel; If We All Pull Together (We Will All Pull Through); Pull Together, Canada; The Man With Two Pearls; We Shall Build Again; Drugstore Revolution; *Music:* The Bells Must Ring (Rutgers Univ football song); Have You a Place for Me Up There?; Sorry Is a Magic Little Word; You Can Defend America; Ol' Man Devil Gotta Go Some; You Can Fight for Canada (Ont Second Victory Loan song); Songs for a New India (comn by Mahatma Gandhi's grandson); Don't Underestimate You; The Arm Behind the Army; It's a Great Idea; Uncle Bottleneck; Ol' Man Mose; The Seven-Colored Rainbow (Nana Iro-no Niji); Jersey, Isle of Destiny. *Instrumental Works:* Arch Rock (A Rock Excursion for Two Pianos). *Scores:* Bway Shows: Space Is So Startling; You Can Defend America; Pull Together, Canada; Drugstore Revolution; Take It to the World; The Good Road; Turning of the Tide; Pickle Hill; Battle Together for Britain; The Crowning Experience (contrib); Film/TV: Out of the Frying Pan (Into the Fight); Calling All Nations; Year of Victory; Days of Decision; Road From Ruin. *Albums:* Space is So Startling; The Good Road; The Haddens.

HADDRILL, PHILIP HEILEMAN   ASCAP 1969
composer, teacher
b Oxford, Mich, Jan 20, 17. Educ: Oxford High Sch, Mich; Eastern Mich Univ, Ypsilanti, BS(music); Univ Mich, Ann Arbor, MMus. Instrumental music dir, Huron Valley Schs, Milford, Mich, 38-59 & Dearborn Pub Schs, Mich, 59-78; band teacher of the yr, Dist 12, Mich Sch Band & Orch Asn, 77-78; dir emer, Mich Sch Band & Orch Asn, 78. *Songs:* Michigan, the Water Wonderland (winner of contest for best Mich song); Song of Freedom (band, orch, chorus, vocal solo); God First!; Calling Our Continent to Christ; Peace and Good Will. *Instrumental Works:* Recitation (woodwind quintet); Bright, Sweet, and Beautiful (clarinet trio).

HADLEY, HENRY   ASCAP 1917
composer, conductor
b Somerville, Mass, Dec 20, 1871; d New York, NY, Sept 6, 37. Educ: Studied music with Stephen Emery, George Chadwick & Eusebius Mandyczewski; Tufts Col, MusD. Instr music, St Paul's Sch, Garden City, NY, 1896. Cond, US, Europe, SAm & Japan. Founded, Nat Asn for Am Comp & Cond, 32 & Berkshire Fest, 33. Cond, Seattle & San Francisco Orchs; assoc cond, NY Philh. Mem, Nat Inst Arts & Letters; Am Acad Arts & Letters & French Inst. Awarded Order of Merit, French Govt. *Songs & Instrumental Works:* Piano Concertino; Mirtil in Arcadia (choral); Resurgam (oratorio); Music, An Ode (cantata); Orch Suites: San Francisco; Streets of Peking; Suite Ancienne; five symphonies (No 2, Paderewski Prize, New Eng Cons Prize); two string quartets. *Scores:* Film: When a Man Loves; Operas: Safie; Azora; Bianca (William Wade Hinshaw Prize); Cleopatra's Night; A Night in Old Paris.

HAENSCHEN, (WALTER) GUSTAVE   ASCAP 1925
composer, conductor
b St Louis, Mo. Educ: Washington Univ, BS. Radio cond, 25-, "Maxwell House Show Boat"; "Chevrolet Series"; "American Album of Familiar Music"; "Saturday Serenade." *Songs:* Rosita; Manhattan Merry-Go-Round; Silver Star; Lullaby of Love; Easy Melody; Under the Japanese Moon.

HAFNER, ROBERT JOHN   ASCAP 1960
composer, author, singer
b Coatesville, Pa, Aug 4, 32. Began guitar playing, 47, with band, 49. Actor, dir, writer & stage mgr in theatre, 50's. Songwriter, for film "The Outcasts," 60's, & recording artist, 58-64. Chief Collabr: K C Reeth. *Songs:* Brenda Lee; Georgia

Lee Brown; Music: Rock 'n Billy; Vesuvius; Endless Love; Turn Him Down; The Walls of Yuma. *Instrumental Works:* Johnny Sorrow; Bright Star; I Wanna See You; Big Jack.

HAGEMAN, RICHARD   ASCAP 1950
composer, conductor, pianist
b Leeuwarden, Holland, July 9, 1882; d Los Angeles, Calif, Mar 6, 66. Educ: Scholarships; Brussels Cons; Royal Cons of Amsterdam; Brussels, MusD. Concert pianist at age 6. Accompanist, Royal Opera Co, Amsterdam. Cond, 1899. Came to US, 06, citizen, 15. Asst cond, Metrop Opera, 08, cond, 14-32. Cond, Sunday Night Concerts, 8 yrs. Head, Opera Dept, Curtis Inst, 4 yrs. Music dir, Chicago Civic Opera & Ravina Park Opera, 7 yrs. Cond, Philadelphia Orch summer concerts, 4 yrs. Guest cond, symph orchs, US. Went to Hollywood, 38. Cond, Hollywood Bowl, 6 seasons. Officier de l'Instruction Publique (French govt). *Songs:* Do Not Go My Love; At the Well; Miranda; Music I Heard With You; The Night Has a Thousand Eyes; Christ Went Up Into the Hills. *Songs & Instrumental Works:* The Crucible (oratorio); I Hear America Calling (baritone, orch); Overture in a Nutshell; Suite for Strings. *Scores:* Opera: Caponsacchi (David Bispham Mem Medal); Film background: Stagecoach (Acad Award, 39); The Long Voyage Home; The Shanghai Gesture; If I Were King; Mourning Becomes Electra; She Wore a Yellow Ribbon.

HAGEN, JOHN MILTON (STERLING SHERWIN)   ASCAP 1924
composer, author
b Omaha, Nebr, Dec 3, 02; d. Educ: Stanford Univ, BA; Cleveland Cons. Service, US Inf, World War I & USCG, World War II. Writer for newspapers, magazines; wrote songs for films, US & Eng; author, "The Shrewd Nude and Other Light Verse—and Dark" & "I Am In Iambics." *Songs:* Collections: Singin' In the Saddle Songs; Songs of the Roundup; American Cowboy Songs; Songs of San Francisco (Golden Gate songbook); Bad Man Songs of the Wild and Woolly West; Mac's Songs of the Road and Range; Railroad Songs of Yesterday and Today; 50 Years from Now.

HAGER, CLYDE   ASCAP 1925
composer, author
b Mitchell, SDak, Dec 2, 1886; d Harrisburg, Pa, May 22, 44. Educ: Stearn's Acad, Chicago. Vaudeville entertainer; created character "The Pitch Man"; radio announcer & sports commentator. Chief Collab: Walter Goodwin. *Songs:* That Wonderful Mother of Mine; Back in the Old Neighborhood; I'm Going Over the Hills to Virginia; Tell Them You're from Virginia; That's What's Calling Me Back.

HAGGART, ROBERT SHERWOOD   ASCAP 1953
composer, musician, arranger
b New York, NY, Mar 13, 14. Educ: Great Neck High Sch, 28-29 & 31-32; Salisbury Prep Sch, 30-31. With Bob Sperling Orch, 33-35 & Bob Crosby Orch, 35-42. Free-lance musician-bass player, arr & comp, New York, 42-68, radio recording, DECCA, 51-57, on "Perry Como Show," 17 yrs, NBC staff "Tonight Show," 63-69. Co-leader World's Greatest Jazz Band, 68- Free-lance in NY, 80- Chief Collabrs: Ray Bauduc, Johnny Burke, Jack Lawrence, Johnny Mercer. *Songs:* Music: South Rampart Street Parade; Big Noise From Winnetka; What's New?; My Inspiration (Gone But Not Forgotten); Dog Town Blues; I'm Prayin' Humble; What Else Is New?; Dixieland Shuffle; March of the Bobcats; Smokey Mary; Call Me a Taxi; I Hear Ya Talkin'; The Mark Hop; Takin' It Easy; Billie's Boogie; Mardigras Parade.

HAGMAN, MARIE MARGARET   ASCAP 1964
composer, pianist, organist
b Boston, Mass, Mar 8, 11. Educ: Everett High Sch; New Eng Cons music, BM(magna cum laude), 54; studied comp with Warren Storey Smith. Church organist, choir dir & singer, churches, radio & clubs. Teacher pianoforte & organ & supvr music, pub schs, Reading, Mass. Mem, Pi Kappa Lambda. *Songs:* The Beatitudes Song; The Message of the Bells; The Road to Calvary; Children's songs: It's Spring!; The Grandfather Clock; The Spelling Lesson; Valentine: A Plea; Guess Who?

HAGUE, ALBERT   ASCAP 1952
composer, teacher, performer
b Berlin, Ger, Oct 13, 20. Educ: Studied with Arthur Perleberg, Berlin; Royal Cons of St Cecilia, Rome, scholarship with Dante Alderighi; Univ Cincinnati, BMus, scholarship with Dr Sidney Durst & Maestro Conus. USAF, WW II. Came to New York, 46. Wrote first Bway show song in "Dance Me a Song," first incidental score "Madwoman of Chaillot." Nightclub act with wife Renee Orin, Hague & Hague; teacher theater auditioning; lectr, career building. Actor playing part of prof music in MGM motion picture "Fame." Chief Collabrs: Arnold Horwitt, Dorothy Fields, Allan Sherman, Emlyn Williams, Barbara Fried, Dr Seuss. *Songs:* Music: Young and Foolish; This Is All Very New to Me; Follow Your Heart; Plenty of Pennsylvania; I Feel Merely Marvelous; Look Who's in Love; My Girl Is Just Enough Woman for Me; 'Erbie Fitche's Twitch; Did I Ever Really Live; All of My Laughter; Light One Candle. *Scores:* Bway Show: Plain and Fancy; Redhead (Tony & Grammy Awards); The Figleaves Are Falling; Cafe Crown; Miss Moffat; Surprise! Surprise!; Film/TV: How the Grinch Stole Christmas (Dr Seuss CBS spec); The Funniest Man in the World; Coney Island USA.

HAHN, CARL   ASCAP 1925
composer, conductor, cellist
b Indianapolis, Ind, Oct 23, 1874; d Cincinnati, Ohio, May 13, 29. Educ: Cincinnati Col Music, with Otto Singer, Lino Mattioli, C Van Broekhoven & Frank Van der Stucken. Cellist, Van der Stucken, Anton Seidl & Theodore Thomas Orchs; cond, San Antonio Symph, 12 yrs; cond, Tex State Music Fest, NY Arion Soc, 14-20, NY Mozart Soc, 17-20 & NY Euphony Soc, 20-23; guest cond, NY Philh. *Songs:* Voice of the Chimes; Little Road Through Nazareth; Trees; Little Bunch O' Honeyness; The Green Cathedral; Rain Song.

HAID, WILLIAM   ASCAP 1936
composer, pianist
b Hamilton, Ohio, Apr 2, 01; d New York, NY, Dec 11, 73. Educ: Ohio State Univ; Radio TV Inst; studied piano with Olga Kuntz & Herman Wasserman. Wrote songs for Ohio Univ Scarlet Mask Club. Mem, Lido Venice Orch, London, Brussels, Berlin, Paris & Madrid, 24-25. Electronic & radio engr, WW II. *Songs:* Ohio State; Ohio Buckeye; 'Tain't Good - Like a Nickel Made of Wood; Nearer and Dearer to You; Silvery Moon and Golden Sands; Meet Me at the Football Game; Tell Santy I Live in a Shanty; I Picked a Flower the Color of Your Eyes.

HAIEFF, ALEXEI   ASCAP 1951
composer
b Blagoveschensk, Russia, Aug 25, 14. Educ: Pvt study with Constantine Shredov, 32-34 & Nadia Boulanger, 38-40; Juilliard Grad Sch, with Rubin Goldmark & Fred Jacobi, 34-38. Am Acad in Rome Medal, 42; Lili Boulanger Mem Award, 42; John Simon Guggenheim Fels, 46 & 49; NY Music Critics Award, 53; UNESCO Prize, 58. Guest cond, Woody Herman Band, 46; fel, Am Acad in Rome, 47-49, comp-in-residence, 52-53 & 58-59; prof-in-residence, Univ NY, Buffalo, 62 & 64; Mellon prof, Carnegie Inst Technol, 62-63; with Univ Utah, 67-70; Levi Found, Venice, Italy, 78. Pianist & cond own music. *Instrumental Works:* Divertimento; Piano Concerto; Symphony No 2; Violin pieces; Bagatelles (oboe & bassoon); Ballet in E; Sonata (two pianos); Piano Concerto No 2; Cello Sonata.

HAIG, BERNARD
See Edwards, Clara

HAIGHT, JOHN LEWIS   ASCAP 1971
composer, author, organist
b Texarkana, Tex, Aug 13, 02. Educ: Tex High Sch, Texarkana; Univ Tex, BA; Southern Methodist Univ; Tex Christian Univ. Pres: J L Haight & Co, 42 yrs; H&H Investment Corp, 3 yrs; Texstar Records, 10 yrs; Comp, Authors & Artists of Am, 2 terms. Rec'd President's Award, Composers, Authors & Artists of Am, 78; also 8 Blue Ribbon Awards for creative work in art, music & lit. Singer; real estate appraiser. *Songs:* If You Like Pretty Women; The Carlye Waltz; Lulabel Can't See the Likes of Me; Fantasy; The Rock That Wouldn't Roll.

HAILEY, EDWARD NEBRASKA (VALDEZ)   ASCAP 1975
composer, author, singer
b Martinsville, Va, June 20, 46. Educ: George Washington Carver High Sch; Universal Songwriting Sch, Hempstead, NY; Nashville Songwriting Sch, Fla. Singer-songwriter, actor, fashion model, DJ, dancer, comedian, comp-arr, producer, performer, dir. Chief Collabrs: Martin Pomerantz, Vince Vallis. *Songs:* Do the Hammer (Parts 1 & 2); Wear a Smile; The Feeling That I Have Inside for You; The Cookie Jar (Parts 1 & 2); Anytime Child.

HAILSTORK, ADOLPHUS C   ASCAP 1970
composer
b Rochester, NY, Apr 17, 41. Educ: Howard Univ, BMus(theory), 63, studied comp with Mark Fax; Am Inst, Fountainebleau, France, summer 63, studied comp with Nadia Boulanger; Manhattan Sch Music, New York, BMus(comp), 65, studied with Ludmila Ulehla, Nicholas Flagello & Vittorio Giannini, MMus(comp), 66, studied with David Diamond; Mich State Univ, East Lansing, PhD(comp), 71, studied with H Owen Reed; Electronic Music Inst, NH, summer 72; State Univ NY Buffalo, seminar on contemporary music, summer 78. Capt, USA, WGer, 66-68; piano teacher summer youth prog, Mich State Univ, East Lansing, 69, dir male chorus, 69-70, teacher comprehensive theory, summer 70, teaching fel, 70-71; asst prof music, Youngstown State Univ, 71-76, assoc prof, 76; assoc prof music & comp-in-residence, Norfolk State Col, 76- *Songs & Instrumental Works:* Celebration! (orch, comn by JC Penney); Suite for Organ; Sonatina for Flute and Piano; Bagatelles for Brass; Cease Sorrows Now (madrigal); Out of the Depths (band); Anthology of Black Art Songs; Mourn Not the Dead (Ernest Bloch Award for choral comp, 70-71); Bellevue (orch prelude, comn by Southern Baptists Convention); Spiritual (comn by Edward Tarr for Edward Tarr Brass Ens in Europe); American Landscape No 1 (comn by Boardman High Sch Band, Ohio); Out of the Depths (Belwin-Mills Max Winkler Award, Col Band Dirs Nat Asn, 77); Statement, Variations and Fugue; Epitaph: For a Man Who Dreamed.

HAINES, EDMUND   ASCAP 1956
composer
b Ottumwa, Iowa, Dec 15, 14; d. Educ: Eastman Sch Music, MM, PhD; Columbia Univ; studied with Aaron Copland & Otto Luening. Comp-in-residence, La Napoule Art Found, France, 57-58. Prof music, Sarah

Lawrence Col, 48. Grants: Pulitzer, 2 Guggenheim, Fulbright. *Instrumental Works:* Symphony No 1; Toccata for Brass Instruments; Dialogue From Job (women's chorus); Informal Overture; 3 Dances for Orchestra; Concertino for 7 Instruments, Orchestra (Ford Found comn); Promenade, Air and Toccata (Am Guild of Organists Award); Rondino and Variations for Orchestra; 4 string quartets; 2 piano sonatas.

HAINES, JAMES A ASCAP 1960
author
b Utica, NY, May 17, 25. Educ: Syracuse Univ, BA. Wrote spec material for "Connie Francis Show," TV. Copywriter for advert agencies, 52- *Songs:* When You Make Your Wish.

HAIRSTON, JESTER JOSEPH ASCAP 1956
composer, author, arranger
b NC, July 9, 01. Educ: Tufts Univ, music; Juilliard Cons, NY, music theory; hon PhD(music), Univ of the Pacific, 64, Tufts Univ, 72, Univ Mass, 72 & Lutheran Col, Iowa, 80. Joined late Hall Johnson Choir, NY, 30, asst cond, 33. Did music for Bway musicals, "Hello Paris", "America Sings," Shubert Shows & Roxy Presentations. Came to Hollywood, 36; did background music for "Green Pastures" & choral arr with Dimitri Tiomkin for "Lost Horizons." *Songs:* Amen; Mary's Boy Child; Elijah Rock; Poor Man Lazrus; Rocka My Soul.

HAJOS, KARL ASCAP 1929
composer
b Budapest, Hungary, Jan 28, 1889; d Hollywood, Calif, Feb 1, 50. Educ: Univ Budapest; Acad Music, Budapest. To Hollywood, 28. Wrote operettas in Europe & US, incl "The Black Pierrot"; "The Red Cat"; "Natja"; "White Lilacs"; "America Sings". *Songs:* Falling Leaves; Beautiful Dawn; Melodies Within My Heart. *Instrumental Works:* Phantasy for Piano, Orchestra; Rhapsody in Waltztime. *Scores:* Film: Beggars of Life; The Loves of an Actress; Morocco; Four Frightened People; Summer Storm; The Man Who Walked Alone; It's a Small World.

HALDEMAN, OAKLEY ASCAP 1949
composer, author, publisher
b Alhambra, Calif, July 17, 09. Gen mgr, music publ co. *Songs:* Here Comes Santa Claus; Brush Those Tears From Your Eyes; I Wish I Had Never Met Sunshine; Tho' I Tried; Pretty Mary; Texas Polka; Honey Child; Vict'ry Train; Last Mile; Texans Never Cry.

HALE, EUGENIA
See Woolsey, Maryhale

HALE, JAMES LEE ASCAP 1979
composer, author
b Clarksdale, Miss, Sept 19, 44. Educ: Aggie High Sch. Played with Lonnie Jordan & Freddie King. Chief Collabr: Karl Schiffmann. *Songs & Instrumental Works:* I Love You for This Reason; I'm So Into Your Love; You're More Than a Lady; Your Morning Smile; Today's Dream Is Tomorrow's Future.

HALE, LEROY FRANKLIN (LEE) ASCAP 1966
composer, author
b Tacoma, Wash, Mar 25, 23. Educ: Lincoln High Sch, Tacoma, Wash; Wash State Univ, BAMus. Sang with var vocal groups, vaudeville, radio, TV & commercials, NY. Choral dir, Carol Burnett Specials, "The Entertainers." Spec musical material, Dean Martin TV Show, 65-80. Producer, Dean Martin Specials, Bob Newhart Specials & Music Country USA. Chief Collabrs: Geoff Clarkson, Van Alexander. *Songs:* And the Bells Rang; Lyrics: It's a Time to Be Jolly.

HALE, MARK
See Gearinger, Lemuel Cyrus

HALE, MARY
See Woolsey, Maryhale

HALE, REGINALD
See Hermann, Ralph J

HALEY, BILL ASCAP 1955
composer, author, singer
b Highland Park, Mich, July 6, 25. Educ: Boothyne High Sch. Made many records with own group, Bill Haley and His Comets. Appeared in film, "Rock Around the Clock." *Songs:* Crazy Man Crazy; Rock-a-beatin' Boogie; Green Tree Boogie; Sundown Boogie.

HALL, ANNE ASCAP 1970
author
b New York, NY, Mar 11, 16. Educ: St Agatha's Sch for Girls, New York. Author bk poems & lyrics, "Love and Protest." Chief Collabrs: David Ian Jenkins, Scott Seeley. *Songs:* Lyrics: Tomorrow.

HALL, ARTHUR EDWIN ASCAP 1963
composer, professor
b Bellview, Ky, July 22, 01; d Houston, Tex, Mar 14, 78. Educ: Yale Univ, MusB, 24, with Paul Hindemith, 41; NY Inst of Musical Arts, 28; Colo Col, with Roy Harris & Nicholas Slonimsky, 47; Baylor Univ, MMus, Daniel Sternberg. Organist & choir master, St Paul's Episcopal Church, Wallingford, Conn, 20-24 & Christ Church, Danbury, Conn, 30-36; organist, Christ Church, Norwich, Conn, 24-25; organist & choir dir, Christ Church Cathedral, Houston, 46-52. Choral arr, Benton & Bowles Agency, Palmolive Beauty Box Theatre & "Fred Allen Show," 30-33. Assoc dir, Yale Glee Club, 30-42. Music master, Westminster Sch, Simsbury, Conn, 25-28; chmn, Shepherd Sch Music, Rice Univ, prof of music, 53-73, emeritus prof, 73-78, also mgr, Chamber Music Series. Chief Collabr: Fairfax Downey. *Songs:* Music: High Barbary; Wade in De Water; The Infant Christ; Sourwood Mountain; Cindy; Christ Is Risen; Sing With the Spirit. *Instrumental Works:* String Quartets Nos 1, 2, 3, 4, 5 and 6; Suite for Piano; Alterations (piano); This Is Ilyria, Lady; Symphony Nos 1 and 2. *Songs & Instrumental Works:* Toccata on C; Sounds of Christmas; Christmas Tryptich; Seven Preludes to the Nativity.

HALL, CAROL ASCAP 1970
composer, lyricist, singer
b Abilene, Tex, Apr 3, 36. Educ: Sarah Lawrence Col, BA, 60; pvt study with Meyer Kupferman, John Singer, 2 publ albums of own material on Elektra Records. Writer, music & lyrics, "Free to Be You and Me," incl bk, albums & TV & "Best Little Whorehouse in Texas." Lyricist, "Sesame Street"; produced theater pieces at La Mama, Lion Theatre Co, Playwright's Horizons. Performer, Bway production "I'm Getting My Act Together and Taking It on the Road." *Songs:* Jenny Rebecca. *Scores:* Film: The Best Little Whorehouse in Texas.

HALL, CHARLES JOHN ASCAP 1970
composer, author
b Houston, Tex, Nov 17, 25. Educ: Andrews Univ, BA, 52; Univ NMex, masters, 60, studied with Charles Garland; Mich State Univ, PhD(comp), 70, studied with H Owen Reed, Paul Harder. Taught music, high schs in NMex, Mo & Mich, 56-67. Grad student, Mich State Univ, 67-69. Prof of music, Andrews Univ, 69-; producer, fine arts radio prog, "Hall's Musical Years"; host, radio prog "Concert Preview" & announcer for concerts, South Bend & Twin Cities, Mich & Elkhart Symphonies. Author bk, "Hall's Musical Years, 1900-1979." *Instrumental Works:* Ulalume (after Poe, narrator, mezzo-soprano, orch); Five Microscopics for Large Orchestra; Symphony; Recitative for Orchestra; Three Symphonic Chuckles for Orchestra; Babylon, a Suite for Band (& orch); City in the Sea (soli, chorus, orch); Port Royal (symph poem); Scherzo, Just for Fun (orch).

HALL, DANNIE BELLE ASCAP 1974
composer, singer, pianist
b Pittsburgh, Pa, Oct 6, 38. Educ: Mt Mercy Col, AA(educ & home economics). Started own group at age 11, Dannie Belles. Sang with Andre Crouch and the Disciples, 73; toured with Billy Graham Crusades & others, Europe & Asia. Teaches song writing seminars, var cols & church groups. Has had 5 silver recordings; co-produces & does background arr; solo artist. *Songs:* Ordinary People; Because I'm Me; This Moment; Keep Holding On; All Things Work Together.

HALL, EDMOND ASCAP 1959
composer, clarinetist
b New Orleans, La, May 15, 01; d. Clarinetist in bands led by Buddy Petit, Mat Thomas, Alonzo Ross, Billy Fowler, Charlie Skeets, Claude Hopkins, Lucky Millinder, Billy Hicks, Zutty Singleton, Joe Sullivan, Red Allen, Teddy Wilson, Eddie Condon, Lionel Hampton. Toured US, Australia, Europe with Louis Armstrong, 55. Had own orch. Played & taught in Ghana, 59. *Instrumental Works:* Celestial Express; Uptown Cafe Blues.

HALL, GERTRUDE (SUGAR) ASCAP 1959
composer, author
b Sparta, Ga, June 6, 12. Educ: High sch. Chief Collabr: Edgar Redmond. *Songs:* School Day Blues; It's a Doggone Shame; Day Train; Sadie Lou; That's Why I Cried; Survival Stomp.

HALL, HELEN (TEDDY) ASCAP 1945
composer, author, singer
b New York, NY; d Aug 16, 77. Educ: Bus sch; studied voice. Appeared in vaudeville; organized vocal groups for radio shows. Wrote songs for films; also for Bway musicals, incl "Hellzapoppin"; "New Faces." Teacher & accompanist to singers. Author, "Uncle Don's Book for Children." *Songs:* So Tall a Tree, So Small a Man; Get a Horse, Get a Buggy; We Won't Let It Happen Here; Monkey on a String; Ridin' on a Rainbow.

HALL, JIM ASCAP 1963
composer, author, singer
b Houston, Tex, Feb 28, 40. Guitarist, singer & songwriter with Gidget Starr. Recording artist, Dynamite & Deadwood Records. Worked with Rod Morris, Dusty Rhodes, Dallas Turner & Ernest Tubb. Mem band, Tune Twisters. Chief Collabr: Gidget Starr. *Songs & Instrumental Works:* House of Glass; Truck

Driving Sam; Yesterday Ended Last Night; What's Your Game?; A Kiss for Every Birthday; I'm Glad I Met You After All; Gone Gone Gone; Buying Love; I'm Having a Ball Without You.

HALL, WENDELL WOODS ASCAP 1934
composer, author, singer

b St George, Kans, Aug 23, 1896; d Mobile, Ala, Apr 2, 69. Educ: Univ Chicago Prep Sch. WW I service. Sang & played ukulele in radio, 22, known as Red-Headed Music Maker. Made world radio tour, 24-27; vaudeville appearances, 27-28. Broadcasting dir, Majestic Theatre of the Air, CBS, 29; featured on "Fitch Band Wagon," NBC, 32-35. Song leader, Original Community Sing, CBS, 36-37. Advert exec & originator of Adsongs, 41-48. Author, "Love Poems" & "Ukulele Method." Chief Collabs: Haven Gillespie, Peter De Rose, Harry Woods, Carson Robison. *Songs:* Will You Forget Me While I'm Away?; It Ain't Gonna Rain No Mo'; Underneath the Mellow Moon; Land of My Sunset Dreams; My Carolina Rose; Whispering Trees; Your Shining Eyes; My Dream Sweetheart; Miss American Legion; Collections: Jingle Tunes; Fast Favorites; My Old-Fashioned Scrap Book.

HALLETT, EDWARD MERRIHEW, JR (MAT) ASCAP 1969
composer, author

b Newton, Mass, Oct 20, 06. Educ: Newton Country Day Sch; Wesleyan Univ; studied piano with Guy Maier, Thompson Stone, Pasquali Talarico, Henrick Gebhardt & Nadia Boulanger, Paris. Played piano in sch dance bands; in col with Wesleyan Serenaders. Wrote many songs for amateur musicals, played score & dir. Chief Collabs: Warren Ordway, Arlyne Freedman, Betsy Allen, Missy Darack, Mim Lewis, Laurence C Hobbs. *Songs:* One Gentleman; Le Ballet; Music: Love Like Ours; The Married Man's Lament; Sharing; Love Me Now; Give Us This Day; Love Walked Out; To Thine Own Self Be True.

HALLETT, JOHN C ASCAP 1959
composer, author, conductor

b Binghamton, NY. Educ: Moody Bible Inst; NY Univ; studied with Erik Leidzen. Music dir radio, "Children's Bible Hour," 2 yrs. Co-founder & chmn dept music, Northeastern Bible Col, Essex Fells, NJ. Music ed, Rodeheaver Hall Mack Music Co. Dir, John C Hallet Chorale & Orch. Minister music, Long Hill Chapel, Chatham, NJ & First Baptist Church of Lakewood, Long Beach, Calif. *Songs:* Sacred: There's No Disappointment in Jesus; Thank You Jesus; My Song of Songs; Praise My Soul, the King of Heaven; I Heard the Voice of Jesus Say; Music: Bless the Lord, O My Soul; He Made the Blind to See; America, You're Beautiful to Me.

HALLUM, ROSEMARY NORA ASCAP 1970
composer, author, teacher

b Oakland, Calif. Educ: Univ Calif, Berkeley, BA; Calif State Univ, San Jose, MA; Walden Univ, PhD; piano study with Elizabeth Simpson & Wilbert Baranco. Soloist & accompanist for dancers, singers & instrumentalists, age 13; taught piano, age 19, joined union, age 21. Specialized in music & dance in elem sch teaching career. Author publ relating to music & dance; nat, state & local teacher training workshops in music & dance; educ consult on music & dance. Author, "Music in Early Childhood"; "Beginnings." Chief Collabr: Henry (Buzz) Glass. *Albums:* Educ Recordings: Perceptual Motor Rhythm Games; Rhythm Stick Activities; Aerobic Disco Dancing.

HALPERN, ADELAIDE GARDNER ASCAP 1964
composer, author

b Chicago, Ill, June 21, 04; d Los Angeles, Calif, Aug 27, 76. Singer known as Baby Adelaide while with mother Adelaide Steeg Kline on all Balaban & Katz circuits of vaudeville. Started writing as a teenager with Frank Magine & Jack Gardner. Wrote for TV children series "Time for Beany" with Bob Clampett, later with daughter Joan Gardner Janis, wrote "Checkerboard Plays." Author of series of bks "Growing With Music." Chief Collabs: Joan Gardner Janis, Bob Clampett, Bob Mitchell. *Songs:* Music: Toy Piano Boogie; Good Ship Rock and Roll; Spelling Rock 'n Roll; Church Music: Mass of the Resurrection (Cath); The Lord Is My Shepherd; Happy Are You Who Fear the Lord.

HALSMAN, DAVID
See Fass, Bernie

HAM, ALBERT WILLIAM ASCAP 1958
composer

b Malden, Mass, Feb 6, 25. Educ: Amherst Col, 46; Columbia Univ, studied comp & orchestration with Otto Leuning & Henry Brandt. Arr, Tex Beneke, Glenn Miller & Tony Pastor Orchs. Producer, Columbia Records & Metromedia Records. Chief Collabs: Marilyn & Allan Bergman, Loonis McGlohon, Walter Liss. *Songs & Instrumental Works:* I Believed It All; The Music of Your Life; TV themes: Move Closer to Your World; Part of Your Life; Home Country.

HAMBLEN, BERNARD ASCAP 1925
composer, author, pianist

b Yeovil, Eng, July 14, 1877; d London, Nov 13, 62. Came to New York, 17. Accompanied own works at Hollywood Bowl, NY Hippodrome, Aeolian Hall & Albert Hall, London. *Songs & Instrumental Works:* Cast Thy Burden; Roses of Memory; The Road That Brought Me to You; Smile Through Your Tears;

Trust in Him; The Blind Mendicant; Bells Over Jordan; Restless Sea; Pickwick Sketches; Reverie; Cantatas: The Babe of Bethlehem; The Heavenly Child; Tragedy to Triumph.

HAMBLEN, STUART
composer, author, singer

b Kelleysville, Tex, Oct 20, 08. Educ: Crowell High Sch; McMurray Col, Tex. Radio artist, 25- Recording artist for all major labels. Speaker & singer for churches, clubs & TV. Ran for US Pres, prohibition ticket, 52. First to transport a racehorse by air. Bandleader; songwriter. With Voss Records. *Songs:* It Is No Secret (What God Can Do); Remember Me (I'm the One Who Loves You); This Ole House; Open Up Your Heart (And Let the Sun Shine In); The Lord Is Counting on You; Until Then; How Big Is God; Known Only to Him; He Bought My Soul At Calvary; Of God I Sing; My Mary; I Won't Go Huntin' With You, Jake (But I'll Go Chasin' Wimmin); Texas Plains; They That Wait Upon the Lord (Teach Me, Lord, to Wait); Ridin' Old Paint, and Leadin' Old Bald; It's a Brand New Day; Golden River; The Good Old Days; In My Dreambook of Memories; His Hands; I've Got So Many Million Years; Go on By; Transportation; Little Old Rag Doll; A Few Things to Remember; What Can I Do For My Country.

HAMBLEN, SUZY ASCAP 1957
composer

b Gage, Okla. Educ: Col. Writer songs & producer films with husband, Stuart Hamblen, incl "The Birth of a Song", "Cowboy Church", "Home With the Hamblens" & "Stuart's Scrapbook." *Songs:* Come Unto Me; Help Thou My Unbelief; There's a Place in God's Heart; Be Happy Today; You'll Always Be Mine.

HAMBLIN, FRANK C ASCAP 1970
composer, author, teacher

b Omaha, Nebr, June 15, 18. Educ: Early piano training with Cora Ippish; Orlando Acad Music, studied piano, organ, accordion, also, theory, harmony & writing, 46-50. Accordionist with several combos, Fla & dance combo, The Pacemaker's, Los Angeles, Hollywood, Ventura. Music teacher, Melbourne, Fla, 57-60 & 60-64. Owned music studios, Hawthorne & Los Angeles, 60-64. Publ, sheet music. *Songs:* Rosie the Happy Reindeer; The American Wedding Song; Signs in the Sand; Those Lonely Nights; Santa Claus Came to Town.

HAMILL, PAUL ASCAP 1965
composer, editor, publisher

b Tobyhanna, Pa, June 10, 30. Educ: Boston Univ, studied comp with Gardner Read, BMus, 52; Am Guild Organists, ChM, 54; Wesleyan Univ, studied comp with Richard Winslow, MA, 56. Instr, Adelphi Univ, 60-65. Music ed, Am Book Co, 65-78. Publ, Gemini Press, Inc, 77- Ed-in-chief, Summy-Birchard Music, 78- *Songs & Instrumental Works:* Choral: Tenebrae; A Candlelight Carol Service; Hallelujah; Giving Thanks; A Festival of Lessons and Carols; A Call to Praise; Organ: The Two Manual Organ; Aria da Chiesa; Antiphon I and II; Foundation (choral prelude).

HAMILTON, ARTHUR ASCAP 1955
composer, author

b Seattle, Wash. Educ: Spec studies incl piano with Dr Homer Grunn, comp with Dr Wesley LaViolette & theory with Gregg Smith. Wrote music and/or lyrics for many theatrical films & TV specials. Vpres, ASCAP & Acad Motion Picture Arts & Sci; mem exec bd, Composer & Lyricists Guild of Am; past pres, Calif Copyright Conf; mem, Dramatists Guild & Am Guild of Authors & Composers. Chief Collabs: Johnny Mandel, David Grusin, Roger Kellaway, David Raksin, Jerry Fielding, Riz Ortolani, Gilbert Becaud, Armando Manzanero, Stan Worth, Benny Carter, Mike Melvoin, Luchi DeJesus, Robert Ragland. *Songs:* Cry Me a River; He Needs Me; Sing a Rainbow; Rain Sometimes; Lyrics: You'll Remember Me; Till Love Touches Your Life.

HAMILTON, BOB ASCAP 1944
composer, author, organist

b Bridgeport, Conn, Oct 11, 1899; d. Educ: Studied with John Bowerhan, Pietro Yon. Organist, theatres throughout US. Staff organist, radio networks, New York & Hollywood. Organist, "Ice Capades," 60-61. Writer, films; recording artist. *Songs:* The Military Polka; Hello and Not So Long; I Confess; Gotham Fantasie; Grateful Am I; Love Wail; The Greatest Love; Second Honeymoon.

HAMILTON, EDWARD LESLIE (TED) ASCAP 1972
composer, author, singer

b Sydney, Australia, Feb 12, 37. Educ: Cons Music, Sydney. Commenced career as big band singer, TV perf & stage actor, 55; writer, 58- Moved to Los Angeles in 75. *Songs:* On This Road; Get On With Your Livin'; I Believe in Xmas; Citizen John; Don't Leave Me Babe; You Can Never Go Home.

HAMILTON, FRANK S ASCAP 1967
composer, music teacher, guitarist

b New York, NY, Aug 3, 34. Educ: Los Angeles City Col, studied comp & dance band arr with Robert MacDonald; Calif State Univ, Northridge; Roosevelt Univ Chicago Musical Col. Accompanist; studio musician on recordings; solo performer; mem group, Weavers, 62-63. Vpres, cofounder & head teaching staff, Old Town Sch of Folk Music, Chicago, 57-62; guitar instr, Univ Calif, Los

Angeles Exten Div, 63-69 & Santa Barbara Exten Div, 76-78; guitar instr, Music World, Hollywood, Calif, 70-73; pvt instr, 73-80. Chief Collabrs: Ernie Sheldon, Dianne Hildebrande, Nathaniel Miller, Walter Brough. *Songs:* Music: I Feel It; And We Were Strangers; Telling Me Lies; Baby, What I Mean; Don't Wait for Me; We Shall Overcome. *Scores:* Film: Funeral for an Assassin; Surfers; A Time Out of War.

HAMILTON, GEORGE (SPIKE)   ASCAP 1944
composer, conductor

b Newport, Vt, Jan 13, 01; d New York, NY, Mar 31, 57. Educ: Dartmouth Col. Led Barbary Coast Orch. Cond orch, Chicago Opera, 4 yrs; also hotel orchs throughout US. Appeared in films: "George White's Scandals"; "Sunday Night at the Trocadero." *Songs:* Bye Bye Pretty Baby; Wild Honey; Here Comes Your Pappy; Lovely While It Lasted; I Feel Sorry for the Poor People; There's Never Been a Love Like Ours; Hat Check Girl; You Can Say That Again; Iowa Corn Song.

HAMILTON, L HILL   ASCAP 1963
composer, author

b Covington, Ky, June 5, 17. Educ: Columbia Mil Acad, Univ South; Bowling Green Bus Univ. *Songs:* I Dreamed That I Was Santa Claus; I Wish.

HAMILTON, NANCY   ASCAP 1940
composer, author

b Sewickley, Pa, July 27, 08. Educ: Miss Dickenson's Sch, Sewickley, Pa; The Sorbonne, Paris, France; Smith Col, Mass. Actor, author, song writer & producer. Musical revues: "And So On", "New Faces", "One for the Money", "Two for the Show", "Three to Make Ready" & "Three to One." Film writer & producer, "Helen Keller in Her Story" (Acad Award); "This Is Our Island." Spec material for Mary Martin, Cyril Pritchard, Beatrice Lillie, Billie Burke, Kitty Carlisle, Kaye Ballard, & others. Chief Collabrs: Martha Caples, Morgan Lewis. *Songs:* Lyrics: How High the Moon; The House With the Little Red Barn; The Old Soft Shoe; I Hate the Spring; The Old Gavotte; Lovely Lazy Kind of Day; Clambake; Music: A Horse Called Marg'ret.

HAMLISCH, MARVIN F   ASCAP 1959
composer

b New York, NY, June 2, 44. Educ: Prof Children's Sch; Prep Div, Juilliard Sch, grad; Queens Col, NY, BA. Comp, songs & scores for Bway plays & films. *Songs:* What I Did for Love; They're Playing Our Song; The Way We Were; Nobody Does It Better; Sunshine, Lollipops and Rainbows. *Scores:* Bway show: A Chorus Line; They're Playing Our Song; Films: The Way We Were; The Spy Who Loved Me; Take the Money and Run; The Sting.

HAMMACK, BOBBY   ASCAP 1958
composer, lyricist

b Brookston, Tex, Jan 22, 22. Educ: Univ Tex. Music dir, ABC network, 58-63; then cond & pianist, NBC. *Songs:* I'm Going Home; Eliza; You Bug Me.

HAMMEL, WILLIAM CARL, JR   ASCAP 1976
composer, author, pianist

b New York, NY, Dec 4, 44. Educ: C W Post Col, Long Island Univ, BA, MS; Univ Wis, PhD; studied with Raoul Pleskow, Stefan Wolpe. Prof of mathematical physics. Bicentennial comn for "Three Movements in Concerto Form"; recording artist. *Instrumental Works:* Orexis, Variations for Strings and Timpani; Five Fragments from Comus (soprano, sextet); De Canticorum Solomonis (voice, orch); Symphony (1977-1979); (violin).

HAMMER, JACK
See Burroughs, Earl S

HAMMER, JAN   ASCAP 1977
composer, author

b Prague, Czech, Apr 17, 48. Educ: Acad Muse Arts, Prague, 64-65; Berklee Sch Music, Boston, Mass, 68-69. Began playing piano at age 4; solo recording career began in Czech, 64. Scholarship to Berklee Sch Music, 66; moved to US, 68. Arr, cond & pianist for Sarah Vaughan, 70. Formed the Mahavishnu Orch with John McLaughlin. Started solo recording career in US & formed the Jan Hammer Group; worldwide tours, 76-77; recording artist, 78-79. Chief Collabr: Jeff Beck. *Songs:* Earth/Still Our Only Home; Full Moon Boogie. *Instrumental Works:* Darkness (Earth in Search of a Sun); Blue Wind; Oh Yeah; Star Cycle; You Never Know; Too Much to Lose. *Albums:* Black Sheep; Hammer; Inner Mounting; Flame; Birds of Fire; Between Nothingness and Eternity; The First Seven Days; Wired; Melodies.

HAMMER, ROBERT   ASCAP 1964
composer

b Indianapolis, Ind, Mar 3, 30. Educ: Mich State Univ; Manhattan Sch Music. *Songs:* The Strut; Charleston Hoot; Blue Bongo.

HAMMERMAN, HERMAN   ASCAP 1963
composer, cantor

b Brooklyn, NY, July 4, 12. Educ: Boys High Sch; St John's Univ; Brooklyn City Col. Worked for fed govt, 16 yrs. Cantor, Los Angeles, 50, retired, 70. Chief Collabrs: Murray Schwimmer, Sidney Sornoff, Joseph Auslander. *Songs &*

Instrumental Works: Take God By the Hand; The Wall; Happy Is the Man; Soldier Weeping at Western Wall; L'Chayim (10 songs); Tell the World.

HAMMERSTEIN, ARTHUR
composer

b New York, NY; d Oct 12, 55. Producer of operettas incl, "Naughty Marietta", "Fire Fly", "Rose Marie" & "Sweet Adeline."

HAMMERSTEIN, OSCAR, II   ASCAP 1923
author, producer, publisher

b New York, NY, July 12, 1895; d Doylestown, Pa, Aug 23, 60. Educ: Columbia Univ; Columbia Law Sch. Hon degrees: Columbia Univ, Drury Col, Univ Mass & Dartmouth Col. Columbia Medal for Excellence; Alexander Hamilton Award. Dir, ASCAP, 39-60. Wrote, acted, Columbia Varsity Shows. Began career as stage mgr for uncle. Co-produced Bway productions: "I Remember Mama"; "Annie Get Your Gun"; "Happy Bithday"; "John Loves Mary"; "The Happy Time." Co-founder, Williamson Music, 45. Mem: Nat Inst Arts & Letters; Authors League (pres, 50). Author, "Lyrics by Oscar Hammerstein, II." Biographies: "Some Enchanted Evenings" by Deems Taylor; "The Rodgers and Hammerstein Story" by Stanley Green; "Getting to Know Him" by Hugh Fordin; "Rodgers and Hammerstein Fact Book," ed by Stanley Green. Chief Collabrs: Richard Rodgers, Jerome Kern, Sigmund Romberg; Others: Rudolf Friml, George Gershwin, Herbert Stothart, Vincent Youmans, Arthur Schwartz, Otto Harbach. *Songs:* Bambalina; Wildflower; The Mounties; Indian Love Call; Totem Tom-Tom; Sunny; Who; Two Little Bluebirds; Cossack Love Song; Song of the Flame; Riff Song; Romance; The Desert Song; One Alone; One Flower Grows Alone in Your Garden; Make Believe; Ol' Man River; Can't Help Lovin' Dat Man of Mine; Life Upon the Wicked Stage; You Are Love; Why Do I Love You?; Nobody Else But Me; Softly, As in a Morning Sunrise; Lover, Come Back to Me; Stouthearted Men; One Kiss; Wanting You; The One Girl; Here Am I; Why Was I Born; Don't Ever Leave Me; You Will Remember Vienna; I've Told Every Little Star; And Love Was Born; In Egern on the Tegern See; The Song Is You; When I Grow Too Old to Dream; I Won't Dance; Just Once Around the Clock; I'll Take Romance; Can I Forget You?; The Folks Who Live on the Hill; One Day When We Were Young; All the Things You Are; That Lucky Fellow; All in Fun; Heaven in My Arms; In the Heart of the Dark; The Last Time I Saw Paris (Acad Award, 41); The Sweetest Sight That I Have Seen; How Can I Ever Be Alone?; Tennessee Fish Fry; Your Dream; Dat's Love; Dere's a Cafe on de Corner; Beat Out Dat Rhythm on a Drum; My Joe; Oh, What a Beautiful Mornin'; The Surrey With the Fringe on Top; I Cain't Say No; People Will Say We're in Love; Out of My Dreams; Oklahoma; It's a Grand Night for Singing; It Might As Well Be Spring (Acad Award, 46); That's for Me; All Through the Day; You're a Queer One, Julie Jordan; When I Marry Mr Snow; If I Loved You; June Is Bustin' Out All Over; Soliloquy; You'll Never Walk Alone; What's the Use of Wond'rin'?; A Fellow Needs a Girl; Money Isn't Everything; So Far; The Gentleman Is a Dope; You Are Never Away; A Cockeyed Optimist; Some Enchanted Evening; There Is Nothin' Like a Dame; Bali Ha'i; I'm Gonna Wash That Man Right Outa My Hair; A Wonderful Guy; Younger Than Springtime; Happy Talk; This Nearly Was Mine; Honey Bun; Carefully Taught; I Whistle a Happy Tune; Something Wonderful; Hello, Young Lovers; We Kiss in a Shadow; Getting to Know You; Shall We Dance; A Kiss to Build a Dream On; I Haven't Got a Worry in the World; Marriage-Type Love; No Other Love; I'm Your Girl; All at Once You Love Her; The Next Time It Happens; Everybody's Got a Home But Me; Ten Minutes Ago; Do I Love You Because You're Beautiful?; In My Own Little Corner; A Hundred Million Miracles; You Are Beautiful; I Enjoy Being a Girl; Love, Look Away; The Sound of Music; Do Re Mi; My Favorite Things; Climb Ev'ry Mountain; Maria; Edelweiss. *Scores:* Bway Stage (librettist or co-librettist); Always You; Sweet Adeline; Oklahoma! (Pulitzer Prize, 44); Carmen Jones; Carousel (NY Drama Critics Award, 45); Tickle Me; Wildflower; Mary Jane McKane; Rose-Marie; Sunny; Song of the Flame; The Desert Song; Golden Dawn; New Moon; Show Boat; Music in the Air; Ball at the Savoy (London); Three Sisters (London); Very Warm for May; Sunny River; Rainbow; East Wind; The King and I (Tony Award, 52); Me and Juliet; Pipe Dream; South Pacific (Pulitzer Prize; Tony, NY Drama Critics Awards, 50); Flower Drum Song; May Wine; American Jubilee; The Sound of Music (Tony, Grammy Awards, 60); Good Boy; Film Scores: The Night Is Young; Give Us This Night; The Great Waltz; Screenplays: Viennese Nights; High, Wide and Handsome; State Fair; TV Score (libretto): Cinderella.

HAMMETT, PAUL DEAN (JUSTIN CASE)   ASCAP 1967
composer, author, singer

b Kansas City, Mo, Nov 8, 15. Radio staff, WHB, Kansas City & KSD, St Louis. Mem & arr vocal trio, Rhythm Rockets; appeared radio, stage & nightclubs. Had own band, Hap Hazard & his Orchestra. Chief Collabrs: Bess Brigham, Wade Listerman, Jim Cain. *Songs:* What Is Love?; I'll Go on Loving You With a Broken Heart; Have a Nice Day; With Each Passing Day; I Think We Can Make It If We Try; Music: Myrtle the Turtle Race Queen; Desert Rose.

HAMMITT, ORLIN   ASCAP 1964
composer, author, musician

b SDak, Sept 9, 16. Educ: High sch. Owner, C&H Music Store, Flagstone Music Co. Chief Collabrs: Norman Malkin, John Colonna, George Wilfong. *Songs:* Are You Ready?; Sugar Lips; You Guessed It; The Quiver; Here Comes Mary Christmas.

HAMMOND, CLEON E   ASCAP 1951
composer, author
b Peoria, Ill, Aug 13, 08. Educ: Univ Minn; Univ Ore. Product dir (surgical field), Johnson & Johnson; bus exec. Col, USMCR. Author, "The Marine Corps." Pres, Hopewell Museum, NJ. Mem, Sons of Am Revolution. Chief Collabrs: Larry Wagner, Jimmy Eaton. *Songs:* Turn Back the Hands of Time.

HAMMOND, WILLIAM G   ASCAP 1942
composer, organist
b Melville, NY, Aug 7, 1874; d New York, NY, Dec 22, 45. Organist, Dutch Reformed Church, Brooklyn, 14-45. *Songs:* The Lovely Month of May; When Into Thine Eyes I Gaze; I Fain Would Outpour All My Sorrows; When Thou Commandest Me to Sing; Behold the Master Passeth By; Lochinvar (chorus).

HAMPTON, PAUL   ASCAP 1958
composer, lyricist, actor
b Oklahoma City, Okla, Aug 20, 40. Educ: Dartmouth Col, BA. Rock & roll pioneer; started writing with Hal David & Burt Bacharach; wrote a series of classics, 59-68; wrote & perf theme for TV show, "My Mother the Car"; has written for Eddie Arnold, O C Smith, Sammy Davis, Jr, Don Gibson & others. Co-starred with Diana Ross in the movie, "Lady Sings the Blues" (the story of Billy Holiday). Has appeared on many TV talk shows, incl Ed Sullivan & Johnny Carson. *Songs:* Oklahoma City Time; After the Long Drive Home; Juarez; Sea of Heartbreak; You Don't Know What You've Got (Until You Lose It); Donna Means Heartbreak; You Can't Lie to a Liar.

HANDEL, DARRELL DALE   ASCAP 1972
composer, educator
b Lodi, Calif, Aug 23, 33. Educ: Univ of the Pac, BM, 55, MM, 57, studies with S R Beckler & J Russell Bodley; Eastman Sch Music, PhD, 69, studies with Allen McHose & Wayne Barlow. Prof theory, Univ Kans, 66-71; prof theory & comp, Univ SC, 71-76 & Univ Cincinnati, 76- *Instrumental Works:* Three Balloons for Harp; Suzanne's Animal Music; Erschienen Ist Der Herrlich Tag (brass); Chamber Concerto for Harp; The Poems of Our Climate.

HANDMAN, LOU   ASCAP 1923
composer, pianist
b New York, NY, Sept 10, 1894; d Flushing, NY, Dec 9, 56. Toured in vaudeville, Australia. Served USA, WW I. Pianist, music publ firms; accompanist to vaudeville singers. Chief Collabrs: Archie Gottler, Harry Harris. *Songs:* Give Me a Smile and a Kiss; My Sweetie Went Away; I Can't Get the One I Want; Are You Lonesome Tonight?; I'm Gonna Charleston Back to Charleston; What Good Would It Do?; Is My Baby Blue Tonight?; No Nothing; Me and the Moon; Was It Rain?; Don't Ever Change; Baby Me; Puddin' Head Jones; Blue.

HANDY, WILLIAM CHRISTOPHER (W C)   ASCAP 1924
composer, bandmaster, cornetist
b Florence, Ala, Nov 16, 1873; d New York, NY, Mar 28, 58. Educ: Pub schs; hon degree: Wilberforce Univ. Was sch teacher; worked in iron mills. Cornet soloist in quartet he organized. Cornetist in Mahara's Minstrels. Organized own dance band. Bandmaster & music teacher, Normal, Ala A&M Col. Went to Clarksdale, Miss, taught K of P band & orch. Became music publ, Memphis, Tenn, 13. Ed: "Blues, An Anthology" (coll 37 negro spirituals); "Unsung Americans Sung"; "A Treasury of the Blues"; "Negro Authors and Composers of the United States." Autobiography: "Father of the Blues." Film biography: "St Louis Blues." Mem, NAACP. *Songs & Instrumental Works:* Memphis Blues; Jogo Blues; St Louis Blues; Yellow Dog Blues; Joe Turner Blues; Beale Street Blues; Hesitating Blues; Ole Miss; Aframerica Hymn; Harlem Blues; Basement Blues; Loveless Love (Careless Love); Chantez Les Bas; Aunt Hagar's Blues; East St Louis Blues; John Henry; Annie Love; Hail to the Spirit of Freedom; Big Stick Blues March; Atlanta Blues; Blue Destiny; Shoeboot's Serenade; Sundown Blues; Southside; Ape Mister Eddie; Darktown Reveille; Chicago Gouge; Sounding Brass and Tinkling Cymbals; Ever After On; Friendless Blues; Blue Gummed Blues; Golden Brown Blues; The Birth of Jazz; Pasadena; Who's That Man; Wall Street Blues; Mozambique; Negrita; Woo-Loo-Moo-Loo Blues; Beale Street Serenade; I'm Telling You in Front (So You Won't Feel Hurt Behind); Vesuvius (There's a Red Glow in the Sky Above Vesuvius); Way Down South Where the Blues Began; Negro spirituals: I'll Never Turn Back No More; Nobody Knows the Trouble I See; I've Heard of a City Called Heaven; Shine Like a Mornin' Star; The Rough Rocky Road; For mixed voices: The Bridegroom Has Done Come; Going to See My Sarah; Hist D E Eindow Noah; I'll Be There in the Morning; Give Me Jesus; Steal Away to Jesus; I'm Drinking From a Fountain; Go Down Moses; 'Tis the Old Ship of Zion; Stand on That Sea of Glass; Stand on the Rock a Little Longer; They That Sow in Tears (Shall Reap in Joy); Musical settings: Opportunity (Walter Malone poem); Gettysburg Address.

HANEY, JOE TOM   ASCAP 1973
composer, band director
b Colorado City, Tex, Aug 19, 27. Educ: Marlin High Sch; Southern Methodist Univ, BM; Sam Houston State Univ, MA. High sch band dir, 22 yrs; band dir, Tex A&M Univ, 72- *Songs:* The Trailways Blues. *Instrumental Works:* Noble Men of Kyle; Braso Brillante; Gig 'Em.

HANEY, (GERALD) RAY   ASCAP 1954
composer, author, pianist
b Salesville, Tex, Mar 15, 21. Educ: NY Univ, studied Schillinger Syst; NTex State Univ, BM, MM. Wrote spec material for TV & nightclubs. Pianist in dance bands, theatres, churches & nightclubs; also with Ace Dinning Quartette, 47-50. Had own daily radio show, NBC, Washington, DC, 2 yrs. Music dir, Norwood Records, 58- Cond, singer & arr. *Instrumental Works:* Symphony No 1; String Quartet No 1; Brazos Suite; Rocker Revival; Demon Rum; Cold Porter; Jazz Toccata; A Street Called Summer; The Seafarers; Scene One, Take Two; The Bar Fly; The Eli Whitney Waltz; Overture for a Waitress Working Overtime. *Scores:* Film background: The Air Force Story; TV film series: The Shadow.

HANIGAN, CAROL HOVEY
composer
b Ft William McKinley, Philippines. Educ: Univ Calif, Los Angeles, BA; San Francisco Cons Mus. Songwriter. *Songs:* Got It Down to Two; In Paradise.

HANIGHEN, BERNARD D   ASCAP 1935
composer, author
b Omaha, Nebr; d. Educ: Harvard Col, BS; pres, Harvard Dramatic Club, wrote Hasty Pudding & Pi Eta Club shows. Dir, record cos. Newscaster, CBS short wave, WW II. Wrote spec material for orchs incl Glenn Miller. Wrote additional lyrics for revival, "The Chocolate Soldier Soldier"; wrote for films. Chief Collabrs: Raymond Scott, Johnny Mercer, Cootie Williams, Harold Adamson, Neal Hefti. *Songs:* When a Woman Loves a Man; If the Moon Turns Green; The Weekend of a Private Secretary; Bob White; The Little Man Who Wasn't There; Me and the Ghost Upstairs; Two Little Fishes and Five Loaves of Bread; 'Round Midnight; House of Joy; Tired Teddy Bear; Mountain High - Valley Low; See the Monkey; Where You Are; My Old Man; Dixieland Band; Fare-Thee-Well to Harlem; Air-Minded Executive; Blue Fool; Baby Doll; Here Come the British; Poor Mr Chisholm; Show Your Linen, Miss Richardson. *Scores:* Bway stage: Lute Song.

HANLEY, JAMES FREDERICK   ASCAP 1917
composer, author, pianist
b Rensselaer, Ind, Feb 17, 1892; d Douglaston, NY, Feb 8, 42. Educ: Champion Col; Chicago Musical Col. Wrote & produced Army show, "Toot Sweet", 82nd Div, WW I. Accompanist in vaudeville. Under contract to film studios. Chief Collabrs: B G DeSylva; Eddie Dowling. *Songs:* Back Home in Indiana; The Little White House (At the End of Honeymoon Lane); Gee, But I Hate to Go Home Alone; Rose of Washington Square; Second Hand Rose; No Foolin'; Little Log Cabin of Dreams; Just a Cottage Small by a Waterfall; Sleepy Valley; Zing! Went the Strings of My Heart; Breeze (Blow My Baby Back to Me); Dig a Little Deeper; I'm a Lonesome Little Raindrop; Half a Moon; Jersey Walk; Mary Dear; Wherever You Are; Dreams for Sale. *Scores:* Bway stage: Jim Jam Jems; Spice of 1922; Big Boy; Honeymoon Lane; Sidewalks of New York.

HANLON, BERT   ASCAP 1923
composer, author, actor
b New York, NY; d New York, Jan 13, 73. Educ: City Col New York. Appeared in vaudeville, Bway musicals & films. Wrote spec material, dialogue dir in films. In publicity dept, Yonkers Raceway. Chief Collabrs: Walter Donaldson, James Hanley, Al Bryan, Harry Tierney, Harry Akst, Milton Ager. *Songs:* M-I-S-S-I-S-S-I-P-P-I; Round on the End, High in the Middle; Far Far Away in Rockaway; I'd Love to Be a Monkey in the Zoo; Four Little Walls and Me; Omaha; Vamping Rose; The Coat and Pants Do All Work But the Vest Gets All the Gravy; Steven Got Even; Six Times Six Is Thirty Six; Listen to the Knocking At the Knitting Club; He Left Her Behind Before.

HANLON, RICHARD BRENDAN   ASCAP 1974
writer
b Boston, Mass, July 9, 36. Educ: Boston Latin Sch; Emerson Col; Smith Col; Univ Calif, Los Angeles Annual Entertainment Tax Inst; Irish studies with Horace Reynolds, playwriting with Denis Johnston, special make-up techniques with Bob O'Bradoulch. Performed as clown, 4 yrs; legitimate actor, 7 yrs; with Agony Trio in var nightclubs. Tax practitioner for performing New York. Writer, var mag articles on performing arts taxes, bk, "A Guide to Taxes and Recordkeeping for Performers, Directors and Designers." Chief Collabr: Oatis Stephens. *Songs:* Ketchup, Indiana.

HANNA, R PHILIP   ASCAP 1952
composer, actor, singer
b River Forest, Ill, Oct 9, 10; d Jackson Heights, NY, July 20, 57. Educ: Los Angeles Men's Col. Singer & actor in films, TV & theatre. Wrote for TV show "Bride and Groom." Chief Collabr: Al Jacobs.

HANNAY, ROGER DURHAM   ASCAP 1964
composer, teacher, conductor
b Plattsburg, NY, Sept 22, 30. Educ: Syracuse Univ, BMus, 52; Boston Univ, MMus, 53; Eastman Sch Music, PhD, 56; student of Howard Hanson & Lukas Foss; Tanglewood, Berkshire Music Ctr, 59; Princeton Univ, summer 60. Teacher, Col/Univ, 56-; prof music in comp, electronic music & new music ens, Univ NC, 66-, chmn div fine arts, currently. Grants: Nat Endowment for the Arts & Kenan Found. Recordings, Golden Crest Records. *Instrumental Works:*

Pied Piper; Sphinx; Fantome; Symphony No 4 (Am Classic); Serenade (ARP & piano); Elegy.

HANNER, DAVID N   ASCAP 1978
composer, singer, guitarist
b Pittsburgh, Pa, Feb 22, 49. Educ: Ford City High Sch; Indiana Univ, Pa. Professional musician, nightclubs & some TV, 70-; recording artist, Columbia Records, 2 yrs. *Songs:* Long Gone Blues; Beautiful You; Proof of My Love.

HANSEN, AKSEL H   ASCAP 1954
composer, arranger, teacher
b Stavanger, Norway, Nov 9, 19. Educ: Los Angeles Cons, MM. Arr, dance bands, 37-41. Worked for Spec Services, WW II. Teacher, Los Angeles Cons, 12 yrs. Chief Collabrs: Johnny Mercer, Don Craig, George Howe. *Songs:* Hoping; One Way Street; Open the Door to Your Heart; My Faith.

HANSEN, EDWARD DUANE
author, producer
b Walker, Minn, Jan 30, 37. Educ: Fremont High Sch; Univ Calif, Berkeley; Stanford Univ, studied broadcast advert. Script ed, feature films, Kling Studios, Los Angeles. Producer, copywriter & lyricist, KBSC-TV, Medford, Ore. Radio/TV producer, Young & Rubicam, San Francisco. Radio/TV producer & copywriter, Doyle Dane Bernbach, Los Angeles. Musical producer/copywriter, Gold Star Productions, Hollywood. Co-owner, producer, A&R, Edge Records, Studio City. Owner production co, Ed Hansen & Assocs, Los Angeles. Chief Collabrs: Charles (Casey) H Anderson, Billy Adems. *Songs: Lyrics:* Miss Kitty's Leaving the Long Branch.

HANSEN, LAWRENCE WILLIAM (BILL)   ASCAP 1957
composer, author, publisher
b Jersey City, NJ, Aug 23, 05; d Newport Beach, Calif, Mar 24, 68. Educ: Hong Kong Mil Acad; NY Univ; Univ Calif Los Angeles. In early network radio, 26-42. Worked in films. Publ asst to Fred Waring, 42-48, Charles Hansen & Ethel Smith, 53-64. Chief Collabrs: Jerry Livingston, Noble Sissle, Charles O'Flynn, Jack Fulton. *Songs:* Dreaming of My Indiana Sweetheart; Doin' the Twist; Palladium Twist; White Sails; Torture of Love.

HANSEN, ROBERTA ANN   ASCAP 1978
author, teacher
b Edgerton, Wis, Dec 21, 36. Educ: Univ Colo, BS, 64. Worked as registered nurse. Singer, pianist, clarinettist & homemaker. Lyricist for many popular songs. Chief Collabr: Ted Hansen, husband. *Songs: Lyrics:* Christmas Is for Love; So Near and Yet So Far; Tears; Looks Like It's the Real Thing; First the Good News; And So You'll Never Know; I'll Meet You There; Far Into the Night; Alright, Hello; What Can You Do to Get Me There; Love You So; Some Sunday in June; It's Got to Be a Losing Game; Take Time to Listen; The Summers Gone; Somebody Cured the Blues Last Night; Love Is Someone New; She'll Say Goodbye; Rain May Come Tomorrow; Memories of Yesterday; Just Thought I'd Drop By; Looks Like It Will Be One of Those Days; I Laugh Away the Pain.

HANSEN, THEODORE CARL   ASCAP 1975
composer, professor
b Denver, Colo, Feb 5, 35. Educ: Univ Colo, Boulder, BM(piano), 64; Ariz State Univ, MM(comp), 67; Univ Ariz, AMusD(comp), 74. Asst prof music, Ariz State Univ, 67-74. Assoc prof music, Univ Tulsa, 75- Chief Collabr: Bobbie Hansen, wife. *Songs: Music:* The Summers Gone; Christmas Is for Love; I Laugh Away the Pain; So Near and Yet So Far; And So You'll Never Know. *Instrumental Works:* Symphony No 1; String Quartet; Coloration in Brass; Contrasts for Woodwind Quintet; Suite for Brass Quintet; Toccata for Winds; Collage (vibraphone, 2 flutes, oboe, clarinet); Configuration for Flute and Piano; Nocturne for Clarinet and Piano; Cavatina for Flugelhorn and Piano; Configuration for Trumpet and Piano; Aria for Trombone and Piano; Elegy for Organ; Four Sketches for Piano; Montage for Violin and Piano; Suite for Viola and Piano; Three Movements for Orchestra; Configuration for Piano; Elegy for Saxophone and Piano.

HANSON, ALFRED E (BUD)   ASCAP 1967
composer, author, musician
b Manistique, Mich, June 8, 23. Professional musician at age 14, musician, actor, arr with Repertoire Shows; staff musician, WBAY-TV, Green Bay, Wis. Recordings with var orchs, played with duos & trios in clubs throughout US. *Songs:* A Country Lovin' Heart; Dreamin'; *Music:* Stomp Stomp Polka; Tico Tico Polka.

HANSON, DARYL L   ASCAP 1974
composer, conductor, pianist
b Belmond, Iowa, Feb 17, 24. Educ: Iowa State Univ; Univ Northern Iowa, BA; Eastman Sch Music, MMus; Univ Southern Calif; Columbia Univ Teachers Col; comp teachers, Bill Latham, Alan Hovanhess & Aaron Copeland. Cond of choral & instrumental music; piano recitalist; univ prof; organist-choir dir; comp of choral, instrumental & theatre music. Chief Collabr: Bert Stimmel. *Songs:* There Is a Baby;

HANSON, ETHWELL IDAIR (EDDY)   ASCAP 1950
composer, author, pianist
b New London, Wis, Aug 1, 1893. Educ: Am Col of Music, studied with Frank Van Dusen; Lawrence Col, studied with Mason Slade; Chicago Col of Music, studied with Clarence Eddy; Northwestern Univ, Evanston; Bush Cons, studied organ with Kimball Hall; studied with Adolph Weidig, piano with Julia King, Fannie Bloomfield Zeisler, harp with Clara Louise Thurston, Dorothy Bell, Marie Ludwig. Saxophone soloist with John Philip Sousa Band. Accompanist for Geraldine Farrar, 23. First radio organist, WDAP, Chicago, 23. Staff organist, WBBM, WLS, WCFL-NBC, 24-48. Pianist in supper clubs. Solo organist, Chicago, Tivoli & Uptown Theatres, Chicago. Hon mem, Automatic Musical Instruments Collectors Asn. *Songs:* At the End of the Sunset Trail; Only a Weaver of Dreams; Rattlesnake Rag; California Moon; Thunderbird March; The World Needs a Heart Full of Love; The Joy and the Pain of Love; Weeping Waters; Golden Melody; True Love Is Forever; Song of Life; There's a Land Beyond the Rainbow.

HANSON, HOWARD   ASCAP 1938
composer, conductor, educator
b Wahoo, Nebr, Oct 28, 1896. Educ: Juilliard; Am Acad (Prix de Rome); Keuka Col, LittD; hon MusD: Univ Nebr Sch Music, Northwestern Univ, Syracuse Univ, Horner Inst, Augustana Col & Theol Sem, Am Cons, Columbia Univ, Capital Univ, Shurtleff Col, Hartt Col Music, New Eng Cons, Temple Univ, Newcomb Col, Tulane Col & Univ Mich; LLD: Ill Wesleyan Univ & Col of the Pac; LHD: Drury Col & Valparaiso Univ. Mem fac, then dean, Cons of Fine Arts, Col of the Pac, 19-24. Dir, Eastman Sch Music, 24-64; founder & dir, Inst Am Music, 24-78. Inaugurated Am Composers Concerts. Mem, Nat Inst Arts & Letters, Nat Acad Arts & Letters & Am Philosophical Soc; fel, Royal Acad Music, Swed. Awards: Pulitzer Prize; Ditson; Peabody. Pres, Nat Asn Schs Music, Music Teachers Nat Asn & Nat Music Council; chmn, Adv Music Comn, Oberlaender Trust; mem, Examining Jury, Am Acad, Rome; mem, Adv Comt Music, State Dept; mem, US Comn, UN Educ, Sci & Cultural Orgn. Made many records. *Instrumental Works:* 5 symphonies (No 4, Pulitzer Prize, 44); Lament for Beowulf; Mosaics (comn by Cleveland Orch); Serenade for Flute, Harp, Strings; Pastorale for Oboe, Harp, Strings (comn by UN Educ, Sci & Cultural Orgn); Elegy (comn by Koussevitzky Found); Song of Democracy (comn by Nat Educ Asn, 100th anniversary & Music Educators Nat Conference, 50th anniversary); Chorale and Alleluia; Drum Taps; String Quartet (comn by Coolidge); Concerto de Camera; Piano Concerto in G (comn by Koussevitzky Found); Summer Seascape (comn by New Orleans Philh; solo viola, string orch); Fantasia on a Theme of Youth; For the First Time; Symphony No VI; Symphony No VII (Sea Symphony; chorus & orch); Variations on an Ancient Hymn (string orch); New Land, New Covenant (oratorio for soloists, mixed chorus, children's chorus & orch); Streams in the Desert (chorus & orch); Lumen in Christo (chorus & orch); The Mystic Trumpeter (chorus, orch & narrator); Young Composer's Guide to the Six-Tone Scale (solo piano & wind ens); Dis Natalis (wind ens); Laude (wind ens); Centennial March (wind ens). *Scores:* Opera: Merry Mount (comn by Metrop Opera); Ballet: Nymphs and Satyrs.

HANSON, JO
See Johanson, Ernest Robert

HANSON, LLOYD THEODORE   ASCAP 1979
author
b Bend, Ore, Mar 8, 26. Educ: Willamette Univ, BA; Univ Ore, MA. Prof humanities, Ore Col Educ, 60- Chief Collabr: A Laurence Lyon. *Songs: Lyrics:* Soft, Soft; Consolation: I Am a Child of God.

HARADON, VIRGINIA   ASCAP 1956
composer, author
b Redfield, SDak, July 27, 13. Educ: MA; MEd; M Social Work. *Songs:* When Are You Comin' Home, Joe?.

HARBACH, OTTO ABELS   ASCAP 1914
author
b Salt Lake City, Utah, Aug 18, 1873; d New York, NY, Jan 24, 63. Educ: Knox Col, BA, MA & DHL; Columbia Univ. Prof English, Whitman Col, 95-01; newspaper writer, NY, 02-03; in advert agencies, 03-10. Dir, ASCAP, 20-63, vpres, 36-49, pres, 50-53. Co-author play, "Up in Mabel's Room." Chief Collabrs: Karl Hoschna, Rudolf Friml, Louis Hirsch, Herbert Stothart, Vincent Youmans, Jerome Kern, George Gershwin, Sigmund Romberg, Oscar Hammerstein, 2nd. *Songs:* Cuddle Up a Little Closer, Lovey Mine; Every Little Movement Has a Meaning All Its Own; Giannina Mia; When a Maid Comes Knocking At Your Heart; Love Is Like a Firefly; Sympathy; Something Seems Tingleing-eling; Katinka; Not Now But Later; Allah's Holiday; Rackety Koo; The Ticle Toe; Going Up; The Love Nest; Mary; Cutie; Wildflower; Bambalina; Rose-Marie; The Mounties; Indian Love Call; Totem Tom-Tom; No, No, Nanette; I've Confessed to the Breeze; Sunny; Who?; Two Little Bluebirds; D'Ye Love Me?; Cossack Love Song; Song of the Flame; Riff Song; Romance; The Desert Song; One Alone; One Flower Grows Alone in Your Garden; The Night Was Made for Love; She Didn't Say 'Yes'; One Moment Alone; Try to Forget; A New Love Is Old; I Watch the Love Parade; You're Devastating; Yesterdays; The Touch of Your Hand; Smoke Gets in Your Eyes; I Won't Dance; Your Dream; Let's Begin; Something's Got to Happen. *Scores:* Bway

Stage (librettist or co-librettist): Three Twins; Madame Sherry; The Firefly; High Jinks; Katinka; Going Up; Tumble In; The Little Whopper; The Cat and the Fiddle; Roberta; You're in Love; Tickle Me!; Mary; The O'Brien Girl; The Blue Kitten; Molly Darling; Wildflower; Rose-Marie; No, No, Nanette; Sunny; Song of the Flame; Criss-Cross; The Desert Song; Golden Dawn; The Crinoline Girl; Nina Rosa; Kid Boots; Kitty's Kisses; Oh, Please!; Good Boy.

HARBERT, JAMES K
ASCAP 1961
composer, author

b Okla, Mar 29, 30. Educ: Curtis Inst Music; Univ Okla; Oklahoma City Univ. Asst account exec, Campbell-Ewald Co. Producer, Columbia Records. Wrote scores for revues and musicals, Las Vegas, Paris & London. Chief Collabrs: John Williams, Andre Hornez. *Songs:* This Was My Love; Give Him Love; Hang Ups; Merci Beaucoup; Allez Lido. *Scores:* Revues: Hello Hollywood; Hallelujah, Hollywood; Lido De Paris (MGM); Musicals: Thomas and the King; Ballet: Ballet Rhapsody (Ice Capades, 67).

HARBURG, E Y (YIP)
ASCAP 1930
lyricist, playwright

b New York, NY, Apr 8, 1896. Educ: Townsend Hall High Sch, New York, dipl, 14; City Col New York, BS, 18; hon LittD, Univ Vt, 71; hon DA, Columbia Col, Chicago, 78; hon DFA, City Univ New York, 79. Ed col mag; proprietor elec appliance co. Wrote light verse for newspaper. Theatre lyricist, "Earl Carroll's Sketchbook," 29; "The Garrick Gaieties (3rd ed)," 30; "Earl Carroll's Vanities (8th ed)," 30; "Shoot the Works," 31; "Ballyhoo of 1932," 32; "Americana (3rd ed)," 32; "Walk a Little Faster," 32; "The Ziegfeld Follies," 34; "Life Begins at 8:40"; "Hooray for What," 37; "Hold on to Your Hats," 40; "Bloomer Girl," 44; "Darling of the Day," 68. Lyricist & co-librettist: "Finian's Rainbow," 47; "Flahooley," 51; "Jamaica," 57; "The Happiest Girl in the World," 61. Film lyricist: "The Sap From Syracuse," 30; "Queen High," 30; "Moonlight and Pretzels," 33; "Leave it to Lester," 33; "The Count of Monte Cristo," 34; "Take a Chance," 33; "The Singing Kid," 36; "Gold Diggers of 1937," 36; "Andy Hardy Gets Spring Fever," 37; "The Wizard of Oz," 39; "The Marx Brothers' Day at the Circus," 39; "Babes on Broadway," 41; "Ship Ahoy," 42; "Cairo," 42; "Rio Rita," 42; "Song of Russia," 43; "Cabin in the Sky," 43; "Meet the People," 44; "Hollywood Canteen," 44; "Can't Help Singing," 44; "Kismet," 44; "Centennial Summer," 46; "Stage Struck," 46; "California," 46; "Gay Purree," 61. Authored two books of verse, "Rhymes for the Irreverent," 65 & "At This Point in Rhyme," 76. Awards: Henderson Award Best Musical Comedy, "Finian's Rainbow," 47-48; nomination, Entertainment Hall of Fame, 76; Townsend Harris Award, City Col New York, 50 & James Hackett Award, 72; Horatio Alger Award, 79; Humanity in Arts Award, State of Mich & Wayne State Univ, Detroit; Philadelphia, Pa, 79. Mem Dramatists' Guild; Screen Writers Guild; Am Guild Authors & Comp. Chief Collabrs: Fred Saidy, Henry Myers. *Songs:* Over the Rainbow (Acad Award, 39); Brother Can You Spare a Dime; Happiness Is a Thing Called Joe (Citation, 43); April in Paris; It's Only a Paper Moon; What Is There to Say; Suddenly; Last Night When We Were Young; I'm Yours; Isn't It Heavenly; You're a Builder Upper; Ah But Is It Love; More and More; Evelina; Old Devil Moon; How Are Things in Glocca Mora; We're Off to See the Wizard; Right as the Rain; On That Great Come and Get It Day; When You're Not Near the Girl You Love You Love the Girl You're Near; Look to the Rainbow (Tribute, Univ Calif Los Angeles); You're the Cure for What Ails Me; I Like the Likes of You; Down With Love; God's Country; If I Only Had a Brain; Lydia the Tattooed Lady; The World Is in My Arms; The Same Boat Brother; If This Isn't Love; Something Sort of Grandish; The World Is Your Balloon; Ain't It the Truth.

HARDEE, LEWIS J, JR
ASCAP 1978
composer, author, teacher

b Wilmington, NC, Jan 17, 37. Educ: Southport & Key West High Schs, 50-54; Univ NC, Chapel Hill, BA(radio-TV), 59, MMus, 71; Columbia Univ, comp studies with Dr Jack Beeson, 72. Wrote & produced shows during serv with US Army, 60-62; instr music, Am Acad Dramatic Arts, New York, 70- . Compositions incl six musicals & revues plus numerous contributions to night club acts, revues, etc. Chief Collabrs: Ethan Ayer, Donald Butler. *Songs & Instrumental Works:* Playthings of the Wind (song cycle); Burden and Glory (cantata for chorus & orch); Beatrice's Song (song cycle for soprano & chamber orch). *Scores:* Revolution (musical drama); Pudding Lane (musical comedy).

HARDEN, BOBBY L
singer

b England, Ark. Mem, Harden Trio; sang over radio & TV stations, Little Rock, Ark, Springfield, Mo, Shreveport, La, Grand Old Opry, Nashville, also Columbia Records.

HARDER, PAUL OSCAR
ASCAP 1962
composer, educator

b Indianapolis, Ind, Mar 10, 23. Educ: Butler Univ, BM, 44; Univ Rochester Eastman Sch Music, MM, 45; Ecole des Beaux Arts de Fontainebleau, summer 48, studied with Nadia Boulanger; Univ Iowa, PhD, 59. Music fac, Mich State Univ, 45-73. Dean, sch of arts & humanities, Calif State Col, Stanislaus, 73-76, acad dean, 76- . Author, texts in music theory, "Basic Materials in Music Theory" & "Harmonic Materials in Tonal Music." *Instrumental Works:* Romanze (baritone horn, piano); Sonata (clarinet, piano); Sonata (oboe, piano); Contention (concert band); Refractions (concert band); Prisms (concert band); The Pleasant Truth (orch); Sinfonietta (chamber orch); A Wisp of Time (string

orch); Trio (violin, viola, cello); Quintet (woodwind quintet); Quartet (string quartet).

HARDIN, LOUIS THOMAS (MOONDOG)
ASCAP 1970
composer, author

b Marysville, Kans, May 26, 16. Educ: Iowa Sch for Blind; mainly self-taught. Drummer, New York, 49; recording artist, 50- ; first orch album, 69. Radio concert, Ger, 74; wrote & recorded. Now recording "The Creation." Chief Collabr: Ilona Goebel. *Songs:* What's the Most Exciting Thing; All is Loneliness; Nero's Expedition; Be a Hobo; Maybe; Bells Are Ringing. *Instrumental Works:* Ode to Venus; Stamping Ground; Good for Goodie; Mini Sym; Bird's Lament; Witch of Endor; Portrait of a Monarch (Symphonique No 1); Theme; Viking; Procession of the Aesir; Heimdall Fanfare; In Vienna; Chaconne in G; Logrundr (organ); Here's to J! W! Hardin; Do Your Thing; I'm This, I'm That; Choo Choo Lullaby; Pigmy Pig; I'm in the World.

HARDT, RICHARD
See Kapp, Paul

HARDT, VICTOR H
ASCAP 1966
composer, teacher, conductor

b Youngstown, Alta, Apr 29, 19. Educ: Concordia Teachers Col, BS; Vandercook Col Music, BM; Univ Minn, MM; Columbia Univ EdD; studied cond with Norval Church & H A Vandercook, comp with Milake, Buchtel & W Damrosch. Studied piano & trombone at early age. Band & orch dir, after WW II. Mus dir, Symphonic Singers, Stout Col, Wis. Dir, marching & concert bands, Ark State Univ. Chmn, Music Educ Dept, Chicago Musical Col. Comp many works for band, brass ens, solo piano & mixed chorus. Guest cond & adjudicator, South, Midwest & Mex. *Songs & Instrumental Works:* Chorale and Fugue for Band; Suite for Brass Sextet; Chorale and Fugue in Lavender (band); Praise and Dedication (chorus, band); Concertino for Band.

HARDWICK, ARCHER F
ASCAP 1963
composer, author, playwright

b Sacramento, Calif, Nov 5, 18. Educ: Christian Bros High Sch; Sacramento City Col; studied piano, organ, violin & comp. Music teacher, theatre organist, radio & TV. Guest artist at lodges, churches & political lunches. Wrote books for musicals, "Seven Rock Hill", "Rum Dum", "Alaskan Waters", "Mrs Hutchison" & "Piccadilly Willie." Author comedy, "Fuddy Duddy." Chief Collabrs: William E James, Amy Smith Porter, Florence W Underwood, Ethel E Griffith. *Songs & Instrumental Works:* Let's Tie Our Sails to a Sailboat; Sing O'Rolling River; Beautiful Sweetheart; Who'll Send Me Love; (I'm in Love) Can't You Tell; My Dream Boat; Sand on the Desert; When Spring Comes (pastorale). *Scores:* Musicals: Seven Rock Hill; Rum Dum; Alaskan Waters; Mrs Hutchison; Piccadilly Willie.

HARDY, WESTON VERNON, III (CHIP)
ASCAP 1976
composer

b Scott City, Kans, Oct 1, 51. Educ: Scott Community High Sch, grad, 69; Fort Hays State Univ, Kans, bachelor degree(special educ, music educ). Bass guitarist with Fort Hays State Jazz Ens, 3 yrs. Publ dir, Bobby David Int (I & I Music), 76, with Mandy Music, 77; writer, Haus Music, 77-79; staff writer, Tree (Cross Keys Music), 79- . Chief Collabrs: Danny Hice, Bobby David, Richard Leigh, Sam Lorber, Rick Carnes. *Songs:* Next Best Feeling; Feeling Old Feelings; Only Diamonds Are Forever; Wishin' Well; Over and Over (I Fall in Love Again).

HARGIS, REGINALD J
composer, musician, singer

b Austin, Tex, Jan 8, 51. Educ: Morris Brown Col. Singer & lead guitarist with group, Brick. Chief Collabrs: Edward Irons, Jr, James B Brown, Raymond L Ransom, Jr. *Songs:* Dazz; Dusic; Ain't Gonna Hurt Nobody.

HARING, ROBERT
ASCAP 1942
composer, author, conductor

b Montclair, NJ, Aug 21, 1896; d Barryville, NY, Feb 18, 75. Educ: Univ Wash; Seattle Cons. Music dir, radio, record cos. Music ed, publ co. *Songs:* Dawn of Tomorrow; Concerto for Two; My Midnight Star; Fanny Tinkle.

HARJU, GARY ANDREW
ASCAP 1976
composer, author

b Davenport, Iowa, May 26, 48. Chief Collabrs: Steve Dorff, Larry Herbstritt. *Songs:* Born Believer; Lyrics: Fire in the Morning; Cowboys and Clowns; Pirate.

HARKIN, EDWARD BRANDON, JR
ASCAP 1972
composer, author, singer

b Mt Kisco, NY, Dec 10, 48. Educ: Pvt study. Worked on Atlantic, Epic, Elektra, Arista & Capitol Records; record producer. Chief Collabrs: Starz (group). *Songs:* Cherry Baby; Fallen Angel.

HARKNESS, REBEKAH
ASCAP 1952
composer

b St Louis, Mo, Apr 17, 15. Educ: Studied music & comp with Nadia Boulanger, France; Dalcroze Sch, New York; orch studies with Lee Hoiby. Hon Degrees: DFA, Franklin Pierce Col, NH; DH, Lycoming Col, Pa. Composer & orchr music. Founder, pres & artistic dir, Harkness Ballet Found; pres, William Hale

Harkness Found; established, Harkness House for Ballet Arts, New York. Sponsored dance events in US & Europe. *Instrumental Works:* Orchestrations: Rachmaninoff's Suite No 1 for Two Pianos Opus 5, Cello Sonata, Scherzo, Waltz & Bar Carole; Schubert's Variation in B Flat & Adantino Varie and Two Marches. *Scores:* Opera/Ballet: Safari; Journey to Love; Musical Chairs; Gift of the Magi; Barcelona Suite; Letters to Japan; Elements; Macumba.

HARLINE, LEIGH ASCAP 1940
composer, conductor
b Salt Lake City, Utah, Mar 26, 07; d Long Beach, Calif, Dec 10, 69. Educ: Univ Utah; studied music with J Spencer Cornwall. Arr of first transcontinental broadcast from Los Angeles, 31. Joined Walt Disney staff, 32. Free-lance for film studios, 41. Chief Collabr: Ned Washington. *Songs:* When You Wish Upon a Star (Acad Award, 40); Hi-Diddle-Dee-Dee; Give a Little Whistle; Jiminy Cricket. *Instrumental Works:* Civic Center Suite. *Scores:* Films: Pinocchio (Acad Award, 40); Snow White and the 7 Dwarfs; You Were Never Lovelier; The Sky's the Limit; The Wonderful World of the Brothers Grimm; Film background: Pride of the Yankees; Johnny Come Lately; 7 Faces of Dr Lao; Strange Bedfellows.

HARLING, W FRANKE ASCAP 1926
composer, conductor
b London, Eng, Jan 18, 1887; d Sierra Madre, Calif, Nov 22, 58. Moved to US, 1888. Educ: Grace Church Choir Sch, New York, NY; London Acad Music; studied with Theodore Ysaye. Organist & choir dir, Church of the Resurrection, Brussels, 07-08; US Mil Acad, 09-10. Incidental music to plays: "Deep River"; "Paris Bound"; "Machinal"; "Outward Bound"; "In Love With Love"; "The Outsider." Chief Collabrs: Leo Robin, Richard Whiting, Sam Coslow. *Songs:* The Corps (West Point hymn); West Point Forever (off march); Beyond the Blue Horizon; Where Was I?; Sing You Sinners; Always in All Ways; Give Me a Moment, Please. *Instrumental Works:* A Light From St Agnes (1st Am opera produced in France; David Bispham medal); Alda (opera); A Bible Trilogy; Three Elegiac Poems (cello, orch); Monte Cassino (tone poem); Before the Dawn; Oh Captain, My Captain; At the Tomb of the Unknown Soldier (tone poem); Ava Maria (voice, harp, cello, orch); God Save America. *Scores:* Film Background: Stagecoach (Acad Award, 39); Penny Serenade; So Red the Rose; Men With Wings; The Scarlet Empress.

HARMAN, BARRY MICHAEL ASCAP 1978
author
b Brooklyn, NY, Mar 14, 50. Educ: Westbury High Sch, 68; Harvard Univ, cum laude, 72. Writer, "The Carol Burnett Show" & "All in the Family," Emmy Awards for each show. Author bk & lyrics, Off-Bway musical, "Telecast." Author lyrics for musicals, "Every Thursday Night" & "Amphitryon...Again!"

HARMATI, SANDOR ASCAP 1954
composer
b Budapest, Hungary, July 9, 1892; d New York, NY, Apr 5, 36. *Songs & Instrumental Works:* Little Caprice (violin, piano); Largo (choral); Songs: Bluebird of Happiness.

HARMER, JACK P ASCAP 1953
composer, author
b London, England, July 7, 1884; d Santa Cruz, Calif, Mar 1, 62. To US, 1886. US Army, WW I. Contact man for Will Rossiter, 17 yrs. *Songs:* Old Kishwaukee River; It Was Cherry Blossom Time; You're Sweeter Than Any Bouquet; Some Day; I Want to Go Back to Wisconsin; I'm in Love With You; I Lost My Way.

HARMEYER, MICHAEL RICHARD
composer, author, teacher
b New Orleans, La, Feb 10, 51. Educ: Guitar study with Hank Mackie; Univ New Orleans, BA(music theory). Player in bands & shows; solo performer. 2nd violin/perc, New Orleans Civic Symph. Teacher music at home studio, Metairie Guitar Studio. *Songs:* Highway 49.

HARMON, JOHN HENRY (JAY) ASCAP 1978
composer, author, saxophonist
b Columbus, Ohio, Aug 20, 52. Educ: Linden McKinley High Sch; Ohio State Univ Sch Music, studied saxophone with Steve Genteline, 67-70. Played with bands from Columbus area incl Crowd Pleasers & IRS. Free lance, var jazz artists, Ohio. *Songs:* Now It's You and Me.

HARNELL, JOSEPH ASCAP 1959
composer, conductor, pianist
b Bronx, NY, Aug 2, 24. Educ: Christopher Columbus High Sch; Univ Miami, Fla; Trinity Col Music, London, Eng; Tanglewood, 4 yrs, studies under Aaron Copland, Leonard Bernstein, Darius Milhaud & Tibor Serly. Cond/arr, Peggy Lee, Frank Sinatra, Marlene Dietrich, Robert Goulet, Anthony Newley, Shirley MacLaine & Pearl Bailey. Musical dir, Gray Advertisong, 3 yrs. Fourteen record albums on Kapp, Jubilee, Epic, Columbia & Motown. Chief Collabrs: Mitchell Parrish, Eddie Heyman, Paul Francis Webster, Lennie Bleecher. *Songs:* Music: Cinderella Brown; A Little Bit Older; Song Without a Name; Far Away From You; The Lonely Man Theme; piano preludes, chamber works & art songs. *Instrumental Works:* Passacaglia for Orchestra; Concerto for Piano and Orchestra; String Quartet; London Suite; music for harp & flute. *Scores:* August on Seventh Street (theatrical movie); Film/TV: Mike Douglas Show;

Bionic Woman; The Andros Targets; Cliffhangers; Incredible Hulk; Death in the Family; Married; The Murder That Wouldn't Die!; Alone At Last.

HARP, NOLA JAY
See Kudera, Lottie A

HARPER, ARTHUR LEE ASCAP 1968
composer, singer, actor
b Melbourne, Fla, Sept 8, 51. Educ: Chapman Col, BA(music); studied voice. Recording artist, LHI Records & Nocturne Records. *Songs:* Valentine Gray; Dreams and Images; Strange Song; Open Up the Door; New Day. *Albums:* Dreams and Images; Love Is the Revolution.

HARPER, BILLY R ASCAP 1970
composer, tenor saxophonist
b Houston, Tex, Jan 17, 43. Educ: Frederick Douglas Elem Sch; Emmett Scott Jr High; Evan E Worthing High Sch; NTex State Univ, 61-65. Recording artist. Joined group Art Blakey Jazz Messengers, 66-68. In NBC documentary, "The Big Apple," 67. Played in Gil Evans Orch, 67-75 & Thad Jones-Mel Lewis Orch, 69-75; worked with Lee Morgan, 70-72 & Max Roach, 70-78. Played in Billy Harper Quintet, 79- Concert tours to var countries, incl Japan, Russia, Finland, France, Holland, Italy & Morocco. *Instrumental Works:* Croquet Ballet; Capra Black; Soran Bushi, BH; The Awakening; Cry of Hunger.

HARPER, C PAUL ASCAP 1970
composer, pianist, organist
b St Francisville, Ill, Oct 30, 27. Educ: Asbury Col, BA; Northwestern Univ, MMus & PhD. Teacher music, high schs & elem schs, 10 yrs, col, 19 yrs. Organist & choir dir, 25 yrs. Singer & trumpeter. *Songs:* Music: Four Sacred Choral Responses; His Truth Endureth; How Manifold Are Thy Works; The Lord Is Faithful; Thou Art Fair, My Love; The Voice of My Beloved; Break Forth and Sing for Joy; Too Late I Stayed; The Cuckoo; Amazing Grace.

HARPER, MARJORIE ASCAP 1937
composer, author, pianist
b St Paul, Minn, Apr 26, 1895. Educ: Studied music with Alexander Lambert, Julia Glass, Rubin Goldmark & H R Wilson. Made concert tour of US with Tito Guizar, playing own songs. Mem: Nat Asn Am Composers & Conductors; Composers & Authors Guild; Concert Pianist League. *Songs & Instrumental Works:* La Playa de Malaga; Pancho's Serenade; Cuevas de Granada; Guitarras de Sevilla; Blessed Is He; Jealous of You; Tango della Gelosia; My Pet Brunette (Negra Consentida).

HARPER, MARK ANTHONY ASCAP 1978
composer, author, teacher
b Clarksville, Tenn, Jan 6, 52. Educ: Bonneville High Sch, Idaho Falls, Idaho; Idaho State Univ, studied voice perf with David Williams, 73-74 & 75-78; Boise State Univ. Choir Mem, soloist, recitals & concerts. Mem, Am Fedn Musicians. Chief Collabrs: Douglas Lawrence, Kathleen Battle.

HARPER, MAURICE COE (REDD) ASCAP 1955
composer, author, singer
b Nocona, Tex, Sept 29, 03. Educ: Muskogee High Sch, Okla; Univ Okla, 23-26; music mostly self-taught. Began with dance band, The Sooners. With radio, Oklahoma City, Detroit, Des Moines & Hollywood. Radio prog, "Redd Harper's Hollywood Round-Up," 45-51. Performer films, "Mr Texas", "Oil Town, USA", "Sunday on the Range", "Mr Texas at Teen Ranch", "God Loves People", "The Gospel According to Most People" & "Apache Fire." Mem, Sacred Music Hall of Fame, 80. Chief Collabs: Dr Oswald J Smith, Walt Huntley. *Songs:* (I'm Following Jesus) Each Step of the Way; Lord Keep Your Hand on Me; My Testimony Song; What Would I Do Without Jesus; God Loves People; The Good Life; The Gospel According to Most People; Only God's Love; God Branded My Soul; A Quiet Time; I'm a Happy, Happy Christian; I Walk the Glory Road; The Answer Man; See What God Can Do; Five Minutes More; Come Alive With Jesus; Just Smile and Praise the Lord; Music: He Changed My Life; The Happy Band; Come With Your Heartache; I'm Singing for My Lord; My Heart Would Sing of Jesus; Dumb Ole Country Boy; Shoutin Glory; You Can't Take It With You; Something Special.

HARPER, WALLY ASCAP 1970
composer, conductor, arranger
b Akron, Ohio, Sept 8, 41. Educ: New Eng Cons Music; Juilliard Sch Music. Theater work; dance music for plays: "Company", "Irene", "Mack and Mabel" & "Peter Pan." Musical dir: "The Grand Tour", "A Day In Hollywood, A Night In the Ukraine" & 1980 revival "Brigadoon." Has done TV specials, incl "Mary Tyler Moore" & "Julie Andrews Invitation to the Dance." Has done song arr & albums for Barbara Cook, currently pianist & cond. *Songs:* Music: Sing a Song With Me. *Scores:* Sensations (off Bway Musical).

HARRELL, GORDON LOWRY ASCAP 1974
composer, arranger, conductor
b Galveston, Tex, Sept 10, 40. Educ: Baylor Univ, BBA, 62 & BM, 64; pvt tutoring cond & arr with Lehman Engel, 68-74. Arr, Bway show "Sergeant Pepper" (Beatles); cond, "Jesus Christ Superstar"; arr & cond, "Dancin'." Chief Collabrs:

Edward Villella, Bob Fosse, Tom O'Horgan. *Songs & Instrumental Works:* Harlequin (Emmy Award); Dance of Athletes (Emmy nominee); Three Percussion Pieces for Dancin'.

HARRINGTON, AMBER R
See Roobenian, Amber

HARRINGTON, ROBERT MAXON   ASCAP 1961
composer, author
b Marshfield, Wis, Jan 30, 12. Played drums & vibes, Red Nichols, Bud Freeman, Muggsy Spanier, 30-45; played piano with Charlie Barnet, Vido Musso, Georgie Auld & Red Norvo; accompanist with Vikki Carr & Ann Richards; toured with Stan Kenton & Count Basie, 60 & Ann Richards; recorded with Charlie Barnet, own quartette & Anita O'Day; pianist with Ben Webster; pres, Garlon Music Co. Chief Collabrs: Estelle Vicki (deceased), Bobby Charles. *Songs:* Music: Young Man on the Way Up; Beyond the Moon; I'm Goona Find Out; The Last Blade of Grass; Blues for the Bull.

HARRINGTON, VICKI (VICKI ESTELLE)   ASCAP 1961
composer, author
b Des Moines, Iowa, Mar 15, 11; d Los Angeles, Calif, Dec 22, 71. Educ: Univ Calif, Los Angeles, studied lyric writing. Formed Garlon Music Co with husband. Chief Collabrs: R M Harrington (husband), Bobby Charles, Red Wootten. *Songs:* Ten Years of Tears; I'm Gonna Find Out; Music: Young Man on the Way Up; The Last Blade of Grass; Lyrics: Beyond the Moon.

HARRINGTON, VICTOR B   ASCAP 1957
composer, author
b Antigonish, NS, June 6, 15. Educ: Univ. Saxophonist in dance bands. With War Shipping Admin, Int Freighting Corp (US), WW II. Music copyist, Bway musicals. Chief Collabrs: Harold Marquess, Hal Blake, Don Canton, Stan Rich, Hank Fort. *Songs:* The Hen Is in the Haymow; Arirang; Rikki-Tikki-Toon; Blue Willow; You and Me; Here We Are.

HARRINGTON, WILLIAM CLARK   ASCAP 1942
composer, author
b Worcester, Mass, June 28, 05. Educ: New Eng Cons Music, Boston, 29-30. Position with CBS to verify the performance rights of all music planned for broadcast or telecast on the CBS network and local New York networks, of special lyrics for performers & dirs, & special music for others. Chief Collabrs: Amber R Harrington, Lily A Strickland, David Guion. *Songs:* One Word From You; My Grandfather Used to Hum. Music: Alas That Spring Should Vanish; My True Love; Lyrics: Mother Never Told Me (It Was Anything Like This); There's a Love Knot In My Lariat; Vigil (female choral work); Oh, God Whose Love Is Endless (hymn); In an Old English Garden; Love's Supremacy; Unveil Your Eyes. *Instrumental Works:* Faun Call (orch); Candlelight Prelude, for Piano Solo.

HARRINGTON, WILLIAM O   ASCAP 1950
composer, author, musician
b Indianapolis, Ind, May 31, 18. Educ: Arsenal Tech High Sch; Arthur Jordan Cons; Cincinnati Cons. Pianist & accordionist in dance bands throughout US, 33-43. Vocalist on Cincinnati radio staff, 43; WW II service. Vocalist with Alvino Rey Orch. Moved to New York, 46, had own radio prog, 3 yrs; then TV. Singer. *Songs:* Wendy; Open Parachute; Looking for a Dream; Just We Two; Texas Lullaby; I Made Myself a Promise; Drop a Jitney in the Juke Box.

HARRIS, ALBERT
composer, orchestrator, conductor
b London, Eng, Feb 13, 16. Educ: New York Col Music, doctorate, 44; studied comp & orch with Eugene Zador & cond with Richard Lert. Prof musician, London, 32; played in clubs & radio progs, NBC, CBS, New York & Los Angeles, 37-42; asst music dir, NBC, 3 yrs; started working with mgj studios as cond, comp & orchr; musical dir, "Barbra Streisand Special," ABC; arr, "Cher" on album & Roberta Flack on concert. Also teaching many pvt students; teacher, Univ Calif, Los Angeles; lectr. Presently at Universal. *Songs & Instrumental Works:* Variations on Theme of Handel; Concertino the California (Comn by, Carlos Barbosa-Lima); Sonnatina for Solo Guitar.

HARRIS, CHARLES K   ASCAP 1914
composer, author, publisher
b Poughkeepsie, NY, May 1, 1867; d New York, NY, Dec 22, 30. Began career as banjo player; wrote spec material for vaudeville acts. Became music publ, Chicago & NY. Wrote silent film scripts & plays. Autobiography: "After the Ball: 40 Years of Melody." Charter mem, ASCAP. *Songs:* After the Ball; I'm Trying So Hard to Forget You; There'll Come a Time; Better Than Gold; Just Behind the Times; I've Just Come to Say Goodbye; Break the News to Mother; Mid the Green Fields of Virginia; For Old Time's Sake; I've a Longing in My Heart for You, Louise; Hello Central, Give Me Heaven; Always in the Way; Would You Care?; The Best Things in Life; Nobody Knows, Nobody Cares; Songs of Yesterday.

HARRIS, DONALD   ASCAP 1973
composer
b St Paul, Minn, Apr 7, 31. Educ: Univ Mich, MusB, 52, MusM, 54. Music consult, Am Cult Ctr, USIS, Paris, 65-67; mem teaching fac depts comp & music lit, New Eng Cons Music, Boston, 67-77, asst to pres for acad affairs, 67-71, vpres, 71-74, exec vpres, 74-77; lectr, Schoenberg Inst, 74; comp-in-residence, prof music & chmn comp & theory, Hartt Col Music, Univ Hartford, 77-, dean, 80. Recipient comns from Fest Contemporary Am Music at Tanglewood, 65, French Nat Radio, 72, Boston Musica Viva, 73, Cleveland Orch, 75, Serge Koussevitzky Music Found, 77, Elizabeth Sprague Coolidge Found, 77, Goethe Inst, 78, Conn Pub Radio, 79 & Hartford Symph Orch, 80; Louisville Orch Award, 54; Prince Rainier of Monaco Comp Prize, 60. Fulbright scholar, 56; Guggenheim fel, 65; grantee-in-aid, Rockefeller Found, 69 & Chapelbrook Found, 70. Mem: League Int Soc Contemporary Music; Int Alban Berg Soc; Am Soc Univ Composers. *Instrumental Works:* Piano Sonata; Fantasy for Violin and Piano; Symphony in Two Movements; String Quartet; Ludus for Ten Instruments; Ludus II for Five Instruments; Charmes for Voice and Orchestra; On Variations; For the Night to Wear (mezzo-soprano & 7 instruments); Balladen for Solo Piano; Of Hartford in a Purple Light (soprano & piano).

HARRIS, EDWARD C   ASCAP 1936
composer, author, pianist
b Elizabeth, NJ, Feb 16, 1899; d. Educ: East Liberty Acad, Pittsburgh; studied with James Jordan, Charles Boyd, Joseph Gittings, Adolph Foerster. Accompanist to Lawrence Tibbett & Georges Enesco; music critic, San Francisco Bulletin, 28-29; soloist on tours, Can, Australia, NZ, Africa, Caribbean & SAm; organist, Plymouth Church of the Pilgrims, 43-46. Vpres, Am Guild Musical Artists, 43-47; vpres, NY Singing Teachers Asn, 45-47, pres, 48-50; admin asst to Rep James Delaney, 53-62; had own vocal studio; organist & teacher. *Songs:* Winter; It Was a Lover and His Lass; Vanished Summer; Agatha Morley; Someone Came Knocking; When I Am Dead My Dearest; Moan. *Songs & Instrumental Works:* Piano: Croon; The Gallant Music Box. *Scores:* Stage: Birds of Rhiannon.

HARRIS, ETHEL RAMOS   ASCAP 1959
composer, author, pianist
b Newport, RI. Educ: Hans Schneider Piano Sch; New Eng Cons; Boston Univ; Carnegie Inst; Tanglewood; Harvey Gaul Scholarship; Am Christian Palestine Community scholarship. Appeared as Sophisticated Lady on KDKA radio, 2 yrs; also on WTAE. Singer on TV & in supper clubs. *Songs & Instrumental Works:* I've Been in the Storm So Long; Stan' Steady; Paquita Mia; Yolanda; The Girl Friend's Hymn; There'll Be a Jubilee.

HARRIS, GALE S
See Sullivan, Gala

HARRIS, HARRY   ASCAP 1928
composer, author
b Chicago, Ill, Feb 12, 01. Educ: Jewish Training Sch, Chicago; self-taught in music. Popular song-writer for feature motion pictures incl "The Joker Is Wild", "The Sheriff of Fractured Jaw", "Snow White and the Three Stooges", "Madison Avenue" & others; & special songs for Joe E Lewis, Sophie Tucker, Ted Lewis, Jimmy Durante & Harry Richman. Chief Collabrs: Joe Goodwin, Julie Stynes, Sammy Cahn, Larry Shay, Lou Pollack, Lou Handman, Archie Gottler, Tommie Maley, Jack Stanley & Chummy MacGregor. *Songs:* In the Valley of Love; If The San Francisco Hills Could Only Talk; A Place Called Happiness; When I'm Walkin Down the Lane with Jimmy; If Mother Could Only See Us Now; Annabelles Bustle; Be Yourself; The Milk Song; I Said It Then, I Say It Now; Lyrics: Highways Are Happy Ways; Baby Me; I Had Someone Else Before I Had You, and I'll Have Someone After You're Gone; Where Did You Learn to Love; Why Don't We Say We're Sorry; It's Lovin' Time; Strollin' Down the Lane With Bill; You're One in a Million; Chidabee, Chidabee, Chidabee; Music: I'd Love to Call You My Sweetheart.

HARRIS, HOWARD C, JR   ASCAP 1973
composer, author, educator
b New Orleans, La, June 18, 40. Educ: Southern Univ, La, BS(music educ), 63; La State Univ, MMusEd(comp), 69; North Tex State Univ, studied comp, trumpet & jazz, 71; studied comp with William S Fisher, New York; trumpet with Bobby Bryant, Los Angeles; jazz technics with Alvin Batiste, Southern Univ. Music educr, free-lance comp & arr, 63-69. Music instr, Delaware State Col, 70-71. Assoc band dir, comp, arr-in-residence & prof jazz, Tex Southern Univ, 71-76. Musical producer, comp, arr & author "Augmentations to Jazz and Funk Improvisations", 77- *Songs:* Hell of a Fix. *Instrumental Works:* Black Roots and Passion (jazz ens). *Songs & Instrumental Works:* Folk Psalm and an American Music Tree (orch).

HARRIS, J ROBERT (BOB)   ASCAP 1955
composer, pianist, teacher
b New York, NY, Sept 27, 25. Educ: Studied with Teddy Wilson, 48-49; also studied in Paris. Early piano studies at age 5. Started music career playing piano & clarinet with band. Joined Army, played several camp & USO shows; also joined group Soldier Show Company. Co-wrote show "Could Be" which toured Europe. Partner, Hillcrest Music Publ Co, 51-53. Mgr, Suzanne Dennie. Own radio show, CBS-KXLY, Spokane, Wash; also variety show on TV. Wrote love

themes for motion pictures, "Star of India" & "Lolita" & theme for "Spider Man." Original composer of Bway show "Tourich." With Cameo Records/Chappel Music Co, 62-64. Currently writing theme for movie "Chosen." Chief Collabrs: Sol Parker, Sammy Gallopp, Sunny Skylark, Kay Toomey, Frank Readon, Redd Evans. *Songs:* Music: Lovelight; Too Soon. *Scores:* Movies: Sandy the Seal; Jack of Diamonds; Childrens Show: Icabod Crane of Sleepy Hollow.

HARRIS, JAY MORTON ASCAP 1961
author
b Brooklyn, NY, Apr 30, 28. Educ: Col. Short story writer. *Songs:* Wedding of Two Hearts.

HARRIS, JEFF STEVE ASCAP 1963
composer, author
b Brooklyn, NY, June 10, 35.

HARRIS, JERRY WESELEY ASCAP 1962
composer, choral music teacher
b The Dalles, Ore, Oct 21, 33. Educ: Lewis & Clark Col, Ore, BMusEd & MMusEd; Univ Ore Sch Music, DEd. Pub sch music teacher, 56-; music educ consult, Ore State Dept Educ, 4 yrs; Univ Idaho Sch Music, 2 yrs; conductor community choral orgn, Salem & Beaverton, Ore. Active choral music adjudicator & fest conductor. *Songs:* Choral Music: Behold I Stand At the Door; Be Strong in the Lord; Like as the Culver on the Bared Bough; You May Bury Me in the East; As Lately We Watched; O God How Wonderful Thou Art; O Eyes of My Beloved; A Carroll; Lo In the Time Appointed; Rise Up My Love; The Earth Is the Lord's; Three Christmas Scenes; Lord, in Thy Resurrection; The Heavens Rejoice, the Earth is Filled With Gladness; Our Thanksgiving Song to God; Music When Soft Voices Die; A Song of Salvation.

HARRIS, JOSEPH B ASCAP 1963
composer, designer
Educ: Pratt Inst. Art dir, Dancer, Fitzgerald & Sample Advert Agency, New York; partner, Total TV Productions, Inc; independent producer, Old Greenwich, Conn, currently. Chief Collabrs: Tread Covington, Chet Stover, Watts Biggers. *Songs:* Tennessee Tuxedo and His Tales; Underdog; The Beagles. *Scores:* TV Cartoon Series: King Leonardo and His Short Subjects.

HARRIS, KENNETH L ASCAP 1967
composer, teacher, musician
b Rockdale, Tex, July 5, 36. Educ: Southwestern Univ, BME(music educ); NTex State Univ. Teacher pub schs, 58- Writer original tunes for high sch bands; comps for marching & stage bands. Partner publ co, Harris Publ Co, Ft Worth. *Instrumental Works:* Back to the Jungle; Another Excuse to Play the Blues; "A" Rock; Bread Man; Doggie's Bag; Disco Dude; Bluff Creek Woman.

HARRIS, LEON A, JR ASCAP 1953
author
b New York, NY, June 20, 26. Educ: Phillip Acad, Andover, grad, 43; Harvard Col, grad, 47. Chief Collabr: Bob Miller. *Songs:* Lyrics: Twas the Night Before Christmas in Texas; Merry Texas Christmas You-All.

HARRIS, MYRON ASCAP 1963
author
b Brooklyn, NY, Dec 28, 22. Educ: City Col New York. *Songs:* Apron Strings; Two Pretty Lips; Wedding of Two Hearts.

HARRIS, RANDY DAVID ASCAP 1976
composer, author, singer
b Reading, Pa, July 21, 53. Educ: Pvt training. Began studying piano at age 6, began writing at age 12. First record released on FFO Records, 76. Touring, 77- Second record released on Malvern Records. *Songs:* Sweet Silent Lady; Heavy Love; Wasting My Time.

HARRIS, REMUS ANTHONY ASCAP 1941
author
b Atlanta, Ga, June 6, 16. Educ: Univ Sch, Atlanta. Chief Collabrs: Irving Melsher, Russ Morgan, Terry Shand. *Songs:* Roses in the Rain; Y-O-U (Spells the One I Love); The Georgian Waltz (off state waltz); So Long; Don't Cry, Sweetheart; White Dove of Peace; Cry, Baby, Cry; I Wanna Wrap You Up; A Rose and a Prayer; With This Ring; Always Keep Your Promise; My First and My Last Love.

HARRIS, RONA (RONA JANUARY) ASCAP 1960
composer, author, editor
b New York, NY, Jan 20, 36. Educ: Lincoln High Sch; studied voice with John Crosby, 57-59, piano with Madam Rosa, Fla, 72-74. Wrote complete musical show at age 14. Writer for newspapers, TV & fan mag. Author: "Life Is a Four-Letter Word." Writer of several columns for music, Platter Chatter, Musical Memos & Needle Fever. *Songs:* Why Can't It Happen to Me; Suddenly You Know; The Sack; Some Lazy Day; Rock and Roll Beat.

HARRIS, RONALD S ASCAP 1969
composer, author, arranger
b Los Angeles, Calif, Dec 16, 41. Educ: Univ Calif, Los Angeles, BA, 66. Arr, USA Band, 3 yrs & in Washington, DC. Music dir for Carol Lawrence, 4 yrs. Songwriter, 69- Chief Collabrs: Claire Cloninger, Stormie O'Martian, Carol Harris. *Songs:* Mirror; Special Delivery; Praise the Lord, He Never Changes; All the Time in the World; Friend of the Father. *Albums:* Friend of the Father; Special Delivery.

HARRIS, THEODORE ASCAP 1963
composer, educator
b New York, NY, Dec 8, 12. Educ: Studied piano with Harry Anick, harmony with Joseph Schmid. Pianist, club dates & nightclubs; singer, radio stations WHN & WNYC; comp music to off-Bway show "Meet Peter Grant" & "Bumpo the Ballerina", "Crying in the Street" & the opera, "The First President." Chief Collabrs: Carlos Williams, Elliot Arluck, Howard Finkelstein, Sam Matter. *Songs:* Hanukkah; If You Have a Dream. *Instrumental Works:* The Circus; Piano Concerto; Symphony.

HARRIS, VICTOR ASCAP 1914
composer, conductor, teacher
b New York, NY, Apr 27, 1869; d New York, Feb 15, 43. Educ: City Col New York, studied with Carl Blum & Frederick Schilling. Asst to William Courtney, singing teacher, then opened own studio; coach, Metrop Opera, 1893, became asst dir; organized & dir of original St Cecilia Club concerts. *Songs:* I Little Know Or Care; Way Down South; Wind of the Western Sea; The Hills of Skye; Morning; Invocation to St Cecilia.

HARRIS, VICTOR FRANCIS (EDDIE V) ASCAP 1964
composer, author
b Bonnie Terre, Mo, Jan 6, 11. Educ: Pvt instr. Co-founder & producer, Omega Records. Recorded & studied with Jack Teagarden. *Songs & Instrumental Works:* Sax 5th Avenue; Midnight at Malibu; Soft Lights; Paint the Big City Blue.

HARRIS, WILL J ASCAP 1937
composer, author, director
b New York, NY, Mar 14, 1900; d Chicago, Ill, Dec 14, 67. Educ: Morse Code Telegraphy Sch. Vaudeville dir, 21-34. Staged musical productions, civic & nat orgn, USO. Wrote spec material; coached singers. Chief Collabr: Victor Young. *Songs:* Pretty Cinderella: Sweet Sue Just You; I Wish I Knew I Knew; Boys Town; Please Don't Lean on the Bell; Games of Childhood Days; Some Night.

HARRIS, WOODY ASCAP 1957
composer, author, band leader
b New York, NY, Nov 1, 11. Educ: James Madison High Sch; Art Schs; pvt music studies, 14 yrs. Led band & wrote spec material for many big acts; wrote the Jerry Lester Show on ABC-TV. Partner, Darwood Music Corp; publ, Tweed Music Co. Chief Collabrs: Bobby Darin, Eddie Deane, Al Byron, Paul Evans, Peter Daniels. *Songs:* Rock a Billy; Queen of the Hop; Early in the Morning; Clementine; You Must Have Faith; Dix-A-Billy; I Want You With Me; Some of My Best Friends Are the Blues; Now See How You Are; Lyrics: Splish Splash; Was There a Call For Me?.

HARRISON, CASS ASCAP 1958
composer, pianist, conductor
b New York, NY, Apr 25, 22. Educ: NY Univ; Juilliard Sch Music; Univ Pa. Was concert pianist. Appeared at first Jazz Concert, Panama, 53. Has made records. Exec producer with Meyer Davis. Chief Collabr: Laura Manning. *Songs:* Midnight; Party Line; Once Upon a Love; Life Is a Wheel; Igloo for Two; Take a Tip From Mama. *Scores:* Stage: Look Around Tomorrow.

HARRISON, EUGENE DONALD ASCAP 1973
composer, author, singer
b New York, NY, Oct 14, 49. Educ: John Adams High Sch, Queens; Bethel Bible Inst, BDS; Queens Col, BA. Recording artist; performed with singing group, The Brothers, on radio, TV, cols & nightclubs; producer of gospel albums for church choirs; played organ, piano & synthesizers; keyboard artist. *Songs:* He Will Be There; Softly and Tenderly; Secret Place; Do What the Lord Say Do; Heaven.

HARRISON, KENNETH RICHARD ASCAP 1977
composer
b Toronto, Ont, Mar 31, 52. Educ: Valley Col. Pvt piano lessons, age 8. From librarian to supv copyist, CBS Studio Ctr. Orchr, Jerrold Immel & Bruce Broughton. Composer episodes: "Fantasy Island", "Salvage I", "Dallas", "Hawaii Five-O" & "Culpepper."

HARRISON, THOMAS JAMES ASCAP 1967
composer, author, singer
b Hawaii, July 4, 08. Educ: East Denver High Sch; Sierra States Univ Chiropractic Sch. Prof musician from age 12; played dance bands. Comp Hawaiian music, 34- Movie casting dir, Hawaii, 60-70. Chief Collabrs: Johnny Noble, Randy Oness, Art Fine, Bobby Worth. *Songs:* My Little Grass Shack in Kealakekua; Sentimental Moon; Happiness is Hawaii; Lyrics: Kalapana.

HART, BOB
See Trace, Albert J

HART, BRUCE ASCAP 1959
author
b New York, NY, Jan 15, 38. Educ: Syracuse Univ, AB, 59; Yale Law Sch, JD, 62. Comedy writer, 59-62; songwriter for var films & TV pilots, 62- Writer, lyricist, dir, co-author, producer & co-exec producer, var TV series incl "Sesame Street", "Free to Be...You and Me", "Psychology Today", "Sooner or Later", "Hot Hero Sandwich", 80- Chief Collab: Stephen Lawrence. *Songs:* Lyrics: Can You Tell Me How to Get to Sesame Street; Free to Be...You and Me; Who Are You Now; For Those in Love; One Way Ticket; You Take My Breath Away; Simply Jessie; You're a Hero, Too; Bang the Drum Slowly.

HART, CYNTHIA MARY KATHLEEN (CELETA FELBY) ASCAP 1972
composer, author
b Brit WI. Educ: Boarding sch, Edgehill, NS; Royal Acad Music, London, Eng, cert in theory. *Songs:* Glories in the Skies; Genevra of the Dawn; Good-bye I'll Never Say to You; This Land That Is So Verdant and Vast; Lyrics: Wherever You May Be; It's Only Because I Love You.

HART, FRANCES
See Tishman, Fay

HART, HENRY CLAY, III ASCAP 1959
composer, author, singer
b Providence, RI. Educ: Moses Brown Sch; Amherst Col, BA(theatre arts & music). Singer night clubs. Featured performer, Lawrence Welk Show, 69-75; on tour fairs, conventions, concerts, 75-; commercials nat TV. *Songs:* Sing Me a Love Song; Child of the Wind; Colors and Lines; Give Me Your Love; Bring Me Down Slow.

HART, KEN WOODROW ASCAP 1942
author
b New York, NY, May 7, 17. Aviation cadet, USAF, Editor & publ, Ky Coal J; lobbyist coal indust, Ky. Chief Collabr: Bert Gold. *Songs:* Lyrics: Dogface Soldier.

HART, LISA
See McNeil, Libby

HART, LORENZ ASCAP 1926
author
b New York, NY, May 2, 1895; d New York, Nov 22, 43. Educ: Columbia Univ. Wrote Columbia Varsity Shows. Began professional career translating Ger plays for Shubert bros. Film biography: "Words and Music." Chief Collabr: Richard Rodgers. *Songs:* Any Old Place With You; Manhattan; Here in My Arms; The Girl Friend; The Blue Room; Mountain Greenery; A Tree in the Park; A Little Birdie Told Me So; Where's That Rainbow; My Heart Stood Still; Thou Swell; You Took Advantage of Me; Moon of My Delight; With a Song in My Heart; Why Can't I?; A Ship Without a Sail; Ten Cents a Dance; Dancing on the Ceiling; I've Got Five Dollars; Mimi; Isn't It Romantic?; Lover; You Are Too Beautiful; Vilia; Merry Widow Waltz; Blue Moon; Soon; Easy to Remember; How Can You Forget?; The Most Beautiful Girl in the World; My Romance; Little Girl Blue; There's a Small Hotel; On Your Toes; Quiet Night; Glad to Be Unhappy; Where Or When; I Wish I Were in Love Again; My Funny Valentine; Johnny One Note; The Lady Is a Tramp; Have You Met Miss Jones?; I Married an Angel; I'll Tell the Man in the Street; Spring Is Here; At the Roxy Music Hall; Falling in Love With Love; This Can't Be Love; Sing For Your Supper; Love Never Went to College; I Didn't Know What Time It Was; You're Nearer; It Never Entered My Mind; I Could Write a Book; Bewitched, Bothered and Bewildered; Happy Hunting Horn; Zip; Wait Till You See Her; Everything I've Got; Careless Rhapsody; Nobody's Heart; To Keep My Love Alive. *Scores:* Bway stage: Poor Little Ritz Girl; The Garrick Gaieties (2 ed); Dearest Enemy; The Girl Friend; Peggy-Ann; A Connecticut Yankee; Present Arms; Spring Is Here; Heads Up!; Simple Simon; America's Sweetheart; Jumbo; I'd Rather Be Right; The Boys From Syracuse (Obie Award, 62); Too Many Girls; Higher and Higher; Pal Joey (NY Drama Critics Award, 52); also co-librettist: On Your Toes; Babes in Arms; I Married an Angel; By Jupiter; London: Lido Lady; One Dam Thing After Another; Ever Green; Films: Love Me Tonight; The Phantom President; Hallelujah; I'm a Bum; The Merry Widow; Mississippi.

HART, LUCILLE (BABE) ASCAP 1954
composer, author
b Sidney, Nebr, July 29, 17. Educ: Univ Colo, Boulder, BA(languages), 39; Hunter Col, NY, broadcasting courses; Univ Calif, Los Angeles. Wrote songs for col shows; comp & coproducer of children's musicals; wrote songs & arr for choral groups. Owner bk publ co, Baja Books; author & publ "Speedy" Language Bks in six languages. Chief Collabrs: Frank Lamarr, Mari Valentin, Art Waner, Al Trace. *Songs:* What a Feeling Is This!; When You Saw Him Last; Taking a Walk With My Sweetheart; The Light of Love; Suzanne; With All My Love; Lyrics: To Love; Follow Me.

HART, MAURICE ASCAP 1954
composer, author
b New York, NY, Jan 6, 09; d. Educ: Bus col. Stock broker, 7 yrs. Radio & TV announcer, 30 yrs. Wrote musical commercials, 12 yrs. Chief Collabrs: Al Hoffman, Walter Kent, Al Stillman, Bob Emmerich. *Songs:* Believing; Starlite and Music; One Misty, Moisty Morning; Snerling Through the Flowers.

HART, WELDON ASCAP 1956
composer, teacher, violinist
b Bear Spring, Tenn, Sept 19, 11; d East Lansing, Mich, Nov 20, 57. Educ: Peabody Col, BS, 33; Ward-Belmont Cons, dipl violin, 33; Univ Mich, MMus, 39; Eastman Sch Music, PhD(comp), 46. Dir music, Western Ky State Col Training Sch, 34-38, dir orch & theory, 38-43, head music dept, 46-49; teaching fel, Eastman Sch Music, 43-46; violinist, Rochester Philh Orch, 44-46; dir, Sch Music, WVa Univ, 49-57; head music dept, Mich State Univ, 57. Chief Collabrs: John Jacob Niles, Patrick Gainer. *Instrumental Works:* John Jacob Niles Suite (orch); Symphony No 1; Song and Celebration (band); Stately Music for Strings; Concerto for Violin and Orchestra.

HARTFORD, CHAPIN
See Foster, Paula Hartford

HARTIG, HERBERT A ASCAP 1961
composer, author, actor
b New York, NY. Educ: Brooklyn Col, BA(magna cum laude). Performed with "The Living Theatre." Cartoonist & illustrator. Wrote spec material for Ronny Graham, Pat Carroll, Dick Shawn, Jules Munshin, Phil Leeds, Kaye Ballard, Henry Morgan & others. Appeared in nightclub act, New York, St Louis, Mo, Dallas, Tex, Bermuda. Did TV commercials, voice-overs, film narrations. Writer-in-residence, Tamiment, Green Mansions; NBC staff writer, 56-57. Wrote sketches & songs, "New Faces"; Julius Monk revues; "Shoestring '57"; "Medium Rare" (Chicago); "Spread Eagle" (Washington); "Up Tempo" (Montreal); "Bottoms Up" (Las Vegas); "Graham Crackers"; "Wet Paint." Wrote sketches & songs for TV, "That Was the Week That Was"; "Comedy Tonight"; "The David Frost Revue"; "Living Together"; adaptation, "Rappaccini's Daughter" (Hawthorne), for "The American Short Story" (PBS). Chief Collabrs: Milton Delugg, Gerald Alters, Sol Berkowitz. *Songs:* My Mother's Neighbor's Blues; Lyrics: Surabaya-Johnny (transl); Let It Go; West 83rd Street; Love Power; Here We Are Again; Ulysses; A Graceful Exit; This Time Will Be the Last Time. *Scores:* Stage: Fat Tuesday (Ford Found grant); Our Hearts Were Young and Gay; Joley.

HARTLEY, FREDERICK JAMES ASCAP 1969
author
b Philadelphia, Pa, Feb 21, 45. Educ: Northeast Cath High Sch. Chief Collabr: Ronnie Booner. *Songs:* Lyrics: Love Was Never Far Away; Sunshine Today and Tomorrow; Billy Tell; Mother's Day; Philadelphi Polka.

HARTLEY, RAYMOND OSWALD ASCAP 1955
composer, author, teacher
b Perth, Australia, May 26, 29. Educ: St Joseph's Convent, Western Australia; Conservatorium Music, Sydney, Australia, AMusA, piano studies with Nancy Salas; Royal Acad Music, London, LRAM, piano studies with Harold Craxton & comp with Margaret Hubicki. Command perf for Queen Elizabeth, Victoria Palace Theatre. Accompanist to singer Sam Browne & movie comedian Terry-Thomas. Recording artist, RCA Victor. Pianist, Waldorf-Astoria, Sheraton Ctr, Regency & St Regis-Sheraton Hotels. Chief Collabrs: Desmond O'Connor, Tommie Connor, Jack Lawrence. *Songs:* The Miracle of Christmas; Music: Let's Do It Again; Welcome Home; Whispers in the Wind; The Dawning of Love; Darling He's Playing Our Song. *Instrumental Works:* French Fries; Sleepy Grasshopper; Mouse on the Mezzanine; Twilight in Chinatown. *Scores:* Film/TV: Portobello.

HARTLEY, WALTER SINCLAIR ASCAP 1959
composer, pianist, teacher
b Washington, DC, Feb 21, 27. Educ: Eastman Sch Music, Univ Rochester, BMus, 50, MMus, 51, PhD, 53; studied with Bernard Rogers & Howard Hanson. Teacher at several cols & Nat Music Camp; prof music, State Univ NY Col, Fredonia, 69- Composer of over 100 publ works, mostly instrumental, predominantly featuring wind instruments; several recorded works. *Instrumental Works:* Concerto for 23 Winds; Sonata Concertante (trombone & piano); Suite (unaccompanied tuba); Duo (alto saxophone & piano); Sinfonia No 4 (wind ens); Sonata (tuba & piano); Double Concerto (alto saxophone, tuba & wind octet); Concerto (piano & orch); Metamorphoses (clarinet & piano); Symphony No 2 (large wind ens). *Songs & Instrumental Works:* A Psalm Cycle (voice, flute & piano); Canticles (soloists, chorus & wind ens).

HARTMAN, DIANE
See Smith, Diane Hartman

HARTMAN, DON ASCAP 1935
author, producer, actor
b New York, NY, Nov 18, 1900; d Palm Springs, Calif, Mar 23, 58. Educ: Pub schs. Stage mgr & actor, Dallas Little Theatre. Played "Andy Hardy" in Bway play "Skidding." To Hollywood, 33; wrote songs for films, screenplays incl

"Road to Singapore", "Road to Zanzibar", "Nothing But the Truth", "My Favorite Blonde", "Road to Morocco" & "Up in Arms", also producer-dir "It Had to Be You" & "Every Girl Should Be Married." Became exec producer, Paramount. *Songs:* I Found a Dream; Love at Last; Readin', Ritin', Rhythm; If I Knew You Better; Okolehao; Ting-a-Ling-a-Ling.

HARVEY, LUCY QUINN (ADELLE QUINN)   ASCAP 1978
composer, author, singer
b Magnolia, NC, Mar 14, 32. Educ: Studied voice with Don Warner, Richmond, Va. Music writer. *Songs:* That's the Way the Ball Bounces; Don't Toy With My Affection.

HARVEY, NICHOLAS   ASCAP 1958
author
b Riga, Latvia, June 10, 01. Educ: High sch, Riga. Verse transl of Eng hit songs into Ger or Russian. Writer, song lyrics for European vaudeville acts. Chief Collabrs: Nat Mysior, Harry Green, Wayne Shenklin. *Songs:* Lyrics: In a Small Forgotten Town; Pizza Polka; Isabella; I Found a Livin' Doll in Dallas; Just an Old-Fashioned Fandango.

HARWELL, WILLIAM EARNEST (ERNIE)   ASCAP 1965
composer, author
b Washington, Ga, Jan 25, 18. Educ: Emory Univ, BA. Sports announcer; with major league baseball; CBS football announcer; NBC golf announcer. Mag writer. Chief Collabrs: Sammy Fain, Phillipe Wynne, Jose Feliciano, Deon Jackson, Chuck Boris, Bill Slayback & Will Hatcher. *Songs:* Whatever Happened to Forever?; Lyrics: I Don't Know Any Better; Nobody's Perfect; Our One Sweet Summer; Talking Back to Echoes; Why Did it Take You so Long; Wake Up Wiser; Elsie; Move Over Babe, Here Comes Henry; Only a Fool; Upside Down; Super Bowl.

HARWOOD, BENJAMIN   ASCAP 1968
composer, author, performer
b Los Angeles, Calif, Mar 6, 46. Played piano & guitar since grade 4. Lead singer, comp & rhythm guitarist for rock group Treehouse, 67-68. Var short films, educ films & songwriting. Chief Collabrs: John Cassavetes, Booker T Jones. *Songs:* Almost; Count to Ten; Everybody's Talkin' About You; Play It Again; Pete Kazoo; Rainy Fields of Frost and Magic. *Scores:* Film/TV: Minnie and Moskowitz; A Woman Under the Influence (main theme); The Killing of a Chinese Bookie; Opening Night (main theme); The Bach Train (main theme); The Dawn of Man.

HASKELL, BURT
See Brisman, Heskel

HASKELL, JIMMIE   ASCAP 1955
composer, arranger, conductor
b Brooklyn, NY. Educ: Fairfax High Sch, Los Angeles, Calif, studied harmony; Los Angeles City Col, studied orchestration & counterpoint with Robert P MacDonald; studied basic music educ with Jimmie DeMichele, harmony & orchestration with Lyle (Spud) Murphy. Arr & A&R man, Imperial Records. Producer & arr of 9 gold records with Rick Nelson; went independent, 63. Scored films with Paramount Pictures. Rec'd 3 Grammy Awards as best arr, "Ode to Billy Joe", "Bridge Over Troubled Waters" & "If You Leave Me Now"; rec'd Emmy Award as best comp of dramatic music score TV film, "See How She Runs." Did original scores for 25 motion pictures & 50 TV films. Scoring theatrical & TV films. Started own record co, Horn Records.

HASKIN, ABBY
See Mascolino, Dolores Abigail

HASLAM, HERBERT   ASCAP 1964
composer, author, educator
b Philadelphia, Pa, Apr 23, 28. Educ: Temple Univ, Juilliard Sch Music, BS, MS. Fac mem, Bronx House Music Sch & The Barker Sch. Comp & mem, Composers Circle, New York. Comp-in-residence, Riverdale Country Schs; exec assoc, Riverdale Schs Music. Coauth, "Riverdale Plan," music educ curriculum, 1st-12th grades. *Instrumental Works:* Haiku Set.

HASSELL, JON   ASCAP 1978
composer, trumpeter
b Memphis, Tenn, Mar 22, 37. Educ: Univ Rochester Eastman Sch Music, BM & MM; Cath Univ Am, doctoral candidacy in musicology; electronic music & comp studies with Karlheinz Stockhausen, Germany; Kirana style Indian classical music studies with Pandit Pran Nath, India. Awards: Ger Govt, 65-67; Rockefeller Found, 67-69; NY State Coun Arts, 75; NEA, 77. Chief Collabrs: LaMonte Young; Terry Riley; Brian Eno. *Instrumental Works:* Solid State; Vernal Equinox; Earthquake Island; Possible Musics.

HASTINGS, HAROLD (HAL)   ASCAP 1959
composer, author, conductor
b New York, NY, Dec 19, 16; d Larchmont, NY, May 30, 73. Educ: NY Univ, BS, MA. Music dir, radio & TV shows. Comp background music & musical commercials, also comp music, cond & arr movie "A Thousand Clowns."

Scores: Bway Musicals: Top Banana; The Pajama Game; Damn Yankees (Tony Award); New Girl in Town; Once Upon a Mattress; Fiorello!; A Funny Thing Happened on the Way to the Forum; She Loves Me; Baker Street; It's a Bird...It's a Plane...It's Superman; The Making of a President.

HASTINGS, ROSS RAY (JOE FORTUNE)   ASCAP 1956
composer
b Los Angeles, Calif, Feb 26, 15. Educ: Alhambra High Sch, Calif; Univ Southern Calif, studied with Ray Hastings, Los Angeles Philh. Free-lance arr & comp; choral cond; staff arr & orchr, Hollywood Bowl, 57-62; ed-in-chief, Warner Brothers Publ, 62-70; dir publ, Bourne Co, 73-79; comp 80- *Songs:* Music: Prayer of St Francis (SATB, chorus, narrator). *Instrumental Works:* Emissary Fanfare (band); Overture to a Celebration (band); Flourish and Ceremonial March (band); Let Freedom Sing (band, chorus); Sinfonia Brevis (orch); Chorale: America Loves a Melody. *Scores:* Opera: The Rich Young Ruler.

HATHAWAY, CHARLES   ASCAP 1942
composer, conductor, arranger
b Sparta, Ill, Aug 10, 04; d Los Angeles, Calif, Feb 3, 66. Educ: NY Univ; studied with Joseph Schillinger. Cond, theatre orchs. Chief arr, music publ firms. Comp & cond, radio progs. Founded own publ co. *Songs:* Johnny Get Your Horn; Be Sure; Rock Island Flag Stop; Twilight Romance; My True Story.

HATLEY, JEARLD JAYE   ASCAP 1971
composer, singer
b Manila, Ark, Oct 19, 37. Educ: Manila Pub Sch. Performer, TV & nightclubs, 60- Writer, 67-; recording artist, Hi Records, Columbia & Mega Records, 67- Chief Collabr: Larry Rodgers. *Songs:* When Morning Comes to Memphis; What's Left Never Will Be Right; Love Me Till the Morning Comes; I Didn't Hear a Thing; We Don't Love Anymore.

HATLEY, THOMAS MARVIN   ASCAP 1952
composer, author, arranger
b Reed, Okla, Apr 3, 05. Educ: Univ Calif, Los Angeles; studied harmony & counterpoint with Edmund Ross; studied cond with Arthur Kay & Albert Coates. Prof vaudeville drummer, silent motion pictures at age 9. Became pianist & trumpeter at age 13. Played 20 musical instruments & one-man band, vaudeville, 28. Musical dir, Hal Roach Studios, Hollywood, Calif, 30-40. Chief Collabrs: Charlie Chase, James Parrott, Billy Gilbert, Eddie Dunn, Walter Bullock, Portia Lanning, Louis Herscher, Walter Weems, Frank Terry, Gus Meins, Billy Blecher, Jeff Moffit & King Zany. *Songs:* Ku-Ku (Laurel & Hardy theme); Honolulu Baby; I Wake Up With a Song; Music: Will You Be My Lovey Dovey?; Aunt Emma's Got Ants in Her Pantry; Nobody's Baby; Blame It on Love; Now That We're Alone; I've Dreamed About This; Look What You Do to Me; Don't Start Frettin'; Jumpin' Down at Carnegie Hall; The End of the Trail; Woogie Hula; Goin' to Town. *Scores:* Film/TV: Way Out West; Blockheads; Chump at Oxford; Saps at Sea; Sons of the Desert; Bonnie Scotland; Zenobia; Captain Fury; Topper; Merrily We Live; There Goes My Heart.

HATTON, ALMA W   ASCAP 1960
composer, author
b Waterford, NY, Apr 3, 17. Educ: Troy Sch of Art. Artist, free-lance & for dept store, Albany. Chief Collabr: George Geiger. *Songs:* Violino; Our Wedding Prayer.

HAUGHTON, JOHN ALAN   ASCAP 1942
author
b Baltimore, Md, Sept 23, 1880; d New York, NY, Nov 11, 51. Educ: Johns Hopkins Univ, BA; Modern Language Sem; Peabody Cons (spec scholarship, renewed 4 times), Teacher's cert; studied with Oscar Saenger. On fac, Peabody Cons, 05-13. On ed staff, Opera Mag, 16-17 & Musical Am, 17. Sgt, US Tank Corps, WW I. *Songs:* The Crystal Gazer; Your Eyes; The Stork and the Skylark; Come Raggio di Sol; March of the Toys; The Song of the Flea; Moon Magic. *Songs & Instrumental Works:* Translations Schubert's War in the Household; Fra Diavolo; Orpheus in Hades; A Waltz Dream; The Bartered Bride; The Poacher; Abu Hassan; Consecration of the Arts.

HAUSCHILD, RICHARD CURTIS (BULLDOG)   ASCAP 1978
author
b Elmhurst, Ill, Jan 3, 49. Educ: Libertyville High Sch, Ill; Nebr Wesleyan Univ, BA(Eng), 71. Founded, Red Ripple Music Publ Co, 78- Chief Collabr: Jim Krueger. *Songs:* Lyrics: Trinidad; Run for Cover; Sweet Salvation; It's All About You; You Cut So Deep.

HAVEMANN, WILLIAM G   ASCAP 1961
composer
b Chicago, Ill, May 31, 23. Educ: Chicago Cons, studied with Bernard Dieter. Chief Collabr: Margaret Havemann (wife). *Instrumental Works:* Trumpet Beguine; Peace Corps March and Anthem.

HAVEZ, JEAN   ASCAP 1914
author
b Baltimore, Md, Dec 24, 1874; d Los Angeles, Calif, Feb 12, 25. Charter mem, ASCAP. Press agent, Lew Dockstader's Minstrels. Writer, spec material for

musical comedy, vaudeville & scenarios for Charlie Chaplin, Buster Keaton & Harold Lloyd. *Songs:* Everybody Works But Father; When You Ain't Got No Money Then You Needn't Come Around; I'm Looking For an Angel; Do Not Forget the Good Old Days; Darktown Poker Club; You're on the Right Road, Sister; He Cert'ny Was Good to Me.

HAWK, EDDIE
See Mravik, Edward E

HAWKINS, CHARLOTTE   ASCAP 1958
composer, author
b Boston, Mass. *Songs:* To Whom It May Concern; With You on My Mind.

HAWKINS, EDWARD RANDOLPH   ASCAP 1964
composer, author, singer
b Atlanta, Ga, May 26, 30. Educ: Cass Tech High Sch, Detroit, Mich; Katherine Dunham Sch Perf Arts, New York. Concerts & TV; perf in Europe, 51- *Songs & Instrumental Works:* Missa Nobis; Piccola Scala.

HAWKINS, ERSKINE   ASCAP 1945
composer, conductor, trumpeter
b Birmingham, Ala, July 26, 14. Educ: Ala State Teachers Col, BS; pvt music study. To New York, 36; debut as band leader, Harlem Opera House. Recording artist. *Songs & Instrumental Works:* Tuxedo Junction; You Can't Escape From Me; Gin Mill Special.

HAWKINS, FLOYD WESLEY   ASCAP 1957
composer, author, minister
b Pullman, Wash, Nov 20, 04. Educ: Walla Walla High Sch, grad; Univ Pacific Cons, studies in theory & comp; spec study under John W Bixel. Pastoral ministry, Wash, Ore & Calif, 19 yrs; music ed, Lillenas Publ Co, Kansas City, Mo, 18 yrs. Publ works for use mostly in evangelical churches (solos, duets, choral numbers, cantatas, children's works & prog materials). *Songs:* I've Discovered the Way of Gladness; The Crystal Fountain; Let Thy Mantle Fall on Me; Willing to Take the Cross; God's Great Grace; This Pair of Hands; Not for the Righteous; Let the Beauty of the Lord Our God Be Upon Us (invocation); Music: I Met God in the Morning; Lyrics: Discovery (musical).

HAWKINS, JASON
See Powell, Jack

HAWLEY, CHARLES BEACH   ASCAP 1929
composer, conductor, singer
b Brookfield, Conn, Feb 14, 1858; d Eatontown, NJ, Dec 29, 15. Educ: Cheshire Mil Acad. Music dir & organist, Cheshire Mil Acad; soloist, Calvary Episcopal Church; soloist & music dir, Bway Tabernacle, 18 yrs; St James Church, Elberon, NJ. *Songs:* Because I Love You Dear; Ah, 'Tis a Dream; My Little Love; The Sweetest Flower; Noon and Night; Come Unto Me. *Songs & Instrumental Works:* The Christ Child (cantata); chorus: Trisagion and Sanctus; Margareta.

HAWLEY, WILLIAM PALMER   ASCAP 1977
composer
b Bronxville, NY, Nov 4, 50. Educ: Ithaca Col Sch Music; Calif Inst Arts, BFA, 74, MFA, 76; studied comp with Morton Subotnick, James Tenney, Harold Budd, Alan Chaplin & Earle Brown. Had works performed in New York, Los Angeles, Minneapolis, Darmstadt, Utrecht & Frankfurt; also broadcast over NPR, KRO Dutch radio, Hessischer Rundfunk, KPFK & other radio stas. *Songs & Instrumental Works:* Seven Steps (two pianos); Wave (electronic); Sobetsu (chamber ensemble); Nara; Del Verbo Divino (women's voices, harp).

HAWORTH, ROGER A (RAJAH)   ASCAP 1974
composer, author, pianist
b Brooklyn, NY, July 12, 39. Educ: Manual Training High Sch, Brooklyn; piano & comp with Cy Walter & Sanford Gold; arr with Tony Alliss; singer presentation with Leamen Engleman; actg with Sanford Meisner; dance with Hanya Holms. Performing musician for 22 yrs, incl 3 yrs at Persian Room (nightclub), New York. Wrote first rock opera, "Rajah and the Rah People," 63. Original jazz music performed in concert with all star jazz greats. Composed 4 songs in Silver Burdett Music Textbooks. ASCAP Popular Award, 75-76 & 76-77. Chief Collabr: Mark Barkan. *Songs:* Sunny Side Man; Will We Make It Tonight?; A Friend in Need; Soul Saver. *Instrumental Works:* Rajah.

HAWRYLO, FRANK ZYGMUNT   ASCAP 1963
composer, arranger, teacher
b Trenton, NJ, Feb 16, 36. Educ: Trenton Catholic High Sch; Am Accordionists Asn, certified teachers dipl, 63; Thomas A Edison Col, BS(materials sci), 79. Accordion-Cordovox, nightclubs, radio & TV; recording artist with var cos. *Instrumental Works:* Chocolate Candy; Ride'm Nice; Sweet Girl; From Here; Mood Madness.

HAWTHORNE, GRACE   ASCAP 1972
author
b Salem, NJ, Aug 11, 39. Educ: La State Univ, BA(jour). Copywriter, State Times/Morning Advocate, Baton Rouge, La. Pub rels, Independent Oil Publ,

Houston, Tex. Copy ed, "Time/Life Books," New York. Creative dir, Triune Music, New York. Free lance writer, Atlanta & New York. Chief Collabrs: Buryl Red, Susan Elliott, Tom Fettke, Paul Johnson, John Barbe, Charles F Wilson. *Songs:* Lyrics: It's Cool in the Furnace (children's musical); The Small One (children's musical); The Electric Sunshine Man (children's musical); The Runaway (musical). *Scores:* Opera/Ballet: The Last Sacrifice (adult oratorio).

HAYDEN, JOY LAVONNE   ASCAP 1977
composer, singer
b Effingham, Ill, Sept 4, 41. Country & western singer; entertainer at county fairs & blue grass fests, 59- Writer & recording artist. *Songs:* Cotton Sheets and Faded Gown; Let's Give It One More Try; Movin On; Blues Stay Away From Me.

HAYDEN, RUSSELL MICHAEL   ASCAP 1965
composer, author
b Chico, Calif, June 10, 10. Actor, producer & director. Chief Collabr: Hal Hopper. *Songs & Instrumental Works:* The Story of 26 Men.

HAYES, BILLY   ASCAP 1948
composer, author, guitarist
b New York, NY, Feb 17, 06. Educ: New York Schs. Vocalist, guitarist, performer in nightclubs, hotels, prof music man; mgr, Dawn Music Publ. Chief Collabrs: Milton Leeds, Jay Johnson, Jack Rollins, Bob Hilliard, Ray Whitley, John Redmond, Marty Symes. *Songs:* Blue Christmas; Blue Snowflakes; Hawaiian Christmas; Christmas Kisses; Abbott the Rabbit; Who Shot the Hole in My Sombrero; Got a Ring Around Rosie's Finger; A Whistle and a Whisker Away; You Laughed and I Cried; Yesterdays Kisses; Whittlin'; Who-Else; Tomorrow's Just Another Day to Cry; Landslide of Love; Keep Smilin; The Black and White Pigeon with the Eight Red Toes; Little Wedding Bells; Think It Over; Play-Fair; Poison-Ivy; You Never Know When You'll Need a Friend; A Smile Will Chase Away a Tear; That Miss from Mississippi; The Santa Claus Thing; The Pied Piper Polka Story; Sit Down and Tell Me Where I Stand with You; Proud Papa Polka; Peaceful; Little Hula Honey; Montana; My Oklahoma Rose; Sleep Little One Sleep; Broncho Boogie; Slow Horses and Fast Women; Who's Your Honey.

HAYES, BONNY-ADELE   ASCAP 1978
composer, author, singer
b St Louis, Mo, Dec 5, 53. Educ: Fontbonne Col, BM(cum laude), 74; Washington Univ, Mo; Univ Calif, Los Angeles. Created role of Marie in Am premiere of "13 Rue De L'Amour." Singer/actress, stage, TV & radio. Recording artist, Bonnet Records. Lead roles in many musicals & plays. Producer & dir original music revue, "Jubilee." Chief Collabr: Helen McMillian. *Songs:* Love Remembers; I Have Spoken; Outside My Window; Part Butterfly; You Caught Me With Your Smile.

HAYES, DANA
See Macarthur, Dana Beth Hayes

HAYES, EDGAR JUNIUS   ASCAP 1955
composer, conductor, pianist
b Lexington, Ky, May 23, 05; d. Educ: Fisk Univ; Wilberforce Univ, BM. Pianist in Louis Deppe Orch, 4 yrs; show dir, Alhambra Theatre, New York, 4 yrs. Cond, Irving Mills Blue Rhythm Band; cond, own orch, toured US & Europe; made records. Pianist, Somerset House, Riverdale, Calif, 11 yrs; also Reuben's restaurants, Calif. Past exec council mem, Los Angeles Pacific Col. *Songs:* Someone Stole Gabriel's Horn; Love's Serenade; Out of a Dream.

HAYES, ERNEST W   ASCAP 1973
composer, pianist, arranger
b New York, NY, Feb 12, 29. Educ: New York Col. Did commercials & pop recordings, 59- Pianist with artists, incl Nat King Cole, Lena Horne, Connie Francis, La Verne Baker, Dinah Washington & Aretha Franklin. *Songs & Instrumental Works:* Quad (flute suite); Vaya; Flowers of the Night.

HAYES, GLORIA
See Kremer, Gloria Hayes

HAYES, JACK JOSEPH   ASCAP 1956
composer, arranger, orchestrator
b San Francisco, Calif, Feb 8, 19. Educ: San Francisco State Col; Los Angeles Cons Music; instrs incl, Mario Castelnuovo-Tedesco, Dr Albert Sendry & Ernst Krenek. Orchr, arr & cond films for maj motion picture studios, 46-80; comp TV shows. Chief Collabr: Louis Bellson. *Instrumental Works:* A Piece for Pantomime; Shave and a Haircut; Caranby Street; Peacock Strut; Let Me Walk My Own Walk; Snow Flower; Cornucopia; War Prayer (narration with orch); String Quartet; Fantasy for Trombone and Orchestra; Concerto for Trumpet and Orchestra; Rhapsody for Two Pianos.

HAYES, LARRY RAY
See Ray, (Hayes) Larry

HAYES, LINDA JOYCE   ASCAP 1971
composer, author
b New York, NY, July 12, 47. Educ: Erasmus Hall High Sch. Chief Collabr: Billy Hayes. *Songs:* A Whistle and a Whisker Away; I've Got a Present for Santa; A Love Like This; It's Kid Time Again; Winter in Vermont; Blue Print for Love; Tic-Tac-Toe; Playthings; Try; Let Me Be the One; Blue Ribbon Heartache; Trust Me.

HAYES, PETER LIND   ASCAP 1956
composer, author, entertainer
b San Francisco, Calif, June 25, 15. Educ: High sch. Toured in vaudeville with mother, Grace Hayes. Served, USAF, World War II, recipient 2 Battle Stars & Bronze Star. Appeared on TV, films, nightclubs, theatres & on radio with wife Mary Healy. Author, "Twenty-five Minutes From Broadway." Chief Collabrs: Robert Allen, Nacio Herb Brown, Frank Loesser. *Songs:* Come to Me; Why Do They Call a Private a Private?; When You Used to Dance With Me (Alone); Cool Alaska Rock and Roll.

HAYES, REA
See Symon, Rea Janet

HAYES, THEODORE, JR (TED ERNEST OSAZE)   ASCAP 1977
composer, author, singer
b Cleveland, Ohio, Oct 20, 51. Educ: Cleveland Inst Music; Cleveland State Univ. Road mgr, Roberta Flack Enterprises, 76. Writer, Yeah, Inc, 77-78. Songwriter & producer, Haymarc Music Enterprises, 78-80. Producer, Funky Constellation, 80. Chief Collabrs: Walter Dixon, Melvin Van Peebles, Mtume Eric Saaed, Paul Chaplin, Moses Cartagena, Justice Butler. *Songs:* Street-Talk (Madam Rapper); Eat That Thing.

HAYMAN, RICHARD WARREN JOSEPH (M E DALY, RAY HOWARD, RICHARD SAVAGE)   ASCAP 1956
author, arranger, orchestrator
b Cambridge, Mass, Mar 27, 20. Educ: Pvt studies with Arthur Fiedler, Sixten Ehrling, Harry Ellis Dickson, Victor Young, Alfred & Lionel Newman, Georgie Stoll, Franz Waxman & Max Steiner. Joined the Borrah Minevitch Harmonica Rascals, world tour, 38; free lance arr/orchr, Hollywood, 48. Arr & entertainer & musical dir, Vaughn Monroe Orch, TV shows & recordings. Arr, Arthur Fiedler & The Boston Pops Orch, 49-79. Solo recording artist, Mercury Records, 51, A&R dir, Mercury NY Off, 52. Toured with own orch, 53, disbanded orch to concentrate on comp, arr & solo work, 56. Musical dir emcee for artists incl Bob Hope, Jack Benny, Red Skelton. Formed the Manhattan Pops Orch, 63. Guest cond maj orchs. Principal pops cond, Detroit Symph Orch, St Louis Symph Orch, Birmingham Symph, Hartford Symph & Vancouver Symph. Chief Collabrs: Mitchell Parish, Richard Ahlert, Lee Daniels, Arden Clar, Sol Parker, Jim Tyler, Bobby Mellin, John Sbarra, Joe DiBuono, Ettore Stratta. *Songs:* Music: Dansero; Suzanne; Huckleberry Finn. *Instrumental Works:* No Strings Attached; Skipping Along; Serenade to a Lost Love; Carriage Trade; Valse d'Amour (The Waltz of Love); Marianne; Voodoo Suite; Pop's Hoedown; Harmonica Concerto No 1 in B Flat; Regency Waltz; The Girls of Monte Carlo; Oo-La-La; Blue Beguine; Maryellen; Olivia; Serenade for Suzanne; I Will Write You a Song; What Then; Samba de Victoria; Follow the Crowd. *Scores:* Film/TV: Pain Is My Enemy; The Ballad of the Iron Horse; The Golden Age of the Automobile.

HAYNES, KENNETH D
author
b Louisville, Ky, Nov 22, 42. Radio announcer, many years. Wrote one publ song. *Songs:* Music: Strollin.

HAYNES, LINCOLN MURRAY   ASCAP 1970
author
b Los Angeles, Calif, Aug 10, 24. Educ: Univ Calif, Los Angeles, BA, 47; Calif State Univ, Northridge, MA, 75; studied comedy writing with Abe Burrows. Ed, New York Daily News, Los Angeles Times, Saturday Evening Post, etc; publicist for CBS-TV; writer of mag & spec comedy material. Writer-broadcaster of satiric commentary of KSUL-FM. Col instr in print & broadcast journalism. Chief Collabrs: Myron Roberts, Sasha Gilien. *Songs:* Lyrics: Begatting of the President (Grammy nominee, best comedy record, 71).

HAYNIE, WILLIAM S   ASCAP 1961
composer, author
b Clinton, Miss, Mar 18, 18. Educ: Memphis State Univ, BS; Univ Ala; George Peabody Col, MS. Music teacher, Tenn, Fla & Miss. USMC, 42-46; state supvr music, Miss, 48-56; vpres, Prentice-Hall, Inc, 58-61; music ed, Holt, Rinehart & Winston, Inc, 61- *Songs:* Shake the Papaya Down; Music: Cottleston Pie; Pooh's Song; Summer Morning. *Instrumental Works:* March Mississippi.

HAYS, BILLY SILAS   ASCAP 1942
composer, author, conductor
b Philadelphia, Pa, June 13, 1898; d. Educ: Temple Univ. Led own orch, 25. Chief Collabrs: Morty Berk, Harry James. *Songs:* Nine O'Clock Sal; Dream Buddy; Pretty Face; Looney Little Tooney; Lazy Silv'ry Moon; Mary, the Prairie and I; From the Bottom of My Heart.

HAYS, DORIS (QUINSKA)   ASCAP 1971
composer, concert pianist
b Memphis, Tenn, Aug 6, 41. Educ: Univ Chattanooga, Cadek Cons, BM, 63, comp with Arthur Plettner; Munich Sch Music, artist dipl, study with Friedrich Wührer & Hedwig Bilgram, 63-66; Univ Wis, MM, 68; study with Paul Badura-Skoda; Univ Iowa Ctr New Music, electronic music with Robert Shallenberg, 69; pvt study with Hilde Somer, 77. First Prize, Int Competition Interpreters New Music, Rotterdam, 71; soloist at Europ fests & radio stas & Am campuses such as Syracuse Fest Am Piano Music. Recording artist, Finnadar/Atlantic Records, albums new piano music, 77 & 80. Activist in concerts of music by women. Asst chairperson, Int League Women Comp. Lectr electronic music & new piano music. *Instrumental Works:* Tunings (string quartet and/or six other solo instruments); Characters (harpsichord or piano & string quintet, 3 winds); Pamp (piano, tape & bird whistles); Sunday Nights (piano); Pieces From Last Year (16 strings, winds, piano); Breathless (bass flute); Only (multiple pianos & tapes). *Songs & Instrumental Works:* Southern Voices (tape & narrator); Hands Full (chorus & tape); Sensevents (prog lights, sculptures, 6-9 musicians); Uni (ballet suite, string quartet, flute, tape, chorus).

HAYTON, LEONARD GEORGE (LENNIE)   ASCAP 1953
composer, conductor, arranger
b New York, NY, Feb 13, 08; d Palm Springs, Calif, May, 71. Pianist in jazz groups incl Frankie Trumbauer, Bix Beiderbecke, Red Nichols, Joe Venuti & also with Paul Whiteman Orch. Music dir, MGM, 40-53, also for Lena Horne (wife). *Songs & Instrumental Works:* Flying Finger; Mood Hollywood; Midnight Mood. *Scores:* Films: The Harvey Girls; The Pirate; On the Town (Acad Award, 49); Singin' in the Rain.

HAYWARD, CHRISTOPHER ROBERT   ASCAP 1949
composer, author, singer
b Bayonne, NJ, June 19, 25. Began writing words & music, mid-40's; singer, solo & with big bands, late 40's; TV show writer. Chief Collabrs: Dick Hazard, Alan Schrader, Murray MacEachern, Frank Sinatra, Bob Staver, Sam Schultz. *Songs:* One Way Ticket; The Hills of California; It Never Rains in Honolulu; Lyrics: Sheila; Amber Moon; Summer Snow; Snowfall; Things. *Instrumental Works:* The Sweetheart Waltz.

HAZELWOOD, E CLAYTON (CLATE)   ASCAP 1964
author
b Malden, Mass, Sept 17, 03. Educ: Fifth grade grammar sch; self-taught. Newspaper columnist, upstate NY; pub speaker; author of five bks of verses; theatre mgr, Boston Theatre & University Theatre, Harvard Sq, Cambridge, Mass. Radio star, 34-47; radio, Boston & Syracuse, NY; poetry & music progs. Chief Collabrs: Leo Friedman, Lindsay McPhail, Cornel Tanassy, George Liberache. *Songs:* Lyrics: I Want a Dog for Christmas; When We Gather 'Round the Campfire of the Lord; I Wish My Mind Would Leave My Heart Alone; Santa's Mommy Must Have Had Quintuplets; Bless Your Heart; The Boatman's Prayer; I Want a Turtle for My Daddy; I Can't Live Forever in Dreamland.

HAZLEWOOD, LEE   ASCAP 1965
composer, author, singer
b Mannford, Okla, July 9, 29. Educ: Port Neches High Sch, Tex; Southern Methodist Univ. Record producer for all maj labels, 56-72; written and/or produced for Duane Eddy, Nancy Sinatra, Frank Sinatra, Dean Martin, Elvis Presley, Waylon Jennings, Eddy Arnold. Co-wrote TV specials for Jose Feliciano, Lena Horne & others. Wrote and/or produced TV & films, 72-78. Recording artist, MCA Records, 80- *Songs:* The Fool; Houston (Going Back To); These Boots Are Made for Walking; Sugar Town; Summer Wine; Some Velvet Morning. *Scores:* Film/TV: The Sweet Ride; Tony Rome; The Moonshine War; Golden Spurs.

HAZZARD, PETER PEABODY   ASCAP 1971
composer, conductor, teacher
b Poughkeepsie, NY, Jan 31, 49. Educ: Millbrook Sch; Boston Univ; Berklee Col Music, BM(comp), 71; comp studies with John Bavicchi & William Maloof, cond studies with Jeronimus Kacinskas. Comp film scores & chamber & orchestral music. Fac mem, Berklee Col Music, Boston, 71-, chmn dept music hist & analysis, 78-, cond symphonic band. Conduct local civic orchs. Comp comn by, Metropolitan Wind Symph, Jacksonville State Univ Symphonic Band, Ala, Concord Band, Mass Inst Technol Concert Band & Reeds at Play Chamber Ens. *Instrumental Works:* Weird Sisters, Opus 9 (7 percussionists); Sonata No 2, Opus 23 (clarinet & marimba); Clarinet Quartet, Opus 15; Suite for English Horn, Opus 26 (English horn with string quartet); Concerto for Clarinet and Band, Opus 43; Children's Circus; A Festival Overture, Opus 40 (concert band); Canzona and Overture, Opus 27 (concert band). *Scores:* Laughing Till It Hurt (film biography of Charlie Chaplan); The Death of Faust, Opus 37 (cantata for 10, bass, SATB & band); Elegy, A Symphonic Portrait, Opus 47 (cantata for soprano, narrator, TTBB & band).

HEAGNEY, WILLIAM H   ASCAP 1926
composer, author, pianist
b Clinton, Mass, July 11, 1882; d New York, NY, July 14, 55. Educ: Pub schs. Led own orch. Staff comp, music publ firms. Music dir, light opera cos; mem, 2-piano team in vaudeville. Wrote stage scores. *Songs:* Roll Along, Kentucky

Moon; Tipperary Rose; Shadows in the Canebrake; Moon Over London; Just an Old Birthday Present.

HEARD, RICHARD MARTIN (RICHMOND DEVEREAUX)   ASCAP 1964
composer, author
b Little Rock, Ark, Dec 15, 36. Educ: Little Rock High Sch; Little Rock Jr Col; Univ Ark; USN Journalist Sch; Jochi Univ, Tokyo, BS(econ, world hist), 59; NY Univ Grad Sch. Pub relations, 62. Free lance songwriter, 62-67. Prof mgr, April-Blackwood Music, New York, 67-68. Founder & pres, Royal Am Records, Nashville, 68-71. Pres, Nashville Copyright Mgt, 68- Gen mgr, Metromedia Country Records, Nashville, 71-74. Co-founder, Blue Moon Music, 73. Vpres & gen mgr, GRT Records, Nashville, 74-78. Awards: Nashville Songwriter's Asn, 69; Producer of the Year, Soc Europ Stage Authors & Composers, 73; 25 ASCAP Awards. Chief Collabrs: Eddie Rabbitt, Van Trevor, Hank Hunter, Earl Conley, Mark Barkan, Jimbeau Hinson, Frank Slay, John Gluck, Bobby G Rice. *Songs:* Kentucky Rain; Smokey Mountain Memories; Lovin' on Borrowed Time; Indian Giver; You've Been So Good to Me; Abigail Beecher; Luziana River; The Whole World's Making Love Again Tonight; Make It Feel Like Love Again; All American Girl; A Woman's Kind of Love; The Sounds of Goodbye; Tears and Roses; The Bed; Souvenirs; A Letter a Day; When All the Clowns Go Home; Something Wonderful.

HEATH, BOBBY   ASCAP 1943
composer, author, pianist
b Philadelphia, Pa, Dec 1, 1889; d Philadelphia, Mar 3, 52. Accompanist in vaudeville, then vaudeville producer. *Songs:* My Pony Boy; You Never Can Be Too Sure About the Girls; In the Sweet Long Ago; Roll 'Em Girls; You Can't Cry Over My Shoulder.

HEATH, WALTER HENRY (HY)   ASCAP 1941
composer, author
b Oakville, Tenn, July 9, 1890; d Los Angeles, Calif, Apr 3, 65. Educ: Pub schs. Comedian in musical comedy, vaudeville, minstrel & burlesque shows; wrote spec material for traveling shows & comedy acts. Chief Collabrs: Fred Rose, Johnny Lange. *Songs:* Mule Train; Clancy Lowered the Boom; Somebody Bigger Than You and I; There'll Be No New Tunes on This Old Piano; Take These Chains From My Heart; The Little Red Fox; Loaded Pistol; Uncle Remus Said; The Covered Wagon Rolled Right Along; Benny the Beaver; Deacon Jones; Every Hour, Every Day; Be Goody Good Good to Me; I'll Never Stand in Your Way; Faithless Johnny Lee; Run Boy!; Jole John; Heartless Romance; I Gave My Wedding Dress Away; I Hope My Divorce Is Never Granted; When Johnny Toots His Horn; Up Jumped the Devil; Keep the Bible in Your Heart; Baby, Won't You Come Back Home; Bob and Joe Song Book (15 songs); St Patrick's Day Parade.

HEATON, WALLACE DUNGAN, JR   ASCAP 1953
composer, teacher, conductor
b Philadelphia, Pa, Jan 31, 14. Educ: Studied organ with Rollo F Maitland & theory with Henry Gordon Thunder; Philadelphia Musical Acad, MusB & MusM; Combs Col Music, MusD(hon). Organist, First Reformed Church, First Methodist Church & Messiah Lutheran Church, Philadelphia; organist, First & Central Presby Church, Wilmington, Del. Conductor, Choral Soc of Philadelphia & The Fortnightly Club. Dir music, Drexel Univ, Philadelphia, 45-79, cond 4 concert tours with Varsity Singers to Europe. *Songs:* Fanfare for Christmas; Captain Noah; Cantata: Great Among Nations; Music: God My King; Piece Heroique; Arr: Were You There?; Rock A My Soul. *Instrumental Works:* Arr: America the Beautiful (orch & chorus).

HEAVENER, DAVID B   ASCAP 1972
composer, author
b Louisville, Ky, Dec 22, 53. Educ: Jefferson Community Col, Ky. Songwriter, artist & record promoter. *Songs:* Tip Toe to the Gas Pumps; Taste of Love; Let the Music Play; Back in Ol' Mexico; Porter Waggoner and Sad Country Songs.

HEBERT, JOSEPH GILBERT, JR   ASCAP 1972
composer
b New Orleans, La, Mar 26, 40. Educ: Loyola Univ, New Orleans, BME; Manhattan Sch Music, MM; Univ Southern Miss, PhD. Prof musician, New York, 63-65; high sch band dir, 65-69; prof, Loyola Univ, 69- *Instrumental Works:* Vidac; Point on Point.

HECHT, KEN   ASCAP 1957
composer, author, comedy writer
b New York, NY, Dec 2, 14. Lyricist, comp & spec material writer, Vaughn Monroe, Desi Arnaz, Louis Armstrong, Russ Morgan, Ted Weems Orch, Red Buttons, Sammy Kaye Orch, Noro Morales Orch, Lisa Kirk, Harry Richman, Pinky Lee & others; music publ & record producer, Kenco Records; creator of "The Name Game," a newspaper feature, appearing in publ throughout US, Can, Australia, NZ & Eng, 76- Chief Collabrs: Leonard Whitcup, Sid Bass, Harry Revel. *Songs:* It's Eight O'Clock; It's Illegal, It's Immoral; Myrtle, the Amorous Turtle; The Second Tuesday in November Blues; French Pastry; Lyrics: No One Knows; Julida Polka; Polka Dot Polka; Merry Christmas Polka; When the Moon Bids the Sun Goodnight; Rum and Soda; Minnie the Moocher's Daughter.

HEFNER, KEITH   ASCAP 1958
composer, author
b Chicago, Ill, Jan 5, 29. Educ: Northwestern Univ, BS. *Songs:* Time for Fun; Finger Song; I Like to Fly; Safety Song.

HEFTI, NEAL PAUL   ASCAP 1953
composer, author
b Hastings, Nebr, Oct 29, 22. Educ: North High Sch, Omaha, Nebr; Juilliard Sch Music, trumpet studies with Jimmy Smith. Trumpeter high sch orch/band & Woody Herman Orch. Recording artist, New York & Los Angeles. Cond, CBS/ABC Network, NY. Film comp, Los Angeles. Chief Collabrs: J Mercer, S Styne, E Sheldon, S Cahn, B Troup, L Mattis, R Evans, J Livingston & D Black. *Songs:* Music: Barefoot in the Park; Cute; Duel at Diablo; Fred; Girl Talk; I Knew Jesus; Lonely Girl. *Instrumental Works:* Batman Theme; Coral Reef; Gotham City Municipal Swing Band; The Kid From Red Bank; Lil Darlin'; Plymouth Rock; Repetition; Why Not?. *Scores:* Film/TV: Harlow; How to Murder Your Wife; Last of the Red Hot Lovers; Sex and the Single Girl; Lord Love a Duck; Synanon; The Odd Couple; Oh Dad, Poor Dad; P J; Won Ton Ton-The Dog That Saved Hollywood; Boeing-Boeing.

HEIDER, FREDERICK HOLLAND   ASCAP 1952
composer, author
b Milwaukee, Minn, Apr 9, 17. Educ: Notre Dame Univ; Goodman Theatre, Chicago, Ill. TV show producer incl "Voice of Firestone", "Bell Telephone Hour", "Music for a Summer Night", "Miss America Pageant." Actor with Mercury & Globe Theatres. Author, "Superstitions" & "The Romance of Food." Chief Collabr: Carl Kress. *Songs:* Christmas Chopsticks; Train Out for Dreamland; We're in Love.

HEIFETZ, JASCHA   ASCAP 1937
violinist, composer
b Vilna, Russia, Feb 2, 01. Educ: Sch of Music, Vilna (entered at age 5, grad, age 9); St Petersburg Cons, studied with Leopold Auer; hon MusD, New York Col of Music & Northwestern Univ. First prof appearance at age 7; in concert, Berlin, 12, Carnegie Hall, New York, 17 & throughout world. To US, 17, citizen, 25. Recording artist with many records. Recipient, Comdr Legion of Honor, France. *Songs:* When You Make Love to Me; So Much in Love (written under pseudonym Jim Hoyl). *Instrumental Works:* Transc for violin & piano: El Puerto (Albeniz); Prelude (Bach); Sea-Murmurs (Castelnuovo-Tedesco); Beau Soir (Debussy); Hora Staccato (Dinicu); Humoreske (Dvorak); Jeanie With the Light Brown Hair (Foster); Alt-Wien (Godowsky); Sweet Remembrance (Mendelssohn); Estrellita (Little Stars) (Ponce); March (Prokofieff); Daisies (Rachmaninoff); Oriental Sketch (Rachmaninoff); The Bumble-Bee (Rimsky-Korsakoff); The Swan (Saint-Saens).

HEIFETZ, VLADIMIR   ASCAP 1962
composer, conductor, pianist
b Russia, Mar 28, 1893; d. Educ: St Petersburg Cons. Accompanist to Feodor Chaliapin on tour of Russia. Moved to US, 21. Orch cond, Schenley Theatre, Pittsburgh, Pa. Arr for Don Cossack Chorus. Cond, Heifetz Singers, appeared on radio; US tour, 35; fest, Israel, 52; Cantor's Concert Ens. Accompanist & arr, radio, TV & films. *Songs & Instrumental Works:* The New Era; The Golem (oratorio); Biblical Suite (piano); Cantatas: Yiddishe Legende; President Roosevelt's Message; Ani Yehudi; Lehern Mire. *Scores:* Opera: Pharaoh; Children's opera: Le Mizele Maizele; Film background: Potemkin; Green Fields.

HEIM, EMERY   ASCAP 1946
composer, conductor, arranger
b Budapest, Hungary, Feb 22, 06; d Hollywood, Calif, Aug 1, 46. Educ: Acad Music, Budapest. Wrote scores for musicals & films in Hungary. Moved to US, 39, citizen, 43; staff mem, Spec Services, USA, WW II. Scored films in Hollywood. *Songs:* Szabadkai Udvaron (off Hungarian army song); Time and Time Again; Don't Look At Me the Way You're Lookin'; My Ol' Ten Gallon Hat; Rather Do Without You, Baby; Down the Gypsy Trail; While the Music Plays On; Fighting Wild Cat March (off song, 81st Div); Give It Your Best (off song, 13th Armored Div).

HEIN, BEVERLY J (JAC)   ASCAP 1956
author, director, producer
b Hastings, Nebr, June 24, 20. Educ: High sch. Vocalist with orch, 38-41. USAF fighter & test pilot, World War II. Writer, radio shows & musical commercials, 45-49. Dir & prod, NBC-TV shows "Milton Berle Special", "Broadway Open House", "Dave Garroway Show", 49-59. Pres, production co, Cine-Dyne. Free-lance dir & producer. *Songs:* Midnight Breeze; Angelique.

HEIN, SILVIO   ASCAP 1914
composer, conductor
b New York, NY, Mar 15, 1879; d Saranac Lake, NY, Dec 19, 28. One of 9 founders, charter mem, dir, ASCAP, 14-28. Chief Collabrs: George V Hobart, E Ray Goetz, A Seymour Brown, Harry B Smith. *Songs:* Don't Be What You Ain't; All Dressed Up and No Place to Go; Arab Love Song; He's a Cousin of Mine; Some Little Bug; Old Man Noah; Hottentot Love Song; 'Twas in September; I Love the Last One the Best of All; Heart of My Heart; I Adore

the American Girl; My Queen Bee. *Scores:* Bway Shows: Moonshine; The Boys and Betty; The Yankee Girl; A Matinee Idol; When Dreams Come True; Flo Flo; Look Who's Here.

HEINDORF, RAY JOHN ASCAP 1945
composer, arranger, conductor
b Haverstraw, NY, Aug 25, 08; d. Educ: Troy Cons. *Songs:* Some Sunday Morning; I'm in a Jam; Some Sunny Day; Hollywood Canteen; Melancholy Rhapsody; Pete Kelly's Blues; Sugarfoot. *Scores:* Films: Yankee Doodle Dandy (Acad Award, 42); This Is the Army (Acad Award, 43); Hollywood Canteen; Up in Arms; Rhapsody in Blue; Wonder Man; Night and Day; Romance on the High Seas; Look for the Silver Lining; The West Point Story; Young Man With a Horn; The Jazz Singer; Calamity Jane; A Star Is Born; The Music Man (Acad Award, 63).

HEINZ, JOHN F ASCAP 1955
author
b Allentown, Pa, Feb 16, 26. Educ: Phillips Andover Acad; Lehigh Univ; Brown Univ, BA; Univ Pa, LLB. Ensign, USN, overseas in World War II. Advert writer, joined Bethlehem Steel Co, 53; author of weekly column in Call-Chronicle, Allentown, Pa. Chief Collabr: Robert Lissauer. *Songs:* Lie Detector; High Steel.

HEISS, JOHN C ASCAP 1974
composer, flutist, conductor
b New York, NY, Oct 23, 38. Educ: Pvt study flute with Hosmer & Lora, 54-62; Lehigh Univ, BA(math), 60; Aspen Music Sch, comp with Milhaud & flute with Tipton, 62 & 63; Columbia Univ, grad studies in music & comp with Luening & Beeson; Princeton Univ, MFA(music), 67, comp with Babbitt, Cone & Kim. Comp & flutist, 60-; works performed in US & abroad in all instrumental & vocal media; recitals & free-lance perf, incl Boston Symph, ballet & opera; principal flutist with Boston Musica Viva, 69-74. Wrote articles on contemporary perf techniques & on Stravinsky; wrote article on multiphonics for flute, "Perspectives of New Music", 66. Mem Bd: Kodaly Musical Training Inst; Collage; Nat Flute Asn. Works Premiered: Speculum Musicae; Collage; Boston Musica Viva; Da Capo Chamber Players; Aeolian Chamber Players; Tanglewood Fest. Awards: Guggenheim Found; Nat Inst Arts & Letters; NEA; Rockefeller Found; Fromm Found. Teacher. Chief Collabrs: Comp & Cond: Gunther Schuller, Milton Babbitt, Elliott Carter, Otto Luening, Earl Kim, Joseph Schwantner, David Stock, Henry Brant, Mario Davidovsky, Betsy Jolas, Barbara Kolb, Donald Martino, Benjamin Zander, David Gilbert; Flutists: Doriot Anthony Dwyer, James Pappoutsakis, Fenwick Smith, Lois Schaefer, Paul Fried, Paul Dunkel, Harvey Sollberger, Patricia Spencer. *Songs:* Music: Songs of Nature; From Infinity Full Circle. *Instrumental Works:* Four Short Pieces for Piano; Four Lyric Pieces for Solo Flute; Four Short Pieces for Orchestra; Five Pieces for Flute and Cello; Four Movements for Three Flutes; Quartet for Flute, Clarinet, Cello and Piano; Inventions, Contours and Colors; Capriccio (flute, clarinet & perc); Chamber Concerto; Eloquy; Etudes for Flute Solo. *Songs & Instrumental Works:* Three Choral Songs.

HELBIG, OTTO H ASCAP 1960
composer, author, conductor
b New Haven, Conn, Oct 28, 14. Educ: Yale Univ Sch of Music; Columbia Univ, MA, EdD; studied with Richard Donovan, David Smith, Hugo Kortschak. Field artillery, World War II. Violinist, symph orchs; cond, Trenton State Orch. Instr & dir of bands, Kamehameha Schs, Honolulu. Assoc prof of music, Trenton State Col, 49- *Instrumental Works:* Concert band works: Introduction and Tango; Prelude and Beguine; Short Piece for Band.

HELFER, WALTER ASCAP 1941
composer, educator
b Lawrence, Mass, Sept 30, 1896; d New Rochelle, NY, Apr 16, 59. Educ: Harvard Univ, BA; Columbia Univ, MA; studied with Stuart Mason, George Cassuade & Ottorino Respighi; Endicott Prize, New Eng Cons; fellowship, Am Acad Rome. WW I, Signal Corps, AEF. Language teacher, Mitchell Mil Sch, Lowell, Mass, 22-24; dir music, Deane Sch, Santa Barbara, 24-25; asst prof, Hunter Col, 29, asst prof, Hunter Col, 29, assoc prof, 39, dept chmn, 38-50. Mem, Adv Comt Music, Fulbright Div, Inst of Int Educ, Soc for Publ Am Music; Academia Nac de Artes y Letras, Havana. *Songs & Instrumental Works:* Nocturne for Piano; String Quartet in G; Appassionata for Violin, Piano; Elegiac Sonata (piano); Soliloquy (cello, piano); In Modo Giocoso (orch); Fantasy on Children's Tune; Water Idyl; Prelude to "A Midsummer Night's Dream" (Paderewski Prize); Concertino Eligiaco.

HELFMAN, MAX ASCAP 1957
composer, author, educator
b Poland May 25, 01; d Dallas, Tex, Aug 9, 63. Educ: David Mannes Music Col; Curtis Inst; studied with Rosario Scarelo & Fritz Reiner. To US in 09. Cond, Temple Emanuel, Paterson, NJ, 26-39, Temple B'nai Abraham, Newark, 40-53, Bach-Handel Soc, Westfield, 39-43 & People's Philh Chorus, 37-49. Music dir, Brandeis Youth Found, 44-61, Temple Sinai, Los Angeles, Calif, 54-57, Hillel Found, Univ Calif, Los Angeles, Univ Southern Calif, 54-59 & Hebrew Congregation, DC, 58-62. On fac, Hebrew Union Col, Sch Sacred Music, NY, 49-52. Founder, Dean Col of Fine Arts, Univ Judaism, 61. Chief Collabr: Norman Corwin. *Songs:* Music: Grant Us Peace; O Merciful God; May the Words; Voice of My Beloved; Set Me As a Seal Upon Thy Heart; Ana Dodi;

Lady With the Lamp; Music for a Mourner's Service (collection); Ahavat Olam; Haben Yakirli; Kedusha; Areshes; Uv'Shofar Gadol; Shabat M'Nuchah (Friday Evening Service). *Songs & Instrumental Works:* Shabbat Kodesh; Aron Hakodesh; Sh'ma-Kolenu; Ani Maamin; Song of Dedication; Od Chai; Brandeis College of Israeli Songs; Brandeis Friday Service; 2 Hana Senesh Songs; New Exodus (Naye Hagade; chorus); B'rosh Hashono; Maoz Tzur; Main Rue Platz; Yism'Chu. *Scores:* Ballet: Benjamin III (choral). *Albums:* Passover Melodies; Magic of Max Helfman.

HELLER, ALFRED E ASCAP 1964
composer, conductor, pianist
b New York, NY, Dec 8, 31. Educ: Syracuse Univ, BM(magna cum laude), 52, studied comp with Ernst Bacon; Manhattan Sch of Music, MM, 54, studied piano with Robert Goldsand; Fulbright scholarship, Rome Opera, studied conducting with Luigi Ricci, 54; Ind Univ, DM, 74, studied conducting with Tibor Kozma. Works performed throughout world; protege of Heitor Villa-Lobos. Cond, symph concerts in Budapest, Riga, Kazan & NC, opera in Linz & Venice, shows in New York, Ohio, Fla & Mich. Accompanist for Jan Peerce, John Brownlee, Avon Long & Frank Guarrera. Chief Collabrs: Sarah Anderson, George Patterson. *Songs:* Music: Reach Out to Me; A New Home for Art; & 2 Heine songs. *Instrumental Works:* Petit Bourgeois (incidental music); Symphony No 3.

HELLER, JOEL HARRISON ASCAP 1971
composer, author
b New York, NY, July 5, 31. Educ: Syracuse Univ, MS(sci TV prog). With CBS news, 24 yrs, exec producer, Broadcasting News Dept, 10 yrs. Wrote words to theme, "In the Know"; co-author music to theme, "In the News." Chief Collabr: Eugene Cines.

HELLER, ROBERTA
See Rosenthal, Roberta (Heller)

HELLER, WILLIAM CLARKE ASCAP 1978
composer, author, producer
b New York, NY, July 13, 51. Educ: New Sch, studied music. Bass player, sev rock & rhythm & blues recording acts. Assignment writer, E B Marks Music. Formed publ pro-duction co, Canove Music, Inc, with Ron Carran, Bob Held &, Richie Taninbaum. Wrote songs for "Don't Go in the House." Chief Collabr: Bob Held. *Songs:* Late Night Surrender; What You Won't Do for Love; This Night Is Ecstasy. *Scores:* Film/TV: A Matter of Love; Hot T-Shirts.

HELLERMAN, FRED (FRED BROOKS, ASCAP 1960
PAUL CAMPBELL)
composer, author, singer
b Brooklyn, NY, May 13, 27. Educ: Brooklyn Col, BA; Columbia Univ. Co-founder & mem, The Weavers, 48-63; record producer, "Alice's Restaurant"; recording artist. Chief Collabrs: Norman Gimbel, Fran Minkoff. *Songs:* I'm Just a Country Boy; I Never Will Marry; Music: The Honeywind Blows; Come Away Melinda. *Scores:* Film: Lovin' Molly (film); Bway Show: New Faces of '68.

HELMS, JAMES HERMAN ASCAP 1968
composer
b Norfolk, Va, Sept 14, 33. Educ: San Diego High Sch; San Diego State Col, BA(Span), 57; Univ Calif, Los Angeles, 58-60, guitar studies with Howard Roberts. Studio/film work, 8 yrs; guitarist & arr with Rod McKuen, 64-67. *Songs:* Music: Midnight Train. *Instrumental Works:* Quintet for Electric Guitar and String Quartet; Music for Flute and Cello Octet. *Scores:* Kung Fu (TV series).

HELMS, NORMA HALE (NORMA GREEN) ASCAP 1967
author
b Manhattan, NY. Educ: Univ Md; Univ Chicago. Lyrics for film scores incl, "Straight Time" & "The Old Man's Place," also lyrics for commercials. Chief Collabrs: Mitch Bottler, Charles M Jones, Ken Hirsch. *Songs:* Lyrics: Saturday Night/Sunday Morning; Cold; Color of Snow; Soon as I Touched Him.

HEMMENT, MARGUERITE ESTHER ASCAP 1964
composer, author
b Carlyle, Ill, Apr 19, 08. Educ: Wis Sch Music, studied violin at age 8; high sch; Wash Univ, pub health courses; Univ Wis Ext, jour course. Worked in health field, but always experimented with music & writing. Began "Puppetunes" in 77; wrote musical puppet plays & sketches. *Songs:* Measures to Health; Lion and Mouse Melodies; Grandma for Rent.

HEMMER, EUGENE ASCAP 1962
composer, educator
b Cincinnati, Ohio, Mar 23, 29; d. Educ: Cincinnati Col Music, BM, MM, studied with Felix Labunski. Chmn, Music Dept, Chadwick Sch, Rolling Hills, Calif. Awards: 3 Hartford Found; MacDowell Col; 2 Dumler, Comp of the Yr twice, Ohioanna Lib Asn. Hon mem, Liberal Soc Comp Tokyo. *Instrumental Works:* The School Bus (comn by Thor Johnson for Cincinnati Symph); Introduction and Dance (2 pianos); American Miniatures (piano); Remembrance of Things Present (2 pianos).

HENDERSON, CHARLES E   ASCAP 1931
composer, author, conductor
b Boston, Mass, Jan 19, 07; d Laguna Beach, Calif, Mar 7, 70. Educ: Roxbury Latin Sch; Harvard Univ, BA(cum laude), studied with Walter Piston, Ernst Toch & Victor Bay. Pianist-arr-vocal arr for orchs, musicals & radio; comp-arr-music dir, film studios, also TV producer, 49-51. Created & cond Las Vegas nightclub acts; writer of spec material. Author "How to Sing for Money." Chief Collabs: Francis Ballard, Rudy Vallee, Tom Waring, Edward Heyman, Mack Gordon, Alfred Newman. *Songs:* Deep Night; So Beats My Heart for You; Carefree; This Is a Chance of a Lifetime; Hold Me in Your Arms.

HENDERSON, (JAMES) FLETCHER   ASCAP 1948
composer, conductor, arranger
b Cuthbert, Ga, Dec 18, 1897; d New York, NY, Dec 29, 52. Educ: Atlanta Univ. To NY, 20; pianist in WC Handy Orch; then with Black Swan Records. Toured as accompanist to Ethel Waters. Led own band in nightclubs, theatres. Made many records. Arr for orchs incl Isham Jones, Dorsey Bros, Benny Goodman. Pianist in Goodman Orch, 39. Reformed orch, 44; orch arr, 46. Led orch & sextet, 50. *Songs & Instrumental Works:* Stampede; It's Wearing Me Down; No, Baby, No; Down South Camp Meeting; Wrapping It Up; Bumble Bee Stomp. *Scores:* Stage: The Jazz Train.

HENDERSON, HAZEL JUANITA   ASCAP 1979
composer, author, singer
b Corsicana, Tex, Nov 1, 29. Educ: Long Beach Community Col, AA, studied piano with Willard McDaniels, 7 yrs. Began piano study at age 6. Church musician at age 12. Organized several singing groups, incl gospel singing group, Major Maker Chorale, perf on local TV. Writer & dir for church choir, 52- Recording artist. *Songs:* He Giveth; Bring Back the Joy of My Salvation; Heaven, Heaven, Heaven; Who Is This Man Called Jesus; God Is Moving; 'Pete' the Parakeet; Illusion; Funny Situation.

HENDERSON, HORACE W   ASCAP 1950
composer, author, bandleader
b Cuthbert, Ga, Nov 23, 14; d. Educ: Atlanta Univ; Wilberforce Univ, BA. With Wilberforce Univ band, 30's. Pianist & arr, Fletcher Henderson. Arr, Charlie Barnet Band & Jimmy Dorsey. Pianist, Lena Horne, 4 yrs, Billy Holiday & Catalina Island Band, summers, 60's. Cond, Broadmore Hotel, Colorado Springs, Colo, 4 yrs. Under contract, Columbia OK Records. Living alumni, Newport Jazz Fest, New York. Cut 2000 ft of tape for History of Am Music, Smithsonian Inst. *Instrumental Works:* Christopher Columbus; Big John's Special.

HENDERSON, JOSEPH RAYMOND   ASCAP 1963
composer, author, vocal coach
b Charleston, WVa, Dec 30, 29. Educ: Univ Southern Calif; studied with Lillian Steuber, Ernst Toch & Benjamin Britten. Exchange prof comp, Cons Moscow, worked with Shastokovich, Khatchaturian, Kabalevski. Chief Collabs: Christopher Isherwood, Burgess Meredith, Charles Laughton, Carroll O'Connor, Dory Previn, Rod McKuen, Ray Bradbury, James Thurber. *Songs:* The Dog Beneath the Skin; Music: The Wonderful O. *Scores:* Bway Show: Winter Quarters; Film/TV: Happy Anniversary 2116.

HENDERSON, LUTHER, JR   ASCAP 1956
composer, conductor, pianist
b Kansas City, Mo, Mar 14, 19. Educ: Juilliard Sch. Pianist in var orchs incl Leonard Ware, Mercer Ellington. Pianist & music dir for Lena Horne, 47-50. Writer of special material. Appeared on TV; recording artist. Arr, Bway musicals "Do Re Mi" & "Funny Girl." *Songs:* Hold On; Solitaire; Ten Good Years.

HENDERSON, PATRICK   ASCAP 1973
composer, author, singer
b Dallas, Tex, Jan 15, 49. Educ: Joseph J Rhoades Elementary Sch; Franklin D Roosevelt High Sch; Southern Conn State Teachers Col; Bishop Col, Tex. Church organist, 68- Pianist, Leon Russell Band, 73-75 & Nils Lofgren Band, 76-77. A&R Dept staff producer, Warner Brothers Records. Chief Collabrs: Mike McDonald, Al Jarreau, Gary Wright. *Songs:* Open Your Eyes; Lay It on the Line; Fall in Love Again; Heart of Fire; Music: Real Love.

HENDERSON, RAY   ASCAP 1923
composer, author, pianist
b Buffalo, NY, Dec 1, 1896; d Greenwich, Conn, Dec 31, 70. Educ: Chicago Cons. Pianist in dance bands; also arr with New York publ cos, in vaudeville. In 25, joined B G DeSylva & Lew Brown as song writing team & music publ. Sold publ firm, 29; went to Hollywood under contract to 20th Century Fox; film biography, "The Best Things in Life Are Free." Publ & producer. Dir, ASCAP, 42-51. Chief Collabs: Mort Dixon, Sam Lewis, Joe Young, Billy Rose, Bud Green, Ted Koehler, Jack Yellen, Irving Caesar. *Songs:* That Old Gang of Mine; Alabamy Bound; Don't Bring Lulu; Five Foot Two, Eyes of Blue; I'm Sitting on Top of the World; Too Many Parties and Too Many Pals; Lucky Day; Birth of the Blues; Black Bottom; Bye Bye Blackbird; It All Depends on You; Manhattan Mary; The Best Things in Life Are Free; Good News; The Varsity Drag; Just Imagine; Lucky in Love; Broken Hearted; Just a Memory; So Blue; I'm on the Crest of a Wave; You're the Cream in My Coffee; Button Up Your Overcoat; You Wouldn't Fool Me, Would You?; Sonny Boy; Together; My Sin;

I'm a Dreamer, Aren't We All?; Sunny Side Up; If I Had a Talking Picture of You; Little Pal; Without Love; Thank Your Father; Red Hot Chicago; You Try Somebody Else; My Song; The Thrill Is Gone; Life Is Just a Bowl of Cherries; This Is the Missus; Strike Me Pink; Say When; When Love Comes Swinging Along; My Lucky Star; Oh You Nasty Man; My Dog Loves Your Dog; Hold My Hand; Why Did I Kiss That Girl?; If I Had a Girl Like You; Bam Bam Bamy Shore; Animal Crackers in My Soup; When I Grow Up; Life Begins At Sweet Sixteen; Love Songs Are Made in the Night.

HENDERSON, SKITCH   ASCAP 1958
composer, arranger, pianist
b Halstad, Minn, Jan 27, 18. Educ: Univ Calif; Juilliard; studied with Malcolm Frost, Roger Aubert, Albert Coates, Fritz Reiner & Arnold Schoenberg. Pianist in dance bands, then theatre orchs, films & radio on WCoast. Accompanist to Judy Garland on tour. Served, USAF, WW II. Music dir radio, Bing Crosby. Toured with own dance band, 47-49. Music dir TV, "Tonight," 61- Music dir, "Street Scene" (New York opera). Guest cond, symph orchs incl New York Philh & London Philh. Made many records. *Instrumental Works:* Skitch's Blues; Minuet on the Rocks; Skitch in Time; Come Thursday; Curacao. *Scores:* TV background: American Fantasy; Film background: Act One.

HENDLER, HERB   ASCAP 1948
author
b Philadelphia, Pa, June 17, 18. Educ: West Philadelphia High Sch; Bullis Naval Acad Prep Sch; Univ Southern Calif; NY Univ. Dir A&R, RCA Victor. Mgr, Ralph Flanagan & Buddy Morrow Orchs. Admin asst to pres, Warner Bros Records; vpres, Beechwood Music Corp, Capitol Records, Inc. Co-producer, "Rock Carmen." Now playwright, Roundhouse, London, Eng. Chief Collabrs: Jerry Gray, Ralph Flanagan, Buddy Morrow, Michael Hughes, Doug Arthur, Henri Rene. *Songs:* Lyrics: Hot Toddy; The Kid's a Dreamer; The Magic Tree. *Scores:* Musical Show Lyrics: Rock Carmen; Hashbury.

HENDRICKS, FREDERICK WILMOTH   ASCAP 1957
(WILMOUTH HOUDINI)
composer, author
b Port of Spain, Trinidad, BWI, Nov 25, 01; d New York, NY, Aug 6, 73. Educ: St Mary's Col of the Immaculate Conception, Trinidad. To US in 17. Brought calypso music to US. Since 25 had been recording in US. *Songs:* Stone Cold Dead in the Market; Johnny Take My Wife; Gin and Cocoanut Water; The Calypso Way; Don't Do That to Me. *Songs & Instrumental Works:* Welcome of There Majesty; Harlem Alley Cat; Million Dollar Pair of Feet; Married Life in Harlem; Hot Dogs Made Their Name.

HENDRICKS, JON CARL   ASCAP 1956
composer, author, singer
b Newark, Ohio, Sept 16, 21. Educ: Univ Toledo. Performer in radio, 29. Served, WW II. Sang in Europe; had own vocal quartet. Went to New York, 52. Mem vocal team, Lambert, Hendricks & Ross; later Lambert, Hendricks & Bavan. Formed new group, Jon Hendricks & Co, 64. Made many records. *Songs:* I Want You to Be My Baby; Don't Get Scared; Minor Catastrophe; Four Brothers; The Duck; Hi-Fly; Moanin'; Night in Tunisia; One Note Samba; I'll Die Happy; Desafinado; Gimme That Wine.

HENDRICKS, WILLIAM L   ASCAP 1965
composer, author
b Grand Prairie, Tex, May 3, 04. Writer & producer films & cartoons, Warner Brothers; lyric & music song writer for films. Chief Collabrs: Heinz Roemheld, William Lava, Buzz Adlam, Denny Gould. *Songs:* Lyrics: Happy Song; That's US in the USA; Vaya Con Dios, Amigo; Roadrunner Theme; Speedy's Fiesta; Winter Song; Speedy's Mariachi Band; Paris Je T'aime; Hollywood!; also lyrics for three short films.

HENDRIKS, FRANCIS MILTON   ASCAP 1949
composer, pianist, educator
b New York, NY, Nov 20, 1881; d Santa Monica, Calif, Feb 3, 69. Educ: Studied music with Mademoiselle Schubert, Leopold Godowsky & Hugo Kaun; Denver Col Music, MA. Recitals in Belgium, Eng, France, Italy & Spain. Dir of piano, Scott Sch Music, Wolcott Cons & Denver Col Music. Adv to music group & dir, Civic Music Guild, Santa Monica. *Songs:* Resignation; Flieder. *Instrumental Works:* 4 Preludes; 12 Etudes; Spanish Dances; Piano Concerto; Distant Bells; Suite in 4 Movements; Piano Sonata; Eight Preludes for Piano; Eighty-six Symmetrically Inverted Studies for Piano; The Jester, Sketch for Piano; Sonata for Piano, Opus 59 (3 movements); A Sicilian Spring, Opus 35 (22 page Legend for medium voice & piano); The Night-Bird Song (vocal; high in B, medium in G); Prelude in A Major (violin); Prelude in A Major (cello); Serenade Espagnole (violin & cello); Five Tone Pictures; Four Preludes; Concert Etude in B Flat Minor; Dances Esthetiques: Tristess de la Lune; Exotic Fragrance; Fate; Sunbeams; For Piano: Danse Bizarre; Intermezzo, Opus 39, No 1; Caravan; Berceuse, Opus 40; Vieux Rondel, Opus 40; Pages Fugitives; Fantoches, Opus 38; Fete Galante, Opus 36; Drifting Clouds, Opus 32; Forest Legend, Opus 30; Valse Caprice; In Autumn; Caprice in Double Notes; Valse Arabesque; Octave Etude in F; Twelve Etudes; Dreams to Remember (4 solos for piano); Cloches dans la Brume.

HENIGBAUM, NANCY (HONEYTREE) ASCAP 1973
composer, author, singer
b Davenport, Iowa, Apr 11, 52. Began writing gospel songs in 70, recorded first album, 73. With Word Records, Waco, Tex, have recorded six albums. Toured US, Ger, Eng, Wales, Can, NZ & Australia. Guitarist. *Songs:* Clean Before My Lord; I Don't Have to Worry; Live for Jesus; Searchlight; Heaven's Gonna Be a Blast.

HENN, RICHARD A ASCAP 1969
composer, teacher
b Santa Monica, Calif, Oct 31, 46. Educ: Mt St Marys Col, Los Angeles, BMus(comp); Calif Inst of Arts. Began as a drummer in grammar sch. Arr & comp for stars, incl Helen Reddy. Scored 5 feature films & 2 short films. Cond & comp, Fest of Arts, Laguna Beach, Calif, 2 yrs. Record producer. Cond, Prague Radio Symph for movie proj. *Songs:* I Live for the Sun; Andrea.

HENNAGIN, MICHAEL ASCAP 1965
composer, music professor
b The Dalles, Ore, Sept 27, 36. Educ: Aspen Music Sch, study with Darius Milhaud, 60-61; Tanglewood, study with Aaron Copland, 63; Curtis Inst of Music, BM, 63. Comp & orchr for motion pictures & TV, 57-65; music dir, Lester Horton Dance Theatre, Los Angeles, Calif, 58-60; comp-in-residence, Detroit Pub Schs, 65-66; prof music, Emporia State Univ, Kans, 69-72; prof music, Univ Okla, Norman, 72- *Instrumental Works:* Jubilee (symphonic band); Dance Scene (symphonic band); Sonata (piano). *Songs & Instrumental Works:* Walking on the Green Grass; The Unknown; The Family of Man; The House on the Hill; Psalm 23; Five Children's Songs; Three Emily Dickinson Songs; By the Roadside; Under the Greenwood Tree; Hosanna.

HENNINGER, GEORGE R ASCAP 1947
composer, conductor, organist
b Binghamton, NY, Mar 11, 1895; d West Hempstead, NY, Dec 28, 53. Educ: Univ Pittsburgh; studied music with Dudley Fitch & James Ford. Music dir & organist in theatres & radio, St Petersburg, Fla; free-lance organist, New York, 36; on ABC staff; dir, "Ladies Be Seated" & "Ethel and Albert." *Songs:* Old Prairie Wagon; Little Darlin'; God Is Everywhere; In Suniland; In Flanders; Sunset Lullabye; Our Graduation Waltz; St Patrick's Bells. *Scores:* Film background: Chloe; Hired Wife; Playthings of Desire.

HENRY, CAROL M ASCAP 1979
composer, author, pianist
b Newark, NJ, July 8, 28. Educ: Juilliard, BS(piano), 51; Sarah Lawrence Col, MFA(theatre), 69; studied music comp with Meyer Kupferman. Pianist/comp, Medicine Show Theater Ens, Margot Colbert Dance Co; founder, choreographer, dir/pianist, The Innermost Soc (Inter-media Theatre Co). Music therapist & teacher. *Songs:* I'll Always Want You Near; Lyrics: Day Dreams; Music: Even if it Breaks My Heart.

HENRY, CHEVON C ASCAP 1978
composer, author, singer
b Kingston, Jamaica, Dec 16, 53. Educ: Taft High Sch; York Col; self-taught musician (12 instruments). First TV perf, Jamaica, 71. Performer with band, Chevon & Flagstone, clubs & cols. Several TV shows, US. Recording artist, Jay Bird Records, several recordings. *Songs:* I've Made It to Broadway; Disco Island Lady; A Reggae Rock; Isn't There a Place?; Farewell, My Lovely.

HENRY, FRANCIS ASCAP 1948
composer, author, guitarist
b London, Ont, Jan 5, 05; d New York, NY, Jan 25, 53. To US, 23, citizen, 38. Educ: Pub schs. Guitarist, Guy Lombardo Orch, 21 yrs, Ray Miller Orch & Isham Jones Orch. *Songs:* Little Girl; Ain't It a Shame; Granada Stomp; Sugar Bun.

HENRY, MICHAEL EARL ASCAP 1973
composer author, teacher
b Springfield, Ohio, Mar 17, 42. Educ: Anderson Col, BA, 67; Wright State Univ, MA, 73; Wittenberg Univ Sch of Music. Taught language arts, pub schs, Clark County & Springfield, Ohio. Mem, local & state pub teachers prof orgn. *Songs:* Free At Last; He's the One; There Is a Name; Jesus, Savior, Lord Divine; Love; Hiding Place.

HENRY, S R
See Stern, Henry

HENRY, WILL
See Davies, William Henry

HENSLEY, HAROLD GLENN ASCAP 1965
composer, author, teacher
b Whitetop, Va, July 3, 22. Educ: Los Angeles Cons Music; Los Angeles Valley Col. Musician radio, theaters, auditoriums, TV & Grand Ole Opry, Nashville; also TV films & 73 movies, Hollywood. Chief Collabrs: Hal Southern, Hank Penny & Merle Travis. *Songs:* You'll Find Her Name Written There; Boodle Dee Beep; Lyrics: Muskrat.

HENSON, JAMES MAURY
puppeteer, television producer
b Greenville, Miss, Sept 24, 36. Educ: Univ Md, BA, 60. Creator, The Muppets, 54; producer, Sam and Friends, Wash, 55-61; puppeteer, Rowlf on Jimmy Dean Show, New York, 63-66; numerous TV guest appearances & creator numerous TV commercials; creator, Sesame Street Muppets, 69- & Muppet Show, 76-; producer, The Muppet Movie, 79; producer & dir TV shows. Pres, Henson Assocs. Pres & bd dirs, Am Ctr of Union Internationale de la Marionnette, 74- Rec'd Emmy Award for Best Entertainment Prog, Wash, 58; Emmy Award for Outstanding Individual Achievement in Children's Programming, 73-74 & 75-76; Entertainer of Year Award, Am Guild Variety Artists, 76; TV Acad Award, 78. Mem: Puppeteers of Am (pres, 62-63); Am Fedn TV & Radio Artists; Dirs Guild Am; Writers Guild; Nat Acad TV Arts & Sci; Screen Actors Guild.

HENSON, NORRIS CHRISTY ASCAP 1961
composer, saxophonist, producer
b College Park, Ga, Dec 25, 18. Educ: US Sch of Aeronautics, Memphis. Saxophonist with dance orch. Formed own dance group. Served, ATC, World War II. A&R dir for record co. *Songs:* Eight, Skeight an' Donate. *Albums:* Confession; Ballads Blues and Boleros; King of Ivories.

HERBERT, FREDERICK ASCAP 1953
lyricist
b New York, NY, June 4, 09; d Encino, Calif, Sept 2, 66. Educ: Pub Sch No 46, New York; DeWitt Clinton High Sch; NY Univ; studied piano & music theory with L Leslie Loth. Cub reporter on The New York Times, 27-29. Music ed & lyricist, 20th Century-Fox, MGM, Universal Int & Revue Productions. Supvr of post production & lyricist, Universal Studios. Comp, musical cues for TV series incl "The Virginian", "Wagon Train", "G E Theatre", "Cimarron City", "Checkmate", "M-Squad" & others. Chief Collabrs: Arnold Hughes (Schwarzwald), Milton Rosen, Frank Skinner, Dimitri Tiomkin, Henry Mancini. *Songs:* Lyrics: Magnificent Obsession; The World in His Arms; The Thrill of It All; Meet Me At the Fair; Man Without a Star; Laramie; Headin' Home; Empty Arms; The Far Country; True Love; Time for Love; Hop on the Band Wagon; Handle With Care; Settle Down; Drift Along; Black Angus McDougal.

HERBERT, HERBIE
See Swartz, Herbert

HERBERT, JEAN ASCAP 1935
composer, author
b New York, NY, Mar 8, 05. Educ: Princeton Univ; Juilliard Sch; Casey Jones Sch of Aeronautics. Writer, special material for singers, songs for Bway revues. Chief Collabrs: James Hanley, Billy Rose. *Songs:* Blue Dawn; Let's Dream Again; Ridin' on a Rainbow; Love, Honor and Oh Baby; Gotta See a Man About His Daughter; Clover Blossoms; Too Busy Makin' Money.

HERBERT, VICTOR ASCAP 1914
composer, conductor, cellist
b Dublin, Ireland, Feb 1, 1859; d New York, NY, May 26, 24. Educ: Stuttgart Cons; studied with Bernhard Cossman & Max Seifriz. Cellist in symph orchs, Ger & Austria, also with Court Orch of Stuttgart, 5 yrs. To US in 1886, as a mem of Metropolitan Opera pit orch; cellist symph orchs of Theodore Thomas & Anton Seidl. Cond, 22nd NY Nat Guard Band & Pittsburgh Symph, 1898-04; own orch, 04. One of 9 founders, charter mem, dir, vpres, ASCAP, 14-24. Wrote songs for "Ziegfeld Follies," 21, 23; comp first original background film score for "The Fall of a Nation." Chief Collabrs: Harry B Smith, Robert B Smith, Glen MacDonough, Ride Johnson Young, Henry Blossom, B G DeSylva, Al Dubin, Stanley Adams. *Songs:* Romany Life; Gypsy Love Song; I Can't Do the Sum; Go to Sleep, Slumber Deep; March of the Toys; Toyland; Absinthe Frappe; Al Fresco; Kiss Me Again; I Want What I Want When I Want It; When You're Pretty and the World Is Fair; Every Day Is Ladies Day With Me; The Streets of New York; Moonbeams; Because You're You; Tramp! Tramp! Tramp!; 'Neath the Southern Moon; Italian Street Song; I'm Falling in Love With Someone; Ah! Sweet Mystery of Life; To the Land of My Own Romance; Sweethearts; Every Lover Must Meet His Fate; Pretty as a Picture; When You're Away; Neapolitan Love Song; Thine Alone; The Irish Have a Great Day Tonight; A Kiss in the Dark; I Might Be Your Once-in-a-While; Yesterthoughts; Indian Summer; My Dream Girl. *Songs & Instrumental Works:* Cello Concerto in E; Irish Rhapsody. *Scores:* Bway Shows: The Wizard of the Nile; The Serenade; The Fortune Teller; The Singing Girl; Babes in Toyland; It Happened in Nordland; Wonderland; Mademoiselle Modiste; The Red Mill; Dream City and the Magic Knight; Little Nemo; The Prima Donna; Old Dutch; Naughty Marietta; The Enchantress; The Lady of the Slipper; Sweethearts; The Madcap Duchess; The Only Girl; The Princess Pat; The Century Girl; Eileen; The Velvet Lady; Angel Face; My Golden Girl; The Girl in the Spotlight; Orange Blossoms; The Dream Girl.

HERBSLEB, CATHERINE (CATHY O'SHEA) ASCAP 1978
composer, author, singer
b Kansas City, Mo, July 20, 41. Educ: East Los Angeles Jr Col; Calif State Col, Los Angeles. Singer, nightclubs, concerts & TV; recording artist. *Songs:* Broken Dolls Need Love Too.

HERBSTRITT, LARRY W ASCAP 1975
composer, singer
b Coudersport, Pa, July 4, 50. Educ: Mansfield State Col; Berklee Col Music, Boston. Chief Collabrs: Gary Harju, Steve Dorff & Basil Temchatin. *Songs:* Easy Love; Music: I Just Fall in Love Again; Fire in the Morning; Dancin' Like Lovers; Cowboys and Clowns.

HEREDIA, RENE CORTES ASCAP 1977
composer, teacher, concert guitarist
b Granada, Spain, Jan 27, 39. Educ: High sch; studied guitar with Sabicas, Jose Heredia & Miguel Garcia, Spain. Started guitar at age 10; mem, La Familia Heredia, gypsy dancers from Granada, age 13 to 17; first guitarist, Carmen Amaya Ballet, 4 yrs & Jose Greco Ballet, 2 seasons; concert flamenco guitar soloist, 65- *Instrumental Works:* Flamenco Guitar: Alborada Flamenca; Guajiro y Gitano; Alhambra; Flamenco Jam; Gypsy Jam; Jose; Rosasas del Puerto; El Gato; Inspiracion Gitana; Nostalgia Flamenca; Carmen Amaya.

HERMAN, JERRY ASCAP 1963
composer, author
b New York, NY, July 10, 33. Educ: Univ Miami, BA, 53; Parsons Sch Design. Script writer for TV. Grammy Award, 64 & 67; Variety Poll Award for best music & best lyrics, 66; Order Merit, Univ Miami, 71. *Songs:* Jolly Theatrical Season; Your Good Morning; Your Hand in My Hand; Show Tune in 2/4 Time; Shalom (WPAT Award); There's No Reason in the World; That Was Yesterday; I Will Follow You; Milk and Honey; It Only Takes a Moment; Hello Dolly! (Grammy & Antoinette Perry Awards, 65); Ribbons Down My Back; So Long, Dearie; Mame; If He Walked Into My Life; Hello Lyndon (Pres Lyndon B Johnson's campaign song). *Scores:* Stage: Night Cap (nightclub); Off-Bway: I Feel Wonderful; Parade; Bway: Milk and Honey; Hello Dolly! (Tony & NY Drama Critics Awards, 64); Mame; Dear World; The Grand Tour; Mack and Mable.

HERMAN, PINKY (HERB PINKERT, HERMAN PINCUS) ASCAP 1934
composer, author
b New York, NY, Dec 23, 05. Educ: Chelsea High Sch, Mass; Yonkers High Sch, NY; NY Univ. Music ed, "Radio Daily," 43-45; "Motion Picture Daily"; mem, Writers Adv Comt, ASCAP, 50-62; charter mem, Am Guild Authors & Composers, mem coun, 55-62. Chief Collabrs: Irving Caesar, Buddy Valentine, Lou Handman, William Barry, Michael Cleary, Arthur Swanstrom, Paul Taubman, Maurice Chachkes, John Kamano, Bernard Maltin, Harry Stride. *Songs:* Manhattan Merry-Go-Round; Seven Days a Week; I'm Still in Love With You; Havin' a Wonderful Time; Face the Sun; A Wonderful Night; Lucky; If I Had a Million Dollars; Mademoiselle Hortensia; Come Back to Me, My Love; Got a Gal in Town; It Must Be L-U-V; Bride and Groom; When a Girl's in Love; Looking for a Dream; Yip Yip Yowie, I'm an Eagle; My Heart is Yours for the Asking; My Song Reached Your Heart; Masquerade of Love; Where Can You Be?; Never Leave A Lady When She Loves You; Myrtle the Turtle and Flip the Frog; Acapulco (By the Sea); Texas Lullaby; My Fav'rite Initials are USA; Little Sweetheart of the Mountains; Lighthouse in the Harbor; Franklin D Roosevelt (Presidential campaign song); Sing Something Irish; It's a Co-incidence; The Bible My Mother Left to Me; I'd Like to Kiss Susie Again; Good-Lookin', It's Good Lookin' at You; Now (I Don't Have to Dream); Music Sets Me Free; Poor Little Doll; Lost Romance; Heart to Heart; The Cowboy Isn't Speakin' to His Horse; Talkin' to the Tulips (About the Two Lips I Love); It's a Wonderful, Wonderful Feelin'.

HERMAN, WOODROW WILSON (WOODY) ASCAP 1945
composer, conductor, clarinetist
b Milwaukee, Wis, May 16, 13. Educ: Marquette Univ. Clarinetist & saxophonist in dance bands, incl Joey Lichter, Harry Sosnik, Gus Arnheim & Isham Jones. Formed own orch & appeared in hotels, theatres & ballrooms. Toured Europe, 54, Latin Am (US State Dept), 58 & Gt Brit. Has made many records. Appeared in films: "What's Cookin'?"; "Winter Time"; "Sensations of 1945"; "Earl Carroll's Vanities." Author, "Teaching Folio" & "Clarinet Digest." Chief Collabrs: Chubby Jackson, Ralph Burns. *Songs & Instrumental Works:* Apple Honey; River Bed Blues; Goosey Gander; Northwest Passage; Blues on Parade; Blowin' Up a Storm; Music by the Moon; At the Woodchoppers' Ball; Early Autumn; A Kiss Goodnight; Your Father's Moustache; Wild Root; I Remember Duke; Misty Morning.

HERMANN, RALPH J (REGINALD HALE) ASCAP 1954
composer, conductor
b Milwaukee, Wis, Feb 9, 14. Educ: Milwaukee Pub Schs; high sch grad; advan comp studies with Vittorio Giannini; cond studies with Reiner, Monteaux. After high sch went on road with big name bands. Staff arr, NBC, New York. Piano soloist with Paul Whiteman. Staff cond/arr radio & TV, ABC, 17 yrs. Wrote & cond much of score for first Cinerama. Winner two int prizes for jazz-symphonic orch works, Italy. Writer for educ field, many yrs; over sixty band publ, also many comns & col sems. Guest cond orchs & bands. *Instrumental Works:* Kiddie Ballet; Ballet for Young Americans; North Sea Overture; Lincoln Center Overture; Concerto for Band; Clarinet on the Town; Ode; Arlington Overture; Belmont Overture; Clarinet Cake; Concerto for Horn; Trumpet Concerto; Concord Overture; The Great Gong; Winterset; Pied Piper of Hamlin; Springtime Overture; Texas Portrait; Train in the Night; plus over 90 original works for the Muzak wired services.

HERRERA, HUMBERTO ANGEL (ANGELO ASCAP 1958
D'UMBERTO, ARTHUR O REEMHBER)
composer, author, conductor
b Guatemala City, Guatemala, Sept 20, 1900. Educ: Nat Inst of Guatemala City; Nat Cons Guatemala City. Traveled as pianist & cond with opera & operetta companies Cent Am, SAm & Europe. Dir, Brazilian Orch, Treasure Island's World Fair, 39-40. *Songs:* Spana; Cuerdas Rotas; Ven A Mi; Sambaina; Music: The Time and the Hare; Hilda. *Instrumental Works:* Brazilian Pavilion; A Tango Chantant; Batucando; Media Noche en Buenos Aires; Nacho Piedra Santa; Sud Americana.

HERRICK, LYNN ASCAP 1976
composer, author
b Cincinnati, Ohio, Sept 26, 36. Educ: Northwestern Univ, Evanston, BA; Am Acad of Dramatic Arts, New York, 62. Actress, singer, arr & copyist, New York, 63-65; writer TV & radio commercials, Chicago, 66-72; writer advert copy, Omaha, 73-75; actor, singer, comp-in-residence, lyricist & playwright, Omaha Magic Theatre, 77-80. Comp music for "American King's English for Queens", "Goona Goona" & "Running Gags." Chief Collabrs: Gracie Lee, Megan Terry, Verna Safran, Lyn Riley.

HERRICK, PAUL YOUNG ASCAP 1949
composer, author
b St Petersburg, Fla, Mar 2, 10; d Los Angeles, Calif, Jan 27, 58. *Songs:* That Soldier of Mine; You Make Me Nervous, Mr Jones; Can You Look Me in the Eyes?; You and My Mother-in-Law; When the White Roses Bloom; 1400 Dream Street.

HERRING, JOHN ASCAP 1962
composer, author, publisher
b Memphis, Tenn. Educ: USAF Radar & Radio Sch. Writer, special material for nightclub acts, Las Vegas. Co-founder, publ firm, Sawtell & Herring, 62. Chief Collabrs: Louis Prima, Paul Sawtell. *Songs:* The Shepherd Man; What Have I Got of My Own?; Go Into the Mountains; Young Guns of Texas.

HERRMAN, DANIEL W, JR ASCAP 1963
composer, author
b New York, NY, June 4, 10. Educ: Leonard Da Vinc Art Sch. Songwriter, 50-72; painter; poet. *Songs:* Wings of a Wild Goose; Lavender Eyes; My But I Love You; Golden Brown Eyes; Oh Sacred Heart; Gray Misty Day; Beneath The Hand; Little Blue Scooter; Anchusa Italica; Adeline; Four Seasons; My White Rose Ireland; Wandering Along the Gay White Way; Santa Comes; Machine Gun March; Love Love Love; Artistic Dream; Where There Is Love; Dream Boy; A Rose Close to My Heart.

HERRMANN, RONALD LEE ASCAP 1976
composer, percussion author, teacher
b Chicago, Ill, Jan 26, 47. Educ: VanderCook Col Music, BME(music educ), postgrad work, 70. Performer, USMC Field Bands, 71-74. Perc author & arr, McCormick's Enterprises, Inc, 74-79; ed, The Marching Band Director. Chief Collabr: Clifford Colnot. *Instrumental Works:* Arr for Marches: Auld Lang Syne; Chump Change; Malaga; Summer of '42; Theme From "The Fox."

HERRON, JOEL ASCAP 1950
composer, author, conductor
b Chicago, Ill, Jan 17, 16. Educ: Univ Chicago. Music dir, WMGM, 46-56; "MGM Theatre of the Air"; "MGM Musical Comedy Theatre of the Air"; "Jane Froman Show"; US Treasury "Guest Star" prog. Music dir, pianist & arr for TV shows, incl "Robert Montgomery Show", "Broadway Angels", "Jaye P Morgan Show" & "Jimmy Dean Show" (also assoc producer), 48-59. Cond own orch in nightclubs & hotels. Comn to write score for Repub Theatre Party, 55. Writer of musical commercials. Has made many records. *Songs:* Take My Love; I'm a Fool to Want You; Sierra Nevada; Destiny's Darling; Closer, Closer; I Push My Heart Through a Horn; Too Many Times; Sh'lom Bait; Across the Sea; Shocka-Boom. *Scores:* Stage: Go Fight City Hall; Film Cartoon: Muggy Doo; Put the Paper Down Harry!; Fluky Luke.

HERSCHER, LOU ASCAP 1920
composer, author, conductor
b Philadelphia, Pa, Apr 19, 1894; d Beverly Hills, Calif, Mar 12, 74. Educ: Pub schs; studied music with father, Cantor Eliss Herscher. Wrote for films; lectr songwriting, Univ Calif, Los Angeles; comp & music dir, TV films & TV film series, "Featurettes." Author: "Successful Songwriting." Publ & music dir; co-owner, Accadia Music Co. Chief Collabrs: Frank Loesser, Joe Burke, L Wolfe Gilbert, Benny Davis, Jules Loman, Ruth Grahm (daughter), Mitchel Parish. *Songs:* You're Free to Go (ASCAP Award, 77); Sapphire of the Tropics (Hawaiian Nani Award, 79); Dream Daddy (first radio hit song); There Are Just Two I's in Dixie; Wake Up Little Girl; Nestle in Your Daddy's Arms; Valparaiso; Chilpancingo; Where Were You?; I Didn't Believe I'd Fall in Love; Grasshopper; I'm Free From the Chain Gang Now; Old Love Letters; When Jimmie Rodgers Said Goodbye; Orange Blossoms; Are You Lonely?; One More Kiss Then Good Night; Garden of the Moon; Down Home Blues; Mahalo, I Thank Thee; Lost a Man's Best Pal; Sing Low Sweet Harriet; If; Mama Never Said a Word About Love; In the Park; Fifty Games of Solitaire; Elmer the Knock-Kneed Cowboy; The Best Years in Our Lives; Years Ago; On My

Ukulele. *Albums:* Edgar Guest's Poetic Gems; The Adventures of Tom Sawyer; Hollywood Kiddie Dittles; Little Orphan Annie; The Entertainer; The Princess and the Commoner (operetta).

HERSH, ARTHUR B   ASCAP 1959
composer, author, pianist
b Staten Island, NY, Sept 22, 00. Educ: Pub schs; studied piano & accordion. Served, USA & USN, World War I. Merchant seaman, 15 yrs. Taught music. *Songs:* You Go Well With My Heart; I'll Release You From My Heart; Is Everybody Happy Polka; Mortgage Polka; OK Professor.

HERSH, EVELYN S   ASCAP 1960
composer, author
b Brooklyn, NY, Dec 25, 11. Educ: Col. Exec with shoe mfg co. *Songs:* Have Faith.

HERSOM, FRANK E   ASCAP 1924
composer
b Fair Haven, Mass, May 19, 1894; d Jamaica, NY, Oct 26, 41. Educ: New Eng Cons. *Instrumental Works:* Spring Blossoms; Babylonian Dance; Love Notes; Heads Up; Nymphs of the Nile; Braziliana; Toy Town Tales (suite).

HERST, JEROME P   ASCAP 1939
composer
b Chicago, Ill, May 28, 09. Educ: Townsend Harris Hall, New York; Western Mil Acad, Alton, Ill; Northwestern Univ, Evanston; Univ Calif, Berkeley; Hastings Col Law, San Francisco, JD; Conservatoire de Musique, Paris; studied comp with Frederick Schiller, Mario Castelnuovo-Tedesco & Alexandre Tansman. Radio & nite club pianist during col & law sch; practiced law, 35-42; active duty, USNR, WW II; referee & hearing officer, State of Calif, 47-75; musical comp & songwriting, 75- Chief Collabrs: Al Jacobs, Jack Sharpe, Felton Kaufmann, Richard O Kraemer. *Songs:* Music: So Rare; The Call of Tarzan; The Darling of the Campus; We'll Get a Bang Out of Life; As Long As I Still Have You; Shower of Kisses; Meand'rin'. *Instrumental Works:* A Child's Garden (suite for symph orch); The Golden Spike (overture). *Scores:* Musicals: The Musical Adventures of Tom Sawyer; The Legend of Bret Harte; Ozma of Oz.

HERTZ, FRED   ASCAP 1958
composer, author, producer
b New York, NY, Dec 16, 33. Educ: Amherst Col. Publicity writer for mag. Representative for radio & TV. Vpres, Gotham Recording Corp. *Instrumental Works:* The Marine Corps March (radio theme); Until Niagara Falls; Keep Freedom in Your Future; Senior Year. *Albums:* Monster Rally; Peter Meets the Wolf in Dixieland.

HERZIG, JAMES MARTIN   ASCAP 1976
composer, author
b New York, NY, May 1, 44. Educ: Lafayette Col, Pa, grad, 66; Harvard Law Sch, Mass, grad, 69. First record at age of 13. Wrote music for numerous radio & TV commercials & TV programs incl "Captain Kangaroo."

HESS, CLIFF   ASCAP 1919
composer, author, publisher
b Cincinnati, Ohio, June 19, 1894; d Tex, June 8, 59. Pianist on Miss River boats. Mem staff, music publ firms. Secy to Irving Berlin, 13-18. Exec & publ, recording cos. *Songs:* Homesickness Blues; Huckleberry Finn; Freckles; Don't You Remember the Day?; I Used to Call Her Baby; When Alexander Takes His Ragtime Band to France; I'm in Heaven.

HESS, DAVID ALEXANDER (DAVID HILL) ASCAP 1956
composer, author, singer
b New York, NY, Sept 19, 36. Educ: Putney Sch, 49-53; Ithaca Col, 55; Columbia Univ, 57-63; Juilliard Sch Music, 59-61, studied with Vincent Persechetti. Started writing songs in high sch. Head A&R, Kapp Records, 61-63 & Veejay Records, 66-68 (West Coast). Starred in "Last House on the Left." Chief Collabrs: Bobby Steveson, Aaron Schroeder, Vic Milrose, Alan Bernstein, John Corrigliano, Steven Schlaks. *Songs:* I Got Stung; Speedy Gonzales; Come Along; Daddy Roll 'Em; Frankie and Johnny; Your Hand, Your Heart, Your Love; Hammer and Nails. *Scores:* Opera/Ballet: The Naked Carmen (Grammy nomination); Film/TV: Last House on the Left.

HEST, JEFFREY   ASCAP 1970
composer, author, musician
b New York, NY, July 20, 43. Educ: Masters degree in comp & theory; doctoral studies, also pvt studies. Vpres, head A&R & chief musical arr, Project 3 Records, New York, 68-78. Arr & cond music for Bway shows. Comp, arr & cond music for many TV commercials & industrial films. Comp of original pop, jazz & classical music. Has own co, The MusicWorks, New York. Guest lectr music, var cols in New York area. Originator of a series of re-creations of many Big Band arr from the 30's & 40's, United Artists Music Publ. Cond & singer. Chief Collabrs: Lisa Hest, Merry Aronson.

HESTER, CAROLYN   ASCAP 1965
composer, folksinger
b Waco, Tex, Jan 28, 37. Educ: Studied voice with Paul Gavert & music with Wallace House, New York, 60-65; attended Am Theatre Wing, New York. Dir, Kerrville, Tex, Annual Folk Fest; appeared at maj music fests, incl Edinburgh, Mariposa & Newport; recorded albums; had own TV spec in Europe; had col concerts. *Songs:* My Little Sister, Donna; Kingdom for a Kiss; Warnin'; Ascending Woman; Comin' on Back to You; Stay Not Late; Dorsey's Bar and Grill; The New Jerusalem; Lyrics: King Kong; Sleep My Love.

HESTER, WESLEY HESTER (HAL)
composer, author, singer
b Paducah, Ky, June 9, 33. Educ: Cincinnati Cons Music, Ohio, BM(piano, comp). Recording artist, singer & pianist, var recording cos. Chief Collabrs: Danny Apolinar, Sol Parker, Benjamin Bradford, Chandler Warren. *Scores:* Bway Shows: Your Own Thing (Drama Critics Circle Award—Best Musical, 68; Outer Circle Award; Grammy nomination); Cowboy (Athena and the Cowboy). *Albums:* The Island and the Sea.

HEUSSENSTAMM, GEORGE   ASCAP 1968
composer, educator
b Los Angeles, Calif, July 24, 26. Educ: Univ Calif, Los Angeles, 44-46; Los Angeles City Col, 47-48; Los Angeles State Col Applied Arts & Sci, 61-62; studied with Leonard Stein, 61-62. Comp of many publ works; mgr, Coleman Chamber Music Asn, the oldest continuing chamber music series in US; copyist; critic; lectr; pvt teacher; fac, music theory, Calif State Univ, Dominguez Hills, 76- Awarded 8 nat & int comp competition prizes & Nat Endowment of Arts fel grant, 76. Mem, Am Soc Univ Comp, Int Soc Contemporary Music, Western Alliance of Arts Adminr. *Instrumental Works:* Score, Opus 46 (4 saxophone quartets, 4 perc); Ensembles for Brass Quintet, Opus 58; Tubafour, Opus 30; Playphony, Opus 56 (alto saxophone, perc); Double Solo, Opus 26 (clarinet, perc); Three Pieces, Opus 61 (trombones); Holiday for Percussion, Opus 51; Saxoclone, Opus 42 (saxophone, stereo tape); Tetralogue, Opus 36 (clarinets, perc); Seven Etudes, Opus 17 (oboe, clarinet, bassoon); Windgate, Opus 14 No 1 (flute); Monologue, Opus 50 (clarinet); Die Jugend, Opus 10 (clarinet); Periphony No 2, Opus 63 (4 octets, 5 perc); Brass Quintet No 3, Opus 64; Seventeen Impressions from the Japanese, Opus 35 (chamber orch); Poems from the East, Opus 52 (woodwind quartet, soprano); Stream, Opus 55 (clarinet, cello, piano).

HEVAR, HEDY   ASCAP 1957
composer, pianist
b Berlin, Ger; d Elmhurst, NY, Nov 5, 75. Educ: High sch; studied music with Krause, Georg Bertram, Leonid Kreutzer, Will Gross. Concert pianist. Writer, operetta scores. Mem, Societe Italienne des Auteurs et Editeurs & Nat Asn for Am Composers & Conductors. Chief Collabrs: Lillian Krugman, Arlene Levy, Allan Walker, Sigmund Spaeth. *Songs:* Ducks on Parade; Jack in the Box; The Ballad of Abe Lincoln; Moi Aussi; Perhaps Tomorrow; Israel So Beautiful; Women of America.

HEWES, HARRY E, JR   ASCAP 1952
composer, author
b Boston, Mass, May 27, 10. Educ: Northeastern Univ. Won nat TV contest, Steve Allen's "Songs for Sale," 52. Retired. *Songs:* You May Be the Sweetheart of Somebody Else; A Sweetheart Is Someone From Heaven; I Could Tell You; Don't Fall in Love; Santa's on His Way.

HEWETT, RUSSELL CHARLES   ASCAP 1979
composer, singer, guitarist
b Dover-Foxcroft, Maine, Nov 6, 54. Berklee Col Music, BM(magna cum laude). Numerous TV & concert appearances performing contemporary Christian songs. *Songs:* My Yoke Is Easy; Land of Promises; Rain; It's Time to Grow.

HEWITT, HARRY D
composer
b Detroit, Mich, Mar 4, 21. Comp, symphonies, string quartets, piano sonatas, operas & concerti.

HEWITT, JOSEPH F   ASCAP 1942
composer, author
b New York, NY, Jan 24, 1886; d New York, June 8, 57. Educ: Princeton Univ, BA. In securities bus, 08-57. Businessman. *Songs:* The Princeton Cannon Song; Crash on, Artillery; Princeton Forever; Wings of Gold; The Living God (anthem). *Instrumental Works:* Twilight Mood (violin, piano).

HEWITT, ZOE ADELINE   ASCAP 1972
composer, author
b Roseau, Minn, Apr 10, 07. Educ: Ore Col of Educ, Monmouth; Bemidji State Teachers Col, Minn. Composer & author. Organ & piano perf, radio, TV, dance combos & clubs. Chief Collabrs: Nat Vincent, Norm Davis, Jack Sharpe. *Songs & Instrumental Works:* Oakland, the Beautiful (first off song); Whose Arms Are You Missing?; Give Me Valleys and Mountains Out West; Don't Be Sorry; Kisses Tell.

HEYMAN, EDWARD ASCAP 1931
author, producer, lyricist
b New York, NY, Mar 14, 07. Educ: Univ Mich. Wrote col musicals; wrote songs for films, Hollywood, 39-54. WW II, USAF; wrote musical "At Your Service." Producer, Eng-speaking theatre group, The Players. Mexico City, 54-61. Chief Collabrs: Vincent Youmans, Victor Young, Dana Suesse, Morton Gould, Nacio Herb Brown, John Green, Rudolf Friml, Sigmund Romberg, Arthur Schwartz, Ray Henderson, Oscar Levant, Carmen Lombardo. *Songs:* Body and Soul; Out of Nowhere; Hello, My Lover, Goodbye; Drums in My Heart; Through the Years; Kinda Like You; You're Everywhere; My Silent Love; I Wanna Be Loved; You're Mine, You; I Cover the Waterfront; Blame It on My Youth; After All, You're All I'm After; You Oughta Be in Pictures; Easy Come, Easy Go; Moonburn; When I Grow Up; To Love You and to Lose You; It's High Time I Got the Low-Down on You; Love and Learn; Seal It With a Kiss; Boo-Hoo; They Say; Have You Forgotten So Soon?; The Sky Fell Down; Love Letters; Strange Love; If I Steal a Kiss; When I Fall in Love; Blue Star; No More Shadows; All Yours; The More I See of Lisa; This Is Romance; Jonny; Roses in the Sky; Seattle's World Fair Theme; Songs for films: That Girl From Paris; Curly Top; Kissing Bandit; Delightfully Dangerous; Northwest Outpost. *Scores:* Bway Shows: Here Goes the Bride; Through the Years; She Loves Me Not; Murder at the Vanities; Pardon Our French; Bluebird of Happiness.

HEYWARD, DUBOSE ASCAP 1936
author
b Charleston, SC, Aug 31, 1885; d Tryon, NC, July 16, 40. Educ: Pub schs; hon degrees: Univ NC, Col Charleston & Univ Southern Calif. Author, poems "Carolina Chansons", "Skylines and Horizons" & "Jasbo Brown", novels, "Porgy", "Angel", "Mamba's Daughters" (dramatized), "The Half Pint Flask", "Peter Ashley", "Lost Morning", "Star Spangled Virgin" & "Brass Ankle." Biography, "DuBose Heyward" by Frank Durham. Chief Collabrs: George Gershwin, Ira Gershwin. *Songs:* Summertime; My Man's Gone Now; Bess, You Is My Woman Now; I Loves You, Porgy; I Got Plenty o' Nuttin'; A Woman Is a Sometime Thing. *Scores:* Opera: Porgy and Bess.

HEYWARD, SAMUEL EDWIN, JR ASCAP 1959
composer, author, violist
b Savannah, Ga, Mar 26, 04. Educ: New Eng Cons; St Emma Col; studied with Philip Mittel, Andre Berty, Caesar Finn, Chauncey Lee, Everett Barkesdale, Frank Butler, James Loguen. Appeared in classical & folklore concerts; violist, symph orchs & chamber music groups; singer. Chief Collabrs: Langston Hughes, W Waring Cuney. *Songs & Instrumental Works:* Freedom Train; Lament; Tired As I Can Be; Got to Live; Six Shades of Blue; The Penta Blues Suite; Calypso Folk Sing (collection); Ballad for Harry Moore; Cradle to Grave (cantata); The Love Cycle; Suite for Violin; The Elfin Ballet.

HEYWOOD, DONALD ASCAP 1934
composer, author, conductor
b Trinidad, BWI; d New York, NY, Jan 13, 67. Educ: Queens Royal Col, Trinidad; Fisk Univ; Northwestern Univ Med Sch; Mordkin Moser Cons, NY; also pvt study; Caribbean Col Music, Hon MusD. Dir, traveling theatrical orchs, mem, Will Marion Cook's Am Syncopated Orch. Wrote songs for Rosa Raisa & Schumann-Heink; organized Negro Theatre Guild, 37-38; produced "How Come Lawd," also wrote for films. Author "The West Indies, Its Men, Music and Manners." Trained & presented singers incl Leslie Uggams & Marie Young. Merrick Award for greatest contribution of Negro to Am music, 48. *Songs:* I'm Coming Virginia; Smile; Emaline; Where Are You Now; There's a Spirit in My Heart; Morning; No Need to Tell Me That You Love Me; Home Beyond the River; Stop Beating Those Drums. *Scores:* Ballets: The Wrong God; Spring Is Blue; Virgin Drums; Ballet of the Imps; Bway Shows: Africana; Blackberries of 1932; Hot Rhythm.

HIBBARD, BRUCE ALAN ASCAP 1976
composer, author, singer
b Dallas, Tex, June 2, 53. Educ: U S Grant High Sch; Oklahoma City Univ, 1 yr. Keyboardist in groups with Phil Keaggy; bass player in 5 other prof groups. Studio musician, 4 yrs, recording artist, Word Inc, 2 albums. Songwriter for Emmaus Road Publ. Singer, incl TV appearances. Chief Collabrs: Hadley Hockensmith, Kelly Willard. *Songs:* Questions; Hem of His Garment; All That I Want to Be; All of Me; You're So Good to Me; How the Years Pass By; Never Turning Back; Forgiven (I'm Forgiven); It's a Shame; That Day; (In) Over My Head; Some Day.

HIBBELER, RAY OSCAR ASCAP 1965
composer, author, singer
b Chicago, Ill, Nov 20, 1892. Educ: Elem sch & high sch. Songwriter, 11-; also feature story writer for nat mag; story writer for paperback bks. Chief Collabrs: Fred Strasser, Ray Egan, Jean Walz, Harry D Squires, W R Williams (Will Rossiter), Frank C Polak, Harry Geise, Jerry Sullivan, Casper Nathan, Erwin R Schmidt, Walter M Anderson. *Songs:* Tell Me You'll Forgive Me; Melancholy Lou; I Wish I Were Back in My Cradle; Wand'ring Sparrow; Lost-My-Baby Blues; What Makes My Baby Cry; Oklahoma Indian Jazz; A Window a Light and a Tear; Havana Rose; There's a Spark of Love Still Burning (in My Heart for You); Weeping for My Baby Tonight; If Tears Were Pearls; Lonesome Butterfly; There's a Sad Little Girl for Every Happy Little Boy; Lyrics: You

Won My Heart; I Crave You; Only a Broken String of Pearls; Abie's Got A' Irish Molly O; Bungalow Love.

HIBLER, WINSTON ASCAP 1954
author, director, producer
b Harrisburg, Pa, Oct 8, 10. Educ: Am Acad Dramatic Arts. Actor, Bway & Hollywood, 28-38. Owner & dir, Hollywood Acad of the Theatre. Writer for radio & films, 38-42. Producer, dir & writer for TV & films, incl "Seal Island", "Bear Country", "Beaver Valley", "Water Birds", "Men Against the Arctic", "Melody Time", "Ichabod and Mr Toad", "Vanishing Prairie", "Secrets of Life" & "Those Calloways," 42- Chief Collabrs: Walter Schumann, Oliver Wallace, William Lava, Paul Smith, Gill George, Ted Sears, Ralph Wright. *Songs:* Following the Leader; Break of Day; Now to Sleep; Together Time; Stingaree; We'll Smoke the Blighter Out; I Wonder; A Boy Is a Curious Thing; I'll Remember.

HICE, DANIEL D ASCAP 1976
composer, author
b High Point, NC, Sept 22, 42. Educ: North Mecklenburg High Sch, Charlotte, NC. Began writing, 70, prof, 76. Started Hice House Music Publ, 78. Chief Collabrs: Ruby Hice, Chip Haroy, Tom Chmielewski. *Songs:* Feeling Old Feeling; Sunday School to Broadway; A Good Thing and Goodbye; Til God Moves Out of His Heaven; A Little Less Than Love.

HICE, RUBY F ASCAP 1976
composer, author
b Osceola, Ark. Educ: Matthews High Sch, Mo. Began writing, 54. Songs recorded, 64- Chief Collabrs: Danny Hice, Kim Morrison. *Songs:* Sunday School to Broadway; Best I Ever Had; Love Between a Woman and a Man.

HICKMAN, ART ASCAP 1948
composer, conductor
b Oakland, Calif, June 13, 1886; d San Francisco, Calif, Jan 16, 30. Led orch, St Francis Hotel, San Francisco. Con own orch in early "Ziegfeld Follies"; first dance band featured in a Bway production. Appeared in theatres, ballrooms & nightclubs, US & Europe. *Songs:* Rose Room; Dry Your Tears; Without You; Hold Me; Come Back to Georgia; June, I Love No One But You; Love Moon; You and I; Dream of Me.

HICKMAN, ROGER M ASCAP 1956
composer, author, conductor
b Ash Grove, Mo, Nov 28, 1888; d Lakeland, Fla, Feb 25, 68. Educ: Moody Bible Inst. Was gospel singer, 15-42; minister of music in churches, 43-62. Chief Collabr: Oswald Smith. *Songs:* From the Upper Room to Mount Olivet (Easter cantata); Sacred: Saved; Break Forth Into Joy.

HICKS, REV JOHN B, SR ASCAP 1964
composer, author, singer
b Cleveland, Ohio, May 28, 34. Educ: Case Western Reserve Univ, Sch Applied Social Sci; East Cleveland Bible Inst, Christian Tabernacle Bible Inst, grad as minister. Founder & evangelist, Love Evangelistic Ministry; comp & dir, Nat Convention of Gospel Choirs & Choruses, Inc, US; singer, pianist & organist as recording artist. *Songs:* I Shall Over Come; My Friend Is Jesus; I Thank the Lord; I'm So Happy, Happy in Jesus; I Fell In Love With God.

HICKS, VAL J ASCAP 1971
composer, arranger, lecturer
b Provo, Utah, Feb 6, 33. Educ: Univ Utah, BS, 56, PhD, 71; Univ Southern Calif, MM, 69. Music teacher, elem sch, middle sch, high sch, col & univ. Arr for vocal groups, incl Osmonds, Disneyland's Dapper Dans. Wrote articles for var jour, incl Music Educr Jour, Music Educr Nat Conference. Music adjudicator & clinician. Lectr musicianship & choral arr, Univ Manchester, Eng. Consult on recording project, Smithsonian Inst. *Songs:* That Summer When We Were Young; When the Showboat Came to Town; I'll Be a Song and Dance Man Again. *Songs & Instrumental Works:* The Star Spangled Banner (arr, male voices).

HIDEY, HAL SMITH ASCAP 1974
composer, author, keyboardist
b Cleveland, Ohio. Educ: Western Reserve Acad; Baldwin Wallace Cons, Cleveland; Univ Calif, Santa Barbara. Has worked in nightclubs, studios & made recordings. TV theme comp.

HIGGINBOTHAM, IRENE EVELYN (IRENE H PADELLAN) ASCAP 1944
composer
b Worcester, Mass, June 11, 18. Educ: Pvt piano lessons. Songwriter. Chief Collabrs: Ervin Drake, Dan Fisher, Sammy Gallop, Fred Meadows, Andy Razaf, Bob Hilliard, Syd Shaw, Jay C Higginbotham. *Songs:* This Will Make You Laugh; Music: Goodmorning, Heartache; No Good Man; That Did It, Marie; Typewriter Serenade; Harlem Stomp; Boogie Woogie on a Saturday Night. *Songs & Instrumental Works:* It's Mad, Mad, Mad.

HIGGINS, ESTHER S ASCAP 1967
composer, teacher
b Elmer, NJ, Oct 29, 03. Educ: Spec instrs. Played in silent theatre moving picture houses, 19-30; worked for an organ store, 59; teacher, 59- Played concerts for organ dealers. Author: "Introductions, Breaks, Fills and Endings," All Organ Series No 18 & No 40. *Songs & Instrumental Works:* Song for Mother's Day; Spring Song; Theme From Third Violin Concerto (arr Saint-Saens); Morning Mist; Melodie; Flute Song; Elegy; Reverie; Morning Song; Virgins Lullaby; Grand Chorus; Festival March; In a Pensive Mood; Love Is of God; Theme Concerto No 2 (Wieniawski arr); Passiontide; Worship; First Nowell; Berceuse; Christmas Reverie; Aria; Pastorale (Cliaminade arr).

HIGGINS, JOHN MICHAEL ASCAP 1969
composer, teacher, publisher
b Chicago, Ill, Sept 27, 48. Educ: Univ Mich, BME, 69; Northwestern Univ. Band comp & arr, also teacher & educ clinician. Ed, Hal Leonard Publ, 74-76. Vpres, Jensen Publ, 76- *Instrumental Works:* America '76; The Winner's Circle; Peaches; El Dorado; Advance of the Sponges; Night Coach; Departure One.

HIGGINSON, JOSEPH VINCENT (CYR DE BRANT) ASCAP 1936
composer, organist, teacher
b Irvington, NJ, May 17, 1896. Educ: Manhattan Col; NY Univ, BA, MA; Juilliard Sch; Pius X Sch of Liturgical Music; studied with Richard Biggs, A Mandeley Richardson, Percy Goetschius, Marion Bauer, Albert Stoessel, Philip James, Charles Haubiel. Organist & choirmaster, St Catherine of Alexandria Church, Brooklyn. Managing ed, Catholic Choirmaster. Taught, pvt schs; fac, Pius X Sch of Liturgical Music. Fel, Hymn Soc of Am. *Songs:* Sacred: There Will Be Rest; Unsung Hour; Rain; Pie Jesu; The Lamp; The Holy King. *Instrumental Works:* Magdalen (tone poem).

HIGH, FREEMAN ASCAP 1961
composer, author, singer
b Havana, Ill, Dec 13, 1897; d. Educ: Univ Southern Calif. Was instr, vocal & instrumental groups, Univ Southern Calif. Singer in concerts & theatres. Formed male quartet. Staff arr, KFI (NBC) & KHJ (CBS). Staff arr & choral dir, radio & films. Music dir & arr, "Snow White and the Seven Dwarfs." Cond, Elks' Chorus, Long Beach, Calif. Chief Collabr: Katharine Bainbridge. *Songs:* A Friend or Two. *Instrumental Works:* Pirate's Song (octavo, R L Stevenson text).

HIGH, MILES
See Narmore, Edgar Eugene

HIKEN, NAT ASCAP 1959
author, producer
b Chicago, Ill, June 23, 14; d. Writer & producer "Sergeant Bilko," TV; also other shows. Chief Collabrs: George Bassman, Gordon Jenkins, Dick Stutz. *Songs:* Close to Me; Irving; Fugitive From Fifth Avenue.

HILDERBRAND, DIANE
See Skye, Diane S

HILL, AL
See Twomey, Kathleen (Kay) Greeley

HILL, CHARLES LEE ASCAP 1953
band composer, arranger, teacher
b Houston, Tex, Nov 15, 10. Educ: Nacagdoches High Sch; Stephen F Austin Univ, BS, 33; NTex State Univ, MMusEd, 48; NY Univ & Univ Houston, postgrad study, 48-50. Band cond, Stephen F Austin Univ, (summers), 34-35, Troup High Sch, 34-35 & Overton High Sch, 35-42. Music activities, USA, 42-45. Assoc prof music, Sam Houston State Univ, 48-53. Band cond & vocal music, Lovelady High Sch, 53-59. Instrumental-vocal teacher-cond, North Forest ISD, Houston, 59-66; sch librarian, 66- *Instrumental Works:* Red Rhythm Valley; At the Gremlin Ball; Prairie Jump; Charles Lee Hill's Band Folio; Mars at Midnight; Little Boy Blues; Swinging on the Range; Time Out for Jazz; Varsity Ramble; Deep in Dixie; Little Joe the Wrangler; Space City, USA March.

HILL, DAVID
See Hess, David Alexander

HILL, DEDETTE LEE ASCAP 1940
author
b Lynchburg, Va, Nov 2, 1900; d Hollywood, Calif, June 5, 50. Chief Collabrs: Billy Hill (husband), Johnny Marks. *Songs:* There's a Little Box of Pine on the 7:29; Put on an Old Pair of Shoes; Old Folks; We Speak of You Often; Address Unknown; I Can't Find Anything to Suit My Mood; There's Someone Else in My Place Now.

HILL, EDWARD BURLINGAME ASCAP 1948
composer, educator
b Cambridge, Mass, Sept 9, 1872; d Francestown, NH, July 9, 60. Educ: Harvard Univ, BA; New Eng Cons; studied with John Paine, B J Lang, Frederic Bullard, G W Chadwick, Charles Widor, Paris & Arthur Whiting. Assoc prof, Harvard Univ, 18-28, prof, 28-36, Ditson prof music, 36-60, chmn & dir music, 28-34.

US rep, Int Jury for Musical Competition, Olympic Games, Paris, 24. Awarded Chevalier Legion of Honor. Mem: Nat Inst Arts & Letters & Am Acad Arts & Sci. *Songs & Instrumental Works:* Sextet for Piano, Winds; Prelude for Orch; Violin Concerto; Sonata for Clarinet, Piano; String Quartet; Lilacs (tone poem based on Amy Lowell's poem); also 4 symph.

HILL, GEORGE BYRON ASCAP 1975
composer, author
b Atlanta, Ga, Dec 12, 53. Educ: Appalachian State Univ. Music teacher, Winston-Salem, NC, 75-78; writer & professional mgr, Welbeck Music Corp, 78- Chief Collabrs: Arthur Kent, Dennis Knutson, Bernie Wayne, Michael B Reid. *Songs:* Out of Your Mind; Heal It (title song).

HILL, HENRY (HINERANG) ASCAP 1953
composer, violinist, teacher
b Warsaw, Poland, June 12, 07. Educ: Russian, Ger & Polish State Schs & Gimnasium; Warsaw Cons Music, grad, 22; studied comp with Karol Szymanowski; studied violin with Karl Flesch, Berlin. Started as a violinist at age 6 playing concerts in Poland, Ger & Western Russia; in the 20's, became interested in Am Jazz and made many recordings as violinist & arr. Moved to US, 34; settled in Los Angeles, 36; arr, Victor Young's radio progs, also played violin; mgr, Victor Young's Orch. Violin & music theory teacher. Chief Collabrs: Ned Washington, Don Raye, Phil Zeller. *Songs:* Music: Don't Count the Stars; Do You Wonder. *Instrumental Works:* With All My Love; Bonjour Madame; The Hills Are Green Again.

HILL, JACKSON (STEPHEN) ASCAP 1974
composer, educator, ethnomusicologist
b Birmingham, Ala, May 23, 41. Educ: Univ NC, Chapel Hill, Morehead scholar, AB, 63, PhD(musicol), 70; comp study with Iain Hamilton & Roger Hannay; res grants & study, Oxford, UK & Japan. Instr music theory, Duke Univ, 66-68; mem music fac, Bucknell Univ, 68-, chmn dept, 80-; mem, Nat Coun of Am Soc Univ Comp. Res publ on musical instruments & on Japanese Buddhist Liturgical Music. Comp of more than 80 works. 16 comp prizes & awards incl NYC/AGO Prize, 78 & McCollin Prize, 79. *Songs:* Music: Third Song of Isaiah; An English Mass; Six Mystical Songs. *Instrumental Works:* Three Mysteries; Entourage; Sonata (violin); Four Studies (trumpet & piano); Serenade; Variations for Orchestra; Sangraal (orch); Mosaics (orch); Whispers of the Dead (flute); Sonata: By the Waters of Babylon (piano).

HILL, JAMES LAWRENCE ASCAP 1963
composer, trombonist
b Spirit Lake, Idaho, June 16, 28. Educ: USN Sch Music, DC; Westlake Col, Hollywood, Calif, grad. Played trombone with dance bands, incl Perez Prado, Billy May, Sam Donahue & Les Brown, 52-56. Wrote albums. Musical arr for Bob Hope TV, 57- & Dean Martin, 65-68. Musical dir on three Mitzi Gaynor TV specials. *Songs:* Hello Forever; Music: Just Lucky; Blues on a Count; Bone Voyage; Apple Valley.

HILL, JOHN M ASCAP 1971
composer, lyricist
b Mt Holly, NJ, Sept 23, 42. Educ: Temple Univ, MMus; Berklee Col Music, Boston; Univ Pa, studied Indian music. Record producer for Columbia Records; formed own music house for advert jingles. Chief Collabrs: Charlie Allen, Austin Roberts.

HILL, MILDRED J ASCAP 1940
composer, author, pianist
b Louisville, Ky, June 27, 1859; d Chicago, Ill, June 5, 16. Educ: Studied music with father, Calvin Cady & Adolph Weidig. Church organist & concert pianist. Authority on Negro spirituals. Author: "Song Stories for the Kindergarten and Primary School." *Songs:* Good Morning to All; Happy Birthday to You.

HILL, W ALEXANDER ASCAP 1934
composer, author, conductor
b Little Rock, Ark, Apr 19, 06; d North Little Rock, Feb 1, 36. Educ: Col. Led own orch; also cond orch in silent films. Pianist in jazz bands, recordings. Arr for orchs incl Benny Goodman, Cab Calloway & Duke Ellington. Chief Collabrs: Fats Waller, Clarence Williams, Irving Mills. *Songs:* Heart of Stone; I'm Crazy 'Bout My Baby; Dixie Lee; Delta Bound; Armful o' Sweetness; Let's Have a Jubilee; Shout, Sister, Shout; Long About Midnight; Draggin' My Poor Heart Around; Our Love Was Meant to Be; When Hannah Plays Piano; A Song; Devil in the Moon; He Wouldn't Stop Doin' It.

HILL, WILLIAM J ASCAP 1929
composer, author, pianist
b Boston, Mass, July 14, 1899; d Boston, Dec 24, 40. Educ: Pub schs; studied violin with Carl Muck. Worked with surveyors in Death Valley. Violinist, pianist in dance halls; led first jazz band in Salt Lake City. Violinist, conductor. Chief Collabrs: Peter DeRose, Dedette Hill (wife), Victor Young, William Raskin, Edward Eliscu, J Keirn Brennan. *Songs:* They Cut Down the Old Pine Tree; Have You Ever Been Lonely; The Last Round-Up; Wagon Wheels; Empty Saddles; In the Chapel in the Moonlight; The Call of the Canyon; On a Little Street in Singapore; The Old Man of the Mountain; The Old Spinning Wheel;

Lights Out; There's a Cabin in the Pines; Put on an Old Pair of Shoes; The Glory of Love.

HILLBURN, RAYMOND   ASCAP 1978
composer, author, singer
b Montgomery, Ala, July 1, 40. Played guitar in clubs, Houston, Tex, 58 & Nashville North, Cals Pub & The Blue Star Lounge, Chicago, Ill, 62-80. *Songs:* Bedroom Eyes; Just Another Rhinestone.

HILLEBRAND, FRED   ASCAP 1942
composer, author, actor
b Brooklyn, NY, Dec 25, 1893; d New York, NY, Sept 15, 63. Educ: St Joseph's Acad; Juilliard Sch Music. Musical comedy actor, 25 yrs; wrote own material, also wrote stage scores. *Songs:* How Many Dreams Ago?; Please Return My Heart; I'll Meet You at Duffy Square; Shake the Hand of the Man; I Worry 'Bout You; Will There Be Room for All of Us in Heaven?. *Scores:* Opera: Southland; Operetta: The Swing Princess; TV: Ghosts of Broadway.

HILLER, LEJAREN ARTHUR   ASCAP 1963
composer
b New York, NY, Feb 23, 24. Educ: Princeton Univ, BA, 44, MA, 46, PhD, 47; comp studies with Milton Babbitt & Roger Sessions; Univ Ill, MMus, 58. Res chemist, E I du Pont de Nemours, Va, 47-52; with dept chem, Univ Ill, 52-58. Composed music as an avocation primarily. Prof comp & dir experimental music studio, Univ Ill, 58-; Frederick B Slee prof comp, State Univ NY, Buffalo, 68-. Chief Collabrs: Playwrights, Webster Smalley, Christopher Newton & Frank Parman; comp, John Cage & Robert Baker; technicians, Leonard Isaacson & Ravi Kumra. *Instrumental Works:* String Quartet No 4 (Illiac Suite); String Quartet No 5 (in quarter-tones); Twelve-Tone Variations (piano); Scherzo (piano); Sonata No 3 (violin & piano); Malta (tuba & tape); Persiflage (flute, oboe & perc); Theater: An Avalanche (pitchman, prima donna, percussionist & pre-recorded playback); Multi Media: HPSCHD (1 to 7 harpsichords & 1-56 tapes); five Appalachian ballads for voice & guitar; computer cantata for soprano, tape & instruments; machine music for piano, perc & tape; computer music for percussion & tape.

HILLER, PHYLLIS UNGER (FIBBY)   ASCAP 1963
composer, author, singer
b Petaluma, Calif. Educ: Univ Calif, Berkeley, AA; San Francisco State Col, AB, 49; Peabody Col-Vanderbilt Univ, MS, 76; studied piano with Bernard Abramowitcz, psychol with Bob & Mary Goulding & Carl Rogers, Calif. Taught elem schs, Calif; became music curriculum specialist. Comp, 61- Exec dir, Oak Hill Music Publ Co & Creative Materials Libr, 71-; started C&M Records, 71. Pianist, actor, counselor. Developed new effective educ approaches using music with psychology, also new music material for personal growth & transactional analysis. Writer for United Methodist Publ House. Instr psychology of adjustment, Tenn State Univ. Did one woman show of 11 original songs, poems & soliloquy, "My Name is Fibby," 79. *Songs:* Hole In the Sky (story with 8 songs); Love Is a Circle; I'm Worth It!; It's Easier When They Are Little; The Sun Will Shine Tomorrow; Can a Child Be a Parent To a Man?; Children Are People; It's Much Easier; Making Room In the World (Int Yr of the Child song for Nashville, Tenn, 79); Songs as a Medium of Transactional Analysis and Personal Growth (bk of 16 songs & cassette recording); My Lucky High Heels; Funny World. *Albums:* Ramo-Song-Story.

HILLIARD, BOB   ASCAP 1950
author
b New York, NY, Jan 28, 18; d Los Angeles, Calif, Feb 1, 71. Chief Collabrs: Carl Sigman, Jule Styne, Mort Garson, Sammy Mysels, Dick Sanford, Milton Deluga, Philip Springer, Lee Pockriss, Sammy Fain. *Songs:* Jacqueline; The Coffee Song; The Big Brass Band from Brazil; Civilization (Bongo Bongo Bongo); The Thousand Islands Song; A Strawberry Moon; Red Silk Stockings and Green Perfume; Mention My Name in Sheboygan; Careless Hands; Chocolate Whiskey and Vanilla Gin; Dear Hearts and Gentle People; Dearie; Stay With the Happy People; Boutonniere; Be My Life's Companion; Shanghai; Don't Ever Be Afraid to Go Home; How Do You Speak to an Angel?; Everybody Loves to Take a Bow; Every Street's a Boulevard in Old New York; Somebody Bad Stole de Wedding Bell; Money Burns a Hole in My Pocket; In the Wee Small Hours of the Morning; I'm in Favor of Friendship; Sailor Boys Have Talk to Me in English; The President on the Dollar; Wrong Joe; Moonlight Gambler; Seven Little Girls; My Little Corner of the World; Any Day Now; My Summer Love; Young Wings Can Fly; Baby, Come Home; Everyday's a Holiday; Our Day Will Come; Imagination Is a Magic Dream; You're Following Me; Tower of Strength; Au Revoir; Don't You Believe It. *Scores:* Bway Shows: Angel in the Wings; Hazel Flagg; Film: Alice in Wonderland.

HILLIARD, JACQUELINE DALYA   ASCAP 1971
composer, author, actress
b New York, NY, Aug 3, 18. Educ: Walton High Sch, NY; NY Univ, BA; Central Commercial Bus Col (costume design); studied acting with Sherman Marks, Francis Lederer. Acted in many Bway shows & motion pictures, 37- Gen mgr, Bob Hilliard Music Co, 52-62. Pres, Garson, Hilliard & Day Music Publ, 63-65; artist gallery shows, 66- Music publ, writer & co-producer, Robert Hilliard Productions & founder & pres, Hilliard Audio Visual Studios, 67-70. Lyricist for var artists, 71- Chief Collabrs: Leon Ware, Mark Rael, Bob Hilliard.

Songs: Lyrics: Africa (You Laughed About Love); Come Live With Me, Angel; Euphoria; Here I Come to You With Love; Instant Love; In the Middle of My Time; In the Morning of Love; Lovin' Ain't Like Bizniz; Opportunity; Out of the Past; Party Time; Phantom Lover; Rolling Down a Mountainside; Sweetbreads and Wine; Wait 'til Tomorrow; We Could Make Love; Who's Looking for a Lover; The 3; Wide Awake; A Woman Being Loved.

HILLIGARDT, FREDERICK PHILLIP   ASCAP 1976
composer, author, producer
b St Louis, Mo, Aug 17, 47. Staff writer, Motown Records & Gwen Glenn Productions. Writer TV & radio jingles. *Songs:* Look At This Face; Michael; Hollywood Lovers. *Instrumental Works:* The Boogie Machine.

HILLMAN, MARCIA   ASCAP 1967
author
b New York, NY, June 20, 32. Educ: Brooklyn Col, BA, 54; Columbia Univ; Northwestern Univ. Poet, lyricist, non-performing musician & singer. Original material & lyrics, Am Fedn TV & Radio Artists Showcase, 71. Chief Collabrs: Jon Mayer, Jimmy Curtiss. *Songs:* Lyrics: Now; One More Ride; Pity the Child.

HILLMAN, RICHARD PAUL   ASCAP 1951
author, composer, educator
b Sparks, Nev, Apr 27, 17. Educ: Princeton Univ; Univ Southern Calif; Univ Calif, Berkeley; Univ Hawaii; San Jose State Univ; San Francisco State Univ; Univ Nev; MA(Eng & speech). Taught, Univ Hawaii, high schs in Bay & San Francisco area. Professional pianist & organist in clubs & major shipping lines worldwide. Announcer, NBS, KGU, Hawaii, 3 yrs. Author, poetry & travel story. Chief Collabr: Richard Kraemer. *Songs & Instrumental Works:* I Must Have Been Dumb; White Waves and Grey Gulls; Bon Voyage; also 300 songs written.

HILLMAN, ROSCOE VANOS (ROC)   ASCAP 1942
composer, author, teacher
b Arvada, Colo, July 13, 10. Educ: Univ Colo, jour maj; Calif Acad Music. Reporter, The Denver Post. Vaudeville with father in late 20's. Played guitar with original Dorsey Brothers Band, Jimmy Dorsey, Paul Whiteman, Kay Kyser & Skinnay Ennis Bands, also with orchs at Columbia, Paramount & RKO Studios, Hollywood. Musical dir, TV Channel 13, Hollywood. Chief Collabrs: Barclay Allen, Johnny Napton. *Songs:* Come Runnin'; I Bought a Wooden Whistle; My Serenade; You Keep Me in Hot Water; Pushin' Sand; Wasted Tears; I Met Her in a Revolving Door; Our United States; Music: Long May We Love; Just Lately; Lyrics: My Devotion; Cumana; I Found a Friend; It Began in Havana; The New Look; Timbales; The Copacabana Revue.

HILS, CLIFFORD A   ASCAP 1961
composer, musician
b Pittsburgh, Pa, Nov 5, 18. Educ: High sch. Professional musician, 36-

HILTON, HERMINE
lyricist
b Los Angeles, Calif. Educ: Univ Calif, Los Angeles. Began career as writer for hotel shows, musical theatre & nightclub performers. Collaborated on numerous films & TV shows; lyricist for many well known commercials. Lyricist for TV themes incl "Police Woman," "Hawaii Five-O" & "Popi." Chief Collabrs: Marvin Hamlisch, David Grusin, David Shire, Charles Fox, Morton Stevens, Lalo Shifrin, Artie Butler, Maurice Jarre, Gerald Fried, Frank Devol, Neal Hefti, Aldemaro Romero, Frank Pourcel, John Elizalde, Greg Nicoloff, George & Edward del Barrio. *Songs:* Lyrics: Melissa's Eyes; There Was a Time; Crack in My World; Sister Sunday; You Can Count on Me; I Gotta Know You; Get the Music to the Children; He Called Her Lady; Corey; Mollie (The First Time); Si Lo Quiere Dios; I Don't Want to Hear the Bugles; Touch Me Softly, Love; The Taste of My Tears; Night Eyes; Jennifer and Jamie; Take Me to Morning; The Color of the Wind Is Cold. *Scores:* Lyrics for TV: The Forever Tree; The City; I Want to Keep My Baby; Coffee, Tea or Me; Love American Style; Cannon; Apple's Way; Lyrics for Films: The Heart Is a Lonely Hunter; Vigilante Force; The Moonshine War; Hustle; W-USA; The Killing of Sister George; Illusions.

HILTON, LEWIS BOOTH   ASCAP 1978
composer, author, teacher
b Bulyea, Sask, Nov 21, 20. Educ: Univ Northern Iowa, BA, 42; Columbia Univ Teachers Col, EdD, 51; comp studies with Wallingford Riegger. Teacher elem schs, Belleville, NJ; musician, US Coast Guard; teacher, Drake Univ, 46-49 & Washington Univ, 51- Author, "Learning to Teach Through Playing the Woodwinds." *Songs:* Music: Yet Do I Marvel (baritone & piano). *Instrumental Works:* Glen and Katja (trombone & piano); Polarities I (brass quintet); Polarities II (alto saxophone, flute & harpsichord piano); Etudes for the Intermediate Clarinetist; Arr: Andante Cantabile (Beethoven; for bassoon); Allegro and Minuet (Beethoven; 2 clarinets); variations on La Ci Daren La Mano (Mozart-Beethoven; saxophone trio); Allegro and Minuet (Beethoven; 2 flutes); transc for sax quartet, Sonatine, first movement (Kabalersky).

HILTON, WAYNE EDWARD　　　　　　　　ASCAP 1972
composer, singer
b Wyandotte, Mich, Oct 21, 47. Educ: Southgate High Sch; NCent Bible Col, BA; Ft Wayne Bible Col; Detroit Bible Col. Began Christian music background, 66. Began writing, 70. Working in studio as mgr, vocalist & arr, Nashville, 73. Active in church music. Chief Collabr: Gordon Jensen. *Songs:* We're Together Again; He's Changing Me.

HIMBER, RICHARD　　　　　　　　　ASCAP 1940
composer, author, conductor
b Newark, NJ, Feb 20, 07; d New York, NY, Dec 11, 66. Educ: Col; pvt music study. Cond for Sophie Tucker, also vaudeville & revues. Led own dance orch in ballrooms, theatres, on radio. Has performed as a magician. *Songs:* After the Rain; Haunting Memories; Time Will Tell; Am I Asking Too Much; Moments in the Moonlight; It Isn't Fair; I'm Getting Nowhere Fast With You.

HINDERER, EVERETT ROLAND (SHORTY COOK)　　　ASCAP 1952
composer, author, singer
b Lagrange, Ind, Nov 18, 14. Radio, 20 yrs; on TV, 15 yrs; bass & steel guitarist. Recording artist; recorded 144 transc for M M Cole. Author, song bks & sheet music. Chief Collabrs: Billy Hayes, Guy Campbell, Slim Coxx, Joe Leggo, Bill Haley. *Songs:* Music: Yodel Polka; Landslide of Love; Keep Smiling; Out Where the West Winds Blow; Who's Gonna Kiss You When I'm Gone; Counting Tears.

HINES, EARL KENNETH (FATHA)　　　　　ASCAP 1949
composer, author, pianist
b Duquesne, Pa, Dec 28, 05. Educ: Schenley High Sch, Pittsburgh, Pa. Forms trio, 21; own band, Chicago, 24; tours with Carroll Dickerson Band, Calif, 26; with Louis Armstrong, Chicago, 28 & 48; records classic perf, first solo records & opens with own band for 12 yr stay, Chicago, 28. Solo concerts at New York's Little Theatre. Frequently toured in Europe, Latin Am, Australia & Japan, as well as Soviet Russia for US State Dept. Chief Collabrs: Charles Carpenter, Henri Woode, Reginald Foresythe & Billy Eckstine. *Songs:* My Monday Date; When I Dream of You; One Night in Trinidad; Straight to Love; Piano Man; Music: Rosetta; Apex Blues; You Can Depend on Me; Everything Depends on You; Jelly Jelly Blues; Stormy Monday Blues; Ann; Cavernism; Pianology; Rhythm Sundae; Deep Forest; Love at Night (Is Out of Sight); Jitney Man; The Father Jumps; Father Steps In; Bubbling Over. *Instrumental Works:* Blues in Thirds; Brussels Hustle; The Cannery Walk; 57 Varieties; Stanley Steamer.

HINES, GEORGE THOMAS　　　　　　　ASCAP 1957
composer, author, musician
b New York, NY, Jan 14, 16. Singer & orch leader, The City Hotel, Radio Splendid & El Mundo, Buenos Aires, Argentina. To US; with Enoch Light, Sammy Kaye & Guy Lombardo. Recorded for Mitch Miller & Percy Faith. With "Arthur Godfrey Show," 1 yr; music dir, Roney Plaza, Hollywood Beach & Yankee Clipper Hotels. Convention & free-lance work. Chief Collabrs: Tony Cabot, Mack David, May Singhi Breen. *Songs:* Hawaiian Cha Cha Cha; My Enchanted Island; One Kiss From You; You're My Only Love Song; Music: My Hawaiian Love.

HINES, JEROME　　　　　　　　　　ASCAP 1963
composer, author, singer
b Hollywood, Calif, Nov 8, 21. Educ: BA(chem & math); studied comp with Arthur Lange. Soloist, Metrop Opera, 34 yrs. Own opera, "I Am the Way," was produced in maj theaters, incl Metrop Opera, Indianapolis Symph, Dallas Symph & others. Singer many recitals & in most maj opera houses, incl: La Scala, Milan; Teatro Colon, Buenos Aires; Bolshoi, Moscow; Festsprelhaus, Bayreuth. *Songs:* Music: The Lord's Prayer.

HINTON, MILTON JOHN
composer, bassist
b Vicksburg, Miss, June 23, 10. Educ: Wendell Phillip's High Sch, Chicago, 29; Crane Jr Col, Ill, Assoc Music, 31. Worked in Chicago with Zutty Singleton & Erskine Tate, early 30's; bassist, Cab Calloway Orch, 36-51 & Louis Armstrong, 51-52. Played on radio & TV for Polly Bergen, Patti Page, Dick Cavett, Jackie Gleason & others; performed at Newport Jazz Fest, Nice Jazz Fest, Kansas City Jazz Fest & other fests; concert tours with Pearl Bailey, Bing Crosby, Diane Caroll, Paul Anka. Studio performer in New York with jazz & popular recording artists, 53- Teacher, Hunter Col, Baruch Col & Clinics at cols & univs, 70's. *Instrumental Works:* The Judge Meets the Section; Mona's Feeling Lonely; Sometime's I Wonder.

HIRSCH, LOUIS ACHILLE　　　　　　　ASCAP 1914
composer, publisher
b New York, NY, Nov 28, 1887; d New York, May 13, 24. Educ: City Col New York; Stern Acad, Berlin, studied with Rafael Joseffy. Staff pianist, Gus Edwards, Shapiro & Bernstein Music Cos. Wrote songs for Lew Dockstader Minstrels. Staff comp, Shubert bros, 12-14. Partner, Victoria Publ Co. One of 9 founders, ASCAP, charter mem, dir, 17-24. Chief Collabrs: Harold Atteridge, Otto Harbach, Edward Madden, Irving Caesar, Gene Buck. *Songs:* The Gaby Glide; Always Together; My Sumurum Girl; Mary; Hold Me in Your Loving Arms; Love Is Like a Red Red Rose; Hello, Frisco, Hello; When I Found You; Beautiful Island of Girls; Garden of Your Dreams; My Rambler Rose; 'Neath the South Sea Moon; The Tickle Toe; Going Up; The Love Nest; I Am Thinking of You; Annabel Lee. *Scores:* Bway stage: He Came From Milwaukee; Revue of Revues; Vera Violetta; Passing Show of 1912; Ziegfeld Follies (4 ed); Going Up; The Rainbow Girl; Oh, My Dear!; See Saw; Mary; The O'Brien Girl; Greenwich Follies (22, 23); Betty Lee.

HIRSCH, WALTER　　　　　　　　　ASCAP 1921
author
b New York, NY, Mar 10, 1891; d. Chief Collabrs: Al Goering, Frank Magine, Fred Rose, Spencer Williams. *Songs:* Strange Interlude; Who's Your Little Whoosis; Save the Last Dance for Me; That Little Boy of Mine; Carolina Sunshine; Holding My Honey's Hand; Deed I Do; Marie; Lullaby in Rhythm; If It's Good (Then I Want It).

HIRSHHORN, NAOMI CARYL　　　　　　ASCAP 1963
composer, singer
b New York, NY. Educ: Feagin Sch; Univ Southern Calif. Songwriter & singer for play "Spoon River." Chief Collabr: Charles Aidman. *Songs:* Spoon River; I Am, I Am.

HIRT, CHARLES CARLETON　　　　　　ASCAP 1966
composer, author, arranger
b Los Angeles, Calif, Nov 4, 11. Educ: Occidental Col, BA, hon DrMusic; Univ Southern Calif, MSci & PhD; Westminster Col, hon DFA; Pacific Univ, hon LHD. Cond & music educr, secondary schs & community cols, 10 yrs; fac mem, Univ Southern Calif, 36 yrs, cond & head (founder), Choral Dept. Guest cond & choral clinician in Am & Europe. Comp, author & ed. *Songs & Instrumental Works:* Lyrics: Farewell My Love (arr); I Know a Young Maiden (Lassus, arr); Since My Tears and Lamenting (Morley, arr); Alleluia! Sing Praise (J S Bach, arr); Three Gypsy Songs (Brahms, arr); The Conversion of St Paul (from oratorio Paulus, Mendelssohn, arr, vocal scores, choral parts); Come My Soul, 'Tis Time for Waking (Mendelssohn, arr); Sing We Noël (Chesrakov, arr); As a Choir Celestial (Bortnianski, arr); Kyrie Eleison (from Imperial Mass by Haydn, arr); Now Sing We All This Day (Hassler, arr).

HITE, LES　　　　　　　　　　　ASCAP 1953
composer, author, conductor
b Du Quoin, Ill, Feb 13, 03; d Santa Monica, Calif, Feb 6, 62. Bandleader until early 40's. Became booking agent, Calif. *Songs:* T-Bone Blues; That's the Lick.

HOAGEY, CATHERINE YEAKEL　　　　　ASCAP 1962
composer, author, teacher
b Perkasie, Pa, July 16, 08. Educ: Perkasie High Sch; Philadelphia Musical Acad; Temple Univ, BM(piano) & teacher's cert; Neff Col of Oratory, grad; Univ Mex, sem; studied theatre organ with Irving Cahan, Stanley Theatre, Philadelphia. Organist, theatres, 7 yrs & for church. Taught, piano & organ, Jacobs Hammond Studio, Philadelphia, Charilli & Allentown. Founder & operator, 3 schs of musical kindergarten for children age 2 to 5, 30 yrs. Comp of songs & music appearing in many mags incl Instructor, Highlights, Ranger Rick & Children's Activities. Writer of official centennial songs for Perkasie & Sellersville, Pa. Author, "English Around the World," containing 18 children's songs & on record & tape for use in schs.

HOBART, GEORGE V　　　　　　　　ASCAP 1914
author
b Port Hawksbury, NS, Jan 16, 1867; d Cumberland, Md, Feb 1, 26. Moved to US, 1874. Managing ed, Sunday Scimitar, Cumberland, 55. Wrote "Dinkelspiel" papers, Baltimore News, 14 yrs. Author, "John Henry" bks (15 vols). Playwright: "Wildfire"; "Our Mrs McChesney"; "Experience." Librettist: "A Yankee Circus on Mars"; "Merry Widow Burlesque"; "The Ham Tree"; "Over the River"; "Hitchy-Koo of 1919"; "Buddies"; "Music Box Revue" (21, 22); "Greenwich Village Follies of 1922." Charter mem, ASCAP, dir, 14-20. Chief Collabrs: Reginald DeKoven, A Baldwin Sloane, Victor Herbert, Silvio Hein, Raymond Hubbell. *Songs:* The Lovelorn Lily; Alma, Where Do You Live?; When I Love; I Want a Man to Love Me. *Scores:* Bway stage: The Hall of Fame; Mother Goose; The Rogers Brothers in Ireland; Old Dutch; Broadway to Tokyo (librettist); The Wild Rose (librettist); The Boys and Betty (librettist); The Yankee Girl (librettist); Alma, Where Do You Live? (librettist); Ziegfeld Follies (6 ed; also librettist).

HOBBS, JERRY DAVID　　　　　　　ASCAP 1978
composer, singer
b Lindsay, Calif, Apr 13, 41. Educ: Strathmore High Sch, Calif, grad. Interested in songwriting & singing career as a young boy; played rhythm guitar. *Songs:* I'm Gonna Be a Better Man; If You Ever Pass This Way, Pass Me By.

HOBSON, RICHARD H　　　　　　　　ASCAP 1975
composer, author
b Philadelphia, Pa, Oct 12, 44. Educ: Park Col, BA; Pa State Univ, MA, PhD. Regional theatre, wrote incidental music, "Brecht on Brecht" & "Of Mice and Men"; author & comp, "The Overland Rooms." Off-Bway, author & comp, "Memphis is Gone."

HOCHER, WILLIAM (BILLY)　　　ASCAP 1972
composer, author, singer

b Flushing, NY, July 3, 43. Educ: Orch training high sch; pvt study guitar with Tom Catalano 5 yrs; studied bass with Pete Roberts 3 yrs. Singer/musician night clubs, concert tours, radio & TV. Recording artist, RCA, MCA, Epic, Budda, Kama Sutra & Columbia. Mem groups, Bulldog, Pepper & Sajobi. Staff writer, Love-Zager. Chief Collabrs: Eric Thorngren, Debbie Gurney, Doug Frank, John Turi & Doug James. *Songs:* Moon is the Daughter of the Devil; When the Bell Rings (Come Out Dancin'). *Songs & Instrumental Works:* No; Flamingo; Sunshine Hotel; Are You Really Happy Together; Have a Nice Day.

HOCKENSMITH, HADLEY　　　ASCAP 1971
composer, author, studio musician

b Atlanta, Ga, Nov 15, 49. Started playing guitar at age 13; started own rock band at age 14. Played bass for Righteous Bros at age 15. Joined first jazz group, age 17. Began writing music, age 21. Began playing in Christian Jazz Rock group Sonlight, toured with Andrae Crouch. Played on records for Mike McDonald & David Gates, toured Europe with Gates. Active in Contemporary Christian Records. Produced & co-wrote songs on "Never Turnin' Back" album. Chief Collabrs: Bruce Hibbard, Kelly Willard. *Songs:* In Remembrance; Your Love; One Step Closer; Never Turnin' Back; The Savior Came Into My Life; Still in Love; Calling; Forgiven.

HODAS, DOROTHY GERTRUDE　　　ASCAP 1959
composer, teacher

b Perth Amboy, NJ, Feb 23, 12. Educ: Newark State Teachers Col; Monmouth Col; Brookdale Col. Former sch teacher. Chief Collabrs: Mack Wolfson, Gordon Hodas. *Songs:* Music: Love of My Life; The Harem; Torn Between Two Lovers; Gypsy Dance; Unlock Your Heart.

HODES, SOPHIE
See Kellem, Milton

HODGES, CHARLES EDWARD, SR　　　ASCAP 1969
composer

b Memphis, Tenn, June 29, 47. HI-Recording Studio, Memphis. *Songs & Instrumental Works:* The City; Always; I'd Rather Be Blind; Please Forgive; Nobody But You; Let Yourself Go; Music to My Ear; On the Loose; Super Star.

HODGES, JAMES S　　　ASCAP 1951
composer, author, producer

b New York, NY, May 24, 1885; d. Educ: High sch. Appeared in Liberty Theatres, WW I; produced own shows. Entertainer, camps, hospitals & USO, WW II. Publ. *Songs:* It Wasn't in the Cards; Lonely Nights; Blackberry Jelly Nellie; Some Day You'll Want Me to Want You; Dear Old Girl of Mine; Ding Dong Bell.

HODGES, JOHNNY　　　ASCAP 1945
composer, saxophonist

b Cambridge, Mass, July 25, 07; d New York, NY, May 11, 70. Educ: Pub schs. Saxophonist in dance orchs; joined Duke Ellington, 27. Has made many records. Chief Collabr: Duke Ellington. *Songs & Instrumental Works:* I'm Beginning to See the Light; Hodge Podge; Jeep's Blues; Jitterbug's Lullaby; Wanderlust; Mood to Be Wooed; Wonder of You; Crosstown; Squatty Roo; It Shouldn't Happen to a Dream; Harmony in Harlem; What's It All About?; Shady Side.

HODOWUD, EDWARD FRED　　　ASCAP 1964
composer, author, conductor

b Plains, Pa, Mar 12, 24. Cond, accordionist & bassist with own band. Chief Collabr: Robert Scherman. *Songs:* Always Forever; Telephone; Fun to Be With; Run Little Sheba; I'd Love to Live in Your House; Jamaican Shorts; Love Don't Pay.

HOFF, VIVIAN BEAUMONT　　　ASCAP 1963
composer, author, teacher

b Fountaintown, Ind, Dec 17, 11. Educ: Studied piano with Bomar Cramer & Thelma Todd; Butler Univ, (harmony), studied comp with William Pelz; studied voice with Elma Igleman. Comp, progs of original compositions throughout US & at Nat League of Am Pen Women meetings. Songs used by Purdue Glee Club, Jerry Barnes at Clowes Hall with Indianapolis Symph, Wilshire Methodist Church, Los Angeles, San Diego & Washington, DC, Nat Fedn Music Clubs & on cable TV. Former piano teacher & choir dir. Music ed, Nat League of Am Pen Women, 4 yrs; elected to Nat Fedn Music Clubs' Who's Who of Ind Musicians. *Songs & Instrumental Works:* Father in Heaven; Keep the Star-Spangled Banner Waving; I Look to My Lord; Be of Good Courage; Spring Fever (piano); & 300 songs & piano compositions & a violin solo.

HOFFER, BERNARD　　　ASCAP 1968
composer, arranger, conductor

b Zurich, Switz, Oct 14, 34. Educ: St Benedict's High Sch, NJ; Univ Rochester Eastman Sch Music, BS & MS; studied comp with Wayne Barlow & Bernard Rogers. Arr, USA Field Band, Washington, DC, 58-62; free-lance musician, New York area, 62-; played piano with Sammy Kaye, Buddy Morrow, Warren Covington & others. Cond & arr, club acts for Phyllis Newman, Melba Moore, Sergio Franchi & others, 68-; wrote and arr jingles, background scores, commercials, TV shows & films, 70- *Instrumental Works:* Theme for MacNeil-Lehrer Report, PBS; Theme for NBC Studio 8H; Concerto for Saxophone and Wind Orch; Variations on a Theme of Stravinsky for Saxophone Quartet; Preludes and Fugues for Saxophone Quartet and Brass Quintet. *Scores:* Film/TV: The Ivory Ape; The Old Country.

HOFFER, JAY　　　ASCAP 1969
composer, author

b Brooklyn, NY. Educ: NY Univ, BA, 46, MBA, 54; Columbia Univ, MA, 48. Worked 30 yrs in broadcasting; operations mgr, KERE, Denver; vpres prog, Hercules Broadcasting, Sacramento; mgr nat advert, ABC-TV, New York; promotion mgr, WJAR-AM & TV, Providence; sales promotion dir, WICC-AM & TV, Bridgeport. *Songs:* It's Gold; The Thirteen Colonies.

HOFFMAN, AL　　　ASCAP 1930
composer, author

b Minsk, Russia, Sept 25, 02; d New York, NY, July 21, 60. To US in 08. Educ: Franklyn High Sch, Seattle, Wash. Led own band, Seattle; drummer in nightclub bands, NY, 28. To Eng, 34-37. Chief Collabrs: Al Goodhart, Maurice Sigler, Ed Nelson, Sammy Lerner, Dick Manning, Jerry Livingston, Milton Drake, Mack David, Mann Curtis, Leo Corday, Leon Carr, Bob Merrill, Walter Kent. *Songs:* Heartaches; I Apologize; Auf Wiedersehn, My Dear; Fit As a Fiddle; Black-Eyed Susan Brown; Jimmy Had a Nickel; Who Walks in When I Walk Out?; I Saw Stars; Why Don't You Practice What You Preach?; Little Man You've Had a Busy Day; Roll Up the Carpet; I'm in a Dancing Mood; Without Rhythm; There Isn't Any Limit to My Love; Everything Stops for Tea; From One Minute to Another; I Can Wiggle My Ears; Say the Word; Everything's in Rhythm With My Heart; Let's Put Some People to Work; Gangway; Lord and Lady Whoozis; She Shall Have Music; Romance Runs in the Family; Apple Blossoms and Chapel Bells; Goodnight, Wherever You Are; The Story of a Starry Night; Close to You; O Dio Mio; What's the Good Word, Mr Bluebird?; I Must Have One More Kiss Kiss Kiss; I Ups to Her and She Ups to Me; Mairzy Doats; Fuzzy Wuzzy; I'm a Big Girl Now; I Had Too Much to Dream Last Night; Chi-Baba, Chi-Baba; There's No Tomorrow; I'm Gonna Live Till I Die; Bibbidi-Bobbidi-Boo; A Dream Is a Wish Your Heart Makes; If I Knew You Were Comin' I'd 've Baked a Cake; Takes Two to Tango; Gilly Gilly Ossenfeffer Katzenellenbogen By the Sea; Papa Loves Mambo; Don't Stay Away Too Long; Allegheny Moon; Hot Diggity; Mama, Teach Me to Dance; Ivy Rose; Are You Really Mine?; Oh, Oh, I'm Falling in Love Again; Secretly; Hawaiian Wedding Song; You're Cheatin' Yourself; If You Smile at the Sun. *Scores:* London Stage: This'll Make You Whistle; Going Greek; Hide and Seek; Hollywood: Cinderella; British Films: Come Out of the Pantry; First a Girl; When Knights Were Bold; She Shall Have Music; Gangway.

HOFFMAN, ALLEN　　　ASCAP 1972
composer, educator

b Newark, NJ, Apr 12, 42. Educ: East Orange High Sch; Hartt Col, BMus, 65, MMus, 69, studied with Arnold Franchetti. Instr & adminr, theory & comp, Hartt Col & Hartford Cons, 67-77. Performances, US, Can & Europe; Hartford Symph Premiere, 78. MacDowell Colony fel, 68-72. *Songs & Instrumental Works:* Chorals: Mass...for the passing of all shining things...; Madrigals.

HOFFMAN, CARY　　　ASCAP 1968
composer, author, singer

b New York, NY, Apr 24, 40. Educ: Self-taught. Singer, piano & guitar player. Co-writer of two songs on Country Charts. Jingle writer; comp of music for NBC-TV Special. Chief Collabr: Ira Gasman. *Songs:* Congratulations (You Sure Made a Man Out of Him); The Last Person to See Me Alive; Anything for a Laugh; You, You I LoveYou; Come on Daisy. *Scores:* Off-Bway Musical: What's a Nice Country Like you Doing in a State Like This?

HOFFMAN, EDITH RITTER　　　ASCAP 1970
composer, author, organ-piano teacher

b New York, NY, Dec 27, 14. Educ: Pvt studies with Gregory Ashman & Marie Wilson, 10 yrs & with Albert De Vito, Westbury, NY, 3 yrs; studied at Art Students League & New York Sch Fine & Applied Arts. Prof artist. Prof teacher of piano & organ, 15 yrs; was on staff, Wurlitzer & Hammond Organ Cos. Author bks: "The Latin American Organist," series, "The Pop Organist" & "The Pop Organist Goes Latin." Illustrated music covers for publ. *Songs & Instrumental Works:* The Face of Love; Minnie Mambo; Music for Swamp Angel; Music for Give Us This Day; My Blue Winter Love.

HOFFMAN, JACK　　　ASCAP 1952
author

b Buffalo, NY. Educ: Bennett High Sch; State Teachers Col, Buffalo; Univ Calif, Los Angeles. Orch leader, musician, music publ & record producer. Chief Collabrs: Jimmy MacDonald, Jimmy McHugh, Bebe Blake, Babe Russin, Jerry Livingston, Richard Froeber. *Songs:* Dreamboat; I Thank God; Dreamy Eyes; Bird of Paradise; Lyrics: Teresa; I Love the Sunshine of Your Smile; The Navy Swings; I Wanna Say Hello; Back in the Good Old Days; One Step (Toward the Lord); I'll Always Remember You; I Wish You the Very Best Luck in the World; Walking in the Light of the Lord; Tres Chic; Welcome to Hawaii.

HOFFMAN, JAMES SENATE (BUDDY LANDON)   ASCAP 1959
composer, author, singer
b Kansas City, Mo, June 9, 22. Educ: Studied trumpet with John D'Andelet. Chief Collabrs: Eddie Dean, Janis Landon. *Songs:* Another Time, Another Place, Another World; I Found It (slogan, Campus Crusade for Christ); The Loneliest Day of The Year (Christmas song); Does He Wonder Where You Are; Lyrics: Little Boy Tracks.

HOFFMAN, JOEL HARVEY   ASCAP 1977
composer
b Vancouver, BC, Sept 27, 53. Educ: Univ Wales, Gt Brit, BM; Juilliard Sch, New York, MM & DMA; studied with Easley Blackwood, Elliott Carter & others. As composer performed by Chicago Symph Brass, BBC Welsh Orch, Juilliard 20th Century Music Ens, Parnassus & others. Soloist var chamber groups & orch. Comn from Tanglewood, WGUC-FM, Cincinnati & others. Solo pianist with Chicago Symph, Belg Radio Symph, Fla Gulf Coast Symph & others. Mem fac comp, Col/Cons Music, Univ Cincinnati, 78- *Instrumental Works:* Variations (violin, cello & harp); September Music (double bass & harp); Concerto (violin, viola, cello & orch); Music from Chartres (brass); Chamber Symphony; Fantasy Pieces (piano solo); Divertimento (string quartet, harp & piano).

HOFFMAN, OLIVIA WATSON   ASCAP 1958
composer, author
b Newport, RI. Educ: Newport Art Asn Sch; Scudder Sch. Writer, poetry for radio, articles on art for newspapers. Author, poetry "The Four Seasons." Mem, Philadelphia Art Alliance, Nat League Am Pen Women. Chief Collabr: George Stork. *Songs:* Monte Carlo Moon; Nobody Knows; I Still Dream; The Ballad of Paul Bunyan (1st prize, Jewish Nat Fund contest).

HOFFMAN, RICHARD
See Ascher, Everett

HOFFMAN, STANLEY DAVID   ASCAP 1959
composer, author, singer
b Danville, Va. Educ: Univ Calif, Los Angeles, BA(music); Westlake Col Music, dipl. Wrote music, Hollywood Studio Club Revues, 56 & 58; musical partner, Chuck Blore Creative Services (radio & TV commercials), 63-73; producer. Chief Collabrs: Johnny Mercer, David Man, Dick Allen, Stanley Styne, Hermine Hilton, Jerry Gladstone, Bernadine Grifman, Jay Kholos. *Songs:* My Love Is Like a Red Red Rose; Music: Touch Me Softly; One Is a Lonesome Number; You Can Take It From Me; Try Again (theme from the Hollywood Radio Theater); I Didn't Fall In Love Again Today; Til Now; Winter In Salzburg; My Love for You; Please World Stay Open All Night; Nothing Is Lost. *Instrumental Works:* Rhapsody in Art Deco. *Scores:* Off Bway Show: Adults Only, No Pets; Hollywood Studio Club Revues. *Albums:* Love at Last.

HOFFMAN, WILLIAM M   ASCAP 1965
author
b New York, NY, Apr 12, 39. Educ: City Col New York, BA, 60. Playwright & lyricist, stage, TV & radio; author musical plays, incl "Gulliver's Travels", "A Book of Etiquette" & "A Quick Nut Bread to Make Your Mouth Water." Rec'd Guggenheim fel & NEA grants. Teacher, Univ Mass & Hofstra Univ. Working on opera comn by Metrop Opera for Centennial celebration in 83-84 season, will be based loosely on "The Guilty Mother." Collabr: John Corigliano. *Songs:* Lyrics: The Cloisters.

HOFFMANN, ADOLF G   ASCAP 1959
composer, conductor
b Cincinnati, Ohio, May 30, 1890; d Chicago, Ill, Jan 19, 68. Educ: Cincinnati Col Music (Reuben Springer Medal); studied with Adolf Brune, Adolf Weidig. Cellist with string quartet; joined Chicago Symph, 12, later Chicago Grand Opera Co. Orch mgr, cellist, chief arr & cond, Chicago Theatre, 21. On staff, WMAQ, 30; cellist & arr, WGN, then WGN-TV, 34. Fac, De Paul Univ & Am Cons. *Instrumental Works:* Symphony in E; Prelude and Fugue for String Quartet, Harp, Celeste; String Quartet in E Flat; Sarabande and Allegro; Chicago Theatre of Air Theme; Suite for Bassoon, Piano.

HOFFMANN, MAX   ASCAP 1939
composer, conductor, arranger
b Gnesen, Poland, Dec 8, 73; d Hollywood, Calif, May 21, 63. Educ: Pub schs. To US 1875; violinist, Minn Symph; cond vaudeville theatres, wrote songs for "Ziegfeld Follies of 1907." Staff comp, Klaw & Erlanger; dir first Russian ballet in US, featuring wife, Gertrude Hoffmann. Chief Collabrs: George V Hobart, Harry B Smith, Edward Madden, Harold Atteridge. *Songs:* A Bunch of Rags; Dixie Queen; By the Sycamore Tree; San Francisco Bay; If You Want to Learn to Kiss Me; In Washington; Panama; The Gertrude Hoffmann Glide.

HOHMAN, GEORGE C   ASCAP 1979
author, publisher
b Polar, Wis, Oct 19, 12. *Songs:* The Hobo; Drifting; Los Angeles; The Lumber Jack.

HOIBY, LEE   ASCAP 1952
composer, pianist
b Madison, Wis, Feb 17, 26. Educ: Univ Wis, BA; Mills Col, MA; Curtis Inst, grad; pvt studies with Egon Petri & Gunnar Johansen. Began as pianist, then at 22 switched to composition. Worked for 20 yrs as composer. Made successful debut as pianist in Alice Tully Hall, New York. Chief Collabrs: Lanford Wilson, Harry Duncan, William Ball. *Instrumental Works:* Piano Concerto. *Scores:* Summer and Smoke (opera); Natalia Petrovna (opera); The Scarf (opera); After Eden (ballet).

HOIER, JOHN CHARLES   ASCAP 1972
composer, musician, recording engineer
b Los Angeles, Calif, Mar 25, 49. Educ: Univ Wis. Writer & producer, 72-, Motown Records, 72-75, independent, 76- Chief Collabrs: Heyward Collins, Mike Morgan. *Songs:* That's the Way a Woman Is; Fantasy; It's the Same Way Now; The Trouble Is You.

HOKANSON, MARGRETHE   ASCAP 1949
composer, organist, pianist
b Duluth, Minn, Dec 19, 1893; d. Educ: Am Cons, Chicago; Margaret Morrison Sch, with Josef Lhevinne; studied with Heniot Levy, Arthur Anderson, Marcel Dupre, Wilhelm Middelschulte. Won first prize for orch work, Nat Fedn Musical Clubs, Minn. Dean, Organ Dept, St Olaf Col; dir, Northland Choral Group; founded Nordic Choral Ens, 39-43; assoc prof music, Allegheny Col, 44-54; arr, educr & cond. *Songs:* In the Primeval Forest; Ring Dans; Nordic Song; A Summer Idyl; Song Without Words; Song of the Shepherd; Ring Noel; Snow; Tribute; Gethsemane; Come, Close the Curtains of Your Eyes. *Songs & Instrumental Works:* O Praise Him (choral); Arr: Butterflies at Haga; The Arkansas Traveler.

HOLBEN, LAWRENCE ROBERT   ASCAP 1972
author, lyricist
b Los Angeles, Calif, Sept 2, 45. Writer of lyrics for about 40 songs. Chief Collabr: William Tewson.

HOLCOMBE, WILFORD LAWSHE, JR   ASCAP 1972
composer, flutist, saxophonist
b Trenton, NJ, Nov 9, 24. Educ: Juilliard Sch, studied harmony with George Wedge, orchestration with Vitorio Gianinni & flute with Arthur Lora; Univ Pa, BM(music), with hons, 48; studied comp & theory with William Happich, Robert Elmore & Constant Vaudain; pvt study arr with Dick Jacobs, 49. Played & arr for Tommy Dorsey, 49. Staff musician, WMGM, Atlantic City, NJ, 50-53; comp scores for feature & documentary films, late 50's. Arr & comp, "101 Strings" records, 61-69. Staff arr, Dallas Symph Orch, 70-71. Comp & arr music for band & orch, 70- Clarinetist. *Instrumental Works:* Concert Band: American Suite (Western descriptive piece); Overture in Pop Style (pop, rock legit style piece); Jazz Band: Charter Jazz Suite; Grand Central Suite; Band: Good Tidings of Great Joy (serious fantasy, well known carols); Orch: American Celebration Overture. *Scores:* Film: What Is a Painting.

HOLDEN, PAUL   ASCAP 1975
composer, author, performer
b West Terre Haute, Ind, Mar 25, 40. Educ: Naval Cons, Anacostia, Md; Ind State Univ, Terre Haute, BA. Began writing, 64- Entertainer & actor with Barbra Streisand, Joe E Brown, June Havoc, Virginia Mayo & others. Chief Collabr: Don MacPherson. *Songs:* The Musical Adventures of Tom Jones; Moll Flanders; Fanny Hill; The Love Doctor; How the West Was Lost; The Musical Dracula.

HOLDEN, SIDNEY   ASCAP 1925
composer, author
b Montreal, Que, Sept 17, 1900; d San Francisco, Calif, Dec 8, 47. Served in Can AF, WW I. *Songs:* Yankee Rose; Tell Me Why You and I Should Be Strangers; More Than Words Can Tell; San Domingo Bay; Two Lips on a Path of Roses; Americans All for All.

HOLDRIDGE, LEE ELWOOD   ASCAP 1978
composer
b Port-au-Prince, Haiti, Mar 3, 44. Educ: Manhattan Sch Music, comp studies 2 yrs; studied comp with Henry Lasker, 3 yrs; violin with Hugo Mariani, 5 yrs. Arr for Neil Diamond; scored episodes for TV, incl "McCloud" & "Hec Ramsey"; also scored films "Jeremy" & "Jonathan Livingston Seagull" with Neil Diamond. Symphonic & chamber works performed & recorded. Chief Collabrs: Molly-Ann Leikin, Alan & Marilyn Bergman, Rod McKuen, Joe Henry, John Denver. *Songs:* Music: Eight Is Enough (TV show theme); Moment By Moment; Beautiful Sadness; Rainbow Round; Noel: Christmas Eve 1913; Sierra; The Higher We Fly; Follow Your Restless Dream. *Instrumental Works:* Concerto No 2 for Violin and Orchestra; Scenes of Summer; Ballet Fantasy for Strings and Harp; Concertino for Violoncello and Strings. *Scores:* Opera/Ballet: Lazarus and His Beloved; Summerland; Film/TV: The Other Side of the Mountain Part II; Moment by Moment; Oliver's Story; French Postcards; American Pop; Mustang Country. *Albums:* Holdridge Conducts Holdridge.

HOLIDAY, JIMMY EDWARD ASCAP 1968
composer
b Durant, Miss, July 24, 34. Recording artist on TV; singer, nightclubs & concerts; writer & producer. Chief Collabrs: Ray Charles, Jackie DeShannon, Eddie Reeves. *Songs:* God Bless the Children; Baby I Love You; Put a Little Love in Your Heart; All I Ever Need Is You; Peace of Mind.

HOLIDAY, MARVA JEAN ASCAP 1972
composer, author, singer
b San Jose, Calif, Aug 30, 48. Educ: Merritt Col, harmony, musicianship & piano; Los Angeles City Col; Univ Southern Calif; studied voice, Sanford Shire, 73. Staff writer, Jobete Music, 71-74; singer, nightclubs, 74-76; now writing with Tony J Williams, R&B, Pop & original score for "The Soul of Nat Turner," (play). Chief Collab: Tony J Williams (Sherlie Mathews). *Songs:* It's Written All Over My Face; Hang Around; Black Magic; Lyrics: Woman in My Eyes; Is the Challenge Over; Hey Little Girl Do You Want Some Candy?; Hook, Line and Sinker; Carbon Copy. *Albums:* Where Love Is.

HOLIEN, DANNY LEROY ASCAP 1971
composer, author, guitarist
b Red Wing, Minn, Jan 29, 49. Professional musician, 64-; recording artist, singer, guitarist, 71- *Songs:* Colorado; Red Wing; Wella Wella Isabella; Hick; The Strange One; Satsanga; Labor Man; Home; A Song of Thanksgiving; Lino the Wino; Joshua Brown.

HOLINER, MANN ASCAP 1933
author, actor
b Brooklyn, NY, June 7, 1897; d Hollywood, Calif, Oct 29, 58. Educ: Cornell Univ; Am Acad Dramatic Arts. Actor in stock, vaudeville & on Bway. Writer of spec material. Maj, USA, WW II, chief radio serv, Prog Section. Radio advert exec. Chief Collab: Alberta Nichols (wife). *Songs:* There Never Was a Town Like Paris; Sing a Little Tune; Come on and Make Whoopee; You Can't Stop Me From Loving You; What's Keeping My Prince Charming?; Until the Real Thing Comes Along; I Just Couldn't Take It, Baby; Your Mother's Son-in-Law; I'm Walkin' the Chalk Line; A Love Like Ours; Why Shouldn't It Happen to Us?; also songs for Luckee Girl; Rhapsody in Black & Blackbirds of 1933. *Scores:* Bway Shows: Gay Paree; Angela; Boom Boom.

HOLLANDER, RALPH ASCAP 1959
composer, violinist
b Brooklyn, NY, Nov 9, 16. Educ: Juilliard Sch of Music & Grad Sch, studies in violin; Manhattan Sch Music, MA(comp). Violin soloist, US & Europe; mem, Casal's Fests, Prades, France; concertmaster, NBC Opera Orch. *Songs & Instrumental Works:* Psalms of David for Violin and the Spoken Word (2 cycles); Gitane (violin & piano); Elegie (string orch); Sonata (violin alone); five songs on poems by Charles Erskine Scott Wood.

HOLLER, JOHN ASCAP 1941
composer, arranger, organist
b New York, NY, Jan 13, 04; d. Educ: Studied music with Walter Fleming, Charles Banks, David Williams, Norman Coke-Jephcott. Assoc ed music publ co; organist & choirmaster, St Marks Church, New York. Nat treas, Am Guild Organists. *Songs & Instrumental Works:* Choral: Jesus, Meek and Gentle; Praise My Soul; Our Shepherd; Saviour, Teach Me; Benedictus es, Domine; While Shepherds Watched Their Flocks; The King of Love.

HOLLIDAY, DEREK MICHAEL ASCAP 1971
composer, author, singer
b Indianapolis, Ind, Nov 19, 47. Educ: Emmerich Manual High Sch, 65; studied woodwinds, clarinet, alto & tenor saxophone with William D Kleyla, drama with Michael Mark, Hollywood, Calif; self-taught piano & guitar. Began performing & writing in India

HOLLINGSWORTH, LAYNE RUSKIN ASCAP 1978
composer, author, poet
b Colon, Nebr, Feb 6, 18. Chief Collabr: Yvette Mathews. *Songs:* Up in the Stars; A Bedtime Story; Hamlet; Pops; Take a Trip.

HOLLINGSWORTH, THELKA ASCAP 1928
composer, author
b Lake Rollins Plantation, La; d. Educ: Maddox Sem. Near East Relief spec rep in Europe, Palestine & Egypt, over 8 yrs. Mem adv dept, New York Times. *Songs:* Oh, Miss Hannah; Comin' Home; Oh Lucindy; Awake Beloved; On Wings of Memory; I Lift Mine Eyes Unto the Stars; Lady Moon; Joy; Cawn Bread; When I Hear Thy Call.

HOLLIS, MURRAY COBB, III ASCAP 1973
composer, singer, instructor
b Winfield, Ala, May 20, 40. Educ: Univ Ala, studied radio & TV; Va Commonwealth Univ, BS(advert); pvt vocal instr with Clinton Clark, Rolling Hills, Calif. Worked in sales, Del Monte Foods, Inc; did quality assurance presentations for McDonald-Douglas Aircraft Corp; dir advert (mobile & recreation products), Boise Cascade, Inc; road mgr, The Gospel Lads Quartet; pres, Christian Friends Agency (talent). Chief Collabr: Mel Taylor. *Songs:* I Love People; God's Good Country; Heavenly Days; He Is Jesus; Gift of Love;

Lyrics: Praise God; Please Care; In Just a Little While; Regal Splendor; Let's Put It Together Children.

HOLLODAN, DAMASKAS
See Hollombe, Daniel Ephraim

HOLLOMBE, DANIEL EPHRAIM (DAMASKAS ASCAP 1979
HOLLODAN)
composer, author
b Los Angeles, Calif, Nov 28, 57. Most of musical career has been spent working and writing for famed DJ Dr Demento. *Songs:* Making Love in a Subaru; Window Shopping; Dentist Chair Blues; My Girl's Got Three Legs; Sister Carolina.

HOLLOWAY, HELEN JOYCE (JOYCE ASCAP 1967
BARTHELSON, JOYCE BARTHELSON STEIGMAN)
composer, author
b Yakima, Wash, May 18, 1900. Educ: Oakland Tech High Sch, Calif; Univ Calif, Berkeley, 2 yrs; studied comp with Julius Gold & Otto Cesana, orchestration with Nicolas Flagello. Mem, Arion Trio & staff pianist, NBC, San Francisco, Calif, 24-35; asst cond, Women's Symph, New York, 36-38; comp-in-residence, Western Md Col, 39-41; mem, Concert Tours, Leigh Lect Bur, 41-44; co-founder, Hoff-Barthelson Music Sch, Scarsdale, NY, 44-67, comp-in-residence, 67- Chief Collab: Walter Ehret. *Songs & Instrumental Works:* The Pilgrims (SATB); Christmas, 1620 (SSA); Choral Series Famous Early Americans: Meriwether Lewis (SATB); Benjamin Franklin (SATB); Buffalo Bill (SATB); Daniel Boone (SATB); Father Junipero Serra (SSA); Betsy Ross (SSA); Pocahontas (SSA). *Scores:* Opera & Libretto: The King's Breakfast; Chanticleer (Nat Fedn Music Clubs-ASCAP Award, 67); The Devil's Disciple; Feathertop; Greenwich Village, 1910; Lysistrata.

HOLLOWAY, ROBERT CHARLES ASCAP 1959
composer, arranger, orchestrator
b Baltimore, Md, June 20, 27. Educ: Baltimore Polytechnic Inst; Holloway Inst of Music; studied orchestration with John Hefti, 50-51. Arr for ABC-TV, Radio City Music Hall, Skitch Henderson, Richard Hayman, Boston Pops, Enrique Madriguera, Buryl Red Productions, Caterina Valente, Larry Kert, Connie Francis, Denver Symph Orch, San Antonio Symph Orch & New Jersey Symph Orch. *Instrumental Works:* Busybody; Southern Suite; Eastern Slope (jazz/swing); Wildcat! (jazz/swing); The Authentic Original Genuine Imitation Kansas City Jazz Band Stomp.

HOLM, JOHN CECIL ASCAP 1965
author, playwright, actor
b Philadelphia, Pa, Nov 4, 04. Educ: West Philadelphia High Sch; Perkiomen Sch; Univ Pa, 24-25; Southeastern Mass Univ, hon DFA, 75. Began actg in Mask & Wig, Univ Pa, 25; actor in New York plays: "The Front Page", "Whirlpool", "Penal Law 2010", "The Up and Up", "Wonder Boy", "Dangerous Corner", "Mary of Scotland", "Blue Denim", "A Mighty Man Is He", "Midgie Purvis", "Mr President", "South Pacific" (Jones Beach), "The Advocate", "Xmas in Las Vegas", "Philadelphia, Here I Come!" & "Forty Carats." Author bks: "Sunday Best" & "McGarrity and the Pigeons." Playwright: "Three Men on a Horse", "Best Foot Forward", "Brighten the Corner", "Gramercy Ghost", "The Southwest Corner" & "Sweethearts" (rev version). Chief Collabrs: George Abbott (playwright), John Sacco (comp). *Songs:* Lyrics: Fanfare for Americans; Are You Running With Me, Lord?

HOLMES, DONALD BERT ASCAP 1978
composer, author, musician
b Los Angeles, Calif, Nov 12, 31. Educ: John C Fremont High Sch. Musician in nightclubs. Chief Collabr: Rube Goldberg. *Songs:* Sooner Or Later (You Always); Time of My Life.

HOLMES, G E ASCAP 1941
composer, conductor, arranger
b Baraboo, Wis, Feb 14, 1873; d Chicago, Ill, Feb 10, 45. Educ: Studied music with G Mitchell, W F Heath, Vandercook, Rosdon, Lattimer & Weldon. Cond & arr, John Vogel minstrels. Harmony & instrumentation teacher, Prior's Cons, Danville, Ill; Vandercook Sch Music, Chicago. Toured in Smith Spring-Holmes Quintet. *Songs:* Night Comes and the Day Is Done. *Instrumental Works:* Marches: The Prospector; Southland; Heroic; March Courageous; Colorado; Victory and Fame; War Correspondent; Safari; Trojan Prince; Overtures: Calvacade; Diane.

HOLMES, JOHN GRIER (JAKE)
composer, author
b San Francisco, Calif, Dec 28, 39. Educ: Hofstra Col; Juilliard Sch Music; Bennington Col. Started in theater revival of Golden Apple. Played clubs, Bitter End, Mr Kelly's, Playboy, Troubadour. Toured Europe. Made five albums; wrote album for Four Seasons & Frank Sinatra. Produced musical, "Sidewalkin" (nominated Drama Dist Award). Chief Collabrs: Bob Gaudio. *Songs:* So Close; How Are You; Paris Song; I Can Heal You.

HOLMES, (ALVIN) LEROY　　　ASCAP 1953
conductor, composer, arranger
b Pittsburgh, Pa, Sept 22, 13. Educ: Hollywood High Sch; Los Angeles Jr Col; Northwestern Col Music; Juilliard; studied with Ernst Toch, Ivan Boutnikoff, Joseph Schillinger. Lt(jg), USN, WW II, Pacific Theatre. Arr for Harry James Orch. Music dir, MGM & United Artists Records. *Songs & Instrumental Works:* The Mole; Viva Maria; I've Got a Song for You; I Wrote a Symphony on My Guitar. *Scores:* Motion Picture: Smile; TV Spec: I'm a Fan.

HOLMES, MARTY　　　ASCAP 1959
composer, arranger, musician
b Brooklyn, NY, Feb 7, 25. Educ: High sch. Musician & arr with dance bands incl Les Elgart & Tito Puente. *Songs:* Was There a Call for Me? *Scores:* Stage show: Keep It Clean.

HOLMES, RUPERT　　　ASCAP 1968
composer, author, recording artist
b Cheshire, Eng, Feb 24, 47. Educ: Syracuse Univ; Manhattan Sch Music. Songwriter. Wrote & arr for the Drifters, Platters & Gene Pitney; arr TV shows for Carol Burnett & Engelbert Humperdinck; arr & produced for Barbra Streisand. Touring the US & Can, performing at major clubs; guest on "Tonight Show", "Merv Griffin", "Mike Douglas" & "Soundstage"; has been guest host for "Midnight Special." Won the Cashbox & DJ Award for Most Promising Male Vocalist for 1980. *Songs:* Escape; Timothy; Echo Valley; Partners in Crime; Him; Answering Machine; Get Outta Yourself; In You I Trust; The People That You Never Get to Love; Nearsighted; Lunch Hour; Drop It; Less Is More; Show Me Where It Says; Speechless; Cradle Me; So Beautiful It Hurts; Let's Get Crazy Tonight; Bedside Companions; Guitars; The Long Way Home; Town Square; The Old School; The Last of the Romantics; Who, What, When, Where, Why; Weekend Lover; I Don't Want to Get Over You; You Make Me Real; Escape; Aw Shucks; For Beginners Only; Touch and Go; Annabella; Rifles and Rum; Terminal; Letters That Cross in the Mail; Studio Musician; I Knew You When; Queen Bee; Everything; Lullaby for Myself; My Father's Song. *Albums:* Widescreen; Rupert Holmes; Singles; Pursuit of Happiness.

HOLOFCENER, LAWRENCE　　　ASCAP 1956
author, playwright, poet
b Baltimore, Md, Feb 23, 26. Educ: Univ Md; Univ Wis; City Col New York; Thomas Edison Col, BA. Wrote lyrics for NBC TV "Show of Shows," 50-53; wrote scripts, TV Shows, Kate Smith, Ray Bolger & others, 53-56. Ed, Rhyming Dictionary, 61. Actor on Bway, "Stop the World," 63 & "Hello Dolly," 65; wrote radio play "Day of Change," Nat Pub Radio, 80. First One-Man Exhibition Sculpture, Gibbes Museum, Charleston, SC, 79. Chief Collabrs: Jerry Bock, Irving Joseph, Edward Scott. *Songs:* Lyrics: I've Been too Busy; Without You I'm Nothing; Bye Bye. *Scores:* Bway Shows: Mr Wonderful; Catch a Star; Ziegfeld Follies; Plays: Before You Go; The Shepherd.

HOLSTER, RUSTY REID　　　ASCAP 1976
composer, author, singer
b Midland, Tex, Aug 31, 52. Educ: Univ Houston, BA(communications), 75. Songwriter & demo singer, Peer-Southern Music, Nashville, 72; band mem, Southern Cross, 75-76; formed, Brown Moon Music Publ, 76; band leader, The Unreasonables, 78- Chief Collabr: Jon Stone. *Songs:* Hot As a Pistol; The Sunrise of Our Love; My Troubles Have Just Begun; Impatient; You're Not the One.

HOLT, DAVID JACK　　　ASCAP 1950
composer, author
b Jacksonville, Fla, Aug 14, 27. Educ: Westlake Sch Music, Hollywood, 50's; studied harmony, theory, arr, orchestration & scoring with Lyle (Spud) Murphy; Saddleback Community Col, Mission Viejo, Calif, equal internal syst, orchestration & cond. Danced & sang with Al Jolson & Ted Lewis, legitimate theatre, age 3; under contract to Paramount Pictures, Hollywood, 36-, starred in films incl, "The Adventures of Tom Sawyer", "The Last Days of Pompeii", "The Human Comedy" & "Courage of Lassie." Wrote first publ song at age 14. Chief Collabrs: Arthur Hamilton, Robert Wells, Johny Mercer, Paul Frances Webster, Sammy Cahn, Bob Hilliard. *Songs:* Mobile; Music: The Christmas Blues; What Every Girl Should Know; Anyone Can Fall in Love; I'd Gladly Make the Same Mistake Again.

HOLT, WILL　　　ASCAP 1956
composer, author, singer
b Portland, Maine, Apr 30, 29. Educ: Phillips Exeter Acad; Williams Col; Richard Dyer Bennet Sch Minstrelsy. Singer & guitarist in nightclubs; toured for Columbia Concerts. Co-founder, folksinger & comp, Crystal Palace, St Louis; performer, Village Vanguard & Blue Angel, New York. Has sung on TV & records. Wrote, produced & appeared in off-Bway revue, "Signs Along the Cynic Route"; appeared in & dir, "The World of Kurt Weill in Song"; writer for theatre revues, "Come Summer", "The Me Nobody Knows", "Over Here", "Me and Bessie", "Music Is" & "Platinum." Playwright, "That 5 am Jazz." Dir, "Leonard Bernstein's Theatre Songs." Chief Collabrs: Gary William Friedman, David Baker, Richard Adlev. *Songs:* Sinner Man; Raspberries, Strawberries; Daddy, Roll 'Em; Lemon Tree; The Pergola; Till the Birds Sing in the Morning; Watching the World Go By; Adieu, Madras; Days of the Waltz; Luv; Those

Were the Days; Marieke; Lyrics: One of Those Songs; Bilbao Song; Caesar's Death; Sailor's Tango. *Scores:* Bway Show: Light Sings.

HOLTON, ROBERT W　　　ASCAP 1958
composer
b Dolgeville, NY, July 8, 22. Educ: Wesleyan Univ, BA. Writer, special material for nightclub singers. Mgr, opera & symph div, music publ co. *Scores:* Stage shows: Great Scott; A Real Strange One; Hi, Paisano.

HOLTSCLAW, BENNIE CHARLES　　　ASCAP 1977
composer, author, singer
b Neodesha, Kans, Feb 18, 36. Educ: Clements High Sch, Kans. Composer & author; country-gospel singer, concerts & revivals, using own music, 5 yrs; recording artist, Music Tower, Good & Wings Records. *Songs:* Daddy I Wanna Be a Cowboy; Bring Me My Wings Lord; He's Just As Close to Heaven As He Wants to Be; No Vacancy; Search in Matthew, Mark, Luke and John; Won't You Come Unto Me.

HOLTZMAN, JONATHAN CRAIG　　　ASCAP 1979
composer, author, singer
b Neptune, NJ, July 30, 53. Educ: NY Univ, BA(music, bus), 74; studied arr with Don Sebesky, Jimmy Guiffre, voice with Harry Garland. Singer, songwriter then comp. Writer, music & coauthor, lyrics for show "Foxfire." Creator, workshop & showcase nightclub, New York. Creator of New York Songwriting Contest. Mem, New York Task Force, Am Guild of Authors & Composers. Chief Collabrs: D L Byron, Jonathan Helfand, Susan Cooper. *Songs:* Stop Telling Me No; Sympathy; My Feet Took 'T Walking'.

HOLZER, HANS　　　ASCAP 1958
composer, author, producer
b Vienna, Austria, Jan 26, 20. Educ: Columbia Univ; London Col Applied Sci, PhD(philosophy); training in archaeology & jour; studied harmony & music with Franz Mittler; brief studies at Juilliard. Author of 62 bks incl, "Haunted Hollywood", "ESP and You", "Patterns of Destiny", "Possessed", "The Clairvoyant" & "The Unicorn." TV writer/producer & TV personality. Producer off Bway shows. Wrote columns, features & articles for var mag & newspapers. Wrote & produced NBC's "In Search of...," Alan Landsburg Productions, 76-77; wrote & produced TV spec for Metromedia, RKO Gen, CBS, PBS, Miniseries for ABC News & hosted radio prog for season on WMCA, New York, as well as on WWDC, Washington, DC. Now in production of documentary spec, TV pilot progs & films, as well as prof TV/radio appearances on local, regional & nat progs. Pres of film production co, Aspera Ad Astra, Inc, New York. Prof parapsychology, NY Inst Technol, 70-; vis instr, LaVerne Col, Los Angeles; rec'd Presidential Citation, West Los Angeles Col, Calif; S Hurok Lectr. Res dir, NY Comt Investigation Paranormal Occurrences. Mem: Am Asn Advancement Sci; NY Acad Sci; NY Historical Soc; Archaeological Inst Am. *Songs:* Mom's Asittin' By the Window; Bewitched Am I!; Sewanee Sweatheart; Laugh It Up!

HOLZMANN, ABRAHAM　　　ASCAP 1923
composer
b New York, NY, Aug 19, 1874; d East Orange, NJ, Jan 16, 39. Educ: New York Cons. Staff comp & mgr, band & orch dept, music publ firms. Adv mgr, "International Musician." *Songs & Instrumental Works:* Smoky Mokes Cake Walk; The Whip; Loveland Waltzes; First Love Waltz; Symphia Waltz; Blaze Away; The Spirit of Independence; Old Faithful; Uncle Sammy (march); Blaze of Glory (march).

HOMER, BENJAMIN　　　ASCAP 1945
composer, arranger
b Meriden, Conn, June 27, 17; d Reseda, Calif, Feb 12, 75. Educ: New Eng Cons. Arr for dance orchs, incl Jimmy Dorsey, Tommy Dorsey, Benny Goodman & Les Brown, also for films, records & TV. Chief Collabr: Bud Green. *Songs & Instrumental Works:* Shoot the Sherbet to Me Herbert; Sentimental Journey; Joltin' Joe Di Maggio; Bizet Has His Day; Ridin' on the Gravy Train; Goin' Home; New Mexico.

HOMER, SIDNEY　　　ASCAP 1924
composer, educator
b Boston, Mass, Dec 9, 1864; d Winter Park, Fla, July 10, 53. Educ: Studied music with Chadwick & Rheinberger; hon MusD: Rollins Col; Curtis Inst. Taught harmony & counterpoint, Boston. *Songs:* Sweet and Low; Thy Voice Is Heard; Dearest; Sheep and Lambs; Banjo Song; also 17 Children's Songs. *Instrumental Works:* Quintet for Piano, Strings; 2 string quartets; Trio (piano, strings); 2 violin sonatas; Introduction and Fugue (organ); 20 Little Piano Pieces; Organ Sonata.

HOOD, ALAN　　　ASCAP 1955
composer, author, singer
b Marion, SC, Dec 28, 24. Educ: High sch. Singer, radio, burlesque, nightclubs, films & with bands. Worker in defense plant, World War II. Writer, special material & radio & TV commercials; talent mgr. Chief Collabrs: Gene de Paul, Richard Loring, Alan Copeland. *Songs:* Summertime Lies; Love Me Now; That's the Way I Feel; Try My Arms; Stranger; Joanie; I Know She's Mine; Happy Birthday, My Love; Go Back to Him.

HOOKER, BRIAN ASCAP 1923
author, educator
b New York, NY, Nov 2, 1880; d New London, Conn, Dec 28, 46. Educ: Yale Univ, BA, MA. Asst prof Eng, Columbia Univ, 03-05; instr, rhetoric, Yale Univ, 05-09; lectr, Columbia Univ extension. Literary ed, New York Sun, 17. Author, "The Right Man", "The Professor's Mystery" & "Morven and the Grail"; transl, "Cyrano de Bergerac." Mem, Nat Inst Arts & Letters. Chief Collabrs: Rudolf Friml, Hugo Felix. *Songs & Instrumental Works:* Through the Years (libretto for stage); Give Me One Hour; Huguette Waltz; Only a Rose; Regimental Song; Some Day; Tomorrow; Song of the Vagabonds; Love Me Tonight. *Scores:* Bway shows: June Love; Marjolaine; The Vagabond King; Operas: Mona (Metrop Opera award); Fairyland (Metrop Opera award).

HOOKS, JERRY ASCAP 1957
composer, author
b Okla, Aug 20, 11. Educ: Tatums High Sch, studied Eng. Writer & record producer, 37- Owner of label & publ co. *Songs & Instrumental Works:* You Wrecked My Life; Don't Blame My Dreams; Why Did You Hurt Me?; Let's Make Up; Oh, Larry, My Darlin'; Sweet Disco; Spectrum; House Rent Party; Love Me, Baby; Big Eyes Watching; Non-Support, That What the Judge Say; Who's to Blame for His Crime; I'm in Heaven; Oh, Darlin'; Every Lover Have a Heartache; If You'd Treated Me Right; My New Telephone No Is 62300; Raindrop Blues; Mem'ries of Oklahoma; I Won't Have to Cry; God Is Still Working Miracles; The Lord Lifted Me; Lonely Plains; Sit Thair Mama; 13 Highway; I'm Putting All My Love on the Line.

HOOPER, BUDDY ASCAP 1975
composer, author
b Paxton, Tex, Sept 23, 33. Educ: Univ Houston. *Songs:* You Do Me.

HOOVEN, JOSEPH D ASCAP 1954
composer, author
b Weatherly, Pa; d. Educ: High sch; pvt music study. Trumpeter, arr, Ted Weems Orch, 10 yrs; staff arr, ABC, Chicago & Los Angeles, 10 yrs; arr for records. Chief Collabrs: Marilyn Hooven (wife), Jerry Winn, By Dunham. *Songs:* Any Way the Wind Blows; Oh What a Beautiful Dream; Baby, Baby, Wait for Me; La-bou-laya; Jesse James; Little Nathan; George Washington; Ben Franklin; Jim Bowie; Billy Budd; Cannonball. *Scores:* TV Background: Not for Hire; Outlaw; Beachcomber; Cannonball; Lassie; Boston Blackie.

HOOVEN, MARILYN ASCAP 1954
composer, author, singer
b Aurora, Ill, Oct 17, 24. Educ: Pub & pvt schs. Singer with Ted Weems Orch, 34-44; on radio, incl "Steve Allen Show," also in films & on records. Chief Collabrs: Joseph Hooven (husband), Inez James, By Dunham. *Songs:* Any Way the Wind Blows; Oh, What a Beautiful Dream; Baby, Baby, Wait for Me; La-bou-laya; Jesse James; Lucky Duck; It'll Be a Merry Christmas.

HOOVER, KATHERINE
composer, flutist
b Elkins, WVa, Dec 2, 37. Educ: Eastman Sch Music, BMus(theory, hons), performer's cert flute, 59; Manhattan Sch Music, MMus(theory); studied flute with J Mariano & William Kincaid. Rec'd NEA comp grant & ASCAP award. Comn by the Rogeri Trio, Ariel & New York Bassoon Quartet. Has appeared as flutist in all of New York's major halls, on radio & TV; had recorded for five companies. Founded & dir the nationally broadcast Festivals I, II & III of Women's Music for Women's Interart Ctr. Mem fac, Manhattan Sch Music. *Songs & Instrumental Works:* Trio (violin, cello, piano); Sinfonia (4 bassoons); Homage to Bartok (wind quintet); Divertimento (flute, violin, viola, cello); Trio for Flutes (3 flutes); Two Dances (oboe, guitar); Variations on Welt, ade by Bach (brass quintet); Duets (2 flutes); Set for Clarinet; Selima or Ode on the Death of a Favourite Cat, Drowned in a Tub of Goldfishes (soprano, clarinet, piano); To Many a Well (mezzo or soprano, piano); Lullay, Lullay (soprano, piano); Wings; Acceptance (soprano, flute, clarinet, violin, piano); Proud Songsters (soprano, flute, clarinet, violin); Auspex (soprano, flute, clarinet, violin, piano); Seven Haiku (soprano, flute); Four Carols (soprano, flute); Concerto (flute, with strings & perc); Nocturne (flute, strings, perc); Three Carols (SSA, flute); Songs of Joy (SATB, 2 trumpets, 2 trombones); Four English Songs (SATB, oboe, Eng horn, piano); Syllable Songs (SSA, woodblock); Canons; Lake Isle of Innisfree (SATB, piano).

HOOVER, WILLIS DAVID (BILL) ASCAP 1968
composer, author, singer
b Independence, Mo, Sept 28, 45. Educ: Shenandoah Pub High Sch, Iowa; Cent Mo State Univ. Recording artist, Monument & Epic Records. Wrote theme & featured song for MGM Motion Picture "Tick, Tick, Tick." Chief Collabr: Richard (Kinky) Friedman. *Songs:* All That Keeps Ya Goin' (ASCAP Award, 70); Set Yourself Free; Freedom to Stay; Leave That for Memories; That's How a Woman's S'pose to Be; Jesus Don't Drive No Fast Back Ford.

HOPE, WYN SWANSON ASCAP 1966
composer, author, singer
b Springfield, Ill, Feb 26, 09. Educ: Pendleton High Sch, Ore, grad; Ellison-White Cons, vocal studies with Ted Roy, Lloyd Stille & Wesley La Violette. Comp/lyricist, 27-60; writer, 27-; concerts, 41-42; with community

theatre, 42 & vaudeville, 45-49; lyricist/collabr, 66-; researcher, Bob Hope Museum, presently. Author bk, "Tell It to The Mafia" (by Joe Donato as told to Wyn Hope). Chief Collabrs: Scott Seely & Aime Maurice Verucke. *Songs:* Lyrics: Soft Strings; Quiet Time; Rolling Waters; Hungry Eyes.

HOPKINS, CLAUDE D ASCAP 1944
composer, conductor, arranger
b Washington, DC, Aug 24, 06. Educ: Howard Univ, BA, MA. Organized sch band; joined Wilbur Sweatman orch. To Europe as musical comedy dir. Organized own band, 29, appearing in ballrooms, FDR Presidential Ball & films. Toured US, Europe, SAm & Asia. Made many records. Pianist. Chief Collabrs: J C Johnson, Joe Thomas, Bud Freeman. *Songs:* I Would Do Anything for You; Crying My Heart Out for You; Blame It on a Dream; Vamping a Co-ed; Washington Squabble; Count Off; Low Gravy; That Particular Friend of Mine; Dancing to the Hop; Deep Dawn; Sand Fiddler; Is It So?

HOPKINS, JAMES FREDRICK ASCAP 1974
composer
b Pasadena, Calif, Apr 8, 39. Educ: Univ Southern Calif, BM, 60, studied comp with Halsey Stevens; Yale Univ, MM, 62, studied comp with Quincy Porter; Princeton Univ, PhD, 68, studied comp with Edward T Cone. From instr to assoc prof, Northwestern Univ, 62-71. Assoc cond, Santa Fe Opera, 62-63. Organist-choirmaster several churches, 62- Assoc prof & prof, Univ Southern Calif, 71- *Instrumental Works:* Symphony No 2 (wind orch); Diferencias sobre un tema original (piano trio); Phantasms for large orchestra; Symphony No 4, Visions of Hell. *Songs & Instrumental Works:* Choral: Hodie Christus natus est (SATB); My God, My Portion (SATB); Psalm 121.

HOPKINS, SMITH ANDERSON (LITTLE HOP) ASCAP 1969
composer, author, singer
b South Fulton, Tenn, Sept 13, 20. Educ: Pub sch, Bremerton, Wash; Lincoln Ridge High Sch, Ky; Lincoln Inst, Plumbing & Janitorial Certificate; Midwestern Cons Music, Chicago. Played alto sax, Navy Rhythm Band, World War II. Disabled railroad car man, Chicago. Songwriter, publ; owner Hop's Music Co. Popular Awards winner, ASCAP. Chief Collabr: Bill Carroll. *Songs:* A Stool Pigeon for Jesus; Testimony of Understanding; Take It From the Top; Peace At Last; I Know My Jesus Walks By My Side; I'll Give Up My Bottle for Your Breast; Firemen of Chicago.

HOPPER, HAROLD S (HAL) ASCAP 1949
composer, author
b Oklahoma City, Okla, Nov 11, 12; d Sylmar, Calif, Nov 2, 70. *Songs:* There's No You; Mind If I Love You?; The Riddle Song; With All My Heart; Colt 45.

HOPSON, HAL HAROLD ASCAP 1976
composer, conductor
b Mound, Tex, June 12, 33. Educ: Baylor Univ, BM; Univ Erlangen, Ger; studied organ with Helmut Schuller; Southern Methodist Univ, studied conducting with Lloyd Pfautsch. Dir, Armed Forces Choir; comp; guest cond, var fests each year. Rec'd ASCAP Award from the Standard Awards Panel, 79. *Songs & Instrumental Works:* Cantatas: God With Us; The People of God; A Night for Dancing; The Singing Bishop; Moses and the Freedom Fanatics.

HORN, BOB ASCAP 1975
composer, singer, lyricist
b Tel Aviv, Israel, Dec 22, 49. Educ: Peabody Sch Music (on scholarship), 60-63; Pimlico Jr High Sch; Northwestern Sr High Sch; Community Col Baltimore (violin); Md Univ. Entertainment chmn, Cerebral Palsy Del-Ray Ctr. Recording singer & lyricist, 73- *Songs:* You've Gotta Try a Little Love; Static Free; Shine; You Are; By Myself; She Does.

HORNBERGER, MARY LOU ASCAP 1975
author
b Indianapolis, Ind, Oct 5, 35. Educ: Eastman Sch of Music, 2 yrs; pvt instr with Dr Leonard B Smith. Exec asst & production mgr, Detroit Concert Band, Mich. *Songs:* Lyrics: Stand Up For America (march).

HORNSBY, JOSEPH LEITH (LEE THORNSBY) ASCAP 1955
composer, author
b Carbon Hill, Ala, July 2, 07. Educ: Howard Col; George Washington Univ; NY Univ; Columbia Univ; studying jour, music & advert. Advert for training with Batten, Barton Durstine & Osborn Inc. Became copywriter in radio & TV specializing in words & music for commercials. Wrote songs & incidental music for Bway show, "Tall Story." Chief Collabrs: Ted German, Ben Allen, Gerry Teifer, Budd White. *Songs:* Chuck Wagon Song; Forever Yours; Call Me Lucky; Bunny Rabbit Hop; Blue Wiggle; Judgment; Custer Alma Mater; Would You Believe?; The Doodlin' Noodlin' Soup Man; Banana! What a Crazy Fruit!; Rock Team, Roll Team; Running; Music: I Got a Cold for Christmas; Flying Up to Europe; Heavenly Holiday; *Instrumental Works:* Kettle Drum Hop.

HOROWITZ, ANTHONY ASCAP 1971
composer, author, musician
b New York, NY, Sept 16, 45. Educ: Los Angeles Valley Col, AA. Began playing trumpet professionally at age 17 with Jimmy Wakely; then later appeared with Louis Bellson, Pearl Bailey, Ray Charles, Lou Rawls, Raquel

Welch & Louis Prima. Now work in studios in Hollywood; also serve as mem of trial bd, Am Fedn Musicians. Teacher, Dick Grove Sch Music. Mem of Sigma Alpha Phi. *Songs:* Alone; Morning After; There's No Time for Love; Music: Tomorrow; Lyrics: A Kind of Happy.

HOROWITZ, CAROLINE (CAROLYNE HOWARD)　　ASCAP 1964
composer, author, teacher
b Brooklyn, NY, Nov 12, 09. Educ: Morris High Sch; Columbia Univ, Manhattan Sch Music, studied piano; studied improvisation & piano with Teddy Wilson. Played & sang own songs on radio progs; taught music. Singer. Hon mem, US Bandsmen's Asn. *Songs & Instrumental Works:* In the Memory of This Night With You; The Fifty Stars and the Red, White and Blue (mil march); The Chesapeake and the Ohio; The Old Carousel; Look in the Mirror; Don't Be Afraid to Love Me; On Sunset Hill; I'll Dream No More; I Found You; I Know Why; The Music Box Song.

HOROWITZ, DAVID J　　ASCAP 1978
composer, arranger
b New York, NY. Educ: Juilliard Sch Music. Jazz musician, played keyboards, New York. Free-lance arr for music production cos; arr on records. Owner of jingle writing bus, David Horowitz Music Assocs, Inc, New York, 78-

HORSTMAN-PERSON, LU ANN　　ASCAP 1978
composer, author
b Princeton, Minn, Jan 5, 39. Educ: Univ Calif, Los Angeles; New Sch of Social Res; guitar & comp studies. *Songs:* Ramblin' Gal; Shopping Bag Woman; You're the One; New York Man; Sisters and Brothers; Old Woman Blues; Junkie Woman; Children in the Office. *Albums:* Lu Ann Horstman at Whole Wheat 'n Wild Berrys.

HORTON, ELIZABETH　　ASCAP 1963
composer, author, teacher
b Philadelphia, Pa, Mar 10, 02. Educ: Univ Calif, Los Angeles. Piano teacher, adult educ, Los Angeles Sch Systems; also pvt teacher. Was professional singer. Author "Adult Education Piano Method," 2 vols. *Songs:* I'm Proud to Be an American.

HORTON, GEORGE VAUGHN　　ASCAP 1945
composer, author, arranger
b Broad Top, Pa, June 5, 11. Educ: Robertsdale High Sch, Pa, 29; Penn State Extension. Formed first band in high sch. Group with bro, Roy Horton, The Pinetoppers. Wrote spec material for Joe E Lewis, Homer & Jethro, Roy Clark, Joe Frisco & Elton Britt. Chief Collabrs: Gene Autry, Denver Darling, Milt Gabler, Lionel Hampton, Jimmie Rodgers, Jerry Smith, Artur Beul, Lenny Dee, Jerry Murad. *Songs:* Mockin' Bird Hill; Sugarfoot Rag; Teardrops in My Heart; Hillbilly Fever; Till the End of the World; Choo Choo Ch' Boogie; Come What May; Address Unknown; Charlie was a Boxer; (Isn't It a) Small World; Bar Room Polka; Metropolka; Swiss Lullaby; You'd Better Stop Telling Lies About Me; Jolly Old St Nicholas; An Old Christmas Card; The Lawrence Welk—Hee Haw Counter-Revolution Polka; Dixie Cannonball; Proxy Love Affair; Lyrics: Mule Skinner Blues; Toolie Oolie Doolie; Truck Stop; Harmonica Boogie; Plantation Boogie; Julida Polka; Strollin'.

HORTON, LEWIS HENRY　　ASCAP 1958
composer, author, conductor
b Youngstown, Ohio, Nov 8, 1898; d. Educ: Oberlin Col, BA; Ohio State Univ, MA. Grants: Carnegie Found & Transylvania Col. Taught voice & piano, 23-26; cond choir, glee club & orch; music supvr, jr & sr high schs, Dayton, Ohio, 26-30; head, Music Dept, Morehead State Col, 30-42; asst prof & choir dir, Univ Ky, 42-46 & Transylvania Col, 46-51, appt composer-in-residence; music critic, Lexington Herald & Sunday Herald Leader, 55; organized choirs & festivals. Charter mem, Am Guild Organists; mem, Music Critics Asn; educr & arr. *Songs & Instrumental Works:* Choral: A Cappella Primer; A Cappella Frontiers; Folk Cantatas: White Pilgrim; An Appalachian Nativity; Octavos: Mother Goose Suite; Ancient of Days; Weep You No More Sad Fountains; Madam, I Have Come a-Courtin'.

HORTON, PHILIP　　ASCAP 1960
composer, author, pianist
b Philadelphia, Pa. Educ: Curtis Inst, with Josef Hofmann; also studied with Arnold Happich. Arr, Jan Savitt Orch. To Hollywood, 38; wrote for night clubs, dance bands & singers. Head piano dept, Gillette Sch Music. With Eddie Bergman's Cocoanut Grove Orch, 2 yrs. Pianist, arr & asst cond, Leighton Noble's "Bandstand Review," TV, 54-56; joined Manny Harmon Orch, 57; music dir, Miss Calif Beauty Pageant, 74; pianist, Republican Nat Conventions, 76 & 80; active in theatre & TV films. Chief Collabrs: Joe Rizzo, Red Skelton, Harper MacKay. *Songs:* Be Yourself; Beside the Bay of Napoli; Ho-Ho-Ho; Thanksgiving; I'm So in Love; Lyrics: It's the First Time; Dancing Clown; Twirl, Twirl, Twirl; It's Halloween; You're Just What I Want for Christmas. *Instrumental Works:* The Flea; Jumpin' Bean.

HORVATH, BELA IMRE　　ASCAP 1975
composer
b St Louis, Mo, July 7, 50. Educ: NY Col Music; Manhattan Sch Music; New York Univ, BS(comp), 72; comp with Vladimir Padwa & Ursula Mamlok; piano

with Dennis Russell Davies & Roland Hanna; trumpet with Lynn Berman. Performance with numerous popular & classical ens. Performed with Bronx Community Symph & Queens Symph Orch, Brook Benton, Tex & Beneke. Comp/arr for many New York & Central Fla groups.

HORVIT, MICHAEL M　　ASCAP 1974
composer, teacher
b Brooklyn, NY, June 22, 32. Educ: Yale Univ, BM & MM; Boston Univ, DMA; studied comp with Aaron Copland, Walter Piston & Lukas Foss. Teacher, New Eng Cons, 58, Southern Conn State Col, 59-66 & Univ Houston, 66- Awards: NEA; Houston Symph; Houston Ballet; plus others. *Songs & Instrumental Works:* Antiphone I (saxophone & electronic tape); Antiphone II (clarinet & electronic tape); Antiphone III (piano & electronic tape); Antiphone IV (perc & electronic tape); The Gardens of Hieronymus (orch). *Scores:* Moonscape (electronic ballet); Adventure in Space (chamber opera for children).

HORWITZ, MURRAY LEE　　ASCAP 1979
author, actor, director
b Dayton, Ohio, Sept 28, 49. Educ: Kenyon Col, Ohio, AB, 70. Started as clown in Ringling Bros, Barnum & Bailey Circus, 70-72. To New York, 73; co-author & assoc dir of play "Ain't Misbehavin'," Manhattan Theatre Club & Bway, 78. Writer, dir, performer & lyricist, satirical comedy revue "Hard Sell," New York Shakespeare Fest, 80. Music programming consult, Manhattan Theatre Club. Chief Collabrs: Richard Maltby, Jr, John Lewis, Hank Jones, Arvell Shaw. *Songs:* Lyrics: Handful of Keys; Tain't Nobody's Biz-ness If I Do; That Ain't Right; Spreadin' Rhythm Around.

HOSCHNA, KARL　　ASCAP 1930
composer, oboist, arranger
b Kuschwarda, Bohemia, Aug 16, 1877; d New York, NY, Dec 22, 11. Educ: Vienna Cons, Grand Prize. Oboist in Austrian Army Band. To US in 1896. Played in Victor Herbert Orch, arr for Witmark Music. Chief Collabrs: Otto Harbach, Benjamin Hapgood Burt. *Songs:* Cuddle Up a Little Closer, Lovey Mine; Yama Yama Man; Bright Eyes; Every Little Movement Has a Meaning All Its Own; Girl of My Dreams; The Fascinating Widow; I Want a Regular Man; The Smile She Means For Me; The Mood You're In. *Scores:* Bway Stage: Three Twins; Madame Sherry; The Girl of My Dreams; The Fascinating Widow; The Wall Street Girl.

HOSEY, ATHENA　　ASCAP 1958
composer, author
b New York, NY, July 27, 29. Educ: Barnard Col, FIT, BA. Pianist in nightclubs, 48-52. Then millinery designer; free-lance artist. Chief Collabrs: Hal Gordon, Guy Wood. *Songs:* Someone Else's Boy; Saturday Dance; Scene of the Crime; Highway of Love; Lonely Road; The Glide; Making Time; Saga of Tom Dooley; Tribute to the Pioneers.

HOSMER, LUCIUS　　ASCAP 1924
composer, conductor, organist
b Acton, Mass, Aug 14, 1870; d Jefferson, NH, May 9, 35. Educ: New Eng Cons; studied with J B Claus & George Chadwick. Cond, theatre orchs, Boston; church organist. *Songs:* I Doubt It; Love Was Born That Starry Night. *Instrumental Works:* For Orch: On Tiptoe; Chinese Wedding Procession; Southern Rhapsody; Northern Rhapsody; Ethiopian Rhapsody. *Scores:* Operas: The Walking Delegate; The Koreans; The Rose of the Alhambra.

HOSTE, CATHERINE M L　　ASCAP 1977
composer
b Frankfort, Mich. Educ: Cent & Cathedral High Schs, Duluth, Minn; Superior State Teachers Col, Wis; Am Cons Music, Chicago, BMus, 52, scholarship in piano with Allen Spencer, studied fugue with Leo Sowerby & comp with Stella Roberts; De Paul Univ, Gregorian chant with Msgr Meter. Pianist & arr, Venetian Trio, Minn. Church & choir dir, Detroit, 14 yrs; teacher pvt classes, 25 yrs. *Songs:* Arrowhead Moon; The Things That You Do; Minnesota Chant.

HOSTETLER, FRED ST JOHN　　ASCAP 1978
composer, author, singer
b Goshen, Ind, Mar 2, 45. Educ: Goshen High Sch; Goshen Col, BA. Rock singer & guitarist in clubs & concerts; recording artist. Chief Collabrs: Karen Lawrence, Billy Squier, Mark Kreider, Eric Troyer. *Songs:* Who Knows What Love Can Do; Please Standby...; Lyrics: Don't Break It Up.

HOUDINI, WILMOUTH
See Hendricks, Frederick Wilmoth

HOUGH, WILL　　ASCAP 1937
author, lyricist
b Chicago, Ill, Aug 23, 1882; d Carmel, Calif, Nov 20, 62. Educ: Univ Chicago. Writer of special material for vaudeville acts. Chief Collabrs: Joe Howard, Frank Adams, Harold Orlob. *Songs:* I Don't Like Your Family; Blow the Smoke Away; When You First Kiss the Last Girl You Love; Honeymoon; Be Sweet to Me, Kid; I Wonder Who's Kissing Her Now; Tonight Will Never Come Again; Cross Your Heart; It's Lonesome Tonight; And the World's All Wrong Again; Goodbye Everybody; Don't Be Anybody's Moon But Mine; Some Golden Day. *Scores:* Bway, Chicago Stage: The Land of Nod; The Time, the Place and the

Girl; The Girl Question; A Stubborn Cinderella; The Goddess of Liberty; The Prince of Tonight; A Modern Eve; The Heartbreakers; The Umpire; The Girl At the Gate.

HOVDESVEN, ELMER ARCHIBALD ASCAP 1963
composer, author, educator

b Marshall, Minn, May 4, 1893. Educ: St Olaf Col, Minn, BA; Univ Toronto, BMus, DMus; Inst Art, New York, cert; Fontainebleau Cons, France, cert; studied organ with Widor, Paris. Organ recitalist, Mercersburg Acad, Pa. Fac, Wittenberg Univ, Ohio, North Tex State Univ & Wartburg Col, Iowa. Concert organ recitalist & dir concert choirs on tours; comp for orch, band, chorals, organ & piano. Assoc Royal Col Organists; fel, Can Col Organists. Chief Collabrs: Myrtle Wilson, G J Neumann, Hugo Norden. *Songs:* Got a Boat (SATB); With You, My Own (SAB); Music: Call of the Sea (SATB); Within My Garden Wall (SSA); Youthful Jollity (SATB); Olive Tree Lullaby (SATB); Nightingale Carol (SATB, flute); Fold to Thy Heart Thy Brother (organ); My Heart Is a Manger (SATB); Blessed Is the Nation (SATB); Book of Remembrance (SAB); Wonderful News Tonight (SATB). *Instrumental Works:* Concerto-A minor for Organ and Orchestra; Out of This Prairie (chorus, winds, perc); Passacaglia for Concert Band; Symphony in A minor (orch); Scenes Martian (concert band); Organ: Meditation to a Rose Window; Three Bell Preludes; Three Poetic Preludes; From Psalm 66 (7 pieces); Invocations Extempore (3 pieces); Et Resurrexit (3 pieces); Song Cycle (4 pieces); Three Christmas Carols.

HOVER, LARRY ROBERT ASCAP 1972
composer, author, guitarist

b Detroit, Mich, Feb 1, 51. Educ: East Detroit Cons Music; Wayne State Univ; studied guitar with Joe Fava. Performed in var nightclubs throughout Mich; other concert performances include '75 & '76 Mich State Fair, Grande Ballroom, Detroit, 76; did Outdoor Christian Gospel Concerts, Ontario, 76-78; singer. *Songs:* You, You, You; Everything Under the Son.

HOVEY, CAROL
See Hanigan, Carol Hovey

HOVEY, SERGE ASCAP 1959
composer

b New York, NY, Mar 10, 20. Educ: Studied piano with Richard Buhlig & Edward Steurmann, comp with Joseph Achron, Arnold Schönberg & Hanns Eisler. Musical dir, Bertolt Brecht's "Galileo." Comp, ballet "Fable" performed by Philadelphia Orch & scores for var award-winning documentary films. Completed definitive collection of Robert Burns' songs. Recipient, NEA grant for recording Burns' songs. *Scores:* Off-Bway shows: Tevya and His Daughters; The World of Sholem Aleichem. *Albums:* The Songs of Robert Burns, I & II.

HOWARD, ANNA G ASCAP 1965
composer, author

b New York, NY, Apr 10, 1893. Educ: Morris High Sch, Bronx, NY; pvt piano lessons, 3 yrs. Played piano in silent movie theatres many years; taught ragtime at Christensen Sch of Popular Music, New York. Dep sheriff, Civil Div, County of Los Angeles, 27-56. Chief Collabr: Frank D Grace. *Songs:* M'm, M'm, That's Good; Where's Ben Been?; Lyrics: Who Was That Woman; Flying Dollars; You're My VIP; Inflation Blues.

HOWARD, BART
See Gustafson, Howard Joseph

HOWARD, BEATRICE THOMAS ASCAP 1959
composer, author

b Eutaw, Ala, Mar 7, 05. Educ: High sch; teacher's training. Sch teacher & principal, 20 yrs. Writer, dir, local shows; also for films & TV. *Songs:* Christ Is My Pilot; Naughty Winds; Burnt Sand; We Will Come Rejoicing; Let Us All Give Thanks; In Bethlehem; Mary, Mother of Jesus.

HOWARD, CAROLYNE
See Horowitz, Caroline

HOWARD, DICK
See Dietz, Howard

HOWARD, EDDY ASCAP 1941
composer, conductor, guitarist

b Woodland, Calif, Sept 12, 14; d Palm Desert, Calif, May 23, 63. Educ: San Jose State Col; Stanford Univ Med Sch. Sang with dance bands incl Dick Jurgens, then led own band in 41. Leader, singer, NBC radio, "Carton of Cheer." Made many records with own band, also appeared in hotels & nightclubs. *Songs:* My Last Goodbye; A Million Dreams Ago; Careless; If I Knew Then; Now I Lay Me Down to Dream; Something Old—Something New; For Sale; So Long for Now; With Love; Lonesome Tonight; Lynn.

HOWARD, FRED
See Wright, Fred Howard

HOWARD, GEORGE SALLADE ASCAP 1961
composer, author, conductor

b Reamstown, Pa, Feb 24, 03. Educ: Conway Band Sch, Ithaca Cons, NY, hon grad; Ohio Wesleyan Univ, AB; NY Univ, AM; Chicago Cons, Ill, BMus, MMus & MusD. Dean music, Ernest Williams Sch Music, Brooklyn, NY & Mansfield State Teachers Col, Pa; dir band, orch & sch chorus, Pa State Univ, 21 yrs; dir, US Air Force Band & Orch, Washington, DC; retired, 63. Chief Collabrs: Floyd Werle, Fred Kepner & Serge de Gastyne. *Songs:* Cougars Victory March. *Instrumental Works:* Alfalfa Club March; The Exhibition March; Immer Kleiner (clarinet solo); My Missouri; Bachelors of the Sky; American Minstrels March; Festival Music for a Crown Prince; Flieger Marsch; General Spaatz March.

HOWARD, JOHN ALVIN ASCAP 1977
composer, author, guitarist

b Moscow, Idaho, Nov 13, 44. Educ: Potlatch High Sch; Univ Idaho; Am Sch. Started playing guitar & singing in high sch at sch functions; played guitar & lead singer, country & western bands in nightclubs, Northern Idaho & Eastern Wash. Formed own band, Cripple Creek Cowboys, 73. Recording artist. *Songs:* Honky Tonk Fever; It's Alright; Bottle of Wine; I Wear the Blues.

HOWARD, JOHN TASKER ASCAP 1926
composer, author

b Brooklyn, NY, Nov 30, 1890; d West Orange, NJ, Nov 20, 64. Educ: Williams Col, hon MA; studied music with Paul Tidden, Howard Brockway & Mortimer Wilson. Music ed: McCall's Mag, 28-30; music div, US George Washington Bicentennial Comn (award, 33); music div, US Constitution Sesquicentennial Comn; Cue Mag, 37-38. Curator, Americana Music Col, New York Pub Libr, 40-64. Advert ed, Encyclopedia Americana, 50. Lectr, Columbia Univ, 50-53. Author: "Our American Music"; "Stephen Foster, America's Troubadour"; "Our Contemporary Composers"; "American Music in the 20th Century"; "The World's Great Operas"; "This Modern Music." Ed & compiler: "Program of Early American Piano Music"; "Treasury of Stephen Foster"; "Scribner Radio Music Library" (vol 9). Mem: Soc Am Historians; Authors League; Nat Asn for Am Comp & Cond (vpres, 47-50). Dir, ASCAP, 45-58, secy, 53-57. *Songs & Instrumental Works:* There Is Sweet Music There; O Did You Hear the Meadow Lark?; In the Valley At Home; Others Call It God; Beyond the Stars; The Farmer's Son; Fantasy on a Choral Theme (piano, orch); Foster Sinfonietta; March of the Grenadiers; Mosses From an Old Manse; From Foster Hall (string quartet); Piano: Intaglio Waltzes; Pastorals; Still Waters; Serenade en forme d'etude; Minuet on an Old Song; Cloud Banks; Calendar Suite; Choral: Early American Lullaby; St Augustine's Prayer; Most Holy and Gracious God; I Will Lift Up Mine Eyes; O Master, Let Me Walk With Thee; The Virgin's Cradle Hymn.

HOWARD, JOSEPH A ASCAP 1958
composer, author, educator

b Cleveland, Ohio, Jan 23, 28. Educ: Cleveland Inst Music, piano study with Leonard Shure; Western Reserve Univ, BA, 50, Case Western Reserve Univ, PhD, 78; Kent State Univ, MA, 67. Staff pianist, NBC, WTAM-WNBK-TV, 50; piano recitals, 50- Musical dir, Scripps-Howard WEWS-TV, 59-64. Guest piano soloist, Cleveland Orch, 60, 70 & 71. Comp-cond films, "History of Photography" for Defense Dept/Eastman-Kodak, 67, "Dateline, Ohio" for Ohio State Bd Educ, 76 & "Climate for Learning," 77. Prof music, Cuyahoga Community Col, 69-; head dept jazz studies, Cleveland Music Sch Settlement, 72-; vis Fulbright-Hays sr prof music, Univ Philippines, 78-79. Chief Collabrs: Joseph A Hendrich, Kenneth E Baker, George Kemp. *Songs:* A Thought; Little Angel; Christmas Prayer; Music: Dorioso; Candy Cane; Old Fashioned Christmas. *Scores:* TV: Littlest Angel.

HOWARD, JOSEPH EDGAR ASCAP 1921
composer, author, actor

b New York, NY, Feb 12, 1878; d Chicago, Ill, May 19, 61. Singer, age 11, vaudeville. Toured with stock co in "Little Eva." Produced and dir var stage scores. Entertainer, nighclubs, theatres, radio & TV. Autobiogrpahy, "Gay Nineties Troubadour." Chief Collabrs: Frank Adams, Will Hough, Harold Orlob. *Songs:* Hello, My Baby; Goodbye, My Lady Love; There's Nothing Like a Good Old Song; Somewhere in France Is the Lily; On a Saturday Night; Can't Get You Out of My Mind; Love Me Little, Love Me Long; Montana; Silver in Your Hair; Whistle a Song; On the Boulevard; San Francisco Frizz; An Echo of Her Smile; I Don't Like Your Family; Blow the Smoke Away; What's the Use of Dreaming?; When You First Kiss the Last Girl You Love; Honeymoon; Be Sweet to Me, Kid; I Wonder Who's Kissing Her Now; Tonight Will Never Come Again; Cross Your Heart. *Scores:* Bway shows: The Land of Nod; The Time, the Place and the Girl; The Girl Question; A Stubborn Cinderella; The Goddess of Liberty; The Prince of Tonight.

HOWARD, MEL ASCAP 1950
author

b Bahamas, May 20, 12. To US, 41. Citizen, 43. Educ: NY Univ. WW II, USA. *Songs:* There Ought to Be a Society; Go Now; On the Island of Oahu; Minnequa.

HOWARD, PAUL MASON ASCAP 1953
composer, author
b Burr Oak, Mich, Oct 10, 09; d Los Angeles, Calif, Jan 21, 75. Educ: Col. Led jazz band, 24; appeared in vaudeville & nightclubs. Wrote for newspapers & advert agencies, also writer of musical commercials. Chief Collabrs: Jimmy McHugh, Paul Weston, Buddy Ebsen. *Songs:* Shrimp Boats; A Cowboy Needs a Horse; The Gandy Dancers Ball; Snow Shoe Thompson; Ninety-Nine Years Is a Long Time; Baby All I Need Is You; Catch Me Fish; Milk Train; Hole in the Sky; Zither Blues.

HOWARD, RANDALL LAMAR ASCAP 1974
composer, author, singer
b Macon, Ga, May 9, 50. Educ: Lanier Northeast High Sch, dipl; Macon Jr Col. Night club entertainer. The Buddy Knox & Randy Howard TV Shows. Recording artist, Utopian Records. Chief Collabrs: Tracy Parker, Elroy Kahanek. *Songs:* God Don't Live in Nashville, Tennessee; She's a Lover; Don't Ask Me for Tomorrow; All American Redneck; Johnny Walker Home.

HOWARD, RAY
See Hayman, Richard Warren Joseph

HOWARD, RICHARD ASCAP 1942
composer, author
b Keene, NH, Oct 10, 1890. Educ: High sch. Minstrel & vaudeville performer, 5 yrs; wrote own material. WW I, Yeoman, USN. *Songs:* In the Town Where I Was Born; Somebody Else Is Taking My Place; Put Me to Sleep With an Old-Fashioned Melody; I've Lost You, So Why Should I Care?; Shut the Door, They're Coming Through the Window.

HOWE, GEORGE WARREN ASCAP 1950
composer, author, publisher
b Kansas City, Mo, Oct 5, 09. Educ: Long Beach Poly High Sch, studied voice with Nel Durigin; studied vaudeville with Noodles Fagin. Child actor in silent films & vaudeville, singing & dancing. Radio singer in 1930's. Nightclub performer. Toured with orchs in US. Produced shows in USN, WW II. Talent mgr, record producer & founder, Admiral Music, 62- Music supvr for films. Chief Collabrs: Russ Morgan, Al Sherman, Dave Franklin, David Gussin, Danny Gould, Bobby Burns, Hal Hopper, Randy Cate, Ray Sawyer. *Songs:* Ring My Finger; My Loneliness; Lyrics: Down the Lane; Now-Now-Now (Is the Time); Count Your Blessings; Acapulco Polka; The Waltz That Made You Mine; Rootee-Tootee; The Polkarina; To Love You Is Madness; Goodtime Charlie; Pigskin Polka; Tell Me You Love Me; In His Name; My Faith; Take Command of My Heart; If Somebody Breaks Your Heart; Ain't Love Good Tonight; In Hamburg When the Nights Are Long; Roses Remind Me of You; It's December Again; My Little One; Aglow; Will You Still Be Mine?; The Island Love Song.

HOWE, MARY ASCAP 1940
composer, pianist
b Richmond, Va, Apr 4, 1882; d Washington, DC, Sept 14, 64. Educ: Peabody Cons; Hon MusD, George Washington Univ; Hon Fellow, Music Dept, Am Univ. Toured in 2-piano recitals with Anne Hull, also soloist, 20-35. Mem, Nat Asn Am Comp & Cond; Int Soc Contemporary Music & League of Comp; fellow & bd mem, Nat Fedn Music Clubs; hon mem, Nat League Am Pen Women. Former vpres, Friends of Music, Libr of Congress; bd mem, Bennington Col. Co-founder & hon vpres, Nat Symph. Author of English, French & Ger Texts "Seven Volumes of Songs" (piano accomp). *Songs & Instrumental Works:* Paean; Sand; Spring Pastoral; Dirge; Stars; Potomac; American Piece; Agreeable Overture (Nat Gallery Comn); Castellana (2 pianos); Little Suite (strings); Suite Melancolique (violin, cello, piano); Sonata for Violin; Violin, Piano; Ballade Fantasque (cello, piano); Choral: Chain Gang Song; Prophecy; Spring Pastoral; Song of Palms; Song of Ruth; A Devotion; Catalina; Let Us Walk in the White Snow; Irish Lullaby; Great Land of Mine; Transcriptions for 2 pianos (Bach).

HOWE, MAUDE JOHNSON
See Chenette, Maude Johnson Howe

HOWELL, GENE MAC
See Bartles, Alfred Howell

HOWELL, ROBERT B
composer, author
b Portland, Ore, Nov 20, 44. Educ: Univ Ore. Toured with band, 63-64. Translr & lyricist with Oslo music publ. *Songs:* Since I Lost Your Love.

HRUBY, DOLORES MARIE ASCAP 1973
composer, choral conductor
b Chicago, Ill, May 9, 23. Educ: As a child, studied piano with Louise Robyn; Am Cons Music, BM, studied with Leo Sowerby; Mich State Univ, MM, studied with H Owen Reed & Jere Hutchinson. Had cond church choirs & other choral groups; taught piano. *Songs:* Come and Praise the Lord With Joy; I Lift My Hands to the Lord Most High; He Whom Joyous Shepherd Praised; For the Least of My Brothers; Gather Around the Christmas Tree; Lord Let Your Hands; My Spirit Rejoices (Bach, arr). *Instrumental Works:* Piano: Sea-Gulls; Sailing; Greek Dance.

HUBBELL, FRANK ALLEN ASCAP 1963
composer, author, conductor
b Denver, Colo, May 9, 07; d. Educ: Univ Southern Calif Music Sch; Boguslawski Col Music; studied with Edmund Ross, Albert Coates & Vladimir Balaleinikov. Trumpeter & arr with Henry Halstead & Anson Weeks orchs; musician, comp & arr, radio & films. Founder & cond, Los Angeles Symphonette. Music dir, record co & children's theatre. Guest cond, symph orchs incl San Diego, Bakersfield, Santa Monica (also co-founder) & Burbank. Music dir, comp & author, for Wayne Dailard; then for Music Spectaculars; Death Valley Cent; "The California Story" (Hollywood Bowl, 50, 56, 57 & 58); "The Oregon Story," 59; "The Kansas Story," 61; also for Miss Int Beauty Congress, 63-64 & chamber music concerts, Long Beach Museum Art. *Instrumental Works:* California Eldorado Suite; Passacaglia and Scherzo; Theme and Variations.

HUBBELL, RAYMOND ASCAP 1914
composer
b Urbana, Ohio, June 1, 1879; d Miami, Fla, Dec 13, 54. Educ: Pub schs; studied music in Chicago. Led own dance orch; staff comp, Chicago publ co. One of nine founders, ASCAP, dir, 14-41, treas, 17-28. Chief Collabrs: Robert B Smith, Glen MacDonough, Harry B Smith, E Ray Goetz, George V Hobart, John Golden, Anne Caldwell. *Songs:* Poor Butterfly; The Ladder of Roses; Hello, I've Been Looking for You; Jealous Moon; Chu Chin Chow; Melodyland; Just My Style; Life Is a See-Saw; Little Girl in Blue; What Am I Going to Do to Make You Love Me?; Look At the World and Smile; Yours Truly. *Scores:* Bway stage: The Runaways; Fantana; Mexicana; A Knight for a Day; The Midnight Sons; The Jolly Bachelors; The Never Homes; Ziegfeld Follies (11, 12, 13 & 14); A Winsome Widow; Hip Hip Hooray; The Big Show; Cheer Up; The Kiss Burglar; Happy Days; Good Times; Yours Truly; Three Cheers.

HUBBLE, MARTIE
See Bernhart, Martha Ann

HUBER, CALVIN R
composer, teacher, arranger
b Buffalo, NY, July 12, 25. Educ: Univ Wis, BA, MA, 49; NY Univ, 50-51; Univ NC, Chapel Hill, 56-59, PhD, 64; studied with Curt Sachs, Gustave Reese, Martin Banstein, Glen Haydon, William S Newman & Donald S Reinhardt. Trombonist & arr for many yrs in jazz & big bands, Skitch Henderson Orch & others. Teacher, 52- Teacher, Carson-Newman Col; teacher & dept chmn, Wake Forest Univ; teacher & dir grad studies music, Univ Tenn; vis teacher, Univ Wis; vis teacher, Univ NC, Greensboro, asst, Chapel Hill. *Songs & Instrumental Works:* Four Humorous Songs (bass-baritone, piano); Profunditties (woodwinds in pairs); Band: Bossa Nova Holiday; Four Impressions of a Woodland Pond; Fanfare for a Ceremony; Festival Hymn and March; Orch & Band: Pussilanimous Pussycat; Ancient Dances in Time of Mourning.

HUCKO, MICHAEL ANDREW (PEANUTS) ASCAP 1966
composer, clarinettist, orchestrator
b Syracuse, NY, Apr 7, 18. Educ: Studied with Reginald Kell & Leon Russianoff. Played with J Jenney Orch, Will Bradley, Charlie Spivak, Maj Glenn Miller Air Force Band, B Goodman, E Condon, J Teagarden & L Armstrong. Appeared with "Lawrence Welk TV Show." Led Glenn Miller Orch, 74. Concert tours with Columbia Artists Corp. Touring solo, Europe, 75-76 & 78-80. With Syd Lawrence, Eng. Appeared radio & TV with radio orchs, Stuttgart, Zurich, Hamburg & Stockholm. Chief Collabr: Louis Tobin. *Songs:* A'Bientot; Till I See You Again; First Friday; Raggedy Ann; Tremont Place; Falling Tears; Sweet Home Suite; Sweet One.

HUCKS, WILLIAM RICHARD, JR (DICKSON HUGHES) ASCAP 1958
composer, author, conductor
b Akron, Ohio, Dec 14, 22. Educ: John R Buchtel High Sch, Akron; Univ Redlands, Calif, BA, 48; studied piano & comp with Joseph Zoellner, conducting with Thomas Schippers. Indust show producer & creator, 62-78; regional prof stock cos in var US cities, 62-80. State Dept-sponsored tour of "Carousel" & "Showboat" in SAm, 66. Cond, Sacramento Civic Light Opera, 66-72; lectr on Am Musical Comedy, major US cities & Am Embassy, Paris, 68-80. Comp productions "Like It Is" & "Vive Les Girls" in Las Vegas; singer & pianist at var nightclubs, TV & concert stage. Chief Collabrs: Edward L Alperson Jr, Les Baxter, Bob Lees. *Songs:* Lyrics: Angelita; The Donkey Game; Never Alone; The Restless Breed; Joy Is Born Today; My Friend God; A Child's Prayer; How Can I Let Him Know?; Let's Turn on to Love.

HUDAK, ANDREW, JR ASCAP 1959
composer, arranger, conductor
b Cleveland, Ohio, Oct 16, 18. Educ: High sch; Cleveland Inst Music, studied with Cliff Barnes. Accordionist & soloist with dance orchs; teacher, Wurlitzer Music Sch; founded Hudak's Cons Music, Parma, Ohio; mem & soloist, 8th Armored Div Band, Yuma, USAAF Band, 684th USAAF Band; also featured soloist with band on, "The Coast to Coast Coca-Cola Show," which toured all the army camps, WW II. Staff accordionist, WNBK TV; TV, radio & recording artist. Pres, Cleveland Accordion Teachers Asn; vpres, Cuyahoga Music Dealers Asn. *Instrumental Works:* Samba Impromptu; Twitchy Fingers; Velocity in Reeds; Flipside Boogie; Van's Bounce; Scandinavian Polka; Melody Petite; Charie Waltz; Butterfingers; Look Out Look Out; Flying Clarinets.

HUDDLESTON, FLOYD HOUSTON
ASCAP 1949
author

b McComb, Miss, Aug 19, 19. *Songs:* He's Just My Kind; Highway to Love; You Started Something; Just for Laughs; You Can't Do Wrong Doin' Right; Of All Things.

HUDSON, HELEN LOUISE
ASCAP 1979
composer, author, teacher

b Sydney, Australia, Jan 19, 53. Educ: Am Acad of Dramatic Arts (drama & voice); Orme Sch; Ariz State Univ; Stanford Univ, BA(communications, cum laude), 73; Sherwood Oaks, Calif, 78, studied with Lucille Ball; Will Geer's Theatricum Botanicum, studied with Ellen Geer. Prof model, age 12, New York. Taught Eng, high schs, 2 yrs. Dir, alumni affairs, pvt boarding sch. Writer, performer, radio & TV progs, singer, recording artist, Los Angeles, 5 yrs. Mem, Equity, Am Fedn of TV & Radio Artists, Screen Actors Guild, Country Music Asn, Acad of Country Music, Nat League of Am Pen Women & Nashville Songwriters Asn Int. Semi-finalist, NAm Song Fest, 78. *Songs:* One More Guitar; Nothing But Time; I Never Meant to Love You; This Feeling in My Heart; Don't Ever Let On You're No One.

HUDSON, WALTER
See Hutchison, (David) Warner

HUDSON, WILL
ASCAP 1934
composer, author

b Barstow, Calif, Mar 8, 08. Educ: Southeastern High Sch, Detroit; Juilliard Sch Music, grad & postgrad dipl, 52-53; studied orch & comp with Wallingford Rieger, Henry Brant & Vincent Persichetti. Comp, popular songs. Writer, orchestrations & instrumental comp for music publ. Wrote orchestrations for var dance bands, 30's & 40's; co-leader, Hudson-DeLange Band, 36-38; cond own band, 39-40. WW II, USAF. Chief Collabrs: Eddie DeLange, Mitchell Parish. *Songs:* Tormented; You're Not the Kind; Music: Moonglow; Organ Grinder's Swing; Sophisticated Swing; Mr Ghost Goes to Town; Popcorn Man; White Heat; Jazznochracy.

HUDSPETH, WILLIAM G (GREG WILLIAMS)
ASCAP 1968
composer, author, singer

Educ: Studied with Max Rabinowitz & Leonard Pennario. Recording artist, Sidewalk Productions, Capitol Records & 20th Century Fox Records. Platinum Record, 74. Record of the Year, Record World Mag. Mem band, The Factory, Hollywood & in POP groups. Perf score for short subject movie, "The Bet" (winner Cannes Film Fest). Chief Collabrs: Mike Kennedy, Jeff Barry, Patricia Hudspeth. *Songs:* Heartbeat It's a Love Beat (ASCAP Award); Baby You Don't Know How Good You Are; Is Anybody There?; Moonchild; In the Movies; Gemini Girl; Bright and Shiny Day; Satin Manhattan Lady.

HUESTON, BILLY (BRUCE MORGAN)
ASCAP 1935
composer, author, publisher

b West New York, NJ, Aug 18, 1896; d Hollywood, Calif, Dec 5, 57. Educ: NY Univ. Service, US Army, WW I, received Croix de Guerre. Sold music for publ firms, then on prof staff. Founder & first pres, United Radio Entertainers Asn, 27; publ & ed mag, The Radio Entertainer. Had own booking off, 29-32; assoc with booking off in Boston & Chicago; prod shows for radio & nightclubs; founded music publ co, 47. *Songs:* Call Around; With Tears in My Eyes I'm Laughing At You; Plant a Little Seed of Kindness; Nobody Knows But My Pillow and Me; Throwin' Stones At the Sun; The Doodlebug Song; Cupid.

HUFFAM, PELENTON (TEDDY) LEMUEL, (JR)
ASCAP 1979
composer, singer

b Richmond, Va, Nov 6, 40. Educ: Armstrong High Sch, grad; Fayetteville State Univ, NC; Va Commonwealth Univ, degree. With fed govt, 61-79, retired; minister music, Mt Calvary Holy Church. Recorded for Skylite & Canaan Records. *Songs:* Enter My Heart; So Many Years; You Can't Take These Things With You; Take Another Chance on Me; Living in the Light; Not a Moment to Lose.

HUGHES, ALFRED REA
ASCAP 1967
composer, organist, teacher

b Cleveland, Ohio, Oct 21, 25. Educ: Univ Sch (prep); Dana Sch Music, Youngstown Univ, BA, 48. As organist played in var hotels in Phoenix & Scottsdale, Ariz, resort area. Chief Collabr: William Kerr. *Songs:* Holly; Music: One Million Dollars; A Prayer of Thanksgiving; Lost; Evening Chapel Bells.

HUGHES, DICKSON
See Hucks, William Richard, Jr

HUGHES, ERNEST
ASCAP 1960
composer, author, pianist

b Wilkes-Barre, Pa, May 25, 15. Educ: Wilkes-Barre Pub Schs; Los Angeles Cons Music; studied piano with Oscar Wagner, Juilliard; orchestration & comp with Mario Castelnuovo-Tedesco, SC; comp with Ernest Kanitz. Pianist in var name bands; pianist & arr for many record cos; comp cues for motion pictures & TV specials. Teaching & studying electronic music, 76- Chief Collabrs: Herschel B Gilbert, Nelson Riddle, Earl Hagen. *Songs:* Lyrics: Grand Canyon Suite (special narration); Music: many cues for films & TV. *Instrumental Works:*

Double Fugue for Three Wood-Winds; Introduction and Allegro for Spanish Guitar; Elegie for Piano; also other works.

HUGHES, FLOYD KEITH
ASCAP 1978
composer, author, musician

b Pomona, Calif, Jan 28, 58. Educ: Upland High Sch, grad, 76; Chaffey Col; Azusa Pac Col. Gospel comp/lyricist; active in gospel music, age 14; traveled throughout US & Can performing & recording. Asst dir music, New Life Community Church, Upland, Calif. *Songs:* Music Is My Life (You Gave the Song); Coming in the Clouds; Ruins of a Soul; Three Little Sheep; Tower; I'd Do It All for You.

HUGHES, GLENN VERNON
ASCAP 1969
composer, author, singer

b Los Angeles, Calif, June 18, 27. Educ: San Rafael High Sch, Calif; Compton Col; Univ Calif, Los Angeles; Pasadena Playhouse. Entertainment dir, USA, 45-47. Author, comp & star, col musicals "Musical Masquerade" & "From Out the Night," 47 & 48. Comp, words & music, musical "Shotgun Wedding," 49. With Music Corp of Am, Paramount TV Productions & Hawaiian Village Hotel, 52-64. Co-producer, Paradise Records, Hawaii; soloist with Dynasty Records. Chief Collabr: Carl Suessdorf. *Songs:* The House By the Sea; My Polka Dot Tie; Right Or Wrong (You Belong to Me); Houseboat on the Mississippi; Music: Sittin' on the Railfence; Lyrics: Live and Let Love; The City of the Angels.

HUGHES, (BROTHER) HOWARD LEO, SM
ASCAP 1972
composer, organist, choir director

b Baltimore, Md, June 28, 30. Educ: Univ Dayton, BS, 51; Western Reserve Univ, MA, 65; Univ Fribourg, Switz; Alliance Francaise, Paris; Institut Catholique de Paris; harmony study with Modena Scovill Lane, 65-67; organ study with Robert F Twynham, 71-72. Marianist teaching Bro; choral cond high schs, 18 yrs; organist/choir dir, 51-; mem, Collegiate Chorale under Abraham Kaplan, 65-71; in several concerts with NY Philh under Steinberg, Maazel, Ozawa & Bernstein; mem, Baltimore Choral Arts Soc, 71-80; working full-time liturgical music, presently. *Songs:* Music: San Jose Mass; Let Earth Rejoice; I Know That My Redeemer Lives; Psalm 141: Let My Prayer Rise Like Incense; The Lord's Prayer; Psalm 139: Guide Me, Lord; Behold Your Mother: Evening Prayer for Feasts of Mary; Processional Alleluia. *Songs & Instrumental Works:* For Liturgy of the Hours (psalms, responsories, etc; comn by Int Comn on Eng in the Liturgy); Praise God in Song (psalms, canticles, etc).

HUGHES, LANGSTON
ASCAP 1936
author

b Joplin, Mo, Feb 1, 02; d. Educ: Columbia Univ; Lincoln Univ, BA; hon LittD, Lincoln Univ, Howard Univ & Western Reserve Univ. Wrote newspaper columns, Chicago Defender & New York Post. Taught creative writing, Atlanta Univ, 47; poet-in-residence, Lab Sch Univ Chicago, 49. Lectr, high schs, univs, Stratford Fest, Berliner Festwochen; USIS tour of Africa, Europe, Asia & West Indies. Mem: Author's Guild; Dramatists Guild; PEN; Nat Inst Arts & Letters; Am Acad Arts & Sci. First poem, "The Negro Speaks of Rivers," 21. Awards: Opportunity Poetry Prize; Palms Intercollegiate; Harmon; Witter Bynner Undergrad; Anisfield-Wolfe; Free Acad Arts, Hamburg; Spingarn Medal. Grants: Guggenheim, Rosenwald & Am Acad Arts & Letters. Author: "Weary Blues", "The Dream Keeper", "Shakespeare in Harlem," (poetry); "Fight for Freedom"; "The Ways of White Folks"; "Not Without Laughter"; "Simple Speaks His Mind"; Autobiographies: "The Big Sea"; "I Wonder As I Wander." Author Bway plays: "Mulatto; Don't You Want to Be Free"; "Shakespeare in Harlem." Chief Collabrs: Howard Swanson, Jean Berger, Albert Hague, William Grant Still, David Martin, Kurt Weill, Margaret Bonds, Jobe Huntley. *Songs:* Moon-Faced, Starry-Eyed; What Good Would the Moon Be?; Somehow I Never Could Believe; Wouldn't You Like to Be on Broadway?; We'll Go Away Together; Lonely House; Remember That I Care; Did You Ever Hear the Blues; Good Old Girl. *Instrumental Works:* The Glory Around His Head; The Ballad of the Brown King; Concert settings: Freedom Road; Songs to the Dark Virgin. *Scores:* Stage (librettos): Street Scene, Simply Heavenly; Tambourines to Glory; Black Nativity.

HUGHES, LAVAUGHN RACHEL
ASCAP 1960
composer, author, conductor

b Hilliards, Ohio, Sept 7, 19. Educ: Wurlitzer Music Sch. Pianist in Wurlitzer Band; organist. *Songs:* God's Ten Commandments.

HUGHES, ROBERT E
ASCAP 1968
composer, arranger, conductor

b New York, NY, Oct 29, 34. Educ: Manhattan Sch Music, NY, comp major, 54-58, studied comp with Vittorio Giannini. Started as pianist on Bway, New York; music dir, WCBS-TV, New York, 2 yrs; moved to Los Angeles; cond several summer stock shows all over the country; did arr for Vic Damone, Shirley Bassey, Bob Hope, Pat Boone, Jerry Lewis TV Show & Marilyn Maxwell; music dir & arr for Rich Little, incl Rich Little TV series & all TV specials, 71-; commercial writer. Chief Collabr: Ric Marlow. *Songs & Instrumental Works:* A World Full of Laughter; Love on the Rocks; I Move Around; Between Five and Six.

HUGHES, ROBERT JAMES (JAMES DENTON,   ASCAP 1957
JOHN JOHNSON, JAMES MAFFATT)
composer, author
b Toronto, Ont, May 30, 16. Educ: Royal Cons Music, Toronto, grad, Assoc Toronto Cons Music; Trinity Col Music, London, Eng, grad, Licentiate Trinity Col, London; Ont Dept Educ, Cert in vocal & instrumental; Oxford Univ, Eng, Doctorate. Organist-choirmaster for church in Toronto; Bandmaster, Royal Can Air Force, WW II; choir dir; now sr ed, Lorenz Publishing Co. *Songs:* Music: Man and His World (comn for Expo 67, World's Fair, Montreal). *Songs & Instrumental Works:* Christmas Cantatas: King Forever; Joy to the World; Call Him JESUS; wrote 12 full length cantatas and numerous church works.

HUGHES, RUPERT   ASCAP 1924
composer, author, director
b Lancaster, Mo, Jan 31, 72; d Los Angeles, Calif, Sept 9, 56. Educ: Adelbert Col; Western Reserve Univ, BA & DLitt; Yale Univ, MA; studied with Wilson Smith, Edgar Kelley & Charles Pearce. Author "Contemporary Am Composers", "Love Affairs of Great Musicians" & "Music Lover's Guide." Film scenarist, dir, radio sketch writer & commentator. Bks adapted for films incl "The Cup of Fury", "The Thirteenth Commandment", "Within These Walls", "Souls for Sale", "The Patent Leather Kid", "Empty Pockets" & "The Old Nest." *Songs:* Cain; The Roustabout; Soul of My Soul; Tomorrow.

HUGHES, SHERRIE
See McCall, Sherrie Hughes

HUHN, BRUNO   ASCAP 1924
composer, conductor, pianist
b London, Eng, Aug 1, 1871; d New York, NY, May 13, 50. Educ: Studied music with Sarah Taunton & John Pointer; Trinity Col, London; also with S B Mills & Louis Alberti. Concert tours, Australia, 1889-91. Debut as pianist, Steinway Hall, New York, 1896. Cond, New York Banks' Glee Club, 14 yrs. Assoc founder & cond, New York Jr League Glee Club, Choral Club, Forest Hills, Long Island. *Songs & Instrumental Works:* Courage; We Fight for Peace; Seafarers; God Is Enough; Destiny; Song Cycles: The Divan; Love's Triumph; Invictus; Cantatas: Christ Triumphant; Praise Jehovah.

HUKVARI, EUGENE   ASCAP 1976
composer, educator, musicologist
b Torokbalint, Hungary, Feb 11, 08. Educ: Royal Liszt Acad, Budapest, state artist & prof dipl, studies with Castha, Kodacy, Fleischer & Hammerschlag. Theatre & concert cond, Hungary, Chicago, Cleveland & Detroit. Many concerts in over 40 countries. Author, "Music Shorthand." *Songs & Instrumental Works:* Rapsodi (concert bass band); Indian Symphony; harp solos; string quartet; saxophone trio; voice & piano duets. *Scores:* Aratas (ballet); Vorosmarthy (opera).

HULL, DOROTHY SPAFARD (DOROTHY DANZIG)   ASCAP 1972
composer, teacher, pianist
b Brooklyn, NY, May 9, 24. Educ: Vassar Col, 2 yrs; Juilliard Sch Music, 1 yr; Am Sch Music, Fontainebleau, France; Calif State Univ, Northridge, BA, MA(music); studied with Jakob Gimpel. Concert pianist, East Coast, 40's & 50's. Teacher & lectr, West Coast, 60's & 70's. Docent, Los Angeles Philh, 71; mem, Music Honor Soc. Comp children's pieces, songs & band arr for TV series & Movie of the Week. Piano coach for upcoming major motion picture. *Songs:* Music: Brindley Girls Quintet; Rally March.

HULT, EVE   ASCAP 1965
composer, author
Chief Collabr: Ayre Thea Hult. *Songs:* Beer Can Drag; Love Me Darling; A Prayer (Light the World With Love); It Is Love; Lincoln's Gettysburg Address; Philippine Patrol; It's the Time.

HULTEN, GEORGE P   ASCAP 1950
composer, arranger
b San Francisco, Calif, Mar 17, 1891; d. Educ: Pub schs. Assoc, Sherman Clay Music Co, San Francisco, 07-56, became dept mgr. *Songs:* Old New England Moon; Evening Hour; Winding Trail.

HUMES, HELEN   ASCAP 1945
composer, author, singer
b Louisville, Ky, June 23, 13. Started with Basie Band, 38-42; wrote blues tunes at recording sessions. Now a performer in clubs & fests, also a recording artist. Chief Collabrs: Joseph Williams (cousin), Rudy Render. *Songs & Instrumental Works:* Eee Baba LeBa or BeBopa Leba; Married Man Blues; Loud Talking Woman; Contact Me Papa; Jet Propelled Papa or Drive Me Daddy; I Ain't Gonna Quit Cha Baby; Today I Sing the Blues; Helen's Advice or Million Dollar Secret; He Maybe Your Man; Living My Life My Way; Airplane Blues; I Don't Know His Name; Woojama Cooja; Knock Myself Out; Blues for Jimmy; Flippity Flop Flop.

HUNDLEY, CRAIG L   ASCAP 1968
composer, synthesist, pianist
b Hollywood, Calif, Nov 22, 53. Educ: Studied epistemology with J Samuel Bois; studied microtonality with Ervin Wilson. Mem jazz trio at age 14, tours, nat TV & records. Concert pianist with symphonies at age 17. Developed many instruments such as the Bar, the Tubulong & the Chromatone. Became featured session player. Started comp & collaborating on movies, ballets, plays & occasionally full scores & spec music. Chief Collabrs: David Shire, Paul Chihara, Hans Jurgen Bauer. *Songs:* Music: That's No Reason; Lola (Roadie love theme); Dream Lover; Arrival; You and Me; Birth; Alien.

HUNDLEY, RICHARD   ASCAP 1963
composer, pianist
b Cincinnati, Ohio, Sept 1, 31. Educ: Cincinnati Col Cons; studied with Israel Citkowitz, Harold Knapik. Accompanist, vocal dance studios; also organist, teacher, choirmaster, music copyist. *Songs:* Softly the Summer; Maiden Snow; Postcard From Spain; Just Why Johnnie Was Jimmie.

HUNGATE, WILLIAM LEONARD
composer, author
b Benton, Ill, Dec 14, 22. Educ: Bowling Green High Sch, Mo; Cent Methodist Col, Fayette, Mo; Univ Mo, Columbia; Univ Mich, Ann Arbor; Univ Pa, Philadelphia; Harvard Law Sch. With Club Royal, 39-40, Charlie Armstead, 40-41, 377th Inf Regimental Band, 44-46 & Sonny Lefholz, 48-52. Prosecuting atty, Lincoln Co, Mo, 51-55; spec asst, Mo Atty Gen, 58-64; US Rep, Mo, 64-77; US Dist Judge, Mo, 79- *Songs:* Down at the Old Watergate; When I'm the President.

HUNKINS, EUSEBIA SIMPSON   ASCAP 1959
composer, author
b Troy, Ohio, June 20, 02. Educ: Juilliard Sch Music, Found fellowship, with James Friskin, Rubin Goldmark & Albert Stoessel; studied with Ernest Hutcheson & Darius Milhaud; Ohio Univ, with Ernest Von Dohnanyi; Tanglewood; Salzburg. Music teacher, Cornell Col, 2 yrs & Barnard Sch for Boys. Cond, Lyndon-Wright Choral Soc, Yonkers, NY. Dir, comp workshop, Philadelphia Camp, Leesville Lake, Ohio. Chmn, Jr Comp Ohio Fedn of Music Clubs. Ed, Ohio Junior Composers. Mem: Nat Fedn of Music Clubs, Am Folklore Soc & Nat Asn Comp & Cond. *Instrumental Works:* Wondrous Love (choral drama); Octavos: What Wondrous Love; Hey Betty Martin; Shenandoah; Old Sister Phoebe; Why; Rosa; Forest Voices; Shall I Marry. *Scores:* Folk Opera: Smoky Mountain; 1-Act Operas: Mice in Council; Reluctant Hero; Maniian; Young Lincoln (Knox Col comn); Young Lincoln II; Spirit Owl.

HUNSBERGER, DONALD R   ASCAP 1964
composer
b Souderton, Pa, Aug 2, 32. Educ: Univ of Rochester Eastman Sch of Music, BMus, studied orchestration with Bernard Rogers, arr with Rayburn Wright, master of music literature, 59, studied conducting with Fred Pennel, DMA, 63, studied trombone with Emory Remington. Trombone soloist & chief arr, USMC band, Washington, DC, 54-58. Assoc prof, low brass, orchestration & theory, State Univ NY Col Potsdam, 59-61. Cond & recording artist, Univ Rochester Eastman Sch of Music wind ens, 65-, US State Dept tour of Far East, 78. Arr, ed & transcriber. Cond, 30 all-state fests, univ clinics & workshops. Prof of conducting, Univ Rochester Eastman Sch of Music. *Instrumental Works:* Emory Remington Daily Warmup Routine; Clef Studies for Trombone (ed); Transc for wind band: Festive Overture Opus 96 (D Shostakovitch); Passacaglio and Fugue in C minor (J S Bach); Three Dance Episodes—Spartacus (I Khatchaturian); Overture to Colas Breugnon (D Kabalesky); Excerpts from Mass (L Bernstein).

HUNSECKER, RALPH BLANE   ASCAP 1941
composer
b Broken Arrow, Okla, July 26, 14. Educ: Broken Arrow Elem Schs; Central High Sch, Tulsa, Okla; Northwestern Univ; studied with Estelle Liebling, New York. Singer, show "Hooray for What." Co-vocal arr for many shows incl "Too Many Girls", "Dubarry Was a Lady", "Louisiana Purchase", "Pal Joey", "Cabin in the Sky", "Very Warm for May", "Three After Three", "Stars in Your Eyes" & "Sugar Babies," 79 & 80. Formed songwriting partnership with Hugh Martin; organized mixed quartet, The Martins & appeared on Fred Allen Show & did background for Judy Garland & Mickey Rooney in "Wizard of Oz," New York. Co-music writer, "Best Foot Forward." With var Hollywood studios, 43-, writer of musicals, TV shows & choral works. Recipient of 2 Acad Award nominations; named official Okla Ambassador of Goodwill. Chief Collabrs: Hugh Martin, Harry Warren, Harold Arlen, Joe Myrow, Bob Wells, Roger Edens, Kay Thompson, James Gregory, Peter Garey. *Songs:* Buckle, Down, Winsocki!; Everytime; Shady Lady Bird; What D'Ya Think I Am; Wish I May; You're Lucky; Alive and Kicking; Have Yourself a Merry Little Christmas; The Boy Next Door; The Trolley Song; Skip to My Lou; Girls Were Made to Take Care of Boys; Love; Pass That Peace Pipe; An Occasional Man; Balboa; I Don't Know What I Want; All the Colors of the Rainbow; I Like the Feeling; It's a Wishing World; My Heart's Darlin'; Lyrics: Someone Like You; My Dream Is Yours; Stanley Steamer; Afraid to Fall in Love; Weary Blues; Spring Isn't Everything; The French Line; Lookin' for Trouble; Any Gal From Texas.

HUNT, MICHAEL FRANCIS   ASCAP 1971
composer
b New Castle, Ind, Nov 28, 45. Educ: St Louis Inst Music, BM, 68; Washington

Univ, Mo, PhD, 74. Performed with Los Angeles Philh & St Louis Symph Orchs, as well as numerous chamber performances across the US. Mem fac, Fontbonne Col, St Louis.

HUNTER, ALBERTA ASCAP 1952
composer, author, singer
b Memphis, Tenn, Apr 1, 1897. Educ: High sch. Early singer on records. Appeared in London production, "Show Boat," also at Palladium, London & throughout Europe & Egypt. Had own NBC radio prog. WW II, toured Europe & Pacific entertaining troops; later, Korea & Japan. Appeared in Bway plays, "Mamba's Daughters" & "Mrs Patterson." Practical nurse at Goldwater Mem Hospital, NY. *Songs:* Down Hearted Blues; Chirping the Blues; Down South Blues; My Castle's Rocking; I Want to Thank You, Lord; You Got to Reap Just Reap What You Sow; Will the Day Ever Come When I Can Rest; Kind Treatment; What's the Matter Baby?.

HUNTER, B J
See Bedell, Lew

HUNTER, EVAN ASCAP 1958
author
b New York, NY, Oct 15, 26. Educ: Cooper Union; Hunter Col, BA. Author "The Blackboard Jungle", "Second Ending, Strangers When We Meet" & "Mothers and Daughters." Chief Collabr: Norman Monath. *Songs:* Second Ending.

HUNTER, KEVIN
author
b Montreal, Que, June 2, 39. *Songs:* Lyrics: For Awhile.

HUNTER, ROBERT CHRISTIE
composer, singer, lyricist
b Arroyo Grande, Calif, June 23, 41. Lyricist for Grateful Dead; bandleader & lead singer with Roadhog. Wrote lyrics for American Beauty, Working Man's Dead, Aoxomoxoa & other Grateful Dead Albums. Publ: Grateful Dead, 73. Gold Records, 70, 71, 72, 73. Plays Highland Bagpipes. *Songs:* Lyrics: Truckin'; Uncle John's Band; Friend of the Devil; Gugarae; Playing in the Band; It Must Have Been the Roses; Jesse James; Casey Jones; Stella Blue; Wharf Rat. *Albums:* Tales of the Great Rumrunners; Tiger Rose.

HUNTLEY, JOBE ASCAP 1962
composer, singer
b Monroe, NC, Aug 18, 18. Educ: High sch; Mabel Horsey's Sch Music, NY; Borough of Manhattan Col, NY. Billed as Bway's first gospel comp, 63. Recorded for Folkway Records. Chief Collabrs: Langston Hughes & Herbert R Carr. *Songs:* This is My Prayer; Since You've Been Gone; God Is With You; It's So Amazing; Music: Life is Fine; My Last Long Rest; On a Christmas Night. *Scores:* Bway Show, "Tambourines to Glory": As I Go; Moon Outside My Window; I Have Sinned; Scat Cat; Let the Church Say Amen; When I Touch His Garment; Lord Above; Upon This Rock; New York Blues; Home to God; A Flower in God's Garden; Back to the Fold; I'm Gonna Testify; Devil Take Yourself Away; Thank God I Have the Bible in My Hand; Tambourines to Glory; Love is On The Way; God's Got a Way.

HUPFELD, HERMAN ASCAP 1931
composer, author, singer
b Montclair, NJ, Feb 1, 1894; d Montclair, June 8, 51. Educ: High sch. Served in USN, WW I. Sang own songs in Bway revue, "Ziegfeld's Midnight Frolic" (12). Wrote songs for musicals: "A la Carte"; "The Little Show"; "Second Little Show"; "Everybody's Welcome"; "Murder at the Vanities." Songs for films incl, "Take a Chance." Singer, pianist throughout US & Europe. Entertained in camps & hospitals, WW II. Pianist. *Songs:* Sing Something Simple; As Time Goes By; When Yuba Plays the Rhumba on the Tuba; Let's Put Out the Lights and Go to Sleep; Are You Making Any Money?; Savage Serenade; Down the Old Back Road; A Hut in Hoboken; Night Owl; Honey Ma Love; Baby's Blue; The Calinda.

HUPP, DEBORAH KAY ASCAP 1978
composer, author
b New Albany, Ind, Aug 7, 48. Started out with five rough demo tapes in Nashville, Tenn, 69, three of which were publ. Wrote for Johnny MacRae, Screen Gems, 2 1/2 yrs. Now independent comp-author, 77- Chief Collabrs: Bob Morrison, Johnny MacRae. *Songs:* Are You on the Road to Loving Me Again; Jason; My Side of Town; Music Maker; Gravel on the Ground; You Decorated My Life.

HURD, BARRY T ASCAP 1976
composer
b Highland Park, Mich, Aug 25, 49. Educ: Wayne State Univ, BA(TV, radio, film). Prof musician, guitarist & keyboardist, 65-70. Wrote TV scripts, articles & plays, 68- Writer, producer & lyricist for children's show, "Hot Fudge Show," 75- Creator, Consolidated Tele-Communications, 80- Chief Collabr: Larry Santos. *Songs:* You Can't Buy; Feelings Are Funny; Two Sides to Every Story; Take the Bows; Friendship Is a Two-Way Street.

HURD, DANIEL GEORGE ASCAP 1946
composer, arranger, pianist
b Fitchburg, Mass, May 9, 18. Educ: Wash Square Col, NY Univ, BA, 51; studied with Sam Saxe, Teddy Wilson, Lennie Tristano, Rudolf Schramm & Philip James. Pianist & arr with dance bands, Hal McIntyre, Jimmy Dorsey, Lee Castle, Claude Thornhill, George Paxton & Curtis Bay (USCG) Dance Band; teacher, NJ Music Col & pvt pract; rehearsal pianist & dance music arr for "Perry Como Show", "Jimmy Dean Show", "Dick Van Dyke Show" & the "Other Woman" (TV spec); assoc cond, "Henry Sweet Henry"; new orchestrations, "Golden Boy, 68"; musical dir, "Hair," Los Angeles, Acapulco, Paris, Tokyo & Paramus, NJ; co-orchr, Via Galactica; comp & musical dir of Buick & other indust shows; music coordr for "Milliken Breakfast Show." Chief Collabrs: Tom Moore, Lawrence Dukore, Fred Tobias. *Songs:* Music Lonely Days (and Nights More Lonely); Lovers' Quarrel; You Can't Spell Buick Without U and I. *Instrumental Works:* Strange Mood; Rockin' and Ridin'; Jumpin' Jubilee; Dixieland Mambo; The Awakening of Pedro.

HURLBURT, GLEN ASCAP 1950
composer, author
b Portland, Ore, Aug 29, 09; d San Francisco, Calif, Apr 20, 61. *Songs:* Leprechaun Lullaby; Senor O'Shaughnessy; Cable Car Concerto; Beautiful Land of My Dreams.

HURRELL, CLARENCE E ASCAP 1959
composer, conductor, publisher
b Johnstown, Pa, Sept 11, 12; d Johnstown, Pa, Feb 7, 75. Educ: Curtis Inst, scholarship; USA Music Sch; Ind State Col, studied music with Gordon Nevin & Gustave Strube. Joined USA Band as trombone soloist, 33. Chief arr & comp, Army documentary films, also commercial film, "The US Army Band." Became WO Band Leader. Founder & cond, Mil District of Wash Band, Ft Myer, Va. Founded Hurrell Music Shop & studio, Johnstown, 46; co-founder, pres & gen mgr, Somerset Music Press, 51. Cond, Johnstown Munic Concert Band; dir music, Mercy Hospital Sch Nursing. Dir, Instrumental Music Educ Prog, Johnstown-Altoona Diocese. Band dir & instr in parochial schs; also taught privately. *Instrumental Works:* Band: Pan American Overture; The Boy Friends (cornet trio, band); Elmer the Elephant; Snowfall; Serenade Moderne.

HURT, MARY KATHRYN ASCAP 1970
author, singer, musician
b Anniston, Ala, Oct 13, 40. Educ: Birmingham Cons Music, BME; scholarship, Transylvania Music Camp, Brevard, NC. Began music studies at 6; Pittsburgh Playhouse, 1 yr. Worked in the South on radio & TV until 61. Toured in "Gypsy", "Camelot" & "My Fair Lady." Had own trio in New York, 8 yrs; owner, Audible Advert Productions. Studio singer & musician comedy material; performer of unusual instruments; announcer for country spots. Chief Collabrs: Fannie Flagg, Anne Bryant. *Songs:* Yes, You; Tip Toe Thru the Kumquats; If I Were You; When You Say Goodbye.

HURTE, LEROY EDWARD ASCAP 1965
composer, author, conductor
b Muskogee, Okla, May 2, 15. Educ: Thomas Jefferson High Sch, Los Angeles; Los Angeles City Col; Juilliard Sch Music, studied with Felix Prohuska; Nat Orchestral Asn, studied conducting with Leon Barzin; Tanglewood Workshop, studied conducting with Seymour Lipkin. Cond, Angel City Symph Orch, 58-68; guest cond, Los Angeles Community Symph Orch, Calif Jr Symph & Fresno Philh; publ, Bronze Lyric Publ Co; arr, Davis & Schwegler Transcriptions & Walter Lantz Cartoons; vocalist, radio, TV & motion pictures; choral dir, Hanford Choral Soc, Wings Over Jordan & var other church choirs; singer. *Songs:* O When You Touch Me; Look Always to Thee; Prayer. *Instrumental Works:* Concerto for Violin and Orchestra; Nobody Knows the Trouble I've Seen (spiritual arr for string orch).

HUSTAD, DONALD PAUL ASCAP 1966
composer, teacher, organist
b Echo, Minn, Oct 2, 18. Educ: John Fletcher Col, Iowa, BA, 40; Northwestern Univ, MMus, DMus; Am Guild of Organists, AAGO; Royal Col of Organists, FRCO. Ed, comp & arr, Hope Publ Co, 50- Dir, sacred music dept, Moody Bible Inst, Chicago, 50-63. Organist, Billy Graham Crusades, 61-67. Prof, church music, Southern Baptist Theol Sem, Louisville, 66- *Songs & Instrumental Works:* Prayer Before Singing (choral); Celebration of Discipleship (cantata); The Gospel Bard (cantata); Spirit of God (vocal solo); & many arr of hymns & anthems.

HUSTON, CARLA A (CAARON) ASCAP 1964
composer, author, conductor
b Glendive, Mont, May 11, 44. Educ: Univ Mont, BA; Columbia Univ, MA, MEd, 75, EdD, 77; studied ballet & modern jazz with Eugene Louis; studied acting with Lee Strasberg. Actress; had lead role in Off-Bway show, "The Fantasticks" & in Bway shows, "Once Upon a Mattress" & "Harold." Acted in Stratford, Conn, Shakespeare productions, "As You Like It", "Mac Beth", "Troilus and Cressida"; also appeared in TV dramas such as "Untouchables." Singer with City Center Opera, TV shows, Perry Como & Bob Hope. Author of scholarly articles & music critic for Music Jour. Author of bk, "Olivier Messiaen." Dir music & dance, Trinity Sch, New York. Chief Collabr: Aaron Bell. *Songs:* Let Me Cry Your Tears, Love; Reflection; Ode to Martin Luther

King; Soft Is the Light; Lyrics: Let the Rain Fall on Me; Sifting Sand; I Was Just Thinkin' About You; Katanga; Love Is the Color. *Instrumental Works:* Variations; Suite for a Greek Festival.

HUSTON, FRANK C ASCAP 1948
composer, author, music minister
b Orange, Ind, Sept 12, 1871; d Jacksonville, Fla, Oct 14, 59. Educ: Moody Bible Inst, studied with D B Towner & W C Coffin. Choir dir & cond singing schs. Taught pub schs, Ind; became publ. Served in 150th Field Artillery, WW I. Served in USCG, WW II. Minister of music, Jacksonville Gospel Tabernacle; chaplain, Jacksonville Chap, Coast Guard League. *Songs:* It Pays to Serve Jesus; The Christ of the Cross; Keep on Believing; Wonderful Land of Tomorrow; For the Honor of Old Purdue.

HUSTON, STEVEN CHARLES ASCAP 1974
composer, singer, drummer
b Centralia, Ill, Nov 17, 49. Educ: Woodlawn High Sch, Ill; Kaskaskia Col, AA; Eastern Ill Univ. Performer, nightclubs, col bars, concerts & TV. Recording artist, A&M Records. *Songs:* Jefftown Creek; City of Gold; Open Up the Door; Keep a Secret; Look to the Sky.

HUSTON, WILLIAM DALE ASCAP 1954
composer
b Rantoul, Ill, Aug 28, 18. Educ: Univ of Ill. USAF service. Has been realtor; car dealer, 45- Chief Collabrs: Sammy Gallop, Chester Conn. *Songs:* Saving a Dream for a Rainy Day; Just Like Before; Light House By the Sea.

HUTCHESON, RONITA MARLENE (RONI BELL) ASCAP 1977
composer, singer
b Omaha, Nebr, Mar 10, 45. Singer & accompanist, weddings, musicals, church services & sch progs, age 12. Prof singer, age 15. Comp, church play & var songs, 75-

HUTCHINS, DARYL ASCAP 1947
composer
b Sterling, Colo, Aug 25, 20; d Walnut Creek, Calif, July 2, 71. NBC radio announcer. Correspondent, WW II. Author story bk "Filbert, the Bird With Tailspinitis." *Songs:* I Wonder, I Wonder, I Wonder; The Wiggily Song; I'm Looking for a Sweetheart; Empty Mansions.

HUTCHISON, (DAVID) WARNER (WALTER HUDSON) ASCAP 1969
composer, author, educator
b Denver, Colo, Dec 15, 30. Educ: Univ Denver Lamont Sch Music, 48; Rockmont Col, Denver, 49-51; Southwestern Baptist Theol Sem Sch Church Music, Ft Worth, Tex, bachelor church music(comp), 54; NTex State Univ, MMus(comp), 56, PhD, 71; Univ Rochester Eastman Sch Music, 59; Ind Univ Sch Music, 58; studied with Samuel Adler, Merrill Ellis, Roy Harris, Kent Kennan, Wayne Barlow, French horn with Thomas Holden, Morris Secon, Clyde Miller. Dir of bands, instr of music, Houghton Col, NY, 56-58, instr of comp, theory & brass, band dir, Union Univ, Tenn, 59-66; prof music, head music dept & dir electronic music laboratory, NMex State Univ, 67- Guest cond, var choirs & bands; adjudicator, high sch music fests in Tenn, NY, Tex & NMex. Ed, Proceedings, Am Soc Univ Composers; comp works for band, choral, orch, electronic instruments, ballet & chamber ens. Mem exec bd, Am Soc Univ Composers, 73-; recipient, MacDowell Colony fels, res grants in electronic & computer music & Pulitzer Prize nomination, 71. Chief Collabrs: Joseph Caldwell, Mark Medoff, Erskine Caldwell. *Instrumental Works:* Apocalypse: 1979 (brass quintet, tam-tam, bells); Ceremonies (ballet & for oboe, prepared & amplified piano, electronic tape); Choral Fantasy (horn, organ); Dirge and Hosanna (symph band); Fantasy-Variations (symph band); Five Miniatures on Love (choral, piano); Hornpiece I (French horn, electronic tape); Hymntune Suite (organ); A Joyful Psalm (choral, organ); Mini-Suite for Brass Trio; Monday Music (electronic: synthesizer, piano); Nativity Hymn (choral, organ); Prairie Sketch (orch); Psalm 135 (choral, organ); Sonatina for Baritone Horn; The Strife is O'Er (choral, organ); Suite for Clarinet Choir; Death-Words From the Cherokee (orch, mezzo-soprano solo, tape); Homage to Jackson Pollock (narrator, solo perc, tape, slides); Chrysalis (5 flutes); Fanfare for Easter (brass quartet, carillon); Let Us Be Grateful (text by J F Kennedy, chorus, orch); Equus (incidental music). *Scores:* Opera: Sacrilege of Alan Kent (baritone solo, tape, orch).

HUTNER, HERBERT L ASCAP 1974
composer, author
b New York, NY. Educ: Columbia Col, BA; Columbia Law Sch, JD. First violinist, Columbia Symph Orch, while at Col. Lawyer; partner in New York stock exchange firm; pres, NE Life Insurance Co; chmn of board & dir for var cos. Comp, sports songs & standards. Chief Collabr: Jacqueline Getty. *Songs:* Go Rams Go; The Pride of Morningside; Music: The Super Bowl Song; The Racing Song; Juli; Kansas City Chiefs; The Safari Song; This Life With You.

HYATT, WILLARD CLARK ASCAP 1977
author, singer
b Libertyville, Ill, June 7, 07. Educ: Carleton Col, BA, 33; Northwestern Univ, 34; Whitewater State Teachers Col, 37; voice studies with Dwight E Cook, 27-29 & Florence Morsbach, 32-33. Music critic, News-Sun, Waukegan, Ill,

40-45; pvt sch teacher, Chicago, Ill, 10 yrs. Publ 9 bks of poetry. Free-lance writer, tutor & music critic, Music Jour, New York. Chief Collabrs: (Comp) Eugene Zador, David Morton & Clyde Allen. *Songs:* Lyrics: The Light; Silence; three songs based on the poems of Willard Hyatt (song cycle).

HYDE, ALEXANDER ASCAP 1937
composer, author, conductor
b Hamburg, Ger, Feb 17, 1898; d Santa Monica, Calif, July 7, 56. Moved to US, 1898, citizen. Educ: New York pub schs; studied music with Sascha Coleman, Michael Svedrofsky; hon MusD. Bandmaster, USN, WW I. Cond, theatres, cafes, NY & Europe. Comp & bandleader, USAAF, WW II. Scored films, consult to Miklos Rozsa. Author: "The Key to Harmony"; "American Wings Band Book". *Songs:* Oh, Say Can You Swing; With Thee I Swing; My Heart Is in a Violin; Poor Robinson Crusoe; Picture Me in a Picture With You; I Love You From Coast to Coast.

HYDE, MADELINE ASCAP 1948
composer, author
b Chicago, Ill, Dec 13, 07. Educ: Principia Sch, St Louis, Mo; finishing sch, Paris. Writer, special material for nightclub acts. *Songs:* She Fell in the Fall of the Year; Little Girl; It's Happened Again; My Stubborn Heart; New York Nostalgia; Music: Liana; Lullabye-Bye Blues.

HYMAN, JACKIE D ASCAP 1966
author
b Menard, Tex, Apr 3, 49. Educ: Brandeis Univ, BA; studied poetry writing with Howard Nemerov & playwriting with William Gibson. Lyricist, playwright & journalist; wrote play, "Fantasies" & musical, "Song of the Unicorn." Staff mem, The Associated Press, Los Angeles, 80- Chief Collabrs: Teddy Bart, Betty Lougaris Soldo. *Songs:* Lyrics: Rainy Streets; Song of the Unicorn.

HYMAN, RICHARD R ASCAP 1955
composer, pianist, organist
b New York, NY, Mar 8, 27. Educ: Columbia Col, 48; studied piano with Anton Rovinsky. Jazz pianist, New York; Benny Goodman Europ tour, 50. Staff pianist & organist, WMCA, NBC, New York. Free-lance studio musician, arr & cond. Music dir, Arthur Godfrey progs, 59-62. Recording artist; cond, var TV progs. Comp, TV film scores, concert works & light instrumental pieces. Musical dir, New York Jazz Repertory Co on tour of Soviet Union, 75. Performer, jazz fests & clubs. Orchestrator, "Sugar Babies", 79 & "Black Broadway", 80. Cond & pianist, Twyla Tharp Dance Co. Performer, "History of Jazz Piano." Chief Collabr: Seymour Reiter. *Songs:* Love Is for Amateurs; So Easy; Back With the Human Race; Music: It Was a Lover and His Lass (songs from Shakespeare's plays). *Instrumental Works:* Concerto for Piano and Orchestra (Concerto Electro); Ragtime Fantasy for Piano and Orchestra; Organix for Pop Organ and Orchestra; Suite for Moog Synthesizer (incl The Minotaur); Mountain Mist; Song for Sid; What's the Matter?; Duets in Odd Meters and Far-out Rhythms; Sugarloaf; Stars and Echoes; The Man From O.R.G.A.N.; Little Brother; Happy Ever After; Slow Bus to Oswego; A Letter From My Brother in Brazil; The Flower Road; Beat the Clock (underscore cues). *Scores:* TV films: King Crab; The Last Tenant; Scott Joplin, King of Ragtime; Operetta: Joan and the Devil.

I

IAN, JANIS ASCAP 1970
composer, singer, musician
b New York, NY, Apr 7, 51. Self-taught orchestration & scoring, 69-73. Chief Collabrs: Giorgio Moroder, Albert Hammond. *Songs:* Society's Child; Jesse; Stars; In the Winter; Love Is Blind; At Seventeen; Watercolors; Music: The Other Side of the Sun; Lyrics: Fly Too High.

IANNACCONE, ANTHONY ASCAP 1973
composer
b Brooklyn, NY, Oct 14, 43. Educ: Manhattan Sch Music, MM; Eastman Sch Music, PhD, studied comp with Samuel Adler, Vittorio Giannini, Ludmila Ulehla, Nicolas Flagello & David Diamond; studied cond with Hugh Ross, Anton Coppola. Taught at Manhattan Sch Music, 67-69; prof music, Eastern Mich Univ, 71- Awards, Fels & Comns: NEA, Nat Music Teachers Asn, Mich Music Teachers Asn, East & West Artists of New York, Nat Found Phi Mu Alpha Sinfonia, Univ Mo, State Univ NY at Potsdam, Eastman Sch Music, Prix du Centenaire & ASCAP. Distinguished Fac Award, Eastern Mich Univ, 78. *Songs & Instrumental Works:* Rituals for Violin and Piano; Trio for Flute, Clarinet and Piano; Antiphonies (band); The Prince of Peace (cantata for chorus, soloists & wind ens); After a Gentle Rain (band); Of Fire and Ice (band); Lysistrata (full orch); Scherzo (band); String Quartet; Parodies for Woodwind Quintet; Partita for Piano; Bicinia for Flute and Alto Saxophone; The Sky is Low, the Clouds Are Mean (SATB, chorus); Remembrance for Viola and Piano; Sonatina for Trumpet and Tuba; Three Mythical Sketches for Brass Quartet; Keyboard Essays; Anamorphoses for Brass and Percussion; Solomon's Canticle (SATB); Hades (brass quartet); Night Song (bassoon & piano); Interlude for Wind Ensemble.

IANNELLI, THERESA ROSE   ASCAP 1963
composer, author
b Philadelphia, Pa, Aug 4, 36. Educ: Notre Dame Acad. *Songs:* Secret Sorrow.

IATAURO, MICHAEL ANTHONY   ASCAP 1970
composer, author, educator
b New York, NY, Feb 26, 43. Educ: High Sch of Music & Art, New York, dipl, 60; Manhattan Sch of Music, BM, 66; Cent Mich Univ, MM, 68; Univ Colo, DMA, studied with Vittorio Giannini, David Diamond. Free-lance musician, New York & east coast, 60-66. Instr, Biviano Sch of Music, New York, 62-65. Grad teaching asst, Cent Mich Univ, 66-68; assoc instr, Univ Colo, 69. Supvr & dir, pub schs, South Routt, Colo, 69-76. Acting chmn, dept fine arts, NMex Inst of Mining & Technol, 76-77, head, dept of music, 76- *Instrumental Works:* Two Pieces for String Bass and Piano; Children's Pieces for Adults; Symphony No 1 (symph band).

IDE, HAROLD   ASCAP 1961
composer, author
b Troy Hill, Pa, Oct 9, 17. Educ: Univ of Pittsburgh, BS. Pianist, arr with Buzz Aston Orch. Toured with Ice Capades, 40. Mem, Baron Elliott Orch, 43-46. Worked on Ind Hygiene Found, air pollution proj, Mellon Inst. *Instrumental Works:* Tango Elite.

IDRISS, RAMEZ   ASCAP 1947
composer, author, musician
b New York, NY, Sept 11, 11; d Los Angeles, Calif, Feb 5, 71. Educ: Los Angeles City Col. Musician in dance orchs on radio, records & in films. TV scriptwriter; wrote spec material for Ritz Bros, Eddie Cantor, Jimmy Durante & Marion Hutton. *Songs:* The Old Chaperone; Worry, Worry, Worry; The Woody Woodpecker Song; Take a Letter, Miss Smith; This Is It; I'll Wait; Leave It to Joan.

IJAMES, MARY TUNSTALL (MARION SUNSHINE)   ASCAP 1933
composer, author, actress
b Louisville, Ky, May 14, 1894; d New York, NY, Jan 25, 63. Educ: St Joseph Acad, Mt Vernon, NY. Mem of sister team, Tempest & Sunshine; appeared in melodrama, "Two Little Waifs", age 5; in production of "Richard III." Toured Vaudeville, US & Can; writer of own acts & special material for Fanny Ward, Harry Richman, Hildegarde. Appeared in "Ziegfeld Follies", 07, First & Second Winter Garden Shows, "The Beauty Shop", "Going Up", "Stop! Look! Listen!", "The Blue Kitten", "Daffy Dill" & "Capt Jinks." Sponsored Don Azpiazu Orch & introduced Latin Am music to US & Europe. Marion Sunshine Scholarship established at Juilliard Sch, 63. *Songs:* The Peanut Vendor; Havana's Calling; Voodoo Moon; Cuban Belle; Nina; Los Timbales; Playtime in Brazil; Here Comes the Conga; The Happy Bird; The Color of Her Hair; My Cuban Sombrero; I'm on My Way; Bossa Nova Stomp; El Sopon; Mary, You're a Little Bit Old-Fashioned; I've Got Everything I Want But You; Baby Sister Blues; I Got a Guy; Have You Seen My Love?; MacPherson Is Rehearsin'.

IMIG, WARNER   ASCAP 1963
composer
b Sioux City, Iowa, Feb 12, 13. Educ: Yankton Col, BA; Univ Colo, MME; Stanford Univ; teaching DePauw Univ. Ed assoc, J of Res in Music Educ. Lectr, Stanford Univ; guest lectr, Univ SDak, Kans State Univ, Tex Western State Col, Western Wash Col of Educ & Highlands Univ. Prof of music & dean of Col of Music, Univ Colo. Nat chmn, Choral Comn, Music Teachers Nat Asn, 58- Life mem, Am Choral Dir Asn, pres, 62-64. Author "Music in Our Time." *Songs:* American Folk and Play Songs.

INDELLI, WILLIAM   ASCAP 1961
composer, author
b Chicago, Ill, Nov 16, 24. Chief Collabr: L Leslie Loth. *Songs:* You'll Never Guess; There's So Much to Remember; Lyrics: Brave Hearts of America; Don't Cry My Heart; A Cowboy's Hope and Prayer; Miracle of Love; I Mustn't; Billy the Kid; Prison Blues.

INGE, CLINTON OWEN   ASCAP 1962
composer, author
b Geiger, Ala, Feb 25, 09. Educ: Miss Baptist Sem; Am Baptist Theol Sem. Minister, New Hope Baptist Church, Meridian, Miss. Dir, Religious Educ for East Miss State Baptist Convention. Acting dean, Meridian branch, Miss Baptist Sem. *Songs:* At the End of the Day; Whisper a Prayer; Shadows Will Flee; God Is Love.

INGE, JOSEPH DARRELL   ASCAP 1969
composer
b Culver City, Calif, Aug 16, 41. Educ: Univ Calif, Los Angeles, BA(music), 64; studied comp with Roy Harris & Colin McPhee; Calif State Univ Northridge, MA(music), 68; studied comp with Aurelio DeLaVega. Had comp played over KPFK Radio, Los Angeles, 65 & at Composers' Symposium held at Brigham Young Univ, Provo, Utah, 66. Librarian. Chief Collabr: Keith R Williams. *Songs:* Music Cues TV Series Shows, "Roaring Twenties", "Colt 45", "Bronco" & "Sugarfoot", incl: Two Bad Like; Intense City; Mister Donlikem; Ketch 'Um; Chase Down; String Time; Edgy Tato. *Instrumental Works:* Bagatelles for Piano

(four pieces); Three Brief Pieces (woodwind quintet); String Quartet; Seven Chamber Pieces.

INGERSON, RICHARD WAYNE   ASCAP 1979
composer, author, singer
b Brunswick, Maine, Sept 25, 52. Eight yrs of singing in bands, along with five yrs of music writing; played in country show circuit, Maine, three yrs. Mem, Int Fan Club Orgn, Colo. Recording artist; rhythm guitarist. Chief Collabr: Rusty Scott. *Songs:* Daddy's Cryin', Mama's Gone; Going Back Home (To My Baby); Red Red Roses.

INGRAHAM, HERBERT IRVING   ASCAP 1940
composer, author, conductor
b Aurora, Ill, July 7, 1883; d Saranac Lake, NY, Aug 24, 10. Bro of Roy Ingraham. Educ: Valparaiso Univ. Music dir, touring theatre cos; led own orch, 05; staff comp, Shapiro, Bernstein. *Songs:* Because I'm Married Now; Roses Bring Dreams of You; You Are the Ideal of My Dreams; When I Dream in the Gloaming of You; All That I Ask Is Love; Don't Wake Me Up, I Am Dreaming; Goodbye Rose.

INGRAHAM, (EDWARD) ROY   ASCAP 1938
composer, author, singer
b Whiting, Ind, Dec 6, 1895. Educ: Whiting grade & high schs. Studied violin, age 8. Own orch, Whiting Theatre, Ind, age 10, Los Angeles, 23-26 & New York, 28. First song publ, age 17. Toured vaudeville, 4 yrs. Contract writer, Berlin, Inc & Witmark & Sons. Broadcast over CBS Network, 29-31. Writer for several motion pictures. Wrote spec material for Sophie Tucker, Marion Harris & Edith Clifford. Chief Collabrs: Harry Tobias, Al Hoffman, Dave Oppenheim, King Zany. *Songs:* Topper; Music: I've Got a Cross Eyed Papa (But He Looks Straight to Me); Deep in the Arms of Love; No Regrets; Love Is a Beautiful Thing; A Girl Like You, a Boy Like Me; Sunny Side of the Rockies; Stars Over the Desert.

INGRAM, ALLYN CHERYL   ASCAP 1977
author, singer
b Jacksonville, NC, June 23, 51. Educ: Mich State Univ; Wayne State Univ; Lee Col. Traveled with contemporary gospel band, Alpenglow, six yrs, recording with Paragon Records, Nashville, Tenn & Housetop Records. *Songs & Instrumental Works:* Brand New Way of Loving; It's You Lord; He's Coming Again; My Delight.

INGRIS, EDUARD   ASCAP 1967
composer, author, conductor
b Zlonice, Bohemia, Feb 11, 05. Educ: Univ Prague; Prague Cons Music, MMus(comp & cond), studied with V Novak, O Sin, K B Jirak, J Kricka & M Dolezil. Cond, comp & music dir theaters, Prague, 20 yrs; cond symph for movie studios, Prague; cond symph orch, Lima, Peru. Capt & chief on rafts Kantuta I & II, voyages across Pacific, Peru to Polynesia. Explored Amazon Region & many SPac Islands. Wrote over 60 light operas, operettas, musicals for var theaters in Prague, incl "Capricious Mirror", "Endless Triangle" & "Melody of the Hearts." Wrote music for 11 movies, incl "The Gallant One."

INNES, BETTY K   ASCAP 1979
composer, teacher, performer
b St Louis, Mo, Mar 3, 41. Educ: Florissant Valley Community Col, Mo, AA, 71; Univ Wis, Madison, BMus, 76; Fla A&M Univ, MEd, 79. Professional performer, keyboard & vocal, 50-64; keyboard teacher, 64-68; composer, educator, accompanist, vocalist, dancer & theater work, 68-80. Chief Collabr: (Arr) Max Myover. *Songs:* Have a Very Merry Merry Christmas.

INNES, ROBERT BURNS   ASCAP 1974
composer, author
b Cortland, NY, Aug 8, 41. Educ: Mich State Univ, BS, 63, MA, 65; Univ Mich, PhD(educ & psychol), 71. Assoc prof & dir child develop specialist prog, Peabody Col, Vanderbilt Univ. Chief Collabrs: Darrell Statler, Francis McElvoy. *Songs:* Willie Sing Your Song; More Or Less.

IRESON, JOHN BALFOUR (JOHN WILDER)   ASCAP 1965
composer, singer
b Jefferson, NC, Sept 24, 37. Educ: Lees McRae Col, AA; Westminster Choir Col, Princeton, NJ, BA; Acad del Arte, Florence, Italy. Performer, Radio City Music Hall, 64 & concert tours. Comp, sound tracks for 12 western movies, Rome, Italy, 65-70. Recording artist with RCA Victor, Italy. Europ tour, 65-70. Chief Collabr: Wayne Parham. *Songs:* Candy Castles; Ma Te Che Ne Fai; Themes: Nuggets; Happys Hour. *Albums:* Wanted Dead Or Alive.

IRICK, JOHN   ASCAP 1971
author
b Johnson City, Tenn, Feb 15, 23. Educ: Watauga Acad, Tenn, GED dipl; Guinn Guitar Sch, Tenn, 69. Singer & harmonica player with family, friends & church groups. Chief Collabr: Nedra Guinn. *Songs:* Lyrics: Our Love Will Always Abound; Solid and Sound.

IRONS, EARL D ASCAP 1950
composer, author, conductor
b Sulphur Springs, Tex, Mar 10, 1891; d. Educ: US Army Band Sch; Chicago Cons; hon MusD, Zoellner Cons. Cornet soloist, violinist in theatres. Sgt, World War I; asst cond, Replacement Camp Band, Camp McArthur, Tex; cond, Greenville, Tex Am Legion Band, 22-25; head, Violin Dept, Burleson Col; head, Fine Arts Dept & band dir, Arlington State Col, Tex, 25-58; guest cond, adjudicator in state & nat contests & festivals; musician & educr. Author, "Development of the Embouchure." Charter mem & past pres, Tex Bandmasters Asn & Am Bandmasters Asn; mem, Tex Music Educrs Asn. *Instrumental Works:* Emerald Isle; Everglades; Cedarvale; American Grandeur; Tradition.

IRONS, EDWARD D, JR
composer, musician, singer
b Tallahassee, Fla, Jan 24, 54. Educ: Morehouse Col. Singer & drummer with group, Brick. Chief Collabs: James B Brown, Reginald J Hargis, Raymond L Ransom, Jr. *Songs:* Dazz; Dusic; Ain't Gonna Hurt Nobody.

IRWIN, GENE ASCAP 1941
composer, pianist
b Chicago, Ill, Jan 11, 16; d Philadelphia, Pa, Dec 25, 66. Educ: Brown Prep Sch; studied piano with Joseph Angert, D Sokoloff. Mem, piano duo Mann & Irwin. Pre-flight instr, USN, World War II. *Songs:* It Ain't Being Done No More; Sweet Night; Five O'Clock Whistle; Melinda the Mousie; The Widow Brown; The Tailors' Song.

IRWIN, LOIS ASCAP 1961
composer, author, pianist
b Westmont, Ill, July 29, 26. Educ: Pub schs. Musician, gospel singer with husband in evangelistic progs. *Songs:* Let Me Be Worthy; The Healer; It Was Jesus; He'll Make a Way; The Most Important Thing; There'll Be an Answer Bye and Bye.

IRWIN, WILLIAM ASCAP 1964
composer, author, teacher
b New York, NY, Sept 18, 23. Educ: High sch; pvt music study. Began teaching piano, 40. Has been pianist, organist, throughout US. Had own radio show, 3 yrs. Cond, Teachers Workshops. Producer, organ pops concerts, Hammond Organ Co, US & Can, also technical adv, Hammond TV film series. Organ ed, Hansen Publ. Has made records. Author "Chord Construction Magic", "Rhythm Accompaniment Magic", "Modern Melody Magic", "Bass Pedal Magic" & "Diminished Chord Magic."

IRWIN, WILLIAM C K ASCAP 1937
author, musical director
b San Francisco, Calif, Feb 3, 07. Educ: Louisville Cons Music, piano studies; Inst Musical Art, New York, BA, studied piano with James Friskin & comp with A Madley Richardson & Leopold Mannes. At fifteen won a summer scholarship with Percy Grainger in Chicago, Ill. Worked as comp & musical dir in musical theatre in New York; spent six yrs with Rodgers & Hammerstein. Choral dir, staff comp & musical dir, Radio City Music Hall, New York, 59-79. Chief Collabrs: Norman Zeno, E Y Harburg, Albert Stillman. *Songs:* Rhythm in My Hair; Long as You've Got Your Health; I'm Not Me, I'm You; Swiss Chalet; Love, Come Take Me; What a Dummy Love Has Made of Me. *Songs & Instrumental Works:* In a Little Swiss Chalet; Two Get Together.

ISAAC, MERLE JOHN (JOHN MERLE) ASCAP 1957
composer, author, arranger
b Pioneer, Iowa, Oct 12, 1898. Educ: VanderCook Col Music, BMus; Lewis Inst, Ill, BS; Northwestern Univ, MA. Prof organist, 19-29; high sch music educator, orch dir, 29-43; elementary sch principal, 43-64. Taught part-time, cols & univs; adjudicator, music contests & fest; cond at clinics & fest throughout US. Mem: Music Educr Nat Conference, Ill Music Educr Conference, Nat Sch Orch Asn, Am String Teachers Asn. *Instrumental Works:* Apollo Suite; Festive Holiday Overture; Mexican Overture; Overture Russe; Poppin' Corn; Rhythms and Styles; Rumanian Overture; Russian Chorale and Overture; South American Overture; Espana Cani (Span); Quinto-Quarto Suite; Arr: Berceuse and Finale (Stravinsky); Brandenburg Concerto, No 3 (Bach); Brandenburg Concerto, No 5 (Bach); Caprice Italien Tschaikowsky; Fidelio Overture (Beethoven); Hungarian Dance, No 4 & No 6 (Brahms); March and Procession of Bacchus (Delibes); March of the Boyars (Halvorson); Nutcracker Suite (Tschaikowsky); Procession of the Nobles (Rimsky-Korsakov); Russian Sailors' Dance (Gliere); Swedish Rhapsody (Alfven); Tritsch-Tratsch Polka (Strauss); Ballet Parisien (Offenbach).

ISAACS, ALVIN KALANIKAUIKEALANEO ASCAP 1956
(ALVIN KALEOLANI)
composer, author, singer
b Honolulu, Hawaii, Sept 9, 04. Educ: Self-taught musician. Formed own group, Royal Hawaiians, on stas, KGU, KGMB & KPOI, 28-33; also had group, Hawaii Calls Serenaders. Toured with Harry Owens throughout US & Can, 4 yrs; later worked with group known as The Royal Hawn Serenaders, 47-51. *Songs:* Kauionalani (The Beauties of Heaven); Nalani (The Heavens); Auhea Oe (Where Art Thou); Moon of the Southern Sea; Analani E (Hi! Ann); Leimomi

(My Wreath of Gems); Hula Mai Oe (Won't You Dance the Hula?); E Mau (Long Live Hawaii); Aloha Kuu Pua (You're My Favorite Flower); Nani Wale No Oe (You're Beautiful); My Island Love Song; Kuu Ipo (My Sweetheart); Manowaiopuna (Where the Cool Waters Meet); Aloha Nui Kuu Ipo (The One I Love Most); Nani (Beautiful); Kuulani (My Heaven); Pua Kaleponi (My California Rose); Ke Kaupu (The Magic Over Things); Tahaua La (You and I); Hooheno (Someone You Admire); Alawai Hula (A Song to the Alawai Place); Ke Kumuhana Nui (Object of My Affection); Music: Goodnight Kuu Ipo (Goodnite, Sweetheart); The Story Starts; Dance the Hula in the Sea; Lyrics: Milimili Hula (Fondle Me); Na Pua O Hawaii (The Flowers of Hawaii).

ISAACS, CLAUDE REESE ASCAP 1941
composer, author, teacher
b Johnstown, Pa, June 23, 01; d New York, NY, Sept 11, 53. Educ: Syracuse Univ, law. Soprano as youth, concert tours of eastern US. Recording artist at age 12. With Greenwich Village Follies, toured NY to Fla. Staff artist, CBS, 18 yrs. *Songs:* All Dressed Up With a Broken Heart; Bouncy Bouncy Bally; Noche Buena; Vacilando (Fancy Free); Riendo (Merry Mambo); How Will I Know?; Gonna Give Myself a Pat on the Back; The Luck of the Irish; Idaho Ida.

ISLER, HELEN J ASCAP 1964
composer
b South Range, Mich. *Songs:* This Side of Paradise.

ISLER, JUSTUS F ASCAP 1964
composer
b Detroit, Mich. *Songs:* Just One Girl in All This World.

ISLEY, ERNEST
arranger, instrumentalist
With brothers in group Isley Brothers. *Albums:* Take Some Time Out for the Isley Brothers; Isley Brothers, Doin' Their Thing; Isley Brothers Do Their Thing; Isley Brothers Live at Yankee Stadium; It's Your Thing; Soul on the Rocks; This Old Heart of Mine; Twist and Shout.

ISLEY, MARVIN
bass player
With brothers in group, Isley Brothers. *Albums:* Take Some Time Out for the Isley Brothers; Isley Brothers, Doin' Their Thing; Isley Brothers Do Their Thing; Isley Brothers Live at Yankee Stadium; It's Your Thing; Soul on the Rocks; This Old Heart of Mine; Twist and Shout.

ISLEY, O KELLY
vocalist
b Dec 25, 37. Recorded for Teenage, Gone & Motown labels. Mem, T-Neck Production Co. With brothers in group, Isley Brothers. *Albums:* Take Some Time Out for the Isley Brothers; Isley Brothers, Doin' Their Thing; Isley Brothers Do Their Thing; Isley Brothers Live at Yankee Stadium; It's Your Thing; Soul on the Rocks; This Old Heart of Mine; Twist and Shout; Live It Up; The Heat Is On; Fight the Power; Harvest for the World; Go for Your Guns.

ISLEY, RONALD
vocalist
b May 21, 41. Recorded for Teenage, Gone & Motown labels. Mem, T-Neck Production Co. With brothers in group, Isley Brothers. *Albums:* Take Some Time Out for the Isley Brothers; Isley Brothers, Doin' Their Thing; Isley Brothers Do Their Thing; Isley Brothers Live at Yankee Stadium; It's Your Thing; Soul on the Rocks; This Old Heart of Mine; Twist and Shout; Live It Up; The Heat Is On; Fight the Power; Harvest for the World; Go for Your Guns.

ISLEY, RUDOLPH
vocalist
b Apr 1, 39. Recorded for Teenage, Gone & Motown labels. Mem, T-Neck Production Co. With brothers in group, Isley Brothers. *Albums:* Take Some Time Out for the Isley Brothers; Isley Brothers, Doin' Their Thing; Isley Brothers Do Their Thing; Isley Brothers Live at Yankee Stadium; It's Your Thing; Soul on the Rocks; This Old Heart of Mine; Twist and Shout; Live It Up; The Heat Is On; Fight the Power; Harvest for the World; Go for Your Guns.

IVANOFF, ROSE
See Brignole, Rosa

IVES, BURL ASCAP 1949
author, singer, arranger
b Hunt Township, Ill, June 14, 09. Educ: Eastern Ill State Teachers Col; NY Univ Sch of Music; pvt study. Bway appearances: "Sing Out Sweet Land"; "Paint Your Wagon"; "Show Boat"; "Cat on a Hot Tin Roof". Films incl: "Our Man in Havana"; "Sierra"; "East of Eden"; "Smokey"; "The Power and the Prize"; "The Big Country" (Acad Award, 58); "Let No Man Write My Epitaph." Has given folk music concerts throughout the world, also on TV & in nightclubs. Author: "Sailing on a Very Fine Day"; "Tales of America"; "The Burl Ives Song Book"; "America's Musical Heritage-Song in America." Autobiography, "The Wayfaring Stranger." *Songs:* Arrangements: Blue Tail Fly; Foggy Foggy Dew; Sow Took the Measles; The Fox; Wayfarin' Stranger; Come All Ye Good Fellers; Bold Soldier; Henry Martin; I'm Sad and Lonely;

Jolly Farmer; Lord Thomas and Fair Elinore; Robin; Ten Thousand Miles; Tibbie Dunbar; Turtle Dove; Where Is the Old Man; On the Grand Canyon Line; Woolie Boogie Bee.

IVEY, JEAN EICHELBERGER　　　　　　　ASCAP 1969
composer, author, pianist
b Washington, DC, July 3, 23. Educ: Trinity Col, DC, AB(magna cum laude); Peabody Cons, MMus(piano); Univ Rochester Eastman Sch of Music, MMus(comp); Univ Toronto, MusD(comp). Comp of works incl orchestral, vocal, piano, chamber, opera, electronic, for live performers with tape, theatre, films & educ use. Piano recital incl own works, US, Mex & Europe. Founded, electronic music studio, Peabody Cons, Baltimore, 69, dir & teacher of comp. Subject of film documentary; author, numerous articles. *Instrumental Works:* Testament of Eve (mezzo, orch, tape); Tribute: Martin Luther King (baritone, orch); Sea-Change, (orch, tape); Hera, Hung From the Sky (mezzo, 7 winds, 3 perc, piano, tape); Prospero (bass voice, horn, 1 perc, tape); Terminus (mezzo, tape); Aldebaran (viola, tape); Skaniadaryo (piano, tape); Three Songs of Night (soprano, 5 instruments, tape); Solstice (soprano, flute, piccolo, 1 perc, piano); Crossing Brooklyn Ferry (baritone, piano); Sonata for Piano; Overture for Small Orchestra.

J

J, TREBLA SENO (ALBERT JONES)　　　　　ASCAP 1977
composer, author, lyricist
b Catron, Mo, Nov 29, 39. Writer social comments newspaper, Sikeston Standard. Awards from Clover Int Poetry competition. Poetry: Adios to Mr Charlie; Before Dawn; The Three Chicks Fight.

JABUSCH, WILLARD FRANCIS　　　　　　ASCAP 1979
composer, author
b Chicago, Ill, Mar 12, 30. Educ: St Mary of the Lake, MA; Chicago Cons; Loyola Univ, MA; Univ London; Northwestern Univ, PhD. Parish priest, campus chaplain, sem prof; author, hymns & songs. Chief Collabrs: Robert E Kreutz, Stanley Rudcki. *Songs:* Whatsoever You Do; What a Joy; Every Day Is a Hymn of Beauty; The Walls of Jericho; What More Could I Do?; Such a Proof of Love; Lyrics: The King of Glory; Song of Good News.

JACEY, FRANK
See Cicatello, Frank Domenick

JACKMAN, ROBERT KENNETH　　　　　　ASCAP 1956
composer, author
b Brockville, Ont, Feb 24, 15. Educ: Univ Rochester; Leland Powers Sch of Theatre, Boston, studied with pvt instrs. Musician, songwriter, actor & playwright; head, music dept of Walt Disney Productions, 25 yrs. Chief Collabrs: Buddy Baker, Frank Marks, Marvin Ash, Bill Lava. *Songs:* Dreams; Capri; Napoli; Zorro Themes; I Love the Fall.

JACKSON, GREIG STEWART (CHUBBY)　　　ASCAP 1956
composer, conductor, bassist
b New York, NY, Oct 25, 18. Bassist in dance bands incl Mike Riley, Johnny Messner, Raymond Scott, Jan Savitt, Terry Shand, Henry Busse, Charlie Barnet, Woody Herman. Has led own band; appeared on TV. Chief Collabrs: Ralph Burns, Woody Herman. *Instrumental Works:* Northwest Passage.

JACKSON, HANLEY　　　　　　　　　　ASCAP 1970
composr
b Bryan, Tex, June 7, 39. Educ: Calif State Univ, Northridge, BA, 66; Calif State Univ, Long Beach, MA, 68; studied theory & comp with Gerald Strang & Aurelio de la Vega. Assoc prof music & comp-in-residence, Kans State Univ, 68- *Songs & Instrumental Works:* A Child's Ghetto (chorus, tape); Tangents II (orch, tape); Tangents III (band, tape); Vignettes of the Plains (chorus, tape); Tangents IV (piano, tape).

JACKSON, HARRY CONRAD
composer, author, actor
b Pelham, NY, Oct 12, 27; d 1974. Writer, New York, 46- Producer, with Jackson Wesson Productions, film, Hollywood, 54. Actor, Bway show "Teahouse of the August Moon," 50's. Writer & comp, 60-70.

JACKSON, HOWARD MANUCY　　　　　　ASCAP 1944
composer
b St Augustine, Fla, Feb 8, 00; d. *Songs:* Lazy Rhapsody; Let's Be Frivolous; He's Mine; Hearts in Dixie; The First Spring Day.

JACKSON, JOHN CALVIN
composer, author, pianist
b Philadelphia, Pa, May 26, 19. Educ: Began piano study with Carl Diton, age 4 yrs; studied with Joseph Lockett through sr high sch, Philadelphia; Juilliard Grad Sch Music, 4 yr fel, studied with Madame Raissa Kauffman & Effie Kalisz.

Guest cond & pianist with var symph orch; asst musical dir at MGM; toured with own 31 piece orch & trio; Oscar nominee, Peabody & Maj Armstrong Awards for Radio Documentaries. *Songs & Instrumental Works:* The Carl Sandburg Suite for Symphony Orchestra; Profile of an American for Symphony Orchestra (piano solo); Suite in the Classic Design for Symphony Orchestra and Jazz Orchestra; A Musical Anthology of Jazz for Symphony Orchestra and Jazz Orchestra; Metropolis Per Diem for Symphony Orchestra and Chorale; Themes and Explorations for Symphony Orchestra and Jazz Orchestra (piano solo); The Capacabana Cakewalk for Symphony Orchestra and Piano Solo; Maria Chapdelain (ballet); The Loon's Necklace (ballet); various musical motion pictures, television shows and recordings with original compositions.

JACKSON, LEWIS JAMES　　　　　　　ASCAP 1976
composer, author, guitarist
b Rockford, Ala, Nov 12, 36. *Songs:* Baby, Baby I Had a Dream; I Need a Little Kiss; Hello Baby; Come on Everybody Let's Do a Fast Dance; Sad I Am Thinking of Today.

JACKSON, MARILYN　　　　　　　　ASCAP 1974
composer, author, studio singer
b New York, NY. Educ: Music & Art High Sch; Manhattan Sch of Music. Studio singer, 47-; top variety TV shows, movies, records & commercials. Nat trustee, Nat Acad Recording Arts & Sci. Chief Collabrs: John Cacavas, Richard B Williams. *Songs:* Lyrics: Movin' Groovy.

JACKSON, MIKE　　　　　　　　　　ASCAP 1943
composer, author, pianist
b Louisville, Ky, Dec 23, 1888; d New York, NY, June 21, 45. Educ: Pub schs. Entertainer in theatre, radio & films. WW I, Sgt. Accordionist. *Songs:* Knock Me a Kiss; Slender, Tender and Tall; Whoop It Up; Louisville Blues; Ain't My Sugar Sweet?; Keyboard Express; Blue Black Bottom; Bounce the Ball; Let's Beat Out Some Love.

JACKSON, WILLIAM E　　　　　　　　ASCAP 1963
composer, author, record producer
b Media, Pa, May 22, 38. Producer, Cameo-Parkway Records & Columbia Records. Chief Collabrs: Jimmy Wisner, Kenny Gamble, Leon Huff, J Renjetti, Tommy Bell. *Songs & Instrumental Works:* So Much in Love; Don't Throw Your Love Away; As the Years Go By; Red China Blues; Sha La Bandit.

JACKSON (MILLER), JILL　　　　　　　ASCAP 1954
composer, author, publisher
b Independence, Mo, Aug 25, 13. Educ: Kansas City Jr Col, Mo. Began career as an actress in radio; appeared in films, Hollywood, 34-37; TV writer, 49; sole owner of publ co, Jan-Lee Music; speaker to groups about peace song activities. Chief Collabr: Seymour Miller (husband). *Songs:* Wonderful Child (God Made Our Hands); High Upon a Mountain; The Lord Loves a Laughin' Man; It's Up to You and Me; Lyrics: Let There Be Peace on Earth (Let It Begin With Me) (George Washington Honor Medal, Freedoms Found, Valley Forge, 58; Georgia's Official Bicentennial Song; City of Lakewood float theme, 1980 Tournament of Roses Parade).

JACOB, HELEN
See Fody, Ilona

JACOB, PATTI
See Shor, Pat

JACOB, WILLIAM JACOB　　　　　　　ASCAP 1968
composer, pianist
b Newark, NJ, July 20, 29; d New York, NY, May 24, 70. Educ: Weequaic High Sch; Juilliard Sch Music; Miami Univ; studied piano with Mary Lou Williams. Wrote, produced & cond, indust shows, radio & TV spots; pianist with Louis Prima, Ray McKinley & Buddy Morrow; toured with Bob Hope; orch leader of Latin Quarter; musical dir, Eastern Div, IBM; personal music dir & cond for Florence Henderson, Marilyn Maxwell, Bobby Rydell, Diana Dors & Dion. Chief Collabrs: Marianne Moore, Marty Brill, Patti Jacob (Pat Shor). *Songs:* Music: That Holiday Feeling; Eugene, the Space Machine; Give My Regards to All of the Stars; The Man in the Moon. *Scores:* Opera/Ballet: Vive Les Girls; Bway shows: I Only Wanna Laugh; What's Out There; Jimmy; When You Elect Me Mayor; Tigers of Tammany Hall; Will You Think of Me Tomorrow; The Walker Walk; Charmin Son of a Bitch; The Little Woman; Riverside Drive; Five Lovely Ladies; Life Is a One-Way Street; It's a Nice Place to Visit; The Darlin of New York; Film/TV: One Day At a Time.

JACOBI, FREDERICK　　　　　　　　ASCAP 1924
composer, conductor, educator
b San Francisco, Calif, May 4, 1891; d New York, NY, Oct 24, 52. Educ: Studied music with Paolo Gallico, Rafael Joseffy, Rubin Goldmark; Hochschule fur Musik, Berlin, with Paul Juon; studied with Ernest Bloch. Asst cond, Metrop Opera, 13-17. WW I, saxophonist, Army Band. Taught harmony, Master Sch of United Arts, 27; taught comp, Juilliard Sch of Music, 36-50. Lectr, Univ of Calif, Mills Col & Julius Hartt Musical Found. Mem adv bd, League of Comp; charter mem, Am Music Guild; dir, Int Soc for Contemporary Music; mem, Jewish Acad Arts & Letters. Twice winner, Soc of Publ of Am Music Award.

Instrumental Works: The Pied Piper; A California Suite; The Eve of St Agnes; 3 Preludes for Violin, Piano; String Quartet; Indian Dances; Sabbath Evening Service; Cello Concerto; Piano Concertino; Violin Concerto; Rhapsody (harp, string orch); Ode (orch); From the Prophet Nehemiah; Meditation for Trombone, Piano; Music Hall Overture; Violin Ballade; Viola Fantasy; Hagiographa (string quartet, piano); 3 string quartets. *Scores:* Opera: The Prodigal Son (David Bispham Award).

JACOBS, AL T (MERCDES GABRIL)   ASCAP 1936
composer, author
b San Francisco, Calif, Jan 22, 03. Educ: Stanford Univ; studied with Lew Brown. Was piano salesman; taught piano. Staff pianist, KGO radio; singer, pianist & disc jockey, KJBS radio, San Francisco. Mgr, Wurlitzer Music Sch, San Francisco. Prof mgr, Crawford Music Co, Melrose Music Co & Sherman Clay & Co, New York; gen mgr, Sherman Clay & Co; bus mgr, Miller Music Co. Writer for films, incl "Dancing Daughter", "Seven Wonders of the World" & "Kon Tiki." Chief Collabrs: Jimmie Crane, Joseph Meyer, Gerry Granahan, Benny Davis, Eddie Snyder. *Songs:* No More Rivers to Cross; Crime and Punishment; Surprise; Come Back When You're a Woman; It's Been a Long Time Comin'; Never Again; I Need You Now; Hurt; If I Give My Heart to You; Ev'ry Day of My Life; My Believing Heart; Did I Ever Say; The Last Ones on the Floor; All I Want Is a Chance; Kon Tiki; Just One Time; Please Believe Me; When the Roses Bloom Again; Make a Wish; Honolulu; Music: I'm a Lucky Devil; Twilight Interlude; Rosie the Redskin; Mickey Darlin'; Glad; This Is My Country; I'm Just an Ordinary Human; There'll Never Be Another You; I'm Glad I Wait for You; Lyrics: Time Stands Still; Will o' the Wisp; Sugar Plum; My Sailor Boy; But I Did; A Heart Filled With Love; Taint No Good; Forty Five Men in the Telephone Booth; Fortune for a Penny; Anybody's Love Song; The Last Polka; Scalawag.

JACOBS, DICK   ASCAP 1956
composer, conductor
b New York, NY, Mar 29, 18. Educ: NY Univ. Music dir "Hit Parade," TV, 57-58. A&R dir, record cos; record exec.

JACOBS, JACOB
composer, lyricist
b Hungary, Jan 1, 1889; d New York, NY, Oct 14, 77. Began as song & dance man. Songwriter. Actor, writer of music & lyrics for Yiddish plays. Chief Collabrs: Alexander Mshanetsky, Abe Eilstien, Joseph Rumshensky. *Songs:* Lyrics: Bie Mein Bistu Shain; My Shtellelo Betty; That Wonderful Girl of Mine; You and the Sun and Stars; Say It Again.

JACOBS, JAMES HAROLD   ASCAP 1972
composer, author, playwright
b Chicago, Ill, Oct 7, 42. Educ: Chicago City Col, 2 yrs. Rock-n-roll musician & singer, Chicago, 56-63; amateur actor plays & musical comedy, Chicago, 63-70; professional actor films, theatre, Chicago & New York, 69-72. Co-author, lyricist & comp, "Grease," 71. Chief Collabr: Warren Casey.

JACOBS, MORTON PHILIP   ASCAP 1955
composer, author
b New York, NY, Dec 17, 17. Educ: George Washington High Sch; Haaren High Sch; City Col New York, hon DMus; Philathea Col, Windsor; Univ Calif, Los Angeles Extension, studied film music & orchestration with Eddy Lawrence Manson. Pianist with Bob Zurke Orch; relief pianist with Teddy Wilson Orch; with Milt Herth Trio, film, TV, records, George Burns, Alexis Smith, Ray Bolger, Ethel Merman, Dorothy Dandridge & Margaret Whiting. Principal in Chevrolet Dealers of Chicago Commercial; comp & coordinator, Desilu Studios, 6 yrs. Mem: Am Soc Music Arr; Screen Actors Guild; Am Fedn Musicians; Am Guild of Authors & Comp; Local 802; life mem Local 47 (bd dirs & chmn of Social Serv Comt, 2 yrs). Chief Collabrs: Irving Taylor, Doc Stanford, Milt Raskin, Cully Richards, Eddie Buzzell, Everett Greenbaum, Floyd Huddleston. *Songs:* Left Bank; Music: Tell Me More; Lefty Louie; To Hear You Laugh and See You Smile; Indianapolis Rag.

JACOBS, WILLIAM B (WILL GERARD)   ASCAP 1972
composer, author, actor
b Tex, July 14, 41. Educ: Lamar Univ, BA, 63; Univ Calif, Los Angeles, MFA, 68. Was in Bway production, "Mother Earth" & Off-Bway, "Your Own Thing"; appeared in movies, TV shows & commercials. Wrote lyrics for two albums on Bell Records. Chief Collabrs: Hod David Schudson, Marc Allen Trujillo. *Songs:* Lyrics: By Love I Mean; Aimee.

JACOBS-BOND, CARRIE MINETTA   ASCAP 1925
composer, author, pianist
b Janesville, Wis, Aug 11, 1862; d Hollywood, Calif, Dec 28, 46. Educ: Janesville pub schs; Univ Southern Calif, hon MMus. Formed The Bond Shop, to publ own music, 1894. Appeared in vaudeville; sang at White House for Pres Theodore Roosevelt; also gave concerts in Army Camps, WW I. In 41, selected by Gen Fedn Women's Clubs as one of two comp, representing progress of women during half century. Author: "The Roads of Melody" (autobiography); "The End of the Road" (poetry collection). Publisher & singer. Chief Collabrs: Poets, Paul Laurence Dunbar, Frank Stanton, Elizabeth Barrett Browning, Mary Norton Bradford, Bert Healy, W G Wilson. *Songs:* A Perfect Day; I Love You Truly; God Remembers When the World Forgets; I've Done My Work; Roses Are in Bloom; A Little Pink Rose; Because of the Light; Shadows; The Golden Key; A Vision; His Buttons Are Marked 'U.S.'; Half Minute Songs (collection of 12 brief songs); Music: Just A-Wearyin' for You; His Lullaby; A Little Bit O' Honey.

JACOBSEN, EUNICE
See Stearns, M Eunice

JACOBSON, KENNETH
composer
b Waterville, Maine. Educ: Colby Col, BA; New Eng Cons of Music; Boston Univ. Comp, musicals incl "Fables of Our Time", "Show Me Where the Good Times Are" & "Hot September," TV progs incl "That Was the Week That Was", "Partridge Family" & "People." Staff comp for Valando Music, 6 yrs. Vpres Am Guild of Authors & Composers, 80. Chief Collabrs: Rhoda Roberts, Tony Romeo. *Songs:* Music: Put a Light in the Window; Lyrics: Every Day; Swinging Shepard Blues.

JACOBSON, SIDNEY   ASCAP 1958
author
b Brooklyn, NY, Oct 20, 29. Educ: NY Univ, BA. Lyricist & record producer music industry; ed mags & comic mags; writer TV, films & humor bks; novelist. Chief Collabrs: Jimmy Krondes, Lou Stallman. *Songs:* Lyrics: At the End of a Rainbow; Warm; Thirty Days Hath September; A Boy Without a Girl; Don't Pity Me; I've Come of Age; Yogi; Wonderful You.

JAFFE, BEN   ASCAP 1953
composer, author, pianist
b New York, NY, Oct 14, 02. Pianist in theatres. Writer of radio & TV musical commercials. Chief Collabrs: Michael Stoner, Jack Zero. *Songs:* Please No Squeeza Da Banana; Find 'Em, Fool 'Em and Forget 'Em. *Scores:* Stage: Red Hot and Roman.

JAFFE, JOEL   ASCAP 1977
composer, author
b Ft Bragg, NC, Nov 21, 43. Educ: Deerfield Acad; Swarthmore Col, BA, 65; Temple Univ Sch Med, MD, 70. Singer & guitarist for numerous rock bands. Studio musician, Paris, France, 65-66. Physician & songwriter. *Songs:* Red-Winged Blackbird; Maybe I Could Use That in a Song; Rockabilly Band; Drinking Wine Alone; Last of a Dying Breed.

JAFFE, MOE   ASCAP 1929
composer, author
b Vilna, Russia, Oct 23, 01; d Creskill, NJ, Dec 2, 72. To US, 02. Educ: Wharton Sch; Univ Pa Law Sch. Wrote Mask & Wig shows. Wrote songs for Bway musicals, incl "A Night in Venice" & "A Wonderful Night." Author, "How to Produce an Amateur Show." Chief Collabrs: Clay Boland, Nat Bonx, Richard Hardt, Ludwig Flato, Dwight Latham, Ted Weems, Fred Waring, Jack O'Brien, Larry Fotine, Jack Fulton, Henry Tobias, Larry Vincent. *Songs:* Collegiate; Bell Bottom Trousers; The Gypsy in My Soul; If You Are But a Dream; I'm My Own Grandpaw; If I Had My Life to Live Over Again; Oh You Sweet One; An Apple a Day; Actions Speak Louder Than Words; The Morning After; High School; These Things Are Known; Pray; Get Together With the Lord; Just Whisper; My Lady Won't Be Here Tonight; That Kind of Love Is Not for Me; They Can't Make a Lady Out of Me; Let Me Love You; On the Island of Catalina; Poetry; Something Has Happened to Me; Thanks to You Mother; Watch That First Step; When You Love; Yum-Yum.

JAGER, ROBERT EDWARD   ASCAP 1967
composer, teacher, conductor
b Binghamton, NY, Aug 25, 39. Educ: Univ Mich, BM, 67, MM, 68. Staff arr, Armed Forces Sch Music, 63-65. Dir of Bands, Old Dominion Univ, 68-71; dir comp & theory, Tenn Technical Univ, 71- Awards: Roth, 64 & 66; Ostwald, 64, 68 & 72; Distinguished Service to Music Medal, Kappa Kappa Psi, 73; Volkwein, 76; Friends of Harvey Gaul, 76. *Instrumental Works:* Symphony Nos 1 & 2 for Band; Second & Third Suite for Band; Diamond Variations; Variations on a Theme of Robert Schumann; Concerto No 2 for Alto Saxophone; Concerto for Bass Tuba; Sinfonia Noblissima; Pastorale and Country Dance; Sinfonietta; Apocalypse; Shivaree; Chorale and Toccata; Three Pieces for Orchestra; Variants on a Motive By Wagner (tuba trio); Japanese Prints; Psalmody; A Child's Garden of Verses.

JAISUN, JEF   ASCAP 1970
composer, author, singer
b Seattle, Wash, Mar 24, 46. Educ: Univ Wash. Pianist from age 5; guitarist, from age 17; began writing blues & rock music while in jr high sch; performer, producer & arr, var albums, 69-; play electric bass & harmonica; European tour, 80. *Songs:* Friendly Neighborhood Narco Agent; Brand New Rose; Iggy's Tune; Gonna Hold Out Till My Food Stamps Come; I Smell Like 90 Weight; Apricot Wine; Dollar Bills; Heartbeat Is Risin'; See You in Awhile; The Empress; It's Ragtime; Sierra Saturday; Gunrack Billy; No Motor Down; Sirens of Rock and Roll; Salazar Cards; Fourteen; Heartline; Mailman Blues.

JAMES, ALAN
See Burgdorf, James Alan

JAMES, ALLEN
See Lorenz, Ellen Jane

JAMES, BILLY   ASCAP 1924
composer, author, conductor
b Philadelphia, Pa, July 3, 1895; d Philadelphia, Pa, Nov 18, 65. Educ: Southern High Sch. In vaudeville, 14-24. WW I, Inf. Pianist, arr & music dir, radio, 26-54, incl "Horn and Hardart Children's Hour," 28-54. WW II, entertainer with USO. Had own music publ co. Chief Collabrs: Al Dubin, Bobby Heath. *Songs & Instrumental Works:* Carolina Mammy; Cut Yourself a Piece of Cake; I'm Saving Up Coupons; Easter Morning; Broadway Lament; Angel Eyes; What a Sweet Sensation; Breakin' the Piano; Better Luck Next Time.

JAMES, FREEMAN KELLY, JR   ASCAP 1963
composer
b Miami, Fla, Oct 21, 27. Educ: Univ Calif, BA; Univ Calif, Los Angeles, MA. Chief Collabrs: Jerry Livingston, Bill Hansen, Lar Best. *Songs:* Sons of Westwood; Fight On, Men of Westwood; Hymns to America. *Instrumental Works:* The California Rag; UCLA March; That's the Time; Bruin Band Rock; March Investiture; Rag Tyme; Grand Rock Entrance; Pom Pom Parade; Charioteers Parade; Victory Prelude; Bruin Triumphal.

JAMES, HARRY HAAG   ASCAP 1943
composer, conductor, trumpeter
b Albany, Ga, Mar 15, 16. Educ: Studied with father, Everette James. Left circus & became trumpeter with local Tex band; with Ligon Smith, Hogan Hancock, Joe Gill, Herman Waldman & Ben Pollack's Big Band, 35. Joined Benny Goodman Orch, 37-39; formed own band, 39. *Songs & Instrumental Works:* Two O'Clock Jump; Ultra; Trumpet Blues; Flight of the Bumblebee; Concerto for Trumpet.

JAMES, INEZ ELEANOR   ASCAP 1946
composer, author, pianist
b New York, NY, Nov 15, 19. Educ: Studied piano, age 7; Hollywood Cons of Music & Arts. Wrote first comp, age 11. Under contract, Universal Pictures, 10 yrs; writer, var artists incl Donald O'Connor, Peggy Ryan & Doris Day. Chief Collabrs: Larry Russell, Buddy Pepper, Sidney Miller. *Songs:* Vaya Con Dios; Come to Baby Do; What Good Would It Do; I'm Sorry But I'm Glad; I Can See It Your Way; That's the Way He Does It; Walk It Off; For Parents Only; What Are Parents Made Of; Why Do I Have to Go to Bed; The Kid on the Corner; I'll Be Three; Blanket and Thumb; Cry Baby Polka; It's Christmas; Music: Yonder; Strange, Strange, Sally; I Miss You Howard; Archie-Frazer-Nash; Lucky Duck; In the Wee Small Hours of the Morning; Good Bye Romance; Lyrics: It'll Be a Merry Christmas. *Scores:* Film/TV: Samba Sue; The Captains Kids; The Gremlin Walk; The Pirate Song; Yippi-I-Voot!; Daddy Surprise Me?; What Do I Have to Do; All to Myself; Don't Move; Dobbin and a Wagon of Hay; Something Tells Me; Are You With It?; Musical Chairs; Pillow Talk; Portrait in Black; Ol' St Nicholas; This Must Be a Dream; Ok'l Baby Dok'l; Thee and Me; Letter From an Unknown Woman; When You Bump Into Someone You Know; One of Us Has Gotta Go; Fella With the Flute; A Little Imagination; I'm Looking for a Prince of a Fella; I've Got to Give My Feet a Break; All the Things I Want to Say; It Was the Sullivans; It'll All Come Out in the Wash.

JAMES, JEAN EILEEN   ASCAP 1963
author
b Burlington, Wis, Nov 6, 34. Chief Collabr: Sverre S Elsmo. *Songs:* Lyrics: It's All Over Town.

JAMES, LANCE COLAN   ASCAP 1978
composer, teacher
b Chicopee, Mass, Oct 16, 51. Educ: Penney High Sch, grad; Hartt Col Music, 3 yrs. Served in 76th Div Mil Reserve Band. Writer, performer; owner, Guitorn Record Co. Chief Collabr: Jackie Mclean. *Songs:* The Right Star; It's Gotta Be We (Gotta Be Us); Music: Love King.

JAMES, LEE
See Gillette, Leland James

JAMES, MARION
See Price, Marion James

JAMES, MYRON
See Cohn, James Myron

JAMES, PETE
See Fortini, James

JAMES, PHILIP   ASCAP 1928
composer, author, conductor
b Jersey City, NJ, May 17, 1890; d Southampton, NY, Nov 1, 75. Educ: NY Univ, MusD; Trinity Col, London; studied with Rubin Goldmark, Homer

Norris, Elliott Schenck & Rosario Scalero. Music dir, Victor Herbert, Winthrop Ames productions, 11-16. WW I, 2nd Lt Inf, USA; bandmaster, AEF Headquarters Band. Cond, NJ Symph, 22-29, Brooklyn Orch Soc, 27-30. Taught music, NY Univ, 23-55, prof music & dept chmn, 33-55, then prof emeritus; Columbia Univ, 31-33. Cond, Bamberger Symph broadcasts, 7 yrs, NBC Symph & CBS Symph. Mem: Phi Beta Kappa; Nat Inst Arts & Letters; MacDowell Asn (past vpres); MacDowell Colonists (past pres); Am Guild Organists. Chief Collabrs: Frederick Martens, Charles Hanson Towne. *Songs:* I Am the Vine; Ballad of Trees and the Master; Home Over the Hill; Transit; Nightingale of Bethlehem (cantata); World of Tomorrow (cantata); By the Waters of Babylon (anthem). *Instrumental Works:* Song of the Night (1st prize, Women's Symph); Bret Harte Overture (NY Philh Award); Suite for Orch; Suite for String Orch (Juilliard Found Publ Award); Station WGZBX (NBC Orch Award); Overture in Olden Style on French Noels; Symphony No 1; Symphony No 2; 1 string quartet; 1 piano quartet. *Songs & Instrumental Works:* Meditation on St Clothilde (organ); Gwilym Gwent (choral); General William Booth Enters Into Heaven (choral).

JAMES, ROBERT MCELHINEY   ASCAP 1963
composer, pianist, arranger
b Marshall, Mo, Dec 25, 39. Educ: Univ Mich, MMus(comp); studied comp with Leslie Bassett, Ross Lee Finney, piano with Mrs R T Dufford, Franklin Launer, Ava Comin Case. Composer, musical comedies "Land Ho" & "Bartholome Fair," Bway musical & TV series. Recording artist, CTI Records, 74-, Columbia Records 77-; record producer. Chief Collabrs: Jack O'Brien, Kenny Loggins, Grover Washington, Jr. *Instrumental Works:* Angela; Westchester Lady; The Chicago Theme; Touchdown. *Scores:* Bway show: The Selling of the President; TV: Taxi.

JAMES, WILL   ASCAP 1950
composer, conductor
b Shelbyville, Ill, Dec 29, 1896; d. Educ: Northeast Mo State Col; studied with John Biggerstaff. Salesman in dept store. Served in AEF, WW I. Dir of church choir, Springfield. Mem, Music Educators Nat Conf. Adjudicator, choral fests & music contests, 35. Operated Will James Music Serv, 25-61. *Songs:* Sacred: Hear My Prayer; Jesus Our Lord, We Adore Thee; Almighty God of Our Fathers; Sing and Rejoice; Come Ye Disconsolate; Dark Water; Blow Trumpets Blow; The Little Jesus Came to Town; Hymn of Joy; Alleluia; Holy Lord God; Peace I Leave With You; numerous others.

JAMESON, ROBERT (ROBERT JAMGOCHIAN)   ASCAP 1967
composer
b Detroit, Mich, Mar 29, 47. Educ: Eastern Mich Univ, BA, 70, MA, 80; studied with Dorothy James, Tom Mason & Anthony Iannaccone. Comps publ by Carl Fischer. Performances as pianist/comp in USSR, Eng, Can, US. Cond of pit orchs for musicals, 75-78. Rock comp & instr comp/theory/harmony. *Songs:* Give Me a Little Smile. *Instrumental Works:* Symphony No 1, Yerevan; Piano Concerto No 1; Piano Concerto No 2; A Symphonic Awakening; Symphonic Cadenza for Piano and Orchestra; Portraits (orch).

JAMGOCHIAN, ROBERT
See Jameson, Robert

JANIS, BEVERLY
See Shapiro, Beverly Myers

JANIS, ELSIE
See Bierbower, Elsie

JANIS, JOAN GARDNER   ASCAP 1964
composer, author, actress
b Chicago, Ill, Nov 16, 26. Educ: Fairfax High Sch, Los Angeles; Los Angeles City Col, Calif, 1 yr. Worked as production asst for Stokey & Ebert TV, "Pantomime Quiz" & "Detective," 48. Wrote, acted in & wrote music for TV series, "Time for Beany," 49. Wrote & acted in cartoon series, "Adventures of Spunky and Tadpole." TV cartoon specials, "Here Comes Peter Cottontail", "Santa Claus is Coming to Town" & "Valley of the Dinosaurs." Wrote screenplay, "Monster From the Surf." Wrote screenplay & music for motion picture, "A Man for Hanging." Music written for several radio commercial jingles. Author, "Growing with Music" & "Checkerboard Plays." Worked for UPA, "Gay Puree", "Magoo's Xmas Carol" & "Adventures of Mr Magoo" series. Chief Collabrs: Adelaide Gardner Halpern, Jaime Mendoza-Nava. *Songs:* House of Evil (background music); Toy Piano Boogie; Holly Time; Lyrics: Dark of Night; Spelling Rock 'n Roll; Learnin' to Rock; Good Ship Rock 'n Roll.

JANNS, ROSE
See Johns, Rosalinda Jill

JANS, ALARIC (ROKKO, RICKY)   ASCAP 1978
composer, author, pianist
b St Louis, Mo, Jan 27, 49. Educ: Germantown Friends Sch; Francis W Parker High Sch; Harvard Univ. Writer & performer, with Ned, Rokko & the Hat & nightclubs & concerts. Music dir, St Nicholas Theatre Co. Comp, incidental music, musicals, childrens' musicals & theatres in Chicago & on Bway. Chief

Collabrs: John Stasey, James Quinn, Nick Talantis. *Songs:* Time; Above the Storm; Money and Outer Space. *Scores:* Bway shows: The Water Engine; Do Black Patent Leather Shoes Really Reflect Up?

JANSE, DONALD L   ASCAP 1969
composer, author, conductor
b Williamson, NY, Nov 28, 29. Educ: Crane Dept Music, State Univ NY, Potsdam, BA, grad study; Eastman Sch Music, grad study. Vocal soloist, USCG Band, 52-58, dir, comp & arr, Cadet Musical Activity Groups, 53-60; wrote materials for appearances incl, Bell Telephone Hour, White House State Dinner, Joint Session of Congress for Lincoln Sesq, Mass for St Patrick's Cathedral, New York, 53-60; wrote two MGM albums & three Design-Pickwick albums, 53-60; had own chorale group & Children's Chorus which recorded albums with Design-Pickwick & Ambassador, 60-67. Now dir, comp & arr, USCG Cadet Musical Activity Groups, 67-; incl writing & arr materials for TV shows, incl, "Today", "Mike Douglas", "Truth or Consequences", "Saturday Night" TV shows, CBS Radio show, "Cavalcade of Christmas"; comp & arr for appearance, "White House" 74. *Songs:* Sad the Day (SATB); In Bethlehem My Joy is Stayed (SATB); Man to Man (TTBB, bk); My Soul Shall Sing My Heart's Delight (SATB); Yesterday Santa Claus; Let's Take a Trip to Toyland; Brothers Gather and Rejoice; Harken to the Flights of Christmas Angels.

JANSON, HUGH MICHAEL (SPIKE)   ASCAP 1975
composer, pianist
b Tulsa, Okla, May 4, 36. Educ: Univ Miami, BBA, 58; Westlake Col Music, 59-60; Berklee Col Music, 69-71; studied piano with Pete Jolly & Walter Bishop, Jr. Pianist & accompanist in night clubs & recording studios; composer films-TV. Best Jazz Comp Award, Lighthouse Collegiate Jazz Fest, 60. Chief Collabrs: Ben Oakland, Roy Alfred, Judee Sill, Michelle Wiley & Bob Klimes. *Songs & Instrumental Works:* Annies Theme; Chanson, Chanson; Theme for Tesch; We Came Close; Roberta's Theme; Blues March; I'll Pay You When I Get It; Lucile Can Hold Her Own; Walkin' So Free; Miz (Just Call Her); Chikubucho; Senior Peace; Waltz for Robin; Texas is Where I Want to Be; Saul Fisch Returns; Vo-Do-Di-Ot; Bad Aspects; Little Rotti Cotti; We Don't Have to Tune Up (Cause We're Gon'na Play Hawaiian Music); Gambitus; The Dragon Lady; Blues for Horace; Blues for Mr Montes; Back Home, Down Under, Good Time Bummer Blues; Let it Happen; Mr Montuno.

JANSSEN, DAVID
See Meyer, David Harold

JANSSEN, WERNER   ASCAP 1923
conductor
b New York, NY, June 1, 1899. Educ: Leipzig Cons; Phillips Exeter Acad; Dartmouth Col; Am Acad in Rome; Juilliard Fellowship, Prix de Rome; studied with Ottorino Respighi, Arthur Friedheim, Hermann Scherchen. Cond major orchs throughout world & US. Assoc of Arturo Toscanini, New York Philh. Head: Baltimore Orch, Salt Lake City Orch, Portland Orch, each 2 yrs; Janssen Symph, Los Angeles, 12 yrs. Cond, Gen Motors Radio Orch, NY & Standard Oil Symph, Los Angeles & San Francisco. Cond for RCA Records & Columbia Masterworks, 200 classical recordings. Comp of many songs. Wrote scores for var motion pictures; many shorts on TV & 7 musicals on Bway, incl Ziegfeld Follies. *Songs & Instrumental Works:* New Year's Eve in New York; String Quartets, Nos 1 & 2; Obsequies of a Saxophone; Louisiana Symphony; Quintet for Ten Instruments. *Scores:* Film: The General Died At Dawn; Blockade; The Southerner; Uncle Vanya; Lights Out in Europe; A Night In Casablanca; Robin Hood.

JANUARY, HERB
See May, Robert Arden

JANUARY, RONA
See Harris, Rona

JAPHET, CLIFTON, SR (CLIFF)   ASCAP 1976
composer, author, musician
b Cortland, NY, Oct 20, 09. Educ: Cortland High Sch; Cortland Cons Music, Nick Mayer. Mem, Polly Jenkins Musical Plowboys, vaudeville & screen novelty musical instrumental group. Appeared with Vernon Dalhart in stage revues & with western musical group Bromcho Busters. Formed Western Aces & Saddle Pards & Rodeo Kings & Dixie Stars, radio, show & TV groups. Recording artist, Lamb, Fidelity, Acetone, Down Home & Arzee labels. Singer. Chief Collabrs: Elmer Wickham, Dallas Turner. *Songs:* I'm Goin' West to Texas; A Mi Amigo; Blue River Blues; Just A Tumble Down Ranch in the Valley; Lonely Renfro Valley Rose; Please Tell Me Why; (If I Could Have) Christmas With You; Country Dee-Jay Blues; Jumpin' for Jesus; I've Had My Way.

JARVIS, AL   ASCAP 1954
author
b Russia, July 4, 09; d Newport Beach, Calif, May 6, 70. Educ: Univ Southern Calif; Pasadena Community Playhouse. Was world's first DJ; had own radio prog; discovered many stars; created the forerunner of the USO using stars to entertain troops; originated TV's first daily talk-music show; was first to integrate Navy artists on a music show; one of the first record store owners; also

actor & did many movies. Chief Collabrs: Johnny Mercer, Leo Diamond. *Songs:* Make Believe Ballroom; Shtiggy Boom.

JARVIS, BRIAN TAYLOR   ASCAP 1969
composer, author, singer
b Milwaukee, Wis, Feb 17, 53. Educ: NY Univ; Recording Engineering Inst; studied with Gary Chester. Singer & drummer with territory bands & jazz & rock groups, mid-western US; performer & recording artist of original material. Performing in jazz clubs currently. *Songs:* Believe in Yourself; Anonymous; Sweet Lady; Ann's Plan; Giant Paw; If My Life Depended on It; Wayne's Gotta Go.

JARVIS, JANE   ASCAP 1965
composer, author, arranger
b Vincennes, Ind. Educ: Vincennes Univ; Bush Cons; Chicago Cons; De Paul Univ Sch Music; Pace Univ, BS. Staff pianist at age 13, WJKS-WIND, Chicago, later WOC-TV & WTMJ-TV (NBC). Organist for Milwaukee Braves & New York Mets. Former vpres, Muzak Corp. As performing artist has recorded with Lionel Hampton, Clark Terry, Richie Kamuca, Bill Berry, Grady Tate, George Duvivier & others. Mem, Overseas Press Club, Nat Acad Recording Arts & Sci, Universal Jazz Coalition & Consortium of Jazz Orgn; bd mem, Int Art of Jazz & House That Jazz Built. Chief Collabrs: Steve Allen, Roy Eldridge, Brian Jarvis, Richie Kamuca, Bill Berry, Johnny Hodges. *Songs:* Music: Ann's Plan; Art Deco; Bottom Line; Dawn; Deepest Dream; If My Life Depended on It; Jazz Musem; Kentucky; Little Jazz Talks; Men From the Boys; My Mind Is Up in Curlers; Other Side of the Story; Roseland; Slipped Disco; Zircon.

JASON, ALFRED P   ASCAP 1958
composer, author
b Chicago, Ill, Dec 16, 14. Educ: Northwestern Univ Dental Sch. Dir, Acad of Gen Dentistry. *Songs:* An Orchid From Hawaii; Chapel in the Valley; We're All Children of the Lord; Young Love Is As Old As Time; A Book, a Candle and a Prayer; Pals; Golden Jubilee March (Girl Scout songs).

JASON, DANIEL
See Gorney, Jay

JASON, WILL   ASCAP 1933
composer, author
b New York, NY, June 23, 10; d. Educ: High sch. Wrote songs for films. Chief Collabr: Val Burton. *Songs:* Isn't This a Night for Love?; And the Big Bad Wolf Is Dead; If It Isn't Love; Dilly Dally; Rhythm in My Heart; It Can Happen to You; Buy a Kiss; Romantic; Penthouse Serenade; When We're Alone; You Alone; Out of the Blue; Sincerely Yours; Josephine; Always You.

JAVITS, JOAN
See Zeeman, Joan Javits

JAY, ARNOLD
See Capitanelli, Arnold Joseph, Jr

JAYE, JERRY
See Hatley, Jearld Jaye

JEAN, ELSIE   ASCAP 1941
composer, author
b New York, NY, May 14, 07; d New York, June 9, 53. Educ: Columbia Univ; Nat Cons (scholarship). Won Carl Schurz Soc prize. Cond own radio prog, 5 yrs. Newspaper writer. Author: "Sing With Mother Goose"; "A Merrie Menagerie"; "Adventures of Fairy Tinkle Toes"; "Old Fables and Pictures"; "Wild Flowers and Elves." *Songs:* I Love You So; Song of My Heart; Come Love Me; On Hills of Freedom.

JEDYNAK, EDDIE STANLEY   ASCAP 1963
composer, author
b Chicago, Ill, Mar 27, 22. Educ: Joliet High Sch. *Songs:* Our Wedding Day; Count the Tear Drops on My Pillow; Wish I Had a Girl Like You; It's Time to Say Goodnight.

JEFFERS, RUSSELL LEE   ASCAP 1973
composer, singer
b Oak Ridge, Tenn, Mar 23, 46. Educ: Tenn Temple Col; pvt vocal instr. Worked summer shows, Knoxville & Gatlinburg, Tenn, 70-74; with Opryland USA, Nashville, 74-80. Commercial work, TV & movie actg. *Songs:* Smoky Mountain Love Affair; Roll Wheels Roll; Luzianne; When the Blue in My Grass Turns Green; Does Anybody Want to Sing My Songs; Smoky Mountain Sunshine; Lyrics: Dear Old Dixie.

JEFFERY, WILLIAM   ASCAP 1975
composer
b Dallas, Tex, June 23, 49. Educ: Calif State Univ, Los Angeles, grad, 73; studied film scoring with Buddy Collette, contemporary technique with Byong Kim. Free-lance writer, comp, arr & producer, At Home Productions & Little Brother Productions, 76- Chief Collabr: Ronnie Laws. *Songs:* Friends and Strangers;

Always There. *Instrumental Works:* Jenne (soprano, saxophone, piano); Polynation (perc ens); Hybrids (orchestral work).

JEFFORDS, FRANCES
See Adair, Frances Jeffords

JEFFREY, NAT
See Seligman, Nat Jeffrey

JEFFRIES, JAY
See Matlick, Jay Jeffries

JELLINEK, GEORGE ASCAP 1966
composer, author, broadcaster
b Budapest, Hungary, Dec 22, 19. Educ: High sch & jr col, Budapest, grad; Lafayette Col, Pa, 43. Pursued creative & bus careers in music simultaneously. Dir prog services, Sesac Inc, 55-64; recording dir, Muzak, Inc, 64-68; music dir, Radio Sta WQXR, New York, 68-; adj asst prof, NY Univ. Author bk, "Callas, Portrait of a Prima Donna." Contributing ed, Stereo Rev, 58-; contributor, Sat Rev, Opera News & other mag. Chief Collabs: Eugene Zador (operas), Dick Hyman, Bill Snyder, Earl Sheldon, Emanuel Vardi (songs). *Scores:* The Magic Chair (one-act opera); The Scarlet Mill (full length opera).

JENKINS, ARTHUR E, JR
composer, author, musician
b New York, NY, Dec 7, 36. Educ: High Sch Performing Arts, New York, grad, 55; Baldwin-Wallace Col, Ohio, 56-58. Music dir for Johnny Nash, New York, 60-69. Arr & cond for two recording artists. Arr, recording session, Belafonte Enterprises, 67-69, arr & toured with Harry Belafonte, summer, 69. Arr for "Melba Moore and Clifton Davis Show," 72. Instrumentalist, has made records. Free-lance musician for TV jingles; prof recording musician with John Lennon & Yoko Ono. Chief Collabr: Supership. *Songs:* The Only Time You Say You Love Me (Is When We're Making Love); There's Always Something Missing.

JENKINS, CLARENCE C (CAL) ASCAP 1971
composer, author, singer
b Charleston Heights, SC, June 22, 42. Eudc: Bond-Wilson High Sch. Songwriter for high sch band & glee club. *Songs:* Jenkins Got a Funky Thing; Superman; Who Do You Belong To?; Please Don't Think About Tomorrow.

JENKINS, DAVID IAN ASCAP 1970
composer
b Croydon, England, July 20, 49. Educ: Lowell High Sch, San Francisco, 64-67; Univ San Francisco, 67-69; San Francisco State Univ, BA(music), 72; studied arr with Dick Grove, 74-75 & film scoring with Eddy Manson, 79. As pianist, worked with var singers & groups in nightclubs & recording studios. Comp, arr, orchestrator, copyist & cond. Comp music for documentary film "One Way to Change" & other short films. Worked on pianocorder proj as engr/programmer. Programmed music for radio & airline progs. Chief Collabrs: Anne Hall, David Lopez, Hal Blair. *Songs: Music:* Tomorrow.

JENKINS, ELLA L ASCAP 1963
composer, author, singer
b St Louis, Mo, Aug 6, 24. Educ: Du Sable High Sch; Wilson Jr Col, AA; Roosevelt Col; San Francisco State Col, BA(sociology). Singer, children's camps, schs, librs, nursery schs, day care centers; composer, music educr, for children. *Songs:* You'll Sing a Song and I'll Sing a Song; Play Your Instruments and Make a Pretty Sound; My Street Begins At My House; If I Were an Animal; A Neighborhood Is a Friendly Place; I Got a Job; Good Day, Everybody; Hello; And One and Two; On a Holiday; I Like Animals in the Zoo; It's the Milkman; That's the Way Things Are; I Climbed a Mountain; A Long Time; A Man Went Down to the River; Wake Up, Little Sparrow; The World Is Big, the World Is Small; I Like the Way That They Stack Hay; Tah-Boo; Jambo; I Looked Into the Mirror; This Is Your Year, Children; In the Peoples' Republic of China; *Music:* Miss Mary Mack; Did You Feed My Cow?.

JENKINS, GORDON HILL ASCAP 1935
composer, author
b Webster Groves, Mo, May 12, 10. Arr, Isham Jones, Benny Goodman, Vincent Lopez, Rubinoff, Lennie Hayton & Andre Kostalanetz. Cond Bway show, "The Show is On," 37 & for Judy Garland in London, 57. With, Paramount Pictures, 38-39; musical dir, NBC Hollywood, 39-44, Dick Haymes Radio Show, 44-48; headlined, Capitol Theatre, NY, 49-51, Paramount Theatre, 52; appeared, Thunderbird, Las Vegas, 53 & Riviera, 60; TV producer, NBC, 55-57; comp shows, Tropicana, Las Vegas, 56-60; concert, Hollywood Bowl, 64. Chief Collabrs: Tom Adair, Johnny Mercer. *Songs:* Goodbye; Married I Can Always Get; San Fernando Valley; This Is All I Ask; Homesick, That's All; How Old Am I?; But I Loved You; That's All There Is, There Isn't Any More; I've Been There; Manhattan Tower; Seven Dreams; The Letter; What It Was, Was Love; The Future; *Music:* PS, I Love You; You Have Taken My Heart; When a Woman Loves a Man; *Lyrics:* Blue Prelude; Blue Evening. *Instrumental Works:* Concerto for Clarinet. *Scores:* Film/TV: Bwana Devil.

JENKINS, JOSEPH WILLCOX ASCAP 1957
composer, author, arranger
b Philadelphia, Pa, Feb 15, 28. Educ: St Joseph's Col, BS; Eastman Sch Music, BM, MM, studied with Tom Canning, Wayne Barlow, Bernard Rogers & Howard Hanson; Cath Univ, PhD; studied with Vincent Persichetti. Rec'd Ford Found grant. USA service; arr, Army Field Band. On music staff, Cath Univ, 53-54, grad fel until 56. Arr for Army chorus, 56-59. Music ed, publ col, 60-61. Asst prof, Music Sch, Duquesne Univ, 61- *Instrumental Works:* American Overture (band); Charles Country; Cumberland Gap (Otswald Award); 3 Images for Band.

JENKINS, LOUIS (WOODY) ASCAP 1970
composer, author
b Baton Rouge, La, Jan 3, 47. Educ: La State Univ, BA(journalism), juris doctor in law. Mem, La House of Rep, 72- Delegate, La Constitutional Convention, 73, Democratic Nat Convention, 72, 74, 76 & 78. Democratic Nat Committeeman from La, 80-84. Coauthor of "Declaration of Rights, Louisiana Constitution of 1973." *Songs:* Ballad of Pete Maravich.

JENNINGS, JOHN ASCAP 1963
composer, author
b Evansville, Ind, Dec 7, 33. Educ: Vanderbilt Univ; pvt music study. Wrote 4 shows in col, 1 in Navy, 56. To NY, 58. *Songs:* Sew the Buttons On; Pardon Me While I Dance; Wishing Song. *Scores:* Off-Bway Stage: Riverwind.

JENNINGS, WILLIAM STEWART ASCAP 1960
composer, singer, arranger
b Plainfield, NJ, Oct 30, 42. Educ: Plainfield High Sch; Bloomfield Col, NJ; pvt instr in harmony, theory & classical guitar. Singer, musician & arr, night clubs & TV; recording artist, Decca & MGM Records; radio jingles & commercials; owned & operated own recording studio. Chief Collabrs: Carmine Lombardo, Vic Mazurkiewicz, Stephen Shohfi. *Songs:* Music: Seems Like Only Yesterday; At the End of Each Day; Tropical Weekend; Can't Get Over Losing You.

JENSEN, GAIL PATRICIA ASCAP 1974
composer, author
b Sanger, Calif, Oct 5, 49. Educ: Pasadena Playhouse Col of Theater Arts; Los Angeles Valley Col; Univ Calif, Los Angeles. Appeared on TV shows incl "McCloud", "Merv Griffin", "Spiderman", "Wolfman Jack" & "Class of 65," in films, "The Long Riders", "Doberman Gang", "Don't Answer the Phone." Recording artist with var other artists. Chief Collabr: David Somerville. *Songs:* Boogie Woogie Woman; You Say You Love Me; Fancy; Starry Eyes; *Lyrics:* Prairie Dog Blues.

JENSEN, GORDON ASCAP 1970
composer, singer
b Windsor, Ont, May 8, 51. Writing music for the past 10 yrs, during which time he has written over 300 songs, some of which have been nominated for the Doubleworth Award for either Song of the Yr or Songwriter of the Yr. Records with Impact Records. *Songs:* Redemption Draweth Nigh; I Should Have Been Crucified; Jesus Will Outshine Them All; Bigger Than Any Mountain.

JENSEN, RONALD SCOTT ASCAP 1975
composer, singer, musician
b Long Beach, Calif, Sept 14, 51. Educ: Self-taught. Writer, performer & musician in nightclubs; recording artist, solo & with groups Pony, Bullit & Ron Jensen Blues Band. Chief Collabr: Daniel P Milner. *Songs:* Till I Met You; Now That I've Found You Love; Baby It's Me; Sunny Day.

JENTES, HARRY ASCAP 1915
composer, pianist
b New York, NY, Aug 28, 1897; d New York, Jan 19, 58. *Songs & Instrumental Works:* Put Me to Sleep With an Old-Fashioned Melody; I Don't Want to Get Well; At the Fountain of Youth; Honor Thy Father and Mother; He May Be Old, But He's Got Young Ideas; California Sunshine.

JEROME, HENRY P ASCAP 1951
composer, author
b New York, NY, Nov 12, 17. Educ: Pub sch; Norwich Free Acad, Conn; Juilliard Sch Music; studied trumpet with Max Schlosberg & comp & orchestration with Bill Vacchiano. Formed own orch while in high sch; group performed on Mediterranean cruise ship, clubs, hotels, ballrooms & theaters throughout US, 37-; on radio & TV, 40-59; on var record labels. A&R dir, Coral, Decca & MCA Records, 59-68 & United Artist Records, 68-70; pres, Green Menu Music Factory, 71- Chief Collabrs: Kim Gannon, Leonard Whitcup, Bobbi Martin, Norman Simon, Angelo Musulino. *Songs:* Stay With Me; For the Love of Him; Have a Good Day; Oh How I Need You Joe; There Are No Rules; Nice People; Night Is Gone; I Love You So; I Love My Mama; Song of Exodus (Let My People Go); Even a Clown Can Cry; Singing a Happy Song; Kiss Me Goodnight; Rock Billy Boogie; The Christmas Party of the Eight Reindeer; I Think of You; Tomorrow; John F Kennedy Was His Name; The Game of Life (It's the Only Game in Town); Give a Woman Love; You're Undecided; *Lyrics:* You Are Mine (canto alla vita). *Instrumental Works:* Brazen Brass (theme); Tipica Serenada; Until Six; Soupy's Theme; The Soupy Shuffle; Lullaby in Dixieland; Henry's Trumpets.

JEROME, JEROME   ASCAP 1936
composer, author
b New York, NY, June 1, 06; d New York, NY, Aug 27, 64. Educ: Cornell Univ, BA. *Songs:* Mama, I Wanna Make Rhythm; Country Boy; So Red the Rose; Love Is Like a Cigarette; Over a Bowl of Suki Yaki; I Saw a Ship a-Sailing; The Harlem Waltz; Under the Woo Woo Tree; I'm Gonna Ask the Bobolink; A Portrait of a Lady; Moonlight Masquerade; There's a Moon on the Mountain; L'Amour C'est La Vie; Sweet Love Remembered.

JEROME, M K   ASCAP 1920
composer, publisher
b New York, NY, July 18, 1893. Educ: High sch; pvt music study. While in high sch, pianist in vaudeville, film theatres; then staff pianist, Waterson, Berlin & Snyder. To Hollywood, 29; wrote theme songs for early film musicals; with Warner Bros, 18 yrs. Founded own publ firm, NY, 11. Chief Collabrs: Jack Scholl, Ted Koehler, Joe Young, Sam Lewis. *Songs:* My Wild Irish Rose; Daughter of Rosie O'Grady; Casablanca; San Antonio; Yankee Doodle Dandy; Thoroughly Modern Millie; Red, White and Blue (Nat Am Legion revue); Just a Baby's Prayer At Twilight; Old Pal Why Don't You Answer Me?; Bright Eyes; Jazz Baby; Dream Kisses; Thru the Courtesy of Love; My Little Buckaroo; The Old Apple Tree; You, You Darlin'; Sweet Dreams, Sweetheart; The Wish That I Wish Tonight; Would You Believe Me?; Some Sunday Morning; Bombardier Song; It's Victory Day (Treas Dept Silver Medal); Mary Dear.

JEROME, MAUDE NUGENT   ASCAP 1944
composer, author, actress
b Brooklyn, NY, Jan 12, 1877; d New York, NY, June 3, 58. Educ: Pub schs. Wife of William Jerome. Appeared in vaudeville; actress in Bway shows incl "The Thoroughbred", "The Empire Show" & "Town Topics." *Songs:* Sweet Rosie O'Grady; Mamie Reilly; I Can't Forget You Honey; Mary From Tipperary; There's No Other Girl Like My Girl; Somebody Wants You; Love and You; Down at Rosie Reilly's Flat; My Pretty Little China Maid; My Lady Peggy Waltz; The Donkey Trot; Down Among the Roses.

JEROME, WILLIAM   ASCAP 1914
author, actor, singer
b Hudson, NY, Sept 30, 1865; d New York, NY, June 25, 32. Charter mem, ASCAP, dir, 14-25. Husband of Maude Nugent Jerome. Appeared in minstrel shows; music publ. Chief Collabrs: Walter Donaldson, Louis Hirsch, Jean Schwartz, Harry Tierney, Harry Von Tilzer. *Songs:* Chinatown, My Chinatown; Get Out and Get Under the Moon; And the Green Grass Grew All Around; Bedelia; Row Row Row; Mr Dooley; My Pearl Is a Bowery Girl; Picture Me Down Home in Tennessee; On the Old Fall River Line; Old King Tut; That Old Irish Mother of Mine. *Scores:* Bway shows: Piff! Paff! Pouf!; Lifting the Lid; The Ham Tree; Up and Down Broadway.

JERRETT, JEAN (JEAN JERRETT POLSTON)   ASCAP 1962
composer, author, bassist
b Oak Park, Ill, Dec 7, 24. Educ: Col. Former DJ; bassist & singer with trio The Tiaras. *Songs:* You Are My Cha Cha Baby.

JESSEL, GEORGE   ASCAP 1937
author, entertainer, actor
b New York, NY, Apr 3, 1898. Educ: Pub schs. Singer with Gus Edwards' acts, age 9; toured Eng, 15; known as "Boy Monologist" in vaudeville, 17. Appeared in Bway shows incl "The Shubert Gaieties", "George Jessel's Troubles", "The Jazz Singer", "The War Song" (& co-author), "Joseph and His Brethren" & "High Kickers," & in films incl "Lucky Boy." With Eddie Cantor on vaudeville tour; after-dinner speaker. Producer, films incl "The Dolly Sisters", "Nightmare Alley", "When My Baby Smiles at Me", "Oh, You Beautiful Doll" & "Dancing in the Dark." Columnist, Las Vegas Sun & other Nev papers. Founder, Friars Club of Calif & Emeritus; Friars of NY. Author, "So Help Me", "Hello Mama", "This Way, Miss", "Elegy in Manhattan" & bks "Turn to Any Page" & "Here's to the Greats." Chief Collabrs: Harry Ruby, Ben Oakland, Herbert Magidson, Milton Drake, Roy Turk, William White. *Songs:* Stop Kicking My Heart Around; And He'd Say Oo-La-La Wee Wee; My Mother's Eyes; Oh How I Laugh When I Think How I Cried About You; Roses in December; You'll Be Reminded of Me; If I Ever Lost You; Julie; Dreamland Rendevous; As Long As I Love.

JESSYE, EVA   ASCAP 1957
composer, author, conductor
b Coffeyville, Kans, Jan 20, 1895. Educ: Pub schs; grad, Western Univ Quindaro, Kans & Langston Univ, Okla; studied with Will Marion Cook, Percy Goetschius. Dir of music, Morgan Col, 20, Md State Col, 68. Choral cond, Bway shows, 26-36; music dir, council of churches show "Hallelujah," Capitol Theatre, 29. Featured on radio WOR, 30-32 & NBC, CBS & WMCA. Toured US cols. Choral dir with own choir, Eva Jessy Choir, incl such works as "Four Saints in Three Acts" & "Porgy and Bess," 35-70. Artist-in-residence, Pittsburg State Univ, 79-80. Author, "My Spirituals"; "Paradise Lost and Regained" (text by Milton); "Chronicle of Job"; "Life of Christ in Spirituals." *Songs:* Carried the Key and Gone Home; E-I-O; Handcar Blues; Who Is That Yonder; I Belong to That Band; Rock, My Sinai.

JEWELL, WILLIAM A   ASCAP 1975
composer
b Parsons, Tenn, June 19, 32. Educ: LaSalle Univ, law, 57-69. Chief Collabrs: Bill Rhodes, Frances Rhodes, Rayburn Anthony, Tony Austin. *Songs:* I've Been Loved By You Today; Your Memory Travels Fast; I Can't Find My Way; Lock Me in Your Heart.

JOBE, BEN ANDERSON   ASCAP 1969
composer
b Paris, Tenn, Oct 17, 45. Educ: George Peabody Col for Teachers, BA, 67; Murray State Univ, MS, 76; Southern Baptist Theol Sem, MCM, 80, studied comp with Phillip Landgrave, 77 & 79. Commercial music comp, Atlanta, Ga, 71-74. Wrote TV themes. Accompanist & minister of music. Chief Collabr: Denise George. *Songs:* He Loves You; His Song (sacred cantata). *Instrumental Works:* Atlanta Brave (TV theme); Atlanta Hawks (TV theme).

JOCHSBERGER, TZIPORA H   ASCAP 1965
composer, teacher, administrator
b Leutershausen, Ger, Dec 27, 20. Educ: Palestine Acad Music & Music Teachers Sem, Jerusalem, dipl, 42; Sem Col Jewish Music, Jewish Theol Sem, NY, SMM, 59, SMD, 72. Fac mem, Arab Womens' Teachers Col & New Jerusalem Cons & Acad of Music, Jerusalem, 42-50. Bd mem, Rubin Acad Music, Jerusalem, 47-50. Asst prof music educ, Cantors Inst & Sem Col Jewish Music, Jewish Theol Sem of Am, NY, 54-73. Instr music educ, Teachers Inst, Jewish Theol Sem of Am & Yeshiva Univ Womens' Teachers Inst, NY, 54-68. Founder & dir, Hebrew Arts Sch, NY, 52- *Songs:* Hallel (psalms of praise for cantor, choir & children's voices); *Music:* Bekol Zimra (collection Jewish choral music for mixed voices, a cappella); A Woman of Valor (voice & flute); four Hebrew madrigals to texts of Rahel, SATB, a cappella; two Yehuda Halevi songs for voice, flute & violin. *Instrumental Works:* Moods (piano); Blessings (suite for unaccompanied violin); Hava N'Halela (method for recorder based on Israeli folk songs); Melodies of Israel (duets & trios for recorders or other melody instruments; Hebrew Folk Melodies (piano).

JOEL, WILLIAM MARTIN   ASCAP 1978
musician, songwriter
b Bronx, NY, May 9, 49. Popular recording artist. *Songs:* Just the Way You Are (Grammy Awards for record & song). *Albums:* Piano Man; Streetlife Serenade; Turnstiles; The Stranger; 52nd Street (Grammy Awards); Glass Houses.

JOHANSON, ERNEST ROBERT (JO HANSON)   ASCAP 1966
composer, music director, arranger
b New York, NY, Dec 9, 28. Educ: Jamestown High Sch, New York; Boston Univ. Scored several films, Los Angeles, 64-68; wrote radio & TV commercials; scored many educ TV progs for Can TV; comp & arr all music for "Calgary Stampede Grandstand Shows." Chief Collabrs: Randy Avery, Duke Yelton. *Songs: Music:* Put on the Whole Armor of God (sacred cantata); I Will Praise (anthem). *Scores:* One-act Opera: The Bear.

JOHNNY
See Kamano, John Nakula

JOHNS, AL   ASCAP 1947
composer, author
b Washington, DC, June 4, 1878; d Paris, France, June 16, 28. Entertainer in nightclubs, New York & London. Wrote spec material for May Irwin, then music dir of her theatre co. *Songs:* If I But Thought You Cared for Me; In Spite of All I'll Always Love You; I See Your Face in Everything; We Can't Always Have the One That We Love; Sometime, Someday, Somewhere; The Mississippi Bubble; That Is All; In Dahomey; Go Way Back and Sit Down.

JOHNS, ERIK (HORACE EVERETT)   ASCAP 1960
author, lyricist
b Hollywood, Calif, June 7, 27. Educ: Los Angeles City Col Art Sch; Lester Horton Dance Theatre, Los Angeles. Visual arts interior decorator, NY, 58-; decorations for inaugural parties for President Carter, 76. Ed of review & contributor of poetry & other writings, "White Pond Reflections." Wrote librettos: The Tender Land; Sonata Allegro; Days on Earth. Chief Collabrs: Aaron Copland, Jack Gottlieb, John Schlenck, Bernard Westman.

JOHNS, ROSALINDA JILL (ROSALINDA JILL DEMARCO, ROSE JANNS)   ASCAP 1970
composer, author, singer
b Wheeling, WVa, Dec 29, 50. Educ: Univ Louisville, BA, 72; Univ Ill, Chicago Circle Campus, postgrad studies, 76-77; Chicago Cons Music, vocal instr, 77; studied piano with Alan Swain, Chicago, 77-78. Singer, nightclubs; musician in local production, "Grease"; recording artist. Chief Collabr: J Petach. *Songs:* My World; Come on Back to Beer; The City; Two-Timin' Woman; Ain't No Big Thing Anymore. *Albums:* Flying Up Through the Sky.

JOHNSEN, STANLEY ALLEN (SKIP)   ASCAP 1977
composer, author, singer
b Rensselaer, NY, Jan 4, 55. Educ: Bus Acad of Music, Conn, studied with Marty Kugell. Leader of group, Circus; songwriter. *Songs:* There's No Better Love; I've Been Thinking of You; My Friend John/I Like You; YOU; When

Love Comes On; OH YEAH; Everybody Needs Love; I'm Alive; Arizona Cowboy; I Can't Believe My Eyes; Yesterday, Today and Tomorrow; I'm Free; Everything Will Be Alright; One Night Stand; I Got You; Just Contact Me; Looking for Peace of Mind; Razor Eyes; You've Got It Made; Everything Is You; Making Ends Meet; She'll Try; Forgive and Forget; Always Alone; Everyday; Waiting for a Dream.

JOHNSON, ALBERTUS WAYNE (ALAN WAYNE)　　　ASCAP 1967
composer, singer
b Eldorado, Ark, Sept 7, 42. Educ: Eldorado High Sch; Los Angeles Pierce Col, Calif. Wrote songs for TV shows, "Run for Your Life", "Dean Martin" & "Sonny & Cher." Recording artist; singer night clubs & TV. Chief Collabrs: Hank Capps, Dennis Weaver. *Songs:* Hollywood Freeway; I'm the Lucky One; Hey There Johnny; What's the Use of Living; Music: We Should Have Been; Lyrics: Mary's Near.

JOHNSON, ANN M (ANN ROGERS)　　　ASCAP 1976
composer, author
b Providence, RI, Mar 13, 21. Educ: Washington Irving High Sch; Norfolk State Col. Producer & publ with Annjay Records. *Songs:* Laugh a Little Louder; If I Couldn't Dream; What Must I Do?; You Say.

JOHNSON, ANNE SPEAR　　　ASCAP 1968
author
b Philadelphia, Pa, Apr 14, 16. Educ: Simon Gratz High Sch, 34. Lyricist of over 100 songs. Received appreciation award for "New Horizons" telecast from City of Cape May, NJ. Chief Collabrs: J George Johnson (husband), Benny Meroff. *Songs:* Lyrics: The Laughing Samba; Only the Broken Hearted; A Penny for Your Thoughts; My Bad Boy; This Is My Song; If You Care; Farewell to Spring; Your Kiss; Love You So; I Would Have Loved You; Have a Heart; New Horizons; Romance in Central Park; I Get Hungry for Your Kisses; I Like Philadelphia; Have a Heart for the Children; Mister Frank Rizzo Cha Cha; That's the Story; Good News, Friend; Merry Christmas; It's Never You; I'd Rather Die.

JOHNSON, ARNOLD　　　ASCAP 1925
composer, conductor, arranger
b Chicago, Ill, Mar 23, 1893; d St Petersburg, Fla, July 25, 75. Educ: Chicago Musical Col; Am Cons; studied with Emil Liebling, Silvio Scionti & Adolph Weidig. Toured RKO, Paramount, Loew & Fox circuits with own band. Music dir, Bway musicals. Made film shorts. Music dir & producer, radio network shows. Entertained US troops in Europe, WW II. Pianist. Chief Collabrs: Byron Gay, Mitchell Parish, Benny Davis, Dorothy Fields, Jimmy McHugh. *Songs:* Oh Does Your Heart Beat for Me?; Sweetheart; Don't Hang Your Dreams on a Rainbow; Goodbye Blues; The Lovelight in Your Eyes; Lilliokalani; Tear Drops; All for You; Oh.

JOHNSON, CHARLES　　　ASCAP 1964
author
b Philadelphia, Pa, July 29, 28. Educ: High sch. USN service. Chief Collabr: Frank Bossone. *Songs:* My Heart Is Yours; Alone.

JOHNSON, CHARLES L　　　ASCAP 1941
composer, pianist
b Kansas City, Kans, Dec 3, 1876; d Kansas City, Mo, Dec 28, 50. Educ: Pub schs. Pianist in Kansas City orchs, hotels & theatres, 20 yrs. Staff comp & arr for publ cos. *Songs:* Iola; Dill Pickles; Dream Days; Our Yesterdays; In the Hills of Old Kentucky; Sweet and Low; When Clouds Have Vanished; Crazy Bone Rag; Jubilee in the Sky; Shadow Time.

JOHNSON, CHARLES LAVERE　　　ASCAP 1956
composer, author, instrumentalist
b Salina, Kans, July 18, 10. Educ: Pvt study, cert of grad, Charles D Wagstaff, Salina, 19-26; Col of Fine Arts, Univ of Okla, 28-29. Pianist, instrumentalist & vocalist with bands incl Frank Williams, Herb Cook, Clarence Tackett, Etzi Covato, Sam Robbins, Roy Ingraham, Marshall Van Pool, Tracy Brown, Boyd Schreffler, Johnny Dorchester, Wingy Manone, Eddie Neibaur, Dell Coon, Rico Marcelli, Joe Sanders, Henry Busse, Paul Whiteman & Frank Trumbauer, 28-39; radio work with Skinnay Ennis, John Scott Trotter, Gordon Jenkins, Ray Noble, Bob Crosby & others; was on many TV shows, 39-49. Accompanist to Bing Crosby, 39-47 & George Burns, 59-61. Led own LaVere's Chicago Loopers on records & in personal appearances, 45-50; vocalist, Decca Records, 47-54. Co-writer "Golden Horseshoe Revue." Pianist, Disneyland, 55-60; asst cond, Melodyland Theatre, 63. Single & nightclub work, Las Vegas, 61-67. Mem, Russ Morgan Orch, 67-68. Duo with wife Lois, 79. Chief Collabrs: Bonnie Lake, Tom Adair, Paul Mason Howard, Steve Shoemaker, Glenn Hughes. *Songs:* The Blues Have Got Me; Hello Everybody; It's All in Your Mind; Mis'ry and the Blues; Boogaboo Blues; Music: Cuban Boogie Woogie. *Instrumental Works:* Very 8'n Boogie; Ubangi Man.

JOHNSON, DAVID EARLE　　　ASCAP 1974
composer, author, singer
b Florence, SC, Apr 10, 38. Educ: Berklee Sch Music, dipl, arr & comp; studied with master percussionist, Carlos Mejia. Recording artist. Chief Collabr: Sam Hammer. *Instrumental Works:* Bamba Forest; Night; Safes. *Albums:* Time Is Free; Skin Deep-Yeah!; Hip Address.

JOHNSON, EDWARD　　　ASCAP 1948
composer, trombonist, arranger
b Baltimore, Md, July 12, 10; d Bronx, NY, Oct 26, 61. Educ: Pub schs; pvt music study. Trombonist, 20 yrs. Wrote spec material for Ethel Waters, Tiny Bradshaw, Cootie Williams & Lucky Millinder. Chief Collabrs: Tiny Bradshaw, Robert Bruce. *Songs:* The Jersey Bounce; Salt Lake City Bounce; I May Be Crazy But I'm No Fool; Saturday Night.

JOHNSON, EMANUEL　　　ASCAP 1976
composer, author, singer
b Detroit, Mich, Sept 1, 52. Educ: Pershing High Sch; studied vocals with James Fraizier. Performer, nightclubs, TV, radio & in Bway show "Talking About Love." Singer with group Enchantment, 15 yrs, songwriter for group, 5 yrs & var other artists; recording artist. *Songs:* Gloria; Sunshine; Know What You're Doing to Yourself; Where Do We Go From Here; You and Me. *Scores:* Film: Deliver Us From Evil.

JOHNSON, HALL　　　ASCAP 1952
composer, author, conductor
b Athens, Ga, Mar 12, 1888; d. Educ: Knox Inst; Atlanta Univ; Allen Univ; Univ Southern Calif; Hahn Sch Music; Univ Pa; New York Inst Musical Art; studied with Percy Goetschius; hon MusD, Philadelphia Musical Acad. Formed Hall Johnson Choir, 25; appeared in concerts, theatre, radio, recordings, TV & films. Arr & music dir, Bway production, "Green Pastures" (in which choir appeared). Organized Fest Negro Chorus of Los Angeles, 36. Appeared in Int Fest of Fine Arts, Berlin, toured Ger & Vienna for US State Dept, 51. Rec'd New York City Citation, 62. Mem, New York City Citizens Adv Comt Cultural Affairs. *Songs & Instrumental Works:* Son of Man (cantata). *Scores:* Bway stage: Run, Little Chillun.

JOHNSON, HAROLD VICTOR　　　ASCAP 1959
composer, teacher, conductor
b Omaha, Nebr, May 16, 18. Educ: Univ Calif, Los Angeles; Santa Monica City Col, studied comp with Wesley LaViolette; Los Angeles City Col, studied piano & conducting with Fritz Zweig. Freelance comp & cond, Los Angeles film/TV indust, incl, MCA TV, Inc, Columbia Records, Liberty Records & others; now head, Comp Dept, Southern Calif Cons Music, Sun Valley. Chief Collabrs: Lurrine Burgess, Mary Chaudet, Martin Denney, Anna Hunger, Ed Penney, Judy Vaccaro. *Instrumental Works:* Three Symphonies for Orchestra; Four String Quartets; Chorale Symphony (libretto based on a work by Lord Byron). *Scores:* Opera: Judas; Cinderella; The Barnyard Quartet; The Pied Piper; The Little Mermaid; The Children of Boston (Oratorio).

JOHNSON, HOWARD E　　　ASCAP 1917
author
b Waterbury, Conn, June 2, 1887; d New York, NY, May 1, 41. Educ: High sch; pvt music study. Pianist in Boston theatres; staff writer, NY publ co. WW I, USN. Chief Collabrs: Milton Ager, Walter Donaldson, Fred Fisher, George Meyer, Joseph Meyer, Jimmy Monaco, Harry Warren, Percy Wenrich, Harry M Woods, David Brockman, James Kendis, Archie Gottler, W Edward Breuder. *Songs:* Ireland Must Be Heaven for My Mother Came From There; Sweet Lady; I Scream, You Scream, We All Scream for Ice Cream; What Do You Want to Make Those Eyes At Me For?; M-O-T-H-E-R; What Do We Do on a Dew Dew Dewy Day; When the Moon Comes Over the Mountain; Where Do We Go From Here, Boys?; Bring Back My Daddy to Me; There's a Broken Heart for Every Light on Broadway; I Don't Want to Get Well; Siam; Georgia; A Word That Means the World to Me; Feather Your Nest; Love Me Or Leave Me Alone; Am I Wasting My Time on You?

JOHNSON, HUNTER　　　ASCAP 1954
composer, educator
b Benson, NC, Apr 14, 06. Educ: Benson High Sch; Univ NC, 24-26; Univ Rochester Eastman Sch Music, BMus, 29; studied comp with Alfredo Casella, 34. Taught comp, Univ Mich, 29-33, Univ Man, 44-47, Cornell Univ, 48-53, Univ Ill, 59-65 & Univ Tex, 66-71. Awarded Rome Prize, 33, & Guggenheim fels, 41 & 54. Chief Collabr: Martha Graham. *Instrumental Works:* North State; Past the Evening Sun; For An Unknown Soldier; Piano Sonata; Trio for Flute, Oboe and Piano; Letter to the World; Deaths and Entrances; The Scarlet Letter.

JOHNSON, J C　　　ASCAP 1932
composer, author
b Chicago, Ill, Sept 14, 1896. Educ: Phillips High Sch. Pianist & cond, Chicago. Lt, USA Ambulance Corps, NY, WW II. Wrote nightclub revues, Bway & Europ stage scores. Chief Collabrs: Fats Waller, Andy Razaf, George Whiting, Nat Burton. *Songs:* Trav'lin All Alone; Empty Bed Blues; The Joint Is Jumpin'; Patty Cake, Patty Cake, Baker Man; The Spider and the Fly; Black Mountain Blues; Me and Gin; Music: Little Black Boy; Louisiana; Dusky Stevedore; Guess Who's in Town?; Rhythm and Romance; Beloved; Believe it, That's How Rhythm Was Born; Don't Let Your Love Go Wrong; Without a Shadow of a Doubt; Yankee Doodle Tan; Lonesome Swallow; Lyrics: Yacht Club Swing; How Ya' Baby?; Inside This Heart of Mine; Cryin' My Heart Out for You; My Particular Friend. *Songs & Instrumental Works:* Do What You Did Last Night.

JOHNSON, J GEORGE   ASCAP 1952
composer, author, arranger
b Philadelphia, Pa, Sept 17, 13. Educ: High sch grad. Pianist with orchs & combos; arr for singers & shows for synagogues, high sch & other orgn. Songs performed & instrumentals played on radio, TV & sound systs. Chief Collabs: Anne Spear, Benny Meroff. *Songs:* Ev'rytime; Summer Serenade; Music: The Laughing Samba; Only the Broken Hearted; Curtain Time Suite; Drifting Sampans; Romance in Central Park; Greenwich Village; My Bad Boy; I Would Have Loved You; Farewell to Spring; That's the Story; Good News, Friend; I'd Rather Die; It's Never You; Mister Frank Rizzo Cha Cha.

JOHNSON, JAMES A   ASCAP 1962
author, publisher
b Los Angeles, Calif, Aug 8, 17; d Thousand Oaks, Calif, Jan 9, 76. Educ: Univ Calif, Los Angeles, BA. Joined Walt Disney Studios, 38. WW II, USA, Maj USQMC. In merchandising, publ, record depts, then pres, Walt Disney Music Co. Chief Collab: Tutti Camarata. *Songs:* The Battle of San Onofre; Maybe Tomorrow; Sammy the Way-Out Seal; The Little Train; The Submarine Street Car.

JOHNSON, JAMES P   ASCAP 1926
composer, pianist
b New Brunswick, NJ, Feb 1, 1891; d New York, NY, Nov 17, 55. Educ: New York pub schs; pvt music study. Professional debut as pianist, 04. Pianist in summer resorts, theatres, films & nightclubs; formed own band, Clef Club, 20's; toured Europe with "Plantation Days." Accompanist to Bessie Smith, Trixie Smith, Mamie Smith, Laura Smith & Ethel Waters. Pianist & comp for films, incl "Yamacraw." Mem, League of Comp & Nat Asn for Am Comp & Cond. Chief Collabs: Mike Riley, Nelson Cogane, Cecil Mack. *Songs:* Old Fashioned Love; Don't Cry Baby; Charleston; If I Could Be With You One Hour Tonight; Stop It Joe; Mama and Papa Blues; Hey, Hey; Runnin' Wild; Porter's Love Song to a Chambermaid; Snowy Morning Blues; Eccentricity Waltz; Carolina Shout; Keep Off the Grass. *Instrumental Works:* Symphonic Harlem; Symphony in Brown; African Drums; Piano Concerto in A-flat; Mississippi Moon; Yamacraw (Negro rhapsody); Symphonic Suite on "St Louis Blues"; City of Steel. *Scores:* Opera: Dreamy Kid; De Organizer (folk opera); Operetta: Kitchen Opera; The Husband; Ballet: Manhattan Street Scene; Sefronia's Dream.

JOHNSON, JAMES WELDON   ASCAP 1914
author, educator
b Jacksonville, Fla, June 17, 1871; d Wiscasset, Maine, June 26, 38. Educ: Atlanta Univ, BA, MA. Principal, Stanton Sch. Founder & ed, Daily American, first Negro daily in US. Self-educ in law; admitted to Fla bar. Appointed US consul, Puerto Cabello, Venezuela & Corinto, Nicaragua. Asst ed, New York Age. Visiting prof of creative literature, Fisk Univ; trustee, Atlanta Univ. Dir, Am Fund for Pub Service; nat secy, Nat Asn for Advancement of Colored People, 14 yrs. Author: "Negro Americans, What Now?"; "Black Manhattan"; "God's Trombones"; "St Peter Relates an Incident"; "The Book of American Negro Poetry"; "The Books of American Negro Spirituals." Autobiography: "Along This Way"; "The Autobiography of an Ex-Coloured Man." Translated Enrique Grandos' opera, "Goyescas," produced by Metrop Opera Co, 15. Founding mem, ASCAP. Chief Collab: Rosamond Johnson (brother). *Songs:* Under the Bamboo Tree; Lift Every Voice and Sing; Since You Went Away; The Maiden With the Dreamy Eyes; Nobody's Lookin' But the Owl and the Moon; Tell Me, Dusky Maiden; My Castle on the Nile; Congo Love Song; The Young Warrior; The Awakening; Two Eyes; Morning, Noon and Night; The Old Flag Never Touched the Ground.

JOHNSON, JAY W   ASCAP 1948
composer, author, entertainer
b Ellis, Kans, Mar 23, 03. Educ: WWaterloo High Sch, Iowa; Iowa State Col, BS(sociol); mem, Sigma Delta Chi & Musician's Union. 55 yrs in show bus, vaudeville, cocktail lounges, nightclubs, radio & TV. Fred Waring Show (NBC radio & CBS-TV), 6 yrs. Kate Smith Show (NBC-TV), 1 yr. Galen Drake Show, Jack Sterling Show, educ TV, cable TV. Wrote 4 radio drama series, 3 dramas for community theater, spec lyrics for Fred Waring choral numbers, 1000 shows for radio syndication. Chief Collabs: Harry Simeone, Billy Hayes. *Songs:* Blue Christmas; Peaceful; Lyrics: The Emperor's New Clothes; Whittlin'; Little Boy of Mine; Waltz of the Flowers; Mendelssohn's Spinning Song.

JOHNSON, JOHN
See Hughes, Robert James

JOHNSON, (JAMES) LAMONT   ASCAP 1976
composer, author, teacher
b New York, NY, Oct 1, 41. Educ: Mt Morris Music Sch; piano-comp studies with Dr Franz Bueschler, WGer & improvisation studies with Joseph D Jackson. Started with Star-Time Studios as original Star-Time Kid, (NYC-TV), performing with Annunciation Choir. Appeared at local New York clubs as teenage balladeer. Toured mil bases, Europe, 62. Built first recording studio, Downeast Studios, Lower East Side, 67. Commercials & jingles with MBA Music. Concertized through 68. Formed Sun, Moon & Stars, producing var entertainment projs. Formed Artisan Releasing Corp, 72-73. Duke Ellington Comp-Arr Award, 77. Started Masterscores Acad, to train musicians production of records, 80. *Instrumental Works:* Symphony Number Two in

Blues; Interstellar Suite (orch & jazz ens); Big Ben's Voice; Calypso After Nine; Nine; Beverly; Europa; Libra's Longing; Erdu. *Scores:* Film/TV: Thunderfist; Fastest Six Weeks in Your Life; Weekend in Reserves; School of Military Sciences, Officers; Drift Away; WAF Airman; Children of Freedom.

JOHNSON, LUCILE   ASCAP 1950
author, singer
b Tukwila, Wash, Oct 26, 07. Educ: Univ Wash; Art Inst of Chicago; pvt music study. Singer, Bway musicals, Billy Rose's Diamond Horseshoe & other nightclubs & hotels. Singer, USO unit overseas, World War II. Writer, short stories, novels & children's bks (& illustrator). Chief Collab: Ray Carter (husband). *Songs:* Sagebrush Serenade; Cara, Cara, Bella Bella; All Right, Louie, Drop the Gun; Little Mr Big; The Cuckoo Who Lived in a Clock; Merry-Go-Round; Little Switch Engine.

JOHNSON, MARGARET (CORKY ROBBINS)
author, singer, pianist
b Lincoln, Nebr, 1923; d 1967. Educ: Drury Col, Mo, BA, 45; Cincinnati Cons Music, grad. Staff pianist & organist, WLW-TV, Cincinnati & WOR, New York. Comp, "Queen City Sweet," performed at May Fest, 60. Performed on local TV stas with Ted Steele, New York. *Songs:* The Whispering Winds; Conquest; Release Me; Church Twice on Sunday; Don't Hurt the Girl.

JOHNSON, MARK
See Mercer, W Elmo

JOHNSON, PAUL ALAN   ASCAP 1970
composer, record producer, publisher
b Seattle, Wash, Sept 22, 46. Educ: Walla Walla Col, BA(theol); Dick Grove Music Workshop. Comp gospel songs; arr & producer of contemporary gospel albums. Pres, Paul Johnson Music Production Inc, publ div, Sonlife Music. Chief Collabs: Michael Omastran, Chris Christian, Grace Hawthorne, Rick Dees, Shanalee Lucas. *Songs:* You Took My Heart By Surprise; Here Comes the Son; Lord, Take Control of Me; Love Theme (The Greatest of Them All); That the World May Know; Finders Keepers. *Scores:* TV: 700 Club TV Themes; Masada (TV drama).

JOHNSON, PAUL HARLEN   ASCAP 1964
composer, musician
b Mason City, Nebr, Feb 1, 17. Educ: Completed sch through 8th grade. Semi-prof musician, 35-; comp & songwriter, 40- Worked with local & territory dance bands in Nebr, Kans, SDak, Wyo & Colo. Chief Collabs: Samuel A Short Jr, Charlie Buck, Ted Burgeman, Tommy Hand. *Songs:* Music: If the Moon Could Tell; Wonderful You; We Dipped Our Hearts in Stardust; When Twilight Falls.

JOHNSON, PETE K H   ASCAP 1964
composer, pianist
b Kansas City, Mo, Mar 24, 04; d Buffalo, NY, Mar 23, 67. Educ: Grammar sch. Pianist with singer, Joe Turner; team was in "Spirituals to Swing" concerts, New York, 38. Appeared as single & with Meade Lux Lewis & Albert Ammons, in nightclubs & concerts, 40's & 50's. Appeared at jazz fests; made Europ tour. Has made many records. Chief Collab: Meade Lux Lewis. *Songs & Instrumental Works:* Wee Baby Blues; Boogie Woogie Prayer; 627 Stomp; Johnson and Turner Blues.

JOHNSON, RICHARD HOWIE   ASCAP 1975
composer, author, entertainer
b Hartford, Conn, Feb 11, 52. Educ: New Eng Cons of Music. Professional entertainer, age 16; on col concert & lect circuit. Founder, Stonefinger Music, 74, Plum Island Records, 78. Writer, recording artist & tours US; produces jingles for radio advert. *Songs:* Old Man Adams; Plum Island National Anthem. *Instrumental Works:* Plum Island; Ocean Song: 3 AM; The Bell Tower.

JOHNSON, ROCK
See DiGiovanni, Rocco

JOHNSON, ROGER   ASCAP 1969
composer, teacher, writer
b San Mateo, Calif, Nov 12, 41. Educ: Univ Wash, BA, 63, studied with George McKay; Yale Univ, MM, 66, studied with Mel Powell, Bulent Arel; Columbia Univ, studied with Chou Wen-Chung, Otto Luening. Serious & experimental comp, works performed in US & Europe. Recorded on Angel & CRI. Col teaching, 66- Collected and ed "Scores: An Anthology of New Music." *Instrumental Works:* Ritual Music for Six Horns; Wind Quintet; Suite for Six Horns; Cycles (orch); Echo (flugel horn & piano); Five Miniatures; 3' 08" (Greene Street Music); Extension (flugel horn, strings & tape).

JOHNSON, VIRGINIA D (GINNY)   ASCAP 1968
composer, author
b Guide Rock, Nebr, Apr 5, 26. Chief Collabs: Frank Stanton, Andy Badale, Claudia Carson. *Songs:* Lyrics: There Hangs His Hat; Let Me Down Easy; All Night Long; Nashville Beer Garden; Take My Love; I Wanna Share My Pillow; One Day Down (And a Lifetime to Go); Rainy Day Lovin'; He Loves Me Right Out of My Mind; Touch You With My Mind.

JOHNSON, WILLIAM ASCAP 1941
composer
b Jacksonville, Fla, Sept 30, 12; d New York, NY, July 5, 60. Chief Collabr. Robert Bruce. *Songs & Instrumental Works:* Dolimite; Tuxedo Junction; Uptown Shuffle; Weddin' Blues; Country Boy.

JOHNSON, WOODROW WILSON (BUDDY) ASCAP 1964
composer, conductor, pianist
b Darlington, SC, Jan 10, 15; d. Cond & pianist small group; later large orch. Appeared in nightclubs, theatres & on records. *Songs:* Stop Pretending; Since I Fell for You; Please, Mr Miller.

JOHNSTON, ALBERT CHANDLER, JR (BUCK) ASCAP 1955
composer, author
b Boston, Mass, Dec 19, 25. Educ: Univ NH, BA(musical theory & comp), 49. Numerous performances of classical works for film & TV. Businessman, sales mgr for retail stores in Honolulu, Hawaii. Pianist/comp. Chief Collabrs: Richard P Crew, Leon Rene. *Songs:* God Gave Us Christmas; Autumn Has Come and Gone; Suez Canal; Guess I'm Thru With Love; Dig That Crazy Santa Clause!; Gabi; Music: Taj Mahal. *Instrumental Works:* Tanganyika (2 piano); Scherzo (F-minor for piano); Nocturne (E-major for piano); Mysterious Prelude (piano); Rhapsody (D flat for piano & orch); Solitude (violin and piano).

JOHNSTON, ARTHUR JAMES ASCAP 1927
composer, conductor, pianist
b New York, NY, Jan 10, 1898; d Corona del Mar, Calif, May 1, 54. Educ: Pub schs. Pianist in film theatres; pianist & arr, New York publ co. Pianist for Irving Berlin, music dir for his stage productions. To Hollywood, 29. WW II, 351st Inf; wrote Army show, "Hut-Two-Three-Four." Chief Collabrs: Johnny Burke, Sam Coslow, Gus Kahn. *Songs:* Mandy, Make Up Your Mind; Dixie Dreams; I'm a Little Blackbird Looking for a Bluebird; Just One More Chance; Learn to Croon; Down the Old Ox Road; Moon Struck; Thanks; The Day You Came Along; Moon Song; Cocktails for Two; Ebony Rhapsody; My Old Flame; Troubled Waters; Thanks a Million; Two Together; One, Two, Button Your Shoe; Pennies From Heaven; So Do I; Let's Call a Heart a Heart; The Moon Got in My Eyes; All You Want to Do Is Dance; It's the Natural Thing to Do; Song of the South; Live and Love Tonight; If I Only Had a Match. *Scores:* Film: College Humor; Too Much Harmony; Hello, Everybody; Murder at the Vanities; Thanks a Million; Pennies from Heaven; Double or Nothing.

JOHNSTON, BENJAMIN BURWELL, JR ASCAP 1963
composer, teacher
b Macon, Ga, Mar 15, 26. Educ: Col William & Mary, BA; Cath Univ, Cincinnati Cons Music, MMus; Univ Calif, Berkeley; Mills Col, MA; Univ Ill, Urbana-Champaign; comp study with Darius Milhaud, Harry Partch, Burrill Phillips, Robert Palmer & John Cage. Teacher, Univ Ill, Urbana-Champaign, 51-, now prof. Guggenheim Fel, 59-60. Grants: Nat Found Arts & Humanities, 66; Univ Ill Res Bd, 58- Assoc mem, Univ Ill Ctr Advanced Studies. Polish radio comn, 78; Fromm Found Comn, 80; Am Music Ctr Comn. Chief Collabrs: Wilford Leach, Merce Cunningham, Sibyl Shearer, Jaap Spek. *Songs:* Music: Mass; Sonnets of Desolation (Hopkins); Two Sonnets of Shakespeare; Songs of Innocence (Blake). *Instrumental Works:* Quintet for Groups (symph orch); Nine Variations for String Quartet; String Quartets No 2, No 3, No 4, No 5, No 6; Knocking Piece (2 perc & grand piano); Duo for Flute and String Bass; Duo for Two Violins; Diversion (eleven instruments); Sonata for Microtonal Piano; Suite for Microtonal Piano; Casta. *Scores:* Opera/Ballet: Gambit for Dancers and Orchestra; Gertrude, Or Would She Be Pleased to Receive It?; Carmilla, A Vampire Tale.

JOHNSTON, BOB
composer, producer
b Ft Worth, Tex, May 14, 32. With Clyde Otis' Publ Firm, then Kapp Records. Signed with Hill & Range Publ; then went to CBS, Nashville. Went independent. Chief Collabr: Joy Johnston.

JOHNSTON, DONALD O ASCAP 1974
composer, teacher
b Tracy, Minn, Feb 6, 29. Educ: Macalester Col; Northwestern Univ Sch Music, BM, 51, MM, 54; Ind Univ; Eastman Sch Music, Univ Rochester, AMD, 61; studied comp with Philip Warner, Robert Mills Delaney, Bernard Rogers & Howard Hanson. Served in the Mil during the Korean War; teacher, Col Idaho & Ripon Col, Wis. Comp-in-residence & comp teacher, Univ Mont. *Instrumental Works:* Essay for Trumpet (band or orch accomp); Fourth Symphony; Time and Space Studies in Three Aspects (orch); Concatenation (woodwind quintet & piano); Band: Montage; Symphonic Rondo for Winds; Ritual for Band; Fantasy in the Baroque Manner; Prelude for Band. *Songs & Instrumental Works:* Sonnets From the Barracks (chorus & orch); A Time of Darkness (liturgical drama); Windows on America (soprano, chorus, orch); Choral: The Eyes of the Lord Are Upon the Righteous; Praise the Lord; Sing to the Lord.

JOHNSTON, FRANK RODERICK ASCAP 1979
composer, author
b Des Moines, Iowa, Dec 1, 31. Educ: Pub schs, Des Moines; Grinnell Col, 49-51; Drake Univ, (Eng), 51-53. Writer, bks & lyrics of 2 original comedies,

high sch, lyrics for 2 shows while in col, for several parodies, also actor & singer, Ad Club Gridiron Shows, Des Moines. Involved in insurance & indust sales; free-lance writer for insurance indust at var publ. *Songs:* Never Asking for More.

JOHNSTON, GENE ASCAP 1960
composer, publisher
b Florence, Colo, May 11, 00; d Los Angeles, Calif, June 22, 66. Educ: Univ Southern Calif. Wrote col shows. Music publ, 34-40. Chief Collabr: Milo Sweet. *Songs:* Trojan Marching Song; Hail Our Mighty Trojans (both for Univ Southern Calif); Stairway of Dreams; Tune in on My Heart.

JOHNSTON, JOY A (JOY BYERS)
composer, author, singer
b Springtown, Tex, May 19, 37. Educ: NTex State Univ; Univ Vanderbilt. Records with Aretha Franklin & Johnny Cash. Writes lyrics & music for many singers. Chief Collabrs: Bob Johnston, Charlie Daniels, Johnny Cash. *Songs:* It Hurts Me; Please Don't Stop Loving Me; Hey Little Girl; Hard Knocks; I've Got to Find My Baby.

JOHNSTON, MARY
See Matthews, Mary Ann

JOHNSTON, PATRICIA ASCAP 1943
author
b Kansas City, Mo, Oct 24, 22; d New York, NY, Nov 24, 53. *Songs:* I'll Remember April; Music and Rhythm; Ode to Victory.

JOHNSTONE, GORDON ASCAP 1919
author, actor
b Newport, RI, Sept 16, 1876; d New York, NY, Apr 21, 26. Educ: Pub schs. With Theodore Roosevelt's Rough Riders, Span-Am War. Actor in Bway plays. Author, "There Is No Death." *Songs:* The Living God; The New Christ; The Unknown Soldier; Laddie O' Mine; The Great Awakening.

JOHNSTONE, THOMAS A ASCAP 1924
composer, author
b Evanston, Ill, Mar 3, 1888; d. *Songs:* Up in the Clouds; Betsy Ross; Happiness; Mellow Moon; Plain Jane; Only You; When You Smile; Only a Paper Rose. *Scores:* Bway Stage: Up in the Clouds; Molly Darling; Plain Jane; I'll Say She Is.

JOLLEY, FLORENCE WERNER ASCAP 1954
composer, author, educator
b Kingsburg, Calif, July 11, 17. . Educ: Calif State Univ, Fresno, AB, music choral & piano instr; Univ Southern Calif Los Angeles, MMus; Nova Univ, DEd; Eastman Sch Music, spec study theory & comp. Organist, pianist & choral cond; choral comp & arr; lectr & pianist on improvisation. Prof music theory, piano & comp, Los Angeles City Col, 62- Instrnl develop in music educ & developer self instrnl text with cassettes. *Songs:* Music: Gloria in Excelsis; All People That on Earth Do Dwell (8 part arr).

JOLLY, PETER ASCAP 1957
composer, pianist
b New Haven, Conn, June 5, 32. Educ: Pvt teachers, Conn & New York. Pianist, studios & jazz concerts. With var artists, TV films, motion pictures & records. Recording artist for var cos. Chief Collabr: Dick Grove. *Songs:* Music: Unconcerned. *Instrumental Works:* Little Bird (Nat Acad of Recording Arts & Sci nomination); Three, Four, Five; Skating.

JOLSON, AL ASCAP 1920
composer, author, singer
b Russia, May 26, 1886; d San Francisco, Calif, Oct 23, 50. Moved to US, 1890. Educ: Pub schs. Sang in New York saloons, vaudeville; later with Lew Dockstader's Minstrels. Appeared in Bway musicals incl: "La Belle Paree"; "The Whirl of Society"; "Robinson Crusoe, Jr"; "Sinbad"; "Bombo"; "Big Boy"; "Wonder Bar"; "Hold on to Your Hats." Appeared in films incl: "The Jazz Singer" (first part-sound); "The Singing Fool"; "Mammy"; "Hallelujah, I'm a Bum"; "The Singing Kid"; "Go Into Your Dance"; "Rhapsody in Blue"; "Rose of Washington Square"; "Swanee River." Had own radio show in 30's. Entertained troops during WW II, Korean War. Biography, "The Immortal Jolson", by Pearl Sieben. Film biographies: "The Jolson Story"; "Jolson Sings Again." Actor. Chief Collabrs: Harry Akst, Joseph Meyer, Jean Schwartz, Ray Henderson. *Songs:* Avalon; California, Here I Come; Every Day Can't Be Sunday; Me and My Shadow; 'N' Everything; Back in Your Own Back Yard; All My Love; Sonny Boy; There's a Rainbow 'Round My Shoulder; The Egg and I; You Ain't Heard Nothin' Yet; Yoo-Hoo; Keep Smiling At Trouble; Anniversary Song.

JONES, AGNES
See Sharp, Robert Louis, Jr

JONES, ALBERT
See J, Trebla Seno

JONES, ARTHUR   ASCAP 1950
composer, author
b Liverpool, Eng, May 6, 09. To US, 12, citizen, 23. Educ: High Sch of Commerce, New York; studied music with H Durig. Writer, revues for Princeton Theatre, songs for films & Bway musicals. Author, "How to Crash Tin Pan Alley", "Great Waltzes", "Great Composers" & "The Life of Stephen Foster." *Songs:* Where Could I Go?; Thank You Thanksgiving; West Point Hop; Funny Little Bunny; Tally Ho; I Fell All Over Myself; One Rainy Day, One Lonely Night.

JONES, BETTY HALL   ASCAP 1963
composer, pianist, singer
b Topeka, Kans, Jan 11, 11. Educ: Hollywood High Sch, grad 26; Washburn Col, Topeka, Kans, 1 yr. Started as entertainer in Kansas City in 36 with Bus Motens Band; worked with bands in Los Angeles area several yrs; has had duos, trios & Dixie Land bands; entertainer with Roy Milton's Band, 5 yrs & briefly with Paul Howard & Bud Scott Bands. Full-time entertainer. Chief Collabr: Jester Hairston. *Songs:* Gossip-Gossip.

JONES, BIFF   ASCAP 1960
composer, author
b Cape Girardeau, Mo, Aug 10, 30. Educ: Tex A&M; Univ Southern Calif; Ben Bard Drama Sch. Former film actor. Writer, special material for Edith Piaf, Gogi Grant, Ella Fitzgerald, HiLo's, Andy Williams, Jo Stafford & Lawrence Welk, & for Hotel Riviera shows. Chief Collabr: Charles Meyer. *Songs:* Suddenly There's a Valley; Too Young for the Blues; Island of Desire.

JONES, CHARLES   ASCAP 1953
composer
b Tamworth, Ont, June 21, 10. Educ: Inst Musical Art, NY, grad violin, 32; Juilliard Grad Sch, grad comp, 39, studied with Bernard Wagenaar. Taught at Mills Col, Calif, 39-44, then at Music Acad of the West, Santa Barbara, Calif; now teacher comp & related subjects, Aspen Summer Sch, Colo; winters, chmn comp dept, Mannes Col Music, New York & mem fac, Juilliard Sch. *Instrumental Works:* Three Pieces for Piano; String Quartet No 2; Little Symphony for the New Year; Lyric Waltz Suite (woodwind quartet); Introduction and Rondo (string orch); String Quartet No 6; Sonata Piccola (piccolo & harpsichord); Four Symphonies; Seven String Quartets. *Songs & Instrumental Works:* Three Settings of the Text, "Piers the Plowman" (Middle Eng for voices & var instrumental groups).

JONES, CHARLES MARTIN
author, producer, director
b Spokane, Wash, Sept 21, 12. Educ: Chouinard Art Inst, Los Angeles, grad, 31. Animator, Warner Bros, 33-38, dir, 38-63; creator, Road Runner, Coyote, Pepe le Pew & other animated characters; writer, producer & dir TV specials for ABC & CBS, incl "The Cricket in Times Square", "How the Grinch Stole Christmas", "Rikki-Tikki-Tavi", "Bugs Bunny in King Arthur's Court", "Raggedy Ann and Andy in the Great Santa Claus Caper." Teacher & lectr schs & cols throughout US. Recipient Acad Awards, 50, 65 & 76. First Prize, Tehran Fest Films for Children, 77; Brit Film Inst Tribute, 79. Mem: Nat Coun Children & TV; Acad Motion Picture Arts & Sci; Screen Writers Guild; Acad TV Arts & Sci; Screen Actors Guild.

JONES, CLARENCE M   ASCAP 1940
composer, conductor, pianist
b Wilmington, Ohio, Aug 15, 1889; d New York, NY, June 1, 49. Educ: High sch; studied music with Albino Garni, Van der Stucken, Louis Adler & Charles Singer. Had own orch, Sultan of Syncopation; performed in Owl Theatre & Metrop Theatre, Chicago; also had orch at Moulin Rouge Nite Club, Chicago. Had own radio prog, KYW & WBCN, Chicago. To New York, 31; joined NBC; pianist & arr for Southernaires, until 39; then worked at Harlem Salvation Army Canteen. *Songs:* One Wonderful Night; Twilight, the Roses and You; Old Home; Swanee in Spring; Under the Same Old Moon; My Old Swanee Home; Autumn Colors; Walkin' Thru Mockin' Bird Lane; The Lord's Prayer; Tom Tom Dance; Mid the Pyramids.

JONES, DAVID HENRY, JR   ASCAP 1971
composer, producer, singer
b Detroit, Mich, Aug 27, 49. Educ: Wilberforce Univ, Ohio. Songwriter for var recording artists while in col. Staff writer, Jobette, 71-78. Producer, singer & arr of own album. Chief Collabrs: Wade Brown, Jr, Johnny Bristol. *Songs:* Love Me for a Reason; We've Come Too Far to End It Now; That's How Love Goes; E Ne Me Ne Mi Ne Moe; It's Gotta Be That Way; Full Speed Ahead; Try My Love.

JONES, DAVID HUGH   ASCAP 1942
composer, author, organist
b Jackson, Ohio, Feb 25, 00. Educ: Guilmant Organ Sch, New York; Am Cons, Fontainebleau, France, studied with T Tertius Noble, Henry Libert, Marcel Dupre, Andre Bloch, Charles Widor; Washington & Jefferson Col, MusD; Beaver Col, MusD. Church organist, Ohio & New York, 17-26. Chmn, organ dept, Westminster Choir Col, Dayton, 26-29, comp dept, Westminster Choir Col, Ithaca, NY, 29-32, Princeton Univ, 32-51. Dir of music, Princeton Theol Sem, 34-37, assoc prof, 47-51, prof, 51- Visiting prof of music, Seminario

Evangelico de Teologia, Mantanzas, Cuba, 55-56. Ed-in-chief, The Hymnbook; music ed, Armed Forces Hymnal. Mem, Am Guild of Organists, exec comt, Hymn Soc of Am. *Songs:* Sacred: Build Thee More Stately Mansions; Faith; Life Has Loveliness to Sell; O Holy Light; O Praise the Lord; God Thou Art Love; Hymns and Anthems for Children, Sets I, II, III.

JONES, ELVIN LEE   ASCAP 1972
composer, author
b Point Pleasant, Mo, Dec 13, 39. Educ: Catron High Sch; Lansing Bus Univ; Detroit Col of Bus; San Diego City Col; Nat Univ. Writer, poetry, age 10, with var awards, short stories, age 13, songs, age 17- Chief Collabrs: Jeanetta V Jones (wife), William Akins. *Songs:* It's So Hard (to Say Good-Bye); God Bless This Ring; All the Way Lord; Daddy, I Miss You So; Lyrics: Roly-Poly; God Bless the Child; Christmas Now and Forever; Music: I Got a Little Boy; Please Don't Let Her Hurt Me Again; Sixteen Reasons (to Say Good-Bye). *Instrumental Works:* Mean Woman-Evil City.

JONES, GEORGE THADDEUS   ASCAP 1964
composer, educator
b Asheville, NC, Nov 6, 17. Educ: Univ NC, AB, 38; Eastman Sch Music, Univ Rochester, MA, 42 & PhD, 50; pvt study with Nadia Boulanger & Nicholas Nabokov. Instr, US Navy Sch Music, 42-46; prof music, Cath Univ, Washington, DC, 50-; Fulbright res grant, Italy, 53-54; US State Dept Cult Exchange, Romania, 67-68. Composer & author textbks music theory & comp. Chief Collabr: Leo Brady. *Instrumental Works:* Piano Sonata; The Deadly Garden (piano trio). *Songs & Instrumental Works:* Choral: The Beatitudes; Canticles, Prayers and Psalms. *Scores:* Opera: The Cage.

JONES, GLORIA R   ASCAP 1970
composer, record producer, singer
b Cincinnati, Ohio. Educ: Los Angeles High Sch; studied classical piano with C Pappy, 12 yrs. Started as singer; recorded for 7 yrs, Los Angeles. Mem original cast "Hair." Wrote "If I Were Your Woman," which rec'd Grammy Nomination. Worked with Marc Bolan the key boardest of the rock group FREX. Wrote & produced for Motown Records & EMI, London, Eng. Mem, Nat Piano Playing Soc. Chief Collabr: Ray Gibson. *Songs:* Haven't Stopped Dancing; Music: My Mistake; Christmas Won't Be the Same This Year.

JONES, GORDON G
See Krunnfusz, Gordon

JONES, HENRY Z, JR   ASCAP 1961
composer, author, singer
b Oakland, Calif, June 3, 40. Educ: Stanford Univ, BA. Recording artist for RCA Records; regular cast mem, Ernie Ford Show; actor in TV shows, incl "Mork & Mindy", "Love Boat", "The Jeffersons", "My Three Sons", "Love-American Style" & "Emergency"; actor in films, incl "Tora-Tora-Tora", "Young Warriors", "Village of the Giants", "Girl Happy" & eight movies for Walt Disney; author, "The Palatine Families of New York." Publisher. Chief Collabrs: Larry Ray, Dean Kay. *Songs:* Midnight Swinger; Ain't Got a Nickel; Wishin' Well; Someday, Somebody's Gonna Stop Sandy; What a Mess You Made Outa Me; Star-Light, Star-Bright; I'll Stand on My Own; Big City Life; Train-Train-Train; You're Talking to a Man Who Knows; Let It Happen Again; Who's It Gonna Be.

JONES, HEYWOOD S   ASCAP 1944
composer, conductor
b Bangor, Maine, May 24, 1891; d Bangor, Maine, Aug 20, 59. Educ: Phillips Andover Acad; Dartmouth Col, Delta Kappa Epsilon, Phi Beta Chi; 32nd Degree Mason. Chem Warfare Serv, WW I. Bandmaster, Am Legion Boy's Band. Mem, Bangor Symph; dir, Anah Temple Shrine Band & Bangor City Band; pres, Kiwanis & Tarratine Clubs, Chamber of Commerce & Bangor City Govt. Taught piano & accordion. *Instrumental Works:* On the Way; Libertas; Hot Sands; Right in Step; Pride of Maine; Brass on Parade; Army Ground Forces Band; Music Camp; 4 Rhythmic Dances; A Gypsy Carnival; At the Circus; At the Minstrel Show; Woodland Fantasie; Wake Up, America; The Honeymoon Express; The Alarm Clock (trio with band); Bangor 1-2-5; Lynn Centennial Suite; band arr for Czardas.

JONES, ISAIAH, JR (IKE)
composer, author, pianist
b St Louis, Mo, Mar 10, 40. Educ: Sumner High Sch, 57; Calif State Univ, Los Angeles, BA(music), 72; Talbot Theol Sem, MDiv(theol), 77; studied voice with Florence Russell & Zebolon King; studied piano with Bertha Smith, Wynetta Lindsey, P C Smith, Lionel Taylor, Winifred Chastek & Madame Donche Dikova. Mem of Epilson Alpha Gamma; mem of cast, "Black Nativity," 64-65; contribr articles, Lyric Mag, 65-; vpres, Talbot Theol Associated Student Body, 74-76, dir student serv, 76-77. Music comp & dir for play, "Time for a Big Celebration"; music dir, Calif State Univ, Los Angeles, production, "Tambourines to Glory," then organized gospel choir. Acted in "Don't Bother Me I Can't Cope," Mark Taper Forum, Los Angeles & was solo artist on a gospel prog with piano & vocal only, 75; featured artist, Forest Home Christian Conference Ctr, 74-80. Accompanied on piano, arr for, sang with & comp for the following: Lorraine Adams, Willie Mae Ford Smith, Alex Bradford Singers, Art Reynolds Singers, Bessie Griffin, Cassietta George, Friends of Distinction,

James Cleveland, Art & Honey, Marc Copage, Tony Bennett, Robert Anderson, Lloyd Oldham, McGruder Choraliers, Fifth Dimension, Mahalia Jackson, Watts 103rd Rhythm Band, Doris Akers, Caravans, Issac Douglas, Incredibles, Calif State Univ Concert Choir, Los Angeles City Col Concert Choir & many others. Performed on TV Shows: "Mike Douglas Show", "Joey Bishop Show", "Operation Entertainment", "White Front Special", "Pat Boone Show", "Dr Schuller's Hour of Power", "Rosy Grier Show", "Woody Woodbury Show" & others. Performed at Loyola Univ, Chicago & Los Angeles; Ariz State Univ; Univ Chicago; Calif State Univ, Los Angeles & many others in US, Mex, NZ, Australia. Performed in nightclubs, incl: Caesar's Palace, Las Vegas; King's Hotel, Lake Tahoe; La Fontana, Mexico City, Mex; Ad Lib Room, Los Angeles; Troubadour, Los Angeles & many others around the world. Appeared in the Billy Graham Crusade, San Diego Stadium, 76. Was minister for prisons in Mo, Ill, Calif, NJ & other states; was minister music, People's Tabernacle of Faith, Los Angeles; was minister of youth & music, First Southern Baptist Church, Compton, Calif. Now dir, Youth & Young Adult Ministries, First United Presby Church, Los Angeles; singer & arr. *Songs:* Fill My Cup (Best Song Writer, Acad Gospel Singers, 73); God Has Smiled on Me (Best Song, Acad Gospel Singers, 74; Grammy Nomination, 75); Abundant Life (Grammy Winner, 79); Make Me an Example; Keep Me in Your Care; Until Whenever & Through Whatever; Thank You Lord for Blessing Me Again; We Are One; Music: Give It to Me (Grammy Nomination, 76).

JONES, ISHAM ASCAP 1924
composer, conductor, pianist
b Coalton, Ohio, Jan 31, 1894; d Hollywood, Fla, Oct 19, 56. Educ: Pub schs; pvt music study, Chicago. Saxophonist in dance bands. Led own orch in nightclubs, hotels, theatres & ballrooms throughout US & Europe. Made many records. Chief Collabr: Gus Kahn. *Songs:* On the Alamo; Swingin' Down the Lane; It Had to Be You; I'll See You in My Dreams; Indiana Moon; Spain; The One I Love Belongs to Somebody Else; There Is No Greater Love; My Best to You; You've Got Me Crying Again; It's Funny to Everyone But Me; I'll Never Have to Dream Again; Why Can't This Night Go on Forever; All Mine-Almost.

JONES, JONATHAN (JO) ASCAP 1960
composer, conductor, drummer
b Chicago, Ill, Oct 7, 11. Educ: Pvt music study. With carnival, toured Chautauqua circuit. Drummer, var orchs & bands incl Count Basie Orch, 35-48, Illinois Jacquet, Lester Young, Joe Bushing. With Ella Fitzgerald & Oscar Peterson, toured Europe, 57. Leader, own trio in nightclubs, jazz fests & on records. *Songs & Instrumental Works:* Vamp 'Til Ready; Mozelle's Alley.

JONES, KENNETH EUGENE (BUCKY) ASCAP 1974
composer
b Bainbridge, Ga, Aug 5, 42. Educ: Univ Ga. Began writing prof, 71. With Jim Reeves Enterprises, 74-76, Warner Brothers Music, 76-79 & Tree Int, 79- Chief Collabrs: Jimmie Johnson, Curly Putman, Royce Porter. *Songs:* The Most Wanted Woman in Town; Barroom Pals and Goodtime Gals; Bridge for Crawlin' Back; The Best Day of the Rest of Our Love; I Love That Woman (Like the Devil Loves Sin).

JONES, LEE
author
b Metter, Ga, July 13, 08. Educ: Savannah High Sch, Ga; Yale Univ Sch of Music, MusB. With NBC, New York; music librarian, producer, dir & mgr, WNBC-FM radio station. Chief Collabrs: Buddy Kaye, Larry Wagner, Al Stillman, Pinky Herman. *Songs:* Music: Battle of the Little Big Horn; I'll Know My Love; It's Time to Sing.

JONES, LINDLEY A (SPIKE)
composer, conductor, drummer
b Long Beach, Calif, Dec 14, 11; d Los Angeles, Calif, May 1, 65. Educ: Chaffee Jr Col. Drummer in nightclubs, with touring bands & on records. Mem, John Scott Trotter Orch, "Kraft Music Hall," radio, also in orchs, Al Jolson, Burns & Allen, Bob Burns shows. Appeared in film "Thank Your Lucky Stars." Led own orch, Spike Jones & His City Slickers; toured US & abroad; made many records. Had own TV series "Spiketaculars." *Songs:* Der Fuehrer's Face.

JONES, MARJORIE ASCAP 1968
composer, singer, teacher
b Portland, Ore. Educ: Univ Southern Calif, MA, studied with Leon Kirchner. Author song bks "The Marjorie Jones Song Book", "The Songs of Marjorie Jones", Vols 1 & 2, "A Study in Colossians" & "Hosanna We Sing (for choir)," also Four Short Solos. *Songs & Instrumental Works:* Two Encore Solos: It Couldn't Be Done; Rain; Choir Music: A Sense of Him; What Can I Give Him; Shine; Hosanna We Sing (cantata). *Albums:* The Music of Marjorie Jones.

JONES, OLIVER ASCAP 1969
author
b Heath Springs, SC, Feb 25, 25. Educ: Heath Springs High Sch, SC. Songwriter, 56- Chief Collabrs: Lew Tobin, Jack Curry, Larry Allen. *Songs:* Lyrics: Walk With Me; Mademoiselle; Calypso Blues; Love Me Forever; Where Was My Love; Joan; She Made Foul Outer Me; I'm Waiting for Someone; You Are My Love; All of You; Judy My Love.

JONES, QUINCY ASCAP 1955
composer, conductor, arranger
b Chicago, Ill, Mar 14, 33. Educ: Seattle Univ; Berklee Sch Music, scholarship; Boston Cons; studied with Nadia Boulanger & Olivier Messiaen. Trumpeter & arr, Lionel Hampton orch, 50-53. Arr for orchs & singers, incl Ray Anthony, Count Basie, Sarah Vaughan & Peggy Lee. Organizer, trumpeter & arr, Dizzy Gillespie orch for State Dept tour of Near, Middle East & SAm, 56. Music dir, Barclay Disques, Paris, 2 yrs; "Free and Easy" (toured Europe). Led own orch Eur tour, concerts, TV & radio, 60; US nightclubs, ballrooms & hotels. Music dir, Mercury Records, 61, vpres, 64. Arr for film, "The Boy in the Tree," Sweden; cond for films, "The Pawnbroker," "Mirage" & "The Slender Thread." Comp & actor, "Blues for Trumpet and Koto," TV, Tokyo; comp & arr, industrials, TV & records. Rec'd awards incl Grammy, Ger Jazz Fed & Edison Int, Sweden. *Instrumental Works:* Kingfish; Stockholm Sweetnin'; Jessica's Day; The Midnight Sun Will Never Set; For Lena and Lennie; Evening in Paris; Meet B B; The Boy in the Tree Theme; Li'l Ol' Groovemaker; Kansas City Wrinkles; Pleasingly Plump; I'm Gone; Je ne sais pas; You're Crying; Jasmin; Falling Feathers; Plenty, Plenty Soul; Rat Race; The Big Walk; Muttnik; Blues Bittersweet; I Needs to Be Bee'd With. *Scores:* Film Background: The Boy in the Tree; The Pawnbroker; Mirage; The Slender Thread.

JONES, RICHARD C ASCAP 1957
composer, pianist, arranger
b Como, Miss, May 1, 06. Educ: WTenn State Col, studied with Theodore Bohlmann; Juilliard Sch, studied with Bernard Wagenaar. Pianist, accompanist & arr, 31-35. Pianist & arr, Tommy Dorsey & Glen Gray Orchs, 35-42. Served, USN, ETO, with Artie Shaw & Sam Donahue Bands, SPacific, World War II. Arr, Benny Goodman & Harry James Orchs. A&R producer, Capitol Records, 48- *Songs:* To the Legion.

JONES, RICHARD M ASCAP 1942
composer, author, conductor
b New Orleans, La; June 13, 1892; d Chicago, Ill, Dec 8, 45. Pianist in New Orleans, 08-17. On staff, Chicago publ co, 19. Became publ, cond & record mgr. Publisher. *Songs & Instrumental Works:* All Night Blues; Twenty Ninth and Dearborn; Trouble in Mind; Remember Me?; Ball o' Fire; Dark Alley; Jazzin' Babies Blues; Riverside Blues; Red Wagon.

JONES, ROBERT CARROLL ASCAP 1970
composer, teacher, performer
b Muscatine, Iowa, June 10, 31. Educ: Depauw Univ, BM, 53, MM, 55; Univ Iowa, PhD, 65; Univ Rochester Eastman Sch Music, summers 70, 79 & 80, studied with Rayburn Wright & Manny Albaun. Taught, pub schs, Ind, Colo, Iowa & Mo. Teaching asst, Univ Iowa; assoc prof, Southeast Mo State Univ, 65-75, Culver-Stockton Col, 78- Owner, Kendall-Lee Recording Studio, 75-77; performer with var prof groups; writer & arr for var styles & media. *Songs:* Music: Three Songs for Soprano and Piano. *Instrumental Works:* Just Be Yourself; Blues for the Duke; Moonchild; Juli's Mood; Sheridan Drive; Sonata in F major (alto saxophone, piano); Four Studies for Flute, Clarinet and Violoncello; Canzona for Band; Suite for Jazz Ensemble and Orchestra; March, April, May (orch).

JONES, ROBERT WILLIAM ASCAP 1970
composer, teacher
b Oak Park, Ill, Dec 16, 32. Educ: Oak Park High Sch, 46-50; Chicago Cons, pvt instr in organ & theory, 51; Univ Redlands, BM, 59, MM, 60; self-taught in comp. Ford Found-CMP comp-in-residence, West Hartford, Conn, 65-69 & Livonia, Mich, 69-72; instr, Schoolcraft Col, Livonia, 72- *Songs:* Music: Hist Whist; Christmas Calypso; To Men of Good Will. *Instrumental Works:* Toccata Concertante; Revelations; Passion; Trombone Sonatina.

JONES, ROBIN C ASCAP 1975
author
b Kansas City, Mo, Apr 1, 33. Educ: Scarsdale High Sch; Yale Univ, BA, 55. Lyricist for revues & cabarets; co-lyricist, off-off Bway musical "Gulp" (ASCAP Award); librettist, opera "Dr Jekyll and Mr Hyde" (finalist, Nat Competition, New York Opera). Prof awards as advert copywriter. Chief Collabrs: John Glines, Sam Pottle, Fred Albitz, Barry O'Neal. *Songs:* Lyrics: Moving On (oratorio); Sing Out for the Season of Love; Sweet Tranquility (anthem, sacred setting as chorus of Mozart trio); I Am Full of Imperfections (anthem).

JONES, SAMUEL ASCAP 1971
composer, author, conductor
b Inverness, Miss, June 2, 35. Educ: Millsaps Col, Miss, BA, 57; Univ Rochester Eastman Sch Music, MA, 58, PhD, 60; studied conducting with Richard Lert & William Steinberg, comp with Howard Hanson, Bernard Rogers & Wayne Barlow. Dir instrumental music, Alma Col, 60-62. Cond, Saginaw Symph, 62-65; assoc cond, Rochester Philh Orch, 65-70, cond, 70-72. Founding dean & prof music, Shepherd Sch Music, Rice Univ, 73- Guest cond: Detroit Symph, Houston Symph, Pittsburgh Symph, Buffalo Philh, Iceland Symph, Prague Symph, Flint Symph & others. Comns: Houston Symph Am Symph Orch League, Shenandoah Fest, Utica Symph, Saginaw Symph & others. Founder, Alma Symph, Delta Fest. Artistic adv, Flint Inst Music. *Instrumental Works:* Let Us Now Praise Famous Men; Elegy for String Orchestra; Overture for a

City; Symphony No 1; Chaconne and Burlesque; In Retrospect; Meditation and Scherzo. *Scores:* A Christmas Memory.

JONES, SAMUEL TURNER   ASCAP 1963
composer, teacher
b Pottsville, Pa, Sept 28, 09. Educ: NY Univ, BS(music), 32, MA, 36, DEduc, 59. Music teacher in pub sch, Valley Stream, NY, 29-31; music instr & cond orch & band, Juniata Col, 36-42; music teacher, State Teachers Col, Indiana, Pa, 43-45; asst prof music & dir, Men's Glee Club, Ala Polytech Inst, 47-50. Music dir, radio station WDAD, Indiana, Pa, 45-47. Exec secy, Music Teachers Nat Asn, 51-63; Eastern Div rep, Sohmer & Co, piano makers, NY, 63-65. Owned & managed furniture retail store, 65-73. Sold real estate, 73-79. *Instrumental Works:* Suite Moderne (4 B flat clarinets); Theme and Variations on a German Folk Tune (piano solo).

JONES, STAN   ASCAP 1949
composer, author, actor
b Douglas, Ariz, June 5, 14; d Los Angeles, Calif, Dec 13, 63. Educ: Univ Calif, MA(zoology). US Nat Park Ranger, 15 yrs. Wrote for radio & TV; originated & acted in "Sheriff of Cochise" series; wrote & narrated "Standard School Broadcast," radio, 59-60. Screenplays: "Rio Grande" & "The Rainmaker." Wrote songs for films. *Songs:* Riders in the Sky; Wringle Wrangle; Wagons West; The Searchers; Hannah Lee; Cowpoke; The Awakening; Whirlwind; Cheyenne (TV theme); Texas John Slaughter; Triple-R Song; Windmill; You Mean So Much to Me; Sons of Old Aunt Dinah. *Albums:* Creakin' Leather; This Was the West; Songs of the National Parks.

JONES, STEPHEN OSCAR   ASCAP 1923
composer, author, arranger
b New York, NY, July 12, 1880; d New Rochelle, NY, Apr 12, 67. Educ: New York Ger Cons; studied with Gottfried Kritzler, John Von Brockhoven. Arr, Bway musicals incl "Lady, Be Good", "Wildflower", "No, No, Nanette", "The Bunch and Judy" & "The Blue Kitten." Songwriter for play "Toni," London, "Marjorie", "Talk About Girls" & "Yes, Yes, Yvette." Chief Collabrs: Irving Caesar, B G DeSylva, William Cary Duncan, Clifford Gray. *Songs & Instrumental Works:* What Do You Do Sunday, Mary?; My First, My Only Love; Bygone Days; Summer Breeze; Bees; Rondo a la Breve; Rondo; Appassionata; String Quartet; String Sonata; Alaska Overture; Top Brass; Serenade and Valse; Evensong (male chorus). *Scores:* Bway shows: Captain Jinx; Poppy.

JONES, THADDEUS JOSEPH
jazz musician
b Pontiac, Mich, Mar 28, 23. Played trumpet, cornet & fluegelhorn, Count Basie, 54-63, Gerry Mulligan, 64, George Russell, 64 & Thad Jones/Mel Lewis Orch, 65- Winner, Downbeat Mag Readers Poll, 72-77 & Downbeat Critics Poll, 74-77. *Songs & Instrumental Works:* Mean What You Say; Don't Git Sassy; Fingers; Tiptoe; Central Park North. *Albums:* The Magnificent Thad Jones; Thelonious Monk, Brilliance; Thad Jones-Pepper Adams, Mean What You Say; Thad Jones & Mel Lewis: Monday Night At the Village Vanguard; Central Park North; Consummation; Potpourri; Thad Jones-Mel Lewis; Suite for Pops; New Life.

JONES, TOM   ASCAP 1959
author
b Littlefield, Tex, Feb 17, 28. Educ: Univ Tex, BFA, 49, MFA, 51. Wrote col musicals. Began writing for Julius Monk & Ben Bagley Revues. Wrote spec material for Tom Poston & Ronny Graham. Chief Collab: Harvey Schmidt. *Songs:* A Seasonal Sonatina (New York Is a Summer Festival); Mister Off-Broadway; Race of the Lexington Avenue Express; Soon It's Gonna Rain; They Were You; Is It Really Me?; Much More; Love, Don't Turn Away; Simple Little Things; A Man and a Woman; Lyrics: Try to Remember; My Cup Runneth Over; songs for "Shoestring Revue." *Scores:* Demi-Dozen (nightclub); Bway Shows: I Do! I Do!; 110 in the Shade; Celebration; Off-Bway Shows: The Fantasticks (longest running musical in world); Colette; Philemon.

JONES, WENDY VICKERS   ASCAP 1970
composer, author, singer
b Princeton, NJ, Mar 15, 49. Educ: Finch Col, NY; Univ Philippines, Manila. Perf, col campus tours & on TV incl "Wendy Vickers in Concert," 70's. Recipient, pre-Grammy nomination & ASCAP Popular Songwriters awards. *Songs:* Get on Board; Come to My Table; Go in Peace; High Time; Lord Gave Me a Song; Keep the Faith; The Miracles of Cana; The Love Hymn; Bands of Gold; Candlelight; In Christ We Love; To Love; Music: Glory to God; Holy, Holy. *Albums:* Sow a Seed; The Wedding Gift.

JONES, WILLARD WOOD, JR   ASCAP 1967
composer, author, arranger
b Rochester, NY, Jan 20, 19. Educ: Hofstra Col, BA, 40, pvt study in comp with Paul Yartin, Mario Castelnuovo-Tedesco, Ernest Kanitz & George Tremblay. Trumpet player & orchr; arr for Victor Young, Tommy Dorsey, Axel Stordahl, Nelson Riddle, & others. Active in film & TV scores, 50's & 60's. Music copyist & librarian, MGM. Mem, Comp & Lyricists Guild of Am, Am Soc Music Arrangers, Musicians Local. *Songs:* We Are the World; Chapel of God; The

Christmas Day Is Here. *Scores:* Films/TV: FBI; Barnaby Jones; House of Sand; plus documentaries.

JONGENEELEN, MARGARETHA AUGUSTINA   ASCAP 1969
singer
b Jakarta, Indonesia, Sept 30, 30. Educ: Studied voice with Mrs Cobi Riemersma, Neth. Dancer; recording artist, Columbia Records, Fontana, Neth. Chief Collabr: Ben Hamax de La Brethonier. *Songs:* Believe in Me; Midnight Gypsy; Tomorrow's Love.

JOPLIN, JANIS   ASCAP 1967
composer, author, singer
b Port Arthur, Tex, Jan 19, 43; d Los Angeles, Calif, Oct 4, 70. Educ: Port Arthur Col; Univ Tex, Austin; Lamar Univ. Joined group, Big Brother & The Holding Co, 66; performed as white blues singer, Monterey Pop Fest, Calif, 67; recording artist, 68-70; leader bands, Kozmic Blues Band, 69 & Full Tilt Boogie Band, 70. *Songs:* Mercedes Benz; Kozmic Blues; Women Is Losers; Down on Me; Move Over.

JOPLIN, SCOTT   ASCAP 1942
composer, conductor, pianist
b Texarkana, Tex, Nov 24, 1868; d New York, NY, Apr 4, 19. Educ: Studied music with Louis Chauvin. Pianist in St Louis cafes; cond orch, Chicago World's Fair, 1893; entertainer in vaudeville as early ragtime pianist. *Instrumental Works:* Maple Leaf Rag; Palm Leaf Rag; Sunflower Rag; Euphonic Sounds; Pineapple Rag; Sugar Cane Rag; Country Club Rag; Wall Street Rag; Pleasant Moments; Solace; Frolic of the Bears; Kismet Rag; Entertainer Rag; Original Rag. *Scores:* Opera: Tremonisha.

JORDAN, ALICE (MRS FRANK B JORDAN)   ASCAP 1976
composer
b Davenport, Iowa, Dec 31, 16. Educ: Des Moines, Iowa, pub schs; Drake Univ, BMusEd, grad work comp with Francis Pyle. Free lance comp of organ, choral & vocal works; active in church, cultural, sch & community orgn. Rec'd Alumni Distinguished Service Award, Drake Univ, 70. *Songs & Instrumental Works:* Worship Service Music for the Organist; A Season and a Time (organ collection); Hymns of Grateful Praise (organ collection); Music: Take Joy Home (song for voice & piano); The Fifth Psalm (song for voice & organ).

JORDAN, ARCHIE PAUL   ASCAP 1976
composer, arranger, musician
b Augusta, Ga, Nov 5, 51. Educ: Aiken High Sch; Univ SC, BM(comp). Played guitar on road for group, The Tams. Writer, Bang Records, Atlanta, 73, Pi-Gem & Chess Music, Nashville, 75. Record producer; produced & arr 2 Grammy Award albums, "Happy Man" & "You Gave Me Love." Chief Collabrs: Hal David, John Bettis, Naomi Martin. *Songs:* What a Difference You've Made in My Life; Music: It Was Almost Like a Song; Let's Take the Long Way Around the World; I Never Said I Love You; In No Time At All.

JORDAN, CYRIL H G   ASCAP 1969
composer, author, singer
b San Francisco, Calif, Aug 31, 48. Educ: Self-taught. Started at 17 yrs old as professional musician in rock group Flamin' Groovies; signed to var record cos, 68- Chief Collabr: Chris Wilson. *Songs:* Shake Some Action; Yes Its True; Jumpin' in the Night; Slowdeath; I Can't Hide.

JORDAN, JOE   ASCAP 1939
composer, author, conductor
b Cincinnati, Ohio, Feb 11, 1882; d Tacoma, Wash, Sept 11, 71. Educ: Lincoln Inst, Mo. Music dir, Chicago Theatre, 03; also Bway prod, "Bandana Land." Arr for Ziegfeld; toured Europe leading own orch; appeared in vaudeville. Capt, USA, WW II. Mem fac, Modern Inst Music, Tacoma; background music for stage productions, "Macbeth" & "Haiti." Arr & teacher. *Songs & Instrumental Works:* Oh, Say!; Wouldn't It Be a Dream!; Got to Have My Toddy Now; I Want to Sing About You; Take Your Time; Sweetie Dear; Brother-in-Law Dan; Go, Giants, Go (off Tacoma Giants song); State of Washington; That Teasin' Rag; Lovey Joe; Double Fudge (ragtime two-step); Nappy Lee (a slow drag); Pekin Rag (intermezzo). *Scores:* Bway show: Brown Buddies.

JORDAN, LEROY (LONNIE)   ASCAP 1970
composer, singer
b San Diego, Calif. Started playing keyboards in nightclubs, East Los Angeles, 64; started group, The Creators, 65; with group, Eric Burden & War, 69 & group, War, 72-80. Chief Collabrs: Papa Dee Allen, Howard Scott, Harold Brown, Ronnie Hammond, Luther Rabb, Lee Oskar, Pat Rizzo, B B Dickerson, Charles Miller. *Songs:* All Day Music; Low Rider; Cisco Kidd; Why Can't We Be Friends; Summer; The World Is a Ghetto; Spill the Wine; Slippin Into Darkness.

JORDAN, ROY   ASCAP 1941
composer, author
b New York, NY, Aug 17, 16. Writer for Billie Holiday, Count Basie & for TV, radio, films & nightclubs. Chief Collabrs: Sid Bass, Gene DePaul, Peter De Rose, Paul Taubman, Ulpio Minucci. *Songs:* The Booglie Wooglie Piggy; The Pattycake Man; The Old Soft Shoe; Why Go On Pretending?; You Bring Me Down; Hezekiah; Stars Over the Campus; I'm Gonna Move to the Outskirts of

Town; The 627 Stomp; I'm in a Low Down Groove; My Love's a Gentle Man; My Impression of Janie; I'll Never Know; One Man Woman; Greatest Feeling in the World; Pine Tree Pine Over Me; Broken Homes and Broken Hearts. *Scores:* Stage show: Three Bags Full.

JORDAN, VICTOR HOWARD ASCAP 1969
composer, instrumentalist
b Washington, DC, Oct 19, 38. Educ: Selt-taught. Worked on road as instrumentalist until 74. Recording artist on rhythm guitar & banjo for var producers, 74- Chief Collabrs: Gladys Flatt, Roland White. *Instrumental Works:* Pickaway; Lil' Dave; Cedar Hill; Vic's Ride; Jordan's Hornpipe; Big Dave.

JOSEFOVITS, TERI ASCAP 1947
composer, author, pianist
b Hartford, Conn, Sept 9, 09; d Yonkers, NY, Nov 23, 58. Educ: Lake Erie Col; Cons with Dean Wade; Cleveland Inst Music, with Beryl Rubinstein, Walter Scott, Roger Sessions & Ernest Bloch. Child actor in stock cos & films; pianist on radio, steamships & hotels; staff mem, Paramount Theatre, New York, 36-47; also radio stations, Cleveland, New York & Venezuela; conductor & organist. *Songs & Instrumental Works:* A New Day Prayer; Love Is Ev'rywhere; Last Night I Kissed a Dream; Au Revoir Again; Caribbean Serenade; Bagatelle.

JOSE-PERIERA, FERNANDO ANTONIO
See Pearson (Jose-Periera), Fernando Antonio

JOSEPH, IRVING ASCAP 1958
composer, pianist, arranger
b New York, NY, Mar 3, 25. Educ: Studied with David Saperton, Adele Marcus & Sari Biro; studied theory & comp with Elie Siegmeister, Stefan Wolpe & Hall Overton; studied chamber music playing & accompaniment with Emanuel Vardi. Started prof career playing piano & trombone & arr for USN Band, Washington, DC, WW II. Worked with most of maj dance bands of the period, incl Tommy Dorsey, Glenn Miller Band & others; played the Paramount Theatre stage shows, 2 yrs. Worked with artists incl Tony Bennett, Rosemary Clooney, Billy Eckstine, Pearl Bailey & Frank Sinatra; began cond & playing for singers, incl Lena Horne. Cond for stage shows: "Three-Penny Opera", "See-Saw", "Jesus Christ, Superstar" & CBS TV Series, "Our American Musical Heritage." Cond for Josephine Baker, Palace Theatre. Chief Collabrs: Will Holt, Larry Holofcener, Murray Schisgal. *Songs:* Music: Bye-Bye; Raining, It's Raining; Wailing Waltz; Thoughts; Always and Always; What Man Has Made of Man; M F O'Brien; The Brothers' Frenski (stage show). *Instrumental Works:* A Christmas Memory (incidental music); Divertimento for Flute and Piano. *Scores:* Bway Show Theme: Sherlock Holmes; Luv; Typist and the Tiger. *Albums:* Murder, Inc.

JOSEPH, RAY
See Shayne, Larry

JOSEPH, SAL
See Salviuolo, Joseph Anthony

JOST, PAUL J ASCAP 1971
composer, author, singer
b Vineland, NJ, Aug 31, 52. Educ: Berklee Col Music, Boston; pvt instr with Arthur Harvey, George Small & Tony Davilio. Wrote TV sound track for an NBC Special; also studio work for producers, Stan Vincent, Ted Macero, Genya Ravan, Michael Barbiero, Dave Collins, George Small, Tony Davilio, Harvey Goldberg & Robert Maxwell. Currently working clubs/casinos, Atlantic City. Chief Collabr: George Small. *Scores:* Movie: Last Rites (Dracula's Last Rites).

JOSTEN, WERNER ASCAP 1939
composer, conductor, educator
b Elberfeld, Ger, June 12, 1885; d New York, NY, Feb 6, 63. To US, 21. Educ: Studied music with Rudolf Siegel & Jacques-Dalcroze; hon MusD, Colby Col. Cond in Geneva & Paris. Prof music, Smith Col, 23-49; cond, joint Amherst, Smith Col orch. Dir, opera fest, Northampton, Mass. Rec'd Juilliard Publ Awards. Guest cond, Lewisohn Stadium Concerts, New York. *Instrumental Works:* 2 symphonies; Jungle; String Quartet; Concerto Sacro, I, II; Serenade; Piano Sonata; Sonata for Violin, Piano; Sonata for Cello, Piano. *Songs & Instrumental Works:* Choral: Crucifixion; Hymnus to the Quene of Paradys; Ode to St Cecilia's Day; Songs. *Scores:* Ballet: Joseph and His Brethren; Endymion.

JOTHEN, MICHAEL JON ASCAP 1978
composer, author
b Abington, Pa, Jan 11, 44. Educ: Joliet Township High Sch; St Olaf Col, BA, 67; Case Western Reserve Univ, MA, 72; Ohio State Univ, PhD, 78. Vocal instr, pub schs, Mich & Ohio; prof, Denisson Univ, Ohio State Univ, Newark, Univ Northern Colo. Church musician, Mich & Ohio; choral workshops, clinician & lectr in Ohio, Md, Colo, Wyo & Fla; comp. *Songs:* God Made Me; Sing Hosanna; This Is the Day; Music: Cantate Domino; Radiator Lions.

JOUARD, PAUL E ASCAP 1957
composer, conductor, arranger
b Mt Vernon, NY, May 28, 28. Educ: Yale Univ, BM, MM; Juilliard Sch; studied with Percy Grainger, Clarence Adler. Concert pianist. Music dir, AFRS. Recording artist; piano roll arr. Cond, orch of Lake Placid Club, 49- *Instrumental Works:* Prelude and Fugue in E; Modal Variations on a French Air; Sonata Romantica; Playland Suite.

JOY, LEONARD W ASCAP 1955
composer, conductor, producer
b Claremont, NH, Aug 12, 1894; d New York, NY, Nov 21, 61. Educ: Dartmouth Col. Pianist & arr, vaudeville circuit, Boston & New York, NBC-radio shows. A&R dir, Victor Records, 33, Decca Records, 44. *Songs:* Mavis; Vision of Bernadette; When Shadows Fall; Moonlight Melody; Affectionately Yours.

JOYCE, DOROTHEA
See Vaquer, Dorothea Joyce Buchalter

JOYCE, FONDA M ASCAP 1975
composer, singer
b New York, NY, Apr 18, 46. Educ: Our Lady of Perpetual Help Bus Sch; Am Acad Dramatic Arts; studied under Mata & Hari. Back-up singer, demo recordings. Chief Collabr: Roger Joyce. *Songs:* Lyrics: Peppermint Candy World; I May Be Your Baby; I Wanna Sing With You.

JOYCE, ROGER ASCAP 1970
composer, singer, musician
b New York, NY, June 29, 43. Recording artist, Warner Bros; singer/musician nightclubs; words & music for film score "Big Thumbs." Chief Collabr: Teddy Randazzo. *Songs:* You're Right for What's Wrong in My Life; It Feels So Good, to Be Loved So Bad; Love at First Sight; There's No Good in Goodbye; One Night Affair.

JUAREZ, SAVERIA IRMA ASCAP 1976
composer, author, singer
b Dugenta, Italy, Apr 8, 30. Educ: High sch, 4 yrs; col, 2 yrs. Began singing prof in Hawaii, 75; produced first album as performing artist, 75; comp lyrics & music, producer, recording artist & distributor; own music has been played on Italian & Am passenger ships, in-flight airlines, movie houses & local radio stas in Hawaii. *Songs:* My Magic Stars; Ho, Ho, Sailor Boy; Kailua by the Sea; In Blue, Golden Hawaii; I Borrow My Days; The Islands and This Magic Green; Chi Chi Chi; Good Morning World; Once More; In the Sky, There's a Cloud; Hawaii, Hawaii, Hawaii; It's Happened to Me; Angel Where Are You?; My Heart Burns With Love; Tomorrow, Tomorrow; My Kamani Tree; The Moon Is A-Shinin'; Quando La Luna Brilla (Top Ten Quarter Finalist, Am Song Fest/Int Song Writers Competition, 77; Panel Popular Song Award, ASCAP, 79); Song of the Sea; Domani, Domani, Domani; It Was in Kailua; Every Night and Day; Hauula Way; Here Is the Key to My Heart; Luna Lunatica; Hawaiian Love; Hawaiian Sun Tropical; Love, Love, Love; I Need Love to Be With You; Ti Voglio Bene (I Love You); Free to Fall in Love. *Albums:* Good Morning World; Free to Fall in Love; Here Is the Key to My Heart.

JUEN, JOSEPH P ASCAP 1961
composer, author
b Detroit, Mich, June 15, 02. Educ: High sch. *Songs:* A Heaven for Both of Us; Dreams of Jacqueline.

JUHL, JERRY R
composer, author
b Minn. Educ: San Jose State Univ, BA. Began with Punch and Judy & Puppet Shows, 62, Ed Sullivan Show, 64, Sesame Street, 69; head writer for Muppet Show, England, 80- Co-wrote "The Muppet Movie." Chief Collabr: Jim Hensen. *Scores:* Film/TV: Emmet Otter's Jugband Christmas; The Big Orange Thing.

JULIAN, EDWARD JOSEPH ASCAP 1965
composer, author
b New Rochelle, NY, Jan 8, 18. Educ: Harrison High Sch, NY. With The Les Brown Orch, 38-39, Alvino Rey and the King Sisters, 40-41, Vaughan Monroe Orch, 42-43. Served, USA, World War II. Returned to Vaughan Monroe Orch, 45, with orch until disbanding, 53. Toured with Vincent Travers & orch, Gen Motors Motorama, 6 months. Performer, ocean liner Independence for 2 trips to Europe. Toured with Russ Morgan Orch, 54; joined Bob Ellis Orch in Las Vegas; played major hotels in Las Vegas, 54-71; joined Jack Morgan & Russ Morgan Orch, Dunes Hotel, Las Vegas, 71- *Songs:* Going to Helldorado (off song for annual Helldorado celebration, Las Vegas); Christmas Is the Best Time of the Year; Judy (First Lady of Gambling).

JULIANO, ANTHONY RAYMOND, JR ASCAP 1977
composer, author, singer
b Philadelphia, Pa, July 31, 47. Educ: Upper Darby High Sch, studied vocals & harmony with Clyde R Dengler; Temple Univ, BSEd; studied with vocal coach, Harold Singer, Philadelphia. Vocalist, instrumentalist, comp & author for var record cos, 64-79. Performer, "Jerry Blavat TV Show" & "Ed Hurst TV Show," in Philadelphia at Spectrum, Tower Theatre, Bijou Cafe, Main Point,

Philadelphia Folk Fest, Valley Forge Music Fair, Bottom Line, New York, The Cellar Door, DC, & var clubs, theatres, cols & outdoor fests throughout northeast US & radio shows. Vocalist, instrumentalist, comp, author, arr & producer, radio advert, incl McGovern's campaign theme "Come Home America" & "Regional Campaigns," Ford Motors & Kinney Shoes. Mem, Am Fedn of TV & Radio Artists. Recipient, 2 Clio finalist awards. Chief Collabrs: John Jackson, Chris Darway, Bob Lenti. *Songs:* Pushed Around Too Long; Paradise; Guilty; Alfredo; Wrap Me Up.

JURGENS, DICK HENRY   ASCAP 1941
composer, author, orchestra leader

b Sacramento, Calif, Jan 9, 10. Educ: Marshall Grammar Sch; Sacramento High Sch & Jr Col; Univ Calif, Berkeley, 1 yr. Played Lake Tahoe resorts many yrs beginning 22. Organized own orch, 25. Featured in ballrooms, night clubs, hotels & theaters throughout US; also in films, on radio, TV & commercial shows. Mem first off entertainment unit, USMC, WW II, toured 59 islands in SPac. Featured at Aragon Ballroom, Chicago, 10 yrs & Casino Ballroom, Catalina Island, 5 yrs. Recorded for Columbia Records, over 20 yrs. Chief Collabrs: Elmer Albrecht, Lou Quadling, Eddie Howard, Ronnie Kemper. *Songs & Instrumental Works:* Elmer's Tune; Careless; One Dozen Roses; If I Knew Then (What I Know Now); A Million Dreams Ago; Day Dreams Come True At Night (band theme).

JURMANN, WALTER   ASCAP 1938
composer

b Austria, Oct 12, 03; d. To US, Hollywood, 35, writer, film scores. Chief Collabrs: Bronislaw Kaper, Gus Kahn, Jack Brooks, Serge Walter. *Songs:* All God's Chillun Got Rhythm; Blue Venetian Waters; Tomorrow Is Another Day; You're All I Need; You and the Waltz and I; When I Look at You; Is It Really Love?; In the Spirit of the Moment; Just for a While; San Francisco; Someone to Care for Me. *Scores:* Films: Three Smart Girls; Escapade; Mutiny on the Bounty; A Day at the Races; Presenting Lily Mars.

K

KAAPUNI, SAMUEL KEANINI   ASCAP 1961
composer, author, guitarist

b Kamuela, Hawaii, Nov 2, 15; d Santa Monica, Calif, Dec 17, 68. Educ: Univ Hawaii, music & art major; communication courses while in the Army. Began career as guitarist & arr with Royal Hawaiian Hotel Orch. Capt, Inf, WW II. Joined Dan Stewart's Hawaiian group, 45; later formed group, Sam K's Polynesians. Comp & arr, motion pictures, TV & record albums. Scored dances for film, "Gidget Goes Hawaiian"; also scored many musical arr for Webly Edward's radio show. Chief Collabrs: Gerda, Dan Stewart, William Loose. *Songs:* Ualani; Island Moon; Kou Kino Mambo; Farewell and Aloha; Music: There Is Still a Lot of Steam in Kilauea. Ualani.

KABAK, MILTON   ASCAP 1950
composer, author, teacher

b New York, NY, Mar 9, 26. Educ: Manhattan Sch Music, BMus; Columbia Univ Teachers Col, MA. Trombonist & arr, Louis Prima & Stan Kenton Orchs; band dir, Westlake High Sch, 52- Chief Collabrs: Louis Prima, Joe Riccitelli & Irving Joseph. *Songs:* Oh Babe!; Yeah, Yeah, Yeah; An Old Fashioned Picture; Angelina Zooma Zooma; And No One Knows.

KACHER, DEL   ASCAP 1967
composer

b East Chicago, Ind, Dec 28, 37. Educ: Univ Pittsburgh; Ind Univ. Performed as guitarist with Three Suns, Ray Coniff Orch; movies, "Roustabout" & "The Patsy." Produced NBC theme, Los Angeles. Sacred music for playons in "Chico and the Man." Music dir, "Our Town" TV Show. *Instrumental Works:* Lady in the Night; After the Affair.

KADISON, PHILIP   ASCAP 1945
composer, author

b New York, NY, Dec 1, 19. Educ: Harvard Univ, 41; Juilliard Sch, summer session, studied with Ferde Grofe. Coauthor, first musical comedy telecast "A Nice Place to Visit." Writer, music & lyrics, TV prog "Show of Shows." Writer, cartoon stories, music & lyrics, "Captain Kangaroo Show." Chief Collabr: Thomas B Howell. *Songs:* Music: A Trout, No Doubt; A Trip Doesn't Care At All.

KAECK, ALEXANDER PAKI   ASCAP 1960
composer, conductor, arranger

b Honolulu, Hawaii, July 12, 26; d Los Angeles, Calif, Dec 7, 71. Educ: High sch. Led own group. Arr for vocal group, The Invitations, also for Poncie Ponce & Lani Kai. Chief Collabr: Kui Lee. *Songs:* We Have a Date (Andy Williams TV theme); Wake Me When It's Over; Little Island; Kuu Aina; Oceans Away; Keanani; Just for Tears; Six Men.

KAHAL, IRVING   ASCAP 1927
author

b Houtzdale, Pa, Mar 5, 03; d New York, NY, Feb 7, 42. Educ: Cooper Union, art scholarship. Singer with Gus Edwards' Minstrels. Wrote songs for films incl, "The Big Pond", "College Coach" & "Dames." Chief Collabr: Sammy Fain. *Songs:* I Left My Sugar Standing in the Rain; Let a Smile Be Your Umbrella; Wedding Bells Are Breaking Up That Old Gang of Mine; You Brought a New Kind of Love to Me; When I Take My Sugar to Tea; By a Waterfall; Ev'ry Day; I Can Dream, Can't I?; I'll Be Seeing You; There Ought to Be a Moonlight Saving Time; The Night Is Young and You're So Beautiful; Such Stuff as Dreams Are Made Of; Hikin' Down the Highway; Don't Look Now. *Scores:* Bway Stage: Everybody's Welcome; Film: Footlight Parade; Sweet Music.

KAHN, BERNARD MAURICE   ASCAP 1959
author

b Brooklyn, NY, Apr 26, 30. Educ: Univ Mich, BA & MA. Chief Collabr: Bebe Starr. *Songs:* Lyrics: Because of My Pride; Gone Gone Gone; A Love for a Love; A Heart Divided; In the Beginning.

KAHN, DAVE   ASCAP 1958
composer, arranger, musician

b Duluth, Minn, Oct 14, 10. Educ: Studied with Ernst Toch & Ernst Krenek. Musician & arr for dance bands, also for films & TV, 45- Comp themes for TV series: "Mike Hammer"; "Leave It to Beaver"; "Restless Gun"; "Bachelor Father"; "Flight."

KAHN, DONALD GUSTAVE   ASCAP 1947
composer, author, arranger

b Chicago, Ill, July 17, 18. Educ: Pomona Col, BA; studied with Mario Castelnuovo-Tedesco, Maurice Zam & Lella Simon. Started as a dance band pianist & arranger. Arr for Jan Savitt & Skitch Henderson. With Gus Kahn Music Co, 52-; writer, "Sesame Street," currently. Chief Collabrs: Stanley Styne, Johnny Mercer, Jack Elliot & Sammy Cahn. *Songs:* Sam's Got Him; Music Makes Your Life More Fun (The Muzak Song); Music: A Beautiful Friendship; A Chip Off the Old Block; The Name's The Same; I Love When It Rains; Nobody Else Ever Could Be You; Single-O; Lay That Rifle Down; Carolina Cannonball. *Instrumental Works:* Dream on a Summer Night.

KAHN, GRACE LEBOY   ASCAP 1930
composer

b Brooklyn, NY, Sept 22, 1890. Educ: High sch; pub sch, Elgin, Ill. Chief Collabr: Gus Kahn. *Songs:* Music: I Wish I Had a Girl; Everybody Rag With Me; Good Ship Mary Ann; Dream a Little Longer; Peace of Mind; and others.

KAHN, GUS   ASCAP 1921
author

b Coblenz, Ger, Nov 6, 1886; d Beverly Hills, Calif, Oct 8, 41. To US 1891. Educ: Chicago pub schs. Wrote spec material for vaudeville acts. Wrote songs for "Sinbad", "Passing Show of 1922" & "Greenwich Village Follies of 1923." Wrote songs for films, incl "One Night of Love", "Three Smart Girls", "Let's Sing Again", "San Francisco" & "Ziegfeld Girl." Film biography, "I'll See You in My Dreams." Dir ASCAP, 27-30. Chief Collabrs: Grace LeBoy Kahn (wife), Egbert Van Alstyne, Richard Whiting, B G DeSylva, Al Jolson, Raymond Egan, Walter Donaldson, Ted Fiorito, Isham Jones, Ernie Erdman, Neil Moret, Vincent Youmans, George Gershwin, Ira Gershwin, Harry Akst, Harry Woods, Edward Eliscu, Victor Schertzinger, Arthur Johnston, Bronislaw Kaper, Walter Jurmann, Sigmund Romberg, Harry Warren. *Songs:* I Wish I Had a Girl; Everybody Rag With Me; Evening; You Gave Me Everything But Love; 'Twas Only a Summer Night's Dream; Think of Me; Memories; I'll Say She Does; Sailing Away on the Henry Clay; Pretty Baby; Some Sunday Morning; Where the Morning Glories Grow; My Isle of Golden Dreams; Ain't We Got Fun?; My Buddy; Carolina in the Morning; Side by Side; Toot, Toot, Tootsie, Goodbye; On the Alamo; Nobody's Sweetheart; Swingin' Down the Lane; No, No, Nora; I'll See You in My Dreams; Charley My Boy; It Had to Be You; The One I Love Belongs to Somebody Else; That Certain Party; Yes, Sir, That's My Baby; I Never Knew; Ukulele Lady; Let's Talk About My Sweetie; Beside a Babbling Brook; Just a Bird's Eye View; Love Me or Leave Me; Your Eyes Have Told Me So; Chloe; Who's That Knockin' at My Door?; Who Am I?; You Tell Me Your Dreams; I'm Bringing a Red Red Rose; Makin' Whoopee; Little Orphan Annie; Beloved; Coquette; Liza; The Waltz You Saved for Me; I'm Through With Love; Goofus; Dream a Little Dream of Me; My Baby Just Cares for Me; Guilty; Lazy Day; A Little Street Where Old Friends Meet; Flying Down to Rio; Music Makes Me; The Carioca; Orchids in the Moonlight; Ha-Cha-Cha; An Earful of Music; One Night of Love; Waitin' at the Gate for Katy; Thanks a Million; I'm Sittin' High on a Hilltop; Someone to Care for Me; I've Got a Heavy Date; Tomorrow Is Another Day; A Message From the Man in the Moon; Blue Venetian Waters; All God's Chillun Got Rhythm; A Love Song of Long Ago; Shadows on the Moon; Who Are We to Say?; Josephine; How Strange; You Stepped Out of a Dream; It's Foolish But It's Fun; When April Sings; Day Dreaming. *Scores:* Bway Stage: Kitty's Kisses; Whoopee; Show Girl; Film: Flying Down to Rio; Kid Millions; Thanks a Million; A Day at the Races; Everybody Sing; The Girl of the Golden West; Spring Parade.

KAHN, MARVIN IRVING　　　　　　　　　　　ASCAP 1950
composer, author, pianist
b Chicago, Ill, Mar 31, 15; d. Educ: Univ Ill, BA; Juilliard Sch Music, BS; Columbia Univ, MA. Pianist on TV & for commercials. Comp, Copacabana shows, New York, 56-60. Cond music workshops & lectured at univs. Teacher with Guy Maier, 4 yrs. Educ consult, M Hohner, Inc. Fac mem & adjudicator, Nat Guild Piano Teachers; mem, Music Teachers Nat Asn. Author, music instr bks incl "The Westmoreland-Kahn Piano Course." Chief Collabrs: Redd Evans, Gladys Shelley. *Songs & Instrumental Works:* Blue December; I Wasn't There With You; Amusement Park Waltz; Take It Easy, Arthur; Ma Chere Amie; Take Me Back Again; You'll Always Be the One for Me; Engagement Waltz.

KAHN, ROGER WOLFE　　　　　　　　　　　ASCAP 1941
composer, conductor
b Morristown, NJ, Oct 19, 07; d New York, NY, July 12, 62. Educ: St Bernard's Prep Sch; pvt music study. Led own orch in New York theatres, nightclubs & hotels, 9 yrs. Toured in vaudeville, 24. In 26, opened band & artist booking office; also operated nightclub, New York, featuring own orch. From 41, test pilot & dir service & production, Grumman Aircraft. Mem: Inst Aeronautical Sci; Nat Aeronautic Asn. Wrote songs for "Americana", "9:15 Revue" & "Vogues of 1924." Chief Collabr: Irving Caesar. *Songs:* Crazy Rhythm; Imagination; Following You Around; All By My Lonesome; Good Time Charlie; I Love You Sincerely; Nobody Loves Me; Life As a Twosome; He's Mine; No Place Like Home. *Scores:* Bway stage: Here's Howe.

KAHN, SHERMAN　　　　　　　　　　　ASCAP 1959
composer, author, musician
b New Haven, Conn, Oct 14, 34. Educ: Yale Univ Music Sch, BM; Teachers Col, Columbia Univ, MA. Musician in dance bands; taught music. *Songs:* You Touch My Hand; Solo a Te; Was I Dreaming.

KAHN, SI　　　　　　　　　　　ASCAP 1974
composer, author, singer
b Boston, Mass, Apr 23, 44. Educ: Harvard Univ, AB, 65. Author & comp of over 300 songs. Comp & lyricist of musicals "If I Live to See Next Fall" & "200 RPM." Fest appearances incl Univ Chicago, Vancouver, Winnipeg, Hudson River, Old Dominion & Wheatlands. *Songs:* Aragon Mill; Gone Gonna Rise Again; Truck Drivin' Woman; People Like You; Sunrise; Brookside Strike; Go to Work on Monday; Black Gold; Blue Ridge Mountain Refugee; Rubber Blubber Whale. *Albums:* New Wood; Home; Doin' My Job.

KAHN, WALTER B　　　　　　　　　　　ASCAP 1973
composer, author
b Philadelphia, Pa, Apr 9, 48. Educ: Temple Univ, BS, 70. Writer, jingles & songs, 65-; disc jockey, WIFI, Pa. Chief Collabr: Julie Carter. *Songs:* Can You Feel It; What Is Everybody Doin'; (I Wanna) Make It With You; Gotta Get Next to You; Tell the Truth; My Way Or Hit the Highway; Couldn't Get on the Plane; Gettin' Back to Nature; Where Do We Go From Here; Flow of Love; Phillies Fever.

KAIN, EDDIE
See Kimmel, Edwin Howard

KAISER, JAMES EDWARD　　　　　　　　　　　ASCAP 1977
composer, singer, saxophonist
b Valentine, Nebr, Feb 20, 44. Educ: Nebr Weleyan Univ, BME, 66; Northwestern Univ, MMus, 68, saxophone studies with Fred Hemke; Ind Univ, DMusA, 80, studied saxophone with Eugene Rousseau; Paris Cons, saxophone studies with Daniel Deffayet. Composer, singer & saxophonist nightclubs & TV; recording artist, Music Tower Records, Nashville. Chief Collabr: Bill Kaiser. *Songs:* Lovin' You, Lovin' You; Thinnin' on Out; I Wanna Be in Tennessee; Nashville, Nashville; Hot Springs Tonight, Deadwood Tomorrow.

KAISER, KURT
composer, arranger, producer
b Dec 17, 33. Educ: Northwestern Univ, BA, MMus. Dir of music & vpres music publ co Word, Inc, Waco, Tex, 59- Arr, producer, cond & comp for sacred recordings with var recording artists throughout US & world. Recording artist with 5 albums; gives religious music concerts. Co-authored folk musicals incl "Tell It Like It Is", "Natural High", "I'm Here, God's Here, Now We Can Start", "God's People" & "Just for You," 79. Chief Collabrs: Ralph Carmichael, Charles F Brown. *Songs:* America the Beautiful; Angels Shall Keep Thee; Are You In Control, Lord; As a Little Child; At the Name of Jesus; Be Joyful; Bow Your Heart; Bring Back the Springtime; Commit Thy Way; Conform; Early in the Morning; From Out Here; Go Now and Live for the Savior; God Loves So Much; The Golden Rule; The Good Old Days; Hallelujah! Jubilee!; He Became What We Are; He Brought New Life to Me; He Careth for You; Hear the Right, Lord; The Heart Is a Rebel; Help Me Care; His Will Our Own; The House of the Lord; Hush, the Baby Is Sleeping; I Am Willing, Lord; I Cannot Hide From God; I Heard About Him; I Will Lift Up My Eyes; I'm All Thumbs; I'm Here, God's Here, Now We Can Start; It Is Finished; It's Our World; Jesus Has Been So Good to Me; Just for You; Let All Things Praise the Lord; Let It Ring, God Is Here Right Now; Let Your Light Shine; Limericks; The Long, Long Trail; The Lord Himself Has Built the Church; The Lord Whom We Love; Lost and Found; Love Is a Simple Thing; Master Designer; The Moment of Truth; My Song for

You; Oh, How He Loves You and Me; Our Father; Pass It On; The Plan of God; (Makes You Wanna Sing) Praise to the Lord; Reach Your Hand; Rosy Tinted Glasses; Rough Old Roads; The Sequence of Events; Sing, O Heaven, and Be Joyful; Softly and Tenderly; Sunday Mornin'; People Team Work; Tell It to Jesus; Thank You, My Lord; That's for Me; That's the Way It Is; This One's for You Precious Savior; To My Son; Too Bad About Ginny; Unto the Hills; Wanted—A Portrait; We're On Our Way; What Are Fathers Made Of; What This World Needs; What's God Like; Where Shall I Run?; Arr: Wooden Cross; Where Could I Go; When the Saints Go Marching In; When I Survey the Wondrous Cross; When I Met the Savior, When I Kneel Down to Pray; What a Friend We Have in Jesus; Wayfaring Stranger; The Way of the Cross; This Is My Father's World; Someday; Robe of Calvary; On My Journey Home; No One Understands Like Jesus; My Heavenly Father Watches Over Me; Marvelous Grace; Love; Love's Answer; The King of Love; Jesus Paid It All; Jesus, I Am Resting; It Means Love; In the Garden; In a Silent World; If Your Heart Keeps Right; I Would Be Like Jesus; I Lay My Sins on Jesus; I Can't Live That Way; How Gentle God's Commands; His Eye Is on the Sparrow; Hey, Little Girl; He Hideth My Soul; Have You Any Room for Jesus; Guide Me, Oh Thou Great Jehovah; Goin' Somewhere; God Is So Wonderful; Fill My Cup, Lord; Farther Along; Don't Go Away Without Jesus; Day Is Dying in the West; Crown Him With Many Crowns; Closer Than a Brother; Church in the Wildwood; Cathedral of Peace; Bring Them In; Blessed Redeemer; Beneath the Cross of Jesus; Abide With Me; A Day Like Today.

KALAJIAN, BERGE　　　　　　　　　　　ASCAP 1968
composer
b West New York, NJ, Jan 29, 24. Educ: Performing Arts High Sch, 40; Manhattan Sch Music, BM, 62. *Instrumental Works:* Sonata (flute & piano); Suite for Piano; Trio for Flute, Viola and Piano. *Songs & Instrumental Works:* Mission Mars Feature; Candy Man Feature.

KALANZI, BENNY　　　　　　　　　　　ASCAP 1973
composer, author, professor
b Villa Maria, Uganda, Aug 10, 38. Educ: Univ Cambridge, Bukalasa Sem, cert, 55; Katigondo Major Sem, MA, studied philosophy, music, theology & pedagogy; Fribourg & Berne Univ, studied musicol, piano, Ger & French, 63-66; Univ Cologne, Doctorate in African Music, musicol & Ger, Marius Schneider, 66-69. First prize, Int Folk Music Contest, Cologne, 67. Prof of African music, Manhattan Community Col, 74- Performer, singer & dancer, TV, radio, cols, museums & others; also musician. CAPS Fellowship for comp of African music in modern notation, 76. ASCAP popular awards for music comp, 77-80. Chief Collabrs: Carlos Garnett, Mauricio Smith, Al Gordon, Ron Freeman. *Songs:* Kasadde Kampeko; Nze Mbalamusa; Muno Muno Omwa Tundu; Sikutendera Bulaya; Wuyo Nankya; Sematimba-Kikwabanga (Potato Song); Kyalema Nakato (Warrior's Song); Ono Si Yegu (Flu); Omusango Gw'ennyama (Song About Food); Omugenyi Agenda (Farewell Song); Mukyala (Good Wife); Bibi Yangu (My Lady); Mafabi (As You Loved Me); Kagutema (The Brewer's Song); Guno Muka (Carousing Song).

KALAPANA, JOHN
See Edwards, Webley Elgin

KALEOLANI, ALVIN
See Isaacs, Alvin Kalanikauikealaneo

KALINICH, STEPHEN JOHN　　　　　　　　　　　ASCAP 1970
composer, author
b Endicott, NY, Jan 18, 42. Educ: Syracuse Univ; Harpur Col; Univ Calif, Los Angeles. Artist-writer, Beach Boys, 67-75; writer, A&M Publ, 75-76; staff writer, Motown, 77-79; writer, 79- Chief Collabrs: Brian Wilson, Dennis Wilson, Roger Nichols, Art Munson, Steve Nelson, Kevin Kaufman. *Songs: Lyrics:* Little Bird; Be Still; Child of Wintcr; Only Your Love Song Last; Rainbows; You Dance My Heart Around the Star; When All the Love Songs Have Been Written; Love Is Just a Touch Away.

KALLMAN, CHESTER SIMON　　　　　　　　　　　ASCAP 1950
author
b Brooklyn, NY, Jan 7, 21; d Athens, Greece, Jan 17, 75. Educ: Brooklyn Col, AB, 41; Univ Mich, Ann Arbor, MA(English), 42. Poet & librettist; author bks verse: "Storm at Castelfranco", "Absent and Present" & "The Sense of Occasion." Rec'd grants from Am Acad Arts & Letters, 55 & Merril Found, 64. Chief Collabr: W H Auden. *Scores:* Opera/Ballet (English transl): The Tuscan Players; Anna Balena; Falstaff; Blaubert; The Coronation of Poppen; The Rake's Progress; Elegy for Young Lovers; The Bassarids; Don Giovanni; Magic Flute; Mahagonny; Seven Deadly Sins.

KALLMAN, HERBERT E　　　　　　　　　　　ASCAP 1960
composer, author
b Worcester, Mass, Oct 20, 12. Educ: Col. Former detergent manufacturer. *Songs:* There's a Valley; A Cry in the Dark; Crossroads; By Grace Alone.

KALMAN, EMMERICH　　　　　　　　　　　ASCAP 1943
composer, conductor
b Siofok, Hungary, Oct 24, 1882; d Paris, France, Oct 30, 53. Educ: Musical Kössler Acad, Budapest, studied with Hans Kössler. Cond, Concertgebouw

Orch; also cond in London, Vienna, Budapest & Copenhagen. Cond own operettas at Kalman Fest, Italy, 36. Moved to US, 40. In US, cond concert of own works with Toscanini NBC Symph, 40. Produced Viennese operettas on Bway: "Ein Herbstmanoever" (The Gay Hussars); "Gold gab ich fur Eisen" (Her Soldier Boy); "Fraeulein Susi" (Miss Springtime); "Der Zigeunerprimas" (Sari); "Die Czardasfuerstin" (The Riviera Girl); "Die Bajadere" (The Yankee Princess); "Die Graefin Mariza" (Countess Mariza); "Die Zirkusprinzessin" (The Circus Princess). Awards: Swedish Nordstar; Great Golden Austrian Cross of Merit; Danish Dannebrog Order; French Legion of Honor; Hungarian Dist Service Cross. Biographies: "Emmerich Kalman," by J Bistron; "Emmerich Kalman," by R Oesterreicher; "Ganz ohne Ungarn geht die Chose nicht!", TV show, Ger, 79. Chief Collabrs: Alfred Gruenwald, Charlotte Cushing, P G Wodehouse, B G DeSylva, Harry B Smith, Otto Harbach, Oscar Hammerstein, 2nd. *Songs:* Just a Little Bid for Sympathy; Throw Me a Rose; Ha-Za-Za; My Faithful Stradivari; Love's Own Sweet Song; Love Has Wings; The Lilt of a Gypsy Strain; Will You Forget?; In the Starlight; I Still Can Dream; The Waltz Is Made for Love; Play Gypsies, Dance Gypsies; Love Has Found My Heart; I'll Keep on Dreaming; The One I'm Looking For; Dear Eyes That Haunt Me; We Two; Sigh By Night; Here in the Dark; The Whip; You're on My Mind Again.

KALMANOFF, MARTIN (MARTY KENWOOD)　　ASCAP 1948
composer, author, pianist

b New York, NY, May 24, 20. Educ: Harvard Univ, BA, cum laude, MA; comp studies with Walter Piston. Over 2000 perf of 42 of his 52 works for the musical theatre, performed in 32 states of US, Can & Europe. Winner of Robert Merrill Contest for Best Opera. Second Prize Winner in Harvey Gaul Contest for Best Opera. Ten operas performed with orch incl two with Detroit Symph. Concert music performed on NBC, CBS & ABC TV & radio networks & in concert. Grants: Rodgers & Hammerstein Found, NY State Coun on the Arts & Am Music Ctr. Wrote word & music for original musical comedy version of "The Fourposter." Writer articles on music, Opera News; writer opera reviews, Show Business. Chief Collabrs: Aaron Schroeder, Lewis Allan, Saroyan, Ionesco, Gertrude Stein, Eric Bentley. *Songs:* Just Say I Love Her; At a Sidewalk Penny Arcade; The Big Bell and the Little Bell; Young Dreams; First Name Initial; Music: Pictures in the Fire; Brandy Is My True Love's Name; The Lord Is My Shepherd; George Washington Comes to Dinner; Lamento Di Puccini; The Way of Life (cantata for voice & 11 instruments); Kaddish for a Warring World (30 minute work for tenor, baritone, chorus & orch); Sacred Service (voice, chorus & orch; comn by Temple Emanuel). *Scores:* Operas: The Insect Comedy; Opera, Opera; The Bald Prima Donna; Photograph-1920; The Harmfulness of Tobacco; The Victory at Masada; Bway Show: Young Tom Edison.

KALMAR, BERT　　ASCAP 1920
author, publisher

b New York, NY, Feb 16, 1884; d Los Angeles, Calif, Sept 18, 47. Child magician in tent show. Dancer, Kalmar & Brown, Orpheum & Keith Circuit. Comedian & spec material writer in vaudeville. Co-produced Bway show, "Top Speed." Wrote songs for films, incl "Check and Double Check", "The Cuckoos", "Horsefeathers"; wrote songs & screenplay, "The Kid From Spain." Screenplays: "Look for the Silver Lining"; "Bright Lights"; "Duck Soup." Film biography, "Three Little Words." Chief Collabrs: Harry Ruby, Ted Snyder, Oscar Hammerstein, 2nd, Fred Ahlert, Harry Akst, Con Conrad, Herbert Stothart, Harry Tierney, Pete Wendling, Edgar Leslie. *Songs:* Oh, What a Pal Was Mary; All The Quakers Are Shoulder Shakers; Since Maggie Dooley Learned the Hooley Hooley; He Sits Around; So Long, Oo-Long; Take Your Girlie to the Movies; The Sheik of Avenue B; She's Mine, All Mine; The Same Old Moon; The Vamp From East Broadway; My Sunny Tennessee; I Gave You Up Just Before You Threw Me Down; Who's Sorry Now?; It Was Meant to Be; All Alone Monday; Thinking of You; Up in the Clouds; I Wanna Be Loved By You; Watching the Clouds Roll By; Three Little Words; Hooray for Captain Spaulding (Groucho Marx theme); Nevertheless; I Love You So Much; Everyone Say's I Love You; The Egg and I; A Kiss to Build a Dream On; Omaha, Nebraska; Show Me a Rose; also The Kalmar and Ruby Song Book. *Scores:* Bway Stage: Helen of Troy, NY; The Ramblers; Lucky; The Five O'Clock Girl; Good Boy; Animal Crackers; Top Speed; High Kickers.

KAMAE, EDWARD L　　ASCAP 1970
composer, arranger, musician

b Honolulu, Hawaii, Aug 4, 27. Played in many Waikiki nightclubs; featured in concerts in Hawaii & on the mainland; went to the Orient on a cultural exchange. Musical dir films, "Christmas Time With Eddie Kamae and the Sons of Hawaii" (won IRIS Award), "Bring Wood and Build a House" (documentary) & "Hana Ho'olaulea" (documentary). Researcher of traditional Hawaiian music, 11 yrs; developed a unique style of ukulele playing. Pres, Palolo Sunrise, Inc & Hawaii Sons, Inc. Mem, Musicians' Asn Hawaii. Bd dir, Hawaiian Music Found. Rec'd the Living Treasure of Hawaii Award, 79; Eddie Kamae and the Sons of Hawaii were selected by Nat Geographic as best rep of true folk music of Hawaii. *Songs:* I Love Christmas; Alone Once More; No Matter If You're Late; Christmas Long Ago; Dreams; We Have Two of Those; Ke Ala A Ka Jeep; Morning Dew; Ka'upulehu; Halepule Ma Ke Kai. *Albums:* This Is Eddie Kamae; Sons of Hawaii (four); Eddie Kamae Presents the Sons of Hawaii (six).

KAMAE, MYRNA
songwriter

b Springville, Utah, Oct 13, 42. Educ: 3 yrs of col, majoring in elem educ. Voter educ coordr & media specialist, Off of Lt Gov, currently. Vpres, Hawaii Sons

Publ Co. Coauth three songs in Christmas spec "Christmas Time With Eddie Kamae and the Sons of Hawaii," which rec'd int recognition in New York Int Film Fest, then won an Iris Award. Chief Collabr: Eddie Kamae (husband). *Songs:* I Love Christmas; Alone Once More; No Matter If You're Late; Christmas Long Ago; Dreams; We Have Two of Those; Sunshine in Between the Rain.

KAMAKAHI, DENNIS DAVID　　ASCAP 1976
composer, singer

b Honolulu, Hawaii, Mar 31, 53. Educ: Kamehameha Sch for Boys High Sch; Leeward Community Col. Singer, entertainer, Hawaiian nightclub. Nani Award, Hawaiian Music Acad, 77. Ordained minister, 78. *Songs:* Pua Hone (Honey Flower); Wahine 'Ilikea (Fair Skin Woman); Christmas Memories; Dear St Nick; Hihiwai; Sweet Weuweu; Hualalai; Golden Stallion; Sweet By and By.

KAMANO, JOHN NAKULA (JOHNNY)　　ASCAP 1947
composer, author, singer

b Honolulu, Hawaii, Aug 24, 04. Educ: Pohukaina & Royal Schs. Musician & band leader, Hollywood Ice Review, Radio, TV, Night Clubs & Vaudeville. Chief Collabrs: Andy Iona Long, Billy Faber, Marvin Kahn, William (Billy) Reid & Pinky Herman. *Songs:* I'm a Lonely Little Petunia (In an Onion Patch); If I Had a Million Dollars; Too Long; Along the Pineapple Trail; Here Comes Santa in a Red Canoe; Hawaiian Nights; Blue Kahana Lullaby.

KAMES, BOB
See Kujawa, Robert V

KAMINSKY, LUCIAN JOHN　　ASCAP 1961
composer, author, producer

b New York, NY, Jan 30, 26. Educ: Dewitt Clinton High Sch; Rutgers Univ, BA; NY Univ, MA. Writer of spec material for films/TV & for Jackie Gleason TV show; produced, wrote & appeared in TV series; independent writer, comp, author, film/TV; producer, writer for instructional TV/films & Multi-Media. Chief Collabrs: Jack Spear, Marvin Marx, Dennis Marks, Jack Winter, Robert Kaminsky, Peter Kaminsky. *Songs:* Pip the Piper (song catalogue).

KANE, BERNIE
See Aquino, Frank Joseph

KANE, PETER T
composer, teacher

b Rockville Center, NY, Nov 11, 42. Educ: Hofstra Univ, BA, MA, MS, studied music with Stefan Wolpe; C W Post Col, Long Island Univ. Played in rock band, ages 15-17 yrs. Grad asst, Hofstra Univ; also lectr. Writer of chamber music & popular music. Teacher music, pub schs. Photographer, Manhattan.

KANNER, JEROME H　　ASCAP 1940
composer, violinist, publisher

b New York, NY, Nov 17, 03. Educ: Columbia Univ Sch of Music, BA, BS; New York Sch of Music & Arts (magna cum laude); Paris Col of Music, MA; London Lyceum, MM (summa cum laude); Berne Inst, PhD; hon MusD, Kenyon Col; hon LHD, Boston Col; studied with Franz Kneisel, Paul Stoeving, Leopold Auer, Edward Kilenyi, Walter Damrosch, Albert Stoessel, Maurice Ravel. Debut, age 8, Carnegie Hall. Concertmaster, var orchs incl NBC Symph, Victor Recording Orch. Asst cond, Victor Herbert concert orch. Concert tours, US & Europe, 10 yrs. Music adv, New York Jr Symph Soc. Writer & dir, film studios; writer, radio & producer, TV. Pres, Top Music, Network Music Publ Cos, Chief Phonograph Record Corp; treasurer, Kanner Music; secy, Spin Phonograph Record Co. Author, "Birth and Growth of Symphony Orchestras", "History of Violin Music", "Practical Treatise on Orchestral Conducting", "Poets and Musicians" & "From Paganini to Heifetz." Awards: Sociedade do Brasil Trophy, Debussy Ribbon (Paris); Verdi Prize, Prix de Rome, Ravel award, Paris. *Songs & Instrumental Works:* Psalm of the Soul; Hazel (Purcell award); Christmas in My Heart; The Black Cat; Pebbles in the Pond; Key to My Heart; Free; Topsy-Turvy Moon; Symphony No 1, 2; Tribute to Kreisler; String Quartet in B; Homage a Debussy; Minute at the Spinet (Gold Medal of Rome); The Rubayat (symph poem); 37 French Concert Songs; Songs of Hope and Regret (Purcell award); Sonnets for Ruth; The Riper Years (choral).

KANTER, NANCY REED　　ASCAP 1953
composer, singer, pianist

b Pittsburgh, Pa, May 29, 28. Educ: Juilliard Sch. Band vocalist with Hal McIntyre, Skitch Henderson & Benny Goodman Sextet European tour, 50. Appeared on daily TV shows incl "Morey Amsterdam Morning Show", "Dinner Date", "Bill Silbert Show"; guest appearances on "Frank Sinatra Show", "Songs for Sale" & "Paul Winchell Show"; harpist. Club date at Le Reuban Bleu, New York. Distinguished Service award, UCP. Chief Collabrs: Bob Hilliard, Moose Charlap, Lee Adams, Jack Murray, Debbie Reynolds. *Songs:* Toodle-Ee-Yoo-Do; The Balboa; The Purtiest Little Tree; Sleepy Little Space Cadet; Buy a Bond (Israel bonds song); Music: Look At Us, We're Walking (Nat Cerebral Palsy Telethon theme); Just a Little Girl; The Apple, Wind and Stream; I Wanna Talk About Texas.

KANTOR, JOSEPH ASCAP 1965
composer, organist, pianist
b New York, NY, Nov 22, 30. Educ: Queens Col, BA(music; hon), 54, studied comp with Karol Rathaus; Columbia Univ, MA, 56, studied comp with Otto Luening. Church & temple organist & choir dir, 56- Pianist/accompanist; flutist. *Songs:* Music: By the Rivers of Babylon (SATB); Entreat Me Not to Leave Thee (SSA); Where Shall My Soul Repose? (SATB); Psalm 121 (SATB); Come Ye to the Lord (SATB). *Instrumental Works:* Woodwind Serenade (flute, oboe, clarinet, bassoon); Dialogue for Flute and Piano.

KAONOHI, DAVID (JOHNNY PINEAPPLE) ASCAP 1962
composer, conductor
b Honolulu, Hawaii. Educ: Ore State Univ; Juilliard Sch Music. Entertained troops at army bases, WW II. Has led band in hotels, nightclubs, theatres, radio & TV. *Songs:* I Hear Hawaii Calling; Ginger Flower; It Happened in Honolulu; Pua Mohala; Klililei; Little Hula Girl; Don't Shake My Cocoanuts.

KAPER, BRONISLAW ASCAP 1902
composer, conductor
b Warsaw, Poland, Feb 5, 02. Educ: Univ & Cons, Warsaw. Wrote concert music, songs & film music in Warsaw, Berlin, Vienna, London & Paris. To Hollywood. Chief Collabrs: Gus Kahn, Paul Francis Webster. *Songs & Instrumental Works:* Someone to Care for Me; You're All I Need; A Message From the Man in the Moon; All God's Chillun Got Rhythm; Follow Me; Tomorrow Is Another Day; Invitation; Somebody Up There Likes Me; Hi Lili, Hi Lo; On Green Dolphin Street; Just for Tonight; The Next Time I Care; Take My Love; San Francisco; Cosi-Cosa; Don't Go Near the Water; I Know, I Know, I Know; The Glass Slipper (concert suite); Bataan (concert suite). *Scores:* Red Badge of Courage; Don't Go Near the Water; Film Song: A Day at the Races; Film Background: Gaslight; Our Vines Have Tender Grapes; The Stranger; Mrs Parkington; Green Dolphin Street; Invitation; Lili (Acad Award, 53); The Glass Slipper; The Swan; Auntie Mame; Green Mansions; Butterfield 8; Somebody Up There Likes Me; Mutiny on the Bounty; The Brothers Karamazov (Laurel Award); Lord Jim; Bway Stage: Polonaise.

KAPLAN, ABRAHAM ASCAP 1975
composer, conductor, professor
b Tel Aviv, Israel, May 5, 31. Educ: Israel Acad, Jerusalem, dipl, 54; Juilliard Sch Music, dipl, 55, PG dipl, 57. Cond, Kol Israel Chorus, radio, 53-54; guest cond, numerous appearances with maj orchs, US & abroad, 59-; founder & cond, The Camerata Singers, New York, 61- Dir choral music, Juilliard Sch Music, 61-77; prof, dir of orch, chorus & opera, Univ Wash, Seattle, 77- *Songs & Instrumental Works:* Glorious (SATB); Arvit Leshabat (Sabbath Evening Service) (SATB); Psalms of Abraham (SSA); 12 Inventions for Piano; 12 Duets for Two Flutes; Encore (Run, Run-arun-a run) (mixed chorus & piano); The Lord's Prayer (mixed chorus & piano); Who Is Like Thee (Mi Chamocha) (mixed chorus & piano).

KAPLAN, ARTHUR WILLIAM ASCAP 1972
composer, author, singer
b Brooklyn, NY, Oct 28, 35. Educ: Lafayette High Sch, New York. Saxophone player with Ralph Flanagan Band, 54; also worked with Tony Tastor & Dick Cantino. Sideman in recording studios, New York, 60's. Writer of spec material for musical theatre, New York, 70's. Chief Collabrs: Bob McAllister, Norman Simon. *Songs:* Music: Harmony; Oh Gee, It's Great to Be a Kid; Bensonhurst Blues; The American Dream; Living Ain't So Easy; Lyrics: Harmonica Boogie.

KAPLAN, ELLIOT ASCAP 1965
composer
b Boston, Mass, July 14, 31. Educ: Yale Univ Music Sch, BMus, 53, MMus, 54, studied comp with Quincy Porter, theory with Paul Hindemith; Cons National de Paris, dipl cond, 57, studied comp with Nadia Boulanger, 55-58. Rec'd Fulbright Scholarship to France, 55. Began comp & recording film music. Comp feature films, short films, documentaries & incidental music to stage plays. Active in TV & film music, Hollywood, 69- Has done ballet adaptation scores for "Joffrey Ballet," 78- Chief Collabrs: Easley Blackwood, Frank Lewin. *Songs:* Music: 6 Etudes for Voice and Piano (songs to E E Cummings poems). *Instrumental Works:* Suite for Woodwind Trio. *Scores:* Opera: Gulliver; Ballet: Suite Saint-Saens; Choura: Concertino; Airs de Ballet; Film/TV: Griff; Banacek; Fantasy Island; Ironside; You Lie So Deep My Love; Bridger; Passages From James Joyce's Finnegans Wake; Food of the Gods; Cry Blood, Apache; The Playground; The Square Root of Zero.

KAPLAN, SHARON LYNNE ASCAP 1970
composer
b Brooklyn, NY, Jan 19, 41. Educ: High sch & col, Brooklyn; studied piano. Chief Collabr: Bob McAllister. *Songs:* Music: Kids Are People, Too; Exercise, Exercise; The Make Up Song.

KAPLAN, SHELDON ZACHARY ASCAP 1956
composer
b Boston, Mass, Nov 15, 11. Educ: Boston Latin Sch, 28; Yale Col, BA(hon), 33; Oxford Univ, BA(jurisprudence), 37, MA, 45; Harvard Law Sch; Univ Paris Sch Law; Dr(honoris causa), San Martin de Porres Univ, Peru, 79. Mem, Yale Glee Club. Practiced law, Boston, Mass, 40-42. Capt, USA, 42-46, served overseas; asst to Legal Adv, US Dept State, 46-49; staff consult, House Foreign Affairs Comt, US Congress, 49-57. Practiced int law, 57- Republican candidate for US Congress, 8th Congressional District, Md, 74. Chief Collabrs: Earl S Shuman, Alden Shuman. *Songs:* Music: Dominique; Run; Red Shutters.

KAPLANE, DARCY ANNE ASCAP 1974
composer, singer, actress
b Stamford, Conn, Aug 9, 54. Educ: Eastside High Sch; Film Actors Workshop, Burbank Studios, 72-73. Appeared, nightclubs & film "Getting It Over With." Does voice-overs & children's records; semifinalist, KSCN vocal contest; Miss Variety Club pageant, 74; Am Song Fest, 77. Mem, Am Guild of Variety Artists. *Songs:* Searching; Rock 'n' Roll Tommy; Parking Meter.

KAPP, DAVID ASCAP 1944
composer, author, record executive
b Chicago, Ill, Aug 7, 04; d New York, NY, Mar 1, 76. Bro of Paul Kapp. Owned music store with bro, Jack Kapp, Chicago, 21-31. Vpres, Decca, New York, 35-52; A&R dir, RCA, 52-53. Founder & pres, Kapp Records, 54-67 when label was sold to MCA. Pioneered idea of recording original casts of Bway musicals. Was instrumental in signing many top recording artists, incl Bing Crosby, Andrew Sisters, Perry Como, Eddie Fisher & Gene Autry. Chief Collabr: Charles Tobias. *Songs:* Should I Be Sorry?; Big Boy Blue; Dance With a Dolly; For the First Time; Just a Prayer Away; 160 Acres; Open the Door, Richard; Far Away; Let's All Sing a Song for Christmas.

KAPP, PAUL (J TUCKER BATSFORD, MULLEN ASCAP 1950
BOYD, RICHARD HARDT)
composer, author, producer
b Chicago, Ill, Aug 5, 07. Educ: Chicago Piano Col, studied piano with Mark Wessel & Franz Pfau; Northwestern Univ, BA, 29. Played prof piano from age 15; worked with Louis Panico Orch in Chicago ballrooms; staff mem, Radio Dept, MCA, 30-33, played piano at Blackhawk Cafe, Chicago; set up own management firm, specializing in radio, 33-38; worked for Consolidated Radio Artists, New York, 38; then worked as personal mgr for musical artists; also went into music publ bus as adj to management; now work for Gen Music Publ Co, Inc; record producer & ed. Chief Collabr: Moe Jaffe (d). *Songs:* Jackson Scott, the Astronaut; You and I Are "We"; These Things Are Known; Oh, You Sweet One; Children's Songs: A Cat Came Fiddling; Cock-a-Doodle-Doo; A Blessing; Arthur Samuel Huntley Hayter.

KAPROFF, DANA ASCAP 1975
composer, conductor, orchestrator
b Los Angeles, Calif, Apr 24, 54. Educ: Univ Calif, Los Angeles; Univ Calif, Berkeley; studied with Paul Chihara, Andrew Imbrie & George Trembley. Started by doing mini series, "Once An Eagle," NBC. Has done many episodic shows, incl "Hawaii Five-O", "Ellery Queen", "Bionic Woman" & "Delvecchio." TV movies, incl "Belle Starr" & "Scared Straight." Theatrical films, incl "The Late, Great Planet Earth", "When a Stranger Calls" & "The Big Red One." Mem, Exec Music Branch, Acad Motion Picture Arts & Sci.

KARANT, ZOEY BRYNA (ZOEY WILSON) ASCAP 1962
composer, author, actress
b Chicago, Ill. Educ: Chicago Art Inst, BFA; studied voice with John Mace & Wally Harper, acting with Stella Adler. Actress & singer, theatre, TV, motion pictures & nightclubs. Chief Collabr: Eddie Leonetti. *Songs:* Boomer's Theme Song; Lyrics: Hey Jennie; New York City Too Far From Tampa Blues; Duffy Moon; Over Seven Theme Song.

KARLIN, FREDERICK JAMES ASCAP 1960
composer, author
b Chicago, Ill, June 16, 36. Educ: Amherst Col, BA(cum laude), 56; studied with William Russo, Rayburn Wright, Tibor Serly. Extensive comp-arr, Radio City Music Hall, Benny Goodman, William Russo & others, New York, 58-68. Began scoring films "Up the Down Staircase", 67 & "The Sterile Cuckoo", 69. Chief Collabrs: Lyrics, Meg Karlin (Tylwyth Kymry), Robb Roger, James Griffin, Norman Gimbel. *Songs:* Music: Come Saturday Morning; For All We Know (4 Oscar nominations, Oscar for Best Song). *Scores:* Film/TV: Westworld; Ike; The Autobiography of Miss Jane Pittman (5 Emmy nominations, Emmy for Best Score); Minstrel Man (Image Award).

KARMEN, STEVE D ASCAP 1969
composer, author
b New York, NY, Jan 31, 37. Creator of music & lyrics for advertising. *Songs:* Advertising Jingles: You've Said It All (Budweiser Beer); That's Incredible (Ford); Sooner or Later You'll Own Generals (General Tire); You're Good for More (Beneficial Finance); Hi Ho Pimlico (Pimlico Racecourse); Hershey Is (Hershey Chocolate Bar); The Burry's Blues (Burrys Cookies); Here Comes the King (Budweiser Beer); Energy for a Strong America (Exxon); Nationwide Is on Your Side (Nationwide Insurance); Weekends Were Made for Michelob (Michelob Beer); also jingles for: The Nevele, King Cola, Jack-in-the-Box, WCBS (radio) New York, Michelob Light, I Love New York, Eureka Vacuum Cleaners & You've Got to Pitch In.

KARP, MICHAEL   ASCAP 1978
composer
b Manhattan, NY, May 7, 52. Educ: Univ Rochester, BA(music comp), studied comp at Eastman Sch Music with Samuel Adler & Warren Benson, orchestration & arr with Rayburn Wright & Joseph Schwautner, cond with Robert DeCormier & Gustave Meier. Composed, arranged & produced music for film, radio & TV. Wrote theme for "You," also commercials. Chief Collabr: Rick Cummins. *Scores:* Film/TV: Olympic Moments; NBC Golf Tournament Themes; ABC Sunday Afternoon Movie Theme.

KARR, ELIZABETH R   ASCAP 1964
author, publisher
b New Haven, Conn, Sept 23, 25. Partner, Realm Records & Rolls Music Co. Chief Collabr: Joe Williams. *Songs:* Look of Love; Loverbug; Ladybug; Hide and Seek; Paris This Spring; The Far Apple.

KARR, HAROLD   ASCAP 1954
composer, pianist
b Philadelphia, Pa, Oct 31, 21; d Philadelphia, Pa, Dec 22, 68. Educ: Temple Univ, DDS; Philadelphia Musical Acad; studied piano with David Sokoloff & Leo Ornstein. Appeared on Horn & Hardart children's prog, radio; became professional pianist in dance orchs. Has written spec material for Lena Horne & Delores Gray, also for nightclub, hotel revues & TV. Wrote songs for "New Faces of 1956." Chief Collabr: Matt Dubey. *Songs:* Mutual Admiration Society; New Fangled Tango; If'n; This Is What I Call Love; Just Another Guy; The Game of Love; The Greatest Invention; How You Say It?; I'd Do Anything; Where Did He Go?; Here Today and Gone Tomorrow Love; The Song of the Sewer; How Does the Wine Taste?. *Scores:* Stage: Happy Hunting (Bway); After Hours (nightclub).

KASHA, AL   ASCAP 1972
composer, author, librettist
b Brooklyn, NY, Jan 22, 37. Educ: NY Univ, BS(Eng), 58. Songwriter; 13 Gold Records. A&R dir, producer, CBS Records, 69. Wrote songs for films: "The Cheyenne Social Club"; "The Grasshopper"; "The April Fools"; "Freaky Friday"; "Speedway"; "The North Avenue Irregulars"; "Hot Lead and Cold Feet." Adapted musical stage version, "Seven Brides for Seven Brothers" & Bway musical, "David Copperfield." Co-auth bk, "If They Ask You, You Can Write a Song." Has done continuing column for Songwriters Mag, 3 yrs. Judge for Am Song Fest. Chief Collabrs: Joel Hirschhorn, Charles Aznavour. *Songs:* There's Room for Everyone (UN theme honoring UNICEF); The Morning After (Acad Award & Golden Globe Award nomination); Candle on the Water (Acad Award & Golden Globe Award nomination); We May Never Love Like This Again (Acad Award, Golden Globe nomination); Will You Be Staying After Sunday?; Don't Wake Me Up in the Morning, Michael; Your Time Hasn't Come Yet, Baby; Wake Up; The Old-Fashioned Way; Show Time; Let's Start All Over Again; Irresistable You; One More Mountain to Climb; My Empty Arms; I Stand Accused; Stay and Love Me All Summer; A, My Name Is Alice; Sweet September; I'd Like to Be You for a Day (Golden Globe nomination); Mickey Mouse Birthday Song; I Have Lived. *Scores:* Films: Pete's Dragon (2 Acad Award nominations).

KASHA, PHYLLIS L (LORRAINE PHILLIPS)   ASCAP 1963
author
b New York, NY. Educ: City Univ New York, BA. Composer, 62-75; casting dir TV, motion pictures & theater, 75-80. *Songs:* Lyrics: Sweet September.

KASHANSKI, RICHARD PAUL   ASCAP 1975
composer, musician
b New London, Conn, Feb 2, 47. Educ: New Eng Cons of Music, BA(perc). With Boston Espanade Orch & Honolulu Symph; comp, Honolulu Theatre for Youth. *Instrumental Works:* Etude in Rock; Collage "A Tribute to American Indians." *Scores:* Ballet: Koi; Last Unicorn.

KASS, GERALD H   ASCAP 1967
composer, teacher, pianist
b Staten Island, NY, Aug 10, 43. Educ: Calif State Univ, Northridge, BA; studied composing & musicol with George Skapski, Gregory Stone & Aurelio de la Vega, accordion with Jerry Cigler, Vivian Coffman, Anthony Galla Rini, Frank Marocco & Gregory Stone, piano with Martin Canin, Daniel Pollack, William Richards, Adrian Ruiz & Gregory Stone. Elem teacher & music engraver. Involved in esoteric audio equipment field. Ed of Neofonic Music & Recording Co & Portative Publ. Performer participate in Eduardo Delgado's Los Angeles Master Class, 75.

KASSEL, ART   ASCAP 1930
composer, author, conductor
b Chicago, Ill, Jan 18, 1896; d Van Nuys, Calif, Feb 3, 65. Educ: High sch; Chicago Art Inst. WW I, overseas. Organized band, 24; appeared on radio, 27-50. Reformed orch, 60; appeared on TV & Myron's Ballroom, Los Angeles. Singer & saxophonist. Chief Collabrs: Gus Kahn, Mack David, Irving Caesar, Sammy Gallop. *Songs:* Doodle Do Do; Hells Bells; Around the Corner; Silvery Moonlight; Sobbin' Blues; Don't Let Julia Foolya; Chant of the Swamp; Beautiful One; Golden Wedding Day; The Guy Needs a Gal; You Ain't Got No Romance; You Never Say Yes, You Never Say No; Bundle of Blue; In 1933 (off

Chicago World's Fair song); I'm Thinking of My Darling; I've Got a Locket for My Pocket; Little Leaguer (off Little League song); Ship That Never Sailed.

KASSIN, ARTHUR ROBERT   ASCAP 1953
author
b New York, NY, Nov 13, 17. Educ: Brooklyn Col, BA. Writer, articles & verse for mags. Worked on ships, 34-39. *Songs:* Dynamite in Blue Dungarees; Square Wheels; Tell It to the Jury; Where Were You Last Night; My Tears; Station G-O-D; Say You Love Me; Softly.

KASTLE, LEONARD   ASCAP 1956
composer, author
b New York, NY, Feb 11, 29. Educ: Curtis Inst, studied with Isabelle Vengerova, Rosario Scalero & Gian Carlo Menotti. *Scores:* Opera: Deseret; The Swing; Pariaha (Deerfield Found comn); Whale Songs from Moby Dick (Intercol Musical Council Barter prize).

KATZ, BENJAMIN (BENNY KAYE)   ASCAP 1963
composer, author, singer
b New York, NY, Dec 5, 15. Educ: Brooklyn Cons Music. Sang at Carnegie Hall at age 12, under the baton of Walter Damrough and his symph orch. Singer, nightclubs, supper clubs. Chief Collabr: Sally Moss. *Songs:* The Long Hard Road; I've Got a Feeling I Could Fall for You; Blood and Guts Patton; My Heart Is Not a Plaything; This World, But Once; Coney Island; I Wasted My Love on You; What Good Is Alimony; Mister Spike.

KATZ, FRED   ASCAP 1955
composer, conductor, teacher
b Brooklyn, NY, Feb 25, 19. Won scholarships & fels in cello & piano. Music dir, 7th Army Headquarters, also for Lena Horne, Mindy Carson, Vic Damone & Frankie Laine. Cellist & comp, Chico Hamilton Quintet. A&R dir, Decca Records. Wrote for films & TV. Prof ethnic music, Univ San Fernando. *Songs & Instrumental Works:* Cello Concerto No 1; Viola Sonata; To Paul Klee (No 1 and 2); Adagio (string quintet); Madrigal (choir, cello); Prelude to a Jazz Poet (piano); Lord Randall (quintet); Clarinet Rhapsody; Blues for Piatigorsky (cello, piano); Violin and Cello Duet; Word Jazz; Son of Word Jazz; Satan Wears a Satin Gown; Toy That Never Was; Pastorale; The Moment of Truth. *Scores:* Stage: First Born.

KATZ, MORTON   ASCAP 1976
composer, author
b Pittsburgh, Pa, Apr 13, 25. Educ: Wrote & studied with Arthur Mancini. Mem, Acad Country Music. Started Eagle Rock Music Co, 76. Chief Collabr: Don Borzage. *Songs:* Carter for President (campaign song); 1980 Lady; We're the Young Ones (First Youth & Film Award Show); Baby, Get Your House in Order; Something Deep Inside Me; The Baby Shower.

KATZ, REUBEN   ASCAP 1975
composer
b Pittsburgh, Pa, July 29, 16. Educ: Peabody High Sch. Mem, Acad Country Music, Hollywood, Calif. Chief Collabr: Morton Katz (bro). *Songs:* Carter for President (of the USA); Lyrics: The United States Army is Grand; Carter-Begin-Sadat and Me; You're Good Luck to Me.

KATZ, WILLIAM   ASCAP 1952
composer, author
b New York, NY, Sept 11, 26. Chief Collabr: Ruth Roberts. *Songs:* It's a Beautiful Day for a Ball Game; Mr Touchdown, USA; Meet the Mets.

KAUER, GUENTHER MAX (GENE)   ASCAP 1961
composer
b Weida, Ger, July 30, 21. Educ: Studied comp, music history, piano, French horn & violin with Dr Bruck, music sch, Buckeburg, Ger, 6 yrs. Bandleader & arr, radio & nightclubs. Chief Collabr: Douglas Lackey. *Songs:* Music: Life; Summer Dream; The Sounds of Love; Snow Flakes. *Instrumental Works:* Concerto for Horn and Orchestra; Horn Quartet; 5 Pieces for Woodwinds; Symphonia—Septet (4 bassoons, violin, cello, piano). *Scores:* Bway Show: The Fan Tan King; Film/TV: Faces of Death; Wilderness Family No 1 and No 2; Across the Great Divide; Brother of the Wind; The Great American Wilderness.

KAUFMAN, ALVIN S   ASCAP 1938
composer, author
b Wilkes-Barre, Pa; d. Educ: St Thomas Prep. Writer, special material for Georgie Price, Rubinoff & Maurice Chevalier. Co-comp, first Radio City Music Hall stage production. Chief Collabrs: Marty Symes, Sol Marcus, Edward Seiler, Irving Gordon, Mann Curtis, Richard Himber. *Songs:* How Many Hearts Have You Broken?; Me, Myself and I; Moments in the Moonlight; Heartbreak Hill; Ever So Often, Baby; Secretly; A Wonderful Winter; May the Angels Be With You; And Then It's Heaven; I'm Gonna Make Believe; A Little Love; Ask Anyone Who Knows; Heart of Stone; Romance Still Lives in Paris; You Can't Hide Your Heart; Somehow Days Go By; Ah Dee Ah Dee Ah!; The Outside World; It All Begins and Ends With You. *Scores:* Stage: Belmont Varieties.

KAUFMAN, BILL MYRON (BILLY KAY)　　ASCAP 1963
composer, author, singer
b Cleveland, Ohio, Dec 30, 30. Educ: Pvt tutoring on trumpet 20 yrs; Los Angeles City Col, 2 yrs. Worked in show business, Los Vegas, 20 yrs. Chief Collabrs: Stan Worth, Robert Atillas. *Songs:* Ver Vase; Lyrics: Beauty Is Just Skin Deep; Ring That Bell; Cup 'O Tea.

KAUFMAN, MARTIN ELLIS (WHITEY)　　ASCAP 1961
composer, author, conductor
b Lebanon, Pa, Sept 5, 1899. Educ: Lebanon Valley Col. Toured with own orch. Mgr, Hotel Kaufman, Lebanon, Pa. *Songs:* When Sweet Susie Goes Steppin' By; Louisiana Lullabies; My Girl; Hurry Back Sweetheart of Mine.

KAUFMAN, MEL B　　ASCAP 1924
composer
b Newark, NJ, Apr 23, 1879; d New York, NY, Feb 21, 32. *Songs & Instrumental Works:* Meow; More Candy; Bing Bing; Stop It; Play Ball; Step With Pep; Taxi; Shoot; Happy Go Lucky; also many more.

KAUFMAN, MORRIS (PIUTE PETE)　　ASCAP 1978
author, square dance caller
b New York, NY, Mar 14, 11. Educ: Coop Recreation Sch, New York; NY Univ, recreation sem; Mass State Col, scholarship. Square dance caller, Village Barn, New York, 50's & CBS "Around the Corner," 70's. Author "Piute Pete's Down Home Square Dance Book."

KAUFMAN, PAUL　　ASCAP 1970
composer, author, piano teacher
b Brooklyn, NY, Jan 27, 36. Educ: James Madison High Sch; Brooklyn Col, BA, 59. Song writer, recording artist, Dimension Records. Prof mgr, Premier Publ Co & Rabbits Foot Music. Record producer & singer. Chief Collabrs: Mike Anthony, Jerry Harris, Howard Greenfield. *Songs:* There's No Living Without Your Lovin'; My Town, My Guy and Me; At the Edge of Tears; When the World Was Beautiful; My First and Only Lover; Music: Poetry in Motion; Trouble in My Arms.

KAUKE, HELEN LUCAS　　ASCAP 1977
composer, author
b Needles, Calif, May 21, 26. Educ: Pvt violin instr; high sch grad; self-taught, piano & organ. Church pianist & organist from age 15; comp. *Songs:* Americans!; 200 Percent!; I'm Simply Not a Candidate!; I "N" Double "E" Need Needles!; There Was a Man!

KAY, BILLY
See Kaufman, Bill Myron

KAY, DEAN
See Thompson, Dean K

KAY, EDWARD J　　ASCAP 1946
composer, conductor
b Brooklyn, NY, Nov 27, 1898; d Los Angeles, Calif, Dec 22, 73. Educ: Col of Dental, Oral Surgery, NY; pvt music study. Cond, vaudeville musicals & operettas & arr for radio. Songwriter for films "Under Arizona Skies" & "Alaska." Chief Collabrs: Louis Herscher, Eddie Maxwell. *Songs:* Tahiti Sweetie; Forget If You Can. *Scores:* Films: Sunbonnet Sue; Swing Parade of 1946; Lady, Let's Dance; Klondike Fury; Lure of the Islands.

KAY, HERSHY　　ASCAP 1955
composer, arranger, orchestrator
b Philadelphia, Pa, Nov 17, 19. Educ: Curtis Inst Music scholarship. Arr for concert artists, films, TV & nightclub acts. *Instrumental Works:* Deck the Halls; Joy to the World; Pat a Pan; From the East. *Scores:* Opera/Ballet: L'Inconnue; Who Cares; Union Fair; Grand Tour; The Clowns; Winters Court; Meadowlark; Bway Shows: Evila; Chorusline; 1600 Pennsylvania Avenue; Carmelina; On the Twentieth Century; Music Is; Candide (2nd production); Film/TV: Bite the Bullet.

KAY, JULIAN　　ASCAP 1942
author
b Elizabeth, NJ, Jan 16, 10; d Van Nuys, Calif, May 1, 75. Educ: High sch. Staff writer, music publ co. Music & talent advisor for radio. *Songs:* When the Circus Came to Town; Dear, Dear, What Can the Matter Be?; The Dum Dot Song (Dye Dut Da Denny in Da Dum Dot or I Put a Penny in the Gum Slot); Ole King Cole; Little Buffalo Bill; Ruby Red Lips and Baby Blue Eyes; Let 'Er Go; Run for the Roundhouse, Nellie, He'll Never Corner You There; 'S Good Enough for Me; Mr Jinx; Prove It; At Last I'm First With You; Happy Cobbler, Manuelo; Listen, Listen; Old Town-Crier; Summer Rhapsody; Money in the Bank; Television; I Lied Because I Didn't Want to Lose You; I'll Get Along Somehow; Call Me Darlin', Do; Don't Break My Heart Again; Hollywood; Jolly Jingle Song; Happy Holiday; Don't Ever Leave Me; Let Freedom Ring; Smile; Nite Beat; Lipstick, Powder 'N Paint; Use Easter Seals; Wunderbar, Wunderschoen; Putadechum; How Do You Mend a Dream; Maybe It's Not Love, But It's Lovely.

KAY, MACK H　　ASCAP 1949
composer, author
b Chicago, Ill, Jan 1, 17. Educ: Crane Jr Col; Henry Street Settlement Music Sch, New York; Hartnett Sch Music, New York, studied music & received 4-yr dipl. First prize, Benny Davis amateur song-writing, 38. Signalman 2nd Class, USN, WW II, NAtlantic Convoys. Mem, Disabled Am Vet. Banker, Irving Trust Co, 51-78. Profiled in Bayside Times, New York, 58 & Irving World, 75. Chief Collabrs: Fred Patrick, Julius Schein, Aaron Schroeder. *Songs:* I'm on a Sit Down Strike for Love; Walking Through Heaven Last Night; Thank Your Lucky Stars and Stripes You Live in the USA; What This Country Needs Is Foo; My Pony's Hair Turned Grey; Good-Bye Dear, I'll Be Back in a Year; On Accounta Because I Love You; The Wrong Party Again; Disappointed; Lover Come What May; Under the Tonto Rim; Down in Brown County (IND); Music: Please, Louise; I'll Always Thank You for the Sunshine; The Heart of Paree Is a Song; Lyrics: One Raindrop Doesn't Make a Shower; Provenza By the Sea; Ten Swedes; Nothin's Too Good for My Baby; Someday Soon.

KAYATTA, GEORGE N　　ASCAP 1970
composer, author
b Brooklyn, NY, Apr 25, 44. *Songs:* Santa Ana Woman; Can't Find No Love; I Listen to the Sky; She Is My Woman; Best You Can; The Good Times Are Comin'; Too Many Petals That Fall; Sleepy Girl; Little World of Once Upon a Time; Wake Up Your Mind; Move On; Hey Girl; Time to Wonder Why; Lady; Good Times; Candle River; Seems So Long; Comin' Back Strong.

KAYDEN, MILDRED　　ASCAP 1957
composer, author, radio commentator
b New York, NY. Educ: Juilliard Sch Music, Preparatory Ctr, dipl; Vassar Col, BA; Radcliffe Col, Harvard Univ, MA, post grad; studied comp with Ernst Krenek, Walter Piston & orch with Don Walker. Instr, Music Dept, Vassar Col; lectr, Scarsdale Adult Sch & Vassar Club of New York for Metrop Opera Benefits. Hostess, WEVD-NY for "Musically Speaking." Wrote music & lyrics for specials "Strangers in the Land"; music & lyrics for film, "The Pumpkin Coach"; music for "Leavin' for the Cities" & "The Procession"; music for theater, "The Riddle of Sheba", "The City Scene", "Exhibition", "Pequod", "Mardi Gras", "The Last Word", "Sepia Star", "Storyville", "Ionescopade" & "Absurdities." Chief Collabrs: Morton Wishengrad, Virginia Mazer, Carl Carmer, Russell Baker, James Broughton, Frank Gagliano, Eugene Ionesco, Ed Bullins, Melvin Van Peebles. *Songs & Instrumental Works:* Piano Sonata; Psalm 121; Call of the Prophet.

KAYE, BARRY L　　ASCAP 1969
composer, author, record producer
b Los Angeles, Calif, Apr 24, 46. Educ: Calif State Univ, Northridge, BA, 68; piano studies with Mr Abbey Fraser, 71-77 & voice with Adele Khoury, 75-77. Record producer, 69-, product released on MCA, 20th Century & Capital Records. Songwriter; finalist, Castlebar Int Song Contest (Ireland), 73. *Songs:* Freedom's Coming; Morning Sunshine; Holding on to a Memory; The Quest; Turn the Page.

KAYE, BENJAMIN M　　ASCAP 1961
author
b New York, NY, Aug 15, 1883; d New York, Mar 25, 70. Educ: Columbia Col; Columbia Law Sch. Sr partner of law firm, Kaye, Scholer, Fierman, Hays & Handler. Author of plays "She Couldn't Say No", "I Want My Wife", "The Curtain Rises" & "On Stage." Chief Collabr: Mana-Zucca.

KAYE, BENNY
See Katz, Benjamin

KAYE, BUDDY　　ASCAP 1941
author, saxophonist, producer
b New York, NY, Jan 3, 18. Educ: James Madison High Sch, Brooklyn; pvt music studies. Saxophonist, clubs & cruises. Recording artist with Buddy Kaye Quintet on MGM Records. Lyricist; publ, Budd Music Corp & Budd Music Ltd, 51- Producer of albums; senior extension teacher, Univ Calif, Los Angeles & Los Angeles Valley Col. Coauthor, "The Gift of Acabar"; author, "The Complete Songwriter" & originator "Method Songwriting." Chief Collabrs: Charles Aznavour, Georges Garvarentz, Jimmy McHugh, Jimmy Van Heusan, Ben Weisman, David Pomerantz. *Songs:* Lyrics: Till the End of Time; Full Moon and Empty Arms; Quiet Nights (Corcovado); A-You're Adorable; Speedy Gonzales; Not As a Stranger; The Treasure of Sierra Madre; Hurry Sundown; Twist Around the Clock; Little Boat (O Barquinho); Change of Habit; I Dream of Jeannie; What You See Is Who I Am; My Address Book; The Uninvited Guest; Cloud of Music; The Old Songs; Little Lulu; Banjo Boy; I'll Close My Eyes; Don't Be a Baby, Baby; This Is No Laughing Matter; In the Middle of Nowhere; A Penny a Kiss, a Penny a Hug; Christmas Alphabet; All Cried Out; Her Little Heart Went to Loveland; Conversation in the Street. *Instrumental Works:* Cross-Wits (theme).

KAYE, FLORENCE　　ASCAP 1953
author
b New York, NY. Writer for Elvis Presley Movies, Everly Bros, Bobby Darin & others. Chief Collabrs: Bernie Baum, Bill Grant. *Songs:* You're the Devil in Disguise; Ask Me; Sound of Your Cry.

KAYE, GERRY
See Klug, Geraldine Dolores

KAYE, JAMES R ASCAP 1957
composer, author, producer
b Green Bay, Wis, Jan 29, 29; d Green Bay, Dec 22, 69. Educ: Univ Wis; Daykarhanova Sch. Founder & dir, Lutheran Church Advent Players. Producer, TV prog "Frontiers of Faith," 61-69. Chief Collabrs: J Russel Robinson, Tony Cabot. *Songs:* Ring of Keys; The Other Woman; Bella Roma; After Six.

KAYE, LEONARD JAY (LINK CROMWELL) ASCAP 1976
composer, author, guitarist
b New York, NY, Dec 27, 46. Educ: Rutgers Univ, BA; NY Univ, MA. Recording artist, 66. Lead guitarist with Patti Smith Group, 71. Chief Collabr: Patti Smith. *Songs:* Music: Free Money; Redondo Beach; 'Til Victory; Rock and Roll Nigger; Ghost Dance; Broken Flag. *Albums:* Crazy Like a Fox.

KAYE, MILTON JAY ASCAP 1960
composer, pianist
b Brooklyn, NY. Educ: City Col New York, BA; Columbia Univ, MA; NY Univ, EdD; Juilliard Grad Sch Music. Comp over 60 songs for Silver Burdette series, "Music for Living." Comp & musical dir, children's prog, "Rootie Kazootie"; also "Concentration." Comp, 7 scores for musical theatre & numerous pop songs. Piano soloist, NY Philh & Philadelphia Symph. Accompanist to Jascha Heifetz. Did ballet, "Legs of Lamb." Chief Collabrs: Edward Heymann, Edward Eliscu, Michael Brown, Gladys Shelley. *Songs:* Music: My, My, How Time Goes By; Cuernavaca; I'm Holding on to My Love. *Instrumental Works:* A La Mode; Your Ticket to Jazz. *Scores:* Camera 3.

KAYE, NORMAN
See Knowles, Norman George

KAYE, RONNIE ASCAP 1976
writer
b New York, NY, June 9, 54. Talent agent, William Morris Agency. Co-writer of the TV show "Crosswits." Working in TV prod, 4 yrs.

KAYE, SAMMY ASCAP 1964
composer, author
b Lakewood, Ohio, Mar 13, 10. Educ: Rocky River High Sch; Ohio Univ, BS(civil eng). With col band, 33. Engagements, Bill Green's Casino, Pittsburgh, Pa & Pt Pleasant, NJ. With Tommy Dorsey, Commodore Hotel, 38. Played in major hotels incl: Essex House, Waldorf, Pennsylvania, Hotel Astor Roof, New Yorker. Recording artist, RCA, Columbia & MCA Records. Made two movies, "Iceland" & "Song of the Open Road." On commercial radio & TV shows, "Sunday Serenade," NBC, "So You Want to Lead a Band," ABC & CBS & "Music from Manhattan," ABC. Chief Collabrs: Mitchell Parish, Sunny Skylar. *Songs:* Sammy Kaye Theme; Remember Pearl Harbor; Wanderin; Until Tomorrow; Hawaiian Sunset; You; Music: Moondust.

KAYE, WILLIAM ASCAP 1955
author
b New York, NY, July 7, 17. Educ: Col. WW II, USA. Wrote & produced operas for children for Classic Records, Inc. Librettist, children's records. Wrote songs for "Huckleberry Hound" & "Popeye the Sailor Man," Golden Records. Wrote bk & lyrics for "Pimpernel" (off-Bway). Chief Collabr: Irving Schlein. *Songs:* Gotta See a Dream About a Girl; Hawaiian Sunset. *Scores:* A Child's Introduction to Outer Space; The Ticket (opera); Blue Grass (stage); Eng translations: Le Mariage Aux Lanternes (Offenbach); Der Apotheker (Haydn).

KAYLIN, SAMUEL
composer, director, violinist
b Melitople, Russia, Jan 18, 1892. Educ: Studied with Morton Mason, Ignaz Zemlinski, Arnold Schoenberg; hon DMus, London Inst for Applied Research. Violin prodigy, ages 9-17. Professional 'cellist, ages 17-21. Cond, silent motion pictures, 21-29; comp & musical dir, 20th Century-Fox Studios, 29-41. Comp of over 40 serious works for orch, chamber ens, piano, voice, violin & 'cello, 41-79. *Songs:* Music: Christ and Christmas (voice, piano); Twenty-third Psalm (voice, piano); The Lord's Prayer (voice, piano). *Instrumental Works:* Symphonic Fantasy on Stars and Stripes Forever (Sousa); Fugue Four (orch); Violin Suite; Zingareska (violin, piano).

KAZ, ERIC JUSTIN ASCAP 1974
composer, author, singer
b New York, NY, Jan 21, 46. Songwriter, var artists incl Linda Ronstadt, Bonnie Raitt, Anne Murray, Joan Baez, Tracy Nelson, Rita Coolidge. Solo recording artist, 72-74, with group American Flyer, 75-76 & duo with Craig Fuller, 78. Chief Collabrs: Tom Snow, Craig Fuller. *Songs:* Love Has No Pride; Blowing Away; When You Come Home; I'll Always Love You; Gamblin' Man; Cry Like a Rainstorm. *Scores:* Films: Hi Mom; Greetings.

KAZ, JOHN PETER ASCAP 1978
composer, author
b New York, NY, Aug 6, 28. Educ: NY Univ; Ohio Univ. *Songs:* Loving Caring Heart; My Shiny Rocket Machine.

KEAN, EDWARD GEORGE ASCAP 1956
composer, author, pianist
b New York, NY, Oct 28, 24. Educ: Franklin Sch, New York, grad, 41; Cornell Univ Midshipman Sch, grad, 43; Columbia Col, grad, 47. Lt (jg), USNR, 43-46. Co-producer & writer of scripts & songs, "Howdy Doody TV Show," 47-56; writer, "Gabby Hayes TV Show," "Super Circus TV" & "Going Places," jingles for Quaker Oats, Mars Candy & Int Show. Merchandising for Jackie Gleason & Lassie. Stockbroker, Wall St, 56-70. Publ relations & advert exec with Woody Kepner Assoc, Miami, Fla, 70- Writer, commercials & jingles; pianist, Miami Beach hotels. Chief Collabr: Buffalo Bob Smith. *Songs:* Where Is Sam; Don't Eat Me; It's Howdy Doody Time; Animal Song; Be Kind to Animals; Brush Your Teeth; Clarabell Song; Do Do a Howdy Doody Do; The Friend Song; Goodbye Song; A Howdy Doody Christmas; Hurray for Santa Claus; Howdy Doody for President; Howdy Doody One Man Band; I'm For Howdy Doody; It's a Howdy Doody World; Laugh and Be Happy; Meatballs and Spaghetti; Please, Thanks, Yes; Popcorn Song; Yell Howdy Doody; Toy Piano Song; Your Face May Not Be Handsome.

KEATING, JOHN HENRY (LYN UDALL) ASCAP 1942
composer
b Council Bluffs, Iowa, Feb 4, 1870; d Downey, Calif, Dec 5, 63. Educ: Notre Dame Univ & Cons. *Songs:* I Love to See My Poor Old Mother Work; Just As the Sun Went Down; Just One Girl; Stay in Your Own Back Yard; Zizzy Zee Zum Zum.

KEATS, DONALD H(OWARD) ASCAP 1964
composer, teacher, pianist
b New York, NY, May 27, 29. Educ: Manhattan Sch Music; Yale Univ Sch Music, MusB, 49, comp & theory studies with Quincy Porter & Paul Hindemith; Columbia Univ, MA(comp), 51, studied with Otto Luening, Douglas Moore, Henry Cowell & Jack Beeson; Staatliche Hochschule für Musik, Hamburg, Ger, comp studies with Philipp Jarnach, 54-56; Univ Minn, PhD(comp), 62, studied with Paul Fetler & Dominick Argento. US Army service, 52-54; Fulbright Scholar in music-comp, 54-56; from asst prof to prof & chmn dept music, Antioch Col, 57-75; Guggenheim Fel music-comp, 64-65 & 72-73; vis prof music, Sch Music, Univ Wash, 69-70; vis prof, Lamont Sch Music, Univ Denver, formerly, prof music & composer-in-residence, 75-; participated in concerts as pianist, London, Tel Aviv, Jerusalem & New York. *Songs:* Music: A Love Triptych; Tierras del Alma; The Hollow Men (chorus & instruments). *Instrumental Works:* Polarities (violin & piano); Dialogue (piano & winds); Diptych (cello & piano); Branchings (orch); Musica Instrumentalis (9 instruments); two symphonies; two string quartets; piano sonata; theme & variations for piano; concert piece for orchestra.

KECHLEY, DAVID STEVENSON ASCAP 1978
composer, bassist, teacher
b Seattle, Wash, Mar 16, 47. Educ: Univ Wash, BA, BMus, 70, MM(comp), 74; Cleveland Inst of Music, DMA(comp), 79. Works performed by var orchs throughout US. Asst prof, Univ NC. Recipient, John Simon Guggenheim Mem Found award, 78, NEA, 76 & 79, Opus 1 Chamber Orch Ohio comp contest winner. *Songs:* Music: Five Ancient Lyrics on Poems By Sappho (soprano, harp, strings). *Instrumental Works:* Lightning Images (orch); Concerto for Violin and Strings; Fanfares and Reflections (winds, perc); The Funky Chicken (string orch).

KECHLEY, GERALD ASCAP 1959
composer, professor
b Seattle, Wash, Mar 18, 19. Educ: Univ Wash, BA, 46, MA, 50, studied music comp under George F McKay; spec studies with Aaron Copland. Mem fac, Univ Mich; dir music, Centralia Jr Col; mem fac, Sch Music, Univ Wash, 53-67, prof theory & comp, 67-, asst dir, Collegium Musicum & Madrigal Singers, 77-79, dir, 79-; rec'd Guggenheim fels. Chief Collabrs: Librettists, Elwyn Kechley, Ralph Rosinbum. *Songs:* Music: Three Choruses from "The Golden Lion"; Sing No Sad Songs; In the Lonely Midnight; Pleasure It Is; Res Miranda. *Instrumental Works:* Antiphony for Winds; Suite for Concert Band; Variants; Piano Trio (comn by Eastern Wash Historical Soc); March Incognito. *Songs & Instrumental Works:* Daedalus and the Minotaur (comn by Seattle Symph Orch & George Gershwin Mem Found); For Men Yet Unborn (comn by Univ Portland); First Symphony (comn by Seattle Women's Symph); Drop, Slow Tears; Carol of the Birds; Psalm 150 (comn by St Mary's Sem, Baltimore, Md); The Dwelling of Youth (comn by Wash Music Educr Asn); Suite for Brass and Percussion; Cantata for St Cecilia's Day. *Scores:* Opera: The Golden Lion.

KEDEN, JOE ASCAP 1952
composer, pianist, arranger
b Long Island, NY, Aug 10, 1898. Educ: Virgil Cons New York. Began musical career as a piano player with own orch, Weber's Hotel, Coney Island, 15, played in New York area with own orch, 20's. Staff writer with Waterson, Berlin & Synder, later with Shapiro & Bernstein, 20's. Pioneer in radio, appeared on all radio stations in New York as Keden on the Keys; regular on Bernarr MacFadden's radio prog "Early Bird Exercises" on WOR. Appeared with Helen Kane on nat radio broadcasts, incl shows such as Ed Sullivan, Gem Razor, White Owl Cigar & Nestles, 30's. Appeared with Graham McNamee on first radio show with live studio audience. Accompanist & arr with Helen Kane in all her Nat & Can theatre tours, radio shows, Hollywood films & Victor recordings,

30's. Made many piano rolls for Connorized. Chief Collabrs: Abner Silver, Sam Coslow, Billy Noll, Art Boehn. *Songs:* Music: Pass the Sugar; I'd Go Barefoot All Winter Long; Pipe the Piper; I Don't Wanna Be Loved By Anyone But You. *Instrumental Works:* Tipsy Topsy; The Brownies Frolic; Mousie in the Piano; Off the Elbow; Exquisite.

KEEGAN, JAMES MAGNER, JR (SKY)　　ASCAP 1975
composer, author
b New York, NY, July 24, 50. Educ: Robert E Lee High Sch, Houston, Tex. Joined as a songwriter, Claridge Music Inc, 75, became producer, 79; rep on Nat R & B Charts, 77, 78 & 80. *Songs:* Rock Your Box (Wanna Rock Your Radio); 42nd Street; Steal the Night; That's the Way the Wind Blows; Blue Vibrations.

KEENE, KAHN　　ASCAP 1942
composer, author, trombonist
b Cotton Plant, Ark, Nov 1, 09. Educ: Pub schs, Kans; Wyandotte High, Kans, 28; Univ Kans, 29-31; Horner Cons, Kansas City; pvt music teachers; studied comp & arr with Tom Timothy, NY. With Univ Kans Symph & var name bands, incl New York Roxy Theater Orch. Drafted, 43, joined Glen Miller's Army Air Corps Band. With Roxy Theater Orch, Skitch Henderson & free-lance recording orchs, 46-57. Trombonist, Savannah Symph, Ga, 57, became symph bus mgr & principle trombonist. Resigned, organized own dance orch; leader of Kahn Keene Kwintet & River Street Ramblers, 80- Chief Collabr: Johnny Burke. *Songs:* The Key to My Heart; Throw Your Heart in the Ring; That's What I Like About You; They'll Never Take the Texas Out of Me; Tell Me the Truth; Too Late; Believe in Me; Tell Me; Over the Meadow; Say When; Music: Scatterbrain; Charming Little Faker; Moonlight and You; Over the Hills and Through the Woods; Lyrics: Juke Box Roundelay. *Instrumental Works:* April Fool; I Remember You From Somewhere; Bossa Nova Blues; Hominy Grits.

KEENE, LELA
See Gilbert, Lela

KEENE, ODETTE　　ASCAP 1961
composer, author, vocal coach
b Andrew, Iowa, Sept 11, 1897. Educ: Pvt teachers. Began writing orchestrations for shows at age 13; pianist with concert orch on Chautauqua at age 18; violinist with musical act in vaudeville at age 19, New York; Four Violinettes, Dave Harris Variety Land, orchestrations; in Hollywood, 42- Wrote arr, orchestrations & original material for singers, dancers & others, mostly nightclub performers. *Songs:* So I Said Yes; When This Is Over; Candle Glow and Mistletoe; A Bad Man Brings Out the Best in Me.

KEENEY, CLAIRE HANDSAKER　　ASCAP 1969
author
b Jasper, Ore, Sept 13, 1899. Educ: Univ Ore Extension, 22. Actor, playwright & lyricist. Chief Collabrs: Milo Sweet, Gene Johnston, Charles N Fielder. *Songs:* Lyrics: Oregon Battle Song; A Toast to the Team; Football in the Air; Football Builds the Buildings; Never Let a Sucker Make a Sucker Out of You; If You've Got Time to Worry; It's Great to Play the Races.

KEHNER, CLARENCE　　ASCAP 1953
composer, author
b Atlantic, NJ, July 3, 26. Worked as song plugger, Philadelphia, Pa. Worked for Miller Int Record Co & Daval Publ Corp. Chief Collabr: Russell Faith. *Songs:* Somewhere in Your Heart; Christmas and You; Bobbysox to Stockings; Snowbound. *Instrumental Works:* Theme for a Brokenheart.

KEINER, FERN SYBIL　　ASCAP 1971
composer, author, publisher
b New York, NY. Educ: Performing Arts High Sch; Boston Univ; Columbia Univ; Johns Hopkins Univ; Alliance Francaise, France, BA & MA equivalence. Author of "Children of the Rainbow," music bk used as subject matter & curriculum content for teaching children beginning reading words through music in schs under grants; also had taught at grad level, Hunter Col, on music & the creative process. Author of "Love Songs," bk of seven songs. Comp, lyricist & publ; wrote five bks. *Songs:* Rainbow Lady; Children of the Rainbow; Up Above the Clouds; I Like to Feel the Rain; Prayer Dance; Love-Songs; Chosen Lovers; Love on My Mind; School of Love; When You Went Away; Lazy Sunday Afternoon; Forgive Me, I'm Sorry.

KEISER, ROBERT
See King, Robert A

KEITH, MARILYN
See Bergman, Marilyn Keith

KEITHLEY, E CLINTON　　ASCAP 1950
composer, author, trumpeter
b Greenville, Ind, Nov 15, 1880; d Tampa, Fla, Apr 7, 55. Educ: Pub schs. Mem, theatre orch, Louisville, Ky, 10 yrs. Radio singer, 23; formed radio quartet, The Chicagoans. *Songs:* A Garland of Old-Fashioned Roses; When Shadows Fall; In the Shadow of the Roses; Blue Grass of Kentucky; I'll Return Mother Darling to You; One Wonderful Night You Told Me You Loved Me.

KELLAWAY, ROGER W
composer, pianist
b Waban, Mass, Nov 1, 39. Educ: New Eng Cons Music, studied comp; studied classical piano, 14 yrs; studied comp with George Trembley. Comn by George Ballanchine of New York Ballet Co to compose ballet, 71. Arr music for Walton's Christmas Album, Roger Kellaway Cello Quartet. Piano accompanist, producer to var singers & artists. Comp music for TV, recordings & var chamber ens. *Scores:* Film: A Star Is Born; Paper Lion; The Extraordinary Adventures of the Mouse and His Child (animated cartoon).

KELLEM, MILTON (JIMMY CRAIG, SOPHIE HODES) ASCAP 1952
composer, author
b Philadelphia, Pa, Feb 6, 11. Educ: Villanova Univ, BS(economics), MA(educ). Singer with bands; played guitar, violin, saxophone & clarinet; cond orchs for NBC, CBS & ABC Networks. Chief Collabrs: Al Hoffman, Abner Silver. *Songs:* Gonna Get Along Without Ya Now; There But for the Grace of God Go I; The Game of Love; Tonight Love; Before It's Too Late; Teardrops on My Pillow; Where You Go, Go I; Aladdin's Lamp; The E I O Song; This Is You.

KELLER, CONNIE
See Merlow, Connie

KELLER, JAMES WALTER (JACK)　　ASCAP 1968
author
b Brooklyn, NY, Nov 11, 36. Educ: Pvt instr piano & accordion with Roger Warren; Lafayette High Sch, Brooklyn, studied cello. Exclusive songwriter under Don Kirshner, 60. Writer of theme songs, "Bewitched", "Gidget", "Hazel", "Camp Runamuck", "Wackiest Ship in the Army" & "Here Comes the Bride," 64-65. Record producer with The Monkees, 66-67. Prof mgr, CBS Publ Co, 72-74 & United Artists, 74-78. Chief Collabrs: Gerry Goffin, Howard Greenfield, Ernie Sheldon, Diane Hildebrand. *Songs:* Everybody's Somebody's Fool; My Heart Has a Mind of It's Own; Breaking in a Brand New Broken Heart; Venus in Blue Jeans; Run to Him; Just for Old Times; One Way Ticket; Easy Come, Easy Go; Just Between You and Me.

KELLER, JERRY PAUL　　ASCAP 1958
composer, author, singer
b Ft Smith, Ark, June 20, 37. Educ: Univ Tulsa. To NY, 57; singer & recording artist for var cos; TV appearances & European concerts. Lyricist for films incl "A Man and a Woman", "Almost There", "I'd Rather Be Rich" & "What's So Bad About Feeling Good." Actor in films incl "You Light Up My Life" & "If Ever I See You Again," 78. Chief Collabrs: Gloria Shayne, Dave Blume. *Songs:* Here Comes Summer; Turn Down Day.

KELLER, SHELDON B　　ASCAP 1956
composer, author
b Chicago, Ill, Aug 20, 23. Educ: Univ Ill; Univ Md. TV writer for Sid Caesar, Danny Thomas, Bing Crosby, Dick Van Dyke, Art Carney, Dinah Shore, Mary Martin & Danny Kaye. Chief Collabr: Mel Tolkin. *Songs:* I Just Got Somethin' in My Eye.

KELLEY, BIRTIE MAE　　ASCAP 1969
composer, author, teacher
b Athens, Ga, July 22, 1898. Educ: Pvt schs. Chief Collabrs: L L Loth, Harold Potter. *Songs & Instrumental Works:* Land of Dreams America; Heavenly Blue Eyes and Freckles Too; Little Cabin in Shenandoah Valley; Tomorrow World; Don't Baby Me; Don't Steal My Kisses and Skidoo; I'll Never Wait Again.

KELLEY, EDGAR STILLMAN　　ASCAP 1942
composer, author, educator
b Sparta, Wis, Apr 14, 1857; d New York, NY, Nov 12, 44. Educ: Stuttgart Cons, with Seifritz, Kruger, Speidel & Finck; hon degrees: Miami Univ & Univ of Cincinnati. Organist, Oakland & San Francisco, Calif. Cond, touring opera cos, 1890-92. Taught piano, organ & comp, NY & Calif. Music critic, San Francisco Examiner, 1893-95. Lectr, NY Univ, 1896-97; acting prof of music, Yale Univ, 01-02. Taught comp, Berlin, 02-10. Dean of comp, Cincinnati Cons, 10-44. Author "Chopin, the Composer", "Musical Instruments." *Songs:* Israfel; Eldorado; The Lady Picking Mulberries. *Instrumental Works:* Theme and Variations (string quartet, piano quintet); Wedding Ode; Aladdin; Confluentia; The Pilgrim's Progress (musical miracle play); Suites: Alice in Wonderland; The Pit and the Pendulum; also 2 symph. *Scores:* Opera: Puritania (comic).

KELLIN, MIKE　　ASCAP 1967
composer, author, actor
b Hartford, Conn, Apr 26, 22. Educ: Trinity Col, Conn, BA; Yale Univ, Dept Drama. Actor in theatre, film & TV. Music has been my sideline. Received OBIE for performance in "American Buffalo," 76; Tony nomination for performance in "Pipe Dream." *Scores:* Off Bway Show: Riff Raff Revue (ASCAP Award, 79). *Albums:* And the Testimony's Still Comin' In.

KELLIS, LEO ALAN
composer
b Los Angeles, Calif, Aug 17, 27. Educ: J C Fremont High Sch; Univ Calif, Los Angeles; studied piano with Niel McKie, Herman Wasserman, comp with Julius Gold. Concert pianist; teacher. *Instrumental Works:* Variations on a theme of

Rachmaninoff; Rhapsody Arevelian; Impromptu in F; Fantasy in A minor (2 pianos); Rhapsody on a Children's Tune; Suite En Valse (2 pianos); Hello From the Zoo (piano); Variations on a theme of Balakirev; Two Concert Etudes.

KELLOGG, CHARLES W ASCAP 1974
composer, author, trumpet player
b Rochester, NY, Dec 23, 05. Educ: Syracuse Univ, BA, 31. Trumpet player, Steel Pier Dance Hall, Atlantic City, 33-40. Writer of song lyrics, 35- Played club dates in Rochester, 38- Had my own band for 4 yrs. Became insurance salesman. Chief Collabrs: Vic Lewis, Jack End. *Songs:* Lyrics: Insomnia Ho-Hum; Once Upon a Time.

KELLOGG, LYNN ASCAP 1971
composer, author, singer
b Appleton, Wis, Apr 2, 43. Educ: Univ Wis, 61-64. Guitarist & actress; appeared in original Bway cast of "Hair" & on cast album, 68. Many TV appearances, nightclubs & variety shows. Hosted three Kraft Music Shows. Acted in movie "Charro." On TV show, "Animals, Animals, CBS, 75-, songwriter for show, 75- Tours with Gordon Lightfoot as opening act, 76- Chief Collabr: Lanny Meyers. *Songs:* Every Mother's Son; Just Something to Do; The Sanity Song; Cruel and Unusual Punishment; Arm's Length; The Letters I Never Sent; Kindred Spirit; Being Honest.

KELLY, CASEY
See Cohen, Daniel

KELLY, JOHN ALLEN (JAK)
composer, singer, entertainer
b Washington, DC, Jan 25, 51. Educ: Guitar with James Crabtree at age 9. Entertainer, clubs, concerts, TV & radio; recording artist, Monument Records. *Songs:* Noone Ever Listened to the Opry Any More; Darlin'; Same Old Story; Sean Song; Hey Lady.

KELLY, MONTGOMERY JEROME (MONTE) ASCAP 1968
composer, author, arranger
b Oakland, Calif, June 8, 10; d Mar 15, 71. Trumpeter in var orchs incl Griff Williams, Tom Coadey & Buddy Marino. With CBS, San Francisco. First trumpeter & arr, Paul Whiteman Band. Served in USA Ordnance Band, joined Bob Hope Show as asst music dir & arr. To New York, 50's; free-lance writer & arr with NBC. Scored record albums. *Instrumental Works:* Tropicana; Tibia; Country Rock; Discotheque; Puerto Vallarta; Taorming; Mandolinos Espanol; Noche en Maloga; Sunday in Seville; Tango Gitano; Falmenco Fantasy; Cantina de Los Gitanos; When Will We Know; Malibu Sun; Rio Del Mar; Spanish Candle; Bahia De Acapulco; Encanto Del Caribe; A Love Like Ours; If We Could Spend Each Night Like This; Blues of Guru; Stone Baroque; Strings for Ravi; St Tropez in June; When Love Is All; Maybe It's Love; Summer Love. *Albums:* Karma Sitar.

KELLY, SHERMAN ASCAP 1970
composer, author, singer
b Washington, DC, Oct 27, 43. Educ: Cornell Univ, BA, 66. Singer & keyboard player, nightclubs, concerts & TV; recording artist. Chief Collabrs: Wells Kelly, David Robinson. *Songs:* Dancin in the Moonlight; Vaea (Vy-Ya); Oughta Daughta (Think I Will); Isn't It Easy; Bustin Loose.

KELLY, WELLS ASCAP 1973
composer, author, musician
b Boston, Mass, Apr 7, 49. Educ: New Eng Cons, studies in theory & piano; music summer camp instr in arr, drums & dance band. Played piano in jazz bands & bass fiddle in folk bands, Ithaca, NY; played drums in rock-n-roll bands. Performed own songs & instrumental pieces with groups, King Harvest & Orleans. Chief Collabrs: Sherman Kelly, Chris Kelly. *Songs:* Mountain; Siam Sam; The Bum; Isn't It Easy; Oughta Daughta; Bustin Loose; Dukies Tune.

KELMAN, CHARLES ASCAP 1976
composer, author
b New York, NY, 1930. Started writing music before col. Has appeared on "Johnny Carson Show." *Songs:* To See a Butterfly; Le Petit DeJeuner.

KEMMER, GEORGE W ASCAP 1948
composer, organist, choirmaster
b New York, NY, Oct 11, 1890; d. Organist & choirmaster, Grace Church, Orange, NJ, 11-23 & St George's Episcopal Church, New York, 23-55. *Songs:* Sacred Songs & Arr: Be Calm and Peaceful; When Thou Art Near; Lord I Want to Be; Steal Away; Nobody Knows the Trouble I've Seen; Were You There?

KEMNER, GERALD EUGENE
composer, author, professor
b Kansas City, Mo, Sept 28, 32. Educ: Kansas City Univ, BA(piano), 53; Yale Sch Music, MM(comp), 55, studied with Quincy Porter; Eastman Sch Music, DMA(comp), 62, studied with Henry Cowell, Bernard Rogers, Howard Hanson. Teaching career combined with performing and composing in a wide variety of media. Chief Collabrs: John Obetz, Eph Ehly, James Rothwell. *Songs:* Ezekiel! (SATB, electronic sounds). *Instrumental Works:* Quotations (organist, asst & narrator); Holiday Fantiasies (7) (organ); Scherzophrenia (accordion).

KEMPER, RONOLD VIVIAN ASCAP 1952
composer, author, pianist
b Missoula, Mont, Aug 1, 12. Educ: Studied piano with Hazel Pritchard, also with Zue Geary Pease, Sacramento. Helped form Dick Jurgens Orch in Sacramento & played for many yrs. Joined Horace Heidt Orch; then had own band briefly before joining 100th Div Artillery Hq Battery, France & Ger; after war, had own TV & radio show in Hollywood, "Kemper's Kapers." Brought show to K-G-O-TV in San Francisco. Later did pianist-singer in nightclubs incl Surcouf, Algeria; Geneva, Switz; Cairo, Egypt; French Lick, Ind; Biloxi, Miss; Victoria, BC. Chief Collabrs: Roc Hillman, Mort Green, Frankie Carle, Jack Elliott, Dick Jurgens. *Songs:* It's a 100-2-1 I'm in Love; Knit One, Purl Two; Music: The Doodle Bug Song; Downhearted Blues; In a Blue Canoe.

KEMPINSKI, LEO A ASCAP 1927
composer, conductor
b Ruda, Ger, Mar 25, 1891; d Hampton, Conn, May 25, 58. To US, 08. Educ: Breslau Univ; Juilliard Sch; studied with Julius Gloger, Percy Goetschius. Church organist, Philadelphia. Music dir, theatrical circuit, 13 yrs. Ed, music publ co, 3 yrs. Writer, film music & background music for radio shows. Cond, "Army Hour," 43-46. Staff comp & cond, NBC. *Songs:* Our Faith Shall Live; Gracious Lord Who Givest Blessing; The Call of the Highroad; Land of Faith, Land of Hope; For the Red, White and Blue; Flag of Hope; Somewhere, Sometime, Somehow; Wonderful Night. *Instrumental Works:* Victory Concerto (piano, orch); Marches: The Fifth Army March; The Flaming Sword of Freedom; Corregidor; Heroes of the Pacific; All Hail to Our Heroes; Spirit of America; Old Glory Forever.

KENBROVIN, JAAN
See Vincent, Nathaniel Hawthorne

KENDIS, JAMES ASCAP 1914
composer, author, publisher
b St Paul, Minn, Mar 9, 1883; d Jamaica, NY, Nov 15, 46. Educ: Philadelphia Pub Schs. Formed Kendis & Paley Music Corp, Kendis & Brockman Music Corp & Kendis Music Corp. Charter mem, ASCAP. Chief Collabrs: David Brockman, Howard Johnson, Charles Bayha. *Songs:* I'm Forever Blowing Bubbles; If I Had My Way; Feather Your Nest; I Know What It Means to Be Lonesome; Cheer Up, Mary; Nat'an, For What Are You Waiting, Nat'an?; When It's Night Time in Italy, It's Wednesday Over Here; Billy; Listen to That Jungle Band; Angel Eyes; My Little Kangaroo; Golden Gate; Come Out of the Kitchen, Mary Ann; And Tommy Goes Too.

KENNAN, KENT WHEELER ASCAP 1950
composer, author, teacher
b Milwaukee, Wis, Apr 18, 13. Educ: Univ Mich, 30-32; Eastman Sch Music, BM, 34, MM, 36; studied with Pizzetti, Rome, 38; Am Acad at Rome, 37-39. Prix de Rome in music, 36. Taught theory & piano, Kent State Univ, 39-40, theory & comp, Univ Tex, 40-46 & 49-, theory, Ohio State Univ, 47-49 & comp & orchestration, Eastman Sch Music, 54 & 56. WW II Serv, 42-45. Numerous comp in var media; orch works performed under Toscanini, Ormandy, Stokowski, Hanson & others by NY Philh, Philadelphia Orch, NBC Symph & others. Author of 2 music texts. *Songs:* Music: The Unknown Warrior Speaks (cappella male chorus). *Instrumental Works:* Night Soliloquy (flute, piano, strings, wind ens, harp, guitar, vibraphone); Scherzo, Aria, and Fugato (oboe, piano); Sonata for Trumpet and Piano; Two Preludes (piano); Three Preludes (piano).

KENNEDY, JAMES MICHAEL ASCAP 1971
author
b Oil City, Pa, Jan 1, 47. Educ: Youngstown State Univ, BA, 69, MA, 75. Songwriter, 70. Actor, lyricist & comp. Chief Collabr: Maureen McGovern. *Songs:* Lyrics: Midnight Storm; If I Wrote You a Song; All I Want (All I Need); Little Boys and Men; Memory.

KENNY, CHARLES FRANCIS ASCAP 1936
composer, author
b Astoria, NY, June 23, 1898. Educ: Pub Sch; Longuelle Col, Montreal; McGill Univ, music. Started writing while in USN, 19; wrote shows, battleship; transl classics to Eng lyrics for Robbins Music; wrote songs for Mills Music; staff writer, Berlin & Feist. In show "Student Prince Road," 26; did vaudeville tour. Wrote "Shubert Passing" show, 32 & "Herndon New Faces" show. With Whiteman & Speckt Orchs, Munson Line & SAm countries. Chief Collabrs: J Fred Coots, Nick Kenny (bro), Bill Covell, Tommy Dennis, Frank Perkins. *Songs:* Gold Mine in the Sky; Gone Fishin'; Beyond the Purple Hills; Cathedral in the Pines; Music: While a Cigarette Was Burning; The Magic Piper; When You Look in the Heart of a Shamrock; Lyrics: Love Letters in the Sand; Laughing at Life; That's Beaver; Sunday Drivers; It's a Lonely Trail; Funny Little Snowman; Ev'ry Street Is Canal Street in Venice; I Wear My Glasses to Bed Ev'ry Night (So I Can See You in My Dreams); I'm Planting Little Onions (So I Can Cry Over You); Why Do They Call It a Drug Store?; There's Music in the Sky; Handy Little Handful; The Back Seat of a Taxi With You; In My Apartment on Park Avenue; White Sails; Shall We Gather at the Rhythm?; Mississippi Mansion.

KENNY, GEORGE
See Whitcomb, Kenneth George

KENNY, NICK A
ASCAP 1932
author

b Astoria, NY, Feb 3, 1895; d. Educ: Columbia Univ. Served in USN, WW I; then joined US Maritime Service. Newspaper reporter, Bayonne, NJ; Boston, Mass; New York, NY. Radio ed, New York Mirror, 30-63; also columnist. Produced early radio amateur show. Chief Collabr: Charles Kenny (bro). *Songs:* Laughing At Life; Love Letters in the Sand; Every Minute of the Hour; There's a Goldmine in the Sky; Little Old Cathedral in the Pines; While a Cigarette Was Burning; It's a Lonely Trail When You're Traveling All Alone; Make Believe Island; Running Through My Mind; Leanin' on the Old Top Rail; Beyond the Purple Hills; Gone Fishin'; Carelessly; Just a Letter From Home; Little Skipper; I Met God on the Highway; I Heard a Voice From the Infinite Sky; Violins Were Playing; Paradise Valley; Nobody Knows the Power of Prayer; Save Me a Dream; Drop Me Off in Harlem.

KENT
See Fox, Walter Kent

KENT, ARTHUR
ASCAP 1942
composer

b New York, NY, July 2, 20. Educ: City Col New York, BS; Teachers Col, Columbia Univ, MA; studied electrical engineering & music educ. Began piano lessons at age 5; won medals in city-wide contests at age 10. WW II, USAF. Comp col & service musicals. Pianist in dance orchs, nightclubs & hotels; pianist & vocal coach for New York music publ. Accompanist & cond for singers. Piano teacher & choir dir. Made piano arr for print. Chief Collabrs: Ed Warren, Sylvia Dee, Sammy Gallop, Frank Stanton, Johnny Mercer. *Songs:* We Go Well Together; Wonder When My Baby's Coming Home; You Never Miss the Water Till the Well Runs Dry; Don't Go to Strangers; Mighty Lonesome Feelin'; It Happens to Be Me; Take Good Care of Her; Ring-a-ling-a-lario; The End of the World; Millions of Roses; The Bird of Bleeker Street; I'm Coming Back to You; Bring Me Sunshine; I Taught Her Everything She Knows; Happy Songs of Love; I Never Get Thru Missing You; Take One Step; Nearer, My Love, to You; He's My Lover; I Want to See Me in Your Eyes.

KENT, GARY
See Wright, Carter Land

KENT, RICHARD LAYTON
ASCAP 1979
composer, teacher

b Harris, Mo, Jan 23, 16. Educ: Drake Univ, BME, 40; New Eng Cons of Music, MM, 47; Boston Univ, DMA, 61; Harvard Univ summer sch, studied musicology with Curt Sachs, Donald Grout & Gustave Reese. Taught, music & Eng, Larrabee High Sch, Iowa, 40-42. Pilot & fighter pilot instr, USAAF, 42-46. Prof music, chmn fine arts dept, chmn cultural events comt, pres fac asn, Fitchburg State Col, Mass, 47- *Songs & Instrumental Works:* Five Carol Preludes (organ); Windows of Song (children's song bk); Choral works: The Thing About Cats; To Music; Four Housman Songs; Alleluia; As the Hart Panteth; Set Me As a Seal.

KENT, SANDRA
ASCAP 1951
composer, author, actress

b New York, NY, May 1, 27. Educ: Brooklyn Col. Singer with dance bands, 45-52. Appeared in summer stock & in road co of "Brigadoon." Mem, Phoenix Theatre repertoire co. *Songs:* I Never Had a Worry in the World; Little Pink Toes; Li'l Ole You; Once I Loved You; Oh, Mr Romeo; More Than Anything; I'm on a SeeSaw of Love.

KENT, WALTER
ASCAP 1934
composer, author

b New York, NY, Nov 29, 11. Educ: City Col New York: Juilliard Sch Music, scholarship; advanced violin studies with Leopold Aver & Samuel Gardner. Cond own orch on radio & in theatres. Free lance comp, Hollywood, 43. Wrote music for musical pictures, incl Walt Disney's "Johnny Appleseed" (Melody Time) which won Critic's Circle Award. Comp songs for Bway musicals, incl "The Ziegfeld Follies." Chief Collabrs: Kim Gannon, Milton Drake, Mann Curtis. *Songs:* I'll Forget You; Oh, That Rhythm; An Innocent Affair; These Things Are You; Music: Little Trouper; I Cross My Fingers; Something Called Love; The Beat Generation; For Whom the Bells Toll; I'll Be Home for Christmas; The White Cliffs of Dover; I'm Gonna Live 'Till I Die; Mama I Wanna Make Rhythm; Country Boy; I Never Mention Your Name; I Cross My Fingers; Ah! But It Happens; Love Is Like a Cigarette; I Just Kissed Your Picture Goodnight; The Last Mile Home; Harlem Waltz; Who Dat Up Dere; When the Roses Bloom Again; Pu-leeze! Mr Hemingway!; Yokel Boy; The Lord Is Good to Me; Here It Is Monday; Summertime Is Summertime; After All It's Spring; Apple Blossoms and Chapel Bells; Come Rain Come Shine; Too Much in Love; Coney Island Moon. *Scores:* Bway Show: Seventeen; TV: Lucille Ball's Christmas Show.

KENTON, STANLEY NEWCOMB
ASCAP 1946
composer, conductor, teacher

b Wichita, Kans, Feb 19, 12; d Los Angeles, Calif, Aug 25, 79. Educ: Bell High Sch, Los Angeles; studied with Charles Dalmores. Pianist, nightclubs & dance orchs. Asst music dir, Earl Carroll's Theatre Restaurant; comp for films & radio. Organized own orch, 41, reorganized, 47. Appeared with var orchs in many concerts & theatres throughout US, Europe, Mex, Australia & Japan. Founded Kenton Workshop for teenage musicians, Ind Univ, 59; cond clinics at Redlands Univ, Calif, Mich State Univ, Southern Methodist Univ, Drury Col, Mo, Calif State Univ, Sacramento, Orange Coast Col, Calif & Univ Tex, Arlington. Organized var orchs, incl Neophonic Band, 64. Recorded on own record label, Creative World; pres, Creative World Music Publ; founder & pres, Int Acad Contemporary Music. Third person named to Jazz Hall of Fame. Chief Collabrs: Joe Greene, Lawrence, Joe Garland, Peter Rugolo. *Songs & Instrumental Works:* Artistry in Rhythm; Eager Beaver; Southern Scandal; Concerto for Doghouse (a Setting in Motion); Opus in Pastels; Concerto to End All Concertos; Painted Rhythm; Jump for Joe; Artistry Jumps; Artistry in Tango; Brasilia; Build It Up, Paint It Nice, Tear It Down; Capitol Punishment; Changing Times; Etude for Saxophones; Fantasy; Flamenco; Guess Where I Used to Work Blues; Harlem Folk Dance; Harlem Holiday; Interchange; June Christy; Kentonova; Lazy Daisy; Loco-Nova; Memphis Lament; Mexican Dance; Montage; Night Watch; Number One; 007; Reed Rapture; Reflection; Riff Rhapsody; Sentimental Serenade; Shelly Manne; Something New; Sophisticated Samba; Special Delivery; Sunset Tower; Theme for Jo; Theme for Sunday; Tribute to a Flatted Fifth; Trumpet Symphonette; Variations on Artistry in Rhythm.

KENWOOD, MARTY
See Kalmanoff, Martin

KEPNER, CHARLES FRED
ASCAP 1960
composer

b Waynesboro, Pa, Sept 26, 21. Educ: Catawba Col, NC; Juilliard Sch Music; Manhattan Sch Music. Began arr & comp at 16 yrs old; pianist in eastern territorial bands, 36-39. Military service, World War II; joined USAF Band as chief arr, 47. Organized & lead group, Airmen of Note, 50-55. Retired from USAF, 66. Teacher & writer, 80-; 30 publ in educ, band & orch music. *Instrumental Works:* Cuban Fantasy; Oasis; Stillness at Appomattox; What's Up Tiger (theme, PBS radio, 10 yrs); Lonely Town; When a Flower Blooms. *Scores:* Films: El Paso Story; Mt Rainier; Skyline Drive.

KERBY, PAUL
ASCAP 1948
composer, author, conductor

b Johannesburg, SAfrica, Jan 9, 03; d. Educ: In Eng. US citizen. Dir musical presentations, Capitol Theatre, New York. Assoc dir, Salzburg Fest, 27. Dir off Austrian prog, Chicago Centennial, 34. Under contract to film studio, Hollywood, 37-41. *Songs:* Viennese Memories; Rosalinda, Love of Mine; Oh Jiminy, Oh Jiminy; Laughing Song; Csardas; Melodrama.

KERGER, ANN J
ASCAP 1963
composer, author

b Vienna, Austria, May 25, 1894. Homemaker. *Songs:* Lyrics: Take Me in Your Arms; That Rose; The Wide Blue Sky; You Took My Heart With You; The Little House on the Hill.

KERKER, GUSTAVE A
ASCAP 1914
composer, conductor

b Herford, Westphalia, Ger; Feb 28, 1857; d New York, NY, June 29, 23. Moved to US, 1867. Cond, Casino Theatre, New York; also for Lillian Russell. Founder & charter mem, ASCAP, dir, 14-23. Chief Collabrs: R H Burnside, Harry B Smith, Joseph Herbert. *Songs:* Castles in the Air; Is It a Dream?; In Gay New York; It's Forty Miles From Schenectady to Troy; They Call Me the Belle of New York; They All Follow Me; Teach Me How to Kiss; La Belle Parisienne; Bonjour Monsieur; The Good Old Days; Loud Let the Bugles Sound; It's Nice to Have a Sweetheart; You're Just the Girl I'm Looking For; Old Man Manhattan. *Scores:* Bway stage: The Pearl of Pekin; Castles in the Air; Kismet; In Gay New York; An American Beauty; The Whirl of the Town; Yankee Doodle Dandy; The Belle of New York; The Girl From Up There; The Billionaire; The Social Whirl; The Tourists; The White Hen; Fascinating Flora.

KERN, JAMES V
ASCAP 1955
author, singer, director

b New York, NY, Sept 22, 09; d. Educ: Fordham Law Sch. Singer with George Olsen Trio; appeared with Olsen orch in "Good News." Writer for Yacht Club Boys, 28-39; in 39 became screen writer; then dir of films incl "April Showers", "Never Say Goodbye" & "Two Tickets to Broadway." TV dir; shows incl "Colgate Comedy Hour", "Ann Sothern Show", "I Love Lucy", "77 Sunset Strip" & "My Three Sons." *Songs:* Lover, Lover; Little Red Fox; Shut the Door; Easy Street.

KERN, JEROME
ASCAP 1914
composer

b New York, NY, Jan 27, 1885; d New York, Nov 11, 45. Educ: New York Col of Music, studied with Alexander Lambert, Albert von Doenhoff, Paolo Gallico, Austen Pearce. Charter mem, ASCAP, dir, 24-29 & 32-42. Writer, musical scores, London, on staff, T B Harms Co & Bway scores, Princess Theatre, New York, 15-18. To Hollywood, 34. Mem, Nat Inst Arts & Letters. Biography, "The World of Jerome Kern" by David Ewen; film biography, "Till the Clouds Roll By." Chief Collabrs: P G Wodehouse, Clifford Grey, Anne Caldwell, Oscar Hammerstein 2nd, Otto Harbach, Johnny Mercer, E Y Harburg, Dorothy Fields, Ira Gershwin. *Songs:* How'd You Like to Spoon With Me?; Same Sort of Girl; They Didn't Believe Me; The Magic Melody; Babes in the Wood; On the Shore at Le Lei Wi; Some Sort of Somebody; You Know and I Know; Have a Heart; Til the Clouds Roll By; You Never Knew About Me; Cleopatterer; The Crickets Are Calling; Leave It to Jane; The Siren's Song; Just You Watch My Step; Go Little Boat; The Land Where the Good Songs Go; Bullfrog Patrol; Whose Baby Are You; Left All Alone Again Blues; Look for the Silver Lining; Whip-poor-will; Wild Rose; Sally; Blue Danube Blues; Ka-Lu-A; Raggedy Ann; D'Ye Love Me?; Two Little Bluebirds; Sunny; Who?; Make Believe; Ol' Man River; Bill; Why Do I Love You?; Life Upon the Wicked Stage; Can't Help Lovin' dat Man; Till Good Luck Comes My Way; You Are Love; Why Was I Born?; Here Am I; Don't Ever Leave Me; She Didn't Say 'Yes'; The Night Was Made for Love; I Watch the Love Parade; A New Love Is Old; One Moment Alone; Try to Forget; And Love Was Born; There's a Hill Beyond a Hill; In Egern on the Tegern See; The Song Is You; I've Told Every Little Star; Smoke Gets in Your Eyes; The Touch of Your Hand; You're Devastating; Yesterdays; I'll Be Hard to Handle; Lovely to Look at; I Won't Dance; Lonely Feet; We Were So Young; I Dream Too Much; The Jockey on the Carousel; I Have the Room Above; I Still Suits Me; The Way You Look Tonight (Acad award, 36); Bojangles of Harlem; Waltz in Swing Time; A Fine Romance; Pick Yourself Up; Never Gonna Dance; Our Song; High, Wide and Handsome; The Folks Who Love on the Hill; Can I Forget You; Just Let Me Look at You; You Couldn't Be Cuter; All the Things You Are; All in Fun; Heaven in My Arms; In the Heart of the Dark; That Lucky Fellow; The Last Time I Saw Paris (Acad award, 41); Day Dreaming; Remind Me; Dearly Beloved; I'm Old-Fashioned; You Were Never Lovelier; Long Ago (and Far Away); Sure Thing; Can't Help Singing; Californ-i-ay; More and More; The Sweetest Sight That I Have Seen; All Through the Day; Up With the Lark; In Love in Vain; Nobody Else But Me. *Scores:* Bway shows: La Belle Paree; The Red Petticoat; Oh, I Say!; The Girl From Utah; 90 in the Shade; Nobody Home; Very Good Eddie; Have a Heart; Love O'Mike; Oh, Boy!; Leave It to Jane; Oh, Lady! Lady!; Head Over Heels; Rock-a-bye Baby; She's a Good Fellow; The Night Boat; Sally; Good Morning Dearie; The Stepping Stones; Sitting Pretty; Sunny; The City Chap; Criss Cross; Show Boat; Sweet Adeline; The Cat and the Fiddle; Music in the Air; Roberta; Very Warm for May; Films: I Dream Too Much; Swing Time; High, Wide and Handsome; The Joy of Living; You Were Never Lovelier; Cover Girl; Can't Help Singing; Centennial Summer.

KERNELL, WILLIAM B   ASCAP 1921
composer, pianist
b New York, NY, Feb 21, 1891; d Los Angeles, Calif, July 12, 63. Educ: High sch; studied music with Samuel Jospe, Milan Blanchet & Edward Kilenyi. Pianist with music publ. WW I, with French Ambulance Service. Comp scores for films, Hollywood & London. Chief Collabr: Dorothy Donnelly. *Songs:* The Latin Quarter; Sally of My Dreams; A Pair of Blue Eyes; The Village Belle; Steppin' Along; Beware of Love; Can't Get Along Without You. *Instrumental Works:* Carnival (opera in film, "Charlie Chan at the Opera"). *Scores:* Bway stage: Elsie Janis and Her Gang; Hello, Lola.

KERNER, DEBORAH M (RETTINO)   ASCAP 1971
composer, author, singer
b Los Angeles, Calif, Dec 1, 51. Educ: Univ Calif, Riverside, BA(music). Started composing & singing solo, 69; co-writer & co-producer with husband (Ernie Rettino). *Songs:* Amen, Praise the Lord; Jesus; Changed Into His Image; Mary's Song; Friends; You'll Be Mine; Throne of God; Good News Gospel Ragtime; The Wa-Wa Song.

KERNOCHAN, MARSHALL   ASCAP 1927
composer
b New York, NY, Dec 14, 1880; d Edgartown, Mass, June 9, 55. Educ: Studied music with Ivan Knorr; Juilliard Sch Music, studied with Percy Goetschius. *Songs:* Smuggler's Song; We Two Together; Lilacs; Ah, Love, But a Day; Portrait; Serenade at the Villa. *Instrumental Works:* The Foolish Virgin (cantata); Out of the Rolling Ocean (orch, baritone).

KERNOCHAN, SARAH MARSHALL   ASCAP 1974
composer, author, novelist
b New York, NY, Dec 30, 47. Educ: Sarah Lawrence Col. Co-wrote column in "Village Voice." Co-produced & dir film "Marjoe," Oscar for best documentary, 73; also wrote theme song. Performed & wrote songs for 2 RCA albums, "House of Pain" & "Beat Around the Bush." Publ novel "Dry Hustle," 77. Wrote book for musical "Night-Lites." *Songs:* Biology and You; Pranks for Warped Children. *Scores:* Opera: Night-Lites.

KERR, ANITA
See Grob, Anita Jean

KERR, HARRY D   ASCAP 1922
author
b Santa Rosa, Calif, Oct 8, 1880; d Los Angeles, Calif, May 20, 57. Educ: Albany Law Sch, LLB. Practiced law until 20. Charter mem, Am Guild of Authors & Composers. *Songs:* Do You Ever Think of Me?; Neapolitan Nights; Paradise; Love Me; Counting the Days; Have You Forgotten?; That's My Girl.

KERR, JAMES E (JAY)   ASCAP 1968
composer, author, musical director
b New York, NY. Educ: Princeton Univ, AB(English), with honors; Calif State Univ, Northridge, MA(mass communications). Directed & created mil touring shows, Vietnam. Vocal coach, HB Studio, New York. Wrote & produced children's theatre, Bway, off-Bway & TV; directed children's theatre, Hollywood; wrote & directed "WASP—A Musical Revenge," Los Angeles & New York. Chief Collabr: Geoff Peterson. *Scores:* Shows: Arthur! A Boy Becomes King; Pinocchio; Little Red Riding Hood (ecological feminist musical).

KERR, JEAN   ASCAP 1959
author
b Scranton, Pa, July 10, 23. Educ: Catholic Univ. Playwright, incl "Jenny Kiss'd Me", "King of Hearts", "Mary, Mary", "Finishing Touches" & "Poor Richard." Author of "Please Don't Eat the Daisies", "The Snake Has All the Lines", "Penny Candy" & "How I Got to Be Perfect." Chief Collabrs: Leroy Anderson, Jay Gorney, Walter Kerr (husband), Joan Ford. *Songs:* This Had Better Be Love; It'll Be All Right in a Hundred Years; Be a Mess; The Pussy Foot; Save a Kiss; I Never Know When to Say When. *Scores:* Bway shows: Touch and Go (also libretto); Goldilocks (also libretto).

KERR, PHIL   ASCAP 1954
composer, author
b Los Angeles, Calif, Sept 1, 06; d Glendale, Calif, Aug 31, 60. Educ: High sch. Evangelist, toured US; cond, Phil Kerr Monday Musicals, Pasadena, Calif, 15 yrs. *Songs:* Sacred: In Love With the Lover of My Soul; Melody Divine; Over in Glory; Patiently; Thine Alone; Why Should I Care If the Sun Doesn't Shine.

KERR, WALTER   ASCAP 1959
author, teacher
b Evanston, Ill, July 8, 13. Educ: Northwestern Univ. Fac, Catholic Univ. Drama critic, New York Herald Tribune, 51-66, New York Times, 66- Librettist & dir, "Sing Out, Sweet Land." Author, "How Not to Write a Play", "Pieces At Eight", "The Theatre in Spite of Itself", "The Decline of Pleasure, Tragedy and Comedy", "The Silent Clowns", "Thirty Plays Hath November" & "Journey to the Center of the Theatre." Chief Collabrs: Leroy Anderson, Jay Gorney, Jean Kerr (wife), Joan Ford. *Songs:* This Had Better Be Love; It'll Be All Right in a Hundred Years; Be a Mess; The Pussy Foot; Save a Kiss; I Never Know When to Say When. *Scores:* Bway shows: Touch and Go (librettist & dir); Goldilocks (librettist & dir).

KERR, WILLIAM J   ASCAP 1959
author
b Warren, Ohio, Nov 22, 1890; d. Educ: Hiram Col; Youngstown Col. Service, 380th Motor Supply Co, World War I; pres, W J Kerr Sign Co, 50 yrs; sales supvr, Atwood Corp, Warren; founder, amateur songwriters radio show, "A Salute to Talent." Author bks of poetry: "Love Lines, Images of Imagination", "Zany Zoo." Chief Collabr: Fred Mann. *Songs:* Rainy Evening Sweetheart; The Answer's Only You; I'm Getting Absent Minded; Hi-Ya-Hello-Ohio; One Million Dollars; I Surrender.

KESLER, LEW   ASCAP 1959
composer
b Millville, NJ. Educ: Curtis Inst; Bucknell Univ. Pianist, Bway shows; coordr, Cole Porter Estate. Chief Collabr: June Carroll. *Songs & Instrumental Works:* Rinka Tinka Man; That's Judy; Four Folios: Sleeping Beauty; The Littlest Clown; Thief of Bagdad; Mother Goose on the Loose.

KESNAR, MAURITS   ASCAP 1941
composer, conductor, violinist
b Amsterdam, Neth, July 8, 1900; d Carbondale, Ill, Feb 22, 57. Educ: Cons, Amsterdam; Hochschule für Musik, Berlin; Univ Iowa, MA, PhD. Violin soloist in Neth, Ger & US; chmn, Music Dept, Southern Ill Univ; educr. *Songs & Instrumental Works:* String Quartet in D; Symphony in C; Sinfonietta; Poem (orch); Sundown; The Indian Flute; Mass in E flat.

KESSEL, BARNEY   ASCAP 1957
composer, conductor, guitarist
b Muskogee, Okla, Oct 17, 23. Guitarist in dance bands, incl Chico Marx, Charlie Barnet, Hal McIntyre & Artie Shaw. Mem, Oscar Peterson trio. Cond, "Bob Crosby Show," TV, 54; also cond other shows in TV, films & on records. *Songs & Instrumental Works:* Latin Dance No 1; Everytime I Hear This Song; Twilight in Acapulca.

KESSLER, JASCHA FREDERICK   ASCAP 1962
author
b New York, NY, Nov 27, 29. Educ: Univ Heights Col Arts & Sci, NY Univ, BA, 50; Univ Mich, MA, 51, PhD, 55. Teaching fel English, Univ Mich, 52-54; instr English, NY Univ, 54-55, Hunter Col, 55-56. Asst dir, Curriculum Res, Harcourt, Brace & World, 56-57. Asst prof English, Hamilton Col, 57-61; prof English, Univ Calif, Los Angeles, 61-; Fulbright res fel, Florence, Italy, 63-64. Prof Am Lit, Fulbright Prog, Italy, 70. Author: Poems: "Whatever Love Declares," 69; "After the Armies Have Passed," 70; "In Memory of the Future," 76; Anthology of Poetry: "American Poems: A Contemporary Collection" 64

& 72; Fiction: "An Egyptian Bondage," 67; "Death Come for the Behaviorist," "Rapid Transit," 80; "Bearing Gifts," 80; Translations: "The Magician's Garden" (24 Stories from the Hungarian of Geza Csath), 80; "The Face of Creation" (14 Hungarian Poets in Translation), 80; "Bride of Acacias" (Selected Poems of Forugh Farrokhzad), 80; "Under the Sign of Gemini" (Selected Poems of Miklos Radnoti), 81. Fellowships, Honors & Awards: Major Award in poetry, Avery Hopewood Contests, Univ Mich, 52. Poetry Prize, Heptagon Club New York, 54 & Ellis Bush Found, NY, 58. Fels in writing: Yaddo Found, NY, 58, Danforth Found, 60, Helen Wurlitzer Found, NMex, 61; D H Lawrence, Univ NMex, 61; Inst Creative Arts, Univ Calif, 63-64, 68 & 74; NEA, 74-75. Nominated for Oscar, narration of documentary film, "A Long Way From Nowhere," Motion Picture Acad Am, 72. Fel playwriting, The Am Place Theatre, New York, 67. Popular Panel Award Prize, ASCAP, 68-75. Visiting poet, Israel, 70. Regents Humanities fel, Univ Calif, 77; fel. Rockefeller Found, 79. Translation Award, 78. Hungarian PEN Mem Medal, 79. Scores: Libretto: The Cave.

KESSLER, RALPH
composer   ASCAP 1956

b New York, NY, Aug 1, 29. Educ: Juilliard Sch Music, MS; pvt comp & orchestration study with Tibor Serly & George Tremblay for 3 yrs. Established Ralph Kessler Productions in 67. Won Clios for "Sanka," "Polaroid" & "Benson and Hedges"; comp background music, "Buck Rogers", "Quincy", "Barnaby Jones", "Police Story" & other TV prog. Responsible for all musical treatments to score of "Man of La Mancha." Instrumental Works: Benson and Hedges; Yuban (Dessert).

KESTNER, JOHN NELSON (JOHN CLIFTON)
composer, author, director   ASCAP 1977

b Pittsburgh, Pa, June 13, 35. Educ: Carnegie Mellon Univ, BFA. Comp-lyricist off Bway "A Quarter for the Ladies' Room", regional theatre, "Starshine", "Fiesta" & "Mama"; contributor-orchr Bway "The Madwoman of Central Park West"; orchr off Bway "A Bistro Car on the CNR." Chief Collabrs: Ben Tarver, Phyllis Newman, Mark Rosin, Barry Glasser. Songs: Man With a Load of Mischief; Music: A Song of Lists; My Mother Was a Fortune Teller.

KETTER, PAUL STEPHEN
composer, author   ASCAP 1973

b Chicago, Ill, Dec 6, 32. Educ: Northwestern Univ; Washington & Jefferson Col; Marshall Univ; Tex Christian Univ. Began writing song poems age 14. Won poetry contest sponsored by sch. Began to write commercially, 68. Began own production & publ cos, 74. Chief Collabrs: Jim Webb, Joe Johnson, Bunnie Mills. Songs: Lyrics: The Things I Left Behind; The Games Grownups Play; Nashville Lights; Buddy Do You Need a Friend; Midnight Butterfly; The Badge; Put a Buck-and-a-Half in the Jukebox.

KETTLE, RUPERT
composer, teacher, instrument maker   ASCAP 1973

b Grand Rapids, Mich, Jan 13, 40. Educ: Union High Sch; studied perc with Donald Patterson, 50-58, Henry Adler, 58-62, Doug Allen, 60-62, Alfred Friese, 61; comp with Ted Maters, Henri Gibeau, J R Fortner, 55-62. Prof percussionist; teacher of perc instruments; author of articles on those instruments in various mag & jours. Author: "Drum Set Reading Method" & "9 Solos for Drum Set." Currently teaching privately & in affiliation with Aquinas Col & Grand Valley State Col. Instrumental Works: 9 Solos for Drum Set; Too, Max Dances (perc duet); Partchment (1 to 23 perc soloists); Vide (voice, vibes, vihuela, var perc); To Max: Dances (perc ens).

KEVESON, PETER
composer, author   ASCAP 1954

b New York, NY, June 6, 19. Educ: NY Univ, BA; Columbia Univ. Vpres & creative dir for adv agencies. Writer, TV commercials. Author, novel "Tubie's Monument."

KEVESS, ARTHUR S
author, arranger   ASCAP 1962

b New York, NY, July 17, 16; d New York, Jan 23, 73. Educ: City Col New York. WW II service. Author: "German Folksongs," 51 traditional ballads & songs in Ger & Eng from medieval times to present; "Tumbalalaika," collection of 17 Jewish songs in Eng. Chief Collabr: Teddi Schwartz. Songs: Ariran; Die Gedanken Sind Frei; Dona Dona Dona.

KEY, JAMES R
author

b Quinton, Okla, July 21, 25. Educ: McAlester High Sch, Okla, dipl 43; East Cent State Col, BS. Performing & writing gospel music, 50- Songs: Gospel: The Hem of His Garment; God Let Jesus Come Again; I'm Counting on You, Lord; I Met Sunshine When I Met Jesus.

KEYAWA, STANLEY J
composer, author, pianist   ASCAP 1958

b Oshkosh, Wis, Aug 15, 20. Educ: Chico State Univ, music; pvt study with Bruno Cesana, Wesley La Violette, Rubin Raksin. Began career writing-composing 3 col musicals. World War II, 3 yrs. Comp spec material for the Jack Benny Sportsmen Quartet, The Hi-Lo's, The Modernaires, Margaret Whiting, Charlie Chaplin Jr, Ben Blue. Comp main theme & title for 205 films of "Rin Tin Tin." Comp music for "Rescue 8", series, "Ford Theater" & "Tales

of the Texas Rangers." Comp spec material "NBC Chevy Show" for entire season, featuring Edie Adams, Janet Blair, John Raitt, Rowan-Martin, Dorothy Kirsten, Shelley Berman, Stan Freberg. Chief Collabrs: Barney Ide, Tom Adair. Songs: Anything Can Make You Sing; Come Back Music; The Silent Stranger; Lots of Folks; Available Me; The Fable of the Cable Car; No No Roulette; Music: Twelve Past Midnight; Make Mine the Same; Hula Hoops; The Sand Dance; Seeing Things for the First Time. Instrumental Works: The American Panorama. Scores: Musicals: Ready or Not; High and Dry.

KEYES, BARON
composer, author   ASCAP 1962

b Greenwood, Wis, Oct 2, 1898; d Gardena, Calif, Sept 26, 76. Educ: High Sch; Art Inst. Promotion writer, Milwaukee Journal, 20. On staff, Leo Feist, Inc; writer of special material, Van & Schenk, Olsen & Johnson, Blossom Seeley & Benny Fields. Writer, prod & performer in early radio; originated "Clickety Clock" (children's radio, then TV show). Writer, radio & TV plays & for Harman-Ising, MGM, Walt Disney Studios. Chief Collabrs: Darrell Calker, Scott Bradley, Clarence Wheeler, Nick Bolin, Vernon Leftwich. Songs: Sweet Someone; Mister Sippi; Ripsaw Blues; Sandy; Toy Land Broadcast; The Harvest Mouse.

KEYES, LAURENCE
composer, author, pianist   ASCAP 1960

b Kansas City, Mo, Dec 12, 14. Educ: Col. Organist, arr & teacher.

KEYES, NELSON
composer   ASCAP 1971

b Tulsa, Okla, Aug 26, 28. Educ: Univ Tex, Austin, BM, MM; Univ Southern Calif, DMA; studied with Ingolf Dahl, Halsey Stevens, Arnold Schoenberg. Pianist & teacher; comp, Louisville Orch First Ed records, ballets for Lester Horton Dance Theater & comp-in-residence, Louisville Ballet Co, & for piano, vocal, chamber & band. Ford Found, comp-in-residence, Louisville, 61-65; comp-in-residence, Univ Louisville. Instrumental Works: Hardinsburg Joys (brass quintet); Bassooneries (bassoon duets); Bandances (concert band); Three Love Songs (piano); Music for Monday Evenings; Abysses, Bridges, Chasms; Concerto for Bass Trombone, Winds and Percussion.

KHOURY, EDWARD A
composer, author   ASCAP 1950

b New Castle, Pa, Oct 9, 16. Educ: High sch. Writer, poetry for mags; assoc ed, Al-Phoenician; correspondent, Baton mag. Served, USMC, World War II. Bus mgr, Philadelphia prisons. Chief Collabr: Thomas Gindhart. Songs: Moon Over Tahiti; Country Music; Lullaby of the Trail; Juke Box Jenny; Fantasy; Orchids in the Snow; My Silent Prayer.

KIEFER, J
See Dant, Charles (Bud) Gustave

KIERLAND, JOSEPH SCOTT (JOSEPH SCOTT)
author, playwright, screenwriter

b New York, NY, Aug 6, 32. Educ: Univ Conn, BA; Yale Univ Drama Sch, MFA, studied with John Gassner; Brandeis Univ, drama, studied with N Richard Nash. Playwright, "Sunday", "Hocus-Pocus", "The Patriot Game", "Playsongs." Numerous playwrighting awards: Chicago Univ, Brandeis Univ, Cornell Univ, Town Theatre, Yale Univ, Hunter Col, New England Theatre Conference & others. Chief Collabr: Bobby Scott. Songs: Lyrics: Half a Crown; Johnny.

KIEVMAN, LOUIS
author, teacher, violist   ASCAP 1967

b Naugatuck, Conn, Aug 13, 10. Educ: Inst Musical Art, teaching cert; Juilliard Sch Music, studied with Franz Kneisel, Sascha Jacobsen, Leopold Auer & Dr Demetrius Dounis. Violist of Musical Art String Quartet. Violist & charter mem, NBC Symph. Violist & co-founder, Stuyvesant String Quartet. Principal viola at Columbia Pictures & NBC Hollywood. Pres, Los Angeles Am String Teachers Asn. Ed, Viola Forum, a feature of AST Mag. Contributor: The Strad-Instrumentalist; Violin Soc Bulletin; Viola Soc Quarterly; Nat Symphony Orchestra Asn Bulletin. Instrumental Works: Virtuoso Violin Technique (all works are string educ bks); Practicing the Violin, Mentally-Physically; Practicing the Viola, Mentally-Physically; Introduction to Strings (beginning manual for all strings); Building String Technique.

KILENYI, EDWARD, SR
composer, author, conductor   ASCAP 1927

b Hungary, Jan 25, 1884; d Tallahassee, Fla, Aug 15, 68. Educ: Hungarian State Col, BA; Nat Music Sch, Rome, studied with Mascagni; Cologne Cons; Columbia Univ, MA, PhD, fel with Rybner & Mason. Moved to US, 08, citizen, 15. Author, many articles on music. Teacher of George Gershwin. Music dir, film theatres, New York. Comp, music dir & supvr, film studios, Hollywood, 30 yrs. Pvt teacher, Los Angeles. Instrumental Works: String Quintet; String Quartet.

KILHAM, GENE ASCAP 1958
composer, author
b Rio Vista, Calif, Sept 23, 19; d. Educ: Pasadena City Col. Announcer, engr, writer, prod & account exec, KROY, KOA, WOR, WBZ, WWOR; sales rep, WCRB, Boston; mem fac, Cambridge Sch Radio-TV, Boston. *Songs:* Actress of the Year; Will-O-The-Wisp; The Bug; Gonna Put You Down; How Lonely Can You Get.

KILLGO, KEITH WESLEY ASCAP 1977
composer, vocalist, percussionist
b Baltimore, Md, Jan 30, 54. Educ: Calvin Coolidge High Sch, dipl 71; Bradley Univ, 71-73; Howard Univ, 73-76; studied comp with Russell Woollen, dance with Louis Johnson & performance with Donald Byrd. Recording artist, 73- Appeared on "American Bandstand" & "Soul Train." Rec'd Hon Citizen, Atlanta, Ga; Key to City, Detroit, Mich; Hon Citizen, Los Angeles. Chief Collabrs: Joe Hall, III, Kevin Toney, Orville Saunders. *Songs:* Mysterious Vibes; Time is Movin'; Rock Creek Park; In Life. *Instrumental Works:* Love Is Love; Something Special.

KILMER, JOYCE ASCAP 1950
author
b New Brunswick, NJ, Dec 6, 1886; d Seringes, France, July 30, 18. Educ: Rutgers Col; Columbia Univ, BA. Ed asst "Funk and Wagnall's Standard Dictionary"; literary ed "The Churchman"; poetry ed Literary Digest; contributor, NY Times Sunday Magazine & Warner's Library of the World's Best Literature. Lectr, NY Univ Sch of Jour. In 165th Inf, USA, WW I. Author "Summer of Love", "Trees and Other Poems", "Main Street and Other Poems" & "Literature in the Making." Ed "Verses" & "Dreams and Images." *Songs:* Poems Set to Music: Trees; Roofs; Memorial Day; Slender Your Hands; The House With Nobody in It; Christmas Eve; Gates and Doors; Stars; The Peacemaker; Lullaby for a Baby Fairy; The Constant Lamp; When the 69th Gets Back; Fairy Hills of Dream.

KIMBALL, NARVIN HENRY ASCAP 1967
composer, vocalist
b New Orleans, La, Mar 2, 09. Banjoist, 27-35 & with Preservation Hall Jazz Band, 63-; played guitar & bass violin, 35-63. Chief Collabrs: Harry Godwin, Mrs Lillian H Kimball. *Songs:* My Memphis Baby; Let's All Join Hands; Don't Let Old Age Creep Up on You.

KIMBRELL, WALTER CARROLL ASCAP 1979
composer, author, singer
b Pea Ridge, NC, Sept 3, 29. Educ: New Prospect High Sch; Jones Col, BS, 78. Musician & singer at nightclubs. Chief Collabrs: Cal Davis, Bill Bellew, Jim Lusk. *Songs:* Rice Paddie Lou; Lyrics: Picture in the Hallway.

KIMES, KENNETH F ASCAP 1954
composer, pianist, arranger
b Gillespie, Ill, June 3, 20. Educ: High sch, studied music with Ivy Metzler, Lydia Henninger; St Louis Inst of Music; Wash Univ, BM, studied with Leo Sirota, William Nelson; Northwestern Univ, MM. Pianist & arr with dance orch. Bandmaster, USN, WW II. Managing ed, Summy-Birchard Co, 3 yrs, advert production mgr, 52- *Instrumental Works:* Two Piano Boogie; Rainbow Concerto.

KIMMEL, EDWIN HOWARD (EDDIE KAIN) ASCAP 1956
composer, author
b Brooklyn, NY, Sept 11, 26. Educ: Queens Col-City Univ New York; Chiropractic Col NY, DC, 49. Instr, William Hargraves Metrop Opera. Singing & tap dancing, Radio WMIL & WEVD, New York, at age 3. Appeared on "Horn & Hardart Hour," 30's, "Uncle Don," 30's. Entertainer, Catskill Resorts, New York. Studied with Mabel Horsey, Eddie Lowe. Chiropractic orthopedist. Chief Collabr: Al Vann. *Songs:* Take a Bow; Lyrics: Why Did You Kiss Me?.

KINCAIDE, ROBERT DEANE ASCAP 1960
composer, arranger, orchestrator
b Houston, Tex, Mar 18, 11. Educ: Self-taught. Arr for bands of the Big Band Era, incl Ben Pollack, Benny Goodman, Tommy Dorsey, Fred Waring, Ray Noble, Alvino Rey & Ray McKinley, also for Kate Smith, Jackie Gleason, Lawrence Welk, Johnny Carson, Walt Disney World & Pop Symph. *Songs:* A Batch of Bud; Check the Chick; Music: Seven Spirituals. *Instrumental Works:* Boogie Woogie.

KING, AL ASCAP 1953
composer, musician
b Italy, Oct 27, 04. Educ: Pub schs. Musician with dance bands, 23-; mgr & theatrical agent.

KING, BONNIE B
See Berndt, Julia Helen

KING, CHARLES E ASCAP 1940
composer, author, educator
b Honolulu, Hawaii, Jan 29, 1874; d Elmhurst, NY, Feb 27, 50. Educ: Pub Schs; Oswego State Normal Sch. Leader in music educ in Hawaii & authority on Hawaiian songs. Taught, Kamahemeha Pub Schs. Inspector of schs, Territory of Hawaii. Cond, Royal Hawaiian Band. Senator, Hawaiian Legislature, early 20's. Author bks, "King's Book of Hawaiian Melodies", "Songs of Hawaii", "Favorites From the Hawaiian Operettas", "The Prince of Hawaii" & "Hawaiian Favorites for the Piano." *Songs:* Na Lei O Hawaii (Song of the Islands); Imi Au la Oe (Serenade); Beautiful Kahana; Ke Kali Nei Au (Hawaiian Wedding Song); Me Nei? (How About Me?); Paauau Waltz; Dreaming, Aloha, of You; Lei Aloha, Lei Makamae; Forevermore; Home in Hawaii.

KING, EDWARD C ASCAP 1967
composer, musician, guitarist
b Los Angeles, Calif, Sept 14, 49. Educ: Hoover High Sch, Glendale, Calif. Started writing, 67. Mem groups, Strawberry Alarm Clock & Lynyrd Skynyrd, 72-75. Chief Collabr: Ronnie Van Vant. *Songs:* Music: Sweet Home Alabama; Saturday Night Special. *Albums:* Pronounced Lynyrd Skynyrd; Second Helping; Nothing Fast; First and Last; Gold and Platinum.

KING, JACK (ALBERT) ASCAP 1935
composer, pianist, singer
b Tacoma, Wash, May 6, 03; d Hollywood, Calif, Oct 26, 43. Educ: Studied music with E Enna, Gabrilovitsch, Camille Decreus, Benjamin Fabian, Ernest Schilling & Isidore Philippe; Am Cons, Fontainebleau, France. Debut as child concert pianist, 10; gave concerts until 21. Europ debut, Berlin. Asst dir, Univ Calif Glee Club, 21, 2 yrs. Appeared in vaudeville & nightclubs. Singing coach. Wrote film scores. *Songs:* How Am I to Know; Any Time's the Time to Fall in Love; Everything's Been Done Before; Paramount on Parade; I'm True to the Navy Now; You Still Belong to Me; Live and Love Today; All I Know Is You're in My Arms.

KING, PETE ASCAP 1957
composer, conductor, arranger
b Greenville, Ohio, Aug 8, 14. Educ: Univ Mich; Cincinnati Cons. Arr for singers & orchs; cond "Fred Allen Show"; "Summer Family Hour"; "Hobby Lobby." Comp, cond & arr for records, TV & films. Pres, Nat Acad of Recording Arts & Sci, 67-68. *Songs:* A Night Out; The Wide Open Spaces; Whim of Fancy; The Breaking Point; The Mood I'm In. *Instrumental Works:* Lovers Rhapsody. *Scores:* Films: The Family Jewels; Which Way to the Front?; Badge 373; The Pied Piper; The Last of the Secret Agents.

KING, ROBERT A (ROBERT KEISER, MARY EARL, ASCAP 1920
R A WILSON, MRS RAVENHALL)
composer
b New York, NY, Sept 20, 1862; d New York, Apr 14, 32. Educ: Pub schs. Staff comp, Leo Feist; then Shapiro, Bernstein, 08-32. Appeared in vaudeville. Chief Collabrs: Ballard MacDonald, Billy Moll, Ted Fiorito, Howard Johnson, Gus Kahn. *Songs:* Why Did I Kiss That Girl?; The Fountain in the Park; Beyond the Gates of Paradise; Lafayette, We Hear You Calling; Anona; Beautiful Ohio; Apple Blossoms; Toot Toot, Tootsie, Goodbye; I Ain't Nobody's Darling; I Scream, You Scream, We All Scream for Ice Cream; Moonlight on the Colorado; Love Bird; Just Like a Rainbow; Dreamy Alabama.

KING, STANFORD
composer, teacher
b New York, NY, June 21, 12. Educ: Manhattan Sch Music; Inst Musical Arts, Juilliard Sch Music, studied theory & comp; comp with Aaron Copland. Mem ed staff, Theo Presser Co, Philadelphia, Pa, 42; reviewer educ dept, Mills Music Inc; arr, several CBS prog. Fac, USN Sch Music, 44 & Nat Guild of Piano Teachers, 50. Pvt piano-organ teacher, New York, 46- & San Diego, Calif, 69- *Songs & Instrumental Works:* Here's Boogie Woogie; I'm Playing Ragtime; A Girl and Her Piano; A Boy and His Piano; Stanford King Showcase.

KING, STODDARD ASCAP 1941
author
b Jackson, Wis, Aug 19, 1889; d Spokane, Wash, June 13, 33. Educ: Yale Univ. Press mgr, Yale Dramatic Asn & ed, Yale Record. Columnist in Spokesman-Review, Wash. Served, 3rd Wash Inf, World War I. Author bks of poetry, "What the Queen Said", "Grand Right and Left", "Listen to the Mocking Bird" & "The Raspberry Tree." Mem, Phi Beta Kappa. Chief Collabr: Zo Elliott. *Songs:* There's a Long, Long Trail A-Winding; There's a Wee Cottage on the Hillside; Enchanted River; Oh Oh Abdullah; Roll Along, Cowboy; Tiddledidee-o.

KING, T S
See Blume, David Nason

KING, WALTER
See Kosakowski, Wenceslaus Walter

KING, WALTER RILEY ASCAP 1978
composer, author, teacher
b Lexington, Mass, Feb 8, 51. Educ: Barrets Chapel High Sch; Tenn State Univ, BS, 72. Performed, nightclubs, Opryland USA, in concert with var artists incl Dells, O'Jays, Nancy Wilson & B B King on tour in Europe, Japan, Mex & Can, 2 yrs. Appeared on TV show "That Nashville Music." Chief Collabrs: Cato Walker, Jim Ashenden. *Songs:* Slice of Heaven; Don't Go Away.

KING, WAYNE   ASCAP 1933
composer, conductor, clarinetist
b Savannah, Ill, Feb 16, 01. Educ: Valparaiso Univ. Played prof football; former insurance salesman, garage & railroad mechanic. Clarinetist, Del Lampe Orch. Leader, own orch, Aragon Ballroom, Chicago, 9 yrs, made tours. Recording artist. *Songs:* Josephine; Annabelle; The Waltz You Saved for Me; That Little Boy of Mine; Baby Shoes; Blue Hours; With You Beside Me; So Close to Me; I'd Give My Kingdom for a Smile; Beautiful Love.

KING, WILLIAM ATWELL, JR
composer, author, singer
b Birmingham, Ala, Jan 30, 49. Educ: Rosedale High Sch; Tuskegee Inst, BS(bus mgt). Prof musician since ninth grade; now with the Commodores. *Songs:* Time; Too Hot to Trout; Thumping Music; Underground Aces; Lyrics: Brick House.

KINGERY, LIONEL BRUCE   ASCAP 1967
composer, author
b New Albany, Ind, June 13, 21. Educ: Wayne State Univ, BA(history), MA(guidance & counseling); USA Infantry Officer's Sch, Ft Benning, Ga, grad; Wash State Univ Labor Sch. Gen Motors factory worker, 40-, rep, Int Union, United Automobile, Aerospace & Agricultural Implement Workers Asn, Educ Dept, 64-, union bargainer/grievance handler/educr. Served term as councilman-at-large, Kokomo, Ind, active in Democratic politics, 30 yrs. WW II overseas vet, retired, Reserve Army officer, 20 yrs serv. Mem: NSAI, Am Fed Musicians; Am Guild of Authors & Comp; Poetry Soc Am; Int Acad Poets; Poetry Soc Mich & Fla; Int Belles-Lettres Soc; assoc mem NAm Mentor; Phi Delta Kappa; Adult Extended Learning Adv Council, Mich Dept Educ; labor mem bus, Indust Labor Adv Council to Mich Council for Arts. Active in Labor & Int Union, United Automobile, Aerospace & Agricultural Implement Workers Asn, 50- Gold Card Mem, Am Fedn Musicians. Chief Collabrs: Al Dero, Jeffrey Lavender, Sally Pavey, Dan Naborczyk, Howard F Graham, Henry Gaines, Joe Corso, Norman Clymer. *Songs:* Canticle in Meditation; Lyrics: In My Shangri-La.

KINGSFORD, CHARLES (CHARLES COHEN)   ASCAP 1939
composer, pianist, teacher
b New York, NY, Aug 16, 07. Educ: Pub & high schs, York, Pa, 25; Lebanon Valley Col, 22-24, studied with Edward Baxter Perry; Juilliard Grad Sch, 25-29, comp fel; studied with Harold Triggs, Rosina Lhevinne, piano with Rubin Goldmark. Composed songs performed by var artists in concerts, radio & TV, 34- Comp Bway shows "Boy Meets Girl", 35, & "Good-Bye, My Fancy," 49. Performed at Saratoga Spa Fest in "And Already the Minutes", 37; pianist, teacher & music therapist. *Songs & Instrumental Works:* Wall-Paper (For a Little Girl's Room); Down Harley Street; Alas, That Spring Should Vanish With the Rose; The Ballad of John Henry; Eros; Comin' Thro' the Rye (arr); Clovers; Command; Let It Be You.

KINGSLEY, EMILY PERL   ASCAP 1970
author, writer
b New York, NY, Feb 28, 40. Educ: Queens Col, BA, 60. In TV script research, CBS, "East Side/West Side." In production "John Geilgud's Ages of Man" & "Diary of Anne Frank." Assoc producer, ABC, "Everybody's Talking." Research interviewer, "The Dick Cavett Show." In research for Arnold Perl's film documentary "Malcolm X." Talent coordr, 22nd Annual "Emmy Awards Show." Writer, "Sesame Street," 70- Chief Collabrs: Joe Raposo, Jeff Moss, Sam Pottle, Dave Conner, Lee Pockriss. *Songs:* Lyrics: Sesame Street TV Show: Song of the Count; High, Middle, Low; No Matter How You Count Them; The Adding Song; The Count's Lullaby; Beep; Counting Is Wonderful; Fear; Ankle, Shoulder, Knee; Noise; When I Was As Little As You Are; Bellybutton Silly Song; Cooperation Song; Planning Song; City/Country Song; Hey! I'm President Bird; C-C-C-Cold; Run; Two; Ow I; You Are What You Eat.

KINGSLEY, GERSHON GARY   ASCAP 1968
composer
b Bochum, WGer, Oct 28, 25. Educ: Los Angeles Cons, BM; Juilliard Sch; Columbia Univ. Bway cond; arr of electronic music & founder of Moog quartet. Religious music & music dir, Ger TV shows; writer, major commercials. Recipient, Emmy awards, Clio awards. Chief Collabrs: Norman Simon, Robert C Larimer. *Songs:* Music: Shepherd Me Lord. *Instrumental Works:* Popcorn; Concerto Moogo. *Scores:* Opera/Ballet: God and Abraham; Religious musicals: The Fifth Cup; Sabbath for Today.

KINYON, JOHN L   ASCAP 1960
composer, professor, conductor
b Elmira, NY, May 23, 18. Educ: Eastman Sch Music, BM, 40; Ithaca Col, MS, 49. Taught music in pub schs, 20 yrs; was in mil, 4 yrs; educ dir, Warner Bros Music, 6 yrs; prof music, Sch Music, Univ Miami, 69-; clinician. *Instrumental Works:* Tangotoon (orch); Concert Band: Cherokee (a suite); North by Northwest (concert march); American Embassy (concert march); Festival Fanfare; March Bombastique; Panama Rock; Valse Moderne; Mellow Pudding; Let the Trumpets Ring; Dial 135-6421; The Big Rock; Concerto for Drum Pads; The Blue Rock; Happy Band Rag; Ocala March; Overture in Blue; Percussion on Parade; Rocko Poco; Royal March; Smoky Mountain Suite; Timpatico; The Pittipat Parade; Little Devil March; The Dragons of Komodo; Appalachian Suite.

KIPNIS, IGOR   ASCAP 1971
harpsichordist
b Berlin, Ger, Sept 27, 30. Educ: Westport Sch Music, Conn, 41-48; Harvard Univ, AB, 52. Debut radio sta WNYC, 59; solo debut, New York Historical Soc, 62; concerts, recitals & orchestral appearances throughout US & Can, 62- European tours, 67-, also tours of SAm, 68, 75 & 76, Israel, 69, Australia, 71 & 79. Host of weekly radio prog "The Age of Baroque," WQXR, 66-68. Fac, Berkshire Music Ctr, 64-67, Fairfield Univ, 71-77, Fest Music Soc & Early Music Inst, Indianapolis, summers, 74- Did many LP recordings for Angel, CBS, Nonesuch, Vanguard, London, Decca, Intercord, Kapp, Grenadilla & Golden Crest. Six Grammy nominations; Deutsche Schallplatten Prize, 69; Stereo Review Record of the Year Awards, 71, 72 & 75. Publ, "A First Harpsichord Book", "Concerto No 8 in D Minor" (JS Bach; reconstruction), "The Sufferings of the Queen of France, Opus 23" (Dussek), "Overture in E Flat for Harpsichord" (Telemann; from the Andreas Bach Bk).

KIRBY, CHARLES D, II   ASCAP 1976
composer, author, singer
b West Monroe, La, June 27, 30. Educ: Lafayette High Sch, La; Univ Southwestern La, 46-47; Southern Col Optometry, OD, 49; New Orleans Baptist Theol Sem, BSM, 55, MSM, 56. Practiced optometry, 2 yrs. Entered the ministry, 52; served as minister of music, Southern Baptist Churches in La, Miss, Ala, Tenn, Fla, Ga & Ark; presently serving the West Helena Baptist Church, Ark; have been choral dir and/or fac mem at numerous youth & children's music camps; served in several denominational music positions. Chief Collabr: Barbara L Kirby (wife). *Songs:* No Mountain High Enough; More Like My Jesus; It Is Good to Give Thanks; Music: Peace Like a River (arr); Have Thine Own Way; God's Love; Let Me So Live; The Seven Last Words of Christ in Hymns (cantata); Lyrics: Our Father.

KIRK, ANDREW D   ASCAP 1963
composer, author, conductor
b Newport, Ky, May 28, 1898. Educ: High sch. Cond, own orch, Clouds of Joy, 29- Recording artist. Chief Collabr: Arthur Terker. *Songs & Instrumental Works:* Cloudy; Wednesday Night Hop; Mind If I Remind You.

KIRK, THERON WILFORD   ASCAP 1960
composer, conductor, educator
b Alamo, Tex, Sept 28, 19. Educ: Baylor Univ; Roosevelt Univ; Univ Rochester Eastman Sch of Music. Comp of choral, orchestral & band works. Cond, choral fests throughout US. Chmn, music dept, San Antonio Col, Tex. Pres, Am Choral Dirs Asn, 68-70. *Songs & Instrumental Works:* Prayers From the Ark; Sonatine (piano); Te Deum (piano); String Trio; Smoky Mountain Suite (symph band); Aylesford Variations (symph band); Concerto Grosso for Piano and Strings; Symph orch works: Intrada; Vignettes; Adagietto; Hemisdance; Symphony No 2; Concerto for Orchestra; Choral works: King David's Deliverance (with orch); Night of Wonder (with orch); Noel (with brass ens); Easter Canticle (with brass ens); Four Seasons Songs; Five Shakespearean Songs; Four William Blake Songs; Nonsense Songs; & 1000 publ short choral works for sch & church.

KIRKLAND, MIKE JAMES (BO)   ASCAP 1975
composer, singer
b Yazoo City, Miss, Oct 11, 46. Educ: Dorsey High Sch; Los Angeles Valley Col, AA(liberal arts); Calif State Univ, Los Angeles. Lead singer, three man group, Mike and the Censations, late 60's; soloist, early 70's. Signed, Claridge Records, 75; teamed with Ruth Davis, 76. Chief Collabrs: Frank Slay, Robert Kirkland, Leon Haywood. *Songs:* Your Gonna Get Next to Me; Stay Out of the Kitchen; That's a Bet; Stay By My Side; Grandfather Clock.

KIRKLAND, WILLIAM HOMER   ASCAP 1972
composer, author, singer
b New Haven, Conn. Educ: Ithaca Col; Manhattanville Col, BA, 76. Recording artist for var record cos; producer. *Songs:* Jennifer; Memorize Your Number; Paradise; The Love We Need.

KIRKPATRICK, DONALD A   ASCAP 1964
composer, author
b Ft Sill, Okla, Feb 17, 28. Educ: Univ Tex, BBA; Am Theatre Wing. Served, Korean War, writer, scores for 2 USA revues. Chief Collabrs: Paul Kirk, Ray Hartley. *Songs:* Who's Afraid of Virginia Woolf?

KISCO, CHARLES (CHARLEY) WILLIAM   ASCAP 1936
composer, pianist, musical conductor
b Bridgeport, Conn, Nov 2, 1896. Educ: Bus Col. At age 7, studied with father; later with John Adam Hugo; at age 14, pianist for Poli Theater, Vaudeville Orch & "George White Scandals," 23. Recorded & ed player piano rolls. Music dir & pianist for Duncan Sisters, MGM films, "It's a Great Life," 24-29. Comp, pianist, music supvr, Film Studios, 30-60. Chief Collabrs: Harry Tobias, Henry Tobias, Ralph Freed, Sam Coslow, Leo Robin, Neil Moret, Al Hoffman, Jack Scholl, Harry Pease, Haven Gillespie, Pinky Tomlin. *Songs:* Music: It's a Lonesome Old Town; The Daughter of Peggy O'Neil; Song of Troy (Univ Southern Calif); Love in the Moonlight; Wedding of the Birds; It's Not a Secret Any More; Love Is a Dream; Cuckoo in the Clock; When It's Harvest Time, Sweet Angeline; You Really Started Something; The Laundromat Song; Gee! I'd Love to Be Your Sweetheart; I'll Always Love You; Way Down in My Heart;

Somewhere in Monterey; Promise With a Kiss; Rose Bowl; Annapolis Farewell; On the Cuff; Spring Is in the Air; The Sweetness of It All; Sons of Sierra; Waltz of the Chimes.

KISS, JANOS   ASCAP 1977
composer, educator, conductor
b Hosszupalyi, Hungary, Mar 20, 21. Educ: Bela Bartok Cons of Music, Budapest, Hungary, teaching dipl, 54; People's Educ Inst, Budapest, conducting dipl, 56; Franz Liszt Acad of Music, Budapest, 54-56. Taught brasses, Cleveland Music Sch Settlement, 64-79. Chmn, music dept, St Luke Sch, Lakewood, Ohio, 66-70. Dir of orch, comp-in-residence, teacher of instruments, Western Reserve Acad, Hudson, Ohio, 67-72. Instrumental teacher, comp-in-residence, St Edward High Sch, Lakewood, 68-74. Comp-in-residence, Lutheran High Sch, Rocky River, Ohio, 73-76. Chmn, music dept, Holy Family Sch, Parma, Ohio, 74-, St Ann's Sch, Cleveland Heights, 74-75. Co-founder, cond & music dir, The West Suburban Philh Orch, 69- *Songs & Instrumental Works:* Symphonic works: Interlude 40 (organ solo with orch); Western Legend (rhapsody for harp with orch); Concerto for Violoncello and Orchestra; Suite in Stilo Antico (orch); Via Lactea (The Galaxy) (symph fantasy); Sinfonia Atlantis (orch); Rhapsody for Cimbalom and Orchestra; Las Vegas (The Meadows) (cimbalom solo with orch); Chamber orch: Josepha (alto recorder solo with chamber orch); Chamber music: Osiris Nonet (flute, Eng horn, clarinet, bassoon, French horn, violin, viola, string bass & harp); Silent Presence (poem for clarinet, viola, piano); Episode (oboe, French horn, bassoon, harp); Winter's Sonnet (flute, harp, organ); Harp ensembles: Four Bobbing Masts in High Seas; Spring—At Last!; Vocal: Let Me Be Near (voice with orch accompaniment); Brass ens: In the Court of King Matthias (brass quintet); Processional and Recessional (2 trumpets, 2 trombones, organ); Brass solos: Impression (trumpet & piano); Trumpet Concerto (with piano); Solo for Bass Trombone (Or Tuba) With Harp; Woodwind ens: Two Pictures (woodwind quintet with harp); Evening Sounds (woodwind quintet with piano or harp); Woodwind solos: Flute Concert (piano accompaniment); On the Wing (flute & guitar; prize winner); Violin solos: Meditation (violin solo with organ or piano); Andante (violin with 4 trombones); Arr: Fugue (C Major) (by J S Bach); Concert band: Tableaux D'une Exposition (by M P Mussorgsky); Le Carneval Romain, Overture Opus No 9 (by Hector Berlioz); Till Eulenspiegel's Merry Pranks, Symphonic Poem, Opus 28 (by Richard Strauss).

KLAGES, RAYMOND W   ASCAP 1923
author
b Baltimore, Md, June 10, 1888; d Glendale, Calif, Mar 20, 47. Educ: Baltimore City Col. Appeared in vaudeville, minstrels & road shows; also wrote spec material. Served in 108th Field Artillery, WW I. On staff, New York music publ co. Wrote for films. Chief Collabrs: Louis Alter, Harry Carroll, Jesse Greer, Al Hoffman, Howard Quicksell, J Fred Coots, Jimmy Monaco, Vincent Rose. *Songs:* Doin' the Raccoon; Just You, Just Me; Blue Shadows; Pardon Me, Pretty Baby; Tonight or Never; Had I But Known; $21 a Day—Once a Month; What's Gonna Be With Ya and Me?; I Wonder Why; Time Will Tell; Roll Up the Carpet. *Scores:* Bway stage: Sally, Irene and Mary.

KLAGES, THEODORE   ASCAP 1946
composer, violinist, arranger
b Los Angeles, Calif, Jan 24, 11. Educ: High sch; studied with Fannie Dillon, Harry Schoenefeld, Charles Wakefield Cadman. Violinist & arr with dance orchs. Served, USA, World War II; violinist & arr for Maj Meredith Willson, AFRS, Los Angeles. Cond, Ream Gen Hospital orch, Palm Beach, Fla. *Songs:* Gimme Back My Nickel; The Lip; Lightnin'; The Wishing Well; Under the Harvest Moon.

KLATZKIN, LEON S   ASCAP 1950
composer, author
b New York, NY, June 19, 24. Educ: Studied trumpet with Benjamin Klatzkin, comp & arr with Mario Castelnuovo-Tedesco & Arthur Lange. Trumpet player, Universal Studio, Warner Bros & Columbia. Comp, cond & arr, Hal Roach Studio, 8 yrs, Bing Crosby Entertainment, "4 Star Playhouse", CBS, "Telephone Hour", motion pictures, TV shows & commercials. Chief Collabrs: Marilyn & Alan Bergman. *Songs:* Pink Shoes; Music: Sleep Well Little Children. *Scores:* Film/TV: Superman; Gunsmoke; 4 Star Playhouse; Gale Storm Show; Rawhide; Dennis O'Keefe Show; Telephone Hour.

KLAUBER, MARCY   ASCAP 1943
author
b Budapest, Hungary, Nov 19, 1896; d Hollywood, Calif, Feb 12, 60. Educ: Columbia Univ, Sch Jour; Nat Acad Music, Budapest. Wrote music for films in Hollywood, 30-60. *Songs:* I'm a Little Nobody That Nobody Loves; Goodbye Old Pal Goodbye; I Get the Blues When It Rains; O How I Adore You; Farewell; Gigolette; Rhythm of Paree; Juanita.

KLAUSS, NOAH   ASCAP 1961
composer, conductor, violinist
b Lebanon, Pa, Oct 14, 01; d State College, Pa, Dec 15, 77. Educ: Harrisburg Cons; Elizabethtown Col; studied with Hans Nix, Franz Zinner, Max Pollikoff, Zerline von Bereghy, Ottokar Cadek. Violinist in theatres, radio, TV & symphonies. Taught violin, 40 yrs. Dir of orchs, Elizabethtown area sch dist, Pa,

38-69, Elizabethtown Col, 58-61. Asst dir, Harrisburg Symph, Pa, 48-67. Founder & former dir, Harrisburg Youth Symph.

KLEIN, DEANNE ARKUS   ASCAP 1961
author
b New York, NY, June 3, 34; d New York, Apr 7, 75. Educ: Queens Col, BA, MA; Sorbonne, doctorate, 70; Juilliard Sch, scholarship; Fulbright grant. Promotion dir & press representative, Nat Artists Corp, 55-57. Assoc ed, Musical Courier, 57-60. Free-lance writer, ed & publicist, 58-75. Dir, West Side Symph, Eger Youth Concerts. Prog dir, Int Music Council, UNESCO, Paris. Developer of UN Symph Orch; staff critic for The American Record Guide & Review of Recorded Music. Mem, Music Critics Asn, exec bd, Metrop AV Asn. *Songs:* Sidewalk Santa.

KLEIN, JOHN M   ASCAP 1953
composer, arranger, carillonneur
b Rahns, Pa, Feb 21, 15. Educ: Philadelphia Music Acad; Ursinus Col; BA, BMus; Hochschule für Musik & darstellende Kunst (Mozarteum), Salzburg, Austria; studied with Paul Hindemith, Ger & US, Nadia Boulanger, Paris, Marcel Dupre, Paris. Church organist, 33-42; professional arr & comp, New York & Hollywood, 42-57. Carillonneur, concerts & recordings, 58-77. Author, bks "The First Four Centuries of Music", 2 vols & "The Art of Playing the Modern Carillon." Chief Collabrs: Hal Richardson, Elfrida Norden, Stan Rhodes. *Instrumental Works:* Cranberry Corners (symph band); Yellow Stone Suite (3 movements; symph band, chorus); African Suite (6 movements; symph orch); All Around the Christmas Tree; The Bells of Peace; & 65 var comps for handbells & choirs for schs & churches.

KLEIN, LOTHAR   ASCAP 1965
composer
b Hannover, Ger, Jan 27, 35. Educ: Univ Minn, MA, 56; Hochschule für Musik, Berlin, 58, studied with Boris Blacher; Free Univ of Berlin; Univ Minn, PhD, 62; Tanglewood, Berkshire Music Ctr. Comp, symph music performed by maj US, Can & Europ orchs & conductors, film & theater scores. Teacher; chmn grad studies in music, Univ Toronto, 72. Guest-prof, Hochschule für Music; consult, CBC documentary film "Stravinsky." Recipient, Rockefeller New Music Awards, 65, 67 & 68, Am Acad of Film Sci, Golden Reel Award; Fulbright fel, 58-69, MacDowell Colonly fel. *Instrumental Works:* Musique a Go-Go (a symphonic melee, orch); Symmetries for Orchestra; Design for Orchestra; Paganini Collage; Janizary Music; Masque of Orianna (chorus, orch); Musiqua Antiqua for Consort and Orchestra; Three Symphonies, Two Concerti (violin, cello); Philospher in the Kitchen (contralto, orch); Hachcava (voice, perc ens).

KLEIN, LOU   ASCAP 1914
author
b Albany, NY, Oct 11, 1888; d Hollywood, Calif, Sept 7, 45. Educ: Pub schs. Charter mem, ASCAP. *Songs:* If I Had My Way; Little Good for Nothing; Mama's Holiday; Now That We're Sweethearts Again; Little Shanty in Ypsilanti; Honeymoon Express; There's Someone More Lonesome Than Me; A Gay Caballero.

KLEIN, MANUEL   ASCAP 1914
composer, author, conductor
b London, Eng, Dec 6, 1876; d London, June 1, 19. Educ: London. Music dir, New York Hippodrome, 05-14 & Gaiety Theatre, London, 15-19. Charter mem, ASCAP. *Songs:* Moon Dear; Meet Me When the Lanterns Glow; Lucia; Home Is Where the Heart Is; If I Love You; I'm Looking for a Sweetheart; In Siam; Loving; Temple Bells; Ho! Every One That Thirsteth (anthem). *Scores:* Hippodrome stage: A Society Circus; Pioneer Days; The Auto Race; Sporting Days; A Trip to Japan; The International Cup; Around the World; Under Many Flags; America; The Wars of the World.

KLEIN, ROBERT ARNOLD   ASCAP 1970
author
b Syracuse, NY, Apr 10, 28. Educ: Univ Mich, BA. Producer, NBC, New York, 51-54, TV progs, Hollywood, 54-57; gen mgr, Freberg, Ltd, 57-60; partner, Klein/Barzman Productions, 60-69; pres, Klein Creative & Production Services, 69- Chief Collabrs: Bob Bain, Tom Bahler, Dick Hamilton, Larry Muhoberac. *Songs:* Lyrics: Have a Happy Day; We're For (You); Things Are Looking Up; Here's To; Call It Home; People Like You; The One and Only; We Light Up the Bay.

KLEINER, RICHARD   ASCAP 1957
author
b New York, NY, Mar 9, 21. Educ: Rutgers Univ, LittB. Army service. Writer for newspapers, feature syndicates; Hollywood columnist, Nat Endowment of the Arts. Chief Collabrs: June Douglass White, Hank Sylvern, Hugo Montenegro. *Songs:* Say Hey; It'll Get Worse.

KLEINMAN, ISADOR I   ASCAP 1961
composer, violist, violinist
b New York, NY, Jan 25, 13. Educ: High sch; Damrosch scholarship, 20-30. Mem, Roxy Theatre Orch, 46-49. Played in Bway theatre orchs; also with Hollywood Ice Show, indust shows. First violist, Am Symph of NY, 54-; with

Little Orch Soc, 58. *Instrumental Works:* Musical Offering; Suite for String Orch; Tone Poem Tel Aviv; Violin Concerto; Viola Concerto.

KLEINSINGER, GEORGE ASCAP 1946
composer, conductor

b San Bernardino, Calif, Feb 13, 14. Educ: NY Univ, BS, studied music with Philip James, Marion Bauer & Charles Haubiel; Juilliard, fel, studied with Frederick Jacobi & Bernard Wagenaar; also with Harrison Potter. Music dir, CCC camps. WW II, music supvr, 2nd Service Comn, ASF. Chief Collabrs: Paul Tripp, Joe Darion. *Songs & Instrumental Works:* Life in a Diary of a Secretary (Nat New Theatre Prize); Victory Against Heaven; Scherzo for Orchestra; Fantasy for Violin, Orchestra; Symphony No 1; String Quartet; Overture on American Folk Themes; Western Rhapsody; Clarinet Quintet; Street Corner Concerto; Sonatina for Flute, Cello, Piano; Pantomime; Westward Ho!; Joie de Vivre; Cantatas: Brooklyn Baseball Cantata; Farewell to a Hero; I Hear America Singing; For children: Tubby the Tuba; Story of Celeste; Pee Wee the Piccolo; Pan the Piper; Johnny the Stranger; Christmas Is a Feeling in Your Heart; Toujours Gai; The Growing-Up Tree; The Toy Box; Lollipoptree. *Scores:* Bway Stage: Shinbone Alley (from archie and mehitabel); TV Background: Greece—the Golden Age; John Brown's Body; Film Background: M D International; Kaiser to Fuehrer; The Inheritance.

KLEMM, GUSTAV ASCAP 1930
composer, arranger, educator

b Baltimore, Md, Feb 6, 1897; d Baltimore, Md, Sept 5, 47. Educ: Peabody Cons, studied with Gustave Strube; scholarship in cello with Bart Wirtz. Bandmast, World War I, Camp Holabird. Cond, City Park Band, Baltimore, 22-25. Prog dir & asst mgr, radio station, 25-38. Cond, Little Symph; music critic for the Baltimore Sun, 20-32. Ed, var music publishers; arr for concert orch. Head of prep dept, Peabody Cons. *Songs & Instrumental Works:* A Hundred Little Loves (Chicago Singing Teachers Guild prize); A Child's Prayer; London Rain; Love, You Are My Music; O Sing Again!; Prayer for a Home; Sounds; September Day; Weary Goin'; Three Moods and a Theme (piano; The Etude Prize).

KLEMM, ROBERTA KOHNHORST ASCAP 1973
composer, author

b Louisville, Ky, Nov 29, 1884; d Louisville, Aug 8, 75. Educ: Louisville Girl's High Sch; Univ Chicago; Univ Louisville Sch Music. Teacher, Louisville Pub Sch Syst until 09. Active in civic affairs. Mem: Woman's Club of Louisville; Filson Club; Nat Asn Am Composers & Conductors. Ky Col, also publ poet. Author poetry: "Quest and Other Poems." Chief Collab: Edward G Klemm, Jr. *Songs:* They Never Told Me. *Instrumental Works:* Souvenir; Holiday in Napoli; Shadows.

KLENNER, JOHN ASCAP 1932
composer, author, pianist

b Ger, Feb 24, 1899; d New York, NY, Aug 13, 55. Arr. *Songs:* Just Friends; Japansy; Window of Dreams; I'm Still Caring; Down the River of Golden Dreams; Heartaches; Crying Myself to Sleep; With Love in My Heart; Don't Cry Little Sweetheart; On the Street of Regrets; Smoke Dreams; Driftwood on the River. *Instrumental Works:* Fantasia (viola, orch); Variations (string orch); Squares and Rounds on "My Old Brown Fiddle" (string orch).

KLICKMANN, F HENRI ASCAP 1921
composer, arranger, accordionist

b Chicago, Ill, Feb 4, 1885; d. Educ: North Chicago Col Music; studied with Ernest Louffer (uncle), Louise Harmon, Mrs Walter Stein, Armin Hirsch & Alfred Piatti. Arr, Bway musicals, music publ & dance bands; also for Eddie Cantor, 6 Brown Bros, Sophie Tucker, Ben Lyons & Bebe Daniels. Prof violinist & pianist. Mem gov bd & former vpres, Am Accordionists' Asn. Chief Collabrs: Will Callahan, Al Dubin, Andy Razaf, Joe Davis, Bob Miller, Roger Lewis, Clinton Keithley. *Songs & Instrumental Works:* Sweet Hawaiian Moonlight; Weeping Willow Lane; Sing Me the Rosary; Just a Dream of You, Dear; Mindinao; Floating Down to Cotton Town; In Flanders Field; Sabbath Chimes.

KLING, HEYWOOD WOODY ASCAP 1970
author

b New York, NY, Apr 14, 25. Educ: Wesleyan Univ, BA with honors & high distinction in creative writing. Writer, Milton Berle's "Texaco Star Theatre" & "Carol Burnett Show." Exec producer, "All in the Family" & "Hot L Baltimore." Creator, TV Series, "A Year At the Top." Winner of two Emmy Awards. Chief Collabrs: Buddy Arnold, Dick de Benedictis. *Songs:* Lyrics: We Are the Men of Texaco.

KLOHR, JOHN N ASCAP 1939
composer, author, trombonist

b Cincinnati, Ohio, July 27, 1869; d Cincinnati, Feb 17, 56. Educ: Pub schs. Trombonist in bands, Cincinnati. Head of band & orch dept, music publ co. Author, "The Apex Band Book." *Instrumental Works:* Marches: The Billboard; Men of Valor; Soaring Eagle; Heads Up; Vigilance; Torch of Liberty; Peace and Progress; Arch of Steel; Fellowship.

KLOSS, ERIC ASCAP 1972
composer, saxophonist

b Greenville, Pa, Apr 3, 49. Educ: Western Pa High Sch for Blind Children; Duquesne Univ, BA, 72. Recording artist, has produced albums; comp & recorded sound tracks for films, 3rd place, Int Chicago Film Fest. *Instrumental Works:* Celebration (1st place, Seventh Annual World-Wide Competition); The Goddess, Gypsy and the Light; We Are Together; The Wise Woman; Afterglow; Now; Autumn Blue; The Force; Heavy Connections; Blue Delhi; Joni; Lady; Waves; Gentle Is My Lover; Morning Song; Love; Quasar.

KLOTMAN, ROBERT H ASCAP 1961
composer, author, teacher

b Cleveland, Ohio, Nov 22, 18. Educ: Ohio Northern Univ, BSMusEd; Western Reserve Univ, MM; Teachers Col, Columbia Univ, DME. Supvr music, Dola, Ohio, 40-41. Teacher instrumental & vocal music, Cleveland Heights, Ohio, 46-59; dir music educ, Akron Pub Schs, Ohio, 59-63; divisional dir music educ, Detroit Pub Schs, 63-69; prof music & chmn music educ dept, Indiana Univ Sch Music, 69- . Author "Action With Strings," method bk & "Learning to Teach Through Playing: String Techniques and Pedagogy," col string text. Chief Collabrs: Ernest Harris, Lawrence Burkhalter. *Instrumental Works:* String Literature for Expanding Technique; Concerto No 1 in A Minor for Violin and Orchestra (Accolay; orch accompaniment); Herald Quartet; Student Concerto (L Mendelssohn; orch accompaniment, viola solo); Four Violins in Concert.

KLOTZ, LEORA (LEORA NYLEE DRETKE) ASCAP 1961
composer, conductor, arranger

b Canton, Ohio, Oct 17, 28. Educ: Mt Union Col, BM, BPSM; Western Reserve Univ, MA. Soprano soloist, church choirs, Canton Symph; cond & arr, Canton Player's Guild; dir, Civic choirs. Vocal music supvr, Canton pub schs. Head of vocal dept, high schs, Louisville, Ohio, dir, adult church choir. Won Ohioana Authors & Comp Award. Mem: Am Guild of Organists, Am Choral Dir Asn. *Songs:* Sacred: Sing Alleluia! Christ Is Born; Sing We Now for Christ Is King; In Praise and Adoration.

KLUCZKO, JOHN (JOHNNY WATSON) ASCAP 1967
composer

b Newark, NJ, Sept 24, 12; d Las Vegas, Nev, Mar 23, 77. Educ: Curtis Music Inst Philadelphia. With Jan Savitt Band, Vaughn Monroe Orch & Gen MacArthur's Army Band. Cond, Johnny Watson's Kampai Kings, Japan. Chief Collabrs: Jan Savitt, Vaughn Monroe. *Songs:* Music: Racing With the Moon; 720 in the Books; It's a Wonderful World.

KLUG, GERALDINE DOLORES (GERRY KAYE) ASCAP 1967
composer, author, performer

b Allegheny, Pa, May 26, 15. Self-taught comp, performer. Professional beautician; entertainer; model for TV commercials, also photographer's model for commercials, newspaper & mag. Did shows for nightclubs, senior citizen groups & clubs. *Songs:* Lonely and Blue; You Gotta Have Love; Little Old Church; Hangup Blues; I'll Try Not to Cry; High in the Mountain.

KLUND, RICHARD ASCAP 1972
composer

b Eau Claire, Wis, Nov 18, 30. Wrote songs for Miami Dolphins football team. Chief Collabr: Johny Boudreau. *Songs:* Lyrics: Dolphins Go; Meet the Team.

KNAPE, GERALD BEARNDT
composer, author, singer

b Austin, Tex, Mar 6, 12. Educ: Austin High Sch; Univ Tex, 29-31, Univ Tex Glee Club under Dr Schram, studied under Mrs Morris, J Campbell Wray, Ethel Moseley Wallace & George Moody. With First Southern Presby, Memorial Methodist & Cent Christian Church choirs. With newspaper "Texas Poston" (Swedish-Am Newspaper; 84 yr old weekly). Mem, Cavalry, Tex Nat Guard, 31-34; 2nd, then 1st Lt, Tex State Guard, retired. Drummer, pianist, organist. Hon mem, Vasa, Sweden; 50th Award, Tex Press Asn; named hon commodore, Tex Tidelands Guard, 53. *Songs:* Honky Tonk Gals From Wilbarger Creek; In the Mist and Fog I See a Light; Just Let Me Forget.

KNEE, BERNIE ASCAP 1962
composer, author, singer

b New York, NY, Feb 14, 24. Educ: NY Univ, BA(music), 48; Columbia Univ, advanced musical educ; studied Schillinger Syst with Rudy Schramm, 48-50. Began career as guitarist; later leader in USN Seabee Band, World War II. Singer-guitarist, New York area, 48-50; made records for songwriters & publ; commercials, 51-; writer, 60-; made Bway debut in "Ballroom," 79; occasionally works in New York nightclubs; sings as cantor during High Holy Days. Chief Collabrs: Herb Miller, Horace Linsley. *Songs:* Without Your Love; Someone to Love; Music: Love Isn't Just for the Young; Give Me Another Chance; I Don't Feel Like Singing Anymore; Lovin' You, Lovin' You.

KNIGHT, ERIC W ASCAP 1976
composer, arranger, orchestrator

b Brooklyn, NY, Oct 24, 32. Educ: City Col New York, BA, 54, Mark Brunswick & William Gettel; Columbia Univ, MA, 60, Otto Luening & Henry Cowell. Arr, Arthur Fiedler & Boston Pops, 71-78; Pops cond with major symph orchs, 76-; now principal Pops cond, Baltimore Symph Orch. *Instrumental Works:* Symphony in Four American Idioms; Earth, Water, Space: Three Elements for Orchestra; Americana Overture.

KNIGHT, GARY
See Temkin, Harold P

KNIGHT, GLADYS (MARIA)
singer
b Atlanta, Ga, May 28, 44. Educ: High sch, grad. First pub recital, Mt Mariah Baptist Church, Atlanta, 48; toured with Morris Brown Choir, 50-53. Winner grand prize, Ted Mack's Amateur Hour, 52. Jazz vocalist, Lloyd Terry Jazz Ltd, 59-61; mem, Gladys Knight and the Pips, 53-; concert appearances in England, Australia, Japan, Hong Kong & Manila; appearances on TV. Recording artist, Brunswick, Fury, Everlast, Maxx and Bell, Motown & Buddah. Winner six gold records. Two Grammy Awards; named Top Female Vocalist, Blues and Soul Mag, 72. Other awards incl: Clio, Am Guild Variety Artists, Am Music, NAACP Image, Ebony Music, Cashbox, Billboard, Record World, Rolling Stone, Ladies Home Journal. *Songs:* Lyrics: I Don't Want to Do Wrong; Do You Love Me Just a Little Honey; Daddy Could Swear I Declare; Me and My Family; Way Back Home.

KNIGHT, JAMES B   ASCAP 1963
composer, author, singer
b Waverly, Ala, July 18, 29. Songwriter, novelist, guitarist & inventor. Started own record, bk & music publ cos. *Songs & Instrumental Works:* The Valley of Love; I'm an Educated Lover; You Got the Churn, and I Got the Dasher; Loving Is My Birthmark; Wake Up Old Hen.

KNIGHT, MORRIS   ASCAP 1963
composer, author, professor
b Charleston, SC, Dec 25, 33. Educ: Univ Ga, 55. Research grant from Ball State Univ. Broadcaster in Atlanta & San Francisco, 10 yrs. Founder of the first Int Brass Symposium, Atlanta, 63. Coauthor, "Aural Comprehension in Music" (text & records). Originator of forty discrete audio channels. Has done chamber music. Prof music, Ball State Univ. *Songs:* Music: Four Brass Quientets; Music for the Gobal Village.

KNIGHT, VICK RALPH, JR   ASCAP 1976
composer, author
b Lakewood, Ohio, Apr 6, 28. Educ: Univ Southern Calif, BS, 52; Calif State Univ Los Angeles, MA, 58. Educr; dir of develop, Children's Hospital, Orange County, Calif. Author, children's bks, adult non-fiction & articles for prof journals & periodicals. Chief Collabr: Vick Knight, Sr. *Songs:* Lyrics: Brass Bottle; The Squirrel Song; The Night the Crayons Talked. *Scores:* Film/TV: Send for Haym Salomon!

KNIGHT, VICK RALPH, SR (TOM FELL)   ASCAP 1940
author, composer, writer
b Moundsville, WVa, Aug 5, 08. Educ: Cleveland Prep Sch. Ad agency exec & poet; producer, dir, writer of broadcast progs: Fred Allen, Kate Smith, Eddie Cantor, Rudy Vallee, Gangbusters, Amos 'n' Andy. Screen, TV, mag writer & textbks; bk ed. Field comn USA, 44; decorations, Bronze Star Medal with Oak Leaf Cluster, Order of Brit Empire. Chief Collabrs: Walter Schumann, Henry Russell, Bud Dant, Johnny Lange, Edgar Fairchild, Hoagy Carmichael. *Songs:* We've Got a Job to Do; Savin' Myself for Bill; Clancy; I Love Coffee; My Valentine; Can't Say I Blame Her; When Linda Walks By; Boogie With Your Boody; Lyrics: Halls of Ivy; Melancholy Mood; The Lip; The Fiftieth State; Powder River; I Walk Alone; Junior Miss; Tom, Tom, the Piper's Son; The Only Thing I Want for Christmas; Serenade to Gabriel; Are You Listenin' Joe?; Honey Baby; Mocking Bird Lament; Moment in Sorrento; Dixie; Send Me; Coffee Break; Dear Mr Deejay.

KNISS, RICHARD LAWRENCE   ASCAP 1966
composer, string bass player
b Portland, Ore, Apr 24, 37. Educ: Self-taught. Played jazz, New York, 59-64; worked with show bands & dance bands incl, Woody Herman, Si Zetner; played jazz with Herbie Hancock, Donald Byrd, Pepper Adams, Don Friedman & Attila Zoller; worked with Peter, Paul & Mary, 64-70 & 80-; worked with John Denver, 70-77. Chief Collabrs: Paul Stookey, John Denver. *Songs:* Whatshername; On a Desert Island (With You In My Dreams); Music: Sunshine on My Shoulders; Season Suite; Song Is Love.

KNOPF, EDWIN H   ASCAP 1952
composer, author, producer
b New York, NY, Nov 11, 1899. Educ: BA. Producer & dir, MGM films. Chief Collabrs: Leo Robin, Jack King, Bronislaw Kaper, Harold Adamson. *Songs:* Everything's Been Done Before; Thank You Very Much; Through.

KNOPF, PAUL   ASCAP 1974
composer, pianist
b Bronx, NY, Feb 3, 27. Educ: Juilliard Sch Music; NY Univ, BA, 51; prominent instrs, Josef Schmid & Bohuslav Martinu. Jazz composer appearing mostly in concert halls performing own compositions, incl operas. Appearances on radio, TV & in night clubs. *Songs:* Faith of a Radical; When You Call Me. *Instrumental*

Works: Strontium 90; Blues on a Wet Thursday. *Scores:* The Murder of Agamemnon (opera).

KNOWLES, NORMAN GEORGE (NORMAN KAYE)   ASCAP 1960
composer, manager
b San Luis Obispo, Calif, Nov 8, 38. Educ: San Luis Sr High Sch; Calif Polytech State Univ, studied with H P Davidson. With Big Band until 58; formed group The Revels, 58. Produced surfing albums incl Wipe Out & Surfer Girl. Managed various groups incl The Sentinels until 66; personal mgr, Johnny Barbata. Chief Collabrs: Johnny Barbata, Tommy Nunes. *Instrumental Works:* Church Key; Rampage.

KNOX, CHARLES   ASCAP 1969
composer, teacher
b Atlanta, Ga, Apr 19, 29. Educ: Atlanta Pub Schs; Univ Ga, BFA, 51; Indiana Univ, MMus, 55, PhD, 62. Began as trombonist in Atlanta Symph Orch & Third Army Band. Prof music, Ga State Univ. Mem: Southeastern Composers' League, Am Music Ctr, Col Music Society. *Songs:* Music: Psalm of Praise; Festival Procession; Sing We to Our God Above. *Instrumental Works:* Solo for Trumpet with Brass Trio; Solo for Tuba with Brass Trio; Symphony for Brass and Percussion; Voluntary on Hyfrydol; Voluntary on Lauda Anima; Paseos; Symphony in D-Flat; Music for Brass Quintet; Sonata for Marimba.

KNOX, HELEN BOARDMAN   ASCAP 1924
author
b South Lawrence, Mass, Mar 7, 1870; d Blawenburg, NJ, Nov 10, 47. Educ: Pub schs; pvt music study. Exec secy, Am Acad Arts & Sci, Boston, late 20's. *Songs:* Hush, Ma Honey; Iljinsky Cradle Song; My Love of Londonderry; Carita; The Silent Hour; Autumn; The Russian Nightingale.

KOBRICK, LEONARD   ASCAP 1958
composer, author
b New York, NY, Dec 9, 12. Educ: NY Univ, BS; studied music with Felix Barenblatt. Cond, arr, Ted Lewis, Ernestine Mercer. WW II, USA, Inf; dir, Headquarters First USA; writer, comp & dir of musicals for annual tours of mil installations. Author "We Ripened Fast," div combat history; Bronze Star. *Songs & Instrumental Works:* Jumpin' Jupiter; Waiting for Jody; Once Over Lightly; It Ain't Like Texas; Item: Madison Avenue; The Branches of the Army; It's Talent That Makes the Difference; So Long, Good Bye.

KOCH, FREDERICK   ASCAP 1961
composer, author, pianist
b Cleveland, Ohio, Apr 4, 23. Educ: Cleveland Inst Music (scholarship), BM, 49, studied piano with Beryl Rubinstein & Arthur Loesser, comp with Gardner Read; Case-Western Reserve Univ, MA(music), 50, studied piano with Leonard Shure, comp with Arthur Shepherd; Univ Rochester Eastman Sch of Music, DMA, 70, studied comp with Herbert Elwell, Henry Cowell, Bernard Rogers. Began piano study with mother, age 6. Served in Armed Forces, comp 2 all-soldier shows, 43-46. Founder, Koch Sch of Music, 52; co-founder, Rocky River Chamber Music Soc & West Shore Concerts, Cleveland. In concert, as soloist & with Cleveland Orch cellist Albert Michelson; piano soloist with Cleveland Chamber Orch. Comp performed by Nat Gallery Orch, DC, Cleveland Orch, Orch of Am, New York, Columbus Symph, Lima Symph & Carnegie Mellon Symph & by soloists & chamber ens throughout US; cond. With Great Lakes Shakespeare Theater, Cleveland Playhouse, Berea Summer Theater, Lakewood Beck Ctr, 73- Winner, Comp Press Contest, 46 & Homer B Hatch Award in Comp, 50; recipient, NEA grants, Am Music Ctr Cleveland Arts Prize, 77; mem, Ohio Arts Coun. Chief Collabrs: Barbara Angell, Margaret Merryman. *Songs & Instrumental Works:* Dance Overture; String Quartet No 2 (with voice); Trio of Praise (voice, viola, piano); Sound Particles (piano, perc, reciter); Barometric Readings (perc quartet, tape); 12/12 (2 pianos); Children's Set (song cycle); Music for the Theater (brass quintet); City Moon (flute, vocalist, piano); Sonic (piano solo); Be Not Afraid; Feed My Lambs; Five Sacred Songs; Concertino (saxophone, orch/band); Symphonic Suite (voice, orch); Concerto (2 pianos, orch); Analects for Saxophone (quartet); Cantata: Violence No More (mixed choir, 2 sopranos, baritone, narrator, string quartet, rock trio perc, tape); Original music comp for: Comedy of Errors (Shakespeare); Italian Straw Hat; Good Woman of Setzuan (Brecht); Abelard and Heloise; Thurber Carnival; Girls of the Garden Club (Patrick); Hamlet (Shakespeare); Richard III (Shakespeare).

KOCH, HERBIE   ASCAP 1958
composer, organist, carillonneur
b Louisville, Ky, Aug 27, 03. Educ: Louisville Cons; Schulmerich Sch, Westminster Choir Col; studied with Arthur Becker, Robert Whitney & Marcel Dupre. Solo organist, Paramount Pictures, throughout US, London, Paris & Cuba, 12 yrs. With WHAS radio 23 yrs, WHAS-TV, 7 yrs; CBS prog "Keyboard and Console," 2 yrs. Carillonneur, Liberty Nat Bank & Trust Co, Louisville, World's Fair, Seattle & NY World's Fair, 64. Mem, Am Guild of Organists. *Instrumental Works:* Sabbath Evening Service; In Memoriam (J F Kennedy); Waltzing With Mary (32 vols of organ arr).

KOCH, JOHN JAMES, JR   ASCAP 1955
composer, author
b Amsterdam, NY, Jan 20, 20; d. Educ: High sch. Served in USAF, Europ Theatre of Operations, WW II. Worked as car salesman. *Songs:* I Want You All to Myself; Just You.

KOCH, JUDITH
See Ecker, Judith K

KOEBNER, RICHARD   ASCAP 1962
composer, oboist, teacher
b Wiesbaden, Ger, May 5, 10. Educ: Univ Wis. Music teacher, oboist, 30- Author "Oboe Method." Chief Collab: Joseph Skornicka. *Albums:* Music Educator's Elementary Orchestra.

KOEHLER, TED   ASCAP 1926
author, pianist
b Washington, DC, July 14, 1894; d. Educ: Pub schs. Photo engraver. Pianist in film theatre; producer, nightclub shows. Writer, special material, vaudeville singers & songs for Bway musicals incl "9:15 Revue", "Earl Carroll Vanities" 30 & 32 & "Americana." Chief Collabrs: Harold Arlen, Harry Barris, Duke Ellington, Rube Bloom, Sammy Fain, Jay Gorney, Ray Henderson, Burton Lane, Jimmy McHugh, Jimmy Monaco, Sammy Stept, Harry Warren. *Songs:* Get Happy; Between the Devil and the Deep Blue Sea; Kickin' the Gong Around; I Love a Parade; I Gotta Right to Sing the Blues; I've Got the World on a String; Minnie the Moocher's Wedding Day; Happy As the Day Is Long; Stormy Weather; Let's Fall in Love; As Long As I Live; Ill Wind; Some Sunday Morning; When the Sun Comes Out; The Moment I Laid Eyes on You; Now I Know; Tess's Torch Song; Wrap Your Troubles in Dreams; I Can't Face the Music; Don't Worry 'Bout Me; Animal Cracker in My Soup; Stop, You're Breaking My Heart; I'm Shooting High; Spreadin' Rhythm Around; Lovely Lady; Good for Nothin' Joe; My Best Wishes. *Scores:* Stage: Cotton Club Parade; Say When; Films: Let's Fall in Love; King of Burlesque; Up in Arms.

KOENIGSBERG, ROBERT MORRIS   ASCAP 1970
composer, author, publisher
b Lynwood, Calif, Nov 23, 51. Educ: Calif State Univ, Dominguez Hills (worked as student aide, music dept); El Camino Jr Col, Torrance, Calif. Singer of contemporary Christian music, soloist & with groups; formed own label, 77; writer & arr, special material for other artists. *Songs:* Reunion; He Helps Me; God Really Is Good; He Is Here, He Is Worthy; Any Old Stick.

KOFF, CHARLES   ASCAP 1951
composer, conductor, arranger
b Duryea, Pa, May 1, 09; d. Educ: James M Coughlin High Sch; studied music with Michael Fiveisky. Mem, George Olsen pit orch in Bway musicals incl "Good News" & "Whoopee." Arr, NBC, CBS & Paramount Theatre Orchs & music publ. To Hollywood, 42, comp for films & TV incl "The Man From Planet X" & "Topper" (series). Ed, Acoustics "The Applied Musical Acoustics of Michael M Fiveisky." *Songs:* The Man From Planet X; Sword of Venus; Captive Women. *Instrumental Works:* Spinning Song of India (trumpet, symph band); Arr: The Rafael Mendez Trumpet Solos.

KOGEN, HARRY   ASCAP 1937
composer, conductor, violinist
b Chicago, Ill, Dec 18, 1895. Educ: Studied violin with Franz Kneisel; Juilliard Sch Music, Percy Goetschius. In service, WW I. Toured Chautauqua with string quartet. Cond, violinist in theatres. Joined NBC, 28; cond, ABC & NBC until 48. *Songs & Instrumental Works:* Los Bomberos; Caprice Americana; Pictures in Pastel; A Toy Suite; Sons of Freedom; Tzing Boom; Convention City; March of the Blue; 5 Star General; Merlin; Let's Sail to Dreamland; Laddies; 3 Characteristic Moods (string orch).

KOHANIM, SHOKROLLAH SHOKIE (LOTFOLLAH)   ASCAP 1970
composer, teacher
b Tehran, Iran, Feb 9, 20. Educ: Am Cons of Music; Northwestern Univ, MM, 53; studied with Leo Sowerby, Jeanne Boyd, Stella Roberts, 46-53. Prof of music, Tehran Cons of Music; works perf by Am, Persian & Israeli artists & by Am symph orchs. Mem, Educ Music Inc; participated in Olympic Hymn award competition, artists Concurs Musical Int Rein Montcarlo, De Belgique-Bruxelles & Neil Elizabeth Mem award competitions, Chicago. Chief Collabrs: Russell Harvey, Richard Brittain, Elaine Skorodin Fohrman, David Wexler, R H Gordon, Rew Marnie Koski. *Songs:* Chicago Is My Town (voice, piano & stage band); Music: Song of Myself; Olympic Hymn; A Lover's Dream; Unfaithful; Divine Master; I Will Dwell in the House of the Lord for Ever; Ah, My Beloved, Fill the Cup That Clears. *Instrumental Works:* Tehran Souvenir; The US Championers March (concert band); Persian Overture (concert & symph band); String Quartet; Sonata Da Camera (solo violin); Triangle Concerto (violin, orch); Sonata in A major (violin, piano); Legend (violin & piano).

KOHLMAN, CHURCHILL   ASCAP 1952
composer, author
b Pittsburgh, Pa, Jan 28, 06. Educ: High sch; correspondence courses in business & law, also var civil serv courses. Held State & Fed positions. *Songs:* Cry;

Peddler of Dreams; I Hurt So Easy; There's No Escape; Just Another Smile; Bungalow of Dreams; Lonesome Lane; Cross at the Crossroads.

KOHLMANN, CLARENCE   ASCAP 1940
composer, arranger, organist
b Philadelphia, Pa, Sept 24, 1891; d Philadelphia, Dec 13, 44. Educ: Pub schs; pvt music study. Ed, collections of sacred music. Organist, auditorium, Ocean Grove Camp Meeting Asn Methodist Hosp Philadelphia & Mem Baptist Church, Philadelphia, 25 yrs. Editor.

KOHN, KARL   ASCAP 1963
composer, pianist, conductor
b Vienna, Austria, Aug 1, 26. Educ: NY Col Music, artist's cert, 44; Harvard Univ, BA, 50, MA, 55. Fulbright Res Scholar in Helsinki, 55-56; Guggenheim fel & grantee, Howard Found, 61-62; Mellon Found grant in humanities, 74; fel-grants, Nat Endowment for the Arts, 75, 76 & 79. Fac, Berkshire Music Ctr, Tanglewood; now Thatcher prof music & comp in residence, Pomona Col. Made contributions in performance of medieval, Renaissance & 20th century music. With his wife, Margaret, gave two-piano concerts throughout US & Europe. Serves on bd dirs, Monday Evening Concerts, Los Angeles. His works have been performed by Los Angeles Philh, Buffalo Philh Orch, Oakland Symph & in concerts & broadcasts throughout US & abroad. *Instrumental Works:* Castles and Kings, A Suite for Children (orch); Three Scenes for Orchestra; Concerto Mutabile (piano & chamber orch); Interludes (orch); Episodes for Piano and Orchestra; Esdras-Anthems and Interludes (chorus & orch); Centone per Orchestra; Concerto for Horn and Small Orchestra; Waldmusik-Concerto for Clarinet and Orchestra; Innocent Psaltery (colonial music for orch, symph, winds, perc); Serenade II (concert band); Concert Music I (12 wind instruments); The Prophet Bird-Concert Music II (chamber ens); Impromptus for 8 Wind Instruments; Encounters I-VI (solo instruments, piano); Paronyms (flute(s), piano); Paronyms II (saxophone(s), piano); Quintet for Brass; Three Descants from Ecclesiastes (chorus, brass); Sensus Spei (chorus of mixed voices, piano, intruments); also, music for piano, organ, harp, chorus & chamber music.

KOHN, RONALD THOMAS   ASCAP 1978
composer, author, singer
b Calumet, Mich, June 20, 48. Educ: North Platte Jr Col, Nebr; Chadron State Col, Nebr. Concert promoter; ballroom mgr; lounge owner; booking agent; singer; TV sports announcer. *Songs:* Are We There Yet?; Steele Street Revenge; Music: Uptown Tonight; Lyrics: Give It to Me.

KOKER, DANIEL N   ASCAP 1976
composer, author, producer
b Detroit, Mich, Dec 17, 33. Educ: Webb Cons of Music, Detroit; Fred Warington Sch, Del. Writer, gospel & inspirational music, for Rex Humbard, 20 yrs. *Songs:* Get the People to All Join Hands; Somebody Here Needs a Prayer; Knowing Jesus; Perhaps Today; Believe in Me; I Care.

KOKINACIS, ALEXANDER (NICK ALEXANDER)   ASCAP 1965
composer, author
b Lowell, Mass, Mar 11, 17. Educ: Lowell High Sch; studied law at Univ Suffolk. Personal mgr for wife's singing-acting career on radio, TV & films. Owned & operated large supper club with bros. Chief Collabr: Patsy Garrett (wife). *Songs:* Listen to Lacy (Jack Lacy theme song); This Is Forever; Top of the Hill; Christmas Is Being With Your Friends. *Albums:* A Walk With Mr Peeps (Storybook for children).

KOLDENHOVEN, DARLENE JOAN   ASCAP 1978
composer, author, singer
b Chicago, Ill, Oct 9, 50. Educ: Chicago Cons Col, BMEd, 71, MM(voice), 76; piano study with Joanne Grauer, 80; voice study with Virginia Parker, 66-71 & 74-76 & Ron Anderson, 80. Past mem, Chicago Symph Chorus; vocal solo with Chicago Symph Orch; lead & background vocals on albums of Ramsey Lewis, Abbe Lane & Pat Boone; vocals on TV show theme song "St Peter." Solo piano & voice in var Los Angeles nightclubs; vocals for TV & radio commercials incl United Airlines, RCA TV, McDonalds & others. Pianist; teacher. Chief Collabr: Bob McGilpin. *Songs:* I'm Not Alone Without You.

KOLE, ROBERT
See Kolodin, Robert

KOLODIN, ROBERT (ROBERT KOLE)   ASCAP 1963
composer, singer
b New York, NY, May 22, 32. Educ: Henry Street Settlement, studied voice & theory; Yale Univ, studied voice with Ben Deloace, 3 yrs. Singer, Bway shows, "Top Banana", "Wonderful Town", "Almanac", "Plain and Fancy", "Pajama Game" & "Mr Wonderful"; replacement lead actor in "West Side Story." Nightclub singer, 62- Wrote music for the musical version of "The Ghost and Mrs Muir" which had been optioned for Bway. Chief Collabrs: Sandi Merle, Vicki Lee, Dick Curry. *Songs:* Music: Laughing Is a Funny Way to Cry; Why, Tell Me Why; I Am Yours.

KOMEDA
See Trzcinski, Krzysztof

KOMPANEK, RUDOLPH W ASCAP 1974
composer, pianist, teacher
b Cumberland, Md, Sept 29, 43. Educ: WVa Univ, BM(theory & comp), 65; Eastman Sch Music, MM(theory), 72; studied comp with Samuel Adler & piano with Brooks Smith. Taught music theory at Eastman Sch Music; pianist for Mel Torme, Diahnn Carroll, Shirley MacLaine & others. Performed as pianist, arr & comp with Denver Symph, Milwaukee Symph, Montreal Symph & Rochester Philh Orchs. Chief Collabr: Elissa Viggiani. *Songs:* Music: Believe in You; Turtle-Wise; I'm Glad for You. *Instrumental Works:* The Seven Ages of Music.

KONDOROSSY, LESLIE ASCAP 1976
composer, writer
b Pozsony, Hungary, June 25, 15. Educ: Franz Liszt Acad Music, Budapest, Hungary, comp; Western Reserve Univ, music educ sci; Sophia Univ, Japanese theater, music & language. Cantor, violinist & cond, Hungary & Ger, 32-51. To US, 51. Citizen, 57. Founder, Am New Opera Theater Soc, 53. Teacher, Cleveland Cultural Arts Bureau, 54-71; pvt teacher & choral dir. Cond "Opera of the Air," WSRS radio sta, 55-57. Rep abroad, WCLV Fine Arts Sta, 66-70. Awards: Cultural Decoration Medal, Hungarian World Fedn, Budapest, 68; with wife Elizabeth Davis Kondorossy, received Martha Holden Jennings Found Award, 70. Chief Collabr: Lyrics & librettos, Elizabeth Davis Kondorossy. *Instrumental Works:* Ammophila Arundinacea (piano); Meditation for Organ; Kalamona and the Four Winds (children opera-oratorio, children's voices); Two Pieces for Organ, Chimes and Bell; Harpsichord Trio (alto recorder, flute, harpsichord); Son of Jesse (oratorio); Suite for Violin and Piano; Fantasy for Organ. *Scores:* Operas: The Voice (one act); Ruth and Naomi (one act).

KONING (KONINGSBERGER), HANS ASCAP 1969
author
b Amsterdam, Holland, July 12, 24. Educ: Univs of Zurich & Paris. Writer, 46-; radio producer & assoc producer for var motion pictures. Novelist & playwright. Chief Collabr: Michael Small. *Songs:* Lyrics: The Revolutionary; A Walk With Love and Death.

KONSTAN, MICHAEL ALLAN
composer, author, singer
b New York, NY, Apr 3, 46. Educ: Hunter Col, 1 yr. Composer/lyricist, 62- Staff writer, var publ cos. RCA Album. Chief Collab: Dorothy Horstman. *Songs:* Long Before; Back in a Little While; Meantime; Summer Love; I Will Rise Again.

KONTE, FRANK EARL (SKIP) ASCAP 1969
composer
b Canon City, Colo, Oct 2, 47. Educ: Alaska Methodist Univ; Univ Alaska. Worked at KTVA-TV, Anchorage, 67-68. Appeared on local shows throughout US, 68-73. Formed group, Blues Image, recorded for Atlantic Records, 70. Formed & produced, recording group Manna. Formed Konte Music Publ Co & Konte Productions. Joined group, Three Dog Night, recorded & involved creatively & technically with stage shows & video, 73-76. Pres, gen mgr of production & producer of artists, Int Automated Media, 76- Chief Collabrs: Dennis Correll, Sherwood Ball, Michael Pinera. *Songs:* Ride Captain Ride (gold record, 72); Midnight Flyer.

KOONSE, JOHNNY ASCAP 1972
composer, author, singer
b Kansas City, Mo. Educ: Port Allen High Sch; La State Univ. Played in first band in high sch; lead guitarist for Davis show bands & pianist for Grand Ole Opry road bands; tuner for piano & other musical instruments. Chief Collabrs: Bobby P Barker, Johnny Bell. *Songs:* (All Together Now) Let's Fall Apart; It Started With a Smile; Music: That's Just My Truckin' Luck; Nosey.

KOPITA, MURRY ASCAP 1950
composer, author
b New York, NY, Mar 10, 03. Educ: Commercial High Sch, Brooklyn, NY; bus admin & indust eng, NY Univ. Learned to play piano at age 10. Comp over 200 songs; on radio, TV. *Songs:* Olga By the River Volga; Send Our Regards to the Boys Over There; Sarabara; My Adorable One; God Bless the Land of Israel; Irene; I'll Never Forget the Night We Parted; Muchacha Mia; Come Back My Love; Ah! My Mama; Is It True What They Say About You.

KOPLOW, DONALD H ASCAP 1953
composer
b Cleveland, Ohio, May 11, 35. Educ: High sch. Sales engr. *Songs:* Oh Happy Day.

KOPP, FREDERICK EDWARD ASCAP 1964
composer, author, conductor
b Hamilton, Ill, Mar 21, 14. Educ: Carthage Col, BA; Univ Iowa, MA; Univ Rochester, Eastman Sch Music, PhD; cond studies with Pierre Monteux; cond-comp studies with Gustav Strube; cond-opera studies with Louis Hasselmanns. Vis prof, Southeastern La Col, 40-41; 1st Lt (CAC) & radar instr,

US Army, 41-45; cond, Baton Rouge Civic Symph, 46-48; vis prof, NY State Univ Col, Fredonia, 48-49; assoc prof, Univ Ga, 50-52; asst prof, Calif State Univ, Los Angeles, 59-62; free lance comp & cond, Film Studios, Hollywood, 62-; part-time fac mem, Moorpark Col, 69-72. *Songs:* The Denial of St Peter (oratorio); The Songs of David (cantata); We Thank Thee, Lord (motet); Dance Mass in Latin-American Rhythms. *Instrumental Works:* Symphony No 1 in One Movement; Symphony No 2 in A; Trilogy (orch); Terror Suite (winds, brass & perc); Conversations (woodwind quintet); October '55 (clarinet & strings); Three Movements (woodwind quintet); Portrait of a Woman (flute & piano); Five Sketches (piano & string quartet); Passacaglia in the Olden Style; five choral preludes for organ; two choral preludes for organ. *Scores:* Pepito (light opera for children); Bway Show: That Woman's Gotta Hang!!; Film/TV: The Smile of Recife; The Creeping Terror; Air Freight Specialist.

KOPP, RUDOLPH GEORGE ASCAP 1919
composer, conductor, teacher
b Vienna, Austria, Mar 22, 1887; d Calabasis, Calif, 1971. Educ: Studied voice & operatic literature, Frankfurt & Bayreuth. First violinist with orch, Folks Opera, Vienna; first chair violist & soloist with Los Angeles Symph; violist, Brahms Quintet, 12-23. Musical dir & cond, Wis Theatre, Milwaukee; musical dir with 5 piece band, comn to open Grauman's Million Dollar Theatre, Los Angeles, also musical dir, Milwaukee Athletic Club & Milwaukee Journal Radio Sta. Cond of orchs at Tivoli & Chicago Theatres. Co-founder, Young People's Orch, Milwaukee. Comp, arr & scorer, Paramount Pictures. Film score credits incl "The Sign of the Cross", "This Day and Age", "Cleopatra" & "The Crusades." Asst to Nat W Finston, MGM Studios; played for Franz Joseph. Entertainer, Huntington Mansion.

KOPPELL, ALFRED BALDWIN ASCAP 1943
composer, author
b New York, NY, May 6, 1898; d New York, May 31, 63. Educ: Pub schs. Gen mgr, Irving Caesar, Inc, 32-63. Chief Collabrs: Fred Fisher, Con Conrad, Irving Caesar, Irving Actman, Frank Loesser, Mitchell Parish. *Songs:* Popeye the Sailor Man; Be a Good Soldier While Your Daddy's Away; That Old Red Flannel Shirt My Father Wore; If I Took You Back Again; That and a Nickel Will Get You a Cup of Coffee; The Lord Knows What He's Doing; All the Girls Think I'm Wonderful.

KORB, ARTHUR ASCAP 1953
composer, author
b Boston, Mass. Educ: Boston Latin Sch; Harvard Univ, AB & MA(music); studied comp with Walter Piston. Naumburg fel, 1 yr. Writer & producer for Peter Pan Records. *Songs:* It Takes Time; Go On With the Wedding; Acres of Diamonds; Annie Oakley; The Fool of the Year; Just for You; Gone; A Lifetime Isn't Long Enough (To Be in Love With You); Goody Good Mornin'. *Scores:* Films: Demo Derby; Feelin' Good. *Albums:* Children's stories with songs: Widgy the Walking Whale; The Owl That Didn't Give a Hoot; Christopher Todd and the Foof; Little Toot.

KORMAN, GERALD ASCAP 1960
composer, author, singer
b New York, NY, June 19, 36. Educ: NY Univ, BS; Brooklyn Law Sch, JD. Singer & guitarist, nightclubs & hotels. Recorded for Paramount Records. Now practicing law, Orlando, Fla. *Songs:* Blue Denim; Hurry Back; Runaround; Blind Date Fate.

KORN, MITCHELL ASCAP 1978
composer, concert guitarist
b New York, NY, Jan 3, 50. Educ: Bard Col, BA, 73; Vassar Col, MA, 74; studied with Ellie Yarden, Ravi Shankar, Garcia Luis Renart, Roswell Rudd. Comp of dance works for Alwin Nikolais, Diane Germaine & Hannah Kahn. Original works performed with ensembles at Lincoln Ctr, Museum of Modern Art, Art Inst of Chicago & Memphis in May Fest. Artistic dir of Comp-in-Residence Inc; artistic rep to bd of dirs, Affiliate Artist, Inc. As 12-string guitarist, named world's best by Chicago Tribune & int concert artist of yr by Amsterdam Concert Asn. *Instrumental Works:* Purple Martin; The Ocean Floor; Aviary Pulse; Hot Fudge Eyes; Hotel Nicaragua; Piecentennial; Idiots Rag; Seabirds; Strolling; Flight and Migration; Haven. *Scores:* Films: Purple Martin; Piecentennial; Flight and Migration.

KORN, PETER JONA ASCAP 1954
composer
b Berlin, Ger, Mar 30, 22. Educ: Berlin Hochschule für Musik, at age 9; Edmund Rubbra, Eng; Jerusalem Cons, Stefan Wolpe; Univ Calif, Arnold Schoenberg & Ernest Toch. Cond, sch production of opera at age 13. To US, 41. Asst cond, Univ Southern Calif Symph Orch & Los Angeles Grand Opera Co. Cond, orchs incl Vienna Symph, Philh Hungarica, Munich Philh & Malmo (Sweden) Symph. Founded New Orch of Los Angeles, 48. Louisville Orch comn. Awards: Hartford Found fellowships; 2 Frank Huntington Beebe Fund Award. *Instrumental Works:* Concertino for Horn; Stings; Piano Sonata; In Medias Res (overture); Variations on Tune From The Beggars Opera; Rhapsody for Oboe, Strings; Violin Concerto; Exorcism of a Liszt Fragment; Trumpet Concerto; Beckmesser Variations; 3 symphonies. *Scores:* Opera: Heidi in Frankfurt.

KORNBLUM, ISIDORE BENJAMIN   ASCAP 1942
composer
b St Louis, Mo, June 21, 1895. Educ: Los Angeles High Sch; Univ Calif, Berkeley. Writer, songs & musical production in high sch & Univ Calif. Admitted to Calif State Bar, 18; pract law in Los Angeles, Hollywood & Beverly Hills while writing songs & scores. Chief Collabrs: Zion Myers, Clifford Grey, L Wolfe Gilbert. *Songs:* If I Were King; When Gramercy Square Was Uptown; The World We Love Will Live Again; Nobody's Lost on the Lonesome Trail. *Scores:* Bway: Blue Eyes; Twinkle Toes; China Toy; Patsy.

KORNGOLD, ERICH WOLFGANG   ASCAP 1939
composer, conductor
b Brünn, Czech, May 29, 1897; d North Hollywood, Calif, Nov 29, 57. Educ: Studied music with Fuchs, Zemlinsky, Grädener. To US, 34. Music adaptor & cond, Max Reinhardt's production of "A Midsummer Night's Dream" & "Die Fledermaus" & "Die Schöne Helena." To Hollywood, scored var films & wrote incidental music for "Much Ado About Nothing." *Instrumental Works:* Violin Concerto in D: Rosalinda (J Strauss); Piano Concerto for the Left Hand; Symphony in F sharp, Symphonic Serenade for Strings; Piano Trio; Piano Sonata in E; Three Quartets, Sextet, Quintet; Three Piano Sonatas; also var songs. *Scores:* Film: Anthony Adverse (Acad award, 36); The Prince and the Pauper; The Adventures of Robin Hood (Acad award, 38); The Private Life of Elizabeth and Essex; Juarez; The Sea Hawk; King's Row; Of Human Bondage; A Midsummer Night's Dream; Bway show: Helen Goes to Troy (from Offenbach); Operas: The Dead City; Der Ring Des Polycrates; Violanta; Das Wunder Der Heliane; Die Kathrin.

KORTE, KARL   ASCAP 1962
author, professor
b Ossining, NY, Aug 25, 28. Educ: Juilliard Sch Music, BS, 53, MS, 56; spec study with Otto Luening & Aaron Copland. Free lance trumpet player, New York, 49-53. Asst prof music, Ariz State Univ, 63-64; assoc prof music, State Univ NY, Binghamton, 64-69; prof music, 69-71; prof comp, Univ Tex, Austin, 71- Ford Found comp-in-residence, Oklahoma City, 61-62 & Albuquerque, NMex, 62-63; 2 Guggenheim fels & the Prix du Gouvernement Belge (Gold Medal), in Queen Elizabeth Int Competition, 69. *Instrumental Works:* Symphony No 2 and No 3; Matrix (wind quintet, piano & perc); Introductions (brass quintet); Remembrances (solo flute and tape); Four Blake Songs (women's voices, piano); Aspects of Love (mixed chorus, piano); Pale Is This Good Prince (oratorio for chorus, soloists, 2 pianos, perc); Symmetrics (saxophone, 4 percs); Concerto for Piano and Wind Ensemble; Concertino for Bass Trombone and Eight Winds; String Quartet No 2; Terry's Tune (theme from Metamorphosis; jazz ens).

KORTLANDER, MAX   ASCAP 1920
composer, pianist
b Grand Rapids, Mich, Sept 1, 1890; d New York, NY, Oct 11, 61. Educ: Oberlin Cons; Am Cons of Music, Chicago; pianist with many piano-roll recordings, 16. Exec, record co, pres, 31. Chief Collabr: J Will Callahan. *Songs:* Tell Me; Any Time, Any Day, Any Where; Red Moon; Bygones; Keep on Raining.

KOSAKOFF, REUVEN   ASCAP 1961
composer, author, teacher
b New Haven, Conn, Jan 8, 1898. Educ: Studied adv comp with Horatio Parker, Yale Sch Music; studied piano with Rudolf Ganz, Carl Friedberg & Earnest Hutcheson, Inst Musical Art; also studied with Artur Schnabel, Berlin, Ger. Concertized in US with famous cantors; organist, music dir & comp, Jenesis Hebrew Ctr, Crestwood, NY. Taught piano & comp. *Songs:* Cabalists (based on story by I L Peretz); Music: Jack and the Beanstalk (full orch, narrator); Song of Songs (text from the Bible; soprano, full orch); Violin and Piano Sonata; Lichvod Shabbat (Sabbath serv comn by Cantor Putterman, Park Ave Synagogue).

KOSAKOWSKI, WENCESLAUS WALTER (WALTER   ASCAP 1964
KING, WINSLOW WATERS)
composer, author, banjoist
b Toledo, Ohio, Aug 2, 11. Educ: Penguin music, Jack Spratts music & Shornack music; Toledo Univ, William & Mary Col. Studied music-comp & played with Paul Spor Orch. Served in Navy, WW II. Worked as draftsman & mechanical floor checker, Doehler Jarvis Div of NL Co. Retired. Chief Collabrs: Robert Stuart, Olenik, Dolly O-Curran, Howard Vokes, Loretta P Jackson, Miss Miskel. *Songs & Instrumental Works:* My Polka Lovin' Gal; The Polka From Outer Space; Just a Sunny Smile; Teardrops; Just a Little Corner in Your Heart; Now I Know Why; Katilinka Polka; Champagne Polka; Why Can't I Stop Dreaming; I May Be Wrong; Honey Street; Cheatin' Lips; Honeyed Kisses; Without You By My Side; Forget; Sugar Plum; Happy Valley; Teenager's Lament; Tan Ya Polka; You Took My Heart Away; Don't Say Good Bye; I Know I Know; I Need Love; Someone to Love; All the Time; Somebody Up There.

KOSLOFF, LOU   ASCAP 1956
composer, conductor
b Chicago, Ill, Jan 1, 04. Educ: Pub schs. Comp & cond, radio shows "Life of

Riley", "Sherlock Holmes", "Quirt and Flagg", "Blondie" & "There's Always a Guy." *Instrumental Works:* People's Choice (TV theme).

KOSSOW, GOLDIE FALK   ASCAP 1966
composer, lyricist
b Woonsocket, RI, June 13, 38. Educ: Bryn Mawr Col; Washington Univ, BA; Cath Univ; studied acting with Ella Gerber, New York. Partners, Dick Hyman & Patricia Friedberg. Chief Collab: M S Anthrope. *Songs:* Lyrics: Pretty Polly.

KOSTAL, IRWIN JAMES
composer, conductor, orchestrator
b Chicago, Ill, Oct 1, 11. Educ: Studied piano with Edward Vlaciha; Am Cons of Music, Chicago, 2 yr scholarship with Esther Payne; studied conducting with Nicolai Malko, comp with Stefan Volpe, New York, piano with Joseph Prostakoff, New York. In Chicago, pianist with var orchs; pianist-accompanist for Buddy Clark, Skip Farrell & others, with Art Van Damme. Orchr, Ted Weems, 2 yrs, var hotels, nightclubs, revues, floor shows & radio "Design for Listening Show." To New York; orchr & comp, TV shows incl "Your Show of Shows," 5 yrs, "Pat Munsel Show" & "Washington Square." Cond & orchr, "Garry Moore Show," 5 yrs (Emmy award winner). Orchr for Bway shows incl "Fiorello", "A Funny Thing Happened on the Way to the Forum", "Tenderloin", "Archy and Mehitabel", "Sail Away With Noel Coward" & "Westside Story." Cond, TV shows incl "Brigadoon" (Emmy award), "Julie and Carol at Carnegie Hall" (Emmy award), "Julie Andrews With Gene Kelly" (Emmy award) & "Carol Burnett" (Emmy award), movies incl "Westside Story" (Acad award), "Mary Poppins" (Acad award nomination), "The Sound of Music" (Acad award), "Bedknobs and Broomsticks" (Acad award nomination), "Pete's Dragon" (Acad award nomination), "Half a Sixpence", "Charlotte's Web", "Chitty Chitty Bang Bang" & "The Magic of Lassie." Chief Collabrs: Sid Ramin, John Green, David Heneker. *Songs:* The Race (Is On); This World Is Mine; Music: Gun Smoke; Million Dollar Dixie Deliverance. *Instrumental Works:* Concerto-Lights and Shadows; Petite Papillon.

KOSTECK, GREGORY WILLIAM   ASCAP 1977
composer
b Plainfield, NJ, Sept 2, 37. Educ: Univ Md, BM, 59, studied with Joel Berman; Univ Mich, MM, 61, DMA, 64, studied with Leslie Bassett, Ross Lee Finney; Cons Amsterdam, Neth, studied with Ton de Leeuw. Taught: Washington Jefferson Col, East Carolina Univ, Appalachian Univ, Columbia Univ & Univ Tenn. Composing, Knoxville, Tenn. Awards: Nat Asn Am Comp & Cond, 64; Int Spoleto Fest Two Worlds, 67; Pa Soc Arts & Letters, 67; World Libr Publ, 67; Ohio State Univ, 67; Sigvald Thompson Orch Comp, 68 & 72; Int Prix Musicale Concours Reine Elizabeth de Belgique Silver Medals, 69; Am Guild Organists, 69; San Jose State Col, 70; Int Delius Comp, 71; NC Fedn Music Clubs, 71; Distinguished Comp Citation of Music Teachers Nat Asn, 73; Calif Cello Club, 74; Int Premio Oscar Espla (Alicante, Spain), 76; Int Soc Contemporary Music, 76; Univ Tenn Fac, 77; Harvey Gaul Asn Opera Competition, 77; Nat League Am Pen Women, 77; Nat Endowment Arts, 77; Minn Orch Asn Competition, 78; Inter-Am Music Contest (San Jose, Costa Rica), 78; NY State Arts Council Travel Grant, 79; Int Wieniawski Competition (Poznan, Poland), 80. *Instrumental Works:* String Quartet No 4; Mini-Variations for Tenor Saxophone and Piano; Counterpoint for Indefinite Pitched Percussion Quartet; Chromatic Fantasy for Saxophone Alone; Violin Concerto; Clarinet Concerto. *Scores:* Opera: Maurya.

KOTA, LU
See Kudera, Lottie A

KOTTKE, LEO   ASCAP 1973
recording artist, guitarist
b Athens, Ga. Educ: High sch, grad. Started playing guitar during teens. Joined USN, Submarine Service. Played guitar in Minneapolis. Recording artist with Oblivion, Takoma, Capitol & Chrysalis Records. Performer, annual Europ tours, also throughout US. *Albums:* Leo Kottke: Twelve String Blues; Circle Round the Sun; Six and Twelve String Guitar; Mudlark; Greenhouse; My Feet Are Smiling; Ice Water; Dreams and All That Stuff; Chewing Pine; Leo Kottke; Did You Hear Me? (compilation); Burnt Lips; Balance.

KOUGUELL, ARKADIE   ASCAP 1962
composer, pianist, teacher
b Russia, Dec 25, 1897. Educ: St Petersburg Cons; Vienna Cons. Dir & teacher, Crimea Imperial Cons, Simferopal, 18-21; cond, NE Symph Orch, Beirut, 23-48. Piano soloist, US, Europe, Russia & Middle East. Founder & dir, Inst Music, Am Univ Beirut. Fac mem, Ecole Normale de Musique, Paris. Mem: Examining jury, Schulamith Cons Music, Tel Aviv (also pres); Concours Artistique de Paris; Paris Nat Cons; also int contests. Awards: Star & Cross Medal, Am Int Acad; Chevalier de L'Ordre, France; Officier d'Acad de la Repub Francaise; Medal of Honor, Lebanese Repub. *Songs & Instrumental Works:* Poeme (harp, cello; Calif Harpist Asn Award); Ballade (soprano, orch; Artistic Asn Paris Award); Suite Ancienna (viola, piano); Intermezzo (trumpet, piano); Danse Hebraique (cello, piano); Piano, Cello Concertos; Piano, Violin, Cello Sonatas; also chamber music for var combinations.

KOUNTZ, RICHARD   ASCAP 1927
composer, publisher
b Pittsburgh, Pa, July 8, 1896; d New York, NY, Oct 14, 50. Wrote weekly prog, KDKA, Pittsburgh. Exec, New York publ co, 27-39. *Songs:* The Sleigh; Be With Us Still; By Love Alone; Come Thou At Dawning, My Love; Come Thou At Night, My Love; Cossack Love Song; Elf Dance.

KOURY, REX   ASCAP 1952
composer, organist, conductor
b London, Eng, Mar 18, 11. Educ: Battin High Sch, Elizabeth, NJ; studied with Jesse Crawford & Bauman Lowe, comp with Wesley Laviolette & Ernst Toch. Featured organist with radio, Keith & Orpheum Theatres, 29-33. Pianist & arr with Veloz & Yolanda Orch, 36-38. Solo organist & pianist, NBC, 39-42. USAAF, 42-46. Organist & musical dir, ABC, WCoast, 47-58. Owner & operator radio sta, Coeur d'Alene, Idaho, 58-62. Musical dir, NBC, WCoast, 63-70. Wrote theme for "You Don't Say"; also theme, cues & underscores for "Gunsmoke." *Songs:* Music: Shooting Star; Waltzing on a Cloud.

KOUTZEN, BORIS   ASCAP 1947
composer, conductor, violinist
b Uman, Russia, Apr 1, 01; d Pleasantville, NY, Dec 10, 66. Educ: Moscow State Cons, studied with Leo Zeitland, Gliere; hon MusD, Philadelphia Cons of Music. Comp from age 6, prof debut at age 11. First violinist, Moscow State Opera House Orch & joined Moscow Symph under Serge Koussevitzky. To US, 23; with Philadelphia Orch as mem of 1st violin section, 23-27. Head, violin dept, Philadelphia Cons of Music & cond of orch, 25-62. Toured US in concert. Mem, NBC Symph under Arturo Toscanini, 37-45. Taught violin, Vassar Col & cond orch, 44-66. Organized & cond Chappaqua Chamber Orch, NY, 58-66. Comp of var works performed by maj symph orchs, chamber music ensembles & soloists. *Instrumental Works:* Symphonic works: Solitude (Poem-Nocturne); Valley Forge (publ award from Juilliard Found, 44); Symphony in C; From the American Folklore (concert overture); Sinfonietta; Divertimento for Orchestra; Rhapsody for Symphonic Band; Elegiac Rhapsody for Orchestra; Fanfare, Prayer and March; Concertos: Symphonic Movement for Orchestra and Violin Obligato; Concerto for Five Solo Instruments and String Orchestra; Concerto for Violin and Orchestra; Concerto for Viola and Orchestra; Morning Music (flute, string orch); Concertino for Piano and String Orchestra; Concertante for Two Flutes and Orchestra; Concerto for Full Chorus and Symphony Orchestra; Chamber Music: String Quartet No 1; Sonata No 1 for Violin and Piano; Trio for Flute, 'Cello and Harp; String Quartet No 2 (publ prize, The Soc for Publication of Am Music, 44); Concert Piece for 'Cello and String Orchestra; Serenade for Saxophone, Bassoon and 'Cello; Duo Concertante for Violin and Piano; String Quartet No 3; Trio for Piano, Violin and 'Cello; Sonata No 2 For Violin and Piano; Sonata for Violin and 'Cello; Landscape and Dance (wind quintet); Poem for Violin and String Quartet; Piano & organ: Feuille D'Album; Enigma; Sonatina for Piano; Sonatina for Two Pianos; Sonnet for Organ; Eidolons; Violin solos: Legende (violin, piano); Nocturne (violin, piano); Holiday Mood (violin, piano); Music for Violin Alone; Arr: Malaguena (Sarasate); Octave Study (Kreutzer); Russian Dance (Tchaikovsky); Cadenzas: Boccherini 'Cello Concerto in B flat; Haydn Violin Concerto in C; Mozart Violin Concerto No 3 in G Major. *Songs & Instrumental Works:* An Invocation (women's voices, orch); Lethe (medium voice); Words of Cheer for Zion; Dreamland (mezzo-soprano, piano); Violin Method (found of violin playing); Clown's Reverie and Dance (piano); Legende (Russian folksong, elem sch band); Melody with Variations (violin, clarinet, piano); Pastorale and Dance (violin, piano). *Scores:* Operas: The Fatal Oath; You Never Know.

KOVACH, GEORGE DANIEL   ASCAP 1978
composer, author
b Fairfield, Calif, Dec 29, 51. In nightclubs, also TV & radio shows. Recording artist & poet. Chief Collabr: Bill Duncan. *Songs:* Lyrics: Silence; Prelude of Revere; As Night Now Enters; When White Roses Turn Brown; Picked You Up (Frisco to Fresno).

KOVACS, ERNIE   ASCAP 1957
author, producer
b Trenton, NJ, Jan 23, 19; d Hollywood, Calif, Jan 13, 62. Educ: New York Sch of Theatre. Performer in radio, TV, films & nightclubs; comedian & actor. Author, "Zoomar." Rec'd Sylvania TV Award. *Songs:* Ugly Duckling; The Patty Cake; The Irving Wong Song.

KOY, PAUL
composer
b Ger, June 8, 09; d Honolulu, Hawaii, Feb 5, 64. Exec chef, Royal Hawaiian Hotel.

KOZINSKI, DAVID B   ASCAP 1956
composer, author, conductor
b Wilmington, Del, July 29, 17. Educ: Univ Del; West Chester State Col, BS; Univ Pa, MS, studied comp with A Constant Vauclain; Army Music Sch, Warrant Off Jr Grade; studied with Nadia Boulanger, Am Schs Arts, Fontainebleau, France, 69-71. Bandleader, 100th Infantry Div Band, WW II, 2nd Armored Div Band; cond, Wilmington Opera Soc, Mozart Singers, Wilmington Symph; guest cond, Bucks County Orch, USA Band. Now music dir & cond, The Brandywine Pops Orch, Wilmington; music critic,

News-Journal Papers. Arranger. Mem, Music Critics Asn, Am Music Ctr. *Songs:* Polish Carols (SATB): Glory to God in Heaven; Loola Jesu; Wonder! Wonder!; Five Miniature Polish Carols; Angels to the Shepherds Say; New Year Comes Flying; Glorious King Triumphant Today; Christ Is Risen; Shepherds, Tell Us All; When Our Lord Comes Living; Holy Messiah; What Tender News Ye Bring; Let Us Hasten to the Manger; Brothers All Rejoice; Shepherds' Chorus; In a Hut Lowly; Raise Your Voices and Rejoice; Sing a Carol; Sweet Hay; To Bethlehem; The Wise Men; Music: Sing Mary's Lullabye (SSA & piano); The Sky Became Silent (SSA & piano); O Praise the Lord, All Ye Nations (SATB). *Instrumental Works:* Suite for Strings; Project Percussion (13 perc instruments, timpani & orch); Variations for String Orchestra; A Children's Suite (five miniatures for orch); Polish-American Fantasy (orch).

KRAEMER, RICHARD O   ASCAP 1964
author
b Portland, Ore, Oct 22, 19. Educ: Stanford Univ, BA, 41. Chief Collabrs: Harry Warren, Sammy Fain, Jerry Herst, Ted Grouya, Joe Leahy, Al Rickey.

KRAFT, LEO ABRAHAM   ASCAP 1961
composer
b New York, NY, July 24, 22. Educ: Queens Col, BA, 45, comp with Karol Rathaus; Princeton Univ, MFA, 47, comp with Randall Thompson; comp study with Nadia Boulanger, Fulbright grant, 54-55. Prof, Queens Col, NY. Bd dirs, League-Int Contemporary Music, 73-79; pres, Am Music Ctr, 76-79; exec bd, Soc Music Theory, 78-79. NEA fels, 76 & 79. *Instrumental Works:* Line Drawings (flute, perc); Partita No 1 (piano solo); Partita No 3 (wind quintet); String Quartet No 2; Variations for Orchestra; Strata (8 instruments).

KRAFT, WILLIAM   ASCAP 1962
composer, conductor, timpanist
b Chicago, Ill, Sept 6, 23. Educ: Columbia Univ, BS, 51, MA, 54; studied with Otto Luening, Vladimir Ussachevsky, Jack Beeson, Henry Cowell, Boris Orr, Cambridge Univ, Eng. Music fac, Immaculate Heart Col, 59-60, Univ Southern Calif, 69-72. Asst cond, Los Angeles Philh Orch, 69-72; music dir, Young Musicians Found, 70-72. Instr, comp, contemporary ens & timpani, Calif Inst of the Arts, 73-74. Comp-in-residence, Univ NC, 75-76; comp & cond-in-residence, Univ Wis, 76-77. Visiting prof in comp, Univ Southern Calif, 77-78. Principal timpanist & percussionist, & guest cond, Los Angeles Philh Orch. Musical dir, Los Angeles Perc Ens & Chamber Players. Co-cond, contemporary chamber ens The New Muse; cond, Los Angeles Group for Contemporary Music. Chmn, west coast chapter, Int Soc for Contemporary Music; bd of dirs, Am Music Ctr. Recipient, Anton Seidl fel in comp, 52 & 53, Huntington Hartford fel, 64, Guggenheim fel, 67 & 72, resident scholar, Found at Villa Servelloni, Italy, 73, Ford Found Comn, 72-73, NEA award, 75, 77 & 79. *Instrumental Works:* Concerto for Four Percussion Soloists and Orchestra; Encounters II (tuba), III (trumpet, perc), IV (trombone, perc); Fanfare 1969; Morris Dance (perc solo); Nonet for Brass and Percussion; Theme and Variations for Percussion Quartet; Triangles: Concerto for Percussion and Ten Instruments; In Memoriam Igor Stravinsky (violin, piano); Des Imagistes; Double Trio; Soliloquy (solo perc, tape); Comns: Concerto (George Solti, Los Angeles Philh Orch, 62); Silent Boughs (Marilyn Horne, 63); Momentum (Nat Asn Col Wind & Perc Instrs, 66); Configurations (Ludwig Drum Co, 66); Contextures (Zubin Mehta, Los Angeles Philh Orch, 67); Games: Collage I (Encounters Comt, Pasadena Art Museum, 69); Cadenze (Charles Boone, BYOP Series in San Francisco, 71); Concerto for Piano and Orchestra (Ford Found, 72); Concerto for Tuba and Orchestra (Roger Bobo, Los Angeles Philh Orch, 75); Requiescat (Ralph Gierson, 75); Encounters I (Karin Ervin, 75); Ombres (Young Artists Series for Mona Golabek, 75); The Sublime and the Beautiful (The Boston Collage, grant from NEA, 79); Piece for Symphonic Wind Ensemble (Univ Mich Wind Ens, 79); Piece for Solo Percussion (Kenneth Watson, 79); Piece for Trumpet and Chamber Ensemble (Mario Guarneri, 79). *Scores:* Ballet: Birthday of the Infante (comn, Minn Dance Co, 79).

KRAH, EARL EDWARD (EDDIE RICHARDS)   ASCAP 1959
composer, author
b Pittsburgh, Pa, Feb 10, 21. Educ: Brentwood High Sch; Univ Pittsburgh; Los Angeles Pierce Col; Allegheny County Community Col. Band mgr, 36-39, leader, 40-41; first songwriting contract, 41-42. USA, 43-47 & 57-72, songwriting, promotion & distribution of recorded music & equipment. Wrote lyrics for gospel, also CW, MOR, popular & rock. Mem, Nat Acad Popular Music. Chief Collabrs: Sol Lake, Harry Green, Nat Mysior. *Songs:* Voo Doo Dolly; That Is How Things Are; Lyrics: Just a Guy to Love Me.

KRAL, IVAN   ASCAP 1970
composer, author, singer
b Prague, Czech. Educ: Prague High Sch; State Univ NY Col, Genesco, BA, 70. Musician & singer, var bands incl Luger, Shaun Cassidy, Blondie, Patti Smith & Iggy Pop, on TV, in clubs, concert halls & stadiums. Recording artist for var cos. Filmmaker, "The Blank Generation," 75. Chief Collabrs: Patti Smith, Lenny Kaye, Richard Sohl, Jay Daugherty, James Osterberg, Kathy Chamberlain. *Songs:* Music: Kimberly; Birdland; Ask the Angels; Ain't It Strange; Pissing in the River; Pumping (My Heart); Space Monkey; 25th Floor; Dancing Barefoot; Revenge; Citizenship; Seven Ways of Going. *Scores:* Films: Unmade Beds; The Foreigner.

KRAMER, A WALTER
ASCAP 1917
composer, editor

b New York, NY, Sept 23, 1890; d New York, Apr 8, 69. Educ: City Col New York; studied music with Maximilian Kramer (father), Carl Hauser & Richard Arnold. Staff, Musical America, 10-22; ed-in-chief, 29-36. Music supvr, CBS Network, 27. Managing dir & vpres, Galaxy Music, 36. Co-founder, Soc for Publication of Am Music, 19; pres, 34-40. Mem adv bd, League of Comp, 34-40 & US Section, Int Soc for Contemporary Music. Dir, ASCAP, 41-56. Pres, Musicians Club of NY, 58-59. *Songs:* The Last Hour; The Great Awakening; Pleading; Clouds; Swans; The Faltering Dusk. *Songs & Instrumental Works:* 2 Symphonic Sketches; Symphonic Rhapsody in F (violin); Elegy in G (cello); Organ: Eclogue; Processional; Piano: Epilogue; Intermezzo; Toward Evening; Cypresses; Choral: Beauty of Earth; In Normandy.

KRAMER, AARON
ASCAP 1969
author, educator

b Brooklyn, NY, Dec 13, 21. Educ: Brooklyn Col, BA, 41, studied with Abraham Maslow, Frederic Ewen, Howard Selsam, MA, 51, studied with Vernon Loggins, Alan Walker Reed; NY Univ, PhD, 66, studied with Leon Edel, John Russell Brown, M L Rosenthal, Charles W Dunn, Jess Bessinger. Co-ed, Brooklyn Col Observer, 40-41, West Hills Rev, 79- & Paumanok Rising, 80; publ in many mags & jours. Staff contribr, Harlem Quart, 49-50, Sing Out, 50-53 & Village Voice, 63-64. Prof Eng, Dowling Col, 61- Pioneer in field of poetry therapy, New York Guild for Jewish Blind & Hillside Hosp, 56-60, Cleary Sch for Deaf & Cent Islip State Hosp, 69-78 & others. Over 60 radio progs, WNYC, WBAI, since 61; publ readings, Carnegie Hall, New York Town Hall, Provincetown Playhouse, Wilshire Ebell Theatre, Los Angeles, Univ Kans, Univ London & Donnell Libr (annually since 64). Author 26 vols poetry, criticism & transl of Heine, Rilke, Peretz, Rosenfeld & others. Author "The Prophetic Tradition in American Poetry, 1835-1900", "On Freedom's Side: American Poems of Protest", "On the Way to Palermo", "Carousel Parkway", "Rumshinsky's Hat." Many awards & fels. Chief Collabrs: Lukas Foss, Charles Wakefield Cadman, Donald Swann, Earl Robinson, Pete Seeger, Michael Sahl, Richard Neumann, Arnold Black, Irwin Heilner, Waldemar Hille, Serge Hovey, Michael Cherry, Betty Sanders, Eugene Glickman, Pauline Konstantin. *Songs & Instrumental Works:* Denmark Vesey (oratorio); A Ballad of August Bondi (cantata for choir, orch); United Nations Cantata (choir, orch); Monticello (political rev); Chelm: A Madrigal Comedy; The Ghosts of Amsterdam (oratorio); Moses (oratorio); Lyrics for: Partisan Hymn; Prothalamium; A Song for Peace; In Contempt; October Song; Marching Song (The Road I Have Taken); Lullaby; My Poems Are Full of Poison; Ballad of Jesus; Neruda in Hiding. *Scores:* Opera: The Emperor of Atlantis (transl); Film/TV/BBC radio scripts: The Mattress (short film); The Tinderbox (verse drama with music); Death Takes a Holiday; The Neglected Poems of Herman Melville. *Albums:* Serenade: Poets of New York; On Freedom's Side: The Songs and Poems of Aaron Kramer.

KRAMER, ALEX CHARLES
ASCAP 1942
composer, author, pianist

b Montreal, Que, May 30, 03. Educ: Pvt piano study with Dunev, Gardner & Hungerford, Montreal. Dir, ASCAP, 54-59. Pianist with var dance orchs, nightclubs, hotels, Paris, Palm Beach & vaudeville theatres. Vocal coach for Aileen Stanley. Led own band, Canadian Network. Publ, Kramer-Whitney Inc & Whitney-Kramer-Zaret Music Co. Former exec vpres & chmn housekeeping comn, Am Guild of Authors & Composers, co-founder & 4-term pres, Veterans Hospital Radio & TV Guild. Chief Collabrs: Joan Whitney (wife), Mack David, Hy Zaret. *Songs:* Far Away Places; Candy; No Man Is an Island; High on a Windy Hill; Ain't Nobody Here But Us Chickens; Love Somebody; It's Love, Love, Love; It All Comes Back to Me Now; My Sister and I; So You're the One; Money Is the Root of All Evil; TV themes: So Long for Awhile; A Room in Paris. *Scores:* Films: Second Greatest Sex; How Lonely Can I Get; Meet Miss Bobby Socks; Come With Me My Honey; Simon; Far Away Places.

KRAMER, ALEXANDER MILTON
ASCAP 1950
composer, arranger, cellist

b New York, NY, Sept 13, 1893; d New York, Aug 25, 55. Educ: Pub schs; pvt music study. Served in USN, WW I. Cellist in theatre orchs; arr for vaudeville & musical comedy singers, 20 yrs. Arr & librarian for Maj Bowes. Compiler, arr of 12 music folios. *Songs:* Everybody Clap Hands; Nickel Serenade; Dear Old Donegal; Derry Dun; Let's Make Love; Longer Than Forever; When Hearts Are in Harmony.

KRAMER, ZOE PARENTEAU (JOAN WHITNEY)
ASCAP 1942
composer, author, singer

b Pittsburgh, Pa, June 26, 14. Educ: Carnegie Tech, Pa; Finch Col, NY. Daughter of comp Zoel Parenteau. Featured singer with own show, CBS Network. Recorded with var artists incl Leo Reisman, Will Osbourne & Enric Madriguera. Appeared, Bway musical "The Great Waltz," 2 seasons. Staff writer, Sun Music; co-founder, publ firm Kramer-Whitney Inc, 47 & record co, Southside Records, 61. Chief Collabrs: Alex Kramer (husband), Hy Zaret. *Songs:* Far Away Places; Candy; No Man Is an Island; High on a Windy Hill; It's Love, Love, Love; Ain't Nobody Here But Us Chickens; Love Somebody; Money Is the Root of All Evil; I Only Saw Him Once; Behave Yourself; Before I Loved You; Summer Rain; That's the Beginning of the End; The Way That the Wind Blows; Christmas Roses; Come With Me My Honey; Comne Ci-Comme Ca; It All Comes Back to Me Now; My Sister and I; No Other Arms-No Other Lips; You'll Never Get Away; What's This World A-Comin' Too?; TV themes: So Long for Awhile; A Room in Paris. *Scores:* Second Greatest Sex; Meet Miss Bobby Sox; Far Away Places.

KRANCE, JOHN PAUL JR
ASCAP 1960
composer, arranger, conductor

b Bridgeport, Conn, June 25, 34. Educ: Univ Rochester Eastman Sch Music, BM, 55; French horn player, Eastman Symph Orch & Eastman Wind Ens, cond, Student Chamber Orch. Worked for radio stas, Rochester, NY & Washington, DC. Instr French horn, Transylvania Music Camp; mem, Brevard Fest Orch. USA, 55-58, arr, Army Field Band, Washington, DC, also made concert tours with band. Ed asst, MPHC, Warner Bros, 58-59; music dir radio sta WPAT, New York, 63-67; arr for recordings & music supvr for "All My Children," ABC-TV, 68-71. Music teacher, Arlington & Fairfax Pub Schs, Va, 71-73; assoc prof, Syracuse Univ, 73-75. Free-lance musician, comp, arr & consult in music media, 75- *Songs & Instrumental Works:* Permian Earth Song (symph orch & mixed chorus); Scenario for Band; Introduction and Satire (woodwind quintet); Symphonic Fanfares (concert band); Dialogue for Trumpet and Band; Regalia Fanfare (herald trumpets); Epitaphs for Orchestra; Band Arr: Broadway Curtain Time; Broadway Minstrel Medley; Five Miniatures (Turina); An American in Paris (Gershwin); Carousel Waltz (Rodgers); Danzon from "Fancy Free" (Bernstein); Drummers' Delight (Mancini); Cuban Overture (Gershwin); Jalousie (Jealousy) (Gade); Days of Wine and Roses (Mancini); Highlights from "Mame" (Herman); Second Prelude (Gershwin); Harlem Nocturne (Hagen); Overture to "Titus" (Mozart); Selections from "Mr Lucky" (Mancini); various Cole Porter songs.

KRANE, DAVID MARC
ASCAP 1971
composer

b Brooklyn, NY, Feb 14, 53. Educ: High Sch Music & Art, 69; Mannes Col Music, Prep Dept, 69; Curtis Inst Music, BM(comp) & Leonard Bernstein Found grant, 74. Comp, arr, cond & musical dir; comp score for pub TV spec, "Silent Dancing"; dance arr for Bway productions of "Peter Pan" & "Carmelina" & Am Ballet Theatre's, "Top Hat & Tails"; musical dir, Am Dance Machine; cond Meryl Streep in Bway production, "Happyend." Chief Collabr: William Wauters. *Songs & Instrumental Works:* Little Suite for Harpsichord; A Pretty a Day (chorus); A Vagabond Song (female chorus); Celebration: A Liturgical Experience (chorus). *Scores:* Opera: Columbus (cantata for chorus & instruments).

KRANE, SHERMAN M
ASCAP 1960
composer, teacher

b New Haven, Conn, Nov 18, 27. Educ: Hartt Col of Music, BM, MM; Mich State Univ, PhD. Taught at Hotchkiss Sch for Boys & Con pub schs. Teacher asst, Hartt Col, Mich State Univ. Visiting lectr, Virgin Islands Exp Col; dir music, Bernard Horwich Jewish Comn Ctr, Chicago. *Scores:* Opera: The Giant's Garden; Film Background: Village of My Fathers; The World of Lindsey Decker.

KRASNOR, DAVID
ASCAP 1953
composer, author

b Boston, Mass, May 21, 21. Educ: Berklee Sch Music, orchestration & piano, 1 yr; studied classical piano for 9 yrs with var teachers & popular music with Josef Rysman for 3 yrs. Chief Collabrs: Ted Rosan, Jordan Ramin. *Songs:* Herkimer, the Homely Doll.

KRASNOW, HERMANN (HECKY) (STEPHEN GALE, STEVE MANN)
ASCAP 1953
composer

b Hartford, Conn, Feb 15, 10. Educ: Juilliard Sch Music; studied violin with Leopold Aver. Violinist, Bway musical shows. Wrote & produced children's records; dir, Columbia Records Children's-Educ Dept, 49-56. Free lance writer & producer. Chief Collabrs: Joe Darion, Bill Lovelock, Jimmy Kennedy, Leo Paris. *Songs:* Music: Chilly Winds Don't Blow; Mad Love Blues; Little Train A-Chuggin'; Rendevous d'Amour; Lyrics: Little Red Monkey. *Instrumental Works:* The Happy Cobbler; Swinging Ghosts.

KRAUS, JOHN FREDRICH
ASCAP 1970
composer, arranger

b Apple Creek, Ohio, Oct 29, 31. Educ: Modesto Jr Col; Bob Jones Univ; Azusa-Pacific Col, BSM; pvt concert piano study with Egon Petri; San Francisco Cons of Music, postgrad work. Solo pianist, 3 performances with Modesto Youth Symph during high sch. Piano concert recitals in Can, US & Cent Am. Appeared on cable TV; recording artist. Concert performer, World Vision Int. Author, "Sacred Music Duets (Piano)," levels 7 & 8, "Sacred Music Solos (Piano)," levels 7 & 8. Chief Collabrs: David Carr Glover, Herbert Tovey. *Songs:* Music: Christmas Lullaby (vocal solo). *Instrumental Works:* Improvisations on Six Hymn Tunes Opus 68.

KRAUS, PHILIP CHARLES
ASCAP 1961
composer, author, teacher

b New York, NY, July 24, 18. Educ: DeWitt Clinton High Sch; Juilliard Sch Music. Staff percussionist, WNEW, New York, 39-41 & 45-54; percussionist, Army show, "This Is the Army," 42-43; free-lance percussionist, NBC, CBS,

ABC, Columbia Records, RCA Victor, Decca & others; made commercial jingles. Teacher, 47-; perc instr, Rice Univ, 79- Personnel mgr, Houston Symph, 78- *Instrumental Works:* Just Flippin; Jan; Vibes for Beginners; Marching Bells; Modern Mallet Method (bks I, II, III).

KRAUSE, KENNETH CHARLES   ASCAP 1974
composer, author, teacher
b Belleville, Ill, Apr 17, 29. Educ: Northwestern Univ, Evanston, BMusEd & MMus; studied marimba with Clair Omar Musser; studied comp with Edwin Gerschefski; studied electronic music with Gilbert Trythall. Musician; percussionist, Grant Park Orch, Chicago, 52-56; dir band & orch, Southwest High Sch, Atlanta, Ga, 52-64; percussionist, Atlanta Symph Orch, 52-57; percussionist, arr & asst cond, Atlanta Pops Orch, 55-69; dir band & chorus, Lakeside High Sch, Decatur, Ga, 64-67; drummer & percussionist, shows & nightclubs in Atlanta, 52-69; percussionist, Nashville Symph, 70-; asst prof music theory, Belmont Col, Nashville, Tenn, 70- Chief Collabr: Roxie Gibson. *Songs:* Children's Musical: Hey God, Listen; Hey God, What is Christmas?; Hey God, Hurry; Choral Anthems: Help Me Be Me; Come Praise the Lord; Psalm 123. *Instrumental Works:* Little Suite (perc instruments); Toccata (marimba).

KRAUSHAAR, RAOUL   ASCAP 1952
composer, author, director
b Paris, France, Aug 20, 08. Educ: Columbia Univ. With Hugo Riesenfeld, 26. Arr with Ted Fiorito, 36. Cond & writer, for var performers incl Gene Autry & Roy Rogers, Republic Studios. Music writer for Frank Capra, 43. With Republic Studios, TV shows incl "Lassie", "Mr Ed", "Bonanza", "Untouchables" & "Fibber McGee and Molly," 45, "Invaders From Mars", "Abbott and Costello TV Series", "Captain Kidd", "30 Foot Bride From Candy Mountain" & "Delta Factor," 51-58. Chief Collabr: Minette Alston. *Songs:* Blue Gardenia; Six Pack Annie. *Scores:* Musical: Magnificent Matador.

KRECHMER, WILLIAM FREDERICH   ASCAP 1959
composer, author
b Millville, NJ, Aug 25, 09. Educ: Curtis Inst, BA(music) & hon doctorate. Toured with many name bands; started recording for Brunswick Records, 29; opened the Billy Krechmer Club, Philadelphia, 38, owned, operated & starred in the club as jazz clarinetist, 38-66, retired, 66. Chief Collabr: Horace Gerlach. *Songs:* Tonight My Sweet; Our Song; Carole; Music: Penn State Hop; Windy Bay; My Violin; Ranstead St Parade; Ranstead St Retreat; Billy's Lament; Pyle of Jack.

KREISLER, FRITZ   ASCAP 1924
composer, arranger, violinist
b Vienna, Austria, Feb 2, 1875; d New York, NY, Jan 29, 62. Educ: Vienna Cons, entered at age 7, studied with Auber, Hellmesberger, gold medal at age 10; Paris Cons, studied with Massart, Delibes, grad at age 12, Grand Prix. US debut, Steinway Hall, NY, 1888; toured with pianist Moriz Rosenthal, 1889. Returned to Europe, studied med, Vienna, art, Rome & Paris. Served in Austrian army, resumed concert career, 1899 & made world tours. Capt, Austrian army, World War I. Concert appearances, US, 14; French citizen, 38; US citizen, 43. Recording artist with many records. Recipient, Comdr French Legion of Honor. Author, bk "Four Weeks in the Trenches"; biography, "Fritz Kreisler" by L P Lochner. *Songs:* The Second Violin; Stars in My Eyes. *Songs & Instrumental Works:* Caprice Viennois; Tambourin Chinois; Recitativo and Scherzo; Schoen Rosmarin; Liebesfreud; Liebesleid; Violin Concerto in C; Chanson Louis XIII and Pavane; La Precieuse; Study on a Choral; Menuet; Sicillienne and Rigaudon; Praeludium and Allegro; String Quartet in a Preghiera; Aubade Provencale; Allegretto in G; The Old Refrain; Violin transc of Dvorak, Tartini, Corelli, Wieniawski, Granados, Albeniz. *Scores:* Operettas: Apple Blossoms; Sissy.

KREMENLIEV, BORIS ANGELOFF
composer, author, educator
b Razlog, Bulgaria, May 23, 11. Educ: DePaul Univ, Chicago, BM, MM; Univ Rochester Eastman Sch of Music, PhD, studied with Howard Hanson, comp with Roy Harris, conducting with Modest Altschuller. Music dir, South Ger Network. Prof of comp, Univ Calif, Los Angeles. Comp of music for films, stage & TV. Music critic. Author, "Bulgarian-Macedonian Folk Music," ethnomusicology articles in prof journals. Recipient, grants & fels for comp & res, ASCAP awards for serious music. Chief Collabr: Dr Elva Kremenlieve. *Songs:* Music: Crucifixion; Tell-Tale Heart. *Instrumental Works:* String Quartet; Sonata for String Bass; Bulgarian Rhapsody.

KREMER, GLORIA HAYES   ASCAP 1972
composer, author
b Philadelphia, Pa, Apr 30, 24. Educ: Temple Univ. Wrote & directed indust shows; comp original music & lyrics for indust; wrote album for Muzak; wrote TV & radio shows for political campaigns; wrote music, lyrics & scripts for children's educ records, Instructo Corp & McGraw Hill, plus series on pet-care for children, Pet Productions, Princeton. *Songs:* Sing My Name (TV series); Horatio and Me (TV series); Captain Noah (TV series); Pied Piper of Hamelin (opera); The Fun and Care of a Puppy, Cat, Gerbil, and Others; The Kingdom of Kabalakaboo (educ records); We Fell In Love to Music By Muzak.

KRENGEL, JOSEPH PHILIP   ASCAP 1963
composer, poet
b New York, NY, June 22, 15. Educ: Pub schs & high sch; Pratt Inst, advanced art, 36; piano with Lucille Scheiman. Commercial artist & technical illustrator, 37-71. Animator, Columbia Pictures, 46, learned of Latin Am Music, 46. Chief Collabs: Louis Herscher, Harry Atwood, Eileen Herbster. *Songs:* O Chuca-Chuca (samba); Music: Christmas in Paris; Irish, As Irish Can Be; Lyrics: Music Box Waltz. *Instrumental Works:* Tokyo Taxi.

KRESA, HELMY   ASCAP 1943
composer, music arranger
b Meissen, Ger, Nov 7, 04. Educ: Dresden Cons, studied with Tibor Serly. Music arr for Irving Berlin, 26- *Songs:* Music: That's My Desire.

KRESKY, JEFFREY JAY   ASCAP 1969
composer
b Passaic, NJ, May 14, 48. Educ: Columbia Univ, BA, studied with Otto Luening, Charles Wuorinen & Harvey Sollberger; Princeton Univ, MFA & PhD, studied with Milton Babbitt, J K Randall & Peter Westergaard. Teacher, Princeton Univ, Mannes Sch & William Paterson Col; author, "Tonal Music: 12 Analytic Studies"; cond & keyboard player with groups for contemporary music, speculum musicae & others; won ASCAP Awards; Tanglewood fel; Nat Endowment grant. *Instrumental Works:* In Nomine; Night Music; Music At Night; Bell Music; Anita's Dance; Aria da Capo; Musica Renata; Dos Tientos de Cabezon. *Songs & Instrumental Works:* Cantata I; Cantata II; Cantata III. *Scores:* Opera/Ballet: Puppets; Chiaroscuro.

KRESS, CARL W   ASCAP 1957
composer, guitarist
b Livingston, NJ, Oct 20, 07; d Sparks, Nev, June 10, 65. Educ: Newark High Sch. With Paul Whiteman Orch, 28-30; free-lance, records & radio. On TV "Garry Moore Show," 51-58. Mem of guitar team with George Barnes, 61-65; was in concert, Town Hall, 64. Chief Collabrs: Dick McDonough, Tony Mottola. *Songs:* Music: Afterthoughts; Love Song; Peg Leg Shuffle; Sutton Mutton; Stage Fright; Danzon; Chicken Ala Swing; Jazz in G; Sarong Number; Praise Be!

KREYMBORG, ALFRED   ASCAP 1961
author, teacher
b New York, NY, Dec 10, 1883; d Stamford, Conn, Aug 14, 66.' Educ: Morris High Sch. Founder, mag Others, 14-17; co-ed mag Broom & American Caravan (anthology). Taught, New Sch for Social Research, New York, Univ Kansas City; Breadloaf Sch of Eng; Olivet Col. Mem of Nat Inst Arts & Letters; pres of Poetry Soc of Am; Pulitzer poetry prize judge, 14 yrs. Recipient of 2 Carnegie Found grants; author, "Troubadour," autobiography & 30 publ vols of poetry, prose & plays. Chief Collabrs: Joseph Wagner, Alex North, Elie Siegmeister, Virgil Thomson. *Songs & Instrumental Works:* Ballad of Brotherhood (poem set to music).

KRICH, HERMAN   ASCAP 1965
composer, author
b Vineland, NJ, Nov 28, 14. Educ: Morton St & Barringer High Sch; studied violin with Prof Novac. Started to play violin at age 4; played first violin in sch orch; own music played by Israel Broadcasting Authority. Chief Collabr: Irving Fields. *Songs:* Forsaken; Let Us Dance; David Slew the Giant; The Women's Liberation Movement; Pussy Cat Be Good; People Were Born to Dream; Play That Piano Mr Fields; Jerusalem Jerusalem; Lord Lord Lord. *Instrumental Works:* Melody of the Gypsies.

KRIEG, RICHARD CHARLES (DICK CHARLES)   ASCAP 1942
composer, author
b Newark, NJ, Feb 24, 19. Educ: Glen Ridge High Sch, NJ, grad; studied piano, harmony & theory under Ernest Stevens. Writer-dir, NBC & ABC, 42-54; dir radio & TV progs, Paul Whiteman. Owner-engr, Dick Charles Recording Serv, New York, 54-79; retired. Wrote special material for Dinah Shore & Patti Page. Chief Collabrs: Larry Markes, Eddie Waldman, John Neary, Gloria Shayne Regney. *Songs:* Along the Navajo Trail; This is My Song; May You Always; (I'm Gettin') Corns for My Country; Mad About Him, Sad Without Him Blues; It Takes a Long Long Train to Carry My Blues Away; The Man on the Carousel; (Ave Maria) That Warm Christmas Feeling; Music: As the World Turns (theme); The Man on the Carousel.

KRIEGER, HENRY   ASCAP 1970
composer
b New York, NY, Feb 9, 45. Educ: Am Univ, Washington, DC; Columbia Univ. Musician & arr for "Tourquoise Pantomime," 74. Writer, music for "The Dirtiest Musical" & songs for TV prog "Captain Kangaroo," 75 & "The Tap Dance Kid," 80. Chief Collabrs: Michael Bennett, Lindsay Kemp, Tom Eyen, Robert Lorick, David Csontos. *Songs:* My Best Friend Is a Toad; Sailing; Can You See; Dancing in My Dreams.

KROEBER, ALAN MATTHEW   ASCAP 1977
author
b Berkeley, Calif, Oct 27, 48. Educ: Occidental Col, BA(Eng lit), 70. Working as lyricist. Chief Collabrs: Lisa Nemzo, Eric Tempke. *Songs:* Lyrics: Short Cut.

KROEGER, KARL   ASCAP 1971
composer, author, music editor
b Louisville, Ky, Apr 13, 32. Educ: Univ Louisville, BM, 54, MM, 59, comp studies with Claude Almand & George Perle; Univ Ill, MS, 61, comp studies with Gordon Binkerd; Brown Univ, PhD, 76. Composer, musicologist & music ed. Curator, Americana Collection, New York Pub Library Music Div; dir, Moravian Music Found; ed complete works, William Billings, Moramus Ed & Moravian Music Series. Taught at Ohio Univ, Moorhead State Univ & Wake Forest Univ. Comp in residence, Ford Found Grant, pub sch, Eugene, Ore. *Instrumental Works:* Divertimento (concert band); Variations on a Hymn (concert band); Pax Vobis (fest cantata for soloists, mixed chorus, orch); Suite (orch); Sinfonietta (string orch); Dramatic Overture (orch); Concerto Da Camera (oboe, string orch); Two String Quartets; Duo Concertante (violin, cello); Three Canzonas (brass sextet); Six Organ Pieces on Moravian Chorales.

KROFFT, SID
producer
b Athens, Greece, July 30, 29. Educ: Pvt tutoring. Started as puppeteer, 36; world tour. Worked with adult show, Les Poupees de Paris, 9 yrs & Six Flags & family shows, 9 yrs. TV producer: "Pufnstuf"; "Land of the Lost"; "Donny and Marie Show"; "The Brady Bunch"; "Barbara Mandrell"; "Middle Age Crazy"; "The Last Desperado." Chief Collabr: Marty Krofft. *Songs:* Lyrics: Lidsville.

KROLIK, MARY STUART   ASCAP 1970
composer, author, singer
b Miami, Fla. Educ: Tulsa Cent High Sch. With Warner Bros, MGM & Columbia, movies, 47-50; TV, 51-, ongoing series, "Search for Tomorrow." Recording artist & writer, Columbia Records, 55 & Bell Records, 73. Author: "Both of Me." Chief Collabrs: Brian Koonin, Michel LeGrand. *Songs:* The Bells of Christmas; Green Coffee; Don't Look Back; Lyrics: Tiny Band of Gold.

KROLL, WILLIAM   ASCAP 1946
composer, violinist, teacher
b New York, NY, Jan 30, 01; d Boston, Mass, Mar 10, 80. Educ: Royal Acad, Berlin; Juilliard Sch Music, Morris Loeb Prize. Debut as violinist, NY, 15. Mem Elshuco Trio, 23-29; first violinist, Coolidge Quartet, 35-45; founded own quartet, 45. Soloist, Boston, Philadelphia, San Francisco & Baltimore Symphonies. Teacher of violin & chamber music, Mannes Col Music, New York, 43-77 & Peabody Inst, Baltimore, 47-65; head of chamber music, Tanglewood, 49-79; head of string dept, Cleveland Inst Music, 64-67; mem fac, Queens Col, NY, 69-74; Boston Univ, 77-80 & Longy Sch Music, Cambridge, Mass, 78-80. Soloist with Nat Symph, The White House, DC, 66. *Instrumental Works:* Pieces for String Quartet, Chamber Orchestra, Solo Violin and Solo Piano.

KRONDES, JAMES JOHN   ASCAP 1958
composer, author, musician
b New Rochelle, NY, Aug 18, 25. Educ: New Rochelle High Sch; Davidson Col, USAF Cadet Prog Navigator, Bombardier; Officer Candidate Sch, Maxwell Field, Montgomery, Ala; Iona Col, BBA. Violin student, age 7. New Rochelle Symph under direction of Grosskoff, age 12. French horn & violin, Championship New Rochelle High Sch Band & Orch under direction of Harry Haigh. With RKO-Unique Records, promotion, nat promotion mgr, nat sales mgr & became head of A&R. Became free-lance writer, 15 yrs. Also produced, managed & publ. Gen prof mgr of RCA, Metromedia, Bourne & ABC Music Publ. Chief Collabrs: Sid Jacobson, Al Stilman. *Songs:* Music: Theme song for "How to Survive a Marriage." *Instrumental Works:* Warm; At the End of a Rainbow; Thirty Days Hath September; Bounty Hunter.

KRUEGER, BENJAMEN   ASCAP 1952
composer, saxophonist, arranger
b Newark, NJ, July 17, 1899; d Orange, NJ, Apr 29, 67. Educ: South Side High Sch, Newark, grad; self-taught on many instruments; formal study of violin. Played supper clubs in NY incl Reisenwebers-Delmonicos & Parody Club; MC, Uptown Theatre, Chicago. Cond orch, radio progs incl "Drene Show", "Phillip Morris Show" & "Pick and Pat Show"; radio shows; cond for "Rudy Vallee Radio Shows." Comp music. Recording artist with Brunswick Recording Co. Cond ASCAP 8th Prog, Carnegie Hall, 39. Chief Collabrs: Lou Davis, Jules Stein, Will J Haris. *Songs & Instrumental Works:* Wild Papa; Sunday; Maybe I'm Wrong.

KRUEGER, SOL RICHARD   ASCAP 1975
composer, author, teacher
b Olympia, Wash, Apr 27, 45. Educ: Studied comp, Leonard Klein, 70-71; classic guitar, Fred Gibson, 69-71 & Rey de la Torre, 77-78. Classical & jazz guitarist & singer, nightclubs & concert; recording artist, Sol Anna Music. Chief Collabrs: Rich Corrin, Michael Bardossi. *Songs:* On Becoming a Butterfly (collection); Francis. *Instrumental Works:* October 28, 1973; collections: compositions for solo guitar & guitar & violin.

KRUGER, LILLY CANFIELD   ASCAP 1958
composer, author, teacher
b Portage, Ohio, Apr 13, 1892; d. Educ: Univ Toledo, BA, BEd; studied music with Mary Willing. Pub sch teacher. *Songs:* The Easter Bunny Comes Hopping

to Town; The First Psalm; 128th Psalm; He Lives; Christmas Pastorale. *Instrumental Works:* Piano: Rondino; Summer Sunset.

KRUGMAN, LILLIAN D
composer, author, lyricist
b New York, NY, Dec 4, 11. Educ: Brooklyn Col. Secy; housewife & mother; real estate broker. Chief Collabrs: Hedy Hevar, Marc Friberg, Herb Strizik. *Songs:* Little Calypsos; Song Tales of the West Indies; Lyrics: Pretty Pretty; Ballad of Abe Lincoln; Ducks on Parade; Animals, Bird Songs for Children; Say Auf Wiedersehn; Weeping Willow; Now We Are Six.

KRUMBEIN, MAURICE
See Carter, Ray

KRUNNFUSZ, GORDON (GORDON G JONES)
composer, author, organist
b Elgin, Ill, July 22, 31. Educ: NCent Col, BMusEd; Northwestern Univ, Evanston, Ill, MMus. Pub sch music teacher for 13 yrs. Now guidance counselor in schs. Church organist; pianist & organist in dance group. *Songs:* Calypso Noel; My Christmas Wish for You.

KUBIK, GAIL   ASCAP 1945
composer, conductor, lecturer
b South Coffeyville, Okla, Sept 5, 14. Educ: Eastman Sch Music, scholarship at age 15; Am Cons, Chicago, MA, Leo Sowerby; Harvard Univ, Walter Piston & Nadia Boulanger. Taught violin & comp, Monmouth Col & Dakota Wesleyan Univ, comp & music history, Teachers Col & Columbia Univ, 37. Staff comp, NBC, NY, 40-41. Music dir, Motion Picture Bureau, Office War Info, USAF, WW II. Guest prof, Univ Southern Calif, 46. Has written background scores for radio & TV. Lectr, UNESCO auspices, 66. Comp-in-residence, Scripps Col, Claremont, Calif, 70-80. Fellowships: Guggenheim (first post-service grant) & Am Prix de Rome. *Instrumental Works:* Scenario for Orchestra; Scherzo for Large Orchestra (Chicago Symph Golden Jubilee Award); Symphony Concertante (Pulitzer Prize, 52); Symphony No 2; Symphony No 3; In Praise of Johnny Appleseed (cantata); Litany and Prayer (men's chorus); Folk Song Suite; Piano Sonata; Boston Baked Beans (opera piccola); Bennie the Beaver (for children); Celebrations and Epilogue; Piano Sonatina; Divertimenti Nos 1, 2; Sonatina for Clarinet; Piano; 2 violin concertos (No 2, Heifetz Prize); Symphony for Two Pianos; Prayer and Toccata for Organ and Two Pianos; Magic, Magic, Magic (chorus; Tex Bi-Centennial comn). *Scores:* Films: The Memphis Belle (NY Film Critics Award, 44); Thunderbolt; Earthquakers; Air Pattern Pacific; The Miner's Daughter and Gerald McBoing-Boing (cartoon, Acad Award; British Film Inst Award, 50); Transatlantic (Edinburgh Film Fest Award); Film Background: The World At War (Nat Asn Am Comp & Cond Citation); The Desperate Hours.

KUBY, BERNARD F   ASCAP 1957
author
b Cincinnati, Ohio, Sept 6, 23. Educ: Univ of Cincinnati. Has been copywriter for mag, radio & TV commercials, 47- Chief Collabrs: Jerry Myrow, Alfred Engelhard. *Songs:* Lead on, Mr President; My Angelina; March of Freedom. *Scores:* Chicago Stage: Analysis in Wonderland; Tongue in Chic.

KUDERA, LOTTIE A (NOLA JAY HARP, LU KOTA)   ASCAP 1964
composer, author
b Ideal, SDak, Nov 30, 20. Own publ co with Lela K Love. Chief Collabrs: Lela K Love, Fred Booth, Ara Belle Bennett, Joe W Mills, Nellie McBrayer, Louise M Bush, Gloria Ann Orndorff, Lola Hildebrand, Bob D Jackson. *Songs:* Music: Hail the Infant King; Bubbling Over; Street of Dreams; I Built a Wall Around My Heart.

KUEHN, BERNARD R   ASCAP 1965
author
b Milwaukee, Wis, Aug 28, 16. Educ: High Sch; Univ Wis-Milwaukee, 12 unit cert. Baker, 3 yrs; prof photographer, 4 yrs; record shop owner, 15 yrs; advert exec, 5 yrs; salesman, 5 yrs. Chief Collabr: Joe De Cimber. *Songs:* Lyrics: Schatzie; One, Two, Three for You My Love; Dixieland Polka; Yankee Polka.

KUHN, LEE   ASCAP 1946
composer, author, conductor
b Chicago, Ill, Aug 8, 12; d New York, NY, Dec 1, 55. Served in US Maritime Service, WW II. Led own dance orch, 45-55. *Songs:* Thanksgiving at Home; Who Said There's No Santa Claus; There's a Tear in My Beer; All That Glitters Is Not Gold; Pvt Billy; Along About Evening; Never Felt Better and Never Had Less.

KUHN, RICHARD S   ASCAP 1941
composer, author, conductor
b New York, NY, Jan 1, 07; d Hollywood, Fla, May 3, 73. Educ: St John's Law Sch, LLB; pvt music study. Admitted to NY Bar, 31; practiced to 35. Cond orch, NY hotel, 38-44. Became music publ & record co exec. *Songs:* Christmas in My Heart; In Old Kalua; Meet Me At the Astor; Featherhead; Miss Peach; Uncle Mistletoe.

KUJAWA, ROBERT VALENTINE (BOB KAMES)   ASCAP 1953
composer, author, musician
b Milwaukee, Wis, Apr 21, 25. Educ: Midwestern Cons Music, Chicago, Ill; studied with Lou Webb. Recording artist, 15 yrs. Creator of the Happy Organ. Music dealer, Milwaukee; owner & pres, Bob Kames & Assoc, Inc, Hammond Organ & Piano Studios, 60- Chief Collabrs: Roy Kaiser & John Meyer. *Songs:* You Are My One True Love; High Life Polka; Fraidy Cat; Henrietta Polka; It's the Little Things in Life That Count; Light of the World.

KUKOFF, BENJAMIN (BERNIE)   ASCAP 1965
writer, producer, actor
b Brooklyn, NY, Apr 23, 33. Educ: Univ Conn, BA; Yale Drama Sch, MFA; studied with Lee Strasberg. TV comedy writer, "Jackie Gleason"; "Phyllis Diller"; "Candid Camera" & "Roger Miller," 65; producer, "Pat Boone"; "Steve Allen"; "Jimmy Durante"; "Lennon Sisters Show"; "Operation Petticoat." Originator, "Different Strokes"; 20 "Wide World of Entertainment Specials"; Comedy News; "Unofficial Miss Las Vegas Showgirl Contest" (ABC). Chief Collab: Jeff Harris. *Songs:* Music: Operation Petticoat (theme); Detective School (theme); Unofficial Las Vegas Showgirl Contest.

KULLER, SID C   ASCAP 1939
composer, author, director
b New York, NY, Oct 27, 10. Educ: Thomas Jefferson High Sch, Brooklyn; Columbia Univ, NY. Head writer, producer, dir, "Colgate Comedy Hour," NBC. Head writer, "Donald O'Connor Show", NBC, "Saturday Nite Revue", NBC, "Jackie Gleason Show," CBS. Wrote sketches, "Ziegfeld Follies", "Earl Carroll Vanities." Musical writer for MGM, 20th Century Fox, Sam Goldwyn, Paramount Pictures, Mary Bros, Bob Hope, Ritz Bros. Co-wrote & dir "Jump for Joy." Chief Collabrs: Duke Ellington, Lyn Murray, Jerry Fielding, Erich Wolf Horngold, Benny Carter, Jerry Dolin. *Songs:* Lyrics: Jump for Joy; Tenement Symphony; I Wish I Wuz. *Songs:* Bway Shows: Rosalinda; Prisoner of Zenda.

KUMMER, CLARE
See Beecher, Clare Rodman

KUNITZ, RICHARD E   ASCAP 1963
composer, author
b Pittsburgh, Pa, May 29, 19. Educ: Univ Miami. Accountant, 55 & in banking, 63, then examr, NY State Bank. Chief Collabrs: Mack Kay, Marc Fredericks. *Songs:* Rockin' Roly Poly Santa Claus; Get Off That Phone!

KUNTZ, JOHN B   ASCAP 1964
author, actor, director
b Dayton, Ohio, Sept 15, 38. Educ: Oakwood High Sch, Dayton; Ohio State Univ. Actor, staff writer, Joy Music, 64; founding mem, Center Stage, Baltimore, Md, 65; theatrical mgr, business mgr, San Francisco's Actor's Cons Theatre, 67; actor var musical comedies, "Now" & others. Chief Collabrs: Lor Crane, George Goehring, Jim Wise, Arthur Rubinstein, John Aman. *Songs:* Lyrics: Whispers on the Wind; Lady Audley's Secret; Michael-John.

KUPELE, DAVID M   ASCAP 1959
composer, author, musician
b Molokai, Hawaii, Oct 7, 21. Educ: McKinley High Sch. Was with war shipping admin. WW II, USMS. Musician in orch, Hawaiian Village Hotel, 50- *Songs:* Lehuanani; South Pacific Moonlight.

KUPFERMAN, MEYER   ASCAP 1952
composer, teacher, conductor
b New York, NY, July 3, 26. Educ: Self-taught in comp; studied theory, harmony & ear-training, High Sch Music & Art; Queens Col. Fac mem, Sarah Lawrence Col, 51-, chmn dept music, currently, cond, Sarah Lawrence Improvisation Ens, 15 yrs. Comns & Fels: Nat Endowment for the Arts, Guggenheim Mem Found, Ford Found, New York Philomusica, Martha Graham Dance Co & Pearl Lang Dance Co. Clarinetist, Music by My Friends Ens. Originated, "Cycle of Infinities," 61. Chief Collabrs: Gertrude Stein; Alistair Reid; Paul Freeman; Martha Graham; Pearl Lang. *Instrumental Works:* Little Symphony; Fourth Symphony; Lyric Symphony; Concerto (cello, tape & orch); Moonchild and the Doomsday Trombone; Infinities 22; Fantasy Sonata; Sonata on Jazz Elements; Concerto for Cello and Jazz Band; Prometheus; Ostinato Burlesco; Superflute; Jazz String Quartet; Sculptures for Orchestra; Libretto for Orchestra; The Red King's Throw; Tunnels of Love; Sound Phantoms I (on Beauty and the Beast); Abracadabra; Infinities No 25 (string orch); Infinities No 12 (chamber orch). *Scores:* Opera: In a Garden; Draagenfut Girl; Persephone; Icarus; Film/TV: Hallelujah the Hills; Blast of Silence; Black Like Me.

KUPKA, STEPHEN MACKENZIE (DOCTOR)   ASCAP 1970
composer, author, performer
b Los Angeles, Calif, Mar 25, 46. Educ: Univ Calif, Santa Barbara, 64-66; Univ Calif, Berkeley, 66-68. Joined pop group, Tower of Power, 68. Placed songs on var albums; plays baritone saxophone; studio musician. Chief Collabrs: Emilio Castillo, Frank Biner. *Songs:* You're Still a Young Man; So Very Hard to Go; What Is Hip; You Ought to Be Havin' Fun; Down to the Nightclub; This Time

It's Real; Only So Much Oil in the Ground; Below Us, All the City Lights; You're So Wonderful, So Marvelous; The Soul of a Child; Sparkling in the Sand.

KURC, ADOLF (EDDY COURTS)   ASCAP 1970
composer
b Radom, Poland, Apr 17, 13. Piano & harmony lessons in home town. First compositions publ in Warsaw, Poland at age 19. Songwriter, Polish Chanteuse Vera Gran, then in Paris, 34-40 & for Boston & Providence Singers. Chief Collabrs: Richard Severs, Monika Severs, Tom Hunter. *Songs:* There's a Feeling of Love; Music: List-La Lettre; I Think I'm Ready Now.

KURKA, ROBERT FRANK   ASCAP 1954
composer
b Cicero, Ill, Dec 22, 21; d New York, NY, Dec 12, 57. Educ: Columbia Univ, MA(comp), 48; studied with Otto Leuning & Darius Milhaud. 1st Lt in command of language detachment, Mil Intelligence, Tokyo, Japan, WW II. Mem fac, Music Dept, City Col New York, 48-51, Queens Col, 54-56 & Dartmouth Col. Comns: Little Orch Soc, 52; Paderewski Fund for Am Composers, 52; Musical Arts Soc La Jolla, 53; San Diego Symph, 55. Awards: Gershwin Mem Award, 50; Guggenheim Fel, 51 & 52; Nat Inst Arts & Letters Grant, 52; Brandeis Univ Creative Arts Award, 57. *Instrumental Works:* Concerto for Marimba and Orchestra; Concerto for 2 Pianos, String Orchestra, Trumpet; Concerto for Violin, Orchestra; 4 violin sonatas; 5 string quartets; The Good Soldier Schweik Suite; Symphony No 2; 3 Piano Sonatas; Ballad for French Horn, Strings. *Scores:* Opera: The Good Soldier Schweik.

KURTZ, EMANUEL (MANNY) (MANN CURTIS)   ASCAP 1936
author
b Brooklyn, NY, Nov 15, 11. Educ: High sch; Brooklyn Evening Col, 2 1/2 yrs. Writer for Vitaphone Studios; staff writer, Mills Music Co & Santly-Joy Music Co. Chief Collabrs: Vic Mizzy, Al Hoffman, Walter Kent. *Songs & Instrumental Works:* Let It Be Me; My Dreams Are Getting Better All the Time; The Whole World Is Singing My Song; The Story of a Starry Night; Anema e Core; The Jones Boy; I'm Gonna Live Till I Die; In a Sentimental Mood; With a Hey and a Hi and a Ho-Ho-Ho; Romance Runs in the Family; You Meet the Nicest People in Your Dreams; I Don't Care (Only Love Me); I Ups to Her and She Ups to Me; Summer Colors; One Pair of Hands; I'm Still Not Thru Missing You; I Had a Little Talk With the Lord; Pretty Kitty Blue Eyes; Look Out I'm Romantic; Did 'Ja Ever; Apple Blossoms and Chapel Bells; Play Me Hearts and Flowers; A Prairie Fairy Tale.

KURTZ, MARJORIE   ASCAP 1952
composer
b New York, NY, June 21, 42. Educ: Brooklyn Col. *Songs:* Snowflakes.

KUTZ, JAMES FULTON   ASCAP 1961
composer, author, pianist
b Vallejo, Calif, June 14, 1880; d Santa Rosa, Calif, Nov 6, 76. Educ: Univ Calif; studied piano with John Metcalf; Naval War Col, grad, 01. Commissioned naval officer, USN, 03; retired as Capt, 46. *Songs:* Fair Hawaii; Hymns: Near to Me; Musical Setting: Ten Commandments. *Scores:* Stage: The Love Game.

KWAS, TONE   ASCAP 1973
composer, performer
b Brooklyn, NY, May 29, 34. Educ: NY Univ, BS, 27, studied comp with Vincent Jones; Hofstra Univ, MA, 65; studied trumpet with William Vacciano & Ray Crisara. Songwriter & trumpeter var shows incl Bob Hope, Frank Sinatra, Tony Bennett & Dinah Shore, 30 yrs. Played in big bands, incl Vaughn Monroe & Harry James. With Bway show, "Dancin'." *Instrumental Works:* Inward Feeling; Look At the Sky; A Delicate Balance; Pot Luck. *Scores:* Ballet: An American Jazz Ballet.

KWEDER, CHARLES J   ASCAP 1961
composer, author
b Pittsburgh, Pa, Aug 16, 28. Educ: Tech Sch. USA, 51. Printer, Pittsburgh. Chief Collabrs: Al Pikelis, Hal Ide. *Songs:* I'm Still in Love With You.

L

LA BARBARA, JOAN
See Subotnick, Joan Lotz La Barbara

LACEY, MARY   ASCAP 1958
author
b Yorkshire, Eng, July 30, 09; d Costa Mesa, Calif, Aug 27, 78. Educ: High sch. Lived in Can, to Calif, 47. Writer of TV dramatic shows & high sch musicals incl "Swinging High", "Get Up and Go" & "Take It Easy." Chief Collabr: Paul Werick. *Songs:* Cha-Cha Polka; Outer Space Santa.

LACHOFF, SOL (SOL LAKE)   ASCAP 1959
composer
b Chicago, Ill, Dec 19, 11. Educ: Chicago Musical Col, grad, studied piano & all phases of harmony & comp. Had combo in Chicago, 30-42, San Antonio, 42-45, Los Angeles, 45-60; had combo with Herb Alpert as trumpeter. Wrote song for film "Pillow Talk." *Songs:* Music: Roly Poly. *Instrumental Works:* The Lonely Bull; El Lobo; Crawfish; Marching Thru Madrid; Crea Mi Amor; Mexican Shuffle; Winds of Barcelona; Salud Amor y Dinero; Adios Mi Corazon; Green Peppers; Bittersweet Samba; El Garbanza; El Presidente; Mexican Road Race; More and More Amor; Memories of Madrid; Cantina Blue; Bobo; Cowboys and Indians; A Beautiful Friend; She Touched Me; Country Lake; Marjorine; Montezuma's Revenge.

LACKEY, DOUGLAS MYRON   ASCAP 1963
composer
b Sacramento, Calif, Aug 10, 32. Educ: Univ Calif, Los Angeles. Musical scores for motion pictures, TV films, TV commercials & educ films. Chief Collab: Gene Kauer. *Songs:* Music: The Wilderness Family; To Touch the Wind; Snowflakes; Brother of the Wind; Zachariah Coop. *Scores:* Film/TV: The Wilderness Family; Across the Great Divide; Further Adventures of the Wilderness Family; Brother of the Wind; The Treasure Chase; Man Against the Sea; Montezuma's Lost Gold; The Curse of the Mayan Temple; Creatures of the Amazon; The Amazing Apes; The Great American Wilderness; Vanishing Africa; The Secret World of Reptiles; Ride the Tiger; The Proud and the Damned; Agent From HARM; Fortress of the Dead; From Hell to Borneo; Guerillas in Pink Tights; TV series: Animal World; The Cliff Wood Avenue Kids; World of the Sea; Safari to Adventure; Littlest Hobo; Gumby; The Chuckle Heads.

LADA, ANTON   ASCAP 1920
composer, conductor, musician
b Chicago, Ill, Sept 25, 1890; d Santa Monica, Calif, Aug 25, 44. Educ: Pvt music study. Musician in Milwaukee Symph. Led own band, Lada's Louisiana Five, in theatres, vaudeville & night clubs throughout US. *Songs & Instrumental Works:* Arkansas Blues; Church Street Sobbin' Blues; Yelping Hound; Swanee Dream; Golden Rod Blues; He's My Man; I'll Get Him Yet; Yesterday, Now and Forever.

LADERMAN, EZRA   ASCAP 1963
composer
b New York, NY, June 29, 24. Educ: High Sch of Music & Art; Brooklyn Col, BA; Columbia Univ, MA; studied with Otto Luening, Douglas Moore & Stefan Wolpe. Pres, Am Music Ctr; comp-in-residence & prof, State Univ NY Binghamton, 71-; dir music, NEA, 79- Awards: Three Guggenheim grants; Prix de Rome; Rockefeller grant; Ford Found comn. Chief Collabrs: Joe Darion, Ernest Kinoy, Archibald MacLeish, Norman Rosten, Clair Roskam. *Instrumental Works:* Violin Concerto (CBS-TV comn); The Eagle Stirred (oratorio); Symphony No 1; Theme, Variations and Finale; 2 string quartets; 3 piano sonatas; piano trio; 2 duos for violin, cello; 2 song cycles; 5 string quartets; 4 symphonies; 2 violin concerti; concerto for string quartet and orchestra; Summer Solstice; 2 violin, cello duos; cello partita; oboe concerto; elegy and other voices for viola; oboe quartet; bassoon concerto; woodwind quintet; piano concerto; Cadence. *Scores:* Operas: Columbus—Visions; Shadows Among Us; Mass for Cain; Film: Questions of Abraham; Operas & Film/TV: Handful of Souls; An Eagle Stirred; Esther; Sarah; Jacob and the Indian; Goodbye to the Clown; Hunting of the Shark; Film Background: Image of Love; The Eleanor Roosevelt Story; TV Background: Grand Canyon.

LAFFERTY, KAREN   ASCAP 1973
composer, singer
b Alamagordo, NMex, Feb 29, 48. Educ: Eastern NMex Univ, BME, 70. Nightclub singer, Dallas, Scottsdale, New Orleans, 70-71, Los Angeles, Calvary Chapel of Costa Mesa, 71. Involved in Missionary work in Holland, concerts for Youth With a Mission. Founder, Musicians for Missions, 80. *Songs:* Seek Ye First; Father of Lights; Nothing Can Separate; Beautiful Day; Sweet Summer Rain.

LAFORGE, FRANK   ASCAP 1932
composer, pianist, educator
b Rockford, Ill, Oct 22, 1879; d New York, NY, May 5, 53. Educ: Studied music with Harrison Wild, Leschetizky, Labor & Navratil; hon degree, Detroit Found Music Sch. Accompanist to Johanna Gadski, Marcella Sembrich, Schumann-Heink, Matzenauer, Lily Pons & Richard Crooks. Co-founder, La Forge-Berumen Studios, New York, 20. Among pupils taught: Bori, Matzenauer, Anderson, Otero, Crooks, Tibbett, Lily Pons & Madame Alda. Made first piano recording for Victor. *Songs:* Retreat; To a Messenger; Before the Crucifix; Hills; also many other secular as well as sacred songs. *Instrumental Works:* Valse de Concert; Improvisations; Gavotte and Musette; Romance.

LAFORGE, JACK   ASCAP 1963
composer, pianist
b New York, NY, Aug 8, 24; d Apr 28, 66. Educ: BS(accounting); LLB; pvt piano study. Pianist in nightclubs, hotels, concerts & on records. *Songs & Instrumental Works:* My Nemesis; Like Latin; Blue on Velvet; Orchid Twist.

LA FRENIERE, CHARLES F   ASCAP 1942
author
b Brooklyn, NY, Jan 12, 14. Educ: Harvard Univ, BS; studied music with Emma La Freniere (mother), Frederick Schneider (grandfather), Herman Annable. Chief Collabrs: Emma La Freniere, Hugo Rubens. *Songs:* A Valley in Valparaiso; White Sands; Mia Venezia; Suitcase Susie; You Can't Escape From Me; Strolling on the Boulevard; The Tide Has Turned At Last.

LA FRENIERE, EMMA P   ASCAP 1936
composer, author, pianist
b Brooklyn, NY, Sept 23, 1881; d Hempstead, NY, Sept 11, 61. Educ: Leipsig Cons; also studied with father, Frederick Schneider. Asst to father. Accompanist to Emma Calve & Blanche Duffield. Concert pianist, Brooklyn Acad Music. Cond orchs, Brooklyn & London. Became music publ. Chief Collabrs: Charles La Freniere (son), Hugo Rubens. *Songs:* A Valley in Valparaiso; White Sands; Mia Venezia; Long After Midnight; Midnight Kiss; Meet Me At the Football Game; Suitcase Susie; Strolling on the Boulevard; The Tide Has Turned At Last; Blue Illusion; My Margarita; Dancing 'Til Dawn; Dog House Polka.

LAHM, DAVID FIELDS   ASCAP 1964
composer, author, jazz pianist
b New York, NY, Dec 12, 40. Educ: Amherst Col, BA(Eng), 63; Ind Univ, MA(Eng), 67; Sch Jazz, Lenox, Mass, 59-60; pvt study, jazz comp with George Russell, 59-60. Jazz pianist with Dave Baker, Jamey Aebersold, Buddy Rich, Attila Zoller, Ted Curson, Richie Cole & own band. Accompanist with Janet Lawson, Lainie Cooke, Michael Moriarty, Sylvia Syms, Judy Kreston. Piano soloist in New York restaurants. Chief Collabr: Richie Cole. *Songs:* Music: Hope You're Having a Swell Noel; Lyrics: I Guess You've Proven Your Point; (Eddie) Jefferson Memorial; Harold's House of Jazz. *Instrumental Works:* And That's Why They Call It Fiction; You're a Blossom (Thanks, Mr Banks); Our Municipal Anthem; Straight Ahead; Ballad '79; Half Moon Bay; I'm Taking the Day Off; T&V (There Certainly Will Be Hell to Pay When the Red Guard Meets the Green Beret); Fanfares; Strapless; The Jersey Jaunt; Rush Hour.

LAINE, FLORA SPRAKER   ASCAP 1963
composer, author
b New York, NY. Educ: High sch grad. Comp, author, realtor & distributor for int oil co. *Songs:* No More; How Many Times Must We Say Goodbye; Come to Majorca; I Can't Let You Go.

LAINE, FRANKIE   ASCAP 1952
composer, author
b Chicago, Ill, Mar 30, 13. Educ: Lane Tech. Singer in nightclubs, theatres, films & TV incl "Frankie Laine Time" & "The Frankie Laine Show" (film series). Has made many records. Chief Collabr: Carl Fischer. *Songs:* What Could Be Sweeter; My Love, My Love; It Only Happens Once; Deuces Wild; We'll Be Together Again; Love of Loves; Only If We Love; Satan Wears a Satin Gown.

LAKE, BONNIE   ASCAP 1952
composer, author, singer
b Waterloo, Iowa, Mar 10, 20. Educ: Spec tutoring. Began career as comp lyricist. Singer & actress, radio. Vocalist with bands, Artie Shaw, Johnny Richards, Jack Jenney. Worked in pictures. Dubbed sound tracks at major motion picture studios. Appeared on var radio & TV shows. Recorded for RCA-Victor, MGM, Decca, Liberty. Chief Collabrs: Edgar DeLange, Mack David, Buddy Ebsen. *Songs:* Man With a Horn; St Francis of Assisi; San Francisco de Assisi (Span version); Sandman; Handsome Stranger; Sad Eyes; Love Means Love; As Simple as That; Come on In; Give Me a Shoulder to Cry On; Harlem Swing; Cuban Boogie Woogie; I've Got Your Number; Gracias; Wild Card; July and I; Original Joe; Rainy Day; Red Nose; Katy (theme song).

LAKE, MEYHEW LESTER   ASCAP 1924
composer, author, conductor
b Southville, Mass, Oct 25, 1879; d Palisades, NJ, Mar 16, 55. Educ: New Eng Cons; studied with Julius Vogler. Violinist, Boston Symph; cond, theatre orchs, 1896-10. Music dir, Payret Theatres, Havana; comp, arr & ed of band music for music publ. Taught arr, NY Univ. Author, bk "The American Band Arranger." *Songs & Instrumental Works:* The Evolution of Dixie (overture); American Rhapsody; Love Suite; Indian Summer Suite; New Orleans Sketches; The Tempest; Evolution of Yankee Doodle. *Scores:* Opera: Salem.

LAKE, OLIVER EUGENE   ASCAP 1979
composer, musician
b Marianna, Ark, Sept 14, 42. Educ: Lincoln Univ, Mo, BMEd; studied with Ron Carter, Oliver Nelson. Formed Oliver Lake Quartet, 67. Organized Black Artist Group with other St Louis musicians, actors, dancers & poets, 68, leader of group, toured Europe, 72. To New York, 74; recording artist. Formed World Saxophone Quartet, 77. Recipient, NEA composer grants, 76 & 79, Creative Artists Publ Service grant, 77. Chief Collabrs: Julius Hemphill, David Murray, Hamiet Bluiett, Leroy Jenkins, Baikida Carroll, Pheeroan Ak Laff. *Albums:* B A G in Paris, '73; Passin' Thru; Heavy Spirits; Ntu: Point From Which Creation Begins; Holding Together; Joseph Bowie/Oliver Lake Duo; Life Dance of Is (Quartet and Quintet); Shine; Buster Bee.

LAKE, SOL
See Lachoff, Sol

LAKSO, EDWARD JOSEPH   ASCAP 1970
composer, producer
b San Francisco, Calif, 1932. Educ: Univ Calif, Los Angeles, MA(music). Producer var shows incl "Charlie's Angels," 7 yrs; presently working on Bway show.

LAMARE, HILTON (NAPPY)   ASCAP 1958
composer, conductor, guitarist
b New Orleans, La, June 14, 10. Guitarist with bands incl, Ben Pollack, 30-35 & Bob Crosby, 35-42; co-leader with Ray Bauduc, Dixieland Band, 55-; toured Far East, 55-56. *Songs & Instrumental Works:* Dixieland Shuffle; Swinging at the Sugar Bowl; March of the Bob Cats; Loopin the Loop; My Inspiration.

LAMARGE, JIMMIE   ASCAP 1951
composer, author, guitarist
b Orange, NJ, Nov 2, 05; d New Providence, NJ, Jan 19, 71. Educ: High sch. Guitarist in dance orchs; singer in radio. Music teacher.

LA MARR, FRANK
See La Motta, Frank Joseph

LAMARRE, RENE T   ASCAP 1949
composer, author, conductor
b Milwaukee, Wis, Apr 5, 07. Educ: Univ Utah; pvt music study. Music dir, record co, 6 yrs; also talent scout. *Songs:* Love Me, Love Me, Love Me; Honey, Honey, Honey; The Unfinished Boogie; Do It Over and Over Again; Baby (Won'tcha Let Me Know); I Wonder, I Wonder, I Wonder; Dainty Brenda Lee.

LA MARRE, RICHARD DUANE   ASCAP 1966
composer, author
b Stockton, Calif, Sept 13, 12. Educ: Balboa High Sch, San Francisco; Univ Calif, Berkeley, music theory & comp. Saxophonist & clarinetist; formed own orch, 34, played in ballrooms in San Francisco & Oakland area. Arr music for var dance orchs, 30's & 40's. Chief Collabr: Robert Henri La Marre (brother). *Songs:* It's Written All Over Your Face; Champs Elysees; Never in My Life!; Seems Like Only Yesterday; Leaf in the Wind; Monte Carlo; You'll Never Get Out of This World Alive!; It Doesn't Cost You Anything to Dream; Hawaii; Where in the World?; Lyrics: For the First Time in My Life; Summertime in Paris; July in the Afternoon; You Can't Win 'Em All; In This Life; Brighter Day. *Instrumental Works:* East Wind.

LA MARRE, ROBERT HENRI
composer, author
b San Francisco, Calif, Nov 10, 17. Educ: Balboa High Sch, San Francisco; Univ Calif, Berkeley, 2 & 1/2 yrs; studied music & theory comp. Started music career as singer, KROW radio, Oakland Calif, 34; appeared on many radio stas incl KLS, KWBR, KSFO, KYA, San Francisco & KRKD, Los Angeles. Singer, Jan Garber's Orch, 38-39. Wrote first song at age 15. Worked in San Francisco nightclub circuit Bimbo's, Topsy's Roost, Kit Kat & Rochambeau's. Appeared on "Steve Allen's Show," NY, 51; pianist, many restaurants & clubs throughout US. Chief Collabr: Richard Duane La Marre (brother). *Songs:* For the First Time in My Life; Summertime in Paris; Champs-Elysees; Yvette Or Marie?; Music: July in the Afternoon; In This Life; It Seems Like Only Yesterday; Monte Carlo; Brighter Day; You Can't Win 'Em All; It Doesn't Cost You Anything to Dream; Wild Cherry; It's Written All Over Your Face; You Stayed Away Too Long; I've Always Been a Dreamer; Kitty; Where in the World?; Here's Looking At You; Dame Este Momento (Give Me This Moment). *Instrumental Works:* East Wind (Vent du L'Est; bolero); Blue Mirage (jazz); Standing Room Only (jazz).

LAMB, ARTHUR J   ASCAP 1942
author
b Somerset, Eng, Aug 12, 1870; d Providence, RI, Aug 11, 28. Moved to US in youth. Appeared in minstrel shows. On staff, music publ. Actor. Chief Collabrs: Ernest Ball, Albert Von Tilzer, Harry Von Tilzer. *Songs:* Asleep in the Deep; A Bird in a Gilded Cage; Jennie Lee; When the Bell in the Lighthouse Rings Ding Dong; The Bird on Nellie's Hat; You Splash Me and I'll Splash You; When You've Had a Little Love, You Want a Little More; The Spider and the Fly; The Mansion of Aching Hearts.

LAMB, JOSEPH F   ASCAP 1960
composer
b Montclair, NJ, Dec 6, 1887; d Brooklyn, NY, Sept 3, 60. Educ: St Jerome Col. Chief Collabrs: Scott Joplin, Amelia Lamb. *Songs & Instrumental Works:* American Beauty Rag; Top Liner Rag; Nightingale Rag; Sensation Rag; Reindeer Rag; Contentment Rag; Bohemia Rag; Excelsior Rag; Ethiopia Rag; Patricia Rag; Alabama Rag; Artic Sunset; Bird Brain; Blue Grass; Chimes of Dixie; Cottontail Rag; Firefly Rag; Good and Plenty; Hot Cinders; The Old Home Rag; Ragtime Bobolink; Thoroughbred Rag; Toadstool Rag; The Alaskan Rag; The Ragtime Special; Greased Lightning; The Bee Hive Rag; Rapid Transit; The Jersey Rag; Joe Lamb's Old Rag.

LAMB, MARVIN LEE   ASCAP 1971
composer, teacher, trumpeter
b Jacksonville, Tex, July 12, 46. Educ: Sam Houston State Univ, BMus; NTex State Univ, MMus; Univ Ill, Champaign-Urbana, DMusArts(comp/theory); studied with John Butler, William P Latham & Paul Zonn. Asst prof music, Atlantic Christian Col, 73-77 & George Peabody Col, 77-79; assoc prof music, Southern Methodist Univ, 80- Major perf, Lincoln Ctr, Brooklyn Museum, Electronic Music Plus Fest, World Saxophone Congress, Music Educr Nat Conf, NC Bicentennial Radio Series, Christ Episcopal Church, Nashville, Tenn, Southeastern Composers League New Music Forum & Cubiculo Theater, New York. Chief Collabr: David Cassel. *Instrumental Works:* Prairie Suite (brass quintet); In Memoriam, Benjy (saxophone quartet); Solowalk (flute alone). *Songs & Instrumental Works:* Professor March and Rag (spoken voice ens).

LAMBERT, BERTRAM BUDDY   ASCAP 1964
author, keyboard musician
b New York, NY, Nov 4, 31. Educ: DeWitt Clinton High Sch, Bronx, NY; studied harmony & comp with Svend Tollefsen, also accordion & piano with Tollefsen, Joe Biviano, Danny Hurd & Anthony Zainer. Professional accordionist, New York. Appeared in movie "The Godfather" (Part I). Played in maj hotels, clubs & TV. Lyricist for movie theme songs. Chief Collabrs: Alf Nystrom, Marty Gold. *Songs:* Lyrics: The Seasons of Love; We Got a Good Thing Going; Roaring Sam the Snowmobile; Simmer Down Susie; Remember I'm Still Young; Heat Wave; Little Girl; Inside Amy.

LAMBERT, DAVE   ASCAP 1947
composer, author, singer
b Boston, Mass, June 19, 17; d Westport, Conn, Oct 3, 66. Educ: High sch. Vocalist, drummer & trumpeter, Hugh McGinnes Trio, 36-38. Served, USA, World War II. Vocalist & arr, Gene Krupa Orch, & leader, vocal group with Johnny Long, 43-45. Contractor & arr for vocal groups, 47-57; singer & arr, Lambert Hendricks & Ross, 57-64. Appeared in Bway musical, "Are You With It?", recording artist with many records. *Songs:* What's This?; Lyrics: Avenue C; Little Pony; Sandman.

LAMBERT, EDWARD J   ASCAP 1942
composer, author
b New York, NY, May 25, 1897; d New York, Feb 13, 51. Educ: Pratt Bus Col. Writer of films & revues. *Songs:* A Vous Tout de Vey a Vous; La Dee Doody Do; Love in Springtime; I'll Never Fail You; Beat the Bongo; Mister Paganini Swing for Minnie; Nautch Girl From Cuba; Panama; Smile at Me; Is This the End; I'm Dreaming While We're Dancing; Doin' the Truck; You're a Magician.

LAMBERT, JERRY
See La Torraca, Gerard

LAMBERT, LANNY BRUCE   ASCAP 1973
composer, author
b Brooklyn, NY, Dec 28, 47. Educ: Great Neck North High Sch; NY Univ Sch of Arts, BFA, 70. Staff writer while in col at MRC Music, 68, Buddah Music, 70-72, Famous Music, 73, ABC Music, 74. To Los Angeles, 74; co-writer at April-Blackwood Music. Songs recorded by var artists, producer. Chief Collabrs: Robert (Bobby) Flax, Joey Carbone. *Songs:* Lyrics: You've Got Your Mama's Eyes; All I Need Is Your Sweet Lovin'; The Stuff Dreams Are Made Of; White Lies, Blue Eyes; Do You Know What Time It Is; Rock You to Your Socks; Bed and Board; Single Woman, Married Man; Not Tonight I've Got a Heartache.

LAMBRO, PHILLIP   ASCAP 1962
composer, conductor
b Wellesley Hills, Mass, Sept 2, 35. Educ: Began studying music in Boston, later in Miami & Fla; scholarship to the Music Acad West, Calif, studied with Donald Pond & Gyorgy Sandor. His music has been performed by Leopold Stokowski, Philadelphia Orch, Rochester Philh, Baltimore Symph Orch, Indianapolis Symph, Miami Symph, Oklahoma Symph & others in US, Europ, SAm & Orient. Comp & cond music for motion pictures incl "Energy on the Move" & "Mineral King" on which he won the Nat Bd Review Award for best music. *Songs & Instrumental Works:* Miraflores (string orch); Dance Barbaro (perc); Two Pictures (solo perc & orch); Four Songs for Soprano & Orchestra; Toccata for Piano; Toccata for Guitar; Parallelograms (flute quartet, jazz ens); Music for Wind, Brass & Percussion; Obelisk for Oboist and Percussionist; Structures for String Orchestra; Fanfare and Tower Music for Brass Quintet; Night Pieces for Piano; Biospheres for Six Percussionists; Trumpet Voluntary; Eight Little Trigrams for Piano

LAMM, ROBERT WILLIAM   ASCAP 1970
composer, keyboardist, singer
b Brooklyn, NY, Oct 13, 44. Educ: Roosevelt Univ, Chicago, Ill. Original mem of jazz rock ens Chicago. Contributing comp of var albums. *Songs:* Saturday in the Park; Does Anybody Really Know What Time It Is; Twenty Five; 25 or 6 to 4; Another Rainy Day in New York City.

LAMONT, VICTOR
See Maiorana, Victor E

LA MONTAINE, JOHN
ASCAP 1955

composer, pianist

b Chicago, Ill, Mar 17, 20. Educ: Eastman Sch Music, BM (scholarship); Juilliard Sch Music. WW II, USN. Was concert pianist; then mem, NBC Symph, under Toscanini. *Instrumental Works:* Piano Sonata; Sonata for Cello, Piano; Piano Concerto (Am Music Ctr comn, Pulitzer Prize, 59); Canons for Orchestra; Ode for Oboe, Orchestra; 5 Sonnets of Shakespeare; Songs of the Nativity; Songs of the Rose of Sharon; Fuguing Set for Piano; String Quartet; Santuary (cantata); From Sea to Shining Sea; Novellis, Novellis; Birds of Paradise (piano, orch).

LA MOTTA, FRANK JOSEPH (FRANK LA MARR)
ASCAP 1941

composer, author

b New York, NY, Jan 24, 04. Educ: Pvt schs, studied saxophone & clarinet. Asst cond, Isham Jones Orch & Ferde Grofe Orch. Had own orch, 30-40, played Yoeng's Rest, NY, 37, Roseland Ballroom, 38 & toured US, Europe & SAm, 39. Chief Collabrs: Carmen Cavallaro, Jose Melis, Johnny Graham, Babe Hart. *Songs:* You Are the One in My Heart; Lyrics: At Twilight Time; Shame-Shame-Shame-on You; Dolores, My Own; While the Night Wind Sings; I Never Was the One; What a Feeling Is This; When You Saw Him Last (Did He Mention Me?); Dancing With a Dream; A Lover's Lullaby.

LA MOTTA, WILBUR L (BILL)
ASCAP 1957

composer, author, teacher

b Christiansted, VI, Jan 13, 19. Educ: Christiansted High Sch, VI; Juilliard Sch Music; Merchant Marine Acad, NY. Self taught piano & harmony during childhood; scholarship to Juilliard Sch Music, studied major comp & piano. Began writing classical music, then popular; started playing prof with small combos. Formed own combo, traveled in US. Served in USN, World War II. Wrote arr for var Latin bands, incl Xavier Cugat. Recording pianist, playing clarinet, organ, piano prof; pres, Westindy Music Co. Goal, to classicize folk music of Caribbean. Chief Collabrs: Aaron Schroeder, Jack Wolf Fine, Bennie Benjamin. *Songs:* Pig Knuckles and Rice; Music: Come Back to the Virgin Isles; I'll Always Thank You for the Sunshine; Virgin Islands, USA; Alma By the Sea (alma mater of VI Col); Kings Point Victory (marching song, US Merchant Marine Acad); With Cindy; Carnival in St Thomas; Prayer for the Virgin Islands (hymn); Have You Thanked the Lord (calypso hymn); Charlotte Amalie; Dance Calypso; Mills of Old St Croix. *Instrumental Works:* Society Mambo; Dawn From a Window in Paradise (symphonic tone poem); The Last Bamboula (symphonic tone poem); Don Pablo's Bolero (string quintet); Bill La Motta (His Classical Piano Works); Concert Band: Echoes of the Virgin Islands; Spirit of the Virgin Islands; Winds on a Psychic Sea; Caribbean Salute to the USA.

LAMPE, J BODEWALT
ASCAP 1914

composer, conductor

b Ribe, Denmark, Nov 8, 1869; d New York, NY, May 26, 29. Educ: Studied music with Frank Danz & Carl Lachmund (scholarship). To US, 1873; ASCAP charter mem. First violinist, Minneapolis Symph Orch at age 16. Organized Lampe's Grand Concert Band, 1890. Music dir, Court St Theatre, Buffalo. Ed, band & orch dept, Jerome H Remick Publ Co, 06-23. In charge of orch, Trianon Ballroom, Chicago, 23-29. *Songs & Instrumental Works:* Vision of Salome; Home Sweet Home the World Over; Sunny South; Daughters of the American Revolution; Love's Garden; Dream Sprites; Regrets; Day Dreams Waltz.

LAMPERT, DIANE CHARLOTTE
ASCAP 1956

author

b Bronx, NY, Sept 25, 24. Lyric writer for country, pop, soul, rock, folk opera, jazz, theatre, TV, nightclubs & motion pictures. Author of 50 hit songs. Awards: Italian Song Fest; 2 gold records, Australia. Chief Collabrs: Julian "Cannonball" & Nat Adderley, Peter Schickele, Sammy Fain, Tom Springfield, Bernard Herrmann, Richard Loring, David Saxon, Peter Farrow, Scott Turner, Joe Seneca, John Gluck Jr, Fred Spielman, Leon Pober, Robert Allen, Jimmy Haskell, Dominic Frontiere. *Songs:* Lyrics: Big Man (Legend of John Henry); Silent Running (Oscar nomination); Break It to Me Gently; Your Name Is Beautiful; I'll Take Sweden; Toby Tyler; Snow Queen; Wizard of Baghdad; O'Halloran's Luck; Operation Petticoat; The Olive Tree; Ten Girls Ago; The Worryin' Kind; Let's Go Calypso; Fun Lovin' Baby; Love You 'Till I Die; Ain't Nothin' Shakin'; Where Mary Go; Blue Ribbon Baby; Can't Wait for Summer; Our Kind of Music; Is It Ever Gonna Happen?; I'm Past Forgetting You.

LAMPL, CARL G
ASCAP 1944

composer

b Cleveland, Ohio, Nov 4, 1898; d Cleveland, Sept 12, 62. Businessman. Chief Collabrs: Buddy Kaye, Morrey Davidson, Al Hoffman, Jerry Livingston. *Songs:* Close to You; Mississippi Holiday; Thoughtless; Where in the World; Are You Fooling; Get 'Em in a Rumble Seat; There's Something in My Heart; Hat Check Girl; You Can Say That Again.

LANCASTER, WILLIAM KINZEA
ASCAP 1977

composer, singer

b Roanoke, Va, July 2, 57. Educ: Killian Sr High Sch; Miami-Dade Community

Col; Fla Int Univ. Writer, 75-; first publ work, 77. *Songs & Instrumental Works:* You Are All I Need; Free the Duck.

LANCE, PETER
ASCAP 1960

composer, conductor, arranger

b Superior, Wis, Aug 20, 14. Educ: Superior State Teachers Col; studied music with Franz Hoffman; Otto Schact. Arr for Rudy Vallee Orch, 3 yrs. WW II, arr for USCG Band. Led vocal group, The Lancers. Vocal dir, Lawrence Welk Orch, TV, Hollywood, 4 1/2 yrs. Has own music & drama studio.

LANCE, VICTOR LEWIS
ASCAP 1969

composer, author, singer

b Baltimore, Md, May 8, 39. Educ: Self-taught. Mem, Screen Comp of Am & Am Fedn TV & Radio Artists. Directed 3 documentary films & acted in 12 films. Stage credits for "Happiest Millionaire"; record releases "Christmas Lullaby Rock", "Secrets" & "I'm Coming Home." Dance teacher, audio sound engr & instrumentalist. Wrote music for commercials; sang on records; script work for movies. Won awards, Cannes Film Fest, 69 & 71. *Scores:* Films: Weekend Lovers; Lila Mantis in Lace; The Notorious Cleopatra; The Joys of Jezebel; Booby Trap.

LANDAU, SIEGFRIED
ASCAP 1960

composer, conductor

b Berlin, Ger, Sept 4, 21. Educ: Stern Cons, Berlin; Guildhall Sch Music & Drama, London, LGSM(comp), 40; Mannes Col, New York, own dipl, 42. Cond: Kinor Symphonietta, 45-54; Brooklyn Philh, 55-71; Chattanooga Opera Co, 59-73; Westphalian Symph Orch, WGer, 74-76. Cond music for Westchester Symph Orch, 61- *Songs & Instrumental Works:* Friday Eve Service; Choruses.

LANDEROS, PEPE
ASCAP 1956

composer, author, violinist

b Durango, Mex, Mar 19, 10. Educ: Cons of Music, Mex. To US, 42. WW II, 101st Airborne Div. Arr, Jack Fina Orch, 46-50. *Songs:* Samba Caramba; Si Te Vas; Chango; Mentira.

LANDESBERG, STEVE
actor

b New York, NY. Mem comedy group, The New York Stickball Team; regular on TV series: "Bobby Darin Amusement Company," 72-73, "Paul Sand in Friends and Lovers," 74-75 & "Barney Miller," 76-; guest appearances on TV shows: "Ed Sullivan Show" & "Johnny Carson Show."

LANDESMAN, FRAN
ASCAP 1959

author

b New York, NY, Oct 21, 27. Educ: Columbia Univ, 40; Temple Univ, 49. Began lyric writing, 52. To London, 64, writer special material, BBC-TV, "The West-End Show" & "Je Vous Aime." Performer & singer, own material, cols, jazz fests & cabarets, Eng, New York & San Francisco. Performer, Nat Theatre, London, twice, Young Vic, London, twice & Ronnie Scott's Jazz Club (only poet to have performed 2 yrs in a row). Author, 3 bks of lyrics, publ, Eng, 75, 78 & 79. Chief Collabrs: Tommy Wolf, Bobby Dorough, Dudly Moore, Georgie Fame, Jason McAuliff, Steve Allen, John Simon, Roy Kral, Alec Wilder, Richard Rodney Bennett, Lee Prockress. *Songs:* Lyrics: Spring Can Really Hang You Up the Most (Oh You Know!); The Ballad of the Sad Young Men; It Isn't So Good; Listen Little Girl; Season in the Sun; There Are Days; This Life We've Led; Nothing Like You; Winds of Heaven; Brontasaurus Named Bert; When Love Disappears; Before Love Went Out of Style; Small Day Tomorrow; The Man Who Used to Be; Poems to Eat. *Scores:* Bway shows: The Nervous Set; A Walk on the Wild Side; Molly Darling; London stage: Don't Cry Baby, It's Only a Movie; Loose Connections.

LANDON, ALLAN
ASCAP 1977

composer, author, pianist

b New York, NY, Mar 28, 50. Educ: Manhattan Sch Music, studied with John Abbott & Daniel Ricigliano. Produced, "First Rush," Atlantic Records, 73; songwriter; wrote, arr & produced, "Magic in the Music" & "Let's Not Rush It" for Buddah-Arista Records. Singer. Chief Collabrs: Doug Lenier, Arnold Ahlert. *Songs:* (Sending Out an) SOS; I Love You More Than Ever; Love Conquers All; Beware the Night; Let Go.

LANDON, BUDDY
See Hoffman, James Senate

LANDON, STEWART
See Wilson, Roger Cole

LANDRY, RONALD L
ASCAP 1970

author

b New Orleans, La, Oct 24, 34. Educ: Roanoke Col; Univ Va. Started career in radio, 53; worked at numerous radio stations. Currently working at KFI, Los Angeles; writing & producing "Flo." Made 5 comedy albums, one of which was nominated for Grammy. Chief Collabr: Bob Hudson. *Songs:* Soul Bowl; Lyrics: Ajax Liquor Store; Ajax Airlines; The Prospector; Bruiser Larue.

LANE, BURTON
ASCAP 1933

composer, author

b New York, NY, Feb 2, 12. Educ: High Sch of Commerce; Dwight Acad; studied with Simon Bucharoff. Staff writer, Remick Music Co, age 15. Songwriter for "Three's a Crowd" & "Third Little Show." Pres, Am Guild of Authors & Composers, 57-66. Chief Collabrs: Harold Adamson, Ralph Freed, Ted Koehler, Al Dubin, E Y Harburg, Frank Loesser, Alan Jay Lerner, Ira Gershwin, Dorothy Fields. *Songs:* Tony's Wife; Heigh Ho, the Gang's All Here; Look Who's Here; Let's Go Bavarian; Everything I Have Is Yours; Have a Heart; I Want a New Romance; Swing High, Swing Low; Stop, You're Breaking My Heart; Madame, I Love Your Crepe Suzettes; Howdja Like to Love Me?; Moments Like This; The Lady's in Love With You; Says My Heart; Smarty; Would You Be So Kindly?; There's a Great Day Coming Manana; Don't Let It Get You Down; Swing High! Swing Low; Thc World Is in My Arms; I Hcar Music; How About You?; Feudin' and Fightin'; How Are Things in Glocca Morra?; The Begat; If This Isn't Love; Look to the Rainbow; That Old Devil Moon; Something Sort of Grandish; When I'm Not Near the Girl I Love; Too Late Now; You're All the World to Me; I Left My Hat in Haiti; Open Your Eyes; How Could You Believe Me?; It Happens Every Time; Applause Applause; On a Clear Day You Can See Forever; Come Back to Me; Melinda; Hurry, It's Lovely Up Here; Wait Till You're Sixty-five; She Wasn't You; Go to Sleep, Go to Sleep; It's Time for a Love Song; One More Walk Around the Garden; Someone in April; The Image of Me; Signora Campbell; I'm a Woman; Carmelina. *Scores:* Bway shows: Earl Carroll Vanities of 1931; Hold on to Your Hats; Laffing Room Only; Finian's Rainbow; On a Clear Day You Can See Forever (Grammy award, 65); Carmelina (Toni nomination); Films: Dancing Lady; College Swing; St Louis Blues; Babes on Broadway; Ship Ahoy; Royal Wedding; Give a Girl a Break.

LANE, EASTWOOD
ASCAP 1925

composer

b Brewerton, NY, Nov 22, 1897; d Central Square, NY, Jan 22, 51. Educ: Syracuse Univ. Asst dir, Wanamaker Concerts, New York, 23 yrs. *Instrumental Works:* Sea Burial (tone poem); Piano suites: In Sleepy Hollow; Adirondack Sketches; 4th of July; 5 American Dances; Sold Down the River. *Scores:* Ballet: Boston Fancy.

LANE, EDWARD
ASCAP 1946

author, publicist

b Newark, NJ, Feb 19, 15; d Sands Point, NY, June 5, 59. Educ: NY Univ; Oberlin Col, BA (scholarship); Oberlin Cons of Music. Business exec, Abe Lyman Orch. Advert & publicity exec for var music publishers. *Songs:* Bless You; Let's Dream This One Out; Let's Play House; When the Lilacs Bloom Again; Lovely; It's Always You; Lyrics By My Lips, Music By My Heart; Lyrics: You're the Only Pebble on the Beach; Night of Memories; (When the Moonlight Fell) on the Waterfall; Candlelight and Kisses. *Songs & Instrumental Works:* The Sample Song (voice, piano). *Scores:* Children's operetta: Little Tommy Tinkle, The Little Bell Who Found a Big Job.

LANE, IVAN
ASCAP 1961

composer, conductor, arranger

b New York, NY, Aug 5, 14. Educ: NY Univ, BA; Guildhall Sch Music & Art, London, Eng. Arr for dance bands incl Sammy Kaye, Blue Barron & Guy Lombardo, 37-43 & 46-48; also for ice shows & nightclubs. Comp for films & TV. Chief Collabrs: Kermit Goell, Jerry Gladstone. *Songs:* Long May We Love; Qu'est Que C'est L'amour.

LANE, JAMES W (DEMON SPIRO)
ASCAP 1958

composer, author, singer

b Oakfield, Ga. Educ: Glenside Music Sch, Pa; studied piano with father. WW II, USN. Sang with own group, The Sugartones. Arr for Philadelphia record co. A&R dir, Dee Records; then arr, cond, Warwick Records. Recorded with own trio. Music dir "Jazz At Home Club." *Songs:* Railroad Boogie; Shades of Ivy; It's Just the Mood I'm In; Francine; Help Me to Pray; Say Okay; They Call Me the Champ.

LANE, KERMIT
ASCAP 1959

composer, author

b Brooklyn, NY, Dec 20, 12. *Songs:* Everybody Loves Somebody.

LANE, RICHARD BAMFORD
ASCAP 1960

composer, teacher

b Paterson, NJ, Dec 11, 33. Educ: Eastman Sch Music, BM, 55, MMus, 56. USA, 2 yrs. Comp-in-residence, Rochester, NY, 59-60, Lexington, Ky, 60-61, under Ford Found. Pvt teacher, piano & comp, NJ. Accompanist for local choruses, NJ. Writer. *Songs:* Music: A Hymn to the Night (soprano, alto, tenor & bass chorus); Cradle Song (sopranos & alto chorus); Rejoice in the Lord (voice & piano). *Instrumental Works:* Four Songs for Mezzo-Soprano and Orchestra; Sonata No 1 for Flute and Piano; The Penguin (piano solo); Suite for Alto Saxophone (saxophone & piano); Passacaglia for String Orchestra; String Song (string orch).

LANE, RICHARD JOSEPH
ASCAP 1976

author, singer

b Butte, Mont, Mar 17, 38. Educ: Longfellow Sch, Butte; Butte High Sch. Writer & author of songpoems & one novelette. Custodian, Crippled Children's Hosp, Tempe, Ariz. Chief Collabr: Lew Tobin. *Songs:* Lyrics: Bicentennial USA; Brown Eyes; Love Bug.

LANE, WALTER

See Cohn, Gregory Phil

LANEY, LUTHER KING
ASCAP 1952

composer, author

b Chesterfield, SC, Aug 23, 16. Educ: Jr col; studied piano & violin. Vocalist, guitarist in Lew Douglas Orch & radio, Mich, 35-38. Officcr, USA, Inf, Air Force, WW II. Promotion dir, GM. Collabr: Lew Douglas *Songs:* Why Don't You Believe Me?; Don't Call Me Sweetheart Anymore; Love Lies; Clay Idol; Maybe Next Time; Wait and See.

LANG, EDDIE (SALVATORE MASSARO)
ASCAP 1955

composer, guitarist

b Philadelphia, Pa, Oct 25, 02; d New York, NY, Mar 26, 33. Guitarist, dance orchs incl Joe Venuti, Dorsey Brothers, Mound City Blue Blowers & Paul Whiteman. Accompanist to Bing Crosby; recording artist with many records. *Songs & Instrumental Works:* Perfect; Wildcat; Jet Black Blues; Stringing the Blues; In the Bottle Blues.

LANG, PHILIP JOSEPH
ASCAP 1942

composer, author, orchestrator

b New York, NY, Apr 17, 11. Educ: Ithaca Col, BS (music); Juilliard. World War II musical consult, Office War Information; in charge of music, Ensign, US Maritime Service. Orchestrations for Morton Gould, Alfred Wallenstein, Arthur Fiedler, Andre Kostelanetz. Radio & TV. Assoc prof orchestration, Univ Mich, summers, 49, 50, 51, Univ Colo, summer, 55. Ed educ music, E H Morris & Co. Partner, Lawson Gould Music Publ. Mem of Am Bandmasters Asn. *Songs & Instrumental Works:* Over 100 originals & arrangements publ for educ music, band, orch & chorus. *Scores:* Orchestration for 75 Bway musicals, incl High Button Shoes, Annie Get Your Gun, Carnival, Camelot, Hello Dolly, Mame & Annie.

LANGDON, VERNE LORING (J S BORK)
ASCAP 1973

composer, author

b Oakland, Calif, Sept 15, 41. Educ: James Lick High Sch, San Jose, Calif; San Jose City Col, Calif; San Jose State Col, Calif, MA, studied piano with Thomas Ryan. Disc jockey, radio KLOK, San Jose, 59-62. Record producer, songwriter, 63- Albums incl "An Evening With Boris Karloff and His Friends", "Musical Menopause", "Circus Clown Calliope", vols 1 & 2, "Poe With Pipes." Chief Collabrs: Milt Larsen, David B Roberts. *Songs:* Carousel Dreams; Carnival of Souls. *Instrumental Works:* Echos of the Organ (Phantom of the Organ Suite); Baby Bear Suite; Bork Shuffle.

LANGE, ARTHUR
ASCAP 1924

composer, author, arranger

b Philadelphia, Pa, Apr 16, 1889; d Washington, DC, Dec 7, 56. Educ: Pvt music study; hon doctorate, 55. Arr for dance orchs incl Dardanella & var Bway musicals. Head music dept, MGM, 29, & music dir for var other studios. Contributed to recording techniques in studios. Produced Co-Art Records; publ mag Keynote & Co-Art Turntable. Organized, past pres, Am Soc Music Arrangers; pres Native Am Composers Crescendo Club. Conducted Hollywood Bowl Orch, 30. Taught, pvtly & at Los Angeles Cons of Music & Arts. Organized & conducted Santa Monica Civic Symph, 47-56. Author bks, "Arranging for the Modern Dance Orchestra", "Harmony and Harmonics" & "Spectrotone Chart." Motion picture Acad awards for "The Great Victor Herbert" & "The Great Ziegfeld." *Songs:* America Here's My Boy; We're Going Over; In a Boat; In the Valley of the Moon; On the Old Front Porch; and many others. *Instrumental Works:* Atoms for Peace; A Gosling in Gotham; Antelope Valley; Arabesque for Harp and Orchestra; Big Trees; Divertimento for Strings; The Fisherman and His Soul; Mount Whitney; Symphony No 1; Four Symphonic Murals; Symphonette Romantique; Symphonette Spirituelle; In the Evening; Water Whispers Suite (piano). *Scores:* Films: Hollywood Revue of 1929; The Woman in the Window; Along Came Jones; Casanova Brown; On the Avenue; Cavalcade; Belle of the Yukon; and many others.

LANGE, HENRY W
ASCAP 1924

composer, pianist

b Toledo, Ohio, July 20, 1895. Educ: Pub schs; studied harmony, counterpoint, theory & comp with Arthur Kortheur & Max Ecker, piano & comp with Herman Wasserman, New York. Pianist, Paul Whiteman Orch, 20; played Palais Royale & Ziegfeld Follies, also toured Europe, 20-24. Recording artist, var record cos, 20-28 & for player piano rolls for Ampico & Duo Art, 21-25. Cond, stage production for Whiteman of "Lucky." Comp for Rudolph Valentino. In London, gave command performances before Duke of Windsor, Lord & Lady Mountbatten. Performed as 1 of 3 pianists in premiere of George Gershwin's "Rhapsody in Blue," 24. Organized own orch, 25; music dir, Baker Hotels, Dallas, Tex, 25-30. Toured in vaudeville; dir, radio sta, 36; consult for radio & TV, 40-53. Hon mem, Automatic Musical Instrument Collectors Asn. *Songs:*

Hot Lips; Page Mr Pianist; Sweet; Regret; When Night Comes; Yes Sir, That's Lazy-bones; Oh, What She Does to Me; On Sunday Night. *Instrumental Works:* Classicana; Cho-Piano; Symphanola.

LANGE, JOHNNY   ASCAP 1940
composer, author
b Philadelphia, Pa, Aug 15, 09. Educ: SPhiladelphia High Sch, grad. Writer, spec material & songs for acts & nightclub singers; wrote songs for motion picture studios, 37-47 & for Ice Capades, 50; also wrote songs for many motion pictures. Chief Collabrs: Henry "Hy" Heath, Eliot Daniel, Lew Porter, Leon Rene, Vick Knight, Dick Loring, Fred Glickman. *Songs:* Mule Train; Uncle Remus Said; Chapel in the Valley; The Little Red Fox (Nyah, Nyah, Ya Can't Catch Me); Benny the Beaver; There'll Be No New Tunes on This Old Piano; I Fell in Love With a Dream; Toyshop Jamboree; I Lost My Sugar in Salt Lake City; Somebody Bigger Than You and I; St Patrick's Day Parade; Git Along Mule; I Aint Gonna Change; Is It Better to Have Loved and Lost (Than Never to Have Loved At All); Madrid; I Asked the Lord; I Found the Answer; Someone's in the Kitchen With Dinah; I Am Not Alone; The Only Thing I Want for Christmas; The Angelus Ring Again; Deacon Jones; Annabella; Be Goody-Good-Good to Me (I'll Be Goody-Good-Good to You); Christmas Carols By the Old Corral; Easter Sunday on the Prairie; Elmer and the Bear; I Don't Want the World With a Fence Around It; (I'm Gonna Hurry You Out of My Mind and) Cry You Out of My Heart; It's All Over Now, I Won't Worry; Loaded Pistol (And Loaded Dice); From the Rim of the Canyon; Up Jumped the Devil (In a White Night Gown); Nora Me Darlin'; Santa Claus Is Ridin' the Trail; You Can't Go on Forever Breaking My Heart; When They Pass Around the Basket; A Miracle Happened to Me; Merci Beaucoup; He Loves Everybody (In This Whole Wide World); There's Someone to Help You; Music: Hail Mister Touchdown; We Had the Best Band There; Lyrics: Bluebirds Keep Singing in the Rain; Hawaiian Serenade; Hula Twist; Blue Shadows on the Trail; Pecos Bill; Without Your Love; I Got It Bad; It's Crazy, But Baby It's Love.

LANGENUS, GUSTAVE   ASCAP 1939
composer, clarinetist, conductor
b Malines, Belg, Aug 6, 1883; d Commack, NY, Jan 30, 57. Educ: Malines Music Sch; Royal Cons Brussels, studied with Poncelot, Hanon. Clarinetist in Queen's Hall Orch, 00-10, Duke of Devonshire's Orch, Eastbourne, Eng. To US, 10. Toured Europe with Sousa's Band. First clarinetist, New York Symph & New York Phil Orchs. Soloist, NBC symph orch. Clarinetist, Perole, Budapest & Gordon String Quartets. Co-founder, New York Chamber Music Soc. Taught, Juilliard Sch, Nat Music Camp, Interlochen, Mich, Peabody Col, Dalcroze Sch of Music & NY Univ. Organized Langenus Woodwind Ens. Guest cond, New York Police Band, City Park Concerts. Ed, Woodwind News. Author, "Langenus Clarinet Method." *Instrumental Works:* Swallows Flight (scherzo for flute, clarinet, orch); Donkey Ride; Chrysalis; Scale Waltz; Irish Serenade; In Cowboy Land; Old New Orleans; Examinations; Indian Mother Song; The Commuters Express; In the Forest; Lullaby; Mount Vernon Minuet; Grand Duo Concertante, Opus 48 (transc for 2 clarinets); & var arr & transc for clarinets & other instruments.

LANGLEY, CORDES JEFFREY   ASCAP 1975
composer, educator, pianist
b Ukiah, Calif, May 2, 51. Educ: Studied piano with Siegfried Schultze, 62-69; Univ Calif, Berkeley, undergraduate work, 69-72; Juilliard, BM, MM, studied comp with David Diamond, 76-80. Comp many songs. Recorded 3 record albums, Redwood Records. Toured extensively in concert, US & Asia. Fac mem, Juilliard, 80- Chief Collabr: Holly Near. *Songs:* Old-Time Woman; Santa Monica Pier; Song to a Melody; Winner Takes All; Damn the Poets; Put Away; Music: Don't Take My Sunday Paper; Faces; Water Come Down; Feeling Better; It's My Move; Someday One Will Do; Nicolia; You've Got Me Flying; You Can Know All I Am. *Instrumental Works:* Lyric Essay for Orchestra; Piano Sonata, The Son (cantata for soprano, cello & piano); Variations for Orchestra. *Scores:* Bway show: Saralinda.

LANGLEY, LEANNE   ASCAP 1977
composer, musicologist, teacher
b Coral Gables, Fla, Jan 29, 53. Educ: Baylor Univ, BM(theory, comp); Univ NC, Chapel Hill, PhD(musicol). *Songs:* A Most Unusual Champion; Wonderful Surprises; Music: It Is Well With My Soul; Like a River Glorious.

LANGNER-SAKS, GITLE
See Saks, Gitle Langner

LANGSTROTH, IVAN   ASCAP 1947
composer, pianist, educator
b Alameda, Calif, Oct 16, 1887; d. Educ: Royal Acad Music, Berlin, 10-14; studied with Paul Juon, Rudolf Krasselt & Josef Lhevinne; Royal Acad Arts, Berlin, master class for comp, scholarship with Engelbert Humperdinck. Choirmaster, Kiel Opera, Ger, 14-15; Am Church, Berlin, 16-17. Concert pianist, Sweden & Denmark, 17-21. Prof comp & theory, New Vienna Cons, Vienna, 21-23; Austro-Am Int Cons, 32-34. Head comp dept, Chatham Square Music Sch, New York, 40-43. Lectr, instr & cond, City Col New York, 42-43 & Brooklyn Col, 43-45. Pvt teacher. Mem: Austrian Soc Comp; Austrian Comp League; Austrian Teachers Soc; Am Guild Organists. *Songs & Instrumental Works:* Fantasie and Fugue (Haussermann prize); Piano Sonatina; Piano

Concerto; String Quartet; Aria for Soprano, Orchestra; A Cappella Mass; Toccata and Double Fugue (Am Guild Organists prize); Theme With Variations; Introduction and Fugue (Am Guild Organists exam piece); Choral: Cradle Song; Butterfly.

LANIER, VERDELL (CONSTANCE NORMAN)   ASCAP 1977
composer, author, singer
b Detroit, Mich, June 11, 57. Educ: MacKenzie High Sch, dipl; Mich State Univ; Detroit Bible Col. Independent songwriter, 76-78; practicing publisher, 80- Chief Collabs: Michael Stokes, George Vary & Rudy Robinson. *Songs:* It's You That I Need; If You're Ready (Here it Comes); You Must Be an Angel; Up Higher; You, You're the One.

LANOUE, CONRAD (TEE)   ASCAP 1960
composer, pianist, arranger
b Cohoes, NY, Oct 18, 08; d Albany, NY, Oct 15, 72. Educ: Pub schs. *Songs:* Souvenir.

LANSKY, PAUL   ASCAP 1975
composer
b New York, NY, June 18, 44. Educ: Queens Col; Princeton Univ, Ba, MFA, PhD; studied with George Perle, Hugo Wersgall, Milton Buffy. Work in instrumental & electronic media. Former mem, Dorion Wind Quintet. *Instrumental Works:* Crossworker; Model Fantasy.

LANZA, ALCIDES E   ASCAP 1967
composer, educator
b Rosario, Arg, June 2, 29. Educ: Rosario Indust Sch, elect eng; Di Tella Inst, Buenos Aires, music comp studies with Albert Ginastera, Vladimir Ussachevsky, Aaron Copland, Bruno Maderna & Olivier Messiaen. Coach, Teatro Colon, Buenos Aires, 60-65; Guggenheim Fel, 65-66; Ford Found grant, 67-; assoc prof & dir electronic music studio, McGill Univ, Can, 71-; artist-in-residence, Berlin, Ger, 72-73. *Instrumental Works:* Penetrations VI (1972-II; singer, tape, instruments); Plectros II (1966-I; piano & electronic tape); Acufenos I (1966-III; trombone & four instruments); Interferences II (1967-I; perc ens & electronic tape); Eidesis II (1967-II; 13 instruments); Eidesis III (1971-II; orch & electronic tape).

LANZARONE, BENJAMIN ANTHONY   ASCAP 1969
composer
b Brooklyn, NY, Oct 28, 38. Educ: Brooklyn Cons Music; High Sch Music & Art; Manhattan Sch Music, BM, MM & MMusEd; piano with Dora Zaslousky; comp with Nicholas Flagello. Pianist, studio work; featured on album Bhen Lanzaroni in Classic Form; solo recital at Carnegie Recital Hall; soloist on tour with Longines Symph. Arr, many recordings; arr/orchr 2 Bway shows; cond Bway & many name acts; comp & arr many jingles. Chief Collabr: Bob Alan. *Songs:* Music: Are You Ready for This; Let's Make Love. *Scores:* TV shows: Love Boat; Happy Days; Laverne and Shirley; Mork and Mindy; Shirley; Out of the Blue; Good Time Girls; Traditions of Easter.

LAPELL, DOROTHY
See Subota, Dorothy LaPell

LAPLANTE, CHARLES
See Douglas, Charles

LAPO, CECIL ELWYN   ASCAP 1953
composer, teacher, choral director
b Flint, Mich, Mar 12, 10. Educ: Westminster Choir Col, Princeton, NJ, BM; Mt Union Col, Alliance, Ohio, DM. Minister music in churches, Hornell, NY, Trumansburg, NY, Newtown, Pa, Cuyahoga Falls, Ohio, Wichita Falls, Tex, Oklahoma City, Okla, 30 yrs. Exec, Methodist Bd Educ, dir of ministl music, 9 yrs. Exec dir, Choristers Guild, Dallas, Tex. *Songs:* Music: Choral music for church use.

LA PORTA, JOHN DANIEL   ASCAP 1953
composer, author
b Philadelphia, Pa, Apr 13, 20. Educ: Manhattan Sch Music, BM, 56, MMusEd, 57; pvt clarinet study with Herman Pade, William Dietrich, Joseph Gigiotti & Leo Russianhoff; flute with Robert Morris; comp with Ernst Toch & Alexei Haieff; jazz improvisation with Lennie Tristano. All Am Youth Orch under Leopold Stokowski & Sylvan Levine; concerts & recordings under Walter Hendl, Igor Stravinsky, Alexei Haieff, David Broekman, Ralph Shapey, Gunther Schuller & Leonard Bernstein. Played & arr for Bob Chester, Woody Herman & Charles Mingus; musical dir, Comp Workshop, 52-54 & Jazz Found of Am; performer & comp "Music in the Making"; performed & recorded own Quartet, Quintet & Septet, also the premier of 6 contemporary comp comn by Brandeis Fest, 57; soloist, New York Philh Symph Orch; mem & comp, Berklee Fac Saxophone Quartet, 73-; recorded, Metronome All Stars; jazz concerts performances with Herb Pomeroy Quintet, 75-; performed series of concerts with Berklee Bicentennial Fac Orch, 76, also performed series of radio broadcasts "Modern Jazz vs Figs"; played & arr, Herb Pomeroy Orch, 76- Taught clarinet, flute, saxophone, music dictation, comp, band & ens, Parkway Music Inst, 48-51, clarinet, flute & saxophone, Oyster Bay High Sch, 54-58 & jazz workshop classes, Manhattan Sch Music, several yrs; pvt teaching of

clarinet, saxophone, theory, comp & improvisation, 48-; fac mem, Nat Stage Band Clinics, 60-; fac, Berklee Col Music, 62-; dir, Boston Youth Band, 64-65; reed consult & asst music dir, Newport Youth Band & Newport Int Youth Band; jazz improvisation clinics, Nat Music Educ Nat Conf Conventions. *Songs & Instrumental Works:* Jazz Comp: Non Alcoholic; Mother's Invention, True to Myself; Reunion; Flotsam and Jetsam; Remember Mingus; Reap the Harvest; and many others; Educ Works: Developing the School Jazz Ensemble (22 vols); A Guide to Jazz Phrasing and Interpretation (3 bks, records); Developing Sight Reading Skills in the Jazz Idiom (3 bks); A Guide to Improvisation (4 bks, records); Ear Training Phase I (bk); Spanish Rhapsody (saxophone quartet); Tonal Organization of Improvisational Techniques (4 bks with 4 LP's); Functional Piano for the Improvisor (bk); Jazz Ear Training (4 bks, record); Rhapsody for Trumpet (dedicated to Doc Severinsen); Essay for Clarinet Alone; also a number of original comp for stage band.

LARDNER, RING W   ASCAP 1933
author
b Niles, Mich, Mar 6, 1885; d East Hampton, NY, Sept 25, 33. Educ: Armour Tech. Reporter on Niles, Chicago & Boston newspapers; columnist, Chicago Tribune, 13. Sportswriter & short story writer. Author "Bib Ballads", "You Know Me, Al", "Gullible's Travels", "How to Write Short Stories", "Round Up", "Big Town" & "First and Last." Chief Collabr: Vincent Youmans. *Songs:* June Moon; Little Puff of Smoke, Goodnight; How Far Is Heaven From Here?; Teddy, You're a Bear; Prohibition Blues; Montana Moon; If I Were You, Love. *Scores:* Bway plays: June Moon; Elmer the Great; Bway Stage: Smiles.

LARGE, DONALD E   ASCAP 1951
composer, author, conductor
b Can, Nov 15, 09. Educ: Jacksonville Col of Music; also pvt music study. Cond dance orch, Windsor, Can; singer in Detroit, 32-39. Choral dir, WJR, 40-44 & 46-61, Wayne King Orch, 53-59 & Univ of Detroit, 63- Comp scores for GM indust shows. *Songs:* If We All Said a Prayer; Hayride.

LARIMER, ROBERT WALKER   ASCAP 1963
author
b Pittsburgh, Pa, June 24, 29. Educ: Carnegie Inst Technol, musical productions. Pres & creative dir, Nadler & Larimer Advert Agency, 64-, accounts with Faberge, Self Mag & CBS Toys, Lily of France, NY State Lottery & Austin Nichols. Chief Collabrs: Vinette Carroll, George Panetta, Burt Keyes. *Songs:* You Fabulous Babe (advert); Today Is Your Brutday; Hugo the Hippo (animation musical); But Never Jam Today; King of the Whole Damn World (off Bway musical); I Will, I Will for Now (movie lyrics); You're a Self Made Woman (commercial); For the Love of Life (commercial); The World Goes Rolling On (Newark Boys Choir).

LARKIN, MARY   ASCAP 1974
composer
b Tuskaloosa, Ala, Feb 27, 44. Educ: Univ Ala. Chief Collabr: Earl Conley. *Songs:* Lyrics: This Time I've Hurt Her More Than She Loves Me; The Devil and Miss Jones.

LAROCCA, DOMINICK JAMES (NICK)   ASCAP 1936
composer, conductor, cornetist
b New Orleans, La, Apr 11, 1889; d New Orleans, Feb 22, 61. Educ: High sch. Cornetist, leader & mgr, Original Dixieland Jazz Band. Played at Reisenweber's, New York, World War I. Toured throughout US & Europe. Recording artist with many records; building bus, 38-58. *Instrumental Works:* Tiger Rag; Dixieland One Step; Lazy Daddy; Skeleton Jangle; Fidgety Feet; Some Rainy Night; Barnyard Blues; Ramblin' Blues; At the Jazz Band Ball; Lasses Candy.

LARRIN, JAY
See Dodd, J D

LARSEN, ELIZABETH B (LIBBY)   ASCAP 1976
composer
b Wilmington, Del, Dec 24, 50. Educ: Univ Minn, BA, 71, MA, 75, PhD, 78, studied with Dominick Argento, Paul Fetlex. Co-founder, dir of Minn Comp Forum, 73- Produced operas "Some Pig," 75, "Words Upon the Windowpane," 78, "Silver Fox," 79, "Tumbledown Dick," 80. Comn by St Paul Chamber Orch, "Weaver's Song and Jig," 77. Wolf Trap Fel, 78. Minn State Arts Bd Individual Fel, 80. NEA new performance panelist. Founding mem New Music Alliance. Nat Opera Inst comp/librettist project, 80. Chief Collabrs: John Olive, Vern Sutton. *Songs:* Double Joy; Dance Set (chorus, & instrumental ens); Soft Pieces (choral); Music: Rilke Songs (voice & guitar). *Instrumental Works:* Bronze Veils; Weaver's Song and Jig; Three Cartoons. *Scores:* Opera/Ballet: The Silver Fox; Tumbledown Dick.

LARSEN, NEIL ROBERT   ASCAP 1975
composer, pianist
b Cleveland, Ohio, Aug 7, 48. Studio musician, worked on road with bands as keyboardist, New York, 70-78. Recorded 2 solo albums, A&M Records, Los Angeles, 78. First album for Warner Bros, 80. Grammy nomination, best instrumental rock performance, 79. Chief Collabrs: Allee Willis, Richie Ingvi, Charlie Ingvi, Kellny Gamble. *Instrumental Works:* Windsong; Sudden Samba; Midnight Pass; High Gear; Jungle Fever.

LARSON, JACK EDWARD   ASCAP 1966
author
b Los Angeles, Calif, Feb 8, 33. Educ: Montebello High Sch; Pasadena City Col. Began career as actor, poet, playwright. Performed on stage, in films, TV. Played Jimmy Olsen in "Superman." Verse plays off-Bway, Los Angeles, London. Chief Collabrs: Virgil Thomson, Ned Rorem, David Diamond, Gerhard Samuel, Paul Chihara. *Songs:* Lyrics: Marsyas; Sun-Like; Poems of Love and the Rain; Do I Love You; The Peace Place; Love Songs for Two Monsters; Egmont, Beethoven-Goethe, adaptation, concert drama, comn Los Angeles Philh; Lelio, Berlioz, adaptation, translation, comn Los Angeles Philh; The Soldier's Tale, Stravinsky-Ramuz, adaptation, comn Los Angeles Philh. *Scores:* Opera/Ballet: Lord Byron (libretto); The Relativity of Icarus; Orpheus Times Light 2.

LARSON, LEROY   ASCAP 1974
composer, author, entertainer
b Bagley, Minn, Sept 4, 39. Educ: Bemidji State Univ, BS(music educ); Ind Univ, MS(music educ); Univ Minn, PhD(musicol). Pub sch music teacher, 7 yrs; prof banjoist & entertainer, 10 yrs; founder & pres, Banjar Records, Inc. *Songs:* Banjo on My Mind; Banjo Drifters; Life Is a Spree; Red Winged Blackbird; Music: Harry's Old Time Waltz.

LARSON, NICOLETTE   ASCAP 1979
composer, author, singer
b Helena, Mont, July 17, 52. Educ: Bishop Hogan High Sch; Univ of Mo, Kansas City. Toured as back-up singer, Hoyt Axton, 75-76; New Commander Cody Band, 76-77; session vocalist, Neil Young, Linda Ronstadt, Christopher Cross, Amy Lou Harris, Doobie Bros, Van Halen, Graham Nash & Dirt Band, 75- Recording artist, Warner Bros. Chief Collabrs: Hoyt Axton, Ted Templeman, Laureen Wood. *Songs:* Old Greyhound; I Light This Candle; Just in the Nick of Time.

LARUE, D C
See L'Heureux, David Charles

LASKY, PAUL S   ASCAP 1954
author, lecturer
b Philadelphia, Pa, Aug 10, 24. Chief Collabrs: Stanley Appelbaum, Bob Sadoff. *Songs:* Lyrics: Suddenly; Santa Brought Me Choo Choo Trains; My Love Belongs to You; Firth of Forth; Democracy for Little Boys.

LASLEY, DAVID ELDON   ASCAP 1974
composer, author
b Sault Ste Marie, Mich, Aug 20, 47. Educ: Mason County Eastern High Sch, Custer, Mich, 65. Recorded first with vocal group, 66; other recordings, Detroit, 66-68; wrote songs & sang background vocals, Detroit recording studios, 68-70. In Bway shows, "Hair" & "Dude," 70-72. Wrote songs & sang background vocals, New York, 73. Formed vocal group Rosie, recorded 2 albums; also sang vocals for var artists. Four nat tours as background vocalist with James Taylor. Chief Collabrs: Allee Willis, Lana Marrano, Peter Allen, Don Yowell, Roxanne Seeman, Boz Scaggs, Kiki Dee, Gary Wright, Luther Vandross, Zane Buzby. *Songs:* Lead Me On; Love Me Again; The Blue Side; I Don't Go Shopping; Somebody's Angel; Come What May; Take Your Heart; Treat Willie Good; Dark Side of Your Soul; Jojo; Selflessly; Back On the Street Again; Like A Promise; I Should Have Been You; Small Town Change; Out of Pawn; I See Home; The Word's Don't Matter; You Bring Me Joy; It Must Have Been Love; Music: Roll Me Through the Rushes; Safe Harbor; Your Voice.

LASSWELL, MARY
See Smith, Mary Lasswell

LASZLO, ALEXANDER   ASCAP 1942
composer, pianist, conductor
b Budapest, Hungary, Nov 22, 1895; d. Educ: Budapest Acad of Music, grad; studied with A Szendy, A Kovacs & V Herzfeld; Univ Munich, PhD, 24. At age 14, taught piano & composition, also composed for movies; went to Ger, comp, did concerts & taught, age 18; concert pianist, age 19; concert tours, Europe & US. Piano soloist, Bluthner Orch, Berlin, 15. Gave piano recitals, Europe, 21-23. Invented Colorlight, machine to reproduce music & color. First perf, Kiel Music Fest, 24. Recitals in opera houses, Ger, 25-26. Music dir, Munich Cinema Art Studios, 27-33. Prof film music, Ger Stage & Film Sch & Univ Munich, 27-33; vis prof, Univ Hamburg. Head music dept, Hungarian Film Office. Exec producer documentary film for Hungarian Govt, 33-38. Came to US, 38, became citizen, 44. Music prof, Inst Design, Chicago, 38. Went to Hollywood, scored films, 44-48. Appeared as soloist, Hollywood Bowl, 46. With Paramount, Columbia & Republic. Comp motion pictures in Budapest, Europe & Hollywood. Music dir, NBC radio. *Songs & Instrumental Works:* Fairytale (dance); For Colorlight: 11 Preludes; Sonatina; Dreams; Improvisations on Oh Susannah (symph orch); Mechanized Forces (orch); 4D-122 (piano, orch); Hollywood Concerto; Structural Music; Mana Hawaii; Pacific Triptych; This World—Tomorrow; Secret Music of China; Century 21st; This Is Your Life; My Little Marge; Waterproof.

LATHAM, DWIGHT B ASCAP 1948
composer, author, singer
b New Britain, Conn, May 24, 03. Educ: High sch. Formed Jesters Trio; sang on radio, TV & in films, 23-50. Made many records. Wrote musical commercials. WCoast rep, Hansen Publ, 50. Became mgr, Carl Fischer, Inc, WCoast, 68-78, later promotional & adv work. *Songs:* MacNamara's Band; I'm My Own Grandpaw; Poetry; Hiawatha's Mittens; Bread and Gravy; It's the Same the Whole World Over; I Had But Fifty Cents.

LATHAM, WILLIAM P ASCAP 1959
composer, educator
b Shreveport, La, Jan 4, 17. Educ: Cons Music Univ Cincinnati, BS(music educ), 38; Col Music Cincinnati, BMus, 40, MMus(comp), 41; Eastman Sch Music, PhD(comp), 51; studied comp with Eugene Goossens, 39-41 & Howard Hanson, 49-51. Mem fac, N Tex State Teachers Col, 38-39 & Eastern Ill State Teachers Col, 46; mem fac, Univ Northern Iowa, 46-59, prof, 59-65; prof & coordr comp, N Tex State Univ Sch Music, 65-, dir grad studies, 69-, distinguished prof, 78- Chief Collabr: Thomas Holliday. *Songs:* Music: Epigrammata (a cappella choir). *Instrumental Works:* Suite for Trumpet and String Orchestra; Suite for Trumpet (transc for wind ens); Brighton Beach (concert march for band); Proud Heritage (concert march for band); Three Chorale Preludes (band); Court Festival (band); Passaglia and Fugue (band); Concerto Grosso (2 saxophones & wind ens); Concerto Grosso (transc for orch); Five Atonal Studies (solo clarinet); Dodecaphonic Set (band); Concertino (alto sax & wind ens); Concertino (transc for orch); March 5 (band); Prayers in Space (band); Sisyphus 1971 (alto sax & piano); SBF (bass flute solo); Preludes Before Silence (flute/piccolo solo); Bravoure (piano); Eidolons (euphonium & piano); Ex Tempore (alto sax solo); March 6 (band); Symphony No II (orch); Fusion (band); Jubilee 13/50 (orch). *Songs & Instrumental Works:* Te Deum (chorus & wind ens). *Scores:* Orpheus in Pecan Springs (ballad opera).

LATIMER, JAMES H ASCAP 1963
composer, author, percussionist
b Tulsa, Okla, June 27, 34. Educ: Ind Univ, Bloomington, BM, 56; Boston Univ, MM, 64; Berkshire Music Ctr. Founding mem, Madison Marimba Quartet; mem, New Boston Perc Ens; timpanist, Madison Symph Orch, Wis. Head perc dept, Univ Wis-Madison, 68-; music dir, Wis Youth Symph Orchs, 72-78. Current ed, "Who's Who in the World of Percussion, USA." *Songs:* Let's Do It; Mood of the Nation. *Instrumental Works:* Motif for Percussion; Variations on Westminster Clock Theme; FAMU March Cadences 11 and 12. *Scores:* Film/TV: Assignment Prison; Opera/Ballet: Epic of Man.

LA TORRACA, GERARD (JERRY LAMBERT) ASCAP 1963
composer, author, pianist
b Newark, NJ, Nov 23, 35. Educ: Montclair State Teachers Col, BA(music educ); pvt piano study with Sylvia Rabinoff & Narciso Figueroa; comp & arr with Hall Overton. Author of musical play "Crispus." Played for Billy May Band, Ann Maria Albrighetti, Cab Calloway, Emelio Pericoli, George Gobel, Red Buttons, Henny Youngman, Bob Newhart, Phyllis Diller & Van Johnson. Mem: Dramatist Guild & Authors League. Chief Collabrs: Saul Fish, Jerry Green, Bruce Williamson. *Songs:* Music: The Loving Tree.

LATOUCHE, JOHN ASCAP 1940
author
b Richmond, Va, Nov 13, 17; d Calais, Vt, Aug 7, 56. Educ: Richmond Acad Arts & Sci; Columbia Univ. Wrote sketches for Bway revue, "Pins and Needles." Chief Collabrs: Vernon Duke, Earl Robinson, Duke Ellington, Jerome Moross, Bronislaw Kaper, Douglas Moore. *Songs:* Cabin in the Sky; Honey in the Honeycomb; Love Turned the Light Out; Takin' a Chance on Love; Do What You Wanna Do; Yellow Flower; Summer Is a-Comin' In; Tomorrow Mountain; Just for Tonight; Lazy Afternoon; It's the Going Home Together; Wind Flowers; My Love Is on the Way; Strange. *Instrumental Works:* Ballad for Americans (cantata; first sung in Bway revue, "Sing for Your Supper"). *Scores:* Opera: The Ballad of Baby Doe; Bway stage: Cabin in the Sky; Ballet Ballads; Polonaise; The Golden Apple (NY Drama Critics award, 54); songs for Candide.

LATTANZI, JOSEPH W ASCAP 1976
composer, author, singer
b Philadelphia, Pa, Sept 4, 50. Educ: South Philadelphia High Sch; studied with Harold Rehrig, comp with father. Started recording, singing background vocals, Philadelphia, at age 10. Began writing, age 13. Performer, nightclubs on East & West Coasts. Chief Collabrs: Vincent Montana, Bud Ross, Major Harris. *Songs:* Put It in Love; You Want It, You Got It; Caribbean Lady; Brazilian Paradise; What a Big Thing; Love Means Everything. *Albums:* Fania All Stars (Grammy nomination).

LATTANZI, PEPPINO WILLIAM ASCAP 1955
composer, author, arranger
b Philadelphia, Pa, May 19, 26. Educ: Girard Col; Univ Pa, studied with William Hoppich; Knecht Sch Music, studied with Harold Rehrig, Clarence Borden. Wrote & played trumpet for major nightclub acts & recording cos; comp & arr songs for Columbia Pictures. Chief Collabrs: Freddie Bell, Jackie Lee, Paul Lasky. *Songs:* Giddy Up a Ding Dong; We're Gonna Teach You to Rock; Take the First Train Out of Town; Everyone Wants to Be Remembered.

LAUBER, TERRY DONALD ASCAP 1974
composer, singer, musician
b Minot, NDak, July 29, 49. Educ: Shelton High Sch; Olympic Col, bus, 69. Nightclub performer, guitar, piano, steel pedal, singer. Writer & performer for radio & TV commercials. Studio musician & vocalist. Recording artist, comp for ABC Records, 75, 76, Epic Records, 78, 79. Comp workshop instr. *Songs:* Martha (Your Lovers Come and Go); Future; Maybe; Annie; Life in the City.

LAUFER, BEATRICE ASCAP 1964
composer
b New York, NY, Apr 27, 23. Educ: Juilliard Sch, studied comp with Roger Sessions & Marion Bauer, orchestration with Vittorio Giannini. Comp of works for var media. *Songs & Instrumental Works:* Symphony No 1; Second Symphony; Cry!: An Orchestral Trilogy incl Cry!, In the Throes, Resolution; Percussion (SATB, perc instruments); Soldier's Prayer (baritone, piano); SATB choruses: Under the Pines; Do You Fear the Wind?; Spring Thunder; He Who Knows Not; Everyone Sang; and Thomas Jefferson Said...(baritone solo, 2 choral groups, orch); Violin and Viola Concertante with Orchestra. *Scores:* Opera: Ile; Ballet: The Great God Brown.

LAUREL, BOBBY
See Lessnau, Robert Gerald

LAURENCE, MICHAEL ASCAP 1959
author, director, producer
b New York, NY, Dec 30, 28. Educ: Yale Univ; Oxford Univ; New Sch of Social Res, New York. Producer, dir & writer, theatre, films & TV. Pub relations consult. Chief Collabr: Stephen Richards, Jr. *Songs & Instrumental Works:* Oratorio: The Ballad of Ruth.

LAURENCE, VICTOR
See Buchtel, Forrest Lawrence

LAURIDSEN, MORTEN JOHANNES ASCAP 1969
composer
b Colfax, Wash, Feb 27, 43. Educ: Whitman Col; Univ Southern Calif, DMA, 74; studied comp with Ingolf Dahl, Halsey Stevens, Robert Linn & Harold Owen. Won Sam & Harriette Stark Fel & Alchin Fel. Comn by Univ Southern Calif Chamber Singers, Yoav Chamber Ens & others. Did recordings on Orion Records. Currently assoc prof music theory & comp, Univ Southern Calif. *Songs & Instrumental Works:* A Winter Come (song cycle; Santa Barbara competition prize); Sonata for Trumpet and Piano; Symphony I (Jimmy McHugh Comp Prize); Four Madrigals on Renaissance Texts; Te Deum for Chorus and Orchestra; Be Still, My Soul, Be Still.

LAURIE, LINDA ASCAP 1968
composer, author, singer
b Brooklyn, NY. Educ: Lincoln High Sch; NY Univ. Singer with rock & roll band, toured throughout world, 3 yrs. Writer & singer, ABC, Screen Gems & Paramount, 68- Pres, Brooklyn Music Co, Los Angeles. Producer. Chief Collabrs: Jerry Ragavoy, Terri Etlinger. *Songs:* Ambrose; Crystal Clean; I Love What You Did With the Love I Gave You; When You Find Out Where You're Going Let Me Know; Life Is a Trippy Thing; Who Knows; Burn Your Bridges Behind You; Tune; Ruby Redress; You Got It.

LAVA, WILLIAM ASCAP 1948
composer, arranger, conductor
b St Paul, Minn, Mar 18, 11; d Los Angeles, Calif, Feb 20, 71. Educ: Northwestern Univ; studied conducting with Albert Coates. Ed of Northwestern Commerce Magazine & assoc ed for Purple Parrot. To Hollywood, 36; arr for radio. Chief Collabrs: Stan Jones, Harry Tobias, Sammy Cahn, Max Steiner, Franz Waxman, Henry Mancini, Frank Skinner, Ray Heindorf. *Songs:* The Moonrise Song (It Just Dawned on Me). *Scores:* Films: A Boy and His Dog; Embraceable You; I Won't Play; Star in the Night; The Good Guys and the Bad Guys; Chubasco; PT 109; Assignment to Kill; Chamber of Horrors; TV series: Cheyenne; Zorro; The Dakotas; The Treasury Department.

LAVALLE, PAUL ASCAP 1950
composer, conductor, music director
b Beacon, NY, Sept 6, 1908. Educ: Juilliard (scholarship), grad. Clarinetist & saxophonist, NBC Symph Orch under Toscanini. Creator & organizer many radio progs incl "Chamber Music Society of Lower Basin Street", "Highways of Melody" & "The All-Stradivari Orchestra." Organized The Band of America, 48, official band, New York World's Fair, 64-65. Guest cond, Voice of Firestone, World's Fair Symph Orch, Radio City Music Hall Symph Orch, New York Philh Symph, NBC Symph, CBS Symph, ABC Orch & Rochester Philh Orch. Dir music & principal cond, Radio City Music Hall Symph Orch, 68. Creator & organizer, All-Am High Sch Band. Cond, int musical fests in Europe. Cond for many albums. Recipient, Christopher Award, Man & Boy Award, Alfred I Du Pont Award & many ASCAP annual comp awards. *Instrumental Works:* Band of America March; Dwight D Eisenhower March (theme song, presidential campaign, 52); Cities Service Triumphal March; Big Brass Band (motion picture theme); S S Walton Jones March; US Air Force (tone poem, received citation from USAF Asn); United States Overture; Pitter Pat Parade;

Jolly Coppersmith; Ballyhoo March; United Press March; Land of Our Fathers (tone poem); All American High School Band March; Newspaper Boys on Parade; Dance of the Woodwinds; Memoirs of a Dilemma; March of the Jibyugs; Buzzards' Bachanal; Boys' Clubs of America; Bugle Calls'-a-Plenty; Big Joe the Tuba; Symphonic Rhumba; Manhattan Rhapsody; Sophisticated Sophomore (orch, band); Melody in the Night; Silhouettes in Blue; The Bullfrog and the Robin; Evergreen; Horns'-a-Plenty; Piquant Concerto for Clarinet; Suzanne; Arr: God of Our Fathers (orch, band); O Holy Night; When the Saints Come Marching In; Dream of Love (Liszt); When Yuba Plays the Rhumba on the Tuba (Herman Hupfeld; tuba soloist); South Rampart Street Parade (Ray Bauduk); & symph arr for music of Jerome Kern, Gershwin, Richard Rodgers & Lerner & Loewe. *Scores:* Film: Symphony of Deadly Fathoms.

LAVERE, CHARLES
See Johnson, Charles LaVere

LA VERE, FRANK
composer
b Chicago, Ill, June 21, 17; d Oct 21, 76. *Songs:* Have You Heard; Quanto; Drift Board; Progress; Who Am I to Say; Don't Let It Go to Your Head; Purple Shades; Pretend.

LAVERNE, ANDREW MARK
composer, keyboardist
b Brooklyn, NY, Dec 4, 47. Educ: Juilliard Sch Music; Ithaca Col; Berklee Sch Music; New Eng Cons; pvt study with Bill Evans, Don Friedman, Jaki Byard & Richard Bierach. Pianist/comp with Woody Herman, 72-75, Bill Watrous, Miroslau Vitous, John Abercrombie, Ted Curson & Lee Konitz, 75-77 & Stan Getz, 77-80. Recording artist, Columbia Records, Fantasy, Inner City, Steeple Chase & others. *Songs:* Music: Pretty City; Sabra; Keep Dreaming; Chappaqua; Shells; Europa; Academy of Love; Come to Me; Jet Lag; Metropolis; Another World; Museum; Designed Desires; Aqua; Lake Taco.

LAVOIE, ELIZABETH
See McNeil, Libby

LAVOIE, ROLAND KENT   ASCAP 1970
composer, singer
b Tallahassee, Fla, July 31, 43. Performed 12 chart records as Lobo. Owner of Boo Publ Co, 74. 12 million records in last 10 yrs. Co-produced & co-publ Jim Stafford's music hits, 74. *Songs:* Me and You and a Dog Named Boo; I'd Love You to Want Me; Don't Expect Me to Be Your Friend; How Can I Tell Her; It Sure Took a Long Long Time; Let Me Down Easy.

LAVSKY, PHYLLIS   ASCAP 1967
composer
b New York, NY, Feb 9, 48. Educ: High Sch of Music & Art, acad dipl in art; Hunter Col, BA(sociology). Co-comp musical score for "Brighty of the Grand Canyon." Wrote background music for many TV & radio commercials & short films. Pianist & singer, nightclubs & restaurants, New York. Chief Collabr: Richard Lavsky.

LAVSKY, RICHARD HARRY   ASCAP 1965
composer
b New York, NY, Dec 16, 40. Educ: Dewitt Clinton High Sch; New York City Col, BA(music comp), 63. Percussionist for many entertainers, 56-70; music editor & recording engr, Musifex, Inc, 62-67; formed Dick Lavsky's Music House. Comp, arr & cond music for many TV commercials & specials. Awards: Clio; Cannes Film Fest; Int Film & TV Fest Grand Award; Hollywood Radio & TV Soc; Am Fedn TV & Radio Artists; Screen Actors Guild. *Scores:* Films: Brighty of the Grand Canyon; Gizmo; People Soup; Face to Face; No Can Do.

LAW, ALEX W   ASCAP 1952
composer, author, conductor
b Swansea, Wales, Jan 10, 09. Educ: Pub schs. To US, 29. Violinist, NZ & Australia, with NBC, San Francisco & Horace Heidt Orch. Comp, arr & violinist, films & radio, Hollywood. Cond, Am Pres Lines. Orch mgr & arr, "Ice Follies."

LAWLOR, CHARLES B   ASCAP 1930
composer, singer
b Dublin, Ireland, June 2, 1852; d New York, NY, May 30, 25. To US, 1870, citizen, 1884. Soloist in churches, Dublin & US; traveled with opera cos. To New York 1887. Wrote songs for own vaudeville act & other performers. Chief Collabr: James Blake. *Songs:* The Sidewalks of New York; The Irish Jubilee; The Mick Who Threw the Brick; The Man in the Moon Is a Lady; Doolin and His Bike; Pretty Jennie Slattery; In Alabama.

LAWNHURST, VEE   ASCAP 1932
composer, singer, teacher
b New York, NY, Nov 24, 05. Pianist, singer for early radio. Mem of original Roxy's Gang. Comp of instrumental piano solos. Mem, 2-piano team of Pollock & Lawnhurst, on radio several yrs. First hit song, 32. Contract with Famous Music Corp as comp, 35-37. Chief Collabrs: Tot Seymour, Mack David. *Songs:* Music: I'm Keepin' Company; And Then Some; Accent on Youth; Please Keep Me in Your Dreams; Cross Patch; When the Leaves Bid the Trees Goodbye; Johnny Zero.

LAWRENCE, CORNELIUS C (NEIL)   ASCAP 1942
composer, author, publisher
b Brooklyn, NY, Dec 11, 02. Educ: Univ Pa; Temple Univ. Actor in plays. Co-author, play "Ethiopia." *Songs:* Curfew Time in Harlem; Abdullah; Sing Chilun Sing; You've Got Me Voodoo'd; Ink Spink Spidely Spoo; You're Gonna Reap What You Sow; Baby, Baby, Baby Blues.

LAWRENCE, EDDIE
See Eisler, Lawrence

LAWRENCE, ELLIOT (ELLIOT LAWRENCE BROZA)   ASCAP 1945
composer, conductor
b Philadelphia, Pa, Feb 14, 25. Educ: Univ Pa, BM; studied music with Harl McDonald, Leon Barzin. Won state contests for high sch pianists. Led dance orch; toured throughout US. Music dir, Bway musicals incl "How to Succeed in Business Without Really Trying" & "Golden Boy." *Songs:* Heart to Heart; Sugartown Road; Hunter and Three Dears; Five O'Clock Shadow; Once Upon a Moon; Box No 155; Brown Betty. *Instrumental Works:* Tone Poem (Thornton Oakley Prize).

LAWRENCE, HAROLD   ASCAP 1940
composer, author
b Narrowsburg, NY, Sept 3, 06. Educ: Deposit High Sch, NY; NY Univ (prelaw); Dickinson Col Law, grad. Admitted to NJ Bar, 30; Capt, USA, WW II. Helped found Gift Raps, Inc, Houston, Tex, 48, pres & chmn bd, retired, 64. Chief Collabrs: Isham Jones, Don Redman, Jay Milton, Nathaniel Shilkret, Basil Adlam, Sammy Kaye, Leonard Whitcup & Harry Horlick. *Songs:* Gardenias; Waiting; Little Lad; Downstream; Shame on You; Angry River; Another Night, Another Dream; Darkness; In the Same Old Way; I'll Forsake All Others; Lyrics: Let Me Be the One in Your Heart; You Will Cry; Ay, Ay, Ay (English transl); Cielito Lindo (English transl); La Golondrina (English transl); Whisper to Me.

LAWRENCE, JACK   ASCAP 1933
composer, author, conductor
b Brooklyn, NY, Apr 7, 12. Educ: Thomas Jefferson High Sch; Long Island Univ First Inst Podiatry, DrPod. WW II, 41-45, chief petty officer, USCG, transferred to USN-US Maritime Serv as Ensign; as head officer organized serv bands, welfare & morale units, network broadcast recruitment progs; served overseas as Lt Sr Grade. Wrote for films & shows either solo or in collaboration. Preparing Bway productions, "The Peanut Man" & "Tallulah, Dahling!" Chief Collabrs: John Barry, Hoagy Carmichael, John Green, Eric Coates, Sammy Fain, Arthur Altman, Nicholas Bordzsky, Clara Edwards, Raymond Scott, Charles Trenet, Margaret Monot, Victor Young, Ted Shapiro, Mary Lou Williams, Walter Gross. *Songs:* Heave Ho, My Lads, Heave Ho (off US Maritime Serv song); All or Nothing At All; Almost; Big Boy Blue; Faith; Foolin' Myself; If I Didn't Care; In the Moon Mist; It's Funny to Everyone But Me; Linda; My Bel Ami; The Other Half of Me; Fickle Finger of Fate; Yes My Darling Daughter; Susan Slept Here; What Would People Say?; My Love Has Two Faces; Talk to Me 'Bout the Hard Times; Lyrics: A Handful of Stars; Beyond the Sea; Boy Scout in Switzerland; Ciri-Biri-Bin; Delicado; Hold My Hand (Acad Award Nomination); Huckleberry Duck; In an 18th Century Drawing Room; Johnson Rag; Moonlight Masquerade; Never Smile at a Crocodile; No One But You; Passing By; Play Fiddle Play; Pawnbroker Theme; Song of the Barefoot Contessa; Sunrise Serenade; Sleepy Lagoon; Symphony; Tenderly; Valentino Tango; What Will I Tell My Heart?; With the Wind and the Rain in Your Hair; What's Your Story Morning Glory?; Poor People of Paris; Trembling of a Leaf. *Scores:* Bway Shows: I Had a Ball; Courtin' Time; Ziegfeld Follies; Crazy With the Heat; Films: Torch Song; Dinner at Eight; Lady Eve; Peter Pan; Valentino; Sleeping Beauty; Manhattan Merry-Go-Round; Susan Slept Here; Only Game in Town; Bachelor's Daughters; Affairs of Bel Ami; Flame and the Flesh; Deadfall; Fedora; The Pawnbroker. *Albums:* Come to the Circus.

LAWRENCE, JEROME   ASCAP 1953
author, playwright, director
b Cleveland, Ohio, July 14, 15. Educ: Ohio State Univ, BA(Phi Beta Kappa), DHL; Univ Calif, Los Angeles, grad study; Villanova Univ, DFA; Fairleigh Dickinson Univ, DLit; mentors in songwriting Frank Loesser, Sigmund Romberg, Johnny Mercer. Mem, playwriting team of Lawrence & Lee, plays incl "The Night Thoreau Spent in Jail", transl into 31 languages, "Inherit the Wind", "Auntie Mame", "The Gang's All Here", "Only in America", "Sparks Fly Upward", about Evita Peron, "Jabberwock", "The Crocodile Smile", "The Incomparable Max", "First Monday in October"; author of books for musicals "Look, Ma, I'm Dancin'", "Mame", "Shangri-La", stage & TV, "Dear World", "Actor", TV-PBS. One of founding fathers, Armed Forces Radio Service. Writer army-navy progs for D-Day, Vet Day, VJ Day. Co-founder, pres, Am Playwrights Theatre. Awards: 2 Peabody, many Tony, Donaldson, Critics (New York & London), Am Theatre Assoc Lifetime Achievement (for distinguished service to theatre). Bd mem of Dramatists Guild, Authors League, Master Playwright, NY Univ. Visiting prof at Ohio State Univ, Baylor Univ. Sem in Am studies, Salzburg, Austria. Sole playwright on US State Dept Cultural Exchange

Comt, traveled more than 50 countries as specialist. *Scores:* TV: Actor (PBS spec); Bway show/Film/TV: Shangri-La; Auntie Mame (incidental music & lyrics); also 239 Railroad Hour Musicals.

LAWRENCE, LOU   ASCAP 1969
composer, author
b New York, NY, Apr 9, 13; d New York, NY, Dec 5, 78. Educ: City Col New York, grad. Writer, bk of poetry, age 16. Reporter with New York Times. Pub relations, WPA theatre, Art World's Fair. Writer of plays. *Songs:* Jump It Mister Parachute Joe; The Rhumba Polka; Bingo Jim; Lyrics: Mm-Mm, It's Time to Say Hello; Two Little Birds and Tree Top; Cheer Up for the Best Is Yet to Come; She's the Sweetheart of the Army; Blue Star; No More Mama's Boy; Hi Ya Chum, Where Ya From; We'll Meet Again in Old Hawaii; Man With the Musical Saw; Isn't That Just Like a Woman; You're Ev'rything I Dreamed You'd Be; (I've Got Those) Lonesome Blues; The Mermaid Song; Prayer; Gimme What's Mine.

LAWRENCE, MARK   ASCAP 1961
composer, producer
b Washington, DC, Jan 14, 21. Educ: Princeton Univ (pres, Triangle Club, 41-42). WW II, USN. Vpres & dir of radio, TV, MacManus, John Adams (adv); 51-61. Founded Mark-L Enterprises, 63. Advert consultant & copywriter, 68-Produced film background score "David and Lisa" (Venice Film Fest prize, 2 awards from San Francisco Int Film Fest); wrote incidental music to Bway play "The Owl and the Pussycat"; co-produced "The Passion of Joseph D." *Songs:* The More I See of Lisa; Wouldn't You Really Rather Have a Buick? (commercial); Christmas Magic.

LAWRENCE, MICHAEL STEPHEN   ASCAP 1975
composer, flugelhornist
b Yonkers, NY, Dec 3, 45. Educ: NTex State Univ, 63-65. Performed & recorded two albums with Joe Henderson, 67-69 & three albums with Larry Coryell, 74-75; also performed with Gil Evans, 68, Horace Silver, 73 & Bob James, 77-80. Performed with own jazz group featuring own comp. *Songs:* Music: No Can Do; What Kind of Love. *Instrumental Works:* The Other Side; Roberta.

LAWRENCE, MORRIS JOSEPH, JR   ASCAP 1975
composer, author, Afromusicologist
b New Orleans, La, May 14, 40. Educ: Xavier Univ La, BSME; studied clarinet with Ronald DeKant, Orlando Tognizzi, Richard Saylor, Alvin Baptist, Theodore Purnell; Univ Mich, MM, studied with W D Revelli, Albert Luconi, W Stubbins & Ross Lee Finney; Bernadean Univ, Van Nuys, Calif, PhD. Lead tenor saxophonist, Royal Dukes of Rhythm Big Band; contra-bassist, Ypsilanti Greek Theatre, 66; article writer, The Instrumentalist, LeBlanc World Music Mag; sang in Begat Trio in Finnian's Rainbow, Ann Arbor Civic Theatre; created a new musical sci, Afromusicology; founder & pres, Afromusicology Soc; taught at Univ Mich; adj lectr, Washtenaw Community Col, Ann Arbor, Mich; leader, Afromusicology Ensemble, toured Brazil, Salvador de Bahia, Rio, Haiti, New Orleans Jazz Heritage Fest. Publ & author, Afromusicology J; gave Afromusicology perf, WDCN-TV, Nashville, Tenn. *Songs & Instrumental Works:* I Still Love You; A Constant Feeling; You Were Someone Else's Love; Tyimba (anthem for NCA); Sunday Morning; Never Look Behind; Big Band Jazz: For the First Time (anthem); Cherryl Jean; Portrait of a Drummer; Candice; Zimbabue; Move Me. *Scores:* Bway shows: What Does It Matter; The Psychiatrist.

LAWRENCE, PAMELA
See Military, Pamela

LAWRENCE, SIDNEY JASON   ASCAP 1974
composer, author, director
b New Rochelle, NY, Oct 28, 09. Metrop Music Sch; Columbia City Col; piano with Aube Tserko, comp with Wallingford Reigger. Pres, Neighborhood Music Sch, NY, 41-52. Was assoc ed "The Musical" mag, 43-45. Author of teaching textbks "Everyone's Music," 46, "Remedial Sightreading for Piano Student," 68, "This Business of Music Practicing," 68, "Profiles of the Piano Student," 78 & "Challenges in Piano Teaching," 78. *Instrumental Works:* Driftwood (flute, piano); Tandem (piano); Vintage, 1950 (voice); Dance You Bastards (voice); A Short Opera (voice); Wondrous World (voice); Aire for Strings (strings, piano); Pieces for Teens (piano).

LAWRENCE, STEPHEN   ASCAP 1967
composer
b New York, NY, Sept 5, 39. Educ: Hofstra Univ, BA, 61; studied piano with Leonid Hambro, Mary Lou Williams & comp with Elie Siegmeister, Meyer Kupferman. *Songs:* Music: You Take My Breath Away; Free to Be...You and Me; Who Are You Now?; One Way Ticket. *Scores:* Film/TV: Bang the Drum Slowly; It Happened One Christmas; Sooner Or Later.

LAWRENCE, STEVE   ASCAP 1957
composer, author
b Brooklyn, NY, July 8, 35. Educ: Thomas Jefferson High Sch; studied piano & saxophone. Mem, Steve Allen's "Tonight" show, TV. Army service, 58-60; vocalist with USA Band Orch, Ft Myer, Va. Singer in TV, hotels & nightclubs;

has made many records, as single and with wife, Eydie Gorme. Appeared in Bway musical "What Makes Sammy Run?" *Songs:* Two on the Aisle; Blue Angel; Hi-Ho, Stev-o.

LAWS, MAURY   ASCAP 1965
composer, arranger, conductor
b NC, Dec 6, 23. Educ: Pvt studies with Tom Timothy & Tibor Serly. Guitarist, singer & arr, groups & bands incl Vaughn Monroe Orch & vocal quartet Hi-Lo-Jack and the Dame. Performed on many TV shows. Arr & cond for var record labels. Wrote, scored & sang TV & radio commericals. Comp, arr & cond movies & TV specials, 65- *Scores:* Films/TV: The Hobbit (Peabody award, 77); The Return of the King; The Daydreamer; The Bermuda Depths.

LAWS, RONALD WAYNE   ASCAP 1975
composer, singer, saxophonist
b Houston, Tex, Oct 3, 50. Educ: Robert E Lee High Sch; Stephen F Austin Col, music major, 2 1/2 yrs. Performed in stage bands, big bands & nightclubs, Tex & Calif. Became recording artist, did 1st album with group Pressure, 75. Performed with Walter Bishop Jr, Hubert Laws (brother), Earth, Wind & Fire & Hugh Masekela. Chief Collabrs: William Jeffrey, Wayne Henderson. *Songs:* Friends and Strangers; Love Is Here; Every Generation. *Instrumental Works:* Always There; Let's Keep It Together.

LAWSHE, WILFORD
See Holcombe, Wilford Lawshe, Jr

LAWSON, TEDD
See Lehrman, Theodore Howard

LAWTON, JIMMY
See DeGraw, Jimmy Dwaine

LAYNE, RUTH
See Gordon, Ruth L

LAYTON, BARBARA SOEHNER   ASCAP 1967
composer, singer, actress
b Brooklyn, NY, May 5, 45. Educ: Marjorie Webster Jr Col, AA(speech, drama), 64; studied singing with Helen Hobbs Jordan. Voice-overs, radio & TV commercials, incl Woolite, 7Up & Tickle deodorant. Appeared in nightclubs; recording artist. Chief Collabrs: Barbara Morr, Michael Zager, Jhon Christopher. *Songs:* And I'd Like to Say I Love You; You Never Bought Two Pillows; Lyrics: Wish That Love Was Magic; Love Is Something That Leads You; Music Fever; I'm Not a Shoulder for Your Tears; Talk About Lovin. *Instrumental Works:* Jerry's Theme.

LAYTON, BILLY JIM   ASCAP 1924
composer
b Corsicana, Tex, Nov 14, 24. Educ: New Eng Cons of Music, BMus, 48; Yale Univ Sch of Music, MMus, 50; Harvard Univ, PhD, 60; studied comp with Francis Judd Cooke, Quincy Porter, Walter Piston, musicology with Otto Gombosi, Nino Pirrotta. Fac, New Eng Cons of Music, 59-60, Harvard Univ, 60-66, State Univ NY Stony Brook, 66-, chmn, music dept, 66-72. Recipient, Rome Prize, 54, Nat Inst of Arts & Letters grant, 58, creative arts award, Brandeis Univ, 61, Guggenheim fel, 63, Thorne Music Fund grant, 68. *Songs & Instrumental Works:* Five Studies for Violin and Piano; An American Portrait, Symphonic Overture for Orchestra; Three Dylan Thomas Poems (mixed chorus, brass sextet); String Quartet in Two Movements; Three Studies for Piano; Divertimento for Violin, Clarinet, Bassoon, Cello, Trombone, Harpsichord and Percussion; Dance Fantasy for Orchestra.

LAYTON, EDWARD   ASCAP 1953
composer, organist
b Philadelphia, Pa. Educ: West Chester State Teachers Col; studied Schillinger Syst of Comp with Jesse Crawford. Staff organist for CBS-TV shows incl "Love of Life", "Secret Storm", "Guiding Light", "Where the Heart Is" & "Love Is a Many Splendored Thing." Int soloist with Hammond Organ Co; performer occasionally at Radio City Music Hall. Now organist at Yankee Stadium & Madison Square Garden. *Songs:* Music: Bright Lights of Brussels—Cat Walk; The Lover; original music for CBS-TV daytime soap operas.

LEAF, ANN   ASCAP 1950
composer, pianist, organist
b Omaha, Nebr. Educ: Omaha Grammar & Central High Sch; Inst Musical Art, New York; piano with Sigmund Landsberg & Jean Duffield. Played organ for silent films in Los Angeles, Calif. Was chosen to open & close CBS network, 29, then was on "Nocturne Show" & others with Tony Wons, Ted Malone, Fred Allen, Easy Aces & Mr Keene; many soap operas; had own organ shows, New York. Have done pipe organ concerts & electronic organ concerts throughout the US & Can, 62- Recorded for Westminster, Warner, Concert, Doric & others. Have accompanied revivals of silent films in theaters & art museums. Comp scores, piano & organ novelties. Chief Collabrs: Lyrics, Tot Seymour, lyrics, Kermit Goell, Hugo Winterhalter. *Songs:* Music: In Time; Here Comes the Bride on a Pinto Pony; Blue Hours. *Instrumental Works:* Waltz on a Cloud;

Tango At Midnight; Aristocrat in the Automat; Fantasy; Tragic Interlude; Near Miss; Satire; Mirage on the Desert.

LEAHY, JOSEPH J
arranger
b Dorchester, Mass, July 25, 16; d Sept 12, 74. Educ: Boston Cons of Music. Sound engr. *Songs:* The Magnificent Christ Called Jesus.

LEASE, ANTHONY F   ASCAP 1963
author
b Pittsburgh, Pa, June 5, 25. Educ: Seattle Univ, BA. Creator of radio shows "Lease on Life" & "Voice of the Pacific." Founder, Tony Lease Tours, Lease on Life Tours. Author, "Take Time for a New Lease on Life." Chief Collabr: Bernie Kaai Lewis. *Songs:* Just Like Being in Hawaii; Liana.

LEAVITT, RAFAEL ANGEL (RAPHY)   ASCAP 1978
composer, author
b San Juan, PR, Sept 17, 48. Educ: Col San Agustin; Univ of PR, BBA; George Kudirka Accordion Acad. Founder, leader & composer of Orchestra La Selecta, 71- *Songs:* Payaso; Te Equivocaste; Amor y Paz; Soldado; Jibaro Soy; La Cuna Blanca; Cafe Colao; Duena y Senora; Herido; Lamento Jibaro; Voces Del Africa; El Buen Pastor; Balada a Un Loco; Carnaval; Cosquillita; Corazon Malvado.

LE BARON, WILLIAM   ASCAP 1933
author, producer
b Elgin, Ill, Feb 16, 1883; d Santa Monica, Calif, Feb 9, 58. Educ: Univ Chicago; NY Univ. Staff writer & prod asst, Jesse Lasky; managing ed, Colliers, 18-19; gen dir, Cosmopolitan Prods, 19-24; to Hollywood, 24; prod films, "Humoresque", "Beau Geste", "Cimarron", "She Done Him Wrong", "I'm No Angel", "Kiss the Boys Goodbye" & "Weekend In Havana." *Songs:* It's Never Too Late to Learn; Twixt Love and Duty; On Miami Shore; You Are Free; When the Wedding Bells Are Ringing; The Second Violin; Star of Love. *Scores:* Bway stage (librettos): The Echo; Her Regiment; Apple Blossoms; The Love Letters; The Yankee Princess; Moonlight.

LE BLANC, ROGER J   ASCAP 1976
composer
b New Bedford, Mass, Oct 4, 45. Wrote several songs for the Cates Sisters. Chief Collabr: Joe H Hunter. *Songs:* Out of My Mind; Love Can Make the Children Sing; Boogiewoogieities; Can't Help It; Mr Guitar.

LEBOW, LEONARD STANLEY   ASCAP 1962
composer, teacher
b Chicago, Ill, Feb 25, 29. Educ: Roosevelt Univ, BMus(comp), 52, studied trumpet with Renold Schilke, comp, Karel Jirak; Chicago Musical Col, MMus(comp & educ), 59, studied with R Schilke, Karel Jirak. Worked way through col playing trumpet, 47-52. Trumpet player, arr for Sahara Hotel Productions, Las Vegas, 52. Teacher in Chicago Pub Schs, 54. Teacher, pub schs, Los Angeles, 64. Trumpet player, teacher, comp & arr, commercial & educ music. *Instrumental Works:* Suite for Brass (march, blues, reel); Popular Suite for Brass Quintet; Ride the Matterhorn (for Disneyland Productions); Western Suite for Brass Quintet; Midwest Landscape (allegro energico, for brass quintet).

LEBOWSKY, STANLEY R   ASCAP 1964
composer, conductor
b Minneapolis, Minn, Nov 29, 26. Educ: Univ Calif, Los Angeles, BA(music-theatre); studied orchestration with Russ Garcia, ear training, Asher Zlotnik, conducting, Leon Barzan. Pop music, late 50's, early 60's. Bway, TV & film scores. Cond of many Bway shows incl "Irma La Douce", "Half a Sixpence", "Pippin", "Jesus Christ Superstar", "Chicago", "The Act." Music coordr for film "All That Jazz." Chief Collabr: Fred Tobias. *Songs:* Music: The Wayward Wind; Tender Love and Care; Don't Go Home; Take Off With Us; Crusade (oratorio). *Scores:* Bway show: Gantry; Film/TV: Gift of the Magi; Quincy's Quest.

LECKRONE, MICHAEL   ASCAP 1975
composer, author, arranger
b North Manchester, Ind, July 30, 36. Educ: Butler Univ, BM & MM; Ind Univ. Began teaching theory, trumpet & arr, Butler Univ, 58, band dir, 66-69. Involved in var performing & writing projects, Indianapolis. Rec'd Eli Lilly Grant, 62. Became mem fac, Univ Wis, 69, dir bands & prof music, 75-, Bascom Professorship, 80. Guest cond, clinician & adjudicator, US & Can. Extensive arr & comp, high sch & col bands. Mem, Am Bandmasters Asn. Author: "Koncert Kaleidoscopes on the March" & "Quicksteps to Arranging." *Instrumental Works:* Avatara; Matrix; Analogue; Theme and Montage; Apokryphos; Tower of the Americas; Paradox; Cousteau's Underwater World; Dithyramb; Harlequinette; Three Moods in Two Movements; Epeisodians; Alpheus: Concert March; Permutations; An American Anthem.

LEDEEN, RAYMOND
See Leveen, Raymond

LEDERER, CHARLES   ASCAP 1958
author, director, producer
b New York, NY, Dec 31, 10; d Los Angeles, Calif, Mar 5, 76. Educ: Univ Calif. Maj, USA, World War II. Producer of musical "Kismet"; writer, dir & prod for films, stage & TV. *Songs:* Love Has Nothing to Do With Looks; Kiss It and Make It Well; It Started With a Kiss.

LEDOUX, CHRIS LEE   ASCAP 1973
composer, author
b Biloxi, Miss, Oct 18, 48. Educ: Casper Col; Sheridan Col; Eastern NMex State Univ, art major. Started as professional rodeo cowboy, 68; winner, Nat Col Rodeo Championship; became world champion professional rodeo cowboy on bareback broncs in 76. Cut first album in 72. Began career in ranching in Northern Wyo, 78- Songwriter & sculptor. *Songs:* Lean, Mean and Hungry; This Country Boy's Going Home; Grange Hall Dance; The Yellow Stud; I've Got to Be a Rodeo Man; Hoka Hey Lakotas!; The Old Timer; Time; Our First Year; I'm Country.

LEE, BARBARA MCCORMICK   ASCAP 1978
author
b Hermitage, Tenn, Dec 6, 39. Educ: Univ Tenn, Nashville. Free-lance songwriter; was in gospel movie, "Sing a Song for Heaven's Sake." Chief Collabr: Jim Whiting. *Songs:* We Kissed Our Good Intentions Goodbye; Shared in the Wearing; Lyrics: The Look of Love in Your Eyes; Butterfly Blue; You've Been Touched By Love.

LEE, CRAIG
See Sigman, Carl

LEE, DAI-KEONG   ASCAP 1945
composer, conductor
b Honolulu, Hawaii. To US, 37. Educ: Univ Hawaii; scholarship with Roger Sessions, New York; Juilliard Sch Music, fellowship with Frederick Jacobi; scholarship with Aaron Copland; Columbia Univ, MA, 2 Guggenheim grants. USA, 5th AF, WW II. Guest cond, Sydney (Australia) ABC Symph. Mem, League of Comp; Allied MacDowell Club; bd of dir, Am Music Ctr. *Instrumental Works:* Prelude and Hula; Hawaiian Festival Overture; Introduction and Allegro for Strings (CBS comn); Golden Gate Overture; Violin Concerto (Albert Metz comn); String Quartet No 1; Polynesian Suite; Pacific Prayer; Overture in C; Children's Caprice (ballet suite); Concerto Grosso; 2 symph; Symphonic Suite; Canticle of the Pacific (chorus & orch); Mele Ololi (joyous songs soli chorus & orch). *Scores:* Operas: Open the Gates; Poet's Dilemma (Inst Musical Art comn); Phineas and the Nightingale; Ballad of Kitty the Barkeep (one act); Film Background: Letter From Australia; Musical Play: Shiny Little Pebbles.

LEE, DAVID   ASCAP 1964
composer
b Shelby, NC, May 3, 36. *Songs:* If Everybody; The Frog; Dom De Dom; Let It Rain; Have You Seen My Baby?; How I Love My Baby.

LEE, FLETCHER
See Little, Dudley Richard

LEE, JAMES
See Gillette, Leland James

LEE, JOHN BARROW   ASCAP 1978
composer, author
b San Antonio, Tex, Nov 26, 48. Educ: Baylor Univ, BME & MM; Lamar Univ, pre-doctoral. Toured world as dir, singer, instrumentalist, Continental Singers, 68-72. Studio singer, Dallas; comp, arr for several publ. *Songs:* Thine Be the Glory; Branches of the Vine; Mountain Song.

LEE, JONATHAN BUTLER (JACK)   ASCAP 1970
composer, author, musician
b Milwaukee, Wis, Oct 27, 47. Educ: Univ Wis, BA. Mem group, Mother Earth, 71-73; mem "Earl Scruggs Revue", 73-74; recorded for Columbia Records, 76-80; session musician, Los Angeles. *Songs:* Slow Fall; Goin' to Tennessee; Letting the Memory Fade.

LEE, KATIE L   ASCAP 1950
composer, author, singer
b Tucson, Ariz, Oct 23, 19. Educ: Tucson Grade Sch, Jr High Sch & High Sch; Univ Ariz, BFA(drama); studied with Burl Ives & Josh White. Actress in stock movies & TV. Folksinger & actress, NBC Radio & shows "Halls of Ivy", "Railroad Hour", "The Great Gildersleeve." Dir folkmusic, TV show, "Hellen Parrish Telephone Hour." Entertainer, nightclubs, incl "Mocombo", "Hungry I," "Gate of Horn," "Blue Angel," "Downstairs at the Upstairs." Recording artist, own record co. Filmmaker, pub TV, "The Last Wagon"; auth book, "Ten Thousand Goddam Cattle." CINE Int Golden Eagle Award, 72. *Songs:* Pore Colly Raddy; Muddy River; Lyrics: The Boatman's Song. *Instrumental Works:* Baby Did You Hear; Nine Hundred Miles. *Scores:* Folk Musical: Maude, Billy & Mr D.

LEE, LESTER   ASCAP 1942
author
b New York, NY, Nov 7, 05; d Los Angeles, Calif, June 19, 56. Educ: Manual Training High Sch. Songwriter, Bway musicals. Under contract, film studio, Hollywood, 43-44 & 47-56. Writer, special material for radio, 45-46. Chief Collabrs: Ned Washington, Allan Roberts, Zeke Manners, Bob Russell. *Songs:* Poor Little February; Pennsylvania Polka; Dreamer With a Penny; Naughty Angeline; Christmas Dreaming; I Wish I Knew the Name; How Do You Know It's Real?; Chico's Love Song; The Heat Is On; Hear No Evil-See No Evil; Sadie Thompson's Song; Film title songs: Man From Laramie; Prize of Gold; Fire Down Below; Blue Gardenia.

LEE, LORA
See Doro, Grace

LEE, LOYE
See DiNino, Louis Lee

LEE, MARJORIE LEDERER   ASCAP 1956
author
b Long Island, NY, June 28, 21. Educ: Sarah Lawrence Col, BA, 44; creative writing with Horace Gregory, Hortense Flexner King. Publ work includes novels, short stories, poems & nonfiction bks on popular psychology. *Songs:* Lyrics: What Have You Done All Day?

LEE, MARVIN   ASCAP 1937
composer, author, publisher
b Chicago, Ill, Aug 15, 1880; d Chicago, Jan 25, 49. Music publ exec. Writer, special material for vaudeville. *Songs:* Hey, Hey, Hey; That Was a Grand Old Song; When I Dream of Old Erin; Casey Jones Went Down on the Robert E Lee; Cheer Up, Daddy; Call on Me, Gal of Mine.

LEE, PEGGY   ASCAP 1947
composer, author, singer
b Jamestown, NDak. Educ: Pub schs. Was vocalist with Benny Goodman Orch; then as single in hotels, nightclubs, radio & TV; appeared in films "The Jazz Singer" & "Pete Kelly's Blues" (Audience, Laurel, Film Critics Awards). Wrote songs for "Tom Thumb." Chief Collabrs: David Barbour, Victor Young, Cy Coleman. *Songs:* It's a Good Day; Bella Notte; Peace on Earth; Goin' Fishin'; Embrasse-Moi; I Don't Wanna Leave You Now; This Is a Very Special Day; You Was Right, Baby; What More Can a Woman Do; I Don't Know Enough About You; Manana; The Gypsy With Fire in His Shoes; Where Can I Go Without You?; He's a Tramp; How Strange; Happy With the Blues; I Love Being Here With You; In Love Again; Johnny Guitar (theme); Then Was Then, Now Is Now. *Scores:* Film: The Lady and the Tramp.

LEE, ROBERT CHARLES   ASCAP 1950
composer, pianist, teacher
b Youngstown, Ohio, Mar 22, 27. Educ: Univ Wichita, BA, BM, MM; pvt music study; fels: Ind Univ, Univ Colo, Univ Wash. Taught music, Ind Univ, cols & pvt schs; pvt teacher. Piano recitalist & lectr. *Instrumental Works:* Transc: Scarlatti sonatas; Liszt piano solos; Extemporaneous Fugue (Scarlatti).

LEE, ROBERT E   ASCAP 1953
composer, author
b Elyria, Ohio, Oct 15, 18. Educ: Pasadena Playhouse Col; Ohio Wesleyan Univ, LittD. Writes in collaboration with Jerome Lawrence; radio & TV shows incl "Railroad Hour," 5 yrs. Awards: 2 Peabody; Press Club; Variety Showmanship & British Playwrights. Collabr: Harry Warren. *Songs:* Second Time in Love; Lost Horizon. *Scores:* Bway plays: Inherit the Wind; Auntie Mame; The Gang's All Here; Only in America; A Call on Kuprin; Opera: Familiar Stranger; Co-Librettist: Look Ma, I'm Dancin'; Shangri-La (also score); Mame.

LEE, RONNY
See Leventhal, Ronald

LEE, SAMUEL JAMES, II   ASCAP 1975
composer, author, publisher
b Houston, Tex, Jan 6, 42. Educ: Univ Tex, BA & LLB. Park ranger, summers, 63-64. USAF, 66-67; USN, JAGC Ready Reserve, 67-68. With Trust Dept, Morgan Guaranty Trust Co of NY, 67-69. Attorney, 70-; songwriter, record producer & publ, 75- Mem, CMA & Nashville Songwriters Asn. Chief Collabrs: Luther Goff, Dennis Thacher. *Songs:* We'll Just Fall in Love Again; I've Been Hurtin' So Long That Lonesome's a Friend; Love 'em and Lose 'em; Lyrics: Good Day for Laughter; Those Old Country Songs.

LEE, SCOTTY
See Blevins, Scotty Lee

LEE, VERNON
See Goldsen, Michael H

LEE, WILLIAM FRANKLIN, III   ASCAP 1964
composer, author, professor
b Galveston, Tex, Feb 20, 29. Educ: N Tex State Univ, BM, 49, MS, 50; Univ Tex, MM, PhD, 56; Conservatorio Nacional de Musica, Lima, Peru,

MusD(hon), 68; Eastman Sch Music, Univ Rochester, 62; pvt comp study with Nadia Boulanger, Fontainebleau & Paris, France, 65. Trumpet, Houston Symph Orch, 44. Double bass, Dallas Symph Orch, 49. Pianist, comp & arr for Gene Krupa, Artie Shaw, Charlie Parker, Gerry Mulligan, New York, 50-51. Prof music, St Mary's Univ, San Antonio, Tex, 52-55. Instr in theory-comp, asst to dean of Fine Arts, Univ Tex, 55-56. Dir music, Sam Houston State Univ, Huntsville, Tex, 56-64. Dean, Sch of Music & prof theory-comp, Univ Miami, 64- ASCAP Serious Comp Awards, annually 68-80. Pulitzer Prize, Music Nomination, 76. Author of "Music Theory Dictionary", "The Nature of Music", "Modern Musical Instruments", "The Art and Science of Music", "1002 Jumbo All-American Jazz Book", "Bill Lee's Jazz Dictionary" & "Stan Kenton-Artistry in Rhythm." *Songs & Instrumental Works:* Three Reflections (alto saxophone & piano, solo literature); Nocturne for Flute and Piano (solo literature); Soliloquy (French horn & piano or string orch, solo literature); Mini Suite for Trumpet and Piano (classical guitar, solo literature); Interlude (classical guitar, solo literature); Scherzo for Viola and Piano (solo literature); Earth Genesis (string orch); Eight Vignettes for a Festive Occasion: I Consciousness, II Being, III Freedom, IV Consideration, V Understanding, VI Happiness, VII Joy, VII Love; Concerto Grosso for Brass Quintet and Orchestra (orch); Alamjohoba (concert band); Suite for Brass (brass choir with perc); Four Sketches for Brass (brass choir with perc); Fanfare for Ralph (brass quintet); Piece for Brass (brass quintet); Mosaics (brass quintet); Regimentation (brass quintet); Allstex (jazz band); Woodwind Quintet No 1; Woodwind Quintet No 2; Spring Carnival (piano); Festival (piano); Thirteen Original Teaching Pieces (piano); Songs for the Classroom (teacher & student song book); Songs for Sunday School (teacher & student song book); Songs for Folk Singing (teacher song book); I Want to Play Tuba (educ music).

LEECH, BRYAN JEFFERY   ASCAP 1974
composer, author, editor
b Buckhurst Hill, Eng, May 14, 31. Educ: London Univ, dipl theory; Barrington Col, BA; North Park Sem, Chicago, spec studies. Came to US, 55- Served Ministry Evangel Covenant Church Am, Boston, Montclair, NJ, San Francisco & Santa Barbara, for 16 yrs. Broadcasting, dramatic writing, comp & lyric writing, 74. Chief Collabrs: Jan Sanborn, Fred Bock, Tom Fettke, Ovid Young. *Songs:* The Hiding Place; Lately, Have You Seen the Sun?; Hymns for the Family of God; Simon; Ebenezer; Let God Be God; Can't You See the Dawning?; God Has Given You to Me; Can Two Walk Together?; When Winds Are Blowing; Safely Through the Night; Children Are the World's Tomorrow; All My Heart Is in Jerusalem; This He Did for Love; Walk Through the World With Me; Ring the Bells Now; Lyrics: The Covenant Hymnal; We Are God's People; Three Times I Asked Him; No Longer a Baby.

LEECH, LIDA SHIVERS   ASCAP 1945
composer, author, pianist
b Mayville, NJ, July 12, 1873; d Long Beach, Calif, Mar 4, 62. Educ: Pub schs; studied with Helen Leaming & Elmer Fink, Columbia Cons, Temple Univ; Moody Bible Inst. Taught music. Organist, Bethany Methodist Episcopal Church, Camden, NJ. Pianist in evangelistic services. *Songs:* Gospel Songs: I Have Redeemed Thee; No Fault in Him; God's Way; God's Morning; What Will It Matter Then?; When the Veil Is Lifted; Some Day He'll Make It Plain.

LEEDS, CORINNE   ASCAP 1958
composer, author
b New York, NY, Dec 5, 09. Educ: High sch; pvt music study. *Songs:* Pray Today; Kissless Blues; In a Million Years.

LEEDS, MILTON   ASCAP 1942
author
b Omaha, Nebr; Dec 4, 09. Educ: Northwestern High Sch, Detroit, Mich. Wrote special material for radio & nightclubs. In USA, WW II. *Songs:* Perfidia; Misirlou; Slipping Thru My Fingers; Dear Diary; Bells of San Raquel; You're Only in My Arms to Cry on My Shoulder; Guilty Heart; You Laughed and I Cried; You You You Are the One; All the Bees Are Buzzin' Round My Honey; Yesterday's Kisses.

LEEDS, NANCY BRECKER   ASCAP 1959
author
b New York, NY, Dec 22, 24. Educ: Rosemary Hall, grad, 42; Pine Manor Jr Col, 44. Author of lyrics for pop songs, country songs & children's sch books. Chief Collabrs: Gwen Lynd, Bee Walker, Don McAfee, Joe Clonick, Fred Silver, Stan Harte Jr. *Songs:* Lyrics: Take Me Away From the Crowd; No Turning Back. *Scores:* Bway show: Great Scot.

LEEDY, G FRANK   ASCAP 1974
composer, author, pianist
b Fairmont, WVa, Apr 14, 31. Educ: Greenbrier Mil Sch, 45-49; WVa Univ, BA(psychol), 53; New York Inst Photography, grad cert, 78. Studied piano, 14 yrs. Leader of 12 piece band, 48-49; wrote theme for motion picture, "The Treasure of Tayopa." Music writer, 72- Chief Collabr: Bob Cawley.

LEES, BENJAMIN   ASCAP 1954
composer
b Harbin, China, Jan 8, 24. To US, 25. Educ: Univ Southern Calif, 46-48; pvt shcolarship student of George Antheil, 49-54. Served in signal corps, World War

II. Recipient, Guggenheim & Fulbright fels. *Instrumental Works:* Symphony No 1, No 2 (comn, Louisville Orch, Arnold Bax Soc medal), No 3 (comn, Detroit Symph Orch, 69); String Quartet No 1 (Fromm Found award, 53), No 2 (UNESCO award), No 3 (comn, New World Quartet, 78), No 4 (comn, Tokyo String Quartet, 79); Prologue, Capriccio and Epilogue (comn, Portland Jr Symph); Concerto for Orch; Cyprian Songs; Six Ornamental Etudes (piano); Concertante Breve; Sonata for Two Pianos (Fromm Found award); Violin Concerto; Profile for Orchestra; Moment da Camera (cello, piano, flute, clarinet; Copely Found award); Sonata Breve (piano); Divertimento-Burlesca (Thor Johnson comn, Peninsula Music Fest); Interlude for String Orchestra; Piano Concerto No 1, No 2; Vision of Poets (comn, Seattle Symph); Sonata for Violin and Piano No 1, No 2 (comn, McKim Fund, Libr Congress, 75); Oboe Concerto; Invenzione (solo violin);Passacaglia for Orchestra (comn, Nat Symph, 76); Concerto for Woodwind Quintet and Orchestra (comn, Detroit Symph, 76); Etudes for Piano and Orchestra (comn, James Dick); Variations for Piano and Orchestra (comn, Music Teachers Nat Asn, 76); Concerto for String Quartet and Orchestra (comn, Kansas City Philh, 64); Spectrum (comn, Musical Arts Soc, 63); Concerto for Oboe and Orchestra (comn, John DeLancie, 63); Labyrinths (comn, Univ Ind Wind Ens, 75); Scarlatti Portfolio (orch suite based on 7 Scarlatti keyboard sonatas); Mobiles (comn, Ft Worth Symph, 79); Collages (comn, Univ Wis Milwaukee Sch of Fine Arts, 73); The Trumpet of the Swan (narrator, orch); Staves (soprano, piano); Odyssey (solo piano). *Scores:* Opera: Medea in Corinth.

LEESS, STAN   ASCAP 1964
composer
b New York, NY, May 24, 26. Educ: Rochester Univ Eastman Sch Music, NY. Prof performer on piano. Chief Collabrs: Hal Fischman, Gerry Flesher. *Songs:* Music: Don't Smile That Smile; A Wonderful Thing; My Mistake.

LEFCO, SEYMOUR   ASCAP 1958
composer, author
b Milwaukee, Wis, Jan 26, 15. Dentist. *Songs:* Kindergarten Hero.

LEFLEUR, LEO   ASCAP 1956
composer, conductor, pianist
b Russia, Aug 28, 02. Educ: Imperial Sch of Music, Russia; Berlin Royal Acad of Music. To US, 22, citizen, 28. Concert tour, US & Can. Cond, orchs in hotels & at Plaza Hotel, New York, 16 yrs. Toured with Continental Ens. *Instrumental Works:* Nocturne Arabe; Oriental Festival; Wedding of the Violins; Valse Pizzicato; Daily Double Gallup; Bashful Eyes; Castellana Samba; Flea Circus; Christmas Joy Ride.

LEFTWICH, VERNON   ASCAP 1943
composer, arranger
b London, Eng, June 19, 1881; d Los Angeles, Calif, Mar 8, 77. Educ: Guildhall Sch Music, London; studied with Orlando Morgan. Comp & arr for films. Charter mem & secy, Am Soc Music Arr; charter mem, Bohemians. Secy, Musicians Guild. *Songs:* When You Are Near; Within the Temple of My Soul; Autumn Leaves; Little Ranchero; How Softly the Rain Falls; Beside the Sea of Galilee. *Instrumental Works:* Reverie (string orch); Elegy; Cello Concerto; Seven Ages (baritone, orch); What the Moon Saw (suite); Sunken Ships (tone poem); Nocturne (Nat Comp Clinic award); Valse de Ballet (I, II); Symphonic Overture; Festival Overture; Symphony No 1; Sonata for Cello, Piano; Septet (string quartet, winds); String Quartet; Little Eileen; Lion and the Mouse (tone poem); Woodwind Quintet; String Quintet; Musical Forum; Nonet for Wind, String Quartet; Requiem for Brass Ens; Three Pieces for Violin, Viola, Cello; Seranade for Flute, Violin, Viola; Three Pieces for Flute, Clarinet, Bassoon; Marches: Emblem of Victory; Varsity Spirit; Symphonic Triumphal.

LEGLAIRE, SOPHIA (SONNY)   ASCAP 1957
author
b New York, NY, Aug 11, 15. Educ: Mt Sinai Hospital, Philadelphia, RN; Coe Univ, NBC-TV production. RN, World War II, Korean War. Nursing home & hospital surveyor for City of New York. Show writer for nursery sch & army units. Traffic mgr, WFDR-FM, 50. Chief Collabrs: Harriet Bocean, Horace Leinsly, Gracien Ovecotte. *Songs:* Fool's Paradise; Lyrics: Miracle Man; Who But You; Bamboo Rock and Roll; My Crying Hour; Cha Cha Cha Cho Cho San.

LEHAC, NED   ASCAP 1943
composer
b New York, NY, Sept 3, 1899. Educ: City Col New York, studied with Carl Friedburg. Wrote songs & spec material for "Garrick Gaieties", 30 & Billy Rose Productions, 30-31. Wrote several comp for "3rd Little Show", "9:15 Revue", Federal Theater Revue & "Sing for Your Supper", 39. Chief Collabrs: Allen Boretz, Edward Eliscu, Billy Rose, Harold Rome. *Songs:* Music: You Forgot Your Gloves.

LEHRER, THOMAS ANDREW
composer, author, singer
b New York, NY, Apr 9, 28. Educ: Harvard Univ, BA & MA. Entertainer, night clubs & concerts, 53-60 & 65-67. Recording artist, Lehrer Records & Reprise Records, 53- Author & comp of humorous songs. Pianist. *Songs:* Be Prepared; The Irish Ballad; Poisoning Pigeons in the Park; The Masochism Tango; The Vatican Rag; Pollution; Silent E.

LEHRMAN, LEONARD JORDAN   ASCAP 1978
composer, translator, conductor
b Ft Riley, Kans, Aug 20, 49. Educ: Pvt study with Elie Siegmeister, 60-67; Harvard Univ, BA(cum laude), 71, studied with David Del Tredici, Earl Kim, Leon Kirchner; Ind Univ, BM & MM equivalency, 75, studied with John Eaton, Donald Erb, Tibor Kozma; Cornell Univ, MFA, 75, DMA(piano, comp, cond), 77, studied with Robert Palmer & Karel Husa; Salzburg Mozarteum; Paris Ecole Normale de Musique, certs, 72, studied with Nadia Boulanger, 69, 71-72; pvt study with Leonard Bernstein, 74. Mem fac, Cornell Univ, Empire State Col, Metrop Music Sch, Univ Md & others, 73-79; asst chorus master & asst cond, Metrop Opera, 77-78; cond, comp, pianist & translr, Bel Canto Opera, 77-79; asst cond, repetiteur & comp, Heidelberg Theatre, 79-80; repetiteur & comp, Augsburg Theatre, 80; repetiteur & cond, Basler Theatre, 80-81. Recipient, comns & fels, Nat Fedn of Music Clubs, 68 & 77, Fontainebleau Cons, 69, Bennington & Wellesley Cols, 70, Goldovsky Opera, 71 & 78, Goethe Inst, 71 & 73, French Govt, 71-72, Cornell Univ, 72-75, B'nai Brith Hillel Found, 76, NY State Coun on the Arts, 78, Meet the Comp, 78-79, Bel Canto Opera, 79, ASCAP, 78-80. Chief Collabrs: Marc Blitzstein, David Aizman, Bernard Malamud, Barbara Tumarkin Dunham, Orel Odinov, Dachine Rainer, Jack P Eisner, Etienne Bellay, Gesa Valk, Bill Castleman, Edgar H Lehrman. *Songs:* Music: Four Shelley Songs; Three Girls' Love Songs (Blake, Rosetti, Tennyson); The Bourgeois Poet (8 song cycle on Karl Shapiro poems). *Instrumental Works:* Sonata for Piano and Tape; Sonatas for Oboe, for Flute and Piano, for Violin and Piano; String Trio; Piano Trio; Chamber Symphony. *Scores:* Opera/TV: Tales of Malamud; Idiots First; Karla; Sima; Hannah; Rembrandt; The Survivor; Bway Show: Growing Up Woman. Transl: The Days of the Commune (play by Brecht); Speech to the Danish Workers (poem by Brecht); The Roundheads and the Pointedheads (play by Brecht); Getting Married (opera by Musorgski after play by Gogol); A Life for the Czar (opera by Glinka); Mistress Bailey, Song of a Working Mother, and others (songs by Brecht & Eisler); Karla (trans into Ger); My University (Mayakovsky poem set to music); Songs of Birds (song cycle on poems of Fet, Krylov, Derzhavin); Benediction (setting of Blok poem).

LEHRMAN, THEODORE HOWARD (TEDD LAWSON)   ASCAP 1955
composer, author, singer
b Brooklyn, NY, Dec 28, 29. Educ: Boys' High Sch; NY Univ, BS, 50. Recording artist, Roulette Records. Teacher social studies, New York sch syst, 21 yrs. Initiated first student songwriter workshops, Grover Cleveland High Sch, Queens, NY, 72. Pres, Songwriter Sem & Workshops, New York. Chief Collabrs: Leonard Whitcup, Phil Sheer, Soupy Sales, Libby Bush, Redd Evans, Alfie Davison. *Songs:* No Man Is an Island; The Mighty Sons of Hercules; When I Go Home; Pie in the Face; Where Have You Been, My Love?; Love Is Serious Business; The Apple Don't Fall Far From the Tree; One Way Love; The Flower and the Weed; Wasteland; Life Is Just a Bed of Neuroses; It Makes a Difference to Me.

LEIBER, JERRY
lyricist
With var groups incl the Coasters, the Drifters & Stealer's Wheel, 70's. Writer for Willie Mae Thornton & Elvis Presley movies incl "Loving You" & "Jailhouse Rock." Chief Collabr: Mike Stoller. *Songs:* Hound Dog; Two Days Away. *Albums:* Riot in Cell Block No 9; There Goes My Baby; Stand By Me; Stuck in the Middle With You; Pandora's Box; Procol's Ninth.

LEIBERT, RICHARD WILLIAM   ASCAP 1945
composer, organist
b Bethlehem, Pa, Apr 29, 03; d Cape Coral, Fla, Oct 22, 76. Educ: George Washington Univ; Peabody Cons, scholarship. Organist, Radio City Music Hall, New York, since opening. *Songs & Instrumental Works:* Maryette; Valse Rhythmique; You Were a Dream; Sailing Suite; Come Dance With Me; Ride, Son, Ride; Pray for Me; Where I Could Smoke My Pipe; In a Little Clock Shop; Once in a Dream; Rosemaria.

LEIDZEN, ERIK
composer, conductor, arranger
b Stockholm, Swed, Mar 25, 1894; d New York, NY, Dec 20, 62. Came to US, 15. Educ: Royal Cons, Stockholm. Head, Theory Dept, Ernest William Sch Music, 8 yrs. Teacher, Univ Mich summer sch, Nat Music Camp, Interlochen & NY Univ. Guest cond & arr, Goldman Band, arr & ed, music publ cos. Wrote piece for band contest, Manchester, Eng, 55. Author: "An Invitation to Band Arranging." *Instrumental Works:* Irish Symphony; Swedish Rhapsody; Suite for String Orchestra; Spring Journey (women's chorus); The 4 Heralds (cornet quartet); The Foursome (brass quartet); Alpine Fantasy (horn quartet); Fugue With Chorale; Symphony in the Sky; The Happy Warrior (US Mil Acad Comn); Springtime Overture; Autumn Overture; Romantic Overture; Storm King Overture.

LEIGH, CAROLYN (PAULA)   ASCAP 1955
author
b New York, NY, Aug 21, 26. Educ: Hunter Col High Sch; Queens Col; NY Univ. Began writing, 51. Copywriter, radio sta & advert agency. Wrote TV specials, incl "Heidi." Has written songs for films, "The Cardinal" & "Father Goose." Performer, "Stage 73" & "The Ballroom." Now working on Bway show "Flyers." Mem, Dramatists Guild. Chief Collabrs: Mark "Moose" Charlap, John Richards, Philip Springer, Elmer Bernstein, Morton Gould, Lee Pockriss,

Cy Coleman. *Songs:* Lyrics: Young at Heart; Witchcraft; Hey Look Me Over; Step to the Rear; The Best Is Yet to Come; Pass Me By; How Little We Know; Real Live Girl; I've Got Your Number; Here's to Us; On the Other Side of the Tracks; A Doodlin' Song; It Amazes Me; I've Gotta Crow; I Won't Grow Up; I'm Flying; Stay With Me; Something to Do (cantata, Bicentennial comn by US Dept Labor); I'm a Fan; The Rules of the Road; On Second Thought; In the Barrio; I Walk a Little Faster; Firefly; You Fascinate Me So; Playboy Theme; Stowaway; Westport; Bouncing Back for More. *Scores:* Bway Shows: Peter Pan; Wildcat; Little Me; How Now Dow Jones.

LEIGH, GERRI J   ASCAP 1975
  composer, author, teacher
b Manhattan, NY, July 27, 57. Educ: Christopher Columbus High Sch; Am Acad Dramatic Arts, NY Univ, PhD; Rosicrucian Univ, MA. Performed on Bway "The Treatment"; asst producer Bway "Dance With Me"; producer TV "Joe Franklin Show" & "Live At the Factoria in NY." Singer in clubs, stage, commercial, TV & radio; plays violin, piano, guitar & ukulele professionally. Chief Collabr: Billy Revel. *Songs:* Strike While the Iron Is Hot; Lock Out the Four Walls; Time and Space; Martin Paint Jingle. *Instrumental Works:* Senseless Organ.

LEIGH, MITCH   ASCAP 1964
  composer, arranger, producer
b Brooklyn, NY, Jan 30, 28. Educ: Yale Univ, BA, MA. Founder, pres & creative dir, Music Makers, Inc; pres & dir, Sound Makers, Inc. Has written & produced TV & radio musical commercials. Incidental music for Bway productions "Too True to Be Good", "Never Live Over a Pretzel Factory." Awards: Am TV Commercial Fest & Venice Int Adv Film Fest. Chief Collabr: Joe Darion. *Songs:* The Impossible Dream. *Scores:* Stage: Man of la Mancha.

LEIGH, RICHARD C
  composer, author
Chief Collabr: Archie Jordan. *Songs:* I'll Get Over You; Don't It Make My Brown Eyes Blue; In No Time At All; Your Old Cold Shoulder.

LEIGHTON, BERT (JAMES ALBERT LEIGHTON)   ASCAP 1945
  composer, author, singer
b Beacher, Ill, Dec 29, 1877; d San Francisco, Calif, Feb 10, 64. Educ: Pub schs. Mem vaudeville team with brother Frank. Became realtor. Chief Collabrs: Boyd Bunch, Ren Shields. *Songs:* Steamboat Bill; Frankie and Johnnie; Ain't Dat a Shame; Fare Thee, Honey, Fare Thee Well; I Got Mine.

LEIGHTON, HERB
See Leventhal, Herbert

LEIKIN, MOLLY-ANN   ASCAP 1972
  author
b Ottawa, Ont, Oct 11, 48. Educ: Royal Cons Music, Toronto; Univ Toronto, BA; Sorbonne, MA; Univ Calif, Los Angeles. Can Council grant, 71; staff writer, Almo Music, 74-77 & Interworld Music, 77-; instr songwriter's workshop, Univ Calif, Los Angeles; author of music bus novel, "The Man in the Moon Will See Me Home," 80. *Songs:* Buick Jingle; Lyrics: Two Steps Forward and Three Steps Back; Silver Wings and Golden Rings; Let Me Love You Once Before You Go; Moment By Moment; Eight Is Enough; It's Time to Say I Love You; You Set My Dreams to Music; Beautiful Sadness; Where Do You Go When You Dream. *Albums:* Step Into the Sunshine (children's)

LEINER, RANDY DALE   ASCAP 1978
  composer, author
b Cape Girardeau, Mo, Aug 9, 53. Educ: Scott City High Sch; Southeast Mo Univ, BSEd(art); Recording Workshop, sound engr apprentice cert. Played in local bands, 12 yrs. Singer. Chief Collabrs: Sam Blackwell, Steve Duniphan. *Songs:* Hot Box Blues; Little One; One to One; Do You Love; Some Day.

LEISER, ERIC   ASCAP 1950
  composer, author
b Brooklyn, NY, July 9, 29. *Songs:* Till Death Do Us Part; You Don't Need Her; Can Spring Be Far Behind?

LEISY, JAMES FRANKLIN   ASCAP 1973
  composer, author
b Normal, Ill, Mar 21, 27. Educ: Southern Methodist Univ, BBA, 49. Field rep & ed var publ, 49-56; co-founder, Wadsworth Publ Co, 56, pres, 56-77, chmn bd, 77- Free lance writer songs, spec material, bks & musical shows. Chief Collabrs: Charles Randolph Grean, Marvin Moore, Carl Eberhard, Marjorie Farmer. *Songs:* A Little Old Lady in Tennis Shoes; Clemen Who?; Tell Me Why; Lyrics: Keep a Little Christmas in Your Heart. *Songs & Instrumental Works:* The Good Times Songbook; Songs for Swinging Housemothers; Hootenanny Tonight; Musical Plays for Children's Theater. *Scores:* Opera/Ballet: Scrooge; Alice.

LEMING, WARREN EWING   ASCAP 1970
  composer, author, banjoist
b Oak Park, Ill, May 30, 41. Co-founder, Wilderness Road, a satirical & rock group & Painter Band. Co-wrote & appeared in "A Christmas Commercial," one act musical. Albums on Columbia & Warner Bros. Has appeared professionally

on TV & radio; now produces, writes & performs political satire, Nat Pub Radios, "All Things Considered" prog. Chief Collabrs: Paul Sills, Nate Herman, Jerry Sullivan. *Songs:* Revival; AMA; Sunday/Sunday; Mouth-Jive; The Authentic British Blues; Lyrics: Reno.

LEMMON, CHRISTOPHER BOYD   ASCAP 1979
  composer
b Los Angeles, Calif, Jan 22, 54. Educ: Univ Miami, Sch Music; Calif Inst of the Arts, Sch Music, BFA. Appearances as an actor in "Airport '77", "Class of 65", "Brothers and Sisters" (13 episodes), "Hooray for Hollywood" & "Seems Like Old Times," & as musician in "Johnny Carson Show", "Merv Griffin Show" & "Dinah!" Chief Collabrs: Dean Rod, Victor Garvey, Gary Benjamin. *Songs:* Marie; Please Don't Say No; All in the Course of a Day; Music: The Soft Touch.

LEMONIER, TOM   ASCAP 1942
  composer
b New York, NY, Mar 29, 1870; d Chicago, Ill, Mar 14, 45. *Songs:* America, Land of Promise; Hello, Mr Moon, Hello; Better Days Will Come Again; You Are Up Today and Down Tomorrow; Praise God We're Not Weary; Just One Word of Consolation; Is Everybody Happy?

LEMONT, CEDRIC WILMOT   ASCAP 1949
  composer, author, teacher
b Fredericton, NB, Dec 15, 1879; d New York, NY, Apr 27, 54. To US 1899; citizen 33. Educ: Univ NB; Faelten Piano Sch; New Eng Cons; Capitol Col, MM. Taught piano & theory in cols, also privately; choirmaster & organist. *Instrumental Works:* Lotus Bloom; At Eventide; Dream Pictures; Serenade Mexicaine; Creole Sketches; Spanish Fiesta; To My Valentine.

LENGSFELDER, HANS JAN (HARRY LENK)   ASCAP 1942
  composer, author, record exec
b Vienna, Austria, Oct 19, 03; d Hallandale, Fla, Feb 6, 79. Educ: Col in Vienna; Univ Brunn, Czech. Comp & author of operettas, revues & plays, incl "Why Do You Lie, Cherie?," Vienna. Rec'd Czech Broadcasting Co Award. Came to US, 39, became citizen, 44. Founder, Your Theatre, Inc, pres, 45-48. Chief Collabrs: Ervin Drake, Paul McGrane, Irwin Rowan, Joe Darion. *Songs & Instrumental Works:* Red Moon of the Caribbean; Pound Your Table Polka; Hayfoot-Strawfoot; Perdido; Washington Waltz; Tyrolean Tango; If a Man Answers, Hang Up; There's a Big Blue Cloud Next to Heaven; God's Green Acres; BWI Express; The Typewriter Concerto.

LENK, HARRY
See Lengsfelder, Hans Jan

LENOX, JOHN THOMAS   ASCAP 1974
  composer
b Ft Worth, Tex, July 23, 46. Educ: Southern Methodist Univ. Producer/dir, motion picture-TV; wrote numerous cues for "The Odd Couple", "Laverne and Shirley" & "Happy Days." Chief Collabr: Lloyd J Schwartz. *Songs:* Music: Three Trees in Texas. *Scores:* Musical: The Life and Legend of Arnie Bates.

LENTI, ANNA   ASCAP 1969
  composer, author
b Santa Monica, Calif, Jan 28, 12; d Rockville Centre, NY, Feb 28, 75. Educ: St Mary's Sch, Los Angeles, studied piano, theory & harp; advanced study with pvt teachers in Italy; coached by father, Vincent Rose. Wrote material for spec occasions, pub & pvt schs. Author folio, "A Spring Sing." *Songs:* The Mouse Who Loved Strauss; Charley the Horse; If You Want to Be Birds; Norbert the Rat; The Snail. *Albums:* Animal Songs.

LEON, BOBBY
See Dunbar, Robert Leon

LEON, TANIA JUSTINA
  composer, music director, pianist
b Havana, Cuba, May 14, 44. Educ: Peyrellade Cons Music, Havana, BA(piano & theory), 63; Nat Cons Music, Havana, MA(music educ), 64; Univ Havana, BA(acct), 65; NY Univ, BS(comp), 71, MS, 73. Piano soloist, Cuba, 64-67; TV music dir, Havana, 65-66; piano soloist, NY Col Music Orch, 67, NY Univ Orch, 69 & Buffalo Symph Orch, 73; staff pianist & cond, Dance Theatre of Harlem, 68-, music dir, 70-78; founder, Dance Theatre of Harlem Orch, 75; founder concert series "Meet the Performer," 77. Guest cond, Genova Symph Orch, Italy, Juilliard Orch, Spoletto Fest, Symph New World, Royal Ballet Orch, BBC Orch, Buffalo Philh Orch, Concert Orch of Long Island & London Universal Symph. Royal command performer, London Palladium, 74 & 76. Concert pianist, Sta WNYC-FM, 68-70. Cond coordr, Music by Black Composers Series, Brooklyn Philharmonia, 78-79. Cond & musical dir, "Godspell," NY Univ, 78, "Carmencita," 78 & "The Whiz," 78. With PR Traveling Theatre. Recipient Young Composers Prize, Nat Coun Arts, Havana, 66; Cintas Award in Comp, 74-75, 78-79. NEA fel, 75. Mem: French Soc Composers; Am Fedn Musicians; Int Artists Alliance; Am Women Composers. *Songs & Instrumental Works:* Tones (piano concerto); Namiac Poems (voice, chorus & orch); Spiritual Suite (2 sopranos, chorus & mixed ens with narrator);

Concerto Criollo (concerto for piano, 8 timpanies & orch); Pet's Suite (flute & piano); I Got Ovah (soprano, piano & perc). *Scores:* Haiku (ballet); Sailor's Boat (musical); Dougla (African ballet); La Ramera de la Cueva (musical).

LEONARD, ANITA
See Nye, Anita Leonard

LEONARD, EDDIE (LEMUEL GORDON TONEY)　　ASCAP 1937
composer, author, singer
b Richmond, Va, Oct 18, 1875; d New York, NY, July 29, 41. Was professional baseball player, then joined minstrel shows. Served in Spanish-Am War. Sang at Tony Pastor's, other variety theatres. Mem, Primrose & West Minstrel Show, 02; appeared in films; acted in Bway musical "Roly Boly Eyes." Last professional engagement, Billy Rose's Diamond Horseshoe, 40. Autobiography "What a Life." *Songs:* Ida, Sweet As Apple Cider; Roly Boly Eyes; Just Because She Made Them Goo-Goo Eyes; Oh, Didn't It Rain?; I'm on My Way; I Lost My Mandy; Sweetness; Don't You Never Tell a Lie; Mandy Jane; Sugar Baby; Beautiful; Molasses Candy; I Wish I Was Some Little Girlie's Beau.

LEONARD, ROBERT DUKE　　ASCAP 1943
composer, singer, actor
b Utica, NY, Oct 23, 01; d Miami Beach, Fla, Nov 19, 61. Educ: Utica Free Acad; Utica Cons. Appeared in musical comedy, vaudeville & nightclubs. *Songs:* Light a Candle in the Chapel; With a Pack on His Back; Sam, You Made the Pants Too Long; Taking the Trains Out; Josephine, Please No Lean on the Bell; When I Gets to Where I'm Going; I Wanna Wienie With the Works; Singing Hosanna As I Fly; It's Time to Go to Church Again.

LEONARD, STANLEY S　　ASCAP 1975
composer, musician
b Philadelphia, Pa, Sept 26, 31. Educ: Northwestern Univ; Eastman Sch Music, BA, performer's cert. Principal timpanist, Pittsburgh Symph Orch, 56- Has toured with Pittsburgh Symph Orch in maj cities of world; also appeared as timpani & perc soloist in its subscription concerts. Has comp works for solo perc & perc ens. Was sr lectr perc instruments & perc ens, Carnegie-Mellon Univ, 58-78. Has own perc music performed throughout the world. *Instrumental Works:* Symphony for Percussion; Dance Suite; Fanfare and Allegro; Prelude for Four Marimbas; Solo Dialogue; Antiphonies; Suite of Psalms; Two Contemporary Scenes.

LEONE, GENNARO CYPRIAN, JR　　ASCAP 1974
composer, author
b Camden, NJ, July 6, 52. Educ: Camden Cath High Sch; Camden County Col, AA; Glassboro State Col, BA(communications). Played drums at age 6. Drummer, leader of jazz, concert & marching bands; recording artist, MGM Records, 74. Recording engr, 75-; chief engr, Alpha Int Recording Studios, Philadelphia. Chief Collabrs: Richie Rome, Gayle Kerry, Bob Sworaski, Juliano Salerni, Steve Leone. *Songs:* She's a Lady.

LEOPOLD, J WALTER　　ASCAP 1942
composer, author, pianist
b Brooklyn, NY, July 27, 1890; d Hollywood, Calif, Dec 28, 56. Educ: Pratt Inst; Columbia Univ; Heffley Inst (civil engr). Pianist in Brooklyn & New York theatres; also for music publ co. Appeared in vaudeville with Bert Lewis & Emma Carus. Became publisher, 22. *Songs:* Take Me Back to Dreamland; Oh, How She Can Dance; Is It a Sin?; Beautiful Mother of Mine; Plant a Little Garden in Your Own Back Yard; Everybody Loves the Irish; You Wouldn't Fool a Friend; There's Something in the Wind.

LEPORE, LOUIS PHILIPPE　　ASCAP 1978
composer, author, musician
b New York, NY, June 20, 55. Educ: Bayside High Sch; Queens Col, 75; Mannes Prep, 73; studied guitar, Howard Morgen, 73-76. Guitarist & singer, nightclubs, concert halls & TV; guitarist for Cherry Vanilla. Chief Collabr: Cherry Vanilla. *Songs:* Music: The Punk; You Belong to Me; Moonlight; Liverpool; No More Canaries.

LERNER, AL　　ASCAP 1957
composer, pianist, conductor
b Cleveland, Ohio, Apr 7, 19. Educ: Cleveland Inst of Music; pvt music study. Pianist, Harry James, Charlie Barnet & Tommy Dorsey Orchs. Music dir, Dick Haymes, Frankie Laine & Dennis Day. Chief Collabrs: Victor Corpora, Frankie Laine. *Songs:* So Until I See You (Jack Paar theme); Torchin'; Annabelle Lee.

LERNER, HOWARD MARSHALL　　ASCAP 1964
composer
b Brooklyn, NY, Apr 16, 27. Educ: Brooklyn Col, BA; additional studies at NY Univ, City Col New York & Am Nat Theatre & Acad. Gen mgr, Music Library, Sam Fox Publ Co; pres, Siri Music Library; advert dir, Mills Music Inc, Sam Fox Publ & Carl Fischer Inc; consult for Chappell Music, Shapiro-Bernstein Music, Plymouth Music & Big Three Music. *Instrumental Works:* Three Moods for Trumpet; Three Moods for Oboe.

LERNER, SAMUEL MANUEL　　ASCAP 1931
composer, author, publisher
b Saveni, Romania, Jan 28, 03. Educ: Detroit Cent High Sch; Wayne State Univ. Writer, spec material for many vaudeville acts, original scripts & songs for Paramount shorts, also theatre organists stunts for audience participation. Lyricist, Bway & London stage productions, also films in London & Hollywood. Mem, Dramatists Guild, Am Guild Authors & Comp; ASCAP Adv Comt; Acad Motion Picture Arts & Sciences. Chief Collabrs: Richard Whiting, Gerald Marks, Irving Caesar, Abel Baer, Burton Lane, Hoagy Carmichael, Ben Oakland, Al Hoffman, Al Goodhart, Jay Gorney, Dana Suesse, Al Skinner. *Songs:* I'm Popeye the Sailor Man (theme of "Popeye" cartoon); Is It True What They Say About Dixie?; Lyrics: (Oh, Suzanna) Dust Off That Old Pianna; Falling in Love Again; Judy; In the Hush of the Night; I Promise You; I Don't Know Your Name (But You're Beautiful); Saskatchewan; You'll Never Get Up to Heaven That Way; Ev'rybody's Laughing; Intrigue; Sittin' in the Sand a-Sunnin' (Atlanta City Prize song); The Pump Song (It's Hard to Tell the Depth of a Well By the Length of the Handle on the Pump); By the Sign of the Rose; Lord and Lady Whoozis; The Rhyming Song (You'll Find a Rhyme for Ev'rything But Orange); The Eyes of the World Are on You; My Dear Public; Hold It; Hello Paris; Lyrics for stage productions: Going Greek; Hide and Seek; Swing Is in the Air; Trans-Atlantic Rhythm; Lyrics for films, London: Love From a Stranger; Gangway; The Lady Vanishes; A Shilling for Candles; Jack of All Trades; Splinter in the Air; Good Morning, Boys; Rhythm Racketeer; Bicycle for Two; Sunset in Vienna; Hollywood: Laugh It Off; Blondie Meets the Boss; Flame of New Orleans; The Lady From Cheyenne; It Started With Eve; Margie; La Conga Night; Charlie McCarthy Detective; Ma! He's Makin' Eyes At Me; A Little Bit of Heaven; Rhapsody in Stripes; The Impostor; His Butler's Sister; Golden Girl; Anne of the Indies; Betty Boop Cartoons; songs in Thumbs Up, White Horse Inn, Three's a Crowd & Ziegfeld Follies, 35.

LERTZMAN, CARL MYRON (COLEMAN MONOSHA)　　ASCAP 1956
composer, author
b Odessa, Russia, Feb 22, 08. Educ: East Tech High Sch, Cleveland, Ohio. Elec contractor & designer. Have many patented electrical products, Ford Transistor Radio, Musical Light Switch, Automobile Aerial & Link Switch. Songwriter, 48; writer of many articles on ESP. Has traveled to the Orient & has designed products for manufacturers, 75- Chief Collabrs: Danny Gould, Mills, Al Delory. *Songs:* He's a Rockin' Horse Cowboy; The Last Supper; Siberian Sunset; The King James Twist; The Beetles Will Getcha; Trip One; Trip Two; Baby Baby Baby; Pretty Little Girl; Forever and Ever; X-mas Candles; Poor Little Bird; I'll Always Be Yours; Good-By Darlin; Santa Claus Jr; The Spirit of 76.

LESEMANN, FREDERICK
composer, teacher
b Los Angeles, Calif, Oct 12, 36. Educ: Oberlin Col, BM, 58, studied with Joseph Wood & Richard Hoffmann; Univ Southern Calif, MM, 61, DMA, 72, studied with Ingolf Dahl; Stanford Univ, workshop computer music, 77. Lectr music theory & comp, Univ Southern Calif, 66-71, asst prof, 71-76, dir, Electronic Music Studio, 74-, assoc prof music theory & comp, 76- Grants & Awards: Univ Southern Calif Friends of Music Outstanding Teacher Award, 73; Martha Baird Rockefeller Fund grant, Am Music Ctr, 73; ASCAP Award, 75; NEA comp grant, 76. Author, "Comprehensive Musicianship Training," 69, "Caoine, Music for Brass," 74 & "Symph in Three Movements," 74. *Songs & Instrumental Works:* Paradiso XXI (five visions from Dante); Phase Music; Legends; Cantata: The Garden of Proserpine; The Knight's Tour; Two Pieces for Four Trombones, Percussion and String Bass; Suite for Two Percussion Choirs; Symphony in Three Movements; Caoine, Music for Brass; Theme and Fourteen Variations in Three Movements for Violin, Violoncello and Piano; Chamber Concerto for Solo Violoncello and Woodwind Quintet; The Chain of Lethe; Sonata for Clarinet and Percussion; Fantasy for Piano Solo; Nataraja (prepared piano).

LESHAY, JEROME　　ASCAP 1957
composer, director
b New York, NY, Feb 28, 26. Educ: NY Univ, BA; studied with Sam Saxe. Served, USAAF, World War II. Producer, CBS-TV; assoc dir, Television City, Hollywood. Writer, TV background music. *Songs:* The Sands of Time; When You Love; Bonjour La Vie.

LESLIE, EDGAR　　ASCAP 1914
composer, author, publisher
b Stamford, Conn, Dec 31, 1885; d. Educ: Cooper Union, New York. Wrote spec material for Nat Wills, Julian Rose, Belle Baker, Lew Dockstader, James Barton & Joe Welch. Became publ. Wrote songs for films. Charter mem, ASCAP, dir, 31-41 & 47-53. Chief Collabrs: Joe Burke, Fred Ahlert, James Monaco, Walter Donaldson, Archie Gottler, Maurie Abrams, Joe Young, Harry Warren, Irving Berlin, George Meyer, E Ray Goetz, Pete Wendling. *Songs:* Sadie Salome - Go Home; That Italian Rag; When Ragtime Rosie Ragged the Rosary; Lord, Have Mercy on the Married Man; Where Was Moses When the Lights Went Out?; He'd Have to Get Under; Put It on, Take It Off; When the Grown Up Ladies Act Like Babies; America, I Love You; Hello Hawaii, How Are You?; Since Maggie Dooley Learned the Hooley Hooley; In the Gold Fields of Nevada; For Me and My Gal; Come on Pappa; All the Quakers Are Shoulder Shakers; Oh What a Pal Was Mary; Take Your Girlie to the Movies; Take Me to the Land of Jazz; On the Gin Gin Ginny Shore; Oogie Oogie Wa Wa; Rose

of the Rio Grande; Home in Pasadena; Dirty Hands, Dirty Face; I'll Take Her Back If She Wants to Come Back; Blue and Broken Hearted; Hay Hay Farmer Gray (Took Another Load Away); Among My Souvenirs; Me and the Man in the Moon; Mistakes; Kansas City Kitty; 'Tain't No Sin; Romance; I Remember You From Somewhere; By the River Sainte Marie; You've Got Me in the Palm of Your Hand; Crazy People; I Wake Up Smiling; The Moon Was Yellow; Moon Over Miami; In a Little Gypsy Tearoom; On Treasure Island; Cling to Me; A Little Bit Independent; Midnight Blue; Robins and Roses; It Looks Like Rain in Cherry Blossom Lane; At a Perfume Counter; We Must Be Vigilant ("American Patrol"); You're Over the Hill; Oky Doky Tokyo.

LESLIE, WALTER
See Levinsky, Walter

LESSER, JEFFREY DAVID ASCAP 1978
composer, author, producer
b New York, NY, June 27, 47. Educ: High Sch Music & Art, New York, grad, 64; State Univ NY Buffalo, 68. Film soundman & recording engr, Media Sound, New York, 68-74; record producer & comp, 74- Has produced the following artists: Barbra Streisand, Rupert Holmes, Pat Travers, Head East, Strawbs, Sailor, Hounds, Sparks, Starcastle & Viva Beat. Engineered: Climax Blues Band, Kool & the Gang, Stylistics, Van McCoy, Renaissance & many others. Chief Collabrs: Pat Travers, Rupert Holmes. Songs: Heat in the Street; Killers Instinct; Love Minus One; Nobody's Fool; So Here We Are; She; Can I Make You Say Ooo?

LESSNAU, ROBERT GERALD (BOBBY LAUREL) ASCAP 1968
composer, author, performer
b Detroit, Mich, Jan 8, 38. Educ: Holy Redeemer High Sch; Wayne Univ Col Music & Drama; Univ Detroit Col Music & Drama; Detroit Inst Musical Arts. Performer, weddings, pvt parties, major clubs, radio & TV. Writer & performer, MGM Records, 69. Actor; producer motion picture, "The Rosary Murders," 80. Formed Murray Hill Publ-Grant Records, 72; pres, Take One Productions, TV motion picture production co. Chief Collabrs: John Meyers, Ernie Harwell, James Bruce, Joseph Sievers. Songs: I Don't Want to Hurt You Anymore; It's Over Now; You'll Come Running Back; Seek; He'll Never Be Me; Tomorrow Is Another Day; Being Alone; Winning Isn't Everything; Whatever Happened to Heroes; I Think I Like You. Scores: Film: The Rosary Murders; Theme From Room 1394.

LESSNER, GEORGE ASCAP 1953
composer
b Budapest, Hungary, Dec 15, 04. Educ: Royal Acad Music, Budapest, grad, studied with Dohnanyi, Kodaly, Siklos, Santo, Bartok. Began composing at age 7. Comp for motion pictures in Hollywood for var major studios, 35-41. Comn by NBC to write radio opera, 39. Comp of symphonic orchestral compositions, concert songs, chamber music, operas, ballet pantomines, piano pieces, choral numbers & violin compositions. Chief Collabrs: Russell Maloney, Miriam Battista, Bud Fishel, Alice Hammerstein Mathias, Nicholas Bela, Victor MacLoed. Instrumental Works: Sunrise (symphonic poem); In Memoriam (symphonic); Merry Overture (symphonic); Symphonic Poem in D Minor. Scores: Opera/Ballet: The Nightingale and the Rose; Bway shows: Sleepy Hollow; Mr Strauss Goes to Boston; & others.

LESTER, ALBERT BUDDY ASCAP 1966
composer, author
b Chicago, Ill, Jan 16, 17. Educ: High sch. Singer at age 10, The Granada Theatre, Chicago; comedian, night clubs. Songs: You're Twice As Nice; Hear My Heart; According to the Stars, I'm in Love; All My Friends Are Turning Grey; Don't Buy Blues.

LESTER, EDWARD LEE ASCAP 1972
composer, author, singer
b Shawsville, Va, July 26, 46. Educ: Alleghany Dist High Sch. Singer, commercials, TV; recording artist; actor. Chief Collabrs: Jim Hall, J D Stephenson. Songs: Blue Crystal Mornin'; Uptown; I Just Can't Believe; Disco Donna; Rollin' Waters of '72; Jesus Makes It Right; Tennessee Sunshine Queen; What Ever Happened to Clifton Clowers?; I Was Born to Rock 'n' Roll; Turning Tangent; Popular Holler; I'm Gonna Shout, I'm Gonna Sing. Instrumental Works: Donkey Dew; Pennsylvania Polka.

LEVANT, LILA ASCAP 1965
author, singer
b NJ, May 29, 33. Educ: Washington Irvine High Sch, fine & applied arts dipl; studied singing with Brooks Alexander, Nat Jones, Virginia Harper. Singer, nightclubs. Appeared stage & film shows, 70-79. Chief Collabrs: Lorenzo Fuller, Jack Barker, Jack Labow. Songs: Lyrics: All My Tomorrows; Has the Music Stopped Playing for Me. Scores: Off Bway Show: Speed Gets the Poppys; Anybodys Child; Pay the Piper; Felicia; Jasper; Ms Leona Lyon; Clifford; Film/TV: Once Around the Universe; The Story of a Music Note.

LEVANT, OSCAR ASCAP 1930
composer, author, pianist
b Pittsburgh, Pa, Dec 27, 06; d Beverly Hills, Calif, Aug 14, 72. Educ: High sch; studied music with Sigismund Stojowski, Arnold Schoenberg & Joseph Schillinger. Pianist in Rudy Wiedoeft Band & in play, "Burlesque." Has given many concerts of George Gershwin music. Soloist with major orchs, incl The New York Philh, The Philadelphia, Boston, Cleveland & Pittsburgh Symph Orchs & The NBC Symph Orch with Arturo Toscanini. Appeared in films, "Dance of Life", "Rhapsody in Blue", "The Barkleys of Broadway", "An American in Paris", "The Band Wagon", "Humoresque" & others. Mem panel, "Information Please" prog, radio. Has appeared on TV & made many records. Autobiographies: "A Smattering of Ignorance", " Memoirs of an Amnesiac" & "The Importance of Being Oscar." Chief Collabrs: Irving Caesar, Stanley Adams, Edward Heyman. Songs: Lady Play Your Mandolin; Don't Mention Love to Me; Wacky Dust; Blame It on My Youth; We've Got the Moon and Sixpence; Lovable and Sweet; My Dream Memory; If You Want the Rainbow. Instrumental Works: Piano Sonatina; 2 string quartets; Piano Concerto. Scores: Bway stage: Ripples (with Albert Sirmay); Films: Street Girl (first RKO film); Tanned Legs.

LEVEEN, RAYMOND (RAYMOND LEDEEN) ASCAP 1934
author
b Newark, NJ, Nov 28, 1893. Educ: New York Schs. Chief Collabrs: Maria Grever, Murray Mencher. Songs: Lyrics: I See God (sang by Mahalia Jackson at Democratic Nat Convention, Chicago); Ti-Pi-Tin; Make Love With a Guitar; In a Shelter From a Shower; I Wonder; The Magic of Believing; I Will Be Home Again; Blue Fantasy; By Blue Hawaiian Waters; Continental Nights; Figaro; Goodnight Mother; He Never Knew She Lived Next Door; Grandma's Birthday Party; You Gotta Live With a Beat; Jealous Moon; When You Live Down South; Vienna in Moonlight; Violins and Violets; Time and Time Again; Tear It Down; Sunday Is Daddy's Day With Baby; Rag Picker; Petootie Pie; Christmas Candles (Am version); folio 48 songs of the 48 states, also lyrics to many children's songs. Scores: Bway Show: Viva O'Brien (eleven songs).

LEVEN, MELVILLE ABNER ASCAP 1959
composer, author, writer
b Chicago, Ill, Nov 11, 14. Educ: Carl Schurz High Sch, 33; Chanute Field, USAF, specialist/instr, 42; Westlake Col Music, grad, 51; studied music with Alfred Sendry, Dave Robertson. Wrote songs in educ & health films for TV's "Wonderful World of Disney," also theatrical shorts. Stories, songs & voices in TV's "Boing Boing" show & theatrical "Ham and Hattie," Acad nominate, 57. Songs, stories, voices for "Sesame Street" & "Electric Co," Emmy & Peabody Awards, also TV singles incl "Bring Home the Good Webers Bread, Fred." Spec material for Nat King Cole, Mario Lanza, Andrew Sisters, 4 Lads, Les Baxter, Annette, Dennis Day, Gordon McCrae, Ray Anthony, Tex Ritter, Les Brown, Les Elgar, Molly Bee, Peggy Lee, Jerry Lewis, Dean Martin. Songs: It's Tough to Be a Bird, Acad Award, 69; Litterbug, Shame on You; 101 Dalmations, all songs; Ev'ry Time; Lady Says No, theme; Lyrics: Tell Me All About Yourself; Carmens' Boogie; Babes in Toyland, all songs, new lyrics & libretto.

LEVENSON, BORIS ASCAP 1924
composer, conductor
b Ackermann, Russia, Mar 10, 1884; d New York, NY, Mar 10, 47. To US 21; citizen, 27. Educ: Imperial Music Sch, Odessa; Imperial Cons, St Petersburg, studied with Rimsky-Korsakov. Debut as cond, Odessa, 01; cond opera, symph orchs, St Petersburg & Moscow, 07-12; Scand tour, 15; also gave concerts in London. Songs & Instrumental Works: Hebrew Folk Tunes; Night in Bagdad; Hebrew Fantasy; Song of the Orient; Andante Tragico; Hebrew Suite; Elegie Russe; 2 string quartets; Poem (violin, piano; 1st prize, Nat Fedn Music Clubs); David and Abraham (oratorio); Stalingrad (overture). Scores: Opera: Woman on the Window.

LEVENSON, ROBERT
composer
b Boston, NY, Jul 19, 1897; d Rome, Italy, Apr 21, 61. Educ: Boston Latin Sch; studied voice, Harvard Univ. Wrote & performed, WW I. Songwriter, then went into advert. Chief Collabrs: Vincent C Plunkett, George L Cobb, Ted Garton. Songs: My Little Gypsy Wanda; My Pretty Poppy; When the Sun Sets in Galway; Baby Dreams; Music: In the Sweet Bye and Bye; The Angel God Sent From Heaven; Lyrics: My Belgian Rose; Pretty Little Rainbow; Salvation Rose; Sweet Kentucky Sue; Good Bye Dixie Lee; I'm Knitting a Rosary; plus many more.

LEVENTHAL, HERBERT (HERB LEIGHTON) ASCAP 1949
composer, author
b New York, NY, Nov 18, 14. Educ: New York Pub Schs; City Univ New York. Became associated with Irving Berlin Music Co, 38. After serving in WW II joined a music publ co as song plugger & prof mgr. Chief Collabrs: Hank Fort, Buddy Kaye, Hugo Taiani, Edward Ballantine, Frank Como, Sylvia Dee, Ivory Joe Hunter. Songs: I Didn't Know the Gun Was Loaded; The Things You Left in My Heart; A Written Guarantee; If I Give You My Love; His Arms Are Open to Everyone; Too Much; House of Prayer; God Is Near.

LEVENTHAL, RONALD (RONNY LEE) ASCAP 1963
composer, author, arranger
b New York, NY, Mar 2, 27. Educ: William Howard Taft High Sch; RCA Inst Technol, 47-49; NY Univ, 69-71; studied guitar privately with Shadow Ferber, Anthony Antone, John Sigelitto, Nicholas DeBonis, Hy White, Charles Ruoff & Juan De La Mata. At age 16, appeared regularly as guitarist on radio sta, WNEW, New York; author of guitar instr bks & charts; arr music for guitar for

Hansen, Roslyn, Chappel, Leo M Cohan, Robbins & Frank. Has performed on records, club dates & with New York Philh. Adjudicator at music fests. Pres, Sunrise Publ Co, Inc. Teacher, lectr & performer. Author instr bks: "Jazz Guitar Method" (vols I-II); "Folk Strums for Guitar"; "More Folk Strum for Guitar"; "Classic Guitar Method"; "Beginner's Chord Book for Guitar"; "Electric Bass Guitar Method"; "Flamenco Guitar Method"; "Step By Step Guitar Method" (vols I-VII); "Step By Step Chord Method for Guitar" (vols I-IV); "Advanced Chord Playing for Guitar" (vols I-III); "The Guitar Band" (vols I-II).

LEVER, BEATRICE RAE
ASCAP 1959
composer, pianist, singer

b Manchester, Eng, May 27, 1897; d. Educ: London Col Music. Concert pianist & singer until 15; then returned to music, 51. Chief Collabrs: Paul Francis Webster, Mary Sar Sarlow. *Songs:* A Gypsy Romance; Our Wedding Song; The Lord Has His Arms Around Me (Song of the Yr award, 60); I'll Be There; Gone; Give Me Time to Think It Over; Trying So Hard Not to Fall.

LEVEY, HAROLD A
ASCAP 1925
composer, conductor, clarinetist

b New York, NY, June 17, 1898; d. Educ: Nat Cons (scholarship at age 10); studied with Soffaroff, Joseffy. First clarinetist, New York Symph. With Victor Herbert, many yrs. Cond, Bway musicals; comp & cond, film co, 5 yrs. Songwriter, "Greenwich Village Follies of 1925." Comp & arr, radio shows incl "Cavalcade of America", "Armstrong Theatre" & "Theatre Guild of the Air." Cond, NBC Symph, 49-50. Chief Collabrs: Zelda Sears, Owen Murphy, Kenneth Webb. *Songs:* Just Plant a Kiss; Love Needs No Single Word; The Clinging Vine; First Last and Only; Rainbow; Lovely Lady. *Scores:* Bway shows: Lady Billy; The Clinging Vine; Rainbow Rose; Lovely Lady.

LEVIN, EDWARD EMANUEL
ASCAP 1977
composer, author, singer

b Minneapolis, Minn, Feb 26, 52. Educ: Univ Minn, educ major. Started writing songs & lyrics, 60; rock piano player, lead vocalist, 66-80; piano technician/studio musician, 70; comp & released first single, 77 & first album, 80, own label, Pragmatic Records Inc, 77. *Songs:* Good Time Comin' On; Quite a Time; Opus 140 No 1; Grocery Store; G H P; Song for Linda; Who's the One?; Don't Go Now; Lightweight Lover Nineteen Time Loser; Late Winter Dream. *Albums:* Live Game.

LEVIN, IRA
ASCAP 1965
author

b New York, NY, Aug 27, 29. Educ: Horace Mann Sch; Drake Univ; NY Univ, BA. Author "A Kiss Before Dying" (novel); plays: "No Time for Sergeants", "Interlock" & "Critic's Choice." Chief Collabr: Milton Schafer. *Songs:* He Touched Me. *Scores:* Bway Stage, Libretto: Drat the Cat!

LEVIN, LOUIS
composer, pianist

b New York, NY, May 6, 52. Educ: N Hollywood High Sch; State Univ NY Stony Brook; Berklee Col Music, pvt study with Charles Banacas. Recording artist for John Payne Band. Albums for Arista/Freedom & Mercury Records. Recorded "Power" with John Hall, Columbia Records. Toured with John Hall, 1 yr. Pianist for Rupert Holmes. Play with own band Nightfire. *Songs:* Before the Dawn; Thinkin' of You. *Instrumental Works:* Dreams/Zone 9; Free Falling; Touchdown Cafe; Woman in the Shadow; The Razor's Edge; New Spaces; Song for Love; African Brother; Lonely Space Person.

LEVIN, MORRIS ALBERT (MARK NEVIN)
ASCAP 1962
composer

b Newark, NJ, Mar 3, 00. Educ: Barringer High Sch; Princeton Univ; studied piano with Alexander Berne, harmony & comp with James Bleecker; Juilliard, studied theory. Teacher, Newark & Maplewood, NJ, until 62. Comp piano teaching material & gave workshops for piano teachers. Writer solos, duets & duo-piano works. Author: "Mark Nevin Piano Course" (6 vols) & "Piano for Adults" (2 vols). *Songs & Instrumental Works:* Buzzing Bee (solo); Hopak (solo); Tokyo Toccatina (solo).

LEVINE, ABE (AL)
ASCAP 1953
composer, author, singer

b Denver, Colo, Nov 9, 15. Educ: North Denver High Sch; special sem in criminal investigation & law, Denver Univ & Denver District Attorney's Off, 47-67. Police detective, Denver Police Dept, 41-66; dist attorney investigator, Denver Dist Attorney's Off, 66-73. Started writing songs while in high sch, 30; local minstrel & radio shows during 50's. Merit Award, Am Legion; for outstanding police work, Denver Post Newspaper Hall of Fame. Chief Collabrs: L Wolfe Gilbert, Ray Perkins, Morey Bernstein. *Songs:* I Love to Eat Chili in Chile; Music: The Man Behind the Badge; Lyrics: Don't Say You're a Dream; Keep the Faith; Today Is Your Birthday; The Shadow of the Blues; I Ain't Gonna Worry No More.

LEVINE, DAVID MYER
ASCAP 1976
author

b New York, NY, Feb 4, Educ: Forest Hills High Sch, 66; studied poetry writing with Paul Blackburn; City Col New York, BA, 71, MA, 72; K Lardes, Joel Opfenlecher. Has written lyrics for songs with David Forman, 66- & poetry since high sch; has won many awards. Translr of lyric poetry; songwriter. Author

of bk "Fellow Travelers" (2 vols); now working on new play & novel. Chief Collabrs: David Forman, Daniel Troob, Charles Haldeman. *Songs:* Lyrics: A Train Lady; Smokey China Tea; Seven Sisters; Winnsboro, Louisiana; Losing; Thirty Dollars; No Rhyme or Reason; Let It Go Now; Painted in a Corner; Now That I Told You; Arethusa; Travel Light; Sleeping on Her Doorstep; East New York; On My Mind; Five Danish Pastries.

LEVINE, HENRY
ASCAP 1962
composer, author, pianist

b Boston, Mass, Jan 2, 1892; d New York, NY, Nov 10, 76. Educ: Harvard Univ, BA(cum laude). Concert pianist & teacher. Boston music critic, Musical America, 20-27. Music ed, publ. Cond workshops, Sci & Art of Piano Playing. Ed, "Rhapsody" (Gershwin). Wrote many classical music arrangements for piano. Author: "Henry Levine's Piano Course" & "Know Your Scales." *Instrumental Works:* Arr: Gotham Classics.

LEVINE, JEFFREY LEON
ASCAP 1970
composer

b Brooklyn, NY, Sept 15, 42. Educ: Brown Univ, BA; Yale Univ, MMus; Accademmia Chigiana, Italy, with Franco Donatoni. Comp, string bassist & teacher. Works performed in Europe & US. Performed extensively on bass, New York. Mem of the Performing Arts Orch. Also cond the Concordia Chamber Orch. Taught at Rutger's Univ, Univ Calif, Berkeley; fac mem, Bennington Col, Vt. *Instrumental Works:* Divertimento (for 10 strings); Piano Trio; Crystals (ballet); Form for Two Pianos; Concertante per 28 Tromboni.

LEVINE, JOSEPH
ASCAP 1970
orchestra conductor

b Philadelphia, Pa, Aug 14, 12. Educ: Curtis Inst Music, Philadelphia, MusB(cond & piano), cond studies with Fritz Reiner & Artur Rodzinski, piano with Josef Hofmann & harpsichord with Wanda Landowska. Mem fac, Curtis Inst, 33-40; asst cond, Philadelphia Grand Opera Co, 38-40; founder & cond, New Ctr Music Orch, Philadelphia, 40-43 & Chamber Opera Soc, Philadelphia, 46-50; pianist, Philadelphia Orch, 40-43 & 46-50. Cond, USAAF Tactical Air Ctr Symphonette, 43-45. Piano accompanist with Joseph Szigeti, 46-50; music dir & cond, Co-Opera Co, Philadelphia, 47-50, Am Ballet Theatre, New York, 50-58, Omaha Symph Orch, 58-69 & Bremerton Symph, 79-; fac mem, Cornish Sch Allied Arts, Seattle, 69-73 & 76-79, mem, Cornish Trio, 69-73; music dir, Omaha Civic Opera Soc, 61-69 & Omaha Starlight Theatre, 61. Assoc cond, Seattle Symph Orch, 69-73, Hawaii Opera Theatre & Honolulu Symph Orch, 73-76. Am cond, Royal Ballet Eng, 63-65. Recipient Citations: Dana Col, 61, Creighton Univ, 62 & Mercian Medal, Col St Mary, 67.

LEVINE, LUCY SIMON
composer, author, singer

b New York, NY, May 5, 40. Educ: Fieldston High Sch; Bennington Col; Cornell Univ, BS. Performed & recorded with sister Carly Simon as The Simon Sisters. Solo recording artist; producer of record album. Chief Collabrs: Jonathan Schwartz, Carole Bayer Sager. *Songs:* From Time to Time to Time; Sally Go Round the Sun; Music: Wynken, Blynken and Nod; The Lobster Quadrille. *Albums:* In Harmony.

LEVINE, MARKS
ASCAP 1947
author, manager

b New York, NY, Aug 19, 1890; d New York, May 28, 71. Educ: Jr col (gymnasium), Russia; Cooper Union, NY, BCE. Mining, highway & civil engr, 13-21. Concert mgr, 22-55. Toured throughout world with Mischa Levitski (bro), Dusolina Giannini & Kirsten Flagstad. Consult to musical orgn. *Songs:* Do You Remember?; When I Love You; Spring Came; We Love and Dream; I Looked At a Tulip.

LEVINE, STANLEY MARK
ASCAP 1973
composer

b Los Angeles, Calif, Jan 14, 47. Educ: San Francisco State Univ, BA; Calif Inst Arts, MFA, studied with Mel Powell, Leonard Stein, Mort Subotnick. Comp electronic & acoustic music for documentary & short films. Own electronic music studio. Teacher, Los Angeles community cols. *Instrumental Works:* Crystalline Cave and Other Explorations; Four Moments in Time. *Scores:* Film/TV: To Be Me; City, City; Stranger Than Fiction.

LEVINGER, LOWELL VINCENT (BANANA)
ASCAP 1968
composer, author, singer

b New York, NY, Sept 9, 44. Educ: Boston Univ, theatre div. Musician; formed the Proper Bostonians, 63 & Banana & The Bunch, 73. Joined, The Youngbloods, 65. With Mimi Farina & The Fabulous Fenders. Recording artist, RCA & Warner Bros. *Songs:* Fool Me; My True Life Blues; Hippie From Olema; Faster All the Time; Jonah; New Sail Away Ladies; Music: On Sir Francis Drake; On Beautiful Lake Spenard; Lagonda; Big Party; Corduroy Creepers.

LEVINSKY, RONALD FREDERICK
ASCAP 1979
composer, author, singer

b Bronx, NY, Feb 11, 51. Educ: Bronx High Sch of Sci; John Jay Col Criminal Justice, BA, 75. Singer & recording artist, Doval Records. Chief Collabrs: Judy Hinger, Tyrone M Powell. *Songs:* When Fortune Smiles; Music To My Ears; I

Can't Remember Yesterday; Slowly But Surely; Robinwood; Lyrics: Local Lover.

LEVINSKY, WALTER (WALTER LESLIE) ASCAP 1955
composer, conductor, instrumentalist
b River Edge, NJ, Apr 18, 29. Educ: Lebanon Valley Col, 51; pvt comp & orch study with Tibor Serly; studied cond with Samuel Kratchmalnick. Saxophonist & clarinetist with Benny Goodman, Tommy Dorsey & Skitch Henderson Orchs. Asst cond & arr "Tonight Show," 6 yrs & "Dick Cavett Show" (ABC), also comp theme song. Comp original scores for many NBC & PBS documentaries. Orchr on "Just Tell Me What You Want"; also for many Bway shows. Arr, Doc Severinsen; musical dir, Richard Harris; comp & arr many commercials. Appeared on over 4000 recording sessions as cond, comp, arr and/or instrumentalist. On bd trustees, Lebanon Valley Col, currently. Awards: 4 Emmy Awards. *Songs:* Music: Jalopy; Night Flight to Madrid; Walking on Ice; Gribbenes; Jon's-Walt's (theme). *Scores:* Film/TV: Breaking Up; Everglades; The Great Barrier Reef; Outerscope; 3-2-1 Contact.

LEVINSOHN, LAWRENCE JAY ASCAP 1970
composer, author
b Los Angeles, Calif, July 20, 49. Educ: Calif State Univ, Northridge, BA(tele-communications). Quarter finalist, Am Song Fest Lyric Competition. Chief Collabrs: Jim Zrake; Dennis McCarthy. *Songs:* Lyrics: A Matter of Time; Days of My Life; Memories Better Left Alone; For Everyone; Echoes in a Memory; Another Page Torn From Our Lives.

LEVINSON, JOHN M (JACK)
See Bradford, John Milton

LEVINSON, PAUL ASCAP 1969
composer, author, professor
b Bronx, NY, Mar 25, 47. Educ: Studied psychol, City Col New York, 63-66; NY Univ, BA(jour), 75, PhD(media theory), 79; studied media with Marshal McLuhan, Univ Toronto. Songwriter & record producer, 66-73; radio production asst, Murray the "K" & Wolfman Jack, WNBC-radio, 72-74. Writer of pieces on popular music & culture, publ, 71- Prof mass communication & media theory, Fordham Univ, 75-77 & Fairleigh Dickinson Univ, 75- Chief Collabr: Edward Fox. *Songs:* Sunshine Mind; Looking for Sunsets (in the Early Morning); The Soft of Your Eyes; Lyrics: Merri-Goes-Round; The Isle of Skorpios.

LEVINSON, ROBERT WELLS
See Wells, Robert

LEVIT, ALLEN BERNARD ASCAP 1970
composer, author, arranger
b Philadelphia, Pa, Apr 21, 34. Educ: Central High Sch, Philadelphia, Pa, dipl; Temple Univ, BS(bus admin); studied piano with David Sokoloff. Leader, arr, comp & author. Now indust consult, progs for handicapped & human resources develop. Dir & author educ materials, Life Skills/Information. Chief Collabr: Sir Joseph Lodato. *Songs:* In Spring; I Wish I Really Knew; In My Own Quiet Way; Let Me Be Free; You Brighten Up My Day.

LEVITCH, LEON ASCAP 1971
composer, author, pianist
b Belgrade, Yugoslavia, July 9, 27. Educ: Conservatorio di Musica, Lecce, Italy, 44; Los Angeles City Col, AA(music), 49; Los Angeles State Col, BA(elem educ), 52; Univ Calif Los Angeles, MA(music comp), 70; studied piano with Vera Levinson & Jakob Gimpel, comp with Erich Zeisl, Mario Castelnuovo-Tedesco, Darius Millhaud & Roy Harris. Arrived in US, 44. Awards: Scholarship to study at Aspen, Colo, 57 & 60; second prize comp, Atwater-Kent Competition for String Quartet, 68. *Songs:* Of Plants and Humans, Opus 9 (cantata). *Instrumental Works:* Little Suite for Piano, Opus 1/2; Sonata for Flute and Piano, Opus 1; Trio for Flute, Clarinet (or Viola) and Piano, Opus 2; Quartet for Flute, Viola, Cello and Piano, Opus 3; First Piano Sonata, Opus 4; Quintet for Flute and Strings, Opus 5; Sonata for Violin and Piano, Opus 6; Suite for Flute, Harp, and String Orchestra, Opus 7; Of Plants and Humans, Opus 9; Sonata for Viola and Piano, Opus 11; Phantasy for Oboe and Strings, Opus 12; First String Quartet, Opus 13; Sonata for Violin, Opus 14; First Symphony, Opus 15; Ricordo di Mario, Opus 16 (piano or guitar solo or guitar duet).

LEVITT, ESTELLE ASCAP 1964
composer, author
b Brooklyn, NY, Dec 18, 41. Educ: Hunter Col. Joined staff, Blackwood Music, 63. Chief Collabrs: Lee Pockriss, Tommy Goodman, Camille Monte. *Songs:* In the Name of Love; I Can't Grow Peaches on a Cherry Tree.

LEVITZKI, MISCHA ASCAP 1940
composer, pianist
b Krementchug, Russia, (Am parents), May 25, 1898; d Avon-by-the-Sea, NJ, Jan 2, 41. Educ: Juilliard Sch Music, with Stojowski; Berlin Hochschule, with Dohnanyi. Twice awarded Mendelssohn piano prize. Piano debut, Berlin, at 15 yrs of age & in New York, 16; gave concerts throughout the world. *Songs & Instrumental Works:* Waltz in A; Valse Brilliante; Gavotte; Cadenza to Beethoven's 3rd Piano Concerto; Arabesque Valsante; Valse Tzigane. *Scores:* Ballet: The Enchanted Nymph.

LEVY, DAVID (DON LITTLE) ASCAP 1955
author
b Philadelphia, Pa. Educ: Univ Pa, BS(economics), MBA. Assoc dir radio/TV dept & vpres Young & Rubicam. Vpres in charge of network progs & talent, NBC. Author of novels "Chameleons", "Gods of Foxcroft", "Network Jungle." Chief Collabrs: Vic Mizzy, George Tibbles. *Songs:* Lyrics: Never to Know; A Creepy, Shhh, Happy Halloween.

LEVY, DONALD BENJAMIN ASCAP 1975
composer, author, singer
b Brooklyn, NY, Mar 21, 49. Educ: Eastchester High Sch; Am Univ, Washington, DC, BA, 72; Iona Col, NY. Performed in acoustic NY trio; comp TV commercial; worked with Lee Pockriss in production as artist. Formed Sugar 'n' Soul Music, Inc, & served as pres; mgr, record producer. Chief Collabrs: Mark Sameth, Stephen Epstein, Michael Berm, Alan Bernstein. *Songs:* Music: (You're the) Morningstar; Can't Take the You Outa Me; Midnight Madness.

LEVY, FRANK EZRA ASCAP 1962
composer, cellist
b Paris, France, Oct 15, 30. Educ: High Sch Music & Art, New York, 44-48; Juilliard Sch Music, BS, 51; Univ Chicago, MA(musicol), 54; studied comp with Hugo Kauder & cello with L Rose & J Starker. Played with many orch incl St Louis Symph, Ballet Theatre Orch & NY Philh. With Radio City Music Hall Orch, 61-, principal cellist, 68- *Instrumental Works:* Sextet for Winds and Strings; Concerto for Oboe, Horn, Bassoon, Timpani and String Orchestra; Suite for Unaccompanied Viola or Violoncello; Ricercar for Four Violoncelli; Fantasy for Brass Quintet and Timpani; Suite for Horn or Bassoon and Piano; Concerto for Bassoon and String Orchestra; Concertpiece for Brass Quartet; Quintet for Flute and String Quartet; Trio for Clarinet, Horn and Bassoon; Fanfare for Brass Quintet; Dialogue for Tuba, Harp, Timpani and String Orchestra; Brass Quintet; Sonata for Clarinet and Piano; Symphony No 1 (small orch); Duo for Two Violins; Symphony No 2 (16 brass & 4 perc); Sonata Ricercare for Viola and Piano; Adagio and Rondo for Two Clarinets and Bass Clarinet; Serenade for Flute, Clarinet and Cello; Trio for Flute, Horn and Harpsichord; Toccata for Organ; Adagio and Scherzo for Four Saxophones; Seven Bagatelles for Oboe, Cello and Harp; Symphony No 3; Sonata for Violin and Piano. *Songs & Instrumental Works:* Specks of Light (cycle for soprano & 6 instruments); Lament (narrator, oboe, strings & perc); Go Down, Death (narrator, trumpet, harp & solo dancer).

LEVY, HAL ASCAP 1951
author, publisher, teacher
b Los Angeles, Calif, Oct 18, 16; d Sherman Oaks, Calif, Sept 29, 70. Educ: Univ Calif, Los Angeles. USAAF, WW II. Story analyst, ed & writer, film studios. Wrote radio shows, incl "Mike Malloy" & "Starr of Space"; TV shows, incl "Chevy Show" & "Sheriff of Cochise." Teacher pop lyric writing, Univ Calif, Los Angeles. Co-owner & mgr, Mark Warnow Music; owner & gen mgr, Leeway Music. Chief Collabrs: Paul Atkerson, Gladys Rosenthal, Irving Gertz, Sid Kuller, Alvy West. *Songs:* Whoo-ee Lou-ee-siana; Thanksgiving Song; Listen to the Rockin' Bird; He Was a Man; Bang Bang Boogie; Peppermint Stick; The Wrong Door; My Love and I; First Traveling Saleslady; A Corset Can Do a Lot for a Lady; Come on Back; Lullaby Baby; When You're Young; Lonely People.

LEVY, JONATHAN F ASCAP 1973
author
b New York, NY, Feb 20, 35. Educ: Harvard Col, AB; Columbia Univ, MA, PhD. Taught & wrote plays, 60- Wrote & translated librettos. Chief Collabrs: Bruno Maderna, William Bolcom. *Songs:* Lyrics: Boswell's Journal (cantata for tenor & orch).

LEVY, MARVIN DAVID ASCAP 1958
composer
b Passaic, NJ, Aug 2, 32. Educ: NY Univ, studied with Philip James; Columbia Univ, with Otto Luening. Awards: Rome Prize; Guggenheim; Ford; Damrosch & Hartford grants. *Instrumental Works:* Chassidic Suite; Festival Overture; For the Time Being (Christmas oratorio); Symphony No 1; Sabbath Service. *Scores:* Operas: The Tower; Escorial; Sotoba Komachi; Mourning Becomes Electra (Ford Found grant; Metrop Opera comn).

LEVY, PARKE ASCAP 1957
author
b Philadelphia, Pa, July 15, 08. Educ: Col. Writer for films & radio incl "Duffy's Tavern", "My Friend Irma" & "Baron Munchausen", also for Ben Bernie & Al Jolson; for TV created "December Bride", "Peter and Gladys" & "Many Happy Returns." Chief Collabr: David Rose.

LEVY, SOL PAUL ASCAP 1942
composer, clarinetist, publisher
b Chicago, Ill, July 22, 1881; d New York, NY, Feb 14, 20. Educ: All Hallows Col; studied music with father, also Anton Petersen. First clarinetist in John Philip Sousa & Arthur Pryor bands. In charge of Foreign Orchestrating Dept,

Victor Records. Co-founder, Belwin Music. *Songs:* That Naughty Waltz; Roses That Die Bloom Again; Because You Say Goodbye; Why?; Memories; Hunka-Tin; Cannibal Carnival. *Scores:* Films: Sealed Orders; The Barrier.

LEWALLEN, JAMES C　　　　　　　　　　　　ASCAP 1972
composer, author, performer
b Indianapolis, Ind, Sept 14, 26. Educ: Jordan Cons, Indianapolis, BMME, 50; Butler Univ, MM, 52, studied comp with William Pelz & Norman Phelps. Cond/musician spec serv, USA, 45-46. Col performing musician, theater, jazz, dance & others, 46- Cond, performer, 67, 79 & 80. *Songs:* Realization (tenor, piano); The Word Is Love; song cycle incl: The Word; God Bless Us Everyone; The Beatitudes; The Lord's Prayer; Hymn to Love; Expect a Miracle; Psalm 23; With This Kiss; Serenity Prayer; In Perfect Love; One Day At a Time; Attitude of Gratitude. *Instrumental Works:* Sonata Rondo (piano, sonata, concert piece); Fantaisie; Country Dance; Notturno; Poeme Petite; Andantino; Valse Romantique; Taurus; Watergirl Blues; Moon Child; Aries; March II. O Give Thanks Unto the Lord (anthem, chorus, brass, organ). *Scores:* Opera/Ballet: Who'll Pay the Rent?

LEWINE, RICHARD　　　　　　　　　　　　ASCAP 1947
composer, author, producer
b New York, NY, July 28, 10. Educ: Franklin Prep; Columbia Univ; NY Univ, studied Schillinger Syst. Capt, Signal Corps, World War II. Dir, special programs, CBS-TV, 9 yrs. Producer, var shows incl "Cinderella", "Aladdin", "Blithe Spirit", "Hootenanny" for ABC-TV, Leonard Bernstein's "New York Philharmonic Young Peoples Concerts", "My Name Is Barbra" for CBS-TV. Songwriter, "Ziegfeld Follies" & "Star and Garter." Co-ed, "Encyclopedia of Theatre Music." Chief Collabrs: Ted Fetter, Arnold Horwitt. *Songs:* Let's Hold Hands; I Like the Nose on Your Face; Do My Eyes Deceive Me?; Saturday Night in Central Park; Love Makes the World Go Round; I Fell in Love With You; Gentleman Friend; Mother Isn't Getting Any Younger; Doing the Waltz; Old-Fashioned Girl; Home By the Sea; Hootenanny Saturday Night; I Gotta Have You; Lolita; A Pretty Girl. *Instrumental Works:* A Little Theatre Music (7 pieces for clarinet & piano). *Scores:* Bway shows: The Fireman's Flame; Naughty-Naught; The Girl From Wyoming; Make Mine Manhattan; The Girls Against the Boys; Film background: The Days of Wilfred Owen.

LE WINTER, DAVID　　　　　　　　　　　　ASCAP 1953
composer, conductor, teacher
b New York, NY, Oct 28, 08; d Hollywood, Fla, Jan 22, 76. Educ: Chicago Musical Col. Asst cond, Bway musicals. Vocal coach for Gertrude Lawrence, Mary Martin, Al Jolson, Danny Kaye, Alfred Drake. Music dir, USO tours with Jack Benny, Ingrid Bergman. Orch cond, Pump Room, Ambassador East Hotel, Chicago, 23 yrs. Booking agent for orchs & entertainers. *Songs:* Day Dreams; Mi Prieta; You're the Prettiest Thing I've Seen Tonight; Hand to Mouth Boogie; Rozana.

LEWIS, ADEN G　　　　　　　　　　　　ASCAP 1961
composer, author, choral arranger
b Frostburg, Md, Nov 11, 24. Educ: Frostburg State Col, BS; Pa State Univ, MEd; Juilliard; Columbia Univ; Danube Bend Univ, Hungary. Music teacher, Alleghany County, Md pub schs. Coordr music educ, Mountainside, NJ pub schs. Comp, author & arr for numerous choral compositions. Pianist, accompanist, music dir. Prof music, Kean Col, Union, NJ. Chief Collabr: Jack E Platt. *Songs:* Choral arrangements: African Noel; Just Three; All Join In; Textbook series: Listen, Look and Sing; Basic Skills Through Music.

LEWIS, AL
composer, author, singer
b Cleveland, Ohio, Sept 9, 24. Educ: Pvt music training; studied accordion; Cleveland Sch Art, BA. Produced, created & executed own TV show "Uncle Al Show," 30 yrs. Musician, performer & artist. Accordion soloist, nightclubs. *Songs:* Children's Songs: It's a Happy Day; Lucky the Clown Song; Prayer Song; Here Comes the Happy Mailman; The Happy Birthday Song; The Exercise Song; children's album of many songs.

LEWIS, AL　　　　　　　　　　　　ASCAP 1927
composer, author, publisher
b New York, NY, Apr 18, 01; d New York, Apr 4, 67. Educ: Univ Mich. Chief Collabrs: Al Sherman, Richard Whiting, Larry Stock. *Songs:* Now's the Time to Fall in Love; Gonna Get a Girl; 99 Out of 100 Wanna Be Loved; Sweet Child; Slowly But Surely; All American Girl; No! No! A Thousand Times No!; You Gotta Be a Football Hero; Over Somebody Else's Shoulder; Blueberry Hill; Rose O'Day; Way Back Home; Why Don't You Fall in Love With Me?; Cincinat-ti Dancing Pig; You're Irish and You're Beautiful; The Breeze (That't Bringing My Baby Back to Me; Tears on My Pillow; Got the Bench, Got the Park, But I Haven't Got You; Invitation to a Broken Heart; The Finger of Suspicion Points at You; Lyrics: When I'm the President; Start the Day Right; Under Blue Canadian Skies; Adoration Waltz.

LEWIS, BERNIE KAAI　　　　　　　　　　　　ASCAP 1959
composer, author, conductor
b Hakalau, Hawaii, Sept 14, 21. Educ: Univ Chicago, MA. Staff comp, cond & arr, NBC, San Francisco. To Los Angeles, 42. Served, World War II. Arr for Dorothy Lamour, 50-56. Comp & arr for films, radio, TV & records. Chief

Collabrs: Joseph Moshay, Tom Powers. *Songs:* Josie; Glow-Worm Cha-Cha; My Hawaiian Home.

LEWIS, BILL
See Simon, William Louis

LEWIS, BOB
See Ruse, Robert Louis

LEWIS, C HAROLD　　　　　　　　　　　　ASCAP 1934
composer
b Derby, Conn, July 27, 1892; d Los Angeles, Calif, Aug 25, 55. Educ: Univ Syracuse. First Lt, Am Expeditionary Forces, World War I. *Songs:* This Little Piggie Went to Market; Hey, Hey, We're Gonna Be Free; There's Something in the Air; Sophisticated Baby; Pardon Me; What About You and Me?; You Do.

LEWIS, DONNELL JOY　　　　　　　　　　　　ASCAP 1978
author
b Mobile, Ala, Oct 17, 61. Educ: Hendersonville High Sch, Tenn, grad 78; student, Nashville State Tech Inst, 80- Secy & bookkeeper. *Songs:* Lyrics: Dreamin' About You; Sweet Memories.

LEWIS, EDNA　　　　　　　　　　　　ASCAP 1959
composer, author
b Brooklyn, NY; d. Chief Collabr: Beverly Ross. *Songs:* I Wish That We Were Married; Judy's Turn to Cry; Lipstick on Your Collar; Folk Ballads From the World of Edgar Allan Poe.

LEWIS, EDWARD A　　　　　　　　　　　　ASCAP 1939
composer, author
b Eagle City, Okla, Jan 22, 09. Educ: High sch, music classes & studies. Trumpeter, Bennie Motens KC Victor Recording Orch, 24-31, Thaymon Hayse, Kansas City Rockets, 32-35, Harlan Leonard, 35-37 & Count Basie Orch, 37-47. *Songs & Instrumental Works:* It's Sand Man; Jump the Blues Away; Doctor Blues; Love Is a Pleasure.

LEWIS, JACK B　　　　　　　　　　　　ASCAP 1961
composer, author
b Ft Worth, Tex, Jan 27, 24; d Thousand Oaks, Calif, Dec 30, 64. Educ: Tex Christian Univ. Capt & bomber pilot, WW II. Commercial airlines pilot. *Songs:* Green Finger; Charm Bracelet; Bad Case of Love; Sunflowers; Teenage Idol.

LEWIS, JANET
See Winters, Janet Lewis

LEWIS, JOHN LEO　　　　　　　　　　　　ASCAP 1956
composer, organist, teacher
b Chicago, Ill, May 11, 11; d. Educ: Am Cons, studied with Edward Eigenshenk, Frank Van Dusen & Leo Sowerby; De Paul Univ, BA, MA. Organist & choirmaster, Christ Episcopal Church, River Forest, Ill, 41-44 & Trinity Episcopal Church, Aurora, Ill, 50; minister of music, St Paul's Union Church, Chicago, 44-50; music instr, Elmhurst Col, 48-61. Fel, Am Guild Organists. Chief Collabr: Marion James. *Songs & Instrumental Works:* For Organ: Meditation on "St Flavian"; Orientis Partibus; Prelude on "Annunciation"; Toccata on "Duke Street"; Verdant Pastures; Choral: Awake My Heart; Be Strong, O Ye Children; Caedmon's Hymn; Come and Hear; Lord of All Power and Might; O God Who Art the Truth; Praise to the Living God; Remember Now; We Sing of God (AGO, H W Gray Anthem prize); Prayer of St Francis (Ascension Anthem prize); I Tooted a Horn (Drexel Choral prize); Lord Throughout All Generations; Prayer for the Seven Gifts (Harvey Gaul award).

LEWIS, LEON (A LEON BLOOM)　　　　　　　　ASCAP 1956
composer, conductor, pianist
b Kansas City, Mo, Mar 30, 1890; d Beverly Hills, Calif, Oct 5, 61. Educ: Vienna Cons, studied with Leschetizky, Graedener & Thern. As pianist & cond, concertized in Europe, Can & US. Teacher, Chicago Cons. Initiated CBS radio network classic music orchestral progs. Comp & arr, var TV shows. Scored movies for United Artists, Warner Bros & Pathe. *Songs:* Humayun to Zobeida; Ma Vie; Near the Sea. *Instrumental Works:* Jessica - A Portrait (orch & piano, or 2 pianos); Israeli Suite (large orch: The Prophet Speaks, The Freedom March, Pastorale, Romance & Hora); Cello Concerto No 1; Nocturne & Moonsprites (perc & small orch or piano); Cello Sonata; Quartetto Americana (string quartet); Wind and the Willow (piano, violin, cello); God's Image (baritone solo, choir, orch); var piano solos.

LEWIS, LILLIAN　　　　　　　　　　　　ASCAP 1979
author, publisher
b Brooklyn, NY, June 21, 39. Educ: Hunter High Sch, dipl. Had written int publ slogans, greeting cards, brochures, copy, interviews & many other things; then became lyrics writer. Record promotion, radio & pub rel. Publ, Dripping Bullets Music. Chief Collabrs: Jack Perricone, Steve Fechtor. *Songs:* Lyrics: We Keep Getting Closer (to Being Farther Apart); Morning Noon and Night; I Need to Be in Love; One More Night With You; Ridin' on a High.

LEWIS, MEADE (LUX)   ASCAP 1942
composer, pianist
b Chicago, Ill, Sept 5, 05; d Minneapolis, Minn, June 7, 64. Pianist in nightclubs & concerts; made many piano rolls & records. Popularized boogie-woogie. Appeared with Albert Ammons & Pete Johnson. *Instrumental Works:* Yancey Special; Honky Tonk Train Blues; Six Wheel Chaser; Yancey Goes Honky Tonk; Bass on Top; Bearcat Crawl; Boogie Woogie Prayer; Glendale Glide; Boogie Tidal; Lux Boogie; Rockin' the Clock; Whistlin' Blues; Doll House Boogie; Two's and Fews.

LEWIS, (WILLIAM) MORGAN, JR   ASCAP 1940
composer
b Rockville, Conn, Dec 26, 06; d. Educ: Univ Mich; studied music with Hans Pick. Songs for "Second Little Show", "Third Little Show" & "New Faces." Chief Collabrs: Nancy Hamilton, Ted Fetter, Edward Eliscu, E Y Harburg. *Songs:* How High the Moon; You Might As Well Pretend; 'Cause You Won't Play House; Teeter Totter Tessie; House With a Little Red Barn; The Old Soft Shoe; Barnaby Beach; With All My Heart; I Only Know; Once Upon a Time; At Last It's Love; Lazy Kind of Day. *Scores:* Bway stage: One for the Money; Two for the Show; Three to Make Ready; Film background: The Unconquered (Helen Keller, Her Life; Acad Award documentary film, 55).

LEWIS, OVID BARTON   ASCAP 1972
composer, author, violinist
b Ottumwa, Iowa, Aug 11, 05. Educ: Ottumwa High Sch; Juilliard Sch Music; Columbia Univ, BS & MS; studied violin with B O Worrell, Arcule Sheasby & Beno Rabinof, cond with William Von Hoogstraten, dir New York Philh. Author bk & writer lyrics musical comedy, "Nagshead." Violinist, prof road shows, TV & talk shows. Record producer, O'Barton Records. Cond, symph orch. *Songs:* You're the One; Manhattan Blues; Music Box; G-I-R-L; Wonderful Son; All He Sees Tis a Dame in His Eyes; Bob Tailed Shay. *Scores:* Musical comedy: Nagshead.

LEWIS, ROBERT ALAN   ASCAP 1973
composer, instrumentalist
b Oshkosh, Wis, Jan 23, 36. Educ: Univ Wis-Madison, MM. Began comp & arr, 60. Recording studio musician, Chicago, 64- Two comp fel grants from Nat Endowment for Arts. Author of commercials, record dates, brass works, songs, jazz arrangements & compositions. *Songs:* By Night. *Instrumental Works:* The Trumpet Section (suite, 4 movements); Incantation; Wilderness; La Casa Del Forefronte; Reverberations; Trumpetry (suite, 3 movements).

LEWIS, ROBERT HALL   ASCAP 1968
composer, conductor
b Portland, Ore, Apr 22, 26. Educ: Univ Rochester Eastman Sch of Music, BM, 49, MM, 51, PhD 64; Paris Cons, dipl in conducting, 53; Vienna Acad of Music, dipl in theory & comp, 57; studied with Hans Erich Apostel, Vienna, 55-57. Comp-in-residence, Am Acad in Rome, 80-81. Prof of music, Goucher Col; prof of comp, Johns Hopkins Univ Peabody Inst. Recipient, Koscivszko Found Chopin Award, 51, Fulbright Scholarship, Vienna, 55-57, Guggenheim fel, 66 & 79, Walter Hinrichsen Award for Composers, 73, Acad of Arts & Letters Award, 76, NEA fel, 76, Koussevitzky Found Award, 77. *Instrumental Works:* String Quartets I and II; Music for Twelve Players; Symphonies I and II; Music for Brass Quintet; Three Pieces for Orchestra; Toccata for Violin and Percussion; Nuances II for Orchestra; Concerto for Chamber Orchestra; Osservazioni I for Flutes, Piano and Percussion; Osservazioni II for Winds, Harp, Keyboard and Percussion; Serenades for Piano Solo; Serenades II for Flute, Piccolo, Cello and Piano; Combinazioni I; Combinazioni II; Moto for Orchestra.

LEWIS, ROGER   ASCAP 1925
composer
b Colfax, Ill, Apr 3, 1885; d Chicago, Ill, Jan 1, 48. Educ: High sch. *Songs:* Oceana Roll; Down By the Winegar Woiks; When I Was a Dreamer and You Were a Dream; One Dozen Roses; Down Home Rag; Torpedo Jim.

LEWIS, RUSSELL ROOSEVELT   ASCAP 1970
composer, author, singer
b St Louis, Mo, Sept 26, 41. Educ: Webster Groves High Sch; Douglass High Sch; Meramec Community Col. Recorded for Monument Records, Westbound Records & Gold-Future Records. Has own production co, Gold-Future Productions & publ co, Best-Bet Music. Chief Collabrs: Herman Davis, Audie Phipps, Sid Wallace, Terry Willis. *Songs:* Groovy Situation (nominated for Grammy 70); Body Language. *Instrumental Works:* Loving You.

LEWIS, SAMUEL M   ASCAP 1914
author
b New York, NY, Oct 25, 1885; d New York, Nov 22, 59. Educ: Pub schs. Began career singing in cafes. Songs for films, incl "Spring is Here." Charter mem, ASCAP & The Friars. Chief Collabrs: lyric-writing, Joe Young, comp, Fred Ahlert, Walter Donaldson, Bert Grant, Harry Warren, Jean Schwartz, George Meyer, Ted Fiorito, J Fred Coots, Ray Henderson, Victor Young, Peter DeRose, Harry Akst. *Songs:* When You're a Long, Long Way From Home; My Mother's Rosary; Come on and Baby Me; Arrah, Go on, I'm Gonna Go Back to Oregon; If I Knock the 'L' Out of Kelly; Where Did Robinson Crusoe Go

With Friday on Saturday Night?; I'm All Bound 'Round With the Mason-Dixon Line; Why Do They All Take the Night Boat to Albany?; Hello, Central, Give Me No Man's Land; Rockabye Your Baby With a Dixie Melody; Just a Baby's Prayer at Twilight; How Ya Gonna Keep 'Em Down on the Farm?; Baby Blue; Don't Cry, Frenchy, Don't Cry; You're a Million Miles From Nowhere; Who Played Poker With Pocahontas When John Smith Went Away?; I'd Love to Fall Asleep and Wake Up in My Mammy's Arms; My Mammy; Tuck Me to Sleep in My Old 'Tucky Home; Five Foot Two, Eyes of Blue; I'm Sitting on Top of the World; Dinah; In a Little Spanish Town; King for a Day; Laugh, Clown, Laugh; Then You've Never Been Blue; Got Her Off My Hands But Can't Get Her Off My Mind; Cryin' for the Carolines; I Kiss Your Hand, Madame; Telling It to the Daisies; Too Late; Just Friends; Street of Dreams; Lawd, You Made the Night Too Long; One Minute to One; For All We Know; I Believe in Miracles; A Beautiful Lady in Blue; Put Your Heart in a Song; Gloomy Sunday; Gonna Hitch My Wagon to a Star; I Heard a Forest Praying; What's the Matter With Me?; Have a Little Faith in Me.

LEWIS, TED
See Friedman, Theodore Leopold

LEWIS, WAYNE I   ASCAP 1978
composer, author, singer
b Valhalla, NY, Apr 13, 57. Educ: Woodlands High Sch; studied jazz improvisation with Bill Ellington, vocal improvisation with Barbra Feller, theory & harmony with Evelyn LaRue Pittman; Westchester Cons Music, studied classical piano with Mr Pollen; pvt lessons in classical piano with Wilma Machover. Musician, off Bway plays & TV commercials; singer & keyboardist, nightclubs, concerts & TV; recording artist. Chief Collabr: David E Lewis. *Songs:* Stand Up; (Let's) Rock n' Roll; Fallin in Love With You; Losin' You; Being in Love With You Is So Much Fun; Straight to the Point.

LEWIS, WILLIAM CHRISTOPHER   ASCAP 1976
composer, author, singer
b New York, NY, Sept 17, 53. Educ: William Floyd High Sch; Crane Sch of Music, Potsdam, NY. Singer in nightclubs. Recording artist, ETC Records, Starbase Records. Pianist. *Songs:* Music in My Soul; One Year Older (Happy Birthday Dad).

LEWISOHN, ARTHUR
See Mazlen, Henry Gershwin

LEYDEN, JAMES A   ASCAP 1958
composer, author, singer
b Springfield, Mass, June 12, 21. Educ: Pleasantville High Sch; Pa State Univ, BS(music educ), 42; Am Theatre Wing, 46-47. Mem, Pa State Thespian Soc & vocal groups, Moonlight Serenaders, Three Beaus & Peep. Recording artist, RCA, EPIC & Columbia Records. Coauth of musicals, "Rough 'N' Ready", "Ballad of Brawn Michael" & "Bayou Flute." Pioneer in steel drum movement; dir of first steel drum orchs to perform in Romania, USSR & Poland. Arr & teacher. Chief Collabrs: Lee Benjamin, Merril Staton Ostrus. *Songs:* Lonesome Whistles; Nittany Lion. *Scores:* Off-Bway Shows: Rough 'N' Ready; The Ballad of Brawn Michael; Bayou Flute.

L'HEUREUX, DAVID CHARLES (D C LARUE)   ASCAP 1962
composer, author, singer
b Meriden, Conn, Apr 26, 48. Educ: Cheshire High Sch; Cheshire Acad; Univ Conn; Yale Univ; Pear Sch Fine Art. Appeared in, "Goggles", "Discotheque Holiday" & "Thank God It's Friday." Recording artist, ABC Paramount, Septer, Decca, Philips, Kirshner, Claridge, Pyramid & Polydor/Casablanca. Art director & performer. Chief Collabrs: Crewe, Slay, Levitt, Heard, Schefrin, Christie, E Z Epstein, Esty & Corbetta. *Songs:* Nashville, Tennessee; Cathedrals; Do You Want the Real Thing; Let Them Dance; On Your Knees.

LIBBEY, DELORES R (DEE)   ASCAP 1957
composer, author
b De Land, Fla. Educ: Stetson Univ, BMus; pvt study in advanced music with Leo Sowerby; Am Cons, Chicago, studied comp 4 summers. Writer pop songs, symphonic scores, ballet & choral works & religious songs. Creator of dishes for gift shops. Chief Collabrs: Syd Wayne, Charles Tobias. *Songs & Instrumental Works:* Mangos; Silver Bird; Essence and Distractions (orch score in rental); The Lost Forest; Impressions of a Leaking Faucet; Choral: Tolling Bells; Wee Little Boy.

LIBERACE, GEORGE J   ASCAP 1958
composer, violinist, conductor
b Menasha, Wis, July 31, 11. Educ: Northwestern Cons Music; Chicago Cons; studied with Maurice Werner, Detroit Symph. With Milwaukee Philh, Milwaukee Theatres & Liberace Award Winning TV Series. Violinist, Orrin Tucker Orch & Anson Weeks Orch. Owner, George Liberace Orch. Admnr, Liberace Museum. Chief Collabr: Turk Prujan. *Songs:* Music: La Cherie Jolie; Paris at Dawn; The Natives of Hawaii; Our Hawaiian Love; Hawaiian Water Fall; Champs Elysees; Parisian Skies; Thanks. *Instrumental Works:* Bull Frog on a Spree; Mi Amour; George Liberace Mambo.

LIBERACE, WALTER VALENTINO (LIBERACE)　　　ASCAP 1954
composer, pianist, actor
b Milwaukee, Wis, May 16, 19. Educ: High sch; studied piano with Florence
Kelly. Concert debut at age 11, Milwaukee; piano soloist, Chicago Symph. To
NY, 40; nightclub pianist, NY. Toured with USO shows. World pianist,
nightclubs, hotels, concerts & theatres. Had own TV show; has made many
records. Acted in films "Sincerely Yours" & "The Loved Ones." *Instrumental
Works:* Rhapsody By Candlelight; Boogie Woogie Variations.

LIBLICK, MARVIN　　　ASCAP 1964
composer, author, pianist
b Detroit, Mich, Mar 16, 29. Educ: High sch. Founded own publ & record cos.
Film & TV technician. *Songs:* A Little Less Talk; If I Had a Sweetheart; Mr
Fortune Teller; You Taught Me How to Remember; How'd You Like to Fall
in Love; I'm Afraid of Tomorrow.

LICHTER, CHARLES　　　ASCAP 1959
composer, conductor, violinist
b Philadelphia, Pa, Jan 15, 10. Educ: Ethical Culture Sch; Juilliard Sch. Staff
violinist, cond & music consult, CBS, 36- Music coordr, "Bell Telephone Hour."
Instrumental Works: Romantic Suite.

LIEB, ZISKIND R (DICK)　　　ASCAP 1963
composer, arranger, orchestrator
b Gary, Ind, Mar 7, 30. Educ: Eastman Sch Music, BMus, 53, studied trombone
with Emory Remington, comp & arr, Rayburn Wright, comp, Stefan Wolpe.
Bass trombonist, writer & arr with Kai Winding, Radio City Music Hall & NBC
Staff, incl "Tonight Show." Have comp & arr for the "Tonight Show", "Sesame
Street" & Muzak system. Arr, orchr for TV, Bway shows, recordings. Pieces
publ for solo instruments with concert band, brass quintet, string quintet. Also
many stage band arr of standards. *Songs & Instrumental Works:* Muppet Film
(theme); Sesame Street Christmas Special (theme, 78); HBO Puppet Spectacular
(theme, 79); Song and Dance for Solo Trombone and String Quartet; Short
Ballet for Saxophone and Concert Band; Feature Suite for Brass Quintet and
Organ; also over forty originals used in Muzak system.

LIEBER, DOODLES
See Lieberstein, Marcus Edward

LIEBERMAN, ERNEST SHELDON　　　ASCAP 1963
composer, author, singer
b Brooklyn, NY, Jan 24, 30. Educ: Brooklyn Tech High Sch; Brooklyn Col.
Guitarist, folksinger; mem singing groups, Gateway Singers, Limeliters &
others. Record producer; has done albums for Columbia, RCA & Mercury.
Wrote songs for films, TV & radio. Co-auth of bk "Dirty Money." Awards:
Western Heritage Award; Nat Advert Council; Ohio State Univ Radio. Chief
Collabrs: Elmer Bernstein, Jack Keller, Quincy Jones, Neal Hefti, Jerry
Goldsmith, Frank Hamilton, Carol Connors, Fred Karlin. *Songs:* Wouldn't
You?; Mighty Joe Magarac; When We Sing; (If You Open Up) The Windows
of Your Mind; I Love to Look At Animals; Bring Me a Rose (How Easy We
Forget); Time to Move On; No Man Is an Island; The Best Is Yet to Come;
Music: Ballad of Murder, Inc; Lyrics: Baby the Rain Must Fall; Seattle; Sons
of Katie Elder; I Feel It; Hallelujah Trail; Duel at Diablo; Glass; Yours, Mine
and Ours; Children of the Summer; Love Me True; Baby What I Mean; Bound
for Glory; And We Were Strangers; Another Time, Another Place; If You Want
Love; There Is a Place for Lovers; Sunday's Gonna Come on Tuesday; Love Will
Keep Us Going; I'll Build a Bridge; (Let the Lovelight in Your Eyes) Lead Me
On; Wish I Knew; Lord Love a Duck.

LIEBERMAN, FREDRIC
composer, professor
b New York, NY, Mar 1, 40. Educ: Eastman Sch Music, BMus; Univ Hawaii,
MA; Univ Calif, Los Angeles, PhD. Asst prof music, Brown Univ, 68-75. Assoc
prof music, Univ Wash, 75- Ed, "Ethnomusicology," 78- *Songs & Instrumental
Works:* Two Short String Quartets; Suite for Piano; Sonatina for Piano; Leaves
of Brass; Symphony for Small Orchestra; By the Rivers of Babylon (SATB).

LIEBERMAN, PETER　　　ASCAP 1976
composer, author
b Paterson, NJ, Dec 30, 54. Educ: Eastside High Sch; Montclair State Col, BA,
76. Singer, pianist & recording artist. *Songs:* Lorelei; Go With It; Kick in the
Head; Beautiful Girls; Boring; Just Not Worth It; Wait for Me.

LIEBERSON, GODDARD　　　ASCAP 1964
composer, author, musician
b Hanley, Staffordshire, Eng, Apr 5, 11; d May 29, 77. Educ: Univ Wash,
studied with George Frederick McKay; Eastman Sch Music, with Bernard
Rogers; hon degrees, Temple Univ & Cleveland Inst Music. Record exec; joined
Masterworks Dept, Columbia Records, 39. Dir dept & vpres, Masterworks
A&R, exec vpres, 49, pres, 56-66. Was vpres & mem, CBS bd dirs, until 77;
mem, CBS Found. Chmn, spec Yale Univ Libr Comn; hon curator, Yale Col
Literature Am Musical Theatre; chmn, Music Adv Comn, Hopkins Ctr,
Dartmouth. Pres, CBS Columbia Group, 66-77. *Instrumental Works:* String
Quartet; Piano Pieces for Advanced Children or Retarded Adults.

LIEBERSTEIN, MARCUS EDWARD (DOODLES LIEBER) ASCAP 1975
composer, author, teacher-musician
b East St Louis, Ill, Dec 1, 33. Educ: Russell S Rigden Jr High Sch; studied
trumpet from age 9 to age 19; studied bass viol with Henry Lowe. Started
playing trumpet at age 9; won ribbons at State Ill Dist competition for trumpet
soloists at ages 15 & 17. First chair trumpeter, Army Band, Ft Leonard Wood,
Mo; toured country with own group, Sherry Drake & the Marksmen; high career
point, The Dunes, Las Vegas, Nev, alternated on bandstand with Freddy
Martin's Orch, 68. Now playing in St Louis area; musical dir, "Carousel",
"Pajama Game" & "King and I," 63, 64 & 65; played prominent St Louis
entertainment areas incl Gaslite Square & Laclede's Landing. Plays flugelhorn
& drums; choral dir. *Songs:* On the Beat; The Sign; The
Workin' Man; This Is My Feeling for a Christmas Eve; Thank You Prayer; Fear;
The Struggle. *Instrumental Works:* Trifle Thoughts.

LIEBERT, WILLIAM EDWARD　　　ASCAP 1962
composer, arranger, conductor
b Detroit, Mich, Apr 18, 25. Educ: Studied music, accordion & piano with James
Bruzzese, Detroit, 34-41; Los Angeles Cons Music & Arts, 49-50; studied
orchestration, comp & conducting with Lionel Taylor. Entertainer for
nightclubs in Detroit; on tour with show, 42-43. Served in USN, 43-45. Dance
band work, Los Angeles, 46; musical dir, Cliffie Stone's "Hometown Jamboree"
for radio & TV, 47-54; musical dir, arr & musician var shows, incl Tennessee
Ernie Ford, Curt Massey & TV spec, 54-68. Produced, wrote & cond, first
"Academy County Music Show," 65. Producer, comp & cond, John Wayne
Album, "America, Why I Love Her." Joined Sons of the Pioneers, 74.
Recording artist, 46- Chief Collabrs: Howard Barnes, Hal Blair, John Mitchum,
Stan Freberg, Bell Ezell. *Songs:* Music: So Much to Remember; Face the Flag;
Theme for John and Marsha; The People; Dust on the Snow; The Good Things;
Mis Raices Estan Aqui; Whoever You Are (CBS Repertoire Workshop, bk
musical); The Hyphen.

LIEBLING, ESTELLE　　　ASCAP 1950
composer, author, singer
b New York, NY, Apr 21, 1884; d New York, Sept 25, 70. Educ: Hunter Col;
Stern Cons, Berlin; studied with Nicklass Kempner & Matilde Marchesi; hon
degrees, Boguslawski Col Music & Fairleigh-Dickinson Col. Debut as Lucia in
"Lucia Di Lammermoor," Dresden Opera House. Soloist with John Philip
Sousa Band on world tour. Decorated by King Edward VII of Eng. Soloist with
NY Philh, Boston Symph, Detroit Symph, Philadelphia Orch & Leipzig
Gewandthaus Orch. Teacher; pupils incl Galli-Curci, Frieda Hempel, Maria
Jeritza, Jessica Dragonette, Gertrude Lawrence, Adele Astaire & Beverly Sills.
Author: "Estelle Liebling Coloratura Digest." *Instrumental Works:* Arr:
Carnival of Venice; Blue Danube Waltz; Souvenir Waltz; Invitation to the
Dance; Waltz of the Flowers; Ombre Legere.

LIEBLING, HOWARD　　　ASCAP 1959
author
b Rockford, Ill, Jan 25, 28. Educ: Northwestern Univ Sch Speech. Chief
Collabrs: Marvin Hamlisch, Ray Ellis, Charles Aznavour. *Songs:* Lyrics:
Sunshine, Lollipops and Rainbows; California Nights; 'Cause I Believe in
Loving; Carnival; The Travelin' Life; Too Little Time; To Die of Love; All Night
Market.

LIEBMAN, JOSEPH H　　　ASCAP 1961
composer, author
b Philadelphia, Pa, Nov 5, 11. Educ: Univ Pa, BA. Sr vpres of sales promotion,
R H Macy, New York, dir, Bamberger Div. *Songs:* Strange Feeling; My Secret
World. *Instrumental Works:* The Harmony of Man (concerto); *Scores:* Films:
Rooftops of New York; Force of Impulse; Light Fantastic; *Albums:* Light
Fantastic.

LIEBMAN, MAX　　　ASCAP 1950
author, producer, director
b Vienna, Austria, Aug 5, 02. Writer, sketches; dir, summer hotel shows.
Discovered Danny Kaye, Sid Caesar, Betty Garrett, Imogene Coca & Jules
Munshin. Producer, TV revue, "Your Show of Shows," 49 (annual TV award,
Look mag, 51-53), Bway revue, "From the Second City." Created NBC-TV
spectaculars, 54. Songwriter, Bway musicals "Let's Face It", "Make Mine
Manhattan", "Tickets Please", "Crazy With the Heat", "Along Fifth Avenue,"
films incl "Up in Arms", "Kid From Brooklyn", "The Ziegfeld Follies." Chief
Collabr: Sylvia Fine. *Songs:* Melody in 4-F; Say It After Me; Lobby Number;
That's My Idea of Heaven; Sittin' on the Moon; Love Is Gone; Honey Is Sweet
on Me; World Weary; Eileen; No Other Love; Love Me Tonight; Poet's Heart.

LIEF, MAX　　　ASCAP 1931
author
b New York, NY, Feb 22, 1899; d Westwood, Calif, Mar 6, 69. Educ: NY Univ,
BS. Reporter, columnist & drama ed, New York Daily News, 21-30. Writer,
films & TV, Hollywood, verse & short stories for Saturday Evening Post & New
Yorker. Playwright, "Champagne for Everybody" & "Two for Tonight."
Songwriter, "Earl Carroll's Vanities of 1931", "Third Little Show", "Shoot the
Works" & "Grand Street Follies." Author, novel, "Hangover," verse,
"Bachelor's Guide to the Opposite Sex." Co-author, "The Missouri Traveler
Cookbook." Chief Collabrs: Nathanial Lief (brother), Michael Cleary, Sholom

Secunda, Maurie Rubens, Manning Sherwin, David Snell, Joseph Meyer, Arthur Schwartz, Louis Alter, Sammy Fain, Muriel Pollock. *Songs:* I'll Putcha Pitcha in the Paper; I'm Back in Circulation Again; It's in the Stars; Dream of Me; I'll Always Remember; Poor Little Doorstep Baby; My Impression of You; His Servant; How Long Will It Last?; Under the Stars. *Scores:* Bway shows: Luckee Girl; Greenwich Village Follies of 1928; Pleasure Bound.

LIEF, NATHANIEL   ASCAP 1931
author
b New York, NY, Jan 1, 1896; d New York, Dec 21, 44. Educ: NY Univ Col Dent. First Lt, AEF, WW I, Lt Comdr, USNR, WW II. Wrote songs for "Earl Carroll's Vanities of 1931", "Third Little Show", "Shoot the Works" & "Grand Street Follies." Chief Collabs: Max Lief (brother), Michael Cleary, Sholom Secunda, Maurie Rubens, Arthur Schwartz, Louis Alter, Sammy Fain, Muriel Pollock. *Songs:* I'll Putcha Pitcha in the Papers; I'm Back in Circulation Again; It's in the Stars; Dream of Me; I'll Always Remember; Poor Little Doorstep Baby; My Impression of You. *Scores:* Bway: Luckee Girl; Greenwich Village Follies of 1928; Pleasure Bound.

LIEURANCE, THURLOW   ASCAP 1934
composer, educator
b Oskaloosa, Iowa, Mar 21, 1878; d Boulder, Colo, Oct 9, 63. Educ: Col Music, Cincinnati, MusD; Cons de Musique, France; Fontainebleau, scholarship. Bandmaster, 22nd Kans VSVI, Span-Am War. Hon by Am Sci Res Soc for music res among Am Indians. Recorded Am Indian songs. Author, "To Dance, Live, Love and Sing." Toured in concerts with wife, singer Edna Woolley Lieurance, 18-27. Prof, Univ Sch Music, Lincoln, Nebr. Dean fine arts, Univ Wichita, 27-47. *Songs:* By the Waters of Minnetonka; Reverie; Blue Mist; At Parting; Purple Pines; Among the Pines; And I Ain't Got Weary Yet; The Good Rain; From the Old Homestead; In Mirrored Waters; Hymn to the Sun God; Holiday Pleasures; Irish Spring Song; I Wonder Why; Came the Dawn; If I Hadn't Had You; The Sandman; Sunbeams; A Prayer. *Instrumental Works:* Colonial Exposition Sketches; Scenes Southwest; Prairie Sketches; Water Moon Maiden; Fantasia for Violin, Piano; Six Songs; Conquistador; 11 Song Cycles.

LIGGINS, JOSEPH CHRISTOPHER   ASCAP 1945
composer, author, pianist
b Guthrie, Okla, July 9, 16. Educ: Royal Brown Cons Music, San Diego, 37-39; San Diego State Col, 2 yrs. Worked in nightclubs, 35-39. Leader of Joe Liggins & Honeydripper Band, 45- Recording artist, Exclusive, Specialty & Mercury Records. *Songs:* The Honeydripper; I've Got a Right to Cry; Pink Champagne; Tanya; Little Joe's Boogie.

LIGHT, BEN   ASCAP 1954
composer, author, pianist
b New York, NY, Apr 23, 1894; d Pacific Palisades, Calif, Jan 6, 65. Educ: High sch. Pianist for singers; made many records.

LIGHT, ENOCH   ASCAP 1951
composer, conductor
b Canton, Ohio, Aug 18, 07; d New York, NY, July 31, 78. Educ: Johns Hopkins Univ, BA; NY Univ, MA; Mozarteum, Salzburg, Austria. Cond own orch, Light Brigade, in theatres, hotels & radio; toured Europe for 3 yrs. Taught at NY Univ, 59. Pres, Award Record Co & Total Sound Inc, 66-78. Managing dir, Command Records until 65. Mem, NY Fac Club & Nat Acad Am Comp & Cond. *Songs & Instrumental Works:* Cinderella; Rio Junction; Daniel Boone, the Daddy of Them All; Carribe; Via Veneto; Private Eye Suite; Big Ben Bossa; Chuggy the Choo Choo; Ca C'est Paris; C'mon, C'mon Don't Be Timido; The Love I Give to You; Pussy Foot.

LILLENAS, BERTHA MAE   ASCAP 1889
composer, author
b Hanson, Ky, Mar 1, 1889; d Tuscumbia, Mo, Mar 13, 45. Educ: High sch; pvt music study. Ordained minister, Church of the Nazarene, 12. *Songs:* Sacred: Jesus Took My Burden; Jesus Is Always There; He Will Not Forget; Are You Watching His Star?; Saved by the Blood; Leave Your Burden at the Place of Prayer; His Grace Is My Strength and My Song.

LILLENAS, HALDOR   ASCAP 1938
composer, author
b Bergen, Norway, Nov 19, 1885; d Calif, Aug 18, 59. To US, 1887. Educ: Pacific Bible Col; studied voice with Daniel Protheroe, Adolph Rosenbecker; hon MusD, Olivet Nazarene Col. Elder, Church of the Nazarene, 12, pastor, 15 yrs, singing evangelist, 10 yrs. Music ed for publ; own publ. *Songs:* It Is Glory Just to Walk With Him; Jesus Will Walk With Me; How Can I Be Lonely?; Wonderful Peace; Where They Need No Sun; The Garden of My Heart; Peace That My Saviour Has Given; The Theme of My Song; I Know a Name; I Have Settled the Question.

LILLEY, JOSEPH J   ASCAP 1947
composer, author, director
b Providence, RI, Aug 16, 14; d. Educ: New Eng Cons; Juilliard Sch Music; Schillinger Syst. Wrote radio shows, NBC & CBS; moved to Hollywood; film dir; cond; also TV writer. *Songs:* Jingle Jangle Jingle; Friendly Mountains; Don't Tell Me That Story; The Windshield Wiper; Here's to a Wonderful Christmas; You're Here, My Love; Take Me in Your Arms. *Scores:* Films: Red Hot and

Blue; Sailor Beware; Seven Little Foys; Anything Goes; The Mating Season; That Certain Feeling; Paris Holiday; White Christmas; G I Blues; Li'l Abner; Blue Hawaii; Papa's Delicate Condition; The Disorderly Orderly.

LILLIE, JESSIE   ASCAP 1950
composer, author
b Elk Point, SDak, June 4, 1890; d Torrington, Wyo, Dec 24, 76. Educ: SDak State Univ; pvt music study. Taught, county schs, 2 yrs. Chief Collabr: Ray Magee. *Songs:* Way Out West In Wyoming; When the Cowboys Gather Home; Song of a Pioneer; There's Something 'Bout the Prairie; Just a Prairie Song at Twilight; Is It Wrong?; Seven Reasons.

LIMPIC, GERALD RICHARD   ASCAP 1977
composer, author, singer
b San Diego, Calif, Sept 2, 51. Educ: Helix High Sch; San Diego State Univ, BA(history, speech communications & relig studies). Toured with groups, Random Sample, Gabriel & Limpic & Rayburn. Chief Collabr: Rob Mehl. *Songs:* Sunshine in My Soul; Crossfire; Mary's Song; Domino; Come to the River; Gentle Touch of Your Love; Music: The First Step. *Albums:* Gentle Touch.

LINARD, SIDNEY LEE
composer, singer
b Birmingham, Ala, May 7, 36. Started singing & writing while in USAF; performed at Air Force bases, radio, TV & night club circuit. Recording artist, Ovation & Vulcan Records. Chief Collabs: Johnny (Chance) Jones, Nilda Daniels. *Songs:* I Gave Up Good Morning Darlin'; Saving Up Sunshine; Nashville Mirrors; Message to Khomeini; Jack Daniels Kinda Day.

LINDEMAN, EDITH
See Calisch, Edith Lindeman

LINDEMANIS, HARALDS   ASCAP 1963
composer, teacher
b Valka, Latvia, Feb 25, 21. Educ: Cons, Riga, Latvia; Cons Music, Stuttgart, Ger. Church organist; choir dir; comp; theatre music dir, Ger. Organ piano & accordion teacher. *Songs:* Music: Kiss Me Goodby Tomorrow; Just Playing Games; Careless Man.

LINDEMUTH, WILLIAM I   ASCAP 1961
composer, musician, arranger
b Harrisburg, Ill, June 3, 15. Educ: Studied with John Wummer, William Kincaid, Tom Timothy. Musician, Mich Fox Theatres & with dance orchs incl George Olson, Gordon Jenkins. With pit orchs, Bway musicals. With staff orch, Mercury Records. Arr, Westbury Music Fair, 4 seasons. Staff writer, Kali-Yuga Music Press. *Songs & Instrumental Works:* Pixie Polka; Tangier; Kokeshi Doll; Forty Fabulous Fingers; Grenadilla Waltz.

LINDSAY, BRYAN EUGENE (GENE LYND)
composer, author, teacher
b Brooklyn, NY, Sept 19, 31. Educ: Fairhope High Sch, Ala, 49; Troy State Col, Ala, BA(music educ, Russian), 56; Peabody Col, MA(music ed, related arts), 62, PhD(fine arts, humanities), 66. High sch choral & jazz ens dir, 56-61. Prof writer & arr, played with bands, Nashville, 61-65. Chmn, Humanities Dept & developer, Music Prog, Okaloosa-Walton Jr Col, 65-69. Joined fac, Eastern Ky Univ, 69-72; joined staff, Ctr Humanities, Converse Col, Spartanburg, SC, 72-76. Assoc prof, Univ SC, Spartanburg, 76-80. Writer & poet publ, several jour, Poet in the Schools, SCAC PITS Prog. Exec secy, Nat Asn for Humanities Educ; consult. Chief Collabs: Alfred Bartles, Jr, Ian Mitchell, Richard Law, Glenn Baxter, Ray Griff. *Songs:* Soul Dance; Southside Soul Society, Chapter No 1; Big Green Indian; Lyrics: Come Ride the Wind With Me; I Just Can't Look Sunday in the Eye; Sunchild; Teach Me to Swim. *Instrumental Works:* The Loser; Muddy Bottom; Maggie's Drawers; Hello, There!; General Funky.

LINDSEY, MORT   ASCAP 1957
composer, conductor, pianist
b Newark, NJ, Mar 21, 23. Educ: Columbia Univ, BA, MA, EdD. Staff pianist, NBC, 48-51. Arr, "Arthur Godfrey Show," 51-53; music dir, "Pat Boone Show", "Andy Williams Show", "Judy Garland at Carnegie Hall" (Grammy award), "Judy Garland Show", "Barbra Streisand in Central Park" (Emmy award), 69, 2 Barbra Streisand TV specials & "The Merv Griffin Show" (3 Emmy nominations), 64- Comp & cond, films incl "Gay Purr-ee", "I Could Go on Singing", "The Best Man", "40 Pounds of Trouble", "Stolen Hours" & "Real Life." Arr, Bway musical "Bajour." Chief Collabs: Marilyn & Alan Bergman, Johnny Mercer, Noel Sherman. *Songs:* Lorna; Stolen Hours; Steve's Theme. *Scores:* Ballet: The Seven Ages of Man.

LINK, DOROTHY (DOROTHY DICK)   ASCAP 1932
composer, author
b Philadelphia, Pa, Nov 29, 1900. Educ: Sternburg Sch Music, Philadelphia; Acad Arts; Acad Design. Chief Collabrs: Mort Fryberg, Chauncey Gray, Nick Kenny, Harry Link, Bert Lown, Albrecht Marcuse, Bert Reisfeld, Max Steiner, Al Van. *Songs:* Until We Meet Again Sweetheart; By My Side; Please; In a Boat Out to Sea; The Kiss That You've Forgotten; Call Me Darling; I Was Introduced to Heaven (When I Was Introduced to You); Kiss Me Once More; Let's Go Back to Where We Started; Modern Melody; Jealousy; The Moment I Looked

in Your Eye; It's Love Time!; Must We Say Goodnight So Soon; A Star is Born; You're Out of This World to Me; Peelin' the Peach; There is No Breeze; All the World is Mine; I May Hate Myself in the Morning (For Fallin in Love Tonight); Donn' Ama'; Please Tell Me That You Love Me; Remember Tonight.

LINK, HARRY　　　　　　　　　　　　　　　　　ASCAP 1930
　composer, publisher
b Philadelphia, Pa, Jan 25, 1896; d New York, June, 1957. Educ: Wharton Sch, Univ Pa. Gen mgr, music publ cos. *Songs:* These Foolish Things; I'm Just Wild About Animal Crackers; I've Got a Feeling I'm Falling; Until We Meet Again, Sweetheart; The Kiss That You've Forgotten; Tell Me While We're Dancing; You're the One I Care For; I've Got a New Love Affair; The Miracle of the Bells; Wonderful You; Boo Hoo Hoo (You're Gonna Cry When I'm Gone); Daddy's Wonderful Pal; No One Loves You Better Than Your Mammy; Sweet Papa Joe; Red Nose Pete; Where is My Love; Me, Myself and I; Hoodle De Doodle Do; Steppin Fool; Old Ironsides; Along Came Ruth; Don't Take That Black Bottom Away; Hello Swanee Hello; Talk About Dixie; For Mary and Me; Someone Had to Steal You Away; You Are Just a Little Different; Who's to Blame; Gone; By My Side; Please Tell Me That You Love Me; In a Boat Out to Sea; I Was Introduced to Heaven (When I Was Introduced to You); There's a Ring Around My Rainbow; Take it Easy!; Night Wind; Peelin' the Peach; Between You, Me and the Floor Lamp.

LINK, PETER
　producer, writer, director
Educ: Neighborhood Playhouse Sch of Theatre, studied with Sanford Meisner. Began career as actor; was in Bway "Hair" & on TV prog "As the World Turns," 2 yrs. Comp & performed on "Salvation," rock musical (Drama Desk Award). In concert, Delacorte Theater, 73 & Ens Studio Theater, Central Park, 76 & 77. Theatrical works incl, "Iphigenia", "Older People", "The Orphan", "Comedy of Errors" & "Trelawney of the Wells," all with The New York Shakespeare Fest & on Bway, "Lysistrata", "Ulysses in Nightown", "The Mighty Gents" own original musical "King of Hearts." Orch & arr Stephen Foster themes for bicentennial ballet, "Drums, Dreams and Banjos." Songwriter, record producer, artistic dir & performer. Now with proj development of rock act, Jenny Burton & The Other Birds Band, in New York top rock clubs. Writer of pop material for own publ co, Shaker Music Group Ltd. *Songs:* Vegetable Soup (title song & theme; Asn Int Film Animation Awards); The Good Doctor (Tony Award nomination); If You Let Me Make Love to You, Then Why Can't I Touch You? *Songs & Instrumental Works:* Island; On the Road to Babylon. *Scores:* Bway: Much Ado About Nothing (Tony Award nomination); TV: Nightmare; The Great Niagara; High Feather (children's series).

LINN, RAY LAWRENCE, JR　　　　　　　　　　　ASCAP 1969
　composer, author, singer
b Burbank, Calif, Oct 19, 14. Educ: Woodrow Wilson High Sch; Chapman Col, BA, 42; studied voice with Ted Novis, Sarah Farrar. Staff vocal dir, arr & singer, CBS; vocal dir, arr, contractor & singer, Warner Bros & Republic Pictures; vocal dir, comp, arr & singer, Shipstads & Johnson Ice Follies. Free lance singer & arr in radio, TV, motion pictures, commercials & phonograph records. Choral group mem with Ken Darby, Norman Luboff, Johnny Mann, Roger Wagner, Jack Halldran, Ray Conniff, Harry Simeone, Fred Waring, Andre Kostelanitz. Pianist & singer for nightclubs. Chief Collab: Richard A Friesen. *Songs:* Town Meeting; Hockey-Canucks (Vancouver Canucks); Four Bare Walls; Say What You Feel; Ice Follies: Sea World of Fantasy (also Sea World); Honey, Be My Little Honey Bee; Tip Your Hat to a Carrot; TLC (Tender Loving Care); Soil, Seed, Sun and Rain; Shoo, Fly Crows; Mr Bell; Happy Factory; The Fun Barrel; Bad News Report; Gotta Move; Sour Grapes Theme; A Child Is a Horses Best Friend; Spark Plug Blues March; The Riddle Song; What Kind of Animal Is That; Through the Eyes of Your Imagination. *Instrumental Works:* Rhapsody of Sounds in Motion; Showers of Diamonds.

LINN, RAY S　　　　　　　　　　　　　　　　　ASCAP 1979
　composer, trumpeter, bandleader
b Chicago, Ill, Oct 20, 20. Mem, Tommy Dorsey, Woody Herman, Jimmy Dorsey, Artie Shaw, Boyd Raeburn Bands, 40-45. In radio, motion pictures, TV & recording in Hollywood for 30 yrs. Has own band, Ray Linn & The Chicago Stompers, last 5 yrs. Chief Collab: Chuck Niles. *Instrumental Works:* Bix's Bugle; North Side Blues; Where's Prez?; Blop-Blah.

LINN, ROBERT　　　　　　　　　　　　　　　　　ASCAP 1960
　composer, educator
b San Francisco, Calif, Aug 11, 25. Educ: Mills Col, Univ Southern Calif, BM, MM; studied with Darius Milhaud, Halsey Stevens, Roger Sessions & Ingolf Dahl. Past pres, Los Angeles Chapter, Nat Asn Am Comp & Cond. Mem music fac, Univ Southern Calif, 58-, from asst prof to assoc prof music theory & comp, 61-73, prof music & chmn dept music theory & comp, 73- *Instrumental Works:* Clarinet Sonata; 5 Pieces for Flute, Clarinet; String Quartet No 1 (1st prize, Nat Fedn Music Clubs); 3 Madrigals (SATB, 1st prize, Nat Fedn Music Clubs); Overture for Symphony Orchestra (Louisville Orch Award); String Trio; Adagio and Allegro for Chamber Orchestra; An Anthem of Wisdom (Friends of Music; Univ Southern Calif comn); March of the Olympians (1961 Winter Olympics comn; CBS theme); Olympic Anthem; Theme of the Master Plan (Univ Southern Calif comn); Saxophone Quartet; Quartet for Saxophones; Piano Sonata No 1; Duo for Clarinet and Cello; Symphony in One Movement;

Concerto Grosso (trumpet, horn, trombone & wind orch); The Hexameron (3 pianos & orch, from 1837 piano version by Liszt, Thalberg, Pixis, Herz, Czerny, Chopin); Quintet for Brass Instruments; Woodwind Quintet; Piano Sonata No 2; Elevations (wind orch); Dithyramb (8 cellos); Concertino for Violin and Wind Octet; The Pied Piper of Hamelin (speaker, tenor, chorus, orch); Propagula (wind orch); Duo for Cello and Piano; Sinfonia for String Orchestra; Concertino (oboe, horn, percussion & string orch); Toccatina (organ); Five Preludes for Piano; Vino (violin & piano); Fantasia for Cello and String Orch; John Burns of Gettysburg (ballad for oboe, clarinet, bassoon, trumpet, horn, trombone, double bass, piano, perc); Saxifrage Blue (baritone saxophone & piano); Trompe L'oeil (bass trombone & piano); Diversions for Six Bassoons; Trombosis (12 trombones); Partita (wind ensemble); Concerto for Flute and Winds.

LINSKY, JEFFREY JAMES　　　　　　　　　　　ASCAP 1977
　composer, guitarist
b Whittier, Calif, Apr 12, 52. Educ: Self-educated; pvt study with Maestro Vicente Gomez. Played jazz guitar as youth in Los Angeles; later studied classical guitar & began comp music for guitar. Began recording original comp, 77. Concertize on solo guitar & with group worldwide. *Instrumental Works:* Wintersuite (solo guitar); A Contemporary March (solo guitar); Inspiration.

LINTON, KENT RANDALL　　　　　　　　　　　ASCAP 1976
　composer, author
b Logan, Utah, July 24, 47. With barbershop quartets in 60's. Began writing songs, 69. Awards, Am Song Fest & CB Song Contest, 76 & 77. *Songs:* After All the Songs; Nashville Boy; Lorenzo's Theme (theme song); Song Magic; I've Got My Style.

LIPKIN, STEPHEN BARRY (STEVE BARRI)　　　ASCAP 1967
　composer, author
b Brooklyn, NY, Feb 23, 41. Educ: Fairfax High Sch. Writer & producer, ABC/Dunhill Records & Music Publ, 64-75. Producer for Warner Bros Records; writer/producer for own Golden Clover Productions. Chief Collabrs: Phil Sloan, Michael Price, Dan Walsh. *Songs:* Eve of Destruction; Secret Agent Man; You Baby; Where Were You When I Needed You?; Glory Bound; A Must to Avoid; I Wouldn't Treat a Dog (The Way You Treated Me); Who's Foolin' Who; Bella Linda; (Here They Come) From All Over the World.

LIPPMAN, SIDNEY　　　　　　　　　　　　　　　ASCAP 1943
　composer, author, publisher
b Minneapolis, Minn, Mar 1, 14. Educ: Univ Minn, BS(educ); Juilliard, scholarship in comp; studied with Bernard Wagenaar. Music arr, Irving Berlin Inc. Chief Collabrs: Sylvia Dee, Buddy Kaye, Fred Wise. *Songs:* Music: Too Young; Chickery Chick; 'A'—You're Adorable; My Sugar Is So Refined; Laroo Laroo Lili Bolero; A House With Love in It; That's the Chance You Take; Little Lulu (theme of Little Lulu cartoons); These Things You Left Me; After Graduation Day; In These Crazy Times. *Scores:* Red Devil Battery Sign; Mr Popularity; Bway Show: Barefoot Boy With Cheek.

LIPSITZ, HILARY J　　　　　　　　　　　　　　ASCAP 1965
　author
b Baltimore, Md, June 23, 33. Educ: Ahoskie High Sch, NC; Mercersburg Acad; Princeton Univ. Pres, Sunday Productions, BBDO Advert. Collaborated in writing several Pepsi-Cola campaigns; wrote songs for Carol Burnett Show & Melanie. Chief Collabr: Peter Cofield. *Songs & Instrumental Works:* Everybody's Gotta Be Someplace; Dance the Night Away; What Do I Keep, What Do I Throw Away.

LIPTON, JAMES　　　　　　　　　　　　　　　　ASCAP 1963
　author
b Detroit, Mich, Sept 19, 26. Educ: Wayne State Univ. TV writer, incl, "US Steel Hour," "Night of Betrayal" & "The Charley and the Kid"; dir "The Doctor in Spite of Himself." Chief Collabrs: Laurence Rosenthal, Sol Berkowitz. *Songs:* Nowhere to Go But Up; Baby Baby; When a Fella Needs a Friend. *Scores:* Stage: The Doctor in Spite of Himself; Miss Emily Adam; Bway: Nowhere to Go But Up.

LIPTON, LENNY　　　　　　　　　　　　　　　　ASCAP 1963
　author
b Brooklyn, NY, May 18, 40. Educ: Cornell Univ, AB(physics), 62. Worked as ed at Time Inc & Popular Photography, New York. Moved to Calif, became film critic & filmmaker, 65. Wrote several books on motion picture technol. Inventor of a three-dimensional filmmaking system. Chief Collabrs: Peter Yarrow, Bernie Krauss, Mike Mirabella. *Songs:* Lyrics: Puff the Magic Dragon; Doctor Fox; I Used to Be Shy.

LISBON, KENNETH
　See DeVito, Albert Kenneth

LISBONA, EDWARD (EDDIE PIANO MILLER)　　　ASCAP 1951
　composer, author, pianist
b Manchester, Eng, July 16, 15. Educ: Manchester Univ; London Col Music. Pianist in dance orchs, Eng, also accompanist to singer. US citizen, 35. To Hollywood, wrote for films, 49. Made many piano recordings. Chief Collabrs: Art Berman, Leo Pearl. *Songs:* It's My Mother's Birthday Today; Jump on the

Wagon; I Get Up Ev'ry Morning; Don't Fall in Love; Crystal Ball; Don't Leave Me Now; Symphony of Spring; Shoemaker's Serenade; Mary Contrary; Angelina.

LISI, ALBERT   ASCAP 1968
composer, author, singer
b New York, NY, Oct 10, 29. Educ: Seward Park High Sch, New York; Art Students League; Am Art Sch; Mexico City Col; City Col New York, BA. Painter, New York City, Mexico, Italy, Guatemala; had several showings. Started writing songs, 60. *Songs:* Forgive Me.

LISSAUER, ROBERT   ASCAP 1955
composer, author, theatrical producer
b New York, NY, May 1, 17. Educ: The Franklin Sch; Juilliard Sch Music, 34-37; NY Univ, studied Schillinger Syst of Musical Comp with Rudolf Schramm; studied comp with Bernard Wagenaar, 36-39; teaching cert, 49. Music publ, 40-42 & 55-80; record producer. Irving Berlin's "This Is the Army," 42-43; command, all-soldier show, "Yanksapoppin'," Pacific Area, 44-45. Fac, NY Univ, Eastern Cons Music & Newark Cons, 48-52; gen mgr, Vincent Youmans Co, 62- Chief Collabrs: Langston Hughes, John Jacob Loeb, Eddie Deane, Jack Heinz. *Songs:* I Feel So Low When I'm High; Promises, Promises; Hello and Goodbye; Music: Lie Detector; Too True; Double Solitaire; Make Me Thrill. *Instrumental Works:* String Quartet; Sinfonietta; Quartet for Woodwinds; Two Preludes for Concertina and Piano. *Scores:* Off-Bway Show: Just a Little Simple.

LITKEI, ANDREA FODOR   ASCAP 1958
author, poet
b New York, NY, Apr 28, 32. Educ: Fordham Univ, NY, (psychol, Eng). Soloist with Metrop Opera Ballet & Sadler Wells (Royal Ballet). Songwriter for film "The Golden Cage." Artist, one man oil painting exhibition given; poetry readings. Author 2 vols poetry, "Thalassa" & "Plums From a Tree"; author "ESP an Account of the Fabulous in Our Everyday Lives" & var articles in prof mags. Mem, (lifetime) Songwriters Hall of Fame & Nat Acad of Music. Chief Collabr: Ervin Litkei. *Songs:* Lyrics: Oh Madchen Oh Madchen; Tonight I'm Not Just Pretending; Cleopatra; I Waited By the Chapel Door; John Fitzgerald Kennedy March; President Lyndon Baines Johnson March; President Ford March; President Harry Truman March; President Roosevelt March; Bicentennial March; Salute to the First Lady March; Jimmy Carter March; The First Lady Waltz; The Walt Disney World March; The Captured Fifty; Bermuda Serenade; Have You Got Any Dreams for Sale?

LITKEI, ERVIN   ASCAP 1964
composer, author
b Budapest, Hungary, Dec 19, 21. Educ: Univ Hungary; Music Cons of Hungary; studied with Franz Lehar. Writer & publ, Hungary. Songwriter for Ilona Massey. Producer, film "The Golden Cage." Pres, Olympia Record Industs Inc; Arovox Record Co; Galiko Music & Film Productions Enterprises. Chmn of bd, Hanlit Publ Inc. Producer, Bicentennial Concert, 76. Translator of hit songs from Eng to Hungarian. Mem, NARM, Recording Indust Asn of Am; charter mem, Songwriter's Hall of Fame & Nat Acad of Music. Chief Collabr: Andrea Fodor Litkei. *Songs:* Ich Bin Very Happy; The Captured Fifty; Music: I Waited By the Chapel Door; Cleopatra; The John Fitzgerald Kennedy March; President Lyndon Baines Johnson March; President Ford March; President Harry Truman March; President Roosevelt March; Bicentennial March; Salute to the First Lady March; Jimmy Carter March; The First Lady Waltz; The Walt Disney World March; Bermuda Serenade; Laguelo Beach Blues; Have You Got Any Dreams for Sale? *Instrumental Works:* Peace and Remembrance (piano concerto).

LITMAN, NORMAN L   ASCAP 1961
composer, musician
b Duluth, Minn, Nov 19, 17. Educ: Duluth State Teachers Col, studied music. Musician; writer of spec material, radio shows, NBC & motion picture performance. Chief Collabrs: Sammy Gallop, Art Kassel. *Songs:* Music: Thats the Moon My Son; What Would Annie Say; He's a Hillbilly Gaucho With a Rhumba Beat; If You're Happy So Am I; Who's Who in Your Heart?

LITTEE, RAMON   ASCAP 1972
composer, teacher, arranger
b Paris, France, Aug 11, 05. Bandleader at Trocadero, Hollywood, La Conga, NY. Arr for Paul Whiteman, Mark Warnow Lucky Strike Hit Parade, Paul Lavalle Saludos Amigos Prog, NBC & CBS Libr, New York, Xavier Cugat. Recorded for Columbia, Anza, Tic-Tac, Coda, specialized in Continental & Latin music. *Songs:* Music: Sunday in Old Santa Fe; Rumba Jubile; All Aboard Boogie; Vive La Vie, Vive L'Amour; For Love.

LITTLE, DON
See Levy, David

LITTLE, DUDLEY RICHARD (BIG TINY LITTLE,   ASCAP 1956
DUDLEY TINY LITTLE, FLETCHER LEE)
composer, pianist, singer
b Worthington, Minn, Aug 31, 30. Educ: McPhails Cons, Minneapolis; Midwestern Univ, Wichita Falls, Tex. With var bands, 45-50. Joined USAF, 50;

with Japanese jazz group, Tokyo, 52-54. With "Lawrence Welk Show," 55-59. Orch leader of own group, Las Vegas & Reno, 60- Chief Collabrs: Larry Fotine, George Cates. *Songs:* Marla My Love; Honky Tonkin Love Song; Music: Sidewalk Serenade; Jackrabbit Rag; Tinys Tinkle Piano; Here Tis; Make Room for Tiny; Shake Them Bones; Centipede Walk; Toe Teasin Rag; Honky Tonk Train; Bulldoggin the Keys; Margarita Maid with Tequila; Razzle Dazzle; Santa's Chopsticks; Angela.

LITTLE, GEORGE A   ASCAP 1921
author
b St Louis, Mo, Nov 25, 1890; d New York, NY, June 2, 46. Educ: Christian Bros Col. Mem staff, music publ cos, Chicago & New York. *Songs:* Mother O' Mine; When I Was a Dreamer and You Were My Dream; Hawaiian Butterfly; Sweet Sugar Babe; Sweet Mama, Your Papa's Getting Mad; You're in Kentucky, Sure's You're Born; They Needed a Songbird in Heaven, So God Took Caruso Away; I'm Knee Deep in Daisies; So Tired.

LITTLE, (LITTLE) JACK   ASCAP 1928
composer, author, conductor
b London, Eng, May 28, 00; d Hollywood, Fla, Apr 9, 56. Came to US in youth. Educ: Univ Iowa (pre-med). Organized univ band. Toured US with orch, appearing in hotels, nightclubs & on radio. *Songs:* A Shanty in Old Shanty Town; Hold Me; Jealous; I Promise You; You're a Heavenly Thing.

LITTLE, RICHARD ANTHONY   ASCAP 1977
composer
b St Louis, Mo, Apr 6, 48. Writer, Gene Chandler's Publ Co. *Songs:* Get Yourself Together; Desperate for Your Affection; This Time; I Miss You; Music: La! La! I Love You.

LITTLETON, BILLY JOE
composer
b Oklahoma City, Okla, Aug 14, 35. Educ: Classen High Sch, Oklahoma City, grad, 53; Okla Baptist Univ, Shawnee, BA, 57; Univ Okla, MMusicEd, 59; studied voice with Eva Turner. Music minister: First Baptist Church, Crutcho, Okla, 51-53 & Atoka, Okla, 53-55; Crestwood Baptist Church, Oklahoma City, 55-60; Bethany Baptist Church, Kansas City, Mo, 60-62; Olivet Baptist Church, Oklahoma City, 62-64; First Baptist Church, Borger, Tex, 64-66; Eastwood Baptist Church, Tulsa, Okla, 66- Had comp & arr performed in Africa, SAm, Japan, Korea, Taiwan, Switz, WGer & US. *Songs:* Reach Out; One Way; Love's a Word; Music: Come We That Love the Lord; Christ the Lord Is Risen Today; Come, Holy Spirit; Behold the Lamb of God; Christian Men Rejoice; Do You Love My Lord?; I Love Thee; I'm Troubled; Worthy Is the Lamb; The Master Hath Come; Alleluia! Alleluia!; Amazing Grace; Away in a Manger; I'm a Gonna Walk; Jesus Loves Me; Lord, Love; My Jesus, I Love Thee; Pleading Savior; Rise, Shine; See Now the Lamb of God; Surely He Hath Born Our Griefs; That's Enough for Me. *Instrumental Works:* Bells for Evangelism (handbell collection).

LIVINGSTON, ALAN WENDELL   ASCAP 1949
composer, author
b McDonald, Pa, Oct 15, 17. Educ: Univ Pa; Wharton Sch Finance & Commerce, BS(economics). Capitol Records, Inc, writer, producer, 46-50, vpres, A&R, 50-55, pres, chmn of bd, 60-68. Vpres TV programming, NBC, 55-60. Pres, Capitol Industries, Inc, 60-68. Pres, chmn of bd, Mediarts, Inc, 68-76. Pres, Atlanta Investment Co, Inc, 80- Chief Collabr: Billy May. *Songs:* I Taut I Taw a Puddy Tat; Bozo's Song; Sparky's Magic Piano; Woody Woodpecker's Picnic; Henery Hawk; Bozo at the Circus; Rusty in Orchestraville; Yosemite Sam; That's All Folks.

LIVINGSTON, HELEN   ASCAP 1965
composer, author
b New York, NY, Mar 26, 00. Educ: Bus Col. Chief Collabrs: Oscar Wach, Helene Wach. *Songs & Instrumental Works:* Kaddish Or a Prayer.

LIVINGSTON, HUGH SAMUEL, JR   ASCAP 1978
composer, author, music editor
b Maryville, Tenn, Aug 17, 45. Educ: Maryville Col, BA(music educ); Carson-Newman Col; Sch Church Music, Southern Sem, Louisville, Ky, grad study. Pub sch music teacher. Piano/organ demonstrator, McKeehan-Rose Music Co, Tenn. Church musician, 15 yrs. Now ed/comp, Lorenz Industs, Dayton, Ohio. *Songs:* When the Angels Carry Me Home; Sing, All Ye Folk of His Creation; Let Us Sing Praise Unto the Lord Forever; The Secret Place; Music: The Holly and the Ivy; Frankie and Johnny; The Morning Trumpet; Swing Low, Sweet Chariot; Stand By Me.

LIVINGSTON, JAY   ASCAP 1945
composer, author, pianist
b McDonald, Pa, Mar 28, 15. Educ: Univ Pa, BA; studied piano with Harry Archer, orch with Harl McDonald; Univ Calif, Los Angeles, studied orch, film scoring with Leith Stevens & Earle Hagen. Organized col dance band; played local nightclubs, proms & cruise ships. Pianist & vocal arr, radio. Wrote spec material for Olsen & Johnson, New York. Under contract to Paramount Pictures, 45-55; free lance for all major studios. Has written spec material for

TV & nightclub acts, also many film themes & title songs. Co-owner, publ co. Chief Collabrs: Ray Evans, Henry Mancini, Max Steiner, David Rose, Percy Faith, Neal Hefti, John Addison, Jimmy McHugh, Victor Young, Leith Stevens, Franz Waxman, Allan Sherman, Sammy Cahn. *Songs:* G'Bye Now; Wish Me a Rainbow; Buttons and Bows (Acad Award, 48); Mona Lisa (Acad Award, 50); Silver Bells; Almost in Your Arms (Acad nomination); As I Love You; Stuff Like That There; Never Let Me Go; All the Time; You're So Right for Me; Red Garters; I'll Always Love You; His Own Little Island; Through Children's Eyes; Warm and Willing; Song of Delilah; Wait Until Dark; Song of Surrender; Dreamsville; A Thousand Violins; Home Cookin'; Surprise; Marshmallow Moon; Havin' a Wonderful Wish; Brave Man; A Dime and a Dollar; Haven't Got a Worry; Just an Honest Mistake; Femininity; The Ruby and the Pearl; Streets of Laredo; The Cat and the Canary (Acad nomination); A Square in the Social Circle; My Love Loves Me; Angeltown; The Morning Music of Montmartre; Maybe September; In the Arms of Love; Bye-Bye; Song from "Harlow"; Films: To Each His Own; Tammy (Acad nomination); Dear Heart (Acad nomination); Golden Earrings; Never Too Late; Copper Canyon; The Man Who Knew Too Much; Houseboat; The Lemon Drop Kid; The Paleface; Sorrowful Jones; Tammy and the Bachelor; The Blue Angel; Son of Paleface; What Price Glory; TV Themes: To Rome With Love; Bonanza; Mister Ed; Mr Lucky. *Scores:* Film: My Friend Irma; Here Come the Girls; Here Comes the Groom; Red Garters; All Hands on Deck; Aaron Slick from Punkin Crick; The Stars Are Singing; Bway Shows: Oh Captain!; Let It Ride.

LIVINGSTON, JERRY ASCAP 1933
composer, author, pianist

b Denver, Colo. Educ: Univ Ariz, music major, studied piano, harmony, theory & comp. Played piano in Denver orchs during high sch; organized dance orch in col; first score comp for col musical. Pianist in dance orchs, New York, 32; organized orch, 40. Writer, many popular songs, also Bway revues, incl Hollywood Revels & Bright Lights of 44. Has written many theme songs for films & TV. Former pres, Songwriters Guild Am; mem, Dramatists Guild. Comp in religious & educ fields. Chief Collabrs: Mack David, Al Hoffman, Al G Neiburg, Marty Symes, Milton Drake, Paul Francis Webster, Leonard Adelson, Ralph Freed, Dan Shapiro, Mann Curtis, Mitchell Parish, Helen Deutsch, Bob Merrill, Allen Roberts, Sammy Gallop, Carolyn Leigh. *Songs:* Music: When It's Darkness on the Delta; Oh, Oh, What Do You Know About Love; It's Sunday Down in Caroline; Under a Blanket of Blue; Sixty Seconds Got Together; Just a Kid Named Joe; The Story of a Starry Night; Blue and Sentimental; Close to You; Chi-Baba Chi-Baba; I'd Give a Million Tomorrows (For Just One Yesterday); It's the Talk of the Town; I've Got an Invitation to a Dance; I'm a Big Girl Now; Fuzzy Wuzzy; What's the Good Word, Mr Bluebird?; I Had Too Much to Dream Last Night; Mairzy Doats; Rose of Santa Rosa; A Dream Is a Wish Your Heart Makes; So This Is Love; The Work Song; Bibbidy-Bobbidy-Boo (Acad Award nomination); The Sounds of Christmas; Wake the Town and Tell the People; The Unbirthday Song; Don't You Love Me Anymore?; Sweet Thursday; The Ballad of Jack and the Beanstalk; The March of the Ill-Assorted Guards; The Stowaway; The Twelfth of Never; My Last Night in Rome; Shenandoah Rose; Baby, Baby, Baby; Who Are We?; Young Emotions; What a Wonderful Life; Adios, Amigo; My Destiny; Sons of Westwood (Univ Calif, Los Angeles fight song); Films: Alice in Wonderland; Glory Alley; Follow That Dream; Sergeant Rutledge; Those Red Heads From Seattle; The Hanging Tree (Acad Award nomination); Guns of the Timberland; For Those Who Think Young; The Ballad of Cat Ballou (Acad Award nomination); TV title songs: Hawaiian Eye; Surfside 6; Lawman; Broncho; Bourbon Street Beat; The Roaring Twenties; The Bugs Bunny Theme (This Is It); Casper, The Friendly Ghost; Dreams Are Made for Children; The Alaskans; 77 Sunset Strip; Room for One More. *Songs & Instrumental Works:* Young Man of Manhattan. *Scores:* Bway Show: Molly (musical); TV: Jack and the Beanstalk; Shirley Temple Storybook; Jackie Gleason; Danny Kaye; Films: Cinderella; At War With the Army; Sailor Beware; Jumping Jacks; The Stooge; Scared Stiff. *Albums:* A World of Miracles; A Man Named Moses; Hail Mary; The President.

LIVINGSTON, JOSEPH A (FUD) ASCAP 1946
composer, saxophonist, arranger

b Charleston, SC, Apr 10, 06; d New York, NY, Mar 25, 57. Educ: Citadel Col. Saxophonist & clarinetist in dance bands; arr for Paul Whiteman, 5 yrs; then Freddy Rich & Andre Kostelanetz. To Hollywood, scored films. *Songs & Instrumental Works:* I'm Through With Love; Lorraine; Au Reet; Without a Penny in Your Pocket; Any Old Time; Saxophone Solos: Feelin' No Pain; Imagination; Humpty Dumpty.

LIVINGSTON, STEPHEN SCOTT ASCAP 1975
composer

b Los Angeles, Calif, June 3, 50. Educ: Aviation High Sch, Manhattan Beach, dipl; El Camino Jr Col, 2 yrs; Long Beach State Col, music, 2 yrs. Studied piano from age 5 yrs with pvt teachers. Played many nightclubs, TV & radio shows. Started into TV & motion picture music editing at 18. Co-owner Damask Productions Inc (music editing serv). *Scores:* TV Underscore Cues: Charlie's Angels; Starsky and Hutch; S.W.A.T.; Family; Vega$; Mothers and Daughters; Shampoo.

LIVINGSTON, WILLIAM ASCAP 1935
composer, author, director

b Los Angeles, Calif, Jan 14, 11. Educ: High sch. Producer & dir, radio & TV. West coast representative, advert agency Warwick & Legler. Coordr, radio & TV for film co. Songwriter for films incl "Frankie and Johnny" & "Having a Wonderful Time." Chief Collabr: Victor Young. *Songs:* Having a Wonderful

Time; My First Impression of You; Get Rhythm in Your Feet; The Popcorn Man; The Lord Has Given Me a Song; If You Want My Heart; It's You I Adore; Friends.

LLOYD, ASHTON
See Coates, Carroll

LLOYD, GERALD JOSEPH ASCAP 1968
composer, music administrator, teacher

b Lebanon, Ohio, Sept 6, 38. Educ: Univ Cincinnati, Col Cons Music, BM, 60, MM, 62; Eastman Sch Music, PhD, 67, studied with Scott Huston, Bernard Rogers. Performances with Eastman-Rochester, Huston, Syracuse, Detroit, Comn-Kalamazoo symphonies & Contemporary Chamber Ens. Chamber performances, Univ Ill, Univ Cincinnati & others. Two Rockefeller Found sponsored performances. *Instrumental Works:* Three Sketches for Tuba and Piano; L'Evenement for Trumpet and Piano; Concertino for Piano and Orchestra.

LLOYD, JACK ASCAP 1955
composer, author, actor

b Duisburg, Ger, Dec 23, 22; d Los Angeles, Calif, May 21, 76. Moved to US, 39. Educ: Sch in Holland; Ohio Univ. Was actor in radio, New York & Hollywood; became dir. Served in USA Ski Troops, WW II. Moved to Hollywood, 51; writer for "Bob Crosby Show", TV, 3 yrs; "Giselle MacKenzie Show", "Red Skelton Show", since 58. Director. Chief Collabrs: David Rose, Ernest Gold, Alan Copeland, Victor Young, Hal Dickinson, Hoagy Carmichael, Al Pellegrini. *Songs:* You've Never Been in Love; Summer Kisses, Winter Tears; Love Is a Wonderful Thing; Candlelight Conversation; Wishing Well; The Silver Waltz; Darling, Darling, Darling; Two Kisses; Ring of Brass; The Little White Light; Warm and Tender; Don't Look Back; Two Strangers in the City; The Greatest Gift; On the Carousel; The Blues Make the Nights Too Long.

LLOYD, MICHAEL J ASCAP 1963
composer, author, record producer

b New York, NY, Nov 3, 48. Educ: Studied classical piano age 4-17; 5 yrs theory, harmony & orch; pvt instruction with Harold Johnson. Numerous Platinum & Gold albums & singles earned in US & abroad for work with a group of artists, incl Maureen McGovern, The Ballamy Bros, Shaun Cassidy, Lou Rawls, Debby Boone, Leif Garrett, The Osmonds & Pink Lady. Featured in Walt Disney's production "North Avenue Irregulars." Vpres in charge of A&R, MGM Records, 69-73. Grammy Award for production of "Natural Man," 70. Independent producer, 73-79; partner, Michael Lloyd Productions, 79- Chief Collabrs: Al Kasha, Joel Hirschhorn, Howie Greenfield, John D'Andrea. *Songs:* I Was Made for Dancin'; Kiss in the Dark; Is It Because of Love; The Umbrella Song; I Can Sing I Can Dance; Don't Play With the One Who Loves You; If I Said You Had A Beautiful Body, Would You Hold It Against Me?; Sugar Daddy; Music: Charlie I Love Your Wife; I Was Lookin' for Someone to Love; Lyrics: Something in Return. *Scores:* Film: Take This Job and Shove It; Far Out Space Nuts; Lost Saucer; Land of the Lost.

LLOYD, NORMAN ASCAP 1957
composer, teacher, conductor

b Pottsville, Pa, Nov 8, 09. Educ: Braun Sch Music, Pottsville, cert; NY Univ, BS, 32, MA, 36; piano study with Robert Braun & Abbey Whiteside, comp with Vincent Jones & Aaron Copland. Teacher, NY Univ, Sarah Lawrence Col, Juilliard Sch Music. Dean, Oberlin Col Cons Music. Dir arts & humanities, Rockefeller Found. Comp & cond dance scores, Am modern dancers, exp & doc film scores & "The Billy Rose Show," ABC-TV. Author, "The Golden Encyclopedia of Music"; co-author, "Creative Keyboard Musicianship", "The Complete Sightsinger", "The Fireside Book of Folk Songs" & "The American Heritage Songbook." Chief Collabr: Ruth Lloyd. *Instrumental Works:* A Walt Whitman Overture (band); Three Pieces for Violin and Piano; Sonata for Piano; Episodes for Piano; Rememories (wind symph); An American Sampler (chorus, wind symph). *Scores:* Ballet: La Malinche; Lament for Ignacio Sanchez Mejia.

LOBODA, SAMUEL R ASCAP 1956
composer, conductor

b Coy, Pa, May 21, 16; d Oakton, Va, June 13, 77. Educ: Ind State Teachers Col, BS & hon DLitt, 75; Army Music Sch, 43. Army Inf, WW II; exec officer & assoc bandmaster, USA Band, 46-64; organized The USA Chorus, 56, leader & commanding officer, USA Band, 64; exec officer, Army Music Sch. Pres, Am Bandmasters Asn, 65; promoted to Colonel, 70. Received special bronze statue of George Washington, Bd Trustees of Freedoms Found which reads: Exemplary patriot, soldier, distinguished composer and director. Mil decorations incl: Legion of Merit, Meritorius Service Medal & the Army Commendation Medal with oak leaf cluster. *Instrumental Works:* Your Army; Fan-Fare; The Monument and the Sword; Medal of Honor; Anti-Freeze; Presidential Procession; The Prince and Mermaid (harp); Procession to Delphi; Dharma; Marches: Broadcasters March; Newspaper Boys March; Band: For God and Country (Off Am Legion March); The Screaming Eagles (101st Airborne Div comn); The Honor Guard; The 101st Airborne March; Freedoms Foundation; Choral: Lift Up Your Heads; The Story of the Stranger. *Scores:* Christmas Opera: Night of the Miracle (Emmy Award, 64); Film: O'er the Ramparts We Watch (story of our Nat Anthem); Film Background: We're a Team; Retreat; Headquarters, USA.

LOBUONO, JOHN ANTHONY ASCAP 1963
composer, author

b Lancaster, Ohio, Feb 22, 30. Educ: Glendale High Sch, Calif; Univ Calif, Berkeley, BA, 50. Teacher's asst Eng literature, Univ Calif, Berkeley, 50-51; news reporter & feature writer, Eureka, Calif & St Louis, Mo; wire service correspondent, 54-60; advert copy writer, ad agencies, St Louis, 60-68; musical commercial producer for radio & TV incl 50 nat jingle productions, Pet Milk, Sheaffer Pen, Lion Oil Co, Bardenheier Wines, Falls City Beer & many others. Independent music consult to ad agencies; ad agency owner in Paducah, Ky, 68- Music publ & founder, Neverly Music Co, 69- Chief Collabrs: Beasley Smith, Frank "Pete" Thompson, Mark Dinning, Louis Nunley. *Songs:* Land of the Midnight Sun; Ev'rett the Friendly Evergreen; Music: Ev'rett's Tune; Lyrics: Everybody Wants Love; When's He Gonna' Wash His Feet; Warming Love of You.

LOCKHART, EUGENE (GENE) ASCAP 1925
composer, author, actor

b London, Ont, July 18, 1891; d Santa Monica, Calif, Mar 31, 57. Educ: De La Salle Inst, Can; Brompton Oratory Sch, London, Eng. US citizen, 39. Playwright; toured country in recital-revue with wife, 27-31. Instr, Dept Stage Technique, Juilliard, 32. To Hollywood, 34, appeared in many films incl, "Algiers"; "Going My Way"; "The House on 92nd Street." Stage appearances incl, "The Riviera Girl"; "Happily Ever After"; "Ah Wilderness"; "Death of a Salesman." *Songs:* The World Is Waiting for the Sunrise; In Your Wedding Gown; Love's Riddle; Moon Dream Shore; Road to Jericho; Mother of All; By Lo; Midsummer's Day.

LOCKHART, RONALD STUART ASCAP 1969
composer

b Pittsburgh, Pa, Apr 6, 46. Educ: Emerson Col; Berklee Sch Music; studied with John Mehegan. Musical asst to Mitch Leigh, 66. Producer, Columbia Record Club, 67-73. Comp for Herman Edel Assoc, commercials, 67-73. Pres & creative dir for Ron Lockhart Inc, 73- Chief Collabrs: Charles Harding, Hal Friedman, Richard Druz. *Songs & Instrumental Works:* We Want to Help You Do Things Right; Where's Merlin; Basic Things.

LOCKLAIR, DAN STEVEN ASCAP 1976
composer

b Charlotte, NC, Aug 7, 49. Educ: Mars Hill Col, NC, BM(cum laude); Sch Sacred Music, Union Theol Sem, New York, MSM; New Eng Cons Music, Boston, Mass; State Univ NY, Binghamton, studied with Ezra Laderman; Int Summer Sch, Univ Edinburgh; doctoral candidate, Eastman Sch Music, Rochester, NY, studied with Samuel Adler & Joseph Schwantner. Church musician, past 17 yrs, now at Binghamton's First Presby Church; col teacher, past 7 yrs, now part-time lectr music, Hartwick Col, Oneonta, NY. First works publ, 74; founder, Binghamton Music Series, "Abendmusiken," 77. Chief Collabr: Suzanne Locklair. *Songs:* In Praise of Easter (cantata); Anthems: Prayer of Supplication and Thanksgiving; Jubilate Deo; Grace. *Scores:* Opera: Good Tidings From the Holy Beast.

LOCKWOOD, LARRY PAUL ASCAP 1976
composer, author, conductor

b DuLuth, Minn, June 18, 43. Educ: Manhattan Sch Music, BS, 67, MM, 69; Cornell Univ, DMA, 73; studied comp with Mario Davidovsky, David Diamond & Robert Palmer; studied conducting with Karel Husa & Hugh Ross; studied theory with Ludmila Ulehla. Comp vocal & instrumental works; founded The New York String Ensemble, 77; had works performed in concert halls & on radio; also had works publ & recorded. Grants: NEA, 76; Ludwig Vogelstein Found; Zorn Found; Meet the Comp. *Songs & Instrumental Works:* Landscapes (voice, vibraphone, marimba); Epithalamia (five songs for voice, violin, piano); Four Psalms (tenor & baritone solos, SATB chorus, orch); Tifillot (Prayers) (voice, piano); Four Songs for Voice and Piano; Six Haiku (voice, flute, viola); Hanishamah Lach (The Soul Is Thine) (anthem, SATB, organ); several song cycles; Concerto for String Orchestra; Quartet for Strings; Serenade for Strings; Quartet for Two Pianos and Two Percussionists; Canzona (strings, piano & cymbals); Choral Partite (vibraphone-marimba); Duets for Two Percussionists; Simple Music (two treble instruments & piano); Ricercar (flute, piano); Trio 3 (ampl piano, electric harpsichord, perc); Symphony for Orchestra; Trio Variations (flute, clarinet, violin); Octet for Woodwinds; Divertimento for Orchestra.

LODICE, DON ASCAP 1956
composer, author

b Corona, NY, Oct 25, 19. Educ: Newtown High Sch; studied music with father, Bartolo Logiudice. Tenor saxophonist with orchs of Bunny Berrigan & Tommy Dorsey. Played woodwinds with MGM staff orch, Stan Kenton Neophonic Orch, Merve Griffen TV Show, Frank Sinatra TV, records & concerts. Chief Collabr: Matt Dennis. *Songs:* Lyrics: We Belong Together.

LOEB, DAVID ASCAP 1964
composer, teacher

b New York, NY, May 11, 39. Educ: Cornell Univ; Mannes Col Music, BS; Yale Univ Sch Music, MusM; Columbia Univ, studied with Peter Pindar Stearns, Aaron Copland, Wolfgang Fortner, Lutold Witoslawski, Quincy Porter, Francis Judd Cooke, Yehudi Wyner, Otto Luening. Extensive comp for instruments,

performed by leading soloists & groups in Japan, 78. Many comp for early instruments. Fac theory & comp, Mannes Col Music, Curtis Inst Music. *Songs: Music:* Three Hiroshima Songs (soprano, koto, piano). *Instrumental Works:* Concerto da Camera; Octet for Stings; Suite for Guitar; Concerto (8 winds, string orch); Jiuta (viola da gamba); Fantasia e Due Scherzi (2 viole da gamba); String Quartet No 4; String Quartet No 8; Tanigawa no Haru (20 string koto); Nocturnes and Meditations (perc); Concerto da Camera No 5 (perc); Dotaku Hankyo (shakuhachi, viola da gamba); Symphony (chamber orch Japanese instruments); Nachttaenze (viola da gamba, string orch); Ancient Dutch Landscapes (large orch); Three Chinese Legends (large orch).

LOEB, JOHN JACOB ASCAP 1932
composer, author

b Chicago, Ill, Feb 18, 10; d Woodmere, NY, Mar 2, 70. Educ: Woodmere Acad. Won USO Award entertaining in hospitals, WW II. Chief Collabrs: Carmen Lombardo, Paul Francis Webster, Edward Lane. *Songs:* Masquerade; Reflections in the Water; Boo Hoo; The Kid in the Three Cornered Pants; A Sailboat in the Moonlight; It's Never Too Late; It's Easier Said Than Done; Some Rainy Day; Rosie the Riveter; Sweetie Pie; Seems Like Old Times; Boulevard of Memories; Horses Don't Bet on People; On the Waterfall; Where Are You Gonna Be When the Moon Shines?; Our Little Ranch House; Get Out Those Old Records; How Long Has it Been?; A Thousand and One Nights; A Whale of a Story; Teeny Weeny Genie; Marry the One You Love; The Hero of All My Dreams; Paradise Island; The Coconut Wireless. *Instrumental Works:* Jazz Bolero. *Scores:* Stage: Arabian Nights; Paradise Island; Mardi Gras! (all Jones Beach, NY).

LOEB, STEVEN M ASCAP 1969
composer, author, publisher

b New York, NY, June 14, 51. Educ: Dewitt Clinton High Sch, Bronx; Univ Hartford. With AVCO Embassy Records, 69-; played with Ten Wheel Drive, 70. Founded Anacrusis Music/Bandora Music, 71, Fire Sign Ltd & finally the Big Apple Recording Studios. Chief Collabrs: Billy Arnell, J Gordon. *Songs:* Good Morning Captain; Sleepy Head; Second Chance; By Your Side. *Instrumental Works:* ABC-TV News.

LOEHNER-BEDA, FRITZ ASCAP 1946
author

b Wildenschwerd, Czech, June 24, 1883; d Auschwitz (concentration camp), Poland, Oct, 42. Educ: Univ Vienna (law). Wrote poems in newspapers & books. After WW I, staff writer, music publ co. Joined AKM (Austrian Performing Right Soc), 24, vpres, 32-38. Chief Collabrs: Franz Lehar, Paul Abraham; Alfred Gruenwald (co-lyricist). *Songs:* Drunt' in der Lobau; Ich Hab' Mein Herz in Heidelberg Verloren; O Donna Klara; Valenzia; Sonja; O Katherina; Dein Ist Mein Ganzes Herz (Yours Is My Heart Alone); Oh, Maiden, My Maiden (O Maedchen, Mein Maedchen); Schoen Ist Die Welt; Meine Lippen Sie Kussen So Heiss; Blume Von Hawaii; Lyrics: Theo Wir Fahren Nach Lodz; (Das) Alte Lied; Du Schwarzer Zigeuner.

LOES, HARRY DIXON ASCAP 1955
composer, author, singer

b Kalamazoo, Mich, Oct 20, 1892; d Chicago, Ill, Feb 9, 65. Educ: Moody Bible Inst; Am Cons, Chicago Musical Col; Okla Baptist Univ. Toured US & Can as gospel singer. Minister educ & music, 2 churches, Okla, 12 yrs. Instr music, Moody Bible Inst, 26 yrs. Joined staff, Rodeheaver Music, 60. Author: "A Church-Wide Music Program." Chief Collabr: George Schuler. *Songs:* Gospel: Blessed Redeemer; Love Found a Way; Jesus Won My Heart; Everybody Ought to Love Jesus; Hallelujah! I'm Saved; Every Moment of the Day; Sing Along; All Things in Jesus; Song Books: Gospel Choir Medleys; Let Youth Sing; Sing, Boys and Girls (2 vols); Singable Songs for Children.

LOESSER, FRANK ASCAP 1934
composer, author, publisher

b New York, NY, June 29, 10; d New York, July 28, 69. Educ: Townsend Harris Hall; City Col New York. Wrote songs for col shows. Newspaper reporter; pianist; singer; caricaturist in vaudeville act. Ed, trade newspaper. Wrote songs for Army shows, USA, WW II. Chief Collabrs: Burton Lane, Hoagy Carmichael, Jimmy McHugh, Jule Styne, Victor Schertzinger, Arthur Schwartz. *Songs:* The Moon of Manakoora; I Fall in Love With You Every Day; Moments Like This; I Go for That; Says My Heart; Small Fry; Heart and Soul; Two Sleepy People; The Lady's in Love With You; Strange Enchantment; Hey, Good Lookin'; See What the Boys in the Backroom Will Have; You've Got That Look; Little Joe; I've Been in Love Before; My, My; Say It; I Hear Music; Dolores; White Blossoms of Tah-ni; I Said No; I Don't Want to Walk Without You; Sand In My Shoes; Kiss the Boys Goodbye; I'll Never Let a Day Pass By; Jingle Jangle Jingle; Praise the Lord and Pass the Ammunition; A Touch of Texas; Can't Get Out of This Mood; Love Isn't Born; They're Either Too Young or Too Old; How Sweet You Are; The Dreamer; In My Arms; What Do You Do in the Infantry; Murder, He Says; Let's Get Lost; Leave Us Face it, We're in Love; First Class Private Mary Brown; Spring Will Be A Little Late This Year; The Ballad of Rodger Young; Rumble Rumble Rumble; Poppa, Don't Preach to Me; I Wish I Didn't Love You So; Tallahassee; What Are You Doing New Year's Eve?; That Feathery Feeling; On a Slow Boat to China; My Darling, My Darling; Make a Miracle; Lovelier Than Ever; Once in Love With Amy; Baby, It's Cold Outside (Adac Award, 49); I'll Know; A Bushel and a Peck; If I Were a Bell;

I've Never Been in Love Before; My Time of Day; Luck Be a Lady; No Two People; Thumbelina; Inchworm; Anywhere I Wander; A Woman in Love; The Most Happy Fella; Big 'D'; Joey Joey Joey; Warm All Over; Standing on the Corner; Summertime Love; Faraway Boy; I Believe in You; The Company Way; Brotherhood of Man. *Scores:* Films: College Swing; Destry Rides Again; Seven Sinners; Buck Benny Rides Again; Kiss the Boys Goodbye; Seven Days Leave; Thank Your Lucky Stars; Happy-Go-Lucky; The Perils of Pauline; Variety Girl; Let's Dance; Hans Christian Andersen; Bway stage: Where's Charley?; Guys and Dolls (NY Drama Critics, Tony Awards, 51); The Most Happy Fella (also librettist; NY Drama Critics Award, 57); Greenwillow (also co-librettist); How to Succeed in Business Without Really Trying (Pulitzer Prize; NY Drama Critics, Grammy Awards, 62).

LOEWE, FREDERICK   ASCAP 1941
composer
b Berlin, Ger, June 10, 01. Educ: NY Univ, Hon Doctorate; Redlands Univ, Hon Doctorate; studied music with Ferruccio Busoni, Eugene D'Albert, N Reznicek. Piano recital, Carnegie Hall, 42. Awarded Hollander Medal, Berlin. Co-producer, "Camelot." Chief Collabr: Alan Jay Lerner. *Songs:* A Waltz Was Born in Vienna; A Jug of Wine; The Heather on the Hill; Almost Like Being in Love; There But for You Go I; Come to Me, Bend to Me; I Talk to the Trees; They Call the Wind Maria; I Still See Elisa; Another Autumn; Wouldn't it Be Loverly; I Could Have Danced All Night; The Rain in Spain; With a Little Bit of Luck; I've Grown Accustomed to Her Face; Get Me to the Church on Time; On the Street Where You Live; Gigi (Acad Award, 58); The Night They Invented Champagne; I Remember It Well; Thank Heaven for Little Girls; I'm Glad I'm Not Young Anymore; If Ever I Should Leave You; Camelot; How to Handle a Woman; Follow Me. *Scores:* Film/TV: My Fair Lady (NY Drama Critics Tony Awards, 47); Camelot; Gigi (Acad Award, 58); Brigadoon; Paint Your Wagon; Day Before Spring (NY Drama Critics Award, 47).

LOEWY, BENJAMIN WILFRED   ASCAP 1975
composer, author, singer
b New York, NY, Dec 14, 15. Educ: Vocal training with Emilio Roxas, New York. Began singing career at a very early age; became radio & stage star. At age 17 sang over the principal radio networks, Nat Broadcasting Co, coast to coast & Can, & Mutual Broadcasting Co. As soloist has performed leading roles in many major musical productions; as a leading tenor toured the country in musical comedy & plays with Schubert Co & performed in many of the famous operettas with Victor Light Opera Co on tour. Played leading roles in "New Moon", "Student Prince", "Showboat", "Boy Meets Girl" (also directed), "Merry Widow" & many others. Performed in "Hiawatha," 35, also performed in grand opera, Manhattan Opera House, New York Hippodrome & New York Civic Opera Co, late 30's & early 40's. Gave concert performances, Carnegie Hall. Mem, Nat Opera Asn, 43, 44 & 45. Wrote several musicals & produced own works to stunning revues. Dir "Marriage Proposal"; produced & dir own musical comedies "Gypsy Fantasia", "America Let's Sing", "Sweet Music" & original operetta "Princess Yvette." Produced wide variety of phonograph records. Was the first to introduce Columbia's long-playing records, 48; also first to produce & release stereo albums, 57. Artist, dir, producer, Columbia, Paramount, Hollywood, Hallmark, Variety, Heritage, Societe De Musique D'or & Top 18 Hits. Comp of popular songs, innumerable religious & liturgical selections; has written musical arr for many performers. Author "Tone Placement for the Professional Singer." Voice teacher. *Songs:* If I Should Ever Lose You; Oh God of Love and Goodness; Messe Sollennelle (Gounod, adaptation & transl); Lyrics, English Version: The Nock, Opus 129 No 2; Tom the Rhymer, Opus 135; Blossoming Angel, Opus 143.

LOFGREN, NILS
pianist, guitarist
Born of Swedish/Italian parentage; grew up in Chicago, Maryland & DC. As a teenager he played in a succession of bands before forming group Grin. Other groups incl Crazy Horse. *Albums:* Grin; 1 Plus 1; All Out; Gone Crazy; Nils Lofgren; Cry Tough; Back It Up!!; I Came to Dance.

LOGAN, FREDERICK KNIGHT   ASCAP 1917
composer, conductor
b Oskaloosa, Iowa, Oct 15, 1871; d June 11, 28. Educ: Pvt music study. Music dir, theatre cos. Chief Collabr: Virginia Logan (mother); others, James Shannon, Jesse Glick. *Songs:* Over the Hills; In Fancy's Bower; Fallen Leaf; Rose of My Heart; Oh, Vision Fair; Thru the Night; A Song for You and Me; Moonlight Waltz; Blue Rose Waltz; Missouri Waltz; Pale Moon; Choral: Songs of Cupid.

LOGAN, VIRGINIA KNIGHT   ASCAP 1922
composer, author
b Washington County, Pa, May 23, 1850; d Oskaloosa, Iowa, Nov 27, 40. Chief Collabr: Frederick Logan (son). *Songs & Instrumental Works:* Over the Hills; In Fancy's Bower; Fallen Leaf; Rose of My Heart; Oh, Vision Fair; Thru the Night; A Song for You and Me; Moonlight Waltz; Choral: Songs of Cupid.

LOGGINS, DAVID A   ASCAP 1971
composer, singer
b Mountain City, Tenn, Nov 10, 47. Educ: Va High Sch, Bristol, Va, grad, 65; E Tenn State Univ. To Nashville, songwriter, 70-; recording artist, 72- Comp, songs for var artists & performer of original works. *Songs:* Pieces of April; You've Got Me to Hold On To; The Fool In Me; Sunset Woman; Goodbye

Eyes; Please Come to Boston; One Way Ticket to Paradise. *Albums:* Country Suite; David Loggins Album; One Way Ticket to Paradise; Please Come to Boston.

LOGGINS, KENNETH CLARKE
singer, songwriter
b Everett, Wash, Jan 7, 47. Educ: Pasadena City Col. Mem groups, Second Helping, Loggins and Messina & Electric Prunes. Recording artist, Columbia Records. Songwriter, ABC/Wingate Music Publ Co. Hon chmn, Los Angeles County March of Dimes. Rec'd Rock N Roll Sports Classic Gold Medal. Mem, Nat Asn Recording Arts & Sci.

LOKE, MELE
See Roes, Carol Lasater

LOMAN, JULES   ASCAP 1934
author
b Elizabeth, NJ, June 29, 10; d New York, NY, Oct 19, 57. Educ: George Washington High Sch. Was film co exec. *Songs:* All Over a Cup of Coffee; It Doesn't Cost a Thing to Dream; The Love in My Life; The Tea Leaves Say Goodbye; With a Dollar in My Pocket; Goodbye Sue; Lyrics: Mambo in the Moonlight; Christmas Alphabet.

LOMBARDO, ADELE J   ASCAP 1974
author
b Elizabeth, NJ, Jan 18, 34. Educ: Jersey City Med Ctr, RN, 54; Seton Hall Univ, BSN, 60. Writer. Chief Collabr: Comp, Mario Lombardo. *Instrumental Works:* Drakestail.

LOMBARDO, ANTHONY M   ASCAP 1962
composer, author, musician
b Anita, Pa, May 29, 05. Educ: Col. Formerly with own group. Appeared in films. Musician with orch incl TV prog "Dick Powell Theatre," 2 yrs, Bob McGrew & var hotels. Chief Collabr: Karleen Carley. *Songs & Instrumental Works:* Beson Perdidos; Keep This in Mind; Penn Polka.

LOMBARDO, CARMEN   ASCAP 1929
composer, author, singer
b London, Ont, July 16, 03; d North Miami, Fla, Apr 17, 71. Educ: Pub sch. Saxophonist & singer in orch cond by Guy Lombardo (brother). Appeared on radio, in hotels & films; made many records. Chief Collabrs: John Loeb, John Green, Gus Kahn, Charles Newman. *Songs:* Coquette; Sweethearts on Parade; Snuggled on Your Shoulder; Jungle Drums; Wake Up and Sing; Address Unknown; Powder Your Face With Sunshine; Return to Me; Boo Hoo; A Sailboat in the Moonlight; It's Never Too Late; It's Easier Said Than Done; Some Rainy Day; Seems Like Old Times; Where Are You Gonna Be When the Moon Shines?; Our Little Ranch House; Get Out Those Old Records; How Long Has It Been?; A Thousand and One Nights; A Whale of a Story; Teeny Weeny Genie; Marry the One You Love; The Hero of All My Dreams; Paradise Island; The Coconut Wireless. *Scores:* Stage: Arabian Nights; Paradise Island; Mardi Gras! (all Jones Beach, NY).

LOMBARDO, MARIO D   ASCAP 1959
composer, pianist, teacher
b Elizabeth, NJ, May 30, 31. Educ: Began study piano at age 9; Thomas Jefferson High Sch; Seton Hall Univ, BA, 53, MA, 56; Columbia Univ Grad Sch Music, studied piano, harmony, theory & conducting, 56. Asst prof Eng, Seton Hall Univ, 56-64. Staff comp, Shapiro-Bernstein Music Publ, 63; comp, Chappell Music Co, 76. Received grant award, NJ State Coun on the Arts. Mem: Am Fedn Musicians; Am Symph Orch League; Am Asn Univ Prof. *Songs:* Music: Roxanne; Symphony of Love; Does Your Heart Hurt a Little; My Heart Belongs to Karen. *Instrumental Works:* Rock'n Rhapsody; Variations in a Mod Mood; Revival; Symphonic Ode; Winter Frolic; Drakestail; A Citizen Song; America! The New Promised Land! *Scores:* Ballet: Ode, Blues and Revival; Bway show: Display a Little Style; It's Worth Your While!

LONDON, EDWIN   ASCAP 1971
composer
b Philadelphia, Pa, Mar 16, 29. Educ: Central High Sch, Philadelphia, 46; Oberlin Col Cons, BMus, 52; Univ Iowa, PhD, 60; comp study with Luigi Dallapiccola, P G Clapp, Phillip Bezanson, Darius Milhaud. Comp, 52-; mem, Orquesta Sinfonica de Venezuela, 57 (French horn) & Oscar Pettiford Orch, 57-58. Comp/arr, Radiotelevisione Italiana, Rome, Italy, 58. Mem fac, Smith Col, 60-68, cond, Smith-Amherst Orch & Amherst Community Opera; summers, mem fac, Tanglewood Berkshire Music Ctr, 64 & comp in residence, Cummington Sch for Arts, 66-68. Mem fac, Univ Ill, 68-78. Cond, Univ Contemporary Chamber Players. Founder/dir, The Ineluctable Modality & chmn, Comp-Theory Div. Prof music & chmn dept, Cleveland State Univ, 78- Chmn nat council, Am Soc Univ Comp, 77-81. Chief Collabr: Donald Justice. *Songs & Instrumental Works:* Portraits of Three Ladies (American); Brass Quintet; Day of Desolation (chorus); Death of Lincoln; Iron Hand (oratorio); Pressure Points; Woodwind Quintet; Psalm of These Days I (with women's voices); Psalms of These Days II (4 solo voices); Psalm of These Days III; Psalm of These Days IV (with tape); Psalm of These Days V (band & chorus); Viola

Sonatina; Three Symphonic Movements for Band; Paraleipsis for Orchestra; Praising Thy Worth (with women's voices); Tala Obtusities.

LONDON, JOE
See Darmanin, Joseph

LONDON, JULIE ASCAP 1958
composer, author, singer
b Santa Rosa, Calif. Singer, nightclubs & TV; recording artist. Appeared in films incl "The Great Man", "Saddle the Wind" & "Wonderful Country." *Songs:* Voice in the Mirror; The Freshman.

LONG, CANDACE LOWE ASCAP 1976
composer, author, singer
b Gainesville, Ga, Oct 3, 45. Educ: Converse Col, BA; Univ Ga. Sang & performed on col campuses, 70-75; top 40 DJ, 76-77; performer, 77-78; free-lance jingle writer & producer, Denver, Colo; also songwriter. *Songs:* Rejoice in Today; I Want to Come Home; I Never Get Tired of Hearing (Jesus Loves Me); Like a Gentle Breeze; To Me You're Like.

LONG, NEWELL HILLIS
composer, professor
b Markle, Ind, Feb, 12, 05. Educ: Ind Univ, AB(math), 28, MA(mus comp), 39, EdD(higher educ), 65; Northwestern Univ, 34; studied comp with Winfred B Merrill & Robert L Sanders. Played trombone prof, with Ray Williams Orch, France, 28-29. Directed sec sch bands & orchs, Ind, Mich & Ill, 10 yrs. Taught low brasses, conducting, arr & music educ courses, Ind Univ, 35-75; retired, conducted Bloomington Community Band. Pres, N Cent Div Music Educ Nat Conf, 49-57 & Nat Asn Col Wind & Perc Instrs, 56-57. Guest cond sch bands fest; judged musical contests. Music, comp, Huntington Hartford Found resident fel, 61 & 65. Chief Collabr: Eleanor R Long (wife). *Songs:* Journey Toward Freedom (chorus, orch). *Instrumental Works:* Concertino for Woodwind Quintet and Band; Art Show (band); 'Twas the Night Before Christmas (band, narrator); Lincoln Lyric Overture (band); Christmas Rhapsody (band, orch); Symphonic Variations on Yankee Doodle (band); Three Bears (band novelty, orch); Stephen Foster Rhapsody (band); American Rhapsody (band); Chaccone in D Minor (brass quartet); Undercurrent (bass clarinet solo); Rubank Elementary Method for Trombone; Newell Long Brass Sextet Album; Devotional Solos (wind instruments); Salute to Corell (band); Merry Street Musicians (string quartet, narrator); Raintree Rhapsody. *Songs & Instrumental Works:* The Music Hater (instant opera); Politics on Parade.

LONGO, ALFRED ASCAP 1954
author
b Bovino, Italy, Nov 18, 1896. Educ: Pvt study with Luigi Santorio, Vincenzo Cafaro, Italy. Solo trumpet player, band master, Italy. Asst band master, Olympic Park, Irvington, NJ, 27-65. Chief Collabrs: Joe Basile, Joe DeMasi. *Songs & Instrumental Works:* Chilean Tango; Big Time March; Appian Road Overture; Valse Triste; Egyptian Suite; Ave Maria; Yankee Doodle and Dixie (march); Fandango (Span dance); Pilgrimage to the Shrine (symphonic march); Madrilena Beguine; Lisbon Beguine; Andalusia Mazurka Di Concert (B flat clarinet); Aurora Borealis Fantasy; Stizzosetta Polka Brillante; Redemption (symphonic march); Napoletan Tarantella; Spanish Paso Doble; I Prima Albori Rimembranza.

LONSDALE, MARY MARTHA ASCAP 1971
composer, author, teacher
b Los Angeles, Calif, Aug 7, 28. Educ: Woodrow Wilson High Sch, Los Angeles; Univ Calif, Los Angeles & Santa Barbara; Calif State Univ, Northridge, BA, 65. Teacher & writer of children's music, over 15 yrs. *Songs:* I Pledge Allegiance; Listen to the Wind; Wheels Are Turning; Color Song; One and One.

LOOMIS, CLARENCE ASCAP 1942
composer, pianist, organist
b Sioux Falls, SDak, Dec 13, 1888; d Aptos, Calif, July 3, 65. Educ: Dakota Wesleyan Univ, BM; Am Cons, Chicago, MA & MusD; Royal Acad, Vienna, Austria; studied with Schreker & Godowsky; Kimball Gold Medal (piano); Adolf Weidig Gold Medal (comp); J K Lilly Found grant. Am Expeditionary Force, WW I. Mem fac, Am Cons, 14 & Chicago Musical Col, 29. Head, Theory Dept, Arthur Jordan Cons, 30-36. Head, Piano & Organ Dept & teacher theory, Highlands Univ, 45-55. Lectr, Jamestown Col, NDak, 55-56. Rec'd bronze plaque presented by Nat Music Coun, NMex Fedn Music Clubs & Exxon, unveiled during bicentennial at Highlands Univ. *Songs & Instrumental Works:* Operas: The Captive Woman; A Night in Avignon; The White Cloud; The Song of Solomon; David; Yolanda of Cypress (Bway; David Bispham Mem Medal); Fall of the House of Usher; The Passion Play; Gaelic Suite, No 1 & 2; Alabado al Amor (oratorio); Susanna Don't You Cry (Bway); 3 string quartets; Cantatas: Dream Fantasy; A Mother's Lullaby; Hymn to America; Song of the White Earth; Choral: White Birches in the Rain; Dancer of Dreams; Ebb and Flow; Rose Fantasia; The Missive; Thou, O Father; The Harp and the Willow; The Joyful Sound; Ballets: The Flapper and the Quarterback; Oak Street Beach.

LOPATNIKOFF, NIKOLAI ASCAP 1944
composer, educator
b Reval, Russia, Mar 16, 03; d Pittsburgh, Pa, Oct 7, 76. Came to US, 39, became citizen, 44. Educ: Cons of Petrograd; Technol Col (civil engr); Cons of Helsingfors; studied with Ernst Toch. Mem, Bd of Int Soc Contemporary Music, Berlin. Head, Theory & Comp Dept, Hartt Col Music & Westchester Cons; prof music, Carnegie Tech, 45. Awarded 2 Guggenheim fels. Elected to Nat Inst Arts & Letters, 63. *Instrumental Works:* 4 Symphonies; Introduction & Scherzo; Sinfonietta; Violin Concerto; Opus Sinfonicum (1st Prize, Cleveland Orch); Danton (opera); Concerto for 2 Pianos, Orch (Vronsky & Babin comn); Festival Overture (Pittsburgh Plate Glass Co comn); Divertimento for Orch; Music for Orch (Louisville Orch comn); 2 violin sonatas; 3 string quartets (No 2, Belaieff Prize); 2 sonatas for violin, piano; Variations & Epilogue for Cello, Piano; Variazioni Concertanti (Pittsburgh Bicentennial Asn comn); Vocalise for Mixed Chorus (Pittsburgh Int Music Fest comn); Concerto for Orch; Concerto for Wind Orch; Concertino for Orch; Fantasia Concertante (violin, piano); Melting Pot (ballet).

LOPEZ, JEFFREY ASCAP 1971
composer
b Teaneck, NJ, May 28, 55. Finalist, first annual Am Song Fest. Writer, Tuffy Music/Mel Tillis Enterprises. *Songs:* Pretty Lady; Come on Home; Apologies to Mom.

LOPEZ, VINCENT ASCAP 1941
composer, author, conductor
b Brooklyn, NY, Dec 30, 1898; d Miami Beach, Fla, Sept 20, 75. Educ: St Mary's Monastery; Kissick's Bus Co. Organized orch, appeared in vaudeville & dance halls. Began broadcasting, 21. Gave jazz concert, Metrop Opera House. Orch leader, Hotel St Regis, 8 yrs & Hotel Taft. Author "Lopez Speaking", "Numerology", "What's Ahead" & "Modern Piano Method Books 1, 2, 3 & 4." Gave concerts & lectures on numerology; also Trends of Music. US Treas Dept Citation (for selling US Bonds). Chief Collabrs: Joseph Cohen, Johnny Messner. *Songs & Instrumental Works:* Silver Head; Piano Echoes; Three Sisters; Sky Ride; Rockin' Chair Swing; Since Nellie Came Back from the City; Capricorn; Knock, Knock, Who's There?; What's Your Business?; Does a Duck Like Water?; Clarabel; The World Stands Still; Bell Bottom Trousers; The Chauffeur and the Debutante; Charlie Was a Sailor; Charlie Was a Boxer.

LO PRESTI, RONALD B ASCAP 1962
composer
b Williamstown, Mass, Oct 28, 33. Educ: Eastman Sch Music, BM, 55, MM, 56. Instr of theory, Tex Tech Col, 59-60. Ford Found Comp, Winfield, Kans Pub Schs, 60-62. Asst prof music, Ind State Col, Pa, 62-64. Asst prof theory-comp, Ariz State Univ, 64- *Instrumental Works:* The Masks (for orch); Suite for 8 Horns; Pageant Overture (band); Elegy for a Young American (band); Llano Estacado (The Staked Plain) (orch); Suite for 5 Trumpets; A Festive Music (band); Introduction, Chorale and Jubilee (band); Tundra (symphonic band); 1st Symphony (orch); 2nd Symphony (orch). *Scores:* Opera/Ballet: Scarecrow (cello orch, chorus, 3 solo dancers); TV: Southwestern Indian Artists (6 documentary series).

LORD, STEPHEN
See Loyacano, Stephen Jacob

LORD, WALTER ASCAP 1951
author
b Baltimore, Md, Oct 8, 17. Educ: Princeton Univ, BA, 39; Yale Univ, LLB, 46. Author non-fiction books, incl "A Night to Remember" & "Day of Infamy." Chief Collabr: Anton Karas. *Songs:* Lyrics: The Third Man Theme.

LOREN, RANDY
See DiLorenzo, Randy Paul

LORENTZON, VENDLA
See Shepard, Vendla Lorentzon

LORENZ, EDMUND SIMON ASCAP 1938
composer, publisher, educator
b North Lawrence, Ohio, July 13, 1854; d Dayton, Ohio, July 10, 42. Educ: Otterbein Col, BA, MA & MusD; Yale Divinity Sch, BD; Berlin & Leipzig Univs; LLD, Lebanon Valley Col. Pres, Lebanon Valley Col, 1887-88. Founder, Lorenz Publ Co. Author, "The Gospel Workers' Treasury"; "Getting Ready for a Revival"; "Practical Church Music"; "Practical Hymn Studies"; "The Singing Church." *Songs:* Sacred: Tell It to Jesus Alone; Joy Cometh in the Morning; The Name of Jesus Is So Sweet; Thou Thinkest, Lord, of Me; I Want My Life to Tell; The Angels' Song; The Cathedral Bell; I'm a Pilgrim. *Instrumental Works:* Cantatas: The Lord's Anointed; The Easter Eve Angel.

LORENZ, ELLEN JANE (ALLEN JAMES) ASCAP 1938
composer, author
b Dayton, Ohio, May 3, 07. Educ: Wellesley Col, BA, 29; studied with Nadia Boulanger, Paris, 31-32; Wittenberg Univ, MSM, 71; Union Grad Sch, PhD, 78. Music teacher, Akron West High Sch, 29-31; instr sacred music, United Theological Sem, 71- Ed, Lorenz Publ Co, 32-68. Cond, lectr & clinician. *Songs:*

Music Anthems: The Love of God; Stand in Awe; Ring a Bell of Joy; A Festal Alleluia; Cantatas: Christmas/Folk Style; Carols of Christmas; Christ Is Born; Handbell Music: Bell Jubilee; Carillon; Bell Largo; Bell Joyance; Bells Play Early American Folk Tunes; Handbells in the Sanctuary; Operettas: Up on Old Smoky; D Boone Killed a Bear; Johnny Appleseed.

LORENZO, ANGE   ASCAP 1940
composer, conductor, pianist
b West Branch, Mich, Feb 5, 1894; d Saginaw, Mich, Apr 22, 71. Educ: High sch. 28th Coast Artillery Band, WW I. Pianist for publ. Mem, singing team Jack & Jerry, WJR, Detroit; pianist in Jean Goldkette & Seymour Simons Orchs. Formed own orch, Tunesters; music dir, A B Marcus shows. Chief Collabrs: Richard Whiting, Raymond Egan, Gus Kahn, Joseph Alden. *Songs:* Sleepy Time Gal; Dreamy Dream Girl; Sweet Forget-Me-Not; I've Waited for This; Watching for Your Shadow.

LORING, RICHARD EDWIN   ASCAP 1955
composer, author, teacher
b Chicago, Ill, July 23, 27. Educ: Cincinnati Cons Col of Music; Am Cons of Music, Chicago; Univ Cincinnati; Univ Chicago. To Los Angeles, worked in production dept, NBC; in music dept, Paramount Pictures; voice coach & writer, Universal Pictures. Song & music writer for var theatre productions incl "Bonds for Israel Show", "I Must Go to a Quiet Place", "Great Scot", "A Big Kiss", "The Gym" & TV film, "I Am a Rainbow" & special, "The Freedom Spectacular." Teaching mem of fac, Am Operatic Lab, Westlake Col of Music & Calif Inst of Arts. Coauthor, "The Note" & "I Am a Rainbow." Chief Collabrs: Diane Lampert, Rod McKuen, Dorothy Wayne, Patrick Mitchell, Roy Stuart, Edward Heyman, Ned Washington, Leonard Adelson, Alan Hood. *Songs:* Music: Deacon Jones; Be Goody-Good-Good to Me; A Touch of Pink; Biddle-Dee-Dee; Summertime Lies; Very Warm; You Can't Win; The Hamill Camel; House on Haunted Hill; also songs in var other films incl "Toby Tyler", "The Snow Queen" & "Up Jumped the Devil."

LOTZENHISER, GEORGE WILLIAM
composer, conductor, professor
b Spokane, Wash, May 16, 23. Educ: NCentral High Sch, Spokane, Wash, dipl, 41; Eastern Wash Univ, Cheney, 41-42 & 46-47, BA(music, cum laude) & BAEd(social sci); Univ Mich, Ann Arbor, MMus, 48; Univ Ore, Eugene, EdD(music & higher educ), 56. Trombonist, NCentral High Sch, 37-41, Spokane Civic Symph, 41, Eastern Wash Univ, 41-42 & 46, Radio Sta KHQ, 46, Spokane Philh, 46-47, Univ Mich, 47-48, Tucson Symph Orch, Ariz, 48-60, Tucson Symphonietta, 50-60 & Spokane Symph, 60-62. USNR, 42-46 & 50-52, Rear Admiral, 77-; trombonist, USN Band, Pasco, Wash, 42-43 & dir, USN Band, Saipan & Tinian, 45; sr seminar admin, Indust Col Armed Forces. Asst to dir, NCentral High Sch Band, 46; instr brass, Sch District No 81, Spokane, 46-47; adjudicator throughout US, 46-; cond, Massed Bands & Orchs All State, Western US, 46-; dir, Am Legion Post No 9 Band, 46-47. Asst to dir & instr brass, Eastern Wash Univ, 46-47, pub rels asst, 46-47, head, Div Music, 60-61, prof music, 60-69, dir, High Sch Creative Arts Summer Series, 60-61 & Div Creative Arts, 61-69, chmn, Dept Music, 61-69, dean, Sch Fine Arts, 72- Teaching fel brass & asst drillmaster Marching Band, Univ Mich, Ann Arbor, 47-48. Asst band dir & drillmaster, Univ Ariz, 48-49 & 52-54, instr brass, 48-49, from asst prof to assoc prof music, 48-56, dir ROTC band, 48-55, cond univ symph orch, 49-50, cond symph brass choir, 52-60, chmn, Regional Music Fest, 54-56, asst to Dean Fine Arts & dir, High Sch Fine Arts Summer Session, 57-60. Teaching asst & grad admin asst to dean, Sch Music, Univ Ore, 55-56, supvr Pract Teachers in Music, 55-56. Pres, Chamber Commerce, Cheney, Wash, 62-63; chmn, Res & Develop Comt & deacon, Westminster Congregational Church, 64-68; chmn, Boy Scout Troop No 356, 65-70. Adminr & consult, High Sch Music Theory, Fed Project 6-285, 66-68; reader, Evaluation Music & Educ, Fed Projects, US Dept Health, Educ & Welfare, 70- Guest lectr, Conservatoria, The Netherlands, 69-70. Sr admin, Nat Security Seminar, Spokane, 73 & Missoula, Mont, 74. Mem staff, NCentral Asn Accreditation Comt, 57-60; chmn & mem staff, Nat Asn Schs Music Accreditations Comts, 60-; mem staff, NW Asn Accreditation Comts, 61- & Western Asn Schs & Cols Comts, 76- Mem, Grad Res Council, Western Div, Music Educr Nat Conference, 57-59 & Higher Educ Comt, NW Div, 61-64, chmn, Res Council, NW Div, 61-65, & Nat Comt Historical Ctr, 65, mem, Nat Music Educr Res Council, 65-70. Pres, Eastern Wash Music Educrs, 65-67; mem, Wash State Music Adv Comt, 67-; chmn, Wash State Music Guide Comt, 67-69. Mem exec comt, Alliance for Arts Educ, John F Kennedy Ctr & US Dept Health, Educ & Welfare, 72- Mem bd dirs, Tucson Symph Orch, 56-60, Tucson Fest Soc, 58-60, Spokane Philh Orch, 60-62, Greater Spokane Music & Allied Arts Fest, 60-64; mem bd dirs & pres, Tamarack Fest, 72-74; mem bd dirs, Spokane Riverfront Fest Arts, 76-, Arts Alliance Wash State, 76- & Allied Arts Wash State, 77- Author book, "Music-A Programmed Music Theory Text-200." *Instrumental Works:* Solos: Minuet Miniature D-E (clarinet); Poco Waltz II C-D (E flat alto saxophone); Accelerando Waltz C-D (E flat alto saxophone); Petit Valse (cornet or trumpet); Marion Waltz D-E (cornet or trumpet); Autumn Dream E (French horn); Petit Valse E (trombone or baritone); Desert Shadows E-D (trombone or baritone); Interlude D (trombone or baritone); Hornpipe D-E (tuba); Solitude D-E (tuba); Yankee Doodle Paradiddle (snare drum); She'll Be Flamin' Round the Mountain (snare drum); Turkey in the Snare (snare drum); Arkansas Flamsdiddle (snare drum); Parade of the Clicking Sticks (snare drum); Drummer's Nightmare (snare drum); Trumpet Trio: Junior Trumpeteers C-D

(with piano); The Happy Trumpeters; The Three Pyramids; Trumpet Quartet: March Militaire B-C; Marcia Grandioso B-C; Scherzetto D; Trombone Quartet: Folk Song Album C-D (with tuba); Rakoczy March A-B; Dance and Prayer; March of the Marionettes B-C; Trombumba; All Through the Night; Horn Quartet: The Call and Hunt; Morning Prayer; Brass Quartet: Canzona A-B; At an Old Trysting Place; Three Hungarian Folk Songs; Brass Sextet: Chorale and March C; Minuet; Rienzi Prayer and March; String Orch: Minuet in C (with piano).

LOUCHHEIM, STUART F   ASCAP 1952
composer
b Philadelphia, Pa, Jan 15, 1892; d Philadelphia, Jan 19, 71. Educ: Penn Charter Sch; Univ Pa, BS. Maj, USA, WW I. Vpres, later pres, S B & B W Fleisher, Inc. Treas, later pres, Motor Parts Co. Pres, Stuart F Louchheim Co. Chmn bd, Nuclear Electronics Corp. Dir, Acad Music Philadelphia, 52, later pres. Dir, Philadelphia Orch Asn. *Songs:* Mixed Emotions; You're After My Own Heart; What Can I Lose?.

LOUGHNANE, LEE DAVID
trumpeter
b Chicago, Ill, Oct 21, 46. Educ: DePaul Univ, Chicago, 64-66; Chicago Cons Music, 66-67. Mem musical groups, The Big Thing, 67 & Chicago, 67-; vpres, Chicago Music, Inc. Named Entertainer of Year, People's Choice Awards, 74; group named Best Instrumental Band, Playboy Mag, 71-75; Three Grammy Awards, 77. Mem: Am Fedn TV & Radio Artists; Nat Acad Recording Arts & Sci; Screen Actors Guild. Recording artist, Columbia Records.

LOUIS, GENE (GENE L QUACIARI)   ASCAP 1979
composer, author, producer
b Chester, Pa, Jan 31, 50. Educ: Salesianum & William Penn High Schs; Univ Del, BA, 71. Musician & singer, nightclubs & TV. Record & jingle producer. Tech supvr for theatre productions of "South Pacific", "Music Man", "Come Blow Your Horn", "Sound of Music" & "Jubilee on Ice," 79-80. Production crew, "Elixir of Love." Chief Collabrs: Stout, Benicky, Brower, DeLuke, Hawkins. *Songs:* Teddy Bears and Laughter; More Than a Fool; Music: Deliver Me; The Writer. *Instrumental Works:* Radio Spooky.

LOVE, LUTHER HALSEY (LUDY VAN LOVE)   ASCAP 1956
composer, violinist
b Millville, NJ, Feb 25, 04. Educ: Ithica Cons Music; studied violin with Caeser Thompson. Played in Keith Vaudeville, 15 yrs, Mastbaum Theater, Philadelphia & occasionally with Philadelphia Orch & many hotels. Played on Steel Pier, Atlantic City, NY. Teacher. Chief Collabrs: William A Dillon, Margaret Love, Henry Tobias. *Songs & Instrumental Works:* Hot Cakes and Sausage; I Love Everybody; Only Just a Little Puppet.

LOVE, RANDOLPH DEYO   ASCAP 1979
composer
b Sandusky, Ohio, June 15, 50. Educ: Ohio State Univ, BM, 72; Univ Cincinnati, MM, 74, DMA, 78. Fac assoc trumpet, Wright State Univ, 74-78. Grad asst theory, Univ Cincinnati, 75-77. Actg dir bands, Phoenix Col, 79. Coordr instrumental activity, Columbia Col. *Instrumental Works:* Theme and Variations for Trumpet and Piano; Ter Fato Obire for Wind Ensemble; Translucent Notions for Two Solo Flutes; Fantasy for Solo Violin; Three Impressions for Euphonium (trombone, perc); Quartet No 2 (clarinet, trumpet, piano, perc); Bicinium (Vis 1) for Horn and Euphonium.

LOVEDAY, CARROLL   ASCAP 1942
composer, pianist, author
b Salem, Mass, Sept 23, 1898; d New York; NY, June 19, 55. Educ: Harvard Univ; pvt music study. USN, WW I. Pianist in film theatres. Wrote spec material for vaudeville & nightclubs. Chief Collabrs: Helmy Kresa, Fred Hall. *Songs:* The Shrine of St Cecilia; That's My Desire; I Had Trouble With You Before; As Long As We Still Have Each Other; My Pipe, My Slippers and You; Here's a Rose for Your Birthday; One Little Glance; Zany Zoo; I'm So Alone; I'll Let That Be My Consolation; I Never Knew How Wonderful You Were.

LOVEJOY, ADDISON RAY   ASCAP 1968
composer, author, teacher
b Buffalo, NY, Apr 1, 16. Educ: Nichols Sch, Buffalo, NY; Lafayette High Sch, Buffalo, NY; Fredonia State Teachers Col, NY. Pvt teacher, 33- Owner-operator of Add Lovejoy Studios, Cincinnati. Partner-owner Municorn Music Co, Cincinnati. Prof perf churches, nightclubs, theaters, lounges, 31- Stadium organist for Cincinnati Reds baseball team, 73- Chief Collabr: Michael Stoner. *Songs:* The Baseball Song; The Johnny Bench Songbook; Some Songs for Boys; Music: Cheers for the Boys of Baseball; Soda Pop, Hot Dogs and Baseball; also over 30 additional publ works, incl Instruction Series for piano & organ & liturgical music.

LOVELACE, AUSTIN COLE   ASCAP 1973
composer
b Rutherfordton, NC, Mar 26, 19. Educ: High Point Col, AB, 39, MusD, 63; Sch Sacred Music, Union Theol Sem, NY, MSM, 41, DSM, 50. With Holy Trinity Episcopal & Univ Nebr, 41-42, Queens Col & Myers Park Presby, Charlotte, NC, 42-44; USN, 44-46; with First Presby, Greensboro, NC, 46-52,

First Methodist Church, Garrett Sem, Evanston, Ill, 52-62, Christ Methodist & Union Theol Sem, New York, 62-64, Montview Blvd Presby, Iliff Sem, Colo Woman's Col, Denver, 64-70, Lovers Lane Methodist, Dallas, Tex, 70-77. Wellshire Presby & Iliff Sem, Denver, 77- *Songs:* Music: God Is My Strong Salvation; What Shall I Render to My God; Job of Uz; Christmas Gloria; Go in Peace.

LOVELLO, TONY
See Lovullo, Anthony

LOVETT, COLLEEN ASCAP 1958
composer, author, singer
b Dallas, Tex, Nov 3, 46. Educ: North State Univ, BA; Berklee Sch Music. Performer & recording artist since age six. Toured US, Orient & Europe; arr; much TV work, nightclubs & Bway shows. *Songs:* Freckle-Face Soldier; Asleep in His Arms; To Tommy With Love; Wait for Me Sue; Love's Melody; Birds With Broken Wings.

LOVETT, GEORGE ASCAP 1975
composer, orchestrator, drummer
b Chicago, Ill, July 29, 32. Educ: Cleveland Inst of Music, studied perc with C S Wilcoxon, Cloyd Duff; Senior Dramatic Workshop; studied voice with Margaret Taylor. Began as jazz drummer; turned to serious composing, early 60's, comp of modern music for concert band. Cond of workshops & symposiums; works performed by Paul Lavalle at Interlochen Arts Acad & Am Concert Band. Actor, var films incl "Death Wish", "Taxi Driver", "Badge 373", "Madigan", "Super Cops" & "Prisoner of 2nd Avenue." Recipient, grant from Meet the Comp & NY State Coun on Arts, comns from var schs & cols. *Instrumental Works:* The Greatest City in the World, New York Symphonic Suite; A Joyful Noise (concert band); The Great American Overture for the Bicentennial; Stevenson: A Call to Greatness (in memory of Adlai E Stevenson); Project: Band Power, 1980.

LOVINGOOD, PENMAN, SR ASCAP 1963
composer, author, singer
b Marshall, Tex, Dec 25, 1895. Educ: Samuel Huston Col, Tex; Temple Univ; studied with William Happich at Symph Club, Philadelphia & with J Rosamond Johnson, New York, 4 yrs. Singing debut at Town Hall, New York, 25; had own orchestral works performed. Author of "Practical Method of Voice Culture." *Songs & Instrumental Works:* Song of the Free (Wanamaker Prize, 30); Saturday's Child (Christmas Carol); Christus Natus Est (Christmas Carol); Lament of the Passionate Pilgrims (chorus); The Romance of Noah (cantata); Supreme Deliver (cantata); San Juan Overture; Vitania Suite for Orchestra; Les Oisean (The Birds) Orchestra; Prelude in E flat (piano, orch); Mass in B flat (Latin & Eng text); Summertime for Piano; Ballade for Violin and Piano; Pavan for a Beautiful Lady (piano); A Legend for Violin and Piano; Collection of 12 Spirituals. *Scores:* Opera: Menelik of Abbysinnia (folk; Griffith Music Found Medals for singing & comp); A Tale of Acadie.

LOVULLO, ANTHONY (TONY LOVELLO) ASCAP 1961
composer, musician, accordionist
b Buffalo, NY, Dec 17, 32. Educ: Manual Arts High Sch, Los Angeles; Los Angeles City Col; Univ Southern Calif. Began career in 39; former mem musical trio, The Three Suns; mem, "The Arthur Godfrey Show," TV; had appearances on "Hee Haw," TV show; now retired from show bus & recordings, 75. Chief Collabrs: Darla Hood, Frank Ricchio, Lorraine Moodie. *Songs:* Music: Amore Mio; Your Tender Kiss; Dreamy Serenade; I've Never Cried Before; I Can't Find the Song; Love Song.

LOWDEN, ROBERT WILLIAM ASCAP 1970
composer, arranger, conductor
b Camden, NJ, July 23, 20. Educ: Temple Univ, music educ. Arr & played trombone, US Army band; arr, Claude Thornhill, Ruby Newman & Oscar Dumont; teacher instrumental music, pub schs, Camden, 10 yrs; chief arr, 58-68; free lance arr, comp, educ field, 68- Concert band, stage band, orch, small ens work, Warner Bros, Columbia Pictures Publ, Hal Leonard Publ, C L Barnhouse Co, Big 3 & others. *Songs & Instrumental Works:* Star Wars (marching band); Rocky (concert band); Happy Hobo (101 strings); My Valley (101 strings).

LOWDEN, RONALD DOUGLAS, JR ASCAP 1965
composer, author
b Forrest Hills, Mass, Dec 8, 28. Educ: Univ Pa, 53-57, BArch, 57. Pianist with bands, combos & solo, nightclubs, recording studios, rehearsals & concerts, 46-; Radio Sta WKOX, 46-50. USA, 50-51. Song plugger, 51-53; comp & transc manuscripts, 51- Comp & auth musicals, Mask & Wig Club, Univ Pa & var dramatic orgns, Philadelphia area, 54- Winner, ASCAP Popular Awards Prog, 3 yrs. Chief Collabrs: Stephen De Baun, James Philip Struthers, Lemuel P Schofield III, William Link, Robert Levinson & Sol Parker. *Songs:* The Wild Wind; Music: Keep Your Dreams; Pocketful of Promises; All Alone.

LOWE, BERNARD ASCAP 1956
composer
b Philadelphia, Pa, Nov 22, 17. Educ: Studied piano & comp. Pianist, Meyer Davis Orch, Howard Lanin Orch & var nightclubs. Cond, Paul Whiteman TV Orch, 7 yrs. Pres, founder & chief producer, Cameo-Parkway Records, Inc; writer of var comps; arr. Chief Collabr: Kal Mann. *Songs:* Music: Teddy Bear;

Butterfly; Teenage Prayer; Wild One; We Got Love; South Street; I'll Make You Mine; Please Let It Be Me; I Love to Twist; Twenty Miles; Remember You're Mine; Swingin' School; Good Time Baby.

LOWE, MUNDELL ASCAP 1956
composer, guitarist
b Laurel, Miss, Apr 21, 22. Educ: High Sch; pvt study in orch & comp with var teachers, incl Hall Overton, Water Piston, Marion Evans & Ernest Kanitz. Started as a country guitar player; played with small groups, New Orleans, at age 13; mem, Pee Wee King Orch for "Grand Old Opry," radio. With touring bands, WW II, USA. Guitarist in bands & orchs, incl Ray McKinley, Dave Martin, Benny Goodman, Sauter-Finegan. Mem, NBC staff, 50-58; comp, Columbia Pictures. Actor & guitarist, off-Bway plays. Led own quartet. Has made many records. *Instrumental Works:* Guitar Suite; Night Line. *Scores:* TV: Love on a Rooftop; Hollywood TV Theater; Wild Wild West; FBI Special; Starsky and Hutch; Andy Griffith Specials; over 300 episodes of var TV series; Films: Everything You Always Wanted to Know About Sex; Billy Jack; Sidewinder One; Satan in High Heels.

LOWE, RUTH ASCAP 1939
composer, author
b Toronto, Ont, Aug 12, 14. Educ: Pub schs. Pianist with CBC radio & Ina Ray Hutton's all girl orch, 37-39. With music publ co, Chicago. Radio performer in Toronto. *Songs:* I'll Never Smile Again; Ode to an Alligator; Won't Somebody Please Write a Song; A Touch of Love; A Short, Short Story; Take Your Sins to the River; Music: Too Beautiful to Last; Lyrics: Put Your Dreams Away for Another Day.

LOWELL, EUGENE ASCAP 1965
composer, author, singer
b New York, NY, Apr 12, 07. Educ: Univ Rochester, BA, 28, Eastman Sch Music, BM, 31; Curtis Inst Music, BM, 35; teachers, Emilio de Gogorza, Fritz Reiner. Singer for operas & concerts. Cond, Longines Symphonette, Radio WOR. A&R vpres, Longines Symphonette. Chief Collabr: Sid Bass. *Songs:* Mexico a Go Go; Howdy Pardner.

LOWELL, JACK ASCAP 1974
composer, singer, guitarist
b Riverbank, Calif, Sept 19, 24. Educ: USAF Band, 1 1/2 yrs; studied voice technique with Glenn Raiks, 1 1/2 yrs. Began singing on "The Children's Hour," radio station KTRB, Modesto, Calif, 38-41. USA, 7 yrs. To Hollywood, joined trio "The Bel-Aires," 5 yrs. Began solo singing & acting. *Songs:* Take Time to Pray; Ben Marble; Music: Sundown.

LOWN, BERT ASCAP 1942
composer, conductor, producer
b White Plains, NY, June 6, 03; d Portland, Ore, Nov 20, 62. Educ: High sch. Salesman, sales exec, 21-26. Had own theatrical booking off, NY, 26-28. Led orch, NY Biltmore Hotel, 30's, also in hotels throughout US, 34-37; broadcast over radio. Toured SAm. Exec, WW II, Red Cross, Nat War Fund, USO, British War Relief, United China Relief. NY State Mgr, Comn for Economic Develop, 44-46. Vpres & sales mgr, Radio-TV Div, Muzak, 46-52; with CBS-TV, 52-62. Chief Collabrs: Harry Link, Chauncey Gray, Dorothy Dick, Fred Hamm, David Bennett, Theo Turros. *Songs:* Bye Bye Blues; You're the One I Care For; By My Side; Tired; I'm Disappointed in You; My Heart and I; Today and Tomorrow; Let Me Fill Your Day With Music.

LOWREY, NORMAN EUGENE ASCAP 1977
composer, author, teacher
b Midland, Mich, Jan 13, 44. Educ: Tex Christian Univ, BMus; Eastman Sch Music, MM, 70, PhD, 74; pvt comp study with Samuel Jones, 64-65. Comns: Saginaw Symph, Saginaw Community Theater, Midland Symph, Tex Christian Univ. Vis composer-in-residence, San Diego State Univ, 71-72. Prof humanities, Stephens Col, 72-76. Chmn, Music Dept, Drew Univ, 77- *Songs & Instrumental Works:* Breaking Open for Women's Chorus and Orchestra; A Child's Christmas in Wales for Narrator and Orchestra; Riff Ram (concert overture); Solitary Gestures for Solo Trumpet and Narrator.

LOY, S J
See Loyacano, Stephen Jacob

LOYACANO, STEPHEN JACOB (STEPHEN LORD, S J LOY) ASCAP 1973
composer, author
b New Orleans, La, Dec 14, 26. Educ: Holy Cross High Sch; Univs of Notre Dame, Tulane & Loyola of South; Pasadena Playhouse; BA, 51. Bandleader, arr & pianist, 43-49; nightclub performer, 49-54; TV writer, dir & producer, 54-57; TV writer/producer, "Johnny Ringo", "June Allyson Show", "Zane Grey Theatre" & "Death Valley Days," plus five taped syndicated series; wrote over 200 scripts for TV series & movies incl "McCloud", "Ironside", "Fantasy Island", "Bonanza" & "Virginian"; directed others; theatrical movies as author incl "From Hell to Eternity", "Beyond and Back", "Bermuda Triangle" & "House of Usher"; as playwright, incl "The Chinaberry Tree", "Love and Learn" & "Analog 7." *Songs:* Lonely Town; Marry Me. *Instrumental Works:*

Interludes At Twilight; Transcendency. *Scores:* Bway show: Autumn Fever; Opera/Ballet: Tonette.

LUBAN, FRANCIA　　　　　　　　　　　　ASCAP 1940
author
b Kiev, Russia, Dec 1, 14. *Songs:* Orticinas; On the Beach of Havana; Tango of Roses; Champagne Tango; Say Si Si; Gay Desperado; El Choclo; La Chaparrita; Altenitas.

LUBIN, ALLENE BERNE (ALLI)　　　　　　ASCAP 1973
composer, singer, music teacher
b Brooklyn, NY, Mar 26, 49. Educ: Gateway Sr High Sch, Monroeville, Pa; Duquesne Univ, studied voice; Smith Col, studied voice, 66-68; Barnard Col, BA, 70; studied with Dorothy Stahl. Singer, nightclubs in Southern Vt; produced "The Wizard of Oz," Derry Community Theater, 76; wrote original song for "Catch My Soul," feature film & also played an extra; mgr, West Bank Restaurant & Tavern, 76-77; recording artist; teacher of guitar, flute, piano, voice, comp & aerobic exercise & dance. Chief Collab: Chuck Harris. *Songs & Instrumental Works:* Hard of Hearing; Forgotten Hitchin Posts; Time on Our Side; Sweet Loving Man; All in This Together.

LUBIN, ERNEST　　　　　　　　　　　　ASCAP 1955
composer, pianist, teacher
b New York, NY, May 2, 16; d. Educ: Manhattan Sch Music (scholarship); Teachers Col, Columbia Univ, BS, MS; studied with Roger Sessions, Ernest Bloch & Darius Milhaud; won Bearns prize. Teacher, High Sch Performing Arts, New York. Arr. Mem, MacDowell Col. *Songs & Instrumental Works:* Songs of Innocence (Blake); Suite in the Olden Style (string orch); Wayfaring Stranger (fantasy for band); 3 Piano Pieces; Pavane for Flute, Strings; Harpsichord Suite (Purcell; transc). *Scores:* Bway stage: Sing Out, Sweet Land.

LUBOFF, NORMAN　　　　　　　　　　　ASCAP 1953
composer, conductor
b Chicago, Ill, May 14, 17. Educ: Chicago Univ; Central Col, BA; Am Cons, Chicago, with Leo Sowerby. In US Signal Corps, WW II. Teacher theory, Central Col. Singer, arr & coach for radio shows, Chicago; assoc with Lyn Murray, Ray Bloch & Al Goodman, NY. To Hollywood, 48 for "Railroad Hour," then with Warner Bros. Has led own choral group in concert & on records. Co-ed & arr "Songs of Man." Chief Collabs: Alan Bergman, Marilyn Bergman. *Songs:* Yellow Bird; Warm; It's Some Spring; How Come; Jole John; Paul Bunyon; Arr: Christmas Carols; Sweet and Low; All Through the Night; Go to Sleepy.

LUBOSHUTZ, PIERRE　　　　　　　　　　ASCAP 1960
composer, pianist
b Odessa, Russia, June 22, 1894; d. Mem piano team, Luboshutz & Nemenoff. *Songs:* In the Springtime; We Love and Dream. *Songs & Instrumental Works:* 7 Variations on Theme by Mozart; The Bat (themes from Die Fledermaus); Transc: Moussorgsky, Bach, Handel, Glinka, Gluck, Mendelssohn, Prokofieff, Weber, Shostakovich, Beethoven & Johann Strauss.

LUCAS, CARROLL W　　　　　　　　　　ASCAP 1947
composer, author, conductor
b Oakland, Calif, Apr 23, 09; d St Petersburg, Fla, July 10, 79. Educ: Peddie Sch, Hightstown, NJ. Arr for dance orchs incl Sammy Kaye, Art Mooney, Ozzie Nelson & Leo Reisman. Led own orch, 35-41. *Songs:* How Soon?; There's a Music Box on the Moon; Make Believe Cowboy; If You Were Mine; You Promised Me; Go, Dartmouth, Go; Give, Give, Give, Give Your Share (Community Chest Song); Island Music; I'll Ride Across the Purple Sage; Yippie-Ki-Aye. *Instrumental Works:* Dartmouth Suite. *Scores:* Stage: Spacecapade.

LUCAS, CHRISTOPHER NORMAN (NORMAN DAVIS) ASCAP 1955
composer, author, conductor
b Manchester, Eng, Sept 17, 12; d San Francisco, Calif, Dec 5, 70. Educ: San Francisco Cons. Music dir, radio sta. Led jazz group, played in hotels, resorts & ballrooms, then dance orch; wrote for singing groups incl Limeliters. A&R dir, Talent Records. *Songs:* Charlie the Midnight Marauder; Marvin; Whose Arms Are You Missing?; Tell Him, Tell Him; You Were My First Affair; Sugar Let's Dance Tonight; Merry Christmas I Love You.

LUCAS, GENE　　　　　　　　　　　　ASCAP 1953
composer, author
b Hungary, May 8, 1886; d. Educ: Univ Budapest (law); pvt music study. Comp & arr for theatre, films, radio & TV. *Songs & Instrumental Works:* Moments Enchanting; A Tragedy in Porcelain; A Norse Dance; How Can I Tell You?; Oh No—Not Much.

LUCAS, SHARALEE　　　　　　　　　　ASCAP 1975
composer, author, singer
b Ft Lauderdale, Fla, Aug 13, 49. Educ: Oral Roberts Univ; pvt violin lessons, 13 yrs, vocal lessons, 6 months. Singer, with group Spurrlows, Chrysler Road Show, 67-69, World Action Singers, Oral Roberts Univ, 69-70, Pat Boone Family Show, Las Vegas & Orient tour, 70 & TV prog "Stand Up and Cheer," 70-74. Recording vocally, commercials incl Clairol, Sanka, Ford, Chevrolet &

Copper Penny, 74-80. Recording artist. Author, bk "Always Becoming." Chief Collabrs: John Thompson, Ron Harris, Shane Keister. *Songs:* Feed My Sheep; You Make Me Feel Like a Woman; May Your Love Grow; Glory Forevermore; I'm Gonna Be Quiet; Portrait; In Answer to Your Cry; Lone Voice; Does the Rain Have a Father; Spring Song; Music: Last Night; Lyrics: Praise You Just the Same; Doesn't That Surprise You; Ain't No Way; The Christmas Reason. *Albums:* Jesus You Are My Friend; Daughter of Music; Sharalee; Finally Him, Finally Me.

LUCCIOLA, JOHN (JOHNNIE LUCE)　　　ASCAP 1964
composer, author
b Jersey City, NJ, May 28, 26. Educ: Seton Hall Univ; John Marshall Col, studied with Otto Cesana. Saxophonist with many orchs; led own band, USN, after WW II. Wrote background music, "Seeburg," Chicago, Ill, 63-68; 2 recordings, Danny Thomas Tape "Satin Strings." Chief Collabrs: Pat Noto, Joseph Darmanin. *Songs:* For Your Eyes Only; Nocturnal Mist; Ellen; Eva; Miracle of Love; El Vida; Chi Puo Dimenticar; A Taste of True Love; Portrait in Black; Marilyn's Dream; Ostinato; Maracaibo; Eileen; Lu-Ann; Barcelona; Margaret-Ann; Tierra Del Fuego; Farewell; South of Panama; Punta Mala; Moonrise; Desire; Gypsy Prelude; Madonna; Rapture.

LUCE, JOHNNIE
See Lucciola, John

LUCE, WILLIAM　　　　　　　　　　　　ASCAP 1961
author, playwright
b Portland, Ore, Oct 16, 31. Educ: Boston Univ; Univ Wash; Lewis & Clark Col; studied with Amparo Iturbi. Toured as singer with Gregg Smith Singers, Norman Luboff Choir. Sang with Roger Wagner Chorale. Author, "The Belle of Amherst," rec'd three Christopher Awards, Tony Award & Grammy Award for record album. Author play, "Currier Bell, Esquire," which won Peabody Award, 79. Author bk Bway musical, "Sayonara." Chief Collabs: Martin Broones, Clement Barker. *Songs:* Lyrics: Let No Walls Divide; Be Still and Know; The Prodigal Son; I Was a King at Jesus' Birth.

LUCIOTTI, BONITA L　　　　　　　　　ASCAP 1979
composer, teacher
b Lebanon, Pa, June 8, 43. Educ: Lebanon Valley Col Cons (scholarship, ages 7-18), studied with Isabella Sant Ambrogia, Steinway Hall (ages 11-13). Piano soloist local civic band, Perseverence Band, ages 9-11. Cocktail pianist on road for ACA, Milwaukee, Wis, 65-69. Church organist & choir dir, St John's UCC, Fredericksburg, 72- Teacher, Yamaha Electone Course group organ classes, piano & improvisation. *Songs & Instrumental Works:* Serenity (organ; sacred); Melodia Sacra (organ; sacred); Soul's Voice (organ; sacred); Jesus, He Died for Me (SATB anthem).

LUCONTO, FRANK X　　　　　　　　　　ASCAP 1959
composer, author, performer
b Allston, Mass, Mar 26, 31. Educ: Rindge Tech Sch, Cambridge, Mass. In Morning Radio Show, with bros Pete & Art, Boston, Mass, 49. In Special Serv, GI show in Korea, USA, 52-54. Mem, Lane Bros (also known as Luconto Bros), nat known singing group on TV, recordings & movies; recorded with RCA Victor, 57 & Tambourine Records, 69. Appeared in "Black Sunday," "I'm the Greatest" & "The Godmother." Nat & int tours with bros, appearing in clubs, concerts & conventions. Co-host, Luconto Bros, Cerebral Palsy Telethon, 78. Pres, Luconto Productions & FXL Sound Studios, Inc. Prof singer, entertainer, songwriter, actor & master of ceremonies. Mem: Am Guild of Variety Artists, Am Fedn of Musicians, Country Music Asn, Screen Actors Guild, Sales and Marketing Execs, Nat Asn of Record Manufacturers & Advert Fedn of Ft Lauderdale. *Songs:* You've Gotta Believe in America; Hialeah, Hialeah; Why Don't You Give Jesus a Try; Texas One More Time; Long Time.

LUDLOW, BENJAMIN, JR　　　　　　　　ASCAP 1957
composer, conductor, pianist
b Ardmore, Pa, Mar 27, 10. Educ: Swarthmore Col, BA. Leader, orch, cruise ships & hotels. Comp & arr, records, radio, TV & musical commercials. *Instrumental Works:* Christmas Fantasy; El Silbador.

LUDLUM, STUART D　　　　　　　　　　ASCAP 1956
author, director, producer
b Swarthmore, Pa, Apr 2, 07. Educ: Yale Univ. Former football coach, Univ Mex. Writer, newspaper; on staff, Buena Vista Distributing Co. Writer, musical commercials. Chief Collab: James MacDonald. *Songs:* Somebody's Gotta Lose; Let's Dance At Disneyland; Old Tuscara; Nouvel Amour.

LUDWIG, NORBERT　　　　　　　　　　ASCAP 1953
composer, accordionist, organist
b Luck, Russia, Dec 28, 02; d New York, NY, Oct 29, 60. Educ: Vienna Cons; Juilliard Sch Music. Organist, Rivoli, Roxy & Paramount Theatres, New York. Accordionist in hotels. Also taught music. *Songs & Instrumental Works:* Blue Scarecrow; Dancing Checkers; My One and Only Love.

LUDWIN, RICK ASCAP 1977
composer, author, producer
b Cleveland, Ohio, May 27, 48. Educ: Miami Univ, BA; Northwestern Univ, MA. Assoc producer, "Mike Douglas Show" & "Jerry Lewis Telethon"; producer, "The Bert Convy Show" & "America Alive"; TV writer, Bob Hope, "America 2Night." *Songs:* This Week With You.

LUKE, RAY EDWARD ASCAP 1961
composer, conductor, teacher
b Ft Worth, Tex, May 30, 28. Educ: Tex Christian Univ, BM, 49, MM, 50; Eastman Sch Music, PhD(theory & comp), 60, studied comp with Bernard Rogers. Univ teacher & cond, 51-63; prof instrumental music & cond univ band & orch, Oklahoma City Univ, 63-; music dir & cond, Oklahoma City Lyric Theater, 63-67; assoc cond, Oklahoma City Symph Orch, 68-73, music dir & cond, 73-74, principal guest cond, 74-78. Gold Medal & Premiere Prix, Queen Elizabeth of Belg Int Comp Competition, 69; First Prize, Rockefeller Found/New Eng Cons Am Opera Competition, 79. Chief Collabrs: Carveth Osterhaus, Wong May, Conrad Ludlow. *Instrumental Works:* Symphonies No 1, 2, 3 & 4; Compressions for Orchestra; Bassoon Compressions 2 for Orchestra; Orchestra and Concerto; Orchestra and Piano Concerto; Symphonic Dialogues for Violin, Oboe and Orchestra; String Quartet; Four Dialogues for Organ and Percussion; Suite for Orchestra; Second Suite for Orchestra; Incantation for Violoncello, Harp and Strings; Concert Overture-Summer Music; Trio for Flute, Clarinet and Piano; Septet for Winds and Strings; Symphonic Songs for Mezzo Soprano and Orchestra. *Scores:* Tapestry (ballet); Medea (opera); ten scores for Canadian TV.

LUNCEFORD, JAMES MELVIN ASCAP 1942
composer, conductor, saxophonist
b Fulton, Miss, June 6, 02; d Seaside, Ore, July 13, 47. Educ: Fisk Univ, BA; City Col New York. Taught in high sch, New York. Saxophonist & flutist in Fletcher Henderson & Wilbur Sweatman orchs. Formed own orch, 29; toured US & Europe. Made many records. *Songs & Instrumental Works:* Rhythm in My Nursery Rhymes; Rhythm Is Our Business (theme); Dream of You; Uptown Blues.

LUND, ALAN KEITH ASCAP 1978
composer, author
b Primghar, Iowa, Mar 8, 48. Educ: Iowa State Univ, BSME. Comp & author, assoc with regional touring artist. Recording artist, 75- *Songs:* You Can't Do That (To Me); Just in Time; Tobacco Road; I Love to Boogie.

LUND, EDDIE ASCAP 1952
composer, author, conductor
b Vancouver, Wash, Oct 12, 09; d Los Angeles, Calif, Dec 4, 73. Educ: High sch; studied piano with Alfred Cortot. Pianist in film theatre, also radio & nighclubs. Became partner in nightclub, Tahiti; organized orch with native players; record exec, did records under own label. *Songs:* Farewell (For Just Awhile); Tangi Tika; Tahitian Cowboy; Far Lands; E Piko; Na Te Moana; Oriori Cha Cha.

LUNDE, LAWSON (LONNY) ASCAP 1974
composer, entertainer, pianist
b Chicago, Ill, Nov 22, 35. Educ: Northwestern Univ, BA, 57, studied comp with Robert Delaney; Chicago Musical Col, studied comp with Vittorio Rieti. As child, gave piano recitals & soloed with Chicago Symph Orch. Mem panel, music & sports specialist, NBC radio & TV show "The Quiz Kids," 44-50. Chicago-based entertainer in subsequent yrs. *Songs:* Music: My Wonderful Mother. *Instrumental Works:* Sonata No 1 (saxophone & piano); Sonata No 1 (unaccompanied saxophone); Sonata (saxophone duo). *Songs & Instrumental Works:* Choral: Psalm 120; The Beatitudes.

LUNDIN, NILS O ASCAP 1972
composer, accordionist
b Gestrickland, Sweden, Oct 30, 21. Educ: Quincy Cons, Mass. Playing as soloist & dance orch accordionist, over 40 yrs, mostly Scand or Europ ethnic type music. *Songs:* Music: American Wooden Shoe Polka; Little Carols Vals; Darrin's Vals; Jularbo Polka; Gurka Hambo.

LUNDQUIST, MATTHEW NATHANAEL ASCAP 1942
composer, educator, conductor
b Chicago Lake, Minn, June 24, 1886; d Chisago City, Minn, Sept 28, 64. Educ: Augustana Col; Broadview Col, BA; Cobbs Col Music, BM; St Bonaventure Col, MA; studied with Percy Goetschius; Chicago Musical Col, MusD; Niagara Univ, PhD. Prof music, Taylor Univ, Susquehanna Univ, Muskingum Col, Gustavus Adolphus Col, Blue Mountain Col, Chicago Col Music, Hartwick Col, Salem Col, Niagara Univ & Concordia Teachers Col.

LUNSFORD, JAMES CAMILLE ASCAP 1970
composer, author, singer
b Waynesville, NC, Oct 12, 27; d Sept 13, 78. Educ: Lee Edwards High Sch. Fiddler, country music, radio, stage & TV. Served as entertainer, Spec Services of Armed Forces. With Roy Acuff's Smokey Mountain Boys; recording artist. Singer with Lunsfords. Stage performer, nightclubs & TV. *Songs:* Blue Ridge Mountains Turning Green; Streets of Gold; The Web of Time; I'm in a Jam, Jim;

Meet Me in Reno; Texas Lonesome; Music: Next Year Finally Came. *Instrumental Works:* Dixie Breakdown; Luns Waltz.

LUPBERGER, PAULINE ASCAP 1963
composer, author
b St James, Mo, Jan 15, 31. Educ: High sch. *Songs:* Violins Roses and Rainbows; Star of Gold; Chimes of Love; Hidden Violins; Whistlin' Red Bird's Love Call; Hidden Gold.

LUSSI, MARIE (MARI MITALE) ASCAP 1945
author
b Santa Clara Valley, Calif, Oct 4, 1892; d Kingston, NY, Sept 4, 68. Educ: Cathedral Col; Hunter Col. Writer, newspapers & mags. Chief Collabr: David Guion. *Songs:* Mary; Mam'selle Marie; Greatest Miracle of All; Little Pickaninny Kid; Love Is Lord of All; Li'l Black Rose; Resurrection; Life and Love; Compensation; In Galam; De Massus and de Missus.

LUSTBERG, ARTHUR (ARCH) ASCAP 1959
author
b New York, NY, July 5, 25. Mem fac, Speech & Drama Dept, Cath Univ, Washington, DC, 52-62, dir, musicals & operas for Music Sch. Dir spec proj, Chappell & Co, Inc, 66-70. Co-producer Bway musical, "Don't Bother Me, I Can't Cope" & off-Bway musical, "Tuscaloosa's Calling Me, But I'm Not Going." Dir-producer album, "Gallant Men" (Grammy Award). Producer album, "The Voice of the People." Chief Collabrs: Jean Anne Lustberg, John Cacavas.

LUSTBERG, JEAN ANNE ASCAP 1959
author, actress
b Portland, Ore, June 3, 27. Educ: Marymount Col Kans, BA(drama); Cath Univ Am, postgrad drama studies. Author/actress, Off Bway show, "A Political Party," 63; wrote script for record album, "The Voice of the People," narrated by Helen Hayes & E G Marshall for US Capitol Historical Soc. Author: "Angelica", "Theodosia", "Eliza" (trilogy subtitled, "The Torment of Aaron Burr"), "Willow Grove" (Gothic Novel of Year Award by West Coast Rev Bks) & "Valago Crest." Chief Collabrs: John Cacavas, Phil Ramone, William Graves, Guy Wood *Songs:* Claudia; Lyrics: The Citadel of Freedom. *Scores:* Musical Plays for Children: Aladdin; Gulliver; Libretto: The Juggler. *Albums:* Letters to a Black Boy; And Me, I'm Ed McMahon.

LUTCHER, NELLIE ROSE ASCAP 1948
composer, author, singer
b Lake Charles, La, Oct 15, 15. Educ: Rec'd early training in piano at Lake Charles. Moved to Los Angeles, 35; discovered by Dove Depteo of Capitol Records, 47. Pianist. *Songs:* Hurry on Down; He's a Real Gone Guy; The Pig Latin Song; You'd Better Watch Yourself, Bub; The Lake Charles Boogie.

LUTZ, ABBOT ASCAP 1964
author
b New York, NY, Aug 14, 17. Educ: Trinity Col of Music, London, Eng. Chief Collabr: James Timmens. *Songs & Instrumental Works:* A Child's Introduction to Musical Instruments.

LUTZ, MICHAEL GEORGE ASCAP 1969
composer, author
b Ann Arbor, Mich, June 15, 49. Educ: Eastern Mich Univ. Has been with band, Brownsville Station, 70's. Chief Collabrs: Cub Koda & Henry Weck. *Songs:* Smokin' in the Boys Room; Kings of the Party; Mama Don't Allow No Parkin'; They Call Me Rock'n'Roll; Martian Boogie; Waitin' for the Weekend.

LUX, LILLIAN SYLVIA (LILI AMBER, LILLIAN BURSTEIN) ASCAP 1975
composer, author, actress
b New York, NY, June 20, 18. Educ: Girls High Sch; Professional High Sch; New York Sch Music; City Col New York. Began as actress at age 6; started in Yiddish Art Theatre. Joined husband, Pesach Burstein, traveling worldwide with Yiddish Theatre. Wrote words & music to 7 operettas. Appeared in every Yiddish-speaking country. Chief Collabr: J Russel Robinson. *Songs:* Your Heart and Mine; Macanooda; The Chasidic Twist; The World Loves an Actress; Vie Bistu Gevein; Ich Hob Dich Lieb; Tel-Aviv; Vie Nemt Men Di Tzaitn Fin Amul; Der Chusen Iz Klein; A Nacht in Tiberius; Farvus Hob Ich Dich Nisht Bagegnt Frier; Out of Sight; Come to the Discoteque; Shpielt Kezmurim; Herbst (Autumn). *Scores:* The Rebitzin From Israel; My Mama the General.

LYALL, MAX DAIL ASCAP 1978
composer, arranger, pianist
b Mazie, Okla, Feb 14, 39. Educ: Okla Baptist Univ, BM; Univ Okla, MM; Peabody Cons Music, DMA(piano), studied with Leon Fleisher. Music arr & ed for Broadman Press & Baptist Sunday Sch Bd, Nashville, Tenn, 63-66; active in commercial/sacred recording bus, Nashville, 63- Mem fac, Music Dept, Belmont Col, Nashville, 66-74; fac mem, Church Music Dept, Golden Gate Baptist Theol Sem, Mill Valley, Calif, 74- Piano & harpsichord soloist, Nashville Symph Orch & Nashville Little Symph, 70's; frequent contributor to musical publ, Broadman Press & Tribune Music Co, Nashville. Singer & teacher. Chief

Collabrs: William J Reynolds, Buryl Red. *Songs & Instrumental Works:* Symphony of Song; Music From Way Back When; Favorite Hymns for the Piano.

LYDE, CECIL ORLANDO (CISCO)　　　ASCAP 1973
composer, author, singer
b Chicago, Ill, Sept 20, 48. Educ: Univ Southern Ill, studied music & communications; Santa Monica Col, studied radio & TV; Los Angeles Valley Col, studied music. First recording, Chess Records, 65. Recording artist, Capital Records, 73. Writer, United Artist & Mercury Records, 76. Producer, recorder & writer, Home Boy Music Co & Aladdin Records, 80. Chief Collabrs: Bruce Fisher, Rick Giles. *Songs:* Money's Funny, When Will I See You.

LYMAN, ABE　　　ASCAP 1929
composer, conductor, singer
b Chicago, Ill, Aug 4, 1897; d Beverly Hills, Calif, Oct 23, 57. Drummer in silent film theatres. Wrote theme music for early sound films. Led own dance orch, The Californians; toured country, playing in theatres, hotels, nightclubs & radio. Appeared in films; made many records. *Songs:* Mary Lou; After I Say I'm Sorry; Faithfully Yours; I Don't Want You to Cry Over Me; I Cried for You.

LYMAN, EDWARD PARSONS, JR　　　ASCAP 1968
composer, author, singer
b St Albans, NY, Mar 25, 32. Educ: Rutgers Univ, BS; Hunter Col, sociol; Adelphi Col, sociol; voice training, Neville Landor, Juilliard, Ladislaus Gamauf, Hollywood, Calif & Samuel Margolis, New York; John Brown Univ, DMus(hon). Children's radio broadcast, "Uncle Win's Children's Hour," WNEW, New York; children's TV prog, "Storytime," New York; radio & TV, Armed Forces, Bermuda, Panama, Canal Zone; Riverside County, Arabian Nights Musicals, 4 yrs. Recordings, RCA Victor, Word Records, Supreme Records, Zondervan Records, Hope Recordings & Forge Records. Rutgers Univ Glee Club & Univ Choir, Gold R Award. Pres, Buena Vista Missionary Asn & Shenandoah Bible Col. Ed, Noteworthy Mag; author musical meditations, "Singing Your Song" & "The Layman Leads." Chief Collabr: Fred Bock. *Songs:* All My Troubles; In a Silent World; God's Matchless Love; The Man of Steel; The Sounds Alive; I Have a Melody; I Have a Song to Sing; Once; Once I Had a Love; There Are Times; I'll Raise My Voice to Sing; They're All Gone; Escape Into Emptiness; The Clock Song; I Evermore Shall Sing; Drifting; Why, Oh, Why; A New Life for Me; The Shifting Sands; There Were Songs I Had Not Sung; Communion Service; Lyric: Poor Little Lost Lamb.

LYND, GENE
See Lindsay, Bryan Eugene

LYNN, GEORGE　　　ASCAP 1956
composer, choral conductor, organist
b Edwardsville, Pa, Oct 5, 15. Educ: Westminster Choir Col, BMus, 38, studied comp with Roy Harris, organ, Carl Weinrich, conducting, J F Williamson & Paul Boepple; Princeton Univ, MFA, 47, studied comp with Randall Thompson; LLD(hon), Harding Univ, 59. Organist, choir dir in churches, NJ, Calif, Pa, Colo. Prof, choral & voice, Univ Colo, Westminster Choir Col, Loretto Heights Col, Colo Sch of Mines. Visiting comp-in-residence at Univ NMex. Choral workshops throughout the country. Major works incl 3 symphonies, 2 operas, 4 string quartets, 2 overtures, over 100 songs, over 50 piano pieces, chamber music, 3 choral symphonies. Chief Collabrs: Donald Sutherland, Aileen Fisher. *Songs:* Music: Sing Unto the Lord; Clap Your Hands; There is a River; Psalm 150; O Magnify the Lord With Me; Lonesome Valley; I Want Jesus to Walk With Me; Let Us Break Bread Together; Gently Little Jesus. *Instrumental Works:* Gettysburg Address (chorus, baritone solo & symph orch).

LYNN, JOHNNY
See Birch, Peter

LYON, KATHERINE EDELMAN　　　ASCAP 1971
composer
b Kansas City, Mo, July 20, 15. Educ: Cath Parochial Sch; Cent High Sch; Kansas City Jr Col, assoc degree; Cons Music, Univ Mo, Kansas City, studied comp & arr. Accompanist for voice soloists & radio performances in 30's; background music for many philanthropic affairs. Mem, Diversifiers, group of Kansas City poets; mem, Kansas City Keramic Club. Chief Collabrs: Katherine Edelman (mother), Eugene Butler, David Smart. *Songs:* Music: Winds of Judea (2 arr SATB & male voices).

LYONS, DAN D
See Diasio, Daniel Joseph

LYONS, JOSEPH CALLAWAY (JODIE)　　　ASCAP 1975
composer, author, arranger
b Jacksonville, Fla, Jan 3, 30. Educ: Andrew Jackson High Sch; NTex State Univ, BM, 59; USAF Bandsman's Training Sch, Washington, DC. Touring instrumentalist, singer, arr & woodwind instr, NTex State Univ & Tex Woman's Univ, Denton. Comp, arr, orchestrator, cond, producer & singer, nightclubs, TV, radio, records & commercials, Dallas, Los Angeles & Can. Comp, arr & cond, films, records, radio & TV, Los Angeles. Pres, Score One Music, Hollywood. Mem: Am Fedn Musicians; Am Fedn TV & Radio Artists; Am Soc Music

Arrangers; Composers & Lyricists Guild of Am. *Songs:* If You Ever Need Somebody; Home At Last; Don't Mind the Years; The Last Time; Maybe You Could Find a Way. *Instrumental Works:* Radio themes: The Beach Boys: A California Saga; The Fleetwood Mac Story; Presenting the Eagles; The Electric Light Orchestra Story; Frankie Valli and the Four Seasons. *Scores:* Movies: Terror on the Hill; A Falling of Bells; Nagasaki and One Man's Return; The Search; Other Trumpets.

LYONS, RUTH　　　ASCAP 1957
composer, author, pianist
b Cincinnati, Ohio. Educ: Univ Cincinnati Cons of Music. Writer, musicals while in col. Pianist, organist, music librarian in radio, 29; music dir, radio station, 33, prog dir. Joined WLW-radio, 42; hostess of own show "50-50 Club" simulcast. *Songs:* The Ten Tunes of Christmas; Wasn't Summer Short?; Let's Light the Christmas Tree; This Is Christmas; Christmas Is a Birthday Time; Sing a Song (collection of original works).

LYTELL, JIMMY　　　ASCAP 1958
composer, conductor, clarinetist
b New York, NY, Dec 1, 04; d. Mem, original Dixieland Jazz Band, later toured with original Memphis Five. Cond & clarinetist in musicals & on radio. Music dir: NBC; MCA for "Coca Cola Show," 4 yrs; "Perry Presents," TV. *Songs:* A Blues Serenade; The Moon Is My Pillow; Restless; I Know Now.

M

MAASS, ARLENE FOURNIER (CHARLEE)　　　ASCAP 1978
author
b Thunder Bay, Ont, Apr 17, 40. Chief Collabr: Marilyn Berglas. *Songs:* Lyrics: Touching Me With Love.

MAASS, MARGARET HARTMANN　　　ASCAP 1966
composer, teacher, arranger
b Livingston, NJ. Educ: High sch; Juilliard Sch Music; NY Univ; studied with Alexander Raab, Henry Levine, James Bleecker & Raymound Burroughs. Piano class teacher, West Orange Pub Schs, NJ, 15 yrs; pvt teacher of piano, organ & harmony; accompanist, West Orange Symph & NJ Symph. Chief Collabr: Andrew J V Klein. *Songs & Instrumental Works:* Where the Mountains Meet the Moon; The Magic Pool; Music: A June to Remember.

MABLEY, EDWARD HOWE　　　ASCAP 1961
author, director
b Binghamton, NY, Mar 7, 06. Educ: Wayne Univ. Playwright, "Temper the Wind" & "Glad Tidings," on Bway; radio & TV scriptwriter, all networks; radio & TV dir, CBS & NBC. Chief Collabrs: Comp, Elie Siegmeister & Vera Brodsky Lawrence. *Songs:* Lyrics: The Plough and the Stars; Night of the Moonspell; The Mermaid in Lock No 7; I Have a Dream (cantata). *Songs & Instrumental Works:* Dick Whittington and His Cat (orch & narrator).

MACALUSO, LENNY　　　ASCAP 1973
composer, author
b Philadelphia, Pa, June 5, 47. With group, The Rockin' Horse, 5 yrs. Lead guitarist & bandleader with Tina Turner, 4 yrs. Chief Collabrs: Pat Somerson, Donna Weiss, Booker T Jones. *Songs:* Night Dancin'; Trust It All to Somebody; Down to the Wire; Love Explosion; Music Keeps Me Dancing; Love Do Me Right; You Got My Love; Mighty Good Love; Dancing to the Music; I Can Give You Love Power; Didn't I Give You Love; Love Can Bring You Down; Didn't I.

MACARTHUR, DANA BETH HAYES (DANA HAYES)　　　ASCAP 1979
composer, author, artist
b Lake Charles, La, Jan 7, 48. Educ: Harbor Fields High Sch, Greenlawn, NY; Wilson Technol Sch Beauty Culture, 67; NY Univ, Farmingdale, studied commercial & graphic arts. First song released, Soul Country & Blues/Cross Country Label, 79. Songwriter & artist, writer, screenplays. Writer & illusr, children's bk. Chief Collabrs: Greg Wohlegemuth, Tom Stanley. *Songs:* Poor Baby Lonely; Bedroom War; Motel Cowboy; Lyrics: One Man Away From Bein' Alone.

MACBOYLE, DARL　　　ASCAP 1925
author, singer
b Waverly, Iowa, Feb 12, 1880; d Glen Cove, NY, Sept 2, 42. Was circus acrobat; soldier in Arg army; vaudeville singer. Wrote spec material for own acts & others. Chief Collabr: Albert Von Tilzer. *Songs:* To Have, to Hold, to Love; Forever Is a Long, Long Time; Bring Back Those Wonderful Days; We Are With You, Tommy Atkins; Since Johnny Got His Gun; I Want a Daddy Like You; Texas Never Seemed So Far Away.

MACBRIDE, DAVID HUSTON   ASCAP 1972
composer
b Oakland, Calif, Oct 3, 51. Educ: Univ Calif, Berkeley; Hartt Col Music, BM, 73; Columbia Univ, MA, 76, DMA, 80; studied comp with Ed Diemente & Jack Beeson. Comp music for concert, theatre, dance & film. Arr, Bradley Publ & Warner Bros. Freelance pianist & violinist. *Songs & Instrumental Works:* Four Sonnets (chamber orch); Tantum Ergo (SAA, organ); Envelop (solo perc); Up in the Air (carillon); Poet in New York (countertenor, 2 lutes, 2 vielles).

MACCARTHY, HECTOR   ASCAP 1957
composer, author, pianist
b Toronto, Ont, May 17, 1888; d. Educ: Ottawa Col; Ottawa Cons; Juilliard Sch Music; studied voice with Dudley Buck. Accompanist & soloist, Metrop Opera tours; joint recitals with Orville Harrold, Caroline White, Craig Campbell & Louise Gunning; music supvr & asst dir music, NY Bd Educ; wrote music in educ field; educr.

MACDERMID, JAMES G   ASCAP 1922
composer, organist
b Utica, Ont, June 10, 1875; d New York, NY, Aug 16, 60. Became US citizen. Educ: Studied music with Belle Saunders, Alfred Williams & George Hamlin. Weekly organ concerts for many yrs. Accompanist to wife, Sibyl Sammis. *Songs:* My Love Is Like the Red Red Rose; Charity; If I Knew You and You Knew Me; Ninety-First Psalm; Arise, Shine for Thy Light Is Come; Behold What Manner of Love; Whither Shall I Go From Thy Spirit.

MACDONALD, BALLARD   ASCAP 1914
composer, author
b Portland, Ore, Oct 15, 1882; d Forest Hills, NY, Nov 17, 35. Educ: Princeton Univ; Sorbonne, Paris. Wrote spec material for vaudeville artists; wrote play "Battling Butler"; songs & spec material for motion pictures. Wrote songs for "George White Scandals of 1924"; "Ziegfeld's Midnight Frolic"; "Love Birds"; "Harry Carroll's Pickings"; "Le Mairs Affairs." Chief Collabrs: Harry Carroll, James Hanley, Con Conrad, Joseph Meyer, Sigmund Romberg, Albert Von Tilzer, Victor Herbert, Lewis Muir, Walter Donaldson, George Gershwin. *Songs:* Somebody Loves Me; Beautiful Ohio; Back Home in Indiana; Trail of the Lonesome Pine; Play That Barber Shop Chord; On the Mississippi; Bend Down Sister; Clap Hands, Here Comes Charlie; Parade of the Wooden Soldiers.

MACDONALD, JAMES LEE   ASCAP 1954
composer, author, pianist
b Jersey City, NJ, Mar 4, 21. Educ: NY Univ; Hartford Found fel. Bassist, Mendelssohn String Orch; pianist, hotels & ballrooms. Arr, films, radio & TV commercials. Owner, Royal Lion Restaurant. Dir & entertainment chmn, Roorag, Inc. Chief Collabrs: Jack Hoffman, Stuart Ludlum. *Songs:* We Love the Sunshine of Your Smile (Eisenhower campaign song); At a Sidewalk Penny Arcade; I Wanna Say Hello; It's So Laughable; Crocodile Tears; I'll Always Remember You; Gotta-Seeya Once More; Back in the Good Old Days.

MACDONALD, RUBY   ASCAP 1959
composer, author, actress
b Quincy, Mass. Educ: Prep sch; finishing sch. Former Conover model. Singer, Moonmaid, with Vaughn Monroe Orch. Actress, TV, radio, commercials, indust shows & summer stock. Recording artist; writer, musical commercials & column, Woman's World. Chief Collabr: Ruth Ogilvie, George Macdonald.

MACDONOUGH, GLEN   ASCAP 1914
author
b Brooklyn, NY, Nov 12, 1870; d Stamford, Conn, Mar 30, 24. Educ: The Gunnery & Manhattan Col. One of 9 founders, also charter mem & dir, ASCAP, 14-23. Chief Collabrs: Victor Herbert, John Philip Sousa, Raymond Hubbell, Joseph Meyer, A Baldwin Sloane, Cole Porter. *Songs:* I Can't Do the Sum; Go to Sleep, Slumber Deep; Absinthe Frappe; The Knot of Blue; Ask Her While the Band Is Playing; Rose of the World; My Firefly Lady; Forgive and Forget. *Scores:* Bway Stage & Librettos: Chris and the Wonderful Lamp; Babes in Toyland; It Happened in Nordland; Wonderland; The Midnight Sons; The Jolly Bachelors; The Summer Widowers; Eva; Queen of the Movies; Hitchy-Koo (17, 18 & 20); The Kiss Burglar; Librettist: The Hen Pecks; The Never Homes; The Count of Luxembourg.

MACDOWELL, EDWARD ALEXANDER   ASCAP 1937
composer, pianist, educator
b New York, NY, Dec 18, 1861; d New York, Jan 23, 08. Educ: Studied with Juan Buitrago, Paul Desvernine & Terese Carreno; Paris Cons with Marmontel & Savard; Frankfort Cons, with Carl Heymann & Joachim Raff; hon MusD, Princeton Univ & Univ Pa. Taught piano, Darmstadt Cons, Ger, 1881 & Frankfurt Univ, 1884. Returned to US, 1888. Am piano debut, Boston. Performed at Paris Exposition Am Concert, 1889. First piano recital, Boston, 1891. First head of music dept, Columbia Univ, 1896-1904; made col credits available for music classes in US. Cond, Mendelssohn Glee Club, 2 seasons. Charter mem, Am Acad Arts & Letters. MacDowell Col, Peterborough, NH, named in his honor. Biographies by Lawrence Gilman & Thomas Trapper. *Songs & Instrumental Works:* Orch: Hamlet and Ophelia; Lancelot and Elaine; Lamia; First Suite; Indian Suite; Romance (cello); also 2 piano concertos; Piano: Prelude and Fugue; Serenata; Forest Idyls; Marionettes; Sea Pieces; Fireside

Tales; New England Idyls; Moon Pictures; also 2 Modern Suites; 2 Fantastic Pieces; 6 Idyls After Goethe; 6 Poems After Heine; 12 Studies; 12 Virtuoso Studies; 4 Sonatas; Woodland Sketches (incl To a Wild Rose & To a Water Lily); 3 poems & songs & part-songs.

MACE, RAYMOND ARTHUR   ASCAP 1964
composer, author, teacher
b Salt Lake City, Utah, Sept 3, 13. Educ: Univ Utah; McCune Cons, studied piano with Mable Borg Jenkins, William Peterson, theory & piano with Dr Nathaniel Dett. With dance bands, 27- Arr, 30- Music dir, NBC, Salt Lake City, 42. Rehearsal pianist, 20th Century Fox, 45. Music supvr, MGM, 66. Cond, orchr. *Songs:* Always on My Mind; Cute Redhead; Not Comin' Home; Dreaming; And Love. *Instrumental Works:* Misty Monday Mood; Flamenco; Round on Every Side; Monday Suite; Symphony to Normandy '44; Cameos and Intaglios; Quartet in B minor; Impromptu in G; New York Pastorale. *Scores:* Film/TV: Daktari; Courtship of Eddie's Father.

MACELL, JERRY   ASCAP 1961
composer, author, singer
b Chicago, Ill, Aug 30, 1899. Educ: Crane Tech High Sch. Singer & harmonica player, vaudeville. *Songs:* Tattle Tale Moon; I Guarantee; I'm Dancing With Mazie Tonight; Welcome Arms.

MACFARLANE, WILL C   ASCAP 1945
composer, organist
b London, Eng, Oct 2, 1870; d North Conway, NH, May 12, 45. Educ: Pub schs; studied music with father, Duncan Macfarlane & S P Warren; hon MA & MusD, Bates Col. Debut as organist, Chickering Hall, New York, 1886. Organist, All Souls Church, New York, 1889-1900, Temple Emanuel, 1898-1912 & St Thomas Church, 00-12. Cond, Yonkers Choral Soc, 02-12. Munic organist, Portland, Maine, 12-19. Concert tour, 15. Founder & winner, Clemson Medal, Am Guild Organists. *Songs & Instrumental Works:* Organ: Meditation; Reverie; Spring Song; Cradle Song; Scotch Fantasia; Cantata: The Message of the Cross; Setting to America the Beautiful. *Scores:* Operettas: Little Almond Eyes; Swords and Scissors.

MACFAYDEN, ALEXANDER   ASCAP 1939
composer, pianist, teacher
b Milwaukee, Wis, July 12, 1879; d Milwaukee, June 6, 36. Educ: Chicago Musical Col; hon MusD, Chicago Cons. Pianist in recitals & with symph orchs. Teacher, Wis Col Music & Chicago Cons. Wis Fedn Music Clubs established Macfayden Mem Prize for state winner piano comp, Nat Fedn Music Clubs. *Songs:* Cradle Song; Inter Nos; Just for You; Home; Love and Wait; Love's Springtide; Sing It Mother, Sing It Low; Oh Let Me Ever Know.

MACFOY, EMMANUEL KAYASI (ABEODUN OJU)   ASCAP 1979
composer, author
b Freetown, Sierra Leone, Dec 23, 48. Educ: State Univ NY, Plattsburgh & Buffalo; Univ Md. Ace drummer, Golden Strings Music Group, Freetown, Sierra Leone, 10 yrs, Charlie Bird, Freetown, 69, Circus Kirk, 70, Newport Jazz Fest, 73, Alice Tully Hall, Carnegie Hall, 73, ZNRT, 74-75 & Dizzy Gillespie, Hilton, Buffalo, 76. Chief Collabrs: Dizzy Gillespie, Charlie Bird, Norman Connors, Dee Dee Bridgewater, Pharoah Sanders. *Songs & Instrumental Works:* Aunty Sally; Leone Stars USA.

MACGIMSEY, ROBERT   ASCAP 1938
composer, author, singer
b Pineville, La; d Phoenix, Ariz, Mar 13, 79. Educ: Juilliard Sch Music; Los Angeles Cons, MusD; studied with Cesare Sodero, Oscar Seagle. Secy to US Sen Ransdell. After yr's practice in law, became prof whistler. Appeared on radio, made many records. *Songs:* Shadrack; Sweet Little Jesus Boy; Down to de Rivah; Trouble; Thunderin'; Wonderin'; Daniel in the Lion's Den; Old Slave; Jonah and the Whale; I Saw You There in the Moonlight; My Child Asleep.

MACGREGOR, IRVINE THOMAS (SCOTTY)   ASCAP 1961
composer, author, teacher
b Portobello, Scotland, Apr 4, 15. Educ: Brooklyn Technical High Sch; Bay Ridge High Sch; Dobbins Vocational Sch; Univ Fla; Fordham TV Workshop, NY. Worked in nightclubs, radio & TV as singer, master of ceremonies, producer, recording engr & promotion man; worked for small radio stas, WNEW & CBS-TV. Writer & publ of guitar instr bks. Wrote & publ "Watergate" Poetry Bk featured on nat shows. *Songs:* Wilbur the Wiggily Worm; Willy the Spider; The Land of Hatchy Milatchy; Don't Forget Me; Crash Bang He's Out of Bed Again; Fox and His Friends; Song of the Cave; Don't Shoot Those Guns Anymore; The Ant and the Elephant; Mommy's Birthday; Volunteer Fire Engine Song.

MACGREGOR, J CHALMERS (CHUMMY)   ASCAP 1943
composer, author, pianist
b Saginaw, Mich, Mar 28, 03; d. Educ: Univ Mich. Pianist & arr with dance orchs, Detroit, Chicago & New York. To Europe 27; scored revues for Cafe des Ambassadeurs, Paris; pianist & arr, Glenn Miller orch, 36-42; with film studios. *Songs:* I Sustain the Wings (Miller's AF band theme); Simply Grand; Doin' the Jive; Sold American; Moon Dreams; Mr Lucky Me; It Must Be Jelly ('Cause

Jam Don't Shake Like That); Why Don't We Say We're Sorry?; Get Me to Kansas City; It's Lovin' Time; A Little Bit Longer; Saturday Night Mood. *Scores:* Film: The Glenn Miller Story.

MACGREGOR, MARY A ASCAP 1979
composer, author, singer

b St Paul, Minn, May 6, 48. Educ: Grade Sch, St John's, St Paul, Minn; St Joseph's Acad for Girls, St Paul; Univ Minn, Minneapolis. Commercial jingle singer, night clubs, TV. Recording artist with Ariola Am, 76-79 & RSO Records, 80- Chief Collabrs: Peter Yarrow, David Bluefield. *Songs:* Benjamin; Music: Love in the Afternoon; Lyric: This Girl Has Turned Into a Woman.

MACHADO, LENA ASCAP 1962
composer, author, singer

b Honolulu, Hawaii, Oct 16, 07; d Honolulu, Jan 22, 74. Educ: Sacred Heart Convent. Entertained servicemen, WW II; singer nightclubs & hotels; Hawaii rep, San Francisco World's Fair, 39-40; soloist, Royal Hawaiian Band. Made many records. *Songs:* Mom; Kaulana O Hilo Hanakahi; Kaooha Mai; Ui Lani; Ei Nei; None Hula; Hawaii Aloha; Pua Mamane; Kuu Wa Lilii; Hoohaehae; Moani Ke Ala Ana Pua Makahikina; Holo Waapa; Mai Lohilohi; E Kuu Baby Hotcha Cha; Hoonanea; Kamalani O Keaukaha; Pohai Kealoha; Nuku O Nuuanu; Lei Kiele; Kuu Pua Pakalana I Lualualei; Kaiuilani; Sweet Nite Blooming Cereus; Radio Hula; Holau; I Walani; Puakea; E Maliu Mai Oe Ke Kanaka U'i; Aloha No; Home Nanea; Hawaii Eo Mai; Hawaii No Eka Ai; Nonosina; Na Wahi Kaulana O Kanai; Home Nanea; Noho Olu; Charms of Kehaulani; Kukui O Lono Paka; Keaukaha; Kuu Lei Paukea Kolona; Piilani; U-Umi Au A Hiki Ole; Kuu Pua Nani; Nani Nuuanu; No More Tears Momii; Hula Lesson; Kala O Kona.

MACHAN, BENJAMIN A ASCAP 1944
composer, conductor, pianist

b Cleveland, Ohio, Sept 11, 1894; d Woodbury, Conn, Feb 14, 66. Educ: Studied piano & comp with father. At 5, debut as piano soloist with Cleveland Symph. Served in USA Infantry in France, WW I; formed jazz band in Paris. Toured US with concert group. Comp & pianist, Rochester Philh. Moved to New York; wrote for films & radio shows incl: "Helen Hayes Theatre"; "Lucky Strike Hit Parade"; "We the People." Served in USCG, WW II. *Songs:* America Speaks; Soldiers of God (off song, USA Chaplain Corps); Little White Church; Fairy Princess Song; Fleecy, the Lamb; Chubby, the Pig; Yippy, the Chick; Squawky, the Duck; Perky, the Pup; Frisky, the Horse; Balky, the Mule; Cuddly, the Cat; musical setting to Pledge of Allegiance. *Instrumental Works:* Night Music; American Concerto (violin, piano); American Suite (symph); Rhapsody in Jazz; Nutmeg Suite; Connecticut Hymn. *Scores:* Documentary Film: Seeds of Destiny (Acad award, 44).

MACHITO
See Grillo, Frank R

MACINNIS, DONALD (DONALD GARLAND, DON ASCAP 1964
SINNICAM)
composer, author, teacher

b New York, NY, Apr 4, 23. Educ: Lincoln Sch Teachers' Col, high sch dipl, 41; Princeton Univ, BA, 48, MFA, 50, studied with Milton Babbitt, Bohuslav Martinu, Roger Sessions & Randall Thompson; Berkshire Music Ctr, studied conducting with Leonard Bernstein; Columbia Univ, studied electronic music with Vladimir Ussachevsky. Cond concert band & Freshman Glee Club, Princeton Univ, 48-50; mem fac theory & comp, Music Dept, Univ Va, 50-, cond, Univ Singers, 56-67; dir, Electronic Music Studio, 70- Researcher in electro-acoustic music, 65-; cond. Pres, Southeastern Comp League, 64-66; comp-in-residence, Atlanta Symph, 68-69; mem, Nat Coun, Am Soc Univ Comp, 66-69 & 71-76. Music Comp Prizes: Scholastic Mag, 41, Princeton Univ, 49, Ga State Univ, 68 & Bowdoin Col, 73. Comns: Ga State Univ, 69; Va Music Teachers' Asn, 71; Kindler Found, 71. Grants: Ford Found, 67; Rockefeller, 68; Univ Va, 65, 70, 72, 73, 76 & 80. *Instrumental Works:* String Quartet; Canto Giocoso (concert band); Variations on a Theme by Webern (cello, tape); Toccata for Piano and Tape; Dialogues for Orchestra; Variations for Brass and Percussion; Intersections for Tape Recorder and Orchestra; Collide-a-Scope (12 brass instruments, tape); Sonogram I (5 instruments); Sonogram III (12 brass instruments); In Memoriam John Fitzgerald Kennedy; Two Pieces for Woodwind Sextet; Four Miniatures for String Orchestra. *Songs & Instrumental Works:* Death By Water (male chorus, strings, piano). *Scores:* Opera: The Bear (based on story by William Faulkner); Ballet: Quadrilith (electro-acoustic tape, dancers); Dance Movements (brass quintet, vibraphone, slides, solo dancer); Bway show: Taming of the Shrew.

MACK, AL ASCAP 1959
composer, arranger, pianist

b Milwaukee, Wis, July 29, 12. Educ: Marquette Univ. Writer & arr, dance bands, nightclubs, radio & TV. Writer, special music for ballet "Red Mill" & for TV specials incl Gene Kelly, Donald O'Connor & Mitzi Gaynor. Music dir for Donald O'Connor, 51-; music supv, MGM, Hollywood, 60-; cond. *Songs & Instrumental Works:* The Cinderella Waltz.

MACK, NOREEN
See O'Flynn, Honoria

MACK, RICHARD R ASCAP 1963
composer, author, producer

b New York, NY, Dec 14, 1900; d. Educ: St Lawrence Univ, BA. Writer for Edgar Bergen & W C Fields, radio; wrote spec material for Fanny Brice, Ritz Bros, Carolyn Richter, Groucho Marx, Danny Kaye, Eddie Cantor, John Barrymore, Abbott & Costello, Martin & Lewis, Dinah Shore & Kenny Baker; writer & prod, "Joan Davis Show," radio, TV, 12 yrs; wrote "Pabst Blue Ribbon" commercial. Chief Collabrs: Lyn Murray, Leonard Whitcup, Walter Samuels & Robert Emmett Dolan. *Songs:* Nize Baby; I Married Joan (theme); Baby.

MACK, TOM H ASCAP 1959
composer, author, arranger

b Worcester, Mass, July 2, 14; d. Educ: Bowdoin Col. Taught languages, 2 yrs. Trombonist, arr & mgr orchs, incl Glenn Miller, Artie Shaw & Claude Thornhill. WW II Service. A&R producer, Decca & Capitol Records. Vpres, Dot Records. Chief Collabrs: Ray Gilbert, Sonny Burke. *Songs:* Music: We Love But Once; Lyrics: Oodles of Boodles; Chi Chi Cha Cha Cha.

MACKAY, HARPER ASCAP 1962
composer

b Boston, Mass, Oct 13, 21. Educ: New Eng Cons Music, piano; Harvard Univ, AB(comp), 42; Univ Southern Calif, MA(comp), 48, PhD, 54. Comp, arr, conductor in films, TV & musical theatre, 55- Musical dir, Los Angeles Civic Light Opera Music Theatre Workshop, 62-80; wrote theme for NBC Follies; comp music for var Warner Bros cartoons & films for TV, also spec material songs for film & TV performers. *Instrumental Works:* Symphony No 1; Overture for Orchestra; Six Minutes for Six Pieces; Chamber works for var instruments. *Scores:* Bway shows: Forty Thieves; Major Barbara; Myles Standish.

MACKAY, HUGH ASCAP 1958
composer, author

b New London, Conn, Dec 22, 07. Educ: Norwich Univ, BS; Harvard Law Sch, LLB. Mem, Mass & Conn state bar. Lectr, trust councils throughout US. Writer, special material for radio incl "Chamber Music Society of Lower Basin Street." *Songs:* Sunday in Savannah; Shoemaker's Holiday; Backstage At the Ballet; For Whom the Bell Tolls; It's Almost Summer.

MACKENZIE, LEONARD C, JR ASCAP 1947
composer, author, producer

b Westport, Conn, June 28, 15. Educ: Union Col, BA; pvt music study. 1st Lt, USA, World War II, 41-44. Writer & producer, musical commercials, 45. Creative dir, Faillace Productions, Inc. *Songs:* Chiquita Banana; Watching for Your Shadow; I'm Singing to You; Army Fighting Song; Honey Bear Boogie; Time Table Mabel.

MACLEAN, T ROSS ASCAP 1947
composer, author, singer

b Burghead, Scotland, Apr 9, 04. Educ: Studied singing, opera with Arthur J Foxall, Los Angeles. Opera singer, vaudeville, Publix Circuit, "George White's Scandals," NBC Radio Stations WEAF, WJZ, Chase & Sanborn, Nestle Chocolate & Ponds Cream hours, nat programs & supper clubs. Chief Collabrs: Howard Johnson, Arthur Richardson. *Songs:* Too Fat Polka; Old Arm Chair; My Baby Said Maybe; I Gotta Go Now; Mind Your Own Business; Above Timberline; She Makes Me Feel Like a Man; Royal Canadian Mounted Police Song; The Business of Sex; The Old Soft Shoe; Remittance Man; Mutually; Sourdoughs and Chechakos; Gold; The Weather; Musical Chairs; Horsefly; Love is Born; Keep a Song in Your Heart; Especially Little Girls.

MACLEISH, ARCHIBALD ASCAP 1942
poet, author

b Glencoe, Ill, May 7, 1892. Educ: Yale Univ, AB, 15, hon LittD, 39; Harvard Univ, LLB, 19, hon LittD, 55; hon MA, Tufts Col, 32; hon LittD: Wesleyan Univ, 38; Colby Col, 38; Univ Pa, 41; Univ Ill, 46; Washington Univ, 48; Columbia Univ, 54; Rockford Col, 53; Univ Pittsburgh, 59; Brandeis Univ, 59; hon LHD: Dartmouth Col, 40; Princeton Univ, 65; hon LLD: Johns Hopkins Univ, 41; Univ Calif, 43; Queens Col, Ont, 48; Carleton Col, 56; Amherst Col, 63; hon DCL: Union Col, 41; Univ PR, 53; hon DHL, Williams Col, 42. Served, from Pvt to Capt, USA, World War I, 17-19. Librarian of Congress, 39-44; dir, US Office of Facts & Figures, 41-42. Rede lectr, Cambridge Univ, Eng, 42. Asst dir, Office of War Information, 42-43. Asst Secy of State, 44-45. Am delegate to Conference of Allied Ministers of Educ, London, 44. Chmn, Am delegation to London conference for drawing up UNESCO constitution, 45; chmn, Am delegation, 1st Gen Conference, UNESCO, Paris, 46; 1st Am mem, exec council, UNESCO. Boylston prof, Harvard Univ, 49-62. Simpson lectr, Amherst Col, 63-67. Recipient: Comdr Legion of Hon, France; Encomienda Order el Sol del Peru; Bollingen prize, poetry, 53; Nat Book Award, poetry, 53; Pulitzer prize, poetry, 32 & 53; Pulitzer prize, drama, 59; Antoinette Perry award, drama, 59; Presidential Medal of Freedom, 77; Nat Medal for Literature, 78; Am Acad gold medal, poetry, 79. Mem, Am Acad Arts & Letters, pres, 53-56. Author: verse: "The Happy Marriage"; "The Pot of Earth"; "Streets in the Moon"; "The Hamlet of A MacLeish"; "New Found Land"; "Conquistador"; "Frescoes for Mr Rockefeller's City"; "Collected Poems";

"Public Speech"; "Land of the Free"; "America Was Promises"; "Act Five"; "Collected Poems, 1917-1952"; "Songs for Eve"; "A Continuing Journey"; "The Wild Old Wicked Man and Other Poems"; "The Human Season"; "New and Collected Poems 1917-1976"; Verse plays: "Noboddady"; "Panic"; "The Fall of the City" (radio); "Air Raid"; "J B"; "Herakles"; "The Great American Fourth of July Parade"; Prose: "The Irresponsibles"; "The American Cause"; "A Time to Speak"; "A Time to Act"; "American Opinion and the War"; "Poetry and Opinion"; "Freedom Is the Right to Choose"; "Poetry and Experience"; "Eleanor Roosevelt Story" (bk; motion picture, 65, Acad award, 66); "Riders on the Earth"; Prose play: "An Evening's Journey to Conway Massachusetts"; "Scratch"; Broadcasts: "American Story." *Scores:* Ballet: Union Pacific; Libretto: Magic Prison.

MACPHERSON, HARRY   ASCAP 1942
author
b Topeka, Kans; d. Educ: Friends Univ Reporter, Wichita Eagle & other newspapers. Wrote verse for San Diego Sun. Has written radio, TV & film scripts. Author, novels: "Poison Island"; "The Dangled Old Dude"; also verse: "Squared Circles." Chief Collabrs: Albert Von Tilzer, Ted Fiorito, Glenn Spencer. *Songs:* Let's Go Places and Do Things; Lover, I Cry Over You; Roll Along, Prairie Moon; Ridin' to the Rhythm of the Round-Up; When a Cowboy Goes to Town; Drifting; Ai Viva Tequila; Sundown on the Prairie; Sierra Moonlight; That Moon's in My Heart; My Madonna of the Trail; I'm Praying to St Christopher; Rolling Along for a Hundred Years.

MACRAE, FRED AYLOR (JOHNNY)   ASCAP 1970
composer, singer, record producer
b Independence, Mo, Feb 15, 29. Nightclub entertainer with Rockabilly Band, late 50's; recording artist, 60's; backup singer. Chief Collabrs: Bob Morrison, Johnny Wilson. *Songs:* I'd Love to Lay You Down; Let Me Be Your Baby; That's What You Do to Me; God Made Love; You Lift Me Up; You're Just About to Lose Your Clown; Where Does a Little Tear Come From.

MADDEN, EDWARD   ASCAP 1914
author
b New York, NY, July 17, 1877; d Hollywood, Calif, Mar 11, 52. Educ: Fordham Univ. Wrote spec material for singers incl Fanny Brice. Was charter mem, ASCAP. Chief Collabrs: Ben Jerome; Dorothy Jardon (wife); Joseph Daly, Gus Edwards, Julian Edwards, Louis Hirsch, Theodore Morse, Percy Wenrich, Jerome Kern. *Songs:* By the Light of the Silvery Moon; Moonlight Bay; Down in Jungle Town; Blue Bell; Look Out for Jimmy Valentine; Ain't You the Wise Ole Owl?; My Only One; What Could Be Sweeter?; The World Can't Go 'Round Without You; Red Rose Rag; Silver Bell; Arra Wanna; I've Got a Feelin' for You; A Little Boy Called Taps; I'd Rather Be a Lobster Than a Wise Guy. *Scores:* Bway Stage: Rogers Brothers in Panama; The Mimic World; The Girl and the Wizard; He Came From Milwaukee (also co-librettist); La Belle Paree; Little Boy Blue.

MADDEN, FRANK   ASCAP 1941
composer, author
b New York, NY, July 19, 1900; d San Francisco, Calif, Nov 18, 64. Educ: New York Col of Music. *Songs:* Maybe; If Your Sweetheart Met My Sweetheart; I'm a Son of a Legionnaire; Thrill From Brazil; Okechobee; The Birthday Song.

MADDOX, FANNIE BELL   ASCAP 1963
composer
b Detroit, Mich, Sept 21, 22. Educ: Wayne State Univ, BS(elem educ). *Songs:* Because You've Been So Good to Me; He Satisfies My Soul; Jesus What a Wonderful Friend.

MADDY, JOSEPH EDGAR   ASCAP 1960
composer, conductor, musician
b Wellington, Kans, Oct 14, 1891; d Traverse City, Mich, Apr 16, 66. Educ: Bethany Col; Wichita Col; Columbia Sch Music, Chicago. Violist & clarinetist, Minneapolis Symph, 09-14 & St Paul Symph, 14-18. Supvr, instrumental music, pub schs, Rochester, NY, 18-20 & Richmond, Ind, 20-24. Instr, Earlham Col, 22-24. Prof music educ, Univ Mich, 24-62, then emer prof. Co-founder, Nat Music Camp, Interlochen, Mich, 28. Founder & cond, Nat High Sch Symph. Founder, Interlochen Arts Acad, 62 & Interlochen Arts Fest, 64. Mem, Music Educ Nat Conference, pres, 36-38, 1st vpres, 38-40; mem, Music Educ Res Council. *Instrumental Works:* Andante; Music Makers March; Festival Finale; also Symphonic Band Folio.

MADEIRA, PAUL
See Mertz, Paul Madeira

MADISON, NATHANIEL JOSEPH   ASCAP 1938
composer, author
b South Boston, Mass, Mar 15, 1896; d South Boston, Jan 28, 68. Educ: Pub schs, Boston. On prof staff, music publ, 20 yrs. Wrote "Organlogues." With quartet, in vaudeville, 2 yrs. Writer of radio scripts, TV musical commercials. Chief Collabr: Al Frazzini. *Songs:* My Cabin of Dreams; Summers End; When It's Autumn in the Mountains; Sheila; Pug Nose; I'd Give the World to Love You; The Girl of My Dreams; You Can Count on Me; Pal of My Lonesome Days; Lucky Days (Were Always Meant for Me); As You Are; I'se Regusted.

MADRIGUERA, ENRIC   ASCAP 1963
composer, author, conductor
b Barcelona, Spain, Feb 17, 04; d. Educ: Barcelona Cons; studied with Leopold Auer & Juan Manen. Concertized, Spain & France, also in New York, Boston & Chicago; violin soloist, NBC. Violinist. Organized Latin-Am Orch, appearing in hotels & on radio. Rec'd title, Music Ambassador of the Americas, from US Congress. *Songs:* Adios; The Minute Samba; Take It Away. *Instrumental Works:* Follies of Spain (ballet). *Scores:* Stage: The Moor and the Gypsy.

MADURO, CHARLES   ASCAP 1931
composer
b Curacao, DWI, Oct 5, 1883; d New York, NY, Oct 4, 47. *Songs:* Filigrane; Melodie Creole; Curacao; I Love the Rain; In Old Granada.

MAEKELBERGHE, AUGUST R   ASCAP 1960
composer, conductor, organist
b Oostende, Belgium, Jan 15, 09; d Mt Clemens, Mich, Aug 8, 75. Educ: Notre Dame Col; Acad Music, Oostende; Royal Cons, Ghent, Belgium; Detroit Inst Musical Art, MM. Has given annual concerts, Europe, US & Can. Organist & music dir, St John Episcopal Church; cond, Madrigal Club; dir, Nurses Chorus, Mercy Schs Nursing, Detroit. Prof organ, Wayne State Univ. *Songs:* In Paree Just for a Lark; Tira-lira-lira. *Instrumental Works:* Triptych; Fantasia; Night Soliloquy; Impromptu-Etude; A Flemish Prayer; A Plain Song Prelude; Let All Mortal Flesh Keep Silent; De Profundis Clamavi; Elegy for Organ; Elegy for String Orch; Toccata Prelude for Organ; Verlangen (Desire; strings, organ); Organ: Puer Natus (improvisation); Toccata, Melody in Blue and Fugue; Three Chorale Preludes; Three Hymn Preludes; Ostinata Malinconia; Choral: Communion in D; Christ Is Risen (anthem); A Christmas Suite (choir, string orch, harp); also transc of Bach organ works.

MAEL, RUSSELL   ASCAP 1971
composer, author, singer
b Santa Monica, Calif. Educ: Univ Calif, Los Angeles, BS(theatre arts). Mem, Brit based band, Sparks; many Brit & Europ hit records. Chief Collabr: Ron Mael. *Songs:* This Town Ain't Big Enough for Both of Us; Beat the Clock; No 1 Song in Heaven; Amateur Hour; Young Girl.

MAESCH, LAVAHN K   ASCAP 1972
composer, organist, choral director
b Appleton, Wis, Oct 15, 04. Educ: Lawrence Col, BMus; Univ Wis; Univ Mich; Eastman Sch Music, MMus; studied organ with Palmer Christian, Abel Decaux, Harold Gleason & Marcel Dupre, comp with Herbert Elwell & Bernard Rogers. Dean emer, Lawrence Univ Cons Music. Guest prof: Univ Mont; Univ Idaho; Univ Southern Calif. Assoc, Am Guild Organists; past pres, Music Teachers Nat Asn; past vpres, Nat Asn Sch Music. Distinguished Service Awards, Lawrence Univ & Univ Wis. Now pres, Music Teachers Nat Asn Scholarship Found. Mem, Pi Kappa Lambda; hon life mem, Sinfonia. *Songs:* Music: Ho, for Slumberland (medium voice); Six Junior Choir Anthems; Birds Are Singing (children's chorus); Chorus: Prayer After Triumph; Dese Bones Gwine to Rise Again; Waking Time.

MAGANINI, QUINTO   ASCAP 1932
composer, conductor, flutist
b Fairfield, Calif, Nov 30, 1897; d Greenwich, Conn, Mar 10, 74. Educ: Univ Calif; studied music & eng, US & Europe; Am Cons, Fontainebleau; studied flute with Georges Barrere & comp with Nadia Boulanger; two Guggenheim fels. Flutist in orch, Armed Forces, WW I. Flutist, San Francisco Symph, New York Symph, Sousa's Band, Metrop Opera Orch, Chicago Opera Orch & Russian Symph. Cond Silvermine Music Fest, Norwalk Symph; also children's concerts, Norwalk, Greenwich, Conn & Scarsdale, NY. Taught orchestration & counterpoint, Columbia Univ. Pres: Kingsbury Machine Works; Am Schs, Fontainebleau, France; Edition Musicus, Inc. Publisher & businessman. *Instrumental Works:* Tuolumne (rhapsody for trumpet, orch; Pulitzer award, 27); Southwind; Sonate Gaulois (flute, piano); The Argonauts (opera cycle; David Bispham Medal); A Sylvan Symphony; A Suite of Music by Royalty; Ladies of the Ballet; Genevieve (rhapsody for orch); The Cathedral at Sens (chorus, cello, orch); An Ornithological Suite.

MAGEAU, MARY JANE   ASCAP 1971
composer, pianist, music lecturer
b Milwaukee, Wis, Sept 4, 34. Educ: DePaul Univ, BMus, 63, studied comp with Leon Stein; Univ Mich, MMus(comp), 69, studied with Ross Lee Finney, Leslie Bassett; Composer's Fel Prog, Berkshire Music Ctr, Tanglewood, 70, studied with George Crumb. Awards: Louis Moreau Gottschalk Centenary Competition Silver Medal, 70, Univ Honolulu & Minn Composer's Competition Prizes. Comp Grant from The Australian Council, Sydney, 80. Harpsichordist with Univ Mich Collegium Musicum & Brisbane Baroque Trio. Chamber music pianist performing in NAm & Australia. Music lecturer, Scholastica Col, Duluth, Minn, Univ Wis, Superior, Kelvin Grove & N Brisbane Cols of Advanced Educ, Queensland, Australia. *Instrumental Works:* Three Pieces for Organ; Mass for Our Lady of Victory; Contrasts (for solo cello); Forecasts (for solo piano); Australia's Animals (for solo piano); Adventures in Time and Space (contributor 5 vol set); Montage (for symph orch); Dialogues (for clarinet, cello & piano); Statement and Variations (for solo viola); Fantasy Music (for violin & piano); Sonate Concertate (for flute, cello & harpsichord).

MAGEE, RAY ASCAP 1961
author
b Sharon, Pa, Oct 20, 1897; d. Educ: Pub schs. Was a painter & interior decorator. *Songs:* Farrell Polka; Could Happen; Let's Dream; Do You Mind?

MAGID, LEE (DIANE ALEXIS) ASCAP 1957
composer, author, publisher
b New York, NY, Apr 6, 26. Educ: Theodore Roosevelt High Sch, Bronx, NY; studied trumpet with Kestenbaum & Emil Shulman; studied harmony, theory & arr with Otto Cessana & Ernie Cornicelli. Worked as trumpet player with var bands in New York area, age 14 to 20; songplugger, Sam Fox Music Publ, 44, Music Publ Holding Corp (Harm Inc), 44-46, Mills Music, 47 & Hudson Music, 47-48; began Alexis Music, 49; songwriter, record producer & promoter for Nat Records, Jubilee Records, Savoy Records; became personal mgr for Al Hibbler, Ralph Young, Della Reese, Lou Rawls, O C Smith, Earl Grant, Sam Fletcher & others. Chief Collabs: Max Rich, Bobby Marcus, Mack Kay. *Songs:* I Played the Fool; Blues for the Weepers; The Parade Has Passed Me By; So Soon; Gladly.

MAGIDSON, HERBERT ADOLPH ASCAP 1929
composer, author
b Braddock, Pa, Jan 7, 06. Educ: Braddock High Sch; Univ Pittsburgh, jour. Brought to New York by Sophie Tucker, 28; wrote spec material for music publ; moved to Hollywood, 29, under Warner Bros contract. Songs for films incl, "The Gay Divorcee", "The Great Ziegfeld", "Show of Shows", "No, No, Nanette", "Here's to Romance", "Music for Madame", "Hers to Hold", "Song of the Thin Man", "Little Johnnie Jones", "Tiger Rose", "King Solomon of Broadway", "Bright Lights", "Lilies of the Field", "Gift of Gab", "George White's Scandals 1935", "Priorities on Parade" & "Sleepy Time Gal." Songs for Bway revues incl, "George White's Scandals of 1939-40", "George White's Music Hall Varieties", "The Gay White Way" & "Michael Todd's Peep Show." Elected, Songwriter's Hall of Fame, 80. Chief Collabs: Con Conrad, Allie Wrubel, Sammy Fain, Ben Oakland, Jule Styne, Carl Sigman, Sam Stept, Michael Cleary, Burton Lane, Jimmy McHugh, Joseph Meyer, Jack Yellen, Ned Washington, Lou Pollack, Joe Burke, Felix Bernard, Matty Malneck, Dick Manning, James V Monaco, Al Hoffman, Cliff Friend. *Songs:* Black-Eyed Susan Brown; My Impression of You; Linger in My Arms a Little Longer, Baby; Lyrics: The Continental (First Acad Award, 34); Music, Maestro, Please; Gone With the Wind; Enjoy Yourself (It's Later Than You Think); I'll Buy That Dream (Acad Nomination); I'm Afraid the Masquerade Is Over; Midnight in Paris; Here's to Romance; I'll Dance At Your Wedding; Something I Dreamed Last Night; Singin' in the Bathtub; Say a Prayer for the Boys Over There (Acad Nomination); I'm Stepping Out With a Memory Tonight; Roses in December; I Can't Love You Any More (Any More Than I Do); Good Night, Angel; A Needle in a Haystack; Hummin' to Myself; According to the Moonlight; Twinkle, Twinkle, Little Star; H'lo Baby; Conchita, Marchita, Lolita, Pepita, Rosita, Juanita Lopez; A Pink Cocktail for a Blue Lady; Violins From Nowhere; Barrelhouse Bessie From Basin Street. *Scores:* Film: Radio City Revels; Life of the Party; Music in Manhattan; Hats Off; Sing Your Way Home; The Forward Pass.

MAGNANO, ANTHONY SALVATORE ASCAP 1968
composer, author, pianist
b Waterbury, Conn, Apr 9, 29. Educ: Wilby High Sch, Waterbury; Marietta Col; Univ Conn, BA, 54; Southern Conn State Col, master's prog, 61; studied piano & comp with Tony Barbieri. Pianist & writer, 45- Mgr, Playmates, 54-58; pianist & orch leader in clubs, hotels & radio. Singer. *Songs:* Island Girl; Evolution; Sing Bahama Mamma; Bagdad Daddy; Barefoot Girl; Lot of Money.

MAGNANTE, CHARLES ASCAP 1952
composer, author, accordionist
b New York, NY, Dec 5, 05. Educ: High sch; studied music with father. First accordionist to play with symph orch & to give full accordion concert, Carnegie Hall, 39. Performed on radio & TV. Recording artist with many records & radio transc; in concert throughout US; cond teacher workshops. Pres, Am Accordion Asn. *Instrumental Works:* Accordiana; Waltz Allegro; Accordion Boogie; Swingyana; Tantalizing; Waltz in Blue; Greenlight; Holiday for Basses; Holiday for Chords; Perpetual Motion; La Bella Teresa Polka.

MAGOON, EATON, JR (BOB) ASCAP 1955
composer, author
b Honolulu, Hawaii, June 24, 22. Educ: Yale Univ, BA. *Songs:* Fish and Poi; My Waikiki Girl; Two Senators From the 50th State; Lyrics: Coconut Willie; Number One Day of Christmas. *Scores:* 13 Daughters musical comedy); Heathen (Bway musical comedy); Aloha Lord (musical comedy).

MAHAN, MARILYN MCADAMS ASCAP 1975
composer, author
b Salinas, Calif, May 5, 28. Educ: Salinas High Sch; Stanford Univ, BA, 61, MA, 63. Chief Collabrs: Mary W Lacey, Paul Weirick. *Songs & Instrumental Works:* Love Was Born in a Manger.

MAHER, WILLIAM MICHAEL ASCAP 1978
author
b Lynn, Mass, May 31, 47. Educ: Emerson Col, BS(speech), 69, MS(speech), 74. Actor, singer, playwright & musician, Off-Bway, regional, stock & dinner theatres. Chief Collabr: Bill Brohn.

MAHLER, GUSTAV ASCAP 1946
composer, conductor
b Kalischt, Czech, July 7, 1860; d Vienna, Austria, May 18, 11. Educ: Studied music with Viktorin & Brosch; Vienna Cons, studied with Julius Epstein, Robert Fuchs & Franz Krenn; Vienna Univ. Opera cond: Summer theatre, Hall, Austria, 1880; Laibach, 1881; Olmutz, 1882-83; Cassel, 1884; Prague, 1885; Leipzig, 1886-88. Dir, Royal Opera House, Budapest, 1888-91. Cond, Hamburg Opera, 1891-97; German opera troupe, London, 1892. Dir, Imperial Opera House, Vienna, 1897-1907. Cond, Metrop Opera House, New York, 07; New York Philh, 08-11. Biographies by: Bruno Walter; Paul Bekker; Alma Mahler; H L de La Grange; Paul Stefan; Kurt Blaukopf; Donald Mitchell; Otto Klemperer; Guido Adler; Ludwig Karpath; G Specht; Nat Bauer-Lechner. *Songs & Instrumental Works:* Ten Symphonies; Song Cycles & Songs: Songs of a Wayfarer; Youth's Magic Horn; Five Songs From Ruckert; Kindertotenlieder; Song of the Earth; Cantata: Das klagende Lied.

MAHONEY, JACK FRANCIS ASCAP 1925
author
b Buffalo, NY, Oct 10, 1882; d New York, NY, Dec 26, 45. Educ: High sch. Writer, special material for var artists incl Nat Wills, Sam Bernard, Raymond Hitchcock, Eddie Foy, Frank Crumit, Blanche Ring, Lew Dockstader. Chief Collabrs: George Meyer, Theodore Morse, Percy Wenrich. *Songs:* When You Wore a Tulip and I Wore a Big Red Rose; He's a College Boy; Goodbye, Betty Brown; If This Rose Told You All It Knows; That's Why the Violets Live; Kentucky Days; When It's Moonlight in Mayo; Goodbye, Summer, So Long Fall, Hello Wintertime; Bing, Bang, Bing 'Em on the Rhine; Summertime; Snow Deer.

MAHR, HERMAN CARL (CURLEY) ASCAP 1943
composer, arranger
b Boston, Mass, May 23, 01; d Reseda, Calif, Feb 27, 64. Educ: New Eng Cons. Pianist in dance orch; to Europe with band, 28; arr in radio, 30; accompanist & arr for Landt Trio, 7 yrs; had own vocal group, CBS, 3 yrs; vocal arr for films & singing coach, Hollywood, 40; returned to radio, 44. *Songs:* Have You the Time?; Wake Up a Robin; Thank Your Lucky Stars and Stripes; Sons of the Navy; With a Pack on His Back; The Little Red Hen; If You're Ever in My Arms Again.

MAIDEN, TONY
composer, author, vocalist
b 1949. Lead male vocalist & songwriter for group, Rufus. *Songs:* Music: Walk the Rockway; Once You Get Started; Ain't Nobody Like You; Sweet Thing. *Albums:* Pleasure Dome.

MAIER, BETTY ASCAP 1970
composer, author
b US. Educ: Columbia Univ; Hunter Col. Mem, Authors League Am, Inc. Author children's stories; linguist in German, Span & French. Chief Collabrs: Russ Taylor, George Thorn, Jean Kaufman, Lincoln Chase. *Songs:* You Started a Fire; Light the Candles on the Christmas Tree; Wish I Were Tied to You; Lyrics: My Unfinished Symphony; The Lonesome Christmas Tree.

MAIETTA, ANGELO LEONARD ASCAP 1959
composer, author
b Boston, Mass, Apr 28, 05. Educ: Tufts Col; Sch Med, Middlesex Univ, MD. Physician, 30-; chief allergy, Carney Hospital, Boston; clin instr med, Tufts Univ Sch Med; assoc staff, Tufts New Eng Med Ctr, Boston. *Songs:* The Christmas Message.

MAILMAN, MARTIN ASCAP 1961
composer
b New York, NY, June 30, 32. Educ: Univ Rochester Eastman Sch Music, BM(comp), 54, MM, 55, PhD, 60; studied comp with Louis Mennini, Wayne Barlow, Bernard Rogers & Howard Hanson. Taught at USN Sch Music, 55-57; Ford Found Young Comp Project comp-in-residence, Jacksonville, Fla, 59-61; prof music & comp-in-residence, East Carolina Univ, 61-66; prof music & coordr comp, N Tex State Univ, 66- Guest comp & cond, cols, univs & numerous regional, state & nat orgn. Chief Collabr: Richard B Sale. *Instrumental Works:* Liturgical Music, Opus 33 (band); Symphony No 1, Opus 46 (orch); In Memoriam Frankie Newton, Opus 50; Requiem, Requiem, Opus 51 (chorus, orch & soloists); Decorations, Opus 54 (Music for a Celebration); Symphony No 2, Opus 63 (orch). *Scores:* The Hunted, Opus 11 (one act opera).

MAINENTE, ANTON EUGENE ASCAP 1964
composer, author, conductor
b Paterson, NJ, Nov 5, 1889; d Auburn, Maine, Aug 18, 63. Educ: New Eng Cons; studied with Francis Casadesus, Andre Gedalge, Andre Caplet. Cond, Doree Grand Opera Co. Flutist, Boston Pops Orch. Taught, New Eng Cons, Gould Acad, Hebron Acad. Founder, Mainente Sch of Music, 21. 2nd Lt,

taught, AEF Bandleader's Sch, World War II; cond, USA Band. Officer d'Academie Francaise. *Instrumental Works:* Symphony America; Impressions of an Afternoon; Reminiscences; Prelude for Organ.

MAIONE, JOHN GUY　　　　　　　　ASCAP 1978
　　composer, lyricist
b Pittsburgh, Pa, June 12, 53. Educ: Univ Pittsburgh, BA; studied with Joseph H Negri, 3 yrs. Worked in shows, Don Brockett Productions, Norman Roth Productions & Tom Smith, Pittsburgh area. Free-lance jazz/pop guitarist with var bands & shows, Pittsburgh area. Writer & arr. Wrote music for "Pook Family Jamboree." Songplugger. Chief Collabrs: Norman E Roth, John Mascio, Richard Infante, Janet Scuro, Angel Tucciarone. *Songs:* All the Love in the World; Put Your Faith in the Lord; Good Morning Glory; Cheatin' Frame of Mind; A Love Song Just Won't Do; Come to Me As Children; Every Man Needs a Forever Woman; Music: Do the Pook; The World Is But a Small Town; Lady Fox's Theme; Always in Love With You.

MAIORANA, VICTOR E (VICTOR LAMONT)　　ASCAP 1959
　　composer, pianist, organist
b Palermo, Italy, July 20, 1897; d New York, NY, Oct 18, 64. To US as child. Educ: Pub Schs; pvt music study. Organist in film theatres. Ed, Sam Fox Music Co, 37-49; then free-lance. *Instrumental Works:* Reflections on the Lake; Legend of the Canyon.

MAISTER, ALEXANDER　　　　　　　　ASCAP 1950
　　composer, author, teacher
b Lida, Russia, Sept 18, 03. Came to US, 05, became citizen. Educ: Bentley Sch, Boston. Saxophonist & clarinetist in dance orchs, New Eng, 25 yrs. Teacher of clarinet & saxophone. Wrote radio continuity & publicity; also humor column. Author: "An-am-ated Verse." Chief Collabrs: Bernardo Fazioli, Lew Tobin, Maury Goldsmith, Jack Neiburg, Sherm Feller. *Songs:* If You're Ever Gonna Leave Me; The Baigel Song; Music: Does a Duck Like Water?; Over Here; Am I a Passing Dream?.

MAKEBA, MIRIAM ZENZI　　　　　　　ASCAP 1951
　　composer, singer
b Johannesburg, SAfrica. Educ: Kilmerton Training Inst, Pretoria, SAfrica. Mem vocal group Black Mountain Bros, 2 1/2 yrs, then with revue, 18 months. Appeared in stage musical "King Kong" & in film "Come Back Africa." Sang on BBC-TV, London. US debut "Steve Allen Show," 59; appeared in nightclubs, concerts, alone & with Harry Belafonte. Has made many records. Grammy Award, 65. *Songs:* Unhome; Amampondo Dubula; Pole Mze; Mangwene Mpulele; Boot Dance.

MAKRIS, ANDREAS　　　　　　　　　ASCAP 1967
　　composer
b Salonika, Greece Mar Mar, 7, 30. Educ: Nat Cons, Greece, grad, violin & comp, prize student, 50; Kansas City Cons, 51-53; Mannes Col Music, grad, artist honors, 56; Aspen Music Fest, 56-57; studied with Boulanger, France, 58. Comp-in-residence, Nat Symph Orch, Kennedy Ctr, musical adv to Rostropovich. Exchange student scholarship, Damrosh Grant, NEA Arts Assistance & Martha Baird Rockefeller Award. First contemporary comp to be performed in Kennedy Ctr Concert Hall with the Nat Symph Orch & Antal Dorati. *Instrumental Works:* Aegean Festival (orch & wind ens); Anamnesis (orch); Efthymia (orch); Mediterranean Holiday (wind ens); Chromatokinesis (orch); Variations for Orchestra; Viola Concerto; Concerto for Strings; String Quartet in One Movement; Voice Quintet (for soprano & string quartet); Fantasy and Dance (saxophone & piano); Concertino for Trombone and Strings; Five Miniatures (strings); Schertzo for Violins (4 parts).

MALATESTA, JOHN PAUL　　　　　　ASCAP 1962
　　composer, author, singer
b Wilmington, Del, Aug 10, 44. Educ: High sch; Sch for Ind Electronics. Singer, vocal group Tradewinds. Co-owner, Starsun, Ltd (Brandywine Records, Big "T" Music Co). Chief Collabrs: David Malatesta, Carmine Poppiti, Walter Mateja. *Songs & Instrumental Works:* Wildwood Twist; The Snake; Congo Beat; I'd Be Surprised; Jump; Tea Room; Aba-Daba-Do Dance.

MALIJEWSKI, PETER MARTIN　　　　ASCAP 1975
　　composer, author, pianist
b Ludenscheid, Ger, Apr 23, 46. Educ: Pvt study with Germaine Kozak, Chicago; Pasadena City Col; USN Sch of Music. With, 5th Army Band, 67-68. Pianist, var groups & artists incl Supremes, 69, Monte Rock III, Ray Coniff, Brenda Lee, Bill Medey & Bobby Caldwell, 74. Cond & pianist, Billy Joe Royal, 71; asst cond & pianist, "Two Gentlemen of Verona," 73. Music dir, Disney Studios incl TV specials "I Believe," 77 & "Our Heritage Our Hope," 78. Vocalist & arr. Chief Collabrs: Marc Ray, David Talisman, Bobby Caldwell. *Songs:* Climb a Beam to a Dream; Let's Go Dry; Surprise Day; Who, What, Where and Why; Show Time; Our Heritage Our Hope; Mouse Le Dance Disco.

MALIN, DONALD FRANKLIN　　　　　ASCAP 1953
　　composer, editor, translator
b Tama, Iowa, Nov 16, 1896. Educ: Iowa State Univ, BS, 18. Service in WW I. Did newspaper work, 19-25. Prog dir, WLS Radio Sta, Chicago, 26-30. Educ dir, Lyon & Healy, 30-43; with C C Birchard & Co, 44, pres, 50-56; educ dir,

Mills Music, E B Marks Music Corp & Belwin-Mills Publ Corp; ed consult for Belwin-Mills Publ Corp. *Songs & Instrumental Works:* Madrigals for Treble Voices (arr & ed); Let the Song Be Begun; Rediscovered Madrigals (ed); Renaissance Choral Music (ed); Songs of the Late Renaissance (series of ed); Choruses From Dramatic Works (series of ed); Renaissance Choral Series (ed).

MALLORY, MASON　　　　　　　　　ASCAP 1956
　　composer, author
b Los Angeles, Calif, Aug 29, 16. Educ: Pasadena City Col; Univ Wash. Joined Western Airlines, 41, sales promotion mgr. Writer, musical commercials. *Songs:* Batter Up, Batter Up, Batter Up; Minneapolis At Aquatennial Time; Hubert Humphrey March; Your Travel Agent Is Your Very Best Friend.

MALLORY, ROBERT　　　　　　　　ASCAP 1962
　　author, editor, publisher
b Rochester, NY, Apr 16, 20. Educ: High sch. Sgt, USA, World War II. Former publ; owner, demo record co. Ed & publ Songsmith Mag, 56-62. Chief Collabr: Cal De Voll. *Songs:* Second Heaven; Tired of Me?.

MALNECK, MATTY　　　　　　　　　ASCAP 1931
　　composer, violinist, director
b Newark, NJ, Dec 9, 03. Educ: Manual Training High Sch; Univ Denver, (accounting); studied violin with Henry Ginsbury. Violinist & arr with Paul Whiteman, 10 yrs; leader, own orch, 35. Free-lance work, radio, TV & movies. Music dir, Al Jolson, var radio shows & movies. Recording artist, solo & with var artists. Chief collabrs: Gus Kahn, Johnny Mercer, Frank Loesser. *Songs:* Music: Stairway to the Stars; Goody-Goody; Shangri-la; I'm Through With Love; If You Were Mine; I'll Never Be the Same; Pardon My Southern Accent; Eeny Meeny Miny Mo; Hey, Good Lookin'.

MALOOF, WILLIAM JOSEPH　　　　　ASCAP 1967
　　composer
b Boston, Mass, May 19, 33. Educ: Boston Univ, BMus, grad studies. Chmn of comp dept, Berklee Col Music, 67- Author of textbooks on theory, counterpoint & notation. Extensive conducting appearances. Compositions, chamber, choral, band & orch widely performed, incl performances by Boston Symph, youth concerts & Indianapolis Symph Orch. *Songs:* Music: I Sing of Brooks, Blossoms, Birds and Bowers, for A cappella women's voices; Gloria, for chorus, brass choir & organ. *Instrumental Works:* Prelude and Chaconne for Solo Viola; Homage to Bali (for 8 percussionists); Essay for Band; Sinfonietta Concertante (for symph orch); In Tribus Linguis (concerto for rock, jazz & symph orchs). *Scores:* Opera: The Centurion.

MALOTTE, ALBERT HAY　　　　　　ASCAP 1936
　　composer, author, organist
b Philadelphia, Pa, May 19, 1895; d Hollywood, Calif, Nov 16, 64. Educ: Pvt music study. Concert organist, US & Europe. Founded sch for theatre organists, Los Angeles, 27; wrote for early sound films. Music dir, Walt Disney Studios, 4 yrs. Song bk, "Music By Albert Hay Malotte," publ 74. *Songs:* The Lord's Prayer; Twenty-Third Psalm; Song of the Open Road; Sing a Song of Sixpence; Ferdinand the Bull; The Ugly Duckling; For My Mother; Bob-o-Link; My Fascinating Girl; Melancholy Moon; Maybe Perhaps; The Beatitudes; David and Goliath; Little Song of Life; Upstream; Fiesta; My Friend; I Am Proud to Be an American; Golfer's Lament; It's Good to Know; Faith; Understanding Heart. *Instrumental Works:* Ballets: Little Red Riding Hood; Carnival of Venice; Musical Play: Lolama; Choral: The Ninety-First Psalm; Voice of the Prophet. *Scores:* Film background: Dr Cyclops; Enchanted Forest; Stage: Fanfare; The Big Tree; Limbo.

MALTBY, RICHARD E　　　　　　　ASCAP 1954
　　composer, conductor, trumpeter
b Chicago, Ill, June 26, 14. Educ: Northwestern Univ. Cornetist, dance bands. With staff orch, WBBM, Chicago. Network cond & arr. To New York, 45. Cond, own orch; recording artist. *Instrumental Works:* Six Flats Unfurnished; What's Your Hurry?; Manhattan Discotheque; Hail to the Fleet; Fugue in 5 Flats; Threnody; Requiem for John F Kennedy.

MALTIN, BERNARD　　　　　　　　ASCAP 1936
　　composer, pianist
b New York, NY, June 17, 07; d New York, Apr 10, 52. Educ: Juilliard Sch Music. Pianist in dance orchs, Ben Bernie & Ray Heatherton. Accompanist for Connee Boswell. Served in USMS, WW II. *Songs:* Afraid; You Are Music; I'm Good for Nothing But Love; Because of Once Upon a Time; Don't Count Your Kisses. *Instrumental Works:* Professor Spoons; U A Like No A Like; Finesse; Keeper of the Keys; Happy Fingers. *Scores:* Bway Stage: Bamboola.

MALVIN, ARTHUR　　　　　　　　　ASCAP 1958
　　composer, author, singer
b New York, NY, July 7, 22. Educ: George Washington High Sch; NY Univ, 2 yrs; Am Theatre Wing, studied voice & Solfeggio. Vocalist with Claude Thornhill Orch; organized vocal group, The Crew Chiefs for Maj Glenn Miller's Army Air Force Orch; soloist with Glenn Miller Orch; writer of spec musical material for Carol Burnett Show for 11 seasons; winner of Emmy in collaboration with Stan Freeman for spec musical material in 78; nominated for

Tony Award for additional music & lyrics for "Sugar Babies." Chief Collabrs: Stan Freeman, Glen Miller, Hal Dickinson, Bill Conway. *Songs:* Lyrics: I'm Headin for California; The Blues of the Record Man.

MAN, DAVID   ASCAP 1979
composer, author, singer

b Philadelphia, Pa, Apr 29, 38. Educ: Am Univ; Am Theatre Wing; studied with Ellis Larkins & Lehman Engel. Films as actor incl "Medical Center", "Love Boat", "Chips", "Rookies" & "Cannon." Bk, lyrics & dir, "The Woyzeck Follies," 74, "Elves in Bondage," 75, "Soap" & "Adults Only, No Pets," 79 (ASCAP Award for lyrics). Performed, wrote & dir 2 concerts of original material, Lincoln Ctr, New York, 80. Chief Collabrs: Aaron Egigian, James Abruzzo, Stan Hoffman, Michael Korie. *Songs:* The Good Stuff; Lyrics: Small Mistakes; Do You Come Here Often?; Aunt Ida; Please Bring Me the World Tonight.

MANA-ZUCCA   ASCAP 1925
composer, pianist, singer

b New York, NY, Dec 25, 1894. Educ: Univ Miami, degree; studied piano with Alexander Lambert & Godowsky Busoni, orchestration with Herman Spielter & Vogrich, voice with Von Zur Muhlen. Piano debut at age 8 with NY Philh. Toured US & Europe. Appeared in Europ & Am operettas, debut in "The Count of Luxembourg," 14. Concertized, incl own works in progs. Gave war bond concerts, WW II. *Songs:* I Love Life; Rachem; Big Brown Bear; Nichevo; Zonaves Drill; There's Joy in My Heart; Honey Lamb; Time and Time Again. *Instrumental Works:* Piano Concerto; Violin Sonata; Trio for Piano, Violin, Cello; My Musical Calendar (365 piano pieces); Sonata for Piano No 3; Sonata for Cello and Piano; Concerto for Piano and Orchestra; Concerto for Violin and Orchestra. *Scores:* Hypatia (one act Chinese opera).

MANCHESTER, SUSAN   ASCAP 1970
composer, singer

b New York, NY, Mar 16, 42. Educ: Pembroke Col; NY Univ. Singer with group, New York, 60's; club engagements late 60's; wrote songs incl rock-n-roll & country, 70's; studio work & commercials also. Chief Collabrs: Charles Silver, Annie Sutton. *Songs:* Music: Standing Room Only.

MANCINI, ALBERT   ASCAP 1959
composer, conductor, musician

b Potenza, Italy, Apr 23, 1899. Educ: High sch. With Nat Soldiers Home Band, Johnson City, Tenn, 10-14. Musician in dance bands, 11-23. Traveled with Chautauqua, 15. Served USA, WW I, 15-19. With US Marine Band, 23; Detroit Symph, 23-45; Los Angeles Symph & Hollywood Bowl, 45-65. Cond, Oakland County Symph, 38-43. Cond, Am Legion Band, Knights Templar & Elks Band. *Instrumental Works:* US Marines on Parade; March of the Champions; BPOE March; Sheer-Zadah March; Symphonic Trios for 3 Trumpets; Daily Studies for Trumpet; Trumpet Studies With Modernistic Rhythms; Symphonic Quartets for Brass; Etudes and Caprices in the Modern Manor; Trans: Divertissements (trumpet); 12 World Famous Concertos (trumpet).

MANCINI, FELICE   ASCAP 1970
author, singer

b Burbank, Calif, May 4, 52. Educ: Univ Denver, studied music; Univ Calif, Los Angeles, studied music; studied voice with Lee & Sally Sweetland. Backup singer for various recording artists & on TV. Chief Collabr: Henry Mancini (father). *Songs:* Lyrics: Sometimes.

MANCINI, HENRY   ASCAP 1952
composer

b Cleveland, Ohio, Apr 16, 24. Educ: Pvt study with Max Adkins, 38-40; Juilliard Inst Music, 41; pvt study with Mario Castelnuovo-Tedesco, Ernst Krenek & Alfred Sendry. WW II service, 42-45. Pianist-arr, Tex Beneke-Glenn Miller Orch, 45-47. Staff comp, Universal Studios, 52-58. Has cond most major symph orchs in US & abroad. Author "Sounds and Scores." Has made many records. Former mem exec bd, ASCAP; mem exec bd, Comp & Lyricists Guild Am. Recipient of 20 Grammy Awards & 6 gold albums. Honorary Alumnus, Univ Calif, Los Angeles; DMus, Duquesne Univ; LHD, Mount St Mary's Col. Chief Collabrs: Johnny Mercer, Leslie Briscusse, Don Black, Alan & Marilyn Bergman, Livingston & Evans, Bob Wells, Felice Mancini. *Songs:* Music: Moon River (Acad, Grammy Awards, 61); Days of Wine and Roses (Acad, Grammy Awards, 62); Charade; Dear Heart; The Sweetheart Tree; Moment to Moment; In the Arms of Love; Two for the Road; Darling Lili; Sunflower; All His Children; Send a Little Love My Way; Once Is Not Enough; It's Easy to Say; Sometimes. *Instrumental Works:* Peter Gunn; Mr Lucky (Grammy Award, 50); Pink Panther; Soldier in the Rain; The Great Race March; The Molly Maguires theme; Oklahoma Crude; Beaver Valley '37 (concert suite); Mystery Movie theme; What's Happening? theme. *Scores:* TV: Peter Gunn (Grammy Award, 58); Mr Lucky; Films: Touch of Evil; The Glenn Miller Story; Breakfast at Tiffany's (Acad Award, 61); Days of Wine and Roses; Hatari; Charade; The Pink Panther (and all sequels); Darling Lili; The Molly Maguires; Sunflower; The White Dawn; The Silver Streak; 10; The Benny Goodman Story; High Time; Bachelor in Paradise; Man's Favorite Sport; A Shot in the Dark; The Great Imposter; Mr Hobbs Takes a Vacation; Experiment in Terror; Soldier in the Rain; Dear Heart; The Great Race; Moment to Moment; Arabesque.

MANDEL, JOHNNY ALFRED   ASCAP 1956
composer, conductor, trumpeter

b New York, NY, Nov 23, 25. Educ: Started studying arr at age 13 with Van Alexander; Juilliard; Manhattan Sch Music; pvt study with Stefan Volpe, Bernard Wagner, Mario Castelnuovo-Tedesco & George Tremblay. Started as jazz trombone player & arr with bands, incl Count Basie, Buddy Rich, Woody Herman, Georgie Auld, Jimmy Dorsey & Joe Venuti. Has worked in records with Frank Sinatra, Peggy Lee, Mel Torme & others. Staff comp "Your Show of Shows," TV. Chief Collabrs: Johnny Mercer, Paul Francis Webster, Arthur Hamilton, Hal David, Paul Williams, Peggy Lee. *Songs:* The Shining Sea; Close Enough for Love; Music: The Shadow of Your Smile (Acad, Grammy Awards, 65); Suicide Is Painless; A Time for Love; Emily. *Instrumental Works:* Straight Life; Not Really the Blues; Hershey Bar; Pot Luck; Tommyhawk. *Scores:* TV: Markham; GE Theatre; Films: You're Never Too Young; I Want to Live; The Americanization of Emily; The Sandpiper (Grammy Award, 65); The Russians Are Coming, the Russians Are Coming; Harper; An American Dream; Mash; Pretty Poison; Summer Wishes Winter Dreams; Agatha; Being There.

MANDEL, JULIE   ASCAP 1956
composer, author

b Brooklyn, NY, Sept 12, 27. Educ: Los Angeles City Col, music; Univ Calif, Los Angeles, music; studied comp with Ernst Krenek & Eric Zeisl. Wrote revues at Green Mansions, off-Bway & summer stock productions of musical based on Kaufman & Hart's "Once in a Lifetime." Musical revue, "2," done in dinner theatre & in part on British TV. Wrote two children's musicals "Pari and the Prince", "Danny Dunn and the Homework Machine." Choral works done in schs throughout the country. Wrote Nat Book Week theme song, radio commercials, Ambre Solaire. *Songs:* Junk Food; Cathy; Pizza; The Human Brain; A Teenager Takes Stock; Cars; Summer TV; Think Metric; Books Now, Books Wow; In or Out; Cat—Sentence; Address: Moon; Lyrics: Back in My Arms. *Scores:* Off-Bway shows: Dear Mr Greene; Two Pieces of Bread; Two Points of View; Two is What It's All About; Lucky, Lucky.

MANERI, JOSEPH GABRIEL
composer, teacher

b New York, NY, Feb 9, 27. Educ: Studied harmony, counterpoint & comp with Josef Schmid, 46-58. Prof clarinetist & saxophonist, weddings. Jazz musician, concerts. Comp microtonal music, 72- *Songs & Instrumental Works:* Metanoia (concerto for piano, orch); Maranatha (woodwinds, brass, perc); Ephphatha (clarinet, trombone, tuba, piano); And Death Shall Have No Dominion (voice, piano).

MANGEL, CARLOS A   ASCAP 1975
composer, author

b San Jose, Costa Rica. Studied piano with Crisanto Murillo, guitar with Rafael Solano; Manuel Aragon Sch Commerce, Costa Rica; M A Castro Carazo Accounting Sch, Costa Rica; ICS, Scranton, Pa, studied advert; Univ Miami, studied English. Founder, C Mangel Co & Publicidad Mangel. Dir-promoter, Miss Universe Beauty Contest, Costa Rica, Nicaragua, Honduras, Salvador & Guatemala, SAm, 55-60. Founder & pres: Gala Records, Miami; Gala Int; Gala Americas Inc; United Exporters, Miami, Fla. *Songs:* Ballads: Pasional; Mientes; Desilusion.

MANGES, KENNY   ASCAP 1960
author

b Lyons, NY, July 9, 13. Gag writer; puzzlemaker. Chief Collabrs: Ray Rivera, Tony Mazzola. *Songs:* Lyrics: Donkey Got Drunk; Let Me Kiss You Goodnight; Calypso Cat; When a Woman Is Blue; Thank You My Lord; What Am I Doing Here.

MANGUAL, JOSE LUIS, JR   ASCAP 1977
composer, author, singer

b New York, NY, Jan 11, 48. Educ: Pvt lessons, 3 yrs; Jr high sch music prog, 3 yrs; High Sch Commerce, New York, studied theory, 2 yrs. Started playing with neighborhood groups, early 60's. Played with Willie Colin & Hector Laval. Accompanist, Rubin Blades, Celia Cruz & Ismael Miranda. Percussionist & back-up singer, later lead singer & bandleader. Writer & comp, original material, dance halls, theatres, TV & radio. Chief Collabrs: Jose Mangual, Sr, Luis Mangual. *Songs:* Campanero; Salta Perico; Amigo Infiel; Matrimonia Feliz; Negrita.

MANION, MARY ENDRES   ASCAP 1962
composer, author, singer

b Philadelphia, Pa, Feb 16, 07. Educ: Annunciation Sch; Stephen Girard Sch; Edgar Allan Poe Sch; SPhiladelphia High; Peirce Bus Col; studied voice with A Moore. Secy, City of Philadelphia, retired 67. Secy to chief, Div Preventive Med, Dept Pub Health; chief, Div Educ; Philadelphia Museum Art. *Songs:* Shadow in Love; Darling Will You Marry Me; Welcome to Philadelphia; I Wish I Were Twins; I Long to Be Back in Your Arms.

MANK, CHARLES (CHAW)   ASCAP 1935
composer, author, singer

b Staunton, Ill, Sept 30, 02. Educ: Studied piano with David Silverman; studied voice. Started first fan club, 10. Theatre organist, age 14. Had own band, 58 yrs, retired, 79. Teacher piano & songwriting. Has own record co, Blue Ribbon

Record Co. Publicity mgr for Cowboy Copas, 8 yrs. Mem, 265 fan clubs, pres, 22 clubs. Author: "Garbo"; "Valentino"; "Chaw Mank's Psychic Diary"; "My Favorite Prayer." Chief Collabrs: Cowboy Copas, Johnny Dollar. *Songs:* Bringing Mary Home; Rose of Oklahoma; Down in Nashville, Tenn; I Saw Jim Reeve's Up There; Counterfeit Kisses; First Degree Burns; This Woman Is Mine; The Country Gentleman; Let's Say Hello to Reno; I'd Like to Be 16 Again (And Know What I Know Now).

MANN, AARON ASCAP 1959
composer
b Tornalja, Hungary, May 31, 1899. *Songs:* Hand in Hand; Wedding Prayer.

MANN, CHARLES MAYNARD ASCAP 1971
composer, author, singer
b Atlanta, Ga, Dec 29, 49. Educ: Harper High Sch; Morehouse Col, BA(music comp), 77; studied voice & harmony with Wendell P Whalum, comp with T J Anderson, harmony with Joyce Fynch Johnson. Recording artist, ABC/Dunhill Records. Performer in nightclubs, New York & Atlanta. Appeared on TV, "Mike Douglas Show" & "Soul Train." Collab musical comedy, "Dr B S Black," performed in Atlanta. Chief Collabrs: Dave Crawford, Carlton & Barbara Molette, Roberta Flack, Donny Hathaway. *Songs:* Be Real Black for Me; Say You Love Me Too; Very Lonely; You Came Out of Nowhere; Lyrics: I Like to Live the Love.

MANN, DAVID A ASCAP 1949
composer, author, teacher
b Philadelphia, Pa, Oct 3, 16. Educ: Univ Pa; Villanova Univ, MA; Curtis Inst Music, studied with David Saperton, Fritz Reiner & Rosario Scalero. Began broadcasting career while in high sch, CBS, Philadelphia. As pianist joined Charlie Spivak Orch; later with Jimmy Dorsey as pianist & arr. Served in USA, WW II; off pianist for Pres Truman. After arr, arr many broadcasts, 20th Century Fox Studios & Bway shows. Began writing ed columns for local newspaper, 71; now syndicated in several suburban papers. Taught in Walden Sch, NY, as head music dept. Now preparing musical version of hit farce "Room Service." Journalist. Chief Collabrs: Bob Hilliard, Redd Evans, John Murray. *Songs:* Music: There, I've Said It Again; Dearie (You're Much Older Than I); Somebody Bad Stole de Wedding Bell; In the Wee Small Hours; No Moon At All; Don't Go to Strangers; Boutonniere; Downhearted; It Might As Well Rain; These Will Be the Best Years of Our Lives; Come Down to Earth, Mr Smith.

MANN, HERBERT JAY ASCAP 1959
composer, author, musician
b Brooklyn, NY, Apr 16, 30. Educ: Abraham Lincoln High Sch, Brooklyn; Manhattan Sch Music; studied flute with Frederick Wilkins. Played with Mat Mathews, 52; flutist in Pete Rugulo's band, 54; played with Tony Bennett, 55; leader of own group, 56-; toured Africa for State Dept, 60 & toured Turkey, Cyprus & Scandinavia, 71. Recorded over 75 albums as leader for Verve, Prestege, Savoy, Bethlehem, Columbia, Riverside & Atlanta. Performer in concerts, nightclubs & TV; wrote scores for 2 plays & 56 TV shows, NBC. *Songs:* Yellow Fever; Music: Bedouin; Mushi Mushi; My Little Ones; Sports Car; Sudan; Today; Turkish Coffee; Challil; Paradise Music; Body Oil. *Instrumental Works:* Memphis Underground; Yesterdays Kisses; Push Push; High Above the Andes; Mediterranean; Concerto Grosso in D Blues; Paradise Beach; Miss Free Spirit; Waltz for My Son; Don't You Know the Way; The Piper; Birdwalk; Sunbelt; Pele; Oh How I Want to Love You.

MANN, JEROME ASCAP 1952
composer, author, actor
b New York, NY, Aug 1, 10. Educ: Prof Children's Sch. Former child actor. Writer, radio, films & TV. *Songs:* Shakin' Jamaican Rum-ba; It Ain't the Cough; A Liberal Education.

MANN, JOHN RUSSELL ASCAP 1963
composer, author, musical director
b Baltimore, Md, Aug 30, 28. Educ: Baltimore City Col; Peabody Cons, Baltimore. Formed vocal groups, Baltimore & Philadelphia, 49-51; played trombone, sang & arr, USA Field Band, 51-53. Moved to Hollywood, 53; orchestration for seven feature films at Columbia, Warner Bros, 20th Century Fox; choral dir, NBC's "Comedy Hour." Johnny Mann Singers had 35 albums in release, two Grammy winners & five nominations. Musical dir, "Joey Bishop Show"; starred in own TV series, "Stand Up and Cheer" (86 shows); created & produced hundreds of commercials & radio station ID's. Singer & arr. Chief Collabrs: Lynn Mann, Paul Sawtell. *Songs:* The Voice of Freedom; Joey Is the Name; Stand Up and Cheer; Music: Sing a Song of Love; Lyrics: Texas Lady.

MANN, KAL ASCAP 1956
composer, author, record producer
b Philadelphia, Pa, May 6, 17. Educ: Overbrook High Sch, grad, 34. Started as comedy writer. Became successful with writing parodies. Asked to write lyrics to original melodies. Became successful as songwriter. Produced records. Discovered, recorded & managed Chubby Checker, Dee Dee Sharp, The Dovells, The Orlons & others. Chief Collabrs: Dave Appell, Bernie Lowe. *Songs:* Let's Twist Again; Slow Twistin'; Twistin' USA; Kissin' Time; Lyrics: Bristol Stomp; Dancing Party; Hully Gully Baby; Limbo Rock; Popeye Waddle; Ride!; South Street; Wah-Watusi; You Can't Sit Down; Teddy Bear; Don't Hang Up; Dinner With Drac; We Got Love; Wild One.

MANN, LYNN
See Dolin, Lynn Marie

MANN, PAUL ASCAP 1940
composer
b Vienna, Austria, Sept 3, 10. Educ: Acad Music, Vienna, studied with Joseph Marx. Wrote songs for stage & film, Austria & Berlin, Ger until 33 & US, 37- Chief Collabrs: Stephan Weiss, Al Lewis, Ruth Loew, Al Jacobs, Kim Gannon, Edward Heyman, Sid Tepper, Roy Bennet, Eddy De Lange, Sammy Cahn. *Songs:* Music: Put Your Dreams Away; The Finger of Suspicion; They Say; Angel in Disguise; When You Look in Your Looking Glass; Make Love to Me; The Woodchuck Song; And So Do I; Anybody's Love Song.

MANN, ROBERT E (BERT) ASCAP 1944
composer, author, comedian
b Los Angeles, Calif, Mar 18, 02; d New York, NY, Jan 15, 78. Educ: High sch. Comedian, theatres, films & radio. Writer, spec material for vaudeville acts. Chief Collabrs: Jesse Greer, Eugene West, William Faber, Joe Rosenfield, Jr. *Songs:* Why Do Peanuts Whistle?; Caught in a Dream; I Didn't Think You Cared; If I Misunderstood You; Dream Another Dream; Need I Say?; Two Broken Hearts; I Fell and Broke My Heart; The Happiness Exchange; I've Got Cousins By the Dozens; When Good Folks Get Together; Be a Big Pal to a Little Pal (off PAL song); Give to Leukemia & The City of Hope (off City of Hope songs); Wrong; Waltz With Me; He's a Carousel Cowboy; Tango of Hearts; Here Comes Tomorrow (off Girl Scouts song); Have a Heart and Save a Heart (off Deborah HOSO song).

MANN, STEPHEN FOLLETT (CLIFF DIAMOND) ASCAP 1971
composer, arranger
b Oak Park, Ill, Oct 21, 45. Educ: Studied with Robert Mann (father); Kendall Col, studied music theory & harmony with Jim Bohart; Northwestern Univ, studied orchestration technique. Orchestrator for three albums & many singles. Comp music for Quaker Oats, 3 yrs. Recording artist, West Records. Some TV; arr, films & live shows. *Songs:* Diane in the Sunshine; Low Are the Tides.

MANN, STEVE
See Krasnow, Hermann (Hecky)

MANN, SY ASCAP 1959
composer, pianist, organist
b Binghamton, NY, June 13, 20. Educ: NY Univ, BS(music educ), 46; studied conducting with Tibor Serly. Chief warrant officer & bandleader, 44th Inf Div, AUS, WW II. Staff musician with WNEW, New York, 49-53 & CBS, New York, 54-73; musical dir, pianist & arr, Arthur Godfrey Show, 61-73; pianist, organist & arr, commercial jingles, recordings, film, TV & theater. Mem: Life mem Phi Mu Alpha-Sinfonia. Chief Collabrs: Hy Glaser, Remus Harris, Sy Muskin. *Songs:* Coronado 1-2-3; Music: Here Am I Without My Valentine; My Number One Song; Let's Tell Them Now; Disenchanted; I'm Old Enough; Warm, Sweet, Tender and Dreamy; Betty; When the Tide Went Out. *Instrumental Works:* Metropole; Nocturne; Etude; Reflections.

MANNE, SHELLY ASCAP 1959
composer, jazz musician
b New York, NY, June 11, 20. Educ: Studied drums with Billy Gladstone. Jazz musician with var bands, incl Bobby Byrne, Bob Astor, Joe Marsala, Raymond Scott, Will Bradley & Les Brown, 39-42. Served with USCG, 42-45. Musician, NBC & CBS Studios, 52nd Street Jazz Clubs, Stan Kenton Band, Charlie Ventura, Jazz at Philh & Woody Herman Orch, 45-52. Free lance musician, Los Angeles, 52-55; formed own band, 55. Made recordings for Capitol Records, 54- Owner, The Manne-Hole, Hollywood nightclub, 60- Tech adv & actor in motion pictures. Guest star on numerous TV shows. Comp score, Centre Theatre Group production, Shakespeare's Henry IV, Part I, Los Angeles. Rec'd awards from var mag. *Songs:* Music: Tall Story; Parthenia (A Year of Youth); Grasshopper. *Instrumental Works:* Pastorale. *Scores:* Film/TV: T-Bird Gang; The Proper Time; Daktari; Trial of Catonsville Nine; Trader Horn; Young Billy Young; The Box.

MANNERS, MAXINE ASCAP 1952
composer, author, singer
b Los Angeles, Calif, Sept 7, 20. Educ: Fairfax High Sch; Santa Monica City Col. Songwriter from age 16. Writer, spec material for Harry Richard & Louise Hovak, songs for Earl Carroll's Hollywood Theatre Revue "Let Freedom Ring," & 2 films. Chief Collabr: Sid Kullen. *Songs:* You're the Answer to My Prayer; Don't Let Them Write Another Polka; Gotta Have It; Music: Oh, Brother; Lyrics: You're My Destiny.

MANNERS, ZEKE (LEO MANNES) ASCAP 1942
composer, singer
b San Francisco, Calif, Oct 10, 11. Leader, own group of country entertainers; featured on radio. Served, World War II. *Songs:* There Was a Time; Pennsylvania Polka; That's Why I Waited So Long; Don't Do It, Darling; An Olden Melody.

MANNES, LEO
See Manners, Zeke

MANNEY, CHARLES FONTEYN   ASCAP 1926
composer, conductor, editor
b Brooklyn, NY, Feb 8, 1872; d New York, NY, Oct 31, 51. Educ: Brooklyn Polytech; studied with William Arms Fisher, J Wallace Goodrich & Percy Goetschius. Asst ed, then chief ed, Boston music publ, 1898-30. Choral cond, MacDowell Club. *Instrumental Works:* A Shropshire Lad; O Captain, My Captain; Cantatas: The Resurrection; The Manger Throne.

MANNING, DICK   ASCAP 1946
composer, author
b Gomel, Russia, June 12, 12. Educ: Juilliard Cons. Has been concert pianist, cond, arr, vocal coach & accompanist. Music dir, radio. Chief Collabrs: Al Hoffman, Al Stillman, Buddy Kaye, Kay Twomey. *Songs:* Takes Two to Tango; Morningside of the Mountain; Pussycat Song (Nyot Nyow); Allegheny Moon; Papa Loves Mambo; La Plume de Ma Tanta; Gilly Gilly Ossenfeffer; Secretly; Treasure of Sierra Madre; Oh-Oh I'm Falling in Love Again; I'm Never Gonna Tell; I Can't Tell a Waltz From a Tango; I Still Feel the Same About You; Jilted; Mi Casa Su Casa; Belonging to Someone; O Dio Mio; Ivy Rose; Are You Really Mine?; Like I Do; Mama Teach Me to Dance; Johnny Jingo; Lyrics: Fascination; Hawaiian Wedding Song; An Empty Glass; Hot Diggity; Rosanne; Torero; Underneath the Linden Tree. *Instrumental Works:* Nightbird (symphonic rhapsody).

MANNING, KATHLEEN LOCKHART   ASCAP 1932
composer, pianist, singer
b Hollywood, Calif, Oct 24, 1890; d Hollywood Mar 22, 51. Studied music with M Moszkowski, Jaques Coini, Regina de Sales & Elizabeth Eichelberger. Concert tours, Eng & France, 09-14. Sang with Hammerstein Opera Co, London, 11-12. Gave concerts, US, 26. *Songs & Instrumental Works:* Sketches of Paris; Sketches of London; Songs of Egypt; Four Songs of Bilitis; Sketches of New York; Water-Lily; Autumn Leaves; Shoes; Nang-Ping; Pagoda Bells; In the Luxembourg Gardens.

MANNING, LAURA   ASCAP 1955
composer, author, singer
b Brooklyn, NY, Sept 24, 36. Educ: S J Tilden High Sch; Brooklyn Col; studied voice with James Woodside, Greta Stuckgolde & Estelle Liebling, piano with Isadore Franzblau, guitar with Bill Suyker & accordion with Billy Costa. Started singing with soc orchs, incl Lester Lanin, Meyer Davis & Ray Bloch. Wrote songs, incl off-Bway show & children's albums. Writer of act for Donald O'Connor & Sid Miller, material for Redd Foxx, children's shows & pilots for Toni Tennille. Writer for MGM. As a singer traveled all over, incl trip to Vietnam. Chief Collabrs: Alan Greene, Cass Harrison, Henry Tobias, Alf Nystrom. *Songs:* Lyrics: A Woman Is Love; Room for Everybody; The Old Lady of Threadneedle Street; Since You Looked At Me; All That's Left; Just for Me; Bridges; My Garden; Singer; What Do You Say After You Say Hello?; If a Bug Won't Eat It, Why Should I?. *Scores:* Bway Shows: Antiques; Go Like Sixty. *Albums:* Know Your Body From Head to Toe; What Can the Difference Be?.

MANNING, RICHARD   ASCAP 1946
composer, singer
b London, Eng, Aug 30, 14; d Vienna, Austria, July 8, 54. Educ: Oxford Univ; Juilliard Sch Music, fel. Mem, Metrop Opera Co; also sang at City Center, New York. *Songs:* I Been Waitin'; A Kentucky Riddle; Shenandoah; Santa Maria; What Is This Fragrance; Wife Trouble; Vielle Chanson de Chasse; Le Montagnard Exile; La Guajira; Serrana; Since First I Saw Your Face; Down by the Riverside.

MANNO, TONY   ASCAP 1957
composer, author
b Chicago, Ill, June 17, 12. Educ: High sch. Chief Collabr: Ed Ballantine. *Songs:* More Than Ever; Be Mine My Love.

MANONE, JOE (WINGY)   ASCAP 1953
composer, author, conductor
b New Orleans, La, Feb 1900. Educ: Pub schs. Toured & recorded with dance bands. Led own small groups, 34-41. Appeared in radio & films. Autobiography, "Trumpet on the Wing." Trumpeter & singer. *Instrumental Works:* Tar Paper Stomp; Nickel in the Slot; Tailgate Ramble.

MANSFIELD, MARIE MOSS   ASCAP 1953
composer, author, pianist
b Pittsburgh, Pa. Educ: Morton's Bus Col; studied piano with Antoinette Brosky, Father Raymond Balka. Staff pianist, WCAE, 8 yrs; pianist, KDKA. Mgr, music dept, G C Murphy Dept Store. Leader, own trio, Park Schenley Restaurant, Pittsburgh, 53- *Songs:* Until Sunrise; Rhapsody on the Loose; Don't Say You Love Me; It Happened in My Heart; Please Leave Me Alone; Look Out for Santa Claus; Rhumba Boogie.

MANSFIELD, SCOTT JOEL   ASCAP 1975
composer, author
b Evanston, Ill, Mar 23, 49. Educ: Boston Univ; NY Univ, BA. Wrote screenplay for motion picture "Deadly Games." *Songs:* Lyrics: Lost in Love Again, theme. *Scores:* Bway shows: Once I Saw a Boy Laughing; Le Belly Button.

MANSON, EDDY LAWRENCE   ASCAP 1958
composer, author, conductor
b New York, NY, May 9, 22. Educ: Juilliard Sch Music, hon grad, clarinet/comp maj, 42; City Col New York, 51; NY Univ Sch Radio, TV & Film, cert, 53; Univ Calif, Los Angeles, 73-75; pvt study: comp with Vittorio Giannini, Howard Brockway & Rudy Schramm; orchestration with Adolf Schmid & Vittorio Giannini; electronic music with Jimmy Carroll & Philip Springer; clarinet with Jan Williams; conducting with Albert Stoessel & Louis Bostelmann; harmonica with Borrah Minnevitch. Performer & cond, USO Camp Shows, 43-45; leading int harmonica virtuoso, 45-, soloist, Brentwood Symph Orch & Calif Chamber Symph Orch & had recitals & appearances with Los Angeles Mandolin Orch. Became film composer in 53; comp/producer commercials, 56- Pres, Am Soc Music Arr, NY, 56-58. Pres, Eddy Manson Productions, Inc & Margery Music, Inc, 58- Music dir, Synagogue of Performing Arts, Los Angeles, 73-75; sr teacher, Univ Calif, Los Angeles Ext, 75-, prof scoring music film & arr & orchestrating. Pres, Am Soc Music Arr (Nat), 77- Founder, Am Soc Music Arr, Comp/Arrs' Workshop, Los Angeles, 80-; founder-dir, Manson Ensemble, 80- Mem bd, Music & Arts Found Am & Comp & Art Found Am. Mem adv bd, Songwriters Resources Service. Mem: Acad Motion Picture Arts & Sci; Nat Acad Recording Arts & Sci; Am Guild Authors & Comp; Am Fedn Musicians; The Bohemians; Nat Asn Comp, USA; Juilliard Alumni Asn. Awards & Prizes: The Elizabeth Sprague Coolidge Prize Comp; ASCAP Panel Awards; 16 CLIOS for TV Commercials; 5 Venice Film Festival Awards; Golden Eagle; shared Acad Award, "Day of the Painter", 60. Arr. Chief Collabrs: Carl Sigman, Hal Hackaday, Al Stillman, George Weiss, Fred Ebb. *Songs:* Song of Lorena (adaptation); Oh No!; Music: Joey's Theme. When He Was Young; But Give Me Time; The Cliff Dwellers (theme); If She Were Mine; The Family Way. *Instrumental Works:* Boy on a Carousel; Night Beat; Coney Island; Lovers and Lollipops (theme); Peggy's Theme; Ezra's Theme; Join Up, Join In (Am Red Cross); Haunted Heart; Runaway Star; Fandango; Paisano; Cornball No 1; Cornball Rag. *Scores:* Film: Little Fugitive (Venice Film Festival award, 53); Day of the Painter (Acad Award, 60); Weddings and Babies; Lovers and Lollipops; Three Bites of the Apple; The Supermarket; The Boudoir; What Time Is It Now; The Cliff Dwellers (Acad Award Nominee); King of the Ice; The Woman Inside; Documentary Film/TV: The River Nile (Emmy nomination Best Music); American Spectacle; Polaris Submarine (Venice Film Festival award); The Capitol: Freedom's Chronicle (Golden Eagle Award); US 1: American Profile (Venice Film Festival award); Al Smith Story; 73 Who Served; Mirror in the Mountains; TV: A Love Affair: The Eleanor & Lou Gehrig Story; Crash: The True Story of Flight 401; The Bugs Bunny Christmas Special (79, cond); Firehouse (ABC Series); Night Train to Terror (ABC Wild World of Entertainment); Slattery's People; The Virginian; Ben Casey; Harvey (Dupont Theater; Emmy nomination, Best Music); Ed Sullivan's Invitation to Moscow; Armstrong Circle Theater; Kraft Theater; Johnny Jupiter (series); Wonderful World of Little Julius; Lamp Unto My Feet. *Albums:* Grimm's Fairy Tales; Black Beauty; Little Songs That Teach; Snow White and the Seven Dwarfs.

MANTIA, JOE   ASCAP 1962
composer, conductor, pianist
b Chicago, Ill, Aug 30, 14. Educ: Col; pvt music study. Pianist, nightclubs & hotels; had own group. Pianist & cond for Forrest Tucker. Chief Collabr: Johnny Schiller. *Songs:* Back to Rome; I Look for You.

MANUPPELLI, ANTONIO   ASCAP 1960
author
b Panni, Italy, June 7, 1892; d St Petersburg, Fla, Aug 2, 72. Educ: High sch. Served, USA, World War I. Vpres, Am Legion, 30 yrs. Author, poetry bks "Whispers From My Heart (Sussurri Del Mio Cuore)." *Songs:* Bimba Mia; Regina Mia.

MANUS, FAY WHITMAN   ASCAP 1953
author, poet
b Little Falls, NY, June 14, 26. Educ: Midwood High Sch, Brooklyn, NY. Wrote spec material for Carl Brisson, also poetry & light verse in McCall's, NY Times & Weight Watcher's Mag; poet-in-schs; writer workshops, poetry readings; ed consult, Harvest Mag. Chief Collabrs: Jack Manus, Helen Miller. *Songs:* Lyrics: The Doodle Song; Am I Asking Too Much; You Don't Know What You're Getting; Where the Bongos Play; Say Hello for Me; Be I Bumblebee Or Not; It's Funny.

MANUS, JACK   ASCAP 1947
composer, author, publisher
b Philadelphia, Pa, Sept 9, 09. Educ: Syracuse Univ. USAAF, WW II. Staff writer for Shapiro, Bernstein. Chief Collabrs: Guy Wood, Bernard Bierman, Leonard Joy. *Songs:* Lyrics: Vanity; Midnight Masquerade; When Paw Was Courtin' Maw; Forget If You Can; My Cousin Louella; Am I Wasting My Time?;

This Is the Inside Story; Unless It Can Happen With You; Cuban Mambo; What More Can I Ask For?; Jump Through the Ring; The Bridge.

MANZAREK, RAYMOND DANIEL   ASCAP 1968
composer
b Chicago, Ill, Feb 12, 39. Educ: De Paul Univ, BA(economics); Univ Calif, Los Angeles, MFA(cinema). Mem rock groups: The Doors & Nite City. Recording artist for Mercury Records; presently producer of rock bands for New Way Productions. Chief Collabrs: Jim Morrison, Robby Krieger, John Densmore. *Songs:* America; Music: Light My Fire; The End; When the Music's Over; L.A. Woman; Entire Doors Catalogue. *Albums:* The Golden Scarab; The Whole Thing Started With Rock & Roll Now It's Out of Control; Nite City.

MAR, JEFFREY KENNETH   ASCAP 1976
composer, author
b Palo Alto, Calif, July 3, 53. Educ: Cubberly High Sch; Univ Calif, Los Angeles, BA, 76. Musical dir, The Sophisticates & the Lettermen.

MARAFFI, LEWIS FREDERICK (FRITZ)   ASCAP 1977
composer, author, conductor
b Northampton, Pa. Educ: State Col High Sch; Oberlin Cons, BMus, 66; Oberlin Col, AB(English), 66; Univ Cincinnati Cons Music, MM(orchestral cond), 67; studied theory with Richard Hoffman, theory & comp with Marcel Dick & Scot Huston; Chautauqua Inst; Cleveland Inst Music. Guest cond-in-residence, Richmond Symph, Va. Musical dir & cond, Utica Symph, AIH ROMA Orch, Italy & Rome Fest Orch, Italy. Cond, Orchestra da Camera di Santa Cecilia, Rome & New York String Ens. Col teacher, 6 yrs. Guest cond maj orchs, US, Mex, Italy, Ireland, Poland, Greece, Romania, Denmark & USSR. With Pan Records & Pentaphon Records, Europe & VOX Records, US. Comns: State Univ NY Res Council; Pentaphon Records; Bradley Publ; Am Harp Soc. *Songs:* Timeless Afternoons (song cycle). *Instrumental Works:* Movements for Orchestra; Symphony No 1; Solo Sonata for Violoncello.

MARAIS, JOSEF   ASCAP 1942
composer, author, violinist
b Sir Lowry Pass, SAfrica, Nov 17, 05; d Los Angeles, Calif, Apr 27, 78. Educ: SAfrican Col Music (scholarship); Royal Acad, London. Mem, Capetown Symph. Early translr of Afrikaans & other folk songs. First US radio series "African Trek" (Blue Network), 40-42; with OWI, as dir, Afrikaans, later Dutch broadcasts for Voice of Am. Gave many concerts with wife, Miranda, also made many records. Author "Folk Song Jamboree", "World Folksongs", "Koos the Hottentot," co-author "Long Live the Brueghel People" (play with music). *Songs & Instrumental Works:* Marching to Pretoria; Henrietta's Wedding; Sugarbush; Pretty Kitty; Around the Corner; Brandy Leave Me Alone; The Crickets; The Zulu Warrior; Tony Beaver (opera); Africana Suite; Songs From the Veld (14 songs); The Bangalorey Man (for children); Booboo, the Baby Baboon; Hebraic Rhapsody (quintet for strings, French horn, piano). *Scores:* Film: Rio Grande.

MARC, RONALD
See Wolfson, Maxwell A

MARCELLI, NINO   ASCAP 1944
composer, conductor, educator
b Santiago, Chile, Jan 21, 1892; d San Diego, Calif, Aug 4, 67. Educ: Nat Cons of Chile; Univ of Chile. US citizen, 17. Dir, instrumental music, San Diego, Calif schs. Guest lectr, Univ Southern Calif, Univ of Idaho, Western State Col of Colo & Calif Music Col. Hon mem, fac of fine arts, Univ of Chile. Founder, cond, San Diego Symph, 25-37. Guest cond, Hollywood Bowl, Los Angeles Philh & San Francisco Symph. Cond, Ford Symph, Calif-Pacific Int Expos, 35-36. *Songs:* Solitude; Deep in the Forest; Harp of Sunset; Song of the Andes; Light Opera; Music: Song of Thanks. *Songs & Instrumental Works:* Suite Araucana (Am Comp Prize); Symphony; Suite for Strings; March Processional; Ode to a Hero; Music Box Minuet; 2 Christmas Processionals; Holy, Holy, Holy (for a capella, mixed chorus with opus, chimes).

MARCH, MYRNA FOX   ASCAP 1960
composer, author, singer
b Los Angeles, Calif, Nov 9, 35. Educ: High sch. Writer, special material. Singer & actress, nightclubs, films & TV. *Songs:* Crying Up a Storm; Why?

MARCHESE, ANDREW L   ASCAP 1956
composer, conductor, trumpeter
b Pensacola, Fla, Dec 29, 22. Educ: De Paul Univ. Led 607th USAF dance band, WW II. Trumpeter in bands incl Jack Teagarden & Frankie Masters; has led own dance band; head music dept, St Procapeni Col, Acad, Ill; educr. *Songs:* Lover's Lullaby; Baby Buggy Boogie; Little Gates; I'm Saving You for Me.

MARCHESE, HECTOR D   ASCAP 1952
composer, author
b West Springfield, Mass, Sept 1, 01. Played woodwinds in dance bands, radio, recordings, transcs, Bway musicals. Recorded for Muzak; led own band. Chief Collabr: Ray Trotta. *Songs:* I Should Have Told You Long Ago; What Could Be More Beautiful; Kitty Kat's Party; Tuxedos and Flowers; Play Ball; Happy

Little Island; Dance of the Candy Dolls; I'm from Texas; I'm Gonna Miss Ya; Bugles and Drums; Lovely Lady; Lyrics: Rozina; Don't Wait for Sunday to Pray.

MARCHFIELD, RUDY   ASCAP 1960
author, drummer
b Chicago, Ill, May 29, 07. Educ: Col. Drummer, dance orchs, nightclubs, theatres & tours. Chief Collabr: Frank Lavere. *Songs:* If I Could Have You Back Again; Who Am I to Say.

MARCO, SANO   ASCAP 1943
composer, author, singer
b Russia, Dec 10, 1898; d New York, NY, Sept 20, 70. Educ: High sch. Former mem, Metrop Opera Co; vocal teacher. Chief Collabr: Walter Hirsch. *Songs:* May I Never Love Again; Hoya; He Wants It That Way; Black Silence; Dig Down Deep (war bond song); Don't Cry Anymore (Non Piagere Piu); The Comedy Has Ended; Don't Say You Love Me.

MARCONE, STEPHEN F
composer, author, educator
b New York, NY, July 19, 45.

MARCOVICCI, ANDREA   ASCAP 1969
composer, author, singer
b New York, NY. Educ: Marymount Col. Actress on stage, film & TV; recording artist; appeared on film: "The Front"; "Airport '79"; "The Concorde"; "The Hand"; appeared on stage: "Hamlet"; "Nefertiti"; "Ambassador." *Songs:* Lost Angeles; I Do Believe I Love You.

MARCUCCI, ROBERT   ASCAP 1953
author, manager, record executive
b Philadelphia, Pa, Feb 28, 30. Educ: Columbia Inst, jour. Mgr, Frankie Avalon & Fabian; pres, Chancellor Records. Chief Collabr: Peter De Angelis. *Songs:* You Are Mine; Why; With All My Heart.

MARCUS, ADA BELLE   ASCAP 1929
author, pianist, educator
b Chicago, Ill, July 8, 29. Educ: Studied piano with Sergei Tarowsky, 41-46, comp with S Lieberson, 41-46; DePaul Univ (scholarship), 41-46, studied comp with Alexander Tcherepnin, 61-62, BMus, 77, MMus, 79; Cincinnati Cons Music, studied piano with Robert Goldsand, 48-49; Am Cons Music, studied comp with Leo Sowerby, 54-55; Roosevelt Univ, studied comp with Karel B Jirak, 59-60. Concertized in Midwest; soloist with symph orchs, in recitals & TV. Prolific comp, contemporary style incl piano, vocal, choral, chamber, concerti, operatic & orchestral works. Teacher piano, theory & comp, Chicago Cons Col. Mem: Am Music Conference; Chicago Artists Asn; Musicians Club of Women, Nat Fedn Music Clubs; Int Soc Contemporary Music; Chicago Fedn Musicians; League of Women Composers; Am Women Composers; Am Soc Univ Composers. Performed original piano works, "Meet the Composer," WNYC radio, New York, 78. *Instrumental Works:* Song for Flute (flute with piano); Blue Flute (flute with piano); Theme and Variations (piano solo); Etude Erotique (piano solo); A Child's Day (suite; piano solo); American Song Cycle (Robert Frost, text; Int Soc Contemporary Music Comp Award).

MARCUS, SOL   ASCAP 1942
composer, author, conductor
b New York, NY, Oct 12, 12; d Linden, NJ, Feb 5, 76. Educ: Col. Led own orch until 41; pianist. Chief Collabrs: Edward Seiler, Al Kaufman, Bennie Benjamin, Guy Wood. *Songs:* I Don't Want to Set the World on Fire; When the Lights Go on Again All Over the World; Till Then; Ask Anyone Who Knows; You're Gonna Fall and Break Your Heart; Cancel the Flowers; Small World; Fishin' for the Moon; And Then It's Heaven; The Girl From Jones Beach; Because You Love Me; To Remind Me of You; If Every Day Would Be Christmas; If All Begins and Ends With You; You Can't Hide Your Heart; Somehow Days Go By; Ah Dee Ah Dee Ah!; Strictly Instrumental; Lonely Man; Of This I'm Sure; Anyone Can Fall in Love; You're All I Want for Christmas; Don't Let Me Be Misunderstood.

MARES, PAUL JOSEPH   ASCAP 1946
composer, trumpeter
b New Orleans, La, June 15, 1900; d Chicago, Ill, Aug 18, 49. Educ: St Aloysius Sch. Trumpeter, USMC, WW I. Formed New Orleans Rhythm Kings, Chicago, 19. Producer jazz concerts, Chicago. *Songs & Instrumental Works:* Milenberg Joys; Farewell Blues; Tin Roof Blues; I'm Goin' Home; Make Love to Me.

MARGARETTEN, WILLIAM J   ASCAP 1959
composer, author
b Brooklyn, NY, Dec 30, 30. Educ: NY Univ; Manhattan Sch of Music; studied with Emil Friedberger, Elie Siegmeister. Former arr & copyist. Chief Collabrs: Milton Greene, Denes Agay, Clay Boland, Jr, Jerry Bresler. *Songs:* Going Steady With the Moon; Forever Now; A Thousand Dreams; Like This; Fallin'; Yours to Love; Love Me Fortissimo.

MARGERUM, MICHAEL BRAD   ASCAP 1979
composer, musician
b Chicago, Ill, Apr 14, 51. Guitarist rock, blues & jazz, nightclubs in Detroit & Ann Arbor, Mich. Comp, Jobete Publ Co. Chief Collabr: David Jones. *Songs:* Music: Come on and Try My Love; I Get So Used to Being Around.

MARGOULEFF, ROBERT J   ASCAP 1968
composer, singer
b New York, NY, Aug 8, 40. Educ: Manhattan Sch Music, 2 yrs; summer study with Boston Symph at Tanglewood. Producer in Synthesis of Music. Engr & co-producer of Stevie Wonder's first 5 albums. Grammy Award winner. Assoc producer, Isley Bros albums. Currently producer, Arista Records.

MARGULIS, CHARLES A (CHARLES MARLOWE)   ASCAP 1960
composer, musician
b Minneapolis, Minn, June 24, 03; d Apr, 67. Educ: North High Sch, Minneapolis; Univ Minn, 2 yrs; Juilliard Sch Music. At age 10 was in boys band, Minneapolis. While in high sch & univ, played in local theaters & dance pavilions. With Vincent Lopez Red Caps, Lopez Pa Hotel Orch; first trumpeter with Paul Whiteman, movie "King of Jazz," 30. Radio shows, Kate Smith, Jack Benny & Fred Allen, later TV. Had own radio prog "Accent on Brass." Chief Collabrs: Linda Santoni Parker (daughter), Marjory Jastrey (daughter), Willie Berg. *Songs:* Linda Rosa; Another Day. *Instrumental Works:* March Berg. *Songs & Instrumental Works:* O My Papa. *Albums:* Marvelous Margulis; Solid Gold Horn.

MARIN, RICHARD ANTHONY (CHEECH)
writer, actor
b Los Angeles, Calif, July 13, 46. Educ: Calif State Univ, Northridge, BS. Co-founder improvisational group, City Works, Vancouver; formed comedy duo with Tommy Chong, called Cheech and Chong; appeared in clubs throughout US incl Carnegie Hall. Co-writer & co-star, "Up in Smoke," 78 & "Cheech and Chong's Next Movie," 80. Rec'd Grammy Award, 73. *Albums:* Cheech and Chong; Big Bambu; Los Cochinos; The Wedding Album; Sleeping Beauty.

MARINAN, TERRENCE RICHARD (TERRY RICHARDS) ASCAP 1971
composer, singer
b Cleveland, Ohio, Oct 26, 45. Worked for local TV, early teens; mem, The Four Coins; also group, Chase, until 74; currently working hotels, Las Vegas. Chief Collabr: Bill Chase. *Songs:* Music: Get It On; River Suite.

MARINI, PEER
See Piermarini, Clito L

MARINO, ALBERT RALPH   ASCAP 1960
composer, author
b Washington, Pa, Dec 31, 11. Educ: Univ Pittsburgh; Calif State Teachers Col, Pa. Taught graphic arts, 14 yrs. Principal, Boys Sch, Youth Develop Ctr, Canonsburg, Pa. Cartoonist & writer for publications; commercial artist. Chief Collabr: Louis Popiolkowski. *Songs:* Everytime We Kiss; Break the Glass and Ring the Bell; Coming Home From School.

MARINO, SEV F   ASCAP 1957
composer, author, guitarist
b New York, NY, Feb 28, 15; d. Educ: High sch; pvt music study. Appeared on "Morning Show," CBS, 3 1/2 yrs & "Jack Paar Show," 5 yrs. Mem, Jose Melis Orch, for recordings & concert tours. Writer of musical commercials. Chief Collabr: Jose Melis. *Instrumental Works:* I-M-4-U (Jack Paar theme).

MARION, GEORGE, JR   ASCAP 1930
author
b Boston, Mass, Aug 30, 1899; d. Educ: La Villa Sch, Lausanne, Switz; Harvard Univ. Wrote film scenarios, "Love Me Tonight", "The Big Broadcast"; librettist, "Too Many Girls." Chief Collabrs: Fats Waller, Richard A Whiting, Johnny Green, Emmerich Kalman & Sammy Fain. *Songs:* The Steam Is on the Beam; My Sweeter Than Sweet; My Future Just Passed; There's a Man in My Life; Love Is a Random Thing. *Scores:* Bway stage (librettos): Beat the Band; Marinka.

MARION, KARL
See Blackman, Michael Bruce

MARK, ANDREW PEERY   ASCAP 1972
composer
b Philadelphia, Pa, July 18, 50. Educ: Lafayette Col, AB(hon French). Played guitar professionally in small folk group at age 12, also played through col. Pres, Philadelphia Music Works, jingle production co. Chief Collabr: Jeffrey Calhoon. *Scores:* Film/TV: Some Gotta Lose.

MARK, OTTALIE   ASCAP 1952
composer, editor, consultant
b New York, NY; d New York, Nov 13, 79. Educ: Washington Irving Art Sch; NY Prep Sch; NY Univ, pre-law; studied with Sunya Samuels & Michael Sciapiro. Staff, Capitol Theatre, NY. In charge of music libr, Copyright Dept, Vitaphone Pictures. To Hollywood as first supvr, Electrical Res Products, Inc,

29, then supvr, Music Rights for Music Copyright Bureau. Copyright consult & head of Copyright Res Dept, 41-47. In charge of Music Copyright Res, NY. *Songs:* The Ring on My Finger; I Walk With God.

MARKAY, BARBARA   ASCAP 1975
composer, author, singer
b New York, NY. Educ: Juilliard Sch Music, BM(comp), studied piano with Ania Dorfman, comp with Roger Sessions. Toured cols with band, Eng, 73. With Warner, Electra & Atlantic Records, Holland. Pres, Hot Box Records & Hot Box Publ. First record album released, 76. *Songs:* I'd Rather Be With Cowboys Than Queens; Wooden Rose; Women in Jail. *Albums:* Hot Box.

MARKES, LARRY   ASCAP 1953
composer, author
b Brooklyn, NY, Sept 24, 21. Educ: Univ Miami. Capt, USAF, WW II, rec'd Distinguished Flying Cross, Legion of Merit, Air Medal & 3 oak leaf clusters. Writer for radio & TV shows: "Chesterfield Supper Club", "Chamber Music Soc of Lower Basin Street", "The Flintstones", "Room for One More" & "Jonathan Winters Show"; screenplay, "Three on a Match." *Songs:* Mad About Him Sad About Him, How Can I Be Glad Without Him Blues; Along the Navajo Trail; May You Always; Save Your Confederate Money Boys, the South Shall Rise Again; A Nightingale Can Sing the Blues; To a Sleeping Beauty. *Scores:* London stage: Strike Me Pink.

MARKOE, GERALD JAY   ASCAP 1975
composer
b Brooklyn, NY, Mar 22, 41. Educ: Juilliard Sch Music, 60-62; Manhattan Sch Music, BM, 66, MM, 68. Comp-in-residence, Perry Street Theater, 75-77. Chief Collabrs: Michael Colby; Paul Rawlings; Kathy Hurley. *Scores:* Opera/Ballet: Ludlow Ladd (The Poor Little Orphan Boy, Christmas opera); Faust; Bway Shows: Fair Play for Eve; Another Time; Alice in Wonderland; He Who Gets Slapped; The Marriage of Mr Mississippi; Indulgences in the Louisville Harem; Cinderella; Androcles and the Lion.

MARKOWITZ, PHILIP L   ASCAP 1979
composer
b Brooklyn, NY, Sept 6, 52. Educ: Eastman Sch Music, BM. Founder, Petrus; Best New Jazz Group, Newport, Fest, 75. Played & recorded with jazz artists incl Chet Baker, Miroslav Vitous, Joe Chambers, Joe Williams, Toots Theiumans, Thad Jones & Jeremy Steig. Recordings, radio & TV. Producer of solo tapes by original comps. *Songs:* Music: Sno'Peas.

MARKOWITZ, RICHARD ALLEN   ASCAP 1959
composer, pianist, singer
b Los Angeles, Calif, Sept 3, 26. Educ: Santa Monica High Sch; Los Angeles Cons Music, 46-47; Ecole Normale de Musique, Paris, 48-50; studied comp with Mario Castelnuovo-Tedesco, 40-42, Arnold Schoenberg, 47, Arthur Honneger, 48-50 & George Tremblay, 75. Dance band leader & pianist, 40-44; pianist & singer, nightclubs & records, Paris & London, 48-53 & nightclubs, Los Angeles, 55-58; arr, BBC, 51-52; comp, cond & pianist, Katherine Dunham Ballet Co, 53-55; comp & songwriter for feature films/TV, 58- Arr/producer album, Michael Franks, 73. Chief Collabrs: Andrew J Fenady, K Lawrence Dunham, Katherine Dunham, Haru Yanai. *Songs:* Music: The Rebel, Johny Yuma; Can't Ever Go Home Again; From Day One; Why Don't You Walk Away; Themes: The Wild, Wild West; Joe Forrester; Hondo; The Runaways; Drs Private Lives. *Scores:* Feature Films: The Boss' Son; Face to the Wind; The Wild Seed; Bus Riley's Back in Town; Ride Beyond Vengeance; The Shooting; The Hoodlum Priest; Face in the Rain; The Magic Sword; Black Veil for Lisa; Road Racers; Operation Dames; Stake-Out on Dope Street; The Hot Angel; Cry of Battle; One Man's Way; TV Films: Mayday-40,000 Feet; Brinks-the Great Robbery; Girl on the Late, Late Show; Panic on the 5:22; The Hanged Man; Cutman Caper; One Plus One; The Iron Horse; The Stranger; Voyage of the Yes; Crisis; Custer; Hondo; Weekend of Terror; Winner Take All; Mask of Alexander; Washington Behind Closed Doors (parts 4, 6); Standing Tall; Hunters of the Reef; Death Car on the Freeway; Confessions of a Lady Cop; The Neighborhood; TV Series: Streets of San Francisco; Barnaby Jones; Police Story; Mannix; Mission Impossible; Joe Forrester; The Quest; The FBI; Hunter; The Wild, Wild West; Hondo; The Invaders; Dan August; Tales of the Unexpected; Hawaii Five-O; Quincy; The Runaways; Buck Rogers 25th Century; Drs Private Lives; Ben Casey; Breaking Point; Slattery's People; Dr Kildare; Jamie McFeeters; Chrysler Bob Hope Theatre; Empire; Philip Marlowe; The Rebel.

MARKS, CHARLES BAREND   ASCAP 1949
composer, author, publisher
b Brooklyn, NY, Jan 26, 1890. Educ: High sch; pvt music study. Pianist in film theatres at 16, Portland, Maine; later pianist & organist, Loew, Keith & Fox Theatres. Staff pianist, Harry Von Tilzer, Remick publ cos. Wrote spec material for vaudeville singers. Prog dir, WMCA, 7 yrs. Music publ, 10 yrs. Became comptroller, Acme Carriers, NY. Chief Collabr: Harry Warren. *Songs:* Where Do You Work-a John?; Waitin' for You; Triplets in Black and White; Eng Lyrics: Panis Angelicus; Ave Maria; Come Back to Sorrento; Dark Eyes; La Cumparsita; Estrellita.

MARKS, ELIAS J (ELI DAWSON)　　ASCAP 1921
composer, author, singer
b New York, NY, Nov 2, 1880; d New York, Oct 11, 60. Educ: Pub schs. Worked for music publ, then vaudeville singer, comedian. Appeared in Bway musicals "Welcome Stranger", "Canary Cottage", "Mary", "George White's Scandals." Wrote, produced & appeared in show for 150th anniversary, Grand Lodge, State of NY, 31; George Washington celebration, 32. Founded publ firm, 43. *Songs:* Goodnight, Mr Moon; Pucker Up Your Lips Miss Lindy; That's Big Business for Me; Beautiful Danube No Wonder You're Blue; He Told Her to Wait; Busy Body Moon; Mazie; Roll Along Silvery Moon to Slumberland; Rika Jika Jack; Little Red Riding Hood's Christmas Tree.

MARKS, FRANKLYN　　ASCAP 1950
composer, author, pianist
b Cleveland, Ohio, May 31, 11; d Sherman Oaks, Calif, July 12, 76. Educ: Dartmouth Col, BA; studied with Joseph Schillinger. Pianist & arr for dance bands, radio (37-42), Chamber Music Soc Lower Basin St (43). Served in USA, 97th AGF Band, WW II. Arr, Bway musicals, TV, films & records. With Walt Disney Studios, 55-76. Did orchestrations for film & TV: "The Great Locomotive Chase"; "The Light in the Forest"; "Pollyanna"; "One Hundred and One Dalmatians"; "The Absent-Minded Professor"; "The Parent Trap"; "Babes in Toyland"; "The Sword in the Stone"; "That Darn Cat"; "The Wild Country." Arr, cond & teacher. *Songs & Instrumental Works:* Suite for Flute and Strings; Flamingo; Lullaby to a Lampost; Evening in Pakistan; Trajectories; I Can't Carry a Tune; Climb the Mountain; Night and the Sea (guitar); Dialogue (guitar); West Virginia (symph). *Scores:* Ballet: The Bridge; Film/TV: Charlie the Lonesome Cougar; Elfego Baca; Hacksaw; Hog Wild; How to Have an Accident in the Home; How to Relax; Hurricane Hannah; In Shape With Von Drake; Justin Morgan Had a Horse; Lefty the Dingaling Lynx; Legend of the Boy and the Eagle; Outlaw Cats of Colossal Cave; Pluto's Day; Saludos Amigos; Scrooge McDuck and Money; Sancho the Homing Steer.

MARKS, GERALD　　ASCAP 1932
composer
b Saginaw, Mich, Oct 13, 1900. Educ: High sch. Led own orch. In Armed Forces, WW II. Wrote songs for "White Horse Inn" & "Ziegfeld Follies." Wrote for films also; mem ASCAP group touring US Army installations, Europe & Africa, 54. Cited by Defense Dept, Am Heritage Found, Am Legion, Chapel of 4 Chaplains & B'nai B'rith. Mem bd dirs, Songwriters Hall of Fame; asst secy, ASCAP. Chief Collabrs: Irving Caesar, Sammy Lerner, Seymour Simons. *Songs:* All of Me; You're the One (You Beautiful Son-of-a-Gun); I Can't Write the Words; The Night Shall Be Filled With Music; Mr Lincoln and His Gloves; Mr Longfellow and His Boy; Today and Tomorrow (off B'nai B'rith Youth Orgn song); Give Me Your Hand; Dig Down Deep; Oh Suzannah, Dust Off That Old Pianna; It's a Wonderful Thing to Be Loved; That's What I Want for Christmas; Is It True What They Say About Dixie?; Love Is Such a Cheat; Mountain Gal; When You Reach the Age of 21; Is Your Name in the Book?; Sing a Song of Safety; Nine Days for Americans. *Instrumental Works:* Religious: The Ten Jewish Holidays; Ten Catholic Holy Days; The Ten Protestant Days; The A-B-C Stories of Jesus. *Scores:* Bway: My Dear Public; Hold It!.

MARKS, JEANNE MARIE　　ASCAP 1974
composer, author
b Wenonah, NJ, Feb 9, 19. Educ: Friend's Select Sch, Philadelphia, Pa, 36; Spring Garden Col, 38; studied with Frederick Starke, Philadelphia. Music & art, Little Theatre Leagues, Conn. Gospel music, art & alto, Methodist churches, 30 yrs. *Songs & Instrumental Works:* I Gave Myself to Jesus; On Your Hand and Face; Around the Clock.

MARKS, JOHNNY (JOHN D)　　ASCAP 1939
composer, author, publisher
b Mt Vernon, NY, Nov 10, 09. Educ: Colgate Univ, Trustee, BA; Columbia Univ; studied music in Paris. Producer radio progs, coached singers. 26th Spec Service Co, produced army shows, overseas, World War II; Bronze Star, 4 Battle Stars. Formed St Nicholas Music, 49. Ed "Christmas Community Lyric Book." Mem Phi Beta Kappa. *Songs:* Rudolph the Red-Nosed Reindeer; Rockin' Around the Christmas Tree; I Heard the Bells on Christmas Day; A Holly Jolly Christmas; Don't Cross Your Fingers, Cross Your Heart; Address Unknown; We Speak of You Often; She'll Always Remember; What've You Got to Lose But Your Heart; A Merry Merry Christmas; The Night Before Christmas Song; Everyone's a Child at Christmas; Summer Holiday; Neglected; Who Calls?; Happy New Year Darling; When Santa Claus Gets Your Letter; I Guess There's an End to Everything; How Long is Forever; Free; Chicken Today and Feathers Tomorrow; Silver and Gold; There's Always Tomorrow; The Most Wonderful Day of the Year; Anyone Can Move a Mountain; To Love and Be Loved; Everything I've Always Wanted (ASCAP Award); Is It Only Cause You're Lonely. *Scores:* TV: Rudolph the Red-Nosed Reindeer; Ballad of Smokey the Bear; The Tiny Tree; Rudolph's Shiny New Year; Rudolph and Frosty.

MARKS, WALTER　　ASCAP 1960
composer, author
b New York, NY, Jan 15, 34. Educ: New York High Sch Music & Art; Amherst Col, BA; Columbia Univ, grad work in musical comp. Has written indust shows & spec material for nightclubs & revues. *Songs:* I've Gotta Be Me; Getting On (Emmy Award); We Got Us; Love, Here I Am; Love Is a Chance; Must It Be Love?. *Scores:* Bway Shows: Bajour; Golden Rainbow; Film/TV: Pinnocchio; That's Life; The Wild Party; Getting On.

MARLEY, ROBERT NESTA　　ASCAP 1970
composer, author, singer
b St Ann, Jamaica, Feb 6, 45. Educ: Self-taught musician & comp. Leading Jamaican recording artist & promoter of reggae music, worldwide. First hits, 64; toured US, 73. Worked on sound track of Swedish film, early 70's. Recipient of United Nations Peace Medal, 79. Chief Collabrs: The Wailers, Aston Barrett, Carlton Barrett, A Patterson, Tyrone Downie, Al Anderson. *Songs:* I Shot the Sheriff; Stir It Up; Guava Jelly; Is This Love; Concrete Jungle; Slave Driver; Get Up, Stand Up.

MARLOW, ERIC　　ASCAP 1962
composer, author, singer
b New York, NY, Dec 21, 25. Educ: Woodmere High Sch, grad, 44; NY Univ, 44. Began singing & acting at age 8. USA, World War II. Recording artist, Liberty Records, 56. Worked nightclubs, NY, radio, theatre, films & TV, 59-Actor for more than 135 TV shows. Wrote several movie theme songs. Chief Collabrs: Bobby Scott, Luchi de Jesus, Michele Rubini, Bronislav Kaper. *Songs:* Lyrics: A Taste of Honey; Slaughter, theme; Mi Amor, love ballad; Kisses, theme; Summer's Child.

MARLOWE, CHARLES
See Margulis, Charles A

MARLOWE, JEFFRY R　　ASCAP 1969
composer, pianist, teacher
b Westerly, RI, July 28, 39. Educ: Temple Univ, BS(music educ), 61; pvt study piano with Pierre Luboshutz & Genia Nemenoff. Duo pianist with Ronald Marlowe; performed many concerts, US & Can. Performed with Philadelphia Orch, New York Philh, Pittsburgh Symph, Dallas Symph & others. TV perf with Milton Berle, Johnny Carson, Steve Allen, Gary Moore, Mike Douglas, Sam Levenson & others. Artist with Devon Records. Chief Collabr: Ronald Marlowe, twin bro. *Instrumental Works:* Arr: Wedding Day at Troldhaugen (Grieg); Esurientes from "Magnificat" (Bach).

MARLOWE, LINDA R (LINDA MARLOWE PARKER)　　ASCAP 1958
composer, author
b Greenwich, Conn, July 6, 36. Educ: Syracuse Univ. Col revues; author bk, "Just Bring Vanilla." Had short stories publ; ghosted for several writers; writer for CBS, 60-71; later free lance for J Rivers & D Garroway. Chief Collabrs: Alice Luongo, Charles Margulis. *Songs:* Music: Another Day; Linda Rosa; March Berg.

MARLOWE, RONALD M
composer, pianist, teacher
b Westerly, RI, July 28, 39. Educ: Temple Univ, BM, 61; pvt piano study with Pierre Luboshutz & Genia Nemenoff. Artist with Nat Music League, toured US & Can. Extensive concerts with Columbia Mgt & Alkahest Attractions. TV perf with Johnny Carson, Milton Berle, Arthur Godfrey & others. Symph perf with New York Philh, Philadelphia Orch, Dallas Symph & others. Chief Collabr: Jeffry Marlowe, twin bro. *Instrumental Works:* Arr: Wedding Day at Troldhaugen (Grieg); Esurientes from "Magnificat" (Bach).

MARMELZAT, JEFFREY ALAN　　ASCAP 1975
composer, author
b Cleveland, Ohio, Apr 30, 48. Educ: Univ Calif, Los Angeles, BA, 69; Tulane Univ, MD, 73. Had first song recorded at age 17. Wrote while in col; songs recorded by var artists. Recorded album of original songs for Columbia Records while in med sch. Wrote songs for film "Report to the Commissioner" & var artists. Chief Collabrs: Paul Anka, Spencer Proffer, Vernon Burch. *Songs:* Loving You Gets Better With Time; Crazy About You; Sunrise; Temptation, Temptation; I Remember the Rhymes; All Over Again. *Instrumental Works:* Prelude.

MARRYOTT, RALPH E　　ASCAP 1950
composer, organist, choir director
b Jamesburg, NJ, Apr 15, 08; d. Educ: Peddie Sch. Minister of music, Presby Church, Jamesburg; dir, Choral Soc Jamesburg, 29-36; dir music, Jamesburg schs; choir dir, Calvary Methodist Church, 43-61; dir, Monmouth Glee Club, Keyport, 45-53; organist, Temple Anshe Emeth, New Brunswick, 46-49. *Songs:* Sacred Songs: Hosanna! Blessed Is He; Christmas Street; The Praise Carol; The Searching Carol; Alleluia of the Bells; Christmas Roundelay; Come, Shepherds, Come; One Early Easter Morning. *Songs & Instrumental Works:* Carols for the Christ Child (organ suite).

MARSALA, ADELE GIRARD
b Holyoke, Mass, June 25, 13. Educ: Springfield pub schs, Mass; studied harp with Marcel Granjany, Joseph Vito & Mario De Stefano. Harpist with Harry Sosnik & Dick Stabile dance bands; joined Joe Marsala jazz, Hickory House, 36-45. Own TV show, "Easy Does It," NBC, 47-48; staff harpist, CBS, Chicago, 1 yr. Chief Collabrs: Joe Marsala & Johnny Mercer. *Songs:* Little Sir Echo; Only In Heaven; Champagne and Tears; I Think We Need a Drink.

MARSALA, JOE   ASCAP 1949
composer, author, conductor
b Chicago, Ill, Jan 4, 07; d Santa Barbara, Calif, Mar 3, 78. Educ: Pub schs; studied with Clarence Warmelin & Duke Rehl; Cons of Milan, with Alfredo Di Grazia. Clarinetist in dance bands, Chicago; led own band, Hickory House, NY, 36-45; first musician to lead an integrated band, 37. Music publ, NY, 54. Wrote show, "I've Had It." Chief Collabrs: Adele Girard Marsala, also Sunny Skylar. *Songs & Instrumental Works:* Don't Cry Joe; And So to Sleep Again; Little Sir Echo; Hot String Beans; The Little Christmas Tree; Music: You're Not the One and Only Lonely (One); Lyrics: Champagne and Tears; You'd Make a Wonderful Stranger; Snow Bunnie.

MARSH, CHARLES HOWARD   ASCAP 1946
composer, organist, educator
b Magnolia, Iowa, Apr 8, 1885; d San Diego, Calif, Apr 12, 56. Educ: High sch, studied with Walter Hall, A J Goodrich, J Christopher Marks; Fontainebleau Cons, studied with Widor, Libert, Philipp, Decreus. Head, piano dept, Bible Inst, Los Angeles; fac, Univ Redlands, 19; prof, organ & theory, Orlando Col. Substitute organist & choirmaster, Am Church & Am Cathedral, Paris. US pres, European Sch of Music & Art. Organist & choirmaster, First Presby Church, Ft Wayne, Ind, St James-by-the-Sea Episcopal Church, La Jolla, Calif, 26-56. Organist, Univ Fla, 33. Dist supvr, Federal Music Proj, San Diego, 36-40; music ed, newspaper, La Jolla Light, 45-56. Mem, comn on church music, Episcopal Diocese, Los Angeles. *Songs & Instrumental Works:* Choral: In This Place Will I Give Peace; Benedictus Es Domine; Jubilate Deo; Benedic Anima Mea; Christus Natus Est; Te Deum; Ballad of the Christ Child; Organ: Four Color Prints; Scherzo; Legend Triste; Beside Still Waters (nocturne).

MARSH, DONALD T   ASCAP 1970
composer, arranger
b Camden, NJ, Oct 24, 43. Educ: Nyack Col, BA(music), 65; Glassboro State Col, MA(music), 70. Teacher comp, Baptist Bible Col, Clarks Summit, Pa. Dir publ, Benson Publ Co, Nashville. Free-lance comp, "Jerry Falwell's Old Time Gospel Hour." *Songs:* I Want Jesus More Than Anything; I Want to Thank You, Jesus. Musicals arr: Go Tell Your World; Greater Is He; Noel Jesus Is Born; God Has Always Had a People.

MARSH, JANE   ASCAP 1979
lyricist
b Iowa Falls, Iowa, Oct 16, 44. Educ: Nyack Col, BA(English). *Songs:* Lyrics: I Want to Thank You Jesus; I Could Go a Day.

MARSH, RUDY
See Schramm, Rudolf R A

MARSHALL, EDWARD HARRY   ASCAP 1960
composer, author
b Baltimore, Md, Mar 28, 32. Educ: Settlement Sch, Philadelphia, Pa; studied with Romeo Cascarino. Began writing songs in serivce & continued after discharge in 52. Chief Collabrs: Joan Bender, Jerry Ragovoy, George Goehring, Tony Hughes, Jack Ackerman, Desmond Robinson, Ronnie Scalair. *Songs:* Venus; Hello, My Love; Long Before; Music: Here's to My Jenny; Lyrics: A Wonderful Dream; A Little Bit Now. *Scores:* Film/TV: Adventures of Huckleberry Finn.

MARSHALL, HENRY I   ASCAP 1914
composer, author, director
b Boston, Mass, Feb 22, 1883; d Plainfield, NJ, Apr 4, 58. Educ: New Eng Cons. Charter mem, ASCAP. Actor & dir, "The Runaways." Vaudeville pianist & accompanist. Radio producer & dir; mgr, chain of music stores; gen mgr, New York publ house. Presented first amateur radio show, WBMS, New York, 29; producer of radio show, "Calvalcade of Youth" for US Treasury Dept (Billboard award, best teenage show). Author, allegorical playlet, "White Coupons." *Songs:* Bless Your Ever Lovin' Heart; Be My Little Baby Bumble Bee; Cuddle Up and Cling to Me; On the 5:15; If You Ever Get Lonely; Somebody Wrong; Baby Sister Blues; Mary, You're a Little Bit Old-Fashioned; I Want to Linger; Oh, Miss Flanegan; I Wish There Was a Window in Heaven.

MARSHALL, PAUL
See Solomon, Paul Marshall

MARSHALL, PEGGY   ASCAP 1956
composer, author
b Birmingham, Ala, Aug 30, 16. Educ: Columbia Univ; arr with Bennett Rich, Juilliard Sch Music; piano, Mabel Corey, Watt Sch, Brooklyn, NY; pvt studies, Michael Field & Michael Shelby. Vocal arr & lead singer, had various vocal groups incl, The Marshalls & The Holidays. On many radio & TV shows, also own shows on NBC, CBS & others. Wrote many commercial jingles incl Lipton Tea, Borden Products, Sterling Salt, Woodbury-Jergens, Motts Apple Sauce & others. Peggy Marshall & the Holidays, Arthur Godfrey Talent Scouts, 6 1/2 yrs. DJ with husband Tom Eldridge, WFBG, Altoona, Pa, 3 yrs. Solo & group singer, vocal arr, also wrote special songs for quartet on show "Land of the Lost," children's prog, NBC & MBS. Supper clubs; Rainbow Room, Hotel Biltmore. *Songs:* Let's Walk Once Again Through the Blue Grass; So Live; Bayou Baby; Come Back; There's an Ache in My Heart; Don't Feel Sorry for Me; Blue Bell.

MARSTERS, ANN   ASCAP 1958
author, publisher
b Boston, Mass, Mar 1, 18. Educ: Miss Haskells Sch; Child Walker Sch of Art. Film ed & columnist, Chicago American, 50. Vpres, Marsters Sound Music. Chief Collabr: Bill Snyder. *Songs:* My Pony Macaroni; This Town of New York; Be Sure to Tell Him; Teresa Smiles.

MARSTERS, NANCY L
composer, author, teacher
b Newberg, Ore, Aug 22, 37. Educ: Willamette Univ, BMed; Fla State Univ, comp studies with Carl Nosse. Chief Collabr: Jack DeMello. *Songs:* The Wonderful World of Aloha; Thou Art Groovy; Love in The Music.

MARSZALEK, HENRY   ASCAP 1962
composer, author, pianist
b East Chicago, Ill, Jan 19, 22. Former shipper, painter & decorator. *Songs:* Yo Yo Twist; As My Heart Weeps; About This Thing Called Love; I Got the Best; It's Your Fault; Since I Met You; Don't Give Me This Night; Anyone Can Tell You.

MARTEL, THOMAS OLIVER   ASCAP 1971
composer, author
b Long Beach, Calif, Sept 28, 49. Educ: Mar Vista High Sch; US Int Univ, San Diego, BA, 71. Won Best Comp Award, Intercollegiate Music Fest, St Louis, Mo, 71. Mem cast, nat touring co, "Jesus Christ, Superstar," 71-72. Author & lyricist Bway production, "Hard Job Being God," 72. Performer in nightclubs & TV. Recording artist, GWP Records. Chief Collabr: Bob Phelps. *Songs:* A Psalm of Peace; It's All Been Said; Shalom! L'Chaim!; What Do I Have to Do?. *Scores:* Bway stage: Hard Job Being God.

MARTELL, HELEN HERON   ASCAP 1955
composer, author, singer
b Tulsa, Okla; d. Former singer & secy. Chief Collabr: Tom Glazer. *Songs:* Take Possession; Fallen Angel; Let Me Give the Bride Away; Poor Fool; If You Love Me, Tell Me; Runnin' Away From Love; Time After Time.

MARTELL, PAUL   ASCAP 1957
composer, author, violinist
b Italy, Jan 6, 05; d. Educ: High sch. Led own dance orch in hotels, ballrooms & radio, 36; accordionist, pianist & conductor. Chief Collabrs: Milton Berle & Ervin Drake. *Songs:* I Wuv a Wabbit; Suspense Tango.

MARTELL, RALPH   ASCAP 1956
composer, author
b Brooklyn, NY, Mar 6, 34. Scored several commercials; produced albums for Star Power Records; transcribed songs for "Push Button Song Book." Rec'd Popular Panel Awards, ASCAP, 4 yrs. Chief Collabr: Morna Murphy. *Songs:* Little Boy Lost; It Won't Be Easy; Other Peoples Windows; It's Not Supposed to Happen. *Scores:* Stage Musicals: Shelley; Henry and Lucy and Susan B; Mumbo Jumbo; Oh What a Night; The Musical Book; Only a Woman.

MARTENS, FREDERICK HERMAN   ASCAP 1914
author
b New York, NY, July 6, 1874; d Mountain Lakes, NJ, Dec 18, 32. Educ: Pvt music study. Charter mem & dir, ASCAP, 24-32. . NY correspondant "London Musical Record"; contributor to music bks & periodicals. WW I, dir, Soldiers and Sailors Club, Trinity Church Serv Club, NJ. Author "Leo Ornstein, The Man - His Ideas - His Work", "Violin Mastery", "Talks With Master Violinists and Teachers", "Little Biographies", "A Thousand and One Nights of Opera" & "Book of the Opera and Ballet." Chief Collabrs: Charles Wakefield Cadman, Francesco De Leone, B G DeSylva, Philip James, Will MacFarlane, N Clifford Page, Oley Speaks, Charles G Spross, Lily Strickland, Harriet Ware, Pietro Yon. *Songs & Instrumental Works:* America (anthem, 1st prize, Nat Contest, Brooks Bright Found); Gesu Bambino; Librettos: Contest of the Nations; Old Plantation Days; Ballad of the Golden Sun; Spring in Vienna.

MARTH, HELEN JUN   ASCAP 1963
composer, author, choir director
b Alton, Ill, May 24, 03. Educ: Alton High Sch; Washington Univ; studied organ & comp; studied with C Albert Scholin, piano with W D Armstrong. Traveled as accompanist, Cadman Chautauqua Co. Vernon Henshie organist. Storybook lady on radio, used original music & songs for children. Dir, 3 children's choirs & 4 bell choirs. Lectr, 46 yrs. Actress, Little Theatre. *Songs & Instrumental Works:* The Triumph of Christ (cantata); Sing Oh Ye Heavens (cantata); Melodies for Handbells; I Saw Three Ships Come Sailing (choral); also Worship in Song (bk for young people & children).

MARTIAL, MICHAEL
See Bonagura, Michael John, Jr

MARTIN, BARBARA ANNE (BOBBI)　　ASCAP 1968
composer, author

b Brooklyn, NY, Nov 29, 43. Educ: Attended sch, Baltimore, Md; studied voice & guitar with pvt instrs. As teenager played & sang with local groups, Baltimore. Recording artist, Maypole, Coral, United Artists, Buddah & Green Menu Records. Appearances TV variety & talk shows; personal appearances, US, Europe, Japan, Philippines, Formosa, Thailand, Hong Kong, Santa Domingo, Haiti, Aruba & Australia & with Bob Hope Christmas Tours. Chief Collabr: Henry Jerome. *Songs:* For the Love of Him; Give a Woman Love; A Place for Me; John F Kennedy was His Name; Tomorrow; Tell Him I Love Him; Goin' South; Don't be Down On Me; I Think of You; Stay With Me; Lisa Marie.

MARTIN, BILLY　　ASCAP 1954
composer, author, musician

b New York, NY, Mar 14, 08. Educ: High sch. Owned & operated Met Recording Studios. Wrote songs for New York World's Fair exhibits, 64. Chief Collabr: Larry Martin (son). *Songs:* Till We Two Are One; Five; Old Shoes and a Bag of Rice; My Heart's on a Fast Express; Miami Dolphins Go, Go, Go; A Man; Charlotte NC; Israel Is Forever; One Small Voice.

MARTIN, CHARLES E　　ASCAP 1967
composer, author

b NJ, Mar 1, 30. Educ: NY Univ; NJ Law Sch; studied music with var teachers. Began as writer on "March of Time." Wrote 50 screenplays for var major studios. Dir 10 motion pictures. Wrote musical for Bway & play "White Harlem Boy." Chief Collabrs: Sammy Fain, Paul Sanders. *Songs:* A Man Has to Love; Can't Make it With the Same Man Twice; I Have Loved You in Other Worlds; Search; Here You Are.

MARTIN, DAVID　　ASCAP 1957
composer

b New York, NY, Oct 5, 07; d New York, May 4, 75. Chief Collabr: Langston Hughes. *Songs:* Did You Ever Hear the Blues?; When I'm in a Quiet Mood; Good Old Girl. *Scores:* Bway Stage: Simply Heavenly.

MARTIN, ENOCH, II (SIR ENOCH)　　ASCAP 1961
composer, author, singer

b Rockmart, Ga, Oct 12, 21. Educ: Barringer High Sch, Newark, NJ; Wilberforce Univ, BA, 42. Recording & working club dates. *Songs:* Lucom Plow; You're Like Old Age Wine; Easy Baby; One Day; I'm Henpecked.

MARTIN, GARY WILLIAM (PEPPER)　　ASCAP 1970
composer, author, singer

b Lubbock, Tex, May 7, 47. Did nightclub & TV perf. Recording artist, Decca Records. Chief Collabr: Buzz Cason. *Songs:* Revolt of Emily Young; Don't Let the Angels Come; Seeing's Believing; Buy the House a Round; Little Miss America.

MARTIN, GILBERT M　　ASCAP 1968
composer, author, conductor

b Southbridge, Mass, Jan 6, 41. Educ: Mary E Wells High Sch; Westminster Choir Col, BMus, 68; studied organ with Donald McDonald & Alexander McCurdy, piano with Mathilde McKinney, cond with George Lynn. Arr/cond musical theatre, "Just for Fun-The Music of Jerome Kern" (Off-Bway) (Off-Bway), "Serenade" (Cami) & "Broadway Encore" (Cami). Music ed, Lorenz Indusls, 68-75. Choral clinician; freelance cond/arr/comp. Chief Collabr: John Jakes. *Songs:* No Golden Carriage, No Bright Toy; The Jesus Gift; Music: When I Survey the Wondrous Cross. *Scores:* Musicals: Mother Goose...Now!; One Family...Some Friends.

MARTIN, GORMAN O　　ASCAP 1960
author

b Drift, Ky, Aug 28, 34. Educ: Col. *Songs:* I'm Through With Love.

MARTIN, HUGH　　ASCAP 1941
composer, author, singer

b Birmingham, Ala, Aug 11, 14. Educ: Birmingham Southern Col; studied with Edna Gussen, Dorsey Whittington. Vocal arr, Bway shows incl "Hooray For What!", "The Streets of Paris", "The Boys From Syracuse", "Cabin in the Sky", "Gentlemen Prefer Blondes", "Top Banana", "One for the Money", "Stars in Your Eyes", "Too Many Girls", "DuBarry Was a Lady" & "Louisiana Purchase," MGM films incl "Girl Crazy", "Broadway Rhythm" & "Presenting Lily Mars." Leader of vocal quartet The Martins. Accompanist, Judy Garland during first Palace Theatre perf & Eddie Fisher, Palladium, London. Music dir, Bway show "Sugar Babies," 79. Chief Collabrs: Ralph Blane, Timothy Gray. *Songs:* Buckle Down Winsocki; That's How I Love the Blues; Shady Lady Bird; Ev'rytime; The Three B's; What Do You Think I Am; Just a Little Joint With a Jukebox; Love; Connecticut; The Trolley Song; The Boy Next Door; Have Yourself a Merry Little Christmas; Pass the Peace Pipe; An Occasional Man; Venezia; I Don't Know What I Want; You Are for Loving; Shauny O'Shay; Suits Me Fine; When Does This Feeling Go Away?; Hello, Springtime; Was She Prettier Than I?; Home Sweet Heaven; If I Gave You; Forever and a Day; You'd Better Love Me; It's Christmas Time All Over the World. *Scores:* Bway shows: Best Foot Forward; Look, Ma, I'm Dancin'; Make a Wish; High Spirits; Love

From Judy (London); Films: Meet Me in St Louis; Athena; The Girl Most Likely; Grandma Moses Suite (New England Suite); TV: Hans Brinker.

MARTIN, HUGH E　　ASCAP 1961
composer, arranger, singer

b Gaffney, SC, Apr 26, 29; d York, SC, Dec 23, 76. Educ: Furman Univ; Erskine Col, SC; Juilliard Sch Music, NY. Band dir, Bartow High Sch, Fla, 52-57. Singer/bass player with John LaSalle Quartet, New York, 59-61. Instrumentalist (trumpet & stringbass) *Songs:* Blue Is the Color of Her Eyes; Class Rings; The Day John Glenn Came Home; The Dee Die Doe; Jumpin' At the Left Bank; Arr: Clementine.

MARTIN, JEAN LEONARD　　ASCAP 1974
composer, author, singer

b Columbus, Ohio, July 5, 31. Educ: Peace Jr Col; Meredith Col, BA(primary educ); Transylvania Music Sch Camp, studied with Mr & Mrs James Christian Pfolh; pvt study piano with Sally Charles Cheetham; Brevard Community Col, studied paramedics. Began playing accordion at age 8. Played for var civic groups, toured with USO shows, performed on radio & played live from music store window, ages 10-13. Opera singer; church organist. Gospel concert soloist & barbershop gospel quartet, Rays of Sonshine. Mem, Sweet Adelaides. Sound judge & banjo instruction. *Songs:* God's Wonderful Love; My Saviour, My Master, My Friend; Welcome Home; If You Love the Lord; Lyrics: A Broken Heart.

MARTIN, LARRY　　ASCAP 1954
composer, author

b New York, NY, Jan 6, 33. Educ: Brooklyn Col Law Sch, LLB. Child singer in radio; practicing lawyer. Chief Collabr: Billy Martin (father). *Songs:* Till We Two Are One; Five; Old Shoes and a Bag of Rice; My Heart's on a Fast Express; The Sparrow Sings; Dear Diary.

MARTIN, OLIN E (FREDDY)　　ASCAP 1971
composer, author, singer

b Jackson City, Ind, June 16, 04. Educ: Rose Polytech Inst; Fogeed Hardeman Christian Col; Phoenix Jr Col. Singer, dancer & actor, 23. Appeared in "Dancing Honeymoon Show," 3 seasons, "Passing Falling Revue," 1 season, Dublix & Loew's Picture Theatres, 2 seasons, "Holland Importations," 1 season & "A Symphony of Songs & Dances," 1 season. *Songs:* My Rhapsody; My Love for Life; Say a Prayer With Our Boys; Our Dear Old America (Opus 1 & 3); I Come to You With Songs (a prologue); Singing Souls With Dancing Feet; Westward Ho (Doin a Bee-Bop Bounce); Nashville Tennessee The Music City; The Maricopa Tapioca; My Own American Rose; Out to Sun Valley Idaho; Dreaming Dreams; Down on Our Old Home-Place; Arizona Moon; His Love Is the Greatest; A Song Is Born; Mother of Mine; God Bless the USA (You and Me); A United Nations Song; A National Boy Scout Song; The New Waltz. *Scores:* The American Vanities Revue; A Composer Dreaming Dreams.

MARTIN, PETER
See Malijewski, Peter Martin

MARTIN, RALPH EUGENE　　ASCAP 1975
composer, lyricist

b Los Angeles, Calif, May 12, 34. Educ: Sch Radio & TV Arts & Sci, Hollywood, with Don Martin; Sch Music, Meglin Dance Studio, Calif, with Dick Grove. Played violin & danced on radio, age 3. Learned to play piano at an early age. Started writing songs, late 50's. Chief Collabr: Bill Fox. *Songs:* Rio de Janeiro; Lovelier Than You in Spring Time; Never Kiss Your Dreams Goodbye; Poor Little Girl; Oh Please Forgive Me; Simplicity.

MARTIN, RICK
See Capellan, Richard Victor

MARTIN, RUTH KELLEY　　ASCAP 1955
author, editor

b Jersey City, NJ, Apr 14, 14. Educ: Smith Col, BA; Columbia Univ; Univ Munich; Salzburg Mozarteum; studied also in Budapest & Vienna. Has written articles for New York Times, music mags; ed & translator, bks on music. Chief Collabr: Thomas Martin (husband). *Instrumental Works:* Eng versions of Mozart: The Magic Flute; Abduction From the Seraglio; The Marriage of Figaro; Don Giovanni; Cosi Fan Tutti; Eng versions of Verdi: La Traviata; Rigoletto; Eng versions of Puccini: La Boheme; Madame Butterfly; Eng versions of Johann Strauss: Die Fledermaus; A Night in Venice; Eng versions of Rossini: Barber of Seville; An Italian Girl in Algiers; Eng version of Bizet: Carmen.

MARTIN, SAM　　ASCAP 1947
composer, author

b New York, NY, June 18, 08. Educ: High sch grad; studied botany under Dr Moldenke & William J Robbins & Harold W Rickett. Wrote many country & western songs. Chief Collabrs: Fred Rose, Al Trace, Dave McEnery (Red River). *Songs:* You Call Everybody Darling; You're Not My Darling Anymore; Wagon Trail; Thorn in My Heart; Why Should I Feel Sorry for You Now; Tears From the Sky.

MARTIN, T
See Cavanaugh, Thomas Martin

MARTIN, THOMAS PHILIPP   ASCAP 1955
author, conductor, director
b Vienna, Austria, May 28, 09. Educ: Vienna Cons; also pvt music study. Asst cond, St Louis Grand Opera & Chicago Opera; cond, New York City Opera, 44-56; assoc chorus master, Metrop Opera, 58; cond, Central City Opera Fest. Author, "Treasury of Grand Opera Librettos." Chief Collabr: Ruth Martin (wife). *Instrumental Works:* Eng versions of Mozart: The Magic Flute; Abduction From the Seraglio; The Marriage of Figaro; Don Giovanni; Cosi Fan Tutti; Eng versions of Verdi: La Traviata; Rigoletto; Eng versions of Puccini: La Boheme; Madame Butterfly; Eng versions of Johann Strauss: Die Fledermaus; A Night in Venice; Eng versions of Rossini: Barber of Seville; An Italian Girl in Algiers; Eng version of Bizet: Carmen.

MARTIN, VERNON   ASCAP 1962
composer
b Guthrie, Okla, Dec 15, 29. Educ: Univ Okla; Juilliard Sch Music; Columbia Univ; Studied Schillinger Syst, 49-51; Univ Salzburg, Austria (scholarship). Comn, Staten Island Symph, 61. Compiled bibliography writings on electronic music, 64. Prepared exhibits, Lincoln Ctr Library of Performing Arts, 65. Music librarian, NTex State Univ, 66-70. Head, Art & Music Dept, Hartford Pub Library. Chief Collabrs: Gertrude Stein, Walt Kelly. *Songs:* Music: We Have Met the Enemy and He Is Us. *Instrumental Works:* Orchestra Piece With Birds, Symphony and Magnetic Tape. *Scores:* Film/TV: Cabinet of Dr Caligari; Opera: Ladies Voices.

MARTINEZ, LORENZO P   ASCAP 1975
composer, author
b Cuba, Jan 25, 44. Educ: Wash State Univ, BA(music), 67; Manhattan Sch Music, MA, 69. Head theory dept, 92nd St Y Music Sch; lectr, City Univ New York. Comp & producer for TV commercials. *Songs:* Music: The Circus (bk of children's songs); Does It Really Matter? (Capt Kangaroo TV Show). *Albums:* The Circus.

MARTINI, BENNIE
See Azzara, Bennie Anthony

MARTINI, CATHERINE
See Ruthenberg, Jane Catherine

MARTINO, RALPH JOHN   ASCAP 1968
composer, author, arranger
b Sewaren, NJ, Feb 16, 45. Educ: Manhattan Sch Music, BM, 66, MM, 68. Comp & arr staff, Navy Band, Washington, DC. *Songs:* The Journey; Little Flower. *Instrumental Works:* Bacchanal.

MARTINO, RUSS NORMAN   ASCAP 1965
composer, pianist, conductor
b Stamford, Conn, Jan 25, 32. Educ: Julius Hartt Col of Music; Univ Hartford, BME(piano), 53; Manhattan Sch of Music, MME(music educ), 57; Univ Nev, admin cert & teacher's cert; Calif & Conn state teacher's cert. Served, USA Band, Fort Mason, Calif. Pianist, organist & accompanist at var hotels, Las Vegas; also cond. In concert throughout US & on TV. Performed at var hotel-supper clubs throughout US incl Las Vegas, Florida, Conn, Calif, NY, Pa & in Can. Presently asst cond, Casino De Paris, Dunes Hotel, Las Vegas, Nev. Mem, Am Fedn of Musicians, locals 369, 47 & 802. *Songs & Instrumental Works:* El Dorado Sam; Suite for Jazz Orchestra; Innovation (concert band); Beguine Modernique; Conception; Also Sprach Zarathustra (arr; Richard Strauss); Sch stage band works: Speak Easy; Solid Soul; Pellom Place; Torrey Pines; Soul Brother; Soul Sister; Michael Way; Lakewood Drive; Charleston West; Eau De Groove; Cast a Spell; Grooveh; Sploophy; Choral arr: Fugue No 2 (J S Bach); Prelude No 23 (J S Bach); Invention No 1 (J S Bach); Prelude No 11 (J S Bach); Prelude No 9 (J S Bach).

MARTINS, JAY
See Tener, Martin Jack

MARTONE, DON   ASCAP 1963
composer, conductor, violinist
b US, Apr 15, 02. Educ: High sch; music sch. 1st violinist, Philadelphia Orch. Music dir, instrumental groups; recording artist. *Songs & Instrumental Works:* Angelina Polka; Mazurki-Providenza; Mazurka alla Palermitana.

MARTUFI, PEARL GERTRUDE (PEARL G ADAMS)   ASCAP 1969
composer, writer, poet
b Wise, Va, Mar 31, 1897; d Bellflower, Calif, Nov 23, 77. Educ: Wise High Sch; Theodora Kane Sch Art, DC, 49-52; George Washington Univ, 55-58; Cath Univ Am, 59-60; Corcoran Art Sch, 61-62; Chapman Col; USS Universe Campus Afloat, 71; special studies, Rome, Babylon, Palestine & Ikebana, Japan; Cypress Col, AB(English), 73; Univ Calif, Fullerton, BA(English), 75; Univ San Francisco, MA(secondary educ), 77. Hotel mgr, 18-20. With US Govt, 38-63; US Inf spec, 63. Free-lance writer, ed, music & lyrics, lectr, 43. Adv bd, May Co, 69. Founder, Holy Yr Pilgrims, 50 & Writers Anonymous Club, 66; dir,

Movieland Wax Mus & Palace of Living Art. Hon dir, Japanese Village, Buena Park, Int Platform Asn, 68. Calif State pres, Nat League Am Pen Women, 68-70, Buena Art Guild, 69, Buena Park Playhouse, 69, Nat Asn Parliamentarians, 70, Int Toastmistress Club, Cath Daus of Am. Established the Pearl G Martufi Award, 77. Gold Medal Award, Int Poetry Shrine, 70. Mem, Professional Writers Club, 50-55. *Songs:* Bella Primavera; A Hui Hou Kaua (Until We Meet Again); Seas and Safaris (col style).

MARTZ, JASUN ALLAN   ASCAP 1968
composer, author, performer
b Camp Kilmer, NJ, June 18, 53. Educ: Univ Calif, Los Angeles; Calif State Univ, Northridge; Univ Calif, Santa Barbara, BA, 75. First recording/publ contract at age 15; then extensive recording, production, radio & TV performances. *Songs:* Disguise; Vicissitudes. *Scores:* Film/TV: Follow the Leader. *Albums:* The Pillory; Lusion.

MARVIN, JOHNNY   ASCAP 1940
composer, author, singer
b Butler, Okla, July 11, 1897; d North Hollywood, Calif, Dec 20, 44. Educ: Pub schs. Had own radio show, NBC, NY, 5 yrs; was on Victor Records for many yrs. To Calif, wrote for Gene Autry films, formed music publ co with Gene Autry. His collection is in the Univ Wyoming's Rare Bks & Spec Collections Div as an example of 20th Century Contemporary Music. *Songs:* There's a Little Deserted Town; I've Learned a Lot About Women; As Long As I Love My Horse; Goodbye, Pinto; Rhythm of the Hoofbeats; Listen to the Rhythm of the Range; Old November Moon; Goodbye Little Darlin'; Dude Ranch Cow Hands; At the Close of a Long Long Day.

MARVIN, MEL WILLIAMS   ASCAP 1969
composer
b Walterboro, SC, Nov 24, 41. Educ: Washington & Lee Univ; Col Charleston, BS, 62; Columbia Univ, MA, 65. Theater comp. Chief Collabrs: David Chambers, Robert Montgomery, Ron Whyte, Bob Satuloff, Christopher Durang. *Scores:* Opera/Ballet: An American Theater Mass; Bway Shows: A History of the American Film; Yentl; Funeral March for a One-Man Band; The Portable Pioneer and Prairie Show; Off-Bway Shows: Green Pond; Tintypes; Film/TV: The Prince of Hamburg; Journey.

MARX, HARPO (ARTHUR)   ASCAP 1951
composer, comedian, harpist
b New York, NY, Nov 23, 1893; d Hollywood, Calif, Sept 28, 64. One of the 4 Marx Bros, appeared in vaudeville, Bway musical comedy "I'll Say She Is", "The Coconuts", "Animal Crackers", also in films "Monkey Business", "Horsefeathers", "Duck Soup", "A Night At the Opera", "A Day At the Races", "At the Circus", "Go West", "The Big Store", "A Night in Casablanca" & "Love Happy." Autobiography, "Harpo Speaks." *Songs & Instrumental Works:* Guardian Angels; Lullaby Doll; Moon Tune.

MASCARI, JOSEPH ROCCO (RED MASCARA)   ASCAP 1959
composer, author
b Phillipsburg, NJ, July 20, 22. USAF, WW II. Chief Collabrs: Parke Frankenfield. *Songs:* Seek, Seek, Seek; I'm From New Jersey (state song); People In Love; My Lucky Day; The One for Me.

MASCHEK, ADRIAN MATHEW (BOB BRANNON,   ASCAP 1963
ROD POWERS)
composer, author
b New Orleans, La, Feb 27, 18. Educ: Nat Inst Violin. Coordinator & welding instr for Boilermakers Local No 37, Welding & Training Sch, New Orleans, La. *Songs:* Dear Lord and Santa Claus; God Bless Santa Claus; Blue Angel.

MASCIA, MADELINE THERESE   ASCAP 1964
composer, author
b Port Chester, NY, Jan 28, 28. Educ: Col New Rochelle, NY, AB; Oxford Univ, Eng, studied Shakespeare with A L Rowse. With US Foreign Service in London, Eng, Bonn, Ger, Oslo, Norway & Rome, Italy. Chief Collabrs: Grace Morgan, Virgilio Volpe, Alberto Di Miniello. *Songs:* Ciao For Now; Madonina Di Loreto; Lyrics: Diece Giorini D'Estate.

MASCOLINO, DOLORES ABIGAIL (ABBY HASKIN)   ASCAP 1960
lyricist
b Chicago, Ill, Aug 21, 16. Educ: Northwestern Univ, studied advert & copy writing; Am Cons Music, studied voice, 3 yrs. Chief Collabr: Ray Willow. *Songs:* This Is the Time of the Year; Should Have Been—Could Have Been; Have You Ever Wondered Why?.

MASON, DANIEL GREGORY   ASCAP 1933
composer, author, educator
b Brookline, Mass, Nov 20, 1873; d Greenwich, Conn, Dec 4, 53. Educ: Harvard Univ, BA; studied with Chadwick, Goetschius & Vincent D'Indy; hon DLitt, Tufts Col; hon MusD, Oberlin Col, Rochester Univ. Son of Henry Mason, founder of Mason-Hamlin Co. Prof music, Columbia Univ, 10-42, MacDowell prof, 29-42, then prof emeritus. Mem, Nat Inst Arts & Letters. Author: "From Grieg to Brahms"; "Beethoven and His Forerunners"; "The Romantic Composers"; "Contemporary Composers"; "The Orchestral Instruments";

"Tune in, America"; "The Chamber Music of Brahms"; "The Quartets of Beethoven." Autobiography, "Music in My Time, and Other Reminiscences." *Instrumental Works:* Suite After English Folk Songs; Clarinet Sonata; Prelude & Fugue for Piano, Orchestra; Chanticleer (A Festival Overture); Three Symphonies; Scherzo-Caprice; Songs of the Countryside (choral); Quartet for Piano, Strings; Pastorale (violin, clarinet, piano); String Quartet; Serenade (string quartet); Sentimental Sketches.

MASON, HAROLD E   ASCAP 1978
composer, author, singer
b Susquehanna, Pa, Feb 17, 32. Educ: Laurel Hill Acad; Mansfield State Teachers Col, Pa; Ithaca Col, NY, BS(music, drama), 63, MS, 66. Conductor, singer; stage dir & managing dir, var opera cos, US. Ed & arr, Plymouth Music. Chief Collabr: Don Craig. *Songs:* The Birds of Christmas; Music: Show Me Thy Ways.

MASON, HARVEY W   ASCAP 1973
composer, author
b Atlantic City, NJ, Feb 22, 47. Educ: Berklee Col Music, Boston, 2 yrs; New England Cons of Music, 2 yrs; BA(music educ). Composer & studio musician, 70; solo artist, Arista Records, 74; record producer, 75-76; drummer, percussion instrumentalist & writer, 76- Chief Collabr: David Foster. *Songs:* So Won't You Stay; Till You Take My Love.

MASON, JACK   ASCAP 1947
composer, arranger
b Cleveland, Ohio, Jan 18, 06; d New York, NY, Dec 28, 65. Educ: Oberlin Cons; Univ Chicago; Univ Wis, BM. Chief arr, Famous Music, 30-33; then free-lance arr in films & radio; comp-arr, TV incl commercials. Arr, Boston Pops Orch, 52-65. *Songs & Instrumental Works:* With All My Heart; I've Got a Date at Eight; Two of a Kind; Just for Tonight; And Still I Care; Candlelight Waltz; Pops Polka; Enchanted Sea; Odalisque; Suite in 4 Movements.

MASON, JAMES HOWARD   ASCAP 1967
composer, author
b Mason City, Iowa, Mar 30, 42. Educ: Central High Sch, Battle Creek, Mich; Western Mich Univ; W K Kellogg Community Col. Left col to pursue singing group career, 63. Performed in Chicago, San Francisco & in New York for 12 yrs. Artist career on Fantasy, Columbia, RCA, ABC Dunhill Record Labels. Record production, 69- Chief Collabr: Paul Stookey. *Songs:* I Dig Rock'N'Roll Music; Hymn; Tiger.

MASON, KENNETH JAY
composer
b Atlantic City, NJ, Feb 1, 55. Educ: Atlantic City High Sch; New Eng Cons Music (scholarship), BME(trumpet, educ), 77. In high sch, mem, county & all-state band. Performer, Boston. Went to Los Angeles, 77. Toured with var acts; did freelance studio work on trumpet. Later began arr & comp for var persons and/or groups. Chief Collabr: Harvey W Mason, Jr. *Songs:* Never Give You Up; Music: Groovin You; The Mase. *Instrumental Works:* When I Am With You.

MASON, ROBERT PAUL   ASCAP 1972
composer, synthesist, keyboardist
b New York, NY, June 26, 46. Educ: Mannes Cons, studied comp with William Sydeman; High Sch Music & Art, studied comp with Eric Salzman; Oberlin Col, BA, studied music comp with Richard Hoffman; NY Univ Dept Intermedia, studied with Morton Subotnik; Columbia-Princeton Electronic Music Ctr. Invented polyphonic synthesizer keyboard; toured clubs & auditoriums; produced & comp, Hayden Planetarium's first musical sky shows, New York; recording artist with Columbia Records, Elektra Records & Columbia Masterworks Records; built RPM Sound Studios (recording electronic music); comp "SoundMurals" speaker installations for museums & art galleries. *Instrumental Works:* Stardrive; Dr Tandem Takes a Ride; Intergalactic Trot; Everything At Once; Rushes; Pulsar; Ballad; Journey; Electronic: Plantar Audition; Psychoalchemy.

MASON, SANDY
See Theoret, Sandy Mason

MASONE, PATRICK T   ASCAP 1960
composer, guitarist, teacher
b Jamaica, NY, Mar 29, 28. Educ: Brooklyn Tech High Sch. Wrote instruction bks for guitar. Has made records. Teacher of guitar. *Songs:* Let Me Take You By the Hand; Sleepy Guitar.

MASSARO, SALVATORE
See Lang, Eddie

MASSE, LAUREL ANNE   ASCAP 1978
composer, author, singer
b Holland, Mich, Dec 29, 51. Educ: Int Sch Brussels, 67-68; Abbot Acad, 69; studied voice with David Collyer, New York, 73-76 & Seth Riggs, Los Angeles, 76-80. Founding mem, The Manhattan Transfer, 72-79, traveled and performed internationally. Started writing seriously, 79, solo artist & writer, 80- Chief Collabrs: Peter Leinheiser, Elliott Randall, Marty Kupersmith.

MASSER, MICHAEL
composer, producer, lyricist
b Chicago, Ill, Mar 24, 41. Educ: Univ Ill, BA, Law Sch. Began writing & producing with Motown Records, then Arista Records & Screengem Records. Under contract with Columbia. Chief Collabrs: Gerry Goffin, Carol Conners, Carol Bayer Sager, Ron Miller, Hal David, Randy Goodrum, Pam Sawyer.

MASSEY, D CURTIS   ASCAP 1954
composer, author, singer
b Midland, Tex, May 3, 10. Educ: Horner Cons. Bandleader, 30, featured on own show, radio & TV. Music dir & comp, var TV series, incl "Petticoat Junction" & "Beverly Hillbillies." *Songs & Instrumental Works:* The Honey Song; Ridin' Down That Texas Trail; Dude Cowboy; I've Been a Fool Again; Draggin' the Bow; Baby Guitar; Petticoat Junction (theme); We'll Sing the Old Songs (theme).

MASSEY, MARIA
See Pelikan, Maria

MASTERS, ARCHIE
See Akers, Howard Estabrook

MASTERS, DAVID
See Burger, David Mark

MASTERS, FRANKIE   ASCAP 1948
composer, author, conductor
b St Mary's, WVa, Apr 12, 04. Educ: Univ Ind. Toured Orient in univ band. Organized own orch, featured in nightclubs, hotels & theatres throughout US; also in films, on radio & TV shows incl "Fitch Band Wagon", "Lucky Letters" & "The Walgreen Open House." Chief Collabr: Johnny Burke. *Songs:* Scatterbrain; Sweet Dream of You; Moonlight and You (theme); Charming Little Faker; What a Heavenly Night for Love; Lovers Lullaby.

MASTERS, WILLIAM RUSH   ASCAP 1975
composer, performer, singer
b Wichita, Kans, Sept 15, 50. Educ: Began playing guitar at age 6; studied with Chips Hoover, 76-77; studied harmony, theory & studio guitar, Dick Grove Sch Music, Studio City, Calif, 77. Learned Chuck Berry type rock & roll by 60; formed rock groups' acts during high sch & col. Began writing contemporary gospel music for The Archers, 70, joined them & toured 7 yrs. Now involved with contemporary Jesus music with focus on teaching. Chief Collabrs: Don Alderidge, Judy Masters, Tim & Steve Archer, Nancye Short Tsaparlis. *Songs:* Fresh Surrender (nominated for Dove Award, 79); God's Love; You Are My Inspiration; Brand New Day; Music (Things We Deeply Feel).

MASTREN, CARMEN   ASCAP 1956
composer, guitarist, conductor
b Cohoes, NY, Oct 6, 13. Educ: Cohoes High Sch. Banjoist, then guitarist in Wingy Manone Jazz Group, later with Tommy Dorsey Orch, also arr, asst cond. WW II, USAF, comp, arr & guitarist, Glenn Miller Orch, 43-45. Accompanist, cond for Morton Downey. NBC staff musician, 53. Has made many records. Chief Collabrs: Carl Severinsen, Sheldon Cohen, Albert Harris. *Songs & Instrumental Works:* Lament in E; Minuet in Miniature; Tempo for Two; Two Moods; Para Mi; Banjo Rock; Interlude; Trumpet Lament; Arr: Black Eyes; Liebestraum; Goin' Home; Melody in F.

MATESKY, RALPH   ASCAP 1961
composer, author, violinist
b New York, NY, Jan 4, 13; d Seattle, Wash, Mar 3, 79. Educ: Teachers Col, Columbia Univ, BS; Juilliard (scholarship, Coolidge award); Univ Southern Calif, MM; studied with Michel Piastro, Edouard Dethier, Bernard Wagenaar, Ernest Kanitz, Roger Sessions & Paul Creston. Violinist, arr & comp for radio, TV & films. In 31, began teaching in music schs & cols. Contract violinist, Enterprise Motion Pictures, 46-48. Founder-musical dir, Compton Civic Symph & Compton Youth Orch, 47-63. Supvr instrumental music, Compton City Schs, Calif, 49-63. Fac mem, Univ Southern Calif Sch Music, 57-63. Cond, Idyllwild High Sch Youth Symph, Grad Chamber Orch, 58-64. Cond, Idyllwild Tour Orchs in: Eng, 64; Scandinavia, 65. Music dir, Stockton Symph, 63-67; assoc prof music, Univ Pacific, 63-67. Founder-cond, San Joaquin Youth Symph, 63-67. Prof music & dir string orch, Utah State Univ, 67-77. Cond, Northern Wasatch Youth Symph, 67-73 (two tours of Mex, 70 & 72). Cond & teacher. Assoc ed, Am String Teacher, 59-64; mem, Music Educ Nat Conference Copyright Comn, 60-66; Nat pres, Am String Teachers' Asn, 70-72, publ chmn, 74-78. Hon mem, Japanese String Teachers Asn, 73. Hon Awards/Medals: State of Calif, 62, Ysaye Found, Brussels, Belg, 70, Venice, 71 & Distinguished Service Award, Am String Teachers Asn, 78. Co-Author: "Playing and Teaching Stringed Instruments" (2 vols); "Learn to Play in the Orchestra" (2 vols); "Learn to Play a String Instrument" (3 vols, with Ardelle Womack). *Instrumental Works:* Cowboy Rhapsody; Train Ride; Welsh March; The Concertmaster Series; Finger Families for Orchestra; Prayer for Peace (chorus, orch); Odyssey in Strings (2 vols, string orch); Wonderful World of Strings-Romantic Period (string orch); Choreo Primo (orch); Variations on a Famous Theme by Paganini (orch); Concertino for Violin Solo With Piano Accompaniment; Mozartino Violin Solo With Piano Accompaniment; The Well

Tempered String Player (violin, Viola, Cello, bass, piano); Fiddlers Day (orch); Variations on a Theme By Beethoven (orch); The Holly and the Mistletoe (orch); Jig-O-Rama (orch); Polacca Moderne (orch); When Johnny Comes Marching Home; Transcriptions: Finale From Beethoven's Fifth Symphony (sch orch); Bach's Chorale & Invention; Vivaldi's Two Concerti Grossi; Brahms Hungarian Dance No 1; Beethoven's Romance in G major.

MATHEWS, JAMES SNOOKIE (JOHNNY NOVEMBER) ASCAP 1963
composer, author
b Richmond, Va, Feb 3, 19. Educ: Benedictine Col. Longshoreman, seaman & DJ. Chief Collabr: Edith Lindeman. *Songs:* Five A M; Some Other Town; Pudjy; Music: Hannukah; Dismal Swamp. *Instrumental Works:* Moonmist.

MATHEWS, PATRICK ASCAP 1976
author
b Belfast, Ireland, Feb 6, 34. Educ: McGill Univ, Montreal. Screen writer for TV incl "Switch", "Quincy" & "Wonder Woman"; also special occasion lyrics for "Switch." Chief Collabr: Jimmy Dibasquale.

MATHEWS, RAY
See Matousek, Raymond Anthony

MATLICK, JAY JEFFRIES (JAY JEFFRIES) ASCAP 1971
author
b New York, NY, Oct 3, 41. Educ: NY Univ, BS. Revue lyrics & sketches for The Upstairs at the Downstairs, New York, Washington Theatre Club, DC, Madeira Club, Provincetown, Mass & others. Chief Collabrs: Harrison Fisher, Don McAffe, Rod Warren, Richard Gessner. *Songs:* Lyrics: Peppermint Fugue; Peaceable Kingdom; Mistmatched; Aesop and His Animal Crackerss(12 Crackers (12 song cycle); Ransom of Redchief; The Manhattan Arrangement.

MATLOCK, JULIAN C (MATTY) ASCAP 1957
composer, conductor, clarinetist
b Paducah, Ky, Apr 27, 07; d Van Nuys, Calif, June 14, 78. Educ: High sch. Clarinetist in Beasley Smith Orch, 5 yrs, Ben Pollack, 29-34, then with Bob Crosby. To Los Angeles, 43. Clarinetist in radio & TV; made many records. *Instrumental Works:* March of the Bob Cats; Dixieland Shuffle; Paducah Parade; Sugar Daddy Strut.

MATOS, ALEXANDER ASCAP 1961
composer, accordionist
b Bronx, NY, June 15, 29. Educ: Studied music with William Rivelli. WW II, entertained with Am Theatre Wing groups throughout US (Am Theatre Wing Coun Citation). Guest appearances. Town Hall debut, 50. *Instrumental Works:* Flame Dance; Spanish Dance; Busy Carpenter; Southern Festival; Red Hot; White Hat.

MATOS, MANUEL GARCIA ASCAP 1944
composer, author, conductor
b Seville, Spain, July 18, 04. Educ: Studied with Reverend Eduardo Torres, Manuel de Falla. Mem, Orquesta Betica de Camera. Cond, Paris, Madrid, London; comp, music dir, film studios, Hollywood & Mex. Dir, Latin Am Ballet. *Songs & Instrumental Works:* An Incan Song; From Peru; A Venezuelan Dance; Claveles Rojos; Rumor Andaluz; Seguiriya Gitana; Silueta Cubana; Barrio Santa Cruz; Rapsodia Celta; Milagro de Dios; Caminito de Sevilla.

MATOUSEK, RAYMOND ANTHONY (RAY MATHEWS) ASCAP 1970
b Cleveland, Ohio, Feb 26, 26. Educ: Pvt study harmony, theory, comp, choral arr & piano with Clifford P Barnes, vocal with Francis J Sadlier. Guitarist & pianist in pvt clubs, also church organist. Arr, local bands. Songwriter of choral, pop & country music. *Songs:* A Song for Judy; It's Always Christmas (In My Heart); If You Believe in Make-Believe; Don't Send Me Roses.

MATSUDAIRA, RENKO ASCAP 1960
composer, arranger
b Tokyo, Japan. Educ: Kunitachi Sch Music, Tokyo; San Francisco Cons; Hammond Organ Studio with Hal Shutz. *Songs:* Blue Shadow; The Red Balloon; Soliloquy; Hawaiian Love Song; Teddy Bear Polka.

MATTHES, BETSY DURKIN
author, actress
b Ft Benning, Ga, Mar 11, 47. Educ: High sch grad; Am Theatre, studied with Daniel LeGrant & Olympia Dubabis; Sch Am Ballet, studied with Luigi. Actress, Bway show ("Cactus Flower"), First Nat Co ("Mary Mary"); in TV commercials, 75-80; in daytime soap opera ("Dark Shadows"); in films ("Husbands"). Chief Collabrs: Patrick Adams, Jerry Raganoy, Steven Schoenberg, Barbara Mann, Mark Barhan, Michael Zager. *Songs:* Lyrics: Love Express; Pleasure Man; Love Is Holding On; Let's Get Down to Doin' It Tonight.

MATTHEWS, DONALD EDWARD ASCAP 1973
composer
b Troy, Ohio, June 22, 35. Educ: Ohio State Univ; Univ Mich BM(comp); studied with Ross Lee Finney, Leslie Bassett & George B Wilson; Ball State Univ, MA(music). Began piano study at age 8. Cornet study, age 9 with pvt study, age 13. French horn study, age 11. Began comp tunes, age 12.

Accompanist for modern dance classes, Univ Ill, 63-65. Worked in gen music store, 65-69. 2nd Place, Nat Comp Award, 67. First Publ Comp, 69. Worked for dealer & publ printed music, 69. Chief Collabr: John Wilson. *Songs:* In Jesus' Name; Praise Jehovah. *Instrumental Works:* Stonehenge (orch); The King's Pipes (flute trio or trumpet trio).

MATTHEWS, HARRY ALEXANDER ASCAP 1935
composer, conductor, educator
b Cheltenham, Eng, Mar 26, 1879; d Middletown, Conn, Apr 12, 73. Educ: Studied with John Matthews (father), George West & W W Gilchrist; hon MusD, Muhlenberg Col, Univ Pa. To US 1900. Citizen, 23. Organist, choirmaster, Philadelphia churches, 16-54. Cond & co-founder, Clarke Art Soc, Philadelphia, 22-34 & Univ Glee Club of Philadelphia, 35-44. Dir music, Univ Pa, 22-31. Cond, Philadelphia Music Club Chorus, 29-54. Head theory, Organ Depts, Clarke Cons, 34-54. *Songs & Instrumental Works:* Cantatas: The Story of Christmas; The Triumph of the Cross; The City of God (Lutheran Church of Am Comn); The Conversion; The Life Everlasting; The Eternal Light; Gethsemane to Golgotha; Hades, Inc (comic opera); Play the Game (opera); also works for organ, piano, vocal solos & choral works.

MATTHEWS, MARY ANN (MARY JOHNSTON) ASCAP 1958
composer, author
b Oakland, Calif, Feb 2, 22. First woman comp in Hawaii to be elected to ASCAP. Has had many songs recorded by var artists. Wrote campaign song for Pres Kennedy, 60 & Hawaiian Gov Burns, 62. Chief Collabr: Tony Todaro. *Songs:* Music: Keep Your Eyes on the Hands; Somewhere in Hawaii; My Hawaiian Dream; Hula Cop Hop; Ukulele Island; Flowers of Paradise; Pleeza No Peencha Da Hula Girls; A Lei, A Kiss and Aloha; Color Our Love Hawaii; Waikiki Farewell; Malialani; Around the Island in 80 Shakes; Hula Belle; Go to Sleep, My Kuulei; Hawaiian Santa; Aloha Week Parade (theme song); Sweetheart of Waikiki; Blue Hawaiian Skies; My Love Will Wear Plumeria; Steel Guitar Prayer.

MATTHEWS, MARY JO
See Rush, Mary Jo

MATTHEWS, T
See Prisco, Thomas Matthews

MATTHIAS, JACK WILLIAM
composer, arranger
b Brooklyn, NY, Apr 5, 15. Educ: Erasmus Hall High Sch, Brooklyn, NY; NY Univ. Arr, pianist & leader of own orch; arr & pianist, Jerry Blain Orch; arr, Harry James Orch, 39-44. Chief Collabr: Harry James. *Songs:* Music: Trumpet Blues (and cantabile); Trumpet Rhapsody; James Session; Dodgers Fan Dance.

MATTIS, LILLIAN ASCAP 1963
author
b New York, NY, Dec 6, 24. Educ: Roosevelt High Sch, NY; Hunter Col, NY. Spec material lyricist for Jerry Lewis, 61-, singer, actress & original lyrics for "Jerry Lewis Muscular Dystrophy Telethon," 73- Chief Collabrs: Louis Yule Brown, Neal Hefti. *Songs:* Lyrics: Three on a Couch (theme song); We've Got a World That Swings; I Must Know; How to Murder Your Wife; Think Pink.

MAULE, LEROY ERNEST (ABE)
composer, author, instrumental teacher
b Payette, Idaho, Jan 5, 04. Educ: Payette High Sch; Univ Idaho, 21-22; Univ Southern Calif, 51-56, BM, 56; Univ San Francisco, 56-59, MS. With Glen Oswald Orch, 22-25, saxophonist & leader, Hank Halstead Orch, 25-26, Fanchont Marco Stage Shows, 26-28, Jean Goldkette, Detroit, 28-32. WGM cond, 32-34, Ted Weems, 35-36, Ben Bernie, 38-42. Free-lance work, Paramount, Fox, Warner Bros, Jimmie Dorsey, Phil Harris, Victor Young, Glen Gray, Freddie Bergin & Glen Miller, USAAF. Chief Collabrs: Merle Tonning, Del Porter. *Songs:* Ridin' Fence All Day; Music: Moon River; The Milk Man Said Good Morning. *Instrumental Works:* Just a Shade Corn.

MAULTSBY, CARL
composer, author, arranger
b Orlando, Fla. Educ: Lake Forest Col, BA; Columbia Univ, studied with Vladamir Ussachevsky, Paul Leunning, Mario Davidovsky. Arr, dance music for Bway show "It's So Nice to Be Civilized." A&R staff producer, RCA Records. Cond & keyboardist, with Vivian Redd & Eddie Kendricks & musicals incl "Don't Bother Me, I Can't Cope", "Bubblin' Brown Sugar", "Timbuktu" & "Eubie." Chief Collabr: Vivian Reed. *Songs:* Gotta Get Away; Don't Boom Boom; The Signs Were Wrong; Terrie; Love Shack (Opened Up a Shop Called 'Love'); Reviviscence; Half of Your Heart; It Keeps Getting Better; How Does It Feel.

MAULTSBY, PORTIA KATRENIA ASCAP 1977
composer, teacher, arranger
b Orlando, Fla, June 11, 47. Educ: Jones High Sch; Univ Salzburg, Austria, studied piano, 66; Benedictine Col, BM(piano, theory), 68; Univ Wis-Madison, MM(musicology), 69, PhD(ethnomusicology), 74. Asst prof & dir/producer, Soul Revue, Ind Univ, 71- Musical dir & keyboard player, nightclubs & TV.

Chief Collabrs: Marcellus Lawrence, Lillian Dunlap, Carl Maultsby. *Songs:* Music Is Just a Party; Music: You! Bringin' Me Good Vibes. *Instrumental Works:* Tell Me 'Bout It.

MAUPIN, REX   ASCAP 1960
composer, conductor, musician
b St Joseph, Mo, Nov 25, 1886; d Iowa, Kans, July 28, 66. Educ: Kans State Univ; studied music with Nicolai Malko. Organized dance band; appeared in hotels, theatres & nightclubs. Cond studio orch, KYW, 29-35; cond-arr, NBC, 36-43; music dir, ABC, 43. *Songs & Instrumental Works:* Night Magic; Scenes; Yodel Polka; May God Be With You; Limpy Wimpy; Shades of Blue; Sons of the Soil; Esquire March; Oracle March; Struck in the Groove; Mood and the Melody.

MAURADA, MAC   ASCAP 1957
composer, author
b Millville, NJ, Sept 18, 02; d Hollywood, Calif, Dec 7, 63. Educ: William & Mary Col. Reporter, Philadelphia Inquirer & Ledger, Wilmington Star. Ed, Woodbury Constitution (NJ) & Culver City Citizen (Calif). Writer spec material for Sophie Tucker, Ted Lewis, Harry Richman, Ritz Bros & Pearl Bailey. *Songs:* Hilarity in Hollywood.

MAURICE, CECIL
See Chachkes, Maurice

MAURICE-JACQUET, H   ASCAP 1947
composer, pianist, conductor
b St Mande, France, Mar 18, 1886; d New York, NY, June 29, 54. Educ: Paris Nat Cons; studied with Thome, De Beriot, Rougnon, Pessard, Gedalge, Massenet, Luigini, Vidal, Hugo Rieman & Arturo Nikish. Piano debut at 9 yrs of age; toured Europe as cond, comp & soloist; founder & dir, Union des Femmes Artistes Musiciennes, Paris; accompanist to Grace Moore; music dir, Sch Vocal Arts, New York, Acad Vocal Arts, Philadelphia & Am Cons Music, Drama & Dance, New York; publ. Order, Legion of Honor, France. Former mem, Soc for Advan Continuing Educ for Ministry. *Songs & Instrumental Works:* American Symphony; Spanish Love; The Mystic Trumpeter (cantata). *Scores:* Ballet: Les Danses de Chez Nous (French Ministry of Fine Arts, Opera Comique Fest comn); Operas: Romanitza; Messaouda; Operettas: Le Poilu; La Petite Dactylo.

MAURY, LOWNDES   ASCAP 1955
composer, pianist
b Butte, Mont, July 7, 11; d Encino, Calif, Dec 11, 75. Educ: Univ Mont, BA; Chicago Musical Col; Malkin Cons; scholarship with Wesley LaViolette & Arnold Schoenberg. Pianist, 20th Century Fox Studios; radio & TV; comp for films incl, "Mr Magoo," USAF cartoons. Bd mem, Nat Asn Am Comp & Cond. Univ Mont, LHD, 74. *Songs & Instrumental Works:* Night Life (cello, piano); Sonata for Harp and Cello; Suite for Solo Cello; Reflections (flute, harpsichord); Variations on a Beethoven Theme for Igor Kipnis (harpsichord); Summer of Green (flute, piano, alto flute, cello or orch); Flute and Three Guitars; Changes for Seven Flutes; Prelude and Fugue (piano with trombone or double bass); Sonatina (violin, basson, piano); Blues (string quartet); Scene de Ballet for String Quartet and Alto Piccolo; Speculations for Piano, Violin, Viola and Cello; Springtime Digressions (flute, string quartet, piano); Trios for Educational Concerts (violin, cello, piano); Three Pieces for Woodwind Quintet; Eleven Sketches (piano trio); Cock of the Walk (saxophone or clarinet quartet); Song Without Words (clarinet, piano); Three Essays in Style (woodwind quintet); Trio Scherzando (three flutes, concert band); Three American Songs (brass sextet); Scarlattiana (5 sonatas, woodwind quintet); Concerto for English Words, Brass and Percussion (spec orch, chorus); Proud Music of the Storm (orch, chorus); Concerto for Violin and Orchestra; Waltz Rhapsody (orch); Rhapsody for Alto Flute and Chamber Orchestra; Concerto for Piano and Orchestra; Sonata No 1 (violin, piano); Sonata No 2 (violin, piano); Choral Prelude (organ); Chorale Aria (organ); Three Affirmations (organ); In Memory of the Korean War Dead (organ); Mountain in the Mist (piano); On Quiet Waters (piano); Three Poets: Homage to E E Cummings, Robert Frost, Lorca (piano); Three-Voice Invention (piano); Christmas Legend (piano); Windsweep (piano); New Soundings (3 vols, piano); Magic Lines and Spaces (instr & repertoire bks, piano); Six Changes for Two Pianos; For Two Flutes (flute, piano); Serious Cereal (flute, piano); Flute Now (12 pieces, flute, piano); The House of Dust (mezzo, string quartet); When Daisies Pied and Violets Blue (duet for mezzos, piano); A Christmas Carol (high voice, organ or piano); Lullaby for Jeremy (high voice, piano); Three Elemental Songs (high voice, piano); Arabesque (high, low voices, piano); Four Songs (high, low voices, piano); Farandole (high, low voices, piano); Three Miniatures for Voice and Piano (high, low voices); The Hills of Old County Brome (low voice satire, piano); Cynara (mezzo-soprano, viola, piano); Book of Hours (mezzo-soprano, string quartet); A Lover's Day (mezzo-soprano, song cycle, piano); Irish Rhapsody (tenor, piano); I Cannot Wait Another Day (tenor, piano); The End of July (tenor, piano); The Bicycle (tenor, piano); Christmas Prayer (women's voices, organ); Three Songs for A Cappella Chorus; He Shall Learn Earthliness (SATB, organ); Sabbath Eve Service (SATB, organ); Man Is My Song (5 soloists, full chorus, 2 piano, string bass and perc); Songs for Female Chorus Accompanied by Two French Horns and Harp (Brahms, Opus 17). *Scores:* Opera: The Celebration (one-act).

MAVES, DAVID W   ASCAP 1974
composer
b Salem, Ore, Apr 3, 37. Educ: Univ Ore, BM, 61, comp with Homer Keller; Univ Mich, MM, 63, AMusD, 71, studied with Ross Lee Finney, Lesslie Bassett. USA, 55-57. Comp in residence, Ford Found Grant, Raleigh, NC, 63-65; Rockefeller Perf Grant; Sigma Alpha Iota Inter Am Awards, 74-77. Teacher, Univ Mich & Duke Univ; now chmn fine arts, Col Charleston, SC. *Songs:* Music: Bestiary (woman's chorus). *Instrumental Works:* Piano Sonata No 1; Piano Sonata No 2; Symphony No 3; Trio Oktoechos (clarinet, horn, perc).

MAVES, VICTOR HENRY ARTHUR   ASCAP 1975
composer, teacher, organist
b Milwaukee, Wis, Jan 10, 1897. Educ: Wis Col Music, dipl; Milwaukee State Teachers Col, dipl; Christiansen Sch Music, cert; Fred Waring Sch Music, cert. Teacher organ, Wis Col Music, 14 yrs. Organist, Wesley Methodist Church, 11 yrs, First Baptist Church, 7 yrs & Fox Theatres, Milwaukee, 12 yrs. Organist & dir, United Church of Christ, Milwaukee, 40 yrs. Made 2 albums of organ music. *Songs & Instrumental Works:* Statement of Faith (4 part choral).

MAXWELL, CHARLES   ASCAP 1953
composer, author, arranger
b Leipzig, Ger, Oct 25, 1892; d Los Angeles, Calif, Aug 20, 62. Educ: Leipzig Cons, studied piano, theory, comp & orchestration, 08-11; studied comp with Max Reger, Ger. Came to US, 11. Arr-orchestrator, music publ firms, incl Feist, Berlin & Schuberts, until 29. With MGM Motion Picture Studios, Calif. Free lance, 20th Century-Fox, Columbia, Universal, Warner Bros & others. Worked on many film presentations at major studios. Charter mem, Am Soc Music Arrangers. Mem: Screen Composers Asn; Composers & Lyricists Guild; Nat Asn Composers & Conductors. Chief Collabrs: Arthur Lange, Hugo Friedhofer, William Lava, Ernest Toch, Oscar Levant, Dimitri Tiomkin, Walter Scharf, Lowndes Maury. *Instrumental Works:* Caprice (piano solo); Symph: Congo Spirituale; Overture Plymouth Rock; Stephen Foster Overture; Punch and Judy Overture; Moto Perpetuo; Prelude and Scene; Chamber music: David and the Lord; Trio for Flute, Horn and Bassoon; Trio for Flute, Clarinet and Bassoon; Idyls of Four Goblins (bassoon quartet); Voice in the Wilderness. *Scores:* Films: The Gay Caballero; In Old Sacramento; Scotland Yard Investigator; Secrets of Scotland Yard; Fire; Tree Farm; Casanova Brown; The Woman in the Window; Along Came Jones; Dixie Dugan; Quiet Please, Murder; Storm Over Lisbon; Lake Placid Serenade; Charlie Chan at the Opera.

MAXWELL, EDDIE (EDDIE CHERKOSE)   ASCAP 1942
author
b Detroit, Mich, May 25, 12. Service, WW II. Writer radio scripts; songs for films incl "Rose of the Rio Grande" & "Melody Ranch"; wrote songs, radio TV scripts for "Beany and Cecil", "Donald O'Connor Show", "Spike Jones Show", "Abbott and Costello", "Danny Thomas", "Jimmy Durante" & numerous others; plus songs for Ritz Bros on film. Chief Collabrs: Charles Rosoff, Jacques Press, Jule Styne. *Songs:* Song of the Rose; A Cowboy's Life; What Care I?; How Was I to Know?; Rhythm of the Islands; In Buenos Aires; Love At Last; Torpedo Joe; Rodeo Rose; Melody Ranch; I'm Gonna Swing My Way Up to Heaven; Lyrics: Breathless; Pico and Sepulveda; Tap Happy; There's a Brand New Baby At Our House.

MAXWELL, ELSA   ASCAP 1958
composer, author
b Keokuk, Iowa, May 24, 1883; d New York, NY, Nov 1, 63. Educ: High sch, San Francisco, Calif. In vaudeville as actress & pianist; became hostess & party-giver; organized Monte Carlo Beach Club in 20's; wrote newspaper column. Autobiographies: "My Last 50 years"; "R S V P." *Songs:* Tango Dreams.

MAXWELL, HARRY PHILIP   ASCAP 1951
author, editor
b Greencastle, Ind, Aug 16, 01; d Countryside, Ill, Jan 12, 74. Educ: DePauw Univ, BA, hon LittD; hon MusD, Sherwood Music Sch, Cosmopolitan Sch of Music & Chicago Cons. Made travelogue films with wife, Helen Maxwell. Dir, annual Chicagoland Music Fest. Worked on newspapers, Ind & Ky; joined Chicago Tribune, 29, became ed promotion mgr. Author, poetry "One, Two, Three, Strike!" Chief Collabrs: Helen Purcell Maxwell, Noble Cain, Richard Bowles. *Songs:* Wheels a-Rolling (theme, Chicago Railroad Fair Pageant); Toast to Music; Let's Sing to Victory; All My Love, Dear; Autumn Ballet; Campus Days; Give Us a Campus; I'm a Christmas Tree; Hawaiian Holiday; Oh, Lord, Don't Turn Away From Me; Indiana; There's Something About a Band.

MAXWELL, RICHARD WILLIAMS   ASCAP 1945
composer, author, conductor
b Mansfield, Ohio, Sept 12, 1896; d East Stroudsburg, Pa, Sept 4, 54. Educ: Georgetown Univ; Kenyon Col, BA & MA, (Phi Beta Kappa); Chicago Musical Col; studied voice with Ruffo, Sacerdote, Trevisan, Marafiotti, Bristol, Behr & Alberti. Radio singer, 23-50; soloist, Seth Parker broadcasts. Sang in Bway 1st & 2nd Music Box Reviews, "Greenwich Village Follies" & "The Lady in Ermine." Co-founder, music publ firm, 46, which later became Richard Maxwell Publ. Compiler & ed, volumes of hymns & gospel songs. Dir, Sacred Music, Shawnee Press, 52-54. *Songs & Instrumental Works:* Mine; Dear Friends and

Gentle Hearts; Ask for a Kiss; Smile Awhile; Can't I Just Pretend?; All for a Song; Don't Trouble Trouble; Peace I Leave With Thee; I Love The Lord; The Holy City; Lyrics: Do Unto Others; Thank You Lord; God Bless You and Keep You; Thank God; One Moment of Prayer; Peace That Passeth All Understanding; Thank You Prayer; Angel of God; Dear Lord, Sweet Savior; Go to Your Children and Give Them a Kiss; Let's Go to Church Next Sunday; My Master Was So Very Poor; Prayer for Peace; Cantorio series, The Word of God: The Generation. The Incarnation, The Glorification, The Light of the World; Arise United Nations (int anthem); Collections: Goodwill Songs; Smile Songs; Wonderful Words of Life.

MAXWELL, ROBERT   ASCAP 1953
composer, author
b New York, NY, Apr 19, 21. Educ: Juilliard, studied with Giannini & Grandjany. Jazz harpist in concerts, cafes, theatres & TV. Mem, NBC Symph under Toscanini at age 17. Toured extensively as nightclub act. Comp, many TV specials. Musical dir & comp, NBC Children's Theatre, incl "The Me-Too Show," 65-75. Has made many records. Chief Collab: Carl Sigman. *Songs:* Music: Ebb Tide; Shangri-La; Song of the Nairobi Trio. *Scores:* Film/TV: The Treasures of Tut-Ank-Ha-Men; Bill Cosby Special.

MAXWELL, SANDERS
composer, jazz pianist
b Germantown, Pa, Dec 8, 17. Educ: Princeton Univ, BA, 39; Columbia Univ, 39-40. Creative & account mgt positions in advert agencies incl Young & Rubicam, Inc & J Walter Thompson Co, 40-; composed var jingles; jazz pianist with own & other groups, NY/NJ areas. *Songs:* Just Because; Better Than Average Girl; Take It Away; Can It Be True?

MAXWELL, SPENCER   ASCAP 1966
author
b Los Angeles, Calif, Feb 1, 37. Educ: Pub schs, Salt Lake City, Utah; Univ Calif, Los Angeles, lyric writing with Hal Levy. Performed, wrote & directed shows, Bryce Canyon & Zion Canyon Nat Parks, while in high sch. Began writing songs prof, 63. Spec material for Raquel Welch & Barbara Luna. Publ poetry, 73. Chief Collabrs: Gene Di Novi, Larry Marks, Percy Faith, Pat Williams, Howlett Smith. *Songs:* Lyrics: Christmas Is (Christmas seal campaign theme); The Grass Is Greener; I Can Hear the Music; Brand New Morning; My Very Own Person; Boy Do I Have a Surprise for You; Waitin'; Lonely Afternoon; Walk an Autumn Day With Me; A Quiet Day; Peppermint Hill and Strawberry Lane; Meadows and Flowers; It's Time for Me; A Warm Summer Day; Home; The Other Girl; Morning.

MAY, DARYL
composer, author, singer
b Potomac, Ill, Feb 25, 36. Educ: Studied voice two yrs. Entertainer, comedian & guitarist. *Songs:* The Gator Bar.

MAY, EDWARD CHARLES
composer, teacher
b Rochester, NY, June 21, 1900. Educ: Eastman Sch Music; studied with Tom Grierson & Janette Fuller. Played for silent movies, hotel dining rooms, lounges, concerts & club dates. Teacher of piano, organ, theory, harmony, counterpoint, fuge, invention & comp. *Instrumental Works:* Installation March; Marching Song; Victory Song.

MAY, ROBERT ARDEN (HERB JANUARY)   ASCAP 1978
composer, author
b Dayton, Ohio, July 28, 48. Educ: Greenville High Sch; Tri-State Col, studied bus, lit, music; Univ Calif, Berkeley, BA(philosophy). Began playing guitar, age 14, piano, age 16. Recorded with group, The Raging Winds. Went to San Francisco, 70. Worked with nightclub corp, incl entertainment & promotion. Went to Nashville, 77. Chief Collabrs: Paul Hotchkiss, Anthony Crawford, Arbus Madden. *Songs:* For That Summer (Barn Swallow); I Really Don't Feel Like Dancing; Can It Be Love?; If You Don't Love Me By Now.

MAYER, ARTHUR E   ASCAP 1963
composer, author, arranger
b Rockaway Beach, NY, Nov 19, 18. Educ: NY Univ, BA; Brooklyn Law Sch, LLB; Cornell Univ; Adelphi Col; pvt music study with R Schram, Irving Dwier & Sal Nicosia. Regional adv, Dept Housing & Urban Develop. Writer of special material & arr. Played drums, vibes & guitar with bands during swing era; wrote arr for bands & singers. Now writer of ballads & arr for singers. Chief Collabrs: Thelma Mayer, Jimmy Downs, Rose Warshauer. *Songs:* Has the Romance Really Ended?; I Need You; Anything; Music: I Miss You So; Lonesome and Blue; Little Things Mean So Much; Angel; Cherie; Nothing Stays the Same; My World's an Empty Place.

MAYER, LORI   ASCAP 1974
composer, author
b Wilmington, Del, June 3, 60. Educ: State Univ NY Stony Brook. Writer of lyrics & music, children's educ songs; also rock groups. Chief Collabrs: Hy Glaser, Jamie Glaser. *Songs:* The Weatherman; Music: So What If I'm Not Perfect; Lyrics: Take Me Through the Night; Chanukah.

MAYER, THELMA   ASCAP 1967
composer, author
b New York, NY, Mar 13, 32. Educ: High Sch Music & Art; New York Inst Technol; studied music with Rudolph Schramm. Prof artist & designer, writer of poetry, illusr of children's bks, lyricist & comp. Chief Collabrs: Arthur Mayer, Irving Fields. *Songs:* Lost Without You; I Miss You So; Nothing Stays the Same; Lyrics: I Reached for a Star; Little Things Mean So Much; Cheire; Angel; Wild Little Firefly; Now.

MAYER, WILLIAM ROBERT   ASCAP 1956
composer, author
b New York, NY, Nov 18, 25. Educ: Yale Univ, BA, 49; Mannes Col Music, dipl music theory & comp, 52; pvt study comp with Roger Sessions, 49 & Otto Luening, 53. Comp orchestral, vocal & chamber works. Writer contemporary music, New York Times & other publ. Chmn, Comp Recordings, Inc, 4 yrs. Awards: Guggenheim & MacDowell Fels. Grants: Ford Found; NEA. *Songs & Instrumental Works:* Octagon (piano, orch); Spring Came on Forever (soloists, chorus, orch); Hello, World!; Two Pastels (orch); Overture for an American; Dream's End; Enter Ariel; Messages; Brass Quintet; Eight Miniatures and Two News Items (voice, chamber ens); Eve of St Agnes (soloists, chorus, orch); Essay for Brass and Winds; La Belle Dame Sans Merci (solo, chorus); Festive Alleluia; Khartoum; Always Always Forever Again; Paradox; Piano Sonata; Country Fair (brass trio); Andante for Strings; Toccata (piano). *Scores:* Opera/Ballet: A Death in the Family; The Snow Queen; One Christmas Long Ago; Brief Candle (micro-opera).

MAYERS, BENEDICT   ASCAP 1953
author, educator
b Chicago, Ill, Oct 7, 06. Educ: Univ Chicago, PhB; Ill Tech, BS; Roosevelt Univ, MA; De Paul Univ; Univ of London, PhD. Was instr, Armed Forces Educ Ctr. Child guidance counselor, Cook Co Pub Schs; dir, Cook Co Juvenile Bur, 6 yrs. Assoc prof of political sci, admin asst to pres, dir of col prep prog, Roosevelt Univ, 9 yrs. Personnel syst planning, res, Statistics, US Govt, State of Ill, 7 yrs. WW II, Korean War service. Dir, Dept of Spec Educ, Leyden area, Chicago. Trustee, Olivet Inst, Chicago, Ill Acad of Criminology & Med Corps Convalescent Ctr, USA Reserves; youth consult, Skokie, Ill Police Dept.

MAYHEW, WILLIAM   ASCAP 1956
composer, author
b Emmitsburg, Md, May 22, 1889; d Nov 17, 51. *Songs:* It's a Sin to Tell a Lie.

MAYO, CASS
See Stevens, Casandra Mayo

MAYS, CARL W   ASCAP 1975
composer, author, professional speaker
b Humboldt, Tenn, Dec 6, 43. Educ: Humboldt High Sch; Murray State Univ, BS(speech & jour); Memphis State Univ, grad work in speech & jour; New Orleans Sem, MA(communications). Speech & drama instr & football coach. Writer & announcer for TV & radio. City-wide youth dir for New Orleans & Columbus, Ga presenting dramas, musicals & talks. Pres, Creative Living, 72- Author of 4 bks, 6 plays & 2 musical-dramas. Ed, monthly newsletter "Creative Living." Chief Collab: Comp & arr, W Elmo Mercer. *Songs:* From Musical Drama The Clown: We Can Live; Winter Rain; Jesus Has the Power; With Me in Paradise. *Scores:* Musical Drama: The Clown.

MAYS, WILLIAM ALLEN   ASCAP 1971
composer
b Sacramento, Calif, Feb 5, 44. Educ: San Diego State Univ; Palomar Col, studied with Victor Aller & Phil Cohen; Pierce Col; USN Sch Music. USN music, 61-65. Prof musician, San Diego, 65-69; recording musician & comp, Los Angeles, 69- *Instrumental Works:* Great American Rag; Suite for Flute and Piano; Euterpe; No Hurry; Linsong.

MAZLEN, ANN (ANN SHEPARD)   ASCAP 1950
composer, author
b Brooklyn, NY, Aug 17, 18. Educ: Seward Park High Sch; pvt study piano. Writer lyrics, occasionally music. Chief Collabrs: Henry Gershwin Mazlen, Roger G Mazlen, Kenneth M Mazlen, Gene Autry. *Songs:* Abraham Lincoln; All Aboard; It's Fat; Bring Back the Good Old Days; Cindy Lou; Sticky Fingers; Brother Daniel in the Lion's Den; Out of the Frying Pan (And Into the Fire); A Rose Is a Rose Is a Rose; Impact of Love; Lyrics: I Just Saddle My Pinto and Ride.

MAZLEN, HENRY GERSHWIN (ARTHUR LEWISOHN)   ASCAP 1950
composer, author, publisher
b Manhattan, NY, Mar 1, 12. Educ: James Monroe High Sch; Nat Univ, Washington, DC. Songwriter since early teens. Comp-author motion picture, "Ecstasy." Tune detective as musical consult, Walt Disney Enterprises. Fed Civil Serv, 40 yrs, retired, 66. Staff, Bus Off, Brooklyn Col, 70-74. Chief Collabrs: William Colligan, Roger G Mazlen, Felix Maly, Hans Haas, Gene Autry, Ann Mazlen, Wilhelm Licht, Hadju Imre, Al Sanders, Kenneth M Mazlen, Victor Thomas, Cedric Poland, Herman Leopoldi. *Songs:* I'm Sure It's Love; It's Fat; All Aboard; Lyrics: I Just Saddle My Pinto and Ride.

MAZUR, ALBERT　　　　　　　　　　　ASCAP 1961
composer, teacher
b Schenectady, NY, Oct 21, 29. Educ: Kingsborough Community Col, Brooklyn, NY. Musician with USO, nightclubs & resorts; piano, accordion & guitar teacher; written from Holy Scriptures: Isaiah 53, Romans 10, Psalm 2 & John 3:16; had pub performances. Chief Collabr: Marion Turner Mazur (wife). *Songs:* Music: Bar Mitzvah Song; Tennessee Rock (theme song on radio); It Was Nice Loving You. *Scores:* Play: Marriage Anyone?.

MAZUR, MARION CLAIRE
author
b Brooklyn, NY, Jan 25, 20. Educ: Girls Commercial High Sch, Brooklyn, grad. Songwriter; wrote 18 songs for play, "Marriage-Anyone?"; had written religious songs, sch & occasion songs for income tax day, Christmas & Mother's Day. Chief Collabr: Albert Mazur (husband). *Songs & Instrumental Works:* Tennessee Rock (theme song on radio); It Was Nice Loving You; Why Mothers' Cry (Mother's Day song); It's Xmas Time Again (Xmas Song); Bachelor's Lament (income tax song); I Promise..! (religious song); Lyrics: Bar Mitzvah Song & Speech.

MCALLISTER, DAVID
See Wood, Douglas Albert

MCALLISTER, ROBERT CHARLES　　　　　ASCAP 1968
author, teacher
b Philadelphia, Pa, June 2, 35. Chief Collabrs: Joe Raposo, Arthur Kaplan. *Songs:* Lyrics: Kids Are People Too; The Exercise Song; Good News; Fingelheimer Song; Gee, Its Great to Be a Kid.

MCARTHUR, EDWIN　　　　　　　　　ASCAP 1953
composer, conductor, pianist
b Denver, Colo, Sept 24, 07. Dir, Wagnerian repertory, Metrop Opera Co. Guest cond, US Symph Orchs. WW II, toured SW Pac area with chorus of 1500. Accompanist to John Charles Thomas, Ezio Pinza & Kirsten Flagstad. Music dir, St Louis Municipal Opera, 17 yrs; also radio progs, St Louis, 12 yrs (had own prog, 59-61). Music dir, Harrisburg Symph, Pa, 49-

MCAULIFFE, WILLIAM LEON　　　　　　ASCAP 1959
composer, musician, author
b Houston, Tex, Jan 3, 17. Educ: John Reagan High Sch, Houston. First guitar at age 14; first play for pay at age 15, Tex Qualify Network (radio) & first recordings, Brunswick, age 16. Joined Bob Wills Band, age 18. Did many records, Columbia, 8 yrs, 10 movies, Columbia & Monogram; also shows, dances, KVDO radio. USN, WW II. Had own band until 65, also own TV show, record co, radio sta & ballroom. *Instrumental Works:* Steel Guitar Rag; Blue Bonnet Rag; Panhandle Rag.

MCBETH, WILLIAM FRANCIS　　　　　　ASCAP 1964
composer, author, teacher
b Ropesville, Tex, Mar 9, 33. Educ: Hardin-Simmons Univ, BMus, 54, DMus, 73; Univ Tex, MMus, 57, studied with Kent Kennan & Clifton Williams; Eastman Sch Music, 59-64, studied with Howard Hanson & Bernard Rogers. Prof music, teacher, resident comp & chmn dept theory & comp, Ouachita Univ, Ark, 57-; cond, Ark Symph Orch, Little Rock, many yrs. Composer Laureate, State Ark. Performed in Ger, France, Italy, Eng, Scotland & Iceland. Conducted in 40 of the 50 states, Can & Japan, averaging 40 concerts a yr. *Instrumental Works:* Chant and Jubilo; Masque; Battaglia; Kaddish; Joyant Narrative; Drammatico; Divergents; Seventh Seal; To Be Fed By Ravens; Canto.

MCBRIEN, ROGER RALPH (ROD)　　　　ASCAP 1971
composer, singer, producer
b Amityville, NY, June 20, 43. Educ: Amityville High Sch. Audio engr, recording artist, A&R dir, staff writer & arr at record co. Has own record co, Rod McBrien Productions, Inc. Writer, producer & singer of commercials, incl Coca-Cola & Burger King. Winner, First Am Song Fest. Chief Collabrs: Hal Hackady, Hal Friedman, Bill Backer, Billy Davis, Joe Rock, Estelle Levitt, Sarah Daly. *Songs:* Music: Isn't It Lonely Together; Look Up America; Let Yourself Go to Pizza Hut.

MCCABE, CHARLES HENRY, III　　　　　ASCAP 1978
composer, author, singer
b Pensacola, Fla, Aug 24, 44. Performer, nightclubs & USO tours, Vietnam & Southeast Asia. Recording artist, Capitol, ABC, GRT & Woodshed Records. Chief Collabr: Gary Dahl. *Songs:* Sailor Beware; Our House; Music: That Old Pet Rock of Mine.

MCCALL, LEONARD　　　　　　　　　ASCAP 1952
composer, author
b Florence, SC, July 7, 10. Chief Collabrs: Boris Cherney, Al Albert, Gus Braun. *Songs:* Two Little Kisses; Wanted; Dance With Me; Arizona Moon; Forgive Me; You Are My One Love.

MCCALL, SHERRIE HUGHES　　　　　　ASCAP 1970
composer, author, singer
b Nashville, Tenn, May 13, 47. Educ: Belmont Col, Nashville. Theatrical performer, Nashville. Recorded with Dial Records. Songwriter, country/western, gospel & pop music. Chief Collabr: Jan Wilson. *Songs:* Happy Day.

MCCAREY, LEO　　　　　　　　　　ASCAP 1957
author, director, producer
b Los Angeles, Calif, Oct 3, 1898, d Santa Monica, Calif, July 5, 69. Dir, Hal Roach film comedies. Writer-dir-producer of films incl "The Kid From Spain", "Duck Soup", "Ruggles of Red Gap", "The Milky Way", "The Awful Truth", "Love Affair", "Going My Way" (Acad Award, 44), "The Bells of St Mary's", "An Affair to Remember", "Rally 'Round the Flag, Boys" & "Satan Never Sleeps." Chief Collabrs: Harry Warren, Harold Adamson. *Songs:* An Affair to Remember.

MCCARRON, CHARLES　　　　　　　　ASCAP 1914
author, singer, pianist
b Janesville, Wis, Oct 6, 1891; d New York, NY, Jan 27, 19. Educ: High sch, Winthrop, Mass. On staffs of music publ firms; appeared in vaudeville; also wrote for performers. Chief Collabr: Albert Von Tilzer. *Songs:* Blues My Naughty Sweetie Gives to Me; I'm Glad I Made You Cry; Down Where the Swanee River Flows; When Old Bill Bailey Plays His Ukulele; Oh, Helen; Poor Pauline; When the Sun Goes Down In Dixie; Down In Honky Tonky Town; Oh How She Could Yacki Hacki Wicki Wacki Woo.

MCCARTHY, CHARLES J (PAT)　　　　　ASCAP 1938
composer, author, pianist
b New York, NY, Jan 31, 03; d New York, Mar 2, 60. Educ: Cathedral High Sch. Wrote parodies for Van & Schenck. Was businessman, then pianist. *Songs:* Paradise Lane; When Your Old Wedding Ring Was New; At Least You Could Say Hello; I'm Afraid to Love You; Dreams Are a Dime a Dozen; The Address Is Still the Same; I'm All That's Left of That Old Quartet.

MCCARTHY, CHARLOTTE ELLEN　　　　ASCAP 1964
composer, author
b Tangier, Ind, Sept 12, 18. Educ: Colo Woman's Col. Started writing songs at age 12. *Songs:* I Don't Want to Be Hurt Anymore; Can't You See I'm Sorry?.

MCCARTHY, JOSEPH　　　　　　　　　ASCAP 1914
author
b Somerville, Mass, Sept 27, 1885; d New York, NY, Dec 18, 43. Educ: Malden Pub Schs. Began as singer in cafes. Music publ, Boston; then mem prof staff, Feist & other publ. Wrote songs, screenplays for films incl, "High Society Blues." Charter mem, ASCAP, dir, 21-29. Chief Collabrs: Harry Tierney, Harry Carroll, Fred Fisher, James Monaco. *Songs:* You Made Me Love You; Beatrice Fairfax; In All My Dreams I Dream of You; What Do You Want to Make Those Eyes At Me For?; They Go Wild, Simply Wild, Over Me; Through; If We Can't Be the Same Old Sweethearts; Ireland Must Be Heaven for My Mother Came From There; I Found the End of the Rainbow; Oui, Oui, Marie; I'm Always Chasing Rainbows; My Baby's Arms; I'm Crying Just for You; I Miss You Most of All; Alice Blue Gown; Irene; Castle of Dreams; Journey's End; If Your Heart's in the Game; Someone Loves You After All; Rio Rita; The Kinkajou; The Rangers Song; If You're in Love You'll Waltz; You're Always in My Arms.

MCCARTHY, JOSEPH ALLAN　　　　　　ASCAP 1948
author, editor, publisher
b Pelham, NY, Aug 18, 22; d New York, NY, Nov 7, 75. Educ: Juilliard Sch Music; NY Univ. Son of Joseph McCarthy. Assoc with J J Robbins & Son. Wrote songs for Bway revues "John Murray Anderson's Almanac" in 53 & "Ziegfeld Follies" in 56, also for TV. Chief Collabrs: Cy Coleman, Marvin Fisher. *Songs:* Why Try to Change Her Now?; Rambling Rose; The Riviera; Cloudy Morning; No Fool Like an Old Fool; I'm Gonna Laugh You Right Outa My Life; The Champion (film theme).

MCCARTHY, KEVIN JAMES　　　　　　ASCAP 1976
composer, author
b Shawnee, Okla, May 4, 44. Educ: Loyola High Sch; Santa Clara Univ, BA. Played duo with Paul Kantner. Wrote religious music. Taught high sch, 9 yrs. Built soundtrack studio, Nev. Chief Collabrs: David Petrucci, Tom Wargo. *Songs:* Do It in the Dirt; The Meter Song; Please Remember Me; Lyrics: Save Me in Time; You Make Me Feel Like a Woman Should.

MCCARTHY, ROBERT SYLVESTER, III　　ASCAP 1968
composer, author, singer
b Salem, Mass, Jan 31, 49. Educ: Cambridge Sch Broadcasting. Started writing at age 13. Performer, Boston & New York area. Minister & writer of gospel songs. Chief Collabrs: Keith Lambert, Laurie McCarthy. *Songs:* Working on the Main Line; Can't Live Without Your Love.

MCCARTY, JOE LAWRENCE　　　　　　ASCAP 1974
author
b Denver, Colo, Mar 26, 05. Educ: Sacred Heart High Sch, 23; Notre Dame Univ, BA, 28. With radio shows, "Benny Goodman Camel Caravan" & "Jack

Oakie Col Musical Knowledge"; stage show, "Everyday's a Holiday." Chief Collabrs: Harry Barris, Matty Malneck, Barclay Allen, Jimmy Dorsey, Will Back. *Songs:* Lyrics: Naturally; This Night Is Our's!; Just Lately; 'Leven Pounds of Heaven. *Scores:* Film/TV: Swing That Cheer.

MCCATHREN, DONALD EUGENE   ASCAP 1959
author, conductor, arranger
b Gary, Ind, July 6, 24. Educ: Ind State Univ, BS(music educ); Chicago Musical Col, MM; Ind Univ; Boston Univ; Tufts Univ; USN Sch of Music; Harvard Univ; studied with Rudolph Ganz, Daniel Bonade, Victor Polatschek & Thor Johnson; Hon Doctorate, Huron Col. WW II, Ensign USN, mem, US Navy Broadcast Band, Washington, DC. Instr woodwind instruments, Chicago Musical Col; grad asst, Ind Univ. Dir of res & educ serv, G Leblanc Corp. Dir of bands, chmn of wind ens dept & prof music, Duquesne Univ; assoc dir, Sch Band of Am (annual European tours). Vpres, Student Leaders of Am; music dir, WDUQ. Ed for publ. Author "Playing and Teaching the Clarinet Family", "Organizing the High School Stage Band", "Improving the Soprano Clarinet Section" & "The Saxophone." Chief Collabrs: Alfred Reed, Noah Klauss, Fred Kepner, Marcel Frank. *Instrumental Works:* Arr: Minute Waltz (Chopin; clarinet, piano); Serenade (Pierre).

MCCLEARY, FIONA
See Warndof, Fiona McCleary

MCCLINTIC, LAMBERT GERHARDT, JR (GARY)   ASCAP 1964
composer, author, singer
b Lansing, Mich, Aug 13, 46. Educ: Spring Arbor Col, BA(music), 68; Mich State Univ, comp & arr studies. Recording artist, Capitol Records; singer concerts, night clubs & TV; arranger; master of ceremonies; concert pianist. *Songs:* Carousel of Life; I'm Your Dancin' Man; This Is Your Night; You Were Meant For Me; Through It All; Special Friends.

MCCLINTOCK, HARRY KIRBY   ASCAP 1940
composer, author, singer
b Knoxville, Tenn, Oct 8, 1882; d San Francisco, Calif, Apr 24, 57. Educ: Calif Sch Fine Arts, San Francisco. Became folk singer on radio in 25; had own prog, Mac's Haywire Orchestra, until 36. *Songs:* The Big Rock Candy Mountain; The Bum Song; Fifty Years From Now; Lonesome Trail; Fireman, Save My Child; If I Had My Druthers; The Hobo Spring Song; The Trusty Lariat.

MCCLINTON, OSBIE BURNETT   ASCAP 1973
composer
b Senatobia, Miss, Apr 25, 40. Educ: Rust Col, BS(educ). Singer & songwriter. *Songs:* You've Got My Mind Messed Up; A Man Needs a Woman; Black Speck; Foot Prints on the Windshield; It's So Good Lovin You; Happy Day Inn Room 309; Just in Case; Miss Sara Lee; Soap.

MCCLURE, RONALD DIX   ASCAP 1974
composer, bassist, arranger
b New Haven, Conn, Nov 22, 41. Educ: Hartt Col Music, BM, 63; studied with Joe Iadone & Hall Overton. Played bass with Buddy Rich, Maynard Ferguson, Charles Lloyd, Wes Montgomery, Wynton Kelly, Joe Henderson, Stan Getz, The Pointer Sisters, David Liebman, The Fourth Way, Blood, Sweat & Tears, 63. Teacher, Berklee Col, 71-72 & Nat Stage Band Summer Jazz Clinics, 77-80. Chief Collabrs: Mike Nock, David Liebman. *Instrumental Works:* Mirror Image; No Show (nominated for Grammy Award, 75); Sunburst; Farewell, Goodbye.

MCCOLLIN, FRANCES   ASCAP 1942
composer
b Philadelphia, Pa, Oct 24, 1892; d Philadelphia, Feb 20, 60. Educ: Inst for the Blind; Bryn Mawr Col; studied music with William Gilchrist & H Alexander Matthews. Lectr & chorus cond, Burd Sch, Philadelphia, 22-33 & Swarthmore Col, 23-24. Mem, Nat Asn Am Comp & Cond; life mem, Nat Fedn Music Clubs. *Songs & Instrumental Works:* The Winds of God (Soc Arts & Letters Prize); The Midnight Sea (Nat Fedn Music Clubs Prize); Caprice (organ); Madrigals: The Nights o' Spring; What Care (both Chicago Madrigal Club Prize); Anthems: O Sing Unto he Lord (Philadelphia Ms Soc Prize); The Lord Is Kind (Clemson Award); Then Shall the Righteous Shine (Mendelssohn Club Prize); Now the Day Is Over; Come Hither Ye Faithful (Dayton Westminster Choir Prize); Peace I Leave With You (Capital Univ Prize); O Little Town of Bethlehem (Harvey Gaul Prize); Cantata: The Singing Leaves; Choral: Spring Is Heaven (Nat Fedn Music Clubs Prize); The Coming of June; The Shepherds Had an Angel (Sigma Alpha Iota Prize); Christmas Bells (Pa Fedn Music Clubs Prize).

MCCONNELL, GEORGE BURNHAM   ASCAP 1921
composer, author, pianist
b Philadelphia, Pa, Mar 10, 1894. Educ: High sch. Pianist, Philadelphia music publ cos. In vaudeville, 3 yrs. WW I, USCG. Ed, Morton Downey's Song Folio, Frank Luther's Hillbilly Folio, Pappy Ezra & Zeke's Hillbilly Folio, Lani McIntyre's Hawaiian Song Folio. Wrote spec songs for many productions, incl "Willie & Eugene Howard Passing Show of 1921", "Clayton Jackson & Durante", "Ziegfeld Follies, 1929," also songs for many vaudeville performers. Chief Collabrs: Al Dubin, Al Bryan, Howard Johnson, Lew Brown, Jimmy McHugh, Morton Downey, Andrew B Sterling, Johnny Klenner, Mort Dixon,

Fred Fisher, Joe Goodwin, Harry Pease, Edgar Leslie, Jack Yellen. *Songs:* You Wanted Someone to Play With (I Wanted Someone to Love); When Mother Played the Organ; That's How I Spell I-R-E-L-A-N-D; Mickey Donohue; Sweet Hawaiian Chimes; Marion You'll Soon Be Marryin' Me; I'm in Love With a Beautiful Baby; Dream Moon Valley; When I Tell You I Love You Believe Me Dear; 'Twas Only an Irishman's Dream; I Ain't Got Nothing for Nobody But You; Your Country Needs You Now (recruiting song, WW I); I'll Take Care of Your Cares; Lazy Silvery Moon; Between the Dances; Let's Drift Away on Dreamers Bay; Winter in Havana; Hearts Are Never Blue in Blue Kalua; Would You?; After I Took You Into My Heart; Moon or No Moon, I Love You; More Than Words Can Tell; Here's a Rose for You; That's the Way We'll Say Good-bye; When It's Moonlight on the Levee; The Lovelight in Your Eyes; Get the Right Little Girl in the Right Kind of Place; There Never Was a Girl Like Mary; I Can't Keep My Eyes Off You; Those Beautiful Eyes; Where Are You Love?; You Remind Me So Much of My Mother; It Happens Every Night; When I Get Back to Old Virginia; My Mother, My Dad and My Girl; Won't You Give Me One More Waltz?; When the Sun Goes Down in Switzerland; When the Sails Are Set for Home; I Just Made Up With That Old Girl of Mine; I'm the Last One Left of That Old Quartette; Oh Ya Ya; I Can't See the Beautiful Sea; Tell Your Troubles All Good-bye; Thanks; When the Rest of the World Don't Want You; She Wore a Little Dimple on Her Chin; Next Door to Heaven; I'm Out of My Mind; With You in My Heart; Heaven's Little Doorway; To-day's Your Anniversary; So Long But Not for Long Aloha;

MCCORD, WILLIAM PATRICK (BILLY VERA)   ASCAP 1969
composer, author, singer
b Riverside, Calif, May 28, 44. Educ: Archbishop Stepinac High Sch, White Plains, NY, 62; Fordham Univ. Singer & recording artist for Atlantic Records; singer, TV, theaters & nightclubs. Chief Collabrs: Chip Taylor, L Russell Brown, Steve Cropper, Ted Daryll. *Songs:* I Really Got the Feeling; Storybook Children; Make Me Belong to You; Mean Old World; At This Moment.

MCCORMICK, CLIFFORD   ASCAP 1957
composer, pianist, music educator
b Belleville, Ont, Sept 18, 09. Educ: Royal Cons of Music, Toronto; Royal Col of Music, London, Eng, Canadian scholar. Taught music at Dalton Sch, New York, Bennett Jr Col, NY & William & Mary Col, Va. Choral dir, US Navy Music Sch, DC. Founder & first cond, Norfolk Civic Chorus. *Songs:* Sacred Music for SATB Chorus: On the Morning of Christ's Nativity; If God Be for Us; Seek and Ye Shall Find; Early in the Morning; Go Ye Into All the World.

MCCOY, CHARLES R
instrumentalist
b Oak Hill, WVa, Mar 28, 41. Mem, Stonewall Jackson's Touring Band & Area Code 615. Recording artist, Monument Records. CMA Instrumentalist of the Year, 72 & 73. *Albums:* Real McCoy; Charlie McCoy; Fastest Harp in the South/Goodtime Charlie's Got the Blues; Nashville Hit Man; Charlie My Boy; Harpin' the Blues; Christmas Album; Stone Fox Chase.

MCCOY, HOBART R   ASCAP 1962
composer, author, teacher
b Holyoke, Mass, May 27, 1897; d Buffalo, NY, Nov 2, 77. Educ: New York City Music Sch. Comp, music, words & songs, age 60. *Songs:* This Day Is Mine; Skiing on a Mountain Lake; We All Need God.

MCCOY, LARRY GENE   ASCAP 1975
composer, author, singer
b Middletown, Ohio, May 18, 40. Educ: Cons Music, Cincinnati; Univ Cincinnati, BA(political sci); Ga State Univ, MBA(economics). Pianist with Johnny Cash Show, 73-75. *Songs:* The Revelation of Jesus.

MCCOY, PAUL BUNYAN (BULLFIGHTER)   ASCAP 1969
composer, author
b Chapel Hill, La, Apr 25, 30. Educ: Merrit Col, studied piano. Chief Collabr: Emma L McCoy, wife. *Songs:* Such a Fool; Stop, Lover Stop; Bad Paul; Yuletide Comes But Once a Year.

MCCRAY, DELBERT H   ASCAP 1978
composer, author, singer
b Nelsonville, Ohio, Mar 14, 30. Educ: Self-taught. Writer, gospel songs. Singer, church gatherings, fests, radio & some TV. *Songs & Instrumental Works:* Baby Rose; Jailhouse Song; Sweet Love Is Christmas and You; Jesus (gospel); I Feel Rhythm (gospel).

MCCREE, JUNIE   ASCAP 1939
author, actor
b Toledo, Ohio, Feb 15, 1865; d New York, NY, Nov 17, 18. Circus performer; then actor in vaudeville, stock cos. Appeared in Bway musicals, "The Wild Rose", "Babes in the Wood", "The Time, the Place and the Girl" & "The Girl Question." Wrote special material for himself & other performers. Charter mem, pres, White Rats (vaudeville actors union), 09-13. Chief Collabr: Albert Von Tilzer. *Songs:* Put Your Arms Around Me Honey; Take Me Up With You, Dearie; Why Doesn't Santa Claus Go Next Door?; How Do You Do, Miss Josephine?; Nora Malone; Blind Pig; Just Out of My Teens. *Scores:* Bway Show: The Happiest Night of His Life.

MCCREERY, WALKER (BUD)　　　ASCAP 1957
composer, author

b Benton, Ill, May 17, 21. Educ: High sch; pvt music study. Has written special material for Beatrice Lillie, Dorothy Shay & Kay Thompson. Wrote songs for Julius Monk nightclub revues, also "Shoestring Revue" & "Shoestring '57." *Songs:* The Style to Which I'm Accustomed; Mink Mink Mink; Guess Who Was There; The Sitwells; Renoir, Degas and Toulouse-Lautrec; Tranquilizers; Steel Guitars and Barking Seals; The Time Is Now; Requiem for Everybody.

MCCRIMMON, DANIEL BRUCE　　　ASCAP 1969
composer, author

b Amarillo, Tex, May 25, 42. Singer/songwriter; performer night clubs, concerts & TV; recordings on ABC-Probe & Biscuit City Records. Chief Collabr: Steven Fromholz. *Songs:* Don't Go to Mexico; Kansas Legend; Weaver's Song.

MCCULLER, ARNOLD　　　ASCAP 1976
composer, singer

b Cleveland, Ohio, Aug 26, 50. Educ: John F Kennedy High Sch; Kent State Univ; studied voice with Keith Davis & Seth Riggs. Nat tour, "Hair," 2 yrs. Performed, recorded & wrote with male vocal group, Revelation, RSO & Atlantic Records, 76. Back-up singer, James Taylor, Todd Rundgren & Melissa Manchester, 77-79. Chief Collabrs: Len Ron Hanks, Zane Grey, David Lasley, Jan Alejandro. *Songs:* Lyrics: Never Had a Love Like This Before; Get Ready for This.

MCCULLOH, BYRON B　　　ASCAP 1973
composer

b Oklahoma City, Okla, Mar 1, 27. Educ: Eastman Sch Music, BM(comp), MM(comp), Performer's Cert trombone. Bass-trombonist with Oklahoma City Symph, 51-52, St Louis Symph, 52-56, Pittsburgh Symph, 56- & Chautauqua Symph, summers 59-69. Artist lectr trombone, Carnegie-Mellon Univ, 69- Vis assoc prof trombone, Eastman Sch Music, 77-78. *Songs & Instrumental Works:* Symphony No 1, Six Songs on Poems of Ric Masten; Sinfonia for Brass and Battery; Concertino No 1 for Large Trombone and Small Orchestra; Concertino No 2 for Large Trombone and Small Wind Ensemble.

MCCURDY, EDWARD P　　　ASCAP 1962
composer, author, singer

b Willow Hill, Pa, Jan 11, 19. Educ: High sch; military sch; col. Studied opera & art song. Sang hymns on WKY, Oklahoma City, 38. Baritone singer & master of ceremonies, vaudeville, clubs & burlesque shows. Radio announcer, producer, actor & writer. Worked with children's TV shows in Canada & NY. Has recorded folk, sacred & children's songs. *Songs:* Last Night I Had the Strangest Dream; The Kings Highway; An Irish Song; If I Check Out Before You Do; Whiskey.

MCDANIEL, MEL H　　　ASCAP 1974
composer, singer

b Checotah, Okla, Sept 6, 42. Educ: Okmulgee High Sch, Okla, 61. Mem high sch band. Performed in many nightclubs, Okla, Ark & Kans; had nightclub act, Anchorage, Alaska, 70-72 & Nashville, Tenn, 73-74; staff writer, Combine Music, 74; artist, Capitol; recording artist, 80- Chief Collabrs: Dennis Linde, Roy Bourke. *Songs:* God Made Love; Grandest Lady; Good-bye Marie; I Could Sure Use the Feeling; Roll Your Own.

MCDIARMID, DON　　　ASCAP 1949
composer, author, conductor

b Stockton, Calif, June 10, 1898; d Kailua, Hawaii, Feb 27, 77. Educ: Stanford Univ. WW I Service. Trumpeter in theatres, films, radio. Warner Bros Studios, 33. Moved to Hawaii, 34; led orch, Royal Hawaiian Hotel, nightclubs, 10 yrs. Taught music in Honolulu schs, 10 yrs. Rep for text bk publ. Trumpeter & teacher. Chief Collabrs: Robert Wiley Miller, Lee Wood, R Alex Anderson. *Songs:* Hilo Hattie; Paradise Found; Little Brown Gal; Hula Town; Evening in the Islands; Hana; Do the Hula; Spring Spends the Winter in Hawaii; Haina Ia Ma'i Kapuana; South Sea Sadie; My Wahine and Me; Aloha Nui Loa, Dear; Old Kamaaina From Lahaina; Cast Your Cares to the Tradewinds; Aloha Malihini; Malihini Molly; Black Coral; My Tropical Garden; Kanaka Meka Umi Umi Umi Loa Kea.

MCDONALD, HARL　　　ASCAP 1937
composer, pianist, organist

b Boulder, Colo, July 27, 1899; d Princeton, NJ, Mar 30, 55. Educ: Univ Redlands; Univ Southern Calif, BA; studied music with Vernon Spencer, Ernest Douglas, Jaroslawde Zielinski & Augustus Steiner; Leipzig Cons, studied with Robert Fichmuller. Instr, Academie Tournefort, Paris, 22; also concertized as piano soloist, accompanist, 23-24. Taught at Philadelphia Musical Acad; prof then dir, Dept Music, Univ Pa, 26-46. Elected to Sigma Ki. Mgr. Philadelphia Orch, 39-55. Educr. *Songs & Instrumental Works:* Four Symphonies; Fantasy for String Quartet; Festival of the Workers; My Country at War; Violin Concerto; An Overnight Scout Hike; God Give Us Men (cantata); Song of Free Nations (soprano, orch); Dirge for Two Veterans (women's chorus, orch); From Childhood (harp, orch); Concerto for Two Pianos, Orchestra; Two Piano Trios; Quartet on Negro Themes.

MCDONALD, MICHAEL HANLEY
composer, author, singer

b St Louis, Mo. Educ: McCluer High Sch, grad. Studio musician; performer in clubs, Los Angeles. Mem of group Doobie Bros. Recording artist. Chief Collabrs: Kenny Loggins, Patrick Henderson, Carol Sager, Pat Simmons, Burt Bacharach. *Songs:* Takin' It to the Streets; What a Fool Believes; Minute By Minute.

MCDONOUGH, JACK　　　ASCAP 1974
composer, author

b Scranton, Pa, Aug 10, 44. Educ: King's Col (Pa), BA(Eng), 66; Univ NC, Chapel Hill, MA(Eng), 68. Instr in Eng, Wake Forest Univ, 68-70. Free-lance writer, San Francisco area, 70-80. San Francisco correspondent for Billboard, 74-80. Chief Collabr: Boz Scaggs. *Songs:* Lyrics: Angel Lady.

MCDONOUGH, MEGAN (MARY)　　　ASCAP 1971
composer, recording artist, musician

b Elgin, Ill, Nov 21, 53. Educ: High sch; studied voice with Harvey Ringle; Am Cons Music. Recorded first album at age 17. Has had own bands, 3 1/2 yrs; has toured US working as opening act for many artists. Chief Collabrs: Barry Fasman, Ed Tossing, John Allan. *Songs:* Lady in Love; Guitar Picker; If Love Is a Dream; Pocketful; Lyrics: Love Comes and Love Goes.

MCDOW, WILLIAM DAYTON (PEEVY)　　　ASCAP 1974
composer, singer

b Leoma, Tenn, July 14, 30. Began singing & playing guitar for country square dances, age 13. Worked with Ernie Ashworth, radio, 47-48. With Tenn Tune Twisters, 48-56. Nightclubs & personal appearances, 70. Warm-up show for George Jones, Conway Twitty, Earl Green, Guy Drake, 76. Appeared, "The Wake Up Show," Memphis, 76. *Songs:* The Possum Song; He's Just a Friend; Don't Bother Me.

MCDUFF, JACK　　　ASCAP 1969
composer, organist, pianist

b Champaign, Ill, Sept 17, 26. Educ: New York Tech. Served in USN, 45; played for School Boy Porter, 46, Lester Shackleford Band, Jimmy Coe & Willis Jackson, 58-59; own group, 59- *Instrumental Works:* Rock Candy; Electric Surf Board; A Real Goodun'; Pocket Change; Screamin'.

MCELHINEY, BILL　　　ASCAP 1958
arranger, composer

b New Orleans, La. Educ: High sch; trumpet studies. With WSM Radio, Nashville; active in recording indust. Has written arr for Brenda Lee, Charlie Rich, Tammy Wynette & many albums for Floyd Cramer. Co-producer & arr recordings for Danny Davis and the Nashville Brass. *Instrumental Works:* Dream Country; Cookin' Country.

MCELROY, LEO　　　ASCAP 1963
author, librettist

b Los Angeles, Calif, Oct 12, 32. Educ: Loyola High Sch; Loyola Univ, BS, 53. Radio & TV newsman, CBS & ABC; investigative & political reporter. Wrote musical, "Mermaid Tavern." Chief Collabrs: J Russell Robinson, Randy Van Horne. *Songs:* Lyrics: Melanie Goodbye; The Wanderin' Song.

MCELWAINE, JAMES WILLIAM　　　ASCAP 1976
composer, author, teacher

b Galveston, Tex, May 18, 47. Educ: N Tex State Univ, BM(cum laude), 69; Yale Univ, MM(cum laude), 71. Prof music, Hampshire Col, 72-76 & State Univ NY Col Purchase, 76-80. Arr, Springfield Symph & Mohawk Trail Concerts. Producer, arr & artist, Vanguard Records, Midsong Records & Ocean/Ariola Records. Musical dir, Ridiculous Theatre & off-Bway shows. Founder, Musical Elements, contemporary chamber ens, New York. Clarinetist, saxophonist & pianist. Chief Collabrs: Charles Ludlam, Dolores Allen. *Songs:* Whatcha Do to Me (disco); Oh Sweat (rhythm & blues); Music: Evil in Your Eyes (disco). *Instrumental Works:* Dance Changes (solo piano); The Lords and the New Creatures (rock cantata). *Scores:* Der Ring Gott Farblonjet (parody/opera); King Lear (chamber opera).

MCENERY, DAVID LARGUS (RED RIVER DAVE)　　　ASCAP 1914
composer, author

b San Antonio, Tex, Dec 15, 14. Educ: Self-taught. Created the Country Western character Red River Dave, performed singing & playing world wide. With Decca & MGM Records, TV, movies, folk festivals, etc. *Songs:* Amelia Earharts Last Flight; Is the Range Still the Same Back Home?; The Ballad of Patty Hearst; Song of the US Hostages; The Watergate Blues; The Ballad of Marilyn Monroe; Flight of Apollo II; It's for God and Country and You Mom; Cotton Eyed Joe; I'd Like to Give My Dog to Uncle Sam; There's a Star Spangled Banner Waving No 2 (the ballad of Francis Powers); I Won't Care A (Hundred Years From Now); Vietnam Guitar; The Red White and Blue Christmas; John Wayne; God's Game of Checkers; God's Secret Weapon.

MCENERY, VELMA LEE (LEE REYNOLDS)　　　ASCAP 1979
composer, author, singer

b Burnsville, Miss, Mar 18, 29. Educ: San Antonio Col. Appeared on stage, radio & TV with Red River Dave McEnery. Played guitar & sang harmony on Reveal

Records. Worked as single with var backup bands. Co-owner with Red River Dave McEnery of ASCAP Publ Co, Scriptomuse Publ. Chief Collabrs: Red River Dave McEnery (husband); Jimmy & Ruth Kish. *Songs:* Playboy; The Cheater of the Year; Night Plane to Nashville; I Just Want to Be Singing Amazing Grace When Jesus Calls Me Home; Jesus Is the Only Way to the Other Side of Sin.

MCFARLAND, GARY RONALD   ASCAP 1960
composer, arranger, vibraharpist
b Los Angeles, Calif, Oct 23, 33; d. Educ: Univ Ore, 52; Sch of Jazz, MA, 59; Berklee Sch of Music. With Jerry Mulligan, Modern Jazz Quartet, Dizzy Gillespie, Szabo, Bill Evans, Lena Horne, Cal Tjader & Barbra Streisand. Music dir, "To Live Another Summer" & "To Pass Another Winter." Chief Collabr: Lou Savary. *Songs: Scores:* Films: Who Killed Mary What's Her Name?; 13; Jazz ballet: Reflections of the Park. *Albums:* America the Beautiful; October Suite; Point of Departure; Scorpio and Other Signs.

MCFARLAND, JOHN DENNIS   ASCAP 1976
composer, author, singer
b Los Angeles, Calif, July 19, 46. Composer & nightclub performer. *Songs:* Fly Away; Better Side of Thirty; Babe It Ain't Easy; Against a Crooked Sky; Rosie's Last Ride; Rodeo Cowboy.

MCFEETERS, RAYMOND   ASCAP 1952
composer, pianist, organist
b Rushville, Ill, Dec 11, 1899; d. Educ: Occidental Col; Juilliard Sch Music, studied with Carl Friedberg; also with Paolo Gallico & Rudolph Reuter. Pianist & organist; accompanist throughout US & Can. Chief Collabr: Marion Kerby. *Songs:* A Psalm of Praise; Exultation; Hear the Nightingales Sing; Redeemed; Gentle Mary; The Manger Song of Mary; A Mother's Song; Light of Our Nation.

MCGARRIGLE, KATE   ASCAP 1974
composer, author, singer
b Montreal, Que, Feb 6, 46. Educ: McGill Univ, BA(sci); classical piano studies, 6 yrs. Began as songwriter, early 70's; currently recording with sister, Anna McGarrigle. *Songs:* The Work Song; Talk to Me of Mendocino; Kiss and Say Goodbye; First Born Son; NaCl (Sodium Chloride).

MCGHEE, HOWARD   ASCAP 1961
composer, conductor, trumpeter
b Tulsa, Okla, Feb 6, 18. Clarinetist in dance bands incl Lionel Hampton, Andy Kirk & Coleman Hawkins. Led own group, 45-47; also at Paris Jazz Fest, 48. With Oscar Pettiford in tour of Far East. Has made many records. *Instrumental Works:* McGhee Special; Strollin.

MCGIBENY, RUTH T   ASCAP 1961
author
b Chicago, Ill, Feb 10, 1896. Educ: Col. Author of children's verse; also "Ali of Baku." Chief Collabr: Rica Moore. *Albums:* Zoo Songs; Childhood Memories.

MCGINNIS, DONALD R   ASCAP 1971
composer, author, producer
b Miami, Fla, July 29, 39. Educ: Coral Gables High Sch; Univ Miami; studied film comp with Albert Harris, 60. With Univ Miami Symph. Bassist & keyboard player, nightclubs, TV & studios. Recording artist; producer & arr for var artists. Chief Collabrs: Gene Eccles, Jerry Winn. *Songs:* The Young and the Restless; Days of Our Lives; Ginger in the Morning; Jessi's Girls; The Fakers; Silent Treatment; Questions; Music: How Do I Love You. *Instrumental Works:* Sensuous Woman; Cosmic Sea.

MCGINNIS, JAMES DOUG   ASCAP 1950
composer, singer, actor
b Monroe, NC, Dec 24, 22. Educ: Indian Trail High Sch; Actor Sch, Baltimore, Md. In stage shows & nightclubs. Movie stuntman, Telemont Pictures. Emcee for Jackie Coogan, Russell Hayden & Lash La Rue. Chief Collabr: Russ Hayden. *Songs:* Leaving the Moon Over Texas; Angele; Wrong Number; Teach Me to Forget; Pack My Bags; You're Always Just in Time to Be Too Late; Pretty Thing; It's About Time; Women Drivers; Everything Is Coming Back to You; Behind the Iron Curtain; I Care No More; Baby You're Always Right.

MCGONIGAL, ALEXANDER ANDREW (ZAN DERR)   ASCAP 1971
composer, author
b Brooklyn, NY, Apr 2, 15. Educ: New Utrecht High Sch, Brooklyn; Brooklyn Col, studied piano & music theory. Worked for Repub Steel Corp, Brooklyn Div Production, eng & payroll depts, 30 yrs. Chief Collabrs: Edde King, Bobbi Baker. *Songs:* Where Are You; Music: Alone At Christmas; Lyrics: Pocono Polka.

MCGONIGLE, MARY   ASCAP 1978
author, singer
b Glasgow, Scotland, May 24, 37. Movie, "Sinful Davey & Darling Lilli" & TV show, "Up the Irish." Host of "Going Back to Ireland," radio. Concerts in Carnegie Hall with Slim Whitman & Royal Albert Hall, Eng. Performed in nightclubs throughout Eng, Scotland, Wales, Ireland & US. Recording artist, Glenside Records, Ireland & MGD Records, US. Chief Collabr: Dermot O'Brien. *Songs:* Lyrics: My Hometown in County Mayo; I'm Going Back to Ireland; My Ireland.

MCGOWAN, JAMES EDWARD   ASCAP 1967
composer, author, singer
b Kansas City, Mo, July 11, 35. Educ: Westlake Col Music, 1 yr; Whittier Col, Calif, studied voice with Jerold Sheppard; studied piano with Dick Grove, 3 1/2 yrs. Professional entertainer as singer, Hollywood; teamed with John Rusk, show lounges, 7 yrs. Chief Collabr: Durwood Haddock. *Songs:* The Perfect Love Song (ASCAP Awards); Every Night Sensation.

MCGOWEN, FRANK S (RICHARD CARROLL)   ASCAP 1970
composer, author, teacher
b Strawn, Tex. Educ: Univ Southern Calif, BS in Ed & MA. Former bandleader & singer, playwright, poet. Author of "Poems of Love and Passion," 77. *Songs:* I Cannot Change My Heart; Florida, the Beautiful; I Wish You Happiness; Thank God for America; By the Light of the Pale Blue Flames; My America; The Gospel Songs of Frank McGowen (bk form); The Love Songs of Frank McGowen (bk form).

MCGRANE, PAUL JAMES   ASCAP 1943
pianist, composer, recording artist
b Hanover, Ger, Oct 22, 02. Educ: NY Pub Schs; Inst Musical Art; NY Univ, studied with Rudolph Schramm, 24-28. Pianist in pit orch with Glenn Miller, Red Nichols, Jimmy Dorsey, Benny Goodman & Gene Krupa. Accompanist for Gertrude Niesen, Jackie Gleason & others. Bway musical productions incl "Guys and Dolls" & "The Boy Friend." Vpres, Gem Records, Inc, 48-50. Publ & producer, Clipper Records, 50. Chief Collabrs: Al Stillman, Jimmy Eaton, Ervin Drake, Harry Lenk. *Instrumental Works:* Whirlpool; Ballet Music for One Flea; Thumbmusic for a Hitchhiker. *Songs & Instrumental Works:* It's You I Want; One Sunday Morning in June; To Be Continued; Rockettes in a Row; High Flying; Rhythm Talk; Sweet Are the Tulips; Ho-Ho-Kus, N J; Stars on Ice; Juke Box Saturday Night; Little Jack Frost; Gin Rummy, I Love You; The Cavalier Cat; You're Awfully Smart; Big Broad Smile; Breaking the Ice; The Peddler's Serenade; There's a Big Blue Cloud (Next to Heaven); Powder Blue; Hayfoot, Strawfoot; I Love You in Any Language; To Bed Early; Baby's in Bermuda; If a Man Answers, Hang Up!; Alabam'.

MCGRATH, DAVID FULTON (FIDGEY)   ASCAP 1956
composer, author, pianist
b Superior, Wis, Dec 6, 07; d Hollywood, Calif, Jan 1, 58. Child prodigy, Orpheum Circuit Tour at age 14 and at 15 was youngest mem of Musicians Union-Duluth local, then pianist arr for own "Pit Orchestra" until finished with high sch. Came to New York, 29, became the most recorded pianist in New York; in addition to records, was the "Famous Musak Pianist"; staff pianist, NBC, New York, 35-43, CBS, Hollywood, 45-54 & Riviera Hotel, Las Vegas, 56-57. Original pianist & arr for Red Nichols & His Five Pennies & the original Dorsey Bros Band; played & recorded with Jimmy Dorsey, Red Norvo, Artie Shaw, Joe Venuti, Benny Goodman, Adrian Rollini, Glen Miller, Sidney Bechet, Bunny Berrigan, Horace Heidt, Paul Whitman, organist Milt Hirth & singers Connie Boswell, Boswell Sisters, Mildred Bailey, Lee Wiley, Ethel Waters, Bing Crosby & others. Chief Collabrs: Johnny Mercer, Jimmy Dorsey. *Songs:* Mandy Is Two; The Town That Time Forgot; Shim-Sham-Shimmy.

MCGRAW, CAMERON   ASCAP 1967
composer, author, pianist
b Cortland, NY, Apr 28, 19. Educ: Middlebury Col, BA, 40; Cornell Univ, MA, 63; piano study with Egon Petri & John Kirkpatrick, musicology with Otto Kinkeldey & Donald Grout, comp with Roy Harris, Robert Palmer & Hunter Johnson. Pianist & music dir, Halprin-Lathrop Dance Theatre, San Francisco. Co-founder with Monroe Levin, Jenkintown Music Sch, Pa, 54, later co-dir sch & teacher of piano & theory. New York debut in piano-duettist team, Levin & McGraw, Carnegie Recital Hall, 58. Co-author: "Doors Into Music"; author: "Piano Duet Repertoire." Chief Collabr: Jean Reynolds Davis. *Songs & Instrumental Works:* Dance Suite (orch); Three French Noëls (SATB); These Things Shall Be (fest piece for mixed chorus, organ, brass, tympani).

MCGRAW, GEORGE DONALD   ASCAP 1958
composer, author, producer
b Carabou, Maine, Sept 17, 27; d Salem, Va, Nov 15, 69. Educ: Pub Sch. DJ, WRVA, also produced, "Jolly Jamboree," synd radio show. Owner record shop & recording studio. *Songs:* Happy Birthday, Jesus; Don't Let Them Take the Bible; Following Footsteps; Woo-Hoo.

MCGREGOR, THEODORE ROOSEVELT   ASCAP 1964
composer, author, clown comedian
b McGregor, Pa, Oct 27, 02. Started as entertainer at church social; joined circus at age 16; later joined Ital & Am Vagabond Comedy. Organized own show, "The Ramblin' Hobos"; also had band & did comedy work. Performer of acts & comedy songs at hillbilly parks. Has traveled throughout US. Auto mechanic; has worked in mines & logging woods. *Songs:* Why Don't You Write to Me?; Rose Malone; Time and Tide Waits on No One; Work for Jesus; You Can't Lose; Walton Mountain; Hobo Last Call; She Was Painting a Picture; Pretty Little Swedish Queen; Truck Driver's Down the Line; Set Me Free; All the Way.

MCHUGH, CHARLES RUSSELL
composer
ASCAP 1975

b Minneapolis, Minn, Aug 5, 40. Educ: Univ Minn, BA, MA, PhD, 70; studied comp with Dominick Argento & Paul Fetler. Taught music theory, form & comp, Univ Minn, 65-70 & Carleton Col, 73; now work with sr citizens in the Congregate Dining Project. *Songs & Instrumental Works:* Prayer (SATB); Peace I Leave With You (SATB); Psalm 100 (SATB); Beloved Let Us Love One Another (SATB, organ); Jubilate Organum (organ); Symphony No 1; Symphony No 2; Symphony No 3; Quintet for Flute, Clarinet, Violin, Violoncello, Piano; Seventy-Three for Horn, Trumpet, Trombone and Percussion; Matrix-Plus 1 (woodwind quintet).

MCHUGH, JIMMY
composer, pianist, publisher
ASCAP 1922

b Boston, Mass, July 10, 1894; d Beverly Hills, Calif, May 23, 69. Educ: St John's Prep; Holy Cross Col; Los Angeles City Col, hon MusD. Was rehearsal accompanist, Boston Opera House. Exec, New York publ cos. Founded Jimmy McHugh Polio Found, 51; later, Jimmy McHugh Charities, Inc. Founded own publ co, 59. Mem bd dirs, Beverly Hills Chamber of Commerce, pres, 50-52. Dir, ASCAP, 60-69. Awards: Pres Cert Merit (WW II); Foreign Press Asn; Court of Hon, Am Legion. Chief Collabs: Dorthy Fields, Harold Adamson, Ned Washington, Johnny Mercer, Frank Loesser. *Songs:* When My Sugar Walks Down the Street; My Dream of the Big Parade; I Can't Believe That You're in Love With Me; I Can't Give You Anything But Love, Baby; Diga Diga Doo; I Must Have That Man; Porgy; Doin' the New Low Down; On the Sunny Side of the Street; Exactly Like You; Blue Again; Cuban Love Song; Hey, Young Fella; My Dancing Lady; Dinner at Eight; Don't Blame Me; Thank You for a Lovely Evening; Lost in a Fog; Lovely to Look At; I'm in the Mood for Love; I Feel a Song Coming On; Lovely Lady; I'm Shooting High; Spreadin' Rhythm Around; There's Something in the Air; Banjo on My Knee; Hey, What Did the Bluejay Say?; Let's Sing Again; You're a Sweetheart; Where Are You?; You're as Pretty as a Picture; For the First Time; Is It Possible?; Rendezvous Time in Paree; South American Way; Robert the Roue From Reading, Pa; Say It Over and Over Again; My, My; You've Got Me This Way; I'd Know You Anywhere; On the Old Park Bench; Clear Out of This World; Can't Get Out of This Mood; A Touch of Texas; Comin' in on a Wing and a Prayer; I Couldn't Sleep a Wink Last Night; A Lovely Way to Spend an Evening; The Music Stopped; Let's Get Lost; Murder, He Says; Fuddy Duddy Watchmaker; Sing a Tropical Song; Say a Prayer for the Boys Over There; In a Moment of Madness; How Blue the Night; Here Comes Heaven Again; Hubba Hubba Hubba; Buy, Buy, Buy a Bond (7th War Bond Drive song); We've Got Another Bond to Buy (8th War Bond Drive song); It's a Most Unusual Day; I Got Lucky in the Rain; As the Girls Go; You Say the Nicest Things, Baby; There's No Getting Away From You; Love Me as Though There Were No Tomorrow; Warm and Willing; I Just Found Out About Love and I Like It; Too Young to Go Steady; Dream, Dream, Dream; The Star You Wished Upon Last Night; Where the Hot Wind Blows; The First Lady Waltz; Massachusetts; I'm Keeping Myself Available for You; Sally; A Good Old Burlesque Show; In Louisiana; You Can't Blame Your Uncle Sammy; Immigration Rose. *Scores:* Cotton Club Revues (nightclub); Bway Shows: International Revue; Hello Daddy; Streets of Paris; Keep Off the Grass; As the Girls Go; Film: Hooray for Love; Let's Sing Again; Every Night at Eight; King of Burlesque; Buck Bunny Rides Again; You'll Find Out; Higher and Higher; Happy Go Lucky; Doll Face; Film Background: Jack the Ripper.

MCILVAINE, HOWARD
composer, author
ASCAP 1973

b Warren, Ohio, Sept 12, 19. Wrote first song at age 13. *Songs:* Wishin'; Bananas; Blue Grass State; The South Has Made It's Call; Friday.

MCILWAINE, FRANCES ELLEN
composer, author, singer
ASCAP 1973

b Nashville, Tenn, Oct 1, 45. Educ: Canadian Acad, Kobe, Japan; King Col, Tenn; DeKalb Community Col, Ga. Recording artist var companies. *Songs:* I Don't Want to Play; Underground River; Secret in This Lady's Heart. *Instrumental Works:* We the People; Sliding; Losing You. *Albums:* Fear Itself; Honky Tonk Angel; We the People; The Guitar Album; The Real Ellen McIlwaine; Ellen McIlwaine.

MCINTIRE, LANI
composer, conductor, singer
ASCAP 1940

b Honolulu, Hawaii, Dec 15, 04; d New York, NY, June 17, 51. Educ: Col Hawaii. Mem, USN Band. Singer with own orch. Scored early sound films in Hollywood; appeared in nightclubs, hotels & radio; also in film "Waikiki Wedding." Guitarist. Chief Collabs: Dick Sanford, George McConnell. *Songs:* The One Rose That's Left in My Heart; Sweet Little Sweetheart; Aloha; Hilo Serenade; Meet Me in Kahina; My Little Red Rose; I Picked a Flower in Hawaii; Aloha, Hawaii, Aloha; Next Door to Heaven; Sailing Away From the Islands; Sweet Hawaiian Chimes; Hearts Are Never Blue in the Blue Kalua.

MCINTOSH, MICHAEL D
composer, author, singer
ASCAP 1977

b Sacramento, Calif, Nov 14, 50. Performer in clubs; played in large halls, late 60's; worked in clubs, 70's. Started doing session work, mid 70's. Wrote theme songs. Chief Collab: Steve Olitsky. *Songs:* The Entertainer Who Entertains Entertainers; Let's Be Alone Together.

MCINTYRE, MARK W
composer, pianist
ASCAP 1953

b Navasota, Tex, July 20, 16; d Los Angeles, Calif, May 15, 70. Educ: Baylor Univ. Pianist in dance orchs until 43; moved to Hollywood, appeared on radio shows, "Fibber McGee and Molly" & "Duffy's Tavern." Pianist for film studios, 4 1/2 yrs. Producer-cond popular recordings, TV-radio jingles & spec show material, 55-70. *Songs:* The Money Tree; The Trouble With Harry; Tucumcari; Never Like This; Bimini; When I Was a Child.

MCKALIP, MANSELL BROWN (TODD MCKAY)
composer
ASCAP 1969

b Freeport, Pa, Sept 8, 15. Educ: Carnegie Inst Technol; Pittsburgh Inst Music. Played saxophone & clarinet, dance bands, combos & others, 30's & 40's, Pittsburgh area. Had own music performed by San Fernando Symph Orch & Beach Cities Symph. Retired as music ed, motion picture & TV indust. Now music writer. Chief Collabs: Eddie Roberts, Maryhale Woolsey, Ada M Dransfeldt. *Songs & Instrumental Works:* Central Park South (symph orch, piano solo); A Children's Ballet Suite (based on Sicilian legend; scored for symph orch); Reflections At Christmas (symph orch, full chorus, vocal soloists & children's chorus); Group of Religious Songs; Theme and Variations for Piano; Three Shades of Aqua (symph orch, piano).

MCKAY, ALBERT PHILLIP
composer, author, singer
ASCAP 1970

b New Orleans, La, Feb 2, 48. Educ: Los Angeles High Sch. Has worked with Ike and Tina Turner, H B Barnum, Watt 103rd Street Band, Sammy Davis Jr, Sylvers, Isaac Hayes, Earth Wind and Fire. Chief Collab: Maurice White. *Songs:* Best of My Love; Sing a Song; Saturday Night; September; I'll Write a Song for You.

MCKAY, FRANCIS HOWARD
composer, teacher
ASCAP 1946

b Harrington, Wash, Mar 7, 01. Educ: Eastman Sch Music, violin scholarships under Vladimir Reznikoff, 22-24; Univ Wash, BM, 24, MA, 31, comp with Carl Paige Wood. Former mem, Rochester Philh, Eastman Theater Orchs. 45 yrs in educ, incl Univ Ore, Ore Col, Wash State Univ, Univ Southern Calif, Los Angeles Cons Opera Orch & var levels of pub sch teaching. *Instrumental Works:* Brass Quartet (4 pieces, second suite); Four Horns in F (divertimento, suite for 4 horns); Four Trombones (pageant march, fest prelude); Brass Sextet (10 titles incl Romantic Mural); Clarinet Quartet (McKay Clarinet Quartets, 8 titles bound); Woodwind Quintet (Bainbridge Island Sketches, 5 titles); Symphonic Band (from Foxen's Glen, an Irish Rhapsody); many other instrumental ens & pieces for piano, pipe organ & instrumental solo, as well as jr solo series.

MCKAY, GEORGE FREDERICK
composer, educator
ASCAP 1941

b Harrington, Wash, June 11, 1899; d Lake Tahoe, Nev, Oct 4, 70. Educ: Eastman Sch Music, BM, studied with Sinding & Palmgren. Prof music, Univ Wash. *Songs & Instrumental Works:* Sinfoniettas (I, II, III & IV); Quintet for Woodwinds; Organ Sonata (Am Guild Organists prize); Violin Concerto; To a Liberator; Sonata for Trombone, Piano (comn by Nat Asn Schs Music); Symphonie Evocation (comn by Seattle Arts & Music Found); Song Over the Great Plains (comn by Ind Symph); Suite for Harp, Flute (Northern Calif Harpists Asn 1st prize); Two Suites for Violin, Piano; Lincoln Lyrics (cantata); Four String Quartets; The Big Sky (comn by Great Falls High Sch); Suite on Children's Themes; Suite for the Bass Clef Instruments (Publ prize, Nat Asn Wind & Perc Instrs); Six Pieces on Winter Moods and Patterns (Harvey Gaul prize); Suite on Northwest Indian Songs & Dances.

MCKAY, RODERICK NEIL
composer
ASCAP 1963

b Ashcroft, BC, June 16, 24. Educ: Univ Western Ont, BA, 53; Eastman Sch Music, MA, 55, PhD, 56. Can Navy Band, 44-46. Arr, cond, performer, Can radio, 46-53. Prof music, Univ Wis, Superior, 57-65, Univ Hawaii, 65- Fel of MacDowell Colony, 61, 63, 78. Chief Collabs: Grady Smith, Samuel Taylor Coleridge, Edgar Allan Poe. *Songs:* Honolulu; Music: A Dream Within a Dream. *Instrumental Works:* Four Miniatures (for piano); World(s) (for solo koto or harp); Parables of Kyai Gandrung (for symph & Javanese gamelan); Ring Around Harlequin (opera); Echoes (12 flutes & perc); Band: A Sketch of the West; Gamelan Gong; Evocations; Dance Overture; Fanfare & Ceremonial; Orch: Symphony; Dance Overture; Fantasy on a Quiet Theme; Chamber: String Quartet; Kaleidoscope; Kubla Khan (with soprano); Trioloque.

MCKAY, TODD
See McKalip, Mansell Brown

MCKEAN, WILKIN JOSEPH MARTIN
composer, author, singer
ASCAP 1976

b New Orleans, La, Oct 24, 52. Performed in nightclubs; recording artist. *Songs:* When Was the Last Time; I'm So Glad You're Mine.

MCKEE, ARTHUR W
composer
ASCAP 1951

b Worcester, Mass, Oct 15, 1891; d Winona Lake, Ind, June 7, 53. Educ: Colby

Acad; Moody Bible Inst. Dir music, Moody Mem Church, Chicago; wrote gospel songs. Chief Collabr: B D Ackley.

MCKEE, FRANK W   ASCAP 1914
composer, conductor, cornetist
b Prescott, Wis, July 21, 1867; d Hollywood, Calif, Jan 30, 44. Educ: Pub schs; studied piano, violin, drums & cornet. Won interstate drum championships in Ill, Iowa, Mo & Ind. Leader & cornet soloist in theatre orch; band dir. Bandmaster, 3rd Regiment, Ill Nat Guard, 6 yrs; also cond, operas. Charter mem, ASCAP. *Songs & Instrumental Works:* Millicent; Minor and Major; Cecile; My Clarabelle; Perdita; Rosalie; In Wintertime; Riverside Bells; Youth and Beauty; Yearning for You; Irresistible; The Miracle of Love; Danse de la Pierrette (ballet).

MCKELVY, JAMES MILLIGAN   ASCAP 1978
composer, editor
b Detroit, Mich, Oct 31, 17. Educ: Oberlin Cons Music, BM, BMusEd, 41, MMusEd, 47; Univ Southern Calif, DMA, 57. Choral dir, Shurtleff Col, Dakota Wesleyan Univ, Whittier Col, Chapman Col, Occidental Col, Univ Calif, Berkeley, Northern Mich Univ & Slippery Rock Col, 39-73; also dean of students & chmn, Music Dept. Army band leader, WW II. Cond col bands, Dakota Wesleyan Univ & Whittier Col. Founder, owner & ed, Mark Foster Music Co, 62. *Instrumental Works:* Laetatus Sum; Star Spangled Banner (choral); Arr: Deck the Halls; Gute Nacht (SATB); also about 50 choral arr, comps & eds.

MCKELVY, LIGE WILLIAM   ASCAP 1950
composer, author, saxophonist
b Milan, Tenn, Nov 4, 04; d Augusta, Ga, Jan 5, 65. Educ: Bliss Bus Col; pvt music study. Saxophonist in dance bands; wrote spec material. Clarinetist. Staff writer, Orchestra World, 5 yrs. Was mgr, dance orchs. Appeared in "This Is the Army," WW II. Chief musical commercial writer, Tele-Sound Prod, Washington, DC. Co-owner, Ransom Records. *Songs:* No, No, No; Mothballs; That Old Sweetheart of Mine; Withering Words; Yesterday's Love; Boogie Woogie Train; Pick It Up.

MCKENNA, DAVID   ASCAP 1964
composer, pianist
b Woonsocket, RI, May 30, 30. Educ: High sch. Pianist in orchs incl Charlie Ventura, Woody Herman, Gene Krupa, Bobby Hackett, Buddy Morrow & Stan Getz.

MCKENNA, WILLIAM J   ASCAP 1925
composer, author, conductor
b Jersey City, NJ, Feb 28, 1881; d Jersey City, Mar 4, 50. Educ: St Peter's Col; Stevens Tech; studied music with John Vernon, William Redfield, J Bodewalt Lampe & Edward Cupero. Actor in minstrel shows, musical comedies & vaudeville. Writer & dir radio. Cond, arr & dir Bway musicals. *Songs:* Mandy Lane; Down in the Old Neighborhood; Lady Love; Has Anybody Here Seen Kelly?; Everybody Loves an Irish Song; Toodles; My Broken Rosary. *Instrumental Works:* Operettas: The Bride Shop; The Midnight Kiss; Puss in Boots.

MCKILLEN, ARCH ALFRED
composer, author
b Chicago, Ill, Feb 25, 14. Educ: St Xavier Col Music, Ill, 30-32. Played bassoon with de la Salle Band & 106th Cavalry, Black Horse Troop; played violin & bassoon with var little symph orch. Author Poems: Nicholas Mouse (a poem of the sea in 5 cantos); The Death of the Scharnhorst; The Wee Christmas Mouse. *Songs:* A Star and a Stable; Lyrics: Last Call; Pillar of Salt. *Instrumental Works:* Various instrumental duets for flute or oboe and bassoon. *Scores:* Bway show: Lady Windermere's Man (musical comedy); Opera: L'Alfabeto Arabo (in Eng, with several arias in Ital).

MCKINLEY, RAYMOND FREDERICK   ASCAP 1947
composer, author
b Ft Worth, Tex, June 18, 10. Drummer & singer with Dorsey Bros Orch, Jimmy Dorsey Orch; co-leader, drummer & singer, Will Bradley Orch; drummer & singer with Glenn Miller USAAF Band, cond band following Maj Miller's death; leader, Ray McKinley Orch, 46-52; on TV & radio, 52-56; leader, New Glenn Miller Orch, 56-66; still active part-time. Chief Collabrs: Mel Powell, Don Raye, Hughie Prince. *Songs:* Hoodle Addle; Howdy Friends; Lyrics: My Guy's Come Back; Beat Me, Daddy-Eight to the Bar.

MCKINNEY, ALENE   ASCAP 1954
composer, conductor, musician
b Lincoln, Nebr; d Los Angeles, Calif, Mar 12, 78. Educ: Nebr Wesleyan Univ. Staff musician, WIBW, KFAB. Music dir, KBIG, 53-62, KMPC, 63-78. Chief Collabrs: Richard Loring, Alan Copeland. *Songs:* That's the Way I Feel.

MCKINNEY, JOHN E, JR   ASCAP 1976
composer
b Dallas, Tex, June 13, 47. Educ: Southwest Methodist Col, BA(music). Music direction & vocal arrs, "Tintypes" (off-Bway), orchestration, "Tintypes" (Bway), incidental music: Idiot Delight, Monseiur Amircare; Don Juan Is Back

From the War; Twelfth Night; Marathon '33; The Death and Life of Jesse James; Music Hall Sidelights; Enchanted Cottage; music for "Vegetable Soup" (children's show); "NBC Weekend"; Will Rogers Found; plus industrial films & commercials.

MCKINNOR, NADINE THERESA   ASCAP 1971
composer, author
b Chicago, Ill, Nov 23, 41. Educ: Hyde Park High Sch, Chicago; Southeast; Kennedy King Col; Wilson Col; Olive-Harvey Col; Univ Ill Chicago Circle Campus. Began writing poems in col that became songs. Chief Collabr: Donny Hathaway. *Songs:* This Christmas; Lyrics: Take a Love Song; The Sands of Time and Changes.

MCKUEN, ROD MARVIN   ASCAP 1957
composer, author, singer
b Oakland, Calif, Apr 29, 33. Educ: Self-taught harmony, theory & orch; West Lake Sch of Music, Los Angeles; orch music with Stravinsky; studied with Henry Mancini & Arthur Greenslade. Comp & performed for Bay area clubs incl Purple Onion & others, San Francisco, 54. To Hollywood, 55. Wrote songs for films, Universal & Twentieth Century Fox, 50's & 60's. Scored CBS TV Workshop, New York. Wrote for Kington Trio, Glen Yarbrough & others, also wrote complete album for Frank Sinatra. Comns incl: Menniger Found, Royal Philh Orch, Pittsburgh Ballet, Am Dance Ens & Edmonton Symph Orch. Awards: Grand Prix du Disc, Paris, 66, Golden Globe Award, 69, Motion Picture Daily Award, 69, Entertainer of Year Award, Los Angeles, 75, Freedom's Found Award, 75, Horatio Alger Award, 76, Emmy Award, 77, Humanitarian Award, First Amendment Soc, 77 & Carl Sandburg Poetry Award, 78. Chief Collabrs: Henry Mancini, Anita Kerr, John Williams, Jacques Brel, Gilbert Becaud, Lee Holdridge, Francis Lai, Leo Ferre, Bruce Johnston, Petula Clark, Georges Moustaki, Mort Garson, Hildegarde Knef. *Songs:* Ally Ally Oxen Free; Lonesome Cities; Doesn't Anybody Know My Name; Toward the Unknown; Jean (Acad Award nomination); The World I Used to Know; Love's Been Good to Me; I'll Catch the Sun; Listen to the Warm; Soldiers Who Want to Be Heroes; A Cat Named Sloopy; Champion Charlie Brown; I've Been to Town; Everybody's Rich But Us; Moment to Moment; Rock Gently; Stanyan Street; Children One and All; The Lovers; Lyrics: The Wind of Change; If You Go Away; Seasons in the Sun; I Think of You; The Importance of the Rose; The Ever Constant Sea; We; (The Port of) Amsterdam; I'm Not Afraid; That Golden Summer By the Sea; The Lonely Things. *Instrumental Works:* Something Beyond; Symphonies No 1-4; Concertos No 1-7. *Scores:* Operas/Ballets: The Black Eagle; The City (Pulitzer Prize nomination; comn by Louisville Orch); Americana, RFD; Volga Song; The Minotaur; 7 Elizabethan Dances; TV/Films: The Prime of Miss Jean Brodie (Acad Award nomination); Joanna; Heidi; Scandalous John; Me, Natalie; The Borrowers; Lisa Bright and Dark; Emily; Say Goodbye; A Boy Named Charlie Brown (Acad Award nomination); Forever Young, Forever Free; The Unknown War; The Loner.

MCLAUGHLIN, JOHN   ASCAP 1930
composer, author, pianist
b Lynn, Mass, Feb 17, 1897; d. Educ: Holy Cross Col; New Eng Cons; studied with John Orth, Felix Fox & Isadore Phillip. Mem, 602nd Engrs, Am Expeditionary Force, WW I. Pianist & cond for George M Cohan Productions, 20 yrs. *Songs:* At the End of the Day With You; Stepping on the Ivories; Little Brown Shoes; I Can't Forget; I'm Tired of Making Believe; When the Moon Is High; I'll Let the World Know I Love You; One Kiss, One Smile, One Tear. *Instrumental Works:* Broadway Rhapsody (symph).

MCLEAN, BARTON KEITH   ASCAP 1966
composer, professor, director
b Poughkeepsie, NY, Apr 8, 38. Educ: State Univ NY Col Potsdam, BS, 60; Eastman Sch Music, MM, 65; Ind Univ, MusD, 72; comp study with Henry Cowell. Performance tours by electronic music duo, The McLean Mix, with wife, Priscilla, in midwest, 73-74 & east coast, 79. Instr music comp & theory, Ind Univ, 69-76. Instr music comp & theory & dir, Electronic Ctr, Univ Tex, Austin, 76- Works recorded by CRI, Orion, Folkways & Advance Records. Producer, "Radiofest, New American Music," Am Soc Univ Comp. Grants: MacDowell Colony Fel; NEA; univ summer fels for comp; Pres Council on the Humanities. *Instrumental Works:* Metamorphosis for Orchestra; The Purging of Hindemith (orch); Trio for Violin, Vocal, Piano. Electronic music: Heavy Music for 4 Crowbars; Song of the Nahuatl; The Sorcerer Revisited; Spirals (electronic); Genesis. With instruments: Dimensions I for Violin and Tape; Dimensions II for Piano and Tape; Dimensions III and IV for Saxophone and Tape; Dimensions V and VI for Piano and Tape; Mysteries From the Ancient Nahuatl-Excerpts & Complete (chorus, instruments, electronic).

MCLEAN, HAMILTON GORDON   ASCAP 1966
composer, author
b Barbados, West Indies, Aug 18, 06. Educ: Calif Inst Music, Los Angeles; studied orchestration with Mary Carr Moore & Arthur Carr, choral writing technique with W A Goldsworthy & organ with Clarence Mader. Came to US, 22. Began singing bass in quartets & choral groups; sang with Vincent Youman's "Great Day," 29 & Schubert's musical "Hello Paris," 30; Went to Hollywood with Hall Johnson Choir to work in picture "The Green Pastures" for Warner Brothers. *Songs & Instrumental Works:* Pastorello (organ); Rondo for Woodwind Quintet (chamber music); Serenade for Orch; Spirit of the Crusaders

(concert overture); Promenade for Woodwind Choir; Four Psalm Verses for String Quartet; Choral: Rejoice! This Glorious Day; The Merry Easter Bells; Holy Spirit of God.

MCLEOD, JAMES (RED)
composer, arranger
b Virginia, Minn, Jan 12, 12. Educ: Virginia High Sch, grad with honors, 23; Virginia Jr Col, grad with honors, 30; Univ Minn, degree in educ, grad with honors, 32. Professional saxophone & clarinet player, leader & arr for band, 47-62. Musical dir & arr for Golden Strings, Radisson Hotel, Minneapolis, 63-; entertainment dir for Minn Vikings, 63- Arr for col bands; commercial arr, theaters, radio, TV, local musical shows, dance bands & old time music. *Songs:* Skol Vikings (Minn Viking theme). *Songs & Instrumental Works:* Zing March (Kansas City Chief's song); Fiddlin' Fancy (orch); Explorations (band); Big Band Bash (band); Divertissment (band); State Street Strut (dixie combo with band or orch); Radio Rag (dixie combo with band or orch); PDQ Dixie (vocal combo with band or orch); 4 Series of Dixieland Tunes for Dixie Combo.

MCLEOD, KEITH   ASCAP 1943
composer, author, director
b Loveland, Colo, Apr 6, 1894; d Beverly Hills, Calif, Oct 15, 61. Educ: Denver Univ, BA; Denver Law Sch; pvt music study. Music supvr, NBC; prod & dir progs incl "GM Concerts", "An Evening With Sigmund Romberg" & "The Red Skelton Show." Dir, progs in Hollywood Bowl & other concert halls throughout US. *Songs:* Slumber On; My Reveries; On the Velvet Wings of Night; In Acapulco; Careless Love; Haitian Rose; Mem'ries and Old Refrains.

MCLEOD, MARILYN   ASCAP 1973
composer, author, singer
b Detroit, Mich, May 22, 42. Educ: Started pvt piano lessons at age 9; Northeastern High Sch, Detroit; Los Angeles City Col. Pianist & singer. Writer, 70- Recording artist, Motown & Fantasy Records. Producer, own publ co. Chief Collabrs: Pam Sawyer, Mel Balton. *Songs:* Walk in the Night; Love Hangover No 1; You Can't Turn Me Off; Pops, We Love You; Different Kinda Different.

MCLOUD, HARRY HAYWOOD   ASCAP 1978
composer, author, background vocalist
b Dayton, Ohio, Jan 3, 50. Educ: Roosevelt High Sch; Cent State Univ, BS, 72. Prof guitarist & songwriter; wrote two songs for Capital group, Sun, 73-74; asst road mgr, Ohio Players, 75-77; guitarist with Atlantic group, Faze-O, 78-80. Guitarist with Electra Asylum group, Shadow, 80- Songwriter for local prominent talent in Dayton, 80- Chief Collabrs: Michael Jennings, Ralph Jones, Clarence Willis, Deborah L McLoud. *Songs:* Love Is Never Sure; The Show Is Over.

MCMANUS, JOHN L   ASCAP 1956
composer, conductor
b Peabody, Mass, July 11, 1891; d New York, NY, Apr 20, 63. Educ: Boston Cons; studied with Joseph Schillinger. Cond, Bway musicals "5 Ziegfeld Follies", "Tonight At 8:30", "Hellzapoppin", "Sons o' Fun", "The Streets of Paris" & "You'll Never Know," also for opera cos incl St Louis Municipal, Pittsburgh Civic & Detroit Civic, Atlanta. Cond, Maxwell House series TV & also Arthur Schwartz radio show. Comp, Bway stage scores. *Songs:* Castles in the Air; I'll Tell the World; Havana; Wonder Why; Happy As a Lark; Mr Harding, We're All for You (campaign song).

MCMULLEN, DOROTHY   ASCAP 1960
author, singer
b Florida, NY, June 9, 26. Educ: High sch. Singer in vaudeville, nightclubs & TV; also made many records. Chief Collabr: Edwin McMullen (husband). *Songs:* The Game of Broken Hearts; Moon Song; Four Season Sweetheart.

MCMULLEN, EDWIN D   ASCAP 1953
composer, author, conductor
b New York, NY, Oct 21, 11; d. Educ: Law Col, LLB. Actor, singer, cond, arr, teacher & guitarist; featured on radio & TV; Service, World War II, Europ Theatre Opers, received Purple Heart, 2 Battle Stars. Chief Collabr: Dorothy McMullen (wife). *Songs:* The Game of Broken Hearts; Four Season Sweetheart; Tipica Serenade; Two-Timin' Gal.

MCMURRAY, VANCE   ASCAP 1961
composer, guitarist
b Scott County, Va, Sept 6, 10. Educ: Pub schs. *Songs:* The Drunken Driver; The Rising Sun; The Little Message.

MCNABB, MICHAEL DON   ASCAP 1979
composer, teacher, computer music consultant
b Salinas, Calif, July 5, 52. Educ: Salinas High Sch; Stanford Univ, BA(music), 74, MA(music comp), 75, DMA, 80, studied with Leland Smith & John Chowning; Nat Cons, Paris, 75-76. Georges Lurcy fel, Paris, 75. Taught music theory, 76-78. Comp & teacher at Ctr for Computer Res in Music & Acoustics, Stanford Univ, 76- Rec'd League-Int Soc for Contemporary Music Comp Award, 78, mention, Bourges Exp Music Fest, 79 & NEA fel, 79. *Instrumental Works:* Dreamsong (computer-generated tape); Having Lost My Sons, I Confront the Wreckage of the Moon; Laughing Buddha; Love in the Asylum.

Scores: Film/TV: Mars in 3-D (computer-generated music); Altered States (computer-generated music).

MCNAIR, JACQUELINE HANNA   ASCAP 1979
composer, author, teacher
b Norfolk, Va, May 25, 31. Educ: Duke Univ, BA, 52. Pvt piano studio, 58-66. Coordr of children's choir, Vineville United Methodist Church, Macon, Ga, 62-77. Concert columnist, Macon Telegraph, 65- Instr music, Macon Jr Col, 72- Recital & theatrical accompanist. *Songs:* Anthems: Jubilate; Come and Rejoice With Us; Al-le-lu (Hawaiian carol); If I Were a Fifer; He Is the Delight of Our Days; God Is in His Heaven; Whosoever Shall Come to Me; Cantatas: Hear Ye! Be Joyful!; Fanfare for the King; A Thousand Hosannas; Again We Tell the Story.

MCNEELY, JERRY CLARK   ASCAP 1963
author, producer, director
b Cape Girardeau, Mo, June 20, 28. Educ: Southeast Mo State Univ, BA; Univ Wis, MA, PhD. Writer of network TV progs; series creator, "Owen Marshall", "Lucas Tanner" & "Three for the Road." Producer/writer & dir, MTM, Universal & Paramount. Chief Collabrs: Jerry Bock, Harry Sukman, Gerald Fried, Michael Small, Jon Epstein. *Songs:* Lyrics: Ballad of the Valley; What Is Different About Today?; Lonely Street, Winter Day; Smiles From Yesterday; The First Day of Your Life.

MCNEELY, LARRY P
banjoist, musician
b Lafayette, Ind, Jan 3, 48. Worked for Roy Acuff on "Grand Ole Opry," 3 yrs, "Glen Campbell TV Show" & tours, 4 yrs; feature, "Smothers Bros" & "Burl Ives" shows. *Instrumental Works:* Pyrannes Suite; Banjosaurus; Bethe; Juarez; Number Five (Beethoven on banjo).

MCNEIL, LIBBY   ASCAP 1963
composer, author, teacher
b Chicago, Ill, July 18, 17. Educ: Elliot Jr High Sch, music & drama; Pasadena Jr Col; special training with the Dominicans. Staff writer, Mills Music; writer of music & words, Am Acad of Music. Syndicated column, Eight to the Bar, musical advert. Conducted music arranging studio, Hollywood. Promoted opening, Old Alcazar Theatre, San Francisco, then managing dir, Alcazar Theatre Assoc; shows incl "Moon Is Blue", "Gigi", "Lady's Not for Burning", "Remains to Be Seen" & others. Songwriter team with husband Stephen H McNeil, 50-80. Publicity for Vincent Price, Eva Gabor, Audrey Hepburn, Allen Jenkins, Pat O'Brien, Christopher Plummer, Roddy McDowell & others. *Songs:* Lyrics: San Francisco-My Enchanted City; The French Poodle; San Francisco; It's God's Country.

MCNEIL, STEPHEN (PHIL STECMAN, JACK   ASCAP 1963
SPAULDING)
composer, author, teacher
b San Francisco, Calif, Feb 27, 07; d Apr 18, 80. Educ: Mission High Sch; Samuel Gompers Radio Sch; studied with Fred Sapman, Darius Milhaud & Julius Gold. Had own band. Prog dir, Henry Kaiser; musical dir, Indigo Records & Oliver Records; musical advert, Foote & Cone & Belding. Radio shows "Face the Music", "Graveyard Gaieties", "Cottage for Sale" & "Dial Tunes." Author "Innovator Allen's Harmony System and Countachord Method" & "Count to 15 and Play." Staff arr, Republic Studios; co-producer of opening, Alcazar Theatre, 52. Staff artist for var advert firms; songwriting team with wife Libby McNeil, 50-80. Former mem, Locals 6 & 47, Am Fedn of TV & Radio & Artist Dramatist Guild. *Songs:* Smooth Sailing (Off launching song); Looking for a Dream Beyond the Hill; Music: The French Poodle; San Francisco-My Enchanted City; San Francisco; It's God's Country; All the Days of My Life (23rd Psalm).

MCNEILL, DONALD T
composer
b Galena, Ill, Dec 23, 07. Host ABC radio, "The Breakfast Club," 33-69; comp themes, songs & hymns. Chief Collabr: Walter Blaufuss. *Songs:* Music: My Cathedral.

MCNULTY, FRANK FREMONT (SCOTT FREEMAN)   ASCAP 1956
composer, author, producer
b Park Rapids, Minn, Aug 31, 23. Educ: DePaul Univ, studied with Samuel Liberson; also pvt music study. Joined NBC music div, 43. Music rights dir, ABC, Chicago. Writer & producer of commercials & themes, TV. Chief Collabrs: James Krum, Bert Pollock. *Songs:* Bye Bye Baby, Goodbye; To Be With You; Moonlit Night; Gonna Leave Tomorrow; Music: I'm Not Alone; A Beautiful Girl to Make Love To; Take My Love; Glad Glad Glad; If I Cry; What Puts the Go in Chicago; Chicago, USA. *Instrumental Works:* Tic Toc Melody; Cats 'n Kittens; Bahia Bay; Marches: Flat Tops on Parade; Sons O' Guns; On the Midway; Sport of Kings; Step Lively; High Steppers; The Mighty Saratoga; Sports Final; Air Cadets; Astronauts March; Space Command; Triple Threat; Sunshine Special; Strutalong. *Scores:* TV specials: Illinois Sings; The Flight Brothers; Stage: Jody Boy; The Lighter Side; Chicago, USA; Faces and Places; The Flight Brothers.

MCNUTT, MARSHALL
ASCAP 1966
composer, instrumentalist
b Emporia, Kans, Sept 11, 35. Educ: Emporia State Univ, AB(music); studied trumpet with Armando Ghitalla, James Stamp, Harold Mitchell & Lou Maggio. Played trumpet with bands of Henry Busse, Perez Prado, Jimmy Dorsey/Lee Castle & Les Elgart. Played featured trumpet solo on record "Cherry Pink & Apple Blossom White," 55. *Songs:* Sweet Tooth; The Brave Ones; Country Cornet.

MCPARTLAND, MARIAN
ASCAP 1957
composer, pianist
b Slough, Eng, Mar 20, 18. Educ: Guildhall Sch Music, (scholarship) teacher's degree. Mem, piano team with Billy Mayerl; moved to US, 46; toured Europe for USO, WW II; played in group with husband, Jimmy McPartland, 46; formed own trio, 50; had own radio show, WOR. Recording artist. Chief Collabrs: Margaret Jones, Walter Marks. *Songs:* With You in Mind; So Many Things; There'll Be Other Times; Castles in the Sand.

MCPHAIL, LINDSAY
ASCAP 1935
composer, author, conductor
b Chicago, Ill, Nov 9, 1895; d Tupper Lake, NY, Mar 3, 65. Educ: Columbia Sch Music, Chicago, BM; pvt music study. AEF, WW I; Silver Star Citation. Pianist. Cond, all-soldier show, "Front Page Revue." Arr, Paramount Theatre, Los Angeles, 26 & Paul Whiteman Orch, 3 yrs. Cond own orch, Dr Alan Dafoe Prog, CBS, 36-37. Wrote music for radio & films. Chief Collabrs: Al Neiburg, Walter Michels, Harry Kerr, Lenora McPhail. *Songs:* San; Flag That Train; Foolish Child; Some Little Bird; The Swing Waltz; Danbury Fair; I Want a Dog for Christmas; Reconciled; Orange Suspenders; You Can't Make Honey; There's a New Gang on the Corner; Fishin' With the Angels; New Orleans Town; Wanna Know Somethin'; Down in Charleston.

MCQUEEN, JODI
ASCAP 1971
composer, singer, musician
b Oklahoma City, Okla, Jan 28, 45. Educ: Univ Kans. Model actress. Songwriter, 70- Chief Collabrs: Bobby Gosh, Mark Keller. *Songs:* Is She More Beautiful; Cowboys Never Cry; How Would You Like It?; Rollin' With Emotion.

MCRAE, THEODORE
ASCAP 1945
composer, author, publisher
b Philadelphia, Pa, Jan 22, 08. Educ: North Philadelphia High Sch; Temple Col, studied medicine; pvt music study. Organized band with bros, 28. Musical dir/arr & instrumentalist, Chick Webb Orch, 36-40, Ella Fitzgerald, 44-45 & Louis Armstrong & his Orch. Organized own orch, 46. Chief Collabrs: Chick Webb, Artie Shaw, Bud Green. *Songs & Instrumental Works:* Broadway; All Night Long; You Showed Me the Way; Back Bay Shuffle; Traffic Jam; Jumpin' in a Julep Joint; Santa Rosa; You're Too Lovely to Last; Paper Boy; Cincinnati; You're Too Sharp to Be Flat; Groovin'; Ding-Dong Boogie; Bang Your Box.

MCREYNOLDS, DENNY E
ASCAP 1959
composer, arranger, pianist
b Tulsa, Okla, Nov 17, 29; d Tulsa, Sept 12, 78. Educ: Anacosta High Sch, Washington, DC; Peabody Cons Music. Violinist & arr, Air Force Symph, 49-52. Pianist, nightclubs throughout US. Arr & comp, films, commercials, records & TV, 24 yrs. Chief Collabr: Karen O'Hara. *Songs:* Music: It's a Great Life; Make the World a Little Younger; If I Were Free; Old Glory; A Great Golden Day; Where Old Friends Meet; This Is You and Me; Hello World; I Can Only Wish You Love; The Wind and Sea; The World Belongs to You; For Old Times Sake; Did I Ever Really Know Him.

MCREYNOLDS, KAREN
See O'Hara, Karen

MCSHANN, JAY (JAMES) COLUMBUS
ASCAP 1965
composer, author
b Muskogee, Okla, Jan 12, 16. Educ: Kansas City Cons Music. Started with Elmer Hopkins Duo, Kansas City, 37; played with Dee Stewart band, 37; organized own 5 piece combo, 38 & big band, 39-40. Drafted into USA, 44. After discharge from service, with small combos. Chief Collabrs: Skip Hall, Charley Parker, Walter Brown. *Songs:* Music: You Say Forward, I'll March; Lonely Boy Blues; Vine Street Boogie; Jumpin' the Blues; Bottle It; Merry Go Round; Bad Tale Boogie; Confessin' the Blues; Walkin' Blues; Hard Working Man; When I've Been Drinking; McShann's Boogie Blues; Shipyard Woman Blues; Crown Prince Boogie; Hootie Blues; Garfield Avenue Boogie; Wrong Neighborhood; Home Town Blues; Hot Biscuits; My Chile; The Man From Muskogee; Blues for an Old Cat; Doo Wah Doo; Dexter Blues; Jay's Jam.

MEAD, EDWARD GOULD
ASCAP 1961
composer, organist
b Reading, Mass, June 26, 1892. Educ: Harvard Univ, BA; Yale Univ, BM; Fontainebleau, France, with Nadia Boulanger; Royal Col Music, London, with Harold Darke. Organist & choir dir, Cornell Univ, 27-28; mem fac, Miami Univ, Ohio, organist & head organ dept, 29-57, comp-in-residence, 57-60. Has played organ recitals in var cols & univs. Fel, Am Guild Organists. Organist, Retirement Home, 74- *Songs & Instrumental Works:* Choral: God Is My Strong

Salvation (SATB & TTBB); Great Is the Lord (SATB); Americans, Oh Cherish These (SATB); Bread of the World (SATB); Bells in the Rain (SSA); I've Put Away a Little Dream (SSA); Organ: Prelude on Duke Street; Fantasy on Sine Nomine; Prelude on Old 124th; Prelude on Puer Nobis; Prelude on Heinlein; Prelude on Grace Church.

MEAD, GEORGE
ASCAP 1943
composer, author, conductor
b New York, NY, May 21, 02. Educ: Trinity Col, Columbia Univ, BA, MA(music), MusD(hon); studied voice with George Bowden, piano with Ann Lockwood Fyffe, organ with Channing Lefebvre. Cond, The Glee of the Friendly Sons of St Patrick, 37-, The Downtown Glee Club, 41-, Radio Choir of Trinity Church & others. Dir music & organist, Trinity Church, NY, 41-68. Teacher & lectr, Hofstra Col, Union Sem, Western Reserve Univ & others. Var original works for chorus; numerous comp arr for chorus. Opera translr. Assoc, Am Guild of Organists. Chief Collabr: Phyllis Mead, wife. *Songs & Instrumental Works:* Fantasy for Organ (Diapason Prize); Anniversary Anthem (chorus & orch; comn by Trinity Church); With Instruments of Music (chorus & orch; comn by Trinity Church); Choral: No Man is an Island (comn by Intercollegiate Music Council); Proclaim Liberty; City of Ships; Let Us Keep the Feast; Composed Arr: When Johnny Comes Marching Home; Once to Every Man and Nation; Down in the Valley; I Saw Three Ships; Prayer From "Lohengrin"; Cantata: The Shepherds. *Scores:* Opera; The Broker's Opera; English Opera Transl: Amelia Goes to the Ball (Menotti); The Last Savage (Menotti); The Barber of Seville (Rossini); Rita (Donizetti); Martha (Flotow; libretto); Manon (Massenet); Faust (Gounod; libretto); Romeo and Juliet (Gounod; libretto); Der Freischütz (Weber; libretto).

MEADOWS, FRED
See Gordon, Ben

MECHEM, KIRKE LEWIS
ASCAP 1964
composer, author, conductor
b Wichita, Kans, Aug 16, 25. Educ: Topeka High Sch, Kans; Stanford Univ, BA, 51; Harvard Univ, MA, 53, comp studies with Walter Piston & Randall Thompson. Taught & conducted, Stanford Univ, San Francisco State Univ & Lone Mountain Col/Univ, San Francisco. Awards: Boott Prize, Harvard Univ; Am Music Award, Sigma Alpha Iota; Nat Endowment for the Arts. Symphony No 2 comn by Josef Krips after premiere of Symphony No 1 with San Francisco Symph, 65. *Songs:* Music: Goodbye, Farewell and Adieu (song cycle). *Instrumental Works:* Sonata for Piano; Whims for Piano; Piano Trio; Divertimento for Flute and String Trio; String Quartet No 1; Symphony No 1; The Jayhawk (overture). *Songs & Instrumental Works:* Singing is So Good a Thing (an Elizabethan recreation; chorus, solist & chamber orch); The King's Contest (cantata, chorus, soloists & orch); Seven Joys of Christmas (chorus a cappella or chamber orch); The Winds of May (choral cycle); Five Centuries of Spring (choral cycle); Epigrams and Epitaphs (catches & canons); Tourist Time (choral cycle); The Shepherd and His Love (chorus, piano, piccolo & viola); Christmas Carol (chorus & guitar); The Children of David (chorus & organ); Make a Joyful Noise Unto the Lord (chorus); Give Thanks Unto the Lord (chorus); Songs of Wisdom (chorus); I Will Sing Alleluia (chorus, piano, flute); American Madrigals (choral cycle; instruments accompanied ad lib); The Winged Joy (women's chorus & piano). *Scores:* Opera: Tartuffe (score & libretto).

MECUM, DUDLEY C
ASCAP 1955
composer, author, pianist
b Hamilton, Ohio, May 20, 1896; d Hamilton, Ohio, Mar 6, 78. Educ: Wash State Col. Served USN, WW I. To Chicago; accompanist to Duncan Sisters, Ruth Etting & Helen Morgan. Pianist in Don Bestor Orch, 25, then New Orleans Rhythm Kings. Rejoined Bestor. Pianist in cocktail lounge, Hamilton, 58-78. *Songs:* Angry; It's Always Raining; Gee But I Hate to Say Goodnight.

MEDEMA, KENNETH PETER
ASCAP 1975
composer, author, performer
b Grand Rapids, Mich, Dec 7, 43. Educ: Mich State Univ, BA(music), 65, MA(music), 69. Music therapist, Ind & NJ; occasionally performed, 65-72. Performer, singing original compositions & traveling in US & abroad, 73- *Songs:* Moses (choral anthem); Lead the Way; Sonshiny Day; Come Let Us Reason; Lord, Listen to Your Children Praying; Story Tellin' Man.

MEDINA MENDEZ, CARMEN
ASCAP 1964
composer, author, pianist
b Matanzas, Cuba, Mar 11, 19. Educ: Amelia de Vera, Havana; Santa Cecilia Music Sch; Normal Sch Kindergarten, grad; Havana Univ, DEduc. Played piano since 8 yrs old; played recitals at Carnegie Hall, 78 & 79. Auxiliary teacher, Kindergarten; pianist. Author: "Cantos y Juegos Para Kindergarten," 1st ed, title changed to, "Cantos y Juegos Para Escolares," 2nd ed. Was in TV "Romper Room," in different countries. *Songs:* Music: God's Love.

MEEHAN, DANNY
ASCAP 1957
composer, author, singer
b White Plains, NY; d. Educ: High sch; Am Acad Dramatic Arts. Appeared in summer theatres, TV & nightclubs; also in Bway musicals: "Whoop Up" &

"Funny Girl." Actor & dancer. Chief Collabr: Colin Romoff. *Songs:* Lookout for Love; Something Makes Me Want to Dance With You.

MEEHAN, MARTHA (MARTHA CAROLIN, MARTY CAROL)　　ASCAP 1968
composer, author, pianist
b Siler City, NC, Apr 19, 23. Educ: Siler City High Sch; Louisburg Col; Univ NC, Greensboro; studied piano with mother. Comp of church music. *Songs:* My Friend; A Special Day; Steadily On; Prayer for America; You Are Very Close to Me.

MEEK, FRANCES MCCULLOUGH　　ASCAP 1972
author, teacher
b Hico, Tex, Jan 15, 34. Educ: Univ Tex, Austin, 51; vocal studies with Robert Sewell, Odessa, Tex. Chief Collabrs: Bob Hughes. *Songs:* Lyrics: What Shall I Leave You.

MEEKS, LARRY MONROE　　ASCAP 1957
composer, author, pianist
b Pine Bluff, Ark, Apr 15, 30. Educ: Memphis Cons Music; USN Sch Music; NY Univ, with Rudolf Schramm. Comp-author, "Prairie Navy" musical for USN, pianist, Admiral's Band, US 6th Fleet Flagship, 50-52. With RKO-Teleradio-Unique Recording Co, 3 yrs; publicity writer with Mike Hall Assocs, 3 yrs; press secy to Benny Goodman, 4 yrs. Currently pianist with Denver Orch-combos; conducting-pianist for Denver shows with Helen O'Connell & others; comp-arr, Carousel Productions, Denver & audiovisual shows, commercials & productions. Chief Collabrs: Maryruth Weyand, Gladys Shelley. *Songs:* Me and My Bestest Feller; I Heard Ya the First Time; Music: Make Those Miracles Happen; The Moment; Darned Good Country; Butterscotch Morning; Bossa Nova Scotia; Wicked Western; Denver Time; One Day At a Time. *Instrumental Works:* Benny Happy Returns; Shoppin' Spree; The Code.

MEEROPOL, ABEL
See Allan, Lewis

MEGLIN, NICK　　ASCAP 1967
author
b Brooklyn, NY, July 30, 35. Educ: Stuyvesant High Sch; Brooklyn Col & Sch Visual Arts, BFA. Author of 12 bks & many articles for Opera News, American Artist, New York News Sunday Mag, Quarterback Mag, Tennis Mag & others. Writer, TV, spec material, comedy albums & others. Ed, Mad Mag, 20 yrs. Chief Collabr: Norman Blagman. *Songs:* Love's Short Day; Shadows; Lady, Make Nice to Me; Snow Bunny; What More Is There? (Love, Love, Love); Hello, Son; Images; Millions of Faces; Good Morning to You; Vinegar Where Once Was Wine.

MEHR, SHELDON MARSHALL　　ASCAP 1975
composer, teacher, conductor
b Chicago, Ill, Sept 18, 31. Educ: Northwestern Univ, 49-51; Univ Calif, Los Angeles, BA, 54; Calif State Univ, Los Angeles, MA, 59, Northridge, grad; Univ Southern Calif; trumpet study with Louie Maggio & Robert Divall. Professional trumpeter, Chicago area, 46-51. Free lance, Los Angeles area, 51-60. Teacher music, Los Angeles City Schs, 55-70. Mem fac, Moorpark Col, 70- Writer, brass chamber music, concert band works, songs & works for chorus & instruments. *Songs:* No, My Darling Daughter.

MEINKEN, FRED　　ASCAP 1950
composer
b Chicago, Ill, July 10, 1882; d San Diego, Calif, May 1, 58. *Songs:* Wabash Blues; Virginia Blues; Clover Blossom Blues.

MEISNER, RANDY
composer, guitarist, singer
b Scottsbluff, Nebr, Mar 8, 46. With original Eagles Group, 10 yrs. Independent soloist, CBS Records, 77. *Songs:* Music: Take It to the Limit; Try and Love Again.

MEISTER, THEODORE HENRY (TED DARYLL)　　ASCAP 1970
composer, author, record producer
b Mt Vernon, NY, Jan 5, 40. Educ: Archbishop Stepinac High Sch, White Plains, NY, dipl; Sal Mosca Piano Studio, Mt Vernon, NY. Staff songwriter for several firms, incl Koppelman/Rubin Asn, 62-67. A&R staff producer, RCA Records, 68-70. Prof mgr, E B Marks Corp, 75-77. Owner, ASCAP firm, October Moon Music. Writing/producing independently for record labels, incl Ariola & Reflections Records. Chief Collabrs: Chip Taylor, Billy Vera. *Songs:* She Cried; Shadow of Your Love; You Put the Music in Me; Hey Mr Paul; Music: Country Girl/City Man (Just Across the Line); Tommy; Lyrics: Sneakin' Up on You.

MEJIA, CARLOS ANTHONY　　ASCAP 1963
composer, musician
b Bogota, Colombia, Sept 20, 23; d Los Angeles, Calif, May 24, 69. Educ: High sch. Musician in pit orchs, Bway musicals; also in orchs incl Jose Curbelo, Noro

Morales, Xavier Cugat & Peggy Lee. Chief Collabr: Eddie Cano. *Songs:* Panchita; Listen to My Heart.

MELARO, H J M (JERRY)　　ASCAP 1960
composer, author, producer
b Sewickley, Pa, Dec 28, 31. Educ: Pa Mil Col, Chester; Univ Pittsburgh Law Sch; LaSalle Extension Univ Law Sch. Author: "The Viet Nam Story," 68; "Factor Ten," 76, 2nd ed, 80. Screenwriter: "Astro Cosmo", "Youngstars in Outer Space", "The Viet Nam Story" & "The Exiles." Int lawyer. Chief Collabrs: Bob Bunton, Donna M Meyer. *Songs:* Ciao, Baby, Ciao; Gonna Mean a Lot to Somebody Else; It Always Happens to Me; That Old Pair—Me and You; You Just Can't Win Them All; Youngstar Space Theme; For the Thrill of It; Senorita; Down Memory Lane; I Cry Again; I Want to Walk With You; What Have We Now?.

MELIS, JOSE
See Guiu, Jose Melis

MELLENBRUCH, GILES EDWARD (JOHNNY GILES)　　ASCAP 1960
composer, author, trumpeter
b Hiawatha, Kans, May 9, 11. Educ: Wyandotte High Sch, Kansas City, Kans, grad, 27; Kansas City Kansas Jr Col, grad, 30; Univ Kans, 32; Univ Kansas City, BA, 42. Band leader, Kansas City clubs & ballrooms, 27-43; bandleader & songwriter, Hollywood, Calif, 44-64. Recording artist, Hollywood. Chief Collabr: Russel Trost. *Songs:* Bye Bye Baby Blues; I've Tried to Forget; Music: Love Is a Wonderful Thing; Lyrics: Enchanted Isle, Hawaii; Betty.

MELLENCAMP, JOHN J (JOHN COUGAR)　　ASCAP 1976
singer, songwriter
b Seymour, Ind, Oct 7, 51. Educ: Seymour Senior High Sch; Vincennes Univ, 2 yrs. Did world tours; also made several albums, 76, 77, 79 & 80. *Songs:* I Need a Lover; A Little Night Dancin'; Small Paradise; This Time; Ain't Even Done With the Night.

MELROSE, RONALD KEITH LASONDE
composer, author, arranger
b Urbana, Ill, June 29, 54. Educ: Harvard Univ, BA, 76. Summer stocks, commercials, industrial shows, music for gymnastics, dance & choir. Arranger, film & Bway. Spec material, club acts. Novelty singles. Composer/lyricist, "Unicorn" & "Odyssey." Composer, "Fourtune" & "Tots in Tinseltown." Chief Collabrs: Andrea LaSonde, Mark O'Donnell.

MELROSE, WALTER　　ASCAP 1927
composer, author, publisher
b Sumner, Ill, Oct 26, 1889; d. Educ: High sch. In music bus since 12. Served in USAF, WW I. *Songs & Instrumental Works:* Tin Roof Blues; Milenburg Joys; High Society; Sugar Foot Stomp; Copenhagen; Asia Minor; Spanish Shawl; Make Love to Me; That Same Old Way.

MELSHER, IRVING　　ASCAP 1943
composer, conductor, pianist
b Charleroi, Pa, Nov 12, 06; d New York, NY, May 3, 62. Cond & pianist, Atlanta radio sta. Singer & accordionist, Arrowhead Inn, Yonkers, NY, 8 yrs. Chief Collabrs: Remus Harris, Russ Morgan, Cy Coben. *Songs:* Roses in the Rain; Y-O-U (Spells the One I Love); The Georgian Waltz (off state song); So Long; Don't Cry, Sweetheart; Let's Have an Old-Fashioned Christmas; Starlight Trail; Lollypop Ball; There's No Wings on My Angel; Cry, Baby, Cry; The Man Who Paints the Rainbow in the Sky.

MELTZER, RICHARD BRUCE (MR VOM)　　ASCAP 1970
author, singer, disc jockey
b New York, NY, May 10, 45. Educ: Far Rockaway High Sch; State Univ NY Stony Brook, BA, 66. Lyricist, Stalk-Forrest Group & Blue Oyster Cult; singer, punk-rock group Vom; disc jockey, "Hepcats From Hell" show, KPFK-FM, Los Angeles; author rock bks, "Aesthetics of Rock" & "Gulcher". Chief Collabrs: Albert Bouchard, Allen Lanier, Donald Roeser, Eric Bloom. *Songs:* Lyrics: Arthur Comics; What Is Quicksand?; Stairway to the Stars; She's As Beautiful As a Foot; Teen Archer; Cagey Cretins; Harvester of Eyes; Death Valley Nights; Dr Music.

MELVOIN, MICHAEL
pianist, organist
b Oshkosh, Wis, 1937. Educ: Studied piano at age 3; Dartmouth Col, 59. Played with Gerald Wilson, Paul Horn Quintet, Terry Gibbs Combo & others during 60's. Toured New Zealand with Gene McDaniels, 64.

MELYAN, THEODORE　　ASCAP 1965
composer, performer, teacher
b Newark, NJ, Nov 20, 17. Educ: Columbia Univ, BS & MA(music & music educ); Eastman Sch Music, advanced arranging courses; studied comp with Normand Lockwood. Began prof music career at age 18; pvt teacher keyboards, 37- Arr for var dance bands, New York area; cond amateur musical shows; supvr music educ, Clifton Pub Schs, NJ. *Instrumental Works:* Soliloquy; Cha Cha for Band; Debonair for Trumpet; Gypsy Campfires; Free and Easy.

MENCHER, T MURRAY ASCAP 1931
composer
b Boston, Mass, Oct 5, 04. Educ: Pvt study. Recorded for piano rolls. Song plugger. Started to write songs, 30. Coach for Eddie Cantor. Part owner of children's record co, Voco, 47-52. Reviews for clubs. Chief Collabrs: Charlie Tobias, Benny Davis, Charlie Newman, Al Lewis. *Songs:* Music: Throw Another Log on the Fire; You Can't Pull the Wool Over My Eyes; Merrily We Roll Along; Don't Break the Heart That Loves You; I'll Follow the Boys; Whose Heart Are You Breakin' Tonight?; Flowers for Madame; Alice in Wonderland; Poor Cinderella; I Want a Little Girl; Ro Ro Rolling Along; I See God; Let's Swing It; Tonights My Night; Sweet Varsity Sue; Moonlight and Violins; Children Songs; Children Records; Baby's First Christmas. *Instrumental Works:* Intrigue; Gringola. *Scores:* Bway stage: Earl Carroll Sketch Book.

MENDENHALL, RALPH G ASCAP 1963
composer, musician, teacher
b Minneapolis, Minn, Sept 28, 21. Educ: Univ Minn, BS, MEd; USN Sch Music. Band dir on ships; teacher in high sch & cols, 47-; cond, Minn Vikings Football Band, 61- *Songs & Instrumental Works:* Twin Cities; Orbital Flight; Spirit of the Vikings; Battle Cry.

MENDEZ, RAFAEL G ASCAP 1951
composer, trumpeter
b Jiquilpan, Mex, Mar 26, 06. Educ: Mexico City Cons. At age 10, trumpeter for Pancho Villa; soloist, univ orchs, Los Angeles Symph & also in theatres. Recording artist. *Instrumental Works:* The Elf Trumpeter; Valse Suriano.

MENDOZA, DAVID ASCAP 1929
composer, violinist, conductor
b New York, NY, Mar 13, 1894; d. Studied music with Franz Kneisel, Rubin Goldmark, Percy Goetschius. Concertmaster, Victor Talking Machine Orch, Russian Symph & NY Symph; music dir, Capitol Theatre, New York, 9 yrs; also radio & films; later Radio City Center Theatre; wrote scores for films, 30-39; guest cond, Philadelphia Orch & NY Philh. *Songs:* Flower of Love; I Loved You Then As I Love You Now; In a Little Hideaway; I Found Gold When I Found You; Love Brought the Sunshine; Cross Roads; Live and Love.

MENKES, DORIS
See Rubin, Doris Anne

MENNIN, PETER ASCAP 1946
composer, educator
b Erie, Pa, May 17, 23. Educ: Oberlin Cons; Eastman Sch Music, BM, MM; Univ Rochester, PhD; studied with Howard Hanson & Serge Koussevitzky. Served in USAF, WW II. Fac mem, Juilliard Sch Music, 47, pres, 62- Dir, Peabody Cons, 58-62. Awards: Am Acad Arts & Letters; first George Gershwin Mem; 2 Guggenheim; Columbia Records Chamber Music; Naumberg; Bearns prize, Columbia Univ; Centennial Citation, Univ Rochester. Comns: Koussevitzky Found; Coolidge Found; Robert Shaw Chorale; also Dallas, Erie, Louisville & Cleveland Symph Orchs; Juilliard Musical Found; Nat Fedn Music Clubs; NBC & ABC networks. Mem: Bd dirs, Am Music Ctr; Comp Forum, Naumburg Found; State Dept Adv Comn on the Arts; Nat Inst Arts & Letters. *Songs & Instrumental Works:* Seven Symphonies; Two String Quartets; Canzona for Band; Sinfonia for Chamber Orch; Sonata Concertante for Violin, Piano; Folk Overture; Flute Concertino; Fantasia for Strings; The Christmas Story (cantata); Partita (piano); Four Choruses Based on Chinese Texts; Canto and Toccata; Canto for Orchestra.

MENNINI, LOUIS ALFRED ASCAP 1955
composer, teacher, administrator
b Erie, Pa, Nov 18, 20. Educ: Oberlin Cons, 39-42; Eastman Sch Music, BM, MM & PhD, studies with Howard Hanson. Prof comp, Univ Tex, 48-49 & Eastman Sch Music, 49-65; dean, Sch Music, NC Sch Arts, 65-71; dir, Sch Music, Mercyhurst Col, Pa, 73-; artistic dir, D'Angelo Young Artist Competition. Awards from Nat Inst Arts & Letters, Koussevitzky Found, NEA, plus others. *Instrumental Works:* Arioso (strings); Sonatina (cello); Symphony No 2 (da Festa); Allegro Energico (orch); Tenebrae (orch); String Quartet. *Scores:* Opera/Ballet: The Rope.

MENOTTI, CARLO ASCAP 1966
composer, voice teacher
b Sao Paulo, Brazil, June 21, 09. Educ: Univ Liberal Arts Theatre, Paris, France; Cons Bellini, Catania, Italy. Began as film & stage actor. Prof debut as baritone singer with Louis Teichner, Town Hall, 43. Sang overseas with USO. Concertize & teach voice. Chief Collabrs: Comp, Billy Ver Plank, Rudy Schramm, Frankie Avalon. *Songs:* Music: Braziliero.

MENZA, DONALD JOSEPH ASCAP 1974
composer, author, musician
b Buffalo, NY, Apr 22, 36. Educ: Self-taught. Wrote, comp & played with Maynard Ferguson, Buddy Rich, Stan Kenton, Woody Herman, Louie Bellson, Henry Mancini & Burt Bacharach; has played in local jazz clubs. Clinician for high sch & col jazz educ progs. Has big band & small group. Best Tenor & Best Soloist Awards, Notre Dame Col Fest. *Songs:* Groovin' Hard. *Albums:* Horn of Plenty; First Flight.

MERCER, JOHN H (JOHNNY) ASCAP 1933
composer, author
b Savannah, Ga, Nov 18, 09; d Los Angeles, Calif, June 25, 76. Educ: Woodbury Forest Sch, Orange, Va. Was actor in little theatre groups. Singer, MC with Paul Whiteman Orch & Benny Goodman Orch, 38-39. Dir, ASCAP 40-41; pres, TV Acad, 56-57. Founded Capitol Records; made many records. Chief Collabrs: Harold Arlen, Richard Whiting, Hoagy Carmichael, Harry Warren, Gene dePaul, Victor Schertzinger, Henry Mancini, Matty Malneck, Bernard Hanighen, Jerome Kern, Robert Emmett Dolan, Gordon Jenkins, Rube Bloom, Arthur Schwartz, James Van Heusen. *Songs:* Out of Breath; Wouldja for a Big Red Apple?; Whistling for a Kiss; Satan's Li'l Lamb; Lazybones; Fare-thee-well to Harlem; Pardon My Southern Accent; Moon Country; When a Woman Loves a Man; PS I Love You; If You Were Mine; Eeny Meeny Miny Mo; I'm Building Up to an Awful Let Down; Jamboree Jones; Goody-Goody; I'm an Old Cowhand; Lost; Love Is a Merry-Go-Round; Bob White; Night Over Shanghai; Sentimental and Melancholy; Too Marvelous for Words; I'm Like a Fish Out of Water; Silhouetted in the Moonlight; Hooray for Hollywood; Love Is on the Air Tonight; You've Got Something There; We're Working Our Way Through College; Have You Got Any Castles, Baby?; The Weekend of a Private Secretary; Ride Tenderfoot, Ride; Love Is Where You Find It; The Girl Friend of the Whirling Dervish; Jeepers Creepers; Mutiny in the Nursery; You Must Have Been a Beautiful Baby; You Grow Sweeter As the Years Go By; Show Your Linen, Miss Richardson; Day in—Day Out; I Thought About You; Blue Rain; In a Moment of Weakness; And the Angels Sing; The Rhumba Jumps; Ooh! What You Said; I Walk With Music; Fools Rush In; Mister Meadowlark; You've Got Me This Way; I'd Know You Anywhere; The Air-Minded Executive; Says Who? Says You, Says I!; Blues in the Night; This Time the Dream's on Me; You're a Natural; Arthur Murray Taught Me Dancing in a Hurry; The Fleet's In; If You Build a Better Mousetrap; Tangerine; Not Mine; I Remember You; Skylark; Dearly Beloved; You Were Never Lovelier; I'm Old Fashioned; That Old Black Magic; Hit the Road to Dreamland; My Shining Hour; One for My Baby; GI Jive; Travelin' Light; Dream; How Little We Know; Ac-Cent-Tchu-Ate the Positive; I Promise You; Let's Take the Long Way Home; On the Atchison, Topeka and Santa Fe (Acad Award, 46); Laura; June Comes Around Every Year; Out of This World; Cakewalk Your Lady; Any Place I Hang My Hat Is Home; Come Rain Or Come Shine; I Wonder What Became of Me; Ridin' on the Moon; Legalize My Name; I Had Myself a True Love; Midnight Sun; The Big Movie Show in the Sky; Autumn Leaves; Fancy Free; In the Cool Cool Cool of the Evening (Acad Award, 51); When the World Was Young; When I'm Out With the Belle of New York; Seeing's Believing; Oops; Early Autumn; Lonesome Polecat; When You're in Love; Sobbin' Women; Something's Gotta Give; You Can't Run Away From It; Temporarily; Namely You; Jubilation T Cornpone; If I Had My Druthers; The Country's in the Very Best of Hands; Love in a Home; Bernadine; Satin Doll; Joanna; A Game of Poker; Goose Never Be a Peacock; The Man in My Life; Moon River (Acad Award, 61); Two of a Kind; Just for Tonight; Days of Wine and Roses (Acad Award, 62); Talk to Me, Baby; I Wanna Be Around; Emily; Moment to Moment. *Scores:* Bway Stage: Walk With Music; St Louis Woman; Texas Li'l Darling; Top Banana; Li'l Abner; Saratoga; Free and Easy (Blues Opera); Foxy; Films: Ready, Willing and Able; Hollywood Hotel; Varsity Show; Cowboy From Brooklyn; Garden of the Moon; Going Places; Naughty But Nice; You'll Find Out; Blues in the Night; Navy Blues; The Fleet's In; You Were Never Lovelier; Star Spangled Rhythm; The Sky's the Limit; Here Come the Waves; The Harvey Girls; Out of This World; The Belle of New York; Seven Brides for Seven Brothers; You Can't Run Away From It; Daddy Long Legs; Merry Andrew.

MERCER, W ELMO (MARK JOHNSON) ASCAP 1957
composer, author
b Pollock, La, Feb 15, 32. Educ: Winnfield High Sch, La, grad, 50; attended Peabody Col, Nashville. Wrote first song at 14. Became staff writer for John T Benson Publ Co, Nashville, 51, music ed, 61. Arr in gospel music field. Mem: Gospel Music Asn (bd dirs); Nashville Songwriters Asn; int mem Nat Acad Recording Arts & Sci. ASCAP Standard Awards. Chief Collabrs: Oswald J Smith, Carlton C Buck, John T Benson, Jr. *Songs:* Gospel & Sacred Songs: Each Step I Take; Lonely Road Up Calvary's Way; The Way That He Loves; The Time Is Now; Do You Need a Friend?; I Found It All in Jesus; Sittin' Around the Table of the Lord; Nailing My Sins to His Cross.

MERCURIO, PAUL
See Rivelli, Pauline

MEREDITH, ISAAC H ASCAP 1938
composer, singer, conductor
b Norristown, Pa, Mar 21, 1872; d Orlando, Fla, Nov 9, 62. Educ: High sch; studied music with Irenee Berge. Wrote songs for Sunday schs. Choir dir, NY; with Cent Presby Church, Brooklyn, 5 yrs. Worked with evangelists. Co-founder, Tuller-Meredith Publ Co, 1899. *Songs:* Sacred Songs: My Jesus, I Love Thee; In Heavenly Love Abiding; The Valley of Peace; Keep Smiling Through; Love's Rainbow; Seal Us, O Holy Spirit!; Blue Skies Will Come Again; For the Man of Galilee; Beautiful Words of Jesus; Building, Daily Building.

MERETTA, LEONARD V ASCAP 1954
composer, conductor, trumpeter
b Keisers, Pa, Sept 5, 15. Educ: Ernest Williams Sch of Music; Univ of Mich; studied music with Del Staigers, Ernest Williams, Mayhew Lake, Erik Leidzen,

Clifford Lillya & Philip Lange. Toured US as trumpet soloist, Maj Bowes group. Taught in pub schs, Lenoir, SC. Fac music, Univ of Mich, 41; dir of bands & instr of wind instruments, Western Mich Univ, 45- Cond concerts in midwest. Guest cond, Univ of Mich Band, Goldman Band & Belle Isle Band. Mem: Am Bandmasters Asn. *Instrumental Works:* Tioga, Men of Might (marches); Holiday (cornet trio).

MERIAN, LEON ASCAP 1959
composer, conductor, trumpeter
b South Braintree, Mass, Sept 17, 25. Educ: Columbia Univ, BS, MA; Sorbonne, Paris; also studied with R Robinson & Dean Meyer. Trumpeter in dance orchs incl Boyd Raeburn, Lucky Millinder, Elliot Lawrence, Gene Krupa & Pete Rugolo; also cond own group; arr. *Songs:* Something Sentimental.

MERKUR, JACOB LOUIS ASCAP 1954
composer, teacher
b Czernowitz, Austria, Apr 7, 1895. Educ: Damrosh Inst Art; Stuyvesant High Sch. Musician, composer, arr, 1 & 2 piano duets. Chief Collabrs: Grant Clarke, Sidney Mitchel, Dorothy Frank. *Songs & Instrumental Works:* Rosie Make It Rosy for Me; Honey Suckle (piano); Valse Tina (saxophone solo); Chasing the Fox; Holy Men of India; Tiger, Tiger; Lost in the Amazon Forest; Potemkin; Devils Playground; To Night; Flying the Lindberg Trail; Dynamic Suite; Birthday Greetings; Land of Dreams; Magic Carpet; Bob-o-Link; Hats Off to Ice; Prologue to Diane; Precision Fanfare; Medieval Fanfare; Man About Town; Boogie Woogie; Hoe Down; Up Front; Step By Step; The News Ticker; Along the Way; Free an' Easy.

MERLE, GEORGE ASCAP 1914
composer, author
b Brooklyn, NY, Feb 13, 1874; d Brooklyn, June 11, 45. Educ: High sch. In US Postal Serv, 40 yrs. Charter mem, ASCAP. *Songs:* Down in My Bungalow; I Should Worry; Turkey Trot Rag; Ragtime Dixie Band; My Old Dad; Aeroplane Built for Two.

MERLE, JOHN
See Isaac, Merle John

MERLOW, CONNIE (CONNIE KELLER) ASCAP 1969
composer, author
b Baltimore, Md, Dec 3, 20. Prof dancer, 22 yrs. Own TV show "Let's Write a Song," WNBT, New York. Writer, songs & 23 film scores. Chief Collabrs: Michael Merlow, Vic Lance.

MEROFF, BENNY ASCAP 1941
composer, author, singer
b New York, NY, Apr 19, 01; d. Educ: Pub sch. Mem vaudeville trio with mother & sister; then appeared as single; formed dance band; cond & master of ceremonies in theatres, hotels; with Eddie Cantor, Palace Theatre, New York; toured with USO, World War II; prod musical, "Funzafire"; entertainer with wife, Kathleen McLaughlin. Chief Collabrs: Walter Hirsch, Sam Coslow, Billy Rose, James Van Heusen, Jule Styne, Walter Donaldson & Gus Kahn. *Songs:* That Little Boy of Mine; Lonely Melody; What's the Use of Crying the Blues?; Wherever You Go.

MERRILL, BLANCHE ASCAP 1936
author
b Philadelphia, Pa, July 23, 1895; d Jackson Heights, NY, Oct 5, 66. Educ: Teacher Training Sch. Wrote spec material for Eva Tanguay, Fanny Brice, Belle Baker, Nora Bayes, Willie Howard; also for musicals. Chief Collabr: Leo Edwards. *Songs:* Poor Little Cinderella; Trailing Along in a Trailer; Bye and Bye; Oh That Heavenly Man; I'm From Chicago; I'm an Indian; Just Around the Corner From Broadway; Becky Is Back At the Ballet; I Can't Do This I Can't Do That; There Is Life in the Old Boy Yet; A Little Wigwam for Two; My Little Dancing Heart; Why Didn't I Meet You Long Ago; Love Is an Old-Fashioned Feeling; Page Mister Cupid; We Take Our Hats Off to You Mr Wilson; Good Night Blue Eyes; Dippy Doodle-Um; This Is the Day; Melodious Jazz; Toodle-Oodle-Oo; Coat of Mine; Jake, Jake, the Yiddish Ball Player; Where is Love - Where Is the Song; I'm a Little Butterfly; Make 'Em Laugh; Ain't That Always the Way; Fanny Brice's Comedy Songs; Jazz Baby; On the Morning After the Night Before; The Ragtime Drama; Gentlemen Be Cheated; Give an Imitation of Me; (The) Tanguay Rag; Money; Tanguay Tangle; Egotistical Eva; I Can't Help It; Neath the Light of the Twinkling Star; Shadowland; Russian Art; I Had a Hard Job Gettin' Him (I Can't Be Losin' Him Now); Becky Is Back in the Ballet; If You Love Me as I Love You; Here's to You, My Sparkling Wine.

MERRILL, BOB ASCAP 1951
composer, author
b Atlantic City, NJ, May 17, 21. Film writer; TV producer; Bway comp, lyricist; bk writer. Chief Collabr: Jule Styne. *Songs:* Honeycomb; Love Makes the World Go 'Round; How Much Is That Doggie in the Window?; It's Good to Be Alive; If I Knew You Were Comin' I'd Bake a Cake; Mambo Italiano; Make Yourself Comfortable; Tina Marie; Pittsburgh Pennsylvania; My Truly Truly Fair; Belle Belle My Liberty Bell; Lyrics: People; Don't Rain on My Parade; I'm the Greatest Star. *Scores:* Bway shows: Take Me Along; Funny Girl.

MERRILL, BUDDY
See Behunin, Leslie Merrill, Jr

MERRILL, IDAHO
See Tonning, Merrill D

MERRILL, RAY ASCAP 1960
composer, author, conductor
b Woburn, Mass, June 30, 16. Educ: High sch. Singer, guitarist in radio, films & nightclubs, 30-41. Orch leader, singer, dir, producer, arr & writer of special material, TV, 45-59. Mgr of Big Tiny Little, 60- *Songs:* Round-Up Polka; I'm in a Mellow Mood.

MERRIMAN, THOMAS W
composer
b Chicago, Ill, Mar 20, 24. Educ: Ind Univ, BM; Juilliard Sch, grad work. *Instrumental Works:* Theme and Variations (brass ens).

MERRITT, DICK
See Obegi, Richard

MERRITT, O O ASCAP 1954
composer, author, comedian
b Phenix City, Ala, Dec 27, 19. Educ: High sch; Grupp Sch of Music, NY. Was nightclub comedian, WW II. Worked for ARC. Chief Collabrs: Redd Evans, Louis Prima, Dave Lambert, Vin Roddie. *Songs:* Bon Voyage; That's Why I Was Born; The World That We Live In; I Love to Dance the Polka; Thinking and Drinking; Playboy; With the Good Lord Willing; Put Something in My Hand; Lovin' Machine; I'm Making Love to You.

MERSEY, ROBERT ASCAP 1958
composer, conductor, arranger
b New York, NY, Apr 7, 17. Producer, Epic records. *Songs:* My Mother Doesn't Like Me; Susie's Theme; Busy Butterfly.

MERTZ, PAUL MADEIRA ASCAP 1952
composer, author, arranger
b Reading, Pa, Sept 1, 04. Educ: Univ Detroit; Tex A&M Univ; Los Angeles City Col. Began playing local gigs with theatre orchs, dance bands, etc, 18; toured with Dorsey Bros Wild Canaries, 22; mem, Goldkette's Graystone Ballroom Band & Book-Cadillac Orch. Arr, Goldkette & Red Nichols groups. Joined, Fred Waring's Pennsylvanians & Irving Aaronson's Commanders. Pianist & chief arr, Horace Heidt. Worked for Paramount, Columbia Pictures & MGM Films. Free-lance arr-comp & music coordr for film indust, 54- *Songs:* I'm Glad There Is You; Music: Merry Ann; Learn to Love; Good-Bye Blues. *Instrumental Works:* Piano Solos: Hurricane; Ennui; Erratique.

MESANG, TED ASCAP 1955
composer, conductor, educator
b Eau Claire, Wis; Dec 7, 04; d Corvallis, Ore, Oct 26, 67. Educ: Univ Wis, BM; Univ Minn, MEd. Clarinetist in military bands, theatres & dance orchs. Dir instrumental music, pub schs, Ashland, Wis; dir bands, Ore State Univ, 49. *Instrumental Works:* Symbol of Honor; Overture Triumphant; Orion; Magic Mountain; Tip Top Band Books; Sportunes; Time Out; Mighty Mite; The Cascades; Bright Star; The Champ; FB Melodie; Vagabond.

MESHEL, WILBUR ASCAP 1968
composer, author, singer
b Brooklyn, NY, May 2, 39. Educ: Cooper Union, fine arts. Singer, songwriter & publ, S Mountain Music, 65, Vicki Music, 66, H&L Music, 67, L F Music, 68, Famous Music, 70 & Arista Music, 77. Chief Collabrs: Arthur Altman, Chris Montez, Teddy Randazzo, Phil Barr. *Songs:* Dear Mrs Applebee, L David Sloane; Aye No Digas (Oh Don't Tell Me); Loco por Ti; If You Can Put That in a Bottle.

MESKILL, JACK ASCAP 1924
composer, author
b New York, NY, Mar 21, 1897; d. Educ: High sch. Played prof baseball; wrote spec material for vaudeville & films. Chief Collabrs: Vincent Rose, Jack Stern, Jean Schwartz, Al Sherman, Albert Von Tilzer, Pete Wendling, Abner Silver, Cliff Friend, Archie Gottler, Con Conrad, Larry Stock, Ted Shapiro, Alex Beller. *Songs:* Smile, Darn Ya, Smile; There's Danger in Your Eyes, Cherie; I Was Lucky; Au Revoir, Pleasant Dreams; Pardon Me, Pretty Baby; When the Organ Played 'O Promise Me'; On the Beach At Bali-Bali; Were You Sincere?; One Little Raindrop; You'll Be Reminded of Me; Blue Hoosier Blues; Rhythm of the Rain; Singing a Happy Song; Don't Let This Waltz Mean Goodbye; I Sent a Letter to Santa; Oh Gee, Georgie; The Day You Said Goodbye to Old Hawaii; What, No Women; Cheer Up and Smile; Tonight or Never; Adios, My Madonna; Mama Macushla; Santa Claus Is Riding the Trail; I've Been Around.

MESSENHEIMER, SAM ASCAP 1948
composer, pianist, arranger
b Columbus, Ind, Mar 4, 1898; d. Educ: High sch. Saxophonist, Vincent Rose, Paul Whiteman, Abe Lyman, Art Hickman & Max Fischer orchs; piano arr for composers; music adv & arr for films, "The Great Ziegfeld", "The Wizard of

Oz", "Idiot's Delight", "Cover Girl", "Strike Up the Band", "Born to Dance", "The Women", "Down to Earth", "Romeo and Juliet." Chief Collabrs: Gus Kahn, Val Burton & Alfred Bryan. *Songs:* Perfume; When Romance Wakes; Idolizing; Singing a Vagabond Song; My Universe Is You; We Laughed At Love; Sing a Little Love Song; Waitin' for the Springtime; Lady of the Morning.

MESSINA, JAMES M
composer, author, singer

b Maywood, Calif, Dec 5, 47. Musician & singer, with first rock band, ages 13 to 17. Recording engr at age 18; engineered, produced & dir, Buffalo Springfield, age 19. At age 21, co-found, engineered, produced, sang & performed with group Poco, also did 3 LP's. Began publ career as writer & publisher; co-found, performed, produced, wrote, arr & sang with Loggins & Messina, Columbia Records. *Songs:* Your Mama Don't Dance; My Music; Listen to a Country Song; Be Free; Angry Eyes; You Better Think Twice; Talk to Me; Changes; Lahaina; Keep Me in Mind; Lately My Love; You Need a Man; Nobody But You; Pathway to Glory; Pretty Princess; Same Old Wine; Thinking of You; New and Different Way; Travelin' Blues; Watching the River Run; Do You Wanta Dance; Magic of Love; Love Is Here; Seeing You (for the First Time); Trilogy: Lovin' Me; Make a Woman Feel Wanted; Peace of Mind.

MESSINA, SYLVESTER J (CHICO)   ASCAP 1953
composer, author

b Cerami, Italy, Sept 12, 17. Educ: High sch music & self-taught. Worked with quartet, Nocturnes, 14 yrs; sang & played guitar; sang in seven languages. *Songs & Instrumental Works:* Giuseppe's Serenade; Sing It Paisan.

MESSNER, JOHNNY   ASCAP 1951
composer, author, saxophonist

b New York, NY, Oct 13, 09. Educ: Juilliard Sch Music, scholarship. Saxophonist in orchs, incl Walter Damrosch, Frank Black. WW II, USA; led band, Special Services Sch. Has led own orch in resorts, nightclubs & hotels throughout US. Has made many records. *Songs:* Stuff; Johnny's Messin' Around; Rich Or Poor; What Can I Tell My Heart?

METIS, FRANK W   ASCAP 1959
composer, author, arranger

b Gruenberg, Ger, Aug 8, 25. Educ: NY Univ, studied comp & orch. Authorized teacher, Schillinger Syst of Musical Comp. Comp, pop & educ material. Arr, pop, rock, jazz piano & choral publ. *Songs:* Music: The Enchanted Sea; Educ Publ: Rock Modes and Moods; Multi-Piano Compositions and Arrangements (incl Easy Together, Good 'n' Groovy, Kid 'n' Keyboards & Festival Fingers).

METIVIER, PAUL ROBERTS   ASCAP 1943
composer, author, singer

b Dorchester, Mass, Mar 30, 15. Known as "Paul and Ann Roberts Show" with radio broadcasts out of Bangor, Maine, 30's & 40's. WW II, USA. Specialized in country music with personal appearances throughout Maine & NB, Can. Chief Collabr: Bob Miller. *Songs:* There's a Star Spangled Banner Waving Somewhere; She Taught Me to Yodel; If I Could Only Learn to Yodel; A Prisoner of War; Did You Ever; Acapulco; Flight Two Thirty Three.

METZ, THEODORE A   ASCAP 1932
composer, author, conductor

b Hanover, Ger, Mar 14, 1848; d New York, NY, Jan 12, 36. To US in youth. Educ: Music sch, Hanover; studied music with Joachim, Beissenberz. To Indianapolis, instr in swimming, gymnastics; then concertmaster, Metrop Theatre. To Chicago, violinist, then cond, traveling musical shows incl McIntyre & Heath. Became music publ. *Songs:* There'll Be a Hot Time in the Old Town Tonight; Ta-ra-ra-Boom-de-ree; Mother's Dear Old Face; When the Roses Are in Bloom; Merry Minstrels; There's a Secret in My Heart. *Instrumental Works:* Poketa (operetta).

MEYER, ALAN HASKEL
author

b Houston, Tex, May 5, 22. Educ: Yale Univ; Columbia Univ Grad Sch Jour. Advert writer, N W Ayer, Y&R, BBDO, Tracy-Locke & Bozell & Jacobs, Dallas, 30 yrs. Wrote many singing commercial lyrics. Chief Collabrs: Dick Boyell, Tom Merriman, Don Zimmers, Otis Conner. *Songs:* Lyrics: Spectrum; The Abilene Jingle (Imperial Sugar); Warmth Is a Shore (Pearl Beer); You'll Never Do It Sooner (Fine Jeweler Guild).

MEYER, CHARLES   ASCAP 1960
composer, author, pianist

b San Antonio, Tex, Apr 28, 24. Educ: Univ Calif, Los Angeles; Westlake Col of Music. Pianist & entertainer in nightclub. Writer of special material. Chief Collabr: Biff Jones. *Songs:* Suddenly There's a Valley; Too Young for the Blues; As Children Do.

MEYER, DAVID HAROLD (DAVID JANSSEN)   ASCAP 1977
author, actor

b Naponee, Nebr, Mar 27, 31; d Feb 13, 80. Educ: Fairfax High Sch; Univ Calif, Los Angeles. Served, USA, 52-54. Actor, incl TV shows "Richard Diamond," 57-60, "The Fugitive," 63-67, "O'hara US Treasury," 72, "Harry-O," 74-76, movies incl "Hell to Eternity", "My Six Loves", "The Green Berets", "Shoes

of the Fisherman", "Where It's At", "Marooned", "Generation", "Macho Callahan", "Once Is Not Enough", "Two Minute Warning", "The Swiss Conspiracy", "A Sensitive Passionate Man", "Stalk the Wild Child", "Mayday at 40,000 Feet", "Nowhere to Run" & "Golden Gate Murders"; guest star on var TV progs. Songwriter. Recipient, TV Guide award, TV-Radio Mirror award, 64, Emmy nominations, 64 & 66, Spec Editor's award, Photoplay Mag, 65, Golden Globe award, Hollywood Foreign Press Asn, 65, Gold Camera award as most popular star in SAm, Ecran Mag, 66, Western Heritage Wrangler award; selected Man of Year on TV by Radio-TV Daily, 64. Mem, Am Fedn of TV & Radio Actors, Acad Motion Picture Arts & Sci, Acad TV Arts & Sci, Am Guild of Variety Actors, Screen Actors Guild & Artists Equity Asn. Chief Collabr: Carol Conners. *Songs:* Lyrics: My Sensitive Passionate Man; Freestyle (Sesame Street).

MEYER, DON   ASCAP 1958
composer, author, director

b Chicago, Ill, Feb 8, 19. Educ: High sch. In vaudeville as mem of team, Three Mike Frights; in "Pins and Needles," Bway & on tour; also on radio. WW II, USA, wrote training films & off AAF radio shows. Wrote special material for nightclubs, Tamiment Playhouse. Dialogue dir, 20th Century Fox & Universal Studios. Writer of special production material, TV. Chief Collabrs: Sherman Edwards, Lee Pockriss, Dewey Bergman. *Songs:* For Heaven's Sake; Nobody's Home At My House.

MEYER, GEORGE W   ASCAP 1914
composer

b Boston, Mass, Jan 1, 1884; d New York, NY, Aug 28, 59. Educ: Roxbury High Sch. Worked in accounting depts, Boston & New York dept stores; then songplugger. Songs for films incl "Footlights and Fools." Charter mem, ASCAP, dir, 20-23 & 32-59. Chief Collabrs: Sam Lewis, Joe Young, Grant Clarke, Roy Turk, Arthur Johnston, Al Bryan, Edgar Leslie, E Ray Goetz, Pete Wendling, Abel Baer, Stanley Adams. *Songs:* Lonesome; When You're a Long, Long Way From Home; My Mother's Rosary; Come on and Baby Me; Since Maggie Dooley Learned the Hooley Hooley; There's a Little Lane Without a Turning; Where Did Robinson Crusoe Go With Friday on Saturday Night?; For Me and My Gal; Everything is Peaches Down in Georgia; Bring Back My Daddy to Me; In the Land of Beginning Again; Beautiful Annabelle Lee; Now I Lay Me Down to Sleep; Tuck Me to Sleep in My Old 'Tucky Home; Sittin' in a Corner; Way Down in Iowa; Brown Eyes, Why Are You Blue?; I'm a Little Blackbird Looking for a Bluebird; Mandy, Make Up Your Mind; Dixie Dreams; I Believe in Miracles; There Are Such Things; If I Only Had a Match; In a Little Book Shop; The Story of Annie Laurie. *Scores:* Bway Stage: Dixie to Broadway.

MEYER, JOHN LAWRENCE   ASCAP 1953
composer, author, choral director

b Sheboygan, Wis, Aug 17, 11. Educ: Univ Notre Dame & Univ Wis. Started singing with duo & later as quartet over WHBL, 29-36; first song publ, 29; played with var combos & orchs, 36-49. Directed, Sheboygan Sweet Adeline Chorus, 18 yrs as well as Manitowoc & West Bend Choruses, also Sheboygan Barbershop Chorus & St Peter Claver Church Choir, 10 yrs. Vocal arr for many choruses & quartets, coached & arr for Chordettes. Chief Collabrs: J V DeCimber, Jack Lynch, Tom MacWilliams. *Songs:* Honey Bee Waltz; When Otto Plays a Polka; Wake Up With a Whistle; Billy My Billy; The Prettiest Girl in Idaho; Music: Lyin' Lips; Lyrics: Schatzie; Yes Dear; How Can My Heart Forget You.

MEYER, JOSEPH   ASCAP 1922
composer

b Modesto, Calif, Mar 12, 1894. Educ: Lowell High Sch, San Francisco; studied violin in Paris & harmony & counter point. Served in USA, World War I. Brief business career. To New York, 21. Chief Collabrs: B G Dylva, Irving Caesar, Mann Curtis, Joseph McCarthy Jr. *Songs:* Music: California Here I Come; If You Knew Susie; Crazy Rhythm; Clap Hands Here Comes Charley; A Cup of Coffee, A Sandwich and You; Idle Gossip; How Long Will It Last?. *Scores:* Bway shows: Big Boy; Just Fancy; Here's Howe; Lady Fingers; Stage play: That's a Good Girl (London); Film: George White Scandals.

MEYER, SOL   ASCAP 1942
author

b Jersey City, NJ, Dec 28, 13; d New York, NY, Aug 12, 64. Educ: NY Univ. Wrote songs for radio, nightclub singers; also for films (40-42), radio & TV. Served with Glenn Miller Unit, USAAF, WW II. *Songs:* Reminiscing; Tahiti Honey; After All; Guy With the Polka Dotted Tie; Puddin' Head; I'd Like to Sing a Love Song; Brownie With the Light Blue Jeans; Rainbow in the Night; Songs of Good Behavior.

MEYERS, BILLY   ASCAP 1927
author, singer

b Louisville, Ky, July 29, 1894; d. Educ: St Anthony's Sch, studied music with Leo Kolleras. Vocalist in vaudeville, radio & nightclubs. *Songs & Instrumental Works:* Nobody's Sweetheart; Bugle Call Rag; Spanish Shawl; House of David Blues; Everybody's Stomp; Suite Sixteen; Blue Grass Blues; I Found a Horseshoe; Railroad Man.

MEYERS, LANNY DOUGLAS
composer, author

Educ: Hunter Col, NY, BS(music); Univ Calif Los Angeles, MA(music comp). Vpres, Not-Just-Jingles of NYC Inc. Underscored music for "Search for Tomorrow" & "Edge of Night." *Songs:* St Joan of the Microphone; Sweet Beginning; Michelangelo's Dance Party; Music: You Can Love Again; Lyrics: Blindfold.

MEYERS, WARREN B — ASCAP 1962
composer, author, musical director

b New York, NY, Oct 29, 29. Educ: Horace Mann High Sch; Columbia Col, BA, 52; Juilliard Sch Music. Composer/musical dir for Diahann Carroll, Marlene Dietrich, Jose Ferrer, "The Hallmark Hall of Fame" & Bway production of "Lenny." Bway appearances, "Me and Juliet" & "Compulsion." Leader numerous jazz groups, currently Octagon. Chief Collabrs: Julian Barry, Timothy Gray, Robert Alan Bernstein. *Scores:* Bway Shows: Lookin' for the Man; Tam O' Shanter; Educ TV: The Strawberry Book of Colors; The Strawberry Book of Noses and Toes; The Little House on the Prairie; The Little House in The Big Woods.

MEYN, THEODORE A — ASCAP 1953
composer, author, organist

b Kansas City, Kans, Aug 20, 1901; d St Petersburg, Fla, Sept 23, 75. Educ: Bus col; pvt music study. Prof organist, age 12. Featured in Loew's Theatres, 27 yrs. One-Man-Wonder-Trio, hotels & nightclubs. Chief Collabrs: Charles Tobias, Murray Mencher, Larry Stock. *Songs:* Raise the Window Down; Wag-ga-shoe; My Thrill Is Loving You; Roundup Time for Love; There's No Right Way to Do Me Wrong; More of the Same Sweet You; Ol' Lonely; Why Is My Little Redhead Blue?

MIAMI, JOE
See Ballard, Louis Wayne

MICH, THOMAS ALEXANDER, JR — ASCAP 1979
composer, author, singer

b Detroit, Mich, Feb 2, 58. Educ: Cody High Sch, 75. Instrumentalist. *Songs:* D-Day 1980.

MICHAEL, ELAINE — ASCAP 1960
composer, author

b New York, NY, Jan 9, 30. Educ: Long Island Univ; Brooklyn Col. Chief Collabrs: Hal Gordon, Bill Schulman. *Songs:* They're Playing Our Song; Little Boy; Drink to a Fool; Don't Say Goodbye; Make Believe Island of Dreams. *Albums:* Moonlight Magic.

MICHAEL, GILBERT F — ASCAP 1975
musician

b Lee County, Miss, Aug 30, 33. Educ: Memphis State Univ. Pvt music instructors during childhood. Free-lance musician; plays steel guitar & fiddle, Bill Black's Combo. Chief Collabrs: Larry Rogers, Bob Tucker. *Instrumental Works:* Boilin' Cabbage; Fire on the Bayou.

MICHAEL, JEFF
See Prescott, Norm

MICHAEL, MIKE
See Cassone, Michael, Jr

MICHAEL, ROBERT — ASCAP 1969
composer, author, pianist

b Niagara Falls, Ont, Oct 10, 01. Educ: Berkeley High Sch. US citizen, 41. Led own orch in night clubs. Wrote background words & music for TV. Asst mgr, Hilton Hotel, Los Angeles. *Songs:* When You Are Mine; It's Never Too Late to Dream; Santa Barbara; Music: Just Adoring You.

MICHAELS, D(ENNIS) Z
See Zuvich, Dennis Michael

MICHAELS, LEE
instrumentalist, vocalist

b Los Angeles, Calif, Nov 24, 45. Mem band, Sentinels. Formed Lee Michaels Band; own group played Bay Area clubs & fests. Recording artist, A&M & Columbia Records. *Albums:* Carnival of Life; Recital; Lee Michaels; Live; Barrel; 5th; Space and First Takes; Nice Day for Something; Tailface.

MICHAELS, STEPHEN — ASCAP 1969
composer, author, actor

b Los Angeles, Calif, July 14, 45. Educ: N High Sch, Torrance, Calif; Am Sch Dance, Hollywood, studies with Al Gilbert; El Camino Jr Col; UCLC; studies with Ballett Russe, Luigi, David Le Grant in New York & Lehman Engle, Los Angeles. Movies, "Bye Bye Birdie" & "The Trouble With Girls" & Bway "Funny Girl," stock, nat cos, night clubs & TV. Screenplays for "Young Lady Chatterley", "Racquet", "Gas Station", "Made in Hollywood" & D H Lawrence's "Lady Chatterley's Lover." Chief Collabrs: John Rubinstein, Bob Ecton, Nelson Riddle, Don Bagley. *Songs:* Time; Don't Cry Anymore; Tryna

Get Some Love On; (You're) My Reverie (adapted from Debussy); Lyrics: The Bigger The Love; Thanks To You; The Way You Are.

MICHALOVE, EDWIN BENNETT — ASCAP 1950
composer

b Atlanta, Ga. Educ: Yale Univ, BA. Chief Collabr: Joseph Schuster. *Songs:* Lyrics: I Kissed a Girl; The Wheel Turns; What I Never Had, I'll Never Miss!.

MICHALSKY, DONAL RAY
composer, teacher

b Pasadena, Calif, July 13, 28; d Balboa, Calif, Jan 1, 76. Educ: Univ Southern Calif, BMus, 52, MMus, 57, DMusA, 65, student of Ingolf Dahl. US Air Force, 53-56. Fulbright scholarship to Ger, State Acad Music, Freiburg, 58. Prof music, Calif State Univ, Fullerton, 60-76; co-dir, Ford Found Contemporary Music Proj, 66-67; sabbatical leave in Ger for comp, 67. Chief Collabr: Paul Obler. *Instrumental Works:* Divertimento for Three Clarinets; Variations for Accordion; Four Pieces for Accordion; Trio Concertino; Sonata for Two Pianos; Concertino for Trombone and Band; Fantasia a Due for Horn and Bass Trombone; Three Times Four; Fantasia alla Marcia; Fanfare After 17th Century Dances; Elegy Concerto; Sonatina for Flute and Clarinet; The Wheel of Time (choral symph). *Scores:* Opera/Ballet: Der Arme Heinrich.

MICHELS, LLOYD
See Bergman, Lloyd Michel

MICHELS, WALTER — ASCAP 1943
composer, author, pianist

b Chicago, Ill, Apr 17, 1895. Educ: Univ of Wis; pvt music study. WW I, 56th Engrs, France; entertained troops after Armistice. Pianist, accompanist to singers. Chief Collabrs: Lindsay MacPhail, Will Rossiter. *Songs:* San; Until You Came; That Day Will Come; The Paper Doll Parade; The Garden of Tomorrow; There's a New Gang on the Corner; Danbury Fair; Cowboy's Honeymoon; Fishin' With the Angels; You Can't Make Honey.

MICHLIN, SPENCER
composer, author

b New York, NY, Dec 11, 41. Educ: Studied with pvt teachers. Writer of speeches & non-fiction articles; through advertising got into writing well-known jingles. *Songs:* You've Got Alot to Live, Pepsi's Got Alot to Give (jingle); Maxwell House, Good to the Last Drop (jingle); Hello Sunshine, Hello Mountain Dew (jingle); Borrowed Time; All My Choices; Gumbo Jones; Get the Dog Outta the Room.

MICHROVSKY, STEFAN
See Miron, Issachar

MIDDENDORF, J WILLIAM, II
composer, author

b Baltimore, Md, Sept 22, 24. Educ: Holy Cross Col, BS(naval sci), 45; Harvard Univ, AB, 47; NY Univ, MBA, 54. Eng & communications officer, USN, 45-46; with, Chase Manhattan Bank & Wood, Struthers & Co, 47-61; partner ins stock firm, 62-69; US Ambassador, Neth, 69-73; Under Secy & Actg Secy Navy, 73-74, Secy of the Navy, 74-77; pres & chief exec officer, Financial Gen Bankshares, Inc. Hon Doctor of Letters from Sch Ozarks & Am Christian Col. *Songs:* Stand Up For America; US Capitol March; Music: Old Ironsides March; Big Brass Band March; American Spirit March.

MIDDLETON, LAVINIA JOANN — ASCAP 1974
composer, author

b LeCompte, La, Jan 18, 34. Educ: La Col, 51; La Tech, BA in Ed(music), 54. Church organist-comp, 27 yrs. Pub sch music teacher; pvt teacher of piano, voice & organ. Accompanist for professional soloists & singing groups for state & nat Southern Baptist conventions. Teacher-accompanist for summer workshops. Dir of vocal, instrumental & handbell groups. *Songs:* Sand, Sea, Sky and Me (folk musical for young people). *Instrumental Works:* Golden Sounds of Ringing (21 arr for handbells); The Sound of Bells (9 arr for handbells).

MIDDLETON, OWEN — ASCAP 1971
composer, guitarist

b Mobile, Ala, Aug 28, 41. Educ: Fla State Univ, MMus(comp), studied with John Boda & Carlisle Floyd; pvt classical guitar study with Alexander Bellow, New York. Comp, performer & teacher. Guest comp, Am Music Forum, 74. Artist-in-residence, Franklin & Marshall Col, 75. Comn to comp incidental music for play, "Buchanan Dying" (John Updike). *Instrumental Works:* Solo Music for Guitar; Five Studies; Suite for Solo Guitar.

MIDGLEY, CHARLES WILLIAM — ASCAP 1965
composer, author, publisher

b Salt Lake City, Utah, Dec 17, 1899. Educ: Oakland Tech High Sch, Calif; Stanford Univ, Palo Alto, AB(economics); Inst Musical Art, New York; studied musical comp with Dr Percy Goetschius. Original pianist with Horace Heidt, Oakland, 27-28; rehearsal asst with Shuberts & Earl Carroll, New York, 28-29; comp, arr & coach with Paramount Studios, Hollywood, 29-30. Chief Collabrs: Daniel W Evans, J C Lewis, Jr, Bert Van Cleve, Don C Krull, George L Evans. *Songs:* The Donkey Song; Hymn of Peace; The Sweetheart of Sigma Nu; Thank

You, Dear Father; The Waltz of Wichita; Music: A Brooklet and a Pretty Maid; The Girl Who Wears the Five-armed Star; Hymn of Praise; I Want to Major in Love; A Mountain Song; Who Cares Anyhow?; You Have an Invitation to Take the Ozone With Me. *Instrumental Works:* Boy Scouts of America March; Cuban Serenade; Korean Story; Lullaby for Christmas; The Potluck Polka.

MIEIR, AUDREY MAE ASCAP 1972
composer, author, pianist

b Leechburg, Pa, May 12, 16. Educ: Olga Steeb Sch Music, Riverside, Calif; LIFE Bible Col, Los Angeles. Minister of music, 45 yrs; comp & dir large choirs, US; dir, Mieir Ministries Inc, music & support of missions, Orient. Active in Christian TV, 52-; host, TV Show (satellite), Trinity Broadcasting Network, Los Angeles. *Songs:* His Name Is Wonderful; I'll Never Be Lonely Again; It Matters to Him; When You Pray; To Be Used of God; Don't Spare Me; Because He Touched Me; All He Wants Is You; I Heard God Today; Consume Me; God's Great Love; So Soon It Is Over; Untold Millions; Real Peace; Fear Thou Not; Let My Heart Be Broken.

MIESCER, A STEPHEN ASCAP 1960
composer, author, teacher

b Monongah, WVa, Nov 22, 03. Educ: Ithaca Col; Eastman Sch Music; Dana Sch Music; Youngstown Univ, BM, MM, MusD; Univ Pittsburgh; Pa State Univ; Univ Fla. Clarinetist, Rochester Little Symph, Am Opera Orch & Pat Conway Band; clarinetist-saxophonist & asst cond, Royal Scotch Highlander Band; organizer-dir, Mt Lebanon High Sch Band, Pittsburgh, Pa & Baker High Sch Band, Fla; dir, Wash & Jefferson Col Band; co-organizer & first pres, Pa Music Educators Asn, 35. *Instrumental Works:* Pride of the Navy March; PSMA March; Naomi; La Chiquita.

MIGLIORE, TONY ASCAP 1974
composer, studio musician, producer

b New York, NY, Oct 12, 44. Educ: Juilliard Sch Music; Eastman Sch Music, BM; Columbia Univ Teachers Col, studies in improvisation with Jaki Byard & arr with Mort Lindsey. Played with var travelling jazz groups. Pianist with USMA Band, West Point. Dir several local productions, "Most Happy Fella" & "Annie Get Your Gun." Studio musician & record producer, Nashville, 70-*Instrumental Works:* Moon Pie; Finger Prints.

MIKETTA, BOB (ROBERT MORRIS) ASCAP 1945
composer, arranger, teacher

b Cincinnati, Ohio, Apr 3, 11; d Cincinnati, Ohio, Oct 7, 75. Educ: Littleford Sch Bus. Fac mem, Cincinnati Col Music. Arr for dance orchs. Staff arr, Louis Prima, also NY radio sta & WLW, Cincinnati. Pvt music teacher; also freelance arr. *Songs:* Robin Hood; Angels Are All Asleep; Next to the 'X' in Texas; One, Two, Three O'Leary; You Can't Do That to Me.

MILAZZO, CHARLES JOSEPH ASCAP 1971
composer, author

b New York, NY, Mar 20, 09. Educ: Bay Ridge Evening High Sch; Columbia Univ, studied acad & jour; studied narrative technique with Thomas Uzzell. Served USA. Writer, soldier shows, 41- Wrote musical comedy, "Grin and Bear It." Chief Collabrs: Arnold Gibbs, Alec Siniavine, Harry Haggett, Walter Bernstein, Roland Wolpert, Don Williamson. *Songs:* Sayonara; O'Brien's Gone Hawaiian; Grin and Bear It; There's Laughter in Paris Again; Lyrics: Have a Good Time in Your Prime.

MILBURN, ELLSWORTH ASCAP 1972
composer

b Greensburg, Pa, Feb 6, 38. Educ: Univ Calif, Los Angeles, BA; Mills Col, MA; Col Cons Music; Univ Cincinnati, DMA. Music dir, Committee Theater, San Francisco, 63-68; wrote for Imagination Inc, San Francisco. Asst prof, Col Cons Music, 70-75. Dir, Contemporary Music Series. Assoc prof, Rice Univ, Houston, Tex, 75- Chief Collabrs: C E Cooper, Allyson Brown; Arthur Gottschalk. *Instrumental Works:* String Quartet; Spiritus Mundi; Soli I-IV; Revenants.

MILES, ALFRED HART ASCAP 1943
author

b Norfolk, Va, Nov 3, 1883; d Norfolk, Oct 6, 56. Educ: William & Mary Col; US Naval Acad. Choir leader; organized glee clubs & musicial shows. Naval officer, USN, WW I; submarine comdr; dir, Armed Guard, Norfolk. WW II, constructed & commanded Naval Section Base, Little Creek, Va. Stationed in Philippines & China; commandant, Guantanamo, Cuba. Retired as Capt, 45. *Songs:* Anchors Aweigh.

MILES, BARRY ASCAP 1963
composer, conductor, musician

b Newark, NJ, Mar 28, 47. Led own jazztet on TV & in concerts. Made Europ tour for US State Dept. *Songs & Instrumental Works:* Dialogue for 2 Drums and Orchestra; Dee Weet; Color the Lady Pink; Terry; Top Coates; 12 Themes and Improvisations.

MILES, C AUSTIN (A A PAYN, G W PAYN) ASCAP 1925
composer, author

b Lakehurst, NJ, Jan 7, 1868; d Philadelphia, Pa, Mar 10, 46. Educ: Philadelphia Col Pharm; Univ Pa. Choir dir, 40 yrs; dir music, NJ Conf of Camp Meeting Asn, 25 yrs; also at conventions & fests. Ed & mgr, Hall-Mack Co, 37 yrs. Ed, bks of sacred songs. *Songs & Instrumental Works:* Sacred Songs: In the Garden; If Jesus Goes With Me; Come Rest a While; In the Upper Garden; Dwelling in Beulah Land; He is Mine; Still Sweeter Every Day; Cantatas: The Red Santa Claus; Mary.

MILES, GEORGE (BUDDY)
drummer, singer, writer

b Omaha, Nebr, Sept 5, 46. Rock drummer; played professionally at age 15, backing the Ink Spots; later played in Wilson Pickett's back up band. Joined Electric Flag, later formed own Buddy Miles Express, which ended when he worked temporarily with Jimi Hendrix in the Band of Gypsies; later formed Buddy Miles Band; went back to reformed Electric Flag in 74 which lasted a short time & in 75 was back solo. *Albums:* Chapter VII; Booger Bear; All the Faces of Buddy Miles; More Miles Per Gallon; Bicentennial Gathering of the Tribes; Roadrunner; The Buddy Miles Express; Santana/Miles.

MILES, RICHARD ASCAP 1946
composer

b Dorchester, Mass, Nov 3, 16. Educ: New Eng Cons. Chief Collabrs: Bob Hilliard, Mack Discant, Jack Segal. *Songs:* I'll Remember Suzanne; Jose Gonzales; The Coffee Song; Lover, Are You There?; It Was Nice While the Money Rolled In; In the Land of the Buffalo Nickel; I'll Cry Tomorrow; Someday Somewhere; Morning, Noon and Night.

MILES, ROBERT ASCAP 1962
composer, author

b Roanoke, Va, June 26, 20. Educ: Univ Ky, BA, 42, MA, 48; Juilliard Sch Music; studied comp with Lewis Henry Horton, Esther Williamson & John Mehegan. Wrote revues & resorts, Columbia Law Sch. Stage scores, "Alice in Wonderland" & "Four O'Clock Children." Wrote music reviews for Herald-Leader, Lexington, Ky. Chief Collabrs: William K Hubbell, Richard Diamond, Chandler Warren, Shirley Shore, George Cole, Arnold Falleder, Bobbie Kassan. *Songs:* Music: My Life Begins with You; When Man Moves In; Twenty-One Miles from Home (First Prize Winner); Another Day with You (First Prize Winner). *Instrumental Works:* Jazz Themes 1, 2, and 3; Background Themes 1 and 2; Sirod. *Scores:* Cantata: Portrait of a Patriot.

MILES, WALTER E ASCAP 1925
composer

b Grand Rapids, Mich, May 10, 1885; d Ft Lauderdale, Fla, May 9, 61. Educ: Pub schs; pvt music study. Pres, Walter Miles Coal Co, 20-38. Moved to Ft Lauderdale, 41. *Instrumental Works:* Sparklets; Curl-i-cues; Painted Clouds; Valse; Danseuse; Blue Mist; American Students March; Birdland Sketches (suite).

MILITARY, FRANCIS PHILIP (FRANK) ASCAP 1961
composer, author

b New York, NY, Oct 26, 26. Educ: Lafayette High Sch, Brooklyn, NY. Worked in talent dept for Marvin Schenck & Louis B Mayer, MGM, New York, age 18. Co-mgr for Dean Martin, 5 yrs. Mgr for Alan Dale & Eileen Barton. Worked with Frank Sinatra, Calif, 11 yrs. Prof mgr, Bregman, Vocco & Cahn. Pres own co, Music Maximus. Vpres, Music Publ Metromedia & Chappell Music. Chief Collabr: Mann Curtis. *Songs:* Christmas Auld Syne.

MILITARY, PAMELA (PAMELA LAWRENCE) ASCAP 1976
author

b Paterson, NJ, Oct 21, 24. Educ: Ohio State Univ, Montclair State Col, BA. Chief Collabrs: Bennie Benjamin, Michael Sternberg, Neil Wolfe. *Songs:* Lyrics: Traces of You; The Nominees; Nothing Can Hold Me.

MILKEY, EDWARD T (MARTIN ALBERT, TED TALBERT) ASCAP 1951
composer, teacher

b Turners Falls, Mass, July 2, 08. Educ: Turners Falls High Sch, 26; NY Univ Sch Educ, BS, 30, MA, 35. Music supvr, pub schs, Mountain Lakes, NJ, 30-45. Educ rep, G Inc, 45-52, Mills Music, Inc, 52-55 & Big 3 Music Corp, 55-61. Dir choral music & theory, pub schs, Parsippany, NJ, 61-73. Dir, Community Church Choir & Men's Glee Club, Mountain Lakes. Chief Collabrs: Carl J Bostelmann, Wilbur Weeps, Eugene Pillot. *Songs & Instrumental Works:* Suite for String Orchestra; Christmas Is Coming; The Glee Club; 'Tis Weary Waiting; I Must Go Forth Into the Morning.

MILLAY, EDNA ST VINCENT ASCAP 1934
author

b Rockland, Maine, Feb 22, 1892; d Austerlitz, NY, Oct 19, 50. Educ: Vassar Col, BA. Hon degrees: Tufts Col, Russell Sage Col, Colby Col, Univ Wis & NY Univ. Mem, Am Acad Arts & Letters. First woman to receive Pulitzer Prize for Poetry, 22. As actress, appeared in "Bonds of Interest." Author bks poetry "Renascence"; "Second April"; "A Few Figs From Thistles"; "The Harp-Weaver and Other Poems"; "The Buck in the Snow"; "Poems Selected for Young People"; "Wine From These Grapes"; "Fatal Interview"; "Huntsman,

What Quarry?"; "Make Bright the Arrows"; "Collected Sonnets"; "Collected Lyrics"; "Mine the Harvest"; "Collected Poems." Author plays & verse plays incl "The Princess Marries the Page"; "Two Slatterns and a King"; "The Lamp and the Bell"; "Aria da Capo"; "The King's Henchman"; "Conversation At Midnight"; "The Murder of Lidice." Chief Collab: Deems Taylor. Poems set to music: Elaine; God's World; Thursday; First Fig; The Return From Town; A Prayer to Persephone; Afternoon of a Hill; Epitaph; City Trees; Moritorus; Departure; Humoresque; Pity Me Not; Conscientious Objector; Three Songs of Shattering; Songs of the Nations; Alms; The Betrothal; Elegy Before Death; Journey; The Strawberry Shrub; Recuerdo; For You There Is No Song; Come Back to Us in April; My Heart Being Hungry; Rain Comes Down; One, Two Three; Mariposa; Oh, Little Rose Tree Bloom; Bridal Song; The Snare; Sun's Comin' Out!; Let the Little Birds Sing; Children's Song; Interrupted Song.

MILLER, ADAM S   ASCAP 1970
composer

b Washington, DC, Feb 24, 47. Educ: St Albans, DC; Pierrepont, Frensham, Eng, 65; Hampden-Sydney Col, Va. Recording artist as singer, 71. Songwriter with Chelsy Records, 71. Producer for Wes Farrell & Cashman & West, 73. Comp & writer for var artists, commercials & TV shows, 80. Chief Collabr: Wes Farrell. *Songs:* Westwind Circus; Have You Just Stopped Loving Me; Even If I Could Change; Storybook Love.

MILLER, ARNOLD E, JR   ASCAP 1959
composer, arranger, singer

b San Francisco, Calif, Feb 21, 21. Educ: Beacon Sch; Harvard Col; Univ NC; studied with Eric Zeisl. Arr/performer with vocal groups, San Francisco & Los Angeles. Chief Collabr: Connie Pearce. *Songs:* Music: No Sad Songs for Me; Night Time Was My Mother; Christmas Heart; Ring a Merry Bell; Sorry to See You Go; The Little Star; Hang Them on the Tree; The Merriest; This Time of Year; Seven Shades of Snow; The Magic Gift; Winter's Got Spring Up Its Sleeve.

MILLER, BOB   ASCAP 1933
composer, author, singer

b Memphis, Tenn, Sept 20, 1895; d New York, NY, Aug 26, 55. Educ: Southern Cons; Chicago Cons. Prof pianist at age 10. Led Steamer Idlewild Orch on showboats, 15. Sang on radio from first Memphis sta. To NY, 22; arr for music publ, then formed own publ co, 33. Wrote under many pseudonyms. *Songs:* 'Leven Cent Cotton, Forty Cent Meat; Chime Bells; There's a Star-Spangled Banner Waving Somewhere; Conversation With a Mule; Seven Years With the Wrong Woman; Twenty-One Years; Rockin' Along in an Old Rockin' Chair; New River Train; When the White Azaleas Start Blooming; Uncle Bud; Gonna Have a Big Time Tonight; In the Blue Hills of Virginia; Sweet Pal; Little Red Caboose Behind the Train.

MILLER, CARL S(AMUEL)   ASCAP 1975
composer, arranger

b Bay City, Mich, Feb 20, 17. Educ: Cent High Sch, Detroit, Mich; Yale Univ Sch Music, MusB, 47, MusM, 48, studied with Paul Hindemith. Ed, arr, publ designer, production mgr & educ dir, Assoc Music Publ, Inc, 48-55, Chappell & Co, Inc, 55-74 & Bourne Co, 74- Chief Collabr: Vladimir Bobri. *Songs & Instrumental Works:* Two Guitars; A Musical Voyage With Two Guitars; Sing Children Sing; Rockabye Baby.

MILLER, CHARLES   ASCAP 1953
composer, violinist, conductor

b Russia, Jan 1, 1899. Moved to US, 01. Educ: Juilliard Sch Music, studied with Hans Letz, Franz Kneisel; also studied with Percy Goetschius, Leopold Auer, Carl Flesch & Alfredo Casella. Cond, concerts in Paris & Budapest; violinist, Philadelphia Orch, 41- *Songs & Instrumental Works:* Symphony; Appalachian Mountains (orch rhapsody); West Indies Suite; Cubanaise for Violin; String Quartet; New Orleans Street Crier (mixed voices).

MILLER, CHARLES EDWARD   ASCAP 1969
composer, author

b New Orleans, La, Dec 11, 29. Educ: St Mary's Sem, Mo, grad philosophy; Univ Southern Calif, MA(communications). *Songs:* The Christmas Star (Disney).

MILLER, CONNIE H (CONNIE PEARCE)   ASCAP 1959
author, singer

b Toledo, Ohio, July 20, 20. Educ: Austin High Sch, Chicago; poetry/music workshops, Los Angeles City Col. Writer/performer with vocal groups, San Francisco & Los Angeles. Chief Collabr: Arnold Miller. *Songs:* Lyrics: No Sad Songs for Me; Night Time Was My Mother; Christmas Heart; Ring a Merry Bell; Sorry to See You Go; The Little Star; Hang Them on the Tree; The Merriest; This Time of Year; Seven Shades of Snow; The Magic Gift; Winter's Got Spring Up Its Sleeve.

MILLER, EDDIE PIANO
See Lisbona, Edward

MILLER, EDWARD RAYMOND   ASCAP 1957
composer, musician

b New Orleans, La, June 23, 11. Educ: Warren Easton High Sch, New Orleans. Saxophonist, Bob Crosby & Paul Whiteman Orchs; with Pete Fountain, New Orleans, 10 yrs; free lancing, Los Angeles; yearly concert tours, Europe. Chief Collabrs: Johnny Mercer, Bob Haggart. *Songs:* Music: Love's Got Me in a Lazy Mood; March of the Bob Cats; Cajun Love Song; Gotta Be On My Way.

MILLER, FLOURNOY E   ASCAP 1950
author, actor

b Nashville, Tenn, Apr 14, 1887; d Los Angeles, Calif, June 6, 71. Educ: Fisk Univ. Wrote songs for Pekin Theatre, Chicago, 07. Toured US & Europe in vaudeville with partner, A L Lyles. Wrote & starred in, "Shuffle Along", "Runnin' Wild", "Rang Tang" & "Keep Shufflin'." Co-librettist, "Amos & Andy," TV series. Appeared in Bway musical, "Running Wild." Wrote "Amos 'n' Andy" radio series; starred in Vincent Youman's "Great Day," Schuberts' "Great Temptations" & "Ziegfeld Roof," 40. Organized hosp shows, WW II. Chief Collabrs: James P Johnson, Ford Dabney, Dudley Brooks, Sherman Crothers, Noble Sissle, Eubie Blake. *Songs:* You Can't Lose a Broken Heart; Got to Get the Gittin'; Keep 'Em Guessing; Peace, Sister, Peace; Stay Out of the Kitchen; My Sweet Hunk o' Trash; No Labor in My Job. *Scores:* Stage: Sugar Hill; The Oyster Man.

MILLER, FREDERICK S   ASCAP 1967
composer

b Lima, Ohio, Dec 12, 30. Educ: Northwestern Univ, BME, MM; Univ Iowa, DMA. Teacher band & music theory, Univ Ark. Teacher band & music theory, Northwestern Univ, assoc dean, Sch Music, 70-76. Dean, Sch Music, DePaul Univ, 76- Comp & arr for concert & marching band. *Songs & Instrumental Works:* Procession and Interlude (concert band); Sea Pieces, By Edward MacDowell; Willie's Rock (marching band).

MILLER, (ALTON) GLENN   ASCAP 1964
composer, conductor, trombonist

b Clarinda, Iowa, Mar 1, 04; d Dec 15, 44. Educ: Univ Colo. Trombonist in orchs incl, Boyd Senter, Ben Pollack, Paul Ash, Red Nichols, Dorsey Bros (also arr) & Ray Noble. Formed own orch, 38; appeared in cols, hotels, theatres & films, "Orchestra Wives"; "Sun Valley Serenade"; made many records. Capt, USAAF, WW II; led USAAF Orch; killed in plane crash. Film biography, "The Glenn Miller Story." *Songs & Instrumental Works:* Moonlight Serenade; Sometime; Wham; Sold American; Boom Shot; Annie's Cousin Fanny; Room 1411.

MILLER, H(ENRY) THOMAS   ASCAP 1960
composer, author, conductor

b Morristown, NJ, Apr 8, 23. Educ: Bernards High Sch, Bernardsville, NJ, 41; Rutgers Univ Extension Div, 41; voice scholarship with Charles A McLain, New York, 41; NY Univ Sch Educ, 41, 42 & 45; Hunter Col Night Div, 44; pre-col spec studies in voice with Frances B & Baldwin Allan, Allen, NJ, 5 yrs; Theodora Irvine Sch of Theatre, New York, 45; voice, repertoire & oratorio, George Rasely, 45-49; coaching with Romano Romani, 45-46, piano, Esther Lundell, 45-46 & cond & arr, Max Rudolf, 45-46. Instruments: Piano, organ, trumpet, tympani & cello. Asst dir music, St Bernard's Episcopal Church, Bernardsville, NJ, 41-42; organized & pres, Somerset Singers, 41-42; tympanist, Somerset County Civic Orch, 41-42; soloist, vocal recitals, Metrop New York area, 41-42. Mil service with USCG, 42-45. Teacher singing, Metrop New York, 45-; staff mem, Pace Col, 50-55; teacher voice, Turtle Bay Sch Music, 63-69. Cond var employee choral groups, New York, 45-69; dir music, Wadsworth Avenue Baptist Church, New York, 47-48; organized & cond, Community Singers of Queens, Flushing, NY, now comd emeritus; assoc ed, "Choral and Organ Guide," 48-55; cond, The Chaminade, Brooklyn, 51-52; pres, Int Choir Dirs League; mem bd dirs, Choral Cond Guild Am. Mem: NY Singing Teachers Asn & Nat Asn Teachers Singing. Chief Collabr: Dorothy R McCarthy (Beard). *Songs:* Let All the Bells Ring Out; A Silence Came O'er Bethlehem; Dreams; Choral Salutation; It's Merry Christmas Time; God Fills the World With His Love; Hear Our Prayer, O Lord!; The Green Hills of Ireland; Wond'ring; Music: A Prayer; Dance Song; Passing By. *Scores:* Off-Bway Prod: Backstage Fantasy.

MILLER, HARRY S   ASCAP 1944
composer, author, singer

b New York, NY, July 30, 1895. Educ: New York Pub Schs; Juilliard, keyboard harmony & Schillinger Syst Music; also studied briefly with Wallingford Reigger, Otto Cesano & Ted Royal. Singer, dancer, comedian in Bway musical comedies & vaudeville, 14-30; full-time writer, 30-; served in US Army, WW I & WW II, wrote many shows for troops, notably "America's Marching Again" & "Great Scott." Chief Collabrs: Lew Pollack, Dave Stamper, Mike Cleary, Frank Signorelli, Robert Katcher, Leo Russotto, Louis Alter. *Songs:* I'm Hittin' The Trail for Home; Out on the Lone Prairie; Oh Lord, Show Me The Way; Memories on Parade; The Dreams I Dreamed (In My Childhood Days); There's a Wishing-Well in the Moon; Mother Goose Swings It!; Between You and Me and The Lamppost; I Wanna Be a Minstrel Man; I've Got a Date With an Afterbeat; Night; The Magic of a Moonbeam (In Your Eye); Lyrics: A Soldier's Pray'r; Wake Up The Gypsy In Me; A Wonderful Night; Your Love; It's Because You're Beautiful.

MILLER, HERB ASCAP 1962
composer, author, teacher
b New York, NY, Jan 21, 15. Educ: Juilliard Sch Music, BS; Columbia Univ Teachers Col, MA. Taught in pub schs, Tex, 38-40, NJ, 41-42 & NY. US Army, WW II. *Songs:* Night; Love Isn't Just for the Young; Next Time the Band Plays a Waltz; Valerie's Theme; I Possess; Never Turn Back; What Will My Future Be?.

MILLER, IRVING ASCAP 1942
composer, conductor, arranger
b New York, NY, Sept 2, 07. Educ: Columbia Univ; studied music with Vladimir Drozdoff & Paul Yartin. Piano soloist with symph orchs; joined NBC staff, 28, became cond. To Hollywood, 44; comp, cond & arr, radio & TV films. *Songs:* The Bells of Normandy; Homeward Bound; Shadows on the Moon; Just Like That; My Little Prairie Flower; Soldier and the Soldierette; Desert Night; Heart to Heart; In a Blue Mood; Charlie Is My Darling; The Black Cat. *Instrumental Works:* Aquarelles (piano suite).

MILLER, JACQUES ASCAP 1963
composer, pianist, teacher
b Russia, Aug 4, 1900. *Instrumental Works:* Fantasie; Scherzo Miniature; Impromptu Elegante; Impromptu in E Flat.

MILLER, JAMES M ASCAP 1954
composer, arranger, pianist
b Pittsburgh, Pa, Aug 30, 07; d Pittsburgh, Nov 6, 70. Educ: Carnegie Tech, BA; Dusquesne Univ, MA. Concert pianist, 30-45. Music teacher, Pittsburgh Pub Schs. Organist & dir, Bethseda Church. *Songs:* I Wanna Be Ready; Didn't My Lord Deliver Daniel?; I Am Seeking for a City; You Gonna Reap; Daniel; So Fades the Lovely Blooming Flow'r; Please Don't Drive Me Away.

MILLER, JOSEPH (TAPS) ASCAP 1961
composer, author, singer
b Indianapolis, Ind, July 22, 15. Educ: St Rita High Sch. Worked with Isham Jones, Hal Kemp & Count Basie. Was given personal trumpet of Louis Armstrong. Originated dance, Suzie-Q. Toured Italy with Frank Sinatra. Appeared in musical comedies in New York & Eng. Toured with USO shows & with own band. *Songs:* Wham; Hot Dogs; Hold Tight; Stop the Red Light's On; You Lied to Me; Loan Me Two Til Tuesday; Sheridan Square.

MILLER, LEWIS MARTIN ASCAP 1970
composer, teacher
b Brooklyn, NY, Sept 4, 33. Educ: Queens Col, BA(music), 54, studied with Karol Rathaus; Manhattan Sch Music, MM(comp), 61, studied with Vittorio Giannini; North Tex State Univ, PhD(theory, comp), 65, studied with Samuel Adler. With Fourth Div Spec Services, Frankfurt, Ger, 55-56. Resident comp grant, Ford Found Young Comp Proj, Elkhart, Ind & El Paso, Tex, 61-63. Prof music, Ft Hays State Univ. Named Kans Comp of the Yr, 77; winner of the Nat Sch Orch Asn/Scherl & Roth orch comp award, 79. *Songs:* Music: Here on the Mountain; The Faucet. *Instrumental Works:* Just Desserts; Overture: King Henry V; Overture to Tartuffe.

MILLER, MARION C ASCAP 1968
composer, pianist
b St Louis, Mo, Sept 20, 28. Educ: St Joseph High Sch, St Louis, Mo; Kroeger Sch Music & Arts, St Louis, piano. Played with trio, travelling, local radio & TV, 10 yrs; piano bar performer, 54; composer, 60-; performer, Godfather's Restaurant, St Louis, Mo. Chief Collabr; Bob Ragan. *Songs:* Hey, Mrs Jones; Love Is a Living Thing; I'm Your Slave.

MILLER, MICHAEL KENNETH ASCAP 1975
composer
b The Hague, Holland, Sept 11, 55. Educ: Ygnacio Valley High Sch; Univ Calif Los Angeles, BA, 77; studied comp with Paul Chihara, 75-77. Winner song contest, Warner Bros "Ode to Billy Joe." Frank Sinatra Award. Composed song for "Airport '77." Arr music for Paul Anka, Mac Davis, Carol Burnett, Susanne Somers & Florence Henderson. Composed for "Barnaby Jones" series. Chief Collabrs: Mac Davis, Monica Riordan. *Songs:* Music: I Will Always Love You; Beyond Today. *Instrumental Works:* Mike's Tune (Broken Dreams).

MILLER, NED ASCAP 1924
composer, author
b London, Eng, Aug 2, 1899. Educ: Chicago pub schs. Mgr, Leo Feiss Music Co, Chicago, 17 yrs; songwriter. Chief Collabrs: Jule Styne, Chester Conn. *Songs:* Oh What a Gal Is My Gal; Lyrics: Why Should I Cry Over You; Crying for You; Don't Mind the Rain; Sunday; You Don't Like It, Not Much; Kiss and Make Up; What'll You Do; Too Busy; My Supressed Desire; My Victory (Was Conquering Your Heart); Little Joe; Winter Moon; You're Always There; Sicilian Tarantella.

MILLER, ROBERT WILEY ASCAP 1955
composer, arranger, radio executive
b Philadelphia, Pa, Mar 6, 25. Educ: Univ Calif, Los Angeles; studied with Joseph Schillinger, Jesse Crawford & Franklyn Marks. Arr, Xavier Cugat Orch, 45-48; scored & arr films for Samuel Goldwyn, Warner Bros & Wayne-Fellows,

48-58; mgr & chief engr, Radio Call Service, Ltd, Honolulu, 59-64; pres, Cambridge Broadcasting Corp (KWIP), Merced, Calif. *Songs:* Island in the Sky; Big Jim McLain; Man From Monterey.

MILLER, RON D (GRAYSON RHODES) ASCAP 1975
composer, author, singer
b San Antonio, Tex, Mar 24, 54. Worked in original band, Wakefield, 70-75; did road work with Narvel Felts, Tony Jo White, Elvis Wade & others; did studio work in Nashville, 74- Made jingles, demo work; worked with var producers. *Songs:* Raintree County.

MILLER, RON S ASCAP 1959
author
b Chicago, Ill, Jan 3, 36; d. Educ: Los Angeles State Col, BA. Writer of spec material for nightclubs, also singing group, The Wayfarers; bk critic, Los Angeles Times. Collabr: Hylton Socher. *Songs:* Low Bridge; The Good Times.

MILLER, RONALD ASCAP 1961
author
b Middletown, NY, Dec 7, 34. Educ: S J Tilden High Sch, Brooklyn, NY; City Col New York, Eng major. Associated with publ, Al Sears. Former saxophonist with Duke Ellington Orch. Chief Collabr: Lee Porter. *Songs:* Lyrics: The Good Times; He's a Lover; Not for All the Money; Handful of Memories; Girls Need Lovin' Care.

MILLER, SEYMOUR (SY) ASCAP 1950
composer, author, pianist
b New York, NY, Feb 9, 08; d Los Angeles, Calif, Aug 17, 71. Educ: Cornell Univ; NY Univ. Accompanist in vaudeville, 31; later wrote acts. Served in USA, WW II. Wrote spec material for nightclubs (also prod), radio & TV. Producer. Chief Collabr: Jill Jackson (wife). *Songs:* My Very Good Friend, the Sandman; I Like to Ride on My Bike; Listen to the Wind; Once Upon a Summertime; High Upon a Mountain; Ask Your Heart to Show the Way; Wonderful Child (God Made Our Hands); It's Up to You and Me; Music: Let There Be Peace on Earth (Let It Begin With Me) (used in Crusade for Peace prog; also in USIA film for Japan; Freedoms Found George Washington Honor Medal, 58; Brotherhood award; Ga's Bicentennial Song; City of Lakewood float theme, 1980 Tournament of Roses Parade).

MILLER, SHELLEY ROBBINS ASCAP 1972
composer, author, singer
b New York, NY, Sept 23, 47. Educ: Rosemary Hall & Dalton High Schs; Carnegie Inst Technol; NY Univ, BA(Eng), 69. Wrote song for "Free to Be You and Me" (album, bk & TV spec); also other album & musical material. Chief Collabr: Stephen Lawrence. *Songs:* Lyrics: When We Grow Up.

MILLER, SIDNEY ASCAP 1946
composer, author, actor
b Shenandoah, Pa, Oct 22, 16. Educ: LeConte Jr High Sch, Hollywood; Hollywood High Sch; Lawlors Prof Sch. Began as child singer & actor, WJZ radio, NY. Went to Calif & appeared in films, "Mayor of Hell", "Wild Boys of the Road", "Boystown", "Men of Boystown", "Strike Up the Band" & "Babes in Arms." Appeared in many movies & TV shows, incl "Lucille Ball Special." Performed with Donald O'Connor, "Colgate Comedy Hour," 9 yrs. Dir, TV shows. Chief Collabrs: Mickey Rooney, Inez James, Ray Gilbert, Bob Wells, Stanley Cowan, Donald O'Connor, Sid Kuller, Sammy Cahn, George Tibbles, Don Wolf, Bernie Wayne. *Songs:* Come to Baby Do; Lora Belle Lee; I Waited a Little Too Long; I Realize Now; What Do I Have to Do to Make You Love Me; There They Are; My Fickle Eye; Walk It Off.

MILLER, STEVEN H composer, author, singer
b Milwaukee, Wis. Educ: Univ Wis; Univ of Copenhagen. While in col, formed band, Ardells, which became Fabulous Knight Train, incl Boz Scaggs. Moved to San Francisco, 66, formed Steve Miller Band, with Capitol Records, 68- *Songs:* Living in the USA; The Joker; Fly Like an Eagle; Take the Money and Run; Rock 'n Me; Swingtown; Shu Ba Da Du Ma Ma Ma Ma. *Albums:* Children of the Future.

MILLER, SUNNIE PERLMAN ASCAP 1975
author, copywriter, lyricist
b New York, NY, June 30, 29. Educ: High Sch Music & Art; NY Univ; Acad Moderne, Boston, Mass. Promotion copy chief, Seventeen Mag, 50-64; free-lance copywriter; sales presentations, lyrics for musical radio commercials & top 40 music, fashion shows, brochures. Presented musical scores, "Owed to Radio" & "Pals." Chief Collabr: Elissa Schreiner. *Songs:* Lyrics: Alone on Christmas Eve; Home At Last. *Scores:* Off Bway: Once Upon a Vine (received ASCAP Award); Sneakers.

MILLER, WILBER H ASCAP 1963
author, producer
b Nampa, Idaho, Oct 29, 06. Saxophonist in dance bands; asst to head of music dept, Paramount Pictures, 3 yrs; head recording dept, Capitol Records, 45; A&R producer, 54. Chief Collabrs: Webley Edwards, Eddie Dunstedter. *Songs:* Island Paradise; Pi-Kaaki.

MILLET, KADISH (KAY)　　　　　　ASCAP 1959
composer, author, publisher
b Brooklyn, NY, Apr 21, 23. Educ: Brooklyn Col, BA; NY Univ, MA. WW II service; teacher sch syst, New York; publ, Blue Umbrella Music Publ Co, 70. Valley Forge Honor Cert for song folio. Cert of Recognition, Nat Conf Christians & Jews, 75; Valley Forge Teachers Medal, Freedoms Found, 75. *Songs:* What's More American; Valentino; Soldier of Fortune; Voulez-Vous Cha Cha; Hats Off to Brooklyn; Deep Are the Roots (of a Heart Born in Freedom); Always and Forever; Brooklyn College Victory March; The NYU Rouser; Football! USA!; My First Family Favorites (collection of children's songs); Music: Who Can Build a Mountain?.

MILLET, NANCY LYNNE　　　　　　ASCAP 1966
b Brooklyn, NY, July 12, 54. Educ: State Univ NY Stony Brook, BA, 75; Univ Cambridge, comparative law, 78; Univ Miami Sch Law, JD, 80. Chief Collabrs: Kadish Millet, Steven Millet. *Songs:* The Poky Puppy; Tiger on the Pampas; Deep; Adieu, Adios, Auf Wiedersehen; Lyrics: Who Can Build a Mountain?.

MILLET, STEVEN RICHARD　　　　　　ASCAP 1968
composer, author
b Brooklyn, NY, May 4, 56. Educ: Col of Insurance, BS(actuarial sci), 79. Chief Collabrs: Kadish Millet, Nancy Millet. *Songs:* The Poky Puppy; Deep; Adieu, Adios, Auf Wiedersehen; Tiger on the Pampas.

MILLIGAN, ROY HUGH　　　　　　ASCAP 1960
composer, author, arranger
b New Rochelle, NY, Sept 4, 22. Educ: Ernest S Williams Sch Music, prof degree, 43; NY Univ, BS, 47, MA, 49; special studies with Erik Leidzen. Asst dir, Lenoir High Sch Band, NC, 46-48; dir bands, Mineral Springs Schs, Winston-Salem, NC, 48-55; dir music educ, East Islip Schs, Long Island, NY, 55-; comp. Original Comp Awards: First prize, Kingsville, Tex, 47; first & second place awards, NC Composers Contest, 49. *Songs & Instrumental Works:* Dreams of Karen; March Sherwood; On the March; Sa-Ris; A Christmas Anthem.

MILLMAN, JACK M　　　　　　ASCAP 1958
composer, author, conductor
b Detroit, Mich, Nov 21, 30. Educ: Univ Calif, Los Angeles; studied music with Eric Zeisl, Shorty Rogers & Rafael Mendez. Trumpeter in orchs incl Glen Henry, Stan Kenton, Perez Prado; also Southern Calif Jr Symph. Mem, Sixth Army Band, San Francisco. Formed jazz quartet, quintet & sextet. Cond band on "Strictly Informal," TV, Los Angeles, 59-60. Chief Collabs: Frank Erickson, Spud Murphy, Shorty Rogers, Johnny Mandel. *Songs & Instrumental Works:* Pink Lady; Tom and Jerry; Thinking of Russ; Groove Juice; Too Much; Ballade for Jeanie; Butterfingers; Four More.

MILLROSE, VICTOR D　　　　　　ASCAP 1965
composer, author, record producer
b Boston, Mass, May 25, 35. Educ: Boston Univ Sch Pub Rels, BA(communications arts), 57. Writer for Elvis Presley, Louis Armstrong, Jack Jones, Dusty Springfield & Gary Puckett. Producer for most maj labels. Free-lance writer & record producer. Chief Collabrs: Tony Bruno, Alan Bernstein. *Songs:* Last Exit to Brooklyn; This Girl Is a Woman Now; I'll Try Anything to Get You; Smokey Mountain Boy; Startin' Tonight; Two of a Kind. *Scores:* A Day in the Life of a Dinosaur (children's musical); Film/TV: The Plastic Dome of Norma Jean. *Albums:* On the Seventh Day; Rocky and ChyAnne.

MILLS, ALVIN MARVIN　　　　　　ASCAP 1972
composer, author, conductor
b Chicago, Ill, Feb 2, 22. Educ: Univ Calif Los Angeles, BA, hons in music, 48; Mt St Mary's Col, MA, 60; studied cond with Pierre Monteux, L'Ecole Monteux, Hancock, Maine; Acad of the West Scholarship. Founded Lompoc Symph, Calif, 49; founder & dir, Brentwood-Westwood Symph; cond, Los Angeles Doctor's Symph, 62-64. Initiated young artists concerts, 72. Prepared & cond all ASCAP composers concerts with the Brentwood-Westwood Symph Orch, 77-80. Chief Collab: Josefa P Mills. *Songs:* Music: Canciones Folkloricas Infantiles de Espana; Canciones de Navidad; Diary for May. *Instrumental Works:* Elegy for Strings; Spanish Rhapsody; An American in Spain.

MILLS, CARLEY　　　　　　ASCAP 1941
composer, author
b Deal, NJ, Sept 9, 1897; d New York, NY, Oct 20, 62. Author "A Nearness of Evil." *Songs:* Why Pretend?; On the Outside Lookin' In; No Foolin'; Poor Moon; I Take to You; The Things You Said Last Night; Time and Time Again.

MILLS, DONN LAURENCE　　　　　　ASCAP 1968
composer, conductor, educator
b Indianapolis, Ind, Dec 7, 32. Educ: Northwestern Univ, BMus; Univ Rochester Eastman Sch Music, MMus; cond study with Pierre Monteux, Leopold Stokowski, Sixten Ehrling & Max Rudolf. Cond, Charleston Symph, SC. Music dir, Royal Winnipeg Ballet of Can. Dir orchs, Univ Okla. Am educ dir, Yamaha Music Found. Guest cond, US & abroad. Author bks & mag articles. *Songs:* Cat Tales. *Instrumental Works:* Overture Giocoso; Kinetics; Perspectives; Far Horizon; Suite for Strings; Music For a Festive Occasion;

Reflections; Canonic Designs; Nautical Overture; Toccata for Piano. *Songs & Instrumental Works:* Over 100 educational songs and piano pieces. *Scores:* Opera/Ballet: Unwritten Letters, Unspoken Words.

MILLS, FREDERICK ALLEN (KERRY)　　　　　　ASCAP 1932
composer, author, violinist
b Philadelphia, Pa, Feb 1, 1869; d Hawthorn, Calif, Dec 5, 48. Educ: Pvt violin study. Prof music & head, Violin Dept, Univ Mich Sch Music, 1892-93; also had own studio, Ann Arbor; music publ. *Songs:* Rastus on Parade; At a Georgia Camp Meeting; Meet Me in St Louis, Louis; Red Wing; Whistling Rufus; When the Bees Are in the Hive.

MILLS, IRVING　　　　　　ASCAP 1920
composer, author, singer
b New York, NY, Jan 16, 1894. Educ: Pub schs. Began as song plugger, 10. Formed Mills Music Inc with bro, Jack, 19. Started to build own orch combinations & recorded for many labels, 20. Developed Duke Ellington Band, Cab Calloway & his Orch, Mills Blue Ribbon Band, Irving Mills & his Hotsy Totsy Gang & others. Organized first All Girl Jazz Orch. Co-producer, "Stormy Weather." Pres, Cotton Club Productions, New York, Am Acad Music & Mills Artists. *Songs:* Lyrics: Caravan; When My Sugar Walks Down the Street; Sophisticated Lady; In My Solitude; Mood Indigo; I Let a Song Go Out of My Heart; Minnie the Moocher; Lovesick Blues; Moon Glow; It Don't Mean a Thing (If it Ain't Got That Swing); Blues in My Heart; If Dreams Come True; Hard Boiled Rose; Prelude to a Kiss.

MILLS, JACKIE
drummer
b Brooklyn, NY, 1922. With Harry James, 40's & 50's & Harry Edison Combo, 60's; played with Charlie Barnet, Tommy Dorsey, Boyd Roeburn, JATP, Dizzy Gillespie, Billie Holiday, Ella Fitzgerald & others; worked in & wrote sketches for motion pictures while working with Jack Cole & Herman Pan. Record co executive.

MILLS, JOSEFA PRIMO (PEPA)　　　　　　ASCAP 1976
author, teacher, graphic artist
b Valencia, Spain, Mar 10, 38. Educ: Nat Inst San Vicente Ferrer High Sch; Normal Sch Magisterio, BA, 54; draftsman dipl, 70; standard designated teaching credential, Span, 78; studied theory, voice & piano with Amparo Serrano, 5 yrs. Wrote bilingual songs; bk illustrator; graphic artist; Span teacher; painter & publ. Author: "Bilingual ABC Plus a Fundamental Reading System for the Spanish Language" (with cassette); "Bilingual ABC Copy Book"; "Arte, Culture y Trajes Tipicos de Mexico-Art, Culture and Typical Dress of Mexico." Chief Collabrs: Alvin Mills, Josef Marais. *Songs:* Canciones Folkloricas Infantiles de Espana-Children's Folk Songs From Spain (bk, with cassette); Canciones de Navidad-Christmas Songs (bk).

MILLS, KENNETH THOMAS　　　　　　ASCAP 1971
composer, author, music teacher
b Eldorado, Ill, May 3, 28. Educ: Southern Ill Univ, BM, 54, MME, 56. Concert violinist & violist, nightclubs & TV; violinist & violist, symph orchs; jazz violinist. *Songs:* Giddy Up Reindeer; Christmas in Nashville.

MILLS, PAUL (LEE RICKS)　　　　　　ASCAP 1946
composer, author
b Philadelphia, Pa, Jan 9, 21. Educ: Rutgers Prep Sch; Riverside Mil Acad, grad; Abraham Lincoln High Sch, Brooklyn. Radio combat correspondent, USMC, WW II. West Coast prof mgr, Mills Music Inc, 45-65. Pres, Solo Music Inc, 66- Chief Collabrs: Slim Gaillard, Josef Myrow, Louis Castellucci, Freddy Morgan. *Songs:* Cement Mixer (Putti-Putti); Down By the Station; Yep Roc Heresi; Hawaii (I Hear You Calling); Lyrics: Ode to a Marine; Gioia Mia.

MILLS, STANLEY　　　　　　ASCAP 1968
producer author, publisher
b New York, NY, Feb 18, 31. Educ: Woodmere Acad; Swarthmore Col. General prof mgr, Mills Publ Co, 63-65, E D Marks, 65-67. Started own bus, 67. Mem, East Coast Publ Adv Comn, bd of dirs, Nat Music Publ Asn & bd of review, ASCAP. *Songs:* Reaching for a Star; Sweet September.

MILLS, VERLYE　　　　　　ASCAP 1961
composer, harpist
b St John, Kans, Dec 16, 16. Educ: Paris Cons, scholarship; Curtis Inst. Harp soloist, Chicago Symph; first harpist, Cleveland Symph. Appeared in films, TV & theatres.

MILLS, WILLIAM R　　　　　　ASCAP 1943
composer, conductor, pianist
b Flint, Mich, Sept 6, 1894; d Glendale, Calif, Oct 19, 71. Educ: Univ Syracuse; Univ Mich. Wrote col musicals. Bandmaster, 31st Field Artillery, WW I. Arr for Isham Jones Orch; formed own orch, Chicago, 22. Organized chain of orchs playing throughout southern Mich. On radio, WFDF, Flint, 25. To Chicago, 27; arr & asst cond, Frank Westphal Orch; pianist, Balaban & Katz. Music supervr, CBS, Chicago, 33. Gen music dir for Western Div, 34. To NBC, 38, music dir, "Fibber McGee & Molly," 38-55. *Songs & Instrumental Works:* Wing Wing to Wing; We Two; One Magic Hour; I Sang a Song; I'm in Love With the Sound

Effects Man; 99 Years Is a Long Time; Fidoodlin; Mister Rainbow; California Sketches (organ suite); Flint Centennial March; American Heroes (children's songs).

MILNER, DANIEL PAUL   ASCAP 1975
composer, arranger, producer
b San Diego, Calif, June 17, 52. Educ: Studied bass with Carol Kaye, 1 yr. Played in nightclubs; staff songwriter for Warner Bros Records; then recording artist, 20th Century Records, 3 1/2 yrs; became staff recording engr, Studio West; then recording engr & producer for rock group, Stallion. Presently producer & writer for var acts. Musician & singer. *Songs:* It Keeps Breaking My Heart; Something's Wrong; You; It's Such a Lonely Feeling. *Scores:* TV: Ace Diamond Private Eye (TV theme).

MILO, PHIL
See Puco, Philip Milo

MILSAP, RONALD LEE   ASCAP 1975
singer, recording artist
b Robinsville, NC. Educ: Young-Harris Jr Col, AA, 64. Country music singer; recordings for RCA Records. Mem, Country Music Asn (Male Vocalist of Yr, 74, 76, 77; Album of Yr, 75, 77, 78; Entertainer of Yr, 77), Nat Acad Recording Arts & Sci (Country Male Vocalist of Yr, 74, 76).

MILTON, JAY   ASCAP 1941
composer, author, pianist
b Auburn, NY, Feb 15, 10. Educ: Syracuse Univ, BS. Pianist in dance bands & film studio orchs, Hollywood. USAAF, WW II. *Songs:* Shame on You; Angry River; Laughing Up My Sleeve; Downstream; Gardenia; Little Lad.

MIMAROGLU, ILHAN   ASCAP 1973
composer
b Istanbul, Turkey, Mar 11, 26. Educ: Columbia Univ, MA, 66; studied comp incl electronic music with Vladimir Ussachevsky, Edgard Varese & Stefan Wolpe. Rockefeller fel, 55; Guggenheim fel, 71. Comp affiliate, Columbia-Princeton Electronic Music Ctr, 63-; producer, Atlantic Records, 69-; founder-dir, Finnadar Records, 72- *Songs & Instrumental Works:* Pieces Sentimentales; Le Tombeau d'Edgar Poe; Intermezzo; Bowery Bum; Preludes for Magnetic Tape; Music Plus One; Sing Me a Song of Songmy; Music for Dubuffet's Coucou Bazar; Tract; To Kill a Sunrise; Rosa; Sleepsong for Sleepers.

MINELLI, CHARLES   ASCAP 1969
composer, conductor
b Virginia, Minn, Sept 4, 14. Educ: Univ Minn, BS(educ), 40, MEd, 48; Cincinnati Cons Music, spec study with Fausto Cleva. Prof music, Ohio Univ, Athens, dir bands & cond, Fine Arts Theatre Orch, 25 yrs. Now cond, Lakeland Community Band, Fla. *Instrumental Works:* Rhumbango; Ballad for Winds; Marche Regalis; Sunset Glow; Neopolitan Love Song.

MINEO, ANTOINETTE (TONI)   ASCAP 1957
composer, author, choir director
b Tacoma, Wash, Nov 6, 26. Educ: Studies with Carl Svedberg, Eugene Lindon, Lennard Anderson & Prof Lento. Choir dir, 30 yrs; musical dir, Cath Church, 5 yrs. Music publ with husband, Mineo & Mineo Music Publ Co; pianist & composer with husbands orch; written over 400 original songs with husband. Co-founder music sch & music teacher, 25 yrs. Chief Collabrs: Attiolio Mineo (husband), Pat Noto, Lou Monte. *Songs & Instrumental Works:* Rhapsody 21; Century 21; six masses, SATB & full orch; original music & official theme, Seattle World's Fair, 61 & 62.

MINEO, ATTILIO (ART)   ASCAP 1958
composer, author, singer
b Brooklyn, NY, Aug 28, 18. Educ: Studied with Simon Condosta, William Colburn & Liotti; studied comp, theory, harmony & arr. Band leader, 28 yrs. Played with Buddy Raye, Alan Fielding, Anthony Trini, Chauncey Gray, Charlie Barnett & Gene Darrow. Piano & bass arr for dance & stage bands. Co-founder of govt sch, Inst Modern Music. Wrote plays: "One Man's Life"; "Wild Is My Love"; "Baby Mine"; "Murder for Passion." Chief Collabrs: Antoinette Mineo (wife), Pat Noto, Lou Monte. *Songs & Instrumental Works:* Solo Per Te; Non Sai; 5 symphonies; 4 string quartets. *Scores:* Plays: Little Mary's Little Lambs; TV background: Portrait of a Great American.

MINEO, SAMUEL H   ASCAP 1942
composer, author, pianist
b Buffalo, NY, Jan 23, 09. Educ: Sherwood Music Cons, 24; studied with John Ingrahm. Radio shows in New York. Orch mem, V Lopez, Larry Clinton & Paul Whiteman, 30's. Staff pianist & asst cond, NBC. Assoc with Ray Sinatra, New York & Greek Theatre, CBS, Los Angeles. Personal cond for Jane Froman, Mae West & Dorothy Lamour. *Songs & Instrumental Works:* Evangeline (tone poem); Trust in the Lord (fest anthem); California Rhapsody (piano concerto); Tarantella (folk dance).

MINER, LAWRENCE A (LARRY THOMAS)   ASCAP 1971
composer, author, publisher
b Galveston, Tex, May 23, 43. Educ: Polytech High Sch, San Francisco, grad, 61; Los Angeles City Col, 2 yrs; studied music theory & harmony with David Tiplitz. Played piano at age 10, switched to trumpet, at age 13, to all perc, age 15. Played with Vegas show band, Brooks & Co, Kodiak, Alaska, 66; teacher perc, 5 yrs. Chief Collabrs: Johnny Guitar Watson, Cat Anderson, Jerry Hooks. *Songs:* Muhammad Ali; Brown Butter; Who Is That; Do You Wanna Be My Girl; Road Runner 076; The Theme to No More Joy. *Albums:* Brown Butter Album.

MINKOFF, FRANCES MYRA   ASCAP 1962
author
b New York, NY, Feb 5, 15. Educ: Brooklyn Col, studied with John Latouche, BA. Teacher drama technique, Lafayette & Madison High Schs, Brooklyn. Adaptations of Yiddish, Hebrew & French songs publ & recorded. Writer additional lyrics to folk songs for several artists. Author & writer lyrics radio show, "Once Upon King Solomon's Nose." Wrote lyrics for musical, "Out on a Limb" (Thurber). Chief Collabrs: Fred Hellerman, Jay Gorney. *Songs:* Lyrics: Come Away, Melinda; The Honey-Wind Blows; Quiet Room.

MINOGUE, DENNIS MICHAEL (TERRY CASHMAN)   ASCAP 1968
composer, author, singer
b New York, NY, July 5, 41. Educ: Rice High Sch, 55-59; City Col New York, BA, 64; studied piano with Norman Gold, 77-79. Recording artist with The Chevrons for Brent Record Inc, 58-60; prof mgr, ABC Music, 66-68; recording artist for Cashman & West, 67-76; record producer, 66- Chief Collabrs: Gene Pistilli, Tommy West. *Songs:* Sunday Will Never Be the Same; But for Love; Medicine Man; A Song That Never Comes; Sweet City Song; All Around the Town; Hello Jack; A Friend Is Dying; Only a Moment Ago; She'd Rather Have the Rain; Sausalito; Oscuerita; Sandy When She's Sleeping; Baby Baby I Love You; King of Rock'n'Roll; There's Nothing Else on My Mind; I'll Never Get Enough of Your Love; Songman; Son of a Lovin Man.

MINUCCI, ULPIO
composer, pianist
b Campobello, Di Mazzara, Italy, June 29, 21. Educ: Studied comp with Ennio Porrino. Came to US as newsman, 50, then switched to music in New York. Dir, April Black-Wood Music Publishing Div, CBS, Inc. A&R person motion picture TV spec projs. Chief Collabrs: John LaTouche, Roy Jordan, Tony Velona. *Songs & Instrumental Works:* My Love's a Gentle Man; The Deep Blue Sea; Celicia; I'll Never Know; Forgive Me. *Scores:* TV: Saga of Western Man (which incl, Leonardo DiVinci, Venice a City in Danger & Robert Scott and the Race for the South Pole); Film: Love I Think.

MIRIKITANI, ALAN MASAO (AL TANI)   ASCAP 1977
composer, author, singer
b Lynwood, Calif, Mar 1, 55. Educ: Warren High Sch, Downey, Calif, 73. Started saxophone lessons at 8 yrs; self-taught on guitar at 13 yrs; formed band at 15 yrs; began playing nightclubs at 17 yrs; some writing and recording; performer, nightclubs; group name, Liquid Blue. *Songs:* Ain't That What You Want.

MIRKIN, BARRY W   ASCAP 1957
author
b Boston, Mass, Jan 31, 16. Educ: Univ Ala. Production asst, MC, Metrop Theatre, Boston, 53, Strand Theatre, NY, 38; mgr traveling production, MCA, later band & personal mgr. WW II serv. Formed finance co in Los Angeles. *Songs:* Majolie; Give Me a Sign; Can't Wait.

MIRON, ISSACHAR (STEFAN MICHROVSKY)   ASCAP 1966
composer, author, conductor
b Kutno, Poland, July 5, 20. Educ: Liceum Col, Poland, BA, 36; Univ Cons Music, Poland, MA, 39. Officer-in-chief humanities, arts, music & entertainment, Israel Def Forces, 40-44. Nat deputy dir music, Israel Ministry Educ & Culture, 50-53. Music ed, Israel Ministry Educ & Culture 10th Anniversary Vol of Songs, 50. Trustee, Am for Music Libr in Israel, Chicago, 51-62. Sr vpres, ACUM Societe D'Auteurs, Compositeurs et Editeurs de Musique En Israel, 51-60. First vchmn, Israel Composers League, 53-59. Dir gen com for cultural music progs, Am Israel Cultural Found, Israel, 53-61. Chief music ed Israel monthly magazine, Zemiroth, 53-60. Chmn, Israel Composers League Publ, Inc, 51-60. Creator, music educ progs, 53-62. Came to US, 61, naturalized, 68. Vchmn, Am-Israel Music Alliance, New York, 61-65. Assoc prof & chmn music fac, Jewish Teachers Sem & Peoples Univ, 63-73. Exec vpres, Int Cultural Ctrs for Youth, New York, 65-67 & Star Records Enterprises, Inc, 67-68. Nat dir, Creative & Educ Progs, United Jewish Appeal, New York, 73- Awards: Laureate of Engel Prize, Israel, 59; Kavod Award, Cantor's Assembly of Am for Distinguished Contribution to Jewish Liturgical Music, 64; Deems Taylor Award, 70. Chief Collabrs: Yehiel Haggiz, Mitchell Parish, Joe Darion, Lan O'Kun, Natan Alterman, Hayim Hefer, Dan Almagor, Yehiel Mohar, Avraham Soltes, Tsipora Miron. *Songs & Instrumental Works:* Golden Gates of Joy (oratorio); I Remember (six poems for cello, piano); Psalms of Israel (oratorio for orch, choir, tenor); Prothalamia Hebraica; Proverbs Canticles (oratorio for choir, orch); Rock 'n Rest (choir, orch); Proclaim Liberty; Voices of the Household of Abraham (oratorio); High Holidays Service; Juvenilia

Hebraica (cantata); Passacaglia for Moderns (piano); Seven Syncopated Preludes (piano, orch); Triptych for a Klezmer Virtuoso and Orchestra; Profiles of Soul (oboe, piano, orch); Klezmer Reflections (flute, orch or piano); 101 Songs of the Bible; Tzena Tzena Tzena; Whistlin' in the Sunshine; Magic Horn; Singing Marathon; With the Echo of a Dream; No Good Jim; It May Seem Unreal Bizarre; Box of Colors; Stormy Heart; Dawn Before the Day; Southern Happening; Dreaming in the Moonlight; I'm Dying; Ufi Ruach; Hanerot Halalu; Barhu; Kol Chala; Shir Eres Adoshem Oz; Mayim Rabim; Ahavti Ki Yishma; Ki Mitzion; Ze Hayom; Aguda Achat; Shir Shabat; Lecha Dodi; Halleluya; Maoz Tzur; Yigdal; Adon Olam; Kaddish; Kol Nidrei; Ura Dor; Amen; Adonay Malach; Hodu Ladonay; The Night Shall As the Day; We Are One; Partners in Freedom; Klezmer; A Song of Jewish Soul; Music for Film-Documentaries: From Destruction to Redemption; My Brother's Keeper; Silent No More; Jewish Dimensions. *Scores:* Ballet: Wings of Illusion; The Art of Klezmer; Opera: Song of Esther; Purimspiel Opera.

MIRON, TSIPORA (THELMA MOORE) — ASCAP 1965
composer, author, pianist

b Olevsk, Ukraine, Russia, July 27, 23. Educ: N Balfour Col, Tel-Aviv, dipl, 39; Israel Cons Acad Music, BA, 44. Pianist, organist, music publ exec, comp & author; mem piano fac, Israel Cons Acad Music; music ed, Mills Music Inc; pres, Star Record Co, incl McRon Co & Main Floor Music Co; mem, Am Fedn Musicians. Translated from Hebrew & contrib lyrics, Issachar Miron's oratorios & choral works incl, "Hallelujah", "Seven Blessings", "This Is the Day", "And None Shall Make Them Afraid" & "Proverbs Canticles." Teacher. *Songs:* Lyrics: Psalms of Israel (oratorio); Proverb Canticles (oratorio); Juvenilia Herbraica (cantata for Pilgrimage Fests). *Instrumental Works:* Meditation and Dance (clarinet, instrumental ensemble); Lonely Hill (trumpet, instrumental ensemble); Mirages (piano etudes); Oh Riddle (piano).

MISSAL, JOSHUA M — ASCAP 1964
composer

b Hartford, Conn, Apr 12, 15. Educ: Univ Rochester Eastman Sch Music, BM, 37, MM, 38; studied with Roy Harris, 47. Prof music, Wichita State Univ, Univ NMex, Southern Miss Univ, Hartford Cons, Tunxis Community Col & Ariz State Univ. Over 25 yrs prof symph exp, incl principal violist with Wichita Symph, violist with Rochester Philh, Hartford Symph & others. Violist with Olympia String Quartet, Wichita String Quartet & others. Conductor, Southern Miss Symph & Albuquerque Philh; assoc conductor, Wichita Symph, conductor, Scottsdale Col/Community Orch & guest conductor with symph orchs thruout US. Comn by Wichita Pub Schs to write Bi-Centennial Cantata for orch, 2 choirs, 4 bands & narrator; Suite for band by South Mountain High Sch, 79; Cantata "City of the Sun" for chorus, orch & soloists by Wichita State Univ. *Instrumental Works:* Overture (symphonic band); Rondo Caprice (six flutes or flute choir); Jericho Suite (brass choir); Hoedown (perc ens); Three Miniatures (perc ens); Three Miniatures (string orch); Barbaric Dance (perc ens); Gloria in Excelsis Deo (two SATB choruses & brass choir); Three American Portraits (symph orch); In Memoriam (symph orch & soprano); Two Nocturnes (perc ens).

MISSISSIPPI
See Bevel, Charles William

MITCHELL, DON
See Gilkinson, Donald Mitchel

MITCHELL, LOUIS D — ASCAP 1977
composer, author, educator

b New York, NY, June 30, 28. Educ: New York Inst of Educ for Blind High Sch, studied comp, piano & musicol; Fordham Univ, BA, MFA; NY Univ, MA, PhD; Studied with Bassett W Hough, R Strauss & Ernst Von Dohnanyi. Comp words & music for 4 musicals, Fordham Univ, also score & music for 3 musicals. Prof, Univ Scranton. *Songs:* Star of the Morning; Music: Two Songs for Ballad of a Winter Soldier.

MITCHELL, LYNDOL COLEMAN
composer, teacher

b Itta Bena, Miss, Feb 16, 23; d Rochester, NY, Feb 19, 63. Educ: Western Kentucky State Univ, BS(music), 48; Eastman Sch Music, MM(comp, theory), 50, MDA, 61, comp with Howard Hanson. Teacher/comp, Eastman Sch Music, 51-63. Choir dir, Christ Church, Rochester. *Instrumental Works:* Kentucky Mountain Portraits; Concerto Grosso for Three Trombones; Folk Suite; Railroad Suite (band, orch); River Suite (band, orch). *Songs & Instrumental Works:* St Mark's Easter Gospel (SATB, TTBB, trumpet); Arr: When Johnny Comes Marching Home (chorus, orch); Battle Hymn of the Republic (chorus, orch).

MITCHELL, RAYMOND EARLE — ASCAP 1943
composer, pianist

b Milwaukee, Wis, May 31, 1895; d. Educ: Milwaukee State Normal Sch; studied music with Jacob Moerschel & Carl Eppert; Marquette Univ Music (scholarship). Music critic & ed, Hollywood Citizen-News, Musical Courier, 29-35. Mem, Nat Fedn Music Clubs. *Songs:* I Must Go Down to the Sea; Lost in London Town; Love Is the Wind; Phyllis; Sing No Sad Songs for Me; The Tabernacle of God Is With Me. *Songs & Instrumental Works:* Dusty Road; Pastorale Suite; Childhood Scenes; Danae's Garden.

MITCHELL, RODGER MALCOLM — ASCAP 1977
composer, author

b Chicago, Ill, Mar 25, 35. Educ: Univ Ill, MBA. Painter, poet & advert exec. Author of "A Guide to Creativity." Chief Collabr: Joyce Bresnahan. *Songs:* Breaking Free; Long Time Between; Cool Shade on a Hot Summer Day; Aw, to Hell With Love; Ever Since You Said Goodby; Love Is Only; It's Not My Way; Love Is Shinin' in My Eyes; One By One.

MITCHELL, ROSCOE EDWARD
musician, composer

b Chicago, Ill, Aug 3, 40. Educ: Wilson Jr Col, 63. Mem, Englewood High Sch Dance Band, Chicago, 54-58; served with band, USA, 58-61; principle, Roscoe Mitchell Sextet, 65-66, Quartet, 66-67, Art Ensemble, 67-69; multi-instrumentalist & comp, Art Solo & Ensemble, Chicago, 69-; teacher in field & artist in residence, Univ Ill, 77. With Creative Music Studio, Woodstock, NY, 79. NEA comp/performer grantee, 73, comp fel grantee, 75. Mem, Asn Advancement Creative Musicians, Creative Arts Collective (founder, pres). *Albums:* People in Sorrow (French Prix de l'Academie du Jazz, 70); NONAAM (Downbeat Mag Record of Yr Award, 78).

MITCHELL, SIDNEY D — ASCAP 1919
author

b Baltimore, Md, June 15, 1888; d Los Angeles, Calif, Feb 25, 42. Educ: Baltimore Polytech Inst; Cornell Univ. Newspaper reporter, Baltimore, 5 yrs. Exec, NY publ co. Staff writer, Hollywood film studios. Wrote songs for films incl, "Captain January" & "Trail of the Lonesome Pine." Chief Collabrs: Con Conrad, Lew Pollack, George Meyer, Maceo Pinkard, Louis Alter, Archie Gottler, Sam Stept, Raymond Scott. *Songs:* Would You Rather Be a Colonel With an Eagle on Your Shoulder or a Private With a Chicken on Your Knee?; Big City Blues; Walking With Susie; All My Life; Weep No More My Mammy; Early Bird; Moonshine Over Kentucky; At the Codfish Ball; One in a Million; Alone With You; A Melody From the Sky; Twilight on the Trail; The Toy Trumpet; You Turned the Tables on Me; It's Love I'm After; Sugar. *Scores:* Film: Pigskin Parade; One in a Million; Life Begins in College; Rebecca of Sunnybrook Farm.

MITCHELL, WALLACE ORLANDO — ASCAP 1973
composer, author, singer

b New York, NY, Mar 14, 51. Educ: Los Angeles City Col; East Los Angeles City Col; Loopek Music Acad, 59-63. Staff writer, Jobet, 70-71, Joan Jinnie, 72-76 & H D H, 76-78. Mem, 100 Proof Aged in Soul, 76-78 & Expertise, 79-80. Chief Collabrs: Edward & Brian Holland, Richard Davis, Ron & Arnold Patton. *Songs:* We Should Be Lovers; Fun Is Just a Dance Away; The Best Love; Where Did Our Love Go; What Do You Do; Music: Last Night Made My Day; Number One With a Heartache; You and Me Together; One Night Stand; Lyrics: Woman's Time; Darling Judy; Straight From the Gate.

MITCHELL, WILLIAM L — ASCAP 1964
composer

b Birmingham, Ala, Feb 18, 44. Educ: Haren High Sch, grad, 62; Juilliard Sch Music. Med Corps, USAAF; comp & show dir, Concord, Mass; playhouse actor in "Taste of Honey" & "The Last Man." *Songs:* Oh Lord I Want to Grow; Let This Season Last Through the Year; Happiness; Music: Now Is the Time. *Instrumental Works:* Crystal (My True Crystal).

MITCHELL, WIRT MCCLINTIC — ASCAP 1961
author

b Los Angeles, Calif, May 24, 14. Educ: Central Col, BA; Columbia Univ, MS. Writer for newspapers & advert agencies, 25 yrs. Dir, VI Govt News Bur; also writer & creative consult. Chief Collabrs: John Cacavas, Charles Casey. *Songs:* Hush Puppy Lullaby; Taps for Two Brothers; Gone Is My Love; Shipwreck Jackson; The Endless Encore; Love Me, Love My Dog; Hymn to the Free World.

MITCHUM, JOHN NEWMAN — ASCAP 1968
composer, author, singer

b Bridgeport, Conn, Sept 6, 19. Educ: Long Beach City Col; Herbert Wall Sch Music; Univ Calif, Los Angeles, summer sessions. Singer & cond, state fairs, rodeo circuits & spec shows for police circus, St Louis Shriners, Harrisburg. Radio work, Hollywood & Dallas, Tex; motion pictures & TV, 47- Nightclub entertainer & recording artist, RCA. Chief Collabrs: Howard Barnes, Billy Liebert. *Songs:* All the Pretty Horses; Ode to a Mule; Mis Raices Estan Aqui; Story of Taps; Story of Pledge of Allegiance; Why Are You Marching Son?; An American Boy Grows Up; The Good Things; The Hyphen; The People; also title narration for John Wayne's, "America, Why I Love Her."

MITCHUM, ROBERT — ASCAP 1958
composer, author, actor

b Bridgeport, Conn, Aug 6, 17. Actor in films inc: "Bataan"; "The Story of GI Joe"; "Track of the Cat"; "The Night of the Hunter"; "Not As a Stranger"; "Heaven Knows Mr Allison"; "The Sundowners"; "The Longest Day"; "Two for the Seesaw." *Instrumental Works:* Ballad of Thunder Road; The Whippoorwill.

MITRALE, MARI
See Lussi, Marie

MIZE, JOANN ALBERTA ASCAP 1974
author, singer
b Torrance, Calif, Apr 7, 30. Educ: Washington High Sch, Fullerton Jr Col; studied with Inez Montfort Pisani. Prof singer, 20 yrs. Appearances on stage, "Bye, Bye, Birdie" (New York); "The King and I"; "Fiddler on the Roof"; "The Sound of Music"; groups, Ray Conniff, Anita Kerr, Roger Wagner & Nat King Cole; TV, "The Carol Burnett Show"; "The Mary Tyler Moore Show"; "The Mac Davis Special"; "Bell Telephone Hour"; commercials, Toyota; Chevrolet; Hoffy Hot Dogs; Treesweet; Bon Ami; Sea World; operas, "Madame Butterfly"; "Magic Flute"; "Bartered Bride"; "Sour Angelica"; plays, "Bus Stop"; "Silver Whistle"; "Staring Match"; "Cat and Canary." Chief Collabrs: Ron Harris, Fred Bock, Barbara Young. *Songs:* Lyrics: Put Jesus First in Your Life; My Saviors Love; Jesus Was There All the Time.

MIZELL, ALPHONSO JAMES ASCAP 1971
composer, record producer
b New York, NY, Jan 15, 43. Educ: Dwight Morrow High Sch, Englewood, NJ; Howard Univ, BMusEd. Producer & writer, Motown Record Corp. Produced & wrote for The Jackson Five; later producer for Donald Byrd, Bobby Humphries, LTD & A Taste of Honey. Chief Collabrs: Larry Mizell, Freddie Perren, Berry Gordy. *Songs:* I Want You Back; ABC; The Love You Save; Places and Spaces. *Scores:* Film: Hell Up in Harlem.

MIZELL, LAURENCE CLINTON ASCAP 1973
composer, producer
b New York, NY, Feb 17, 44. Educ: Dwight Morrow High Sch, Englewood, NJ; Howard Univ, BSEE, 67; NY Univ, MSEE, 71. Produced & composed LP's. Worked with Blackbyrds, Gary Bartz, Johnny Hammond Smith & Rance Allen. Chief Collabr: Fonce Mizell. *Songs:* Harlism River Drive; You're in Good Hands; Love to the World. *Instrumental Works:* Blackbyrd; Flight Time.

MIZZY, VIC ASCAP 1939
composer, author
b Brooklyn, NY, Jan 9, 22. Educ: Alexander Hamilton High Sch; NY Univ. Served in USN. Writer, variety shows & teacher of Schillinger System, NY Univ. Started songwriting after winning Fred Allen Contest. Arr, leading orchs & singers. Chief Collabrs: Irving Taylor, Mann Curtis. *Songs:* In the Middle, In the Middle, In the Middle; Music: The Whole World is Singing My Song; Three Little Sisters; With a Hey and a Hi and a Ho Ho Ho; Choon Gum; Didja Ever; The Jones Boy; I Had a Little Talk With the Lord; There's a Faraway Look in Your Eyes; My Dreams Are Getting Better All the Time; Take It Easy. *Scores:* TV shows: The Shirley Temple Show; The Addams Family; Kentucky Jones; Green Acres; Don Rickles Show; Richard Boone Series; Quincy; Temperature Rising; Movies of the Week for NBC, ABC, CBS; Films: Easy to Love; A Very Special Favor; The Night Walker; The Reluctant Astronaut; The Ghost and Mr Chicken; The Shakiest Gun in the West; How to Frame a Figg; Did You Hear the One About the Traveling Saleslady; Don't Make Waves; The Busybody; The Spirit Is Willing; The Love God; The Perils of Pauline; The Caper of the Golden Bull.

MOAN, PATTY
See Schauer, Patricia Kay

MOBELL, SIDNEY F ASCAP 1956
composer, author, singer
b Denver, Colo, Apr 10, 26. Educ: Univ Denver. Service, USN. Sales rep for mfg co, Calif. *Songs:* No One to Blame But You; The Myth of Joe Smith (Adlai Stevenson campaign song, 56); At'sa Nice-a; Never Do; Rock-in Chair Roll.

MOBLEY, SYLVIA MAE ASCAP 1975
composer, singer
b Marshall, Ark, Apr 28, 41. Singer & writer; worked several TV shows thruout the mid-south. *Songs & Instrumental Works:* I Give in, Till I Give Out; Let Me In; If I Only Knew; Silent Love.

MOCK, LEWIS E ASCAP 1978
composer
b Dodge City, Kans, Dec 7, 54. Educ: Univ Kans. Professional musician, actor & singer, 15 yrs; has toured extensively playing clubs & concerts. Music teacher & studio musician; owner of Garveland Music publ co; also writer for other cos. *Songs:* Old Man Looking Through a Young Man's Eyes; Whenever I'm Alone; Memories of Love.

MODLIK, HELENE PATRICIA (HELENE VELVETTE) ASCAP 1968
composer, author, arranger
b Cleveland, Ohio, Sept 3, 07. Educ: Sacred Heart of Jesus Sch, Harvard Sch & South High Sch, Cleveland; US Sch Music, New York. *Songs & Instrumental Works:* Count Your Blessings; Are You Asking Me Again?; Moon-Kist Waters!; Don't Ask Me No Questions!; Two Hearts in Love!; I Can't Decide!; Please! Don't Let Me Go!; Love Me! Love Me!.

MOEHLMANN, R L ASCAP 1959
composer
b Madison, Wis, Mar 5, 07; d Cedar Rapids, Iowa, Jan 21, 72. Educ: Univ Wis, BEd; Berlin Staatische Hochschule für Musik; studied with Milton Rusch, Paul Juon, Phillip Clapp. Jazz musician & arr, vaudeville & radio, 20's. Writer, music bks for schs. Cond, Municipal Band, Cedar Rapids, Iowa. Chief Collab: Joseph Skornicka. *Instrumental Works:* Bach transc for concert band.

MOEN, DONALD J ASCAP 1977
composer, author, arranger
b Duluth, Minn, June 29, 50. Educ: Univ Southern Miss; Oral Roberts Univ; studied for BMusEduc, 3 yrs. Traveled with gospel contemporary group, Living Sound, 8 yrs; began writing & arr for group, 74; now music adminr for group. Has also done nat jingle work. Chief Collabrs: Jack Elliot, Larry Dalton. *Songs:* Blessed Be the Name of Jesus; Believe in the Promises; God Can Do It Again; If You Only Knew. *Instrumental Works:* Free.

MOEN, JOHN VINCENT ASCAP 1958
author, teacher
b McIntosh, Minn, June 19, 28. Educ: Univ Calif, Berkeley, studied with Mark Shorer & Ben Lehman, BA(English, French); Occidental Col, PhD(comparative lit); Sorbonne, Paris, 49-50. English/French teacher high sch, Los Angeles, 58-61. Language teacher, Izmir, Turkey & Rabat, Morocco, 61-63. Prof comparative lit, Eisenhower Col, 68- Consult English language teaching, P F Collier, Macmillan Publ Co, Tokyo, Japan, 74-75. Chief Collabrs: Benny Carter, Jack Weeks, Hub Atwood, Leonard Feather, Ed Cuomo. *Songs:* Lyrics: Honey on the Moon; Fountain of Youth; Lasse, Lasse, Litten (Swed folk song); A Song Called Revenge; Canzone D'Amore; Once Upon a Time.

MOEVS, ROBERT WALTER ASCAP 1960
composer
b La Crosse, Wis, Dec 2, 20. Educ: Harvard Col, BA, MA, studied with Walter Piston; Conservatoire Nat, Paris, studied with Nadia Boulanger. Fel, Am Acad Rome; mem fac, Harvard Univ & Rutgers Univ. *Instrumental Works:* Piano Sonata; Pan, for Solo Flute; String Quartet; Variazioni Sopra una Melodia; Musica da Camera I, II; Phoenix (piano); Games of the Past (two pianos). *Scores:* Opera/Ballet: Et Occidentem (chorus and orch); A Brief Mass.

MOFFATT, JAMES
See Hughes, Robert James

MOFFATT, RICHARD CULLEN ASCAP 1965
composer, pianist, conductor
b Colorado, Tex, Apr 14, 27. Educ: Lewis & Clark Col; studied with Robert Stoltze & Lenord DePaur; pvt piano study with Margaret Notz Steinmetz. Music dir, cond, pianist & comp, Portland Park Bureau, 25 yrs. Producer, three original operas: "Rumpelstiltskin"; "Cinderella"; "A Song for Ruby-Jo." Chief Collabrs: Michael Falotico, David Richmond. *Songs & Instrumental Works:* As It Began to Dawn (Easter cantata); I Will Lift Up Mine Eyes Unto the Hills (SATB); Alleluia! Let Us Sing! (SATB); In the Beginning Was the Word (SATB); Alleluia! (SATB); Arr: O Rest in the Lord (Mendelssohn; SATB).

MOFFETT, PERCY S ASCAP 1973
composer, lyric writer
b Memphis, Tenn, Dec 18, 26. Educ: Am Cons Music, BMus; DePaul Univ, MMus; songwriting course with Buddy Kaye. Pianist with Willie Mitchell's Band, 46-47. Taught piano at Southern Univ, Baton Rouge, 55-57; assoc prof music, Jackson State Univ, 57-58; teacher of music in Chicago pub high sch. Chief Collabr: Roger Freeman. *Songs:* Oceans of Love; Let Me Stay; Another You; All the Love I'll Ever Need; Love Attack.

MOFFITT, DE LOYCE (DEKE) ASCAP 1953
composer, conductor, arranger
b Hardy, Ark, Aug 13, 06; d Ft Thomas, Ky, July 13, 76. Educ: Cincinnati Cons. Band organizer & teacher, C G Conn Co & Wurlitzer Co. Mem, Albee Theatre Orch, Cincinnati; then dir. Arr, Armco band. Cond, Beverly Hills Country Club band, 9 yrs. Music dir & arr for Bill Robinson with whom he toured US. A&R dir, King Records; also assoc with Cincinnati Symph, Zoo Opera Co. Dir, Cincinnati Symph "Pops" concert, 60. Cond own band in summer concerts. *Songs & Instrumental Works:* The Little Red Caboose; Swinging the Ingots; Big Time Boogie; Hear That Dixieland Band; Boogie March; Bop She Goes; Hi-Score March; Auditorium Session; Rocking in a Plastic Chair; In the Spotlight; Frisky.

MOGA, SORIN
See Cioroiu, Alexandru Sorin

MOISE, WARREN ASCAP 1979
author, composer, producer
b Bishopville, SC, Feb 4, 53. Educ: Sumter High Sch; Univ SC. Staff arr, Soundation & Masterpiece studios. Nightclub singer. Chief Collabrs: Frank Smoak, Mark Sameth, Andy Anderson, Lee Bogan, Jimi Oates, Joel Johnson. *Songs & Instrumental Works:* You're So Cold I'm Turnin' Blue; Love and Hate.

MOLIN, JAMES   ASCAP 1970
author

b Seattle, Wash, July 2, 35. Educ: Univ Wash, BA, 61. Author of 450 prose poems & lyrics. Chief Collabrs: Don McGinnis, Jess Pearson. *Songs & Instrumental Works:* Highway One; Touch.

MOLINE, ROBERT LLOYD   ASCAP 1973
composer, author, singer

b San Gabriel, Calif, Dec 2, 38. Educ: Valley Jr Col, music & drama, 56-57; studied music & voice with Irene Blades, 62-68. Solo tenor, First Christian Church Choir, North Hollywood, Calif; performer in many nite clubs, Los Angeles. Wrote & made several recordings. Principal role in musical comedy, "That Certain Girl," Las Vegas, 66; lead production singer, "Lido De Paris," Stardust Hotel. Performer, Newporter Inn, Newport Beach, Calif, 10 yrs. Chief Collabrs: Richard G Allen, Chris Randall Stephens. *Songs:* It Could Only Happen at Disneyland (theme song; CLIO Award); Words (Span transl); Hallelujah (choral); Here's to America (Disney/Coca Cola theme); Music: December Child; You Are Now (choral).

MOLL, BILLY   ASCAP 1930
composer, author

b Madison, Wis, Apr 18, 05; d Stoughton, Wis, Jan 17, 68. Educ: High sch. Chief Collabrs: Harry Barris, Bob King, Murray Mencher, Joseph Meyer, Beasley Smith. *Songs:* I Scream, You Scream, We All Scream for Ice Cream; Moonlight on the Colorado; Wrap Your Troubles in Dreams; I Want a Little Girl; Ro, Ro, Rolling Along; Long About Sundown; This Is No Dream: Honeymoon Lane; Me and the Girl Next Door; I Love You in the Same Sweet Way; There's a House on a Hill; At the Close of a Long Long Day; A Man and a Mountain; Learning.

MOMARY, DOUGLAS R   ASCAP 1971
composer

b Paterson, NJ, June 1, 47. Educ: Univ Ariz, BA(playwriting); Calif State Col, Fullerton. Writer, var musicals while at col, incl "Lynell", "What Am I Doing Here" & "Is It Dark Or Light," 66-69. Co-creator, childrens' TV series, "A New Zoo Review," 71; songwriter for series. Comp, theme song for LPGA Golf Tour. With Video Enterprises, Las Vegas, 80. *Songs:* New Zoo Review Theme Song.

MONACO, JAMES V   ASCAP 1914
composer, pianist

b Fornia, Italy, Jan 13, 1885; d Beverly Hills, Calif, Oct 16, 45. To US, 1891. At 17, pianist in cabaret; then in nightclubs, Coney Island. To Hollywood, under contract to Paramount, 36. Wrote songs for films, "Weekend in Havana" & "The Dolly Sisters." Charter mem, ASCAP. Chief Collabrs: Johnny Burke, Joe McCarthy, Mack Gordon, Edgar Leslie, Grant Clarke, Sidney Clare, Mort Dixon. *Songs:* Row, Row, Row; You Made Me Love You; I Miss You Most of All; Beatrice Fairfax; If We Can't Be the Same Old Sweethearts; What Do You Want to Make Those Eyes at Me For?; You Know You Belong to Somebody Else; Through; I'm Crying Just for You; Dirty Hands, Dirty Face; Red Lips, Kiss Those Blues Away; We're Back Together Again; Me and the Boy Friend; Me and the Man in the Moon; Crazy People; You've Got Me in the Palm of Your Hand; You're Gonna Lose Your Gal; My Heart is Taking Lessons; This is My Night to Dream; On the Sentimental Side; I've Got a Pocketful of Dreams; Laugh and Call It Love; Don't Let the Moon Get Away; Go Fly a Kite; An Apple for the Teacher; A Man and His Dream; East Side of Heaven; That Sly Old Gentleman; Sing a Song of Sunbeams; Hang Your Heart on a Hickory Limb; Sweet Potato Piper; Too Romantic; April Played the Fiddle; Meet the Sun Half Way; Six Lessons From Madam LaZonga; Every Night About This Time; Ain't It a Shame About Mame?; I Don't Want to Cry Anymore; I'm Making Believe; There Will Never Be Another You; Once Too Often; Time Alone Will Tell; I Can't Begin to Tell You; Music: Only Forever; I'll Take Care of Your Cares. *Scores:* Film: Dr Rhythm; Sing, You Sinners; East Side of Heaven; The Star Maker; The Road to Singapore; If I Had My Way; Rhythm on the River; Stage Door Canteen; Iceland; Pin-Up Girl.

MONACO, RICHARD A   ASCAP 1968
composer, teacher, conductor

b Richmond Hill, NY, Jan 10, 30. Educ: NY Univ, 48-50; Cornell Univ, BA, MA & DMA; studied with Robert Palmer & Hunter Johnson. Composer chamber music, choral works & songs. Prof music, Western Col for Women, 59-73 & Univ Ill, Chicago Circle, 74-; vis prof, Cornell Univ, 68-69. Cond, Western Col Choir, 59-73 & Oxford Chamber Orch, 64-68. Performer, jazz trombone & piano, 47-. *Songs & Instrumental Works:* The Magnificat (chorus, soloists & chamber orch; NEA comn); Quartet for Piano and Strings; Three Miniatures for Quintet; Five Short Pieces for Flute and Clarinet; Sonata for Trombone and Piano; Blessed Be the Lord (cantata); Duo for Violin and Piano.

MONATH, NORMAN   ASCAP 1952
composer, author

b Toronto, Ont, July 3, 20. Educ: NY Univ, BA, music maj. Wrote songs as a teenager. Ed, Simon & Schuster Bk Publ, also wrote for records. Wrote some songs for Dionne Warwick. Chief Collabrs: Hal David, Kermit Goell, Estelle Levitt, Ray Leveen. *Songs & Instrumental Works:* The Magic of Believing; Silent Voices; The Riddle Song; Don't Sugar Me.

MONELLO, SPARTACO VINDICE   ASCAP 1963
composer

b Boston, Mass, June 20, 09. Educ: Harvard Col, AB, 32, Harvard Univ, MA, 35; Columbia Univ, EdD, 63; studied with Aaron Copland & Roger Sessions. Two Hartford Found fels. Civilian instr, USAF, WW II. Asst prof music & dir orch, William & Mary Col, 43; asst, Dept Music, Univ Calif, 45-47, instr, Univ Ext Div, 46-47. *Instrumental Works:* Sinfonia Accademica (orch); Sicilian Suite (orch); Concerto Grosso (strings and piano); Symphony No 1, 2, 3, 4 (orch); Sinfonia (orch).

MONK, MEREDITH J   ASCAP 1976
composer, singer, director

b Lima, Peru, Nov 20, 42. Educ: George Sch, Bucks County, Pa; high sch; studied comp with Richard Averre; Sarah Lawrence Col, BA, 64; studied voice with Paul Ukena & Vicki Starr, comp with Ruth Lloyd & Glen Mack & vocal chamber music with Meyer Kupferman. Artistic dir, The House Found for Arts, 68- Comp, choreographer & dir of more than 40 works. Awards & Grants: Guggenheim fel, 72; Brandeis Creative Arts Award, 74; CAPS Grant, 77; NEA Grants, 70-80; NY State Council on Arts grants, 70-80. *Songs & Instrumental Works:* Juice (cantata); Key; Our Lady of Late; Songs From the Hill; Tablet; Dolmen Music. *Scores:* Opera: Vessel (epic; Oble award, 72); Quarry (Oble award, 76); Education of the Girlchild.

MONOSHA, COLEMAN
See Lertzman, Carl Myron

MONROE, VAUGHN   ASCAP 1945
composer, author, conductor

b Akron, Ohio, Oct 7, 11; d Stuart, Fla, May 21, 73. Educ: Carnegie Tech; pvt music study. Wis state champion trumpet soloist at 15. Trumpeter in local nightclub bands. Organized own band, 40, appearing in theatres, ballrooms, films, radio & TV. Was "Voice of RCA," for radio & TV progs. Named ambassador from Pa, 49. Trumpeter & singer. *Songs:* Racing With the Moon (theme); Something Sentimental; The Pleasure's All Mine; A Man's Best Friend Is His Horse; Let's Have a Cigarette Together; Caboose on a Slow Freight; Chocolate Choo Choo; I'm Easy to Get Along With; Rasputin's Tootin'; Candy Classy Chassis; Boston Rocker; Singin' My Way Back Home; Mexicali Trail; Cry Cry Cry.

MONTANA, PATSY
See Rose, Rubye B

MONTANA, VINCENT, JR   ASCAP 1976
composer, author, arranger

b Philadelphia, Pa, Feb 12, 28. Played with own group in var nightclubs & for pvt affairs, early 50's. Record producer; helped create hit records which established Philadelphia Sound. Created Salsoul Orch; first to bring fully orchestrated sound to dance-pop market. Awards: Billboards Top Disco Orch, 75, 76 & 77; Arr of Yr, 77; Record World's Top Orch Awards for Rhythm & Blues & Disco, 77; Int Orch of Yr, Canadian Record Pool, 77; 50 gold & platinum, in singles & albums. *Songs:* Chicago Bus Stop (Ooh, I Love It); You're Just the Right Size; Salsoul Rainbow; It Looks Like Love; Dance a Little Bit Closer; It's Good for the Soul; Nice 'N' Nasty; Run Away; It's a New Day; Don't Beat Around the Bush; Ritzy Mambo; Cuchi Cuchi; Only You; Love Is You; More of You; Maybe It's All in My Mind; Put It in Love; Merry Christmas All; Lyrics: Number 1 Dee Jay. *Instrumental Works:* Salsoul 3001; Night Crawler; Samba De Montana. *Songs & Instrumental Works:* Salsoul Hustle; You Know How Good It Is; Magic Bird of Fire; Montana an' Friends.

MONTANI, NICOLA A   ASCAP 1937
composer, organist, choirmaster

b Utica, NY, Nov 6, 1880; d Philadelphia, Pa, Jan 11, 48. Educ: Parochial schs, studied music with Gaetano Montani (bro) & H D Beissenherz. Church organist & choirmaster, St John the Evangelist, Philadelphia, 06-23; St Paul the Apostle, New York, 23-25. Prof & dir, choral music in cols, acad. Liturgical ed, music publ firms; ed, "St George Hymnal" (issued in Braille). Founder & ed, "Catholic Choirmaster," 14-41. App Knight Comdr, Order of St Sylvester, insignia of Count's Cross. Educator. *Songs & Instrumental Works:* Stabat Mater (oratorio); Missa Festiva; Missa Solemnis; The Bells (cantata); White Silence (chorus); St Nicholas Mass (3-part chorus).

MONTGOMERY, BRUCE   ASCAP 1965
composer, author, conductor

b Philadelphia, Pa, June 20, 27. Educ: Germantown Friends Sch, Philadelphia; Bethany Col, Kans, BFA; Univ Pa; studied comp & cond with Hagbard Brase & Arvid Wallin. Dir musical activities & assoc performing arts, Univ Pa, 55- Dir, Gilbert & Sullivan Players, Philadelphia. Frequent lectr & narrator, Philadelphia Orch. Cond choruses throughout US, Soviet Union, Denmark, Eng, Finland, Bulgaria, Peru, Ecuador & others. Mem, Intercollegiate Musical Council, Young Audiences, Inc, Musical Fund Soc, Edwin P Garrigues Found & Pa Pro Musica. *Songs & Instrumental Works:* Fanfare and Wedding March (organ); Learning Love; When Time Takes Your Hand; Let Us Now Praise Great and Famous Men; Lincoln's Gettysburg Address; Candystore; Remembrance; Choral works: Three Haiku; Clap Your Hands; Twelve Choral Amens; O Wüsst Ich Doch Den Weg Zurük (Brahms); The Glendy Burk (Foster); I Know Where I'm Going

(Irish Folk Song); Sometimes I Feel Like a Motherless Child (spiritual); Set It Down (spiritual); He's Gone Away (Am Folk Song). *Scores:* Opera/Ballet: Herodotus Fragments; Thespis (new score); Et in Terra Pax; Off-Bway: The Amorous Flea; Bway stage: Spindrift; Why Me?.

MONTGOMERY, EDYTHE MAY ASCAP 1964
author
b New Bedford, Mass, Mar 23, 08. Educ: Pub schs. *Songs & Instrumental Works:* Tanya; Chickadee Polka; Champagne Polka; Hug and Kiss Me; You Teaser You; Rocks in the Head; Jazztime Beat; Cute Little Ice Cube; Katinka Polka; Lyrics: Cuddlin' There; House of Regrets; Valley of Tears; Blessings of Love; Blue Ribbon Fool; Grand Prize Fool.

MONTGOMERY, KANDEDA
See Brandewine-Montgomery, Kandeda Rachael

MONTGOMERY, MERLE (ALAN CAMPBELL) ASCAP 1961
composer, author, editor
b Davidson, Okla, May 15, 04. Educ: Univ Okla, BFA; Eastman Sch Music, MMus & PhD(music theory); studied with Nadia Boulanger & Isidore Phillip, Paris, 2 yrs. Taught at Univ Okla; head piano & theory, Southwestern State Col, Okla. State supvr, Fed Music Proj. Taught at Eastman Sch Music, Rochester, lect on Schillinger Syst, 5 yrs. Nat educ consult, Carl Fischer, Inc, later, vpres in charge pub rels. Asst mgr music dept, Oxford Univ Press, NY. Pres, Nat Fedn Music Clubs, 71-75; pres, Nat Music Coun, 75-79; chmn bd, 79-; proj dir, Bicentennial Parade Am Music. Author, "Music Theory Papers" (I, II, III); "Music Composition Papers." Transl from French into Eng, Vincent d'Indy's "Cours de Composition Musicale." *Songs & Instrumental Works:* They Dared to Lead (orch); Leisure (SSATBB chorus); The Princess and the Pirates (piano); Air for Two Hands (piano); Stepping Lively (piano); Away I Go.

MONTIEL, URBANO GOMEZ
See Gomez, Urbano

MONTOYA, CARLOS GARCIA ASCAP 1958
composer
b Spain, Dec 13, 03. Educ: Studied with Pepe Barbero at age 8, 1 yr. Flamenco guitarist; played for singers & dancers, Cafe Cantante, Madrid, age 14; toured with La Agentina, Paris, Europe, Asia, NAfrica, North & South Am. First solo recital, New York, 48. Appeared on Today Show, Tonight Show, Mike Douglas Show & many others. Soloist with symphs & orchs. Chief Collabr: Julio Esteban. *Instrumental Works:* Malaga; Tango Antiguo; La Rosa; Gaita Ga Llega; Zambrilla; Duende Flamenco; Nana Del Gitanito; Granaina; Solea Por Medio; Cante De Sevilla; Aires De Genil; Levante; Jaleo; Toque De Cana; Fiesta; Caribe Aflamencao; Variaciones; Fandango; Tarantas; Zambra; Rondena; Jota; Saeta; Tanguillo De Cadiz. *Scores:* Opera/Ballet: Suite Flamenca (Flamenco guitar, symph, orch).

MONTROSE, JACK ASCAP 1957
composer, arranger, instrumentalist
b Detroit, Mich, Dec 30, 28. Educ: Los Angeles City Col, AA; Los Angeles State Col, BA; San Fernando Valley State Col, MA. Record albums on Pacific Jazz, Atlantic & RCA Victor. Numerous other recorded compositions, arrangements & performances with var name jazz artists. Performer all reed instruments, Caesar's Palace House Orch, Las Vegas, Nev. *Songs:* Music: A Little Duet; A Dandy Line; Blues and Vanilla; Finder's Keepers; Dot's Groovy; Two Can Play; The News and the Weather; Listen, Hear; Poeme; Pretty; For the Fairest; Meet Mr Gordon; Pro Defunctus; Ergo; Onion Bottom; The Hornstull; April's Fool. *Instrumental Works:* Lament; Etude de Concert. *Scores:* Opera/Ballet: Street Corner Royalty.

MOODY, PHILIP TREVOR ASCAP 1951
composer, author, pianist
b Southampton, Eng. Educ: St Mary's Col, Southampton; Royal Acad of Music, London. With Jack Hylton Productions, Ambrose Orch, Chappell Music Co, Arthur Rank Film & British Broadcasting Co, Eng, also with Ray Heindorf-Warner Bros & 3 M Co, London & Rome. Shows for Desert Inn Motel, Sahara Motel, Frontier Hotel, Las Vegas, MGM Grand, Reno, Moulin Rouge, Hollywood, Latin Quarter, New York & Miami. Acts for Mae West, Dale Robertson, Eddie Fisher, Betty Grable & others. In concerts, Los Angeles, Las Vegas, Rome & Palm Springs. Chief Collabrs: Pony Sherrell, Ned Washington, Ben Oakland. *Songs:* Pretty Little Girl; You're Something Special; Music: Small Town; Since You've Gone; Three Nuts in Search of a Bolt; I Used to Be a Stripper Down on Main; Little People; The Strongest Men in the World. *Instrumental Works:* The Luna Concerto (piano, orch); Wedding Suite (piano; concert piece); Noon in Napoli; Three Or Four Times. *Scores:* Films: So This Is Paris; Love Me Deadly; Ain't Misbehavin'; The 2nd Greatest Sex; Have You Ever Been to Paris.

MOON, ANTHONY JOSEPH ASCAP 1971
composer, author
b New York, NY, Nov 20, 38. Educ: St Mary's Col; studied classical guitar with Fred Stockton. Lead guitarist & cond for Brenda Lee, 61-64; recording artist, Dante & the Evergreens. *Songs:* You Give Me You; The Water's Too Rough

Tonight; How I Love Those Xmas Songs; More Than a Bedroom Thing; Country Xmas Party.

MOON, JACK
See Elliott, John B

MOON, JOSEPH FREDERICK ASCAP 1962
composer, arranger, accompanist
b Ann Arbor, Mich, Sept 11, 12. Educ: Morrison R Waite High Sch, Toledo, Ohio; Cons of Music, Cincinnati. Pianist in, "Idiot's Delight", "Amphitryon 38", "There Shall Be No Night", "Boys from Syracuse", "Annie Get Your Gun" & "My Fair Lady." Accompanist & coach, Gertrude Lawrence, Julie Andrews & Kitty Carlisle. Composed background scores for "The River Jordan", "The Vatican", "1492", "1898", "1964", "Custer" & "The Pilgrims." Chief Collabrs: Ulpio Minucci.

MOONDOG
See Hardin, Lewis Thomas

MOONEY, HAROLD ASCAP 1936
composer, arranger, A&R recording producer
b Brooklyn, NY, Feb 4, 17. Educ: Jamaica High Sch; St John's Law Sch; spec study with Joseph Schillinger, Castelnuovo-Tedesco & Franklyn Marks. Arr, Hal Kemp & Jimmy Dorsey Orchs. US Armed Serv, WW II. Free lance arr, Los Angeles, 46. Artist & repertoire position with Mercury Records, 57. Music supvr, Universal Studios, 70. *Songs:* Music: Sing, It's Good for 'Ya; If You Leave Me Tonight I'll Cry. *Instrumental Works:* Rigamarole; Swampfire.

MOORE, ART ASCAP 1963
author
b Anaheim, Calif, Aug 13, 14. Educ: Blaine Inst. TV writer. Chief Collabrs: Basil Adlam, Charles Henderson.

MOORE, CARMAN LEROY
composer, author, teacher
b Lorain, Ohio, Oct 8, 36. Educ: High sch, Elyria, Ohio; Oberlin Cons, spec studies; Ohio State Univ, BS(music); pvt comp studies with Hall Overton, Luciano Berio & Vincent Persichetti; Juilliard Sch Music, MS; studied French horn, cello & cond at Oberlin Cons & Ohio State Univ. Assoc with Judson Church concerts & intermedia, early 60's; gave one-man concerts at New Sch for Soc Research, 62 & Judson Church, 67. Has had works comn & performed by San Francisco Symph Orch, 75, New York Philh, 75, Rochester Philh, Am Symph & orchs abroad. Music critic for Village Voice, 65; has contributed to many nat publ. Fac mem, Yale Univ Sch of Music, Queens Col, Brooklyn Col & Manhattanville Col. Mem, NEA New Music Panel & Bd of Am Music Ctr & Comp Forum. Author, "Somebody's Angel Child: Story of Bessie Smith" & "Growth of Black Sound in America." Has written popular music for record albums. Chief Collabrs: Felix Cavaliere, Ishmael Reed, Jerry Lieber. *Songs:* Lyrics: Rock and Roll Outlaw. *Instrumental Works:* Wildfires and Field Songs; Concerto for Percussion and Orchestra; Fixed Do: Movable Sol (intermedia). *Songs & Instrumental Works:* Gospel Fuse. *Albums:* Rock and Roll Outlaw.

MOORE, CHARLES WILLIAM ASCAP 1954
composer, author, musician
b Wilson, NC, Feb 28, 18. Appeared in nightclubs, theatres, radio & TV throughout the world. *Songs:* Out of the Bushes; Ling Ting Tong; All I Have Is You; That Don't Do Me No Good; Don't Lie to Me.

MOORE, DALLAS ASCAP 1973
author
b Como, NC, Nov 4, 29. Started writing for church choir. Chief Collabr: Pete Rote. *Songs & Instrumental Works:* Love and Affection.

MOORE, DONALD IRVING ASCAP 1969
composer, band director, arranger
b Farnhamville, Iowa, Apr 11, 10. Educ: Drake Univ; Carleton Col, AB, 32; Univ Northern Colo, AM, 40; Univ Mich. Dir high sch bands, Charles City & Britt, Iowa; dir jr high bands & All-City High Sch Orch, Dallas, Tex; band dir, Univ Northern Colo; dir bands, Juilliard Sch Music & Columbia Univ; band dir, Baylor Univ, 48-69, emer, 70-; dir and/or judged band concerts in 28 states, Scotland & Switz. *Songs & Instrumental Works:* March Poco; Ides of March; Wagner Showcase; Rise and Shine; Marcho Stereo; Bandwagon; March Winds; America (chorus with and/or orch); March Forth; Requiem for a Hero; Patriotic Oratory for Horn (solo with band or orch); Saul of Tarsus; Psalm 23 (band with optional chorus and orch).

MOORE, DONALD LEE ASCAP 1952
composer
b Mooresville, NC, Nov 30, 10. Educ: Pvt study. Teacher, composer & band dir. Chief Collabrs: Daniel S Twohig, Adelaide Van Wey. *Songs & Instrumental Works:* Organ Works; Piano Works; Sacred and Secular Songs; Smokey Mountain Ballads (collection).

MOORE, DOUGLAS STUART ASCAP 1938
composer, conductor, organist
b Cutchogue, NY, Aug 10, 1893; d. Educ: Yale Univ, BA, BM, studied with Horatio Parker & David Smith; Cleveland Inst Music; Schola Cantorum, Paris, with Vincent D'Indy; also studied with Nadia Boulanger & Ernest Bloch; hon MusD: Cincinnati Cons, Univ Rochester, Yale Univ & Adelphi Col; hon DHL, Columbia Univ. Grants: Pulitzer; Guggenheim. Joined fac, Columbia Univ, 26, prof music & chmn dept, 40-63; educr. Dir, ASCAP, 57-60. Author: "Listening to Music" & "From Madrigal to Modern Music." Mem bd dirs: Am Acad, Rome; Nat Inst Arts & Sci (pres, 46-52); Am Musical Soc; Nat Inst Arts & Letters; Am Acad Arts & Letters (pres, 59-62). Dir, MacDowell Asn. Awards: Huntington Hartford; Eastman Publ; SPAM Publ; Columbia Soc Older Graduates; Henry Hadley Medal, Nat Asn for Am Comp & Cond. *Songs & Instrumental Works:* Four Museum Pieces; Pageant of P T Barnum; Ballad of William Sycamore; Moby Dick; Violin Sonata; Symphony of Autumn; Overture on an American Tune; String Quartet; Adam Was My Grandfather (songs); Quintet for Winds, Horn; Quintet for Clarinet, Two Violins, Viola, Cello; In Memoriam; Symphony in A; Farm Journal; Down East Suite (violin, piano); Village Music; The People's Choice; Cotillion Suite; Chorus: Perchance to Dream; Simon Legree; Dedication. *Scores:* Operas: White Wings; The Devil and Daniel Webster; Giants in the Earth (Pulitzer prize, 51); The Ballad of Baby Doe (comn by Koussevitzky Found; New York Music Critics award, 58); Wings of the Dove (comn by New York City Ctr); Carry Nation; Operetta: The Headless Horseman.

MOORE, ELIZABETH EVELYN ASCAP 1925
author
b Poughkeepsie, NY, June 22, 1891. Educ: Quincy Sch; pvt music study. Winner nat poetry prizes. Music critic, Poughkeepsie Eagle News, 9 yrs; society ed, Rochester Democrat and Chronicle. Chief Collabrs: Charles Spross, Noble Cain, Geoffrey O'Hara, Gustave Klemm, Huntington Woodman, Robert Flagler, Sylvia Dee (daughter). *Songs:* Laroo, Laroo, Lilli Bolero; Moonlight in Old Granada; Let There Be Song; He Could Only Sing a C; Where Heaven Is; Maripo; Let All My Life Be Music; In the Night; Boys; My Rosary of Roses; How Sweet the Bells of Christmas; White Swans; Music of Life; O Sing Again.

MOORE, ELOISE IRENE (TRUDY, EVALYN) ASCAP 1962
composer, author, guitarist
b River Rouge, Mich, Dec 29, 29. Educ: Pub Schs. Mem, Melody Mountaineers; owner, Brok-A-Tears Records. Chief Collabrs: Louise Moore, Lee Jackson. *Songs:* Too Many Tear-Drops; Rainbow Island: Star of Love; A Life Time of Love; Unwanted Love; Tingle, Dingle, Jingle, Tringle; Till I Met You; Every Moment I'm With You; A Girl Like Me Is Never Blue; Where Did My Dream Go?; Please Come Back to Me; I Gave You My Heart; How Can I Get Over You?; All My Tomorrows; You Have Broken My Heart; Someone Is Taking My Place; Sweetheart You'll Forget Me; Lyrics: Somebody Loves Me; I Wonder Why!.

MOORE, FRANCIS ASCAP 1935
composer, pianist, teacher
b El Paso, Tex, July 3, 1886; d Pelham Manor, NY, July 11, 46. Educ: Temple Col; Sherwood Music Sch, Chicago. Taught at Sherwood Music Sch, also in El Paso. Accompanist to Maude Powell, Graveure, Gadski, Kreisler, Elman, Calve & Witherspoon. Debut as concert pianist, NY, 21; gave yearly piano recitals. Concert tour, Europe, 32. Cond own studio, NY & Francis Moore Music Ctr, Pelham, NY. *Songs:* Swing Song; Jay; This Love of Ours; The Devil Take Her. *Instrumental Works:* Meditation (piano); The Promised Land; Piano Arr: Spinning Song (Mendelssohn); Rondo (Haydn); Christmas March (Gade).

MOORE, FRANK ASCAP 1964
composer, author, conductor
b Philadelphia, Pa, Oct 10, 28. Educ: High sch; music cons. Leader group, Frank Moore Four, appeared in clubs, films & TV; made many records. Chief Collabrs: Ray Karol, Henry Sanicola. *Songs:* Seven Days; Alone With a Dream.

MOORE, FRANK LEDLIE ASCAP 1973
composer, author
b Cambridge, Mass, Dec 28, 23. Educ: New Eng Cons Music, studied with Ernst Levy; Dalcroze Sch Music, studied with Paul Boepple; fel drama, Bennington Col, studied with Francis Fergusson. Comp, dir for theatre & var jobs, Washington, DC, 49-57; comp scores for documentary films & prod films, New York, 58-68; comp score for Hartford Symph, New York World's Fair, 62; designed shows for World's Fair, New York & Seattle, Wash; gen mgr, Norello Publ, 74-; comp choral dramas & concert music. *Instrumental Works:* Quartet on B; Captain Shrimp; Wagadougou; Ryan; John Brown. *Scores:* Film/TV: The American Vision; Music Hall Miniature.

MOORE, GEORGE PHILIP, JR ASCAP 1944
composer, author, pianist
b Portland, Ore, Feb 20, 18. Educ: Univ Wash; Cornish Inst. Child piano prodigy. Comp-arr, Hollywood; worked at Metro-Goldwyn-Mayer, Columbia, United Producers of Am & others; organized quartet, New York, early 40's; opened Singers Workshop, Hollywood; writer of acts for singers & comp for TV & films, 73- *Songs:* Shoo, Shoo Baby; I Feel So Smoochie; Music: A Little on the Lonely Side. *Instrumental Works:* Concerto for Piano and

Orchestra; Concerto for Trombone and Orchestra; Moore's Tour (An American in England); My New York Sweet. *Songs & Instrumental Works:* Fantasy for Girl and Orchestra; Portrait of Leda.

MOORE, GLEN RICHARD ASCAP 1970
composer, teacher, performer
b Portland, Ore, Oct 28, 41. Educ: Univ Ore, BS, 64; studied bass with James Harnett, Gary Karr & Ludwig Streicher; studied piano. Bassist in duet with Ralph Towner, Larry Karusa, David Friesen, sideman with Zoot Sims, Chico Hamilton, Ted Kurson, Kenny Burrell, Jeremy Steig, Paul Bley. Made winter concert recording, 70; mem of group Oregon. Chief Collabrs: Ralph Towner, David Darling, Paul Bley, Paul McCandless, Collin Walcott, Jeremy Steig. *Songs & Instrumental Works:* Deer Path; Fall 77; Roots in the Sky; Hawaiian Shuffle; Three Step Dance; Will You Miss Me When I'm Here; Always, Never and Forever; Belt of Asteroids; Flageolet; Love Over Time; Chromatic Blues; Egyptian Tune; Contraire Emotion; At the Hawks Well; Land of Hearts Desire; Spring Is Really Coming.

MOORE, KERMIT ASCAP 1975
composer
b Akron, Ohio, Mar 11, 29. Educ: Cleveland Inst Music, BMus, 50; NY Univ, MA, 51; Juilliard Sch Music; Paris Cons, artists dipl; student of Marcel Dick, Cleveland & Nadia Boulanger, Paris. Fac mem, Hartt Sch Mus, Univ Hartford, 50-53. Concertized, Europe, Asia, Africa & US. Conducted own composition with Fest Orch, UN, 76. Conducted own works at Philh Hall. *Songs:* Many Thousand Gone (chorus, flute & perc). *Instrumental Works:* Concerto for Timpani and Orchestra; Music for Cello and Piano; Music for Viola, Piano and Percussion; Music for Flute and Piano. *Songs & Instrumental Works:* Songs for soprano and piano; four arias adapted for soprano and symphony orchestra.

MOORE, MARY CARR ASCAP 1940
composer, singer, educator
b Memphis, Tenn, Aug 6, 1873; d Ingleside, Calif, Jan 11, 57. Educ: Studied music with Emma Dewhurst, John Pratt & H B Pasmore; hon MusD, Chapman Col. Was concert & choir singer until 1898. Head of theory dept, Olga Steeb Piano Sch, Los Angeles; teacher, Chapman Col; prof of theory, Calif Christian Col. Awards: 3 Chamber Music Prizes, Nat League Am Pen Women. *Instrumental Works:* Chamber Music: Trio for Piano, Violin, Cello; Piano Quintet; Beyond These Hills; Orch: My Dream (chorus); Piano Concerto in F. *Scores:* Operas: Narcissa (David Bispham Medal); David Rizzio; The Shaft of Ku'Pish Ta Ya.

MOORE, MCELBERT ASCAP 1924
author
b Boston, Mass, July 2, 1892; d Newport Beach, Calif, Apr 10, 74. Educ: Mass State Col; Harvard Col; Carnegie Tech. On drama & music staff, Boston Record, 16; drama critic & asst ed, Boston Advert, 17. With 2nd Army, Am Expeditionary Force, WW I. Co-author "Who Can Tell," Army show. Assoc ed, Community Motion Picture Co, 20. Screen writer, Hollywood. Chief Collabrs: J Fred Coots, Jean Schwartz, Roy Webb. *Songs:* Your Voice Is Twilight; Innocent Eyes; Whistle in the Rain; Louisiana; Little Red Book; One Step to Heaven; Night in My Heart; Lady; My Rose; Lorelei; Through the Night; The First Texan. *Scores:* Bway Stage: Spice of 1922; A Night in Paris; Co-Librettist: Plain Jane.

MOORE, MICHAEL JACKSON ASCAP 1971
composer, author, singer
b San Francisco, Calif, July 15, 45. Educ: Univ Southern Calif, BA, 67, studied drama & music, 67-70. Compiled & wrote songs for "Feiffer's People," satirical revue based on Jules Feiffer's cartoons. Actor & singer on many TV shows. Now performer with own band, Los Angeles area. *Songs:* Yellow Roses on Her Gown; Rocked Them to Sleep; Money and a Woman; I Pretend; Monterey Midnights.

MOORE, MILTONA ASCAP 1952
composer, author, pianist
b Joliet, Ill, Feb 7, 02. Educ: Chicago Col Music, MM; The Principia; studied with Leopold Godowsky, Charles Wakefield Cadman & Maurice DePackh. Piano soloist with Chicago Symph; comp educ material. Staff mem dept educ, Univ Calif. Chief Collabr: Kate Hammond. *Instrumental Works:* Piano: Gremlins; Little Ballerina; Jungle Caravan; Island Fantasy; On Venetian Waters; In a Russian Village.

MOORE, RICA OWEN ASCAP 1960
composer, author, piano teacher
b Lake Forest, Ill, Jan 3, 29. Educ: Am Acad Dramatic Arts, New York; studied piano with Margaret Wilson, Lee Pattison & Guy Maier. Piano soloist with Waukegan Philh & Chicago Symph Orch, Ill, 43. Appeared in Bway musicals, "Lend an Ear" & "Make a Wish"; sang in motion pictures, "Funny Girl," "Finian's Rainbow" & others; also in films & TV; sang in numerous recordings; dir & arr singing groups. Soloist, Ray Coniff, 9 yrs. Grammy nomination for best childrens recording, 63. Chief Collabr: Ruth T McGibeny. *Songs:* My Monkey and Me; I Can Do Anything. *Albums:* Mother Goose Rhymes and Their Stories; Legend of Sleepy Hollow and Rip Van Winkle; Best Loved Fairy Tales; Addition and Subtraction; Childhood Memories; Goldilocks and the Three Bears; Zoo Songs; These United States; Multiplication and Division.

MOORE, ROBERT L, JR (ROBIN) ASCAP 1966
author
b Boston, Mass, Oct 31, 25. Educ: Middlesex Sch, 43; Belmont Hill Sch, 44; Harvard Univ, AB, 49. Europ correspondent, Boston Globe, 47. Independent TV producer, New York, 49-52. Dir pub relations, Sheraton Corp Am, Boston, 52-54, dir advert & pub relations, 54-56, dir, 56-65. Served as Staff Sgt, USAAF, WW II; joined US Army Spec Forces as civilian historian, 63. Clubs: Overseas Press, Lambs, Athletic (New York), Harvard, Metrop, Friars. Author: "Pitchman"; "The Devil to Pay"; "The Green Berets"; "The Country Team"; "Fiedler"; "The French Connection"; "The Khaki Mafia"; "The Fifth Estate"; "The Happy Hooker"; "The Banksters"; "Dubai"; "Mafia Wife"; "Rhodesia"; "The Crippled Eagles"; "The Big Paddle."

MOORE, ROBERT S ASCAP 1963
composer, author
b Lisbon, NY. Educ: High sch & bus col; Craine Sch Music; Ithaca Cons of Music, violin studies. Violinist, Craine Symph Orch; wrote music for labor mgt shows, Centennial march for fest & Kiwanis welcome song. Chief Collabrs: Ernie Barnett, Mack David. Songs: Break My Heart; Music: A Ribbon, a Ring and a Rose; Mothers Lullaby; Tears on the Rose; If You See Marie.

MOORE, STEVEN RICHARD ASCAP 1974
composer, author, teacher
b Albert Lea, Minn, Feb 18, 42. Educ: Univ Minn, BS; studied with Lehman Engel. As comp & lyricist, works have been performed by SCoast Repertory Theatre, Costa Mesa & theatres in Southern Calif. First publ play as comp & lyricist, "Alice in Wonderland."

MOORE, THELMA
See Miron, Tsipora

MOORE, THOMAS F ASCAP 1954
composer, author
b New York, NY, Jan 23, 11. Educ: Regis High Sch; City Col New York. Protege & lyric collabr of Lew Brown, 34-36. Worked on Bway shows, Casino de Paree, Manhattan Music Hall, Palm Island Casino & in Hollywood. Lyric writer, 50's. Chief Collabrs: Harry Akst, Sammy Fain, Danny Hurd. Songs: Bierstube Song; Lyrics: You're Waltzing on My Heart; Lonely Days and Nights More Lonely; Lover's Quarrel; I Have You.

MOORE, TIMOTHY HARRISON ASCAP 1974
composer, author, recording artist
b New York, NY. Educ: Tyler Sch Fine Art. Formed band, Gulliver, with Daryl Hall, performing all original songs. Toured major US cities, Britain & Europe, 75. Songs: Second Avenue; Love Enough; Rock and Roll Love Letter; Charmer (Grand Prize Winner, Am Song Fest, 74). Albums: Tim Moore; Behind the Eyes; White Shadows; High Contrast.

MOORE, WARREN THOMAS (PETE) ASCAP 1972
composer, singer
b Detroit, Mich, Nov 19, 38. Educ: Caff Tech High Sch, Detroit, 77; Highland Park Jr Col. Cut first record, 58; with Motown Records & writer, Jobete Publ Co, 58-75; began writing, 63; with CBS Records, 75-77; independent, Grimora Publ, 77-80. Chief Collabrs: Smokey Robinson, Marv Tarplin, Bill Griffin. Songs: The Tracks of My Tears; Ooh Baby Baby; Love Machine; I'll Be Doggone; Ain't That Peculiar; City of Angels.

MOORE, WILMA
See Richter, Ada A

MOPPER, IRVING ASCAP 1950
composer
b Savannah, Ga, Dec 1, 14. Educ: Studied with Minnie Lasnik, Ethel Chasins, Julius Herford, Frederick Transnitz & Oliver Messiaen. Taught at Ralph Wolfe Cons. Chief Collabrs: Linda Roberts, Pat Noto, Mini Stein, Langston Hughes. Songs & Instrumental Works: It's Raining Again; Lost; Ibbity Bibbity Bob; You Make the Living Worthwhile; How Come?; Teenage Bliss; It's Love; Choral: The Mountain of God; Men; Resourceful Mary; The Frog; Love Story; The Lemon-Colored Dodo; Cantatas: The Wonderful Works of God; The Creation (James Hall Comn); The Hand Loved Best of All; Alice in Wonderland (piano suite); Sonatina for Piano, Clarinet; Trio for Strings; also two piano sonatinas. Scores: Operas: The Door (Nat Fedn Music Clubs Prize); George; Nero's Mother.

MORALES, NORO ASCAP 1942
composer, conductor, pianist
b San Juan, PR, Jan 4, 11; d San Juan, Jan 4, 64. Pianist in orch with father & brothers as youth, became official orch of Venezuela pres. To US, 35. Formed own orch, 39, appeared in US hotels, nightclubs & theatres. Recording artist with many records. Songs & Instrumental Works: Bim Bam Bam; Perfume de Amor; If You Only Knew; Walter Winchell Rhumba; Oye Negra; Rum and Soda; Wha' Happen Baby? Mambo Jumbo.

MORAN, EDWARD P ASCAP 1934
author
b Cincinnati, Ohio, Sept 14, 1871; d New York, NY, Sept 20, 56. Songs: Sweetheart of Mine; Dream of You; It Ain't No Lie; Please Mr Conductor, Don't Put Me Off the Train; No Wedding Bells for Me; I Lost Another Chance to Be a Hero; Down on Uncle Jasper's Farm.

MORAN, JAIME
See Aguirre, Jaime Moran

MORAND, EDWARD RAYMOND ASCAP 1973
composer, teacher
b Detroit, Mich, July 21, 38. Educ: St John's Univ, BA(English), 60; Manhattan Sch Music, studied piano with Ernest Ulmer, 59-60; Columbia Univ Teachers Col, studied organ with Thomas Richner, MA, 65; studied organ & harpsichord with Anthony Newman, 70-71. Organist & choirmaster, Most Holy Trinity Church, Brooklyn, 59-60, St Michael's, Jersey City, 60-61, St Peter's Church & Sch, Staten Island, 61-69 & Holy Family Church, 70- Music teacher, cath schs, Staten Island, 61-69 & pub schs, New York, 69- Singer, pianist & free-lance music dir, local music productions. Actor, "A Little Night Music," Staten Island Civic Theater. Wrote sch songs for St Peter's Girl's High Sch, St Joseph-By-the-Sea High Sch & St Louis Acad. Songs: Devotion Solidarity and Honor. Instrumental Works: Arr: Silent Night (Flammer).

MOREHEAD, JAMES T ASCAP 1950
composer, author, producer
b Chattanooga, Tenn, Oct 28, 06. Educ: St Mary's Col; studied music with Triante Kefalas & John Hammond. Actor, singer, musician, arranger & vocal coach. Wrote spec material & producer acts. Produced radio package shows; freelance writer & photographer. Chief Collabrs: Sandra Kent, James Cassin, Albert Morehead. Songs & Instrumental Works: Once I Loved You; Sentimental Me; Satisfied; US Army March; Panorama; Aurora Borealis Suite.

MOREL, JORGE
See Scibona, Jorge

MORENO, JOHN JOSEPH ASCAP 1974
composer, author
b Utica, NY, Aug 24, 17. Educ: Utica Free Acad; Ark State Univ, BA, 47; Syracuse Univ, MA, 52. High sch, jr col & col teacher. Chief Collabr: Bart Allen. Songs: Sweet Ballad Goodnight; Singles Dance Lament.

MORENO, MARCOS
See Shaffer, Lloyd M

MOREY, LARRY ASCAP 1938
author
b Los Angeles, Calif, Mar 26, 05; d Santa Barbara, Calif, May 8, 71. Chief Collabrs: Frank Churchill, Albert Hay Malotte. Songs: Heigh Ho, Heigh Ho; Some Day My Prince Will Come; Whistle While You Work; One Song; Ferdinand the Bull; Lavender Blue. Scores: Walt Disney films: Snow White and the Seven Dwarfs; Ferdinand the Bull.

MORGAN, BRUCE
See Hueston, Billy

MORGAN, CAREY ASCAP 1923
composer
b Brownsburg, Ind, Dec 25, 1885; d Pittsburgh, Pa, Jan 6, 60. Wrote spec material for vaudeville. Songs: Rain; My Own Iona; The Blues My Naughty Sweetie Gives to Me; I'm Glad I Can Make You Care; Wait and See. Scores: Bway Stage: Greenwich Village Follies of 1921.

MORGAN, DANIEL WILLIAM ASCAP 1972
composer, author, singer
b Louisville, Ky, Nov 29, 47. Educ: Eastern Ky Univ, BA(fine arts, educ). Leader, lead singer, writer & guitarist, Apple Butter Band, 70-75; solo artist & writer, 75-80. Songs: Thank You for the Dance; Leave a Light in Your Window; This Heart; Will I Ever Fall in Love Again; I Want You Back.

MORGAN, DAVID ASCAP 1958
composer, author, guitarist
b Chicago, Ill, Feb 15, 42. Educ: Los Angeles Cons. Guitarist & singer with Russ Morgan Orch; appeared on radio & TV. Songs: I Couldn't Stand It; Catalina Moon. Instrumental Works: Choral motets.

MORGAN, DORINDA ASCAP 1954
composer, author, artist
b Cincinnati, Ohio, Nov 25, 09. Educ: Cincinnati Acad Art. Chief Collabrs: Bill Anson, Mike Riley, Al Piantadosi. Songs: Man Upstairs; Confidential; Little Women; Moonlight on the Hudson; Cypress; A Flag Is Born; Lolita; C'est Fini; Anne Frank; Bluer Than the Blues; Fantasy.

MORGAN, FREDDY
ASCAP 1953

composer, author, banjo player

b New York, NY, Nov 7, 10; d. Educ: High sch. Mem vaudeville banjo-duo, Morgan & Stone, 27; toured Europe, 1 yr; in London, 29-44; co-founder, Am Overseas Artists, entertaining troops; took USO show to France after invasion; to Far East, 45; joined Spike Jones orch, 47; appeared on radio, TV & records, 11 yrs; master of ceremonies & entertainment dir, Hesperia Inn, Calif; toured Australia, Asia & Europe, 61-64; at Harold's Club, Reno. Chief Collabrs: Norman Malkin & Eddie Brandt. *Songs:* Hey, Mr Banjo; Japanese Farewell Song (Sayonara); I Love You Fair Dinkum, Shimmy Shake; Er War Ein Schoner Monsieur.

MORGAN, HAYDN
ASCAP 1949

composer, arranger, educator

b Van Wert County, Ohio, Mar 25, 1898. Educ: Wooster Col; Cornell Univ; NY Univ, BSM, MA. Supvr music for pub schs: Bellefontaine, Ohio; Mannington, WVa; Findlay, Ohio; Grand Rapids, Mich; Newton, Mass. Visiting instr music educ: Buffalo State Teachers Col, New Eng Cons, Boston Univ, Univ Southern Calif & Harvard Univ. Head music dept, Eastern Mich Univ, 41- Dir, civic choral socs & church choirs. Life mem, Music Educr Nat Conference. *Songs:* Sacred Songs: Bow Down Thine Ear, O Lord; Song of Friendship; Go Not Far From Me, O Lord; Thy Word Is a Light; God Is the Light of the World; Be Thou My Judge, O Lord; Hide Not Thou Thy Face; Arise O God and Show Thy Might; Arr: Snowflakes; Reverence and Praise.

MORGAN, JESSE HILRAY, JR
ASCAP 1972

composer, author, singer

b Independence, La, Feb 1, 47. Educ: Self-taught. Professional entertainer, concerts, nightclubs & USO, 15 yrs. Has band called Jesse Morgan-High Speed Band. Recording artist for var record labels. Also musician. Chief Collabr: Michael Assadourian. *Songs:* You and Me Baby; What Changed Your Mind; Mr Jive; It's Your Sweet Thing.

MORGAN, JESSICA EMMA
ASCAP 1960

composer, author

b Cheswold, Del, May 25, 29. Educ: Springfield High Sch; Montessori teaching degree. Comp of material for vocal groups & singers. Helper music dept, Montessori Schs. Chief Collabrs: Robert Duke Morgan, William Dubrow. *Songs:* Shake Your Disco Dust; Knockety Knock; Lyrics: Record Me in Your Heart; You Oughta See Me Strut My Stuff; Mister Lee, Come Disco With Me.

MORGAN, MARABEL
ASCAP 1975

author

b Crestline, Ohio, June 25, 37. Educ: Mansfield Sr High Sch, Ohio; Ohio State Univ. Author: "The Total Woman," 73; "Total Joy," 76; "The Total Woman Cookbook," 80.

MORGAN, ROBERT B
ASCAP 1971

composer, teacher

b Houston, Tex, July 31, 41. Educ: NTex State Univ, BA(music), MA(music); Univ Ill, DMusA(comp); studied comp with Samuel Adler, Morgan Powell, Gordon Binkerd & Thomas Fredrickson. Instr, NTex State Univ, 63-65, Sam Houston State Univ, 65-70, 72-76 & Univ Ill, 70-72; chmn music dept, High Sch Performing & Visual Arts, Houston, 76- ASCAP grants, 72-80. *Instrumental Works:* Jazz Ens: Anadge; Market Square; T-Bones; Holden; Naturally!; Flow Past; Bluish; Piece of Eight (perc ens); Arr: Texas (David Guion; concert band); May Day (jazz ens); Sinfonietta (symph); Jazz Cantata on Black Poets (NEA grant, chorus & jazz band).

MORGAN, ROBERT DUKE
ASCAP 1958

composer, author

b Philadelphia, Pa, May 26, 1896. Educ: Stanton High Sch; Strayers Bus Col. Chief Collabrs: Jessica E Morgan, Walte Rossi, Rose Montgomery. *Songs:* Hannah From Havana; I Pulled a Star Out of the Sky; Counting the Stars; Rise Up and Shine Up America; Memories for Sale; America Is Worth It All; Kiss Me Baby; I Saw Stars and Flowers; I'm Thru With You; What You Got Now, You Ain't Got; Who's Gonna Call You Sweetheart; Strut Mummers Strut; What's That Stuff Joe's Got That Goes; New New York Town; Kiss Me Baby on a Disco Beat; Let Freedom Ring; Rocking With My Baby; Here Am I; Knock on My Door; Was I Wrong About Love; The Craziest Thing; One Love for Me; Little Pink Man From Mars; When I Got a Date With Love; United and Smiling To-gether; Robin on the Rainbow; Swinging on the Swanee; Don't Get Lost Mr Santa Claus; Hale Pennsylvania; Tain't No Fun What You've Done; Go Get 'em Soldier Boy; Laughing Tears; Consequently; I'll Never Forget To Kiss You Goodnight; Pretty Girl Pretty Girl; Deep Down in My Soul; Cozy Room; We've Got a War to Win; Baby, That'll Be the Day; Record Me in Your Heart; Steal, Lie and Swear; The Moon Is in Tears Tonight; Shake Your Disco Dust; Everybody's Shaken At My House; Mr Lee, Come Disco With Me; Wrap It Up; I Stopped Crying Over You.

MORGAN, RUSS
ASCAP 1939

composer, conductor, trombonist

b Scranton, Pa, Apr 29, 04; d Las Vegas, Nev, Aug 7, 69. Educ: Pub schs. Arr for Victor Herbert, John Philip Sousa; later Boswell Sisters, Louis Armstrong, Freddy Martin & Ted Fiorito. Music dir, stage productions, Detroit; for Brunswick Records, 34. Leader & trombonist in own orch, 36; appeared in hotels, nightclubs & theatres throughout US. Had own radio & TV shows; also in films. Pianist & arr. Chief Collabrs: Dave Franklin, Eddie De Lange, Joe Venuti, Arnold Johnson, Mitchell Parish. *Songs:* Does Your Heart Beat for Me? (theme); Please Think of Me; Somebody Else Is Taking My Place; You're Nobody Til Somebody Loves You; So Tired; Homespun; So Long; Sweet Eloise; Don't Cry, Sweetheart; Wise Guy; Flower of Dawn; Tell Me You Love Me; Goodnight, Little Angel; This Is the Last Time I'll Cry Over You.

MORGAN, THOMAS R
ASCAP 1964

composer, author, publisher

b Philadelphia, Pa, Feb 4, 36. Educ: Univ Va. Writer for advert agency, N W Ayers & Son, 8 yrs. Formed Blue Star Music, 64; also artists' mgr. *Songs:* Arr: House of the Rising Sun.

MORGAN, TOMMY

See Edwards, Thomas Morgan

MORGIO, GEORGE A (NOEL THATCHER)
ASCAP 1968

composer

b New Haven, Conn, Sept 30, 42. Singer, nightclubs & concerts; recorded with Mr G Records & Epic Records. *Songs:* Black on White; The Rainmaker.

MORIANA, ROCCO ANTHONY
ASCAP 1976

composer

b Wiloughby, Ohio, Nov 5, 27. Educ: Lincoln High Sch, Cleveland, Ohio; Ohio Univ; Univ Southern Calif. Started in motion pictures, Paramount Studios, 49, then to TV series & independent motion pictures. Supvr music & music ed, TV & movies, 12 yrs. Music supvr, Aaron Spelling Productions. Chief Collabr: Steve Livingston. *Songs:* Lyrics: Hop-Skip-Hum; Tweet M and M. *Scores:* Film/TV: Living Time; Street Flute.

MORITT, FRED G
ASCAP 1949

composer, author

b New York, NY, Oct 5, 05. Educ: NY Univ; Brooklyn Law Sch, LLB; pvt music study. Mem, NY State Assembly, 38-44 & NY State Senate, 44-57; also civil court judge, NY. *Songs:* Cansado; I Wrote a Love Song; Oh Willie I'm Waiting; Sing Everyone Sing; Song of December; Prologue to Pagliacci (English transl). *Scores:* Stage: The Third Kiss (basis of London musical, Robert and Elizabeth).

MORITZ, EDVARD
ASCAP 1939

composer, conductor

b Hamburg, Ger, June 23, 1891; d New York, NY, Sept 30, 74. Educ: Studied music with Paul Juon, Nikisch, Flesch, Diemer, Marsick & Debussy. Symph cond, Europe & US. *Instrumental Works:* 4 symphonies; Viola Sonata; 6 violin sonatas; Cello Concerto; Violin Concerto; Concerto for Violin, Cello; Divertimento for Strings, Tympani; Der Klingende Garten (voice, orch); 2 piano concertos; Italian Overture; The Blue Bird (suite); American Overture; The Animated Intervals (piano); 6 string quartets; Quintet for Saxophone, Strings; Divertimento for Three B Flat Clarinets; Scherzo Bassoon and Piano; Andante for Four Saxophones; Pavane for Clarinet B Flat and Piano; Divertimento for Flute, Clarinet (B) and Bassoon; Quintet for Flute, Oboe, Clarinet, Horn and Bassoon; Sonata for Alto Saxophone and Piano No 1 & 2; Saxophone Quartet (altos, tenor & baritone); Sonata for Flute and Piano; Intermezzo for E Flat Alto Saxophone and Piano; Cantata for Alto and String Quartet.

MORO

See Bohn, Walter (Buddy) Morrow

MOROSS, JEROME
ASCAP 1949

composer

b Brooklyn, NY, Aug 1, 13. Educ: NY Univ; Juilliard (fel); also two Guggenheim Fels. Writer for concert, ballet, Bway, opera, films, TV & radio. Chief Collabrs: John Latouche, Edward Eager. *Songs:* Music: You Ain't So Hot; Life Could Be So Beautiful; I've Got Me; My Yellow Flower; Riding on the Breeze; Lazy Afternoon; Windflowers; Store Bought Suit; Goona Goona; It's the Going Home Together; Stay With Me; My Rebel Heart; Another Day, Another Sunset; Shiloh; The Ballad of Stonewall Jackson; Wagons Ho; Have You Seen Him?; I Can't Remember; The Freedom Train. *Instrumental Works:* Symphony No 1; Frankie and Johnny; The Last Judgement; The Big Country; Music for the Flicks; A Tall Story; Variations on a Waltz; Paeans; Biguine; Those Everlasting Blues; Sonatina for Clarinet Choir; Sonatina for Contra Bass and Piano; Sonatina for Woodwind Quintet; Sonatina for Brass Quintet; Sonata for Piano Duet and String Quartet; Concerto for Flute and String Quartet; Recitative and Aria for Violin and Piano. *Scores:* Bway stage: Parade; Ballet/Opera: Susanna and the Elders; Willie the Weeper; The Eccentricities of Davy Crockett; Riding Hood Revisited; Gentlemen, Be Seated; Sorry, Wrong Number; Film background: The Big Country; The Cardinal; Proud Rebel; The Warlord; Rachel, Rachel; TV background: Wagon Train.

MORPHIS, ROBERT C (BOBBY TWINE)
ASCAP 1979

composer, author, singer

b Glendale, Calif, Mar 28, 48. Educ: Burbank High Sch; Los Angeles Valley Col, AA, 68; Army/Navy Music Sch, Norfolk, Va, grad, 70. Drummer & singer clubs

& TV; wrote, produced & recorded albums, singles & commercial jingles. John Philips Sousa Award, 66. Chief Collab: Mark J Seamons. *Songs:* Ice, Fire and Desire; Lyrics: Dreams and Promises. *Albums:* Open Any Door; Harvest.

MORRA, EGIDIO (GENE)
ASCAP 1959
composer, author, conductor
b Panni, Italy, Apr 4, 06. Educ: Studied music with father; Columbia Univ, studied with Percy J Starnes. Euphonium soloist in father's band, toured Italy. Came to US, 22. Featured baritone horn soloist with Giuseppe Creatore Band & New York Symphonic Band. With Manhattan Concert Band & New York World's Fair Band, 39-40; Cities Service Band Am, Paul Lavalle, cond, NBC radio, 10 yrs. Music teacher, Gotham Sch Music, St Regis High Sch, Am Sch Music & Brooklyn Prep High Sch. Dir & teacher, Power Mem Acad, 17 yrs. Featured soloist with many recording cos under dir of Robert R Bennett, Merl Evans, Jack Gleason, Andre Kostelanetz, G Iasilli, A Giammatteo & others. Trombonist, Loew's Theatres, RKO, Century Theatres, Wagner Opera Co, D'Oyly Carte Opera Co & Sigmund Romberg Orch. *Songs & Instrumental Works:* Why Can't I Kiss You Now?; Don't Be a Stranger; Nocturnal Serenade; Bimba Mia; Regina Mia; Non Far Piangere Il Mio Cuore; Romantique; Concertino in B Flat Major; Polka Caprice; Trilogy (trumpet trio); Clara (waltz caprice); Tic-Tac-Toe Polka; Norma (grand fantasy); Bicentennial Salute Overture; Concerto for Euphonium; Love Waltz; My Beautiful; What I Found in You; Lonesome; I Lost The World When I Lost My Girl; I've Changed My Mind About You; Just Waiting to Hear From You; My Fondest Dream; Father, Don't Be Mean; Charms of Love; Lover's Springtide; Sempre Mia; Occhioni Neri; Ave Maria; 24 melodic studies in all major & minor keys.

MORRIS, BERNARD
See Bernikoff, Morris

MORRIS, CHARLES EDWARD
ASCAP 1961
composer, conductor
b Carthage, SDak, Sept 25, 13. Educ: Pub schs. Led own dance band; founded music co, Spencer, Iowa. *Songs:* I'd Like to Change Your Name From Miss to Mrs; You Forgot All About Me; I Think You Did It Just for Me; Oink-Oink-Oink; Say a Prayer for a Buddy Somewhere; Hill Billy Lovin'; Black Hills Moon; This I Know.

MORRIS, COZETTE MARIE
ASCAP 1977
composer, author, singer
b New Orleans, La, Oct 4, 52. Educ: St Francis Xavier High Sch, New Orleans; City Col; studied dramatics in Los Angeles. Started as dancer at age 8. Went to work professionally at age 13. Joined with husband as singer & became duo of Sugar & Sweet. Has done commercial TV work for CBS. Recording artist with Steam Records. Worked in movie, "Lady Sings the Blues." Chief Collabs: Cozette Landry, Mike Goldstein, Edmond Steinerberg. *Songs:* Tonight We'll Get Married; Got Me Crying; Dream Love; Our Wedding Night; Who Is the Fool?.

MORRIS, ELVA AGNES
ASCAP 1963
composer, author
b DeGray, SDak, July 28, 17. Educ: High sch; libr credits. Asst librarian; poetess. Chief Collabrs: Frances Stelzer, Neil Wrightman. *Songs:* I Know That I'm a Fool. *Albums:* Talking to Myself; Making Plans.

MORRIS, HAROLD CECIL
ASCAP 1939
composer, pianist, educator
b San Antonio, Tex, Mar 17, 1890; d New York, NY, May 6, 64. Educ: Univ Tex, BA; Cincinnati Cons, MM, MusD; studied with Godowsky, Rothwell, Scalero. Piano soloist, symph orchs. Fac, Juilliard Sch, 22-39, Teachers Col, Columbia Univ, 39-46 & Castle Sch, Tarrytown. Guest prof, Rice Inst, Duke Univ, Univ Tex. Dir, Int Soc for Contemporary Music, 36-40. Mem, MacDowell Colony, 13 summers; life mem & vpres, Nat Asn for Am Composers & Conductors; life fel, Int Inst of Arts & Letters, Switz. *Instrumental Works:* Poem for Orchestra; Dum-a-Lum; Piano Concerto (Juilliard Publ award); Violin Concerto (Nat Fedn Music Clubs award); American Epic; Sonata for Violin, Piano; Suite for Orchestra (Philadelphia Music Guild award); Piano Quintet; Ballet Music for Woodwinds (Tex Composers award); Trio No 2 for Piano, Violin, Cello (Soc for Publ Am Music award); Passacaglia, Adagio and Finale (Rockefeller Found comn for Louisville Symph); Symphony No 1, No 2, No 3 (Tex Composers award); Piano Sonata No 1, No 2, No 3 (Fel of Am Composers award) No 4 (Nat Asn for Am Composers & Conductors Publ award).

MORRIS, HAYWARD
ASCAP 1954
composer, teacher, orchestrator
b Brooklyn, NY, Dec 20, 22; d New Brunswick, NJ, Mar 2, 77. Educ: Manhattan Sch of Music, BMus, 50; comp with Giannini, Serly & Creston. Comp/arr for numerous TV, radio shows, commercials, documentary & commercial films, theatrical productions, concert stage, ballets & pop tunes. Fac, Manhattan Sch of Music & NY Univ. Awards: Golden Eagle Award, NY & Chicago Film Fest; Cleo Award, Cannes Film Fest. Chief Collabrs: Stone Widney, Renee Morris Spiro. *Songs:* Music: Auctioneer; Love's a Precious Thing. *Instrumental Works:* Gabrielle; You're Crazy; I'm Not a Fool; Breaking Point; The Day Is Long; Theme and Variations for Jazz Orchestra; Phoenix—Brass Ensemble and Percussion; All Birds in Flight (3 flutes). *Songs*

& *Instrumental Works:* Your Own Thing (orchestrations; Merit Award, Drama Circle Critics, 68; NY Art Dir Show Merit Award). *Scores:* Operas: A View From the Bridge; Paradise Lost.

MORRIS, JOHN
ASCAP 1965
composer
b Elizabeth, NJ, Oct, 18, 26. Educ: Arthur Jordan Cons, Ind; Juilliard Sch, piano scholarship; New Sch; Univ Wash, studied piano with Alfred Mirovitch. Comp, ballet music for 27 musicals incl "Bye Bye Birdie", "Bells Are Ringing" & "Mack and Mabel," TV, 25 musical specials incl Anne Bancroft & Jack Lemmon, all Mel Brooks' films & 15 Shakespeare scores for Joseph Papp's NY Shakespeare Fest. Recipient Emmy award. Chief Collabs: Gerald Freedman, Jerome Robbins, Bob Rosse, Michael Kidd, Agnes DeMille, Power Champion, Herbert Moss, Danny Daniels, Anna Sokolow. *Scores:* Bway show: A Time for Singing; Film/TV: The Producers; The Twelve Chairs; Blazing Saddles (Academy Award nomination); Young Frankenstein; Silent Movie; High Anxiety; Sherlock Holmes' Smarter Brother; The World's Greatest Lover; The Bank Shot; The Last Remake of Beau Geste; The In-Laws; The Adams Chronicles; The Scarlet Letter; Julia Child's French Chef (theme); The Tap Dance Kid (Emmy Award best score); Georgia O'Keeffe; In God We Trust; The Elephant Man; History of the World, Part 1.

MORRIS, LEE
ASCAP 1948
composer, author, teacher
b Boston, Mass, Mar 12, 12; d Miami, Fla, Oct 18, 78. Educ: Boston Latin Sch; Colby Col, BA; Boston Teachers Col, MEd. Writer of spec material for singers, hotel and nightclub revues, also musical commercials. History teacher. Chief Collabrs: Bernie Wayne, Dick Manning, Dolores Fuller, Clint Ballard, Jr, Bobby Vinton. *Songs:* If I Only Had a Match; Thirsty for Your Kisses; It All Seems New; Blue Velvet; I Don't Want to See Tomorrow; Night People; Peppermint Stick Parade; Tina.

MORRIS, MARK BENNETT
composer, studio musician
b St Louis, Mo, Apr 24, 42. Educ: Studied with David Rizzo, 50-54, with George Carey, 55-58 & with Jules Mendelson, Cal Berlinner & Tommy Thomas; Univ SFla, BA, 69. Founder & cond, Univ SFla Stage Band. Principal percussionist, Tampa Philh Orch. Tympanist, St Petersburg & WCoast Symphs. Perc instr, Univ Tampa. Recording studio percussionist & comp with Johnny Cash, Porter Waggoner, Dolly Parton, Bobby Goldsboro, Elvis Presley, Larry Gatlin, Joe Tex, Dickie Betts, Allman Bros, John Davidson, Glen Campbell, Ray Charles & Kenny Rogers, Nashville, Tenn, 69- Commercials with 7-Up, Budweiser, Schlitz, Chrysler, Heath, Burger Queen, Libby's, Fab & Lincoln Mercury.

MORRIS, MARSHALL
ASCAP 1977
composer, author, singer
b New Orleans, La, Jan 12, 46. Educ: Booker T Washington High Sch, New Orleans; self-taught in music. Professional singer, songwriter, recording artist & producer. Has traveled & performed throughout US in nightclubs & on TV. Has own publ & record co. Chief Collabs: Mike Goldstein, Edmond Steinerberg, Cozette Landry. *Songs:* Tonight We'll Get Married; Who Is the Fool!?; Dream Love; Our Wedding Night; Got Me Crying.

MORRIS, MELVILLE
ASCAP 1914
composer, pianist
b New York, NY, Oct 5, 1888. Educ: Pub schs. Pianist, J H Remick Co; accompanist to Al Jolson & Blossom Seeley; vaudeville entertainer; mgr, Paul Whiteman Orchs, 23. Charter mem, ASCAP. Chief Collabrs: Gus Kahn, Edward Madden. *Songs:* Ragtime Regiment Band; Kewpie Doll; Tiddle de Wink; Kangaroo Hop; On the Bay of Old Bombay; Cute and Pretty. *Scores:* London Stage: You'd Be Surprised.

MORRIS, ROBERT
See Miketta, Bob

MORRIS, STEVLAND (STEVIE WONDER)
singer, composer, musician
b Saginaw, Mich, May 13, 50. Educ: Detroit Pub Schs; Mich Sch for Blind. Solo singer, Whitestone Baptist Church, Detroit, 59. Recording artist with Motown Records, Detroit, 63-70. Founder music publ co, Black Bull, 70. Appeared in Films: "Bikini Beach" & "Muscle Beach Party." Frequent TV appearances incl "Ed Sullivan Show", "American Band Stand", "Shivaree", "Flip Wilson Show", "Symphonic Soul", "Mike Douglas Show" & others. Awards: Musician of Yr, Down Beat Mag Rock/Blues Poll, 73-75 & 77-78; Best Selling Male Soul Artist of Yr, Nat Asn Rec Merchandisers, 74; rec'd numerous awards for best singer/songwriter; Rock Music Award, 77; Am Music Award, 78. *Songs:* Uptight; I'm Wondering; Everytime I See You I Go Wild; I Was Made to Love Her; Hold Me; Shoo-Be-Doo-Be-Doo-Da-Day; You Met Your Match; My Girl; My Cherie Amour; Never Had a Dream Come True; Signed, Sealed, Delivered I'm Yours; I Wish (Grammy Award, 77); Don't You Worry 'Bout a Thing; You Haven't Done Nothin'; Boogie on Reggae Woman (Grammy Award, 75); Sir Duke; Another Star; You Are the Sunshine of My Life (Grammy Award, 74); Superstition (Grammy Award, 74); Higher Ground; Living for the City (Grammy Award, 75). *Albums:* 12 Year Old Genius; Tribute to Uncle Ray; Jazz Soul; With a Song in My Heart; Signed, Sealed and Delivered; My Cherie

Amour; At the Beach; Uptight; Down to Earth; I Was Made to Love Her; Someday at Christmas; Stevie Wonder's Greatest Hits; Music of My Mind; Innervisions (Grammy Award, 74); Fulfillingness' First Finale (Grammy Award, 75); Songs in the Key of Life (Grammy Award, 77); Stevie Wonder Live; Where I'm Coming From; Talking Book; Journey Through the Secret Life of Plants.

MORRISON, ALEX
See Clark, Allan

MORRISON, JAMES DOUGLAS
composer, author, singer
b Melbourne, Fla, Dec 8, 43; d Paris, France, July 3, 71. Educ: St Petersburg Jr Col, 62; Univ Calif, Los Angeles, cinema arts degree, 66. Joined group, The Doors & performed with group as lead singer, US & Europe. Author poetry bk, "The Lords and the New Creatures." Chief Collabrs: Ray Manzarek, Robby Krieger, John Densmore. *Songs:* Light My Fire; The End. *Albums:* The Doors; LA Woman; Strange Days; Absolutely Live; Waiting for the Sun; American Prayer; Soft Parade; Weird Scenes Inside; The Doors Full Circle.

MORRISON, JULIA   ASCAP 1968
composer, author
b Minneapolis, Minn. Educ: Univ Iowa, BA, MFA; Univ Minn, MA; NTex State Univ, spec study in electronic & computer music. Publ of lyrics. Residence at Yaddo, 14 months. Resident visitor (computer music & films; computerized text manipulation), Bell Laboratories. Blues singer in jazz clubs. Author bk: "Smile to the Bone." Chief Collabr: Dika Newlin. *Songs:* To Mother on Her Day (satire); Musta Been Water Here. *Instrumental Works:* First Thing the Morning (perc). *Scores:* Opera: Rübezahl; Say What (dance); Films: Good Old-Fashioned.

MORRISON, MARSHALL LEE, III   ASCAP 1974
composer, author, singer
b Dyersburg, Tenn, Sept 5, 44. Educ: Bruce High Sch; Howard Univ Sch Music, BM, 68, Col Fine Arts, MMEd, 78, studied voice with LeRoy O Dorsey, 64-68; grad vocal studies with Jeanette Walters-Brown, 77. Lead singer in vocal group, Mayfield Singers; toured eastern US & recorded with group. Comp & studio musician, Curtom Record Co, Chicago. Wrote songs for group, Voices of East Harlem. Background singer & instrumentalist on album Now. Soloist in Univ Chicago production of Leonard Bernstein's "Mass," theater piece for singers, dancers & musicians. Baritone soloist with Howard Univ Concert Choir which appeared occasionally with Nat Symph Orch. Asst cond of Howard Univ Chapel Choir on grad assistantship. Chorister, Grant Park Symph Chorus, Chicago & Chicago Sunday Evening Club Chorale in TV broadcast. Appeared as featured vocalist & part of song team, Colette & Marshall, in nightclubs in Chicago area. Voice teacher & coach. *Songs:* Jimmy Joe Lee; Amazing Love; Take a Little Time to Love; Take a Stand; Lyrics: Just Got to Be Myself; Can You Feel It?.

MORRISON, ROBERT EDWIN   ASCAP 1968
composer, author, singer
b Biloxi, Miss, Aug 6, 42. Educ: Biloxi High Sch; Miss State Univ, BS, 65. Contract actor, Screen-Gems TV. Recording artist, Columbia, Capitol & Monument Records; in var TV commercials. To Nashville, 73; joined Music City Music of combine music group. Formed Southern Nights Music, 79. Songs written for film, "Urban Cowboy." ASCAP Country Writer, 78. Chief Collabrs: Debbie Hupp, Johnny MacRae, Johnny Wilson. *Songs:* The River's Too Wide; You're the One; Let Me Be Your Baby; You'd Make an Angel Want to Cheat; Love the World Away; Music: You Decorated My Life (Grammy Award, country song, 79); Are You On the Road to Lovin' Me Again?; Angels, Roses, and Rain; Lookin' for Love.

MORRISS, RALPH ALEXANDER (RANDY)   ASCAP 1977
composer, author, singer
b St Louis, Mo, July 20, 52. Educ: St Louis Country Day; Aspen Music Sch; Univ Colo, BAMus; studied arr & comp with Wayne Scott. Formed Westworld Productions, 76. Keyboardist, arr, producer & solo entertainer in nightclub act. Chief Collabr: Norman Wells. *Songs:* Java Time; Easy Street; Candle Love; Music: Time Turn Back Again.

MORRISSEY, JOHN JOSEPH   ASCAP 1954
composer, teacher
b New York, NY, Nov 9, 06. Columbia Col, AB, 28, Teachers Col, MA, 32. Instr music, Teachers Col, Columbia Univ, 32-38; prof music & dir bands, Tulane Univ, 38-42. Music Branch, USA, 42-46, Maj. Head dept music, Tulane Univ, 46-68; emer prof musical arts, 68- *Instrumental Works:* Caribbean Fantasy; Viva Mexico; Concerto Grosso for Band; Music for a Ceremony; Soliloquy for Trumpet; French Quarter Suite; Carnival Day in New Orleans; Gala for Band.

MORRISSEY, WILL   ASCAP 1948
composer, author, producer
b New York, NY, June 19, 1887; d Santa Barbara, Calif, Dec 17, 57. Educ: Engineering, Cooper Inst, NY. WW I, AEF. Co-founder, Overseas Theatre League. Wrote spec material for vaudeville acts; prod, wrote scores & librettos for musicals, NY & Hollywood. *Songs:* Covered Wagon Days; Loving You the Way I Do.

MORROW, BUDDY   ASCAP 1951
composer, conductor, trombonist
b New Haven, Conn. Educ: Juilliard Sch Music. Trombonist in orchs incl Paul Whiteman, Artie Shaw, Tommy Dorsey, Vincent Lopez, Bob Crosby & Jimmy Dorsey. USN, WW II. Cond own band, 45-46; then in radio, New York; formed touring orch, 51; made many records. *Songs:* Should I Believe My Heart?; When the Moon Is Gone; Our Song of Love.

MORSE, DOLLY
See Morse, Theodora

MORSE, THEODORA (D A ESROM, DOLLY   ASCAP 1914
MORSE, DOROTHY TERRISS)
author, publisher
b Brooklyn, NY, July 11, 1890; d White Plains, NY, Nov 10, 53. Charter mem, ASCAP, first woman mem. Chief Collabrs: Theodore Morse (husband), Ferde Grofe, Joe Burke. *Songs:* Blue Bell; Another Rag; When Uncle Joe Plays a Rag on His Old Banjo; Bobbin' Up and Down; Three O'Clock in the Morning; Siboney; Hail, Hail, the Gang's All Here; Sing Me Love's Lullaby; Baby Your Mother; Wonderful One.

MORSE, THEODORE   ASCAP 1914
composer, publisher
b Washington, DC, Apr 13, 1873; d New York, NY, May 25, 24. Educ: Md Mil Acad; pvt music study. Worked for Oliver Ditson Music Co; then became publ in partnership with F B Haviland. Charter mem, ASCAP. Chief Collabrs: Theodora Morse (wife), Edward Madden, Howard Johnson, Richard Buck, Al Bryan, Jack Mahoney. *Songs:* Dear Old Girl; Aren't You the Wise Ole Owl?; I've Got a Feelin' for You; Hooray for Baffins Bay; Blue Bell; A Little Boy Called Taps; Keep a Little Cosy Corner in Your Heart for Me; Down in Jungle Town; Good Old USA; Keep on the Sunny Side; He's a College Boy; Another Rag; When Uncle Joe Plays a Rag on His Old Banjo; Bobbin' Up and Down; I'd Rather Be a Lobster Than a Wise Guy; M-O-T-H-E-R; Hail, Hail, the Gang's All Here; Sing Me Love's Lullaby.

MORTON, FERDINAND JOSEPH (JELLY ROLL)   ASCAP 1939
composer, pianist, conductor
b New Orleans, La, Sept 20, 1885; d Los Angeles, Calif, July 10, 41. Began playing piano in New Orleans clubs, 02; later toured country; made many records as soloist and with Morton's Red Hot Peppers; mgr, Washington, DC nightclub, 37-38; singer & arr. *Songs & Instrumental Works:* Jelly Roll Blues; King Porter Stomp; Winin' Boy Blues; The Pearls; Wolverine Blues; Milenberg Joys; Wild Man Blues; Shoe Shiner's Drag (London Blues); The Crave; Buddy Bolden's Blues; Perfect Rag; Frog-i-More Rag; Kansas City Stomp.

MORTON, FRANK
See Ascher, Everett

MORTON, RICHARD   ASCAP 1972
composer, author
b London, Eng, Apr 19, 48. Educ: State Univ Oneonta. Recording artist; also a playwright, US & other countries. *Albums:* Razmataz.

MORTON, VINCENT GEORGE   ASCAP 1967
composer, author, singer
b Lockport, NY, July 15, 33. Educ: Hollywood Prof High Sch; Loyola Univ, Los Angeles; Univ Southern Calif. Studio singer; recording artist for var cos. Actor, Los Angeles; commercials & TV. Arr & cond for Vikki Carr, Connie Stevens, The Letterman & others. Chief Collabrs: Frankie Laine, David Wilson. *Songs:* The World's Filled With Love; Magic Carpet Ride; Wait for Me; Goodbye; Lyrics: Classical Gas.

MOSCA, SALVATORE JOSEPH   ASCAP 1977
composer, author, performer
b Mt Vernon, NY, Apr 27, 27. Educ: NY Col Music, teachers cert; NY Univ, authorized teacher Schillenger Syst; pvt lessons with Lennie Tristano, 8 yrs. With 50th Army Ground Forces Band, USA, 45-47. Teacher jazz improvisation, 41- Made recordings for Atlantic, Prestige, Verve, Choice & Interplay record cos; gave solo concert, Alice Tolley Hall; performer, major jazz clubs incl Birdland, Basin Street, Top of Gate & Village Vanguard. *Songs:* Vitamin Blues; Family Song. *Instrumental Works:* Sal's Line; Oracle; Scrapple Solo; Night Blues; Sal's Stride; Dassy; In There; KLM; MFM; SAM; For LT; For Myself; Tumbles; The Gift; The Flame; Finishing Touch; The Hard Way.

MOSELEY, JAMES ORVILLE (JOB)   ASCAP 1970
composer, author, teacher
b Alcorn College, Miss, Sept 21, 09. Educ: Bolivar County Training Sch high sch; Morehouse Col, AB; Chicago Musical Col, teachers cert; Univ Mich, MM; NY Univ; Univ Southern Calif, doctoral studies; studied with Quincy Porter, Noble Cain, Ross Lee Finney, Eric Delamater, Wesley LaViolette & Halsey Stevens. Adminr, teacher music, comp & author, Natchez Col, Southern Univ, USA, Los Angeles Pub Schs, Calif State Univ, Long Beach & Morgan State Univ. Cond. Chief Collabr: Vivian Moseley. *Songs & Instrumental Works:* Little Wheel A-Turning (SA, arr); Hand Me Down (SSA, arr); Bronze Airmen (band).

MOSHAY, JOE ASCAP 1959
composer, author, violinist
b Norfolk, Va, Dec 1, 08. Educ: Cons Music, Mexico City. Cond own orch in ballrooms, hotels, nightclubs & society balls.

MOSHIER, CARMEN ASCAP 1970
composer, author
b Blockton, Iowa, Nov 19, 32. Educ: Univ Iowa, BA; Univ Houston, MEd. Author: "Say and Sing Your Way to Successful Living." Songs: Let's Be!; Thank God We Live in America!; Tell Them That You Love Them; Life Is for Living; Be!

MOSKOWITZ, SEYMOUR L (CY) ASCAP 1972
composer, author
b New York, NY, Sept 2, 26. Educ: DeWitt Clinton High Sch, dipl; NY Univ, BS; City Col New York, business cert. Co-founded Cy-Del Production Co, 70. Produced jazz concerts for City Col New York, Columbia Univ, churches & clubs. Co-founded CDP Record Co, 79. Produced jazz album, The Soul and Sounds of Del Rae, 79. Active in producing shows & benefits. Chief Collabr: comp, Del Rae. Songs: Lyrics: Contemplation Blues (Grammy nomination); Goodbye Love (Grammy nomination); Sing My Blues Away; Easy to Love You; All We Ever Do Is Cry.

MOSLEY, LAWRENCE LEO (SNUB) ASCAP 1953
composer, author, singer
b Little Rock, Ark, Dec 29, 05. Educ: Gibbs High Sch, Little Rock; Cutair Cons, Cincinnati; studied with Dave Gornston. Entertained troops worldwide. Recording artist for var cos. Featured on stage in clubs & hotels, US & Eng. Songs: Devil Sits on the Throne of Love; Amen, Stolen; Juice Head Willie; Cabo Jo; Blue Memories; Music: Pretty Eyed Baby; Man With the Funny Horn; Snubs Blues.

MOSS, EARL ASCAP 1969
composer
b Dallas, Tex, Jan 6, 40. Educ: Nat Sch Home Study. Recorded with group, The Festivals, for Mercury Records, 63; recorded two songs on a Doc Severensen's album, 76 & worked on road with him, 76. Lead vocalist, The Festivals. Chief Collabrs: Jerry Ross, Al Kline. Songs: I'll Always Love You; You've Got the Makings of a Lover; Baby Show It; Red, Yellow, Brown, Black and White; So in Love; Gee Baby; My Way; Music: You're Gonna Make It.

MOSS, EIVIND ROY ASCAP 1970
composer
b Everett, Mass, May 8, 09. Educ: Kirksville Col of Osteopathic Med, 40. Gen practiner, 44 yrs. Songs & Instrumental Works: Wintertime in Maine; Fetchin' Gretchen Home; Lullaby for Baby.

MOSS, ELLSWORTH FRANCIS (DON RUBE RICHARDS) ASCAP 1975
composer, author, teacher
b Chicago, Ill, Mar 11, 04. Educ: Studied violin with Prof Hart, LaViva Hines & Frank Davidson. Played at age 9 in Lutheran Church recital. Played for many theatrical engagements & revues. Wrote numerous compositions for var acts & performers. Joined Am Fedn of Musicians, 22. Songs: Let's Pretend (There Will Be No Tomorrow); Hurry Back to Me; Happy Birthday, Dear Grandma! (Grandpa); I Sing to You—My Melody of Love; Mia Bella (We All Love You); Mister Bumble Berry (theme song).

MOSS, JEFFREY ARNOLD ASCAP 1965
composer, author
b New York, NY. Educ: Princeton Univ. One of the original creators of TV series, "Sesame Street," also head writer and composer/lyricist. Wrote text, "In the Beginning," book & lyrics, "Double Feature." Rec'd three Emmy Awards. Songs: Many songs for Sesame Street incl Rubber Duckie; The People in Your Neighborhood; I Love Trash; Everyone Makes Mistakes; What Do I Do When I'm Alone?. Scores: Double Feature (musical); Stage: In the Beginning.

MOSS, LAWRENCE KENNETH ASCAP 1966
composer, educator
b Los Angeles, Calif, Nov 18, 27. Educ: Univ Calif, Los Angeles, BA, 49; Eastman Sch Music, MA, 50; Univ Southern Calif, PhD(comp), 57; principal teachers, Leon Kirchner & Ingolf Dahl. Fulbright fel, Vienna. Army serv as German translator, Frankfurt, 54-56. Instr, Mills Col, 56-59. Guggenheim fels, Florence, Italy, 59 & 68. From asst prof to assoc prof, Yale Univ. Morse fel, Rome, 64-65. Prof comp & dir comp, Univ Md, College Park. Chief Collabrs: Eric Bentley, Maren Erskine, John Gracen Brown. Instrumental Works: Remembrances (8 performers); Evocation and Song (alto sax & tape); Symphonies (brass quintet & chamber orch); Songs & Instrumental Works: Unseen Leaves (soprano, oboe, tape, slides, lights). Scores: The Brute (comic opera in one act).

MOSSMAN, BINA NIEPER ASCAP 1969
composer, singer
b Honolulu, Hawaii, Jan 7, 1893. Educ: McKinley High Sch, Honolulu; Phillips Commercial Sch, Honolulu; singing of old time Hawaiian songs with Queen Liliuokalani, last queen of Hawaii. Led, Bina Mossman's Glee Club, 14-44, sang for entertainments for Princess David Kawananakoa, Prince & Princess Jonah Kuhio Kalanianaole, gov of Hawaii & many others; organized entertainment for Pres Roosevelt's visit to Hawaii, 34; dir, Kasehumanu Choral Group, 52-68, group sang at many hotels in Hawaii, toured mainland several times, went to Orient, 66 & Europe, 68, sang at Seattle World's Fair, 62 & New York World's Fair, 64. Secy to exec secy, Hawaiian Homes Comn, 22-25 & Territorial Employees Retirement Syst, 25-34; on staff, Territorial Legislature, var times, 25-49; mem, Territorial House of Rep, 39, 43 & 45; Republican Nat Committeewoman, Hawaii, 40-57; curator, Queen Emma's Summer Palace, 58-68. Songs: He Ono; Niu Haohao; Ka Pua U'i; Mapuana Kuu Aloha; Kuulei; Stevedore Hula; Lae Lae.

MOSSMAN, TED ASCAP 1941
composer, author, pianist
b Chicago, Ill, Apr 6, 14; d. Educ: Chicago Musical Col (scholarship, Gold Medal); Univ Rochester; Eastman Sch Music (fel), BM; Univ Ill; Juilliard Sch Music (scholarship), studied with Rudolph Ganz, Howard Hanson, Hedy & William Spielter & Jules Appielle. Concert debut, Rochester Philh; music dir, Chicago Cube Theatre; also Victory Bond Rallies, World War II; soloist, Carnegie Hall, with symph orch; pianist in supper clubs. Songs: Till the End of Time; Full Moon and Empty Arms; When I Write My Song; The Loveliness of You; Dingbat the Singing Cat; Dream On; What a Lovely Afternoon; Don't You Ever Let Me Go; Six PM; Christmas Comes But Once a Year; The Encounter; Good for Me. Songs & Instrumental Works: Salome (ballet); Chicago, Illinois (overture); Lotus Blue (tone poem); Abraham Lincoln (music drama); Let Freedom Ring (chorus, orch); Three Children's Dances; Piano, Orch: Central Park Romance; Piano Concerto; New York Concerto.

MOTT, HAROLD ASCAP 1947
author, percussionist
b Cortland, NY, May 9, 08; d. Educ: Rutgers Univ; Newark Col Eng. Newspaper reporter, 4 yrs; publicist. Songs: Ho Hum, It's Spring; Go Happy, Go Lucky, Go Love; The Little Wooden Soldiers Go to War; Don't Have to Tell Nobody; So They Tell Me; Wanderlust; Can't Get the Mood; Whistle Down Lane.

MOTTOLA, ANTHONY ASCAP 1952
composer, guitarist
b Kearny, NJ, Apr 18, 18. Educ: Studied comp with Tom Timothy & Stefan Wolpe. Began career as staff guitarist, CBS, New York, age 20; NBC staff guitarist, 20 yrs, working on the "Perry Como Show", "Sid Caesar Comedy Hour", "Sing-Along with Mitch" & 12 yrs on the "Tonight Show." Comp & guitarist, CBS-TV Mystery Drama "Danger," 6 yrs. Free lance studio work, New York. Appeared with Frank Sinata's Tour. Emmy Award for music score, WNEW-TV Special, "My Childhood," 63. Instrumental Works: Jimmy's Blues; I Love, I Live, I Love; Mitzi; Tony's Tune; Lullaby de Espana; Warm Feelings; Maria Nicole; For Two in Love.

MOTZAN, OTTO ASCAP 1914
composer, violinist, conductor
b Hungary, Oct 12, 1880; d New York, NY, Jan 15, 37. Educ: Hungary. To US 07; led own orch; music dir for Belle Baker & Bway stage scores, "The Passing Show", "The Show of Wonders." Songs & Instrumental Works: Bright Eyes; Where are You, Dream Girl?; The Traffic Was Terrific; Mandy and Me; Any Old Night; That's Why My Heart Is Calling You; Fi Fi; Honeymoon Bells; Elegie; Thoughts of Home; Strolling Through the Park One Day. Scores: Nobody Home; Ballet: El Brut.

MOURADIAN, SARKY ASCAP 1974
composer, author
b Beirut, Lebanon, Nov 15, 31. Educ: St Nichan Armenian High Sch; St Gregoire French Col; Cons Musique, Lebanon; Theatre of Arts, Los Angeles. Has written & dir motion pictures. Songs: Tears of Happiness; Sons of Sassoun; Promise of Love; Lebanon (Honorary Award winner, 79); You Are My Sweetheart; I Know It's a Dream; I Have No Smile Without You; The Song of the Waves; Sing Forget.

MOUZON, ALPHONSE
composer, author, drummer
b Charleston, SC, Nov 21, 48. Educ: Bonds-Wilson High Sch; Manhattan Med Asst Sch; City Col New York. Has played & recorded with Roy Ayer's Band, McCoy Tyner's Band, Weather Report Band, Eric Clapton, Carlos Santana, Freddie Hubbard, Herbie Hancock, Stevie Wonder, Roberta Flack, Freda Payne & George Benson. Has done Bway show "Promises, Promises." Produced a group "Poussez," also a band "Beverly Hills." Recorded on United Artist Records, MPS Records & Atlantic Records. Keyboardist, singer & producer. Chief Collabr: Linda Ledesma-Mouzon. Songs: Come on and Do It; Boogie With Me; I'm Never Gonna Say Goodbye; Leave That Boy Alone; You Made My Dream Come True; Making Love.

MOWERY, BOBBY LEE ASCAP 1977
composer, author, singer
b Detroit, Mich, Mar 21, 49. Recording artist, Caprice Records, 74-76; songwriter contract with Sound Corp Music, 74. Songs: I'll Always Love You; I'll Still Need You Mary Ann.

MOYE, DONALD FRANKLIN   ASCAP 1973
composer, author, performer

b Rochester, NY, May 23, 46. Educ: Cent State Univ, Ohio; Wayne State Univ, 67. Began music at early age; has played with drum & bugle corps, blues bands, combos, perc ens, dance cos & big bands. Mem of jazz group, Art Ens of Chicago, 11 yrs. Recipient of NEA grants & awarded best percussionist, Down Beat Poll, 77, 78 & 79. TV performer, recording artist & percussionist. Has made numerous tours. Chief Collabrs: Roscoe Mitchell, Joseph Jarman, Malachi Favors, Lester Bowie. *Songs & Instrumental Works:* Illinstrum; JFM 3 Way Blues, Ode to Wilbur Ware; Folkus; N'Famoudou-Boudougou.

MOZIAN, ROGER KING   ASCAP 1953
composer, conductor, arranger

b New York, NY, June 30, 25; d Yonkers, NY, May 16, 63. Educ: Schillinger Syst, NY Univ; pvt music study. First trumpeter in dance bands; formed own band, 53; made many records. *Songs & Instrumental Works:* Asia Minor; Midnight in Spanish Harlem; Desert Dance; Afterthoughts; Mirror, Mirror; Change Rock; Renegade; Feelin' Kinda Blue; So Soon; Rock Bottom; Dizzy Dame; The Twistin' Shepherd.

MRAVIK, EDWARD E (EDDIE HAWK)   ASCAP 1956
composer, author, singer

b Milwaukee, Wis, Feb 16, 17. Educ: High sch, Lublin, Wis; IIT, 2 yrs. Worked in machine shops at early age, did auto mechanic work. Served USA, 3 yrs, toolmaker, engr & tool cost estimater. Songwriter, played nightclubs, actor, choral group singing, made recordings. Radio & TV repair. *Songs:* I Told You; Season; You Told Me; Tender Heart; Just a Start; Darlin'.

MR BONGO
See Costanzo, Jack J

MR GREEN JEANS
See Brannum, Hugh Roberts

MR ROGERS
See Rogers, Fred

MRS RAVENHALL
See King, Robert A

MUCZYNSKI, ROBERT STANLEY   ASCAP 1960
composer, pianist, professor

b Chicago, Ill, Mar 19, 29. Educ: DePaul Univ, BM & MM; Acad Music, Nice, France; comp with Alexander Tcherepnin, 49-52. First symph, Found Comn, 53; piano soloist, first piano concerto, Louisville Orch Comn, Grant Park Summer Symph & Chicago Symph Orchs, 54. Piano debut, Carnegie Recital Hall, New York, 58. Documentary film background scores. Major chamber & solo piano recording proj, Laurel Records. Prof music, chmn comp, comp-in-residence, Univ Ariz, Tucson. Distinguished Alumni Award, DePaul Univ, 77. Recipient of 2 Ford Found fel grants. *Instrumental Works:* Cavalcade (A Suite for Orchestra); Sonata (flute & piano); Third Piano Sonata; Dovetail Overture; Second Piano Trio; A Serenade for Summer (chamber orch); Dance Movements (small orch); Fantasy Trio (clarinet, cello, piano); Six Preludes for Piano.

MUELLER, CARL FRANK   ASCAP 1940
composer, educator, organist

b Sheboygan, Wis, Aug 12, 1892. Educ: Elmhurst Col, Ill, organ studies with Wilhelm Middleschulte; voice & cond studies with John Finley Williamson. Organist & choirmaster, Grand Avenue Congregational Church, Milwaukee, Wis, 17-27; organist & minister music, Cent Presby Church, Montclair, NJ, 27-53; dir choral music, Montclair State Col, NJ, 27-53; organist & minister music, Tower Hill Presby Church, Red Bank, NJ, 53-62; retired, 63. *Songs:* Choral Music: Create in Me a Clean Heart; A Mighty Fortress is Our God; Now Thank We All Our God; Laudamus Te; The One Hundreth Psalm; Christ of the Upward Way; O God, Our Help in Ages Past; Come Christians, Join to Sing; Lincoln's Gettysburg Address; Salutation to the Dawn; When Thou Prayest; The Lord's My Shepherd; Surely the Lord is in This Place; Organ Music: Faith, Hope and Love; Moments of Reverence; The Organist's Solo Book; Six Preludes on Familiar Hymn Tunes; A Song of Triumph; Echo Caprice; Meditation on Crimond; Praise the Lord; O Worship the Lord.

MUELLER, EDWARD CHARLES   ASCAP 1976
composer, author

b Carlstadt, NJ, June 23, 12. Educ: Stevens Inst Technol, ME, 35; piano instr, K Ruettinger Mueller. Consult music comp with John A Jenkins of Dept Music, Univ Mass. Ed-in-chief, high sch year bk, 31; literary ed, col year bk, 34; did technical writing & ed, 35-41; feature article ed, McGraw-Hill, 60; done applications eng, 48-62; gen engr, technical manual writing & ed, Armament Res & Develop Command, USA, ARRCOM, Dover, NJ. Chief Collabr: Michael F Matushin, Sr. *Songs:* New Jersey State Song.

MUELLER, LARRY ROSS   ASCAP 1973
composer, author, teacher

b San Antonio, Tex, Apr 4, 39. Educ: US Naval Sch Music, 58; studied voice with Walter Bricht, New York, 59; San Antonio Col; Southwestern Univ; Foothill Col; Brigham Young Univ, Univ Utah; Pac Col; Calif State Univ, BA, 68, MA, 73; studied comp with Wilson Coker, 70; extended grad work, Ariz State Univ & Northern Ariz Univ. Played clubs & solo work, 54-58. Soloist, USA Chorus, 58-60 & var opera perf & symphs in col, 60-70. Sch teacher. Pres, Creativity Res, 77- & Am Energy Group, 79- *Songs:* Cycle of Faith (3 part song cycle). *Scores:* Opera: Little Red Riding Hood.

MUELLER, WILLIAM F   ASCAP 1972
composer, author, vocalist

b Detroit, Mich, July 15, 52. Educ: High sch, two yrs of music theory & ear training; Wayne State Univ, one yr of music theory, ear training, classical piano & concert choir. Prof entertainer, singer & musician, 64-; song writer music & lyrics, 65-; road & studio work with Bob Seger; studio musician, 68- Writer & producer of radio jingles & music for TV, also albums & singles. Guitarist, pianist & bass player. Chief Collabr: Marcy Levy. *Songs:* Who'll Miss the Bus; I Am Somebody; No Place Like Home; Bootlace.

MUIR, LEWIS F   ASCAP 1955
composer, pianist

b 1884; d Jan 19, 50. Ragtime pianist, St Louis, 04. Later featured in London. Chief Collabrs: L Wolfe Gilbert, William Tracey, Edgar Leslie, Maurie Abrams. *Songs:* Play That Barbershop Chord; When Ragtime Rosie Ragged the Rosary; Waiting for the Robert E Lee; Take Me to That Swanee Shore; Here Comes My Daddy Now; Mississippi River Steamboat; Ragtime Cowboy Joe; Hitchy-Koo; Mammy Jinny's Jubilee; Hicky-Hoy.

MULL, MARTIN E
comedian, singer

b Chicago, Ill, 1943. Educ: RI Sch Design. Nightclub singer & comedian. Appeared in TV series "Mary Hartman, Mary Hartman", Fernwood 2-Night & Soundstage; guest on TV talk shows; appeared in movie "FM." *Albums:* Martin Mull; Martin Mull and His Fabulous Furniture in Your Livingroom; Normal Days of Wine and Neuroses; Sex and Violins.

MULLIGAN, GERALD JOSEPH   ASCAP 1955
composer, saxophonist, conductor

b New York, NY, Apr 6, 27. Staff comp, WCAU, Philadelphia; saxophonist in orchs incl Gene Krupa, Miles Davis, Elliott Lawrence & Claude Thornhill. Moved to Calif, 52; formed own quartet; cond sextet, Italy & Paris, 56; toured Great Brit, 57; soloist, "Sound of Jazz," CBS-TV, 57; appeared at jazz fests; formed group, 58; appeared on TV; also in films: "Jazz on a Summer Day"; "I Want to Live"; "The Subterraneans." Organized new orch, 60. Recording artist. *Songs & Instrumental Works:* Disc Jockey Jump; Elevation; Walking Shoes; Soft Shoes; Bark for Barksdale; The Blight of the Fumble Bee; Utter Chaos; Bunny; What's the Rush?; A Ballad; Night Lights; A Thousand Clowns.

MUMFORD, THADDEUS QUENTIN, JR   ASCAP 1972
author, writer

b Washington, DC, Feb 8, 51. Educ: Western High Sch, Washington, 68; Hampton Inst, 68; Fordham Univ, 69-71. Staff writer, "The Electric Company," children's TV workshop, 71-76, "Alan King Special," 74 & "Flip Wilson Show," 74-75. Story ed, "That's My Mama," 75, "Maude," 76-77 & "Roots," 78. Exec story ed, "MASH," 79- Chief Collabrs: Joe Raposo, Dave Conner, Christopher Cerf. *Songs:* Lyrics: Phantom of Love; Is It Love?; What Would We Do Without Ed?; Stop; Two Letters.

MUNDY, JAMES L   ASCAP 1967
composer, author, singer

b Muldrow, Okla, Feb 8, 34. Educ: Muldrow High Sch. Singer, nightclubs, radio & TV shows & Can & US tours, 50- Writer of country music, 67- Twenty-five appearances on Grand Ole Opry. Free-lance writer & singer for nat commercials incl Hungry Jack Biscuits, Miller Beer, Pizza Hut & Kentucky Fried Chicken, 78. Chief Collabrs: Peggy White, Buck Moore. *Songs:* Good Ole Fashioned Country Love; What You See Is What You Get; Come Home; She's Already Gone; The River Is Too Wide; Pull My String and Wind Me Up; Country Girl With Hot Pants On; Philadelphia Fillies; Yesterday Once More; Mexico Winner.

MUNDY, JAMES R   ASCAP 1943
composer, author

b Cincinnati, Ohio, June 28, 07. Educ: Northwestern Univ, BA; studied with Dr E Toch. Played tenor sax in Earl Hines Orch. Arr, Benny Goodman, Tommy Dorsey, Duke Ellington, Count Basie, Jimmy Lunceford, Harry James, Glenn Grey & Chick Webb's Orchs; MGM, Columbia, RKO, 20th Century, Warner Bros & Universal Movie Studios. Chief Collabrs: John Latouche, Don George, Charles Carpenter, Johnny Mercer, Joel Seneca. *Songs:* Ram Bunk Shush; Music: Travelin' Light; My One Desire; To Beat, Or Not to Beat; Fiesta in Blue; Fiesta in Brass. *Instrumental Works:* Madhouse; Swing Time in the Rockies; House Hop; Air Mail Special; Solo Flight. *Songs & Instrumental Works:* The Impossible She; I've Always Loved You; Tillie's Tango.

MUNDY, JOHN ASCAP 1950
composer, cellist, teacher
b London, Eng, Dec 19, 1886; d. Educ: Royal Acad Music, London, LRAM, ARAM. Cellist, Royal Opera Orch, Covent Garden, 08 & London Opera House, 11-12; soloist with Ernst Denhof, Scotland; Capt, World War I, Brit Army; prof cello, Royal Irish Acad Music; mem chamber concert group, sponsored by Royal Dublin Soc; to US 21, citizen; cond, Bway prod, "The Beggar's Opera"; mgr & gen agent, Mozart Opera Co; music dir, Radio Counselors, Inc; prod, "Iron Fireman" series; dir & comp, "Am Sch of the Air," CBS; playwright, "The Liar" & songs for Bway musical, "Sing Out, Sweet Land"; mem, CBS Orch, 37-44; mgr, Metrop Opera Orch, 44-57. Chief Collabr: Edward Eager. *Songs:* His Brown-Eyed Mistress; The Secret; Where?; And More Than These.

MUNN, WILLIAM O ASCAP 1959
composer, pianist
b Selma, Ala, Jan 24, 02. Educ: Piano student of Madeline Keipp; Atlanta Cons, with Hazel Wood. Pianist in local dance bands. Pres, Atlanta Music Co, Ga, 44-78, retired, 78. Chief Collabr: Lawrence F Munn (bro). *Songs:* Music: Beloved; From Gay Vienna; March of the Tiny Soldiers; Sleepy Town; Whistling Down the Road I Go. *Instrumental Works:* Prelude Romantique; School and Fraternity March; Singing Tower; Snake Charmer.

MUNSEY, JOEL PORTER
composer, author, musician
b San Gabriel, Calif, Aug 19, 49. Educ: South Hills High Sch; Pasadena City Col. TV controls, 70-71; asst audio engr, 74. Head engr of Hound Dog Recording, 76-79. Recording artist, Grand Theft Music/Organized Crime label; also record producer. *Songs:* Love Is Enough; Crazyman; (More Than) Mother Loves Child; Cops and Robbers; Diamonds and Blonds; In Your Arms; Roll Me Over; Oh That Ballet Dancer; For You; When It's Over; Fire Overhead; Don't You Know?. *Instrumental Works:* The Ice Ray; Laser Man vs the Blond Unit; Still Champion.

MUNSON, EUGENE DALE ASCAP 1976
composer, author
b Whittier, Calif, Jan 28, 55. Educ: Buckley High Sch, grad; Loyola-Marymount Univ, BA. Pvt bass lessons, age 14; played in numerous rock bands; formed rock & roll band, Los Angeles. *Songs:* Ancient Hearts; Be My Love.

MURADIAN, VAZGEN ASCAP 1969
composer, instrumentalist
b Ashtarak, Armenia, Oct 17, 21. Educ: Spendiarian Prof Sch Music, Yerevan, Armenia, 35-39; Benedetto Marcello Cons Venice, Italy, Prof Di Musica, 48; spec studies viola d'amore with Renzo Sabatini & comp with Vittorio Giannini. Taught music, Armenian Col, 45-50; came to US in 50. Has written songs in six languages. Winner of Tekeyan Prize of Beirut, Lebanon, 62. *Instrumental Works:* Concerto Opus 23 (viola d'amore, orch; first in Am music lit); Symphony Opus 58; Concerto Opus 52 (violin, orch); Sonata Opus 42 (solo violin); Concerto Opus 25 (oboe, orch; first in Am music lit); Concerto Opus 57 (oud, orch; first in world music lit).

MURDOCK, JANE
See Roobenian, Amber

MURE, EILEEN DAVIES ASCAP 1963
author
b Wales, Aug 14, 18. Wrote for TV, "Toy Balloons." *Songs:* Lily of the West. *Albums:* What Do You Want to Be When You Grow Up.

MURO, DON ASCAP 1975
composer, author, performer
b Freeport, NY, July 29, 51. Educ: Hofstra Univ, BS(music ed), 73; studied comp with Elie Seigmeister & William Strickland; Queens Col, grad studies, 74-75. Presented concerts of original material, 67. Recording artist, Sine Wave Records. Nat chmn electronic music, Nat Asn Jazz Educators. Mem, Electronic Music Comt, Music Educators Nat Conference. Rec'd ASCAP Awards, 78, 79 & 80. *Songs:* You're the One; Music: I Will Lift Up Mine Eyes. *Instrumental Works:* Badlands Overture; Island in the Sky; Current Events.

MURPHY, BEVERLY KAY ASCAP 1977
singer, writer
b Holdenville, Okla, Apr 3, 47. TV & radio appearances; nightclub entertainer; recording artist. *Songs:* I'll Never Be the Same; Cheatin' Kind.

MURPHY, JAMES FRANCIS ASCAP 1965
composer, author, teacher
b New York, NY, July 23, 10. Educ: Juilliard Inst Musical Art, studied string bass with Fred Zimmerman; Columbia Univ Teachers Col, BS & MA; studied violin with Dante Cavicchioli, Otakar Vycharod, Walter Pfeiffer & Vlado Kolitch. Sch teacher, Louisville, Ky, NJ & New York. Guest lectr & cond summer orch, Ind Univ. Principal violist, NJersey Regional Symph Orch. Violinist/violist with var chamber music groups. Choral dir, Nurses' Chorus, Long Island Col Hosp & Albertus Magnus Col. *Instrumental Works:* Trans: Ten Little Classics (J S Bach; viola).

MURPHY, LYLE (SPUD)
composer, teacher
b Berlin, Ger, Aug 19, 08. Played saxophone, clarinet, flute, oboe & trumpet with var bands, 25-35, arr for Glenn Gray, Benny Goodman & others, 35-41, leader of own band, 38-41. Merchant Marine, 42-46. Worked on many motion pictures, did albums for RCA, Contemporary, GNP & others. Stock arr, Robbins-Feist-Miller & others, 35-50; author of several bks for clarinet, saxophone, harmony, comp, arr & orchestration; teaching own method "Equal Internal System," 49- *Instrumental Works:* Warm Winds (saxophone quartet); Seismograph; Dizzy Dialogue; Lost in a Fugue; Mombasa. *Albums:* Round the World Cruise.

MURPHY, MARK ASCAP 1974
composer, author, teacher
b Syracuse, NY, Mar 14, 32. Educ: Syracuse Univ, drama, music & art studies; studied with Mira Orstova. Recording artist, Decca, Capitol, Riverside & Muse Records. Chief Collabrs: Herbie Hancock, Fredie Hubbard, Oliver Nelson. *Songs:* Come and Get Me; Sausalito; They; Lemme Blues; Lyrics: On the Red Clay; Cantelope Island; Sly; Stolen Moments.

MURPHY, OWEN ASCAP 1928
composer, author, director
b Mt Clemens, Mich, Sept 2, 1893; d Stone Harbor, NJ, Apr 4, 65. Educ: Notre Dame Univ, BA; Univ Pittsburgh, LLB. Author, dir & producer industrial films. Chief Collabr: Jay Gorney. *Songs:* Speak Easy; That's My Baby; Wouldn't You?; It Always Takes Two; I'd Like to Take You Home to Meet My Mother; Feelin' Good; The Wanderer; Then You Know That You're in Love. *Scores:* Bway Stage: Top Hole; Greenwich Village Follies of 1925; Hold Your Horses; Rain or Shine.

MURPHY, PAT ASCAP 1950
composer, author
b Ridgway, Pa, Feb 21, 01; d Pittsburgh, Pa, June 3, 54. Educ: Ky Mil Inst, Mercersburg Acad; Carnegie Tech. Vpres, lumber & millwork business. *Songs:* Tell the Truth; Springtime and You; My Bugle Reverie; Somethin's Got Me Jumpin'.

MURPHY, PAUL ASCAP 1978
composer
b New York, NY, Mar 25, 28. Educ: Harvard Univ, BA(Eng lit). Madison Avenue jingle writer with big agencies & as an independent; words, music & performance. Chief Collabr: Sheila Davis. *Instrumental Works:* A Walk in the Spring Rain.

MURPHY, ROSE ASCAP 1961
composer, pianist, singer
b Xenia, Ohio. Singer & pianist in nightclubs, theatres & on records. *Songs:* Whatcha Gotta Lose?; What Good?.

MURPHY, STANLEY ASCAP 1914
author
b Dublin, Ireland, Nov 29, 1875; d New York, NY, Jan 10, 19. To US, 1883. Educ: Pvt & pub schs. Charter mem, ASCAP. Chief Collabrs: Harry Carroll, Lewis Muir, Albert Von Tilzer, Harry Von Tilzer, Percy Wenrich, Henry Marshall. *Songs:* Put On Your Old Gray Bonnet; Be My Little Baby Bumble Bee; On the 5:15; When We Meet in the Sweet Bye and Bye; Oh How She Could Yacki Hacki Wicki Wacki Woo; I Want to Linger.

MURRAY, BERT
See Slezinger, Herbert Edwin

MURRAY, DAVID ASCAP 1976
composer, saxophonist, bass clarinetist
b Oakland, Calif, Feb 19, 55. Educ: Berkeley High Sch; St Mary's High Sch, grad, 73; Pomona Col, studied with Bobby Bradford, Stanley Crouch. Formed David Murray Trio, 75; recording artist, 76- Formed David Murray Big Band, played at pub theaters, New York, 78. Writer, lyrics & music for var records, 76-80. *Albums:* Flowers for Albert.

MURRAY, GILBERT DONALD, III ASCAP 1955
composer, author
b Orange, NJ, May 26, 30. Educ: Princeton Univ, BA; Univ Geneva, CCEI. Pres, Acco Int. *Songs:* The Charleston Rag; The Steamroller Operators Ball; Gee I'd Like to Wiggle You in My Little Igaloo.

MURRAY, HAYA ASCAP 1973
composer, author, singer
b London, England, Apr 7, 10. Educated in London, England, Düsseldorf, Ger & Rome, Italy; studied bel canto with Giovanni Villa, Rome. Child dancer, London & continental stage, Europe. Studied singing & piano; stage technician & dir, Venice Int Music Fest, 53-55. To US, 58, Citizen, 63. Own transl bur, New York. Lyricist; composer; novelist; nightclub singer. Chief Collabr: Lorenzo Fuller. *Songs:* Gentleman At Heart; Lyrics: Draw on an Inside Straight; Playing the Game; Music: Sailor Man, Sailor Man; Is It Because.

MURRAY, JACK (JOHN) ASCAP 1929
composer, author
b New York, NY. Educ: DeWitt Clinton High Sch; City Col New York; Columbia Univ; Brooklyn Law Sch. Head writer for var comedians; contributor of material to Eddie Cantor, The Marx Bros, Milton Berle, Jack Benny, Ethel Merman & Jack Albertson; scenarist for Metro-Goldwyn-Meyer, Radio-Keith-Orpheum & Paramount Pictures; producer & writer for USA Signal Corps; industrials for Pan-Am, Gulf Oil; contributor of sketches & songs: "Ziegfeld Follies", "Straw Hat Revue", "Americana" & "Meet the People." Coauth: "Room Service" (play) & "Hello Out There" (musical). Author: "The Monkey Walk" (play). Chief Collabrs: Sammy Fain, Ben Oakland, Henry Tobias, Al Hoffman, Dave Mann. *Songs:* It Can't Happen Here; Lyrics: Hello Sunshine Hello; If I Were You (I'd Fall in Love With Me); Oh What a Thrill (To Hear It From You); Have a Little Dream on Me; Flapperette; If I Love Again; Two Loves Have I.

MURRAY, JOHN A ASCAP 1955
composer, author, singer
b Jamaica, NY, Oct 18, 25. Educ: Queens Col, BA; Columbia Univ, MBA. Singer on radio, "Old Gold Party Time"; also in nightclubs. Dancer on TV, "Arthur Murray Party Time." Actor in many maj films, daytime TV & off-Bway. Chief Collab: Gratien Ouellette. *Songs:* Lyrics: Night Life; My Love, Your Love; Faces on the Mountainside.

MURRAY, LYN ASCAP 1943
composer, conductor
b London, Eng, Dec 6, 09. Educ: Juilliard Sch Music; studied with Joseph Schillinger, Victor Bay & Charles Blackman. Staff cond & arr, WCAU, Philadelphia, 31-34. Staff cond, comp & arr, CBS, NY, 34-47. Music for dramatic radio progs incl, "The Adventures of Ellery Queen", "Campbell Playhouse", "Radio Readers Digest", "March of Time", "The Ford Theatre", "Columbia Workshop", "26 by Corwin", "Hallmark Playhouse", etc. Arr choral music for Bway musicals: "Panama Hattie", "Let's Face It", "This Is the Army" & "Finian's Rainbow." Staff comp & cond, Paramount Pictures, 54-57. Chief Collabrs: Norman Corwin, Sid Kuller. *Songs & Instrumental Works:* Camptown (ballet); Cromer (strings); Variations on a Children's Tune (strings); Collage for Clarinet and Orchestra; Incident at State Beach (orch); Ronald Searle Suite (orch); Liberation (cantata); The Miracle (Christmas oratorio). *Scores:* Film Scores: The Prowler; The Big Night; Son of Paleface; Here Come the Girls; The Bridges at Toko-Ri; To Catch a Thief; Threshold of Space; Period of Adjustment; Come Fly With Me; Wives and Lovers; Signpost to Murder; Promise Her Anything; Rosie; Angel in My Pocket; The Sea Gypsies. TV Film Scores: General Electric Theatre; Alfred Hitchcock; Mr Novak; The John Forsythe Show; Dr Kildare; Daniel Boone; The Time Tunnel; It Takes a Thief; The Virginian; Love Hate Love; The Magic Carpet. Documentary Film Scores: The Time of Man; Cousteau; Carl Sandburg's Lincoln; Primal Man; John Glenn in Africa; The Amazon; The Lonely Doryman; Treasure!; The Tigris Expedition; Superliners: The End of an Era. Hollywood TV Theatre Scores: Steambath; Double Solitaire; Incident at Vichy; Requiem for a Nun; Ladies of the Corridor; The Last of Mrs Lincoln.

MURRAY, MARK
See Kopita, Murry

MURRAY, STEPHEN BRUCE ASCAP 1976
composer
b Hartford, Conn, Nov 7, 41. Educ: Univ RI, 59-62; Univ Calif, Los Angeles, 62-65, BA & MA in comp, studies with John Vincent, Roy Hanz & Henri Lazary. Former Peace Corps volunteer. Orch management, Iowa & RI. *Songs:* Music: Three songs by Pablo Nervda. *Instrumental Works:* The Legend of Sleepy Hollow (narrator & orch); Heights of Macchu Picchu (chamber orch); Introduction and Allegro.

MURRELL, IRENE JANET (IRENE CASTLE) ASCAP 1977
composer, author, pianist
b Lynn, Mass, Oct 3, 36. Educ: Lynn English & Hope High Schs, Providence, RI; pvt piano studies. Pianist & vocalist, lounges, jazz rooms, radio & TV; recording artist, Humming Bird label. Author bk, "The World's Greatest Dancer???" *Songs:* Never Say Goodbye (Am Songwriting Fest Award); I'm Without You (Am Lyric Fest Award); What About Love?; Billy's Blues. *Scores:* Bway: The World's Greatest Dancer???.

MURRY, TED
See Mencher, T Murray

MURTAUGH, JOHN EDWARD ASCAP 1962
composer
b Minneapolis, Minn, Oct 30, 27. Educ: Univ Mich, BMus. Began performing & comp, 45. Experience in jazz, classical, pop & electronic music. Chief Collab: Spencer Michlin. *Songs:* Music: Movin' Day; Blues Current; The Connection; The Predators.

MUSIC, LORENZO ASCAP 1958
composer, author
b Brooklyn, NY, May 2, 37. Educ: Univ Minn, Eng major. Writer, TV prog "Smothers Brothers Show," 68-70, theme song for "Bob Newhart Show," 72. Worked with Leslie Uggums & Glen Campbell. Chief Collab: Henrietta Music.

MUSICANT, SAMUEL ASCAP 1959
composer, author
b New York, NY, July 21, 22. Educ: New York Pub Schs; Hartnett Music Studios, New York, studied theory, harmony & guitar. Served in USMC, WW II; worked with popular music publ; production mgr, Song Plugger; covered radio exploitation for musicals, "Mr Wonderful" & "The Body Beautiful." Chief Collabrs: Al Bandini, Al Rainy, Freddie Van. *Songs:* The Church in the Valley; Lyrics: Wykiup; Talk It Over With Your Heart.

MUSOLINO, ANGELO ASCAP 1952
composer, author, teacher
b New York, NY. Educ: Haaren High Sch; arr-orchestration studies with William McGill, comp with Josef Schmid; Empire State Col, BS, 77. Had radio & TV assignments on Theatre Guild of the Air, Hollywood Open House, Winky Dink & You, CBS, Juvenile Jury, NBC, Mike Wallace PM-East, Ed Sullivan, CBS, Sesame Street, PBS & The Elec Co, PBS. Teacher, Brooklyn Cons Music, 53-57 & Adelphi Univ, 78- Asst to Raymond Scott producing radio & TV commercials, 61-65. Cond-arr, Temple Isaiah Chamber Ens of Great Neck, NY, 73- Comns: The Int Trio, Edith Stephen Dance Co & The Descants. Author of over 20 publ music educ bks. Chief Collabrs: Carl Sandburg, Gwyn Conger Steinbeck, Kim Gannon, Henry Jerome, Ralph Baldwin, Bill Kaiman. *Songs:* Music: Red, Red Rose (choral); Tipica Serenada; Ketty; Cafe Paree; Tweety; Nice People; How's the Little Woman?; God Is My Corner; Diamond Heels; Why Pretend to Me?; Carl Sandburg in Song (collection). *Instrumental Works:* Violin and Piano Sonata; Violin Concerto; String Quartet No 2. *Songs & Instrumental Works:* The Last Word (oratorio). *Scores:* Bway Show: April in Canterbury.

MUSSER, WILLARD I (BILL) ASCAP 1964
composer, author, teacher
b Mohnton, Pa, Feb 2, 13. Educ: Mohnton High Sch; Ithaca Col, BS(music educ), 33, MS(music educ), 46. Played prof in symph orchs under Hans Kindler & Saul Caston. Teacher instrumental music, Pa & NY state pub schs. Prof music, Hartwick Col, 53-56 & Crane Sch Music, State Univ NY Potsdam, 56-71. *Instrumental Works:* Arabesque for Band; Globil for Band; Arban; General Music (6 vols); Trans: Sonata for Trumpet; Concerto for Trumpet; Trumpet Sonata.

MYERS, FARLAN I ASCAP 1956
composer, author
b Los Angeles, Calif, July 7, 18. Educ: Univ Calif, Los Angeles, BA; New Eng Cons; Juilliard. USAAF, WW II. In production dept, CBS Radio, 41 & 46-47; in advert, 49-; mgr, J Walter Thompson Co, 56- Chief Collabrs: Hal Levy, Ken Thoren. *Songs:* Little Red Riding Hood; Little Red Riding Hood's Hood; Little Red Hen; Do It Yourself; Little Hiawatha; Do a Good Turn; Music: Fly High and Free; Make This a Slow Goodbye; My Guitar; Fisherman's Chantey; Thanksgiving Song.

MYERS, HENRY ASCAP 1941
author, teacher
b Chicago, Ill, June 24, 1893; d. Educ: Columbia Univ; Damrosch Sch Music; studied with Rubin Goldmark. Reporter, NY Evening Mail; press agent, Shubert bros Bway stage score, sketches, "Meet the People"; author of novels, "Our Lives Have Just Begun", "The Utmost Island", "O King Live Forever", "The Signorina." Taught novel writing, NY Univ. Chief Collab: Jay Gorney. *Songs:* The Stars Remain; Meet the People; The Four Rivers; The Bill of Rights; Juarez and Lincoln; In Chi Chi Castenango.

MYERS, JAMES E (JIMMY DE KNIGHT) ASCAP 1950
composer, author
b Philadelphia, Pa. Educ: High sch. Served in 32nd Inf Div, USA, World War II, comn Lt in field. Cond & arr of own recording group, Knights of Rhythm. Pres, Myers Music Inc; actor, 300 motion pictures & TV shows; producer, film "The Block." Comp, 200 publ songs; author, bk "Hell Is a Foxhole" & syndicated column, "Actors Diary," currently writing bk, "Rock Around the Clock." Mem Am Guild of Authors & Composers, Screen Actors Guild, Am Fedn of TV & Radio Artists & others; recipient of over 50 awards. Chief Collabrs: Ed Gallagher, Max C Freedman, Rusty Keffer. *Songs:* Rock Around the Clock; Why Do I Cry Over You; Blues on the Block; Headin' for Armadgeddon; Ten Gallon Stetson; and many others.

MYERS, RICHARD ASCAP 1927
composer, producer
b Philadelphia, Pa, Mar 25, 01; d Perigueux, France, Mar 12, 77. Educ: Pa Charter Sch. Wrote songs for "Greenwich Village Follies of 1925", "Here Goes the Bride", "Murder At the Vanities", "Americana" & "Earl Carroll Vanities of 1932." Produced Bway plays "My Dear Children", "Margin for Error", "The Importance of Being Ernest", "Goodbye, My Fancy", "Caesar and Cleopatra" & "The Devil's Disciple." Chief Collabrs: Leo Robin, Edward Heyman, Jack

Lawrence, E Y Harburg, Johnny Mercer. *Songs:* Whistling for a Kiss; Hold My Hand; Jericho; My Darling; Say That You Love Me; Music in My Fingers. *Scores:* Bway Stage: Allez Oop; Hello Yourself.

MYERS, RONALD CHARLES　　　　　ASCAP 1968
composer, author
b Hamburg, NY, Mar 31, 33. Educ: NY State Univ Col Teachers, Buffalo, BS & MS; studied band & orch with Joseph Wincenc, vocal with Silas Boyd. Church organist & choir dir. Chorus dir, 1st Training Regimental, USA, Fort Dix. English teacher, 13 yrs. Pvt tutor, Osmonds, 67-68. Wrote theme song, "The Great Brain"; "Krofft Supershow" & Saturday morning TV. Mgr, Tony DeFranco, early 70's. Church music publ. In charge of Osmond Sch-Music proj. Chief Collabrs: Osmonds. *Songs:* If Santa Were My Daddy; In God We Trust; Music: Just the Other Way Around; This I Promise You; Lyrics: You're There. *Scores:* Stage: Alice Adams (Can).

MYERS, STANLEY A　　　　　ASCAP 1953
composer, author
b Buffalo, NY, July 15, 08. Educ: Canisius Col, PhB, MA(economics, history, Eng); studied comp & orchestration with Edward Kilenyi and Mario Castelnuevo-Tedesco. Prof clarinetist & saxophonist, theatres, dance bands, radio & symph while in high sch & col. Music dir & MC at var theatres incl Lafayette Theatres, Buffalo, 1 yr, RKO, Boston, 1 yr, Paramount Theatres, Brooklyn, 1 yr, Fox, Detroit, 1 yr, RKO, Los Angeles, 1 yr & Oriental Theatre, Chicago, 9 months. Music dir, comp & arr for Groucho Marx "You Bet Your Life Show," 2 yrs, Shipstad & Johnson "Ice Follies", Captiol recordings, 4 yrs, Walt Disney & TV commercial spots, childrens' TV series & albums, TV films "Hop-a-Long Cassidy,", 1 yr. Writer & dir, special material & music for var artists & groups at Las Vegas, TV, films, nightclubs & theatres. Formed Samco Music Publ Co, 80. *Songs:* Let's Be Thankful for Thanksgiving Day; Land of the Easter Bunny; Sakatumi; Vote; Sweet Somebody Like You; Look Lord, What You've Done for Me; You Can't Have Your Cake; Graduation Song; Try a Little Prayer; Scottish Lullaby; Samba in F; That Old Barbershop Quartette; The Little Barber; Valley of the San Joaquin; I'm Gonna Wed My Darlin'; Lullaby of the West; Thanks for the Dream; Take a Tip From Mr Bluebird; The Rainbow Trail; Johanna (a Skating Song); Sing a Song of Christmas. *Albums:* Casper the Curious Kitten (childrens').

MYERS, THELDON　　　　　ASCAP 1963
composer, teacher
b Lee County, Ill, Feb 4, 27. Educ: Pub schs, Dixon, Ill; Northern Ill Univ, BS; Calif State Univ, Fresno, MA; Peabody Cons, DMA; Fontainebleau Summer Sch, studied comp with Nadia Boulanger, Arthur Bryon, Stefan Grove & Sandor Veress. Teacher woodwind instruments, Ill & Calif pub sch syst; fac music dept, Towson State Univ, 63-, prof theory & comp. *Songs:* Music: Make a Joyful Noise Unto the Lord (Psalm 99; SATB, chorus, piano, organ); I Will Lift Up Mine Eyes (Psalm 121; SATB, chorus, piano, organ); O Praise the Lord, All Ye Nations (Psalm 117; SATB, chorus, piano, organ). *Instrumental Works:* Concertino for Band; Aubade for Band; Eventura (concert march for band); From an 18th Century Album (band); Chorale and Fantasy (band); Four Carols for Clarinets (clarinet choir); Efflorescence (solo flute); Night Song (clarinet, piano); Andante and Allegro (flute, clarinet, piano); Valse (clarinet, piano); Sonata (clarinet, piano); Sonatine (alto saxophone, piano); Constellation (concert march for band); Arianova (band, orch); Pioneer Pictures (band); Six Little Songs (band); Ceremonial Tribute (band, orch); Intrada (solo harp).

MYKIETYN, JEROME (JAREMA)　　　　　ASCAP 1969
composer, singer, guitarist
b Ochtmannien, Ger, July 7, 42. Educ: Wayne High Sch; Upper Iowa Univ, BA. Recording artist, 63- Performer in nightclubs & TV; owner, L A M Music Publ Co. Chief Collabrs: Vic Piscatello, Len V Mykietyn. *Songs:* Don't Feel Sorry for Yourself; Infatuations; (Feels Like) Makin' Love in the Dark; Let's Boogie Together; China Blue; Music: Midnight Star; Fun on Me; Lyrics: You Gotta Love, Love, Love.

MYLES, WARREN　　　　　ASCAP 1976
composer, author, librettist
b Toronto, Ont, Aug 15, 20. Educ: Hollywood High Sch, 39; vocal studies with Forrest LaBarr, Hollywood. Producer, dir & star, USO Camp Shows, WW II. With production & script dept, Universal Pictures. Film technician, Paramount Pictures. Photographer, Newell Color Lab. Announcer, NBC. Pres, Musical America, Inc. Theatrical producer & music publisher. Chief Collabr: Donald Hansen. *Songs:* The Land That I Love; The Devils Ride; Without Your Love; Tell Me, Please Tell Me; Tell Me Lover; The Call of the Wild; It's You, I Know, It's You!; Once Upon a Time; Lyrics: My True Love; It's Too Late Now; It's a Long, Lonely Day; It Must Be Love; Close to You; Gamblin' Man, Ramblin' Man; It's the Irish Thing to Do; The Legend of Michael Nome; In the Shadows in the Moonlight. *Scores:* Libbretto: Alaska! (Am folk musical-drama)

MYROW, FREDRIC　　　　　ASCAP 1960
composer, pianist, conductor
b Brooklyn, NY, July 16, 39. Educ: Univ Southern Calif, BM; studied with Ingolf Dahl, Darius Milhaud, Muriel Kerr & Gwendolyn Koldolfsky; Santa Cecilia Acad Rome, Fulbright & Italian Govt grants, studied with Goffredo Petrassi. Other grants incl Rockefeller, Kate Neal Kinley & Guggenheim.

Pianist & founding mem, Evenings for New Music, 64. Concertizing & works throughout Europe & US incl maj fests, series & radio broadcasts, 68-69. Composer-in-residence with New York Philh. Dimitri Mitropolous Comn. Began active career as film & TV comp, songwriter, recording artist & producer, 69. Comp for musical theatre incl "Bloomers." *Songs & Instrumental Works:* Theme and Variations for Piano; Four Songs in Spring; Chamber Symphony; Symphonic Variations (Hollywood Bowl-Young Musicians Found comn); At Twilight (soprano, orch); Songs From the Japanese (voice, chamber orch); Musics I and II for Orchestra (Tanglewood-Fromm Found comn); Sand Mountain Symphony (banjo, singer, orch); Palm Canyon; Six Preludes; Triple Fugue for Two Pianos. *Scores:* Film: Soylent Green; Scarecrow; On the Nickel; Phantasm; Leo the Last; A Reflection of Fear; Lolly Madonna; Jim the World's Greatest; The Steagle; Threshold; Stop; Highway; Kenny and Company; TV Film: In Search of America; Message to My Daughter; The Secret Journal of John Chapman; Pray for the Wildcats.

MYROW, GERALD　　　　　ASCAP 1957
composer, author, arranger
b Youngstown, Ohio, June 26, 23; d Park Forest, Ill, Aug 17, 77. Educ: Cleveland Cons; Am Cons; Roosevelt Col Sch Music; Gov State Univ, MA. Musician, USN, WW II. Community prof & lectr notography, Gov State Univ. Has written indust shows & choral arrangements, incl 3 collections of sacred music. Author: "Myrow Notography: A New Concept in Music Manuscript Preparation for the Student and Professional." Chief Collabs: Bernard Kuby, Alfred Engelhard, Walter Rodby. *Songs & Instrumental Works:* March of Freedom; Five O'Clock Rush; Bah-Dee-Bah-Doom; Nobody's Business; It's So Wonderful to Be Young; Open Your Eyes Wide; Benediction for Bluebirds; Hurry Up, Christmas!; Eulogy; Jimbo's Limbo; One for the Boys; Soft, Warm—and Wild!; Song for Suzanne; Warrick's Little Island. *Scores:* Stage: Tongue in Chic; Twist of Lemon.

MYROW, JOSEF　　　　　ASCAP 1940
composer, pianist, author
b Russia, Feb 28, 10. To US, 12, became US citizen. Educ: Philadelphia pub schs; Univ Pa; Philadelphia Cons of Music, 24, scholarship to study piano with Hendrik Ezerman; Curtis Inst of Music, piano & comp, 26, scholarship. Piano soloist with symph orchs incl Philadelphia & Cleveland Orchs. Comp, nightclub revues incl Delmonico's, 34, Earl Carroll Palm Island Revue, 36, Monte Proser's Copacabana Revue, 44 & many songs & motion picture scores. Chief Collabrs: Mack Gordon, Edgar DeLange, Kim Gannon, Bickley Reichner, Ralph Blane, Robert Wells. *Songs:* Five O'Clock Whistle; Endless Love; Love Can Happen Anytime; This Is the Place; Music: Haunting Me; Fable of the Rose; I Love to Watch the Moonlight; The Way That I Want You; On the Boardwalk in Atlantic City; Somewhere in the Night; You Make Me Feel So Young; I Like Mike; Always the Lady; If I'm Lucky; One More Kiss (One More Vote); Bet Your Bottom Dollar; You Do; Kokomo, Indiana; Everytime I Meet You; What Did I Do; By the Way; A Lady Loves; We Have Never Met As Yet; Where Did You Learn to Dance; Life Has Its Funny Little Ups and Downs; It Happens Every Spring; Baby Won't You Say You Love Me; Wilhelmina; Down on Wabash Avenue; If I Love You a Mountain; With a Kiss; Wait 'Til You See Paris; Any Gal From Texas; Well I'll Be Switched; Comment Allez-vous; All About Love; Lullaby in Blue; Someday Soon; Bundle of Joy; A-weepin' And A'wailing Song; If and When; October Twilight; I Never Felt This Way Before; The River and I; Fare-Thee-Well Dear Alma Mater; Ode to a Marine (cantata, baritone, chorus, symph); The C A P Is on the Go (official Civil Air Patrol song); Love Is Eternal; I'm Mad About the Girl Next Door; Nowhere Guy; Quiet Little Place in the Country; Marianne; What is This That I Feel. *Instrumental Works:* Moon of Jade; The Botucada; Exotica; L'Affaire; Saturday Afternoon Before the Game; Follow the Band; Three Quarter Blues; Surrealism; Soft and Warm; Five-Four Blues; Velvet Moon; Autumn Nocturne; Overheard in a Cocktail Lounge. *Scores:* Film: Three Little Girls in Blue; If I'm Lucky; Mother Wore Tights; Wabash Avenue; I Love Melvin; The Girl Next Door; The French Line; Bundle of Joy; One More Tomorrow.

MYSELS, GEORGE　　　　　ASCAP 1950
composer, author, journalist
b Pittsburgh, Pa, Oct 5, 12. Educ: Hartnett Sch Music, New York. Columnist, editorial cartoonist, Le Voix de France, Our Town newspapers. USAF, WW II. Author literary works, "The Voice of the Pigeon" & "The Foundations of Beauty." Chief Collabr: Sammy Mysels. *Songs:* Religious Songs of Stephen Collins Foster (revised); Folios: Aesop's Fables in Song; All About My Toys; Songs of Inspiration; Musical Arr: Lincoln's Gettysburg Address; The Prayer of St Francis of Assisi; Music & Lyrics: One Little Candle; Father Time; Sure-Fire Kisses; It's Good to Know I'm Welcome (In My Old Home Town); Mom; Buy Me Chocolate; Where's-A Your House?; Lyrics: I Want You, I Need You, I Love You; Idaho State Fair; Heaven Drops Her Curtain Down; The Things I Didn't Do.

MYSELS, MAURICE　　　　　ASCAP 1957
composer, author
b Pittsburgh, Pa, May 22, 21; d Pittsburgh, May 25, 79. Educ: Pittsburgh Musical Inst; La Salle Extension Univ, LLB, 73. Served ETO, WW II (6 Bronze Stars). Was jukebox operator, sales & insurance realtor & dist magistrate, Pittsburgh. Chief Collabrs: George Mysels, Sammy Mysels. *Songs:* Time Alone;

Somebody Else's Roses; Wherever There's a Chapel; Heads You Win, Tails I Lose; I Love You Just the Same; Mr Magician.

MYSELS, SAMMY   ASCAP 1935
composer, author, pianist
b Pittsburgh, Pa, Nov 17, 06; d Los Angeles, Calif, Feb 5, 74. Educ: Carnegie Tech (scholarship in sculpture at age 10), asst instr, 3 yrs. Mem prof staff, music publ. Pianist in cabarets, vaudeville & nightclubs. Served in WW II. Chief Collabrs: Dick Sanford, Bob Hilliard, Nelson Cogane, Dick Robertson, George Mysels, Nat Simon, James Cavanaugh, Charles McCarthy, Maurice Mysels, Bella Mysell. *Songs:* Bim Bam Baby; The Singing Hills; We Three; Yesterday's Gardenias; You Forgot About Me; Throwing Stones at the Sun; The Horse With the Lavender Eyes; His Feet Too Big for de Bed; Dreams Are a Dime a Dozen; Mention My Name in Sheboygan; I'm in Love; Red Silk Stockings and Green Perfume; Heaven Drops Her Curtain Down; Chocolate Whiskey and Vanilla Gin; Idaho State Fair; Michigan Bank Roll; Time Alone; Somebody Else's Roses; Walkin' Down to Washington (Democratic campaign song, 60); Strawberry Moon.

N

NABBIE, JAMES ENOCH   ASCAP 1977
composer, teacher, entertainer
b Tampa, Fla, Apr 21, 20. Educ: Bethune-Cookman Col; studied vocally under T Tom Taylor, Chicago. Singer, concert artist & teacher; played bass & vocalist with combo; lead singer, Ink Spots, working maj supper clubs, dinner & cruise ships. Chief Collabr: William (Pat) Best. *Songs:* You Are My Love; Twinkle Eyes; Don't You Run Away (And Leave Me); Lyrics: Sometime, Someplace, Somewhere; I Found Love When I Found You.

NACLERIO, RUTH   ASCAP 1974
composer, singer
b St Louis, Mo, Oct 2, 24. Singer in church choir. Chief Collabrs: Charles Macey, Don Thomas, Sid Bass. *Songs:* Music: Brazilian Impressions; Ruth; Ana Capri; Donna; Change of Heart.

NADEL, WARREN (RANDY STARR)   ASCAP 1958
composer, author, singer
b New York, NY, July 2, 30. Educ: Columbia Col, BA, 51; Columbia Dental Sch, DDS, 54. Songwriter, Elvis Presley films. Recording artist. Chief Collabrs: Dick Wolf, Fred Wise, Frank Metis. *Songs:* The Girl I Never Loved; Who Needs Money; Could I Fall in Love; Old MacDonald; Music: Kissin' Cousins; The Enchanted Sea; Datin'; Adam and Evil; Carny Town; Look Out, Broadway; Lyrics: After School; I Know Where I'm Goin'; Almost in Love; Yellow Rose of Texas.

NAGY, FREDERICK   ASCAP 1963
composer
b Marmarossziget, Hungary, Jan 18, 1894; d. Educ: Budapest Univ; Debrecen Univ, LLD; Budapest Acad Music; pvt music study. Practiced law in Hungary, 25-41; dist judge, 41-44; interpreter, US Occupation Forces, Austria, 45-51. Mem, Am Soc Int Music; hon mem, Magna Charta Dance Soc. *Songs & Instrumental Works:* Serenade (string orch); Choral: Thanksgiving Hymn of the Refugees; Pledge of Allegiance.

NAILE, LINDA LOUISE   ASCAP 1976
composer, singer
b Wabash, Ark, Jan 19, 54. Educ: Elaine High Sch. Performer, Opryland USA, 74-80; guest, Opryland Tours, TV & Grand Ole Opry; recording artist, Paragon & Ridge Top Records. *Songs:* I Am a Woman.

NAKASHIMA, JEANNE MARIE   ASCAP 1971
composer, author, singer
b Chicago, Ill, Sept 23, 36. Educ: Chicago Musical Col; Univ Chicago High Sch; Univ Chicago Col; Loyola Marymount Univ, BFA, 57; Chicago Teachers Col, studied educ & psychol; Univ Calif, Los Angeles, studied music, drama & foreign languages. Performed as a child at classical piano recitals. Began adult songwriting prof career, 71. Formed New Child Music Publ Co, 72, later pres. Wrote & publ songs for Hawaii & Far East music markets. Pres, Makai Records, Hawaii. *Songs:* Chotto Matte Kudasai (Never Say Goodbye); Wakarimasen (I Don't Understand) (Victor Records, Japan Hit Song Award, 72); Ano-Ne (So Much My Heart Wants to Say); Some Day I'll Be With You (If Wishes Could Come True); Tomorrow's Rainbow (Inauguration song, Gov George Ariyoshi, Hawaii, 74); You Spoke of Love; Where Sweet Flowers Grow; My Little Son; Kona Coffee Festival Song (Queen of the Coffeelands). *Instrumental Works:* Classic Mood (piano); Happy Butterfly (piano).

NALLE, BILLY   ASCAP 1954
composer, pianist, organist
b Ft Myers, Fla. Educ: Ft Myers High Sch, Fla, grad; Tampa Bus Univ, Fla, bus cert; studied jazz perf & analysis with Teddy Wilson, New York, 47 & 48;

Juilliard Sch, New York, grad dipl organ-piano, 48. Piano prodigy at age 3. Pianist in combo, dance orch & radio work, Fla. Piano & organ soloist, CBS-TV & NBC-TV Networks, New York; artist-in-residence, Wichita Wurlitzer, Century II Ctr, Kans, 75- Debut organ recording, RCA Label, NY Paramount Theatre, 58; debut concert on organ, Fox Theatre, Atlanta, 66; 26 Nat-Int Music Firsts via Theatre Organ. Chief Collabrs: Joe Darion, Howard Phillips, Alice Remsen. *Songs:* Music: It's a Beautiful Day; Parade Day; April Smiles Again; Mama; Show Business; Helen and Jesse. *Songs & Instrumental Works:* Television March; Arturo Ricardo; Center City Rag; Alles Was Du Bist; Homecoming.

NAMANWORTH, PHILLIP   ASCAP 1968
composer, author
b New York, NY, Jan 11, 45. Educ: City Col New York, BA(music; with hon), 67. Played with Dave Van Ronk & the Hudson Dusters, 67. Player, writer & singer with group, Randalls Island. Wrote ballet for Louis Falcon, 71. Has had own bands. Pianist for Ry Cooder & Roberta Flack. Writer of 5 musical plays for children. Has done songs for "Sesame Street"; also music for films. Chief Collabrs: Benjamin Goldstein, Doc Pomus, Kenny Vance. *Songs:* I Apologize; Fame and Fortune; Mr Performer; Baby; Harvest the Time; Make Me Cry; Talk to Me Nice; Where's the Magic; Rock and Roll City; Music: Upside Down Inside Out. *Instrumental Works:* EM. *Albums:* Fair Is Fair; Getting Ready for School.

NAMETH, MARTHA J
See Bachman, Martha Jeanne

NANCE, LONNIE BEE   ASCAP 1978
composer
b Browns, Ala, Oct 30, 38. *Songs:* Some Honky Tonk in Town; I Wish She Still Was Mine; Lyrics: Seldom Did You Ever See Me Cry; This Coal Mining Man.

NANTON, MORRIS PATRICK   ASCAP 1958
composer, pianist, teacher
b Perth Amboy, NJ, Sept 28, 29. Educ: Juilliard Sch Music, piano maj, 49-53; instr piano, Irwin Freundlich. Played tuba & piano, 5th Armored Div Band, USA, Camp Chaffee, Ark, 53-55; started jazz piano trio, 55; recording artist, 59- Chief Collabrs: Lyricists, Austin Gumbs, Leonard Chetkin. *Songs:* Music: Buzzin; Carry My Books; Tonight's the Night; They Say That a Lover Can Tell. *Instrumental Works:* The Pretty Time; Whistle Stop; Something We've Got.

NAPOLEON, MARTY   ASCAP 1959
composer, pianist, singer
b Brooklyn, NY, June 2, 21. Educ: New Utrecht High Sch, Brooklyn; studied piano with Teddy Napoleon, Gabby Budd & Bruce Steeg; theory with Tom Timothy, Joe Napoleon, Wes Hensel & Marty Holmes. As pianist traveled with Louis Armstrong, Gene Krupa, Charles Barnet, Joe Venuti & others; pianist & singer in clubs, cabarets, radio, TV & recordings with own group & others. Chief Collabrs: Louis Armstrong, Leonard Whitcup, John Cresci, Bob Braman, Jack Ackerman, George Litto. *Songs & Instrumental Works:* Louie's Dream; Napoleon in Paris; Little Marty; M T Blues; But Baby.

NAPOLEON, PHIL   ASCAP 1964
composer, conductor, trumpeter
b Boston, Mass, Sept 2, 01. Cond, original Memphis Five, 20's; appearances at jazz fests. Recording artist. *Instrumental Works:* Just Hot; At Dusk; Anything.

NAPTON, JOHNNY   ASCAP 1943
composer, pianist, trumpeter
b New York, NY, July 10, 24. Educ: Manhattan Sch Music; studied piano with Richard McClanahan & Lennie Tristano. Trumpeter in dance orchs incl Bunny Berigan, Jimmy Dorsey & Paul Whiteman; also radio & films. *Songs:* I'm Not Just Anybody's Baby; My Devotion; Twilight Serenade; The Miracle of Love; I Know a Gal in Nogales; Come on Baby, Let's Dance; What Kind of Love Is This?.

NARDO, DANIEL C   ASCAP 1963
composer, author
b Wilmington, Del, Dec 23, 20; d Wilmington, June 23, 68. Was a barber and inventor with a patent on a revolutionary scissor. *Songs:* Broken Love; Low Cut Sneakers and Bermuda Shorts.

NARMORE, EDGAR EUGENE (MILES HIGH)   ASCAP 1979
composer, author, actor
b Waynesville, NC, Jan 8, 44. Educ: Montreat-Anderson Col; Belhaven Col; New York Col, studied voice with Dee Marquit, 65. Wrote lyrics for Bway musical, "Gotta Go Disco," 79; performed own music; also an artist, an actor & a screenplay writer. Chief Collabr: Betty Rowland. *Songs:* Take Me to Heaven and Take Your Time; Blue Roses; Lyrics: Pleasure Pusher; Takin' in the Light; Hey!.

NASET, CLAYTON E   ASCAP 1955
composer, author, musician
b Stoughton, Wis, May 7, 1895; d Chicago, Ill, Feb 19, 66. Educ: High sch.

Played with Dan Russo & Ted Fiorito orchs, 8 yrs & on WMAQ, with Joseph Gallicchio orch, 6 yrs. Also in pit orchs, Bway musicals. Chief Collabs: Frank Magine, Ted Koehler. *Songs:* Dreamy Melody; Susie; Some Golden Day.

NASH, GRAHAM
ASCAP 1963

composer, singer

b Blackpool, Eng, 1942. Mem Brit group, The Hollies, 63-68. Joined David Crosby & Stephen Stills; formed group, Crosby, Stills & Nash, 69, then with Neil Young, until 71. Soloist & duo with David Crosby, then regrouped with Stephen Stills, 77. Appeared in film, "Woodstock," 70. Rec'd Grammy Award for Best New Artist of Yr, 69. *Albums:* Bus Stop; Stop, Stop, Stop; Hollies' Greatest Hits; Evolution; Dear Eloise/King Midas in Reverse; Crosby, Stills and Nash; CSN; Deja Vu; 4 Way Street; Graham Nash and David Crosby; Wind on the Water; Whistling Down the Wire; Crosby/Nash Live; Songs for Beginners; Wild Tales; Earth and Sky.

NASH, JOHN LESTER, JR
ASCAP 1961

composer, singer, recording artist

b Houston, Tex, Aug 19, 40. Educ: Jack Yates High Sch; Quintannos Sch for Young Prof. Lead vocalist church choir, Progressive New Hope Baptist Church. First regularly featured black performer, KPRC-TV, Houston, 3 yrs. Performer, Arthur Godfrey's Radio-TV Show, 7 yrs. First dramatic role, "Take a Giant Step", at age 17; also appeared in "Key Witness." Producer, arr, performer & co-songwriter, "Love is Not a Game", 70. Rec'd Silver Sail Award, Locarno Film Fest, Switz. *Songs:* I Can See Clearly Now; Hold Me Tight; There Are More Questions Than Answers; My Merry Go Round; What Kind of Love is This. *Albums:* I Can See Clearly Now; My Merry Go Round; Celebrate Life; Tears on My Pillow; What a Wonderful World; Let's Go Dancing.

NASH, N RICHARD
ASCAP 1978

lyricist, librettist

b Philadelphia, Pa. Educ: Univ Pa, BA. Author novels: "Aphrodite's Cave"; "Last Magic"; "East Wind, Rain"; "Cry Macho"; plays: "Rainmaker"; "Echoes"; "Handful of Fire"; "Girls of Summer"; "See the Jaguar"; "Young and Fair"; "Second Best Bed"; philosophy books: "Wounds of Sparta"; "Athenian Spirit." *Scores:* Lyricist & Librettist: 110 in the Shade; Wild Cat; Happy Time; Sara Va.

NASH, OGDEN
ASCAP 1943

author

b Rye, NY, Aug 19, 02; d 1971. Educ: Harvard Univ. Poetry Collections: "Free Wheeling"; "Happy Days"; "I'm a Stranger Here Myself"; "The Face Is Familiar"; "Good Intentions"; "The Private Dining Room"; "You Can't Get There From Here"; "Hard Lines"; "The Primrose Path"; "Many Long Years Ago"; "Selected Verse"; "Versus." Mem, Nat Inst Arts & Letters. Chief Collabs: Kurt Weill, Vernon Duke. *Songs:* Speak Low; West Wind; One Touch of Venus; That's Him; Foolish Heart; I'm a Stranger Here Myself; Wooden Wedding; Madly in Love; You're Far From Wonderful; Roundabout; Out of the Clear Blue Sky. *Scores:* Bway stage: One Touch of Venus; Two's Company; The Littlest Revue (off-Bway).

NASH, ROBERT
ASCAP 1971

composer, author, arranger

b Orange, NJ, Mar 16, 30. Educ: Yale Sch Music, 48-50; Royal Acad Music, London, LRAM & ARCM, 53; pvt comp & cond studies with Michael Fivesky. Professional trombonist, Metrop Opera, Radio City Music Hall, ABC, etc, 54-57; free lance music writer, 57-60; music dir, William Esty Advert, 60-66; vpres & music dir, Foote, Cone & Belding, 66-69; free lance composer/arranger, TV commercials, commercial scoring, documentaries, etc, 69-

NASSAN, SANDER ALAN
ASCAP 1970

composer

b Cincinnati, Ohio, Aug 21, 47. Educ: Univ Cincinnati, comp studies with Dr Scott Houston. Began professionally accompanying vocalists, 65. Writer/publ, Family Owl Music, 70. Solo col concert work & club dates, 10 yrs. *Songs:* Music: J-Am; Captiva; Emily Jane Bell; Music Box. *Scores:* Film: A Legal Crime.

NATALI, ALFRED MAXIM
ASCAP 1973

author, singer, cellist

b Genoa, Italy, Mar 9, 15. Educ: Augustinian Acad, Staten Island, NY; Villanova Univ, BA & MA; St Augustine Col, DC; study & chanter of Gregorian chant & polyphonic music. Asst, Lawrence, Mass; missioner in North Queensland, Australia; pastor, Holy Rosary Church, Lawrence, Mass; asst, St Nicholas, Philadelphia. Chief Collabs: Bob Wishart, Mary Jane Wishart. *Songs:* The Workingman's Prayer; Christmas Forever; America America So Young and Beautiful; The Football Hero; Another Day.

NATALIE, ANGELO MICHAEL
ASCAP 1975

composer, author, musician

b Erie, Pa, Feb 17, 52. Educ: Cathedral Prep Sch, 66-70; Edinboro State Col, Pa, 70-72, music maj. Began playing drums in high sch rock bands, age 14; songwriter throughout high sch & col days. Recorded an album with the band, Clockwise, 76. Started Buon Natalie Music (publ & production), 78. *Songs:* Happy to Be the Moon; Time to Dance; Anthem for His Majesty; Now's the Time; Wandering Star. *Albums:* Anthem for His Majesty.

NATHAN, CHARLES
ASCAP 1959

composer, author

b London, Eng, Apr 17, 21. Educ: Belmont, Hollywood & Metrop High Schs, Los Angeles, Calif; trumpet studies with Lloyd Reece & Louis Maggio, Los Angeles; Am operatic lab under Dr Ed Loe, piano under Larry Greene & Harry Fields, Los Angeles. Started trumpet at age 14; had own band Chuck Denny at age 16; played with Jim Jeffers Band, Weidler Bros Band & many others, Los Angeles, late 30's early 40's. USAF, 42, played with dance bands under Phil Washburn at Lowry Field, Denver, Colo; Kelly Field Band, Tinker Field, Oklahoma City, Okla, arr & wrote comp for Kelly Field Band. Played in marching, concert & dance bands, shows & others; performed on radio, 44. In charge of spec serv & played in local night clubs, Italy, 44. Began song writing. Chief Collabs: Howard David Heisler; Mike Post, Lenny Adelson, Don Robertson, Larry Fotine, Jack Elliott, Sid Flick. *Songs:* Dance If You Want to Dance (Said the Little Moment); Hurry Home to Me; The Foursome; Music: Say You're Mine Again; Somewhere There Is Someone.

NATHAN, LANE
See Cohen, Lane Nathan

NATHAN, ROBERT
ASCAP 1943

author

b New York, NY, Jan 2, 1894. Educ: Harvard Univ, Phillips Exeter. Author of forty novels, of 9 poetry bks; playwright. Chief Collabs: Walter Damrosch, Richard Hageman, Phillip James & others. *Songs & Instrumental Works:* March, America; Dunkirk; Home Over the Hill; Fear Not the Night; I Ride the Great Black Horses; Hush; Atque Vale; Is It You; Rolling Rivers, Dreaming Forests; A Lover's Song (My True Love); Epitaph for a Pact; At Heaven's Door (Am Himmelstor); O Lovely World; The Town (Die Stadt); Beggar's Love (Bettlerliebe); So Love Returns; Il Passa (He Passed By); Nocturne; Here in This Spot With You; The Bird; Watch America (World Music Horizons); Shadows of Autumn; The Blessed Night; Three Songs for Baritone: Evening; Secret; Where Am I Going; Three Songs for Soprano: Epitaph; Bells; Waves.

NAVARA, LEON
ASCAP 1950

composer, conductor, pianist

b Brooklyn, NY; d. Educ: Pratt Inst; Juilliard Sch Music; studied piano with Mrs Thomas Tapper, Edwine Behr, Edith Quale & Harold Bauer. In vaudeville, Keith-Orpheum Circuit, NY, 12 yrs; cond theatre orchs, New York, San Francisco & Los Angeles; also Loew's Circuit, Balaban & Katz Theatres & Skouras Circuit; organized own band, appeared in hotels, theatres & radio, 32; in film shorts, "Leon Navara and His Melody Masters", "Dizzy Fingers." Master of Ceremonies, Strand Theatre, New York & Stanley Theatre, Baltimore; master of ceremonies & mus dir, Capital Theatre Orch, New York. Chief Collabs: Mitchell Parish, Joe Goodwin, Sidney Mitchell, Ned Washington, Stanley Adams & Milton Berle. *Songs:* We're Ridin' for Uncle Sammy Now!; In a Corner of My Heart; To Think That You Belong to Me; Who Do You Have to Know?; Gigolette.

NAVARRA, TINA
ASCAP 1973

composer, author, teacher

b Roswell, NMex, Dec 29, 36. Educ: Amarillo Col, 57. Author two bks. Chief Collabr: A Ray Gardner. *Songs:* The Texas Spy; Hustlin' Hereford Boomer Jump; Hello Judas; The Sound of Goodbye; Castles in Spain.

NAZARIAN, BRUCE CHARLES
ASCAP 1978

composer, author, singer

b Detroit, Mich, Mar 27, 49. Educ: David Mackenzie High Sch; Wayne State Univ, BA(music), 70. Became singer & studio musician, 69. Mem, Brownsville Station, 75-79. Private Stock recording artist, later Epic Records. Producer, studio musician & instr, Recording Techniques for Musicians, Wayne State Univ. Extensive choral experience. Chief Collabs: Lutz, Koda, Weck, Jerome Jones, David Van De Patte, Frank Lee. *Songs:* Martian Boogie; Hot Spit; Waiting for the Weekend.

NEALS, BETTY HARRIS
ASCAP 1979

author

b Newark, NJ, Mar 27, 34. Educ: Kean Col, NJ, BS; NY Univ, MA. Lyricist, Rahsaan Roland Kirk & his Vibration Society. Author two bks poetry, "Spirit Weaving", "Move the Air!" & cassette poetry "Soul, Alleluia." College, nightclub & TV work. *Songs:* Lyrics: Theme for the Eulipions; Giant Steps.

NEAR, HOLLY HOLMES
ASCAP 1976

composer, author, singer

b Ukiah, Calif, June 6, 49. Educ: Ukiah High Sch; voice studies with Connie Cox, 58-65; Perry-Mansfield Sch Performing Arts, Colo, 62; Ramblerny Sch Performing Arts, 65-66; jazz studies with Chan & Phill Woods, 65-66; extensive perf, writing exp & master classes, 67-80. Extensive childhood perf exp from age 7; recorded first song comp in pre-teens; summer stock, age 17; TV/film work began at 19. Formed Redwood Records Co, 73. Chief Collabs: Jeff Langley, Meg Christian. *Songs:* Get Off Me Baby; It Could Have Been Me; Fight Back; Singing for Our Lives; Working Woman-Nine to Five; Ain't No Where You Can Run; Imagine My Surprise; Lyrics: The Rock Will Wear Away; Nina.

NEDROW, JOHN WILSON (WILLEY WORDEN)   ASCAP 1972
singer, lyricist
b Confluence, Pa, Oct 30, 12. Performed in high sch glee club; mem choral group, Col Mountain State & Baltimore City Col; appeared with trio in nightclubs; vocalist with var bands. Chief Collabrs: Walter MacDonald, Brick English, Robert Scherman. *Songs:* Keep a Cozy Corner in Your Heart for Me; My Dream Girl; Lyrics: I'll Be Waiting for You; San Diego Sue; I Remember My Pappy.

NEFF, MORTY
See Weinstein, Morton Neff

NEIBURG, AL J (ALLEN)   ASCAP 1933
composer, author, publisher
b St Albans, Vt, Nov 22, 02; d New Haven, Conn, July 12, 78. Educ: Boston Univ. Worked for Oliver Ditson Co. Wrote songs for films, incl "Gulliver's Travels", "Raggedy Ann and Raggedy Andy", "Popeye." Author: "In the Language of the Songwriter" & "Rhyme and Reason." Chief Collabrs: Milton Ager, Jerry Livingston, Sigmund Romberg, Marty Symes, J Fred Coots. *Songs:* Too Much Mustard; I'm Confessin' That I Love You; It's the Talk of the Town; Under a Blanket of Blue; It's a Hap-Hap-Happy Day; I've Got an Invitation to a Dance; When It's Darkness on the Delta; Sweet Slumber; Moon Nocturne; A Little Bit Later On; The Shag; It's Sunday Down in Caroline; There Is No Peace (Without God); Chimes in the Chapel; Why Let a Lie Break Your Heart; I'm Yours Sincerely; He'll Be Coming Down the Chimney; That's How It Goes; If I Can Count on You; Last Date; It's Always Nice to Be With You; The Snows of Kilimanjaro. *Instrumental Works:* Portrait of a Mood in Blue (piano); Scenario Music to a Matinee Idol (piano concerto).

NEIKRUG, MARC E   ASCAP 1970
composer, pianist, conductor
b New York, NY, Sept 24, 46. Educ: State Univ NY Stony Brook, MA. Concert pianist performing world wide. Comp performed at maj music fests, concerts, radio & TV. *Instrumental Works:* Eternity's Sunrise; Viola Concerto; Violoncello Solo Sonata; String Quartet.

NELHYBEL, VACLAV   ASCAP 1968
composer
b Polanka, Czech, Sept 24, 19. Educ: Musicology, Univ Prague & Freiburg, Switz; comp, Cons Music, Prague. Affil as comp & cond with Radio Prague, 39-46 & with Swiss Nat Radio, 46-50. Musical dir, Radio Free Europe, 50-57. To US, 57. Comp, lectr & guest cond, 57- *Instrumental Works:* Etude Symphonique (orch); Cantus Concertante (string trio and orch); Concerto Spirituoso No 1, 2, 3, 4 (orch, large ensembles); Trio for Brass; Miniatures for String Trio; Piano Brass Quartet; Trittico (symph band); Chorale (symph band); Music for Orchestra. *Songs & Instrumental Works:* Adoratio (voices, a capella); Caroli Antiqui Varii (chorus, a capella); Fables for All Time (chorus, orch). *Scores:* Opera: Everyman.

NELIUS, LOUIS
See Wilde, Cornel L

NELSON, DYER
See Spitzer, Cordelia

NELSON, ED, JR   ASCAP 1952
composer, author
b Bronx, NY, Mar 26, 16. S/Sgt, USA Special Services, World War II; writer & performer in USA shows. Chief Collabrs: Ed G Nelson (father), Steve Nelson (brother). *Songs:* I'm Throwing Rice; My Tormented Heart; With This Ring, I Thee Wed; One Kiss Too Many; Baby, Be Mine; I Wish I Had a Sweetheart.

NELSON, ED G   ASCAP 1921
composer, conductor, pianist
b New York, NY, Mar 18, 1885; d. Educ: High sch; pvt piano study. Pianist in nightclubs & cabarets. Orch leader, 18-24. Coauth vaudeville act, "Inspiration." Wrote songs for films. Chief Collabrs: Harry Pease, Al Goodhart, Al Hoffman, Fred Rose, Howard Johnson, Ed Nelson Jr (son), Steve Nelson (son). *Songs:* When Yankee Doodle Learns to Parlez Vous Francais; Peggy O'Neil; Ten Little Fingers and Ten Little Toes; I Apologize; Auf Wiedersehn, My Dear; Josephine, Please No Lean on the Bell; Hang Your Head in Shame; In a Shady Nook by a Babbling Brook; Why Do They Always Say No?; Light a Candle in the Chapel; Pretty Kitty Kelly; All for the Love of Mike; In a Little Second Hand Store; In the Old Town Hall; The Pal That I Loved Stole the Gal That I Loved; I'm Climbing Up a Rainbow; Red Roses for My Blue Baby; That's My Mammy; There'll Never Be Another You; Setting the Woods on Fire; Nobody's Love Is Like Mine; One Little Kiss Did the Trick; Worried Over You; You're Only in My Arms to Cry on My Shoulder.

NELSON, ERICK   ASCAP 1973
composer, author, singer
b Lynwood, Calif, June 21, 49. Educ: Pomona Col, BA(philosophy). Played Christian music, toured US, Europe & Can, 71- Chief Collabrs: Steve Berg, Don Stalker. *Songs:* Picking Up the Pieces; Flow River Flow; Soldiers of the Cross; He Gave Me Love; The Misfit; The Martyr Song.

NELSON, (REV) FREDERIC JUL   ASCAP 1953
composer, author, singer
b Portland, Ore, May 18, 23. Educ: Univ Ore; Univ Colo; St Thomas Sem; St Francis Sem; Univ NDak, PhD(music); studied with Fred Waring, Roger Wagner & Robert DeCormier. Former concert & opera singer. Ordained Roman Cath priest, 50. Founder, Antonian Choirs of West Coast; founder, Marian Chorus, 54; founder & present dir of continent-wide, Marian Hour Radio Rosary Broadcast; founder & pres, Marycords Record Co; founder & present headmaster, Notre Dame of the Prairies Roman Cath Acad; present ed, Maryfaithful. *Songs:* Hail Mary Hail; Oh My Jesus, Goodnight; Music: Lovely Lady Dressed in Blue; People's Mass. *Songs & Instrumental Works:* Mass of Our Lady of the Prairies (World Premiere, Central City Opera Fest, 57).

NELSON, HARMON OSCAR, JR   ASCAP 1966
composer, singer, musician
b Whitinsville, Mass, July 5, 07; d Pasadena, Calif, Sept 28, 75. Educ: Cushing Acad, Mass; Univ Mass, BA. Formed own band in col, played New Eng area. Own radio show, Boston & New York, late 20's. Joined Tommy & Jimmy Dorsey Band; vocalist, with Irving Aaronson, for recordings, Roy Smeck's Band. Radio producer & dir with Young & Rubicam, Inc, New York. To Calif, re-formed Harmon Nelson Band, played west coast. Bette Davis used name for motion picture Oscar award. Served installing radio stations behind landing forces, Armed Forces Radio Services, S Pacific, WW II, 3 1/2 yrs. With advert co, Roche, Williams Cleary; agent, comp & arr with Berg-Allenberg, Peter Smith Agency, McManus, John & Adams & Stromberger, Lavenem & McKenzie advert agencies. Comp, background music & commercials.

NELSON, JAMES C, JR   ASCAP 1962
composer, author
b Denver, Colo, Nov 10, 21. Educ: Yale Univ, BA. Served, USN, World War II. Marketing & illustration ed, Business Week Magazine, 46-52. Free-lance author, 52-57. Vpres & creative dir, Hoefer, Dieterich & Brown, San Francisco. Writer, musical commercials. Chief Collabr: Don Quinn. *Songs:* Sunrise in Hawaii.

NELSON, LARRY ALAN   ASCAP 1970
composer
b Broken Bow, Nebr, Jan 27, 44. Educ: Univ Denver, BMus, 67, Normand Lockwood; Southern Ill Univ, MMus, 68, Will Bottje; Mich State Univ, PhD, 74, H Owen Reed. MacDowell Colonist, 73, 75 & 76. Nat Endowment Arts grant, 74; Pa Comp Project prize, 74; Norlin Fellow, 76. *Instrumental Works:* Flute Thing; Nocturne; Poem of Soft Music; Variations for Orchestra; Cadenzas and Interludes.

NELSON, OSWALD GEORGE (OZZIE)
composer, author, singer
b Jersey City, NJ, Mar 20, d Los Angeles, Calif, June 3, 75. Educ: Rutgers Univ; NJ Law Sch. Led dance band on radio & records; also toured country. Featured in radio & TV series, "The Adventures of Ozzie and Harriet", with wife, Harriet Hilliard, and sons, Rick and David. Wrote, produced & dir film, "Love and Kisses."

NELSON, PAUL   ASCAP 1959
composer, conductor, arranger
b Phoenix, Ariz, Jan 26, 29. Educ: Phoenix Col; Ariz State Col; Teachers Col, Columbia Univ, BS; Harvard Univ, studied with Walter Piston & Randall Thompson, two Naumburg fels, MA; Univ Vienna; Am Acad, Rome, three Damrosch fels; also studied with Paul Creston, Paul Hindemith & Lukas Foss; Paine fel. Arr for dance bands & records; first trumpeter, Phoenix Symph & Monterey County Symph. Instr trumpet & music fundamentals, USA Band Training Unit, Ft Ord, Calif, 50-51; staff comp & arr, US Mil Acad Band, West Point; cond, Post Chapel Choir, 51-53. Instr comp & theory, Univ Louisville, 55-56. Asst prof theory & comp, Brown Univ, 64- Educr. *Songs & Instrumental Works:* Variations on a Western Folksong (1st prize, Tucson Fest of Arts); Easter Cantata (1st prize, Friends of Harvey Gaul contest); Theme & Passacaglia (Louisville Orch student award); For Theirs Is the Kingdom of Heaven (chorale); Three Songs for Soprano & Eight Horns; Narrative for Orchestra; Trio for Strings; Two Madrigals on Old English Airs (chorus; Francis Boott prize); Divertimento for Clarinet (Contemporary Music Soc, Houston, Tex, comn); The Creation (chorus, narrators, piano, perc); Christmas Cantata (chorus, soloists, piano, flute); Colombes; Gloopy (jazz band); Sinfonietta; Idyll for Horn, Strings; In Bethlehem That Noble Place; Thy Will Be Done.

NELSON, PORTIA   ASCAP 1965
composer, author, singer
b Brigham City, Utah, May 27, 20. Educ: Self-taught. Singer, New York & other cities of the world, 50's; recorded albums & musical comedies for Columbia. Comp, lyricist & arr with revues, recordings, TV spec film scores. Actress in films "The Sound of Music", "Doctor Dolittle", "The Trouble With Angels" & "The Other" & on Bway in "The Golden Apple." Painter & photographer. Author bk "There's a Hole in My Sidewalk." Chief Collabrs: Hal Hackady, Laurindo Almeda. *Songs:* Sunday in New York (off Bway revue, cabaret favorite); I Don't Smoke; So Far It's Wonderful, This Life; Pieces; Winter Moon. *Instrumental Works:* Lady Nelson and the Lords. *Scores:* TV Spec: Sound of

Children; Sleeping Beauty; Midnight Ride of Paul Revere; Off Bway Show: There's a Hole in My Sidewalk. *Albums:* Picadilly Pickle.

NELSON, ROBERT E   ASCAP 1972
composer, author
b Wailuku, Maui, Nov 26, 34. Dir, Hawaiian Professional Songwriters Soc; founder/dir, Comp Workshop, Hawaii. Pres, Mahina Music, Inc & Island Music Productions, Inc. Musician/entertainer, Waikiki. Mem: West Coast Writers Adv Comt & Na Hoku Hanohano Comt. *Songs:* Hanalei Moon (Nani Award, 74, 75); Mau'i Waltz (Na Hoku Hanohano nominations, 77); From Today (Tokyo Music Fest, 78); Fill My Cup With Rainbows; Just a Little Girl.

NELSON, RONALD J   ASCAP 1957
composer
b Joliet, Ill, Dec 14, 29. Educ: Eastman Sch Music, BM, 52, MM, 53, DMA, 56; studied with Howard Hanson & Bernard Rogers; Fulbright grant, Paris, 54-55. Taught at Brown Univ, 56-, chmn, Dept Music, 63-73. Awards: ASCAP, Howard Found, Ford Found & Nat Endowment Arts. Comn from Rochester Philh, Dartmouth Col, Univ Minn, Lima Symph, Sherman Symph, LaSalle Col, Lawrence Univ, New Music Ens & Cincinnati Symph. *Songs & Instrumental Works:* Savannah River Holiday (band); For Katherine in April (Benjamin Award); This Is the Orchestra (Comn by Children's Concert Comt); Jubilee (Comn by Children's Concert Comt); Overture for Latecomers (Comn by Ford Found); Toccata for Orchestra (Comn by Lima Symph); Rocky Point Holiday (band; comn by Univ Minn); Trilogy: JFK-MLK-RFK (Comn by RI Philh Orch); Five Pieces for Orchestra After Paintings by Andrew Wyeth; Meditation and Dance; Six Pieces for Chamber Ensemble; Mayflower Overture (band); The Christmas Story (cantata; SATB, organ, brass, timpani, narrator, orch; comn by Cent Baptist Church); What Is Man? (oratorio; 3 movements, chorus, SATB, orch, baritone, soloists, narrator, brass, perc, organ; comn by Baptist Jubilee Advance); Choral: Fanfare for a Festival (SATB, brass, timpani; comn by Chicago Music Fest); Glory to God (SATB, brass); Christmas Fanfare (SATB, brass; comn by Cent Baptist Church); Hear O Israel (SATB; comn by Am Baptist Assembly); O Lord How Can We Know Thee (SATB; comn by Am Baptist Assembly); He Came Here for Me (SSA, SATB, chime); Behold Man! (TTBB; comn by Brown Glee Club); Sleep Little One (SSA, SATB, TTBB); To God All Praise and Glory (SATB); Will He Remember? (SSA); Red Rosy Bush (SSA); Barbara Allen (SSA); He's Gone Away (SSA); Choral Fanfare for Easter and Christmas (SATB, narrator); Jehovah Hear Our Prayer (SSAA; comn by JTHS Glee Club); Autumn Night (SSAA); Vocalise (SSAA); Five Anthems for Young Choirs (SA); All Praise to Music (SATB, brass, timpani); God, Show Thy Sword (SATB, organ, perc; comn by Methodist Church of Birmingham); Meditation on the Syllable OM (TTBB; comn by Dartmouth Glee Club); Alleluia, July 20, 1969 (SATB; commemorating the voyage of Apollo 11); Thy Truth Is Great; Prayer of Emperor of China on the Altar of Heaven, December 21, 1539; Psalm 95; Prayer of St Francis of Assisi; Oh God, Invent a Name for Us; Four Pieces After the Seasons (SATB); Here We Come As in the Beginning (SSA); Early May (SATB); Wonder and Wild Honey (SATB); Winter Journeyings (SATB); Late September (SATB); Three Autumn Sketches: Beyond the Elm (SATB); Autumn Rune (SATB); Acquiescence (SATB); For Freedom of Conscience (SATB, organ, trumpets). *Scores:* Opera: The Birthday of the Infanta; Films: Eastman Kodak; This Is Russia (March of Time); Baden Street; Piloted Aircraft (documentary); Song Outside Your Window; The Social Security Story; The Long Haul; TV: Before the Day.

NELSON, RONALD JUREZ   ASCAP 1972
composer, author
b Alma, Ga, Aug 9, 37. Educ: Bacon County High Sch; Univ Md, 2 yrs. Radio announcer/writer, Am Forces Korea Network & Far East Network, 10 yrs; com radio & TV announcing-writing-dir in the South, 5 yrs; asst creative dir, wrote, produced, filmed, jingles, TV com, A/V Shows & indust films, W B Tanner Co. Chief Collabrs: William H McMath, Mark Blumberg. *Songs:* She.

NELSON, RONNIE
See Niedhammer, Ronald Edward

NELSON, SANDY
See Egnatzik, Joseph

NELSON, SEENA   ASCAP 1976
composer, author
b New York, NY, May 9, 36. *Songs:* It's Spring Again; Music: Old Ficus Trail; Jubilation.

NELSON, STEVE EDWARD   ASCAP 1945
composer, author
b New York, NY, Nov 24, 07. Educ: Evander Childs High Sch; NY Univ. Wrote country, children & holiday songs. Mem, Nashville Songwriters Hall of Fame. Chief Collabrs: Johnny Burke, Bob Hilliard, Jack Rollins, Benny Davis, Charlie Tobias. *Songs:* Music: Frosty, the Snowman; Peter Cottontail; Bouquet of Roses; Lyrics: Hang Your Head in Shame; Yours and Mine. *Songs & Instrumental Works:* Smokey the Bear (off song for US Forestry Dept).

NELSON, STEVEN DAVID
composer, author, singer
b New York, NY, Dec 2, 47. Educ: Lake Forest Col; NY Univ; Manhattan Sch Music; Songwriting & Recording Workshop, studied with Paul Simon; Music Workshop, studied with Dick Grove. Songwriter, 66-; staff writer, Intersong, 77-79; mgr catalog promotion & writer, 20th Century Fox Music Publ, 79- Chief Collabrs: Michael Morgan, David Wolfert, Diana Canova, Lalo Schiffrin, Melissa Manchester. *Songs:* Songbird; Living Without Your Love; Say You Will; When Love Is Gone; Just Hold Me Tonight.

NEMO, HENRY   ASCAP 1938
composer, author
b New York, NY, June 8, 14. Wrote "Cotton Show," 38; nightclub & vaudeville entertainer; actor in films incl "Song of the Thin Man." Chief Collabr: Duke Ellington. *Songs:* Jump Jump's Here; If You Were in My Place; I Let a Song Go Out of My Heart; Born to Swing; Don't Take Your Love From Me; Blame It on My Last Affair; I Haven't Changed a Thing.

NEMOY, PRISCILLA   ASCAP 1958
composer, pianist
b Chicago, Ill, Dec 12, 19. Educ: Jr City Col. With piano duo; 3 piano concerts. Music copyist, 39. *Songs:* The Christmas Toy.

NEMTZOW, LISA (LISA NEMZO)   ASCAP 1977
composer
b Newport, RI, Jan 12, 52. Educ: Cons of Sydney, Australia, 70-72; Westminster Col, 72-74, studied arr & composing with Ladd McIntosh; studied arr with Albert Harris, Los Angeles, 75-76; studied with vocal & acting coach Margaret Rolfe, 75-80. Singer & songwriter, USO tour, 75; South Pacific "Eugene Jeleshik Show." Nat tour opening act for Kenny Rogers, Tom Waits, Ry Cooder & Martin Mull, 77, Hall & Oates, 79. Recording artist. Chief Collabrs: Jenny Yates, Alan Kroeber, Art Collatrella. *Songs:* Music: Short Cut.

NEMZO, LISA
See Nemtzow, Lisa

NERO, PAUL   ASCAP 1946
composer, conductor, violinist
b Hamburg, Germany, Apr 29, 17; d Hollywood, Calif, May 21, 58. Educ: Curtis Inst, scholarship. To US, 23, Citizen 29. First violinist, Pittsburgh Symph; asst cond, CBS, Philadelphia. USN, WW II, cond Navy Dance Orch, DC. Gave concerts, New York & Los Angeles. Soloist, Chamber Music Soc of Lower Basin Street; also other radio progs. Concertmaster, Greek Theatre Orch. Fac mem, Juilliard Sch Music & Los Angeles Cons. *Instrumental Works:* Concerto for Hot Fiddle; Prelude and Allegro (oboe, strings); Seven Etudes for Violin; The Hot Canary; The Hot Gavotte.

NESTICO, SAMUEL LOUIS   ASCAP 1968
composer
b Pittsburgh, Pa, Feb 6, 24. Educ: Horace Mann Grade Sch; D B Oliver High Sch; Duquesne Univ, 46-50; Cath Univ, 51-52. Staff musician for ABC Radio at age 17, Pittsburgh; arranger for Off USAF Band, DC & the US Marine Band, DC, 15 yrs. Comp several albums for Count Basie, arr for Andre Kostelanitz Orch & Boston Pops. Orchestrated for Universal Studios, 20th Century Fox, Paramount, Walt Disney, MGM & all major movie studios. Have publ arrangements & original comp in the educ field. Distinguished Alumni Award, Duquesne Univ. *Songs:* Music: Have a Nice Day; Vaquero; Dark Orchid; Basie, Straight Ahead; El Dorado; Los Valientes; Apotheosis.

NETO, SEBASTIAO CARVALHO   ASCAP 1968
composer, bassist, singer
b Rio de Janeiro, Brazil, Nov 5, 31. Educ: Rio Cons Music, 59-62; Pro-Arte Sch Music, 62-67, Degree in Gen Arts & Crafts, 74. Started career as self-taught bassist, 58-62, joined the Bossanova Movement, Brazil & the Brazil 66 group with Sergio Mendes. In US, 62-74. Recordings & works with Vince Guaraldi, Shorty Rogers, Bola Sete & Brazil 66 & 77, 66-74. Chief Collabrs: Oscar Neves, Sergio Mendes, Lani Hall. *Songs:* Music: Salt Sea; Celebration of Sunrise; After Sunrise; Mozambique; Let It Go.

NETSKY, RONALD   ASCAP 1978
composer, author
b Philadelphia, Pa, Dec 19, 51. Educ: Philadelphia Col of Art, BFA, 73; Washington Univ, MFA, 75. Chief Collabrs: Steve Netsky, Michael Bacon, Hankus Netsky, George A Wallace, Malick Bachammer. *Songs:* Love Don't Hurt People; Only Love Can Make It Right; Dance the Night Away; What Did Love Ever Do for You?; When It's Right for Love; Hard to Fall in Love; Just Call Me Lover; Handin' Out Emotions; Lyrics: Photograph; Holding On.

NETSKY, STEVE   ASCAP 1979
composer, author
b Philadelphia, Pa, Dec 19, 51. Educ: Temple Univ, BA, 73. Folksinger, Philadelphia area, early 70's. Chief Collabr: Ron Netsky. *Songs:* What Did Love Ever Do for You?; It's the Music; How to Make a Woman Disappear; Bring on the Night; Find It in Your Heart.

NEUBERT, BRUCE ALAN   ASCAP 1979
composer, author, guitarist
b Sioux Falls, SDak, Apr 17, 54. Educ: Stevens High Sch; Brown Inst. Rock guitarist, concerts, sch dances & nightclubs; teacher rock guitar techniques. Chief Collabrs: Dan Birr, Tarver Johnson, Ron Kohn. *Songs:* Steele Street Revenge. *Instrumental Works:* Unspoken.

NEUFELD, MACE   ASCAP 1953
composer, author, producer
b New York, NY, July 13, 28. Educ: Yale Univ, BA; NY Univ Law Sch. Dir, TV progs, 48-50. Producer, "Laugh Line," NBC. Artists' mgr, 52- *Songs:* Smalltown; Bouncy Bouncy Bally; Blues to End the Blues; I Love You a Mountain; Play a Sentimental Tune.

NEUMANN, ALFRED JOHN   ASCAP 1974
composer, accompanist, conductor
b Brooklyn, NY, Dec 15, 28. Educ: Davidson Col, NC, BS; Univ Mich, Ann Arbor, MM; cond studies with Dr James C Pfohl & Dr Maynard Klein, opera coaching with Josef Blatt. Accompanist two Europ tours, Mozart Trio. Three tours as organist/cond, performing in Eng, France, Italy & Austria. Cond two sacred operas on NBC-TV, Washington, DC. Cond choirs at New York World's Fairs, 64 & 65, Riverside Church, New York, White House, Kennedy Ctr Concert Hall, Constitution Hall & Washington Nat Cathedral. Organist & choir dir, Christ Congregational Church, Silver Spring, Md & Washington Hebrew Congregation, DC; accompanist, Washington Performing Arts Concerts Schs Prog. Mem chorus, Washington Opera Soc, 15 yrs. *Songs & Instrumental Works:* Finale from Symphony No 2; Truly, We Shall Be in Paradise With Him; Arr: (Moravian anthems) Praises, Thanks and Adoration; One Thing We Ask, O Lord; Oh Had I Been There and Shared, Lord; Can You Not See Our God; To Us a Child Is Born; Three Responses. *Scores:* An Opera for Christmas.

NEUMANN, JOANNE K NYLUND   ASCAP 1973
composer, author
b Eveleth, Minn. Educ: Eveleth High Sch; Eveleth Jr Col; Winona State Teachers Col; Univ Minn. Teacher, Ithaca, NY & Managua, Nicaragua. Chief Collabrs: Joyce Pritchard, Nancy Underwood, Robert Comstock. *Songs:* Music: You Should; Cherry Blossom Time in Washington, DC; Let's Call the Game; It Isn't Likely; Golden Love.

NEUWIRTH, WILLIAM   ASCAP 1966
composer, author, teacher
b Allentown, Pa, July 30, 15. Educ: Lehigh Inst Music, Allentown. Band dir, Ft Eustis Army Band, 41-44; chief arr, Victor Lombardo Orch; own dance band, Whitey Worth, broadcasting nightly over WOR Mutual, 47; guest cond with var concert bands. Entertainer on a semi-retired basis, Sr Citizen Clubs, 70- Singer. Mem, Kismet Temple Shrine Band; hon mem, Local 802, Am Fedn Musicians. *Songs:* Nix Besser Polka; Majorettes on Parade; Bowling Polka; Beef Beans and Beer Polka; Ilanith; The Sweetheart Song; The World Can Be So Wonderful; Being Just the Two We Are; Sam's Polka; Froehliche Voglein; The Sun's on Top of the Mountain; Hawaiian Honeymoon; Music: The Fifty States March; March of Men and Music; Peace Corps March; General H F Nichols March; "T" Bones on Parade; The Big Fat Cat; Tommy; Candystripers March; Vantage Point March; Noble Ned March. *Instrumental Works:* Hobby Horse; Struttin'; Campers Caravan; Valse Christina.

NEVILLE, MICHAEL DOUGLAS   ASCAP 1971
composer
b Birmingham, Ala, Nov 18, 42. Educ: Birmingham Cons of Music; Auburn Univ; Musical Theatre Workshop with Lehman Engel. Staff comp, Bobby Goldsboro Music, Nashville, Tenn; musical dir, Tim Cahill. Chief Collabrs: Jim David, Marty Hansen, Donald Hillegas, Molly-Ann Leikin. *Songs:* Music: Give Love Time; Holding on for Dear Love; Pieces. *Scores:* Ballet: Five Contrasts; Film/TV: The Girl Who Ran Out of Night.

NEVILLE, RASUNAH ROSANA   ASCAP 1973
author, poet, lyricist
b Morris, Ill, Feb 1, 38. Educ: Western Ky Univ. Writer of poetry & lyrics to songs. *Songs:* Lyrics: Down to Earth.

NEVIN, ARTHUR FINLEY   ASCAP 1924
composer, conductor, teacher
b Edgeworth, Pa, Apr 27, 1871; d Sewickley, Pa, July 10, 43. Educ: New Eng Cons; Klindworth Cons, Berlin; hon MusD, Univ Pittsburgh. Prof of music, Univ Kans, 15-20. Dir, Memphis Municipal Music Dept; cond, Memphis Orch. WW I, dir of music, Camp Grant, Ill. Gave lecture tour. *Songs:* The Secret; Eron; Sleep, Little Blossom; Ah, Moon of My Delight. *Instrumental Works:* Lorna Doone (suite); Hindu Dance; Mother Goose Fantasy; Piano: Southern Sketches; Piano Concerto; Rhapsody; Cantatas: The Djinns; Roland. *Scores:* Operas: Poia; Daughter of the Forest.

NEVIN, ETHELBERT WOODBRIDGE   ASCAP 1925
composer
b Edgeworth, Pa, Nov 25, 1862; d New Haven, Conn, Feb 17, 01. Educ: Williams Cons, Pittsburgh, with von der Heide, William Guenther; Western Univ, studied with S Austin Pierce, BJ Lang & Stephen Emery. Pianist &

teacher, Pittsburgh, 1883; debut as concert pianist, 1886. *Songs:* The Rosary; Wynken, Blynken and Nod; Little Boy Blue; Mighty Lak' a Rose. *Instrumental Works:* Water Scenes (incl Narcissus); The Quest (cantata); Piano Suites: May in Tuscany; A Day in Venice.

NEVIN, GEORGE BALCH   ASCAP 1927
composer, organist, businessman
b Shippensburg, Pa, Mar 15, 1859; d Easton, Pa, Apr 17, 33. Educ: Lafayette Col, MA & MusD(hon). Worked in wholesale paper bus, 27 yrs. Church soloist, 25 yrs. *Songs:* My Bonnie Lass She Smileth; O Mistress Mine; It Was a Lover and His Lass; When the Flag Goes By; Anthems: At the Sepulchre; Hail Gladdening Light. *Instrumental Works:* Organ: The Shepherd's Evening Prayer; Vesper Hour at Sea; Cantatas: The Crown of Life; The Incarnation; The Gift of God; The Angel of the Dawn; The Crucified; The Adoration.

NEVIN, GORDON BALCH   ASCAP 1936
composer, organist, arranger
b Easton, Pa, May 19, 1892; d New Wilmington, Pa, Nov 15, 43. Educ: Studied with Charles Maddock, J Warren Andrews, J Fred Wolle; hon MusD, Westminster Col. Organist, teacher, Easton, Johnstown, Greensburg. Organist, Cleveland, Ohio. Teacher, Hiram Col, 15-17. Music arr, Boston, 17-18. Prof of organ, comp, Westminster Col, 32-43. Author "Primer of Organ Registration", "First Lessons At the Organ" & "The Harp and Chimes in Organ Playing." *Instrumental Works:* Organ: Sonata Tripartite; Pageant Triumphale; Tragedy of a Tin Soldier (suite); Rural Sketches; Sketches of the City; In Memoriam; 16 Postludes; Easy Anthems (3 vols); Behold the Christ (cantata); Following Foster's Footsteps (operetta).

NEVIN, MARK
See Levin, Morris Albert

NEW, JIMMY RAY   ASCAP 1979
composer, author, teacher
b Delta, Ala, Mar 13, 38. Educ: Birmingham-Southern Col, Ala, BM, 59, AB, 61; Auburn Univ, MM, 64, additional study, 64-77; Univ Colo, 70. Piano instr, Birmingham Cons of Music, Birmingham-Southern Col, 60-62; music instr, Randolph County Sch Syst, Ala, 62-63, music supvr, 63-65, dir music, 65-70; music consult for workshops, 65-70; music instr, Southern Union State Jr Col, Ala, 71-80. Music Educr Nat Conf/CMP res grant in music educ, 66. *Songs:* Short Songs for Children's Choir. *Instrumental Works:* Some Quick Pieces for Piano, Vol I.

NEWBORN, IRA   ASCAP 1975
composer
b New York, NY, Dec 26, 49. Educ: Plain View Sr High Sch; NY Univ, BMus; music studies with Lenny Frank, Luther Goodhart & Stuart Scharf. Guitarist, club dates, 64; recording sessions, New York, 67; musical dir for group, Manhattan Transfer, 73; writer for movies, 75-80. Chief Collabr: Liza Fields. *Songs:* Clap Your Hands.

NEWBURY, KENT ALAN   ASCAP 1972
composer, teacher, clinician
b Chicago, Ill, Nov 25, 25. Educ: Ind Univ, BM, 50, MM, 56, theory & comp studies with Bernhard Heiden; DePaul Univ, voice studies with Andrew Foldi; Am Cons Music, comp studies with Leo Sowerby. Choral Workshops: Fred Waring, Olaf Christiansen, Harry Veld & Norman Luboff. Teacher & choral dir elem & high schs, jr col, churches & indust choruses. Guest cond, fests & Ariz Lutheran Youth Coun. Sight-reading clinician for music dealers & Shawnee Press. Comp sight-reading material for Ariz All-State Chorus auditions. Commissioned works, over 230 choral publications. Adjudicator choral & vocal competitions, Ill & Ariz. Mem, High Sch Level Music Comts, Chicago & Phoenix Pub Schs. Chief Collabrs: Gail D Newbury, Lloyd A Whitehead. *Songs:* Music: Psalm 150; Break Forth Into Joyous Song; The Beatitudes; Go Ye Forth, America; Wisdom and Understanding; An Evening Scene; Every Night When the Sun Goes In; For You Shall Go Out in Joy; Prayer of Thanksgiving; Lord, Hear My Cry; Now Songs for the Church Year; Be Exalted, O Lord; Jacob's Ladder; O Give Thanks to the Lord; Sing to the Lord a New Song; With a Voice of Singing; Hallelujah; The Singers; Christmas; Ring Out, Wild Bells; Three Seasons; Rejoice in the Lord; Hosanna.

NEWBURY, MILTON S, JR (MICKEY)   ASCAP 1978
composer, singer
b Houston, Tex, May 19, 40. Served, USAF, 59-63. Writer, 63-; recording artist with var cos, 65- Songwriter for var artists incl Andy Williams, Ray Charles, Elvis Presley, Kenny Rogers, Glen Campbell, B B King & Willie Nelson. Appeared on var TV shows incl "Mike Douglas Show", "Johnny Carson" & others. Chief Collabr: Wesley Rose. *Songs:* Sweet Memories; An American Trilogy; Funny Familiar Forgotten Feelings; Frisco Mabel Joy; Lovers.

NEWELL, ROY
See Raymond, Harold Newell

NEWMAN, ALBERT M   ASCAP 1946
composer
b San Francisco, Calif, Aug 1, 1900; d Los Angeles, Calif, Nov 2, 64. Educ: Univ Calif; Univ Southern Calif, BS. Wrote film scores. Was sound man for films, TV & Hollywood. *Songs:* Blue Island; C'est Vous. *Instrumental Works:* For Piano: Just a Minute; Lock, Stock and Barrelhouse; Riverside Jive; Pop-a-Doo.

NEWMAN, ALFRED   ASCAP 1938
composer, conductor, pianist
b New Haven, Conn, Mar 17, 01; d Los Angeles, Calif, Feb 17, 70. Educ: Studied with Sigismond Stojowski (scholarship), Reuben Goldmark, George Wedge & Arnold Schoenberg. At age 13, piano soloist, Strand Theatre, New York. Pianist & accompanist in vaudeville & concert. Cond in vaudeville; then Bway musicals. Moved to Hollywood, 30. Guest Cond: Cincinnati Symph; Nat Symph; Los Angeles Philh; Hollywood Bowl Symph. Chief Collabrs: Harold Adamson, Otto Harbach, Frank Loesser, Mack Gordon, Paul Francis Webster, Ken Darby, Sammy Cahn. *Songs:* The Moon of Manakoora; Anastasia; The Best of Everything; The Pleasure of His Company; Adventures in Paradise; How Green Was My Valley; Sentimental Rhapsody; Through a Long and Sleepless Night; Music: Airport Love Theme. *Scores:* Films: Nevada Smith; Counterfeit Traitor; Camelot (Acad Award, 67); Airport I; Alexander's Ragtime Band (Acad award, 38); Tin Pan Alley (Acad Award, 40); Mother Wore Tights (Acad Award, 47); With a Song in My Heart (Acad Award, 52); Call Me Madam (Acad Award, 53); The King and I (Acad Award, 56); Film background: Street Scene; Hunchback of Notre Dame; Gunga Din; The Hurricane; The Prisoner of Zenda; Wuthering Heights; The Bluebird; How Green Was My Valley; The Song of Bernadette (Acad Award, 43); The Razor's Edge; Gentlemen's Agreement; Pinky; Come to the Stable; All About Eve; Broken Arrow; The Snows of Kilimanjaro; The Robe; David and Bathsheba; Desiree; The Egyptian; Love Is a Many-Splendored Thing (Acad Award, 55); A Man Called Peter; The Seven Year Itch; Anastasia; A Certain Smile; The Best of Everything; The Diary of Anne Frank; The Pleasure of His Company; How the West Was Won; The Greatest Story Ever Told; Musicals: Flower Drum Song; South Pacific; Carousel; Diamond Horseshoe; Come to the Stable.

NEWMAN, ANTHONY JOSEPH   ASCAP 1970
composer
b Los Angeles, Calif, May 12, 41. Educ: Mannes Col, NY, BS(organ); Harvard Univ, MA(comp); Boston Univ, DMA(organ). Concert career in US & Europe, 69- *Instrumental Works:* Concerto for Violin and Orchestra; Symphony for Organ Solo on the Battle Hymn of the Republic; Variations and Contrapunctus for Guitar Solo.

NEWMAN, BARBARA BELLE (T F OGAL)   ASCAP 1947
composer, author, producer
b Brooklyn, NY, Nov 22, 22. Educ: Richmond Hill High Sch, grad, 40; NY Univ, 44, LaVerne Noyes scholarship; studied piano with several teachers. Winner of Helen Chaplin Mem Medals for piano & musical theory, Brooklyn. Has made several appearances as a piano recitalist. Has written spec material for Louis Armstrong, McFarland Twins, Lucky Millinder, Louis Prima; personal mgr of several artists, incl Louis Prima, Gene Williams & Fran Warren. Pres, Renault Music Co, Inc; vpres, Enterprise Music Corp. Mem, Am Recreational Asn & Songwriters' Protective Asn. Chief Collabrs: Louis Prima, Anita Leonard, Louis Armstrong, Keely Smith, George Greeley. *Songs:* A Sunday Kind of Love; Early Autumn; You Broke the Only Heart That Ever Loved You; Swing You Lovers; Music: Theme From Walter Winchell Album "Story of Murder Inc".

NEWMAN, CHARLES   ASCAP 1929
author
b Chicago, Ill, Feb 22, 01; d Beverly Hills, Calif, Jan 9, 78. Educ: Columbia Univ. Chief Collabrs: Carmen Lombardo, Isham Jones, James Monaco, Joseph Young, Milton Ager, Lew Pollack, Allie Wrubel, Victor Young, Charles Tobias, Murray Mencher. *Songs:* Why Can't This Night Go on Forever?; I Met Her on Monday; Six Lessons From Madam La Zonga; Why Don't We Do This More Often?; You've Got Me Crying Again; You Can't Pull the Wool Over My Eyes; Pigalle; Song of a Lost Love; Summer Souvenirs; The Wooden Soldier and the China Doll; Sweethearts on Parade; Dream Train; Let's Swing It; Flowers for Madame; If You Were Only Mine; I Can't Believe It's True; Silver Shadows and Golden Dreams. *Scores:* Bway stage: Earl Carroll's Sketch Book (1935); Films: That's Right, You're Wrong; Jitterbugs; Tahiti Honey; Lady, Let's Dance.

NEWMAN, GERALD   ASCAP 1967
author, teacher
b New York, NY, May 3, 39. Educ: Stuyvesant High Sch, New York; Brooklyn Col, BA & MFA. Chief Collabr: Louis Schere. *Songs:* Lyrics: This Is the Last of the Wine; Banjo Boy of Washington Square; This Room.

NEWMAN, HERBERT   ASCAP 1955
composer, author
b Los Angeles, Calif, Mar 6, 25; d. Educ: Univ Calif, Los Angeles. Salesman, Mercury & Decca Records; founder & pres, Era Records, Pattern Music. *Songs:* The Wayward Wind; So This Is Love; You're In Love; I Gave You My Heart; The Big Round Wheel; It's Not That Easy; Music City; Rock Bottom.

NEWMAN, MAX   ASCAP 1964
composer, author
b Vienna, Austria, Mar 26, 14; d. *Songs & Instrumental Works:* Requiem Mass (memory of John Kennedy).

NEWMAN, THEODORE SIMON   ASCAP 1977
author
b New York, NY, June 18, 33; d Bay Harbor Island, Fla, Feb 16, 75. Educ: Univ Miami Music Sch, BA, 56; Juilliard Sch Music, BA, 60, MA, 63; studies with Victoria Giannini, Vincent Persichetti, Darius Milhaud, Paul Held & Aaron Copland. Composed music since 9 yrs old. Awards: Edward B Benjamin Prizes, 58-60, Gershwin Scholarship, 59, Ford Found, 60, Guggenheim Fel, 61, Elizabeth Sprague Collidge Chamber Music Prize, 63 & McCollin Award, 64. *Songs & Instrumental Works:* Alleluia (choir, mixed chorus, 8 instruments); Amen (choir, mixed chorus, SATB with piano); Divertimento (chamber orch); Discourse (small orch); Fragemens for Young Orchestra; Suite (band); Three Violin Duets; Psalm (string orch); Presto for Orchestra (symph orch); 'B' for Orchestra (symph orch); Toccata for Orchestra (symph orch); Symphony No I (symph orch); Dance of the Children (perc); Quetzalcoatl (small orch); Cain (full orch); Psalm (a cappella chorus); Epilogue to Memory of JFK, 3 Minutes in Dallas (string & perc).

NEWSOM, THOMAS P   ASCAP 1963
composer, saxophonist
b Portsmouth, Va, Feb 25, 29. Educ: Peabody Cons, BM; Teachers Col, Columbia Univ, MA. Saxophonist & comp, Les Elgart Orch, Ruby Braff Sextet & Benny Goodman Orch; toured SAm & Russia. Mem, Skitch Henderson Orch, "Tonight Show," NBC; wrote for Woody Herman Orch. *Instrumental Works:* Titter Pipes; La Boehm; See-Saw.

NEWTON-JOHN, OLIVIA
singer
b Cambridge, Eng, Sept 26, 48. Singer in Australia, Eng, US, 65- Appeared in film "Grease," 78. Recipient awards, Acad Country Music, 73, Country Music Asn (UK), 74, Country Music Asn, 74, Grammy Awards, 73, 74, Am Guild of Variety Artists, 74, Billboard People's Choice, 74, Record World, 74, 75 & 76, Nat Asn Retail Merchandisers.

NEZ, NITA   ASCAP 1972
composer, author, whistler
b Tex, Jan 15, 30. Educ: Hollywood High Sch; Valley Col; City Col. *Songs:* No Rainbow in the Sky; My America; We're Gonna Drink; Happy Birthday, Happy Birthday; I Miss Him When They Play the Tango.

NIBLOCK, JAMES F   ASCAP 1963
composer
b Scappoose, Ore, Nov 1, 17. Educ: Wash State Univ, BA & BEd; Colo Col, MA; Univ Iowa, PhD; pvt study of comp with Roy Harris & Paul Hindemith, violin with Jascha Brodsky, Louis Persinger & Josef Gingold. Prof music, Mich State Univ, 48-, dir music dept, 63-78. Performer, var string quartets & symph orchs. *Songs & Instrumental Works:* Six Motets (chorus); Entreat Me Not (chorus). Trigon (string orch); Soliloquy and Dance (symphonic band); La Folia (symphonic band); Sonatina (5 & 7 tempered piano); Vanity of Vanities (chorus, organ, brass & perc).

NICHOL, CLARISSA B   ASCAP 1961
composer, author, arranger
b Homestead, Pa, Aug 16, 1895. Originator, "Music Symbol Flash Cards" & "Musical Slip-On-Notes" (piano). Author, "Music Coloring Book" (piano). *Songs:* Sing and Play (collection Am patriotic songs).

NICHOLAS, DON
See De Collibus, Nicholas

NICHOLS, ALBERTA   ASCAP 1933
composer
b Lincoln, Ill, Dec 3, 1898; d Hollywood, Calif, Feb 4, 57. Educ: Louisville Cons, studied with Alfred Calzin & George Copeland. Wrote spec material for vaudeville, also radio theme songs & musical commercials. Chief Collabr: Mann Holiner (husband). *Songs:* There Never Was a Town Like Paris; Sing a Little Tune; You Can't Stop Me From Loving You; What's Keeping My Prince Charming?; Until the Real Thing Comes Along; I Just Couldn't Take It Baby; Your Mother's Son-in-Law; I'm Walkin' the Chalk Line; A Love Like Ours; Why Shouldn't It Happen to Us?. *Scores:* Bway stage: Gay Paree; Angela; songs for Luckee Girl; Rhapsody in Black; Blackbirds of 1933.

NICHOLS, ERNEST LORING (RED)   ASCAP 1956
composer, conductor, cornetist
b Ogden, Utah, May 8, 05; d Las Vegas, Nev, June 28, 65. Educ: Culver Mil Acad. Cornetist in dance orchs, also led own pit orch for Bway musicals, incl "Strike Up the Band" & "Girl Crazy." Later, formed orch, Red Nichols & his Five Pennies. Cond band, Bob Hope's first radio prog. Film Biography: "The Five Pennies." Made many records. *Instrumental Works:* Trumpet Sobs; Bugler's Lament.

NICHOLS, JAMES WALKER ASCAP 1970
composer, teacher, director
b Sheboygan, Wis, Jan 23, 29. Educ: Northwestern Univ, BME & MM; Univ Southern Calif; McGiffin, Nolte, Pottag, Neff, Paynter, Donato & Geiringer. Instrumental & vocal music, Earlville, Ill, 52-56 & Torrance High Sch, Calif, 56-59; band & orch dir, Grossmont High Sch, 59-80. Entertainment dir, San Diego Chargers, 70-, also for Nat Football League. Church choir dir, dance & jazz band dir & trumpet & piano player. Designed numerous shows for Chargers, Rams & Riders. Calif chmn, Nat Basketball Asn. Awards: Second place, Disneyland Holiday Marching Band Contest, 66; Grand Prize, Disneyland Contest, 67; Miami Orange Bowl Play-off Bowl, 68; Shrine East-West Game, 68; Nat Football League Pro-Bowl Games, 62 & 69; All Western Sweepstakes, field competition (7 times), Chaffey Sweepstakes; PTA Serv Award; 2 Calif Life Credentials, Calif State Legislature for excellent music teaching. *Instrumental Works:* American Flag Salute; Charger March; Roman Procession; Triumph of the Blue and Gold; Salute to the New Year; Glory Hallelujah.

NICHOLS, NELLIE MARGARET (NELLIE ROWE) ASCAP 1973
author
b Ewen, Mich, Sept 4, 22. Educ: Ewen High Sch, dipl, 42; LaSalle Extention Univ, speedwriting dipl, 52; Muskegon Bus Col, 76. Songwriter. Chief Collabrs: James Fraser, Will Gentry.

NICHOLS, ROGER STEWART ASCAP 1969
composer
b Missoula, Mont, Sept 17, 40. Educ: Studied violin for 8 yrs; Santa Monica High Sch, 58; Univ Calif, Los Angeles, on basketball scholarship, studied music for 3 yrs. Started writing songs while in high sch. Had vocal group, Roger Nichols & a Small Circle of Friends; signed with A&M Records, 67, exclusive songwriters contract, 68. Have written for movies, TV, also number of TV commercials. Chief Collabrs: Paul Williams, William Lane, Norman Gimble. *Songs:* Music: We've Only Just Begun (commercial; Grammy Award nomination, 70); Rainy Days and Mondays; I Won't Last a Day Without You; Let Me Be the One; Out in the Country; The Times of Your Life (commercial); I Never Had It So Good; To Put Up With You; She's So Good to Me; Someday Man; Treasure of San Miguel; Love So Fine; The Drifter; Song for Herb; Have You Heard the News; I Kept on Loving You; The Olympic Theme; Love Theme from Hart to Hart; No Love Today; Somebody Waiting; When You've Got What It Takes; The One World of You and Me; Trust; It's Time to Say Goodbye.

NICHOLS, TED ASCAP 1964
composer, author
b Missoula, Mont, Oct 2, 28. Educ: Baylor Univ, BMus; Syracuse Univ; Tex Col Arts & Indust, MMus(comp); doctoral studies at Univ Calif, Los Angeles, Univ Southern Calif & Claremont Grad Sch. Cmndg officer, Air Force Band Sch; high sch band & orch dir; univ band dir; musical dir, Hanna-Barbera TV Productions, Hollywood; dir music & creative arts, Western Conservative Baptist Sem, Portland, Ore. Chief Collabr: D Bruce Lockerbie. *Songs:* Religious Choral Music: King of Kings-Triology (choir, brass, perc & organ); His Love; Savior, Like a Shepherd; Life More Abundant; Clap, Shout, Sing and Praise; Music: Carols for Harp, Choir and Brass. *Scores:* Pilgrim's Progress (chancel opera); Film/TV: The Man Called Flintstone.

NICHTERN, DAVID M ASCAP 1974
composer, guitarist, singer
b New York, NY, Feb 19, 48. Educ: Columbia Univ, BA(Eng lit); Berklee Sch Music, studied arr. Played with many prominent folk & pop acts, New York, until 74; then with Maria Muldaur, Los Angeles. Played with Bonnie Raitt, Jerry Garcia & others; also did studio work. *Songs:* Midnight at the Oasis; I Never Did Sing You a Lovesong; Oh Papa; Just Another Broken Heart; Birds Fly South (When Winter Comes); Elona. *Scores:* Films: White Line Fever.

NICOLETTI, JOSEPH ASCAP 1978
composer, author, singer
b Brooklyn, NY, Dec 9, 47. Educ: Lincoln High Sch, Brooklyn, NY; OCC Col, Southern Calif. Recorded & wrote for group Chapter 5, RCA Records, 66 & SSS Int Records, 67. Singer radio & TV spots for commercials; performer in clubs & concert halls, US. Chief Collabrs: Chery Lee Gammon, Barry White. *Songs:* Love Has Come to Stay; Street Wise; Life Time Fantasy Dancer; Lullaby; Gypsy.

NIDAY CANADAY, EDNA VERONICA (EVE ABBOTT, VERONICA CANADAY) ASCAP 1978
composer, author
b Gallipolis, Ohio, Dec 26, 07. Educ: Gallia Acad High Sch, Gallipolis, dipl; Famous Writer's Sch, West Port, Conn, cert; Chowan Col, 27 & 73-79. Sang with church choirs, area musical festivities. A&P Tea Co employee, 10 yrs. Mental health employee, 19 yrs. Chief Collabrs: Cheryl Warner, Barbara Steele, D L Leatherman, Ben Tate, May Redding, Will Gentry, Greg Bane. *Songs:* Lyrics: A Soldier and a Star; When the Golden Rod's in Bloom; My Heart Keeps Singing; Worldly Pleasures; Out of the Dusk; A Love of My Own; Spring and Winter; The Fool; His Love.

NIEBERDING, WILLIAM JOSEPH (WILL DENTON) ASCAP 1971
composer, singer
b Baltimore, Md, Jan 1, 48. Educ: Towson State Col, Md, 2 yrs; NTex State Univ, Denton, BM & MM; studied trombone with Leon Brown & comp with Merrill Ellis. Trombonist with var dance bands; trombonist & comp with rock group, Harvest; comp of choral & instrumental works; writes & records popular songs. Chief Collabr: James Ogilvy. *Songs:* Choral Expressions for Worship (choir); The Ballad of Bigfoot; Lonesome Sorrows; The Mover. *Instrumental Works:* Three lyric pieces for piano.

NIEDHAMMER, RONALD EDWARD (RONNIE NELSON) ASCAP 1975
composer, author, singer
b Scotia, NY, Oct 4, 30. Educ: Self-taught in piano, accordion & comp, 40-80. Composed classical piano works, 44-50; nightclub & radio performer, 48-65; with TV shows, 55-64; performer, "One Man Band" act, 65-80. Chief Collabrs: Paul Lovelace, Robert Kent. *Songs:* Liechtenstein Oh Liechtenstein; Dear Santa Claus; Music: There Goes That Mister Love. *Instrumental Works:* Fire in the Sky.

NIELSON, M SCOTT ASCAP 1974
composer, author
b St Paul, Minn, Jan 15, 43. Educ: Univ Minn, 4 yrs, studied anthropology. Singer & guitarist in coffee houses, Midwest, 60. Has done documentaries for TV, 64-; supv ed, "War Called Peace," CBS; assoc producer, "Lure of the Tall Ship." Songwriter, 70- Wrote for "Captain Kangaroo Show," 74. *Songs:* Children: The Horse of Course; When You Got a Good Book, You Got a Good Friend; William T Goat; Jigsaw Puzzle; Tell Me Your Secret Old Man River.

NIGHTINGALE, MAE WHEELER ASCAP 1957
composer, author, teacher
b Blencoe, Iowa, Dec 30, 1898. Educ: Univ Calif, Los Angeles; Univ Southern Calif; Fresno State Col. Began teaching music, Calif schs, 23; trained teachers for Univ Calif, Los Angeles, Univ Southern Calif & Los Angeles State Col until 59. Teacher, clinician & lectr at var workshops & univ summer sessions. Cond, teenage choruses at fests; adjudicator, choral fests for SCalif Vocal Asn, 40-Recipient, Mancini Award, Calif Music Educr Asn, 64. *Songs & Instrumental Works:* Troubadour Series (2 vols); Folk and Fun Songs; Young Singers' Choir Book; American Heritage Songs; Choral works: Choral Concert Series; Nightingale Choral Series; Arr: My Child Is Gone; Twelve Days of Christmas; Recessional. *Scores:* Operettas: Ride 'Em Cowboy; Queen of the Sawdust.

NILLES, BRAD (CATFISH) ASCAP 1978
composer, author, guitarist
b Winona, Minn, Aug 30, 51. Educ: St Mary's Col, Minn, BA(hist), 73, MA(educ), 76. Author, "Dreams From the Road." *Albums:* Catfish Dreams.

NILSEN, ALEXANDER ASCAP 1962
composer, conductor, pianist
b Chicago, Ill, Jan 24, 03. Educ: Chicago Musical Col; Berklee Sch of Music; studied with Leo Sowerby. Pianist, network & nightclub orchs; cond, own orch. Pianist & arr, CBS-TV prog "Teenage of America." Chief Collabr: Searcy Johnson. *Songs:* Sweet Bird; Ballad of the Thresher.

NIMS, WALTER DAVIS
composer, author
b Cleveland, Ohio, Sept 11, 43. Educ: St Ann's Grade Sch; Heights High Sch; Lakewood High Sch. Played in local bands at age 16, was mem of group the Outsiders, 66, later formed group, Climax. Taught music; worked in computers at a bank. *Songs:* Precious and Few.

NISSENSON, GLORIA DIANE ASCAP 1974
author
b Jersey City, NJ. Educ: Birch Wathen High Sch; NY Univ, BA. Author, "One of Our Millionaires is Missing"; TV Christmas spots, "Give a Little Bit of Your Love"; many songs performed by var artists. Winner, First Am Song Fest, rhythmn & blues category, 74. Chief Collabrs: Marcia DeFren, Hod David Schudson, Ritchie Adams, Don Sebesky, William Goldstein, Lucy Simon. *Songs:* Lyrics: Family Tree; And a Little Child Will Lead Us; I Wouldn't Have It Any Other Way; Sweet Talk; Allison; Angelita (Strummed on My Guitar); The Best of the Rest of Our Lives; Heaven in the Afternoon; Duffy.

NITZSCHE, JACK ASCAP 1976
composer, author, arranger
b Chicago, Ill, Apr 22, 37. Educ: Howard City Elem & High Schs, Mich, 43-55; Westlake Col Music, Hollywood, Calif, 55-57; studied privately with Leonard Stein, 68-69. Began doing lead sheets & copying work, 57; with, Original Sound Records, 59; began arranging in 61. Arr, Phil Spector, 63. Mem group, Rolling Stones, 66. Produced, wrote & scored several works, 76. Chief Collabrs: Sonny Bono, Jackie De Shannon, Buffy Ste Marie, Alan Gordon, Ry Cooder, Russ Titelman. *Songs:* Needles and Pins; Gone Dead Train. *Instrumental Works:* Bongo Bongo Bongo; The Lonely Surfer; St Giles Cripplegate. *Scores:* Film/TV: Performance; One Flew Over the Cuckoos Nest (Acad Nomination); The Exorcist; Blue Collar; Hardcore; Heartbeat; Cruising; Heroes; When You Comin' Back Red Ryder; Sticks and Bones; Greasers Palace; Jive.

NIVERT, TAFFY
See Danoff, Mary Catherine

NIX, KENTON T   ASCAP 1979
composer, author
b Chattanooga, Tenn, July 13, 54. Educ: Jefferson High Sch, Brooklyn, NY, 72; York Col, Queens. Chief Collabrs: Henry Batts, Raymond Reid. *Songs:* Work That Body; Just Be a Friend; We've Got to Work It Out; When You Touch Me; There's Never Been No One Like You;

NIXON, ROGER A   ASCAP 1965
composer, teacher
b Tulare, Calif, Aug 8, 21. Educ: Studied with Roger Sessions, Arnold Schoenberg, Ernest Bloch & Sir Arthur Bliss; Univ Calif, Berkeley, BA, 42, MA, 49, PhD, 52. Instr music, Modesto Jr Col, 51-59; prof music, San Francisco State Univ, 60- Awards: Am Bandmasters Asn Ostwald Award, Fest Fanfare March, 73; first prize, Comp Press/Haubiel Solo Work Comp Contest; two Nat Endowment for the Arts Awards, 68 & 76. *Songs:* Music: Six Moods of Love (song cycle); Bye, Bye, Baby, Lullay (SATB); Firwood (SATB); Ditty (SSAA); Love's Secret (TTBB); To the Evening Star (SATB). *Instrumental Works:* Fiesta del Pacifico; Viola Concerto; Elegy and Fanfare-March; Pacific Celebration Suite (Neil A Kjos Memorial Award, 79); Reflections; Twelve Piano Preludes; Centennial Fanfare-March; Prelude and Fugue; Nocturne; Festival Fanfare-March; Air for Strings; String Quartet No 1 (Phelan Award); A Solemn Processional; Ceremonial Piece for Brass; Four Duos for Flute and Clarinet (oboe); Music for a Civic Celebration; Movement for Clarinet and Piano; Four Duos for Violin and Viola; Mooney's Grove Suite; Psalm for Band. *Scores:* Opera/Ballet: The Bride Comes to Yellow Sky.

NIZER, LOUIS   ASCAP 1956
composer, author
b London, Eng, Feb 6, 02. To US, 05. Educ: Columbia Law Sch. Practicing lawyer. Autobiography, "My Life in Court." *Songs:* David; Elizabeth; Jimmy; Johnny; Mary; Robin.

NOBLE, HARRY   ASCAP 1953
composer, author, singer
b New York, NY, Apr 7, 12; d NJ, Apr 30, 66. Educ: Juilliard; studied with David McKay Williams, Tertius Noble & Lolita Gainsborg. Dir, NY State prize-winning girls' choir, 29. Gave organ concerts in churches. Mem vocal trio, Three Marshalls, NBC, 5 yrs. Formed team, Noble & King, 42, toured the world, 13 yrs. Appeared in films. Minister of Music, First Baptist Church, Jersey City, 58. Had own radio show. Taught organ, Bamberger's Dept Store, Newark, NJ, 62. *Songs:* Hold Me, Thrill Me, Kiss Me; Out of the East; The Love I Never Had; Don't Touch Me; Yodel Waltz; Little White Donkey.

NOBLE, JOHN AVERY (JOHNNY)   ASCAP 1935
composer, author, conductor
b Honolulu, Hawaii, Sept 17, 1892; d Honolulu, Jan 13, 44. Educ: St Louis Col. Led orch, Moana & Royal Hawaiian Hotels, Honolulu, 17 yrs. Went to Los Angeles, 25, directed Hawaiian musical shows & broadcast Hawaiian progs on radio networks. Exec, Mutual Telephone Co, Honolulu. Chief Collabrs: Ted Fiorito, Harold Adamson, Don McDiarmid, Andy Iona. *Songs:* My Little Grass Shack in Kealakekua, Hawaii; Hawaiian War Chant; Hilo Hattie; Hula Blues; Little Brown Gal; King Kamehameha; My Tane; I Want to Learn to Speak Hawaiian; Naughty Hula Eyes; Island Serenade; Tropic Trade Winds.

NOBLE, NICK (NICK VALKAN)
composer, author, singer
b Chicago, Ill, June 21, 36. Educ: Loyola Univ, BSA. Recorded for var recording cos, singer, clubs, TV & theatres, 60- Chief Collabr: Lew Douglas. *Songs:* If We Could Live Our Love Over Again; Stay With Me; Girl on the Other Side; Country Kind of Girl; Big Mans Cafe.

NOBLE, THOMAS TERTIUS   ASCAP 1939
composer, organist, teacher
b Bath, Eng, May 5, 1867; d Rockport, Mass, May 4, 53. US citizen. Father of Ray Noble. Educ: Pvt tutors, Colchester, Eng; Royal Col Music, London, ARCM; studied with Parratt, Stanford & Bridge; hon degrees: FRCO, London, MA, Columbia Univ, MusD, Trinity Col; fel, Trinity Col, London. Organist, All Saints, Colchester, 1881-89 & St John's, Wilton Road, London, 1889-90; asst, Trinity Col, Cambridge, 1890-92, Ely Cathedral, 1892-08, York Minster, 1898-13 & St Thomas Church, New York, 13-43; teacher of organ, Royal Col Music, London, 1889-98; founded York Symph, 1898; cond, York Musical Soc & Hovingham Festival; pres, Nat Asn Organists, 22-24. *Songs & Instrumental Works:* Prelude to Gloria Domini; Toccata & Fugue in F; Introduction & Passacaglia (orch); Choral: Magnificat; Nunc Dimittis in B; Souls of the Righteous; Fierce Was the Wild Billow; Grieve Not the Holy Spirit; Go to Dark Gethsemane; Rise up, O Men of God.

NOBLITT, KATHERYN MCCALL   ASCAP 1964
composer, author, teacher
b Marion, NC, Feb 10, 09. Educ: Marion High Sch, scholarship prize; Greensboro Col, BMus, summa cum laude. Piano teacher, NC & Va, 30-; numerous pub perf as pianist. Several awards as poet. Comp about 160 musical

pieces, incl easy & difficult piano pieces, songs of many types, also suites of music with storyettes. Mem teacher & comp orgns. Chief Collabrs: John W Schaum, Paul B Noble. *Songs & Instrumental Works:* Waltz Mood (piano solo); March of the Americans (piano solo); The Windshield Wiper Rock; Jack Frost Surprised Me!; Doctor Pill to the Rescue; The Old Bell Ringer (piano solo); Twinkling Keys (piano solo); Red Pepper March (piano solo, 3 performers at 2 pianos & symphonic band); Praise to Our Wonderful God! (SATB or SA anthem).

NOCK, MICHAEL ANTHONY   ASCAP 1969
composer, instrumentalist, bandleader
b Christchurch, NZ, Sept 27, 40. First recording, 60; has recorded as leader-comp & sideman, 60- Comp fels, Nat Endowment Jazz, 72, 75 & 78. *Instrumental Works:* Magic Mansions; Casablanca; Mossa Flo; Recollections; California Country Songs.

NOEL, DICK   ASCAP 1957
composer, author, singer
b Brooklyn, NY, May 30, 27. Educ: Cons. Vocalist, dance orchs, nightclubs, radio & TV incl "Tennessee Ernie Ford Show." Co-owner & A&R dir, Fraternity Records, 54-59.

NOLTE, ROY E   ASCAP 1938
composer, organist
b Louisville, Ky, July 25, 1896; d Louisville, Aug 21, 79. Educ: Bus sch; pvt music study. Secy, Louisville & Nashville Railroad Co, 10 yrs. Contributing ed, "Volunteer Choir," 28-57. *Songs & Instrumental Works:* Cantatas: Hosanna; His Natal Day; King All-Glorious; The Easter Alleluia; The Cross of Redemption; The Dawn of Christmas; The Star of Silent Night; Memories of the Manger; Anthems: Lift Up Your Head (Volunteer Choir Prize); I Walked in the Fields With Jesus; By the Waters of Galilee; Christ Walked This Way Before; also 29 Easy Church Voluntaries for the Organ (book).

NOMIS, LOU
See Simon, William Louis

NOON, DAVID   ASCAP 1972
composer
b Johnstown, Pa, July 23, 46. Educ: Pomona Col, BA, 68, studies with Karl Kohn; NY Univ, MA, 70, studies with Gustave Reese & Jan LaRue; Yale Univ, MMA, 72, DMA, 77, studies with Yehudi Wyner & Mario Davidovsky; Aspen Sch Music, 69, 71, 75, 77, 79 & 80, studies with Darius Milhaud & Charles Jones. Fulbright fel in comp, Music Cons Warsaw, Poland, 72-73. Taught music theory & comp, Sch Music, Northwestern Univ, 73-76. Composer-in-residence, Wurlitzer Found, Taos, NMex, 76-77. Young Musicians Found Awards, 68, 71 & 73; ASCAP Awards, 73-79; Aspen Prizes, 69, 71 & 79. Mem: Am Musicological Soc; MLA; Pi Kappa Lambda. *Songs:* Music: Psalm, Opus 17 (tenor, solo chorus, flute, cello & piano); Cantata, Opus 22 (chorus & instrumental octet); Six Chansons, Opus 32 (soprano & chamber ens); Four Medieval Lyrics, Opus 51 (soprano, flute & harp). *Instrumental Works:* Concerto, Opus 23 (cello, 11 winds, piano & harpsichord); Berceuse Seche, Opus 30 (orch); Lost in Transit, Opus 42 (large orch & mezzo-soprano); New Year's Resolution, Opus 48 (doublebass, winds, perc); Promissory Notes, Opus 53 (orch); Broken Blossoms, Opus 56 (large concert band); Inflections, Opus 15 (piano, prepared piano, harp, harpsichord, vibraphone); Introduction, Dirge and Frolic, Opus 18 (wind quintet); Sonata, Opus 21 (clarinet, vibraphone & prepared piano); Fratricide, Opus 27 (instrumental septet); Fantasy, Opus 28 (violin & piano, 4-hands); Cadenzas, Opus 29 (solo violin); Motets and Monodies, Opus 31 (oboe, Eng horn & bassoon); Trope, Opus 34 (solo cello); Quartet No 1, Opus 35 (string quartet); Quartet No 2, Opus 40 (string quartet); Fanfares and Dances, Opus 41 (brass quintet); Quartet No 3, Opus 43 (string quartet); Quintet, Opus 52 (woodwind quintet); Recitatives and Arias, Opus 54 (doublebass & piano). *Scores:* Ballet: Labyrinth, Opus 16 (chamber orch); AI, AI, Opus 20 (orch).

NORBERG, KEVIN MICHAEL   ASCAP 1973
composer, author, singer
b Minneapolis, Minn, June 8, 53. Educ: Bethel Col, 71-74. Teacher, Minneapolis, 74-76; went on concert tour, 76-78; now minister music, Liberty Church & Bible Col, Pensacola, Fla. *Songs:* We Start All Over; Time to Remember.

NORDEN, ELFRIDA   ASCAP 1957
author
b Englewood, NJ, Nov 5, 16. Educ: Univ des Annales, Paris; Beerbohm Tree Acad, London; Alviene Sch of Dramatic Arts, New York. Writer, special material, verse for advert agencies & greeting cards. Chief Collabrs: Marcel Frank, Kenneth Walton, John Klein & Hugo Rubens. *Songs:* Forever Means Always; Carmelita; Good-for-Nothin' Lover; Joy Is Born in My Heart; Starlight Lullaby; Let There Be Light, O Lord; Love Is Waiting in Hawaii; Sing to the World; Hush, My Love; Our God.

NORLIN, LLOYD B — ASCAP 1955
composer

b Sioux Falls, SDak, Mar 23, 18. Educ: Northwestern Univ, scholarship, BM, MM. Comp, music for 16 col shows. Served as tail-gunner, USAF, Italy, World War II. To Hollywood, writer for films. Music dir, Wilding, Inc. Writer, theme songs, indust films incl "The New World of Stainless Steel," off-Bway show "Shoestring Revue." *Songs:* One Fine September; Goodnight; Out of the Silence; Medea in Disneyland.

NORMAN, CONSTANCE
See Lanier, Verdell

NORMAN, FRED — ASCAP 1943
composer, trombonist, arranger

b Leesburg, Fla, Oct 5, 10. Educ: Fessenden Acad; Howard Univ. Trombonist & arr, Elmer Calloway & Claude Hopkins Orchs, 30-40. Arr, WNEW, New York, Benny Goodman & Artie Shaw Orchs & singers incl Connee Boswell, Barry Wood, Billy Eckstine, Dinah Washington & Damita Jo. Chief Collabrs: Walter Bishop, Jack Wolf, Benny Goodman, Eddie Safranski, Cliff Owens. *Songs & Instrumental Works:* Hot Foot Shuffle; Monkey Business; Smoke House; Boulder Bluff; Man That's Groovy; Young and Willing; Keep Moving; Knock It Down; Solid Sam; That's It; Buster's Gang Comes On; High on a Cloud.

NORMAN, ROBERT
See Gardner, Maurice

NORMAN, ROLF
See Elsmo, Ralph Norman

NORMAN, THEODORE — ASCAP 1960
composer, author, classical guitarist

b Montreal, Can, Mar 14, 12. Educ: Studied in Ger, Italy, Spain, also with Adolph Weiss, Willy Hess & Aurio Herrero. US citizen. Composer, classical guitarist & teacher. First violinist, Los Angeles Philh Orch, 35-42. Guitar concert of own works, Paris Radio, 56. Teacher classical guitar, Univ Calif, Los Angeles, 67-, Europ tours with students, 78, 79 & 80, concerts of original works & transc for guitar. Author, "The Classical Guitar, A New Approach"; 20 bks of original works & transc for one or two classical guitars. *Instrumental Works:* Transcribed 8 pieces of Igor Stravinsky for 2 guitars, Hayden trios for 3 guitars, Vivaldi trios for 3 guitars & 24 Paganini caprices for guitar. *Scores:* Metamorphasis (ballet).

NORRIS, PHILIP EUGENE — ASCAP 1979
composer, teacher, arranger

b York, Pa, Jan 27, 54. Educ: Grace Col, BMusEd, trumpet studies with Jerry Franks; Northwestern Univ, MMus (trumpet), studies with Luther Didrickson. Arranger & summer music theatre playing, Col & Post-Col; commercial arranging & playing, Chicago; teacher, Grace Col & Lakeland Christian Acad, 3 yrs. Head instrumental music, Western Baptist Col, Ore. *Instrumental Works:* Sacred Sounds for Band (25 separate titles).

NORTH, ALEX — ASCAP 1947
composer, conductor, teacher

b Chester, Pa, Dec 4, 10. Educ: Curtis Inst, studied with George Boyle; Juilliard Sch Music (scholarship); Moscow Cons (scholarship); studied with Ernst Toch & Aaron Copland; Guggenheim fel. Wrote scores for Fed Theatre Project. Moved to Mex, 39; music dir & comp, Anna Sokolow Ballet; cond concerts, Palace of Fine Arts, Mexico City. Capt in charge of self-entertainment progs in hospitals, WW II. Scored documentary films for Office of War Information, incl "A Better Tomorrow." Taught at Sarah Lawrence, Briar Cliff & Finch Cols. Rec'd Golden Globe Award & 6 Laurel Awards. *Songs:* Loneliness and Love; Unchained Melody; I'll Cry Tomorrow; The Long Hot Summer; A World of Love; The Nile. *Instrumental Works:* Symphony No 1; Symphony No 2; Symphonic Suites for "A Streetcar Named Desire," "Death of a Salesman" and "Viva Zapata!"; Rhapsody for Orchestra, Piano; Revue for Clarinet, Orchestra (comn by Benny Goodman); Morning Star (cantata; comn by New York Herald Tribune); Holiday Set. *Scores:* Ballet: Mal de Siecle (jazz; comn by Marquis de Cuevas); Golden Fleece (ballet for Hanya Holm); American Lyric (ballet for Martha Graham); Streetcar Named Desire (Ballet Theatre); Stage: The Hither and Thither of Danny Dither; Stage background: Death of a Salesman; The Innocents; Coriolanus; Richard III; Film background: Death of a Salesman; Viva Zapata!; A Streetcar Named Desire; Member of the Wedding; Desiree; I'll Cry Tomorrow; The Rose Tattoo; Unchained; The Bad Seed; Four Girls in Town; The Long Hot Summer; The Rainmaker; Hot Spell; South Sea Adventure; The Sound and the Fury; Spartacus; The Misfits; Cleopatra; The Agony and the Ectasy; Who's Afraid of Virginia Woolf?; Africa (documentary); The Shoes of the Fisherman; A Dream of Kings; Hard Contract; Willard; Pocket Money; Shanks; Bite the Bullet; Wise Blood; TV background: The FDR Story; theme for Playhouse 90; Rich Man Poor Man (Emmy Award).

NORTH, JACK KING
composer, music teacher

b Buffalo, Ill, Oct 16, 08. Educ: Ill Wesleyan Univ Sch of Music, MMus. Music teacher, high sch band & choral, Mason City, Ill, 4 yrs, high sch & elem sch band & choral, Pontiac, Ill, 23 yrs. Regional mgr, Field Enterprises Educ Corp, Decatur, Ill, 13 yrs; retired, 73; began composing as a retirement hobby. Chief Collabrs: Festus Paul, Walter Rodby. *Songs:* Alleluia, Noel (SAB); Blow, Heavenly Trumpets (SATB); The Donkey of Galilee (choirs); Every Valley Shall Be Exalted (SATB); For Unto Us a Child Is Born (SAB); Joy to the World (SAB); Lullaby of the Flutes; No Room (SATB); O Zion That Bringest Good Tidings (SAB); Shepherd Boy (SAB); Sing a Song of Joy (SSATB); Where Are You Going Balthasar?; David Swing Your Sling; Shine Down Christmas Star; Here's to America; It's a Glorious Easter; Gideon; Ring That Bell; Man With a Horn; Man With a Piano; Curtain's Goin' Up; Turn It On; Let the People Say Amen; A Song for You; Solfa Calypso; Like a Bee and Honey; For the Freedom of Man; I Can Never Touch a Rainbow; Come and See the Baby; It Must Be Spring; Do You Know What Jesus Said? (SATB); For Everything There Is a Season (SATB); Glory Be to the Father (SATB); Holy Books (SATB); Last Psalm (SSATB); Let Not Your Heart Be Troubled (SATB); A New Song; Praise the Lord O My Soul; Put Your Trust in the Living God; Sing for Heaven's Sake; This Is My Song; Follow Me (SATB); Hallelujah, Amen (SAB); He Was Wounded (SSAATB); O Let Us Sing Hallelujah (SATB); Sing for Joy This Happy Day; Thanks Be to God (SATB); That Day in Jerusalem (SATB); Land of Liberty (SATB); O Give Thanks (SAB); Take This Bread (SAB); Lyrics: Bells of Christmas (SATB); Music: Christmas Prayer; For the Beauty of the Earth (SSATB); Still Waters (SATB).

NORTH, JOHN RINGLING — ASCAP 1951
composer, author, producer

b Barlboo, Wis, Aug 14, 03. Educ: Yale Univ. Pres, Ringling Bros, Barnum & Baily Circus; pres, Rockland Oil Co. Chief Collabrs: J Fred Coots, E Ray Goetz, Irving Caesar, Tony Velona. *Songs:* I Am a Melody; Impossible; Honolulu Bay; Lovely Luawanna Lady; Why'd I Have to Fall in Love With You For?.

NORTON, GEORGE A — ASCAP 1940
author, pianist

b St Louis, Mo, Apr 16, 1880; d Tucson, Ariz, Sept 14, 23. Educ: Peabody Cons. Pianist in vaudeville; also wrote special material. Reporter, advert exec for newspapers throughout US. Chief Collabrs: W C Handy, Ernie Burnett. *Songs:* My Melancholy Baby; Memphis Blues; Sing Me a Song of the South; Two Little, Blue Little, True Little Eyes; Sweetie Be King to Me; That's Gratitude; At the Old Square Dances Down in Arkansas; Where Is My Boy Tonight; The Black Hand Rag; Suicide Blues; 'Round Her Neck She Wears a Yeller Ribbon; I'd Rather Float Through a Dreamy Old Waltz With You, You, You; Sahara; I Love You for Yourself Alone; Tell Me, Moon; They Wouldn't Stand for That in Honolulu; Farewell My Own United States; The Wedding of the Lobster and the Crab; My Nubian Maid; A Sweetheart in Every Port; I'm the Man; Bye and Bye; I'm Sighing for You Honey, All the Time; Down Georgia Way; Down Mobile.

NORVO, KENNETH (RED) — ASCAP 1956
composer, conductor, vibraphonist

b Beardstown, Ill, Mar 31, 08. Cond marimba band, Chicago; mem, Paul Ash orch; toured in vaudeville; staff musician, Victor Young Orch, NBC, Chicago; with Paul Whiteman; formed own band, 35-45; vibraphonist with Benny Goodman & Woody Herman Orchs. Formed sextet, 49 & trio, 50. Overseas tour with Jazz Club USA, 54; cond quintet which became part of Benny Goodman Orch touring Europe, 59. Recording artist. *Songs & Instrumental Works:* Dance of the Octopus; Knock on Wood; Bughouse; Nero's Conception; Steps; Igor; Back Talk; The Night Is Blue.

NORWOOD, WAYNE DENZIL, JR — ASCAP 1974
composer, author, musician

b Pinehurst, NC, Aug 1, 43. Educ: Yale Univ; Univ Calif, Davis, BA, 69; studied with Jack Millman, Hollywood. Nightclub performer, San Francisco, 70-74; publ contract, Music Industries, Hollywood, 74-75; publ & recording contract, Westgate, Hollywood, 75-76 & Music Int, 77-78; performer, Intergalactic Threat group, 78. Chief Collabrs: John Ammirati, Les Marlin, Billy Sheets. *Songs:* You're the Sausage in My Weenie World; Momma's Rock and Roll Job; Honk If You Love Jesus; 3-D Astral Teenage Love; The Ten Monterey; Anna Banana; No Cowabunga Today; Just One; Baby, I'm Tired; Omaha, You're Not Chicago; Everywhere: Blues; Sniffin' Seats on Bicycles; Cigarettes Taste Like Hell; Mafia Rock; Blue Schmuck Shoes; Maybe Someday, We'll Be Poor; Wa-Wa-Wanda Kay; Waterbed Deep; Little Jail Bait; Good Ham; Roller Derby Queen; Prison o' Flesh; Country Wedding; Sonja; This Sad Scenario; La Vie de Boheme.

NORWORTH, JACK — ASCAP 1922
composer, author, actor

b Philadelphia, Pa, Jan 5, 1879; d Laguna Beach, Calif, Sept 1, 59. First appeared in vaudeville as blackface comedian & in Bway musicals, incl "The Great White Way", "Ziegfeld Follies of 1909", "The Jolly Bachelors", "Little Miss Fix-It", "Roly-Poly" & "Odds and Ends." Toured in vaudeville with wife, Nora Bayes. Wrote songs for "The Jolly Bachelors" & "Ziegfeld Follies," also Weber & Fields shows. Established grants to Young Comp Prog, ASCAP Found. Film biography: "Shine on Harvest Moon." Chief Collab: Albert Von Tilzer. *Songs:* Shine on Harvest Moon; Take Me Out to the Ball Game; Good Evening, Caroline; Smarty; Honey Boy; Over on the Jersey Side; Meet Me in Apple

Blossom Time; Come Along, My Mandy; O How He Could Sing an Irish Song; Dear Dolly; Since My Mother Was a Girl; Kitty. *Scores:* Bway stage: Little Miss Fix-It.

NOSWORTHY, MARALD WINNIFRED ASCAP 1978
composer, author, singer
b Winnipeg, Manitoba, Aug 28, 21. Educ: Piano study with Grace Rich, Winnipeg, 6 yrs; Long Beach City Col, voice studies with Pricilla Rameta, 75. Began with amateur singing groups; soloist at weddings. *Songs:* It's Christmas Time; Everything's Going to Be Okay; Hey Suzanne; Remember Their Laughter; Long Beach, California; Songs by Marald Nosworthy (Vols 1 & 2).

NOTO, PAT ASCAP 1950
author
b New York, NY, Nov 5, 22. Educ: City Col NY; Sch Am Music, cert. In Army Signal Corps, WW II, 42; assigned to Soldier Show Co, Paris, 46. Entered US Treasury, Internal Revenue Serv, Manhattan, 62. Chief Collabrs: Edward Scalzi, William Eisenhauer, Joseph Filloramo, John Lucciola. *Songs:* Sweet Kentucky Rose; Lyrics: Hello Baby, Mademoiselle; You Can't Buy Happiness; Time to Be Saying Goodnight; Now; Your Good-for-Nothing Heart; Shalom-Salaam; Ding-a-ling-aling Ding Dong; Little Bit of Love; Wishful Thinking; I'm Gonna Get a Dummy; Italian Lyrics: From the Vine Came the Grape; Now Is Forever; Amor Mio.

NOTT, DOUGLAS D ASCAP 1970
composer
b Yakima, Wash, Feb 27, 44. Educ: Central Wash Univ, BAMusEd, 66, MA(comp), 70, studied with Paul Creston; Univ Ariz, DMA(comp), 79, studied with Robert Muszynski. Teaching staff, div chmn humanities, Yakima Valley Col. Publ 30 opus numbers for band, orch, chorus, solo, instruments & voice. *Instrumental Works:* Cascade (overture, band); Rhapsodie (E flat alto saxophone, piano, band); Theatre on Third Street (orch, chorus); Symphony No 1, Places (orch, chorus); String Quartet No 1.

NOURI, MICHAEL ASCAP 1975
author, singer, actor
b Washington, DC, Dec 9, 45. Educ: Rollins Col; Emerson Col, studied drama, communications. Appeared in films, "Goodbye Columbus", "40 Carats", "Contract on Cherry Street" & "Cliff Hangers." Actor in soap opera, "Search for Tomorrow," 72-76. Appeared in "Last Convertible," 80.

NOVELLO, EUGENE RALPH ASCAP 1950
composer, author
b Scotch Plains, NJ, May 15, 12. Educ: Westfield High Sch; Villanova Univ; Univ Colo, studied music. Songwriter, 30- Chief Collabr: Paul Greenwood. *Songs:* Music: Boulder Buff; Nickleodeon Rag; Hello Mrs Jones; Let Me Tell You 'Bout Suzanne; Road Runner.

NOVEMBER, JOHNNY
See Mathews, James Snookie

NOWAKOWSKI, PERRY CASEY (PERRY DANTES) ASCAP 1968
composer, author, singer
b Torun, Poland, Oct 16, 43. Educ: Univ Wis-Milwaukee; Milwaukee Tech Col; guitar & piano training. *Songs:* Give Me Back My Letters; I Can't Say Good-Bye to San Diego; Claudine; Apollo.

NUGENT, THEODORE ANTHONY (TED) ASCAP 1973
composer, author, singer
b Detroit, Mich, Dec 13, 48. Educ: Oakland Community Col, Mich. Began guitar playing at age 8, first prof perf, age 10, Detroit, formed Royal Highboys, 60, the Lourds, 62. Started Amboy Dukes, 64, recording artist, 67-, US & European tours, 68-; group changed name to Ted Nugent & the Amboy Dukes, 70, then to Ted Nugent, 75- *Albums:* Amboy Dukes; Journey to the Center of the Mind; Migration; Marriage on the Rock/Rock Bottom; Survival of the Fittest; Call of the Wild; Tooth, Fang and Claw; Doctor Sling Shot and the Best of the Original Amboy Dukes; Ted Nugent (platinum album); Free for All (platinum album); Cat Scratch Fever (platinum album); Double Live Gonzo (platinum album); Weekend Warriors (platinum album); State of Shock; Scream Dream.

NUTTYCOMBE, CRAIG ASCAP 1969
composer, author
b Los Angeles, Calif, Mar 24, 47. Recording artist, 70- *Albums:* At Home; As You Will; It's Just a Lifetime.

NYE, ANITA LEONARD ASCAP 1948
author, pianist
b New York, NY. Educ: NY Univ, BS(music), piano studies with Modena Scovill Lane, Bruno Eisner, Herman Wasserman, Comp with Otto Cesana & Wallingford Riegger; New Sch for Social Res, dramatic workshop, acting with Stella Adler. Wrote for varsity shows, NY Univ & City Col New York; ran Choreographer's Workshop, New York; wrote ballet scores for Danny Daniels, Ron Fletcher & "Show of Shows," TV. Staff comp, Camp Tamiment, 3 yrs. Duo-piano team with Deborah Greene; songs for "Dena Revue." Chief Collabrs:

Barbara Belle, Evelyn Caroll, Charles B Fair, Marshall Barer. *Songs:* He's My Baby; Music: A Sunday Kind of Love; Tell Me, Tell Me; Graduation Ring; Letters Tied in Blue; Chitterlinswitch; The Bee Song; Jingle Dingle; William Didn't Tell. *Scores:* Kings in Nomania (children's theatre). Children's Albums: Fox and the Grapes; The Amazing Adventures of Johnny; Little Golden Records.

NYE, DOUGLAS RAYMOND ASCAP 1963
composer, pianist, musical director
b Los Angeles, Calif, Dec 26, 30. Educ: North Hollywood High Sch, grad; Los Angeles City Col; Fresno State Univ; studied piano under Maurice Zam. Asst cond, 562nd Air Force Band. Pianist, Hacienda Hotel, Fresno, Calif, 13 yrs. Vocal group singer & brass instrumentalist. Musical dir for 15 musical comedy productions, San Diego. Chief Collabrs: Randy Sparks, Vikki Leigh (Williams). *Songs:* Music: The Music Box; Think Rain, Think Sunshine; Loving Kindness; Let the Song Begin; Curiosity.

NYE, NAOMI SHIHAB ASCAP 1977
composer, author, teacher
b St Louis, Mo, Mar 12, 52. Educ: Trinity Univ, BA(summa cum laude), 74. Author & poet of 3 bks: "Tatooed Feet"; "Eye-to-Eye"; "Different Ways to Pray." Work as poet in schs & musician, Tex Comn Arts, 74- Chief Collabr: John Paul Walters. *Songs:* Just Like a Recurring Dream; Rutabaga-Roo; The Circus Song; Heroes in the Dimestore; Lyrics: Hondo's Lament. *Albums:* Rutabaga-Roo.

NYSTROM, ALF ASCAP 1964
composer
b Sweden, Jan 4, 27; d. Educ: Brooklyn Cons.

O

OAKES, RODNEY HARLAND ASCAP 1979
composer
b Rome, NY, Apr 15, 37. Educ: San Diego State Univ, BA, 60, MA, 66, studied with David Ward-Steinmann; Univ Southern Calif, DMA, 73, studied with Anthony Vazanna. Music educr elem & sec level, San Diego & Azusa, 61-70; dir, Electronic Music Studios, Los Angeles Harbor Col, 72-; comp chamber, choral & vocal music, musicals & electronic music, 68- Chief Collabr: Larry Heimgartner. *Instrumental Works:* Six By Six; Fantasy for Buccina; Hyporchema; Introspectrum in Six Refractions; Duet; Dialogue for Flute and Tape Recorder. *Scores:* Grab the Ring (2-act musical); Children's Musical: Abadaba; Bumble; Alligator, Alligator; Bwbachs Two; Opera/Ballet: Synergy; Film/TV: Guinea Pigs Is Pigs.

OAKLAND, BEN ASCAP 1934
composer, pianist, producer
b Brooklyn, NY, Sept 24, 07; d Beverly Hills, Calif, Aug 26, 79. Educ: Commercial high sch. Carnegie Hall piano concert at age 9. Vaudeville pianist for Helen Morgan & George Jessel. Wrote songs for Bway revues, incl "Ziegfeld Follies" (1931); "Earl Carroll's Sketch Book", "Hold Your Horses" & "Americana"; also nightclub revues, "George White's Gay White Way", "Cotton Club Parade", "Casino de Paree" & "Paradise Parade". Writer, dir & producer for personal appearances of Van Johnson, Jeanette MacDonald, Tony Martin, Joe E Lewis, Nelson Eddy, Josephine Baker, Nanette Fabray & Gisele MacKenzie. Producer, "George Jessel Show", 2 yrs, "Down Tin Pan Alley" (also appeared in show), TV. Songs for films incl "I'll Take Romance", "The Awful Truth", "My Little Chickadee", "The Big Store" & "Show Business." USO Camp shows, WW II; rec'd 14 citations, incl US Treasury. Past chmn, AGAC(West Coast). Won 2 Global Awards, City of Hope. Elected to Am Music Hall of Fame. Honored by Univ Tel Aviv by having their Am Music Fine Arts Dept named the Ben Oakland Am Music Library. Chief Collabrs: Oscar Hammerstein 2nd, Paul Francis Webster, Herb Magidson, Don Raye, Milton Drake, Bob Russell, L Wolfe Gilbert, Artie Shaw, Tony Martin. *Songs:* I'll Take Romance; If I Love Again; The Champagne Waltz; Java Jive; I'll Dance at Your Wedding; I Promise You; Roses in December; Cool Tango; You're Not So Easy to Forget; Twinkle Twinkle Little Star; Sidewalks of Cuba; I'm Counting on You; Li'l Abner; A Mist is Over the Moon; Puppy Love; A Pink Cocktail for a Blue Lady; Valse Moderne; Happiness; Dimples and Cherry Cheeks; Beau Night in Hotchkiss Corners; Golden Wedding Waltz; Winter Sun; River, River; Congratulations; Music: The Minute and a Half Waltz.

OATES, RONNIE O ASCAP 1979
composer
b Washington, DC, June 16, 40. Educ: Fork Union Mil Acad; East Carolina Univ, BA. US Navy Band, 5 yrs; with own trio, Pensacola, Fla, 2 yrs. Conductor; studio keyboard player; arranger. Chief Collabrs: Lynda K Lance-Oates, Ed Penny, Reba Rambo. *Songs:* Who's Gonna' Love Me Now; Sunshine Saturday; Welcome Stranger; Music: I Sing for Him; also theme from the Exterminator.

OBEGI, RICHARD (DICK MERRITT) ASCAP 1966
producer
Writer of commercials.

OBILO
See Polk, Hersholt Calvin

O'BRIAN, HUGH ASCAP 1957
author, actor, singer
b Rochester, NY. Educ: Roosevelt Mil Acad; Kemper Mil Sch; Univ Cincinnati; Los Angeles City Col. Drill Sgt, USMC, 4 yrs. To London with Wild West Show, 59. Actor, TV plays incl "Wyatt Earp," stage musicals incl "Destry Rides Again" & "Guys and Dolls," plays incl "First Love," films incl "Never Fear." Owner, TV production co. *Songs:* I'm Walking Away.

O'BRIEN, JACK ASCAP 1973
author
b Saginaw, Mich, June 18, 39. Educ: Arthur Hill High Sch, Saginaw; Univ Mich, Ann Arbor, AB, 61, MA, 62. After col joined APA Repertory Theatre doing direction & comp. Has directed "Porgy and Bess" for Houston Grand Opera/Bway, "The Most Happy Fella" for Bway revival, 79 & "Street Scene" for New York Opera, Ahmanson Theatre, Santa Fe Opera, Washington Opera, & others. Chief Collabr: Bob James. *Songs:* Lyrics: The Blue Tattoo. *Scores:* Opera/Ballet: Orpheus in the Underworld (Offenbach, transl & adaptation); Le Coq D'or (Rimsky-Korsakov, transl & adaptation); Bway Show: The Selling of the President.

O'BRIEN, JAMES JOSEPH ASCAP 1963
composer, author
b Brooklyn, NY, Sept 21, 42. Educ: St John's Univ, BA, 66. Singer, musician, accompanist & arr, nightclubs & rock events, early 60's. Chief Collabr: George Taylor. *Songs:* Take You Back Again.

O'BRIEN, ROBERT FELIX ASCAP 1969
director, teacher
b Breese, Ill, June 24, 21. Educ: St Dominic High Sch; Carlyle High Sch; Southern Ill Univ, BS, 47; State Univ Iowa, MA, 49. USN fleet band, Pacific area, 42-46. Teacher, pub schs, Iowa, 47-51 & St John's Univ, Minn, 54-55; assoc prof & dir bands, Univ Notre Dame, 52-54 & 55-, acting chmn music dept, summers 70 & 71 & 80. Has made local & nat TV & radio appearences as univ band dir, also made several recordings with Univ Notre Dame Band. *Songs:* Music: Damsha Bua (Victory Clog); Irish Entrance; Irish Salute; Lullaby; Mourn Thy Servant; Spirit of America.

OCHS, PHIL ASCAP 1964
composer, singer
b El Paso, Tex, Dec 19, 40; d Far Rockaway, NY, Apr 9, 76. Educ: Ohio State Univ. Mem of team, The Sundowners. Appeared in clubs; in concert, Town Hall, Carnegie Hall, NY, Newport Jazz Fest, 63 & 64 & Philadelphia Folk Fest, 64. *Songs:* What's That I Hear?; The Power and the Glory; The Bells; Draft Dodger Rag; There But for Fortune; I Ain't Marching Anymore; Changes; Outside a Small Circle of Friends; Chords of Fame; Pleasures of the Harbor.

OCNOFF, EDWARD EBBER ASCAP 1958
composer, author, arranger
b Boston, Mass, Nov 11, 06. Educ: Harvard Univ, BA, 28, music study with Piston, Hill, Spalding, Ballantine & Davison; cond with Findlay, New Eng Cons, 36-37; comp with Toch & Kanitz & film music with Rozsa, Univ Southern Calif, 46-49; studied with Berkowitz, Christianson & Wienpahl, San Francisco Valley State Col, 68; studied with Slonimsky, Ed Ross, Julius Gold, Albert Coates, Frank Marks & Earl Hagen. Arr, NY, 32-35, on radio prog with Joe Venuti, Tommy Dorsey, Jimmy Dorsey, Arnold Johnson, Frank Tours & Paul Whiteman. Cond-arr, radio prog, Boston, 34, violist arr, theatre, opera & symph, 36-37; comp-arr-violist, radio & motion pictures, Hollywood, 38-42. Cond-arr, choral groups in the Middle East while in WW II, USAAF Weather, 43-45. Comp-arr-violist-librarian, motion pictures & TV, Hollywood, 45-80, comp-arr-librarian, Four Star TV, Hollywood, 59-64, arr, Hollywood, 80-, on TV pictures incl "Knott's Landing" series, "Wild Times", "Texas Rangers" & "Roughnecks." Teacher. Chief Collabrs: Bernard Hirsch, Lee Bishop, Herschel Gilbert, Ernest Hughes. *Songs:* Habeebee Rock; When Two Lovers Get Together; I Want Somebody; Tight White Capris; Zow-wez-nee; Sheik's Palace; Music: Diggin' the Gypsy Rock. *Instrumental Works:* Scherzo (piano); Piece for Flute and Piano; Sudan Suite (orch); Earthbound (orch). *Scores:* Film/TV: Soft Shoe Tessie; Summer Breeze; Humoresque; Western Range; Canyon Gallop.

O'CONNELL, LOUIS P ASCAP 1942
composer, author, lawyer
b Chicago, Ill, Sept 25, 1895. Educ: St Rita Col; Chicago Kent Col of Law, LLM, LLB. Officer, Inf, WW I. Chief counsel, Loeb-Leopold case, 24. Owner of music publ firms. Playwright, "The Missing Tadpole." Chief Collabrs: Victor Herbert, Ted Fiorito, Fred Rose, Frank Magine. *Songs:* Cutest Little Nudist; Stranger in My Old Home Town; I Love the Isle of the Sea; The Cross Upon the Hills; I Send You These Roses; Garland of Old-Fashioned Roses; Unless You're in Love; Fascinating Melody; Part of My Life. *Scores:* Stage: Take It With You; Fantabulous.

O'CONNOR, CARROLL ASCAP 1970
composer, author, singer
b New York, NY, Aug 2, 24. Educ: Nat Univ, Dublin, BA; Univ Mont, Missoula, MA, 56. Acting career incl Irish Edinburgh Fest Players of 1951, Dublin Gate Theatre, Off-Bway & Europ Tour of "Ulysses in Nighttown"; TV Specials: "The Sacco-Vanzetti Story", "The Last Hurrah", "The Funny Papers", "The Carroll O'Connor Special" & "Of Thee I Sing"; 27 feature films; author, dir & star, "Ladies of Hanover Tower." Writer, dir & actor, "All In The Family" & "Archie Bunker's Place," 10 seasons. Four Emmy Awards. *Songs:* Remembering You (closing theme of "All In The Family"); Lyrics: Grey Sundays In (musical drama).

O'CONNOR, DONALD ASCAP 1954
composer, actor, dancer
b Chicago, Ill, Aug 30, 25. With family vaudeville act during early career. Actor, var films incl "Anything Goes", "There's No Business Like Show Business", "Call Me Madam" & "Francis the Talking Mule." Prod & appeared in TV series, "Here Comes Donald," 56. Appeared var TV shows & nightclubs; singer. Chief Collabr: Sidney Miller. *Songs:* Donald's Waltz; Let's Imagine; Dear Old Dad.

O'CONNOR, GILES ASCAP 1955
composer, author, producer
b New York, NY, May 11, 08. Educ: City Col New York. Appeared in vaudeville, 28-31, then films. WW II, USCG; produced recruiting shows; also "Tars & Spars." Producer & dir, army films, 46-53; also for USIA, Wash, 55-59; in NY, 59- Chief Collabr: Howard Phillips. *Songs:* How's the Little Woman?; Wet Paint. *Scores:* Off Bway: My Canary Caught a Cold.

O'CONNOR, ROBERT CARL ASCAP 1967
composer, author
b Newark, NJ, Dec 4, 42. Educ: Barringer High Sch, pvt music lessons; Juilliard. Chief Collabrs: Arnold Capitanelli, Ayn Robbins, Artie Wayne, Joe Reed. *Songs:* Music: Move in a Little Closer Baby; Sweet Marjorene; Big John; Father O'Conner; No Cookies in My Bag.

O'CURRAN, CHARLES ASCAP 1960
composer, author, choreographer
b Atlantic City, NJ, Apr 5, 14. Educ: Atlantic City High Sch. Choreographer & dancer, Int Casino, New York, 35; dancer, Follies Bergere, 41; actor & dancer, Warner Bros pictures, 42; dir & choreographer, Universal, 43; with Paramount, 48; directed musical sequences, arr & cond, 58-67; writer & comp, 67-80. Chief Collabr: Dudley Brooks. *Songs:* Lyrics: We'll Be Together; Mama.

O'DAY, ALAN EARLE ASCAP 1971
composer, singer, entertainer
b Los Angeles, Calif, Oct 3, 40. Educ: Coachella Valley Union High Sch; Pasadena City Col; San Bernardino Valley Col. Scored & dir music for film "Wild Guitar." Singer & musician, nightclubs, USO shows in Europe & Far East. Staff writer with E H Morris & Warner Brothers Music. Recording artist with Pacific Records. Chief Collabrs: Artie Wayne, Johnny Stevenson, Mack David. *Songs:* Angie Baby; Undercover Angel; Rock and Roll Heaven; Easy Evil; The Drum; Flashback; Caress Me Pretty Music; Do Me Wrong But Do Me; Blue Finger Lou; TV theme songs: A Little Love; California Fever.

ODELL, MAMIE
See DeLoriea, Marybelle C(ruger)

ODERMAN, STUART DOUGLAS ASCAP 1976
composer, author, pianist
b Elizabeth, NJ. Educ: Newark State Col, BA; State Univ NY New Paltz, MA; Columbia Univ, 67. Pianist, hotel orchs & nightclubs, Catskill Mountains, 56-63. Silent film pianist for museums, TV & films, 59- Publ, short stories; producer, off-off Bway shows. *Songs:* Music: The Kooky Koo-Koo. *Scores:* Film/TV: The Penny Arcade; The Eternal Tramp; The Dawn of Laurel and Hardy; Laurel and Hardy Laughtunes.

ODLE, MARY ARMINDA ASCAP 1971
author
b Pryor, Okla, Aug 26, 15. *Songs:* Every Moment of the Year; My Star of Love.

O'DONNELL, ROBERT EDWARD ASCAP 1974
composer, author, singer
b Utica, NY, Sept 27, 43. With Windgate Singers, TV show, 64-66, toured NY & New Eng. Soloist, throughout NY. Lectr, folk & country music. In Europe, 67-69; played nightclubs in Berlin, London & Paris; made commercials. Entertainer in clubs; writer & pitching songs, Nashville, 72- Chief Collabrs: John Ham, Bob McCracken, Josh Graves, Billy Troy, Sam Oliva. *Songs:* I Still Get Funny When It Rains; Jimmy; All That Feeling of Greatness Is Gone; You Said Forever.

OEHLER, DALE DIXON ASCAP 1969
composer, producer, arranger
b Springfield, Ill, Oct 1, 41. Educ: Northwestern Univ, BA(music), 63; Univ Iowa, MA(comp), 67, completion of doctoral hours, 69; studied with Earle Hagen & Tom McIntosh. Arr main title of "Trouble Man," film & record; arr

for Freddie Hubbard, Marlena Shaw, Gene McDaniels & O C Smith, 74, Joni Mitchell, A Jarreau, Andre Kostelanetz, Horace Silver, Tavares & others, 75-; producer, 75- *Scores:* Film/TV Incidental Music: Streets of San Francisco; Barnaby Jones; Mod Squad; Trouble Man; And Justice for All.

O'FARRILL, ARTURO (CHICO) ASCAP 1958
composer, conductor, trumpeter
b Havana, Cuba, Oct 28, 21. Educ: Univ Havana Law Sch. Moved to US, 47. Comp & arr for dance bands incl Benny Goodman & Stan Kenton. Moved to Mex, 57. Leader of own band, TV & recordings. Arr for Count Basie & Glen Miller Orch, 66-; has been involved in commercials for radio & TV, 70- *Songs & Instrumental Works:* Havana Special; Carambola; Undercurrent Blues; Shishkabop; Cuban Episode; Ramon Lopez; Three Afro-Cuban Jazz Moods; Oro, Inciensoy Mirra.

O'FLYNN, CHARLES ASCAP 1927
author, publisher
b New York, NY, Aug 12, 1897; d New York, Apr 25, 64. Educ: Fordham Univ; Manhattan Col. Chief Collabrs: Jack Meskill, Max Rich, Larry Vincent, Edgar Leslie, Al Hoffman, Tot Seymour & Carol O'Flynn (daughter). *Songs:* Smile, Darn Ya, Smile; Hay, Hay, Farmer Gray (Took Another Load Away); When You Waltz With the One You Love; Roses Are Forget-Me-Nots; Swingin' in a Hammock; Strangers; Good Evenin'; Early in the Mornin'; Melodies Bring Memories; Jungle Drums; Who Threw Confetti in Angelo's Spaghetti?; Happy Nothing to You; God's Rain; The Angelus; Rosary of Roses (spirituals); American Beauty Series.

O'FLYNN, HONORIA (NOREEN MACK) ASCAP 1963
composer, author, publisher
b Galway, Ireland, Sept 1, 09. Educ: Nat schs, Ireland. Wife of Charles O'Flynn, mother of Carol O'Flynn. *Songs:* I'll Give Up the Late, Late Show for You; Dancing At the Crossroads.

OFMAN, LEE ASCAP 1979
composer, author, singer
b Warsaw, Poland, Mar 9, 46. Educ: Univ Tex, BS(math); law sch. Traveled with 5 to 6 piece band, Las Vegas, Tulsa, Houston, Evansville, etc, 71-76. *Songs:* Houston Oiler Fight Song; Who's Gonna Worry 'Bout You Now; Galveston Winds.

OGAL, T F
See Newman, Barbara Belle

OGILVIE, RUTH SIMMONS ASCAP 1959
composer, author, singer
b Boston, Mass, Apr 5, 20. Educ: Col prep. With twin sister Ruby Simmons appeared as one of Moonmaids with Vaughn Monroe Orch & on TV. Writer, musical commercials. *Songs:* Echoing Mailbox; Chickadee Valley; It's All Over But the Crying; Bacia Ba Lu.

O'HARA, GEOFFREY ASCAP 1914
composer, author, teacher
b Chatham, Ont, Feb 2, 1882; d St Petersburg, Fla, Jan 31, 67. Came to US, 04, became citizen. Educ: Chatham Col Inst; pvt music study; Huron Col, hon MusD, Began career as banker. App by Secy of Interior as instr native Indian music, 13. Armed Forces song leader, WW I. Instr community music & song writing, Teachers Col, Columbia Univ, 36-37 & Huron Col, 47-48. Comp operettas. Charter mem, ASCAP, dir, 42-45. *Songs:* K-K-K-Katy; Give a Man a Horse He Can Ride; There Is No Death; Leetle Bateese; I Walked Where Jesus Walked; Where Heaven Is; The Old Songs (int theme song of Soc for the Preservation of Quartet Singing in Am); Forward to Christ; One World; God's Hand Is There; Your Eyes Have Told Me; Tennessee; Stay Close to God.

O'HARA, KAREN (KAREN MCREYNOLDS) ASCAP 1959
composer, author, singer
b Omaha, Nebr, Jan 30, 33. Educ: Conaty Girls High Sch; Mt St Mary's Col; studied ballet, actg & voice. Singer, nightclubs, Las Vegas, Reno, Lake Tahoe & Los Angeles area, 10 yrs; recording artist, Liberty Records. Chief Collabr: Denny McReynolds. *Songs:* Lyrics: It's a Great Life; If I Were Free; Music: Make the World a Little Younger; Suddenly I'm Sad; Old Glory; A Great Golden Day; Where Old Friends Meet; This Is You and Me; Hello World; I Can Only Wish You Love; The World Belongs To You; For Old Times Sake; Did I Ever Really Know Him.

O'HARA, LINDA ASCAP 1969
composer, author
b Paterson, NJ, Apr 7, 48. Educ: Fullerton Union High Sch; Calif State Univ, Fullerton, Long Beach, BA(cum laude), 73. Collaborated as comp/author of "Mind Odyssey," 69. Chief Collabrs: Dale Burt, Lemoyne Taylor, Lewayne Braun, Leo Potts. *Songs:* Looking for the Tour Guide; Lyrics: The Lady At the Gate; Flying Free; White Light; In the Garden.

OHLSON, MARION ASCAP 1959
composer, author, conductor
b Jersey City, NJ. Educ: NY Univ; New York Col of Music; Juilliard Sch; Guilmant Organ Sch; pvt study. Prof pianist & accompanist; choir dir & church organist. *Songs:* The Victory of Easter; Anthems: The Vigils of Mary; Christ Is Born; Mother-Love; Christ Is Risen; Now Is the Triumph. *Instrumental Works:* Little Piano Concerto. *Scores:* Children's operetta: Three Little Pigs.

OHMAN, PHIL ASCAP 1936
composer, conductor, pianist
b New Britain, Conn, Oct 7, 1896; d Santa Monica, Calif, Aug 8, 54. Educ: High sch. Pianist, demonstrator, then asst organist, New York. Soloist with orchs. Toured as accompanist to concert singers. Mem, 2-piano team with Vic Arden, featured in theatres, radio & Bway musicals incl "Lady, Be Good!"; "Tip-Toes"; "Oh, Kay!"; "Funny Face"; "Treasure Girl"; "Spring Is Here." Cond own orch in night clubs. Guest soloist, symph orchs. Made many records. Wrote film scores in Hollywood. *Songs:* Lazy Rolls the Rio Grande; Each Time You Say Goodbye; Lost; Only One; Hilda; Don't Believe All You Hear About Love; What'll I Use for Money; If You Are There; I Close My Eyes; The Girl With the High-Buttoned Shoes; Dreaming to Music; The Cowboy and the Senorita; Dream Awhile; Strawberry Samba.

OJU, ABEODUN
See Macfoy, Emmanuel Kayasi

O'KEEFE, JAMES CONRAD ASCAP 1922
composer, author, director
b St Louis, Mo, Dec 9, 1892; d Colorado Springs, Colo, July 26, 42. Educ: St Louis Univ; studied music with Charles Kunkel & Ernest Kroeger. Musician, World War I, USNR; to New York, 19; recording mgr, phonograph co, 10 yrs; dir, NBC, 32; head, Film Studio Music Dept, Hollywood, 42. Chief Collabr: Lester O'Keefe (brother). *Songs:* Rosita; Linger Longer Lane; Adorable; What Was I to Do But Fall in Love With You?; Black-Eyed Blues; Tell Me You Love Me; Station March (for USNR); Land o' Dreams. *Scores:* Stage: Leave It to the Sailors; Great Lakes Revue (for Navy Relief Soc).

O'KEEFE, LESTER (TOM FORD) ASCAP 1926
composer, author, actor
b St Louis, Mo, Aug 25, 1896; d Midland Park, NJ, June 19, 77. Educ: Acad & Col of St Louis Univ, BA; studied voice with Albert Jeanotte. USNR, WW I. Went to NY, 19, appeared in Bway musicals & toured vaudeville. Production dir, NBC, 31-43. Mem radio staff, advert agency. Chief Collabrs: James O'Keefe (brother), William Stickles, Idabelle Firestone. *Songs:* Rosita; Linger Longer Lane; Honolulu Moon; Adorable; What Was I to Do But Fall in Love With You?; Tell Me You Love Me; Land o' Dreams; Lalawana Lullaby; Paddy; Love Passed Me By; I Saw a Star Tonight; My Heart Is in the Hills Tonight; In My Garden (Firestone theme, radio, TV); With All My Heart. *Scores:* Stage: Leave It to the Sailors; Great Lakes Revue.

O'KEEFE, WALTER MICHAEL ASCAP 1941
author, actor
b Hartford, Conn, Aug 18, 1900. Educ: Hampton Court, Eng; St Thomas Sem; Notre Dame, scholarship. Served, USMC, World War I. Appeared in New York nightclubs & vaudeville; scenarist & radio producer. Chief Collabrs: Robert Dolan, Harry Archer, Irvine Orton. *Songs:* The Man on the Flying Trapeze; The Tattooed Lady; Little By Little; I'm Gonna Dance Wit de Guy Wot Brung Me; Anything Your Heart Desires; Pretty, Petite and Sweet; Henry's Made a Lady Out of Lizzie; I Love Love; Hand Holdin' Music; When the Sun Goes Down.

O'KUN, LAN ASCAP 1958
composer, author, pianist
b New York, NY, Jan 13, 32. Educ: High Sch of Music & Art; Syracuse Univ; David Mannes Sch; Juilliard; studied piano with Teddy Wilson. Writer/comp for Shari Lewis TV Show, 8 yrs; writer spec material for TV, incl "Tonight", "Barbra Streisand Specials" & "This Was the Week That Was"; also nightclub acts & for records. Music dir, NBC, 5 yrs; music coordr, "Jimmy Dean Show." Author bk, "The Littlest Angel." *Songs:* My Own Personal Bird; The Minute Waltz; Natural Sounds; They're Shooting in the Streets; The Best Gift; Music: That's What God Looks Like to Me. *Scores:* Film/TV: The Littlest Angel; Insight Series; Tales of the Riverbank. *Albums:* 13 Jazz Classics.

OKUN, MILTON THEODORE ASCAP 1958
composer, teacher, author
b Brooklyn, NY, Dec 23, 23. Educ: NY Univ, BMEd; Oberlin Cons Music, MMEd. Taught music in New York pub sch syst. Worked as a singer, cond & arr, Harry Belafonte. Music dir & record producer, Peter, Paul & Mary; musical dir, Brothers Four; musical dir & record producer, Chad Mitchell Trio & John Denver, also Tom Paxton, Miriam Makeba, Paul Robeson & many others. Author & arr of all contents, "Something to Sing About"; ed, "Great Songs of the Sixties", "Great Songs of Lennon and McCartney", "Great Songs of the Seventies", "New York Times Country Music's Greatest Songs" & "New York Times Great Songs of Abba." *Songs:* Arranged & Adapted: Have You Got a Light Boy; Tell It to the Mountains; Sinner Man; Odds Against Tomorrow.

OLCOTT, CHAUNCEY
ASCAP 1914
composer, author, actor

b Buffalo, NY, July 21, 1858; d Monte Carlo, Mar 18, 32. Educ: Christian Bros; studied voice in London. Singer in minstrel shows; acted in Bway musicals incl "Barry of Ballymore", "Isle of Dreams", "The Heart of Paddy Whack" & "Macushla." Film biography: "My Wild Irish Rose." Chief Collabrs: Ernest Ball, George Graff. *Songs:* My Wild Irish Rose; Mother Machree; When Irish Eyes Are Smiling; In the Sunshine of Your Love; I Love the Name of Mary; Goodbye, My Emerald Land; Every Star Falls in Love; Your Heart Alone Must Tell; Wearers of the Green; Laugh With a Tear in It; Day Dreams; Tic Tac Toe.

OLDS, WILLIAM BENJAMIN
ASCAP 1944
composer

b Clinton, Wis, June 3, 1874; d Los Angeles, Calif, Jan 10, 48. Educ: Beliot Col, BA, hon MusD; Oberlin Cons; Am Cons; studied with Oscar Seagle. Taught, Grinnell Col, Ill Col & James Millikin Univ; also taught privately. Supvr, adult chorus, Bureau of Music, Los Angeles, 43-48; cond; organized annual choral fests. *Songs:* Recollection; Nocturne; The Water of Life; The Bread of Life; God Is Love; Ye Shall Know the Truth; The West; Blow, Blow, Thou Winter Wind. *Instrumental Works:* A Christmas Choralogue; A Pastoral Choralogue; A Passion Choralogue; Desert Drums (cantata); Bird Songs for Children (2 vols). *Scores:* Opera: The Feathered Serpent.

OLIVA, FRANK F
ASCAP 1960
composer, author, actor

b Nutley, NJ, Aug 15, 04. Educ: Col. Actor, singer since childhood. Dir, musicals, 58- Interior decorator & paint contractor. Chief Collabr: Ilona Fody. *Songs:* A Woman; Ask for Me; You Are My Love; Angel Face; Legend of the Cowboy Saint; Ring of Virgin Gold; Green Is the Color; Till Eternity.

OLIVADOTI, JOSEPH
ASCAP 1961
composer, oboist, arranger

b Cortale, Italy, Nov 7, 1893; d Long Beach, Calif, Sept 28, 77. Came to US, 11. Music educ in Italy. Toured prov with local band, 6 yrs. In US, toured with Bachman's Million Dollar Band, 20-38. Played in film houses and for musicals, Chicago, 25-41. USN Band, WW II. Mem, Long Beach Philh Orch, Calif, 12 yrs & Long Beach Munic Band. Taught music until 63. *Instrumental Works:* We're the Navy; Cruiser Chicago; Hall of Fame; El Cabellero; National Victors; March of Youth; Scepter of Liberty; Zaragosa; South of the Rio; Enchanted Canyon; Festival of Youth March; Naval Sea Cadet March; Overtures: Carnival of Roses; Ponce de Leon; Pacific Grandeur; Laureate; Triumph of Ishtar; Beau Sabreur; Avalon Nights; Apple Valley Overture; Ensenada Overture.

OLIVEIRA, ALOYSIO (LOUIS)
ASCAP 1945
composer, author

b Rio de Janeiro, Brazil, Dec 30, 14. Musician, 20th Century Fox, 40-50 & Walt Disney Studios, 41-47, producer, EMI, Rio de Janeiro, 56-67. Chief Collabrs: Antonio Carlos Jobim, Ray Gilbert, Badem Powell. *Songs:* Lyrics: Dindi; Tico-Tico; If You Never Come to Me.

OLIVER, RICHARD S
ASCAP 1970
author

b Oakland, Calif, Dec 10, 36. Educ: City Col San Francisco, AA(radio/TV); Univ Calif, Los Angeles BA(motion pictures/theatre), 61. Writer/dir children's story albums, Disneyland Records; co-writer children's musical, "Aladdin and His Genie"; ed dir, Liberty/United Artists Records; co-producer/album note writer of 12 double LP series, "Those Glorious MGM Musicals"; researcher for NBC-TV's "First 100 Years of Recorded Music"; writer of ABC-TV's 13th and NBC-TV's 15th "Academy of Country Music Awards." Twice nominated Grammy Award for best album notes. *Songs:* Lyrics: Look Out At the Rain; Where Are You?; One Time.

OLIVER, THOMAS EDWARD, JR
author, arranger, conductor

b Seabright, NJ, Sept 19, 32. Educ: Gloversville High Sch, NY; Los Angeles City Col, studied arr with Bob McDonald; Univ Calif, Los Angeles, 4 yrs. Wrote musicals, 51. Organized dance band; contract with Warner Bros; arr & cond with Joni Sommers, 58. Music dir TV specials & series: "Donny and Marie Show"; "John Denver Special"; "Name That Tune"; "Lil Abner"; "Laugh In." Wrote theme, "Face the Music." *Songs:* One More Mountain.

OLIVEROS, PAULINE
ASCAP 1978
composer

b Houston, Tex, May 30, 32. Educ: San Francisco State Univ, BA, 57; pvt comp study with Robert Erickson, 54-59. Mem, San Francisco Tape Music Ctr, 60-67; dir, Mills Tape Music Ctr, 66-67. Prof music, Univ Calif, San Diego, 67-Guggenheim Fellow, 73-74. Chief Collabrs: Elaine Summers, Al Chung Liang Huang. *Songs:* Music: Sound Patterns for Mixed Chorus; Rose Moon; Electronic Music: Big Mother Is Watching You; I of IV; Bye Bye Butterfly; Jar Piece; Beautiful Soop. *Instrumental Works:* Meditations on the Points of the Compass; To Valerie Solanas and Marilyn Monroe in Recognition of their Desperation; Double Basses At Twenty Paces; Outline for Flute Percussion and String Bass; Trio for Flute Piano and Page Turner; Willowbrook Generations and Reflections; Aeolian Partitions; El Relicario de los Animales (singer,

instrumentals). *Songs & Instrumental Works:* Crow Two; Sonic Meditations; Bonn Feier (1st prize, City of Bonn, 77).

OLIVER-SLETTEN, MADRA IMOGENE (M RIX SLETTEN)
ASCAP 1959
composer, author, teacher

b Three Rivers, Mich. Educ: Oberlin Col & Cons; Univ Mich, BSM; New Eng Cons; Univ Wis; Claremont Grad Sch, MA; Univ Ill; Univ Nebr. Music teacher elem, jr high & high schs; gave benefit concerts; teacher spec classes in impressionism & expressionism under Nebr Coun Arts; Wis Fel of Poets; Univ Wis Europ choir tour. Chief Collabr: Oliver Faber *Songs:* Music: Folk Song Fantasy (chorus & ens); Whispering Wisconsin (band with trumpet or vocal solo); Seven Songs for Youth; also five modern piano pieces.

OLIVO, BRUNO F(RANCIS)
ASCAP 1972
composer

b Philadelphia, Pa, July 20, 17. Educ: McCall Trade Sch; Army Technol Sch, dipl; Naval Marine Technol Sch, dipl. Self-taught musician. Writer, musical plays while in Army. Performer, stage & radio; soloist on banjo, guitar & piano. *Songs:* A Candle for St Jude; Be Like a Clown and Smile; Oh! What a Wonderful Feeling; You're the World to Me; To Be Without You; You're Everybody's Sweetheart, But Mine.

OLMAN, ABE
ASCAP 1920
composer, pianist, publisher

b Cincinnati, Ohio, Dec 20, 1888. Educ: Pub sch. Office mgr, Gus Edwards Productions, 12; wrote songs, Empire Revue, London, 13; managing dir, MGM Robbins Music Corp, Leo Feist, Inc & Miller Music Corp, 35-56. Dir, ASCAP, 46-56. Co-founder, Nat Acad Popular Music (Songwriters Hall of Fame), 68. Chief Collabrs: Jack Yeller, James Brockman, Ed Rose. *Songs:* Music: Oh Johnny Oh; Down Among the Sheltering Palms; Down By the O-Hi-O; I'm Waiting for Ships That Never Come In; Johnny's in Town; Come Back to Waikiki.

O'LOUGHLIN, ED
ASCAP 1969
composer

b Brooklyn, NY, Jan 9, 45. Writer, producer & music publ. Has written for Carol Douglas, The Critters & others.

OLSEN, ESTHER SIGRID
ASCAP 1975
composer, author

b Rainier, Ore, Dec 9, 21. Educ: Rainier Grade Sch & High Sch; Bremerton Bus Col, studied voice, script writing, piano & art. Chief Collabr: Will Herring. *Songs & Instrumental Works:* Juneau; Peachy Penguin.

OLSHANETSKY, ALEXANDER
ASCAP 1962
composer, conductor

b Russia, Oct 23, 1892; d. Educ: High sch. Wrote for Yiddish Theatre. Music dir for summer resorts. Chief Collabr: Jacob Jacobs. *Songs:* I Love You Much Too Much; That Wonderful Girl of Mine.

OLSON, HENRY RUSSELL
ASCAP 1944
composer, author, pianist

b Moorhead, Minn, Sept 4, 13; d Sherman Oaks, Calif, Apr 14, 68. Educ: Pub schs; Concordia Cons, Fargo, NDak. Organized vocal group, Four Bachelors; toured US & Eng. Pianist, arr & vocalist with orchs; introduced Novachord. Machinist, WW II. Music dir, NBC. Wrote for films. *Songs:* The Madam Swings It; Broadway Caballero; Pete the Piper; I Still Care; We're Going Across; When I'd Yoo Hoo in the Valley; Halls of Ivy; Obsession; Yancy Derringer; Lulu Belle.

OLSON, HENRY RUSSELL
See Russell, Henry

OLSON, LYNN FREEMAN
ASCAP 1966
composer, author, clinician

b Minneapolis, Minn, June 5, 38. Educ: Minnehaha Acad; Univ Minn; New Sch for Music Study, cert; piano & pedagogy studies with Cleo M Hiner & Frances Clark, theory-comp, Glenn Glasow & David Kraehenbuehl, Dalcroze eurhythmics, Martha Baker. Originator & comp, "It's Time for Music" (syndicated radio), with over 200 educ songs comp for series; teacher & lectr in piano pedagogy; listening consult, Silver Burdett Music; consult in keyboard educ, Carl Fischer, Inc; regular columnist, Clavier Magazine; staff lectr, Nat Piano Found. Chief Collabrs: Georgia Garlid; Louise Bianchi & Marvin Blickenstaff; Merrill & Barbara Staton. *Songs:* Topsy-Turvy March; Ebeneezer Sneezer; Milk; Drum and Bugle Corps; Good Morning, Mister Sun; Hello There, Officer; Counting; Build That Building; Rainbows. *Instrumental Works:* Make It Snappy!; Wheels; The Flamingo; Kites; Brief Encounter; Caribbean Blue; Silver Bugles; First Sonatina; Festival in Aragon; Ballad of Don Quixote.

OLSON, ROBERT G (JON ROBERTS, GLENN ROLLINS)
ASCAP 1961
composer, author, teacher

b Minn, May 29, 13. Educ: Univ Iowa; Univ Minn, BA; Eastman Sch Music, Univ Rochester, MA, 39. Teacher, Bemidji State Col. Dir music, Northwood Sch, Lake Placid Club, NY. Dean studies, St Louis Inst Music. Ed-in-chief, Summy-Birchard Publ Co, 52-62. Teacher, Foothill Col & De Anza Col, Calif,

64-80. *Songs & Instrumental Works:* Alleluia, Glorious Is Thy Name (fest choral music); Banners and Bells (concert band); Suite in Brief (two pianos); numerous choral pieces & piano teaching comps; Music and English Literature (prog of text material, 5 recordings & a film strip); Music Dictation (textbook & series of 24 tapes).

O'MALLEY, FRANCIS K   ASCAP 1959
composer, author

b Meadville, Mo, Nov 16, 1896; d. Educ: Kansas City Sch Mech Engr; Fox-Morgan Art Inst; studied violin. Serv, World War II; publ many poems. Mem, Am Guild Authors & Comp. *Songs:* Grotto of Love; Mr Man in the Moon; If There Never Had Been an Ireland.

OMARTIAN, STORMIE SHERRIC   ASCAP 1973
composer, author, singer

b Scottsbluff, Nebr, Sept 16, 42. Educ: Long Beach State Col; Washington Univ; Univ Southern Calif, music; Univ Calif, Los Angeles, music. Studio singing, 66-; back-up singer, Cher, Helen Reddy, Glen Campbell, Mac Davis, Ray Charles & Tom Jones. Wrote songs for Cher, Leo Sayer, The Imperials, Michael & Stormie Omartian albums & Evie. Chief Collabrs: Michael Omartian, Ron Harris, Annie Herring. *Songs:* Lyrics: All the Time in the World; Praise the Lord, He Never Changes; One More Song for You; What I Can Do for You; Fat City; All My Life; Movin' in the Spirit; Ms Past; The Only Thing Missing Is You; Closer Than Ever; Don't Give Up on Jesus; The Builder; Anything You Ask of Me; Dr Jesus; Half Past Three; It All Comes Down to You.

ONDEK, STEPHEN   ASCAP 1957
composer, author, teacher

b Bridgeport, Conn, Feb 1, 1899. Educ: Pub schs. Appeared in vaudeville, burlesque & musical comedy. Appeared in "Castles in the Air" & "Son's of Guns." *Songs:* Roses for You; I Wanna Feller; Tears in the Dark; Oh Baby, Be a Lady; Dear Old Connecticut; The Birth of the T-53; To My Friends of Christ; Gentlest Heart of Jesus; I Thank Thee O My Lord; The Apostles Creed; Christmas Basket; Lovely Christmas Day; My Christmas Gift to You; Christmas Twinkling Bells; Merry Christmas Santa Claus; Christmas Tinsel Time; Christmas Claus I'm Waiting; Christmas Chimes Mean Laurel Time; Christmas Lights; When Christmas Day Is Gone; It's Time to Trim Your Christmas Tree; No One Should Have a Christmas Without a Christmas Tree. *Instrumental Works:* Battre le Mesure (15 minute overtures).

O'NEALE, MARGIE LOUISE   ASCAP 1954
composer, author

b Stanberry, Mo, Nov 25, 23. Educ: Stanberry High Sch. Started writing songs at age 9. Worked for Pacific Telephone Co, 25 yrs. Chief Collabrs: Marvin Charney, Fred Darian, Joe Egner, Johnny Anz. *Songs:* Sin in Satin; Christian Clay; Snowball Arkansan; The Sky Is My Cathedral; She Knows; Lyrics: Water Can't Quench the Fire of Love; Calypso Joe; Mucho Gusto; Strong Man; So Near and Yet So Far; The Diggie Song; The Eucalyptus Tree.

ONEGLIA, MARIO F(RANCESCO) (MARTY ORNELL)   ASCAP 1975
composer, trumpeter, educator

b New York, NY, Sept 23, 27. Educ: Bronx High Sch Sci, NY; Manhattan Sch Music, NY; Columbia Univ; BMus, MArts, DEd degrees; Eastman Sch Music; Berklee Col Music; trumpet studies with Maurice Grupp, Carmine Caruso, William Vacchaiano; cello studies with Shapinsky, Krane; cond & comp studies with Tibor Serly. Began study of music while in high sch; performed with name bands incl, Louis Prima, Vincent Lopez, Ina Ray Hutton, Tito Puente, etc, both as trumpeter & arranger/composer. Teacher, Garden City Pub Schs, several yrs; founded & cond, Garden City Community Orch. App professorship, Montclair State Col, NJ, 63, founded jazz studies, 74, arr & comp music for var student ens. Music dir, Montclair Operetta Club. Composer & arranger educ media. *Instrumental Works:* Brotherman (jazz-rock ens); Rock-Cha-Cha (Latin-jazz ens); Homage A Tibor Serly (cello solo & string quartet); Make Me Love Ever'body (jazz-rock ens); Chamber Music: Music per Mani Cheiro Diversi.

O'NEIL, VINCENT   ASCAP 1972
author

b San Francisco, Calif, Oct 3, 12. Educ: Pub schs, San Francisco; Galileo High Sch. Pianist; 17th & 82nd Airborne Divs, Merchant Marines, WW II. Chief Collabrs: Clarence Freed, Lew Tobin. *Songs & Instrumental Works:* What Happened to Our Love; Merry Christmas; Black and White; Derrier; Lost and Found; For Me There's No Tomorrow; Lost Prayer.

O'NEILL, CHERYL LYNN BOONE (CHERRY)   ASCAP 1968
composer, author, singer

b Denton, Tex, July 7, 54. Educ: Westlake Sch for Girls, 72; Univ Calif, Los Angeles, 2 yrs; piano studies with Marsha Rudolph, 8 yrs. Began writing, age 14; professional singer with family tours, 69-77; with family TV specials, 78-79; personal appearances & writer for radio jingles, 79-80. Chief Collabr: Pam Mark Hall. *Songs:* Father God; Matter of Time; Ruth; Miracle Merry-go-Round; Lyrics: The First Butterfly.

O'NEILL, NORRIS   ASCAP 1959
composer, author, musician

b Montclair, NJ, Feb 7, 39. Educ: Montclair Acad; Georgetown Univ, BA, 61. Organized folk group, Ivy League Trio; recorded for Decca, Coral & Reprise Records; did concerts, nightclubs & TV. Mem, Bitter End Singers; recorded for Mercury Records. Toured with Lyndon Johnson campaign show. Sang for President Johnson & Congress at the White House. Performer, soloist on TV & concerts, Europe. Writer & producer of many educ records for Encyclopedia Brittanica & Kimbo Records. Rec'd Freedom's Found Award for series on Am Music. Original music & lyrics for feature films, documentaries, records & many commercials. *Songs:* If You Go Across the Sea; Lookin' for a Woman Blues; Hey, Young Rider; Bury Me Beneath the Willow. *Scores:* Film/TV: The Berry That Won the West (also background music); Maybe Tomorrow (also background music); also This Is Only the Beginning (theme song & incidental music).

ONIVAS, D
See Savino, Domenico

ONORATI, HENRY V   ASCAP 1959
author

b Revere, Mass, Jan 25, 12. Educ: Revere High Sch, Mass; Lowell Inst, Mass. Newspaper reporter, columnist, 30-33. With RCA, copywriter, promotion specialist, pub relations, record sales rep, pop records promotion mgr, 34-50. Advert mgr, Crossley Div AVCO, 51-52. Producer, radio show "Stars Review the Hits," 52-53. BillBoard Mag staff, 53-55; vpres, Dot Records, 55-58; pres, 20th Century Fox Records, 58-63; vpres, World Broadcasting Syst, 64-69. *Songs:* Lyrics: The Little Drummer Boy; The Bravados.

OPLER, ALFRED M   ASCAP 1942
composer, author

b New York, NY, Aug 30, 1897. *Songs:* Always Yours; My Valley of Memories; Seems I've Always Held Your Hand; Sweet Little Lady Next Door; While We Danced At the Mardi Gras; The Cradle and the Music Box.

OPPENHEIM, DAVID   ASCAP 1931
author

b Dubuque, Iowa, Sept 16, 1889; d New York, NY, Dec 5, 61. Educ: DeWitt Clinton High Sch. Minor League baseball player. Wrote songs for musicals (London, Bway), nightclubs & films. *Songs:* When a Lady Meets a Gentleman Down South; Freddy the Freshman; Hold Me; It's the Girl; The Night When Love Was Born; Thank You, Mr Moon.

OPPENHEIMER, JOSEPH L   ASCAP 1961
author, editor, publicist

b Wurzburg, Ger, June 27, 27. Educ: Wash Univ, BA. Corresponding ed, Int News Service, 49-58. Assoc ed, Forbes mag. Pub relations exec, A A Schechter Asn, 59-62. Ed, Outlook. Chief Collabr: William Simon. *Songs:* Sidewalk Santa.

ORBON, JULIAN   ASCAP 1968
composer, teacher

b Aviles, Spain, Aug 7, 25. Educ: Cons Oviedo, Spain; Cons Havana; Berkshire Music Ctr, Tanglewood; studied with Aaron Copland. Prize, First Latin Am Fest. Guggenheim Fel, 59 & 69. Comns: Serge Koussevitzky Found; Fromm Found. Rec'd Am Acad Arts & Letters Award. Asst of Carlos Chavez, Comp Workshop, Nat Cons Music, Mex. *Songs & Instrumental Works:* Homenaje a La Tonadilla (orch); Tres Versiones Sinfonicas (orch); Concerto Grosso (orch); Monte Gelboe (tenor, orch); String Quartet; Partita No 1 (harpsichord); Partita No 2 (chamber group); Tres Cantigas del Rey (voice, chamber group); Himnus ad Galli Cantun (voice, chamber group); Partita No 3 (orch); Preludio y Danza (guitar).

O'REILLY, JOHN SAMUEL   ASCAP 1970
composer

b Walden, NY, Nov 25, 40. Educ: Newburgh Free Acad High Sch, 58; Crane Sch Music, BS, 62; Columbia Univ, MA, 64; comp studies with Robert Washburn, Arthur Fradunpohl & Charles Walton. Teacher music, East Meadow Pub Schs, Long Island, NY, 62-70; prof music, Nassau Community Col, 71-72. Music ed & comp, Alfred Publ, Sherman Oaks, Calif, 73- *Instrumental Works:* Concerto for Trumpet and Winds; Music for the Cinema; Metropolitan Brass Quintet; Three Episodes for Percussion Ensemble; Arlington Festive Music; Stratford Overture; Jefferson County Overture; Kings Go Forth; Kaleilascope; March for Kim; March for a Rainy Day; Royal Procession; Idyllwild Fantasy; Change of Pace; Modal Overture; Three Kentucky Sketches; Overture for a New Decade; Temple Hill.

ORENSTEIN, LARRY   ASCAP 1955
composer, author, trumpeter

b St Paul, Minn, Aug 30, 18. Educ: Univ Calif, Los Angeles; studied music with Louis Maggio & Richard Cummings. Trumpet soloist & singer with Shep Fields, Paul Whiteman & Ray Noble orchs; mem 1st motion picture unit, USAAF Band, WW II. Studio musician, Hollywood; actor in summer stock & also in "I Love Lucy," TV; wrote TV scripts; also wrote spec material for Donald O'Connor, Guy Mitchell, Danny Kaye, Desi Arnaz, Lucille Ball & Walt Disney Studio. Copy chief, Doyle, Dane & Bernbach, Los Angeles, 58; creative dir,

Kenyon & Eckhart; vpres & creative supvr, Carson Roberts, 63- Advert exec. Bd mem, Comp & Lyricists Guild Am. Chief Collabs: Jeff Alexander, Alvy West. *Songs:* The General Jumped At Dawn; Cross My Heart; Blues About Manhattan; Ballad for Beatnicks; Trouble Man; Holiday in Hawaii; The Winter Waltz; Bachelor Father; Have Horn Will Blow; Nobody Loves the Ump; Horseless Carriage.

ORENT, MILTON H   ASCAP 1946
composer
b New York, NY, Apr 3, 18; d. Educ: NY Univ, BS. *Instrumental Works:* Whirlpool; Wonderful World; Riff Staccato. *Songs & Instrumental Works:* Concerto Grosso.

ORIO, C A   ASCAP 1959
composer, author, accordionist
b St Louis, Mo, Jan 22, 12; d. Educ: Acad Arts & Tech, Paris; studied music with Art Davis & C Graham. Trained in Europe as chef; accordionist & writer in vaudeville; was exec chef steward. Mem, Am Guild Authors & Comp. *Instrumental Works:* River Blues Rhapsody.

ORLAND, HENRY   ASCAP 1969
composer, educator, conductor
b Saarbruecken, Ger, Apr 23, 18. Educ: Univ Strasbourg, France, cert; Northwestern Univ, BMus, 47, MMus, 49, PhD(musicology), 59; cond studies with Nicolai Malko, comp with Anthony Donato & Oswald Jonas. Chmn depts theory-comp, hist-literature, cond orch & chorus & actg dean, St Louis Inst Music; music dir & cond, Maplewood-Richmond Heights Symph Orch; concert series coordr, Florissant Valley Col; literary critic, "Music and Man"; music critic, St Louis Post-Dispatch; artistic dir & cond, Midwest Chamber Ens; comp, Eden Singing Soc; music dir & cond, Brentwood Symph Orch; prof music & chmn dept, St Louis Community Col, Florissant Valley. *Songs:* Music: A Christmas Legend; Elegie; Songs of the Shepherd; Colloque Sentimental; Serenade; Peace; Encounter; Occasional Songs; Drei Lieder; Goethe Balladen; Love and Pity. *Instrumental Works:* Symphony No 3; Symphony No 4; Epigram; Initial; Concerto (bassoon); Double-Concerto (flute & Eng horn); Pre-l-et-ude; Quartet for Strings; String Trio; Brevissime Pretexte, Bagatelle et Etude (piano); Fantasy (piano); Sonata (piano).

ORLICK, PHILIP   ASCAP 1960
composer, author, singer
b Boston, Mass, Sept 22, 40. Educ: Columbia Univ. Appeared, TV show "Ted Steele Show" & in nightclubs. *Songs:* When Alma Mater Was Younger (Pamphratria prize, Columbia Univ); Fraternalism.

ORLOB, HAROLD F   ASCAP 1914
composer, author
b Salt Lake City, Utah, June 3, 1883. Educ: Univ Utah; Brigham Young Univ; Univ Mich, Ann Arbor. Chief Collabrs: Harry B Smith, Frank Adam, Will Hough, Thommy Grey. *Songs:* That's How Dreams Should End; Saint Frances Cabrini; When The Shadows Fall; Nothing But Love; Don't Forget; Music: I Wonder Who's Kissing Her Now; I Will be Waiting. *Songs & Instrumental Works:* Recreation (symphonic suite). *Scores:* Town Topics; Hitchy Koo; Red Canary; Time The Place The Girl; Films: One Third of a Nation; Citizen Saint.

ORMANDY, EUGENE   ASCAP 1954
conductor, violinist, arranger
b Budapest, Hungary, Nov 18, 1899. Educ: Entered Royal Acad Music, Budapest, at 5 (prof's dipl); studied violin with Jeno Hubay; hon degrees: Hamline Univ; Univ Pa; Philadelphia Musical Acad; Curtis Inst; Temple Univ; Univ Mich; Lehigh Univ; Clark Univ; Miami Univ; Rutgers Univ. Concert tours as violinist; also taught at State Cons, Budapest. Cond first concerts with Philadelphia Orch & New York Philh, 30; Minneapolis Symph, 6 yrs. Cond & music dir, Philadelphia Orch, 36- Awards: Bruckner Soc; Order of Merit of Juan Pablo Duarte (Degree of Caballero), Dominican Repub; Knight of the Order of Dennebora; Knight of the Order of the White Rose of Finland; Commandeur, French Legion of Honor.

ORME, DAPHNNIE   ASCAP 1964
composer, author
b Avoca, Iowa, Oct 21, 1889; d Yakima, Wash, Aug 14, 70. Educ: Acad Art; studied music with father. Chief Collabrs: Roy Jackson, Jennie Brockway, Charles Ilvess. *Songs:* Old Fashioned Christmas; Spinning in My Heart.

ORMONT, DAVID   ASCAP 1953
composer, author, educator
b Paterson, NJ, Mar 17, 1898; d Long Beach, Calif, Mar 31, 78. Educ: City Col New York, BA(magna cum laude, Phi Beta Kappa); Columbia Univ, MA. Teacher of French, Eng, Span, Brooklyn high schs; also col adv. Wrote songs for films, Bway musicals & Latin Quarter nightclub. Book reviewer, "Brooklyn Daily Eagle." Author: "Let's Act", "Sports Quizz Book" & bk & lyrics, "Twelve Musical Plays for Children." Chief Collabrs: Henry Tobias, Irving Fields, Jay Blackton, Harry Warren, Dick Manning, Phil Charig, Frank Dale, Erich Wolfgang Korngold, Maurice Sturm. *Songs:* My Kingdom for a Kiss; Two Hearts Divided; Pardon Me, Madame; For Old Atlantic; One Hour Ahead of the Posse; God Walks in My Garden; The Wonder of Your Love; The Story of Engine 1706; Piccolo Polka; Echoes of Love; Wonderful Wyoming; Let's Go

Skiing; A Little Bird Told Me So; Paris By Night; Por La Noche. *Albums:* Let's Go to the Circus; Let's Go to the Zoo; Let's Go to a Mother Goose Jamboree; Aladdin; Beauty and the Beast; William Tell; Dick Whittington; The Pied Piper.

ORNELL, MARTY
See Oneglia, Mario F(rancesco)

ORNISH, NATALIE GENE   ASCAP 1963
composer, author, lecturer
b Galveston, Tex, Feb 15, 26. Educ: Sam Houston State Col, Tex, BA, 43; Northwestern Univ, Evanston, MS, 45. Music performed by the 85-piece Dallas Symph Orch. Chief Collabr: Charlotte Royal. *Songs:* Swing Me, Swing Tree; March of the Toys; You Can Fly; Let's Have a Tea Party; The Sleep Fairy; Sweet Dreams; A Lap Full of Laurie; The Tooth Fairy; You Are a Beautiful Child; Teach Me, Father; People Are More Important Than Things; What Do You Do After School?; Very Normal Twelve Year Old; First Girl on the Moon; I Want to See a Tree; I'm in Between; If You Can't Say Anything Good; Lyrics: The World Loves a Winner; Stand Up for Staubach.

ORSBORN, VICTOR R   ASCAP 1975
composer, singer
b Los Angeles, Calif, Aug 15, 53. Educ: George Washington High Sch, Los Angeles, 70. Wrote high sch class song, 70; mem groups, E Robinson & Youth for Christ Choir, 73-74; wrote gospel songs & performed in churches; writer pop songs, 74; under contract, Jobete Publ, 75-80. Chief Collabr: Eric J Robinson. *Songs:* Lyrics: Dance (Disco Heat); Just Us; Love Has Finally Come.

ORSHAN, HERBERT ALLEN   ASCAP 1963
composer, author, teacher
b Brooklyn, NY, Apr 25, 25. Educ: Brooklyn Col, BA, 49; NY Univ, MA, 50, EdD(music), 59. US Army, 43-46. Performing musician while attending var cols. High sch music teacher, asst principal & principal; retired, 80. *Songs:* Echoing Beguine; Music: How Do I Love Thee; The Kerry Dance; A House By the Side of the Road; The Minstrel Boy; Whither Thou Goest, I Will Go; Songs From Africa; Paean to Peace. *Instrumental Works:* A Festival for Christmas; Six African Songs.

ORTEGA, FRANK   ASCAP 1960
composer, arranger, conductor
b Los Angeles, Calif, Nov 27, 27. Educ: Studied with Edith Knox & Mario Castelnuovo-Tedesco. Pianist/orch leader, 45-, appearing in major hotels, nighclubs, TV shows & others, cond/arr, Ed Ames, Kay Starr, Rosemary Clooney, Margaret Whiting, Rose Marie, Eartha Kitt & Peggy Lee; comp, TV shows incl "King of Diamonds", "Yankee and Son in Mexico", "Magic Circus Specials", "Magic World of Mark Wilson", "77 Sunset Strip", "Roaring 20's" & "Surfside 6", also shows "Showtime America", "Magic of the Globe", "Hall of Magic" & "NY World's Fair." Chief Collabr: Jack Kaplan. *Instrumental Works:* Magic Circus (theme); Magic Wand (theme); Happy Train; Crystal Ball; Gorilla; The Cannon; Magic Moments, Magic Songs; Achemistic; Big W; Backstage Disco; The Los Angeles Suite.

ORY, EDWARD (KID)   ASCAP 1952
composer, author, conductor
b La Place, La, Dec 25, 1886; d. Educ: Pub schs; pvt music study. Led own band, New Orleans, 07-19, then Los Angeles, 19-25. First New Orleans band to broadcast & record. Trombonist in bands incl "King" Oliver & Jelly Roll Morton. Operated chicken ranch, 29. Reformed own band, 40's; led group at Berlin Fest, 59. Has given many concerts. Owner nightclub, On the Levee, San Francisco, 58-61. *Instrumental Works:* Muskrat Ramble; Savoy Blues.

OSAZE, TED ERNEST
See Hayes, Theodore, Jr

OSBORN, ARTHUR H   ASCAP 1945
composer, author, businessman
b Boston, Mass, Dec 26, 1884; d Princeton, NJ, Sept 27, 65. Educ: Princeton Univ, BS. Wrote Triangle Club shows. Was mem, NY Stock Exchange, officer pub utilities corps. Has been coach of Princeton Univ Marching & Concert Band, was active in Glee Club. Chief Collabrs: Herman Hupfield, Joseph Hewitt. *Songs:* Crash on Artillery (comn by Coast Guard Artillery Corps); Princeton Cannon Song; Colgate Marching Song; Here Comes That Tiger; The Guard of Old Nassau; Princeton's Sons; Princeton on Parade.

OSBORNE, CHESTER GORHAM   ASCAP
composer, author
b Portsmouth, NH, Sept Educ: New Eng Cons of Music, dipl(orch, trumpet), 36, MusB, 37; Northwestern Univ, MusM, 50; studied theory with Converse & Delaney, comp with Donato, trumpet with Kloepfel, Walter M Smith, Harry Glantz. Taught music, schs in Lexington, Mass, Burgin, Ky & Center Moriches, NY. With 355th Army Band, World War II. Trumpeter, Boston Opera & Boston Symph. *Songs:* Music: I See the Moon (SSAA chorus); Dumb, Dumb, Dumb (SSAA chorus). *Instrumental Works:* The British Eighth (march, band); Island (overture, band); sextet; Connemara Sketches (suite for band); The Silver Anchor (overture for band); Diversions for (collections for perc); The Piper and

the Captain (suite for band); Aisling (horn, piano); Lowlands (tuba, piano). *Scores:* Play: The Candle.

OSBORNE, DON
See Bergman, Dewey

OSBORNE, JEFFREY   ASCAP 1973
composer, singer
b Providence, RI, Mar 9, 48. Lead vocalist with group LTD, 70. Recording artist for A&M Records, 73. Chief Collabrs: Jimmy Davis, Henry Davis, Billy Osborne. *Songs:* Holding on (When Love Is Gone); We Both Deserve Each Other's Love; We Party Hearty; Where Did We Go Wrong; Stranger; Material Things.

OSBORNE, NAT   ASCAP 1914
composer, pianist
b New York, NY, Apr 23, 1878; d Hackensack, NJ, Mar 13, 54. Educ: City Col New York; NY Univ, Bellevue Med Col; Scharwenka Cons; studied with Hans Strobel. Concert pianist, 2 yrs. Wrote songs for Bway musicals. *Songs:* Take Me Back to Your Garden of Love; That's the Song of Songs for Me; When I Looked in Your Wonderful Eyes; That Wonderful Kid From Madrid; I'm a Fool to Believe in You; Another Good Man Gone Wrong; Everything Must Have an Ending; You Wanted Someone to Play With.

OSBORNE, WILL   ASCAP 1941
composer, conductor
b Toronto, Ont, Nov 25, 06. Educ: St Andrews Col. Organized own orch, 25; has appeared in dance halls, theatres, radio & films. *Songs:* Between Eighteenth and Nineteenth on Chestnut Street; Pompton Turnpike; Woulds't Could I But Kiss Thy Hand, Oh Babe; Dry Bones; Beside an Open Fireplace; Imagine; On a Blue and Moonless Night; Just Think of Me Sometime; The Gentleman Awaits; Missouri Scrambler; Roses Are Forget-Me-Nots.

O'SHEA, CATHY
See Herbsleb, Catherine

OSKAR, KERI CHRISTINE   ASCAP 1975
composer, author
b Sacramento, Calif, Mar 14, 53. Collaborated with rock group War & Lee Oskar, 71-78, now free-lance writer. Chief Collabr: Lee Oskar. *Songs:* More Than Words Can Say; Haunted House; Lyrics: The Way We Feel; Starkite; Sing Song; San Francisco Bay.

OSSER, ABE ARTHUR (GLENN)   ASCAP 1955
composer
b Munising, Mich, Aug 28, 14. Educ: Univ Mich, BMus. Arr for dance bands, incl Bob Crosby, Les Brown, Charlie Barnet & Bunny Berigan. Arr & asst cond, Paul Whiteman, staff cond, ABC, 47-68. Arr & cond on albums with Georgia Gibbs, Roger Williams, Johnny Mathis, Vic Damone, Jerry Vale, Della Reese, Tony Bennett & Robert Goulet. Music dir, "Miss America Pageant," 55- Comp original music for TV, films, commercials & concert band. Chief Collabr: Edna Osser, wife. *Songs:* Music: Ah Yes, There's Good Blues Tonight; Look at Her; Miss America, You're Beautiful; Roseanne; Travelin' Freedom's Road. *Instrumental Works:* Jet Out of Town; Carol; Young Man With the Blues; Beguine for Band; Seascape; Studio One; Hiawathaland; Music for a Summer Night; Holiday for Winds; Bandolers; Tango for Band; 'Beguine' Again.

OSSER, EDNA   ASCAP 1948
composer, author, producer
b New York, NY, Apr 26, 19. Educ: Brooklyn Col. Writer & producer, radio & TV commercials; wrote spec material for radio, TV & records. Lyricist for "Miss America Beauty Pageant." Chief Collabrs: Marjorie Goetschius, Glenn Osser (husband), Les Brown. *Songs:* I Dream of You; I'll Always Be With You; Heavenly; There You Go; The Last Time I Saw You; Ah Yes, There's Good Blues Tonight; Can I Canoe You Up the River; You're Different; Roseanne; Jet Out of Town; Carol; Young Man With the Blues; Comes the Sandman; Look At Her; Miss America, You're Beautiful; What Every Woman Knows.

OSSEWAARDE, JACK HERMAN   ASCAP 1965
composer, organist
b Kalamazoo, Mich, Nov 15, 18. Educ: Kalamazoo Cent High Sch; Univ Mich, BMus, 40, MMus, 41, studied organ with Palmer Christian, comp with Percival Price; Union Theol Sem Sch Sacred Music, 45-47, studied organ with David McK Williams, comp with Harold Friedell & Normand Lockwood; pvt comp with Leo Sowerby. Organist & choirmaster, Calvary Episcopal Church, New York, 47-53 & Christ Church Cathedral, Houston, Tex, 53-58; prog annotator, Houston Symph Orch, 55-58; dir music, organist & choirmaster, St Bartholomew's Church, New York, 58- ASCAP Awards, 70-71 & 72-73. Fel, Westminster Choir Col, 79; assoc, Am Guild of Organists. *Songs:* Anthems: Sing We Merrily; Magnificat and Nunc Dimittis in C; Draw Us in the Spirit's Tether; A Paean of Praise; Carol of the Stork.

OST, ROBERT S (JERRY ROBERTS)   ASCAP 1977
composer, author
b Philadelphia, Pa, Mar 11, 51. Educ: Univ Pa, BA(Eng). Began writing plays, age 15; plays at Annenberg Ctr, Univ Pa, Clark Ctr for Performing Arts, New York & play "Breeders," Nat Theatre, New York, 79. Songwriter, musical "Dogwoods Don't Bite," 73, cabaret show "Three Part Invention," 78 & cabaret singers. Guest, Edward Albee Artist's Found musical "Finale," Bway, 81. Chief Collabr: Jerrold Fisher. *Songs:* If Christmas Isn't Love; Lyrics: Simple Holiday Joys; A Christmas Suite.

OSTERLING, ERIC ALFRED   ASCAP 1956
composer
b West Hartford, Conn, Mar 21, 26. Educ: Hall High Sch, Conn, 44; Ithaca Col, BS, 48. Dir music, pub schs, Portland, Conn, 48- Many comp & arr publ for concert band. Chief Collabrs: John Cacavas, Frank Erickson, James Ployhar. *Instrumental Works:* Bandology; Scandinavian Fantasy; Thundercrest; Totem Pole; Folk Leider Fantasy; Winds on the Run; Showstopper; Charter Oak; Caribbean Celebration; The Nutmeggers; Questar; Sunburst; Blue Mist; Beguine for Flutes; Brass Brilliante; Samba for Flutes; Christmas Ballet; Costa Brava; Overture in C Minor; Trilogy; March of the Madcap Marionettes; Scarlet Hurricane; First Symphony; Nocturne for Winds; Nordic Overture; LeSabre.

OSTROW, HERBERT RAY   ASCAP 1955
composer, author
b Philadelphia, Pa, Mar 28, 11; d. Educ: Temple Univ. Dir, Concert Artists, Inc; mgr of Michel Piastro, violinist; with Melomusic Publ; booking agent, Japan & Far East, 51. Chief Collabrs: Roger King Mozian & Clark McClellan. *Songs & Instrumental Works:* The Black Cat (El Gato Negro); Scotch Heather; Blue Dream.

OSTROW, SAMUEL   ASCAP 1959
author
b Methuen, Mass, Apr 28, 19. Educ: Everett High Sch, Mass; Northeastern Univ; studied aeronautical eng. Worked in credit dept, Sears, Roebuck & Co, 25 yrs. In the consumer loan dept, Shawmut Bank of Boston. Writer musical, "Fourteen Carat Fool." Chief Collabr: Gordon Vanderburg. *Songs:* Lyrics: The Fortune Hunter; Fourteen Carat Fool; It's in the Stars; I'll Always Remember; A Thousand Dreams Ago.

OSTRUS, MERRILL
See Staton, Merrill

OTT, JOSEPH HENRY   ASCAP 1964
composer, teacher, publisher
b Atlantic City, NJ, July 7, 29. Educ: Comp for dance with Louis Horst; comp, Hans Sachssee, Munich, Ger & William Happich, Philadelphia, Pa; Univ Conn, BA; Univ Calif, Los Angeles, MA, Roy Harris. Instrumental comp of concert music & vocal & electronic media. Works have been performed in many univs & cols, also by many orchs & concert bands in US. First Am to win first prize in the Premio Citta di Trieste Int Symph Comp Competition, 63. Comn from performers & musical orgn; first comp to present an all electronic concert at the Nat Gallery of Art, DC. *Instrumental Works:* Suite for Eight Trombones; Toccata for Brass Quintet; Solosforhorn (horn, electronic tape); Africotta II (concert band); Palo Duro (concert band); Premise for Orchestra; Extensions (symph orch, tape); Matrix IV (piano trio); Timbres (brass quintet, electronic tape).

OTTESEN, MILTON F   ASCAP 1964
composer, author, teacher
b Tromso, Norway, Oct 2, 20. Educ: NY Univ, BS, MA. Served, USAF, World War II. Taught, State Univ Col, New Paltz, NY, fac fel. *Songs:* Sleep, Sleep, Jesus; Long Ago Near Bethlehem.

OTTO, ELEANOR   ASCAP 1967
composer, lyricist, dancer
b Rochester, NY. Educ: Rochester, AB; Columbia Univ; Juilliard Sch Music; Manhattan Col Music; Colo Col, Colorado Springs; Hanya Holm Dance Sch. Author, "The Brass Instruments of the Orchestra: How to Start"; three vols poetry, "Winged Rhapsodies", "To the Stars" & "Dreams Lights." Mem: Am Guild of Musical Artists; Composers, Authors & Artists of Am; The NY Poetry Forum (exec bd); Mark Twain Asn of NY; Shelley Soc of NY; Ill State Poetry Soc; Am Women Composers. *Songs & Instrumental Works:* Forsythia; The Song of the Mountain; America, We Love You; Christmas Kindness; One of Your Peers; Forever.

OTTO, HENRY CHRISTIAN   ASCAP 1961
composer, author
b Nuremberg, Bavaria, Sept 28, 03. Journalist & authority on political science; instructor.

OTTO, INGA   ASCAP 1962
composer, author
b Leipzig, Ger, Mar 1, 36. *Songs:* Follow Me; China Surf; Rubino.

OTTO, JOSEPH FRANCIS (ART FRANCIS)   ASCAP 1953
composer, author, publisher
b Buffalo, NY, May 8, 1889. Educ: St John's Parochial Sch, grad; Columbia Univ, pre-med, grad, PhD(music); studied music with Jon Gartland of John Philip Sousa's Band, 4 yrs; studied cornet & trombone under Jay Fay. Soloist, Arthur Pryors Band, 4 yrs. Served in 32nd Div, 213th Aero Squadron, WW I. Appeared in vaudeville; wrote spec material; founded two publ cos. Owner, The Francks Music Publ. Chief Collabrs: Fred Fisher, Jack Meskill, Billy Faber, Frank Magine. *Songs & Instrumental Works:* Frances, Darling Frances; The Beginning of the End; An Old-Fashioned Waltz; To Have, to Hold; You Cried in My Dream Last Night; Mediterranean Lady; I Like to Squeeze Tomatoes ('Cause I Love Tomato Juice); March: Hail to the Legionnaire; To the Fore; Topside; Our National Commander; Issues and Answers.

OTVOS, A DORIAN   ASCAP 1923
composer, author
b Budapest, Hungary, Oct 11, 1890; d Los Angeles, Calif, Aug 25, 45. To US, 21. Educ: Ferencz Liszt Acad of Music, Budapest. Wrote songs & musical comedy scores in Hungary. Wrote for films, also songs for "Greenwich Village Follies" & "George White's Scandals." *Songs:* Tinkle Tune; In the Spring; Love's Sweet Hour; Stars and Moonlight; Yvette; Sailing on the Nile. *Scores:* Bway Stage: Paradise Alley.

OTVOS, RUSSELL EMERY   ASCAP 1976
composer, author, singer
b Chicago, Ill, July 30, 54. Educ: Self-taught; Maine South High Sch, Park Ridge, Ill. Began writing folk music at age 15, later full rock music; recorded album in 75-76, played all instruments; currently working on new album & musical play; singer, pianist, guitarist, bassist & drummer. *Songs:* The Rearrangement; Cool Air; Silver Chain; The Flood; Babe; Shy.

OVANIN, NIKOLA LEONARD   ASCAP 1962
composer, teacher, conductor
b Sisak, Yugoslavia, Nov 25, 11. Educ: Cleveland Inst Music, BM(comp), 39, studied with H Elwell; Western Reserve Univ, BS(music educ), 41, studied with A Shepherd; Hamline Univ, BA & MA(comp), 47, studied with E Krenek; Eastman Sch Music, PhD(comp), 69, studied with H Hanson. Popular dance music performer & arr, age 16-26. Began to compose in late teens. Taught music in schs & cols, USA, 41-77. Cond choral groups, bands & orchs from elementary level to prof level, 41- Received awards for original works, 38, 42, 48, 54, 66, 75 & 79. *Instrumental Works:* Suite (Pleiades; full orch, 7 movements); Dusk (woodwinds, horns, harp & strings); Elegy (small orch); Poem (string orch); Prelude Moderne (concert band); Four Pieces (elem string orch); One Hundreth Psalm (SATB); Hatikvah (orch, also concert band version); Cherubim (trio for violin, viola, piano); The Supreme Miracle (chorus & chamber orch, NEA grant, 79); Sorta Fun (tonal scenario full orch); Third Symphony (Toys; youth symph); Essay One (full orch); Flute Suite (flute, string orch & orch bells, 3 movements); also chamber works, choral works, art songs, piano comps & instrumental educ materials.

OVERALL, ZAN   ASCAP 1960
composer, author
b Henry, Ill, June 11, 26. Educ: Lake Forest Univ; George Washington Univ; Northwestern Univ. Played string bass with Skinny Ennis & others. Owner & supervisor of own music copying serv in Los Angeles. *Songs:* Falling; Love Has Come, Love Has Gone.

OVERGARD, GRAHAM T   ASCAP 1943
composer, author, conductor
b Allen County, Kans, Oct 9, 03. Educ: Ithaca Col, BM; Univ Ill, BS; Capital Col Music, MusD; hon LLD, Ferris State Col. Dir music, Ala Mil Inst, 25-30; instr, Univ Ill, 30-37; prof music educ, Wayne State Univ, 37-68. Dir bands & NBC broadcasts, Nat Music Camp, Interlochen, 31-38, New York World's Fair, 38 & 64; dir, Detroit City Band, 44. Awarded Diamond Medal, Am Fedn Musicians; First Hons, Nat Sch Band Contests, 36, nat judge, 37-67. *Songs & Instrumental Works:* Ballad Bravura (march paraphrase); The Circus (ballet, eleven movements); Side Show, Cody's Cowboys; The Force of Freedom; Fanfare and Fable (march paraphrase); The Peace Corps Song; Fighting Bull Dogs; Motor City Parade; Irish Parade; The Blue and the Gray; Chicago Bears, March On; The Falcons; A Summer Holiday; A Winter Holiday; Gridiron Heroes; Circus Suite No 1 (pageantry); Circus Suite No II (nostalgia); Circus Suite No III (center ring); Oriental Parade.

OWEN, HARRY (ROBERT)   ASCAP 1925
composer, author, director
b O'Neil, Nebr, Apr 18, 02. Educ: St Ignatius Col, grad high sch, 20; Loyola Univ, Los Angeles, grad, 24. Conducted own orch throughout western states; to Hawaii, 34; formed own orch, Royal Hawaiians, toured US & Can, 37-38. To Hollywood, featured in & wrote songs for var films incl "Cocoanut Grove" & "Song of the Islands"; own TV show, CBS, 12 yrs. *Songs:* Sweet Leilani (Academy Awards 37); Linger Awhile; To You Sweetheart Aloha; Hawaiian Paradise; Sing Me a Song of the Islands; Blue Shadows and White Gardenias; Dancing Under the Stars; Hawaiian Hospitality; Hawaii Calls; Let's Go for Broke; Voice of the Tradewinds; Lei Aloha; Maui Girl; O-ko-le Ma-lu-na (Bottoms Up); Princess Poo-poo-ly Has Plenty Papaya; Hula Breeze;

Syncopated Hula Love Song; Palace in Paradise; If Your Aloha Means I Love You; Maunaloa; Take It Easy By Slow; Cool Head Main Thing; Do Unto Others; Little Butch; Timmy; Melinda; Hawaii My Island; Menehune Lullaby; O'Brien Has Gone Hawaiian; Beneath a Banyan Tree; Down Where the Tradewinds Blow; Singing River; Lyrics: My Isle of Love.

OWEN, HELEN
See Bilby, Helen Owen

OWEN, MARY JANE (JENNIE M BROCKWAY)   ASCAP 1963
composer, author
b Mecca, Ohio, Nov 19, 1886; d. Educ: Bus col; pvt music study. *Songs:* Old Fashioned Christmas.

OWEN, RICHARD   ASCAP 1967
composer, author
b New York, NY, Dec 11, 22. Educ: Dartmouth Col, BA; Harvard Univ, LLB; Manhattan Sch of Music, comp with Vittorio Gianinni. Opera comp; Wrote numerous songs to poems. *Songs:* Poems set to Music: The Road Not Taken (Robert Frost); The Hill Wife (Robert Frost); Patterns (Amy Powell). *Songs & Instrumental Works:* Dismissed With Prejudice; A Moment of War. *Scores:* Operas: Mary Dyer (3 acts); A Fisherman Called Peter (1 act); The Death of the Virgin (1 act).

OWENS, D H (TEX)   ASCAP 1955
composer, author, singer
b Kileen, Tex, June 15, 1892; d New Baden, Tex, Sept 9, 62. Educ: High sch. Known as "Radio's Original Texas Ranger"; singer-guitarist, CBS, 10 yrs; also KMBC, Kansas City, 10 yrs. *Songs:* Cattle Call (Eddy Arnold theme); Red Roses Bring Memories of You; Love Me Now; Give Me a Home on the Lone Prairie; Bow Down Brother; Life's Evening Sun; December the 25th Day; With Jesus You Will Win; The Cowboy Call; Shall We All Be Together Up There; When the Savior Comes; Indian Call.

OWENS, DOROTHY
See Fotinakis, Dorothy Owens

OWENS, JACK MILTON   ASCAP 1942
composer, author, singer
b Tulsa, Okla, Oct 17, 12. Educ: Wichita High Sch E, Kans, glee club soloist, studied music theory, harmony & appreciation with Thurlow Lieurance. Sang & played, sch affairs & parties & on Radio KFH, Wichita. Worked on Chicago Radio Stas. Vocalist, Ted Weems & Hal Kemp Orchs. Sang on Breakfast Club, Radio NBC, 2 yrs & nightclubs in Calif. Songwriter, 40- Headliner, Statler Hotels & Decca Records. *Songs:* The Hut Sut Song; Hi Neighbor; The Hukilau Song; By-u, By-o (Louisiana Lullaby); I'll Weave a Lei of Stars; I Love You More, More Every Day; The Luau Song; I Dood It; The Kid With the Rip in His Pants; Lyrics: How Soon?; Cynthia's in Love.

OWENS, MARGARET ANN   ASCAP 1978
composer, author, singer
b Anniston, Ala. Started writing songs at early age; grew up singing & playing guitar; entertained at concerts, nightclubs & mil bases, US, Europe & UK. Recording artist. *Songs:* Alabama Lady; Country Pickin' Singin' Fool Like Me; You're Gonna Love Me; Waitin' On You, Babe; Kansas Back to Nowhere; Meet Me 'Round the Block By Ten; You Never Got to Know Me; Joker Saloon; Here It Comes Again; North Carolina Country Girl; Song for Hoss; Tangled Up and Torn; Songs on the Radio; Hound Dog Jack; Waiting.

OWENS, ROCHELLE   ASCAP 1973
composer, author, playwright
b Brooklyn, NY, Apr 2, 36. Educ: New York Pub Schs; New Sch Social Res; Yale Sch Drama, fel film-making; studied with Stanley Kaufman. Author, many controversial plays, eight books of poetry & three collections of plays, several of which are incl in "The Best Short Plays" series. Produced plays throughout the world & presented at fests in Edinburgh, Berlin, Paris & Avignon. Feature-length film, "Futz." Recipient, Guggenheim, Yale Sch Drama, CAPS, Rockefeller & NEA fels. Founding mem, New York Theatre Strategy. Sponsor, Women's InterArt Ctr Inc. Mem, Dramatists Guild & Author Guild. Chief Collabrs: Galt MacDermot, George Quincy. *Songs & Instrumental Works:* The Joe 82 Creation Poems (theatre piece with music & words); The Joe Chronicles Part 2 (selections performed in solo with mountain Dulcimer); Shemuel (selections performed in solo with flute). *Scores:* Play: The Karl Marx Play.

OWENS, TERRY WINTER   ASCAP 1968
composer, harpsichordist, teacher
b New York, NY, Aug 13, 36. Educ: City Univ NY, BA(music), 57; studied piano with Lisa Grad, comp with Ralph Shapey. *Instrumental Works:* Fünf Kompositionen für Altblockflöte; Adagio for Recorder and Piano; Nocturne (piano); Confetti (piano); Caprice (piano).

OWSLEY, B BRISTOW   ASCAP 1961
composer, author
b Paducah, Ky, Mar 13, 1882; d Los Angeles, Calif, Nov 23, 67. Educ: Pub & pvt shcs; New York Sch of Graphic Art. Mgr, Swift & Co, Chicago. Chief

Collabrs: Victor Herbert, Frank Westphal. *Songs:* The Island of Sweet Sixteen; Yours; Play Me an Old-Fashioned Waltz; Rock-a-Bye Baby, There in the Manger; Baby Bunting Lullaby; A Song Feast of Spirituals.

OWSTON, CHARLES EDWARD (SNAKE)   ASCAP 1978
composer, author, singer
b Braddock, Pa, July 29, 42. Ky Christian Col, AB, 65, BTh, 67. With band, The Tempests, 60-63. Entered Christian ministry, 65-76, performed as gospel & folk singer. Formed Fannin St Blues Band, 76; publ first song, 77. Performed with group Rockabilly, 79-80. *Songs:* Mysterious Lady; My Daddy Was an Outlaw; Midnight Queens; Rockin' at the Midnight Grill; Rattlesnake Woman; Outlaw on the Run; Heroin Lady; Down Home Southern Fried Rock 'n' Roll; Home Fried Blues; Springtime; Vampire Eyes; Autumn Afternoon; Indian Summer Daydream; Goodbye, Amy; Neon Nightmare.

OYSHER, MOISHE   ASCAP 1956
composer, author, cantor
b Bessarabia, Mar 7, 08; d New Rochelle, NY, Nov 27, 58. Educ: European schs. Cantor as youth. Singer & actor, stage & films; gave concerts. *Songs:* Amar, Amar; H'Alevey; I Love This Land; Oh, My Mamma. *Scores:* Films: Singing in the Dark.

P

PABLO, JUAN
See Sifler, Paul John

PACE, DAVID ALLEN   ASCAP 1979
composer, author, singer
b Hammond, Ind, Sept 20, 54. Educ: Russellville High Sch, Ala; scholarship in Ikard. Artist & writer, Muscle Shoals Music Asn. Owner & operator, Morrilou Records; owner, publ co, Keep Up the Pace Music. *Songs:* Don't Give Up Love; When Will They Learn; Losin My Love to You; Respond to Me; One Mistake Is All It Takes.

PACE, PAT (PASQUALE) JOSEPH   ASCAP 1979
composer, pianist
b Akron, Ohio, Feb 19, 30. Educ: Juilliard Sch, grad, 50 (scholarship), studied piano with G Tracey, comp with V Persichetti, choral with R Shaw & improvisation with Leonid Hambro; studied with R Mann, Harold Miles, Kent, orchestration with Lane & master class with Nadia Boulanger. Began piano studies with Rena Wills; first recital, age 10; in jazz & improvisation, 45- Performed with Cleveland, Akron & Atlantic Symphonies, & as soloist of own works. Performed, jazz concerts with own quartet & solo, throughout Ohio; comp, pvt teacher. Comn from Akron Symph & Cleveland Chamber Music Soc. Chief Collabr: Louis Lane. *Songs:* Music: Lusty Angel; Son of Firebird; The Good Apple; Minor Yours?; Devil's Dance; Lullaby for Adam Sorcerer; The Crow's Flight; The Ally; The Warrior; & other jazz tunes. *Instrumental Works:* Concertino for Piano and Orchestra; Music for Winds (woodwinds, brass, perc); Quintet (comn, Cleveland Chamber Music Soc, flute, clarinet, bassoon, bass, piano); Piano Sonata; Piano Improvisations; Three Movements for Piano with Orchestra. *Scores:* Film/TV: Feeling Fine, The Story of Pat Page (7 awards).

PACE, THOMAS M   ASCAP 1976
composer, author, singer
b Boise, Idaho, Jan 13, 49. Educ: Pocatello High Sch; Idaho State Univ, 2 yrs; studied piano with Evelyn McLeod, 12 yrs & Cecil Simmons, 5 yrs. With bands, The Strangers, 65-69, Thom Pace & the Turning Point, 68-71, Thom & Dave, 71, Thom Pace Band, 74-79. Wrote music & lyrics for "Life and Times of Grizzly Adams," 74. Has been writing, singing & recording albums, 74- Chief Collabr: Maria Hegsted Pace. *Songs:* Maybe; Belong to Someone; Don't Kid Yourself; Waiting for Their Time.

PACK, LORENZO
composer, author
b Detroit, Mich, Aug 24, 16. Educ: Univ Mich. Won Golden Gloves championship, 33-35; prof boxer, 35-41. Chief Collabrs: Sammy Gallop, Ray Leveen. *Songs:* I Bet You Do; Are You Foolin'?; Petootie Pie; Chance of a Lifetime; You Must Be Blind; Five Times Twice; Once a Year; Gonna Trade My Saddle; Be a Sweetheart; Nowhere Guy; Peek-a-Boo; Talk to the Lord.

PADELLAN, IRENE H
See Higginbotham, Irene Evelyn

PADGETT, STEPHEN THOMAS   ASCAP 1973
composer, author, singer
b Fullerton, Calif, Oct 6, 53. Educ: Biola Col, Calif, BA, 77; studied voice with Christopher Beatty, 73-76. Writer, singer, recorded with Shiloh; with The Padgett-Klingberg Band, 80- Chief Collabr: Paul Klingberg. *Songs:* Hole in My Britches; Wear Your Burden.

PADILLA, MARIO RENE   ASCAP 1978
composer, author, pianist
b Detroit, Mich, Oct 4, 49. Educ: High sch & col; rhythm & perc, Albert (Rags) Anderson, 58-62; comp & theory with Marcel Padilla, 69-; Ohio State Univ, BS(orchestration, piano), 71; orchestration & arr, Ken Harrison, 74- Played piano & perc in var jazz groups. Began writing songs, 70. Wrote original musical score for plays, "A Rainbow in the Night," 77 & "Richard III," 78, Hollywood Ctr Theatre, Los Angeles; stage comp-pianist, "Suicide in B Flat," The Odessey Theatre, Los Angeles, 79; percussionist, "Angel City," Los Angeles Production, 80; completed ballet for Los Angeles Ballet Co. *Songs:* Give It Up; Looking Back; Don't Stop; Because of You; I'm in Love With a Stranger; Lady Show Biz; Old Promises; Queen of the Night. *Instrumental Works:* Thanks for Nothing/Images: After Midnight (jazz orch). *Scores:* Ballet: La Giungla; Harbinger of Evolution.

PADWA, VLADIMIR   ASCAP 1955
composer, author, teacher
b Krivyakino, Russia. Educ: Imperial Cons, Petrograd, Russia; Hochschule für Musik, cert, Berlin, Ger; State Cons, dipl(Reifezeugniss), Leipzig, Ger, studied with Ferruccio Busoni; hon DMus, Thiel Col, 78. Founder & fac mem, State Cons, Tallinn, Estonia. World concert tours; accompanist to Mischa Elman, 34-40, Zino Francescatti & others. Co-founder & mem of First Piano Quartet, 41-50. Fac & head of piano dept, New York Col of Music, 45-67. Assoc prof, NY Univ, 67- Awards: Madrigal Soc, Peabody, Accademia Int Di Roma. *Instrumental Works:* Symphony in D; String Symphony; Concerto in the Form of Variations for Two Pianos With String Orchestra; Electric Rag. *Scores:* Ballet: Tom Sawyer; Opera: Compartment No 7.

PAGAN, RICARDA   ASCAP 1978
composer, author
b Aguas PR, June 5, 19. Songwriter, 66- *Songs:* Navidad Triste; Ritmo Navidemo; Sin Corazon Vivir; Porque; No Me Ilusiones.

PAGE, JAMES PATRICK   ASCAP 1975
composer, author
b Heston, Eng, Jan 9, 44. Began as a session musician, London, mid-sixties; became one of the leading mem of band, The Yardbirds. Founded & lead guitarist of band, Led Zeppelin; producer of all Led Zeppelin albums & writer of original material for group. Chief Collabrs: Robert Plant, John Baldwin, John Bonham. *Songs:* Good Times Bad Times; Dazed and Confused; Communication Breakdown; Whole Lotta Love; Thank You; Heartbreaker; Living Loving Maid; Immigrant Song; Since I've Been Loving You; Black Dog; Rock and Roll; Stairway to Heaven; The Song Remains the Same; Over the Hills and Far Away; Dancing Days; D'Yer Mak'er; No Quarter; Trampled Under Foot; Kashmir; In the Light; Ten Years Gone; Night Flight; Achilles Last Stand; Nobody's Fault But Mine; Candy Store Rock; In the Evening; Fool in the Rain.

PAGE, NATHANIEL CLIFFORD   ASCAP 1940
composer, arranger, editor
b San Francisco, Calif, Oct 26, 1866; d Philadelphia, Pa, May 12, 56. Educ: Pub & pvt schs; studied theory with Edgar Stillman Kelley. Wrote stage scores; music ed, Oliver Ditson Co, Carl Fischer, Theodore Presser; taught orch, Columbia Univ, 20-28. Life mem, Nat Asn Am Comp & Cond. *Songs & Instrumental Works:* Contest of the Nations; Old Plantation Days; also cantatas.

PAGE, PAUL
See Brown, Paul D

PAGE, PAUL F   ASCAP 1976
composer, teacher, singer
b San Francisco, Calif, Aug 6, 47. Educ: St Patrick's Col, Calif, BA(philosophy); San Jose State Univ, BA(music, sec teaching credential). Taught high sch, Calif, 7 yrs. Music dir & organist, St Lucy's Church, Calif, 14 yrs. Music ed, Resource Publ, Saratoga, Calif, 8 yrs & producer, arr & dir, var albums, 8 yrs. Ed & publ "Gather Round" & "Gather Round, Too," 76-77. *Songs:* With Songs of Gladness; Simple Gifts; Picture the Dawning; Look for the Savior; Come, My Friend; Each One's Joy; Blest; Music: Six for Song; Donde Hay; Blessing.

PAGE, RAYMOND EDISON   ASCAP 1969
composer, author
b Waxahachie, Tex, Feb 23, 29. Educ: Sunset High Sch; Southern Methodist Univ, studied piano with Annette Walsh. Pianist, nightclubs; recording artist, Atlantic Records, record producer & musical arr, 59. Wrote & produced own comp, also for other writers. Chief Collabr: Mary Popplewell. *Songs:* Heart Full of Tears; The Best Friends Money Can Buy; Just in Time for Christmas; The Only Thing; How Softly a Heart Breaks; It's a Cryin' Shame. *Instrumental Works:* The Downtown; Kon-Tiki; Navajo Rock; Lay the Good News on Me; The Best of My Life (Just Slipped Away); Iron Bar Hotel; Green Eyed Monster; I Pretend You're Coming Back (But I Know You Never Will).

PAGENSTECHER, BERNARD (JAMES BREDT)   ASCAP
composer
b New York, NY, Apr 2, 07. Educ: Taft Sch, grad, 25; Yale Univ, BA(harmony, comp, piano), 29. Studied piano, 5 yrs. Songwriter for Jr Follies, 37. Mgr, incl print, radio & TV, Young & Rubicon Inc, 45-67. Writer, score for "Sure Sign

of Spring," 57-58. Chief Collabrs: Edward Eager, Tony Tanner, Don Reid. *Songs:* The Face of Love; It's Almost Too Good to Be True. *Scores:* Off-Bway show: Happy Hypocrite.

PAICH, DAVID FRANK   ASCAP 1963
composer, author, arranger
b Burbank, Calif, June 25, 54. Educ: Univ Southern Calif. Played piano, age 8, singer at age 14; pianist for "Ironsides." Formed Toto, 78; two gold albums to date. Recording artist, Columbia Records. Chief Collabrs: Marty Paich, Boz Scaggs & Cher. *Songs:* Lowdown; Lido Shuffle; Georgie Porgie; 99; Prisoner; Hold the Line; Houston (I'm Coming to See You); Girl Goodbye; Hydra; Got to Be Real; The Way I Am; It's Over; What Can I Say; Light the Way (Emmy Award); I'll Supply the Love; Rock Maker; Mama; All Us Boys; White Sister; St George and the Dragon; Manuela Run; Child's Anthem.

PAICH, MARTIN LOUIS   ASCAP 1953
composer, arranger, pianist
b Oakland, Calif, Jan 23, 25. Educ: San Francisco State Univ; Cons Music & Art, Los Angeles, MA(music comp); Univ Southern Calif; Chapman Col; Calif State Col; studied with Mario Castelnuovo-Tedesco. Pianist/cond for Peggy Lee. Arr for Frank Sinatra, Sammy Davis, Jr, Ella Fitzgerald, Andy Williams, Ray Charles, Lena Horne, Andre Previn, Jack Jones, Bing Crosby, Anita O'Day, Al Hirt, Mel Torme, Dinah Shore, Dean Martin, Mahalia Jackson, Astrud Gilberto, Glen Campbell, Antonio Carlos Jobim & others. USAAF band leader, WW II. Chief Collabrs: David Paich, Paul Francis Webster. *Songs:* Money Girl; Music: Light the Way. *Instrumental Works:* Gray Flannel; Suze Bluze; Color It Brass. *Scores:* Film/TV: Yogi Bear Motion Picture; The Swinger; Lady and the Tramp.

PAIGE, FRANCES
See Sukman, Frances Paley

PAIGE, ROGER   ASCAP 1957
composer, author, musician
b Astoria, NY, Mar 18, 28. Educ: High sch; pvt sch. Sang on radio. Musician in dance bands. Chief Collabrs: Leo Talent, George Arlotta, Danny Hurd. *Songs:* What Should a Teen Heart Do?; Please Daddy.

PAISLEY, WILLIAM MERRELL   ASCAP 1941
composer
b Hamburg, Ark, Aug 6, 03; d. Educ: Univ Ark, BA, also Sch Music. Dir, Music Libr, NBC, New York. *Songs:* Razorback Rootin' Song; Just Like You; Beautiful Dreams; Write Home to Mother; Razorback Pep Song; La Carumba; I Sing; Dust on Your Picture; Once I Heard a Song; In Old Rincon; Do Ya S'pose; How Do I Know?

PALAD, GELSA
See Paladino, Gelsa Theresa

PALADINO, GELSA THERESA (GELSA PALAD)   ASCAP 1977
composer, author, teacher
b New York, NY, Nov 2, 44. Educ: Performing Arts High Sch, New York; Los Angeles Valley Col; studied songwriting with Buddy Kaye; ASCAP Workshop; SRS; Dick Grove's Music Sch. Prof singer in US, Can & Mex, 26 yrs; movie actress & songwriter; teacher, SRS; performer in clubs & records independently. Chief Collabrs: Roger Kellaway, Michael Kohl, Doug Thiele, Bent Myggen. *Songs:* I Am Music; I Never Lied to You; You're Leavin' Me; Who Were You?; Far Away.

PALANGE, LOUIS S   ASCAP 1953
composer, conductor, arranger
b Oakland, Calif, Dec 17, 17; d Burbank, Calif, June 8, 79. Educ: Studied comp with father, also with Dr Brecia, Wesley La Violette. Led own band, 33-35; clarinetist in Oakland Municipal Band, bassoonist with Oakland Civic Symph. Comp, arr & asst cond, Los Angeles Co Band; arr & musician for film studios & radio. Arr for Werner Janssen Symph, 36-42. WW II, USN; comp & cond, USO shows, also "Anchors Aweigh," radio, San Diego, Calif. Comp, documentary films, DC. Musician, TV shows incl "Hallmark Playhouse" & "Dragnet," 46-62; also wrote for films. Cond, Beach Cities Symph, 6 yrs, Sons of Am Legion Band, 10 yrs, Redondo Beach Symph, Hollywood Am Legion Band & Los Angeles Philh Band. Founder, dir, West Coast Opera Co. *Songs & Instrumental Works:* A Pair; Brass Woodwind Clique; Navy Forever; Jazz Rhumba; Driftwood; Southern Four; Intrigue; Evangeline (tone poem); Romantic Piano Concerto; Symphony in Steel; 2nd Violin Concerto; Overture Domesticania; Campus Bells (overture); Sunset Strip Polka; Queen of Hearts; The Southern Four; Intrigue; Palanges Little Italy; Pan American Fiesta; A Shadow of a Fortress; Beginning of Time (suite, tone poem); Hollywood Panorama (tone poem); Snow Race; Hollywood Wolf; Story of London Bridge; Park Bench Serenade; The Piedpiper; Five Cops on a Beat; The Real Cool Fazool; Little Sir Echos, Echo!; Boy Scouts Jamboree; Saxolo; So Much More (trombone solo); Danzon Bolero; Fan Fares for Introductions and Presentations; Dizzy Fingers (accordion & band); Stella By Starlight; Dutch Dances; Marches: Sons of the American Legion; 50th State Salute; Imbroglio (symphonic); Honor and Dignity; March of the Day; Bicentennial USA; Violin & Band: Zigeunerweisen; Valse Bluette; Saxophone Solo: Valse Vanite; Valse Erica;

Harlem Nocturne; Vocal Arr: Un Bel Di; Seguedille; Si Mi Chiainano Mimi; In Quelle Trine Morbide; Arietta; Una Voce Poco Fa; Caro Nome; Adeles Laughing Song; Vissi Darte; La Danza; Voi Lo Sapete; Othello's (finale solo); Othello and Desdemone (1 act duet); Othello and Jago (2nd act duet); Othello Ave Mario (3rd act); Othello Credo; Romance. *Scores:* Films: My Japan; Midnight; Iwo Jima; Voice of Truth; Radar; 954 or Guam; Dark Venture; Juvenile Delinquent.

PALEY, HERMAN   ASCAP 1914
composer, publisher, radio executive
b Moscow, Russia, Apr 5, 1879; d Los Angeles, Calif, Nov 4, 55. Educ: City Col New York, BA; Columbia Univ, studied with David MacDowell; NY Cons, studied with Alexander Lambert & Jacob Danielson; also studied with Edward Kilenyi & Carl Hambitzer. Teacher, NY high schs, 2 yrs. Staff comp with music publ; then publ exec. Organized entertainment unit touring camps in Europe, WW I. Dir music shows, New York Stage Door Canteen, WW II. Talent scout, test dir & comp, Fox Films, 30-32. Radio exec & mgr, Artists Bur, Mutual Broadcasting Co, 33-45. Went to Hollywood, 45; motion picture agent & comp. One of the organizers of ASCAP. *Songs:* Everybody Gives Me Good Advice; Cheer Up, Mary; Just a Little Fond Affection; Is It Warm Enough for You; A Friend of Mine Told a Friend of Mine; How Could You; Deutschland; There's Not Enough Gold to Buy Him; When a Poor Relation Comes to Town; I'd Love to Have You Love Me Just As Much As I Love You; Ain't You Glad You've Come Home, Mary; Why Don't You Answer, Dearie; May Fuzzy; Everybody Likes the Girl I Like; Keep on Smiling; I Couldn't Make a Hit With Molly; I'm the Man Who Kept Her Waiting At the Church; If Somebody Loved Me; I'd Like to See You Get Along; I'll Teach You How; Don't Go Away; Welcome Home; And More Yet Besides; My Little Kangaroo; Angel Eyes; Don't Kill the Goose That Lays the Golden Eggs; Listen to That Jungle Band; You Ain't Got the Girl Til the Ring Is on Her Finger; What Good Is Water When You're Dry; Say But It's Lonesome, Kid; Sonny; Lucky Boy; You Can Tell Her Anything Under the Sun (When You Get Her Under the Moon); The Whisper Song; When the Pussy Willow Whispers to the Catnip; Tannenbaum; Blueberry Lane; Bachelor Life; Hello; Howdya Do; Dolores; Havana; Springtime Brings Roses and You; If You Promise to Behave; Love Me With Your Big Blue Eyes; When You're in Love With Someone Who's Not in Love With You; I Like You Just the Same; Jungle Glise; Billy; Lize, Lize, Lize I Know Another Lize Just Like You; Hawaiian Love Song; You Can Bet Your Life I Would; Little One; Yawning; Whose Heart Is He Breaking Tonight; I Like You Just Because You're Not Like Anyone Else I Know; I Miss Him All the Time; Every Night You'll Find Her Painting New York Town; Think It Over; And Then; The Parisian Ball; All Aboard That Ocean Baby; Amorita; Broadway; I Should Have Met You a Long Time Ago; Oh Mrs Fortune Teller Please Find My Lovin' Man; On the Boat That Sails Next Wednesday; Poor Little Rich Girl; Say Goodbye to Gay Paree; Providing; Beautiful Eggs; Bingen on the Rhine; She's Going Mad; Georgie; What Did Romeo Say to Juliet; When It's Night Time Down in Burgundy; Sweetest Girl in Monterey; There's One California for Mine; What Would You Do for Fifty Thousand Dollars; Dancing the Jelly Roll; I Didn't Raise My Dog to Be a Sausage; I Want You; Just You; Twilight of Love; Sweet Little Buttercup; Cheer Up Father; Cheer Up Mother; Outside; Come Back to Arizona; Don't Cry Dolly Grey; I Wouldn't Steal the Sweetheart of a Soldier Boy; Mother She's Good Enough to Vote With You; I Can Hear the Ukuleles Calling Me; Parisienne Walk; Sail on to Ceylon; She's Good Enough to Be Your Baby; Down South Everybody's Happy; Be Yourself; The Song the Moonlight Sang to Me; I'd Love to Live the Old Days Over; Love Is the Same; Texas Never Seemed So Far Away; There's Nothing Left to Say Except Goodbye; When He Took a Look in His Little Red Book; Feather Bed Lane; Golden Sands of Waikiki; It Must Be You; Found at Last; Long Ago; Silver Song Bird; Goodnight Night Owl; Two Eyes of Brown Are Looking Blue; Oh, What I'd Give to Bring You Back; I Can't Believe the Tales of Hoffman.

PALLADINO, RALPH FRANCIS (RALPH DINO)   ASCAP 1971
composer, singer, musician
b Philadelphia, Pa, Apr 26, 38. Educ: Logan Sch Music; Dale Levin & Artie Singer. Singer, nightclub performer, voice & percussion in TV & radio commercials; recording artist, 20th Century Fox, Date, Columbia & A&M. Album producer, comp, poet, lyricist, comedy, concert & TV performances. Chief Collabrs: John Sembello, Leiber & Stoller, Hugo Montenegro, Larry Di Tommaso. *Songs:* Viva Max March; Don't Turn Back; Paula's Theme; Pearl's a Singer (top ten Eng); Dancing Jones; One More Lie; Best Thing; Midnight Lovers; See the Light; Sweet Lady; Words; Only Yesterday; Jug of Wine; Who Would Ever Think That I Would Marry Margaret; Somebody You Love. *Albums:* Dino and Sembello.

PALLARDY, THOMAS PATRICK   ASCAP 1972
composer, author, teacher
b St Louis, Mo, Nov 26, 47. Educ: Presentation Sch, 61; Mercy High Sch, St Louis, 61-65, dipl(honor roll); St Louis Univ, 65-66; St Louis Inst of Music, 66; Southern Ill Univ, BMus(educ), 68. Began playing music, 57, professionally, 59. While in col, started song writing, 67. Taught music, grade schs, 69-75. To Nashville, 75; writer, co-writer, producer, publ & arr; performer, clubs, TV & radio; recording artist. Chief Collabrs: Mike Anthony, Judy Mehaffey, Sharon Tricamo, Betty Gallup, Caroline George. *Songs:* You Bring Out the Best in Me; After Every Goodbye; I'll Be There; The Lackadaisy Song Music: Champagne From a Paper Cup; Songwriter's Blues.

PALLOCK, RUTH   ASCAP 1972
composer, author, teacher
b Los Angeles, Calif, Sept 1, 26. Educ: Roosevelt High Sch, studied with Anita Priest; Los Angeles City Col, studied with Mr Peterson. Began at 5 yrs old, played solo harmonica & sang on radio station KYER. Entertainer, songwriter, radio performer, incl own children's prog "Auntie Ruthie Someone Cares." Writer for Learning Systs, sing-along bks for schs & many works for country western, gospel, popular music for var media. Organist & accordian player. *Songs & Instrumental Works:* You're Walking Down Sunshine Lane (Sunshine Lane); O Lord You Made the Rainbow; No One Ever Told Me; Tenderly Jesus Loves You (lullabye); Someone Somewhere Needs a Prayer; Someone Cares About You; Dear Lord (Can You Tell Me); Wait for the Lord; My Little Girls, or Boys First Christmas; Just One More Time; My Little Cowboys Song; Call Me If You Need Me; O Lord Remember Me; When You Pray God Will Answer; When You Dream At Twilight; In the Mornin' Time; Ask the Lord; High on a Mountain Top; Tell Me; Happiness Is Loving the Lord; Come Home, Come Home to God; If I Could Know; Come to the Chapel; Jackalena Polka; She Prayed to God and Then She Made Some Chicken Soup.

PALLOTTA, LORRAINE   ASCAP 1963
composer
b Chicago, Ill, Mar 8, 34. Educ: High sch. *Songs:* I Think of You.

PALMER, BISSELL B   ASCAP 1946
composer, author
b New York, NY, Feb 4, 1889; d. Educ: NY Univ Col Dentistry. Capt, AEF, WW I. Pres, New York Acad Dentistry, 23-25 & Am Col Dentists, 33-34. Attending oral surgeon, Polyclinic Med Sch & Hosp, 29-40 & Flower & 5th Ave Hosp, 30's. Pres, Group Health Insurance Inc, 48-62; chmn bd, Group Health Dental Insurance Inc. Pres, William J Gies Found; vchmn, Wagner Col Develop Council. Chief Collabrs: Mana Zucca, Helmy Kresa, Tibor Serly, Paul Weiner, Victor Young, Mart Freiberg. *Songs:* Head on My Pillow; I Do; One God; Be the Good Lord Willin'; Today Is Mine; Little Patch O' Land.

PALMER, JACK   ASCAP 1926
composer, author
b Nashville, Tenn, May 29, 1900; d Waterbury, Conn, Mar 17, 76. Educ: Christian Bros Col. Worked in father's piano store, wrote spec material for local shows. Went to NY, pianist in clubs. Staff writer for music publ firms. Wrote songs for revues, incl "Ziegfeld Follies", "George White's Scandals" & "Earl Carroll's Vanities." Wrote for films & nightclub acts. Chief Collabrs: Harry Woods, Marty Symes, Willard Robison, Spencer Williams, Jimmy Cavanaugh, Dick Sanford, Little Jack Little, Teddy Powell, Hughie Prince, Cab Calloway. *Songs:* Everybody Loves My Baby; I Found a New Baby; Jumpin' Jive; Silver Dollar; Boogit; Geechy Joe; 920 Special; Sentimental Baby; Juke Box Jive; 'Taint Me; I'll Take the South; Don't Tell a Man About His Woman; Dream Street; You Dreamer, You; Love Doesn't Grow on Trees; I Love to See the Evening Sun Go Down; It All Begins and Ends With You; Are You Making Believe You Love Me?; Hi-De-Ho Man; Oh, My Achin' Heart; Are You All Reet?; Let's Go Joe.

PALMER, SOLITA BIRDENIA   ASCAP 1958
composer, author, singer
b Kansas City, Kans, Dec 10, 05. Educ: Kansas City Grade & High Schs, piano & harmony; pvt study voice with Marjorie Rose Ryan; Chicago Musical Col, voice with Eduardo Sacerdoti, 2 yrs; voice with Robert Hosea, New York, 2 yrs; studied ballet with Madame Mikalova, New York, 2 yrs; comp, New York. Musical shows, New York. Clubs, Atlantic City, New York, Philadelphia, Detroit. Worked with Jimmy Durante, Ben Bernie, Billy Rose & others. Radio soloist, WOR & WJZ. Movies, Paramount, Warner Brothers, Fox & Independent. Recordings for Brunswick & Radio Transc. Wrote official march, "Little League," used in 10 little league films. Wrote music scores for 35-40 documentary films. Chief Collabrs: Emerson Yorke (husband), Gene Lockhart. *Songs:* It's Christmas; Music: This is Baseball; Tangoroa (intermezzo, E flat). *Scores:* Film: Our Heritage.

PALMER, WILLARD A, JR   ASCAP 1962
composer, author, accordionist
b McComb, Miss, Jan 31, 17. Educ: Millsaps Col, BS; Univ Houston. Mem concert trio; has given concerts; cond workshops with William Hughes Jr. Pvt music instr, Univ Houston, 47- Coauth, "Palmer-Hughes Accordion Courses."

PALMER, WILLIAM J   ASCAP 1955
composer, author
b LeRoy, Minn, Aug 20, 1890. Educ: Univ Minn; Univ Southern Calif, BA, JD. Began law practice, 13. Jurist. Judge, Superior Court, Los Angeles, 30 yrs, retired. *Songs & Instrumental Works:* Choral: The Lord Is My Shepherd; I Love the Night.

PALUMBO, CAMILLE MARIE (JEAN MARIE EVANS)   ASCAP 1977
composer, author, singer
b Boston, Mass, Feb 8, 30. Educ: New Eng Cons of Music (voice & piano); Emerson Col (acting, dir & scriptwriting); Boston Col, BA(journalism); voice scholarship, Maria Pardo Calvarese, Boston & Christina Garden Mem; studied with Frederic Mario Fiorello. Soprano soloist with Boston Symph Orch, Boston

Pops, People's Symph, Willis Page Chorale & European concert tour. Performed, radio & TV; appeared, Bway & off-Bway shows & in films incl cameo role in "Roseland"; journalist. *Songs:* New York, the City of the Future; Crazy 'Bout Our Yankee's Team; Goggomobile (TV commercial); What Is Music? (taped, illustrated narrative for children).

PALUMBO, JOHN   ASCAP 1975
composer, author, singer
b Steubenville, Ohio, Jan 13, 51. Educ: Marshall Univ, studied psychology. Formed & wrote all the material for Crack the Sky; author of film "Ruby and Me" & novel "Never Finished High School." Chief Collabrs: Sal Anzalone, John Vasil, Rick Witkonski. *Songs:* Ice; Surf City; She's a Dancer; Hot Razors in My Heart; Nuclear Apathy; All American Boy. *Albums:* Innocent Bystander; White Music; Crack the Sky; Animal Notes; Safety in Numbers; Live Sky.

PANCOAST, ASA (ACE)   ASCAP 1952
composer, author, organist
b Philadelphia, Pa, Jan 14, 05. Radio staff organist, Philadelphia; with "American Bandstand," Dick Clark shows. Head teaching dept, Lowrey Organ Studios, Philadelphia; teacher.

PANDEL, TED (PRAXITELES)   ASCAP 1958
composer, author, pianist
b McKeesport, Pa, Jan 30, 35. Educ: Juilliard Sch Music (scholarship), studied with Beveridge Webster. Won youth & adult auditions, Pittsburgh Concert Soc. Had debut, Carnegie Hall, 63. Has given concerts with symph orchs; appeared on TV. Chief Collabr: Bruce Haack. *Songs:* Satellite; I Like Christmas; Seashell. *Scores:* Stage background: The Kumquat in the Persimmon Tree.

PANDOLFO, JOSEPH   ASCAP 1977
composer, author, violinist
b New York, NY, July 28, Educ: Grammar & bus sch, 06-12; pvt violin studies, New York, 08-14. Prof violinist, var restaurants, New York, 17; recital violin soloist, appearances in hotels & concert halls. Staff violinist, radio station, New York; concert & orch leader, 30-35; songwriter. *Songs:* All Things New. *Instrumental Works:* Duo for One Violin; In a Moonlit Garden (violin); Italian Serenade (piano); Indian Moon (piano).

PANICO, FRANK PORKY   ASCAP 1959
composer, author, trumpeter
b Chicago, Ill, June 23, 24. Educ: High sch. First trumpeter & arr, WBBM, 20 yrs. Arr for vocalists & performers. A&R dir, record co, 3 yrs. *Songs:* Andrea; Francesque; More Brothers; Sunny and Cool; Vic's Boogie.

PANKOW, JAMES CARTER
composer, musician
b St Louis, Mo, Aug 20, 47. Educ: Quincy Col, Ill, 65-66; DePaul Univ, 66-68. Mem musical group, Chicago, 67- *Songs:* Make Me Smile; Colour My World; Feeling Stronger Every Day; Just You 'n' Me; Old Days; I've Been Searchin' So Long.

PANTANO-SALSBURY
See Salsbury, Ronald Foster

PAPAI, RAY ANDREW   ASCAP 1975
composer, author, teacher
b South Bend, Ind, Dec 15, 32. Educ: Ind Univ, BA; Northwestern Univ, MA; studied clarinet with Clark Body, Henry Gulick & Jerome Stowell, bassoon with Leonard Sharrow, flute with Don Peck, Walter Kujala & Ernest Liegel, oboe with Ray Still & Darrel Stubbs, orchestration & comp with Thomas Beversdorf, Bernard Heiden & Jean Martinon. Extra woodwind, Chicago Symph, Lyric Opera, Indianapolis Symph, Bolshoi Ballet, Kirov Ballet, Royal Ballet & Am Ballet. Teacher, Triton Col, Northeastern Univ & Mich Univ, Interlochen. Performer, NBC, ABC, CBS, WGN-TV & WTTW-TV. Musical dir, Mill Run Theater, Arlington Park Theater, Contemporary Arts Quintet, Chicago Chamber Music Ens & Nirvanova. Pres, Ultra-Nova Publ & Records, Inc. Artist, Columbia, RCA & Vox Records. Chief Collabr: Pam Purvis. *Songs & Instrumental Works:* Lonely Love; Once Upon a Spring; Love Touches All; New Child; Power Comes From Within; Our Happiness in Love; Seeds of Papai; Take My Hand; Pick a Papai; The Reason We Love; Changing Clouds; Love Groove.

PAPARELLI, FRANK   ASCAP 1962
composer, author, pianist
b Providence, RI, Dec 25, 17; d Beverly Hills, Calif, May 24, 73. Educ: Brown Univ, BA. Pianist in dance orchs; also soloist, nightclubs. Comp, writer & arr, music publ. Ed, Leeds Music. Appearances on TV. Writer of musical commercials; also teacher. Chief Collabrs: Raymond Leveen, Dizzy Gillespie. *Songs & Instrumental Works:* Polonaise in Boogie; Night in Tunisia; Blue 'n' Boogie; Petootie Pie; Ooh Oooh, My My, Oh Oh!; Kind Treatment; Music books: Eight to the Bar; The Blues; Two to the Bar; Boogie Woogie for Little Fingers; Four to the Bar.

PAPPALARDI, FELIX ALBERT, JR
composer, producer, arranger

b New York, NY, Dec 30, 39. Educ: Diller-Quaille Sch Music; High Sch Music & Art; NY Univ, baroque & pre-baroque counterpoint; Univ Mich Sch Music, studied cond with Maynard Klein; also with Hans T David. Instrumentalist on many albums, 63-64. Production, The Youngbloods & Cream, awarded Platinum Record, first in recorded music history. Producer-leader, bass, lead singer & writer, Mountain Production, Hot Tuna & The Dead Boys. Two solo albums as vocalist, A&M. Musical dir & comp NBC series, "Hot Hero Sandwich." Chief Collabr: Gail Collins. *Songs:* My Lady; Music: Nantucket Sleighride; Mississippi Queen; Strange Brew; World of Pain; Show Your Love; Busy Dreamin'; Pride and Passion; The Laird; One Last Cold Kiss. *Songs & Instrumental Works:* Still Theme from Weekend World.

PAPPALARDI, GAIL COLLINS
composer, author   ASCAP 1968

b Baltimore, Md, Feb 2, 41. Educ: St John's Col, Md; tutored in music history & theory by Felix Pappalardi. Lyricist for Cream; comp & lyricist for Mountain; co-producer & writer for Japanese band Creation; production assoc, Double Dose; asst to musical dir, "Hot Hero Sandwich," hour series, Emmy Winner, NBC. Chief Collabs: Felix Pappalardi, Leslie West. *Songs:* Summer Days; Lyrics: Nantucket Sleigh Ride; World of Pain; Strange Brew; Pride and Passion.

PAPPIN, MALCOLM C
composer, author, arranger   ASCAP 1967

b Albany, NY, Feb 9, 25. Educ: Albany High Sch, NY; Ill Wesleyan Univ, BMus; State Univ NY, Albany, MSc(sch admin). Musical dir, San Diego Starlight Theatre & San Diego Adult Sch Productions; comp/arr/dir, Hudson Valley Community Col. Bandleader, Adj Gen Corps, USA. Comp/arr, Chargers, Rams, Giants & Packers. Arr, Cabaret Theatre, San Diego. Trumpeter with Gordon McRae, Don Ho, Wayne Newton & others. Col lect, Musical Creativity. *Songs & Instrumental Works:* Let's Have Music (choral); Our Summer Romance (choral); Blessed Is Thy Holy Name (religious/choral); Panorama (orch bk); YBarra Band Book; Tiajuana Trolley; March Miniature; Gigue; Mysterioso; Dorian Daybreak; The Phantom Trumpeter; A Modern Mass (sacred); And Away We Go; Taco Taco.

PARCHMAN, GEN LOUIS
composer, arranger, lecturer   ASCAP 1960

b Cincinnati, Ohio, May 2, 29. Educ: High sch; Cincinnati Cons, BM & MM; Tanglewood, studied with Kirshner, Copland & Foss. Musical arr, Phyllis Diller, Gene Krupa & symph orchs; bassist, Cincinnati Symph Orch; pianist, Bankers Club, Cincinnati. Has received comns from Cincinnati Symph Orch, George Gabor, Univ Ind, Miami Symph Orch, St Paul Symph, San Francisco Symph, USM Band & Jazz/Rock Symph Maynard Ferguson. Symphonic composer & popular song composer; author of bk "Tomorrow Always Comes"; lectr, Univ Cincinnati. Chief Collabr: Librettist, Dallas Wiebe. *Songs:* Day-Dream Me; The Kiddle of Your Love; Children's Song; In a Yesterdaze; I've Met Barbra; Soft Fluid Nights; Cheerful Santa Claus; Birthday Song; All My Flaws of Yesterday; I'm Snow Blind; Roll On; Leonore; All My Senses. *Instrumental Works:* 5th Symphony for Reduced Orch; 3rd Piano Concerto; Concerto for Soprano and Orchestra; History of Music (narrator & orch); Symphony for Chorus and Orchestra; 3rd Violin Concerto; also 7 symph perc ens & 2 concertos for perc ens & orch.

PARENTE, SISTER ELIZABETH
composer, educator   ASCAP 1957

b Cambridge, NY. Educ: Georgian Court Col, studied with Prof Thompson; New York Col Music, with Leslie Hodgson; Cath Univ; also studied with William Pollack. Superior & head music dept, Villa Victoria Acad, Trenton, NJ, 45- Choir, piano, voice & organ teacher. Led choir on radio & TV; gave annual concerts. Mem: Trenton Symph Bd; NMEA; MCMEA; Cath Broadcasters Asn. *Songs & Instrumental Works:* Sunrise (arr of Serenade of the Roses); Ave Maria (for centenary of Our Lady of Lourdes); Waltz With Me; Silver Waters; Sunbeams; Fairyland Waltz; Frolic; Mitzie's Rendezvous; Mass in Honor of Our Lady of Victory.

PARISH, MITCHELL
composer, performer, author   ASCAP 1929

b Shreveport, La. Educ: NY Univ, BA (Phi Beta Kappa); Tusculum Col, DLit; Univ Charleston, DHL; elected to Songwriters Hall of Fame. Staff writer for music publ. Author bk "For Those in Love" (verse). Served apprenticeship as song plugger, special material; writer for stage & screen. Chief Collabrs: Hoagy Carmichael, Duke Ellington, Peter DeRose, Frank Perkins, Leroy Anderson, Sammy Fain, Glenn Miller, Will Hudson. *Songs:* Lyrics: Stardust; Deep Purple; Stars Fell on Alabama; Hands Across the Table; Syncopated Clock; Ruby; Stairway to the Stars; Sophisticated Lady; The Lamp is Low; Moonlight Serenade; Does Your Heart Beat for Me?; Organ Grinder's Swing; Sweet Lorraine; Take Me in Your Arms; One Morning in May; Sentimental Gentleman From Georgia; Volare; Emaline; Cabin in the Cotton; Sleighride; Blue Tango; Serenata; All My Love; Blue Skirt Waltz; Don't Be That Way; Let Me Love You Tonight; The Starlit Hour; Belle of the Ball; Corrine Corrina; Sidewalks of Cuba; Sophisticated Swing; Mr Ghost Goes to Town; The Scat Song; Who Blew Out the Flame?; Lilacs in the Rain; The Moon Is a Silver Dollar; Lazy Rhapsody; Riverboat Shuffle; Angel; Tzena Tzena Tzena; Dream

Dream Dream; Ciao Ciao Bambino; My Window Faces the South; Turn Back the Clock; You Excite Me; Blue September; I Hear America Singing; Blues Serenade; Mademoiselle de Paris; The Blond Sailor; Christmas Night in Harlem; The White World of Winter; Forgotten Dreams.

PARISSI, ROBERT W
composer, producer, singer   ASCAP 1972

b Steubenville, Ohio, Dec 29, 50. Educ: Jefferson County Tech Inst, Steubenville. Singer & guitarist with Bobby Vinton, age 14, 2 yrs. Formed group Wild Cherry; writer under Terry Knight, Brown Bag label, 3 yrs. Songwriter, signed with CBS. *Songs:* Play the Funky Music (White Boy); Hold On; I Love My Music; Don't Wait Too Long; Sitting Alone.

PARK, STEPHEN
composer, educator   ASCAP 1963

b Austin, Minn, Sept 23, 11. Educ: Univ Nebr, BA; Univ Mich, MM; studied with Ross Lee Finney; Berkshire Music Ctr; Aspen Music Ctr, with Darius Milhaud. Teacher & high sch principal, Nebr pub schs, 29-36. Fac mem, Univ Mich, Lincoln Col, 3 yrs. Assoc prof music & comp-in-residence, Univ Tampa, 39- Pres, Fla Comp League; state chmn, Fla Fedn Music Clubs, 48-51. Charter pres, Tampa Philh Asn, 52-53. Mem: Nat Asn Am Comp & Cond; Music Teachers Nat Asn; charter mem, Southeastern Comp League. Minister music, Univ Christian Church, Tampa. *Instrumental Works:* Pastorale for Flute, Strings; Pavanne for Two Violins, Piano; Teaching pieces: Toboggan Ride; Trees; Shadows; Holiday; There Was a Crooked Man; At the Ballet.

PARKER, ALICE
composer   ASCAP 1955

b Boston, Mass, Dec 16, 25. Educ: Smith Col, BA, 47; Juilliard Sch Music, MS, 49; Hon DMus, Hamilton Col, 79. Arr, Robert Shaw Chorale, 48-67. Self employed comp & cond; pvt teacher; workshops, sem & master classes, Meadowbrook, Aspen & Blossom Fest Schs, 67-73, also at cols, univs, prof orgn, civic & church groups. Chief Collabr: Robert Shaw. *Songs:* Songs for Eve; Echoes From the Hills; Of Irlaunde. *Songs & Instrumental Works:* Cantatas: Commentaries; Journeys: Pilgrims and Strangers; Gaudete; The Day-Spring; Melodious Accord; The Time of Ingathering; A Serman From the Mountain; An Easter Rejoicing; Children, Saints and Charming Sounds; Choral Suite: There and Back Again; Love Songs; Phonophobia; A Play on Numbers; Psalms of Praise. *Scores:* Opera: The Martyrs' Mirror; The Family Reunion; Singers Glen; also many publ arrangements of folk songs, hymns, carols & spirituals.

PARKER, DOROTHY
author   ASCAP 1961

b West End, NJ, Aug 22, 1893; d New York, NY, June 7, 67. Educ: Miss Dana's Sch; Blessed Sacrament Convent. On staff, "Vogue," 16-17; drama critic & on staff, "Vanity Fair," 17-20. Taught at Los Angeles State Col. Free-lance writer; wrote bk reviews for "Esquire." Rec'd O'Henry short story award, 29. Author of volumes of verse: "Enough Rope"; "Sunset Gun"; "Death and Taxes"; "Collected Poems-Not So Deep As a Well." Also short stories: "Laments for the Living"; "After Such Pleasures"; "Here Lies." Collected works, "The Portable Dorothy Parker." Co-auth of plays: "Close Harmony"; "The Coast of Illyria"; "Ladies of the Corridor." Wrote songs for Bway musical, "Candide." Mem, Nat Inst Arts & Letters. Chief Collabrs: Ralph Rainger, Leonard Bernstein, Jack King. *Songs:* I Wished on the Moon; Gavotte; How Am I to Know?.

PARKER, HELEN K
composer, author

b Waimea, Hawaii, Aug 1, 1889; d Nanakuli, Hawaii, July 30, 54. *Songs:* Akaka Falls; Hilawe Falls; Ka Lei Hoohie (Fascinating Lei); Maunaia Kikala Nui; Flowers of the Sea (Kai Puu A'o Makapala); Kai Pii Ao Makapala; Kaua Kikoni Ili; Kuu Aloha Mauna Lei; Lani Kuhonua; Maikai Waimea; Haaheo Eka Wai Pili Ili; Mauna Loa; Olu O Puulani; Ka Le Hoohie Hula.

PARKER, HORATIO WILLIAM
composer, educator   ASCAP 1934

b Auburndale, Mass, Sept 15, 1863; d Cedarhurst, NY, Dec 18, 19. Educ: Studied with John Orth, Stephen Emery & George Chadwick; Royal Col, Munich, studied with Josef Rheinberger; hon MusD, Cambridge Univ, Eng. Became organist, choirmaster; taught counterpoint, Nat Cons, NY. Organist, Trinity Episcopal Church, Boston. Prof music, Yale Univ, 1894. Cond, New Haven Symph. Mem, Am Acad Arts & Letters. *Songs & Instrumental Works:* Dream-King and His Love (cantata); Hora Novissima (oratorio); Mona (opera; Metrop Opera prize); Fairyland (opera; Nat Fedn Music Clubs prize); Concerto for Organ, Orchestra; Star Song; Ca'hal M'or of the Wine-Red Hand; Adstant Angelorum Chori; A Wanderer's Psalm; The Legend of St Christopher; 7 Greek Pastoral Scenes; The Morning and Evening Service (Episcopal Church); Union and Liberty.

PARKER, JOHN CARL
composer, conductor   ASCAP 1960

b St Paul, Minn, Oct 15, 26. Educ: High sch. Led own jazz group, 40's & 50's. Arr for dance orchs, incl Benny Goodman & Bob Crosby. Comp, cond, arr & trumpeter, radio & TV, "Arthur Godfrey Show," music dir, 67- Comp & cond TV: "Gunsmoke"; "Medical Center"; "Cannon"; "Then Came Bronson";

"Police Woman"; "Police Story"; "SWAT"; "The Rookies"; "Love Boat"; "How the West Was Won"; "Dallas"; "CHIPS"; "Trapper John, MD." Comp & cond feature films: "The Man Who Died Twice"; "Darker Than Amber"; "The Glitter Palace"; "Secrets of Three Hungry Wives"; "Strange Homecoming"; "Secret Night Caller"; "Cutter's Trail"; "The Further Perils of Laurel and Hardy"; "Laurel and Hardy-Laughing 20's"; "Corky"; "Witches' Brew." Songs: Bum Deedle Um Bo; Little Jimmy From Texas; The Pity Pot; Verlie Mae; I'm Leaving; Cinderella Jones; I Remember Louis; Who Am I?; Witches' Brew.

PARKER, JONATHAN (JOHNNY) — ASCAP 1956
composer, author, singer
b New York, NY, May 12, 22. Educ: James Monroe High Sch. Vocalist with dance bands, incl Les Brown, Les Elgart, Gene Krupa, Hugo Winterhalter, Charley Ventura and others. Featured in nightclubs, TV & radio. Capitol Records & Coral Records. Chief Collabrs: Carl Sigman, Roy Alfred. Songs: Baby Sittin' Boogie; Tra La La; I Wanna Love You; Can't Seem to Laugh Anymore; The Way I Feel. Songs & Instrumental Works: Keep it Movin'; Nothin' to Do; With This Pen; Just Plain Struttin'; Ooh, How I Love Ya; They Remind Me of You; I Will Still Love You; Alphabet Rock; Jackie, My Darlin'; A Lot in Common; There I Was in Love.

PARKER, LINDA MARLOWE
See Marlowe, Linda R

PARKS, ANNE RAIFORD — ASCAP 1967
composer, author
b Atlanta, Ga, June 29, 35. Educ: Bass High Sch; Ga State Univ, 2 yrs; Newspaper Inst Am, studied with Jack B Cherwin, dipl. Secretarial free-lance writer with "The Atlanta Times", "Georgia Mag", "Atlanta J-Constitution Mag" & "The Lutheran Standard." Chief Collabr: John C Stedman.

PARKS, GORDON
director, author, composer
b Ft Scott, Kans, Nov 30, 12. Educ: Md Inst, AFD; Kans State Univ, LittD, 70; St Olaf Col, HHD, 73; hon degrees: Fairfield Univ, 69, Boston Univ, 69, Macalester Col, 74, Colby Col, 74 & Lincoln Univ, 75. Photographer, FSA, 42-43, OWI, 44, Standard Oil Co, NJ, 45-48 & Life Mag, 48-72. Color & black & white consult, motion picture productions, US & Europe, 54- Writer, producer & dir "The Learning Tree." Dir movie "Shaft", "Shaft's Big Score", "The Super Cops" & "Leadbelly." Ed dir, Essence Mag, 70-73. Author "A Choice of Weapons" (autobiography), "A Poet and His Camera", "Whispers of Intimate Things", "Born Black", "In Love", "Moments Without Proper Names", "Flavio" (Christopher Award for Outstanding Biography) & "To Smile in Autumn" (autobiography). Mem: Urban League of New York, Nat Assoc for Advancement of Colored People, Newspaper Guild, Asn Comp & Dirs Guild (nat dir), Dirs Guild NY & Am Soc Mag Photographers. Awards: Rosenwald Fel, 42-43, Frederic W Brehm Award, 62, Syracuse Univ Sch Jour, 63, Am Soc Mag Photographers, 63, Nat Coun Christians & Jews, 64, Philadelphia Mus Art, 64, NY Art Dirs Club, 64-68, Univ Miami, 64, Carr Van Anda Jour Award, Ohio Univ, 70 & Spingarn Award, NAACP, 72. Instrumental Works: Piano Concerto; Tree Symphony; 3 piano sonatas; modern works for piano & wind instruments.

PARKS, RICK — ASCAP 1976
composer
b Wheeler, Tex, Nov 12, 45. Educ: McMurry Col, Abilene, Tex, BS(music); Hunter Col, New York, MA(music), studied cond with Clayton Westermann; Mannes Col of Music, studied comp with Frederick Werle, NY Univ. Performed with BAFFA Symph Orch, Bayport, NY. Choirmaster & organist, Aldersgate Methodist Church, Abilene, Tex, Wynnewood Presby Church, Dallas, Tex & Bethany Reformed Church, New York. Instrumental Works: What Is This Lovely Fragrance? (organ prelude); Abide With Me Still; Organ arr: Overture to Die Meistersinger (Wagner); Promenade (Moussgorsky); Entrata in D major (Karg-Elert).

PARMAN, CLIFF — ASCAP 1951
composer, author
b London, Ky. Educ: High sch. In USN, WW II. Trumpeter & arr with dance orchs incl Henry Busse & Lawrence Welk, then arr for singers incl Eddy Howard, Al Morgan, Joni James, J P Morgan, Damita Jo & Connie Francis. Songs: Pretend; Where the Red Roses Grow; It Took a Dream to Wake Me Up; Sands of Gold; Our Love Affair; After School; Abernathy's Serenade.

PARMENTIER, C A J
composer, organist
b Belgium. Educ: Studied with bro, Firmin; Univ Philotechnique, Brussels. Concert perf in Holland, Belgium & Eng. Came to US, 16. Performed with Melchiore Mauro-Cottone, Paul Whiteman, Eugene Ormandy & Frank Black, 20's. Theatre organist, silent films. Organist debut, Capitol Theatre, 22. Presided at dual consoles of Largest Wurlitzer Theatre Organ, with Richard Leibert, Radio City Music Hall Opening, 32. Featured in numerous organ recitals, some on radio, late 30's. Organist, Waldorf-Astoria Hotel, New York; perf at important functions, New York Americana, Hilton & Plaza Hotels. Songs & Instrumental Works: Fifteen Compositions Written for the Silent Movies; Supplication; Pastorale; Edward Grieg Album; Adoration; Deep River; Sunset

in Damascus; Chant Triste; Desert Caravan; Arr: Over the Rainbow; Knightsbridge March (Eric Coates); Stranger in Paradise; Menuet (Beethoven); Theme From Love Story; The Lost Chord (A Sullivan); 'S' Wonderful; Second Hungarian Rhapsody in a 1920 Classical Jazz (Franz Liszt).

PARNELL, LEE ROY — ASCAP 1979
composer, author
b Abilene, Tex, 21, 56. Worked, clubs & studios in Dec New York, Nashville, Muscle Shoals, Ala & Tex. Formed own band, The Roy Parnell Band, 79. Songs: Texas Fever; Show Bizness; Catch a Train; Can't Stop Runnin'; Everybody Gets the Blues.

PARNES, PAUL — ASCAP 1958
composer, author
b New York, NY, Jan 25, 25. Educ: NY Sch Printing; Sch Am Music. On staff, Golden Records, 4 yrs; writer of special material, TV incl "Yogi Bear", "Mr Ed", "Dennis the Menace" & "The Flinstones." Song writer for TV shows, "Captain Kangaroo", "Sesame Street" & Sesame Street Records. "Stories of the UN" & "Hans Christian Andersen Stories." Chief Collabr: Paul Evans. Songs: We Three Believe in Safety; Quick Draw's A-Comin' to Clean Up This Town; Piano Tuner's Tango; Autumn Rain; I Could Conquer the World; Happiness Is (Kent commercial); Our World; A Child's Introduction to French (16 songs); A Child's Introduction to Spanish (12 songs); Feelin'; The Last Happy Song; The Next Step Is Love; The Masterpiece (theme); Disneyland Daddy.

PARRIOTT, JAMES DEFORIS — ASCAP 1976
composer, author, writer
b Denver, Colo, Nov 14, 50. Educ: Univ Denver, BA, 72; Univ Calif, Los Angeles, MFA(film), 74. Staff writer, Universal TV, 75. Producer, "Bionic Woman", 76. Supv producer, "Incredible Hulk," 78. Supv producer/writer, movie for TV, "The Legend of the Golden Gun," 78. Producer/writer, "Nick and the Dobermans," 80. Chief Collabrs: Joseph Harnell, Jerrold Immell. Songs: Friends; Lyrics: Lisa's Song; Moonbeam's Song.

PARRIS, HERMAN M — ASCAP 1953
composer
b Russia, Oct 30, 03; d Philadelphia, Pa, Jan 14, 73. Educ: Philadelphia Cons; Jefferson Med Col, MD. Physician & surgeon in pvt practice, Philadelphia. Served, USA, World War II. Songs: Blue Roses; All the Love in the World. Instrumental Works: Suite for Violin and Viola; Fantasy for Quintet; Woodwind Minatures; Suite for Piano and Strings; Four Etchings for Orchestra; Violin Concerto; Hebrew Rhapsody for Large Orchestra; Hospital Suite; Suite for Trumpet and Strings; Symphony No 1, 2, 3 & 4; Nocturne and Burlesca for Bass, Clarinet and Piano; 29th Psalm of David (orch, women's voices); Break, Break, Break (voice, orch); Three Preludes for Piano; Brass Quartet; Rhapsodies for Brass Ensemble; Solitude (piano).

PARRISH, AVERY — ASCAP 1959
composer, pianist, arranger
b Birmingham, Ala, Jan 26, 17; d New York, NY, Dec 10, 59. Educ: Pub schs, Birmingham; A H Parker High Sch, grad, 32; Ala State Teachers Col, studied music with Willis Lawrence James. Pianist for & toured with Bama State Revelers. Pianist & arr with original Bama State Collegians, which became Erskine Hawkins' orch. Songs & Instrumental Works: Because of You; So Tired; After Hours; Blackout.

PARSONS WILLIAM — ASCAP 1959
composer, singer
b Crossville, Tenn, Sept 8, 33. Educ: High sch. Singer in nightclubs & on TV throughout US. Songs: All American Boy.

PASATIERI, THOMAS — ASCAP 1968
composer
b New York, NY, Oct 20, 45. Educ: Juilliard Sch Music, BMus, 65, MS, 67, DMus, 69. Mem fac, NC Sch Arts, Siena, Italy, 67, Juilliard Sch, 67-69 & Manhattan Sch Music, 69-71. Teacher, master classes throughout the US. Recipient var prizes, fels, grants & awards. Artistic dir, Atlanta Civic Opera, app 80; distinguished vis prof, Cincinnati Col Cons, app 80. Songs: Over 600 songs & song cycles, incl: Three Poems of James Agee; Heloise and Abelard; Rites de Passage; Day of Love; Three Sonnets From the Portuguese; Far From Love. Scores: Operas: The Trysting Place; Flowers of Ice; The Women; La Divina; Padreivia; The Penitentes; Calvary; The Trial of Mary Lincoln; Black Widow; The Seagull; Signor Deluso; Ines de Castro; Washington Square; Before Breakfast; Three Sisters; The Goose Girl; Music for Bway Production: Romeo and Juliet.

PASCAL, JEFFERSON
See Wilde, Cornel L

PASCAL, MILTON H — ASCAP 1940
author
b New York, NY, Jan 21, 08; d. Educ: City Col New York, BA; Columbia Univ, LittB. Wrote spec material for vaudeville & films. Chief Collabrs: Phil Charig, Dan Shapiro. Songs: Swing Low, Sweet Harriet; I Wanna Get Married; Twelve

O'Clock and All Is Well; Gotta Go to Work Again; Call It Apple Fritters; Waitin' for a Street Car; Santo Dinero; Running a Temperature.

PASCALE, PALMA ANNE   ASCAP 1977
composer, author, singer
b Brooklyn, NY, Nov 1, 50. Educ: Hofstra Univ, BA(music, magna cum laude), Phi Beta Kappa; Manhattan Sch Music, studied films & commercials with Heywood Morris; Eastman Sch Music, studied arr with Manny Albam & Ray Wright. Cond, Hofstra Drama & Grey Wig Productions, 70-76; studio singer & pianist; pres, comp-lyricist, Pasland Music Publ Co; two-time winner, Am Song Fest. Adj asst prof songwriting, Adelphi Univ. Featured vocalist on "Songs That Tickle Your Funny Bone." Chief Collabs: Gary Portnoy, Charles Calello. *Songs:* Love Me for What I Am. *Scores:* Bway Show: What the Hell, Nell; Bachelor Buttons.

PASCOE, RICHARD W   ASCAP 1938
author, singer
b Penzance, Eng, Dec 5, 1888; d Detroit, Mich, Dec 23, 68. To US, 07. Educ: Thorne's Abbey Sch, Penzance. Mem vocal group, Red Apple Club, WJR, Detroit; introduced own songs. Was realtor, 11-68. Chief Collabs: Monte Carlo, Alma Sanders, H O'Reilly Clint, Will Dulmage. *Songs:* That Tumble Down Shack in Athlone; Little Town in the Ould County Down; Faded Love Letters; That Dear Old Mother of Mine; When It's Night Time in Nevada; Tenderly Think of Me; Holding Hands; I Like to Go Back in the Evening; If I Were a Rose in Your Garden.

PASKMAN, DAILEY   ASCAP 1922
author, producer
b Philadelphia, Pa, July 24, 1897; d. Educ: Columbia Univ; Philadelphia Cons; studied with Alfred Robyn. Was newspaper writer & theatre agent. Coproducer: "Chu Chin Chow"; "Mecca"; "Aphrodite"; "The Miracle." Playwright, "This Side of Paradise." Founded radio sta, 24; early leader in chain broadcasting. Wrote songs for Balieff's "The Honey Boy"; "The Yama Yama Girl." Screenplays: "The Honey Boy"; "The Yama Yama Girl." Author: "Gentlemen, Be Seated"; "Blackface and Music." Adapted Dickens' "A Christmas Carol" for records. Chief Collabs: Rudolf Friml, Peter DeRose, Victor Young, Lionel Barrymore. *Songs:* Chansonette; On the Blue Lagoon; In Love With Love; Give Me a Song to Remember; The Answer in Your Eyes; Whistle a Happy Refrain; You, My Love; Anuschki; So Waits My Heart; Our Prayer; Somewhere in My Heart. *Instrumental Works:* Hallowe'en (musical fantasy). *Scores:* Stage: Two Hearts in 3/4 Time (also libretto); Bublitchki (Bway).

PASQUET, JEAN   ASCAP 1962
composer, author, conductor
b New York, NY, May 31, 1896; d Martinsburg, WVa, Jan 24, 77. Educ: Studied with George Wilson, Cecil Berens, Ossip Gabrilowitsch, J C Marks, Tertius Nobel & Max Rudolph. Rec'd William Mason scholarship. Educ dir, Aeolian Co. Gave recitals. Dir, Orch da Camera & Munson-Pasquet Music Studios, Garden City, NY. *Songs & Instrumental Works:* A Lenten Meditation (choral); O God Our Help in Ages Past (with descant & brass); Angels We Have Heard on High (arr of French carol); Jesus Christ Is Risen Today (with descant & brass); Praise to the Lord (with descant & brass); The Blessed Day; Carol of the Nativity (with hand bells); Woodwind Quartet (arr of courante by Muffat); Lord, Make Thy Word a Lantern; Light of the World (A Lenten Service); May the Grace of Christ Our Saviour; A Psalm of Worship; Fifteen Short Preludes for Organ; Baroque Master Series (Bach Vol I, II, III & Handel I, II); The Church Musician (organ or piano); Bless Thou the Lord; Create in Me a Clean Heart; Come Ye Thankful People, Come (with descant & brass); Twelve Service and Recital Pieces for Organ; Lord, Sanctify Me Wholly.

PASSALAQUA, JOSEPH A
musician
b New Brunswick, NJ, Jan 13, 29. With Tony Pastor Orch & Ray McKinley Orch, 44-48, also with Duke Ellington, Ella Fitzgerald, Dizzy Gillespie & Oscar Peterson. Recording artist. Author "Guitar Methods." Mem: Am Fedn Musicians & Nat Acad Recording Artists. Recipient of Grammy Award & Down Beat Mag Award; winner, Jazz Group European Jazz poll, 74.

PASTERNACKI, STEPHAN   ASCAP 1959
composer, author
b Detroit, Mich, Sept 11, 1891. Educ: Mich Cons Music; also pvt study. Song plugger, Waterson Berlin, Snyder Publ & Kalmar & Puck, New York, 12-14, leader dance band, Detroit, 14. Bandmaster of 85th Regiment during WW I, 19-29. Cond dance band on radio, Detroit. Joined as music adv-comp-arr, Paramount Music Dept, 29, later as music librarian, Paramount, Columbia & Walt Disney Studios; organizer & first pres, Calif Copyright Conference. Chief Collabs: Richard Whiting, Ray Egan, Seymour Simons, Egbert Van Alstyne. *Songs:* Music: Little Girl; Precious; There's a Boatman on the Volga; Just One Kiss; Let's Waken the World With a Love Song. *Instrumental Works:* Vignettes Polonaise.

PASTERNAK, JOSEPH H   ASCAP 1954
composer, author, director
b Szilagy-Somlyo, Hungary, Sept 19, 01; d. To US 21. Began as asst film dir; assoc with Carl Laemmle; prod films in Europe, 8 yrs. To Hollywood, 36; joined

MGM, 41; dir & prod of films including, "Three Smart Girls", "One Hundred Men and a Girl", "Destry Rides Again", "Anchors Aweigh", "In the Good Old Summertime", "The Great Caruso", "Love Me or Leave Me", "Please Don't Eat the Daisies", "Jumbo", "A Ticklish Affair" & "The Horizontal Lieutenant." *Songs:* The Horizontal Lieutenant.

PASTORIUS, JOHN FRANCIS (JACO)   ASCAP 1975
composer, author, musician
b Norristown, Pa, Dec 1, 51. Educ: Self-taught. With bands, Woodchuck, 69-70, Tommy Strand, 70-71, Wayne Cochran, 71-72, Ira Sullivan, 73-74, Peter Graves Orch, 74-75. Teacher bass, Univ Miami, Fla, 73. Joined Weather Report, 76. Chief Collabs: Josef Zawinul, Wayne Shorter, Herbie Hancock, Michael Gibbs, Joni Mitchell, Pat Metheny, Michael Knuckles. *Songs:* Music: Come On Come Over. *Instrumental Works:* Continuum; Kuru; Portrait of Tracy; Opus Pocus; Okonkole y Trompa; (Used to Be a) Cha-Cha; Forgotten Love; Barbary Coast; Teen Town; Havona; River People; Punk Jazz; Slang; Las Olas.

PATRICK, FREDERICK   ASCAP 1948
composer, author
b London, Eng, Mar 27, 1896. Educ: Pvt piano study; King's Col, London; Univ Lille, France, studied French & piano. Music arr & songwriter, New York. Chief Collabs: Claude Reese, Jack Val, George Snow Hill, Arthur Richardson, Mack Kay, Jimmy Durante. *Songs & Instrumental Works:* All Dressed Up With a Broken Heart (top song in Europe & Eng); Invisible Hands (gospel song); Hot Potato Mambo (top song in Eng); Little Old Man With a Green Thumb; Some Day Soon; Mama Cara Mama; Misers Serenade (in revival of Zeigfeld Follies); also many more songs.

PATRICK, KIRK
See Gillette, Leland James

PATTEN, ROBERT FLETCHER   ASCAP 1976
composer, author, singer
b Washington, DC, July 18, 46. Appeared, nightclubs & local TV; writer, recording artist & producer of own music. Formed The Soc for the Prevention of Frustrated Musicians, 76. Chief Collabs: Fred Patten, father & Stephen Patten, brother. *Songs:* Back to My Girl; Now That It's Over; Gonna Catch a Train; Memory Is Gone; Music: It's a Silly Thing.

PATTERSON, KARIN G
b Los Angeles, Calif, Dec 3, 50. Educ: Los Angeles City Col, music; Calif State Univ, Los Angeles; Dick Grove Music Workshops. Singer with Helen Reddy, Mac Davis, Diana Ross, Leslie Uggams, Carol Burnett, Rich Little & Seals & Crofts. Chief Collab: Greg Wright. *Songs:* Lyrics: You Were the One; He's My Man; Never Say I Don't Love You; Happiness Is; Triflin'; Don't Worry 'Bout My Love.

PATTERSON, RUTH CLEARY
See Cleary, Ruth

PAUL, CHARLES F   ASCAP 1953
composer
b New York, NY, Aug 23, 02. Educ: New York Col of Music, grad; Royal Cons of Music, Leipzig, studied piano with Teichüller, conducting with Nikisch, comp with Ludwig; grad studies in comp with Mortimer Wilson, Joseph Shillinger. Conducted opening of Loew's 5 Presentation Movie Palaces, New York. Cond for Bob Hope, Bing Crosby, Jack Benny, Danny Kaye & Sophie Tucker, at the Valencia, 6 yrs. Staff organist, cond & comp, CBS, New York, 4 yrs. Recording artist for var cos. Cond, "All Gershwin" & summer series with New York Philh, Paris Conservatoire, London Philh, Copenhagen Philh & Katonah Fest. *Songs:* Theme songs: Martin Kane, Private Eye; As the World Turns; Somerset; General Hospital. *Scores:* Bway shows: On Baile's Strand; First Love.

PAUL, DORIS A   ASCAP 1961
composer, author, teacher
b Upland, Ind, Aug 16, 03. Educ: Amboy High Sch, Ind; Taylor Univ, BA, 26, BMusEd, 31; Northwestern Univ Sch Music, 3 summers; Univ Mich, MM, 35; attended summer workshops with Fred Waring & Olaf Christensen. Taught music, Ind & Mich Pub Schs, 26-30. Instr music educ & dir, Glee Clubs, Iowa State Teachers Col, 31-32; supvr music, Douglas County, Wis, 33-35. Instr music educ & dir, Choral Groups, Univ Denver, 45-47. Dir, Matinee Musical Chorus, Lansing, Mich, 48-64. Chief Collabr: Esther Mary Fuller (sister). *Songs:* Thou Art My Lamp (octavo); Remember Now Thy Creator (octavo); We Give Thee Thanks (octavo); Christmas Bells (octavo); Let's Sing to God (book of songs for children); Of Such is the Kingdom (full-length prog for children); Seasonal Songs for Children (book of songs for children); Altar of Christmas (full-length prog for children); 38 Introits and Responses.

PAUL, EDMUND
See Zerga, Joseph Louis Edmund

PAUL, EDWARD
composer, author, conductor
b Rensselaer, NY, Aug 24, 1896. Educ: Juilliard. Music dir, Roxy Theatre, New York, Brooklyn Paramount Theatres & Paramount Radio Hour. Music dir, Jerry Fairbanks Productions, Hollywood, 38-76; retired in 76 at age 80. Has written film background scores. Chief Collabrs: David Rose, Charles Koff, Al Stewart, Roy Ingraham. *Songs:* Ski Yodel; Land of the Pecos; The Great Outdoors; Harbor of Mystery; Topper Theme; Mr and Mrs North Theme.

PAUL, JIMMY
See DeMaio, James Paul

PAUL, JOHN
See Curnutt, John Paul

PAUL, LYNN
See Ram, Samuel

PAULETTE, JANE   ASCAP 1958
composer, author, singer
b Claremont, NH. Educ: High sch. Singer with The Paulette Sisters. *Songs:* Why; Eustis the Useless Rabbit.

PAULINI, JOSEPH JOHN   ASCAP 1973
composer, author
b Newton, Mass, Mar 22, 25. Has been a singing host & singing bartender. Manages a liquor mart & writes gospel songs. Chief Collabr: Mike Dinapoli. *Songs:* She's Got to Be a Saint; In My Own Little Way I Pray.

PAULL, BARBERI PLATT   ASCAP 1976
composer, author, director
b New York, NY, July 27, 45. Educ: Academics, Univ Fribourg, Switz; pvt study piano, Am music & jazz with Leonid Hambro & Billy Taylor; studied theatre, Herbert Berghof Studios, 58-60; eurhythmics, Dalcroze Sch, 67-68; psychol, Columbia Univ, 67-69; Juilliard Sch Music, BA(comp), 73; Manhattan Sch Music, 73-74. Early years spent touring & studying. Rehearsal pianist for Jose Limon. Comp of commercial music, incl jingles, educ, illus songbooks, popular songs & film scores. Awards: Rockefeller, Delius, Segall, Nat Endowment for the Arts & others. Dir, Barberi Paull Music Theatre & Cavu Music Assocs. Chief Collabrs: Elise Breton, Jarrett Kroll, Saeko Ichinohe. *Songs:* America, You Touch Me to My Soul; Lay Beside Me Now. *Instrumental Works:* O Wind (string quartet with middle voice). *Scores:* The Home of the Gum Drop King (full-length musical for young people); Ballet: Time (electronic).

PAULL, E T   ASCAP 1921
composer, author
b Gerardstown, WVa, Feb 16, 1858; d New York, NY, Nov 25, 24. *Songs & Instrumental Works:* The Ben Hur Chariot Race; The Burning of Rome; Sheridan's Ride; Custer's Last Charge; Battle of Gettysburg; Main Street Hoe Down.

PAULSON, GUY
See Giasson, Paul Emile

PAUNETTO, ROBERT VINCENZO   ASCAP 1974
composer, author, teacher
b New York, NY, June 22, 44. Educ: DeWitt Clinton High Sch; Berklee Col Music, BM(comp), 73; studied with Gary Burton, Allen Dawson, vibraharp with Dave Samuels, comp with Jeronimus Kachinkos, William Maloof, John Bavicchi, jazz comp with Herb Pomeroy, Lynne Oliver, John Laports. Served in USA, 65-67; recording artist; owner & pres, Pathfinder Records, Inc, producer of two albums, "Paunetto's Point" (Latin-Jazz, rec'd Grammy nomination, 75-76) & "Commit to Memory." Taught at Berklee Col Music, Boston, Mass, 72-73; pvt teacher of jazz comp & improvisation. Performed with Cal Tjader, Buddy Rich, Tito Puente, Clare Fischer, Mongs Santamaria & John (Pompeo) Rae. *Songs:* Give Me Your Eyes to Dry; From Broadway to Rivers Flow. *Instrumental Works:* Brother Will; In Time's Time; El Catalan.

PAXTON, GARY S
songwriter
Artist. Head of several publ, production & record cos; also part owner of studio. Co-producer "No Shortage" (Dove Award). Has won Grammy for his own album. With own TV show "The Gary S Paxton Christian Grit Revue." Has plans for production of Christian animated cartoons for use in churches as teaching tools for young people. Touring, appearing in concerts.

PAXTON, GLENN   ASCAP 1959
composer
b Chicago, Ill. Educ: Chicago Musical Col; Princeton Univ. Comp for Bway musical, opera, film, TV & concert music. *Instrumental Works:* Four Character Pieces for Piano. *Scores:* Opera: The Adventures of Friar Tuck; Bway Show: First Impressions; Film: When the Legends Die; TV: Willa Cather's America.

PAXTON, TOM   ASCAP 1962
composer, author, singer
b Chicago, Ill, Oct 31, 37. Educ: Univ Okla, BFA, 59. Folk singer, Greenwich Village Coffee Houses, 60. Self-composed first album, Elektra Records, 64. Concert artist in US, Britain, Europe, Australia & New Zealand. *Songs:* The Last Thing on My Mind; Ramblin' Boy; The Marvelous Toy; Jimmy Newman; I Can't Help But Wonder Where I'm Bound.

PAYMER, MARVIN E   ASCAP 1961
composer, author, pianist
b New York, NY, May 23, 21. Educ: City Col New York, BS; Univ Hartford, BM; Queens Col, NY, MA; City Univ New York, PhD. Fels: Nat Endowment for Humanities; Andrew W Mellon Found. Taught at York Col, City Univ New York, asst prof, Hunter Col, assoc dir, Pergolesi Res Ctr, Grad Ctr; managing ed, "The New Pergolesi Ed" (26 vols); musicologist, pianist, comp & arr. Ed: "String Trio No 7" (Josef Haydn); "Sinfonia to Flaminio"; "Laudak pueri Dominum"; "Questo e il Piano"; "The Instrumental Works." Author: "G B Pergolesi: A Thematic Catalogue of the Opera Omnia"; "The Instrumental Music Attributed to G B Pergolesi: A Study in Authenticity." Coauthor: "The Pergolesi Hand: A Calligraphic Study." Chief Collabr: Barry S Brook. *Instrumental Works:* Caprice for Strings.

PAYN, A A
See Miles, C Austin

PAYN, G W
See Miles, C Austin

PAYNE, FRANK LYNN   ASCAP 1971
composer
b Asheville, NC, Nov 29, 36. Educ: Univ Ark, BM, 59; NTex State Univ, MM, 61; studied comp with Samuel Adler & William Latham, 65-70. Instr, Texarkana Col, 61-65; grad fel, NTex State Univ, 65-67; assoc prof music, Oklahoma City Univ, 67- *Instrumental Works:* Toccata for Three Flutes; Quartet for Tubas; Toccata for Alto Saxaphone and Piano; Images I and II for Oboe and Piano; Concerto for Brass Quintet and Wind Ensemble; Sonata for Tuba and Piano; Concert Suite for Trumpet and Trombone; Brass Quintet; Pavanne and Ostinato for Flute Ensemble; Trio for Flute, Oboe and Clarinet; Miniatures for Clarinet Choir.

PAYNE, WILLIAM H   ASCAP 1971
composer, author, singer
b Waco, Tex, Mar 12, 49. Educ: Classical training, 15 yrs. Mem group, Little Feat, 10 yrs; recordings with numerous stars. Chief Collabrs: Fran Pane, Lowell George. *Songs:* Oh Atlanta; Time Loves a Hero; Give a Little; Strawberry Flats; Day Or Night.

PAYTON, LENNY   ASCAP 1954
composer, author, guitarist
b Philadelphia, Pa, Nov 22, 21. Educ: Temple Univ. Guitarist in dance orchs; then toured with own group. Became radio & TV arr, then producer & panelist. Teacher, Music City; music dir, Music Study Ctr, Philadelphia. *Songs:* Sweetheart of Mine; Who's the Guy With the Mink Bow Tie?.

PEACE, GEORGE J   ASCAP 1961
composer, author
b New York, NY, Feb 17, 09. Educ: High sch. Craneman with Carpenter Steel Co, Reading, Pa. *Songs:* Holiday From Love; Turn Back the Dawn.

PEAKE, DONALD G   ASCAP 1969
composer
b Los Angeles, Calif, June 7, 40. Educ: Los Angeles City Col, 2 yrs; studied music with Dr Albert Harris, Paul Glass, Elliott Kaplan & S Krachmalnick. Started out as guitarist accompanying acts, also for Ray Charles Band; recording musician & arranger; currently scoring films. *Scores:* Film/TV: In the Region of Time (Acad Award); Strange Fruit (Acad nomination); The Hills Have Eyes (Int Award); Walk Proud; The Prey.

PEAKS, MARY JANE
See Polk, Mary Jane

PEARCE, CONNIE
See Miller, Connie H

PEARL, LEO J (LEE)   ASCAP 1945
composer, author
b New York, NY, May 20, 01; d New York, NY, Aug 21, 77. Chief Collabr: Art Harry Berman. *Songs:* A Second Lieutenant Is No 1 Tenant in My Heart; I've Got a Cookie in Kansas; Don't Say You're Sorry Again; Just You Wait and See; The Scissors Grinder's Serenade; When It's Tulip Time in Amsterdam; It Happened in the Mountains; If I'm Lucky; Half-way to Montana; It'll Take a Little Time; I Know Something I Won't Tell Ya; More Than Anything Else in the World; If I Had Only Known; Symphony of Spring; With the Help of the Lord; Mad Love; White Roses; Slow Poison; Love Is a Beautiful Thing; Hot Dogs and Roses; The Freedom Song; Bang 'Em One for Me; It's Not the Same

Old Corner; Rumpus in Columbus; I Hate to See the Evening Sun Go Down; She Didn't Lay That Pistol Down; Suzanne; The Russians Are Crushin' the Prussians; Down in Old Wyomin'; Natina.

PEARLSTEIN, DAVID BLUEFIELD   ASCAP 1970
composer, author, keyboardist
b Los Angeles, Calif, Sept 13, 47. Educ: Univ Calif, Los Angeles, BA, 69; San Francisco State Grad Sch, 70, studied with John Handy; San Francisco Cons of Music, 70; studied orchestration with Lyle Murphy, 74-78; Aspen Music Fest, 78. Keyboardist & writer for var rock bands, 67-69. Recording artist with group Kindred & writer, arr & co-producer of 2 albums; toured with group 3-Dog Night. Producer of commercials for Frito-Lay, 74-76. Writer of cues & themes for Columbia Pictures Music incl "Close Encounters", "Cover Girls" & "Father Knows Best 25 Year Reunion," 76-79. Started mail-order demo bus, Hollywood Demos, 77. Formed group Bluefield, 78. Keyboardist for var artists & groups. Writer & arr, ABC-TV commercial "There's More to Love in the Afternoon," 79; writer, arr & producer of commercials for Kloster Beer of Thailand, 80. Chief Collabrs: Marty Rodgers, Gerry Robinson, David James Holster. *Songs:* Memories; Secretly (award winner, Am Song Fest, 78); What's the Use; Power of Love.

PEARSON (JOSE-PERIERA), FERNANDO ANTONIO   ASCAP 1976
composer, arranger
b Panama City, Panama, Oct 30, 51. Educ: Brooklyn Tech High Sch; Juilliard Sch Music, 75-76; pvt study with Lawrence Widdoes, 74-76. Composed background music for off-Bway production, "Talk to Me Like the Rain"; composed background libr music, Valentino Music, 76; TV commercials, NY, 76 & Los Angeles, 78 & 80; with Southern Libr of Music, Los Angeles, 78; produced var recording artists, 79. Scores for Am Film Inst "Sophies Choice." *Instrumental Works:* Boogie-Olin (theme).

PEASE, FREDERICK TAYLOR (TED)   ASCAP 1970
composer, teacher, drummer
b New York, NY, May 17, 39. Educ: Cornell Univ, BA(Eng), 61; Berklee Col Music, BM, 65; studied jazz comp with Herb Pomeroy & Ray Santisi, perc with Alan Dawson. Drummer in Boston area with musicians such as Herb Pomeroy, Ray Santisi, Charlie Mariano, John LaPorta, Red Norvo & Lee Konitz. Comp & arr for Buddy Rich Orch. Co-founder, co-leader, comp & cond of fac concert jazz orch, Berklee Col Music, 71-77, chmn arr dept, 68-, chmn jazz comp dept, 79- *Instrumental Works:* Cornerstone; Are You Ready?; Cold Country Mornings; Dusk to Dawn; One More Time.

PEASE, HARRY   ASCAP 1925
composer, author, singer
b Mt Vernon, NY, Sept 6, 1886; d New York, NY, Nov 8, 45. Educ: Pub schs. Singer in vaudeville, known as "Boy with the Golden Voice." Also wrote spec material. WW I, Signal Corps. To Hollywood, 29; wrote songs for films. Chief Collabrs: Edward G Nelson, Howard Johnson, Vincent Rose, Larry Stock, Harry Jentes. *Songs:* I Don't Want to Get Well; Peggy O'Neil; Ten Little Fingers and Ten Little Toes; Josephine, Please No Lean on the Bell; In a Shady Nook by a Babbling Brook; Why Do They Always Say No?; Light a Candle in the Chapel; Pretty Kitty Kelly; All for the Love of Mike; In a Little Second Hand Store; Moon at Sea; In the Old Town Hall; The Pal That I Loved Stole the Gal That I Loved; I'm Climbing Up a Rainbow; Red Roses for My Blue Baby; When the Sun Says Goodnight (The French Song); That's My Mammy.

PECK, MURRAY   ASCAP 1963
composer, musician
b Russia, Feb 6, 03. Educ: High sch; Naval Air Sch Photography. Formed own instrumental group, Peck's Bad Boys; toured US. Aerial photographer, USN, WW II. Wrote for films. Chief Collabrs: Gordon Clifford, Gus Arnheim, Paul Francis Webster, Lawrence Welk. *Songs:* Was It Wrong?; When Paris Smiles.

PECK, RAYMOND W   ASCAP 1914
author
b Jackson, Mich, July 3, 1875; d New York, NY, Mar 15, 50. Chief Collabrs: Percy Wenrich, Zoel Parenteau. *Songs:* The Trials of a Simple Maid; The Rainbow of Your Smile; The First Kiss of Love; Land of Romance; Baby; New York (You're the Best Town in Europe); Lantern of Love. *Scores:* Bway Stage, Librettos: The Right Girl; Castles in the Air.

PECK, RUSSELL JAMES   ASCAP 1971
composer, teacher
b Detroit, Mich, Jan 25, 45. Educ: Ferndale High Sch; Eastman Sch Music; Univ Mich, BM, 66, MM, 67 & DMA, 72. Ford Found comp-in-residence, Herricks Pub Schs, Long Island & City of Indianapolis. Mem fac, Northern Ill Univ, Eastman Sch Music & NC Sch Arts. Performer of children's concerts for major symph orchs. Chief Collabrs: Kurt Carpenter, Bill Bleich. *Instrumental Works:* Who Killed Cock Robin?; Jack and Jill at Bunker Hill; Cave; Lift-Off; American Epic; In the Garden.

PEDERSON, TOMMY   ASCAP 1964
composer, teacher, player
b Watkins, Minn, Aug 15, 20. Educ: Pvt study all over Am & with Castelnuovo-Tedesco. Played piano & drums at age 4, violin at age 7, trombone

at age 13; played trombone with Orrin Tucker, Gene Krupa, Woody Herman, Tommy Dorsey, Charlie Barnet, Benny Goodman, 41-45; records, movies, TV, Hollywood Studios, 45- *Instrumental Works:* Bosco Rosco; She Has Gone; Farm Girl; Mexican Monday; I've Been Workin' on the Trombone; All the Little Girls; 50 unaccompanied solos for tenor trombone & 50 unaccompanied solos for bass trombone; concertos for tenor trombone, bass trombone, 2 tenor trombones, tenor & bass trombone; elem, medium & advanced etudes for tenor, bass trombones.

PEDROSKI, WALTER J (LEFTY)   ASCAP 1974
composer, singer
b New Kensington, Pa, Apr 25, 48. Educ: Washington Township High Sch, Apollo, Pa; Indiana Univ, Pa. TV actor. ASCAP Popular Awards, 74-; mem, West Coast Writers Adv Bd, ASCAP. Chief Collabr: Pat McManus. *Songs:* No Love in the Room; Baby, Hang Up the Phone; Brooklyn. *Albums:* No End in Sight; Captain of Your Soul; The Next Time That I See You; Houston.

PEEK, CATHERINE LOUISE   ASCAP 1975
author
b Jacksonville, Fla. Educ: London Cent High Sch; Old Dominion Univ, 2 yrs; studied acting, voice with Margret Rolfe, Hollywood, Calif, 77-78. Acted in amateur productions; co-wrote several songs with husband, Dan Peek. Chief Collabr: Dan Peek. *Songs:* Lyrics: Lonely People; Olde Virginia; Jet Boy Blue.

PEEK, DANIEL MILTON   ASCAP 1972
composer, author, singer
b Panama City, Fla, Nov 1, 50. Educ: London Cent High Sch, 69; Old Dominion Univ, 70-71. Began piano lessons at age 7, Japan; self-taught guitar & began semi-professional band, Peshawar, Pakistan at age 12. Formed group America, London, 70, solo career, 77. Chief Collabr: Catherine Peek. *Songs:* Lonely People; Don't Cross the River; Today's the Day; All Things Are Possible; Ready for Love; Divine Lady; Don't Cry Baby.

PEEK, THOMAS RANDALL   ASCAP 1979
composer
b Bellville, Ill, Aug 18, 48. Educ: Univ Md. Performed, var bands; comp & lyricist for Christian Soldier Music. Chief Collabr: Dan Peek. *Songs:* Lighthouse.

PEERY, ROB ROY   ASCAP 1935
composer, author, conductor
b Saga, Japan, Jan 6, 1900; d Dayton, Ohio, Sept 18, 73. Son of Am missionaries. To US, 02. Educ: Midland Col, BA, hon MusD, Oberlin Cons, BM; Sch Sacred Music, Union Theol Sem, NY; Wittenberg Col, hon MusD; studied with Rubin Goldmark. Toured as music dir with film, "Four Horsemen of the Apocalypse," 20-21. Mem fac, Leonoir-Rhyne Col, 22-23, Catawba Col, 26-28, 29-31. Publ mgr, Theodore Presser Co, 32-49; assoc ed, Lorenz Publ Co, 50-65. Church organist & choirmaster, St Matthew's Lutheran, Philadelphia, 32-44, Trinity Lutheran, Germantown, 44-49; dir music, First Lutheran, Dayton, 50-65. Ed music section, "Etude," 42-49. Awards: "Etude" piano comp; Ohio State; "Homiletic Review"; Dartmouth; Franklin Mem; Schulmerich Organ. Author: "Very First Violin Book"; "Easiest Orchestra Collection"; "Young People's Choir Book"; "Singing Children of the Church"; "Chancel Choir Book"; "Master Melodies From the Great Symphonies"; "Master Melodies From the Great Concertos"; "Famous Sacred Transcriptions." Mem, Am Guild Organists. Chief Collabrs: Meredith Willson, Frederick Martens. *Songs:* I Want to Walk With God Today; I Met the Master; The Lord's Prayer; The Lord Is My Shepherd; This Be My Song. *Songs & Instrumental Works:* Cantatas: America My Wonderful Land, Lead Thou My Soul; God Shall Wipe Away All My Tears; That Quartet in Our Old Barn; Joy Is in My Heart; Slumber On; Give Me This Day; A Star in the Sky; Night of the Star; Behold the Star; The Wonder of the Star; Easter Cantatas: The Empty Tomb; The Crown of Life; The Risen King; The Last Words of Jesus. *Scores:* Operetta: The Nightingale.

PEGRAM, WAYNE FRANK   ASCAP 1975
composer, music professor
b Nashville, Tenn. Educ: Tenn Tech Univ, music educ degree, 59; Univ Tenn, Knoxville, masters in flute & comp, 65; Univ Northern Colo, doctorate of arts in comp & conducting, 75. Prof woodwind performer in regional dance bands, touring shows & symph orchs. Instrumental music teacher. Arr & comp. *Instrumental Works:* Big Band Boogie; Polovetsian Production Number; Processional Entrance; March Slav; Shostakoirch Finale.

PEHRSON, JOSEPH RALPH   ASCAP 1976
composer
b Detroit, Mich, Aug 14, 50. Educ: Univ Mich, BA, MMus, DMusA, studied with Leslie Bassett, William Albright; Univ Rochester Eastman Sch Music, postgrad studies with Joseph Schwantner, Wayne Barlow. Works performed at Univ Mich Composers' Forums, by Univ Philh Orch & by Contemporary Chamber Ens, Eastman Sch Music; publ of works, 76- *Instrumental Works:* Regions (orch); Entropic Latitudes (ens); De Rerum Natura (ens, voice); Approaches (trombone); Entelechies (2 violas, clarinet); Fractio Modi.

PELIKAN, MARIA (MARIA MASSEY)
translator
b Vienna, Austria, Feb 7, 20. Educ: Realgymnasium, MM, 13, Vienna, grad, 38. Translated art bks, photography bks, one children's bk & Diary of Paul Tillich, 36; now a literary scout for publ in Ger, Spain, Denmark & Norway. *Songs:* Eng Translations of: Melusine (Aribert Reimann); Daphne (Richard Strauss); The Donkey's Shadow (Richard Strauss); Capriccio (Richard Strauss); Salome (Richard Strauss, singing in Eng); The Stag King (H W Hentze); The Moon (Carl Orff); The Seven Last Words of Christ (Haydn); Wunderhorn Songs (Mahler); Animal Songs (A V Beckerath); Selected Songs (Sibelius); Six Folksongs From Yugoslavia (Alojz Srebotnjak); Pastimes of Youth (Hindemith); Julius Caesar (Handel; not for singing, libretto translation only).

PELL, DAVE ASCAP 1955
composer, musician, teacher
b New York, NY, Feb 26, 25. Played in bands of Les Brown, Harry James, Benny Goodman, Ray Anthony, Bobby Sherwood, Tony Pastor & Bob Astor; with West Coast Studios; leader of Dave Pell Octet. *Songs & Instrumental Works:* Dance for Daddy; Prom to Prom; Suze Blues; Sandy Shoes.

PELLEGRINI, AL
See Pellegrino, Alfred R

PELLEGRINO, ALFRED R (AL PELLEGRINI) ASCAP 1951
composer, arranger, pianist
b Buffalo, NY, Oct 25, 21. Educ: Hutchison High Sch, NY; Westlake Col Music, Calif; studied comp with Alfred Sendry. Played reed instruments, CBS, Buffalo, NY, 42. Served in USA, World War II, discharged 45. Played reeds with var performers in Los Angeles, 45-50. Music dir, Mel Torme Show, 50-55, Bob Crosby, 56-57 & Jimmy Dean; arr & pianist for several TV shows, 58-60. Chief Collabrs: Sammy Gallup, Jack Lloyd, Bobby Troup. *Songs:* Christmas Is Magic; Music: Why Did You Call It Love; Two Kisses; One In a Million; Loving You; I Think of Paris. *Songs & Instrumental Works:* Heroes Die Young; Say It With Music.

PELLEGRINO, JOSEPH VITO, JR ASCAP 1968
composer, author
b Brooklyn, NY, May 8, 44. Pres, Pellegrino Record Co, Inc; songwriter, arr & recording engr. Chief Collabrs: Al Diaco, Daniel J Soccorso, Dino P Ascari. *Songs:* On My Way to Colorado; Well, It's Alright; Mr Maestro; Everywhere I Go; Dance the Jerk; I Can't Dance.

PELLISH, BERT JAY ASCAP 1955
composer, author, arranger
b Denver, Colo, Feb 14, 14. Educ: High sch; Univ Denver, studied piano & comp with Edward B Fleck. Wrote songs for Tex Ritter films, spec material for Donald O'Connor TV shows & Las Vegas shows, also spec material for acts for Shelly Winters, Rhonda Fleming, Dorothy Dandridge. Cond & pianist for Jerry Wallace. Chief Collabrs: Ray Gilbert, Milton Berle, Sidney Miller, Sidney Kuller, Mitchell Tableporter, Buddy Feyne, Jack Hoffman. *Songs:* Do You Know What It's Like to Be Lonesome (ASCAP No 1 Chart Award); Ginger; I Don't Hear the Music Anymore; Music: Diamonds and Horseshoes; His Greatest Reward; Would It Make Any Difference to You; At Last I'm Free; Lost in Your Love; Living With Love; Frozen Tears; Then It's Summertime; Sweethearts' Lullaby; Things Have Changed a Lot.

PEMBERTON, ROGER ASCAP 1965
composer, studio musician, clinician
b Evansville, Ind. Educ: Univ Evansville, Ind, BME, 53; Ind Univ, MMus(woodwinds), 61; Hon DMus, Newberry Col, SC, 76. Played & recorded with big bands incl Woody Herman, Maynard Ferguson. Taught saxophone & jazz comp, Ind Univ, 60-64. Lead alto saxophonist & arr, Merv Griffin TV Show, 65-70. Clinician, bandleader, studio musician, 70- *Instrumental Works:* Whiskey Waltz; Doodlebug; Marshal; Ode to Sister Sue; Bossa Fuego; Easy Cookin'; Another Shade of Blue; Barely Bossa Nova; Monk's Mood; Anyway You Slice It.

PENA, PAUL ASCAP 1972
composer, author, singer
b Hyannis, Mass, Jan 26, 50. Educ: Perkins Sch for Blind, Mass; Clark Univ; Cape Cod Cons Music; studied guitar with Felix Perez, Spain, 66. Performed at Contemporary Comp Workshop, also at Newport Film Fest with James Taylor, Joni Mitchell & Van Morrison, 69. Played guitar with T-Bone Walker, 3 yrs. *Songs:* Jet Airliner; I'm Gonna Move. *Albums:* Pena.

PENA, RALPH R ASCAP 1962
composer, bassist
b Jarbidge, Nev, Feb 24, 27; d Mexico City, Mex, May 21, 69. Educ: San Francisco State Col, BA. Bassist in orchs, incl Billy May, Woody Herman, Shorty Rogers, Pete Jolly & George Shearing. Had own group, Stars of Jazz, appearing on TV; also ens in concerts, theatres, nightclubs. Chief Collabr: Peggy Lee. *Songs & Instrumental Works:* Algo Novo; My Star.

PENINGER, JAMES DAVID ASCAP 1965
composer, teacher, singer
b Orangeburg, SC, Dec 27, 29. Educ: Chicora High Sch, Charleston, SC, grad, 46; Col Charleston, BS(Eng), 51; The Citadel, teacher cert, 54; Converse Col Sch Music, BMus(vocal perf), 57, MMus(vocal perf), 59. With 82nd Airborne Div, USA, Ft Bragg, NC, 51-53. Taught music, chorus, speech, dramatics, fine arts, guitar, jr high level, pub schs, Spartanburg's Dist Seven, 58-77; dir choral activities, Dorman High Sch, Spartanburg's Dist Six. 77-; part-time teacher pvt voice & assisted with sch Glee Club, Wofford Col, 5 yrs; taught two summer sessions pvt voice, Converse Col. Former asst minister of music, Spartanburg First Baptist Church; dir music, Morningside Baptist Church; now minister of music, Fernwood Baptist Church, Spartanburg. Has sung with SC Opera Workshop, Converse Col Opera Workshop, Spartanburg Music Fest, Charlotte Opera Asn, Spartanburg Little Theatre, Chautauqua Opera Asn, Southern Baptist Centurymen Chorus (charter mem), Charleston Choral Soc & Stephens Col Concert Series; concertized in NC, SC & Ga. Mem: Southern Baptist Church Music Conference; Nat Educ Asn; SC Educ Asn. Named to ASCAP Standard Awards List, last 5 yrs. *Songs:* Little Things That Creep and Crawl and Swim and Sometimes Fly (for children's voices, SA, SSA, 4 song cycle). *Songs & Instrumental Works:* Christmas Quodlibet (SATB & piano). *Scores:* The Door (youth music drama for church use, SATB).

PENN, ARTHUR A ASCAP 1920
composer, author, publisher
b London, Eng, Feb 13, 1875; d New London, Conn, Feb 6, 41. Educ: Pvt schs, Eng. To US, 03; had own publ firm, 06-10; staff comp with publ co, New York, 14. *Songs:* Smilin' Through; Carissima; Magic of Your Eyes; When the Sun Goes Down; Nobody Else; Mighty Lonesome; Your Spirit Dwells with Me; The Lamplit Hour. *Scores:* Bway Stage: Yokohama Maid; Your Royal Highness.

PENN, WILLIAM ALBERT ASCAP 1969
composer
b Long Branch, NJ, Jan 11, 43. Educ: State Univ NY Buffalo, BFA(applied music), 64, MA(theory & comp), 67; Mich State Univ, PhD(theory & comp), 71. Mem fac theory & comp, Eastman Sch Music, 71-78. Wrote original scores, Folger Theatre's Shakespeare Productions, NY Shakespeare Festival, spacearium scores, Smithsonian Inst, solo record albums, Crystal Rainbows & The Music of Shakespeare, Vol I, scores for Am Wind Symph, Eliot Feld Ballet & Atlanta Symph Orch. Nat Endowment for Arts grants comp. Chief Collabrs: Craig Impink, Edward Berkeley, Louis Scheeder. *Instrumental Works:* Fantasy (solo harpsichord).

PENNA, DENNIS ROY (RYCHARD; TONY D) ASCAP 1963
composer, author, singer
b New York, NY, Mar 24, 47. Educ: Thomas Jefferson High Sch; Univ Calif, Los Angeles, teaching credential. Singer, nightclubs & TV; recording artist. Film "The Only Way to Spy"; author bk "The Russ Columbo Story."

PENNARIO, LEONARD ASCAP 1954
composer, concert pianist, recording artist
b Buffalo, NY, July 9, 24. Educ: Los Angeles High Sch; Univ Southern Calif, 1 yr; studied piano with Olga Steeb, Guy Maier & Isabelle Vengerova, comp with Ernst Toch, orchestration with Lucien Caillet. Prof debut with Dallas Symph at age 12; New York debut with Philh under Artur Rodzinski, 43; Europ debut, 52. Has been soloist with every major orch in US & abroad, incl Chicago, Philadelphia, Boston, Berlin, Vienna, Paris & 8 of Brit's leading orchs; has played recitals in all 50 states. Made many TV & radio appearances. Performed his own pieces in many concerts. *Songs:* Midnight on the Cliffs; numerous popular songs. *Instrumental Works:* March of the Lunatics (piano solo); March of the Lunatics (2 pianos); Fireflies (2 pianos); Concerto (piano & orch); Arr: Minute Waltz (Chopin, 2 pianos); Transc: Emperor Waltz (Strauss, piano solo).

PENNEY, EDWARD JOSEPH, JR ASCAP 1959
composer, author, producer
b Cambridge, Mass, Aug 21, 25. Educ: Emerson Col, Boston. Disc jockey, Boston, 49-59; independent record promotion & pub rels, New Eng area for Ed Penney & Assoc, 59-71; writer, publ & producer, Nashville, Tenn, 71- *Songs:* Who's Gonna Love Me Now?; Let Me Be the One; That's All I Wanted to Know; Where Do You Go?; Wasted Love; Lyrics: That's What Friends Are For; Two Lonely People; There's Nobody Home on the Range Anymore; Queen of the Senior Prom; What Is Christmas?; Welcome Stranger.

PENNINO-COPPOLA, ITALIA ASCAP 1972
composer, author
b New York, NY, Dec 12, 18. Educ: Madison High Sch, Brooklyn; Putnam Sch Bus; trained with poet father. Lyricist. Translated father's neapolitan songs. Worked with Nino Rota on lyrics for "The Godfather," also worked with Carmine Coppola on various songs for "The Godfather, Part II." Chief Collabrs: F Pennino, C Coppola. *Songs:* Lyrics: Nina Nanna; Italian Eyes; Sophia; Teresa; Come Back to Love; Come Back to Naples; Evrytime I Look in Your Eyes; Theme from Black Stallion.

PENNY, LEE
See Goddard, Leroy A

PENROD, JERRY LOUIS   ASCAP 1978
composer, singer, musician
b Mesa, Ariz, Aug 7, 51. Educ: Mesa High Sch; Mesa Community Col, studied classical guitar. Singer, musician & arr, nightclubs & TV; recording artist for pvt label. Chief Collabr: Michael C Dukes. *Songs:* Again; Music: If You've Got Ten Minutes; Luscious Lucy.

PEPPER, BUDDY   ASCAP 1948
composer, author, conductor
b La Grange, Ky, Apr 21, 22. Educ: George Rogers Clark Sch; Mar-Ken Professional Sch, Hollywood; studied piano with Alma Steedman, Westminster Choir Sch, Princeton, NJ. Child actor in vaudeville & radio, 37-41, actor in films & on Bway. In USAAF, WW II. To Hollywood under contract to Universal. Wrote songs for films incl "When Johnny Comes Marching Home", "Top Man", "This Is the Life" & "The Hucksters." Accompanist to Margaret Whiting, Judy Garland & Marlene Dietrich. Chief Collabr: Inez James. *Songs:* Don't Tell Me; Nobody But You; What Good Would It Do?; Ol' Saint Nicholas; Sorry; I'm Sorry But I'm Glad; Now You've Gone and Hurt My Southern Pride; That's the Way He Does It; The Marge and Gower Champion Strut; Vaya Con Dios; It's Christmas; Film title songs: Pillow Talk; Portrait in Black. *Scores:* Film: Mr Big.

PEPPERS, WILLIAM ANDREW   ASCAP 1955
composer, author
b McAlester, Okla, Aug 9, 21; d Gardena, Calif, Nov 5, 61. Aircraft mechanic. *Songs:* My Lips Are Sealed; I Was the One.

PERAZZO, JOSEPH WILLIAM (JOSEPH   ASCAP 1970
WILLIAM WEST)
composer, singer, guitarist
b Philadelphia, Pa, Dec 30, 43. Worked with local club bands. Joined in comp with Clifford Henrickson, 68. Did studio work under Hally Moffit, New York & Philadelphia; soloist. Chief Collabr: Clifford Henrickson. *Songs:* Faith Healing Remedy; Gimme'; Corn Stalk; Home; Bad Water.

PERERA, RONALD CHRISTOPHER   ASCAP 1971
composer, teacher
b Boston, Mass, Dec 25, 41. Educ: Harvard Col, AB, 62; Harvard Univ, MA, 67; Univ Utrecht, electronic music, 68; comp with Leon Kirchner, Gottfried Michael Koenig, Randall Thompson & Mario Davidousky. Assoc prof music & dir electronic music studio, Smith Col; taught at Dartmouth Col & Syracuse Univ. Grants & Awards: Nat Endowment Arts, Mass Arts & Hummanities Found, Paderewski Fund, Goethe Inst & ASCAP. Chief Collabr: Jon Appleton. *Songs:* Electronic Music: Alternate Routes (tape). *Instrumental Works:* Reverberations (organ, tape); Reflex (viola, tape); Fantasy Variations (piano with live-electronics); Chanteys (full orch); Bright Angels (organ, perc, tape); Tolling (two pianos, tape); Vocal Work With Instruments: Apollo Circling (soprano, piano); Three Poems of Günter Grass (soprano, chamber ensemble, tape). *Songs & Instrumental Works:* Children of the Sun (soprano, horn, piano).

PERETTI, HUGO   ASCAP 1952
composer, author, producer
b New York, NY, Dec 6, 16. Educ: Studied comp, orchestration & conducting with Tibor Serly. Trumpeter in pit band; also arr for Bway musical "Hellzapoppin." Played in dance orchs & on radio. With Luigi Creatore, formed writing, arr & production unit for records & musical commercials; A&R dir, Mercury, RCA, Roulette, Avco & H&L Records. Chief Collabrs: Luigi Creatore, George David Weiss. *Songs:* Bimbombey; Can't Help Falling in Love With You; The Lion Sleeps Tonight; Wild in the Country; Oh, Oh, I'm Falling in Love Again; Secretly; A Walkin' Miracle; And Now; Let's Put It All Together; I Can't Give You Anything But My Love; Love Is the Answer; Star on a TV Show; Good Times; Maggie Flynn; Why Can't I Walk Away; Thank You Song; Mr Clown; Smile Smile Smile; You Are Beautiful; Carnival; Are You Really Mine?.

PEREZ, LOUIS A   ASCAP 1959
composer, author
b New York, NY, June 21, 28. Educ: Haaren High Sch; Rhodes Prep Sch; Harnett Sch Music, rec'd cert; studied Joseph Schillinger Syst Musical Comp with John Schaffer Smith, arr & comp with S Addeo & Marc Fredricks, piano with Marc Fredricks, flute with Harold Bennet & Harry Zlotnik, perc with Ted Reed. Led own musical aggregation, 20 yrs. Recorded for Columbia Records, Ajay Records, Parnaso Records & Tico-Fania Records. Played in exclusive clubs & hotels, incl Waldorf Astoria, Sheraton Hilton, Americana Hotel, Roseland Ballroom, Chateau Madrid. Chief Collabrs: Sunny Skylar, Bert Douglas, Mickey Stoner, Don Canton, Bert Mann, Vic Abrams. *Songs:* Bon Bon De Chocolate; Jugue y Perdi; Music: Barrio; Rain in New York; Lyrics: Guatanamera (spec arr & lyrics). *Instrumental Works:* African Fantasy; Our Heritage; Fire Island; Pintame Un Son; De Todo Un Poco; Tumba, Bongo y Claves; Yo No Soy Del Monte; I'll Call Her Monday.

PERITO, NICK   ASCAP 1959
composer, director, conductor
b Denver, Colo, Apr 7, 24. Educ: North Denver High Sch; Denver Univ, Lamont Sch Music; Juilliard Sch Music, studied cond, also piano with Jeanne Behrend, orchestration with Bernard Wagenaar; pvt orchestration study with Marion Evans & Don Costa. Pianist, radio sta KLZ, Denver, 40-42, also for all major networks & recording cos, New York, 49-64. All Perry Como's TV specials, 64-; arr, cond record albums with Jane Morgan, Julius La Rosa, Steve & Eydie, Shirley Bassey Perry Como & others. Hons, Kennedy Ctr, 79. Musical dir, cond & arr, TV specials with Andy Williams, Bing Crosby, Steve Lawrence & Eydie Gorme; music dir, cond & arr for "The Big Show," NBC-TV, 80. *Songs:* Music: Stay With Me; Sounds of Summer; Take the Time; We Are Love; also many more songs & themes used on numerous TV specials. *Scores:* Film: Don't Just Stand There.

PERITZ, BERNICE PERRY   ASCAP 1970
composer, author, publisher
b Elizabeth, NJ, Jan 27, 24. Educ: Thomas Jefferson High Sch, Brooklyn, NY; Pace Univ, New York. Dancer & actress, on stage; TV producer & dir; own TV talk-variety show, 7 yrs. *Songs:* In the Hush of a Lifetime; Say Yes, My Love; Love You're Everything; I Can See You in the Distant Light; For I Could Not Forget You.

PERKINS, FRANK S   ASCAP 1933
composer, conductor, arranger
b Salem, Mass, Apr 21, 08. Educ: Brown Univ, PhB, 29; var pvt studies incl comp & cond with Tibor Serly, 45. With music publ, 29-34; arr, Waring's Pennsylvanians, 34-38; arr, comp & cond, Warner Bros Pictures Inc, 38-52, as comp-arr, 61-66. Free lance, TV, 52-61. Nominated Acad Award for scoring "Gypsy," 62. Two albums of instrumentals with Decca. Chief Collabrs: Mitchell Parish, John Bradford. *Songs:* Music: Stars Fell on Alabama; Sentimental Gentleman From Georgia; Emaline; Fandango. *Instrumental Works:* Kentucky Trotter; Escapade; Feliciana.

PERKINS, HUEL DAVIS   ASCAP 1969
composer, teacher, administrator
b Baton Rouge, La, Dec 27, 24. Educ: Southern Univ, La, BS; Northwestern Univ, Ill, MMus & PhD; studied clarinet with George Waln, Domenico DeCaprio. Music instr, Lincoln Univ, 48-50; dir, Music Div, Southern Univ, La, 50-68, dean, Col Arts & Humanities, 68-78; deputy dir educ progs, Nat Endowment for Humanities, Washington, DC, 68-69; asst vchancellor academic affairs, La State Univ, Baton Rouge. *Songs:* Southern Univ Fight Song; Southern Univ Pep Song; Alpha Phi Alpha Sweetheart Song.

PERKINS, RAY   ASCAP 1921
composer, author, pianist
b Boston, Mass, Aug 23, 1896; d Bradenton, Fla, Jan 31, 69. Educ: Columbia Univ, BA; Juilliard; Denver Univ; also pvt music study. Reserve officer, USA. WW I & II, awarded Bronze Star, Order of Crown of Italy; retired as Col. Began in radio, 24, New York: made piano recordings for Edison Records; also piano rolls; radio producer & MC, KFEL, Denver, 46-59. DJ, WTRL & WSPB, Fla. *Songs:* Under a Texas Moon; Down the Old Church Aisle; Bye-Lo; Scandinavia; Stand Up and Sing for Your Father; Tessie; Smiling Irish Eyes.

PERKINSON, COLERIDGE-TAYLOR
composer
b New York, NY, 1932. Educ: Manhattan Sch Music, BA, 53 & MM, 54; Tanglewood; Salzburg Mozarteum; Nederland Radio Union Hilversum; Berkshire Music Ctr. Assoc cond, Symph of New World, 65. Rec'd commission from Ford Found; NY State Coun on the Arts grant, 74. *Instrumental Works:* Song of the Lusitanian Bogey; God Is a Guess What?; Man Better Man; Attitudes; Viola Concerto; Concerto for Viola and Orchestra; Sinfonietta No 1 (string orch); Grass (piano, strings); Blues (violin); The McMasters; Together for Days.

PERL, LOTHAR   ASCAP 1954
composer, conductor, pianist
b Breslau, Ger, Dec 1, 10; d New York, NY, Apr 28, 75. Educ: Univ; cons. Has given piano recitals; accompanist to musicians, dancers & singers. Teacher at Los Angeles City Col & Adelphi Col, NY. Comp & cond for films, TV, theatres & nightclub. Comp ballets for David Lichine, Ballet Russe & Trudi Schoop. *Instrumental Works:* Dance Suite; Four American Variations on a Theme by Paganini (piano). *Scores:* Film: Three Daring Daughters; Unfinished Dance; This Land Is Mine.

PERLA, GENE AUGUST   ASCAP 1972
composer, author
b Hackensack, NJ, Mar 1, 40. Educ: Park Ridge High Sch; Pascack Valley Regional High Sch; NY Mil Acad; Univ Toledo; Berklee Col Music; Boston Cons Music; Inst Audio Res. Began piano at age 5; classical studies for 10 yrs; began trombone at age 13, studied for 5 yrs. To New York, 67. Performed & recorded with Willie Bobo, Nina Simone, Woody Herman, Sarah Vaughn, Elvin Jones & Sonny Rollins. Has made music with many artists, incl Dizzy Gillespie, Miles Davis, Nancy Wilson, Joni Mitchell, Chick Corea, Chuck Mangione, Frank Sinatra, plus others. Began own music publ co, 72. Head engr, Secret

Sound Studios, New York; owner of Red Gate Studio with partner, Jan Hammer. Began own recording co, P M Records, 73. Co-leader of group, Stone Alliance. Musician, comp, arr, band leader, agent, music publ, producer, record co & studio owner, engr & recording artist. Chief Collabr: Lorraine Feather. *Songs:* Music: Destiny; Can't Sleep; Miss T; Namuh; On the Mountain; PP Phoenix; Aunt Remus; Taking a Good Long Look.

PERLE, GEORGE   ASCAP 1965
composer, musicologist, teacher
b Bayonne, NJ, May 6, 15. Educ: NY Univ, PhD. Prof, Queens Col, 61-; Guggenheim fels, 66-67 & 74-75. Elected to Am Acad & Inst Arts & Letters, 78. Author: "Serial Composition and Atonality"; "Twelve-Tone Tonality"; "The Operas of Alban Berg." *Songs:* Music: Thirteen Dickinson Songs. *Instrumental Works:* A Short Symphony; Concertino for Piano, Winds, and Timpani; Three Movements for Orchestra; Etudes for Piano.

PERRAULT, JOHN PAUL   ASCAP 1977
composer, author
b Biddeford, Maine, Nov 20, 42. Vocalist & banjo player, Nonesuch River Singers, 62-66. Writer, vocalist & guitarist, John Perrault Group, 70-80, performed New Eng clubs, cols & schs, TV & radio progs & folk fests in Vt, NH & Maine. *Songs:* Wounded Knee; Minnesota Mornin'. *Albums:* Thief in the Night.

PERREN, CHRISTINE YARIAN
author
b Sept 15, 44. Educ: Marshall Univ, studied nursing. Nurse, 65-70. Free-lance writer, 70-76. Adminr several music cos, 76- Chief Collabr: Freddie Perren. *Songs:* Lyrics: Hallelujah Day; Don't Let It End; Till You Let It Begin; Do It Baby; It's So Hard to Say; Goodbye to Yesterday.

PERREN, FREDRICK   ASCAP 1975
composer, author, arranger
b Jersey City, NJ, May 15, 43. Educ: Dwight Morrow High Sch, Englewood, NJ, grad; Howard Univ, DC, BA(music). Music teacher, DC Sch Syst, 66-67; keyboard player, arr & cond with Jerry Butler, 68-69; producer & songwriter, Motown Records & Jobete Music, 69-75; owner & pres, Grand Slam Productions, Inc, 75-80. Pres, MVP Records. Owner, Mom & Pops Company Store (recording studios); also owns Perren-Vibes Music Inc. Billboard Pop Producer's Award, 76. Chief Collabrs: Dino Fekaris, Keni St Lewis. *Songs:* I Will Survive (Grammy Award & Nat Music Publ Award, 79); Reunited; Shake Your Groove Thing; Makin' It; Heaven Must Be Missing an Angel; Boogie Fever; Don't Take Away the Music; Hot Line; Funtime; One Child of Love.

PERRI, ROMANO   ASCAP 1968
composer
b Plati, Italy, Aug 24, 28. Educ: Liceum Sch Music, Omegna, Italy, cert, Cameri, Italy, comp & music theory cert; Musical Liceum Naples, Italy, comp cert; Gozzano Col, studied strings & brass. Began studies with pvt teachers at age 6; joined symph band in Omegna at age 8. Played several instruments with different bands in Italy & US. Moved to US, 48. Played trumpet, guitar & violins. Played guitar solo on radio, WRYO, Rochester, Pa, 48-52. Chief Collabrs: Marjorie Baderak, Joe Freman, Ed Ihlefeldt. *Songs:* Hurt Me; Today Was Tomorrow Yesterday; Play My Guitar; If You Remember; Love Is Made for Us to Share; Love of Long Ago; I Remember New York; Mediterrenean Madness; Tango Rock; You Broke Our Wedding Date; Sad Song; Music: Pain; You Can't Keep a Good Love Down.

PERRIN, JUAN   ASCAP 1976
composer, guitarist
b Pasadena, Calif, Jan 27, 27. Groton Sch, Groton, Mass; Yale Univ, BA, 51; studied flamenco guitar, Madrid, Spain, 49-55; Cons Superior de Musica de Malaga, Spain, currently studying classical guitar & harmony. Accompanist, group Los 4 Vargas, & appeared on TV progs incl "Ed Sullivan Show" & "Garry Moore Show," 54-55. Appeared in film "One-Eyed Jacks," 59. With Carmen Amaya Co, 2 nat tours incl US & Can, 55-58. Accompanist, Leonor Amaya, Mex & Cent Am, 62-67. Appeared in "Camino Real," Ctr Theatre Group, Los Angeles Music Ctr. Comp & arr, production of "Los Tarantos," Cons Superior de Musica, Artes Dramaticas y Danza de Malaga, 80. Flamenco guitarist & accompanist, Cons de Malaga dance dept, nightclubs, TV & Theater, US, Mex, Cent Am, Can, Dominican Repub & Spain. Chief Collabr: Don Ferris. *Instrumental Works:* Fantasia por Soleares en Fa Sostenido menor; Impresiones por Seguiriyas; Fantasia por Soleares en Dos Tonos; Fantasia por Seguiriyas en Dos Tonos; Fantasia por Farruca en Mi menor.

PERRIN, LESLEY DAVISON   ASCAP 1962
composer, author, singer
b London, Eng, Sept 7, 30. Educ: Brown Univ, BA; studied guitar with Ivor Mairants & Angel Iglesias, harmony with Malcolm Williamson. Contributor to 11 Julius Monk revues at "Upstairs at the Downstairs" & "Plaza 9"; also revues at "Crystal Palace", Aspen, "Wit's End", Atlanta, "Pheasant Run", Chicago & others. Writer for TV shows: "Rowan and Martin's Laugh In"; "Dean Martin Show"; "Johnny Carson"; "Merv Griffin"; "Mike Douglas"; "Jack Paar"; "Steve Allen"; "Ed Sullivan Shows"; "Not So Much a Programme," BBC; "Mavis Bramston Show," Australia. Five albums recorded. Writer for indust shows, DuPont, McDonald's & Ship 'n Shore. Singer at "Blue Angel", "Playboy

Club", "Janice Mars Baq Room", "In Boboli" & "Coonamessett Inn." Writer of spec material for Ruth Buzzi, Joanne Worley & Mabel Mercer. Contributor of lyrics to var bks & mag. Comedienne & guitarist. *Songs:* Alma Whatsa Mater (The Peace Corps); Ping Pong; The Joy of Sex; The Jackie Look; I Want a Secret Serviceman for Christmas; Lady Bird; Cook's Tour; Marching for Peace; Las Vegas East; Club Mediterranee; Ten Percent Banlon; Scotch on the Rocks; Lust in My Heart; Peanuts; Billy Beer; The Power Behind the Throne; Travolta Fever; Cries in the Common Marketplace; The Silent Majority Waltz; M for Medicare; Hollywood Sheik; The Final Days; Mrs Johnson; The Music of Broadway; Mommie Dearest; Megalopolis.

PERRON, JEAN   ASCAP 1973
composer, author
b Buffalo, Mo, Mar 23, 16. Educ: Buffalo High Sch, Mo. Entered a talent show using the name Mama Hooch, 74. Did two Gong Shows for TV, 77. Performed in motion picture for Universal "Melvin and Howard," 79. Writer of musical comedy "The Second Half." Chief Collabr: Jeanette Sue Davis. *Songs:* Looking At the Bad Side of Me; Takes a Lot of Lovin; It Aint Fittin to Be Hurtin Like I Am; The Next Two Hundred Years ('Gonna Be All Right).

PERRONE, VALENTINA   ASCAP 1960
author, teacher
b Bronx, NY, Feb 14, 06; d. Educ: Col Mt St Vincent; Fordham Univ, MA. Taught Eng & music, pub schs, New York. Chief Collabr: Virginia De Neergaard. *Songs:* Sleep Precious Babe.

PERROTTA, SOSSIO   ASCAP 1979
composer, conductor,
b Naples, Italy, Dec 16, 10. Educ: Elem sch, Italy; Cons Naples, bachelors degree. First trumpeter, San Carlo Opera, Wagner Opera Co, 55, New York Metrop Opera, 59. Cond, var concerts, Town Hall & Carnegie Hall, & in var parks, New York. Leader, Italian feast band, New York. Taught, New York Sch of Music; recreation dir in music, New York Dept of Social Services. *Songs:* Music: Senior Citizens March; Campagnola (Country Girl); Luna Chiara. *Instrumental Works:* A Gina (sinfonic march, band); Fantasy for Trumpet (with piano).

PERRY, ALFRED   ASCAP 1954
author
b Berlin, Ger, Sept 1, 10. Univ Berlin; Univ Munich; Univ Wuerzburg; dramaturgy with Leopold Jessner. Wrote spec material & poetry in midteens, performed by the leading performers of the theater, the cabaret & radio. Came to US in 38. Worked as music ed, wrote first English lyric for Max Steiner, theme from "Caine Mutiny" & "Full Speed Ahead." Chief Collabrs: Music, Georg Duning, Ernest Gold, Herschel Gilbert, Hugo Friedhofer, Dimitri Tiomkin, Rudi Schrager. *Songs:* Brindisi; songs from The Guns of Navarone & Judgment at Nuremberg; songs from var segments of the Rifleman, The Big Valley, The Dick Powell Show & The Corrupters; title song, The Rifleman & Beyond a Reasonable Doubt. *Scores:* Librettist: Volpone (opera); Penelope (opera); The Rise and Fall of the Third Reich (dramatic cantata).

PERRY, ALFRED JAMES   ASCAP 1969
composer, author, pianist
b Montreal, Que, Oct 1, 31. Educ: Piano lessons at age 10; studied comp & songwriting with Gordon Woodford; studied accounting at McGill Univ & Sir George Williams Univ. Wrote poetry, lyrics, own songs, words & music, played piano & sang, film actor, 79-80. Mem: Nat Acad Popular Music; Songwriters Hall of Fame. *Songs:* Sweet Sweet America (in Songwriters Hall of Fame; song comp for US Bicentennial, 76); Disco Girl; Need Your Love; You Don't Know; Comes the Loneliness; Don't Cry Now; I Love, Lovely Chinese Girl; I've Got a Million Songs to Sing to You; I Tried So Hard not to Cry; I Never Want to Lose Your Love; My Heart Is in Canada; I Want You to Have My Baby.

PERRY, BERNICE
See Peritz, Bernice Perry

PERRY, JACK   ASCAP 1953
composer, author
b Brooklyn, NY, Jan 10, 20. Educ: Eastern District High Sch. Sales rep, photography studio. Chief Collabr: Harry Sims. *Songs:* Love Me Again; What Kind of an Animal Are You?; Sandy the Sandman; Upsy Down Town; Sure Fire Kisses; Soda Pop Parade; I'm Wired for Lovin'; Suspense; Must I?; This Is the Time; His Arms Are Open to Everyone.

PERRY, PHIL   ASCAP 1950
composer, author
b New York, NY, Nov 24, 14; d Bay Shore, NY, Nov 10, 72. Educ: High sch. *Songs & Instrumental Works:* Christmas Symphony; Teenage Rose; My Promise to You.

PERRY, ROGER LEE   ASCAP 1965
composer
b Davenport, Iowa, May 7, 33. Educ: Grinnell Col, BA. Actor; wrote two children's musicals & "You Never Can Tell." Chief Collabrs: Johnny Melfi, Jim Ploss, Jo Anne Worley. *Songs:* Music: A Kid Again; We Do It.

PERRY, SAM A   ASCAP 1923
composer, author, pianist
b Russia, Mar 28, 1884; d Los Angeles, Calif, Nov 1, 36. Educ: Royal Acad of Music, Vienna. Staff comp & music dir, Hollywood film studios, 28-36. Wrote incidental music & theme songs for films. Author piano instr bks. *Songs & Instrumental Works:* Chant d'Amour; The Wanderer's Plaint; And Then You Came; The Furies; Fiesta in Seville; Battle in the Air; Chinese Patrol; La Fiesta.

PERSE, JUNE (JUNE REIZNER)   ASCAP 1963
composer
b Pittsburgh, Pa, June 29, 27; d Oct 17, 78. Educ: Northwestern Univ, studied theatre & drama. Wrote comedy revues, Pittsburgh Playhouse; wrote advert campaign, Southeast Dairy Inst, 65. Won six Addy Awards, 65-68. Wrote comedy sketches, Wits End Nightclub, Atlanta; wrote musical comedy, Upstairs At the Downstairs, New York, 66-69; wrote & contributed to revues, Julius Monk's Plaza Nine, Plaza Hotel, New York; wrote musical material & nightclub acts for Gordon & Sheila McRae, Jack Carter, Jackie Wilson & Everly Bros. Wrote spec musical numbers for TV, Alan King, "Comedy Is King," I & II, "Alan and His Buddy." Her material has been performed on Ed Sullivan, Johnny Carson, Jack Paar Spec, Red Skelton, Merv Griffin, Mike Douglas & Jackie Gleason shows. Chief Collabrs: Bill Brown, Ted Simon. *Songs:* Barry's Boys; The '68 Nixon; Your Friendly Liberal Neighborhood; Ku Klux Klan.

PERSICHETTI, VINCENT   ASCAP 1947
composer, author, pianist
b Philadelphia, Pa, June 6, 15. Educ: Combs Cons of Music, BM(comp), studied with Russell King Miller; Philadelphia Cons of Music, MusD, studied with Olga Samaroff; Curtis Inst, dipl in conducting, studied with Fritz Reiner; 6 hon doctorates. Organist, Arch St Presbyterian Church, 32-48; comp fac, The Juilliard Sch, 47-; publ consult, Elkan-Vogel Co, 52-; comp-in-residence in over 200 univs; over 100 publ works. Brandeis Creative Arts Award & 3 Guggenheim fels; mem of Nat Inst of Arts & Letters. *Instrumental Works:* Symphony No 9; Divertimento for Band; Eleventh Piano Sonata; Fourth String Quartet; Parable XXI for Solo Guitar; The Creation (solo quartet, chorus, orch); Symphony for Band; Harmonium (cycle of 20 songs, voice, piano); Mass (a cappella); Hymns and Responses for the Church Year.

PERSKIN, SPENCER MALCOLM   ASCAP 1970
composer, author, singer
b Brooklyn, NY, Oct 6, 43. Educ: Spec child student, Southern Methodist Univ, Dallas, 51-61. Founder/leader, Shiva's Headband, 67. Producer for Capitol Records. Founder, Armadillo Records, 69, founder & 1st pres, Armadillo World Headquarters, Austin, Tex, 70. Founder & pres, Ape Records, 78. Chief Collabrs: Suzy Perskin, Shawn Siegel. *Songs:* Kaleidescoptic; Take Me to the Mountains; Country Boy; North Austin Strut; Song for Peace.

PERSKIN, SUSAN ELIZABETH   ASCAP 1970
composer, author, singer
b Joliet, Ill, Dec 7, 46. Educ: Musical Col Joliet, five yrs. Folk singer, Houston Jewish Community Ctr; singer, comp & instrumentalist with Shiva's Headband, Austin, Tex, 67- Co-founder, Armadillo World Headquarters, Austin, 70. Chief Collabr: Spencer Perskin. *Songs & Instrumental Works:* Homesick Armadillo Blues (instrumental); Lyrics: 'A' Rockslide; Don't Blame Me.

PETE, PIUTE
See Kaufman, Morris

PETERIK, JAMES MICHAEL   ASCAP 1970
author, singer, guitarist
b Berwyn, Ill, Nov 11, 50. Educ: Piano lessons, ages 6 to 9; saxophone, sixth grade through high sch; self-taught on guitar, age 12. Started career as mem of rock band The Shondels, which became The Ides of March, 66, followed by new group Survivor. *Songs:* Rockin' Into the Night; San Pedro's Children; Rebel Girl. *Songs & Instrumental Works:* Vehicle; You Wouldn't Listen; Somewhere in America.

PETERS, MITCHELL THOMAS   ASCAP 1978
composer, teacher, performer
b Red Wing, Minn, Aug 17, 35. Educ: Univ Rochester Eastman Sch of Music, BM, 57, MM, 58, performer's cert in perc. Timpanist, 7th USA Symph Orch, 58-60. Principal percussionist, Dallas Symph Orch, 60-69. Drummer, Dallas Summer Musicals, 62-69; formed own publ co specializing in perc music, 68. Perc instr, Calif State Univ, Los Angeles, 70-80, Univ Calif, Los Angeles, 79- Co-principal timpanist & percussionist, Los Angeles Philh. *Instrumental Works:* Sonata Allegro; Yellow After the Rain; Theme and Variations for Marimba and Piano; Sea Refractions; Piece for Percussion; A la Samba.

PETERS, WILLIAM FRANCIS   ASCAP 1960
composer, educator
b Brooklyn, NY, Dec 18, 1895. Educ: Pub sch. Worked as salesman, elevator operator, Wall St messenger, custodian, restaurant owner, song writer; soldier in World War I, 16-25. Chief Collabr: Robert Kimberly. *Songs:* Al for All All for Al; All the Time; As We Grow Older; Baby I Love You So; Baby When We Meet; Cherish; Church on the Hill; Drums of Cayuga; Everything's Rosy; Gamble with My Heart; I Lived a Million Years Last Night; I'm Gone; I'm the

Boy I'm the Girl; It Happened with You; Keep Me Faithful; Look What You've Done; Lost in a Love; Mountain Song to the Valley; My Own Sweet Love; My Tears of Love Are Tears of Happiness; My Thoughts of You; My Wish for You; Naughty Boy; New World; Oh Where Are You Tonight; On A Day When I Was Walking; Out Where the High Winds Blow; Please Do; Pop My Papa Tonight; Shade of the New Apple Tree; Shirley; The Celebration Waltz; The Guatemala Glide; The Kissing Waltz; The Love Songs They Sang At That Old Singing Bee; The Ole Singin' Bee; The Subject Is You; The Way It Goes; Wanting You; When in Doubt Do Without; Whether Or Not. *Scores:* Off-Bway: Breath Waite and the Genie.

PETERSEN, MARIE (MRS ROBERT SCHWARTZ)   ASCAP 1952
composer, author, dancer
b St Louis, Mo. Educ: Univ Tenn; ballet sch; drama sch. Has been ballerina; led own group, appeared in Balaban & Katz theatres. Ballet mistress, St Louis Munic Opera. Artist; has had exhibits of paintings, Tenn Art League Show. Bd mem, Nashville Ballet Soc & Tenn Art League. Chief Collabr: Beasley Smith. *Songs:* Tennessee Hillbilly Ghost; Hillbilly Heaven; Lucky Lou.

PETERSEN, ROBERT E   ASCAP 1965
composer, author
b Omaha, Nebr, Nov 27, 37. Labor & checker for Wometco, Coca Cola Inc, Nashville. Worked for 2 defense plants. Songwriter. Chief Collabr: John W Pulignano.

PETERSON, BETTY J (MRS LOUIS BLASCO)   ASCAP 1948
composer, author, publisher
b Spurgeon, Mo, June 15, 18. Educ: Business col; pvt voice study. Staff mem, music publ co, Kansas City. Singer with local bands, 35-38. With Jenkins Music Co, 38-44. Partner, Blasco Artist Bureau, Blasco Music Co Inc, 44-48, vpres & mem bd, 48-54; partner, Midland Music, 44-54, sole owner, 54. Pres, Happiness Music Corp, 54- *Songs:* Sailing on a Moonbeam; My Happiness (Cash Box Award); The Meaning of a Lonely Heart; I Want It in Black and White; That's the Place for Me; You Can't Go Wrong; Crying My Heart Out for You; I'm Coming Back; Pearly Gates; You Say You Love Me.

PETERSON, HAROLD VAUGHAN   ASCAP 1974
composer, teacher, studio musician
b Oak Park, Ill, June 23, 48. Educ: San Jose State Univ, BA, 69; Stanford Univ, MA, 71, DMA, 73, studied with Leland Smith & Gyorgy Ligeti. Music educr, arr, music ed & publ. *Songs & Instrumental Works:* Symphony (synthesizer & orch); Reflections (prolog, jazz sextet); Passing By (instrumental-vocal jazz ens); Kyrie Eleison (SATB choir & keyboards); Four Geometries (woodwind quintet); Sangria; Sonatina (horn & piano); The Charismatic Bassist.

PETERSON, HAZEL SHIRLEY
composer, singer
b Morganton, NC, June 12, 52. Educ: NC Cent Univ, 2 yrs; John Robert Powers Sch of Modeling & Drama; Los Angeles City Col, music. Began as singer at age 8; songwriter at age 11; participated in bands at age 16. Toured Europe with band Beverly Hills, 77. Did studio recording; now touring Europe as mem of Gwen Brisco Review. Chief Collabr: Kenneth Stover. *Songs & Instrumental Works:* I Want to Dance With You; I Love to See You Dance.

PETERSON, IVOR   ASCAP 1959
composer, teacher, conductor
b Högsby, Sweden, Mar 29, 05. Educ: High sch; pvt violin study in Stockholm, Sweden; NY Univ, studied with Prof Erb. Recording artist, US & Europe; wrote songs for Bway play, "Stepping Sisters"; appeared in concerts & radio, Boston. Accordion soloist, McAlpin (hotel), New York, 30-37, Waldorf Astoria, 37-42, with USO Shows, 51 & also in nightclubs. *Songs:* Shadows Were Falling; Your Loving Arms. *Instrumental Works:* Rattling Keys; Waltz Continental; Bubble Waltz; Skating Queen; Dancing Snowflakes; Castaneta; Morning Mist; Niagara Falls; Whirlpool; Florita Tango; Patriotic America.

PETERSON, JAMES NEWELL   ASCAP 1923
composer, author, arranger
b Eveleth, Minn, July 2, 11; d Apr 26, 67. Educ: Univ Minn; Univ Rochester Eastman Sch of Music; Columbia Univ; studied with Dr Frank Black, NBC. In concert as pianist & organist. Vocal coach & arr for var groups. With NBC, CBS, ABC & Roxie Theatre. Orchr & arr with var opera, light opera & pop stars. Music dir, own NBC show "Hymns of All Churches," "Ice Capades," 60-65, play "Man of La Mancha," 66-67. Recording artist.

PETERSON, LELAND ARNOLD (ERNIE)   ASCAP 1962
composer, author
b Galva, Ill, Mar 1, 11. Educ: Galva High Sch; Univ Ill. Mem of var orchs; played saxophone & clarinet in clubs in Midwest & South; also played on luxury liners to Europe & SAm. *Songs:* I Want to Be the Only One.

PETERSON, SPENCER C   ASCAP 1975
composer, author, singer
b Minneapolis, Minn, July 6, 48. Educ: Self-taught. Coauthor songs, recorded on Columbia & Glacier Records. Mem group, Northern Light. Duo guitarist.

Chief Collabr: David Stewart. *Songs:* Minnesota; Think Snow; Be My Woman; Can't Walk Away; Runnin'.

PETERSON, WAYNE TURNER
composer, pianist
b Albert Lea, Minn, Sept 3, 27. Educ: Univ Minn, BA, MA, PhD; Royal Acad Music (Fulbright scholar), 53-54; studied comp with Lennox Berkeley & Howard Ferguson, piano with Harold Craxton. Started as jazz pianist, on road, 45-48. Has rec'd many awards & comns. *Songs & Instrumental Works:* Free Variations for Orchestra; Exalation, Dithyramb and Caprice (comn by Ford Found); Earth Sweet Earth (chorus); Psalm 56; Spring; Can Death Be Sleep (chorus); Metamorphoses for Wind Quintet; Clusters and Fragments (string orch); Cataclysms (music from a Greek tragedy; orch); Caprice for Flute and Piano; Trialogue (piano, violin, cello); Diatribe (violin, piano); An Interrupted Serenade (flute, harp, cello); Dark Reflections (cycle of 4 songs for high voice, violin, piano).

PETITE, E DALE (DARRYL PRICE) ASCAP 1970
composer, author
b Vancouver, Wash, Aug 10, 26. Educ: Lincoln High Sch, Seattle; Univ Wash, BS, 49, studied chromatic harmony with John Verrall; Ariz State Univ, MNS, 65. Science teacher incl physics, chemistry & biology, Seattle Pub Schs, 29 yrs. Mem, Allied Songs Inc, Seattle, 53-59. Pres & mgr, Petite Film Co, educ film producers, Seattle, 54- Chief Collabr: Art Benson. *Songs:* Lost and Found; When I Think of You; Reassurance; Home on a Star; Sweet Prairie Bride; Music: The Thrill Is Gone; Lyrics: My Love Was Meant for You.

PETKERE, BERNICE ASCAP 1932
composer, author
b Chicago, Ill, Aug 11, 06. Educ: Englewood High Sch, Chicago, 2 yrs; Henshaw Cons Music, scholarships voice; self-taught in piano. As a child toured in vaudeville; pianist for music publ firm, New York; wrote score for MGM "Ice Follies of 1938." Wrote scenario for "Sabotage Squad"; wrote shooting script "Columbia Pictures." Chief Collabrs: Joseph Young, Ned Washington, Marty Symes, Walter G Samuels. *Songs:* Close Your Eyes; By a Rippling Stream; A Mile a Minute; Happy Little Farmer; Our Love; Oh Moon; Half a Mile Away From Home; That's You Sweetheart; Music: Lullaby of the Leaves; My River Home; Stay Out of My Dreams; Did You Mean What You Said Last Night?; It's All So New to Me; Hats Off, Here Comes a Lady; The Lady I Love; Barcelona Goodbye; Tell the Truth; Dancing Butterfly.

PETRIE, HENRY W ASCAP 1929
composer, singer
b Bloomington, Ill, Mar 4, 1857; d Paw Paw, Mich, May 25, 25. Appeared in minstrel shows. *Songs:* Asleep in the Deep; I Don't Want to Play in Your Yard; Davie Jones' Locker; Where the Sunset Turns the Ocean's Blue to Gold; When the Twilight Comes to Kiss the Rose Goodnight; Dreaming of You.

PETRILLO, CAESAR ASCAP 1943
composer, trombonist, conductor
b Chicago, Ill, Aug 1, 1898; d Chicago, Ill, Nov 22, 63. Educ: Pub schs; studied music with Ignacio Izzo, James Sylvester & Edward Geffert. Trombonist in Chicago theatre orchs & dance orchs. WW I, Field Artillery. Led own orch. Music dir, WBBM, Chicago, 37-63. *Songs:* Jim; We'll Never Know; Smile the While We Say Goodbye; Without a Nickel in My Pocket; United National March to Victory; My Thoughts Take Wing; Song of the West; We, Darling You and I; Miss Americana; No Words of Mine; Face to Face; Looks Like a Cold Cold Winter.

PETRONE, JOSEPH ASCAP 1976
composer, teacher
b Pietrelcina, Italy, Jan 12, 28. Educ: Liceo Musicale & Cons, licensed in solfeggio & harmony; pvt comp study. Prof musician since age 16. Plays trumpet, drums, accordion, mandolin & piano; leader of quartet, appearing at local clubs & on TV. *Songs:* Music: My Little City. *Instrumental Works:* Anna Maria (symph march); Maria Rosaria (symph march); Cich e 8 (mil march); Mom's Serenade (mazurka).

PETTY, FRANK ASCAP 1953
composer, author, singer
b Chelsea, Mass, Jan 12, 16. Educ: Boston Cons. Singer in radio, 40's; also sang with Guy Lombardo orch. Entertained servicemen, Pacific, 45. Formed own trio, 51; toured US & Can; also made many records. Entertainer, Sherry Biltmore Hotel, Boston, 48- Chief Collabr: Mike Di Napoli. *Songs & Instrumental Works:* Big Ben Boogie; Pino Pantaloni; Would It Make Any Difference to You?

PETTY, VIOLET ANN ASCAP 1959
composer
b Clovis, NMex, Sept 17, 28. Educ: Univ Okla; studied piano & organ. *Songs:* Someone, Someone.

PEVSNER, LEO ASCAP 1959
composer, author
b Russia, Dec 7, 06. Educ: Chicago City Col; DePaul Univ; Univ Chicago. Wrote songs for Don McNeil's "Breakfast Club" radio network show, 11 yrs; wrote spec material for local radio shows, nightclub & theatre performers. Musical commentator, Nat Pub Radio, now writer & singer of songs about nat & int events. Rec'd two Cash Awards, ASCAP. Chief Collabrs: Henry Pevsner, Naomi Hene Diamond, Eddie Ballantine, Pat Ferreri. *Songs:* Diamond Ring; Without You; All the Time; I Wanna Be Somebody; Rainy Kisses; Happy New Year; Don't Be a Drop Out; Gimme the Car; Alas, Alas, Give Me a Pass; Give the United Way (spec Citation from Chicago Crusade of Mercy); No Better Way to Die; Mama Don't Like to Fly; Little Fat Sam; ABC; Cherry Tree; Aleph Bet Gimmel; Mary's Little Lamb; What Does a Young Man Know 'Bout Making Love; Open Eyes; Haifa (Mee Hoo Hee Shee); Two Hundred Years; Let It Rain; I Don't Care; Bo Pajamas; Family; Shoes Under My Bed. *Instrumental Works:* Daivd and Paula.

PEYRONEL, DANIEL AUGUSTO ASCAP 1976
composer, author, singer
b Buenos Aires, Arg, Nov 15, 53. Educ: Manuel Belgrano Col, BA; studied piano with Sacha Grümberg, 58-68; studied comp with Jose Marti-Llorca, 70-71; Juilliard, 72. Keyboard player/harmony vocals, touring US & Europe with Heavy Metal Kids, Atlantic Records, 73 & UFO, Chrysalis Records, 75-76. Formed The Blue Max, Charisma Records, 77-79; solo career, 80- *Songs:* Martian Landscape; I Know You're There; Silent Woman; Love Me Like a Child; Lyrics: It's the Same.

PFAUTSCH, LLOYD ALVIN ASCAP 1958
composer, teacher, singer
b Washington, Mo, Sept 14, 21. Educ: Elmhurst Col, Ill, AB, MusD(hon), 59; Union Theol Sem, New York, MTh & MSM; Ill Wesleyan Univ, LHD(hon), 78. Choral cond; mem, Robert Shaw Chorale, 3 yrs; mem fac, Ill Wesleyan Univ, 48-58 & Southern Methodist Univ, 58-; vis prof, Union Theol Sem, 52 & 59 & Univ Ill, 56-57. *Songs:* Music: Songs Mein Grossmama Sang; Sing Praises; Reconciliation; Musick's Empire; Go and Tell John; I Hear America Singing; David's Lamentation; A Wondrous Mystery; Music When Soft Voices Die; I Thank You God; Seven Words of Love; In Music God Is Glorified; Who Hath a Right to Sing. *Instrumental Works:* A Day for Dancing; I'll Praise My Maker; Gloria; Befana; Christmas in the Straw; Christ Is the King; Requiem.

PFEIFER, DIANE PATRICIA ASCAP 1976
composer, author, singer
b St Louis, Mo, Nov 4, 50. Educ: Notre Dame High Sch; Col, chem maj, 2 yrs. Lead guitar in all-girl rock group. Singer & voice-over on commercials. Awards: UPI & 2 Emmys for original comps. Staff writer for MCA, 2 yrs. Capitol recording artist. *Songs:* Free to Be Lonely Again; Just When I Needed A Love Song; Roses Ain't Red; Sing You to Sleep; Wishful Drinkin'.

PHAGAS, DIMITMOS
See Fagas, James Jimmie

PHELPS, SANDRA SUE ASCAP 1965
composer, author, singer
b Cresco, Iowa, Sept 19, 40. Educ: Univ Northern Colo, music maj, voice; studied voice with Prudence Clark; studied guitar with Dale Brunning. Shortly after leaving col, embarked on folksinging career, 7 yrs; appeared in cols & coffee houses throughout US incl, Bitter End, New York, Troubador, Los Angeles & Ice House, Pasadena; appeared on TV, "Let's Sing Out," CBC; made two records of own comp. DJ for KFML-Denver, KRNW-Boulder & KTCL-Ft Collins, Colo, prog own radio show music, interviews & comedy, 70- Guitar player. *Songs:* Early Morning; Talk Talk Talk; Juke Box Junkies.

PHILLIPPE, ROY TAYLOR ASCAP 1976
composer
b Cleveland, Ohio, Feb 27, 50. Educ: Kent State Univ, BM, 72, studied comp & orchestration with Phil Rizzo, 66-72; studied piano with Leon Machan & Ruth Laredo. Arr for var big bands, incl Count Basie & Louie Bellson. Associated with Stan Kenton, 72-77. Arr-orchestrator for recordings, film & TV. Play-ons for TV series, "Every Day." Chief Collabr: David Luell. *Instrumental Works:* Shadow Play (Los Angeles Express).

PHILLIPS, BURRILL ASCAP 1947
composer, educator
b Omaha, Nebr, Nov 9, 07. Educ: Denver Col Music, 24-28; Eastman Sch Music, BMus, 32, MMus, 33, studied with Bernard Rogers & Howard Hanson. Teacher theory, orchestration & comp, Eastman Sch Music, 33-49; Guggenheim fels, 42-43 & 61-62; prof music, Univ Ill, 49-64; Fulbright lectr, Univ Barcelona, Spain, 60-61; prof comp, Eastman Sch Music, 65-66, Juilliard Sch Music, 68-69 & Cornell Univ, 72-73. Chief Collabr: Librettist, Alberta Phillips. *Songs & Instrumental Works:* Selections From McGuffey's Reader (suite for orch); Concert Piece (bassoon & string orch); Piece for Six Trombones; Trio for Trumpets; Return of Odysseus (baritone, chorus & orch); Triple Concerto (clarinet, viola, piano, orch); Piano Concerto (piano & orch); Canzoma III (7 instruments & reader); Second String Quartet; Quartet for Oboe and Strings; That Time May Cease (TTBB chorus & piano); Huntingdon Twos and

Threes (flute, oboe, cello); Music for This Time of Year (woodwind quintet); The Recesses of My House (soprano, clarinet, perc & piano. *Scores:* Opera Buffa: Don't We All; Film: Nine From Little Rock (Oscar Award, 65).

PHILLIPS, FRED ASCAP 1925
composer, author
b Boston, Mass, Oct 17, 1890; d New York, NY, Oct 13, 56. Educ: Pub schs. *Songs:* Lily of the Nile; Havana Bay; Ragtime Jim; Goodbye, Little Girl of My Dreams; Got the Bench, Got the Park, But I Haven't Got You; Got Her Off My Hands But Can't Get Her Off My Mind; Stop Kickin' My Heart Around; There's Heaven in Your Eyes; Sweet Little You; Walking Around in Circles; Slappin' the Bass; There's a Blue Ridge 'Round My Heart Virginia; I Am Always Building Castles in the Air.

PHILLIPS, HOWARD BARON ASCAP 1945
composer, author
b New York, NY, Apr 12, 09. Educ: Keene State Col; Goddard Col, masters degree in counseling & psychotherapy. As singer, "Ziegfeld's Rosalie"; as leading man, "Billy Rose's Sweet & Low"; as soloist, NBC, CBS, Coconut Grove, Rainbow Room, Paramount Theatre, Strand Theatre & Radio City Music Hall. Led band at Hotel Taft, Boston & Hotel Brunswick. Made records with Leo Reisman, Ray Noble, Fiorito, Johnny Green & Joe Venuti; winner, Maj Bowes' spec contest for service men. Chief Collabrs: Joe Meyer, Redd Evans, Eddie Delange, Bob Carroll, Dudley Wilkinson, Don Meyer, Ruth Lowe, George Leeman. *Songs:* Will You Promise; Fate, Spin Me a Dream; Stay Here (Beside Me); Are You Somebody Else's Dream?; Music: Livin' Lovin' Laughin'; Lyrics: Holiday Forever (theme, Randy Brooks); Bachelor & Bobby Soxer; Carry on Brother; Lonesome for You; I'd Do It All Over Again; It Used to Be Me; Where in the World Is Love; Before Tonight; I'm Getting Nowhere Fast; Summer Rain; Hook & Ladder Co 94; When I Carried Your Books Home From School; Joe's Cozy Corner; Take Me Back; Thanks for Caring; I Ain't Talkin, (Though It's All Over Town); Peanuts & Kisses.

PHILLIPS, J C ASCAP 1967
composer, author, singer
b Philadelphia, Pa, Oct 21, 53. Educ: Haverford Sch, Pa; Wesleyan Univ, AB, 67, studied with Ravi Shankar; New Sch Music, Philadelphia; Temple Univ Sch Broadcasting. First recording made in Philadelphia at age 14. Managed or produced, The Turtles, Dave Mason, Sugarloaf, Stonebolt, Sweet Pain, Jonathan Cain & The Handcock Bros. Artist, writer & producer, Atlantic Records. Chief Collabrs: Jerry Corbette, Bob Wahler. *Songs:* Green Eyed Lady; Sail On; The Cheap Show; Colorado Jones; Windy City Breakdown; Rock It Down; Highway 101; Mother Natures Wine; Midnight Preacher; Kona Lady.

PHILLIPS, JOHN E A
singer
b Parris Island, SC, 41. Educ: Univ Va; George Washington Univ. Formed the Smoothies with Scott McKenzie; later both joined Richard Weissman to form The Journeymen. Was Papa John of the Mamas & the Papas. *Albums:* Mamas and the Papas; Mamas and Papas Deliver; Mamas and Papas Golden Era; Papas and Mamas; Crashon Screamon All Fall Down.

PHILLIPS, KATHERINE ASCAP 1945
composer
b Brenham, Tex, Mar 22, 12. Educ: Studied voice with Mrs John Wesley Graham, Houston, Tex. Songwriter, 40's. Chief Collabrs: George Olsen, Cliff Friend, Bill Turner, Babe Fritch. *Songs:* Gonna Build a Big Fence Around Texas; Sweethearts of Aggieland; Six Shooter Junction Lil; Violets and Violins; Border Town.

PHILLIPS, KENNETH JAY ASCAP 1970
b Detroit, Mich, June 28, 49. Educ: Univ Mich, BA(speech communications), 71. Songwriter, 70-; wrote numerous song parodies for DJ Dick Puston, Detroit, 75-78; with morning shows on Radio WXYZ-AM & CKLW-AM. *Songs:* Where Strangers Meet; Lyrics: Liquidate Ohio State (parody); On Eight Mile (parody); It Never Rains At Pine Knob in the Summer (parody).

PHILLIPS, LORRAINE
See Kasha, Phyllis L

PHILLIPS, LOUIS JAMES ASCAP 1973
author
b Lowell, Mass, June 15, 42. Educ: Stetson Univ, BA, 64; Univ NC, Chapel Hill, MA(radio, TV, motion pictures); City Univ New York, MA(English, comp lit). Poet, lyricist & playwright, whose plays incl "The Last of the Marx Brothers' Writers", "The Envoi Messages" & "The Ballroom in St Patrick's Cathedral." Author of book & lyrics for numerous musical shows, incl "Byron: A Masque" & the opera "Gulliver." Chief Collabrs: Thomas Pasatieri, Jim D'Angelo, Robert Karmon, Frank Lewin. *Songs:* Lyrics: Heloise and Abelard; Rites de Passage; Three American Songs.

PHILLIPS, MILDRED
See Pressman, Mildred

PHILLIPS, MURRAY ASCAP 1973
composer, author, singer
b New York, NY, Jan 8, 10. Educ: Col of City of New York, BS, 32; Columbia Univ, MA, 33. Taught, Sch, New York, 32-37, New York high schs, 37-72, Harriman Col, 73-75, Ridgewood, NJ, 80- Appeared in folk concerts incl McMillin Theatre Series, Columbia Univ, Rutgers Univ, Sarah Lawrence Col, McGill Univ, Univ PR, high schs, elem schs, throughout the US & in folk fests. Dir of summer concerts, Hillsdale, NJ; recording artist. *Songs:* Your Love; Bye and Bye; Sailor Man No Good; Tides of Lindisfarne; Music: the The Ocean. *Albums:* Murray Phillips Sings.

PHILLIPS, SHAWN ASCAP 1967
composer, author, performer
b Ft Worth, Tex, Feb 3, 43. Recording artist, A&M, RCA, VA & Columbia; did movie soundtracks for "Run With the Wind", "Una Macchia Rosa" & "Com'e L'Amore." *Songs:* Second Contribution; Collaboration; Furthermore.

PHILLIPS, TEDDY STEVE (TEDD SIMMS) ASCAP 1950
composer, author, conductor
b Chicago, Ill, June 15, 16. Educ: Oak Park High Sch; pvt lessons. Played saxophone for Ben Bernie, Ted Weems, Lawrence Welk, ABC & CBS networks. Formed Teddy Phillips Orch. Had own TV Show, Chicago, 56-57. Chief Collabr: Al Trace. *Songs & Instrumental Works:* Cloudburst; Thankful; Camel Hump; Don't Call Me Sweetheart Anymore.

PHILLIPS, WILMA SUSANNE ASCAP 1970
composer, author, singer
b Oakland, Calif, June 26, 41. Educ: Brigham Young Univ, BA(Eng); San Jose State Univ, teachers cert. Singer & bassist with group, Dave & Susanne, 66-79. Chief Collabr: David A Phillips. *Songs:* La Poloma; Lyrics: What Happened to Forever; Master Plan; Seattle in the Rain; Play Me Like a Guitar.

PHOEBUS, FRANK COLEMAN ASCAP 1966
composer, teacher
b Plainfield, NJ, Aug 7, 1899; d Sussex, NJ, Dec 3, 68. Taught piano & organ. Chief Collabrs: Eddie Connors, Dave Ringle. *Songs:* My Schoolday Sweetheart.

PIANO, ANTHONY A ASCAP 1959
composer, author, record executive
b Brooklyn, NY, July 26, 26. Educ: Harvard Univ, BA. Radio producer, 49-57. A&R dir, Columbia Records, 57-60. Independent producer, 60- *Songs:* The Story of My Love; Cherie.

PIANTADOSI, AL ASCAP 1914
composer, pianist, publisher
b New York, NY, July 18, 1884; d Encino, Calif, Apr 8, 55. Educ: St James Sch. Pianist in nightclubs & resorts; on staff, music publ co. Toured vaudeville theatres throughout US with Anna Chandler. Became publ; retired, 30. Charter mem, ASCAP. Chief Collabrs: Al Bryan, Grant Clarke, Henry Fink, Joseph McCarthy, Joe Goodwin, Edgar Leslie. *Songs:* The Curse of an Aching Heart; I Didn't Raise My Boy to Be a Soldier; Pal of My Cradle Days; That's How I Need You; Baby Shoes; When You're in Love With Someone; Send Me Away With a Smile; If You Had All the World and Its Gold; On the Shores of Italy; In All My Dreams I Dream of You; I'm Tired of Making Believe; Where Was Moses When the Lights Went Out?; That Italian Rag.

PICARDO, THOMAS R (TOMMY WEST)
record company executive
b Jersey City, NJ, Aug 17, 42. Educ: Villanova Univ, BS(social studies), 63. Dir music, radio WRIB, Long Branch, NJ, 63-66. Served with USA, 64. Staff promotion ABC, ABC Records, New York, 66. Producer & writer, Cashwest Productions & Lifesong Records, record commercial productions, New York, 68- Music publ, Blendingwell Music. Free-lance singer on radio & TV commercials. Mem: Nat Acad Recording Arts & Sciences; Screen Actors Guild; Am Fedn TV & Radio Artists; Nat Songwriters Asn; Country Music Asn. Comp, "American City Suite," 72. Producer of Jim Croce, Dion, Gail Davies, Voltage Bros, Nina Kahle, Ed Bruce, Corbin & Hanner records. *Albums:* Hometown Frolics.

PICARIELLO, FREDERICK ANTHONY ASCAP 1963
(FREDDY CANNON)
composer, author, singer
b Lynn, Mass, Dec 4, 39. 22 chart hit records. Dick Clark Specials, TV & "Hollywood Squares." Europ appearances. Chief Collabrs: Bob Crewe, Frank Slay, Jerry Goldstein, Russ Reagan. *Songs:* What's Gonna Happen When Summer's Done?; Beechwood City; Tallahassee Lassie; You Know; Patty Baby; Betty Jean.

PICCININNI, JEANETTE M ASCAP 1979
composer, author, guitarist
b New York, NY, Dec 6, 56. Educ: Grover Cleveland High Sch; pvt music study with Joseph Fuoco. Guitarist & singer in nightclubs. Free-lance work; pvt music teacher. Owner, retail music bus. Chief Collabr: Joseph Fuoco. *Songs:* Summerfields; I Am Here; Bad Man; Children In the Lane; As You Wanted.

PICKELL, EDWARD RAY
ASCAP 1972
composer, author, arranger

b Detroit, Mich, Oct 4, 1934. Educ: Albion Col, BA(music theory), 56, senior recital in voice; Mich State Univ, MMus(music educ), 67, graduation recital in voice. Pres, Phi Mu Alpha Sinfonia, Albion Col, 56, pres col band & orch, 56; formal vocal & instrumental music study, age 8; vocal soloist, WXYZ, Detroit Mich; comp studies with col & univ fac; studied voice with Mrs William Neidlinger, 65-66; choral workshop study with Norman Luboff, Frank Pooler, 72. Lyricist. Songword semi-finalist, Am Song Festival, 77, Lyric V winner, 78. Music educator for pub sch & col, 56-80; conductor. Mem: Music Educator's Nat Conference; Nashville Songwriter's Asn, Int; Mich Sch Band & Orch Asn (secy-treas, 58); Mich Music Educators Asn; Mich Sch Vocal Asn; Southwestern Mich Vocal Asn & Festival (pres elect, 70); Ill Music Educator's Asn; Ill Grade Sch Music Asn; Nat Orch Asn; charter bd mem, Ill Cent Col Performing Arts Ctr. TV vocal soloist. Songs: It's the Time of the Year; O'Dove of Peace; Christmas Is for Kids; Through the Eyes of a Child; Christmas Time in America; Three Wisemen Came to Bethlehem; Christmas Morn (contemporary spiritual); Christmas Rag; Give Me An Old-Fashioned Christmas; Waltz of the Snowflakes; A Special Star; What a Beautiful Christmas; Christmas Is a Comin' (contemporary spiritual); The Santa Claus Song; The Littlest Christmas Tree; Mary Had a Baby Boy (contemporary spiritual); Just Give Me All Your Love; Christmas Is Love; The Christmas Waltz; The Saga of "Disco Tex"; Whenever I Pray I See Love; Lyrics: Don't Save Your Love (semi-finalist award, Am Song Festival, 77). Instrumental Works: Percussion Manual for Improving Snare Drum Rolls.

PICKER, GERALDINE LEE
ASCAP 1969
composer, author, teacher

b Manhattan, NY, May 10, 45. Educ: Gen Douglas MacArthur High Sch, Best Musician Award, 63; King's County Hosp Ctr, RN. Comp & lyricist for recording artists & own recordings, 68- Comp, lyricist, singer, guitarist & music dir for several shows, clubs & TV; best known, "Brewery Puppets." Chief Collabr: Marsha Andrea. Songs: I Love Him So; Pleasures; My Man; Music: Music Is the Word; Mighty Fine Town.

PIERCE, (ANNE) ALEXANDRA
ASCAP 1975
composer, teacher, pianist

b Philadelphia, Pa, Feb 21, 34. Educ: Univ Mich, BMus, New Eng Cons of Music, MMus; Radcliffe Col, MA(music); Brandeis Univ, PhD(theory, comp). Danforth Assoc, Antioch Col; prof of music, Univ Redlands Sch of Music; taught movement for performers & Heller Method Training; piano recitalist. Author articles, relationship of structure & movement in music to structure & movement in human body. Chief Collabrs: Fred Strickler, Robert L Stuart, Milton Miller. Instrumental Works: Three Pieces for Clarinet and Piano; Buffalo Bill (voice, tape, clarinet); The Great Horned Owl (kelon marimba); Job 22:28 (clarinet duo); Behemoth (orch); Blending Stumps (prepared piano); Orb (prepared piano); Maola (harp); The Lost River, Sevier (piano).

PIERCE, BETTYE
See Volkart, Bettye Sue

PIERCE, NAT
See Blish, Nathaniel Pierce, Jr

PIERCE, WEBB
performer, actor, singer

Became movie & TV star, TV appearances incl "Kraft Suspense Theatre", "Patti Page Show", "Dick Clark Show", "Steve Allen Show", "Perry Como Show" & "To Tell the Truth" show; headliner, ABC-TV, "Oskar Jubilee Show." Received four triple Crown Awards, Billboard Magazine. Was one of the founders of Cedarwood Publ Co, now owner of two publ facilities incl several Ga radio stas. Songs & Instrumental Works: Wondering; I Ain't Never; More and More; I Don't Care; There Stands the Glass; Walking the Dog; Slowly & many more.

PIERMARINI, CLITO L (PEER MARINI)
ASCAP 1963
composer, teacher

b Leominster, Mass, Dec 21, 27. Educ: Leominster High Sch; Northwestern Univ, BM; Sorbonne, Paris; Santa Cecilia Cons, Rome. Comp, movie scores, New York; singer & pianist, Las Vegas. Songs: TV theme: The Late Show.

PIESTRUP, DONALD J
ASCAP 1966
composer

b Santa Cruz, Calif, Dec 19, 37. Educ: Univ Calif. Writer, big band charts for Buddy Rich, TV & radio commercials.

PIKET, FREDERICK
ASCAP 1956
composer, conductor, organist

b Istanbul, Turkey, Jan 6, 03; d New York, NY, Feb 28, 74. Educ: Music Col, Berlin; Vienna State Cons; Berlin Music Hochschule (Masterclass). Cond, opera in Ger & Switz. Came to US, 40, became citizen. Music dir, Free Synagogue, Flushing, NY. Arr, Sch Sacred Music, Hebrew Union Col. Teacher, NY Col Music, NY Univ. Songs & Instrumental Works: Sea Charm (choral suite); Curtain Raiser to an American Play (orch); The Seventh Day (Friday Evening Serv); Symphony in B; Prelude & Triple Fugue for 6 Woodwinds; Sonata in C (piano); Concerto for Orchestra; The Funnies (suite); How Do I Love Thee?; If

Thou Must Love Me (a cappella); Legend and Jollity (three clarinets); Reflexion and Caprice (four clarinets); Dance and March (two trumpets & two trombones); Eso Enai and V'Ohavto; Trio (flute, clarinet, bassoon); Twinkle, Twinkle Little Star (variations for band); Love? Nay, Nay! (male chorus); The Speaking Silence (female chorus); Kavod La-Torah (Torah Serv for Sabbath Eve); Sim Sholom (solo voice & organ); Ahavas Olom (solo voice & organ); Six High Holiday Selections (cantor, choir, organ); Three Biblical Songs; Memorial Service; Shire B'Ne Y'Shurun (Short Hills Service); Friday Eve Youth Service; Three Songs of Faith; T'Fila; Shire Bet Sinai; The Three Festivals; Seven Sabbath Selections; Shiru Landonai Shir Chadash; Service for Rosh Hashana Eve; Service for Rosh Hashana Morning; This is My God; Music for Yom Kippur, Evening and Morning; Service for Yom Kippur Afternoon and Conclusion; Six Hebrew Prayers; Four Choral Prayers; All Day I Hear; Adonai Malach; In the End; Mixed chorus: 6 About Love; Only for God Does My Soul Wait; Out of the Depths I Cry; Wake Me to Bless Thy Name; It Hath Been Told Thee.

PILLER, EUGENE SEYMOUR
ASCAP 1950
author

b New York, NY, Jan 12, 18. Educ: Univ Calif, Los Angeles, BA. Writer for motion pictures & mag, 39-53; lyric writer, 45- Chief Collabrs: Ruth Roberts, William Katz. Songs: Lyrics: Mr Touchdown, USA; It's a Beautiful Day for a Ball Game; Malaya; Partners; True Blue.

PILLIN, BORIS WILLIAM
ASCAP 1968
composer, teacher

b Chicago, Ill, May 31, 40. Educ: Univ Calif, Los Angeles, AB, 64, studied comp with John Vincent; Univ Southern Calif, AM, 67, studied comp with Robert Linn; pvt comp study with Leonard Stein, 62-65. Comp; pvt music theory teacher; engraver, sheet music. Instrumental Works: Sonata for Clarinet and Piano; Scherzo for Woodwind Quartet; Duo for Percussion and Piano; Three Pieces for Double-Reed Septet; Suite for Flute, Oboe, Clarinet and Organ; Sonata for Cello and Piano; Serenade for Piano and Woodwind Quintet; Tune in C Minor for Piano and Percussion; Scherzo Barbaro for Bass Clarinet and Piano; Four Scenes for Three Trumpets and Piano; Sonatina for Guitar.

PILTZECKER, TED
ASCAP 1974
composer, vibraphonist

b Passaic, NJ, May 22, 50. Educ: Eastman Sch Music, BM, 72; studied with Ray Wright, Warren Benson & Chuck Mangione. Teaching asst, Ohio State Univ; toured as vibraphonist with George Shearing Quintet, 2 yrs; NY State Arts Council & NEA comp grants; mem fac & recitalist, Aspen Music Fest; ASCAP Popular Awards Panel Awards; residencies in seven states as first jazz musician, Affiliate Artists Prog; guest artist & clinician in cols throughout US; leader quartet, Young Audiences, Inc; leader, Ted Piltzecker Ens. Songs: Through My Smile. Instrumental Works: Bus; North High Street Parade; Stepping Out; Pesos, Besos.

PINARD, LANCELOT VICTOR (SIR LANCELOT)
ASCAP 1970
composer, author, singer

b Cumuto, West Indies, May 24, 02. Educ: Western Boys Parochial, Jr Druggist Certificate. Pharmacist; calypso singer & comp, 40- Signed by CBS for var movies, incl "Two Yanks in Trinidad", "Happy Go Lucky" & "Brute Force." Comp music for films & commercials; singer, toured Europe & Asia, 8 yrs; recorded var albums. Songs: I Bawled, I Bawled (Old Lady With the Rollin' Pin); St Martin De Porres (Black Saint of Peru); Carnival in Trinidad; Music: Shame and Scandal in the Family; The Lord's Prayer (Our Father).

PINCUS, BUCK
See Simon, George Thomas

PINCUS, HERMAN
See Herman, Pinky

PINE, ARTHUR (JAY RICHARDS)
ASCAP 1960
composer, author

b New York, NY, Apr 20, 17. Educ: City Col New York, BBA. Pub relations, 38-68; literary agent, 68- Songs: The Three Funny Bunnies.

PINEAPPLE, JOHNNY
See Kaonohi, David

PINERA, MICHAEL CARLOS
ASCAP 1969
composer, singer, guitarist

b Tampa, Fla, Sept 29, 48. Educ: Jefferson & Tampa Catholic High Schs. With Atlantic Records, 66-75; soloist, Capricorn Records, 77-80; main writer, vocalist & guitarist, Spector Records, 77-80. Songs: Ride Captain Ride; Pay My Dues; Take Me to the Sunrise; Reality Does Not Inspire; Butterfly Blue; Stone Believer; Best Years of Our Life; Heart Song; Daddy Ain't Gone; Alone With You; Isla; Can't You Believe in Forever; Goodnight My Love Goodnight; I Am the Bubble.

PINERO, JOSE JUAN — ASCAP 1977
composer, author, bandleader

b Trujillo Alto, PR, Aug 29, 42. Educ: Inter-Am Univ, PR, degree in arts. Bandleader, musical ens Pijuan Sextet, 15 yrs. Keyboard player; TV personality & host. Author, comp, arr & singer. *Songs:* Descargra Pijuan; Que Bueno El Boogaloo; Shake It But Don't Break It; Do Your Shing-a-Ling; Ya estoy en Humacao; Me Voy Pa Carolina; Mi Bomba; Me Encanta Estar por el Libro; Que Sera de Mi Dona; Vamos Toditos Pa San Juan; Increible; Compartimos El Mismo Botiguin; Y Un Chorrito de Pitorro; En El Campo Se Gosa Mas; De Boringuen a Panama; Soy Estudiante; El Soncro Mayor; La Supertrulla; Eating Go Fio; Cancion de Mi Tierra; Mi Alumna Mas Avanzada; Ensalada de Amores.

PINGATORE, FRANK J — ASCAP 1955
composer, author, arranger

b West Chester, Pa, Aug 8, 30. Educ: Juilliard. Arr many rock & roll hits of the 50's; producer. Chief Collabr: Bill Haley. *Songs & Instrumental Works:* Razzle Dazzle; Dim the Lights; Hound Dog; Happy Baby; Tasty Lips; Well Now Dig This; Midnight; Everybody Out of the Pool; Do the Bop; Peppermint Twist; Teen Age Tango.

PINKARD, EDNA BELLE — ASCAP 1946
composer, author

b Ottumwa, Iowa, Mar 19, 1892; d. *Songs:* Sugar Granny; You're in Wrong With the Right Baby; Does My Sweetie Do?; When Love Comes Along; I'll Always Remember Livin' High; Make Those Naughty Eyes Behave.

PINKARD, MACEO — ASCAP 1921
composer, author, publisher

b Bluefield, WVa, June 27, 1897; d July 21, 62. Educ: Bluefield Inst. Toured with own orch; founded theatrical agency, Omaha, Nebr, 14; prod musical, New York; pres, Pinkard Publ, New York. *Songs:* Sugar; Gimme a Little Kiss, Will Ya Huh?; At Twilight; Them There Eyes; Sweet Georgia Brown; Here Comes the Show Boat; Sweet Man; I'll Be a Friend (With Pleasure); Don't Cry Little Girl, Don't Cry; Congratulations; Is That Religion?; Liza; Lila; There Must Be Somebody Else; Okay Baby; That Wonderful Boy Friend of Mine; Let's Have a Showdown; My Old Man; Mammy o' Mine. *Scores:* Bway Stage: Liza.

PINKERT, HERB
See Herman, Pinky

PINKERTON, WILLIAM CHARLES — ASCAP 1969
composer, author

b Alpena, Mich, Feb 16, 36. Educ: Univ Calif; Univ San Francisco, BS, 67; Stanford Univ; San Francisco Acad Music; Niles Bryant Sch Piano Tuning; Alice Bredeson Sch Music. Managed groups, did concerts, worked in creative broadcast media. Chief Collabrs: Ralph Pinkerton, Gary Heins, Gale Wyley, Shota Osabe, Constance Hunt. *Songs:* Come See, Little One; Ride My Lima Bean; Christmas Family; Lyrics: Little Toymaker.

PINTO, MAURICE — ASCAP 1973
composer, author

b Amsterdam, Neth, Aug 4, 07. Educ: Acad Music, Belg. Lead saxophonist & arr, Tushinski, Amsterdam, Neth; with Josephine Baker, 33-34. Formed group, Pinto & His Pintonians; Jack Kluger & His Pintonians; now Pintonian Productions. Mem, Societe Belge des Auteurs, Compositeurs et Editeurs de Musique. Chief Collabrs: Jack & Lorris de Vries, Max Tak, Melle Weersma, Josephine Baker, Ken Little. *Songs:* Time's a Healer; One More Time; I Couldn't Care Less; My Old Pal; Princess; I Recall; I Would Love to Be With You.

PINZ, SHELLEY — ASCAP 1969
composer, author, singer

b Brooklyn, NY, Nov 20, 43. Writer, Pebblestone Productions, Bob Crewe Productions, Buddah Records & E H Morris. Chief Collabrs: Lee Pockris, Paul Leka, LeRoy Glover, Jr. *Songs:* Green Tambourine; Rice Is Nice; Jelly Jungle of Orange Marmalade; Shoemaker Leatherware Square; Without Her; Shoeshine Boy; Tell Me Who I Am; My Rocking Chair; I Need Some; Pink Lemonade; Pretty Thing; I Wrote a Song; Now You Belong to Me; The Way of Love; also Penthouse movie theme; plus commercials.

PIPIA, MIMMO — ASCAP 1961
composer, author, teacher

b Italy, Jan 11, 02. Educ: In Italy. *Songs:* L'Astronauta; Coco Coco; Regina; Doretta; Un Topo in Paradiso; Il Paradiso; Il Presidente Kennedy; La Bella Indiana.

PIRON, ARMAND JOHN — ASCAP 1942
composer, author, conductor

b New Orleans, La, Aug 16, 1888; d New Orleans, Feb 17, 43. Educ: St Agnes Sch; studied music with Albert Piron (brother) & Charles Eldger. Cond own orch, New Orleans. *Songs:* Mama's Gone Goodbye; Brown Skin; I Wish I Could Shimmy Like My Sister Kate; Let It End; Mama's Got It; Purple Rose of Cairo; America They're Both for You; Day by Day.

PISACANE, MARCI (MARCI SUTIN) — ASCAP 1972
author

b New York, NY, Jan 14, 46. Educ: High Sch Performing Arts, theatre major. Auth bk & lyrics for off-Bway show, "Tokyo Diary," at Cafe La Mama, 71; author bk & lyrics for Bway option show, "Crazy Love." Songwriter in Tokyo, 5 yrs. Writer pop songs in NY. Author musical teaching cassette "Images," Bantam Bks. Chief Collabrs: Istsuro Shimoda, Tetsugi Hayashi, Marsha Mallamet. *Songs:* Lyrics: If I Have to Go Away; After All This Time; When You've Gone; Still a Boy. *Albums:* Love Songs and Lamentations.

PISTILLI, GENE — ASCAP 1968
composer, author, singer

b Fairview, NJ, Mar 27, 47. Educ: Cliffside Park High Sch, NJ. Partner, Cashman, Pistilli & West, writers, singers & producers, 67-70. Founding mem, Manhattan Transfer, 70-72. Chief Collabrs: Terry Cashman, Tommy West, Tom Anthony, Pat Rosalia, Walter Murphy. *Songs:* Sunday Will Never Be the Same; But for Love; Sold My Soul to Rock 'n' Roll.

PISTRITTO, JOHN (JOHNNIE TRITT) — ASCAP 1969
composer, author, singer

b New York, NY, June 24, 20. Educ: Paulding High Sch; Hartnett Music Sch, studied voice & guitar, 49-54, BA, dipl, 54. Country & western singer, nightclubs & radio weekly prog. Chief Collabr: Henry Boyd. *Songs:* I Love You, My Little Sweetheart; A Letter for Mother; What Have I Done?; The Man in the Moon; I Love No One But Mother.

PITMAN, WILLIAM — ASCAP 1967
composer

b Belleville, NJ. Educ: Self-taught. Arr for jazz bands; wrote 2 instr bks. Arr 2 original tunes for Art Pepper Band. *Instrumental Works:* San Fernando Valley.

PITTMAN, EVELYN LARUE — ASCAP 1963
composer, author, choral director

b McAlester, Okla, Jan 6, 10. Educ: Highland Park High Sch, Mich, dipl; Spelman Col, BA, 33; Okla Univ, MMus, 54; pvt study comp with Nadia Boulanger, Paris, France, 56-57. Taught music in Okla City Pub Sch System, 35-36, Greenburg District Pub Sch System, 58-76. Choral cond many award winning choirs incl Evelyn Pittman Choir, 38-52; cond 350-voice interdenominational choir, 48-56; guest cond, Westchester All-County Jr High Festival, White Plains, NY, 64; dir, Woodlands High Sch Choir, 66, 71-76. *Songs:* Rich Heritage (bk 21 songs, short stories & pictures); Music: Rocka-Mah Soul; Any How; Sit Down Servant; Joshua. *Scores:* Folk Opera: Cousin Ester; Drama: Freedom Child; Jim Noble.

PITTS, GERTRUDE ELIZABETH — ASCAP 1968
composer, author

b Philadelphia, Pa, Aug 10, 32. Educ: Philadelphia Musical Acad; Temple Univ; Juilliard Sch Music; Conn Col Women, BM, teachers cert. Traveled in US, Europe, Can, Bermuda & the Carribean, performing on piano and organ. Also vocals with own group, Trudy Pitts & Mr C. Have performed with Sonny Stitt, Gene Ammons, Ben Webster and others. Recorded under own name, also with Rahsaan Roland Kirk, Willis Jackson & Pat Martino. Performed in clubs, concert halls, cols, radio & TV. Chief Collabrs: Bill Carney, Rahsaan Roland Kirk. *Songs:* The Ghetto Song; Christmastime; Clouds. *Instrumental Works:* Anysha; Mean Perspectives; My Thang; Moon Stones; Colorless Wind; Freedom Child; Old Shoes; Steppin' in Minor; My Waltz; Git-it, Git-it; Siete; Come Dawn; Le Neo-Leo; Just Doin' It; A Whole Lotta Amen.

PITTS, VINCENT CLIFFORD — ASCAP 1962
composer, trumpeter

b St Louis, Mo, Jan 29, 35. Educ: High sch. Trumpeter in dance bands; with 423rd USA Band, 59-60. *Songs & Instrumental Works:* Trudie's Delight; Trane Stop; Blue Rocky; Interlude; Soul Blues; Outside Blues.

PLACE, MARY KAY — ASCAP 1969
composer, author, singer

b Tulsa, Okla, Sept 23, 47. Educ: Univ Tulsa, BA, 69. Wrote many songs for TV show "Mary Hartman, Mary Hartman," also sang songs on show in role of Loretta Haggers, Emmy Ward, 77. Wrote "If Communism Comes Knocking At Your Door" for episode in "All in the Family," also sang & performed. Script writer for many TV comedy shows, incl "Mary Tyler Moore Show," "Mash," "Phyllis" & "Maude." Developed & wrote many pilot scripts & variety shows. Acted in var TV shows, incl "Mary Tyler Moore Show," "All in the Family," "Mash" & "Saturday Night Live." Host "John Denver Special" & others; features: "Bound for Glory," "New York, New York," "More American Grafatti," "Private Benjamin," "An Act of Love" & "Starting Over." Recorded albums for Columbia Records "Love Tonite At the Capri Lounge," "Aimin' to Please" & "Almost Grown." *Songs:* Baby Boy; Vitamin L.

PLANO, GERALD PETER — ASCAP 1969
author

b Los Angeles, Calif, Mar 15, 38. Educ: Pasadena Playhouse. Began career as prod stage mgr, Off-Bway musicals. Creator & producer of recorded direct mail collections until 63; A&R coordr, Premium Dept, RCA Victor Records, mgr spec music proj, RCA Music Serv. Author of novel, "Hollywood Postcards."

Recipient of several gold albums created or produced; author, NBC-TV doc, "Tornado-Xenia, Ohio." Chief Collabrs: R C Garrison, R Gorobetz, J Krondes, S Zabka, P Giasson. *Songs:* Lyrics: Handful of Happy New Years; Gone (Where Did a Lifetime Go?); Flying Home for Christmas; That's What a Dance Floor Is For; Look Ahead With Me; I Will Be With You (On Christmas Day); Moving Day; Interlude; Meditation.

PLANT, ROBERT ANTHONY   ASCAP 1968
composer, author
b West Bromwich, Eng, Aug 20, 48. Began as lead vocalist with group Band of Joy. Became lead singer for Led Zeppelin, does harmonica work & writer of original material recorded by band. Chief Collabs: Jimmy Page, John Paul Jones, John Bonham. *Songs:* Good Time Bad Time; Dazed and Confused; Communication Breakdown; Whole Lotta Love; Thank You; Heartbreaker; Living Loving Maid; Immigrant Song; Since I've Been Loving You; Black Dog; Rock and Roll; Stairway to Heaven; The Song Remains the Same; Over the Hills and Far Away; Dancing Days; D'Yer Mak'er; No Quarter; Trampled Under Foot; Kashmir; In the Light; Ten Years Gone; Night Flight; Achilles Last Stand; Nobody's Fault But Mine; Candy Store Rock; In the Evening; Fool in the Rain; All My Love.

PLATTHY, JENO   ASCAP 1976
composer, author, conductor
b Dunapataj, Hungary, Aug 13, 20. Educ: P Pazmany Univ, teacher's dipl, 42; Ferenc Liszt Cons, 43; Ferencz J Univ, PhD, 44; Catholic Univ of Am, MS, 65; studied with Bela Bartok & Zoltan Kodaly. Debut, Bruxelles, 39. Music reviewer for Nouvelle Europe & INFO, Tokyo. Exec dir, Fedn of Int Poetry Asn of UNESCO; mem of var foreign academies, insts & socs; recipient, 2 laureateships & 3 hon doctorates; nominated twice for Nobel Prize. *Instrumental Works:* Concertum Lyrae (Opus 11); Christmas String Quartet (Opus 80). *Scores:* Opera: Bamboo.

PLAYMAN, GORDON   ASCAP 1975
composer
b St Croix Falls, Wis, Jan 29, 22. Educ: Univ Minn, BA, 47, studied comp with Donald N Ferguson; Tanglewood, 47, studied with Honegger, Copland, Barber; Univ Calif, Santa Barbara, grad studies, 72. Spec agent, Federal Bureau Investigation, serving in Okla, Philadelphia, Minn, Los Angeles, Santa Barbara & Honolulu, 48-72, retired. Comp, 48- *Songs:* Music: Eleven Dickinson Songs. *Instrumental Works:* Sisyphus Symphony; Theme and Aliases; Two Scenes from Dante. *Scores:* Ballet Score on Three Levels.

PLEIS, JACK K   ASCAP 1950
composer, conductor
b Philadelphia, Pa, May 11, 20.

PLUMB, EDWARD H   ASCAP 1948
composer
b Streator, Ill, June 6, 07; d Studio City, Calif, Aug 18, 58. Educ: Dartmouth Col, BA; Univ Austria, PhD. Began with Walt Disney Studios, 37; arr background music for "Fantasia", "Dumbo", "Bambi", "Pinnochio", "Snow White and the 7 Dwarfs", "Cinderella", "Lady and the Tramp", "Sleeping Beauty", "Peter Pan" & "Nature Series." *Songs:* Music: Raindrops.

PLUMB, (BENJAMIN) NEELY   ASCAP 1961
producer, arranger, conductor
b Augusta, Ga, Nov 17, 12. Educ: Acad of Richmond County, Augusta; Ga Tech, mechanical eng; studied harmony & comp with Sigvart Hofland, Chicago, Julius Gold, San Francisco; self-taught, arr & orch. Had campus band at Ga Tech, Neely Plumb & His Georgia Tech Ramblers; first alto saxophonist & arr with Anson Weeks, 30's, Artie Shaw, 40, Ray Noble & Victor Young; mem staff recording orch, Universal Studios, MGM Studios & RKO Studios, Hollywood, 15 yrs; head West Coast A&R, RCA Records, 58-68; independent record producer, 68- Composer & cond for records & albums; clarinetist/saxophonist. Chief Collabrs: Ron Kramer, Leon Pober, Eddie Maxwell, Arthur Hamilton. *Songs:* Paco Peco (Span lyric); For You (dramatic score narrative long play); Aloha Hawaii; Happy Sad Song; My Funky Valentine; Massage Parlor; How Will It Be; What Ever Happened?; Together Again, For the First Time; Along El Camino Real; That Half-Hacienda of Mine.

PLUMBY, DONALD   ASCAP 1959
composer, author, conductor
b Martins Ferry, Ohio, Nov 8, 19. Educ: Univ Ky. Musician & arr with dance bands, 40-55. Tech Sgt, USA, WW II; led Army dance band. Asst cond & arr, Latin Quarter, New York, 5 yrs. Asst cond Bway musical, "Bye Bye Birdie"; assoc cond, "Zizi" (revue); cond, "Once Upon a Mattress." *Songs:* Samson; Porch Swing.

PLUMMER, ELDORA FITE   ASCAP 1968
composer, author
b Novelty, Mo, Oct 13, 15. Educ: Pvt piano lessons, 8 yrs; voice lessons, 2 yrs; Northeast Mo State Univ. Won first place in amateur songwriting contest & performed number on organ, 67; career has been in bus; comp, a side-line. *Songs:* I Wanna Be Happy.

PLUMMER, HOWARD   ASCAP 1957
composer, author, publisher
b New York, NY, Jan 29, 21. Educ: Yale Univ, BA. Author, comp & producer musical commercials, 49- Founder, HAP Music. Bd mem, Musical Commercial Producers Asn & Am Bosch Arma Corp. *Songs:* May Santa Fill Our Hearts (This Christmas); Hearts Are Funny Things; A Man About Town (That's Me!); Who Takes My Hand?; Learning to Love; Watch Out for Your Heart; Naive; You Know; Too Bad Baby; Commercials: There's No Catching Plymouth (Nat Asn Radio-TV Broadcasters award); Suddenly—It's 1960 (Radio Advert Bur award). *Scores:* Stage: Sconset Heyday.

PLUMMER, JEAN VINCENT   ASCAP 1955
composer, pianist, arranger
b Lyle, Wash, Mar 22, 13. Educ: Col. Pianist, CBS, NBC radio & TV; also film studio orchs. Has recorded with Meredith Willson, Carmen Dragon. Orch mgr & pianist, Melodyland Theatre, Anaheim, Calif.

POBER, LEON   ASCAP 1954
composer, author
b Springfield, Mass, Mar 24, 20; d Los Angeles, Calif, May 31, 71. Educ: High sch. Wrote spec material for Margaret Whiting & Jerry Lewis. Wrote for films; also wrote theme from TV show "Ben Casey." Chief Collabr: Bud Freeman. *Songs:* Evening Rain; La La Colette; The Ski Song; Moonlight Mountain; Walk to the Bull Ring; Tangi Tahiti; Gunslinger; Pearly Shells; Beyond the Rainbow; Tiny Bubbles. *Scores:* Bway Stage: Beg, Borrow or Steal; Hardly a Kind Word About Anybody. *Albums:* Songs of Couch and Consultation; Almost Authentic Folk Songs.

POBLINER, HARRIET   ASCAP 1967
composer
b New York, NY, Aug 7, 43. Educ: George Washington High Sch, New York; NY Univ. Started writing music & lyrics at age 15. Hired by Al Caiola to work for his publ co. Did lyrics for Phil Bodner, Boldex Productions. *Songs:* Bossa Nova Noel; Lyrics: No More Tears.

POCHON, ALFRED   ASCAP 1924
composer, author, violinist
b Yverdon, Switz, July 30, 1878; d Switz, Feb 26, 59. Educ: Studied with Cesar Thomson. Asst prof, Brussels, 1896; first violinist, Ysaye Orch; organized Flonzaley Quartet, 03 & Stradivarius Quartet, 29; US citizen, 28; dir, Cons of Lausanne, Switz, 41. Decorated by French Govt; Order Knight of the Crown of Roumania; author, "A Progressive Method of Quartet Playing", "Jean-Jacques Rousseau, Musician"; educator. *Songs & Instrumental Works:* Indian Suite; Ballade; Andante Sostenuto; Theme Varie (with Paderewski; for string quartet); Passacaglia (viola).

POCKRISS, LEE J   ASCAP 1955
composer, author, pianist
b New York, NY, Jan 20, 27. Educ: Brooklyn Col, BA; NY Univ, MA; Tanglewood; studied with Stefan Wolpe, Aaron Copland. Wrote shows at Camp Tamiment, also wrote ballet music for Bway musicals "Top Banana" & "Three Wishes for Jamie." Chief Collabrs: Paul Vance, Bob Hilliard, Anne Croswell. *Songs:* Catch a Falling Star; Itsy Bitsy Teeny Weeny Yellow Polka Dot Bikini; My Little Corner of the World; A Handbag Is Not a Proper Mother; A Wicked Man; My Very First Impression; My Heart Is an Open Book; What Is Love?; The Only One; Wait for Me; I Know the Feeling; All for You; Seven Little Girls (Sitting in the Back Seat); Calcutta; Starbright; Johnny Angel; Go Chase a Moonbeam; Marie, Marie; Hey Love; Jimmy's Girl; I Don't Know; A World Without Sunshine; In My Room; Stagecoach to Cheyenne.

PODDANY, EUGENE FRANK   ASCAP 1952
composer, film editor
b Harbin, China, Dec 23, 19. Educ: Hollywood High Sch, 37; studied comp with Dr Ernst Toch, comp & orchestration with Mario Castelnuovo-Tedesco. Film ed & comp, Leon Schlesinger Productions incl Bugs Bunny, Daffy Duck & Porky Pig cartoons, Walter Lantz Productions, incl Woody Woodpecker cartoons & Metro-Goldwyn Meyer Animation incl Tom & Jerry cartoons; comp, John Sutherland Productions, live action-animation documentary films & var specials incl Dr Seuss' TV specials "How the Grinch Stole Christmas" & "Horton Hears a Who," Walt Kelly's "Pogo's TV Special Birthday Special" & Norton Juster's "The Dot and the Line," short subject Academy award, 66; sculptor. Chief Collabrs: Irving Bibo, Dr Seuss. *Songs:* Music: Woody Woodpecker March; Andy Panda Polka; Oswald the Rabbit Hop; Dr Seuss songs: The Cat in the Hat Songbook; The Super-Supper March; My Uncle Terwilliger Waltzes with Bears; In My Bureau Drawer; The No Laugh Race; Plinker Plunker; Hurry Hurry, Hurry; Cry A Pint; Ah-A-A-A-A-A-H; I Can Figure Figures; Somebody Stole My Hoo-to Foo-to Boo-to Bah; Rainy Day in Utica, New York; Lullaby for Mr Benjamin B Bickelbaum; Happy Birthday to Little Sally Spingel Spungel Sporn; My Uncle Terwilliger Likes to Pat; Yawn Song; The Left Sock Thieves; Drummers Drumming; Party Parting.

PODELL, ARTHUR M   ASCAP 1961
composer, singer, producer
b New York, NY, Oct 2, 36. Educ: Studied classical guitar with Rolando Valdez-Blaine, NY; Columbia Univ. Solo folk musician, New York, prior to 58;

in duet of Art & Paul, 58-60; songwriter with Henry Mancini Co, 60-61; primary mem, New Christy Minstrels, 61-66; producer & writer motion picture music & publ, 66- Chief Collabrs: Walter Schorr, Rod McKuen, Barry McGuire. *Songs:* Everybody Loves Saturday Night; Music: You Know My Name; Lark Day; Miss Katy Kruel; So Long, Stay Well.

PODOLSKY, LEO S
pianist, teacher
b Odessa, Russia, May 24, 1891. Educ: Studied with George Lalewicz, Odessa, until 06; studied in Cracow, Poland, 06-12; Vienna State Acad, Austria, scholarship, 12-14. Pianist, recitals, concerts & as soloist with major symph orchs, Europe, Am & Asia. Mem, artist fac, Sherwood Music Sch, Chicago, 26-; visiting prof, St Mary's Col, Notre Dame, 18 yrs; guest fac, Mozarteums, Salzberg, Austria. Clinician; conducts master classes at var cols & univs, jr master classes & workshops. Music ed, var classical piano publs; ed of bks: "The Moving Hand"; "The Stationary Hand, Bks A & B"; "The Fixed-Hand Position, Bks A, B, C & D"; "Rhythms and I-V 7th Chords"; "Chords, Cadences and Transposition"; "Dances in Major and Minor"; "Lower Elementary Bks One & Two"; "Upper Elementary Bks One & Two"; "Lower Intermediate Bks One & Two"; "Intermediate Bk One"; "Higher Intermediate Bk One"; principles of pedaling incl "Select Sonatinas"; "More Select Sonatinas"; "Duet Playing"; classic sonatas from 18th century composers incl "Introduction A"; "Introduction B"; "Advancing"; "Advanced"; "Piano Progress"; "A 20th Century New Piano Method, Bks I, II & III"; "Piano Sonatinas"; "The Piano Way to Music"; "The Music Speller"; "The Music Reader, Bks I, II & III"; & other piano solos, fest pieces & sonatas. Recipient, Liszt & Anton Rubenstein prizes. Chief Collabr: June Davison.

POE, HORACE COY   ASCAP 1950
author
b Huckaby, Tex, Dec 20, 07. Educ: Tex Christian Univ; Univ Okla; PhD(clinical psychology), PhD(criminal psychology). Comp songs for many films; produced many shows with var artists. Practicing psychologist. *Songs:* Lyrics: The Trouble With Me Is You; Don't Be Afraid to Tell Your Mother; If It Wasn't for the Moon; The Object of My Affection; What's the Reason I'm Not Pleasin' You; That's What You Think.

POHLMAN, M RAY   ASCAP 1962
composer, musical director, arranger
b Melvin, Iowa, July 22, 30. Educ: Manual Arts High Sch, Los Angeles, Calif; pvt instr. Jazz guitarist, 50. Musical dir, TV & films. Grammy nomination for best arr. *Scores:* Stage: Catch My Soul.

POLA, EDWARD   ASCAP 1940
composer, author, teacher
b New York, NY, June 23, 07. Educ: Univ London, MA. Assoc mem, Inst Elec Engrs, Eng. Producer for radio & TV in US & Eng, 33-64; exec with Granada TV, Eng, 54-64. Film actor & writer, Eng. Teacher of English. Chief Collabrs: George Wyle, Eddie Brandt, Franz Steininger, Freddie Spielman. *Songs:* I've Got a Note; I Love the Way You Say Good-Night; Lyrics: Marching Along Together; The Most Wonderful Time of the Year; My Canary Has Circles Under His Eyes; The Kazoo Song; You Broke Your Promise; Quick Silver; I Didn't Slip, I Wasn't Pushed, I Fell; I Said My Pajamas; The Longest Walk; She'll Always Remember. *Scores:* Bway Show: Woof-Woof; Here's Howe.

POLEDOURIS, BASIL KONSTANTINE   ASCAP 1970
composer
b Kansas City, Mo, Aug 21, 45. Educ: Studied piano with Dorothy Judy Klein & Lillian Stuber, comp with David Raksin; Univ Southern Calif, BA(film). Scored student films, became film ed for educ & indust films, left editing & film making, 70, now scoring of theatrical motion pictures. *Songs:* Music: The Blue Lagoon (love theme). *Scores:* Films: Big Wednesday; The Blue Lagoon.

POLIN, CLAIRE   ASCAP 1964
composer, flutist, musicologist
b Philadelphia, Pa. Educ: Philadelphia Cons Music, BMus, MMus, DMusA, 55; Juilliard Sch Music; Temple Univ, Pa; studied comp with V Persichetti, P Mennin, R Sessions, L Foss & flute with William Kincaid. Leverhulme fel to Gt Brit; lectr in Europe & Israel. Prof, Rutgers Univ & dir univ exchange concerts. Free-lance flutist, records for var record cos; musicologist & comp. Mem, Pan-Orphic Duo, flute & harp; comn & perf, Seoul Philh, New York Philh, Gregg Smith Singers, Ken Dorn, William Kincaid, Karen Phillips. Awards, Ga State Univ, 70, Delta Omicron, twice, Gedok (Ger) & Vercelli (Italy). *Instrumental Works:* First Flute Sonata (flute, piano); Death of Procris (flute, tuba); O, Aderyn Pur (flute, alto saxophone, tape); Scenes from Gilgamesh (flute, string orch); Ma'alot (viola, perc quartet); Owain Madoc (brass quintet); Cader Idris (brass quintet); Summer Settings (solo harp); Infinito (soprano, alto saxophone, narrator, dancers, SATB); Paraselene (soprano, flute, piano); Windsongs (soprano, guitar); Makimono (mixed); Sonata (flute, harp); Margoä (solo flute); Structures (solo flute).

POLISTINA, ANTHONY THOMAS   ASCAP 1975
composer, lyricist, pianist
b Orange, NJ, June 29, 44. Educ: Cranford High Sch; Union Col, BS(psychol); Mannes Col of Music, BA(comp), studied piano with Frances Marantz; New

Sch for Social Research, (theatre), studied comp with Robert Hebble. Pianist, in concert throughout NY, NJ & Conn. Comp & arr, music for industrials. Writer, bk, music & lyrics for 5 musicals. *Songs:* And Rejoice; A Charles Dickens Christmas; There Is a Child; See the Child; Run; A Child; A Joyful Noise (comn, 76) concert series incl: Love Is Like Nature; As Long As I Remember Love; John; For Now; Lyrics: Incline Thine Ear; A Goodly Time to Be Dancing; Midnight Sleighbells; One Hundred Years (comn, S New Eng Bell, 77). *Scores:* Bway show: A Fine and Private Place.

POLITTE, CHARLOTTE
See Gilmore, Charlotte Politte

POLK, HERSHOLT CALVIN (OBILO)
composer, author, singer
b Chicago, Ill, Jan 5, 42. Educ: Frances E Willard Elem Sch; Tilden Tech High Sch; Kennedy King Col. Actor in several plays & films. Songwriter & producer with Jerry Butler Songwriters Workshop, 5 yrs. Singer, actor in numerous commercials for radio & TV. Artistic dir & assoc producer, Black Arts Celebration, Chicago. Chief Collabrs: Homer Talbert, Donald Whitehead. *Songs:* If You Move, You Lose; Lyrics: Ain't Understanding Mellow; She's a Real Live Stepper; Said a Mother, Said a Father; As the Seasons Change; Were We Lovers, Were We Friends.

POLK, MARY JANE (MARY JANE PEAKS)   ASCAP 1953
composer, author
b New York, NY, Aug 19, 16. Educ: Univ Pa, DDS; Columbia Univ, cert in orthodontics; NY Univ, cert in interior design. Dental practice specializing in orthodontics. Mem, Am Dental Asn, Am Soc of Orthodontists & Fel of Royal Soc of Health. *Songs:* I Told a Lie.

POLL, RUTH   ASCAP 1948
author
b New York, NY, June 10, 1899; d New York, Mar 14, 55. *Songs:* I'm a Military Man; Weary Little Fellow; I'd Love to Make Love to You; These Things Money Can't Buy; I'm Wearing a New Shade of Blues; It Was So Good While It Lasted; If Yesterday Could Only Be Tomorrow.

POLLA, W C   ASCAP 1926
composer, conductor, arranger
b New York, NY, Aug 12, 1876; d New York, NY, Nov 4, 39. Educ: Chicago Cons; NY Col Music. Cond & arr, Bway musicals & radio. Chief Collabrs: Phil Ponce, Cliff Friend, Charles Tobias. *Songs:* Dancing Tambourine; The Troubadour; When Evening Shadows Fall; Dear Heart; The Melody That Made You Mine; Some Day; Carmencita; Old Mother Hubbard; The Gondolier. *Instrumental Works:* America My Homeland; Symphonic Idyl; Pilgrimage to Mecca.

POLLACK, BEN   ASCAP 1954
composer, conductor, drummer
b Chicago, Ill, June 22, 03; d Palm Springs, Calif, June 7, 71. Drummer with New Orleans Rhythm Kings. Formed own band, 25. Had own record co during 40's. Appeared in film, "The Glenn Miller Story." Restaurant & bar owner in Palm Springs & Hollywood. *Songs & Instrumental Works:* Tin Roof Blues; Make Love to Me.

POLLACK, LEW   ASCAP 1920
composer, author, singer
b New York, NY, June 16, 1895; d Hollywood, Calif, Jan 18, 46. Educ: DeWitt Clinton High Sch. Boy soprano in Walter Damrosch Choral Group. Singer & pianist in vaudeville. Wrote theme music for silent films incl "What Price Glory" & "Seventh Heaven." Chief Collabrs: Sidney Mitchell, Erno Rapee, Paul Francis Webster, Sidney Clare, Ned Washington, Ray Gilbert, Jack Yellen. *Songs:* Charmaine; Diane; Angela Mia; That's a-Plenty; Two Cigarettes in the Dark; In the Middle of a Kiss; I'm Missin' Mammy's Kissin'; Weep No More My Mammy; Early Bird; Moonshine Over Kentucky; At the Codfish Ball; One in a Million; Alone With You; Miss Annabelle Lee; Reap the Wild Wind; Sing, Baby, Sing; The Right Somebody to Love; Cheatin' on Me. *Scores:* Film: Pigskin Parade; One in a Million; Life Begins in College; Rebecca of Sunnybrook Farm; Captain January.

POLLOCK, BERT D   ASCAP 1955
author, actor, teacher
b Pittsburgh, Pa, June 30, 23. Educ: Carnegie Tech, BFA, MFA, scholarship. WW II, USAAF. Dir of drama dept, Berea Col, 49-50. Staff entertainment dir, 5th USA area, 50-57. Stage mgr, off Bway production "Leave It to Jane." Chief Collabrs: Hugh Martin, Ralph Blane, Frank McNulty, John Miller. *Songs:* If I Cry; So Goes My Love; Tonight Is the Last Time; It's the Army; I'll Be Following You; Dear Diary; I'm Not Alone; A Beautiful Girl to Make Love To; Glad, Glad, Glad; Athena (film title song).

POLLOCK, CHANNING   ASCAP 1914
author
b Washington, DC, Mar 4, 1880; d New York, NY, Aug 17, 46. Educ: Bethel Mil Acad; Polytechnique, Prague; Colgate Univ, hon LittD; Northeastern Univ, LLD. Began as press reporter for theatrical producers; then became playwright.

Drama critic, 05-19. Charter mem, ASCAP. Author: "Star Magic" (novel); "Synthetic Gentleman" (novel); "Guide Posts in Chaos" (essays); "Harvest of My Years" (autobiography). Playwright: "Roads of Destiny"; "The Crowded Hour"; "The Sign on the Door"; "The Fool"; "The Enemy"; "Mr Moneypenny"; "The House Beautiful". Librettos: "The Red Widow"; "The Beauty Shop"; "My Best Girl"; wrote songs for "Ziegfeld Follies" (15, 21). *Songs:* My Man (Eng lyric); Marie Odile; I Love Love.

POLLOCK, MARTIN
See Gardner, Maurice

POLLOCK, MURIEL   ASCAP 1933
composer, pianist
b Kingsbridge, NY; d Hollywood, Calif, May 25, 71. Staff organist, NBC. Wrote songs for play, "Pleasure Bound." *Songs:* Mood in Blue; Lost in Love; In Allah's Garden; Love Is a Dancer; Ode to a Man About Town; Children's "talking books": Cinderella; Sleeping Beauty; Little Black Sambo; Jack and Jill. *Instrumental Works:* Spanish Suite; Hispana; Reminiscence.

POLSTON, JEAN JERRETT
See Jerrett, Jean

POMERANZ, DAVID HYMAN   ASCAP 1977
composer, author, singer
b New York, NY, Feb 9, 51. Educ: Roosevelt High Sch, Stamford, Conn; Univ Cincinnati; Lehman Engel Musical Theater Workshop. Recording artist, 71- Record producer. Film actor in "Americathon." Appeared on "Dinah" & "Midnight Special." Toured, more than 500 concerts & clubs. Chief Collabrs: Buddy Kaye, Spencer Proffer, John Barry, Dominic Frontiere, Lisa Cohen. *Songs:* It's in Every One of Us; Trying to Get the Feeling Again; Daybreak; If You Walked Away; Gold Theme; Don't You Ever Say "No"; Let It Be Now; Music: What You See Is Who I Am; Theme for Gumball Rally; Lyrics: Are You in There? (theme for King Kong).

PONCE, ETHEL   ASCAP 1951
composer, singer, pianist
b New York, NY. Daughter of Phil Ponce. Mem of singing duo, Ponce Sisters; sang in vaudeville, on radio, also records; then pianist in small groups. Music teacher in pvt sch. *Instrumental Works:* 3 Dialogues for Piano, Orch; Happy Landing; Holiday; Blue Haze; A Light in the Window; also Bell Telephone commercial.

PONCE, PHIL   ASCAP 1929
composer, author, publisher
b Cambridge, Mass, Apr 15, 1886; d New Haven, Conn, Aug 21, 45. Exec, artists' bureau of nat radio chain; professional mgr singing groups; music publisher, New Haven. Chief Collabrs: W C Polla, Dan Dougherty. *Songs:* Dancing Tambourine; I'd Rather Cry Over You Than Smile at Somebody Else; Oh, You Have No Idea; Oh the Last Rose of Summer Was the Sweetest Rose of All; Let's Don't and Say We Did; Underneath the Palms; Sugar Rose.

POOLE, DONN H   ASCAP 1976
composer
b Houston, Tex, Feb 6, 45. Educ: E Tex Baptist Col, BA, 68; Southwestern Sem, Tex, MMus, 70. Studied classical & folk guitar; began composing, 72; concerts & singing engagements, 75- Studying Am folk, bluegrass & country music; developing composing technique for country music writing, 80- *Songs:* Sweetest Thing I Know; God Is There; There Was a Man; I Met the Christ Who Took My Place; I Love You (for Changing My Life); He'll Give You a Reason to Live; Sail Away; Edgar the Ant; Out-a-Sight Out-a-Mind; Life Gets Better and Better; Brand New Morning.

POOLE, GEORGE E   ASCAP 1960
composer, conductor, flutist
b Columbus, Nebr, Nov 21, 04. Educ: Pvt tutors. Flutist in dance bands; then with WGN, Chicago, 10 yrs & ABC, Hollywood, 15 yrs. Leads own band.

POOLER, FRANK   ASCAP 1970
composer, author, teacher
b La Crosse, Wis, Mar 29, 26. Educ: St Olaf Col, BM; State Univ Iowa, MA & MFA. Teacher, Shimer Col, Mt Carroll & New Trier Township High Sch, Winnetka, Ill. Dir music, First Lutheran Church, Albert Lea, Minn; dir choral studies, Calif State Univ, Long Beach. Cond, The Carpenters. Chief Collabr: Richard Carpenter. *Songs:* Music: Thou Art Worthy; Be Thou My Vision; Man of Sorrow; The Desert Shall Rejoice; I Will Be As the Dew; Praise Him With Trumpets; The Face of God; Two Christmas Songs; Lyrics: Merry Christmas Darling.

POPE, T L   ASCAP 1964
composer, author
b Statesboro, Ga, Aug 23, 04. Educ: Savannah State Col, BSA. Works in mfg dept, Western Electric Co, 43- Chief Collabrs: Harry Stitz, Millie De Rosa. *Songs:* Please Tell Me Now; This Eventide; Lord, My Heart Cries to Thee.

POPE, WILLIAM T   ASCAP 1963
composer, author, actor
b Ramsey, Ill, Mar 25, 24. Educ: NY Univ, BS, 52, MA, 60, studied with Gerald Cook & Rudolph Schramm, New York & Giuliano Pomerantz, Rome, Italy. Solo singer & dancer, "Diamond Horseshoe," 50. Appeared in Bway musical "Fanny," 54-56; actor, "Biribri," RAI-TV, Italy. Singer, dancer & guitarist, 63. Teacher, Spanish, sr high sch, New York. *Songs:* I Don't Cry.

POPIOLKOWSKI, LOUIS JOHN   ASCAP 1963
composer
b Canonsburg, Pa, Sept 1, 27. Educ: Univ Pittsburgh, BA, masters degree. Pianist & arrangement writer with var big bands incl Russ Romero, Lee Barrett & Rio Richerts, 35 yrs. Arrangement writer, group Four Coins; songwriter. Chief Collabr: Al Marino. *Songs:* Music: Every Time We Kiss; Break the Glass; Coming Home From School; A Silver Medal; My One Mistake.

POPPLEWELL, MARY PAGE   ASCAP 1962
composer, author
b Italy, Tex, Oct 15, 20. Chief Collabr: Raymond Edison Page. *Songs:* It's a Cryin' Shame; How Softly a Heart Breaks; The Only Thing; Someone Else's Hands; There's a Time.

POPWELL, ROBERT LEE (POPS)   ASCAP 1975
composer, author, instrumentalist
b Daytona Beach, Fla. Educ: Bethune Cookman Col; Los Angeles Mission Col. Staff musician, Capricorn Records, Macon, Ga & Atlantic Records, Miami, Fla. Toured with The Rascals, Dr John, The Crusaders, Larry Carlton, Al Jarreau, Tom Scott. Chief Collabrs: Larry Carlton. *Songs:* Be on the Real Side; Lyrics: Feel It. *Instrumental Works:* Feeling Funky; The Way We Was; Cosmic Reign.

PORAT, YORAM   ASCAP 1978
author
b Tel Aviv, Israel, Aug 16, 39. Educ: Studied in Israel; Gene Frankel Workshop, Actors Studio & Stela Adler Theatre Studio, New York. Has been awarded by Israeli Broadcasting Authority for Best Radio Play & by Council of Art & Culture for Best Play of Yr. Chief Collabr: Shlomo Gronich. *Scores:* Amerika (musical); The Golem (last play); Chemdat (culinary opera).

PORTER, ANDREW BRIAN   ASCAP 1978
author
b Cape Town, SAfrica, Aug 26, 28. Educ: Diocesan Col, Cape Town, studied comp with Albert Coates, 40-46; Univ Col, Oxford, BA & MA. Played organ for col serv & cond col choir & orch, Univ Col, 47-50. Music critic, The Financial Times, London, 52-72 & The New Yorker, 72-; ed, The Musical Times, 60-67. Translator of English singing version, Wagner: "Tristan", "The Ring"; Verdi: "Macbeth", "Rigoletto", "La Fuerza del Destino", "Othello", "Falstaff"; Richard Strauss: "Intermezzo"; Mozart: "The Magic Flute"; Rossini: "The Turk in Italy"; Thomas: "Hamlet" & many others.

PORTER, B L
See Ballard, Clint C, Jr

PORTER, COLE   ASCAP 1931
composer, author
b Peru, Ind, June 9, 1891; d Santa Monica, Calif, Oct 15, 64. Educ: Worcester Acad; Yale Univ, BA; Harvard Law Sch; Harvard Sch Music; Schola Cantorum, Paris; studied with Vincent d'Indy. War relief work in France; attached to French Foreign Legion & US Embassy; in Europe until 28. Biographies: "Cole Porter: The Life That Late He Led" by George Eells; "The Cole Porter Story" by Richard Hubler; "Cole," ed by Robert Kimball; "Cole Porter," by Charles Schwartz; film biography, "Night and Day." *Songs:* Yale Bulldog Song; Bingo Eli Yale; I've a Shooting-Box in Scotland; An Old-Fashioned Garden; I'm in Love Again; Two Little Babes In the Wood; Let's Do It; The Laziest Gal in Town; Let's Misbehave; Which?; You Do Something To Me; You've Got That Thing; Find Me a Primitive Man; The Tale of an Oyster; What Is This Thing Called Love?; Looking at You; Miss Otis Regrets; Love for Sale; Where Have You Been?; Let's Fly Away; After You; Night and Day; How's Your Romance?; I've Got You on My Mind; Experiment; Nymph Errant; I Get a Kick Out of You; All Through the Night; You're the Top; Anything Goes; Blow, Gabriel, Blow; Why Shouldn't I?; Begin the Beguine; Just One of Those Things; Down In the Depths; It's De-Lovely; Red, Hot and Blue; Goodbye Little Dream Goodbye; Ridin' High; Easy to Love; I've Got You Under My Skin; In the Still of the Night; Who Knows?; Rosalie; At Long Last Love; Get Out of Town; Most Gentlemen Don't Like Love; From Now On; My Heart Belongs to Daddy; Do I Love You?; Well, Did You Evah!; Katie Went to Haiti; But in the Morning No; Friendship; It Was Written in the Stars; I Concentrate on You; I've Got My Eyes on You; I've Still Got My Health; Let's Be Buddies; Make It Another Old-Fashioned, Please; So Near and Yet So Far; Dream Dancing; Ev'rything I Love; Ace In the Hole; Don't Fence Me In; You'd Be So Nice to Come Home To; Something For the Boys; Hey Good-Looking; By the Mississinewah; Sing to Me, Guitar; I Love You; Ev'rytime We Say Goodbye; Pipe-Dreaming; Love of My Life; Be a Clown; Another Op'ning, Another Show; Wunderbar; So in Love; Were Thine That Special Face; Why Can't You Behave?; Too Darn Hot; Brush Up Your Shakespeare; Always True to You in My Fashion; Where Is the Life That Late I Led?; Where, Oh Where; I Am Loved; From This Moment On;

Use Your Imagination; Nobody's Chasing Me; C'est Magnifique; I Am in Love; It's All Right With Me; I Love Paris; Paris Loves Lovers; All of You; Without Love; You're Sensational; I Love You Samantha; True Love; Ca, c'est l'amour; Come to the Supermarket. *Scores:* Bway Stage: See America First; Hitchy Koo, 1919; Greenwich Village Follies of 1924; Paris; Fifty Million Frenchmen; Wake Up and Dream; The New Yorkers; Gay Divorcee; Nymph Errant (London); Anything Goes; Jubilee; Red, Hot and Blue!; You Never Know; Leave It to Me; DuBarry Was a Lady; Panama Hattie; Let's Face It!; Something for the Boys; Mexican Hayride; Seven Lively Arts; Around the World In Eighty Days; Kiss Me, Kate (Tony award, 49); Out of This World; Can-Can; Silk Stockings; Film: The Battle of Paris; Born to Dance; Rosalie; Broadway Melody of 1940; You'll Never Get Rich; Something to Shout About; The Pirate; High Society; Les Girls; TV: Aladdin; Ballet: Within the Quota.

PORTER, LEO BERNARD (LEE)   ASCAP 1962
composer, orchestrator, arranger
b Montreal, Que, Feb 8, 30. Educ: Wayne State Col; Detroit Cons Music. Choirmaster, vocal coach & arr for recordings & films; spec material, nightclub acts also Off-Bway show, "The Golden Kazoo" & revue, "The Orphans of the Storm." Chief Collabr: Ronald Miller. *Songs:* Music: The Good Times; A Handful of Memories; Fifty-Fifty; Like the Honey for the Bee; Girls Need Loving Care; He's a Lover; You've Got Your Mind On Other Things; When a Woman's in Love; Not for All the Money.

PORTER, LEW   ASCAP 1938
composer, director
b New York, NY, Feb 4, 1892; d North Hollywood, Calif, Jan 30, 56. *Songs:* Wake Up, Virginia; They Needed an Angel in Heaven; Romance in the Rain; In Elk Valley; Romance in Rio; The Little Red Fox; Ashes of Roses.

PORTER, ROBERT MORRIS (PACO GATSBY)   ASCAP 1968
composer, arranger, singer
b Berkeley, Calif, Nov 12, 24. Educ: Berkeley High Sch; Univ Calif, Berkeley, BA(music), 49, studied comp with Roger Sessions; Westlake Sch Music, comp with Russ Garcia & Alfred Sendry. Orchr for Darrell Calker & Nathan Scott, "Lassie Show." Baritone-arr, Lancers Quartet, records, TV & nightclubs, arr, "Donald O'Connor Show", studio singer, Ray Conniff & others. To Guatemala for Baha'i Faith, 70. Musical dir, Dila Record Co, arr, dir, producer of records, jingles & documentaries. Chief Collabr: Mickey McMahan. *Songs:* Music: Release the Sun; Bubble Shuffle; Walking Alegre; Estelares.

PORTER, ROY L   ASCAP 1975
composer, author, drummer
b Colorado Springs, Colo, July 30, 23. Educ: Wiley Col, (journalism, music). Started prof playing, 43. Recorded, with Charlie Bird Parker, 46, & drummer, with Dexter Gordan, Earl Bostic, Louis Jordan, Perez Prado. Recording artist with own group. *Songs:* Lonesome Mood; You Do This to Me; Love You; Got a Funny Feeling; Music: Summer Night. *Albums:* Grazin'.

PORTNOFF, MISCHA   ASCAP 1942
composer, pianist, teacher
b Berlin, Ger (Russian parents), Aug 29, 01; d. Educ: Stern Cons, with father; Royal Acad Stockholm. Mem, Swed Royal Acad. Had own music studio, Brooklyn. Background music & Theatre Guild prod, "Merry Wives of Windsor." Chief Collabr: Wesley Portnoff. *Instrumental Works:* Marches for Tomorrow; Piano: Murals; Prelude; Improvisations et Ruga Libera; Piano Sonata; Quartet for Piano, Strings; For 2 Pianos: Perpetual Motion on a Theme of Brahms; Brief Flirtation; Playful Leaves; March of the Imps; Song Cycles: From a Bayou Cabin; From Temple and Tepee; Lodge Fire Tales. *Scores:* Stage: The Royal Blush; Happy as Larry.

PORTNOR, RALPH B   ASCAP 1960
composer
b Indianapolis, Ind, Jan 29, 19. Radio correspondent, WW II. Comedy & song writer & announcer on radio & TV. Radio voice for Lawrence Welk Champagne Music in over 5000 broadcasts. Dir sales, Hollywood Palladium for 18 yrs. Speaker to hundreds of serv clubs, women's clubs, management groups & churches. Chief Collabrs: Zeke Manners, Joe Rizzo, Myron Floren. *Songs:* You Stand Tall When You Kneel to Pray; Lyrics: Secretary Polka; Petticoat Polka; There is This Need; Mother Nature's in Love.

POSEGATE, MAXCINE WOODBRIDGE   ASCAP 1970
composer, author, teacher
b Modesto, Calif, June 5, 24. Educ: Wheaton Col, Ill, BS; Calif State Univ, Long Beach, MA, studied with Leon Dallin. Taught music in pub & pvt schs. Teacher music theory & class piano, Northwestern Col, St Paul, Minn. Church choir dir & organist, pvt piano teacher. *Songs:* The Gift of Love; Holy, Lord of Hosts; Procession to Jerusalem; Lead on Softly; The Fiery Furnace (manuscript cantata).

POSNACK, BLANCHE   ASCAP 1953
composer, author, teacher
b Brooklyn, NY, Oct 30, 12. Educ: NY Univ, BA; Univ Maine, MA. Songwriter of children's songs and plays performed throughout the sch system. Chief Collabr: George Posnack. *Songs:* Don't Ever Marry for Money (Only for Love);

It's a Wonderful Life; Sing a' Day (bk children's songs & playlets); You're a Lucky Little Fellow (Am Acad Award for best war song).

POSNACK, GEORGE   ASCAP 1950
composer, pianist
b Brooklyn, NY, July 31, 04; d. Educ: NY Univ Law Sch. Pianist, Warner Bros Brooklyn Studio, 10 yrs; also for Rodgers & Hart Bway musicals, 37-42 & at Capitol & State Theatres. Piano salesman. Chief Collabr: Blanche Posnack (wife). *Songs:* Don't Ever Marry for Money; It's a Wonderful Life.

POTTER, ARTHUR WAYNE   ASCAP 1979
composer, arranger, producer
b San Antonio, Tex, Dec 9, 53. Rec'd prof training on job & worked with producer Bob Mackenzie, arr John Coates, musician Gordon Twist & others in recording studio. Music dir, trombonist & vocalist for contemporary Christian road group, Eternity, 73-79, also recorded ten albums with them; music dir, Fla Bible Church, Hollywood, 80- Producer & arr for groups & churches in the area. *Songs:* I Love to Sing (His Song of Love); More Than Words; The Coming of the Lord.

POTTER, NEVILLE   ASCAP 1972
author
b Birmingham, Eng, Sept 10, 41. Educ: Moseley Sch Arts & Crafts, Eng; Birmingham Col Arts & Crafts, Eng. First Prize Silver Medal for Engraving & Silversmithing, City & Guilds of London Inst. Designer; hand engraver; artist. Lyricist & writer. Chief Collabrs: Chick Corea, Stanley Clarke. *Songs:* Lyrics: 500 Miles High; What Game Shall We Play Today?; Open Your Eyes You Can Fly; You're Everything; Butterfly Dreams; Sea Journey; Sometime Ago; San Francisco River; Times Lie; Looking At the World.

POTTLE, SAM   ASCAP 1962
composer, pianist
b New Haven, Conn, May 8, 34; d New York, NY, July 4, 78. Educ: Phillips Exeter Acad, 51; Yale Univ, BA, 53, MA, 59. Chief Collabrs: David Axelrod, Charles Choset, Tom Whedon. *Songs:* What's the Name of That Song?; A Shaker Patchwork; Jabberwocky; Moving On; Be Kind to Your Neighborhood Monsters; Muppet Show Theme. *Scores:* Off-Bway Stage: All Kinds of Giants; Money; TV: America, Be Seated.

POTTS, JOHN R   ASCAP 1979
composer, author, singer
Educ: Univ Okla, BBA. Songwriter, Nashville, 5 yrs. ASCAP Award, 79. *Songs:* She's Been Keepin' Me Up Nights; I Don't Talk to Strangers.

POTTS, WILLIAM ORIE   ASCAP 1967
composer, recording engineer, teacher
b Arlington, Va, Apr 3, 28. Educ: Washington-Lee High Sch, Arlington; Cath Univ Am. Recording engr & arr, USA Band, 49-56. Chief comp-arr for Willis Conover's Orch. Cond & arr for album "The Jazz Soul of Porgy and Bess." Arr & cond own albums, "Bye Bye Birdie" & "How Insensitive." Piano and/or arr-comp for Buddy Rich, Woody Herman, Count Basie, Stan Kenton, Phil Woods, Quincy Jones, Al Cohn/Zoot Sims & Lester Young. Piano arr-cond for Paul Anka, 64-68. Recording specialist & teacher of jazz arr, Montgomery Col, Rockville, Md, 73- Recording artist for United Artists, VIK, Decca & Pablo. *Instrumental Works:* Big Swing Face; Standing Up in a Hammock; Eesom; Brazilville; Light Green; Pill Box; Playground; Willis; The Opener; High Steppin Bizzles; Dry Chops in the Moonlight; Frank the Barber; Pottsville USA; Blixed; Hags; Strange Again; Flute Cocktail; Crazy Head; Dingle Bird; Half Breed; Happy Blues.

POWELL, BRYCHAN B   ASCAP 1948
author
b Scranton, Pa, Aug 24, 1896. Educ: Mansfield State Teachers Col. WW I, USA. Mem, Scranton Bd of Educ, 33. Managing ed, Scranton Tribune & The Scrantonian, 38-64. Chief Collabrs: Frances Williams, Philip James. *Songs:* The Song My Heart Will Sing; Gwilym Gwent.

POWELL, DAVID (DAVID DAVID, WILL DAVID)   ASCAP 1975
composer, author, singer
b Cleveland, Tex, Sept 4, 34. Educ: San Francisco State Univ, BA, 59; Highlands Univ, MA, 66; Southern Ill Univ, PhD, 70. Served in USA, 55-57; mathematics, history & literature teacher, 59-65; univ prof language & literature, 65- *Songs:* Cottonfield Sun; Song of Melchior (Holy Child); Mystic Air; Mary's Boy; Devil Man; Fable; Away, Away; Waterline; Lyrics: Ebenezer; Bornin' Tonight.

POWELL, JACK (JASON HAWKINS)   ASCAP 1977
composer, author, singer
b Scott County, Mo, Aug 12, 41. Educ: Sikeston High Sch; Oxford Univ, mil sci. Served in var African armies, several yrs. Country & western songwriter. Pres & head producer, Foxfire Records. Promoter. Chief Collabrs: Jennifer Foxx, C Allen Powell. *Songs:* Middle Aged Fool; Love Is; A Song That I Can Sing; She Only Loved You for the Dream; My Last Dream.

POWELL, JOHN   ASCAP 1930
composer, pianist
b Richmond, Va, Sept 6, 1882; d Charlottesville, Va, Aug 15, 63. Educ: Univ Va, BA; studied music with F C Hahr, Leschetizky & Nawratil. Concert debut as pianist, Berlin, 07; toured Europe 4 yrs, Am debut, Richmond, 12 & Carnegie Hall Concert, 13; gave 25th anniv benefit concert, Carnegie Hall, 38; piano soloist, symph orchs throughout US. Mem, Nat Inst Arts & Letters. *Songs & Instrumental Works:* Green Willow; Jockie to the Fair; Pretty Sally; In Old Virginia; Natchez On the Hill; From a Loved Past; Sonata Virgianesque; In the South; Virginia Symphony (Symphony in A).

POWELL, JOHN LEONARD   ASCAP 1975
composer, author, singer
b San Diego, Calif, July 20, 44. Educ: Univ Ill, BS(forestry), 66; Univ Mo, MS(forest econ), 69; Southern Ill Univ, MS(elem educ), 71. Singer gospel music, 66- Sch teacher & prin, 69-78. Songwriter, 73- Cabinetmaker, 78- *Songs:* Miracle Worker; The Angel's Gonna Shout It; Satisfied; Harvest of Blessing; Thank You Lord for the Day.

POWELL, LAURENCE   ASCAP 1923
composer, organist, choirmaster
b Birmingham, Eng, Jan 13, 1899. Educ: Ratcliffe Col, Leicester; Ushaw Col, Durham; scholarships: Birmingham & Midland Inst Sch of Music; Birmingham Univ, BM; Univ of Wis, MA; studied with Bantock; Fellow, Trinity Col of Music, London. WW I, British Army, RAF. Music critic, Boston Transcript, 23-24. Instr, Univ of Wis, 24-26; assoc prof of theory, Univ of Ark, 26-34; head of music dept, Little Rock Jr Col, 34-39. Organized & cond, Little Rock Symph; cond, Grand Rapids Symph, Mich, 39-41 & Rio Grande Symph, 61. Organist & choirmaster, St Andrews Cathedral, Grand Rapids, 39-47; St Mary's Church, Victoria, Tex, 47-52 & St Francis Cathedral, Santa Fe, NMex, 52- *Instrumental Works:* Concertino for English Horn, Small Orch; The Ogre of the Northern Fastness (suite); Keltic Legend; Deirdre of the Sorrows; Variations on an Original Theme; Charivari; County Fair; Sam Houston; Duo-Concertante (recorders, orch); The Santa Fe Trail (Rio Grande Symph comn); Mass in Honor of St Andrew; Canticle for Soprano, Recorder & Piano; also 2 symph.

POWELL, MEL   ASCAP 1956
composer
b New York, NY, Feb 12, 23. Educ: Studied comp with Ernst Toch & Paul Hindemith; Yale Univ, MusB & MA. Teacher, Yale Univ, chmn comp fac, 54-69; dean, Sch Music, Calif Inst Arts, 69-72, provost & vpres acad affairs, 72-76, inst fel, 76- *Songs & Instrumental Works:* Filigree Setting (string quartet); Haiku Settings (voice & piano); Immobiles I-IV (orch & tape); Stanzas (orch); Divertimento (violin & harp); Divertimento (five winds); Setting (cello & orch); Settings (soprano & chamber group); Little Companion Pieces (soprano & string quartet).

POWELL, MORGAN EDWARD   composer
b Graham, Tex, Jan 7, 38. Educ: NTex State Univ, BM, 59, MM, 61, comp studies with Samuel Adler; Univ Ill, Urbana, 65-67, comp studies with Kenneth Gaburo. Jazz arr & comp, Dallas, Tex, 58-63; taught jazz comp, NTex State Univ, 61-63; taught jazz comp & related courses, Berklee Sch Music, Boston, 63-64; taught theory/comp, Univ Ill, Urbana, 67-, presently full prof music & chmn comp div. Grants: Fromm Found, Univ Ill, Univ Ill Ctr for Advan Study & NEA. Comns from the Spoleto Fest, 77. Recordings of music on Advance Records, Crystal Records & University Brass Recording Co. *Instrumental Works:* Midnight Realities; Inacabado; Alone; Faces; Darkness II (brass quintet); Brass Quintet No II.

POWELL, ROBERT JENNINGS   ASCAP 1965
composer
b Benoit, Miss, July 22, 32. Educ: La State Univ, BM(organ-comp), 54; Union Theol Sem Sch Sacred Music, MSM, 58. Asst organist-choirmaster, Cathedral of St John the Divine, New York, 57-59; organist-choirmaster, St Paul's Episcopal Church, Meridian, Miss, 60-65; dir music, St Paul's Sch, Concord, NH, 65-68; organist-choirmaster, Christ Church (Episcopal), Greenville, SC, 68- Fel & choirmaster, Am Guild Organists. Chief Collabr: Billie Echols. *Songs:* Music: Apperception (cantata for 2 choirs); Of the Father's Love Begotten (cantata); Jesus! Name of Wondrous Love (anthem, SATB); Let Faith Be My Shield (anthem, SS). *Instrumental Works:* Free Hymn Accompaniments (for organ).

POWELL, TEDDY RAYMOND   ASCAP 1933
composer, author, bandleader
b Oakland, Calif, Mar 1, 06. Educ: San Francisco Cons. Musician, Abe Lyman Orch, 17 yrs. With advert agency, 35-40. Formed own band, 40-46, appeared throughout US in nightclubs, hotels, theatres & films. Made pictures incl "Jam Sessions," Columbia Pictures; videophone shorts for Warner Bros; also recorded for Victor Records, 4 yrs & Decca Records. Now in music publ bus, Tee Pee Music Co Inc. Chief Collabrs: Lenny Whitcup, Bob Merrill, Tony Starr, Walter G Samuels, Claude DeMetruis. *Songs:* Take Me Back to My Boots and Saddles; I Couldn't Believe My Eyes; March Winds and April Showers; Heaven Help This Heart of Mine; The Snake Charmer; If My Heart Could Only Talk; Love

of My Life; Bewildered; Unsuspecting Heart; With Faith in Your Heart; All I Need Is You; Always Look Up; April Give Me One More Day.

POWERS, MELVIN   ASCAP 1974
composer, author
b Boston, Mass, Apr 23, 32. Educ: Boston Univ. Writer of country-western songs. Chief Collabr: Tommy Boyce. *Songs:* Who Wants a Slightly Used Woman?; Mister Songwriter; Willie Burgundy; Devil Man; I Wanna Believe in Love.

POWERS, ROD
See Maschek, Adrian Mathew

POWERS, THOMAS EDWARD   ASCAP 1978
composer, author, singer
b Washington, DC, June 10, 48. Educ: Manchester West High Sch, NH; Keene State Col, NH, 3 yrs. Singer, pianist, night clubs & concerts; recording artist, Big Tree Records. *Songs:* It Ain't Love; Thoughts of You; Rise and Shine; Willie.

POZDRO, JOHN WALTER   ASCAP 1965
composer, educator
b Chicago, Ill, Aug 14, 23. Educ: Am Cons Music, Chicago, studied piano with Edward Collins; Northwestern Univ, BMus, 48, MMus, 49, studied comp with Robert Mills Delaney; Univ Rochester Eastman Sch Music, PhD, 58, studied with Howard Hanson, Bernard Rogers, Alan Hovhaness; studied piano & theory with Nina Shafran, Chicago. Served in USA, World War II. First prof orch perf, 50. Third Symphony, comn by Oklahoma City Symph under Ford Found grant; Sonata No 4 funded with Nat Endowment for Arts grant, 75. *Instrumental Works:* Third Symphony; Piano Sonata No 2; They That Go Down to the Sea in Ships; All Pleasant Things; Waterlow Park; Landscape II.

PRAGER, SAMUEL   ASCAP 1963
composer, pianist
b Jersey City, NJ, Mar 22, 07; d. Educ: Inst Musical Art, Juilliard Sch Music, with Carl Friedberg. Accompanist to Bing Crosby, Kate Smith, Morton Downey, Frank Sinatra, Lanny Ross & Danny Kaye. *Instrumental Works:* Piano: Poinsetta; Purple Pastel.

PRATER, JOHNNIE LEE   ASCAP 1972
composer, author, singer
b Spencer, Tenn, Apr 3, 06. Nightclub singer. *Songs:* Country Music: Green Southern Boogie; So Lonely Today; Wildcat Still; If I Could Feel Your Lips Pressing to Mine.

PRATT, ANDREW SEARS   ASCAP 1971
composer, author, singer
b Boston, Mass, Jan 25, 47. Educ: Westminster Sch; Harvard Col. Recording artist, Columbia Records & Newspun Records. Chief Collabr: Mark Doyle. *Songs:* Avenging Annie; That's When Miracles Occur; Savior; All I Want Is You.

PRATT, LOUIS TRUETT   ASCAP 1975
composer, author, singer
b San Antonio, Tex, Oct 22, 49. Educ: Thomas Jefferson High Sch, San Antonio, Tex; Baylor Univ. With var gospel groups; with group Brotherlove, 70; entertainer, nightclubs & TV; recording artist, Pratt & McClain for Columbia, ABC Dunhill & Warner Bros; instrumentalist. Chief Collabrs: Steve Barry, Bob Alcivar, Jerry McClain, Michael Omartian. *Songs:* California Cowboy; Summertime in the City; When My Life Is Over; Rock and Roll Fever.

PRATT, SAMUEL ORSON   ASCAP 1965
composer, author
b El Paso, Tex, Mar 20, 25. Educ: Brigham Young Univ; Eastman Sch Music, flute, Joseph Mariano; Univ of Utah, BA, MA; Columbia Univ, EdD. Flute & harp accompanist for Roberta Peters, 17 yrs; principal flute, Utah Symph, 5 yrs; flutist, New York, also others. Soloist, Los Angeles Chamber. Winner, Friends of Harvey Gaul. Featured on "Ed Sullivan TV Show", "Mike Douglas Show" & "Dick Cavett Show." Author, "Affairs of the Harp." *Instrumental Works:* Concerto No 2 in B minor (harp & orch); Harp Solo: The Little Fountain; Sonata in Classic Style; 5 Preludes; numerous collections of music for harp. *Scores:* Opera/Ballet: The New Song (oratorio).

PRESCOTT, NORM (JEFF MICHAEL)   ASCAP 1967
composer, author
b Boston, Mass, Jan 31, 27. Educ: Pub Latin High Sch; Emerson Col. DJ, WHDH, Boston, 47-50, WNEW, New York, 55-56 & WBZ, Boston, 56-59. Prog dir, WORL, Boston, 50-55. Vpres, record producer & publ, Music Embassy Pictures, 59-61. Producer feature film musical, "Journey Back to Oz." Comp, writer & producer of over 30 different animated network TV series. Chief Collabrs: Yvette Blais, Dean Andre. *Scores:* Animated TV series: Fat Albert; Archie; Tarzan; Tom and Jerry; Lone Ranger.

PRESS, JACQUES   ASCAP 1951
composer, conductor, arranger

b Tiflis, Russia, Mar 27, 03. Educ: Studied piano at age 6; local high sch & cons; studied comp with Nadia Boulanger, Paris, France, 22-23, orchestration with Leo Zeitlin, trumpet with Max Schlossberg, NY. Improvisational pianist, silent movies, age 14. To Istanbul, Turkey, 20, Paris, 22. Toured Europe, own orch, 24-25. To US, 26; arr, Roxy Theatre, NBC, Capitol & Music Hall with Erno Rapee, Frank Black & J Bonime; invited to White House for concert, 36. Writer, scores & songs, numerous motion pictures, Hollywood, 38-50; suprvr, TV music, NY, 50. Associated with Boston Pops with Arthur Fiedler, Richard Hayman, Andre Kostelanetz & Richard Goldman. Music coordr, Bolshoi Ballet video taping, Los Angeles, 59; pianist & teacher. Chief Collabs: Eddie Maxwell, Stanley Cowan, Frank Loesser, Sol Meyer. *Songs:* Music: Breathless (Was No 4, Lucky Strike Hit Parade); Love At Last; I'm Gonna Swing My Way Up to Heaven; Zig Me Baby With a Gentle Zag (piano boogie woogie); How Was I to Know; Olivia; Tap-Happy; Talkin' to the River; Rhythm of the Islands; What in the World?; After All These Years; Music Is the Heart of Me; Can I Stop Loving You?; Hallucination; Information Please!; This Time Tomorrow. *Instrumental Works:* Hasseneh (suite for orch); Wedding Dance; Prelude and Fugue, in Jazz; Disconcerto (piano, orch); Polka Coloratura (orch); Polka in C (2 harps); Blues Nostalgia (piano); Spice-Cakewalk (orch); Israeli Festival March; Russian-Gypsy Dance; Jig-Jag. *Scores:* Spanish Interlude. *Albums:* Children's: Songs About History.

PRESSER, WILLIAM HENRY   ASCAP 1964
composer

b Saginaw, Mich, Apr 19, 16. Educ: Alma Col, BA, 38; Univ Mich, MM, 40; Univ Rochester, Eastman Sch Music, PhD, 47, studied comp with Roy Harris. Played violin & viola with Rochester Philh, 44-46. Teacher in Iowa, Fla, Ala, Tex & Calif Cols, 47-52. Teacher, Univ Southern Miss, 53- *Instrumental Works:* Chorale Fantasy (high sch level orch); The Devil's Footprints (band); Rhapsody on a Peaceful Theme (violin, horn & piano); Second Brass Quintet; Suite for Six Tubas; Sonatina (tuba & piano); Third Brass Quintet; Second Sonatina (tuba & piano); Symphony No 2 (band). *Songs & Instrumental Works:* Songs of Love and Death (mezzo-soprano & string quartet or string orch); Song of Simeon (bass voice & string orch); Four Herrick Songs (soprano, horn & piano); Seven Southern Songs (chorus & orch); Concerto (wind quintet & strings).

PRESSLEY, ALLEN ANDREW   ASCAP 1976
composer, choirmaster

b Columbus, Ohio, June 16, 18. Educ: Hammond Sch Music, grad, 51; Wurlitzer Sch Music, studied organ, 54. Played piano, WJOB Radio Sta, Hammond, Ind, 52-55. *Songs:* Jesus, He Prayed Alone; Think of Christ; Jesus, I'm Keeping Him on My Mind; Mighty Good God; The Voice of God; Once Again; When I Get Home.

PRESSMAN, AILENE
See Goodman, Ailene Sybil

PRESSMAN, HARRY   ASCAP 1960
composer, author

b Philadelphia, Pa, Dec 24, 07; d Philadelphia, Jan 15, 73. Educ: Drexel Tech. In clothing mfg business. *Songs:* Red Hot; Nobody Nowhere; The Red Dress.

PRESSMAN, MILDRED (MILDRED PHILLIPS)   ASCAP 1955
composer, author

b Philadelphia, Pa. Educ: High sch; bus col. Writer of many recorded & publ songs for movies, concerts, plays, & one-woman shows; appeared on TV & radio interviews. Chief Collabrs: Jimmy De Knight (James E Myers), Steve Carpenter, Jim Ayre, Len Lewy, Miriam Roberts, Bud Brees, David Saturen, Leroy Lovitt. *Songs:* Mambo Rock; Head Home Honey; Teenage Kids; The Wrong Guy; Lyrics: If You're Not Completely Satisfied; My Heart Is Not a Toy; Never Will I Forget; I Dig 'Em All; Where There's a Will. *Albums:* Happy Holidays (ASCAP award).

PRESTON, WALTER H   ASCAP 1942
author, singer, producer

b Quincy, Ill, Feb 9, 01. Educ: Pace Inst of Accountancy; studied music with Sergei Klibansky; Juilliard Sch Music, 3 yrs scholarship with Francis Rogers. Singer in radio, 25; also on stage & in films. Wrote & produced "The Show Shop," WOR, NY. Dir of radio, Columbia Concerts, 43-48. Had own talent agency, NY. News ed, The Produce News, trade paper; publisher, 44- Won Gold Medal, NY Music Week Asn; 1st place, NY State Fedn Music Clubs annual competition. *Songs:* Southern Skies; All Day Long; Slumber On; Lamp of Love; Mississippi Lament; Cute and Sweet; So Long; The Kiss I Stole From You; My Dream of Love; Dance of the Gypsies.

PREVIN, ANDRE   ASCAP 1952
composer, arranger

b Berlin, Ger, Apr 6, 29. Educ: Cons in Berlin & Paris; studied with Mario Castelnuovo-Tedesco. To US, 39. At age 17, arr for MGM, Hollywood. In service, USA, 50-52. Comp many film scores, four Acad Awards. Cond, Houston Symph, 67-69, London Symph Orch, 68-79 & Pittsburgh Symph, 76- Chief Collabrs: Philip Larkin, Alan Jay Lerner, Johnny Mercer. *Songs:* Music:

Five Songs for Soprano; Every Good Boy Deserves Favour; Coco; The Good Companions. *Instrumental Works:* Portrait for Strings; Violin Sonata; Overture to a Comedy; Two Serenades for Violin; The Invisible Drummer; Pages From My Calendar; Concerto for Guitar and Orchestra; Concerto For Cello and Orchestra; Five Soundings for Brass Quintet; Wind Quintet; Matthew's Piano Book; Peaches for Flute; Principals for Orchestra; Summer Music for Orchestra; Concerto for Trumpet and Orchestra; Impressions for Piano. *Scores:* Ballet: Invitation to the Dance (Screen Comp Asn Award).

PREVIN, CHARLES   ASCAP 1953
composer, conductor, pianist

b Brooklyn, NY, Jan 11, 1888; d. Educ: New York Col Music; Cornell Univ, BA; hon MusD, Ithaca Cons; studied with Joseph Schillinger. Pianist, music publishers. Cond, vaudeville, road shows & Bway musicals, St Louis Munic Opera; also in film houses, St Louis, Chicago, Philadelphia & NY. Head music dept, Universal Studios, 7 1/2 yrs. *Scores:* Films: 100 Men and a Girl (Acad Award, 37); Mad About Music; First Love; Spring Parade; Buck Privates; It Started With Eve.

PREZIOSI, REMO J   ASCAP 1967
composer, author, accompanist

b Naples, Italy, July 31, 11. Educ: Theodore Roosevelt High Sch, 29; studied piano at Frank Damrosh Inst Music, piano & harmony with Ferdinand Ligoth, pvt studies in opera coaching, harmony & comp with Luigi & Antonio Dell Orefice; studied organ with A Carbone, NY Univ; music librarian with Gustane Haenschen, NBC Orchestra. Taught pvt piano, harmony & opera coaching; vocal coach & asst condr, Lyric Grand Opera Co, New York. Accompanist to Amelia Sanandres of WQXR. Chief Collabrs: Luigi Dell Orefice, Carlo Tomanelli. *Songs:* The Golden Sun Will Ever Shine; My Peaceful Mountain Home; Matenat' E Primmavera; I'll Put a Rose in Your Hair; Ti Vorrei Dire (Canzone Tango); Love in May; Till the End; Lyrics: Let Me Dream; Yearning (A Song of Lament); Dormi; Hour of Love; Hail MacArthur; Music: Your Kiss; You're Still My Love.

PRICE, BENTON
See Wilson, Roger Cole

PRICE, DARRYL
See Petite, E Dale

PRICE, FLORENCE ANNE   ASCAP 1973
composer, author, singer

b Muskegon, Mich, Dec 13, 31. Educ: Bob Jones Acad, grad, 49; Owosso Col; studied voice 4 yrs & piano 6 yrs. Singer in concert throughout US, Can & Europe, 60- Rec'd Nat Evangel Film Found Award for best vocalist, 62 & 70. Lead roles in 6 gospel films; wrote 3 cookbooks. Hostess of nationally syndicated children's TV show "Tree House Club," 72-; also writing & recording children's musicals. Chief Collabr: Melody Price. *Songs:* Bright New World; He's Listening; Trusting Is Believing; Smile, God Loves You; My Times Are in Thy Hand; Gonna Wake Up Singing; Lyrics: Lookin' to Find; Musicals: Our House; I Like the Sound of America; And That's the Truth!; The Best You Can Be; Christmas 2001; What's New, Corky?

PRICE, FLORENCE B   ASCAP 1940
composer, pianist, organist

b Little Rock, Ark, Apr 9, 1888; d Chicago, Ill, June 3, 53. Educ: New Eng Cons, studied with Cutter, Chadwick & Converse; Am Cons; Chicago Musical Col; Chicago Teachers Col; Cent YMCA Col; Lewis Inst; Chicago Univ; studied with Henry Dunham, Charles Dennee, Arthur Andersen & Gail Haake. Teacher, Shorter Col, Clark Univ. Mem, Nat Asn Am Comp & Cond. *Songs & Instrumental Works:* Symphony in E (Wanamaker Prize); Symphonic Tone Poem; Piano Concerto; Violin Concerto; Quintet for Piano, Strings; Concert Overture on Negro Spirituals; The Wind and the Sea (chorus, orch); 3 Little Negro Dances; Lincoln Walks at Midnight (chorus, orch); Rhapsody for Piano, Orch; Negro Folksongs in Counterpoint (string quartet); Moods (flute, clarinet, piano); Organ Sonata; Passacaglia & Fugue (organ).

PRICE, GEORGE E   ASCAP 1923
author, comedian

b New York, NY, Jan 5, 1900; d New York, NY, May 10, 64. Educ: Prof Children's Sch. As youth, mem Gus Edwards vaudeville act, "Schoolboys and Schoolgirls." Comedian in vaudeville, nightclubs & Bway musicals, incl "Spice of 1928", "Artists and Models" & "A Night in Paris." Appeared in radio & TV. Founder & past pres, Am Guild Variety Artists. Became mem of New York Stock Exchange, 34. *Songs:* Angel Child; Sing Me a Song of the South.

PRICE, HARVEY ALAN (MICHAEL)   ASCAP 1972
composer, author

b Los Angeles, Calif, Sept 15, 47. Educ: Fairfax High Sch. Mem of Arkade; recording artist with var cos. Production work with Steve Barri. Chief Collabr: Dan Walsh. *Songs:* Heaven Knows; Temptation Eyes; Glory Bound; Ain't No Love (in the Heart of the City); It Ain't the Real Thing; I Just Wanna Be the One; The Morning of Our Lives; Love Pains.

PRICE, JOHN ELWOOD   ASCAP 1970
composer, author, teacher
b Tulsa, Okla, June 21, 35. Educ: Tulsa Pub Schs, 39-53; studied piano & theory with Horace F Mitchell; Lincoln Univ, Mo, BMus(comp, piano), 57, studied comp with O A Fuller & piano with Gwendolyn Eichelberger; Univ Tulsa, MMus(comp), 63, studied comp with Bela Rozsa; Washington Univ, St Louis, studied comp with Robert Wykes & Harold Blumenfeld, 67-68. Started comp, 43; had piano lessons at age 5 & continued with same teacher in theory & comp until 53; staff comp-pianist, Karamu Theatre, Ohio; comp-in-residence, Fla Mem Col, 67-74; had works performed by Oakland Youth Symph, Contemporary Chamber Players (Rutgers), Donald Tracy, Barbara Sullivan, Dewitt Tipton, Gayle Kowalchyk, Jeff Hunter, Ann Armstrong, Richard Barta, Virginnia Di Bianco & Nancy Uptmor at Eastern Ill Univ; did film scores for films of Joe Heumann & Linda Smorgor; had works listed for contestant use in Vocal, Woodwind & String Competitions sponsored by Nat Asn Negro Musicians. Writer of instrumental & choral works. Chief Collabrs: Lewis Allan, Robert Chute, John Tagliabue. *Songs & Instrumental Works:* Invention I (piano); Two Typed Lines (voice, piano); Spirituals for the Young Pianist (bk I); Scherzo I (clarinet, orch); The Damnation of Doctor Faustus (tenor solo, small chorus, orch); A Ptah Hymn (cello).

PRICE, LLOYD
composer, author, singer
b Kenner, La, Mar 9, 33. Educ: Tutored on the road until high sch educ was finished.

PRICE, MARION JAMES   ASCAP 1957
author
b Aurora, Ill, Feb 3, 13. Educ: Vassar Col, BA. Reporter & columnist, Aurora Beacon News; ed, Trinity Episcopal Newsletter. Church secy, Westminster Presby Church; lyricist, sacred & secular works. Author, 2 bks of verse, juvenile poems & stories & local histories. Chief Collab: John Leo Lewis. *Songs:* Lyrics: Camel Carol; God of the Small Things; Mother, I Didn't Bring Home the Fish; I Am the Boat; The Innkeeper; I Tooted a Horn (Drexel Inst prize); Prayer for the Seven Gifts (Harvey Gaul prize); Lord Throughout All Generations (2nd prize, Moravian Contest, Bethlehem, Pa).

PRICE, PENNY
See Watts, Mayme

PRICE, WALTER
See Wilson, Roger Cole

PRIESING, DOROTHY M   ASCAP 1958
composer, author, teacher
b Nantucket, Mass, July 31, 10. Educ: Juilliard, dipl piano, 30; teachers' dipl piano, 34; Columbia Univ, BS & MA; studied with James Friskin, Rubin Goldmark & Nadia Boulanger. Instr, Keene State Normal Sch, NH, Columbia Univ Teachers Col & Juilliard Sch Music; chmn piano dept, Shimer Jr Col, Mt Carroll, Ill; assoc prof music, Montclair State Col. *Songs:* Now Is the Carolling Season; Carol of the Children; Music: Preludes for Piano.

PRIGMORE, JAMES   ASCAP 1974
composer
b Bingham, Utah, Feb 9, 43. Educ: Univ Utah, 61-65; studied comp & piano with Ardean Watts. Started comp at age 12; comp-in-residence, Pasadena Playhouse, Calif, 65-66. Comp, pianist & arr, Continental Army Band, USA, 66-68. Musical dir, Repertory Dance Theatre, Salt Lake City, 68-70; musical dir, Pioneer Memorial Theatre, Salt Lake City, 70- Chief Collab: Murray MacLeod. *Songs:* Music: Four Seasonal Songs (voice, piano). *Instrumental Works:* Psalmic Episodes for Piano; The Tarot (suite for piano); Preludes From the Book of Mormon (piano); Orch Works: Concertino for Piano and Chamber Orchestra; Rhapsody on Redeemer of Israel (string orch, harp, soprano); Alma in the Wilderness (variations for large orch); Choral Works: Palmyra (cantata for chorus & orch with baritone solo); Requiem for a Martyred Prophet (scenic cantata for soloist, chorus, orch). *Scores:* Operas: Richard Strauss and the Heavenly Choir; The Rise of the Gods (Or the Downfall of Wagner); Ballets: Woman Remembered; The Little Mermaid; Dracula; Musicals: Belle Starr; Butch and the Kid; The Sabine Women; Robinhood; Sweet Betsy From Pike; Bordello Banditos; TV: The Rookies; Starsky and Hutch; The Lazarus Syndrome; The New Land; Evil Roy Slade; Can Ellen Be Saved; The Savages; Run Simon Run.

PRIMA, LOUIS   ASCAP 1941
composer, author, conductor
b New Orleans, La, Dec 7, 11; d New Orleans, La, Aug 24, 78. Educ: Jesuit High Sch. Trumpeter & singer in New Orleans theatre; then trumpeter in nightclubs, New York; appeared in films. Formed own band, 40. Had own record co; also produced for other cos. *Songs:* Sing Sing Sing; Sing a Spell; Little Boy Blew His Top; Brooklyn Boogie; Robin Hood; Marguerita; Bridget O'Brien; Where Have We Met Before; It's the Rhythm in Me; Boogie in Chicago; Alone; Boogie in the Bronx; New Aulins; A Sunday Kind of Love.

PRIMATO, FRANK PETER   ASCAP 1976
composer, singer, arranger
b New Hyde Park, NY, Jan 31, 56. Educ: Mineola High Sch, grad, 74; Hofstra Univ, BS(music educ), 79; studied contemporary arr with Don Sebesky. Player, arr & jingle writer, club & studio work; producer. Started publ co with partner, Primatunes Enterprises, Ltd, 80- Chief Collab: Teresa Wiater (lyricist). *Songs:* Christmas Time With You; This Song Is for the One I Love; Morning, Noon and Night; Will We Ever Share a Love Song?.

PRINCE, HUGH DURHAM (HUGHIE)   ASCAP 1940
author
b Greenville, SC, Aug 9, 06; d New York, NY, Jan 15, 60. Managed radio script agency. *Songs:* Beat Me Daddy Eight to the Bar; Rhumboogie; Yodelin' Jive; Sweet Mollie Malone; Pipe Dreams; Let George Play It; Rock A Bye the Boogie; Sadie Hawkins Day; Boogie Woogie Bugle Boy.

PRINCE, ROBERT
composer
b New York, NY, 1929. Comp ballets, also dance music for Bway shows & TV incl "Dr Faustus," 64 & "Half a Sixpence," 65. *Scores:* Ballets: New York Export; Opus Jazz and Events; Meet the Band.

PRINCE, WILLIAM F
composer
b Albemarle, NC, May 25, 38. Educ: Wayne State Univ, BS(educ); Fla Atlantic Univ, MMusicEd; Univ Miami, DMA. Played prof with Pee Wee Hunt, Billy Maxted & Buddy Rich; mem, NORAD Band, USA, 61-63; teacher, Fla Atlantic Univ, 68-73, 74- Teacher, Univ Colo, Denver, 73-74. *Instrumental Works:* C'est Le Gasse; Waltz Scene; Palmetto Bug; Little Willie Pentasonic.

PRIOLO, JOSEPH   ASCAP 1953
composer, author
b New York, NY, Oct 10, 18. Educ: City Col New York; Sch Am Music, New York; studied arr with Leon Addio & Ross Gorman. Chief Collabrs: Ross Gorman, Pat Noto, Andy Sannella. *Songs:* All Night Long; Birthday Waltz; Music: Now; Say It to My Heart; Lyrics: Careless Kisses.

PRISCO, THOMAS MATTHEWS   ASCAP 1954
singer
b New York, NY, Mar 16, 31. Educ: St Francis Erasmus High Sch. Recorded for King, Mercury & Epic Records. Chief Collabrs: Steve Allen, Sammy Mysels, Claude DeMitrus. *Songs:* Till Today.

PRITTS, ROY A   ASCAP 1970
composer, teacher
b Denver, Colo, Dec 17, 36. Educ: East Denver High Sch, 55; Univ of Denver, BMEd, 66, MA, 74; studied with Normand Lockwood, Dennis Cam. Arr staff, Stan Kenton & Martha Raye, 57-59. Dir, electronic music, assoc prof & past acting asst dean, Univ Colo, Denver. Comp-in-residence, Gates Planetarium, Denver. Author, articles on electronic music for "Downbeat", "AES Journal" & "IEEE Journal." Chief Collabrs: Russell Hunter, Keith Aurdon, Dennis Tenney. *Instrumental Works:* Wheel of Fortune; Celebration for the Comet 'Kehotec'; Bronco Kickor; On Base 9; Child of the Twentieth Century; 4-to 5 to 4; Starspan; Star Flight; The Last Question; Vision Beyond Time; Solarian System. *Scores:* Films: UFO's (Strangers in the Night?); Whirlpools of Darkness.

PRIVAL, MAX   ASCAP 1932
composer, author
b New York, NY, Mar 19, 1889; d New York, Dec 17, 57. Educ: Pub schs. Was buyer, merchandise mgr for music depts of retail stores. *Songs:* Lullaby Land; I'm Waiting for Tomorrow to Come; Only a Dream; Somebody Misses Someone's Kisses; Am I Wasting My Time?; I Fell in Love With You; May God Bless You, Mother.

PROBERT, GEORGE ARTHUR, JR   ASCAP 1978
composer, musician
b Los Angeles, Calif, Mar 5, 27. Educ: Alhambra High Sch; Univ Southern Calif; Stanford Univ, BA, 48; grad work, Stanford Univ & Univ Calif, Los Angeles. Jazz musician on clarinet & soprano saxophone with Bob Scobey, Kid Ory & Fire House Five Plus Two; toured Europe as guest star at var jazz fests, 70's. Asst dir animation & music ed, motion pictures & TV, 54-; music ed for "Dallas"; has written source cues for "Charlie's Angels" & "Starsky & Hutch."

PROCHUT, LOUIS, JR   ASCAP 1959
composer, author, accordionist
b Chicago, Ill, May 14, 31; d. Educ: High sch; pvt accordion study. Accordionist throughout country; world tour as USMC rep. Played at Carnegie Hall, 54; mem staff, WLS, Chicago, 3 1/2 yrs. Writer TV prog, "Polka-Go-Round," ABC, 4 yrs. Won Am Accordion Asn Award. *Instrumental Works:* Polka-Go-Round (theme); Playtime Polka; Busy Fingers Polka; Choo Choo Train Polka; Folios: Original Polkas for Accordion; International Favorites for Accordion.

PROFFITT, JOSEPHINE MOORE
See Dee, Sylvia

PROMETHEUS GEMINI
See Smith, Clifford

PROTO, FRANK   ASCAP 1968
composer, arranger, double bassist
b Brooklyn, NY, July 18, 41. Educ: High Sch of Performing Arts, New York; Manhattan Sch of Music, bachelor & masters degrees, studied double bass with David Walter, comp self-taught. Double bassist, Princeton Chamber Orch & Cincinnati Symph. Comp-in-residence, Cincinnati Symph Orch, incl works performed by orchs throughout the US for young people's & pop's concerts; comp, chamber music for double bass, string quartet & for small orch & perc. Recording artist & leader, symph jazz ens. *Instrumental Works:* Concerto for Double Bass and Orchestra (No 1); Concerto for Violin, Double Bass and Orchestra: Casey at the Bat, an American Folk Tale for Narrator, Orchestra and Tape; Three Pieces for Percussion and Orchestra; Concerto for Cello and Orchestra; The Four Seasons, for Tuba, Percussion, Strings and Tape; Concerto No 2 for Double Bass and Orchestra. *Albums:* The Sound of the Bass, Vol 1 & 2.

PROVISOR, DENNIS ERROL
composer, author, singer
b Los Angeles, Calif, Nov 9, 43. Educ: Col in Santa Monica, 3 yrs; Woodbury Bus Col; studied piano with Miss Headson, 3 yrs. With Four Sounds, 2 yrs, Al & The Originals, 1 yr, The Persuaders, 3 yrs, Shock, 1 yr, Grass Roots, 6 yrs, Association, 3 months & Providor, 6 months. *Songs:* Walkin' Through the Country; Glory Bound; City Life; Rock Sugar; When Will It Be?

PRUJAN, TURK   ASCAP 1959
composer, author, producer
b Detroit, Mich, Apr 3, 09. Educ: Law Sch. Mgr & prog dir for Johnnie Ray. Producer & dir, USO shows, benefits & concerts. MC, entertainer in concerts, radio, TV, films & theatres. Owner & mgr, night clubs in Detroit & Hollywood. Chief Collabr: Pat Kennedy. *Songs:* Nice Talking to You, Baby; Don't Cry on My Shoulder; To Me; If I Painted Your Picture; Crazy Heart; Paris At Dawn; Hawaiian Waterfall; Aloha to You; Walk in the Sun; Kamahula; Here Comes the Fool; I Paid the Penalty.

PRYOR, ARTHUR   ASCAP 1914
composer, bandmaster, trombonist
b St Joseph, Mo, Sept 22, 1870; d West Long Beach, NJ, June 18, 42. Educ: Studied music with father, bandmaster. Trombone soloist & asst cond, John Philip Sousa Band; made 3 Eur tours. Organized own band; first NY concert, 03. Cond, Asbury Park, 25 summers, Miami, Fla, 11 winters. Charter mem, ASCAP. *Songs & Instrumental Works:* The Whistler and His Dog; The Victor; Heart of America. *Scores:* Operettas: Jingaboo; On the Eve of Her Wedding Day; Uncle Tom's Cabin.

PUCO, PHILIP MILO   ASCAP 1974
composer, author
b New York, NY, Sept 24, 26. Screenwriter. *Songs:* Friendly People (Merry Christmas).

PUENTE, ERNEST ANTHONY (TITO)
composer
b New York, NY, Apr 20, 23. Educ: Juilliard Sch; NY Univ, studied Schillinger Syst. Orch leader, appeared in var nightclubs, hotels & resorts throughout world, 49- Hosted weekly TV show, "Grand Marshall Puerto Rican Day Parade," 68. Served USN, 42. Recipient, Bronze Medallion, City of New York, 69, Key to Cities of Los Angeles, Boston, Hartford & Miami; named King of Latin Music, Prensa Newspaper, Best Latin Orch, New York Daily News, 77-79; bd of gov, Nat Acad of Recording Arts & Sci, 78-80. *Songs:* Para Los Rumperos; Oye Como Va; & 200 other compositions & 1500 arr for Latin Am music.

PUGLIESE, CARLOS ANIBAL (CHARLIE TONTO)   ASCAP 1971
composer, author, singer
b Mar del Plata, Arg, Dec 12, 44. Educ: St George's Col, Arg; Escuela Argentina Modelo; Univ Buenos Aires, diplomat as attorney at law. Chief Collabr: Nono Pugliese. *Songs:* Alla Viene y Soy Feliz; Chica de Verano; Tiritando.

PULLEN, OLIVE DUNGAN (MRS CLAUDE PULLEN)   ASCAP 1938
composer, teacher, pianist
b Pittsburgh, Pa, July 19, 03. Educ: Pittsburgh Inst Musical Art, studied piano & comp with Charles N Boyd; studied organ with Anton Koener; studied piano with Emily Byrd; Univ Miami, studied comp with Franklin Harris; pub sch music, Univ Ala. Piano debut at age 7 with Pittsburgh Fest Orch. Entertained in hospitals during WW II. First recipient, Chi Omega Bertha Foster Award, 53. Theta Sigma Phi Community Headliner Award, 69. Chief Collabrs: Vivian Laramore Rader, Gertrude Gore, Harriet Grey Blackwell, Hannah Kahn, Ruth Enck Engle. *Instrumental Works:* Tropic Night Suite (single & duo, White Jasmine, Enchantment & Magnolias in Moonlight); Impression of the Argentine; The Everglades; The Peacock; Fun and Fancies (collection of 7 pieces). *Songs & Instrumental Works:* Eternal Life; I Will Lift Up Mine Eyes

(anthem); I Will Love Thee; White Jade; Be Still and Know That I Am God; The Christ Child; Stranger; Tropical Tunes for Tiny Tots; Character Studies for Young Folks. *Scores:* Operetta: The Mysterious Forest.

PULLINS, CARL LEROY   ASCAP 1965
composer, singer
b Elgin, Ill, Nov 12, 40. Educ: High Sch; trained by Billy Edd Wheeler. Recording artist. *Songs:* I'm a Nut (nominated for Grammy Award for best country record, 66).

PUMPIAN, PAUL H   ASCAP 1976
comedy writer
b Baltimore, Md, Oct 18, 28. Educ: Univ NC, Chapel Hill, 53-54, radio-TV-motion picture studies. TV writer, Los Angeles & New York, primarily TV variety, 56- *Songs:* Lyrics: Police Chorale.

PURDY, WILLIAM T   ASCAP 1960
composer, pianist, teacher
b Aurora, NY, Feb 28, 1882; d Aurora, Dec 31, 18. Educ: Auburn High Sch; Hamilton Col. Studied piano extensively as child & youth. Leader, Glee Club. Organist & head, Mandolin Club, Hamilton Col. Went to Chicago; teacher piano & voice, Drexel Cons Music. Ran musical agency; comp. *Songs:* Music: On (Univ Wis march song; off state song); March of the Maroons; Let's Linger Longer Love; No One Knows But Noah. *Instrumental Works:* Cabaret Rag; Mam'selle Coquette; Valse Caprice.

PURIFOY, JOHN DAVID   ASCAP 1976
composer
b Camden, Ark, Sept 30, 52. Educ: Univ Ark, BM(piano performance); studied music theory, Univ Tex Grad Sch, 1 yr. Joined as music ed, staff arr & composer, Word Inc, 75, now dir, Music Publ. Chief Collabr: Tina English. *Songs:* Walkin' in the Light of His Love; Teach Me, Lord; Here Am I, Send Me; Someday My Lord Will Come; In Wonder of Your Love; When in Times Like These; A Son Is Given (cantata); Faith, Hope, and Love; In My Way; Music: Come to Me All Who Labor; In My Father's House.

PURIFOY, LYDIA M   ASCAP 1978
author
b Bluff City, Ark, June 28, 42. Educ: Lafayette High Sch; Philander Smith Col, BS, 64. Home economist & off mgr, ICA Records. Chief Collabr: Pearl Smith. *Songs:* Lyric: Come Fly With Me.

PURNELL, ALTON   ASCAP 1964
composer, author, musician
b New Orleans, La, Apr 16, 11. Educ: Pub schs. *Songs:* Buster Anderson's Blues.

PURPURA, CRAIG JOHN   ASCAP 1979
composer, saxophonist
b Boston, Mass, July 20, 51. Educ: Ridgewood High Sch, 69; Univ Wis, 69-71; studied with Cecil Taylor, 3 1/2 yrs. Performed with Cecil Taylor Ensemble, 70-74; performed with Roy Meriwether Trio, Dayton, Ohio, 73; performed on soundtrack for movie, "Methadone, an American Way of Dealing," 73; performed with Paul Jeffery Big Band, 77-79; played baritone saxophone on a Charles Mingus album, 78; produced own record as leader, 79. *Instrumental Works:* Fifth Floor Walk-Up.

PURVIN, THEODORE V   ASCAP 1979
composer, author
b Bridgeport, Conn, Sept 8, 18. Educ: Univ Ill, BA, 41. Comp, many years; started record cuts, 79; comp, show tunes, pop, dance music & country music. Chief Collabr: Jack Grayson. *Songs:* You Can't Remember and I Can't Forget; Don't Turn Around; Yesterday I Sent You a Dozen Roses; The Stores Are Full of Roses; A Little Tear Came Down My Cheek; I'll Always Walk in Your Shadow; It's Fun to Go to Grandma's House (and Trim the Christmas Tree); Step Aside; Don't Burn All Your Bridges.

PURVIS, CHARLIE EDWARD   ASCAP 1956
author
b McKenzie, Tenn, Nov 4, 09. Educ: Pub schs. Chief Collabrs: Arthur Korb, Al Kennedy, Olive Dungan, Arthur Kent. *Songs:* Lyrics: Go on With the Wedding; You Can't Divorce a Loving Heart; Green Pastures.

PUTSCHE, THOMAS   ASCAP 1968
composer, author, teacher
b Scarsdale, NY, June 29, 29. Educ: Univ Chicago, BA, 50; Juilliard Sch Music, 51; Hartt Sch Music, BA, 54, MM, 55, studied with Aaron Copland, Milton Babbitt, Arnold Franchetti, Isadore Freed & Vittorio Giannini. Instr, Hartt Col, 55-58, chmn, Hartford Cons, 59-60, asst prof, Hartt Sch Music, 60- Chmn, Int Soc Contemporary Music, 64-66 & ICAM, 64-70. Scholarships to Tanglewood, fellowships to MacDowell Colony & Princeton Seminar. Comn by Tanglewood, Rockefeller, Plainville Chorale. Mem, MacDowell Colony Fellows; Am Soc Univ Comp & Soc for Music Theory. *Instrumental Works:* Three Bugs for Piano; Three Bugs for Orchestra; Six Preludes for Piano; Wind Quintet; Three Studies for Flute and Clarinet; Twelve Studies for Piano; Theme and Variations for Six

Saxophones; Hexachord Fantasies (Nineteen Pieces for Piano); Mass for Mixed Chorus. *Scores:* Opera/Ballet: The Cat and the Moon.

PYKE, HAROLD IRVINE   ASCAP 1964
composer, author
b Kentville, NS, May 24, 03. Educ: Rindge Tech Sch, Cambridge, Mass. Author, special material for radio & vaudeville acts. Chief Collabs: Bob Ellsworth, Dick Howard. *Songs:* Music: Did I Make a Mistake in You?; It Won't Be Long Till You Belong to Me; Carmelita; Sorry.

PYLE, FRANCIS JOHNSON   ASCAP 1963
composer, educator
b South Bend, Ind, Sept 13, 01. Educ: South Bend High Sch, 19; Oberlin Col, AB, 23; Univ Wash, MA, 33; studied theory & comp with George McKay, 28-33; Univ Rochester Eastman Sch, PhD, 45, studies with Bernard Rogers, Howard Hanson, Herbert Elwell, 37-45. Asst prof music, Cent Col, Wash, 29-37; prof & chmn depts theory & musicology, Drake Univ Col of Fine Arts, 37-72, emer prof, 72-; vis prof, Univ Calif, Los Angeles, summer 55; pvt studio, theory & violin, 72-; staff mem, Cent Col, Iowa, 73-78. *Songs:* Music: Canticle of the Sun (mixed chorus, brass sextette); Three Psalms (mixed chorus, symph orch); Three Amusements (women's chorus); A Mountain Tarn (SSA, piano); The Fall (SSA, piano); O Love That Sings (SSA, piano); I Have Chosen Thee (SATB, a cappella); Full Stature (SATB, a cappella); Mixed Choruses: Father We Praise Thee; I Hear No Voice; High Upon a Hilltop; Children of the Heavenly Father; Winds Through the Olive Trees; Sail Forth. *Instrumental Works:* Quintet for Woodwinds (flute, oboe, clarinet, French horn, bassoon); Sonata for Three (clarinet, piano, perc); Sonata for Clarinet and Piano (From the Middle Border); Sonata for Flute and Piano; Sonata No 1 for Free Bass Accordion; Eight Etudes in 20th Century Idioms (free bass accordion or piano solo); Sonata No 2 for Free Bass Accordion or Piano Solo; Suite for Puppeteers (piano solo); Pictures for Suzanne (string orch); Frontier Sketches (elem string orch); Edged Night (flute solo, 19 winds & perc); Far Dominion (concert band); Symphony No 1 (symphonic band); Trumpet Concerto (symphonic band); Sinfonietta No 1 (chamber orch; comn by St Paul Chamber Orch); Set of Six (duos for 2 B-Flat clarinets); Reprints of Currier and Ives (flute clarinet & bassoon).

Q

QUACIARI, GENE L
See Louis, Gene

QUADLING, LEW   ASCAP 1942
composer, arranger, author
b Cedarville, NJ, June 7, 08. Educ: Pub Sch; High Sch; Curtis Inst. Big Band Era pianist with Ted Weems, Anson Weeks, Dick Jurgens, Bob Crosby & Phil Harris. Staff arr, WBBM, Chicago. USA, 43-45, comp, arr & cond all Signal Corps movies at Long Island Studios. Arr & cond record dates for Dean Martin, Eydie Gorme, McGuire Sisters, Eddy Howard & others. Chief Collabs: Johnny Mercer, Mack David, Jack Elliott. *Songs:* I Do, Do You?; Music: Careless; A Million Dreams Ago; Do You Care?; Sam's Song; The Lights of Home; It's Snowing in Hawaii; So Long Train Whistle; I Haven't Been Home in Three Whole Nights; I'm Not Good Enough for You; College November. *Instrumental Works:* Plenty of Brass; Trumpet Rag; Double Shuffle.

QUEENER, CHARLES CONANT   ASCAP 1967
composer, pianist
b Pineville, Ky, July 27, 21. Educ: Univ Tenn; pvt study in comp/orchestration with Paul Creston. Jazz pianist with many groups in New York, incl Benny Goodman. First Symph was one of ten works chosen when Goucher Col inaugurated its Performing Arts Ctr, 68 & was performed by Baltimore Symph Orch. *Instrumental Works:* Suite (orch); Symphony No I, II; Two Orchestral Dances; Introduction and Dance (symphonic band).

QUENZER, ARTHUR   ASCAP 1940
author
b New York, NY, Oct 20, 05. Educ: Columbia Univ, cert law. Musician reeds & violin; free lance lyricist. With Irving Aaronson's Commanders, 26-32, Vincent Lopez Orch, 33-35, Ben Bernie Orch, 36-38; radio & recording musician for David Rose, Phil Harris, Gordon Jenkins, Victor Young, Paul Newton & others, 40-54; real estate broker, 54-75. Two acad award nominations. Chief Collabs: Alfred Newman, Lionel Newman, Artie Shaw, Phil Charig, David Rose, Mickey Bloom, Lou Bring, Franklyn Marks. *Songs:* Lyrics: Moonray; So It's Love; The Cowboy and the Lady; Merrily We Live; Trade Winds.

QUILLEN, CHARLES W   ASCAP 1973
composer
b Lee County, Va, Mar 21, 38. Started writing while in Vietnam, 66. *Songs:* Music: Back on My Mind Again; My Heart; It Don't Hurt to Dream; They Never Lost You.

QUINCY, GEORGE   ASCAP 1973
composer, keyboard player
b McAlester, Okla, Sept 8, 44. Educ: McAlester High Sch; Okla Univ; Juilliard Sch Music, BS & MS; piano study with E Freundlick & J Carlson. Artistic adv to Martha Graham, 4 yrs; fac mem, Juilliard Sch Music, 4 yrs. Keyboards for many recordings, jingles, etc. Chief Collabs: Thayer Burch, Rochelle Owens, Myrna Lamb, Leon Katz, Tom Everett. *Songs:* Music: Give My Heart an Even Break; Man; Magic; High Intensity Times; Promises of Love; I Can't Come Down. *Scores:* Bway Show: Mandrake the Magician; Opera/Ballet: Zodiac; The Mummy; Flowerstone; Film/TV: The Hiest.

QUINE, RICHARD HARDING   ASCAP 1956
composer, director
b Detroit, Mich, Nov 12, 20. Motion picture dir, producer & writer; actor, singer & dancer, vaudeville, stage & screen. On Bway, "Very Warm for May", "My Sister Eileen"; MGM contract player, "Babes on Broadway", "Words & Music", "For Me and My Gal" & others; dir musicals, "All Ashore", "Sound Off", "Sunny Side of the Street", "So This Is Paris"; films dir, "The World of Suzie Wong", "Solid Gold Cadillac", "Hotel", "How to Murder Your Wife", "Operation Mad Ball", "Bell, Book and Candle" & others. Chief Collabs: George Duning, Fred Karger. *Songs:* Sex and the Single Girl; Lyrics: Strangers When We Meet; The Morning After; I'm a Runaway; Full of Life; Going Steady.

QUINLAN, FRED J   ASCAP 1958
composer, author
b Chicago, Ill, Nov 2, 25. Chief Collabs: Al Trace, Lew Douglas, Cliff Parman. *Songs:* Where the Red Roses Grow; Why Cry; Sunshine and Flowers; Why Go Home; Aba Da Aba Du; Honky Tonk Melody; The Old Church Organ; Believe in the Lord; Sticks and Stones.

QUINN, ADELLE
See Harvey, Lucy Quinn

QUINN, DON   ASCAP 1958
author, artist
b Grand Rapids, Mich, Nov 18, 1900; d. Educ: USN Gunners' Mates' Sch; art schs; Univ Calif, Los Angeles. Was commercial artist, 10 yrs. Creator & writer, "Fibber McGee and Molly," radio, 35-52 & "The Halls of Ivy," radio, 3 yrs, TV, 2 yrs, Peabody Award. Pres, AdStaff, Inc, 5 yrs. Chief Collabs: Martin Sperzel, Bill Howe, Gene De Paul, Henry Russell, Jimmy Sheldon, Ken Darby. *Songs:* Yancey Derringer; Two on the Isle; Tiana; Detroit News (commercial).

QUINN, JAMES FRANCIS, III (CHRISTOPHER)   ASCAP 1967
composer, author, singer
b Chicago, Ill, Aug 19, 52. Educ: John Muir High Sch; Pasadena City Col; Sherwood Oaks Exp Col, studied record producing with Richard Perry & sound recording with Alan O'Day. Won first place, Calif Educr Statewide Youth Talent Search, 64. TV regular on dance shows, Los Angeles, 60's. Staff writer, Warner Bros Music, 67-77 & Gary Wright, 78. Recording artist, Mercury, Excello & Velvet Hammer Records; formed Velvet Hammer Records, 79. Has written lyrics for motion picture themes by Henry Mancini, Lalo Shiffrin & Alexjandro Jodowrowsky. Worked with "Alternitave Chorus." First double-platinum song "Let It Out." Producer, publ, arr, keyboardist & drummer. Chief Collabs: Sherri Thomas, Gary Wright, Alan O'Day, Michael Laurence, Juregun Drews, Joachim Kuhn, Michelle Polnareff, Bohemile Klemish, Lynn Farr. *Songs:* Mother Natures' Man; Thief of Love; Lady Los Angeles; Men Without Women; Honky-Tonky-Tea; San Francisco Summer; Feelin' It; Seventeen Sycamore Street; More of You; Superbitch; Tunin' Me Up; Dream Theme; Lyrics: Let It Out; Night-Ride; Stay Away; Something Very Special; Can't Get Above Losing You; Keep Love in Your Soul; All About Her; Mister Memory; Georgia Sun; Theme from El Topo; Theme from Our Time; Theme from the Omega Man; Make Love With Me Again; Love Me Good-bye.

QUINN, JERREL H   ASCAP 1978
composer, author, singer
b Magnolia, NC, Mar 12, 34. Songwriter. *Songs & Instrumental Works:* That's the Way the Ball Bounces; Don't Toy With My Affection.

QUINN, LAWRENCE A   ASCAP 1976
composer, singer, producer
b Troy, NY, Aug 31, 52. Educ: Troy High Sch, grad, 70; State Univ NY Fredonia Ctr for Audio Studies, cert, 79. Began singing with bands, 65; wrote first songs, 66; recorded first record, 76 & first LP, 78; worked in nightclubs, 5 yrs; now free lance producer. *Songs:* 15/20; You Make Me Real; Disco Must Die; Oh Linda.

QUINSKA
See Hays, Doris

QUITTENTON, MARTIN   ASCAP 1972
composer, guitarist
b Ashford, Eng, Apr 22, 45. Educ: Pvt study of basic theory, reading & guitar, 57-62, studied classical guitar technique with Julian Byzantine, 69-72 & extensive self study, 70- Electronic guitarist with Steamhammer, 69; accompanied Freddie King on British tour, 70; worked with Rod Stewart on 5

solo albums, 70-75; session work for Carl Davis, 76. Chief Collabrs: Rod Stewart, Judy Dyble. *Songs:* Music: Velvet to a Tone; Maggie May; You Wear It Well; Farewell. *Instrumental Works:* Water.

R

RABBIT, SAMUEL
author   ASCAP 1964

b Bronx, NY, Sept 14, 11. Educ: High sch. *Songs:* Juke Box Luke.

RABINOVITCH, FISHEL
See Rovin, Felix A(sher)

RACHMANINOFF, SERGEI VASILYEVICH
composer, conductor, painist   ASCAP 1925

b Oneg, Russia, Apr 2, 1873; d Beverly Hills, Calif, Mar 28, 43. Educ: St Petersburg Cons; Moscow Cons (Gold Medal), studied with Zverev. Made 2-piano arr of Tschaikowsky's "Manfred Symph" at age 14; cond, Bolshoi Theatre, Moscow, 04-06; to Dresden, 3 yrs; concert tours, 07; to US, 17; gave 26 concerts in Am, 09; resumed Am tours, 18; made many records. *Songs & Instrumental Works:* Morceaux de Fantasie; 4 piano concertos; 5 Piano Pieces; Prelude in C-Sharp; 3 symphonies; 6 Moments Musicaux; Sonata for Piano, Cello; The Spring (cantata); Isle of the Dead; 2 piano sonatas; 13 Piano Preludes; The Bells (choral symph); Variations on a Theme by Corelli; Rhapsody on a Theme of Paganini; Symphonic Dances; Symphonic Poem; Mass and Vesper Services; 2 suites for 2 pianos; The Rock (tone poem); Trio Elegiaque (piano, violin, cello). *Scores:* Operas: The Miserly Knight; Aleko; Francesca da Rimini.

RACKLEY, LAWRENCE
See Smith, Lawrence Rackley

RADCLIFFE, P STERLING
composer, author   ASCAP 1954

b New York, NY, May 30, 29. Song writer of music & lyrics; producer of records; country artist. Chief Collabrs: Stan Gardner, Barry White. *Songs:* Why Don't You Believe Me; Have You Heard; The Seventh Day; You're the First, the Last, My Everything; They're Playing Our Song; Don't Let It Break Your Heart; The Lovely King of Rock n' Roll; Roamer; Piano Bar; Black Superman; I'll Be Waiting for You; Pretend; also many others.

RADFORD, DAVE
composer, author   ASCAP 1941

b Galt, Ont, Feb 26, 1884; d. Chief Collabr: Richard Whiting. *Songs:* It's Tulip Time in Holland; Where the Black-Eyed Susans Grow; My American Beauty Rose; It's Lilac Time in Lover's Lane; My Rose of Palestine; Where the Four-Leaf Clovers Grow; In the Valley of the Nile; I'm Glad You're Sorry.

RADICE, MARK
composer, musician

b Newark, NJ, Nov 23, 57. First single at age 9; recorded an album with Paramount at age 14. Toured with Donovan & Aerosmith. Fill-in keyboardist in bands. *Songs:* The Answer Is You.

RADO, JAMES
See Radomski, James

RADOCCHIA, EMIL (EMIL RICHARDS)
composer, musician   ASCAP 1959

b Hartford, Conn, Sept 2, 32. Educ: Julias Hartt Sch Music (Univ Conn); Hartford Sch Music; Hylliard Col, AA(music). Joined Hartford Symph while in high sch under Arthur Fieldler; asst band leader, First Cavalry Army Band, 4 yrs; with Geo Shearing Quintet. World tour with Frank Sinatra, Stan Kenton Neophonic Orch, Paul Horn Quintet & Roger Kelloway Quintet. Mem, The Orch, awarded Percussionist Award, 73-79. Film recording with all maj comp. Recording musician, film studios. *Songs:* Music: Oh Very Well; It's Ten to Five; A Sixey Feeling; Mashavu; Fremptz; Hot Fudge Sunday; Yazz Per Favore; Maharinaba; Enjoy Enjoy; Bliss; Mantra; Journey to Bliss (parts 1-6); Underdog Rag; Celesta; Garnet; Amethyst; Blood Stone; Diamond; Emerald; Moon Stone; Ruby; Opal; Sardonyx; Sapphire; Topaz; Turquoise.

RADOMSKI, JAMES (JAMES RADO)
composer, author   ASCAP 1972

b Jan 23, 42. Chief Collabrs: Gerome Ragni, Galt MacDermot. *Scores:* Bway: Hair; Off-Bway: Rainbow.

RADY, SIMON (SI)
composer   ASCAP 1955

b New York, NY, Oct 17, 09; d New York, Mar 9, 65. Record exec, RCA Victor, Decca & Project Records Inc. Joined Capitol as dir of creative serv, 63. *Songs:* Music: Little Tune That Ran Away; Genie the Magic Record; Littlest Angel.

RAGLAND, ROBERT OLIVER
composer   ASCAP 1956

b Chicago, Ill, July 3, 31. Educ: Began piano study at age 5 with Wilbur Held, later Margaret Borchers & Nicholas Sothras; Univ Ill, 49-50; Northwestern Univ, Evanston, BA(bus admin), 53; Acad Music & Dramatic Art, Vienna, studied cond with Hans Swarofsky, comp with Karl Schiske & piano with Fran Wang; also studied with Nadia Boulanger, Paris; Am Cons Music, Chicago, BA & MA, studied comp with Leo Sowerby, Grace Welsh, Karel Jirak, Alexander Tcherepnin & William Russo; last 10 yrs studied with George Tremblay, Woodland Hills, Calif & Paul Glass. Started career with father; played with Dixie & Bop bands in Chicago area through col. Arr for Count Basie, Tommy & Jimmy Dorsey, Ralph Marterie & Dick Contino. Played many dances & pvt parties. Worked in advert bus, 57-70. Began scoring films in Los Angeles, 70; since then have scored 41 features, also many TV shows. Nominated for Oscar Awards in Best Song & Best Score category, 76. Chief Collabrs: Sid Wayne, Carol Conners, Arthur Hamilton, Janelle Webb. *Songs:* Life Is So Beautiful (Best Song of 1980, Film Adv Bd); theme songs: Only a Dream Away; There's a New World Comin'. *Scores:* Film/TV: Seven Alone; Grizzly; Pony Express Rider; Jaguar Lives; Mountain Family Robinson; High Ice; Return to Macon County; Shark's Treasure; Mansion of the Doomed.

RAGNI, GEROME
composer, author   ASCAP 1972

b Pittsburgh, Pa, Sept 11, 36. Chief Collabrs: James Rado, Gait MacDermont. *Scores:* Bway Show: Hair.

RAGONESE, DON (DON RODNEY)
composer, singer, musician   ASCAP 1950

b Bridgeport, Conn, May 26, 20. Educ: Pvt music study. Singer, musician in dance orchs; has had own radio prog. *Songs:* That's What Every Young Girl Should Know; Funny Little Money Man; Peculiar; Four Winds and the Seven Seas.

RAGOVOY, JERRY
composer, author   ASCAP 1972

b Philadelphia, Pa, Sept 4, 30. Songwriter & producer for var productions incl Garnet Mimms, Howard Tate, Miriam Makeba, Dionne Warwick, Bonnie Raitt, Paul Butterfield. Chief Collabrs: Bert Berns, Len Roberts. *Songs:* Stay With Me; Piece of My Heart; Time Is on My Side; Get It While You Can; Ain't Nobody Home; Phata Phata; You Got It; Cry Baby; You're So Good You're Bad; Move Me No Mountain; Eight Days on the Road; Look At Granny Run Run; All Night Lover.

RAHIM, EMMANUEL KHALIQ (EMMANUEL JUAN AMALBERT)
composer, arranger, instrumentalist   ASCAP 1975

b New York, NY, Feb 20, 34. Educ: Cardinal Hayes High Sch; Kathrine Dunham Sch Perc; studied perc with Dr "Sticks" Evans, 52-56; studied arr with William Billy Strayhorn, 60-65; Berklee Sch Music, 69-71; Pacific Col, BA, 72, PhM, 76. Music dir, Hollywood Pavilion 64, World's Fair; bandleader with The Latin Jazz Quintet on Prestige Records & Cobblestone Records; accompanist for Josephine Baker, The Duke Ellington Orch, Clark Terry Band, Diana Ross, Ester Williams, The Four Tops, John Coltrane, James Moody, Art Blakey, Jimmy Cliff, Don Shirley, Shirly Scott & Thad Jones' Eclipse; now performer with own group, Times At Hand, touring Europe & on Danish radio & TV. Chief Collabrs: William Edward Ellington, Sonny Henry, Ralph Sawyer. *Songs & Instrumental Works:* Total Submission; Times At Hand; The Knower; Al-Haqq; Oh-Pharaoh Speak; Daria; Alpha and Omega; Spirit of Truth; Ps and Qs; Haarlem; Ritmo Son; Midnite Montuno. *Scores:* Opera/Ballet: The Ball.

RAHMAN, YUSUF NAFEESUR
teacher, arranger, conductor   ASCAP 1971

b Pittsburgh, Pa, May 27, 42. Educ: George Westinghouse High Sch; USMC Drum & Bugle Corps; studied theory & comp with R G Chandler, string bass with Anthony Bianco. Began as trombonist at age 5. Played with prominent jazz groups, New York & on ECoast. Went to Los Angeles, mid 60's. Comp & arr, Watts 103rd Street Rhythm Band. Producer records, 70's. Arr, Stevie Wonder, Bill Withers, Wilson Pickett, Charles Wright, Robert J Conti & others. Chief Collabrs: Judith Claire, (Raifman) Charles Wright, Robert Conti, Wilson Pickett, Sheila Wilkerson. *Songs:* The Promise; Higher Consciousness; Hard Sometimes; Again; Gone; Music: Tell Me What You Want Me to Do; Lyrics: Comment. *Scores:* Film/TV: Up River; The Jinnii and the Fairy.

RAIANI, ALBERT GEORGE (AL RAINY)
composer, author, teacher   ASCAP 1957

b New York, NY, Feb 17, 17; d New York, May 13, 62. Educ: High sch, grad, 34; Brooklyn Cons of Music, 49-52. Guitarist, local clubs & pvt parties. With McGraw-Hill Book Publ. Chief Collabrs: Lee Russell, Joe Turrano, G Romero, H Stride. *Songs:* Gather Your Dreams; Get That Golden Key. *Albums:* Religious: Someone Walks Beside Me; Healing Hands; Tablets of Stone.

RAINGER, RALPH
composer, pianist, arranger   ASCAP 1931

b New York, NY, Oct 7, 00; d Palm Springs, Calif, Oct 23, 42. Educ: Damrosch Cons (scholarship); Brown Univ Law Sch, LLB; studied music with Paolo

Gallico, Clarence Adler & Arnold Schoenberg. Was prof pianist; mem, two-piano team in "Ziegfeld Follies." Arr & accompanist to Libby Holman & Clifton Webb. Went to Hollywood under contract to Paramount, 30-38 & 20th Century Fox, 38-42. Chief Collabr: Leo Robin; others, Howard Dietz, Sam Coslow, Dorothy Parker. *Songs:* Moanin' Low; Please; Here Lies Love; In the Park in Paree in the Spring; Give Me Liberty or Give Me Love; Take a Lesson From the Lark; Love in Bloom; With Every Breath I Take; June in January; Here Is My Heart; Miss Brown to You; Double Trouble; I Wished on the Moon; I Don't Want to Make History; Here's Love In Your Eyes; La Bomba; Blue Hawaii; In a Little Hula Heaven; Sweet Is the Word for You; Easy Living; What Have You Got That Gets Me?; You're Lovely, Madame; Blossoms on Broadway; Ebb Tide; Thanks for the Memory (Acad Award, 38); You Took the Words Right Out of My Heart; Joobalai; The Funny Old Hills; I Have Eyes; Sweet Little Headache; Bluebirds in the Moonlight; Hello, Ma! I Done It Again; Oh, the Pity of It All; If I Should Lose You. *Scores:* Films: A Bedtime Story; Little Miss Marker; Here Is My Heart; The Big Broadcast (35, 37, 38); Waikiki Wedding; Paris Honeymoon; Gulliver's Travels; Moon Over Miami; Coney Island; My Gal Sal.

RAINY, AL
See Raiani, Albert George

RAITT, BONNIE
singer, musician
b Burbank, Calif, Nov 8, 49. Educ: Radcliffe Col. Performer, blues clubs, East Coast. Concert performer, toured Britain, 76 & 77. *Albums:* Bonnie Raitt; Give It Up; Takin' My Time; Streetlights; Home Plate; Sweet Forgiveness; The Glow.

RAKOV, PHILIP H   ASCAP 1955
composer, author surgeon
b Syracuse, NY, Aug 23, 03. Educ: Syracuse Univ, Col of Medicine. Practicing surgeon, 31- Chief Collabrs: Alan Shurr, Charles Shaw. *Songs:* Let's All Sing; I Found a Lucky Penny; Will You Take a Walk?; I Take Thee; Tears; A Kiss to Say Hello.

RAKSIN, DAVID (JOHN SARTAIN, JR)   ASCAP 1945
composer, author
b Philadelphia, Pa, Aug 4, 12. Educ: Central High Sch, Philadelphia; Univ Pa, BFA, MusB; studied with Harl McDonald, Isadore Freed, Arnold Schoenberg. Played, arr & conducted dance bands; arr, radio, records & Bway musicals. To Hollywood, 35, assisted Charlie Chaplin with score of "Modern Times"; comp, var film scores, 300 TV progs, incl "Ben Casey." Conductor, concerts & recordings; lectr; producer of recordings. Adj prof music & fac, Ctr for Pub Affairs, Univ Southern Calif; fac music, Univ Calif, Los Angeles. Radio series, "The Subject Is Film Music"; own film music prog at Libr of Congress; subject of oral histories by Yale & Southern Methodist Univs. Chief Collabrs: Johnny Mercer, Mack Gordon, June Carroll, Paul Francis Webster, Sammy Cahn, Arthur Hamilton, Kermit Goell, Bob Wells, Jay Livingston, Ray Evans. *Songs:* Music: Slowly; You Can't Run Away from Love; Rainbows in the Night; You Above All; Until They Sail (title song); Love Song; Ballad of Al Capone; Lonely Rider; Some Days Seem So Beautiful; My Name Is Love; If You Remember Me; Laura; The Bad and the Beautiful; Forever Amber; Mother Courage; Wind in the Willows; A World I Never Made (chorus); If the Shoe Fits; Hasten the Day. *Instrumental Works:* Force of Evil-Nocturne and Finale (orch); A Song After Sundown (tenor saxophone, orch); Litany (orch); Train to Exile (orch); Serenade (recorder quartet); Theme from Ben Casey (orch); Hoofloose and Fancy Free (chamber orch); Grande Polonaise (orch); Morning Revisited (ens of horns, perc); Life with Father (concert band, theme); Toy Concertino (orch). *Songs & Instrumental Works:* Too Late Blues. *Scores:* Films: Laura; Forever Amber; Force of Evil; The Bad and the Beautiful; The Redeemer; Opera/Ballet: Feather In Your Hat; Inspiration; Mother Goose-Step.

RALEY, GLENN   ASCAP 1976
composer, author, trumpeter
b Cincinnati, Ohio, Feb 17, 44. Educ: Cleveland Inst of Music, 65-68; Los Angeles City Col, 67, studied trumpet, piano, music theory & comp. Scored music for Palatine Concert Band, Ill & Tulsa Community Band, Okla, then performed as trumpeter & cond. Played in dance bands & orchs. *Songs:* I Wish I Had You (ballad). *Albums:* The Now Sounds of Today.

RALKE, DONALD EDWARD   ASCAP 1962
composer, arranger
b Battle Creek, Mich. Educ: Univ Southern Calif, BM & MM. Comp, arr & cond, Hollywood, 25 yrs; arr & cond 44 hit singles, incl 6 gold records; comp & arr for TV & movies. *Songs:* Music: It Shall Come to Pass; Just 'Round the Riverbend.

RALPH, RALPH J
See Schuckett, Ralph Dion

RALSTON, GILBERT A   ASCAP 1963
author
b Los Angeles, Calif, Jan 5, 12.

RAM, SAMUEL (BUCK) (ANDE RAND, LYNN PAUL)   ASCAP 1940
composer, producer, arranger
b Chicago, Ill, Nov 21, 07. Educ: Violin, self-taught; studied arr & writing songs with Joseph Schillinger. Completed law sch, passed bar & never practiced. Moved to New York, became arr, Mills Music. Traveled with bands, incl Ina Rae Hutton, Duke Ellington, Count Basie & Dorsey Bros. Discovered Ella Fitzgerald in amateur show, Apollo Theatre. Recorded Savoy Jazz Masters, 43-44. Producer, Three Suns. Wrote scores for Grand Terrace & Cotton Club Reviews. Writer & producer, The Platters. Chief Collabrs: Al Stillman, Will Hudson, Don Redman, Count Basie, Cab Calloway, Hot Lips Page. *Songs & Instrumental Works:* Only You; Great Pretender; Twilight Time; I'll Be Home for Christmas; I'm Sorry; Remember When; Enchanted; For the First Time (Come Prima); (You've Got) The Magic Touch; Wish It Were Me; My Dream (Fest Winner); My Serenade (Shubert); Rock All Night; You Lovable You; Sonata; Where; After Glow; Heaven on Earth; At Your Beck and Call; On My Word of Honor; Have Mercy; But Not Like You; Sweet Sixteen; One in a Million; You'll Never Never Know; Sleepless Nights—Restless Days; Adorable; Benfica (Bossa Nova); Sad River (Rio Triste); I Wish (Quero Te Assim); It's Raining Outside (Chove La Fora); Whispering Wind (Ta Petite Guele); These Precious Moments; Goodbye My Foolish (Sayonara); I Must Be Dreaming; Sorans Song (Seran Bushi); Town of Falling Snow (Yuki No Furu Machi O); Twilight in Tokyo (Tokyo Tasagare); Vigil By the Sea (Es Singen Nach Immer Die Walder); The Big Dream (Il Grande Segna); Ram Session; Swing Street; Twilight in Tehran; Aladdin's Lamp; Headin' Home; I Complained; You'll Know (When the Time Comes). *Albums:* Most Beloved of Women; Shimabara Lullabye; Snow on the Mountain; Japanese Noodle Man; Song of Gion; Song of the River (Kitakami Yakyoku).

RAMBO, JOYCE REBA (DOTTIE)   ASCAP 1977
composer, singer
b Madisonville, Ky, Mar 2, 34. Mem, Singing Rambos, 25 yrs of full-time travel. Children's musical, "Down By The Creek Bank." 50 LP records & 1000 songs written. *Songs & Instrumental Works:* He Looked Beyond My Faults; Remind Me; If That Isn't Love; Glory in the Cross; Behold the Lamb; Tears Will Never Stain the Streets of That City; Never Been This Homesick Before.

RAMIN, JORDAN STANLEY   ASCAP 1955
composer
b Boston, Mass, Mar 7, 30. Educ: Berklee Col Music, Boston, BA, 50; studied clarinet with Emil Arcierro. Vpres, Liza Music Corp, publ of music from "Around the World in 80 Days," 57-71. Comp title song & music for cinerama film "Holiday in Spain." Recorded jazz albums with Doc Severinsen & worked in var capacities as musician, songwriter, publ with Neil Sadaka & Melissa Manchester. Has written numerous music articles for mag High Fidelity, After Dark, Record World & others. Signed with Valando Orgn for TV proj titled "Crato's Original Stone Age Jazz Band," 80-81. Chief Collabrs: Robert Share, Frank Stanton, Murray Semos. *Scores:* Herkimer the Homely Doll (on Captain Kangaroo, CBS-TV); Around the World of Mike Todd (ABC-TV spec); Look Where I'm At (off-Bway musical). *Albums:* The Worst of Morris Garner (comedy jazz); JUNK (comedy jazz).

RAMIN, SID   ASCAP 1955
composer, conductor
b Boston, Mass, Jan 22, 24. Educ: Boston Univ; Columbia Univ. Comp & arr, "Milton Berle Show," 49-56; comp, cond & arr, RCA Victor; arr, Bway musicals "West Side Story" (Grammy Award & Acad Award for film, 61); "Gypsy", "Wildcat," "I Can Get It for You Wholesale" & "A Funny Thing Happened on the Way to the Forum." Music dir, "Patty Duke Show" & "Candid Camera," TV. Cleo Award for Johnson & Johnson commercial. *Songs & Instrumental Works:* Simon Says; Where There's a Man; Ecstasy Waltz; Music to Watch Girls By; Come Alive (Pepsi-Cola commercial).

RAMIREZ, ROGER J (RAM)   ASCAP 1950
b San Juan, PR, Sept 15, 13. *Songs:* Lover Man; Mad About You; I Just Refuse to Sing the Blues.

RAMSAY, EUGENE SPURGEON   ASCAP 1955
composer, author
b San Antonio, Tex, Apr 1, 18. Educ: Northwestern Univ, Sch Music, BME, 41; began as a piano student at age 9. Began writing songs at age 13; wrote one hit song for a col musical; learned to fly in 41; airline pilot, 42; flew for Eastern Air Lines, 33 yrs, retired, 78. Songwriter. Chief Collabr: Jay Hathaway (lyricist). *Songs:* I'll Try; I'm Gonna Throw Away My Little Black Book; You Taught Me to Love Again; You and Me; Music: Love With No Tomorrow.

RAMSEY, CURTIS LYNFORD   ASCAP 1960
composer, arranger, trumpeter
b Grand Meadow, Minn, Oct 1, 16. Educ: Pub schs, La Crosse, Wis; La Crosse State Teachers Col; Am Cons, Chicago. Trumpeter in dance bands. Musician, USS Shangri-La, USN, WW II. Musician, joined Lawrence Welk, 49, later to production staff, TV show, 30 yr mem. Chief Collabrs: Lawrence Welk, Myron Floren, George Thow, Joe Rizzo. *Songs:* Music: Keep a Song in Your Heart; On With the Show; Just Another Dream; Ragtime Piano Gal; Just Lucky I Guess. *Instrumental Works:* Stop Time; Lovable Doll; Happy Norwegian Polka; Whirlaway.

RAMSEY, NORMAN
See Rodby, Walter

RAMSEY, WILLIS ALAN   ASCAP 1972
composer, singer, recording engineer
b Birmingham, Ala, Mar 5, 51. Educ: Univ Tex. Performer, folk clubs, Tex area, 70 & col coffee house concert, 71. Recording artist, 72; recorded sound track for Hal Ashly's film "Second Hand Hearts," 79-80. *Songs:* Muskrat Love; The Ballad of Spider John.

RAMSIER, PAUL   ASCAP 1961
composer, pianist, educator
b Louisville, Ky. Educ: Univ Louisville, BM; Juilliard, spec studies, grad; Fla State Univ, MM; NY Univ, PhD; studied piano with Beveridge Webster, piano & comp with Ernst V Dohnanyi & comp with Alexei Haieff. Comp, symphonic, chamber, opera & dance music with spec interest in virtuoso double bass. Currently prof comp, NY Univ; also engaged in psychotherapy practice devoted to problems of creative artists. Has been comn by & performed in Louisville Orch, Am Ballet Theatre, Chicago Symph, Toronto Symph, Minn Orch & St Louis Symph. *Songs:* Music: The Moon and the Sun (SSA, Old Eng text); Eden (SATB, Old Eng text); Wine (Old Eng text). *Instrumental Works:* Divertimento Concertante on a Theme of Couperin (double bass & orch); Road to Hamelin (double bass, narrator & orch); Eusibius Revisited (double bass & orch); Pied Piper (piano suite). *Scores:* Opera/Ballet: The Man on the Bearskin Rug.

RAN, SHULAMIT
composer
b Tel Aviv, Israel, Oct 21, 49. Educ: Mannes Col Music, studied with Norman Dello Joio & Nadia Reisenberg, dipl, 67; Tanglewood, studied with Aaron Copland & Lukas Foss, 63; Darmstadt, 70; comp study with Ralph Shapey, piano with Dorothy Taubman. Grants, Awards & Comn: Martha Baird Rockefeller Fund, Ford Found, Am-Israel Cultural Found, Fromm Music Found, NEA, Guggenheim Fel & others. Recorded by Vox-Turnabout Records. Appeared extensively as pianist. Assoc prof comp, Univ Chicago. *Songs & Instrumental Works:* Capriccio for Piano and Orchestra; Seven Japanese Love Poems (voice, piano); Hatzvi Israel Eulogy (voice, instruments); O The Chimneys (voice, instruments); Concert Piece for Piano and Orchestra; Three Fantasy Pieces for Cello and Piano; Ensembles for 17; Double Vision (two wind quintets, piano); Hyperbolae for Piano (obligatory piece, 2nd Arthur Rubenstein Piano Competition); For an Actor: Monologue for Clarinet; Apprehensions (voice, clarinet, piano).

RAND, ANDE
See Ram, Samuel

RAND, LIONEL
See Clouser, Lionel Randolph

RANDALL, BRUCE
See Rodby, Walter

RANDALL, GERALD ROBERT   ASCAP 1973
composer, author
b Summittville, NY, May 27, 36. Educ: Studied with Maceo Jefferson. Free lance writer, 57-; served with USA, 59-61; lyricist & comp, 65-; independent record producer & personal mgr musical groups, 67- Pres, H&G Randall Inc (publ) & Randall Records, 72- Vpres, P J Reilly Funeral Homes Inc, Middletown, NY. Chief Collabrs: Maceo Jefferson, Samuel Turiano, Tobias C Frey, Howard Russell, John Frost, Michael Schwab, Terry Wilhelm, Eva Bonn, De Dona Bonn. *Songs & Instrumental Works:* Why Is Your Love Haunting Me?; Hangout Pete; Right On; J, the Jack; Mac Jefferson's Song; Eternal Love; Sahib Sam; I've Got Feelings, Too; Boom Billy Coo; There's One More Adventure Left in Me; Zodiac Zoo; I'm an Astrologer, Too; That's the Way You Are, My Love; The Toby's Song; What Happened to Us; Do I Know You?; No Name Blues; Why Me Blues; Playing Games With the Blues; Satyr's Tears; There Is Only One Special You; Bagnew Dixon; If What the People Say Is True; Fate's Mystery; Be My Destiny; We're Movin'.

RANDLE, DODIE
See Flournoy, Roberta Jean

RANDLE, EDWARD EARL   ASCAP 1979
composer, singer
b Indianola, Miss, Mar 1, 47. Educ: Gentry High Sch; Miss Indust Col, 64-65; Los Angeles City Col, 66-67. Wrote tunes for group, Natural Four, San Francisco, 68. Worked in French clubs with house bands, Montreal, 70. Wrote for Syl Johnson, 71; with Twinight Label, Chicago, 71-80. Joined Willie Mitchell & Hi Records, 71. Songwriter, A&R man & publ consult, JEC & Fi Publ Co. Chief Collabrs: O V Wright, Syl Johnson, Al Green, Willie Mitchell, James Shaw, Russ Allison, George Jackson, Patrick Simmons. *Songs:* Echoes of Love; Come to Papa; About to Make Me Leave Home; God Blessed Our Love; I'm Gonna Tear Your Playhouse Down; Somebody's on Your Case; Anyway the Wind Blows; Come to Mama; I'm Doing Fine; Slow and Easy; I Didn't Take Your Man (You Gave It to Me).

RANEY, CAROLYN
See Schechtman, Carolyn R

RANNO, RICHARD B   ASCAP 1976
composer, guitarist, singer
b New York, NY, Jan 21, 50. Musician with rock groups, Bungi, 70-73, Stories, 73-74, Stasz, 75-79 & Hard Core, 79- Chief Collabr: Gene Simmons. *Songs:* Fallen Angel; Pull the Plug; Nightcrawler; Boys in Action; Cherry Baby; Sing It, Shout It; Violation; Steady; Hold on to the Night; I'll Be There; Third Time's the Charm; Johnny All Alone; X-Ray Spex; Last Night I Wrote a Letter; Take Me; No Regrets. *Instrumental Works:* Coliseum Rock.

RANSOM, RAYMOND L, JR   ASCAP 1972
composer, musician, singer
b Waycross, Ga, Dec 27, 50. Educ: Morris Brown Col, grad. Singer & bass guitarist with group Brick, currently. Chief Collabrs: James B Brown, Reginald J Hargis, Edward Irons, Jr. *Songs:* Dazz; Dusic; Push Push; Get Started; Let Me Make You Happy; Don't Ever Lose Your Love; Waiting on You; Free; Sweet Lips; Get Fired Up; Hello; Living From the Mind; We Don't Wanna Sit Down, We Wanna Get Down; Raise Your Hands; Dancin' Man; To Me; Stoneheart; By the Moonlight; Life Is What You Make It.

RAPEE, ERNO   ASCAP 1923
composer, conductor
b Budapest, Hungary, June 4, 1891; d New York, NY, June 26, 45. Asst cond, Dresden Opera House; then cond opera houses in Magdeburg, Kattowitz. Concert tours of SAm & Mex, 12; then US. Cond, Rivoli Theatre, first NY film theatre with symph orch. Assoc with S L Rothafel (Roxy) in musical presentations, NY theatres. Gen music dir, NBC. Dir-in-chief, Radio City Music Hall. Film background scores & themes incl, "Seventh Heaven" & "What Price Glory." Chief Collabr: Lew Pollack. *Songs:* Charmaine; Diane; Angela Mia; Ever Since the Day I Found You; Among the Stars; Rockettes on Parade.

RAPH, ALAN   ASCAP 1964
composer, author
b New York, NY, July 3, 33. Educ: NY Univ, BSMusEd; Fontdinbleau, Paris, France, studied with Nadia Boulanger; Teachers Col, Columbia Univ, MAMusEd. Commercial recording bassist & trombonist. Leader, Chamber Brass Players & The Seventh Century. Trombone soloist & clinician; fac, NY Univ & Teachers Col, Columbia Univ. Charter mem, Am Symph Orch, Stokowski & Gerry Mulligan Concert Jazz Band. *Songs:* Wedding Song; Do You Know. *Instrumental Works:* Dance Band Reading and Interpretation (method); The Double Valve Bass Trombone (method); Caprice (trombone). *Scores:* Ballet: Trinity; Sacred Grove on Mt Tamalpais.

RAPH, THEODORE E   ASCAP 1955
composer, author, conductor
b Boston, Mass, Sept 24, 05. Educ: Juilliard; pvt study with Youry Bilstin & Samuel Gardner. Dixieland trombonist; arr for name bands, theatres & singers. Comp, arr & cond, nat radio, TV, films & recordings. Consultant, USA, WW II (with commendation). Author, "The Songs We Sang." *Songs:* Judge a Human; There'll Be Good Times Comin'. *Instrumental Works:* No Parking; Bouncin' 'Round; Devil Dog Marines; March of Dimes; Parade of the Clams; Cock of the Walk.

RAPHLING, SAM
composer
b Ft Worth, Tex, Mar 19, 10. Educ: Chicago Musical Col, MM, studied with Rudolph Ganz; Hoch Sch Music, Berlin, studied with Leonid Kreutzer. Performed with Chicago Symph Orch under Toscanini, Rachmaninoff & Stock. Gave piano concerts. Won 1st prize for "Suite for Strings" & "Lively Overture." Taught at Chicago Musical Col. *Songs:* Music: Dream Keeper (cycle songs on poetry of Langston Hughes); Four Poems of Carl Sandburg (voice & piano); Spoon River Anthology (poems of E L Masters; voice & piano). *Instrumental Works:* Symphony No 1, 3 & 4 (full orch); Piano Concerto No 1 & 3; Ticker-Tape Parade (overture for orch); I Hear America Singing (cantata for soli-chorus & orch); Concerto for Trumpet & Strings; Concerto for Piano & Percussion; Warble for Lilac-Time (flute solo & strings); Israel Rhapsody (piano solo & orch); Sonata No 3 (violin & piano); Sonata (french horn & piano); Sonatas I, III, V & VI (piano); Involvement (concert band); Carnival of the Mind (8 pieces for full orch); Rhapsody for Ondes Martinot & Orch; String Quartet No 2; Transc: Rite of Spring (Stravinsky; piano solo of complete ballet). *Scores:* Opera: President Lincoln (4 acts); Nathan the Wise (1 act); Johnny Pye and the Fool-Killers (2 acts; S V Benet story); Liar, Liar (children's opera).

RAPOSO, JOSEPH G   ASCAP 1961
composer, author
b Fall River, Mass, Feb 8, 37. Educ: Harvard Univ, AB, 58; Ecole Normale de Musique, Paris, France, 60, studied with Nadia Boulanger. Resident comp, Harvard Univ Loeb Drama Ctr & head, music theatre dept, Boston Cons. Original music dir & composer lyricist, "Sesame Street" & "The Electric Company." Comp & lyricist, special projects, CBS, NBC & ABC incl Dr Seuss specials & "The Muppet Show." Comp, lyricist & music dir, var Bway & off-Bway productions incl "You're a Good Man Charlie Brown", "Half a Sixpence", "Play It Again, Sam", "The Mad Show" & "The Office." Chief

Collabrs: Hal David, Sheldon Harnick, Jim Henson, Jeff Moss. *Songs:* Sing; Bein' Green; Somebody Come and Play; You Will Be My Music; Winners; Blue; I'm No Girl's Toy; Candy Hearts; TV show theme Three's Company. *Scores:* Film: Raggedy Ann and Andy.

RAPTAKIS, KLEON   ASCAP 1963
composer, author, conductor
b Andros, Greece, May 25, 05. Educ: Juilliard Sch Music; Columbia Univ. WW II service. Mem, symph bands in concerts & on radio. Has had own music sch, 52- *Instrumental Works:* Book of Greek Songs and Dances (incl Music History of Greece); The Hero; Sonata for Strings; Piano Quintet; also 3 symph, 2 piano sonatas & 2 piano suites.

RASBACH, OSCAR   ASCAP 1932
composer, pianist
b Dayton, Ky, Aug 2, 1888; d. Educ: Pub schs; studied music with Ludwig Thomas, Julius Jahn, Jode Anderson, A J Stamm & Hans Thornton. Has been accompanist, piano soloist, teacher & choral dir. Chief Collabr: Joyce Kilmer. *Songs:* Trees; The Red Woods; Mountains; A Wanderer's Song; The Look; Laughing Brook. *Scores:* Operettas: Dawn Boy; Open House.

RASCH, RAYMOND P   ASCAP 1954
composer, conductor, pianist
b Toledo, Ohio, Mar 1, 19; d Hollywood, Calif, Dec 23, 64. Educ: St Louis Inst of Music. Led own orch in hotels; pianist in dance bands; also wrote spec material. Chief Collabrs: Paul Francis Webster, Ray Gilbert, Sid Miller, Bob Russell, Dotty Wayne. *Scores:* Films: Limelight; Stage: I'm With You. *Albums:* Wild Is Love; The Nina, the Pinta, the Santa Maria.

RASCHI, EUGENE G   ASCAP 1963
composer, author, singer
b Springfield, Mass, Oct 24, 29. Educ: Pub schs; Pekins Sch for the Blind. Wrote musical commercials. Chief Collabr: William Taylor. *Songs:* My New Year's Wish; Missouri; Hot Dog; Branded By Love; Friendship Ring; Sharon, Oh Sharon; My Misty Illusion.

RASKIN, EUGENE   ASCAP 1961
composer, author, teacher
b New York, NY, Sept 5, 09. Educ: Columbia Univ, BA & MA(Arch); Univ Paris, cert. Mem duo Gene & Francesca, did concerts & recordings, 50-70. Songwriter, 40- Recordings with Elektra, Apple, RCA Victor, Columbia & Deutschegramafon. *Songs:* Those Were the Days; Bambu; Hello Love; Other Birthdays Other Years; Kretchma. *Instrumental Works:* 47.50. *Scores:* Film/TV: Gigantor; Big World of Little Adam.

RASKIN, WILLIAM   ASCAP 1924
author
b New York, NY, Nov 3, 1896; d New York, Apr 8, 42. Educ: Pub schs. Song writer with music publ cos. Wrote songs for early sound films & spec material for vaudeville acts. Chief Collabrs: Sammy Fain, Irving Kahal, Billy Hill. *Songs:* They Cut Down the Old Pine Tree; Wedding Bells Are Breaking Up That Old Gang of Mine; I'm Waiting for Ships That Never Come In; Fifty Million Frenchmen Can't Be Wrong; I'll Buy That Ring and Change Your Name to Mine; I Found a Rose in the Devil's Garden; That's When Your Heartaches Begin.

RATHAUS, KAROL   ASCAP 1953
composer, pianist, educator
b Tarnopol, Poland, Sept 16, 1895; d New York, NY, Nov 21, 54. To US, 38. Educ: Univ & Acad Music, Vienna; Hochschule fur Musik, Berlin. WW I, officer, Austrian army. Comp, incidental music to plays & films, Ger. To Paris, then London, 34-38. Comp, film scores, Hollywood. Prof comp, Queens Col, 40-54, chmn dept, 44-46. *Songs & Instrumental Works:* Le Lion Amoureux (Ballet Russe comn); Polonaise Symphonique (New York Philh comn); Vision Dramatique; Uriel Acosta Suite; Salisbury Cove Overture; Sinfonia Concertante; Prelude for Orch (Louisville Orch comn); Piano Concerto; Trio Serenade (piano, violin, cello); The Last Pierrot (ballet); String Quartets No 4 (Soc for Publ Am Music Award) and No 5; Suite Opus 27 (violin & piano or orch); 2 Violin Sonatas (violin & piano); Trio (clarinet, violin, piano); Three English Songs (voice & piano); Three Choral Songs Opus 70 (SATB); Ballade (piano); Piano Sonata No 3; Diapason (oratorio); Choral Pieces: Lament, Requiem and Rondeau (SATB); Greek Lament (from Iphigenia; SATB & French horn); Boris Godunov (Mussorgsky, revised orchestration).

RAVEN, EDDY
See Futch, Edward Garvin

RAVEN GREY EAGLE
See Florio, Andrea Nicola

RAVOSA, CARMINO C   ASCAP 1959
composer, lyricist, playwright
b Springfield, Mass, Jan 29, 30. Educ: Hartt Col of Music; Teachers Col, Columbia Univ. Songwriter, TV prog "Captain Kangaroo Show," 75- Comp-in-residence, Dalton Sch, New York. Comp, women's rights musical

"Seneca Falls," Carnegie Hall, 77. Command perf for Pres & Mrs Carter & staff of musical "Ghosts in the White House," at the White House, 78. TV spec for children "The Story Song Man." *Songs:* Ladder of Love. *Scores:* Stage shows: Laff Capades of '59; Johnny Appleseed.

RAWITZ, STEVEN JEFFREY   ASCAP 1975
composer, trumpet/flügelhorn player
b Mineola, NY, Sept 5, 54. Educ: Univ High Sch, West Los Angeles, 69-72; Calif State Univ, Northridge, 72-73. Studio trumpet/flügelhorn player; comp & arr TV & radio jingles, incl C&H Sugar, Schlitz Beer, Bob's Big Boy, Coors Beer & others; staff music arr, Merv Griffin Show, 76-78; comp musical cues, John Davidson Show; arr music, Benny Goodman's Carnegie Hall Concert, 78. *Instrumental Works:* Step Right Up; Alternate Roots; Brush Off; No Soap; Sew Dare; Theme for a Pretty Lady; Peppermint; Factory Aire; Mira No Mas!; How's Bayou?; Nosmo King; Winter; Enter Stage Left; Stella by Carlight; Spy Guy; The Umpire Strikes Back; A Night of Amnesia; A Little Traveling Music; But Seriously Folks.

RAY, JOHN ALVIN (JOHNNIE)   ASCAP 1952
composer, author, singer
b Dallas, Ore, Jan 10, 27. Was singer on radio, Portland, then in nightclubs & theatres throughout US, also in films. Has made many records. *Songs:* The Little White Cloud That Cried; A Sinner Am I; Whiskey and Gin.

RAY, MARC B   ASCAP 1976
author
b Klamath Falls, Ore, May 17, 40. Educ: Hofstra Univ, BA; Columbia Univ, MA. Writer, producer & dir. Wrote new music for New Mickey Mouse Club, Disney Studios. Chief Collabr: Peter Martin. *Albums:* The Mickey Mouse Club.

RAYBURN, MARGIE   ASCAP 1961
composer, author, singer
b Madera, Calif. Educ: Hollywood High Sch. Vocalist with dance bands incl Ray Anthony. Toured with Gene Autry. Appeared on TV shows, also in nightclubs throughout US. *Songs:* Hello, Mr Heartbreak; I've Tried So Hard Not to Love You.

RAYBURN, MARK LYNN   ASCAP 1977
composer, author, singer
b Alton, Ill, Dec 20, 47. Study: Eastern NMex Univ, commercial art & graphic design. Christian concert artist, singer, guitarist, recording artist, Myrrh Records, div of Word, Inc. *Songs:* Where Are You Going?; Love Songs (To the Father); Freedom and Peace; Empty Words; Love You.

RAYE, DON
See Wilhoite, Donald MacRae, Jr

RAY (HAYES), LARRY   ASCAP 1960
composer, author, novelist
b Alamosa, Colo, Feb 29, 40. Educ: Air Univ (Air Force); George Washington Univ, Air Force Cadet Prog; San Mateo Jr Col; Univ Calif, Los Angeles. Songwriter. Gen mgr, ABC Records; chief operating officer, Elektra Records, West Coast; co-partner with Bill Szymczyk forming Tumbleweed Records Inc/A G&W Co. Wrote 4 screen plays. Author, "Rock and Roll, A Novel." Chief Collabrs: Hank Jones, Dean Kay, Terry Miller. *Songs:* Lyrics: Let it Happen Again; Ain't Gotta Nickel; Born Lonely; Wishin' Well; Last Letter Home.

RAYMOND, GEORGE   ASCAP 1963
composer, author
b Cleveland, Ohio, Oct 7, 03. Educ: Morningside Col, Iowa, AB; studied with Rudolph Schramm, Schillinger Syst Composing. Chief Collabrs: Harry Stride, Andy Bazaf, Jack Scholl, Betty Brown, Jimmy Franklin, Jack Owens. *Songs:* The Flag You Wave May Be the Flag You Save; I Want My Sweetheart Back Again; Rest in Peace; Left Over Love; God Needs America; Don't Make Me Cry Anymore; Would You Mind; The Sweetest Story Ever Told; I Don't Care What the Words Are if it Just Has a Tune; Behind Your Back; Betty Brown; Live All You Can Today; City Patrol Song; Be My Guest; Love Me Now; Live to Love and You'll Love to Live; If You Could Fall in Love With Me the Way I Fell in Love With You; You Gotta Love Somebody to be Somebody; I Wish I Could Live Forever; Love is Eternal; Santa Claus Will Be Here Tonight; In Old Antigua; Count Me In; I Still Love New York; I Can't Get Away With a Thing; You're the Girl; Thanksgiving Day; You Are My Minimum Daily Requirement; Kingdom Come; When Will We Learn?; Last Night I Dreamt I Was Back Home Again; I Often Wonder; Music: The Church By the Side of the Road; Play That Honky Tonk Tune; Mother's Little Man; I Lost My Heart in Paradise.

RAYMOND, HAROLD NEWELL (ROY NEWELL)   ASCAP 1936
composer, author, publisher
b Chicago, Ill, Sept 26, 1884; d Denville, NJ, Dec 12, 57. Educ: Am Acad Dramatic Arts; studied violin. Became publ, 32. Mem, Am Guild Authors & Comp. *Songs:* I'm Alone With My Dreams of You; Old Clothes; Ring the Bell; At a Little Country Tavern; Hi, Beautiful; Unsophisticated Sue; Kisses.

RAYMOND, LEWIS ASCAP 1964
composer, pianist, arranger
b Newark, NJ, Aug 3, 08; d Los Angeles, Calif, May 19, 66. Educ: NY Col Music; studied with Felix Deyo, Bernard Wagenaar, Max Rudolf, Herbert Weiskopf. Organist, silent film theatres; pianist, New York & Brooklyn Paramount Theatres. Toured with Maj Bowes orch. Bandsman, USAAF, WW II. Arr, Tommy Dorsey Orch; staff arr, WOR, also for Bway musicals. *Instrumental Works:* First String Quartet; Suite for Brass Quartet; 4 Designs for Various Solo Instruments and Piano; Divertissement for 3 Flutes; Chorale in Gregorian Style (clarinet choir); transc of Gershwin's Piano Preludes.

RAYMOND, WALKER X
See Walker, Raymond

RAZAF, ANDY (ANDREA PAUL RAZAFKERIEFO) ASCAP 1929
author
b Washington, DC, Dec 16, Son of Malagasy nobleman. Educ: Pub sch; also pvt study. Wrote many nightclub revues. Cited by US Treas Dept for War Bond Drive songs. Chief Collabrs: Fats Waller, Eubie Blake, J C Johnson, James P Johnson, Paul Denniker, Joe Garland. *Songs:* Ain't Misbehavin'; Honeysuckle Rose; In the Mood; Stompin' At the Savoy; Memories of You; 12th Street Rag; Black and Blue; S'posin'; Make Believe Ballroom; Christopher Columbus; Milkman's Matinee; Concentratin' on You; You're Lucky to Me; Porter's Love Song; Knock Me a Kiss; Dusky Stevedore; My Special Friend; That's What I Like 'Bout the South; Keepin' Out of Mischief Now; Blue Turning Gray Over You; Shoutin' in the Amen Corner; Gee, Baby, Ain't I Good to You?; On Revival Day; Stealing Apples; How Can You Face Me?; Massachusetts; My Handy Man; My Fate Is in Your Hands; The Joint Is Jumpin'; I'm Gonna Move to the Outskirts of Town; If It Ain't Love; The Burning Bush of Israel; Am I My Brother's Keeper?; Seeds of Brotherhood; Precious Rosary. *Scores:* Bway stage: Keep Shufflin'; Hot Chocolates; Blackbirds of 1930.

RAZAFKERIEFO, ANDREA PAUL
See Razaf, Andy

REA, DAVID ERNEST ASCAP 1968
composer, author, singer
b Akron, Ohio, Oct 26, 46. Educ: Silver Lake Sch; Cuyahoga Falls High Sch; Kimball Union Acad, studied music hist; studied classical music with Irene Drake, Kent State Univ. Guest speaker ethnomusicology, Dartmouth Col at age 16. Guitarist for Gordon Lightfoot, Ian & Sylvia, Judy Collins, The Chaney Bros, Jesse Winchester, Tom Rush, Fred Niel & Doug Kershaw. Recorded 3 solo albums; appeared numerous TV shows. Hon teacher advanced Eng. Chief Collabrs: Ian & Sylvia, Leslie West, Felix Pappalardi, Bob Wier, Mike Seeger, Charles Lloyd, Wayne Moss, Robbie Robertson. *Songs:* For Yasgur's Farm; Flowers of Evil; Juanita Tonight; Blueberry Eyes; Learn to Lose; Fish for the Table. *Scores:* Opera/Ballet: Emperor Norton; Film/TV: Mississippi Queen; David and Goliath.

REACH, ALICE SCANLON ASCAP 1963
composer, author
b Buffalo, NY. Chief Collabr: Anthony Scibetta. *Songs:* Spring in Manhattan.

READ, DONALD ASCAP 1962
composer, author, singer
b Saugus, Mass, Sept 19, 14. Educ: Boston Univ, BA, MA; Juilliard Sch Music. Tenor soloist in concert & oratorio. Teacher at Juilliard Sch Music, also privately. Mem, NY Singing Teachers Asn; dir, UN Singers. *Songs:* United Nations Singers Folk Song Series (compiler, arr, translr).

READ, GARDNER ASCAP 1945
composer, author
b Evanston, Ill, Jan 2, 13. Educ: Eastman Sch Music, BM & MM, pupil of Howard Hanson & Bernard Rogers, 32-37; advanced studies with Ildebrando Pizzetti, Rome, 39 & Aaron Copland, Berkshire Music Ctr, 41. Hon DMus, Doane Col, 62. Taught at Nat Music Camp, 40. Head, Theory & Comp Depts, St Louis Inst Music, 41-43; Kansas City Cons Music, 43-45 & Cleveland Inst Music, 45-48. Head, Theory & Comp Depts, Boston Univ Sch Music, 48-78, emer prof, 78- Cromwell Traveling Fel, 38-39. Lect & cond grants, Int Educ Exchange Serv, Mex, 57 & 64. Comns from Ravinia Fest, Pittsburgh Int Contemporary Music Fest, Cleveland, Indianapolis & Louisville Orchs & Kindler Found. Chief Collabr: James Forsyth. *Instrumental Works:* Sketches of the City, Opus 26; Symphony No 1, Opus 30; Night Flight, Opus 44; Symphony No 2, Opus 45; The Temptation of St Anthony, Opus 56; First Overture, Opus 58; Pennsylvania Suite, Opus 67; Symphony No 3, Opus 75; Symphony No 4, Opus 92; Toccata Giocosa, Opus 94; Vernal Equinox, Opus 96; Prelude and Toccata, Opus 43; Sound Piece for Brass and Percussion, Opus 82; Concerto for Cello and Orchestra, Opus 55; The Prophet, Opus 110; Villon, Opus 122; String Quartet No 1, Opus 100; Los Dioses Aztecas, Opus 107.

READE, CHARLES FASO ASCAP 1951
composer, pianist
b Naro, Sicily, May 1, 11. To US as child. Educ: High sch; studied piano with Gilda Ruta. Pianist in dance groups; also appeared as single. Chief Collabrs: Sy Taylor, Joe Candullo, Chauncey Gray, Monica Stuart, Marie Manovil, Phil

Perry. *Songs & Instrumental Works:*Sweet Potato Polka; Christmas Symphony; I Had Too Much to Dream Last Night; Te Amo; Friendship Ring; Everyone Knows I Love You; I Can't Make Up My Mind; No More Rain; Sentimentos; Stocking Full of Blues.

REAL, LOUIS ALBERT, II ASCAP 1970
composer, singer, guitarist
b Kerrville, Tex, Apr 6, 51. Educ: Schreiner Col, Kerrville, Tex. Singer in nightclubs since age 18. Mem of Justice Band, then of Cactus Rose Band; appeared at Kerrville Folk Fest, 79. Now appearing with Cactus Rose Band, Ga & Tex. Chief Collabrs: Greg Cox, Cindy Cox, Dave Wood, Mike Gones, Wells Young. *Songs:* Lady of My Life; Sweet Potato Pie; Little Butterfly; White Horses; Come Over to My Side.

REARDON, FRANK C (VERNON CROSS) ASCAP 1954
composer, author, singer
b New York, NY, Mar 14, 25. Educ: John Adams High Sch. Contract writer, Theodore Presser Co, 49 & Mills Music Corp, 51. Wrote lyrics for Bway musical, "Rumple." Chief Collabrs: Sammy Cahn, Ernest G Schweikert, Robert Harris, John Pocorobba. *Songs:* Same Old Saturday Night; In Times Like These; Somebody Cares; How Do You Say Goodbye; Lolita; My Symphony; All Dressed Up and No Place to Go; also two musical comedy scores.

REARDON, JACK ASCAP 1957
composer, author
b Lowell, Mass, Apr 29, 34. Educ: Lowell High Sch; Boston Univ. Writer of special material & plays. Chief Collabrs: Paul Evans, Sacha Distel, Eddie Layton. *Songs:* When; La Strada Del'Amore; Twilight Roses; Worried Guy; Lyrics: The Good Life (Grammy nomination, best song, 63); The Lover.

REBILLOT, PATRICK E ASCAP 1974
composer, pianist
b Louisville, Ohio, Apr 21, 35. Educ: Mt Union Col, studied piano & organ, 49-53; Cincinnati Cons of Music, studied piano with Jeno Takacs; Univ Cincinnati, BS(music educ), 57. Church organist, ages 12-17, Louisville. Accompanist to classical singers & instrumentalists, Cincinnati Cons. Arr & pianist, USA special services, toured world, 58-60. To NY, 60; with var artists & led own groups, 60's. Worked with Gary Burton & Herbie Mann, 70's; session-man, New York studios. Chief Collabr: Pat Kirby. *Songs:* Music: Easter Rising; Violet Don't Be Blue; Let Me Know; Song for the New Man; Thank You, Mr Rushing; The Beautiful Bend Ahead; In a Melancholy Funk. *Albums:* Free Fall.

REDD, ALONZA THOMAS ASCAP 1978
composer, singer
b New Bern, NC, Feb 12, 50. With Nantucket Rock Group, 11 yrs. *Songs:* Heartbreaker; Gimme Your Love; California; (Don't Hang Up) On Me Baby; Is It Wrong to R&R.

REDDICK, WILLIAM J ASCAP 1926
composer, author, conductor
b Paducah, Ky, June 23, 1890; d Detroit, Mich, May 18, 65. Educ: Cincinnati Col Music; Cincinnati Univ; studied with Clarence Adler, Ernest Hutcheson, Rudolf Ganz & Oliver Denton. Pianist & accompanist; organist & choir dir, Cent Presby Church, New York, 20-37; choral dir, Soc Friends of Music, 4 yrs; music dir, New York Opera Co, 5 yrs; dean music & music dir, Bay View Summer Univ & Chautauqua, 12 summers; mem fac, Brooklyn Music Sch, Neighborhood Music Sch, Master Inst United Arts, New York & Marygrove Col; founder & music dir, "Ford Sunday Evening Hour," radio, 36-46; prod, NBC Symph Series; guest cond, Philadelphia Orch; taught voice, Detroit; dir, Birmingham, Mich Chorale. Author, "The Standard Repertoire." *Songs:* Velvet Darkness; Red Bombay; To a Little Child; Standin' in de Need of Prayer (arr); Love in a Cottage (song cycle). *Albums:* Roustabout Songs of the Ohio River.

REDDING, EDWARD CAROLAN (BUD) ASCAP 1962
composer, author
b Louisville, Ky, Aug 17, 15. Educ: Louisville Male High Sch; Univ Louisville; pvt study piano; pvt study comp with Paul Creston. Musicals for professional Children's Theatre & scores of musical commercials, in asn with Phil Davis. Cocktail pianist. Chief Collabrs: Joseph George Caruso, Dorothy Hodapp, Sidney Lipman. *Songs:* The End of a Love Affair; The Golden Palomino (LP); The Silver Button (musical); Huckleberry Finn (musical); Jefferson Davis Tyler's General Store; Twelve Good Men and True; The Grapevine; Lyrics: Summer Photographs.

REDDING, NOEL DAVID ASCAP 1968
composer, author, musician
b Folkestone, Eng, Dec 25, 45. Educ: Self-taught guitarist. Started songwriting, 67; performing & recording vocalist & guitarist with groups, Loving Kind, Jimi Hendrix Experience, Fat Mattress, Road & Noel Redding Bands; also did session work for many others. Chief Collabr: David Clarke. *Songs:* She's So Fine (She's in With Time); Little Miss Strange; Mr Moonshine; Music: I Don't Mind; Born to His Name; If I Had.

REDFORD, JONATHAN ALFRED CLAWSON   ASCAP 1978
composer
b Los Angeles, Calif, July 14, 53. Educ: Skyline High Sch, Salt Lake City, Utah, grad 71; Brigham Young Univ, 71-72; pvt study trombone, Marion Albiston, 62-71, comp with Harold V Johnson, 79- & conducting with Fritz Zweig, 80- Performed in var bands, 66- Comp art music, 71- Musical dir & arr for var singers, 75- Studio musician, Los Angeles; comp for films TV & theatre & cond, 76- Teacher with artists in schs, 77-78. Chief Collabrs: Carol Lynn Pearson, Murray MacLeod. *Songs:* Music: 5 Sonnets of E E Cummings (soprano & pianoforte; 2nd Place Award, Utah Composer's Guild Contest, 76). *Instrumental Works:* Jessie Lee (jazz band & dulcimer); Selmer Award Outstanding Comp, Orange Coast Jazz Fest, 76 & Best Instrumental Work & Best of Show Award, Utah Composer's Guild Contest, 77); Here's Brother Brigham. *Scores:* Bway Show: Don't Count Your Chickens Until They Cry Wolf; Film: Stingray; TV: 240 Robert; Starsky and Hutch; James at 15/16.

REDMAN, DON   ASCAP 1942
composer, conductor, arranger
b Piedmont, WVa, July 29, 00; d New York, NY, Nov 30, 64. Educ: Storer's Col (admitted at 14); Boston Cons. Mem prof band at age 6. Saxophonist & arr with dance orchs, incl Paul Whiteman, 35 yrs. Formed own band; later accompanist to Pearl Bailey. Appeared in Bway musical "House of Flowers." Made many records. *Songs & Instrumental Works:* Gee, Baby, Ain't I Good to You?; Save It, Pretty Mama; Cherry; My Girl Friday; How'm I Doin'; Chant of the Weed; How Can I Hi De Hi?; If It Ain't Love; Down, Down, Down; If It's True; The Flight of the Jitterbug; You Ain't Nowhere; Carrie Mae Blues; Who Wants to Sing My Love Song?; Frantic Atlantic.

REDMAN, WALTER DEWEY   ASCAP 1972
composer, author, teacher
b Ft Worth, Tex, May 17, 31. Educ: Prairie View A&M Univ, BS, 53; N Tex State Univ, MEd, 59. Saxophonist & clarinetist. Played & recorded with Ornette Coleman, 4 yrs & Keith Jarrett, 3 1/2 yrs. Has own group appearing in US & Europe, 70- *Albums:* Look for the Black Star; The Ear of the Behearer; Coincide; Tarik; Sound Signs; Musics; Old and New Dreams.

REDMOND, JOHN   ASCAP 1936
composer, author
b Clinton, Mass, Feb 25, 06. Educ: High sch; studied voice. Sang on radio network prog. In USN, WW II. Has own music publ co. Past pres, Songwriters Guild of Am; pres, Religious Music Guild. Chief Collabrs: Frank Weldon, James Cavanaugh, Nat Simon, Lee David, Arthur Altman, Duke Ellington, Hal Aloma, Dick Sanford, Allan Flynn, Charles McCarthy. *Songs:* Sweetheart of Mine; I Let a Song Go Out of My Heart; The Man With the Mandolin; The Gaucho Serenade; The Big Apple; Dream, Dream, Dream; Christmas in Killarney; Crosstown; You're Breaking My Heart All Over Again; Give, Give, Give (Off song, March of Dimes, 47); One Fold and One Shepherd; I Came I Saw I Conga'd; On a Simmery Summery Day. *Albums:* American Booties on a Musical Cruise; Songs of Brotherly Love; 12 Songs on the Apostle's Creed.

RED RIVER DAVE
See McEnery, David Largus

REDWINE, WILBUR (SKIP)   ASCAP 1957
composer, author
b Marshall, Ark, Oct 31, 26. Educ: Hendrix Col; Southern Methodist Univ; Univ Southern Calif. Pianist & cond for June Havoc, Linda Darnell, Elsa Lanchester. Pianist for TV & Bway musicals. Chief Collabrs: Ray Gilbert, Jack Lloyd, Rod McKuen, Ron Stephenson. *Songs:* Promises, Promises; Honky-Tonk Heart; What to Do; Take Me Home Again.

REED, ALFRED   ASCAP 1956
composer, conductor
b New York, NY, Jan 25, 21. Educ: Juilliard Sch Music, student of Vittorio Giannini, 46-48; Baylor Univ, BM(cum laude) & MM(cum laude), 53-55; Int Cons Music, Lima, Peru, Hon MusD. 529th USAAF band during WWII. Free lance comp & arr, NBC, ABC, CBS & RCA Victor records, New York. Exec ed, Hansen Publ, New York & Miami, 53-66. Prof music theory-comp & dir, Music Merchandising Prog, Univ Miami Sch Music, 66- Cond, Univ Miami Wind Ens, 80. Guest comp-cond in 46 states, Can, Mex, SAm & Europe. *Instrumental Works:* A Festival Prelude (concert band/wind ens); Russian Christmas Music (concert band/wind ens); Armenian Dances (concert band/wind ens); Second Symphony (concert band/wind ens); Rhapsody for Viola and Orchestra (Luria Prize, 59); Othello (a symphonic portrait for concert band); Punchinello (overture to a romantic comedy); music for Hamlet; First Suite for Band; Symphony for Brass and Percussion; Greensleeves (fantasy for band; orchestral setting); The Music-Makers (a concert overture for wind ens); Alleluia! Laudamus Te (a celebration hymn for winds); The Enchanted Island (after Shakespeare's "The Tempest"); The Hounds of Spring (concert overture for winds, after Swinburne); Second Suite for Band; Prelude and Capriccio (wind ens); A Symphonic Prelude (concert band/wind ens); Passacaglia (concert band/wind ens); Choric Song (mixed voices & winds); Ode for Trumpet (solo trumpet & band); A Festive Overture (concert band/wind ens); Seascape (solo baritone & band); A Sacred Suite (concert band/wind ens).

REED, DAVID   ASCAP 1934
composer, author, singer
b New York, NY, July 30, 1872; d New York, Apr 11, 46. Educ: Pub schs. Banjo soloist & actor in vaudeville; wrote spec material. Staff writer, New York music publ firms. Chief Collabr: Ernest Ball. *Songs:* My Hannah Lady; Love Me and the World Is Mine; In the Sunshine of Your Love; On a Good Old Time Straw Ride; Below the Mason Dixon Line; Sailing On the Good Ship Sunshine; Take Me Back to Melody Lane.

REED, H OWEN   ASCAP 1953
composer, author, educator
b Odessa, Mo, June 17, 10. Educ: Univ Mo-Columbia, studied theory & comp with James Quarles & Scott Goldthwaite, 29-33; La State Univ, Baton Rouge, BM(theory, with distinction), 34, MM(comp), 36, BA(French), 37; Univ Rochester Eastman Sch Music, Guggenheim fel, 38-39, PhD(comp), 39, studied comp & orchestration with Howard Hanson & Bernard Rogers; Berkshire Music Ctr, Lenox, Mass, studied comp with Bohuslav Martinu, contemporary music with Aaron Copland, Leonard Bernstein & Stanley Chappel, summer 42; pvt study with Roy Harris, Colorado Springs, summer 47; studied comp & folk music in Mex, 48-49, folk music, summer 60; studied folk music, Caribbean islands, winter 76 & Scandinavian countries, summer 77. Mem fac, Mich State Univ, 39-76, emer prof theory & comp, 76- Awards: Resident fels, Huntington Hartford Found, Pacific Palisades, Calif, 60 & Helena Wurlitzer Found, Taos, NMex, 67; Mich State Univ Distinguished Fac Award, 62; George Romney & Greater Mich Found Citation for Distinguished Contributions to the Arts, 63; Annual ASCAP Awards; Neil A Kjos Mem Award For The Unfortunate, 75; Phi Mu Alpha Orpheus Award, 76; hon mem, Kappa Kappa Psi, Tau Beta Sigma & Mich State Band & Orch Asn. Mem: Am Soc Univ Comp; Nat Asn Comp, USA (nat council mem); Am Music Ctr; Mich Orch Asn; Teatro Int; Phi Mu Alpha; Kappa Sigma; Music Educr Nat Conference. Author: "A Workbook in the Fundamentals of Music" & "Basic Music"; Coauth: "Basic Contrapuntal Techniques", "Scoring for Percussion" & "The Materials of Music Composition." Chief Collabrs: Joel Leach, Paul Harder, Robert Sidnell, Forrest Coggan, Hartley Alexander, Merrick F McCarthy. *Instrumental Works:* La Fiesta Mexicana (band or orch); For the Unfortunate (band); The Turning Mind (orch); Spiritual (band); The Touch of the Earth (band); Overture for Strings. *Songs & Instrumental Works:* Ut Re Mi (orch & taped men's voices). *Scores:* Opera in Two Acts: Peter Homans Dream; Chamber Operas Based on Indian Spirit Legend: Earth Trapped; Living Solid Face; Butterfly Girl and Mirage Boy.

REED, JOHN MARSHALL   ASCAP 1978
composer
b Port Hueneme, Calif, Mar 11, 54. Educ: Lorenzo High Sch, Tex; Angelo State Univ; Tex Tech Univ. Studied tuba, 6 yrs; plays guitar, harmonica & piano; singer. *Songs:* Have You Kissed Any Frogs Today?; I Believe There's Somebody Greater.

REED, NANCY
See Kanter, Nancy Reed

REED, NANCY BINNS   ASCAP 1952
composer, author
b Palo Alto, Calif, Dec 11, 24. Educ: Univ Calif, Davis & Berkeley, AB, 45; grad work as trumpet player, singer, sch band, orch, choir, and others. Wrote music as child. Music written for shows, schs, scouts and others in Am, Korea & Ger. Wrote several marches. ASCAP Awards, 77-78 & 78-79. Mem, Nat League Am Penwomen, Friday Morning Music Club, Washington, DC. Author & illusr, "The Sun and the Moon", "The Magic Gourds" & "A Tale of the Heidelberg Lion." *Songs:* Oh, Happy Day; Our Lions; Music: March Civilian. *Scores:* Musicals: Tocqueville (Washington, DC); Ali Baba and the Forty Thieves (Lake Braddock, Va).

REED, ROBERT B   ASCAP 1945
composer, conductor, organist
b Philadelphia, Pa, Mar 25, 1900; d Washington, DC, Dec 26, 68. Educ: Univ Pa, BM; studied with Hugh Clark, H Alexander Matthews, Robert Elmore. Colleague, Am Guild of Organists. Organist & choirmaster, St Martin's Church, Radnor, Pa, 25-32, 42-48. Cond, Girard Trust Co Glee Club, Philadelphia. On staff, Library of Congress, DC. *Songs:* Rise Up, O Men of God; Let Us Now Praise Famous Men; God Bless Thy Year; I Hear America Singing; Sea Dreams. *Instrumental Works:* The Incarnate Word (Christmas pageant); The Easter Story (cantata); Shadow March; A Series of Christmas Carols; The Arkansas Traveler (male voices).

REEKER, CECILIA   ASCAP 1970
composer, author, music teacher
b College View, Nebr, Mar 8, 1897. Educ: Univ Lincoln, Nebr; North Side Sch Music. Teacher, North Side Sch Music, 52-62; songwriter. Chief Collabrs: George Gershwin, Robert Russell Bennett, Ed Rose, George Ahlborn, Billy Baskette. *Songs:* Pretty Soon; Memories Precious Memories; Playing Ball With Time; The Moon Was Cold; Music: Peace on Earth; Carolina Lullaby.

REEMHBER, ARTHUR O
See Herrera, Humberto Angel

REESE, CLAUDE
See Isaacs, Claude Reese

REESE, DELLA
See Early, Delloreese Patricia

REESE, WENDEL
See Rusch, Harold W

REEVE, FOX
See Elliott, Marjorie Reeve

REICHEG, RICHARD   ASCAP 1967
composer
b Brooklyn, NY, May 26, 37. Educ: Brooklyn Col, BA & MA. Performed as folksinger in nightclubs, cabarets & concert halls, early 60's; writer spec material for other performers, 60-; writer popular songs & acting in films, TV & stage productions. *Songs:* Looking for an Echo; For the Sake of the Children (from film "Nashville"); Capture the Moment; Everybody's a Masterpiece; Love Songs and Romance Magazines.

REICHERT, HEINZ   ASCAP 1940
author
b Vienna, Austria, Dec 27, 1877; d Los Angeles, Calif, Nov 16, 40. Educ: Real-Gymnasium, Vienna. Actor in Berlin, then journalist, Ullstein Verlag, Berlin. Returned to Vienna, 06, became playwright. Came to US, 38. Dir, AKM. Chief Collabr: Erich Wolfgang Korngold. *Scores:* Stage, librettos: Das Dreimaederlhaus (Blossom Time); The Great Waltz; Frasquita; The Czarwitsch; La Rondine (Puccini).

REICHERT, JAMES   ASCAP 1960
composer
b Toledo, Ohio. Educ: Oberlin Cons, BMus; Eastman Sch Music, MM; Berkshire Music Ctr, Tanglewood. Began as music dir with CBS-TV shows "20th Century", "Camera Three", "The Play of the Week", "Dupont Show of the Month", also many spec incl "Dial M for Murder", "Heaven Can Wait", "Of Mice and Men", "The Heiress" & "Fallen Idol." Engr/dir, Gotham Recording, comp with Tod Docksadter "Omniphony I" (symph with electronic transmutations), then went into theater as comp/mus dir for "The Effect of Gamma Rays on Man- in-the-Moon Marigolds" (Pulitzer Prize). Has written extensively for Boosey & Hawkes Background Music Libr. Fellow, MacDowell Colony. Now composer. *Songs:* Music: Exposition '67 (Air Canada); All My Children (ABC-TV; 3 Emmy Nominations). *Songs & Instrumental Works:* Other Voices Other Rooms; also var mime theaters.

REICHNER, S BICKLEY (BIX)   ASCAP 1938
composer, author, publisher
b Philadelphia, Pa, Apr 6, 05. Wrote scores for Mask and Wig Shows, Univ Pa, 30-44. Sang in Schubert Musicals. Reporter, Philadelphia Evening Bulletin, 22 yrs. Owner, Malvern Music Co, Pa. Chief Collabs: Clay Boland, Elliot Lawrence, John Benson Brooks, Al Cohn. *Songs:* Stop Beating 'Round the Mulberry Bush; You Better Go Now; Papa Loves Mambo; Midnight on the Trail; Stop It's Wonderful; When I Go A Dreaming; The Red We Want Is the Red We've Got (In the Old Red, White and Blue) (Freedom Found Award); If You Know the Lord; Don't Wait For the Hearse to Take You to Church; Cathedral of Peace; The Fable of the Rose; Mambo Rock; I Need Your Love Tonight; Teenage Prayer; The Ballad of Valley Forge; Nightfall; Heart to Heart; Dixie Danny.

REID, DONALD   ASCAP 1942
composer, author, director
b Montreal, Que, Sept 28, 15. Educ: Studied music & voice pvtly, ages 5-16; joined Vanderpoll choir, studied with Vanderpoll, ages 16-18; coached by & studied with Alex Kramer, Can; grad Mt Royal, Baron Byng & McGill Univ. Began prof radio career as soloist on weekly radio show, Can; appeared on many CBC, CFCF & CKAC progs. Singer & musician, recorded & appeared with var artists, US. Featured soloist, weekly show, "Al Pearce & His Gang", "Sammy Kaye for Camels", CBS & "Jack Kirkwood Show", NBC. Recording artist on var labels. Creator, producer & dir, award winning documentaries, "The Second Elizabeth" & "The Life and Times of Eisenhower." Creator, writer & producer, "College Bowl", winner of var awards incl Emmy & Peabody, 28yrs, "Alumni Fun", 5 yrs, CBS, "Dream House", ABC-TV, 3 yrs, "Anything You Can Do", 4 yrs, CTV, Can, "University Challenge", Granada TV, Gt Brit, NZ, Holland & Nigeria, 20 yrs; syndicated progs, "High Q", "Scholastic Challenge", "High School Bowl" & "Dollars for Scholars." Chief Collabrs: Arthur Altman, Henry Tobias, Guy Wood, Milton Berle, David Terry, Sammy Kaye. *Songs:* Remember Pearl Harbor; Land of Dreams; Hurry Hurry Hurry; I Still Feel the Same About You.

REID, JOYCE GREEN   ASCAP 1973
composer, author
b Egg Harbor City, NJ, Aug 30, 03. Educ: Egg Harbor City pub schs & high sch; studied music with Miss Rothholtz, Atlantic City & Gustave Ronfort, Miami, Fla. Started comp at age 9; first lessons with local teacher. Then won two out of nine songs in Dade County Comp Contest, 48 & was performed at Miami Bandshell. Wrote & produced musical play, "Some Happy Day," in Coral Gables, Fla; also wrote & produced three religious musicals at First Presby Church, Miami. State Music Chmn, Nat League Am Pen Women, 74-78, also won first place for musical play, "New Day Dawning," which was collab with Margaret M Matlack, 76. Author bk, "Jesus and the Inn Keeper." *Songs:* Some Happy Day; Something Tells Me; Lovely You; Golden Spring—My Mother's Praying for Me; Are You Looking at the Moon Tonight; I Was in Love With Love; Sitting and Dreaming of You; Don't Be Naive; Down Miami Way; Sitting and Thinking of You; It's Maypink Time; I'll Send You a Love Song; Dixie First and Dixie Last; I Am Free Again; You're Wonderful; The Word of God Shall Stand Forever; He Is Risen As He Said; Why Must You Go; Land of Lovely Spring; Jesus Birthday Song; Books of the Bible; You Caught Me in the Tub, Darling; October; A Child's Morning Prayer; It's a Time of Miracles.

REID, REIDY   ASCAP 1946
composer, author
b Roanoke, Va, Sept 26, 1889; d New York, NY, Oct 25, 46. On prof staff, music publ firms. *Songs:* Yankee Doodle Rainbow; 3,121 Miles Away; You've Got Me Stopped; Just Love; Don't Ever Change Your Mind; A Sweetheart's Prayer.

REID, WILLIS WILFRED (BILLY)   ASCAP 1972
composer, author, teacher
b La Poile Bay, Nfld, Sept 19, 10. Educ: Studied with George Ernst; Dalhousie Univ, studied with Dennis Farrell. Radio career, CHNS, Halifax, NS, 29-65; played CBC Dominion Network, until it closed, 63. Ran own sch of music, 40 yrs; teacher, 75- Singer, arr & musician. Chief Collabr: Johnny Kamano. *Songs:* Blue Paradise; Whispering Aloha to You; Until Today; Hawaii My Hawaii; Maka Ke Aloha; Over the Blue Pacific.

REIF, PAUL   ASCAP 1948
composer
b Prague, Czech, Mar 23, 10; d. Educ: Vienna Acad Music, with Bruno Walter, Richard Strauss & Franz Schalk; Sorbonne Univ, PhD; studied violin with Erica Morini. Comp for theatre & films in Sweden, Austria & France. Moved to US, 41, citizen, 43; served in USA Intelligence Corps, WW II. Chief Collabrs: George David Weiss, Jack Lawrence, Don George, Duke Ellington. *Songs & Instrumental Works:* I'm Just a Poor Street Singer; The Sun Never Sets on the AEF; A Prairie Lullaby; Takes Two; They All Wanted You for Me; One Way to Love Me; Dirty Gertie From Bizerte; No Time for Tears; Cowboy Rhumba; You Stole My Wife, You Horse Thief; I Can't Remember; Petticoat Waltz; Dream Concerto (piano, orch); Spirituals for Male Sextet; Birches (orch, voice; Robert Frost poem); Goat Song (comn by Equity Lib Theatre; incidental music to play); A Murderer Among Us (incidental music to play); Five Finger Exercises (T S Eliot poems; comn by Giorgio Tozzi; song cycles); And Be My Love (song cycles); Cantatas: Triple City; Requiem to War (comn by New York Lyric Ensemble); Letter From a Birmingham Jail (Martin Luther King text); Chamber Music: Reverence for Life (comn by Schweitzer Hosp Fund); Monsieur le Pelican (comn by Schweitzer Hosp Fund); Wind Spectrum (quintet); Philader's Defense (chess game set to music). *Scores:* Operas: Portrait in Brownstone; Mad Hamlet (comn by Giorgio Tozzi).

REILLY, JACK   ASCAP 1972
composer, author, teacher
b New York, NY, Jan 1, 32. Educ: Manhattan Sch of Music, BM, 57, MM, 58; studied comp with Hall Overton, Ludmila Ulehla, Joseph Maneri, jazz with Lennie Tristano, George Russ. Former, fac at Mannes Sch of Music; fac, the New Sch for Social Research. Recording artist of original jazz works. Soloist & with own group, Duende, The Jack Reilly Quartet, 80, toured US, Can, PR, Ireland, Poland, Norway & Italy. Recipient, comn from Catholic liturgical conf, 69 & NEA grant, 72. Author, 3 vol text on jazz "Species Blues." *Songs:* The Great Invocation (A Hymn for All Humanity); Music: Blue-Sean-Green; November; Waltz for Fall; Kyrie. *Instrumental Works:* Suffering/Death/Ressurection (string orch, piano solo); In Memoriam, Ben Webster; Sonata in D minor for Piano Solo; La-Not-IB Suite for Piano with Improvisation; Allegretto for Jazz Trio; Tributes (9 dedicatory pieces for jazz piano); Mass of Involvement; No Name (jazz piano solo); Fantasy for Woodwind Quintet and Piano Improvised; Requiem Mass for Chorus and Jazz Quartet; Oratorio for Church and Chamber Jazz Ensemble; Concerto for Piano and Chamber Orchestra; Rhapsody for Chorus, Orchestra and Piano Solo; String Quartet and Piano Solo; Sonata No 2 in F sharp major for Piano and Trombone; Piano Sonata No 2 & 3; Piano Quintet; Chamber Symphony No 1.

REINACH, JACQUELYN   ASCAP 1963
composer, author
b Omaha, Nebr, Sept 17, 30. Educ: Univ Calif, Los Angeles; Stanford Univ. Pres, Childways Music, music pub & audio production; co-founder, Euphrosyne, Inc, creators of "Sweet Pickles" books. Composer/lyricist of children's songs & author children's books. Chief Collabr: Joe Rene. *Songs:* Liberation Now!; The Reading Works (multi-media educ prog). *Scores:* Theater: Yo-Yo Game;

Gottlieb; Film: An Early Start to Good Health (for the Am Cancer Soc). *Albums:* Music to Read the Pretenders By; Sweet Pickles Pop 26 (children's); It's About Time; Introduction to Reading, Writing and Arithmetic.

REISER, VIOLET   ASCAP 1962
composer, pianist, organist
b New York, NY, July 3, 15. Educ: Col; studied with David Brown, Gary Sheldon, Herman Schwartzman & Clarence Adler. Organist, Loew Circuit, Rialto Theatre & piano teacher; comp of educ pieces, concerts, novelty & popular songs. Awards of Merit, Am Fedn Music Clubs; awards in nation wide song contests. Chief Collabrs: Harold Orenstein, Ray Sterling, Max Smith. *Songs:* Morning in Manhattan; Take Our Love Out of the Shadows; I Won't Play Second Fiddle. *Instrumental Works:* New Dawn Fantasy; Waltzing Ballerina; Motivation; Impromptu; Tiny Toe Dancer; Dancing Sunbeams; Echoes of Vienna; The Gossips; Dance of the Pixies; Indian Lament; Fancy Frolic; Song of the Bobolink; Venetian Village; Jewel in the Sun; Gypsy Strings; Sophisticated Blues; Blue Ballet; Plantation Picnic; Cathedral Chimes; Whirlpool; Valse Celeste; Spanish Serenade; Chromatic Waltz; Ragtime Raggedy Ann. *Songs & Instrumental Works:* Collections: A Bouquet of Violets; Blossoms in My Garden.

REISFELD, BERT   ASCAP 1939
composer, author, journalist
b Vienna, Austria, Dec 12, 06. Educ: Vienna Cons Music, studied with Oscar Dachs & Carl Prohaska; Inst Technol, Vienna, architectural degree. Founded Les Editions Meridian, Paris, 34. Composed film scores, operettas & songs, Vienna, Berlin, Paris, New York & Los Angeles. Journalistic work incl reports on show business, films & concerts for the Brit, Ger, Austrian & Swiss press & radio. Chief Collabrs: Rolf Marbot, George Whiting, Michael Stone, Dimitri Tiomkin. *Songs:* Call Me Darling; Music: You Rhyme With Everything That's Beautiful; The Singing Sands of Alamosa; Lyrics: The Three Bells; Jeder Tag Geht zu Ende (The End). *Instrumental Works:* California Concerto; Modern American Music for Piano. *Scores:* Mein Friseur; Mitzi-Mitzou; Flight Into the Blue.

REISMAN, JOE   ASCAP 1957
composer, producer, conductor
b Dallas, Tex, Sept 16, 24. Educ: Baylor Univ; Univ Tex, El Paso, assoc degree. Comp, instrumental music, TV themes & scores & Bway show. Record producer, cond & arr for var artists; cond & arr, TV shows incl "Oldsmobile Show" & "NBC Shower of Stars" & motion pictures. Recording artist; exec producer & mgr, RCA & Roulette Record Cos. Instrumentalist & arr with bands incl Jack Teagarden, Casa Loma Orch, Sam Donahue & Bob Crosby. Guest lectr, Disney Calif Arts, Golden West Col & Nat Acad Recording Arts & Sci Workshop. Recipient, 14 Gold singles & 8 Gold albums, Grammy nominations, "Record World" poll winner & Randall Am Sweepstakes Award. *Instrumental Works:* Joey's Song; Front Row Center; Skyride; Warm Up; Cheryl's Dream; Chanson De Gail; Jean's Song; Aeromeds Theme. *Scores:* Bway show: Infidel Caesar; Film/TV: Gift of the Magi; Gigi; Pink Panther.

REISMAN, JUDITH (JUDITH BAT'ADA)
composer, teacher, author
b Newark, NJ, Apr 11, 35. Educ: Case Western Reserve Univ, BA, 75, MA(speech communication), 76, PhD(speech communication), 79. With var TV stas in New York, Cleveland, Honolulu & Milwaukee, 67- Writer of many articles & bks. Producer, writer & performer for several TV stas. Mem: Am Fedn of TV & Recording Artists; Am Asn for the Advancement of Sci; Ohio Acad of Sci; Int Communication Asn; NY Acad of Sci; Hastings Ctr/Inst of Society, Ethics & the Life Sci. Awards: 1st place, 13th Pub Relations Competition, Family Serv Asn, 74; Emmy nominee, 76; Action for Children's TV Award, 76-79. *Songs:* New Sounds; Independent; Art Through Music; The Shakers; Scholastic Magazine.

REITER, MELVYN T   ASCAP 1976
composer, author
b Manhattan, NY, Jan 12, 38. Educ: NY Univ, MA, 70; studied guitar with Leon Block. Played Span & Lap Steel guitars; comp songs, 68- Guitar builder, designer & inventor; builder of World's Smallest Steel Guitar. Produced record album, Folk Music of Washington Square. *Songs:* I Found the Lord; Loving You Is All I Need; I Can See the Writing on the Wall; I Don't Want a Teddy Bear; I'm the Moth, She's the Flame.

REITTER, ROSE B (ROSE B WARWICK)   ASCAP 1960
author, teacher, poet
b Brooklyn, NY, Aug 7, 34. Educ: Bard Col, BA, 55; Columbia Univ Grad Fac of Poetical Sci, 56; NY Univ Grad Sch of Educ, 65. Free-lance writer, researcher & ed; copy ed, Appleton-Century-Crofts, Inc, Show Magazine, War/Peace Report & Realm; researcher, Vogue. Taught English at George Washington High Sch, New York. Started & ran poetry prog at Hillside Sch, Hastings. Poet-in-residence, Pocantico Hills & many schs in Westchester. Poetry consult, Children's Village, Dobbs Ferry, NY, 5 yrs. Chief Collabrs: Milt Okun, Irene Olsen. *Songs:* Lyrics: Tina; Chevaliers; Sally Ann; Paddy; Gallows Tree; Hey Nanine; Singing All Night Long.

REIZNER, JUNE
See Perse, June

RENE, JOSEPH   ASCAP 1920
author, composer, trumpeter
b Amsterdam, Holland, Sept 4, 20. To US, 48. Educ: Music Cons. Trumpeter, comp & arr with dance bands; toured throughout Europe. After WW II, comp & arr for radio, Rio de Janeiro. A&R dir, Columbia Records; record exec. *Instrumental Works:* Claudette's Theme; Like Chopsticks; Valse de Montmartre.

RENE, LEON T   ASCAP 1940
composer, author, pianist
b Covington, La, Feb 6, 02. Educ: Xavier Univ; Southern Univ; Wilberforce Univ. To Los Angeles, 22. Bricklayer; led own orch. Wrote songs for films incl "Let Freedom Ring", "She's Got Everything" & "Stormy Weather." Became publ, also owner of record co. Chief Collabr: Otis Rene, Jr. *Songs:* When the Swallows Come Back to Capistrano; When It's Sleepytime Down South; Sweet Lucy Brown; That's My Home; Dusty Road; Someone's Rocking My Dreamboat; I Sold My Heart to the Junkman; It's Sleepytime in Hawaii; If Money Grew on Trees; Chapel in the Valley; I Lost My Sugar in Salt Lake City; Beyond the Stars; Convicted; From Twilight Till Dawn; Gloria; Boogie Woogie Santa Claus; What's the Score?; I Never Had a Dream. *Scores:* Stage: Lucky Day.

RENE, OTIS J, JR   ASCAP 1940
composer, author, publisher
b New Orleans, La, Oct 2, 1898; d Los Angeles, Calif, Apr 5, 70. Educ: Wilberforce Univ, BS; Univ Ill, pharmacy. Owned & operated drug store, Los Angeles, 24-34. Wrote songs for films incl "Let Freedom Ring" & "She's Got Everything." Became publisher, also owner of record co. Chief Collabr: Leon Rene. *Songs:* My California Maid (won amateur song-writing contest); When It's Sleepytime Down South; Sweet Lucy Brown; That's My Home; Dusty Road; Someone's Rocking My Dreamboat; I Sold My Heart to the Junkman; It's Sleepytime in Hawaii; I Woke Up With a Teardrop in My Eye; I'm Lost; I Never Had a Dream; Still Water; Moonrise. *Scores:* Stage: Lucky Day.

RENNA, RICHARD JOSEPH   ASCAP 1967
composer
b St Louis, Mo, Nov 16, 20. Educ: Studied with var keyboard teachers while in teens; course in music after WW II. Played with local bands until 56; House Band, Casa-Loma Ballroom, 56-66; band dir, St Louis Football Cardinals, 60-73 & St Louis Baseball Cardinals, summer season, 8 yrs. Treas, Musicians Local 2-197, 77 & 80. Musician, park concerts, banquets. *Songs:* Music: The Arch March; Big Red Go-Go-Go; Why Lose?; Can't Get Along Without You; Big Red Bird in the Bush.

RENWICK, WILKE RICHARD   ASCAP 1977
composer
b Stockton, Calif, Dec 17, 21. Educ: Longy Sch Music, Cambridge, Mass, sr dipl, 51; New Eng Cons Music, BM(perf), studied horn with Willem Valkenier; Univ Denver, MA(music educ), 71, studied comp with Normand Lockwood. Asst principal horn, Pittsburgh Symph Orch, 51-53; principal horn, Denver Symph Orch, 54-71, assoc principal horn, 71- Co-founder, Denver Brass Ens. Mem fac & brass specialist, Univ Denver, 61-71; mem fac, Colo State Univ, 68- *Instrumental Works:* Dance for Brass Quintet; Encore Piece for Solo Trumpet; Oop's Slipsies (trombone & piano); Facets (string orch); Six Bach Chorales (brass quintet); Prelude, Dodecaphony and Dance (chamber orch).

RESNICK, LEE   ASCAP 1963
composer, violinist
b Livingston Manor, NY, Apr 8, 23. Educ: Ithaca Col, BS. Violinist, Plainfield Symph Orch, NJ. *Songs & Instrumental Works:* I've Got My Heart Set on You.

RESNICOFF, ETHEL   ASCAP 1971
composer, author
b Brooklyn, NY, July 3, 47. Educ: Brooklyn Col, BA & MS. TV writer educ filmstrips, stories & "Captain Kangaroo."

RESTA, FRANCIS EUGENE   ASCAP 1962
composer, teacher, conductor
b Gioia del Colle, Italy, Apr 3, 1894; d Bronx, NY, Aug 16, 68. Educ: Army Bandmasters' Sch, Governor's Island, NY, Clappe, 17-20; Juilliard Sch Music, grad with cert of conductor, Percy Goetschius, 17-20; piano & pedagogy with Cecil Berryman, Omaha, Nebr, 29-32. Clarinet soloist with Goroglione Concert Band, Italy, 10-12; professional clarinetist, Norfolk, Va, 14-17. Bandmaster, warrant officer, USA, 20-34. Was comn 1st Lt, USA, 34, then Lt Col, then retired. Teacher of music & bandmaster, United States Mil Acad, West Point, NY, 34-57. Comp & arr music for many night shows, 34-57; comp marches & songs, also did several transcriptions. *Instrumental Works:* Marches: Le Defi (The Challenge); Hail to Alaska; Color Guard.

RETTINO, ERNEST W   ASCAP 1973
composer, author, producer
b Hackensack, NJ, Jan 23, 49. Educ: Calif Inst Arts. With group, The Young Americans, age 15-18; then joined The Kids Next Door. Back-up singer for Pat Boone; choreographer for Boone Family. Several recordings, contemporary Christian music. Chief Collabr: Debby Kerner (wife). *Songs:* Joseph; Doer of the Word; I'll Never Be Alone Again. *Albums:* Friends; Joy in the Morning; More Than Friends; Changin'; The Best of Ernie and Debby; The Kids Praise Album; The Joy Album.

REVEL, GARY NEAL   ASCAP 1970
composer, author, singer
b Florala, Ala, June 29, 49. Educ: Holmes County High Sch, Fla, grad; USN CLEP; Naval Sonar Sch & intermediate electronics, 52 weeks grad. Singer & guitarist with band, age 15; while in USN, singer in nightclub, San Diego, 68-69; honorable discharge, USN, 69. To Hollywood; recording artist, var cos; writer, Grosvenor House Music, Bee Gee Records & Birthright Music. To Nashville, 73; writer, Miline Music Inc; recording artist. Chief Collabrs: Judy Russell, Juddy Phillips, Mary Noel, Alan Stoddard. *Songs:* Like a Hobo Should; Richie Allan; Little Did We Know (The Ballad of Stringbean); They Slew the Dreamer (The Ballad of Martin Luther King); Land of Make Believe; Peanut Man.

REVEL, HARRY   ASCAP 1934
composer, pianist
b London, Eng, Dec 21, 05; d New York, NY, Nov 3, 58. Educ: Guild Hall of Music, London. To US, 29. Pianist, Hawaiian Band, Paris; joined orch touring Europe. Wrote scores for musicals in Paris, Copenhagen, Vienna & London. Under contract to Paramount, 20th Century Fox, Hollywood. Chief Collabrs: Mack Gordon, Mort Greene, Paul Francis Webster, Arnold Horwitt. *Songs:* Help Yourself to Happiness; Underneath the Harlem Moon; An Orchid to You; A Tree Was a Tree; Did You Ever See a Dream Walking?; She Reminds Me of You; Once in a Blue Moon; May I?; With My Eyes Wide Open I'm Dreaming; Stay as Sweet As You Are; Straight From the Shoulder; Paris in the Spring; Without a Word of Warning; From the Top of Your Head to the Tip of Your Toes; I Feel Like a Feather in the Breeze; You Hit the Spot; A Star Fell Out of Heaven; Goodnight, My Love; In Old Chicago; But Definitely; When I'm With You; It's Swell of You; Never in a Million Years; Wake Up and Live; Afraid to Dream; Danger, Love at Work; You Can't Have Everything; May I Have the Next Romance With You?; An Old Straw Hat; In Any Language; Meet the Beat of My Heart; Just Beyond the Rainbow; It's Just an Old Spanish Custom; Shadows on the Wall; Your Sunny Southern Smile; Walkin' on Air; Hum a Tune; You're a Symphony of Love; My Design for Living; Goodmorning Glory; You're My Past Present and Future; I Love You Pizzicato; Goodnight Lovely Little Lady; In The Good Old Wintertime; Don't Let It Bother You; Rhythm of the Rain; Let Me Sing You to Sleep With a Love Song; Will I Ever Know; You Gotta S-m-i-l-e to be H-a-double p-y; I've Got My Heart Set On You; Please Pardon Us We're in Love; Head Over Heels in Love; That All American Swing; It Never Rains But Pours; I've Got a Date With a Dream; In Copacabana; A Full Moon and an Empty Heart; Sing Your Worries Away; Me for You for Evermore; I'm Like a Fish Out of Water; Livin' in My Own Sweet Way; Remember Me to Carolina; Just the Way You Are; Here I Go Again; This Is My Beloved; That's What Christmas Means to Me. *Instrumental Works:* Perfumes Set to Music (suite). *Scores:* Bway: Meet My Sister; Ziegfeld Follies of 1931; Are You With It?; Film: Sitting Pretty; Broadway Through a Keyhole; She Loves Me Not; College Rhythm; Love in Bloom; Paris in the Spring; Stolen Harmony; Two for Tonight; Stowaway; Poor Little Rich Girl; Ali Baba Goes to Town; Wake Up and Live; You Can't Have Everything; Head Over Heels; Love and Kisses; Four Jacks and a Jill; Love Finds Andy Hardy; Here Comes the Groom; The Dolly Sisters; Stork Club; It Happened on Fifth Avenue; Rebecca of Sunnybrook Farm; Moon Over Burma; Call Out the Marines; Hit the Ice; Rose of Washington Square. *Albums:* Music From Out of the Moon; Music for Peace of Mind; Perfume Set to Music; Music From Out of Space; And So to Sleep.

REVEL, LINDA MARIE   ASCAP 1978
composer, author
b Winter Garden, Fla, May 18, 57. Educ: Ocoee Elem Sch, grad; Ocoee High Sch, grad. Singer-songwriter, Rebel Publ Inc, Nashville, Tenn, 75-78; songwriter, Acuff-Rose, 78- Chief Collabr: Gary Revel. *Songs:* In My Dreams; Peanut Man; She's My Sweet Rock 'N Roller; Mommy When's My Daddy Coming Home; Fallin' in Love With Me Day.

REVUELTAS, SILVESTRE   ASCAP 1946
composer, conductor, violinist
b Santiago, Mex, Dec 31, 1899; d Mexico City, Mex, Oct 5, 40. Educ: Chicago Musical Col, studied with Sametini, Mayott, Borowsky & Sevcik. Cond, theatre orchs, Tex & Ala, 26-28. Asst cond, Orquesta Sinfonica de Mex, 29. Teacher, Nat Cons, Mexico City, 33; also cond cons concerts. Organized Orquesta Sinfonica Nacional, 36. *Songs & Instrumental Works:* Esquinas; Sensemaya; Cuauhnahuac; Homenaje a Frederico Garcia Lorca; Musica Para Charlar; Parian (voices, orch); Toccata (violin, small orch); 2 string quartets; 7 Songs for Children; Duo del Pato y El Canario (voice, piano); Allegro for Piano; Ventanas; Caminos; Alcancias; Planos (pianos, orchs); Redes; Janitzio; Noche de Los Mayas; Itinirarios; Ocho por Radio; Tres Sonetos; Troka; Caminando (voice, orch); Amiga Que Te Vas (voice, orch); No Se Por Que Piensas Tu; Three Little

Serious Pieces (wind instruments); Three Little Pieces for Violin and Piano; Four Little Pieces for Violins and Cello; Quartets: Magueyes. *Scores:* Ballet: El Renacuaja Paseador.

REYNOLDS, CHARLES H   ASCAP 1967
composer, author, teacher
b Manchester, NH, Dec 15, 31. Educ: Pinkerton Acad; Graceland Col, BA; State Univ Iowa; Univ Colo Grad Sch Music; Univ Puget Sound; Alaska Methodist Univ; Univ Alaska, Anchorage; Portland State Univ. USAF vet. Guest clinician: Alaska Methodist Univ, Nome Pub Schs, Alaska, Beaverton Pub Schs, Oregon, Calif State Univ, Fullerton, Music Educ Nat Conf, Atlantic City, NJ, & Chicago, Ill, Music Educ Nat Conf, Northwest Regional Conf, Seattle, Wash. Music teacher, Fort Richardson, Alaska, 62-66; music consult & res teacher, 66-76. Lectr, Anchorage Community Col & Univ Alaska, Anchorage, 68-76. Founder/ed, Joy Mag, 70-74. Coordr music K-8, Anchorage Sch District, 76- Writer for Alaska Music Educators, Music Educators J & The Educational Informer. *Songs:* Prayer for Peace; Three Places in Alaska; The Animal Suite of Alaska (songbk for children); Seeing Ears (RCA theme song for introduction of the telephone to rural Alaska, 76).

REYNOLDS, GEORGE FRENCH (EDMUND FRENCH)   ASCAP 1969
composer, conductor, organist
b New York, NY, June 7, 27. Educ: Brooklyn Cons Music, 46-47; Guilmant Organ Sch, 47-48, studied organ with Willard Nevins, Viola Lang; NY Univ, BS(music educ), 56, MA(music educ), 59; studied comp with Vincent Jones; conducting with Luther Goodhart, Paul Van Bodegraven. Sgt, USMC, 45-46 & 50-51. Clerk & organ demonstrator, Wurlitzer Piano & Organ Co, NY, 48; demonstrator organs, Rybak Organ Co, Bronx, NY, 48-53. Dir vocal music, Baldwin Pub Schs, NY, 56-68; dir music, NCountry Community Col, 68-; organist, St Bernard's Church, Saranac Lake, NY, 70-; organist & choir dir, Adirondack Community Church, Lake Placid, NY, 73- *Songs & Instrumental Works:* The Lord Is My Shepherd (choral & organ); Psalm 67-God Be Merciful (choral & organ); Glory to God from St Luke's Mass; Hodie Christus Natus Est; Gloria from a Festive Mass; Mary's Cradle Song.

REYNOLDS, HERBERT
See Rourke, Michael Elder

REYNOLDS, JACK   ASCAP 1955
pianist, composer
b Minsk, Russia, Oct 6, 04. Educ: Horace Mann & Bayonne High Schs; New York Law Sch. Mem musical trio, Three Hauser Boys; mem duos, Reynolds/Green & Reynolds/McMahon. Single pianist in cocktail lounges & restaurants, Miami Beach, Fla, 20 yrs, incl Key Biscayne Hotel Racquet Club & others, presently Piccolo's Rest. Chief Collabrs: Cliff Friend, Benny Davis, Larry McMahon. *Songs:* Music: Old Man Time; Time; Send Me Jackson; U of M Marching Song; May God Bless You on Easter Sunday.

REYNOLDS, LEE
See McEnery, Velma Lee

REYNOLDS, MALVINA   ASCAP 1957
composer, author, singer
b San Francisco, Calif, Aug 23, 00; d Berkeley, Calif, Mar 17, 78. Educ: Univ Calif, Berkeley, BA, 25, MA, 27, PhD(English, lit), 39. Comp of topical & humorous songs, children's songs used on "Sesame Street" & "Mr Dreesup." Toured extensively in US, Europe & Japan. Subject of film, "Love It Like a Fool." Mem, Am Fedn Musicians, Am Fedn TV & Radio Artists. Author: "Little Boxes and Other Handmade Songs"; "The Muse of Parker Street"; "The Malvina Reynolds Songbook"; "There's Music in the Air"; "Cheerful Tunes for Lutes and Spoons"; "Tweedles and Foodles for Young Noodles." *Songs:* Turn Around; Magic Penny; Bury Me in My Overalls; What Have They Done to the Rain?; Little Boxes. *Albums:* Malvina Reynolds Sings the Truth; Malvina Reynolds; Malvina; Malvina-Held Over; Magical Songs; Mama Lion; Artichokes, griddle Cakes; Funnybugs.

REYNOLDS, VERNE BECKER   ASCAP 1970
composer, teacher
b Lyons, Kans, July 18, 26. Educ: Cincinnati Cons, BM, 50; Univ Wis, MM, 51; Royal Col Music, London, Eng, 53 & 54. Mem, Cincinnati Symph, 46-50 & Rochester Philh, 59-68. Mem fac, Univ Wis, 50-53, Ind Univ, 54-59 & Eastman Sch Music, 59- *Instrumental Works:* Partita for Horn and Piano; Sonata for Flute and Piano; Three Elegies for Oboe and Piano; Suite for Brass Quintet; Sonata for Horn and Piano; Sonata for Tuba and Piano; Concertare I for Brass Quintet and Percussion; Concertare II for Trumpet and Strings; Concertare III for Woodwind Quintet and Piano; Concertare IV for Brass Quintet and Piano; Concertare V for Chamber Ensemble; Four Caprices for Clarinet and Piano; Scenes for Wind Ensemble; Graphics for Trombone and Piano (4 hands); Events for Trombone Choir; Calls for Two Horns; 48 Etudes for Horn; Sonata for Violin and Piano; Sonata for Piano; Sonata for Viola and Piano; Scenes Revisited for Wind Ensemble; Ventures for Orchestra; Xenoliths for Flute and Piano (4 hands); Echo Variations for Oboe and Piano; Florilegium for Piano; Last Scenes for Solo Horn and Wind Ensemble.

REYNOLDS, WILLIAM JENSEN   ASCAP 1955
composer, author, church musician
b Atlantic, Iowa, Apr 2, 20. Educ: Southwest Mo State Col, AB, 42; Southwestern Baptist Theol Sem, MCM, 45; NTex State Univ, MM, 46; George Peabody Col for Teachers, EdD, 61; summer sch, Westminster Choir Col. Minister of music in var churches in Okla, Mo & Tex, 39-55. Church Music Dept, Baptist Sunday Sch Bd, Nashville, Tenn, 55- Music dir, Southern Baptist Convention, Baptist World Alliance & Baptist Youth World Conf. Pres, Harpeth Valley Sacred Harp Singing Asn, 65- Pres, Hymn Soc Am, 78- Comt mem, Dictionary of Am Hymnology. Weekly columnist, Hist of Hymns, The Nashville Banner. Chief Collabrs: Ed Seabough, Mary Lou Reynolds. *Songs:* People to People; Share His Love; Jesus Gives Me Sweet Peace; Give the Lord a Chance; Music: Praise Him, O Praise Him; O God of Might, O Son of Light; There is a Name; In The Beginning; Let Christ's Freedom Ring; It Takes Us All; God's World Today; One World, One Lord, One Witness; New Life for You.

RHEA, CLAUDE HIRAM, JR   ASCAP 1976
composer, singer
b Carrollton, Mo, Oct 26, 27. Educ: William Jewell Col, AB, 50; Fla State Univ, BME, 53, MME, 54, EdD, 58; studied voice with Anna Kaskas, 56-58 & Allen Lindquist, 63-67. Prof & dean, New Orleans Baptist Theol Sem, 54-63; prof & later vpres, Houston Baptist Univ, 63-67; consult in music & mass media, Baptist Foreign Mission Bd, 67-69; recording artist; had concerts in 53 countries; dean Sch Music, Samford Univ, 69- Chief Collabr: Carolyn Rhea, lyricist. *Songs:* Music: A Child's Life in Song (collection of children's songs); Sing While You Grow (collection of children's songs).

RHEA, RAYMOND   ASCAP 1951
composer, musician, educator
b Littleton, Colo, Dec 28, 10; d Carthage, Tex, Feb 7, 70. Educ: Denver Univ; Northwestern Univ, BM, MM; Univ Tex. Soloist in churches & radio in Denver & Chicago. Choir dir, churches in Colo, Mich, Ore, Ill & Tex. Played in dance orchs & instrumental groups. Cond & adjudicator, fests & clinics throughout the west & in Hawaii. Co-author, "Music in Our Life" & "Music in Our Times." Music & voice teacher in schs & cols. Teacher & coordr of music, Corpus Christi, Tex. Head of music dept, Panola Col. *Songs:* Sacred: Let My Soul Rise in Song; Let Music Fill the Skies; Echo Noel; Hail Our Redeemer; O Lord Most Glorious; With Singing Heart.

RHINES, HOWARD M   ASCAP 1958
composer, author
b Hoquiam, Wash, Oct 12, 12. Educ: Bradley Univ, Ill; hon MusD, St Luke's Univ, Havana, 55. Radio announcer, KHQ-KGA, Spokane, Wash, 36-39. Production mgr & prog dir, KMPC, Los Angeles, 39-49. Operations & prog mgr, KFAC & KFAC-FM, Los Angeles, 49-74. *Songs:* Hope and Pray; Music: What Is Love?; Lyrics: Silence. *Instrumental Works:* Concerto for Parted Lovers; Dream and Variation; Not a Sonata.

RHOADS, WILLIAM EARL   ASCAP 1968
arranger, composer
b Harvey, Ill, Aug 5, 18. Educ: Hobart High Sch, Ind; Univ Mich, BMEd, 41, MMusEd, 42. USA Signal Corps, 42-46. Dir bands, Alamogordo Pub Schs, NMex, 46-53; dir bands, Univ NMex, 53-75, chmn dept music, 73-79. Former woodwind teacher. Guest cond, clinician & teacher in numerous states. *Instrumental Works:* Concert Band: Musica Simpatica; Scottish Rhapsody; Tres Danzas; de Mexico; Variations on America (Charles Ives); Oro Quemado; Pickles and Peppers and Cornets; Nativity Songs for Band; Puerto Alegre.

RHODES, GRAYSON
See Miller, Ron D

RHODES, JOSEPH WILLIAM   ASCAP 1968
composer, arranger, tuba player
b Campbell, Mo, Dec 18, 01. Educ: Gideon High Sch, Mo; Miss State Univ; Cincinnati Col of Music; studied harmony & theory with Felix Deyo. Tuba player & arr, Jan Garber Orch, 7 yrs & New York Paramount Theater, 7 yrs. Bassist, Russ Morgan Orch, Fred Waring Orch. Arr & comp, musical commercials, Phil Davis Musical Enterprises. *Songs:* Praise Thee, O God; They Shall See the Glory of the Lord; Responses. *Instrumental Works:* Mystique.

RHODES, ROBERT MILFORD   ASCAP 1976
composer, author, publisher
b Stanley, NDak, June 25, 31. Educ: Univ Kans, BSEE, 56; NY Univ, MEE, 59; studied saxophone with Hayden Moore & Mickey Gillette studios. Saxophonist, Buck Sprague, Clyde Bysom & Ray Effinger orchs; occasional bandleader; arr, original musical for Air Force, 51; comp, author & publ, Synthesis Music, 76- *Songs:* St Augustine Memories; The Fountain of Youth; The Ghost of Jesse Fish; St Augustine Buggy Ride; Walking on the Sea Wall.

RHODES, STAN   ASCAP 1960
composer, author
b New York, NY, May 5, 24. *Songs:* A Sunday Kind of Love; Early Autumn; Monday Again; Tryin' Too Hard.

RHODES, TAYLOR   ASCAP 1974
composer, author
Chief Collabr: Lupe Martinez. *Songs:* Dream Girl of Delta Sigma Phi; The Ushers' Song of Central City, Colorado; Relax, It's No Big Deal; Betty Jean; Lyrics: Music.

RHODES, THOMAS ANTHONY   ASCAP 1974
composer, author, singer
b Sheridan, Wyo, Dec 30, 57. Educ: Mont State Univ, 76; Sheridan Col, 77; Univ Wyo, 78-80. Started songwriting at age 12; turned prof at age 16. Solo singer/guitarist, played conventions, TV & radio. Then at age 19, turned from pop music writer to gospel music writer; currently campus evangelist & agent for other gospel writers. Own publ co, Winds of War Music. *Songs:* Oh, My Jesus; I Can't Make It Without You; Who Is the Child?; Running Out of Time; Only a Few.

RHOTEN, KENNETH DALE   ASCAP 1975
composer, author, singer
b Hammond, Ind, Dec 28, 50. Writer, folk-rock songs, 69; professional songwriting, 73-; guitarist. Chief Collabrs: Dirk Keefner, Rick Dominguez. *Songs:* Pages in a Book of Love; All Night Long; Stretch Me a Road; Make a Dream Come True; Reflection in Your Eyes; The Diamond; Fade Away.

RIBOT, RHODA (RHODA ROBERTS)   ASCAP 1956
author, publisher, producer
b New York, NY. Educ: Lincoln High Sch; NY Univ; Columbia Univ; lyrics with Jay Gorney. Songwriter for records, TV, movie theme & Bway; TV, "That Was the Week That Was"; also TV material for Glen Campbell, Perry Como & Carol Burnett shows; Bway, "Show Me Where the Good Times Are." Chief Collabrs: Kenneth Jacobson, Louis Scheme, Paul Osborne, Leonard Turner. *Songs:* Easy Does It; Put a Light in the Window.

RICCA, JOHN ALBERT   ASCAP 1976
author
b Bisacquino, Italy, Apr 4, 1900. Chief Collabrs: Salvatore Assenza, Dave Ringle, John Dentato. *Songs:* Lyrics: Solo Te; Arriva Lu Tappinaru; Can't You Wait Till We Get Home; My Sweet Marie; Me Ne Vado Sulla Luna; Dove Questo Paese; Fu Fu Fu; I Could Be Laughing With Somebody Else But I'd Rather Cry Over You; La Bicicletta; Bambinella Mia; Fascinatin' Baby; It's You; When You're Tired of Calling Me Sweetheart You Can Always Call Me Pal; Lu Cucciarello Americano; When the Dream in Your Arms Is the Dream in Your Heart.

RICCA, LOUIS   ASCAP 1943
composer
b New York, NY, Oct 10, 09. Chief Collabr: John Redmond. *Songs:* Dream, Dream, Dream; Goodbye Sue; Good Old Moon; I'm Holding the World in My Arms; Gee, I Wish I Knew; I Hope I Hope I Hope; Carnival in Cotton Town; Heavenly Hideaway.

RICCHIO, FRANK THEODORE   ASCAP 1963
composer, musician
b Racine, Wis, Apr 25, 23. Educ: Wash High Sch; Andy Rizzo Sch Music, Chicago, studied comp with the late Carl Eppert. First place accordion categories, Chicago Musicland Festival, 39. Mem, Ricchio Trio, 42- WW II vet, featured accordian soloist with "Gertrude Lawrence War Bond Show." Chief Collabrs: Oscar Ricchio, Frederick Schulte, Ralph Hermann. *Songs:* Last Night; Where in This World; For Eternity; Dreamy Serenade; Sweet Reveria; Stars in the Night; Rolling Stone; Music: Hong Kong Traffic (first place, Wis Composers Contest, piano comp, 68); Holiday for Ten Fingers. *Instrumental Works:* Sambala (accordion solo).

RICCIARDELLO, JOSEPH A   ASCAP 1946
composer, violinist
b New York, NY, Oct 18, 11. Educ: High sch; pvt violin study. *Songs:* The Frim Fram Sauce; 22 Steps; The Wise Old Owl; The Brooklyn Dodgers Jump; Baby, Don't Bother Me; To Si Belle; Laughing Eyes.

RICE, ROBERT GENE   ASCAP 1973
composer, author, singer
b Boscobel, Wis, July 11, 44. Educ: Madison East High Sch, Wis, grad, 62. Started in music bus with family, age 5; active in dances, clubs & radio & TV shows, Wis. First nat chart record, 70. Writer & recording artist, Sunbird Records. Chief Collabrs: Charlie Fields, Don Riis. *Songs:* You Lay So Easy on My Mind; The Whole World's Makin Love Again Tonight; Holidays Are Happy Days; There Ain't No Way Babe; She Sure Laid the Lonelies on Me; What Better Way to Say I Love You.

RICH, CHARLES ALLAN
composer, author, singer
b Colt, Ark, Dec 14, 34. Educ: Univ Ark. Served USAF. Singer, songwriter & performer, TV, clubs, fairs, concert halls & Electra Records. Singer of movie theme, "Benji." Appeared in "Every Which Way But Loose." Sang in movie, "I'll Wake You Up When I Get Home." Chief Collabr: Margaret Ann Rich, wife.

Songs: Lonely Weekends; There Won't Be Anymore; Lord, I Feel Like Going Home; Midnite Blues; On My Knees; Dance of Love; Everytime You Touch Me I Get High; Peace on You; Breakup; Why, Oh Why.

RICH, FREDDIE
composer, conductor
ASCAP 1943

b Warsaw, Poland, Jan 3, 1898; d Beverly Hills, Calif, Sept 8, 56. US citizen, 34. Cond own orch, Astor Hotel, NY, 22-28; first Am band to play Command Perf for King George V, London, 28. Nat music dir, CBS, 28-38. Comp & music dir, Hollywood films. *Songs:* Penthouse; I'm Just Wild About Animal Crackers; Donn-Ama; Cap and Gown; Blue Tahitian Moonlight; Time Will Tell; On the Riviera.

RICH, MAX
composer, author, pianist
ASCAP 1931

b Brooklyn, NY, Aug 22, 1897; d. Educ: Boys high sch. Pianist for silent movies & music publishers. Accompanist to vaudeville singers. Prof mgr, music publ co, 27. To Hollywood, wrote for films. Formed publ firm, Gordon & Rich, with Mack Gordon. Wrote spec material for nightclubs & revues. Chief Collabrs: Mack Gordon, Jack Scholl, Pete Wendling, Jack Meskill, David Oppenheim, Irving Bibo, Henry Creamer, Al Hoffman, Ned Washington. *Songs:* Wonderful You; Smile, Darn Ya, Smile; Making Faces At the Man in the Moon; The Girl in the Little Green Hat; Wake Up, Sleepy Moon; I'll Smile Again; Hold Me Closer; Couldn't You Fall for Me?; I Don't Mind Walkin' in the Rain; Somewhere Beyond the Sunset; In the Wink of an Eye; An Ol' Tin Cup; I Behold You; Shake Hands With a Millionaire; Aintcha; My Bluebird Was Caught in the Rain. *Scores:* Stage: Keep Moving (Bway).

RICH, SELMA
See Brody, Selma Ruth

RICHARD, MAE
author
ASCAP 1965

b Philadelphia, Pa. Educ: Univ Pa, BS(Ed). Wrote lyrics for and produced industrial shows. Pres, Mae Richard Productions, Philadelphia. Collabr with other writers in the musical theatre and TV, New York. Wrote special material, promotional songs and revue material. Chief Collabrs: Elliot Lawrence, Joseph Schrank, Ted Simons, Thomas Tierney. *Songs:* Lyrics: Day Number; Feel; Why Me; One At a Time; A Tune of Our Own.

RICHARDS, DAVE
See Richman, David Alan

RICHARDS, DON (RUBE)
See Moss, Ellsworth Francis

RICHARDS, EDDIE
See Krah, Earl Edward

RICHARDS, EMIL
See Radocchia, Emil

RICHARDS, HOWARD L, JR
composer
ASCAP 1961

b Detroit, Mich, Nov 2, 27. Educ: Culver Mil Acad; Univ of Mich; Rollins Col, BA, BM; Fla State Univ, MM. Wrote musicals in col. With A&R dept, Columbia Records, 4 yrs. Computer programmer, IBM. *Songs:* Who Goes Amid the Greenwood?; Rain.

RICHARDS, JAY
See Pine, Arthur

RICHARDS, NORMAN
composer, pianist
ASCAP 1964

b New York, NY, Feb 21, 31. Educ: High Sch of Music & Art; Queens Col; City Col New York, BBA; Juilliard Sch Music; also pvt music study. Pianist & arr with bands. USAF, Special Serv, wrote Army shows, also in Army band. Pianist in cocktail lounges; accompanist, singing coach. Writes special material, musical commercials. *Songs:* I'd Like to Sing in Five-Four; A Thousand Miles of Mountains; Hello Yellowstone Park; Move On; Shake Hands With the Eastern Crowd.

RICHARDS, STEPHEN
composer, author
ASCAP 1942

b New York, NY, July 21, 08; d. Chief Collabr: Edward Lambert. *Songs:* A Vous Tout de Vey a Vous; La De Doody Do; Love in Springtime; I'll Never Fail You; Beat the Bongo; Mister Paganini Swing for Minnie; Nautch Girl From Cuba.

RICHARDS, STEPHEN (JR)
composer, conductor, arranger
ASCAP 1959

b New York, NY, May 9, 35. Educ: Music & Art High Sch, New York; Brown Univ; NY Univ, BA(music); Columbia Univ, MA(music comp), studied with Henry Cowell & Otto Leuning; Hebrew Union Col-Jewish Inst Religion, Sch Sacred Music, BSacredMusic. Ed, Transcontinental Music Publ; fac mem, Sch Sacred Music, Hebrew Union Col-Jewish Inst Religion; cantor & music dir.

Songs & Instrumental Works: Ki Lekach Tov (Torah service for chorus & bass); Psalm 150 (chorus); Three Sayings of Hillel (solo & chorus). *Scores:* Chamber opera: Ballad of Ruth.

RICHARDS, TERRY
See Marinan, Terrence Richard

RICHARDSON, ARTHUR
composer, pianist
ASCAP 1948

b Bradford, England, Nov 18, 1899; d New York, NY, May 20, 63. Educ: High sch; studied music with Andrew Holroyd. To US 1905; citizen. Pianist in orchs, 20-28; vaudeville, 28-30. Staff mem music publ firms. Toured Alaska, Aleutians, with own show, 43; also with USO shows. *Songs:* Goodbye Again; My Baby Said Maybe; Too Fat Polka; Everybody's Polka; Wasted Words; Wind Song; The Greatest Miracle of All.

RICHARDSON, CLAIBORNE FOSTER
composer, author
ASCAP 1963

b Shreveport, La, Nov 10, 29. Educ: La State Univ, BA, 50. Wrote music for "Shoestring 57"; also songs for several Julius Monk revues; wrote score & lyrics for "Brightest Show on Earth," NY World's Fair, 64; wrote score for "Man and the Polar Regions," Expo 67; wrote incidental music & lyrics for Bway show & PBS TV version of "The Royal Family"; has written many industrials & commercials. Chief Collabrs: Kenward Elmslie, Frank Gagliano, Frank Gehrecke. *Songs:* Come Christmas Time; Happiness Is a Bird; Music: The Rochelle Hudson Tango; Nobody Else Like You. *Scores:* Bway Show: The Grass Harp.

RICHARDSON, DARRELL ERVIN
composer
ASCAP 1970

b Columbia, SC, Sept 17, 11. Educ: Univ SC, BS & BA, 46; Univ Tenn, DDS, 50. Musical arr, Blue Steele, Isham Jones Orchs & Tony Martin, 35-41; WW II & schs, 41-50. Symphonic comp, 50- Chief Collabr: Bernie Burk. *Songs & Instrumental Works:* Elegy (string orch); Behold Thy Son Beloved (string quartet & vocal quartet); Crown Him Lord of All (anthem for youth choir, SAB); That Easter Morn (anthem for choir, SATB); Music: This Is My Song to You.

RICHARDSON, HAL AINSLIE
composer, author
ASCAP 1954

b Pullman, Wash, Aug 26, 13; d San Francisco, Calif, Jan 5, 78. Educ: Washington State Univ; Univ Calif, Los Angeles. Researcher for films until 41. Capt, Gen Staff Corps, USA, WW II. Writer for nightclub acts; under contract to Raymond Scott. To San Francisco, 56. Sci writer & pub info officer, Calif Acad Sci. Chief Collabr: John Klein. *Songs:* Cranberry Corners; So Proudly We Hail; It Takes Two!; Break My Heart Gently.

RICHARDSON, WOODROW P
composer
ASCAP 1969

b Manning, Tex, Oct 30, 19. Producer & publisher, 50- *Songs:* Sundown in Nashville.

RICHENS, JAMES WILLIAM
composer, conductor, teacher
ASCAP 1974

b Memphis, Tenn, Oct 7, 36. Educ: Memphis State Univ, BS(comp), 58; Eastman Sch Music, MM(theory-comp), 60; studied with Bernard Rogers; Eastman, further studies, comp with Sam Adler & electronic music with Wayne Barlow, 69-72. Fac mem comp, electronic music & orchestration, Memphis State Univ, 66-; clarinetist, Memphis Symph, 67-, asst cond, 74- Also active as ballet & opera cond; has comp in all media incl electronic music; had own music performed throughout US, Can, SAfrica, WGer, Eng & other countries. Had many comn works *Instrumental Works:* Fantasia on the Battle Hymn of the Republic (band); Chicano! (band); Prelude and Dance (solo clarinet, band); The Bells (chorus, orch).

RICHMAN, DAVID ALAN (DAVE RICHARDS)
composer, author, entertainer
ASCAP 1975

b Brooklyn, NY, Oct 18, 47. Educ: Nassau Community Col, music maj. Started performing, Greenwich Village, NY, 64. Wrote promotions for WTHE, NY. First record, 67. TV commercials. Local Los Angeles TV concentration. In country field, 74- *Songs:* Just Can't Wait; World of Difference; Candy Store.

RICHMAN, HARRY
composer, author, singer
ASCAP 1926

b Cincinnati, Ohio, Aug 10, 1895; d. Educ: Ohio Mechanics Inst; pvt piano study. Accompanist to Mae West, Nora Bayes & Dolly Sisters. Pianist. Singer on radio, then at own nightclub, Club Richman. Actor. Appeared in Bway musicals "George White's Scandals"; "The International Revue"; "Ziegfeld Follies"; "Say When." Also appeared in nightclubs, radio, films & TV; made many records. Made first trans-ocean round-trip air flight in history; holds world altitude record for single motored amphibious airplanes. Chief Collabrs: Roy Turk, Pete Wendling, Jack Meskill, Fred Ahlert, Little Jack Little, Abner Silver, Irving Kahal, Mack Gordon, Harry Revel, Sam Messenheimer, Val Burton. *Songs:* Walking My Baby Back Home; Muddy Water; There Ought to Be a Moonlight Saving Time; There's Danger in Your Eyes, Cherie; Singing a

Vagabond Song; (I Don't Believe It But) Say It Again; She Came Rolling Down the Mountain; Help Yourself to Happiness; One Little Raindrop; Ro Ro Rolling Along; You Don't Need Glasses to See; I Think You're Wonderful.

RICHMOND, JAMES ERSKINE
ASCAP 1966
composer, author

b Auburn, Ala, Apr 10, 15. Educ: Fairfield High Sch, dipl; Tuskegee Inst Teachers Col; Pepperdine Univ, BA, MA; Univ Calif, Los Angeles, Cert Social Welfare; Sussex Univ, PhD; Los Angeles Cons Music; chorus study under Dr William L Dawson, 3 yrs. Psychol counr, instr, tutor, interviewer & music psychol exp. Assoc prof psychol & coun, Los Angeles Trade Tech Community Col, 4 yrs. Church music dir & minister of music, Los Angeles. *Songs & Instrumental Works:* I'm Proud to Be An American; I Have An Assurance; Tres Flores; Eternal Life.

RICHMOND, KIM ROBERT
ASCAP 1972
composer, instrumentalist

b Champaign, Ill, July 24, 40. Educ: Univ Ill, BS(music educ), BM(music comp); studied comp with Robert Kelly & Tom Fredrickson, clarinet with Harold Wright & Dominic Fera. USAF Airmen of Note, 63-67. Freelance comp, arr & instrumentalist for woodwinds. Has written original scores for several TV series & movies of week. Guest soloist & clinician, col music fests & workshops. With Stan Kenton Orch, 67-68, Clare Fischer Orch, 68-70, Louis Bellson Orch, 69-71, Percy Faith Orch, 73-76; now mem of Bob Florence, Ed Shaughnessy, Bill Holman & Curt Berg Orchs. *Songs:* The The Set-up; Admiral's Lady; For Love of Money; Madonna Legacy; Forbidden City. *Instrumental Works:* Realization (guitar & jazz orch); Tributaries; Fantasia (alto sax & jazz orch); Movements (brass quintet, strings & perc); The Big Sur; Firebush; Score (jazz orch & 3 soloists); Planos; Melon Bells; All Together; Big Mama Louise; Probe; Flapjacks and Maple Syrup; Sojourn; Back a Tad; Under the Loop; Soft Feelings. *Scores: Film/TV:* It Happened at Lakewood Manor (ABC movie of week).

RICHMOND, PAUL DAVID
ASCAP 1973
composer, author

b Greenfield, Tenn, Mar 19, 41. Educ: Greenfield High Sch; Bethel Col. Engr & writer, Mastercraft, Memphis; comp, author & producer in Nashville; engr, Monument Studios, Nashville; mgr, Laurel Tree Studio, Nashville. Chief Collabrs: Ray Riley, Bobby Richmond. *Songs:* Jesus Is the Living End; You've Got to Get Your Ship Together; If He's Really Gettin' to You; *Music:* Do It My Way; Common Law.

RICHMOND, VIRGINIA
ASCAP 1955
composer, author

b New York, NY. Stage, screen, TV & radio star; recording & performing artist; composer, lyricist, producer, playwright, screenplay writer, author & poet. Written & produced over 100 recordings & performed on 47 records. Pres, Chesterfield Records, Collie Music, Mac Heather Music House & head, Queen Features Syndicate; corp exec head, Virginia Richmond Enterprises. Plays written for Bway incl "Cheesecake and Horses", "Elegant Hill" & "The Story of Christmas." Citation from State of Calif for music; commendation from The Nat Fedn Songwriters & Affil Poets & Composers. *Songs & Instrumental Works:* Tippy, the Little Magic Candy Cane; The Anthem of the Astronauts; If You Want to Get You've Gotta Give!; Everybody Loves a Winner.

RICHTER, ADA A (HUGH ARNOLD, WILMA MOORE)
ASCAP 1944
composer, author, arranger

b Philadelphia, Pa. Educ: Philadelphia Music Acad. Pub sch teacher, NJ Teacher Training Schs. Conducted sch music with husband, Merchantville, 40 yrs. Lectr, US, Can & Hawaii, 42- Contributor mag articles in Etude & Clavier. Mem: Musicians Club Am, NJ Fedn Music Clubs, Music Teacher Nat Asns; hon mem, Philadelphia Music Teachers Forum, Haddonfield Music Club, Eugene Field Soc & Music Educ Nat Conf. Author, "The Ada Richter Piano Courses." Arr of Gershwin, Romberg, Herbert and stories with music incl Cinderella, Three Little Pigs, Jack and the Beanstalk, Peter Rabbit, Lion and the Mouse, Nutcracker Suite; also arrangements of hymns, folk songs, Walt Disney and many others. Over 300 publ works. Chief Collabrs: Charles Ware, Lysbeth Boyd Borie, Nancy Hosking, Marie Pentz.

RICHTER, CLIFFORD G
editor, translator

b Pittsburgh, Pa, Mar 6, 17. Educ: Dalcroze Sch of Music; studied viola with Hugo Kortschak. Taught, col & univ, 8 yrs. Ed, var music publishers, 47-, var choral works for publ & transl for many choral texts. Violist, var free-lance orch groups & chamber music orgn; cond, concert & opera. Organizer & music dir, Am Bach Soc, Rockland County, NY.

RICHTER, MARGA
ASCAP 1964
composer, pianist

b Reedsburg, Wis, Oct 21, 26. Educ: Juilliard Sch, BS, 49, MS, 51; studied comp with Vincent Persichetti & William Bergsma, piano with Rosalyn Tureck. Perf by major orchs incl Minn, Milwaukee, Buffalo, Oakland, Ore, Madison, Okla, Tucson & Maracaibo Symph Orchs. NEA grants for major orchestral works; grants & comns from Martha Baird Rockefeller Fund, Nat Fedn Music Clubs, NYSCOA, MGM Records, Carl Fischer & others. Had works recorded on MGM & Grenadilla Records; pianist recording artist on albums of

contemporary music for MGM. ASCAP Standard Awards. *Songs: Music:* Transmutation (song cycle); Psalm 91 (chorus SATB). *Instrumental Works:* Landscapes of the Mind I (piano concerto no 2); Blackberry Vines and Winter Fruit (orch); Lament (string orch); Concerto for Piano and Violas, Cellos and Basses; Music for Three Quintets and Orchestra; Sonata for Piano; Landscapes of the Mind II (violin & piano, selected for repertory list for Kennedy Ctr-Rockefeller Found Int Violin Competition); Landscapes of the Mind III (piano, violin, cello); Requiem (solo piano); Aria and Toccata (viola & strings); Eight Pieces for Orchestra; Darkening of the Light (solo viola or solo cello); Melodrama (two pianos); Variations on a Theme by Latimer (piano 4-hands); Soundings (harpsichord); Remembrances (piano); String Quartet No 2; Sonata for Clarinet and Piano. *Scores:* Abyss (ballet & concert suite, comn by Harkness Ballet); Bird of Yearning (ballet, comn by Harkness Ballet).

RICKER, EARL D
ASCAP 1966
composer, teacher, pianist

b Sterling, Ill, Mar 23, 26. Educ: Oberlin Cons of Music, perf degree piano, 49, advanced study piano; studied with Joseph T Hungate; studied comp with Maurice Weed, Northern Ill Univ, 60-63. Comp, author, pianist, teacher, guest lectr in var cols & teacher groups; former dir preparatory piano, Rock Valley Col; pvt piano & comp teacher, 49- Coauth: "The Church Musician," (primer level & levels 1-6). Chief Collabr: David Carr Glover. *Instrumental Works:* An Old Valentine; Festival of the Clouds; Ice Ballet; Legend of an Ancient Land; Animal Land; Hopscotch (piano; Piano Quarterly, one of 12 Best Piano Comp, 63).

RICKER, RAMON LEE
ASCAP 1973
composer, teacher, performer

b Camp Forrest, Tenn, Sept 16, 43. Educ: Univ Denver, BME, 65; Mich State Univ, MM, 67; Eastman Sch Music, DMA, 73. Mem, Rochester Philh Orch, 74- Asst prof clarinet & saxophone, Eastman Sch Music. Has nine publ bks on jazz improvisation & twelve publ articles on music. Comp grants from NEA, NY State Council on Arts & Creative Artists Pub Service. *Songs:* Heavy Hitter. *Instrumental Works:* The Legend of the Black Swan; Genesis. *Scores: TV:* NYPM Theme; The Mime Workshop.

RICKS, LEE
See Mills, Paul

RIDDLE, R RICHARD
ASCAP 1962
composer, author, singer

b Missoula, Mont, July 16, 40. Educ: Univ Mont, BA. Comp-lyricst, "Cowboy", Goodspeed Opera House; comp-lyricist-dir, "Democrat", Off-Bway; singer, "Three Young Men From Montana", Columbia Records; appeared on Johnny Carson Show, Today Show & others. Actor in commercials; comp-lyricist for musical, "Ox-Bow"; personal mgr, Mission Mountain Wood Band. Chief Collabrs: Jim Lowe, Jess Gregg. *Songs & Instrumental Works:* Mountain Standard Time.

RIDENOUR, VALERIE DUNN
ASCAP 1978
composer, author

b Maryville, Tenn. Educ: Univ Tenn; Univ Chattanooga; Suffolk Univ; pvt study voice with Lelia Hampton Leslie & piano with Alfred Schmied. Prof musician & singer; producer master & demo records; journalist for nat mag. Chief Collabrs: Gary Chase, Lee Morgan, Sonny Smith, Fred Straining. *Songs & Instrumental Works:* Mississippi Pearl; Country Music's Music to My Ears; I Can Feel Another Sad Song Coming On.

RIDGE, BRADLEY B
ASCAP 1974
composer, author, teacher

b San Antonio, Tex, Apr 16, 26. Educ: Univ Tex, Austin, BA, 48; studied with Verna Harder; Stanford Univ, AM, 55; Temple Univ, PhD, 64. Teacher, 26- *Songs:* Too-Short Song No 1 & No 2. *Instrumental Works:* Prelude No 1, No 8 & No 16.

RIDGE, CLYDE HERMAN
ASCAP 1978
composer, author

b Cape Girardeau, Mo, July 11, 14. Educ: Univ Southern Calif, studied classical piano with John Crown; also studied with Jacob Gimpel, Los Angeles. Played piano with Midwest bands in 30's. Moved to Calif, 37; did studio work; staff pianist & arr, KTTV, 3 1/2 yrs; worked at Flamingo Hotel, Las Vegas, 6 1/2 yrs; arr & recorded player piano rolls for Aeolian Corp, New York; had four originals recorded in two albums; also recorded for background music. *Songs:* Don't Ever Change; Only Fools Will Never Love; Don't Forget Me All the Way; Hurtin'; *Music:* Latin Fever.

RIEPE, RUSSELL CASPER
ASCAP 1979
composer, arranger, pianist

b Metropolis, Ill, Feb 23, 45. Educ: Southern Ill Univ, BM(piano), 67; Eastman Sch Music, MA(theory), 69, PhD(comp), 72, studied with Samuel Adler, Warren Benson & Wayne Barlow. Founder-dir electronic music studio, assoc prof music, head of comp-theory progs & piano teacher, Southwest Tex State Univ, San Marcos. Had comp & arr recorded on Columbia & Orion Records; also pianist in recordings of own arr. *Instrumental Works:* Voci Antifonali for

Brass Choir; Three Studies on Flight for Solo Clarinet; Arr for multiple pianos: Stars and Stripes Forever; Thunder and Lightening Polka; Maple Leaf Rag.

RIERSON, RICHARD D   ASCAP 1959
composer, author, arranger
b Winston-Salem, NC, Jan 7, 29. Educ: Draughan Bus Col, Winston-Salem; studied voice with Paul Peterson; pvt piano study. Music dir, First Baptist Church, Winston-Salem, 2 yrs. Mem, Comn on Music, Ritual & Custom (South Province), Moravian Church; chmn, Libr Comn. *Songs:* Sacred: The Holy Will Divine; Arr: I Know the Lord's Laid His Hands on Me. *Scores:* Documentary Film Background: Once Upon a Tanglewood Day.

RIESENFELD, HUGO   ASCAP 1924
composer, conductor, violinist
b Vienna, Austria, Jan 26, 1879; d Hollywood, Calif, Sept 10, 39. Educ: Vienna Cons (scholarship); Univ Vienna; studied violin with Bachreich & Grun. Violinist, Imperial Opera House, Vienna Philh, Mozart Fest, Salzburg, 04 & Bayreuth Wagner Festspiel. Came to US, 07. Concertmaster, Manhattan Opera Co, NY, 07-11. Cond, Bway musical, "Eva." Concertmaster & cond, Century Opera Co, NY, 15. Managing dir, Rialto, Rivoli & Criterion Theatres, NY, 19-25. Dir music, Hollywood studio, 28-30. *Songs:* Westward Ho!. *Songs & Instrumental Works:* Merry Martyr (operetta); Chopin Ballet; Symphonic Epos; Dramatic Overture; Balkan Rhapsody; Etchings of New York; Children's Suite; American Festival Overture.

RIESNER, CHARLES FRANCIS   ASCAP 1957
author, actor, director
b Minneapolis, Minn, Mar 14, 1887; d La Jolla, Calif, Sept 24, 62. Educ: St Joseph's Parochial Sch, Minn. Mem vaudeville team, Riesner & Gores. Appeared in Bway musicals: "Stop, Look, Listen" & "Queen of the Movies." Became film dir; assoc writer & dir with Charlie Chaplin, 8 yrs. Author children's bk, "Little Inch High People." Chief Collabrs: Abe Olman, Jimmy Monaco. *Songs:* Goodbye Broadway, Hello France; Come Back to Old Kentucky; Frisco's Kitchen Stove Rag; Pick a Little Four Leaf Clover; The Garden of Earth; Where the Mississippi River Meets the Gulf of Mexico; Come Back and Mend My Broken Heart; She's All Alone.

RIGGS, JOHN FREDERICK (COUNTRY KOJAC)   ASCAP 1968
composer, author
b Mt Carmel, Ill. Co-host with Ralph Emery, WSM "Opry Spotlight," 5 yrs. articles on var country music artists for several newspapers and magazines. Toured Eng as an artist writer & appeared in US with other artists. *Songs:* Forbidden Angel; You Make Me Feel More Like a Man; Lawyers; The House of Bottles and Cans; Under Cover Man; She Knows What She's Crying About; Sexy Southern Lady; Getting Over the Storm; Victim of My Needs.

RIIS, DONALD L (JOHNNY HOWARD)   ASCAP 1969
composer, author
b Hampton, Iowa, Nov 10, 38. Educ: Britt High Sch, Iowa, grad, 57; Brown's Inst Broadcasting & Electronics, Minneapolis, Minn, grad, 59. Active in radio, KNIA, Knoxville, Iowa, KHAK, Cedar Rapids, KEDD, Dodge City, Kans, WPGC, DC, WMAD, Madison, Wis & WENO, Nashville, Tenn. Record producer, songwriter & publisher. Chief Collabrs: Charles W Fields, Ruby Falls. *Songs:* You Lay So Easy on My Mind; The Whole World's Making Love Again Tonight; Sweet Country Music; He Love's Me All to Pieces; You've Got to Mend This Heartache; Buckdance; If That's Not Loving You; Empty Arms and Teardrops; Somewhere There's a Rainbow Over Texas; Let's Spend Summer in the Country; She Laid the Lonelies on Me; What Better Way to Say I Love You.

RILEY, JAMES R   ASCAP 1976
composer
b Shreveport, La, Sept 2, 38. Educ: Centenary Col, BM, 60; NTex State Univ, MM, 63, studied comp with Samuel Adler; Univ Tex, DMA, 68, studied comp with Hunter Johnson. Perf of symphonic works by Indianapolis Symph Orch, Tex Little Symph & San Antonio Symph Orch; chamber music by Concord String Quartet, Ga Woodwind Quintet & San Antonio Symph Woodwind Quintet. *Instrumental Works:* Dyadics for Flute and Piano; Textures for Trombone and Piano; Visiones (saxophone quartet); Suite for Brass Choir.

RILEY, JAMES WHITCOMB   ASCAP 1939
author
b Greenfield, Ind, Oct 7, 1849; d Indianapolis, Ind, July 22, 16. Educ: Pub schs; hon MA, Yale Univ; hon LHD, Wabash Col & Univ Pa; hon LLD, Ind Univ. Ed, Greenfield newspaper; began contributing to Ind newspapers, 1873. With Indianapolis Journal, 1877-85. Mem, Am Acad Arts & Letters. *Songs:* Poems set to music: The Raggedy Man; When the Frost Is on the Punkin'; Little Orphant Annie; Uncle Sidney; A Life Lesson; Old Trundle Bed; Song of the Road; There Is Ever a Song Somewhere; The Pixy People; Prayer Perfect.

RILEY, MIKE   ASCAP 1940
composer, author, conductor
b Fall River, Mass, Jan 5, 04. Educ: High sch. Trumpeter in orchs incl Rudy Vallee, Ben Bernie, Vincent Lopez & Will Osborne. Appeared in films. Led own band with Ed Farley. Nightclub owner, Hollywood, Calif. Chief Collab: Ed Farley. *Songs:* The Music Goes Round and Round; Ooooh Boom; Not Enough;

Lookin' for Love; Hey, Hey; Looks Like a Cruller, Doughnut; No Nothin'; Laughing Through Tears; Rip Van Winkle.

RINES, JOSEPH   ASCAP 1942
composer, author, producer
b Boston, Mass, Oct 1, 02. Started in radio as entertainer, 21. Led own orch. Music dir, Yankee Network, New Eng, WMCA, New York & NBC Network, New York. Radio producer & dir, "Abie's Irish Rose," Judy Canova & The Andrew Sisters. TV supvr, Colgate Comedy Hour, 6 yrs & The Shirley Temple Storybook. Chief Collabr: Abel Baer. *Songs:* Halo, Everybody, Halo (award); Ajax, the Foaming Cleanser (award).

RINGLE, DAVE   ASCAP 1922
composer, author, pianist
b Brooklyn, NY, Nov 20, 1893; d Brooksville, Fla, June 20, 65. Educ: Commercial High Sch. 1st Sgt, 3rd Machine Gun Battalion, World War I. Contract writer, music publ firms. Pianist in dance orchs, then formed own orch. Appeared in vaudeville, 7 yrs, also in radio, TV & films. Became publisher, 32; partner, Selva-Ringle Record Co. *Songs:* Wabash Blues; Roll On, Mississippi, Roll On; Raggin' the Scales; Blue Eyes; Memory Lane; Any Old Time at All; Changes; After All Is Said and Done; Down in Sleepy Hollow Lane; Sailin' on the Robert E Lee.

RINGWALD, ROY   ASCAP 1944
composer, arranger, orchestrator
b Helena, Mont, Aug 10, 10. Educ: Parochial & pub schs. Singer, dir & arr for vocal groups in radio, theatre & motion pictures. Organist, prog dir, choral dir & violist. Comp/arr, Earl Burtnett, Raymond Paige, Andre Kostelanetz, Billy Rose's "Aquacades, Seven Lively Arts", Fred Waring's Pennsylvanians & Shawnee Press, Inc. *Songs & Instrumental Works:* A Cigarette, Sweet Music and You (Chesterfield Theme); General Electric Theme; Sacred Heart Program Theme; O Brother Man; Heritage; Little Fraternity Pin; Having a Lonely Time; Here It Is Tomorrow Again; The Chocolate Burro; O Listen to the Angels Sing; Affirmation; Greater Love; God Is My Song; A Place in the World; English Text: Five Christmas Songs (Silbelius); Sacred Collections: Praise Him, I & II; The Song of Christmas; The Song of Easter; The Song of America; God's Trombones; Animals (a musical Who's Zoo); The Christmas Crib (a cappella cycle); An American Carol Sampler (choral sequence with chamber orch); Battle Hymn of the Republic (chorus & orch).

RINKER, AL   ASCAP 1949
composer, singer
b Tekoa, Wash, Dec 20, 07. Mem, Paul Whiteman Rhythm Boys, with Bing Crosby, Harry Barris. Made many records. Appeared in film "The King of Jazz." *Songs:* Peter Peter Pumpkin Eater; Dreamsville, Ohio; Suspense; Highway to Love; You Started Something; Just for Laughs; You Can't Do Wrong Doin' Right; Of All Things; My Song to You; Let's Choo-Choo to Idaho; Every Song That I Sing.

RINKER, CHARLES DONALD   ASCAP 1958
author, singer, agent
b Tekoa, Wash, Jan 14, 11. Educ: Glendale High Sch; Glendale Jr Col. Band/group singer, motion pictures & radio. Asst prof mgr, Irving Berlin Music Publ Co; prof mgr, Feist Music & Mercer & Morris. Owner, Charles Rinker Music Publ Co. Radio agent, packager & producer, ABC Network's "Glamour Manor." Wrote for Bing Crosby CBS Radio "Minute Maid" Prog & for Bob Crosby CBS-TV Prog. Chief Collabrs: Gene dePaul, Walter Gross, Al Rinker. *Songs:* Music: What's the Use of Getting Used to You; Lyrics: City Boy; Your Name is Love; Dreamsville, Ohio; Mexican Moon; Don't Let it Throw You; Mother Dear; After Dark; Gypsy; Run For the Hills, Cowboy; Don't I Know You; The Best Part of Me; Sing it Sad and Pretty; Black Roses; Let's Have a Christmas Party.

RIO, ROSA   ASCAP 1954
composer, teacher, arranger
b San Francisco, Calif. Educ: Oberlin Col; Eastman Sch Music. Was featured solo organist, Fox Theatre, Brooklyn, NY & Paramount Theatre, Brooklyn; staff organist, ABC & NBC, 39-59; also on WMCA, WOR, CBS; provided original background music for radio shows, 39-59. Now int theatre organ concert artist; teacher organ & piano, Rosa Rio Sch Music, Huntington, Conn; arr organ-piano for Richard Bradley Publ, New York. Chief Collabrs: Abel Baer, Edward B Marks. *Songs:* Come Rain Come Shine; Gigi, My Fair Lady; Everythings Coming Up Rosa; Music: In My Caravan of Dreams; Just to Be Alone With You; The Moon Is Blue; Mem'ries of the Past; You'll Come Running Back to Me; If I Could Love You; The Lord's Prayer; Dreaming (En Revant).

RIORDAN, MONICA LYNN   ASCAP 1977
author
b San Mateo, Calif, Oct 20, 53. Educ: Univ Calif, Los Angeles, BA(French), 75. Writing lyrics professionally, Warner Bros, MCA & Casablanca, 76-; recording in Rio de Janeiro; preparing a new musical; music dir for jazz radio sta KKGO-FM, Los Angeles. Chief Collabrs: John Elizalde, Mike Miller, Rocky Davis, Gileno Azevedo. *Songs:* Lyrics: Beyond Today; I'll Write My Own Story;

I'll Keep the Memory; Barnaby Jones Episodes CBS-TV: I Don't Try to Understand; Too Much of a Good Thing; More Than I Expected.

RIOS, JAMES   ASCAP 1962
composer
b New York, NY, Jan 7, 31. Educ: Stuyvesant High Sch; City Col New York, BE(chem), 55; studied violin, piano, arr & comp with pvt teachers. Pianist for several Latin-Am bands, made recordings. *Songs:* Sera Charanga; San Francisco; Todo Lo Que Digo; Muchacha Tan Bonita; Que Otra Pachanga; No Bailo Mas; Pa Eso Tu Bebes; Bocoro; A Ti Nomas.

RIPOSO, JOSEPH   ASCAP 1971
composer, teacher, music administrator
b Syracuse, NY, Aug 5, 33. Educ: Syracuse Univ, BME, 56, MME, 69. Dir music educ, Liverpool Cent Schs, NY; jazz coordr, Civic Ctr, Syracuse; adjudicator & clinician for jazz educ & teacher, Onon Community Col; appeared with Ella Fitzgerald, 76, with the Syracuse Symph; appeared in theatre restaurants with Tony Bennett, Nat King Cole, Patti Page, Sammy Davis Jr, McGuire Sisters, Bobby Darin & Paul Anka; had 31 performances, Ice Follies, 56-76. Comn by New York State Sch Music Conference, 68 & Eastern Div Music Educ, New York State Educ Dept, 69; scored the theme for Empire Games, 70. *Instrumental Works:* Crosswinds; Afterglow; All About You; Outer Space; Country Squire; Stage Coach Trail; Two Christmas Carols; Sleepy Hollow; Feeling Soulful; Honey Blonde; Choral and March; Empire Gold (arr for wind ensemble); Jazz Suite.

RISO, RICK   ASCAP 1976
composer
b Monterey, Calif, Aug 10, 50. Educ: Calif State Col, Sonoma; Fuller Theol Sem, Pasadena; studied guitar with Tony Napoli. Performer, 64-; radio & TV performances & interviews; toured throughout US & Can. Chief Collabrs: Si Simonson, Joe Arreguin. *Songs:* Fill Me With Your Spirit; Bringin' the Message; Celebrate; Your Love; Livin' in Love.

RISSER, BRYCE NATHAN (NATHAN DAVID)   ASCAP 1976
composer, author, singer
b Valley City, N Dak, Nov 6, 43. Educ: Valley City High Sch; St Olaf Col, Minn, (music). Songwriter since elem sch; student band, high sch; with combo, high sch & col; writer, music & songs featured on radio & TV & for Bicentennial Pageant for N Dak. *Songs:* Grandma's Upright Grand; Winter Song; Prairie Man; Gentle Carpenter; The Old House.

RITCHIE, JEAN   ASCAP 1964
composer, author, singer
b Viper, Ky, Dec 8, 22. Educ: Viper High Sch; Cumberland Jr Col, Williamsburg, Ky, grad, 43; Univ Ky, AB(social work), 46, Phi Beta Kappa & highest honors. Singer, Greenwich Mews Playhouse & radio sta WNYC, New York. Appeared in many concerts, fests, TV & radio broadcasts in US & abroad. As folklorist, represented US at int folklore conferences, Expo in Can, Cultural Olympics in Mex & Folklife Fest in Washington, DC; was one of seven original dirs, Newport Folk Fest; served 3 yr term on first folklore panel, NEA. Visiting prof folklore, Calif State Univ, Fresno, spring 79. Pres, Geordie Music Publ Co; vpres, Greenhays Recordings. Author, "Singing Family of the Cumberlands," 55 & "Celebration of Life," 71 (nat prize). Awards: Fulbright Scholarship, 52; Univ Ky Founders Day Award & place in Hall of Distinguished Alumni; Burl Ives Award; Nat 4-H Club Cert of Honor. *Songs:* The L&N Don't Stop Here Anymore; Sweet Sorrow in the Wind; Black Waters; West Virginia Mine Disaster; Now Is the Cool of the Day; The Bluebird Song (children's song); One, I Love; Come Fare Away (Marnie); Mountain Born and Country Gentle. *Scores:* Film/TV: Blue Diamond Mines. *Albums:* None But One (Rolling Stone Critics Award as Best Folk Album of Yr, Melody Maker Award, Eng, 80); High Hills and Mountains.

RITENOUR, JOHN DONALD (JAY)   ASCAP 1974
composer, author, guitarist
b New Kensington, Pa, Mar 14, 50. Educ: Univ Pittsburgh, music minor grad, 72; studied jazz guitar with Joe Negri, 70-72. Bass player with numerous rock & country bands, nightclubs & concerts, 69-72; studio guitarist, Nashville, 74; songwriter; lead guitar for two traveling rock bands, Pittsburgh & F-66, 75-; toured Pa, Ohio, NY & WVa. Chief Collabrs: Gary Ritenour, Dean Rutherford. *Songs:* I'm Finally Getting Over You; The Dream's Long Over; Nashville Ain't Far South Enough for Me; Music: Straight From the Heart; Flight 714.

RITENOUR, LEE   ASCAP 1970
composer, arranger, music director
b Los Angeles, Calif, Jan 11, 52. Educ: Rolling Hills High Sch; Univ Southern Calif; studied with Duke Miller, Howard Heitmeyer, Christopher Parkening, Wally Bower, Howard Roberts & Stan Kenton Clinics. Nicknamed "Captain Fingers." Toured with Friendship Band, US, Europe & Japan. Best Studio Guitarist Awards, Guitar Player Mag, 77 & 78. Music dir, Olivia Newton-John "Hollywood Nights" TV Show, 4/80. Chief Collabrs: David Grusin, Don Grusin, Bill Champlin, David Foster, Harvey Mason. *Albums:* First Course; Captain Fingers; Gentle Thoughts; The Captain's Journey; Sugarloaf Express; Feel the Night; Lee Ritenour and Friendship; Lee Ritenour in Rio; Friendship.

RITTENHOUSE, ELIZABETH MAE   ASCAP 1961
composer, author
b Woodlawn, Ala, July 23, 15. Educ: Bible Inst. In ministry, 54- Secy, Akron Ministerial Asn. Chartered Christian Assembly, Inc. Cond, radio ministry Akron & Clarksburg. *Songs:* Sacred: Oh Halleluia Jesus Lives Within; A Soldier for Christ; Memories of By-gone Days; Search My Heart; For My Sake.

RITTER, CHARITY LEE (FORRESTER)   ASCAP 1966
composer, author, publisher
b Marionville, Mo, Sept 29, 17. Educ: Pub schs; Dale Carnegie Pub Speaking; Am Savings & Loan Inst; Lumbeau Sch Real Estate (brokerage & sales); cert, real estate law. Singer with dance band until onset of deafness; pub speaker on deafness; hearing restored, 57. Formed publ corp, pres, 10 yrs. Author & publ, poetry bk, "Life As I See It," & var short works. *Songs:* Credit Card Blues; The Gopher Song; I Know; I Know Where I Am Going; If I Turn Away From Him; You're One of Adam's Ribs; Santa's Alarm Clock Didn't Ring; Los Angeles, City of the Angels; Ecology; Miss California Theme.

RITZ, LYLE   ASCAP 1959
composer, author, instrumentalist
b Cleveland, Ohio, Jan 10, 30. Educ: Occidental Col; Carnegie Inst Technol; Univ Southern Calif; Univ Calif Los Angeles; Art Ctr Col, Los Angeles; studied violin with Ralph Lewando, Pittsburgh. Jazz & big band bassist, Los Angeles. Recording artist, Verve Records. Freelance studio recording musician, 17 yrs. Comp/arr varied records, TV & movie scores. Sem teaching, col level. *Songs:* No Drums No Bugles; When the Live Goes Through. *Albums:* How About Uke; 50th State Jazz.

RIVELLI, PAULINE (ROSE ROSINA, PAUL MERCURIO) ASCAP 1963
composer, author
b New York, NY, Mar 29, 39. Educ: Washington Irving High Sch; Calif State Univ. Founder & publ, Jazz Mag, Jazz & Pop Mag; ed, Words & Music Mag. Pres, Jazz Press Inc, Contact Records, Jazz & Pop Records, JPB Music Corp, PAB Music Corp, Flying D Music Corp & Teder Distributing Co, 62-71. Chief Collabrs: George David Weiss, Milton De Lugg, Tom Scott. *Songs:* Lyrics: Here Is My Heart for Christmas; Andiamo; Father McKenzie; Let Me Be the First to Know; Bell' Amore; (A) Lover's Lament (Eng lyrics, Divorce, Italian Style).

RIVERA, LAWRENCE   ASCAP 1965
composer, author, singer
b Kekaha, Hawaii, Sept 14, 30. Educ: Self-taught. Featured performer at Coco Palms Hotel, 25 yrs. 8 record albums. Composer of over 30 songs, all publ; songbook "Songs by Larry Rivera". Star in musical, "People". Featured singer in TV series, "Fantasy Island", 11/79. *Songs:* Kauai Waltz; The Whole World Looks to Hawaii; Waialeale; Hawaii Belongs to Everyone; Let There Be Hawaii; Jennifer; Puka Puka Road; Coconuts; Kalalau; Kamalani; Live Young As Long As You Live; Today is the First Day of the Rest of My Life; Grace of the Islands; Winona Love; I Searched for Love.

RIVERA, RAY A   ASCAP 1957
composer, author, guitarist
b New York, NY. Educ: Studied guitar with Robert Yelin, Allen Hanlon & Remo Palmieri. Lead own jazz group for 20 yrs. Recorded for MGM, Decca, Mercury & Insight. Appeared on TV, radio & in hotels & night clubs. Played many jazz concerts. Chief Collabrs: Walter Hirsch, Gary Romero, Walter Bishop. *Songs:* You've Been Talkin' About Me Baby; The Right Kind of Woman; Bop Talk; Let Me Hear Some Jazz. *Instrumental Works:* Night Flight to Puerto Rico; Cuchy Frito Man; Nothin' Beats an Evil Woman; Yambo.

RIZO, MARCO   ASCAP 1955
composer, pianist, conductor
b Havana, Cuba, Nov 30, 16. Educ: Nat Cons of Havana; Univ Calif, Los Angeles, MMus; studied comp & orchestration with Mario Castelnuovo-Tedesco, cond with Leo Scheer. Piano soloist with Havana Symph Orch. Played own comp in solo concerts & symph concerts, US & abroad. Pianist-arr with "I Love Lucy" TV Show, 9 yrs. Comp scores for TV & movies. Appeared with own orch at hotels & nightclubs throughout US & Europe. Performed recitals of own works at Town Hall, Carnegie Hall & Lincoln Ctr. Made many recordings. Chief Collabrs: Hal David, Raoul Gonzalez, Kevin Morgan, Michael L Allman. *Songs:* La Charanga; The Chi, Chi, Cha, Cha, Cha; Voulez Vous Cha Cha; Chocolate Merengue; Confesion de Amor; Mi Cuba; Blue Havana Moon; Mi Corazon Estuyo; Nanigo; Noche de Amor. *Instrumental Works:* Chopin Goes to Rio; Broadway Concerto; Sinfonia Cubana; Suite Campesina; Afro-Jazz; Afro-Samba; Mambo Rhapsody; Bossa Moderne; Comparsa Bembe; La Negra Macusa; Rondo a La Turque (arr); Black Madonna (cantata); Tamborito; Suite Espanola; By the Cascades (piano solo); Lucy Cha-Cha.

RIZZI, ALBERTO   ASCAP 1940
composer, conductor, arranger
b Fondi, Vittoria, Italy, Sept 20, 1889; d Brooklyn, NY, Dec 10, 45. To US 08. Educ: Cons of Naples. Cornetist in father's band; later cond. Pianist; gave concerts, taught music in US. Arr for music publishers & symph orchs. *Songs:* Dimmi Fanciulla; On the Shores of Napoli; Mariettina; Night of the Stars;

Sleeping With My Heart Wide Awake; Ammore e Mamma; Vieni; Fides; Carmelita.

RIZZI, TREFONI TONY   ASCAP 1963
composer, teacher
b Los Angeles, Calif, Apr 16, 23. Educ: Los Angeles City Col; Univ Southern Calif; studied Schillinger System of Comp with Franklyn Marks, 12 tone system with George Tremblay & orchestration with Albert Harris. Played violin, 12 yrs; has played guitar mainly studio work, 36 yrs. Writer & performer, 5 Guitar Plus 4, 5 yrs. *Songs & Instrumental Works:* Breakfast Food; Frying Home; Anything But Love; Three for Two; A New Baby; Rose's Loom; I Surrender; He's Got Riddum.

RIZZO, JOE   ASCAP 1961
composer, arranger
b Rochester, NY, Aug 30, 17. Educ: Pvt instr with Vladimir Bakaleinikoff, Los Angeles Cons. Mem, Stan Kenton Band. Arr, many dance bands, incl Ken Baker, Garwood Van, Rudy Friml Jr & others. Arr, Lawrence Welk TV recordings, 23 yrs. Chief Collabrs: Ralph Portnor, Les Kaufman, Mel Brandt, Phil Horton. *Songs:* Music: Be Yourself; You Stand Tall When You Kneel to Pray; Don't Want That Man Around; Flame of Freedom. *Instrumental Works:* Nina.

ROACH, CHRISTINE ENGLISH (TINA ENGLISH)   ASCAP 1974
composer, teacher, singer
b Dallas, Tex, May 21, 52. Educ: Voice training, Southern Methodist Univ, Dallas; Baylor Univ, BS, 74. Mem, Kurt Kaiser Singers & began asn with Word Music, 72. Jingle singer, Pam's, Dallas, 74. Continued comp. Presently doing varied concert work throughout US & sem work for Word Inc. *Songs:* You Are the One; The Lord is the Strength of My Life; Quiet Time; Cast Your Cares; All I Know; What Does Jesus Mean to Me; He's the Kind of Friend You Need; Child of Love; In His Arms.

ROBB, JOHN DONALD   ASCAP 1951
composer, author, teacher
b Minneapolis, Minn, June 12, 1892. Educ: Yale Univ, BA, 15; Univ Minn, 16; Harvard Law Sch, 21-22; Univ Toronto; Juilliard Sch Music; Stanford Univ; pvt study with Nadia Boulanger, Darius Milhaud & Paul Hindemith. Teaching fel biol, Yale Univ, China, 15-16. Officer, 11th Field Artillery, WW I. Practiced law, New York, 22-41. Prof music & head dept, Univ NMex, actg dean, Col Fine Arts, 42, dean, 45-57, retired, 57; comp, author & lectr, 57- *Songs:* Music: Cradle Song; Little Dove (chorus); Hispanic Folksongs of New Mexico; Hispanic Folk Music of New Mexico and the Southwest; The Shepherdess (folk song). *Instrumental Works:* String Quartet No 1; Sonata for Violin and Piano; Piano Sonata; Wedding Music for Violin and Pipe Organ; Dances from Taxco for Two Pianos, Suites No 1 and No 2; Pictures of New Mexico for Young Pianists; Symphony No 1 for Strings; Concerto for Piano and Orchestra; Sonatine for Piano, Three Incidents from Liliom; Symphony No 2 in C for Orchestra; Free Variations on Two Themes for Orchestra; Through the Musical Telescope for Piano; Symphony No 3 in One Movement; Little Suite for Four Double Basses; Two Trios for Soprano, Oboe and Piano; Space Odyssey West (orch & electronic synthesizer); Cogitations, Eight Short Pieces for Piano Solo; Trio for Oboe, Violin and Piano; Sonata No 3 for Violin and Piano; Concertino for Viola and Piano; Little Suite for Flute and Harpsichord; Triangulum for Clarinet and Piano. *Scores:* Little Jo (opera); Dontaro (chamber opera). *Albums:* Electronic Music from Razor Blades to Moog. Piano; Space Odyssey West (orch & electronic synthesizer); Cogitations, Eight Short Pieces for Piano Solo; Trio for Oboe, Violin and Piano; Sonata No 3 for Violin and Piano; Concertino for Viola and Piano; Little Suite for Flute and Harpsichord; Triangulum for Clarinet and Piano. *Scores:* Little Jo (opera); Dontaro (chamber opera). *Albums:* Electronic Music from Razor Blades to Moog.

ROBBERTS, ORIELL
See Wilhelm, Elsie Lee

ROBBINS, CORKY
See Johnson, Margaret

ROBE, HAROLD ATHOL   ASCAP 1919
author
b Syracuse, NY, Feb 20, 1881; d Hempstead, NY, Apr 20, 46. Educ: Buffalo pub schs. Actor in musical comedies; stage mgr, Winter Garden, NY. *Songs:* Tennessee I Hear You Calling Me; From Someone in France to Someone in Somerset; A Rose, a Kiss and You; Dear Old Pal of Mine; Tomasso Rotundo; Glory of the Morn. *Scores:* Stage: Follow the Flag (London).

ROBERDS, FRED ALLEN (SMOKEY)   ASCAP 1963
composer, author, singer
b Leesville, La, Jan 24, 41. Educ: Pasadena Playhouse, grad, 63; chief intern, Tex Chiropractic Col, presently. Over 50 songs recorded. Recording artist with Capitol, A&M & White Whale Records. Appeared in numerous TV & motion pictures incl "Planet of the Apes", "Day of the Wolves" & "Proud and Damned." Chief Collabrs: Murray McLeod, Roger Nichols, Stuart Margolin, Allen Wayne, Mimi Roberds, Howard Beaman, Johnny Cunningham. *Songs:*

Sunshine Girl; Time to Get it Together; A Woman's Way; California Special; Today, I Found You; Good Morn'n Sunshine.

ROBERTS, ALLAN   ASCAP 1926
composer, author, pianist
b Brooklyn, NY, Mar 12, 05; d Hollywood, Fla, Jan 14, 66. Educ: Pub schs. Bookkeeper; wrote spec material for burlesque & nightclubs. Assoc with Mike Todd, 36-40. Under contract to Columbia, Hollywood. Writer for Sid Caesar, Red Buttons, Eddie Cantor, Beatrice Lillie & Herb Shriner. Pianist in nightclubs, Hollywood, Fla. Chief Collabrs: Doris Fisher, Al Kaufman, Irving Gordon, Al Goodhart, Kay Twomey, Al Hoffman, Jerry Livingston, Lester Lee, Robert Allen. *Songs:* Me, Myself and I; Johnny Doughboy Found a Rose in Ireland; Chatterbox; What's the Good Word, Mr Bluebird?; Dreamer With a Penny; To Know You Is to Love You; Wrong Wrong Wrong; You Always Hurt the One You Love; Into Each Life Some Rain Must Fall; Good Good Good; Invitation to the Blues; Tampico; Amado Mio; Put the Blame on Mame; You Can't See the Sun When You're Crying; Tired; I Wish; Either It's Love Or It Isn't; Angelina; They Can't Convince Me; Gee, It's Good to Hold You; That Ole Devil Called Love; The River Seine. *Scores:* Films: Gilda; Down to Earth; Thrill of Brazil.

ROBERTS, AUSTIN
See Robertson, George Austin, Jr

ROBERTS, BILLY JOE
See Barnhill, Joe Bob

ROBERTS, C LUCKEYTH (LUCKEY)   ASCAP 1939
composer, conductor, pianist
b Philadelphia, Pa, Aug 7, 1893; d. Educ: Pvt tutors; studied music with Eloise Smith & Melville Charlton. Singer, dancer & pianist in vaudeville at 5; later made three Europ tours. Had own musical units; also restaurant owner, led orch, music teacher & actor. Pianist for radio progs incl "Moran & Mack." Wrote scores for Bway musicals. *Songs & Instrumental Works:* Moonlight Cocktail; Massachusetts; Elder Eatmore Sermons; Pork and Beans; Music Box Rag; Shy and Sly; Railroad Blues; Helter Skelter.

ROBERTS, CHARLES J   ASCAP 1924
composer, arranger, flutist
b Kassa, Hungary, July 25, 1868; d Albuquerque, NMex, Aug 3, 57. Educ: Budapest Acad Music. To US, 1890; flutist, New York Philh & Mozart Symph Club, 1892-93; dir music, Hoffman House, New York, 1895-10; ed, staff comp & arr, music publ co, 09-40. *Songs & Instrumental Works:* The Language of the Flowers; International March; A Tale of Two Hearts; Cupid's Caress; Swanee River (band arr).

ROBERTS, DAVID BRIAN
composer, author, trombonist
b Prince George, BC, Sept 5, 35. Educ: Courtenay High Sch, grad, 53; Westlake Music Col, 58-59. Trombonist, Les Brown, Stan Kenton & Claude Gordon Orchs & Hollywood studios. Arr for var artists incl Charo, Tom Sullivan, Iris Larratt & groups Climax & Jefferson Starship; songwriter. Chief Collabrs: Verne Langdon, Cort Murry, Gregory H Cline.

ROBERTS, GENE   ASCAP 1952
composer, author
b New York, NY, Jan 16, 18; d New York, Oct 23, 70. Educ: NY Univ. Social worker, Dept Welfare, NY. Chief Collabr: Valerie Brooks. *Songs:* Must Have Your Love; How Could You Forget Me; Just One More Time; Only Yesterday; Lover, Be Careful; Tinsel and Joy.

ROBERTS, GEORGE M   ASCAP 1958
composer, musician
b Des Moines, Iowa, Mar 22, 28. Educ: High sch; Cons. Mem, Gene Krupa & Stan Kenton Orchs. Free-lance musician, Hollywood, 51-

ROBERTS, HOWARD ALFRED   ASCAP 1965
composer, author, conductor
b Burlington, NJ, July 18, 24. Educ: Baldwin-Wallace Col, Ohio; Western Reserve Univ; Cleveland Inst Music, MusB, 50, MusM, 51; studied with Marcel Dick & Mordecai Bauman, also with Maggie Teyte, London, Pierre Bernac, Paris & Marinka Gurewich, NY. Jazz trumpet player, Lionel Hampton & Lucky Millinder Orchs. Singer Bway shows, "Porgy and Bess", "Shinbone Alley." Tenor soloist, Robert Shaw Chorale, Am Concert Choir. Teacher, NC Cent Univ & Morgan State Univ. Musical dir, Harry Belafonte & Alvin Ailey Dance Co. Cond Bway shows, "Raisin", "Guys and Dolls" (revival), "The Wiz" & "Comin' Uptown." Chief Collabrs: Maureen Meloy, Harry Belafonte. *Songs:* Look Over Yonder; Be My Woman, Gal; Shake That Little Foot; Music: Always Left Them Laughing; False Love; Hoe Down Blues. *Scores:* Bway shows: Trumpets of the Lord; Every Night When the Sun Goes Down; A Nation Is Born (sound & light show); TV: Cindy; Young, Gifted and Black; Ballet: Revelations; Blood Memories; Long Remembrance (cantata); Burst of Fists; Film: Lord Shango.

ROBERTS, JASON
See Bock, Fred

ROBERTS, JERRY
See Ost, Robert S

ROBERTS, JON
See Olson, Robert G

ROBERTS, LEE S   ASCAP 1923
composer, pianist
b Oakland, Calif, Nov 12, 1884; d San Francisco, Sept 10, 49. Educ: Pub schs. In piano mfg bus, 11. Developed QRS artist-recorded music rolls & catalogs for player piano, 12. Pianist on radio, 28-36. *Songs:* Smiles; Lonesome, That's All; My Old Piano and Me; A Little Birch Canoe and You; After All; Patches; Drowsy Baby; Broken Moon; Out of the Mist; Mammy's Lullaby; Oklahoma Lullaby; When You Smile.

ROBERTS, LINDA   ASCAP 1955
author
b New York, NY, May 15, 01. Educ: Cornell Univ; Hunter Col, BA; New Sch for Social Res. Has been ed, trade paper. Wrote special material. Author "Two Man Woman," novel. Chief Collabrs: Lawrence Elow, Robert Effros, Gene Mascara, Irving Mopper. *Songs:* Not As a Stranger; Love Wears a Mask; You Should Have Kissed Me Then; Charm Bracelet; Beatnick Boogie; You Make Living Worth While; Castanets; Summer Will Come Again.

ROBERTS, LOU
See Ruse, Robert Louis

ROBERTS, MARION EARL, JR   ASCAP 1976
composer, author, singer
b West, Miss, Aug 28, 45. Chief Collabrs: Lonnie Wright, Randy Calloway. *Songs:* Earl the Pearl; Sharing Sharon's World; Shootin' the Bull; The Hustler Song; Ecstasy; Boots; Passing Seasons.

ROBERTS, MURIEL
See Fendell, Muriel Roberts

ROBERTS, PAUL
See Metivier, Paul Roberts

ROBERTS, RHODA
See Ribot, Rhoda

ROBERTS, RUTH   ASCAP 1948
composer, author
b Port Chester, NY, Aug 31, 30. Educ: Juilliard; Northwestern Univ; Manhattanville Col, NY. *Songs:* It's a Beautiful Day for a Ball Game; Mr Touchdown, USA; Meet the Mets.

ROBERTS, WILFRED BOB   ASCAP 1972
composer, author, instrumentalist
b Detroit, Mich, Feb 26, 21. Educ: Univ Mich, BM(music educ) & BM(theory-comp); studied counterpoint, comp & orch with Erik Leidzen, Alfred S Burt, Rayburn Wright. NY studio musician, arr/performer, 25 yrs; original music & underscoring for many children's recordings. Mgr, Music Projects Div, The Christian Sci Publ Soc. Writer for disc, cassette, radio, slide-tape & others. Author many articles for The Music J, Leblanc Bandsman, The School Musician & New York Brass Conference J. *Instrumental Works:* Three Headlines (brass quintet); Serenade for Trumpet (with chamber orch or piano); Coliseum March; Miniatures for Three Winds; Trouble on the Thames (stage band); Little Tune for a Big Horn (tuba, bass trombone); Woodwind Septet; Duo for Two Winds; And They Two Went On (duo for winds); Transitions (brass quintet); Variations on an English Tune (brass quintet); Crosscurrents (brass quintet).

ROBERTSON, DICK   ASCAP 1941
composer, author, singer
b Brooklyn, NY, July 3, 03; d. Educ: Pub schs. Singer in theatres & nightclubs throughout US, Can, Eng & France. Record exec. Chief Collabrs: Sammy Mysels, Frank Weldon, Nelson Cogane, James Cavanaugh. *Songs:* We Three; A Little on the Lonely Side; At Least You Could Say Hello; Out of Port; Goodnight, Wherever You Are; Yesterday's Gardenias; You Forgot About Me; Dearest Darling; I'd Do It All Over Again; You Can Cry on Somebody Else's Shoulder; Is There Somebody Else?; My Old Gal; If You Cared.

ROBERTSON, DON   ASCAP 1969
composer, author, performer
b Denver, Colo, Apr 4, 42. Educ: Colo Univ; Univ Calif, Los Angeles; Juilliard Sch; studied with comp Morton Feldman, 2 yrs & with Ali Akbar Kahn, 2 yrs. Rock & jazz musician & comp, 64-68. Musician, New York studio, writer & recording artist, 68-70. Researcher, multivolume set of bks on Renaissance & medieval sacred music & effects of music, 71-75. Lectr & performer, 75- Author bk, "Kosman." *Songs & Instrumental Works:* Tabla; Dann.

ROBERTSON, DONALD IRWIN   ASCAP 1955
composer, author, pianist
b Peking, China, Dec 5, 22. Educ: Pvt piano study from age 4; Univ Chicago, AA; Chicago Musical Col; pvt orch & comp study with Mario C Tedesco, cond with Alfred Sendrey, voice with George Morgan. Began composing at age 7. Played in local dance orchs; professional at age 14. Musical arr, Chicago Radio Sta WGN. Played in nightclubs, Los Angeles, 45. Pianist, Capitol Records, Hollywood, 50's. Began songwriting, 53; created piano style known as Country Piano or Nashville Piano. Recording artist with Capitol, RCA & Monument Records; played piano or other keyboard instruments as backup to many recording artists. Featured playing opening song of "Country Bear Jamboree," Disneyland & Disney World. Keyboardist, arr, cond, singer, whistler & comp-author for nightclubs, radio, TV, films & recordings. Chief Collabrs: Howard Barnes, Hal Blair, John Crutchfield, Lou Herscher, Jack Rollins, Harold Spina. *Songs:* Please Help Me I'm Falling; I Can't Help You (I'm Falling Too); Ringo; I Love You More and More Every Day; Born to Be With You; Hummingbird; Does My Ring Hurt Your Finger; I'm Counting on You; Not One Minute More; Anything That's Part of You; There's Always Me; I'm Yours; I Can't Seem to Say Goodbye; You're Free to Go; Ninety Miles an Hour (Down a Dead End Street); They Remind Me Too Much of You; Wallpaper Roses; Honey Eyed Girl; I Stepped Over the Line; Magic Fingers; Go Back You Fool; I've Come to Say Goodbye; Thank You for Loving Me; Stand In; Longing to Hold You Again; One Step Ahead of My Past; Love Me Tonight; Starting Today; Marguerita; I'm Falling in Love Tonight; I Met Her Today; I Think I'm Gonna Like It Here; What Now, What Next, Where To; Music: I Really Don't Want to Know; I Don't Hurt Anymore; Does He Mean That Much to You; The Queen of Draw Poker Town; Condemned Without Trial; I Let Her Go; Lyrics: No More. *Songs & Instrumental Works:* The Happy Whistler; Pianjo. *Albums:* Heart on My Sleeve.

ROBERTSON, GEORGE AUSTIN, JR (AUSTIN ROBERTS) ASCAP 1968
composer, author, singer
b Newport News, Va, Sept 19, 45. Educ: Ferguson High Sch, Newport News, grad; col, 2 yrs. Began writing professionally for AMPCO Music, 68, also recorded for Philips Records. Writer & singer commercials, "Skooby Doo" cartoon series & "Josie and the Pussycats"; also wrote for several movies. Chief Collabrs: Layng Martine, Johnny Cymbal, Buzz Cason, Van Stephenson, Kenny O'Dell, Jeff Silbar, Chris Christian, Milton Blackford, Randy Goodrum. *Scores:* Musicals: Damon's Song; Rachinoff.

ROBERTSON, LEROY   ASCAP 1950
composer, educator
b Fountain Green, Utah, Dec 21, 1896; d Salt Lake City, Utah, July 25, 71. Educ: New Eng Cons, studied with George Chadwick; Brigham Young Univ, BA, MA; Univ Southern Calif, PhD; studied with Ernest Bloch, Arnold Schoenberg, Hugo Leichtentritt, Ernst Toch. Prof & chmn of music dept, Brigham Young Univ, 25-48, Univ Utah, 48-71. Lectr, comp, Univ Calif. Mem, Utah Acad Arts & Letters. *Songs & Instrumental Works:* Endicott Overture (Endicott prize); Quintet for String and Piano (Soc for Publ Am Music prize); Three Concert Etudes for Piano; Rhapsody for Piano, Orchestra (Utah Inst Fine Arts award); Trilogy for Orchestra (Reichhold award); Prelude, Scherzo and Ricercare for Orchestra; Punch and Judy Overture; Violin Concerto; Cello Concerto; Oratorio from the Book of Mormon; Organ Sonata in B minor; Fantasia (organ); Come, Come, Ye Saints (choral); Passacaglia for Orchestra; Hatikvah (choral); From the Crossroads; Motet for Chorus; The Lord's Prayer (choral); All Creatures of Our God and King Alleluia and Choral for Band and Chorus; Novelette for Orchestra; Timpanogas Symphonic Poem; Saguaro Overture; University of Utah Festival Overture; American Serenade (string quartet or string orch); Three Songs from the Shadow (high voice, piano); & many songs & anthems.

ROBIN, LEO   ASCAP 1927
lyricist
b Pittsburgh, Pa, Apr 6, 1900. Educ: Univ Pittsburgh Law Sch; Carnegie Tech Drama Sch. Early career as newspaper reporter. Chief Collabrs: Richard Myers, Vincent Youmans, Clifford Grey, Sam Coslow, Richard Whiting, Franke Harling, Ralph Rainger, Harry Warren, Frederick Hollander, Jerome Kern, Arthur Schwartz, John Green, Harold Arlen, Jule Styne, Sigmund Romberg, Lewis Gensler, Nacio Herb Brown. *Songs:* Lyrics: My Cuties Due At Two to Two Today; Hallelujah; Why Oh Why; Paree; Jericho; Louise; True Blue Lou; It's a Habit of Mine; Wait 'Til You See Ma Cherie; If I Were King; All I Want Is Just One; Beyond the Blue Horizon; It's a Great Life; My Ideal; Prisoner of Love; One Hour With You; Here Lies Love; Please; In the Park in Paree; Give Me Liberty or Give Me Love; Take a Lesson From the Lark; Love in Bloom; With Every Breath I Take; June in January; Here Is My Heart; Love Is Just Around the Corner; Miss Brown to You; Double Trouble; I Don't Want to Make History; Whispers in the Dark; The House Jack Built for Jill; I Can't Escape From You; Here's Love in Your Eye; La Bomba; Moonlight and Shadows; Blue Hawaii; In a Little Hula Heaven; Sweet Is the Word for You; Easy Living; What Have You Got That Gets Me; You're Lovely Madame; Blossoms on Broadway; Ebb Tide; Thanks for the Memory (Acad Award, 38); You Took the Words Right Out of My Heart; Kinda Lonesome; The Funny Old Hills; Joobalai; I Have Eyes; You're a Sweet Little Headache; What Goes on Here in My Heart; Faithful Forever; Bluebirds in the Moonlight; Hello, Ma! I Done It Again; Oh,

the Pity of It All; A Journey to a Star; No Love, No Nothin'; Up With the Lark; In Love in Vain; A Gal in Calico; A Rainy Night in Rio; Oh, But I Do; Through a Thousand Dreams; The Turntable Song; Hooray for Love; For Every Man There's a Woman; What's Good About Goodbye; It Was Written in the Stars; Bye Bye Baby; Diamonds Are a Girl's Best Friend; A Little Girl from Little Rock; Just a Kiss Apart; It's a Hot Night in Alaska; Betting on a Man; Zing a Little Zong; A Flight of Fancy; I'll Si-Si Ya in Bahia; A Little More of Your Amor; Uncle Sam Gets Around; In Paris and in Love; Lost in Loveliness; A Ride on a Rainbow; The Hills of Old Wyomin'; Silver on the Sage. *Scores:* Film: Dance of Life; Monte Carlo; One Hour With You; A Bedtime Story; Little Miss Marker; Here Is My Heart; The Big Broadcast (35, 37 & 38); Rhythm on the Range; Waikiki Wedding; Paris Honeymoon; Gullivers Travels; My Gal Sal; The Time, the Place, and the Girl; Casbah; My Sister Eileen; Just For You; Coney Island; That Lady in Ermine; Meet Me After the Show; TV Score: Ruggles of Red Gap; Bway Stage: Judy; Hit the Deck; Allez-Oop; Just Fancy; Hello Yourself; Gentlemen Prefer Blondes; The Girl in Pink Tights.

ROBIN, SYDNEY
ASCAP 1942

composer, author

b New York, NY, July 12, 12. Special service, WW II. Appeared in Army revue, "This Is the Army." *Songs:* Blind Date; Evelyn; Green Cockatoo; Just Because; My Baby Said Yes; No One to Cry To; Save a Smile; Undecided.

ROBINETTE, JOSEPH ALLEN
ASCAP 1976

author, teacher

b Rockwood, Tenn, Feb 8, 39. Educ: Carson-Newman Col, BA, 60; Southern Ill Univ, MA, 66, PhD, 72. Teacher, Arkansas City Jr Col, 63-64, Southern Ill Univ, 67-71, Glassboro State Col, 71-; chmn dept speech/theatre, 78-79. Playwriting instr, Cape Cod Writers Conference. Awards: Charlotte Chorpenning Cup, 76; Nat Children's Theatre Playwriting Award. Wrote lyrics for children's musicals: "The Fabulous Fable Factory"; "Showdown At the Sugar Cane Saloon"; "The Princess, the Poet and the Little Gray Man"; "Mr Herman and the Cave Company"; "Legend of the Sun Child." Chief Collabrs: Thomas Tierney, James R Shaw. Tierney, James R Shaw.

ROBINSON, AVERY
composer, author

b Louisville, Ky, Jan 21, 1878; d Pittsfield, Mass, May 11, 65. To London in 20's; treas, Royal Philh Soc; to US to operate perfume business with wife in 30's. *Songs:* Water Boy.

ROBINSON, BETTY JEAN
ASCAP 1978

composer, author, singer

b Hyden, Ky. Educ: High sch. Started out in Country Music, 67; wrote first hit, 68. Has Written about 130 country music songs. Voted Country Female Song Writer, Bill Board Mag, 74. Started writing gospel music, 74. Now involved in Christian TV; owns own record co, Brentwood, Tenn. Record label is Melody Mountain Records. *Songs:* Hello Love; On the Way Home; Old Silver Wing; The Shepherd of My Valley; Living Up on the Mountain; A Baby Back Again; A Red Rose From the Blue Side of Town; All I Need Is You; Same Old Story, Same Old Lie.

ROBINSON, EARL HAWLEY
ASCAP 1940

composer, author, conductor

b Seattle, Wash, July 2, 10. Educ: West Seattle High Sch, Wash; Univ Wash, BMus & teaching dipl; studied comp with Aaron Copeland, Hanns Eisler & George Autheil. Joined the Workers Theater of Action & wrote music for Fed Theater Plays, 34-43. Wrote film scores, Hollywood, 43-51. Cond, Europ Tour. Wrote scores for films & TV, Hollywood, 66. Began writing own lyrics-texts, 70. Writing operas & full length musicals, Santa Barbara, 75- Chief Collabrs: Alfred Hayes, John Latouche, Lewis Allan, Millard Lampell, Bob Russell, Harry Schachter, David Arkin. *Songs:* Battle Hymn; The People, Yes; The Pumpkin Who Couldn't Smile; To the Northwest Indians; Music: Joe Hill; Abe Lincoln; Ballad for Americans; The Lonesome Train; House I Live In; Gotta Get Out and Vote; Black and White. *Instrumental Works:* Good Morning; A Country They Call Puget Sound; Concerto for 5 String Banjo; Piano Concerto; My Fisherman, My Laddio, My Love; Uptight. *Scores:* Musicals: Our Fort in America; Earl Robinson's America; Films: Romance of Rosia Ridge; California; Man from Texas; The Roosevelt Story; Giants in TV Land; A Walk in the Sun; TV: Great Man's Whiskers; Maybe I'll Come Home in the Spring; Bway: Sandhog; Opera: David of Sassoun.

ROBINSON, EDWARD
ASCAP 1957

composer, author, pianist

b New York, NY, Jan 28, 05; d. Educ: Columbia Univ, BA, MA, Mosenthal fel; studied music with Alexander Berne & Seth Bingham. Music Critic, Columbia Daily Spectator; ed & publ, Fortnightly Musical Review, 28-29. Columnist & drama critic, United Feature Synd, 34-38. Concert accompanist; piano & comp teacher. Coauth, "Love or Perish." *Songs:* Stop, Look and Listen!; also, A Child's Introduction to Science (song cycle). *Instrumental Works:* Chilmark Suite; Gay Head Dance; The Storekeeper's Daughter; Variations for Piano on a Theme by Beethoven.

ROBINSON, EDWARD ALFRED (SAM BELEFAN)
ASCAP 1964

composer, author, arranger

b Phoenix, Ariz, June 30, 21. Educ: George Washington High Sch, Los Angeles, Calif; studied comp with Lucien Cailliet, 41-42. Arr/comp & instrumentalist,

Big Band Era, film, recording studios. *Songs:* Give Me a Moment With Somewhere; Music: Walk It Off.

ROBINSON, GORDON W
ASCAP 1953

composer

b Toronto, Ont, July 13, 08. Educ: La State Univ, BA, BM, MM.

ROBINSON, HARRY I
ASCAP 1948

composer, author

b New York, NY, June 26, 1888; d Chicago, Ill, May 23, 54. Educ: Bus col; pvt music study. Vaudeville performer, 15 yrs. Wrote for musical productions & vaudeville acts. *Songs:* Is It Within the Law?; As the Years Roll By; Games of Childhood Days; Let's Make Love While the Moon Shines; Just As We Used to Do; I Do-Do You?

ROBINSON, J RUSSEL
ASCAP 1920

composer, author, publisher

b Indianapolis, Ind, July 8, 1892; d Palmsdale, Calif, Sept 30, 63. Educ: Shortridge High Sch; pvt music study. Mem, team Robinson Brothers, played film theatres, 09-18; single act, vaudeville. Mem, Original Dixieland Jazz Band. Toured Europe. Songwriter, var London revues, incl "Bran Pie." Made piano rolls, 18-26. Pianist & vocal coach, radio show "Children's Hour." Honored for contribution to music and entertainment by Ind State House of Representatives. Materials & records of works on file, Traditional Music section, Univ Ind. Chief Collabrs: Al Bernard, Roy Turk, Benny Davis, Addy Britt, Con Conrad, Noble Sissle. *Songs:* Singin' the Blues (Hall of Fame, 77); Margie; Aggravatin' Papa; Rhythm King; Mary Lou; Palesteena; Yeah Man; Beale Street Mama; On the Eight O'Clock Train; Blue Eyed Sally; Let Me Be the First to Kiss You Good Morning; When Dixie Stars Are Playing Peek-a-boo; Hello, Sweetheart, Hello; Is I in Love? I Is; Meet Me at No Special Place; Portrait of Jennie; I Won't Believe It; Memphis Blues; Original Dixieland One-Step; St Louis Gal; Rampart Street Blues; Ringtail Blues; Swing, Mr Charlie.

ROBINSON, JESSIE MAE
ASCAP 1952

composer

b Beaumont, Tex, Oct 1, 19; d. Educ: High sch. *Songs:* Clean Head Blues; Railroad Porter Blues; In the Middle of the Night; Blue Light Boogie; Without a Memory; The Lover Waltz; When I See You; The Bachelor's Tune; You Let My Love Get Cold; The Other Woman; Let's Have a Party; Keep It a Secret.

ROBINSON, MATTHEW THOMAS, JR
ASCAP 1970

composer, author

b Philadelphia, Pa, Jan 1, 37. Educ: Pa State Univ, BA. Began as writer-producer with WCAU-TV (CBS), Philadelphia; produced & wrote songs for series "Sesame Street"; produced musical extravaganza "Save the Children" for Paramount Pictures; wrote & produced comedy "Amazing Grace" for United Artists. Recently completed full-length drama "Matt Robinson's Play." Exec producer for TV series on history of Caribbean. Chief Collabrs: Coleridge-Taylor Perkinson; Joe Raposo. *Songs:* Hey, Big Dancin' Boy (theme song); Roosevelt Franklin Counts; Roosevelt Franklin's Alphabet; Amazing Grace (How Sweet She Be); Just Because; The Safety Boy Blues.

ROBINSON, WILLIAM, JR (SMOKEY)
ASCAP 1971

composer, author, singer

b Detroit, Mich, Feb 19, 40. Educ: High sch grad; jr col, 2 yrs. Formed group Smokey Robinson & the Miracles, 57, performed with group until 72, Detroit nightclubs. Co-founder Tamla record label, 59. Recording artist; songwriter; producer with Motown Records. Actor & movie producer. Chief Collabr: Marvin Tarplin. *Songs:* Shop Around; Bad Girl; Tracks of My Tears; Tears of a Clown; Quiet Storm; Crusin'. *Albums:* A Quiet Storm; Smokey's Family Robinson; Deep in My Soul.

ROBISON, CARSON J
ASCAP 1933

composer, author, singer

b Oswego, Kans, Aug 4, 1890; d Pleasant Valley, NY, Mar 24, 57. Educ: Pub schs. To Kansas City, 20, singer, radio. To New York, 24; made records as whistler for Victor Co. Singer, radio, vaudeville & films. Formed own group, The Buckaroos, 32, toured Eng. *Songs:* Carry Me Back to the Lone Prairie; Barnacle Bill the Sailor; My Blue Ridge Mountain Home; Left My Gal in the Mountains; 1942 Turkey in the Straw; Life Gets Tee'jus Don't It; I'm Going Back to Whur I Came From; Home Sweet Home on the Prairie; There's a Bridle Hangin' on the Wall; The Charms of the City Ain't Fer Me; Goin' Back to Texas; Little Green Valley; New River Train; Wreck of the Number Nine; Settin' By the Fire.

ROBISON, WILLARD
ASCAP 1928

composer, author, singer

b Shelbina, Mo, Sept 18, 1894; d Peekskill, NY, June 24, 68. Writer col musicals; organized Deep River Orch, toured US. Featured on radio; made many records. *Songs & Instrumental Works:* A Cottage for Sale; Peaceful Valley; 'Tain't So, Honey, 'Tain't So; Round House Nellie; Guess I'll Go Back Home; A Woman Alone With the Blues; Six Studies in Modern Syncopation; Rural Revelations; Wake Up, Chillun, Wake Up; Don't Smoke in Bed; Old Folks; What's This World A'Coming To.

ROBYN, ALFRED GEORGE ASCAP 1914
composer, pianist, organist
b St Louis, Mo, Apr 29, 1860; d New York, NY, Oct 18, 35. Educ: Univ St Louis, MusD; studied with father. Charter mem, ASCAP. Prof pianist & church organist. Accompanist to singer Emma Abbot; cond, Apollo Club & Amphion Club, St Louis. Organist, New York theatres. Chief Collabr: Henry Blossom. *Songs:* A Heart That's Free; Answer; You; It Was a Dream; I'm a Gypsy Wild and Free; Amo; Ain't It Funny What a Difference a Few Hours Make?. *Instrumental Works:* Symphony in D; Pompeii (symph poem); Concerto in C; Manzanilla (accordion, orch); The Ascension; The Mass of the Sacred Heart.

ROCHBERG, A GEORGE ASCAP 1953
composer, educator
b Paterson, NJ, July 5, 18. Educ: Montclair State Teacher's Col, BA, 39; Mannes Sch Music, New York, comp scholarship, 39-41; Curtis Inst Music, Philadelphia, BM, 47; Univ Pa, MA, 49. Mem fac, Curtis Inst Music, 48-54. Ed & dir publ, Theodore Presser Co, 51-60. Chmn, Dept Music, Univ Pa, 60-68, prof music, 68-, comp-in-residence, 76, Annenberg prof humanities, 78. Slee prof, State Univ NY Buffalo, 64; guest comp, Tanglewood, summer 66, Temple Inst Music, 69, Oberlin Fest Contemporary Music, 70, Testimonium, Jerusalem, 70-71, Aspen Conference Contemporary Music, summer 72, Grand Teton Fest, Wyo, summer 77 & Santa Fe Chamber Music Fest, summer 79. Honors, Awards & Fels; Fulbright Fel, Italy, 50-51; Am Acad Rome fel, 50-51; Soc Publ Am Music Award, 56; Guggenheim Fels, 56-57 & 66-67; Ital Int Soc Contemporary Music Chamber Music Orch Prize, 59; Nat Inst Arts & Letters grant, 62; Hon Doctorates, Montclair State Col, 62, Philadelphia Musical Acad, 64 & Univ Mich, 80; Prix Italia for NET Lincoln Ctr Spec; Stereo Rev Record of the Yr Award, 73; NEA grant, 73-74. Koussevitsky Found Comn, 57. *Songs & Instrumental Works:* Night Music (Gershwin Mem Award, 52); Symphony No 1; Symphony No 2 (Naumberg Recording Award, 62); Symphony No 3 (double chorus, chamber chorus, soloists & large orch, comn by Juilliard Sch Music); Music for the Magic Theater (small orch); Symphony No 4 (comn by Seattle Youth Orch); Phaedra (monodrama for mezzo-soprano & orch, comn by New Music Ens, Syracuse, NY with assistance from NY State Council on Arts); Violin Concerto (comn by Pittsburgh Symph Orch for Isaac Stern); Chamber Symphony for Nine Instruments (oboe, clarinet, bassoon, horn, trumpet, trombone, violin, viola, cello); Seranate d'Estate for Six Instruments (flute, harp, guitar, violin, viola, cello); Blake Songs for Soprano and Chamber Ensemble (flute, clarinet, bass clarinet, celesta, harp, violin, viola, cello); String Quartet No 2; Trio for Violin, Cello and Piano; Contra Mortem et Tempus (violin, flute, clarinet, piano, comn by Aeolian Quartet); String Quartet No 3 (comn by Concord String Quartet, Naumberg Chamber Music Comp Award, 72); Ricordanza (soliloquy, cello & piano); Piano Quintet (NEA grant, 75); String Quartet No 4 (Friedheim Award, 79, comn by Concord String Quartet); String Quartet No 5 & No 6 (comn by Concord String Quartet); Sonata for Viola and Piano (comn by Brigham Young Univ & Am Viola Soc for William Primrose's 75th Birthday Celebration, Seventh Int Viola Congress); Twelve Bagatelles; Nach Bach Fantasia (harpsichord or piano); Carnival Music; Partita-Variations (piano solo, comn by Etsuko Tazaki through auspices of Washington, DC Performing Arts Soc Bicentennial Series); Songs of Solomon (voice & piano); Three Psalms (mixed chorus, a cappella); Songs in Praise of Krishna.

ROCHEROLLE, EUGENIE RICAU ASCAP 1970
composer, author, pianist
b New Orleans, La, Aug 24, 36. Educ: St Martin's Episcopal High Sch, Metairie, La; Sophie Newcomb Col, Tulane Univ, BA(music), 58; studied with Nadia Boulanger, Paris; pvt band study with Clare Grundman, 70. Professional comp, 65-; widely publ in choral music with original lyrics, also publ in concert band & piano music. *Songs:* Little Train; How Can It Be?; Some Special Place; Baby Boy. *Instrumental Works:* Southern Holiday (concert band); Six Moods for Piano; Montage (piano).

ROCHINSKI, STANLEY J ASCAP 1949
author
b Scranton, Pa, Aug 31, 06. Chief Collabr: Carmen Lombardo. *Songs:* Powder Your Face With Sunshine; Heavenly Honeymoon; Hail to the Legion; My Marine.

ROCK, CHRIS
See Smith, Christopher Alan

ROCK, JOSEPH V ASCAP 1960
composer, author, manager
b Pittsburgh, Pa, May 16, 36. Educ: South Comprehensive High Sch, 52; Schenley Bus Sch, 58. With promotion dept, ABC Paramount Records, nat promotion of Calico Records; record plugger, 57-58. Formed group, Sky Liners, 59, mgr, 59- Songwriter for Otis Redding, The Jaggerz, James Darren, Marcels & others. Co-writer & producer for Calico, Kama-Sutra, Stax, Columbia, Bell, Gateway, RCA & Capitol. Songwriter for motion pictures, "American Graffiti", "American Hot Wax", "Hometown, USA" & "The Line." Chief Collabrs: James Beaumont, Donnie Ierace, Jimmie Ross, Steve Cropper, Rod McBrien. *Songs:* Lyrics: Since I Don't Have You; This I Swear; Lonely Way; It Happened Today; That's My World; (I've Got) Dreams to Remember.

ROCQUEMORE, HENRY ASCAP 1965
composer, author
b Marshal, Tex, Apr 9, 09. Educ: Univ Ariz, BA(music). Record producer; own recording studio, record label & publ co. *Songs & Instrumental Works:* This Can't Be Love; Ball and Chain; Beauty Alone Just Ain't Enough; If This Is Love.

RODBY, WALTER (BRUCE RANDALL, NORMAN ASCAP 1959
RAMSEY)
composer, author, teacher
b Virginia, Minn, Sept 17, 20. Educ: Columbia Univ, MA & prof dipl; London Univ Trinity Col Music; studied perf with Collegiate Chorale, New York & Royal Choral Soc, London. Has been associated with music educ in Ill since 50; mem fac, Joliet Jr Col & Col St Francis; now teaches at DePaul Univ. Cond 4 int concert tours, incl tour of Soviet Union, performing with choral & instrumental groups in some of Europe's greatest cathedrals, auditoriums, radio & TV studios. Choral rev ed, The School Musician Magazine, 25 yrs. Taught choral workshops in 11 States. Chief Collabrs: Jack North, Eugene Butler, Joseph Roff. *Songs:* Song Triumphant; In Praise of Friday; Waltz for Two Left Feet; Goin' Down That Road; Shine on Me; Movin', Rollin'; High Upon the Mountain; Companions All; When Good Men Sing Together; The Blessing of Aaron; Lyrics: A Song for You; Schubert's Horse; Counting Calories; Sol-Fa Calypso. *Songs & Instrumental Works:* Great Choruses for Lent and Easter (choral collection).

RODDE, LEROY WILLIAM ASCAP 1951
composer
b Chicago, Ill, Aug 31, 19. Educ: Brentano Grade Sch; Lane Tech High Sch; Univ Chicago. Discoverer, mgr & record producer, Joni James, 51; discoverer of Johnny Ray; mgt of artists, Aretha Franklin & Trini Lopez. Chief Collabr: Lew Douglas. *Songs:* Lyrics: Why Don't You Believe Me; Purple Shades; Is It Any Wonder.

RODDIE, JOHN W ASCAP 1961
composer, author, publisher
b Poplarville, Miss, Mar 16, 03. Educ: Miss State Col, BS. Reporter, Country Song Roundup Magazine. Vpres & dir, Nat Garment Mfg Co, Hot Springs, Ark; owner, SPA & Caesar Recording Co; pres, Rodie-Miller Music Publ Co. Chief Collabrs: James Monaco, Opal Winstead. *Songs:* All Through the Holidays; Come Get Me Johnny; Love Is Such a Little Word; Last Date; I Walk Alone.

RODEHEAVER, HOMER ASCAP 1941
composer, author, singer
b Union Furnace, Ohio, Oct 4, 1880; d Winona Lake, Ind, Dec 18, 55. Educ: Ohio Wesleyan Univ. Trombonist, 4th Tenn Regimental Band, Span-Am War. Led evangelic community song progs, assoc with Billy Sunday. Founder, summer sch music, Winona Lake. First cond of community sing on radio. Author, "Song Stories of the Sawdust Trail", "Twenty Years with Billy Sunday" & "Singing Black." *Songs:* Somebody Cares; Confidence; Carry On; Good Night and Good Morning; Then Jesus Came; Forgive Me for Forgetting; Prepare Ye the Way of the Lord; O 'Twas in Vain; How It Saves; Pure White Ribbons; He's a Mighty Reality to Me; List to the Bells; We'll Be Waiting When You Come Back; You Must Open the Door.

RODER, MILAN ASCAP 1935
composer, conductor, pianist
b Osijek, Slavonia, Dec 5, 1878; d Los Angeles, Calif, Jan 23, 56. Educ: Vienna Cons (govt scholarship); studied with Hellmesberger, Graedener, Fuchs, Loewe. To US, 14, citizen, 20. Cond, symphonies, operas & operettas throughout Europe. Comp for films, Hollywood. *Songs:* By a Waterfall; In the Afteryears; I Am Proud to Be an American; I Will Sing in the Spring; Sand and Boots; Tonight and Every Night. *Songs & Instrumental Works:* Four Symphonic Sketches; Rondo Capriccioso; Motto Perpetuo; Vindobona (suite); Piano: Lullaby (from Brahms); Vienna Memories (concert waltz); Festival March. *Scores:* Operas: Jelka; Round the World (comic).

RODGERS, JAMES FREDERICK ASCAP 1957
singer, guitarist
b Camas, Wash, 1933. Educ: Studied piano with mother; Clark Col. Served in USAAF, Korean War. Started singing in nightclubs, Vancouver, Wash & Portland, Ore. Starred in 3 films. Did 3 gold albums; wrote "It's Over." Writer; now touring throughout US & world, appearing in major nightclubs. *Songs:* Honeycomb; Kisses Sweeter Than Wine; Oh Oh I'm Falling in Love Again; Bim Bom Bay; Secretly; Are You Really Mine.

RODGERS, JIMMIE ASCAP 1933
composer, author, singer
b Meridian, Miss, Sept 8, 1897; d New York, NY, May 26, 33. Educ: Pub schs. Recorded many of own songs. *Songs:* Blue Yodels; Daddy and Home; Lullaby Yodel; Mississippi Moon; Yodeling Cowboy; Waiting for a Train; Home Call; Never No Mo' Blues; You and My Old Guitar; Why Should I Be Lonely?; Any Old Time; I'm Lonesome Too; In the Jailhouse Now; My Old Pal.

RODGERS, JOHN ASCAP 1961
composer, organist, editor
b Bonham, Tex, Mar 24, 17. Educ: Southern Methodist Univ, BM; NTex State Col, MM; Union Theol Sem, MSM. Organist & choir dir in churches; taught organ & voice in col. Ed in charge of prod, H W Gray Co.

RODGERS, MARTY ASCAP 1979
composer, singer
b Belsen, Ger, Jan 3, 48. Educ: Hamilton High Sch; Los Angeles City Col, 65-67; San Fernando Valley State Col, PhD(nuclear physics), 71. With high sch & col rock bands. Songwriter rock & roll music. Chief Collabr: David Bluefield. *Songs:* Memories.

RODGERS, MARY
See Guettel, Mary Rodgers

RODGERS, RICHARD ASCAP 1926
composer, author, producer
b New York, NY, June 28, 02; d New York, Dec 30, 79. Educ: Columbia Univ; Juilliard Sch; Univ Bridgeport; Univ Md; Hamilton Col; Brandeis Univ; Fairfield Univ; NY Univ; New Eng Cons Music; Philadelphia Col Performing Arts; hon degrees: LLD, Drury Col; DHL, Univ Mass; MusD, Columbia Univ. Dir, ASCAP, 41-47 & 60-74. Writer, Columbia varsity shows. Co-founder, Williamson Music Co, 45. Mem, bd dirs, Philh Symph Soc, bd trustees, Juilliard Sch & Barnard Col. Pres & production dir, Music Theater of Lincoln Ctr, 62-69. Trustee, John F Kennedy Ctr for Performing Arts, DC. Producer, "No Strings," Tony award, 62; co-producer, "I Remember Mama." Mem, Nat Inst of Arts & Letters. Biographies incl "Some Enchanted Evenings" by Deems Taylor, "Richard Rodgers" by David Ewen & "The Rodgers and Hammerstein Story" by Stanley Green; film biography "Words and Music"; autobiography "Musical Stages." Chief Collabrs: Lorenz Hart, Oscar Hammerstein 2nd, Stephen Sondheim, Sheldon Harnick, Martin Charnin. *Songs:* Any Old Place With You; Manhattan; Here In My Arms; The Girl Friend; The Blue Room; Mountain Greenery; A Tree in the Park; A Little Birdie Told Me So; Where's That Rainbow?; My Heart Stood Still; Thou Swell; You Took Advantage of Me; Moon of My Delight; With a Song in My Heart; Why Can't I?; A Ship Without a Sail; Ten Cents a Dance; Dancing on the Ceiling; I've Got Five Dollars; Mimi; Isn't It Romantic?; Lover; You Are Too Beautiful; Blue Moon; Soon; Easy to Remember; How Can You Forget; The Most Beautiful Girl in the World; My Romance; Little Girl Blue; There's a Small Hotel; On Your Toes; Quiet Night; Glad to Be Unhappy; Where or When; I Wish I Were in Love Again; My Funny Valentine; Johnny One Note; The Lady Is a Tramp; Have You Met Miss Jones?; I Married an Angel; I'll Tell the Man in the Street; Spring Is Here; At the Roxy Music Hall; Falling in Love With Love; This Can't Be Love; Sing for Your Supper; Love Never Went to College; I Didn't Know What Time It Was; You're Nearer; It Never Entered My Mind; I Could Write a Book; Bewitched, Bothered and Bewildered; Happy Hunting Horn; Zip; Wait Till You See Her; Everthing I've Got; Careless Rhapsody; Nobody's Heart; To Keep My Love Alive; Oh, What a Beautiful Mornin'; The Surrey With the Fringe on Top; I Cain't Say No; People Will Say We're in Love; Out of My Dreams; Oklahoma; It's a Grand Night for Singing; It Might as Well Be Spring (Acad award, 46); That's for Me; You're a Queer One, Julie Jordan; When I Marry Mr Snow; If I Loved You; June Is Bustin' Out All Over; Soliloquy; You'll Never Walk Alone; What's the Use of Wond'rin'; A Fellow Needs a Girl; Money Isn't Everything; So Far; The Gentleman Is a Dope; You Are Never Away; A Cockeyed Optimist; Some Enchanted Evening; There Is Nothin' Like a Dame; Bali Ha'i; I'm Gonna Wash That Man Right Outa My Hair; A Wonderful Guy; Younger Than Springtime; Happy Talk; This Nearly Was Mine; Honey Bun; Carefully Taught; I Whistle a Happy Tune; Something Wonderful; Hello, Young Lovers; We Kiss in a Shadow; Getting to Know You; Shall We Dance; I Haven't Got a Worry in the World; Marriage-Type Love; No Other Love; I'm Your Girl; All At Once You Love Her; The Next Time It Happens; Everybody's Got a Home But Me; Ten Minutes Ago; Do I Love You Because You're Beautiful?; In My Own Little Corner; A Hundred Million Miracles; You Are Beautiful; I Enjoy Being a Girl; Love, Look Away; The Sound of Music; Do-Re-Mi; My Favorite Things; Climb Ev'ry Mountain; Maria; Edelweiss; Willing and Eager; The Sweetest Sound; No Strings; I Have Confidence in Her; Something Good; Do I Hear a Waltz?; Take the Moment; Someone Like You; I Do Not Know a Day I Did Not Love You; Away From You; You Could Not Please Me More. *Scores:* Bway shows: Poor Little Ritz Girl; The Garrick Gaieties (2 ed); Dearest Enemy; The Girl Friend; PeggyAnn; Betsy; A Connecticut Yankee; Present Arms; Chee-Chee; Spring Is Here; Heads Up!; Simple Simon; America's Sweetheart; Jumbo; I'd Rather Be Right; The Boys From Syracuse (Obie award, 62); Too Many Girls; Higher and Higher; Pal Joey (New York Drama Critics award, 52); Oklahoma! (Pulitzer prize, 44); Carousel (New York Drama Critics award, 46); Allegro; On Your Toes (co-librettist); Babes in Arms; I Married an Angel; By Jupiter (co-librettist, co-producer); South Pacific (co-producer, Pulitzer prize, New York Drama Critics award, Tony award, 50); The King and I (Tony award, 52); Me and Juliet; Pipe Dream; Flower Drum Song; The Sound of Music (Tony award, 60); Do I Hear a Waltz?; Two By Two; Rex; I Remember Mama; London stage scores: Lido Lady; One Dam Thing After Another; Ever Green; Annie Get Your Gun; Happy Birthday; John Loves Mary; The Happy Time; Films: Love Me Tonight; Hallelujah, I'm a Bum; Mississippi; State Fair; TV: Cinderella; Androcles and the Lion; Victory At Sea (USN Distinguished Publ Service award, Emmy award, 53); Winston Churchill—The Valiant Years (Emmy award, 62).

RODNEY, DON
See Ragonese, Don

RODNEY, JOSEPH B ASCAP 1972
composer, teacher
b Feb 14, 17. Educ: Studied comp & arr with William Owens, Paris, France, also Tony Galino, Buffalo, NY & Joseph Sulkowski. Played in Army Bands, Top Hatters Orch, radio & TV. Chief Collabrs: Brad Swanson, Kathryn M Rogers. *Songs:* Music: White Sands of Hawaii; Ragtime 74; Country Girl; Love Me, Kiss Me, Hold Me Tight; Love Is the Thing You Do to Me; Con Man Rag; Cats Meow Rag.

RODOMISTA, VINCENT (VIN RODDIE) ASCAP 1950
composer, author, pianist
b Far Rockaway, NY, June 10, 18. Educ: High sch & drama sch; pvt music studies. Actor summer stock; pianist orchs, US & Can. Featured pianist in night clubs, hotels, radio, TV & Brazil & Arg cruise ships. Chief Collabrs: Mitchell Parish, Sammy Gallop, O O Merritt, Don Canton, Kay Twomey, Ray Rivera. *Songs:* My Heart Is Out of Town; Bon Voyage; That's Why I Was Born; Show Me a Man; Who Kicked the Light Plug (Out of the Socket); Christmas Rings a Bell; Strange Mood; What Kind of Woman?; Buster the Butterfly; Kitty the Kangaroo; Flying Fingers; Cuchy Frito Man; The Lucky Silver Coin; Happiness; Happy Hour; Ocean Serenade.

RODRIGUEZ, ROBERT XAVIER ASCAP 1975
composer
b San Antonio, Tex, June 28, 46. Educ: Univ Tex, Austin, BM, 67, MM, 69; Univ Southern Calif, DMA, 75; pvt study with Hunter Johnson, Halsey Stevens, Jacob Druckman & Nadia Boulanger; master classes with Bruno Maderna & Elliott Carter. Instr, Univ Southern Calif, 73-75. Rec'd comns from Neville Marriner, Antal Dorati & Eduardo Mata. Awards: Guggenheim Fellowship, Nat Endowment for the Arts Bicentennial Grant, Am Acad & Inst Arts & Letters, Lieberson Fellowship, Prince Pierre De Monaco Prize, Prix Lili Boulanger, McHugh Award. Seven works recorded on Crystal & Orion Labels. Assoc prof, head theory-comp progs & dir, Collegium Musicum, Univ Tex, Dallas. Cond, Dallas Chamber Opera Soc. Chief Collabr: Daniel Dibbern. *Instrumental Works:* Favola Boccaccesca (large orch); Sinfonia Concertante (saxophone, harpsichord, chamber orch). *Songs & Instrumental Works:* Canto (soprano, tenor, chamber orch). *Scores:* Favola Concertante (violin/VC, string orch); Opera: Le Diable Amoureux (one-act).

ROE, GLORIA KLIEWER ASCAP 1960
composer, author, singer
b Pasadena, Calif, Jan 5, 40. Educ: El Monte High Sch; Pasadena Col; piano prodigy of Francis Zulawinski. Vocal student of the Sweetlands. Bank of Am Fine Arts Award; NEFF Song of the Year. Dean, Performing Arts Ctr, Bakersfield, Calif, 80- Chief Collabr: Keith Miller. *Songs:* I Hear A New Song; May We Know Peace; Abiding Love; I'm Coming Home; There's Something Special; Does it Make Any Difference?; Unworthy; Surrender; I'm Beginning to Understand; See the Light; He is Coming; To Know Him; Safe in His Hands; Be Calm, My Soul; Music: Joseph Loves Mary; Mary's Song; Joe; Why Can't I Say I'm Sorry?; Why?. *Instrumental Works:* I Am the Way; Keyboard Favorites (Vols 1-6).

ROEMHELD, HEINZ ASCAP 1948
composer, pianist, conductor
b Milwaukee, Wis, May 1, 01. Educ: Wis Col Music, BM; studied with Hugo Kaun, Breithaupt & Egon Petri. Debut as pianist, Berlin Philh, 22; comp & music dir for films, 23-26, Washington, DC, 27-28 & Berlin, 28-45. Chief film, theatre & music section, Inf Control Div, US Forces in Europe, 45. Chief Collabr: Mitchell Parish. *Songs:* Ruby. *Scores:* Film: Strawberry Blonde; Yankee Doodle Dandy (Academy Award, 42); Background: Ruby Gentry; Valentino; The Moonlighter.

ROES, CAROL LASATER (MELE LOKE) ASCAP 1963
composer, author
b Oklahoma City, Okla. Educ: Oberlin Cons Music; Stanford Univ, majored in publ speaking. Songwriter, Eng & Hawaiian songs & spirituals, 55-; started Mele Loke Publ Co, 61; conducts workshops at cols & dance studios, 65- *Songs:* Mahalo Nui (Thank You Very Much); E Kuu Lei (To You My Love); Maui Aloha (Love to Maui); The Counting Song (Kaui, Kaui Pele); Aloha Kakahiaka Means Good Morning.

ROESER, DONALD (BUCK DHARMA) ASCAP 1972
composer, author
b New York, NY, Nov 12, 47. Educ: Smithtown Cent High Sch; Clarkson Col Technol. Lead guitarist, singer, founding mem, CBS, recording artist, Blue Oyster Cult. Chief Collabrs: Sandy Pearlman, Richard Meltzer, Albert Bouchard, Bruce Abbott, Sandra Roeser. *Songs:* Don't Fear the Reaper; Godzilla; I Love the Night; Then Came the Last Days of May; Divine Wind; Deadline; Cold Wind; Music: ETI (Extra Terrestial Intelligence); The Vigil; Mirrors; Cities on Flame With Rock and Roll; Before the Kiss (A Redcap); Harvester of Eyes; Teen Archer.

ROETER, ADA (ADA RUBIN)　　　　　　ASCAP 1964
composer
b New York, NY, July 1, 06. Educ: Carnegie Town Hall, studied with Prof Dahl; studied classical music. Concert pianist, Carnegie Music Hall & Brooklyn Acad of Music. Became jazz performer, 25; in radio for several yrs. Jazz recording artist. Chief Collabrs: Andy Razof, Joe Davis. *Songs:* Music: The Meetin's Called to Order; Fair and Square; Alexander's Back In Town.

ROFF, JOSEPH　　　　　　ASCAP 1975
composer, teacher
b Torino, Italy, Dec 26, 10. Educ: Trinity Col, London, fel organ; Univ Toronto, MusD & MA; studied with Healy Willan. Part-time lectr music, St Joseph Col, Brooklyn, NY; free-lance comp; some anthems performed by Mormon Tabernacle Choir. *Instrumental Works:* Niagara (orch tone poem). *Scores:* Lady of Mexico (off Bway show).

ROGAN, JAMES EDWARD　　　　　　ASCAP 1948
composer, author, violinist
b Perth Amboy, NJ, Oct 28, 08. Educ: Szabo Cons Music, New York, harmony, counterpoint, theory & violin; cello with Sidney Herbert. Musician in radio, film, vaudeville, musical comedy, clubs & others. In musical comedy with Busby Berkeley. Cellist in symph. Chief Collabrs: Emery Deutsch, Dick Smith. *Songs:* When a Gypsy Makes His Violin Cry; Stardust on the Moon; You Started Something; Moonlight Mood; Stars and Soft Guitars; Song of the Cricket.

ROGERS, ANN
See Johnson, Ann M

ROGERS, BERNARD　　　　　　ASCAP 1945
composer, educator
b New York, NY, Feb 4, 1893; d Rochester, NY, May 24, 68. Educ: Inst of Musical Art; studied with Bloch, Goetschius, Bridge & Boulanger. Grants: Pulitzer, Guggenheim & Fulbright Res Grant. Awards: Loeb Prize, Seligman Prize, David Bispham Medal for Opera, Edith Fairchild Award, Mu Phi Epsilon Award of Merit & Philadelphia Music Fund Soc Prize. Hon MusD, Valparaiso Univ & HumD, Wayne State Univ. On staff, Musical America, 11 yrs. Mem, Nat Inst Arts & Letters. Comns: Ford Found; String Soc Cleveland; Columbus Symph; Jewish Folk Choir of Toronto; League of Comp; Am Wind Symph & Louisville Symph. On Fac, Eastman Sch Music, 29-67. Author, "The Art of Orchestration." Chief Collabrs: Charles Rodda & Norman Corwin. *Songs & Instrumental Works:* To the Fallen; The Faithful; 3 Japanese Dances; 2 American Frescoes; The Song of the Nightingale; The Supper at Emmaus; 5 Fairy Tales (Juilliard Publ Award); The Dance of Salome; Soliloquy for Flute, Strings; Hear My Prayer (Temple Emanu-El, NY Comn); Soliloquy for Bassoon, Strings; The Colors of War (ballet); String Quartet; Amphitryon Overture (Juilliard Comn); Leaves From the Tale of Pinocchio; Variations on a Song by Mussorgsky; Dance Scenes; Portrait for Violin, Orchestra; The Passion; The Prophet Isaiah; The Raising of Lazarus; A Letter From Pete; Exodus; Sonata for Violin and Piano (String Soc Cleveland Comn); Light of Man (oratorio); The Colors of Youth; Romance in D Major; Mood; Bells; Five Norwegian Folk Songs; Pastorale (11 instruments); Buona Notte; Psalm 68; Fantasia (horn, timpani & strings); The Musicians of Bremen; Pastorale Mistico; 5 symphonies. *Scores:* Operas: The Marriage of Aude (David Bispham Medal); The Warrior (Ditson Award); The Nightingale; The Veil.

ROGERS, DICK　　　　　　ASCAP 1941
composer, author, conductor
b New York, NY, Sept 23, 12; d New York, Sept 13, 70. Educ: Fordham Prep. Vaudeville entertainer, US & Eng, 28-33. Pianist, Will Osborne Orch, 33-35, leader, 40-45, Jack Hylton Orch, 35-38; toured Europe. Writer of special material for Joe E Lewis, Sophie Tucker, Jerry Lewis, Ted Lewis, Buddy Lester, Betty & Jan Kean. Chief Collabrs: Will Osborne, Hughie Prince. *Songs:* Between 18th and 19th on Chestnut Street; Wouldst Could I But Kiss Thy Hand, Oh Babe; Dry Bones; Pompton Turnpike; Harlem Nocturne; I Guess I'll Get the Papers and Go Home; Spaghetti Rag; Come Back to Sorrento.

ROGERS, EDDY
See Ruggieri, Edmond

ROGERS, FRANCES OCTAVIA (DALE EVANS)　　　　　　ASCAP 1952
composer, author, singer-actress
b Uvalde, Tex, Oct 31, 12. Educ: High sch & bus sch. Singer on radio, CBS Chicago, WFAA Dallas & WHAS Louisville; big band singer, 20th Century Fox, Chase & Sanborn Hour, Jimmy Durante & Jack Carson Radio Shows, Roy Rogers Pictures & Roy Rogers/Dale Evans TV Series. Author 17 bks; featured on variety TV, Christian TV progs & concerts. Chief Collabrs: Frank S Mead, Fleming H Revell, Carale Carlson. *Songs:* Will You Marry Me, Mr Laramie?; Aha, San Antone; Down the Trail to San Antone; Lo Dee Lo Di; T for Texas; Happy Trails; I'm Gonna Lock You Out-a My Heart; Buckeye Cowboy; The Bible Tells Me So; No Bed of Roses.

ROGERS, FRED (MISTER ROGERS)　　　　　　ASCAP 1955
composer, author, producer
b Latrobe, Pa, Mar 20, 28. Educ: Rollins Col, BM; Pittsburgh Theol Sem, BD. Created & produced TV series, "Children's Corner", WQED, NET & NBC network, "Misterogers", CBC network, "Mister Rogers' Neighborhood" & "Old Friends...New Friends", PBS. Ordained United Presby clergyman. Chief Collabr: Josie Carey. *Songs:* Goodnight, God; Won't You Be My Neighbor?; It's Such a Good Feeling; Many Ways to Say I Love You; It's You I Like; You Are Special; Everybody's Fancy; What Do You Do?; Sometimes People Are Good; The Truth Will Make Me Free; Wishes Don't Make Things Come True. *Scores:* Opera/Ballet: Potato Bugs and Cows; Key to Other Land; All in the Laundry; Snow People and the Warm Pussycat; Windstorm in Bubbleland.

ROGERS, HARLAN DALE
composer, musician, arranger
b Oklahoma City, Okla, Sept 17, 43. Educ: Midwest City High Sch; N Tex State Univ, 2 yrs; studied music theory & var music courses. Had early piano training at age 5; played trombone throughout sch yrs; switched to piano & keyboard instruments. Played in nightclubs, 8 yrs; involved in Christian music, 71-Producer, singer & publ. *Songs:* Let Me Have a Dream; Father Me.

ROGERS, JAMES HOTCHKISS　　　　　　ASCAP 1924
composer, organist, author
b Fair Haven, Conn, Feb 7, 1857; d Pasadena, Calif, Nov 28, 40. Educ: Lake Forest Acad; studied music with Clarence Eddy, Guilmant, Widor, Loeschhorn, Ehrlich & Fissot. Organist & music dir, Euclid Ave Temple, Euclid Ave Baptist Church & Unitarian Church, Cleveland, 25 yrs. Own publ firm, 19 yrs. Music ed, Cleveland News & Cleveland Plain Dealer, 15-32. *Songs & Instrumental Works:* Five Quatrains (song cycle, Rubaiyat of Omar Khayyam); In Memoriam; The Man of Nazareth (cantata); Suite for Organ; Concert Overture; The 5th Temple Service; 5 piano sonatas; The Star; At Parting; The Last Song; Autumn; Anthems: Seek Him That Maketh the Seven Stars and Orion; Great Peace Have They; Beloved, If God So Loved Us.

ROGERS, KENNETH
See DeVito, Albert Kenneth

ROGERS, KENNETH RAY
entertainer
b Houston, Tex. Educ: Univ Houston, studied music & commercial art. Appeared on Am Bandstand. Mem, Bobby Doyle Trio, then Christy Minstrels, 66-67, The First Edition, 67-76; performed numerous concerts in US, Can, Eng, Scotland & New Zealand. Starred in own syndicated TV series, "Rollin'"; has made appearances on "Tonight Show." Recording artist with United Artists Records, 76-; has made numerous records. Named Cross-over Artist of Yr, Billboard Mag, 77, Top Male Vocalist. Awards: Country Music Asn Awards, 78-79; Grammy Award, 77; Brit Country Music Asn Award; Acad Country Music Award. *Albums:* Kenny Rogers; Love Lifted Me; The Gambler; Ten Years of Gold; Kenny.

ROGERS, LARRY THOMAS　　　　　　ASCAP 1975
composer
b Corinth, Miss. Educ: Univ Miss, BM. Road musician; studio engineer; record producer. *Songs:* Take Me Back; Let's Put Our Love in Motion; Women Get Lonely.

ROGERS, LEE
See Wilson, Roger Cole

ROGERS, MILT
See Adelstein, Milton

ROGERS, MILTON
composer, author, conductor
b New York, NY, Aug 12, 14. Educ: Manhattan Sch Music, BMus(comp), MA(music educ); Columbia Univ. Comp of songs, orchestral works, opera & chamber music; cond of musicals; col level teacher. Chief Collabrs: Marion Abeson, Jimi Hendrix. *Songs:* Music: Monkey and the Elephant. *Instrumental Works:* Prairie; 10 Minutes of Music. *Songs & Instrumental Works:* Psalm (choral). *Scores:* Opera/Ballet: Young Goodman Brown.

ROGERS, MILTON (SHORTY)　　　　　　ASCAP 1955
composer, author, conductor
b Lee, Mass, Apr 14, 24. Educ: Los Angeles Cons; studied with Wesley LaViolette. With 379th ASF Band, US Army, WW II. Trumpeter, comp & arr for dance bands incl Woody Herman & Charlie Barnet. Formed own band, Hollywood, 54. Writer for TV shows, also scores for UPA cartoons, film. Made many records. *Songs & Instrumental Works:* Cerveza; Jolly Rogers; Steps; Nero's Conception; Kean and Peachy; Wake Up and Shout; Freedom's Coming; Samba do Lorinho; Sugar Loaf; So Voce; Be As Children; Jazz Waltz; Terence's Farewell; The Sweetheart of Sigmund Freud; That's Right. *Scores:* Film/TV: Young Dillinger; Occasional Wife; Mr Deeds Goes to Town; The Partridge Family; The Interns; Gidget Grows Up; The Paul Lynde Show; Temperatures Rising; I Spy; Mod Squad; Gunfight At Abilene; Breakout; The Tiger Makes Out; Fools; The Rookies; Starsky and Hutch; The Love Boat; Vegas.

ROGERS, ROY
See Slye, Leonard

ROGERS, SHARON ELERY   ASCAP 1965
composer, organist, vocalist
b Grosse Pointe, Mich, Mar 4, 29. Educ: Detroit Cons Music; Hillsdale Col,
BA(mus); Wayne State Univ, MM. Began composing and arr as a youngster.
Wrote music for choirs & organ. Dir music for var churches in Mich. Appeared
as solo guest organist in recitals & cond multiple choirs in fest progs. Served as
paid vocalist on radio sta, Detroit, wrote & arr music for progs. Workshop dir
for many musical orgns. Music critic. *Songs:* Born in a Manger; A Chant of
Glory and Praise; Hear the Sound of the Shepherds Piping; That Babe of
Bethlehem; My Lord Was Crucified; O My Dearest Jesus; Now Let Us Sing;
Music: O Brother Man; O Come and Mourn With Me; Liturgical Responses and
Anthems for Special Occasions; New Testament Songs; Come As a Child.
Instrumental Works: Four Keyboard Settings of Folk Tunes; Noel Fantasies;
Contemporary Organ Settings on Familiar Hymns; Festal Hymn Variations for
the Church Year; An Organ Festival of Postludes and Preludes; Solera Toccata.

ROGERS, TIMOTHY LOUIS AIVERUM   ASCAP 1959
composer, author, singer
b Detroit, Mich, July 4, 15. Had own band, 54. Toured in vaudeville &
nightclubs, US & Europe; comedian. *Songs:* If You Can't Smile and Say Yes;
Back to School Again; Fla-ga-la-pa.

ROGERS, WAYNE
See Bacon, W Garwood, Jr

ROHE, ROBERT KENNETH   ASCAP 1959
composer, contrabassist, teacher
b New York, NY, Aug 22, 16. Educ: Peter Cooper Sch Fine Arts, New York,
grad & Highest Award, 39; Nat Orch Asn under Leon Barzin, grad & cert, 42;
studied contrabass with Fred Zimmermann of NY Philh. Played contrabass with
Am Symph under Leopold Stokowski, 44; principal contrabass, New Orleans
Symph, 44- Performed with NBC Symph, New York, under Arturo Toscanini
& Fritz Reiner. ASCAP Comp Awards, 60-; comn, Edward Benjamin Tranquil
Music for "Mainescape," 66. *Songs & Instrumental Works:* Mainescape
(symph); Land of Bottle (fantasy for young audiences, small symph, narrator &
4 soloists blowing on bottles); House in the Bend of Bourbon Street (symph,
narrator, 4 voices, electronic tape); Yerma (symph tone poem); Progam of Eight
Christmas Carols (4 string basses); Trio for Violin, Harp, Contrabass.

ROLFE, WALTER   ASCAP 1931
composer, author, teacher
b Rumford Corners, Maine, Dec 18, 1880; d Brighton, Mass, Jan 18, 44. Educ:
Von Ende Sch Music; also pvt music study. Taught music. Ed, Century Music
Co. *Songs & Instrumental Works:* Kiss of Spring; Cadets on Parade; In an
Old-Fashioned Garden; A Jolly Little Band; The Little Shepherd; Musing.

ROLLIN, ROBERT LEON   ASCAP 1972
composer, conductor, pianist
b Brooklyn, NY, Feb 16, 47. Educ: Juilliard Sch Music, comp & theory, 62-64;
City Col New York, BA, 68, mem, Phi Beta Kappa; Cornell Univ, MFA, 71,
DMA, 73; full scholarships to Bennington Comp Conference, 69 & 71; studied
comp with Mark Brunswick, Karel Husa & Robert Palmer; study in comp with
Elliot Carter, Gyorgy Ligeti, Mario Davidovsky & Donald Erb. Teaching fel,
Cornell Univ; comp fel, Darmstadt Music Fest, Ger; chmn, Midwest Region,
Am Soc Univ Comp. Currently, asst prof music, Dana Sch Music, Youngstown
State Univ. Comp publ by Galaxy Music Corp, Seesaw Music Corp & Media
Press; recorded by Redwood Records & Cornell Univ Records. Author articles,
Musical Quarterly, Proceedings of Am Soc Univ Comp & other jour. Grants:
WGer Govt; NEA; Am Music Ctr; Lilly Endowment; Cornell Univ;
Youngstown State Univ. *Songs & Instrumental Works:* Seven Sound-Images on
Seven Stanzas By a Child (piano, orch); Two Pieces for Solo Flute; Suite for
Woodwind Quintet; Aquarelles for Wind Ensemble; Reflections on Ruin By the
Sea for Trumpet and Piano; For Six in Darmstadt (flute, clarinet, violin, cello,
piano, perc); Thematic Transformation for String Quartet; Concerto for
Woodwind Quintet and Orchestra; Antiphon-Fare for Organ, Antiphonal Brass
and Wind Ensemble; Two Jazz Moods for Alto Sax and Piano; Introduction and
Canon for Two Clarinets; Prelude and Dance for Five (flute, trumpet, French
horn, trombone, contrabass); Sonata for Cello and Piano; Wandrers Nachtlied
(setting of poem by Goethe for mixed chorus, mandolin, flute, Eng horn,
bassoon, piano); Movement in Rupak Tal for Two Violins; Night-Thoughts II
for Solo Piano; Two Studies for Piano; Four Songs of Dreams and Love (settings
of poems by Yeats, mezzo-soprano, baritone & chamber ensemble); The Only
Jealousy of Emer (incidental music to play by Yeats); Fanfare Antiphony (four
low brass, perc); Etude for Solo Guitar; Recollections for Clarinet and Piano;
Gloria Nova (setting of Hopkins' Pied Beauty for chorus a cappella);
Composition for Two Pianos; Canon-Cantabile for Four or More Recorders in
F; Among the Keys for Tuba and Piano.

ROLLINS, GLENN
See Olson, Robert G

ROLLINS, LANIER (JETTE EDWARD)   ASCAP 1967
composer, author, singer
b New Orleans, La, Mar 12, 37. Educ: Chicago Cons Music, 4 yrs; Chicago
Teachers Col, 1 yr; Am Nat Theatre & Acad Performing Arts, 1 1/2 yrs;
Writer's Guild of Am-W, Trade Tech Col, 2 yrs; studied with Richard Loring.
Began radio broadcasting at age 5; radio broadcaster, 16 yrs. Prof gospel singer.
Publ, novel "The Human Race Is a Gang." Dancer, actor & singer for theatre
& arts. Record producer; organized own co, Jette Edward Rollins Enterprise &
BFN Records, Hollywood. Chief Collabrs: Myles Grayson, Renee Hall, Richard
Loring, Earl Smith. *Songs:* Mister Computer; I'm Crying Over You; Return to
Nature; Love to Love; One Love I'm Grateful.

ROLLINS, WALTER E (JACK)   ASCAP 1958
author
b Scottdale, Pa, Sept 15, 06; d Cincinnati, Ohio, Jan 1, 73. Educ: Pub schs. Chief
Collabrs: Steve Nelson, Don Robertson. *Songs:* Peter Cottontail; Frosty the
Snowman; I Don't Hurt Anymore; With This Ring I Thee Wed; Does He Mean
That Much to You; Smokey the Bear; Heart of a Clown; Queen of Draw Poker
Town; The Christmas Cannon Ball; Candyland Parade; Rubber Knuckle Sam.

ROMA, VINNY
See Tozzo, Vincent J

ROMANO, NICK   ASCAP 1960
composer
b Fresno, Calif, May 21, 22. Educ: High sch. Chief Collabrs: Johnny Bradford,
Bonnie Lake, Barbara Hayden. *Songs:* Love Comes Along.

ROMANO, RALPH   ASCAP 1960
composer, author, saxophonist
b Philadelphia, Pa, Apr 29, 28. Educ: Col. Saxophonist in small groups & bands.
USA, Special Serv. Has been realtor; partner in 2 record cos. *Songs:* Learnin';
This Is What I Ask; Streets of Venice; Love Is; The Day That Rock and Roll
Dies; Lucky Coin; Fool Was I.

ROMANO, THOMAS MATTHEW   ASCAP 1963
author
b Brooklyn, NY, June 29, 29. Educ: Univ Ark; Yale Univ. Newsman, ed &
announcer, WABC-radio & TV. Writer, songs for off-Bway show "Sketchbook,"
60 & original nightclub material. Chief Collabrs: Ruth Cleary Patterson, Johnny
Andrews, Mickey Alpert. *Songs:* Lyrics: Serendipity; May in Manhattan; One
Fine Day; Ya' Gotta.

ROMANO, TONY   ASCAP 1952
composer, author, teacher
b Fresno, Calif, Sept 26, 15. Educ: Pvt study violin with Henry Daulton at age
9; George M Smith Scholarship, guitar, age 16. Featured singer with Al Pearce,
32-39. Started comp, 33. Vocal arr, Warner Brothers, 39-41. Guitarist, 20th
Century Fox. Traveled with Bob Hope. Appeared with Johnny Carson, Mike
Douglas & Dinah Shore. Chief Collabrs: Morey Amsterdam, John Bradford,
Paul Frees. *Songs:* My Kind of Music; Christmas in San Francisco; Life Has
Been Good to Me; I Said Hello to a Stranger; The Likes of Two People in Love;
Too Soon to Laugh, Too Late to Cry; Music: Plain Old Me; A Girl; You're
Priceless. *Scores:* Film/TV: Robers Roost.

ROMBERG, SIGMUND   ASCAP 1917
composer, conductor
b Nagy Kaniza, Hungary, July 29, 1887; d New York, NY, Nov 9, 51. Educ:
Polytechnische Hochschule (eng); studied music with Joseph Heuberger,
Vienna. Served in Hungarian army, 07-08. To US, 09, citizen, 12. Cafe pianist,
New York. Cond, own orch, Bustanoby's Restaurant, New York, 12-13. Staff
comp, Shubert Brothers, 13-19 & 21-24. Cond, own orch, toured US, 42-43.
Biography, "Deep in My Heart" by Elliott Arnold; film biography, "Deep in My
Heart." Chief Collabrs: Harold Atteridge, M E Rourke, Rida Johnson Young,
Dorothy Donnelly, Otto Harbach, Oscar Hammerstein 2nd, Dorothy Fields,
Gus Kahn, Leo Robin. *Songs:* Leg of Mutton; Omar Khayyam; Auf Wiedersehn;
Fascination; The Road to Paradise; Will You Remember?; My Springtime Thou
Art; Serenade; Song of Love; Deep in My Heart, Dear; Golden Days; Just We
Two; Drinking Song; Students Marching Song; One Alone; Riff Song; Romance;
The Desert Song; When Hearts Are Young; It; One Flower Grows Alone in
Your Garden; French Military Marching Song; Silver Moon; Your Land and
My Land; Boys in Gray; Lover, Come Back to Me; Softly, As in a Morning
Sunrise; Stouthearted Men; One Kiss; Wanting You; I Bring a Love Song; You
Will Remember Vienna; When I Grow Too Old to Dream; The Night Is Young;
Who Are We to Say?; Somebody Ought to Be Told; Just Once Around the
Clock; I Built a Dream One Day; Close As Pages in a Book; The Big Back Yard;
When You Walk in the Room; April Snow; Lost in Loveliness; in Paris and in
Love; Faithfully Yours; Chinese Lullabye; Zing, Zing, Zoom Zoom. *Scores:*
Bway shows: The Whirl of the World; The Midnight Girl; The Passing Show (7
ed); Dancing Around; Maid in America; Hands Up; The Blue Paradise; A World
of Pleasure; Robinson Crusoe, Jr; Ruggles of Red Gap; The Show of Wonders;
The Girl From Brazil; Her Soldier Boy; Maytime; Doing Our Bit; Over the Top;
Follow Me; Sinbad; My Lady's Glove; The Melting of Molly; Monte Cristo, Jr;
The Magic Melody; Poor Little Ritz Girl; Love Birds; Blossom Time; Bombo;
The Blushing Bride; The Rose of Stamboul; Follow the Girl; The Lady in

Ermine; The Dancing Girl; Caroline; Innocent Eyes; Artists and Models of 1924; Annie Dear; The Student Prince in Heidelberg; Louis the XIV; Princess Flavia; The Desert Song; My Maryland; The Indian Love Call; Rosalie; The New Moon; Nina Rosa; Melody; May Wine; Up in Central Park; My Romance; The Girl in Pink Tights; Films: Viennese Nights; Children of Dreams; The Night Is Young; The Girl of the Golden West; They Gave Him a Gun; Springtime of Youth.

ROME, HAROLD JACOB   ASCAP 1938
composer, author

b Hartford, Conn, May 27, 08. Educ: Trinity Col, Hartford, 24-26; Yale Univ, BA, 29; Yale Univ Law Sch, 29-30, Sch Architecture, BFA, 34; studied comp with Reuven Kosakoff, Tom Timoth & Joseph Schillinger. Wrote music & lyrics for revues incl "Pins and Needles," 37, "Sing Out the News," 38, "Call Me Mister," 46, "Pretty Penny," 48, "Bless You All," 50, also for musicals incl "Wish You Were Here," 52, "Fanny," 54, "Destry Rides Again," 59, "I Can Get It for You Wholesale," 62, "The Zulu and the Zayda," 65, "Scarlett," Tokyo, 70, "Gone With the Wind," London, 72, Los Angeles, 73 & Dallas, 75. Contributed songs to "Star and Garter," 40, "Streets of Paris," 41, "Ziegfeld Follies," 43 & "Peep Show," 50. Served in USA, 43-45. *Songs:* Lyrics: All of a Sudden My Heart Sings; Enlloro; On the Avenue; On Guard; Whisper a Word of Love; United Nations on the March; Dancing With You; Giddy Ap; Goodbye Darling, Hello Friend; Gigolette; Ask Me. *Scores:* Bway Shows: Sunday in the Park; Sing Me a Song With Social Significance; Mene Mene Tekel; When I Grow Up; It's Better With a Union Man; Franklin D Roosevelt Jones; Along With Me; When We Meet Again; The Face on the Dime; South American Take It Away; Take Off the Coat; You Never Know What Hit You When It's Love; Wish You Were Here; Where Did the Night Go; Shopping Around; Fanny; Welcome Home; I Have To; Restless Heart; I Say Hello; Fair Warning; The Money Song; Miss Marmelstein; The Sound of Money; Like the Wind Blows.

ROME, J GUS
See Southard, Mary Ann

ROMEO, JAMES JOSEPH   ASCAP 1978
composer, pianist, conductor

b Rochester, NY, Mar 5, 55. Educ: Mich State Univ, BM(comp), 77, MM(theory), 78; Bowling Green State Univ, MM(music history), 79; Harvard Univ, currently working on PhD in comp; studied with H Owen Reed, Jere T Hutcheson & Leon Kirchner. Dir, New Musical Arts Ensemble, Mich State Univ, 78; rec'd Helene Wurlitzer Found Grant to comp ballet on Am Indian folklore, 79; music dir, Boston Theatre Group, 80; comp numerous concert pieces & music for plays, films & other media; author articles on music, Harvard Inquiry, 80. Chief Collabr: Carol J Pierman. *Instrumental Works:* The Fall: 1831; Fanfare of the Tall Ships: 1980. *Scores:* Opera/Ballet: The Naturalized Citizen; The Gilgamesh Epic; Film/TV: One Brief Moment; Toby; The Iran Film Project.

ROMERO, CELEDONIO P   ASCAP 1978
b Malaga, Spain, Apr 2, 18. Educ: Royal Cons Malaga, Madrid; studied with Joaquin Turina, Angel Barrios, Rivera Pons. Debut, age 10, Lope de Vega Theatre, Seville, Spain; in concert throughout Spain, France & Italy. Immigrated to US, 57. Founder, The Romeros, classical guitar quartet, with sons Celin, Pepe & Angel; tour US cities, appearances with major symph orchs, European concert tours, 70- & 2 White House performances; recording artist. Chief Collabrs: Celin, Pepe & Angel Romero (sons). *Instrumental Works:* Concierto de Malaga for Guitar and Orchestra; Suite Andaluza (Soleares, Alegrias, Tango, Zapateado, Fantasia) for Guitar; Zapateado and Guajiras for Guitar; Tango Angela for Piano; Three Preludes (Granadina, Gaditano, Cartajenero); Fandango for Guitar; Malaguenas for Guitar; Plegaria and Alleluia for Guitar; Dos Canciones de Cuna for Guitar; Dos Valses for Guitar; Dos Sonatas Scarlattas for Guitar; Homenaje a Sors for Guitar; Six Canciones Andaluzas for Guitar; Zapateado Clasico for Guitar; Fota Clasica for Guitar; 22 preludes for guitar; Six Studies for Guitar.

ROMERO, GARY
See Catsos, Nicholas A

ROMOFF, COLIN   ASCAP 1957
composer, conductor, pianist

b New York, NY, Oct 15, 24. Educ: Mannes Sch of Music. Cond, pianist & arr for Bway musicals & TV. *Songs:* Sing Another Song; Something Makes Me Want to Dance With You.

RONELL, ANN   ASCAP 1932
composer, author, conductor

b Omaha, Nebr. Educ: Radcliffe Col. Taught music, coached singers, rehearsal pianist for Bway musicals. First woman to compose, conduct for films. Song writer for films incl "The Three Little Pigs", "Champagne Waltz", "Algiers", "Commandos Strike at Dawn", "The Story of GI Joe", "Love Happy" & "Main Street to Broadway"; comp, cond, "Meeting at a Far Meridian" (first US-USSR feature film under US State Dept Cultural Exchange Prog), Russia, 64; mem, Nat Adv Bd, Interlochen Arts Acad. *Songs:* Who's Afraid of the Big Bad Wolf?; Baby's Birthday Party; Rain on the Roof; Willow Weep for Me; The Woman Behind the Man Behind the Gun; In a Silly Symphony; On the Merry-Go-Round; C'est la Vie; Linda, My Love; Ernie Pyle Infantry March;

Take Me, Take Me to the Moon; Across the Everglades; Don't Look Now But My Heart Is Showing. *Songs & Instrumental Works:* Ship South (Nat Orch Asn comn). *Scores:* Opera: Oh! Susanna (folk); Librettos: Martha; The Gypsy Baron (both Metrop Opera comns); Ballet: Magic of Spring.

RONKA, ILMARI   ASCAP 1963
composer

b Ely, Minn, May 14, 05. Educ: Kans State Teachers Col, cert; Inst Musical Art, New York, cert; studied cond with Pierre Monteux. First trombonist, New York Symph, Cleveland Orch, Cincinnati Symph, Hollywood Bowl Symph, Am Ballet Theatre, London Ballet, New York Ballet, first trombonist & asst cond, Ballet Russe de Monte Carlo. Cond & played in major motion picture studio orchs, Los Angeles. Fac, Los Angeles Cons Music, Westlake Cons, Los Angeles & Chouniard Sch Music, Los Angeles. Founder-cond, San Fernando Valley Symph Orch, Los Angeles; guest cond, Hollywood Bowl, Finnish Broadcasting Co Orch, Helsinki & Finland; cond, Mutual Radio network symph prog. *Instrumental Works:* Method Books: Daily Lip Drills and Studies (trombone); Trumpet Beginning Correctly Method; Modern Daily Warm-Ups and Drills (trombone, euphonium, tuba); Solos for Trumpet/Trombone: Fantasette; Polkette; Transc for Accordion: Finnish Airs.

ROOBENIAN, AMBER (AMBER R HARRINGTON,   ASCAP 1943
JANE MURDOCK)
composer, organist, pianist

b Boston, Mass, May 13, 05. Educ: Eastman Sch Music, majored in concert organ; New Eng Cons Music, organ study with Dunham. Served as organist in principal Armenian church, Boston; played improvised background for silent movies in Brooklyn Theatre. Chief Collabrs: W Clark Harrington (husband), Lily Anderson Strickland, Irwin Rowan. *Songs:* Music: In an Old English Garden; Mother Never Told Me; Two Red Roses Across the Moon; Sere (Armenian song). *Songs & Instrumental Works:* The Willow Tree (Armenian song, vocal & string orch arr); Desert Solitude (string orch).

ROOD, HALE   ASCAP 1959
composer, conductor, arranger

b Merrill, Wis, Feb 2, 23. Pres, Hardric Productions (produce commercials, industrial films & documentaries), New York. Stage band series initiated with Camerica Productions, New York. *Songs:* Wickdippers; Kim's Lament; Nicki; Ballade; Just Plain Bill; Second Floor Please. *Instrumental Works:* Cacti Series (brass sextet); Central Park North-East. *Scores:* TV: NBC Chet Huntley Reports (Emmy Award, prog of yr); The Tunnel (90 min documentary).

ROONEY, JAMES KEVIN   ASCAP 1973
composer, author, singer

b Boston, Mass, Jan 28, 38. Educ: Amherst Col, BA, 60; Harvard Univ, MA(classics), 62; Fulbright fel, 63. Came out of folk music revival, Cambridge, Mass, ran Club 47, 65-68; dir, Newport Folk Found, 66-69; mem, Woodstone Man Revue. *Songs:* Only the Best; The Beginning of the End; Interest on the Loan; Music: One Morning in May; The Knight Upon the Road; Kentucky Moonshiner. *Albums:* Livin' on the Mountain; Sweet Moments With the Blue Velvet Band; Borderline: Sweet Moments and Quiet Desires; One Day at a Time.

ROONEY, MICKEY
See Yule, Joe, Jr

ROONEY, PAT, SR   ASCAP 1951
composer, singer, dancer

b New York, NY, July 4, 1880; d New York, Sept 9, 62. First appeared in vaudeville with sister, Mattie, in act "Two Chips Off the Old Block," Tony Pastor's in NY. Later with wife, Marion Brent in vaudeville & Bway musicals incl "In Atlantic City" & "Love Birds." Last stage appearance, "Guys and Dolls." Also in films, radio, TV & nightclubs. *Songs:* Trolley Ride; Take Me Back to Baby Land; I Got a Gal for Every Day in the Week; You Be My Ootsie, I'll Be Your Tootsie; She's the Daughter of the Daughter of Rosie O'Grady; Goodnight, People; Make Yourself At Home.

ROPER, STEVE
See Dorn, Veeder Van

ROREM, NED   ASCAP 1951
composer, author

b Richmond, Ind, Oct 23, 23. Educ: Northwestern Univ, 40-42; Curtis Inst, Philadelphia, 42-43; Juilliard Sch Music, BA, 47, MA, 49; hon DFA, Northwestern Univ, 77. Sleep prof & comp-in-residence, Buffalo Univ, 59-61; prof comp, Univ Utah, 65-67. Rec'd Gershwin Mem award, 49; Lili Boulanger award, 50; Nat Inst Arts & Letters award, 68; Pulitzer Prize Music, 77. Fulbright fel, Paris, 51-52; Guggenheim fel, 57-58 & 77-78. Comns for US Bicentennial incl Cincinnati Symph, NC Symph, NEA, Am Harp Soc. Author: "The Paris Diary of Ned Rorem"; "Music From Inside Out"; "The New York Diary"; "Music and People"; "Critical Affairs"; "Pure Contraption"; "The Final Diary"; "An Absolute Gift"; also articles for newspapers & mags. Made records for Columbia, Decca, Odyssey, Desto, CRI, Westminster & Orion. *Songs:* Lordly Hudson (Music Libr Asn award, 48); Rain in Spring; Echo's Song; The Nightingale; Early in the Morning; To You; Lullaby of the Mountain Woman;

also Cycle of Holy Songs; Poems of Love and the Rain (song cycle). *Instrumental Works:* Symphony No 1; Symphony No 2; Symphony No 3; Lento for Strings; Design for Orchestra (comn by Louisville Orch); Pilgrims for Strings; Eagles for Orchestra; Lions (tone poem); Ideas for Easy Orchestra; Piano Concerto No 2; 3rd Piano Concerto; Eleven Studies; Water Music; Sun (for voice, orch; comn by New York Philh, 66); Air Music for Orchestra (Pulitzer prize, 76); Assembly and Fall; Sunday Morning for Orchestra; Letters From Paris (chorus, orch; comn by Koussevitzky Found in Libr Congress); Flight for Heaven; Sicilienne; 3 Barcarolles; 2 Psalms and a Proverb; Lovers (narr for harpsichord, oboe, cello, perc); Little Prayers (chorus); Cycles: War Scenes; Six Songs for High Voice and Orchestra; Six Irish Poems; Ariel for Voice, Clarinet and Piano; Last Poems of Wallace Stevens for Voice, Cello and Piano; Serenade for Voice, Violin, Viola and Piano, Women's Voices; The Nantucket Songs; Day Music and Night Music for Violin; Etudes for Piano; Book of Hours for Flute and Harp; A Quaker Reader for Organ. *Scores:* Opera: A Childhood Miracle; Three Sisters Who Are Not Sisters; Fables; Bertha; Miss Julie (Ford Found grantee); Hearing.

ROSALES, MARCO   ASCAP 1956
composer, author, singer
b Bogota, Colombia, Dec 4, 13. Educ: Columbia Univ, BA; studied with Nadia Boulanger, Joseph Schillinger, Felix Deyo, Richard Benda & Tibor Serly. Sang & played guitar on NBC; performed in leading hotels around the country; master ceremonies & singer at La Conga. Inducted into USA, post bandleader, Ft Dix, arr-performer, 11th Airborne Band, Southwest Pac, WW II. Now owner of "The Latin Sound," Span language commercials production co, comp jingles for commercials. Chief Collabrs: Chick Lindgren, Will Copeland, Sylvia Rosales (wife). *Songs:* The Merry Mailman; El Piraguero; Yo Te Tengo A Ti.

ROSALES, SYLVIA (SYLVIA ST CLAIR)   ASCAP 1956
composer, author, singer
b New York, NY, June 14, 17. Educ: Studied piano with Helen Muck; NY Univ, BA, Phi Beta Kappa, 37; musical theatre workshops with Lehman Engel & Fred Silver; studied sight-singing with Maurice Finnell. Wrote & directed, NY Univ Varsity Show, 38; writer for Columbia Workshop, CBS celebrated radio series, 39; mem comn expert consults to Secy War, wrote & produced shows explaining Rehabilitation Prog to convalescent soldiers, 44. Appeared in cabaret revue "The Nite Wits," 39-40; co-writer & producer, TV musical "La Ronda Del Monte," PR & revue "This is Puerto Rico," which gave command performance for Pres Eisenhower, 56. Former comedy writer for Carol Channing, Henry Morgan & Milton Berle. Writer-producer & singer on Span language commercials. Mem: Screen Actors Guild; Am Fedn TV & Radio Artists; Local 802, Am Fedn Musicians. Chief Collabrs: Marco Rosales (husband), Elie Siegmeister, Baldwin Bergersen, Alex North. *Songs:* The Merry Mailman (radio & TV theme); El Piraguero; Yo Te Tengo A Ti.

ROSCOE (BUMPUS), B JEANIE (B J GROH)   ASCAP 1977
composer, teacher
b Wilbur, Wash, Nov 27, 32. Educ: High sch grad; Wash State Univ; Whitworth Col; Univ Wash; Music Teachers Nat Asn, state & nat certification; studied comp with Loran A Olsen, piano with Margaret Saunders Ott; master coaching with Irwin Freundlich, Constance Keene, Randolf Hokanson, Istvan Nadas & others. Had own pvt piano studios, 56-; perf & recitals; adjudicator; teacher of formal (classical) piano through 20th Century serious music; comp, 62- Had works performed in recitals & concerts. *Instrumental Works:* Whimseys for Piano; Dimensions in Color for Piano (2 pieces); Spectrums for Piano, Opus 9: 1 Evolution, 2 Equinox, 3 Imminecy's, 4 Abstractions.

ROSE, BILLY   ASCAP 1923
author, producer
b New York, NY, Sept 6, 1899; d Jamaica, Brit WI, Feb 10, 66. Educ: High Sch of Commerce. Trained in Gregg shorthand, won high speed dictation contest at age 16; shorthand reporter, War Indust Bd, World War I, 17; prod plays: "Jumbo", "Clash by Night", "Carmen Jones", "Seven Lively Arts"; expositions: Ft Worth Centenniel, 36, Aquacade, Great Lakes, Cleveland, 37, World's Fair, New York, 39 & Golden Gate, San Francisco, 40; owner & operator Diamond Horseshoe Nightclub, New York; also Ziegfeld, Billy Rose Theatres; wrote synd column, "Pitching Horseshoes"; author, "Wine, Women and Words." Co-founder, Am Guild Authors & Comp, pres, 3 yrs. Chief Collabrs: Ray Henderson, Mort Dixon, Dave Dreyer, Al Jolson, Vincent Youmans, Harold Arlen, Dana Suesse, Mabel Wayne, Harry Warren. *Songs:* You Tell Her, I Stutter; You've Got to See Momma Every Night; Barney Google; Come On, Spark Plug; That Old Gang of Mine; Does the Spearmint Lose Its Flavor on the Bedpost Overnight?; Follow the Swallow; Too Many Parties and Too Many Pals; I Found a Million Dollar Baby (in a Five and Ten Cent Store); Clap Hands, Here Comes Charley; Don't Bring Lulu; A Cup of Coffee, A Sandwich and You; Me and My Shadow; Fifty Million Frenchmen Can't Be Wrong; Here Comes the Show Boat; Four Walls; Tonight You Belong to Me; Golden Gate; It Happened in Monterey; Happy Days and Lonely Nights; Back in Your Own Back Yard; There's a Rainbow 'Round My Shoulder; If You Want the Rainbow (You Must Have the Rain); I've Got a Feeling I'm Falling; I Got a Code id By Doze; More Than You Know; Great Day; Without a Song; Happy Because I'm in Love; Cooking Breakfast for the One I Love; When a Woman Loves a Man; Overnight; Cheerful Little Earful; Would You Like to Take a Walk?; It's Only a Paper Moon; I Wanna Be Loved; Suddenly; The House Is Haunted; The Night Is Young and You're So Beautiful; Yours for a Song; The Sun Will Shine

Tonight. *Scores:* Bway Stage: Harry Delmar's Revels; Great Day!; Sweet and Low (prod); Crazy Quilt (prod).

ROSE, DAVID   ASCAP 1942
composer
b London, Eng, June 3, 19. Educ: Chicago Musical Col. Comp numerous scores for motion pictures, TV movies & series. Recording artist, Capitol, MGM, Polydor, RCA Victor, Decca & Kapp; guest cond for many orchs. *Songs:* Music: Holiday for Strings; Our Waltz; Dance of the Spanish Onion; One Love; The Stripper; Music for TV series: Little House on the Prairie.

ROSE, EARL ALEXANDER   ASCAP 1972
composer, pianist, arranger
b New York, NY, Sept 5, 46. Educ: McBurney High Sch; Mannes Col Music, BSMus, 70. Began as pianist & arr & acted on many occasions. Asst music cond for "Tonight Show." Comp, arr & co-producer of featured songs for TV series, "Captain Kangaroo." Performer radio & TV, guest artist with symph orchs as well as touring throughout US & Can. Comp scores for TV, motion pictures & recordings. Mem, East Coast Projs Comt, Am Guild Authors & Comp, also Nat Acad Recording Arts & Sci. Chief Collabr: Judy Spencer. *Songs:* Music: Overnight Success; Someone, Somewhere; Linnea, My Love; Wheels; Things That You Want to Do. *Instrumental Works:* Love Theme in Search of a Motion Picture; Waltz for Autumn; To the One You Love; May's Song; Scorpio Rising.

ROSE, ED   ASCAP 1924
author
b Evanston, Ill, Nov 24, 1875; d Evanston, Ill, Apr 29, 35. Educ: Valparaiso Univ. *Songs:* If You Cared for Me; Baby Shoes; Oh Johnny, Oh Johnny, Oh; Everybody Wants the Key to My Cellar; Ukulele Baby; I Don't Want a Doctor; He Walked Right In and Turned Around and Walked Right Out Again; Good Night Moonlight; I'll Buy the Ring and Change Your Name to Mine.

ROSE, FRED   ASCAP 1928
composer, author, singer
b Evansville, Ind. Aug 24, 1897; d Nashville, Tenn, Dec 1, 54. Educ: Pub schs, St Louis. Singer & pianist, Chicago; music publ, Nashville. Chief Collabrs: Hy Heath, Edward G Nelson, Steve Nelson, Walter Hirsch, Gene Autry. *Songs:* 'Deed I Do; Honest and Truly; Red Hot Mama; Don't Bring Me Posies; Roly Poly; Take These Chains From My Heart; I'll Never Stand in Your Way; Hang Your Head in Shame; Crazy Heart; No One Will Ever Know; Be Honest With Me; Blues Eyes Crying in the Rain; Just Like Me; You Know How Talk Gets Around; Texarkana Baby; Kaw-Liga; Before You Call; Setting the Woods on Fire; Worried Over You; Tears on My Pillow.

ROSE, GRIFFITH WHEELER   ASCAP 1974
composer
b Los Angeles, Calif, Jan 18, 36. Educ: Hartt Sch Music, comp with Isidore Freed, 55-56; Freiburger Hochschule, comp with Wolfgang Fortner, 57-59; Basler Akademie, comp with Pierre Boulez, 60-61; studied with Nadia Boulanger & Stockhausen. Performed in Freiburg & Heidelberg, 60; in concerts with The Generation of Music, London, 62; performed with Fluxus Orgn, Ger, 62, also performed in "Complaintes," Ger, 64. Trumpet recital, Salpinx in Town Hall, 66; performances of brass works, Atlanta, 68, 70 & 71. Incidental music for Camus' "Caligula," Sete, France, 69. Several appearances as pianist, Ducal Palace, Venice. Chief Collabrs: Marie-France Rose, Riccardo Licata. *Songs:* Le Mikado; Gedichte Vom Mond. *Instrumental Works:* Piano Concerto (after Mercel Duchamp; piano, baritone, orch); Viola Concerto (Comp Theatre comn, 74); 2nd Viola Concerto (French Ministery of Culture comn, 76); Ziggurat.

ROSE, HARRY   ASCAP 1950
author
b Leeds, Eng, Dec 2, 1893. To US, 05. Citizen. Educ: Pub schs. Appeared in Bway musicals; also in vaudeville, nightclubs. Wrote special material. *Songs:* Kitty From Kansas City; Lonesome Hours; Anna in Indiana; I've Got Some News for You.

ROSE, RONALD FREDERICK   ASCAP 1967
composer, author
b Cleveland, Ohio, Apr 27, 40. Educ: North Hollywood High Sch; Univ Calif Los Angeles, music maj in comp & piano; attended Dick Grove's musical workshops. Pianist nightclubs & studios, Los Angeles area. Featured songs on TV series, "Happy Days." Theme song for TV series, "Brothers and Sisters" & 1980 theme for Am Heart Asn. Chief Collabr: Anson Williams. *Songs:* Children, Children; You Are My Melody; Rodeo; Save Your Last Kiss for Me; Music: Masquerade.

ROSE, RUBYE B (PATSY MONTANA)   ASCAP 1950
composer, singer
b Hot Springs, Ark, Oct 30, 14. Educ: High sch. Country & western singer on radio shows, WLS Nat Barn Dance, 15 yrs & Louisiana Hayride; had guest spots on TV shows; appeared in early films with Gene Autry. Recording artist. Chief Collabr: Lee Penny. *Songs:* I Want to Be a Cowboy's Sweetheart; A Cowboy's Gal; Back on Montana Plains; Give Me a Home in Montana; Homesick for My Old Cabin; I Know the Lord is Watching Over Me; I Want to Be a Cowboy's Dreamgirl; I've Found My Cowboy's Sweetheart; Ireland is Calling; Little Doby

Shack; Little Mountaineer Mother; Me and My Cowboy's Sweetheart; Ridin the Sunset Trail; Sage Brush Soprano; She Buckaroo; Where the Mountains Kiss the Sky; Where the Sagebrush Billows Roll; Sweetheart of the Saddle; The Moon Hangs Low; Deep Water; Music: Shine on My Boots; I Wanna Yodel; Texas Tomboy; Lyrics: My Poncho Pony; Rodeo Queen.

ROSE, VINCENT   ASCAP 1921
composer, conductor, pianist
b Palermo, Italy, June 13, 1880; d Rockville Centre, NY, May 20, 44. Educ: Technical Inst; Palermo Sch of Music (scholarship); studied with Liberati. To US, 1897, citizen. Violinist & pianist, dance orchs, Chicago & Los Angeles. Music dir, west coast hotel chain. Formed own orch. Chief Collabrs: Larry Stock, Jack Meskill, Al Lewis, Ray Klages, James Cavanaugh, B G DeSylva, Richard Coburn, John Schonberger. *Songs:* Avalon; Whispering; Linger Awhile; Love Tales; May Time; Were You Sincere?; Kiss By Kiss; Tonight Or Never; The Umbrella Man; Blueberry Hill; The American Prayer; Raindrop Serenade; Pardon Me, Pretty Baby; Pretty Little Busybody; Moon At Sea; I Sent a Letter to Santa; Ma-Ma-Maria; Slowly But Surely; Creaking Old Mill on the Creek; Whistling in the Wildwood.

ROSE MARIE
See Guy, Rose Marie

ROSEMONT, WALTER LOUIS   ASCAP 1925
composer, producer
b Philadelphia, Pa, Aug 16, 1895; d Whippany, NJ, Feb 22, 69. Educ: Univ Pa; studied piano with mother, then with Robert Tempest, Martin Krause & Richard Hofmann; Sondershausen Cons, with Karl Schroeder. Cond, opera symph orchs, Europe, also Am Philh Soc, NY, Victor Herbert Productions & 6th Regional Pa Band; later led own orch. Taught music. Foreign correspondent, music mag; music ed, publ. Produced operettas & revues. Translr of plays & lyrics. Wrote for Bway productions. *Songs:* The Lord's Prayer; The Lord Is My Shepherd; Fiorita; Why Can't I Sell Myself to You?. *Instrumental Works:* Tone Poems: Troilus and Cressida; Over Hill and Dale; Fughetta; Regrets in a Garden; Scene Orientale; Bird Ballet; The Prophetess; also music for film travelogues.

ROSEN, MILTON SONNETT   ASCAP 1941
composer
b Yonkers, NY, Aug 2, 06. Educ: Inst Musical Art, New York; comp & orchestration with Pietro Floridia, cond with Vladimir Bakaleinikoff. Violinist & orchr for theatres & radio, New York, 24-35, orchr & comp on staff of radio sta WLW, Cincinnati, Ohio, 35-39, comp, orchr, cond & asst head of dept, also comp songs & background music for over 100 pictures, performances of symph works by Cincinnati Symph Pittsburgh Symph, Rochester Symph, Boston Pops Orch & Hollywood Bowl Orch.

ROSEN, THEODORE   ASCAP 1952
author, teacher
b Boston, Mass, Mar 15, 18. Educ: Boston Univ. Chief Collabr: David Krasnor. *Songs:* Herkimer, the Homely Doll.

ROSENBAUM, SAMUEL   ASCAP 1963
composer, author
b New York, NY, June 11, 19. Educ: NY Univ, BA; Damrosch Inst; pvt study. Cantor, Temple Beth-El, Rochester, NY, 46- Exec vpres, Cantors Assembly. Chief Collabrs: Sholom Secunda, Abraham Ellstein, Samuel Adler, Lazar Weiner, Charles Davidson, Gershon Kingsley. *Songs:* The Redemption; If Not Higher; Sing a Song of Israel; Yizkor: In Memory of the Six Million; The Last Judgment; A Singing of Angels; also Sabbath and Festival Songs for the Young Singer; 12 songs from Yiddish folklore. *Instrumental Works:* Fanfare for Muted Trumpets; The Birthday of the World.

ROSENBERG, GEORGE
See Rosey, George

ROSENBERG, JACOB (JACK)   ASCAP 1943
composer, musician
b Austria, Feb 15, 1896; d New York, NY, July 31, 46. Percussionist, New York Philh Symph, 20 yrs, & NBC Symph. With Assoc Musicians of Greater New York, past pres, Local 802. Consult on civic music progs for Mayor La Guardia; on advisory staff, WPA music projects. *Songs:* All for Love; On the Sands of Time; The Same Little Words; Any Day Now; Paris Will Be Paris Once Again; Let's Put Our Dreams Together.

ROSENBERG, JOSEPH ARNOLD   ASCAP 1977
composer, author
b New York, NY, Dec 29, 51. Educ: Rider Col, BS(commerce); Juilliard Sch Music, studied piano. Mem of rock, jazz & blues bands; DJ & music dir, WRNW-FM; producer & songwriter, "The Elements." Songwriter consult. Chief Collabrs: Ingrid Russell, Roz Snyder. *Songs:* I Took a Chance; L A Baby; Music: If You Don't Use It, You're Gonna Lose It.

ROSENBERG, SEYMOUR S
composer
b Memphis, Tenn, Nov 19, 33. Educ: Memphis State Univ, JD. Publ & writer, 20 yrs. *Songs:* Lyrics: From Barrooms to Bedrooms.

ROSENBERGER, MARGARET A   ASCAP 1964
composer, author, educator
b Micanopy, Fla, Oct 30, 21. Educ: P K Yonge Lab Sch, maj bus; John B Stetson Univ, maj music educ; Univ Fla, BAE & MAE. With Mil Personnel, USAF, Camp Blanding, Fla. Taught elem sch, Gainesville, Fla; principal & teacher, Micanopy Jr High Sch; supvr elem educ, then gen supvr, Alachua County schs. Taught at Heidelberg Elem Sch, USA, Ger. Principal, Littlewood Elem Sch, Gainesville & Prairie View Elem Sch. Chief Collabr: Lew Tobin. *Songs:* The Saint Augustine Song; Spanish Town; Bridge of Make Believe; Delta Kappa Gamma Song; Skip and Mitzi.

ROSENFELD, DAVID   ASCAP 1972
composer
b New York, NY, July 6, 33. Educ: Fredonia State Teachers Col, clarinet, Harry Peters, 1 yr; Manhattan Sch Music, clarinet with Joe Allard, Leon Russianoff, Harold Freeman, Herbert Blayman & Sidney Powers; Gino B Cioffi, Boston. Played solo & second clarinet with Michael Piastro; also played 1st & 2nd clarinet in training orch with Leon Barzaw. Played numerous musician trust fund concerts. *Songs:* Music: Oh Here Comes Mr Lovelace.

ROSENMAN, LEONARD   ASCAP 1955
composer
b Brooklyn, NY, Sept 7, 24. Studied with Julius Herford, Bernard Abramowitsch, Roger Sessions, Arnold Schoenberg, Luigi Dallapiccola. Berkshire Music Ctr, Margaret Lee Crofts fel, comp-in-residence, 53. *Songs:* East of Eden Theme; Rebel Without a Cause Theme. *Instrumental Works:* Concertino for Piano and Winds; Violin Concerto; Six Lorca Songs; Piano Sonata; Threnody on a Song of K R; Foci (3 orchs). *Scores:* Films: East of Eden; Cobweb; Rebel Without a Cause; Edge of the City; The Savage Eye; The Chapman Report; TV: Marcus Wellby, MD; The Defenders.

ROSENSTOCK, MILTON MAX   ASCAP 1973
composer, author, conductor
b New Haven, Conn, June 9, 17. Educ: Inst Musical Art, clarinet scholarship; Juilliard Sch Music, fel clarinet, cond & comp; teachers, Albert Stoesse, Simeon Bellison, Vittorio Giannini, Bernard Wagenaar, D C Dounis. Bway original cond & musical dir, "This Is the Army", "On the Town", "Billion Dollar Baby", "Finian's Rainbow", "High Button Shoes", "Gentleman Prefer Blondes", "Make a Wish", "Can-Can", "Bells Are Ringing", "Gypsy", "Stop the World", "Funny Girl" & others; revivals, "The King and I", "Fiddler on the Roof", "Gypsy" & "A Funny Thing Happened to Me on the Way to the Forum." Chief Collabrs: Ogden Nash, John Latouche, Larry Markes. *Songs:* Music: Four Songs of Time and the River; Three Songs for Angie; In Praise of Francois Villon (songs, narration, cantata). *Instrumental Works:* The Facts of Monsieur Valdemar (E A Poe); Berlioz (song cycle & narration). *Scores:* Bway Show: Nash At Nine; Off-Bway Show: Tell the Truth.

ROSENTHAL, LAURENCE   ASCAP 1956
composer, pianist
b Detroit, Mich, Nov 4, 26. Educ: High sch; Eastman Sch Music, BM, 47, MM, 51; Cons Nat Musique, Paris, studied comp with Nadia Boulanger, 48-50; studied cond, Mozarteum, Salzburg, Austria. Served in USAF as chief composer, 1st Documentary Film Squadron, 51-55. After discharge, comp for theater, film & TV, New York, Europe & Los Angeles; music has been performed by NY Philh, Rochester Philh & others. *Scores:* Bway Shows: A Clearing in the Woods; Rashomon; Becket; A Patriot for Me; Sherry (musical); Films: A Raisin in the Sun; Requiem for a Heavyweight; The Miracle Worker; Becket; The Comedians; The Return of a Man Called Horse; Who'll Stop the Rain; Meetings With Remarkable Men; TV: The Power and the Glory; Michelangelo: The Last Giant (Emmy Award, 66); The Missiles of October; Pueblo; 21 Hours at Munich; The Amazing Howard Hughes; FDR (The Last Year).

ROSENTHAL, ROBERTA (HELLER)   ASCAP 1967
composer, author, singer
b Buffalo, NY. Educ: James Madison High Sch, Brooklyn; Adelphi Univ, BA & grad work; studied voice with Fred Steele & acting with Ruth Klinger. Has done work in radio, TV, film & theater. Writer, spec material; has written for & appeared in musical theater. Actress & musician. *Songs:* Lyrics: The Lonely One; Speak, My Love.

ROSETTE, MARION SAVAGE   ASCAP 1958
composer, author, concert pianist
b Baltimore, Md. Educ: Western High Sch; Loyola Col; Johns Hopkins Univ; Peabody Inst, grad teacher & artist's dipl; studied with Harold Randolph, Alfredo Oswald & Gustave Strube. Peabody piano scholarship; gave radio & song-story recitals; soloist with orch. Wrote sch-bk songs, Ginn & Co, also songs for Greeting Card Records. Toured with singers, violinists & ballet dancers as accompanist. Wrote & produced over 100 song-stories for children. Pianist & arr, French Folk Dance Group. Wrote spec material for night clubs & music hall.

Songs: Katie the Kangaroo; City Mouse and Country Mouse; Old Mother Hubbard; Monkey Who Wanted to Fly; Lion and Mouse; Traveling Musicians; Wynken, Blynken and Nod; Old-Fashioned Harmony Party; Who Was the Fella?; Sweet Innocent Smile; Cowboy's Old Horse; Santa Claus Is Flying Through the Sky; 'Twas the Night Before Christmas; My First Christmas Tree. *Instrumental Works:* Busy Bar Rag (honky tonk piano & orch); Summer Love Affair (Dixieland band); Mardi Gras Strut (Dixieland band); The Rose and the Ring (organ); Magic of the Night (organ).

ROSEY, GEORGE (GEORGE ROSENBERG)   ASCAP 1931
composer, arranger, publisher
b Dusseldorf, Ger, Apr 18, 1864; d New York, NY, Feb 19, 36. Educ: In Ger; studied music with Radeke. Came to US, 1883. Comp, arr & exec, music publ co. *Songs & Instrumental Works:* Maybe; Believe; Lovely Caprice; I Love My Girl; The Honeymoon March; The Handicap March; The Anniversary March; King Carnival.

ROSEY, JOE   ASCAP 1919
composer
b New York, NY, Oct 29, 1882; d New York, Dec 20, 43. *Songs:* Someone Else; Suppose. *Instrumental Works:* Ragging the Waves; Waltzing the Bride; Waltzing the Scale.

ROSINA, ROSE
See Rivelli, Pauline

ROSNER, ARNOLD   ASCAP 1975
composer, teacher
b Bronx, NY, Nov 8, 45. Educ: State Univ NY, Buffalo, PhD. Former broadcaster, WNYC. Fac mem, Brooklyn Col & Wagner Col. *Songs:* Music: Nightstone. *Instrumental Works:* A My Lai Elegy; five Ko-ans for orch; six symphonies; five string quartets.

ROSNER, GEORGE   ASCAP 1959
composer, professional pianist
b Krakow, Poland, Jan 12, 09. Educ: Studied piano with Baroness Closman; mem of "Zaiks," Warsaw; Krakow Cons Music. Many songs publ & recorded in Poland featured in movies, incl US movie "Americano." Music dir & pianist for Phoenix Country Club, Ariz, 61- Chief Collabrs: Al Stillman, Xavier Cugat, Tom Smith, Fred Wise, Buddy Kaye. *Songs:* Music: The Americano; Nightingale; I Wish, I Wish. *Instrumental Works:* Children of Rome (plush music); Waltz of Joy (Valse de Joie, plush music).

ROSNESS, JUANITA M   ASCAP 1964
composer, author, singer
b Chicago, Ill, May 13, 1897; d Park Ridge, Ill, Sept 19, 67. Educ: High sch; music degree. Singer, vaudeville, films, light & grand opera. Teacher; rep; musical leader. *Songs:* Window Shopping; Little One; Mists; Fragrance; Music From a Box; Chicago Beautiful; Behold! Tis Day.

ROSOFF, CHARLES   ASCAP 1925
composer
b Brooklyn, NY, May 1, 1898. Educ: Pub schs; pvt music study. Pianist in film theatres & for music publishers. Wrote songs for films; also for "Earl Carroll's Vanities." Chief Collabrs: Leo Robin, Gus Kahn, Eddie Maxwell, Mort Greene, Cliff Friend, Samuel Lewis. *Songs:* When You and I Were Seventeen; Look in the Looking Glass; It's Love; On My Honor; The Most Beautiful Girls; I Can Tell By the Stars; In the Merry Month of May; I've Taken a Likin' to You; Tres Chic; Just an Old Love Affair. *Scores:* Bway Stage: Judy.

ROSS, ARNOLD   ASCAP 1950
composer, pianist, arranger
b Boston, Mass, Jan 29, 21. Educ: Brighton High Sch; studied with Sam Saxe. Glenn Miller, Vaughn Monroe, Harry James & Jimmy Dorsey bands; accompanist for Lena Horne, Billy Eckstine & Frank Sinatra. TV shows with Nelson Riddle Orch. Jazz band, Beverly Hills, Calif; Free-lance studio work as pianist. Chief Collabrs: Jerry Gladstone, Merrylin Hammond, Vaughn Monroe, Freddie Stewart. *Songs:* Music: Shy Ann From Old Cheyenne. *Instrumental Works:* Commodore Clipper; Last Call for Coffee; C E D; N S A; Hugo; Reliable Source; Might Be.

ROSS, BEN   ASCAP 1956
composer
b New York, NY, Apr 28, 11; d Brooklyn, NY, Mar 28, 58. Educ: NY Univ. Co-founder, NJ Philh, 34. Coauthor, "Recorded Guitar Lessons." Chief Collabrs: Sid Press, Harold Solomon, John Murray, Mann Curtis, Nick Kenny, Charles Kenny. *Songs:* One Kiss Ago; I Can Do It; Knock Wood; Penny Carousel; Afraid; The Magic Horn; What Makes It Tick; The Crying Wind.

ROSS, BENNY   ASCAP 1956
composer, author
b New York, NY, Dec 22, 12. Educ: Jr High Sch. Musician, singer, song plugger; prof mgr, var music publ; songwriter. Chief Collabrs: Mack Discant, Helen Ross, Horace Linsley, Roy Straigis. *Songs:* Music: Hold Me Forever; Till You Come Back to Me; What Am I to Do; Love Don't Be a Stranger; I Wanna Be Seventeen All of My Life; I Want a Gal Who Can Dance Me a Cha Cha; I Hope You Won't

Hold It Against Me; Hearts Were Never Meant to Be Broken; Shake Hands With a Guy in Love; Sightseeing; I Can't Help It; Baby Baby Watcha Gonna Do Tonight; Lyrics: Dominique's Discotheque; You Say; Say Auf Wiedersehn; Sailor Boy; Cling to Me; Ten Miles from Nowhere.

ROSS, EDWARD
See Samuels, Milton Isadore

ROSS, HELEN   ASCAP 1956
composer
b New York, NY, July 31, 12. Educ: High sch. Chief Collabrs: Benny Ross, Horace Linsley. *Songs:* Hold Me Forever; Till You Come Back to Me; What Am I To Do?; Love, Don't Be a Stranger; I Wanna Be 17 All of My Life; Shake Hands With a Guy in Love; I Wanna Gal Who Can Dance Me a Cha Cha; I Hope You Won't Hold It Against Me; Hearts Were Never Meant to Be Broken; Sightseeing.

ROSS, JERRY   ASCAP 1950
composer, author
b New York, NY, Mar 9, 26; d New York, Nov 11, 55. Educ: NY Univ; studies with Rudolf Schramm; also with Michael Fivelsky. Child actor, Yiddish Theatre; also in films & on radio. Chief Collabr: Richard Adler. *Songs:* Strange Little Girl; You're So Much a Part of Me; Rags to Riches; Hey, There; Hernando's Hideaway; I'm Not At All in Love; Small Talk; Steam Heat; Once-a-Year Day; There Once Was a Man; Who's Got the Pain?; A Little Brains, a Little Talent; Heart; Whatever Lola Wants; Two Lost Souls. *Scores:* Bway stage: John Murray Anderson's Almanac; The Pajama Game (Tony, Donaldson & Variety Critics Awards); Damn Yankees (Tony, Donaldson & Variety Critics Awards).

ROSS, LANCELOT PATRICK (LANNY)   ASCAP 1941
composer, author, singer
b Seattle, Wash, Jan 19, 06. Educ: Cathedral Choir Sch; Taft Sch; Yale Univ, BA, 28; Columbia Univ, LLB, 31; Juilliard. Began singing on NBC, 28. Engaged on "Show Boat" series, 32-37; "Packard," 38; "Hit Parade," 39, "Franco American," 40-42 & "Camel," 43. WW II, Maj, USA, SPac, 43-46. Musical show on TV, 48-50; disc jockey, CBS, 51-60. Has given concerts, made records & movies. *Songs:* Music in the Evening; Nothing Like the Smile of the Irish; Honomu; Somewhere in England; Brown Eyes; April Is a Woman; Silver Dollar Country; Sleigh-Bell Serenade; Valentine Waltz; Girl With the Silver Smile; Silver Dollar Days; Where the Sky Meets the Mountains.

ROSS, STANLEY RALPH   ASCAP 1958
composer, author, screenwriter
b New York, NY, July 22, 40. Began as songwriter/performer, 58; advert jingle writer, 58-65. Became scriptwriter for TV shows, incl "Batman", "Man From Uncle", "All in the Family" & others; created var TV shows, incl "That's My Mama", "Wonder Woman", "Challenge of the Sexes" & "The Kallikaks"; wrote var TV themes. Writer, producer & actor, TV & motion picture features. Chief Collabr: Jimmy Haskell, Bob Arbogast, Larry Grossman, Charles Fox. *Songs:* Beat the System (NBC TV theme); Chaos; The Fifty Mile Hike; Music: Drowning in the Surf; Lyrics: The Movies (NBC TV theme); The American Working Man (NBC TV theme); Speedy Gonzalez. *Albums:* Did You Come to Play Cards Or to Talk?; My Son the Copycat.

ROSS, WALTER BEGHTOL   ASCAP 1969
composer, educator
b Lincoln, Nebr, Oct 3, 36. Educ: Univ Nebr, BA Mus, 60, MA Mus, 62; Cornell Univ, DMusA, 66, studied with Karel Husa & Robert Palmer; additional study, Inst Torquato Di Tella, Buenos Aires, with Alberto Ginastera, 65. Wrote 48 works for chamber ens, orch, band & voices. Assoc prof music & chmn dept, Univ Va, 73-, orgn & dir series music concerts. Chief Collabr: Ira Rodgers. *Instrumental Works:* Tuba Concerto (tuba solo & band); Trombone Concerto (trombone & orch); Concerto for Wind Quintet and String Orchestra; Six Shades of Blue (preludes for piano solo); Divertimento (flute, oboe, clarinet, horn & bassoon); A Jefferson Symphony (orch, chorus & tenor solo); String Trio (violin, viola & cello); Trombone Quartet; Prelude, Fugue and Big Apple (trombone & electronic tape); Canzona I and II (brass & perc ens); Midnight Variations (tuba, tape). *Scores:* Opera: In the Penal Colony (a chamber, 1-act).

ROSSANA, AUGUSTINE S (GENE ASRO)   ASCAP 1954
composer, author
b Adrian, WVa, Apr 4, 32. Educ: Trenton Cons Music; Hamilton Inst 20th Century Music; Temple Univ, radio & jour major; Bucks County Community Col, Business. USN. With Trentonian United Press. Teaches photography at Carl Sandberg & Bucks County Tech Sch. Owner & operator, Asro Mobil Photo. Chief Collabr: Eddie Hat Rak. *Songs:* Someone Somewhere; I Don't Want to Go on Loving; Lovely Stranger; Remember Your Mother.

ROSSANO, NINO
See Giacobbe, Nello

ROSSI, WALTER   ASCAP 1956
composer, author
b Philadelphia, Pa, Aug 2, 14. Educ: Pub schs; studied violin & guitar. Guitarist in local bands. Chief Collabrs: Lew Hartley, Charles Shaw, Alan Shurr, Robert Duke Morgan. *Songs:* I Found My Old Girl Again; Does Your Heart Tell You; You've Got to Be Tender; Who's Gonna Call You Sweetheart; Kisses Are Better Than Roses; What You Had Now You Ain't Got; That'll Be the Day; Music: Steal, Lie and Swear.

ROSSINI, CARLO   ASCAP 1943
composer, author arranger
b Osimo, Italy, Mar 3, 1890; d Osimo, Aug 6, 75. Educ: Interdiocesan Sem, Fano, Italy, ordained Catholic priest, 13; Pontifical Inst of Sacred Music, Rome, masters degree, studied with Perosi, Casimiri, Dobici, Dagnimo. Chaplain, Italian army, World War I. To US, 21, citizen 29. Assoc with Scalabrinian Fathers of St Charles Borromeo, New York, 21. Organist & choirmaster, Church of Epiphany, Pittsburgh, 23-26, St Paul's Cathedral, Pittsburgh, 27-50. Reorganized Italian St Cecilia Soc, 50-55. Founder, Nat Inst Arts & Crafts for Boys, Osimo, Italy, 56-60. *Songs & Instrumental Works:* Choral Compositions and Arrangements of Liturgical Music for Choirs (10 vols); Liturgical Music Arranged for Reed or Pipe Organ (14 vols); Gregorian Chant for Church and School (7 vols); Catholic Church Music (18 vols); & 22 masses.

ROSTEN, NORMAN   ASCAP 1978
author
b New York, NY, Jan 1, 14. Educ: Brooklyn Col, BA; NY Univ, MA. Author: "Under the Boardwalk" & "Over & Out" (novels); "Mister Johnson" & "Come Slowly, Eden" (plays); "Selected Poems." Awards: Guggenheim fel; Am Acad Arts & Letters Award; Ford Found grant for libretto. Chief Collabrs: Elie Siegmeister, Ezra Laderman. *Songs:* Lyrics: Songs for Patricia (song cycle); Songs of Elie Siegmeister (for my daughters); Who Killed Norma Jean?

ROTE, KYLE   ASCAP 1958
composer, author
b San Antonio, Tex, Oct 27, 28. Educ: Southern Methodist Univ. Professional football player, NY Football Giants. Sports commentator, WNEW, NY. *Songs:* Touchdown; Skating Polka; Wait for Me; Send Me Someone; I Can't Figure You Out; Lonely Christmas Snow; Someone Lovely Just Passed By; Don't Rock and Roll the Polka; Fight You Fighting Giants.

ROTELLA, JOHN W   ASCAP 1954
composer, studio musician
b Jersey City, NJ, Nov 4, 20. Educ: Emerson High Sch; pvt instr on all woodwinds & Schillinger Syst Musical Comp. Saxophonist, Raymond Scott, Tommy Dorsey, Benny Goodman & Jerry Gray Orchs. Mem, 389th ASF Band, Ft Monmouth, NJ, WW II. Studio recording musician. Chief Collabrs: Johnny Mercer, Ray Gilbert, Franz Steininger, Jerry Gladstone. *Songs:* A Lonesome Heart; Time to Say Goodnight; Nothing But the Best; Abbracciami; Per Te-Per Me; Music: The Sky Is Extra Blue; Tormented; Baby-O; Thanks for Nothing; If You Don't Think I'm Leaving; You and Me My Love; I've Waited for a Waltz; How Can I Begin to Tell; Just Close Your Eyes; A Thousand Violins; Do It Now. *Instrumental Works:* Desidero; Walking Through Capetown; Tin Whistle; Chicha; Big Daddy.

ROTH, BERNARD
composer, author
b Gary, Ind, Feb 3, 23. Educ: Ind Univ, 2 yrs. *Songs:* The Show Goes On; Forty Days and Forty Nights; Love, Love, Go Away; Just to Get Back Home With You.

ROTH, MICHAEL STEVEN   ASCAP 1978
composer, author
b Brooklyn, NY, July 23, 54. Educ: Univ Mich, BA(cum laude), 75, studied music comp with William Bolcom; pvt study, Manhattan Sch Music, piano with Hyman Kurzweil. Comp for var off Bway theatres, incl Impossible Ragtime, Am Place & Columbia Univ; comp var songs & chamber pieces, music theatre work & opera. Chief Collabrs: Daniel M Schreier, John Wellman, Norman Plotkin. *Songs:* Things are Looking Up; Train; Music: On the Legacy of Chairman Mao (a two step). *Instrumental Works:* Woodwind Quintet. *Scores:* Opera/Ballet: Hopi Prophecies of the Twentieth Century; Imagination Dead Imagine; Off Bway Shows: The Bird Lovers; Starluster.

ROTH, PETE   ASCAP 1964
composer, author, musician
b Cleveland, Ohio, Oct 30, 1893. Educ: Pub schs. Mem, string groups. Chief Collabr: Roy Jackson. *Songs:* If You Feel the Way I Do.

ROTHBERG, BOB   ASCAP 1936
composer, author
b New York, NY, Oct 28, 01; d New York, Feb 1, 38. Educ: New York Law Sch, LLB; pvt music study. Lyricist, film cartoons. Chief Collabrs: Joseph Meyer, Peter Tinturin, Dave Pollock. *Songs:* Night Wind; And Then They Called It Love; Are You Lovable?; Close to Me; Congratulate Me; Debutante Waltz; Did She Ask for Me?; I'm Gonna Put You in Your Place; It Ain't Right;

Mickey Mouse's Birthday Party; You or No One; There's a Silver Moon on the Golden Gate.

ROTTURA, JOSEPH JAMES   ASCAP 1962
composer, author, performer
b Rochester, Pa, Apr 29, 29; d Jan 18, 80. Educ: Rochester High Sch, Pa; Catholic Univ of Am; Univ of Ariz, BMus; Univ Calif, Los Angeles; Mt St Mary's Col, Los Angeles, Calif, MMus; studied voice, piano & clarinet with Armando Januzzi, Eugene Conley, Diran Akmajian, Ann Melignani. Singer, opera, theatres, clubs, radio & TV. Taught at univ level. Gen mgr, record & publ co. Chief Collabrs: Paul Weston, Marilyn & Alan Bergman. *Songs:* Come Touch My Hand; Chorals: Ballad of Jesse James; The Beatitudes; Christmas on the Trail; Missa Simplex; Parish Mass of St Paul; Overture for Voices; We Sing of America.

ROURKE, MICHAEL ELDER (HERBERT REYNOLDS)   ASCAP 1914
author
b Manchester, Eng, July 14, 1867; d New York, NY, Aug 26, 33. Educ: Monastery sch. Charter mem, ASCAP. Bway press agent; staff writer, music publishers. Songwriter, "The Girl From Utah." Memorabilia in Am music section of archives, Univ Wyo. Chief Collabrs: Jerome Kern, Oscar Nedbal, Sigmund Romberg, Emmerich Kalman. *Songs:* They Didn't Believe Me; Auf Wiedersehn; I Picked a Lemon in the Garden of Love; Throw Me a Rose; What's the Use of Dreaming?; Come Back to Connemara; Lieber Augustin; I Saw the Roses and Remembered You; Half a Moon. *Scores:* Bway shows: The Peasant Girl; The Blue Paradise; Miss Springtime; Rock-a-bye Baby.

ROUSE, ERVIN THOMAS   ASCAP 1935
composer, author, singer
b Craven County, NC, Sept 18, 17. Started writing, 46. With RCA Victor Records, 69. Singer with Glen Miller, Coney Island, Metier Davis Band, Boston & Hamston, Long Island. Appeared on "Johnny Cash Show" & "Grand Ole Opry." *Songs:* Orange Blossom Special; Sweeter Than the Flowers; Craven County Blues; New York Boy Goin' Hillbilly; I'm Getting Grey Hair; When My Baby Cries; We'll Start Love All Over Again; Please Doggies Lead On; Loan Me a Buck; Bum Bum-Blues; North Carolina I'm Coming Home; The Champion; The Silver Meteor; I'm a Lonesome Ranger Now.

ROVIN, FELIX A(SHER) (FISHEL RABINOVITCH)   ASCAP 1965
composer, author, conductor
b Vilna, Lithuania, July 16, 12. Educ: CBK Humanistic Gymnasium, Vilna, dipl, 29; Grad Nat Cons, Vilna, dipl, 33, studied perc with Prof Stempkowski, comp with Prof Galkowski, 33-35. Made debut with Vilna Symph Orch, 33. Mem fine arts fac, Stephen Batory Univ, Vilna, 35-38. With Nat Lithuania Radio Symph & Jazz Ens, Vilna, White Russian & Armenian Philh Orchs, Georgian & Uzbekian Jazz Ens, Soviet Circus, Caucasus & Israeli Radio "Kol Israel" & "Galey Tsahal." Had freelance concerts, recordings & club dates in US. Music dir, cond & founder, Old/New Am Stage/Jazz Orch, New York. Made var recordings of own works in Poland, Lithuania, USSR, France, Israel & US. Drummer, percussionist, tympanist, jazz events producer & music publ. Former mem: Soviet Music Fund; ZAIKS, Poland; CISAC, France; ACUM, Israel. Mem: Am Fedn Musicians; Prof Musicians & Vocalists Asn New Immigrants (founder & chmn); House Congress LSNCC. *Songs:* Money, Money; New York-My Town; The Sinai Saga-Trilogy; Mon Amour (It's You That I Love); Call Me Sweetheart. *Instrumental Works:* Golden Peacock Rhapsody; Yemenite Dance Scene.

ROWE, MITCHELL L   ASCAP 1969
composer, author, singer
b Philadelphia, Pa, Nov 14, 48. Performed TV series, "CBS Children's Hour," 56-60; rock & roll performer, 60-68; songwriter, 68- Chief Collabrs: Bobby Eli, Fred Disipio, Bix Reichner. *Songs:* Fair Skin Man; Gone Is the Laughter of You; Brown Eyed Girl; L-O-V-E Love. *Scores:* Opera: Free the Black Man's Chains.

ROWE, NELLIE
See Nichols, Nellie Margaret

ROWELL, GLENN   ASCAP 1940
composer, author, actor
b Pontiac, Ill, Nov 2, 1899; d Rapid City, SDak, Oct 8, 1965. Educ: Strausberger's Cons. Rag-time pianist, age 13, St Louis; played silent movies, St Louis & Chicago; cabarets, Chicago. On radio, WLS-Chicago, 24; mem of team Ford & Glenn, originated "National Barn Dance" & "National Farm & Home Hour"; with team Gene & Glen with John & Lena on network shows for many yrs. Appeared on TV, WPIX-New York, 2 yrs, WLW-Cincinnatti, 2 yrs, KYW-Cleveland, 2 yrs & KOTA-Rapid City, 8 yrs; originated children's show "Captain Glenn's Fun Wagon." Co-owner, Rowell-McDonald Travel Agency, SDak; pres, Funwagon Products, Inc. Mem, Am Guild of Authors & Composers, Songwriters of Am. Chief Collabrs: Gene Carroll, J Fred Coots. *Songs:* I Wish You Were Jealous of Me; But You Do; Some of Your Sweetness; Help the Kid Around the Corner; Open the Window of Your Heart; Where in the World But in America; Schoolday Sweethearts; Read Your Bible Every Day; I Get the Blues When It Rains; Barbara With the Big Blue Eyes; On a Circular Staircase; and many others.

ROWEN, RUTH HALLE   ASCAP 1959
composer, author, educator

b New York, NY, Apr 5, 18. Educ: Horace Mann High Sch; Bernard Col, BA(Phi Beta Kappa); Columbia Univ Grad Fac, MA, PhD, William Mason & Clarence Barker fels; studied with William John Mitchell, Paul Henry Lang, Erich Hertzmann & Douglas Stuart Moore. Mgr, Educ Dept, Carl Fischer, Inc, 53-63. Prof, Music Dept, City Col New York & City Univ New York Grad Sch, 63- Chmn, NY State, Young Artist Auditions; bd mem, NY Fedn Music Clubs. Author "Early Chamber Music" & "Hearing-Gateway to Music." Chief Collabrs: William N Simon (Bill Simon), Mary Rowen Obelkevich. *Songs:* Jolly Come Sing and Play; Whoa, Mule, Whoa!; Somebody Cares for Me; No "Going Steady" for Me; The Needles Eye; I Love Who Loves Me; I Have Decided to Be an Old Maid.

ROWIN, JOHN WILLIAM   ASCAP 1974
composer, author

b Cincinnati, Ohio, Jan 7, 45. Educ: Grossmont Col; Pacific Christian Col; Harbor Col. Writer, 63- Artist, United Artists Records, 68. Writer of musical play. Chief Collabrs: Jerry Peters, Skip Scarborough, Charlotte Politte, Ralph Melendrez, Melvin Brown, Ted Walters. *Songs:* Every Girl; Hey Little Girl; Baby, Baby, Baby; A Road to Nowhere; It's Your Love; The Journey; It Is Love; Lyrics: Raw Sugar; Funky Business; Sauda; HRD Boogie; Rebop.

ROWLES, JAMES GEORGE   ASCAP 1960
composer, author, pianist

b Spokane, Wash, Aug 19, 18. Educ: Gonzaga Univ, pre-law; pvt piano study with Norm Thue. Mil service, WW II. Accompanist & pianist with Garwood Van, Muzzy Marcellino, Slim & Slam, Lee & Lester Young, Benny Goodman, Woody Herman, Skinnay Ennis, Les Brown, Tommy Dorsey, Jerry Gray, Bob Crosby, Peggy Lee, Evelyn Knight, Vic Damone, Billie Holiday, Henry Mancini, Carmen Macrae, Sarah Vaughan, Carol Sloane & Alberta Hunter & also for 20th Century Fox, Universal & Paramount; own trios & duos in Hollywood & New York; recording artist, 47-; singer. Chief Collabrs: Johnny Mercer, Sheryl Ernst, Tom Adair. *Songs:* Ballad of Thelonius Monk; The Lady in the Corner (Heather); Jam Face; After School; Music's the Only Thing That's on My Mind; Granpa's Vibrato; Myriam; Music: Morning Star; Frasier; My Mother's Love; Looking Back; Shadows on the Sand; The Persian; Pavin' California; Baby, Don't Quit Now (Little Ingenue). *Instrumental Works:* Perk Up (jazz); 502 Blues (Drinkin' and Drivin'). *Songs & Instrumental Works:* The Pygmy Lullaby; American Gardner; The Devil's Day Off; The Peacocks; Old Orleans; We Take the Cake.

ROY, WILLIAM   ASCAP 1958
composer, author, conductor

b Detroit, Mich, May 24, 28. Educ: Studied comp with Edward Kilenyi. Featured roles in some 20 films & many radio appearances. Writer, arr & musical dir, Julius Monk Revues, 7 yrs. Music & lyrics, musical direction & perf many indust shows. Musical dir for Dorothy Dandridge, Mary McCarty, Celeste Holm, Lisa Kirk, Sylvia Syms, Julie Wilson, Portia Nelson, Dolores Gray, Margaret Whiting, Bernadette Peters, Mabel Mercer & Bobby Short. *Songs:* Charm; Chicago, Illinois; Come Away With Me; The World Today. *Scores:* Maggie (Bway); The Penny Friend (Off-Bway).

ROYAL, TED
See Dewar, Ted Royal

ROZARIO, BOB   ASCAP 1975
author, director

b Shanghai, China; June 2, 33. Educ: St Francis Xavier High Sch; studied piano with Mrs Moisef, 5 yrs. Pianist, 60. Cond & arr for Bobby Darin, 67. Music dir for TV "Tony Orlando and Dawn", "Donny and Marie Special" & "Bobby Darin Show," 72- *Scores:* Rock Opera: Judas Maccabeus.

ROZIN, ALBERT   ASCAP 1960
composer, teacher

b Minsk, Russia, June 15, 06. Educ: Studied piano with Nicholas Nicolaeeff & organ with Jesse Crawford. Organist & choir dir, Beth Sholom People's Temple, Brooklyn, NY, 53- Comp of liturgical music. Judge for Annual Nat Student Comp Test sponsored by Am Col Musicians. *Songs & Instrumental Works:* Hebrew Festival Melodies; Traditional Hebrew Songs; Little Concerto (2 pianos); Two Together (duet bk); The Weather Suite (6 piano solos).

RUBEN, AARON
See Gonzalez, Aaron Ruben

RUBENS, HUGO   ASCAP 1940
composer, pianist, organist

b New York, NY, Apr 1, 05; d. Educ: High sch; also studied music with father. Pianist & organist in film theatres & vaudeville. *Songs:* Little Small Town Girl; The Chauffeur and the Debutante; Suitcase Susie; Low Tide; Be Good, Be Careful, Be Mine; It Doesn't Cost a Thing to Dream; Don't You Put the Bee on Me; Cobbler on Cobblestone Road (children's song). *Instrumental Works:* Carnegie Hall Concerto; Scotland Yard Suite; Overture to Love's Labor Lost.

RUBENS, MAURIE   ASCAP 1926
composer

b New York, NY, Dec 25, 1893; d Los Angeles, Calif, July 24, 48. Chief Collabrs: Clifford Grey, J Keirn Brennan. *Songs:* Over the Hill; What's the Reason?; The Promenade Walk; Temptation Strut; Your Broadway and Mine; Beauty Is Vanity; No Other Love; Odle-De-O. *Scores:* Bway Stage: Great Temptations; The Madcap; Greenwich Village Follies of 1928; Music in May; A Night in Venice.

RUBENSTEIN, LOUIS URBAN   ASCAP 1950
composer, author

b Boston, Mass, Jan 1, 08. Educ: Piano study with William Strong; Boston Latin Sch, 26; Brown Univ, BA, 30. Writer of short stories & radio scripts, 30-37. Staff pianist, Jack Yellen Music Publ Co, 31-32; singer & pianist, nightclubs, NY & NJ, 38-41. Sgt, 6th Army, WW II, 42-45. In textile business, 46-51; sales exec, Security Mills, Inc, 51-61, financial analyst & consult, 61- Chief Collabrs: William Kaye, Elliot Jacoby, Gladys Shelley. *Songs:* Here's My Heart; All Night Long; Why Not Try Paradise; Keep America Free; Music: The Merry Ghost of Chatham Square; Twilight (Borodin adaptation); Garden of Allah.

RUBIN, ADA
See Roeter, Ada

RUBIN, AL I   ASCAP 1970
composer, author

b New York, NY, Apr 4, 28. Record distributor & manufacturer. Chief Collabr: Bernie Baum. *Songs:* Red, Red Roses; You're the Girl I've Always Wanted; It's Christmas Time Again (formerly known as "It's Snowing in New York"); Dolly Dimples; Love My Dolly; Absence Makes My Heart Grow Fonder; The Yeaster Bunny.

RUBIN, DIANE GAIL
See Browne, Diane Gail (Daisy)

RUBIN, DORIS ANNE (DORIS MENKES)   ASCAP 1962
author

b Charlottesville, Va, Aug 24, 21. Educ: Duke Univ, BA, 41; Columbia Univ Grad Bus Sch, 42. Copy chief, Bamberger's, NJ, 53-45; advert dir, Gimbels, NY, 65-71; wrote lyrics. Chief Collabr: Comp, Joseph Liebman. *Songs:* Lyrics: My Secret World; Forbidden.

RUBIN, RUTH   ASCAP 1963
composer, author, folklorist

b Montreal, Can, Sept 1, 06. Educ: High sch. Began specializing in Jewish folklore, 44; gave lecture-recitals, US, Can & abroad. On ed bd, NY Folklore Quarterly. Taught at New Sch for Social Res, NY. Author "Treasury of Jewish Folksong", "Voices of a People", "The Story of Yiddish Folksong" & "Singable English Translations," Yiddish songbk. Mem: Am Folklore Soc (past councillor), Can Folk Music Soc (past councillor), NY Folklore Soc & Int Folk Music Coun (secy, US Nat Comn).

RUBINSTEIN, JOHN ARTHUR
actor, composer

b Los Angeles, Calif, Dec 8, 46. Educ: Univ Calif, Los Angeles, 64-67; Juilliard Sch Music, 73-74. Keyboard player & comp for group Funzone. Appeared in numerous TV shows incl "The Virginian", "Ironside", "The Bold Ones", "Storefront Lawyers", "The Young Lawyers", "Mod Squad", "The Psychiatrist", "Mary Tyler Moore Show", "Matt Lincoln", "Hawaii Five-O", "Broadway, My Street", "Barnaby Jones", "The Quest" & "Lou Grant"; appeared in TV movies incl "A Howling in the Woods", "The Streets of San Francisco", "All Together Now", "Roots: The Next Generations", "Happily Ever After" & "The Gift of the Magi"; also appeared in motion pictures incl "Journey to Shiloh", "Getting Straight" & "The Car"; stage show appearances incl "Camelot", "South Pacific" & "Pippin" (Theater World Award). Mem: Am Fedn TV & Radio Artists, Actors Equity, Screen Actors Guild, Comp & Lyricists Guild Am. *Scores:* Films: Paddy; Jeremiah Johnson; Kid Blue; The Candidate; The Killer Inside Me; TV: The New Land; All Together Now; Stalk the Wild Child; Emily; The Fitzpatricks; The New Maverick; Wonderland Cove; Champions: A Love Story; Get Patty Hearst.

RUBY, HARRY   ASCAP 1917
composer, author, pianist

b New York, NY, Jan 27, 1895; d Los Angeles, Calif, Feb 23, 74. Educ: Pub schs. Pianist & song plugger for var publ firms incl Gus Edward & Harry Von Tilzer. Played in vaudeville, nickelodeans & cafes. To Hollywood, 30, songwriter for var films incl "Check and Double Check", "The Cuckoos", "Horsefeathers" & "The Kid From Spain" (also screenplay). Writer of screenplays for "Look for the Silver Lining", "Bright Lights" & "Duck Soup." Film biography, "Three Little Words." Chief Collabrs: Bert Kalmar, Ted Snyder, Oscar Hammerstein 2nd, Edgar Leslie, George Jessel, Rube Bloom, Herbert Stothart, Fred Ahlert. *Songs:* When Those Sweet Hawaiian Babies Roll Their Eyes; What'll We Do Saturday Night When the Town Goes Dry; Daddy Long Legs; And He'd Say 'Oo-La-La-Wee-Wee; He Sits Around; So Long, Oo-Long; The Sheik of Avenue B; She's Mine, All Mine; The Same Old Moon; The Vamp from East Broadway; My Sunny Tennessee; I Gave You Up Just

Before You Threw Me Down; Who's Sorry Now?; It Was Meant to Be; All Alone Monday; Thinking of You; Up in the Clouds; I Wanna Be Loved By You; Watching the Clouds Roll By; Three Little Words; Hooray for Captain Spaulding (Groucho Marx theme); Nevertheless; I Love You So Much; Everyone Say's I Love You; A Kiss to Build a Dream On; Give Me the Simple Life; Another Night Like This; Maybe It's Because; Show Me a Rose; Omaha, Nebraska; The Real McCoys (TV theme); also The Kalmar & Ruby Song Book. *Scores:* Bway shows: Helen of Troy; The Ramblers; Lucky; The Five O'Clock Girl; Good Boy; Animal Crackers; Top Speed; High Kickers.

RUBY, HERMAN   ASCAP 1922
composer
b New York, NY, Mar 15, 1891; d Los Angeles, Calif, July 31, 59. Chief Collabrs: Harry Akst, Con Conrad, Joseph Meyer, Sammy Stept, Harry Woods, Harry Ruby. *Songs:* My Sunny Tennessee; I'll Always Be In Love With You; Cecilia; My Honey's Lovin' Arms; The Egg and I; In a Boat for Two; Stolen Kisses; Flower of Love; Since I Found You; Pals Just Pals; My Sunday Girl.

RUDERMAN, SEYMOUR GEORGE (RUDY)   ASCAP 1955
author, editor
b New York, NY, May 30, 26. Educ: Antioch Col, BA; Yale Univ Grad Sch of Govt. Prog dir, WHK, Cleveland; asst news dir, WNEW, NY. Chief Collabr: William Harrington. *Songs:* Gee, But You Gotta Come Home.

RUGGIERI, EDMOND (EDDY ROGERS)   ASCAP 1947
composer, author, conductor
b Norfolk, Va, Sept 23, 07; d Denver, Colo, Oct 8, 64. Educ: Royal Cons of Naples, Italy, MA, MusD, hon grad; studied with Rubin Goldmark. Concert violinist, US, Europe & SAm; arr, var orchs. Staff cond, NBC, New York & Denver. Comp for Beniamino Gigli, Metrop tenor. Orch leader, Las Vegas, Aragon Ballroom, Chicago & hotels throughout the US. Chief Collabrs: Leonard Whitcup, Enzo Stuarti, Irving Caesar, Albert Gamse, Paul Cunningham, Dave Oppenheim, Pearl Fein, Ted Lehrman. *Songs:* Maria Mia; I Still Believe in God; Bettina; Only You; Hand in Hand; Moon Valley; Farewell My Darling; Hot Springs Jubilee; The Lord Was There; Ain't Gonna Sin; A Church of Wood; Rosie; Music: Them Golden Stairs; Have You Ever Been in Love in Rome; Promise; Colorado Skies; The Hyphen Song; Tropical Breeze; Thou; Now's the Time; Hold Hands With God; C'Est La Vie; Sympatica; Leaves of Gold; Once More; By the Way; Once Upon a Time; Tormented; Without; Peti Jean. *Instrumental Works:* Niagra; Zingaresca; Strings on the Wing; Wingin' the Strings; Tarantella; Cantilena; The Feather Parade; Autumn Twilight; Grand Lake; Modern Air; Shades of Scarlatti; Chatreuse; Tamarindo.

RUGGLES, CARL SPRAGUE   ASCAP 1975
composer
b Marion, Mass, Mar 11, 1876; d Bennington, Vt, Oct 25, 71. Educ: Harvard Univ, music studies under John Knowles Paine. Taught modern comp, Univ Miami, two yrs; active comp & drawing, Winona, Minn, 07-17, founded & directed a symph orch; active in the Int Guild of Comp, New York, 20's; mem, Nat Inst of Arts & Letters. Hon DMus, Univ Vt, 60; Creative Arts Award, Brandeis Univ, 64; Award of Merit, The Nat Asn for Am Comp & Cond. *Songs:* Toys. *Instrumental Works:* Sun-treader; Lilacs; Men and Mountains; Portals; Organum; Evocations; Angels.

RUIZ, ENRIQUE   ASCAP 1960
composer, singer
b Arg, Nov 11, 08; d Green Valley, Ariz, Nov 5, 75. Educ: High sch; pvt music study. Prof debut in "Tosca," Buenos Aires, Arg, 25. Gave concerts for USO, WW II. Has had own radio progs, Buenos Aires & New York. Has made many records; appeared in films in SAm & Europe. Chief Collabr: Helen Steele. *Songs:* Intermezzo; Nuestro Amor de Hoy; Tiri Tomba; El Afilador; Reflejos de Espana; Cancion del Pastor; Campanas de Fiesta; Duerme, Nina Mia; Lagrimas; Donde; Dudosa; La Primavera; El Viajero.

RUMORO, JOE LOUIS   ASCAP 1957
composer, guitarist
b Chicago, Ill, Oct 1, 23; d. Educ: High sch; pvt music study. Led jazz group, 41-43. Guitarist, Boyd Raeburn Orch & Chicago Theatre pit band. Staff guitarist, WBBM, radio & TV, Chicago. Made many records. *Songs & Instrumental Works:* Easy Pickin'; Sorta Blue; Early Ride; Cook's Delight; Unless There's You; Yesterday's Love.

RUMSEY, MURRAY
See Rumshinsky, Murray

RUMSHINSKY, JOSEPH M   ASCAP 1963
composer
b Vilna, Russia, Sept, 1881; d New York, NY, Feb 6, 56. Educ: Europ Cons. Produced musicals in the Yiddish Theatre. *Songs:* Shein Vi Di L'vone; Eishes Chayil; Shloimele-Malkele; Z'chor; Hamavdil; In Meine Oigen Bistu Shein; Es Tziht, Es Briht. *Songs & Instrumental Works:* Oz Joshir (cantata). *Scores:* Opera: Ruth.

RUMSHINSKY, MURRAY (MURRAY RUMSEY)   ASCAP 1960
composer, author, conductor
b New York, NY, June 26, 07. Educ: Damrosch Inst of Musical Art; studied with Lazare Saminsky, Antonio Lora. Comp, cond & pianist in vaudeville, operettas. *Songs & Instrumental Works:* Sabra Square Dance; Music to My Ear; Bazaars of Bagdad; My Philosophy.

RUNNINGBROOK, JIM
See Drawbaugh, Jacob W

RUNYAN, WILLIAM MARION   ASCAP 1952
composer, author
b Marion, NY, Jan 21, 1870; d Galveston, Tex, July 29, 57. Educ: Garrett Biblical Inst, Northwestern Univ; Wheaton Col, LittD, 48. Minister of the Gospel, Methodist Episcopal Church, 24 yrs, retired, 23. Assoc ed, Moody Bible Inst, 26-39. Morning devotional speaker, WMBI radio sta, Chicago, 5 yrs. Ed, Hope Publ Co, 44-48. Writer words & comp music of many hymns of faith. Ed, numerous gospel song books. Lectr, hymnology. *Songs:* Great Is Thy Faithfulness; In the Hollow of His Hand; Lord, I Have Shut the Door; What God Hath Promised; Behold What Love; He Will Hide Me; Jesus, Oh What a Name; Assurance March (WMBI); Jesus Name I Love; Teach Me Thy Will, O Lord.

RUPP, ANNA T   ASCAP 1963
composer, author
b Quincy, Ill, Jan 25, 09. Educ: High sch; bus sch. *Songs:* You Are My Sweetheart; Loving Only You; Janie; Dreaming; It's Love; Love Me.

RUPP, CARL   ASCAP 1925
composer, conductor, pianist
b Chicago, Ill, May 11, 1892; d. Educ: High sch; Metrop Cons; studied with father and Max Kramer. Led own orch in hotels, 11. Great Lakes Training Sta, WW I. Music dir, hotels & radio. Invented elec devices to simplify teaching of piano. *Songs:* I Feel So Good; Arizona Stars; Don't Bother Me; My Sweetie and Me; Lovely Lady; Tonight's the Night; The Flapper Wife.

RUSCH, HAROLD W (WENDEL REESE)   ASCAP 1958
composer, author, arranger
b Wabeno, Wis, Oct 14, 08. Educ: Wabeno High Sch; Univ Wis; Lawrence Univ, BA, 30; studied with Carl Bruebner, 48-49 & Joseph Wagner, 50-51. Teacher; sales personnel; educ consult. Chief Collabrs: J Frederick Muller; Mark R McDunn. *Songs:* The Beat Goes On. *Instrumental Works:* Belwin Band Studies; Hal Leonard Band Methods; Muller-Rusch String Methods; Quick Steps to Note Reading; Methode De Trombone; Methode De Trumpette; Methode De Cor; Korps Metodikk; Handel Suite (band); Nubucco (band); Circa 1900 (band); Rosamunde (orch); Menominee Sketches (symph, orch).

RUSCH, JEROME ANTHONY (JERRY RUSH)   ASCAP 1973
composer, author, trumpet player
b St Paul, Minn, May 8, 43. Educ: Univ Minn, 65. Performer, nightclubs, TV, films & Gerald Wilson Big Band. Jazz trumpet player; teacher; singer. Recording artist. *Songs:* Like They Say in LA; Adams and Eve; Music: Reds Blues; Mode for a Toad; David.

RUSE, ROBERT LOUIS (BOB LEWIS, LOU ROBERTS)   ASCAP 1960
composer, author
b Los Angeles, Calif, Dec 16, 19. Educ: Inglewood High Sch, Calif; Compton Jr Col, Calif; Univ Ariz, BA(Spanish, music). WW II, Ger, 2 yrs; Lt Colonel, pilot, USAF, retired, 70. *Songs:* Men in Blue.

RUSH, JERRY
See Rusch, Jerome Anthony

RUSH, LAWRENCE R   ASCAP 1970
author
b Dayton, Ohio, July 16, 38. Educ: Radio TV Dept, Univ Cincinnati, Ohio, 60. Prof mgr, September Music Corp. Chief Collabrs: Paul Leka, Paul Evans & Lor Crane. *Songs:* Lyrics: Lots of Pretty Girls; Another Year, Another Love, Another Heartache; Falling Sugar.

RUSH, MARY JO (MARY JO MATTHEWS)   ASCAP 1956
composer, actress, singer
b Mannington, WVa, Apr 11, 09. Educ: Mannington High Sch; Fairmont Normal Sch, WVa, 1 yr; WVa Univ, AB; Univ Calif Los Angeles Music Sch. Dancer; appeared in New York musical comedies, Bway, 29-34; appeared in a Hollywood movie for Columbia Studios, 34; was under contract to Metro-Goldwyn-Mayer, 35; had small parts in other films. *Songs:* Chilly Willy; Buenas Noches, Maria; Love Never Changes; Lonely; America's Way of Life; Christmas Prayer; Love is Not a Sometime Thing; Monterey; Night Winds; Sun Down; Music: A Consolation (lyrics, Shakespearean Sonnet XXIV).

RUSHING, JAMES ANDREW   ASCAP 1946
composer, singer
b Oklahoma City, Okla, Aug 26, 02; d. Educ: Wilberforce Univ; studied violin & piano. Singer with bands; joined Count Basie, 35; to New York with band, 36-50. Formed own septet, toured theatres & Savoy Ballroom, until 52. Worked

as single, appeared at jazz fests; made Europ tours. Appeared in film, "Funzapoppin'" & TV shows. Chief Collabrs: Eddie Durham, Count Basie, Lester Young. *Songs:* Goin' to Chicago Blues; Sent for You Yesterday; Bran' New Wagon; Baby, Don't Tell on Me; Good Morning Blues; Don't You Miss Your Baby?; Nobody Knows; Blues in the Dark; Take Me Back, Baby; Undecided Blues; You Can't Run Around.

RUSINCKY, PAUL   ASCAP 1940
composer, author, violinist

b Miskolcz, Hungary, July 10, 03; d Queens, NY, June 25, 79. Educ: Studied with family, also pvt tutors; studied violin with Deszo Szigeti, Eugene Ormandy & Jacques Malkin. To US, 12; violin soloist in recitals. Chief Collabrs: Edward Breuder, Charles Tobias, Al Neiburg, Nathan Van Cleave, Ray Bloch, Alfredo Antonini, Michael Colicchio. *Songs:* Out of the Night; Midnight Moon; Jersey Jungle; I Can't Pretend; If You Were Mine; Elegy of Love; Moondust Rhapsody; Daybreak Serenade; Lydia Waltz; I Travel Alone; Blue and Melancholy Mood; Sam the Vegetable Man; I'm Face to Face With Love; Festival Night in Santa Barbara; Pepito and His Violin; Young Fella You're Ready for Love; Fatima's Drummer Boy; Gee! But You're Cute; America, We're on Our Way!; You Can't Do That to Me; Ev'ry Night Is a Goody Good Night (When I'm With You); Keep Holin'; The Oceana; As Dawning Greets the Day; Skyrocket; Cold Turkey; My Little Mule (Mi Muletto); Mother's Little Helper; Cryin' My Heart Out for You; (The) Big Bass Drum.

RUSKIN, HARRY   ASCAP 1954
author

b Cincinnati, Ohio, Nov 30, 1894; d. Educ: Miami Mil Acad. Wrote songs for Bway musicals; to Hollywood, 30; writer for Paramount, 5 yrs & MGM, 16 yrs; wrote screenplays, "Dr Kildare", "Andy Hardy" series, "The Postman Always Rings Twice." Chief Collabr: Henry Sullivan. *Songs:* I May Be Wrong, But I Think You're Wonderful; I Can't Get Over a Girl Like You.

RUSSELL, ALEXANDER (GEORGE)   ASCAP 1928
composer, organist, pianist

b Franklin, Tenn, Oct 2, 1880; d Dewitt, NY, Nov 24, 53. Educ: Hon MusD & BA, Syracuse Univ, Fine Arts Col; studied with Leopold Godowsky, Harold Bauer & Edgar Stillman Kelley, Cincinnati Cons. Instr piano & organ, Syracuse Univ, 02-06. Debut as pianist, Paris, 08; concertized in US, 08-10. Concert dir, Auditorium Concerts, John Wanamaker, NY, also in Philadelphia, 19-29. Dir of music (Frick Chair), Princeton Univ, 17-35. Supervised construction of organs in 2 Wanamaker stores, also Princeton chapel. Rec'd Order of Crown of Belgium. Mem, Am Guild of Organists. *Songs:* Sunset; The Sacred Fire; In Fountain Court; Lyric From Tangore; Expectations; Puer Redemptor. *Instrumental Works:* Piano: Theme and Variations; Contrapuntal Waltz; Organ: St Lawrence Sketches; Choral: Motet in Memory of Princeton Men Fallen in World War I.

RUSSELL, ANNA   ASCAP 1956
composer, author, singer

b London, Eng, Dec 27, 11. Educ: Royal Col of Music, London. Concert comedienne throughout the world. Wrote, comp & appeared in "Lady Audley's Secret (Or, Who Pushed George)" & "All By Myself." *Songs:* I'm Sitting in the Bar All Alone; Feeling Fine; I Love the Spring. *Albums:* Anna Russell Sings?; Anna Russell Sings? Again!; Guide to Concert Audiences; Square Talk on Popular Singing; Anna Russell in Darkest Africa; A Practical Banana Promotion.

RUSSELL, ARMAND   ASCAP 1965
composer

b Seattle, Wash, June 23, 32. Educ: Lincoln High Sch; Univ Wash, BA, 53, MA, 54; Eastman Sch Music, DMA, 58. Performer double bass, Seattle Symph, Rochester Civic & Philh Orch & Boston Pops Tour Orch. Prof music, Univ Hawaii, 61- *Instrumental Works:* Pas de deux (clarinet & perc); Suite Concertante (tuba & woodwind quintet); Particles (saxophone & piano); Harlequin Concerto (double bass & orch); Second Concerto (perc); Symphony in Three Images. *Songs & Instrumental Works:* A Set of Psalms (choral).

RUSSELL, BENEE   ASCAP 1927
composer, author

b New York, NY, Aug 10, 02; d New York, June 28, 61. Educ: Pub schs. Newspaper reporter, Rochester, NY. Under contract for var music pubs, New York. To Hollywood, staff writer for films. Playwright, "By Appointment Only." Chief Collabrs: Abel Baer, Al Jolson. *Songs:* Lonesome in the Moonlight; Don't Never Do That; Nice Baby; Go Home and Tell Your Mother; A Song Without a Name (Steinway prize); You Didn't Want Me When You Had Me; Katinka; Israel (nat marching song).

RUSSELL, BOB (SIDNEY KEITH RUSSELL)   ASCAP 1942
composer, author

b Passaic, NJ, Apr 25, 14; d Beverly Hills, Calif, Feb 18, 70. Educ: Washington Univ, St Louis, scholarship. Adv copywriter; worked in film studios; wrote spec material. Wrote songs for films incl "That Midnight Kiss"; "Ticket to Tomahawk"; "Affair in Trinidad"; "Banning" (Acad Nomination, 68); "For Love of Ivy" (Acad Nomination, 69); "The Wild Bunch"; "Whatever Happened to Aunt Alice"; "Four Seasons"; "Anatomy of a Murder"; "A Matter of Who." Wrote songs for musicals "All in Fun" & Shootin' Star." Chief Collabrs: Harry

Warren, Duke Ellington, Lester Lee, Carl Sigman, Lou Alter, Harold Spina, Peter DeRose, Bronislau Kaper, Quincy Jones, Bobby Scott, Sol Kaplan, Shorty Rogers, Pete Rugolo. *Songs:* Lyrics: Frenesi; Maria Elena; Brazil; Time Was; Parade (A Banda); Taboo; Don't Get Around Much Anymore; Babalu; Do Nothin' Till You Hear From Me; I Didn't Know About You; Ballerina; You Came a Long Way From St Louis; The Color of Love; Crazy He Calls Me; The Girl Most Likely; No More; Would I Love You, Love You, Love You; Alone Too Long; No Other Love; A Matter of Who; Miserlou; Carnival; I Know, I Know, I Know; I've Been Kissed Before; Circus; He Ain't Heavy, He's My Brother; Just When We're Falling in Love; Blue Gardenia; For Love of Ivy; The Eyes of Love; Mirror of Morning; Interlude.

RUSSELL, BOBBY   ASCAP 1967
composer, author, singer

b Nashville, Tenn, Apr 19, 41. Educ: Univ Tenn; George Peabody Col; Belmont Col, BA & BS. Won Nashville & Nat Songwriter of the Year Awards; Emmy nomination for "Marcus Nelson Murders." Chief Collabrs: Burt Bacharach, Billy Goldenburg. *Songs:* The Night the Lights Went Out in Georgia (DJ Choice of the Yr); Honey (Miden Song of the World, CMA Song of the Yr); Saturday Morning Confusion; Little Green Apples (Grammy Award); The Joker Went Wild.

RUSSELL, CHARLES ELLSWORTH (PEE WEE)   ASCAP 1958
composer, clarinettist

b St Louis, Mo, Mar 27, 06; d New York, NY, Feb 14, 69. Educ: Western Mil Acad; Univ Mo. Clarinettist, with Tex Beiderbecke, Frank Trumbauer, Eddie Condon & Buddy Hackett, in nightclubs, 30's & 40's. Appeared at many jazz fests; made many records. *Songs:* Music: Englewood: Mama's in the Groove; Muskogee Blue; PeeWee Blues. *Instrumental Works:* D A Blues; Pee Wee Squawks; You're There in a Dream; Midnight Blue; Write Me a Love Song, Baby; Cutie Pie; This Is It.

RUSSELL, GEORGE H   ASCAP 1969
composer, guitarist

b Chicago, Ill, Feb 7, 19. Educ: Hyde Park High Sch, Chicago; Chicago Cons, teaching cert; Los Angeles Cons, comp; studied guitar with Vicente Gomez. Entertainer in nightclubs & TV; recording artist, Motion Picture Studios & RCA Int. Chief Collabrs: Jay Livingston, Ray Evans, Dave Taxe. *Songs:* You Will Find Him There; Music: In Laguna; On the Mountain. *Instrumental Works:* I'll Walk With the Rain; Easy Listening; Talk'n Talk'n Talk; Califia; Far Out; Ju Ju; Tears; Sandpipers; Hello My Love; How Incredible; Birthstone-Suite. *Scores:* Ballet: Encounter Near Venus (comn by Lila Zali of Ballet Pacifica).

RUSSELL, HANON W   ASCAP 1960
composer, author

b Springfield, Mass, Nov 10, 47. Educ: Milford Prep. Chief Collabr: Joey Russell (father). *Songs:* Happy Sticks; Our Prayer.

RUSSELL, HELEN EUGENIA   ASCAP 1978
composer, author, singer

b Clearwater, Fla, Sept 9, 56. Educ: Clearwater High Sch; studied with Tony Rodriquez & Llew Horowitz. Actress for Double Image Theatre, New York. Singer & music creator, Opal Studios; recording artist. Chief Collabrs: Anthony Rodriquez, Llew Horowitz, Karen Young, Michael Lee. *Songs:* Lyrics: God Knows I'm Just a Woman.

RUSSELL, HENRY
See Olson, Henry Russell

RUSSELL, JOSEPH E   ASCAP 1960
composer, author, comedian

b Springfield, Mass, July 12, 20. Own show, "Happy the Clown," TV 8, New Haven, Conn, 56-58 & WHNB-TV, NBC, Hartford, Conn, 74-79; resident clown, Grossinger's, 14 yrs & Concord Hotel, 4 yrs. Stand up comic, leading clubs & hotels US, incl Copacabana, New York; put on artist booked for spec events. Role in play, "The Tender Trap." Chief Collabrs: Hanon Russell & Carl Russell (sons). *Songs:* TV Themes: Happy Sticks; Our Prayer; Be Careful.

RUSSELL, LEE   ASCAP 1959
composer, gospel singer

b Cleveland, Ohio, Feb 16, 20. Educ: Studied comp & voice with Bert Rule. Pop singer & comp. Began as soloist in Showboat nightclub, Cleveland, 40. Joined Paul Martell's Orch, New York. Began TV show with Vincent Lopez, 48; featured vocalist with Vincent Lopez Orch, 3 yrs. Recorded country music, RCA with Pee Wee King, MGM & Kapp Records; changed to gospel singer & comp; formed Steeple Tone Records & Steeple-Tone Publ Co. Known as "The Singing Missionary"; traveled around world 6 times. Made nationwide appearances on TV & radio. Chief Collabrs: Al Rainy, Gary Romero. *Songs & Instrumental Works:* Flower of Faith; But for the Grace of God (There Go I); Someone Walks Beside Me; Precious Promises (God Said); Little White Dove; John the Baptist; Let There Be (And It Was So); Turn Around and Go Back (Go Back to the Bible); If I Had the Wings of an Angel; Gos-Pills (Medicine Brewed in Heaven); When I Look Through the Eyes of God; In His Own Quiet Way; Resurrection (Oh What a Day); Brotherly Love. *Albums:* Healing Hands (ASCAP Award).

RUSSELL, LUIS CARL   ASCAP 1967
composer, pianist, bandleader
b Careening Cay, Panama, Aug 5, 02; d Dec 11, 63. Educ: Studied with Felix Alex Russell (father); Univ Chicago, studied Schillinger Syst. Pianist with King Oliver, Chicago. Leader, own band accompanying Louis Armstrong, 35-43. Toured with Joe Louis & Nat King Cole. Recording artist with Apollo & Decca Records. Chief Collabrs: Louis Armstrong, Evelyn Kizer, Henry (Red) Allen. *Songs:* Back in Town Blues; Call of the Freaks; Come Back Sweet Papa; Let Me Miss You; Saratoga Shout.

RUSSIN, IRVING (BABE)   ASCAP 1957
composer, pianist, saxophonist
b Pittsburgh, Pa, June 18, 11. Educ: High sch. Saxophonist in orchs incl Red Nichols, Roger Wolfe Kahn, Benny Goodman & Ben Pollack. On staff, CBS, NY, 36-38. Pianist in Tommy Dorsey & Benny Goodman Orchs. Led own orch. Staff, Bobby Hammack Orch, ABC-TV, Hollywood, 59-60. Appeared in film "The Glenn Miller Story." *Instrumental Works:* Inspiration; Evergreen.

RUSSO, DAN   ASCAP 1925
composer, conductor
b Chicago, Ill, Oct 14, 1885; d Hollywood, Calif, Sept 5, 56. Educ: Pub schs; studied violin with father. Music dir, vaudeville circuit, Mich, cond ballroom orch, Detroit; formed own orch, toured country in ballrooms, hotels, vaudeville. *Songs:* Kentucky Blues; Toot Toot Tootsie, Goodbye; Imagination; Because of You; Night; Oh, Lizzie; Couldn't Help It If I Tried; Lost.

RUSSO, WILLIAM   ASCAP 1957
composer, conductor, director
b Chicago, Ill, June 25, 28. Educ: Senn High Sch, 45; Roosevelt Univ, BA, 55; pvt study with John J Becker, Karel Jirak & Lennie Tristano. Founded & cond own orchs, 47-69. Cond, trombonist, mgr & publicist of group, Experiment in Jazz, Russo Orch, London Jazz Orch & Chicago Jazz Ens. Trombonist, comp & arr with Stan Kenton, 50-54. Comp pieces played by New York Philh, Chicago Symph, Kansas City Philh, Boston, Boston Pops & San Francisco Symph. Cond, Kansas City Philh, Los Angeles Neophonic Orch & Peabody Orch. Teacher, Manhattan Sch Music, Peabody Inst, Antioch Col, Univ Chicago & Columbia Col, Ill, 65- Dir, Ctr for New Music, Columbus Col, 67-75. Comp-in-residence, City & County of San Francisco, 75-76. Has done film work with Faith & John Hubley, 76-78. Chief Collabrs: Jon Swan, Arnold Weinstein, Stuart Douglass, Adrian Mitchell. *Songs & Instrumental Works:* Symphony No 2 in C; Three Pieces (blues band & orch); Street Music; Aesops Fables; Boulevard (Alice B Toklas Hashish Fudge Revue, Paris Lights); Shepherds' Christmas; 23o N/82oW; The Civil War; Antigone.

RUTHENBERG, JANE CATHERINE (CATHERINE   ASCAP 1967
MARTINI)
composer, author, teacher
b Albuquerque, NMex. Univ Calif, Los Angeles, BA(French), 69, studied with Jan Popper, Opera Workshop, 5 yrs. Mem adj fac & instr French, Spanish & Japanese, Pepperdine Univ, Los Angeles, 70-79. Performed in numerous operas as mezzo soprano, Univ Calif, Los Angeles. Principal performer in musical comedy "Go Like Sixty"; singer in concerts. Chief Collabr: Harry Richman. *Songs:* Lyrics: Stop That Girl (theme song).

RUTHERFORD, PARIS N, III   ASCAP 1973
composer, teacher
b Dallas, Tex, Sept 23, 34. Educ: Southern Methodist Univ, MM(comp), 60. Trombonist & orchestrator, Dallas Symph, 60-65; free lance comp & arr of commercial music, Dallas, 65-70; comp TV commercial scores, London, Eng & comp & arr music, WDR Radio, Cologne, 70-73; prof music, Univ Colo, Denver, 73-78. Prof jazz arr & jazz vocal studies, NTex State Univ, 78-

RUTTEN, GARY DONALD   ASCAP 1974
composer, author, singer
b Carroll, Iowa, Sept 29, 42. Educ: Studied voice with Lehman Beck & music with Willard Straight. Seventh Army Soldiers Chorus, Ger; singer, night clubs; recording artist. *Songs:* These Lonely Children; A Place in Life.

RYAN, BEN   ASCAP 1923
author, dancer
b Kansas City, Mo, Mar 30, 1892; d Leonia, NJ, July 5, 68. Educ: New York High Sch. Dancer, with partner George White, vaudeville, then mem of team, Ryan & Lee. Contract writer for films & writer of special material for comedians. *Songs:* The Gang That Sang 'Heart of My Heart'; When Francis Dances with Me; Inka-Dinka-Doo; M-I-S-S-I-S-S-I-P-P-I; Sentimental Feeling; Remember Mother's Day; Love Tales; Ain't Nature Grand; When We Get Together in the Moonlight; Tum-Tum-Tumble Into Love; Down on 33rd and 3rd; Tree Top Jubilee; Steven Got Even; Huckleberry Finnegan; A Ruble a Rhumba.

RYAN, JAMES EDMUND   ASCAP 1971
composer, author, guitarist
b Plainfield, NJ, Nov 17, 46. Educ: Westfield High Sch, NJ; Villanova Univ; Juilliard Sch Music; studied jazz improvisation with Adolph Sandole. Played, sang, wrote & recorded with group The Critters, 64-70 & with Carly Simon, 70-73; session musician, London, Los Angeles, Calif & New York, 73-80;

recorded with group Wondergap, 76. Chief Collabrs: Andy Goldmark, Robin Bateau, Amy Bolton. *Songs:* Don't Let the Rain Fall Down on Me; After You; Music: Summer's Coming Around Again.

RYAN, JOAN MARY   ASCAP 1976
composer, author
b Brooklyn, NY, Dec 8, 40. Educ: Studied guitar with Lawrence Lucie; Brooklyn Cons, piano-reading & writing; studied piano with Jim Carling. Some volunteer singing in Vet Admin Hospitals, Blind Athletic Asn & Light House; some club work singing. Vocal coach on own songs. Chief Collabr: Jimmy Angel. *Songs:* Nobody's Perfect; Country Mornin'; The Comfort of Your Love; Riverside Drive.

RYAN, ROBERT FRANCIS (ROCKET)   ASCAP 1979
composer, author
b Boston, Mass, June 9, 30. Educ: Brown Univ, AB(Eng lit). Copywriter, BBDO Advert & Rumrill-Hoyt Advert; comedy writer, actor & songwriter, "The Madhouse Brigade," comedy TV series. *Songs:* When You're in Love; It's Time to Start Unloading You; Nothing Happened; How Can I Love You; Every Time You Touch Me I Get Tired.

RYDER, MARY E (MARY CANDY, MARY STIEBLER)   ASCAP 1965
composer, author
b Woodhaven, NY, Sept 27, 24. Stand-up comedian. Chief Collabrs: Eddie Deane, Gloria Shayne. *Songs:* Three Little Worms; Lyrics: The Men in My Little Girl's Life; The Girls in My Little Boy's Life.

RYDER, NOAH F   ASCAP 1948
composer, educator
b Nashville, Tenn, Apr 10, 14; d Norfolk, Va, Apr 17, 64. Educ: Hampton Inst, BS; Univ Mich, MM. Music supv, Goldsboro schs, NC, 35-36; dir music dept, Palmer Mem Inst, Sedalia, NC, 36-38, Teachers Col, NC, 38-41. Cond, Hampton Inst Choir, head theory dept, 41-44. Dir of music, Va State Col, Norfolk div, from 47, Bank St Baptist Church. Cond, Harry Burleigh Glee Club, Va & Fedn of Male Glee Clubs of Va. Served, USN, World War II. *Songs:* Sea Suite for Male Voices; Haul Away Mateys We're Almost Home (Navy War writers prize); Gonna Journey Away. *Instrumental Works:* Piano: Five Sketches.

RYDHOLM, RALPH WILLIAMS   ASCAP 1977
composer, advertising creative director
b Chicago, Ill, June 1, 37. Educ: Austin High Sch; Northwestern Univ, BA, 58, MBA prog, 59. With Young & Rubicam Advert, 60-63, Post-Keyes-Gardner Advert, 63, E H Weiss Advert, 63-65 & BBDO Advert, 65-66; sr vpres, J Walter Thompson Advert, 66-, exec creative dir, 76- Chief Collabrs: Tom Hall, Kelso Herston. *Songs:* Schlitz Makes It Great (Schlitz commercial); Erlanger Beer Commercial; Anthem (Burger King commercial); Only Way to Do It (7-Up commercial).

RYE, SVEN (BUSTER B BROWN)   ASCAP 1959
author
b Randers, Denmark; Feb 26, 26. Educ: Univ Denmark; Sorbonne & Alliance Francaise, Paris; Univ, Berlin. Newspaper correspondent, Paris, London, Vienna, Rome, Berlin & Stockholm; also with London Daily Express & Associated Press. Danish vice consul, Los Angeles, 51-62. Pres, Hollywood Foreign Press Asn, 63 & chmn of bd, 63- Correspondent to leading newspapers & mag in Europe. Publ 2 novels. Chief Collabrs: Hugo Telling, Jim Barry, Kield Jargensen, Otto Lington. *Songs:* Bagateller; Vi er venner; Blomstrende Kastanjer; Rent tilfaldigt. *Instrumental Works:* Nattens Symfoni.

RYERSON, FRANK LAYTON   ASCAP 1943
composer, author, teacher
b Paterson, NJ, July 3, 05. Educ: Paterson Sch Syst, Cent High Sch; Manhattan Sch Music, New York; pvt instr with Sigmund G Schertel. Started as trumpet player & arr for Art Landry, Jan Garber, Arnold Johnson, Mal Hallett, Al Donohue, Glen Gray, Alvino Rey, Jack Teagarden & Vaughn Monroe; finished career as head, Instrumental Music Dept, Paramus Sch Syst, NJ, 19 yrs; arr, "Dance Ballerina Dance," Vaughn Monroe Victor Record. Chief Collabrs: Jimmy Eaton, Grady Watts, Vaughn Monroe, Irving Taylor, Paul Cavanaugh, Jack Palmer. *Songs:* The Boston Tea Party (theme song); Music: Blue Champagne; Bottom Man on the Totem Pole; Something Sentimental; Notes to a Classy Chassis; Host Meets Ghost; Rasputin' Tootin; The Pleasures All Mine; The Love That I Have for You; Caboose on a Slow Freight; Nice Dreamin'; Give a Broken Heart a Break; New New Jersey Tercentenary March. *Songs & Instrumental Works:* Lament in D minor (saxophone solo).

RYMAN, BRYAN   ASCAP 1969
author
b London, Eng, July 27, 33. Dancer, West End, London; choreographer TV & stage; writer & producer cabaret worldwide; lyricist, Dunhill/ABC & film theme songs. Chief Collabrs: Gabriel Mekler, Gerry Grant. *Songs:* Lyrics: The President's Clothes; Yesterday Was Mine; The Jesus Trip (theme for film).

RYNEARSON, PAUL FRANKLIN   ASCAP 1977
composer
b Long Beach, Calif, Dec 12, 45. Educ: Calif Inst Arts, BM; Claremont Grad Sch, MA; Univ Southern Calif, DMA. Teacher: Calif Inst Arts; Polytech Sch, Pasadena; Moorpark Col; Pepperdine Univ. Soloist/accompanist. *Songs:* Ode to a City. *Instrumental Works:* Eleven Contemporary Flute Etudes; Geometriphon.

S

SAAR, LOUIS VICTOR   ASCAP 1924
composer, pianist
b Rotterdam, Holland, Dec 10, 1868; d St Louis, Mo, Nov 23, 37. Educ: Kaiser Wilhelm Univ of Strassburg; Royal Acad Music, Munich. To US as accompanist, Metrop Opera Co. Teacher piano, theory & comp, Nat Cons, NY & NY Col Music, 1898-06. Head of theory dept, Cincinnati Col Music, 06-17, Chicago Musical Col, 17-33 & St Louis Inst, 34-37. Awards: Mendelssohn Stipendium, Berlin; Tonkuenstler Prize, Vienna; Kaiser Prize, Baltimore. *Songs:* Little Gray Dove; Some Happy Days; Indian Summer. *Instrumental Works:* Rococo Suite; From the Mountain Kingdom of the Great Northwest; Along the Columbia River; Old German Masters Suite (string orch); Gondoliera (violin, string orch); Choral: Angus Dei (Bizet); Ave Maria (Schubert); Hallowe'en Night; A Song of Consolation; Persian Love Song.

SACCHETTI, CARL SALVATORE (CARL SETTY)   ASCAP 1967
composer, author
b Pittsfield, Mass, Nov 9, 15. Educ: Am Cons Music, Mass. Musical dir TV & radio show, WBRK, Pittsfield, Mass; producer self-owned commercial jingle co. Authored spec material for singers. Chief Collabrs: Gene DiNovi, Gene Morford, Dennis Klein, Joe Rizzo, Evel Knievel. *Songs:* You Gotta Love Me Now; Oceans of Lovin'; Music: Why (Evel Knievel's epic poem); Lyrics: Celestina (Heavenly One); It's That Time Again (My Time to Cry).

SACCO, ANTHONY (TONY SANTOS, TONY STARR)   ASCAP 1942
composer, author, singer
b Waterbury, Conn, Mar 28, 08. Educ: Wilby High Sch; studied violin with William Tinsley; Yale Sch Music, studied harmony & orch, 29-30. Played violin in vaudeville, Palace Theatre, Waterbury, 28-29. Sang with Norman Cloutier Orch, WTIC, Hartford, 28-29. Guitarist & vocalist with Red Nichols World Famous Pennies, 32. As band vocalist made Brunswick, Melotone, Victor-Columbia & Decca Records. Recorded with Dorsey Bros, Benny Goodman-Roy Smeck, Eddie Paul Orchs, Am Recording Co. Joined Enric Madriguera Orch, Waldorf-Astoria, 33. USA, 3 yrs, 2 yrs in Italy, 5th Army, Staff-Sgt, wrote scores for Army show "Stars and Gripes." Pianist in Sarasota. Chief Collabrs: Dick Smith, Fred Coots, Fred Achert, Peter Tinturin, Marty Symes, Al Lewis. *Songs:* Tally Ho; Music: The Breeze (That's Bringin' My Honey Back to Me); The Summer Breeze; Slumbertime Along the Swanee; In a Soda Fountain Mirror; Campus Moon; Two Ton Tony; I Thrill When They Mention Your Name; Army Shows: Mail Call; I Can See My Man With a European Tan; Half a Mile to Honeysuckle Lane. *Songs & Instrumental Works:* Just a Stone's Throw From Heaven; Hey! Goomba.

SACCO, JOHN CHARLES   ASCAP 1941
composer, conductor, pianist
b New York, NY, July 11, 05. Educ: David Mannes Sch of Music, piano scholarship, 23; Columbia Col, BA, 30, Teachers Col, MA, 40; studied comp with Douglas Moore & Deszo D'Antailfy. Comp songs for Columbia Varsity Shows, 29-30. Capt, Spec Services, Army Air Corp, WW II, wrote musical score for all Air Force Show "Highflight." Assoc musical dir, St Louis Municipal Opera; musical dir, Paper Mill Playhouse; exec dir, Starlight Musicals, Indianapolis, Ind; assoc music ed, G Schirmer Music Publ Co. Chief Collabrs: (poets) Sara Teasdale, Willa Cather, Arthur Guiterman. *Songs:* Music: Brother Will, Brother John; Maple Candy; With This Ring; Spanish Johnny; Strictly Germproof; Who Are You (cantata); The Bells Ring Out for Christmas; Six Doves; Railroad Reverie; Fanfare for Americans; The Spelling of Christmas; Jabberwocky; The Holy Day; Luck O' the Road; Alice (operetta); Johnny the One; Mexican Serenade; Never the Nightingale; Let It Be Forgotten; Are You Runnin' With Me Lord.

SACCO, P PETER   ASCAP 1964
composer, teacher, singer
b Albion, NY, Oct 25, 28. Educ: Fredonia State Univ, BS(music), 50; Frankfurt Sch of Music, 51; Eastman Sch of Music, MMus(comp), 53, DMusA, 58; studied with Wayne Barlow, Bernard Rogers & Howard Hanson. Taught gen music classes & cond jr & sr choral groups, 53-55. Dir choir, Aquinas Col, Grand Rapids, Mich; app dir, Hillel Symph Orch, Rochester, NY, 57-58. Joined music fac as comp-in-residence & head composers workshop, San Francisco State Univ, 59. Began voice study & career as vocal soloist in opera & art songs, 64. App dir vocal dept, 69-71. Teacher theory & comp, Univ Hawaii, 70-71. *Songs & Instrumental Works:* Collected Songs, Vols I & II (medium to high voice & piano); Ring Out, Wild Bells, Opus 100 (SATB); The Lord Is My Shepherd,

Opus 120 (SATB); Vanity, All Is Vanity, Opus 134 (bass clarinet); Sequence, Opus 138 (viola); Elegie, Opus 131 (cello); Ancient to Modern, Opus 124 (piano); Moab Illuminations, Opus 146 (solo piano); Symphony No 1, Opus 11 (orch); Symphony of Thanksgiving, Opus 18 (orch); Four Sketches on Emerson Essays, Opus 17 (orch); Piano Concerto No 1, Opus 19 (orch); Violin Concerto No 1, Opus 21 (orch); Classical Overture, Opus 15 (orch); Five Songs, Opus 22; The Hypocrites, Opus 32 (orch); Song of Solomon, Opus 36 (cantata for tenor, soprano & orch); Three Psalms (cantata); Clarinet Quintet, Opus 50; Requiem, Opus 146 (wind quintet); Sonata No 2, Opus 147 (piano). *Scores:* Opera: Mr Vinegar (chamber opera); Solomon (oratorio).

SACK, ALBERT E   ASCAP 1958
composer, conductor, arranger
b New York, NY, Jan 3, 11; d Los Angeles, Calif, Dec 6, 47. Educ: Studied violin with Rudolph Ringwall & Louis Persinger. With NBC, Cleveland, 26. Music dir for Olsen & Johnson, 34-37. Ghosted for Dave Rose, early 40's. Music cond, Blue Network, 43. Writer & arr, radio & films. Doubled as violinist for Leslie Howard in "Intermezzo." Nat music dir, Black & White Records. Cond & arr for var artists. Winner, Orch World's Distinguished Radio award, 46. Chief Collabrs: Alvie West, Ted Travers, Nat Leslie. *Songs:* Music: Poppa's Tune (Stara); Two Dreamers; I Love You Dearly. *Instrumental Works:* Moonlight Memoirs; Midnight Reveries; In a Breeze. *Scores:* Film/TV: Tunnel of Love; Crusader Rabbit; Make Mine Music (& cond); Three Caballeros (& cond).

SADOFF, MELISSA M   ASCAP 1963
composer, author, pianist
b Belgrade, Yugoslavia, May 1, 33. Educ: Music Acad, Belgrade; also studied drama & ballet. Chief Collabrs: Frankie Carle, Dorothy Wayne. *Songs:* Honolulu Honky Tonk; Aloha Paradise; Melissa.

SADOFF, ROBERT   ASCAP 1953
composer, conductor, pianist
b Brooklyn, NY, June 16, 20. Concert pianist; also pianist & cond dance bands. Accompanist & cond for Eddie Fisher, Rosemary Clooney & Vic Damone. Professional mgr, Bourne, Inc. Music coordr, NBC Radio Network; exec producer, "Bert Parks Show"; talent coordr daytime programming. Pres, Liberty Artist Services, Las Vegas, Nev. Chief Collabrs: Steve Allen, Carolyn Leigh. *Songs & Instrumental Works:* The Rockin' Ghost; Lonely Love; I Hear Those Bells; Toot Sweet; Rollin', Rollin' Stone.

SAENGER, GUSTAV   ASCAP 1924
composer, violinist
b New York, NY, May 31, 1865; d New York, Dec 11, 35. Educ: Studied with Richter, Meyer, Leopold Damrosch, C C Muller. Violinist, Metrop Opera House Orch; also symph orchs until 1893. Asst cond, Empire Theatre; then cond. Ed-in-chief, music publ co. Ed, Metronome & Musical Observer, 04-29. *Instrumental Works:* Scotch Pastorale; March of the Tin Soldiers; Springtime Valse; Intermezzo Scherzo; Andantino.

SAFAN, MARK   ASCAP 1976
composer, author, singer
b Los Angeles, Calif, Aug 15, 51. Educ: Beverly Hills High Sch; Univ of Calif, Santa Barbara; San Francisco Inst of the Arts. Recording artist, Warner Bros Records, 76 & Planet Records, 79. *Songs:* I'm on My Way; Skeletons Dancing; Relax Boy.

SAFFER, BOB   ASCAP 1957
composer, author
b Leeds, England, June 12, 10. Chief Collabr: George Mysels. *Songs:* L B J; Happy Democrats Are We; New Frontiers; New Lyrics: Hail to the Chief.

SAFKA, MELANIE
composer, singer
b New York, NY, Feb 3, 47. Educ: Am Acad Dramatic Arts, New York. Wrote title song for Stanley Kramer's movie, "RPM"; wrote music for movie, "All the Right Noises." Recording artist, RCA, Europe, Neighborhood Records, Australia & New Zealand & Portrait Records, US & Can. Maj Fests incl Woodstock, Isle of Sight & many others; 27 albums; sold close to 23 million records worldwide. Numerous charity works world wide; spokeslady for UNICEF, 70 & 71. *Songs:* Look What They've Done to My Song; Brand New Key; Candles in the Rain; Beautiful People; Nickle Song; Peace Will Come; Leftover Wine; Combine Harvester; Bitter Bad.

SAHL, MICHAEL   ASCAP 1970
composer, author
b Boston, Mass, Sept 2, 34. Educ: Studied with Israel Citkowitz, New Lincoln Sch, New York; Amherst Col, BA, 55; Princeton Univ, MFA, 57, studied with Roger Sessions & Milton Babbitt; Berkshire Sch Music, Tanglewood, studied with Aaron Copland & Lukas Foss; Fulbright Fellowship, Europe. Performed & recorded album with Judy Collins, 68-69. Has appeared as piano soloist with Buffalo Ens for New Music, 65-66, Studio C Free Band, 73, Dan Wagoner & Dancers, 74-78 & in concerts in New York & on tour. Artist in residence, Antioch Col, 75; lectr, Inst of Studies in Am Music, Brooklyn Col. Music dir, WBAI-FM, New York & in charge of Free Music Store, also performed, 73-74.

Major credits incl dance scores: "Saltimbocca", "Flamingoes", "Taxi Dances" "Prayer to the Subway", "An Old-Fashioned Girl" & "Variations on Yonker Dingle." Coauthor of bk on popular harmony "Making Changes." *Songs:* Prothalamium. *Instrumental Works:* A Mitzvah for the Dead; Tropes on the Salve Regina; String Quartet 1969; Symphony 1972; Symphony 1973; Piano Sonata 1974; Violin Concerto; The Conjurer; Stauf; Civilization and Its Discontents; Noah. *Scores:* Films: Pig; Khrushchev Remembers; The Empty Nest; America's Cup; The Incredible Torture Show; The Cruise of the Courageous & many others.

ST CLAIR, FLOYD J ASCAP 1924
composer, cornetist, arranger
b Johnstown, Pa, Feb 4, 1871; d Cleveland, Ohio, Aug 23, 42. Educ: Curry Univ; studied with Carl Retter, Charles Gernert, Harry Archer & Adolph Foerster. Cornetist, 25 yrs; also band dir. Church organist, Trinity Congregational, 07 & Hough Ave Congregational, 22. Organist, Cleveland theatre, 13-15. Ed & arr, music publ firm, 25 yrs. Also taught music. *Instrumental Works:* Iron King (march); The Steel King; Andantino; Communion; Descending Night; Dream Melody; March Pompous; Meditation.

ST CLAIR, SYLVIA
See Rosales, Sylvia

SAINTE-MARIE, BUFFY
composer, singer
b Piapot Reserve, Sask, Feb 20, 41. Educ: Univ Mass, BA(philosophy), 62. Appearances at Saladin, Gaslight, Village Gate & Troubedour, also var coffeehouse theatres. Concert appearances at Carnegie Hall, 65, Royal Albert Hall, London, Eng, 65, Newport Folk Fest, 65 & 67, New York Philh, 67, Queen Elizabeth Theater, Vancouver, 67 & Helsinki Music Fest, Finland, 67. Founder, owner & pres, Gypsy Boy Music Inc & Caleb Music Inc. Appeared on TV shows "The Virginian" & "Bronson." Recording artist, Vanguard Recording Soc, MCA & RCA. Adv, Upward Bound. Founder & maj contributor, NIHEWAN Found for Native Am Scholarships. Founder, Native NAm Women's Asn & Creative Native, Inc. Author, comp & illusr "The Buffy Sainte-Marie Songbook." Mem: Am Fedn TV & Radio Artists & Am Fedn Musicians. Awards: Billboard Award, 65, Outstanding Artist of Yr Award, Nat Asn FM Broadcasters, 75 & Premio Roma Award, Italy, for perf at Sistina Theatre. *Songs:* It's My Way; Many a Mile; Little Wheel Spin and Spin; Fire and Fleet and Candlelight; I'm Gonna Be a Country Girl Again; Until It's Time for You to Go (ASCAP Award); Universal Soldier; Piney Wood Hills; My Country 'Tis of the People You're Dying; Now That the Buffalo's Gone.

ST JOHN, KATHLEEN LOUISE ASCAP 1977
composer, pianist, teacher
b Long Beach, Calif, May 28, 42. Educ: Studied piano with Angelon Hoffmeister, Los Angeles; then studied with Sherman Storr & Howard Brubeck; Dorsey & La Jolla High Sch; San Diego State Col, 62-66; Juilliard Sch Music, BM, studied piano with Ania Dorfmann, 66-67, comp with Hugo Weirgall, 67 & Luciano Berio, 68-71; Darmstadt, 68; Tanglewood, studied with Alexander Goehr, 69; Columbia Univ & Princeton Univ, EMC, 68-72, studied with Vladimir Ussachevsky, Bulent Arel, Mano Davidovsky & Alice Shields; Inst voor Sonologie, 76-77; Calif Inst Arts, MFA, studied comp with Mel Powell, 77-79. Music transcriber for Laura Boulton, ethnomusicologist for Columbia Univ, 68-70; residency fel to MacDowell Colony, 71, 73 & 75-76 & Va Ctr Creative Arts, 76-77. Guest lectr: Univ Ottawa, Randolph-Macon Sch Gifted & Sweet Briar Col. Pianist mem, 20th Century Players Ensemble, Calif Inst Arts, 77-79, fac mem, Sch Music, 78-, asst to Leonid Hambro & Alan Chaplin. Rec'd Calif Inst Arts Student Council Production Grant for "The Revelation of St John the Divine," 78-79. Also had many performances. Comn: Astoria High Sch, Ore; individual Juilliard musicians; Nat Arts Ctr, Ottawa; The Music Project Repertory Chamber Ensemble, New York (3); Sweet Briar Col; individual Calif Inst Arts musicians. Awards: Norlin Fel Awardee in tribute to Aaron Copland, MacDowell Colony, 76; Fellow's Fund Awardee, Va Ctr Creative Arts, 76; Irvine Found Scholar, Calif Inst Arts, 77-78, Marie A Lovelace Scholar in Classical Music, 78-79. *Songs & Instrumental Works:* Mosquito (string orch, alto choir, perc); Fragrances (piano, orch); Socrates on the Divination of Swans (Youth Music Found Prize for Orchestral Work, 70; vocal soloists, orch); A Prayer (string orch); The Devil-Bird: A South American Myth (boys' choir, clarinet, marimba solo, perc).

ST ONGE, BILL
See Drawbaugh, Jacob W

SAKAMAKI, BEN (BENNY SAKS) ASCAP 1962
composer, author, pianist
b Olaa, Hawaii, Apr 18, 21. Music dir, Televi-Digest, TV show, 7 yrs; with hotel bands, incl Royal Hawaiian, Moana, Biltmore & Hawaiian Village, 12 yrs; cond, arr & pianist for over 12 record albums; arr & teacher. *Songs:* Black Sands of Kalapana; Hula Eyes; Yacka Hicki Hula Tune; Lovely Kaui; Music: Crushed Flowers.

SAKAYAMA, BOB ASCAP 1969
composer, author, producer
b Tokyo, Japan, Dec 9, 47. Educ: Brown Univ. A&R & staff producer,

Paramount Records, 72; formed original music production co, TNG/Earthling, Inc, 75. *Songs:* Toronto Underground Railroad; Shoeflies.

SAKS, BENNY
See Sakamaki, Ben

SAKS, GITLE LANGNER ASCAP 1970
author
b Philadelphia, Pa. Educ: Univ Calif, Los Angeles; Los Angeles City Col; studied music with Val Chalk & voice with Bob Sellon, 74-78. Writer poetry, 55-60, children's poetry, 60-69 & lyrics, 69- Rec'd two ASCAP Awards. Chief Collabrs: Jan Zackery, Joe Sample, Gordon Brisker. *Songs:* Lyrics: One Way Street; Put Your Lovin' on Me; You Said Call Me; Grass Grows 'Round My Feet; I'll Be All Alone Again Tonight.

SALAT, HOWARD ASCAP 1964
composer, conductor, pianist
b New York, NY, Nov 29, 28. Comp, pianist & arr, radio & TV; also cond & accompanist for entertainers.

SALERNI, GIULIANO ASCAP 1978
composer, arranger, producer
b Milan, Italy, Aug 20, 42. Educ: Liceo Cairoli High Sch, Varese; Cons G Verdi, Milan, studied piano & theory, 62; Philadelphia Music Acad, studied electronic music techniques & comp, 71; Juilliard, studied 20th century comp techniques with Stanley Wolfe. Performer, nightclubs, 8 yrs; band leader & musical dir for Joe Franklin & Mike Douglas TV Shows; accompanist, Sergio Franci Show; writer, arr & producer, Casablanca, 78; arr & producer for Columbia artist Bonnie Boyer, 79; arr for jazz band-orchestration with Andrew Rudin, 79-; arr & producer, Prelude Records, Unidisc, Casablanca, Columbia & RSO. Own publ co, GS EuroAmerican. Chief Collabr: Phil Hurt. *Songs:* Love Is the Ultimate; Touch Me Baby; Ritmo De Brasil; Never Never; Music in My Heart; Dancing in the Night; Love Is a Strange Affair; Bad Connection; Don't Stop the Music; Music: Another Time.

SALES, SOUPY ASCAP 1965
composer, author, comedian
b Wake Forest, NC, Jan 8, 30. Educ: Marshall Col, BA. Radio script writer, Huntington, WVa, also comedian in local nightclubs. Radio DJ; then performer on radio & TV, Cincinnati, Cleveland & Detroit. Had own ABC-TV series, Los Angeles, 60-64; then to NY. Has recorded for ABC-Paramount. Chief Collabrs: Leonard Whitcup, Ted Lehrman. *Songs:* There's Nothing to Do Today; King Kong; You Really Know How to Hurt a Guy.

SALLO, JACOB ASCAP 1967
author
b Chicago, Ill, Jan 7, 20. Educ: John Marshall High Sch. Lyricist. Chief Collabrs: James Charles McNeil, Biff Cannon, Tim Gayle, Sheila Marsh & Jack Moon (John Ebert). *Songs:* Lyrics: Dreams in the Stars; Irish Symphony; When I See Dreams in Your Lovely Irish Eyes; The Magic Touch of Your Beauty; Violins, Orchids, Moonlight and You; Are You Coming Over for Dinner This Christmas Day.

SALPETER, SOPHIE ASCAP 1956
composer, author
b New York, NY, Nov 19, 16. Educ: Brooklyn Col, BA, MA(Eng). Modern dancer with Tamiris & Lillian Shapero, 30's; Dance Project, Workshop Players Art. Law stenographer; off mgr, Harry Von Tilzer Music Publ Co; now Eng teacher, Thomas Jefferson High Sch. Chief Collabrs: John Habash, Art Gordon, Edna Lewis. *Songs:* I've Always Loved You; Climbing Some Other High Hill; Sweethearts and Headaches; Lyrics: Inismore; Gather Up All the Oranges; What Cha Gotta Lose; Spin Me a Riddle.

SALSBURY, HUBERT IVAN (SONNY) ASCAP 1971
composer
b Los Angeles, Calif, Mar 8, 38. Educ: Dorsey High Sch; Pasadena Col. *Songs:* Psalm 19; God Speaking to You; Communion Song; The Father Loves You; Carols by Candlelight; Come and Dine; The Five Little Fingers of God; The First Song I Sing; Good Morning, Lord; Friendship; Sometime; Thanksgiving; Death, Where Is Your Victory; Jesus in the Morning; Can't You See?; Musicals: Backpacker's Suite; Love Came Down; Breakfast in Galilee.

SALSBURY, RONALD FOSTER (PANTANO-SALSBURY) ASCAP 1972
composer, author, singer
b Los Angeles, Calif, Feb 8, 50. Educ: Pasadena City Col, 2 yrs; Point Loma Col, 2 yrs. Christian singer, concerts, TV & nightclubs; recording artist, Word Records & Solid Rock Records. Chief Collabr: Jeffrey David Hooven. *Songs:* Lover of My Soul; I Choose to Follow You; Fill Me, Jesus; I Need You; Magic of the Moonlight; Restore; Oh, My Jesus; Don't Let Jesus Pass You By; Open Your Spiritual Eyes; Lyrics: People Tend to Forget.

SALTER, HANS J ASCAP 1946
composer, conductor
b Vienna, Austria, Jan 14, 1896. Educ: Vienna Acad of Music & Univ; studied with Alban Berg, Schreker & Weingartner. To US, 37. Citizen, 42. Asst cond,

opera cos incl Volksopera, Vienna, Berlin State Opera. Scored films in Berlin; head of music dept, UFA, Berlin. Former mem, AKM. Chief Collabrs: Jack Brooks, Ned Washington. *Songs:* Once Upon a Dream; No Matter Where You Are; So Goes My Love; Blue Danube Dream; Spring In My Heart; A Bedtime Story; Sign of the Pagan; Wichita; The Villa; Theme from Come September. *Scores:* Film/TV: It Started With Eve; Christmas Holiday; This Love of Ours; Bedtime Story; Man Without a Star; Bend of the River; Magnificent Doll; The Spoilers; Autumn Leaves; Hold Back the Night; Come September; If a Man Answers; Beau Geste; The Warlord; Return of the Gunfighter; Wichita Town; The Law and Mr Jones; Wagon Train; The Virginian; Laramie; The June Allyson Show; Dick Powell Theatre; The Third Man; Maya; Lost in Space. *Albums:* The Film Music of Hans J Salter.

SALTER, MARY TURNER   ASCAP 1932
    composer, singer, teacher
b Peoria, Ill, Mar 15, 1856; d Orangeburg, NY, Sept 12, 38. Studied singing with Alfred Arthur, Max Schilling, John O'Neil & Hermine Rudersdorff. Taught singing, Wellesley Col, 1878-81; also choral groups, NY, Boston & Chicago. Appeared in concerts, oratorios. *Songs:* The Cry of Rachel; The Pine Tree; Für Musik; Die Stille Wasserrose; Unseen; Serenity; The Veery; Song Cycles: Love's Epitome; A Night in Naishapur; Lyrics From Sappho; From Old Japan.

SALTER, WILLIAM   ASCAP 1964
    composer
b New York, NY, June 29, 36. Educ: Performing Arts High Sch, New York, 54. String bass player, sch, clubs, Blue Morocco 51; perf with Nancy Wilson, Irene Reed & others, 60-69; world tour with Miriam Makeba; toured with Harry Belafonte, 65-67; partnership with Ralph MacDonald, formed own co, Antisia Music Inc, NY, 68-80. Chief Collabr: Ralph MacDonald *Songs:* Where Is the Love; Trade Winds; When You Smile; No Tears in the End; Mr Magic; When I've Passed On; Super Ship.

SALUCCI, JOSEPH JAMES   ASCAP 1979
    composer, author, drummer
b Brooklyn, NY, May 22, 56. Educ: Self-taught drummer. Formed several bands; then became a songwriter & singer; performed many commercials for radio & TV; presently studio recording for var artists; recording artist. Lead vocalist. Chief Collabr: Meco Monardo. *Songs & Instrumental Works:* Living in the Night; Batman '77; Renee'; Lazer Eyes; Watching You Go By/Rescue Me.

SALVADOR, SAL   ASCAP 1958
    composer, author, guitarist
b Monson, Mass. Educ: Self-taught; aided by Harry Volpe, Johnny Smith & Tal Farlow. Guitarist for var groups, incl Mundell Lowe & Terry Gibbs, New York, 49. Staff musician, Columbia Records. Featured soloist with Stan Kenton's orch, 52-53. Formed own combo, 54 & traveled country playing jazz palaces. Personal accompanist to Robert Goulet & Carol Lawrence; guest artist with Joe Morello's group. Has 2 publ firms. Head guitar dept, Univ Bridgeport, 72- Leader of small group & jazz guitar ens; pvt teaching, New York. Author: "Single String Studies"; "Beginners Book for Guitar"; "Jazz for Two Guitars"; "Complete Chord Book"; "Technique for Beginners"; "Complete Guitar Method"; "Do It Yourself Course"; "Single String Fingerboard System" & "Chord Scales." *Songs & Instrumental Works:* Walkin' Time; Paralellogram; Northern Lights; Love You Are Here.

SALVATORI, ADOLPH   ASCAP 1957
    composer, author
b Galena, Italy, Feb 1, 08. Educ: Grammar sch; typing & accounting, business col. Songwriter. In accounting dept, Metal Trades Industs. Chief Collabr: Frank LaVere. *Songs:* The Girl Who Sat in My Row; Pinky Tail; Lyrics: Follow Me; It All Started With You; The Place I Live In.

SALVATORI, PAUL   ASCAP 1958
    composer, author
b Chicago, Ill, June 19, 12. Contact man for music publ, Chicago, Midwest & NY. Became salesman. *Songs:* My Love for You; America's Prayer; In a Moonlit Chapel; On the Outside Looking In.

SALVIUOLO, JOSEPH ANTHONY (SAL JOSEPH)   ASCAP 1973
    composer, author
b Southbridge, Mass, Sept 16, 40. Educ: Mary E Wells High Sch, grad, 58; Villanova Univ, BSEd, 63; Univ Pa Annenberg Sch Communications, MAC, 64, Univ Pa, MA(folklore), 65. *Songs:* Thursday.

SALWITZ, HARDY   ASCAP 1959
    composer, arranger
b Elbing, Ger, Mar 2, 30. Educ: Manhattan Sch of Music, MM. Free-lance arr, 56- *Songs:* How Many Stamps (for the Girl Behind the Counter)?

SALZEDO, CARLOS   ASCAP 1949
    composer, harpist, pianist
b Arcachon, France, Apr 6, 1885; d Waterville, Maine, Aug 17, 61. Educ: Paris Cons, Premier Prix, piano & harp. To US 1909, citizen, 23. Concert pianist & harpist; solo harpist, Metrop Opera Co. Co-founder, Trio de Lutuce, 13. French Army, WW I. Pres, Nat Asn Harpists, 20; organized annual Nat Harp Fests throughout US. Founder & ed-in-chief, Eolus, 21. Helped organize Int

Composers Guild, 21; also US Sect of Int Soc for Contemporary Music, 23. Founded harp dept, Curtis Inst, 24. Soloist symph orchs throughout US. *Instrumental Works:* Scintillation; Ballade; Desirade; Petite Valse; Dances for Harp; Transcriptions for 2 Harps; Chanson dans la Nuit; The Enchanted Isle; Harp Concerto; Panorama.

SALZMAN, ERIC
    composer, author
b New York, NY, Sept 8, 33. Educ: Columbia Univ, BA, studied with Otto Luening; Princeton Univ, MFA, studied with Roger Sessions & Milton Babbitt; Fulbright Fel, Rome & Darmstadt Univ, Ger. Music critic, New York Times, New York Herald & Stereo Review. Wrote many articles. Author "Twentieth Century Music" & "Making Changes—Guide to Popular Harmony." Music dir, WBAI-FM, 62-63 & 68-72. Founder & dir, Free Music Store; founder & artistic dir, The Electric Ear, New York & New Image of Sound at Hunter Col. Toured alone, also with ens & later with group, Europe, SAm, US & Can, 64- Taught at Queens Col, 66-68. Has done many sem, workshops, artist-in-residencies & guest teaching with emphasis on music theater, many schs in US. With Quog Music Theatre, 70- Producer, Nat Pub Radio & Nonesuch Records. Chief Collabr: Michael Sahl. *Songs & Instrumental Works:* Cummings Set (on poems of E E Cummings; voice & orch or voice & piano); Indian Set; String Quartet: Piano Suite; Partita for Violin; On the Beach At Night; Night Dance; Inventions; Oh, Praise the Lord; In Praise of the Owl and the Cuckoo; Foxes and Hedgehogs (text by John Ashbery); Verses; Larynx Music; Queen's College; Wiretap; The Peloponnesian War; Feedback; Can Man Survive (comn by Am Mus Natural Hist); The Nude Paper Sermon (text by John Ashbery & Wade Stevenson); Ecolog (comn by Artists TV Workshop, WNET); Helix (voice, perc, clarinet, guitar); Voices; Birdwalk; Saying Something; Biograffiti; Lazarus; Accord (accordion solo). Also theater operas or music theater works with Michael Sahl: The Conjurer, Stauf (Faust); Civilization and Its Discontents, Noah; The Passion of Simple Simon, Escape From the Harem (transl of Mozart's Abduction from the Seraglio).

SAMINSKY, LAZARE   ASCAP 1924
    composer, author, conductor
b near Odessa, Russia, Oct 27, 1882; d Rye, NY, July 1, 59. Educ: Univ St Petersburg; studied comp with Rimsky-Korsakoff & Liadoff; studied folk music of Georgia (Caucasia). Dir, People's Cons, Tiflis, Caucasia; also cond symph concerts, 17-18. Music dir, Duke of York Theatre, London, 20. Came to US, 20, became citizen, 26. US debut with Detroit Symph, conducting own works, 21. Dir music, Temple Emanu-El & annual Three Choir Fest, NY. Co-founder & dir, League of Comp. Allied mem, MacDowell Asn. Guest comp & cond, symph orchs, US & Europe. Cond & lectr Am music, SAm tour, 40, Can tour, 41-42 & Europ tour, 49. Author: "Music of Our Day"; "Music of the Ghetto and Bible"; "Living Music of the Americas." *Songs & Instrumental Works:* Vigils; Requiem; Litanies of Women; Songs of 3 Queens (soprano, chamber orch); Chassidic Suite (violin, chamber orch); 5 Symphonies; Choral: King Saul; Songs of Yemen and Palestine. *Scores:* Operas: Julian; The Apostate Caesar; The Vision of Ariel; The Plague's Galliard; Jeptha's Daughter; Ballets: Pueblo; Rachel.

SAMON, GRICO
    See Sampson, James

SAMPSON, EDGAR M   ASCAP 1940
    composer, conductor, violinist
b New York, NY, Aug 31, 07; d Englewood, NJ, Jan 16, 73. Violinist & arr with dance orchs incl Benny Goodman. Organized own orch. *Songs:* Stompin' at the Savoy; If Dreams Come True; Lullaby In Rhythm; Blue Lou; Don't Be That Way; Blue Minor; Serenade to a Sleeping Beauty.

SAMPSON, JAMES (GRICO SAMON)   ASCAP 1972
    composer, teacher
b Baltimore, Md, June 9, 30. Educ: Peabody Prep, 56; studied piano, guitar, accordion, trumpet, saxophone, drums, harmonica & other instruments. *Songs:* Waite for Me; Closer to Me; Down By the Shore; Who Put the Hole in the Doughnut; I've Got My Shoes on the Wrong Feet; Bean Sandwich; What Could It Be.

SAMPSON, LARRY CARL   ASCAP 1972
    composer, author
b Oxnard, Calif, Jan 1, 42. Educ: Fresno State Col, BA(music), 63; studied with Al Kasha, 74. Has been sch teacher for 14 yrs. Now writer of contemporary, commercial & gospel songs. Chief Collabr: Beth Leupp. *Songs:* Lyrics: It's Good Enough for Me; The Upper Room.

SAMUEL, GERHARD   ASCAP 1970
    composer, conductor, educator
b Bonn, Ger, Apr 20, 24. Educ: Univ Rochester Eastman Sch Music, BM, 45; Yale Univ, MM; studied comp with Paul Hindemith, studied with Serge Koussevitsky, Tanglewood, Berkshire Music Ctr, 2 summers; hon doctorate, Calif Col Arts & Crafts, Oakland. Cond, Ballet Ballads, Bway, 48 & Ballets Concertants, Minneapolis Civic Opera, Grand Marcis Music Fest, all in Minneapolis, 49-59. Assoc cond, Minneapolis Symph & Los Angeles Philh, 70-73. Dir, Collegium Musicum, Minneapolis-St Paul, Oakland Symph, Calif,

59-71 & Ojai Fest, Calif, 70. Dir & cond, San Francisco Ballet, 60-71; founder, dir & cond, Cabrillo Music Fest, Aptos, Calif, 62-66. Prof music, Calif Inst of Arts, Valencia, 72-76, Univ Cincinnati Col Cons Music, 76- Recording artist on var labels. Guest cond, symphs & operas incl Poland, Russia, Royal Philh Orch, London, Belg, Mex, Peru, Philippines, Can & US incl San Francisco, Denver, Baltimore, Phoenix, Long Island, Am Symph, Lincoln Ctr-Mozart Fest, New Haven, Opera Co of Philadelphia, Pac NW Dance Co & Nat Orch Asn, New York. Guest fac, Tanglewood, Berkshire Music Ctr, 76. Recipient, 2 comp grants, NEA, 2 grants, Comp's Showcase, New York, ASCAP Annual Standard Award, 71- Mem, Int Soc for Contemporary Music, Congress Indust Orgns-Am Fedn Musicians, Calif Chamber Music Soc, Nat Asn of Comp, USA, Cincinnati Comp's Alliance & Arnold Schoenberg Inst Democrat. *Instrumental Works:* Au Revoir to Lady R (clarinet, cello, piano); Beyond McBean (violin, chamber ens); Cold When the Drum Sounds for Dawn (comn, Los Angeles Chamber Orch); Into Flight From... (orch); Looking at Orpheus Looking (Orch); Requiem for Survivors (And Suddenly It's Evening) (comn, NEA grant, Los Angeles Philh); Three Hymns to Apollo (cello, instrumental ens); On a Dream (viola, chamber orch); Out of Time (A Short Symphony) (orch); String Quartet No 1 (comn, Friends of LaSalle Quartet); In Memorium D Q (cello); Put Up My Lute (comn, Joel Krosnick); Circles (3 perc); And Marsyas (contralto, bass-baritone, instrumental ens); The Relativity of Icarus (comn, San Francisco Chamber Soc, contralto, bass-baritone, instrumental ens, premiered as ballet); Sun-Like (soprano, chamber ens); To an End (mixed chorus, orch); Twelve on Death and No (tenor, mixed chorus, chamber orch); Fortieth Day (soprano, speaker, chamber ens); What of My Music (Soprano, perc, 30 double basses, comn, Int Soc of Bassists); Paul Blake-Icon Maker-Statement (soprano, 4 winds, 3 strings, 2 perc).

SAMUELS, DAVID ALAN   ASCAP 1976
composer, author, performer
b Waukegan, Ill, Oct 9, 48. Educ: Boston Univ, BA, 71. Has made recordings & performances with Gerry Mulligan, Frank Zappa, Double Image, Gerry Niewood, Paul McCandless, Carla Bley & Hubert Laws. Recognized by critics in all major jazz polls in world. *Instrumental Works:* Mist; Veldtland; Sunset Glow; Crossing; Soaring; Night Rain; Masada; Anyo; My Asian Land. *Albums:* Double Image (nominated for Ger Grammy Award, 77).

SAMUELS, MILTON ISADORE (EDWARD ROSS)   ASCAP 1943
composer, author
b Denver, Colo, Jan 28, 04. Educ: Pub sch; self-taught in piano. Played with 5-piece orch, Nebr, 20-25. Played piano, Bibo-Bloeden-Lang Publ, Chicago, 26. Rehearsal pianist & writer spec material, Feist Music Co, 27. Mgr, Bregman, Vocco & Conn, Inc, Calif, 45-68. Chief Collabrs: Johnny Mercer, Jack Fulton, Art Kassel, Nelson Shawn, Caesar Petrillo, Sammy Gallop. *Songs:* I'm Moody; I Hate Music; Music: Jim (Doesn't Ever Bring Me Pretty Flowers); Are Yuh Spoken Fer; Fountain in the Rain; Papa Parakeet; A Friend of Man I'll Be.

SAMUELS, WALTER GERALD   ASCAP 1934
composer, author, publisher
b New York, NY, Feb 2, 08. Educ: DeWitt Clinton High Sch; NY Univ, studied law; studied piano, 8 yrs, classical music with Eugene Bernstein, 15 yrs & harmony with Reubin Goldmark. Music therapist, Vet Admin, 35 yrs. Rec'd award, Nat Red Cross. Comp & entertainer, represented ASCAP, S Pacific, WW II. Chief Collabrs: Buddy De Sylva, Brian Hooker, Ralph Freed, Charles Newman, Leonard Whitcup, Jack Brooks, Morrie Ryskind, Teddy Powell, Allen Boretz, Ed Sullivan. *Songs:* Heaven Help This Heart of Mine; Infatuation; True; If My Heart Could Only Talk; March Winds and April Showers; I Couldn't Believe My Eyes; Blazin the Train (To My Home); Hot Dogs and Sassparella; It's Too Hot for Words; Lady From Fifth Avenue; Little Genius; Tears in My Heart; Clearance Sale; Music: It Isn't a Dream Anymore; There's Nothin' the Matter With Me (That a Kiss Can't Cure); The Swiss Bellringer; It's Way Past My Dreamin' Time; Dark Clouds. *Scores:* Take Me Back to My Boots and Saddle; Fiesta; The Gaucho; Rollin' Plains; Alice in Movieland; Crack O' Dawn; Chap W Chip on Shoulder; Farmer's Daughter; Mr President; Too Soon; Interceptor Command; Hellzapoppin; Night Cruise; Ned Wayburn's Gambols; Tom Tom; Glee Club Swings Alma Mater; Mate; Gonzalez; Dim Marimba; Ride Banderleros; Ali Baba (Eng version); Lamento Guitano; scores to some 20 Gene Autry and Roy Rogers pictures played all over the world.

SANDBURG, CARL   ASCAP 1955
author, guitarist, singer
b Galesburg, Ill, Jan 6, 1878; d. Educ: Lombard Col; hon degrees: LHD, Northwestern Univ, Harvard Univ, Yale Univ, NY Univ, Wesleyan Col & Dartmouth Col; LLD, Rollins Col & Augustana Col; PhD, Upsala Col, Sweden. Service, 6th Inf Reg Ill Vol, Span-Am War; ed col newspaper; first poetry publ in Poetry Magazine, 14; with Off War Info, WW II; toured country reading his own poetry, and as guitarist & ballad singer. Awards: Am Acad Arts & Letters Gold Medal; Poetry Soc Am Gold Medal; Boston Arts Fest; Albert Einstein; Citation (Great Living American) from US Chamber of Commerce; US Medal of Freedom. Author, "Chicago" (poem, Levinson prize), "Cornhuskers" (co-winner, Poetry Soc prize), "Steichen, The Photographer", "The People, Yes", "Abraham Lincoln", "The Prairie Years and the War Years" (Pulitzer prize, 40), "Home Front Memo", "Remembrance Rock" (novel), "Lincoln Collector", "Complete Poems" (Pulitzer prize, 51), "Always the Young Strangers" (autobiography). Mem, Nat Inst Arts & Letters & Am Acad Arts & Letters. *Songs:* Summer Grass; Upstream; Lost; Sunsets; My Shirt; Night Stuff; Calls; Summer Stars.

SANDERS, ALMA M   ASCAP 1923
composer, singer
b Chicago, Ill, Mar 13, 1882; d New York, NY, Dec 15, 56. Educ. Chicago Musical Col (scholarship); studied voice with William Castle. Concert singer, Chicago; wrote dance routines for dance schs, Detroit, 12; wrote songs for music publ. Chief Collabr: Monte Carlo (husband). *Songs:* Hong Kong; That Tumble-Down Shack at Athlone; Little Town in the Ould County Down; My Home in the County Mayo; Two Blue Eyes; The Hills of Connemara; Dreaming of Louise; No One to Care; Ten Baby Fingers; Tangerine. *Scores:* Bway stage: Tangerine, Elsie; The Chiffon Girl; The Houseboat on the Styx.

SANDERS, BONNIE
See Shimkin, Bonnie Lee

SANDERS, BRANCH STEVENS   ASCAP 1969
composer, arranger
b Concord, NH, Feb 13, 47. Educ: Univ NH, BA(music comp), 70; Franklin Pierce Law Ctr, JD, 78. Arr since jr high sch; arr & performed on recordings made by The Spectras in 69, 70. Trombonist, baritone, arr & writer, 590th USAF Band of the East, 70-72. Had own work performed at Int Jazz Fest, Montreux, Switz, 76. *Songs & Instrumental Works:* The Best Years of Our Lives; Vince.

SANDERS, FAREIL
See Glenn, Fareil

SANDERS, JOE L   ASCAP 1923
composer, author, conductor
b Thayer, Kans, Oct 15, 1896; d Kansas City, Mo, May 14, 65. Was pitcher, Kansas City Athletic Club (world strike out record). Co-founder, cond & pianist, Coon-Sanders orch; then formed own band, 34. Made many records. First organized band to broadcast on WDAF radio, Kansas City, Mo. *Songs & Instrumental Works:* Beloved; Little Orphan Annie; Harold Teen; She Loves Me Just the Same; What a Girl, What a Night; Billie; Blue Moonlight; Tennessee Lazy; High Fever; Sluefoot; My Dear; Got a Great Big Date With a Little Bitta Girl; Until Yesterday; Martha; Sweetheart Trail; Blazin'; Hallucinations; The Wail; Improvisation (incl Embers, Intangibility, Inhibition); Southology (piano); Twinkle Toes (piano); Little Feller; Dreaming of Tomorrow; Brainstorm; Louder and Funnier; Roodles; Nighthawk Blues; Lazy Waters; Sittin' and Whittlin'; There's a Love Song in the Air; Right Next Door to Love; Believe Me; Do You Miss Me?; I Want to Go Home; Over the Rim of the Sun; Because You Said I Love You.

SANDERS, PAUL
See Santoro, Paul

SANDERS, RICHARD CHARLES   ASCAP 1975
composer, author
b Bridgeport, Conn, Apr 22, 49. Educ: Yale Univ. Has written music & lyrics for TV & radio jingles, themes, incidental music, AV & indust presentations & other related fields, incl popular music. Comp & arr for several children's TV progs. Awards: Clio Award; Hollywood Radio & TV Soc Award; Advert Club New York Award; Conn Art Dir Club Award; Fairfield County Ad Club Award. Chief Collabr: Stan Davis.

SANDERS, ROBERT L   ASCAP 1948
composer, conductor, pianist
b Chicago, Ill, July 2, 06; d Dec 26, 74. Educ: Bush Cons, Chicago, BM, MM; Prix de Rome (FAAR), 25-29, studied with Ottorino Respighi, Alfredo Bustini, Luigi Dobbici, Guy de Lioncourt, Paul Braud, Arthur Dunham, Eric Delamarter, Frederick Stock; hon MusD, Chicago Cons; Guggenheim fel. Taught, Bush Cons, Meadville Theol Sch, 30-38 & privately. Choral cond, Chicago churches & Ind Univ, 29-34; asst cond, Chicago Civic Orch, 34-36. Prof music & dean, Sch Music, Ind Univ, 38-47; prof music & chmn dept, Brooklyn Col. Pianist in recital & as accompanist. Guest cond, Chicago Symph, New York Philh, Palma de Mallarca, Baleares. Author, bks "Manual for Melody Writing," co-ed "Dictionary of Hymn Tunes in USA." *Songs & Instrumental Works:* Saturday Night: a Barn Dance; Little Symphony No 1 in G (New York Philh award); Little Symphony No 2 in B flat (Louisville Philh Soc comn); Scherzo and Dirge (trombone quartet); Brass Quintet in B flat; Sonata in E flat for Trombone, Piano; Suite for Brass Quartet; Symphony in A (Knoxville Symph comn); Recessional (choral); Chanson of the Bells of Oseney; Ring Out, Wild Bells; An American Psalm; While Shepherds Watched; Truly My Soul Waiteth; A Song of the Spirit; Out of the Cradle; Hymn of the Future; Man's Praise.

SANDGREN, CLYDE D   ASCAP 1979
composer, author
b Provo, Utah, Sept 5, 10. Educ: Provo High Sch; comp, Juilliard Sch Music, New York, 35; Brigham Young Univ, Provo, BS, 38; St John's Univ Law Sch, New York, LLB, 39, JD, 68. Practiced law, New York, 40-46 & Provo, 47-80; nearly 30 yrs, gen counsel, 15 yrs, vpres, Brigham Young Univ. Pres, Council Utah Educ, Inc, 53-54, Utah Educ TV Found, 61-64 & Brigham Young Univ Alumni Asn. Mem, Exec Bd, Nat Asn Col & Univ Attorneys; mem, Exec Comt, Nat Parks Council, Boy Scouts Am. *Songs:* We Two; The Cougar Song; The Old Y Bell; Bulldog Fight Song; Roar for Orem High; Fight On You Thunderbirds; Vivi-Ann's Lullaby; (A Dream of Mine Came True) One Day in Spring; Little

Girl; Is It Love?; Someday You Should See the Valley; Peaceful Old Valley of Home; Never Again; Nevermore; Leaves Are Falling Again; Ann; Near You; Ernie the Elf; Here in Paradise; I'm Pretending; The First Time Mary Sang a Lullaby; Thy Will Be Done; I'll Follow Thee; Spanish Sunset; You're the One I Love.

SANDOVAL, MIGUEL   ASCAP 1940
composer, author, conductor
b Guatemala City, Guatemala, Nov 22, 03; d New York, NY, Aug 24, 53. Educ: Studied music with Eduardo Trucco. To US, 19, citizen, 25. Accompanist to Rosa Ponselle, Gigli, Martini, Baccaloni, Licia Albanese. Martinelli, Leonard Warren & Grace Moore (also music adv). Writer, films & radio. Staff pianist, comp & cond, CBS, New York, 41-47. Gen dir, nat radio station, Guatemala City. Guest cond, Manhattan Opera House, Lewisohn Stadium. *Songs:* Sin tu Amor; Serenata Gitana; Lament; Vola Farfalletta; Novelette; I Come to You; Eres Tu. *Instrumental Works:* Recuerdos en un Paseo (symph poem); Spanish Dance (piano, orch); Petite Valse (piano).

SANDRICH, MARK, JR   ASCAP 1964
composer
b Los Angeles, Calif, Jan 2, 28. Educ: Univ Calif, Los Angeles; studied harmony & counterpoint with Arnold Shermburg. Worked in TV & films. Comp Bway play "Ben Franklin in Paris."

SANDRY, VIN   ASCAP 1948
author
b Liverpool, Eng, Apr 11, 02. US citizen. *Songs:* Yesterday's Roses; Who Are We to Say?; Our Dream; Just to Be With You Tonight; Mississippi Miss, I Miss You; On a Night Like This; I Must Be in Heaven.

SANDS, EVIE   ASCAP 1976
composer, author, singer
b New York, NY. Educ: High Sch of Performing Arts, Tilden. At early age started singing & making records; TV & concerts; songwriting for different artists & projs. Chief Collabrs: Ben Weisman, Richard Germinaro. *Songs:* You Can Do It; I Love Makin' Love to You; Love in the Afternoon; Lady of the Night; As We Fall in Love Once More.

SANFILIPPO, JOSEPHINE ANN   ASCAP 1967
author
b San Jose, Calif, Dec 26, 18. Educ: San Jose State Univ, AB(English), 38, studied poetry, verse writing & foreign languages, 44-46; Stanford Univ, MA(educ), 48; pvt verse writing study, Mills Col. Teacher English in secondary schs, retired. Traveled Europe, Asia, Africa, Middle East, Scandinavian Countries, South Pacific & others. Lyricist for "The Young Orchestra/String Orchestra Concert Book." Chief Collabr: Margherita Sanfilippo. *Songs & Instrumental Works:* Scandinavian Suite; Sketches of Galilee; Seasonal Selections; Saw-Whet Owl; Cricket (Field Cricket); United Nations Processional March; Jamaican Donkey; Children's March; Space Fantasy; Christmas Calypso; Spotted Duckling.

SANFILIPPO, MARGHERITA MARIE   ASCAP 1967
composer, music teacher
b San Jose, Calif, June 4, 27. Educ: San Jose State Univ, AB, 50; Music Spec Sec Teaching Credential, Supvr Credential & Gen Elem Credential; studied with Herold Johnson, Frank Erickson, Robert Aichele, Leonard Klein, Joseph Hoffman, Gibson Walters, Alma Lowery Williams, Allan Wendt, William Erlendson, Valbort Leland, Rodger Nixon, Charlene Archibeque & Anthony Circone. Pvt study, comp, lyric writing, violin, viola, cello, string bass, piano, perc, tuba, French horn, saxophone, flute, oboe, clarinet. Taught in Calif, 29 yrs; teaching in schs, Palo Alto Unified Sch Dist, Calif. Dir, All-City Orch, Palo Alto. Auth two books, "The Young Orchestra/String Orchestra Concert Book" & "Position Studies for Strings." Chief Collabr: Josephine Ann Sanfilippo (sister). *Songs:* The Spotted Duckling; El Burrito, Carlo; Music: Jamaican Donkey; Christmas Calypso. *Instrumental Works:* United Nations Processional March; A Rickshaw Ride; Moreland Overture; Camel Caravan.

SANFORD, DICK   ASCAP 1934
author, singer
b Gloversville, NY, May 28, 1896. Educ: Pub schs. Radio operator at sea, 13 yrs. Conducted early experiments in TV; became radio engr. Chief Collabrs: Sammy Mysels, George McConnell, Bob Hilliard, James Cavanaugh, Lani McIntire. *Songs:* The Singing Hills; Purple Shadows; His Feet Too Big for de Bed; Mention My Name in Sheboygan; The Horse With the Lavender Eyes; Idaho State Fair; Michigan Bank Roll; The Prairie Skies; When Mother Played the Organ; That's How I Spell Ireland; Lonesome Valley Sally; Sweet Hawaiian Chimes; Rural Rhythm; Woe Is Me; Walking Down to Washington; Sailing Away From the Islands.

SANFORD, EDWARD CLARK   ASCAP 1972
composer, author, singer
b Paterson, NJ, Dec 6, 48. Educ: Ocala High Sch; Cent Fla Community Col. Singer & guitarist, nightclubs & TV; producer of demos of Fla rock bands. Columnist, Rock Rites. *Songs:* Distance; Last American Dream; After All the

Words; Hometown Homecoming Queen; Let Me Take You Down. *Scores:* Rock Opera: Requiem.

SANFORD, HERBERT C   ASCAP 1963
composer
b Pontiac, Mich, Aug 8, 05. Educ: Princeton Univ, BS, 27, pres, Triangle Club, pianist & leader of jazz band. Radio, TV dir-producer. Author, "Tommy and Jimmy: The Dorsey Years" & "The Garry Moore Show (Behind the Scenes When TV Was New)." Chief Collabrs: Hoagy Carmichael, Helen Meinardi, Bill Demling. *Songs:* Manhattan in the Spring; I'm in Love With Every Girl in the Universe.

SANG, LANI   ASCAP 1960
composer, author, guitarist
b Honolulu, Hawaii, July 8, 16; d Baldwin Park, Calif, Mar 16, 77. Educ: High sch. Guitarist in local groups; toured with Ray Kinney Orch, 1 yr; to Los Angeles. *Songs:* Mapuana; Sea and Sand; From Hawaii to You; Drums of Tahiti.

SANICOLA, HENRY W (HANK)   ASCAP 1957
composer, publisher
b New York, NY, June 14, 14; d Santa Monica, Calif, Oct 6, 74. Educ: High sch. With var music publ incl Harms, Witmark, Embassy, Seneca. Mgr for Frank Sinatra, 42. Owner of publ firms incl Barton, Sands, Maraville. Chief Collabrs: Frank Sinatra, Dok Stanford. *Songs:* This Love of Mine; Mistletoe and Holly; Mr Success; It Will Never Happen Again; I'm Coming Home Los Angeles; Meet Me At Jilly's.

SANICOLA, JOHN JOSEPH   ASCAP 1964
composer, author
b Brooklyn, NY, Sept 20, 17. Educ: Alexander Hamilton High Sch. Chief Collabr: Oscar Evans. *Songs:* The Same Old Story; Lyrics: Twistin' Away.

SANTARPIA, RALPH C   ASCAP 1968
composer, author
b Brooklyn, NY, Mar 25, 51. Educ: Bishop Loughlin High Sch, Brooklyn; St Francis Col, Brooklyn, BA. Singer, small clubs. Chief Collabr: John Vetere, Jr. *Songs:* Night Time Music.

SANTLY, HENRY   ASCAP 1922
composer, pianist, publisher
b New York, NY, Oct 23, 1890; d New York, Feb 13, 34. Mem professional staff, music publ. Formed own publ firm with bros, Lester & Joe, 29. WW I, 51st Pioneer Inf. Chief Collabr: Pete Wendling. *Songs:* Put Your Arms Around Me Where They Belong; Will You Remember Me?; I'll Find a Way to Forget You; The Day That I Met You; What Good Is Good Morning?; Jelly Roll; I'm Sitting Pretty.

SANTLY, JOSEPH H   ASCAP 1914
composer, pianist, publisher
b New York, NY, Aug 21, 1886; d New York, Aug 28, 62. Educ: Pub schs. Boy soprano in vaudeville; staff mem, music publ, 12. Returned to vaudeville as mem of act Santly & Norton, 14-20. Professional mgr, Remich Co. Formed own publ firm with bros, Henry & Lester, 29. Organized firm, Sanson Music, 60. *Songs:* There's Yes Yes in Your Eyes; Tamiami Trail; Big Butter and Egg Man; At the Moving Picture Ball; Hawaiian Butterfly; Before We Say Goodnight; Friends; Mother, Dixie and You.

SANTLY, LESTER   ASCAP 1924
composer, author, musician
b New York, NY, Apr 2, 1894. Educ: DeWitt Clinton High Sch; studied violin & piano. Musician in dance orchs. Mem professional staffs, music publishers. Formed own publ firm with bros, Joseph & Henry, 29; organized Santly Joy Co. Dir, ASCAP 45-51. Chief Collabrs: Milton Ager, Abel Baer. *Songs:* Heart of Wetona; All That I Need Is You; Hi-lee, Hi-lo; I'm Nobody's Baby; The Sunrise.

SANTORO, PAUL (PAUL SANDERS)   ASCAP 1958
composer, author
b Mt Vernon, NY, Oct 20, 15. Educ: Medford High Sch, Mass; Staley Col, Brookline, Mass. Newspaper columnist. Writer of gags for var early day comics, incl Phil Baker, Joe E Lewis & Jack Benny. WW II, spec services. Wrote spec material for Bing Crosby for many yrs. Chief Collabrs: Sammy Fain, Pat Sullivan, Jimmy Dorsey, By Dunham, Bobby Troup. *Songs:* Talkin' to My Heart; Altar in the Pines; Church Bells; Don't Worry About To-morrow (Be Thankful for To-day) (CBS radio theme song); Believe; Please Save All the Pieces; I'd Never Make the Same Mistake Again; The One Thing I Can't Seem to Do (Is Say Goodbye); It Doesn't Cost a Penny (To Wear a Million Dollar Smile); Music: Don't Turn Your Back on a Broken Heart (Because It Could Happen to You); Lyrics: It's Time to Say Goodbye; Don't Let a Mem'ry Break Your Heart; It's Christmas; Let's Have a Heart to Heart Talk; I'm Gonna Celebrate the New Year (With My Old Friends). *Songs & Instrumental Works:* I Want You (USA WW II conscription song); Make the Whitehouse the Lighthouse of the World (rec'd presidential commendation from Pres Roosevelt).

SANTOS, LAWRENCE E   ASCAP 1963
composer, author, singer
b Oneonta, NY, June 2, 41. Educ: Colgate Univ, BA; studied piano, 8 yrs. Songwriter, 63- Music dir & writer, childrens' show "Hot Fudge." Recording artist. Chief Collabr: Barry Hurd. *Songs:* Candy Girl; We Can't Hide It Anymore. *Albums:* Just Larry Santos; You Are Everything I Need; Don't Let the Music Stop.

SANTOS, TONY
See Sacco, Anthony

SARACENI, RAYMOND R (GENE ADAMS)   ASCAP 1962
composer, author, arranger
b Philadelphia, Pa, Feb 19, 32. Educ: Trombone, Peter Rosano, harmony, Armand DePolis, jazz arr, theory & harmony, Adolph Sandole, vibraharp, Dick S Witzgal; self-taught guitar, banjo & piano; big band arr, Dick Grove Music Workshop. First trombone, Joe Cassiano Orch, Barclay Ballroom, 48-50, Coronet Club, Philadelphia Met, Fort Dix, Coatesville Veteran's Hosp & others, arr for The Four Counts & var Philadelphia clubs. Musical cond & dir, "The Mikado" & "Lucky for Me," LaSalle Col Mask & Wig, 51-53, mus cond, arr & dir, "Watch the Curtain." *Songs:* Italiano; I'm in Love; I Love You 'Cause You're You; Cried a Million Tears; Senza Cuore' Romantica; That's When I'll Be There; I Need Your Love; Top Dawg; The Way You Say I Love You; Goin' Steady; Somewhere; Sam, Sam, Sam; Twist-a-Hip; I Just Don't Love You Anymore. *Instrumental Works:* 1st Symphony in A Flat. *Scores:* Operetta: Watch the Curtain.

SARACENO, JOSEPH   ASCAP 1959
composer, author, producer
b Utica, NY, May 16, 36. Educ: St Lawrence Univ, BA. Independent record producer, Calif. Wrote theme for TV show, "The Sensuous Man," Can. Chief Collabrs: Ernest Freeman, Bob Russell. *Songs:* Beautiful Obsession; Surfer's Stomp; Balboa Blue; Symphony on Wheels; Music: California Hustle.

SARCHE, ED   ASCAP 1955
composer, author
b Chicago, Ill, Mar 14, 07. Educ: High sch. Wrote for stock cos, Chicago, also vaudeville. Mgr of cigar stand, Chicago. *Songs:* I Remember When; Making Believe We're Millionaires; Symphony in Three-Quarter Time; Billy Buck; Tears Never Lie; Francais Francais Baby.

SARDELLA, EDWARD A   ASCAP 1964
composer, author
b Boston, Mass, Dec 29, 28. Educ: Boston Univ; Suffolk Univ; San Francisco State Col. *Songs:* Black Hills Gold.

SARGENT, KAREN
See Schiesser (Rachels), Karen Ann

SARGENT, PAUL   ASCAP 1960
composer, piano teacher, accompanist
b Bangor, Maine, Mar 30, 10. Educ: Eastman Sch Music, BM(piano), 31; studied piano with John Mokrejs, New York, 32-36; Ecole Normale de Musique, Paris, piano degree, 48. Comp & pianist; accompanist for many singers in concerts. Chief Collabrs: Robert Hillyer, Louise Richardson Dodd, Isobel Harris. *Songs:* Music: XXth Century; Hickory Hill; Stopping by Woods on a Snowy Evening; Manhattan Joy Ride; 3 AM. *Instrumental Works:* Piano Suite: Promenade-Night Song-The Sea.

SARGON, SIMON   ASCAP 1974
composer, pianist, conductor
b Bombay, India, Apr 6, 38. Educ: Brandeis Univ, BA; Juilliard Sch Music, MS. Assoc cond, Concert Opera Asn, 62-67; musical staff, New York Opera, 68. Fac, Juilliard Sch Music, Sarah Lawrence Col, Hebrew Univ, Jerusalem; head voice dept, Rubin Acad, Jerusalem, 71-74; music dir, Temple Emanuel, Dallas, Tex, 74- Chief Collabr: Lyrics, Dennis Britten. *Songs & Instrumental Works:* Patterns in Blue (vocal, instruments); V'Shamru (choral); Elvl Midnight (cantata); Star in Haymow (song cycle); Not By Might (oratorio).

SARNOFF, JANYCE LOIS   ASCAP 1964
lyricist
b Dubuque, Iowa, Nov 25, 28. Educ: Clarke Col; Univ Dubuque, BS(med technol); Mercy Hospital, Dubuque, internship; Northwestern Univ, degree. Worked as registered med technologist at Evanston Hospital, Wesley Hospital & Vet Admin Research Hospital, Chicago, 51-55. Joined SHARE (show business charity ladies group), 58. Mem bd dirs, Calif Spec Olympics, 71-73, pres, 73- Chief Collabrs: Ivan Lane, Carol Connors. *Songs:* Lyrics: I Wonder.

SARTAIN, JOHN, JR
See Raksin, David

SATTERWHITE, COLLEN GRAY (TEX)   ASCAP 1959
composer, author, arranger
b Eastland, Tex, Oct 17, 20; d Studio City, Calif, Feb 6, 78. Educ: Tex Tech Col. Trombonist, Dixieland group, with Joe Venuti, Jan Savitt & Tommy Dorsey,

New York. To Los Angeles, comp & arr for singers & orchs incl Lawrence Welk. Chief Collabr: Frank Scott. *Songs:* The Moment of Truth.

SATTINGER, CELIA C   ASCAP 1963
composer
b Brooklyn, NY, Aug 14, 03. Has been writing poetry, lyrics & music for many yrs. *Songs:* Tonite (Our Very Own); You're a Darling; Love's a Wonderful Thing; Thank My Lucky Stars; Tomorrow Will Be Brighter.

SAUER, ROBERT   ASCAP 1943
composer, conductor, educator
b Rammeneau, Ger, Oct 3, 1872; d Provo, Utah, Jan 5, 44. Educ: Pub schs, Ger; music sch; studied with Kretschmer. Came to US, 05. Cond, Brigham Young Univ Band, 06-44. Asst prof music, Brigham Young Univ, 20, prof, 38, emer prof, 43. Chief Collabr: Maryhale Woolsey. *Songs:* When It's Springtime in the Rockies.

SAUNDERS, MILTON   ASCAP 1962
composer, author, conductor
b New York, NY, Mar 2, 13. Educ: City Col New York, BS; NY Univ, MA. Led Army orch, WW II. Cond orch in hotels, radio & TV. *Songs:* In the Midst of Our Love; How's About It, Baby; Tango in the Park; Cha-Cha in the Park.

SAUTER, EDWARD ERNEST (EDDIE)   ASCAP 1952
composer, conductor, arranger
b Brooklyn, NY, Dec 2, 14. Educ: Columbia Univ; studied with Stefan Wolpe, Bernard Wagenaar & Louis Gruenberg. Played in Archie Bleyer's Orch, 32; arr for Red Norvo, Mildred Bailey, 35-39, Benny Goodman, Artie Shaw, Tommy Dorsey, Woody Herman, Ray McKinley. Co-cond with Bill Finegan, Sauter-Finegan Orch, 52. Arr for TV, Bway musicals & records. *Songs & Instrumental Works:* Superman; Benny Rides Again; The Man With the Flaccid Air; I'm Late, I'm Late; Night Rider; A Summer Afternoon; All the Cats Join In; Concerto for Jazz Band and Symphony Orchestra; Focus; Saxophone Quartet; Quintet: Tuba and Saxophone Quartet; Quintet: Woodwinds and Bass Violin; Quintet: Tuba, French Horn, Harp, Oboe, Bassoon; Trio: Bassoon, Oboe, Harp; Quintet: Woodwinds and Tuba; Duo: Harp and Flute; 8 Random Thoughts for Unaccompanied Tuba; Brass Quintet: In Memory of Jim Timmens. *Scores:* Film/TV: Night Gallery; Switch; Beggarman Thief; Film background: Mickey One.

SAVADOVE, LAURENCE D   ASCAP 1972
author
b Camden, NJ, Nov 19, 31. Educ: Harvard Univ, BA, 53. Advert creative dir, McCann Erickson, Int. TV producer, Metromedia Producers Corp; producer, writer & dir for TV & film, Alan Landsburg Productions & Tomorrow Entertainment; pres, Savadove Productions, Inc. Chief Collabr: Gary Geld. *Songs:* Lyrics: It Takes a Lot of Love; Alone and Alive.

SAVAGE, RICHARD
See Hayman, Richard Warren Joseph

SAVARY, LOUIS MICHAEL   ASCAP 1967
composer, author
b Scranton, Pa, Jan 17, 36. Educ: Fordham Univ, AB; Woodstock Col, PhL; Cath Univ Am, PhD & STD. Was teen-age trumpeter & leader dixieland group, Musical Minors, who did network TV shows & toured with Ken Murray's Blackouts, 50-53; performed & recorded on Columbia Records with Woodstock Jesuit Singers, 66-68; wrote lyrics for many Gary McFarland tunes, 67-71; co-founder, Inst for Consciousness & Music, Baltimore, Md, 73; co-authored, "Music & Your Mind," 73; developed concepts of "Creative Listening" for children & "Meditation With Music" for children & adults; leader of many workshops on contemplation & music. Chief Collabrs: Gary McFarland, Leslie J Schnierer, Hank Levy. *Songs:* Lyrics: Sack Full of Dreams; Alone.

SAVINO, DOMENICO (D ONIVAS)   ASCAP 1924
composer, conductor, editor
b Taranto, Italy, Jan 13, 1882; d. To US, 05, citizen, 14. Educ: Royal Cons Naples. Music dir, record co, 15-25. Wrote for films. Chief ed, music publ co. Cond, CBS Symph; guest cond, other symph orchs. *Songs:* Indianola; Kentucky Dream; Arabian Nights; Burning Sands; Anchors Aweigh. *Instrumental Works:* Madrilena; Panorama; 4 Impressions; Vesuvian Rhapsody; Overture Fantasy; Symphony No 1; Venetian Scenes; Piano Concerto.

SAVITT, JAN   ASCAP 1941
composer, conductor, violinist
b Petrograd, Russia, Sept 4, 13; d Sacramento, Calif, Oct 4, 48. Educ: Curtis Inst, scholarship; studied with Carl Flesch, Arthur Rodzinski & Fritz Reiner. To US 1914. Violinist, Philadelphia Orch, age 14. Organized string quartet, 31. Music dir, WCAU, Philadelphia, 34 & KYW, 37. Formed dance orch & appeared on radio & in films. Chief Collabrs: Al Stillman, Harold Adamson, Johnny Watson. *Songs:* Moonrise; It's a Wonderful World; 720 in the Books; Now and Forever; It's the Tune That Counts; It Must Be Love; Beloved Friend; The Nearness of You. *Instrumental Works:* String Quartet Interpretation.

SAVOY, JAMES
See Criscuolo, James Michael

SAWTELL, PAUL   ASCAP 1952
composer, conductor, violinist

b Gilve, Poland, Feb 3, 06; d. To US, 23, citizen, 29. Educ: Cons in Essen, Munich & Berlin; pvt study. Violinist & cond, Chicago; cond, Lubliner & Trintz & Biograph Theatre, 26-28; violinist in radio, concert & opera cos, 28-31; cond, Chicago World's Fair, 33. Mem staff, NBC, Cleveland; arr, Standard Oil Prog & Cleveland Symph. To Hollywood, 35; arr, Andre Kostelanetz, Victor Young & David Broekman Orchs. Wrote for films; cond radio shows incl "Jack Benny." Established TV music dept, Warner Bros, 58. Chief Collabrs: John Herring, Bert Shefter, Louis Diaz, Johnny Mann, Ned Washington. *Songs:* What Have I Got of My Own?; Go Into the Mountains; Young Guns of Texas; Every Day Is Mother's Day; Texas Lady; To Love Once More; Tema-Tangi; Broken Arrow; West of Gallatan. *Scores:* TV background: Cheyenne; Sugar Foot; Colt 45; 77 Sunset Strip; Maverick; Bourbon Street Beat; Hawaiian Eye (also cond). Film background: Big Circus; The Sea Around Us; Voyage to the Bottom of the Sea; Arrowhead.

SAWYER, PAMELA JOAN
composer, lyricist

b London, Eng. Started writing, age 8. Moved to US. Wrote for Motown, 12 yrs. Is now a free-lancer. Chief Collabrs: Marilyn McCloud, Leon Waire, Gloria Jones, Mike Masser, Lorie Burden, Frank Wilson. *Songs:* Lyrics: Love Child; If I Ever Lose This Heaven; Love Hangover; If I Were Your Woman; It's the Way Nature Planned It; Last Time I Saw Him; My Whole World Ended; Better Hold on to This Feeling; I'm Living in Shame; A Different Kind of Different; Ain't Going to Eat My Heart Out.

SAXON, DAVID   ASCAP 1943
composer, conductor

b Brooklyn, NY, July 31, 19; d. Educ: Juilliard Sch Music. Served in USAF, WW II, Spec Services. Wrote spec material for Gordon & Sheila MacRae, Lisa Kirk, Marge & Gower Champion & Eartha Kitt (also cond). Music coordr: Victor Borge, Gene Kelly, Andy Williams & Jane Powell shows. Chief Collabrs: Robert Wells, Sammy Gallop, Buddy Kaye, Robert Cook, Sunny Skylar. *Songs:* Misbehavin' Lady; Do You Miss Your Sweetheart?; Are These Really Mine?; Wish You Were Waiting for Me; I Guess I Expected Too Much; There'll Soon Be a Rainbow; There Must Be a Way; Vagabond Shoes; Ask Me No Questions; Speak a Word of Love; What's My Name; All Year 'Round; Free; On an Ordinary Morning. *Scores:* TV background: O'Halloran's Luck.

SAXON, GRACE   ASCAP 1957
composer, singer

b New York, NY, Nov 23, 12. Educ: NY Professional Sch. Child performer with family act. Mem, Saxon Sisters, appearing in clubs, theatres, radio. To Calif, 35; dubbed voices in films. *Songs:* Ma Jolie; You Were Made for Love; Give Me a Sign; A Christmas to Remember; Why Do I Cry for Joey?; Lonely Christmas.

SAXTON, STANLEY EDWARD   ASCAP 1945
composer, author, teacher

b Fort Plain, NY, Aug 5, 04. Educ: Fort Plain High Sch, 22; Syracuse Univ, BM, 27, scholarship, 28; MM(comp), 42; Fontainbleau Cons, France, organ with Widor & Dupre, comp with Nadia Boulanger, 33. Organist, var theaters, Syracuse, 23-28; pianist, The Collegions with Paul Whitman, 27, Syracuse Symph & Vincent Lopez Club Orch, 27-28. Organist & prof music, Skidmore Col, 28-68. Did var concert tours as organist soloist, Caribbean tour, 58; appeared as comp-soloist with orchs; organ designer & builder, 38- Chief Collabr: Dixie Wilson. *Songs & Instrumental Works:* The Mist and All (solo); The Noble Nature (choral, SSAA); Carol Cantata (SSAA, SATB); Symphonie Byzantine (organ solo, 3 movements); Piano Concerto in A Minor (miniature score, pianos); Christ's Entry Into Jerusalem (organ solo); Mohawk Suite (orch); numerous pieces for organ solo & many songs for soprano.

SAYERS, PETER ESMONDE   ASCAP 1970
composer, author

b Bath, Eng, Nov 6, 42. Singer, instrumentalist & entertainer, WSM TV, 4 yrs. Maj tours, Britain, Middle East & Europe. Organized & dir, Grand Ole Opry, Eng. *Songs:* Picken and a Grinin for the Beeb; Lament for a Flea Pit; Swamp Rat; Chariots of Fire; The Sculptor; Gascoin Gush and Grumble; Trains; Old Pawn Shop Guitar; Thunderbird; Music: Dobro Doins; Banjo Bananas.

SAYLOR, BRUCE (STUART)
composer

b Philadelphia, Pa, Apr 24, 46. Educ: Juilliard Sch Music, BMus, 68, MS, 69, studied comp with Hugo Weisgall & Roger Sessions; Accademia di S Cecilia, studied comp with Goffredo Petrassi, 69-70; City Univ New York, PhD, 78. Juilliard Sch Music, Rodgers & Hammerstein scholarship; Nat Career Award from Nat Soc of Arts & Letters; Charles E Ives Award from Am Acad-Inst of Arts & Letters; Fulbright grant for study in Italy; Nat Endowment for the Arts fels (2). Comn from the Houston Symph Orch, Yale Symph Orch, Pa Opera Fest, The Contemporary Trio & Phyllis Curtin. Publ writings on contemporary music in: "Musical Quarterly", "Musical America", "Inst for Studies in Am Music Monograph Series", "Contemporary Music Newsletter" & "The New Grove's Dictionary." Served on bds of league, Int Soc for Contemporary Music, Composers Recordings, Inc & The Yard, Inc. Teacher, NY Univ, 76-79 & Queens Col, 79- *Songs:* Music: Four Psalm Settings (voice & flute); Loveplay (mezzosoprano, flute, cello or viola); Lyrics (soprano & violin); songs from Water Street. *Instrumental Works:* Turns and Mordents (concerto for flute & orch); Cantilena (string orch); Duo for Violin and Viola; St Ulmo's Fire (flute & harp); Firescreen (flute, cello, piano); five short piano pieces. *Scores:* My Kinsman, Major Molineux (opera in 1 act); Cycle (dance score).

SBARBARO, ANTHONY (TONY SPARGO)   ASCAP 1953
composer, drummer

b New Orleans, La, June 27, 1897; d New York, NY, Oct 30, 69. Began career with Original Dixieland Band, Reisenweber's, NY, 17; made first recording with band. Appeared with band in London, in Charles Cochran revue "Joy Bells" & Billy Rose's Ft Worth Fest, Tex, 36. Drummer in bands incl Miff Mole, Phil Napoleon, Russell Moore, Pee Wee Erwin, Jimmy Lytell & Tony Parenti. Appeared in Katherine Dunham revue, with original group, 43. Chief Collabrs: Nick La Rocca, Larry Shields, DeCosta, Eddie Edwards. *Songs & Instrumental Works:* Tiger Rag; At the Jazz Band Ball; Barnyard Blues; Bluin' the Blues; Clarinet Marmalade; Fidgety Feet; Sensation Rag; Mournin' Blues; Ostrich Walk; Original Dixieland One Step; Livery Stable Blues; Satanic Blues; Lazy Daddy; Mister Clarinet Man; Skeleton Jangle.

SCAFURO, ANTHONY PHILIP   ASCAP 1972
composer, singer

b Paterson, NJ, Sept 26, 48. Educ: Guitar lessons, 12 yrs; classical lessons with Tony Pizzarelli, 4 yrs. Mem groups, Mirrors Image, 12 yrs & Plastic Ono Band, 2 yrs. *Instrumental Works:* Running Scared; Malinda.

SCAGGS, WILLIAM ROYCE (BOZ)
musician

b Ohio, June 8, 44. Educ: Univ Wis-Madison. With Steve Miller's Band, The Marksmen, then his Ardells band (also under name Fabulous Night Train). Formed own rhythm-and-blues band, the Wigs. Rejoined Steve Miller, 67; made 2 albums. *Songs:* Lowdown (Grammy Award, 76). *Albums:* Children of the Future; Sailor; Boz; Boz Scaggs; Moments; Boz Scaggs and Band; My Time; Slow Dancer; Silk Degrees; Down Two Then Left.

SCALZI, EDWARD ANTHONY   ASCAP 1950
composer, author, singer

b Staten Island, NY, Jan 18, 18. Educ: Pvt saxophone study with Merel Johnson & Joe Napolean; Am Sch Music, New York, grad in 50. Played with bands, Tommy Dorsey, Jimmy Dorsey, Art Mooney, Woody Herman, Les Elgart & others, 32 yrs. Cert as Ed Lou Music Publ Co, 79; owner Tonex Record Co. Chief Collabr: Pat Noto. *Songs & Instrumental Works:* You Can't Buy Happiness; As Long As I Have You; Boo Boo in My Heart; Somewhere; Henpecked Joe; The Greatest Gift; Give It to Me Baby; I Told You So; I Love to Be With You; Being With You; Nothing Lasts Forever; Time to Be Saying Good Night; Take Back Your Heart; Singing a Happy Song; Your the One I Love.

SCANTLIN, RAY   ASCAP 1972
composer, author

b Hogansville, Ga, Mar 13, 47. Educ: Performers degree in piano. Screenwriter, currently working on two screenplays. Came to Los Angeles after completing educ, 70. Songwriter; has written plays & musicals.

SCARMOLIN, A LOUIS   ASCAP 1939
composer, conductor, pianist

b Schio, Italy, July 30, 1890; d Wyckoff, NJ, July 13, 69. Educ: New York Col of Music; pvt study. Sgt, USAF, World War I. Cond & accompanist for concert performers. Comp with over 600 publ works for orch, chorus, band, solos, ensembles, piano, organ, sacred & art songs & cantatas. *Songs:* We'll Keep Old Glory Flying; Longing; Gondola Nera; Preghiera. *Songs & Instrumental Works:* Night (prize winner, 47); Dramatic Tone Poem; Two Symphonies; In Retrospect (quintet, ancient instruments, prize from the Am Soc of Ancient Instruments, 39); O, Wisest of Men (choral, 1st prize, Franklin Inst, 38); Two Symphonic Fragments (prize winner, 44); My Creed (a cappella, Tribal Dance prize, Fed of Am Composers); Visions; Sinfonietta in A; Pastorale; Variations on a Folk Song; Minature Symphony No 1, No 2; Lithuanian Rhapsody; String Quartet; Mexican Holiday; Zombies; Introduction and Tarantella; An English Suite; Move Along; Minuet and Rondo; Fanfare (brass quintet); Duet Time (12 pieces for any 2 wood winds); Album Leaf for Four Horns; Lilliput Symphony; The Choristers' Daily Dozen (SATB, SSA); Overtures: Dramatic Marco Polo; Golden Heritage; Melodious Scale Studies (educ material). *Scores:* Operas: The Interrupted Serenade; also 7 grand operas.

SCARPA, SALVATORE (DON DONSON)   ASCAP 1964
composer, author, conductor

b Vineland, NJ, Nov 2, 18. Educ: Granff Sch Music, Philadelphia. Served in USA, Pacific, WW II. Has led own orch in Philadelphia & Atlantic City. Founder, music sch; teacher. Chief Collabr: Clarence Rehner. *Songs:* I Love You Forever; Bella Mia.

SCHACHTEL, IRVING I　　　　　　　　　ASCAP 1950
composer, author
b London, Eng, Mar 2, 09. Educ: Univ Buffalo, BA; Columbia Univ, LLB; Hartwick Col, LLD. Pres, Sonotone Corp; former pres, Nat Hosp for Speech Disorders & Prof Children's Sch. Lawyer.

SCHAD, WALTER C　　　　　　　　　　ASCAP 1928
composer, clarinetist, arranger
b Brooklyn, NY, Aug 24, 1889; d New York, Feb 16, 66. Educ: Juilliard Sch Music; NY Col of Music. Clarinetist in orchs led by Victor Herbert & John Philip Sousa. Staff, NBC musical res dept; ed & arr for music publ firms. Teacher of piano, clarinet, harmony & counterpoint. *Instrumental Works:* Americana; Trio for Violin, Cello, Piano; Overture: Samson, a Legendary Hero. *Scores:* Opera: Plango.

SCHAEFER, HAL　　　　　　　　　　ASCAP 1956
composer, pianist, arranger
b New York, NY, July 22, 25. Educ: High Sch Music & Art; Columbia Univ; studied with Mario Castelnuovo-Tedesco, Henry Brant & Laura Dubman La Marchina. Pianist in orchs, incl Benny Carter, Boyd Raeburn & Harry James; accompanist to singers, incl Peggy Lee, Vic Damone & Billy Eckstine; arr & vocal coach, 20th Century Fox Studios, Hollywood, 48-55. Led own trio & orchs in New York, Los Angeles, San Francisco, Europe & SAm; comp, cond & arr, United Artists Records; arr dance music for Bway shows, "Foxy" & "A Funny Thing Happened on the Way to the Forum." Chief Collabrs: Brenda Schaefer, Bob Larimer, Will Holt. *Songs:* Music: Strange as It Seems; The Lord's Prayer (jazz choir). *Instrumental Works:* Paramax for Percussion; Overture to the Blues (comn by Joseph Eger); Fail Safe; Montevideo; Of Things Gone By; February Fiesta; Let's Have a Cerebration. *Scores:* Ballet: Bop Song (comn by Daniel Nagrin for dance co); Film/TV: Amsterdam Kill; The Money Trap; Ballad for an Ancient Hope (comn by UN, Tenth Anniversary); Their World Is Limited (comn by Nat Asn Retarded Children).

SCHAEFER, ROBERT E　　　　　　　　ASCAP 1960
author
b Salt Lake City, Utah, July 17, 26. TV screenwriter, 50- Co-writer of "Lassie," 63-73, also wrote lyrics for the show. Chief Collab: Eric Freiwald. *Songs:* Lyrics: Ghost Town Rock; Fickle Woman; I Know Where I'm Going; Lassie, the Voyager; Listen With Your Mind.

SCHAEFER, WILLIAM ARKWELL　　　　　ASCAP 1962
arranger, educator, conductor
b Cleveland, Ohio, Feb 28, 18. Educ: Miami Univ, Ohio, BS & MS(educ & music); Univ Mich; Juilliard Grad Sch Music. Army bandleader, WW II. Dir, Kiltie Band & asst prof music, Carnegie Inst Technology, 47-52; prof music, Univ Southern Calif, 52-, lect, Eng Univs & Schs Music & Res in Eng, France & Ger during leaves from univ; fel, Wolfson Col, Cambridge Univ, Eng. Did CBS Prog, "Discovering Music," 62. *Instrumental Works:* Arr for Concert Band: Wellington's Victory Symphony (Beethoven); Overture to the New Year 1758 (Boyce); Chorale and Fugue (Buxtehude); Jeremiah Clarke Suite; Fetes From Three Nocturnes (Debussy); Sonata Pian E Forte (Gabrieli); Concerto for Two Horns (Handel); Music for Two Wind Bands (Handel); Three English Marches (Haydn); Suite for Band (Hook); Symphonie for Band (Jadin); Suite Royale (Lully); Symphony III, first movement (Mahler); Night on Bald Mountain (Moussorgsky); Symphony V, first movement (Prokofieff); Battle Symphony (Purcell); Feste Romane (Respighi); Scherzo for Band (Rossini); Suite From Opera "The Nose" (Shostakovich); Symphony V, first movement (Shostakovich); Symphony IX, three movements (Shostakovich); Petrouchka Suite (Strawinsky); Symphony I, finale (Tschaikowsky); Huldigungsmarsch (Wagner); Marche Ecossaise (Debussy); Four Sketches (Bartok).

SCHAEFER, WILLIS　　　　　　　　　ASCAP 1955
composer
b Kenosha, Wis, Nov 23, 28. Educ: DePaul Univ, BM; Northwestern Univ, Evanston; studied with Leon Stein, Anthony Donato, Ted Royal, Robert Ginzler & Franklyn Marks. Arr, comp & asst cond, Fifth Army Band, Chicago, 3 yrs. Comp & arr 150 works for maj music publ. Comp, arr & produced music for 700 TV & radio commercials. Comp/arr, Disney Studios, Hollywood, 14 yrs. *Instrumental Works:* The Sound of America; Overture: Fanfare and Capriccio; Dimension Six; Fanfare and Processional; Shadings; Series Arr: Ode to Joy (L Beethoven); Unfinished Symphony (F Schubert); Symphony Number Forty (W Mozart). *Scores:* Film/TV: Walt Disney's Wonderful World of Color; Barnaby Jones; The Tonight Show; Gunsmoke; Smile; The New Mickey Mouse Club (120 shows).

SCHAEFFER, DON　　　　　　　　　　ASCAP 1964
composer, author, teacher
b New York, NY, Sept 10, 35. Educ: Morris High Sch; Adelphi Univ, BA, 57, scholarship, 54-56; Columbia Univ, MA, 58, prof dipl, specialist in music educ, 60; Music Acad of West, scholarship, summer, 59; studied trombone with Davis Shuman, Juilliard Sch & John Clarke, Manhattan Sch of Music, voice with Karen Branzell, Metrop Opera, piano with Stanley Hummel. Music fac, South Huntington Sch District, 57- Dir, I H B Prog, summer session, Adelphi Univ, 66. Author, "Encyclopedia of Scales", "Dictionary of Chords & Inversions" & "Folk Song Extravaganza." Ed of "Method of Scales", "Easy Duets" &

"Method of Bass Trombone" by Ernest Williams, "The Jazz Soloist" by Walter Stuart, "Arrangers Workshop" by Angelo Dellaria, "Sightreading Studies" by Gaston Dufresne, "Advanced Studies" by Harry Glantz, "Trombone Rhythms" by Colin-Bower, "New Directions in Tonguing" by James Burke & "Rhythms for F Attachment-Bass Trombone" by Colin-Bower. *Songs:* Concert band arrangements: Polonaise; Symphonic March; Play; Israeli Folk Songs; Christmas Sketches; Tarantella. *Instrumental Works:* Arr: The Award Folio; Yuletide Band Fest; Concert Showcase; Instrumental bks: Duets Are Fun; The Brass Choir; The Clarinet Choir; Instrumental ens: Conversations (trumpet quartet); Renaissance Ballade (trombone trio); Adagio (brass quartet); Jubilation (trumpet quartet); Impressions (clarinet quartet); Double feature band series: Moscow At Midnight; The Heavens Are Telling; In Merry Old England.

SCHAEFFER, MARY　　　　　　　　　ASCAP 1938
composer, author, pianist
b Christianburg, Va, Feb 4, 1893; d New York, NY, July 25, 77. Educ: Montgomery Col; studied with Van Wagner, Brownold. Organist in theatres & radio, Roanoke, Va. Winner, songwriting contest, to NY, 30. Writer, Bway musicals & motion pictures. *Songs:* Little Old Shack in the Mountains; Rockin' Chair Swing; I Long to Belong to You; My Heart Has Wings; Penthouse for Rent; The Heather Is Blooming in Scotland; Dancing With a Broken Heart; Keep the Flag Flying, America; You Little Heart Breaker You; That Flame Is Burning Again; Toy Town Jamboree.

SCHAFER, BOB　　　　　　　　　　　ASCAP 1924
author, singer, publisher
b New York, NY, July 24, 1897; d New York, Sept 28, 43. Educ: Holy Name Sch, New York. Prof staff, music publ co. On radio, with wife, New York; mgr, music publ co, Chicago. *Songs:* Calling Sweetheart for You; Louisiana; Sonya; Tell Me Why You and I Should Be Strangers; Some Other Bird Whistled a Tune; Walk Jenny Walk; I've Got My Habits On; Daddy, Your Mama's Lonesome for You; I Want You to Want Me to Want You; Midnight Moon.

SCHAFER, DANIEL JOSEPH　　　　　　ASCAP 1976
composer, musician, vocalist
b Mt Pleasant, Mich, Oct 5, 52. Recorded with RCA Records, 76-78; started Da Scha Music Publ, 76. Chief Collabrs: Jack Richardson, Don Davis, Gary Lazar. *Songs:* A Day Without You, Dear; You Mean the World to Me.

SCHAFER, HELEN SCHAFMEISTER
See Schafmeister, Helen Louise

SCHAFER, MILTON　　　　　　　　　ASCAP 1957
composer, author, teacher
b New York, NY, Sept 24, 20. Educ: Juilliard Sch Music, 36-39, BS, 52; Am Cons at Fontainebleau, 49; pvt study with Nadia Boulanger, Paris, 49-50; cert, Paris Cons, 50; City Col, MA, 67. Winner Nat Piano Competition, Nat Guild Piano Teachers, 48. Concert pianist in Paris, 49-50; NY Town Hall Debut, 50; 2nd Town Hall Recital, 54. Musical dir & vocal coach, Am Theatre Wing, 54-56; worked with & for Frank Loesser, 56-58; comp music for "Bravo Giovanni," score nomination for Tony Award; also cantata "For the Living." Chief Collabrs: Ira Levin; Ronny Graham; Barbara Fried, Nita Schroeder. *Songs:* I'm Five; Colored Kisses; Mommy Gimme a Drinka Water (children's song cycle); I Like Old People, Don't You?; Playing on the See-Saw; Balloon Balloona; Crazy Barbara; Music: He Touched Me; Ah, Camminare!; The No Color Time of the Day; Today Is a Day for a Band to Play; The Kangaroo; Let's Go; Drat the Cat (voted best score of yr); I'm All I've Got; Steady, Steady; One Little World Apart; Miranda; J'ai Fatigue; I Like Him; Holmes and Watson; Lyrics: The Money Trap.

SCHAFF, JAN　　　　　　　　　　　ASCAP 1964
composer, author, pianist
b Poland, Oct 3, 03; d. Educ: Col & Cons, Poland; studied with Jacobo Ficher, Arg. Mem, SADAIC (Soc of Composers, Arg). Chief Collabr: George Cardini. *Songs:* Stardust of Yesterday; Don't Let It End.

SCHAFF, SYLVIA (VALERIE BROOKS)　　　ASCAP 1953
composer, author
b Brooklyn, NY, Mar 24, 16. Educ: Manhattan Sch Music, piano with Dora Zaslovsky, 35-37; Brooklyn Singer & own piano accompanist for radio stas WEVD & WLTH, New York, 34-36. Wrote Alma Mater for Brooklyn Col, 36. Winner, Song Contest CBS, 51. Music teacher, New York high schs, 58-72. Comp & lyricist. Chief Collabr: Gene Roberts. *Songs:* I Never Noticed the Rain; You Changed; Music: Deny; Just One More Time; Only Yesterday; How Could You Forget Me?; Hey Mister; Lover Be Careful; Tinsel and Joy; I Fell in Love; Hold Me Close.

SCHAFMEISTER, HELEN LOUISE　　　　ASCAP 1967
composer, pianist, teacher
b Ossining, NY, Oct 5, 1900. Educ: Ossining Sch, William Barber; studied with Frank La Forge, Ernesto Berumen, Egon Petri, Charles Haubiel & Emerson Whithorne. Soloist, concerts in Carnegie Hall, Town Hall & Steinway Hall; accompanist & soloist toured NAm & Can; toured Europe, 54; soloist with radio symph orchs; made Philadelphia Symphonette-Duo Art records; originator of The Candle-Light Musicales; played at Waldorf-Astoria, 28 yrs; had songs on

radio. Chief Collabrs: Livio Manucci, Correlis Van Fleet, Federico Longas, Rose Dirman, Maryjane Richardson (poet), Stanley Kimmel (poet), Eleanore Lewis, Norma Regan. *Songs & Instrumental Works:* Brass band: We Are To-Gether; Prairie; A Night Myth; Gypsies; Barnegat Bay; The Music of Your Love; The Jaunting Car; Entreat Me Not; Duet-46th Psalm; The Dawn and You; Reasons; Spring Song; Illusion; Sea Swept Fantasy; Then and Now; Forever; To and From Town.

SCHANTZ, DAVID MATHEW (DAVID CHANCE)   ASCAP 1979
composer, author
b Berkeley, Calif, Mar 13, 53. Educ: Pub sch; pvt lessons; Univ Calif, Berkeley, drama, 1 yr. Began playing locally; produced album for local band, Hammerhead, 75; recording artist, 79- *Songs:* Factory Man; A Real Hot Band; Havin a Good Time; Protest Song.

SCHARF, WALTER   ASCAP 1943
author
b New York, NY, Aug 1, 10. Educ: NY Univ; Damrosch Inst; studied with Ernst Toch. As a youth arr & played piano for Vincent Lopez, Rudy Vallee, Kate Smith & Helen Morgan, then joined Warner Bros as comp, 35-37, 20th Century Fox, 37-41 & Paramount, 41-42. Head music dept, Republic, 42-46, Universal, 46-50, Goldwyn, 50-52- Did many major motion pictures & TV shows. Received 4 Emmy Awards, 1 Grammy Award & 1 Golden Globe Award. Now prof, Univ Wyo; lectr. Chief Collabrs: Lyrics, Sammy Cahn, Don Black, Ned Washington, Mitchel Parish. *Songs:* Music: Ben (ASCAP Plaque, 71); Walking Tall (theme for 3 films); Three Ring Circus (title march song). *Scores:* Opera: The Pilot to Overthrow X-mas; Bway Shows: Maybe That's Your Problem (musical); C'est La Vie (musical); Films: Hans Christian Andersen; The Joker Is Wild; Funny Girl (adaptation); Cheyenne Social Club; Willy Wonka and the Chocolate Factory; Pocket Full of Miracles; Where Love Has Gone; If It's Tuesday This Must Be Belgium; Three Violent People; King Creole; TV: The Man From Uncle; Mission Impossible; The Under Sea World of Jacques Cousteau; National Geographic Specials; Ben Casey; From Here to Eternity; Blind Ambition; Moviola; Slattery's People; Salvage; Adventures of Jamie McPheetens; Adventures of Little Red Riding Hood (special). *Albums:* Legend of the Living Sea; Wilderness Trails (Nat Geographic); Funny Girl; Dreams By the Dozen; My Favorite Places.

SCHARFMAN, NITRA   ASCAP 1974
composer, author
b New York, NY, Aug 21, 38. Educ: High Sch of Art & Design. Co-author & comp of Bway production, "The Lieutenant," which was nominated for four Tony's. Chief Collabrs: Gene Curty, Chuck Strand.

SCHARLACH, ED   ASCAP 1972
author
b San Francisco, Calif, Mar 12, 43. Educ: Beverly Hills High Sch; Univ Calif, Berkeley, BA(sociol). Wrote scripts & lyrics for col shows, 66- TV comedy writer for "That Girl", "Odd Couple", "Happy Days", "Love American Style", "Dean Martin Show", "Bob Hope Show", "John Denver Special", "Neil Sedaka Special", "Mork and Mindy", "3 Girls 3" & others; now producer "Mork and Mindy"; lyrics for original songs in scripts of var shows. Chief Collabrs: Charles Fox, Sheryl Scharlach, Tom Tenowich. *Songs:* Lyrics: You Dropped Your Pencil; Fuzzy-Mountain Breakdown; Shazbot Blues.

SCHAUER, PATRICIA KAY (PATTY MOAN)   ASCAP 1972
composer, author, singer
b Elkhart, Ind, Feb 22, 47. Educ: Goshen High Sch, Ind; Patricia Stevens Career Sch, Chicago, 5 months. Sang with Curtis Bros, 67-74; sang backup with several unknown groups, 73-75. Chief Collabrs: Richard & Michael Curtis. *Songs:* Lyrics: Don't You Mess With a Woman.

SCHAUM, JOHN WALTER   ASCAP 1958
composer, author, teacher
b Milwaukee, Wis, Jan 27, 05. Educ: Univ Wis, Milwaukee, BE, 28; Marquette Univ, BM, 31; Northwestern Univ, MM, 34. Won Nat Fedn Music Clubs-Young Artists Contest Div Piano, 31. Pres, Wis State Music Teachers Asn. Comp of piano teaching materials; cond hundreds of seminars for piano teachers throughout US. Now comp, publ & clinician. *Songs:* Carol of the Birds (revised lyrics); Lyrics: Hail Great Aloha State (off Hawaiian state song); National Anthems of the Americas (off anthems of all NAm & SAm countries plus Caribbean nations, spec Eng transl). *Instrumental Works:* Mountain Concerto (piano & band); Sea Rover Sonata (piano solo); Corsage Waltz (piano solo). *Songs & Instrumental Works:* Fifty Songs-Fifty States (off state songs with spec piano arr).

SCHECHTMAN, CAROLYN R (CAROLYN RANEY)   ASCAP 1964
author, musicologist, critic
b Los Angeles, Calif, Aug 14, 24. Educ: Univ Rochester Eastman Sch Music, BM; Cleveland Inst Music, MM; NY Univ, PhD; studied with Nadia Boulanger, Queena Mario, Enrico Rosati, Clytie Mundy, William P Herman. Singer, concert, opera, oratorio, musicals; premiere, "Mother of Us All"; voice teacher, AMDA & NY Univ, New York. Critic, Baltimore Sunday "Sun" & "Music Magazine"; ed in chief, CMA "Symposium," 4 yrs. Coordr grad studies, Peabody Cons, Baltimore, Md; Fulbright Fel, 63-64. Col dean, East Stroudsburg State Col, Pa; col vpres, Pa State Syst. Choral series ed, "Nine Centuries of

Music by Women," incl works by Caccini, Strozzi, de la Guerre & Reichardt. Chief Collabrs: Saul Schechtman, Antonio Lora.

SCHECHTMAN, SAUL   ASCAP 1966
composer, conductor
b Winchester, Conn, Sept 4, 24. Educ: Brooklyn Col, BA, 47; Juilliard Sch Music, postgrad dipl, 49; studied orch conducting with E Schenkman, D Dixon & J P Morel. Assoc cond, Juilliard Sch Music, 49-51; music dir, Chamber Group 27 & Co-Opera, New York; cond, Omnibus, CBS TV; music dir, Bronx Symph Orch, 53-57 & Teaneck Symph Orch, NJ, 57-61; comp incidental music for "Auntie Mame" (play & film), 57; music dir Bway musicals, "Carnival," 61-63 & "Hello, Dolly," 67-70; music dir, Orch Piccola, Baltimore, 76-80; guest cond var Europ orchs. *Instrumental Works:* Recreations for Piano; Capriccio for Organ; Serenade for Bassoon and Piano. *Songs & Instrumental Works:* O, Lord Our God (choral motet).

SCHECK, GEORGE   ASCAP 1956
composer, author, producer
b New York, NY, Sept 22, 11. Educ: High sch. Dancer, also radio & TV producer. Personal mgr singers, incl Connie Francis.

SCHEIB, CHARLES J   ASCAP 1963
author
b New York, NY, July 27, 1891. Educ: Pub schs. Originated first amateur song contest, Rochester, NY, 28. Chief Collabrs: M K Jerome, Andrew Donnelly. *Songs:* The Song That Made You Mine; By a Mountain Stream; Let's Bend an Elbow; Send New York's Son to Washington (Al Smith campaign song).

SCHEIN, JULIUS   ASCAP 1952
composer, author, publisher
b New York, NY, Sept 21, 10; d New York, Jan 4, 69. Educ: St John's Univ, Sch Law, LLB. Attorney, 35; admitted to US Supreme Court, 47. USN, WW II. Had own publ co, then partner, Music Workshop, NY. *Songs:* Sleepy Mood; Lover Come What May; Under the Tonto Rim.

SCHELL, NORMAN CLARK   ASCAP 1972
composer, author, singer
b Lebanon, Pa, Sept 17, 44. Educ: Shirley Indust Sch Boys; Worcester Jr Col, AA. Band leader, lead vocalist & chief comp for Vanguard recording artists, Clean Living, 68-79. Chief Collabrs: Peter Frizzel, Anthony Rubino, F Fredrick Shaw. *Songs:* Backwoods Girl; Jubals Blues Again; Price I Pay; Charles Street in the Morning; Far North Again.

SCHELLE, MICHAEL   ASCAP 1977
composer
b Philadelphia, Pa, Jan 22, 50. Educ: Villanova Univ, BA, 71; Butler Univ, BM, 74; Hartt Sch Music, Univ Hartford, MM, 76; Univ Minn, PhD, 80; studied comp with Arnold Franchetti, Paul Fetler, Dominick Argento & others. Had works performed by St Paul Chamber Orch, Indianapolis Symph, Orquestra Sinfonica Nacional, SONOR of Univ Calif, San Diego, Pittsburgh New Music Ens & many others. Awards/Prizes: Inter-Am Music Fest Comp Prize (orch), 77; Delius Asn Comp Prize (orch), 78; Am Soc Univ Comp Nat Comp Prize, 78; ASCAP Found Grants, 79 & 80; Harvey Gaul Mem Comp Prize, 80. Other Comp Hons: MacDowell Colony Fel, 77; Wolf Trap Found Grants (comp-in-residence at Wolf Trap, Va), 78 & 79. Comns: Bratnober Fund, Inc; Vale of Glamorgan Music Fest, Cardiff, Wales; Welsh Arts Council. *Instrumental Works:* Masque for Orchestra; Lancaster Variations for Orchestra; Music for the Last Days of Strindberg (9 players); Chamber Concerto for Solo Violin and Three Players; Ubu Roi (wind ens).

SCHELLING, ERNEST   ASCAP 1952
composer, conductor, pianist
b Belvidere, NJ, July 26, 1876; d New York, NY, Dec 8, 39. Educ: First music study with father, Felix Schelling; at age 7, Cons de Paris, with Mathias, studied with Gotschius, Pruckner, Huber, Barth, Moszkowski, Leschetizky & Paderewski. Debut at age 4, Acad Music, Philadelphia; toured Europe. WW I, Maj, US Inf, asst Am mil attache; Dist Serv Medal, US; Legion of Honor, France; Polonia Restituta, Poland; Order of Alfonso XII, Spain. Concert tours. Founder, cond, Concerts for Children & Young People (NY Philh Soc); also in Boston, Philadelphia, Cincinnati, Baltimore, Los Angeles & San Francisco. Cond, Baltimore Symph, 35-37. Coauthor "Oxford Piano Course" (10 vols). *Instrumental Works:* Legende Symphonique; A Victory Ball; Suite Fantastique; Impressions From an Artist's Life; Violin Concerto; Morocco; Divertimento; Tarantelle (string quartet).

SCHER, WILLIAM   ASCAP 1951
composer, pianist, teacher
b New York, NY, Oct 12, 1900; d Brooklyn, NY, June 16, 75. Educ: Pub schs; studied with Lazar Weiner, Arnold Zemachson. Gave piano recitals as child. Taught piano, Brooklyn Cons, 38-46; also pianist with Brooklyn Cons Trio. Wrote primarily in educ field. Taught piano, comp. *Instrumental Works:* Sea Fantasy (2 pianos); Czardas Rhapsody; plus many more pieces & adaptations.

SCHERER, FRANK H ASCAP 1955
composer, conductor, organist
b New York, NY, Dec 5, 1897. Educ: Studied with T Tertius Noble, Rosario Scalero, Clement Gale & Courtland Palmer. Teacher. *Songs & Instrumental Works:* Contemplation on the Crucifixion (oratorio); Good Friday Requiem (cantata).

SCHERMAN, ROBERT ASCAP 1963
composer, author, producer
b Indianapolis, Ind, June 14, 20. Educ: Black Fox Mil Inst; Univ Calif, Los Angeles. Writer & producer of records. Chief Collab: Ralph Freed. *Songs:* All for You; I Promise; Shufflin' Boogie; Love of Bridey Murphy; Fun to Be With; Telephone. *Albums:* Seven Wonders of the World Plus One.

SCHERTZINGER, VICTOR ASCAP 1934
composer, author, violinist
b Mahanoy City, Pa, Apr 8, 1890; d Hollywood, Calif, Oct 26, 41. Educ: Brown Prep, Pa; Univ Brussels Sch of Music; pvt violin study. Violin soloist, Victor Herbert Orch, age 8; gave solo concerts, US & Europe. Cond theatre orchs, Los Angeles; also Bway musicals. Wrote songs for films incl "The Love Parade." Dir many films incl "The Return of Peter Grimm", "Forgotten Faces" & "The Mikado." Chief Collabs: Clifford Grey, Gus Kahn, Johnny Burke, Frank Loesser, Johnny Mercer. *Songs:* Marcheta; Life Begins When You're in Love; Another Kiss; Gotta Be Good; March of the Grenadiers; My Love Parade; Paris Stay the Same; Dream Lover; Love Me Forever; One Night of Love; I'll Never Let a Day Pass By; Sand in My Shoes; Kiss the Boys Goodbye; The Moon and the Willow Tree; Tangerine; I Remember You; Not Mine; The Fleet's In; Arthur Murray Taught Me Dancing in a Hurry; If You Build a Better Mousetrap. *Scores:* Film background: Civilization.

SCHICKELE, PETER (P D Q BACH, WILLIAM BECKER) ASCAP 1961
composer, author
b Ames, Iowa, July 17, 35. Educ: Central High Sch, Fargo, NDak; Swarthmore Col, BA, 57; Juilliard Sch Music, MS, 60. Ford Found Grant, wrote music for Los Angeles Pub Schs, 60-61. Fac, Juilliard Sch Music, 61-65. Free-lance comp, arr & entertainer, 75- Sole discoverer & perpetrator of the music of the highly figmental comp P D Q Bach. Works comn by Smith Col, Philadelphia Art Alliance, Juilliard Repertory Proj, Louisville Symph Orch, St Louis Symph, Pilobolus Dance Theatre, Yale Univ Concert Band & others. Has recorded on Vanguard, Louisville & others. Chief Collabs: Robert Dennis, Stanley Walden, lyrics, Diane Lampert, Brooks Jones. *Songs:* Oh! Calcutta!; The Seasonings (choral); Blaues Gras (Blue Grass Cantata); Iphigenia in Brooklyn (cantata); Music: Rejoice in the Sun; Three Choruses from Cummings (choral). *Instrumental Works:* A Zoo Called Earth (orch); Five of a Kind (concerto for brass quintet, orch); Overture to the Civilian Barber; Hornsmoke (A Horse Opera for Brass Quintet); Concerto for Piano vs Orch; Grand Serenade for an Awful Lot of Winds and Percussion. *Scores:* Opera/Ballet: The Stoned Guest; Hansel and Gretel and Ted and Alice; Film/TV: Silent Running.

SCHIESSER (RACHELS), KAREN ANN (KAREN SARGENT) ASCAP 1973
composer, author, singer
b Glasgow, Mont, Aug 6, 38. Educ: Butte High Sch, Mont; Am Theatre Wing, New York, Matt Dennis. Singer, actress & dancer in Bway "All American", "Little Mary Sunshine", "Carousel", "Bye Bye Birdie", "Showboat", "No No Nannette" & others. Staff, "Name That Tune", "Truth or Consequences", Kenny Rogers Productions, TV & movies. Chief Collabr: Matt Dennis.

SCHILLACI, JOSEPH JOHN ASCAP 1961
composer
b Chicago, Ill, Nov 21, 06. Educ: Pub sch. Chief Collabr: Joe Mantia. *Songs:* Back to Rome; Lover's Quarrel.

SCHILLER, THOMAS BENNETT ASCAP 1979
author
b Los Angeles, Calif, Apr 12, 49. Educ: Studied guitar with Harriet Williams, 58-59; studied actg & voice with Andre Phillippe, 68-69. Writer, actor & film dir for NBC's "Saturday Night Live," 75-; creator of feature shows, "Bad Playhouse" & "Bad Musical." Chief Collabr: Howard Shore. *Scores:* Bad Musicals, incl Leuenhoek (Maybe I'm Too Big for Him), Kinder Kabaret (Velkommen, Tomorrow You Go on the Bus) & Mr Potatoe Head (I Wish Potatoes Weren't So Dumb).

SCHILLIO, EMILE JACQUES ASCAP 1972
composer, arranger, orchestrator
b London, Eng, Sept 19, 09. Educ: Cons Nat Paris; Loyola Univ, BS; Calif State Univ, MA; pvt comp studies with Mario Castelnuovo-Tedesco. Violinist & arr, Publix-Paramount; cond, WWL, New Orleans; asst concertmaster, New Orleans Symph; first violinist with Fort Worth Symph. *Songs & Instrumental Works:* SATB: Down in Trinidad; Oh! Cordelia Brown; African Work Song; Dulcie; Nine Hundred Miles From Home; Band: Jumping Jupiter; Who do Voodoo?.

SCHINE, HILDEGARDE FELDMAN ASCAP 1977
composer, author
b Gloversville, NY, Mar 23, 03. Educ: Castle Boarding Sch, Tarrytown, NY; studied with Prof Portnoff & Marie Calle; Syracuse Univ, fine & liberal arts; Juilliard Sch Music. Supvr music for pub schs, Johnstown, NY. Chief Collabrs: Mrs Lavonne Mouw, Valentine Glockmur. *Songs & Instrumental Works:* Teasin'; I Have Never Lost a Friend; My Mother's Attic; Kiwanis Means We Build; The Renee Waltz.

SCHINSTINE, WILLIAM JOSEPH ASCAP 1964
composer, author, teacher
b Easton, Pa, Dec 16, 22. Educ: Studied with George Hamilton Green & William G Street; Eastman Sch Music, BM, 45; Univ Pa, MS, 52; Temple Univ; West Chester State Col. Percussionist, Nat Symph & Pittsburgh Symph; percussionist & arr, San Antonio Symph & Tamiment Orch. Pub sch music teacher, Pottstown Schs, Pa, 51-78. Owner, S & S Sch Music, Pottstown, 62- Performed with Pottstown Band; founder & exec dir, Cornerstone Fest of the Arts, 79. Clinician in perc; writer for Percussive Notes, Percussionist, School Musician & Instrumentalist. Chief Collabrs: Fred A Hoey, Craig Bennett, Randy Koons. *Instrumental Works:* Basic & Intermediate Drum Method; Southern Special Drum Solos; Futuristic Drum Solos; Little Champ First Year Drum Solos, Piano Accompaniment and Record; 17 Plus One Drum Solos; Adventures in Solo Drumming; Tympendium (timpani solo, band accompaniment); Tympeloro (timpani solo, band accompaniment); Acoustic Suite for Percussion Ensemble; Sonata No 1 for Timpani and Piano; Sonata No 2, 3 for Timpani; The Developing Solo Timpanist; Tymp Tunes; Five Star General March; Drum Primer; Drum Method (vol I); Three Means to An End (drum solo); Scherzo Without Instruments; Bossa Nova Without Instruments; Rock Trap (Without instruments); Centralization; Drumming Together; Four Hands Around (Easy & Difficult) Percussion Duets; Roto Tom Solos for the Melodic Drummer; Cadences for All Occasions. *Scores:* Ballet: The Pennsylvania Farmer.

SCHIRMER, RUDOLPH E ASCAP 1962
composer, author, publisher
b Santa Barbara, Calif, June 18, 19. Educ: Princeton Univ; Curtis Inst, with Rosario Scalero. S/Sgt, Mil Intelligence, WW II. Dir, G Schirmer, New York, 49; also vpres. *Songs & Instrumental Works:* Seven Songs (choral).

SCHLAKS, STEPHEN DAVID ASCAP 1964
composer, author, recording artist
b New York, NY, May 13, 40. Educ: Studied piano with Samuel Seigel, 49-59; Christopher Columbus High Sch; Carle Place High Sch; Hofstra Col; C W Post Col, studied comp & orch with Stefan Wolpe & Raoul Pleskow, 60-62. Began comp rock & pop songs, 58. Produced & arr singles & albums for most top record cos; int recording artist; recorded own comp & songs, Baby Records, Milan, Italy. Chief Collabrs: Charlie Weiss, Mel Glazer. *Songs:* Fantasy Girl; Music: Your Ma Said You Cried in Your Sleep Last Night; I've Got Lovin' on My Mind; Speedway. *Instrumental Works:* Blue Dolphin; Casablanca; Composition in Venice; 3rd Melody; Sensitive and Delicate; Openings; Moon Cake La La.

SCHLEIN, IRVING ASCAP 1950
composer, author, conductor
b New York, NY, Aug 18, 05. Educ: Brooklyn Col Pharmacy, 27; New York Col Music, 28; Inst Musical Art, cert in piano, 30; City Col New York, BA, 36; scholarships in comp with Aaron Copland, Roy Harris, Roger Sessions, Hans Eisler & Wallingford Riegger. Worked as cond & arr with Kurt Weill & Cole Porter; comp symph, stage works & piano works. Recent works, Testament to Freedom & The Common Sch of Literature. Author bk, Slave Songs of US. *Songs:* Heave Away; Let God's Children Come Home; Chariot Wheels Are Rollin'; There's a Meetin' Here Tonight. *Instrumental Works:* Strictly From the Birds (suite for piano solo). *Songs & Instrumental Works:* Dance Overture (First Prize, 47). *Scores:* Opera: Salammbo (based on Flaubert's novel); Bway Show: My Heart's in the Highlands (musical based on Robert Burns).

SCHLITT, JOHN WILLIAM ASCAP 1975
composer, singer
b Lincoln, Ill, Feb 3, 50. Educ: Univ Ill. Formed group Johnny, 80. *Songs:* One Against the Other; The Feeling Is Right; Get Up and Enjoy Yourself; Dance Away Lover; Every Little Bit of My Heart.

SCHLITZ, DON ASCAP 1978
composer, author
b Durham, NC, Aug 29, 52. Singer. *Songs:* The Gambler; Senior Prom.

SCHMERSAL, ARTHUR H
composer
b Baltimore, Md, Dec 24, 35. Educ: Peabody Cons Music, BA(music), MA(music). Teacher & dir, Baltimore Colts Marching Band. Comp music for marching bands.

SCHMID, ADOLF ASCAP 1928
composer, author, conductor
b Hannsdorf, Austria, Nov 18, 1868; d Englewood, NJ, Feb 2, 58. Educ: Vienna Cons. Music dir, His Majesty's Theatre, London, 01-15. To US, 15, citizen, 24.

Cond, British Symph, 12-13, Boston Grand Opera Co & Pavlova Ballet Russe, 15-16, Pavley-Oukrainsky Ballet, 20-37. Chief arr, NBC, 30-45. Taught orchestration & conducting, Juilliard Sch, 32-58. Author bk, "The Language of the Baton" & ed, "Digest of Rimsky-Korsakoffs 'Principles of Orchestration'." *Instrumental Works:* Joseph and His Brethren (suite); Prelude; Caravan Dance; Bacchanalian Dance.

SCHMID, JOHANN C — ASCAP 1936
composer, violinist
b Philadelphia, Pa, Aug 7, 1870; d Philadelphia, Mar 7, 51. Educ: Philadelphia Musical Acad; studied with Richard Schmidt, Martinus Van Gelder, Fritz Braun & Richard Zeckwer. Cond own orch. *Songs:* Garden of Roses; Moonlight, the Rose and You; Vale of Dreams; If I Could Only Make You Care; There's A Warm Spot in My Heart; In the Valley of Contentment; The Passing Caravan.

SCHMIDT, ERWIN R — ASCAP 1924
composer, author, pianist
b Chicago, Ill, Mar 11, 1890; d Boston, Mass, Dec 14, 66. Educ: High sch; studied with William Taegtmeyer, August Harms, Henry Block. Saxophonist, USN, Battalion Band at Great Lakes Training Station, World War I; toured US on Liberty Bond Drives. Pianist, T B Harms, 14-16, vaudeville, radio & concerts. Mgr, New Eng area, Ted Browne Music Co. Chief Collabrs: Walter Hirsch, Haven Gillespie. *Songs:* Spread a Little Sunshine; Always Be Careful-That's the Meaning of Your A-B-C (safety song); Carolina Sunshine; Drifting and Dreaming.

SCHMIDT, HARVEY — ASCAP 1960
composer, author, artist
b Dallas, Tex, Sept 12, 29. Educ: Univ of Tex, BFA. Wrote col musicals. To NY, 55; painter, illusr. Coauthor, "The In and Out Book" & "The Worry Book." Wrote spec material for Tom Poston & Ronny Graham; also songs for "Shoestring Revue." Chief Collabr: Tom Jones. *Songs:* Mister Off-Broadway; The Race of the Lexington Avenue Express; A Seasonal Sonatina (New York Is a Summer Festival); Try to Remember; Soon It's Gonna Rain; They Were You; Much More; Is It Really Me?; Love, Don't Turn Away; Simple Little Things; A Man and a Woman. *Scores:* Demi-Dozen (nightclub); The Fantasticks (off-Bway); 110 in the Shade (Bway).

SCHMIDT, SHARON YVONNE DAVIS — ASCAP 1974
composer, pianist
b North Hollywood, Calif, Sept 30, 37. Educ: Piano study with Lois Skartvedt Drew, 49-52; Univ Southern Calif, piano study with John Crown, BM, 60; Juilliard Sch Music, piano study with Rosina Lhevinne, MSc, 62; Fulbright grant for piano study with Yvonne Lefebure & Nadia Boulanger, Paris. Played duo with cellist-bro, Carnegie Recital Hall debut, 61, toured US & Can, 8 yrs; piano soloist & ens player with many Los Angeles based performing & recording groups, nat & Europe. Vocal coach & accompanist, Univ Southern Calif & Calif State Univ, Los Angeles, 63-64 & 65; principal piano instr, ETex State Univ, 64-66. Recording artist as soloist & chamber player; ed, WIM, Inc, music publ. *Songs & Instrumental Works:* Though Men Call Us Free (soprano, clarinet, piano); Three Poems of William Blake (soprano, solo clarinet, alto, bass, contra-bass); Suite of Wildflowers (flute, oboe, violin, cello, piano, soprano); Three Moods of Emily Dickinson (soprano, violin, cello, piano); Cocktail Etudes (piano solo); Noctune (Chopin; transcribed for oboe, piano); Lamento (DuParc; transcribed for alto clarinet, piano); Etude (Chopin; transcribed for bass clarinet, piano); Prelude in B flat (Chopin; transcribed for mixed clarinet quartet); Sarabande (Debussy; transcribed for clarinet choir); Allegro From Sonata No 3 (Bach; transcribed for ten saxophone, piano); Adagio From Sonata No 3 (Bach; transcribed for ten saxophone, piano); Largo (Bach; transcribed for baritone saxophone, piano); Chopin for the Tuba (Three Etudes, transcribed for tuba, piano); Prelude and Fugue in G minor (Bach; transcribed for oboe, clarinet, viola, cello).

SCHMIDT, WILLIAM JOSEPH — ASCAP 1965
composer
b Chicago, Ill, Mar 6, 26. Educ: USN Sch Music, 44-46; Chicago Musical Col, 46-49; Univ Southern Calif, BM & MM, 55-60, studied comp with Halsey Stevens & Ingolf Dahl. Free-lance performer on woodwinds, 46-52; worked as copyist, CBS, Chicago & motion picture studios, Hollywood, 47-53; free-lance jazz arr, 47-53; comp & music publ, 58- Started Avant Music, 58, then inc with Western Int Music, Inc, in 64, pres, 64- *Instrumental Works:* Concerto (clarinet & symphonic winds); Concerto (trumpet & symphonic winds); Suites No 1, No 2, No 3 & No 4 (brass quintet); Short'nin' Bread Variations (brass choir); Sonata (trumpet & piano); Sonata (horn & piano); Septigrams (flute, piano & perc); Concertino (piano & brass quintet); Music for Scrimshaws (harp & brass quintet); Variations on a Negro Folk Song (brass quintet); Sequential Fanfares (six trumpets & two perc); The Turkish Lady (trumpet & piano); Serenade (tuba & piano); Rhapsody No 1 (clarinet & piano); Sonatina (tenor saxophone & piano); Sonata (baritone saxophone & piano); Duo With Cadenzas (oboe & clarinet); Chamber Music (three brass & piano); Concertino (bass trombone & woodwind quintet); Variegations II (oboe & chamber orch); Sonata in Two Movements (viola & piano); Vendor's Call (piano & clarinet choir); Sonata Breve (flute, clarinet & viola); Partita on "Hammering" (trombone trio); Variations on "St Bone" (trombone & piano); Concertino (two trumpets & organ).

SCHNEIDER, DOROTHY FAY (DOLLI) — ASCAP 1970
author
b Iowa, May 16, 32. Educ: Univ Dubuque, 64; Benson Barrett's Sch for Writers, 66. Produced own weekly poetry prog, "Poetry of the People," KMCR-FM, Phoenix & Mesa, Ariz, 70-80. Compiled, ed & publ on yearly basis a chapbook, "KMCR FM, Poetry of the People, Mini-Anthology." Had poetry in many publ; also wrote articles for Am Astrology mag. State secy, Ariz Pen Women. Mem: Fiesta Branch, Nat League Am Pen Women (branch treas); Gospel Music Asn; Nat Acad Popular Music. *Songs:* Cryin' for My Baby; Everyday; Young Man, Young Girl; Lyrics: A Girl, a Boy, a Summer Night; Beat of the Traps.

SCHNEIDER, GEORGE HERBERT — ASCAP 1978
composer, author, pianist
b Newark, NJ, Sept 29, 43. Educ: Transylvania Col, BA(theatre); Ohio Univ, MFA(theatre, music). Musical dir, Arena Fair Summer Theatre, Wooster, Ohio, 65-69; arr & cond for singing group, The Red Raspberrys, 69-72; asst musical dir, Christopher Ryder House, Cape Cod, 76-78; guest performer, Ragtime Soc, Toronto, 76 & 78. Musical dir, Holland Am Cruises, 78- Chief Collabr: Carmine Stipo. *Songs:* Here We Are Again; Let's Do It Again; Baby Ailene and Her Dancing Elephant; Christmas on the Water; Music: All-American Dixieland Band. *Instrumental Works:* Pussy on the Piano; Wyndham Rag; Bleecker Street Rag No 1; The Furry Lisa; White Rose Rag.

SCHOEBEL, ELMER — ASCAP 1927
composer, pianist, conductor
b East St Louis, Ill, Sept 8, 1896; d. Educ: High sch; studied piano. Pianist & organist in film theatres; later cond orch. Served in WW I. Moved to Chicago, 19. Pianist in orchs incl Friars Soc (New Orleans Rhythm Kings), Isham Jones, Louis Panice & Art Kassel; also led own orch. Inventor & manufacturer, "Tune-O-Matic" radio, 33. Arr for Ina Ray Hutton, 35; chief arr, MPHC, 10 yrs. *Songs:* Nobody's Sweetheart; Bugle Call Rag; Farewell Blues; Everybody Stomp; Ten Little Miles From Town; A Minor Thing With a Major Swing; Prince of Wails; Spanish Shawl; House of David Blues; What Shall We Name the Baby?; There's Dixieland in Heaven.

SCHOEN, VICTOR — ASCAP 1952
composer, author
b Brooklyn, NY, Mar 26, 16. Educ: Self-taught. Began comp & arr with Andrew Sisters, 36; first hit record, 37; comp & arr for many prominent singers & entertainers; comp, arr & orchr for Paramount, 3 yrs; Universal, 4 yrs; free lance comp. *Songs:* Amen; Bei Mir Bist du Schoen; For Dancers Only; The Court Jester. *Scores:* TV: The Shirley Temple Series; The Dinah Shore Show; Bing Crosby Specials; Danny Kaye Specials; Pat Boone Specials; Ethel Merman Specials; Andy Williams Specials.

SCHOENBERG, ARNOLD — ASCAP 1939
composer, educator
b Vienna, Austria, Sept 13, 1874; d Los Angeles, Calif, July 13, 51. Educ: Realschule; studied with Alexander von Zemlinsky. Orch cond, Berlin, 01, taught, Stern Cons, 02. Organized musical group, Vienna, 03; taught, Vienna Acad. Lectr, Berlin; guest cond of own works throughout Europe. Prof, master class, Prussian Acad of Arts, Berlin, 25-33. To US, 33, citizen 41. Taught, Malkin Cons, Boston, 33; prof of music, Univ Southern Calif, 36, Univ Calif, Los Angeles, 36-44. Archives of mss, Arnold Schoenberg Inst, Los Angeles. Mem, Music Teachers Nat Asn, Music Teachers Asn, Calif, hon mem, Acad Santa Cecilia, Rome; recipient of Nat Inst of Arts & Letters Award of Merit. Author bks, "Harmonielehre (Theory of Harmony)", "Letters", "Structural Functions of Harmony", "Preliminary Exercises in Counterpoint", "Fundamentals of Musical Composition" & "Style and Idea" (essays). *Songs:* Music: Brettl-Lieder (cabaret songs); Nachtwandler. *Instrumental Works:* String Quartet in D major; Die Eiserne Brigade; Verklärte Nacht; Gurre-Lieder; Four String Quartets; Chamber Symphony; Book of the Hanging Gardens; Friede auf Erden; Five Pieces for Orchestra; Erwartung; Herzgewaechse; Pierrot Lunaire; Glueckliche Hand; Serenade for Septet; Baritone; Quintet for Wind Instruments; Four Pieces for Orchestra; Canon for Mixed Chorus; Orchestra; Canon for String Quartet; Begleitungsmusik zu einer Lichtspielscene; Violin Concerto; Piano Concerto; Theme and Variation for Band; Variations on a Recitative for Organ; Survivor From Warsaw; Prelude to Genesis Suite; Fantasy for Violin, Piano. *Songs & Instrumental Works:* New Classicism (cantata); Die Jakobsleiter (oratorio); *Scores:* Opera: Moses und Aron.

SCHOENFELD, WILLIAM C (HUGH CONRAD, LOWELL BLAKE) — ASCAP 1960
composer, author, conductor
b New York, NY, Nov 22, 1893; d New York, Jan 8, 69. Educ: Studied trumpet with father, Frederick Ecke, Herman & Philip Egner, Dr Fleck, Domenico Savino. Music dir, vaudeville & silent films. Arr, Sam Fox Publ Co, 35-38; head of dept, Leo Feist, 38-47; chief arr, MPHC, 50-69. Chief Collabr: Belle Fenstock. *Songs & Instrumental Works:* The American Thanksgiving Story; Festival in Madrid; The Presence.

SCHOENLEBEN, RALPH (LOUIS) — ASCAP 1969
composer, author
b Racine, Wis, Oct 27, 15. Educ: William Horlick High Sch. Author of numerous

articles in nat mag; lectr musicol in col; host of concert, WRJN radio, Milwaukee, Racine & Kenosha, 25 yrs. *Songs:* Secretly.

SCHOLIN, C ALBERT   ASCAP 1946
composer, organist, publisher
b Jamestown, NY, May 24, 1896; d Brentwood, Mo, Dec 22, 58. Educ: Am Cons of Music, BM, MM. Served in World War II. Taught organ, piano & theory. Organist & choir dir, Trinity Presby Church, 25 yrs. Past dean, Am Guild of Organists, Mo chapter. Founded music publ co, St Louis. *Songs & Instrumental Works:* Suite for Symphony Orchestra; Pastorale (organ); A Christmas Blessing (cantata); Anthems: God Is a Spirit; Incline Thine Ear; Hear My Cry, O God; Create In Me a Clean Heart; Eye Hath Not Seen; Fear Thou Not; Away in a Manger.

SCHOLL, JACK TREVOR   ASCAP 1932
composer, author
b New York, NY, Mar 19, 03. Staff song writer, Warner Bros Pictures & MGM. Wrote songs for Columbia & Universal Pictures. Chief Collabrs: M K Jerome, Eubie Blake. *Songs:* Lyrics: Loving You the Way I Do; Throw Another Log on the Fire; Making Love Mountain Style; The Old Apple Tree; You, You Darling.

SCHOLZ, PAUL   ASCAP 1958
composer, pianist, arranger
b New York, NY, May 18, 1894. Educ: Pvt music study. Staff mem, music publ cos. Chief Collabrs: Mitchell Parish, Jack Waverly, Frank Stanton. *Songs:* Where the Four Leaf Clovers Grow; Ridin' Toward the Sunset; It Musta Been Sumpin I Et; Happy Birthday in December.

SCHONBERG, CHRIS M   ASCAP 1924
composer, conductor, pianist
b Steinkjer, Norway, July 25, 1890; d Culver City, Calif, June 16, 57. To US, 1892. Educ: Pub schs, Ashland, Wis. Pianist in family band, also in MGM Studio Orch; led orch in nightclubs, Chicago & Hollywood. Accompanist to Nora Bayes, 2 yrs & Eleanor Powell, 6 yrs. Chief Collabrs: Harry Kerr, Abe Lyman, James Brockman. *Songs:* Darling; Somewhere This Summer With You; Roaming Away From Me; 'Neath a Blanket of Stars; Out of the Deep; Chuck-a-Boom; Somebody's Waiting; Croon a Little Lullaby; Her Danny.

SCHONBERGER, JOHN   ASCAP 1925
composer, conductor, violinist
b Philadelphia, Pa, Oct 1, 1892. Educ: Pub schs. Gave violin recitals at age 12. Charter mem, Memphis & Dallas Symph Orchs. Violinist in dance bands; has led own orch. In film indust. Chief Collabr: Gus Kahn. *Songs:* Whispering; Rosemary; Day By Day; Gingham Gown; Havana; Tell Me a Story; Moonlight on the River Danube; I'll Think of You; An Old-Fashioned Girl.

SCHOOLEY, JOHN HEILMAN   ASCAP 1967
composer, author, performer
b Nelson, Pa, Feb 8, 43. Educ: Montrose High Sch; Mansfield State Col, BS, 65; Royal Acad Music, London, Eng, cert, 66; ECarolina Univ, MM, 68; summer studies, Aspen Music Sch, Yale Univ, L'Ecole de Hindemith, Vevey, Switzerland & City Univ NY Grad Ctr; studied comp with Richard Stoker & Charles Jones, tuba with John Fletcher & William J Bell. Instr music, Eastern Kentucky Univ, 68-70; assoc prof music, Fairmont State Col, 70- Coauthor, "A Prospectus for College Theory" (series of 4 bks in music theory). Hons & Awards: First place, instrumental category, Delius Nat Competition, 75; Rotary Int Found Fellow, 65-66; 2 Educ Professional Develop Assistance grants; Ellen Battell Stoeckel Fellow; 4 Fairmont State Col Res grants; Nat Endowment for the Humanities Fellow, 79. Chief Collabr: H Richard Hensel. *Songs:* Music: From a Very Little Sphinx (song cycle of 5 songs); Songs of Victory in Heaven (cantata). *Instrumental Works:* Serenata for Tuba and Piano; Partita for Brass Quartet; Three Dances for Woodwind Trio.

SCHOONMAKER, LLOYD   ASCAP 1970
composer, author
b Billings, Mont, May 31, 39. Teacher, Calif. Worked with Ray Ruff & Mike Curb. Has had 4 chart records. Writer for Gene Kennedy. Chief Collabr: Ray Broome. *Songs:* Baby, Don't Keep Me Hanging On; Julie Ann; All American Rodeo Hero; Fresno Blues. *Albums:* Truth of Truth; Happy Birthday, USA (bicentennial).

SCHOOP, PAUL   ASCAP 1964
composer, conductor, pianist
b Zurich, Switz, July 31, 1909; d Van Nuys, Calif, Jan 1, 76. Educ: Acad & Cons, Zurich; Ecole Normale, Paris; Hochschule für Musik, Berlin; studied with Alfred Cortot, Robert Casadesus, Arthur Schnabel, Paul Dukas, Paul Hindemith, Arnold Schoenberg. Accompanist to sister, Trudi Schoop; concert soloist & mem of duo piano team, US & Europe. Formed Schoop Co, toured with USO, World War II. Writer, films & cartoons, US & Europe. *Songs & Instrumental Works:* Fata Morgana (symph poem); Maria Del Valle (dance drama); Dance a Story (children's educ records); Everything New (Swiss govt comn for Exposition, 39); Wishing Tree (musical fantasy); *Scores:* Stage shows: Three Apple Trees; Schoolmaster's Journey Through Hell; Comic opera: The Enchanted Trumpet; Ballet: Marche Ballet.

SCHRADE, ROLANDE YOUNG
See Young, Rolande Maxwell

SCHRAMM, HAROLD   ASCAP 1964
composer, arranger
b Chicago, Ill, July 3, 35; d. Educ: Chicago Musical Col, BM & MM; studied with Saul Dorfman, Rudolph Ganz & Karel Jirak. Comp & arr, Australian Broadcasting Comn, Sydney, 60-61. Gave lectr-recitals, Hawaii, Hong Kong, Ceylon, India & US. Awards: Berkshire Music Ctr, MacDowell Asn, All India Radio, Bennington Comp's Conf. Creative work in Ethnomusicomposing (synthesizing materials, methods of Eastern & Western musical systems). *Instrumental Works:* Invocation (string orch); Bharata Sangita (piano). *Scores:* Opera: Shilappadikaram.

SCHRAMM, RUDOLF R A (RUDY MARSH)   ASCAP 1950
composer, author, conductor
b Greiffenberg, Ger, July 9, 02. Educ: State Cons, Leipzig, Ger; pvt study with Joseph Schillinger, Max Reger & Steinbach. Cond, State Opera House, Riga, Latvia & Munic Opera, Hirschberg; cond, Louis Bauer Opera Co US Tour; music dir, US Office Educ; coordr of Schillinger Instr, NY Univ, 46-66. Wrote commercials & cond, NBC; author, "Rhythm & Melody"; chief summer course in radio music, Nat Music Camp, Interlochen, Mich. Pianist & organist. *Songs:* Lola Montez; Adam's Apple; Invocation; Heaven's Gate Choir. *Instrumental Works:* Pleasantdale Folks; The President's Birthday Ball; Bowl of Rice for China; Labor Parade; Safety Musketeers. *Scores:* Film/TV: Nanook of the North (18 films in the Air Force Story).

SCHRAUBSTADER, CARL   ASCAP 1955
composer, author
b St Louis, Mo, Apr 26, 02. Educ: St Louis Cons Music, until age 10; Townsend Harris Hall High Sch, New York; Cornell Univ, grad, 24. Was a businessman, now retired. Chief Collabr: Lew Brown. *Songs:* Last Night on the Back Porch.

SCHREIBER, FREDERICK C(HARLES)   ASCAP 1945
composer, teacher, organist
b Vienna, Austria, Jan 13, 1895. Educ: Vienna State Acad Music, studied piano, violin & cello; studied comp with Franz Schreker; studied conducting with Franz Schalk; Univ Vienna, studied musicology with Guido Adler. Church organist; prof comp & music theory, Vienna State Acad Music; teacher comp, organist & choir dir, Broadway Presby Church, New York; winner, First Prizes in int & nat comp contests for orchestral, choral & instrumental works. *Songs & Instrumental Works:* Nine Symphonies (No 4, NC Symph Prize); Sinfonietta in G (Musical Fund Soc Philadelphia Int Contest Prize); Festive Prelude (organ, bells); Concerto Grosso; Music for Orchestra; Dance Suite; Variations on a Folk Tune; Concertino for Two Pianos; Sonata for Piano; Harpsichord Concerto; Christmas Suite; Sonatina for Orchestra; Sonata (organ); Suite (Chicago Organ Work Prize); Variations (Am Guild Organists Prize); Choral: The Beatitudes (symph trilogy); Psalm 42 (male chorus prize); The Intangible (oratorio).

SCHREIBMAN, ALEXANDER (ALLAN SMALL)   ASCAP 1950
composer, music arranger
b New York, NY, May 7, 10. Educ: Thomas Jefferson High Sch, grad, 27; self-taught in harmony, orchestration & comp. Led my own 10-piece dance band, 30-31; worked as music arranger for Andre Kostelanetz, Morton Gould, Paul Whiteman, RCA Victor Records & others. Wrote many educ music bks for Alfred Publ Co. *Instrumental Works:* Teacher's Choice; Very First Piano Solo Book; The Classics; Basic Timing; Blues and How; Blues Piano; Rock Piano; Disco Piano.

SCHREINER, ALEXANDER   ASCAP 1959
composer, author, pianist
b Nuremberg, Ger, July 31, 01. Educ: Univ Utah, AB, PhD & hon LHD; hon DFA, Utah State Univ; hon DM, Brigham Young Univ; Phi Beta Kappa; Phi Kappa Phi. Came to US, 12, naturalized, 20. Studied piano & organ with John J McClellan, Salt Lake City; Louis Vierne, Charles & Marie Widor & Henri Libert, Paris. Chief organist, The Tabernacle, Salt Lake City, 24-77, retired, 77. Organist & lectr music, Univ Calif, Los Angeles, 30-39. Organ broadcasting over nat network, Salt Lake Tabernacle, 29-77. Made annual transcontinental recital tours, 43-65. Fel, Am Guild Organists. Comp & compiler, six vols, "Organ Voluntaries." *Instrumental Works:* Concerto in B Minor for Organ and Orchestra (in 3 movements); The Worried Drummer (humoresque for solo perc & orch).

SCHREINER, ELISSA PAULETTE   ASCAP 1975
composer, teacher, singer
b New York, NY, July 12, 34. Educ: Music & Art High Sch; Hunter Col, BS(music); Delta Omicron. Music supvr, Yonkers Elem through Jr High Schs, 56-57; accompanist for Diahann Caroll, Robert White & others; free lance pianist for film fests, operatic progs, fashion shows, jazz progs & community theaters; did vocals for demo tapes & comp "Top 40 Music"; teacher jazz piano; pop singer; cocktail pianist; comp musical scores, 74- Rec'd ASCAP Award. Chief Collabr: Sunnie Miller. *Songs:* Alone (on Christmas Eve); Home at Last. *Scores:* Off Bway Shows: Once Upon a Vine; Sneakers.

SCHROEDER, AARON HAROLD ASCAP 1948
composer, author, producer
b Brooklyn, NY, Sept 7, 26. Educ: Sch of Music & Art, NY, hon grad. As founder of A Schroeder Int, he sponsored, publ & helped guide to prominence Acad Award winning songwriters such as Hal David, Burt Bacharach, Al Kasha, Joel Hirschorn, Joe Brooks, Irwin Levine, Fred Neil, Randy Newman, John Stewart, Jimi Hendrix, Tony Macaulay, Gene Pitney & Barry White. His songs were recorded by many prominent recording artists. Mem elections bd, ASCAP; mem bd gov, Nat Acad Recording Arts & Sci. Judge in the Am Song Fest Competition. Pres, Musicor Records. First mgr & producer, Gene Pitney & Blood Sweat and Tears. *Songs:* It's Now or Never; French Foreign Legion; I'm Gonna Knock on Your Door; Stuck on You; Twixt Twelve and Twenty; Mandolins in the Moonlight; At a Sidewalk Penny Arcade; Because They're Young; Good Luck Charm; Time and the River; Rubber Ball; Half Heaven-Half Heartache; I Got Stung; Any Way You Want Me; I Was the One; Not As a Stranger; Don't Let Her Go; Move Me No Mountain; She Can Put Her Shoes Under My Bed Anytime; Sure Thing; Love Makin' Music; (Play Our) Love's Theme. *Scores:* Film: Once She Was Mine (main theme); The Four Musketeers; TV: Skinflint (a country Christmas carol); NBC two hour Christmas spec.

SCHUCKETT, RALPH DION (RALPH J RALPH) ASCAP 1970
composer, author, musician
b Los Angeles, Calif, Mar 2, 48. Educ: John Marshall High Sch, Los Angeles; musician, self-taught. Played keyboard for var groups & recording artists, incl Carole King, Todd Rundgren, Bette Midler, James Taylor, Lou Reed, Richie Havens & Ellen Shipley. Studio musician & arr for recordings, New York. Chief Collabrs: Ellen Shipley, John Siegler, Leida Snow. *Songs:* I Surrender; Rhythm Rhapsody; Music: Another Life; Can't We Make It Right Again; Every Step of the Way.

SCHUDSON, HOWARD M (HOD DAVID) ASCAP 1968
composer
b Milwaukee, Wis, Oct 29, 42. Educ: Self taught comp; orchestration with Albert Harris; Northwestern Univ Drama Sch. Folk singer artist, Liberty Records, early 60's; recorded 2 albums of own material, Hod & Marc duo, Bell Records; wrote off-Bway & revues, NY. Began comp & cond for TV & motion pictures, Los Angeles, 74. Chief Collabrs: Gloria Nissenson, Ayn Robbins, Will Jacobs, Tom Paisley, Ben Raleigh, Ray Errol Fox. *Songs:* I'd Love Making Love to You; Music: Here's to Love; Without You; Now You're Comin' Back Michelle; By Love, I Mean; Love Songs Are Getting Harder to Sing; I Wouldn't Have It Any Other Way; Harry; Two Hearts in Perfect Time. *Scores:* Opera/Ballet: Mrs Bab; Off Bway: Cities; Off Bway Revue: Upstairs at the Downstairs; Film/TV: The Girl, the Gold Watch and Everything; Bureau; Very Good Friends (Emmy Award); The Last Resort; Lou Grant Show; Heartbreak Winner; Francesca Baby; Pinballs; Characters; Friends; The Attic.

SCHUH, MARIE ASCAP 1961
composer, author, singer
b Milwaukee, Wis, Apr 17, 22. Educ: Hagen Piano Studio; Weidner Int Cons, Boston; Wis Cons. Singer, St John's Cathedral Choir, Milwaukee. Secy-treas, Wis Songwriters Guild, 2 yrs, vpres, 58- *Songs:* We Can't Bid Our Love Goodbye; Broken Promises; In the Soft Twilight; I Hold Your Picture.

SCHULBERG, BUDD WILSON ASCAP 1958
author, professor, lyricist
b New York, NY, Mar 27, 14. Educ: Los Angeles High Sch; Deerfield Acad; Dartmouth Col, LittD(cum laude), 60. Author Bks: "What Makes Sammy Run?", 41 (Nat Critics Choice as Best Novel of Yr); "The Harder They Fall"; "The Disenchanted"; "Some Faces in the Crowd"; "Waterfront" (Christopher Award); "Sanctuary V"; "Everything That Moves," 80; Nonfiction incl: "From the Ashes"; "The Voices of Watts"; "Loser and Still Champion: Muhammed Ali"; "The Four Seasons of Success"; "Swan Watch" (photos by Geraldine Brooks); Author Screenplays: "On the Waterfront" (Acad Award, 54); "A Face in the Crowd" (Berlin Fest Award); Author Short Story: "Your Arkansas Traveler." Founded the Watts Writers Workshop (his TV report "The Angry Voices of Watts," rec'd an Emmy Award); also founded The Frederick Douglass Creative Arts Ctr, now active in Harlem. Chief Collab: Tom Glazer. *Songs:* Lyrics: A Face in the Crowd; Mama Guitar; Free Man in the Morning; Just Plain Folks; An Old Fashioned Marriage. *Scores:* Bway Show: What Makes Sammy Run?

SCHULMAN, BILLY REVEL ASCAP 1964
composer
b Brooklyn, NY, June 30, 50. Educ: Jr high sch; Chatham Square Sch Music, scholarship. *Songs:* When Winter Comes.

SCHUMACHER, TIMOTHY ALBERT ASCAP 1974
composer, author
b Des Moines, Iowa, Oct 28, 45. Educ: Univ Wis-Madison; Univ Strasbourg, France, French; Wartburg Col, BA(French, speech/drama). Wrote first song at age 10. Began performing prof in 61. Became producer in Colo, 73. Learned studio trade doing jingles. Produced sound tracks for var types of clients, nat & local. Now producing jingles & sound tracks & writing pop songs. Chief Collabrs: Steve Soltow, David Sisson. *Songs:* City of the Silver San Juan; I Believe He's Gonna Drive That Rig to Glory; Come in to Me; If I Gave You;

Colorado Ride; The Ballad of Brady Gray; Lyrics: You Were Beautiful; Questions.

SCHUMANN, WALTER ASCAP 1948
composer, conductor
b New York, NY, Oct 8, 13; d Minneapolis, Minn, Aug 21, 58. Educ: Univ Southern Calif & Law Sch. Organized band while at univ. With Eddie Cantor & Andre Kostelanetz radio shows. Music dir, AFRS, USAF, World War II. Cond, "This Is the Army," New York, & choral group, The Voices of Walter Schumann. Music dir for var films; made many records. Chief Collab: Nathan Scott. *Songs & Instrumental Works:* Melancholy Moon; I Walk Alone; There Was a Little Girl; It's Dream Time; Lonesome Gal; The Sleeping Beauty. *Scores:* Bway shows: Three for Tonight; John Brown's Body; Film: The Night of the Hunter; TV shows: Dragnet (Emmy award, 55); Steve Canyon.

SCHUSTER, IRA (JOHN SIRAS) ASCAP 1921
composer, author, pianist
b New York, NY, Oct 13, 1889; d New York, Oct 10, 45. Educ: Pub schs. Staff pianist for publ co, later publ. Performed on radio. Songwriter for var films incl "Lullaby of Broadway", "Three Faces of Eve", "Mister 888", "Roaring Twenties" & "They Shoot Horses Don't They?" Chief Collabrs: Paul Cunningham, Leonard Whitcup, Joe Young, Jack Little, James Cavanaugh, Larry Stock, Joseph Schuster (brother), Ed Nelson. *Songs:* The Navy Took Them Over and the Navy Will Bring Them Back; I Am an American (Congressional record); Ten Little Fingers and Ten Little Toes; I'm Alone Because I Love You; A Shanty in Old Shanty Town; Did You Ever Get That Feeling in the Moonlight?; Hats Off to MacArthur; You Know You Belong to Somebody Else; Dance of the Paper Dolls; Hold Me; Go Home and Tell Your Mother; Let's Grow Old Together.

SCHUSTER, JOSEPH ASCAP 1928
composer, author, publisher
b New York, NY, Feb 6, 1896; d New York, June 9, 59. Educ: High sch. Appeared as team with John Tucker, The Delivery Boys in theatres, nightclubs & radio. Chief Collabrs: John Tucker, Lee Pearl, Art Berman, Ira Schuster (brother). *Songs:* My Memories of You; Dance of the Paper Dolls; Sleep, Baby, Sleep; Maybe, Who Knows?; I Know Somethin' I Won't Tell Ya; Honest, I'm in Love With You; Winter Interlude; The Christmas Polka; Anything Can Happen When You're Lonesome; I Kissed a Girl and Made Her Cry; I Shouldn't Love You But I Do; Do What Your Heart Tells You to Do.

SCHUSTER, ROBERT JOSEPH, JR ASCAP 1977
composer, author, singer
b Caracas, Venezuela, Aug 19, 50. Educ: St Joseph's Acad, Jacksonville, Fla; Am Sch, Maracaibo, Venezuela & Managua, Nicaragua; Holy Trinity Sch, Mamaroneck, NY; Mamaroneck High Sch; Berklee Sch Music, Boston, Mass, 2 yrs. Began playing guitar & songwriting in late 62; performed & wrote all through high sch. Performer & writer, 70- Chief Collabrs: Pam Miller, Wayne Carpenter, Bob Morse. *Songs:* Saturday Morning; Talk to Me; Baby Goodbye; Lyrics: So Much Love. *Instrumental Works:* Waitin' on Willie; Spinner.

SCHUTTE, MARCUS KAMEHAMEHA, JR ASCAP 1974
composer, author, singer
b Honolulu, Hawaii, Oct 6, 31. Educ: Punahou Sch; Univ Ore; Brigham Young Univ. Started performing professionally as singer, musician & comedian, 66. Coproduced album Paniola Country, 74; also Return to Pan/Country & Hawaiian Railroads. Has had many songs recorded. Conducted comp workshop, Hawaii. Chief Collabrs: Ke'lii Tau'a, John Spencer. *Songs:* Paniolo Country; Kamuela; Come Into My House (E Komo Mai); Waimea Corral; Kamuela Green; Makua to Kahuku; Ball-Lee Iaia; Music: Kaumakapili.

SCHUYLER, PHILIPPA DUKE ASCAP 1960
composer, author, pianist
b New York, NY; d. Educ: Convent of the Sacred Heart; pvt music study. Debut, NY Philh at age 14. Toured throughout world, incl three State Dept tours. Guest artist, Independence Celebrations incl Leopoldville, Ghana, Madagascar. Command perf for Emperor Haile Selassie, King & Queen of Malaya, Queen Elizabeth of Belg. Author: "Who Killed the Congo?"; "Jungle Saints"; "Kingdom of Dreams." *Instrumental Works:* Rumpelstiltskin (Wayne Univ Award); Manhattan Nocturne (first prize, Detroit Symph); White Nile Suite.

SCHWAB, ALBERT L ASCAP 1978
composer, author
b Philadelphia, Pa, Jan 24, 26. Educ: Philadelphia Musical Acad, comp, 1 yr; Drexel Inst Technol, BS. Formed Metronome Music Publ Corp Pa, 78. *Songs & Instrumental Works:* No Forwarding Address; Hang Around; Love Came Along; Sooner or Later; Strange As It Seems.

SCHWANDT, WILBUR CLYDE (DON SWAN) ASCAP 1951
composer, musician, musical arranger
b Manitowoc, Wis, June 28, 04. Educ: Univ Chicago, individual study with Sigvart Hofland; studied with Emil Soderstrom, Ray Noble & Ted Duncan. Arr for several bands & made two tours with "Bob Hope Show," 30-40. Studied Latin music & arr for Xavier Cugat, 20 yrs; also did Latin arr for Freddy Martin,

Harry James, Skinnay Ennis & MGM Studios. Signed with Liberty Records, 57 & made five albums of Latin music. Recorded for C P Macgregor Transcriptions & other recording cos under name Don Swan & His Orch; played at Hollywood Palladium & var other engagements with orch. Arr for var bands. Author of bks, "Cha Cha for the Hammond" & "Tango for the Spinet." Chief Collabs: Fabian Andre, Gus Kahn, Xavier Cugat, Lou Holzer, Joe Guitierrez, Reed Christensen. *Songs:* Dime Dime (Merengue); Music: Dream a Little Dream of Me; Hokey Joe; Ay Que Merengue; Betita (Cha Cha); What's the Meaning of It All; Sheila Shesa. *Instrumental Works:* Dixieland Cha Cha.

SCHWARTZ, ARTHUR — ASCAP 1930
composer, producer
b Brooklyn, NY. Educ: NY Univ, BA & LLD; Columbia Univ, MA; Phi Beta Kappa. Taught English in high schs, NY. Practiced Law. Wrote songs for "The Grand Street Follies" & "The New Yorkers"; also radio score for "The Gibson Family." Produced Bway plays, "Inside USA", "Hilda Crane," also films, "Night and Day" & "Cover Girl." Former pres, New York League of Theatres & Producers; former treasurer, Authors League; former treasurer & now London rep, Dramatists Guild. Chief Collabs: Howard Dietz, Dorothy Fields, Johnny Mercer, Frank Loesser, Oscar Hammerstein, II, Edward Heyman, Ira Gershwin, Leo Robin & Al Stillman. *Songs:* High and Low; One Two Three Four Five; All About Love; The Simple Things of Marriage; I Give This Marriage Just One Day; I Guess I'll Have to Change My Plan; I've Made a Habit of You; Right At the Start of It; The Moment I Saw You; Something to Remember You By; Lucky Seven; Hoops; Confession; New Sun in the Sky; I Love Louisa; Dancing in the Dark; Alone Together; A Shine on Your Shoes; Smoking Reefers; Louisiana Hayride; A Rainy Day; Two-Faced Woman; Fatal Fascination; How High Can a Little Bird Fly?; Under Your Spell; After All You're All I'm After; If There Is Someone Lovelier Than You; When You Love Only One; You and the Night and the Music; Wand'ring Heart; Thief in the Night; Paree; Farewell, My Lovely; What a Wonderful World; Love Is a Dancing Thing; The Hottentot Potentate; Loadin' Time; Get Yourself a Geisha; By Myself; I See Your Face Before Me; Triplets; How Can We Be Wrong?; Seal It With a Kiss; Love and Learn; You and I Know; Goodbye, Jonah; An Old Flame Never Dies; This Is It; It's All Yours; I'll Pay the Check; Just a Little Bit More; Terribly Attractive; A Lady Needs a Change; Tennessee Fish Fry; How Can I Ever Be Alone?; In Waikiki; You're a Natural; Honorable Moon; They're Either Too Young or Too Old; Love Isn't Born; How Sweet You Are; The Dreamer; There's No Holding Me; Don't Be a Woman If You Can; A Rainy Night in Rio; Oh, But I Do; A Gal in Calico; Through a Thousand Dreams; My Gal Is Mine Once More; Haunted Heart; Blue Grass; Rhode Island Is Famous for You; Spring Has Sprung; Look Who's Dancing; I'm Like a New Broom; Love Is the Reason; Make the Man Love Me; I'll Buy You a Star; That's Entertainment; Happy Habit; More Love Than Your Love; When You're in Love; Magic Moment; Come a-Wandering With Me; Why Go Anywhere at All?; Who Can? You Can!; Waiting for the Evening Train; Before I Kiss the World Goodbye; Music: A Silent Song. *Scores:* Bway Stage: The Little Show; The Second Little Show; Princess Charming; Three's a Crowd; The Band Wagon; Flying Colors; Revenge With Music; At Home Abroad; Virginia; Between the Devil; Stars in Your Eyes; Park Avenue; Inside USA; A Tree Grows in Brooklyn; By the Beautiful Sea; The Gay Life; Jennie; Film/TV: That Girl From Paris; Under Your Spell; Navy Blues; Thank Your Lucky Stars; The Time, the Place and the Girl; Excuse My Dust; Dangerous When Wet; You're Never Too Young; High Tor; A Bell for Adano.

SCHWARTZ, CHARLES — ASCAP 1976
composer, author, impresario
b New York, NY. Educ: Studied comp (on scholarship) with Aaron Copland, Darius Milhaud & Roger Sessions; NY Univ Grad Sch Arts & Sci, PhD(musicol), 69. Comp works from solo pieces to symphonic comp. Prof music, Hunter Col, New York. Founder & dir, Composers' Showcase, a leading contemporary music series held at Whitney Museum of Am Art, New York. Author: "Gershwin: His Life and Music" & "Cole Porter: A Biography." *Instrumental Works:* Mother! Mother!! (jazz symph); Professor Jive (jazz symph); Solo Brothers (jazz symph, jazz soloists & orch); Comments (brass, woodwinds, perc); Sounds (chorus, perc); For Coughers, Sneezers and Snorers (chorus); Motion (strings); Passacaglia for Orchestra.

SCHWARTZ, ELLIOTT — ASCAP 1964
composer, critic, teacher
b New York, NY, Jan 19, 36. Educ: Columbia Univ, BA, 57, MA, 58, EdD, 62; Bennington Composers Conference, 61-66. Instr music, Univ Mass, 60-64. Prof, Bowdoin Col, 64-, dept chmn, 75- Vis prof, Trinity Col Music, London, 67 & Univ Calif Col Creative Studies, Santa Barbara, 70, 73 & 74. Vis res fel, Univ Calif Ctr for Music Exp, San Diego, 78-79. Author "The Symphonies of Ralph Vaughan Williams", "Electronic Music: A Listener's Guide", "Contemporary Composers on Contemporary Music" & "Music: Ways of Listening." *Songs & Instrumental Works:* Chamber Concerto No 2; Cycles and Gongs; Texture for Chamber Orchestra; Mirrors; Extended Piano.

SCHWARTZ, FRANCIS — ASCAP 1975
composer, author, performer
b Altoona, Pa, Mar 10, 40. Educ: Juilliard Sch Music, BS & MS, studied with Vittorio Giannini & Lonny Epstein, 61-62; Univ Paris, Diplome des Etudes Approfondis in musical aesthetics, 78. Prof music, Univ PR, 66-80, chmn dept music, 71-80; visiting prof music, Univ Paris, 77-78. Co-founder, Grupo Fluxus

de Puerto Rico, 68. Casal Fest comn, "I Protest," 74; "Mon Oeuf" presentation, Centre Pompidou, Paris, 79; "Cosmos" event, PR, Paris, New York, Brussels, 80. Chief Collabs: Rafael Aponte-Ledee, Eduardo Kusnir, Alberto Ponce, Roberto Aussel, Abel Carlevaro. *Instrumental Works:* Auschwitz; My Eyebrows Are Not Bushy; Cannibal-Caliban; Amistad I, II and III; Mon Oeuf (My Egg); Baudelaire's Uncle; Cosmos; Ergo Sum; The Temple of the Flower; Paz en la Tierra (Peace on Earth).

SCHWARTZ, JEAN — ASCAP 1914
composer, pianist
b Budapest, Hungary, Nov 4, 1878; d Sherman Oaks, Calif, Nov 30, 56. To US in 1888. Citizen 1902. Charter mem, ASCAP. Studied piano with sister. Pianist, Coney Island Band, then worked in sheet music depts & dept stores. Pianist-song plugger for Shapiro & Bernstein. Performed in vaudeville with William Jerome, also accompanist to Dolly Sisters. Wrote songs for musicals incl "Hoity-Toity", "The Wild Rose" & "Sinbad." Chief Collabs: William Jerome, Harold Atteridge, Anne Caldwell, Harry Williams, Al Bryan, Clifford Grey, William Cary Duncan, Grant Clarke, Sam Lewis, Joe Young, Milton Ager, Jack Meskill. *Songs:* Rip Van Winkle Was a Lucky Man; Hamlet Was a Melancholy Dane; Since Sister Nell Heard Paderewski Play; I'm Unlucky; Mr Dooley; Bedelia; Goodnight, My Own True Love; Chinatown, My Chinatown; The Hat My Father Wore on St Patrick's Day; Back to the Carolina You Love; I Love the Ladies; My Irish Molly-O; Hello, Hawaii; Hello, Central, Give Me No Man's Land; Rockabye Your Baby With a Dixie Melody; Why Do They All Take the Night Boat to Albany?; I'm All Bound 'Round With the Mason-Dixon Line; My Yellow Jacket Girl; I'm Tired; You Can't Get Away From It; One Little Raindrop; Au Revoir, Pleasant Dreams (Ben Bernie theme); Trust in Me. *Scores:* Bway Stage: Piff! Paff!! Pouf!!!; Lifting the Lid; The Ham Tree; A Yankee Circus on Mars; Up and Down Broadway; The Honeymoon Express; The Passing Show; When Claudia Smiles; Hello Alexander, Gaieties of 1919; The Century Revue; The Midnight Rounders; Make It Snappy; Topics of 1923; Artist and Models of 1923; Innocent Eyes; A Night in Spain; Sunny Days.

SCHWARTZ, MILTON M — ASCAP 1954
composer, author
b St Louis, Mo, Aug 13, 24. Educ: Northwestern Univ, BA. *Songs:* This Little Town Is Paris; also Sing Along With Jack (songbook).

SCHWARTZ, NAN LOUISE — ASCAP 1979
composer
b Burbank, Calif, Feb 25, 53. Educ: Calif State Univ, Northridge, BA(radio, TV, film), 73; pvt study with Albert Harris & Billy Byers, 75-77. Did arr for "S H A R E Show," a Ray Charles album (80), various big bands, Carmen McRae, "Muppets Go Hollywood" TV spec, "Carol Burnett Show", "Merv Griffin Show" & Al Hirt. Studio singer for TV, commercials & films. Chief Collabr: Nick Ceroli. *Songs:* Music: Collaboration; Jim and Andy's; Sambistro. *Instrumental Works:* Two Woodwind Quintets; One Horn Quintet. *Scores:* Feature Cartoon: Popeye Out West; TV movie: New Adventures of Heidi; TV Series: Barnaby Jones episode, Murder in the Key of C; A Man Called Sloane; Stone; Big Shamus, Little Shamus; Rockford Files; BJ and the Bear.

SCHWARTZ, SEYMOUR — ASCAP 1953
composer, record manufacturer
b Chicago, Ill, Jan 11, 17. Educ: Col. In record bus since 38. Chief Collabr: Sammy Cahn. *Songs:* The Holy Bible; All; I Get a Warm Feeling; How Can You Not Believe; My Hometown Chicago; My Golden Horn; This Is America; United Nations.

SCHWARTZ, SHERWOOD — ASCAP 1963
composer
b Passaic, NJ, Nov 14, 16. Educ: NY Univ, BA(arts); Univ Southern Calif, MS. Writer, producer; creator of TV series. *Songs:* It's About Time; Dusty's Trail; Big John, Little John; Lyrics: Gilligan's Island; The Brady Bunch.

SCHWARTZ, STEPHEN LAWRENCE — ASCAP 1969
composer, lyricist
b New York, NY, Mar 6, 48. Educ: Juilliard Sch Music, 60-64; Carnegie Inst Technol, BFA(drama), 68. Comp/lyricist title song "Butterflies Are Free." Comp music & new lyrics "Godspell." Coauthor (with Leonard Bernstein), Eng Texts for Leonard Bernstein's Mass. Wrote music & lyrics "Pippin", "The Baker's Wife" & "The Magic Show." Author, "The Perfect Peach" (juvenile). Author of 4 songs, adaptation & dir, "Working." Rec'd Grammy Award, 71 (2); Drama Desk Award, 71 & 78; Trendsetter Award, Billboard, 71; Nat Theatre Arts Conference Award, 71. Mem: Dramatists Guild & Nat Acad Recording Arts & Sci.

SCHWARTZ, THEODORA (TEDDI) — ASCAP 1962
author, composer, singer
b New York, NY, July 4, 14. Educ: Pub schs; Manhattan Sch Music. Co-author, arr of Tumbalalaika (English versions of Hebrew & Yiddish songs); folk music workshps; articles; spec material for radio documentaries, New York World's Fair, camp shows & blind chorus. Owner-publ, Tevye Records, recorded Kumt Arayn (Walk Right In), Yiddish versions of 16 Am songs; author-arr of Songs My Grandma Taught Me (Yiddish songs in English, with narration). Chief Collabr: Arthur Kevess. *Songs:* Story of a Man Named Dan; Ballad of Big

Indian; If Not Now, When?!; Lyrics: Dona Dona Dona (English version); Frumke un Yosl (Frankie and Johnny); Alter Donald (Old MacDonald); The Song Snatcher; Beygl Lid (Donut Song); Geven a Tsayt (Those Were the Days); I Had a Little Overcoat; The Wheels Keep Turning; The Seamstress; Music: Ballad of the Child.

SCHWARZWALD, ARNOLD (ARNOLD HUGHES)   ASCAP 1953
composer

b Chicago, Ill, Sept 10, 18. Educ: Studied piano with Lawrence Bernhardt, comp with Constantin Schvcdov, Otto Cesana & Mario Castelnuovo-Tedesco; Calif State Univ, Los Angeles, BA(psychol). Began comp, New York, 37. Wrote film scores for Republic Studios; music ed, Universal Studios. Chief Collabr: Frederick Herbert. *Songs:* The Thrill of It All; A Man Without a Star; Blue Lagoon; True Love; Time for Love. *Instrumental Works:* Tone Poem; The Barrier; Two Rhapsodies for Piano and Orchestra; series of piano pieces transc for orch.

SCHWARZWALD, MILTON   ASCAP 1924
composer, conductor, arranger

b Detroit, Mich, Sept 16, 1891; d Hollywood, Calif, Mar 2, 50. Educ: Chicago pub schs. At age 9, debut as concert violinist. Pianist, theatre mgr & cond, Chicago theatres. Professional staff, Chicago publ co; cond & arr, NY theatres, 20. Gen music dir, Keith-Albee-Orpheum circuit, 26. Music & prog dir, "RKO Theatre of the Air," radio, 28. Exec, music dept film studio, 32-50. Chief Collabr: Earl Carroll. *Songs:* Flora Bella; Give Me All of You; You're the Girl. *Scores:* Bway Stage: Flora Bella; Be Yourself.

SCHWEIKERT, ERNEST G   ASCAP 1956
composer, author

b Brooklyn, NY, Feb 20, 21. Educ: Studied piano with Anna Seredy & violin & arr with Julius Seredy. Songwriter; comp music for Bway show, "Rumple." Chief Collabr: Frank Reardon, lyricist. *Songs:* Color the Children; Music: This Is Heaven to Me; In Times Like These; How Do You Say Goodbye; All Dressed Up and No Place to Go.

SCHWERIN, DORIS HALPERN   ASCAP 1961
composer, author

b Peabody, Mass, June 24, 25. Educ: New Eng Cons Music; Boston Univ; Juilliard Sch Music, dipl; studied with George Antheil, Marian Bower & comp with Stefan Wolpe. Comp for modern dance & theatre music. Author: "Diary of a Pigeon Watcher," 76; "Leanna," 78; "Movie Malone's 200 Days," 80; "Where Did You Put It, When You Had It?" Writing historical novel. Chief Collabrs: Lyrics, Ira Wallach & Rhoda Bellak, Jose Quintero, Norman Geuanthor. *Scores:* Marco Millions; The Orchestra; Off-Bway Show: O' Oysters, Kaboom. *Albums:* From Morning 'Till Night.

SCIANNI, JOSEPH   ASCAP 1955
composer, educator

b Memphis, Tenn, Oct 6, 1928. Educ: Southwestern at Memphis, BS; Eastman Sch Music, MM, DMA, Benjamin Award, comp; studied with Howard Hanson. Began piano at age 5. Formed dance band & did var performances & arrangements while in high sch. Comp for diverse instruments. Arr & recorder, Columbia Records. Producer, Liberty Records, Riverside Records & others. Prof of Music, City Univ New York.

SCIAPIRO, MICHEL (MICHAEL FIELDING)   ASCAP 1941
composer, author, conductor

b Odessa, Russia, Apr 6, 1891; d New York, NY, Mar 3, 62. To US in youth. Educ: Hugo Heermann's master class (scholarship); Otakar Sevcik Paganini scholarship. Concert violinist at age 5; soloist with Berlin Philh & Wiener Konzert Vereins Orch. Mem, Arnhem Symph. Organized own orch. Ed, School of Intonation, Opus XI. *Songs:* Where's My Love?; I Was Waiting for a Dream; Pal; I'll Never Dream a Dream; Paris After Midnight; I'm Wondering Why. *Instrumental Works:* Fantasy for String Quartet (Prague Chamber Music Fest Award); Violin: Fantasia Slav; Serenade Temperamenta; Valse Episode; Sakura; Chiquita; Romance.

SCIBETTA, ANTHONY JAMES   ASCAP 1960
composer, author, pianist

b Buffalo, NY, Jan 9, 26. Educ: Fel to Juilliard Sch Music; also pvt music study. Pianist in radio, TV, nightclubs. Stage scores for "Winnie the Pooh", "Alice in Wonderland" & "Many Moons", Buffalo. Chief Collabrs: John Wallowitch, Alice Scanlan Reach, Johnny Mercer. *Songs:* Lazy Day; Marissa; Music: How Do You Say Auf Wiedersehn; Spring in Manhattan; What's Wrong With Me?; Softly Say Good Bye; Only Know I Loved You; Say Hello for Me; You're for Loving; Something Special; What Do I Care?; One Night.

SCIBONA, JORGE (JORGE MOREL)   ASCAP 1967
composer

b Buenos Aires, Arg, May 9, 31. Educ: Sch for Classical Guitar, Buenos Aires, studied with Pablo Escobar; Univ Advanced Musical Studies, grad; musical research at Juilliard; studied with Manuel Romero (harmony), Rudolph Schramm. Began studying guitar at age 11. Made series of SAm concert & TV appearances. Made US debut at Carnegie Hall, 61. Toured extensively in US. Also appeared in Hawaii & PR. Plays guitar classics, SAm music & Am popular

favorites. *Instrumental Works:* Suite Del Sur (guitar-orch; five movements); Surena (guitar & orch); Olga (guitar & orch); Carinosa (guitar & orch); Spring Theme (guitar & orch); Choro (solo guitar); Cancion and Danza (solo guitar); Variations on a Theme by Gershwin (solo guitar); Romance (solo guitar).

SCLATER, JAMES STANLEY   ASCAP 1968
composer, teacher

b Mobile, Ala, Oct 24, 43. Educ: Univ Southern Miss, BM, MM; Univ Tex, DMA(comp). Music arr, Univ Southern Miss & Univ Tex Marching Bands; coordr music theory, Miss Col, 70-; clarinetist, Jackson Symph, Miss, 71-Ostwald Prize for new band music, 74. *Songs:* Songs of Time and Passing; four songs on texts of Emily Dickinson. *Instrumental Works:* Prelude and Variations on Gone Is My Mistris; Columbia Eagle March; Visions (band); Suite for Clarinet and Piano; Piano Sonata; Mobile Suite (in hon of 275th anniversary of founding of Mobile, Ala).

SCOTT, ALAN ROBERT   ASCAP 1962
lyricist, author, actor

b Haddonfield, NJ, Oct 13, 22. Educ: Univ Pa, BS(econ); Columbia Univ Law Sch, JD. Began as lyricist for musical commercials with wife, Marilyn Scott, New York. Dir, Scott-Textor Productions, Inc & Scott-Textor Music Publ Co. Lyricist & coauthor musical, "Apollo and Miss Agnes." Writes plays & short stories; also many commercials. Did spec material for "The Muppets Valentine Show." Chief Collabs: Marilyn Lang Scott, Keith Textor, Bob Banner, Alice Banner. *Songs:* Lyrics: Air Force Blue; Hold Me; He Has a Way; Sweet Wine of Life; Number Two Song; Smile, You're on Candid Camera.

SCOTT, CHARLES KENNEDY
composer, conductor

b Romsey, Eng, Nov 16, 1876; d London, Eng, July 2, 65. Educ: Studied organ at Brussels Cons, 1897. Established Oriana Madrigal Soc, London, 04, Philh Choir, London, 19 & Euterpe String Players, London, 22. Publ, "Madrigal Singing", "Word and Tone" & "The Fundamentals of Singing." Ed old carols & choral music of the 16th century.

SCOTT, EDWARD NOBLE   ASCAP 1954
composer, author, teacher

b San Jose, Calif, July 4, 19. Educ: Los Angeles City Col, studied piano with Israel Citkovitz & Laura Dubman, comp with Rudolph Schram. Pianist. Comp dance music, "Where's Charley?", "Guys & Dolls" & "Walking Happy"; wrote revues, "That's Life," Hollywood & "Pieces of Eight," London. Has written songs & material for TV shows, incl "Ray Bolger Show", "Patti Page Show", "Garry Moore Show", "Steve and Edie Show", "Phillis Diller Show" & "Jim Nabors Show." Chief Collabs: Larry Holofuener, Sheldon Harnick, Anne Croswell, Lenny Adelson. *Songs:* Music: Funny; You Meet the Nicest People; We're Going to the Moon; Washington Square. *Instrumental Works:* Candid Camera Theme. *Scores:* Off-Bway Shows: The Seducers; Madam Senator.

SCOTT, FRANK R   ASCAP 1959
composer, arranger, pianist

b Fargo, NDak, June 21, 21. Educ: NDak State Univ. Joined Lawrence Welk TV Show, 56 as music coordr, arr, pianist & harpsichordist. Scored over 6000 arr for many orchs & performers. Own band & free-lancing. Chief Collabrs: Tex Satterwhite, Don Roseland, George Cates. *Songs:* Music: The Moment of Truth; Let's Go Dance Again; A Walk in the Glen; Always the Same; This Must Be the Place. *Instrumental Works:* Blue Fountain; Apples and Bananas; Street Corner; A Study in Syncopation; The Now Sound; Crack Up; Dixieland Bar-Be-Que; Riverboat; That's It; Count Me In; Lock-n-Lole; Brocade; Pastel.

SCOTT, HAZEL DOROTHY   ASCAP 1952
composer, pianist, singer

b Port of Spain, Trinidad, June 11, 20. Moved to US, 24. Educ: Juilliard Sch Music. Debut at age 5 with mother's all-girl band, American Creolians. Had own radio series, 36. Appeared in Bway musical, "Sing Out the News." Featured singer & pianist in nightclubs & films. *Songs:* Love Comes Softly; Nightmare Blues.

SCOTT, JAMES A
See Yoder, Paul V

SCOTT, JOHN PRINDLE   ASCAP 1928
composer, author, teacher

b Norwich, NY, Aug 16, 1877; d Syracuse, NY, Dec 2, 32. Educ: Oberlin Cons; also pvt study. Taught singing in Saginaw, Mich. Concert soloist. Awards: State of Nebr; Ohio Univ. *Songs:* Holiday; The Old Road; Come Ye Blessed; Repent Ye; Light; Consider the Lilies; The Secret; The Voice In the Wilderness.

SCOTT, JOHNNIE NEWHALL   ASCAP 1949
composer, teacher

b The Dalles, Ore, May 11, 07; d Los Angeles, Calif, July 25, 63. Educ: Univ Wash, studied music. Musician & pianist, Portland, Ore. Went to San Francisco, worked many places, incl Mark Hopkins Hotel. Accompanist & staff pianist, Fox Studios, Los Angeles, 15 yrs. Chief Collabrs: Sammy Cahn, Harry Ruby, Anson Weeks. *Songs:* Music: I'm Sorry Dear; Maybe It's Because; This Could

Be Forever. *Scores:* Film/TV: Rickey, Tickey, Tickey; My Darling Clementine; Ain't Misbehavin.

SCOTT, JOSEPH
See Kierland, Joseph Scott

SCOTT, KENNETH IRVING   ASCAP 1979
composer, singer
b Boston, Mass. Educ: Studied ballet, Elma Lewis Sch Fine Arts, Boston, ages 12-17; Am Ballet Theater Sch, New York; New York City Ballet Sch; Mannes Col; Yale Univ; pvt study with David Morgan & Mary Ludington. At age 6, he appeared in joint concert with Paul Robeson; was also presented in solo concert. First appeared on stage in "The Country Wife" & Boston production of "Finian's Rainbow." Made Bway debut at age 10 in "The Relapse." Featured vocalist with Earl 'Fatha' Hines, Apollo Theater, New York, at age 11. Toured Europe as dancer & singer in "Jazz Train." Returned to Bway as lead dancer in "The Happiest Girl in the World." Was a principal dancer with Talley Beatty, Alvin Ailey & Donald McKayle dance cos. First Am dancer chosen by Bolshoi Ballet for production, "Spartacus." Toured Europe in "Black Nativity." Then first tenor & lead dancer with the Belafonte Singers. Went to Ger for classical vocal training & returned to US & sang "The Creation" with NJ Philh & performed in NET Opera production, "Rachel La Cubana." Appeared in Bway shows, "Two Gentlemen of Verona" & "Hello Dolly" with Pearl Bailey; had many TV spec appearances incl Ed Sullivan, Carol Burnett, Julie Andrews, Carol Channing, Dick Van Dyke, Joel Grey & Anne Bancroft shows. Comp music for off-Bway productions "Emily T" & "Transcendental Blues." Had many operatic roles. Actor, Bway production, "The Wiz," 3 yrs. Now studying classical music toward an operatic career. Chief Collabs: Denzill Miller, Lynee Daris. *Songs:* Lyrics: I'm in Love With Someone; Feelings Inside.

SCOTT, MARILYN LANG   ASCAP 1962
composer, singer, pianist
b Chicago, Ill. Educ: Chicago Musical Col, studied with Wedertz; Northwestern Univ, BS(speech); Juilliard Sch Music. Writer of musical commercials incl KMart, Dodge Ram Power Trucks; Dodge Cars; Nestles' Chawclit; United Airlines, Lincoln-Mercury & Cheerios. Officer & dir, Scott-Textor Productions & Scott-Textor Music Publ Co. Chief Collabs: Alan Scott, Bob Banner, Stanley Baum, Sidney Sloan, Keith Textor, Alice Banner. *Songs:* Number Two Song (for Sesame Street); Hold Me; Sweet Wine of Life; Air Force Blue. *Scores:* Musicals: Apollo and Miss Agnes; My Dear Commissar.

SCOTT, MOLLY   ASCAP 1966
composer, author, singer
b Wellsville, NY, Jan 11, 38. Educ: Smith Col, BA; voice studies with Dorothy Stahl, Ruth Post, William Horn, Gretchen d'Armand, Rodney Gisick, comp with David Reck, Lewis Spratlin. Early career as singer, actress, comp & poet, clubs, concerts & musical theater; own TV prog WCBS, "Around the Corner"; guest artist & songwriter, "Captain Kangaroo" & "Sesame Street"; also own radio show; theater, "Fantastiks" & "Day of the Dancing"; films, "Psychomania" & "One Plus One" (nominated for Acad Award). Founded ens, Sumitka. Recipient Meet the Composer grant, 80. Mem, Screen Actors Guild; Actor's Equity Asn; Am Women Composers; Am Fedn TV & Radio Artists. *Songs:* Centering Home; Down on the Farm; Poison Treasure; Cows; The Names and the Tree; Wood Dance; Pablo; Honor the Earth; Jesus of the Colors. *Albums:* Waitin' on You; Honor the Earth.

SCOTT, NATHAN GEORGE   ASCAP 1952
composer
b Salinas, Calif, May 11, 15. Educ: Calif Inst Technol; Univ Calif, Berkeley, BA(music), 39. Music dir, Blue Network, West Coast, 42; staff comp, Repub Pictures, 46-52; comp-arr partner of Walter Schumann, var musical proj, 52-59; free lance comp-arr-cond, TV, films & recordings, 59-80. Chief Collab: Walter Schumann. *Songs:* Music: Shall I Compare Thee (Shakespeare sonnet). *Songs & Instrumental Works:* The John Scotter Trot. *Scores:* Dragnet (approx 250 episodes); Lassie (approx 200 episodes); Var features: Wagon Train; Laramie; Twilight Zone; Have Gun Will Travel; My Three Sons; Gunsmoke; Virginian; Untouchables; Family Affair; Frontier Circus; Barnaby Jones; The X-15 Story; Wake of the Red Witch; Galactica (arr); BJ and the Bear (arr); Buck Rogers (arr).

SCOTT, OSCAR EMANUEL   ASCAP 1969
composer, author
b Nov 3, 29. Educ: New Eng Show Case Music, Boston; Combs Col Music, Pa. *Songs & Instrumental Works:* Hold My Hand; I'm Glad I Obey; Evening Glory; It's Later Than You Think; Who Is My Friend, Are You My Friend.

SCOTT, RAYMOND
See Warnow, Harry

SCOTT, ROBERT W (BOBBY)   ASCAP 1961
composer, author, pianist
b Mt Pleasant, NY, Jan 29, 37. Educ: Studied music with Dorothea LaFollette & Eduard Moritz. Pianist in dance bands; toured with Gene Krupa Orch; arr for Bobby Darin, Harry Belafonte, Sarah Vaughn, Fran Jeffries & Betty Madigan; wrote incidental music for Bway play, "A Taste of Honey." *Songs:* Ace of

Diamonds; Only You, My Lady; Nine Hundred Miles From Home; I Gotta Run Now; A Taste of Honey. *Scores:* Stage: Dinny and The Witches.

SCOTT, TOMMY LEE   ASCAP 1963
composer, singer, musician
b Stephens County, Ga, June 24, 17. Educ: Stephens County High Sch. Started career on Old Time Medicine Show, 35- Appears in many different towns in US & Can each yr. Does stage shows, song writing, recording, radio & TV productions. Chief Collabr: Scotty Lee Blevins. *Songs:* The Medicine Man; Rosebuds and You; Exorcism; Rollin' in My Sweet Baby's Arms; Pollution; Snake Oil; Nightmare at Seventeen; Slow Down World; Laughing Song; Peanut Man; Have You Seen Her; Have a Good Day; Don't Blame the Car; Flick My Bic; Write Me a Love Song; Uncle Sam's Got the Flu; Sing, Sing, Sing; Rainbow of My Dreams; Thibodezux; Soldier at Sea; Bluegrass Jam; I'm Gonna Kill Myself O' Lawdy Me; Don't Go Round With a Married Girl; Mississippi Miss; Good Times Are Coming; Hi Dee Ho.

SCOTT-HERON, GIL   ASCAP 1970
composer, author, singer
b Chicago, Ill, Apr 1, 49. Educ: Fieldston Schs Ethical Culture, New York; Lincoln Univ; Johns Hopkins Univ, MA, 72. Author novels, "The Vulture" & "The Nigger Factory" & poetry, "Small Talk at 125th and Lenox." Recording artist, Flying Dutchman Records, 70-72, Strata-East Records, 73 & Arista Records, 74- Chief Collabr: Brian Robert Jackson. *Songs:* The Revolution Will Not Be Televised; Home Is Where the Hatred Is; The Bottle; Johannesburg; Angel Dust.

SCOTTI, WILLIAM   ASCAP 1952
composer, conductor, clarinetist
b Italy, Dec 1, 1895; d. Educ: Cons Music, San Pietro. Organized own orch in US, 25; on NBC radio as Venetian Gondoliers. Also teacher & saxophonist. Chief Collabr: Paul Francis Webster. *Songs:* My Moonlight Madonna.

SCOTTOLINE, MARY ROSALIA   ASCAP 1963
composer, author
b Philadelphia, Pa, Nov 3, 23. Educ: West Cath Girls High Sch, grad, 43. Played piano by ear since age 7; wrote musical for local high sch, "Oh Brother!" 62. Chief Collabr: James Guglielmo (Jimmy Williams). *Songs:* With You; Cara Mia; Beholden; One Little Tear; Lyrics: Half-Way Home.

SCUDDER, WALLACE M   ASCAP 1963
composer, author
b Newark, NJ. Educ: Haverford Col, BA; Harvard Univ, MA. Co-founder & dir, Longy Sch Music, Cambridge, Mass; former bd dir, Chamber Music Asn, Boston. *Songs:* A Kiss for Christmas; Time Out for Christmas. *Instrumental Works:* Christmas Music.

SEA, BERNIE
See Chianco, Bernard V

SEAMAN, WILLIAM HYLAND   ASCAP 1964
composer, author, pianist
b Stoughton, Wis, Mar 25, 10. Educ: Columbus Col; S State Normal; Dak Wesleyan Univ, BA, 31; Univ Wash, postgrad drama & jour; studied under Glenn Hughes, John Ashby Conway & Burton James. Wrote stage score "Pesty," Univ Wash, 33; staff pianist, WNAX, Yankton, SDak; KSOO, Sioux Falls; KGDA, Mitchell. Wrote music score for radio drama, KNX, Seattle, Wash; taught piano & voice; had own band; wrote spec material for stage, radio & TV; pianist, USO, Actors Equity & Red Cross, WW II; dir, high sch chorus, Wash, 34-44 & Community Chorus, Calif, 48-73; jour instr. Life Mem: Locals 47 & 7, Am Fedn Musicians; Orange County Press Club. Mem, Sigma Delta Chi. Chief Collabrs: Tom Herbert, O B Clow, Dan Busath, Art Benson, Marie Seaman (wife). *Songs & Instrumental Works:* Egyptian Ballet; Sammamish (march); To Be Or Not to Be; One White Rose; Where But in America (chorale); For One Day I Am Queen (Halloween TV Spec); Au Revoir (Till Then); I'm Not Asleep I'm Just Dreaming; Zola (Tango); Patty Cake Polka; There's No Yesterday; Love, Love, Go Away; Washington Chant (fight song, Univ Wash); You're a Perfect Picture; Clarabelle.

SEARS, TED   ASCAP 1953
author
b Greenfield, Mass, Mar 13, 00; d Studio City, Calif, Aug 22, 58. Educ: High sch; also studied art & lettering. Began career as cartoonist. Went to Hollywood as writer for Educ Studies, 30's. Joined Walt Disney, 31. *Songs:* Following the Leader; I Wonder.

SEAVER, BLANCHE EBERT   ASCAP 1941
composer, author, teacher
b Chicago, Ill, Sept 15, 1891. Educ: Robert Waller High Sch; Chicago Music Col, 11; Hull House as a protege of Jane Addams; studied music with father, also Amalie Hannig & Brahm van der Berg; hon degrees: LHD, Univ Southern Calif, 66; DFA, Seaver Col, Malibu, 68; LLD, Pomona Col, 70; DBA, Woodbury Col, 70; DH, Oklahoma Christian Col, 72; DPS, MacMurray Col, 73. Piano teacher, accompanist & coach, Hull House, Chicago, 02-19 & Los Angeles, 12-16. Awards: Named Los Angeles Times Woman of the Year, 60;

Jane Addams Award, Rockford Col; Award of Freedom, Young Am for Freedom, 71; Award of Excellence, Patriot of the Year, Christian Freedom Found, 71; Dr Robert Fenton Craig Award, Blue Key, 72-73; Guardian of Freedom Award, Calif Young Am for Freedom, 73; Scroll of Honor, Navy League of the US, 73 & Am Patriot Award, 80; Distinguished Patriot Award, Religious Heritage of Am, 73; Am Humanics Award, 80. *Songs & Instrumental Works:* Just for Today; If God Sent Me You; Remember Me; Calling Me Back to You; Close At Thy Feet, My Lord; Pontifical Mass; The Flower; Stay With Me, O Lord; Alone With Thee; No Llores Yo Volvere; Morrow Rock; Battle Hymn of the Republic (special arr). Mass.

SEBESKY, DONALD J ASCAP 1975
composer, conductor, pianist
b Perth Amboy, NJ, Dec 10, 37. Educ: Manhattan Sch Music, studied comp with Vittorio Giannini. Arr for Dionne Warwick, Wes Montgomery & Peggy Lee, 59-80. Assoc with CTI Records, 14 yrs. *Songs & Instrumental Works:* Bird and Bela in B Flat (Grammy Nomination, 79).

SEBESKY, GERALD JOHN ASCAP 1972
composer, author, teacher
b Perth Amboy, NJ, Sept 8, 41. Educ: Manhattan Sch Music, BM, 62, MM, 63; Kean Col, MA, 69; Columbia Univ Teacher Col, prof dipl, 72; Univ Hawaii, comp with Robert Lincoln & Stephan Wolpe. Comp work for band, orch & chorus. Author: "The Gerald Sebesky Band Method Book I & II" & "The Creative Music Theory Handbook." *Instrumental Works:* The Elementary and Intermediate Stage Band Book; Concepts for Percussion; Passacaglia for Band; Very First Recital for Strings Book; Fundamentals for Beginning Band.

SEBINIANO, MICHAEL P ASCAP 1962
composer, author, musician
b Brooklyn, NY, July 7, 27. Educ: High sch. Singer.

SECRIST, HARLEY WALTER ASCAP 1963
composer, author
b Buchtel, Ohio, Sept 1, 1890. *Songs:* June Time; Just Today; I Want to Stay in Monterey; Place Me in Your Dreams Soldier Boy.

SECUNDA, SHELDON ASCAP 1956
author
b Brooklyn, NY, Jan 5, 29. Educ: Bronx High Sch of Sci; Univ Calif, Los Angeles; NY Univ, BA, 50, MA, 51. Publicist for Bway shows. Dir of TV commercials. Photographer, advert & nat mag covers. Creator & photographer, children's books, "Sesame St Book of Opposites", "What I Want to Be When I Grow Up", "Mr Rogers Tells Us." Chief Collabr: Sholom Secunda. *Songs:* Lyrics: Dana, Dana, Dana; Up on the Mountain; Channukah; There's One Lord for All.

SECUNDA, SHOLOM ASCAP 1954
composer, conductor
b Alexandria, Russia, Aug 23, 1894; d New York, NY, June 13, 74. To US in 1907. Educ: Cooper Union; Columbia Univ; Juilliard Sch Music; studied with Ernest Bloch (scholarship). Band arr, USN, WW I. Comp & cond, opera, burlesque, musical comedy, radio & TV. Music critic, "Jewish Daily Forward." Pres, Soc of Jewish Comp; fellow, Int Inst Arts & Letters, 61. Chief Collabr: Sheldon Secunda (son) *Songs:* Bei Mir Bist Du Schon; Dana, Dana, Dana. *Songs & Instrumental Works:* 3 Symphonic Sketches; String Quartet in C; Kabbalat Shabbat; Shabbat Hamaltah; Friday Evening Service; Oratorios: If Not Higher; Yiskor.

SEDORES, SIL
See Eisenberg, Sylvia White

SEELEN, JERRY ASCAP 1943
author
b New York, NY, Mar 11, 12. Educ: High sch. Wrote songs for Bway musicals: "Star and Garter", "Ziegfeld Follies" & "Priorities." Writer for films, radio, also TV incl "Danny Thomas Show." Head writer, "Revlon Revue" TV series, 60. *Songs:* No Room for the Groom; Poor Little February; How Do I Know It's Real; Chico's Love Song; C'est Si Bon; Hush-a-Bye; Living the Life I Love; I Hear the Music Now.

SEELY, SCOTT BUCKLEY ASCAP 1963
composer, author, producer
b Lyons, Kans, Dec 25, 11. Educ: Bethany Col, Lindsborg, Kans; Chicago Music Cons; pvt training with Wesley La Violette. Started arr & playing piano with bands in Kans, Okla & Tex in 32. Arr for NBC & bands, Chicago & Los Angeles. Started Accent Records, 54 & S & R Music Publ Co, 58. Chief Collabrs: Buddy Merrill, David Garvin, Robin Miller. *Songs:* Music to Make Love By; Music: Hurt, and All Alone; One Earth. *Instrumental Works:* Allegra's Eyes; Perry's Theme.

SEGAL, ERICH ASCAP 1961
composer, author, educator
b Brooklyn, NY, June 16, 37. Educ: Midwood High Sch, Brooklyn; Harvard Univ, AB, 58, AM, 59 & PhD, 65. Novelist & screenwriter: "Sing Muse!" off-Bway musical, 60-61; "Beatles' Yellow Submarine," screenplay, 68; "Love

Story," novel & screenplay, 70; "Oliver's Story," novel, 77; "Man, Woman and Child," novel, 80. Prof of literature. Chief Collabr: Charles Aznavour. *Songs:* Lyrics: Our Love, My Love; Whatever Became of the Wrath of Achilles?.

SEGAL, JACK ASCAP 1947
composer, author, teacher
b Minneapolis, Minn, Oct 19, 18. Educ: Univ Wis, Madison, PhB, 42, political sci studies; New Sch Social Res, Sem Creative Writing, MSc(polit sci), studied with H Glicksberg. Paramount Pictures Music Dept, Hollywood, 44-45; poetry publ, Am Vanguard, 48, TV, "Justice," specials for Harry Belafonte, Paul Winchell & Janet Blair, original musical "A Man's Game," NBC. Teacher songwriting, Calif State Univ, Agac Songshop & Grove Music Sch. Chief Collabrs: George Handy, Marvin Fisher, Evelyn Danzig, Bob Wells, Paul Vance, Ben Oakland. *Songs:* Bye-Bye, Barbara; Laughing Boy; When Joanna Loved Me; This Godforsaken Day; Here's to the Losers; Only Me and You; All the Porches Are Empty; I'll Remember Suzanne; Hard to Get (in top ten Hit Parade songs, 55); Lyrics: Someday-Somewhere We Will Meet Again; Who Told You That Lie (in top ten Hit Parade songs, 46); A Boy From Texas-A Girl From Tennessee (Off song, Madison Square Garden Rodeo); Years and Years Ago (Toselli's Serenade); Scarlet Ribbons (for Her Hair); For Once in Your Life; When Sunny Gets Blue; Too Much-Too Soon; Nothing Ever Changes; May I Come In?; When He Makes Music; Ce Serait Dommage; Summer Is Gone (Jimmie's Gone Home); Man Smart-Woman Smarter; Strings; Woman-Woman (Warm and Wonderful); Forgetful.

SEGALL, BERNARDO ASCAP 1956
composer, pianist
b Campinas, Brazil, Aug 4, 11. Educ: Sao Paulo Cons; Gymnasium Anglo-Americano, Brazil. Piano debut, Rio de Janeiro, age 9. Toured US, Europe & SAm. Soloist, NY Philh, also NBC, Los Angeles, Pittsburgh, Mexico City & Rio de Janeiro Symph Orchs. Awarded Alberte Chiaffarelli Prize, Brazil. Wrote incidental music for plays: "Camino Real"; "Skin of Our Teeth"; "Sound and the Fury." *Songs:* Airforce on Canvas; Gabriella; Europea; It's Only My Heart; Watching the World Go By. *Instrumental Works:* Ballets: As I Lay Dying; Domino Furioso; The Wall; Desperate Heart.

SEGALL, DON ASCAP 1962
author
b Boston, Mass, Aug 11, 33. Educ: Boston Univ, MS(communication arts). Writer-producer numerous TV comedy & variety shows, incl "That's Incredible!", "The Neil Sedaka Touch", "Celebrity Charades", "Out of the Blue", "Olivia Newton-John/Hollywood Nights", "What Every Woman Wants to Know, With Bess Meyerson" & "AM New York" (twice nominated for Emmy Awards). Writer of travel & recruitment films. Author & producer for the theatre. Author of bks, var articles & stories. Producer-writer radio shows; Sigma Delta Chi Award for Pub Service Through Radio Jour, WBUR, Boston. Chief Collabr: Richard B Koerner. *Scores:* TV Musical: Talk Turkey.

SEGALL, RICHARD ROBERT ASCAP 1972
composer, author, singer
b Brooklyn, NY, Oct 7, 47. Educ: High sch. Rock'n'Roll singer, 64-70; with group, Smubbs. Wrote & sang with own family under name, Family Portrait, 70-72. Sang, wrote & performed as Ricky Segall & the Segalls, 72-74. Under contract to Columbia Pictures & Screen Gems TV; wrote spec material for Partridge Family, Merv Griffin & Mac Davis. Appeared on all major talk shows. Through Wes Farrell Orgn wrote many songs for "Capt Kangaroo Show," 75. Chief Collabrs: Dennis McCarthy, Jack Goga, Dick Hamilton. *Songs:* Say Hey Willie; Sooner or Later; Hello, Hello, Hello; A Picture; Sunrise on the Prairie.

SEGER, ROBERT CLARK ASCAP 1966
composer, author, performer
b Ann Arbor, Mich, May 6, 45. Educ: Washtenaw Col, Ann Arbor. Recording artist, Capitol Records. *Songs:* Against the Wind; Back in '72; Beautiful Loser; East Side Story; Famous Final Scene; Katmandu; Mainstreet; Mongrel; Night Moves; Ramblin' Gamblin' Man; Rock and Roll Never Forgets; Rosalie; So I Wrote You a Song; Still the Same; The Fire Down Below; Horizontal Bop; Till It Shines; Travelin' Man; Turn the Page; We've Got Tonite.

SEIDMAN, WILLIAM (WILLIAM SIDEMAN) ASCAP 1976
composer, author, guitarist
b New York, NY, July 13, 53. Educ: Berklee Col Music, studied with William Leivitt, guitar with Steve Khan & John Scholfield, arr with Steve Robbins. Played in var bands, 67-68 & 71-75; played with Chubby Checker on tour, 69-70; staff writer, RCA Publ Div, 76-78; studio musician, 78-80; arr, Ashford & Simpson, US tour. Chief Collabrs: Gordon Grody, Carlotta McKee, Leo Adamian. *Songs:* Lack of Respect; Falling in Love; You're Far Away; Girls Get the Latest Kicks; Kiss Off Tomorrow Tonight.

SEIGENTHALER, WILLIAM ROBERT (ROBERT TREBOR) ASCAP 1979
composer, author
b Nashville, Tenn, Nov 22, 34. Educ: Father Ryan High Sch, Nashville; Univ Tenn; Fisk Univ, teacher spec communications sem. Writer of poetry, TV prog, tribute concert to W C Handy, audio visual shows, jingles & songs. Chief

Collabr: Robert Holmes. *Songs:* Ham on Monday; Am I Too Big to Cry; Lyrics: Frosty Morn; If We Knew, Then. *Scores:* Film/TV: If We Knew, Then.

SEIGHMAN, WILLIAM HENRY   ASCAP 1974
composer, author, singer
b Uniontown, Pa, Jan 13, 38. Educ: Self-taught. Prof entertainer, radio, nightclubs, TV & stage, since late 40's. Writer pop songs. Chief Collabr: Terry Plumer. *Songs:* Back on My Feet Again; Love for a Life Time; You Are My Magic; The Light At the End of the Hall; Lyrics: Conversation Love.

SEILER, EDWARD   ASCAP 1942
author
b Iwonicz, Austria, Mar 14, 11; d Linden, NJ, Jan 1, 52. Worked for newspapers. Chief Collabrs: Sol Marcus, Al Kaufman, Bennie Benjamin, Guy Wood. *Songs:* I Don't Want to Set the World on Fire; When the Lights Go on Again All Over the World; Till Then; Ask Anyone Who Knows; You're Gonna Fall and Break Your Heart; Cancel the Flowers; Small World; Fishin' for the Moon; And Then It's Heaven; The Girl From Jones Beach; Because You Love Me; To Remind Me of You; If Every Day Would Be Christmas; It All Begins and Ends With You; You Can't Hide Your Heart; Ah Dee Ah Dee Ah!; Somehow Days Go By; Strictly Instrumental.

SEINBERG, LILLIAN   ASCAP 1974
composer
b Bridgeport, Conn, Jan 1, 07. Educ: Inst Musical Art, 3 yr cert from Frank Damrosch, New York; studied with Rudolph Gunz, 30, Alton Jones, 31-35, Alberto Jonas, 35-38, piano & comp, William Scher, 52-57, Martha Levitski, 56-58 & Richard McClanahn, 72-79. Piano teacher, pre-sch ages 3-6, 51 yrs. Taught classical music spec courses for adults; lectr on pre-sch teaching & advantages of early start. Comp children pieces, 53- Cert as piano teacher by NY State, 67, Music Teachers Nat Asn, 70 & Fla, 79. *Songs & Instrumental Works:* Masquerade Waltz; Boastful Little Monkey; Jack in the Box; Joyous March.

SEITTER, CHARLES F   ASCAP 1956
composer, author
b Philadelphia, Pa, Sept 21, 1892. Educ: Bus Inst. Led small groups, also taught music, Philadelphia. *Songs:* Tell All Your Day Dreams to Me; Here's Luck to Our Love; Broadway Lament; What a Sweet Sensation; Who's Gonna Bury the Last Mean Dead?; Carolina Lou; I've Got an Easter Hat and an Easter Suit for Easter Morning.

SEKULIDIS, DONNA   ASCAP 1973
author
b Detroit, Mich, Nov 10, 49. Educ: Fordson High Sch, Dearborn, Mich; Wayne State Univ, Detroit. Free lance writer, Detroit & Los Angeles, Calif, 67-; worked with other writers & producers. Chief Collabrs: Tom Baird, Joe Hinton, Hank Cosby, Andreas Neie. *Songs:* Lyrics: Bring Me Home; Yesterday's Love Is Over.

SELBY, PETER HOLLINSHEAD   ASCAP 1960
composer, author
b Austin, Minn, Jan 26, 14. Educ: Principia Col, BA, 36; studied piano & comp, Charles Marsh. Wrote songs for Charles H Blake productions, 45-52, also for Globe Theater shows & for 2 west coast reviews "Up in the Air" & "Bye, Bye, Jupiter." Chief Collabrs: Vic Schwartz, Don Pope, Irving Bibo. *Songs:* This Is Swell; Words Alone Will Never Do; Heads It's Love; So This Is the End; Music: Let's Join the School of Love; Give Ear Oh Ye Heavens; O'er Waiting Harpstrings. *Instrumental Works:* Autumn Afternoon; Free As the Breeze; Offertory. *Scores:* In Murphy Park; Rip Van Winkle.

SELIGMAN, NAT JEFFREY   ASCAP 1979
composer, producer, recording engineer
b Los Angeles, Calif, June 27, 50. Educ: University High Sch, 68; Univ Calif, Los Angeles, BA, 72; Inst of Audio Res, 73. Recording engr for Bob Dylan, The Band, Joe Cocker, Eric Clapton & Neil Diamond; producer & writer, The Marc Tanner Band; music producer & coordr, "The Great American Traffic Jam," NBC TV movie. Chief Collabrs: Marc Tanner, Jeff Monday. *Songs:* Elena; Never Again; She's So High; Getaway.

SELINSKY, WLADIMIR   ASCAP 1956
composer, conductor, violinist
b Kiev, Russia, Feb 15, 10. To US, 25. Educ: Prince Heinrich Gymnasium Music Sch, Berlin, studied violin with Willy Hess & Adolf Busch; Inst Musical Art & Juilliard, scholarships in violin & comp; studied violin with F Kneisel & Leopold Auer, comp with Bernard Waagenar & Michael Feveisky. Began cond at age 4, violin lessons at age 5. Concertized as both cond & violin soloist. Played & cond Bway shows. Began comp & cond for radio, 43 & later for TV, incl "FBI in Peace and War", "The Big Story", "The Jeffersonian Heritage", "Omnibus", "Kraft TV Theatre", "US Steel Hour", "Lux Video Theatre", "General Electric Theatre" & "Hallmark Hall of Fame." Chief Collabrs: lyrics, Mel Mandel & Lester O'Keefe. *Songs:* Music: My Little Boy; Jasmine; Driftwood; All I Touch.

SELLERS, BROTHER JOHN   ASCAP 1962
author, singer
b Clarksdale, Miss, May 27, 24. Educ: Chicago Cons Music, studied with Prof Kecdricks; studied with Mahalia Jackson (godmother) & Hortense Love. Made debut at Oliver Baptist Church, Chicago, 42. Appeared on Bway in "The Roots of the Blues." Appeared on var shows, "Tambourines to Glory", "Ed Sullivan Show", 63, "The Johnny O'Keefe Show", Sydney, Australia, 66, Flemish TV, Antwerp, Belgium, "Lee Phillips Show", Chicago, "Osaka Hour", Tokyo, French TV, Paris, "The Music Hour", plus others. Mem, Local 802 Musicians Union & Am Fedn TV & Radio Artists. Blues, gospel & folk singer; tambourine player. Chief Collabr: Howard Robert. *Songs:* Gospel: You Got to Love Everybody; All These Days Are the Beginning of Sorrow Don't You See?; I Was Blessed and Brought Up by the Lord; Let's Run While the Sun Is Shining; God's Love Is Better Then Told; Going to See the King; Right Now; Oh Lord Don't Let Me Fall; Everybody Needs to Pray. *Songs & Instrumental Works:* Big Boat Up the River; Something Strange Going on Wrong; Oh Little Girl; State Side Ora; Mean 'Ole Frisco; What More Can I Do? (My Loving Baby); Mamie Blues; Children Go Where I Send Thee; House of the Rising Sun; Something's Gone Wrong on the Levee; Shake My Hand; Love Is Just Like Fire; Well That's All Right; Godamighty Gonna Cut You Down; Dark Was the Night; Ding Dong That's a Pretty Girl; Kindhearted Woman (Little Girl).

SELMER, KATHRYN LANDE   ASCAP 1962
composer, author, singer
b Staten Island, NY, Nov 6, 30. Educ: Eastman Sch Music; Juilliard. Singer, comp, NBC, TV show, "Birthday House" & "Captain Kangaroo." Chief Collabr: Wade Denning. *Songs:* Let's Go to the Toy Shop; Collections: For Sleepyheads Only; Let's Have a Party; Songs for Little Folk. *Scores:* Operas: Shoemaker and the Elf; The Princess and the Pea; The Princess Who Couldn't Laugh.

SELSMAN, VICTOR   ASCAP 1942
author
b New York, NY, Feb 9, 08; d Forest Hills, NY, July 26, 58. Educ: City Col New York. Chief Collabrs: Lyn Murray, James Van Heusen, J Russel Robinson, Milton Ager, Jerry Livingston. *Songs:* Deep South; Do You Wanna Jump, Children?; I Won't Believe It; To a Little Boy; Old Moses Put Pharaoh in His Place; You're Letting the Grass Grow Under Your Feet; I've Been a Stranger in My Father's House.

SELVAGGIO, JOHN RALPH (JOHNNY CARLO)   ASCAP 1960
singer
b Cementon, Pa. Educ: Studied voice with Al Barto. Performer, clubs, TV, "Merv Griffin Show"; recording artist. Chief Collabr: Chet Warren. *Songs:* Lyrics: Fish Walk.

SELVIN, ROBERT BRIAN   ASCAP 1978
composer, author, singer
b Los Angeles, Calif, Feb 6, 57. Educ: Studied jazz piano with Matt Dennis, comp with Hal Johnson & conducting with Fritz Zague. Performer in nightclubs & Las Vegas; records producer; scored films; teacher. Chief Collabr: Joe Bandille. *Songs:* The Ballad Bubbles. *Instrumental Works:* Cameoflage; Freedom; Simsiama Land; Just By Chance.

SEMBELLO, JOHN ANTHONY   ASCAP 1971
composer, singer
b Philadelphia, Pa, Feb 22, 45. Educ: Haverford High Sch. Recorded "Who Would Ever Think I Would Marry Margaret"; recording artist, A & M Records. Chief Collabrs: Hugo Montenegro, Koppelman & Ruben-Leiber & Stoller, Ralph Dino. *Songs:* Pearl's a Singer; Dancing Jones; Best Thing; See the Light. *Scores:* Film/TV: Viva Max.

SEMBELLO, MICHAEL ANDREW   ASCAP 1975
composer, author
b Philadelphia, Pa, Apr 17, 54. Educ: Studied with Denis Sandole, Pat Martino, Harry Fields, Seth Rigg, Albert Harris. Played, recorded & wrote songs for var artists, Japanese commercial, Am TV & radio commercials. Chief Collabrs: Stevie Wonder, Sergio Mendes, David Batteau. *Songs:* If and Any Day; Hide it Away; Finally Found a Reason; Lyrics: Saturn; Power Flower.

SEMOLA, ALFONSE J   ASCAP 1970
composer
b Philadelphia, Pa, Apr 18, 19. Educ: Philadelphia Cons Music; Univ Pa. Worked in Las Vegas for many yrs. Arr for many, most notably The Ames Bros. *Songs:* Christmas Is the Warmest Time of the Year.

SEMOS, MURRAY   ASCAP 1950
composer, author
b New York, NY, Aug 3, 13. Chief Collabrs: Jack Val, Buddy Sheppard. *Songs:* It's So Nice to Be Nice; Mm, Mm, Not That; Bella Faccia; Who Do You Think You're Foolin'?; Paree; Sing Sing Sing; Can You Spare a Couple of Minutes?; Gee, It's Tough to Be a Skunk.

SENDAK, MAURICE BERNARD
writer, illustrator

b Brooklyn, NY, June 10, 28. Educ: Art Students League, New York, 49-51. Writer & illusr children's bks, 51- One-man show, Gallery Sch Visual Arts, New York, 64, Ashmolean Mus, Oxford, 75 & Am Cult Ctr, Paris, 78. Author & illusr: "Kenny's Window"; "Very Far Away"; "The Sign on Rosie's Door"; "The Nutshell Library"; "Where the Wild Things Are" (Caldecott Medal, 64). Illusr: "A Hole Is to Dig"; "A Very Special House"; "I'll Be You and You Be Me"; "Charlotte and the White Horse"; "What Do You Say, Dear?"; "The Moonjumpers"; "Little Bear's Visit"; "Schoolmaster Whackwell's Wonderful Sons"; "Mr Rabbit and the Lovely Present"; "The Griffin and the Minor Canon"; "Nikolenka's Childhood"; "The Bat-Poet"; "Lullabies and Night Songs"; "Hector Protector and As I Went Over the Water"; "Zlateh the Goat"; "Higglety Pigglety Pop, Or There Must Be More to Life"; "In the Night Kitchen"; "The Animal Family"; "In the Night Kitchen Coloring Book"; "Pictures By Maurice Sendak"; "The Juniper Tree and Other Tales From Grimm." Writer, dir & lyricist TV animated spec, "Really Rosie," 75. Rec'd Hans Christian Anderson Illustrator's Award (first Am), 70.

SENDREY, ALBERT RICHARD   ASCAP 1946
composer, arranger, orchestrator

b Chicago, Ill, Dec 26, 22. Educ: Herne Bay Col, Eng; Trinity Col Music, London; Univ Southern Calif, Los Angeles; Ecole Normale, Paris; cond studies with A Coates, J Barbirolli & father, Dr A Sendry, comp with Arnold Schoenberg, Gehl & Lovelock, London, orchestration with Marvel Rosental, Paris. Film comp & arr, Paris & London & MGM, Calif. Comp & orchr over 100 films incl, "The Yearling", "Three Musketeers", "Great Caruso", "American in Paris", "Raintree County", "Royal Wedding", "Easter Parade", "Summer Stock" & "Brigadoon." Chief Collabrs: John Green, George Stoll, Harry Sukman, David Rose, Tony Martin, Sid Kuller, Barry de Vorzon. *Instrumental Works:* Sonata for Viola; Symphony (1st; Chicago Symph Prize, 41); Symphony (2nd; Detroit Symph Prize, 48); Symphony (3rd); Johnny Appleseed Overture (Ohio Sesquicentennial Prize, 53); L A Boheme (jazz version Puccini's La Boheme); Elegy for String Orchestra; Symphonic Variations on a Jazz Theme; Spanish Suite; Debussy Ballade; Divertimento; Cello Concerto on Hungarian Themes; Grande Chaconne for Piano; Concertino for Piano; also one string quartet & one woodwind quintet.

SENTER, BOYD LANGDON   ASCAP 1960
composer, author

b Lyons, Nebr, Nov 30, 1898. Educ: Pvt instruction. Went on stage at age 18. Recorded with var cos. Had own band, Boyd Senter & His Senterpedes. Chief Collabrs: Walter Hirsch, Walter Melrose.

SERAPHINE, DANIEL PETER
drummer

b Chicago, Ill, Aug 28, 48. Educ: High sch. Mem musical group, Chicago, 67- Owner nightclub, B Ginnings, Schaumburg, Ill, 74- Owner clothing store, Peabody's, Chicago, 74- Co-comp, "Lowdown", "Devil's Sweet" & "Aire."

SERETAN, STEPHEN HOWARD   ASCAP 1978
composer, author, conductor

b New York, NY, Oct 10, 48. Educ: Univ Calif, Los Angeles, BA(music-comp), 70; studied with Roy Harris. *Songs:* Love, Love Go Away; He's a Part of Me; Come to Me; Love Is All We Need. *Songs & Instrumental Works:* Redemption of the Pariahs (cantata). *Scores:* TV: The Paper Chase; The FBI; National Geographic Society Special.

SERLY, TIBOR   ASCAP 1945
composer, conductor, violinist

b Losonc, Hungary, Nov 25, 1900; d. To US, 03. Educ: Studied music with father; later with Kodaly & Bartok; Royal Acad Music, Budapest, studied with Hubay. Violist, Cincinnati Symph & Philadelphia Orch; charter mem, NBC Symph. Guest cond, orchs including Philadelphia, CBS Symph, Naumberg Concerts & Budapest Philh. US rep & mem bd judges, Bartok Int Competition, Budapest, 48. Author, "Melody, the Core of Music." Cond, Stamford Symph. Taught orchestration & conducting. Arr. *Instrumental Works:* Viola Concerto; 2 Symphonies; Violin Sonata; Fugue for Strings; Suite for Orchestra; Transylvania Suite; Dance Designs; Colonial Pageant; Elegy (orch); Rhapsody (viola, orch); also arr posthumous works of Bela Bartok.

SERRETT, JAMES   ASCAP 1975
composer, author

b New York, NY, Aug 21, 48. Educ: Plainview High Sch; NY Inst Technol, BFA(communication arts), 71. Co-writer on "Love Songs Are Getting Harder to Sing." Chief Collabs: Annette Tucker, Arthur Hamilton.

SETARO, PETER D (LARRY BAXTER)   ASCAP 1955
composer, author

b New Haven, Conn, Nov 29, 24. Educ: East Haven High Sch; Quinnipiac Col. Wrote music for varsity shows, 46, 47, 48 & 52, also plays, 60, nightclubs, 58 & 59, Country Music Fest, 77. Chief Collabs: Everett Hale, Eddie Curtis, Don Canton, Lee Jackson, Sol Parker, Henry Jerome, Patti Gianini. *Songs:* Compare; Indispensable Love; Here and Now; Music: Why a Teenager Cries; Drop It and Run; You Are Mine; Summer Love; Velvet Window; All Summer Long; We Can

Make It Together; Come and Dance With Me; The Me Nobody Knows; Soul Searcher; Living Without You; I'm in Love With the Man Behind the Song; I'll Never Get Over What's Over; Sometimes in Shadows; Song of the Painter; Never Felt a Thing; Living in My Dreams; Sometimes.

SEVERINSEN, CARL H (DOC)   ASCAP 1961
composer, conductor, trumpeter

b Arlington, Ore, July 7, 27. Educ: Studied cornet with father, later with Benny Baker. Trumpeter in orchs incl Ted Fiorito, Benny Goodman, Charlie Barnet, Sam Donahue, Tommy Dorsey, Noro Morales & Vaughn Monroe. On staff, NBC, New York; later asst cond to Skitch Henderson, "Tonight Show." Made many records; concert soloist. *Songs & Instrumental Works:* Dear Ruth; Para Mia; La Puenta del Sol; Cleopatra's Asp; Trumpet Lament.

SEVERN, EDMUND   ASCAP 1924
composer, conductor, violinist

b Nottingham, Eng, Dec 10, 1862; d Melrose, Mass, May 14, 42. To US, 1866. Educ: Studied violin with Edmund Severn (father), Franz Mileke, Bernard Listemann, Emanuel Wirth. Cond theatre orchs; Springfield Orchestral Club, Severn String Quartet & Trio. Pres, NY State Teachers Asn, 09-10. *Instrumental Works:* Lancelot and Elaine; Abelard and Eloise; Festival Overture; Violin Concerto; Violin Sonata; String Trio; Suite for 2 Violins, Piano; From Old New England; Italian Suite; Puck and Titania; 2 Russian Dances; 3 string quartets.

SEVERSON, MARIE   ASCAP 1960
composer, author

b Athens, Wis, Aug 19, 13. Educ: High sch. Writer musical commercials. *Songs:* Ingomar the Walloping Swede.

SEVILLE, DAVID
See Bagdasarian, Ross

SEVITZKY, FABIEN   ASCAP 1954
composer, conductor

b Vichny, Russia, Sept 30, 1893; d Athens, Greece, Feb 3, 67. To US 1923. Citizen 28. Educ: St Petersburg Imp Cons; De Pauw Univ, MusD; hon MusD, Ill Wesleyan Univ, Indiana Univ & Butler Univ. Double bass soloist, St Petersburg Cons Philh Orch, Moscow Imp Theatre & Warsaw State Opera, 11. In Russian Army, WW I. Concert tours, Russia, Poland, Finland, North & SAm. Mem, Philadelphia Orch. Founder & cond, Philadelphia String Chamber Sinfonietta, 25. Gave annual concerts, Philadelphia & NY, also made many tours. Cond, Philadelphia Opera Co & Pa Opera Co, 27-30. Guest cond orchs, US, Can, Europe & SAm. Music dir, cond, Indianapolis Symph, (also founder & dir, Indianapolis Symph Choir), 37-55, San Diego Summer Symph, 49-52 & Univ of Miami Symph, 59. Concerts in Europe, Chile & Guatemala, 61-64. Co-founder, Pro-Mozart Soc of Greater Miami. Awarded Cavalier Order de Boyaca, Colombia. *Songs & Instrumental Works:* Nocturne for Orch; Overture to Opera; Fanfare and Chorale for 3 Trumpets, 2 Horns; Fanfare No 3; My Prayer; Transc: Bach's Toccata and Fugue; Fantasy and Fugue; Giant Fugue.

SEXAUER, ARWIN F B GARELLICK   ASCAP 1966
composer, author, poet

b Richford, Vt, Aug 18, 21. Educ: Pvt study piano, drama, voice, journalism, library & dance; hon DLitt, World Univ; Hon Dipl Arts & Letters, Athens, Greece; Dipl Di Benemerenza, Accademia Leonardo da Vinci, Rome, Italy. Publ poet/lyricist at age 14; radio/theatre monologist at age 17; ed, Vermont Odd Fellow Mag, 59-71. Co-founder, Music Mission for World Peace, Inc, 63. Comp lyrics for all Music Mission songs of ecumenical hymnody. Librarian, 66-76. Author of bk of poetry "Remembered Winds" & 14 musical pageants. Life fel, Int Acad Poets; mem, Int Platform Asn. Rec'd over 100 awards & honors, incl three George Washington Honor Medals, 57, 59, 73; 13 ASCAP Popular Panel Awards for lyrics, 67-78; cert of merit for musical pageant "Golden Scale," Nat Fedn Music Clubs & ASCAP; Distinguished Serv Citation for Poetry, World Poetry Soc. *Songs:* Wedding Day; Profile of a Handshake; Lyrics: Forward Together (Vt State bicentennial song); Patterns for Peace; Men of Apollo; Pray for Peace; A Better World; God Is Not Dead; Universal Friendship Hymn; My Brother's Hand in Mine; I'm the Flag of All the People (George Washington Hon Medal); One Last Coin for Brotherhood; For Some the War Will Never End; For Connecticut; If I Had But One Day to Live (tribute to Robert Kennedy); The People's President; Song of the Shofar; One World-Under God (Dr Arthur W Hewitt Mem Award).

SEYMOUR, HARRY   ASCAP 1953
composer, author, actor

b Brooklyn, NY, June 22, 1891; d. Educ: City Col New York. Staff writer, music publ firms. Appeared in vaudeville & nightclubs; actor in Bway productions: "Follow Me", "Just a Minute", "Mary, Be Careful." Wrote spec material. Actor, dialogue dir in films. Chief Collabrs: Paul Cunningham, Cliff Friend. *Songs:* Sally's in the Movies Now (theme for film); The Yanks Are Coming Again; All You Have to Do Is Smile; What a Fool I've Been.

SEYMOUR, JOHN LAURENCE　　　　　　　　ASCAP 1935
composer, author, professor
b Los Angeles, Calif, Jan 18, 1893. Educ: Univ Calif, Berkeley, AB, 17, MA, 19, PhD, 40; hon DLitt, Southern Utah State Col, 77. Teacher, Hollywood High Sch, Los Angeles, 19-23; chmn, Div Dramatic Art, Sacramento Jr Col, 26-50; lectr, Univ Calif, 28-36; special librarian, Southern Utah State Col, 69- David Bispham Medal, 35. Chief Collabrs: Henry Chester Tracy, Fernando Diaz de Medina, Ralph Birchard. *Songs:* The Poet's Prayer; Music: Nona; The Lord Victorious (choral ode); O Captain! (choral ode) *Instrumental Works:* String Trio "Arizona"; The Arthurian Suite; numerous sonatas for wind & stringed instruments; also many songs and choral numbers. *Scores:* Operas: In the Pasha's Garden; Ramona; Ollanta, el Jeffe Kolla (gold, silver & bronze medals, Bolivarian Games, La Paz, Bolivia, 77); Operettas: The Two Gentlemen of Verona; The Bachelor Belles; Ballets: The Closed Gate; The Maid, the Demon, and the Samurai.

SEYMOUR, TOT　　　　　　　　　　　　　ASCAP 1921
author
b New York, NY; d New York, Aug 31, 66. Educ: Miss Ely's Sch. Staff lyricist, publ co. Wrote spec material for Fannie Brice, Mae West, Belle Baker & Sophie Tucker. Under contract to Paramount, also wrote for radio. Chief Collabr: Vee Lawnhurst, Others: Jesse Greer, J Fred Coots, Pete Wendling, Jean Schwartz. *Songs:* Sunday Go to Meetin' Time; What's the Name of That Song?; Us on a Bus; And Then Some; Accent on Youth; Cross Patch; No Other One; The Bride Comes Home; You Don't Love Right; Please Keep Me in Your Dreams; When the Leaves Bid the Trees Goodbye; Swingin' in a Hammock; I'm Making Hay in the Moonlight; Pretending You Care; Watchin' the Trains Go By; I Miss a Little Miss; Good Evenin'.

SGAMBELLONE, GUIDO VINCENT　　　　　ASCAP 1968
composer, author, teacher
b Reggio Calabria, Italy, Feb 22, 04. Educ: Ginnasium, 5 yrs; Vincent Bellini Sch Music, Naples; studied operatic score with Franco De Gregorio, Antonio Galano. Sang baritone lead & comprimary parts with Quillan & San Carlo Opera Co in Italy & US, 24-31. Opened singing sch, 34-42. Served with 7th USA in Europe, 42-45, Bronze Star, two Presidential Citations. Recorded many songs. Active in music bus, incl composing. Chief Collabr: P J Goody. *Songs & Instrumental Works:* The Road to Love; Searching for a Star; The Calm Before the Storm; Phantom Beauty; There's No Mistaking Love; Novelli; Middle the Road; Calabria; Lord I Am Not Worthy; Rose D'Altri Tempi; This is Your Song; By Midnight Sky (piano concerto); Spring is a Love Song; Faded Kisses; The Stairs; Only Yesterday; Is it Legal to Love You; I'm Gonna Sit Right Down and Cry; One to Love; Follow Me; Nostalgic Tango; Do Not Deceive Me; I Wish I Knew; It Was Almost Like a Song; Picture in the Fire; We March for Victory.

SHACKELFORD, RUDOLPH OWENS　　　　ASCAP 1973
composer, author
b Gloucester County, Va, Apr 18, 44. Educ: Va Commonwealth Univ, BM(magna cum laude), 66; Univ Ill, Urbana, MM(organ), 67, MM(comp), 68, DMA, 71, studied with Gordon Binkerd. Free lance comp of serious concert music & writer of articles on serious 20th Century Europ & Am music, 71- Residence fels: Yaddo, 72, 73, 76 & 77; The MacDowell Colony, 74, 76 & 78; Ossabaw Island Project, 75 & 76; Rockefeller Study & Conference Ctr, Bellagio, Italy, 77. Original comp comn & performed by: Hartt Col Music, Hollins Col, Pa State Univ, Southern Methodist Univ, Cleveland Museum of Art & others. Now under contract with G K Hall & Co, Boston, to write first book-length study of Vincent Persichetti for publ in new Twayne Musical Arts Series. Guest lectr on music at Skidmore Col, Southern Methodist Univ & Ripon Col, Wis. *Songs & Instrumental Works:* Epitaffio (in Memoriam Luigi Dallapiccola, for guitar); Le Tombeau de Stravinsky (harpsichord); Airlooms (suite; harpsichord); Sweelinck Variations (harpsichord or organ); Trio Sonata 1970 (organ); Canonic Variations Vom Himmel hoch, da Komm' ich her (organ; first prize, 74 Spokane World Expo Contest); Nine Aphorisms (organ); Sonata for Organ; Buxtehude Redux (chorale fantasia) (organ); Three Pieces for Contemporary Children or Archaic Adults (piano); Berg im Nebel/Berg im Spiegel (piano); The Light Passages (variations on theme by Beethoven; clarinet, percussion, narration); Olive Tree, First Pilgrim (canticle; trumpet, organ, narration); Wandering (fantasia after Schubert; French horn, piano, narration); String Trio; String Quartet I; The Broken Tower (string quartet II, soprano; texts by Hart Crane, Dante, Shakespeare & comp); Nighthawks (three cityscapes after Edward Hopper; brass quintet, slides, narration); Toccata and Threnody (wind ens); The Crucifix Across the Mountains (wind ens, narration); Variations for Orchestra.

SHACKLEY, GEORGE H　　　　　　　　　ASCAP 1944
composer, author, conductor
b Quincy, Mass, Mar 7, 1890; d St Petersburg, Fla, Oct 25, 59. Studied music with Allen Daugherty, J Treavor Garmey, R Huntington Woodman & Philip James. Gen music dir, MBS, 28-35 & Fed Coun Churches. Minister of music, West End Col Church, NY, 34. Music dir radio prog "Ave Maria Hour." *Songs:* Sacred: Put on the Whole Armor of God; Down a Country Lane; Mother Love; There's a New Road; Let's Go to Church Next Sunday; Dear Savior Bless Us Ere We Go; Alleluia, Alleluia, Alleluia.

SHAFFER, JEANNE ELLISON
composer, author, singer
b Knoxville, Tenn, May 25, 25. Educ: Stephens Col, AA, 44; Samford Univ, BM, 54; Birmingham Southern Col, MM, 57; George Peabody Col, PhD, 70. As a child, had role of Jeannette MacDonald in "Girl of the Golden West." Sang in radio & concert, 15 yrs; soloist with Paul Whiteman's Orch, 2 yrs, also with Vincent Lopez, Rudy Vallee, Glenn Miller; also Louisville, Nashville, Peoria, Birmingham Symph & Spoleto Fest, Charleston, 2 yrs. Teacher, 54- Publ choral music, 51- Head dept visual & performing arts, Judson Col, Marion, Ala, 73-76 & Huntingdon Col, Montgomery, Ala, 76- Chief Collabr: Robert S Barmettler. *Songs & Instrumental Works:* Hymn Tune Meditations (vols I-II, organ); Broadman Organ and Piano Duets; Laudate Dominum, omnes gentes (SATTB, strings & continuo); Boats and Candles (cycle for string quartet, flute, soprano); Eternity (cycle for voice, piano, poems of William Blake); On Gardens, Minutes and Butterflies (cycle for oboe, voice, piano); SATB, Anthem: A Man Went Forth to Die; From Henceforth, O My Lord; Show Me, O Lord; Christmas Cantata: Sing Noel; Lenten Cantata: The Words From the Cross. *Scores:* Ballet: Rainbows (comn by Montgomery Civic Ballet); Chamber Opera: The Ghost of Susan B Anthony.

SHAFFER, LLOYD M (MARCOS MORENO)　　ASCAP 1944
composer, conductor
b Ridgway, Pa, Sept 21, 01. Educ: Allegheny Col; Univ Cincinnati Col Music; cond & comp with Tibor Serly, NY. Cond, all major radio networks & Chesterfield Supper Club with Perry Como; recordings, Capitol, Forecast & others, Hollywood. Chief Collabrs: Lee Allman, John Klemmer. *Songs:* Music: Smoke Dreams; I Want to Be a Star; El Amoria; In This Goodbye; Lyrics: Panama Piano. *Instrumental Works:* Three Etchings (voice, piano, strings); Suite for Multiple Horns (tympani, strings); View From a Satellite (Six Impressions of Space); Ballade for Atlantis (six scenes); Three Dance Designs (orch).

SHAFFER, MAX　　　　　　　　　　　　ASCAP 1961
composer, author
b Atlanta, Ga, Dec 25, 25. Educ: Univ Ga, BCS. *Songs:* Love Me; Bongo Boo Boo.

SHAFFNER, ROBERTA ROSE (BOBBIE)　　ASCAP 1971
composer, author, publisher
b Philadelphia, Pa, Dec 2, 37. Educ: Temple Univ; Univ Pa; pvt music study with Bernard Peiffer. Formed writing, arr, producing & promotion unit with husband for records & musical commercials. Chief promotion for off songs for the City of Philadelphia & Commonwealth of Pa. Mem, Nat League Am Pen Women; founder, Pa Asn for State Song. Hon Citizen's Award, Plains, Ga; hon citation, Pa House of Representatives. Chief Collabr: Henry Shaffner, husband. *Songs:* Philadelphia (Philly, I Love You); Pennsylvania—Gee! It's Great!; America, This Is America; Garlands of Holly; Jimmy Carter; Plains, Georgia; The Two Street Strut; The Phillies Are Winning Again; Scotty's Strut; Pass Up That Cigarette; Children's Songs; The Breath of Spring; You Don't Have to Love Me (Every Minute of the Day); The Colder It Gets (The Warmer Grows My Love for You); God Give Us Men; Paris in the Fall.

SHAFTEL, ARTHUR (BOBB ARTHUR)　　　ASCAP 1957
composer, author, musician
b Brooklyn, NY, June 26, 16. Educ: Boys' High Sch; City Col New York, BSS; clarinet instr with Gerardo Iaselli. Orch leader & vocalist on NY radio stas. Chief Collabrs: Sunny Skylar, Fletcher Henderson. *Songs:* Just a Little Bit South of North Carolina; Atlanta GA; There's That Lonely Feeling Again; Love Is So Terrific; I'm Gonna Love You; Whatta Ya Gonna Do?; The Kiss; Blind Date; Lyrics: Hard to Get. *Scores:* Musical Revue: Fair and Warmer.

SHAFTEL, SELIG SIDNEY
See Skylar, Sunny

SHAHAN, PAUL　　　　　　　　　　　　ASCAP 1958
composer, educator
b Grafton, WVa, Jan 2, 23. Educ: Fairmont State Col, BM; WVa Univ, MM; Peabody Col, MEd; Eastman Sch Music; studied with Weldon Hart, Roy Harris, Kent Kennan, Bernard Rogers & Howard Hanson. Instrumental supvr, Grafton Schs. Staff arr, WSM, Nashville, 51-52. Prof theory & brass, Murray State Col. *Instrumental Works:* Spring Festival; Fiesta en Espana; The City of David; 150th Psalm; The Fountain Head; Brass choir, perc: Spectrums; Leipzig Towers (60th Thor Johnson Award). *Scores:* Opera: Stubblefield Story.

SHANAPHY, EDWARD JOHN　　　　　　　ASCAP 1965
composer, author
b Jersey City, NJ, Mar 8, 38. Educ: Cath Univ of Am, Sch Music, BM & MM; comp studies with Dr George Thaddeus Jones. Pianist/comp/arr; arr, USAREUR, 62-64; with Bobby Hackett, Glenn Miller Orch & Ray McKinley, 64; dir marketing, CBS Columbia House, 65-72; owner & publ, Sheet Music Mag & Virtuoso Mag. *Songs:* Pinocchio; Lyrics: 2000 Year Old Sailor.

SHAND, TERRY — ASCAP 1938
composer, author, conductor

b Uvalde, Tex, Oct 1, 04; d. Pianist in silent film theatres. Cond of one of first orchs on radio. Played piano, sang & recorded for Freddy Martin for several yrs. Had own band during WW II. Chief Collabs: Jimmy Eaton, Bob Merrill. *Songs:* I Double Dare You; I'm Gonna Lock My Heart and Throw Away the Key; Dance With a Dolly; Cry Baby Cry; Why Doesn't Somebody Tell Me These Things?; Your Eyes Are Bigger Than Your Heart; I'm a Whistlin'; The Ukulele Song; I Ain't Gonna Take It Settin' Down; You Don't Have to Be a Baby to Cry; Who Threw Confetti in Angelo's Spaghetti?; My Extraordinary Gal; Stephen Foster's Unfinished Song; If and When I Fall in Love; Just Sittin' Fishing By a Lazy Stream; Music: Wedding of the Birds; You've Got No Time For Me; Table Under a Tree; Maria; Country Boy; Today Didn't Pay to Get Up; Honey Don't You Love Me Anymore?; Am I Talking Out of Turn?. *Instrumental Works:* My Philosophy.

SHAND, WILLIAM — ASCAP 1972
author

b Glasgow, Scotland, Dec 20, 02. Wrote var bks of poetry in Eng; var bks containing translations into Span of US contemporary poetry; bks containing translations into Span of Eng poetry; also var plays which rec'd official awards. Wrote two bks of short stories. Author of libretto for opera by Alberto Ginastera, "Beatrix Cenci," which was presented in The Kennedy Ctr, Washington, 71. Chief Collabr: Alberto Girri.

SHANK, CLIFFORD EVERETT, JR (BUD) — ASCAP 1959
composer, saxophonist, flutist

b Dayton, Ohio, May 27, 26. Educ: Univ NC. Saxophonist, Alvino Rey & Charlie Barnet Orchs; also Stan Kenton's Innovations in Modern Music, Lighthouse All-Stars. Led own group in nightclubs; made many records. *Scores:* Film: Slippery When Wet; Barefoot Adventure; War Hunt.

SHANKAR, RAVI
composer, author

b Benares, 1920. Educ: Studied under Ustad Allauddin Khan; Hon Doctorate, Univ Calif, Santa Cruz. Musician; dir, comp & cond, India Radio, 49-56; founder & dir, Kinnara Sch Music, Bombay, 62 & Los Angeles, 67; res lectr, Univ Calif, Los Angeles, 64 & City Col New York, 67. Staff mem, Calif Inst of Arts. Author, "My Music, My Life." *Songs & Instrumental Works:* Film Music: Charly; Chappaqua; Pather Panchali/Aparajito/The World of Apu; The Flute and the Bow; The Chairy Tale; TV Music: Alice in Wonderland; numerous pieces for var ensembles; Concerto for Sitar and Orchestra (comn by LSO). *Scores:* Ballet: The Discovery of India.

SHANKLIN, WAYNE, SR — ASCAP 1950
composer, author

b Joplin, Mo, June 6, 16; d Santa Barbara, Calif, June 16, 70. Educ: High sch. Chief Collabs: Al Sherman, Red Callender. *Songs:* Jezebel; Little Child; Chanson D'Amour; Primrose Lane; The Big Hurt; West of the Wall. *Scores:* Film background: Angel Baby.

SHANNON, HARRY — ASCAP 1970
composer, lyricist, singer

b Reno, Nev, Dec 4, 48. Educ: Ganesha High Sch, Pomona, Calif. With group, Back Porch Majority, 69; did commercials, Ford Motor Co, 71-72; with bands & clubs, Las Vegas & Tahoe, also nat tours, 72-74; exec staff writer & dir, ATV Music, 75- Chief Collabs: Tom Bahler, Barry Mann, John Lewis Parker. *Songs:* Cowboy; The Other Women; Someday Soon (theme from movie); Lovely Lady; So Good, So Rare, So Fine; Daddy They're Playing a Song About You; Why Don't We Just Sleep on It Tonite; Almost All the Way to Love.

SHANNON, JAMES ROYCE — ASCAP 1938
composer, author, producer

b Adrian, Mich, May 13, 1881; d Pontiac, Mich, May 19, 46. Organized own theatrical co, then toured US & Europe. Mgr, music store chain, Mich; asst mgr-dir, weekly shows, Majestic Theatre, Detroit, 19. Wrote spec material for vaudeville, also dance numbers for Pavlova. Drama critic, Detroit Free Press. *Songs:* Too-Ra-Loo-Ra-Loo-Ral; The Misouri Waltz; Aloha Sunset Land; My Dream of Yesterday; Just an Old Sweetheart of Mine; Mary Was a Real Nice Girl; Raise a Little Army of Your Own; There Is a Red Bordered Flag in the Window; Spanish Rose; Climbing the Stairway of Love.

SHAPERO, HAROLD S(AMUEL) — ASCAP 1952
composer, professor, director

b Lynn, Mass, Apr 29, 20. Educ: Harvard Univ, AB, 41, Naumburg & Paine fels, 42-43; studied musical comp with Slonimsky, Krenek, Piston, Hindemith & Boulanger. Gershwin Prize & Bearns Prize, 45; two Guggenheim fels, 47-48; Fulbright grant, Rome, Italy, 49-50, also senior Fulbright grant, Italy, 62-63; Ford Found Comn, 60; comp in residence, Am Acad in Rome, 70-71 & others. Prof music & dir of Electronic Music Studios, Brandeis Univ, 51- *Songs & Instrumental Works:* Three Sonatas for Piano; Sonata for Piano Four-Hands; Sonata for Violin and Piano; Serenade in D for String Orchestra; Symphony for Classical Orchestra; String Quartet No 1; Sonata in F Minor for Piano; Hebrew Cantata; Partita for Piano and Small Orchestra; also 2 Hebrew songs for tenor, piano & string orch.

SHAPEY, RALPH — ASCAP 1964
composer, conductor, educator

b Philadelphia, Pa, Mar 12, 21. Educ: Univ Pa; Univ Chicago; studied violin with Emanuel Zetlin & comp with Stefan Wolpe. Asst cond, Philadelphia Nat Youth Admin Symph Orch, 38-42; cond, McMillan Theatre, Times Hall, New York, New York Philh Chamber Soc & var other concerts; guest cond, Philadelphia Symph Orch, Buffalo Symph Orch, Chicago Symph Orch & London Symph Orch. WW II, USAF. Comp & cond in residence, Tanglewood. Prof music, music dir, Univ Chicago Contemporary Chamber Players, 64- Rec'd MacDowell Colony fel, 56-58 & Ital Govt grant, 59-60. Awards: Frank Huntington Beebe Award, 53; Brandeis Creative Arts Award, 62; Edgar Stern Family Fund Award, 62; William & Noma Copley Found Award, 62; Arts & Letters Award, 66; Nauremberg Recording Award, 66; Norlin Found Award, 78; ASCAP Award, 78-79; Am Comp Alliance Laurel Leaf Award, 79. *Instrumental Works:* Evocation (violin, piano & perc); String Quartets No VI and VII; Configurations (flute & piano); 21 Variations for Piano; 31 Variations for Piano (Fromm Variations); Ontogeny (symph orch); Invocation (concerto for violin & orch); Rituals (symph orch); Concerto (clarinet & chamber group); Discourse (four instruments). *Songs & Instrumental Works:* Incantations (soprano & 10 instruments); Songs of Ecstasy (soprano, piano & perc); Praise (oratorio for bass baritone, double chorus & chamber group); Dimensions (soprano & 23 instruments); O Jerusalem (soprano & flute); Songs of Eros (soprano, orch & tape); The Covenant (soprano, 16 players & tape); Songs of Songs No I, II, III.

SHAPIRO, BEVERLY MYERS (BEVERLY JANIS)
author, singer, actress

b Ossining, NY. Educ: Boston Cons, voice with Jessie Drew, Alicia Zepilli, Rosalie Snyder & David Craig & acting with Marc Daniels, Sanford Meisner & Betty Cashman. Was original Jenny Hildebrand in opera, "Street Scene." Appeared in theatre, TV, commercials, radio & maj stock productions. Chief Collabs: Irma Jurist, Richard Oliver, Len Maddox. *Songs:* Lyrics: Too Much Loneliness; I Won't Let Myself; Penny People.

SHAPIRO, CARL FREDERICK — ASCAP 1959
composer, author

b Jersey City, NJ, Feb 28, 38. Educ: Self-taught; studied Schillinger Syst Comp & Arr with Richard Benda, 60-61. Author poem, "It's Only a Piece of Cloth," which rec'd Presidential commendation & acclaim by nat patriotic & fraternal orgns. *Songs & Instrumental Works:* Please Be Mine; Choral: Liberty Tree (bicentennial anthem); Psalm 100; 23rd Psalm; The Lord's Prayer.

SHAPIRO, DAN — ASCAP 1942
composer, author, comedy writer

b Brooklyn, NY, Jan 3, 10. Educ: Pub schs. Wrote & directed musicals in summer stock, Upstate NY. Wrote special cafe shows & night club material for Joe E Lewis, Milton Berle, Henny Youngman, Tony Martin. Wrote radio & TV shows for Bob Hope, Eddie Cantor, Danny Thomas, Dean Martin & Jerry Lewis, Jackie Gleason. Bway shows, "Artists and Models", "Follow the Girls", "Michael Todd's Peep Show", "Ankles Aweigh." To Hollywood, 48, films for Universal & RKO. Chief Collabs: Phil Charig, Sammy Fain, Milton Pascal, Jerry Livinston, Sam H Stept, Ben Oakland, Lester Lee, Jerry Seelen. *Songs:* No Room for the Groom; How Do I Know it's Real; Chico's Love Song; Poor Little Feb; Tyrone Shapiro (The Bronx Caballero); Lyrics: I Wanna Get Married; Over a Bottle of Wine; The Next Time Around; An Eleven O'clock Song; Kiss Me and Kill Me With Love; Honeymoon; Where You Are; Shave and a Haircut, Shampoo; Endlessly; When Was the Last Time; Take Me to Town; Nothing Can Replace a Man; Nothing at All; A Man Once Said; I'm Gonna Hang My Hat on a Tree That Grows in Brooklyn; His and Hers; You're Perf; Today Will Be Yesterday Tomorrow; I've Had a Very Good Xmas; A Woman Ages Quicker Than a Man; I Just Need $999,999.99 (to Be a Millionaire).

SHAPIRO, KENNETH STEVEN — ASCAP 1967
composer, author

b Brooklyn, NY, Sept 25, 43. Educ: Calif State Univ, Northridge, BA(drama). Produced, directed & wrote col shows, also produced & wrote spec musical material for TV specials, 67- Chief Collabs: Jerry Bilik, George Wilkins, Dan Shapiro, Jerry Livingston, Dennis Livingston. *Songs:* Questions Children Ask; Sea World Blues; Sittin' on a Bar Stool Blues; Do You Like Yourself?; Lyrics: The Greatest Show on Earth; Something for Everyone (At the Circus); Lookin' Your Best (theme song for Golden Globes Awards); Psychodelic Sally; Candidate for Love; Old Mac Donald; The Shortest Distance; An Old Fashioned Christmas Tree; All You Need for Christmas; Stand Up, Sit Down.

SHAPIRO, MAURICE — ASCAP 1952
composer, pianist, saxophonist

b Washington, DC, Sept 6, 06. Educ: High sch; pvt music study. Chief Collabr: Buddy Feyne. *Songs:* Monte Carlo Melody; Why; For Always; Annabelle; Ne Parley Plus.

SHAPIRO, MICHAEL JEFFREY — ASCAP 1973
composer

b Brooklyn, NY, Feb 1, 51. Educ: Columbia Col, BA, 73; Juilliard Sch Music, MM, 75; studied piano with Consuelo Elsa Clark, comp with Elie Siegmeister, Vincent Persichetti, solfege with Renee Longy. Comp opera, orch works, chamber music, choral pieces and over eighty songs; accompanist, song recitals; broadcast journalist, educr, cond. *Songs:* Music: Canciones (soprano & piano); Dublin Songs (soprano & piano); Songs for American Poets (bass & piano); Erotic Songs (coloratura soprano & piano); Chorals: Three Shakespeare Madrigals (SATB); Three Psalms (SSAA); There Is That in Me (6 soloists, SATB, brass, perc, piano); By The River of Babylon (SATB & organ). *Instrumental Works:* Orch: Concerto for Two Guitars and Strings; Lamentations (large orch); A Declaration of Independence, July 4, 1776 (narrator & orch); Sinfonia Concertante (violin, cello & strings); Pomes Penyeach (symph orch); Chamber Music: Sonata (violin & piano); Sonata (clarinet & piano); Piano: First Sonata; Second Sonata; Songs of the Jewish Ghetto; Mysteries. *Scores:* Opera: The Love of Don Perlimplin and Belisa in the Garden.

SHAPIRO, MICHAEL JOSEPH — ASCAP 1964
composer
b Brooklyn, NY, Nov 10, 40. Educ: Columbia Col, BA; studied comp with Otto Luening, piano with William Beller, cond with Rudolph Thomas. Concert pianist. Has done commercials & sta identifications. Co-owner, ServiSound Inc, New York. Scores indust shows, videotapes & commercials. Chief Collabrs: Frank Levy, Jeff Gusman, Gershon Kingsley. *Scores:* Films: Geronimo Jones; The Longest Journey; The Anatomy of a Parade; Beloved Island.

SHAPIRO, SUSAN — ASCAP 1958
author
b Baltimore, Md, Nov 4, 23. Educ: Monticello Girls Col. Chief Collabr: Ted Shapiro (husband). *Songs:* Ask Anyone in Love; Time; The Merry Christmas Waltz; Your Love Has Made Me Young; All That Any Heart Can Hope For.

SHAPIRO, TED — ASCAP 1924
composer, publisher, pianist
b New York, NY, Oct 31, 1899. Educ: High sch. Vaudeville accompanist to Nora Bayes & Evan Tanguay; music dir, comp & arr for Sophie Tucker, 21-66. Own music publ co, Miami, Fla. Chief Collabrs: Benny Davis, Jack Lawrence & Susan Shapiro (wife). *Songs & Instrumental Works:* He's Home for a Little While; If I Had You; A Handful of Stars; To You; Winter Weather; Far-Away Island; Sitting in the Sand a-Sunnin'; Now I'm in Love; You'll Be Reminded of Me; Starlight Souvenirs; Time; This Is No Dream; Dog on the Piano; Puttin' on the Dog; Music: Ask Anyone in Love.

SHARALEE
See Lucas, Sharalee

SHARBUTT, DELBERT EUGENE — ASCAP 1953
composer, author, announcer
b Cleburne, Tex, Feb 16, 12. Educ: Tex Christian Univ. Studied piano from age 5 to 9; began saxophone & clarinet at age 13. Played in col band & local dance bands. Entered radio while in col, 30; staff announcer, CBS, New York, 34-37. Announcer, big name bands, Bob Hope's first radio prog, Isham Jones' prog, Guy Lombardo's progs, Hit Parades for Lucky Strike, Lanny 'n' Andy, Lanny Ross prog & other nat progs on radio & TV. Worked on commercial progs with Tommy Dorsey, Glen Gray & Artie Shaw. Was commercial spokesman for Campbell's Soups. Did Bob Crosby's Club 15 with Jerry Gray, Andrews Sisters & Modernaires. Musician & singer. Chief Collabrs: Frank Stanton, Dick Uhl, Joseph Lilley, Kim Gannon. *Songs:* A Day at a Time; Why Did You Kiss Me?; My Window on Main Street; Music: Nickel Serenade; Lonely Lullaby; The Best Years of Our Lives; Violins; The Day Will Come; My Love; I'd Love To; Lyrics: A Romantic Guy, I.

SHARP, BARBARA LOU — ASCAP 1974
composer, author
b Harlingen, Tex, Jan 12, 44. *Songs & Instrumental Works:* Your Shoeshine Girl.

SHARP, JOSEPH PERSHING — ASCAP 1966
composer, author, singer
b Madisonville, Tenn. Educ: Self-taught on guitar. Musician; had own band; songwriter. *Songs:* The April Love Song; Missouri Show Me Gal; Poison Honey; The Little White Church; Climbing to the Mountain Top.

SHARP, ROBERT LOUIS, JR (AGNES JONES) — ASCAP 1963
composer, author, singer
b Topeka, Kans, Nov 26, 24. Educ: Greenwich House Music Sch; Manhattan Sch Music, 2 yrs. First song publ, 56. Recorded as singer for Wing & Everest Record Cos. Chief Collabrs: Freddy James, Gerald E Teifer. *Songs:* Unchain My Heart; Don't Set Me Free; Blues for Mister Charlie; Film/TV: Doin' the Impossible; The Little Toy Ship.

SHARPE, CLAUDE — ASCAP 1963
composer, conductor
b Maynardville, Tenn, July 20, 05; d. Educ: Col; cons. Organized Old Hickory Singers, WSM, Nashville, also choir dir, then music librarian. Chief Collabrs: Geoffrey O'Hara, Beasley Smith. *Songs:* Cheer Up World; The Nashville Polka; Lord Send an Angel.

SHARPE, JOHN RUFUS, III — ASCAP 1950
composer, author, music publisher
b Berkeley, Calif, Oct 31, 09. Educ: St Joseph's Acad, West Berkeley; Calif Mil Acad, Los Angeles; Galileo High Sch, San Francisco; Univ Calif Extension, creative writing. Began career as songplugger/writer, 27. First song publ, 28. Sang lead with trio, radio, band, night clubs, casuals, San Francisco, 33-35. Staff writer, music publ exec, Hollywood, 41-43. Passenger agent, Santa Fe Railway, San Francisco, 44-66. Wrote for stage; lyrics & sketches for three revues, San Francisco, "Black and Blue Eagle" (35), "Friskiana" (45), "Dance Anyone?" (53). Formed own publ catalog, Rondo Music Co, 65. Mem, Am Guild Authors & Composers. Chief Collabrs: Jerry Herst, Art Wilson, Johnny Mercer, Michel Michelet. *Songs:* Lyrics: So Rare; Dream Peddler's Serenade; We'll Get a Bang Out of Life; What Would You Like to Do Tonight; Shower of Kisses; Chinoiserie (suite of two songs for voice, two flutes, bassoon, harp, celesta & piano); Newspaper Clippings (suite of four songs for voice & piano); The Headsman's Song (for basso & piano). *Scores:* Libretto: Cathedral Windows (oratorio in four parts for quintet of soloists, choir, & organ or piano).

SHARPLES, WINSTON S — ASCAP 1948
composer
b Fall River, Mass, Mar 1, 09; d Savannah, Ga, Apr 3, 78. Comp, film & TV background music. *Songs:* It's a Hap Hap Happy Day; When You Left Me; What Has She Got That I Haven't Got?. *Albums:* The Mighty Hercules.

SHAVER, FLOYD HERBERT (BUSTER) — ASCAP 1956
composer, dancer, pianist
b Ogdensburg, NY, Feb 7, 05. Educ: High sch; pvt piano study. Had vaudeville act, Buster Shaver & His Midgets; later, Buster Shaver With Olive & George. Performed throughout US, Europe, Australia & SAm. Appeared in Bway musicals: "Earl Carroll's Vanities" (2 ed); "Are You With It?" Vocal coach & pianist, Calif. *Songs:* I Kissed You a Million Times.

SHAVERS, CHARLES — ASCAP 1952
composer, conductor, trumpeter
b New York, NY, Aug 3, 17; d. Educ: Bordentown Mil Acad. Trumpeter & arr with orchs incl John Kirby, Lucky Millinder, Count Basie, Tommy Dorsey & Benny Goodman. Staff mem, CBS, 2 yrs. Toured with Jazz at Philh unit, US & Europe. Has led own quartet; made many records. *Songs & Instrumental Works:* Undecided; Dawn on the Desert; Pastel Blue; A Waltz for Tommy; Why Begin Again?; Don't Be Late; Period of Adjustment; I Kid You Not; Minor Blues; Big Time Blues.

SHAW, ARNOLD (KEN SLOAN) — ASCAP 1947
composer, author, instructor
b New York, NY, June 28, 09. Educ: City Col New York, BS; Columbia Univ, MA; Univ Nev, Las Vegas. Pianist on radio & bandleader. Dir publicity & advert, Robbins, Feist & Miller music corporations, 44. Ed, Swank Mag, 45. Dir publicity & advert, Leeds Music Corp, 46. Vpres & gen professional mgr, Duchess Music Corp, 49, Hill & Range Songs, 53 & Edward B Marks Music Corp, 55-66. Co-ed, "Schillinger Syst of Musical Comp"; ed, "Mathematical Basis of the Arts." Author 9 bks incl, "The Rock Revolution", "Honkers and Shouters", "The Rockin' 50s" & "52nd St: The Street of Jazz"; comp 6 collections modern piano pieces. Nev Comp of the Year, 73. Deems-Taylor/ASCAP Awards, 68 & 79. Pres, Las Vegas Music Teachers Asn, 75-77; chmn, Bolognini Scholarship Fund, 76-; nat adv bd, Fisk Univ Inst for Res in Black Am Music, 79; pres, Univ Musical Soc, Univ Nev, Las Vegas, 80. Chief Collabrs: Rosemary & Stephen Vincent Benet; Peter Lind Hayes; Richard Armour; Charles Tobias; Lou Singer. *Songs:* A Man Called Peter; Dungaree Doll; Acres of Diamonds; A Moth and a Flame; Woman Is a Five-Letter Word; Music: Sing a Song of Americans; What's Cookin'; I Have a Dream. *Instrumental Works:* Night Lights; Mobiles (10 graphic impressions for piano); Stabiles (12 images for piano); Plabiles (12 songs without words for piano); A Whirl of Waltzes; The Bubble-Gum Waltzes (11 young-at-heart melodies); The Mod Moppet.

SHAW, ARTIE — ASCAP 1942
composer, author, conductor
b New York, NY, May 23, 10. Arr & clarinetist in local orchs, New Haven. Formed own orch, 35, appearing in dance halls, theatres, radio, films & nightclubs. Chief Petty Officer, USNR, SPacific, WW II. Film distributor. Has made many records incl 8 golds. Annual lectr adult educ series, Univ Calif, Santa Barbara. Author: "The Trouble With Cinderella" & "I Love You, I Hate You, Drop Dead!" *Songs & Instrumental Works:* Comin' On; Back Bay Shuffle; Any Old Time; Traffic Jam; Non-Stop Flight; Summit Ridge Drive; Nightmare; Chant; Monsoon; Fee Fi Fo Fum; Free for All; Pastel Blue; Concerto for Clarinet; One Foot in the Groove; Moonray; Easy to Love.

SHAW, BARNETT — ASCAP 1955
composer, author
b Joplin, Mo, Dec 10, 14. Educ: Univ Tex, BA; Sorbonne, cert. Actor, play translator. Chief Collabr: Xavier Cugat. *Songs:* Apple, Cherry, Mince and Choc'late Cream; Lyrics: Night Must Fall; Musical: Bettina (London).

SHAW, CHARLES
ASCAP 1948

composer, author, pianist

b New York, NY, July 4, 06; d New York, Feb 13, 63. Educ: Fordham Univ, PhG; studied music with Milton Kraus. Pharmacist, 26-34. Pianist & arr, Lenny Herman Quintet. *Songs:* How Can You Do This to Me; Topsy Turvey Moon; Featherhead; Twenty-Seven Times Around the Block; Blue Sunrise; Poor Duffy; Audrey Goes to the Zoo; Rondo to a Pink Cloud; Samba Chiquita; Will You Take a Walk With Me?

SHAW, CLIFFORD
ASCAP 1954

composer, pianist

b Little Rock, Ark, Sept 19, 11; d Louisville, Ky, Jan 6, 76. Educ: Opportunity Sch, Knoxville; studied piano with Frank Nelson & Frederic Cowles. In music dept, sta WAVE, Louisville, 33. Taught piano; coached singers. Hon mem, MacDowell Music Study Club, Louisville. *Songs:* Arr: Black Is the Color of My True Love's Hair; He's Gone Away; I'm Sad and I'm Lonely; also settings to poems of Walt Whitman, R L Stevenson, Thomas Ford, Christina Rossetti, John Dryden & William Blake. *Instrumental Works:* Third Street Rhumba; Manhattan Barcarolle; Valentine.

SHAW, RICHARD RANDALL
ASCAP 1963

composer, author, singer

b West Stewartstown, NH, Feb 1, 1941. Educ: Kennett High Sch; Univ NH, BA, 63, studied art. Brandywine Singers, 61-66, Hillside Singers, 72-74, The Shaw Brothers, 70- Singer for concerts, nightclubs, TV. Recording artist, Joy, Metromedia, Brandywine & RCA record cos. Chief Collabr: David V Craig. *Songs:* The Day the Tall Ships Came; Ah, Man, See What Ya Done; Take Some Time to Smell the Roses; Happy Birthday, Boston; The Green Years; Katrina.

SHAW, SERENA
See Davison, Lita

SHAW, SYDNEY
ASCAP 1958

author

b Brooklyn, NY, Sept 28, 23; d New York, NY, May 29, 69. Chief Collabr: Alex Fogarty. *Songs:* Will I Find My Love Today?; Five Cups of Coffee; Hot Cha Cha; Dreamy; Lyrics: Heavenly; Evil Spelled Backwards; Faithfully; If You; Love Is a Gamble; I Love Jazz.

SHAW, TOMMY
ASCAP 1976

composer, author, singer

b Montgomery, Ala. With var club bands before joining STYX; guitarist. Chief Collabr: Dennis DeYoung. *Songs:* Fooling Yourself; Blue Collar Man; Renegade; Crystal Ball; Boat on the River.

SHAWN, NELSON A
ASCAP 1944

composer, author

b Chicago, Ill, Apr 19, 1898; d Evanston, Ill, Dec 22, 45. Radio exec with advert agencies. Citations for radio shows from Army & Navy. Chief Collabrs: Caesar Petrillo, Milton Samuels. *Songs:* Jim; Hale and Hearty; Sergeant, Can You Spare a Girl?; A Kiss in the Moonlight; There's One in a Million Like Mary; Don't You Cry for Me.

SHAY, LARRY
ASCAP 1925

composer, conductor, arranger

b Chicago, Ill, Aug 10, 1897. Educ: Bush Cons Music. Organized orch & entertainment unit while in service, WW I. Musical dir, Metro-Goldwyn-Mayer Studios, prog dir, NBC, New York. Chief Collabrs: Joe Goodwin, Haven Gillespie, Charles Tobias, Harry Harris. *Songs:* Walking With the Lord; Music: When You're Smiling (The Whole World Smiles With You); Everywhere You Go; Get Out and Get Under the Moon; Highways Are Happy Ways; Tie Me to Your Apron Strings Again; I'm Knee Deep in Daisies; You're In Kentucky, Sure As You're Born; That's Georgia; Too Tired; Beautiful; I'd Love to Call You My Sweetheart; Gee, But I'd Like to Make You Happy; Our Old Home Team; By the Light of the Stars; Don't Cross Your Fingers, Cross Your Heart; Love Me Sweet and Love Me Long; It Takes So Long to Say Goodbye; The Fly Outflew the Flea; There's a Ranch in the Sky; Who Wouldn't Be Jealous of You?; Our Silver Anniversary; This Holy Love; Twenty-Third Psalm (musical version); The Lord's Prayer (musical version).

SHAYNE, BOB
ASCAP 1974

composer, author

b Paterson, NJ, July 21, 45. Educ: Univ Calif, Los Angeles. Comedy writer incl spec musical material.

SHAYNE, LARRY (RAY JOSEPH)
ASCAP 1941

composer, music publisher

b New York, NY, Nov 22, 09. Educ: NY Univ, 1 yr; Lehigh Univ, 2 yrs. With Famous Music Corp & affiliates, 34-42. Enlisted in USA, 42-46. Returned to Famous Music Corp, 46; joined Paramount Studios, 47, Universal Studios, 55. Started own publ cos, 58. Elected publ mem, ASCAP, 58, mem bd. Chief Collabr: Mack David. *Songs:* Music: A Sinner Kissed an Angel.

SHEEHAN, NEIL JOSEPH
ASCAP 1972

composer, author, manager

b New York, NY, Oct 5, 46. Educ: Carle Place High Sch; Villanova Univ, BS(mech eng), 68; Harvard Univ, grad study, 69; Univ Calif, Berkeley, pre-med, 74-75. Singer, Jagged Edges, 65; judge, Int Song Fest, Sopot, Poland, 72; organizer of pop group the Squares. Chief Collabrs: Joseph Satriani; Leon Martell. *Songs:* Somebody Look Like You (number 3 song in Poland, 72); Lyrics: Is It Real?; I Never Want to See Your Face Again; You Can't Get Away. *Scores:* Bway show: Rox.

SHEEN, MICKEY
ASCAP 1959

composer, author, drummer

b Brooklyn, NY, Dec 13, 27. Educ: High Sch Music & Art; Juilliard; RCA Inst; NY Univ. With Glenn Miller Air Force Band, WW II; studio recording artist. Consult, tech adv & coach, "The Gene Krupa Story," Columbia Pictures. Featured artist in concerts at Carnegie Hall, UN Council Room & Lincoln Ctr; with many name bands, groups & singers. Appeared on TV. Lectr, clinician & performer, schs & cols. Author first textbook in art of drumming, "It's All in the Book." Past chmn perc music, Five Towns Col. Owns pvt music studio. *Songs:* Rock 'n' Roll Espanol; Halloween. *Instrumental Works:* Whistle Your Blues Away; Cha-Cha Blues.

SHEER, PHILIP
ASCAP 1954

composer, author

b New Haven, Conn, Apr 4, 15. Educ: Morris High Sch; studied with Collins Smith. Played from 37-41. USA, 42-46. Studied accordion, harmony & comp at Robotti Accordion Sch. Played club dates & steady band work until 53. Chief Collabrs: Ted Lehrman, Fred Lightner, Don Cauton, Morrie Alin, Neal Grossman, Walter Schanzer. *Songs:* Music: No Man is an Island; When I Go Home (Italian version "Quando Tornare A Casa"); It Makes a Difference To Me; The Flower and the Weed; First October Frost.

SHEETS, WALTER KESTER
ASCAP 1955

composer, arranger, orchestrator

b London, Ohio, Aug 7, 11. Educ: Pub schs & high sch, London; Miami Univ, 1 1/2 yrs; largely self taught in music. Taught popular piano in high sch, also taught in col for 1 yr; taught & arr, Bohemian Club, San Francisco, 5 yrs. Arr & comp, radio, TV & motion pictures; played in dance bands, Los Angeles; orchestrator, Walt Disney Productions, 25 yrs, now free lance.

SHEFTER, BERT ABRAM
ASCAP 1940

conductor, pianist, composer

b Poltaua, Russia, May 15, 04. Educ: Carnegie Tech, scholarship; Curtis Inst Music; Damrosch Inst. Mem famous piano team, Shefter & Gould (Morton). Cond own orch, featuring own comp & arr on numerous radio commercial shows, Sta WOR & NBC. Musical dir, Sta WINS, New York. Guest cond, Philh at Carnegie Hall, 46-47. Recorded for cos, Victor, Decca, Brunswick & made transc & service progs for Assoc Muzak. Chief Collabrs: Paul Sawtell, Mitchel Parish, Peter De Rose. *Songs & Instrumental Works:* The Lamp Is Low; Chopin's Ghost; Burglar's Revenge; The Aeroplane and the Bee; It's Grieg to Me; Haydn Seek; Traffic in Times Square; The Lonely Little Music Box; Moonbeams; Farmer Leaves the Hay; Prairie Portrait; Portrait of the Duke; Portrait of a Ballerina; Portrait of a Child; Lost in a Dream; Self Portrait; S O S; Locomotive; Taming the Devil; Trammin At the Fair; Under the Greenwood Tree; I'll Be Close to You; Toast to Paganini's Ghost; Twilight Serenade; Deserted Desert; Sonata Pathetic; Four Caricatures; Boogie Woogie Etudes. *Scores:* Films: Cattle Empire; Deerslayer; Kronas; Tematangi; The Cosmic Man; Counterplot; The Fly; Machete; Sierra Baron; The Big Circus; A Dog of Flanders; The Last Gun in Durango; The Return of the Fly; The Lost World; The Long Rope; Misty; Five Guns to Tombstone; Jack the Giant Killer; Voyage to the Bottom of the Sea; Wild Harvest; The Big Show; Young Guns of Texas; Cattle King; Motor Psycho; Flesh and Leather; Bandit Island; Scandal Incorporated; Wind Across the Everglades; Gigantis; Villa; Danger Game; Pier 5 Havana; The Last Shot You Hear; The Curse of the Fly; One Too Many; Holiday Rhythm; Leave It to the Marines; The Big Parade; Cross Roads; TV: 77 Sunset Strip; Sugarfoot; Bronco; Bourbon Street Beat; Maverick; The Roaring 20's; Hawaiian Eye; The Alaskans; Colt 45; Surfside Six; Lawman; Cheyenne.

SHELDON, EARL
ASCAP 1961

composer, conductor, arranger

b New York, NY, Jan 1, 15; d New York, Nov 14, 77. Educ: DeWitt Clinton High Sch. Arr for dance bands incl Tommy Dorsey, Tommy Tucker & Harry James. Cond & arr in radio, 45-49, then TV.

SHELDON, ERNIE
See Lieberman, Ernest Sheldon

SHELDON, SIDNEY
ASCAP 1964

author

b Chicago, Ill, Feb 11, 17. Co-librettist, "The Merry Widow" (New Opera Co production); "Redhead." Screenplays incl "The Bachelor and the Bobby Soxer" (Acad award, 47). Writer & producer TV series: "The Patty Duke Show" & "I Dream of Jeannie." Chief Collabr: Sid Ramin. *Songs:* When Love Has Gone;

Open Up Your Heart; I'm a Gamblin' Man; Brooklyn Heights High We Love You.

SHELLEY, GLADYS ASCAP 1941
composer, author

b NY. Educ: Professional schs; Columbia Univ. Ballerina, actress, poet laureate & lyricist. Chief Collabrs: Fred Astaire, Morton Gould, Abner Silver. *Songs:* Clown Town; He Will Call Again (I Will Fall Again); Sing Me a Tune; The Answer Is; Leave It to the Girls; Come on Over (Award); I Believe in Love; You Say Something Nice About Everybody; Flying Can Be Fun; The Show's on Me Tonight; My World Is You; An Old Song Is the Best Song; It Only Takes One Man; Stranger in the Mirror; Cheer-Up Syrup; Pavanne; Just Like Taking Candy From a Baby; Lady Clown; Cycles; If You Don't Know Your Bible (You Haven't Got a Prayer) (Award from Layman's Bible Comt); A Nurse in the US Army Corps (Hon Nurse Award); Ring Ting a Ling (UNICEF Award); Lyrics: How Did He Look?; Lifestyle; You Gotta Have a Man Around the House; Paper Roses; Christmas Is Christmas All Over the World; Peace and Harmony (Award from Brotherhood Soc); Experience Unnecessary.

SHELLY, LOUIS EDWARD ASCAP 1946
composer, author

b New Haven, Conn, Aug 1, 1898; d New York, NY, Oct 15, 57. Educ: High sch. Played semi-professional baseball. *Songs:* Everyone But Me; There's No Yellow in the Red White and Blue; Takin' the Trains Out; Twice in a Lifetime; A Dream Ago; Halfway to Montana.

SHELTON, JAMES H ASCAP 1950
composer, author

b Paducah, Ky, Dec 5, 12; d Miami, Fla, Sept 2, 75. *Songs:* Lamplight; I Dance Alone; Lilac Wine; Our Town; Four Young People; Tea in Chicago; I'm the Girl. *Scores:* Bway Stage: Mrs Patterson.

SHELTON, JERLINE ODELL ASCAP 1974
composer, author, voice instructor

b Chicago, Ill, June 3, 48. Educ: Crane High Sch, 65; Kennedy-King Col. Singer, performer in nightclubs & TV, producer, has own publ co, recording artist with GEC. Chief Collabr: Maurice D Commander. *Songs:* Spank Your Blank Blank; One More Time; Love Jones "75"; Sexy Baby; Hot Spot; Never Stop Dancing; Spank Your Thang; Lyrics: I Can't Seem to Forget You; Goddess of Love; Disco Boogie Mama; Spank with Love; Only Fooling Myself.

SHELTON, LARRY ZANE (ZIGGY WHO) ASCAP 1979
composer, author, singer

b Ft Worth, Tex, Nov 16, 50. Educ: Burleson High Sch; ETex State Univ, mem Phi Mu Alpha Sinfonia Fraternity Am; NTex State Univ; AMI Trade Sch, sales & marketing; Eastman Sch Music, studied trumpet with Conrad Baushka; studied voice with Charles Nelson; Univ Tex, Arlington, studied voice & vocal dir with James E Richards. Has performed prof with gold & platinum recording artists such as Greg Allman, Marshall Tucker, Tiny Tim, Johnnie Taylor, Disco Lady, Archie Bell & the Daells & Walter Scott; now has own act, Zane and Hogan, which records with LeCam Records from Eng. Portray a cartoon & TV character, Freddy, the Disco Frog; also portray Cowboy Hollywood in Bway musical of same name. Has appeared on several TV shows. Chief Collabrs: Johnnie Taylor, Phil Gramm, Jim Wright, Maj Bill Smith, Merrill Ellis, Mr Diulio, Mark Hanby, John Douglas, David Beak, Oral Roberts, Rex Humbard, Jack Van Impe, Mike Borak, Ollie Carson, Marjorie Thamp, Floyd Shelton. *Songs & Instrumental Works:* Studio 54; Happy Trails; Step Into Your Love; Freddy, the Disco Frog; Cowboy Hollywood; Texas Boogie; Space Child (lyric); Tokyo Nights; Latin Nights; Infinity's Child.

SHEPARD, ANN
See Mazlen, Ann

SHEPARD, JOAN ASCAP 1967
composer, author, actress

b New York, NY, Jan 7, 33. Educ: Prof Children's Sch; Royal Acad Dramatic Art. Prof actress since age 7; was in 10 Bway shows, TV & others. Co-founder & producer, The Fanfare Theatre Ens Inc. Chief Collabrs: Evan Thompson, John Clifton, Joe Bousard. *Scores:* Musical Plays for Children: Annie Oakley and Buffalo Bill; Puss in Boots; Rumplestiltskin; Little Red Riding Hood; Alice Through the Looking Glass.

SHEPARD, ROBERT BLOOMFIELD ASCAP 1969
composer, singer

b Phoenix, Ariz, Apr 28, 27. Educ: Riverside Polytech High Sch, Calif; Los Angeles City Col, Calif; Peirce Jr Col, Woodland Hills, Calif; tutored with Roy Reid Brighall, Trinity Col, London, Eng. Arr, comp, orchr, cond; singer, movies, shows, TV; recording singer. Chief Collabrs: Wendell St Clair, Duane Mouer. *Songs:* I Am Not Alone; Music: My Confidence; Love; Give Way to Love; This New Day.

SHEPARD, VENDLA LORENTZON ASCAP 1962
composer, author

b Smaland, Sweden. Educ: Värnamo Högskola; Stockholm Royal Acad Music; Stockholm Borgaschoola of Literature, Language & Eng; Brigham Young Univ;

schs in Calif & Ohio. Songwriter, US & Europe. Did progs for Swed radio & TV. Working on new album. Chief Collabrs: Jan-ake Gareke, Jeremi Garvin. *Songs:* Northern Magic; Touch of Tomorrow; Spring and Lilac; Angel (Hold Me in Your Arms); Pretty Little Girl.

SHEPHERD, ARTHUR ASCAP 1939
composer, educator

b Paris, Idaho, Feb 19, 1880; d Cleveland, Ohio, Jan 12, 58. Educ: New Eng Cons. Cond, theatre orch, Salt Lake City. Mem fac, New Eng Cons, 08. Bandmaster, France, WW I. Asst cond, Cleveland Orch, 20. Prof music, Western Reserve Univ, 27. Mem, Nat Inst Arts & Letters. *Songs & Instrumental Works:* Overture Joyeuse (Paderewski Prize; 2 Prizes, Nat Fedn Music Clubs); Overture to a Drama; Symphony No 1 (Horizons; 1st Juilliard Publ Award); Symphony No 2; Violin Sonata; Quintet for Piano, Strings; Triptych (voice, string quartet); Choreographic Suite; Settings to Psalm XLII (chorus, orch); Fantasy Overture on Down East Spirituals; Violin Concerto; Cantatas: City in the Sea; The Song of the Pilgrims.

SHEPPARD, BUDDY ASCAP 1952
composer, author, conductor

b New York, NY, Dec 20, 03. Educ: High sch. Violinist in dance orchs incl Phil Spitalny. Asst cond, Rudy Vallee Orch, 3 1/2 yrs. Staff violinist, CBS, then cond, 13 yrs. Asst cond, Bway musical, "Where's Charley?"; also Al Goodman radio orch. Violinist in orchs for TV shows incl Perry Como, Bing Crosby & Jack Benny. In bus, Miami, Fla. Chief Collabr: Murray Semos. *Songs:* It's So Nice to Be Nice; How Little You Know; The Minute Minuet; Take a Fool's Advice; Mm, Mm Not That; It Wouldn't Be Christmas Without You.

SHEPPARD, JOSEPH STANLEY ASCAP 1959
composer, teacher, arranger

b New York, NY, Apr 21, 15. Educ: Harvard Univ, BS, 37, MA, 39; Boston Univ; Univ NH, Tanglewood; studied with Walter Piston, Paul Hindemith, orch with E Burlingame Hill, organ with Francis W Snow. Head music dept, St Mark's Sch, Southboro, Mass, 42-76; consult & production mgr, Valente Music Co, 76- Vis comp, Music Dept, Harvard Univ, 2 terms. Organist, choirmaster, St Mark's Church, Southboro. Chief Collabrs: John J Witherspoon, John Jacob Niles. *Songs:* Music: St Mark's School Choral Series (20 titles); De Word; Come Beloved Monarch; Beyond All Comparing; Benedicite, omnia opera Domini.

SHEPPARD, TIMOTHY EDSEL ASCAP 1976
composer, singer

b Ft Worth, Tex, Aug 19, 54. Educ: W W Samuell High Sch; Southwestern Assemblies of God Col; pvt music training, Mrs George Cook, Dallas, Tex, 10 yrs. Won the Amateur Gospel Div Am Song Fest, 75; recording & publ, Greentree Records-The Benson Co, Nashville, Tenn, 76; songs have appeared on Grammy Award winning albums. Now touring US, Can & Europe. *Songs:* Would You Believe in Me; Hosanna; Ever Since the Day; The Fiddler. *Albums:* Diary; Inside My Room; Songtailor.

SHER, JACK ASCAP 1959
composer

b Minneapolis, Minn, Mar 16, 13. Educ: Univ of Minn. Film writer, producer; author of two novels, Bway play. Writer of Bing Crosby TV show. Chief Collabr: Farlan Myers. *Songs:* Make This a Slow Goodbye; Kathy 'O.

SHERBERG, JON ALFRED
composer, author, pianist

b Denver, Colo, Jan 22, 51. Educ: Univ Colo; Univ Northern Colo, studied with Buddy Baker & Richard Bourrasa. Toured US, comp & arr with Christian music, comedy & drama group, Jeremiah People, 74-76. Free lance comp & arr, Nashville, 77 & Los Angeles, 79- Worked in copyright development for Benson Co, Nashville, 78. *Songs:* Where Your Heart Is; Livin' in Your Love; Where Do We Go From Here?; Every Moment of My Life; We Stand With Him.

SHERMAN, AL ASCAP 1925
composer, author

b Kiev, Russia, Sept 7, 1897; d Los Angeles, Calif, Sept 15, 73. Educ: Gymnasium, Prague; pvt music study. Pianist in film studios, during 10's, also with publ cos. To US, 11. Wrote songs for Bway revues incl "Ziegfeld Follies", "George White's Scandals", "The Passing Show", "Earl Carroll's Vanities", also songs for films incl "The Big Pond", "Sweetie", "The Sky's the Limit", "Sensations of 1945." Chief Collabrs: Al Lewis, Abner Silver, Edward Heyman, Harry Tobias. *Songs:* Save Your Sorrow; Pretending; On the Beach at Bali-Bali; Now's the Time to Fall in Love; Me Too; Dew-Dew-Dewy Day; You Gotta Be a Football Hero; Roses Remind Me of You; Over Somebody Else's Shoulder; In God We Trust; For Sentimental Reasons; Comes-a-Long-a-Love; No! No! A Thousand Times No!; The Mood That I'm In; Living in the Sunlight; Ninety-Nine Out of a Hundred; Got the Bench, Got the Park; Woodland Reverie; Never a Dream Goes By; When You Waltz With the One You Love.

SHERMAN, ALLAN ASCAP 1959
author, comedian, producer

b Chicago, Ill, Nov 30, 24; d. Educ: Col. Writer comedy material for Jackie Gleason, Joe E Lewis, Jerry Lester & Frances Faye. Co-creator, TV show, "I've Got a Secret" (produced 6 yrs). Also writer & producer, radio & TV shows incl

"Broadway Open House", "The Steve Allen Show", "Victor Borge Special", "Phil Silvers Special", "Steve Lawrence Special" & "Funnyland" (own show). Appeared in nightclubs, theatres & TV; has made many records. Autobiography, "A Gift of Laughter." *Songs:* Sarah Jackman; Harvey and Sheila; Hello Muddah, Hello Fadduh; The 12 Gifts of Christmas; The Drop-Outs March; The End of a Symphony; Variations on 'How Dry I Am'; The Mouse That Roared. *Albums:* My Son, the Folk Singer; My Son, the Celebrity; My Son, the Nut; Peter and the Commissar; My Name Is Allan.

SHERMAN, GARRY
composer, conductor, orchestrator
b Brooklyn, New York, Dec 28, 33. Educ: NY Univ, BA(humanities); Temple Univ, DPM, 56; studied Schillinger Syst of Comp with Richard Bender, 51, piano with Frank Bernard, cond & comp with Tibor Serly. Studied piano in teens. Became professional arr & comp, 58; first album with Columbia Records, 59; arr & cond over 50 top ten records, 60's. Chief orchestrator for Coca Cola, 65-, Miller Beer, 70-, Lowenbrau, 75-; has written hundreds of TV commercials, incl Coca Cola, Arthur Treachers, IBM, Wendy's, Volkswagon, 6 Flaggs, PSA Airlines, Nat Air Lines, Englenook Wine & Howard Johnsons. Rec'd Am Music Conf Award & numerous Clio Awards. Chief Collabrs: lyrics, Stanley Kahan, Eugene Pistilli & Peter Udell. *Songs:* Music: Comin' Uptown. *Instrumental Works:* Idioms (Pulitzer nomination, 69); Perfpo No 1 (Performance Potential Piece for Classical Guitar). *Songs & Instrumental Works:* Viet Nam Cantata (Pulitzer nomination, 71). *Scores:* Films: Heartbreak Kid; Alices's Restaurant; TV: After the Fall; numerous TV specials & films.

SHERMAN, JOSEPH D   ASCAP 1955
composer, producer, arranger
b New York, NY, Sept 25, 26. Educ: NY Univ, BA; additional training, Juilliard. Musical dir for Tony Bennett, Ames Bros. A&R producer, Epic Records, CBS. Independent recording producer-arranger for Connie Francis, Four Lads, Jerry Vale, Paul Anka, Jack Lemmon, Bette Davis, Jayne Morgan, Nancy Ames, Village Stompers. Scored motion pictures & numerous TV commercials. Chief Collabrs: Noel Sherman, George David Weiss, Sid Wayne, Langston Hughes, Abby Mann. *Songs:* Ramblin' Rose; To the Ends of the Earth; Graduation Day; That Sunday, That Summer; Eso Beso; Por Favor; Toys in the Attic.

SHERMAN, NOEL   ASCAP 1960
author
b Brooklyn, NY, May 5, 30; d New York, NY, June 5, 72. Educ: NY Univ, Phi Beta Kappa. Korean War, USN. Wrote song for Bway revue, "Ziegfeld Follies of 1957," also spec material for Nat King Cole, Georgia Gibbs & Paul Anka. Chief Collabr: Joe Sherman (brother). *Songs:* Ramblin' Rose; Eso Beso; To the Ends of the Earth; Por Favor; Graduation Day; Juke Box Baby; Welcome to the Club; Fantastico; Everlovin'. *Scores:* Films: A Rage to Live; The Glory Guys.

SHERRIC, STORMIE
See Omartian, Stormie Sherric

SHERWIN, MANNING   ASCAP 1954
composer
b Philadelphia, Pa, Jan 4, 02; d Los Angeles, Calif, July 26, 74. Educ: Columbia Univ. Wrote for revues & films, NY & London. Was manufacturer's rep. *Songs:* A Nightingale Sang in Berkeley Square; I Fall in Love With You Every Day; Lovely One; Who's Taking You Home Tonight?; Music for Romance; The Moment I Saw You; Wrap Yourself in Cotton Wool; His Servant; She Came Rolling Down the Mountain.

SHERWIN, STERLING
See Hagen, John Milton

SHERZER, GEORGE   ASCAP 1956
composer
b Philadelphia, Pa, June 14, 16. Educ: High sch. Works as food distributor. *Instrumental Works:* Fantasy Moderne; Sound of the Sea.

SHEVITZ, ARNOLD   ASCAP 1955
composer, instrumentalist
b Los Angeles, Calif, Mar 3, 21. Educ: Pvt instr with Mario Castelnuovo-Tedesco; Music Acad of the West, studied with Darius Milhaud, Richard Lert & Charles Jones; Univ Southern Calif, studied film scoring with Miklos Rozsa. Prof violinist, film recording & local orch performances. *Instrumental Works:* Improvisations for Unaccompanied Flute; Sonata for Flute and Piano; Iberiana (orch); Caribee (orch).

SHIELD, LEROY   ASCAP 1943
composer, conductor, pianist
b Waseca, Minn, Oct 2, 1893; d Ft Lauderdale, Fla, Jan 9, 62. Educ: Univ Chicago; Columbia Univ; hon MusD, Chicago Musical Col. Toured as concert pianist. Cond-arr & mgr, A&R Dept, Victor Talking Machine Co. Comp-cond, Hal Roach Studios, for Laurel & Hardy, Our Gang, Charlie Chase & Thelma Todd series. To Chicago as music dir, NBC radio progs "Roy Shield & Co", "Author's Playhouse", "Phil Baker Show", "Sheaffer World Parade" & "Roy Shield Revue." Cond, Chicago Symph, Chicago Women's Symph & NBC Symph. To NBC, NY, 46; comp-cond, TV shows; cond, NBC concert & symph orchs; also Montreal, Rochester. *Songs:* You Are the One I Love; Rhumba

Rhythm; Happy Anniversary March; Good Morning Breakfast Clubbers; Breakfast Club Makes Life Worthwhile; So Long, You Breakfast Clubbers (all for Don McNeill Breakfast Club); Farm and Home March; Good Old Days; Little Dancing Girl; On to the Show; Metro Goldwyn Mayer Fanfare. *Songs & Instrumental Works:* Union Pacific Suite; Gloucester (tone poem); The Great Bell (tone poem).

SHIELDS, REN   ASCAP 1930
composer, author, actor
b Chicago, Ill, Feb 22, 1868; d Massapequa, NY, Oct 25, 13. Educ: Pub schs. Singer in minstrel shows & vaudeville, 1890-94. Teamed with Max Million until 1897, then featured in Chicago production "Gay Paree". Wrote & produced shows & vaudeville sketches. To NY, 1900; wrote spec material for vaudeville. Chief Collabr: Percy Wenrich, George (Honeyboy) Evans. *Songs:* Let Me Take My Place at Home Again; In the Good Old Summertime; Waltz Me Around Again, Willie; You'll Have to Wait Till My Ship Comes In; Steamboat Bill; The Longest Way Round Is the Shortest Way Home; Frankie and Johnnie.

SHILKRET, JACK   ASCAP 1939
composer, conductor, pianist
b New York, NY, Oct 13, 1896; d New York, June 16, 64. Educ: City Col NY; studied music with Hambitzer & Lowitz, Fla. Brother of Nathaniel Shilkret. Wrote scores for film shorts & US Govt films. Clarinetist, USN Band, DC; led own orch, played in theatres, hotels, nightclubs & radio, also did records. Pianist & cond, Julia Sanderson & Frank Crumit, radio. *Songs:* April Showers Bring May Flowers; On the Isle of Madeira; Copenhagen Love Song; Just Another Kiss; Lazy Summer Moon; She's the Daughter of K-K-K-Katy; Make Believe.

SHILKRET, NATHANIEL   ASCAP 1925
composer, conductor, clarinetist
b New York, NY, Dec 25, 1895. Educ: Bethany Col, MusD; studied with Henius, Hambitzer, Floridia. Mem symph orchs, age 13. Clarinetist in Russian Symph, NY Philh, NY Symph, Metrop Opera House Orch & bands incl John Philip Sousa, Arthur Pryor & Edwin F Goldman. Music dir, Victor Talking Machine Co; organized symph orchs for recordings; cond, early radio broadcasts. Chief Collabrs: L Wolfe Gilbert, Gene Austin, John Klenner, Allie Wrubel, Lew Pollack. *Songs:* Jeannine, I Dream of Lilac Time; The Lonesome Road; Down the River of Golden Dreams; Some Sweet Day; The First Time I Saw You; April Showers Bring May Flowers. *Instrumental Works:* Skyward; New York Ballet; Seasons (4 tone poems); Southern Humoresque (violin); Jealous Ballerina (violin); Firefly Scherzo; Trombone Concerto; Genesis Suite.

SHIMKIN, BONNIE LEE (BONNIE SANDERS)   ASCAP 1976
composer, author, singer
b Far Rockaway, NY, May 8, 41. Educ: Hewlett High Sch; Boston Univ, AD; The New Sch, musical theater writing, Gene Frankel, Kenneth Jacobson. Began writing & singing in high sch. Sang in Murry the K Show. First song publ, 65. Song released by own group, Bonnie and the Clydes, 68. Have written & released many children's songs, incl Sesame Street. Performs own songs in clubs. Chief Collabrs: Susan Green, Jack Perricone, Michele V Pomerantz, Mark Barkan, Lowell Mark, Fran Ziffer, Billy Jackson, Jack Orr, Elaine Mann, Richard Miller, Chuck Gordon. *Songs:* I Got a Song; Blue Skies Apple Pie; Nothin' to Do; Sing Me Your Song; Feel the Music.

SHINDO, TAK   ASCAP 1957
composer, musicologist
b Sacramento, Calif, Nov 11, 22. Educ: Calif State Univ, Los Angeles, BA, 52; Los Angeles City Col, AA, 68, studied with Robert MacDonald; Univ Southern Calif, MA, 72, studied pvt comp with Mikolos Rozsa; studied pvt comp with Lyle Spud Murphy. USA, 44-47, Spec Service Band, Mil Intelligence Service Language Inst. Film comp, technical adv, 49. Cond, comp, "Sayonara", "Cinerama-Seven Wonders of the World", "Stop Over Tokyo", "Dawn of Asia", "Roots of Madness," CBS TV. Recording artist, Japan Victor, Capitol, Mercury & Grand Prix record cos. Prof music, Calif State Univ, Los Angeles, 65- *Songs:* Music: Yesterday's You. *Instrumental Works:* Impression (piano quartet); Mganga.

SHINN, RANDALL   ASCAP 1973
composer
b Clinton, Okla, Sept 28, 44. Educ: Southwestern Okla State Univ, BA (magna cum laude), 66; Univ Colo, MMus, 68; Univ Ill, DMA, 75; studied comp with Benjamin Johnston, Paul Zonn, Herbert Brun. Fac mem, Univ New Orleans, 75-78, Ariz State Univ, 78-80. Chief Collabr: Leven Dawson. *Songs:* Music: Cummings Songs.

SHIRL, JIMMY   ASCAP 1948
composer, author
b New York, NY, Oct 7, 09. Educ: Fordham Univ & Law Sch. Wrote spec material for Jack Haley, Ken Murray, Perry Como, Rosemary Clooney, Nat (King) Cole, Polly Bergen, Tony Martin, Ethel Waters, Tony Bennett, Jane Froman, Janet Blair & Lucienne Boyer. USAF, WW II; wrote for "This Is the Army"; also songs for TV "Sing It Again", "Songs for Sale", "USA Canteen", "The Would-Be Gentlemen" & "To Mamie With Music"; wrote songs for Frankie Laine, Merv Griffin, Patti Page & Jack Carter shows. Chief Collabr: Ervin Drake. *Songs:* Across the Wide Missouri; I Believe; Meet Mr Callaghan; Sonata; Au Revoir; You're Gonna Make a Wonderful Sweetheart; Open Your

Heart (off Heart Asn Song); To Make a Mistake Is Human; One God; My Friend; Beloved Be Faithful; Come to the Mardi Gras; Made for Each Other; Castle Rock; I Remember You, Love; Delilah; Mabel! Mabel!; The Flying Dutchman; Three Things; So Deep My Love; Someone Cares; They're Playing Our Song; Thank You.

SHIVA, H B
See Perskin, Spencer Malcolm

SHMUCKLER, GREGORI — ASCAP 1975
composer, piano & violin teacher

b Rovno, Russia, Nov 22, 1899. Educ: Cons City of Saratov, studied violin with Vicanty Zeits, also with comps Rudolf & Gordon; studied piano with Prof Slivinsky. Started career in violin & piano at age 8; began writing comp at age 16; violin, piano & viola player. Chief Collabr: Juanita W Thomas, lyricist. *Songs & Instrumental Works:* Endless Love (song for mezza soprano, piano); Concerto for Violin and String Orchestra; Concerto for Trumpet and String Orchestra; Fantasy for Piano and Orchestra; Stroll for Orchestra; Romance for Cello and Orchestra.

SHOCKEY, CHRISTIAN ALLEN — ASCAP 1954
composer

b Wheaton, Kans, Dec 25, 10. Educ: Los Angeles Col of Chiropractics. WW II, USAAF. Has been practicing chiropractor, Artesia & Lompoc, Calif. Chief Collabr: Patsy Montana. *Songs:* I Called You Up to Cry on Your Shoulder; The Yodeling Ghost; Water Witch Waltz; Ring Around Rosie's Finger; Relax, Relax, Lovely One.

SHOR, PAT (PATTI JACOB) — ASCAP 1968
author, singer

b Edmonton, Alta, June 12, 28. Educ: Victoria High Sch, Edmonton; studied with Helen Hobbs Jordan. Writer, Bway, TV, nightclubs & recordings. Has written & produced theatre & nightclub presentations for many stars, indust shows, TV & radio commercials. Wrote lyrics for Bway musical, "Jimmy." Originator of "Vive Les Girl!" show & wrote lyrics for "Casino de Paris" show, Dunes Hotel, Las Vegas. Chief Collabs: Riz Ortolani, Luiz Bonfa, Henry Tobias, Alex Alstone, Jerry Goldberg, Bill Jacob. *Songs:* Lyrics: That Holiday Feeling; I Only Wanna Laugh; What's Out There; I Think of You; Sweet Talk; One Day at a Time; Casino de Paris; Vive Les Girls; Jimmy; Keep Thy Faith; Fenwick, the Optimistic Elf; Whatta Land Santa Land Is; When You Elect Me Mayor; You're Not Getting Older, You're Getting Better; Tigers of Tammany Hall; Will You Think of Me, Tomorrow?; The Walker Walk; Here's to New Jersey; Charmin' Son of a Bitch; The Little Woman; I Want It All; Riverside Drive; Five Lovely Ladies; Life Is a One-Way Street; Mama's Gramaphone; Blue Lace.

SHORES, RICHARD — ASCAP 1958
composer, conductor, arranger

b Rockville, Ind. Educ: Ind Univ, BM; Eastman Sch Music, MM(comp); studies with Howard Hanson, Bernard Rogers & Robert Sanders. Cond, Indianapolis Little Symph; bandleader, USA, 4 yrs; cond, comp & arr, NBC & WGN Chicago; to Hollywood, 58; under contract to Revue & CBS-TV. *Scores:* TV: Medical Center; Richard Boone Show; Jericho; Girl from UNCLE; Man from UNCLE; Then Came Bronson; Mannix; Mulligans Stew; Anna and the King; Paper Chase; Richard Diamond Show (theme); Robert Taylors Detectives; Honey West; Dick Powell Show (end theme); Burke's Law; Born Free; Police Woman; Police Story; Medical Story; Risko (theme); Matt Helm; It Takes a Thief; Wells Fargo; Johnny Midnight; Kingston; Wagon Train; Laramie; Alfred Hitchcock Hour; Run for Your Life; Checkmate; The Virginian; Quincy; Hawaii Five-O; Perry Mason; Gunsmoke; Twilight Zone; Men at Law; Storefront Lawyers; Rawhide; Cimarron Strip; Wild, Wild, West; Motion Pictures: Lock in Any Window; Tomboy and the Champ; Run, Appaloosa, Run; The Last Challenge; A Matter of Wife and Death; The Quest; Cover Girls; A Killing Affair; Police Story/Watch Commander; Police Story/Stigma; The Courage and the Passion; Billion Dollar Threat; Walt Disney Movies: The Mystery in Dracula's Castle; Chester, Yesterdays Horse; Cowdog; The Boy and the Runaway Elephant; Twister, Bull from the Sky. *Albums:* Emotions; Music to Read Lady Chatterly's Lover By; Prelude for Eight; Mulholland Suite.

SHORT, NANCYE
See Tsapralis, Nancye Faye

SHOTT, MICHAEL JOHN — ASCAP 1977
composer, music professor

b Berlin, Ger, Apr 7, 28. Educ: Western Mich Univ, BMus, 54; Ind Univ, MMus, 60, PhD, 64. Pvt piano teacher, 45-50; served in USA, 54-56; cost accountant, 56-58. Fac mem, Northern Ariz Univ, 61- Chief Collabr: Randell Shutt. *Instrumental Works:* Romance; Give and Take (vols I & II); Duet Preludes; Galaxy Sonatina.

SHOWALTER, MAX GORDON — ASCAP 1953
composer, author, pianist

b Caldwell, Kans, June 2, 17. Educ: Caldwell High Sch; Pasadena Playhouse, 35-38; studied singing with Eva Gauthier, 46-50. Actor in Bway productions "Knight of Song", "Very Warm for May", "My Sister Eileen", "John Loves Mary", "Show Boat", "Make Mine Manhattan", "Hello Dolly", "The Grass Harp", also in many TV shows & films incl "Niagara", "Bus Stop", "Elmer Gantry", "Summers and Smoke", "How to Murder Your Wife" & "10." As painter had 5 one man shows in Los Angeles & permanent exhib at Shelburne Museum, Vt. Chief Collabs: Ross Bagdasarian, William Howe, Peter Walker, Ken Darby, Robert Lees, Albert G Miller. *Songs:* Hoe That Corn; If I Were You; Silent Picture Rag; Music: Dot's Nice-Donna Fight; We Believe in Love; Vicki (theme song); Cold Fire; My Square Laddie; A Lovely Autumn Day. *Scores:* Bway shows: Little Boy Blue; Joy Ride; Hermione Gingold Revue (debut in US); Go for Your Gun; Films: With a Song in My Heart; Return of Jack Slade; TV: Time for Love (first musical ever televised, NBC, 39); The Ray Bolger Show; The Chevy Show; The Lucy Show; The Stockard Channing Show.

SHOWS, CHARLES W
author

b El Paso, Tex, May 15, 12. Educ: El Paso High Sch; Northwestern Univ, Evanston, Ill. Writer-dir, Paramount Pictures & KTLA TV show "Time for Beany," Acad Award, 50; writer-dir-producer, Walt Disney Studios, 54-62; writer films, Belvision, Brussels, Belgium. *Songs:* Lyrics: Sahara; The Cougar; The African Lion; Children of the World; Balto; Huckleberry Hound; Alice in Wonderland; The Flintstones; The Wizard of Oz; Moon Madness.

SHUKEN, LEO — ASCAP 1949
composer

b Los Angeles, Calif, Dec 8, 06; d Santa Monica, Calif, July 24, 76. Educ: Univ Calif, Los Angeles; studied with Ernest Toch. Chief Collabs: Victor Young, Elmer Bernstein, Henry Mancini, Alfred Newman, Harry Sukman, Quincy Jones, Burt Bacharach. *Songs & Instrumental Works:* The Dorsey Concerto; Theme on a Dream; Majestic Cascades; Summer Silhouettes; Autumn Silhouettes; Spring Madness; Mink Schmink. *Scores:* The Greatest Story Ever Told; Film background: Waikiki Wedding; Stagecoach (Acad Award, 39); Artists and Models Abroad; The Unsinkable Molly Brown (Acad nomination, 64); TV background: Wagon Train; Going My Way; Virginians; River Boat.

SHULMAN, ALAN M — ASCAP 1948
composer, author, cellist

b Baltimore, Md, June 4, 15. Educ: Privately tutored in Baltimore; Erasmus Hall High Sch, Brooklyn; music educ at Peabody Cons, Baltimore; New York Philh scholarship; fel, Juilliard, 32-37, cert. Prof cellist, Kreiner String Quartet, 34-37. Charter mem, NBC Symph, 37-54. Vchmn, Bd of Dirs, Symph of the Air, 54-57. Mem Philharmonia Trio, 62-69. Pres, Violoncello Soc, 67-72. Mem Haydn String Quartet. Fac mem Sarah Lawrence Col, Juilliard, State Univ NY Purchase. Dir Chamber Music Workshop, Johnson Col, Vt. *Instrumental Works:* Theme and Var for Viola and Orchestra; Concerto for Cello and Orchestra; A Laurentian Overture; Waltzes for Orchestra; Suite based on Am folksongs for violin & piano; Threnody for String Orchestra; Suite for Solo Cello; Suite for Solo Viola; Suite for String Orchestra (based on string quartet of Benjamin Franklin); Top Brass (for 12 brass instr); Suite Miniature (for octet of celli); Jazz Grab Bag (for piano); numerous string works for orch, viola ens, cello ens, plus educ works for strings (commissioned by Univ Ill string research project).

SHUMAN, ALDEN — ASCAP 1953
composer, author

b Boston, Mass, Nov 14, 24. Educ: Boston Latin Sch; Cent High Sch, Philadelphia, Pa; NY Univ, BA, Law Sch, 1 yr. Started writing pop songs, movie background music & then into TV drama & documentary background scoring. Chief Collabs: Earl Shuman, Marshall Brown. *Songs:* Seven Lonely Days; The Banjo's Back in Town; Music: See the Cheetah. *Scores:* Films: The Devil in Miss Jones; The Great American Balloon Adventure; Yukon Passage (Nat Geographic Spec); Connecticut Yankee (Peabody Award); Leatherstocking Tales (Emmy).

SHUMAN, EARL STANLEY — ASCAP 1953
author, publisher

b Boston, Mass, Aug 2, 23. Educ: Boston Latin Sch; Yale Univ, BA, 47. Served in WW II, Capt, USMC. Has written many hit songs & many movie title songs, also wrote lyrics for off-Bway musical "Secret Life of Walter Mitty." Now publ/pres, Meat Loaf Publ Co & own Earl Music Co. Chief Collabs: Leon Carr, Alden Shuman (brother), Sherman Edwards, Marshall Brown, Maurice Bower. *Songs:* Seven Lonely Days; Banjo's Back in Town; Lyrics: Hey There Lonely Girl (Boy); Caterina; Left, Right Out of Your Heart; My Shy Violet; Close to Cathy; Hotel Happiness; Clinging Vine; Young New Mexican Puppeteer; Most People Get Married; I Am; Confidence (theme song); Our Everlasting Love; Time, Time; Starry-Eyed; Theme for a Dream; Leaves Are the Tears of Autumn; The River; Disorderly Orderly (movie title theme); Monica (movie theme); I've Been Here; Look!; Marriage Is for Old Folks.

SHUMAN, FRANCIS K — ASCAP 1936
composer

b Boston, Mass, Jan 2, 08. Educ: Georgetown Univ; Harvard Law Sch; studied with Hans Ebel, Otto Straube. WW II, Lt, USAAF. Chief Collabs: Larry Wagner, James Eaton, Jules Loman, Allan Roberts. *Songs:* Doing the Prom; Blue Tahitian Moonlight; It's High Time; With a Dollar in Your Pocket;

Streamline, Dreamline Train; It Took a Little While; Flamenco Love; Penguin At the Waldorf.

SHURE, R DEANE ASCAP 1942
composer, organist, educator

b Chillisquaque, Pa, May 31, 1885. Educ: Oberlin Col, BM; studied music with Felix Draeseke, Alex Wolff & de Blois Rowe. Dir music, Central Univ Iowa, 07-09, Clarendon Tex Col, 09-19, Pa State Teachers Col, 19-21 & Am Univ, 21-25. Dir music, Mt Vernon Place Methodist Church, Wash. Pres, Washington Composers Club, 10 yrs. *Songs & Instrumental Works:* Joyful We Adore Thee; Circles of Washington; Through Palestine (organ suite); Lyric Washington (piano suite); Old Boat Zion; One of God's Best Mornings; Nativity Carol; Galilean Easter Carol; This Is America; 5 symphonies; 75 anthems.

SHURR, ALAN ASCAP 1953
composer, musician

b Brooklyn, NY, Sept 21, 12. Educ: NY Univ; Brooklyn Col of Pharmacy. Mem, Lenny Herman Orch, 40- Comp of musical commercials. *Songs:* I Found My Old Girl Again. *Instrumental Works:* Sempre Canta.

SICURELLA, JOSEPH PAUL
composer, producer

b North Tonawanda, NY, Oct 8, 49. Educ: North Tonawanda High Sch; Ohio Univ, Athens; Ithaca Col, NY; 13 yrs pvt music instr, piano, accordion & drums. Studied radio & TV in col; worked at WOUB Radio & TV & Christian Broadcasting Network. Record & commercial production & writing, Atlanta & Nashville, 5 yrs. Formed Joe Sicurella & Assocs, New York, 77; commercial music production for radio & TV commercials & network themes & logos. *Songs:* Why Not the Best (Pres Carter's election campaign theme, 76); Peacock Club Themes (NBC-TV). *Instrumental Works:* Monday Night Football (ABC-TV themes); Monday Night Baseball (ABC-TV themes).

SIDEMAN, WILLIAM
See Seidman, William

SIDRAN, BEN H ASCAP 1969
composer, author, singer

b Chicago, Ill, Aug 14, 43. Educ: Univ Wis, BA; Univ Sussex, MA & PhD. Recorded 9 albums, Capitol, Blue Thumb, Arista & A&M. Toured, US, Europe & Japan. Taught communication arts, Univ Wis. Produced soundstage TV shows on jazz; wrote articles on music for mag. Chief Collabrs: Steve Miller, James Cooke. *Songs:* Midnight Tango; Feel Your Groove; Song for a Sucker Like You; Broad Day Light; Lyrics: Space Cowboy.

SIEGEL, AL ASCAP 1938
composer, vocal coach

b New York, NY, Aug 27, 1898. Educ: London schs; Art Students League, NY. Began career as accompanist to Sophie Tucker. Gave jazz concerts in Paris. Vocal coach, arr for singers incl Ethel Merman, Lisa Kirk, Martha Wright, Betty Grable, Mary Martin, Carol Channing, Julie Wilson, Irene Dunne, Grace Moore, Joan Crawford, Shirley Temple, Dorothy Lamour, Lucille Ball & Martha Raye. Formed vocal talent dept, Paramount, MGM Studios. Author, "How to Become a Professional Singer." *Songs:* Cry Baby; Vote for Mr Rhythm.

SIEGEL, ARTHUR ASCAP 1952
composer, pianist

b Lakewood, NJ, Dec 31, 23. Educ: Am Acad Dramatic Arts; Juilliard Sch Music. Singer-pianist in nightclubs; accompanist & writer of spec material for Nancy Walker, Georgia Gibbs, Eartha Kitt, Kaye Ballard & Eddie Cantor; also written for Hermione Gingold, Imogene Coca, Beatrice Lillie, Gypsy Rose Lee & Mitzi Green. Singer & pianist on Ben Bagley's record album series. Wrote music for Rosemary Rice's children's record albums. Wrote songs for Bway musicals incl "New Faces" (52, 56 & 62) & "Mask and Gown"; off-Bway, "Shoestring Revue." Chief Collabr: June Carroll. *Songs:* Love Is a Simple Thing; Monotonous; Penny Candy; He Takes Me Off My Income Tax; Where Is Me?; I Want You to Be the First to Know; Tell Her; The Boy Most Likely to Succeed; White Witch of Jamaica; Don't Wait Till It's Too Late to See Paris; Things Are Going Well Today.

SIEGEL, PAUL ASCAP 1948
composer, author, publisher

b New York, NY, Dec 8, 14; d. Educ: Brooklyn Col, BA; NY Univ, MA; Columbia Univ; Juilliard Sch Music, studied with H Seligman & Sidney Sukoenig; Vienna Acad Music, with Josef Marx. Strategic Services Officer, WW II. Became music publ, 53. Has been DJ in Miami, New York, then Berlin. Also record producer & columnist for Berlin Evening News. *Songs:* A Cigarette in Europe; There I Go Again; No More; Nana. *Instrumental Works:* Symphonic Diary; One World Symphony; Four Symphonic Songs; Autumn Concerto; Ballet Nijinsky; Concerto Between Two Worlds.

SIEGEL, SIDNEY EDWARD ASCAP 1955
composer, author, pianist

b Chicago, Ill, Jan 20, 27. Educ: Roosevelt Col, Chicago, BMus(comp). Songwriter in high sch; wrote Sullivan High Sch song, Chicago. Wrote songs for 3 original musicals, Roosevelt Col. Writer, spec material for nightclub acts &

shows, local TV shows; did some popular songwriting. Writer & producer music for radio & TV commercials. Writer musical scores for indust films, songs for indust shows.

SIEGMEISTER, ELIE ASCAP 1952
composer, author

b New York, NY, Jan 15, 09. Educ: Columbia Col, BA(cum laude), 27; studied theory with Wallingford Riegger, 26, theory & comp with Nadia Boulanger, Paris, 27-32; Ecole Normale de Musique (Paris), dipl, 31; Juilliard Sch Music, dipl cond, 38; studied piano with Emil Friedberger. Comp at age 17; did music for Bway, TV & films; works performed by leading Am orchs as well as BBC, London Symph, Moscow State Symph, Cologne, Hamburg Radio Orch, Vienna Symph & others, operas performed in US, France, Belgium & Can. Founder, Am Comp Alliance, 38 & Black Music Colloquium, 80; founder & dir, Am Ballad Singers, 40-47. Prof music & composer-in-residence, Hofstra Univ, 49-76. Mem bd dirs, ASCAP, 77- Author, "A Treasury of American Song", "The New Music Lovers Handbook" & "Harmony and Melody"; comp. Chief Colllabrs: Langston Hughes, Edward Mabley, Lewis Allan, Edward Eager, Norman Rosten. *Songs: Music:* Strange Funeral in Braddock (voice, orch); Madam to You (song cycle); Songs of Experience (song cycle). *Songs & Instrumental Works:* I Have a Dream (chorus, narrator, baritone, orch); A Cycle of Cities (soloist, chorus, orch). *Scores: Opera/Ballet:* Symphony No 3; Symphony No 4; Symphony No 5 (Visions of Time); Miranda and the Dark Young Man; Sextet for Brass and Percussion; Orchestra and Clarinet Concerto; Orchestra and Flute Concerto; Five Fantasies of the Theater (orch); Shadows and Light (orch); Ozark Set (orch); Western Suite (orch); Sunday in Brooklyn (orch); Wilderness Road (orch); String Quartet No 2; String Quartet No 3 (Hebrew Themes); Sonata No 3 for Violin and Piano; The Plough and the Stars (3 act opera); Night of the Moonspell (Shakespeare, 3 act opera); Julietta (Kleist, 3 act opera); Darling Corie (1 act opera); The Mermaid in Lock Number 7 (1 act opera); Fables from the Dark Wood (ballet); plus many more; Bway Show: Sing Out Sweet Land (musical); Film: They Came to Cordura.

SIEMON, CARL (CARL SIMONE) ASCAP 1964
composer, organist, teacher

b Los Angeles, Calif, Dec 8, 18. Educ: Santa Monica High Sch (hon student); Univ Calif, Los Angeles, BA, 42; Univ Southern Calif, MMus, 47; studied comp with Arnold Schonberg. Organist, nightclubs, TV. Recording artist for Capitol Records & Hollywood Artists. Comp & performed "Jet Stream" for dedication of Anchorage Int Airport. *Instrumental Works:* 25 organ solos incl: Song of the Bells; Adoration; Praise Him With the Sound of the Trumpet (var on Russian carol); Cradle Song.

SIENNICKI, EDMUND JOHN ASCAP 1966
composer, author, teacher

b Cleveland, Ohio, Apr 11, 20. Educ: Kent State Univ, BS(educ), 46; Columbia Univ Teachers Col, MA, 48; studied comp with Herbert Elwell, electronic music with David Keane, conducting with Ernest Harris & Norval Church, bassoon with Simon Kovar, arr with Robert Nelson; workshops attended: Thor Johnson, Krenek, Babbitt, McGinnis. Clinician & cond at fests, nat conventions & workshops, for improvisation, keyboard, electronic music, bassoon & music educ, US & Can. Taught music, 30 yrs. Many music publ, for sch & col music groups; works performed throughout world. Author of var bks & articles publ in music educ trade journals. Recipient, Martha Holden Jennings Found Master Teacher award & 2 Nat Sch Orch Asn comp contest awards, & var comns; twice resident comp at MacDowell Colony; established classical electronic music studio in a jr high sch, 67, with Jennings Found grant. Chief Collabrs: Donald E McGinnis, Richard Saunders. *Instrumental Works:* Technical Growth for the Bassoonist (bk); Chorale and Fugue (string orch); Park Avenue Hoedown (orch); Brazilian Holiday (concert band); Orchestral Variations (orch); One By One (concert band); Ensemble Time for Band; Solo Time for Band; Two Duos for Bassoons (col level); Romanze, Two Sketches, and Two Impromptus; many solos & small ens for young performers & pieces for string orch, full orch & band.

SIFLER, PAUL JOHN (JUAN PABLO) ASCAP 1965
composer, choral director, organist

b Ljublajana, Yugoslavia, Dec 31, 11. Educ: Chicago Cons, BM; Westminster Choir Col, MM; studied comp with Robert Sanders & Lee Sowerby. Choirmaster-organist, Chicago area, Trinity Chapel, New York & Christ Church, Oyster Bay. Went to Calif; became choirmaster-organist, St Thomas Church, Hollywood. Organist, concerts, US & Europe. *Songs & Instrumental Works:* De Profundis (solo); Three Puerto Rican Carols: On That Holy Midnight; Hasten Shepherds; Now the Kings Are Coming; Organ: The Despair and Agony of Dachau; The Seven Last Words of Christ; Music for the Holy Night; Four Nativity Tableaux; Sinfonia: Psalm 98; Piano: Three Tall Tales; Young Pianist's Almanac; Sonatina in B Flat; Miniature Sonatina; Second Sonatina in C; Third Sonatina in D; The Ugly Duckling; All Aboard the Iron Horse; Free Wheeling; Marimba: Three Tall Tales; Sonatina; Marimba Suite; Three Miniatures; Choral: On This Night; It Is a Good Thing to Give Thanks; Benedictus Es; Blessed Jesusu, at Thy Word; Gloria in Excelsis.

SIGLER, JAMES HENRY ASCAP 1978
composer, author, jazz keyboardist

b Philadelphia, Pa, Dec 18, 30. Educ: Early jazz studies with Benny Golson, John Simmons & others; Brooklyn Col, BS(music & theatre), 79, studied with

J Scott Kennedy, music, drama, Seymour Reiter, play, lyric writing. Worked with John Coltrane, Lee Morgan, Clifford Brown & others. Accompanist with Dinah Washington, 3 yrs, also Sarah Vaughn, Lou Rawls, The Dells, Esther Phillips & Dakota Staton. Horn & string arrangements for Patti Brooks, Lou Rawls, Bunny Sigler & Instant Funk. ASCAP New Play Award for off-Bway show "Sister's Salutation," 78. Chief Collab: Bunny Sigler. *Songs:* Over the Hump; You'd Better Stop; Leap Tall Buildings; My Number's Up; How Can I Tell Her; Music: He Never Love You Like I Do; Little Red Riding Hood; Since the Day I First Saw Yoo; Dark Vader. *Instrumental Works:* Resorts International.

SIGLER, MAURICE
ASCAP 1934
author, conductor, producer

b New York, NY, Nov 30, 01; d Flushing, NY, Feb 6, 61. Educ: Pub schs, Birmingham, Ala. Banjo player in dance orch, then cond of own band. Owned nightclub. Wrote & produced radio shows, Birmingham; originated "Uncle Remus Show." To Eng, 34-37. Chief Collabrs: Al Hoffman, Al Goodhart, Mabel Wayne, Michael Cleary. *Songs:* Here It Is Monday and I've Still Got a Dollar; Why Don't You Practice What You Preach?; Little Man, You've Had a Busy Day; I'm in a Dancing Mood; Without Rhythm; There Isn't Any Limit to My Love; Everything Stops for Tea; From One Minute to Another; I Can Wiggle My Ears; Say the Word; Everything's in Rhythm With My Heart; Let's Put Some People to Work; She Shall Have Music; I Saw Stars. *Scores:* London Stage: This'll Make You Whistle; Birtish Film: Come Out of the Pantry; First a Girl; When Knights Were Bold; She Shall Have Music.

SIGMAN, CARL (JESSIE BARNES, CRAIG LEE, LEE BURKE)
ASCAP 1941
composer, author

b Brooklyn, NY, Sept 24, 09. Educ: NY Univ Law Sch, BL. Did scores for "Angel in the Wings," also for movies "She's Back on Broadway" & "Stop You're Killing Me," Warner Bros. Chief Collabrs: Bob Hilliard, Bob Russell, Francis Lai, Michel Le Grande, Gilbert Becaud, Peter De Rose, Bert Kaemphert. *Songs:* Dream Along With Me (Perry Como's theme song); The All American Soldier (Off song, 82nd Airborne Div); Robin Hood (TV series theme song); Music: Dance Ballerina Dance; Enjoy Yourself, It's Later Than You Think; Bongo, Bongo, Bongo, (Civilization); Careless Hands; Crazy She Calls Me; Lyrics: Where Do I Begin; What Now My Love; It's All in the Game; Ebb Tide; Till; Pennsylvania 6-5000; My Heart Cries for You; Marshmallow World; You're My World; Shan Gri-La; Arrivederci, Roma; A Day in the Life of a Fool; Summertime in Venice; Over and Over (The World We Knew); The World Outside; Answer Me My Love.

SIGNORELLI, FRANK
ASCAP 1933
composer, pianist

b New York, NY, May 24, 01; d. Educ: Pub schs; studied music with Pasquale Signorelli (cousin). Mem, original Dixieland Jazz Band; leader, original Memphis Five. Pianist in Paul Whiteman orch. *Songs & Instrumental Works:* Stairway to the Stars; A Blues Serenade; I'll Never Be the Same; So At Last It's Come to This; Park Avenue Fantasy; Midnight Reflections; Caprice Futuristic; And Then Your Lips Met Mine; Big Town; You Can't Cheat a Cheater; Love; Fool That I Am; Sioux City Sue; Anything; A Lover's Fantasy; A Serenade to You; Goin' Nowhere Fast; Waltzing With a Dream; Bonnie's Boogie; Rockin' the Bass.

SILBERTA, RHEA
ASCAP 1924
composer, teacher

b Pocahontas, Va, Apr 19, 1900; d New York, NY, Dec 6, 59. Educ: Ethical Culture Sch; Juilliard Sch Music; pvt voice study. Debut as pianist at age 7; toured US. Singer in concert & opera. Vocal coach, 22-59. *Songs:* Yohrzeit; The Message; Wild Geese; Samson Said; Lullaby for Judith; You Shall Have Your Red Rose. *Instrumental Works:* The Nightingale and the Rose (orch, narrator, soloists, chorus); Fantasie Ballade (piano).

SILLMAN, JUNE
See Carroll, June Betty

SILLS, BERENICE
ASCAP 1964
composer, teacher, singer

b Chicago, Ill. Educ: Teachers cert in music at age 14; Chicago Musical Col; Chicago Col Music; Ill Univ, Champaign, medal oratory; Dramatic Art Sch, studied with Lester Alden, Chicago. Piano soloist at age 11, with Chicago Symph Orch. Chief Collabrs: Karl Reckze, Walter Hirsch, Waldo Mayo, Major Bowes. *Songs:* Back Track to San Antone; Music: You Will Never Be Too Old to Love; The Glory of Your Eyes; That Night In Dreamy Havana.

SILVA, LUIS ANTONIO
ASCAP 1978
composer, author

b San Antonio, Tex, Nov 5, 43. Educ: Louis W Fox Technical High Sch, San Antonio, Tex. Started career as night club singer. Directed entertainment for World Hemis Fair in San Antonio, 68. Songwriter for Grever Music & Goldensands Entertainment, vpres of A Side District & Cara Records, 74- Writer of modern & contemporary Span music for group Mazz, 77- *Songs:* Compredo Mi Amor; Algo Bonito; Ayer Y Hoy; No Soy Malo; Manjando Mi Carro; Me Enamore; El; Laura Ya No Vive Aqui; Que Voy Haser Con El El Regalo.

SILVA, YVAN J
ASCAP 1979
composer, author, singer

b Porvorim, Goa, July 8, 36. Educ: Univ Bombay, MD; Vanderbilt Univ; McGill Univ, FRCS(C), FACS. Prof surgery, Wayne State Univ Sch Med; also singer in nightclubs & TV; recording artist; has performed in Bombay, Singapore, Beirut & other countries in Asia; also on radio prog, "Winter Moods," CBC Can. Chief Collabrs: Mark Lashlee, Bootsy Collins. *Songs:* Acapulco Sun; Lyrics: I Want to Love You; Preamble: Song for Jason.

SILVER, ABNER
ASCAP 1922
composer, author

b New York, NY, Dec 28, 1899; d New York, Nov 24, 66. Educ: NY Univ Law Sch. Pianist in dance orch, then for music publ incl Irving Berlin, as apprentice. Wrote songs for films incl "Jailhouse Rock", "King Creole" & "GI Blues." Author "How to Write and Sell a Song Hit" & "All Women Are Wolves." Chief Collabrs: Benny Davis, Al Sherman, Allie Wrubel, Sid Wayne. *Songs:* Angel Child; When Will the Sun Shine for Me?; Say It While Dancing; (I Don't Believe It But) Say It Again; There Goes My Heart; Farewell to Arms; A Typical Tipperary; Step by Step I'm Marching Home to You; My Home Town Is a One Horse Town; Chasing Shadows; How Did He Look?; With These Hands; No! No! A Thousand Times No!; How Green Was My Valley; Not As a Stranger; C'est Vous; Have You Forgotten So Soon?; On the Beach at Bali-Bali; I'm Goin' South; When the Mighty Organ Played "Oh Promise Me"; Make Believe Land; I Laughed at Love; He's So Unusual; Poo-Poo-Pe-Doop; Young and Beautiful; Lover Doll; Tonight Is So Right for Love; What's She Really Like?; My Love for You.

SILVER, CHARLES L (C L WOLFSILVER)
ASCAP 1976
author

b Baltimore, Md, Mar 16, 48. Educ: High sch; Baltimore City Col; Washington Col; St John's Col; Trinity Col, Dublin; Sorbonne Univ, Paris. Voice-over, Cinecitta, Rome. Film maker, Time-Life Films, New York. Advert copywriter, CBS Records, New York. Engineer & producer, Longsilver Music, New York; lyricist, Longsilver Music, Nashville & Baltimore. Chief Collabrs: Susan Manchester, Marvin Hamlisch, Rory Bourke, Jim Rushing, Moses Dillard. *Songs:* Lyrics: Standing Room Only; Hand-Me-Down-Love; Let's Say Goodnight Tomorrow Morning; Everybody Is a Singer; Six-Gun World.

SILVER, FRANK
ASCAP 1927
author, conductor, drummer

b Boston, Mass, Sept 8, 1896; d Brooklyn, NY, June 14, 60. Drummer in Bowery music hall, NY, 11. Toured in Raymond Hitchcock's Hitchy-Koo. Formed own orch, playing vaudeville theatres. Drummer, Loew's Metrop Theatre, Brooklyn; then led touring band; later band contractor. Chief Collab: Irving Conn. *Songs:* Yes, We Have No Bananas; Icky-Wicky-Woo; Gold Digger Blues; What Do We Get from Boston? Beans, Beans, Beans.

SILVER, FREDERICK
See Silverberg, Frederick Irwin

SILVER, HORACE WARD
ASCAP 1957
composer, author, lyricist

b Norwalk, Conn, Sept 2, 28. Educ: Norwalk High Sch; studied piano with William Scofield. Band leader for 28 yrs. Has worked in nightclubs, theatres, fests, concerts & TV. Recording artist, Blue Note Records, 28 yrs. Piano stylist, arr, music publ & record producer. *Songs:* The Preacher; Doodlin'; Senor Blues; Filthy McNasty; Song for My Father; Peace; Sister Sadie; Come on Home; Home Cookin'; Strollin'; Out of the Night Came You; Kissin' Cousins; We All Have a Part to Play; Friends; Inner Feelings; Optimism; Empathy; Togetherness; It's Time; All in Time. *Songs & Instrumental Works:* Opus DeFunk; Nica' Dream; The Tokyo Blues; Silver's Serenade; Gregory Is Here; Nutville.

SILVER, MARK
ASCAP 1951
composer, conductor, teacher

b Russia, July 17, 1892; d Newark, NJ, Jan 23, 65. Educ: Columbia Univ (Mosenthal fel; Pulitzer traveling award). Music dir, YM & YWHA, Newark, NJ, 30 yrs, Temple B'nai Abraham, Newark, 9 yrs & Temple Beth El, South Orange, 9 yrs. Taught music. Award from Cantors Assembly of Am. Mem, Nat Asn Am Comp & Cond. *Songs & Instrumental Works:* 6 Settings of 'Book of 6 V'shomrus'; Biblical Cantata (Psalms 117, 118); 2 Sabbath Eve Services; Peace Be With Thee (solo voice); The Day of Judgment (Hebrew Union Col Award); Uvchein Yiskadash; Havein Yakir Li; Vayechulu; Peace and War (symph).

SILVERBERG, FREDERICK IRWIN (FREDERICK SILVER)
ASCAP 1962
composer, author, pianist

b Brooklyn, NY, Mar 30, 36. Educ: Abraham Lincoln High Sch; Great Neck High Sch; Boston Univ, BM, 57; Juilliard, BS, 59, MS, 61, Gretchaninoff Prize, Freshl Prize (2 yrs), studied comp with William Bergsma, Vittorio Giannini. Won first Rodgers & Hammerstein Award to comp for musical theatre. Publ contract with Williamson Music. Musical dir & contributor to Julius Monk at "Plaza 9." Musical dir for "Upstairs at the Downstairs." Mem of concert duo piano team of DeMaio & Silver. Performed extensively throughout the US. Chief Collabrs: Helen Kromer, Nelson Garringer. *Songs:* The Twelve Days

After Christmas; Freddy Liked to Fugue; A Simple Song; But Not Me; Peter Pipers Fugue; Sterling Silver; The Silver Songbook. *Scores:* Bway shows: For Heaven's Sake; Hannah; Exodus and Easter; Like it Is; Gay Company; Sterling Silver; Film/TV: Snow White Takes a Bite.

SILVERLIGHT, TERRY BENNET   ASCAP 1973
composer, author, drummer
b Newark, NJ, Jan 15, 57. Educ: North Plainfield High Sch; Princeton Univ; studied with Morris Lang, Manny Albam & Olga Von Til. Featured on albums of var artists; TV, radio; Montreaux, Northsea, Berlin, Martinique, Spoleto & Midsummersnight Fests. Co-leader band, Silvermac, with Libby McLaren; auth drum book, "The Featured Drummer." Chief Collabrs: Libby McLaren; Barry Miles; Tom McLaren. *Songs:* City Girl; We Meet Again; Show Emotion; Music Is the Way; Who Do You Think You Are. *Instrumental Works:* Buck Rogers; Vic's Theme; African Chant; Someday; Dayflight.

SILVERMAN, FAYE-ELLEN   ASCAP 1972
composer, pianist, educator
b New York, NY, Oct 2, 47. Educ: Dalcroze Sch of Music; Manhattan Sch of Music; Mannes Col of Music; Barnard Col, BA(cum laude, hon in music), 68; Harvard Univ, MA(comp), 71; Columbia Univ Sch of Arts, DMA(comp), 74; studied comp with Luening, Sydeman, Kirchner, Foss, Ussachevsky, Beeson, piano with Irma Wolpe, Russell Sherman; training in clarinet & viola. Comp, performed works, radio, TV & live concerts, US & abroad. Pianist, chamber music & 20th century works; soloist with Brooklyn Philh Orch. Former fac, City Univ New York; asst prof, Goucher Col & grad fac, Peabody Inst of Johns Hopkins Univ, 77- Winner, Stokowski Comp Contest, age 13. *Instrumental Works:* Yet for Him (flute, cello, piano); Stirrings (chamber orch); Three Movements for Saxophone Alone; Settings (piano). *Scores:* Opera: The Miracle of Nemirov.

SILVERS, DOC
See Silverstein, Herman

SILVERS, DOLORES (VICKI)   ASCAP 1955
composer, author
b Philadelphia, Pa. *Songs:* Learnin' the Blues.

SILVERS, LOUIS   ASCAP 1923
composer, conductor, pianist
b New York, NY, Sept 6, 1889; d Hollywood, Calif, Mar 26, 54. Educ: Erasmus Hall High Sch. Pianist in vaudeville; music dir for Gus Edwards vaudeville productions, 10 yrs; also vaudeville producer; music dir film studios. Chief Collab: B G DeSylva. *Songs:* April Showers; Mother of Mine; Just Snap Your Fingers At Care. *Scores:* Films: The Jazz Singer; One Night of Love (Acad Award).

SILVERS, PHIL   ASCAP 1965
author, comedian, actor
b Brooklyn, NY, May 11, 11. Appeared in vaudeville, burlesque & film shorts. Made Bway appearances: "Yokel Boy", "High Button Shoes", "Top Banana" (rec'd Tony Award); "Do-Re Mi" & "A Funny Thing Happened on the Way to the Forum" (rec'd Tony Award). Actor in films incl "Tom, Dick and Harry", "Cover Girl" & "Summer Stock." WW II, entertained troops, Africa & Italy. Had own TV series, "Sergeant Bilko" (rec'd 8 Emmys in 5 yrs). Chief Collab: James Van Heusen. *Songs:* Nancy (With the Laughing Face).

SILVERS, SID   ASCAP 1929
composer, author, actor
b Brooklyn, NY, Jan 1, 07; d Santa Monica, Calif, Aug 20, 76. Mem staff, music publ co, 2 yrs. Vaudeville comedian with Phil Baker, 8 yrs. Wrote & appeared in films: "Broadway Melody of 1936"; "Born to Dance"; "Broadway Melody of 1938"; co-author: "Babes in Arms"; "For Me and My Gal"; "The Wizard of Oz." *Songs:* Did You Mean It?; Pretty Little Baby; Love and Kisses; I'm in Love With You, You're in Love With Me; Those We Love; When You Dream About Hawaii; Let's Get Friendly; Let's Make a Wish.

SILVERSTEIN, HERMAN (DOC SILVERS)   ASCAP 1968
composer, lyricist, teacher
b New York, NY, Aug 8, 10. Educ: Alexander Hamilton High Sch; studied 2 yrs at NY Univ Sch Music; philh flute scholarship, John Amans. Played piccolo with Brooklyn Hebrew Orphan Asylum Band at age 15; played flute, NY Univ Orch; two flute concerts, Carnegie Recital Hall, NY, also flute concert at Town Hall. Recordings for Army-Armed Forces Radio Prog. Chief Collabrs: Sossio-Perrotta, Irving Fields. *Songs:* Music: Canada, Canada, We Love You; Let's Go Lindsay; Hubie Humphrey, We Love You; Yesterday We Love You (memorial to H Humphrey); Chinese Boy, Chinese Girl; In Puerto Rico; Oh, Mr Nixon. *Instrumental Works:* All the Way With LBJ; The LBJ Waltz; He Cares; Lovey Dovey You; Senior Citizen's March; The Piccolo Cha-Cha; Hello Ronnie!, Goodbye Jimmy!; Hello Jimmy.

SIMA, WILLIAM RICHARD, SR   ASCAP 1961
composer, author, conductor
b Baltimore, Md, May 12, 1892; d Jackson Heights, NY, Sept 26, 65. Educ: Baltimore City Col; Peabody Inst; studied with Franz Fornchein, J Van Hulstein.

Cond, Wilson Theatre Orch, Baltimore; summer concerts, Ocean City, Md, 08-09. Enlisted in USN, 10; band, orch cond, Annapolis, 30 yrs. Music teacher, NY Bd of Educ, also privately. *Songs & Instrumental Works:* Gangway Song; Remember This Night; Lover's Lane; Navy Girl; Navy Victory March.

SIMEONE, HARRY   ASCAP 1949
composer, author, conductor
b Newark, NJ, May 9, 11. Arr for Fred Waring; choral cond; made many records. *Songs & Instrumental Works:* Kiddie Komando; The Magic of Love; Three Mother Geese; Button, Button, Let's Push the Button; Grandma's Thanksgiving; Nursery Rhyme Suite; Rumanian Rhapsody; Flute Cocktail; Trumpet in the Night; It's a Beautiful Day for a Ball Game; Song of the Promised Land; Little Drummer Boy; Christmas Greeting; With Hymn and Prayer; It's Christmas Once Again; Creole Clarinet; Christmas Card; Seville Suite; Can-Can for Band; La Petite Canadienne; Christmas Is the Most.

SIMMONS, ELSIE   ASCAP 1951
author
b London, Eng. Educ: Barnard Col. Writer of lyrics, TV musical, "Alice Through the Looking Glass" & chorale, "The Sound of America." Has written spec material for TV & films. Chief Collabrs: Moose Charlap, Stanley Applebaum, Paul Weirick, Larry Wagner. *Songs:* Lyrics: Backwards Alphabet; Some Summer Day; There Are Two Sides to Everything; I Wasn't Meant to Be a Queen; Come Out, Come Out, Wherever You Are; Jabberwock Song; Keep on the Grass; Through the Looking Glass; Who Are You?; 'Twas Brillig; Alice Is Coming to Tea; The Sound of Love; My Dream; Wrong Again; Sleep, Sleep, Daughter; Legend of the Bells; Charm Bracelet; Come Into My Heart; When You Kiss a Stranger; One Word of Spanish.

SIMMONS, HOMER   ASCAP 1947
composer, author
b Evansville, Ind; d Sunland, Calif, Aug 21, 71. Educ: Studied music with Arnold Habbe; Von Stein Acad Music, with Heinrich von Stein; Univ Southern Calif, BA; studied with Homer Grunn, Ignace Paderewski, Ottorino Respighi, Nadia Boulanger & Gordon Jacob. Toured US as pianist for Hubbard Operalogues. Organized Musical Workshop, Los Angeles, 38. In aircraft indust, WW II. Gave concerts, US & Europe. *Songs:* Carnival; Evening Song; Downtown; Supplication; Nocturne; Tell Me Once More; While Roses Fall; Cradle Song; Serenade to Vida. *Instrumental Works:* Impressions Basques; Panels From a Lacquered Screen (voice, string quartet); For piano & orch: Spanish Caprice; Phantasmania; Piano: Stairways; Alice in Wonderland Suite; Scherzino; The Old Dutch Clock; Evening in Old Vienna (string quartet); Lyra Davidica; The Gingham Dog; The Calico Cat; Three Vignettes: Parting (Auf Wiedersehen); Absence (Abwesenheit); Happy Return (Heimkehr); 2 string quartets. *Scores:* Opera: Red Riding Hood.

SIMMS, ALICE D   ASCAP 1945
composer, author
b New York, NY, Jan 13, 20. Educ: Cornell Univ, BA; Damrosch Inst. Gave concerts at age 11; writer radio scripts. Chief Collabrs: J Fred Coots, Leonard Joy, Jimmie Lunceford & Al Trace. *Songs:* Encore, Cherie; Buzz! Buzz! Buzz!; Foolishly Yours; I Spoke Too Soon; Reserved; Tell the Lord (Christopher Award); Mucho Closer (Cuban Medal); Goombay (Princess Margaret Citation); Island Woman; Like Ma-a-ad; All Suit! No Man!; Basket on Head; Wanna Do Nothin' All Day; Calypso Island.

SIMMS, TEDD
See Phillips, Teddy Steve

SIMMS, WINNIE LEE   ASCAP 1976
lyricist
b Fayetteville, Tenn, Mar 30, 25. Educ: Grade sch. Factory worker & housewife. *Songs:* Lyrics: I Don't Deserve a Mansion.

SIMON, CARLY
composer, singer
Educ: Sarah Lawrence Col; studied with Pete Seeger. Organized vocal duo with sister, Lucy, Simon Sisters. Singer, comp & recording artist, 71- Rec'd Grammy Award for Best New Artist, 71. *Songs:* Nobody Does It Better; Anticipation; You're So Vain; Boys in the Trees; Thats the Way It Should Be; No Secrets. *Albums:* Carly Simon; Anticipation; No Secrets; Hotcakes; Playing Possum; The Best of Carly Simon; Another Passenger; Boys in the Trees; Spy; Come Up Stairs.

SIMON, EDWARD G   ASCAP 1928
composer, author, conductor
b New York, NY, Jan 8, 1871; d Brooklyn, NY, May 17, 34. Educ: Pub schs. Led own orch in theatres & cafes, 10. Music critic, NY Times & Metronome. Ed, music publ firms, NY. *Songs:* Dawnlight, the Rose and You; Cradle Song; Hungarian Dance; Querida; June Rose; Day Dreams; Dancing Doll.

SIMON, GEORGE THOMAS (BUCK PINCUS)   ASCAP 1947
author
b New York, NY, May 9, 12. Educ: Fieldston Sch, New York; Harvard Univ, BA. Joined Metronome Mag, 35, ed, 39-55; TV writing & producing, 55-;

free-lance record producer, also record producer & pres, Bouree Productions. Author bks "The Big Bands" (first Deems Taylor-ASCAP Bk Award), "Simon Says", "Glenn Miller and His Orchestra", "The Big Bands Song Book" & "The Best of the Music Makers." East Coast exec dir, Nat Acad Recording Arts & Sci, 61-71; consult, Acad & Time-Life Records; mem, Newport Jazz Fest Adv Bd; lyricist. Chief Collabrs: Buddy Weed, Joe Ricardel, Alec Wilder (Ace Laramie). *Songs:* Lyrics: The Feeling of Jazz; Willie; A Mother-in-Law Is a Mother Too. *Albums:* Mother Goose for the Swing Set (12 songs).

SIMON, HOWARD   ASCAP 1950
composer, author, pianist
b Victoria, Can, Nov 29, 01; d Grosse Point, Mich, May 8, 61. Educ: Upper Can Col; Toronto Cons; studied with B H Carman & Leo Smith. To US, 21. Citizen, 48. Publ rep, Detroit & on road, 23-27. Organist in theaters, 27-29. Began teaching piano & arr, 29; taught in jr high sch. Author & publ "Simon Systems for Popular Piano and Organ." Chief Collabrs: A R Lewis, Harold Berg, Richard Whiting, Richard Pascoe. *Songs:* Gonna Get a Girl; Sweet Child (I'm Wild About You); As Long As I Have You; Holding Hands; Mary Ellen; Will We Meet Again?; As Long As I Live.

SIMON, JOHN SPIER   ASCAP 1963
composer, author
b Norwalk, Conn, Aug 11, 41. Educ: Piano, Andrew Wuhrer; Norwalk High Sch; Princeton Univ, 59-63, studied theory & comp with Milton Babbitt. Self-taught improvisation; wrote 2 original musical comedies at Norwalk High Sch, also wrote for Princeton Triangle Club Shows, jazz groups & Julius Monk's Plaza 9, New York. Finalist, Georgetown Intercollegiate Jazz Fest, 60; record producer, Columbia Records, 63-67, free-lance, 67-80; arr-orchr of many records. *Songs:* Davy's on the Road Again; My Name Is Jack; Livin' in a Land of Sunshine. *Scores:* Ballet: When We Were Very Young; Film: You Are What You Eat; Last Summer.

SIMON, LUCY
See Levine, Lucy Simon

SIMON, NAT   ASCAP 1934
composer, author, conductor
b Newburgh, NY, Aug 6, 00; d New York, NY, Sept 5, 79. Educ: High sch. Led own orch. Went to New York, became pianist, music publ firms & radio singers. Wrote film scores, London, 38. Chief Collabrs: Charles Tobias, Jimmy Kennedy, Guy Wood, John Redmond. *Songs & Instrumental Works:* The Gaucho Serenade; Little Curly Hair in a High Chair; Little Lady Make Believe; Poinciana; No Can Do; Goody Goodbye; Coax Me a Little Bit; Her Bathing Suit Never Got Wet; The Old Lamplighter; My Bolero; In My Little Red Book; Istanbul; And Mimi; Apple Blossom Wedding; Wait for Me, Mary; The Cocoanut Song; I'm in Love; Every Single Little Tingle of My Heart; Crosstown; I Wish That I Could Hide Inside This Letter; Chapter in My Life Called Mary; My Christmas Prayer; The Sound of Silence; Milwaukee Polka; Sweet Heartaches; Momma Doll Song; Down the Trail of Achin' Hearts; Hurry Back My Love; Red Apple Red; also Crown Jewels (12 instrumentals).

SIMON, NORMAN J   ASCAP 1962
author, librettist
b Brooklyn, NY, Dec 26, 25. Educ: Brooklyn Col, BA; Columbia Univ, MA. Produced records, ABC, Laurie, 20th Century Fox Records; wrote & publ songs; dir off Bway & TV. Chief Collabrs: Gershon Kingsley, Arthur W Kaplon, Ivan A Themmen, Lowell Mark, Ronnie Roullier, Luis Bonfo, Andy Badale, Tommy Goodman. *Songs:* Lyrics: Confessions of a Male Chauvinist Pig; Harmony; Look Around and You'll Find Me There; In My Thoughts of You. *Scores:* Opera: Lucian; Bway shows: A Jazz Requiem for Martin Luther King Jr; The Fifth Cup.

SIMON, PEGGY
See Traktman, Peggy Simon

SIMON, ROBERT A   ASCAP 1934
author
b New York, NY, Feb 18, 1897. Educ: Ethical Culture Sch; Columbia Univ. Wrote songs for Varsity Shows. Feature writer, NY newspapers; music ed, The New Yorker, 25-48. Radio, TV exec. Chief Collabrs: Robert Russel Bennett, Lewis Gensler, Vittorio Giannini, Owen Murphy. *Songs:* I Love Her; No Trouble But You. *Scores:* Operas: Garrick; Maria Malibran; Beauty and the Beast; Rehearsal Call; The Count Ory. Bway Stage: Ups-a-Daisy (also co-librettist); Hold Your Horses; Champagne Sec (Eng version, Die Fledermaus).

SIMON, WALTER CLEVELAND   ASCAP 1924
composer, pianist, organist
b Lexington, Ky, Oct 27, 1884; d New York, NY, Mar 5, 58. Educ: Pittsburgh Col Music, scholarship; New Eng Cons. Played pipe organ in film theatre, Bronx, NY, 12, also for all major circuits of theatres incl Pantages, Keith & Orpheum. First to comp musical score for motion pictures. On Bway, Palace Theatre, New York, also silent films, vaudeville. Played classic, popular & folk music. Hon mem, Am Fedn Musicians. Inventor of registration to allow piano music to be played on pipe organ & the solovox. Chief Collabrs: Mort Eiseman, Alexander Weinberg. *Instrumental Works:* Jack in the Box; Fleur de Lys; Gay Cavalier; For violin: Ecstasy. *Songs & Instrumental Works:* Themes for Organ

& Piano: Hurry; Agitato; Rodeo; Love Themes for Young and Old; Pathetique; Funeral; Marriage and Home Themes; Poverty and Sickness Themes; Negro Themes; Military Music (marches, band); Children's Music; Aged and Infirm Music; High Society and Wealthy Type Music. *Scores:* Film Background: Arrah Na Pough (first original film score); The Hunchback of Notre Dame; Ben Hur; Last Days of Pompeii; The Black Crook.

SIMON, WILLIAM LOUIS (LOU NOMIS,   ASCAP 1960
BILL LEWIS)
composer, author, saxophonist
b Springville, NY, July 1, 20. Educ: Univ Mich. Sr music ed, Bks & Records Div, Reader's Digest; bd dirs, Nat Acad Popular Music. Chief Collabr: Jack Yellen. *Songs:* Just an Old-Fashioned Waltz (For an Old-Fashioned Girl); Music: I Just Can't Wait Till Christmas; Two Left Feet Polka; Time and Again; Remembering Time.

SIMON, WILLIAM N   ASCAP 1956
composer, teacher
b Ste Genevieve, Mo, May 20, 16. Educ: South East Mo State Teachers Col, 2 yrs; Our Lady of the Lake Col, San Antonio, Tex, piano for 2 yrs; Univ Colo, BM & MM; studied with Nadia Boulanger, Fontainbleau, France; counterpoint, Gustav Reese; choral, Peter Wilhousky; comp, Cecil Effinge. Staff pianist & organist, KFVS-CBS & KVOO-NBC, Tulsa, Okla. Music ed, Carl Fischer Inc; choral consult, Big Three Music Corp; organist & choirmaster, Bloomfield Presby Church, NJ. Chief Collabrs: Warner Imig, Vincent Lopez. *Songs & Instrumental Works:* Hi-Fi Hop; Rosalia; Sidewalk Sant; There's No One to Love Me; All Day in the Saddle; UN Charter; America the Beautiful (Beautiful America); Jesus Our Lord Is Crucified; Warm Up and Sing; Prince of Peace; Somebody Cares for Me.

SIMONE, CARL
See Siemon, Carl

SIMONE, ELAINE
See Weisburd, Elaine Simone

SIMONE, NINA
See Wayman, Eunice

SIMONETTI, TED EDDY   ASCAP 1956
composer, author
b Brooklyn, NY, July 10, 04. Educ: Studied trumpet under Giovanni Nappi. At age 19, formed own orch; played & performed in all RKO & Lowe Theatres, nightclubs incl Piping Rock Club, Saratoga & Rivera on the Hudson. Musical dir, RKO Theatres; became mgr of Louis Prima & Keely Smith. Joined promotion staff, 20th Century Fox Records. Pres, Delaware Music; started De-Lite Records; dir & vpres, Delightful Music, Ltd & Double F Music. Chief Collabrs: Frank Davis, Louis Prima, Paul Francis, Johnny Robba. *Songs:* Purple Heart (nat adopted by Order of the Purple Heart); Nothin's Too Good for My Baby; Pray; Bony Bones; To Whom It May Concern (You Will Never Be Missed); I'll Be There.

SIMONS, RUDY   ASCAP 1965
composer, author
b Detroit, Mich, Dec 20, 28. Educ: Univ Mich. Began writing while in advert bus in Detroit, early 50's. Performed on Detroit radio & TV programs. Wrote lyrics for stage reviews while in USA, 52-53. Wrote winning song in competition sponsored by NBC Detroit affiliate WWJ, 53. Wrote lyrics for musical plays, "Bumbles", "Billy the Kid" & musical review for "Bald", also radio & TV commercials. Produced & wrote lyrics for semi-documentary film. *Songs:* Theme: On a Somewhere Sea.

SIMONS, SEYMOUR   ASCAP 1922
composer, author, conductor
b Detroit, Mich, Jan 14, 1896; d Detroit, Feb 12, 49. Educ: Univ Mich, BS. Wrote Mich Union Operas. 2nd Lt, USAAF, WW I. Wrote spec material, London & Paris, 22-23. In radio production; record exec, had booking agency, 28-32. Reorganized orch, 31; appeared on radio; became realtor, 38. Chmn, Detroit USO, WW II. Chief Collabrs: Haven Gillespie, Richard Whiting. *Songs:* Honey; Breezin' Along With the Breeze; All of Me; Tie a Little String Around Your Finger; The One I Love Just Can't Be Bothered With Me; Sweet of Love; Just Like a Gypsy.

SIMONSON, ERNEST LOWELL (SI)   ASCAP 1971
composer, arranger, pianist
b Pittsburgh, Pa, June 1, 53. Educ: Rummel High Sch; Southeastern La Univ; studied comp & theory with Jane Bastien, 67-70. Comp, arr & played keyboards for Messenger; played col & auditorium concerts nat; recording artist, Light Records; pianist, Reba; 3 Grammy nominations. Chief Collabrs: Rick Riso, Ted Pampeyan. *Songs:* Changin' Me; I Still Love You; I Feel Secure; Wings of Salvation; Lyrics: Bringin' the Message.

SIMPSON, EUGENE THAMON   ASCAP 1978
composer, teacher, singer
b North Wilkesboro, NC, Apr 10, 32. Educ: Howard Univ, BM, studied with Mark Fax, Frederick Wilkerson & W Lawso; Yale Univ, BM & MM, studied

with Paul Hindemith, Quincy Porter, H Leroy Baumgartner & Fenno Heath; Columbia Univ, EdD(music), studied with Robert Pace, Thomas Richner, Allen Forte & Harry Robert Wilson. Music instr, New York pub schs, 55-68. USA Spec Serv & Dept Army World Tour Show, 56-59. Piano debut, Judson Hall, 56; vocal debut, Berkshire Music Fest, 65. Pvt voice teacher & coach, Carnegie Hall, 64-68. Dir choral activities, Va State Col, 68-70. Chmn, Div Humanities, Dept Music, Bowie State Col, 70-75. Music chmn, Glassboro State Col, 75-80. Commercial background singer, major labels & for Texaco, Three Musketeers & others. Choral clinician, All-State Fests, Fla, NC, SC & Ga. Contributing & observer cond, Third & Fourth Int Choral Fests, Lincoln Ctr & Kennedy Ctr. *Songs:* Music: Hold On!; Steal Away; Sinnuh Please Don't Let Dis Harves; Nobody Knows De Trouble I've Seen; True Religion; Too Late, Sinnuh.

SIMPSON, MARTIN BLAND, III   ASCAP 1971
composer, author, lyricist
b Durham, NC, Oct 16, 48. Educ: Univ NC, Chapel Hill, BA; piano study with Ed Paloantonio, 79- Chief Collabrs: Jim Wann, Tommy Thompson. *Songs:* These Southern States That I Love; When I Get the Call; Come on Down to the Sea; Bound Away. *Scores:* Off-Bway: Diamond Studs; Hot Grog.

SIMPSON, RONALD WEST   ASCAP 1968
composer, author, teacher
b Seattle, Wash, July 1, 40. Educ: Palo Alto High Sch, 58; Stanford Univ, 58-59; Brigham Young Univ, 59-61, 69-71; Sibelius Acad Music, 64, tutorial work with comp Jouko Tolonen. Began performing & writing, late 50's. Orchestrated & cond Stanford "Gaieties" shows, 64-65. Founded Sound Column Productions & Ronarte Publ, 68. Leader of touring variety group, The Sound Column. Has created musical commercials for radio & TV. Producer & arr. *Songs:* Nancy Drew; Jodie; Live Oak; Lyrics: Brother of the Wind. *Scores:* Films: Snowbird Sunshine (PRSA Award); Gates of Zion.

SIMPSON, VALERIE R
composer, singer, musician
b New York, NY, Aug 26, 46. Recorded with Glover, Sceptor & Motown Records. Songwriter & performer with Nickolas Ashford. Chief Collabr: Nick Ashford. *Songs:* Ain't No Mountain High Enough; Reach Out and Touch; Ain't Nothing Like the Real Thing; Gimme Something Real; Let's Go Get Stoned; Found a Cure; The Boss; Remember Me; It Seems to Hang On; Stuff Like That; I'm Every Woman. *Albums:* Exposed; Valerie Simpson; Gimme Something Real; I Wanna Be Selfish; Come; So, So Satisfied; Send It; Is It Still Good To Ya; Stay Free.

SIMS, HARRY   ASCAP 1951
composer, author
b New York, NY, Nov 6, 08. Educ: Manual Training High Sch, dipl. Stockbroker with Paine Webber, 36-70. Chief Collabr: Jack Perry. *Songs:* You Stole My Wife, You Horse Thief; What Kind of an Animal Are You?; Sandy the Sandman; Upsy Down Town; Sure Fire Kisses; Where-in the World?; Love Me Again; I'm Wired for Lovin'; Cubalita; Must I?; Handful of Rainbows; You Can't Take a Dream From a Dreamer; Too Big to Cry; Soda Pop Parade.

SIMS, JAMES CHRISTOPHER   ASCAP 1977
composer, author, singer
b Oceanside, Calif, Feb 18, 49. Educ: San Diego State Univ; Mira Costa Col. Played prof in clubs & concerts, 63- Recording artist, 71- Chief Collabr: Rob Cammack.

SIMS, JOHN HALEY (ZOOT)   ASCAP 1973
saxophonist
b Inglewood, Calif, Oct 29, 25. Educ: High sch. Saxophonist with Benny Goodman, Woody Herman & Bobby Sherwood Orchs, 41-50; with Stan Kenton, Benny Goodman & Gerry Mulligan, 50-59. Formed Zoot Sims-Al Cohn Quintet, 59, toured Europe & US with Norman Granz, Jazz at the Philh, 66-67, Monterey Jazz Fest, 71, Newport Jazz Fest, 72-77 & 79-80, Montreux Fest, 75 & 77, 1st White House Jazz Concert, 78 & Smithsonian Inst, 78. Served in USAAF, 44-46. Rec'd Grammy Award nomination, 77 & 79; ASCAP Popular Award, 76, 77, 78, 79 & 80. Mem, Defenders of Wildlife Soc & New York Jazz Repertory Co. Made many jazz records. *Songs & Instrumental Works:* Red Door; Dark Cloud; Nirvana; Blues for Nat Cole; Bloos for Louise; Hardav; Wrap Up; Captain Bligh; Morning Fun.

SIMS, LEE   ASCAP 1944
composer, pianist, teacher
b Champaign, Ill, Apr 30, 1898; d New York, NY, May 7, 66. Educ: High sch. Organist in theatres; on radio, vaudeville & clubs with singer Illomay Bailey; made records. Began teaching, 48. Author "Instruction for Modern Piano" (2 vols). *Instrumental Works:* The Moth; Chatter; Similitude; Meditation; Retrospection; Dublin Swing; Improvisation. *Songs & Instrumental Works:* Blythewood (symph tone poem). *Scores:* Film background: Drums; Dinner at the Ritz.

SIMUN, FRANCIS GEORGE   ASCAP 1972
composer, teacher, conductor
b Clairton, Pa, July 3, 44. Educ: Studied violin with grandfather; studied with Michael Uhrinek, piano with Marie Uhrinek (mother), 50 & with Rotilla Rotilli, 52; Univ Chicago, studied with U Howard Talley, 58; Juilliard, studied with

Stanley Wolfe & Jacob Druckman, 60; studied with Luigi Dallapiccolo, Italy, 65; Duquesne Univ, BS, 67, MM, 69. Began musical career at age 5. Cond original works, US & Europe. Chief Collabrs: Robert Moore, Conrad Aiken, Allen Ginsberg, John Milton, Nicomer Parra, Pablo Neruda. *Instrumental Works:* Symphony No 1 in D; Concerto for Violin and Orchestra. *Scores:* Comus (music drama); Ballet: Metamorphosis; Films: Hollywood.

SINATRA, FRANCIS ALBERT (FRANK)   ASCAP 1950
author, singer, actor
b Hoboken, NJ, Dec 12, 15. Educ: Drake Inst. First Prize Winner, Maj Bowes Amateur Hour; also toured with unit. Vocalist with Harry James & Tommy Dorsey Orchs. Singer on radio, TV, nightclubs, theatres & concerts. Made many records; founded Reprise Records. Film appearances incl "Higher and Higher"; "Anchors Aweigh"; "It Happened in Brooklyn"; "The Kissing Bandit"; "Take Me Out to the Ball Game"; "On the Town"; "From Here to Eternity" (Acad Award); "Young At Heart"; "Guys and Dolls"; "Not As a Stranger"; "The Tender Trap"; "The Man With the Golden Arm"; "High Society"; "The Pride and the Passion"; "Pal Joey"; "The Joker Is Wild"; "Some Came Running"; "A Hole in the Head"; "Ocean's Eleven"; "Can-Can"; "The Manchurian Candidate"; "Sergeants Three"; "Come Blow Your Horn"; "Robin and the Seven Hoods"; "None But the Brave"; "Von Ryan's Express." Biographies incl "The Voice" by E J Kahn; "Sinatra and His Rat Pack" by Richard Gehman. *Songs:* This Love of Mine; Take My Love; Mistletoe and Holly; Mr Success.

SINATRA, FRANK W (JR)   ASCAP 1971
author, singer
b Jersey City, NJ, Jan 10, 44. Educ: Univ Southern Calif; Univ Calif, Los Angeles, studied with Feri Roth; Ariz State Univ; studied music, comp & theory, 61-63. Band singer, recording artist & TV artist in US, Can & 41 countries, 62-79. Chief Collabrs: Sam Donohue, Lawrence V O'Brien, Robert T Harrison, Nelson Riddle, Walter V Borys, Jeffrey Morrisson. *Songs:* Spice; Black Night; Believe in Me; What Were You Thinking?; Over-the-Land (Bicentennial celebration song, 76); Trux.

SINATRA, RAY   ASCAP 1947
composer, conductor, pianist
b Gergenti, Sicily, Nov 1, 04. US citizen. Educ: Pub schs; studied music with father, also with DeVoto, D'Allesandro, Riegger, Christ, Schillinger, Waggoner, Grainger, Stoessel & Rianerrie. At age 13, gave piano recital, Symph Hall, Boston; toured New Eng. Organist in Boston theatres; pianist & arr with dance orchs; also for radio. Became cond, 35. To Hollywood, scored films. *Instrumental Works:* Piano Concerto; Central Park Ballet. *Songs & Instrumental Works:* Are You Listenin'?; Miracle of the Bells; Happiness; No One Knows, No One Cares; I'll Never Go to Heaven; Little Church on the Hill; This World of My Own; Hot Ivories.

SINCLAIR, JERRY WAYNE   ASCAP 1972
composer, singer, recording artist
b Calais, Maine, Mar 25, 43. Educ: High sch, Caribou, Maine; Bob Jones Univ, 61-63; Charles Conrad Sch of Acting, 78-79. Recording artist, Capitol Records, 72-75. Has worked in TV, made personal appearances & given concerts. *Songs:* Alleluia; Whenever You Want Me Too (Girl); Jesus Lifegiver; He's the Same; Waters of Shiloh.

SINGER, AMY
See Southard, Mary Ann

SINGER, ARTHUR   ASCAP 1959
composer, teacher
b Toronto, Ont, Feb 1, 19. Educ: High sch; pvt music study. Played in staff orch, CBS, MBS, 10 yrs. With Paul Whiteman, TV Teen Club, 5 yrs. Pvt teacher, Philadelphia. Chief Collabrs: Paul White, Kal Mann. *Songs:* At the Hop; Dottie; Every Sunday Morning; Wind in the Willow.

SINGER, DOLPH   ASCAP 1937
author
b New York, NY, Sept 19, 1900; d Milford, Conn, Dec 8, 42. Educ: Pub schs. *Songs:* I Want My Rib; Just Around the Corner; Sweet to Cheat Jesta Little; That's Where I Met My Gal; Heigh Ho; Summer Wives; On a South Sea Isle.

SINGER, GUY
See Guisinger, Earl C

SINGER, JEANNE WALSH   ASCAP 1975
composer, author, pianist
b New York, NY, Aug 4, 24. Educ: Horace Mann High Sch, 40; Barnard Col, BA, 44; Nat Guild Piano Teachers, Artist Dipl, 54; pvt study in piano with Nadia Reisenberg, 15 yrs; studied theory & comp with Seth Bingham, William Mitchell & Douglas Moore. Concert pianist, solo & with chamber groups. Has given lect-recitals & progs of own works, also radio & TV performances. Pvt teacher for 30 yrs. Has rec'd over 30 awards for comp & var comns. Chief Collabrs: Patricia Benton, Anne Marx, Madeline Mason, Lloyd Schwartz, Frederika Blankner. *Songs & Instrumental Works:* A Cycle of Love (4 songs for soprano & piano); Suite in Harpsichord Style (piano or harpsichord); From the Green Mountains (trio for violin, clarinet & piano); American Indian Song Suite

(4 songs with piano); From Petrarch (voice, French horn & piano); Suite for Horn and Harp; Nocturne for Clarinet and Piano; Composers Prayer (choral SSA & piano).

SINGER, LOUIS C ASCAP 1941
composer, arranger

b New York, NY, Feb 26, 12; d Forest Hills, NY, Dec 30, 66. Educ: Juilliard; Columbia Univ; NY Univ; studied music with Alexander Lipsky, Bernard Wagenaar & Wallingford Riegger. CBS staff arr, 2 yrs. Arr & ed-in-chief, music publ cos, incl Chappel & Schirmer. *Songs:* One Meat Ball; Sleepy Serenade (Film Critics Award); Lass With the Delicate Air; Young and Warm and Wonderful; If I Had a Ribbon Bow; Deep Blues; Song of the Army Nurse Corps (Off anthem, USANC); Wing Ding; Bugler's Dilemma; Night Whispers; Strange Interval; Am I a Toy or a Treasure?; Slipping Through My Fingers; I Will Be Home Again; Don't Make a Memory of Me; Keep Smilin' Keep Laughin' Be Happy; Woman Is a Five Letter Word; also Little Songs on Big Subjects; Little Songs About the UN (UN Comn); Ballads for the Age of Science. *Songs & Instrumental Works:* The Great Assembly Line (US Govt Comn); I Spoke to Jefferson at Guadalcanal; Israel's Freedom Ballad. *Scores:* Ballet: Soliloquy at Midnight; Folk Opera: Patrick Henry and the Frigate's Keel (US Govt Comn).

SINGER, ROBERT MORRIS ASCAP 1955
composer

b Miami, Fla, Sept 2, 30. Educ: Pvt piano instr. Chief Collabrs: James Boothe, Teddy Powell, Joe Shank. *Songs:* Music: Unsuspecting Heart; Lyrics: April Give Me One More Day; Estoril.

SINNICAM, DON
See MacInnis, Donald

SIRAS, JOHN
See Schuster, Ira

SIRAVO, GEORGE ASCAP 1952
composer, arranger, conductor

b Staten Island, NY, Oct 2, 16. Started playing saxophone in his early 20's with various dance bands incl Gene Krupa & Glen Miller. Arr & cond for Vic Damone, Tony Bennett, Frank Sinatra, Dinah Shore & Doris Day, also for movie cos incl MGM, Fox, Warner Bros, 20th Century & Universal.

SIRMAY, ALBERT ASCAP 1933
composer, conductor, editor

b Budapest, Hungary; d New York, NY, Jan 15, 67. Educ: Royal Acad of Music, Budapest; Univ Budapest, MusD. Comp scores for musicals in Budapest & Vienna incl "Dancing Hussars", "Der Puszta Kavalier", "Graf Rinaldo", "Alexandra", "The Gingerbread Heart" & "Tuenderlaki Lanyok." Chief ed, Chappell. Ed bks "A Treasury of Gilbert and Sullivan", "Songs of the Rivers of America", "A Treasury of Grand Opera", "Rodgers and Hart Song Book", "Cole Porter Song Book", "George and Ira Gershwin Song Book", "Jerome Kern Song Book" & "Lerner and Loewe Song Book." *Scores:* London Stage: Bamboula; Lady Mary; Girl on the Film (Bway); Princess Charming (Bway); Bway Stage: Ripples.

SISSLE, NOBLE ASCAP 1922
author, conductor

b Indianapolis, Ind, July 10, 1889; d. Educ: Butler Col. Toured with Thomas Jubilee Singers, 2 yrs; mem, vaudeville team with Eubie Blake, formed 15. Drum maj in Jim Europe's band, WW I; led band after Europe's death. Organized own orch, touring US & Europe. Organizer & first pres, Negro Actors Guild. Actor. Chief Collabr: Eubie Blake. *Songs:* I'm Just Wild About Harry; Love Will Find a Way; You Were Meant for Me; Shuffle Along; Bandana Days; Gypsy Blues; Hello, Sweetheart, Hello; Goodnight, Angeline; Slave of Love; Lowdown Blues; Characteristic Blues; Okey Doke; Yeah Man. *Scores:* Bway stage: Shuffle Along; Chocolate Dandies.

SISSON, KENN ASCAP 1946
composer, author, arranger

b Danbury, Conn, Aug 15, 1898; d Rego Park, NY, May 30, 47. Educ: Parochial schs; studied music with Christian Praetorius. Arr for Ben Bernie Orch. Served in USN, WW I. Organized own orch, appearing in vaudeville & on radio. Had own publ co. Wrote music for radio & films. Arrangements: Swing Low Sweet Chariot; Old Oaken Bucket; Love's Old Sweet Song; Song of India.

SITTIG, ROBERT DONALD ASCAP 1963
composer, author, teacher

b Utica, NY, Mar 18, 19. Educ: Utica Free Acad High Sch; Crane Sch Music; Potsdam Col Arts & Sci; State Univ NY, BS, MS, permanent teaching cert. Began comp & arr, 36. Double bass, Utica Symph, Con Amore Strings & Opera Guild Orch. Tenor saxophone, bass & piano, jazz groups. Traveling musician during Big Band era. Musician, 8 yrs. Teacher pub sch music, 10 yrs. Mem, Am Guild Authors & Comp, Nat Acad Popular Music & Am Fedn Musicians. *Songs:* Holiday; Snow Is in the Air; Let's Have a Halloween Party; Valentine, Valentine.

SIWEK, ROMAN ASCAP 1978
composer, author

b Malkinia, Poland, Feb 28, 35. Educ: SGGW Cols, musical instruments, eng & master degree, 59; Warsaw Music Sch, comp, music theory & clarinet, 63; Acad Music, Warsaw, sound acoustics, Ph degree course, 67. Musician & arr for symphonic, popular & dance music; played in symphonic hall, nightclubs & TV; recording artist in Poland & US; did sci res for musical indust in Poland & US. *Songs & Instrumental Works:* Variation for Clarinet; Hunting Song for Soprano and Orchestra; Bicentennial Happy Birthday; Go to the Races; Me and My Six-Pack.

SIZEMORE, ARTHUR ASCAP 1921
composer, conductor, publisher

b Marion, Ill, Feb 5, 1891; d Chicago, Ill, Sept 24, 54. Pianist with traveling theatrical cos for 2 yrs. Assoc with music publ firm, Chicago, had own publ firm for 2 yrs, then with NY cos. Wrote for films; led own band, appearing in nightclubs & restaurants. Publ of mail order mag "Homeworker." *Songs:* By the Light of the Stars; After the Rain; So Tired; Right or Wrong; Mississippi Shore.

SKAGGS, HAZEL GHAZARIAN ASCAP 1963
composer, author, teacher

b Boston, Mass, Aug 26, 24. Educ: New Eng Cons Music, BA; Fairleigh Dickinson Univ, MA(psychol); Northeastern Univ; Univ Minn; Univ Colo; Univ Hawaii; Univ Wis; studied piano with Clarence Adler. Group piano specialist, 60-; comp educ music in piano, 60-; auth articles, leading music mags. Nat chmn, Comp Test, 64-, adjudicator; pres, Piano Teachers Congress NY, Inc, 65-69; mem ed bd, Leisure Today mag, 78-; dir, Music Counseling Service, 79-. *Songs:* Educational: Little Girl From Mars; Little Invention; Flight to the Moon; Dance of the Martians; Spring Showers.

SKEATH, HAROLD R ASCAP 1940
author, teacher

b Mahanoy City, Pa, May 3, 1899; d Los Angeles, Calif, Mar 17, 42. Music teacher. *Songs:* The Rose and the Butterfly; In the High Hills; Had I But Wings; Harbor; The Bugle Blows; House on a Hillside.

SKELTON, RICHARD RED ASCAP 1964
composer, author

b Vincennes, Ind, July 18, 13. Educ: Ind State Univ, Terra Haute, hon degree. Pantomimes & verbimimes comp; music (marches) played, PBS, also used for parades, political functions & gen audiences. *Songs:* My True Love (theme song); Music: Reds White and Blue March; Grand Marshall March; Sorrento Sunset; Deep Sea.

SKIDMORE, WILL E ASCAP 1935
composer, author, publisher

b Little Rock, Ark, Apr 9, 1880; d El Paso, Tex, Nov 13, 59. Educ: Pub schs. Pianist, calliopist in Ringling's Band. Comp, publ co, Kansas City, Mo. To NY, became publ. Sold co to Shapiro, Bernstein. *Songs:* You Can't Get No Lovin' Where There Ain't Any Love; Pray for the Lights to Go Out; Somebody's Done Me Wrong; When I Gets Out in No Man's Land; Them Has-Been Blues; On the Ozark Trail; Now the Mountains Will See Her Face No More; also Deacon Song Series.

SKILES, MARLIN H ASCAP 1963
composer

b Harrisburg, Pa, Dec 17, 06. Educ: Froehlich Cons, Pa, studies in piano & theory; pvt study in comp with Dr Ernst Toch, Hollywood, 5 yrs, also cond with Albert Coates. Pianist and/or arr with many leading jazz bands, incl Jean Goldkette, Russ Columbo, Aaronsons Commanders, Paul Whiteman & Ben Bernie. Under contract to Fox Film Studios, 33. Radio credits as comp, arr & cond incl, "My Friend Irma", "My Favorite Husband", "Chase and Sanborn Program" & "Pursuit"; TV credits incl, "That's My Boy", "Mister Ed", "The Beachcomber." Comp & music dir TV series, "Death Valley Days", 10 yrs. Assoc with Univ Calif, San Diego Extension teaching music scoring for TV & motion pictures. Former mem bd dirs, San Diego Opera Guild. *Songs & Instrumental Works:* The Play's the Thing (baritone & orch); Ballade of the Duel; You Will Know My Love. *Scores:* Film: Over 21; A Thousand and One Nights; The Jolson Story; Relentless; An Annapolis Story; The Maze; Tonight and Every Night; My Gun Is Quick; Calloway Went Thataway; The Violent Ones; Dayton's Devils; The Resurrection of Zachary Wheeler.

SKILTON, CHARLES SANFORD ASCAP 1924
composer, author, conductor

b Northampton, Mass, Aug 16, 1868; d Lawrence, Kans, Mar 12, 41. Educ: Yale Univ, BA; Royal High Sch for Music, Berlin, with Bargiel & Albert Heintz; Metrop Col of Music, NY, with Harry Rowe Shelley, O B Boise & Dudley Buck; hon MusD, Syracuse Univ. Music dir, Salem Acad & Col, 1883-96 & NJ State Normal Sch, 1898-03. Dean, Sch of Fine Arts, 03-15; prof of organ, theory & history of music, Univ of Kans, 03-41, organized Univ of Kans Orch. Made study of Am Indian music. Pres, Kans State Music Teachers Asn, 14-16. Dean, Kans Chapter Am Guild Organists, 13-35. Mem, MacDowell Col, Nat Acad Am Comp & Cond. Author "Modern Symphonic Forms." *Instrumental Works:* Suite Primeval; American Indian Fantasy (cello, orch); 3 Indian Sketches (piano); The Guardian Angel (oratorio); Ticonderoga (cantata); Overture in E; String Quartet in B. *Scores:* Operas: Kalopin (David Bispham Award); The Sun Bride; The Day of Gayomair.

SKINNER, FRANK   ASCAP 1946
composer, arranger, pianist
b Meredosia, Ill, Dec 31, 1897; d Los Angeles, Calif, Oct 9, 68. Educ: Chicago Musical Col; also pvt music study. Pianist on river boats & in vaudeville. Went to NY, joined Ace Brigode (14 Virginians) orch. Arr, Bway music publ, 24-35. Went to Hollywood, 35. Author of text books: "Arranging for Small Orchestra" & "Underscore - Composing Music for Film Background." *Scores:* Film background: Three Smart Girls Grow Up; Saboteur; Magnificent Obsession; Away All Boats; Written on the Wind; Tammy and the Bachelor; Man of a Thousand Faces; Interlude; Imitation of Life; Back Street; Midnight Lace; Captain Newman, MD; Shenandoah; Madame X; The Ugly American; The Egg and I; Battle Hymn; Tap Roots; Harvey; Bedtime for Bonzo; The Appaloosa; The World in His Arms; Tammy.

SKINNER, JAMES R   ASCAP 1968
composer
b Hartford, Conn, Jan 29, 23. Dir, Cotton Bowl parade, spec events for Tex State Fair & Super Bowl XV pre-game & half time entertainment. Dir of entertainment, Dallas Cowboys. Chief Collabr: Johnny Boudreau. *Instrumental Works:* Go Dallas Cowboys.

SKINNER, WILBUR ALBERT   ASCAP 1955
composer, author, musician
b Meredosia, Ill, Apr 25, 06. Musician, Ill & Miss River boats, 21; formed orch, played midwest, 28-30, hotels & clubs in east, 32-40. Joined Robbins Music Co as songplugger for var artists, 30-32. Started Skinner Music Co; musical score writer, 45- Chief Collabrs: Frank Skinner, Victor Kirk, Charlie Tobias. *Songs:* Let's Harmonize; Heaven's to Betsy; Lyrics: Remember When; Skyline of Old Manhattan; Music: Away All Boats; Singing an Old Refrain; Romeo; Swinging on the Gate; Only a Dream Ago; Lonely Sunday Morning.

SKLEROV, GLORIA J   ASCAP 1973
composer, author, instructor
b New York, NY. Educ: Chatham Square Music Sch; Brooklyn Col, BA; Potsdam State Teachers Col, NY, studied with Anna Landau; Wagner Col, NY. Staff writer, Garrett Music, 74-79; now staff writer, Interworld Music Group. Songwriting instr, Pierce Col & Univ Calif, Los Angeles. Chief Collabrs: Harry Lloyd, Pamela Phillips, Molly-Ann Leikin, Dominick Frontiere, Mark Holden, Peter Threllfall. *Songs:* He Did With Me; Where Did They Go; I Believe I'm Gonna Love You; It Could Have Been Me; Hollywood Seven; Stay; Music: Everytime I Sing a Love Song; Silver Wings and Golden Rings; Lyrics: I Just Fall in Love Again.

SKORNICKA, JOSEPH E   ASCAP 1951
composer, author, conductor
b Birch Creek, Mich, Feb 13, 02; d Houston, Tex, Dec 22, 72. Educ: Univ Wis, Milwaukee, BE; Northwestern Univ, MA; Ore State Univ, EdD. Dir music, Milwaukee Vocational Sch, 22-27. Cond, Milwaukee Engrs Band, 24-30. Supvr & instr music, Milwaukee pub schs, 27-42, later, head of music educ. Maj, USA, WW II. Founder & cond, Milwaukee Civic Band, 39-59. Cond, Milwaukee Civic Orch. Author of educ books. Chief Collabr: Richard Koebner. *Instrumental Works:* Overtures: Eroica; Militaire; Two Admirals; Spring Madrigal; Serenade for Band.

SKORR, MICHAEL   ASCAP 1968
composer, teacher, singer
b Zawaliv, Ukraine, Sept 12, 12. Educ: New York Col Music; NY Univ; Am Acad Dramatic Arts; Queens Col. Recording artist; had vaudeville & nightclub act; musician & actor. Compiled & arr albums: "Ukrainian Folk Dance" (one original comp); "Ukrainian Folk Songs and Dances"; "Russian Folk Songs and Dances"; "Songs and Dances of the Israeli." *Instrumental Works:* Marusia Polka.

SKROWACZEWSKI, STANISLAW   ASCAP 1968
composer
b Lwow, Poland, Oct 3, 23. Educ: Col Lwow, grad, 39; Univ Lwow, 39-44; Music Acad, Lwow, dipl comp & cond, 45; Music Acad, Krakow, Poland, dipl comp & cond, 46; Univ Krakow, musicology, 45-47; studied with Nadia Boulanger. Cond, Wroclaw Opera & Philh Orch, 46-47; Paris Orch Symph, France, 47-49 & Warsaw Nat Orch, 56-59. Music dir, Katowice Philh, Poland, 49-54 & Minneapolis Symph, 62-79. Guest cond, all major orchs worldwide, Vienna & Metropolitan Operas. *Instrumental Works:* Symphony for Strings; Preludium, Fuga, Postludium; Music At Night; Concerto for English Horn and Orchestra; Rice-cari Notturni (saxophone, orch).

SKY, JACK
See Govsky, John M

SKYE, DIANE S (DIANE HILDERBRAND)   ASCAP 1967
composer, author, singer
b Roswell, NMex, Apr 13, 45. Educ: Univ Calif, Northridge, BA(theatre). Songwriter from age 18. Under contract with Central Songs Inc, 2 yrs. Free-lance writer. Signed with Screen Gems & Columbia Music, 8 yrs; songwriter for TV shows incl "The Flying Nun" & "Bridget Loves Bernie." Recording artist. Chief Collabrs: Steven Stone, Jack Peller, Shorty Rogers. *Songs:* He Walks Like a Man; Lyrics: Your Auntie Grizelda; Early Morning Blues and Greens; Easy Come Easy Go; Goin' Down. *Albums:* Early Morning Blues and Greens.

SKYLAR, SUNNY (SELIG SIDNEY SHAFTEL)   ASCAP 1942
composer, author, singer
b Brooklyn, NY, Oct 11, 13. Educ: Elementary sch; James Madison High Sch, Brooklyn. Started writing, 35, band singer with Abe Lyman, Ben Bernie, Paul Whiteman, Ted Lewis & Vincent Lopez, 37-45, then worked as a single act in the Latin Quarter, NY, Versailles, NY, Roosevelt Hotel, New Orleans & others, 45-55; wrote band material for Betty Hutton, also did singing special material (comedic) & others, 42. Singer, artist. Chief Collabrs: Andrew Ackers, Ticher Freeman, Al Frisch. *Songs:* Just a Little Bit South of North Carolina; Gotta Be This or That; Waitin' for the Train to Come In; Hair of Gold, Eyes of Blue; I'd Be Lost Without You; It's All Over Now; Don't Wait Too Long; Atlanta, GA; Lyrics: Besame Mucho; Amor, Amor, Amor; Be Mine Tonight (Noche de Ronde); You're Breaking My Heart; And So to Sleep Again; It Must Be Jelly (Cause Jam Don't Shake Like That); You'll Always Be the One I Love; Vieni Su; Love Me With All Your Heart (Cuando Calienta el Sol); Nola; Carnaval in Costa Rica. *Songs & Instrumental Works:* Fifteen Minutes Intermission. *Albums:* The Hidden Island.

SLACK, FREDERIC CHARLES (FREDDIE SLACK) ASCAP 1955
composer, author, conductor
b La Crosse, Wis, Aug 7, 10; d Hollywood, Calif, Aug 10, 65. Educ: Am Cons, Chicago; also pvt study. Pianist & arr for dance orchs, Chicago; played piano & arr for Ben Pollack's Orch, later with Jimmy Dorsey & Will Bradley. Formed own orch, Los Angeles, 41. Formed his own trio & played clubs & hotels throughout the US, 50-65. Made many records & recorded for Capitol Records. Author "Freddie Slack's Boogie-Woogie Book on 8 Beats." *Songs & Instrumental Works:* Cow Cow Boogie; Strange Cargo; The House of Blue Lights; A Kiss Goodnight; Cuban Sugar Mill; A Cat's Ninth Life; Rib Joint; Mr Freddie's Boogie; Riffette; Beat Me Daddy Eight to the Bar; Celery Stalks at Midnight; Down the Road A-Piece; It's Square But It Rocks; Southpaw Serenade; Butter for the Ducks; You Can Say That Again; O Sole Mio; Lullaby; Celeste Boogie; Think of Me; Chinatown; Small Bunch O Nod; My Mama Never Told Me; An Old Piano (That Played by Itself); Behind the Right Beat; On the Road to Mandolin; Aftersours; Humoresquire; Beating With Chopsticks; Rockin' the Boogie; Bolero to the Moon; Raindrops; Blackout Boogie; Is I Gotta Practice, Ma; Boogie in G; Chopstick Boogie; Back Room Boogie; Beverly Boogie.

SLADEK, PAUL   ASCAP 1960
composer, author, violinist
b Vienna, Austria. Educ: Vienna Pub Sch (violin & 2 yr scholarship); violin study with Gottfried Feist, Fred Toerge, Alois Trnka, David Hochstein, Albert Spalding, Leopold Auer; coached with Fritz Kreisler, Thibaud & Ysaye; Carnegie Inst Tech (one yr scholarship). First violinist to perform a violin solo over radio, KDKA, East Pittsburgh, Pa, 22. Author: "Thirty Minutes a Day." Edited music for Albert Spalding. Researcher of Bach, 5 yrs. Prof violin & comp, Duquesne Univ, 16 yrs. Head, Violin Dept, Carnegie Inst Tech. Pvt teacher, Pittsburgh. Wrote organ pieces for Centennial Anniversary of St Mary's Cathedral, Fargo, NDak. Chief Collabrs: James de la Fuente, Caspar Koch. *Instrumental Works:* Isle of the Mists for Orchestra or for Violin Solo with Orchestra; Fantasy for Piano and Violin (trio, piano, cello & viola); Danse Rustique; Menuet Pompadour (winner, Comp Press Publ Award Contest); The Old Clock (winner, Comp Press Publ Award Contest); Pixie Frolic (violin, piano); Romance; Mazurka; Gavotte Coquette; Berceuse; Mijn Moederspraak (transc); Violin with Piano: Caprice Villageois; Poeme d'Amour Serenade; Paganini Caprice (arr No V); Heidenroslein (transc); Centennial Glory (organ & chorus; comn, Centennial Anniversary Celebration, Fargo, NDak, 80).

SLATER, RICHARD WESLEY   ASCAP 1969
composer, organist, conductor
b Los Angeles, Calif, Feb 28, 31. Educ: Herbert Hoover High Sch; Calif State Univ, Los Angeles, BA, 63, MA, 70; piano study with Gustav Reihard, organ with James Shearer, Byron Arnold & Ladd Thomas. Dir music, St Mark's Episcopal Church, Glendale, Calif, 63-79. Asst prof music theory & hist, Calif State Univ, Los Angeles, 78 & Long Beach, 78-79. Many WCoast organ recitals. Rec'd 1st Prize, Expo Comp Contest, Spokane, Wash, 73. Music comn for Am Guild Organists Regional Convention, Riverside, 77. *Songs:* Shepherds, Pipe Your Melody; Music: 10 Festival Antiphons; O Lord, Thou Hast Searched Me and Known Me; Psalm 66: Make a Joyous Shout to God; Hush! My Dear; A Song of Mary and Jesus; Praise the Lord Through Every Nation; A Christmas Introit; Christ Hath Humbled Himself; Behold the Lamb of God; With Broken Heart and Contrite Sigh; O Day of Rest and Gladness; Blessings; O Praise the Lord, All Ye Nations; Psalm 29: Ascribe Unto the Lord; A Mighty Fortress; An Easter Introit; Gentle Mary.

SLATKIN, LEONARD E
conductor

Educ: Piano study with Victor Aller & Selma Cramer, 55, comp with Mario Castelnuovo-Tedesco, 58, viola with Sol Schoenbach, 59, cond with Felix Slatkin, Amerigo Marino & Ingolf Dahl; Ind Univ, 62; Los Angeles City Col, 63; Juilliard (Irving Berlin fel in musical direction), studied with Jean Morel & Walter Susskind, 64. Began violin study, 47. Cond debut as asst cond, Youth Symph of New York, Carnegie Hall, 66. Asst cond, Juilliard Opera Theatre & Dance Dept, 67. Asst cond, St Louis Symph, 68-71, founder & music dir, 69-, assoc cond, 71-74, assoc principal cond, 79- Debut with Chicago Symph Orch, New York Philh & Philadelphia Orch, 74. Europ debut with Royal Philh Orch, 74; USSR orch debut, 76-77. Principal guest cond, Minn Orch, 74-, summer artistic dir, 79-80. Music dir, New Orleans Philh Symph Orch, 77-78, music adv, 79-80. Guest cond orchs throughout world. Past visiting asst prof music, Washington Univ, Mo; initiated afternoon lect series; hosted weekly radio prog.

SLAY, FRANK CONLEY   ASCAP 1960
composer, author, publisher

b Dallas, Tex, July 8, 30. Educ: Univ Tex, BBA; studied classical piano with Olga Steinman. Independent record producer, 52; music publ with var cos, incl Claridge Music, Inc, Conley Music, Inc, Chicory Music, Inc, 52-61 & 63-66. Head A&R, Swan Records, Philadelphia, 61-63; pres, Claridge Records, Los Angeles, 66-80. Chief Collabrs: Bob Crewe, Freddy Cannon, Chuck Dougherty. *Songs:* Silhouettes; Tallahassee Lassie; La Dee Dah; Jump Over; Lucky Ladybug; Daddy Cool; Bells, Bells, Bells; Buzz, Buzz A-Diddle-It; Happiness; Humdinger; Magic Moon; Mediterranean Moon; Okenfenokee; Pony Express; The Push and Kick; Teen Queen of the Week; Transistor Sister; Twistin' All Night Long; Two Thousand-88; The Urge; Happy Shades of Blue. *Instrumental Works:* Flying Circle.

SLEEK, EARL FOREST   ASCAP 1978
composer, author

b Kansas, Ohio, June 2, 46. Educ: Lakota High Sch; Lincoln Extension Inst, studied bus; Tiffin Univ, assoc degree bus. Served USA, 3 yrs, Nat Guard, 5 yrs. With Bendix Auto Lite Corp, 15 yrs. *Songs:* For a Special Mom and Dad; Two Wrongs Turn Out Right; I Can't Love You the Way You Want Me To; I Wish That We Could Share Those Days Again; You Share the Hurt.

SLEETH, NATALIE WAKELEY   ASCAP 1970
composer, author

b Evanston, Ill, Oct 29, 30. Educ: Joseph Sears Grade Sch; New Trier High Sch, Ill; Wellesley Col, BA(music theory), 52; studied choral arr with Lloyd Pfautsch, Southern Methodist Univ. Pvt organ & piano study, 34-53. Singer sacred & secular choruses, 38-74; church organist, 52-54. Began composing, words & music for choral anthems, 69- *Songs:* Jazz Gloria; Gaudeamus Hodie; Baby, What You Goin' to Be?; Feed My Lambs; Spread Joy; Amen So Be It; God Of Great and God of Small; Jubilate Deo; Little By Little; Love Is a Song; Praise the Lord; Were You There on That Christmas Night?; Joy in the Morning; Little Grey Donkey; Everywhere I Go; Love One Another; Promised Land; A Canon of Praise; A Little Love; Laudamus (collection of sacred songs).

SLETTEN, M RIX
See Oliver-Sletten, Madra Imogene

SLEZINGER, HERBERT EDWIN (BERT MURRAY)   ASCAP 1966
composer, author, singer

b Malden, Mass, Oct 31, 18. Educ: Everett Sr High Sch; music study with Arthur Swartzinger. Travelled extensively with twin bro on USS Lines ocean liners, The Murray Bros, from Can to WI. Worked in nightclubs from Boston to Can. Spent over 15 yrs on radio & TV. Played organ & sang, "Hellzapoppin'," Miami, Fla. *Songs:* What Happened to Our Romance?; Have You Thanked the Lord Today?; Tiny Piney, the Christmas Tree; I Pretend You're Here; Quick As a Wink. *Instrumental Works:* Gliding Waltz (organ solo).

SLIFKA, LEWIS
See Spence, Lew

SLOAN, KEN
See Shaw, Arnold

SLOANE, A BALDWIN   ASCAP 1914
composer

b Baltimore, Md, Aug 28, 1872; d Red Band, NJ, Feb 21 25. Educ: Pub schs; pvt music study. Charter mem, ASCAP. Co-founder, Baltimore Paint & Powder Club. Chief Collabrs: George V Hobart, Edgar Smith, Glen MacDonough, E Ray Goetz, Harry B Smith, John Murray Anderson, Arthur Swanstrom. *Songs:* What's the Matter With the Moon Tonight?; Heaven Will Protect the Working Girl; My Tiger Lily; When You Ain't Got No Money, You Needn't Come Around; It's Love That Makes the World Go 'Round; Toddlin' The Todalo; There's a Little Street in Heaven That They Call Broadway; I Want a Daddy Who Will Rock Me to Sleep; China Rose; Who Am I Thinking Of?; I'm Lonesome for Someone Like You; Where the Edelweiss Is Blooming. *Scores:* Bway shows: Broadway to Tokyo; The King's Carnival; The Hall of Fame; The Wizard of Oz; Seeing New York; Tillie's Nightmare; The Summer Widowers;

The Hen-Pecks; Hokey-Pokey; Hanky-Panky; Roly-Poly; Ladies First Greenwich Village Follies (19 & 20); China Rose.

SLOCUM, EARL A(NDERSON)   ASCAP 1963
educator, composer, arranger

b Concord, Mich, June 17, 02. Educ: Univ Mich, BM, MM; hon DMus, Albion Col; flute study with John Wummer. Dir bands & cond, Univ Symph Orch, Univ NC, prof music pub sch, 33-67. Guest prof, Univ Mich, Univ Ga, Univ KY & Stetson Univ. Past pres, Am Bandmasters Asn. Flute recitals throughout Mich & eastern states. *Songs & Instrumental Works:* Swedish Melody; Transc for concert band: Toccata (Frescobaldi); Marriage of Figaro Overture (Mozart); Good Friday Spell "Parsifal" (Wagner); Enigma Variations (Elgar); Praeludium (Jarnefelt); Introduction and Fugue (Handel); Meditation on a Chorale (Brahms); The High Castle "Vysebrad" (Smetana); Sonata No 3 for Flute and Wind Band (Handel); An American Tragedy (Newman); Finale-Symphony No 3 (Saint-Saëns; organ); Prelude (Frauck); Lyric Interlude (Schreiner); Piano Concert in E Flat (Liszt).

SLONIMSKY, NICOLAS   ASCAP 1952
composer, author, pianist

b St Petersburg, Russia, Apr 27, 1894. Educ: St Petersburg Cons, studied piano with Isabelle Vengerova (aunt), theory with Vassile Kalafati, orchestration with Maximilian Steinberg; pvt study with Gliere, Kiev. Northwestern Univ, Hon DFA, 80. To US in 23. Mem, Eastman Sch Music, 23-25; founded Boston Chamber Orch, active, 27-34; cond, Pierian Sodality, Harvard Univ, 28-30, also cond progs of modern Am music, Paris, 31-32, Berlin & Budapest, 32, Los Angeles, Havana & San Francisco, 33, SAm, 41-42. Lectr under State Dept, Russia, Poland, Bulgaria, Rumania & Israel, 62-63, also lectr on music, Univ Calif, Los Angeles, 64-67. Mem adv bd, Encyclopedia Britannica. Author, "Music Since 1900", "Music of Latin America", "A Thing or Two About Music", "Thesaurus of Scales and Melodic Patterns", "Lexicon of Musical Invective" & "The Road to Music"; ed, "International Cyclopedia of Music and Musicians", "Baker's Biographical Dictionary of Musicians." *Instrumental Works:* My Toy Balloon (variations on Brazilian theme; orch); 4 Simple Pieces for Orchestra; Suite for Cello and Piano; Silhouettes Iberiennes (piano); Yellowstone Park Suite (piano); Studies in Black and White (piano); 51 Minitudes (piano); Gravestones (song cycle; voice); My Little Pool (voice).

SLOTE, GILBERT MONROE   ASCAP 1959
composer, author

b Brooklyn, NY, Sept 12, 29. Educ: Brooklyn Col, BA, 51, MA, 55; Univ Mass, EdD, 73; studied comp with Danny Hurd & Leonard Marker, piano with Sanford Gold & Norman Gold. Songwriter; was sch teacher & principal in New York City pub schs; wrote songs & musical plays for sch children which have been performed on radio & TV, incl Voice of Am. *Albums:* Songs for All Year Long; Gosh, What a Wonderful World; Musical Plays for Special Days; More Musical Plays.

SLOWITZKY, MICHAEL
See Edwards, Michael

SLYE, LEONARD (ROY ROGERS)   ASCAP 1952
composer, singer, actor

b Cincinnati, Ohio, Nov 5, 11. Western star, actor, singer, guitarist; 91 feature motion pictures, 101 1/2 hour TV series. Ten yrs on NBC-TV. Records, RCA, Decca, Capitol & Word. Rodeos, state fairs, radio. Over 6000 charitable appearances. Chief Collabrs: Dale Evans, Tim Spencer. *Songs:* My Heart Went Thataway; Dusty; No Bed of Roses; Buckeye Cowboy; Down Along the Sleepy Rio Grande; Lord, Have Mercy on My Soul; Mavorneen O'Shay; I Ain't A'Worryin'; My Saddle Pals and I; Read the Bible and Pray; Ridin' Ropin'; The Song of the San Joaquin; Think of Me; Why Don't You Love Me?; Wondering Why.

SMALE, ROBERT CLAIRE   ASCAP 1962
composer, author, pianist

b Oakland, Calif, Mar 21, 31. Educ: Univ of Calif, BA. Accompanist & arr for Vic Damone & Mary Kaye Trio. Chief Collabr: Norman Kaye. *Songs:* Bill Bailey Fugue.

SMALL, ALLAN
See Schreibman, Alexander

SMECK, ROY   ASCAP 1959
composer

b Reading, Pa, Feb 6, 1900. Educ: Self taught. Made first talking picture short for Warner Bros, 26. Played banjo, guitar, ukulele & Hawaiian guitar solos. Played at coronation, London, 39, the Palladium, London & Palace Theatre, New York, 30. In vaudeville, 30 yrs. Had name on all instruments played by Harmony Co, Chicago. Wrote over 50 books for banjo, ukulele, guitar & Hawaiian guitar. Made 17 record albums. Chief Collabr: Abel Baer.

SMIT, LEO   ASCAP 1945
composer, author, educator

b Philadelphia, Pa, Jan 12, 21. Educ: Curtis Inst, scholarship, 3 yrs; Moscow Cons, scholarship, studied with Dmitri Kabalevsky; studied with Jose Iturbi &

comp with Nicolas Nabokov. Pianist, Am Ballet Co, 36. Made debut, Carnegie Hall, 39. Mem fac, Sarah Lawrence Col, 47-49, Univ Calif, Los Angeles, 57-63, State Univ NY Col, Buffalo, 63- Rec'd Guggenheim & Fulbright grants, 50 & Boston Symph Merit Award, 53. Chief Collabs: Anthony Hecht, Sir Fred Hoyle, Valerie Bettis. *Songs & Instrumental Works:* Symphony No 1 (NY Critics Circle Award), 56; Symphony No 2; Lenten Is Come (choral); Sonata in One Movement (piano); Fantasy: The Farewell (piano); Three Christmas Tree Carols (choral, instruments); Copernicus; In Woods; Scena Cambiata; At the Corner of the Sky.

SMITH, ALFRED JESSE (BRENTON WOOD)   ASCAP 1965
composer, author, singer

b Shreveport, La, July 26, 41. Educ: Compton High Sch. Songwriter; singer, nightclubs, TV & concerts. Recording artist; has rec'd 2 gold records. *Songs:* The Oogum Boogum Song; Gimme a Little Sign; Baby You Got It; Me and You; Lyrics: Sticky Boom Boom—Too Cold.

SMITH, ALICIA
See Carpenter, Alicia

SMITH, BEASLEY   ASCAP 1945
composer, author, pianist

b McEwen, Tenn, Sept 27, 01; d Nashville, Tenn, May 14, 68. Educ: Peabody Col; Vanderbilt Univ. Led own orch, appearing in hotels, nightclubs & vaudeville, 25-32. Pianist in radio. Music dir, WSM, Nashville, 20 yrs. A&R dir & arr, Dot Records, 5 yrs, also publ. Chief Collabs: Haven Gillespie, Francis Craig, Ralph Freed. *Songs:* That Lucky Old Sun; Beg Your Pardon; The Old Master Painter; God's Country; Night Train to Memphis; Sunday Down in Tennessee; I'd Rather Die Young.

SMITH, C U (OPHELIA MAE CROW BAIT)   ASCAP 1968
composer, author, publisher

b Seattle, Wash, July 29, 01. Educ: Grade sch. Singer, waitress & barmaid, nightclub. Author of poetry bks, "If the Shoe Fits Wear It", "Through Hell in a Hand Basket", "Hello-Hello-Party Line", "The Morning and the Evening", "Ramrod", "Smitty's Shorts", "From an Owls Nest", "Ramrod-2" & "Moving West." *Songs:* The Man From Nowhere; Spider-Spider-Spider.

SMITH, CHRIS   ASCAP 1931
composer, pianist

b Charleston, SC, Oct 12, 1879; d New York, NY, Oct 4, 49. Mem, vaudeville & nightclub act with Edgar Bowman. Chief Collabs: Cecil Mack, James Burris, Luckey Roberts. *Songs:* Ballin' the Jack; Down Among the Sugar Cane; Good Morning, Carrie; He's a Cousin of Mine; You're in the Right Church But the Wrong Pew; Constantly; Never Let the Same Bee Sting You Twice; All in Down and Out; Beans, Beans, Beans; Jasper Johnson, Shame on You; Down in Honky Tonk Town; Come After Breakfast. *Instrumental Works:* Monkey Rag; Junk Man Rag.

SMITH, CHRISTOPHER ALAN (CHRIS ROCK)   ASCAP 1978
composer, author, singer

b San Bernardino, Calif, Aug 27, 47. Singer in nightclubs & TV. Recording artist, CMA Records; guitarist. Chief Collabs: Ken Meyers, Jimmy Haskell. *Songs:* King of the Rock 'n Roll Song; Sweet Country Lady; Hank; Queen of the Broken Hearts; Beautiful Coat.

SMITH, CLAUDE THOMAS   ASCAP 1970
composer, conductor, teacher

b Monroe City, Mo, Mar 14, 32. Educ: Central Methodist Col, Fayette, Mo; Univ Kans, BME. Instrumental dir pub schs, Cozad, Nebr, Center High Sch, Kansas City, Mo & Chillicothe, Mo. Cond, Univ Symph Orch, Southwest Mo State Univ, Springfield. Educ consult, Wingert-Jones Music Inc, Kansas City, Mo; comp, Jenson Publ Inc, New Berlin, Wis. Guest cond & clinician. *Songs:* Meaning of Christmas; My Shepherd Will Supply My Needs. *Instrumental Works:* Emperata Overture; Incidental Suite; Sonus Ventorum; God of Our Fathers (choral-prelude); Eternal Father, Strong to Save; Declaration Overture; Overture on an Early American Hymn Tune; Fanfare and Celebration; Symphony No. 1 (band); Fantasy for Trumpet; Acclamation; Citation; Dance Prelude; Anthem for Winds and Percussion; Moresca: A Symphonie Pantomime; Joyance; Intrada: Adoration and Praise; Chorale and Allegro; Jubilant Prelude; Credence; Prelude for Band; Prelude—Variations; March on an Irish Air; Introduction and Fugato.

SMITH, CLAY   ASCAP 1922
composer, author, musician

b Greencastle, Ind, Aug 6, 1877; d Chicago, Ill, July 18, 30. Educ: Pub schs; pvt music study. Guitarist, Chicago World's Fair, 1893. Asst band dir, mgr & soloist, Liberati Band. Played in showboats, circuses, vaudeville & concerts. Hon Legionnaire. Pres, Int Platform Asn. *Songs:* In the Northland; The Gift Supreme; Dear Little You; Honeysuckle Babe; Waiting Time; Visions of You; One Night When Sorrow Burdened.

SMITH, CLIFFORD (PROMETHEUS GEMINI)   ASCAP 1974
composer, author, concert pianist

b Oregon City, Ore, June 15, 45. Educ: Interlochen Arts Acad, dipl, 63, studied comp with Doy M Baker & piano with Balint Vazsoni, 62-63; Univ Mich, BM, 68, studied comp with Leslie Bassett, 65-68 & piano with Benning Dexter, 67-68. Made extensive concert tours in Europe & NAm. Comp-pianist, concert stage, theatre, radio, TV & films. Carnegie Hall recital, 75. Retired from stage because of illness. Has comp over two thousand musical works. Author, "The Dicta Eide." *Instrumental Works:* Twelve Polyphonic Fantasies (piano); Toccata Perpetua (piano & orch); Visions of the Faerie Queene (tenor & piano); Transport Colloquies (string quartet); Mystery—Masque Lemures (modern ballet); Mystery—Elan Phantasmata, Books I-CXXVIII (piano); Divinations of the Logos-Visitant (opera); Fax-Savoyance Conte (narrator & orch).

SMITH, DAVID LEROY   ASCAP 1967
composer, author, singer

b Balboa, CZ, Jan 28, 15. Educ: Balboa High Sch; Pratt Inst, AID, 35; studied voice with Sigmund Jaffa, New York; coached voice, Joseph Romantini, Hollywood; studied advanced piano, theory & harmony with Roberta Gibbs, Hollywood. Actor in five motion pictures; appeared in Bway productions, "The Fencing Master", "The Waltz King" & "Showboat". Singer, vaudeville, hotel supper clubs, nightclubs & TV; recording artist. Coauth bk for musical adaptation to Bway, "She Stoops to Conquer (Superfluous Silk)." Wrote bk & capsule musical for off Bway, hotel supper clubs & Las Vegas, "Lucky Day" (both music & lyrics). *Songs:* Donna Mia; Hear and See; Hand in Hand; Lend a Hand; Here Is My Song; Back Home for Christmas; The Mother's Lullaby; Sounds of Christmas; Join We the Angeles; Los Angeles; Independence Hall; Lyrics: Malaguena (Lecuona). *Instrumental Works:* Yellowstone Suite.

SMITH, DEREK G   ASCAP 1965
composer, author, pianist

b London, Eng, Aug 17, 31. Educ: Studied in Eng. Pianist in Johnny Dankworth Orch, Eng, 54-55. Came to US, 57. Pianist with Benny Goodman, Art Mooney Orchs. Led own trio in New York jazz spots. Mem Derek & Ray piano team, 64-67. NBC staff pianist, "Johnny Carson Show," 67-74. Bandleader on CBS "Musical Chairs" TV show, 75. Record albums as soloist on RCA, Mercury, Project III & Progressive Labels. Studio musician, New York. *Songs:* Don't Let Go. *Instrumental Works:* Interplay; Honky Tonk Herman; One to Warm Up On; Tristessa.

SMITH, DIANE HARTMAN   ASCAP 1977
composer, author, singer

b Youngstown, Ohio, Dec 28, 35. Educ: Master's degree in ballet; studied music appreciation & dance hist, Am ballet with Leon Danillian & Frederick Franklin. Singer & dancer, Bway. Starred, Copacabana, New York & Desert Inn, Las Vegas, Nev. Appeared on TV shows with Dean Martin, Bob Hope & Jack Benny. Has had own TV shows, London, Paris, New Zealand, Australia, Can & Chile. Choreographer, New York City Opera & Aspen Music Fest. Rec'd Russian Medal for Contribution to Dance. Owner, 10 dance studios for children. Mem, Dance Masters Am; Am Guild Variety Artists; Screen Actors Guild. *Songs:* It's Beddy-Bye Time; I Am a Little Seed; Positive Thinking; Wiggle-Giggle-Wiggle Worm; Wonderful Limitless Happy Me; We Are Happy People; I am a Dolly; What's the Magic Word-Please!. *Albums:* Loving and Learning From Birth to Three; Children's Songs of Joy.

SMITH, DONALD AUMONT   ASCAP 1965
composer, arranger, conductor

b Gap, Pa, July 29, 22. Educ: Oberlin Cons; studied with Miecyslav Munz, Edward Stevermann & Harold Glick. Has been vocal coach & asst cond, New York & Dallas Opera Cos. Dance arr, TV & Bway incl "How to Succeed in Business Without Really Trying." Cond, New York Light Opera Co, also "Bye Bye Birdie" (tour) & "Here's Love" (Bway, tour).

SMITH, EARLE FRANCIS   ASCAP 1972
composer, author, publisher

b Providence, RI, Jan 8, 29. Educ: Pvt piano instr, 5 yrs; pvt saxophone instr, 5 yrs; Hartnell Col, studied music theory, sight reading & music appreciation. Lyric writer, 20 yrs; composer, 10 yrs; publisher & record producer, 5 yrs. Chief Collabs: Steve Waltner, Donald G Pendergrass, William M Layton, Robert Foster. *Songs & Instrumental Works:* Chicano Brown.

SMITH, EDGAR   ASCAP 1914
author, actor

b Brooklyn, NY, Dec 9, 1857; d Bayside, NY, Mar 8, 38. Educ: Pa Mil Acad. Debut as actor, 1878. Librettist & actor, NY Casino Co, 1886-1892. Playwright: "The Spider and the Fly"; "Hands Up"; "Mr Hamlet of Broadway"; "Home Sweet Home" (also producer). Librettist: "Whirl-i-Gig"; "The Girl Behind the Counter"; "Merry-Go-Round"; "The Mimic World"; "Old Dutch"; "Up and Down Broadway"; "La Belle Paree"; "The Kiss Waltz"; "Hokey-Pokey"; "Hanky-Panky"; "The Pleasure Seekers"; "The Blue Paradise." Co-librettist: "Alone at Last." Chief Collabrs: Gus Edwards, Victor Herbert, Sigmund Romberg, A Baldwin Sloane, Gustave Kerker, Al Goodman. *Songs:* When Two Hearts Are One; When in Flanders; Heaven Will Protect the Working Girl; A Great Big Girl Like Me; Come Back Ma Honey Boy to Me; What's the Good; My Neat Little, Sweet Little Girl; He Never Smiled Again; Tell Us Pretty

Ladies; Creole Love Song; Ma Blushin' Rosie. Bway Stage Scores, librettos: Fiddle-Dee-Dee; Hoity-Toity; Twirly-Whirly; Whoop-Dee-Doo; Higgledy-Piggledy; Twiddle-Twaddle; Dream City and the Magic Knight; Tillie's Nightmare; Robinson Crusoe, Jr; The Whirl of New York.

SMITH, EDWARD (TEDD)   ASCAP 1972
composer, author, pianist

b London, Ont, July 18, 27. Educ: Royal Cons Music, Toronto, Ont; Univ Minn; Univ NC; Catholic Univ, DC. Recording artist, RCA Victor Records & Word, ABC Paramount; comp, film scores, musicals, piano & orchestral works & songs. *Songs:* New Vibrations; Requiem For a Nobody; There's a Quiet Understanding; Music: Joni's Prayer. *Scores:* Film: The Hiding Place; Time to Run.

SMITH, ETHEL   ASCAP 1956
composer, organist, publisher

b Pittsburgh, Pa, Nov 22, 10. Educ: Carnegie Tech. Organ soloist with symph orchs; solo appearances in nightclubs, theatres & concerts throughout the world. Appeared in films "Bathing Beauty", "Easy to Wed", "Cuban Pete" & "Melody Time." Has made many records. Founded own publ firm. Author "Hammond Organ Method."

SMITH, FRANK M   ASCAP 1952
composer, conductor, musician

b Dover, Ohio, Feb 2, 06; d Chicago, Ill, May 8, 76. Educ: Miami Univ, Ohio; Cincinnati Cons; Dana Musical Inst, Warren, Ohio. Musician & arr with dance bands; also WLW, 30-32. Staff arr, CBS, Chicago, 32-37, music dir, 41. Comp & arr, radio shows incl "Fibber McGee", "Gene Autry" & "Alec Templeton," Los Angeles, 37-41. Chief Collabr: Jack Fulton. *Songs:* God Has Been Good to Me; Loved and Lost.

SMITH, FREDERICK THEODORE   ASCAP 1961
composer, author, musician

b Cleveland, Ohio, Sept 3, 19. Educ: Western Reserve Univ, BA(music), 50. String bass player, solo & harmony singer for var nightclubs. Played in trios, quartets & full orchs. Co-author/comp of musical "Aloha Hawaii," also Ger version. Chief Collabrs: Peter Lee Zuellner, R Alex Anderson. *Songs:* You Never Can Tell; Aloha (is the Spirit of) Hawaii; Muu Muu Mama; Poi for Two.

SMITH, GARY MILTON   ASCAP 1975
composer, author

b Ontario, Ore, Mar 15, 43. Educ: Pocatello High Sch; Idaho State Univ; Utah State Univ, BS, 67; Marine Officers Candidate Sch & Basic Sch, grad 2nd Lt, 69; Defense Information Sch, 70; studied trumpet with J C Gardner. US Forest & Park Service backcountry ranger. Served in USMC; recording artist, Vanguard Records; featured on ABC 2 hour documentary "Three Young Americans: In Search of Survival"; concerts; fund raising benefits, Multiple Sclerosis Society. Author, bk "Windsinger." *Songs:* Color Crayon Morning; Dick's Song; Something Big; Birds Fly Around Her; Windsinger; The Red Tail; The Cuttin' Horse; One in the Sun; A Mist of Blue; A Simple Waltz for Aspen; The Ghost Herd of Spirit Lake; Hey, What's Happenin'?; The Blue Swan; Wind Is a River; To Marsha, Wherever She May Wander; Gypsy of My Mind.

SMITH, GEORGE M   ASCAP 1959
composer, author, instrumentalist

b New York, NY, Jan 29, 12. Educ: Cerritos Col, AA; studied with Ruth Hanmas, Univ NMex, William Collier, Harvard Univ, Sascha Borisoff, St Petersburgh Cons. Staff guitarist & other fretted instruments, Paramount Studios, 7 yrs, Fox Studios, 7 yrs. Free-lance recording musician, radio, motion pictures & TV. Teaching guitar in high schs & jr cols. Author, "The George M Smith Modern Guitar Method for Rhythm and Chord Improvising." Chief Collabr: David Arkin. *Songs:* The River Is Wide; The Day After Tomorrow; Maybe Song. *Instrumental Works:* Merry Makers; Le Coquette.

SMITH, GREGG   ASCAP 1962
composer, conductor, teacher

b Chicago, Ill, Aug 4, 31. Educ: Univ Calif, Los Angeles, BA & MA; studied music with Leonard Stein & Fritz Zweig. Ford Found grant. Cond, Gregg Smith Singers, West Los Angeles Community Methodist Church Choir, 8 yrs, Los Angeles Doctors Chorus & Columbia Symph Chorus. Taught at Univ Calif, 6 yrs; pvt teacher, 8 yrs. Toured Europe, 58 & 61, NAm, 62-67. Appeared in films & TV. Chief Collabr: Alicia Smith (wife). *Songs:* The Fable of Chicken Little; Bible Songs for Young Voices; Das Lieben Bringt Gross Freud.

SMITH, H WAKEFIELD   ASCAP 1926
composer, author, singer

b England, Nov 10, 1865; d Brooklyn, NY, Nov 4, 56. Educ: Kensington Art Sch, London; studied piano with Mary Stamford. To US, 1893, citizen, 1898. Dramatic reader, toured southern US. *Songs:* Those Songs My Mother Used to Sing; The Gates of Pearl; Roses; Tomorrow; Had I But Known; Watch Thee and Pray Thee; The Lily and the Bluebell; The Hummingbird and the Flower.

SMITH, HARRY BACHE   ASCAP 1914
author

b Buffalo, NY, Dec 28, 1860; d Atlantic City, NJ, Jan 2, 36. Educ: Chicago pub & pvt schs. Music critic, Chicago Daily News; drama critic, Chicago Tribune.

Author of books on Shakespeare & Dickens. Autobiography: "First Nights and First Editions." Chief Collabrs: Reginald DeKoven, Victor Herbert, Gustave Kerker, Raymond Hubbell, Robert Hood Bowers, Jerome Kern, Victor Jacobi, Sigmund Romberg, Karl Hajos, Robert B Smith (brother), Ted Snyder. *Songs:* The Sheik of Araby; Bright Eyes; Yours is My Heart Alone; The Land of Let's Pretend; Romany Life; Gypsy Love Song; To the Land of My Own Romance; Play Gypsies, Dance Gypsies; Dancing Fool; I Wonder Why; I Can't Forget Your Eyes; Drift With Me; Don't Tempt Me; I Wonder If You Still Care for Me. *Scores:* Bway stage: Whirl-i-Gig; The Enchantress; Love o' Mike; Three Little Girls; also librettist: The Begum; Don Quixote; Robin Hood; Jupiter; The Algerian; Rob Roy; The Wizard of the Nile; The Serenade; The Highwayman; The Fortune Teller; The Rounders; Papa's Wife; The Casino Girl; The Strollers; Liberty Belles; The Little Duchess; The Billionaire; The Rich Mr Hoggenheimer; The Persian Model; Ziegfeld Follies (1907, 1908, 1909, 1910, 1912); Little Nemo; Miss Innocence; The Siren; The Doll Girl; The Rambler Rose; Ladies First; The Love Song; Princess Flavia; Naughty Riquette; Countess Maritza; The Circus Princess; White Lilacs; Nearly a Hero; Watch Your Step; Stop! Look! Listen!; Sweetheart Time; also co-librettist: The Wild Rose; The Spring Maid; The Red Rose; The Rose Maid; The Girl From Utah; Sybil; Angel Face; Caroline; The Love Call; The Red Robe; Gaby; Sweethearts; A Lonely Romeo.

SMITH, HOUSTON (HOWDIE)   ASCAP 1963
composer, arranger, pianist

b Kinderhook, NY, July 18, 10. Educ: Stanford Univ, Golden Gate Col, studied music, psychol & bus admin, BA & BS; studied harmony with Bruno Cesana. Studio & dance band arr; pianist, nightclubs. S/Sgt finance, USAF, Spec Services, WW II. Presently accountant, Los Angeles area. Chief Collabr: Frank Slatterly, lyricist. *Songs:* Music: Red Iron Sky; Misty Hill; Love's a Wondrous Thing.

SMITH, HOWARD RUSSELL   ASCAP 1974
composer, singer, musician

b Nashville, Tenn, June 17, 49. Educ: Univ of Tenn; Cumberland Col. With Warner Bros. Chief Collabr: James H Brown Jr. *Songs:* Third Rate Romance; Dancing the Night Away; Amazing Grace; The End Is Not in Sight; Out of the Snow.

SMITH, IRA ALEXANDER
composer, singer

b Kansas City, Mo, Dec 5, 03; d Kansas City, Oct 15, 65.

SMITH, JANET CAROL   ASCAP 1969
composer, author, guitarist

b Dallas, Tex, June 4, 41. Educ: Univ Calif, Berkeley; Oberlin Col; studied theory & arr. Piano & guitar instr in high sch. Operated folk club Il Nocciolo, Rome, Italy, 67-68. Performer, Italian radio & fests, Univ Calif, Berkeley & San Diego fests. Toured Japan, 75. Recording artist. Voice & guitar in commercials. Accompanist for Malvina Reynolds. Owner, Bella Roma Music; co-operator, Smith & Jones Hit Runners. Transc & copywork for GPI Books, Frets Mag, Stefan Grossman Books & others. Chief Collabr: Malvina Reynolds. *Songs:* Talking Want Ad; Sunny's Got Hers; Isometric Love Affair; Johnny's Lullabye; A Little Muscle; Love Is Going Out of Style; More, Please More; The Part of Me That Doesn't Want to Know; I Feel Your Love Shinin' Down on Me.

SMITH, JENNIE
See Callison, Jo Ann

SMITH, JERRY NEIL   ASCAP 1968
composer, educator

b Lefors, Tex, Feb 20, 35. Educ: Beaumont High Sch, Tex, studied with Arnold Whedbee; Univ Tex, BMus, 56, MMus, 57, Performers Certificate in clarinet, 57, studied with Kent Kennan, Clifton Williams, Janet McGaughey, John McGrosso; Univ Rochester Eastman Sch Music, PhD, 63, studied with Frederick Fennell, Herbert Elwell, William S Larson. Taught Tex pub schs, 57-59, Univs of Fla, Southwestern La & Colo, 59-72. Head, Univ Northern Iowa Music Dept, 72-75; dir, Univ Okla Sch Music, 75- Comp, cond, clinician in band music. Soloist, Nat Clarinet Symposium; mem, Eastman Wind Ens. *Instrumental Works:* Big Eight Tribute (band); Epilog (concert band); Fanfare and Celebration; Capriccio (trombone, concert band); Colorado Suite; Death Dancer; Declaration; Tinsel and Foil March; Monday's Child (violin, piano); Dirge and Alleluia (perc ens); Fanfares (band); Essay for Young Americans (orch).

SMITH, JOSEPH COYAL, JR   ASCAP 1977
composer, author

b Huntsville, Ala, Jan 16, 24. Educ: Monrovia High Sch. Songwriter. Chief Collabr: Donn Hecht. *Songs:* Little Bits and Pieces; One Lonely Heart; Is This the Way That Love Starts; Don't Mention His Name; Play Me Down; As Long As I Live.

SMITH, JULIA FRANCES   ASCAP 1945
composer, author, pianist

b Denton, Tex, Jan 25, 11. Educ: NTex State Univ, BA, 30; Juilliard Sch Music, dipl, piano studies with Carl Friedberg, grad sch fel in comp, 33-39, studies with

Rubin Goldmark, Frederic Jacobi, Bernard Wagenaar, Edgar Schenkman; NY Univ, MA, 33, PhD, 52, studies with Marion Bauer, Virgil Thomson, Vincent Jones. Active as orch & solo pianist; contemporary literature lectr, 33-70. Author bks incl "Aaron Copland", "Directory of American Women Composers" & "Carl Friedberg." Hon mem, Sigma Alpha Iota; Am Women Composers; Nat Fedn Music Clubs. Works performed by leading Am & Scand orchs. Chief Collabrs: (Lyricists) Jan I Fortune, John William Rogers, Karl Flaster, Arthur M Sampley, C D Mackay, Josephine F Royle & Bertita Harding; (band & orch) Cecile Vashaw. *Songs:* Invocation (solo or SSA & piano); Music: I Will Sing the Song; The Door That I Would Open; The Love I Hold; God Bless This House (SATB & piano); The Promise; When'er You Make a Promise. *Instrumental Works:* Our Heritage (SSAATB or SSAA, piano; plus band, orch & chorus); Work and Play String Method (2 vols); Characteristic Suite (piano solo); Episodic Suite (piano solo & also large orch); Sonatine in C (piano solo); Suite for Wind Octet; American Dance Suite (2 pianos; also theater orch); Concerto for Piano and Orchestra (3 movements); Quartet for Strings; Trio—Cornwall (violin, cello & piano); Folkways Symphony (chamber or large orch); Hellenic Suite (large orch); Remember the Alamo! (band or orch) optional narrator & chorus); Sails Aloft (band); two pieces for viola & piano. *Scores:* Cynthia Parker (Indian opera); The Stranger of Manzano (one act opera); The Gooseherd and the Goblin (one act opera); Cockcrow (one act opera); The Shepherdess and the Chimneysweep (Christmas opera, one act); Daisy (two act opera).

SMITH, KERMIT STEPHEN   ASCAP 1971
composer, author

b Marion, Ohio, Nov 18, 48. Educ: Ohio Univ, BS(communication-radio & TV) Played music high sch & col, local bands, clubs, singing groups. Songwriter, 71-; toured with group, Steve & Tom, hotel chains through southern US. Worked in Hawaii, 75-; duo with wife Ruth; trio with "Zion Mountain Folk." Christian concert tour, Asia, 3 yrs. Chief Collabrs: Elwood Tom Simpson, Harry Browning. *Songs:* Richard and the Cadillac Kings; Grass Roots Music; We Give Thanks; Bigger Picture of Jesus; I Don't Believe It; Light of His Love; We All Rejoice.

SMITH, LAWRENCE RACKLEY   ASCAP 1969
composer, teacher

b Media, Ill, Sept 10, 32. Educ: Northwestern Univ, MusB, 54, MM, 55; Eastman Sch Music, PhD, 58; studied comp with Robert Mills Delaney, Bernard Rogers & Howard Hanson. Asst prof music, Cent Mich Univ, 57-63; assoc prof music, Kalamazoo Col, 63-76, chmn dept music, 75-, prof music, 76-. *Instrumental Works:* Quintet for Piano and Strings; Discourse, Soliloquy and Concourse (cello concerto); Confluences (orch); Sarasota Sailor Circus March (band); They/You/I/We (concerto for violin and wind ens).

SMITH, LEONARD BINGLEY   ASCAP 1949
composer, conductor, cornetist

b Poughkeepsie, NY, Sept 5, 15. Educ: Poughkeepsie pub schs; NY Mil Acad; NY Univ; Curtis Inst Music; Detroit Inst Technol, DHH; studied music with Ernest S Williams, cornet & trumpet with Mayhew L Lake, Erik W G Leidzen, comp with Rosario Scalero, conducting & solfeggio with Pierre Henrotte. Began playing trumpet at age 8. Played first trumpet, Ford Sunday Evening House, 37-42, Detroit Symph Orch & Philadelphia Orch. Cornet soloist, Goldman Band, summers 36-41. USN, World War II, 3 1/2 yrs. Cond & founder, Detroit Concert Band, 35 yrs. Cond, Blossom Fest Concert Band, Cleveland, 74-. Taught, Wayne State Univ & Univ Detroit. Lectured in over 1000 schs & univs; more than 3800 personal appearances. TV film on life of John Philip Sousa, British Broadcasting Corp; recorded series of all known Sousa marches. Conducting own band in concerts & recording "Gems of the Concert Band," 36 album set preserving Am Band Heritage. Pres, ACBA, mem, Kappa Kappa Psi; recipient of General Booth award, Freedom Found award & comns of var band & orch works. Chief Collabrs: Mary Lou Hornberger, J William Middendorf, II. *Instrumental Works:* Ecstasy (waltz); Spanish Caprice; An American Rhapsodie; Treasury of Scales; Jurisprudence March; Town Crier (march); The Light Fantastic (march), Blue Flame March, The Traveler March; also 350 publ compositions and arrangements for band & 100 publ piano & instrumental solos.

SMITH, MARY CECELIA   ASCAP 1962
author, dancer, teacher

b St Louis, Mo, Feb 23, 13; d. Educ: High sch; pvt dance study. Dancer in Bway musicals, films. Dance dir, Roxy Theatre. Had own dance studio, Hillsdale, NJ. Chief Collabr: John Shaffer Smith, Jr. *Songs:* Now and Then; Navarak.

SMITH, MARY LASSWELL   ASCAP 1966
composer, author, teacher

b Glasgow, Scotland, Feb 8, 05. Educ: Univ Tex, Austin, BS; voice study with Pasquale Amato. Prof singer, Original Roxy Theatre & Victor Herbert Shows, New York, 26-35. Teacher Span & French languages, var schs & cols. Writer, six novels incl "Suds in Your Eye." Began comp, 50. Wrote two musicals. *Songs:* Mis Soledades; Rio Grande. *Scores:* Spankin' Frankie; Lonely Star.

SMITH, OSWALD JEFFREY   ASCAP 1960
composer, author

b Odessa, Can, Nov 8, 1889. Educ: Ont Bible Col; McCormick Theol Sem; Man Col. Minister, First Presby Church, Chicago, Dale Presby Church, Alliance Tabernacle, Toronto, Ont, Can & The Peoples Church, Toronto. Author: "The Man God Uses"; "The Salvation of God"; "The Challenge of Mission"; "The

Passion for Souls"; "The Story of My Life"; "Prophecy—What Lies Ahead?"; "The Endowment of Power"; "The Battle for Truth"; "The Stories of Thomas"; "Men of God"; "Tales of the Mission Field"; "Oswald Smith's Hymn Stories"; "Oswald Smith's Best Songs"; "The Adventures of Andy McGinnis."

SMITH, PATRICIA L
poet, singer, songwriter

b Chicago, Ill, Dec 1946. Began to evolve form of rock 'n' roll poetry, 67; introduced to rock business, 71 & worked on variety of projects incl coauthoring play "Cowboy Mouth," appearing in BBC-TV specials. Poetry reading at St Mark's Church, NY. Works put into print, 71, two vols writing & poems "Seventh Heaven" & "Witt"; poems were set to music & performed in Manhattan Clubs. *Albums:* Horses; Radio Ethiopia.

SMITH, PAUL JOSEPH   ASCAP 1944
composer

b Calumet, Mich, Oct 30, 06. Educ: Col Idaho; Univ Calif, Los Angeles, BA; Bush Cons Music, Chicago, BM; violin scholarship, Juilliard Sch Music. Piano & violin at age 4, harmony at age 9, violin and/or piano soloist during early age. Wrote sch shows & had dance bands, Univ Calif, Los Angeles. Joined as arranger, Walt Disney in 30, started writing scores, Walt Disney Pictures, 33, also wrote radio scores. Acad Award (collaboration) for "Pinocchio," 39. Composer. Chief Collabr: Lyrics, Gil George. *Songs & Instrumental Works:* Sing Out-America. *Scores:* Film background: Beaver Valley: Nature's Half Acre; Bear Country; The Olympic Elk; Westward to the Wagons; Secrets of Life; Pollyanna; The Vanishing Prairie; 20,000 Leagues Under the Sea; The Parent Trap. *Albums:* True Life Adventures.

SMITH, RICHARD B   ASCAP 1947
author

b Honesdale, Pa, Sept 29, 01; d New York, NY, Sept 28, 35. Educ: Pa State Univ. Ed-in-chief col newspaper, Pennsylvania State Froth. Wrote all lyrics for col thespian shows. New York & Chattanooga, Asst theatre mgr, Tenn. Theatre mgr, Waterbury, Conn. Chief Collabr: Felix Bernard. *Songs:* Winter Wonderland; The Breeze; Early to Bed; I Thrill When They Mention Your Name; Me and My Wonderful One; When a Gypsy Makes His Violin Cry; Windmill Willie; The Bluebirds Are Singing a Blues Song; Campus Moon; Slumbertime Along the Suwanee; Under a Ceiling of Stars; Half a Mile to Honeysuckle Lane.

SMITH, RICHARD DREW   ASCAP 1977
composer, author

b New Brunswick, NJ, Aug 1, 49. Educ: Emerson Col, BA(film & TV), 75. Bluegrass musician, clubs & fests. Mandolin & guitar teacher. Recording artist for Revonah, Mountain & Folkways Records. Mag feature writer & reviewer, "Pickin'." Vocalist & instrumentalist for children's films. Chief Collabr: Scott Nielsen. *Songs:* The Little, Old Barber Shop.

SMITH, RICHARD LEMON   ASCAP 1976
composer, author

b Nashville, Tenn, Apr 17, 52. Educ: Aquinas High Sch, Calif; Calif Polytech State Univ, studied theory; pvt piano instr, age 10; performed & wrote in high sch; toured US; recording artist with group War; formed new band, Lemonsmyth. Chief Collabrs: Joe Howard Philips, Wyman Goodloe, Robert Palmer, Mitch McDowell, Morris D Dickerson, Jerry Goldstein. *Songs:* Ride the Rocket; Spirit of 76; Shoot to Kill; The Watchers; After the Rain. *Albums:* Booty People.

SMITH, ROBERT BACHE   ASCAP 1924
author

b Chicago, Ill, June 4, 1875; d New York, NY, Nov 6, 51. Educ: Brooklyn Pub Schs. Reporter, Brooklyn Eagle; press agent, Casino Theatre. Wrote vaudeville & burlesque acts. Chief Collabrs: Victor Herbert, Raymond Hubbell, Robert Hood Bowers, Sigmund Romberg, Harry B Smith (brother). *Songs:* Come Down, Ma Evening Star; Day Dreams, Visions of Bliss; Two Little Love Bees; I Might Be Your Once-in-a-While; Just My Style; Jeanette and Her Little Wooden Shoes; Sweethearts; For Every Lover Must Meet His Fate; The Angelus; Melody of Love; The Little Girl in Blue; Tell Me Lilac Domino; Roses Bloom for Lovers. *Scores:* Bway stage: Twirly-Whirly; Mexicana; The Girl and the Wizard; Sweethearts; The Lilac Domino; The Debutante; Follow Me; A Lonely Romeo; Knight for a Day; The Girl in the Spotlight; Fantana; The Spring Maid; The Red Rose; Angel Face; Gaby.

SMITH, ROBERT LEE   ASCAP 1970
composer, author, musician

b Chico, Calif, Sept 15, 40. Educ: Studied vocals with Judy Davis. Joined musician's union, age 16 & began writing; with Acuff Rose Publ, Nashville. *Songs:* Railroad Jack; Goodbyes Don't Come Easy; Merry Christmas I Love You; The Devil Song; Prophet and a Saint.

SMITH, ROGER   ASCAP 1957
composer, trombonist, teacher

b Mays Landing, NJ, Sept 10, 15; d. Educ: Yale Univ. First trombonist, Metrop Opera Orch. Asst cond, Goldman Band. Fac, Juilliard Sch Music. Author,

"Landmarks of Early American Music." Chief Collabr: Richard Franko Goldman.

SMITH, RUSSELL
composer
ASCAP 1964

b Tuscaloosa, Ala, Apr 23, 27. Educ: Columbia Univ, BS, 51, MA, 53; pvt study with Aaron Copland. Resident of New York until 66, Munich, Ger, 75- Prof music, Univ Ala & Univ New Orleans. Recipient of Nat Inst Arts & Letters citation & grant, 63, NEA, 76-77, Rockefeller Found residence grants, Cleveland Orch, New Orleans Philh. *Songs:* Six Blake Songs (voice, piano). *Songs & Instrumental Works:* Magnificat (orch, chorus, soprano); Orchestral works: Tetrameron; Second Piano Concerto; Sinfonia Concertante; Concerto for Percussion and Orchestra; Symphony for Alto and Orchestra; Symphony in C Major; Choruses: Gloria; Service in G; Three Songs from Emily Dickinson. *Scores:* Opera: The Unicorn in the Garden.

SMITH, STUART SAUNDERS
composer, teacher
ASCAP 1971

b Portland, Maine, Mar 16, 48. Educ: Berklee Sch Music, 66-67; Hartt Sch Music, BMA, 70, MM, 72; Univ Ill, DMA, 77. Instr perc, Hartt Sch Music, 70-73. Asst prof, Univ Md, 75- Recorded on Advance Records, Ubres Records & the ASUS recording series. *Instrumental Works:* Here and There; Faces; Gifts; Links; Links No 2 & No 3; Pinetop; Flight; Blue; Return and Recall; Two Makes Three; One for Syl; Poems I, II, III; Gestures I, II, III.

SMITH, THOMAS ALLEN
composer
ASCAP 1978

b Cleveland, Ohio, Nov 29, 46. Educ: Foothill Jr Col. Guitarist, played in cafes & coffee houses, 8 yrs. Publ first record under own label, 78. *Instrumental Works:* If I Had Wings; Scampers Blues.

SMITH, WALTER A
composer, author
ASCAP 1967

b Bude, Miss, Sept 23, 30. Publ & free-lance writer. Chief Collabr: Jerry Smith. *Songs:* We Got Each Other; The Man They Sweep Up Off the Floor.

SMITH, WALTER WALLACE
composer, pianist, organist
ASCAP 1924

b Johnstown, NY, Aug 30, 1894; d Johnstown, Apr 6, 48. Educ: High sch. Pianist in film theatres. Field Art, WW I. Band sch, Louisville, Ky. Teacher, Johnstown; also theatre organist. *Songs & Instrumental Works:* The Love Refrain; First Call of Spring; Moonlight; The Old Fiddler's Song; River Shannon Moon; Down at the Old Block Dance.

SMITH, WILLIAM H (WILLIE THE LION)
composer, pianist
ASCAP 1942

b Goshen, NY, Nov 23, 1897; d Manhattan, NY, Apr 18, 73. Educ: Howard Univ; studied music with mother & Hans Steinke. Prof debut, Newark, NJ, 14, toured Europe, 17. 350th Field Artillery, WW I. Organized own band, 20. Toured Can & US during 30's & Europe & NAfrica, 49-50. Has made many records. Appeared at jazz fests. Autobiography: "Music on My Mind." *Songs & Instrumental Works:* Echoes of Spring; Passionette; Morning Air; Fingerbuster; I'm Goin' to Ride the Rest of the Way; The Old Stamping Ground; I Ain't Gonna Swing No More; Portrait of the Duke; Contrary Motion; Roll 'Em, Rock 'Em and Weep; Lions Boogie Woogie.

SMOLANOFF, MICHAEL LOUIS
composer

b New York, NY, May 11, 42. Educ: Juilliard Sch Music, BS, 64, MS, 65; Combs Col, MusD, 75. Res asst, Columbia Univ, 65-66. Instr, Juilliard Sch Music, 66 & Philadelphia Music Acad, 68-71. Served in USAF, 66-70. Ed, E B Marks Music Corp, New York, 66-68. Prof music, Rutgers Univ, 71-77. Pres, The Music Press, Collingswood, NJ, 77. Consult, Amherst Electronic Studios. Rutgers Res Coun Grantee, 73. Mem, Nat Asn Am Composers & Conductors. *Instrumental Works:* Concerto for Trombone; String Quartet; Pages From a Summer Journal; Celebration.

SMOTHERMAN, MICHEAL WAYNE
composer, singer, pianist
ASCAP 1971

b Erick, Okla, Dec 17, 52. Educ: Pub schs. To Calif, 70; was pianist, recorded album, RCA, 77. Chief Collabr: Billy Burnett. *Songs:* Can't Turn My Habit Into Love; Can You Fool; I'm Gonna Love You; What Goes Around (Comes Around); California; Nothin' Quite Like Love; Rockin' With Somebody New; Danger Zone.

SMOTHERS, THOMAS B
actor, singer, comedian

b 1937. Educ: San Jose State Col. Nightclub appearances at Harrah's, Lake Tahoe & Riviera, Las Vegas. Co-star half hour TV situation comedy, Smothers Bros Show, 65-66 & Smothers Bros Comedy Hour, CBS-TV, 75. Starred in films, "Get to Know Your Rabbit" & "The Silver Bears"; also starred on Bway, "I Love My Wife," 78-79.

SNELL, DAVID L
composer, conductor
ASCAP 1946

b Milwaukee, Wis, Sept 10, 1897; d Glendale, Calif, Mar 27, 67. Educ: Wis Cons; Wis Col; Meyer Cons. Music dir & comp, stage & films. Has led own orch. *Songs:* Under the Stars; Downstream Drifter; Out of the Deep; Where Were You?; Come Back Little Girl of Mine; Once Over Lightly. *Scores:*Films/TV: Paradin' the Ivories; Lady of the Lake; Bad Bascom; Maisie; Southern Yankee; Billy the Kid; Andy Hardy; Dr Kildare; Dr Gillespie; Pete Smith Shorts; Thin Man.

SNESRUD, ARLIN DUANE
composer
ASCAP 1972

b Rochester, Minn, May 21, 39. Educ: Univ Minn, BS(music educ), 61, MA(music educ), 65, grad study comp, 68-70. Pub sch music teacher, 62-64 & 65-66; admin asst & instr, Music Dept, Univ Minn, 66-72; music copyist, arr, comp & jobbing musician, 72- *Instrumental Works:* Medalist March; Viking Lander (concert march).

SNOECK, KENNETH MAURICE
composer
ASCAP 1978

b Detroit, Mich, Jan 11, 46. Educ: Roseville High Sch; Central Mich Univ, BSEd, 69, MMus, 71. Taught perc, arr & marching band, Central Mich Univ, 69-75; taught Bridgeport, Mich schs, 75-80; clinician & adjudicator throughout US. *Instrumental Works:* Scaramouche, Symphony No 3 (winds, perc); Octet for Keyboard Percussion.

SNOW, LEIDA
author, theatre critic, broadcast newscaster
ASCAP 1976

b New York, NY. Educ: NY Univ, BA(Phi Beta Kappa, cum laude); prof training in dance, sight-singing, piano, singing, acting, theatre history & criticism. Prof experience as actress, singer, dancer in Bway shows, incl "Cabaret." Newswriter, Associated Press, New York. Newscaster, film reviews, host of interview program, WPIX-FM, 78. Theatre critic & ABC Radio News, network anchor, WINS-AM, 79- Publ author, 2 books, several mag articles. Chief Collabrs: Stephen Schwartz, Ralph Schuckett. *Songs:* Lyrics: Manchild Lullabye; Every Step of the Way; Can't We Make it Right Again; In My Loneliness; Double Take.

SNOW, TERRY
See Woolsey, Maryhale

SNOWHILL, GEORGE H
composer, conductor, arranger
ASCAP 1955

b Brooklyn, NY, Mar 17, 11; d. Educ: Lebanon Valley Col, Trenton State Col; Newark State Col; Paterson State Col. Musician in dance bands; also for music publ, radio, TV, records. Instrumental music dir, Hackettstown Sch, NJ.

SNYDER, EDWARD ABRAHAM
composer, author
ASCAP 1951

b New York, NY, Feb 22, 19. Educ: Dewitt Clinton High Sch; City Col New York; Juilliard. Pianist, singer in Miami & Miami Beach, 39-61. Fulltime songwriter 61-71. Chief Collabrs: Larry Kusik, Charlie Singleton, Bert Kaempfert, Nina Rota. *Songs:* Lyrics: A Time for Us; More Than a Miracle; Games That Lovers Play; Strangers in the Night; Spanish Eyes; Music: Talk to Me; What Will My Mary Say?.

SNYDER, KENNETH C T
author
ASCAP 1960

b Evanston, Ill, Feb 28, 25. Educ: Pub Sch 101, Forest Hills, NY; Maine Township High Sch, Park Ridge, Ill; Northwestern Univ, BS, 45; Am Inst Foreign Trade, BFT, 49. Film journeyman, RKO Radio Pictures, Hollywood, Calif, 46; TV/radio creative dir, Batten, Barton, Dustine & Osborn, San Francisco, 50-54 & Stockton, West & Burhart, Cincinnati, 54-55; sr vpres & creative dir, Needham, Louis & Brorby, Chicago, 55-62; founder, Ken Snyder Enterprises, 62; producer, Children's TV Progs: "The Funny Company"; "Roger Ramjet"; "Skyhawks"; "Hot Wheels"; "Big Blue Marble"; produced segments for "Sesame Street" & "Electric Co"; conceived, produced & publ multi-media AV kits, "Learning with Laughter" (54 units), Prentice-Hall, "Amiguitos" (40 projected bilingual, multicultural units), Xerox Educ Publ plus others; coproduced numerous musical pieces. *Songs:* Lyrics: Shrinkin Viollette; Keep Smiling; Peter Peppers Pots'n Pan Band; The Alphabet Song (Sesame Street); Kennedy, Kennedy, Kennedy (political campaign song). *Albums:* Music From a Surplus Store.

SNYDER, TED
composer, publisher, pianist
ASCAP 1914

b Freeport, Ill, Aug 15, 1881; d Woodland Hills, Calif, July 16, 65. Educ: Pub schs, Boscobel, Wis. Was cafe pianist, Chicago. Formed own music publ co, NY, 08. Gave Irving Berlin first job as staff writer, later they became publ partners with Henry Waterson, 30. Opened nightclub, Hollywood, 30. Chief Collabrs: Irving Berlin, Harry B Smith, Bert Kalmar, Harry Ruby. *Songs:* My Wife's Gone to the Country, Hurrah! Hurrah!; Piano Man; That Mysterious Rag; The Sheik of Araby; Who's Sorry Now?; Dancing Fool; Wild Cherry Rag; Kiss Me, My Honey, Kiss Me; Under the Moon; I Wonder If You Still Care for Me; Way Down Home in Dixie.

SNYDER, WILLIAM PAUL   ASCAP 1950
composer, pianist, conductor
b Park Ridge, Ill, July 11, 20. Educ: Chicago Cons Music, BA; Am Cons Music, MA; De Paul Univ, grad degree; studied with Moritz Rosenthal, Herman Klum. Joined CBS radio, staff pianist, at age 14; formed dance band, first appeared in Chicago & first hit recording, 50; other songs produced on var labels. Produced musical "Kingdom Coming," London, 73. Chmn, City Symph Chicago Asn; producer, entertainment dir & performer, 80-; revived jazz in Chicago by creating new jazz showroom. Chief Collabrs: Stanley Allen Baum, Peter De Rose. *Instrumental Works:* My Pony Macaroni; The Chicago Concerto (piano, orch); Piccadilly Circus; Amber Fire. *Scores:* Musical: Kingdom Coming.

SOCHET, WIN H   ASCAP 1976
composer, author, pianist
b New York, NY. Educ: Juilliard Sch Music; Univ Southern Calif, BA; studied comp with Norman Lockwood & jazz piano with Teddy Wilson. Band dir, Eldred Central High Sch; concert pianist, Scranton, Pa; jazz pianist in nightclubs; clinician, pianist, teacher, arranger & vocal coach. Has written over 300 piano solos & songs. Author bks: "Songwriter Court Progression"; "Popular Piano Self-Taught"; "Link to Modern Music"; "50 Years of Popular Piano in USA"; "Win Stormen Pop Jazz Piano Chorus." Chief Collabrs: Ira Kosloff, William Kaye. *Instrumental Works:* Piano: Strutting Down Wabash; Glitters of Dawn; Blue Rain; Cool Autumn; Hong Kong Hustle; The Mississippi Ramble (concert band).

SODERO, CESARE   ASCAP 1936
composer, conductor
b Naples, Italy, Aug 2, 1886; d New York, NY, Dec 16, 47. Educ: Royal Cons, Naples. To US, 06. Cond, Mendelssohn Glee Club, 12 seasons, var opera cos, incl New York Met, 42-47, Eng cos & on radio. Music dir, Thomas A Edison Phonograph Co; with NBC network, 7 yrs. *Instrumental Works:* Preludio Appasionato (violin, orch); String Quartet in D; Morning Prayer (woodwind); Valse Scherzo (woodwind); Invocation (cello, piano); Nocturne (oboe, orch). *Scores:* Ballet: Ombre Russe.

SOEHNEL, RAY   ASCAP 1953
composer
b New York, NY, Aug 31, 00; d. Educ: High sch. Was carpenter. Chief Collabr: Zelma Soehnel (wife). *Songs:* A Heart Full of Love; I'm Looking Forward; Just One More; For Christmas; I'm Going to Saddle My Blues; A Heart Full of You.

SOEHNER, BARBARA
See Layton, Barbara Soehner

SOELL, JOHN B   ASCAP 1950
composer, author, businessman
b St Louis, Mo, May 20, 11; d Little Rock, Ark, 65. Educ: Washington Univ. Salesman in radio, 39-50, then radio & TV sta broker. Gen mgr, TV stas, 56-63. *Songs:* So Tired.

SOKOLE, LUCY BENDER   ASCAP 1952
composer, author
b New York, NY. Educ: NY Univ. Advert exec, R H Macy & Co, Inc, 35-38, Pedlar & Ryan, 43-45 & William Douglas McAdams, 45-47; advert exec, Young & Rubicam, Inc, 39-43, consult, 51-, assoc copy dir, 54-59, casting dir, 59- Advert consult, Pharma-Craft Corp, 48-51. Reading specialist & pub rels, Livingston Sch. Mem, Am Guild Authors & Comp. *Songs:* How Shall I Love You; Love Makes the World Go 'Round; Lyrics: Three Little Fishies; I'm Keepin' Company; Kissable Baby; What Happens Now?; I Just Fell Out of Love; Shall We Love?; There's a Woman With the Man in the Moon.

SOKOLOFF, DAVID   ASCAP 1963
composer, conductor, pianist
b Philadelphia, Pa, Sept 30, 10. Educ: Zeckwer-Hahn Musical Acad, Philadelphia. Soloist with orchs incl Philadelphia, NY Philh & CBS Symph. Has given recitals in Carnegie Hall & Town Hall, NY, also Acad of Music, Philadelphia. Was cond, Stenton Hills Symph. Originator & cond, Pianorama (piano orch); appeared on "Perry Como Show" & "Johnny Carson Show," TV. Pianist & comp, Radio City Music Hall. *Songs & Instrumental Works:* Love Is a Melody; Carnaval Espagnole.

SOLIS, MAX   ASCAP 1959
composer, musician
b Chicago, Ill, Mar 17, 13. Educ: High sch. Mem, Grover Shore Trio, 49- Chief Collabrs: Lanny Shore, Buddy Grover. *Songs:* To Say You're Mine; Immortal Love.

SOLITO DE SOLIS, ALDO   ASCAP 1949
composer, pianist
b Castrovillari, Italy, May 25, 05; d Los Angeles, Calif, May 7, 73. To US, 40; citizen. Educ: Royal Cons Giuseppe Verdi, Milan (Gold Medal); Cons of Leipzig. Concert pianist, Europe & SAm; also Carnegie Hall, New York, 40. Chief Collabrs: Mitchell Parish, Jack Brooks, Joe Rosenfield, Jr. *Songs:* The Same Old Story; Nightfall; April Made a Fool of Me; Everybody's Lullaby. *Instrumental Works:* Fiesta Mexicana; Toccata; Portraits of Spain; Moods of Spain; Capriccio Espanol; Evening in Venice; Paganini Pays a Visit to Bach; Sentimental Clown; Reverie; The Palms and the Stars.

SOLLY, BILL   ASCAP 1976
composer, author
b Hamilton, Ont, Sept 16, 31. Educ: McMaster Univ, BA Hons, 53. Worked in theatre & TV, London, 15 yrs. Writer spec material for Petula Clark, George Burns, "The Two Ronnies," Marty Feldman. Wrote music & lyrics for "Danny La Rue at the Palace" & children's musicals "The Cat in the Castle" & "The Three Magic Mushrooms." *Songs:* (Tell Me Please) Does Anybody Love You?, Crumbs in My Bed; I Could Fall in Love; Lyrics: I'm Gonna Shine Today. *Scores:* Bway shows: Boy Meets Boy; The Great American Backstage Musical; Sweet William; Mrs Moses.

SOLMAN, ALFRED   ASCAP 1921
composer
b Berlin, Ger, May 6, 1868; d New York, NY, Nov 15, 37. *Songs:* If I Had a Thousand Lives to Live; When the Bell in the Lighthouse Rings Ding Dong; There's a Quaker Down in Quaker Town; Mine, Always Mine; In the Sweet Long Ago; The Bird on Nellie's Hat. *Scores:* Stage: Paris By Night.

SOLNIK, TANIA   ASCAP 1969
composer, author, singer
b Miami Beach, Fla, July 19, 56. Educ: Dick Grove Music Workshop. Began singing professionally at age 8, performing in South Fla & Catskill Mountains. Began composing at age 10. Studio demo work, Atlanta, Ga; moved to Calif, currently singing at The Horn & doing demo's. Chief Collabrs: Concha Madrid, Allen Feingold, Joe Glasser. *Songs:* Rainy Day; Seascape in Song; Music in My Head; Spacey Notions.

SOLOMON, HAROLD   ASCAP 1943
composer, pianist
b Brooklyn, NY, Mar 13, 03. Educ: High sch; music study with David Saperton & Angela Diller. Accompanist to Ruth Etting, Frances Langford, Lanny Ross & James Melton. On staff, music publ. Later in investment business. *Songs:* You Came, I Saw, You Conquered Me; Like a Dream; That Minor Melody; It May Be for the Best After All; Hurt; I'd Let You Do It All Over Again; How Can I Pretend.

SOLOMON, JOSEPH   ASCAP 1943
composer
b Chelsea, Mass, Nov 11, 1897; d New York, NY, June 12, 47. *Songs:* Only Just Suppose; Listening; Jes' Dandy; Oh You Little Son-uv-er-Gun; I Wish I Had to Listen to You; Let's Have an Old-Fashioned Christmas; Stardust in the Dawn; I Just Wanna Play With You.

SOLOMON, PAUL MARSHALL   ASCAP 1969
composer, author, teacher
b Los Angeles, Calif. Educ: Univ Calif, Santa Barbara; Univ Calif, Los Angeles; Calif State Univ, Northridge. Recorded & wrote for Mustang Records, 65-66. Folk musician & singer, Santa Barbara, 67-69; lead singer, Strawberry Alarm Clock, 69-71. Writer for SAC; comp for & appeared in film, "Beyond the Valley of the Dolls," 20th Century Fox. Recorded & arr for UNI Records. Bassist with Mary Kay Place & Gaffney-Freeman; bassist & comp for Sideways Jr. Singer, nightclubs & TV. Recording sideman, Columbia Records. Guitarist & producer. Chief Collabrs: Lee Freeman, Lee Gaffney, David Arnold, Butch Hendrix, Lee Kriske, Steve Pouliot. *Songs:* I'm Comin' Home; Girl From the City; Drinkers Hall of Fame.

SOLOMON, SHIRLEY   ASCAP 1967
author
b Detroit, Mich, Oct 4, 19. Educ: Univ Mich. Advert copywriter & pub relations. Author & writer lyrics for musical plays, "The Girl and the Couch", "John Frum" & "Primavera." Chief Collabrs: Nelson Riddle, Eddie Oliver, Ernani Bernardi, Scott Seely, Joan Steel, David Raksin, Gene Kauer. *Songs:* Lyrics: One Earth; The Energy Song.

SOMMERS, JOHN MARTIN   ASCAP 1973
composer, musician, singer
b Los Angeles, Calif, Sept 16, 40. Educ: John Marshall High Sch, 58; Whittier Col, BA, 62. Worked as musician & singer with group Liberty, 71-74 & John Denver, 74-77; now with Wayne Stewart Band. Chief Collabrs: John Denver, Steve Weisberg, Joe Henry. *Songs:* Thank God, I'm A Country Boy; River of Love; In the Grand Way; Music: Love Is Everywhere. *Instrumental Works:* Pickin' the Sun Down.

SOMOHANO, ARTURO   ASCAP 1941
composer, author, conductor
b San Juan, PR, Sept 1, 10; d San Juan, Mar 25, 77. Educ: Acad Cath; studied music with Fr Peridiello, Belen Salgado, Rafael Marquez, Louis Watts, Alexander Borowsky & Bogumyl Sykora. Concert pianist, Cent & SAm. Founder & cond, Philh Orch PR; guest cond in Europe. Hon cond, Madrid Symph. Gave concerts & produced shows for USA Spec Serv, WW II. *Songs:* Waiting for You; La Cancion de las Americas; Medallita; El Flamboyan; Rumbamba; Adios; Dulce Capricho; Oracion Torera; Dime; Mi Casita; Si Tu

Supieras; Vagando. *Songs & Instrumental Works:* Haitian Souvenirs; Puerto Rican Rhapsody; Variations Humoresque; Recuerdos; Caribbean Rhapsody; Fiesta en San Juan; Holiday in Puerto Rico; En el Viejo San Juan; Paseando por Puerto Rico. *Scores:* Stage: Unidas Venceran; El Misterio del Castillo; En Blanco y Negro; Revista Musical de 1944.

SONDHEIM, STEPHEN JOSUHA   ASCAP 1957
composer
b New York, NY, Mar 22, 30. Educ: George Sch; Williams Col, BA; comp & theory with Milton Babbit; Hutchinson Prize for Musical Comp. Incidental music for Bway "Twigs", "Girls of Summer" & "Invitation to a March." Co-author of film "The Last of Sheila" & lyrics for Bway revival of "Candide"; music & lyrics for Burt Shevelove adaptation of Aristophanes' "The Frogs" & "Side By Side By Sondheim." Pres, The Dramatists Guild (Nat Asn of Playwrights, Composers & Lyricists). Composer. Chief Collabrs: Leonard Bernstein, Richard Rodgers, music, Jule Styne, George Furth, James Goldman, Arthur Laurents, Burt Shevelove, John Weidman, librettos, Hugh Wheeler. *Songs:* A Funny Thing Happened on the Way to the Forum; Anyone Can Whistle; Company (Tony Awards); Follies (Tony Awards); A Little Night Music (Tony Awards; NY Drama Critics' Circle Awards); Pacific Overtures (NY Drama Critics' Circle Awards); Sweeney Todd (Tony Awards; NY Drama Critics' Circle Awards); Evening Primrose; Lyrics: West Side Story; Gypsy; Do I Hear a Waltz?. *Scores:* Film: Stavisky (musical).

SONNIER, JOEL   ASCAP 1974
composer, author, singer
b Rayne, La, Oct 2, 46. Started playing French accordion at age 5; sang & performed on KSIG radio & TV, Crowley, Calif at age 8; wrote & recorded "Teeyeaux Bleu" at age 13. Prof accordionist (French & English). Was on Mercury Label, 74; now with Rounder's Records, Summerville, Mass. Chief Collabr: Earl Ball. *Songs:* Louisiana Blues; Knock-Knock-Knock; I Don't Think I Can Take You Back Again; Cajun Born; Country Blues; We Got Fired; My First Time (All Over Again); Cajun Life.

SOPKIN, HENRY   ASCAP 1953
author, conductor
b Brooklyn, NY, Oct 20, 03. Educ: Chicago pub schs; Am Cons, AM & MM, musical training. Head instrumental dept, Am Cons; cond, Chicago schs, 14 yrs, high sch, 6 yrs & Wilson Col, 8 yrs. Cond & founder, Atlanta Symph, 45-66. Writer & comp, Los Angeles, 66- *Instrumental Works:* Orch: Russian and Ludmilla Overture (M I Glinka; transc); Egmont Overture (Beethoven; transc); Perpetuum Mobile (musical humoresque; Johann Strauss; transc); A Night on Bald Mountain (concert fantasy; M Moussorgsky; transc); The Russian Easter (overture; Rimsky-Korsakoff; transc); Capriccio Italien (Tchaikovsky; transc); Oberon Overture (Carl Maria von Weber; transc); Blue Danube Waltz (Johann Strauss; transc); Finlandia (tone poem; Jean Sibelius; transc).

SORCE, RICHARD   ASCAP 1971
composer, author, teacher
b Passaic, NJ, July 29, 43. Educ: Shenandoah Cons Music; Manhattan Sch Music; NY Univ, BS, MA. Comp & songwriter; teacher of theory, harmony, piano, comp & songwriting. Touring musician. Producer of pop recordings. Engr, var recording studios. Has publ many commercial, pop & concert pieces. Chief Collabr: Barbara Norris. *Songs & Instrumental Works:* Do It Tonight; Easy Does It; You're My Only Way of Livin'; Spring and Fall: To a Young Child (SSA); Turn Back O Man (SATB); Fantasy for Brass Quartet; Theme and Variations for Woodwinds; Jam It; Alleluia for Concert Band and Chorus; Admonition (SATB); Two Preludes and Fugues for Three Winds and Four Brass.

SORDEN, MILO TAYLOR   ASCAP 1965
composer, author
b South English, Iowa, Sept 1, 06. Educ: Northwestern Univ Sch Music, BME. Taught pub sch music, SE Iowa, 10 yrs. Started Sorden Music Co, 37, in Ottumwa, Fairfield & Washington, Iowa. Began comp 62. Chief Collabrs: June Kirlin. *Songs:* I Talked With Christ in the Forest; Come Unto Me; I Love Little Girls; The Couple Next Door; The Possum.

SOREY, VINCENT   ASCAP 1961
composer, author, violinist
b Turin, Italy, Oct 3, 1897; d Miami Beach, Fla, Mar 29, 77. Educ: Cons of Turin, first prize. Came to US, 20. First violinist with Toscanini at age 16. Concert violinist, Europe & SAm. Mem, Philh Symph. Music dir, Mutual Radio Network, 24 & CBS, 27. *Songs:* Springtime; Life Forever; My Land of Love; Legenda Appassionata; Lonely Star; That Night When I Found You; Song of My Soul.

SORNOFF, SIDNEY   ASCAP 1956
composer, author
b Chicago, Ill, Nov 24, 21; d Los Angeles, Calif, Dec 8, 62. Educ: Crane Tech High Sch. *Songs:* I Always Have Someone to Turn To; Lovers Dance; My Heart Needs You; Rolling Stone.

SORRENTINO, CHARLES   ASCAP 1958
composer, arranger, violinist
b Sicily, Italy, Aug 13, 06; d. Educ: Manhattan Sch of Music, scholarship; studied with Franz Kneisel, Maximilian Pilzer, Mario Corti, Vittorio Giannini. Comp & arr, CBS, 31-60. *Instrumental Works:* Ameresque for Orchestra; Illusion (voice, orch); Choral: Salem Witches; Humming Bird; Home Is Best.

SOSENKO, ANNA   ASCAP 1946
composer, author
b Camden, NJ, June 13, 10. Educ: Camden High Sch; Pierce Col, Philadelphia. Mgr, dir & producer, Hildegarde. Produced var radio shows incl Raleigh Room, Penguin Room & Campbell Room. Started writing careers of Alan Jay Lerner & Joseph Stein. Producer, annual show tributes, Museum of New York theatre collection incl Oscar Hammerstein, Dorothy Fields, Richard Rodgers, Joshua Logan, George Abbott, Ethel Merman, Mary Martin & Lerner & Loewe. Dealer in musical & theatre autographs & mss. *Songs:* Darling Je vous Aime Beaucoup; Let's Try Again; Time Was; Waltzing With a Dream; Music: Ask Your Heart; Le Coeur est Comme Une Boite a Musique; Lyrics: I'll Be Yours (j'Attendrai);; Why Don't They Leave Us Alone.

SOSNIK, HARRY   ASCAP 1930
composer, conductor, arranger
b Chicago, Ill, July 13, 06. Educ: Am Cons Music; studied with Leo Sowerby, Kurt Waniek, Ernst Toch, Siegfied Landau, Ludmila Uhlele, Vittorio Giannini. Cond & arr for many radio shows, incl Hit Parade, Pall Mall, Danny Kaye, Hildegarde Raleigh Room, Joe E Brown, Hollywood Woodbury Playhouse. Musical dir, Decca Records. Cond & comp, var TV series. Vpres in charge of music for ABC. *Songs:* Concert Band: The Eternal Flame; Overture to a Fanfare; El Paseo Grande; Dancing Puppet; El Mantilla; Starward. *Songs & Instrumental Works:* TV Themes: Producers' Showcase; Philco Playhouse; Jack Carter Series; Kate Smith Series; Musical Comedy Time; Playwrights' '56. *Scores:* TV: Wonderful World of Toys; We, the People; Petrified Forest; Wide Wide World; The Women; The Four Poster; The Skin of Our Teeth; Reunion in Vienna; Yellowjack; Hollywood Woodbury Playhouse.

SOTHERN, ANN   ASCAP 1958
composer, actress, publisher
b Valley City, NDak. Educ: Col. Appeared in Bway musical "America's Sweetheart." In films incl "Let's Fall in Love", "Lady, Be Good", "Words and Music", "Panama Hattie" & "Maisie," series. TV appeareances "Lady in the Dark" & "Ann Sothern Show," series. Owner, A Bar S Music Co & A Bar S Cattle Co; pres, St Francis Productions. *Songs:* Katy (TV theme).

SOULE, EDMUND FOSTER   ASCAP 1967
composer, singer
b Boston, Mass, Mar 4, 15. Educ: Univ Pa, BM, 39, MA, 46, comp, Harl MacDonald, 33-41 & 46; Yale Sch Music, BM, 48, comp, Richard Donovan, 46-48; Eastman Sch Music, PhD, 56; Univ Denver, MLS, 66; piano, Robert Elmore, Philadelphia, 34-41. Pvt piano teacher, 38-41. Played in Army bands, USA, 42-45. Taught theory & music appreciation, Milton Acad, 48-49; piano, theory & comp, Washington State Col, Pullman, 49-51; music appreciation & theory, Eastman Sch Music, 52-53; theory, piano, choir, Salem Col, 55-58; theory, orch & Am folk music, Univ Pac, 58-61; piano, theory & Am folk music, Washington State Univ, 61-65; also high sch summer courses. Music librarian, Univ Oregon Libr, teacher Am folk music, special piano techniques & comp, Sch Music, 66-80. *Songs:* New Wine (song cycle; based on traditional folk texts; voice & piano); Songs From the Psalms (4 songs from bk of psalms, voice & piano). *Instrumental Works:* Concerto for Harp and Chamber Orchestra (4 movements); Concerto for Saxophone (Alto) and Piano (4 movements); Rhapsody for Flute and Harp; A Book of Emily: Or Thirteen Ways of Looking At Miss Dickinson (cycle of 13 songs for voice & piano; Text: Emily Dickinson); War Is Kind (SSAATTBB, soprano, alto solos, reader; Text: Stephen Crane).

SOUSA, JOHN PHILIP   ASCAP 1914
composer, conductor
b Washington, DC, Nov 6, 1854; d Reading, Pa, Mar 6, 32. Educ: Pvt & pub schs; John Esputa Cons; studied with George Benkert; hon MusD, Pa Mil Col, Marquette Univ. At age 17, cond theatrical orch. First violinist, Offenbach's Orch, Philadelphia Centennial Exp, 1876. Leader, USMC Band, 1880-92; music dir, Great Lakes Naval Training Sta, 17-19. Formed own band, 1892, made world tours. Compiled "National Patriotic and Typical Airs of All Lands." Autobiography, "Marching Along." Film biography, "Stars and Stripes." Charter mem, dir & vpres, ASCAP, 24-32. Awards: Medal of the Victorian Order, Britain, Cross of Artistic Merit, First Class, Acad of Hainault, Belgium & Officer of French Acad. *Instrumental Works:* Semper Fidelis; The Thunderer; Washington Post March; High School Cadets; Liberty Bell; Manhattan Beach; The Picador; King Cotton; On Parade; El Capitan; The Stars and Stripes Forever; Hands Across the Sea; Invincible Eagle; Jack Tar; Field Artillery; Fairest of the Fair; New York Hippodrome March; Solid Men to the Front; The Free Lance; Sabre and Spurs; Nobles of the Mystic Shrine; Black Horse Troop; Pride of the Wolverines; Boy Scouts of America; Hail to the Spirit of Liberty; Orch & Band Suites: Last Days of Pompeii; 3 Quotations; Sheridan's Ride.

SOUTHARD, MARY ANN (J GUS ROME, AMY SINGER) ASCAP 1973
composer, author
b Kokomo, Ill, Nov 19, 26. Educ: Turcheck Sch Music, studied piano with Agnes Smith; Kokomo High Sch, grad; Butler Univ, AB. Started comp music & lyrics in high sch; in col contributed to sorority (Kappa Alpha Theta) sings. Comp; first publ work in 73. Writer of ballads, religious songs & children's bks, both music & stories. *Songs:* Is There Room in Your Inn? (religious); Shadows in the Wind (ballad); He's Mine (ballad); To Care for Me (ballad); Elephants Just Don't Happen (children's bk).

SOWERBY, LEO ASCAP 1927
composer, organist, educator
b Grand Rapids, Mich, May 1, 1895; d Port Clinton, Ohio, July 7, 68. Educ: Am Cons, Chicago, MM; studied with Mrs Frederick Burton, Calvin Lampert, Arthur Olaf Andersen & Percy Grainger; Am Acad Rome (first Am Prix de Rome); Univ Rochester, MusD(hon). Debut as concert pianist, Norfolk Fest, Conn, 17. Concertized in recitals as soloist with symph orchs, US & Europe. Lt, USAF, WW I. Bandmaster, 332nd Field Artillery, also serv in France. Mem fac, Am Cons, then head, Comp Dept, 25-62. Organist & choirmaster, St James Church, Chicago. Dir, Col Church Musicians, in asn with Washington Cathedral, DC. Awards: Eastman Sch Publ; Soc Publ Am Music. Mem, Nat Inst Arts & Letters. *Songs:* With Strawberries; Prayer of the Singer; Three Psalms. *Songs & Instrumental Works:* Violin Concerto; Comes Autumn Time; 2 piano concertos; Sonata for Violin, Piano; Prairie; Symph for Organ; Cello Concerto; Organ Concerto; Sonata for Clarinet, Piano; Ballade for English Horn or Viola, Organ; The Canticle of the Sun (cantata; Pulitzer Prize, 46); The Throne of God (cantata); Classic Concerto for Organ, Strings; Sonata for Trumpet, Piano; 5 symphonies; Toccata for Organ; Set of 4; King Estmere; Mediaeval Poem; Irish Washerwoman; Theme in Yellow; Concert Overture; Portrait (fantasy in triptych); Serenade for String Quartet; Quintet for Flute, Oboe, Clarinet, Bassoon, Horn; Suite for Organ; Sonata for Clarinet, Piano; Poem for Viola, Organ; Choral: Vision of Sir Launfal; Great Is the Lord; Te Deum in D; Forsaken of Man; Song for America; All on a Summer's Day.

SPAETH, SIGMUND ASCAP 1925
composer, author, educator
b Philadelphia, Pa, Apr 10, 1885; d New York, NY, Nov 12, 65. Educ: Germantown Acad; Haverford Col, BA, MA; Princeton Univ, PhD; Instr, Philadelphia Musical Acad, 06-08; Asheville Sch, NC, 10-12. Literary & music ed, New York newspapers & mags. Educ dir, Am Piano Co, 20-27. Founder, community concerts, 28, managing dir, 28-31. Dean, Wurlitzer Sch of Music; pres, Songmart. Featured on radio, mem of Met Opera Quiz & as "Tune Detective." Ed, Music Journal, 55-65. Pres, Louis Braille Music Inst of Am; chmn, Nat Fedn Music Clubs AV Educ. Author, column "Music for Everybody"; autobiography, "Fifty Years with Music," bks: "Common Sense of Music", "Barbershop Ballads", "Read 'Em and Weep", "The Art of Enjoying Music", "Great Symphonies", "A History of Popular Music in America", "Music for Everybody", "The Facts of Life in Popular Song", "A Guide to Great Orchestra Music", "Dedication: The Love Story of Clara and Robert Schumann" & "The Importance of Music." Mem, Nat Asn for Am Composers & Conductors, Nat Music Council, Phi Mu Alpha. Recipient, Henry Hadley Medal. Chief Collabrs: Rudolf Friml, Fairfax Downey, Olga Wolf, Johnny Noble. *Songs:* Down South; My Little Nest of Heavenly Blue; Let's Play Every Day; Chansonette; Querida; Madrigal of May; Jabberwocky; Be Fair and Warmer to Me; Our New York; A Song of Freedom; The Old Barber Shop; I Want to Harmonize; Honolulu Luau.

SPAIN, VERNA GALE
See Sullivan, Gala

SPALDING, ALBERT ASCAP 1924
composer, violinist
b Chicago, Ill, Aug 15, 1888; d New York, NY, May 26, 53. Educ: In Florence with Chiti; Univ Bologna; French Cons, Paris; studied with Lefort & Buitrago. Debut as concert violinist, Paris, 05; Am debut with NY Symph Orch, 08. Made many tours, US & Europe. Lt, USAAF, WW I. Known as Maj Sheridan—Father of Italian Partisan Movement, WW II. Awards: Crown of Italy; Legion of Honor, France; Medal of Freedom, US. Mem, Am Acad Arts & Letters. Autobiography: "Rise to Follow." *Songs & Instrumental Works:* 2 violin concertos; Violin Sonata; String Quartet: Suite for Violin, Piano; Etchings (violin, piano); Alabama (violin).

SPAN, NORMAN (KING RADIO) ASCAP 1959
composer, author, singer
b Port of Spain, Trinidad; d. Educ: Inst for the Blind. Toured US, 37; appeared in films & on cruise ships; toured West Indies & SAm. *Songs:* Man Smart, Woman Smarter; Matilda; Mary Ann; Brown Skin Girl; Invasion; Monkey; The Yankees; You Never Miss the Water Until the Well Runs Dry.

SPANGLER, DALE ASCAP 1972
composer, singer, teacher
b Mt Pleasant, Iowa, Feb 6, 19. Educ: Univ Iowa, BSc, grad work in music. In Bway production, "The Student Prince" & road show, "The Merry Widow." Choir dir, St John's Church, Houghton, Iowa, 57-80. DJ, KXGI radio, Ft Madison, Iowa, 60-75. Announcer & account exec, KKSI radio, Mt Pleasant,

Iowa, 75-80. Chief Collabrs: Marjorie Gilbert, Ruth DeLong Peterson. *Songs: Music:* Music Box Serenade; Mass to God the Creator.

SPARACINO, ANGELO ASCAP 1964
composer, author, accordionist
b Monessen, Pa, Mar 10, 14. Educ: High sch. Accordionist in radio, TV, dance bands & nightclubs. Teacher, 44- *Songs & Instrumental Works:* Loco-Loco; Samba.

SPARGO, TONY
See Sbarbaro, Anthony

SPARKS, FELTON ASCAP 1972
composer, arranger
b Columbus, Ga, Aug 21, 31. Educ: Pvt study piano & voice; studied arr with Tommy Newsom. Started playing piano & singing in lounges, 51; comp & arr music for "Tonight Show" orch, NBC-TV; also cond & arr on the road for var prominent singers & orchs. *Instrumental Works:* Sunday PM; Red Beans and Rice; Saundra; Horizons; Madrid; Funky Butt; Tricky Dick; Lovely Lady; Chew Got It; Puerto Vallarta.

SPARKS, JEFF ASCAP 1968
composer, author
b New York, NY, May 31, 05. Educ: Dewitt Clinton High Sch, New York; Nat Acad Art Design/Art Students' League, New York; Oxford Univ. Broadcasting as announcer, producer, writer, station mgr, prog dir, 27- Announcer, NBC, New York. Announcer, producer, writer, WOR, New York. Prog officer, spec projects officer, UN, New York. Prog dir, Am Red Cross, China, Burma, India, World War II. Author, illus of book "Nursery Rhymes for the Time." Broadcasting instr, City Col New York. Chief Collabr: Phillip Lambro. *Songs:* Infatuation.

SPARKS, RANDY ASCAP 1957
composer, author
b Leavenworth, Kans, July 29, 33. Educ: San Diego State Univ; San Francisco State Univ; Univ Calif, Berkeley. Began career as songwriter & singer, San Francisco; toured with Bob Hope; created & dir, New Christy Minstrels, Back Porch Majority. Wrote for films & TV; writer of special material for Burl Ives, John Denver & others. Now a rancher, Calaveras County, Calif, building a museum of Western Americana; touring as Randy Sparks & the Patch Family. Chief Collabrs: Barry McGuire, Nick Woods. *Songs:* Today; A Place to Hideaway; Saturday Night; (Saturday Night in) Toledo, Ohio; The Johnny Horizon Theme Song (Dept of Interior); Payin' Your Dues Again; Mighty Mississippi; Hi Jolly; Green Green; Pete's Cafe; Whiskey; Lyrics: The Singing Nun. *Scores:* Opera: Calaveras Pond; Film/TV: Advance to the Rear; Hang Your Hat on the Wind.

SPARROW, BILI ASCAP 1978
composer, author, performer
b Boston, Mass, Feb 26, 54. Educ: Studied piano with Sheldon Lopathin, theory with William Thompson. Traveled with show groups; performing on stages of maj cities, incl Boston & San Francisco; also Can. Chief Collabrs: Forest Terry, Bruce Nays. *Songs:* Jammin for a Change; Star Wars (That's the Politics); Doobie in the Funk (We Put it There). *Scores:* Cartoon Movie: In the Forest.

SPAULDING, JACK
See McNeil, Stephen

SPAULDING, JAMES RALPH ASCAP 1970
composer, author, performer
b Indianapolis, Ind, July 30, 37. Educ: Livingston Col, BA(music), 75. With Sun Ra Arkestra, 58-59, Sonny Thompson, 58-59, Freddie Hubbard Quintet, 64, Bobby Hutcherson, 66, Randy Weston, 67, Max Roach Quintet, 67 & Leon Thomas, 70. Sideman to Roy Haynes, 65, Pharaoh Sanders, Horace Silver & Art Blakey, 70. In concerts, Newport Jazz Fest, 65 & 70, Theol Sem, 66, Trueblood Col, 66, Town Hall, New York, 67, Requiem Mass of Sacred Music Honoring Dr Martin Luther King Jr, Voorhees Chapel, Douglass Col, NJ, 76 & Tribute to Paul Robeson, 78, Tribute to Wes Montgomery, Indianapolis, 78. Appeared on TV, Nat Educ TV, Boston, Mass, 66, "Black Journal," 68 & "Express Yourself," Trenton, NJ, 76, Reading Col, London, 68, "Dial M," CBS-TV, 69, "Like It Is," ABC-TV, Chicago, Ill, 69. Leader, Loeb Student Ctr Concert, NY Univ, 68, New York City Community Col Concert Series, 68, The East Cultural Ctr, Brooklyn, NY, 69, Cornell Univ Series, 69-70, Jazzmobile, New York, 69-70, Muse, Brooklyn Children's Museum, 70, Vassar Col, Utica Col, Left Bank Jazz Soc & Manhattan Col, 70, Jymie Productions, Rockland State Park, 71. NEA Award, 75 & ASCAP Award, 76. *Songs:* Time to Go (sacred); Uhuru Sa Sa (Freedom Now); The Peaceful Warrior; Give It Up; New World Coming; Ginger Flower; Malcolm.

SPEAKS, OLEY ASCAP 1924
composer, singer
b Canal Winchester, Ohio, June 28, 1874; d New York, NY, Aug 27, 48. Educ: High sch; studied music with Karl Dufft, J Armour Galloway, Emma Thursby, Max Spicker & William Macfarlane. Soloist, St Thomas Church, NY, 4 yrs. Gave recitals throughout East. Co-founder, Musical Art Soc, Columbus, Ohio,

Dir, ASCAP, 24-43. *Songs:* Sylvia; In Maytime; On the Road to Mandalay; My Homeland; Morning; When the Boys Come Home; The Perfect Prayer; Roses After Rain; A Lover's Song; An Evening Song; Memory of You; Now the Day is Over; The Quiet Road; The Star of Hope; Long Ago; Where the Heart Is.

SPEAR, ANNE
See Johnson, Anne Spear

SPEAR, JACK ASCAP 1961
composer, author, actor
b Newark, NJ, Feb 18, 28. Educ: Newark Cons. Army serv, Ft Bragg Band. Coauthor, "Pip the Piper," NBC-TV, NY; also performs on show. Chief Collabrs: Phyllis Spear, Lucian Kaminsky. *Songs:* My Name Is Pip the Piper; The Piper Oath.

SPEARS, JARED TOZIER ASCAP 1972
composer, author, conductor
b Chicago, Ill, Aug 15, 36. Educ: Northern Ill Univ, BSE, 58; Cosmopolitan Sch Music, Chicago, BM, 59, MM(comp), 60; Northwestern Univ, DM(comp), 68; studied comp with Blyth Owen, Alan Stout & Anthony Donato. Drummer with jazz bands during high sch & col, Chicago area & writer, musical scores for col stage shows & pop music, 50's & 60's. Writer of standard publ music, 60- Guest cond & lectr of comp, high schs & univs, 70- Teacher, comp & perc, Ark State Univ. Distinguished Professor award, Ark State Univ, 80. *Instrumental Works:* Symphonic band: Alleluias; Wind River Portrait; Momentations; Meditation and Festival; Kimberly Overture.

SPECHT, DONALD DAVID ASCAP 1963
composer
b Minneapolis, Minn, June 18, 29. Educ: Univ Minn, MA(comp). Jazz trumpeter with var groups, 40's, 50's. Arr for ABC Radio, Chicago, 48-50. Comp, jingle writer, Los Angeles. TV & radio commercials, 60- Film comp, 69-80. Opera comp 80. Comp Awards: Paris Gold Award, Clio, New York, Canne Fest. *Songs:* Nice; Mary's Song. *Instrumental Works:* Animal World (theme); Wandering; Elegy for My Brother; Searchlight Escape; String Quartet, Opus Zero; Study of a Pro: Karen. *Albums:* Kingsmill Suite.

SPEIRS, JOHN V ASCAP 1962
composer, author
b Glenville, WVa, Aug 31, 16. Writer for radio, 47-51. Producer, author, comp, staff, Walt Disney Productions. Chief Collabrs: Oliver Wallace, Paul Smith, Franklyn Marx, George Bruns, Buddy Baker.

SPEIZMAN, MORRIS ASCAP 1963
composer, author
b Paterson, NJ, Aug 31, 05. Educ: Philadelphia Textile Inst. Textile machinery dealer. Chief Collabrs: Joseph Schuster, John Tucker. *Songs:* I Shouldn't Love You But I Do.

SPENCE, JOYCE ANN (JOYE STREET) ASCAP 1969
composer, author, singer
b Waynesboro, Miss, Dec 25, 45. Educ: Beat Four High Sch. Began writing songs at age 12. Singer, nightclubs, TV & church choir. Recording artist, Reena Records, 70. *Songs:* Mississippi Moonshine; Life Ain't Worth Living; That Man of Mine; When You Belong to Me; The Good Book Says Its Wrong.

SPENCE, LEW (LEWIS SLIFKA) ASCAP 1951
composer, author
b New York, NY, June 29, 20. Pianist-singer in supper clubs, Maisonette Room & St Regis Hotel, New York, until 49. Chief Collabrs: Marilyn Bergman, Alan Bergman. *Songs:* That Face; What's Your Name (and Will You Marry Me?); Music: Nice 'N' Easy; Sleep Warm; Philadelphia; I've Never Left Your Arms; That's Him Over There.

SPENCER, FLETA JAN BROWN ASCAP 1920
composer, author, singer
b Storm Lake, Iowa, Mar 8, 1883; d Hillsdale, NJ, Sept 2, 38. Educ: Cincinnati Cons; studied with Fannie Zeisler. Singer in vaudeville, 12 yrs. Chief Collabr: Herbert Spencer. *Songs:* Underneath the Stars; In the Candle Light; Love Make My Dream Come True; Fancies; East of the Moon, West of the Stars; Hearts Desire; Prairie Flower.

SPENCER, GLENN J ASCAP 1955
composer, author, conductor
b Joplin, Mo, Aug 16, 10; d Simi Valley, Calif, Dec 19, 70. Co-founder vocal group, Sons of the Pioneers, publ & producer, radio show. Producer & cond, western films. Founded own publ firm, 61. *Songs:* Gunsmoke (TV theme); To All Generations; Surely, I Can Believe; Song of the Prodigal; Blue Bonnett Girl; Roses Whisp'ring Wind; If Wishes Were Penny's.

SPENCER, HAROLD A ASCAP 1973
author
b Los Angeles, Calif, July 8, 36. Educ: Westmont Col, Santa Barbara, Calif, BA; San Jose State Univ, Calif; Univ Cincinnati, Ohio; Univ Calif Los Angeles. Comp, 58-; pres, Manna Music Publ Co, Burbank, Calif. *Songs:* Jessie (motion

picture theme); The Colored Christmas Lights; I Need You Every Moment of My Life; Praise the Lord, Hallelujah; Beverly.

SPENCER, HERBERT ASCAP 1920
composer, arranger, singer
b Bunker Hill, Ill, May 27, 1878; d St Louis, Mo, Aug 26, 44. Educ: Leipzig Cons; studied voice with Enrico Caruso. In vaudeville, 12 yrs. Soloist, St Louis church; music dir, Irish Village, St Louis World's Fair, 04. Accompanist to Ernestine Shumann-Heink; music arr, Lillian Russell. Staff comp, NY publ co. Chief Collabr: Fleta Spencer. *Songs:* Underneath the Stars; Fancies; East of the Moon, West of the Stars; Hearts Desire; Prairie Flower.

SPENCER, JAMES HOUSTON ASCAP 1944
composer, organist, conductor
b Malone, NY, July 28, 1895; d Adrian, Mich, Sept 3, 67. Educ: New Eng Cons; studied with G W Chadwick, Stuart Mason, Henry Dunham, Wallace Goodrich, Clayton Johns, Lee Pattison; hon MusD, Adrian Col; Cromwell fel. Was head of music dept, Adrian Col. Organist & choirmaster, Trinity Episcopal Church, Toledo, Ohio, 45-50. Founder & past pres, Mich Composers Club; mem, Am Guild of Organists. *Songs:* Sea Fever; Thou Art My Lute; The Cloths of Heaven; Requiem; Cock Crow; My Song; For Whom the Bell Tolls; Prayers of Steel. *Instrumental Works:* The Song of Solomon (orch, chorus, soloists); Chinese Boy and Bamboo Flutes; Symphonesque; String Quartet; Suite for Orchestra; Piano Trio.

SPENCER, JUDY ASCAP 1970
composer, author
b Stamford, Conn. Educ: Columbia Univ, MA; studied comp with Roger Sessions, Elliott Carter, piano with Teddy Wilson. Comp, incidental music, "Hagar and Ishmael," Lincoln Ctr Libr production, of words & music for off-Bway shows, "Cyrano" & "The Real Piece of Parsley" & words for "Love Games." Lyricist & co-producer of songs for TV show & albums, "Captain Kangaroo"; lyricist for var pop & jazz recording artists. Concert perf of jazz songs by Ella Fitzgerald & Duke Ellington, Lincoln Ctr. Chief Collabrs: John Lewis, Earl Rose. *Songs:* Lyrics: Soft Summer Breeze; Walkin'; Checkered Hat; Just My Love and I; Skating in Central Park; A Lovely Way to Die; A Child; Forgetting You; Mirror of Love; Overnight Success; Now I Know the Feeling; The Singer; Wheels; Everytime We Make Love; Winter Snow, Summer Rain. *Scores:* Film: Hello Fool, Goodbye.

SPENCER, KEVIN BION ASCAP 1978
composer, author, singer
b Los Angeles, Calif, June 30, 55. Educ: Los Angeles City Col. Played & sang with var groups in Los Angeles area; bassist for singing group The Sylvers, 1 yr. Held studio sessions, 78-; began writing, 78- Lead vocalist & keyboardist for singing group Dynasty. Chief Collabrs: Leon Sylvers, Dick Griffey, Ricky Smith. *Songs:* Music: Take That to the Bank; Right in the Socket; Let's Find the Time for Love. *Instrumental Works:* Adventures in the Land of Music.

SPENCER, ROBERT E ASCAP 1925
composer, author
b San Francisco, Calif, Feb 15, 02; d San Francisco, Sept 14, 46. Author "Idol." *Songs:* I Wish I Knew; When Night Time Comes; Would You Cry?; Pesticatin'; Every Little Thing; I'm Walking Around in a Dream.

SPIALEK, HANS ASCAP 1941
composer, conductor, arranger
b Vienna, Austria. Educ: Vienna Cons; Moscow Cons. Asst stage mgr, Moscow Bolshoi Theatre, 18-20; cond, Philh & Opera, Bessarabia, 20-22; musical dir, Firebird Theatre world tour, 23-24; arr 147 Bway musicals incl five by Cole Porter & eleven by Rodgers & Hart; comp, cond & arr, GM & Chrysler indust shows; arr radio prog, "Great Moments in Music," 42-47. *Instrumental Works:* Symphonic Suites: The Tall City; Manhattan Watercolors; Sinfonietta; To a Ballerina; Moon Journey; Another Love Story; Overtures: Clarissa; Antigonette.

SPICKOL, MAX ASCAP 1936
author
b Philadelphia, Pa, Aug 2, 13. Educ: High sch. Author of plays. Actor, cartoonist, calligrapher. Writer of spec material for greeting cards. Creator of "Rainbow Rabbitt." Mem Am Guild of Authors & Composers, Philadelphia Calligraphers Soc, Philadelphia Writers Conference. Chief Collabrs: Johnny Fortis, Art Vallee, Pete Deangelis. *Songs:* Lyrics: The Canteen Bounce; He Was Mr Right; The John Bull Boogie; Christmas Tree in Heaven; Honestly; ABC Boogie; Blue Serge Suit; Mary Hartman-Mary Hartman; The House We Pray In; Pennsauken (off city song).

SPIEGEL, LAURIE ASCAP 1975
composer, visual artist, teacher
b Chicago, Ill, Sept 20, 45. Educ: Shimer Col, AB, 67; Oxford Univ, 66-68; Juilliard Sch Music, 69-72; Brooklyn Col, City Univ New York, MA, 75; studied comp with John W Duarte, Jacob Druckman & Emmanuel Ghent. Concert works & music for film, TV, dance & theater. Visual works using musical time-structure. Predominantly electronic & computer media. Instrumental background includes banjo, guitar & Renaissance & Baroque lute. Have taught

at Aspen Music Fest, Cooper Union, elsewhere. CAPS, WNET, ASCAP & other grants & awards. *Instrumental Works:* Electronic: Patchwork; The Expanding Universe; Voices Within. *Scores:* Ballet: Waves (chamber orch & electronic tape).

SPIEGELMAN, JOEL WARREN   ASCAP 1967
composer, conductor, harpsichordist
b Buffalo, NY, Jan 23, 33. Educ: Yale Sch Music, 49-50; Univ Buffalo, BA, 53; Longy Sch Music, Cambridge, Mass, studied harpsichord with Melville Smith; Brandeis Univ, MFA, 56, studied with Harold Shapero, Irving Fine, Arthur Berger; Paris Cons, 56-57; studied comp with Nadia Boulanger, 56-60; Gnesin Inst, Leningrad Cons, 65-66. Made debut as concert pianist with Buffalo Philh, age 13. Compositional career, 55- Received grant from French gov't to study with Nadia Boulanger, 55- Fac mem Brandeis Univ, 61, Sarah Lawrence Col, 66. Established studio for electronic music, Sarah Lawrence Col, 70. Founded New York Electronic Ens, 70. Founded & conducted New Russian Chamber Orch for Russian emigres, 76-79. Comp performed US, France, USSR, Eng, Yugoslavia, Switz, Italy, Israel, Ger, Greece, Holland & Belg. *Instrumental Works:* Kousochki (Morsels) (piano 4 hands); Fantasy No 1 (for string quartet); Fantasy No 2 (for string quartet); Astral Dimensions (for piano, perc, violin, viola, cello); Midnight Sun (for oboe & 4-channel tape); Daddy (for actress, soprano, conga drums, flute, oboe, tape); A Cry, A Song, and a Dance (for string orch). *Scores:* Opera/Ballet: The Possessed.

SPIELMAN(N), FRITZ (FRED)   ASCAP 1941
composer
b Vienna, Austria. Educ: High sch; Acad Music, Vienna, Master Degree in Piano, studied comp with Joseph Marx; Professorship, Austrain Govt, 75. Gave piano recitals & wrote musicals, Vienna. Came to US in 39. Wrote music for motion pictures "Abeline Town", "Torchsong", "Nancy Goes to Rio", "Good Old Summertime", "Luxury Liner", "Tom Thumb" & "Girls, Girls, Girls," Hollywood, 45-51; now composer. Chief Collabs: Janice Torre, Kermit Goell, Mack David, Paul Francis Webster, Eddie Pola, Sammy Cahn, Stanley Adams. *Songs:* Music: Shepherd Serenade; Paper Roses (ASCAP & Billboard Awards & Grammy Nomination, 74); It Only Hurts for a Little While; The Longest Walk; A Purple Cow; If Love Is Good to Me; Yes There Is a Santa Claus; The Birthday Party of a King; An Old Fashioned Christmas; Mankind Should Be My Business; The Christmas Spirit; One Little Boy; It Might Have Been; Golden Dreams; Holly-Ho; The Stingiest Man in Town; One Finger Melody; Go to Sleep. *Instrumental Works:* The Sword and the Rose. *Scores:* Bway Shows: A Lady Says Yes (musical); Take My Heart With You; Off Bway: Peter Rabbit (Joseph Jefferson Award); Toby Tyler; Sleeping Beauty Revised (A Green Fairytale); Films: Spring Came Back to Vienna; You Won't Forget Me; I Don't Want To; After All These Years; Time and Time Again; TV: The Stingiest Man in Town (adapted for stage, Joseph Jefferson Award for Chicago production, 76); Yes There Is a Santa Claus; The Birthday Party of the King; An Old Fashioned Christmas; Mankind Should Be My Business; It Might Have Been; Golden Dreams.

SPIER, DOROTHY
composer, author
b New York, NY, May 23, 38. Educ: Walton High Sch, Bronx, NY. Had brief writing career; now publ.

SPIER, HARRY R   ASCAP 1937
composer, conductor, pianist
b Boston, Mass, Nov 7, 1888; d New York, NY, Jan 20, 52. Educ: Studied music in Europe with Cotogni, DiPietro, Richard Epstein & Frank LaForge. Organist, Church of Atonement, NY. Accompanist to concert singers. Cond, Ctr Glee Club & Carroll Glee Club. Created exercises for vocal students. *Songs:* Ultima Rose; The Clear Midnight; Dusk in June; Sweet Apple; Easter; Garden; The Choice. *Instrumental Works:* Piano: Romantic Study in Double Notes; With Flute: Mohave Sunset; Mesa. *Songs & Instrumental Works:* Choral: The Flight of Time; A Christmas Journey; The Aristocrat; Solo Voice: The Indian Serenade; Come, Come Along; A Hymn for America.

SPIER, LARRY   ASCAP 1925
composer, publisher
b New York, NY, Apr 3, 01; d New York, Nov 10, 56. Educ: Townsend Harris Hall. Co-founder, Spier & Coslow Music Co, sold co to Paramount, 29. Gen mgr, Chappell; then publ, 50-56. *Songs:* Memory Lane; Was It a Dream?; Put Your Little Foot Right Out; Haunting Melody; Golden Wedding Waltz.

SPIES, CLAUDIO   ASCAP 1962
composer
b Santiago, Chile, Mar 26, 25. Educ: Harvard, BA, 50, MA, 57, studied with Irving Fine & Walter Piston; studied with Nadia Boulanger & Harold Shapero. Taught at Harvard Univ, 53-57 & 68, Vassar Col, 57-58, Swarthmore Col, 58-70, Salzburg Sem Am Studies, 76 & Princeton Univ, 70- Mem, Ed Board, "Perspectives of New Music"; founding mem, Am Society Univ Comp & Int Alban Berg Society, Ltd. *Songs:* In Paradisum (chorus a cappella); Animula Vagula, Blandula (4 voices). *Instrumental Works:* Tempi (14 instruments); Viopiacem (duo, viola, keyboard instruments); Impromptu (piano).

SPIKES, BENJAMIN   ASCAP 1942
composer, author, publisher
b Dallas, Tex, Oct 31, 1888. Music publisher, Los Angeles. Chief Collabr: John Spikes (brother). *Songs:* Wolverine Blues; Someday Sweetheart; Some Rainy Day; Love, Love, Why Do You Seem So Hard to Hold?; The Whole World Seems Wrong; That Sweet Something, Dear; Love Divine.

SPIKES, JOHN C   ASCAP 1942
composer, author, conductor
b Dallas, Tex, July 22, 1882; d Pasadena, Calif, June 28, 55. Educ: Col. Toured in medicine show & vaudeville. Organized & dir, Elks Band. Founded own music studio; led all-girl orch. Designed long-hand writing aid for blind. Author, "Until Recognized." Chief Collabr: Benjamin Spikes (brother). *Songs:* Wolverine Blues; Someday Sweetheart; Some Rainy Day; Love, Love, Why Do You Seem So Hard to Hold?; The Whole World Seems Wrong; That Sweet Something, Dear; Love Divine.

SPINA, HAROLD   ASCAP 1933
composer, author
b New York, NY, June 21, 06. Educ: Pub Sch 45, New York; self taught, music. Began songwriting at age 10. Organized neighborhood band at age 15. Joined M Witmark & Sons minstrel dept, 24, then prof dept. Joined Greene & Stept as pianist, vocalist, arr & spec material writer, 29. Prof songwriter, 33. Organized Telefilm, 39. Music publ for Goldwyn, 20th Century Fox, Paramount & MGM Studios, 46. Independent record producer, Capitol, MGM, Liberty, Pickwick, 49. Theater, "Stove Pipe Hat." Chief Collabrs: Johnny Burke, Edward Heyman, Frank Loesser, Walter Bullock, Jack Elliot, Bob Russell. *Songs:* (How Many Different Ways Are There to Say) I Love You; Santa Catalina (Island of Romance); The Velvet Glove; Crystal Chandelier; The Rubaiyat of Khayyam (suite); India's Love Lyrics (suite); The Argentine Fire Brigade; She of the Black Coffee Eyes; Music: It's So Nice to Have a Man Around the House; La Cucaracha (adaptation); Would I Love You (Love You, Love You); Annie Doesn't Live Here Anymore; The Beat O' My Heart; It's Dark on Observatory Hill; I Don't Wanna Be Kissed; I'd Like to See Samoa of Samoa; I Found a Peach in Orange, NJ (in Apple Blossom Time); Lyrics: Cumana; Wallpaper Roses.

SPINELLI, SALVATORE VINCENT   ASCAP 1976
composer
b New Haven, Conn, Jan 1, 1896; d New York, NY, Apr 15, 78. Educ: Yale Univ Sch Music, BA(music); studied violin with Arturo Toscanini. Cond, New Haven Symp Orch, 22, Rudy Vallee & Vaughn Monroe Orchs, Eddie Cantor Radio Show & Schubert Theater, New Haven. First violinist, Arturo Toscanini-NBC Orch & Firestone Orch. Cond, New Frontier, Las Vegas. *Songs & Instrumental Works:* Hall of Hero's March; Impressions From Space.

SPINOSA, TOM   ASCAP 1957
composer, author, conductor
b San Francisco, Calif, June 6, 22. Educ: Col, accounting degree; studied music. WW II, USN; also Korean War. Assoc with Matson Lines & APL. Asst resident auditor, USMC. Asst to comptroller, Kaiser Engrs. Leader of own orch; owner, Cavalier Records, Dexter Music Co & Arrow Printing Co, San Francisco. Accountant, Bd of Educ, San Francisco. *Songs:* Give Your Heart Another Chance; Love Is on a Holiday; Swing a Lullaby; Weekend in Hawaii; Lost Coral Beach; Rockin' Chair Roll; Easter in Hawaii; Dahil Sa Iyo; Dedicated to You.

SPIRE, CHARLES A   ASCAP 1970
composer, conductor
b Gowanda, NY, June 16, 29. Educ: Gowanda High Sch; Boston Univ, BM, MM; Southern Conn State Col; studied piano with Louis Cornell, comp with Gardner Reed & Paul Hindemith, conducting with Arthur Fiedler. Teacher in North Syracuse & Lyndrook, NY; music adminr, Ridgefield, Conn; cond, The Ridgefield Youth Orch. *Instrumental Works:* Gypsy Dance (orch); Now Thank Thee All Our God (orch); Eleven Classic Solos (solos for clarinet, saxophone, oboe, bassoon, flute); Two Moods (piano); Thoughts (piano).

SPIRO, DEMON
See Lane, James W

SPITALNY, MAURICE   ASCAP 1928
composer, conductor
b Tetieff, Russia, Feb 27, 1893. Educ: Berlin Cons Music, 06, studied violin with Prof Henri Marteau. Travelling concert violin soloist with Cleveland Symph, 14-17; musical dir & producer of stage shows at Loews Stillman Theatre, Cleveland, plus concert orch at Statler Hotel; organized Soc Dance Orch; musical dir, NBC Radio Sta KDKA, Pittsburgh, 36-54; organized, Preparatory Div Music, Univ Miami, 63, teacher cond & violin, 16 yrs. *Songs:* Dream Shadows; Parting Kiss; Broken Dreams; Sweetest Girl in All the World; Lost Caravan; Why Must I Dream?; Start the Day Right. *Songs & Instrumental Works:* A Gypsy's Love Is Like a Melody; March Miramar; Garden of India; Woodland Pictures; Song of the Legionnaires; Hebrew Chant.

SPITALNY, PHIL   ASCAP 1942
composer, conductor, clarinetist
b Odessa, Russia, Nov 7, 1890; d Miami Beach, Fla, Oct 12, 70. Educ: Odessa Cons. Toured Russia as child clarinet prodigy. Orch cond, Cleveland & Boston.

Cond own orch, radio, hotels, recordings & TV. Made world tour. Organized all-girl orch, 34, featured on radio show, "Hour of Charm." *Songs:* Madelaine; Enchanted Forest; It's You, No One But You; Save the Last Dance for Me; The Kiss I Can't Forget; Pining for You.

SPITZER, CORDELIA (DYER NELSON)   ASCAP 1964
author

b LaFollette, Tenn. Writer of cantatas, gospel songs, anthems & hymns. Chief Collabrs: John F Wilson, Robert J Hughes, Lani Smith, Floyd W Hawkins, Roger C Wilson, Mosie Lister. *Songs:* Lyrics: Crown Him King (cantata); With Love Untold (cantata); Good News, World (cantata); All God's People (musical); The Joys of Easter (cantata); The Miracle Worker (cantata); Christ Is Risen (cantata).

SPIVACK, LARRY S   ASCAP 1976
composer, author, performer

b Brooklyn, NY, Jan 8, 54. Educ: James Madison High Sch; Brooklyn Col, BA(magna cum laude), 75; Juilliard, MMus, 77; studied with Morris Lang, Saul Goodman, Jacob Druckman & Robert Starer. Began comp at age 14, wrote jingles for radio & TV & concert works. Free-lance percussionist/timpanist, Am Symph, Nat Orchestral Asn & Martha Graham Dance Co, New York. Composer/lyricist for shows, "Frabjous Friends and Alice", "Silent Fantasies" & "Let Down Your Hair!" Chief Collabr: Robert Elisberg. *Instrumental Works:* Four Pieces for Solo Vibraphone; Cowboys; Siciliano; Fip Fop Fuppe; At the Jolly House; Quartet for Paper Bags; Sonata for String Quartet and Vibraphone; Soliloquy (solo vibraphone); Three Duos (vibraphone, marimba). *Scores:* Film: Danger in a Safe Place.

SPOTTS, ROGER HAMILTON   ASCAP 1974
composer, author, arranger

b Cincinnati, Ohio, June 20, 28. Educ: Douglass Elem Sch; Withrow High Sch, Cincinnati; Cent State Col, Wilberforce, Ohio, BS; Univ Southern Calif, electronic music; studied film music with Lyn Murray, Los Angeles. Comp & arr for Armed Services Radio Network, 52-53, also for bands Dizzy Gillespie, Count Basie, Lionel Hampton, Ray Charles, Don Ellis, Al Grey, Papa John Creach, Jefferson Airplane & Johnny Otis. Music dir for Zola Taylor's Platters & Grant's Music Ctr. *Songs:* My Little Girl. *Instrumental Works:* Suite for Orchestra and Jazz Quartet; Octet; String Quartet; The Speechmaker; Woodwind Quartet; Brass Quartet. *Scores:* Film: Too Late for Tears.

SPRECHER, GUNTHER WILLIAM (WILLIAM GUNTHER)   ASCAP 1963
composer, pianist, conductor

b Saarbruecken, Ger, Jan 20, 24. Educ: Pub schs, Saarbruecken, Ger & Tel Aviv, Israel; studied piano with Prof Wittels & Madam Vengerova, comp with Paul Ben-Haim, cond with Georg Singer. Music dir, WEVD radio; founder, music dir & cond, Bronx Philh Symph; music dir & organist, Temple Sholom, Greenwich, Conn. Recording artist of many albums; appeared in 2000 concerts & over 2000 radio programs. Mem of The First Piano Quartet; awarded the Robert Stolz Medallion, Vienna, 73. Chief Collabrs: Jan Bart & Adam Garner. *Songs:* Yinglish (Yiddish-English) (song bk); Music: Three Ghetto Songs. *Instrumental Works:* Jerusalem Concerto (piano, orch); Five Musical Bridges. *Songs & Instrumental Works:* Great Is Thy Faith (biblical cantata).

SPRINGER, A L (LEO FUCHS)   ASCAP 1955
composer, author, actor

b Lvov, Poland, May 15, 11. Educ: Studied in Poland. Wrote stage material, Poland. Mem ZAIKS, Poland. Actor on stage in New York; usually wrote own material. Recorded for RCA, Decca, Batter & Tikua Record Cos. Dir & actor, off-Bway show "Here Comes the Groom." *Scores:* Off-Bway show: Here Comes the Groom.

SPRINGER, PHILIP   ASCAP 1951
composer, author, teacher

b New York, NY. Educ: Columbia Col, BA, 50; NY Univ, MA, 62; Univ Calif, Los Angeles, PhD, 73. Comp music for Columbia Varsity Shows, songs for Bway musicals "Shoestring '57", "Ziegfeld Follies '57" & "Tovarich"; off-Bway musical "Hotel Passionato," also songs for films "Summer Holiday", "Twist Around the Clock" & "New Faces '52." Comp & cond motion pictures "Kill a Dragon", "Impasse", "I Sailed to Tahiti With an All Girl Crew" & "Tell Me That You Love Me Junie Moon," also comp & cond TV shows "Gunsmoke", "Mannix", "Then Came Bronson", "Medical Center " & "The Young Lawyers." Synthesizer scores for TV "The Space Watch Murders"; comp theme & background music for game show "Crosswits." Author, "Switched on Synthesizer." Prof electronic music; music critic, Los Angeles Times. Chief Collabrs: Buddy Kaye, E Y Harburg, Carolyn Leigh, Joan Javits, Richard Adler, Bob Hilliard. *Songs & Instrumental Works:* How Little We Know; Santa Baby; Moonlight Gambler; The Next Time; The Perfect Woman; Time You Old Gypsy Man; Teasin'; Westport; Neverending.

SPRINGSTEEN, BRUCE
composer, musician

b Freehold, NJ, Sept 23, 49. Educ: NJ Community Col. Guitarist, Cafe Wha, Greenwich Village, 65. Formed bands, Steel Mill & Dr Zoom and the Sonic Boom. Solo recording artist, Columbia Records, 72- Formed back-up group, The E-Street Band. *Songs:* Blinded By the Light. *Albums:* Greetings From Asbury Park, NJ; The Wild, the Innocent and E-Street Shuffle; Born to Run (gold album).

SPROSS, CHARLES GILBERT   ASCAP 1925
composer, organist

b Poughkeepsie, NY, Jan 6, 1874; d Poughkeepsie, Dec 23, 62. Educ: Studied music with Adolph Kuehn, Helen Andrus, X Scharwenka & C Lachmund; hon MusD, Capital Univ. Church organist, St Paul's, Poughkeepsie, 7 yrs, Presby, NY, 4 yrs, Second Presby, Paterson, NJ, 8 yrs & Presby, Poughkeepsie, 12-29, then First Congregational. Accompanist to Nellie Melba, Mary Garden, Ernestine Schumann-Heink & Alma Gluck. Soloist, NY Symph. *Songs:* Forever and a Day; Jean; Ishtar; I Love the Lord; Gunga Din; Sweet, Sweet Lady; Asleep; Remember Now Thy Creator; I Do Not Ask, O Lord; Will o' the Wisp.

SPROUT, JOHN WELLS, JR   ASCAP 1978
composer, lyricist, singer

b Princeton, NJ, Apr 12, 52. Educ: The Peddie Sch, Hightstown, NJ, 67-70; Bucknell Univ, BA(psychol), 74. Recording artist, Green Mountain Records. Solo singer & guitar player, clubs from Colo to Vt. *Songs:* To a Friend; Just Like a Song; Angels Everywhere; I'm Singing; Jolie. *Albums:* Angels Everywhere.

SQUIRES, HARRY D   ASCAP 1924
composer, publisher, manager

b Philadelphia, Pa, May 10, 1898; d New York, NY, Dec 19, 60. Educ: Pub schs. Mem staff, music publ firm, Philadelphia & New York. Became publ, operator of music stores. Promoter, mgr of musical units & dir concert tours incl Sigmund Romberg, Phil Spitalny, Paul Whiteman, Duke Ellington, Jarmila Novotna & Victor Borge. *Songs:* Someday I'll Make You Glad; The Heart of a Fool; I Never Miss the Sunshine; Just for Remembrance; Mean, Mean Mama; Rock Me in My Swanee Cradle.

STABILE, JAMES   ASCAP 1967
composer, arranger, conductor

b New York, NY, May 28, 37. Educ: Lafayette High Sch, 55; Nyack Col, dipl sacred music, 63; Manhattan Sch of Music, BM, 62, MM, 63, comp with Vittorio Gianinni; cond with Nicolas Flagello; piano with Pia Sebastiani. Col prof. Arr, cond & producer of sacred music recordings; comp of film scores. *Instrumental Works:* The Greatest of Miracles; Sonata for Tuba and Piano; Suite for Brass Choir; Suite for Brass Quintet; Ballade for Vibraphone.

STAEDTLER, R DARRELL   ASCAP 1968
composer, author

b Llano, Tex, Dec 27, 40. Educ: Southwest Tex State Col, BS(educ), 65. Signed exclusive songwriting contract with Wilburn Bros Co & Bronze Music, 63, with Terrace Music, 69, Jack & Bill Music, 70, King Coal Music, 72, Chappell Music, 73 & Jop Music, 78. Recorded for Dot Records, Polydor Records & Maverick Records. Now composer & author. *Songs:* Blue Collar Job (ASCAP Award); Put Your Lovin' Where Your Mouth Is (ASCAP Award); Honky Tonk Stardust Cowboy (ASCAP Award); I Love the Blues and Boogie Woogie (ASCAP Award); It's Another World (Soc European Stage Authors & Comp Award); I Can't Keep Away From You (Soc European Stage Authors & Comp Award); Touch and Go (Soc European Stage Authors & Comp Award).

STAFFORD, JAMES W   ASCAP 1970
composer, author, musician

b Eloise, Fla. Musician with group. Own show, ABC-TV, summer, 75. Entertainer, actor & comedian, appeared on var TV progs. Recording artist for var cos. Owner, Alad Music Publ Co. *Songs:* Swampwitch; Spiders and Snakes; Wildwood Weed; My Girl Bill.

STAGG, ALAN   ASCAP 1978
composer, author

b Brooklyn, NY, Oct 11, 52. Educ: Brooklyn Col. Played for club dates, incl weddings & bar mitzvahs, then prof songwriter. *Songs:* Good Times.

STALLINGS, CHARLES KENDALL   ASCAP 1971
composer, teacher

b Cape Girardeau, Mo, June 20, 40. Educ: Sikeston Pub Schs, Mo; Cent Methodist Col, Fayette, Mo; Wash Univ, St Louis, Mo, BA, 64, PhD, 69; Cornell Univ; Teylers Museum, Haarlem, The Netherlands; Calif Inst Arts; studied comp with Robert Wykes. Comp & fac mem, Webster Col, St Louis, 67-; comp film music; work in electronic music & microtonal music. Chief Collabrs: Jon Dressel, John & Sondra Camie. *Instrumental Works:* Minimovement (violin, cello & piano). *Scores:* Opera/Ballet: Gas Light Square—A Requiem Celebration; Film/TV: Exchanges I.

STALVEY, DORRANCE   ASCAP 1975
composer

b Georgetown, SC, Aug 21, 30. Educ: Col Music, Cincinnati, Ohio, BM, 53, MM, 55. Comp, concert dir, teacher. Comp chamber music, orch, electronic music, multi-media, theater. Exec-artistic dir, Monday Evening Concerts, 71- Prof music, Immaculate Heart Col. Awards: NEA Comp Grants, 75, 78; ASCAP Awards, 77, 78, 79. Panel mem NEA, 78- *Instrumental Works:*

Points-Lines-Circles; Celebration—Sequent I; PLC—Extract; PLC—Abstract; Celebration—Principium; Celebration—Sequent II; Celebration—Sequent IV; Three Pairs and Seven. *Scores:* Ballet: Agathlon.

STAMPER, DAVID   ASCAP 1914
composer, pianist
b New York, NY, Nov 10, 1883; d Poughkeepsie, NY, Sept 18, 63. Educ: Pub schs. Pianist in Coney Island dance hall, then music publ co. Accompanist to Nora Bayes & Jack Norworth in vaudeville, 4 yrs. Wrote songs for first film operetta in sound, "Married in Hollywood." Charter mem, ASCAP. Chief Collabr: Gene Buck. *Songs:* Daddy Has a Sweetheart (and Mother Is Her Name); In the Cool of Evening; Hello, My Dearie; Sunshine and Shadows; My Rambler Rose; 'Neath the South Sea Moon; Sally, Won't You Come Back?; Lovely Little Melody; Some Boy; Garden of My Dreams. *Scores:* Bway stage: Ziegfeld Follies (13 ed); Ziegfeld 9 O'Clock Revue (2 ed); Ziegfeld Midnight Frolics (11 ed); Take the Air; Lovely Lady; in London: Zig-Zag; Box o' Tricks.

STAMPFEL, HERMANN   ASCAP 1973
composer, author, singer
b Steiermark, Austria, Sept 1, 46. Educ: John Weber Music Sch. Lyricist, comp & recording artist (vocal); also second tenor, Gottscheer Men's Choir. Chief Collabr: John Amos. *Songs:* Poet Who Ran Out of Rhyme; If I Could Only See Your Face (With You); Don't Know Who You Are; I've Loved and I've Lost; Why Can't I Be Loved By You; Not Yet a Widow; Searching for Happiness; The Tears Won't Come; Baby, I Want You Back; Lyrics: Answer My Letter; Learn and Save; Just a Friend; Tra La La La La; Dear Mother.

STANG, ARNOLD   ASCAP 1953
author, performer
b New York, NY, Sept 28, 27. Educ: Townsend Harris Hall; City Col New York. Starred on radio, Bway, motion pictures & TV. Recorded for Columbia, ABC, Epic & RCA Record Cos. *Songs:* Lyrics: Ivy Will Cling; Where Ya Callin' From, Charlie; Come Dance With Me; Peter and the Wolf (revised version); Ferdinand and the Bull (revised version).

STANGER, RUSSELL T   ASCAP 1960
composer, conductor
b Arlington, Mass, May 8, 24. Educ: Berkshire Music Ctr, 48-50, 52; New Eng Cons Music, Boston, Mass, 51-52, BM, MM(theory); studied with Walter Piston, Harrison Keller, Leland Procter, Richard Bergin, Leonard Bernstein & Eleazar de Carvalho. Music dir, Harvard-Radcliffe Orch, 50-53; first Europ tour, 53. Guest cond, Societe des Conserts du Conservatoire & Reims Symph, Notre Dame, Paris, France & Reims Cathedral, Cecilia Soc Boston. Music dir, Pioneer Valley Symph, 53-56. Recordings with var cos, 53-54. Music dir, Boston Univ Orch, 57-59; guest cond var leading orchs, Can & US, 55-58; founder & music dir, Boston Little Orch, New York & Boston concert, 58-60. New York Opera debut, 59; Boston Opera tour US, 60. Asst cond, NY Philh, 60-61 & Minneapolis Symph, Minn, 65-66; music dir, Va Philh, 60- Laureate for Life, regional Europ cond tours, leading orchs. Chief Collabrs: Leonard Bernstein, Benny Goodman. *Instrumental Works:* Buffoons (A Merry Overture), Opus 1; Childhood Images, Opus 2; Rock Opus, Opus 3; Episodes '76 (Dramatic Cantata, full orch & chorus), Opus 4; Fanfare for an unCommon Man, Opus 6.

STANLEY, JACK   ASCAP 1921
author
b Chicago, Ill, June 6, 1890; d Chicago, Jan 30, 36. *Songs:* Keep Tempo; I'm in Love Again; Tenderly; Mother o' Mine.

STANLEY, PAUL   ASCAP 1973
composer, author
b Queens, NY, Jan 20, 52. Educ: Self-taught on rhythm guitar. Mem rock group Kiss, 73- *Songs:* I Was Made for Loving You; Detroit Rock City; Black Diamond.

STANLEY, ROBERT   ASCAP 1944
composer, conductor
b Lancut, Poland, Apr 13, 02. To US, 09. Educ: High sch; studied music wtth Cesare Sodero, Rafael Bronstein & Alexander Block. Cond in vaudeville; staff cond, WOR, NY, 12 yrs. Music dir, Queens Symph, 7 seasons. Cond, musicals on Bway & on tour "Allegro", "South Pacific", "Me and Juliet", "Pipe Dream", "Miss Liberty", "Ankles Aweigh" & "Flower Drum Song." *Songs:* Tropical Gardens; Lamento Tropical; Tropical Palms; Tampa; Mercedes; Se Fue; Tupinamba; Mexican Street Song.

STANO, HENRY   ASCAP 1955
composer
b New York, NY, Sept 16, 08. Educ: NY Univ, BS. Physical therapist, 32-37. Joined Vet Admin, 37; chief physical therapist, Montrose Vet Admin Hosp, NY, 50- Polio Found traveling fellowship, 56. Chief Collabrs: Albert Gamse, Pinky Herman, Jack Rollins, Mary Davies. *Songs:* My Heart Knows Your Heart By Heart; Give, Give, Give.

STANTON, FRANCIS HAYWARD (FRANK)   ASCAP 1950
composer, author
b Norway, Maine, Dec 27, 13. Educ: Mt Hermon Prep Sch, 32; Harvard Univ, AB, 36. Songwriter, 37-; formed publ co with Del Sharbutt, Lanny Ross & Dick Uhl, 40. WWII Army Signal Corps, Europe. Songplugger for major firms. Partnership with Andy Badale began 64. ASCAP SE Writer Adv Comt, 79-80. Chief Collabrs: Andy Badale, Arthur Kent, Larry Fotine, Murray Semos, Fred Patrick, Ginny Johnson. *Songs:* Face It Girl, It's Over; The Nickel Serenade; Nashville Beer Garden; Blue Guitar; Invisible Hands; If We All Said a Prayer; Busy Line. *Scores:* Look Where I'm At (Bway); The Boy Who Made Magic (dinner theaters); Film/TV: Songs from "Framed"; A Romantic Guy, I; 30 children songs on "Captain Kangaroo" TV show.

STANTON, FRANK LEBBY   ASCAP 1929
author
b Charleston, SC, Feb 22, 1857; d Jan 7, 27. Educ: Pub schs. Copy boy, reporter & feature writer, Savannah Morning News; published Smithville News, then on staff, Rome Tribune, Ga. Reporter, then feature writer, Atlanta newspaper, 1889. Georgia's first poet laureate. Collections of verse: "Songs of the Soil", "Comes One With a Song", "Songs From Dixie", "Up From Georgia" & "Little Folks Down South." *Songs:* Poems Set to Music: Mighty Lak a Rose; Just a-Wearyin' for You; Sweet Little Woman o' Mine; Let Miss Lindy Pass; Li'l Feller; Keep on Hopin'.

STANTON ROSEMARY BROWN   ASCAP 1967
author
b Radlett, Eng, Feb 3, 24. Educ: Benenden Sch, Eng. Chief Collabr: Frank Stanton. *Songs:* Lyrics: My Birdfeeder; The Sound of Summer Voices; Sing a Song of Birthdays.

STANTON, ROYAL WALTZ   ASCAP 1961
composer, author, choral conductor
b Los Angeles, Calif, Oct 23, 16. Educ: Univ Calif, Los Angeles, BE, 39, MA(musicol, educ), 46; studied with Arnold Schönberg. Teacher, San Luis Obispo, Calif, 39-41, Pomona, Calif, 42-43, Long Beach Polytech High, Calif, 46-50. USA, 43-46. Head music dept, Long Beach City Col, 50-61; chmn fine arts div, Foothill Col, Los Altos Hills, Calif, 61-67 & De Anza Col, Cupertino, Calif, 67-79. Dir, The Schola Cantorum, Cupertino, 64-80. *Songs:* Music: Forever Blest Is He (SATB); Ev'ry Time (SATB); God's Son Is Born (cantata, SATB); Five Psalm Fragments (SATB, solos); You Fill My Heart (SATB).

STARER, ROBERT   ASCAP 1959
composer
b Vienna, Austria, Jan 8, 24. Educ: State Acad, Vienna, 37-38; Israel Cons, Jerusalem, 38-42; Juilliard Sch Music, PGDipl, 47-49; 2 Guggenheim Fels, 57 & 64. British Royal AF, 43-46. Fac Juilliard Sch Music, 49 & Brooklyn Col, 63. Am Acad Award, 79. Author bk "Rhythmic Training"; now composer. *Songs & Instrumental Works:* For Orch: 3 Symphonies; 3 Piano Concerti; Concerto for Viola; Concerto for Violin and Cello; Concerto a Tre (clarinet, trumpet, trombone, strings); Samson Agonistes; Chorus: Ariel; Joseph; Images of Man; The People Yes; Piano: Sonatas; Sketches in Color; At Home Alone. *Scores:* Operas: Pantagleize; The Last Lover; Apollonia; Ballets: Phaedra; Secular Games (Martha Graham Award); Dybbuk.

STARK, JAMES C   ASCAP 1970
author
b Paterson, NJ, Aug 24, 39. Educ: Xavier High Sch, New York, NY; Georgetown Univ (col) & Georgetown Med Sch; Art Career Sch, New York; Fairleigh Dickinson Dental Sch, Teaneck, NJ. Dentist; lyric writer; involved in athletics, music & art. Chief Collabrs: Ralph Carbone (comp), Tom Douglas (comp), Jack Carroll, Marty Gold (arr), Willie Gilbert (script writer), Lou Toby (arr). *Songs:* Lyrics: Elmer Elf; Hear the Christmas Bells; Crazy Over You, Another Heartache; A Dream Is Not a Dream; Palma (Palma By Midnight).

STARKS, ROBERT   ASCAP 1978
composer, author, vocalist
b Detroit, Mich, May 8, 52. Educ: Studied piano with Mabel Miller, cert, 67, perc, 68-69. In sch & church choirs; later played nightclubs, 69-70. Congal & flute vocalist. Redesigned & patented drum mallet. Chief Collabr: Donald Diamond. *Songs:* Long Time No See; Hot As Erupting Lava; Golden Heart; Razz Matazz. *Instrumental Works:* The Sounds of the 80's. *Scores:* Exhibition Vol 1. *Albums:* The Sounds of the 80's.

STAROYANIS, STRATIS N   ASCAP 1967
composer
b Kalamata, Greece, Dec 27, 37. Educ: Athens-Greece Sch Law, 64; New Sch Social Res, New York, MA(econ), 67; US Sch Music, New York, Cert Award harmony, 67. Lawyer, Athens, Greece; in NY, 64-67; comp mainly Greek songs. Mem, AEPI, Greece. Chief Collabr: Bob Saffer. *Songs:* Music: A Jug of Wine, A Loaf of Bread and Thou; Sagapo Means I Love You.

STARR, MARK   ASCAP 1969
conductor
b New York, NY, Jan 30, 42. Educ: Columbia Univ, BA, 62, MS, 63; Santa Cecilia Cons, Rome, Italy, dipl orchestral & operatic cond, 66; pvt study with

Igor Markevitch, Pierre Boulez, Franco Ferrara, Bruno Maderna & Jean Fournet. Cond, numerous orchs, Europe & US, incl Orchestre Nat of Radio France, Berliner Sinfonieorchester, var Soviet orchs, Phoenix Symph Orch, Mich Chamber Orch, Milwaukee Symph Orch, Wheeling Symph, WVA & others. Dir orchestral activities, Univ Wis, 70-74. Dir orchs & opera, Stanford Univ, 74-78. Cond fac, San Francisco State Univ, 79- Also arr, ed, writer of music, comp, translr libretti & broadcaster. *Instrumental Works:* Il Maestro di Capella (Cimarosa); Grand Duo Concertant No 2 (Bottesini; violincello, double bass, orch); Transc: Deux Paraboles (Ibert; flute & guitar); Elegy (Bartok; flute & piano); Azulejos (Albeniz; symph orch).

STARR, RANDY
See Nadel, Warren

STARR, TAMA LYNN   ASCAP 1971
composer, author, performer
b New York, NY, Nov 12, 46. Educ: Fieldston High Sch; NY Univ, BA, 68; Hebrew Univ, Jerusalem, 69. Recorded "Zero Time" & "It's About Time" with Tonto's Expanding Headband. Performed poetry/dance with Tonto's Expanding Headband, Maui Mud Dance Troupe & The Volcano Players. Chief Collabrs: Robert Margouleff, Malcolm Cecil, Bob Simmons. *Songs:* Lyrics: Riversong; Away; Remembery; Buddha's Blue. *Scores:* Space Opera: Enoch.

STARR, TONY   ASCAP 1948
composer, author, conductor
b Philadelphia, Pa, Nov 9, 14; d Philadelphia, Jan 9, 71. Educ: Pub schs; pvt music study. Led own trio. USA, WW II. Wrote musical shows incl "A-R-M-Y." *Songs:* Rockin' Horse Cowboy; Va Zappa; You're My Treasure; Grin and Bear It; You're the Only One for Me; Ev'ry One But Me; I Stole You From Somebody Else.

STARR, TONY
See Sacco, Anthony

STATLER, DARRELL
See Staedtler, R Darrell

STATON, BARBARA   ASCAP 1975
composer, author, teacher
b Graham, Tex, Feb 4, 33. Educ: Tex Woman's Univ, BA, 54, MA, 67. TV teacher, Ga ETV Network, wrote & produced over 100 videotapes featuring learning music through dance, 65-70; wrote theme songs & related songs for 3 continuing GETV series "Do Re Mi," "Our Musical World" & "Sing It Again"; composer songs for "Captain Kangaroo" (CBS-TV), 75-80. Author instr bk for album Music 1-2-3; composer theme song for album Disco Sing Along; composer/author of "Pot Belly Bear Songs and Stories"; composer songs to go with series of bks "I Can Read." Chief Collabrs: Merrill Staton, Lynn Freeman Olson.

STATON, MERRILL (MERRILL OSTRUS)   ASCAP 1958
author, singer, conductor
b Wiota, Iowa, Jan 13, 19. Educ: Northwestern Mo Univ, BS, distinguished alumni; Columbia Univ, MA, EdD. Served with USNAF, WW II. Choir cond, choral dir of TV shows incl, "Bell Telephone Hour", "Omnibus", "Hallmark Hall of Fame" & "American Musical Theatre." Cond, Merrill Staton Voices, Carnegie Hall & Lincoln Ctr. Record producer, singer. Leader, Merrill Staton Enterprises & The Log Haven Music Publ Co; participating partner in S&K Productions Inc. Writer & recording artist of theme songs for "Music Is the Magic Key" & "Let's Make Music" & radio prog "Group of Nutrition." Songwriter for TV show "Captain Kangaroo." *Songs:* Bit of Logic (Why Study); Lonesome Whistles; Ring the Chimes; Light One Candle; I Want to Be Free; Happy Time Sing Along.

STAUFFER, DONALD WESLEY   ASCAP 1963
composer, author, conductor
b Canton, Ohio, July 30, 19. Educ: Eastman Sch Music, BM, MM & PhD. Musician in orchs, incl USN Band; leader, NY Naval Base Band, 56-58; head, Acad Training Dept, US Naval Sch Music, 58-60; asst leader, USN Band, 60-64. Author, "Intonation Deficiencies of Wind Instruments in Ensemble." Mem: Nat Band Asn; Nat Asn for Am Composers & Conductors. *Instrumental Works:* Fugue 'n Swing; Canine Capers.

STAVIS, BARRIE   ASCAP 1965
composer, author
b New York, NY, June 16, 06. Educ: New Utrecht High Sch, grad, 24; Columbia Univ, 24-27. Foreign correspondent, Europe, 37-38; co-founder & mem bd dirs, New Stages Theatre, 47; mem bd dirs, US Inst for Theatre Technol, 61-64 & 69-72. Novelist, playwright, historian & librettist. Publ plays: "Refuge: A One Act Play of the Spanish War," 38; "Lamp at Midnight: A Play About Galileo," 47; "The Man Who Never Died: A Play About Joe Hill," 55; "Harpers Ferry: A Play About John Brown," 67; "Coat of Many Colors: A Play About Joseph in Egypt," 77. Novels: "The Chain of Command," 45; "Home, Sweet Home!" 49; "The Songs of Joe Hill" (ed with Frank Harmon), 55; "Notes on Joe Hill and His Times," 64; "Joe Hill: Poet-Organizer," 64; "John Brown: The Sword and the Word," 70. Chief Collabrs: Lee Hoidy, Alan Bush. *Songs:* Pilgrim Poor;

Lyrics: Come, All Ye Toilers; Workers of the World, Awaken!. *Scores:* Opera: Joe Hill; Oratorio: Galileo Galilei.

STEALS, MERVIN H   ASCAP 1976
composer
b Aliquippa, Pa, Feb 9, 46. Educ: Cheyney State Col. Started writing in col. Worked with Gable Huff-Bell, Curtis Mayfield & Van McCoy; then went independent. Chief Collabr: Melvin Steals. *Songs:* Music: Could It Be I'm Falling in Love; Honeybee; One Beautiful Day; Trusting Heart; Love Thang.

STEARMAN, DAVID J, III   ASCAP 1977
composer, author, singer
b Louisville, Ky, Nov 1, 49. Educ: Oral Roberts Univ, music & theol majors. Singer var concert situations, 10 yrs. Started writing, 71. Writer, House Top Records, 77; writer & artist, Tempo Records, 79- Chief Collabrs: Stephanie Boasahda, Bob Farrell. *Songs:* He Turned Water Into Wine; There Is a Way; It's Not a Hurry Kind of Day; Lyrics: Coming Home to You; You Were There.

STEARNS, M EUNICE (EUNICE JACOBSEN)   ASCAP 1962
composer, author
b Moira, NY, Feb 3, 19. Educ: Moira High Sch; Champlain Jr Col. Med secy; dining room supvr; demonstration singer. Tarot card reader, Mystic Tea Room, Pittsburgh, Pa; licensed hypnotist. Started writing music & lyrics, 52. Chief Collabr: Lennie Martin. *Songs:* Ring of Sorrow; Wall Around My Heart; Fool of the Year; The Hurtin' Game; After You; Kissin' Cousins; Goodbye Little Angel; Window of Love; Lyrics: Always Stay in Love With Me.

STEBBINS, GEORGE COLES   ASCAP 1943
composer
b East Carlton, NY, Feb 26, 1846; d Catskill, NY, Oct 6, 45. Educ: Albion Acad; Bob Jones Col. Dir of music, First Baptist Church, Chicago, 1870, Clarendon St Church & Tremont Temple, Boston, 1874-76. Evangelical singer with Moody & Sankey; missions to Egypt, Palestine & Europe. Leader of music, Northfield Summer Conference, East Northfield, Mass, 1877-1915. Ed, collection of hymns, "Gospel Hymns (No 1-6)", "Favorite Sacred Songs", "Greatest Hymns" & "New Church Hymnal." Charter mem, Apollo Club, Chicago; mem, Hymn Soc of Am. *Songs:* Sacred: Some Time We'll Understand; Saved By Grace; Take Time to Pray; Have Thine Own Way, Lord; True Hearted, Whole Hearted; Jesus I Come; Take Time to Be Holy; Not Under Law, But Under Grace.

STEBBINS, J A
See Dant, June Anne

STECMAN, PHIL
See McNeil, Stephen

STEDDOM, ART   ASCAP 1971
composer, author, pianist
b Blue Ash, Ohio, Feb 18, 25. Educ: Middletown High Sch, Ohio; DePauw Univ, BA. USAF Pilot Training; WW II pilot. Entered radio broadcasting, 49; pianist-vocalist, 52-70; then started writing songs. Mem, Am Guild Authors. Chief Collabr: Barry Winslow. *Songs:* Get to Know Me; Where There's Love There's Fire; Chariots of the Gods; You've Got the High and Mighties; I Don't Like to Wake Up All Alone.

STEEG, TED H   ASCAP 1967
author
b Indianapolis, Ind, May 29, 30. Educ: Wabash Col, BA; studied harmonics with Bob Mitchum; Columbia Univ, MFA. Writer plots, dialogue & film scripts; became dir films & TV, late 60's; wrote lyrics, 60- Chief Collabrs: Jordy Ramin, Gil Fuller. *Songs:* Lyrics: Coffee House Rendezvous; Summer Rain; When Will Love Sing to Me; Dream Girls.

STEELE, HELEN   ASCAP 1956
composer, author, pianist
b Enfield, Conn, June 21, 04. Educ: Mt Holyoke Col, BA; pvt music study. Accompanist to singers, US & Europe. Voice teacher; also dir & arr of vocal groups. Chief Collabrs: Guido Vandt, Enrique Ruiz. *Instrumental Works:* America, Our Heritage; The Legend of Befana; Duerme; Lagrimas.

STEELE, JON   ASCAP 1958
composer, pianist
b Anderson, Mo, Dec 10, 12. Educ: Fine Arts Sch, Univ of Mo; studied music with Russ Garcia. Pianist in dance bands, nightclubs & hotels.

STEELE, LOIS   ASCAP 1951
composer, author, pianist
b Chilicothe, Ill, Feb 24, 10. Educ: Cosmopolitan Sch Music, Chicago. Concert pianist; taught piano until 42; pianist in nightclubs, hotels & theatres. Chief Collabr: Jack Fulton. *Songs:* Wanted; Ivory Tower; Peace; Make America Proud of You; Sweetie Pie.

STEELE, LOUIS THORNTON (TED)　　　ASCAP 1959
author
b Boston, Mass, Apr 4, 11. Educ: Westminster Sch; Phillips Acad, Andover; Bowdoin Col. Songwriter; exec advert agency, Benton & Bowles, 40 yrs, became chmn bd & retired in 73 as chmn exec comt. Chief Collabr: Matt Dennis. *Songs:* Lyrics: That Tired Routine Called Love; Love Is Wonderful Ev'rywhere.

STEELE, TED　　　ASCAP 1949
composer, author, pianist
b Hartford, Conn, July 9, 17. Educ: Trinity Col; Morse Bus Col; New Eng Cons. Producer & cond, radio & TV incl "Perry Como Show." Has made many records. With CBS, NY. *Songs:* Smoke Dreams; Listening Post; Supper Club; Love Passed By; Danton Walker Rumba; When You Kiss a Stranger.

STEFANO, JOSEPH　　　ASCAP 1956
composer, author, producer
b Philadelphia, Pa, May 5, 22. Educ: High sch. Writer, special material for Sammy Davis, Jr, Eydie Gorme, George Shearing, Karen Chandler & Jack Pleis. Author, screenplays incl "The Black Orchid", "Psycho" (Edgar Allen Poe Award), "The Naked Edge" & "Anni di Brooklyn," TV plays incl "Made in Japan" (Robert E Sherwood & Fund for the Republic Awards), "Mr Novak" & "The Young Juggler," & TV series incl "The Outer Limits." Formed own production co, Villa di Stefano. *Songs:* Give a Fool a Chance; Wonderstruck; Heartbeat; Serenade in Soft Shoe. *Scores:* Stage shows: It's Your Move; Champagne Complex.

STEGMEYER, WILLIAM JOHN　　　ASCAP 1959
composer, clarinetist, arranger
b Detroit, Mich, Oct 8, 16; d New York, NY, Aug 19, 68. Educ: Transylvania Col (scholarship). Clarinetist in dance bands incl Glenn Miller, Bob Crosby. Wrote for Paul Lavalle, "Basin Street" broadcasts. Led own orch; was arr, "Your Hit Parade," 50-58. *Songs:* Symphony for Susan; Music: Love for All Seasons. *Instrumental Works:* The Jazzman Blues; A Pair of Preachers; Blue Manhattan.

STEIG, JEREMY　　　ASCAP 1969
composer, flutist
b New York, NY, Sept 23, 42. Educ: Music & Art High Sch; also studied with Paige Brook, 3 yrs. Recording artist, Columbia, Capitol & CTI Records. Chief Collabrs: Eddie Gomez, Bill Evans. *Albums:* Flute Fever; Jeremy and the Satyrs; What's New; Temple of Birth; Lend Me Your Ears; Rain Forest.

STEIGER, JIMMY　　　ASCAP 1927
composer, pianist
b Syracuse, NY, July 12, 1896; d New York, NY, Aug 5, 30. Accompanist to Lucille Cavanaugh & Jack Rose. Toured in vaudeville, also Eng. *Songs:* Maybe It's All for the Best; Toddle; Learning; Violet; Rambling Rose; Just One More Chance; Burgundy; Rose Colored Glasses.

STEIGMAN, JOYCE BARTHELSON
See Holloway, Helen Joyce

STEIN, HARLENE SHARON　　　ASCAP 1968
author, teacher
b St Louis, Mo, Nov 28, 32. Educ: Lindenwood Col for Women; Yale Univ Music Sch; Univ Calif, Northridge, BA(magna cum laude), MM. Classical singer in opera & concert. Lyricist; writer, short stories & screen plays; teacher of singing. Chief Collabr: Ronald Stein (husband). *Songs:* Lyrics: Beads of Innocence.

STEIN, HERMAN (ANDREW GULLIVER)　　　ASCAP 1952
composer, arranger, orchestrator
b Philadelphia, Pa, Aug 19, 15. Educ: High sch; Univ Pa, 1 yr; studied theory & comp with Mario Castelnuovo-Tedesco. Began arr, age 15. During 30's & 40's, arr for Rubinoff, Gus Haenschen, Vic Arden, Don Redman, Blanche Calloway, Mal Hallett & Tony Pastor. Staff comp, Universal Pictures, 51-58. TV comp: cartoons, commercials & episodes of "Voyage to the Bottom of the Sea", "Lost in Space", "Daniel Boone" & "Gunsmoke." Latest work in field of serious chamber music. Conductor. Chief Collabrs: Frank Skinner, Henry Mancini, Hans Salter, Heinz Roemheld. *Songs:* Music: Toy Tiger; Who's Gonna Sing My Love Song. *Instrumental Works:* Pumpernickel Polka (accordion solo); Sour Suite (woodwind quintet); Mock March (brass quintet); Line O' Jive. *Scores:* Film/TV: The Great Man; The Unguarded Moment; The Lady Takes a Flyer; Quantez; No Name on the Bullet; Backlash; Slim Carter; This Island Earth; I've Lived Before; The Saga of Hemp Brown; The Intruder; It Came From Outer Space; Creature From the Black Lagoon; Tarantula; Abbott and Costello Go to Mars; Abbott and Costello Meet the Keystone Kops; Ma and Pa Kettle At Home; Willie and Joe Back At the Front; The Kettles on Old MacDonald's Farm; All I Desire; The Black Shield of Falworth; Captain Lightfoot; Destry; Female on the Beach; The Glass Web; The Incredible Shrinking Man; Johnny Dark; Man Without a Star; Midnight Lace; Six Bridges to Cross; Walk the Proud Land; East of Sumatra; Joe Dakota; Seminole; The Great Sioux Uprising; Tanganyika; Four Girls in Town; The Lone Hand; Playgirl; City Beneath the Sea; Revenge of the Creature; Riders of Vengeance; So This Is Paris.

STEIN, JIM　　　ASCAP 1972
composer, author
b Los Angeles, Calif, Nov 13, 43. Educ: Beverly Hills High Sch; studied voice with Sy Miller. *Songs:* Lady Bug; Make Love to Life; Songs.

STEIN, RALPH　　　ASCAP 1956
composer, author, arranger
b Irvington, NJ, Sept 10, 19. Educ: Arts High Music Sch, NJ; studied comp with Stefan Wolpe & Tom Timothy Schillinger. Wrote for Louie Prima, Benny Goodman, Kelly Smith & many others, 40's; composed & played piano & organ; joined record cos, Golden Records, Wonderland Records & RCA. Presently producing childrens records for "Captain Kangaroo." Wrote the music & score for the Am Optometric Soc film about color blindness. Chief Collabrs: Sherman Edmunds, Bill Heyer, Sid Wayne. *Songs:* Music: My Favorite Color; The Joys of Noise; I Like All Kinds of People; No Money Down a Lifetime to Play; I'm Just a Guy in Love.

STEIN, RONALD　　　ASCAP 1956
composer, author, arranger
b St Louis, Mo, Apr 12, 30. Educ: Soldan High Sch; Wash Univ, St Louis, BA, 51; Yale Univ, 51-52; Univ Southern Calif, 60-63; studied piano with Margaret Christensen, 38-42 & Leo C Miller, 42-51; studied music with Herbert Fenton, Frank L Harrison, Paul Hindemith & Ingolf Dahl. High sch class song comp, commencement class day chmn, Soldan High Sch. St Louis Munic Opera usher, 43-47, rehearsal pianist, 50, 51, 54. First nightclub music for Marge & Gower Champion, 47. Comp six col musicals, 47-51. USA Spec Serv, 52-54. Asst dir Greek Theatre, 55; 78 Hollywood film scores since 55. Prof music, Calif State Univ, Northridge, 60-62. Assoc cond, Phoenix Star Theatre, 63; adminr, US Educ Films, 67- Vis prof music, Univ Colo, Denver, 80-81. Chief Collabrs: Wayne Arnold, Marilyn & Alan Bergman, Barry Devorzon, Alvin Kaleolani, Bix Reichner, Harlene Stein, Dan Peyton, Marty Kaniger, Caroline Arnell. *Songs:* Of Love and Desire; Road Without End; Raymie; Psych-Out Sanctorum; The Destiny of Love; In Love Before; No Time to Cry; Music: The Beads of Innocence. *Instrumental Works:* Getting Straight; Dime With a Halo; The Rain People; Psych-Out; Jazz in the Joint; The S F Blues; The Bonnie Parker Theme; Gunslinger; In a Living Room; Runaway Daughters. *Scores:* Film/TV: The Premature Burial; The Haunted Palace; Atlas; The Bounty Killer; Dateline Yesterday (TV series); The Attack of the Fifty Foot Woman; Not of This Earth; Arr: The Legend of Tom Dooley.

STEIN, WILLIAM　　　ASCAP 1946
author
b New York, NY. Educ: High Sch Commerce; City Col New York. Appeared in "This is the Army," wrote songs, mem of Spec Services Div, USA, World War II. Contributed material for GI shows, army songbooks & recordings. Wrote for radio & TV. TV producer. Chief Collabrs: Frank Loesser, Milton Delugg, Percy Faith, Woody Herman. *Songs:* Orange Colored Sky; Wave to Me, My Lady; Santa From Santa Fe; Lyrics: Amorada; Eight Babies to Mind; Mother Goose Jumps; Funny Fellow; Pretty Polly Polka.

STEINBERG, ABRAHAM　　　ASCAP 1961
composer, author
b New York, NY, Mar 21, 1897. Educ: High sch. Worked for IRT Subway, New York, 16-66. Appeared on TV & radio. Poems & jingles publ in newspapers & mag. USAF overseas, WW I. Civil Service Career Awards, 61 & 62. Life mem, Song Writers Hall of Fame; mem, Am Fedn TV & Radio Artists. *Songs:* America, I'm for You; Israel, I'm for You; Shalom, Shalom, Shalom; Getting Married in the Subway; I'm Working for the Subway Now; ASCAP, I'm for You; We Are the Boys of Amity; Toby, Toby, Toby.

STEINER, FREDERICK　　　ASCAP 1966
composer, conductor, author
b New York, NY, Feb 24, 23. Educ: Townsend Harris High Sch; Columbia Univ Inst Musical Art; Oberlin Cons Music, BM(comp), 43, studied comp with Normand Lockwood; Univ Southern Calif, PhD cand in musicology, 71- Comp, cond & arr, radio in New York, 43; music dir radio prog "This Is Your FBI." First TV work, CBS, 50; first film work, 50. Major TV credits incl "Andy Griffith", "Danny Thomas", "Gunsmoke", "Have Gun Will Travel", "Hogan's Heroes", "Movie of the Week", "Rawhide", "Star Trek" & "Twilight Zone." Major film credits "Della", "First to Fight", "Hercules", "The Man From Del Rio", "Run for the Sun", "St Valentine's Day Massacre", "Sea Gypsies" & "Time Limit." Comp var transc & pieces for TV & film. Contributor to "Filmmusic Schoenberg Notebook," jour of Arnold Schoenberg Inst & record album notes. Guest lectr film music, Univ Southern Calif, Univ Calif, Los Angeles & others. Restored & cond silent film scores at Filmex, Los Angeles, 78 & 80. Mem: Exec bd, Comp & Lyricists Guild Am; Am Fedn Musicians; Acad Motion Picture Arts & Sciences; Am Musicology Soc. *Instrumental Works:* Dudley Doright Theme (TV); Perry Mason Theme (TV); Navy Log March; Tower Music for Brass and Percussion; Pezzo Italiano for Cello, Piano; Five Pieces for String Trio.

STEINER, GEORGE　　　ASCAP 1960
composer, violinist
b Budapest, Hungary, Apr 17, 1900; d Spring Valley, NY, June 21, 67. Educ: Budapest Acad of Music. Violinist in opera, symph orchs with recitals in Europe

& US. Comp for films, radio & TV. *Instrumental Works:* Rhapsodic Poem for Viola and Orchestra; Serenade Sarcastique for Violin and Cello; Concerto for Saxophone and Band; Hora Burlesca (orch); Introduction and Scherzo for Clarinet and Orchestra; Poeme Hongroise for Harp and Orchestra. *Scores:* Films: The Golden Age of Comedy; In Tune With Tomorrow; Manhattan Rhythm; This Is America.

STEINER, GITTA HANA   ASCAP 1970
composer, author, teacher
b Prague, Czech. Educ: Juilliard Sch Music, artist's dipl, BM, MS; Berkshire Music Fest; studied with Vincent Persichetti, Elliot Carter & Gunther Shuller. Perf & broadcasts with Boston Symph Orch, Univ Mex, Carnegie Recital Hall, Goucher Col, Cortland Univ, Hart Col, Brooklyn Col, The New Sch & Lincoln Ctr. *Instrumental Works:* Fantasy for Clarinet and Piano; Brass Quintet; Five Pieces for Trombone and Piano; Movement for Eleven; Tetrak (string orch); Fantasy Piece for Piano; Concerto for Piano and Orchestra; String Quartet; Percussion Quartet; Three Pieces for Solo Vibraphone; Concert Piece for Seven; Interludes for Voice and Vibraphone (soprano & vibraphone); Concert Piece for Seven No 2; Three Pieces for Piano; Three Poems for Two Percussionists and Soprano; Trio for Two Percussionists and Piano; Four Bagatelles for Solo Vibraphone; Duo for Horn and Piano; Four Songs; Duo for 'Cello and Percussion; Percussion Music for Two; Trio for Voice, Piano and Percussion; Dream Dialogue; Cantos 1975; Dialogue for Two Percussionists; Music for Four Players; Eight Miniatures for Solo Vibraphone; Night Music for Solo Marimba; Percussion Fantasy; Fantasy Piece for Solo Marimba.

STEINER, HERBERT   ASCAP 1952
composer, conductor, pianist
b New York, NY, Dec 25, 1895; d Forest Hills, NY, Mar 17, 64. Cond & pianist with own orch. Co-owner, publ firm. Chief Collabrs: Kyle Rote, Sy Gillis. *Songs:* Fight, You Fightin' Giants (off Giants song); National Football League on Parade; Touchdown.

STEINER, HOWARD IRVING   ASCAP 1942
composer
b New York, NY, Jan 11, 1896. Educ: Winkler Cons, studied with Alex Winkler. Wrote theme song for B29 bomber groundcrew; wrote morale records for US Govt, 42-45. Comp film scores. Had assistance & advice from George Gershwin & Ralph Rainger. Chief Collabrs: Sammy Gallop, Buddy Kaye, Al Dubin. *Songs & Instrumental Works:* Don't Be a Baby, Baby; I'd Cry Like a Baby; Sing a Little Love Song; Tumble Down Ranch in Arizona; Wicked Little Cricket; I Love You More; Grandpa's Gettin' Younger Ev'ry Day; Change the Music.

STEINER, MAX   ASCAP 1934
composer, conductor
b Vienna, Austria, May 10, 1888; d Beverly Hills, Calif, Dec 28, 71. Educ: Imperial Acad Music, studied with Fuchs, Graedener, Mahler & Rose (Gold Medal). At age 14, comp & cond first opera. Cond, Eng, 04 & Paris, 11. Came to US, 14, became citizen, 20. Cond, Bway musicals. Went to Hollywood, 29. Awards: King of Belgium Bronze Medal, Cinema Exhibition, Brussels, 36; Am Exhibitors Laurel Award, 48, First Place Laurel Awards, 49-60; Wisdom Award of Honor, 66; Walk of Fame in Hollywood, 75; Golden Book of Jerusalem, 76. *Songs:* It Can't Be Wrong; My Own True Love; A Summer Place; Someday I'll Meet You Again; As Long As I Live; Kathy; Honey Babe; So Big; On My Way; Sugarfoot. *Scores:* Films: Those Calloways; Film background: A Bill of Divorcement; King Kong; Little Women; The Lost Patrol; The Informer (Acad Award, French govt decoration, 35); The Charge of the Light Brigade; The Garden of Allah; So This Is Paris (Italian medal, 36); A Star Is Born; The Life of Emile Zola; Jezebel; Dark Victory; Four Wives; Gone With the Wind; The Letter; Sergeant York; Casablanca; Now Voyager (Acad Award, 42); The Adventures of Mark Twain; Saratoga Trunk; Since You Went Away (Acad Award, 44); The Corn Is Green; A Stolen Life; Mildred Pierce; Life With Father (Golden Globe Award, 47); Johnny Belinda; Key Largo; Treasure of the Sierra Madre (Statuette Award, Cinema Exhibition, Venice, 48); The Fountainhead; Mrs Mike; The Flame and the Arrow; The Glass Menagerie; So Big; The Caine Mutiny; The McConnell Story; Battle Cry; Band of Angels; Marjorie Morningstar; A Summer Place; The FBI Story; The Dark at the Top of the Stairs; Parrish; Rome Adventure; Youngblood Hawke.

STEINERT, ALEXANDER LANG   ASCAP 1945
composer, conductor, pianist
b Boston, Mass, Sept 21, 1900. Educ: Harvard Univ, hon degree in music, 22; Paris Cons; studied with Loeffler, Gedalge, d'Indy, Loechlin & Ravel; Am Acad, Rome, 27 (Prix de Rome). Debut as pianist with Boston Symph, 25. Cond: Russian Opera Co, 35; "Porgy & Bess," New York & on tour, 35-36; Gershwin Mem Concert, Hollywood Bowl, 37; inauguration, Fine Arts Ctr, Colorado Springs, 36; Nat Youth Admin Orch, Los Angeles, 41. Cond music for stage productions, "Romeo and Juliet", "Porgy and Bess" & "Bambi." Head music, First Motion Picture Unit, USAAF, WW II, scored training & documentary films. Comp & cond, radio incl "CBS Radio Workshop" & "Beyond the Green Door" (series); TV, incl "US Steel Hour" & "Suspense" (series). *Songs & Instrumental Works:* Southern Night (symph poem); Leggenda Sinfonica; Concerto Sinfonico (piano, orch); Barcarole; Rhapsody for Clarinet, Orchestra; Nightingale and the Rose (Oscar Wilde text); Trio (violin, piano, cello); Violin, Piano Sonata; Piano Sonata; Chiaroscuro; Daybreak; Christmas Eve; Adrift;

Behind the Green Door; Perhaps. *Scores:* Film Background: Blondie Knows Best; The Unknown; TV: Tarawa.

STEINFORT, ROBERT EDWIN   ASCAP 1967
composer, author, singer
b Brooklyn, NY, June 18, 46. Educ: Bloomfield Senior High Sch; Montclair State Col; studied voice with Helena W Monbo, 46- Recording artist, Avant Garde Records; comp musicals, choir anthems, hymns, commercials & theme songs; voice & speech teacher; therapist; performer on nightclubs, radio & TV. Free-lance writer. *Songs:* Keep the Rumor Going; With Joy; Confessing Christ Today; Whole Earth, Whole People; Music: Petition; The 23rd Psalm. *Songs & Instrumental Works:* Synergy I (worship setting). *Scores:* Film/TV: The Put Down Generation.

STEININGER, FRANZ K W   ASCAP 1942
composer, conductor
b Vienna, Austria, June 12, 10; d Vienna, Dec 28, 74. Educ: Col; studied music with Josef Marx. Cond, operettas, operas & revues, Vienna, 2 yrs. Guest cond, Metropole Theatre, Berlin, 30. Cond, Palace Theatre, London. Comp, Eng films, 31-34. Came to US, 35. Cond, Billy Rose's Aquacade, Hollywood & New York & light opera cos, Pittsburgh, Los Angeles & San Francisco, incl Greek Theatre, Los Angeles, 56-58, cond, Maurice Chevalier's last performance, 58. Cond, Pittsburgh Light Opera season & "The Great Waltz," Civic Light Opera Asn, Los Angeles & San Francisco. Comp & cond film, "Stage Door to Dances Rock." Guest cond, Mozarteum Orch, Franz Lehar Fest Centennial Concert, Salzburg, Austria, 70. Cond, Bayrische Symph Orch, Munich, Ger, 72. *Songs:* Marching Along Together; One Night in Napoli; Pocket Full o' Pennies; Sleep, My Baby, Sleep; So Beautiful; For Love of You; The Wedding of Mister Mickey Mouse; I Raised My Hat; Again and Again; Song of the Sleighbells; While There's a Song to Sing; Stolen Kisses; The Sky Is Extra Blue; What Good'll It Do Me?. *Songs & Instrumental Works:* Operettas: Song Without Words; Centennial Spectacle (Topeka, Kans). *Scores:* Angelita; Films: Bedelia; Film background: Crazy House; Hold Back Tomorrow; Hit and Run; Paradise Alley; Born to Be Loved; Bway stage: Music in My Heart (based on Tchaikovsky).

STEINKE, GREG A   ASCAP 1972
composer, author, educator
b Fremont, Mich, Aug 2, 42. Educ: Midland Sr High Sch, Mich; Oberlin Col Cons Music, BMus, 64; Mich State Univ, MMus, 67, PhD, 76; Univ Iowa, MFA, 71; studied comp with H Owen Reed, Richard Hervig, Joseph Wood, Lawrence Moss, oboe with DeVeve Moore, Alfred Genovese, Daniel Stolper. Fac, Evergreen State Col, Calif State Univ, Northridge, Univ Md & Univ Idaho; prof music & chmn, Music Dept, Linfield Col, Ore, 80- Comp, chamber, symphonic & contemporary oboe music; oboe soloist. Awards: Mich Fedn Music Clubs, ASCAP, Univ Louisville Comp Contest, Symposium V for New Band Music & research and creative arts awards from Univ Md, Calif State Univ, Northridge & Linfield Col. Mem of Am Soc Univ Comp & ed of "Proceedings." *Instrumental Works:* Six Pieces for Piano; A Music (for oboe, contrabass, perc); Music for Three (oboe, guitar, perc); Tricinium (alto saxophone, trumpet, piano); Episodes (saxophone); Four Desultory Episodes (oboe, tape); Three Sonnets from William Shakespeare (soprano, flute, strings); Ein Japanisches Liederbuch (soprano, chamber ens); Atavism (oboe, bassoon, wind ens); Diversions and Interactions (perc trio); Remembrances (4 trumpets, wind ens); Fantasy Duo Concertante (violin, cello, chamber orch).

STELZER, FRANCES C   ASCAP 1961
composer, author
b Milwaukee, Wis, May 1, 1895. Educ: Columbia Col; NY Univ; Pace Inst. Secretary. *Songs:* I Never Get Enough of You; Keep Me in Love.

STEMPEL, MICHAEL LLOYD   ASCAP 1977
composer, author
b Culver City, Calif, Feb 23, 53. Educ: Miller Music Studio, pvt piano study, 8 yrs; Los Angeles Valley Col, AA(jour). Collab as songwriter, 5 yrs. Started Michael Stempel Mgt, 79. Chief Collabrs: Simon Stokes, Peter Cooper, Dan Foliart. *Songs:* Who Could Have Told You?; Midnight Rendezvous; In Modern Day Vernacular; Lyrics: Perfect Stranger; Nervous Breakdown.

STEPHENS, WARD   ASCAP 1933
.composer, conductor, organist
b Newark, NJ, Sept 9, 1869; d New York, NY, Sept 11, 40. Educ: Rutgers Col; studied music with William Mason, William Sherwood, Samuel Warren, Johannes Brahms, Moriz Rosenthal, Scharwenka, Dreyschock, Breitner, Moszkowski, Vladimir DePachman, Saint-Saëns & Massenet. Debut as pianist, Chickering Hall, NY, age 17 & Paris, 1896. Cond, Mozart Soc; organized Orch des Artistes, Paris. Concert tours of Europe & US with Madame Chaminade, Sibyl Sanderson, Victor Herbert, Kreeiler, Madame Yvette Guilbert, Schuman-Heink & Louise Nikita. Cond, Manhattan Opera House, New York, 3 yrs; Ward Stephens Club, New York. Vocal coach for Lilli Lehmann at Mozarteum, Salzburg. Organized & cond, Mozart Fest, Harrisburg, Pa, 7 yrs. Cond, Philadelphia Orch, New York Symph & Curtis Inst Orch. Church organist & music dir, Holy Trinity Church, Paris; Plymouth, Brooklyn; West End Presby Church & First Church of Christ Scientist, New York; Grace Church, Harrisburg, Pa; St James Episcopal Church, Fordham, NY. *Songs:* Christ in Flanders; Summertime; The Nightingale; Song cycle of James

Whitcomb Riley poems; Someone Worthwhile; The Rose's Cup; In the Dawn of an Indian Sky; The Cry of the Exile; Jesus and His Twelve Apostles; also The Beatitudes; two cantatas: Christmas & Easter.

STEPHENSON, JOHN W ASCAP 1963
composer, author, publisher
b Avery, Tex, Feb 12, 22; d. Educ: High sch. Owned publ & recording co. *Songs:* I'll Come a Callin'; Baldy; I Found the Key; It Was Not You I Hurt; The Legend of Kingua Valley; No One Said a Prayer; Alone With No One But Me.

STEPLETON, JAMES ASCAP 1975
composer
b Muncie, Ind, Apr 28, 41. Educ: Ball State Univ, MMus, 73; Columbia Univ, DMA, expected, 81; studied with Chou Wen Chung, Vladimir Ussachevsky, Allen Forte, George Perle. *Instrumental Works:* Serenade for Solo Guitar.

STEPT, SAM H ASCAP 1926
composer, conductor, pianist
b Odessa, Russia, Sept 18, 1897; d Los Angeles, Calif, Dec 2, 64. Came to US, 1900. Educ: High sch, Pittsburgh, Pa. Staff pianist, music publ co, Pittsburgh. Accompanist to Jack Norworth, Esther Walker & Mae West. Led dance band, Claremont Cafe, Cleveland, 20-25. Organized radio singing group, Record Boys, 25. Went to Hollywood, 29. Wrote songs for films incl "Big Boy", "Baby, Take a Bow", "Having Wonderful Time" & "Laughing Irish Eyes." Chief Collabrs: Bud Green, Charles Tobias, Lew Brown, Ned Washington, Sidney Mitchell, Sidney Clare, Herb Magidson, Herman Ruby. *Songs:* That's My Weakness Now; London on a Rainy Night; Breakin' in a Pair of Shoes; I Came Here to Talk for Joe; Don't Sit Under the Apple Tree; This Is Worth Fighting For; I'll Always Be in Love With You; Please Don't Talk About Me When I'm Gone; Comes Love; Congratulations; When They Ask About You; I Fall in Love With You Ev'ry Day; If You Should Love Me; All My Life; On Accounta I Love You; Every Minute of the Hour; Seems Like Yesterday; Prairie Fairy Tale. *Scores:* Bway stage: Yokel Boy; songs for George White's Music Hall Varieties; Michael Todd's Peep Show.

STERLING, ANDREW B ASCAP 1922
author
b New York, NY, Aug 26, 1874; d Stamford, Conn, Aug 11, 55. Educ: Pub schs. Wrote spec material for vaudeville acts. Chief Collabrs: Harry Von Tilzer, Frederick Allen Mills, James Hanley, Raymond Sterling (nephew). *Songs:* My Old New Hampshire Home; Strike Up the Band; Hello, Ma Baby; Wait Till the Sun Shines, Nellie; On a Sunday Afternoon; When My Baby Smiles at Me; Meet Me in St Louis, Louis; Under the Anheuser Bush; Last Night Was the End of the World; In the Evening By the Moonlight; What You Gonna Do When the Rent Comes 'Round?; All the Boys Love Mary; All Aboard for Blanket Bay; Down Where the Cotton Blossoms Grow; You'll Always Be the Same Sweet Girl; All Aboard for Dreamland; Take Me Back to New York Town; Goodbye, Boys; On the Old Fall River Line; Arthur Murray Waltz; The Frankfurter Song.

STERLING, JEAN
See Taylor, Mary Virginia

STERLING, RAYMOND A ASCAP 1952
composer, author
b New York, NY, Oct 10, 1898. Educ: Nephew of Andrew B Sterling; Stamford High Sch, Conn; Fordham Univ, 2 yrs. Co-publ of "Sunrise Serenade." Publ of many other songs. *Songs:* Arthur Murray Waltz; I've Got My Heart Set on You.

STERN, ALFRED BERNARD
composer, author, director
b Boston, Mass, Dec 6, 20. Educ: Boston Latin Sch; Kings Point, BS(eng); New Eng Cons, theory classes; Univ Calif, Berkeley, BS(bus admin, music); musical studies with Paul Mimart, Boston Symph. Performer, radio WHDH, WBZ & WCOP, Boston, as teenager. Comp of plays, Pioneer Theatre Workshop, Boston. Mem, Mask & Dagger, drama hon soc, Univ Calif, Berkeley, writer of music, lyrics, revue sketches & theatre music. Comp & musical dir of touring productions, East Bay Childrens' Theatre, 18 yrs. Formed Actors' Ens & Fest Theatre, Berkeley. Music arr for Straw Hat Theatre in Bay area. Music writer & lyricist for var revues & plays. Musical dir & performer, Old Chestnut Theatre Summer Stock, Berkeley, 5 yrs. *Songs:* Made to Order; Take a Ride; Open All Night; The Strike Show; Six Hillside Revues. *Songs & Instrumental Works:* Childrens Theatre: Pied Piper; Pinnochio (script); The Pooh Show; The Musicians of Bremen (script); Twelve Dancing Princesses; Rumpelstiltskin; Alladin; Peter Pan; The Emperor and the Nightingale; Adeline and the Pearl; The Magic Mirror; Dick Whittington. *Scores:* Plays: The Vegetable (F Scott Fitzgerald); Boy Meets Girl; Ballet: Peer Gynt; Cartoon: Uppity Albert McGuire. *Albums:* Songs for Growing with Music; 21 Short Songs for Little People; Sing; Up Down All Around.

STERN, HENRY (S R HENRY) ASCAP 1921
composer, publisher
b New York, NY, June 23, 1874; d Dallas, Tex, Mar 13, 66. Educ: City Col New York; Columbia Univ (Sch Mines), PhB. Music publ exec. Cond, play bureau, New York; producer plays & vaudeville sketches. Wrote songs for Bway

musical. "Little Miss Charity." Hon life mem, Variety Club Tex. Chief Collabrs: L Wolfe Gilbert, Ballard Macdonald, Domenico Savino, Frank Warren. *Songs:* By Heck; Indianola; Down at the Huskin' Bee; Kentucky Dream; Now I Know; Down in the Old Cherry Orchard; Au Revoir, Sweet Marie; Polly Prim; I've Got the Time, I've Got the Place, But It's Hard to Get the Girl; Little Miss Charity; S R Henry's Barn Dance; When You're in Love With More Than One, You're Not in Love at All.

STERN, JACK ASCAP 1921
composer, author, vocal coach
b New York, NY, Mar 6, 1896. Educ: DeWitt High Sch, NY. Song-plugger & pianist, Waterson, Berlin & Snyder Music Publ, 14-19. Pianist for var vaudeville performers & 15 motion pictures, 25-35. Vocal coach to many performers, 35-45; pvt educator & vocal coach, 45- Chief Collabrs: Harry Tobias, Jack Meskill, Edgar Leslie, Joe Young, Henry Tobias, Jimmy Durante, Russ Columbo, Sid Caine. *Songs:* I Was Lucky; Rhythm of the Rain; Singing a Happy Song; Aurevoir L'amour; Too Beautiful for Words; When You're in Love; Let's Pretend There's a Moon; I'm Not Ashamed of You, Molly; When I Come Back to You; Tonight, Lover, Tonight; You Can't Lose Me; Happy Landing With Landon; There's a Hole in the Old Oaken Bucket; Remember Pearl Harbor.

STERN, MAX ASCAP 1976
composer, teacher, performer
b New York, NY, Mar 31, 47. Educ: Valley Stream Cent High Sch, 65; Eastman Sch Music, BM, 69, studies with Samuel Adler & Bernard Rogers; First Int Kodaly Sem, post-grad study, 70; Yale Univ, MM, 71, studies with Alexander Goehr; also with Fred Zimmermann, Oscar Zimmerman & Gary Karr. Ethnomusicologist; free-lance musician, New York, 71-76; arr, Am Ballet Theater Orch, 73-76; mem, Jerusalem Symph Orch; comp-in-residence, City of Beer Sheva, Israel, 80- *Songs & Instrumental Works:* Symphony; Sonnet for Orchestra; Song of the Morning Stars; Chamber Music for Children.

STERN, ROBERT LEWIS ASCAP 1962
composer
b Paterson, NJ, Feb 1, 34. Educ: Univ Rochester, BA, 55, Eastman Sch Music, MA, 56, PhD, 62; Univ Calif, Los Angeles, advanced grad study music, 58-59; studied comp with Bernard Rogers, Howard Hanson, Lukas Foss. Prof music & co-dir, Electronic Music Studio, Univ Mass, Amherst. Vis comp electronic music, Hampshire Col, 70-71. Recorded on CRI, ERA, Advance & Opus One labels. Rec'd 6 MacDowell Colony Fels. Grants: Mass Council Arts & Humanities; NEA; ASCAP. *Songs & Instrumental Works:* In Memoriam Abraham; String Quartet No 1; Three Songs (piano & soprano); Symphony; Adventures for One; A Little Bit of Music (two clarinets); Terezin; Three Chinese Poems; Carom; Blood and Milk Songs; Yam Hamelach.

STERN, TONI KATHRIN ASCAP 1973
composer, author, singer
b Los Angeles, Calif, Nov 4, 50. Songwriter for albums; now publ & producing songs. Chief Collabrs: Carole King, Peter Andrews. *Songs:* It's Too Late; It's Going to Take Some Time; Sweet Seasons; When You Lead; No Sad Songs. *Albums:* Tapestry; Music; Rhymes and Reasons.

STERNE, KENNETH
See Stone, Kurt

STERNKLAR, AVRAHAM ASCAP 1971
composer, concert pianist, educator
b Trieste, Italy, Oct 21, 30. Educ: Juilliard Sch Music, 49-54, spec grad dipl chamber music; Philadelphia Cons Music; studied piano with Leo Kestenberg, James Friskin & Edward Steuerman; studied comp with Vittorio Giannini. Studied in Israel; instrumentalist, Israel Broadcasting Sta; soloist, Israel Philh. Moved to US, numerous concerts, US & abroad; now co-dir, Long Island Comp Alliance. Var comns, grants & awards, incl Meet the Composer, NY State Coun Arts; 3 Best of Year awards, Piano Quarterly mag; NEA; Helena Rubenstein Found; scholarships 5 yrs, Juilliard; scholarship, Philadelphia Cons Music. *Instrumental Works:* Montgomery March; Sonatina for Piano; A Promise Fulfilled (piano solo); Sonata for Cello and Piano; Sonata for Violin and Piano; Sonata for Piano, Four Hands; Sonata for Clarinet and Piano; Andante and Rondo for Two Pianos; 12 Duets for Two Violins.

STEVENS, CASANDRA MAYO (CASS MAYO) ASCAP 1962
composer, author, dancer
b New York, NY; d Hollywood, Calif, Jan 8, 66. Educ: Col. Author, "'Twas Ever Thus" (poems). Chief Collabrs: Scott Seely, Lou Bideu, Paula Lewis, Bill Simon, Leo Paris. *Songs:* In Hawaiian Style; Fifteen Only Fifteen; Dear Lord; Two Left Feet Polka.

STEVENS, DAVID ASCAP 1929
composer, author, publisher
b Fitchburg, Mass, Aug 12, 1860; d Boston, Mass, June 29, 46. Educ: Boston Univ Law Sch. Practiced law, Boston & Tacoma, Wash. Exec, Boston music publ co, 32 yrs. Lawyer. Author: "Lyrics of Eliza"; "Ballads of Be-Ba-Boes"; "The Dim Forest." *Instrumental Works:* Opera: Azora; Operettas: The Fire Prince; In Arcady; Bells of Beaujolais; Dragon of Woo Fee. *Scores:* Bway stage: The Madcap Duchess (libretto).

STEVENS, EDWARD GALE ASCAP 1968
composer, author, trumpeter
b Brooklyn, NY, Aug 15, 41. Educ: San Jose Univ, 74-77; pvt study with Kenny Dorham, Cecil Taylor & Sun Ra. Feature artist, 3 albums & band leader, 2 albums, Blue Note Label. Europ tour, 73. Appointed San Jose Ambassador of Jazz, 74. Music workshop dir, Jazz Heritage Soc, Queens, NY, 79-80. Chief Collabrs: Ed Williams, John Carter. *Songs:* The Rain; Fulton Street; A Understanding; The Coming of Gwilu; A Walk With Thee; Black Rhythm Happening; Ghetto Love Night; A Song of Will; Mexico Thing; Look At Teyonda; Ghetto Summer Time; Aferican Sunshine; To Be a Slave.

STEVENS, GLENN ASCAP 1964
composer, author, conductor
b Chesaning, Mich, July 26, 1899; d Bonita, Calif, Apr 28, 74. Educ: Chicago Musical Col; studied with Leopold Auer, Eugene Ysaye. Violinist in orchs incl Isham Jones; cond own orch. *Songs & Instrumental Works:* My Old Michigan Home; Indian Lullaby; Yellow Bird; Naughty Girl; Alone, Alone; Whistler and Donkey; Purple Pants; There's a Swallow 'Neath My Window; Quarte Minute Hop.

STEVENS, MARSHA JEANNE ASCAP 1973
composer, author, singer
b Pomona, Calif, Aug 20, 52. Educ: Scripps Col, 66-69, studied with Val Stuart; Azusa Pacific Col, 70-71; Orange Coast Col, 75-78. Began writing, 69; prof singer, comp & recording artist, six albums with "Children of the Day." Chief Collabr: Peter Jacobs. *Songs:* For Those Tears I Died; Can I Show You; Russ' Song; Where Else Would I Go; Lovin' in the Light; Lyrics: Children of the Day.

STEVENS, MORTON ASCAP 1960
composer
b Newark, NJ, Jan 30, 29. Educ: Juilliard Sch Music, dipl clarinet. Arr & cond for Sammy Davis, Jr, 50-60; film comp, 60- Chief Collabr: Jerry Goldsmith. *Scores:* Film: Wild and Wonderful; Jury of One; Hardly Working; TV: Wheels; Backstairs at the White House; Masada; TV Series Themes: Hawaii Five-O; Policewoman; Apple's Way; 87th Precinct.

STEVENS, PERRY
composer, author
b Cleveland, Ohio, Mar 31, 28. Educ: Ohio Univ; Case Western Reserve Univ, BA. Chief Collabrs: Alan Miller, Shelley Haims. *Songs:* We Go Together; Come Spring; Twenty-One.

STEVENSON, LOUIS C (B W) ASCAP 1971
composer, publisher
b Dallas, Tex, Oct 5, 49. Educ: NTex State Univ, music maj, voice scholarships. Chief Collabrs: Daniel Moore, Chris Christian, B J & Gloria Thomas. *Songs:* Music: My Maria; Chambala; Down to the Station; Special Wish; Headin' Home. *Albums:* B W Stevenson; Live Free; My Maria; Calhbassas; We'd Be Sailin'; Lost Feelings; I'll Miss Christmas Night; Life Line.

STEVENSON, WILLIAM THOMAS ASCAP 1978
composer, author
b Stanford, Ky, Jan 25, 29. Educ: Lincoln High Sch; San Diego City Col, BA; San Diego Vocational Sch, hairdresser & cosmetician license. Voice & piano study, 5 yrs. Wrote poetry, some publ in mags, 5 yrs. Became songwriter, 48. Began own publ co, Sounders Publ Co & own record corp, Krugerran Record Corp, 79. Chief Collabrs: Bob M Guess, Carman M Parish. *Songs:* Forget Me Not; Too Many Dreams; Back to Kentucky; You're My Everything to Me; Moonlight Is Magic; Someday You'll Learn to Love Me; I Know a Valley; Goodbye Cruel World; It's Too Late; One More Hill to Cross; Teardrops Are the Prize for Losing.

STEVENTON, G H (STEVE) ASCAP 1967
composer
b San Diego, Calif, Mar 25, 14. Educ: San Diego High Sch; San Diego State Col; Univ Southern Calif Sch Music. Performing musician alone & with bands incl Ziggy Elman, Red Nichols, Joe Reichman & others. Big Band instrumentalist, band mgr & arr, 32-56. Piano bar pianist & Dixieland clarinet player. Chief Collabrs: Ben Hunter, Phill Upton, Ernie Petrich, Gilbert Hanaike. *Songs:* Maui Boy; Music: Hisako San; Kahului; Mamae Lei; Mexico.

STEWARD, CLIFF ASCAP 1960
composer, author, conductor
b Newport, RI, Oct 10, 16. Originated sing along albums, 54; leader of own orch, Cliff Steward and the San Francisco Boys; recording artist; performer, TV, nightclubs & vaudeville. Chief Collabrs: Vaughn Horton, Rudy Vallee. *Songs:* Saloon; On San Francisco Bay; Good Night Little Girl Good Night; Lyrics: More Than Just a Memory. *Instrumental Works:* Madri; Pompano Rag.

STEWART, AL
singer, songwriter, recording artist
b Glasgow, Scotland, 1945. Played guitar with Tony Blackburn's Band, Bournemouth, Eng; later performed folk music, London, from 65. Switched to rock music performing, 74- Named Compagnon de Vordeaux, 77. *Albums:* Bedsitter Images; Love Chronicles; Zero She Flies; Orange; Past, Present and Future; Modern Times; Year of the Cat; Time Passages.

STEWART, DANIEL KALAUAWA ASCAP 1939
composer, author
b Honolulu, Hawaii, Aug 5, 07; d Honolulu, Apr 9, 61. Educ: Self-taught writing & comp. Musician at age 14, Matson Lines. Came to US. Joined Hawaiian troup, Calif. Worked in the movie indust, Hollywood. Comp music for several movies, engaged in writing for others; was in recording & nightclub entertaining business. Returned to Hawaiian Islands, late 50's, had TV show until 61. Chief Collabrs: Harry Owens, Alfred Alpaca, Gordon Jenkins, Sunny Burke. *Songs:* Flower Girl of Hilo Bay; Koni Koni; Lovely Kawaiian Madonna; Silhouette Hula; U A Like No A Like; Nohea; Faded Ginger Lei; Music: Hawaiian Guitar; Laughing Eyes; Queen's Hula; Whispering Lullaby; Whispering Reef; Maku Kia Kahi Leahi; Tu Felicidad; Lyrics: Island Angel.

STEWART, DONALD GEORGE ASCAP 1971
composer, musician, teacher
b Sterling, Ill, Jan 8, 35. Educ: Sterling High Sch, Ill, Ind Univ, BM(woodwinds), 52-60; Manhattan Sch, New York, 60-61; comp studies with Bernhard Heiden, Roy Harris, Gunther Schuller. Began playing professionally with var pop groups, 50. Birmingham Symph, Ind Univ Orchs, 57-60; wrote first comp. Jazz ens incl David Baker, Ornette Coleman, Sch Jazz/Lewis, New York, 60. Active free-lancer, 60-70. Founder & only continuous mem of the Boehm Quintette. Co-founder, Chamber Music America, 78. First pieces publ, Calif, 68. Taught at Lyndon State & other locations in Vt, mid 70's. Compositional style influenced by jazz & serial techniques. Pieces for var combinations. *Songs:* Music: Tattooed Desert (baritone & ens); Never Leave Me Blue (vocal ens). *Instrumental Works:* Concert Duet for Flute and Bass Clarinet; Scaramouche Suite, Saxophone and Wind Quintet (arr); Piccolo Concerto; 200-Bar Passacaglia (large orch); Angels Arrival (concert wind ens).

STEWART, DOROTHY M ASCAP 1948
composer, author, pianist
b Melbourne, Australia, Mar 21, 1897; d New York, NY, June 18, 54. US citizen. Educ: St Peter's Sch, Lara Col, Melbourne; Juilliard Sch Music, studied music with Hortense Fyffe & Gustave de Chaneet. As pianist & entertainer toured Australia, NZ, US & Can. Had own prog on networks, Australia & US. Am rep, Australian theatres, publ, radio & TV cos. *Songs:* Now Is the Hour; Give Me Your Hand; God Bless Australia; Wedding Bells; Be True; Magic Island; A Rose, a Book and a Ring; Hear These Words.

STEWART, FRANK GRAHAM ASCAP 1970
composer, teacher, pianist
b La Junta, Colo, Dec 12, 20. Educ: Eastman Sch Music, BM(with distinction), 42; Colo State Univ, MAT, 68; Mich State Univ, PhD, 71; scholarship to study with Roger Sessions, summer 39. Comp, arr & pianist in San Francisco & Hollywood, for Temoff Ballet, Celso Hurtado (concert marimbist), Duncan Sisters & Wilbur Hatch, 46-54. Music teacher, Shasta County, 56-58; pvt teacher, 59-65; teacher & grad student, Shasta Col, Calif, Colo State Univ, Univ Mo & Mich State Univ, 65-71. Teacher, Miss State Univ, 71- Clarinetist. Chief Collabr: Robert Ccanzoneri. *Songs:* Music: Tony and Nina; Mississippi. *Instrumental Works:* Toccato for Piano; Suite for Piano on American Indian Songs; Phantom Train of Marshall Pass; Metamorph for Bassoon and Piano; Scene—1970 (band); American Scene (band); Miss Sue Blues (clarinet choir); The First Day (band). *Scores:* Opera: To Let the Captive Go.

STEWART, HERBERT G ASCAP 1963
composer, author, teacher
b Petersburg, Va, May 3, 09. Educ: Col William & Mary; Juilliard Sch Music; Guilmant Organ Sch; studied with Guy Maier, Bernice Frost, Bernard Taylor, Ward Lewis & Williard Nevin. Began prof music career as a jr in high sch. Pianist, Portsmouth Lions Club, 35- With sister, organized Portsmouth Community Concert Asn, 39 & was pres, 5 yrs. Was in Army during WW II & was chapel, post, radio & theater organist for over 2 yrs at var army posts. Had successful audition with NBC, New York, 45. With sister, organized Portsmouth Chap, Am Guild Organists, 52, was first dean. Comp of hundreds of comp for piano, voice, organ & chorus. Mem: Nat Fel Methodist Musicians; Nat Music Teachers Asn; Am Guild Organists; Nat Asn Teachers of Singing, Inc. Was consecrated & certified as Minister of Music, Methodist Church, 60. Music teacher. Has presented radio & TV shows over WTAR, WTAR-TV, WVEC, WVEC-TV, WLOW, WAVY-TV & WGH. Was organist for Portsmouth Bowl, 60. Was off organist for all Tides' home baseball games, Portsmouth Stadium, 61; also Elco Theater organist, 61. *Songs:* Cantatas: Sing Noel!; The Star of Bethlehem; The First Christmas; The Christ Child; The Way of the Cross; Music: God Will Answer Prayer (anthem).

STEWART, JAMES OTTO ASCAP 1970
composer, author, musical director
b San Francisco, Calif, Sept 8, 37. Educ: Col San Mateo, AA; Chicago Sch Music (Cons), BA; Berklee Sch Music; studied guitar with George M Smith, film scoring with Albert Harris & Bway show conducting with Jack Lee. Prof debut at age 15. Arr for many pop singers for records & TV in US & Australia. Musical dir for artists incl Andy Williams, Chita Rivera, Lainie Kazan, John Gary & Ginny Simms. Guitarist with many jazz combos; fests: Monterey, 67-68;

Newport, 68; Univ Calif, Los Angeles, 68. Did records with Louie Bellson, Sonny Stitt, Gabor Szabo, Gary McFarland & many others. Los Angeles studio guitarist; did many TV & feature films incl "Room 222", "Name of the Game", "Charlie's Angels", "Lassie", "Paint Your Wagon", "Topaz" & "Some Kind of Nut." Commercials for Busch Beer, Michelob & Mattel Toys. Wrote numerous articles for music publ. *Songs:* Louise; Once Around the Block. *Instrumental Works:* Concertino for Electric Guitar and Orchestra; A Tribute to Classical Guitar (14 homages); Quintette for String Quartet and Classical Guitar; Castles of Spain; Circle of Fire; Flight to Tel Aviv; Sharyna; Suite for American Jazz Guitar.

STEWART, JAMES RICHARD   ASCAP 1970
composer, author

b Chicago, Ill, Mar 21, 50. Educ: Educational Develop Ctr, cert of merit; Calif Inst Arts, studied guitar, voice & creative writing; studied with Bill Douglas & Leo Hamalian. Singer & guitarist; has performed extensively throughout West as opening act for var name acts, 69-73. Scored parts for film, "Pacific Vibrations," 70. Working club circuit in Pacific Northwest & on album, 80. Chief Collabrs: Mark Achuff, Harry Robinson. *Songs:* When I Get Home to California; I've Been Away From My Baby; It's Good to Be Alive.

STEWART, JOAN BEATRICE (GINGER GREY)   ASCAP 1979
composer, teacher, singer

Educ: High sch & col. With singing duo Lanny & Ginger, New York for 10 yrs; on radio, TV & singing commercials, 5 yrs; with singing duo on WPBR, Palm Beach, Fla, 1 yr & WLIZ, Lake Worth, Fla, 1 yr. Chief Collabr: Lanny Grey. *Songs & Instrumental Works:* That Night of Heaven; Is It True or False; I Never Harmed an Onion.

STEWART, JOSEPH ANTHONY   ASCAP 1975
composer, teacher, pianist

b Buffalo, NY, Nov 11, 24. Educ: Pvt piano lessons with Laura Kelsy; Biarritz Am Univ, piano & comp; Ithaca Col, BS(music educ); Univ Buffalo, MA(music), piano & comp with Livingston Gearhart. Began piano at age 5; starting at age 12, worked clubs; taught music in pub & pvt schs, 29 yrs; also chorale dir-concert & jazz pianist; comp & have had maj instrumental & choral works performed. Now retired from teaching; full-time comp. *Instrumental Works:* Four Dimensions for Flute and Piano; Fantaisies Dun Clown for Oboe and Piano; Tuba (solo tuba, concert band accompaniment); Tone Poems for String Orchestra; La Petite Suite for Clarinet and Piano.

STEWART, LEROY ELLIOTT (SLAM)   ASCAP 1972
composer, author, performing artist

b Englewood, NJ, Sept 21, 14. Educ: Dwight Morrow High Sch; Boston Cons Music. Bassist & singer, jazz groups Slim & Slam, Spirits of Rhythm, Art Tatum Trio; played for Benny Goodman. Played var clubs; recording artist. Worldwide concert tours, Bway, movies, TV, symph orchs, chamber music quartets. Auth book, "Styles in Jazz Bass." Awards: Esquire Silver Award, Down Beat Award best bassist yr, Metronome Award best all-Am Jazz bassist; Ellington Fel, Yale Univ; fel, Newing Col, State Univ NY, Binghamton. Chief Collabr: Slim Gaillard. *Songs:* Flat Foot Floogie; Oh Me, Oh My, Oh Gosh; Slam Mule. *Instrumental Works:* Fish Scales; Slamboree; A Jam With Slam; Foolin' Around; Slam Bam.

STEWART, MEREDITH A   ASCAP 1974
composer, music publisher

b Tulsa, Okla, June 14, 51. Educ: High sch, dipl; George Peabody Col; Watkins Inst. Joined Peer-Southern, 70 & worked under direction of Vaughn & Roy Horton. Worked for Mercury Records in promotion, 72, later in publ under direction of Dianne Petty & A&R under Don Schroeder. Joined Coal Miners Music in secretarial position, 72, gen mgr, 77. Chief Collabr: Theresa Beary. *Songs:* Lyrics: I Can't Feel You Anymore.

STEWART, ORA PATE   ASCAP 1967
composer, author, performer

b Bates, Idaho, Aug 23, 10. Educ: Brigham Young Univ; Univ Utah; studied comp with Emery G Epperson & LeRoy J Robertson, voice with Florence Jepperson Madsen; hon LHD, 72; hon LittD, 77. Taught instrumental, harmony & theory, Rock Springs & Green River, Wyo, Long Island Cons; also taught night courses, Univ Utah & summer courses, Brigham Young Univ. Performer, Int Univ Forums, Graham Lyceum Circuit & Nat Artist & Lect Service, 53- Has written & performed for radio & TV. Founded Sweetwater Cons Music. Mem: Nat Music Bd; Nat League of Am Pen Women; Nat Bd of Dirs for Comp Guild. Chief Collabrs: Sharon Stewart Nielson (daughter), Alfred Lord Tennyson, Nephi J Bott, Jeanne Singer. *Songs & Instrumental Works:* To a Child (solo & SSA, theme song for 2 pageants, Nat First Place); Likewise (solo, chorus & reading to music, Nat First Place); This Is the Land (SATB 42 instruments, Nat First Place); Our Glorious Land (Nat First Place); Pebble Beach (SSA & solo); Golden Promise (SSA); A Tree Stood Tall (SSA); Mother-Song (SSA); Music: Crossing the Bar (SSA, First Place, World Comp); Song of Love (solo & duet, state & nat winner); Lyrics: Blessed Are the Meek (solo, Nat First Place).

STEWART, REX   ASCAP 1957
composer, author, conductor

b Philadelphia, Pa, Feb 22, 07; d. Educ: Col trumpeter in orchs, incl Fletcher Henderson & Duke Ellington. Trumpeter. Formed own group; toured Europe, Australia, 47-51. DJ, prog dir, Troy, NY. Returned to NY, 56. Co-dir & producer, Great South Bay Jazz Fest, 57-58. Made TV appearances, incl "Sound of Jazz" & "Art Ford's Jazz Party." With Jazz at the Philh; Eddie Condon, 58-59. Led own group, NY. *Songs & Instrumental Works:* Boy Meets Horn; Chatterbox; Baby, Ain'tcha Satisfied?

STEWART, ROD
musician, recording artist, lyricist

b London, Eng, Jan 10, 45. Educ: William Grimshaw Sec Modern Sch. Played guitar & banjo at sch events during early teens. Began career in mid 60's with var groups, Eng; lead singer with Jeff Beck Group, late 60's & The Faces, 7 yrs. Recording artist, Mercury Records, 69-74. Made many recordings both solo & with groups. Appeared in rock opera, "Tommy," London, 72. Performed in concerts, US & Eng. Had 2 Gold Albums & 2 Platinum Albums. Chief Collabrs: Ron Wood, Martin Quittenton. *Songs:* Maggie May; The Killing of Georgie; Tonight's the Night; Jo's Lament; Lady Day; Farewell. *Albums:* An Old Raincoat Won't Ever Let You Down; Gasoline Alley; Every Picture Tells a Story; Never a Dull Moment; Sing It Again, Rod; Smiler; Atlantic Crossing; A Night on the Town; Footloose and Fancy Free; Blonds Have More Fun.

STICKLES, WILLIAM   ASCAP 1928
composer, teacher

b Cohoes, NY, Mar 7, 1882; d New York, NY, Oct, 71. Educ: Utica Cons, Syracuse Univ; studied in Europe, 7 yrs. Asst, Isadore Braggiotti, voice teacher, Florence, Italy, 5 yrs. Solo repititeur, Hof Theatre, Munich, with Felix Mottl, 2 yrs. In US, teacher in Boston & New York. *Songs:* Samoan Love Song; The Mither Heart; Expectancy; My Soul Is Athirst for God; I Saw a Star Tonight; My Heart Is in the Hills Tonight.

STICKNEY, KIMBALL PHILIP   ASCAP 1973
composer

b Penn Yan, NY, July 1, 53. Educ: Up With People High Sch, 71; Univ Colo, BS, 76; Goethe Inst of Munich, Cert in Ger, 74; New Eng Cons, MM, 79; studied piano with Francisco Aybar, comp with Normand Lockwood & George Russell. Writer/performer with Up With People, 70-71; made int tours to Europe & SAm; made USO shows tour to Australia & Asia, 75. Teacher, jazz piano, jazz ens & recording techniques, New Eng Cons & Holy Cross Col. *Songs:* Waiting; Music: Ever Lovin' Soul. *Instrumental Works:* Fantasy for Violin and Orchestra; Barcarolle for String Quartet; Nine-Tone Nocturne (jazz band).

STIDMAN, BOBBY   ASCAP 1978
composer, author, singer

b Meridian, Miss, Nov 4, 53. *Songs & Instrumental Works:* Stone Soul Disco.

STIEBLER, MARY
See Ryder, Mary E

STIGLER, ERIC   ASCAP 1967
author

b Newark, NJ, Nov 24, 17. Educ: Crane Tech High Sch; Herzl Col. Advert copywriter, TV & radio, jingles & others; did indust musicals, trade shows & spec assignments; wrote spec material for club performers, singers & comedians. Chief Collabrs: Bernard Yuffy, Dick Marx, Paul Severson, Frank McNulty. *Songs:* Lyrics: You Haven't Seen the USA Until You've Seen Chicago!; What Puts the 'Go' in Chicago?; Recipe for Love; Say You're Mine; Pity Me; Safari; Faith; A Fool in Love; Pay the Piper; My Empty Love Affair.

STILES, NORMAN B
editor, writer

b New York, NY, Dec 4, 42. Educ: Hunter Col, BA, 64. Writer, "Merv Griffin Show," New York, 69-70 & "Sesame Street Show" (Emmy Award, 74), New York, 71-74, head writer, 74-75. Co-creator/story ed, "When Things Were Rotten," Paramount TV, Los Angeles, 75- Co-writer, "Fernwood 2-Night" & "America 2-Night," 78. Co-producer series, "Bad News Bears," 79- Rec'd Gold Album, Sesame Street Fever, 78. Author: "Perils of Penelope"; "Sesame Street 1, 2, 3 Story Book"; "Sesame Street ABC Storybook."

STILL, WILLIAM GRANT   ASCAP 1936
composer, conductor, arranger

b Woodville, Miss, May 11, 1895; d Los Angeles, Calif, Dec 3, 78. Educ: Wilberforce Univ, BS; Oberlin Cons, scholarship; New Eng Cons, studied with George Chadwick & Edgard Varese. Hon degrees: Univ Ark, Pepperdine Univ, New Eng Cons Music, Peabody Cons & Univ Southern Calif; Wilberforce Univ, MM; Howard Univ & Oberlin Col, MusD; Bates Col, LHD. Grants: Guggenheim & Rosenwald. Served in USN, WW I. Musician in dance orchs. Arr, Paul Whiteman & Artie Shaw orch; also Bway musicals. Arr & cond, CBS, WOR. First Negro to cond maj US symph orch (LA, Philh, 36). Cond, New Orleans Philh, 55. Comns: CBS; NY World's Fair, 39-40; Paul Whiteman; League of Comp; Cleveland Orch; Southern Conference Educ Fund; Am Accordionists Asn. Awards: Eastman Publ; Harmon; George Washington

Carver. "William Grant Still and the Fusion of Cultures in American Music," Black Sparrow Press, 72. Chief Collabr: Verna Arvey (wife). *Songs:* Music: Plain-Chant for America; And They Lynched Him on a Tree; A Psalm for the Living; Las Pascuas (Christmas music from the Western Hemisphere). *Instrumental Works:* Ennanga; Afro-American Symphony; Lenox Avenue; From the Delta; Sahdji (ballet); Troubled Island (opera); Symphony in G minor; Poem for Orchestra; The American Scene; Incantation & Dance; Violin & Piano Suite; Festive Overture (Cincinnati Symph prize); Highway 1, USA (opera); Danzas de Panama; To You, America (West Point Sesquicentennial; Freedom Found award); The Peaceful Land (Nat Fedn Music Clubs-Aeolian Music Found award); Symphony No 4 (Autochthonous); Symphony No 5 (Western Hemisphere); From the Black Belt; Old California; In Memoriam: The Colored Soldiers Who Died for Democracy. *Scores:* Opera/Ballet: La Guiablesse; A Bayou Legend; Costaso; Mota; Minette Fontaine.

STILLMAN, AL   ASCAP 1935
  author
b New York, NY, June 26, 06; d New York, Feb 17, 79. Contributed to Franklin P Adams newspaper column. Staff mem, Radio City Music Hall. Wrote song for "The Cardinal." Chief Collabrs: Arthur Schwartz, George Gershwin, Ernesto Lecuona, Robert Allen, Fred Ahlert, Percy Faith, Henry Mancini, Paul McGrane. *Songs:* The Breeze and I; I Believe; Chances Are; It's Not for Me to Say; Moments to Remember; Home for the Holidays; Tell Me That You Love Me Tonight; You Alone; And That Reminds Me; Baby, Don'cha Go 'Way Mad; Bless 'Em All; In Spain They Say 'Si Si'; No, Not Much; Who Needs You?; A Room With a View; My One and Only Heart; When I Am With You; Taboo; You and I Know; An Old Flame Never Dies; If Dreams Come True; Mama Yo Quiero; My Heart Reminds Me; Enchanted Island; There's Only One of You; Jukebox Saturday Night; One, Two, Three, Kick; The Little Boy; Song About Love; Every Step of the Way; I Love You and Don't You Forget It; The Great Escape March; Can You Find It in Your Heart; Teacher, Teacher; Meantime; There's Nothing I Can Say; Truly, Truly True; Happy Anniversary. *Scores:* Stage: Virginia; It Happens on Ice; Stars on Ice; Icetime of 1948; Howdy, Mr Ice; Films: Carnival in Costa Rica.

STILLS, STEPHEN
  composer, musician
b Dallas, Tex, Jan 3, 45. Educ: Univ Fla, political sci. Singer & instrumentalist, local folk-clubs. Performer, var goups incl Au-Go-Go Singers, New York. Formed band Buffalo Springfield with Richie Furay. With group Crosby, Stills & Nash, 68-70, world tour incl Royal Albert Hall, London, 70. Returned to Crosby, Stills, Nash & Young; formed own group Manassas, toured US. Recording artist for var cos. With var other bands. Joined Neil Young for tour & album, 76; reunion set recorded, 77. *Songs:* For What It's Worth; Bluebird; Rock and Roll Woman; Suite: Judy Blue Eyes. *Albums:* Supersession; Stephen Stills; Stephen Stills II; Manassas; Down the Road; Stills; Stephen Stills Live; Illegal Stills.

STINGLE, DAVID ELLOT (DAVID ELLIOTT)   ASCAP 1972
  composer, author
b Washington, DC, Mar 14, 48. Educ: Shenandoah Col & Cons Music. Started playing music age 7. Moved to England, 70. Recorded two albums original music. *Songs:* I'm on Fire for You Baby; On the Loose Again; Blind Love; I Can Take the Weight; You Better Move.

STIPE, THOMAS R, II   ASCAP 1973
  composer, author, singer
b Long Beach, Calif, Oct 10, 50. Educ: Piano & guitar lessons since age 9. Became involved with contemporary gospel music, 70; played in Richie Furay Band, 73-74. Has recorded on Electra Asylum Records & produced about 12 albums. Teacher. Chief Collabr: Richie Furay. *Songs:* Look At the Sun; Over and Over Again; Starlight; Stage Coach; Life in Jesus.

STIRES, ERNEST   ASCAP 1968
  composer
b Alexandria, Va, Dec 17, 26. Educ: Studied with Nicolas Slominsky, Francis Cooke & Robert Erickson. Started comp in '60 & has written about 30 works, incl 5 for full orch & var keyboard, chamber & vocal music; has done music & lyrics for local musical comedies, incl "The Permit", "Tick Tock Bevan" & "Johnny's Town." Taught jazz & comp, Middlebury Col. Collabr: Dutton Smith. *Songs & Instrumental Works:* Song and Dance for Orchestra; Music for Flute and Harpsichord; Jazz for Viola and Piano; Twenty-Two A (orch); Three Songs From China; Twelve by Twelve (violin & piano); Rhapsody for Piano and Orchestra; Emory's Rock (organ sonata).

STITH, LAURENCE   ASCAP 1963
  composer, author, singer
b New Bern, NC, Mar 20, 33. Educ: Univ NC; Juilliard Sch Music; East Carolina Univ, BMus; studied voice with Marion S Freschl, comp with Bernard Wagenaar, vocal coach, Myron Earnhart. Singer & entertainer, var supper clubs, cruise ships & TV; recording artist; commercials & solos for RCA-Victor. Comp musicals; pianist & cond for var entertainers. Mus dir, Eng pantomime, New York Town Hall; church organist & choirmaster; trustee, NC Symph. Chief Collabrs: Richard Everitt, Diane Lampert. *Songs:* Music: It's Just a Matter of Time; Maybe Soon; One Summer Love; Every Time Is the First Time; I Know Not; More Than I Should.

STITZEL, MELVILLE J   ASCAP 1949
  composer, author, conductor
b Chicago, Ill, Jan 9, 02; d Chicago, Dec 31, 52. Educ: Pub schs. Accompanist to vaudeville performers, Orpheum Circuit. Pianist & arr, dance orchs, radio & TV shows. Organized own orch. *Songs:* Doodle-De-Doo; The Chant; Land of Dreams; Tin Roof Blues; I'm Goin' Home; Bittersweet Rag; Make Love to Me; Jackass Blues.

STOCK, DAVID (RIP)   ASCAP 1969
  composer, author, singer
b New York, NY, Nov 7, 47. Educ: Horace Mann High Sch; Univ Pa, BA, 69; St John's Univ Sch of Law, 78. Percussionist & vocalist, Edison Electric Band; recording artist; studio musician; comp; disc jockey; writer & producer, commercial radio spots. Chief Collabr: Mark Jordan. *Songs:* Lyrics: Walked Out My Front Door; No Relief; We Said I Do.

STOCK, LAWRENCE   ASCAP 1927
  composer, author, publisher
b New York, NY, Dec 4, 1896. Educ: Townsend Harris Hall; Inst of Musical Art (Juilliard); studied piano with Clarence Adler & comp with Percy Goetschius. Pianist in concert & with dance bands. Enlisted in USN, 18; accompanied singer David Bispham during Liberty Loan Drive, WW I. Chief Collabrs: Al Lewis, Vincent Rose, James Cavanaugh. *Songs:* Blueberry Hill; You're Nobody 'Til Somebody Loves You; The Umbrella Man; You Won't Be Satisfied Until You Break My Heart; Did You Ever Get That Feeling in the Moonlight?; Navajo Nocturne; Hearts; When You Add Religion to Love; If Wishes Were Kisses; In the Heart of Jane Doe; Lord, Make Him Jealous; All the Pretty Little Horses; The Greatest Sinner of Them All; Song of Devotion; Moon at Sea; I Don't Wanna See You Cryin'; Du bist Mein Liebscho; Dreams of Old Hawaii; Morning Side of the Mountain; Music: The American Prayer; In a Little Dutch Kindergarten; Adoration Waltz; Laughing Sailor; Raindrop Serenade; Tell Me a Story; With All My Heart and Soul; Cradle in Bethlehem; On the Little Big Horn; Slowly But Surely; I Could Swear It Was You; Ma Ma Maria; Pretty Little Busybody; Creaking Old Mill on the Creek; Whisling in the Wildwood; When You Add Religion to Love.

STOCKSDALE, HOWARD MELVIN   ASCAP 1973
  composer, author
b Baltimore, Md, Dec 30, 05. Educ: Md Inst, dipl. Tenor banjoist, var local bands, nightclubs. Chief Collabrs: Lanny Grey, John J Lynch. *Songs:* My Dream of Romance; Music: A Shelf Will Do for Lynn; Hurt Me Gently; You Better Believe in Santa; Lyrics: I'm Thankful.

STODDARD, HARRY   ASCAP 1945
  composer, conductor
b Friedland, Bohemia, Oct 30, 1892; d Los Angeles, Calif, May 7, 51. Moved to US in 10, citizen, 23. Organized orch, played Keith, Orpheum vaudeville circuits throughout US & Can. Scored films; wrote spec material. *Songs:* I Get the Blues When It Rains; O How I Adore You; Farewell; Abadele; Goodbye Old Pal, Goodbye; Without the Man I Love; Never a Beat of My Heart.

STOESSEL, ALBERT   ASCAP 1937
  composer, conductor, violinist
b St Louis, Mo, Oct 11, 1894; d New York, NY, May 12, 1943. Educ: Berlin Hochschule, with Hess, Kretzchmar; hon MA, NY Univ. Debut as violin soloist, Berlin, 15. Toured as mem of Hess Quartet. Lt, Infantry, WW I; leader, 301st Infantry Band. Dir, Am Sch Bandmasters, Chaumont, France. Concert tours in Europe; Am tour with Enrico Caruso. Cond, NY Oratorio Soc, 22, also Chautauqua Symph; music dir, Chautauqua Inst. Founder & head of music dept, NY Univ, 23-30. Was cond, Worcester Music Fest, Mass & head of opera & orch depts, Juilliard. Founder & cond, Chautauqua Opera Asn. Author "Technique of the Baton." *Instrumental Works:* Violin Sonata in G; Suite for 2 Violins, Piano; Suite Antique (2 violins, orch); Early Americans; Hispana; Garrick (opera); Concerto Grosso (piano, strings).

STOKES, ERIC NORMAN   ASCAP 1969
  composer
b Haddon Heights, NJ, July 14, 30. Educ: Haddon Heights High Sch; Lawrence Col; New Eng Cons; Univ Minn. Teacher, Univ Minn, 61- Recorded for Louisville, First Ed, Columbia & Advance Records. Chief Collabr: Alvin Greenberg. *Songs:* Music: Inland Missing the Sea; 4 Songs (oboe & voice). *Instrumental Works:* A Center Harbor Holiday (tuba concerto); 3 Sides of a Town; Eldey Island (flute & tape); On the Badlands-Parables (orch & tape); 5 Verbs of Earth Encircled (orch & narrator); The Continental Harp and Band Report (wind orch); Symphony(s); The Phonic Paradigm. *Scores:* Opera/Ballet: Smoke and Steel (tenor, solo, men's choir, orch); Horspfal; The Jealous Cellist and Other Acts of Misconduct.

STOKES, ROBERTA   ASCAP 1977
  composer
b Chicago, Ill, Jan 20, 27. Educ: Wheaton High Sch, Ill; El Camino Col; Compton Community Col; Southland Col, studied med assistance. Plays piano, self-taught. Chief Collabrs: Kacey Stokes, Bill O'Neill. *Songs:* Lyrics: Chained.

STOLLER, MICHAEL ENDORE   ASCAP 1969
composer, co-author
b New York, NY, Mar 13, 33. Educ: Forest Hills High Sch, New York; Belmont High Sch, Los Angeles, Calif, dipl, 50; Los Angeles City Col; studied comp with Arthur Lange, 50-52 & Stefan Wolpe, 58-60. Comp, songwriter, record producer. Chief Collab: Jerry Leiber. *Songs:* Music: Along Came Jones; Baby, I Don't Care; Black Denim Trousers and Motorcycle Boots; Bossa Nova Baby; Charlie Brown; D W Washburn; Don't; Drip Drop; Fools Fall in Love; Framed; Girls, Girls, Girls; Hound Dog; I (Who Have Nothing); I'm a Woman; Is That All There Is?; I've Got Them Feelin' Too Good Today Blues; Jailhouse Rock; Kansas City; King Creole; Little Egypt; Longings for a Simpler Time; Love Me; Love Potion No 9; Loving You; On Broadway; Poison Ivy; Ready to Begin Again; Ruby Baby; Saved; Searchin'; Smoky Joe's Cafe; Some Cats Know; Stand By Me; That Is Rock and Roll; There Goes My Baby; Treat Me Nice; Trouble; Yakety Yak; Youngblood.

STOLOFF, MORRIS   ASCAP 1950
composer, conductor, violinist
b Philadelphia, Pa, Aug 1, 1898. Educ: Studied with Leopold Auer, Broekhoven, Theodore Speiring. Sponsored in music by W A Clark, Jr. Violinist, in concert throughout US & with Los Angeles Philh. Founder, Stoloff String Quartet. Concertmaster, Paramount Studio Orch; gen music dir, Columbia Pictures, 36. *Songs:* A Song to Remember; Love of a Gypsy; My Consolation; To Love Again; Last Night; There Was a Time; Dream Awhile With Me; Love Comes But Once in a While; It Was a Beautiful Dream; To You, Sweetheart; Song Without End. *Scores:* Films: Cover Girl (Acad award, 44); The Jolson Story (Acad award, 46); The Eddy Duchin Story; Song Without End (Acad award, 60); They Came to Cordura; Gidget; The Last Angry Man.

STONE, BILLY   ASCAP 1930
composer, author
b New York, NY, Aug 23, 1884; d New York, May 18, 31. Mem, music publ co. Worked for civilian morale office, WW I. Wrote & produced Army shows. *Songs:* Indian Butterfly; Perhaps You'll Think of Me; The Kid Next Door; The Cave Man; I Love You Kid; This Is the Wedding Night; Hello Everybody; Rambling in Roses.

STONE, GEORGE
See Wright, Al George

STONE, GREGORY   ASCAP 1941
composer, conductor, pianist
b Odessa, Ukraine, July 20, 1900. Educ: Cons of Odessa, USSR; studied piano with Biber Halperin, harmony & orchestration with Vitold Malischevsky, conducting with Eugene Plotnikoff & Pietro Cimini. Came to US, 23; pianist, arr & cond for var radio programs, 23-35; comp & arr, Paramount Studios, Columbia, Fox, 34-36; comp & cond score, Max Reinhardt's Fest production of Goethe's "Faust", Los Angeles & San Francisco, 37. Radio, symph cond & piano soloist, Mexico City, Buenos Aires & Rio De Janeiro, 45-49; musical dir & cond, radio station Nueva Granada, Bogota, Colombia, 49-51 & Reno Philh Symph Orch. Awards: Concerto Breve, accordion & symph orch, Arcari Found, 1st prize, 56; Appreciation Award, City of Reno, 73; Man of the Yr in Music, Nev Music Teachers Asn, 78; Critics Award for founding prof symph in Nev, 79. Chief Collabs: Toscha Seidel, Efrem Zimbalist, Mishel Piastro, Zino Francescatti & Peter Meremblum. *Songs & Instrumental Works:* Thirteen Articles of Faith; Simon Bolivar Festival; Concertino for 5 Violoncelli and Orchestra; Concierto Venezolano; Transc Gershwin Comp: Rhapsody in Blue (violin, orchestra); I've Got Rhythm; Fascinating Rhythm; Summer Time; American in Paris; Three Preludes; The Man I Love; Strike Up the Band; Embraceable You; Cuban Overture; Symposium on Eight Themes; Overture for a Gershwin Concert.

STONE, HARRY
See Stonum, Harry Francis

STONE, IRA
See Bartelstone, Ira

STONE, JAMES Y   ASCAP 1963
author
b Louisville, Ky, July 11, 29. Educ: Univ Louisville. *Songs:* You're My Dream.

STONE, JON   ASCAP 1969
composer, author
b New Haven, Conn, Apr 13, 31. Educ: Williams Col, BA(music), 52, hon LHD; Yale Univ, MFA, 55. Writer, producer & dir, "Captain Kangaroo", "Children's Film Festival" & "Sesame Street." Chief Collab: Tom Whedon.

STONE, JOSEPH   ASCAP 1957
composer, author
b Everett, Mass, Mar 6, 20. Educ: Boston Univ, BS, BA. Served, USAAF, World War II. Vpres, J Walter Thompson, 45-59, McCann-Erickson, 60-62, Kenyon & Eckhardt, 62 & Kastor Hilton, 64- Advert exec; writer, musical commercials. Chief Collabs: Robert Allen, Charles Tobias. *Songs:* I Just Don't Know; Daffodil Feeling; Kopper Kettle; Red Cross Theme Song; Ford Theme Song.

STONE, JUSTIN FEDERMAN   ASCAP 1947
composer, author, arranger
b Springfield, Ohio, Nov 20, 16. Arr, cond, bandleader & comp, 39-49; served in Air Corps during WW II; author of seven publ bks; had many paintings on exhibit; teacher of Tai Chi Chih movements. Chief Collab: Larry Markes.

STONE, KIRBY   ASCAP 1955
composer, author
b New York, NY, Apr 27, 18. Educ: Grade sch; high sch; US Armed Forces Inst. Organized & led The Kirby Stone Four, 20 yrs. Musical dir & performer for var TV shows incl "Bway Open House" & "Strictly for Laughs." Spec materials author for var entertainers; institutionalized syllable singing for TV & radio commercials. Chief Collabs: Henry Fillmore, Dizzy Gillespie, J Val, Dick Hyman. *Songs:* Take the Lady; Graybeard; Lady, Love Me; Lyrics: Groovin' High; Lassus' Trombone; Buck Dance; Fancy Dan.

STONE, KURT (KENNETH STERNE)   ASCAP 1968
composer, author, pianist
b Hamburg, Ger, Nov 14, 11. Educ: Lichtwarkschule, Ger; Hamburg Univ, 33; Royal Music Cons, Denmark, 38. Taught piano, comp & theory, Ger, 31, Denmark, 33-38, US, 38- Musician, modern dance groups; writer & lectr. Music ed, 42, ed head of orch & band dept, G Schirmer's, 50; ed-in-chief, Assoc Music Publ, Inc, 56; dir of publ, Alexander Broude, Inc, 65-69 & Joseph Boonin, Inc, 69-76. Established, & dir of "Index of New Musical Notation," funded by Rockefeller & Ford Foundations; author of numerous articles & bk, "Music Notation in the 20th Century," funded by Guggenheim grant; ed & annotated (with wife) "The Writings of Elliot Carter"; brought out English transl of "Handbook of Percussion Instruments" by Peinkofer & Tannigel; publ 50 ed of choral music from Dufay to Bruckner with singable English texts. *Songs & Instrumental Works:* Arr & Transl: Suite for Wind Quintet (Crawford-Seeger); Biblical Sonatas for Keyboard (Kuhnau); Parthenia (English collection keyboard music, 1611); Pange lingua (Bruckner, chorus); Command Thine Angel (Buxtehude, chorus & instruments); O vos Omnes (Casals, chorus); Three Settings from the Song of Songs (Franck, chorus); Ab Oriente (Gallus, chorus); Io pur respire? (Gesualdo, chorus); Tenebrae (Haydn, Michal, chorus); Innsbruck (Isaac, chorus); Grant Us Thy Blessing (Loewe, chorus); Veni, Domine (Mendelssohn, chorus); Puer Natus/Lo, a Child (Morales, chorus); Te Deum (Mozart, chorus, instruments); Psallite Praetorius, chorus); La Foi (Rossini, chorus); Gelobet seist Du (Schein, chorus, instruments); Christ lag in Todesbanden (Schein, chorus, instruments); Die Rose (Schumann, chorus); Alleluia (Schütz, chorus); Our Father (Schütz, chorus, instruments); Be Brave, My Friends (Shostakovich, chorus); Absalom (Tomkins, chorus); Ave Maria (Victoria, chorus).

STONE, MAXINE
See Bartelstone, Maxine

STONE, MIRIAM SCADRON (MIMI)   ASCAP 1965
composer
b New York, NY, Feb 23, 16. Educ: Walden Sch, Am Acad Dramatic Arts, Columbia Univ; pvt comp lessons. Actress on "Goldbergs" radio, 2 yrs; comp songs for "Tin Pan Alley." Chief Collabs: William Kaye, Tao Strong, Evelyn Love Cooper, Helen Wartels. *Songs:* The Young in Heart; Lily Hot From Chile; Sargent and the Major's Daughter; Music: This Is Where I Came In. *Scores:* Off Bway show: Pimpernel!.

STONE, NORMAN MILLARD, JR (BUTCH)   ASCAP 1970
composer, author
b Blytheville, Ark, Apr 6, 46. Educ: Univ Ark, Jonesboro. Albums var record cos. Chief Collab: Jim Mangrum.

STONE, PAULA   ASCAP 1970
composer, lyricist
b Detroit, Mich, Aug 6, 45. Educ: Wayne State Univ, BA(creative writing), 72; Ecole Pratique des Hautes Etudes, Paris, cert, Soc of Communication, 74; Univ Calif, Los Angeles, MA(language arts), 76; Ctr Early Educ, 80. Comp since age 5; lyricist for var artists. Chief Collabs: Edu Lobo, Yana Purim, Diane Steinberg, Angelo, Billy Thorp. *Songs:* Stillness; Righteous Life; I Don't Need Nobody; Lyrics: Don't Let Go; Reflection of My Love.

STONE, WILSON   ASCAP 1954
composer, author
b Webster Groves, Mo, Apr 4, 27. Educ: Webster Groves High Sch; Northwestern Univ, BMus, 49. Writer, nightclub revues, films, Bway shows, TV & industrials. Chief Collabs: Victor Young, Burt Bacharach, David Blomquist. *Songs:* Back in the Old Routine; Sabrina; Who's Gonna Be My Sunshine; Who Made the Morning; A World of Dreams; Lyrics: Eyes of Blue; War and Peace; The Three Ring Circus.

STONER, MICHAEL S (MICKEY)   ASCAP 1942
composer, author
b Carnegie, Pa, Aug 1, 11. Educ: Pub schs. WW II service. *Songs:* You Rhyme With Everything That's Beautiful; It's Make Believe Ballroom Time; I Guess I'll Have to Dream the Rest; Jamaican Rhumba; A Dollar Ain't a Dollar Any More; Ding Dong Polka; If Loveliness Were Music; It Was Sex That Made This

Country Great; Lyrics: A Story of Two Cigarettes; I Thought She Was a Local (But She Was a Fast Express); Once to Every Heart; also American History in Song (10 children's songs); The Best in the West (15 songs).

STONUM, HARRY FRANCIS (HARRY STONE)　　ASCAP 1970
composer, author, musician
b St Louis, Mo, Nov 19, 24. Singer, actor & dir. *Songs:* You Smell So Good; The Chiefs Are on the Warpath; We're Number One!; Christmas Is for Children. *Scores:* Bway Show: Chase a Rainbow.

STOOKEY, NOEL PAUL　　ASCAP 1962
composer, author, singer
b Baltimore, Md, Dec 30, 37. Educ: Mich State Univ. Was singer & MC in Greenwich Village nightclub; then mem singing trio, Peter, Paul & Mary, appearing on TV, in nightclubs & concerts throughout US, Can & Europe. Sang at jazz & folk fests; recording artist. Guitarist & arr. Chief Collabrs: Peter Yarrow, Mary Travers, Milt Okun. *Songs:* On a Desert Island; A Soulin'; Talking Candy Bar Blues; Early in the Morning; It's Raining; The House Song; Wedding Song; Building Block; also five solo albums.

STORDAHL, AXEL　　ASCAP 1945
composer, conductor, arranger
b Staten Island, NY, Aug 8, 13; d Encino, Calif, Aug 30, 63. Educ: High sch. Trumpeter & arr, Bert Bloch Orch, 34-36 & Tommy Dorsey, 36-43. Cond & arr, Frank Sinatra, 10 yrs & Eddie Fisher, 4 yrs; also Gisele McKenzie, Nanette Fabray, Dinah Shore, Jack Benny, Dean Martin & Bing Crosby. *Songs & Instrumental Works:* Day by Day; I Should Care; Ain'tcha Ever Comin' Back?; Night After Night; Talking to Myself About You; Recollections; Jasmine and Jade; Return to the Magic Islands; Ride Off.

STORK, GEORGE FREDERICK　　ASCAP 1960
composer, author, pianist
b Philadelphia, Pa, May 18, 13. Educ: Harvard Univ, BA; Univ Pa, MM; studied with Normand Lockwood, Robert Elmore & Arthur Cohn. Taught Eng & variety of acad & music subjects. Writer & ed in electronic & scientific fields. Has done free-lance work in writing & photography. Guitarist, banjoist & former teacher. Chief Collabs: Olivia Hoffman, Charles Wharton Stork (father). *Songs:* One-Two Polka; Giddy-Up, Giddy-Up; Just Ridin' Around; Two Uninhibited People on an Uninhabited Island; Jim White's Cave; The Species We Destroy May Be Our Own; Music: Click with Dick (Nixon campaign song); Crying by the Altar; Have Faith, America; Ballad of Paul Bunyan.

STORY, VAN DYCK　　ASCAP 1960
composer, author
b Hamilton, Va, Feb 19, 17; d. Educ: High sch. Chief Collabr: Laurence Keyes. *Songs:* I Have So Much to Be Thankful For; Time Will Tell; Afraid.

STOTHART, HERBERT　　ASCAP 1923
composer, conductor, pianist
b Milwaukee, Wis, Sept 11, 1885; d Los Angeles, Calif, Feb 1, 49. Educ: Milwaukee Teachers Col, Univ Wis; also music study in Europe. Taught in Milwaukee pub schs; then fac mem, Univ Wis. Music dir, many Bway musicals. Moved to Hollywood, 29; cond & wrote songs for MGM films; then became music dir, MGM. Chief Collabs: Oscar Hammerstein 2nd, Otto Harbach, Clifford Grey, Bert Kalmar, Harry Ruby, Vincent Youmans, George Gershwin. *Songs:* Cute Little Two by Four; Wildflower; Bambalina; The Mounties; Totem Tom-Tom; Why Shouldn't We?; Fly Away; Song of the Flame; The Cossack Love Song; Dawn; I Wanna Be Loved by You; The Cuban Love Song; The Rogue Song; The Donkey Serenade. *Songs & Instrumental Works:* China (musical pageant); Voices of Liberation (cantata). *Scores:* Bway shows: Always You; Tickle Me; Jimmie; Daffy Dill; Wildflower; Mary Jane McKane; Rose-Marie; Song of the Flame; Golden Dawn; Good Boy; Film Background: The Good Earth; Romeo and Juliet; Mutiny on the Bounty; Mrs Miniver; The Green Years; The Picture of Dorian Gray; Treasure Island; Anna Karenina; Warterloo Bridge; Random Harvest; National Velvet; The Yearling; Camille; Via Villa.

STOUFFER, PAUL M　　ASCAP 1961
composer, clarinetist, teacher
b Chambersburg, Pa, Feb 21, 16. Educ: Peabody Cons, clarinet cert, studied with Gilbert Stange; Sch Fine Arts, Univ Pa, BA & MA, studied comp with Andre Vauclaine. Taught clarinet, Philadelphia Musical Acad, pvt & pub schs in Pa, 30 yrs; dir music educ, Springfield, Pa; chmn music dept, Lansdowne Borough Schs, Pa; now retired. Hilda Nitzche Prize, Univ Pa. Life mem, Nat Educ Asn. Chmn, Lansdowne Symph Orch Asn. *Songs:* One Misty, Moisty Morning; Music: Daughter, Will You Marry? (Pa Duteh folk tune). *Instrumental Works:* Concertino for Two (symph orch with clarinet & trumpet soloists); Canzone (symph orch); Celebration Overture (symph orch); Chorale (symph orch); Two Mobiles for Flute and Piano; Three Mobiles for Violoncello and Piano; Conversation for Flute, Clarinet and Piano; Six for Two-Duets.

STOUGHTON, ROY SPAULDING　　ASCAP 1941
composer, editor
b Worcester, Mass, Jan 28, 1884; d Allston, Mass, Feb 1, 53. Educ: Summer music sch. On ed staff, music publ co. *Songs & Instrumental Works:* Can This

Be Love?; A Bowl of Blue; Dark Eyes That Dream; Down the Trail of Dreams to You; April Love; Organ: Persian Suite; Egyptian Suite; In India; Fairyland; Tanglewood Tales; Tales From Arabian Nights; Dreams; A Rose Garden in Samarkand; Within a Chinese Garden; Cantatas: Esther; The Woman of Sychar; The Resurrection and the Life; The Wind of the West. *Scores:* Ballets: The Spirit of the Sea; The Vision of the Aissawa.

STOUT, CLARENCE　　ASCAP 1941
composer, author, conductor
b Vincennes, Ind, Oct 19, 1892; d Vincennes, Oct 29, 60. Educ: Pub schs. Drummer in circus, vaudeville & road shows. Led own dance orch, toured Middle West. Wrote & produced minstrel shows. *Songs:* O Death Where Is Thy Sting; Give Me Liberty or Give Me Death; Brother, You Win; Old Chief Walla Hoo; Jerry the Junker; Death of Smokie Joe; Flop House Fanny; I'm a Hill Billy Boy From the Mountains.

STOUT, GORDON BRYAN　　ASCAP 1979
composer, percussionist
b Wichita, Kans, Oct 5, 52. Educ: Eastman Sch Music, BM, 74, MM(comp), 80; studied perc, John Beck; comp, Samuel Adler & Warren Benson; received performer's cert in perc, 74. Marimba clinician/recitalist, J C Deagan, Div of Slingerland, 76- Played marimba, The Wilder Duo with Robert Levy. Instr perc, Tidewater Music Fest, St Mary's Col, 75-80, music dir, 78; instr music, St Mary's Col Md, 76-79; instr marimba, Birch Creek Farm, Wis, 79-80; asst prof perc, Ithaca Col, 80- Chief Collabs: Robert Levy, David Craighead, Brian Bowman, Paul Smadbeck. *Songs & Instrumental Works:* Two Mexican Dances for Marimba (solo); Five Etudes for Marimba (solo); Suite for Solo Guitar (Alec Wilder, transl for marimba).

STOUT, HERBERT E (BERT)　　ASCAP 1960
composer, author
b West Hoboken, NJ, May 17, 05. Educ: Bus col. Owner, decorative casting studio. Chief Collabrs: Hal Levy, Ray Merrill, Paul Atkerson. *Songs:* Lady Lonely; Peppy, the Peppermint Bear; I Love the Blues; The Other Woman; Ooh! What Santa Said.

STOUTAMIRE, ALBERT LUCIAN　　ASCAP 1972
composer, author, professor
b Broadway, Va, June 19, 21. Educ: Va Commonwealth Univ, BS, 47; Columbia Univ, MA, 53; Fla State Univ, EdD, 60. Teacher music, Richmond Pub Schs, Va, 47-57; also free-lance musician; prof music, LaGrange Col, Ga, 58-61; prof music, McNeese State Univ, 61-; also part-time musician-author-comp. Co-Author: "Band Music Notes"; "Bach-Rock Band Book" (for young sch musicians); "Concert Band Method Book" (for beginning band students); "Stringing Along-String Orchestra Book for Young School Musicians." *Instrumental Works:* Symphonic Sketch (concert band).

STOVER, CHESTER A (CHET)　　ASCAP 1961
composer, author
b Scranton, Pa, Apr 19, 25. Educ: Dickinson Col, BA, 49; Univ Minn, 46; Columbia Univ, 49-50. Advert exec & TV writer, 60-80. Originator TV shows, "Underdog", "Tennessee Tuxedo" & "Kind and Odie." Creative dir, Dancer, Fitzgerald & Sample Advert Agency, New York & William Esty Advert, New York. Partner, Total TV Productions Inc. Currently, free-lance writer; wrote songs & background music for TV cartoon series: "King Leonard and His Short Subjects"; "Tennessee Tuxedo and His Tales" & "The Beagles." Chief Collabs: Tread Covington, Joe Harris, Watts Biggers. *Scores:* Film/TV: Underdog (cartoon).

STOVER, HAROLD M　　ASCAP 1979
composer
b Latrobe, Pa, Nov 26, 46. Educ: Carnegie-Mellon Univ; Juilliard Sch Music, BMus. Organist & choirmaster, Second Presby Church, New York, NY, 68- Comns from leading choirs & organists. *Instrumental Works:* Te Decet Hymnus Deus in Sion; Five Preludes on American Folk Hymns; Jubilate Deo; Forth in Thy Name. *Scores:* The Magic Mime.

STRACHAN, LUCILLE
See Dobrin, Lucille Rebecca

STRADER, RODGER ALLAN　　ASCAP 1975
composer
b Pontiac, Mich, Oct 30, 52. Educ: Waterford Mott High Sch, 70; Grand Canyon Col, BA(music theory), 78. Began writing songs in 73. Now writing with Good Life Productions Inc, Scottsdale, Ariz. *Songs:* King of Love (Christmas musical, 11 songs); Then Came Sunday (Easter musical, 11 songs); Daystar; Why Have You Chosen Me?; Raised of Lovin' Jesus; Let Your Love Flow Through Me; I Praise You; Thank You, Lord, for Lovin' a Sinner; He's Always There; Somebody Prayed for Me; Hand in Hand; He Did It All; Life That's Free; I Want the World to Know; His Love.

STRAIGHT, CHARLEY　　ASCAP 1920
composer, conductor
b Chicago, Ill, Jan 16, 1891; d Chicago, Sept 21, 40. Educ: Wendell Phillips High Sch. Appeared in vaudeville. Music dir, player piano-roll co. Led own orch in

nightclubs & hotels. *Songs:* Everybody Calls Me Honey; I Love You Sunday; Red Rose; Funny Dear What Love Can Do; I'm Going to Stay on Solid Ground; That London Rag.

STRAIGHT, WILLARD   ASCAP 1960
composer, pianist
b Ft Wayne, Ind, July 18, 30. Educ: Univ Kans, BM; Chicago Musical Col, MM; studied with Gene Thompson, Donald Swarthout, Rudolph Ganz, Mollie Margolies, Horszowski, L E Anderson, Vittorio Rieti. Piano soloist, symph orchs incl Chicago, Detroit, Oklahoma City & CBC. Comn from Lyric Wind Ens, New York, Free Concerts Found, Chicago, Edward Benjamin, Washington Square Concerts Asn, New York. *Instrumental Works:* Prelude, Procession and Passacaglia; Piano Concerto; Violin Sonata; Another Summer Gone.

STRANGE, JUSTIN
See Glover, Charles Joseph

STRANGE, WILLIAM E
singer, guitarist
b Long Beach, Calif, 1930. *Songs & Instrumental Works:* Limbo Rock. *Albums:* Great Western Themes; In the Mexican Bag; James Bond Theme; King of the Road; Twelve-String Guitar; Billy Strange With the Challengers.

STRATTA, ETTORE   ASCAP 1960
composer, conductor, record producer
b Cuneo, Italy, Mar 30, 33. Educ: Santa Cecilia Cons Music, degree in piano; comp & cond studies with Tibor Serly, cond studies with Eleazar De Carvalho. Concert pianist, SAm & Europe, 59-60. Conductor orchs, London Symph, Vancouver Symph, Quebec Symph, Hartford Symph, Indianapolis Symph, The Baroque Chamber Orch, plus many more. Composer of over 150 works, pop songs, jazz instrumentals. Winner of 1 platinum & 3 gold albums. Chief Collabrs: Robert Colby, Dick Ahlert, Linda Starr, Ronny White, Sheila Davis. *Songs:* Music: That Ol' Christmas Spirit; When Everything Was Green; I Know What Happens Now; Someone is Waiting; Let It Happen; Carnival Lady; In This Life of Mine; Days of Summer. *Instrumental Works:* Blue Brazil; High Clouds; Good Morning Bahia!; Forget The Woman; A Waltz Dressed in Blue; Pages of Life; Love Scarlatti; City Lights; Of Love Remembered; Portrait of Julia; The Beginning of Our Life. *Scores:* Film/TV: The Lost Galaxy; The Late Planet Love.

STRAUSS, HERBERT   ASCAP 1958
composer, author, director
b Offenbach, Ger, May 22, 29. Educ: Princeton Univ, BA, Phi Beta Kappa, magna cum laude; Columbia Univ, MA. Actor & singer, theatre cos & TV; singer on records. Producer, writer & singer, Armed Forces Radio Service & TV, Ft Dix, NJ, 52-54. Unit mgr, writer, assoc producer, NBC, 55-59. Dir, radio-TV programming, Ben Sackheim, Inc, 59-60; radio-TV producer, head, prog develop Gumbinner-North, 60- *Songs:* Rumbaling; Story of Shenandoah; Come My Pretty Lady; Perhaps; When. *Albums:* Folk Music for People Who Hate Folk Music; Songs and Stories of Jewish Holidays.

STRAUSS, JOHN L   ASCAP 1961
composer, author
b New York, NY, Apr 28, 20. Educ: Dalcroze Sch Music, cert, 43; Sch Music, Yale Univ, MM, 51; studied comp & theory with Paul Hindemith & Quincey Porter. Musical numbers & scores, Bway shows & operas. Fel, MacDowell Colony, 73. Music ed numerous feature films. Chief Collabrs: John La Touche, Kenwood Elmslee, Sheppard Kerman. *Songs:* Car 54 Where Are You (theme); Damages. *Scores:* Opera: The Accused; Film/TV: The Phil Silvers Show; Mikey and Nicky; New York in Ten Hours (short subject film).

STRAUSS, ROBERT IRWIN   ASCAP 1973
composer, author, singer
b Detroit, Mich, Aug 5, 49. Educ: Northwestern Univ, Evanston, BS(speech); studied voice with Warren Barigian. Staff songwriter, Warner Bros Music, 73-79; recording artist; actor. *Songs:* I Will Still Love You; Hold Back the Dawn; If You Could See Through My Eyes; L A Radio; Angeline; Beverly Hills.

STRAVINSKY, IGOR   ASCAP 1940
composer
b Oranienbaum, Russia, June 17, 1882; d 1971. Educ: Univ St Petersburg, Law Sch; studied music with Rimsky-Korsakoff. Wrote scores for Diaghileff Ballet. Cond & recorded many of own works. First Am tour, 25. French citizen, 34; settled in US after fall of France, WW II; US citizen, 45. Mem: Nat Inst Arts & Letters; Am Acad Arts & Letters. Author, "Poetics of Music." Autobiographies: "Conversations With Stravinsky"; "Memories and Commentaries"; "Expositions and Developments". *Songs & Instrumental Works:* Symphony No 1; Fireworks; Three Pieces for String Quartet; Les Noces; Ragtime for Eleven Instruments; L'Histoire du Soldat; Song of the Nightingale; Three Pieces for Clarinet; Piano Rag Music; Symphonies of Wind Instruments; Octet for Wind Instruments; Renard; Piano Sonata; Piano Serenade in A; Le Baiser de le Fee; Capriccio for Piano, Orchestra; Concerto for Piano, Wind Orchestra; Oedipus Rex; Violin Concerto in D; Duo Concertante for Violin, Piano; Concerto for Two Solo Piano; Dumbarton Oaks Concerto; Suite Italienne for Cello, Piano; Symphony of Psalms; Danses Concertantes; Circus Polka;

Concerto Grosso in D; Sonata for Two Pianos; Ebony Concerto; Ode; Norwegian Moods; Russian Maiden's Song; Mass; Symphony in C; Monumentum pro Gesualdo; Concerto in D for String Orchestra; Symphony in Three Movements; Cantata; Canticum Sacrum; In Memoriam Dylan Thomas; Movements for Piano, Orchestra; Epitaphium for Flute, Clarinet, Harp; Double Cannon for String Quartet; Septet; Three Shakespeare Songs; Threni; Abraham and Isaac (cantata). *Scores:* Ballet: The Firebird; Petrouchka; Le Sacre du Printemps; Pulcinella; Persephone; Jeu de Cartes; Orpheus; Agon; The Flood; Opera: Rossignol; The Rake's Progress.

STRAW, ARLEIN FORD   ASCAP 1973
composer, author, teacher
b New York, NY, Jan 15, 20. Educ: Hunter Col, MA(musical comp); Juilliard Sch Music, studied with Fredrich Hart. Piano teacher, pvt studio, 20 yrs; musical mem, New York City Bd Educ, 12 yrs. Chief Collabrs: Helen Williams, Florence V Lucas. *Songs:* I Sing Black America; Music: Two Songs of Freedom. *Scores:* Opera: Bent Twigs.

STRAYHORN, BILLY   ASCAP 1946
composer, pianist, arranger
b Dayton, Ohio, Nov 29, 15; d New York, NY, May 31, 67. Comp & arr, Duke Ellington Orch. Chief Collabr: Duke Ellington. *Songs & Instrumental Works:* Lush Life; Something to Live For; Chelsea Bridge; Take the 'A' Train; After All; Day Dream; Raincheck; Johnny Come Lately; Clementine; Passion Flower; Midriff; Satin Doll; Grievin'; Perfume Suite.

STREET, JOYE
See Spence, Joyce Ann

STREISAND, BARBRA
singer, actress
b Brooklyn, NY, Apr 24, 42. Educ: Yeshiva of Brooklyn. New York theatre debut, "Another Evening With Harry Stoones"; appeared in Bway musicals, "I Can Get It for You Wholesale" & "Funny Girl"; motion pictures incl, "Funny Girl", "Hello Dolly", "On a Clear Day You Can See Forever", "For Pete's Sake", "Funny Lady" & "The Main Event"; star & producer film, "A Star Is Born"; TV spec incl, "Ny Name Is Barbra" (5 Emmy Awards). Recording artist, Columbia Records. Awards: Acad Award, 68; Georgie Award, AGVA, 77; Grammy Awards, 78. *Albums:* People; My Name Is Barbra; Color Me Barbra; Stoney End; Barbra Joan Streisand; The Way We Were; A Star Is Born; Superman; The Stars Salute Israel At 30; Wet.

STRICKLAND, LILY   ASCAP 1924
composer, author
b Anderson, SC, Jan 28, 1887; d Hendersonville, NC, June 6, 58. Educ: Converse Col, LittB; hon MusD; Juilliard Sch Music (scholarship), with Percy Goetschius & William Hummisten. Mem: Nat Asn Am Comp & Cond; Am League of Pen Women; Am League Comp; Music Club Am. *Songs:* Mah Lindy Lou; Dreamin' Time; Jes' My Song; My Lover's a Fisherman; At Eve I Hear a Flute; Here in the High Hills; My Arcady; also Oubangi (African song cycle). *Instrumental Works:* Song of David; St John the Beloved; Moon of Iraq; Sketches From the Southwest; Himalyan Sketches; Dance Moods; Charleston Sketches. *Scores:* Operetta: Jewels of the Desert.

STRICKLAND, WILLIAM BRADLEY   ASCAP 1960
composer
b New York, NY, Aug 21, 29. Educ: Hofstra Univ, BA, 52, studied with Elie Siegmeister; Shillinger Syst with Rudolf Schramm during high sch; with Tibor Serly, 56. Dir of music, Hempstead, NY & Rockville Ctr, NY Pub Sch Systs. Comp of educ music. Founded Consort Music, publ firm. Teacher, Hofstra Univ & Adelphi Univ. Professional comp, scoring music for indust films & TV, 77- Orchr for films & Bway. *Instrumental Works:* Concertino for Trumpet and String Orchestra; The Trumpet Shall Sound! (children's concerts); The Boy Who Hated Music (children's concerts); Sweatshirt Dances; Manahatta (concert march for symph band).

STRIDE, HARRY   ASCAP 1934
composer
b Isleworth, Eng, May 31, 03. Educ: Montreal, Can. Moved to US, 28. Mem, USO Shows, WW II; wrote spec material for nightclubs. *Songs:* Please Handle With Care; Lonely Park; Heaven Only Knows; Bless Your Heart; Me and My Wonderful One; A Hunting We Will Go; More Than Anything in the World.

STRINGER, ROBERT   ASCAP 1962
composer, author, conductor
b Omaha, Nebr, Aug 10, 11. Educ: High sch; pvt music study. Head, music ed, Metro-Goldwyn-Mayer, 28-42. Comp & cond, TV show "American Inventory." Comp, indust films & musical commercials. Writer, Bway revue "New Faces of 1956." *Instrumental Works:* TV theme: The Nurses. *Scores:* Films: The Good Earth; David Copperfield; The Wizard of Oz; Radio shows: Broadway Is My Beat; Studio One.

STRINGFIELD, LAMAR ASCAP 1937
composer, conductor, flutist
b Raleigh, NC, Oct 10, 1897; d Asheville, NC, Jan 21, 59. Educ: Inst of Musical Art; studied with Georges Barrere, Percy Goetschius, Franklin Robinson, George Wedge & Nadia Boulanger; dipl in flute. Army serv, Mexican Border, 16; bandsman, 105th Engrs, 30th Div, France, WW I. Gave up med career for music. Formed Inst Folk Music, Univ NC (for study of native Am music). Founded NC State Symph, music dir, 32-38. Assoc cond, Radio City Music Hall, 38-39. Lectr, Juilliard Summer Sch, 39-41. Music dir, Knoxville Symph, 46-47, Symphonette of Charlotte, 47-48 & Charlotte Symph, 48-49. Flute soloist, guest cond with symph orchs. Author, "America and Her Music." Wrote music for historical dramas, "The Lost Colony" & "Shout Freedom." Chief Collabr: Paul Green. *Instrumental Works:* Indian Legend; From the Southern Mountains (orch suite; Pulitzer award); A Negro Parade; The Legend of John Henry; Moods of a Moonshiner; From the Blue Ridge Mountain; The Mountain Song (opera); Peace (cantata; Marian Sims poem).

STROM, TERRYE
See Coelho, Terrye Lynn

STROUSE, CHARLES ASCAP 1956
composer
b New York, NY, June 7, 28. Educ: New York Pub Sch 87; Townsend Harris High Sch; Eastman Sch Music, Univ Rochester, BM; studied comp with Bernard Rogers, Aaron Copland, Arthur Berger, David Diamond & Nadia Boulanger. Chief Collabrs: Lee Adams, Martin Charin, Sammy Cahn. *Instrumental Works:* Concerto for Piano and Orchestra. *Scores:* Opera/Ballet: Singers; Bway Shows: Bye Bye Birdie; All American; Golden Boy; Superman; Applause; Annie; Charlie and Algernon; Bring Back Birdie; Bo Jangles; Film/TV: Bonnie and Clyde; The Night They Raided Minskys.

STRUZICK, EDWARD HUGH, II ASCAP 1971
composer, author, singer
b Decatur, Ala, Apr 18, 51. Started with Joe Wilson Music, then went to Music Mill Publ, now has own Struzick Music Co. Chief Collabrs: Ana Aldridge, Lenny Le Blanc, Laury Byrom. *Songs:* Sharin' the Night Together; Fallin'; Don't Look At Me That Way.

STRZELECKI, HENRY P (HANK WALLIS) ASCAP 1968
composer, author, musician
b Birmingham, Ala, Aug 8, 39. Played first record session at age 16; two decades of record making; numerous TV shows, "Hee Haw" & "That Nashville Music," plus others. Head, The Nashville Superpickers. Two publ cos; singer, publisher & producer. Chief Collabrs: John Riggs, Bill Barnes. *Songs:* Long Tall Texan; Where Do We Go From Here; I Hate Me for Hurting You; All You Add Is Love; Sexy Southern Lady; Bomb Iran; You and I; I Can't Quit Cheatin' On You.

STUART, MARY
See Krolik, Mary Stuart

STUART, ROBERTA
See Feldner, Roberta Emily

STUART, THOMAS GILMORE (CHRISTOPHER ASCAP 1971
TOBOGGAN)
composer, author, singer
b Tuscaloosa, Ala, Aug 30, 48. Educ: Livingston Univ, BS; Univ Ala, MA. Lead singer & writer, 68-; recorded in England, 75; saxophone soloist appearances as a session player; recording & playing as the Rubberband. *Songs:* Hound Dog Man; If My Life Came Up Again; I Ain't Got Lorraine; In Like Flynn; Love's Lost Flyer.

STUART, WALTER ASCAP 1957
composer, trumpeter, arranger
b Philadelphia, Pa, Sept 28, 25. Educ: Mastbaum Vocal Sch, Philadelphia. Trumpeter, Mal Hallet Orch. Served, 71st Inf Div Band, World War II. Trumpeter & arr, var orchs incl Elliot Lawrence, Hal McIntyre, Buddy Morrow, Billy May, Xavier Cugat, Jerry Fielding & Tex Beneke. Comp, musical commercials & background music for indust films. *Songs & Instrumental Works:* Cerise; This Is Autumn; The Brand New Cha-Cha-Cha; Teen Polka; Wingover.

STUARTI, ENZO ASCAP 1961
composer, author, singer
b Rome, Italy, Mar 3, 25. Educ: Cons of St Cecelia, Rome. Appearances, Bway musicals, hotels, supper clubs & TV. Recording artist.

STUDEBAKER, HOWARD JAMES ASCAP 1979
composer, author, singer
b San Francisco, Calif, Feb 24, 20. Educ: Roosevelt Sr High Sch, Oakland, Calif; studied voice with Sherry, 35-38 & James Corley, 39-41. Began singing in church choirs & PTA meetings, 30; also sch band, musical/comedies, operettas & big bands. Studied piano under sister's tutoring. Formed own band, Howie's Hot-Z-Totsy Swingers featuring Howie & The Six Spark Plugs, 41; played at charity balls, small-time bars & hotels. Began songwriting, 39. Writer musical/comedy, "North Atlantic." Established own publ co, Howard

Studebaker Productions. Chief Collabrs: Nancy Clapham Noyes, Francis Smith, Dixie Cruess Lind, Marty Allan, Ben Herr, Rick Malin. *Songs:* Cupid, You're a Devil; Lyrics: A Politicians' Life (Is Not for Me); Say a Prayer (For Me); Now We're Together Again.

STUESSY, CLARENCE JOSEPH, JR ASCAP 1971
composer, educator
b Houston, Tex, Dec 14, 43. Educ: Southern Methodist Univ, BM; Eastman Sch Music, Univ Rochester, MA, PhD. Asst prof music, Tex Woman's Univ, 69-73; assoc chmn & assoc prof, Div Music, Southern Methodist Univ, 73-79. Chief arr & comp, Dallas Cowboys Band, 74- Dir & prof, Div Music, Univ Tex, San Antonio, 79- *Instrumental Works:* Concerto for Piano & Orchestra; Improvisational Suite (3 soloists & stage band); Polysyntheticisms for Orchestra; Encomium for Band; Homage a P D Q Bach.

STULL, DONALD EARL (MASON FREESOIL) ASCAP 1972
composer, author, singer
b Freesoil, Mich, Apr 26, 27. Educ: Ohio State Univ; Muskingum Col; Ohio Univ, BFA(educ, fine & applied arts). Singer in quartet, octet, glee club & pub choral appearances, incl Handel's "The Messiah" & Mendelssohn's "Elijah" with the Columbus Philh Orch. Mem fac creative arts, Calif Lutheran Col, 64. Teacher, Pub Educ Syst. Local theater show appearances. Co-dir & teacher, Fine Arts Concert. *Songs:* Geneva; Keys to the Kingdom; It's Snowing Here in the Country; Exchange Avenue; Teardrops in Vain; I Look With My Heart.

STURGEON, RUSSELL M ASCAP 1964
composer
b Carrollton, Ky, Jan 16, 21. Educ: Carrollton High Sch; Cincinnati Cons Music, dipl piano technol; studied clarinet with Fredick Lubrani & piano with Leo Paalz. Tuning & rebuilding pianos. Chief Collabrs: Joe Derise, Vikki Dale. *Songs:* Better Late Than Never; Second Fiddle; Strictly for Laughs; My Love's Too Much; Love's a Game; The Wind Was Warm; Little Girl Don't Run Away.

STURM, MAURICE (MURRAY) ASCAP 1925
composer, author
b New York, NY, Apr 12, 1899. Educ: High sch & bus sch; pvt piano study. Writer of spec material; pianist in dance orchs. Chief Collabrs: Jack Meskill, David Ormont, Howard Johnson, Lew Breau. *Songs:* Any Place but Home James, Is Home Sweet Home to Me; We'll Camp on the Campus; You Never Get Nowhere Holding Hands; I'll Never See My Sweetie Anymore; Sumpin' Like This; Have You a Mommy For Sale Today?; What! No Women, What Kind of a Party is This?; Mother Goose Parade; On a Windy Day in March; Have a Heart for Someone; Honolulu Lullaby; Lyrics: I Popped the Question to Her Pop; My High Falutin' Gal; I Want Sp-Sp-Spinach.

STUTZ, CARLTON FRANKLIN ASCAP 1954
composer
b Richmond, Va, Dec 19, 15. Educ: Univ of Richmond, BS, 39; studied violin with Myron Kahn, 35-36. Accountant, Reynolds Metals & Pan Am Airways, 40-47; on-air radio personality with progs of music from Bway, light classics & classics; comp, popular songs, 48-64. Teacher of math, secondary pub schs, 64-79. Homemaker, 79- Chief Collabrs: Edith Lindeman Calisch, Carl Barefoot, Jr. *Songs:* Music: Little Things Mean a Lot; Red Headed Stranger; I Know; Danger, Heartbreak Ahead; Enchanted; Kissing Tree; Blackberry Winter; Jamestown Suite (Jamestown Fest).

STYLES, BEVERLY
See Carpenter, Juanita Robins

STYNE, JULE ASCAP 1931
composer, publisher, producer
b London, Eng, Dec 31, 05; came to US in 1913. Educ: Chicago Col Music, scholarship, Mozart award; Northwestern Univ. Piano soloist with Chicago Symph at age 9; featured with symph orchs; led dance band in hotels & nightclubs, Chicago; vocal coach & writer special material, New York; coached singers, Hollywood; producer of musicals & plays, "Make a Wish", "Pal Joey" (revival; Donaldson, NY Drama Critics award, 52), "First Impressions", "Will Success Spoil Rock Hunter?" & "Mr Wonderful", coproduced, "In Any Language." Chief Collabrs: Frank Loesser, Sammy Cahn, Leo Robin, Betty Comden, Adolph Green, Bob Hilliard, Stephen Sondheim, Bob Merrill, Stanley Styne (son). *Songs:* Sunday; I Don't Want to Walk Without You, Baby; I've Heard That Song Before; I Said No; Victory Polka; I'll Walk Alone; Saturday Night Is the Loneliest Night in the Week; Poor Little Rhode Island (off state song); The Charm of You; I Fall in Love Too Easily; What Makes the Sunset; Guess I'll Hang My Tears Out to Dry; It's Been a Long, Long Time; Let It Snow, Let It Snow, Let It Snow; I'm Glad I Waited for You; The Things We Did Last Summer; Five Minutes More; Time After Time; I Still Get Jealous; Papa, Won't You Dance With Me?; You're My Girl; It's Magic; Bye Bye Baby; Diamonds Are a Girl's Best Friend; A Little Girl From Little Rock; Just a Kiss Apart; How Will He Know?; If You Hadn't But You Did; There Never Was a Baby Like My Baby; Give a Little, Get a Little; How Do You Speak to an Angel?; Every Street's a Boulevard in Old New York; Three Coins in the Fountain (Academy Award, 54); Never Never Land; Captain Hook's Waltz; Long Before I Knew You; Just in Time; The Party's Over; I Met a Girl; Ride on a Rainbow; I Have

You to Thank; Something's Always Happening on the River; Dance Only With Me; Let Me Entertain You; Some People; Small World; You'll Never Get Away From Me; All I Need Is the Girl; Everything's Coming Up Roses; Together; Cry Like the Wind; Make Someone Happy; Adventure; I'm Just Taking My Time; Be a Santa; Ride Through the Night; Comes Once in a Lifetime; People; Don't Rain on My Parade; The Music That Makes Me Dance; I Am Woman; Fade Out—Fade In; Get Acquainted. *Scores:* Bway Shows: High Button Shoes; Gentlemen Prefer Blondes; Two on the Aisle; Hazel Flagg; Peter Pan; Say, Darling; Gypsy (Grammy Award, 59); Do Re Mi; Subways Are for Sleeping; Funny Girl (Grammy Award, 65); Fade Out—Fade In; Hallelujah, Baby!; Darling of the Day; Sugar; Films: Anchors Aweigh; Tonight and Every Night; Tars and Spars; The Kid From Brooklyn; It Happened in Brooklyn; Romance on the High Seas; Two Guys From Texas; It's a Great Feeling; The West Point Story; Two Tickets to Broadway; My Sister Eileen; Meet Me After the Show; TV: Mr McGoo's Christmas Carol; Dangerous Christmas of Little Red Riding Hood; Ruggles of Red Gap.

STYNE, STANLEY H   ASCAP 1956
author

b Chicago, Ill, Oct 24, 30. Educ: Beverly Hills High Sch; Univ Southern Calif. Stage mgr, Bway productions. Film publicist, Columbia Pictures. Music publ prof mgr, Columbia Pictures Music, Robbins-Feist-Miller & Stratford-Chappell Music. Lyric writer for popular recordings, TV, stage productions, indust shows & films, incl "Let's Make Love", "Devil at Four O'Clock", "Pal Joey", "They Came to Cordura", "Four for Texas" & "Jeanne Eagels Story." Chief Collabs: George Duning, Heal Hefti, Donald Kahn, Fred Karger, Barry Mann, Nelson Riddle, Jule Styne. *Songs:* Lyrics: A Beautiful Friendship; Cute; There's No Such Thing (As the Next Best Thing to Love); Open Highway; Gidget Goes Hawaiian; Cry for Happy (Golden Globe Nomination); The Silent Treatment; I Knew Jesus Before He Was a Superstar; Faithfully; Broken Home; All the Young Men; Heidi; All the Way Home; Whip Out Your Ukulele; Shortest Distance Between Two Lips (Is a Kiss).

SUBOTA, DOROTHY LAPELL   ASCAP 1966
composer, author

b Libau, Latvia, Mar 16, 1897. Educ: New York City Grammar Schs, 07-11, pub sch to sixth grade; then to pvt sch, Binghamton, NY, 4 yrs, equivalent to high sch. Started writing poetry while in sch; then songwriting. Chief Collabrs: Lou Halmy, Jesse Hodges, Clarence Freed. *Songs:* You're the Doctor; You're Still on My Mind; Ask Me Baby; Will You Love Me Tomorrow?; You're My Idea.

SUBOTNICK, JOAN LOTZ LA BARBARA   ASCAP 1976
composer, publisher, vocalist

b Philadelphia, Pa, June 8, 47. Educ: Syracuse Univ; NY Univ, BS(music educ); Tanglewood/Berkshire Music Ctr. Developed extended vocal techniques, concerts & sound installations throughout US & Europe; specialist in exp & avant garde voice; workshops on new vocal techniques & comp. Own compositions recorded on var labels; jazz recordings with Don Sebesky & Jim Hall; video artist. Contributing new music ed, mag, "Musical America/High Fidelity," 77- Produced radio series "Other Voices, Other Sounds," KPFK, Los Angeles. *Songs:* Music: Circular Song; Voice Piece: One-Note Internal Resonance Investigation; Vocal Extensions; ShadowSong; Autumn Signal; Klee Alee; quatre petites betes; Twelve for Five in Eight (mixed voices); Erin. *Instrumental Works:* Thunder (6 tympani, voice with electronics); Responsive Resonance with Feathers (piano, voice tape); Ides of March (instruments, voices). *Scores:* Dance: Layers; TV: Signing Alphabet (Sesame Street).

SUBOTNICK, MORTON LEON
composer, teacher, clarinetist

b Los Angeles, Calif, Apr 14, 33. Educ: Univ Southern Calif; Univ Denver, BA; Mills Col, MA; comp study with Leon Kirchner & Darius Milhaud. Pioneer in field of electronic music; innovator in works with instruments & other media also in live electronic manipulation of instruments & voices, creating ghost electronics; extensive work in multimedia. Chmn comp dept, Calif Inst Arts. Co-founder San Francisco Tape Music Ctr & Mills Col Performing Group; music dir, Ann Halprin's Dance Co, San Francisco Actors' Workshop & Lincoln Ctr Repertory Theatre; dir electronic music at original Electric Circus, New York. First comp comn to write electronic comp for phonograph medium. *Songs:* Music: Last Dream of the Beast (voice, ghost electronics). *Instrumental Works:* A Sky of Cloudless Sulphur/After the Butterfly; Liquid Strata (piano, ghost electronics); Two Butterflies (amplified orch); Before the Butterfly (orch); Place (orch); Passages of the Beast (clarinet, ghost electronics); The Wild Beasts (trombone, piano, ghost electronics); Parallel Lines (piccolo, eight instruments, ghost electronics); The First Dream of Light (tuba, piano, ghost electronics); Ten (flute, oboe, trumpet, trombone, piccolos, piano, viola, bass); Mandolin (viola, tape & 16mm film); Play! No 3 (pianist/mime, tape & 16mm film); Play! No 4 (soprano, piano, vibraphone, voice, 2 16mm films). *Songs & Instrumental Works:* Two Life Histories (clarinet, voice, ghost electronics); The Game Rooms (multimedia works). *Scores:* The Caucasian Chalk Circle (incidental music for play); Electronics: Silver Apples of the Moon; Touch; Sidewinder; 4 Butterflies; Until Spring; The Wild Bull; Ballet: Ice Flow.

SUCHOFF, BENJAMIN   ASCAP 1960
composer, author, educator

b New York, NY, Jan 19, 18. Educ: Cornell Univ, BS, 40; NY Univ, MA, 49, EdD, 56; Juilliard Sch Music, postgrad, studied comp with Vittorio Giannini. WW II, USAF, Capt (music officer). Prof, Ctr for Contemporary Arts & Letters,

State Univ NY Stony Brook. Music dir, G W Hewlett High Sch. Musicologist, Bela Bartok Archives, NY. Ed of bks by Bartok, incl "Rumanian Folk Music," 5 vols; author of bks & articles, incl "Guide to the Mikrokosmos of Bela Bartok." Comp & arr of works for chorus, band & var instrumental media. Chief Collabr: Eunice Brown. *Songs:* Song of Peace; Chorus: Three Hungarian Folk Songs; Tumbalalaika; Sleepytime Bach; Bourree for Bach; Evening in Transylvania. *Instrumental Works:* Band: Cavortina; Bartok Centennial Suite.

SUDERBURG, ROBERT CHARLES   ASCAP 1967
composer

b Spencer, Iowa, Jan 28, 36. Educ: Univ Minn, BMus(summa cum laude), 57; Yale Univ, MMus, 60; Univ Pa, PhD, 66. Teacher & cond, Bryn Mawr Col, 60-61, Univ Pa, 61-65 & Philadelphia Music Acad, 63-66. Teacher, cond & co-founder, Contemporary Group, Univ Wash, 66-74. Chancellor, NC Sch Arts, Winston-Salem, 74- Mem music adv panel, NEA; mem bd dirs, Eastern Music Fest, NC Dance Theatre, Southeastern Ctr Contemporary Art & NC Shakespeare Fest. Comp works for orch, cantatas for voice & chamber orch, chamber music, also works for piano, band & choir. Grantee, Houston Symph, 67, Rockefeller Found, 68, ASCAP, 68-, Guggenheim Found, 68 & 74, Am Music Ctr, 69, Hindemith Found, 71 & Nat Found Arts, 73.

SUESSDORF, KARL   ASCAP 1955
composer, author, teacher

b Valdez, Alaska, Apr 28, 21. Educ: Pvt teachers in theory, comp, orchestration & piano. Pianist, arr, comp & author, Hollywood & New York, 40- Chief Collabrs: John Blackburn, Benny Carter, Leah Worth, Nick Cea, Kermit Goell. *Songs:* Moonlight In Vermont; Key Largo; The Good Humor Man; I Wish I Knew; She Doesn't Laugh Like You; Coral Sea; also 30 others.

SUESSE, DANA   ASCAP 1932
composer, author

b Kansas City, Mo, Dec 3, 09. Educ: Elem, Sacred Heart Convent & high sch, Mo; studied privately with Nadia Boulanger, Paris, 47-59. First piano recital, Kansas City, Mo, age 8. Piano studies with Alexander Siloti & comp with Rubin Goldmark. Made debut playing own jazz concerto, Carnegie Hall, 32. Wrote theme song & incidental music for "The Seven Year Itch". Serious music has been played by maj Am symph orchs. Author-comp several musical comedies & a number of straight plays. Chief Collabrs: Eddie Heyman, E Y Harburg, Leo Robin. *Songs:* Music: Whistling in the Dark; My Silent Love; You Ought to Be in Pictures; The Night Is Young and You're So Beautiful. *Instrumental Works:* Young Man With a Harp (comn for Casper Reardon); Concerto Romantico (piano & orch); Three Cities (tone poem); Jazz Concerto in D Major (combo & orch); Jazz Nocturne. *Scores:* 1939 World's Fair Acquacade.

SUKMAN, FRANCES PALEY (LEE FRANCIS, FRANCES PAIGE)
composer, author

b Chicago, Ill. Educ: Chicago pub schs; Am Cons Music, studied piano with Heniot Levy. Pianist-organist, CBS, Chicago; as organist, supplied music for many soap operas. Recording artist; appeared on TV, Chicago, 50's. *Songs:* A Crushed Gardenia; Music: Love on a Merry-Go-Round. *Scores:* Film/TV: Tiger-Tiger.

SUKMAN, HARRY   ASCAP 1954
composer

b Chicago, Ill. Educ: Chicago Pub Schs; Chicago Musical Col; studied piano with Rudolph Ganz & theory & comp with Felix Borowski. Debut as concert pianist, age 12. Concertized in recitals & soloist with symph orchs throughout the US. On music staff as pianist & cond, Mutual Broadcasting Syst, Chicago. Staff mem, Paramount Pictures, Hollywood. Comp/cond of many scores for motion pictures & TV. Recipient of an Acad Award, Oscar. Chief Collabrs: Peggy Lee, Harold Adamson, Paul Francis Webster, Ned Washington. *Songs:* Music: You Are There; The Gold Wedding Ring; I Love Your Gypsy Heart; High Ridin' Woman; Verboten. *Instrumental Works:* Nightfall; Pixie Holiday; Themes: The Eleventh Hour & Gentle Ben. *Scores:* TV Series: The Eleventh Hour; The High Chaparral; Gentle Ben; Dr Kildare; Bonanza; The Monroes; Films for TV: Salem's Lot; Someone's Watching Me; Beyond the Bermuda Triangle; Genesis II; Planet Earth; Motion Pictures: Song Without End; Fanny; The Singing Nun; The Naked Runner; Phenix City Story; Welcome to Hard Times; A Thunder of Drums; Around the World Under the Sea; The Private Navy of Sgt O'Farrell; Forty Guns; Underworld USA; The Hangman; Crimson Kimono; Madison Avenue; Underwater Warrior; A Bullet for Joey; Screaming Eagles; Riders to the Stars; Battle Taxi.

SULLIVAN, ALEXANDER   ASCAP 1922
composer, author

b Boston, Mass, Aug 28, 1885; d Calif, Nov 20, 56. Educ: Boston Latin Sch. Newspaper reporter & ed, Boston & New York. *Songs:* Kisses; Georgia Rose; You'll Find Me Where You Left Me, But I Won't Be Alone; I Want to See My Ida Hoe in Idaho; Give Me a Smile and a Kiss.

SULLIVAN, DAN   ASCAP 1940
composer, author, pianist

b Boston, Mass, May 23, 1875; d Boston, Jan 16, 48. Educ: New Eng Cons. Pianist in father's orch; played in vaudeville; led own band. Wrote spec material for Chauncey Olcott, Fisk O'Hara; songs for Bway musicals. Had own piano co.

Songs: You're As Welcome As the Flowers in May; One Little Sweet Little Girl; Stealing; When It's Springtime in Killarney; Sweet Girl of My Dreams; Macushla.

SULLIVAN, DANE (FORMERLY DANIEL JOSEPH)   ASCAP 1971
composer, author, publisher
b Sherman, Tex, Dec 20, 50. Educ: Sharpstown High Sch, Houston. Has made recordings, 67-; staff songwriter, Am Studios, Memphis; session musician, engr, producer, publ, mgr, consultant & author/ed. Has done other media activities & spec projects dealing with psychology & creative process. Chief Collabrs: Gala Sullivan, Charlie Romans. *Songs:* Ears of Stone; Lamp of Love; Love Shine; Same Old Ride; Lisa Sweetbody; Get It On; Lyrics: World of Complete Beauty.

SULLIVAN, GALA (VERNA GALE SPAIN, GALE S HARRIS)
composer, author, publisher
b Lawrenceburg, Tenn, Nov 28, 39. Educ: Lawrence County High Sch, Tenn; David Lipscomb High Sch, Nashville; George Peabody Col. Made first recording, Am Studios, Memphis, 69; publ, producer, mgr & author/ed. Other media activities & spec projects in psychology & creative process. Chief Collabrs: Dane Sullivan, Richard Mainegra, Robert Walker. *Songs:* Don't Say No; Get It On; One Day; Lovin' Day; Lyrics: Sometimes; Love Shine.

SULLIVAN, GERALD WARDEN   ASCAP 1927
composer, author
b Chicago, Ill, July 21, 1891. Educ: Brentano Grammar Sch; Crane Tech High Sch. Appeared in piano act, Hager & Sullivan, vaudeville, 15-24. Radio dir & announcer, 22-33. Song plugger for band singers. Chief Collabr: Clyde Hagar. *Songs:* Tripping Along; Music: I'm Sorry; Wait'll You See My Gal; All Over You; Everybody Knows; Wonderful Mother of Mine.

SULLIVAN, HENRY   ASCAP 1932
composer, author
b Worcester, Mass; d. Educ: Worcester Acad; Dartmouth Col, BA; studied music with Franz Lehar, Edmund Eysler. WW I, USAAF in France; WW II, USN in Eng. Wrote songs for Bway musicals incl, "A Little Racketeer", "John Murray Anderson's Almanac (1929)", "The Little Show", "Third Little Show", "Thumbs Up" & "Walk a Little Faster." Wrote songs for films incl, "The Greatest Show on Earth." Wrote spec material for Radio City Music Hall, also for Evelyn Laye, Maurice Chevalier & Beatrice Lillie. Wrote songs for Ringling Bros Circus, 48-51. Chief Collabrs: Edward Eliscu, Harry Ruskin, John Murray Anderson, Earle Crooker, Howard Dietz. *Songs:* My Temptation; I May Be Wrong But I Think You're Wonderful; A Nice Cup of Tea; Mona Lisa; Falling in Love; Popcorn and Lemonade; Lily Belle May June; Caught in the Rain. *Scores:* London Stage: Bow Bells; Fanfare; Home and Beauty.

SULLIVAN, JERI KELLI   ASCAP 1952
composer, author, singer
b Jersey City, NJ, Nov 14, 24. Educ: West Seattle High Sch; Univ Calif, Los Angeles; Los Angeles Community Col; studied voice, Carolina Lazzari, New York, Lillian Goodman, Los Angeles, Teacher Louise, Chicago. Singer, radio shows incl "Jimmy Durante-Gary Moore", "Bob Hope", "Jeri Sullivan Show", New York; nightclubs; TV shows incl "Steve Allen", "Johnny Carson"; recording with Les Baxter. Chief Collabrs: Maury Amsterdam, Mario Ruiz Armengol. *Songs:* Rum and Coca Cola; He Loves Me; The Following Sea: A Regular Man; Lyrics: The Christmas Gift.

SULLIVAN, JOSEPH MICHAEL   ASCAP 1943
composer, pianist
b Chicago, Ill, Nov 5, 06; d San Francisco, Calif, Oct 13, 71. Educ: Chicago Cons. Pianist in orchs incl Chicagoans, Red Nichols, Russ Columbo, Louis Armstrong & Bob Crosby. Accompanist to Bing Crosby in films. Has given concerts & appeared at jazz fests & nightclubs; at Hangover Club, San Francisco. *Songs & Instrumental Works:* Little Rock Getaway; Gin Mill Blues; Just Strollin'; In a Minor Mood; Farewell to Riverside; Onyx Bringdown; Star Struck; My Little Pride and Joy; Del Mar Rag; Deep Down.

SULLIVAN, LIAM   ASCAP 1966
author, actor
b Jacksonville, Ill, May 18, 23. Educ: Culver Mil Acad; Harvard, AB(cum laude); Hedgerow Theatre, Philadelphia, acting; studied voice with Keith Davis, New York; Univ Calif, Los Angeles, lyric writing with Hal Levy. Actor, Bway, "The Constant Wife", "The Little Foxes" & "Merchant of Venice", off-Bway, summer stock, dinner theatre, W Coast Theatre, TV. Chief Collabrs: Manos Hajadakis, Forrest Wood, Geoff Clarkson. *Songs:* Lyrics: In the Cool of the Day; Laura Lee; Lonely Road; The Writing on the Wall.

SULLIVAN, THOMAS JOSEPH, JR   ASCAP 1976
composer, author, singer
b Boston, Mass, Mar 27, 47. Educ: Perkins Sch for the Blind; Providence Col; Harvard Univ. Began prof singing during col, then comp. Went to Calif, 73. Performed with Shirley Bassey, Liza Minnelli, Buddy Hackett & Rowan & Martin. Film appearances incl "Airport 77", "MASH" & "Mork & Mindy." Regular spec reporter, "Good Morning America," ABC. Rec'd Most Outstanding Performance Award, Yamaha Music Fest, Tokyo, Japan, 75. Co-author, "If You Could See What I Hear" & "Adventures in Darkness."

Author, "You Are Special." *Songs:* Beauty's in the Eyes of the Beholder; Lady for an Evening; My First Love; I Need You.

SULLIVAN, WILLIAM MICHAEL   ASCAP 1958
composer, author, actor
b Burlington, Vt, Mar 11, 25. Educ: Studied voice & languages in Burlington, Vt, New York, Essen, Ger, Helsinki, Finland; studied theatre with Lee Strasborg, Uta Hagen, acting with Stella Adler. Radio announcer WMFF, New York, WHDH, Boston & Radio Free Europe, Munich. Singer, poetry reader & writer. Speak Finnish, Swedish, Ger & Eng. Volunteer Finnish Army ski troups. Chief Collabrs: Bob Laine, Dixon Devore, Van Dyke Parks. *Songs:* Silent Tears; When I Gave You My Heart; Lyrics: My Pledge to You; Iron Town; New England (With My Love); New Hampshire.

SULTAN, ARNE   ASCAP 1960
composer, author, comedian
b Brooklyn, NY, June 7, 25. Educ: High sch. Comedian, nightclubs, 13 yrs. Writer, comedy material for Martha Raye, Jackie Gleason & Steve Allen. Writer & producer, United Artists Records; writer, Columbia Pictures.

SUMERLIN, MACON DEE   ASCAP 1964
composer, teacher
b Roby, Tex, Oct 24, 19. Educ: Hardin-Simmons Univ, BMus, 40; Eastman Sch Music, 40-41; Univ Tex, MMus, 47; MusD, Tex Guild Comp, 51. Teacher, pub schs, 41-42; served in USAF, 42-45; asst prof comp, Hardin-Simmons Univ, 47-51; assoc prof music, McMurry Col, 52-78, now chmn, Div Fine Arts. *Songs:* Jalapeno; Music: I Am Music; Three Western Songs. *Instrumental Works:* Three Orchestra Pieces.

SUMMER, DONNA
See Gaines, Adrian Donna

SUMMERFIELD, SIDNEY CHARLES   ASCAP 1969
composer, author, singer
b Birmingham, Eng, Nov 2, 1889. Educ: Eng primary & secondary schs; Armour Inst Technol Electrical Eng, 2 yrs. Sang on the concert stage in Eng. Moved to US, became a citizen, 17. Electric engr, Bell Syst, Western Electric Co, Cicero, Ill, 13; engr, Cent Office Maintenance, Ill Bell, Chicago; engr specialist, Machine Switching Telephone Systs, NJ Bell Telephone Co, 18; retired, Bell Syst, 46. Tennis teacher & coach. Mem: Am Electric Eng Asn; Am Inst Electrical Engrs; US Paddle Tennis Asn; US Lawn Tennis Asn; Telephone Pioneers of Am. *Songs & Instrumental Works:* Music: Teach Me How to Pray Lord; Hear Me Dear Lord; American Boy (march).

SUMMERS, ROBERT EUGENE   ASCAP 1968
composer, teacher
b Healdton, Okla, May 3, 29. Educ: Univ Okla, MMusEd, 57. Arr, Air Force Band; band & choir dir; theory teacher; nightclub & show band dir & instrumentalist. *Songs & Instrumental Works:* Colorado Twilight; And I'll Remember You Again; Soft and Blue; The Walkin' Blues; Of Wisdom (vocal suite); Allegro and Andante for Clarinet Choir.

SUMMERSON, PATRICK EUGENE   ASCAP 1978
composer, author
b Nelsonville, Ohio, Apr 20, 51. Educ: Am Acad Dramatic Arts, New York; New Sch Soc Res, New York, studied music theory. Summer stock, New London Players, New London, NH, 70. Recording artist on Crewe Records. Chief Collabr: Lenny Macaluso. *Songs:* Night Dancin'; Love Explosion; Lyrics: You Got My Love; Down to the Wire.

SUNDGAARD, ARNOLD   ASCAP 1951
author, teacher
b St Paul, Minn, Oct 31, 09. Educ: Univ Wis, BA, 35; Yale Univ, drama. Taught drama at Univ Tex, Columbia Univ, Univ Ill, Bennington Col, State Univ NY, Stony Brook. Playwright, "Spirochete", "Everywhere I Roam", "The First Crocus" & "Of Love Remembered." Guggenheim & Rockefeller Fels; NEA Grant. US exchange lecturer, Trinity Col, Dublin. Chief Collabrs: Kurt Weill, Douglas Moore, Alec Wilder, Crawford Gates, Newell Dayley, Fabian Watkinson. *Songs:* Where Do You Go; Douglas Mountain; Jersey Boy; Valley Home; The Wind is a Lion; First You Have a Dream; How Lovely is Christmas; An Axe, An Apple, and a Buckskin Jacket; Boy at a Window. *Scores:* Opera Libretti/Musicals: Down in the Valley; Giants in the Earth; The Lowland Sea; Sunday Excursion; Cumberland Fair; Gallantry; Promised Valley; Brigham; Nobody's Earnest; The Greenfield Christmas Tree; The Truth About Windmills.

SUNSHINE, MADELINE (M CLAIRE FREEDMAN)   ASCAP 1976
composer, author
b Bronx, NY, Oct 6, 48. Writer, childrens' radio progs, WLIR, New York, 71. Song contributor to TV show "Sesame Street." Author of childrens' bks. Chief Collabrs: Frank Cappola, Robert Tepper, Stephen Lawrence, Tom Kellock, Jim Dawson. *Songs:* Lyrics: This Is Love; No One Is Never Gonna Love You; Gentle Women; Mystery Man; Just Imagine; Cowboy; Sunny California...It Can Wait Til; Momi-a Blues; Wonder How It Feels; Round and Round.

SUNSHINE, MARION
See Ijames, Mary Tunstall

SUPA, RICHARD
See Goodman, Richard John

SURGAL, JON   ASCAP 1976
author
b New York, NY, Mar 27, 49. Educ: Columbia Col, Columbia Univ Sch Arts. Playwright; poet; TV writer, dir & producer. Chief Collabrs: Oscar Brand, Billy Cross, Lan O'Kun. *Songs:* The State of Our Union; The Girl I Used to Be; I'm Gonna Make the Big Break Tonight; The Girl Who Sells the Tickets At the Pearly Gates Theater; all the songs from the NBC nighttime special "Howdy Doody and Friends."

SUSA, CONRAD   ASCAP 1961
composer
b Springdale, Pa, Apr 25, 35. Educ: Springdale High Sch, grad, 53; Carnegie Inst Technol, BFA(cum laude), studied with Nickolai Lopatnikoff; Juilliard Sch, MS, studied with Vincent Persichetti, William Bergsma. Staff pianist, Pittsburgh Symph Orch, 58. Comp-in-residence, Nat Shakespeare Fest, San Diego, 59- Cond, Nashville Symph Orch & San Diego Symph Orch, 61. Music dir, Asn Producing Artists, 61-68 & Am Shakespeare Fest, Stratford, Conn, 69-71. Field dir, Lincoln Ctr Dept Educ, 67-71. Recipient, var prizes & awards incl Ford Found fels & NEA grants. Chief Collabr: Richard Street. *Songs & Instrumental Works:* Three Mystical Carols; Hymns for the Amusement of Children; Chamber music: Six Joyce Songs; Pastorale for Strings (orch). *Scores:* Operas: Transformations; Black River.

SUSSMAN, STANLEY BARTON   ASCAP 1975
composer, conductor, pianist
b Brooklyn, NY, June 7, 38. Educ: High Sch of Music & Art, New York; Eastman Sch Music, BM & MM(comp), studied with Bernard Rogers; Tanglewood, studied with Leon Kirshner. Principle cond, Martha Graham Dance Co, 66-; music dir, Jose Limon Dance Co, 74-; comp for dance cos, 69- Guest cond, "Rudolf Nureyev and Friends." *Instrumental Works:* River Drive East (big band). *Scores:* Ballet: I Had Two Sons; Five Songs in August; Robins Dream; Film: Turning Points (documentary).

SUTER, PAUL   ASCAP 1968
composer
b Calgary, Alta, Dec 3, 30. Educ: Western Can High Sch, Calgary, Alta; Westlake Col Music, Hollywood, Calif, 3 yr cert, 58. Piano player, Calgary, 52; band leader, Cave Supper Club, Vancouver, BC, 54; piano player, Los Angeles Area, 58; instrumentalist, piano player & writer; comp for TV shows, 68; comp for Ice Capades, 74-, music supvr, 79- *Songs:* Music: Disney on Parade.

SUTHERLAND, KENNETT BRUCE   ASCAP 1972
composer, author
b New York, NY, Sept 19, 39. Educ: Hill Sch, 58; Carnegie Inst Technol, BFA, 62; Case Western Reserve Univ, MBA, 67. Rock n' Roll bands, 50's & 60's. Started writing as hobby, 70. Finalist in Am Song Fest, 74, semifinalist, 75. Writer, arr & producer, commercial sound tracks, features, TV shows & commercials. *Songs:* Mary Lee; Thanks to You; When Savannah Smiles; Another Dusty Road; Between a Rock and a Hard Place; You've Gone Too Far, You Shot JR.

SUTIN, MARCI
See Pisacane, Marci

SUTTON, DAVID C, SR   ASCAP 1975
composer, author, singer
b Stevenson, Ala, July 31, 25. Educ: Marion County Schs, South Pittsburg, Tenn; Europe, studied songwriting & singing with George Jones & Billy Williams. Gunner, USN, WW II; musician & singer, Air Force/Navy; spec services, USA, Europ occupation. Engr, Luria Eng, Bethlehem, Pa; club singer, South East, Midwest & West Coast; treasure hunter & trapper; author; songwriter; also writer of treasure stories. Chief Collabrs: Johnny Pounds, Milton Rose, Joe Sutton, Billy Williams, Darlene Keimach, Donna Wing, Rose Covington, Raymond Doki, George Jones. *Songs:* Freedom Bells; Battle of Lexington; I Write You This Song; Nashville Here I Come; E S P; I Don't Love You (But I Want To); Dream My Treasure Hunter; Love Song; The Fool Inside of Me; This World.

SUTTON, SONDRA K   ASCAP 1973
composer, author, singer
b St Louis, Mo, Sept 29, 42. Educ: Fox High Sch. Started singing in Fathers Church Choir; sang in many groups in high sch, incl Metrop Singers. Then local bands, St Louis area, for several years. Recorded on the Prof Artist Label, St Louis. Singer with group, Stardom, St Louis. *Songs:* Without One Word Ever Spoken; I Belong to Another; You're My Life; I Don't Like the Way I'm Livin.

SVARDA, WILLIAM ERNEST (BUDDY)   ASCAP 1973
composer, trombonist, arranger
b Middletown, Ohio, Jan 12, 41. Educ: Middletown High Sch, grad; Cons Music, Univ Cincinnati, BS(MusEd); spec comp study with T Scott Huston. Taught part time high sch, worked in nightclubs, concerts, ice shows, circuses, rodeos & one-nighters with road bands incl Buddy Morrow, Ralph Marterie, Warren Covington, 63-69. Arr for singers, bands, educ groups, stage band, marching band, concert band. Began composing for studio P/R, publ in 72. Conducted summer stock of "West Side Story", "Gypsy" & "Hello Dolly." Chief Collabr: Varale Goodman Svarda. *Instrumental Works:* Dissonants for Band (concert band); Chicago 8-5 (marching band); Piece for Six Tubas; The Stinger (marching band); Over and Over (stage band). *Scores:* Film: A Cup of Cold Water; Do You Really Love Me?; Bi-Centennial Wagon Train.

SVOBODA, TOMAS   ASCAP 1971
composer, pianist, percussionist
b Paris, France, Dec 6, 39. Educ: Cons Music, Prague, Czech, perc, comp & cond degrees, 54-62, studies with M Kabelac; Acad Music, Prague, 62-64; Univ Southern Calif, MM, 69, comp studies with Ingolf Dahl. Debut with Prague Symph, 57. Extensive perf & radio broadcasts throughout Czech. US, 64. Works performed by Cincinnati, Buffalo, Utah, San Antonio, Toronto & Ore Symph Orchs. Four ASCAP Standard Awards Panel Citations. *Instrumental Works:* Overture of the Season, Opus 89 (orch); IV Symphony (Apocalyptic), Opus 69 (orch); V Symphony (in unison), Opus 92 (orch); Sinfoniette (a la Renaissance), Opus 60 (orch); Concerto for Piano and Orchestra, Opus 71; Concertino for Violin and Orchestra, Opus 77; Nine Etudes in Fugue Style, Opus 44 (piano); Sonata for Two Pianos, Opus 55; Children's Treasure Box (Vols I, II, III, IV; piano); Pastorale for Flute Solo, Opus 78; Concertino for Oboe, Brass Choir and Timpani, Opus 46; Duo for Clarinet and Cello, Opus 50; Discernment of Time (Gong solo), Opus 74; Passacaglia for Violin, Cello and Piano, Opus 87.

SWACK, IRWIN   ASCAP 1971
composer, teacher
b West Salem, Ohio, Nov 8, 28. Educ: Cleveland Inst Music, BM; Northwestern Univ, MM; Columbia Univ, MSc & PhD; comp studies with Henry Cowell, Norman Lockwood & Vittorio Giannini. Instr, Jacksonville State Univ, Ala & La Tech Univ; adj prof, Nassau Community Col, NY. Concerts in Town Hall, Carnegie Recital Hall & Lincoln Ctr. Ford Found Award. *Instrumental Works:* Fantaisie Concertante; Dance Episodes; String Quartet No 3; Psalm No 8 (tenor, trumpet, strings); Trio (French horn, violin, piano).

SWAIN, PAUL STEVENS   ASCAP 1966
composer, arranger, saxophonist
b New Albany, Ind, Sept 24, 11. Educ: Univ Louisville, AB, studied with Karl Schmidt; studied with Wagenaar. Arr & saxophonist with big bands. Arr & comp for Kate Smith, Ray Block, Ed Sullivan, Jackie Gleason, Music Makers, Mitch Leigh. Comp of cues for Phillip Morris Playhouse.

SWAN, DON
See Schwandt, Wilbur Clyde

SWAN, EINAR AARON   ASCAP 1956
composer, author, arranger
b Fitchburg, Mass, Mar 20, 04; d Greenwood Lake, NY, Aug 8, 40. Educ: In US & Europe. Saxophonist in Vincent Lopez Orch; then arr for radio & concerts. *Songs & Instrumental Works:* When Your Lover Has Gone; A Room With a View; The Trail of Dreams; In the Middle of a Dream; Swan's Serenade; The Spirit of St Louis.

SWANSON, WYN
See Hope, Wyn Swanson

SWANSTON, EDWIN S   ASCAP 1964
composer, author, pianist
b New York, NY, Sept 20, 22. Educ: Manhattan Sch of Music; pvt music study. Pianist, organist, vocal coach & arr for Louis Armstrong, Andy Kirk, John Kirby, Lucky Millinder, Cozy Cole, Dakota Staton, Al Hibbler, Delta Rhythm Boys, Thelma Carpenter, Lucky Thompson & Billy Graham & for record cos. *Songs:* Love's Melody.

SWANSTROM, ARTHUR   ASCAP 1930
composer, author, producer
b Brooklyn, NY, Aug 4, 1888; d Scarsdale, NY, Oct 4, 40. Dancer in vaudeville & nightclubs. Chief Collabrs: A Baldwin Sloane, Louis Alter, J Fred Coots, Arthur Schwartz. *Songs:* Why?; Cross Your Fingers; It's You I Love; Rain; Twenty-Four Hours a Day; Ten o'Clock Town; As Round and Round We Go; Morning, Noon and Night. *Scores:* Bway stage: Greenwich Village Follies (19, 20 & 21); Sons o' Guns (also co-producer); Princess Charming (also co-producer).

SWARTZ, HARVIE J   ASCAP 1975
composer
b Chelsea, Mass, Dec 6, 48. Educ: Berklee Col Music, BA(music comp & accustic bass), 70; pvt study with Orrin O'Brien. Performed with Art Farmer, Yusef Lateef, Stan Getz, Gil Evens, Pat Metheny, Roland Hanna, Dexter

Gordon, Randy Brecker, Joe Farrel, Lee Konitz, Jan Hammer, Sheila Jordan. Recorded with Steve Kuhn, James Brown, Dave Mathews Big Band, Dave Friedman, Double Image, Mark Murphy, Daniel Humair, Eric Kloss, Barry Miles, Bob Degan, Bob Moses. Founder & co-leader, Double Image. Leader of own sextet. Mem of the Jay Clayton Quintet, co-leader with Kirk Nurok & Jay Clayton. Mem of the Harvie Swartz-Dave Friedman Duo Band. Touring world-wide with Steve Kuhn-Sheila Jordan Band. Pvt teacher, comp & accustic bass, 68- Substitute teacher at Manhatten Sch Music. Performed at many major jazz events incl Newport in New York, Berlin, Molde, Monterey Jazz Fests. ASCAP Award for compositions, 79, Meet the Comp Grant, 80. *Instrumental Works:* Islands; Truce; I've Touched Your Soul; Catherine; Firewalk; Dance With the Wind; Passage; Places I Have Never Been; Three Pieces; Rachael's Samba; Woven Thoughts; Ode to Cologne; Perimeters; Circle Waltz.

SWARTZ, HERBERT (HERBIE HERBERT) ASCAP 1962
composer, author
b Chicago, Ill, Aug 13, 26. Educ: Columbia Col, BS; Am Cons, studied music with Leo Sowerby. Worked in newspaper advert & promotion. Chief Collabrs: Al Trace, Lou Herscher. *Songs:* I Said She Wouldn't Do; Never Take Away My Guitar; That Great Big Friendly Town (Chicago); Happy As a Lark; Another Day, Another Heartache; Chicago, Chicago, Chicago; Warm and Tender Loving; Lady of the Rue de la Paix; Winchester; Toy Piano Rock.

SWEATMAN, WILBUR C ASCAP 1917
composer, conductor, clarinetist
b Brunswick, Mo, Feb 7, 1882; d New York, NY, Mar 9, 61. Educ: High sch. Clarinetist in circus bands; then with Mahara's Minstrels. Became vaudeville entertainer. Organized all-Negro orch, Minneapolis, 02-08. Music dir in theatres. Operated theatrical agency for musical units. Made first jazz clarinet recording. *Songs:* Down Home Rag; Old Folks Rag; The Sweat Blues; Virginia Diggins; Battleship Kate; Boogie Rag; That's Got 'Em.

SWEDIEN, BRUCE FREDERIK
composer, author
b Minneapolis, Minn, Apr 19, 34. Educ: Univ Minn, studied elec eng & music. Music recording engr; occasional comp & lyric-writing. Chief Collabrs: Dick Boyell, Quincy Jones.

SWEENEY, CHARLES F, JR ASCAP 1955
composer, author
b Philadelphia, Pa, June 21, 24. Educ: Fordham Univ; Univ Pa. News ed, radio. Pianist in nightclubs; wrote spec material. Chief Collabr: Moose Charlap. *Songs:* Here I Am in Love Again; Young Ideas; What Is the Secret of Your Success? *Scores:* TV: The King and Mrs Candle.

SWEET, DAVID KEVIN ASCAP 1977
composer, author, guitarist
b Wichita, Kans, Aug 3, 54. Educ: Guitar Inst Technol, dipl; studied guitar, theory & arr with Carl Schroeder, Les Wise & Joe DiOrio. Became guitarist at age 15, guitar instr, age 18. Commerical band work, age 19. Began comp, age 19. First publ songs & first recorded album, 77. Started own jingle co, 80. Chief Collabr: Mark Shannon. *Songs:* California Summer Nights; Have You Ever Had the Blues?.

SWEET, GWEN ASCAP 1951
author
b Staffordshire, Eng; US citizen; d. Educ: St Mary's Acad, Can; Univ Calif. Assoc with Milo Sweet Music, Calif. Chief Collabr: Milo Sweet *Songs:* Fight, Vols, Fight; Go on, Bruins; Let's Go, Trojans; Minnesota, March On; Stand Up for the Blue and Gold.

SWEET, MILO ALLISON ASCAP 1941
composer, author, publisher
b Wells, Minn, Nov 20, 1899; d. Educ: Univ Southern Calif, Col of Dentistry; McPhail Sch of Music, Minneapolis, studied voice with Harry Phillips. Toured before & after WW I with male vocal quartet. WW I, solo clarinetist, USA Band. Appeared on radio, 30-35. Had own music publ co, Calif. Chief Collabr: Gwen Sweet. *Songs:* Fight, Vols, Fight; Go on, Bruins; Men of Duke; Let's Go, Tojans; Oregon Battle Song; Fight for Texas Christian; Stand By America Now; I'm Gonna Have a Cowboy Wedding; Minnesota, March On; Stand Up for the Blue and Gold.

SWEVAL, PIETER H (PETE) ASCAP 1971
composer, author, singer
b Glen Ridge, NJ, Apr 13, 48. Educ: Cent Regional High Sch, 66; Rutgers Univ, BA(fine arts), 70; basically self-taught on bass & guitar. Organized rock group, Looking Glass, while in col; after graduation, began recording; then band dissolved in 74. Organized group, Starz, 75, recorded 3 albums on Capitol & then left group, 78. Currently with Skatt Bros. Bass & guitar player. Chief Collabrs: Michael Lee Smith, Richie Ranno, B Harkin, Sean Delaney, David Andez, Richie Fontana. *Songs:* One By One; Violation; Life At the Outpost; Midnight Companion; Music: Cherry Baby.

SWIFT, BASIL
author
b Southport, Eng. *Songs & Instrumental Works:* English texts: Liebeslieder Walzer (Brahms); Waldmärchen (Gustav Mahler); Die Zauberflöte (W A Mozart); Bastien Und Bastienne (W A Mozart); Die Jahreszeiten (Josef Haydn).

SWIFT, FREDERIC FAY ASCAP 1969
composer
b Auburn, NY, Mar 6, 07. Educ: Ithaca Col, MusB, 28; Univ Montreal, MusD, 37; Syracuse Univ, MS(educ), 38. Supvr music, Ilion Pub Schs, NY, 20 yrs; prof music & educ, chmn music dept, chmn educ dept, Hartwick Col, 48-78. Founder & camp dir, NY State Music Camp, 47- Ed, "School Music News," 30 yrs; ed & owner, "Woodwind World-Brass and Percussion," 10 yrs. Exec secy, Asn of Concert Bands of Am, Inc. Author of bks used in music teaching. Has done orch & choral arr.

SWIFT, KAY ASCAP 1931
composer, author, pianist
b New York, NY, Apr 19, 05. Educ: Juilliard Sch Music, fac scholarship; New Eng Cons; studied with Bertha Tapper, Gebhard, Arthur Johnstone & Loeffler. Accompanist to touring concert artists; staff comp, Radio City Music Hall, 2 yrs; first mag radio columnist; script writer for radio progs; chmn music, New York World's Fair, 39. Piano soloist, New York Philh, Lewisohn Stadium. Wrote songs for "Little Show" (29); "Garrick Gaieties" (30); "9:15 Revue"; also songs for film, "Never a Dull Moment"; adapted Gershwin music for film, "The Shocking Miss Pilgrim." Chief Collabr: James Warburg. *Songs:* Can't We Be Friends?; Calliope; Fine and Dandy; Can This Be Love?; Up Among the Chimney Pots; Forever and a Day; A Moonlight Memory; Once You Find Your Guy; I Gotta Take Off My Hat to You; In-Between-Age. *Instrumental Works:* Alma Mater (ballet); One Little Girl (Campfire Girls' 50th Anniversary show); Century 21 (Seattle World's Fair, 62). *Scores:* Bway stage: Fine and Dandy; Paris '90.

SWIFT, RICHARD ASCAP 1967
composer, author, teacher
b Middlepoint, Ohio, Sept 24, 27. Educ: Univ Chicago, MA, 56, studies with Leonard Meyer & Leland Smith; Princeton Univ, Inst Advan Musical Studies fel, 59, 60. Prof music, Univ Calif, Davis, 56-, chmn dept, 63-71; visiting prof, Princeton Univ, 77. Awards: Louisville Orch Young Composers Award, Ford Found, Nat Endowment for the Arts, Am Inst-Acad Arts & Letters & Composers String Quartet Award. *Instrumental Works:* Concerto for Piano and Chamber Ensemble; Summer Notes; Great Praises; String Quartet IV; Stravaganza IX.

SWILLING, DAPHNE ANNETTE ASCAP 1979
composer
b Greenville, SC, Feb 14, 53. Educ: Lee Col, Cleveland, Tenn. Singer for TV; recording artist, House Top Records, Christian Broadcasting Network. *Songs:* Lord, Are You Listening to Me.

SWINDELL, ARCHIE ASCAP 1977
composer, author, singer
b Laurinburg, NC, Sept 13, 31. Studied playing & singing, 39. Began singing, writing & recording own songs. Records on Neon Label. Chief Collabrs: Fred E Sollie, Monte Paul, Don Loving, Orrick A Loacher, Otto Lee January, Nancy Fisher, Jessie Burch, Donald Thompson, Noble D Wilhoite. *Songs:* Gospel: He's Great, He's Almighty, He's My King; When I Think About King Jesus; Contract With the Lord; I'm So Glad Jesus Loves Me; Until I Get Home; I'm Going Home; If God Is for You; Day By Day; God's Greatest Gift; These Are the Last Days; He's My Everything; Are You Walking on Dangerous Ground; Without Faith.

SYBIL, AILENE
See Goodman, Ailene Sybil

SYBIL, FERN
See Keiner, Fern Sybil

SYDEMAN, WILLIAM J ASCAP 1975
composer
b New York, NY, May 8, 28. Educ: Mannes Col Music, BM(comp); Univ Hartford, MM(comp). Comp many chamber & orch works comn & perf for/by groups in the New York area. Awards from Pacifica Found, Nat Inst Arts & Lett, Libr Cong (Koussevitzky Found) & Boston Symph Merit Award. *Instrumental Works:* In Memoriam John F Kennedy (for narrator & orch); Study for Orchestra No II; Study for Orchestra No III; Music for Flute, Viola, Guitar Percussion; Concerto Da Camera No I; Concerto Da Camera No II.

SYLVERN, HENRY ASCAP 1954
composer, conductor, pianist
b Brooklyn, NY, Mar 26, 08; d New York, NY, July 4, 64. Assoc with "DuPont Show of the Week," Arthur Godfrey's radio prog; TV music dir, "Suspense", "This is Show Business", "The Jane Frohman Show", "Man Against Crime" & others. Also wrote musical commercials, notably the Pepsi Cola jingle, "Be

Sociable." Comp, orchestrated & cond the music for the TV series, "Decision," about Harry S Truman, 64.

SYLVERS, EDMUND THEODORE   ASCAP 1973
singer, writer
b Memphis, Tenn, Jan 25, 57. Educ: Collen McCuwin Pvt Sch. Singer, performing in concert halls, US & Las Vegas nightclubs. TV appearances incl "Mike Douglas Show", "Merv Griffin Show", "Dinah Shore Show", "American Bandstand", "Soul Train", "Mac Davis Show", "Dick Van Dyke Show", "Rich Little Show", "Sonny and Cher Show", "Donny and Marie" & others. Solo artist & writer, Casablanca Records. Chief Collabrs: Edmund Sylvers, Leon Sylvers, James Sylvers, Rick Sylvers. *Songs:* Anyway You Want Me; Forever Yours; Don't Stop Get Off; High School Dance; Play This One Last Record.

SYLVESTER, ERICH
See Zwertschek, Erich Sylvester

SYMES, MARTY   ASCAP 1933
author
b Brooklyn, NY, Apr 30, 04; d Forest Hills, NY, June 19, 53. Educ: Erasmus High Sch. Chief Collabrs: Joe Burke, Isham Jones, Jerry Livingston. *Songs:* Under a Blanket of Blue; Darkness on the Delta; It's the Talk of the Town; I've Got an Invitation to the Dance; How Many Hearts Have You Broken?; By the River of the Roses; There Is No Greater Love; It's All So New to Me.

SYMINGTON, JAMES WADSWORTH   ASCAP 1961
composer, author, singer
b Rochester, NY, Sept 28, 27. Son of Sen Stuart Symington & singer Eve Symington. Educ: Deerfield Acad; Yale Univ; Columbia Law Sch, LLB. Folk singer, hotels & TV, 52-53; in USSR, 58. Spec asst to John Hay Whitney, US Ambassador to Gt Brit, 58-60. Deputy dir, Food for Peace, 61; admin asst to Atty Gen Robert Kennedy, 62-64; exec dir, President's Comn on Juvenile Delinquency & Youth Crime, 65-66. US Chief of Protocol, 66-68. *Songs:* One Too Many Times; Christmas Wish; A Child Can Grow; 13 Stripes and 50 Stars; Star-Filled Night. *Albums:* An Evening on Buford Mountain.

SYMON, REA JANET (REA HAYES)   ASCAP 1953
composer, author
b New York, NY. Educ: Pub sch; Lincoln High Sch, Nebr; Lincoln Bus Col. Secy, Mary Margaret McBride, Lincoln Bus Col. Chief Collabrs: Billy Hayes, Guy Campbell, Shorty Cook, Zeb Carver. *Songs:* You Never Know When You'll Need a Friend; Do I Make Myself Clear?; The Santa Claus Thing; The Pied Piper Polka (story); A Little Smile Will Bring a Lot of Sunshine.

SYRCHER, MADELEINE B   ASCAP 1964
composer, author, singer
b Portsmouth, Ohio, May 4, 1896; d Miami, Fla, Mar 21, 73. Educ: Cons; also pvt study. *Songs:* Hold Me Close; Come to Me, My Love; I Believe You; I'm Glad God Gave Me You.

SZABO, ALBERT EDWARD (BURT)   ASCAP 1978
composer, teacher, arranger
b Wellington, Ohio, Dec 28, 31. Educ: Ohio State Univ, BMus; Mich State Univ, MMus & PhD; comp studies with H Owen Reed & Mario Castelnuovo-Tedesco. Teaching & composing, Kalamazoo, Mich, Edinboro, Pa & Orlando, Fla. Prof music, Univ Cent Fla, Orlando. *Songs:* Music: Spring (2 sopranos & instrumental ens); 8 Songs on Chinese Texts (soprano solo, flute & piano). *Instrumental Works:* Diversions of Ares (symph orch); Soundscapes (symph orch).

SZAJNER, ROBERT MARTIN   ASCAP 1978
composer, pianist
b Detroit, Mich, Sept 12, 38. Educ: Chadsey High Sch; Univ Mich. Nightclub performer, Novus Jazz Soc. Recording artist, The Bob Szajner Triad, Seeds & Stems Records. Chief Collabr: Laura Holiday. *Instrumental Works:* Jazz Opus 20/40; Sound Ideas; Afterthoughts; Meeting Competition; Come Back Little Thyroid Gland; September Sunday; Black Monk; The Parson; At My Leisure; Five Flats Up; Side Street; No Bridge in Sight; Strange Change; That's Pretty; Sandbags on Rye; Flying Horace; What's the Matter; Ralph's Groove; Murphy's Law; Reminiscence; Blues in E Sharp; Extra Light; The Goose; 136.5; Mere Formality; 17 Mile Drive; Roger and Out; Anticipation/Apprehension; Royal Outhouse Blues.

SZARVAS, LESLIE L   ASCAP 1969
composer, author
b Pittsburgh, Pa, Apr 25, 30. Educ: Wayne State Univ, Pierce Col. Freelance writer, puppet shows for Krofft, amusement park rides, commercials; spec material writer. *Songs:* London Bridge Is Going Up. *Scores:* Film/TV: Pufnstuf; Lidsville; Sinderella and the Golden Bra. *Albums:* Didja Come to Play Cards or to Talk?

SZIGETY, PAUL   ASCAP 1966
composer
b Budapest, Hungary, May 5, 19. Educ: High sch & cons in Budapest.

Bandleader; musical dir; cond for shows; wrote background music for shows; wrote music for an Australian show at the Tropicana Hotel, Las Vegas.

T

TABACH, BRIAN HENRY   ASCAP 1973
composer, singer, teacher
b Los Angeles, Calif, July 17, 43. Educ: Roosevelt High Sch, Des Moines, Iowa; Univ Iowa, BS(psychol), 66. Singer, nightclubs, concerts & TV. Recording artist, Bell Records. Teacher songwriting workshops, Drake Univ & Adult Educ Prog, Des Moines Sch Syst. Chief Collabrs: Byron Walls, Stephen Dorff. *Songs:* Lovin' Naturally (Eucalyptus-Sassafrass Tea); Elevator Operator; Helpless in Love; Music Machine; Intoxicating Lady; Summertime Sunshine; Just to Be With You Again; The Sideman.

TACONIS, ATZE   ASCAP 1962
composer, author, pianist
b Holland, June 7, 00. Educ: High sch; Merchant Marine Sch. To US, 22. Pianist, radio shows. To Hollywood, 34; writer, films, radio & records.

TAFT, VINCENT   ASCAP 1973
composer, author, producer
b Syracuse, NY, Mar 6, 46. Educ: Syracuse Univ, AB & MS; Erevan State Univ, USSR. Free lance composer & author, 70-75; with own publ & production companies, 75- Chief Collabrs: Dave Appell, Hank Medress. *Songs:* Fancy Meeting You Here Baby; Lyrics: Joygirl.

TAGGART, BARBARA BUDLONG   ASCAP 1975
composer, author, dance instructor
b Rockford, Ill. Educ: Nat Cathedral Sch, DC; Wellesley Col, 2 yrs; Beloit Col, Wis, BA; courses in counterpoint, comp. Mem, Sigma Alpha Iota. Played in dance bands; had own all-girl band during WW II & after. Played calliope, recorded & composed music for calliope & circus bands. Taught dancing & toured US performing authentic Span & Mex dances for sch assembly progs from Utah through the midwest to Long Island. Composed music for shows touring the country, also for circuses & dance bands. Dir, choreographer & accompanist, Fiesta Dancers. Chief Collabr: Ernie Erdman. *Songs:* Rockford, You're Calling Me (off song of Rockford); I'll Hold You in My Dreams. *Instrumental Works:* Sunny Skies; Clowning; Spangleland; Pan American Fantasy.

TAGGART, WILLIAM   ASCAP 1960
composer, author, pianist
b White Plains, NY, Nov 4, 26. Educ: Westchester Cons. Pianist & choral dir, radio progs. Fac, Westchester Cons, 51-53; Iona Col, 54-56; Iona Prep & Grammar Sch. Writer, musical commercials. *Songs:* Draw Me a Sketch of the Autumn; God Bless Mommie.

TAIANI, HUGO EDWARD   ASCAP 1948
composer, author
b Boston, Mass, July 19, 12. Educ: New Utretch High Sch, Brooklyn, NY; studied orchestration & theory with Tibor Serly. Played saxophone with radio sta orchs. Orchestrated & supplied material for "The Breakfast Club" prog. Serviced & worked in the arr depts music publ, TV stas, recording cos, ad agencys, etc. Chief Collabrs: Sylvia Dee, Marty Gold, Sid Ramin, Buddy Kaye, Herb Leventhal. *Songs:* Tender Words; If We Believe; Music: The Things You Left in My Heart; The Tennessee Rock and Roll; The Bright Red Convertible. *Instrumental Works:* Skeedaddlin'; Doggone; Good Morning America; Sambani.

TALBERT, FRED DOUGLAS   ASCAP 1966
composer, pianist, director
b Roanoke, Va, Dec 16, 26. Educ: Jefferson High Sch, Roanoke; studied piano & accordion, 37-41. Pianist with orchs, Charlie Spivak, Neal Hefti, Tommy Dorsey & Dorsey Bros, 49-53; pianist-cond-arr with singer Jack Jones & coordinated & recorded 19 albums, 63-69; pianist-coordr with var TV variety series, 69-75; music dir, pianist arr with var stars of TV & movie screen, 69- Chief Collabrs: Paul Francis Webster, Sammy Cahn. *Songs:* Music: The Snows of Yesteryear; Long Ago, Last Night; Include Me Out.

TALBERT, HOMER ALEXANDER, JR   ASCAP 1971
composer, author, teacher
b Chicago, Ill, Aug 8, 48. Educ: Carver High Sch & Parker High Sch, Chicago; Wilson Jr Col; Teachers Col; Los Angeles City Col, AA; studied piano with Marion Harris. Songwriter, 69- Played piano with Led Feather II Band, 75-77. Record producer, 76- Singer & actor. Chief Collabrs: Hersholt Polk, Patricia Henley Talbert. *Songs:* Ain't Understanding Mellow; I Wanna Do It to You; I'm Music, I'm Your Friend; Suite for Single Girl; What a Pleasant Surprize. *Albums:* Where There Is Smoke.

TALBERT, PATRICIA (HENLEY)   ASCAP 1971
composer, singer
b Chicago, Ill, Mar 26, 48. Educ: Parker High Sch, Chicago; studied with Robert Wooten; voice, piano, drama with Gufaston. Singer in concerts around US, 68; toured with Piperettes of Freedom Group; songwriter, 70-; with Los Angeles Civic Light Opera, 73; sang with backup band, 74; sang with group Quiet Storm, 78. Chief Collabr: Homer Talbert. *Songs:* Where to Now?; I Want to Do It to You; And You've Got Me.

TALBERT, TED
See Milkey, Edward T

TALBOT, PETER HENRY   ASCAP 1977
author
b Spokane Falls, Wash, July 24, 48. Educ: Ketteringham Hall Prep Sch, Eng; City of Norwich Sch, Eng; Lewis & Clark High Sch, Spokane; Eastern Wash State Col. Radio retail & promotion, 12 yrs; also ed publ, short story writing, selling insurance, landscape gardening, entrepreneurial activities. Lyric writer. Chief Collabrs: Neil Peart, Albert Lyon, Ken Kinyon. *Songs:* Lyrics: Closer to the Heart; Florida Queen; Alchemy of Words; Odds and Ends; Sure Ain't Love, Babe.

TALENT, LEO ROBERT (JACK WINTERS)   ASCAP 1950
author
b Hartford, Conn, June 19, 06. Educ: Manchester High Sch, NH; violin studies with Eugene Gruenberg; NE Cons; Tufts Col; Middlesex Sch Med. Violinist orch, Boston; from NE rep to professional mgr, Robbins Music Corp; with Glenn Miller; mgr & co-owner, Mutual Music Soc Inc, 41-50; formed, Leo Talent Inc; joined Jackie Gleason, 53; gen mgr, Songsmiths, Inc; music coordr, Jackie Gleason, 53-77. Chief Collabrs: J Fred Coots, Willard Robison. *Songs:* Lyrics: Me and My Teddy Bear; Little Sally One Shoe; Little Johnny Chickadee; Walter Walter Wallflower; Tweedle Dee the Clown; Everybody Needs a Helping Hand.

TALISMAN, DAVID MICHAEL   ASCAP 1974
composer, singer, screenwriter
b Newark, NJ, Nov 24, 44. Educ: Peirce Jr Col, Pa; Upsala Col, NJ; Rutgers Univ. Started as a studio musician/singer; songwriter, Walt Disney, MGM Records, plus others. Writing credits incl, "The Wonderful World of Disney", "The Jeffersons" & "Hanging on a Star." Produced & composed commercials. Chief Collabrs: Tedd Anasti, Peter Martin, Brian Griffin, Ted Neeley. *Songs:* Friends; Baby Hang Your Love On Me; What Do You Wanna Be; Lady My Love; Sonchild; Go Where the Wind Blows; Lyrics: Ballad of the Peanut Butter Kid. *Instrumental Works:* Shoptalk.

TALLEY, FRANK
See Damico, Frank James

TALMA, LOUISE   ASCAP 1962
composer, author, pianist
b Arcachon, France, Oct 31, 06. Educ: Wadleigh High Sch; Inst Musical Art, 22-30; Fontainebleau Sch Music, 26-39, piano studies with Isidore Philipp & comp with Nadia Boulanger; NY Univ, BMus, 31; Columbia Univ, MA, 33. Taught at Hunter Col, 28-79. Guggenheim Fels, 46-47. Sr Fulbright Res grantee, Am Acad Rome, 55-56; NEA grants, 66 & 75. Mem, Am Acad-Inst Arts & Letters, 74. *Songs:* Music: Terre de France (song cycle). *Instrumental Works:* Piano Sonatas No 1 & 2; Six Etudes for Piano; Sonata for Violin and Piano; Soundshots (20 pieces for piano); Let's Touch the Sky (chorus); Three Duologues for Clarinet and Piano; The Tolling Bell (baritone & orch); Dialogues for Piano and Orchestra. *Scores:* The Alcestiad (opera in 3 acts).

TANEGA, NORMA CECILIA   ASCAP 1966
composer, singer
b Vallejo, Calif, Jan 30, 39. Educ: Scripps Col, Calif, BA; Claremont Grad Sch, Calif, MFA. Recording artist, composer & singer, New York, 62-67; Gene Pitney tour, 66; singer, songwriter & recording artist, London, Eng, 67-72. Chief Collabr: Tom Springfield. *Songs:* Walkin' My Cat Named Dog; I'm the Sky; A Street that Rhymes at 6 AM; Magic Day; Lyrics: Sing Me Sunshine.

TANG, JORDAN CHO-TUNG   ASCAP 1974
composer, conductor
b Hong Kong, China, Jan 27, 48. Educ: Chinese Univ, Hong Kong, BA, 69, studies with K Tuukkanen; Wittenberg Univ, MSM, 71, studies with J Bender & H W Zimmermann; Cleveland Inst Music, MM, 73, studies with M Dick; Univ Utah, PhD, 79, studies with R Cortes, V Ussachevsky & J Rosenstock. Asst cond, Univ Utah Symph, 73-76; assoc cond, Utah Youth Symph, 73-78; music dir, Univ Utah New Music Ens, 76-78 & Southwest Mo State Univ, 78- Fels, MacDowell Colony, Yaddo & Norlin; comns from Springfield Symph, Mo & Utah Symph; perf by Utah Symph. *Instrumental Works:* Timpani Concerto; Psalm of Praise; Little Suite for Woodwind Quartet; Symphony No 2; Refrains; Elegy; Peach Blossom Fountain; Concertino for Violin; piece for violoncello & harp; three Chinese melodies.

TANI, AL
See Mirikitani, Alan Masao

TANNER, JERRE EUGENE   ASCAP 1969
composer
b Lock Haven, Pa, Jan 5, 39. Educ: Univ Iowa, BA, 60; San Francisco State Univ, MA, 70, studied with Roger Nixon. Teacher, Univ Hawaii, Hilo & Univ Hawaii Ctr Continuing Educ & Community Serv; arts coordr, State Found Culture & Arts, Hawaii. Huntington Hartford Found grant; Celia S Buck Award; State Found Culture & Arts grants (3); Hawaii & Nat Bicentennial Comt grants; opera production grants, Nat Endowment for the Arts, Atherton Trust, Castle & Cooke Found & Hawaii Newspaper Asn; Hawaii Ninth Legislature Senate Commendation. Chief Collabrs: Harvey Hess, Leon Siu, Malia Elliott, Phillip Appleman, Kalani Meinecke.

TANNER, MARC LEE   ASCAP 1977
composer, author, singer
b Hollywood, Calif, Aug 20, 52. Educ: Bath Univ London, history maj. Performer in many cover bands & others; recording artist, 77- Chief Collabrs: Nat Jeffray, Ron Edwards, Joe Romersa. *Songs:* Elena; Never Again; She's So High; Getaway; Hot and Cold. *Albums:* No Escape; Temptation.

TANNER, PAUL O W   ASCAP 1962
composer, author, trombonist
b Ky, Oct 15, 17. Educ: Univ Calif, Los Angeles, BA, MA; pvt music study. Served, World War II. Charter mem, Glenn Miller Orch; trombonist, Les Brown & Tex Beneke Orchs. First trombonist, ABC staff, Calif, 51- Taught, Univ Hawaii; fac, music dept, Univ Calif, Los Angeles; asst prof, music dept, San Fernando State Col. Brass clinician, Selmer-Bach-Bundy Instrument Co. Solo trombonist, Europ concert tour, 62. Author, "Practice With the Experts"; co-author, "A Study in Jazz" & "A Study of the Bass Trombone."

TARNER, EVELYN FERN   ASCAP 1971
composer
b Reading, Pa, Sept 3, 12. Educ: Reading High Sch; Kutztown State Teachers Col, BS; Univ Extension Cons, Chicago, harmony cert. Elem teacher, Reading Sch Dist, fifth & sixth grade music. Chief Collabrs: Georgia B Adams, Cordelia Spitzer, Ruth Gibbs Zwall. *Songs & Instrumental Works:* Wedding Prayer; The Steps of a Good Man; Bless the Lord, O My Soul; I Know God Is Love; Music: Show Me a Window; Psalm One Hundred; The Savior Has Come (cantata); The Risen Lord (cantata); Walk With the Years; Dear Little Jesus; God's Little Lamb; The Followers of Jesus.

TARNER, STANLEY PHILIP   ASCAP 1967
composer
b Piraeus, Greece, Mar 10, 23. Educ: East Pittsburgh High Sch; Juilliard, 46-47; Brooklyn Cons Music, 47-48. Freelance musician, arr & comp, 46-55. Producer & dir, ABC, 55-62. Music & film producer commercials with Ted Bates, 62-63 & J W Thompson, 63-79. *Songs:* Music: Is There Anyone Here Who Knows Me; Quiet Love; Warm of Him; Jingles: This is the L&M Moment; Only Mustang Makes It Happen (Ford); The Going Thing (Ford); Let the Good Times Roll (Planter's Nuts); also theme for World of Survival TV Special, "Follow Me."

TARPLIN, MARVIN   ASCAP 1971
composer
b Atlanta, Ga, June 13, 41. Educ: Community Music Sch, Detroit; basically self-taught. Started career with group, Primettes, later, Supreme's. Joined Smokey Robinson and The Miracles, 52-72. Active with Smokey in his solo career & group, Quiet Storm. Chief Collabrs: William Smokey Robinson, Bobby Rogers, Warren Moore, Ronnie White, Al Cleveland, Lanie Bradford Hobbs, Pam Moffett, Donald Whited. *Songs:* Music: Ain't That Peculiar; Baby Come Close; Going to a Go Go Cruisin'; I Like It Like That; I'll Be Doggone; The Love I Saw Was Just a Mirage; My Girl Has Gone; The Tracks of My Tears; Just Soul Responding; Just Passing Through; Wine, Woman and Song; Take This Heart of Mine; Dancing Alright; Fulfill Your Need; Doggone Right; Asleep on My Love; It's Her Turn to Live; Madam X; Open; One More Heartache; Point It Out; Precious Little Things; You're Not An Ordinary Girl.

TARR, FLORENCE   ASCAP 1943
author, monologist
b New York, NY, Mar 14, 07; d New York, May 23, 51. Educ: Columbia Univ; City Col New York; studied piano with Gustave Becker. Perf monologues, wrote lyrics to music by Fay Foster. *Songs:* My Journey's End; God Is Ever Beside Me; I Want an Old-Fashioned Christmas; God Painted a Picture; We Are All His Children; Smoky River; Petroushka From Baroushka; The Place Where I Worship: Margaret O'Brien's Favorite Songs & Stories. *Instrumental Works:* Cantatas: O Wondrous Star; The World of Tomorrow.

TARTAGLIA, JOHN ANDREW   ASCAP 1969
composer, author
b Seattle, Wash, Mar 14, 44. Educ: Los Angeles City Col; Univ Southern Calif. Recording artist for Capitol Records; comp, arr & cond TV movies & series, "Sword of Justice", "McCloud", "Barbary Coast", "Powder Keg", "BJ & the Bear", "Bold Ones" & "Alias Smith & Jones." Composer music for

commercials. Chief Collabr: Sue Collins. *Songs:* It's Love, Love, Love (Grammy nominee); Where Is Someone to Love Me?; Love You and Me; Castles in the Air; Being Me.

TARTO, JOE
See Tortoriello, Vincent Joseph

TARVER, JAMES L   ASCAP 1950
composer, conductor, trumpeter
b Del Rio, Tex, Mar 15, 16. Educ: Sul Ross State Teachers Col, BS; Tex Technol Col; Southwestern Cons; pvt study. Trumpeter, dance orchs, symph orch, mil & civic bands. Former dir of bands, Tex pub schs, incl El Paso; arr. Lt Col, ROTC. *Songs & Instrumental Works:* El Charro; La Donna; El Conquistadore; Two Themes for Band; Palace Guards; Phantom Lake; Purple Horizons; Swing Fanfares for Trumpet and Trombone; Grand Piano Skit; Plantation Memories; Old Woman in the Shoe.

TARZIA, PETER   ASCAP 1961
composer, teacher, singer
b Brooklyn, NY, Aug 26, 08. Educ: Had pvt tutor in gen educ & music. Singer, radio, Italian Broadcasting Co; singer, San Francisco Opera chorus under Gaetano Merola, theatre & nightclubs in Calif & Nev. Played guitar, mandolin & balalaika on radio, theatre, nightclubs & San Francisco TV. Teacher, San Francisco Peninsula Cons Music; also pvt guitar & mandolin teacher, 35- Chief Collabr: Lyricist Eileen Erbe. *Songs:* Questa-Sera T'Aspetter'o; Oh Say Yes; Music: Denise (Marvka); Napoli; Autumn's Here Again; Candlelight Waltz. *Instrumental Works:* Tzigana (Fantaisie Slave); Tango dei baci; Una notte a Parigi; Palpito Dell'estasi.

TATGENHORST, JOHN J   ASCAP 1968
composer
b East Liverpool, Ohio, Aug 22, 38. Educ: East Liverpool High Sch; Ohio State Univ BSc, 61; studied arr & comp with Billy May, 68-71. Arr-comp, Ohio State Univ & Pa State Univ, 64-, Hansen Publ, 71-73, Warner Bros Music, 74- & Columbia Pictures Industs, 75- Founder & pres film & commercial music co, John Tatgenhorst Productions. Partner ASCAP publ co, Beckenhorst Press; owner, Cara Publ. Arr or comp many publ works for concert band, marching band, stage band & orch. Co-author: "The Percussion" (col text bk). Chief Collabr: Maynard Ferguson (jazz). *Instrumental Works:* Somerset; A Little March; A Melody for Margo; Colonial Sam; Coventry; The Pecos; Montage; Tanglewood; Clarion Textures; Acadia; Portrait for Clarinet; Greasy Kids Stuff; American Flyer; Canterbury Suite; The Triumph of Man; Concerto for People; Cambridge; The Cool Dude; Wind Song.

TAU'A, MERRIWELL KELI'I   ASCAP 1977
composer, author, singer
b Kula, Hawaii, July 27, 42. Educ: Brigham Young Univ; Univ Hawaii. Played with several music groups, Hawaii; specialized in writing songs with Hawaiian lyrics & chants. Wrote over 400 songs, 70 recorded. Chief Collabrs: Marcus Sciautte, John Spencer. *Albums:* Hokule'a; Captain Cook: A Bicentennial Tribute; Pele Chants.

TAUBER, DORIS   ASCAP 1943
composer, pianist, singer
b New York, NY, Sept 13, 08. Educ: Elem & high schs, New York. Started musical educ at early age; studied with Prof David Kalish with appearances at Town Hall; joined staff of popular music publ firm. Musical secy to Irving Berlin, 13 yrs. Singer on own radio prog; accompanist & vocal arr to stars on radio, stage & TV. Writer scores for night club revues & musicals. Chief Collabrs: Johnny Mercer, Mitchell Parish, Charles Tobias, Maceo Pinkard, Jack Laurence, Al Stillman, Mann Curtis. *Songs:* Music: Them There Eyes; Drinking Again; Fooled; Who's Afraid; I Was Made to Love You; Why Remind Me; Living Dangerously; Compromise; I Don't Get It; Spinner.

TAUBMAN, PAUL   ASCAP 1952
composer, conductor, arranger
b Winnipeg, Man, May 10, 11. Owner, Penthouse Club, New York; with own All Am Big Brass Band for US State Dept toured 18 countries, 65; recording artist. *Songs & Instrumental Works:* Concerto for Toy Piano; Bomber Command; In the First Place; The Colonel Glenn March.

TAUTENHAHN, GUNTHER   ASCAP 1969
composer
b Kovno, Lithuania, Dec 22, 38. Educ: W H Taft High Sch; pvt study with Leon Kirchner & Edward Applebaum. Author of articles for var magazines. Appt to Cultural Arts Comt, Manhattan Beach, Calif, 80. Has comp music for large orchs, solos & chamber ens. *Instrumental Works:* Symphonic Sounds No 1; Pyramid Four (orch); Tri-Lude (piano); Caprice Elegant (flute & accordion, J Nightingale comn, 79); Suite (solo double bass, B Turetsky comn); Numeric Serenade (piano & orch); Brass Quintet; Concerto (double bass & chamber orch); Dawn Dance (saxophone); Options (flute & double bass); Tone Blocks (clarinet & piano); Elegy (alto saxophone & harp); Double Concerto (horn & trumpet); Quartet (piccolo, 2 flutes, alto flute); The Last Farewell (horn solo); Quintet (clarinet & strings, Young Comp Award, 63); Two October Songs (trumpet & marimba, Int Trumpet Guild comn, 76).

TAYLOR, BERNIE
See Fass, Bernie

TAYLOR, CATHERINE ANNE   ASCAP 1961
composer, author, singer
b Winnipeg, Man, July 26, 44. Educ: Hollywood Prof Sch; Oral Roberts Univ. Singer, 25 yrs. Regular appearances on Christian Broadcast Network, "700 Club." Writer, gospel & children's songs. Named Top Female Vocalist of the Year, Acad Country & Western Music, 68-69. Chief Collabrs: Bill Brock, Stephanie Boosahda. *Songs:* Spread the Name of Jesus; He Is Our Hiding Place; Oh What a Day; Revelation III; You're an Inspiration; At the Feet of Jesus; Oh How I Need You Jesus; Jesus Worked a Miracle; Lyrics: Do It Lord; Child of Mine; All I Really Want to Do Is Love Him More; Gone Fishin'.

TAYLOR, CHARLES RUSSELL SACKETT   ASCAP 1962
composer, author
b Atlantic City, NJ, Jan 12, 15; d Absecon, NJ, July 25, 79. Educ: Studied with Paul Zierold, 30's. Played, famous nightclubs & hotels with trios & solo, also on radio during 30's & 40's. Taught piano & organ. Arr, writer & comp, Robbins Music & Warner Bros. Gave concerts. Chief Collabrs: Joe Beal, Betty Maier, Wayne Sheridan. *Songs:* I Knew You When; Music: Light the Candles (on the Christmas Tree); Winter Champagne; The Lonesome Christmas Tree; Twilight By the Sea.

TAYLOR, CONRAD
See Danowski, Conrad John

TAYLOR, DANIEL DWIGHT   ASCAP 1972
composer, singer
b Bremerton, Wash, Oct 28, 44. Educ: High sch, Tucson, Ariz; Belmont Col. Started playing drums professionaly at age 14. With R&B Group; recorded for Reprise Records. Started singing contemporary Christian music, 69. Started publ co, 80. Chief Collabrs: Mike Johnson, Randy Mathews. *Songs:* Put on a Smile; Hey Man Do You Know My Lord; Pamela; Snatchin' All the Children From the Pits of Hell; Second Coming Sunset; Don't Shake My Hand; Gentile and Jew. *Albums:* Taylor Wade; Live at Carnegie Hall; Time for Love; Mathew-Taylor-Johnson; Double Live Album.

TAYLOR, DAWSON   ASCAP 1958
composer, author
b Detroit, Mich, Nov 14, 16. Educ: Detroit Univ. Lt(jg), in radar, USN, World War II. Auto dealer, Detroit, 45- Chief Collabr: John Cacavas. *Songs:* I Turn the Corner of Prayer; Stars Over My Shoulder; They Said You'd Come Back Running; Moon Struck; Nuit D'Amour; Touch O' the Moon; Moon Madness; The Other Side of the Moon.

TAYLOR, DEEMS   ASCAP 1927
composer, author, editor
b New York, NY, Dec 22, 1885; d New York, July 3, 66. Educ: NY Univ, BA; studied with Oscar Coon. Hon degrees: NY Univ, Dartmouth Col, Univ Rochester, Cincinnati Cons & Syracuse Univ, MusD; Juniata Col, LHD. Asst Sunday ed, New York Tribune, then Paris correspondent, 16-17. Assoc ed, Colliers, 17-19; music critic, New York World, 21-25; ed, Musical America, 27-29; music critic, New York American, 31-32. Music adv, CBS, 36-43; "Encyclopaedia Britannica." Author: "Of Men and Music", "The Well-Tempered Listener", "Music to My Ears", "Some Enchanted Evenings" & "Moments Mousical." Ed, rev ed, "Music Lover's Encyclopedia." Appeared in film, "Fantasia." Commentator radio progs incl, Metrop Opera House & New York Philh broadcasts. Mem: Am Acad Arts & Letters (treas); Nat Inst Arts & Letters (vpres); Am Philosophical Soc. Dir, ASCAP, 33-66, pres, 42-48. *Instrumental Works:* The Siren Song (symph poem; Nat Fedn Music Clubs prize); Fantasy on Two Themes: Through the Looking Glass (orch suite); Elegy for Orchestra; Restoration Suite: Jurgen (symph poem; comn by New York Symph); Circus Day (orch suite; comn by Paul Whiteman); Marco Takes a Walk (orch variations); Operas: The King's Henchman (comn by Metrop Opera); Peter Ibbetson (comn by Metrop Opera); Ramuntcho; The Dragon; Cantatas: The Chambered Nautilus; The Highwayman.

TAYLOR, GLENHALL TAYLOR   ASCAP 1965
composer, author
b Buffalo, NY, June 22, 03. Educ: Lick-Wilmerding Sch Indust Arts, San Francisco, Calif, art maj; pvt instr in piano, harmony & orchestration. Pianist/arr, radio, 22. Leader, first NBC dance band, Pacific Coast Network, 27; dir many radio shows incl, "Silver Theatre", "Burns & Allen" with Paul Whiteman, "California Melodies", "Adventures of Ozzie & Harriet", "Phil Baker Show", "Sherlock Homes", "Sealtest Variety Theater", "Dinah Shore's Open House" & others. Advert agency exec, Young & Rubicam, Inc, 37-46; mgr, Hollywood Office, N W Ayer & Son, Inc, 46-59. Writer for TV, radio, mag, bks, plays & other media. *Songs:* Dream of Love and You; Hawaii, My Island.

TAYLOR, HIRAM EDWIN   ASCAP 1976
author
b Mobile, Ala, Feb 29, 52. Educ: Murphy High Sch, Mobile; Syracuse Univ, BS, studied drama & psychol. Produced Off-Bway musical, "Movie Buff," New

York & "Mobile," Mobile, Ala. Dir & wrote numerous nightclub acts & club revues. Chief Collabrs: John Raniello, Myrtle Peter, Rolf Barnes.

TAYLOR, IRVING   ASCAP 1939
composer, author
b New York, NY, Apr 8, 14. Educ: NY Univ. Started as songwriter, 35. Wrote scripts for TV & radio shows. Writer for Jonathan Winters & "Colgate Comedy Hour." Wrote spec material for Jack Benny, Groucho Marx & Jimmy Durante. Wrote bk & lyrics for original TV musical "The Pied Piper of Hamelin" & "The Lord Don't Play Favorites." Producer, Warner Bros Records. Writer, dir & producer radio & TV commercials. *Songs:* Ain't Nobody's Business But My Own; Kookie, Lend Me Your Comb; Lyrics: Everybody Loves Somebody; Quick Silver; Mambo Jambo; Take It Easy; Three Little Sisters; Onezy-Twozy; Something Sentimental; Swing Mr Charlie.

TAYLOR, JAMES ALVIN   ASCAP 1976
composer, author, singer
b Asheville, NC, Aug 27, 53. Educ: Univ NC, BA(political sci), 75. In duo with Gerry Stone until 79. With Taylor & Stone Band, 79-, toured Netherlands, 80. Songwriter for Gene Kennedy Enterprises until 80. Recording artist for var cos. Chief Collabrs: Gerry Stone, John Allingham. *Songs:* This Time It's Love; Now That Sandy's Gone; Leave Me While You Still Can; Catchin the Morning Train; Fallin' Out of Love; Where Are They Now.

TAYLOR, JEFFREY AYRES   ASCAP 1979
composer
b Geneva, NY, Nov 5, 45. Educ: Morgantown High Sch, WVa; WVa Univ, BM(comp), 67, MM(theory), 68; Peabody Cons, studied film comp with Richard Rodney Bennett, 70; Cath Univ Am, studied comp with Thaddeus Jones, 75. Comp/arr, USN Band, Washington, DC, 69-75, chief arr, 77-79. Dir, USN Band Jazz Ens, 75-77 & 79- Comp, educ concert band & jazz ens works, 75- Free-lance arr, DC area.

TAYLOR, LIONEL (LES)   ASCAP 1960
composer, pianist, arranger
b Provo, Utah, Mar 23, 16. Educ: Calif Inst of Art Sch of Music, BA, MM. Bandleader, CWO, USA, World War II. Instr, Los Angeles Cons, 47-54. Arr & pianist, radio prog "Tennessee Ernie Ford Show," 54-56. With staff orch, CBS-TV, 56-59 & "Red Rowe Show," 60. Free-lance arr, pianist & comp. Part-time educr, San Fernando Valley State Col & Los Angeles City Col. Chief Collabr: Mary Taylor (wife). *Songs & Instrumental Works:* Sleep, My Little Lord Jesus (anthem); Fair Weather Love; Hollywood and Vine; Sunset Strip; Incident At the River (cantata); Adaptations: John Henry; Hosanna, We Build a House.

TAYLOR, MARION CLARISA
See Wilson, Marion T

TAYLOR, MARY VIRGINIA (SUE WOOD, JEAN   ASCAP 1959
STERLING)
author, educator
b Muskogee, Okla, Aug 7, 12. Educ: Northeastern State Col, BA. Taught, var cols; dean, Muskogee Jr High Sch. Chief Collabr: Lionel Taylor (husband). *Songs:* Deck the Hut With Coconut; Sleep My Little Lord Jesus (anthem); Fair Weather Love; Adaptations: John Henry; Hosanna, We Build a House.

TAYLOR, MAUDE CUMMINGS   ASCAP 1964
composer, teacher, organist
b Bermuda, Feb 19, 1897. Educ: Chicago Extension Univ, 25; Columbia Univ; Matlock Col Eng; Mozarteum, Salzburg; Cons Am, Fontainebleau. Mgr, MBC Music Studio. Minister music, Cornerstone Baptist Church, Brooklyn, NY, 41 yrs. *Songs & Instrumental Works:* The Day Is Nearly Done; Music: He Hath Put a New Song in My Mouth; Anthem: They Shall Run and Not Be Weary (SATB).

TAYLOR, PHILLIP HILTON   ASCAP 1971
composer, singer
b Detroit, Mich, Apr 20, 51. Educ: Univ Detroit, BS(bus admin). Singer in Detroit groups, 60's & 70's. Writer & singer, Motown, 71-74. Established own publ firm, Shomary Music, 75. Chief Collabrs: Irving Conwell Jr; E Lamont Jhonson. *Songs:* Time Don't Wait; Master Lover; Heartaches Don't Last Forever; I Never Seen a Stranger; 1999 Air for Sale; Running Through Your Life; Story of My Life.

TAYLOR, SEYMOUR (SY)   ASCAP 1953
composer, author, percussionist
b New York, NY, Nov 3, 12. Educ: Long Island Univ; NY Univ. Percussionist with local orchs. Played vaudeville, hotels, night clubs, cruise ships & radio stas; mem first all-electric orch, NBC. Principal percussionist, Nova-Tamarac Symphonic Pops Orch & Fla Pops Orch. Head musical group touring condominium circuit in SFla. Co-author libretto & lyrics musical play "Miracle of Time." Chief Collabrs: Richard Howard, Charles Reade, Chauncey Gray, Raymond Sterling, Martin F Heller. *Songs:* Spring in Napoli; Rose of the Tennessee Valley; Davie, Is More Than a Little Bit Country; Lyrics: Sweet Potato Polka; I Had Too Much to Dream, Last Night; You Take the Sunshine;

I've Got My Heart Set on You; Jack Be Nimble; Island of Palms; Colorado Columbine; I Can't Make Up My Mind; Starlight Serenade; Free and Easy.

TAYLOR, TELFORD   ASCAP 1959
composer, conductor, author
b Schenectady, NY, Feb 24, 08. Educ: Williams Col, BA, MA, LLD; Harvard Univ, LLB. Former asst to Atty Gen. Chief counsel, Nuremberg war crime trials. Tech adv & narrator, TV play "Judgment At Nuremberg." Cond, original works, Central Park Mall, New York. Practicing lawyer, New York. Author of var bks. *Instrumental Works:* Marches: Italia Eterna; Fifty Stars on a Field of Blue; Farewell to the Cavalry.

TAYLOR, WILLIAM EDWARD
composer, author, pianist
b Greenville, NC, July 24, 21. Educ: Va State Col, BS(music educ); Univ Mass, EdD; studied with Undine S Moore & Richard McClanahan. Worked with Charlie Parker, Dizzy Gillespie, Billie Holliday, Coleman Hawkins, Ben Webster, Eddie South, Don Redman & others. Radio & TV shows, WLIB & WNEW, New York. Musical dir, "David Frost Show" & "Black Journal Tonight"; contributing ed, "Sunday Show." Author articles for contemporary keyboard magazines. Chief Collabrs: Dick Dallas, Ray Rivera, Ben Tucker. *Songs:* I Wish I Knew How It Would Feel to Be Free; Make a Joyful Noise (suite in 6 parts from Psalm 97, comn Tufts Univ); I Think of You (8 voices, comn Jazz Voices, Inc). *Instrumental Works:* Suite for Jazz Piano and Orchestra (comn Utah Symph); Impromptu (jazz comp for symph orch). *Scores:* Film/TV: Letterman (theme & cues); Musical: The Lion and the Jewel; Ballet: Your Arm's Too Short to Box With God.

TAZEWELL, CHARLES   ASCAP 1957
lyricist, author
b Des Moines, Iowa, June 2, 1900; d Chesterfield, NH, June 26, 72. Educ: Des Moines High Sch, Iowa; Am Acad of Dramatic Arts, 20. Bway actor; writer. Winner Edison Award, 57. Chief Collabrs: Victor Young, Carman Dragon.

TCHEREPNIN, IVAN ALEXANDROVITCH   ASCAP 1965
composer, teacher
b Issy-les-Moulineaux, France, Feb 5, 43. Educ: Harvard Univ, BA, cum laude, 64, MA(music), 69; studied comp with Randall Thompson, Leon Kirchner, Karlheinz Stockhausen & Henri Pousseur; cond with Boulez & electronics with David Tudor. Pianist, composer & performer; conducting & electronic perf, as well as performing on Santur & Psalter. Live perf of electronic/instrumental music involving live/electronic a specialty since 66. Teacher, San Francisco Music Cons, 68 & Stanford Univ, 70; teacher & dir electronic music studios, Harvard Univ, 72-; teacher electronic music perf, Dartington, Eng, 79-80. *Instrumental Works:* Wheelwinds (nine wind instruments); Cadenzas in Transition; Summer Brass (brass sextet); Valse Eternelle (piano); Le Va et le Vient (orch).

TCIMPIDIS, GEORGE DAVID   ASCAP 1979
composer, teacher, keyboard artist
b Cincinnati, Ohio, May 21, 38. Educ: Cincinnati pub grade & high schs; Cincinnati Col/Cons Music; Mannes Col Music, New York, BMus, comp studies with Norman Dello-Jois; Queens Col, NY, MA, comp studies with Hugo Weisgall. Col level music instr, principally at Brooklyn Col & The Mannes Col Music; dean, The Mannes Col, 5 yrs. Comp performed internationally. Active as electronic music composer. Numerous off-Bway musical productions. Chief Collabr: Carol Bevan.

TEBELAK, JOHN MICHAEL   ASCAP 1971
composer, author
b Akron, Ohio, Sept 17, 48. Educ: Carnegie-Mellon Univ, BFA & MFA. Chief Collabr: Steven Swartz. *Songs:* Lyrics: Day By Day.

TEDDER, GARY E   ASCAP 1973
composer, author, singer
b Little Rock, Ark, July 25, 52. Educ: Oral Roberts Univ, BS(bus admin). Toured with Living Sound, 28 countries & World Action Singers. Chief Collabrs: Larry Dalton, Stephanie Booshada. *Songs:* Reflection; My Friend Jesus; Lord, I'm Comin' Home Today; Freedom Song; It's Who You Are.

TEDESCO, FREDRIC   ASCAP 1971
composer, teacher, accordionist
b Newark, NJ, Sept 4, 06. Educ: NY Univ, BS(music educ), 30. On radio, WOR, Newark, 32-33; WCBM, Baltimore, 38. Vaudeville, single act, New Eng & Poli Circuits. Conducted sch for accordion, 36-77. *Instrumental Works:* The Gay Matador; Spanish Saffron; Holiday in Paris; Tidewater Concertino; Nocturne.

TEDESCO, PAT LOUIS (STEVE CLAYTON)   ASCAP 1964
composer, singer
b Old Forge, Pa, Sept 8, 34. Educ: Scranton Cons Music; sight singing, Helen Hobbs Jordon, New York; voice, Miriam Spier, New York. Singer, Columbia, Decca & RCA Records, also singer on radio & TV "Mike Douglas Show", "Frank Sinatra & Kate Smith Shows" & "Saturday Night Live." Own shows on WNEW & WINS, New York for several yrs; leading night club & theatres throughout country. Singing voice on many nat radio & TV commercials. Chief

Collabrs: Gladys Shelley, Benny Davis. *Songs: Music:* All I Want; Give Love; Are You Willing to Take a Chance; My Name Is on Your Heart; Loving Without Love; Another Broken Heart.

TEE, RICHARD ASCAP 1977
composer, arranger, musician
b Brooklyn, NY, Nov 24, 43. Educ: High Sch Music & Art, New York. Mem group, Stuff; recording artist, Columbia Records; appeared in movie, "One Trick Pony." Played keyboards on recording sessions for Paul Simon, Quincy Jones, Roberta Flack, Ralph McDonald, Ashford & Simpson, George Harrison, Tom Scott, Bob James, Aretha Franklin, Bros Johnson, Chaka Khan, Andre Kostelanetz, Melissa Manchester, Barbara Streisand, Phoebe Snow, plus many others. Chief Collabrs: Bill Withers, Quincy Jones. *Songs: Music:* Stuff Like That; Love I Never Had It So Good; The Nuts Off of the Screw. *Instrumental Works:* Virginia Sunday; And Here You Are. *Albums:* Strokin; Natural Ingredients.

TEETOR, MACY O ASCAP 1953
composer, author, cornetist
b Hagerstown, Ind, Dec 31, 1898. Educ: Univ Pa, BS; Metrop Sch of Music. Cornetist, Great Lakes Navy Band, 17. Sales mgr, vpres, Perfect Circle Corp, 23-46. Chief Collab: Johnny Mercer. *Songs:* Lost; Tick Tock; I Saw You First; When You Live Down South.

TEGHZE-GERBER, MIKLOS
See Gerber, Miklos Teghze

TEICHER, LOUIS ASCAP 1956
composer, pianist, arranger
b Wilkes Barre, Pa, Aug 24, 24. Educ: Juilliard Sch Music, studied with Carl Friedberg. Teacher, Juilliard, 44-47. Mem two-piano team, Ferrante & Teicher; has given concerts throughout US & Can; also on radio & TV; recording artist. Chief Collabr: Arthur Ferrante. *Songs & Instrumental Works:* You're Too Much; What More Can I Say?; American Fantasy; Dream of Love; Possessed; A Rage to Live (film title). *Scores: Film background:* Undersea Conquest.

TEIFER, GERALD E ASCAP 1957
composer, author, publisher
b Muskegon, Mich, May 28, 22. Educ: Mich State Univ, BA. 1st Lt, Korean War. Prof mgr, April-Blackwood Publ Co. *Songs:* I Don't Care; Poco a Poco; Anniversary of Our Love; Crazy Feelin'!.

TEITELBAUM, JACK ASCAP 1960
composer, pianist
b New York, NY, Jan 4, 02; d New York, Jan 19, 64. Orch cond, vaudeville. Pianist, Jack Delaney's, New York, 33-64.

TEMKIN, HAROLD P (GARY KNIGHT, GARY WESTON) ASCAP 1967
composer, author
b Newark, NJ, June 21, 49. Educ: Piano, self-taught. Writer, Francon Music, 60 & Tash, 63. Mem staff, Saturday Music, 65, Golden Egg Music, Art Kaplan Co, 70, Legacy, 72 & Kirshner Music, 75- Chief Collabrs: Bob Crewe, L Russell Brown, Connie Francis, Irwin Levine, Gene Allan. *Songs:* Vacation; The River Is Wide; Shine on Silver Moon; Breakout; Too Many Rules.

TEMPESTO, LOUIS MICHAEL ASCAP 1963
author
b New York, NY, Mar 30, 05. Educ: Amateur Songwriter Sch Asn. Writer of articles & poems for Literary Digest; wrote short articles for New York World & New York American. Songwriter, 50-72, then retired. Chief Collabrs: Jack Covais, Buddy Bregman, Larry Allen. *Songs: Lyrics:* What Good Are My Dreams; No! He Didn't Descend From Us; Beautiful New Jersey; Abe Lincoln; Spellbound; Down By the Santa Fe Trail; Safety Song; Wishful Thinking; You Planned This Little Game; You're My Darling (Deep Blue Eyes); In Our Paradise for Two; Roll Those Blue Jeans Down; Lead Me to Your Hungry Heart; Living; Why Cry, Little Woman, Why Cry; I'm a Lucky Guy; Violins; The Same Old Things; I'll Never Stop Wishing and Dreaming; You're Something Special; This...Is It; Quaint Cafe in Montevideo; I'll Be Alone This Christmas; That Some Dear Is You; When It's Spring; We're So in Love.

TEMPLETON, ALEC ASCAP 1940
composer, pianist
b Cardiff, Wales, July 4, 10; d Greenwich, Conn, Mar 28, 63. Educ: Worcester Col; Royal Col Music; Royal Acad Music, degree of Licentiate. To US 35, Citizen 41. Gave piano recitals in England. US concert debut, Chicago, 36. Made many radio appearances & records. Concert tours of US, Can & Hawaii. Assoc, Royal Col of Music. Hon Pipe Maj, Seaforth Highlanders, Vancouver & RCAF, Toronto. Chief Collabr: Neville Fleeson. *Instrumental Works:* String Quartet No 1; Trio for Flute, Oboe, Piano; Pocket Size Sonata for Clarinet, Piano; Violin Sonata; Concerto Grosso for Symphony Orchestra, Piano; Hast Thou Not Known (a cappella anthem); Hymn for Easter (chorus, organ); 2 piano sonatas; For piano: Bach Goes to Town; Mendelssohn Mows 'Em Down.

TEMPLETON, WILLIAM B ASCAP 1956
composer, author, director
b San Francisco, Calif, June 2, 18. Educ: Col of Indust Chemistry & Eng, Manila, Philippines. Performer, as youth, announcer, vocalist, writer & dir, radio shows. Served, USN Intelligence, World War II. Dir & producer, Kudner Agency; vpres & dir radio & TV, Cunningham & Walsh, 59; prog consult, Ted Bates, 61. Associated with, Metrop Opera broadcasts, "Milton Berle Show", "Martin Kane, Private Eye" & "Mr and Mrs North." Mem, Radio & TV Exec Soc. *Songs:* America for All; Once Upon a Night in Manila; The Roosts Swing; Little Boy's Bed; Finest Boat; I Never Knew I Had a Heart; The Street of Many Eyes.

TEMPO, NINO ASCAP 1957
composer, author, singer
b Niagara Falls, NY, Jan 6, 35. Educ: Col. Singer, actor & musician in nightclubs, TV & theaters. Has made many records with sister, April Stevens. *Songs:* Teach Me Tiger; Send Someone to Love Me; Swing Me.

TENER, MARTIN JACK (JAY MARTINS) ASCAP 1958
author
b New York, NY, May 13, 35. Educ: NY Univ, BA, MA. Lyricist of Latin-Am songs. Chief Collabrs: Bobby Woodlen, Edgar Sampson. *Songs: Lyrics:* Mambo Inn; Watch Your Step; Why Not Me?.

TENNEY, JACK B ASCAP 1942
composer, author, conductor
b St Louis, Mo, Apr 1, 1898; d Glendale, Calif, Nov 4, 70. Educ: Col Law, Los Angeles Assoc Cols, LLB. Served in USAF, WW I. Pianist, organist until 35. Had own orch, 14 yrs. Mem, Calif State Assembly, 37-43, chmn, Judiciary Comt, 4 yrs; Calif State Senate, 43-55, chmn, Judiciary Comt, 7 yrs. Admitted to US Supreme Court, 47. Lawyer & Legislator. Life mem, Am Fedn Musicians. *Songs:* Mexicali Rose; Some Day I'll Learn to Forget You; Drowsy Moon; Song of the Legionnaire; On the Banks of the Old Merced; A Thousand Years From Now; Little One; Blue Sierra Hills; I Want to Wake Up in Hawaii.

TENNYSON, JAMES J ASCAP 1954
author
b Worcester, Mass, Oct 26, 1898; d. Educ: Holy Cross Col. Taught English at prep schs. Vpres & copy chief, Dancer-Fitzgerald-Sampler, Chicago; copy supvr, Ruthruff & Ryan, NY; vpres, Geyer Adv; vpres, Sullivan, Stuffer, Colwell & Bayles. Chief Collabrs: Jack Fulton, Joe Thomas. *Songs:* Are You Kissin' Someone Else?; I'm Glad I Made You Cry; Green Light; I Took My Grief to Him; Rain Is the Teardrops of Angels.

TENNYSON, WILLIAM J, JR ASCAP 1954
composer
b New Orleans, La, Jan 31, 23; d Hempstead, NY, Apr 8, 59. Educ: Southern Univ; Juilliard Sch. Writer, special material for Louis Jordan, Cab Calloway, Sarah Vaughan, Johnny Mathis. *Songs:* Someone; Salt Pork.

TEOLI, ALBERT G ASCAP 1956
composer, author, publisher
b Wilmington, Del, Feb 25, 15. Educ: High sch; studied saxophone, clarinet & flute with Mike Guerra & Vincent Caruso. Toured Europe & US with dance bands & symph orchs. Pvt teacher; musician & arr. Now writing singing commercials. Chief Collabrs: Jennie Dougherty, Arthur Weinmann. *Songs:* Time; It's So Nice to Dream; Please Handle With Care; *Music:* You Are So Beautiful; *Lyrics:* Voodoo.

TEOLI, GERTRUDE H ASCAP 1966
composer, author, teacher
b Preston, Md, Oct 19, 25. Educ: Western Md Col; Houghton Col, BA; Ohio State Univ; Univ Del, MA. Toured US with choral group; played piano & organ in churches & clubs; sang on TV, 4 yrs; played piano for radio prog; taught sch, 12 yrs; singer; now teach music privately. Chief Collabr: Ruth Sampter. *Songs: Music:* The Doll Who Walks and the Doll Who Talks; The Carol of the Clock; My Cat; I Like to Sit Beneath a Tree. *Albums:* Little Songs for Little People.

TEPPER, ALBERT ASCAP 1965
composer, teacher, conductor
b New York, NY, June 1, 21. Educ: Benjamin Franklin High Sch, New York; New Eng Cons, BMus, 47, MMus, 48; Univ Edinburgh, Fulbright grant, 50-51; Mozarteum, Salzburg, Austria, 51; Princeton Univ, Fromm Sem Advanced Musical Studies, 59. Free-lance arr, New York, 41-42 & 51-52. USN musician, 42-45. Theory instr, New Eng Cons, 47-50; instr, Hofstra Univ, 52-54, asst prof, 54-59, assoc prof, 59-68, prof, 68-, chmn, Music Dept, 54-58, 67-73 & 80- *Songs: Music:* Cantata 1969 (SATB, brass, perc); Five Songs from the Catullus of William Hull. *Instrumental Works:* Sonata for Viola and Piano; Symphony for Strings; Tent Music (suite for symph orch).

TEPPER, SAUL JOEL ASCAP 1941
composer, author
b New York, NY, Dec 25, 1899. Educ: Cooper Union; Nat Acad of Design; Art Student League; Grand Central Sch of Art; Juilliard Sch with Sydney Green. Mag illustrator; illustrated posters for War Dept, World War II. Writer, sketches

for Soc of Illustrators shows, 34-50, official Red Cross campaign song, 60-61. Recipient of awards for paintings & illustrations. *Songs:* My Concerto; Don't Cry, Cry Baby; Slumber Song; I Close My Eyes; The Guy At the End of the Bar; Along 'Bout Sundown; I'll Never Listen to My Heart Again; Good Things Happen When You Give.

TEPPER, SID ASCAP 1947
composer, author
b New York, NY, June 25, 18. Served in spec services, WW II. Staff writer, Mills Music & Hill & Range. Wrote 52 songs for Elvis Presley, incl "Blue Hawaii", "Jailhouse Rock", "King Creole" & other films. Wrote title song for film "The Young Ones," plus 20 other songs. Chief Collabr: Roy C Bennett. *Songs:* GI Blues; New Orleans; Puppet on a String; The Young Ones; When the Girl In Your Arms (Is the Girl In Your Heart); Francis the Talking Mule; Lonesome Cowboy; Travelin' Light; Red Roses for a Blue Lady (Nashville Award, 75); Don't Come Running Back to Me; The Wonderful World of the Young; Eggbert the Easter Egg; Suzy Snowflake; You're Next; Stairway of Love; Jenny Kissed Me; The Naughty Lady of Shady Lane; The Woodchuck Song; My Bonnie Lassie; Twenty Tiny Fingers; Kewpie Doll; Stop and Think It Over; Summer Sounds; Nuttin' for Christmas; Say Something Sweet to Your Sweetheart; If I Had a Girl; Teardrops in the Rain; Hawaiian Sunset; Angel; All That I Am; Take Me to the Fair; Mexico; I've Got a Crush on New York Town; Cap and Gown; Baciagaloop (Makes Love on the Stoop).

TERKER, ARTHUR ASCAP 1936
author
b New York, NY, Sept 28, 1899; d. Educ: High sch. Chief Collabr: Andy Kirk. *Songs:* There's Something Nice About Everyone; Meet Me At No Special Place; Be Good—Be Careful—Be Mine; I'll Close My Eyes to Everyone Else If You'll Open Your Heart to Me; My Favorite Initials Are USA.

TERR, MAX ASCAP 1947
composer
b Odessa, Russia, Nov 16, 1890; d Los Angeles, Calif, Aug 2, 51. US citizen. Began scoring films, 43. *Songs:* The Lord Is My Shepherd; Forever Free; Joyful Hour; Metro News (march theme).

TERR, MISCHA RICHARD (MICHAEL ASCAP 1962
TERRESCO, MANUEL FRANCISCO)
composer, author, publisher
b Odessa, Russia, Apr 1, 1899. Educ: Odessa Imperial Cons; col. Cellist with Imperial Symph, Tokyo; principal cellist var symph orchs; cond local & touring musical shows & TV shows; comp & cond background music for TV shows. Supvr, asst musical dir, Santa Monica Orch; coordr, theatrical & TV pictures; musical dir & supvr musical activities, Independent Motion Pictures Producers Asn, Los Angeles. WW II, music dir & supvr, USO unit & music dir all chapels, Santa Ana AFB. *Songs & Instrumental Works:* Films, incl: Unearthly; House of Monsters; The Attack of Giant Leeches; Red Snow; Dark Venture; Delinquents; Search; Duel in the Sun; I Was an American Spy; Death of a Scoundrel; Stampede; Tuna Clipper; Two Dollar Better; Difference; Flight of Terror; An Old Fashioned Girl; Prejudice; Yukon Manhunt; Tender Grass; Secret Files of Hollywood; World Dancers; Deadwood 76; Spies a Go-Go; Face of Terror; Arson for Hire; Make Mine Love; Phantom of the Sea; King Dinosaur.

TERRANOVA, JOSEPH A (JOE TERRY) ASCAP 1962
composer, singer
b Philadelphia, Pa, Jan 30, 41. With Danny & The Juniors, 57- Chief Collabr: Dave White. *Songs:* Penny for Your Thoughts; Mr Happyness; *Lyrics:* Back to the Hop; Do You Love Me; First Kiss to the Last.

TERRESCO, MICHAEL
See Terr, Mischa Richard

TERRI, SALLI CLEMENTINA
teacher, singer, arranger
b London, Ont. Educ: Wayne State Univ, BA; Univ Calif, Los Angeles, teaching credentials; Univ Southern Calif, MMusEd. Choral arr, singer & teacher, Univ Calif, Los Angeles, Santa Barbara & Irvine, Santa Barbara Community Col & Fullerton Col. Arr for Roger Wagner. Soloist, Roger Wagner & Chorale. Singer, Capitol & Angel Records. Mem: Am Fedn TV & Radio Artists; Screen Actors Guild; Nat Asn Teachers of Singing; John Biggs Consort. *Songs & Instrumental Works:* A Moravian Lovefeast; A Shaker Worship Service; choral arrangements.

TERRISS, DOROTHY
See Morse, Theodora

TERRY, GEORGE N ASCAP 1963
composer
b New Britain, Conn, May 30, 06. Educ: Amesbury High Sch, Mass; studied harmony, counterpoint, comp & cond with Tibor Serly. Played with dance bands. Piano & vocal arr, Famous Music Corp, 38 yrs; free lance work. *Instrumental Works:* Whoopie Stomp; Bisco; Bad Dog Charlie.

TERRY, JAMES ARLIE
composer, singer
b Salina, Kans, Apr 26, 48. Educ: Las Cruces High Sch, grad, 66; NMex State Univ, finance major. Started perc, jr high sch; formed band in high sch. Formed professional group, Creed. Joined professional show group, Country Wine, as drummer, 71; traveled & recorded with group, 4 1/2 yrs. Performer on guitar & banjo in church type settings. Singer & percussionist, nightclubs, TV, recordings. *Songs:* While the Days Are Passing By; Rodeo Girl; Before I First Met You; God Loves You; Jesus, the True Vine.

TERRY, JOE
See Terranova, Joseph A

TERRY, ROBERT ASCAP 1960
composer, author
b Brooklyn, NY, Jan 13, 28; d. Educ: Yale Univ, BA; Columbia Univ, MS; NY Univ. Producer & dir summer stock. Copywriter, advert agency, NY, 51-60. Comp, writer, radio & TV musical commercials; writer, producer records, spec material for entertainers, revues. *Songs:* Adam and Eve; Yesteryear.

TERRY, ROBERT E HUNTINGTON ASCAP 1924
composer, organist
b Hudson, NY, Mar 29, 1867; d Yonkers, NY, May 31, 53. Educ: Pub schs; studied with Philipp Scharwenka, Wenzel Rabach, Dudley Buck. Organist, St Chrysostrom Chapel, Chapel of Transfiguration, New York, Church of Redeemer, Harlem. Organist & choirmaster, St Andrew's Mem Church, Yonkers for many yrs. Mem, Am Guild Organists. *Songs:* The Answer; Song Is So Old; Autumn; Lazin' Along; Early News. *Instrumental Works:* Piano: A Bermuda Suite; Nine Musical Sketches; Phyllis; Organ: Lead on, O King Eternal.

TERRY, WILLIAM PATRICK ASCAP 1975
composer, author
b Marietta, Ga, Feb 17, 52. Formed the Pat Terry Group, 74, traveled extensively in the US performing on campuses & churches. Launched writing career during asn with Word Publ, 75. Recording artist & singer TV. *Songs:* Home Where I Belong; Happy Man; Meet Me Here; I Can't Wait; Enduring Love.

TESSIER, ALBERT DENIS (AL DE TEDLA, TESSIE R ASCAP 1965
ALDEN)
composer, author, pianist
b Las Vegas, NMex, Apr 8, 1900. Educ: Polytechnic High Sch, Los Angeles, 16-20; Fontainebleau Cons, France; Paris Nat Cons; studies with Paul Vidal, Isidor Philipp, Paul S Herard, Saint Saens, Vincent D'Indy, Louis Aubert, Charles M Widor, Egon Petri, Busoni, Kaun & Striegler. Music teacher, 13-; pvt teacher piano, theory, harmony, organ & comp. Theater organist, Calif & Paris. Teacher advan piano, organ & orch, Polytechnic High Sch, Los Angeles, 34-41; retired but active in teaching, performing & composing. Life mem, Am Fedn Musicians Local 47; mem, Mus Teachers Asn of Calif. *Songs:* Davinciana. *Instrumental Works:* Symphonic Concerto in E Flat (piano & orch); Celesta Symphony (orch, organ); Vision (orch); A mosaic orchestral arr of Chopin Fantaisie in F Minor Opus 49 with 15 themes from the works of Chopin.

TEXTOR, KEITH V
composer, author, singer
b Coon Rapids, Iowa, July 21, 21. Educ: St Olaf Col, BA & BM; studied with Tibor Serley. With group, Honey Dreamers, 46-51; with Fred Waring Orgn, 51-54. Partner, Scott-Textor Productions. Has written music for United Airlines, Chevrolet, Ford, Lincoln-Mercury, Chrysler & theme for "Candid Camera" & others. Chief Collabrs: Alan & Marilyn Scott.

TGETTIS, NICHOLAS CHRIS ASCAP 1971
composer, teacher
b Salem, Mass, Sept 1, 33. Educ: Salem High Sch, 51; New Eng Cons Music, BM(comp), 60; Boston Univ, MM(comp), 69; studied with Joseph Block, Franz Reisenstein, D Pinkham. Teacher, piano, comp & music educ in schs kindergarten through 12; free lance comp music in all forms. Chief Collabr: Steve Denson. *Songs & Instrumental Works:* Gaslight (arr & scored); Revere (arr & scored); Cape Ann Suite (string orch); Sonatina for Piano; Sonata-Old South Point; Night Freight (two pianos); Sappho (chamber opera, women's voices, 4 tableaux, orch, narrator solos, chorus, dancers); Celebration of the Eucharest (SATB).

THAMON, EUGENE
See Simpson, Eugene Thamon

THARP, WINSTON COLLINS ASCAP 1955
composer
b Little Rock, Ark, July 28, 05; d Little Rock, May 3, 61. Educ: Univ Ky. Chief Collabrs: Joe Bishop, Gene Gifford. *Songs:* Lyrics: Out of Space; Panic Is On; You've Been Taking Lessons in Love; Square Face; Old Fashioned Swing; Jes' Nat'ully Lazy; Paramour.

THATCHER, HOWARD RUTLEDGE   ASCAP 1939
composer, organist, conductor
b Baltimore, Md, Sept 17, 1878; d. Educ: Peabody Cons, scholarship. Organist & choirmaster, Eutaw Place Synagogue, Baltimore, 05-60 & First Church of Christ, Scientist, 24. Fac, Md Col for Women, 06-23 & Peabody Cons, 11-43. Dir, Meyerbeer Male Chorus, 27-29. Violist, Frank Cahn String Quartet, 32-54. Guest cond, Baltimore Symph & Peabody Cons Orch. *Instrumental Works:* Concert Overture; Legend; Symphonic Fantasy; Lyric Suite; Military Echoes; Elegy (4 cellos, orch); March of the Gargoyles and Marionettes; String Quintet; String Quartet; Piano Quartet; Suite in D (3 violins); Petite Suite (2 violins, piano; Nat Fedn Music Clubs Prize); Violin Concerto; Clarinet Concerto; Viola Concerto; Horn Concerto; Concertino for Violin, Piano; Pastorale (4 violins); Sonatina for Cello, Piano; Duo for Violins; Synagogue Service; Teaching Works: Foundation Studies in Orchestration; Teaching the Fingers to Hear. *Scores:* Opera: The Double Miracle (1-act); Operetta: The King's Jester.

THATCHER, NOEL
See Morgio, George A

THEARD, SAM   ASCAP 1955
composer, author, entertainer
b New Orleans, La, Oct 10, 04. Educ: High sch. Chief Collabr: Timmie Rogers. *Songs:* I'll Be Glad When You're Dead, You Rascal You; Let The Good Times Roll.

THEOFANIDIS, IRAKLIS B (THEO FANIDI)   ASCAP 1965
composer
b Samos, Greece, June 29, 26. Educ: Greek Cons of Athens, master's piano & composing; State Acad of Music, Vienna, Austria, master's piano & conducting; Manhattan Sch of Music, postgrad dipl, piano; Fulbright scholarship. Concert pianist in Europe; comp of musicals & films, Greece. Orch leader in top hotels & comp, songs, musicals & films, US. Chief Collabrs: Paul Zindel, Paul Francis Webster, Sidney Berger. *Songs:* Music: Our Secret Star. *Scores:* Opera/Ballet: Last Temptation of Christ; Four Faces of Love; The Voyage; Bway shows: By Zeus; Speak of the Devil; Mademoiselle from Moleshoe; Film/TV: Naked Brigade.

THEORET, SANDY MASON   ASCAP 1972
composer, singer, ventriloquist
b Tarentum, Pa, Dec 18, 44. Educ: Drama sch; Pittsburgh Playhouse, 2 yrs. Ventriloquist, 12 yrs, TV show, Pittsburgh, 2 yrs. Commercials, NY, 3 yrs. Chief Collabrs: Roger Cook, Bobby Wood, Jim Rushing, Richard Leigh, Charles Cochran, Allen Reynolds. *Songs:* When I Dream; I'd Even Let You Go; You Take Me Home; All I Wanna Do in Life.

THIELE, DOUGLAS M   ASCAP 1979
composer, author, singer
b Jacksonville, Fla, Oct 26, 44. Educ: Walnut Hills High Sch; Ind Univ, BS(piano, English), MA(creative writing); Dick Grove Sch Music, ASCAP Workshop West. Concert pianist, ages 4-17. Pop performer at age 17. Finalist, NAm Popular Song Competition. Past pres, Songwriters Resources & Services. Columnist, The Music Connection; contibuting ed, Songwriter Mag. Mem: Calif Copyright Conference; Country Music Asn. Chief Collabrs: Larry Herbstritt, Mark Jordan. *Songs:* Lyrics: Almost in Love; Dancin' Like Lovers.

THIELE, ROBERT   ASCAP 1955
composer, author
b Brooklyn, NY, July 27, 22. Educ: Pub schs, Sheepshead Bay & Forest Hills, NY; Lawrenceville Sch, NJ; New Forest Sch, Forest Hills, NY. Led own sch, 39-40; formed Signature Records, 39-48; A&R dir, Coral Records, 53-60; producer & vpres, Dot Records, 61-63; producer, Roulette Records, 63 & ABC & Impulse Records, 63-69; formed Hanover Signature Records, 70-72 & Flying Dutchman Records, 73-77. Independent producer for CBS & RCA Records, 77-80. Chief Collabrs: Duke Ellington, George David Weiss, Glenn Osser. *Songs:* What a Wonderful World; Teddy; Gonna Telephone Jesus; There Once Was a Man Named John; We Love You Fats; Mailman, Bring Me No More Blues; Bean's Place; Soul Sauce; Hello Brother; The Sunshine of Love; Gatsby's; Irish Alphabet; Champagne and Music; The Lord Will Understand (And Say Well Done); Merry Christmas to You; The Magic of Hawaii; Umpteen Days Before Christmas; When Lovers Laugh; Lyrics: Duke's Place; The Story of Kevin Barry; Baby Clementine; Blue Piano; Boy From New Orleans (The Satchmo Story). *Instrumental Works:* Warm; Cool; Dear John C.

THIELMAN, RONALD   ASCAP 1964
composer, teacher
b Chicago Heights, Ill, July 27, 36. Educ: Ark State Teachers Col, BME; NTex State Univ, MME. Taught sch bands, Mo & Ark, 6 yrs; asst prof & asst dir of bands, Univ Miss. *Songs & Instrumental Works:* Night Wind and the Conquerors.

THLIVERIS, ELIZABETH HOPE   ASCAP 1978
composer, author, teacher
b San Antonio, Tex, Feb 25, 39. Educ: Clarke Cons, studied piano with Joseph Clarke, comp with H Alexander Matthews; Oberlin Univ, studied comp with Joseph Wood; Univ Tex, BMus & MMus, studied comp with Kent Kennan.

Organist in several churches. Pvt piano teacher. Teacher, Theory-Comp Dept, Univ Tex & Scottsdale Schs, Ariz. Formed a musical group with children, Kid Lit; performed children's musicals based on classical lit for children. *Songs:* Music: The Littlest Angel (musical version); Of Course There Is a Santa Claus; On the Road to Bethlehem; Little Boy Blue; See the Love, Hear the Joy.

THOMAS, BRIAN KEITH   ASCAP 1979
composer
b Conyers, Ga, Mar 28, 57. Educ: The Alliance Theatre, Atlanta. Worked in theatre for several yrs. Began writing for Word Records, 76. Toured with Christian contemporary groups. Writer for Ronnie Milsap Enterprises, 79. *Songs:* It's a Beautiful Thing; Still in Love With You; In My Life; Song for the Heart; Suddenly You Came; I Just Wanna Love You More; Jesus Comforts Me; Don't Let the Water Get You Down.

THOMAS, CHAPMAN SNEAD   ASCAP 1964
composer, author
b Fork-Union, Va, July 23, 09. Educ: Butler High Sch, NJ; Upsala Col, East Orange, NJ. Worked for eng & land surveying cos, 37 yrs. Chief Collabrs: Jimme Dale, Roger Genger. *Songs:* You Didn't Have to Go (and Break My Heart); Struttin'; Got to Get to Nashville (If It's the Last Darn Thing I Do); It's the Infantry.

THOMAS, DICK
See Goldhahn, Richard Thomas

THOMAS, DONALD EDWARD
composer, guitarist, singer
b Weymouth, Mass, Feb 14, 43. Educ: High sch; pvt music instr. Writer, recording musician, commercial writer & producer; inventor of var musical accessories. Chief Collabrs: Estelle Leavitt, Robert Morris, Billy Davis. *Songs:* Mountain Fresh Mountain Pure (Sprite); Hey Catch the Sun (Fanta); Together We Can Change Things (Red Cross); Music: This Door Swings Both Ways; The Music of the World Turnin'; Love Love's to Love Love.

THOMAS, EDWARD   ASCAP 1957
composer, group singer
b Chisholm, Minn, Oct 1, 24. Educ: Studied comp, orchestration & conducting with Tibor Serly. Guitarist & group singer, radio, TV & recordings during early career yrs; leading producer of music for advert. Writer, theatre, films & concerts. Chief Collabrs: Martin Charnin, Anne Croswell, Joe Masteroff, Jerome Coopersmith. *Songs:* Music: Maman; The Bells of Christmas; This Is That Time of the Year; Summer Idyll; A Woman's Love; Cowboy in New York. *Instrumental Works:* Midnight in Madrid; Concerto for Clarinet and Orchestra; First String Quartet. *Scores:* Opera: Desire Under the Elms; Bway show: Ballad for a Firing Squad; Film/TV: Return to Oz.

THOMAS, GENE EDEN   ASCAP 1972
composer, author, singer
b Palestine, Tex, Dec 4, 38. Left high sch to pursue music. Worked as grocery clerk, sawmill worker, iron foundry worker, seismograph crew worker & shipping clerk. Writer, Acuff & Rose Music, 67-72, later Milne Music. *Songs:* Sometimes; Playboy; Perfect Mountain; Lovin' Season; Rings of Gold; Lay It Down; Watching It Go; Kissed by the Rain.

THOMAS, HELEN   ASCAP 1945
composer, author, singer
b East Liverpool, Ohio; d New York, NY, Dec, 73. Educ: New Eng Cons; studied with mother & with Sidney Dietch, Estelle Liebling. Singer in concert, operetta, opera, with symph orchs. Wrote operettas & stage scores. *Songs:* In London Town at Night; When You Come Home Some Day; When I Go Back to Paris; Shelter Lullaby; The Love Song; The Christmas Tree; The Hurdy Gurdy; The Circus; Christmas Carol; also Circus Fantasy (8 songs); Tippie's Tunes (7 songs). *Instrumental Works:* Song of Yesterday (operetta).

THOMAS, JULIUS EARL   ASCAP 1979
composer, singer
b Dallas, Tex, Oct 17, 53. Educ: Comp & voice control, self-taught. *Songs:* No One But You; We Love Each Other.

THOMAS, LARRY
See Miner, Lawrence A

THOMAS, LEON AMOS   ASCAP 1967
composer, author, singer
b St Louis, Mo, Oct 4, 35. Sang with Count Basie; with major groups incl Oliver Nelson & Santana. Had 6 albums on Flying Dutchman/RCA. Performed in Europe at jazz fests. Chief Collabr: Neil Creque. *Songs:* Sun Song. *Songs & Instrumental Works:* Colors; Love Each Other.

THOMAS, MARK STANTON   ASCAP 1975
flutist
b Lakeland, Fla, Apr 24, 31. Educ: Baltimore City Col; Peabody Cons Music; Am Univ; Int Graphoanalysis Soc; studied flute with Emil Opava, Britton Johnson & William Kincaid. With USA Band, Nat Gallery Orch, Nat Symph

& Baltimore Symph. Prof flute, George Washington Univ, Am Univ & Univ Notre Dame. Flute recording artist with Golden Crest & Armstrong Records. Vpres & flute artist-in-residence, W T Armstrong Co. Pres, Elkhart County Symph Asn. *Instrumental Works:* Learning the Flute (Beginner); Learning the Flute (Intermediate); My First Book of Christmas Flute Solos; My First Book of Sacred Flute Solos; My First Book of Popular Flute Solos; Arr: Eighteen Exercises for Flute (Berbiguier); Reverie and Petite Valse (Caplet); Eighteen Exercises for Flute (Andersen); Elegie (Boehm); Air De Ballet (Saint Saens); Minuet and Dance of Blessed Spirits; Allegretto (Godard).

THOMAS, MARY VIRGINIA   ASCAP 1957
composer, author, teacher
b Elkins, WVa. Educ: High sch; pvt tutors; studied with C W Cadman, Frank Antonio Migliaccio, Cora M Atchison, Dave Vining & Jerry Gaddis. Mem of Family Chamber Music Trio, played in concert for women's clubs; demonstrated chamber music for high schs & cols. Had broadcast concerts nationwide; played dinner music in var hotels; played in concert (piano & pipe organ) throughout the South; theatre & church organist, since age 14. Chief Collabrs: James Pasquantonio, Blanche Cuba, L Leslie Loth. *Songs:* Can't Keep From Crying; Pour Me Stardust; Li Geet's Lullabye; Wan Chi (10,000 Talents); The Seeds of Temptation; What Do You Do (In Time of Trouble?); Lyrics: N'a Canzone D'Amore; Tied to a Rainbow.

THOMAS, MAX
See Yoder, Paul V

THOMAS, PAUL LINDSLEY   ASCAP 1969
composer, choral director, organist
b New York, NY, Mar 18, 29. Educ: Trinity Col, Conn, BA, 50; Yale Univ Sch Music, BM, 57, MusM, 58; NTex State Univ, DMA, 79; Am Guild of Organists, AAGO, 53, FAGO, 58; studied comp with Sam Adler & Merrill Ellis. Organist/choirmaster, St George's-by-the-River Episcopal Church, Rumson, NJ, 50-55 & St James Episcopal Church, West Hartford, Conn, 55-60; music dir & organist, St Michael & All Angels Episcopal Church, Dallas, Tex, 60-. *Songs:* Music Anthems: Fanfare and Alleluias; Come See the Place; The Head That Once Was Crowned With Thorns; Shout the Glad Tidings; The Strife Is O'er. *Instrumental Works:* Aberystwyth (organ).

THOMAS, PHILL
See Cappellini, Phillip Thomas

THOMAS, RANDY KEITH   ASCAP 1978
composer, guitarist, vocalist
b Denison, Tex, Nov 15, 54. Educ: Eisenhower High Sch, grad; San Bernardino Valley Col, music major, 1 yr. Made numerous US tours as vocalist & guitarist; with Psalm 150 & Sweet Comfort Bands; recording artist; studio guitarist. Chief Collabrs: Samuel O Scott, Rick Thomson. *Songs:* Childish Things; Good Feelin'; Gotta Believe; We Must Wait; Hold on Tight.

THOMAS, RUFUS   ASCAP 1970
composer, singer, dancer
b Casey, Miss, Mar 26, 17. Educ: Booker T Washington High Sch; Tenn State Univ. Became performer at age 14. *Songs & Instrumental Works:* The Dog; Walking the Dog; Break Down; Push and Pull; Funky Penguin; Do the Funky Chicken; Memphis Train; Jump Back Baby; The World is Round; Sixty Minute Main; Can Your Monkey Do the Dog; Never Let You Go; I Wanna Get Married; 'Cause I Love You.

THOMAS, SUSAN MARIE   ASCAP 1970
composer, author, singer
b Milwaukee, Wis, Oct 10, 46. Educ: Univ Wis, BA, 69; voice training with Estella Anderson, 65-75. Keyboardist & vocalist in var pop music groups. Co-owner of Blue Hour Records. Vocalist on radio & TV jingles. Backup vocalist with Tammy Wynette on tour. *Songs:* Bayou Blue; Romance; Keeping It Warm for You. *Scores:* Film/TV: Ocean Bird.

THOMAS, WILLIAM CARROLL
author
b Los Angeles, Calif, Aug 11, 03. Educ: Univ Southern Calif, BA. Chief Collabr: Bernie Kai Lewis. *Songs:* Lyrics: Tricycles, Mud Pies and Dreams.

THOMAS, WILLIAM SHERWOOD   ASCAP 1975
composer, author, filmmaker
b West Palm Beach, Fla, Feb 27, 44. Educ: Univ RI, BS(econ), 65. Comn officer, USNR, 66. Wrote film score, "Run Before the Wind." Singer night clubs, jingles & TV, Europe. Songwriter, "Captain Kangaroo" & "Sesame Street." Filmmaker, "Captain Kangaroo." *Songs:* Tell Me a Story; Rainy Day Zoo; All the Things That Fly in the Air; Circles; Music: Hands.

THOMASON, ALEXANDER (CHARLIE BYRD)   ASCAP 1976
composer
b Roanoke, Va, June 20, 26. Educ: Stewartsville High Sch, Va; Christian Heinrich Hohmann Violin-Schule Universal-Ed, Wien, Vienna, Austria. With Armed Forces TV & radio; performed at nightclubs; participant, Fiddlers Conventions. *Instrumental Works:* The Virginia Waltz.

THOMPSON, ALFREDA LYDIA   ASCAP 1961
composer, author
b Offerly, Kans, Apr 24, 11. Educ: Golden Eagle Sch. Writer of short stories & poems. Chief Collabr: Chris Henson. *Albums:* Confession; Ballads, Blues and Boleros.

THOMPSON, ALMA I (A BAZEL ANDROZZO)   ASCAP 1970
composer, author
b Harriman, Tenn, Oct 17, 12. Educ: Taught by father to play in all keys at age 5. Now plays piano & writes. *Songs:* If I Can Help Somebody; I Have Something to Give.

THOMPSON, ANN
See Bradford, Sylvester Henry

THOMPSON, BOB   ASCAP 1956
composer
b San Jose, Calif, Aug 22, 24. Educ: Univ Calif, Berkeley. Composer music for TV commercials; documentaries, 60-; songwriter; pres, Yada Corp, 80- *Songs:* Music: Fairyland; Go Go Goodyear; Mr Good Wrench; Kawasaki Makes the Good Times Roll.

THOMPSON, BRIAN MICHAEL   ASCAP 1974
composer
b Baltimore, Md, May 20, 46. Educ: Towson State Univ, BA, 68; Univ Mex, spec studies in Spanish, 67; Los Angeles Community Col & Pierce Col, Woodland Hills, Calif, spec studies in music, 76 & 80. Began songwriting in 70. Joined New York Times Publ Co, 74. Wrote radio commercial. Chief Collabr: Suzie Maddox. *Songs:* Music: Wind Me Up; Look At Our Happy Home; Home Movies; Poor Little Rich Girl; Trapped; One Little Star; Carousel.

THOMPSON, DEAN K   ASCAP 1958
composer, author
b San Leandro, Calif, June 21, 40. Educ: San Jose State Col. Pianist in rock 'n' roll band, 50's. Mem singing team, Hank & Dean, Tennessee Ernie Ford daytime TV show, 61. Recorded for RCA, wrote songs & jingles & produced radio & TV commercials & phonograph records, 60's. Mgr promotional activities, Publ Div, Lawrence Welk, 71, later exec vpres/gen mgr. Chief Collabr: Hal Blair. *Songs:* That's Life; Music: What Have I Done for Her Lately; Crack in My World; I Hope I Lose My Memory Before I Lose My Mind.

THOMPSON, EVAN   ASCAP 1967
author, actor, director
b New York, NY, Sept 3, 31. Educ: Beverly Hills High Sch; Univ Calif, Berkeley, BA, 53. Actor, Bway, off-Bway, film & TV; dir, Fanfare Theatre Ens, 71-; co-author 11 musical plays for children. Chief Collabrs: Joan Shepard, John Clifton, Joe Boresard. *Scores:* Children's Theatre: Huckleberry Finn; Annie Oakley and Buffalo Bill; Alice Through the Looking Glass; East of the Sun and West of the Moon; Puss in Boots.

THOMPSON, FRED W   ASCAP 1954
composer, author, publisher
b Chicago, Ill, Mar 21, 01; d Miami Beach, Fla, Aug 30, 69. Educ: Asbury Col; Columbia Cons, Aurora, Ill, studied with Harry Detweiler & Earl Drake. Served in USN, WW I. Pianist, music publ; in vaudeville. Arr, Waterson, Berlin & Snyder, Chicago. Moved to Hollywood, accompanist, arr & writer for singers. Had own publ firm. *Songs:* Phi Delta Theta Dream Girl; Fight on, War Eagle; The Green Wave; Hail, Red and White; Clap Your Hands; Mem'ries of Pi Beta Phi: Hail, Hail, Hail.

THOMPSON, HARLAN   ASCAP 1924
author, director, producer
b Hannibal, Mo, Sept 24, 1890; d. Educ: Univ Kans, studied eng. Reporter, drama critic & ed, Kansas City Star. Mem, CO 167th Aero Squadron, WW I. Reporter & feature writer, New York World. Co-producer & dir, "Blessed Event." Wrote, dir & produced films. Mem, Signal Corps, in charge of Army training films, WW II. Producer, TV films; in charge of CBS West Coast production. Chief Collabrs: Harry Archer, David Stamper, Lewis Gensler. *Songs:* I Love You; Fatal Fascination; It Must Be Love; Suppose I Had Never Met You; Dance Away the Night; Ending With a Kiss; Open Road; A Man, a Maid. *Scores:* Bway stage: Little Jessie James (libretto); My Girl (libretto); Merry Merry (libretto); Twinkle Twinkle (libretto).

THOMPSON, JENNINGS L, JR (JAY)   ASCAP 1961
composer, author, arranger
b Spartanburg, SC, Dec 27, 27. Educ: Wofford Col; Converse Col, BM; Peabody Cons; studied piano with Conradi; NY Univ. Worked in radio & children's theatre, 39-44; music dir, WAAM-TV, Baltimore, 49-51; vocal coach, accompanist & arr, New York, 54-60; co-librettist, "Once Upon a Mattress." Wrote songs for Julius Monk nightclub revues; pianist. *Songs:* The Intellectuals' Rag; Upper New Jersey Hop; Pill Parade; Career Malice; Circus Sort of Day. *Scores:* Off Bway stage: Double Entry (The Bible Salesman and The Oldest Trick in the World).

THOMPSON, JOAN SHEPARD
See Shepard, Joan

THOMPSON, JOHN EDD, JR
composer
b Mobile, Ala, July 25, 42. Educ: Univ Ala, broadcast & drama major, 60-63. High sch rock & roll singer. Wrote fight song for Univ South Ala. Chief Collabrs: J R Powell, Hal Newman. *Songs:* Can You Think of Anything Better?; Look At Them Jaguars.

THOMPSON, KAY   ASCAP 1951
composer, author, pianist
b St Louis, Mo, Nov 9, 13. Prof debut as piano soloist, St Louis Symph; singer in TV & nightclubs; appeared in film, "Funny Face"; also choreographed film musicals. Author, "Eloise" bks. Music arr, Fred Waring, CBS & MGM. *Songs:* Promise Me Love; This Is the Time; You Gotta Love Everybody.

THOMPSON, LESLIE STEPHEN   ASCAP 1966
composer, singer, teacher
b Long Beach, Calif, June 4, 48. Educ: Northern Va Community Col, studied music. Mem & original founder, Nitty Gritty Dirt Band, 65-75. Wrote for TV specials & theme soundtracks, ABC & nat & regional commercials for Westinghouse & Taco John's; also United Artists Records. *Songs:* Santiago's America; Lovely Lady.

THOMPSON, RANDALL   ASCAP 1940
composer, educator
b New York, NY, Apr 21, 1899. Educ: Harvard Univ, BA, MA; fel, Am Acad, Rome; hon MusD, Univ Rochester; Guggenheim grant; studied with Spaulding, Hill & Ernest Bloch. Asst prof music, Wellesley Col, 27-29; then lived in Switz. Guest cond, Dessoff Choirs, 31-32; wrote survey, "College Music" (Carnegie Fund project); prof music & dir chorus, Univ Calif, 37-38; dir, Curtis Inst Music, 39-41; prof music, Univ Va, 41-45 & Princeton Univ, 45-48. Prof music, Harvard Univ, 48- Mem: Nat Inst Arts & Letters; Am Acad Arts & Sci. Trustee, Am Acad in Rome. *Instrumental Works:* Alleluia; Mass of the Holy Spirit; The Last Words of David (comn by Boston Symph); Testament of Freedom; The Peaceable Kingdom (comn by League of Comp); Tarantella; Symphony No 1 and Symphony No 2 (Eastman Sch publ awards); Symphony No 3 (Ditson award); String Quartet in d (Coolidge Found award).

THOMPSON, ROBERT C
composer, musician
b Converse, SC, July 5, 37. Educ: Self-taught guitar & banjo. Has been playing guitar or banjo since age 18. Wrote background music for "Hee Haw." *Songs:* In God We Trust; Funny Looking Eyes; Violets and Daffodils; Nature's Way of Saying Hi. *Instrumental Works:* Fox Fire.

THOMPSON, ROBERT WICKENS, II (ROBBIN)   ASCAP 1976
singer, songwriter
b Melrose, Mass, June 16, 49. Educ: Melbourne High Sch, Fla, 67; Brevard Jr Col, 68-69; Va Commonwealth Univ, BS, 73. Lead singer in "Steel Mill," 70-71; staff writer/producer, CandyApple Jingle Productions, Richmond, Va, 73-77. Winner prof folk category, Am Song Fest, 75. Recording artist, Nemperor Records, 76- & Richmond Records, 78- Chief Collabrs: Timothy B Schmit, Austin Roberts, Steve Bassett. *Songs & Instrumental Works:* Boy From Boston; Highway 101; Sweet Virginia Breeze; Candy Apple Red; Brite Eyes; Find Out in Time. *Albums:* Robbin Thompson; Together; Two B's Please.

THOMSON, RICK MICHAEL   ASCAP 1976
composer, author
b Cincinnati, Ohio, Mar 15, 54. Educ: Self-taught. Started writing music at age 14. Started playing in Sweet Comfort Band, 73. Chief Collabrs: Randy Thomas, Bryan Duncan. *Songs & Instrumental Works:* Ryan's Song; Children's Things; Get Ready; Got to Believe; Melody Harmony; Good Feelin'; The Lord Is Calling; Hold on Tight; Falling Star; You're the One; Chasin' the Wind; Carry Me.

THOMSON, VIRGIL GARNETT   ASCAP 1945
composer, author
b Kansas City, Mo, Nov 25, 1896. Educ: Cent High Sch, dipl, 14; Harvard Col, AB, 22; comp with Scalero & Boulanger, NY & Paris. Hon degrees from Syracuse, Rutgers, Roosevelt, Fairfield, NY, Mo, Johns Hopkins & Columbia Univs. Taught music at Harvard Univ; choirmaster & organist, King's Chapel, Boston. Music writer, Vanity Fair, Modern Music, NY Rev of Bks & NY Times; chief music critic, NY Herald Tribune, 40-54. Also cond & vis prof. Author of bks, "The State of Music", "The Musical Scene", "The Art of Judging Music", "Music Right and Left", "Virgil Thomson", "Music Reviewed, 1940-54", "American Music Since 1910" & "A Virgil Thomson Reader." Honors incl mem in Am Acad of Arts & Letters, Am Acad of Arts & Sci & Officier in the Legion d'Honneur. Awards incl, Pulitzer Prize, Handel Medallion of City New York, Nat Inst of Arts & Letters Gold Medal for Music, Brandeis Univ Creative Arts Award, MacDowell Award & Guggenheim Fel. Chief Collabrs: Gertrude Stein, Jack Larson, Robert Flaherty, Pare Lorenz, Eric K Hawkins, Lew Christensen, Georges Balanchine, Agnes de Mille. *Songs:* Choral Works: Mass for Two-Part Chorus; Hymns From the Old South; Four Songs to the Poems of Thomas

Champion; Missa Pro Defunctis (Requiem Mass); Dance in Praise; The Nativity as Sung by the Shepherds; The Peace Place. *Instrumental Works:* Orchestral Works: Symphony on a Hymn Tune; Symphony No 2 in C Major; Portraits for Orchestra; The Seine at Night; Wheat Field at Noon; Sea Piece with Birds; Eleven Chorale Preludes (organ); Fugues and Cantilenas; A Solemn Music and a Joyful Fugue; Third Symphony; Five Songs From William Blake; Concerto for Violoncello and Orchestra; Concerto for Flute, Strings and Percussion; Autumn Concertino for Harp, Strings and Percussion; The Feast of Love; Fantasy in Homage to an Earlier England; Cantata on Poems of Edward Lear; Shipwreck; Juan and Haidee; Chamber Music: Sonata da Chiesa; Sonata for Violin and Piano; String Quartet No 1 and No 2; Family Portrait (brass quintet); also more than 100 portraits for piano, some set for chamber ensembles; many songs for soloists or mixed voices, with piano, orch or chamber ens; incidental music for plays. *Scores:* Operas: Four Saints (three acts); The Mother of Us All; Lord Byron; Ballets: Filling Station; Bayou; The Harvest According; Hurrah!; Parson Weems and the Cherry Tree; Films: The Plow That Broke the Plains; The River; Tuesday in November; Louisiana Story (Pulitzer Prize for Music); The Goddess; Power Among Men; Journey to America.

THOREN, KENNETH ALEXANDER   ASCAP 1971
author
b New Rochelle, NY, Dec 22, 26. Educ: Univ Notre Dame. Copy boy, New York Sun. Worked for advert agencies incl Young & Rubicam, J Walter Thompson, McCann-Ericson, Campbell-Ewald. Wrote for Kodak, Ford, Exxon, Goodyear & others. Freelance magazine writer; TV scripts incl "World of Survival", "Incredible Flight of Snow Goose" & "Marcus Welby, MD." Chief Collabr: Farlan Myers. *Songs & Instrumental Works:* Fly High and Free.

THORNHILL, CLAUDE   ASCAP 1947
composer, conductor, pianist
b Terre Haute, Ind, Aug 10, 08; d Caldwell, NJ, July 1, 65. Educ: Cincinnati Cons; Univ Ky. Joined Austin Wiley Orch, Cleveland, then Benny Goodman, New York, 31. Formed own band. Served in Honolulu Navy Band, USN, WW II; toured Pacific with own band. After war, reorganized orch; also arr for Judy Garland films. Made many records. *Songs:* I Wish I Had You; Fare Thee Well; Annie Laurie; Buster's Last Stand; Memory of an Island; Loch Lomond (arr); Snowfall (theme).

THORNSBY, LEE
See Hornsby, Joseph Leith

THORNTON, JAMES   ASCAP 1914
composer, author, entertainer
b Liverpool, Eng, Dec 4, 1861; d Astoria, NY, July 27, 38. Educ: Boston Latin Sch. Moved to US, 1870. Singing waiter, Boston; monologist, singer & comedian in vaudeville, 50 yrs. Also wrote spec material for other acts & for wife, Bonnie Thornton. *Songs:* When You Were Sweet Sixteen; My Sweetheart's the Man in the Moon; She May Have Seen Better Days; The Streets of Cairo; Don't Give Up the Old Love for the New; On the Benches in the Park; There's a Little Star Shining for You; The Irish Jubilee; The Bridge of Sighs; When Summer Comes Again: I'm the Man Who Wrote 'Ta-Ra-Ra-Boom-De-Ay'.

THOW, GEORGE ALBERT   ASCAP 1963
composer, author, trumpeter
b Cleveland, Ohio, July 8, 08. Educ: Cleveland Pub Schs; Harvard Univ, AB, 29. Trumpeter bands, Isham Jones, Dorsey Bros & Jack Teagarden. Recordings with Benny Goodman, Artie Shaw, Ben Pollack & Gordon Jenkins. Mem staff orch, NBC, 41-43 & Warner Bros Studios, 43-45. Free lance musician radio, TV, movies & recordings. Joined Lawrence Welk, 56, mem TV show production staff, 62. Chief Collabr: Curt Ramsey. *Songs:* This is How a Romance Ends; Strasburg Strut; A Quiet Little Guy; Lyrics: Ragtime Piano Gal; Under a Coconut Tree; Just Another Dream; Keep a Song In Your Heart; Just Lucky I Guess; On With the Show. *Instrumental Works:* Tea 'n' Trumpets.

THROCKMORTON, JAMES FRON (SONNY)
songwriter
b Carlsbad, NMex, Apr 2, 41. Educ: High sch, grad; Midwestern Univ. Performer with rockabilly group. To Los Angeles, 62; signed with record co & began songwriting. To Nashville, 64; worked for var publ cos. Signed with Tree Int; country & western music songwriter. *Songs:* When Can We Do This Again; Thinkin' of a Rendezvous; Middle Age Crazy; Knee Deep in Loving You; Yes Ma'am; How Long Has It Been; If We're Not Back in Love By Monday; Here We Go Again; Ordinary Miracle; Easy Look; I Thank God She's Mine; I'm Way Ahead of You; Last Cheater's Waltz.

THURSTON, JANE JACQUELIN (GENE WILLADEN)   ASCAP 1943
author
b Weehawken, NJ, July 24, 15. Educ: Pvt sch, Manhattan, NY; Ned Wayburn's Sch Dancing; drama studies with Theodora Irvine; music studies with Claire Norden. Singer, dancer & magicienne, Big Magic Show, US & Can. Joined Isham Jones Band & worked as lyricist. Chief Collabr: Isham Jones. *Songs:* Lyrics: My Best to You; Just to Be Near You; With No Man of My Own; But I Never Do; Just Like You; I Burned My Bridges.

TIBBLES, GEORGE F   ASCAP 1947
composer, author, writer
b New York, NY, June 7, 23. Educ: Los Angeles City Col; studied piano with Madame Regis Rossini. Mem two piano team with weekly radio show. Began writing songs, 45; wrote spec material for Eddie Cantor, Joan Davis, Ritz Bros & others. Writer, producer & musical dir, TV. Wrote & produced, "My Three Sons", "Betty White Show" & many others. Playwright musical, "Get Out the Madonna" and others. Chief Collabr: Ramez Idriss. *Songs:* The Woody Woodpecker Song; Senora; Worry, Worry, Worry; The Old Chaperone; My Brooklyn Love Song; LLLLA; Something Old, Something New; Beatin', Bangin', Scratchin'; I'll Wait; In All This World; It Ain't Snowin' Outside.

TIERNEY, HARRY AUSTIN   ASCAP 1917
composer, pianist
b Perth Amboy, NJ, May 21, 1890; d New York, NY, Mar 22, 65. Educ: Virgil Cons, New York; also studied with mother & Nicholas Morrissey. Concert pianist, toured US. Staff comp & music publ, London, 15 & Remick, NY, 18. Wrote songs for "Afgar", "Ziegfeld Follies" (19, 20), "Follow Me", "Everything" & "A Royal Vagabond." Under contract to RKO, 31. Wrote songs for films incl "Dixiana" & "Half Shot at Sunrise." Chief Collabrs: Joe McCarthy, Bert Hanlon, Benny Ryan, Al Bryan, Ray Egan, Anne Caldwell. *Songs:* Just for Tonight; If You Can't Get a Girl in the Summertime; M-I-S-S-I-S-S-I-P-P-I; It's a Cute Little Way of My Own; Cleopatra; I Found the End of the Rainbow; My Baby's Arms; Alice Blue Gown; Irene; Castle of Dreams; Journey's End; If Your Heart's in the Game; Someone Loves You After All; Rio Rita; The Kinkajou; The Rangers Song; If You're in Love You'll Waltz; You're Always in My Arms. *Scores:* Bway stage: Irene; The Broadway Whirl; Up She Goes; Kid Boots; Ziegfeld Follies (24); Rio Rita; Cross My Heart.

TIERNEY, HARRY AUSTIN, JR   ASCAP 1978
author
b New York, NY, Mar 20, 34. Son of Harry Tierney, comp. Educ: Duke Univ; Oxford Univ; Royal Acad Dramatic Art. Chief Collabrs: John Cooper, Guido Coen. *Scores:* Opera: The Cry of Abishag; Film: One Brief Summer.

TIERNEY, THOMAS JOHN   ASCAP 1969
composer, author, music producer
b Columbia, Mo, May 25, 42. Educ: Univ Ill, BA, 65, MA, 68; studied comp with Chuck Israels, 74-77. Composer, writer & music producer, New York Telephone Co, 69-75. Composed off-Bway musical, "Ichabod"; composed & co-authored children's musicals, "The Fabulous Fable Factory", "Mr Herman and the Cave Company", "The Stars and Stripes Forever" & "Teddy Roosevelt"; composed two episodes, NBC-TV Series, "Unicorn Tales," 78-79; participant, "Meet the Composer," 3/24/80. Chief Collabrs: John Forster, Mae Richard & Joseph Robinette. *Songs:* Music: A Tune of Our Own (theme song, UNICEF's Int Year of the Child).

TIETJENS, PAUL   ASCAP 1940
composer, pianist
b St Louis, Mo, May 22, 1877; d St Louis, Mo, Nov 25, 43. Educ: Pub schs; studied music with Leschetizky, Fuchs & Bauer. Piano soloist, St Louis Symph, at age 14. Teacher of piano & harmony; accompanist to concert singers. Music dir, Maude Adams productions, 16-19 & 30. *Songs:* Adoration; Blind; Love Is Love; Phantom Patrol; When You Love, Love, Love. *Instrumental Works:* Carnival; Rustic Sketches. *Scores:* Bway Stage: The Wizard of Oz; Incidental Music: Barrie's Kiss for Cinderella; Opera: The Tents of the Arabs.

TIGHE, (JON) KEVIN   ASCAP 1979
author
b Los Angeles, Calif, Aug 13, 44. Educ: Univ Southern Calif, MFA, 70. Chief Collabrs: Lenny Lee Goldsmith, Lee Shapiro. *Songs:* Lyrics: Without Your Love; Needing You; No Love at All; Lead Me Down.

TILLMAN, EDWIN EARL   ASCAP 1955
composer, pianist
b Sheboygan, Wis, May 11, 1900. Educ: Lawrence Cons, Appleton, Wis. Operated E Tillman Song Shop, 26-28. Piano salesman, House of Pianos, Miami. *Songs:* Lonesome and Blue; You Only Want Me When You're Lonesome.

TILLSTROM, BURR   ASCAP 1957
author, puppeteer
b Chicago, Ill, Oct 13, 17. Educ: Univ Chicago. Toured with puppet, marionette & stock shows; mgr, puppet exhibits & Marionette Theatre, Marshall Field, Chicago. Performed on exp TV for RCA; did ship-to-shore TV broadcasts, Bermuda. Creator & writer, "Kukla, Fran and Ollie," 47- *Songs:* Kukla, Fran and Ollie at the Fair; Franny Dear; Moby Dick Blues; The Witches' Ride; Je Vous Aime; Dragon Prep; also opera, St George and the Dragon.

TILTON, GEORGE   ASCAP 1957
author
b New York, NY, Apr 8, 22. Educ: Dartmouth Col, BA. Ed & writer for mag publishers. *Songs:* Lyrics: There's Something in My Eye; Seven Come Heaven; Nine Loves; First Date.

TIMBERG, SAMMY   ASCAP 1942
composer, conductor
b New York, NY, May 21, 03. Educ: Studied music with Rubin Goldmark. Music dir & songwriter for films; producer vaudeville revues; led orch touring film theatres throughout US. Wrote songs for Bway musicals: "Broadway Nights" & "The Street Singer." *Songs:* It's a Hap Hap Happy Day; Just One More Night in Your Arms; Lonely Heart; When I Look in the Book of My Memory; The Rhyming Song; Keep a Little Song Handy; Swingin' the Alphabet; also Popeye Song Folio.

TIMM, KENNETH NICKERSON   ASCAP 1977
composer, teacher, instrumentalist
b San Francisco, Calif, Nov 2, 34. Educ: Calif State Univ, Hayward, BA, 64, comp studies with Glenn Glasow; Mills Col, Calif, MA, 66, comp studies with Darius Milhaud, Luciano Berio & Robert Erickson; Ind Univ, Bloomington, DM, 77, comp studies with Bernhard Heiden & John Eaton. Professional instrumentalist, comp, arr, copyist & cond, 52-80; pub sch teaching, 62-66, univ teaching, 72-80. Currently assoc prof music comp & theory, Eastern Ky Univ. Professional performing experience with "Holiday on Ice", "Barnum and Bailey Circus", Berkeley Symph Orch, San Francisco Cons Artists Ens, Hayward Community Orch, San Francisco Wind Ens & others. *Instrumental Works:* The Joiner and the Die-Hard (five percussionists); Sonata (Other Streams) (four celli); Two Movements for Orchestra; Across a Circle (piano).

TIMM, WLADIMIR   ASCAP 1950
author
b St Petersburg, Russia, Dec 1, 1885; d Hendersonville, NC, Aug 28, 58. US citizen. *Songs:* Beer Barrel Polka (Roll Out the Barrel); Hot Pretzels; The Silver Shenandoah; Holla Lady.

TIMPANO, PAOLA FRANCESCA (IANELLO)   ASCAP 1954
(PAULA FRANCES)
composer, author
b Hoboken, NJ, June 3, 24. Educ: Emerson High Sch, Union City, NJ, grad, 42. Career began as a child performer; sang at var benefits, political rallies, etc. Aspired to a writing career; wrote poetry during childhood & high sch yrs; exec secy for maj music firm. Chief Collabrs: Gary Romero, Joseph Meyers, Ray Rivera & Joseph D D'Agostino. *Songs:* You Gotta Have Faith; My Cup of Life; Baby, I Don't Dig; Lyrics: My True Carrie, Love; I Will Pray; Christmas Roses; Wildflower; Lonesome World; Blue Nocturne; I Blew Out the Flame; Buzzy, The Bumble-Bee; Is It Wrong?; Doodlin'; Broken Promise.

TINTURIN, PETER   ASCAP 1933
composer, author, pianist
b Ekaterinoslav, Russia, June 1, 10. Educ: Vienna Cons; Univ Vienna, BA. Concert debut as pianist at age 9, Russia; made concert tour of Europe. Wrote musicals in Vienna & Paris. Came to US in 1929. USSC, WW II, music dir, 800th Reg, wrote, prod & dir Army shows, organized Army symph orch, wrote When the Hour Has Come (rec'd 7 citations). Music writer for films, Hollywood; mem fac, Chadwick Sch, Rolling Hills, Calif; music & lyrics writer for numerous motion pictures & widely performed pieces for classical guitar, as well as an important concerto for guitar and symphony orchestra. *Songs:* What Will I Tell My Heart; Big Boy Blue; Have You Ever Been in Heaven?; I'll Close My Eyes to Everyone Else; You or No One; Take Me Away; When the Lights Are Soft and Low; The Song Is the Thing; The Monkey and the Organ Grinder; May the Good Lord Take a Liking to You; A New Star Is Shining in Heaven; Saga of the Signal Corps; I'm Sorry. *Instrumental Works:* A Tone Poem (based on Lincoln's Gettysburg Address).

TIPTON, GEORGE ALICESON   ASCAP 1962
composer
b Huntington Park, Calif, Jan 23, 32. Educ: Studied violin from age 4; Beverly Hills High Sch; studied orchestration with Al Harris & conducting with Fritz Zweig. Arr for records; comp for films & TV. Grammy award nomination for arr of song Light My Fire, 68. *Scores:* Film/TV: Phantom of the Paradise (Acad award nomination, 74); Bad Lands; Skidoo; The Gift; Griffin and Phoenix; Hit Lady; The Point; Soap; Benson; The Courtship of Eddie's Father.

TIRRO, FRANK PASCALE   ASCAP 1960
composer, author, educator
b Omaha, Nebr, Sept 20, 35. Educ: Univ Nebr, BME, studied with Robert Beadell; Northwestern Univ, MM, studied with Thor Johnson & Anthony Donato; Univ Chicago, PhD, studied with Edward E Lowinsky, Leonard B Meyer & Howard M Brown. Instrumentalist; performer. Author, "Jazz: A History." Prof, Sch Music, Yale Univ. *Instrumental Works:* American Jazz Mass; American Jazz Te Deum. *Scores:* Opera/Ballet: Masque of the Red Death; Exorcise.

TISHMAN, FAY (FRANCES HART)   ASCAP 1956
composer, author, playwright
b Manhattan, NY, Oct 29, 13. Educ: Julia Richman High Sch; David Mannes Music; NY Univ; Reginald Goode's Provincetown Playhouse. Chief Collabrs: James Whitcomb Riley, Morse Charlap, Dick Charles, Marge Goetschius, Bill Tennyson, Harriet Bailin, Del Serino & others. *Songs:* Spring Rain; Only

Beautiful; Lyrics: I Never Met a Stranger; Moonlight Melody. *Albums:* The Magic of Christmas.

TIZOL, JUAN   ASCAP 1942
composer, trombonist

b San Juan, PR, Jan 22, 1900. To US, 20. Studied music with uncle, Manuel Tizol. Mem, Municipal Band, San Juan. Trombonist in orchs & groups, incl Duke Ellington, 19 yrs, Harry James, Nelson Riddle, Nat (King) Cole, Louis Bellson; free-lance; made many records. Chief Collabrs: Duke Ellington, Charlotte Hawkins. *Songs & Instrumental Works:* Caravan; Perdido; Lost in Meditation; Bakiff; Pyramid; Moonlight Fiesta; Conga Brava; Sphinx; Keb-lah; Home Again; A Sure Sign of Happiness; Rosie; We May Never Meet Again; Sans Souci; Just for Laughs; Lonely Dreams; Night Song; Bagdad; Gypsy Without a Song; You Can't Have Your Cake and Eat It; Zanzibar.

TJADER, CALLEN   ASCAP 1960
composer, author, conductor

b San Francisco, Calif, Mar 26, 1893; d. Educ: High sch. Child actor in stock cos; then in vaudeville. Pub rels officer, Nat Guard; Capt in Reserves. Founded children's theatre, San Francisco, 21. Joined Duncan Sisters in production, "Uncle Tom's Cabin." Staff mem, Dixon-Lane Music Co, St Louis, 24. Producer & writer, vaudeville acts. Founder, dancing & theatrical sch, San Mateo, Calif, 25-37; Tjader's Toy Theatre, produced musical shows. Lt Col, Spec Services, WW II. Assoc ed, Our Army, since 58. Chief Collabr: Larry Connelly. *Songs:* Spring Has Come and I'm Alone.

TOBIAS, CHARLES   ASCAP 1922
composer, author, publisher

b New York, NY, Aug 15, 1898; d New York, July 6, 70. Educ: Worcester pub schs, Mass. Singer on prof staff, music publ; also in vaudeville. Founded own publ firm, New York, 23. Wrote songs for "Earl Carroll's Vanities," 32; "Banjo Eyes," also for films. Husband of Edna Tobias; father of Fred Tobias. Chief Collabrs: Henry Tobias (bro), Harry Tobias (bro), Neil Moret, Gus Arnheim, Jules Lemare, Anson Weeks, Jack Scholl, Cliff Friend, Don Reid, Nat Simon, Sammy Stept, Lew Brown, Al Sherman. *Songs:* Miss You; Two Tickets to Georgia; When Your Hair Has Turned to Silver; Rose O'Day; Don't Sweetheart Me; For the First Time; Time Waits for No One; You Missed the Boat; The Broken Record; Little Lady Make Believe; Somebody Loves You: Little Curly Hair in a High Chair; Trade Winds; We Did It Before and We Can Do It Again; Prairie Fairy Tale; No Can Do; Don't Sit Under the Apple Tree; Coax Me a Little Bit; The Old Lamplighter; That's Where I Came In; Comes Love; Throw Another Log on the Fire: Love Ya; Just a Prayer Away; As Long as I Live; Tomorrow Is Forever; Would You Believe Me; Her Bathing Suit Never Got Wet; Get Out and Get Under the Moon; As Years Go By; What Do We Do on a Dew-Dew-Dewy Day?; In the Valley of the Moon; All Over the World; Those Lazy Hazy Crazy Days of Summer; That's What They Meant By the Good Old Summertime; After My Laughter Came Tears; Faithfully Yours. *Scores:* Bway shows: Hellzapoppin; Earl Carroll's Sketch Book (1935); Yokel Boy (also co-librettist).

TOBIAS, FRED   ASCAP 1953
author

b New York, NY, Mar 25, 28. Educ: Univ Pa. Pub rels, 49-57. Film, "Milliken Breakfast Show" & many other industrial films. Chief Collabs: Stanley Lebowsky, Paul Evans, Clint Ballard, Jr & Charles Strouse. *Songs:* The Children's Crusade (oratorio); Born Too Late; Hello This Is Joannie; Good Timin'; Little Bitty Girl; Johnny Will; My Turn Next Time; Love to Last a Lifetime; One of Us Will Weep Tonight. *Scores:* TV Spec: Gift of the Magi; Quincy's Quest; Bway Musical: Gantry.

TOBIAS, HARRY   ASCAP 1922
composer, author

b New York, NY, Sept 11, 1895. Educ: Pub schs, Worcester, Mass. First song publ, 11. USA, 17-18; to Hollywood, Calif, 29; wrote for films. Mem: Acad Motion Picture Arts & Sci; Nat Acad Recording Arts & Sci; Nat Conf Christians & Jews; Am Guild Authors & Comp; Comp & Lyricist Guild of Am. Chief Collabrs: Charles Tobias, Henry Tobias, Nathan Tobias, Will Dillon, Charles Kisco, Al Sherman, Charles Daniels, Jules Lemare, Percy Wenrich, Roy Ingraham, George Bennett, Pinkey Tomlin, Jack Stern, Nick Kenny, Gus Arnheim, Neil Moret, Phil Boutelje, Harry Barris, Jean Schwartz. *Songs:* All For the Love of Mike; Oooo Ernest (Are You Earnest With Me); Giggling Gertie; Sweet and Lovely; Good Night My Love; I'm Sorry Dear; I'll Keep the Lovelight Burning; Wait For Me Mary; May I Have the Next Dream With You; If I Knew Then (What I Know Now); Moonlight Brings Memories; In God We Trust; Star of Hope; Brother; The Bowling Song; I'm Gonna Get You; Zei Gezunt; Mazzel Tov; Lost and Found; Go to Sleepy Little Baby; Love Is the Thing; On the Sunny Side of the Rockies; Rocky Mountain Express; Call of the Rockies; I'll Have the Last Waltz With Mother; When It's Harvest Time (Sweet Angline); Music: Take Me to My Alabama; That Girl of Mine; Lyrics: National Sports; Hot Roasted Peanuts; Honey Rose; Miss You; It's a Lonesome Old Town; Daughter of Peggy O'Neil; At Your Command; No Regrets; Sail Along Silv'ry Moon; Love Is All; What Is It?; Wedding of the Birds; Good Mornin' (It's Mighty Good to Be Home); Gotta Big Date (With a Little Girl); Ashes of Roses; Mother's Little Sweetheart (Daddy's Little Pal).

TOBIAS, HENRY   ASCAP 1929
composer, author, publisher

b Worcester, Mass, Apr 23, 05. Educ: Pub schs, Worcester & New York; Morris High Sch, New York. Pianist & writer, Mills & Feist Music Cos. Pianist & music dir for Mae West, Eddie Cantor; worked with & wrote for Milton Berle, Sophie Tucker, Groucho Marx, Jackie Gleason, Rudy Vallee & many other stars. Wrote songs for "Earl Carroll's Vanities," 32 & "Earl Carroll's Sketch Book," 35; also for Latin Quarter, New York & nightclubs. Entertainment dir & MC, resort hotels, incl Grossingers, Totem Lodge, Fontainbleau, Eden Roc & Diplomat Hotels, NY & Fla; played vaudeville. Music publ, Tobey Music, Henry Tobias Music, admin by Chappell & Warner Bros. Author, "The Borscht Belt", "Twelve Musical Plays for Children", "How to Produce an Amateur Show." Comp & music dir, sr citizen show "Go Like Sixty," Los Angeles & wrote songs for movies, 79-80. Mem: Am Guild Authors & Comp (council); Am Fedn Musicians; Am Fedn TV & Radio Artists; Am Guild Variety Artists; West Coast Adv Council, ASCAP; Songwriters Hall of Fame. Chief Collabrs: Charles Tobias, Harry Tobias, Billy Rose, Al Dubin, Moe Jaffe, Don Reid, Dan Shapiro, Paul Franics Webster, David Ormont, Ballard McDonald, Laura Manning, Joe Young, Sam Lewis, William Dillon & others. *Songs:* Miss You; If I Had My Life to Live Over; Katinka; If I Knew Then; I Remember Mama; Moonlight Brings Memories; Cooking Breakfast for the One I Love; At Last; Easter Sunday With You; A Man Needs to Know; May I Have the Next Dream With You; plus many others.

TOBIN, LEW   ASCAP 1953
composer, author, conductor

b Boston, Mass, June 21, 04. Educ: Boston Latin Sch; Harvard Col; Suffolk Law Sch; New Eng Cons. Cond & pianist for nightclubs, ballrooms & radio; arr for bands & singers. Practicing attorney. *Songs:* Summer's End; 'Taint Gold in My Pocket; There's a Time and Place for Everything; Sunburst.

TOBOGGAN, CHRISTOPHER
See Stuart, Thomas Gilmore

TOCH, ERNST   ASCAP 1936
composer, pianist, teacher

b Vienna, Austria, Dec 7, 1887; d Los Angeles, Calif, Oct 1, 64. Educ: Univ Vienna, studied med & philosophy; studied piano with Willy Rehberg, Frankfort; Univ Heidelberg, PhD; comp, self-taught. Gave up med career for music. Teacher, Hochschule fur Musik, Manheim, 13. Lt Inf Austrian Army, WW I. Taught privately, Manheim. Toured US under auspices of Pro Musica, 32. Came to US, 34, became citizen, 40. Teacher, New Sch Social Res, 34-36. Prof comp, Univ Southern Calif, 37-48. Pvt teacher; also concertized throughout Europe. Author: "The Shaping Forces in Music." Mem, Nat Inst Arts & Letters. Awards: Mozart Prize; Mendelssohn Prize (twice); Austrian State Prize (4 times); Grand Cross of Merit, Order Govt, WGer Repub. *Songs & Instrumental Works:* 7 symphonies (No 3, Pulitzer Prize); 13 string quartets; Serenade in G; Piano Quintet; Nocturno; Peter Pan; Sonatinetta for Flute, Clarinet, Bassoon; 5 Pieces for Wind Instruments, Percussion; Duos for 2 Violins; Serenade for 3 Violins; Big Ben; Pinocchio; Circus; 2 Piano Concerti; The Chinese Flute; Cello Concerto; String Trio; Poems to Martha; Comedy for Orch; Spitzweg Serenade (2 violins, viola); The Inner Circle (A cappella); Berlesken (piano, incl The Juggler); Geographical Fugue (spoken chorus); Valse (spoken chorus); Cantatas: Das Wasser; Bitter Herbs. *Scores:* Film background: Ladies in Retirement; Peter Ibbetson; Address Unknown; Operas: The Princess and the Pea; Egon and Emile; The Fan; The Last Tale.

TODARO, TONY   ASCAP 1956
composer, author, publisher

h Easton, Pa, May 18, 15; d Honolulu, Hawaii, July 28, 76. Educ: High sch. Originated annual show, ASCAP in Hawaii. Founded publ firm, 62; also mfr's agent, Hawaii. Founded Nani Awards, 76; founded Hawaii Soc Prof Songwriters, 75. Author: "The Golden Years of Hawaiian Entertainment," 74. Chief Collabr: Mary Johnston. *Songs:* Keep Your Eyes on the Hands; I'll See You in Hawaii (off Hawaii Visitors Bureau song); Somewhere in Hawaii; Hula Cop Hop; Mynah Bird; In a Hawaiian Village; There's No Place Like Hawaii; Every Hour on the Hour; Hawaiian Moon; Ukulele Island.

TODD, ARTHUR W   ASCAP 1958
composer, author, singer

b Elizabeth, NJ, Mar 11, 20. Educ: Syracuse Univ; studied banjo & voice. Mem singing team, Art & Dotty Todd in nightclubs, hotels, TV & records. Had own radio show, CBS, 2 yrs & ABC, 2 yrs. Guitarist. Chief Collabr: Dotty Todd. *Songs:* Say You; Joie d'Vivre; Ca C'est la Vie; The Busy Signal Song; Sweet Cha Cha Chariot; The Nearer You Are to Me; Ring-a-ding Feeling; Black Velvet Eyes; I'll Never Leave Hawaii.

TODD, BOB   ASCAP 1971
composer, record producer

b St Louis, Mo, Jan 23, 41. Educ: Chaffee High Sch; Oceanside City Col. Prof mgr, Screen Gems Music, 67-68. A&R vpres, ABC Records & dir publ, ABC Music, 69-70. A&R vpres, Mercury Records, West Coast, 70-72. Independent producer/songwriter, 73-76. Co-owner, Cream Records & dir publ, East Memphis Music, 77- Wrote radio jingles for KRLA, KROQ, KMET & KWST radio & TV. *Songs:* Coming in Out of the Rain; Cryin Shame; Drifting Prophet;

Love Is Gone; Liberated Lady; All That Jazz; What You See Is What You Get; Music: She (Power to Be). *Instrumental Works:* Cosmic Sea; Anyway You Want It; Honey Trippin; Other Side of Midnight; Universal Mind. *Scores:* Film/TV: Days of Our Lives; The Young and the Restless; Spectra Man.

TODD, CLARENCE E   ASCAP 1949
composer, author, singer
b New Orleans, La, Feb 23, 1897. Educ: Pub schs; studied piano with sister. Singer & pianist in orchs incl Sidney Bechet, Buddy Petit & Kid Ory. WW I service. Moved to New York, 21; on staff, music publ & radio; mem, Clarence Williams Trio; pianist in nightclubs, vaudeville & Bway musicals until 47. *Songs:* Oooh Look-a-There Ain't She Pretty; Papa-de-da-da; Sweet 'n' Tender; Chilly 'n' Cold; Love Grows on the White Oak Tree.

TODD, D S
See Billingsley, Derrell L

TODD, DOTTY   ASCAP 1958
composer, author, singer
b Elizabeth, NJ, June 22, 23. Educ: Bus col; studied piano & voice. Mem singing team, Art & Dotty Todd in nightclubs, hotels, TV & records. Had own radio show, CBS, 2 yrs & ABC, 2 yrs. Pianist. Chief Collabr: Art Todd. *Songs:* Say You; Joie d'Vivre; Ca C'est la Vie; The Busy Signal Song; Sweet Cha Cha Chariot; The Nearer You Are to Me; Ring-a-ding Feeling; Black Velvet Eyes; I'll Never Leave Hawaii.

TODD, TOM T   ASCAP 1961
composer, arranger, pianist
b Portland, Ore, Mar 26, 23. Educ: Univ Southern Calif; studied with Harry Kaufman, Mario Castelnuovo-Tedesco & Arnold Schoenberg. Pianist & arr with orchs, Tommy Dorsey, Harry James, Benny Goodman & Billy May; comp & arr, MGM, 46-49 & NBC, 50-52; writer for nightclub revues, films & TV; comp ice ballet for Marji Lee. *Instrumental Works:* Tattle-Tale; Tomfoolery; Trombosis.

TODRIS, MURRAY   ASCAP 1961
author, teacher
b New York, NY, Mar 29, 18. Author of bk, "The Art of Sensual Massage." Chief Collabr: Joseph Ricitelli. *Songs:* Lyrics: Beautiful; The Sound.

TOLBERT, GREGORY JEROME (GERONIMO)   ASCAP 1977
composer, author, singer
b Washington, DC, May 30, 53. Educ: Eastern High Sch; Baltimore Community Col. Mem of Pipeline. Recording artist for Columbia Records. Mem of Universal Robot Band. Worked with Van McCoy, The Choice Four, Disco Tex and Sex-o-Lettes; Faith, Hope and Charity & Musique; also worked with producers, incl Patrick Adams, Billy Jackson, Meco Manado & the Joneses. Chief Collabrs: Woodrow Cunningham Jr, Kathy Mull, Norman A Durham. *Songs:* We've Got Your Sunshine; You're My Music; Rare Pleasure; Baby Love; Do What You Feel Like Doing.

TOLMAGE, GERALD
See Gardner, Maurice

TOMAN, GERALD JOHN   ASCAP 1960
composer, author
b Lansing, Mich, June 7, 37. Educ: Don Lee Studios; Mich State Univ, summer course. Spec Services, USN, 55-58. Road musician with club dates, 58 & 59; pvt instr, 60- Chief Collabrs: Al LaGuire; Richard Garcia. *Songs & Instrumental Works:* Dreamy Rhythm; Trick Or Treat, Halloween; Lonely and Blue (Triste Sin Ti); Help Me Forget; Music: We Love the Green and White.

TOMLIN, LILY
actress
b Detroit, Mich, 1939. Educ: Wayne State Univ; studied mime with Paul Curtis. Appeared, concerts & cols throughout US. TV appearances incl Lily Tomlin specials, CBS, 73 & ABC, 75. Former mem, "The Music Scene" & "Laugh In." Film debut, Nashville, Tenn, 75. Acted in "The Late Show" & "Moment By Moment." Recording artist. Recipient, Grammy award, 71, 3 Emmy awards (for TV specials, 73 & 75), Tony award for one-woman Bway show "Appearing Nitely," 77. *Albums:* This Is a Recording; And That's the Truth; Modern Scream; On Stage.

TOMLIN, PINKY   ASCAP 1936
composer, author
b Eros, Ark, Sept 9, 08. Educ: Univ Okla, studied music, geology & law, 3 1/2 yrs. Sang with Jimmie Grier Orch, Baltimore Bowl; formed own orch & played at Baltimore Bowl, Los Angeles, 39; made cross country tour, played in major hotels & theatres; wrote scores & sang. Author bk, "The Object of My Affection". Made 12 feature movies. Chief Collabrs: Harry Tobias, Johnny Mercer. *Songs & Instrumental Works:* The Object of My Affection; What's the Reason I'm Not Pleasin' You; That's What You Think; The Love Bug Will Bite You, If You Don't Watch Out; Lost and Found; If It Wasn't for the Moon; My, My, Ain't Somethin'; In Ol' Oklahoma; I'm Just a Country Boy at Heart; I Told Santa Clause to Bring Me You; Don't Be Afraid to Tell Your Mother.

TOMS, GRAYDON ARTHUR   ASCAP 1976
composer, author, teacher
b Stroudsburg, Pa, Sept 28, 57. Educ: Chapman Col, 76-78, studied with Alan Oettinger. Rec'd Golden Ear Award (outstanding theory student), Chapman Col, 80. Writer popular songs & piano pieces; nightclub entertainer; singer; pianist. Chief Collabrs: Steven Elwood Siptroth, Jack Fulton. *Songs:* Just a Song; Another Day to Live; Cindy. *Instrumental Works:* The Golden Eagle Fanfare for Band; A Resounding Impact for Band.

TONEY, KEVIN KRAIG   ASCAP 1979
composer, author, instrumentalist
b Detroit, Mich, Apr 23, 53. Educ: Cass Technical High Sch, Detroit; Interlochen Music Acad, scholarship, 65; Howard Univ, BA(music comp), 78; studied comp with Russel Wollen, piano with Thomas Flagg & Arthur Labrew. Performed with Marcus Belgrave & other top musicians, Detroit, 69-71; performed & recorded with var musicians, incl Andrew White, 72-, Donald Byrd and The Blackbyrds, 73-78. Chief Collabrs: Donald Byrd, Andrew White. *Songs & Instrumental Works:* All I Ask; Rock Creek Park; Dreaming 'Bout You; Unfinished Business; Spring Flower; Future Children, Future Hopes; City Life.

TONEY, LEMUEL GORDON
See Leonard, Eddie

TONNING, MERRILL D (IDAHO MERRILL)   ASCAP 1961
composer, author, arranger
b Rathdrum, Idaho. Educ: Fifth grade piano music; self-taught on instruments as well as arr; correspondence courses in arr. First played prof, 27; traveled with vaudeville stage band, 29; has been playing in concert & dance bands, 29- Started writing songs, 29. Worked in grocery stores & show stores; income tax auditor, Internal Revenue Dept, 23 yrs & Idaho State Tax Comn, 5 yrs. Taught band & orch, Grandview, Idaho, 6 yrs. Part-time asst district sales mgr, local daily newspaper. Chief Collabrs: LeRoy E Maule, Antone Iavello, Kenneth F Betzold, Bill Rhodenbaugh, Louie C Ventrella, Lori Wild, Ivan Hooper. *Songs:* We Sing of Idaho (State Centennial March, 63); Idaho Polka (completely rev); Our Home in the Hills; Born in Bethlehem; Charisma; Music: It's Unbelievable; Lyrics: Moon River.

TONTO, CHARLIE
See Pugliese, Carlos Anibal

TORBETT, DAVE   ASCAP 1953
composer, conductor, musician
b Prairie Grove, Ark, Aug 22, 08. Studied with Joseph Schillinger & Ernst Toch. Musician in dance bands, vaudeville, radio & films; also wrote for films; arr.

TORME, MELVIN HOWARD   ASCAP 1946
composer, author, singer
b Chicago, Ill, Sept 13, 25. Educ: High sch. Served in USAAF, WW II. Has sung in nightclubs, hotels, on radio & TV; recording artist. Chief Collabr: Robert Wells. *Songs:* Stranger in Town; The Christmas Song; Born to Be Blue; Willow Road; Magic Town; County Fair; Four Months, Three Weeks, Two Days, One Hour Blues; There Isn't Any Special Reason; Bless You; Lament to Love; It's the Love I Feel for You; Ain't Gonna Be Like That; Welcome to the Club; Reminiscing in Tempo; Whisper Not; A Stranger Called the Blues; Got the Gate on the Golden Gate; The Jet Set. *Instrumental Works:* California Suite.

TORRE, JANICE   ASCAP 1951
author
b New Orleans, La. Educ: Newcomb Col; Tulane Univ; Yale Univ Drama Sch; Univ Tex. Songwriter for films incl "Luxury Liner", "Big City", "In the Good Old Summertime", "Night Song" & "Girls, Girls, Girls." Author, bk & lyrics, TV spec "The Stingiest Man in Town," regional stage & off-Bway musicals incl "Peter Rabbit," Joseph Jefferson award, "Toby Tyler" & "Sleeping Beauty." Recipient, Joseph Jefferson award for stage adaptation of "The Stingiest Man in Town." Chief Collabr: Fred Spielman. *Songs:* Who Killed 'Er?; Merry Christmas; Spring Came Back to Vienna; Paper Roses (ASCAP & Billboard awards & Grammy nomination, 74); Free; I'm Gonna See a Lot of You; Talented Shoes; After All These Years; Magic Boy; I Don't Want To; The Letter; Yes, There Is a Santa Claus; The Birthday Party of the King; An Old-Fashioned Christmas; Mankind Should Be My Business; The Christmas Spirit; One Little Boy; It Might Have Been; Golden Dreams; Holly-Ho; The Stingiest Man in Town; I Saw Eddie Kiss My Sister. *Scores:* Films: Tom Thumb.

TORRES, RICARDO   ASCAP 1979
composer, author, percussionist
b Santurce, PR, Dec 6, 47. Educ: Brooklyn Col, 69; Santa Monica Col, 71; Berklee Col of Music, 72-74; studied vibes with Gary Burton, 72; studied Afro-Cuban perc with Mongo Santamaria, 78. NEA study fel/grant, 78. Percussionist & comp for jazz, Latin, R&B rock groups; also theatre & cabaret acts. Recording artist, Arista-Freedom, Mercury & King Records (Japan). Leader own group, Rimarsan; studio musician, New York. Chief Collabr: Louis Levin. *Instrumental Works:* Nueva Camapana.

TORTORIELLO, VINCENT JOSEPH (JOE TARTO) ASCAP 1953
composer, author, arranger
b Newark, NJ, Feb 22, 02. Educ: Studied tuba & bass with Emil Weber, New York Philh; studied theory, harmony & orchestration with Edward Schaff, Newark, NJ & Tom Timouthy, New York. USA Band, WW I. Launched career in music at age 17. Worked with many radio, movie studio & show bands. Traveled to London with Paul Specht, Paul Whiteman & Vincent Lopez; wrote arr for Don Voorhees, Paul Lavalle, Dorsey Bros, Paul Whiteman, Joe Venuti, Eddie Lang, Al Goodman, Rubinoff, Vincent Lopez, Carmen Cavallero, Ted Staeter, Fletcher Henderson & Chick Webb; played for Betty Boop, Popeye the Sailor & Bugs Bunny TV cartoons; mem staff orchs, NBC, ABC & CBS; played in Off World's Fair Band of Am; tuba player & arr, Essex Brass Ens. Clinician, teacher & adjudicator. Scholarship set up in his name as Joe Tarto Tuba Scholarship Fund, New York Brass Conference for Scholarships, 73. Author Bks: "Banjo Pickings"; "Bass Noodles"; "Modern Method of Improvising"; "Basic Rhythms and the Art of Jazz Improvisation"; "Theory, Harmony, Technique, Shifting Meter Studies for Tuba, Teachers, Composers, Arrangers, Conductors." Chief Collabrs: Paul Lavalle, Al Finnelli, Al Philburn, Ted Bartell, Joe Venuti, Eddie Lang, Tony Collucci. Songs: Go Get That Old Oaken Bucket; Lyrics: Cherie; Whistle Your Blues Away. Instrumental Works: The Trumpet Polka; Big Joe, The Tuba (march); Good Fellowship March; The Dixieland March; El Moresque Cha-Cha-Cha; Shipwrecked; Black Horse Stomp; White Ghost Shivers; Yankees on Parade March.

TOUZET, RENE ASCAP 1953
composer
b Havana, Cuba, Sept 16, 16. Songs & Instrumental Works: Amor de Pelicula; Bolero Time; Minuet Mambo; Let Me Love You Tonight.

TOWNE, CHARLES HANSON ASCAP 1943
author
b Louisville, Ky, Feb 2, 1877; d New York, NY, Feb 28, 49. Educ: City Col New York. Ed & contributor to mags. Author, volumes of poetry; bks: "A world of Windows"; "The Rise and Fall of Prohibition"; "The Bad Man"; "Loafing Down Long Island"; "The Cabin"; "Ambling Through Acadia"; "An April Song"; "Roosevelt as the Poets Saw Him"; "So Far, So Good" (autobiography). Songs & Instrumental Works: La Belle Helene (Eng lyrics); Poems set to music: A Lover in Damascus; The City of Joy; Love's Triumph.

TOWNSEND, BRIGHAM ASCAP 1938
author
b Spokane, Wash, Oct 15, 07. House mgr, Chinese Theatre, Hollywood, 36-38; pub rels & advert dir, Hull Hotels, Calif, 45-64; asst to pres, Gene Autry Hotels, Calif, 64-70; dir publicity & advert, Tropicana Hotel, Las Vegas, Nev. Chief Collabrs: Matt Dennis, George Davolos. Songs: Lyrics: Love Turns Winter to Spring; Little Man With a Candy Cigar; Humpty Dumpty; Pan and Broom Man; Moon Melody.

TOWNSEND, DAVID MICHAEL ASCAP 1974
composer, clarinetist, conductor
b Chicago, Ill, Apr 18, 42. Educ: Ind Univ, BMEd, 65; Mich State Univ, MM, 70; Red Wing Area Voc Tech Inst, wind instrument repair degreee, 79; Univ Ariz, doctoral candidate, 81. Eight yrs col teaching; clarinetist with several community orchs; solo & ens performer, concentrating on chamber music; studio recording; instrument repair technician specializing in woodwinds & customzing clarinets. Instrumental Works: Happy Christmas for Brass (five carols).

TOZZO, VINCENT J (VINNY ROMA) ASCAP 1968
composer, author, singer
b New Rochelle, NY, Nov 2, 29. Educ: Univ Miami, music study; vocal coach, Joseph Brunelli. Singing musician-pianist; worked all prominent clubs, restaurants on East Coast of US. Chief Collab: Jimmy Dale. Songs: Sunset in Rome; The Italian Cowboy; Just Because My Name Is Italian, Don't Call Me the Mafia; The Italian Heart; No Answer; The Lousiest Song in the World; Lyrics: I Saw Her Face Last Night.

TRACE, ALBERT J (CLEM WATTS, BOB HART) ASCAP 1944
composer, author
b Chicago, Ill. Educ: Chicago schs; studied drums & perc with Roy Knapp. Started with own band, Chicago Worlds Fair, 33. Worked in films for Columbia Pictures. Played theatres, hotels & nite clubs, US. With radio network show "It Pays to Be Ignorant." Own TV show, ABC, Chicago, one yr. Recorded on MGM, Mercury & Columbia labels. Chief Collabrs: Ben Trace, Al Hoffman, Oakley Haldeman, Bob Merrill, Abner Silver. Songs & Instrumental Works: You Call Everybody Darling; Wishin'; Brush Those Tears From Your Eyes; If I Knew You Were Comin' I'd've Baked a Cake; Where Did Yesterday Go. Albums: Great Concert in the Sky; Great Big Friendly Town-Chicago.

TRACE, BEN L ASCAP 1949
composer, author, singer
b Chicago, Ill, Oct 15, 1897; d. Educ: Crerar Sch. Staff, music publ co. Singer in nightclubs & vaudeville, 21-32. WW II, US Inf. Chief Collabr: Al Trace. Songs: You Call Everybody Darling; Shh! Don't Look Now; Do You Mind?; Eeny Meeny Miny Mo; I Love Every State of the 48; Everytime You're Steppin'

Out; Sergeant Mike McGinnity; Sweet Dream, Sweetheart; Is This Heaven?; Let's Pretend That We're Sweethearts Again; If I Could Have My Druthers; I'm Through Callin' Everybody Darlin'.

TRACEY, PAUL HUGH LAWRENCE ASCAP 1973
composer, author, entertainer
b Durban, South Africa, June 5, 39. Educ: Malvern Col, Eng; Univ of the Bush, SAfrica. First prof job radio, SAfrica. Bway credits: Revival of "The Boy Friend" & "The Rothschilds." Started to write songs, 72. Own one-man show, "Something Else." Lect/demonstration schs, cols & clubs, "About Africa," US. Artist-in-residence, Affiliate Artists. TV appearances. Songs: The Wishing Song; Dog Walk; Something's Missing; The Ugly Song; The Chicken Song. Scores: Bway Show: Wait a Minim.

TRACEY, WILLIAM G ASCAP 1914
author
b New York, NY, July 19, 1893; d New York, Sept 5, 57. Educ: Pub schs. Mem prof staff, music publ co. Charter mem, ASCAP. Chief Collabrs: Lewis Muir, George Meyer, Maceo Pinkard, Doris Tauber, Nat Vincent. Songs: Gee, But It's Great to Meet a Friend From Your Home Town; Them There Eyes; Bring Back My Daddy to Me; Mammy o' Mine; He's Had No Lovin' for a Long, Long Time; Dixie Is Dixie Once More; Give a Little Credit to Your Dad; Is My Baby Blue Tonight?.

TRACY, DENNIS ARTHUR ASCAP 1971
singer, guitarist, recording artist
b San Jose, Calif, Dec 30, 48. Educ: Willow Glen High Sch; San Jose State Univ, drama major, tutorials prog for gifted students. First songs recorded at age 16. Staff songwriter, CBS, April Music & A&M Records, Almo Music. Recording artist for Janus Records, Columbia Records & Twentieth Century Records. Chief Collabrs: Jan Lucas, Dennis Fridkin. Songs: Showbiz; The Millionaire; In Love Like You and Me; Copenhagen; Dance With the Devil.

TRADER, WILLIAM MARVIN ASCAP 1952
composer, author, singer
b Darlington, SC, May 11, 22. Educ: St Johns High Sch; Nashville Auto-Diesel Col; Florence-Darlington Tech Col; York Tech Col. Grad instr, dept head, indust div head, assoc in applied sci, assoc in indust technol, York Tech Col. End man in minstrel shows; radio DJ; TV, recording artist; promoter, publ & owner of Dixie record label. Chief Collabrs: Noel Durham, Danny Parker, Randy Cottrell. Songs: (Now and Then There's) A Fool Such As I; Don't Wake Me Now; Don't Turn Around; Cherokee Call; Bitter Harvest; I'll Never Fear Tomorrow; Castaway; Veil of Tears; A Song to Sing; Lyrics: Alone At Christmas Time.

TRAINOR, THOMAS WALTER ASCAP 1968
composer, author
b Springfield, Mass, Jan 25, 28. Educ: Am Int Col, Springfield, English; Harvard Col, music appreciation; Univ Chicago, English. Piano, vibraphone, barbershop comp. Songs: Hello Bill; Handys Hot Dogs; Waterfront Mary; Broadway Barney Brown; The Banjo Man.

TRAKTMAN, PEGGY SIMON ASCAP 1963
author
b NY, July 19, 32. Educ: Columbia Univ Sch of Dramatic Arts, BFA. Writer of musicals for children, 59- Has written children's records & musical reviews, all produced. Co-founder & producer, Maximillion Productions. Adaptor of songs for Camarata Singers, Collegiate Chorale. Working on Bway/off-Bway musical, new revue & TV series. Chief Collabrs: Mark Wright, John Clifton, Debra Dargle. Songs: I Love Garbage!; Rainboa; Lyrics: Mr Snow; Who Will Haunt the House?; Wishy Washy Witch; Minute After Midnight; Rattlesnake Soup; Do You Remember?; The Impossible—Just Takes a Little Longer; Wonderful Wailing Wind; Too Many Lovers; 17B; You Were So...; Never Fall in Love.

TRAVERS, MARY ALLIN ASCAP 1963
composer, author, arranger
b Louisville, Ky, Nov 7, 37. Educ: New York pub schs; Art Inst. Sang with Songswappers; later, mem singing trio, Peter, Paul & Mary, appearing on TV, in nightclubs & concerts throughout US, Can & Europe. Singer; has sung at jazz & folk fests; recording artist. Chief Collabrs: Peter Yarrow, Noel Stookey, Milt Okun.

TRAVIS, CAROLYNN D ASCAP 1966
composer, author, teacher
b Orlando, Fla, Aug 10, 22. Educ: Agnes Scott Col, Ga, 2 yrs; Washington Univ, 1 yr; Cook County Sch Nursing, 1 yr; Univ Wyo, BS & MA; law sch, 1 yr. Sec sch teacher sci & Span, 21 yrs; personal mgr rock band, 62-; Pan Am Airlines secy & reservation agent, 2 yrs. Songs: I Beg of the Moon; Gypsy Love; Surf Song.

TRAVIS, ROY ASCAP 1968
composer, author, educator
b New York, NY, June 24, 22. Educ: Columbia Col, BA, 47; Juilliard Sch Music, BS, 49, MS, 50, studied with Bernard Wagenaar; Columbia Univ, MA, 51,

studied comp with Otto Luening; studied with Darius Milhaud at Cons National, Paris, 51-52 & Felix Salzer. Instr, Columbia Univ, 52-53, Mannes Col Music, 52-57; from instr to assoc prof, Univ Calif, Los Angeles, 57-68, prof music, 68- Recent comp reflect interest in using rhythms borrowed from West African dances & concern with problem of creating large-scale tonal coherence with non-triadic vocabularies. Author monograph "Tonal Coherence in the First Movement of Bartok's IVth String Quartet" in Music Forum, Vol II, 70. Fel, Inst Creative Arts, Univ Calif; rec'd two NEA grants & Guggenheim fel, also numerous other awards. *Songs & Instrumental Works:* African Sonata (piano, 4 movements, each based on a different West African dance); Duo Concertante (violin & piano in 5 movements, the first, Gakpa, and last, Asafo, based on Ewe dances from Ghana); Collage (Orch); Piano Concerto (3 movements, finale based on African rhythms); Switched-On Ashanti (live flute & tape, the latter incl African instruments & synthesized sounds with rhythms from different Ashanti dances as recorded by Ashanti (Ghana) master drummer Kwasi Badu on authentic instruments); Five Preludes for Piano; Symphonic Allegro (orch; 1st Prize, 7th Annual Gershwin Awards); Songs and Epilogues (cycle of five songs alternating with four instrumental epilogues & prologues, piano/vocal & orch versions). *Scores:* Opera: The Passion of Oedipus (freely adapted from Oedipus Rex of Sophocles, 2 acts).

TREBOR, ROBERT
See Seigenthaler, William Robert

TREHARNE, BRYCESON   ASCAP 1943
composer, producer, educator
b Merthyr Tydvil, Wales, May 30, 1879; d New York, NY, Feb 4, 48. Educ: Royal Col Music, London (Erard scholarship); studied with Stanford, Franklin, Walford, Davies & Dannreuther; hon MusD, McGill Univ. Taught at Univ Adelaide, Australia, 1900-11. Moved to US, 17. Founder, Adelaide Rep Theatre. Ed, publ to promote theatre arts, US & Italy. Spent 2 yrs in Ger prison camp, WW I. Music lectr, McGill Univ, 23-27. Ed, Boston Music Co, Willis Music Co, 28. *Songs & Instrumental Works:* A Widow Bird; Uphill; Farewell; Choral: Song of Solomon (oratorio); The Banshee; Again in Unison We Stand; Song's Eternity; Mount Your Horses. *Scores:* Operettas: The Toymaker; Abe Lincoln; A Christmas Carol.

TRENNER, DONN   ASCAP 1962
composer, conductor, pianist
b New Haven, Conn, Mar 10, 27. Educ: High sch. Pianist in orchs incl Ted Fiorito, Tex Beneke, Richard Maltby, Charlie Barnet & Les Brown (8 yrs); music dir, Steve Allen TV show, 2 1/2 yrs. Arr. *Songs:* Leave It to Me; Top o' the Morning.

TRENT, JO   ASCAP 1925
author
b Chicago, Ill, May 31, 1892; d Barcelona, Spain, Nov 19, 54. Educ: Univ Pa; City Col New York. Prof mgr, music publ houses. Staff writer & asst dir, film cos; also coach & tutor. Wrote for radio, TV, nightclubs & theatres. Author: "Modern Adaptation of Primitive Tones." Chief Collabrs: Louis Alter, Hoagy Carmichael, Peter De Rose, Ford Dabney. *Songs:* Muddy Water; My Kinda Love; I Just Roll Along, Havin' My Ups and Downs; Wake Up, Chillun, Wake Up; Because I Feel Low Down; Ploddin' Along; Maybe I'm Wrong Again; Here You Come With Love; Got a Feelin' for You; I Want It Sweet Like You; Rhythm King. *Scores:* Bway stage: Rang Tang; Operetta: Peaceful Henry.

TREVOR, VAN
See Boulanger, Robert Francis

TRIGGS, AUBREY LEIGH   ASCAP 1964
composer, author
b Leigh-on-Sea, Eng, May 22, 21. Educ: Durban High Sch, SAfrica; pvt music studies; Univ Calif, Los Angeles Extension Courses, lyric writing with Hal Levy. Singer, drummer, harmonica player on radio in SAfrica. Came to US, 49. Songwriter specializing in African-type songs & ballads. Chief Collabrs: Fred Thompson, Keith R Williams. *Songs:* Jika Jing; Sebenza; Tiares; Bell of Atlantis; Out in the Green, Green World.

TRINKAUS, GEORGE J   ASCAP 1914
composer, editor
b Bridgeport, Conn, Apr 13, 1878; d Ridgewood, NJ, May 19, 60. Educ: Yale Univ. Music ed, New York publ co. Charter mem, ASCAP. *Songs:* Mammy's Little Kinky-Headed Boy; Bells of Killarney: Marceline (Dance of the Clowns). *Instrumental Works:* Two Symphonies; Symphonietta in F; Tribute to a Hero (overture); Sonatina for String Orchestra; Rhapsody for Violin, Orchestra; Overtures for band, orch: The May Queen; The Philosopher; Robin Goodfellow; Souvenir de Rossino; Suites for Orch: The Streets of Bagdad; The Polar Suite; Scenes Pastorale; Night Voices; The Four Winds; Band: Three Humorous Sketches; The Flirtatious Rooster; The Balky Mule; The Buzzing Mosquitoes; Opera: Wizard of Avon.

TRIPP, PAUL   ASCAP 1947
author, actor, singer
b New York, NY, Feb 20, 16. Educ: City Col New York, BA; Brooklyn Law Sch. Bway debut with Hampden's "Cyrano de Bergerac"; active in many Bway shows actg, singing, dir. Signal Corps service, USA, WW II, China. Wrote 30 children's musical record albums, 46-; created, wrote scripts & songs, produced

& starred in "Mr I Magination" (CBS-TV). Starred & produced "On the Carousel" (CBS-TV) & "Birthday House" (NBC-TV). Creator, lyricist & star of perennial children's film classic, "The Christmas That Almost Wasn't" (Grammy Award). Recipient of Peabody Award, Emmy & eight Ohio State Awards. Author five juv bks. Chief Collabrs: George Kleinsinger & Ray Carter. *Songs:* Lyrics: Good Night, Dear Lord. *Instrumental Works:* Peewee the Piccolo; Once Upon an Orchestra; David, Ancient of Kings (symphonic with choir). *Scores:* Ballet: Story of Celeste; The Toy Box; Films: Tubby the Tuba (film script & lyrics).

TRITT, JOHNNIE
See Pistritto, John

TRIVERS, BARRY   ASCAP 1955
author
b Jaffa, Palestine, Feb 12, 12. Educ: NY schs. Was an actor in Bway play "Street Scene." Wrote songs & sketches for "Ziegfeld Follies of 1931." Writer for films & radio; then TV writer, Calif. Author novel, "Blind Man and the Nude." Chief Collabrs: Ben Oakland, Jay Gorney. *Songs:* Two Loves Have I; Do the New York. *Scores:* Stage: Heaven on Earth (Bway).

TRIVERS, JOHN   ASCAP 1970
songwriter
b Buffalo, NY. Educ: Hobart Col, Geneva, NY, BA. Original bass player, Bway show "Grease." Toured with Janis Ian & Peter Allen. Co-writer of songs. Chief Collabrs: Michael Moorcock, Eric Bloom, Elizabeth Myers. *Songs:* I Don't Wanna Know; Nothing to Do; Nightmare; Music: Black Blade; The Great Sun Jester.

TROKER, KATHERINE BEATON   ASCAP 1963
author
b North Sydney, Can, Dec 30, 1891; d. Educ: Bus col; studied nursing. Chief Collabr: Al Avellini. *Songs:* Broken-Hearted Dolly; Don't Ever Break Your Baby's Heart.

TROMBETTA, GAYLE M   ASCAP 1979
author, dancer, teacher
b Philadelphia, Pa, June 30, 47. Educ: Lower Merion High Sch, 65. Chief Collabr: Vincent J Trombetta (husband). *Songs:* Lyrics: I Like Your Style; I'll Never Forget You; Christmas Time.

TROMBETTA, VINCENT J   ASCAP 1967
composer, author, studio musician
b Philadelphia, Pa, Dec 24, 40. Educ: North Cath High Sch; Philadelphia Cons, 60; Philadelphia Musical Acad, BM, 65; studied comp with Vincent Persichetti, Joe Castaldo, Robert Suderberg & Phil Woods; studied saxophone with Tony Dienno, Boots Mazzoli, Guido Mecoli & Phil Woods. Started playing accordion at age 7, saxophone at age 12; prof at age 14. Played & wrote with var bands. Served in USA. Won Best Saxophonist & Charlie Parker Award, Villanova Jazz Fest, 65. Woodwind player, arr & comp, "Mike Douglas Show," 65. Head, Saxophone Dept, Philadelphia Musical Acad, 68-78. Chief Collabr: Gayle M Trombetta (wife). *Songs:* I Am Without You; Here's Mike (theme, Mike Douglas Show); Music: I Like Your Style; Christmas Time. *Instrumental Works:* Rosee; Wind Trio No 1; Fugue.

TROST, RUSSEL G   ASCAP 1957
composer, author, pianist
b Detroit, Mich, June 10, 10. Educ: High sch. With Paramount Studio casting dept, 27; casting dir, Warner Bros, 36-42 & 45-48 & CBS, Hollywood. USCG, World War II. Dir. *Songs:* That's Love; This Night I'll Remember; Miss Pettibone Confesses.

TROTTA, RAYMOND   ASCAP 1953
composer
b Abruzzi, Italy, Sept 6, 1896. Educ: Grade sch. Studied trumpet at age 10; played professionally for silent movies & vaudeville acts at age 17, New Britain, Conn Palace Theatre, later moved to New Haven, Conn & joined the Barney Rapp Band, 7 yrs; staff orch, New Haven Paramount Theatre. Played in radio, WINS, NBC, CBS & WOV, 30's, also Roxy Theatre, New York, 40's; played with Paul Whiteman, Fred Waring & 4 yrs with Tony Pastor. Chief Collabrs: Buddy Kaye, Hal David, Hector Marchese. *Songs & Instrumental Works:* Tira Lira Li; Over and Over; My Topic of Conversation; Don't Wait for Sunday to Pray; Long Ago Last Night; Pucker Uppa; Lovely Lady; Foolin' Around; Gonna Miss You; Bugles and Drums; Happiness.

TROTTER, JOHN SCOTT   ASCAP 1951
composer, conductor, arranger
b Charlotte, NC, June 14, 08; d Los Angeles, Calif, Oct 29, 75. Educ: Univ NC; Univ Calif Los Angeles, studied with classical comp Ernst Toch. Pianist in local band while at Univ; with band when it came to New York, led by Hal Kemp, 25-35. Moved to Hollywood, 36; music dir, Bing Crosby radio shows, "Kraft Music Hall", "Philco Radio Time" & "Chesterfield Show", 37-54; also arr for Kirsten Flagstad, Al Jolson, Mary Martin, Judy Garland & Jose Iturbi. Comp & cond, "George Gobel Show," 54-60. Secy, Los Angeles Chap, TV Arts & Sci, 60-62. Pres, Council of Arts. Had made many records, among them "White

Christmas" with Bing Crosby, one of the first five recordings elected to the Record Hall of Fame. After the 50's, was musical dir, "Peanuts" spec: "The Great Pumpkin", "He's Your Dog, Charlie Brown" & "You're Not Elected, Charlie Brown." Did music for the full length film, "A Boy Named Charlie Brown" which was nominated for an Oscar & Emmy award. Collab with lyricist Tom Adair on musical numbers for TV productions, "Babar the Little Elephant" (Emmy award nomination) & "Babar Comes to America," 68-69; also made numerous indust training films for large cos. Was involved with Disneyland projects with Songfests for Univ Southern Calif for more than 20 yrs. Mem, Orange County Philh Soc. Was nat trustee of TV Acad; pres, Acad Recording Arts & Sci.

TROUP, KENNETH HUGH   ASCAP 1968
composer, author
b Kansas City, Mo, June 21, 06. Educ: Humbolt Elem Sch. Played brass instruments in show bus; songwriter of gospel & popular music. *Songs:* Tear of Happiness; I Left My Sugar in Hawaii; Leota; Jesus Will Return; I Want to Live; The Immigrant; Blue Monday; Desert Moon.

TROUP, ROBERT WILLIAM, JR   ASCAP 1946
composer, author, pianist
b Harrisburg, Pa, Oct 18, 18. Educ: Lancaster Boys High Sch, Pa, 36; Hill Sch, 37; Univ Pa Wharton Sch, BS(econ), 41. Staff songwriter, Tommy Dorsey Orch, 41. Capt, USMC, WW II, 41-46. Wrote scores for, dir & produced service musicals, in US & overseas. Moved to Hollywood, 46, pianist & singer in night clubs, later formed jazz trio. Panel mem, CBS' "Musical Chairs." Recording artist, Capitol, Victor, Liberty, Bethlehem, Decca, Interlude & Mode. Appeared as actor in motion pictures incl "The High Cost of Loving", "Number One", "The Five Pennies", "The Gene Krupa Story" & "The Duchess of Idaho." Wrote songs for films incl "The Great Man", "Rock Pretty Baby", "The Girl Can't Help It", "Voice in the Mirror", "Man of the West." Appeared as regular in NBC's "Emergency," 71-76. *Songs:* Daddy; Snootie Little Cutie; Baby, Baby All the Time; Route 66; Lonely Girl; February Brings the Rain; Now You Know; It Happened Once Before; The Three Bears; Their Hearts Were Full of Spring; You're Lookin' At Me; Julie Is Her Name; This October; One October Morning; Where Did the Gentleman Go?; Bran' New Dolly; I'm Such a Hungry Man; The Meaning of the Blues; Away, Away, Away; Triskaidekaphobia; Lemon Twist; I'd Like You for Christmas; The Girl Can't Help It; Lyrics: My City of Sydney; The Feeling of Jazz; Please Remember; I'm With You; Free and Easy; Girl Talk; Nice Girls Don't Stay for Breakfast.

TROUTMAN, JOHN
See Blake, George M

TROY, HENRY
composer, author
b Birmingham, Ala, Aug 31, 08; d New York, NY, May, 62. Singer, Williams & Walker Troupe. Travelled throughout Europe. Gave command perf for King & Queen of Eng. Chief Collabrs: Chris Smith; Fletcher Henderson; W C Handy; Andy Razoff. *Songs & Instrumental Works:* Gin House Blues; Cake Walkin Babies Back Home; Unsung American Heros Song.

TRUBITT, ALLEN ROY   ASCAP 1979
composer, author, teacher
b Chicago, Ill, Aug 24, 31. Educ: Roosevelt Univ, BMusEd & MusEd, 54; Ind Univ, DMus, 64; cello studies with K Fruh, J Starker & comp with B Heiden & K Jirak. With 7th Army Symph, US Army, 54-56. Asst prof, Indiana Univ of Pa, 57-64; prof, Univ Hawaii, 64-, chmn music dept, 71-75. Co-author, "Ear Training and Sight Singing," (2 vols) & "A Comprehensive Introduction to Music Literature." Chief Collab: Robert S Hines. *Songs:* Music: Madrigal; Eldorado; The Tide Rises, the Tide Falls; What Any Lover Learns; three songs on the shortness of life; three song cycles. *Instrumental Works:* Two symphonies; three piano sonatas; string quartet.

TRUE, CHRISTOPHER MARK
composer, singer, guitarist
b Ipswich, Eng, Jan 5, 54. Educ: Univ Tenn; Belmont Col. Had number 1 record with Crystal Gayle, wrote title cut for her new album. Writer for Ticalic. Chief Collabr: Ted Lindsay. *Songs:* Why Have You Left the One You've Left for the One You're With?; I'll Wait You Out.

TRUED, S(AMUEL) CLARENCE   ASCAP 1961
composer, pianist, church-organist
b Ceresco, Nebr, Apr 20, 1895. Educ: Luther Jr Col, Wahoo, Nebr, AA; Augustana Col, BM & BA; Chicago Musical Col, grad work; instrs, Percy Grainger, Clarence Eddy, Felix Borowski, Matthew Lundquist & Rudolph Ganz. Piano soloist, Augustana Symph & Tri-City Symph. WW 1, France, bandmaster, 123rd Field Artillery Band. Toured with Enrico Rodolfi, NY Opera & with Knute Orstrom, Stockholm Opera; accompa-nist to E Schumann-Heink & Richard Crooks; piano soloist, Dorothy Knight Ballet; directed, Denver Chamber Orch, 10 yrs; cond, Messiah Fest Choruses & Bach Masses in mid-20's in Denver, later in Pasadena, Calif & Roseburg, Ore. Directs music, First Christian Church, Roseburg, Ore; teaches & gives organ & piano recitals. Chief Collabrs: Carlton C Buck, Noble Cain. *Songs & Instrumental Works:* Out of the Depths (tuba & choir concerto); March On, O Church Triumphant (choir, organ & 2 trumpets); Stars of the Morning, So Gloriously Bright (chorus with

keyboard accompaniment); Girl With a Tomahawk (concert choir); Faith, Hope, Love (choral in 5 arr); Cantorio (orch, chorus, solo, narration); O Clap Your Hands (a cappella); The Lord Is My Rock (mixed chorus with organ); Let Us Sing to the Lord a Song of Joy (mixed chorus); Seek the Lord While He May Be Found (a cappella); Remember Also Thy Creator (piano-organ, band or orch); Secular: Blow the Trumpets (SATB); I Saw a Ship A-Sailing (SSA with piano); Old Meg She Was a Gipsy (madrigal type); A Damsel and I (A Janta a Ja); On a Snowy Evening (SATB); Piano Solos: Waters of the Umpqua; Jalopy Junction; Mauricette (organ); Prelude (organ); Sacred Anthems: Father, The Hour Has Come (mixed chorus & organ); He Is Risen! (a festive Easter anthem, with organ); Rejoice, O Zion, Shout and Sing! (Christmas anthem, SATB a cappella); Come Now to His Table (SATB a cappella); Will God Dwell With Man? (organ, 3 trumpets); Marches: The Howitzer Dinger; We're on Our Way.

TRUGLIO, MARIO THOMAS   ASCAP 1974
composer
b New York, NY, May 26, 42. Educ: Juilliard Sch Music, dipl, 64, BMus, 65, MMus, 66; Hofstra Univ, MS, 69, PDEdAdmin, 70; MusD, Santa Cecilia, 72. Comp, cond & arr; staff mem, Warner Bros, Metro-Goldwyn-Mayer & United Artists; worked for NBC, RCA, Kapp, Columbia & Deutch Gramaphone. Mem: Am Fedn TV & Radio Artists; Acad Motion Picture Arts & Sci; Acad TV Arts & Sci; Am Fedn Musicians; Recording Indust Asn Am. *Instrumental Works:* Prelude in G Minor; Serenade for Oboe and Piano; Symphony for Band; Fanfare for Orchestra; Serenade for Cello and Piano; Petit Invention; Consolation in E Flat Major; Serenade for Violin and Piano; Sonata in D Major (piano); Ars Nova (piano or organ). *Scores:* Opera/Ballet: The Moon Singer.

TRUJILLO, ALLEN EUGENE (MARC)   ASCAP 1978
composer, author, singer
b Los Angeles, Calif. Educ: La Puente Union High Sch; Mt San Antonio Col. Singer, Bway shows, night clubs, TV; recording artist, Mercury Records, Bell Records, Pvt Stock Records. Chief Collabrs: Billy Cioffi, Shelly Markham, Monica Pege, Dan Kimpel. *Songs:* Big City Rhythm of Love; Gotta Be the One; Here, Now!; Star Quality.

TRUMAN, EDWARD CRANE   ASCAP 1956
composer, author, coordinator
b Des Moines, Iowa. Educ: Chicago Music Col, piano with Alexander Raab & Boguslawski; piano from mother; Drake Univ, organ & theory; Immaculate Heart Col, BA(English); Univ Redlands, MA(humanistic psychol); Univ Calif, Los Angeles, cert labor studies; AFL-CIO Ctr, cert educ techniques. Staff pianist/organist & asst prog dir, Iowa Broadcasting Co, Des Moines. In broadcast news, WW II, Armed Forces radio serv, Hollywood. Joined network radio with Don Lee Mutual, Los Angeles, 2 yrs, also ABC-TV, 3 yrs; music dir drama progs/films, "Matinee Theatre", "Ellery Queen" & "Cameo Theatre"; adminr phono recording dept & Live TV & com announcements dept, Musicians' Union, Hollywood, 70-78. Free lance comp/consult music, labor & career educ in arts. Co-founder, Artasia/Quest Sem, The Arts Prof Speak Out. Mem, Acad TV Arts & Sci; bd mem: Calif Video Communications, Inc; Musicians' Credit Union; MUSIC Pub Libr charity. Chief Collabrs: Sheldon Allman, Johnny Durham, Bill McMillan. *Songs:* A Song for Builders; Music: The Magic of Believing; Bowie Knife; Safety Songs for Children; Hymns for Children. *Instrumental Works:* Matinee; Across the Sea; Eye of the Storm; Passing Strange.

TRUMBAUER, FRANK   ASCAP 1942
composer, conductor, saxophonist
b Carbondale, Ill, May 30, 01; d Kansas City, Mo, June 11, 56. Began playing saxophone as teenager, St Louis. Musician, 2nd class, USN, World War I. Organized own orch, St Louis, 21; recording artist, New York. Saxophonist with Benson Orch, Chicago, Ray Miller Orch, Gene Goldkette & Paul Whiteman Orch playing a specially made golden Holton C Melody saxophone, 30's. Assoc with movie "King of Jazz." With civilian pilot training prog, Kansas City, Mo, 40. Test pilot, Mo & taught pilots, Can, World War II. With Civil Aeronautics Admin, Kansas City, until 56. Inducted into Hall of Fame, Nat Acad of Recording Arts & Sci, 27, nat pres, 77. *Songs & Instrumental Works:* Trumbology; Krazy Kat; Three Blind Mice; Sunspots; Tailspin; G Blues; The Bouncing Ball; Eclipse; Meteor; Bass Drum Dan; Wringin' and Twistin'; Red Hot; Barb Wire Blues; I'm Glad.

TRUSLER, IVAN   ASCAP 1961
conductor, editor, arranger
b Lake Village, Ark, Aug 10, 25. Educ: Kans State Teachers Col, BS & MS; Columbia Univ, grad fel & PhD. Dir vocal & instrumental music, high schs, Emporia, Kans; also church choirmaster, First Baptist, Hutchinson & First Presby, Emporia. Founder & cond, YWCA Chorus, NY. Platoon leader, USAF, World War II; Bronze Star, 3 battle stars. Cond, Del All-State Chorus, 56, Sussex County Chorus, 57 & Del Vocal Camp, 58; guest cond, choral festivals; dir choral orgn, Univ Del; also choirmaster, Grace Church, Wilmington, Del. Coauth, "Functional Lessons in Singing." Mem, Am Choral Dirs Asn. Chief Collabr: Walter Ehret. *Instrumental Works:* Choral Arrangements: Glory to God; Gentle Jesus; Meek and Mild; Praise Ye the Lord; Jesus Christ Today Is Born; When Jesus Wept.

TRYTHALL, RICHARD AAKER   ASCAP 1969
composer, pianist
b Knoxville, Tenn, July 25, 39. Educ: Univ Tenn, BMus, 61, studied comp with David Van Vactor; Princeton Univ, 63, MFA, studied comp with Roger Sessions; Hochschule für Musik, Berlin, Ger, 63-64, studied with Boris Blacher. Comp of orchestral works, chamber music, electronic & mixed media works. Recipient, Fulbright-Hays fel to Berlin, 63, Rome Prize to Am Acad, Rome, Italy, 64-67, Guggenheim fel, 68, Kranichstein Musikpreis as pianist, 69, Naumburg Recording award, 71. Comn, Fromm Music Found & Dorian Woodwind Quintet. *Instrumental Works:* Continuums (orch); Costruzione (orch); Coincidences (piano); Variations on a Theme By Haydn (woodwind quintet & tape); Omaggio a Jerry Lee Lewis (tape); Penelope's Monologue (soprano & orch); Bolero (4 percussionists); Verse (slides, film & tape).

TRZCINSKI, KRZYSZTOF (KOMEDA)   ASCAP 1968
composer, pianist, arranger
b Poznan, Poland, Apr 27, 31; d Warsaw, Poland, Apr 23, 69. Educ: Poznan Cons, 38-39; Poznan Med Acad, dipl, 56. Komeda Sextet debut perf, 1st Jazz Fest, 56. Wrote & performed "Ballet Etudes," 63. Jazz and Poetry prog, 63. Europ tour with group, 63. Golden Globe Award, Am Movie Press Asn, 68. Chief Collabs: film dirs Roman Polanski, Jerzy Skolimowski, Hennik Carlsen, Buzz Kulik, Rene Utreger, Andrzej Wajda; musicians Tomasz Stanko, Don Cherry, Gato Garbieri, Bernt Rosengren, Michal Urbaniak, Urszula Dudziak, Zbigniew Namyslowski, Kristin Legrand, Eje Thelin; record producer J E Berendt. *Instrumental Works:* Crazy Girl; Alea; Svantetic; Kattorna; Night Time, Day Time, Requiem for Coltrane; Astigmatic; Lullaby from Rosemary's Baby; Ballad from Depart; Ballad from Cul-de-Sac; Ballad from The Knife in the Water. *Scores:* Film/TV: Two Men and the Wardrobe; Sult (Oscar Award); Cul-de-Sac; The Vampire Killers; Le Depart; Rosemary's Baby; Riot. *Albums:* Ballet Etudes: The Music of Komeda; Jazz Greetings From the East; Astigmatic: The Music of Komeda; Meine Susse Europeische Heimat: Dichtung un Jazz—aus Polen; Cul-de-Sac; Le Depart; Rosemary's Baby; Komeda.

TSAPRALIS, NANCYE FAYE (NANCYE SHORT)   ASCAP 1973
composer, singer
b Selma, Calif, Oct 1, 53. Educ: Caruthers High Sch; studied voice & piano. Vocalist with gospel band, The Archers, 5 yrs. Recording artist, Light Records & Benson Records. Background studio vocalist. *Songs:* I'm Gonna Rise; He's My Friend; Change; Truth, Peace, Joy; Sit Yourself Down.

TUBBS, HUBERT ALLEN   ASCAP 1976
composer, singer
b Dallas, Tex, Nov 18, 47. Educ: Franklin D Roosevelt High Sch, Dallas; Foothill Jr Col, Calif. Singer night clubs; recording artist, Columbia Records & Warner Bros; songwriter. Chief Collabs: Steve Kupka, Emilio Castillo. *Songs:* You Ought to Be Havin' Fun; Am I a Fool?.

TUCCI, JOSEPH WILLIAM (ERIC MATTHEW)   ASCAP 1978
composer, author, producer
b Queens, NY, Mar 14, 53. Educ: Elem parochial sch, 8 yrs; pvt accordion lessons, local music sch, 60-65; self taught, guitar; high sch, equivalency dipl. First local band, age 12. Prof musician at age 16. Opened music sch at age 18. Built recording studio. Opened mail-order demo bus. Arr & produced album "Keep on Dancin'." Active in music bus, writing, producing & performing. Chief Collabr: Gary Turnier. *Songs:* Let's Lovedance Tonight; Round and Round and Round; Serenade; Hold On. *Albums:* Keep on Dancin'.

TUCKER, ANNETTE MAY   ASCAP 1970
composer, teacher
b Los Angeles, Calif. Educ: Univ Calif, Los Angeles, music. Has been writing for 17 years. Dir, ASCAP Workshop W, 75- Chief Collabrs: Nancy Mantz, Kathy Wakefield, Jill Jones, Arthur Hamilton. *Songs:* I Had Too Much to Dream Last Night; Green Light; Instant Harry; Love Songs Are Getting Harder to Sing; Get Me to the Wall on Time.

TUCKER, ELIOT   ASCAP 1975
composer, author, singer
b Jacksonville, Fla, Feb 15, 50. Educ: Fla State Univ, BA, 71, best actor studio theatre, 70-71; studied drama with Lela Bliss Hayden, 72-73. Taught actg, Am Col Lucerne, Switz, 71-72; staff writer, Warner Bros Music, 76-79; singer, nightclubs & TV; writer musical theatre. Chief Collabr: Joseph J Bellinghiere, Jr. *Songs:* It's Gone; The Lines of Age.

TUCKER, JOHN A   ASCAP 1924
composer, author, conductor
b New York, NY, June 18, 1896; d. Educ: Epiphany Sch; Delahanty Inst; studied music with Horace Waters & Catherine Nolan. Led own orch in hotels & restaurants. Actg bandmaster, USN, WW I. Joined New York Fire Dept, 20; trombonist, New York Fire Dept Band. With Joe Schuster, appeared as team, The Delivery Boys, in theatre, nightclubs & on radio. Co-founder publ co, Tucker & Marchant. Rejoined New York Fire Dept, 37-58. Pianist & publ. Chief Collabr: Joe Schuster. *Songs:* Dance of the Paper Dolls; Sleep, Baby, Sleep; Maybe, Who Knows?; I Know Somethin' I Won't Tell Ya; Honest, I'm in Love With You; The Christmas Polka; Anything Can Happen When You're Lonesome; I Shouldn't Love You But I Do; Do What Your Heart Tells You to

Do; Maggie, (Yes Ma'am) Come Right Upstairs; The Village Blacksmith Owns the Village Now. *Scores:* Film: Third Alarm.

TUCKER, ORRIN   ASCAP 1953
composer, author, conductor
b St Louis, Mo, Feb 17, 11. Educ: Northwestern Univ; NCent Col. Has led own orch in theatres, ballrooms & throughout US. Made many records. Appeared on "Hit Parade," 1 yr. USN, World War II. Has own TV prog, Los Angeles. *Songs:* Especially for You; Pinch Me; My Resistance Is Low; Would Ja Mind.

TUCKER, TOMMY   ASCAP 1947
composer, author, conductor
b Souris, NDak, May 18, 08. Led own orch in theatres, ballrooms throughout US. Many records made. Asst prof music, Monmouth Col. *Songs & Instrumental Works:* The Man Who Comes Around; Love in June; No, No, No; Cool, Calm and Collected; Stars Over the Campus; Welcome Home; Boogie Woogie Train; Let Him Live; I Love You.

TUFANO, DENNIS S   ASCAP 1972
composer, author, singer
b Chicago, Ill, Sept 11, 46. Educ: St Sylvester's Grammar Sch; Gordon Tech High Sch. Mem vocal group, 64. Lead vocalist band, the Pulsations (later, The Buckinghams), 65; Columbia Records, 66-70. Mem team, Tufano & Giammarese, Ode Records, 72-76. Writer music, Bernie Taupin & Asylum Records, 80. Chief Collabs: Marty Grebb, Carl Giammarese, Bernie Taupin, Tom Scott. *Songs:* Rise Up; Music: The Whores of Paris; Approaching Armageddon; Lyrics: Greed.

TUITAMA, KUKA LEUPENA   ASCAP 1979
actor
b Pago Pago, Am Samoa, Nov 11, 01. Educ: Marist Bros Sch, Am Samoa; LMS Community Col. Worker in studio, 30 yrs. Involved in many activities for movies, also character actor.

TULL, FISHER AUBREY   ASCAP 1964
composer
b Waco, Tex, Sept 24, 34. Educ: NTex State Univ, BMus, 56, MMus, 57, PhD, 65, studied with Samuel Adler. Fac, Dept Music, Sam Houston State Univ, 57-, chmn, 65- Winner 7 prizes, Tex Comp Guild. *Songs:* Music: An Indian Prayer (mixed chorus, piano). *Instrumental Works:* Sketches on a Tudor Psalm (symph band); Concerto No 2 (trumpet, orch); Toccata (symph band; Ostwald Award, Am Bandmasters Asn, 70); The Final Covenant (symph band); Cyclorama I (flute ens); Sonatina (perc ens); Three Bagatelles (trumpet, piano); Variations on an Advent Hymn (brass, perc ens); Sarabande and Gigue (saxophone, piano); Concertino (oboe, string); Three Episodes (orch; Arthur Fraser Award, 79); Segments (trumpet ens); Reflections on Paris (symph band); Studies in Motion (wind ens); Prelude and Double Fugue (symph band); Capriccio (small orch). *Scores:* Ballet: Allen's Landing.

TUMINELLO, PHIL J   ASCAP 1957
composer, singer
b Denison, Tex, May 20, 21. Educ: La State Univ, Baton Rouge, Herbert Wall Sch Music, Los Angeles. Sang with George Givot & Richard Cole Bands, on radio show, WBBM, Chicago & in night clubs, Los Angeles-Whitting Hills. Talent buyer, Walt Disney Studios, also in Casting Off for original "Mickey Mouse Club" TV show. Chief Collabrs: Sammy Cahn, Johnny Lange. *Songs:* Can I Steal a Little Love; Crazy Love; Teach Me How to Cry. *Songs & Instrumental Works:* Step Out of That Dream; I Ain't Gonna Change.

TUNICK, JONATHAN   ASCAP 1969
composer, arranger, conductor
b New York, NY, 1938. Educ: Bard Col, AB, 58; Juilliard Sch Music, MS, 60; comp studies with Paul Nordoff, Vittorio Giannini & Leonard Bernstein. Orchr/arr for Bway musicals: "Sweeney Todd", "Pacific Overtures", "A Little Night Music", "A Chorus Line", "Company", "Promises Promises"; Films: "A Little Night Music" (Acad Award for Best Adaptation Score, 78); "Stavisky", "Young Frankenstein", "Blazing Saddles" & "The Twelve Chairs." Songs for Upstairs at the Downstairs & other revues. Scores for motion pictures & TV. Comns: Pa Ballet, NY Shakespeare Fest & Benny Goodman Orch.

TUOHY, WILLIAM JOSEPH   ASCAP 1972
composer, author
b Chicago, Ill, Aug 1, 41. Educ: Univ Mo, BA, 65. Author of three books of modern poetry. Lyric writer, photographer & have done several films to illus songs. Chief Collabrs: Dion Dimucci. *Songs:* Lyrics: Windows; Soft Parade of Years; Queen of 1959; New York City Song; Running Close Behind You; Pattern of My Lifeline.

TURAN, JERRY
See Turrano, Joseph A

TURETZKY, BERTRAM JAY   ASCAP 1975
composer, author, contrabassist
b Norwich, Conn, Feb 14, 33. Educ: Hartt Col, BM, 55, studied with Willis Page & Joseph Iadone; NY Univ, musical studies with Curt Sachs, Gustave Reese,

Martin Bernstein & Jan LaRue, 55-57; Univ Hartford, MM, 65, contrabass studies with David Walter & perf practice with Josef Marx. Bassist & mem fac, Univ Hartford, 55-68; formed Hartt Chamber Players, first univ new music ens to travel; played in Hartford Symph. Made debut as soloist, New York City, 64; has given concerts all over the world. Recording artist. Author of bk, "The Contemporary Contrabass." Rec'd NEA grant, 78 & ASCAP Comp Prize, 80. *Instrumental Works:* G Timbral Studies; Gamelan Music; Wioste Olowan (NDak Indian love songs for contrabass consort & tape); Collage I (contrabass solo); Collage II (antiphonal double brass quartet); Collage III (flutes, cello, harp & contrabass); Haiku (narrator & bassist); A Braxtonian Collage (tape & amplified contrabass); Celestial Variations on Charles Ives' Serenity (16 channel tape); Poland 1931 (setting of J Rothenberg's poetry for narrator & instruments).

TURK, ROY   ASCAP 1929
author
b New York, NY, Sept 20, 1892; d Los Angeles County, Calif, Nov 30, 34. Educ: City Col New York. Served in USN, WW I. Wrote spec material for Rock & White, Nora Bayes & Sophie Tucker. Staff writer, music publ co. Wrote songs for films. Chief Collabrs: Fred Ahlert, Harry Akst, George Meyer, Charles Tobias, Arthur Johnston, Maceo Pinkard, J Russel Robinson. *Songs:* Gimme a Little Kiss, Will Ya Huh?; I'm Still Without a Sweetheart With Summer Coming On; Walkin' My Baby Back Home; Where the Blue of the Night Meets the Gold of the Day; I'll Get By; Mean to Me: Love, You Funny Thing; Mandy, Make Up Your Mind: Dixie Dreams; I'm a Little Blackbird Looking for a Bluebird; Are You Lonesome Tonight?; Aggravatin' Papa; My Sweetie Went Away; After My Laughter Came Tears; From One 'Til Two; Just Because You're You; Beale Street Mama: Oh How I - Laugh When I Think How I Cried About You; I Don't Know Why.

TURNBULL, GRAHAM MORRISON (SCOTT   ASCAP 1958
TURNER, ALLISON DEWAR)
composer, author, producer
b Sydney, NS, Aug 23, 31. Educ: Stanstead Col Dept Music, Que, degree in music theory. First chair trombonist with Eastern Townships Symph, 48-51. Formed own group, The Raiders, 56. Went to Hollywood with Buddy Holly in 57; then became lead guitarist for Tommy Sands. Joined Guy Mitchell as musical dir & lead guitarist for 2 yrs. Then joined Eddie Fisher Show. In 62, worked for A & M Records; later on as gen mgr for Cent Songs; now head country A&R, Liberty/Imperial & United Artists. Chief Collabrs: Audie Murphy, Nilsson, Mac Davis, John Marascalco, Diane Lampert, Sonny Throckmorton, Larry Butler, Alex Harvey, Bobby Lewis, Jerry Wallace, Slim Whitman, Herb Alpert, Jimmy Bryant, Robert Gordon, Bobby Fischer, Guy Mitchell, Charlie Williams, Samuel Osgood 'Randy' Hoving, By Dunham. *Songs:* The Worryin' Kind; Blue Ribbon Baby; When the Wind Blows in Chicago; Please Mr Music Man; A Travelin' Man; Big City Men; The Moonracers; Simple Days and Simple Ways; Please Buy My Flowers; Hicktown; My Lonesome Room; The Catman; I Just Met a Memory; The Tiffany Waltz; When You Were Sixteen; Put Your Trust in Me; Lyrics: Shutters and Boards; Music: Comin' in the Back Door; The Little Children of Peru; The Mexican Drummer Man.

TURNER, CHARLES   ASCAP 1957
composer
b Baltimore, Md, Nov 25, 21. Educ: Curtis Inst; Juilliard Sch Music. *Instrumental Works:* Encounter; Serenade for Icarus. *Scores:* Ballet: Pastorale.

TURNER, DIANNE GROSS   ASCAP 1970
author
b Jacksonville, Fla, Sept 7, 38. Educ: Fred Waring Workshop; Jacksonville Univ, creative writing; Ridgecrest Baptist Assembly Music Week, NC. Writer, 66-; wrote for several publs. Chief Collabr: Leland (Lee) Turner, Jr (husband). *Songs:* Lyrics: Go Into All the World; Glory, Hallelujah, Jubilee!; Your Life Has a Plan; Give a Cup of Water (In the Master's Name); Thank You for Loving Me; Turn the Other Cheek; Are You the One?; Always a Place at the Table; Jesus Makes the Day Worth Living; God Made These for Us to Love; You Don't Have to Be Alone Anymore; He Was There; The Face of Jesus; Lyrics, Christian Musicals: The Church That God Built With Love; They All Sang Jesus; Great Men of God.

TURNER, HAROLD JOSEPH   ASCAP 1961
composer, author, pianist
b Chicago, Ill, Aug 13, 30. Educ: Northwestern Univ Sch Music, 4 yrs; Berklee Sch Music, 3 yrs; arr/comp studies with Ralph Wilkinson & Bill Russo. Played, arranged & sang for bands, USAF. Worked with name bands, Tex Beneke, Kai Winding & Warren Covington, Tommy Dorsey, Sammy Kaye, Ray McKinley & Glenn Miller Orchs, Peter Duchin & Charlie Barnet. Fronted own orch several yrs, NY. Cond var acts through career. With Hilton Inn, Dallas, 5 yrs. *Instrumental Works:* Toy Piano; The Froogie; El Leoncito; Stay, Love; Sink Or Swim.

TURNER, JOHN C (HAPPY)   ASCAP 1943
composer, author, pianist
b Hannibal, Mo, Oct 18, 1896; d Denver, Colo, Jan 19, 49. Educ: Bus col. Former pianist & singer on radio, incl KOA, Denver. *Songs:* Who Could Ask for More?; Dusty Trail; What Are You Goin' to Say?; A Happy Good Morning to You; Baby Eyes; Midnight Melody; I'm Crying My Eyes Out for You.

TURNER, JOHN DAVID, JR (BO)   ASCAP 1969
composer, author
b Cherry Valley, Ark, June 5, 30. Educ: High Sch GED; Air Univ, courses, Officer Candidate Sch, Admin Officer, Supply Officer, Commercial Transportation Officer, Air Force instr, NCO leadership, mgt for Air Force supvr, automotive maintenance, air conditioning & refrigeration. Songwriter, over 25 yrs. Sales rep, Cherokee Music News; also handling advert & sales, Ozark Talent Register, Div of Ozark Jamboree; sales rep for photo stamp bus. Chief Collabr: Wilks Hinson. *Songs:* Gospel: I'm One of God's People; The Bible Is Our Guide; I Heard the Word Christian; I Work for the Master; Lyrics: Do You Believe?.

TURNER, LELAND (LEE) SMITH, JR   ASCAP 1967
composer, pianist, singer
b Jacksonville, Fla, Nov 22, 36. Educ: Univ Fla, BS(advert), 59; Southern Baptist Theol Sem, BSacred Mus, 61; Fred Waring Workshop, 63 & 67; pvt piano study with Jimmy Knight & Maurice Hinson. Free-lance musician in Jacksonville & Nashville; singer, pianist, arr, cond, comp. Pianist for The Dream Weavers on "It's Almost Tomorrow." Now Minister of music, San Jose Baptist Church, Jacksonville. Chief Collabr: Dianne Turner (wife), Richard Blanchard. *Songs:* Make Every Day a Good Day!; Music: Thank You for Loving Me; Glory, Hallelujah, Jubilee!; The Face of Jesus; Turn the Other Cheek; Who Moved?; Always a Place at the Table; You Don't Have to Be Alone Anymore; Into the Night; Give a Cup of Water (In the Master's Name); May the Road Rise to Meet You; God Made These for Us to Love; He Was There; Lyrics, Christian Musicals: The Church That God Built With Love; They All Sang Jesus; Great Men of God.

TURNER, MILDRED C (MRS HUNTINGTON   ASCAP 1960
M TURNER)
composer, author, teacher
b Pueblo, Colo, Feb 23, 1897. Educ: Univ Wis; studied music with Francis Schwinger, Emil Liebling & Corneille Overstreet. Taught music in pub schs, Wis. *Songs:* Dalmation Lullaby; I Wish They Didn't Mean Goodbye; Geisha.

TURNER, SCOTT
See Turnbull, Graham Morrison

TURNICK, CLEMENT JOSEPH   ASCAP 1975
author
b Blakely, Pa, Dec 1, 13. Educ: St Patrick's High Sch, Olyphant, Pa; Scranton Lackawanna Bus Sch. Wrote essays, poetry & children's stories. Songwriter. *Songs:* Let Me Love You.

TURNIER, GARY RICHARD   ASCAP 1979
composer, author, producer
b Queens, NY, Dec 27, 54. Educ: Grammar sch, High Sch Performing Arts, NY; Queens Col, elem educ degree; studied perc with Brad Spinney. Played prof since age 16. Writer & producer records, 77-; co-producer & writer, "Gary's Gang." Sch teacher. Chief Collabr: Eric Matthew. *Songs:* Keep on Dancin'; Let's Lovedance Tonight; Do It At the Disco; Show Time; Spirits.

TUROK, PAUL HARRIS   ASCAP 1971
composer
b New York, NY, Dec 3, 29. Educ: High Sch of Music & Art, New York; Queens Col, BA, 50; Univ Calif, Berkeley, MA, 51; Juilliard Sch Music, special studies, 51-53. All Turok concert, Tully Hall, Lincoln Ctr, 70. Music & record reviewer, NY Herald-Tribune, Music Jour, Fanfare & Ovation. *Instrumental Works:* Great Scott!; A Joplin Overture; A Sousa Overture; Danza Viva; Aspects of Lincoln and Liberty; Symphony in Two Movements; Chartres West; Two Pieces for Orchestra From Richard III; Homage to Bach; Violin Concerto; Ragtime Caprice for Piano and Orchestra; Canzona Concertante for English Horn and Orchestra; Lyric Variations for Oboe and Strings; Threnody for Strings; Clarinet Trio; Cello Sonata; Horn Sonata; Harp Sonatina; Transcendental Etudes for Piano; Capriccio for Violin and Percussion Ensemble; three songs for soprano and flute; lanier songs for soprano and six instruments. *Scores:* Opera/Ballet: Richard III; A Secular Masque; Scene: Domestic; Antoniana.

TURRANO, JOSEPH A (JERRY TURAN)   ASCAP 1956
composer, author
b Nesquehoning, Pa, June 4, 18. Educ: Hartnett Music Sch, New York; studied harmony with Johnny Smith, piano & sight reading with Mike Shelby. Played piano & sang with groups in Pa, NJ & NY. WW II. Formed instrumental trio & harmony with Al Rainy & Jack Redbird, entertained in hospitals in Europe. Chief Collabrs: Al Rainy, Roger Genger, Harry Stride, Pacheco Costa, Kay Largo. *Songs:* Gather Your Dreams; You're All I Want, Nothing More; Don't Tease Me Now; I'm Ready, Willing and Able; Naiomi.

TURRIN, JOSEPH EDIGIO   ASCAP 1971
composer
b Clifton, NJ, Jan 1, 47. Educ: Eastman Sch Music; Manhattan Sch Music. Comp in residence, Bergen Mall Playhouse, NJ; comp music for "Verna-USO Girl," WNET/Channel 13, New York; "Little Darlings," Paramount Pictures. Instr orchestration, Ctr New Music, Columbia Col, Chicago, 72; artist in

residence, William Paterson Col. Chief Collabrs: Bernard Stambler, Judy Spencer. *Instrumental Works:* Caprice for Trumpet and Piano; Walden Trio (flute, cello & piano, Ann M Alburger Award for Chamber Music); Elegy for Trumpet and String Orchestra; Concertino for Tuba and Wind Ensemble (Am Music Ctr grant); Fanfare for Eight Trumpets; The Steadfast Tin Soldier (orch & narrator); March and Choral (brass choir). *Scores:* Feathertop (2 act opera, NJ State Council on Arts grant, 76); Bway Show: Circle of Love.

TUSTIN, WHITNEY   ASCAP 1963
composer, oboist, teacher
b Seattle, Wash. Educ: Univ Wash; Cons, Nat de Musique, Paris. Oboist, Seattle Symph, 26-42, Kansas City Philh, 46-49 & New York Opera Co. Mem fac, Univ Wash, 35-42 & Kansas City Cons, 46-49; then Mannes Col Music, Dalcroze Sch & Hofstra Univ. Author, "Technical Studies for Treble Woodwind Instruments." *Instrumental Works:* 3 Pieces (recorder, piano); 30 Duets (2 oboes); Solos for the Oboe Player.

TUTHILL, BURNET CORWIN   ASCAP 1942
composer, conductor
b New York, NY, Nov 16, 1888. Educ: Columbia Univ, BA & MA; Col Music, Univ Cincinnati, MM, 45; Memphis Col Music. Librarian, NY Oratorio Soc, 05-13, asst cond, 14-16. Cond, Columbia Univ Orch, 08-13, Bronx People's Choral Union, 13-16 & Southwestern Singers, 24-30. Gen mgr, Cincinnati Cons, 24-30. Prof music & head dept, Southwestern at Memphis, 35-59; dir, Memphis Col Music, 37-59; head music dept, US Army Univ, 58; mem fac, Waddell & Reed, 59-69. Founder, Memphis Symph Orch, cond, 47-58. Retired. *Songs & Instrumental Works:* Bethlehem (pastorale for orch); Nocturne (flute, strings); Symphony in C Opus 21; Big River (soprano, solo, women's voices, orch); Song of the White Horse Vale (solo tenor, male chorus); Overture for Symphony Band; also chamber music for winds & strings.

TUVIM, ABE   ASCAP 1941
author, publicist
b New York, NY, May 10, 1895; d New York, Jan 15, 58. Educ: Pub schs. Was active in Interchange of Musical Artists, US & Latin Am. Was pub rels counsel, Assoc Musicians of Greater New York. US rep, Dept Fine Arts, Mexican Govt. Father of Judy Holliday. *Songs:* How Come Lord?; A Gay Ranchero; Rain Tomorrow, Partly Cloudy; Rainy Day; My Rival; Time Has Wings; Chile Con Conga.

TWINE, BOBBY
See Morphis, Robert C

TWOHIG, DANIEL S   ASCAP 1926
author
b Cork, Ireland, Sept 8, 1883; d Malden, Mass, Dec 9, 61. Educ: Pub schs, Ireland. US dept store mgr, 8 yrs; post office employee, Boston. Chief Collabrs: Geoffrey O'Hara, Henry Hadley, Oley Speaks, Frank Grey, Oscar Fox, David Guion. *Songs:* At Eventime; Loves Magic; I Walked Today Where Jesus Walked; The Fool Hath Said There Is No God; I WAs the Tree; Soft Were Your Hands, Dear Jesus; Art Thou the Christ; He Smiled on Me.

TWOMEY, KATHLEEN (KAY) GREELEY (AL HILL)   ASCAP 1942
author
b Boston, Mass, Apr 27, 14. Educ: Faelten Sch of Music, Boston; New Eng Cons of Music; studied piano & voice for many yrs. Jewelry designer & writer for advert agencies. Contract writer with Aberbach Brothers; songwriter for var motion pictures, Bway show "Girl From Nantucket" & several children's shows incl "Marco Polo." Chief Collabrs: Al Goodhart, George W Meyer, Dick Manning, Don Rodney, Al Frisch, Bee Walker, Richard Addinsell, Fred Spielman, Ben Weisman. *Songs:* Lyrics: Wooden Heart; Serenade of the Bells; Hey! Jealous Lover; Let Me Go, Lover; Johnny Doughboy Found a Rose in Ireland; Robe of Calvary; In the Beginning; Give a Faith to Your Child; A Family That Prays Together; Honey in the Horn; If Hearts Could Talk; OO! What You Do to Me; Lend Me Your Comb; Johnny Jingo; In a Little Kiss Shop; Golden Violins; Satisfaction Guaranteed; Laura's Wedding; Heartbreak Hill; The Bunny Hop!; Ev'ry Prayer Is a Flower; The Rosary of Roses; One Magic Wish; Under Capricorn (movie); A Tiny Little Voice; Who Am I to Cast the First Stone; Ichabod (children's musical). *Albums:* Teen Street.

TYERS, WILLIAM H   ASCAP 1917
composer
b Richmond, Va, Mar 27, 1876; d New York, NY, Apr 18, 24. Educ: Pub schs, New York; pvt music study. Staff arr, var music publ firms. Led own orch, Bretton Woods, NH, 5 summers. Music dir, Rock & White & Vernon & Irene Castle. *Instrumental Works:* Maori; Trocha; Admiration; Call of the Woods; Soliloquy; Mele Hula; Flames and Fancies; Dance of the Philippines.

TYLER, GOLDIE   ASCAP 1956
composer
b Kittrell, NC, Oct 31, 25. Educ: Bus col. Worked in civil serv, US Employment Serv, Philadelphia; then with USAF, New York, 7 yrs. Typist & photographer, Mass. *Songs:* Cause You're My Lover.

TYRA, THOMAS   ASCAP 1963
composer
b Chicago, Ill, Apr 17, 33. Educ: Northwestern Univ, BMusEd, 54, MMus, 55; Univ Mich, PhD, 71. Teacher in pub sch, Iowa, 55-56. Staff arr & rehearsal cond, USN Sch Music, 56-57. Dir musical orgn, Morton Jr Col, Cicero, Ill, 58; dir of bands, La State Univ, Baton Rouge, 59-64; dir of bands & prof music, Eastern Mich Univ, 64-77; prof & head dept music, Western Carolina Univ, 77-Cond, Civic Band, Ann Arbor, Mich, 68-77. *Instrumental Works:* Five Haiku Settings (soprano & chamber ens); Suite for Brass and Timpani; Band: Bedford: An Overture; Intravention; Ceremonial Sketch; Two Gaelic Folk Songs; Three Christmas Miniatures. *Scores:* Film/TV: No Bells At Carville; America's Golden Asset.

TYSON, IAN D   ASCAP 1962
composer, singer
b Victoria, BC, Sept 25, 36. Educ: Vancouver Sch of Fine Art, 58. Recording artist & performer, Ian & Sylvia team; did concerts in all major US & Can Halls, 64-70. Hosted network TV show "Ian Tyson Show," Toronto, 70-75. Now performing, writing & recording. Chief Collabrs: Sylvia Tyson, Joy Wahl. *Songs:* Four Strong Winds; Summer Wages; Someday Soon; Loving Sound; Some Kind of Fool.

TYSON, MILDRED LUND   ASCAP 1944
composer, teacher, organist
b Moline, Ill, Mar 10, 01. Educ: Northwestern Univ, BM; grad study at Northwestern Univ & Columbia Univ, Ithaca Col, summer 79; Eastman Sch Music, studied comp. Soprano soloist, Episcopal Church, Mamaroneck, NY; organist & choir dir, Congregational Church, Sidney, NY. Teacher of piano & voice, Sidney & Unadilla, NY. *Songs & Instrumental Works:* The Great Divide; Chorals: Sea Moods (comn by Schenectady Womens Choral Club); May in Japan; One Little Cloud; The Lilacs Are in Bloom; Like Barley Bending; Keep Loving Me, Dear; Will Spring Be Far Behind?.

TYSON, SYLVIA FRICKER
composer, author, singer
b Chatham, Ont, Sept 19, 40. Mem duo, Ian & Sylvia, 70, now solo with backup band; also on tour. Recording artist, Salt Records. *Songs:* Salt Music.

U

UBER, DAVID ALBERT   ASCAP 1959
composer, teacher, trombonist
b Princeton, Ill, Aug 5, 21. Educ: Carthage Col, BA; Curtis Inst Music (scholarship); Columbia Univ, MA, DEd; studied comp with Harold Morris. First chair trombone with NBC Symph of the Air, NBC TV Opera, NY City Opera Co, NY City Ballet Co, Martha Graham Ballet Co, Joffrey Ballet Co, RCA, Columbia, Decca, Capitol & Crest Records. Prof music, Trenton State Col; dir, Princeton Univ Band also dir ensemble music, Nat Music Camp, Interlochen, Mich & West Minster Choir Col, Princeton, NJ. Recorded on Music Minus One & other recording cos. *Instrumental Works:* Gettysburg Suite (brass choir); Miniature Symphony for Brass Quartet; Beachcomber's Dance-Adventures of a Tin Horn (brass quintet); Sonata for Trumpet (and piano); Evolution I for Brass Choir and Percussion; Double Portraits for Trombone and Tuba; The Power and the Glory (brass choir, timpany); Liturgy for Brass Choir and Timpany; Five Short Sketches for Brass Quintet; Odyssey-A Romantic Overture for Band; Ballets in Brass for Brass Sextet or Brass Choir; Three Settings for Clarinet Choir (masques, antiphonal, parade); A Christmas Festival of Carols-Christmas in Brass (brass choir); Symphonic Fanfare (Three Symphonic Fanfares for Brass Choir); Canzona Moderna for Double Brass Choir); Gloria in Excelsis, 1970 (brass choir); Ballad of Enob Mort (solo trombone, euphonium or tuba); Four River Episodes for Symphonic Band; Exhibitions for Solo Baritone and Baritone Horn Quartet; Sonata for Horn; Sonata for Euphonium; Sonata for Tuba; Antiphonale for Double Brass Choir; Jazz Concerto (trumpet, brass choir and perc); Rhythmic Contours for Solo Tuba and Percussion; Rhythmic Fantasy for Horn and Percussion; Concerto for Brass Choir and Percussion; Sunshower for Brass and Percussion; Musicale for Clarinet Choir. *Songs & Instrumental Works:* Psalms for Antiphonal Choirs (3 brass choirs, 1 vocal choir).

UDALL, LYN
See Keating, John Henry

UDELL, PETER DAVID   ASCAP 1957
author
b New York, NY, May 24, 34. Educ: Great Neck Pub Schs; Univ Chicago. Writer & record producer, 60's. Wrote lyrics & bk for musicals, "Purlie", "Shenandoah", "Angel" & "Comin' Uptown." Chief Collabrs: Gary Geld, Garry Sherman. *Songs:* Lyrics: Sealed With a Kiss; Ginny Come Lately; Save Your Heart for Me; He Says the Same Things to Me; Hurting Each Other; Warmed Over Kisses; Big Daddy; It's Only the Good Times; Let Me Belong to You; I Got Love; Walk Him Up the Stairs; First Thing Monday Morning;

Freedom; Violets and Silver Bells; How Do You Say Goodbye; Beautiful Pair; Tomorrow, I'm Gonna Be Old; Have I Finally Found My Heart?; Born Again.

UHL, ALBERT ALEXANDER, JR   ASCAP 1975
composer, teacher
b Beacon, NY, Dec 6, 30. Educ: Wappingers Cent High Sch; Ithaca Col, BS(music educ), 53, grad work; State Univ NY Col, New Paltz, grad work. Performer on Children's Hour (drums); Navy musician (saxophone & clarinet), 53-57. Pub sch music specialist. *Songs:* Music: Let the Word Go Forth (SATB).

UHL, RICHARD RATHVON   ASCAP 1952
composer, author, producer
b Kingston, Pa, Sept 7, 18. Educ: Princeton Univ, BA(music), 39, comp with Roger Sessions & Milton Babbitt; Juilliard Sch Music, orchestration, 77. Producer/dir, radio, TV & commercials, also "Lanny Ross Radio Show," 39-41 & "Dick Haymes-Gordon Jenkins Show," Hollywood, 46-47. USA, 41-46. Exec vpres & creative dir, SSC & B Advert Inc, 48-76; retired from comp, writing & advert. Chief Collabrs: Tom Adair, Frank Stanton, Del Sharbutt, Walter Mead. *Songs:* A Romantic Guy, I. *Songs & Instrumental Works:* Everybody Every Payday (WW II Loan Song); March for the New Infantry.

UHL, RUTH
See Frank, Ruth Verd

UHR, WILLIAM   ASCAP 1953
composer
b Kiev, Russia, Apr 7, 07; d Hollywood, Fla, May 22, 76. Educ: Univ Pa Law Sch. Songwriter; nightclub owner. Chief Collabrs: Frank Capano, Morris (Buddy) Boardman. *Songs:* Tears; I'd Be Bankrupt; You Can't Take It With You; Rosy; I'm Ruined. *Instrumental Works:* Dear Father in Heaven.

ULFIK, RICHARD JOSEPH   ASCAP 1977
composer, author, arranger
b New York, NY, Oct 20, 49. Educ: Stuyvesant High Sch; City Col New York, BA(music); scholarship & musicianship, Israel Drabkin & Sidney Zolot awards; studied comp & electronic music with Mario Davidovsky. Played for Samantha Sang's first Am concert tour; cond & played keyboards for Ester Satterfield on TV & in concerts; played for Noel Pointer, Jimmy Owens & Bernard Purdie. Recorded on synthesizers & other keyboards for TK, Prelude, Casablanca, Electra Asylum & United Artists Records; arr & played on many commercials incl, Max Factor, Bayer Aspirin, Carolina Rice, General Electric Lamps, Jean Nate, Plymouth Horizon, Magnavox, Viva, Hartford Insurance, Vick's Cough Medicine, Dixieware & Del Taco Restaurants. Chief Collabrs: Cory Braverman, Bob Larro, Richard Grasso, Doug Howerton. *Songs:* Music: Take It or Leave It; Honey I Will Be There; Firesign; With You. *Instrumental Works:* What Do You Say to a Fantasy; Bouncing Billie's Big Time Broadway Strut; Psychodrama.

ULLSTEIN, VLADIMIR MARK   ASCAP 1961
composer, author, pianist
b Kiev, Russia, June 5, 1898; d. Educ: Kiev Music Sch; St Petersburg Cons, with Glazounoff, Esipoff; Stern Cons, Berlin, with Eugene D'Albert, Fidelman. Conductor. Has given piano recitals; accompanied singers incl Feodor Chaliapin. Prof & dir, Western Music Dept, Tsin-Hua Univ; dir, Fine Arts Inst; cond, Peking, Tiotsin & Shanghai Symph Orchs. Guest cond, San Francisco Symph. *Songs:* Weekend in Paris.

UNCLE LUMPY
See Brannum, Hugh Roberts

UNCLE MORRIS
See Janson, Hugh Michael

UNDERWOOD, FRANKLIN ROOSEVELT   ASCAP 1968
composer, author, pianist
b Gilman, Ill, Dec 25, 35. Educ: Rollins Col, BM. With coast to coast cabaret; musical dir & coproducer musical revues in Provincetown & New York. Pianist & singer in New York. Chief Collabrs: Stan Freeman, Fred Silver. *Scores:* Bway Show: Lovely Ladies, Kind Gentleman.

UNGER, GUSTAF   ASCAP 1970
composer, author
b Stockholm, Sweden, Nov 8, 20. Educ: Formal schooling in Stockholm, Sweden, 12 yrs, Sophie Almquist Samskola & Ostermalms Laroverk. Appeared as entertainer on major Europ stages performing own works; recorded own songs for CETRA, Italy; appeared as partner with entertainer Josephine Baker. Came to US as entertainer & produced feature motion pictures, acted in motion pictures & became syndicated foreign correspondent with outlets in var countries in SE Asia & Europe. Mem, Screen Actors Guild & Hollywood Foreign Press Asn. *Songs:* Mad'moiselle; Get Yourself Another Girl; What Have You Done to My Heart?.

UNGER, STELLA   ASCAP 1953
author, producer
b New York, NY, Dec 17, 05; d. Educ: Benjamin Sch for Girls. Columnist, New York Daily Mirror; feature writer, Erwin Wasey advert agency. Writer, producer & commentator, NBC, 10 yrs. Wrote songs for Bway musicals incl "Three Little Girls", "Earl Carroll's Vanities of 1930" & "Continental Varieties"; also songs for films incl "A Date With Judy" & "Where the Boys Are"; theme songs: "The Horizontal Lieutenant"; "The Courtship of Eddie's Father." Chief Collabrs: Fred Fisher, Leopold Godowsky, Victor Young, James P Johnson, Alex Templeton. *Songs:* Alt Wien; All Dressed Up With a Broken Heart; Love Comes Only Once in a Lifetime; Don't Cry, Baby; Presidents on Parade; It's a Thrill All Over Again; C'est la vie; A Man With a Dream; If It's a Dream; Turn Your Frown Upside Down; Have You Met Miss Fandango?; I'm Strictly on the Corny Side; The Story of Life. *Scores:* Stage: Seventh Heaven.

UPTON, DONALD NILES
composer, author
b New York, NY, Nov 15, 25; d Nov 2, 78. Educ: Theodora Irvine Sch for Theater, NY; Hofstra Col, NY; Univ SC, BA. Began composing while actg as guide for NBC, New York; radio WLVA announcer, Lynchburg, Va, then to TV, Augusta, Ga & WIS-TV, Columbia, SC. Dir, OSHA Prog, State of SC. Chief Collabr: Stan Zabka. *Songs & Instrumental Works:* Christmas Eve in My Home Town; Noreen; Funny Little Bunny; Melancholy Wind; So This Is Love; Wouldn't 'Cha Know; What Am I Gonna Tell My Heart; It's New to Me; How Come.

URBANIAK, MICHAL   ASCAP 1973
composer
b Warsaw, Poland, Jan 21, 43. Educ: Acad Music, Warsaw, studied classical violin. Has done several movie sound tracks in Poland, incl "On the Road." Has recorded with own group for Columbia Records, Atlantic, Arista & Motown Records. Chief Collabrs: Norman Simon, Urszula Dudziak. *Instrumental Works:* Atma; Heritage; Butterfly; Body English; Joy; Serenade for the City; Fusion III; Cucoo's Nest; Storks. *Albums:* Serenade for the City.

URBANO, ALFRED J   ASCAP 1948
author
b South Portland, Maine, Jan 20, 11. Educ: Georgetown Univ Clef Award, Am Soc Disc Jockeys, 48. Employed by US War Dept, 35; chief spec investigation, US Immigration Serv, New York, 41; became asst dist dir investigation, Southern Calif; then dist dir, US Immigration & Naturalization, Ore. *Songs:* Serenade of the Bells; I'm Living a Lie; Heartbreaking; Little Poker Face; It's Like a Trip to Tipperary; Hasty Heart; Never Again; The Black Rose.

URBONT, DOROTHY   ASCAP 1978
composer, singer, pianist
b London, Eng, Jan 5, 03. Educ: Peabody Cons, Baltimore, Md; studied voice with Dorothy Godowsky. Singer solo, Henry Hudson Hotel, choral background. Mem, Rodeph Sholem Community Chorus. Staff pianist, WMCA & WNEW; pianist, Baltimore Symphonic orgn. Comp music for progs, ABC-TV & NBC-TV. Chief Collabr: Harry Urbont.

URBONT, ROSALIND ZEINS   ASCAP 1978
composer, author
b Brooklyn, NY, Dec 3, 42. Educ: Hofstra Univ, BA, 74; Brooklyn Col, MA, 76. Author of guide to playground exercise, "Parallel Play," 76. Comp music for var TV progs "Daytime" & "Dinah Shore." *Songs:* Music: Seasons of My Love.

URSTEIN, CARL   ASCAP 1970
composer, teacher, singer
b Jerusalem, Israel, Apr 25, 05. Educ: Vienna Cons. Concert artist; in opera, Vienna. Interpreter of Israeli songs. Cantor of prestigious synagogue, Chicago, 13 yrs & Calif, 32 yrs. Publ vols of liturgical music for choir, organ & soloists, "El Harinah v'el Hat'filah" (Chasidic Service, vol I & II). *Songs & Instrumental Works:* Achare Moti (Hebrew Classic); Sabbath Music At Sinai; The Lord Is My Shepherd (voice, piano); Choir, Soloist & Piano: Psalm-CXXI; Psalm-XXIII.

URWIN, GARY LEE   ASCAP 1979
composer
b Toledo, Ohio, Jan 6, 55. Educ: Oberlin Col, BA, 77; studied trumpet with Louis Davidson & comp with Donald Keats, David Stock, Wendell Logan & Eddy Manson. Staff arr, Pat Longo Orch. Free-lance arr & trumpet playing, Los Angeles area. Winner, UCLA/Frank Sinatra Arr Award, 80. *Instrumental Works:* Chain Reaction.

V

VAGRAMIAN, ARAM (AL VEGA)   ASCAP 1960
composer, teacher, band leader
b Worcester, Mass, June 22, 21. Educ: Chelsea High Sch; New Eng Cons Music. Fac mem, Berklee Col; trio leader & pianist on TV, recordings & nightclubs. Featured on Rod McKuen's TV special, 79 & TV7's "Nightscene." *Instrumental Works:* Marlowe's Mood; Marv's Melody; Sounds in the Night; Just Hankering Around; Sounds for Speed.

VAL, JACK
See Volpato, Jack Albert

VALENCY, MAURICE   ASCAP 1958
composer, author
b New York, NY, Mar 22, 03. Educ: City Col New York, AB; Columbia Univ, AM, LLB & PhD. Admitted to New York Bar, 28. Instr philos, City Col New York, 32-45; asst prof English, Brooklyn Col, 45-46; assoc prof comparative lit, Columbia Univ, 46-53, prof, 53-69, Brander Matthews prof dramatic lit, 69-71, emeritus prof, 71- Dir acad studies, Juilliard Sch, 71- *Scores:* Librettos: La Perichole; The Gypsy Baron; The Reluctant King; Feathertop; Bway shows: The Thracian Horses; The Madwoman of Chaillot (adaptation); The Enchanted (adaptation); Ondine (adaptation); The Apollo of Bellac (adaptation); The Visit (adaptation); Regarding Electra; Conversation With a Sphinx; Savonarola; Film/TV: The Virtuous Island (adaptation); Battleship Bismarck.

VALKAN, NICK
See Noble, Nick

VALLE, MARCOS KOSTENBADER   ASCAP 1966
composer, author, singer
b Rio de Janeiro, Brazil, Sept 14, 43. Educ: Colegio Mello E Souza (Rio); Colegio Santo Inacio (Rio); Colegio Brasileiro de Almeida (Rio); Pontificia Universidade Catolica (Rio); Conservatorio Haydee Lazaro Brant, 12 yrs; Lyle Murphy's Syst Horizontal Comp, 2 yrs. Asn of Critics of Brazil Awards, 64, 65 & 68. Singer & guitarist, Sergio Mendes & Brasil 65, US, 65-66; TV appearances, 67. Brazil rep, Int Song Fest of Mex, 71; first place prize, Int Song Fest of Greece, 72; Brazil rep, Midem Fest Music, France, 73. Writer, TV-Shows, TV-Films, sound scores for movies & commercial jingles, Brazil. Chief Collabrs: Paulo Valle, Ray Gilbert, Norman Gimbel, Alan & Marylin Bergman, Laudir de Oliveira, Leon Ware, Robert Lamm, Danny Seraphine. *Songs:* Life Is What It Is; Music: Summer Samba (So Nice); The Face I Love; Batucada; Gente; If You Went Away; Adam's Hotel; The Answer; With Your Love Now; Crickets Sing for Anamaria; Look Who's Mine; Viola; Love Is a Simple Thing. *Albums:* Marcos Valle Samba de Mais; Marcos Valle Brazilliance; Marcos Valle Samba 68.

VALLEE, HUBERT PRIOR (RUDY)   ASCAP 1930
composer, author, arranger
b Island Pond, Vt, July 28, 01. Educ: Univ Maine; Yale Univ, PhB; hon MS, Suffolk Law Sch. Self-taught in clarinet, drums & saxophone. First professional appearance as saxophonist in film theatre, Portland, Maine. At Yale Univ, organized orch, played in country clubs & cols; also led Yale Univ Band. Organized Conn Yankees, then began long engagement at Heigh Ho Club, NY, 28. Early singer in radio, made many records. Cond, 11th Naval Dist CG Band, USCG, WW II. Toured in nightclubs & hotels throughout US, Can, Panama, Puerto Rico, London, Ger & Hawaii. Autobiographies: Vagabond Dreams Come True & My Time Is Your Time. Appeared in many films incl "Vagabond Lover", "Gold Diggers in Paris", "The Bachelor and the Bobby Soxer", "I Remember Mama", "The Beautiful Blonde From Bashful Bend" & "The Helen Morgan Story"; in Bway musicals incl "George White's Scandals" (31, 36) & "How to Succeed in Business Without Really Trying". Owns 2 music publ firms. Chief Collabr: Charles Henderson. *Songs:* Me Queres (Do You Love Me, English trans); I'm Just a Vagabond Lover; Kitty From Kansas City; Betty Co-ed; To the Legion; The Song of the Navy; The Stein Song; My Cigarette Lady; Toodle-oo, So Long, Goodbye; Violets; Good Night, Sweetheart; Old Man Harlem; There Is a Tavern in the Town (The Drunkard Song); Ask Not; All Right, All Right, All Right; Vieni, Vieni (English trans); The Old Bow Song; Where To.

VAN, GUS   ASCAP 1951
composer, author, singer
b Brooklyn, NY, Aug 12, 1887; d. Mem, comedy team, Van & Schenck; appeared in many ed of "Ziegfeld Follies"; also in vaudeville. Made many records. *Songs:* Red Head Gal; Bran' New Gal of Mine; All She'd Say Was Uhm Hum; Bringing Home the Bacon; Pasta Fazoola.

VAN ALSTYNE, EGBERT ANSON   ASCAP 1923
composer, pianist
b Chicago, Ill, Mar 5, 1882; d Chicago, Ill, July 9, 51. Educ: Chicago Musical Col, scholarship; Cornell Col, Iowa. Joined circus with Harry Williams; toured in vaudeville. Went to New York, 1900; pianist, music publ co. Chief Collabrs: Harry Williams, Gus Kahn. *Songs:* Navajo; Back Back Back to Baltimore; In the Shade of the Old Apple Tree; Won't You Come Over to My House?; I'm Afraid

to Come Home in the Dark; It Looks to Me Like a Big Night Tonight; What's the Matter With Father?; That Old Girl of Mine; San Antonio; Why Don't You Try?; When I Was a Dreamer; Memories; Pretty Baby; Sailin' Away on the Henry Clay; Your Eyes Have Told Me So; Drifting and Dreaming; Beautiful Love. *Scores:* Bway Stage: A Broken Doll; Girlies.

VAN APPLEDORN, MARY JEANNE   ASCAP 1978
composer, pianist, teacher
b Holland, Mich, Oct 2, 27. Educ: Eastman Sch of Music, BMus (piano), MMus (theory), PhD, 66, comp study with Bernard Rogers & Alan Hovhaness. Prof & chmn, Music Theory, Comp & Grad Studies in Music, Tex Tech Univ, 50- Carnegie Recital Hall piano debut, 56. Tex Composers Guild Award, 80. Comns: Women Band Dirs Nat Asn & Nat Kappa Kappa Psi Fraternity. Chief Collabrs: Abba Kovner, Everett A Gillis, Wallace Stevens. *Songs:* Music: Darest Thou Now, O Soul. *Instrumental Works:* Sonnet for Organ; Set of Five for Piano; Concerto Brevis. *Scores:* Cantata: Rising Night After Night.

VAN BRAKLE, JOHN   ASCAP 1956
author, artist, actor
b Brooklyn, NY, Mar 23, 03; d. Educ: High sch. Actor in vaudeville, films & theatre. In advert for many yrs; free-lance writer; marine & landscape painter. Chief Collabrs: Clara Edwards, John Sacco. *Songs:* Ol' Jim; Easter Message. *Instrumental Works:* Who Are You? (cantata).

VAN CAMP, LEONARD WARD   ASCAP 1974
composer
b Wichita, Kans, June 12, 34. Educ: Wichita State Univ, BME, MME; Univ Mo, Kansas City, DMA. High sch & col choral dir, church musician, Wichita, Kansas City, Kans & Decorah, Iowa. Prof music, Southern Ill Univ, Edwardsville, 63- Professional singer (bass-baritone), ed & arr. *Instrumental Works:* Choral Arr: A Cry for Freedom (Billings); O Sing Unto the Lord; Happy Land (southern folk hymn); Begnäbnis Gesange (Brahms, winds & chorus).

VANCE, PAUL J   ASCAP 1956
composer, author, producer
b Brooklyn, NY, Nov 4, 29. Educ: High sch. Was prof prize fighter; writer for films, TV, Bway prods & records; head, ABC-Paramount publ firms. Chief Collabrs: Lee Pockriss, Roy Alfred, Leon Carr, Paul Vance, Perry Cone. *Songs:* Catch a Falling Star; Itsy Bitsy Teenie Weenie Yellow Polka Dot Bikini; What Is Love?; Calcutta; Starbright; Go Chase a Moonbeam; Marie, Marie; On a Cold and Windy Day; Wait For Me; Should I Wait?; Oh, That Feeling; Hey Love; Jimmy's Girl; Gina; What Will My Mary Say?; No Man Can Stand Alone; Bye, Bye Barbara; Then Suddenly Love; I Don't Know; A World Without Sunshine; In My Room; Stagecoach to Cheyenne; Tracy; Leader of the Laundromat; She Lets Her Hair Down; Playground In My Mind; Run Joey Run.

VAN CLEAVE, NATHAN   ASCAP 1946
composer
b Bayfield, Wis, May 8, 10; d Studio City, Calif, July 3, 70. Writer of scores for films & radio. *Instrumental Works:* Daybreak Serenade; Canzonetta; Fantasy for Strings; Trumpet Concerto; American Holiday; Dances From Satanstoe.

VAN CLEVE, BERTRAM DORIAN   ASCAP 1943
composer, author, singer
b San Francisco, Calif, July 18, 1899. Educ: Gen col courses. Born of theatrical parents, spent first seven yrs on the road in father's repertory co coast to coast. Actor in stock, San Francisco & Oakland. Radio DJ, KLX, Oakland. In road show "Road to Rome." Writer, Rex Cole Mountaineers. Partner, Piedmont Music Co. Mem comedy trio, WLW, Cincinnati, 33-34. Chief Collabrs: Arthur Fields, Fred Hall, Guy Wood, Rudy Vallee. *Songs:* There's a Blue Sky Way Out Yonder; I Just Can't Think of Anything But You; Hush, Hush, Lover; The Olive Song (I'm Just Crazy for Olives); The Airplane Song; Frigging in the Rigging; I Took the Last Bus Out of Town; Cyril Isn't Virile Anymore; Teachers Pet; Take Me Somewhere; I Lost My Head in Maiden Lane; Easy Does It; I'm Gonna Get a Bachelor Apartment; He Was a Son of a Bee; Lyrics: I Can't Sleep in the Movies Anymore; Eleven More Months and Ten More Days; Born to Be Loved; Hang It in the Henhouse; Song Without an Ending; Somewhere in Your Heart; Please Squeeze the Coconuts; Shadows on the Trail; When the Sun Sets Over the Rockies; The Persian Pussy; Shadows on the Trail.

VAN DAM, ALBERT   ASCAP 1952
composer
b Amsterdam, Neth, Dec 15, 20. Educ: Comp & counterpoint, Juilliard Sch Music; comp, Brooklyn Col Music; pvt comp study with Felix Deyo & Otto Cesana; Yale Univ. WW II, OSS. Exec, Toy Co & Machine Co. Recorded 4 albums. Chief Collabrs: Sammy Gallop, Lawrence Markes, Al Stillman, Carl Sigman. *Songs:* Music: Circus on Parade; Blue Fedora; Bring Back the Sunshine; The Sentimental Touch; Su-Su; You Were There; If You Ever Go Away; Crazy Horse Saloon; Sleepless Hours; Way Back Home; Disco Cat; Island of Women; The Road to Happiness; Natasha; Not for Just Your Face; Breakfast With the Blues; Mata Hari. *Instrumental Works:* Matto Grosso; Voodoo Doll (Sophisticated Scarecrow); Disco Concorde; Maharajah; Belly Button Bounce; Bubbles Galore.

VAN DAMME, ART   ASCAP 1967
accordionist, teacher
b Norway, Mich, Apr 9, 20. Educ: Studied classical accordion with Pines Caviani & Andy Rizzo, 9 yrs, also harmony & theory. Started prof career as accordionist at age 10. First trio played Chicago night spots, 38-41, joined Ben Bernie band, 41. Worked Chicago night spots as a single; formed trio, played midwest, 41-44; became quartet, with NBC, Chicago, 49-60; became quintet, 45. Recording artist, Capitol Records, 45-52, Columbia Records, 52-65, MPS Records, Ger, 67-78. Opened music studio & store, Chicago, 60. Guest appearances with quintet on var TV & local shows. Working TV, radio, concerts & jazz clubs, US & Europe, 60- *Songs:* Music: Ecstasy. *Instrumental Works:* Selections for Accordion; Play Accordion Like A V D; Modern Jazz Recital; Jazz Magic No 1, No 2; Assorted Solos.

VANDENBURGH, MILDRED M   ASCAP 1968
composer, author, teacher
b Independence, Iowa, May 18, 1898. Educ: Baylor Univ, grad in voice; studied piano with Heniet Levy & voice with D A Clippinger; Am Cons, Chicago; Univ Southern Calif, BSEd(pub sch music) & MSEd(pub sch music). Voice & piano teacher & dir church choirs, 15 yrs; supervised recreational music (harmonica bands) & taught primary through adults, Los Angeles City Schs; taught in insts for boys, Maharashtra, India, 3 short-terms; sang, played & dir groups on var radio & TV progs; spent several seasons in light opera, "Princess Pat", "Robin Hood", "Serenade", "Alone At Last", Aborn Stock Co. Taught two summer sessions, Eastern NMex Univ, Silver City; free-lance writer & soprano. *Songs:* Anthem: Faith; Happy Is the Man That Findeth Wisdom. *Instrumental Works:* Carlsbad Caverns Symphonic Suite; School Band Folio for the Harmonica; Selections for the Chromatic Harmonica. *Albums:* Concert Album for the Chromatic Harmonica; Concert Album for the Super Chromatic Harmonica; Music Education With the Harmonica (series 11).

VANDERBURG, GORDON J   ASCAP 1956
composer, author
b Maywood, Ill, Apr 10, 13. Educ: Am Operatic Lab. Copy boy, Herald Examiner, INS & AP, Chicago. Worked in defense plants, World War II; Seabees. Painter in film studios, Hollywood. *Songs:* Space Needle Twist; Remember Waikiki; Dearest; Nursin' One Beer; Fourteen Carat Fool; Hotel Happiness; Off to Seattle; Silky Sullivan.

VANDERPOOL, FREDERICK W   ASCAP 1920
composer, conductor, singer
b New York, NY, May 8, 1877; d Newark, NJ, Feb 13, 47. Educ: Pub schs; studied music with Louis Koemmenich, R Huntington Woodman, Carl Dufft & Frank Dossert. Asst music dir, De Wolf Opera Co, 01-03. Organist & music dir, Asbury Park, NJ. Asst to Arthur Pryor, bandmaster, 22 yrs. Staff comp, New York publ house; also recorded piano rolls. *Songs:* If; Values; I Did Not Know; Songs of Dawn and Twilight; 'Neath the Autumn Moon; Ma Little Sunflower; The Want of You; Come Love Me; Rejoice My Love; Come Away. *Scores:* Operettas: The King's Highwayman.

VANDERVOORT II, PAUL   ASCAP 1956
composer, author, arranger
b Omaha, Nebr, Aug 2, 03. Educ: Univ courses. Civil service employee. Musician, singer, cond own dance band in Midwest, 20's. Writer bks, mag & newspaper articles, advert copy, nightclub acts, also musical commercials & spec material for radio & TV. Co-author, "Trumpet on the Wing" (biography of Wingy Manone). Auth, "How to Write a Song"; "How to Make Chords"; "How to Play the Ukulele." Mem, Am Guild Authors & Comp; Writers Guild of Am. Chief Collabrs: Benny Carter, Louie Bellson, Al Dero. *Songs:* Lyrics: King Size Papa; Second Hand Love; Rock Me to Sleep; My Kind of Trouble Is You; No Good Man; Never, Never, Never; Tongue-Tied; Talking to Myself; Love Dreams; Let Me Dream (Dejame Sonar); Rain, Rain; Omaha Can Do Songbook (comp for Omaha Chamber of Commerce, Nebr). *Instrumental Works:* Orange County Suite; Strictly Instrumental.

VAN DE VATE, NANCY HAYES   ASCAP 1964
composer
b Plainfield, NJ, Dec 30, 30. Educ: Univ Rochester Eastman Sch of Music, 48-49, summer 50; Wellesley Col, AB, 52; Univ Miss, MM, 58; Fla State Univ, DMus, 68. Fac mem at 9 cols & univs throughout the south & in Hawaii; assoc prof music, Hawaii Loa Col. Founder & chairperson, Int League of Women Composers. Resident fel, Yaddo & Ossabaw Island; recipient, ASCAP Standard awards, 73-, Delius Comp Contest, first place, 75, Stowe Chamber Music Competition, third prize, 75, Los Alamos Chamber Music Competition, first prize, 79 & 3 awards from Meet the Comp & var comns. *Songs:* Music: Two Songs. *Instrumental Works:* Music for Viola, Percussion and Piano; Sonata for Piano; Letter to a Friend's Loneliness (soprano, string quartet); Trio for Strings; Sonata for Viola and Piano; Six Etudes for Solo Viola; Quintet (1975) (flute, violin, clarinet, cello, piano); Adagio for Orchestra; Suite for Solo Violin; Short Suite for Brass Quartet; Quintet for Brass; Concertpiece for Cello and Small Orchestra; How Fares the Night (SSA, piano).

VANDROSS, LUTHER R   ASCAP 1973
singer, songwriter
b New York, NY, Apr 20, 51. Songwriter & singer, 74-; background vocalist. Nat Acad Recording Arts & Sci Most Valuable Player-Best Male Vocalist Award, 79. Chief Collabs: David Lasley, David Bowie. *Songs:* Everybody Rejoice (Brand New Day); Fascination.

VAN EPS, GEORGE   ASCAP 1960
composer, guitarist
b Plainfield, NJ, Aug 7, 13. Educ: Self taught at an early age. Developed own systs & methods of producing music & was teaching at age 15. Started playing banjo, 23, guitar, 27. Theatre tour with Libby Holman & Dean Moore, 28. Joined The Smith Ballew Band, 29, Freddy Martin, 31 & Benny Goodman Band, 34. House musician, Brunswick & Victor Records, 33. With Ray Noble, 35-36; free lance studio on West Coast, 37. Mem, Gordon Jenkins, Paul Weston, Dave Rose & Nelson Riddle Orchs. Author musical text books, "Guitar Method" & "Harmonic Mechanisms," vols I & II. Chief Collabrs: John Van Eps, Ralph Fried. *Songs:* Music: Stop, Look and Listen. *Instrumental Works:* The Chant; Lock It Up; Squattin at the Grotto; A Ducky Dish; Kay's Fantasy; I Wrote It for Jo; Tango El Bongo; All Alone; Scotts Lullaby; Love Theme for Jo; Midnight; Water Fall; Love Theme No 1; Tango; Love Theme No 2; Cross Roads.

VAN EPS, ROBERT   ASCAP 1954
composer, pianist, arranger
b Plainfield, NJ, Mar 10, 09. Educ: Studied piano with William Laurence Calhoun, Vernon Spencer, Calif. Pianist with Red Nichols Band, 28. Pianist & arr, Smith Ballow Band, 30-32, Freddie Martin Band, 32-34 & Dorsey Bros Band, 34, to Calif with Jimmy Dorsey when band split up, 35-37. Under contract with MGM, pianist & picture comp, 35 yrs. Pianist, Paramount Studios, 49-50; free-lance comp, orchr & pianist for other major studios incl Columbia, Disney, Warner Bros, Paramount, Fox & others, 38- Inventor, tone arm to correct tracking errors & eliminate distortion on recorded discs. Author, bk "The Physics of the Piano Technique." *Songs:* Reverie (theme, Smith Bellow Band); Wind in the Chimney; The Cricket on the Hearth; Room Number Nine; Niagara; & many others. *Instrumental Works:* Piano Concerto No 1, 2 (symph orch). *Albums:* The American Suite Within the Piano World of Robert Van Eps (classical); jazz album.

VANEUF, ANDRE
See Cohen, Sol B

VAN FORST, KATHY   ASCAP 1964
composer, author
b Cologne, Ger, Apr 24, 04. Educ: Studied music with Madeline Dietz. Wrote & produced musicals for theatre groups, Europe. WW II, singer with Am Theatre Wing. Chief Collabrs: Arthur Richardson, Fred Patrick, Polly Arnold. *Songs:* The Reason Is Love; Closed for Repairs; Stranger in the Chapel; Tormenting Me; Rosella; Come Out of the Shadows.

VAN HEUSEN, JAMES
See Babcock, Edward Chester

VAN HORNE, HARRY R (RANDY)   ASCAP 1960
composer, singer, arranger
b El Paso, Tex, Feb 10, 24. Educ: Peabody Cons, Baltimore, Md, 45; Tex Western Univ, theory, 47, 48; studies with Albert Harris, Los Angeles, 79- To Calif, then started group The Encores, toured with Billy May Orch; formed jazz chorus, Randy Van Horne Singers, did 6 albums. Wrote music & voice for commercials; was commercial talent agent for 20 months. Now in music comp, songwriting, serious symph & commercial music. Chief Collabrs: Don Raye, Leo McElroy, Ann Nicolaysian. *Songs:* Music: Danny; Melanie Goodbye; The Wanderin' Song; Lonely Places. *Songs & Instrumental Works:* The Running of the Bulls (symph suite).

VAN HULSE, CAMIL   ASCAP 1950
composer, pianist, organist
b St Nicholas, Belg, Aug 1, 1897. Educ: Studied music with Gustave Van Hulse (father), Frans Lenaerts, Edward Verheyden, Lode Mortelmans & Arthur DeGreef; Royal Flemish Cons, Antwerp. Moved to US, 23; gave piano & organ concerts, US & SAm. Moved to Tucson, Ariz; founder, Soc Chamber Music, Symph Orch; church organist & choirmaster until 56. *Songs & Instrumental Works:* Elegy; Variations for Piano; The Beatitudes (cantata); Mass of the Faithful; Missa "Fiat Voluntas Tua"; Christmas Oratorio; Symphonic Mystica; St Louis, Roi de France; Jubilee Suite; 'Twas in the Moon of Wintertime.

VAN INDERSTINE, ARTHUR PRENTICE   ASCAP 1969
composer, teacher
b Oradell, NJ, Apr 16, 20. Educ: Oberlin Col Cons Music, SchMusB, 42, MusEdM, 47; studied voice with Olaf C Christiansen & comp with Normand Lockwood & Herbert Elwell. Choral music dir, Spartanburg High Sch, SC, 46-48; music teacher, East High Sch, Youngstown, Ohio, 48-49; choral music dir, Woodrow Wilson High Sch, Youngstown, 49-78. Choir dir var churches, 46-56; organist, Pleasant Grove UP Church, Youngstown. Publ composer choral

& organ works, 57- *Songs:* Music: O Clap Your Hands; Early in the Morning; God Rest Ye Merry, Gentlemen. *Instrumental Works:* Jesus, the Very Thought of Thee (bk of organ pieces).

VAN LOAN, PAUL S   ASCAP 1953
composer, conductor, trombonist
b San Francisco, Calif, Dec 3, 1892; d July 16, 63. Joined USMC, age 16; youngest bandmaster. Staff comp, Waterson, Berlin & Snyder. Own TV prog "The Prince Albert Hour." With Ben Berney & Paul Whiteman. Music dir, "Burlesque." Comp, 20th Century-Fox, 10 yrs. Music dir with Sonja Henie, 38-52, then Barber & Scott. Chief Collabrs: Ervin Bibo, L Wolf Gilbert, Donna Olson, George Bird.

VAN LOON, GERARD WILLEM   ASCAP 1943
author
b Munich, Bavaria, Jan 16, 11. To US 11; citizen 19. Educ: Eaglebrook Sch, Deerfield, Mass; Glarisegg Sch, Switz; Max Reinhardt Sem, Vienna. Returned to US for theatre & nightclub appearances. Field artillery, USAF, World War II; Brit War Off Intelligence Res; theatre control officer, Infantry Control Div, Bavaria. *Songs:* Liberty Under God; Sing, Sing, Sing; New World on Its Way.

VAN LOVE, LUDY
See Love, Luther Halsey

VANN, AL   ASCAP 1934
composer, author, conductor
b Kiev, Russia, May 21, 1899; d. To US, 09. Citizen, 20. Educ: Pub schs; pvt music study. Boy soprano, Cantor Joseph Rosenblatt's Choir; toured US. Staff mem, music publ cos. Sang in operetta, "The Lady of the Slipper" & in vaudeville. Organized own band. Writer of special material for vaudeville & radio. Publisher, The Music Journal. *Songs:* Falling Star; Must We Say Goodnight?; I Never Care About Tomorrow; Things I Never Knew Till Now; Can I Be Wrong?; Some of Your Sweetness; The Kitten With the Big Green Eyes; Old Man Moon; It's Beginning to Tell on Me.

VANNELLI, GINO   ASCAP 1973
composer, singer
b Montreal, Que, June 16, 52. Educ: Pvt instruction. Began as drummer, played with brother's band. Writer, 69-; standard vocalist, 74- Recording artist with var cos. Chief Collabrs: Rock Vannelli, Joe Vannelli. *Songs:* Wheels of Life; Pauper in Paradise; Brother to Brother; People Got to Move; Where Am I Going; Omens of Love; The War Suite; Powerful People; Storm at Sun Up.

VAN PEEBLES, MELVIN   ASCAP 1976
composer, author
b Chicago, Ill, Aug 21, 32. Educ: Ohio Wesleyan Univ, BA. French delegate to San Francisco Film Fest for film "The Story of a Three Day Pass," 67. Dir & scored film "Watermelon Man"; wrote, dir & scored film "Sweet Sweetback's Baadasssss Song." Writer, bk, music & lyrics, play "Ain't Supposed to Die a Natural Death," nominated for 7 Tony awards, play "Don't Play Us Cheap," nominated for 2 Tony awards. Author, novels "A Bear for FBI", "The Big Heart", "The True American", "Le Chinsois Du XIV" & "Just an Ole Sweet Song."

VAN RONK, DAVID   ASCAP 1963
composer, author, singer
b Brooklyn, NY, June 30, 36. Educ: Richmond Hill High Sch. Guitarist in jazz group, then formed jug band. Singer, NY Folk Fest, Carnegie Hall, 65. Made records. *Songs:* Bamboo; If You Leave Me, Pretty Mama; Frankie's Blues; Bad Dream Blues.

VAN SCIVER, ESTHER   ASCAP 1943
author, editor
b New York, NY, June 11, 07; d Nyack, NY, May 14, 52. Staff writer for newspapers & mag. Ed, All American Bandleader. *Songs:* You Never Know; The Fighting Sun-of-a Gun; I Betcha My Heart I Love You; I Ain't Never Loved Before; The Next Time You Talk to the Lord; In a Little Canning Kitchen.

VAN SLYCK, NICHOLAS   ASCAP 1975
composer, teacher, conductor
b Philadelphia, Pa, Oct 25, 22. Educ: Kent Sch, Conn; Philadelphia Cons; Harvard Col, BA, MA, studied with Walter Piston. Dir, South End Music Centre, Boston, 48-61, Longy Sch Music, Cambridge, 62-76. Cond, Dedham Choral Soc, 55-61, Quincy Symph, 61-67 & Merrimack Valley Philh, 67- Mem fac, Harvard Grad Sch, 64-68. Dir & founder, New Sch Music, Cambridge, 76. *Songs:* Choral: Rhythm Rounds; Song of the Modes; Rain Song. *Instrumental Works:* Passa mezzo Antico (brass); Twelve for Three (wind trios); Fantasia Numerica (unaccompanied bassoon); Sonata for Solo Flute; Suite for Harpsichord.

VAN SPALL, PETER ALEXANDER   ASCAP 1963
composer, pianist
b Brooklyn, NY, Mar 4, 13. Educ: Jamaica High Sch. Led own band; pianist in orchs, US Lines, 56- Chief Collabr: Nola Arndt. *Songs & Instrumental Works:* Please! Speak Softly of Love; American Beauty Waltzes.

VAN STEEDEN, PETER, JR   ASCAP 1949
composer, violinist, conductor
b Amsterdam, Holland, Apr 3, 04. NY Univ, Col Indust Eng, 25; violin with Rudolf Luks, music theory & comp with Paul Yartin, Howard Murphy, Pietro Floridia & Demo Caruso, cond with Norval Church, Columbia Teachers Col. While in col had orch Van and His Collegians, broadcasting over radio sta WEAF, 24. Had engagements in several hotels & restaurants, New York. Cond orchs on radio & TV progs incl "Fred Allen Show", "Duffy's Tavern", "Lucky Strike Hit Parade", "Break the Bank", "Mr District Attorney", "Omnibus", "Jack Pearl-Baron Munchhausen", "George Jessel", "Stoopnagle and Budd", "Abbott and Costello", "Alan Young", "Bob Hawk", "Walter O'Keefe", "Dr Pepper Parade", "What's My Name?", "Christopher Wells", "Tim and Irene", "Claudia and David" & "Ray Perkins Barbasol Program." Chief Collabrs: Geoffrey Clarkson, Harry Clarkson, Albert Miller, Edward Eager. *Songs:* Music: Home (When Shadows Fall); Under the Mistletoe (The Kissing Song); My Dad; The Ballad of Lil; Home for Christmas; Sisters (Gracious Country Life); Conformity; Hand in Hand; Cultivate Your Garden; Jesus My Saviour; while in col wrote songs for varsity shows. *Instrumental Works:* My Children's Waltzes; Themes for Radio Shows: Mr District Attorney; Christopher Wells; Break the Bank (also TV).

VAN VACTOR, DAVID   ASCAP 1955
composer, author, conductor
b Plymouth, Ind, May 8, 06. Educ: Northwestern Univ; Acad Music, Vienna; L'Ecole Normale, Paris; Frederick Stock Scholarship, 39-42; Guggenheim & Fulbright grants. Assoc with Chicago Symph, 31-43; asst cond, Kansas City Philh, 43-46; founder & cond, Kansas City Allied Arts Orch. Latin-Am tours as flutist, cond & lectr. Guest cond symph orchs incl London Philh. Organized Dept of Fine Arts, Univ Tenn, 47, emer prof. Cond, Knoxville Symph. Composer Laureate of Tenn. *Instrumental Works:* Symphony No 4 Walden (chorus & orch); Symphony No 5 (Bicentennial Comn Tenn Endowment for Arts); Suite for Orchestra on Chilean Tunes; Suite for Twelve Solo Trombones; Episodes-Jesus Christ (chorus & orch); Set of Five (band); Elements (band); Economy Band No 1 & 2; Five Songs for Flute and Guitar; Sixth Symphony (orch or band). *Songs & Instrumental Works:* Quintet for 2 Violins, Viola, Cello, Flute (Soc for Publ of Am Music Award); The New Light (Christmas cantata); Symphony No 1 in D (NY Philh Prize); Symphony No 2; Overture to a Comedy No 1; Overture to a Comedy No 2 (Juilliard Publ Prize); Symphonic Suite; Fantasia, Chaconne and Allegro (Louisville Orch Comn); Credo for Chorus, Orchestra; Trumpet Concerto; Music for the Marines; Five Bagatelles; Introduction and Presto; Brass Fanfare; Trojan Women (suite); Cantata for Treble Voices, Orchestra; three songs for soprano, alto flute & bass clarinet.

VAN WINKLE, HAROLD E (RIP)   ASCAP 1963
composer, author
b Indianapolis, Ind, Apr 3, 39. Educ: High sch. Personal mgr, Carole Lancing. *Songs:* Hey, Mr DJ.

VAN WORMER, RANDALL EDWIN   ASCAP 1976
composer, singer
b Denver, Colo, Mar 30, 55. Educ: St Austell Col, Cornwall, Eng. Songwriter, 74- With Albert Grossman Publ, 76 & with Bearsville Records, London, Eng, 77. Now touring US. Chief Collabrs: Ian Kimmet, John Holbrook. *Songs:* Just When I Needed You Most; All We Have Is Tonite. *Albums:* Wormer; Perraform.

VAN ZANDT, MARY O'SULLIVAN   ASCAP 1962
composer, author
b Lee County, Miss, Sept 12, 03. Educ: Southern Female Acad; Harris Cons, BA. Airlines stewardess & music teacher, formerly. *Songs:* It's All Accordin'.

VAN ZANDT, STEVEN   ASCAP 1975
composer, author, producer
b Kingston, Jamaica, Nov 22, 50. Played & worked with Bruce Springsteen Band. Comp 50's revival shows, "Asbury Jukes Playing Oldies Show," 75. *Songs:* I Don't Wanna Go Home; This Time It's for Real; I Played the Fool.

VAQUER, DOROTHEA JOYCE BUCHALTER   ASCAP 1969
composer, singer, performer
b Detroit, Mich, June 1, 43. Educ: Ind Univ Music Sch; Wayne State Univ, BS(music, music educ). Song writer, April Blackwood Music Publ Co; wrote title song lyrics for Cannes Film Fest Winner, "Jeremy"; wrote & performed in off-off Bway one-woman show, "A Woman Now." Singer night clubs & concerts. Performer theater, Apple Pie, The Pub Theater, Mourning Pictures & Bway. *Songs:* Love's, Lines, Angles and Rhymes. *Scores:* Bway: The Fortune Seekers. *Albums:* Enlightenment.

VARELA, DANTE A   ASCAP 1961
composer, conductor, arranger
b Buenos Aires, Arg, Jan 14, 17. To US 52. Educ: Nat Cons, Buenos Aires; studied with Benito Varela (father), Vincenzo Scaramuzza & Ceyetano Marcolli. Organized instrumental group, playing hotels & clubs, Calif & Nev; also cond & arr for films. *Instrumental Works:* Cali; Tintilin; Tangolonga; El Coco; Batuque; The Romantic Cha Cha.

VARLAY, RENE G   ASCAP 1963
composer, author, narrator
b New York, NY, Nov 16, 27. Educ: Allen Stephenson Sch, New York; The Lawrenceville Sch, NJ; Yale Univ, BA, 50; Mary Washington Col, music studies, 78; pvt studies with Sol Berkowitz, Douglaston, NY. Commercial real estate & ins broker, New York, 50-73. Chief Collab: Richard Hyman. *Songs & Instrumental Works:* The Lollipop Songs (children songs); Patrick Henry: Give Me Liberty or Give Me Death (orch setting of speech with narrator); Richmond 200 (symph tone poem).

VARNADO, ALLEAN   ASCAP 1978
composer, singer, writer
b Magnolia, Miss, Dec 29, 47. Educ: Jackson State Univ, BS. Soul Search finalist, KGFJ (LA), 71. USO entertainer, 74; gospel singer & writer; TV recording artist, ICA Records. Chief Collabrs: Clay McMurray, Lydia Purifoy, Pearl Smith. *Songs:* To Be Friends; Lyrics: What Is This Life; Come Fly With Me.

VARNICK, TED   ASCAP 1952
composer, author
b Cleveland, Ohio, Mar 10, 13. Chief Collabr: Nick Acquaviva. *Songs:* In the Middle of an Island.

VARS, HENRY   ASCAP 1950
composer, conductor, pianist
b Warsaw, Poland, Dec 29, 02; d Brentwood, Calif, Sept 1, 77. Educ: Warsaw Cons. Comp & cond for films, theatre, radio, TV & records. Polish Armed Forces, WW II. Entertained front soldiers; rec'd Cavaliere di Croce di Italia. Moved to US, 47. Chief Collabr: William Dunham. *Songs:* Sleep, My Child; Over and Over; Little Shepherd; Good Love; Speak to Me Pretty; Walk With Him; Flipper (TV theme); That's a Cotton Candy World: Daktari (TV theme); Fools Parade (cinema); China Doll (cinema). *Instrumental Works:* Symphony No 1; String Quartet; Sonata for Violin, Piano; Symphonic Suite; Preludes for Piano; Piano Sonata; Piano Concerto; Three Symphonic Poems.

VAUGHAN, CLIFFORD
author, organist
b Bridgeton, NJ, Sept 23, 1893. Educ: Philadelphia Cons Music, grad; studied piano with Adele Sutor & Henric Ezerman; theory, comp, orchestration & choral conducting with Henry Albert Lang; organ with Rollo Maitland, Stanley Addicks & Frederick Schlieder. Organist, Broad & Arch Methodist, Philadelphia. Choral cond, Philadelphia Operatic Soc; mus dir for Ruth St Denis, Ted Shawn & Denishawn Dancers throughout Orient, US & Can. Comp & orchestrator in films, 30 yrs, Hollywood; Congregational Church organist, Hollywood. *Songs:* Bonny Mary; Six Piano Preludes; Service Piece (organ); Revery (harp); Invocation (organ); When Jesus Wept (organ); Contemplation (organ); Reverie (organ); White Jade (var sized orch). *Scores:* Film/TV: Comanche; Flash Gordon; BF's Daughter; New Frontier; Raven; Christmas in Norway; Thousand and One Nights; vol serv music in 7 pieces; also over 200 works for organ.

VAUGHAN, FRANK (PALANI), JR   ASCAP 1975
composer, author, musician
b Honolulu, Hawaii, May 27, 44. Educ: Kamehameha Sch; Univ Hawaii, BFA. Formed Hawaiian Musical group, The Sunday Manoa, 68. Served on active duty with Hawaii Army Nat Guard, 18 months. Singer with The Sons of Hawaii, 70, received No Ka Oi Award; formed own record co, recorded series "Ia'De E Ka La," Vols I, II & III, received Nani Awards, 74 & 75, Na Hoku Hanohano Award, 77. *Songs:* Ka'a Ahi Kahului; Ka Mamakakaua; Voices on the Wind; Kelo Likelike; Ha'aheo; Na Hawaii o'Iolani; Lahaina-Ka'anapali Train; E Ku'u Makamae; Na Kanaka Holo Lio.

VAUGHAN, RODGER DALE   ASCAP 1975
composer, educator
b Delphos, Kans, Feb 2, 32. Educ: Southwestern Col, Kans, 49-50; Univ Kans, BM(theory), 53; Wichita State Univ, MM(comp), 56; Univ Southern Calif, studied comp with Ingolf Dahl & orchestration with Halsey Stevens, 58-69. Instr music, Wichita State Univ, 56-60; lectr music, Univ Southern Calif, 61-63; assoc prof music, Upland Col, 63-65; prof music, Calif State Univ, Fullerton, 65- *Songs:* Christmas Lullaby; Music: Psalm 100; I Will Lift Up Mine Eyes (Psalm 123); Festival Anthem. *Instrumental Works:* Concert Piece No 1 (tuba & piano); Variations for Flute; Suite for Tuba; Quattro Bicinie (clarinet & tuba); American Favorites: Mirafone Arrangements for Tuba Quartet (a collection of old standards).

VAUGHN, JACK   ASCAP 1959
composer, author
b Springfield, Ore, Aug 24, 25. Educ: Univ Ore, BS(communications); Stanford Univ. Started career in radio sta prog; music dir, WBZ, Boston; prog dir, WYZE, Atlanta; production mgr, WNAX, Yankton, SDak; record producer, Scandinavia for 3 yrs. Consult to Japanese radio stas on Am pop music, 20's to 50's; in Japan, 70-80. *Songs:* Goodbye Jimmy, Goodbye; The Toy Drum (With His Drum); How Can You Pick the Roses?; Music: Magic Land; Lyrics: No Beer, No Wine, No Nothin'.

VAUGHN, RICHARD SMITH (BILLY)   ASCAP 1953
composer, author, arranger
b Glasgow, Ky, Apr 12, 19. Educ: Glasgow High Sch; Western Ky Univ. Club musician; organized vocal group the Hilltoppers. Recorded & musical dir for Dot Records also arr for all Dot Records artists. Recording artist, US & abroad. Voted Top Studio Orch. Chief Collabrs: Tom Mack, Harry Tobias, Milt Rogers, Hy Heath, Beasley Smith, Bob Russell, Johnny Mercer. *Songs:* Trying; To Be Alone; Rags (Christmas song); Music: Israeli Nights; Lyrics: I'd Rather Die Young; The Jimtown Road. *Instrumental Works:* Song of the West; Kelli; The Crosseyed Cyclops; Nashville Sunday Morning; Oriental Holiday; A Song for Sage (Sage's Theme); Reggies Theme; Traci's Tracks; Come Along, Sweet Christy.

VAZ DIAS, DAVID
See Egli, David Christian

VAZZANA, ANTHONY E   ASCAP 1963
composer, musician, educator
b Troy, NY, Nov 4, 22. Educ: NY State Univ, BS; Univ Southern Calif, Alchin & Friends of Music scholarships, alumni award, MM & DMA; studied music with Edward Riehl, George Pickering, Frank Catricala, Helen Hosmer, Halsey Stevens & Ingolf Dahl; Bennington Comp Conf scholarship. Cond & musician, USAAF bands, WW II. Taught music, pub schs, 1 yr; music supvr, pub schs, Manhattan Beach, Calif, 49-51; mem fac, Champlain Col, NY State Univ, 51-53, Cortland, NY, 53-54, Danbury State Col, 54-57 & Univ Southern Calif. *Instrumental Works:* Harlequin Suite for Chamber Orchestra; Symphony No 1; Symphonic Allegro (Friends of Music award). *Scores:* Film: Tomorrow May Be Dying (background).

VEGA, AL
See Vagramian, Aram

VELEZDY, JOSEPH   ASCAP 1967
composer, author
b North Braddock, Pa, Mar 11, 12. Educ: Studied violin with father; pvt music study violin, New York; Hungary High Schs, 2 yrs. Chief Collabrs: Mary Velezdy, Emery Marx. *Songs & Instrumental Works:* My Serenade; Small Cafe; If You Love Me Honey; Cynthia; I Can't Live Without You; Last Tango; Dream of Spring; Dancing in a Ballroom; Hat Magyar Dal.

VELEZDY, MARY   ASCAP 1967
author
b Zelienople, Pa, Jan 29, 12. Educ: Pub Schs. Chief Collab: Joseph Velezdy. *Songs & Instrumental Works:* My Serenade; Small Cafe; If You Love Me Honey; Cynthia; I Can't Live Without You; Dream of Spring; Last Tango; Dancing in a Ballroom.

VELIZ, ANDY C   ASCAP 1979
composer, singer, publisher
b Sebastian, Tex, Feb 2, 43. Educ: Lyford High Sch, 61; Tex A&I Univ, BS, 65; Univ Tex, Austin, MEd, 74. Singer, nightclubs & TV, Tex. Recording artist, Skatelands Records & Rique Records, Tex. Owner music co. *Songs:* Lonely Nights Without You; Come Along to Heaven; Tell My Heart; Little Girl; Help Me Write a Song.

VELKE, FRITZ (JOHN ARTHUR), II   ASCAP 1963
composer, author, teacher
b Washington, DC, Sept 10, 30. Educ: Cath Univ Am, BM & MM. Trombonist, USAF Band, DC, 53-57. Teacher instrumental music, Fairfax County Pub Schs, Va, 57- Founded Velke Publ Co, 71. Trombonist & asst cond, Nat Concert Band Am, DC, 76- Ostwald Award for band comp, Am Bandmasters Asn. *Songs:* What Does Music Mean to Me? (children's chorus). *Instrumental Works:* Concertino for Band; Quartal Piece (concert band); Fanfare and Rondo (concert band); Foray At Fairfax (concert band); Plaything (concert band); Caprice and Interlude (concert band); Adagietto for Strings (string orch); Fancy Fiddles (string orch); Concerto Grosso for Brass Sextet and Orch; Godwin Overture (concert band); String Quartet No 1; Tommie Jack Concert March (concert band).

VELMONT, JAMES
See Cross, Frank LeRoy

VELONA, ANTHONY   ASCAP 1957
composer, author
b Jersey City, NJ, Nov 16, 20. *Songs:* Lollipops and Roses; Sad Songs; Oh, Bambino; Two of Us; Lyrics: Music to Watch Girls By; Domani.

VELOSO, ROBERT FLORENDO (ROBERRE)   ASCAP 1975
composer, singer, arranger
b Manila, Philippines, Nov 12, 47. Educ: Silliman Univ, BBA, 69; voice culture studies with Lois Bello. Performer with bands, songwriter & recording, Manila, 64-70; songwriter, arr, producer & performer with bands, San Francisco, 70- *Songs:* I'm All Yours My Love; Thank You; Tell Yourself; Let Our Souls Touch; Tonight Is Party Night.

VELVETTE, HELENE
See Modlik, Helene Patricia

VENE, RUGGERO   ASCAP 1937
composer, conductor, educator
b Lerici, Italy, Aug 12, 1897; d Italy, Aug 18, 61. Came to US, 32, became citizen, 44. Educ: Cathedral of Spezia; Royal Cons (Arrigo Boito) of Parma; Ecole Normale de Musique, Paris, studied with Nadia Boulanger; Royal Cons, St Cecilia of Rome, studied with Ottorino Respighi. Radio cond, Rome. Chorus master, coach & cond, theatres in Italy, France & Belgium. Teacher, New Eng Cons & Malkin Cons, Boston. Asst prof orchestration & music reading, Columbia Univ. Mem fac, Washington Univ; prof of comp. Cond concert choir, Girls Glee Club, Ind Univ. *Instrumental Works:* Rossaccio (symph poem); String Quartet; Quintet for Piano, Strings.

VENTRE, FRANK L   ASCAP 1941
composer, conductor, arranger
b East Weymouth, Mass, Apr 3, 1895; d Huntington, WVa, Oct 12, 66. Educ: New Eng Cons. Youngest bandmaster in US service, WW I, 7th Regiment, US Marine Band. Cond & arr, radio, dance orchs & singers. Comp & cond, background music for TV. Arr, "Sonja Henie Ice Spectacular," NBC, TV; also for "Ice Follies." Music supvr, Roxy Theatre, New York; music dir, "Holiday on Ice," 63-66. Comp, cond & arr of indust shows. Arr for Paul Lavalle Band, New York World's Fair, 64-65. Chief Collabr: Paul Lavalle. *Songs & Instrumental Works:* The Angel God Sent From Heaven; Tropical Palms; That Soothing Melody; If I Should Lose You; Wings of Victory; We Thank You Lord; Our United States; Universities on Parade (comn by Miami Univ); Big Brass Band; Pitter Pat Parade.

VENTURIN, MARGARET ROSS   ASCAP 1968
composer, author
b Newark, NY. Educ: High sch grad plus univ courses. Worked as secy & or admin asst in hospitals, space agency, mental clinics, newspaper offices & as secy in foreign service to Deputy Mission Dir of Liberia. *Songs:* A Christmas Lullabye; Give Him Your Hand; Sa Wa Dee; Lyrics: We Can't Afford to Lose Ford; The Teddy Bear Polka.

VENTURINI, DANTE A   ASCAP 1963
composer
b Genoa, Italy, Mar 25, 22. Educ: Liceo Paganini, Genoa, Italy. With orchs of many steamship cos all over the world & nightclubs of Middle E & SAm. *Songs:* Music: Che Festa; Non Tornar; Pedrito; Gaiety; Esther.

VENUTI, JOE   ASCAP 1940
composer, violinist, conductor
b at sea of Ital parentage, Sept 1, 03; d Seattle, Wash, Aug 14, 78. Educ: Philadelphia pub schs; studied violin with Thaddeus Rich. Violinist in dance orchs, incl Paul Whiteman, 8 yrs. With Eddie Lang, formed Venuti-Lang Orch, 32, toured US & Europe; then organized own band. Made many records. *Songs & Instrumental Works:* Satan's Holiday; Ain't Doin' Bad Doin' Nothin'; Tea Time; Romantic Joe; Goin' Places; Cheese and Crackers; Beatin' the Dog; Stringing the Blues; Wildcat.

VERA, BILLY
See McCord, William Patrick

VERDUCCI, JOHN S   ASCAP 1963
composer
b San Francisco, Calif, Mar 11, 12; d San Francisco, July 12, 77. Educ: High sch. Bldg foreman, Fed Govt. *Songs:* It's Never Too Late for Love; It's Too Late to Tell Me You Love Me.

VERGES, JOE   ASCAP 1928
composer, author
b New Orleans, La, Oct 26, 1892; d New Orleans, Aug 12, 64. *Songs:* I'm Sorry I Made You Cry; When I First Met Mary; Our Bungalow of Dreams; Oh Look At That Baby; The Waltz of Love; Rosy Dreams.

VERKOUTEREN, JOHN ADRIAN   ASCAP 1973
composer, author, teacher
b Washington, DC, July 20, 50. Educ: St Albans Sch, 59-68; studied privately with Leo Sowerby, 64-68; Harvard Col, AB, 72. Choir boy, Washington Cathedral, DC, 59-65, mem men's choir, 65-68 & 72-74. Wrote musical plays for St Albans Sch, Washington, DC, 69 & 71 & other incidental music for plays, teacher music & algebra, 72- *Songs:* Musical Plays: Come, Good Shepherd; James the Dragon Slayer; Music: Missa Brevis; A Boy Was Born. *Instrumental Works:* Incidental Music for The Hobbit.

VERNE, ROBERT
See Vernoff, Robert Arnold

VERNOFF, ROBERT ARNOLD (ROBERT VERNE)   ASCAP 1969
composer, author, singer
b Miami Beach, Fla, July 14, 44. Educ: Fairfax High Sch; Dick Grove Sch Music, studied with Irving Gordon. Wrote first song in 59. Mem of group

Columbus, writing, producing, performing. Chief Collabrs: Jeffrey David Hooven, Stash Wagner, Steve Altman. *Songs:* No Date; Lyrics: Can I Do It 'Till I Need Glasses; Dracula; Georgia Lady; I Wish It Would Rain. *Albums:* Candle.

VERNOR, F DUDLEIGH   ASCAP 1946
composer, organist, teacher
b Detroit, Mich, Aug 21, 1892; d Detroit, Mich, Apr 22, 74. Educ: Juilliard; Berumen Studios, NY; Albion Col, hon MusD. Teacher of piano & theory; head of organ dept, Albion Col, 24-64. Organist & choir dir, First Methodist Church, Jackson, 22-34 & Methodist Church Detroit. Fac, Bay View Summer Col of Music. *Songs:* Sweetheart of Sigma Chi; The Girl I Love; See America First.

VER PLANCK, JOHN FENNO (BILLY)   ASCAP 1951
composer, arranger, conductor
b Norwalk, Conn, Apr 30, 30. Educ: Pub schs, Darien, Conn; high sch. Started playing trombone at age 12; wrote first arr for dance at age 16; played for dance concerts & music clubs until 47. Worked on Navy Band Nat Airs Proj, Navy Sch Music until 49. Played with many bands; studio playing. Chief Collabrs: Carmine Biase, Jim Pollack, Frank Grant, Carlo Minoti, Howard Liebling. *Songs:* Music: This Happy Feeling; Growing Out Gracefully; Red and Yellow Flowers; Thanks for the Misery; Just Sick Blues; Jumping At the Left Bank; Pot Luck Blues. *Instrumental Works:* Brasilano; Chicken Boogie; Zip.

VERSCHAREN, JOSEPH W   ASCAP 1960
composer, author, singer
b Pittsburgh, Pa, Aug 30, 40. Educ: Carrick High Sch, Pittsburgh. With vocal group Skyliners, 59-60; popular recall of group for revival shows & nightclubs incl appearances at Madison Square Garden, Los Angeles Forum, Acad of Music, New York, Celebrity Theatre, Phoenix & Convention Ctr, Miami, 69-75. Chief Collabrs: Joseph V Rock, Walter P Lester, Jr, James L Beaumont, Janet Vogel Rapp, John Taylor. *Songs:* Since I Don't Have You (gold record, 59); This I Swear; It Happened Today; Lonely Way; How Much.

VERST, RUTH   ASCAP 1960
composer, author, singer
b Philadelphia, Pa, July 27, 30. Educ: Philadelphia High Sch for Girls. Singer on radio, TV, records & with bands. *Songs:* I'll Bet You He'll Kiss Me.

VEST, JAMES M   ASCAP 1969
composer, author, singer
b Huntsville, Ala, Feb 15, 41. Educ: Valley High Sch, Louisville, Ky; took music lessons at age 11. Played steel guitar in nightclubs, 54; played with Pee Wee King & The Golden West Cowboys, 60, with David Huston & The Persuaders, 67; started with Billy Walker, 69; formed Nashville Cats, 69-70; worked in Printers Alley, 70-77, Western Room, Johnny Paycheck Club, 77-80. Guitarist in local clubs, writer & producer, 76- Chief Collabr: David Chamberland. *Songs:* I'm Not Easy I'm a Lady (ASCAP Award); Your Sweet Lies Just Turned Down My Sheets Again; Someone Loves Him; From Cotton to Satin; Hank You Tried to Tell Me (About the Mansions on the Hill); It Just Won't Feel Like Cheatin' With You; Land of Cotton; His Little Somethin' on the Side.

VESTOFF, FLORIA   ASCAP 1955
composer, author, dancer
b New York, NY, Apr 6, 1918; d Hollywood, Calif, Mar 18, 63. Educ: Children's Sch, New York. Dancer in nightclubs, hotels, Paramount & State Theatres, New York. Producer, choreographer & dancer in "Old Gold" TV commercials, 49-57 & other commercials. Wrote spec material for Joe E Lewis, Jackie Gleason; also for "Stop the Music", "Old Gold" annual conventions, Chicago & "Union Electric" shows, St Louis. *Songs:* Walkin' Around in Circles; Everyone Was There But Me; If You Change Your Mind; Just a Real Old-Fashioned Sunday; The Show Is On; Somebody Cares; Bugle Woogie.

VIAFORE, S VICTOR   ASCAP 1964
composer, author, musician
b New York, NY, July 4, 10; d Yonkers, NY, Dec 10, 70. Educ: Yonkers High Sch; Manhattan Sch Music, studied perc, xylophone & vibraphone. Taught perc & spec piano chords. Mem, Ben Bernie Orch & Lane Orch. Scout for Ted Mack Amateur Hour. Xylophone performer, radio & TV. Chief Collabr: Rosalie R Viafore (wife). *Songs & Instrumental Works:* I Never Had Love; You'll Be Sorry; Wouldn't You; It's Freedom Time; You're Not Being Fair; Tic Toc Goes the Clock; Your Guess Is Good As Mine; Pizza Polka Time; Every Day; Here Comes Ole Santa.

VICAR, ANTHONY ARNOLD   ASCAP 1963
composer
b Brooklyn, NY, Nov 12, 14. Associated with & involved in all aspects of Charlie Parker Records, Estate Records, Janon & Tad Publ & Record Cos. Chief Collabrs: Del Vicar, Aubrey Mayhew. *Songs:* Have Faith.

VICAR, DEL
See DelVicario, Silvio Patrick

VICARI, JOSEPHINE M (JOSIE CAREY)   ASCAP 1956
author, actress
b Pittsburgh, Pa, Aug 20, 30. Educ: Pittsburgh Playhouse, acting; Univ Pittsburgh, writing; Butler High Sch, Pa. Appeared & created award-winning TV children's prog incl: "The Children's Corner," WQED-TV, PGH, PBS & NBC, 54-72; "Josie's Storyland," KDKA-TV, PGH, "Wheee!," SCE-TV, "Mister Rogers Neighborhood," PBS. Chief Collabrs: Fred Rogers, Johnny Costa, Joe Negri. *Songs:* Lyrics: The Tomorrow Song (closing theme); Good Night God; It's Morning; I'm Looking for a Friend; I Like You As You Are.

VICARS, HAROLD   ASCAP 1930
composer, conductor, arranger
b London, Eng; d Providence, RI, Jan 11, 22. Educ: Kings Col, London; studied music in Ger. Cond, Daly's Theatre, London, 10 yrs; toured provinces with Moody Manners Opera Co. Brought to US by Charles Frohman to cond musicals. *Songs & Instrumental Works:* Song of Songs; Belgium Valse; Meditation; 'Tis Bed Time, Sleepy Head; Looking Seaward; Wonderful One Girl; God Bring You Safely to Our Arms Again. *Scores:* Operas: 49th Star; Zorema.

VICK, DANNY
See Walker, Jeanine Ogletree

VICKERS, JAMES EDWARD   ASCAP 1971
composer, author, singer
b Martin, Tenn, Oct 6, 42. Educ: Jahn Sch, Lane Tech & Lakeview, Chicago. Songwriter, 57-; recording artist, Mo, Tenn, Ill & Mich. *Songs:* I'll Be Glad to Help You Out; People and Their Ways; Too Late; Lonesome Days; Oh If Only; Look At the Sky.

VICKERS, WENDY
See Jones, Wendy Vickers

VIDACOVICH, I J (PINKY)   ASCAP 1954
composer, author, conductor
b New Orleans, La, Sept 14, 04; d New Orleans, July 5, 66. Educ: Pub schs. Music dir, WWL, New Orleans, 19 yrs; musician in dance orchs, incl Horace Heidt. Radio & TV dir, Swigart Co. Chief Collabrs: Ray McKinley, Al Stillman, Eugene West. *Songs:* Arizay; Six Buzzard Feathers and a Mocking Bird's Tail; Gotta Go to de Fais Do Do; I'm on My Way; Pickin' Cotton; Roman Nocturne.

VIDAS, PATRICK JOSEPH   ASCAP 1975
composer, author, trumpeter
b Centerville, Iowa, Dec 19, 53. Educ: Centerville High Sch, Iowa; studied trumpet with John Holeman, Mark Kelly & Robert Weist. Voted First High Sch Jazz Musician, Band Dirs Asn Iowa, 71; Iowa Arts & Perf Scholarship Winner, 71. Toured mid-west with Don Ellis, 72; toured US & Japan as lead trumpet, vocalist & dancer for Sheffields Show Band, 72-73; toured mid-west with Des Moines Big Band, 73; free-lanced shows for Ann Margret, Don Ho, Elvis Presley & others, also miscellaneous comp & commercial arr, Las Vegas, 73-74; toured with D D Smith, 74-75; soloist & clinician with var mid-west schs, 75; toured with show band Three Stories Tall as lead trumpet, vocalist & dancer, 75-76; comp & recorded albums for Capitol Records with own group Flight, 75-76, comp & recorded album for Motown Record Corp with reformed group Flight, 79; developed new instrument, the Polytrumpet, 76-77, issued patent for invention, 79, preparations underway for marketing, 80; invented the Flaming Trumpet, 78-79, patent pending. *Songs & Instrumental Works:* Inca Innuendo; Music: Face to Face; Rhapsody to You; Latin Dippy Doo; Sands of Time. *Albums:* Excursion Beyond.

VIG, TOMMY   ASCAP 1970
composer
b Budapest, Hungary, July 14, 38. Educ: Zenei Gimnazium, Budapest; Acad Music, Budapest; Bela Bartok Cons, Budapest; Juilliard Sch Music. Wrote first songs at age 4; jazz drum at age 7, toured Europe; arr at Hungarian State Radio at age 16. Prof musician & comp arr, US, 57- Now film comp in Hollywood. Chief Collabrs: Phill Thomas Cappellini, Mia Vig (wife). *Songs:* Just for You; Jenny's Song; I Miss You Today; Oriental Bossa Nova. *Instrumental Works:* Sounds for Twelve French Horns; Bagatelle for String Quartet and Xylophone; Bagatelle for Woodwind Quintet and Xylophone; Sounds for Nine Instruments; Budapest 1956 (for marching band); Four Pieces for Neophonic Orchestra; Intro, Largo, Presto and Besame Mucho for Vibraharp and Neophonic Orchestra; Short Story.

VILLA, MANUEL   ASCAP 1958
composer, author, singer
b New Orleans, La, July 22, 17. Educ: Studied with Joseph A Craig, New Orleans; Albert Wicker High Sch, New Orleans; Greenwich House Music Sch, New York. Sang with bands in New Orleans, La, in 30's. Service in WW II; recalled to USA, Korean War, 51. Songwriter, 57- Chief Collabrs: Joe Seneca, David Parker. *Songs:* I'll Change That Too (or I'll Change My Style); Genie; Goodbye Darling; Let Me In; A Stranger in Your Heart.

VILLAREAL, EDMUND   ASCAP 1970
composer, author, singer
b San Antonio, Tex, Oct 5, 47. Educ: Robert E Lee High Sch; San Antonio Col, 65. Singer, nightclubs & TV; recording artist, Bell Records & Big Tree Records. Chief Collabrs: Wanda Watkins, David Callens, Lucy Garber. *Songs:* Music: Feel the Heat; Need a Little Time; Country Wine; Slow Train to Paradise; Down Home Lovin' Woman.

VILLINES, VIRGINIA   ASCAP 1961
author
b Giddings, Tex, Nov 29, 12. Educ: Studied comp with Mary Carr Moore & Calista Rogers, voice with Louis Graveure. Has done singing progs of own comp throughout Calif; church soloist. *Songs:* Bird in the Bamboo; Thoughts; These Are My Hills; Strawberry Wind; I Got a Glory (spiritual); The Trinket; It Must Have Been; The Rain; Serenade to a Child; Sea Call; Chopin at Candlelighting; You're for Whom I Sing; Vagabonds Heart.

VILLONE, LARRY PAUL   ASCAP 1977
composer, author, singer
b Omaha, Nebr, Nov 17, 48. Educ: Creighton Prep High Sch, grad, 67; Univ Nebr at Omaha, BA(psychology), 71. Songwriter & performer. Musician in bands, 63- Built 8 track recording studio, 72. Made album, A Feeling You Can't Hide,

VIMMERSTEDT, SARAH (SADIE) GERMAINE   ASCAP 1963
b Youngstown, Ohio, May 29, 04. Educ: St Ann's Elem; Ursuline Acad, 2 yrs. Sales rep, Elizabeth Arden Cosmetics; now retired. Chief Collabr: Johnnie Mercer. *Songs:* Lyric: I Wanna Be Around.

VINARD, F N
See Vincent, Nathaniel Hawthorne

VINCENT, BOB   ASCAP 1948
composer, author, singer
b Detroit, Mich, Mar 7, 18. Educ: Western High Sch; Wayne Univ; studied saxophone with Larry Teal; Detroit Cons Music, studied vocal coaching. Played with orch in high sch, 36; played & sang at Wayne Univ; sang on the "Happy Hour Club," radio show at WMBD-Radio, 36-38; played & sang with Shorty Sherock's 18 piece jazz-pop orch on East Coast, 42-43; joined Al Trace and the Silly Symphonists, New York, 44, sang hit record, 47; entertainment dir, Harrahs Club, Reno, Nev, 62-65. Author bk, "Show-Business Is Two Words," 79. Musician & teacher. Chief Collabrs: Al Trace, Lee Pines. *Songs:* Cat's Meow; Music: I'm Through Callin' Everybody Darlin'.

VINCENT, JOHN   ASCAP 1954
composer, conductor, educator
b Birmingham, Ala, May 17, 02; d Santa Monica, Calif, Jan 21, 77. Educ: New Eng Cons; George Peabody Col, BA, MA; Harvard Univ Grad Sch, John Payne Fel; Ecole Normal de Musique, Paris; Cornell Univ, PhD. Guggenheim fel. Supvr, instr music, cond, El Paso, Tex, 27-30. On staff, George Peabody Col, 30-33; also cond, Knoxville Symph. Head music dept, Western Ky State Col, 37-45; prof comp, Univ Calif. Music dir, Los Angeles Chamber Symph, 50-55. Dir, Huntington Hartford Found. Exec dir, Calif Inst of Arts, Los Angeles. Guest cond, symph orchs in US & SAm. Author: "Diatonic Modes in Modern Music"; "Music for Sight Reading"; "More Music for Sight Reading." *Instrumental Works:* Symphony in D (Louisville Symph comn); Symphony No 2; Consort for Piano, Strings; Symphonic Poem After Descartes (Eugene Ormandy comn); Nude Descending the Staircase; String Quartet in G; La Jolla Concerto (La Jolla Fest comn); Suite for Orchestra; Overture to "Lord Arling"; Serenade for String Orchestra; Three Jacks (ballet suite, Alfred Wallenstein comn); Piano Quintet; 3 Grecian Songs; Benjamin Franklin Suite; 2 string quartets.

VINCENT, LARRY   ASCAP 1947
composer, pianist, record executive
b San Jose, Calif, Jan 13, 01; d Covington, Ky, Jan 5, 77. Educ: Col. Pianist with L Wolfe Gilbert in vaudeville; pianist & singer in nightclubs & radio. Formed Pearl Record Co, 46. Chief Collabrs: Harry Pease, Moe Jaffe, Charles O'Flynn, Henry Tobias. *Songs:* Oh How I Love That Gal of Mine; When the Sun Says Good Night to the Mountains; If I Had My Life to Live Over; I Used to Work in Chicago; Tender Bartender; I've Come Back to Say I'm Sorry; How's My Baby Tonight?; Trespasser; Is It Too Late to Say I'm Sorry?; Freckle Song; Hay Hay, Farmer Gray (Took Another Load Away).

VINCENT, NATHANIEL HAWTHORNE (JAAN KENBROVIN, F N VINARD)   ASCAP 1922
composer, author, singer
b Kansas City, Mo, Nov 6, 1889; d Burbank, Calif, June 6, 79. Educ: Betts Mil Acad, Stamford, Conn. Was sheet music demonstrator, NY dept stores. Professional mgr, music publ cos. Mem vaudeville teams, Tracey & Vincent and Franklyn & Vincent. Appeared in act, "A Trip to Hitland." Mem of radio recording team, The Happy Chappies, with Fred Howard. Wrote songs for Healy's "Ice Follies", "Palais Royal Revue" & "Cochran Revue," London; also for Bway revues, incl "Show of Wonders", "Passing Shows" & "Ziegfeld's Midnight Frolics." Chief Collabrs: Fred Howard, Herman Paley, Maceo

Pinkard, James Kendis, James Brockman, Russ Morgan, William Tracey, Blanche Franklyn. *Songs:* I'm Forever Blowing Bubbles; When the Bloom Is on the Sage; La Veeda; When Old Bill Bailey Plays the Ukulele; The Strawberry Roan; I Know What It Means to Be Lonesome; Give a Little Credit to Your Dad; Mellow Mountain Moon; Little Girl Dressed in Blue; Pucker Up and Whistle; That Railroad Rag; Down South Everybody's Happy; Pretty Little Cinderella; At the End of the Lane; Liza; My Old Man; I Know Why I Cry; Sitting on the Bank by the River; Nevada Nevada Nevada; It's Great to Love Someone Who Loves You Too; My Pretty Quadroon; Me and My Burro; Old Black Mountain Trail; My Dear Old Arizona Home; It's Time to Say Aloha.

VINCENT, WARREN EDWARD   ASCAP 1959
composer, arranger, conductor
b Elizabeth, NJ, Dec 23, 25. Educ: Princeton Univ (scholarship); Curtis Inst (scholarship); studied comp with Wallingford Riegger (Am Theater Wing 5 yr grant). Arr for records, TV & films, incl Glen Gray, Tommy & Jimmy Dorsey, Ralph Flanagan, Charlie Spivak, Nat King Cole, Connee Boswell, Andre Kostelanetz, "The Ed Sullivan Show", "The Dick Cavett Show" & "The Tonight Show." Producer for Barbra Streisand, Les Elgart & others. Musical dir, Pickwick Sales Corp, 57-60. Vpres & musical dir radio & TV commercials, Audio Designs, Inc, 60-62. Mem A&R staff, Columbia Records, New York, 62-73. Mem A&R staff, CBS Records, Los Angeles, 73- Chief Collabr: Ralph Flanagan. *Songs:* Music: Gin Fizz; Christmas Is for the Family. *Instrumental Works:* String Quartet Moderne; Passacaglia and Fugue. *Scores:* Film/TV: The Magic Moment (orchestration).

VIRTUOSO, FRANK   ASCAP 1957
composer, author, conductor
b Philadelphia, Pa, Jan 29, 23. Educ: Temple Univ. USN, WW II. Led dance band, Bainbridge, Md. Leader group, The Virtues; appeared on TV, US & Canada. *Songs & Instrumental Works:* Cotton Candy; Guitar Boogie Shuffle; Guitar Boogie Shuffle Twist; Guitar in Orbit; Shufflin' Along; Pony Walk.

VITALE, WILLIAM NICHOLAS   ASCAP 1975
composer, author, actor
b Denver, Colo. Educ: Holy Family High Sch, Denver; Cath Univ Am, Washington, DC, BA(drama); Univ Denver, MA(theatre); fel, Univ Calif, Santa Barbara; postgrad study, New Sch, New York. Perf as actor, 40 states, extensively Off-Bway & Eur tour. Artistic dir, Manhattan Theatre Group, The Fantasy Factory. Chief Collabrs: Steve Ross, Ed Kuczewski. *Scores:* Musicals: A Mass Murder in the Balcony of the Old Ritz-Rialto (co-winner with Ed Kuczewski, 1st Prise, NEA New Musical Theatre Competition); Ape Over Broadway; The Gates of Paradise; Hot Voodoo Massage; Indulgences.

VODERY, WILL   ASCAP 1951
composer, arranger
b Philadelphia, Pa, Oct 8, 1885; d New York, NY, Nov 18, 51. *Songs:* Hills of Old New Hampshire; The Unknown Soldier Lives Again; Dearest Memories; Darktown Poker Club.

VOGEL, JANET FRANCES   ASCAP 1960
b Pittsburgh, Pa, June 10, 41. Educ: High sch; finishing sch. Mem singing group, The Skyliners; has toured throughout US & Europe. *Songs:* It Happened Today; Since I Don't Have You; This I Swear.

VOLKART, BETTYE SUE (BETTYE PIERCE,   ASCAP 1969
BETTYE ZOLLER)
composer, singer, teacher
b Kansas City, Mo, Jan 30, 45. Shawnee Mission High Sch; voice study with Verna Brackinreed, 57-65, Stanley Deacon, 57-66 & Lotte Lehman, 64; Univ Minn, 64; Univ Mo, BMus, MMus, 65. Recording artist for RCA; staff writer, Screen Gems EMI Publ. Songwriter; singer, comp/producer, radio & TV jingles; prof singer, nightclubs & TV. Teacher, Dallas County Cols. Winner Am Song Fest; ASCAP Young Comp Awards, 78 & 79; CLIO & ADDY Awards. *Songs:* Girl from Prairie Flats; Another Rainy Saturday; Rollin' Stone and Ramblin' Rose; You Make My World Shine; Rainbow in Your Eyes; Lonely Girl in a Singles Bar; Believe; Flyin' Without You; Sunshine Express; How the Years Have Changed Us All; Make Friends, Make Love, Raise Kids and Raise Some Hell; Gettin' Back to Basics; Feel the Fire; Lyrics: Sweet Song; I'll Give You One More Chance; Body Talk. *Scores:* Film/TV: Los Amigos de las Americas; Kroehler Furniture; Trailways; Sears; US Air Force.

VOLKART, HAZEL O   ASCAP 1966
composer, author, instructor
b Gage, Okla, May 20, 11. Educ: Okla Col for Women, scholarship, studied with John Thompson; studied with Maurice Duminal, Europe; Kans State Univ, studied with Sir Carl Busch, Regina Hall & Wiktor Labunski; Univ Mo, Kansas City, piano degree. Lectr on educ teaching methods for piano. Concert pianist, accompanist & teacher. Mem, Mu Phi Epsilon. Pres, Kansas City Music Teachers Asn. *Songs:* Music: Grandfather Clock; Little Lullabye; Bob-o-Link; Choctaw Indian Dance; Hunters Horn; The Pirate King. *Instrumental Works:* Coral Sea; Reverie; Tarantelle; Victory Entre March.

VOLKMANN, RUDY H   ASCAP 1966
composer
b Kosten, Ger, Oct 10, 42. Educ: Olympic Col, Bremerton, Wash, 59-62; Cent Wash State Col, BA, 64; DePauw Univ, MM(comp), 69, studied comp with Donald White & tuba with Robert Grocock. Construction worker, pop musician & col prof. *Songs:* When Darkness Fills Your Heart. *Instrumental Works:* Fugue in G Minor; Quintet for Brass; Pepper; Trio for Organ.

VOLPATO, JACK ALBERT (JACK VAL)   ASCAP 1946
composer, author, publisher
b Bronx, NY. Educ: High sch; pvt piano study. Mem prof staff, Music Publ Co, 21; became publ in 43. Chief Collabrs: Fred Patrick, Claude Reese, Murray Semos. *Songs & Instrumental Works:* I Was Not so Particular; I'm All Dressed Up With a Broken Heart; I Can't Go on Like This; Just Say I Love Her; I Didn't Come to Say Hello I Came to Say Good-Bye; Home Is Where the Heart Is; Gimme, Gimme, the Miser's Serenade; Buck Dance; Blue Silhouette; Bella Faccia; Dance of the Puppets; Poetry of Love; Red Lips; But Where Is Love; Nobody Cares; Your Chickens Are Coming Home to Roost; Anything Can Happen When You're Lonesome; Lady of Havana; Lazy, Lazy Summer; Misery Highway; New York City Blues.

VOLPE, ALFRED MICHAEL   ASCAP 1967
composer, author, singer
b New York, NY, June 23, 36. Educ: Iona Col, BA; Fordham Univ, MS. Entertainer singer; sch teacher; geriatric dir, Memory Lane Cruises, WOR-TV. Staff singer, Hotel Brickman, South Fallsburg, NY. Chief Collabrs: Joe Bollon, Bob Calilli, Tony Sansone, John Sbarra, Phil Medley. *Songs:* Iona College Fight Song; Lyrics: Surrender.

VOLPE, VIRGILIO A   ASCAP 1964
composer, author, singer
b Norristown, Pa, Aug 11, 35. Educ: Gettysburg Col; Pa State Univ; Middlebury Col Language Sch, BA. Left govt post, SEuropean Task Force for music career. Singer with choral groups, in nightclubs & musical comedies; has appeared on TV, Ger, Italy & US. Chief Collabr: Madeline Mascia. *Songs:* Ciao for Now; Dieci Giorni D'Estate; Se Mi Ami, Chiama; Cos'E La Vita; In Riva Al Mar Con Marion.

VON DER GOLTZ, ERIC   ASCAP 1926
author, publisher
b New York, NY, June 18, 1895; d Westport, Conn, May 12, 77. Educ: Townsend Harris Hall; City Col New York; studied violin with William Doenges & Ernest Bauer. WW I, 308th Inf, 77th Div. Music publ exec. *Songs:* My Heart Is a Silent Violin; Querida; Homecoming; The Song of the Drum; I Sing; Once I Heard a Song; Lyrics: The News Came; The Songs Are Over; Things; My Own Country; The Hawk; Listen, Do You Hear?; My Dream of Vienna.

VON HALLBERG, GENE   ASCAP 1958
composer, arranger, teacher
b Brockton, Mass, July 27, 06; d. Educ: Studied music with Paul Yartin. Comp & arr for radio & TV incl "Arthur Godfrey Show"; "Hit Parade"; "Kraft Theatre" & "Lux Theatre." Arr for music publ, singers, records, indust shows & films. WW II, comp & arr for US Merchant Marine Acad Band & OWI. Co-founder, former vpres, Comp & Lyricists Guild of Am; co-founder, Am Accordionists Asn. Adjudicator at music competitions. Teacher comp & arr, Hollywood. *Instrumental Works:* Behind the Veil.

VON TILZER, ALBERT   ASCAP 1914
composer, publisher
b Indianapolis, Ind, Mar 29, 1878; d Los Angeles, Calif, Oct 1, 56. Educ: High sch. Music dir, vaudeville co. Shoe buyer, Brooklyn dept store. Staff mem, brother Harry's music publ co, Chicago; founded own publ firm with bro, Jack, 03. Wrote songs for films. Charter mem, ASCAP. Chief Collabrs: Jack Norworth, Junie McCree, Lew Brown, Neville Fleeson, Cecil Mack. *Songs:* Teasing; Honey Boy; Smarty; Take Me Out to the Ball Game; Put Your Arms Around Me, Honey; I'm the Lonesomest Gal in Town; Oh, How She Could Yacki Hacki Wicki Wacki Woo; Au Revoir, But Not Goodbye; Take Me Up With You, Dearie; Nora Malone; Why Doesn't Santa Claus Go Next Door?; Give Me the Moonlight, Give Me the Girl; How Do You Do, Miss Josephine?; I May Be Gone for a Long, Long Time; Waters of Venice; Wait Till You Get Them Up in the Air, Boys; Oh By Jingo; My Little Girl; Chile Bean; I Used to Love You But It's All Over Now; I'll Be With You in Apple Blossom Time; Dapper Dan; My Cutie's Due At Two to Two Today; Roll Along, Prairie Moon; I'm Praying to St Christopher; Say It With Flowers.

VON TILZER, HARRY   ASCAP 1914
composer, publisher, producer
b Detroit, Mich, July 8, 1872; d New York, NY, Jan 10, 46. Bro of Albert Von Tilzer. Toured in circus, stock co & burlesque. Moved to New York; wrote spec material for vaudeville singers. Became publ, 02. Wrote & produced musicals. Charter mem, ASCAP. Chief Collabrs: Andrew Sterling, Arthur Lamb, Will Dillon, William Jerome. *Songs:* My Old New Hampshire Home; I'd Leave My Happy Home for You; The Spider and the Fly; A Bird in a Gilded Cage; Down Where the Cotton Blossoms Grow; Down on the Farm; The Mansion of Aching

Hearts; On a Sunday Afternoon; In the Sweet Bye and Bye; Down Where the Wurzberger Flows; Under the Anheuser Bush; All Aboard for Dreamland; Wait Till the Sun Shines, Nellie; What You Gonna Do When the Rent Comes 'Round?; Take Me Back to New York Town; All Aboard for Blanket Bay; I Want a Girl Just Like the Girl That Married Dear Old Dad; They Always Pick on Me; Last Night Was the End of the World; Goodbye, Boys; On the Old Fall River Line; You'll Always Be the Same Sweet Girl; I Remember You; That Old Irish Mother of Mine; When My Baby Smiles At Me; Old King Tut; Just Around the Corner.

VON WAYDITCH, GABRIEL PAUL   ASCAP 1974
composer, author

b Budapest, Hungary, Dec 28, 1888; d New York, NY, July 28, 69. Educ: Royal Acad of Music, Budapest, grad; student of Hans Koessler & Emil Sauer. Cond, Royal Orpheum Theatre, teenager. To US, 1911. As pianist of group, Morningside Trio, gave recitals radio sta WNYC. Chief Collabr: Ivan W von Wayditch (son). *Scores:* Operas: The Caliph's Magician; Jesus Before Herod; Mary Magdalene; Horus; The Catacombs; Sahara; Anthony of Padua; Buddha; The Heretics; Balaton Dreams; Nereida; The Venus Dwellers; Maria Testver; Opium Dreams.

VON WÜRTZLER, ARISTID   ASCAP 1963
composer, harpist, educator

b Budapest, Hungary, Sept 20, 30. Educ: Franz Liszt Acad Music, MM; London Col, DM. Mem, Budapest Philh, until 56. Came to US, 56. Solo harpist, Detroit Symph Orch; harpist, New York Philh Orch. Chmn harp dept, Hartt Col Music, Univ Hartford & State Univ NY; mem fac, Hofstra Univ & New Col, Fla; prof, NY Univ, presently. Founder, dir & soloist, New York Harp Ens. Concertized, US, Can, SAm, SAfrica, Near, Middle & Far East. Recordings with Columbia, Vox, Golden Crest & Musical Heritage Soc. Award of Merit, Nat Fedn Music Clubs; mem int jury, US Harp Competition, Geneva, Israel & Varallo. Performed with New York Harp Ens at spec invitation from Pres Carter at White House Reception for King & Queen of Belg, 80. *Instrumental Works:* Modern Sketches (solo harp & harp ens); Chordophonic (harp ens); XVII Century Hungarian Dances (solo harp); 2 Vol Bartok Selection for Harp; Kodaly Music for Harp Solo; Children Suite for Solo Harp; Space Odyssey for Harp Ensemble; Meditation for Solo Harp; Handel F Major Concerto for Harp and Orchestra (harp solo); Vivaldi D Major Concerto for Orchestra (harp solo); Christian Bach Concerto for Solo Harp and Orchestra (God Save the King); Variations on Theme of Corelli (harp solo); Romantique Etude for Solo Harp; Capriccio for Solo Harp; Canto Amoroso for Solo Harp; more than one hundred arrangements from classical to modern for harp quartet.

VROMAN, JOHN   ASCAP 1962
composer, author, conductor

b Amsterdam, Holland, May 10, 18. Educ: Cons, Amsterdam. Chief Collabr: Sunny Skylar. *Songs:* While We're Dancing; Mia Bella Roma.

W

WADDELL, JAMES LEWIS   ASCAP 1974
composer, author, singer

b Somerville, Tenn, Nov 19, 46. Actor, guitarist, screenwriter & playwright. *Songs:* Nightmares; Soulful Hambone; Tired Fingers.

WADE (JACKSON), MAYBELLE   ASCAP 1960
composer, author

b Bristow, Okla, Mar 5, 14. First started song comp, early 50's. Founded the Richochet Publ Co, 73. Three songs inducted into Songwriters Hall of Fame Museum, 79. *Songs:* Heeby Jeebies; Living in a Dream; Love Love of My Life; Quick Sand; This Is It!; Drip Dry; Loud Perfume; Thomasine; Spreadin Natta What's the Matter?; Sweet and Soothing.

WAGANFEALD, EDWARD JAMES, III (EDDIE FIELDS) ASCAP 1972
composer, author, instrumentalist

b Toledo, Ohio, Oct 16, 34. Educ: Waite High Sch; Ohio Univ; Toledo Univ; Elkins Inst; music studies & radio broadcasting. Instrumentalist night clubs; recording artist with Johnny & The Hurricanes, 60-64. *Songs:* Wine, Women and a Song Turned Me On; Be Completely Mine. *Instrumental Works:* Greens and Beans; Waltz of the Clowns; Pam.

WAGENAAR, BERNARD   ASCAP 1942
composer, violinist, educator

b Arnheim, Neth, July 18, 1894; d. Educ: Studied music with Gerard Veerman, Madame Veerman-Bekker & Johan Wagenaar (father). Teacher & cond, Holland, 14-20. Moved to US, 20, citizen, 27. Violinist, New York Philh, 21-23. Fac mem, Juilliard Sch Music, since 25; also taught privately; cond own works. Chmn, Comn for Neth Music in US, 50. Mem: Int Soc Contemporary Music (bd mem, dir, Am Section); Neth Soc for Contemporary Music; Soc for Neth History Music; MacDowell Asn. *Instrumental Works:* Concert Overture (comn by Louisville Symph); Violin Concerto; Sonata for Violin, Piano (Soc Publ Am Music Award); Concerto for Eight Instruments (comn by League of Comp);

Two Divertimentos for Orchestra (No 1, Eastman Sch Publ Award); Four String Quartets; Triple Concerto (flute, harp, cello, orch); Four Symphonies; Sonatina for Cello, Piano; Piano Sonata. *Scores:* Chamber opera: Pieces of 8 (Alice Ditson Award).

WAGGANER, STANLEY ROBERT   ASCAP 1975
musician

b St Louis, Mo, Nov 10, 56. Bluegrass, 10 yrs; Ozark Opry, 5 yrs, also with Louisiana Hayride & Sassafras. *Songs:* Music: Sleepy Strings; Kentucky Bluegrass Song; Cherokee Pass; Wagganer Wheels.

WAGGONER, LOREN RICHARD   ASCAP 1971
composer, author

b Eldorado, Kans, July 26, 23. Educ: High sch grad, 42; voice & trumpet studies; self taught on organ & piano. Chief Collabr: Richard Cervino. *Songs:* Lyrics: Tell Her So.

WAGNER, DOUGLAS EDWARD   ASCAP 1973
composer, author

b Chicago, Ill, Aug 14, 52. Educ: Mendel High Sch; Butler Univ, BMusEd, 74, MM, 77. Educator; organist; church musician; adjudicator; choral clinician. *Songs:* A Celebration; A Wonderful Noise; Rise Up and Sing; The Legend of the Christmas Rose; Music: Lenten Meditation. *Instrumental Works:* Fanfare and Processional; Impressions on a French Carol.

WAGNER, JOSEPH FREDERICK   ASCAP 1946
composer, author, conductor

b Springfield, Mass, Jan 9, 00; d Los Angeles, Calif, Oct 12, 74. Educ: New Eng Cons, Endicott Prize; Boston Univ, BM; studied with Nadia Boulanger, Alfredo Casella, Frederick Converse, Pierre Monteux & Felix Weingartner; Ithaca Col, hon MusD. WW I service. Supvr, instrumental music, 23, asst dir music, Boston pub schs. Founder & cond, Boston Civic Symph, 25-44. Mem fac, Boston Univ, Col of Music, Rutgers Univ, Univ Okla, Hunter Col & Brooklyn Col; prof & comp-in-residence, Pepperdine Col, 61-73. Guest cond, Orquesta Filharmonica de Habana, 49. Resident music dir, Duluth Symph, 47-50, Orquesta Sinfonica Nacional de Costa Rica, 50-54. Guest cond, symph orchs in Can, Sweden, Finland, Cuba, Chile & Panama. Chmn comp dept, Los Angeles Cons, 61. Author: "Orchestration, A Practical Handbook"; "Workbook for Orchestration"; "Band Scoring, A Comprehensive Manual." Mem, MacDowell Colony & Am Symph Orch League. *Instrumental Works:* 2 sinfoniettas; 3 symphonies; Piano Concerto in G; Rhapsody for Clarinet, Piano, String Orchestra; Northland Evocation; Hudson River Legend (ballet); 2 sonatas for violin, piano; A Fugal Triptych for Piano, Percussion, String Orchestra; Dance Divertissement; Eulogy; American Jubilee (overture); Concerto Grosso (band); Introduction and Rondo for Trumpet, Orchestra. *Songs & Instrumental Works:* Choral: Ballad of Brotherhood; David Jazz; Psalm XXIX; Gloria in Excelsis (Christmas cantata); Missa Sacra.

WAGNER, LARRY   ASCAP 1943
composer, arranger

b Ashland, Ore, Sept 15, 07. Educ: Univ Ore; studied Schillinger System. Arr, Glen Gray Orch, 38-42. USMC, World War II. Co-author of musicals used in high schs throughout US. Chief Collabrs: Jimmy Eaton, Elsie Simmons, Frank Shuman, Frankie Carle. *Songs & Instrumental Works:* No Name Jive; Over the Rhythm of Raindrops; A Lover's Lullaby; Hearts Without Flowers; Penguin At the Waldorf; Turn Back the Hands of Time; Whistler's Mother-in-Law; Flamenco Love; Billy and I; One to Remember; You'll Never Be Lonely; Speak Well of Me; The Sound of America (chorale).

WAGNER, ROGER   ASCAP 1958
composer, conductor, arranger

b LePuy, France, (of Am parents) Jan 16, 14. Moved to US, 21. Educ: Col Montmorency; hon MusD, Univ Montreal. Organist & choral dir, Church of St Ambrose, Los Angeles, at age 12; music dir, St Joseph's Church. In 47, founded Los Angeles Concert Chorale which became Roger Wagner Chorale; appearances in concert, radio, TV & films; Coronation festivities prog, London, 53. Since 55, group has toured US, Can, SAm & Cent Am. Guest cond, choral groups throughout world; dir choral music, Univ Calif; head music dept, Marymount Col; recording artist; educr & organist.

WAGNER, WILLIAM FELKNER   ASCAP 1974
composer

b Warsaw, Ind, Feb 12, 20. Educ: Purdue Univ, 38-41; Univ Calif, Los Angeles, 57. Professional trumpet player, 34-56. Taught at Univ Calif, Los Angeles, 60-63. Personal mgr numerous musical artists. Dir artist relations, Capitol Records, 64-67. Bus rep motion picture & TV film dept, Nat Div, Am Fedn Musicians, Hollywood, 79- Chief Collabr: Page Cavanaugh. *Songs:* Music: Positive; Willoughby-Schmilloughby; Out Back; Jolly; Small Bore.

WAHLE, KENNETH EDWARD   ASCAP 1978
composer, author, singer

b Philadelphia, Pa, Sept 9, 49. Studied under Ralph Neal & Foster & Rice. Night club entertainer, singer & writer; worked with Foster & Rice & John Wesley Ryals; actor. Chief Collabr: Foster & Rice. *Songs:* The Song We Made Love To; Music: Smokey Rooms.

WAINWRIGHT, LOUDON SNOWDEN, III ASCAP 1970
singer, songwriter, actor
b Durham, NC, Sept 5, 46. Educ: St Andrews High Sch; Carnegie Mellon Inst. Singer/songwriter, clubs, concerts & TV; recording artist, 8 albums, Atlantic Records, Columbia Records, Arista Records & Rounder Records. *Songs:* Dead Skunk; The Swimming Song; Wine With Dinner; Down Drinking At the Bar; Final Exam.

WAINWRIGHT, MARY LEE SELLERS ASCAP 1963
composer, author, pianist
b Ruby, SC, Apr 24, 13. Educ: Ruby High Sch; Stetson Univ; Am Christian Col. Am patriot comp. Teacher for Broward County, Fla & Nat Democratic Exec Comt, 58- Author of bk, "The Master Key"; has sung & played ukulele in presenting lect concerts from bk. Mem for 26 yrs & chmn legislative dept, Fla Fedn of Music Clubs; past pres, Hollywood Chapter of Nat Fedn of Music Clubs. Pres, Hollywood Musicale, also Royal Poinciana District. Rec'd annual nat & state awards of merit, blue & gold ribbons for creative works, 23 yrs. Mem, Song Writer Hall of Fame & Nat Police Hall of Fame; mem, Bd of Policy & has rec'd Medal of Honor, Am Security Council. *Songs:* Wake Up America (Oscar Award, 60); Happiness; Down on Papa's Farm; Let the Bells of Freedom Ring; Thank You God; Democracy Is a Gift for You.

WAITS, THOMAS ALAN ASCAP 1973
composer, author, singer
b Whittier, Calif, Dec 7, 49. Songwriter & singer, nightclubs & concerts. With Elektra/Asylum Records, TV & movie appearances & movie scores. *Songs:* Ol' 55; Shiver Me Timbers; San Diego Serenade.

WAKELY, JIMMY ASCAP 1956
composer, author, singer
b Mineola, Ark, Feb 16, 14. Educ: Pub schs. Began career as singer, WKY, Oklahoma City; led own trio on "Gene Autry Show," CBS radio, 41-42; actor & singer in films; had own show, CBS radio, 52-57; also appeared on TV; recording artist. *Songs:* Too Late; You Can't Break the Chains of Love; I'll Never Let You Go Little Darling.

WALCOTT, COLLIN ASCAP 1970
composer
b New York, NY, Apr 24, 45. Educ: Studied square drum with Walter Rosenberger, 58-59; Ind Univ, Bloomington, BM(perc), 66, studied with George Gaber; studied sitar with Ravi Shankar, 67-69; tabla with Alla Rakha, 67- Road mgr, Ravi Shankar, 67-69, also asst in scoring movies "Charly" & "Raga"; performed & recorded with Tim Hardin, 69-70, The Paul Winter Consort, 70-72 & Oregon, 72- Recorded 4 records, ECM Records, 76- *Instrumental Works:* Cloud Dance; Margueritte; Longing, So Long; Grazing Dreams; The Swarm.

WALD, MALVIN D ASCAP 1960
author
b New York, NY, Aug 8, 17. Educ: Brooklyn Col, BA; NY Univ; Columbia Univ; Univ Southern Calif; Woodland Univ, JD. Writer-producer of films & TV. Chief Collabrs: David Raksin, Henry F Greenberg. *Songs:* Lyrics: The Ballad of Al Capone.

WALDEN, STANLEY EUGENE ASCAP 1967
composer, author, singer
b Brooklyn, NY, Dec 2, 32. Educ: Queens Col, BA; studied comp with Ben Weber. Solo clarinetist, 7th Army Symph, 55-57; dance accompanist for Martha Graham; free lance clarinetist, New York; teacher, Juilliard Sch Music, 60-65; mem of open theater; did stage music for "Scuba Duba", "One-Night Stand", "Oh! Calcutta!", "Sigmunds Freude", "Back Country" & others; also ballet, "Image." Chief Collabrs: Jacques Levy, George Tabori, Peter Schickele, Robert Dennis, J C Van Itallie, June Jordan. *Songs:* Oh! Calcutta!. *Instrumental Works:* Circuis; Some Changes. *Scores:* Opera/Ballet: Weewis; Bway shows: Pinkville; Film/TV: The Crazy American Girl; Frohes Fest; Jede Stirbt Sein Leben.

WALDMAN, ROBERT H (HUGH FORRESTER) ASCAP 1960
composer, arranger
b Brooklyn, NY, Feb 16, 36. Educ: Erasmus Hall High Sch; Brown Univ, BA, 57; Juilliard, grad comp, 58. Has done ballets, films, commercials, indust, TV-TW3, "Captain Kangaroo." Publ for children "A Rag Bag" & "A Three-Four Bag." Chief Collabrs: Alfred Vary, Matt Dubey, Earl Shuman. *Songs:* Music: We're a Home; The Waking Up Sun; Deeper in the Woods. *Instrumental Works:* Life in the Theatre; Shadow of Her Sister (ballet). *Scores:* Bway show: The Robber Bridegroom; Here's Where I Belong; Swing.

WALDO, ELISABETH ASCAP 1968
composer, violinist, ethnomusicologist
b Tacoma, Wash, 1923. Educ: Began violin study at age 5; Roosevelt High Sch, Seattle, Wash; violin scholarship, Cornish Sch Music, Seattle; scholarship with Efrem Zimbalist, Curtis Inst Music; special studies in Mexican ethnic music with Carlos Chavez. Was chosen by Leopold Stokowski as one of the leading violinist of All-Am Youth Orch. Cond, Los Angeles Philh Orch, one season; solo tours to Latin Am Capitols, soloist, radio progs, Mexico, 1 yr. Founder, performer, comp & violinst, Pan Am Ens. Recording artist, Crescendo Records; original scores for Nat Educ TV & films. Prof, Univ Calif, Los Angeles, 71-77

& Calif State Univ, Los Angeles, 76; lectr, Univ Southern Calif, Univ Calif, Irvine, Calif State Univ, Northridge & Calif State Univ, Stanislaus. Author of text bks incl "Latin American Music", "Spanish American Folk Songs", "American Folklore" & others. Writer, ASCAP, 68, publ, 73. Awards: Five ASCAP Standard Awards; Gold Medallion, Latin Am Network Announcers/Journalists, Mexico; Sigma Alpha Iota & Historical Soc of Southern Calif. Mem: Am Fedn Musicians; Am Women Comp, Inc; Delta Kappa Gamma Soc (hon) & Nat Acad Recording Arts & Sci. *Songs & Instrumental Works:* El Popol Vuh (ballet music); Concierto Indo-Americana (violin, orch); Realm of the Incas Suite (voices, orch); Misa de La Raza (Mass of the New World; Emmy Award nomination; mixed chorus, chamber orch); Viva California Suite (orch, voices).

WALDO, RALPH EMERSON, III (TERRY) ASCAP 1975
composer, performer
b Ironton, Ohio, Nov 26, 44. Educ: Ohio State Univ, MA, 70; studied piano & comp with Eubie Blake, 72-80. Producer radio series, "NPR—This Is Ragtime," 73. Author bk, "This Is Ragtime." Music dir, Warner QUBE, 78. Chief Collabr: Lou Carter. *Songs:* Music: The Ragweed Rag. *Instrumental Works:* Yellow Rose Rag. *Scores:* Bway: Warren G.

WALDROP, GIDEON W, JR ASCAP 1966
composer
b Haskell County, Tex, Sept 2, 19. Educ: Baylor Univ, BM; Eastman Sch Music, MM & PhD, 52, comp with Howard Hanson & Bernard Rogers. Comns from San Antonio Symph Soc. Air Force Intelligence, 42-46. Awarded Bronze Star, 45. Cond, Waco-Baylor Symph Orch, 46-51; assoc prof, Baylor Univ, 46-51; ed, Musical Courier, 53-58; music consult Ford Found, Young Comp-Pub Sch Proj, 58-61; pres, Juilliard Sch Music, 61-63; dean, 63- Mem, Am Music Ctr, Nat Asn Am Comp & Cond & Toscanini Memorial Archives Comt. *Instrumental Works:* Pressures (string orch); Symphony No 1; Prelude and Fuge; From the Southwest (Suite); Fan Fare.

WALKER, ALLAN ASCAP 1953
composer, author, singer
b Jan 28, 06; d. Educ: Syracuse Univ. Was singer, dancer & producer; also writer of spec material. Appeared in vaudeville, nightclubs, theatres, radio & TV. WW II, USAAF. Assoc producer, writer & actor, "Red Buttons Show," TV, 52-55. Mgr, Am Guild Variety Artists Welfare Fund. Chief Collabr: Red Buttons. *Songs:* Strange Things Are Happening; The Ho Ho Song.

WALKER, BEE
See Wolpa, Bertha Bee

WALKER, BILLY MARVIN ASCAP 1972
composer, author, singer
b Ralls, Tex, Jan 14, 29. With Louisiana Hayride, 52-55, Ozark Jubilee, 55-58 & Grand Ole Opry, 60-80. Recorded for Columbia, 51-65, Monument, 66-70, MGM, 70-75 & RCA, 76-77. *Songs:* Anything Your Heart Desires; Age of Worry; You Turn My Love Light On; A Little Bit Short on Love; Instead of Giving Up (I'm Givin' In); Gone (Our Endless Love); I'm Getting Into Something Good; Love Me Back to Heaven (One More Time); When the Song Is Gone (The Music Dies); I Can't Say No (If She Keeps Saying Yes).

WALKER, DONALD JOHN ASCAP 1947
composer, author
b Lambertville, NJ, Oct 28, 07. Arr for Bway musicals incl "By Jupiter", "Finian's Rainbow", "Miss Liberty", "Gentlemen Prefer Blondes", "Call Me Madam", "Wish You Were Here", "Pal Joey", "Wonderful Town", "The Pajama Game", "Silk Stockings", "Damn Yankees", "The Most Happy Fella", "The Music Man" & "What Makes Sammy Run?" Wrote scores "Memphis Bound" & "Courtin' Time" & music development "The Girl in Pink Tights." *Songs:* Begone My Love; The Way of Dreams; The Magic Highway; The Land and My Music; Let's Go Too Far; Growin' Pains; Old Love; The Nightingale, the Moon and I.

WALKER, DOUGLAS ODELL ASCAP 1977
composer, singer
b Anderson, Ind, Apr 13, 49. Educ: Don Martin Sch Radio & TV, first class FCC license. Songwriter & professional entertainer; entertained, US, Can & Alaska. Recording artist, original material. Chief Collabr: Stan Zucker. *Songs:* Trucker's Prayer; Happy Go Lucky Me; Trav'lin Man; Reap What You Sow; Cowboy's Christmas.

WALKER, GEORGE THEOPHILUS ASCAP 1967
composer
b Washington, DC, June 27, 22. Educ: Oberlin Col, MusB, 41; Curtis Inst Music, artist dipl in piano & comp, 41-45; Univ Rochester, DMA, 57, studied piano with Rudolf Serkin & Rosario Scalero; comp with Nadia Boulanger, 57-59. Town Hall debut as a pianist, 45, also debut with Philadelphia Orch, 45. US & European tours under Nat Concert Artists & Columbia Artists mgt. *Songs & Instrumental Works:* 3 Piano Sonatas; Address for Orchestra; Concerto for Piano and Orchestra; Mass for Chorus, Soloists and Orchestra; 2 Sonatas for Violin and Piano; Sonata for Cello and Piano; Perimeters for Clarinet and Piano; Lyric for String Orchestra.

WALKER, JAMES J ASCAP 1937
author
b New York, NY, June 19, 1881; d New York, Nov 18, 46. Educ: St Francis Xavier Col; NY Univ Law Sch. Elected to NY State Senate, became majority leader. Mayor, New York, 25-32; arbiter, United Garment Indust, 40-44. Pres, record co, 44-46. Lawyer & pub official. *Songs:* Will You Love Me in December As You Do in May?; Good Bye, Eyes of Blue; After They Gather the Hay; In the Valley Where My Sally Said Goodbye; Kiss All the Girls for Me; With the Robins I'll Return; I Like Your Way; Black Jim; There's Music in the Rustle of a Skirt.

WALKER, JEANINE OGLETREE (DANNY VICK)
composer, author, singer
b Laurel, Miss, June 21, 42. Educ: Univ Miss, BA(educ). Elem sch teacher, 64-65; traffic dept & announcer, WLBT-TV & WJDX radio, Jackson, Miss, 66-67; toured with variety group, Kids Next Door, 67-68. Replaced Anita Kerr in her original quartet in Nashville, 68 & still with them as singer. Soloist on sydicated TV prog, "At Home With the Bible." Chief Collabr: Bill Walker (husband). *Songs:* You Were Worth Waitin' For; That's Why I'm Country (Country Music Asn Awards theme); Country Gold; Tell Me About Love (theme for movie, "Going Home"); Lyrics: Music Hall America (theme).

WALKER, JIMMY
See Fortini, James

WALKER, JOHNNY GORDON ASCAP 1971
singer, musician
b New Albany, Miss, Feb 24, 47. Educ: Greenville High Sch. Mem group, Starbuck, 77-79; recording artist; appeared on "Dinah Shore Show", "Don Kirschners Rock Concert" & "Midnight Special." Lead guitarist. Chief Collabr: Bruce Blackman. *Songs:* Lyrics: Mrs Bluebird.

WALKER, MARK FESLER ASCAP 1965
composer, educator
b Alamogordo, NMex, June 5, 18. Educ: Arthur Jordan Cons, BM & MM(comp), studied with Guy Maier, Harold Triggs, Fabien Sevitsky; Ind Univ, PhD(theory), studied with Willi Apel, John White. USAAF band leader, 43-46. Fac, Butler Univ, 46-61; grad fac, Ohio State Univ, 61-68; head theory & comp dept, Youngstown State Univ, 68- publ works include scores for band, brass ens, chorus, string orch & violin quartet. Works comn for perf: Indianapolis Symph; Jordan Ballet; Columbus Symph; Youngstown Symph; Warren Chamber Orch; Ohio Music Educ Asn; Youngstown Univ Wind Ens. Chief Collabrs: Nilo W Hovey, Robert Klotman. *Instrumental Works:* TIPPS for Band; Four Violins in Concert; Ricercare for Orchestra; String Quartet; Arr: Sarabande and Bourree (brass ens); Suite from Dido and Aeneas (band); Overture and Allegro (band); America the Beautiful (orch); Concert Overture (wind ens); Pizzicato Polka (string orch); Carnival Overture (band).

WALKER, MARY LU ASCAP 1973
composer, author, teacher
b Newark, NJ, July 4, 26. Educ: Duke Univ, 45-47. Began songwriting, 71. Has presented workshops for teachers & given concerts in US & Can, 74- Toured Australia under auspices of "A People to Belong To," prize winning children's TV prog in Sydney, 79. *Songs:* Blue Jeans Blues; Lord of the Socks; Zuchinni; Friends; Advent Song. *Albums:* Dandelions; Peaceable Kingdom; Middle-Age, Middle-Class Mama Songs.

WALKER, RAYMOND (WALKER X RAYMOND) ASCAP 1974
author
b Hempstead, NY, Jan 7, 35. Lyricist with var recorded works & musical. Chief Collabrs: Omar Clay, George Kerr. *Songs:* Lyrics: Let's Make Love At Home Sometimes; Disrespect Can Wreck; Look What You Took.

WALKER, ROBERT E ASCAP 1973
composer, author
b Riverside, Calif, Nov 14, 42. Educ: Hanford High Sch, Calif, 60; Ogden Radio Sch, first class radio license, 62. DJ, 62- Chief Collabr: Kent Fox. *Songs:* Lyrics: New York Calling Miami; Tell Me a Lie; Midnight in the Morning; The Eight They Left Behind.

WALKER, TOMMY ASCAP 1956
composer, conductor
b Milwaukee, Wis, Nov 8, 22. Educ: Black Foxe Mil Inst; Univ Southern Calif. Dir, Univ Southern Calif Trojan Band, 48-55 & Toppers Band in Tournament of Roses Parade, 15 yrs; dir talent & entertainment, Disneyland; dir pageantry, 1960 Olympic Games. Chief Collabrs: Dick Winslow, Bob Linn. *Songs & Instrumental Works:* Charge; Parade of the Olympians; Professor Wonderful.

WALKER, WILLIAM JEFFRIE ASCAP 1977
composer
b Sydney, Australia, Oct 23, 49. Educ: Univ Sydney, BEcon. Started writing with Don King, 76- Chief Collabrs: Don King, Dave Woodward. *Songs:* She's the Girl of My Dreams; The Feelings So Right Tonight; Genuine Texas Good Guy; We've Got It All Together; Lady Let Me Love You; Where Were You on My Saturday Nights; I Wonder What It's Like to Be in Love; I'm Gonna Love

You Right Into My Life; She's My Everything; Thanks to You; I Believe in Someone; You Bring Out the Best in Me.

WALKER, WILLIAM STEARNS (WILLIAM BRADFORD) ASCAP 1958
composer, author, pianist
b Chicago, Ill, Aug 28, 17. Educ: Oak Park High Sch, Ill, 35; Amherst Col, BA, 39, studied theory & comp with Vincent Morgan; studied piano with Celia Bender, Chicago Cons Music, Ill, 46. 2nd Lt, Pacific, WW II, 41-45. Arr, pianist, Wayne King, 45-46 & Ted Weems, 46-48; own orch, Chicago, 48-57. Pianist, WGN radio, 50-54. Pres, Bill Walker Musical Productions, Inc, 53- *Songs & Instrumental Works:* Love You So; Half a Heart (Is All You Left Me); The Gettysburg Address (musical setting); Return to Shenandoah (fantasy for symph orch); But for the Grace of God.

WALKER-MALCOSKEY, EDNA ASCAP 1956
author
b Rapides Parish, La; d. Educ: Sacred Heart Convent; pvt tutors. Writer of essays, poems & short stories for mag. Author "The Eternal Variant", "Not Now, My Love", "The Virgin and the Priestess" & "Songs of Greener Pastures." Awards: Long Island Univ; Univ of Chicago Literary Soc; City Col New York. *Songs:* Goodbye Gal - Goodbye; Don't Cry Darlin', Don't Cry; That's Where You Should Be.

WALKOV, SAMUEL ASCAP 1975
composer, author, lecturer
b Philadelphia, Pa, Mar 3, 17. Mem, Author's Guild of Am. Co-composed, "His Son." Chief Collabr: Joe Leahy.

WALLACE, CHRIS ASCAP 1963
composer, author, actor
b Ft Wayne, Ind, June 8, 34. Educ: Ohio Wesleyan Univ, BA. Author of "A Man Passed Our Way," read on NBC by Bill Ryan the day John F Kennedy was buried. Appeared & sang on numerous children's TV shows. Produced "Harlem Cultural Festival," metromedia TV, also produced benefits for var organizations & causes at Amy Fisher Hall, Town Hall & The Apollo Theatre; was on ABC-TV "All My Children"; motion picture & TV career, Los Angeles, 78- *Songs & Instrumental Works:* The Hippo Song; Regina the Laughing Hyena; The Elusive Fly; A Special Thing to Be.

WALLACE, EMETT BABE ASCAP 1965
composer, author, singer
b New York, NY, June 24, 09. Educ: Pub Schs Nos 133 & 9; Manual Training High Sch; studied singing with Jarahal Hall, music with Don Donaldson. Singer, var nightclubs in New York, Can, Europe & Israel. Worked as master of ceremonies; fronted for var bands; song writer. With Les Folies Bergeres, Paris; in film "Stormy Weather,, & Bway show "Guys and Dolls." Chief Collabrs: Walter Hirsch, Ray Ellington, Eddie Bernard. *Songs:* A Chicken Ain't Nothin' But a Bird; The Baseball Song (Game); Bring Enough Clothes for Three Days; You're a Sack O Mappa Dappas; Keep A-Goin'; The Other Fellow's Yard; Song of America; Music That Feeling Is Gone.

WALLACE, JERRY LEON ASCAP 1962
songwriter, singer
b Kansas City, Mo, Dec 15, 28. Educ: Glendale High Sch, Ariz. Recording artist, country singer, Door Knob Records. *Songs:* I Miss You Already; I Bought the House; Your on the Run; Out Wickenburg Way; Paper Madonna; Rosebuds, Rainbows and Wine; I Told the Stars.

WALLACE, JOHN WESLEY ASCAP 1967
composer
b Rock Hill, SC, Mar 11, 14. Started playing piano accompaniment with father & his church choirs, age 8. *Songs:* Chains That Shackle My Heart; A Most Delightful Fellow Is the Bull; Tale of a Tavernkeep; Comes a Lonely Night; Searching for Love; Iris Promenade; The Broken Lei; Verbena Sachet; Springtime; Eternal Spring; Purple Brocade; 'Twixt Here and My Auntie Lucielles; Why Has It Rained All Year?; I Love to Hear the Church Bells Ring; Seventeen; Time; Jose Can't You See?; Red Leaves; Wearing My Love Like a Rose; Misty Island; Come to Monterrey; Lovely Candlelight Affair; Go to Sleep, Sweet; Sweet Little Dreamer; Got the Britches on Ain't I?; Way Up There.

WALLACE, MILDRED WHITE ASCAP 1936
composer, author, singer
b Columbiana, Ala. Educ: Randolph Macon Col; Sullins Col, BA; Birmingham Cons, studied with Ruth Chandler & Clara Harper Steele; Ala Col. On the radio as, The Dixie Bluebird; publ & ed, Shelby County Reporter. Chief Collabr, J Will Callahan. *Songs:* Sometime, Somehow, Somewhere; Close of Day; Black Belt Lullaby; Since Your Path Crossed Mine; I Would Be Near You Then; Alone With Thee; Trust Only in His Love; Dream Boat.

WALLACE, OLIVER GEORGE ASCAP 1940
composer, organist, conductor
b London, Eng, Aug 6, 1887; d Hollywood, Calif, Sept 16, 63. Educ: London schs; pvt music study. To US, 06, citizen, 14. First film accompanist to use pipe organ, Seattle, 10. To Hollywood, 30, comp & cond, Walt Disney studios. Comp of many shorts for cartoons incl "Bearly Asleep", "Bee on Guard", "Beezy

Bear", "Ben and Me", "Canvas Back Duck", "Casey Bats Again", "Chips Ahoy", "Clown of the Jungle", "Crazy Over Daisy", "Dragon Around", "Figaro and Frankie", "Flying Squirrel", "Grandcanyonscope", "Grin and Bear It", "Let's Stick Together", "Lion Around", "No Hunting", "Pigs Is Pigs", "Pluto and the Gopher", "Pluto's Heart Throb", "Pluto's Party", "Primitive Pluto", "Rugged Bear", "Social Lion", "Spare the Rod", "Teachers Are People", "Two Weeks Vacation", "Up a Tree", "Wonder Dog" & "Working for Peanuts." Chief Collabrs: Frank Churchill, Harold Weeks. *Songs:* Hindustan; Der Fuehrer's Face; Rainbow of My Dreams; Louisiana; Other Lips; Indiana Moon; When I See an Elephant Fly; Last Night I Had That Dream Again. *Scores:* Films: Dumbo (Acad Award, 41); Cinderella; Alice in Wonderland; White Wilderness; The Adventures of Ichabod and Mr Toad; Big Red; Darby O'Gill and the Little People; Hans Brinker or The Silver Skates; The Incredible Journey; Lady and the Tramp; The Legend of Sleepy Hollow; Old Yeller; Peter Pan; Sammy, the Way-out Seal; Savage Sam; TV films: Wind in the Willows.

WALLACE, WILLIAM WALTER ASCAP 1973
composer, author
b East Point, Ga, Dec 7, 23. Educ: Self-taught in music; high sch, grad. Has had bands & played in nightclubs throughout Fla; recording artist. Has worked for Southern Bell Telephone & Telegraph, 29 yrs. Teacher of guitar. *Songs:* Blinded By Your Love (Words of Happiness); Big Old Black Dog (Sam Dog); Vicki (Charlie); With Beer in Hand; One for You and One for Your Horse.

WALLACH, IRA ASCAP 1957
author
b New York, NY, Jan 22, 13. Educ: Cornell Univ. Service, WW II; writer of bks, plays & movie scripts; sketches, off-Bway revue, "Phoenix '55"; author: "Hopalong-Freud", "Muscle Beach" & "The Absence of a Cello" (play).

WALLER, THOMAS (FATS) ASCAP 1931
composer, conductor, organist
b New York, NY, May 21, 04; d Kansas City, Mo, Dec 15, 43. Educ: Studied organ at Abyssinian Baptist Church, NY. Singer & pianist in nightclubs; organist in theatres. Accompanist to singers incl Bessie Smith. Pianist in dance bands. Leader, own orch; toured US & Europe. Recording artist. Chief Collabrs: Andy Razaf, Stanley Adams, George Marion, Jr, Clarence Williams. *Songs:* Squeeze Me; My Fate Is in Your Hands; I've Got a Feeling I'm Falling; Honeysuckle Rose; Blue Turning Gray Over You; Zonky; Willow Tree; Ain't Misbehavin'; Black and Blue; Take It From Me; Concentratin' on You; You're My Ideal; Rollin' Down the River; Keepin' Out of Mischief Now; The Joint Is Jumpin'; I'm Crazy 'Bout My Baby; There's a Man in My Life; Georgia Bo Bo. *Instrumental Works:* Minor Drag; Harlmen Fuss; Handful of Keys; Viper's Drag; St Louis Shuffle; Numb Fumblin'; Valentine Stomp. *Scores:* Bway shows: Keep Shufflin; Hot Chocolates; Early to Bed.

WALLINGTON, BILLIE JUNE (HENRY) ASCAP 1955
composer, author
b Wichita, Kans, Nov 1, 34. Educ: Wichita State Univ, BA; pvt music studies. Contributed music articles to jazz journals; dir pub rels, CBS & Warner Bros Records. Chief Collabrs: George Wallington, Maurice Goodman. *Songs:* The Tunnel of Love; Music: My Lover Sho Lied (I Went to the Village); Face to Face; This Is the Time; Middle of Love. *Instrumental Works:* Billie's Tune.

WALLINGTON, GEORGE ASCAP 1954
author, pianist
b Palermo, Italy, Oct 27, 23. Educ: Pvt music studies with Pietro Figlia, father; Mannes Sch Music, New York. Performed as pianist & leader of own jazz ens, has made many record albums. Chief Collabrs: Maurice Bud Goodman, Billie Henry Wallington, Mitchell Parish, Mack David. *Songs:* Lemon Drop; Music: Way Out There; My April Heart; Morning Dew; Hold Me Close. *Instrumental Works:* Godchild; Arrivederci; Christina; Busman's Holiday; Lady Fair; Racing; Variations, Suite for Piano; Cuckoo Round the Clock; Fairyland; Knockout; Among Friends; Summer Rain. *Albums:* Our Delight.

WALLIS, HANK
See Strzelecki, Henry P

WALLOWITCH, JOHN ASCAP 1964
composer, author, coach
b Philadelphia, Pa, Feb 11, 30. Educ: Central High; Temple Univ; Juilliard Sch Music, BA, studied piano with Beveridge Webster, Abby Whiteside & Joseph Prostakoff, comp, Vittorio Giannini. Concert piano debut, 62; State Dept tour of Europe; entertainer, nightclubs; recording artist, Serenus Records. Chief Collabrs: Music, Tony Scibetta, Lyrics, Ira Wallach. *Songs:* Discover Who I Am; Lyrics: Only Know I Love You; What's Wrong With Me. *Instrumental Works:* Sonata for a Windy Day; Four Snappy Pieces for Piano.

WALLS, BETTY DUKE ASCAP 1974
author
b Pontotoc, Miss, Oct 29, 41. Educ: Col. Writer, 65-; with Miss Employment Service, 80- Chief Collabrs: Danny Walls, Dwight Galloway. *Songs:* Who Left the Door to Heaven Open; Living in the Sunshine; So Close to Home; When a Woman Cries.

WALLS, BYRON ROBERT ASCAP 1963
composer, author, singer
b Valley City, NDak, Sept 19, 37. Educ: San Francisco State Univ, BA, MA(music history). Singer: The Travellers, nightclubs; Byron & Howard, comedy singing act; New Cristy Minstrels; Glen Yarbrough and The Limeliters. Songwriter Warner Brothers, 74-77. Chief Collabrs: Brian Tabach, Richard Reicheg, Jim Rushing, Tom Kimmel. *Songs:* Today Is the First Day of the Rest of Our Lives; Lovin' Naturally; Very Fine Lady; Grandma's Letter; The World's A Tuxedo; Pulling Myself Together; Lovesongs and Romance Magazines; Precious Love.

WALLS, ROBERT BOEN ASCAP 1963
composer, author, singer
b Spirit Lake, Idaho, Dec 24, 10. Educ: Moorhead State Univ, BEd, 32; Univ NDak, MS, 36; studied voice with Daniel Preston, Daniel Protheroe & Thomas MacBurney; var choral workshops with Walter Aschenbrenner, Roger Wagner, Fred Waring, Leonard DePaur & Daniel Protheroe. Teacher, East Grand Forks Pub Schs, Minn, 32-36; prof, Valley City State Col, NDak, 36-40 & Univ Idaho, 40-47; dir choral activities, Ore State Univ, 47-74, head music dept, 47-65. Singer in concerts & radio; conductor. Author of bk, "Pronouncing Guide to French, German, Italian and Spanish." Chief Collabrs: Ted Mesang, Archie Jones. *Songs:* Gloria in Excelsis; Shallow Brown; Hymn of Praise; Choral Tune-Ups; Lyrics: The Names of Oregon (narration).

WALLSCHLAEGER, DEAN ANDRE ASCAP 1976
composer, author, singer
b Marinette, Wis, Apr 29, 53. Began working with var artists incl Doc Severinsen, Mike Douglas, Tennessee Ernie Ford & Diana Ross, 70- Writer, music, Bway show & "The Archies," 76, "The Fabulous Funnies," 78. Writer & producer, music, "Mighty Mouse, Heckel and Jeckle Hour," 79, "Sport Billy," 80. Wis All State Honors, orchestra chorus & band; Nat Asn Rudimental Drummers Champion, 70. Chief Collabrs: Danny Janssen, Jeff Michael, Scott Ramsay, Don Wallschlaeger, Marcia Waldorf. *Songs:* Don't Stop; Tower of Love; Hot Pot; Slippin' Away; The Perfect Christmas; It's Christmas. *Scores:* Film/TV: Snow White Christmas Special. *Albums:* Love Rocket.

WALSH, DANIEL ASCAP 1972
songwriter
b Los Angeles, Calif, Feb 21, 48. Educ: Self-taught on piano & guitar. Began playing guitar at age 14; played in bands from age 15 to 20; songwriter since age 17; piano player since age 18. Chief Collabr: Michael Price. *Songs:* Heaven Knows; Temptation Eyes; Ain't No Love in the Heart of the City; I Wouldn't Treat a Dog the Way You've Treated Me; It Ain't the Real Thing; Glory Bound; I Just Want to Be the One in Your Life; Love Pains; It's Your Move.

WALSH, HENRY H ASCAP 1956
author, educator
b New York, NY, July 2, 06. Educ: Nat Acad; Pratt Inst. Artist & art teacher until 40; free-lance radio & TV writer of "Calvacade", "Thin Man" & "You Are There"; taught radio & TV writing, Sarah Lawrence Col; writer, Columbia Records; writer & publ consult, Ittleson Ctr Child Res; dir, Windham Col prog, Communication Arts in Educ. Chief Collabrs: Ray Carter & Hermann Krasnow. *Songs:* Rodeo; Johnny Appleseed; Mamma, Mamma, Mamma; Signing of the Magna Charta.

WALSH, JOSEPH FIDLER
producer, musician
b Wichita, Kans, Nov 20, 47. Educ: Kent State Univ. Recording artist, solo & with var groups incl James Gang, Barnstorm, 71-74 & Eagles, 76-. Mem, Amateur Radio Relay League. *Songs:* Funk 49; In the City; Life's Been Good; Walk Away; Turn to Stone; Rocky Mountain Way. *Albums:* Barnstorm Featuring Joe Walsh; The James Gang; The James Gang Rides Again; The Smoker You Drink, the Player You Get; So What?; You Can't Argue With a Sick Mind; But Seriously Folks.

WALSH, PAULINE ASCAP 1951
composer, author, singer
b Kansas City, Mo, Dec 19, 06. Educ: Wilson Green Sch Music, DC; studied with Oscar Seagle, New York, Jean de Reszke, France, Anita Rio & Edward Harris, New York, Andrei de Segurola, Paris. Soloist, Kansas City Symph & Los Angeles Philh Orch; had own radio show, WOR, NJ. *Songs:* Christmas Story; The Drifter; Thee Lee'le Burro; So Young, So in Love.

WALT, EDWARD JOHN ASCAP 1945
composer, author
b Louisville, Ky, May 23, 1877; d Lincoln, Nebr, Feb 26, 51. Educ: Kansas City, Mo & Lincoln, Nebr pub schs; studied violin with John Behr & August Hagenow. Span-Am War service. Musician in orch, Lansing Theatre, Lincoln. Led own dance band. In retail music bus, 07. *Songs & Instrumental Works:* Lassie O'Mine; A Mother's Croon; Thy Troubadour; Molly Mine; Sleepy Time; Innocent Pranks; March Dignitaire; The Commodore; Midsummer Waltzes.

WALTER, CY ASCAP 1956
composer, pianist
b Minneapolis, Minn, Sept 16, 25; d New York, NY, Aug 18, 69. Educ: Univ Minn. To New York, 34. Pianist, supper clubs, radio, TV, records & at Drake Hotel. Made records. *Songs:* Some Fine Day; Mrs Malaprop; You Are There; Nocturne.

WALTER, EUGENE FERDINAND
librettist, author, actor
b Mobile, Ala, Nov 30, 23. Educ: Pawling Inst; Mus of Modern Art; NY Univ; New Sch Social Res; Alliance Francaise, Paris; Inst Britannique de la Sorbonne, Paris; Istituto Dante Allighieri, Rome; Spring Hill Col, Ala; studied drawing with Edmond de Celle & Yasuo Kuniyoshi, theory with Henry Cowell, ballet with Nikitina, Paris. Toured own marionette theatre; designed Mardi Gras parades & costumes in Mobile. War yrs, Am Airways Communication Syst, Andreanof Islands. To New York after war, designed off-Bway shows, made film with Anaïs Nin, publ poems. Moved to Paris, helped found "Paris Review," worked with "Botteghe Oscure" & seven other reviews. Wrote song in Zefferelli's "Romeo and Juliet," cantata for centennial of Tex, mass sung in St Ignazio & St Peter's, Rome, operette version of "Alice in Wonderland," also opera-bouffes: "Tinsel Time"; "Funnybone"; "The Sneaky-Snacker". Author 12 bks, incl "The Untidy Pilgrim" (Lippincott Prize), "Monkey Poems" (Rockefeller fel), "American Cooking: Southern Style" (Time-Life Series), "Jennie the Watercress Girl", "Shapes of the River", "Love You Good, See You Later", "The Likes of Which" (incl O Henry citation), "Fellini Satyricon" (Eng version). Songwriter, editor, illustrator. Chief Collabrs: Music, Nino Rota, Donald Ashwander, Gail Kubik, Alfredo Di Rocco, David Walker, Taylor Peck, var others; films, Fellini, Zeferelli, Wurtmüller, D Risi & others. *Songs:* Blessed Are the Rich.

WALTER, SERGE ASCAP 1942
composer
b Hungerberg, Russia, July 5, 1896; d Palm Beach, Fla, Oct 8, 76. To US, 25. Citizen. Educ: Pvt schs, St Petersburg, Russia; studied piano & violin with uncle, Victor Walter; St Petersburg Univ, studied law; Army Officers' Sch. Escaped to Finland during revolution. To Paris, 21, as comp & pianist. Wrote songs for Bway musicals & films. Chief Collabrs: Jack Edwards, Bud Brees. *Songs & Instrumental Works:* Gay Parisienne; Tu Sais; Lady Tambourine; The Road Is Calling; If I Could Have My Way; I Talked With God; Tomorrow in the Sky; My Beloved; Lucky Star; Just for Awhile; Who Can Tell?; Lovestruck; Bon Voyage; Monte Carlo; Pour Nous; Avant Vous; Piano Tuner.

WALTERS, CHARLES A ASCAP 1978
composer, author, singer
b Brownsville, Pa, Apr 28, 41. Writer & singer. *Songs:* Breaker Breaker 19; CBer's Christmas Carol; Our Sleeping Love; Your Separate Ways; Lyrics: Alaskan Cowboy.

WALTERS, DAVID L ASCAP 1969
composer
b Youngstown, Ohio. Educ: Miami Univ, BS(music); Fla State Univ, MM(music); hon doctorate, Jacksonville State Univ. Dir band & orch, Hamilton, Ohio, 51; supvr instrumental music, New Bern, NC, 52-60; dir bands, Jacksonville State Univ, 61- Chief Collabr: A E Hoffman. *Instrumental Works:* Fiesta del Rio (band); Episode (solo); Nautical Medley (brass); Fantasy for Trumpet (solo); The Bandsman; 18 Marching Band Arrangements.

WALTERS, HAROLD LAURENCE ASCAP 1956
composer, author, arranger
b Gurdon, Ark, Sept 29, 18. Educ: Little Rock High Sch; Cincinnati Cons Music; Am Univ; Washington Col Music, DMus; advanced study in comp with Nadia Boulanger. Arr & played tuba, Frank Simon's Armco Band, NBC Radio; chief arr, USN Band, Washington, DC, 6 yrs; comp, Fox Movietone news reels, 2 yrs, while orchestrating shows in New York & Sigmund Romberg's Orch. Ed, comp & arr, Rubank Music Publ, 47- Guest cond bands, world wide. Comp and/or arr over 1500 publ works for instrumental music (band, orch, ens, solos & football half-time shows). Chief Collabrs: Karl L King, Paul V Yoder & David Bennett. *Instrumental Works:* Badinage for Brasses; American Folk Suite; Jamaican Folk Suite; Suite Americana; The Third Century; Trumpets Wild; Japanese Folk Suite; Hootenanny; Country and Western; Instant Concert; Bossa Nova; Brasses to the Fore; Civil War Suite; Christmas Suite; La Mascarada; Moonrise; Kneller Hall; TV Suite; Voodoo; Arranger's Holiday; Mariachi; Men of Music; Bands Around the World; Safari; America the Beautiful; Si! Trocadero; Classical Arr: Til Eulenspiegel's Merry Pranks (Strauss); Afternoon of a Faun (Debussy); Finale From the New World Symphony (Dvorak); Band Arr: When the Saints Go Marching In.

WALTERS, ROBERT WILLIAM ASCAP 1958
composer, arranger, conductor
b Tonawanda, NY, Sept 9, 21. Educ: Tonawanda High Sch. Lead clarinet player, Claude Thornhill Orch, Tommy Dorsey Band & Harry James Band. USCG, World War II, 42-45. With Art Linkletter TV show, "House Party," 18 yrs. Head of own big band & casual orch booking office, 80- Chief Collabrs: Earl Brent, Steve Allen, Muzzy Marcellino. *Songs:* Music: Holiday Song; I Love a

Bossa Nova; Do Me Something Different. *Instrumental Works:* Bob's Blues; Relax.

WALTON, JAMES MONROE ASCAP 1965
composer, author
b Charlottesville, Va, Feb 14, 23. Educ: US Sch Music, New York, grad, 48. Singer, night clubs & TV; recording artist, Walton Records; performer motion picture, "The Seduction of Joe Tynan." *Songs:* Chesapeake Girl; It Was True; Since We Drifted Apart; I'm a Little Lonely Boy; Only You.

WALTON, KENNETH E ASCAP 1948
composer, conductor, organist
b Tulse Hill, Eng, Feb 17, 04; US citizen. Pianist in radio. *Songs & Instrumental Works:* Alborada; Snow; St Peter's Rome; Mary; The Autumn Bluebird; I've a Dream; Soliloquy; Christmas Rhapsody (choral).

WALTON, VIVIAN BEATRICE ASCAP 1971
composer, author, educator
b Franklin, Ga, June 5, 34. Educ: Carver High Sch; Tuskegee Inst Ala; Univ Dayton, Ohio, studied with Dr Tag & Mrs Kline; Sinclair Community Col; Awanda Music Studio. Singer, TV, radio & across US & Europe. *Songs:* Muhammad Ali, You Are the Greatest Champ of All; Do It God's Way; Everybody Is a Somebody; Happy 200th Birthday America; There Was A Great Man in Senator Humphrey; Rev Martin Luther King Is Not Dead, Ideas Still Live in Our Hearts; Sadat, Begin the Peace Makers; Dayton the City Beautiful; World Peace Classical Song; There's a New Hope in America; Hawaii is the Paradise; Get It Together with God in Yourself; Bless It, Loose It, Just Let It Go; God Is on the Moon; I Am in Love with God; I Rise High Up in Consciousness, I've Overcome the World; McIntosh and Mortimer Were Men of Action; Love Is the Spirit of Christmas; God Wants Everybody to be Happy; Unite Americans, Unite Today.

WANDERMAN, DOROTHY ASCAP 1963
composer, pianist
b New York, NY, Oct 20, 07. Studied music with Philipp, Saperton & Scoville. *Instrumental Works:* Piano: The Playful Mouse; In a French Cafe; Swiss Alpine Waltz; In a Viennese Garden; Valse Tragic.

WANG, AN-MING (MARION WANG MAK) ASCAP 1978
author
b Shanghai, China. Educ: Cent China Univ, BEd, 47; Wesleyan Cons, BMus, magna cum laude, 50; Columbia Univ, MA, 51; Juilliard Sch Music. Composed for piano, voice, choral ens, strings, woodwind & orch. Many compositions have been performed in the DC area. *Songs:* A Chinese Lullaby; Music: The Nightingale.

WANGBERG, EIRIK WILHELM ASCAP 1969
composer, author
b Hereford, Eng, Jan 19, 44. Educ: Oslo Cathedral Sch, degree; Sacramento State Col, BA; studied record eng with Armin Steiner & record production with Lou Adler. Record producer/engr for many artists, incl Paul McCartney, Diana Ross, Neil Diamond, Olivia Newton John, John Travolta, Carol King, Lalo Schifrin, Mamas & Papas, Beatles. *Songs:* Love Needs the World; I Left My Baby Behind; You Woman; My Marie. *Scores:* Film/TV: Midnight Rider.

WANG MAK, MARION
See Wang, An-Ming

WANN, JAMES CREEKMORE, JR ASCAP 1975
composer, author, singer
b Chattanooga, Tenn, Aug 30, 48. Educ: Univ NC, BA(Eng) with honors in writing. Writer, bk, co-composer, music & lyrics, off-Bway musicals "Diamond Studs", Chelsea Westside, 75 & "Hot Grog", Phoenix, 77. Performer, Jim Wann's Country Cabaret, Manhattan Theatre Club, 78; writer, music & lyrics, "Gold Dust," Louisville, 79; lyrics for "Frimbo," 80. Chief Collabrs: Bland Simpson, Howard Harris, Jon Jory, John Justice, John Foley. *Songs:* Cakewalk Into Kansas City; No Holds Barred; Lyrics: Train Walking.

WARD, CHARLES B ASCAP 1942
composer, singer
b London, Eng, Aug 21, 1865; d New York, NY, Mar 21, 17. Moved to US as youth. Known as Original Bowery Boy in vaudeville; wrote own songs. *Songs:* Strike Up the Band; The Band Played On; How the Irish Beat the Band; In Your Own Town; Maisey, Maisey, Fine and Daisy; While the Band Is Playing Dixie; The Kissing Trust.

WARD, CLARA ASCAP 1960
conductor, singer, arrranger
b Philadelphia, Pa; d. Made many records, appeared in concerts, jazz fests as leader of group, The Ward Singers.

WARD, EDWARD ASCAP 1936
composer
b St Louis, Mo, Apr 2, 1896; d. Educ: High sch; Beethoven Schs of Music, St Louis. Film exec; scored films incl "Cheers for Miss Bishop", "Thanks a

Million", "All American Co-ed" & "Phantom of the Opera." *Songs:* Who Takes Care of the Caretaker's Daughter?; Always and Always; Lullaby of the Bells; Dreaming of Castles in the Air; Anybody Home? *Scores:* Stage: Clowns in Clover (London).

WARD, MICHAEL PHILIP
ASCAP 1977
composer, conductor, arranger
b Chicago, Ill, Jan 18, 49. Educ: Northwestern Univ, BA, 71; studied piano with Alan Swain, John Mehegan, Jack Reilly, comp with Ludmila Ulehla, William Russo, arr with Don Sebesky. Composer, scores for "The Other Cinderella", "Personals", & the opera "Photograph." Music dir, "Haschich Fudge Revu" & "Stamp Act"; mus dir & arr, "Paris Lights"; assoc cond, "Umbrellas of Cherbourg." Song & hymns performed by var artists. Chief Collabrs: Keithen Carter, Herman Wheatley. *Songs:* Here I Am, Lord; Music: I Love You Through Windows; Only Pretty Girls; It's A Lifetime Thing. *Scores:* Opera: Photograph; Bway show: Personals.

WARD, ROY BRITISH
ASCAP 1971
composer, author, singer
b Hertford, NC, Apr 27, 29. Performer, TV, nightclubs, radio & stage shows; recording artist. Chief Collabrs: Lloyd Martin, Joe White, Buddy Powell. *Songs:* A Chance to Try Again; The Whole World Here at Home; I'm the Devil (That Made Her That Way); Passion Is Turning to Love.

WARD, SAM
ASCAP 1924
author
b New York, NY, June 24, 06; d New York, May 5, 60. Educ: Fordham Univ. Writer of spec material for theatre & radio. *Songs:* Your Boy Is on the Coal Pile Now; Not Long Ago; Just Say I Love Her; Bartender's Polka; Kalua Skies; A Little Coat of Tan; I Still Remember; I'm Wrong With the Right Girl.

WARD, WILLIAM REED
ASCAP 1971
composer, author, teacher
b Norton, Kans, May 20, 18. Educ: Eastman Sch Music, BM & BMusEd, 41, Charles S Skilton, MMus, 42, Bernard Rogers, PhD, 54, Howard Hanson. Taught piano & theory, Colo State Univ, 42-44, comp & theory, Lawrence Univ, 44-47, also comp & theory, San Francisco State Univ, 47-, chmn, Music Dept, 54-69, assoc dean, Sch Creative Arts, 77- Nat Arr Award, 47. Dir music var churches; wrote music for 10th Anniversary of founding of UN. Comns by San Francisco Symph Orch, Olympic Club & Lawrence Univ, Chief Collabr: Writer, McKinley Helm. *Songs & Instrumental Works:* In Town Again; Cueca; John Henry and the Steam Drill; Arcs; Lullaby for a Pinto Colt (orch); Suite on Traditional American Songs (orch); Fray Junipero Serra (dramatic oratorio for orch, chorus, soloists, dancers, narrators; performed for 200th Anniversary of founding of City of San Diego); Variations on a Western Tune (band); two woodwind quintets, one string quartet; Listen, Lord; Father, We Praise Thee; Response in Ancient Style: A Vision of the World; Be Thou MY Vision; The Crucifixion; They Shall Rise Up With Wings; Christmas Roundelay; Western Wagons; Hymn Preludes for Organ: O Come, O Come, Immanuel; Lord Jesus, Think of Me; Organ: Passacaglia, Scherzo and Fugue, Variations on St Dunstan's. The American Bicentennial Song Book (2 vols); Examples for the Study of Musical Style.

WARDEN, BRUCE LELAND
ASCAP 1968
composer, author, musician
b Beloit, Wis, July 14, 39. Educ: South Beloit High Sch; Southern Ill Univ, BS, 65; Univ Ill, 68-70; Northern Ill Univ, MS, 70. Played keyboard & brass through high sch & col; musician radio & TV specials, Southern Ill & Ind area; singer, nightclubs & TV; recording artist, WGE Records. Chief Collabrs: Judith A Warden, Lea A Warden. *Songs:* To the Master; Which Way to Go; When You Really Want the Lord; Call Me Anything But Stupid; Music: It's a Bright Sunny Day; Banjo, Lead the Way; I Was a Fool.

WARDEN, JUDITH ANN
ASCAP 1969
composer, author, musician
b Beloit, Wis, Mar 11, 39. Educ: South Beloit High Sch; Northern Ill Univ; Southern Ill Univ, BS, 61; teaching cert. Pvt professional music teacher; music teacher schs. Chief Collabr: Bruce Warden. *Songs:* Lyrics: Just for Judi; I Was a Fool; I Confess to You; I Want You; Day and Night.

WARE, HARRIET
ASCAP 1933
composer, pianist
b Waupun, Wis, Aug 26, 1878; d New York, NY, Feb 9, 62. Educ: Pillsbury Cons, Owatonna, Minn; studied with William Mason, Stojowski, Juliano, Madame Grunewald & Hugo Kaun. Piano soloist, symph orchs; concert tours throughout US. First dir & vpres, Musical Art Soc, Long Island, NY. *Songs & Instrumental Works:* Sir Oluf (cantata); The Artisan; Undine. In an Old Garden (song cycle); A City Child in the Country; Woman's Triumphal March (choral; nat song, Fedn Women's Clubs Am); Boat Song; The Cross; Hindu Slumber Song; This Day Is Mine; The Forgotten Land; The Princess of the Morning; For Piano: Mountain Pictures; Song of the Sea; Victory Prelude; Midnight Waltz.

WARE, JAMES A
ASCAP 1960
composer, author, singer
b Louisville, Ky. Educ: Morgan Prep Sch; George Peabody Col. Cond & vocalist with own band; vocalist with Joe Venuti orch, 29-39; made many records. Chief Collabr: Morton Downey, Jr.

WARE, LEONARD
ASCAP 1947
composer, author, guitarist
b Richmond, Va, Dec 28, 09; d Bronx, New York, Mar 30, 74. Educ: Franklin Sch of Music; Tuskegee Inst. To NY, 37; joined Sydney Beckett Band. Guitarist, Benny Goodman & Count Basie Orchs. Toured with own trio & with Katherine Dunham Dancers. *Songs:* Hold Tight-Hold Tight; Donuts With the Hole in the Middle; I Dreamt I Dwelt in Harlem; Early Hours; Night Train; Baby, I Wanted to Cry.

WARING, FRED
ASCAP 1940
composer, publisher, conductor
b Tyrone, Pa, June 9, 1900. Educ: Pa State Univ. Brother of Tom Waring. Organized dance band, Banjassatra, 18; enlarged group to Waring's Collegians, which became The Pennsylvanians. Appeared in Bway musicals "Hello Yourself" & "The New Yorkers." Film appearances "Syncopation" & "Varsity Show." Began radio shows, 33. Gave concerts throughout US. Began TV prog, 49. Organized Fred Waring Music Workshop, teaching choral singing, also head of Waring Corp (manufacturers Waring Blendor), Shawnee Press, Inc & Shawnee Country Club. Has made many records. *Songs:* Please Don't Tell Me; I Hear Music; Early in the Morning; Song Is the Thing; Spearhead; Bond Jungle; Monday Washing Day; I'm All Fouled Up in Love; The Time Is Now; More Power to America.

WARING, TOM
ASCAP 1935
composer, author, pianist
b Tyrone, Pa, Feb 12, 02; d Shawnee, Pa, Dec 29, 60. Educ: Pa State Univ. Pianist & singer, orch led by brother, Fred Waring. Soloist, Glee Club, Cumberland, Md & Pa State Glee Club. Singer, radio, films & concerts. *Songs:* So Beats My Heart for You; Way Back Home; Jonah; Countin' My Blessings; Desire; Swing Me a Lullaby; When Angels Sang of Peace; Leave It to Me to Remember.

WARNDOF, FIONA MCCLEARY
ASCAP 1955
composer, pianist, lecturer
b Sanderstead, Eng. Educ: St Paul's Girls Sch, London; Royal Acad of Music; Matthay Piano Sch, London, studied with Tobias Matthay; Institute Dalcroze, Geneva, Switz; Trinity Col Music, degree; studied music with R Vaughan Williams, Arnold Bax & Myra Hess. Became US citizen, 30. Prof of music, Brooklyn Col, Col of New Rochelle, Dalcroze Sch of Music, Bank Street Col for Teachers, New York. Teacher, Settlement Schs, Philadelphia, Greenwich House, NY, Westport Sch Music, Briarcliff Jr Col, Barry Col, Miami, Fla Atlantic Univ & pvt classes. Has given concerts in US, Eng, Ger & Switz. Has written teaching material & music for orch, chamber, piano, choral & ballet. Author, "American Song Book for Children." *Instrumental Works:* Trois Melodies; Senart; Melody (cello).

WARNER, BYRON HILBUN, JR
ASCAP 1972
composer, author, singer
b Boston, Mass, July 30, 39. Educ: Athens High Sch, Ga; Marist Col, Atlanta; Univ Ga, BA(English literature), Phi Mu Alpha, pres, Men's Glee Club; studied with father & mother. Founded singing group The Status Cymbal, 66, began solo career, 70. Performed at Bitter End, New York, Gaslight & Gerdes Folk City, Fillmore East, "Ed Sullivan Show" & "Jackie Gleason Show"; did many col concerts. Pres, Ridgewood Productions, Jingle Productions & Ridgewood Place Music. *Songs:* Dixie; Cindy and Me; Modells Memorial; Get Away; Kansas.

WARNER, PHILIP
ASCAP 1950
composer, pianist, teacher
b Chicago, Ill, Nov 6, 01. Educ: Am Cons, BM; Northwestern Univ, MM; studied with Josef Lhevinne, Jan Chiapusso, Kurt Wanieck, Howard Wells, Arnold Anderson & Albert Noelte; taught at Am Cons, Sherwood Music Schs & Northwestern Univ; accompanist to Richard Crooks, Gladys Swarthout, Lauritz Melchior & Richard Tucker; staff pianist, WCFL, Chicago; music dir, WBEZ & Chicago pub schs. *Songs:* Hurdy-Gurdy (Kimbal Award). *Songs & Instrumental Works:* Sarabande-Chaconne (Sinfonia Nat Contest prize); Sinfonietta; Thumbnail Sketches of Chicago; Youth Overture; Green Mansions; The Lake at Dawn; Valse Caprice (saxophone); Cuban Skies (piano); Noel (women's voices).

WARNER, SARAH ANN
ASCAP 1959
composer, author, pianist
b Idaho Falls, Idaho, Oct 16, 1898. Became publ, Long Beach, Calif, 59. *Songs:* Our Engagement Waltz; 'Neath a Blanket of White; Hello, Merry Christmas; So Speaks My Heart; You Stole My Heart.

WARNICK, HENRY CLAY, JR (BUCK)
ASCAP 1947
composer, author, conductor
b Tacoma, Wash, Dec 14, 15. Educ: West Orange High Sch, 31; Colgate Univ, BA, 35; Juilliard Sch Music, 36, studied comp, orchestration & cond with Tibor

Serly, 37-39. Cond & arr for the Shuberts, 39-41, also comp & arr "Ziegfeld Follies", "Three After Three" & "Too Many Girls," 42-44; cond/arr "By Jupiter", "Banjo Eyes" & "A Connecticut Yankee"; comp & vocal arr "Dream With Music," 45-49; cond & vocal dir "Peep Show," 50-54; cond "Once Upon a Matress"; choral dir & vocal arr "Your Show of Shows," 55-61; comp "Marco Polo" for NBC-TV, 62-80. Musical dir & vpres, Young & Rubicam Advert Agency. Chief Collabrs: Don Walker, Edward Eager, Mel Pahl, Mel Tolkin, Max Liebman, Carolyn Leigh, James Whitcomb Riley. *Songs:* The Nightingale, The Moon and I; Tickets, Please; Memphis Band; Old Love; Growin' Pains; Mister Electric Storm; It's Raining; Should a Gentleman Offer; Cigars, Cigarettes; The Dogs Kids Love to Bite; Music: Love at Second Sight; I'm Afraid I'm in Love; Baby, Don't Count on Me; Pick Yourself a Star; I Love to Ramble; Heidi; The Garden of Imagining; You'll Be Seeing Me; Population; Come With Me; Riley Day; When the Frost Is on the Punkin; The Old Swimmin' Hole; An Old Sweetheart of Mine; A Song of Parting; We Are Not Always Glad When We Smile; The Bear Story. *Instrumental Works:* Bermuda Concerto.

WARNKEN, RODNEY GEORGE (ROD WARREN)   ASCAP 1976
composer, author

b Mt Vernon, NY, Feb 9, 31. Educ: Columbia Univ, BA, 52. Spec musical material for nightclubs & TV.

WARNOW, HARRY (RAYMOND SCOTT)   ASCAP 1938
composer, conductor, arranger

b New York, NY, Sept 10, 09. Educ: Juilliard. Pianist, orch of Mark Warnow; staff pianist & comp, CBS, NY. Organized quintet; made many records; wrote for & appeared in films, Hollywood, 37-38. Music dir, CBS, NY, 38-40 & 42-44; appeared on radio, ballrooms & theatres. Toured with dance band, 45; music dir, "Your Hit Parade." *Songs & Instrumental Works:* The Toy Trumpet; In an Eighteenth Century Drawing Room; Twilight in Turkey; Dinner Music for a Pack of Hungry Cannibals; Boy Scout in Switzerland; War Dance for Wooden Indians; Powerhouse; Minuet in Jazz; The Huckleberry Duck; Mountain High, Valley Low; See the Monkey; Where You Are. *Scores:* Bway Stage: Lute Song.

WARREN, DANE
See Colbert, Warren Ernest

WARREN, EDWARD   ASCAP 1959
author

b Norfolk, Va, June 19, 20; d Venice, Italy, Nov 7, 62. Educ: High sch. Writer, special material, Atlanta, Ga. To New York, staff writer, music publ co; artist & advert agency writer. Chief Collabr: Arthur Kent. *Songs:* Take Good Care of Her; One of the Lucky Ones; Adonis; Raisin Sugar Cane; Samma Kanna Wacky Brown; Tonight I Won't Be There; It's Good to Have You Back; Sugar Hill; I'm Coming Back to You.

WARREN, ELINOR REMICK   ASCAP 1936
composer

b Los Angeles, Calif, Feb 23, 06. Educ: Westlake Sch, 1 yr; Mills Col; studied piano with Kathryn Cocke, Paolo Gallico Sr, Ernesto Berumen; studied comp with Clarence Dickinson, Nadia Boulanger; Hon DM, Occidental Col. Toured US with many singers as pianist & accompanist; accompanist to Lucrezia Bori, Richard Crooks, Lawrence Tibbett & others. Orchestral works widely played by leading orchs in US & Europe, also large choral works with orch. *Songs:* Children of the Moon; We Two; Music: White Horses of the Sea; My Lady Lo-Fu; Christmas Candle. *Instrumental Works:* Orch: The Crystal Lake; Suite for Orchestra; Along the Western Shore; Symphony in One Movement. *Songs & Instrumental Works:* Choral & Orch: Abram in Egypt; The Harp Weaver; Chamber Music: Four Sonnets (soprano & string orch or with quartette); Soprano & Orch: Singing Earth; Chorus, Soloists & Orch: The Legend of King Arthur; Requiem; Good Morning, America!; The Passing of King Arthur.

WARREN, FRANK EDWARD   ASCAP 1975
composer, educator

b Norwood, Mass, Feb 27, 50. Educ: Berklee Col Music, BM(comp & music educ), 76; Univ Lowell, MM candidate in music theory & comp; studied trombone with John Coffey, comp & conducting with John Bavicchi & Jeronimus Kacinskas & music theory with Artin Arslanian. Comp, arr, music copyist & educr, 73- Started Frank E Warren Music Service & Publ Co, 80. *Songs & Instrumental Works:* Composition in One Movement, Op 5 (orch); Concerto for Tuba and Concert Band; Leeann: Composition for Solo Tuba; Sonata for Tuba and Piano, Op 1; Sonata for Unaccompanied Clarinet, Op 2; Suite for Three Tubas, Op 3; Three Inventions for Harpsichord Or Piano, Op 6; Quintet for Clarinet and Strings, Op 8c; Trio No 1, Op 10 (flute, clarinet, bassoon); Dodecahadra, Op 12 (for 12 instruments); Tuba Music, Opus 13 (comn by Barton Cummings, 80); Introduction and Canon for Eight Flute, Op 16; Kontrabass, Op 19 (unaccompanied; comn by Wolfgang Freis); Dirge in Woods (small chorus & woodwind quintet); Quatuor Chromatique (flute, oboe, clarinet, bassoon). *Scores:* Opera/Ballet: One Act, Suite for Dancers (original version for 7 instruments; second version for orch); Pathetique Pierott (pantomime for piano, oboe, mime).

WARREN, HARRY   ASCAP 1924
composer

b Brooklyn, NY, Dec 24, 1893. Educ: Self-taught. Rehearsal pianist in silent movies; song plugger for Shapiro, Bernstein Co & Remick Music, 20's; music

writer for Bway shows "Sweet and Low," 30 & "The Laugh Parade," 31; under contract, Warner Bros, 32-39, 20th Century-Fox, 40-44, Metro-Goldwyn Mayer, 44-52 & Paramount, 52-61; free-lance writer, 61- Chief Collabrs: Mort Dixon, Edgar Leslie, Ted Koehler, Al Dubin, Johnny Mercer, Mack Gordon, Arthur Freed, Ralph Blane, Ira Gershwin, Leo Robin, Jack Brooks, Sammy Cahn, Harold Adamson, Richard O Kramer. *Songs:* Music: You're My Everything; Shadow Waltz; Nagasaki; Would You Like to Take a Walk?; You're Getting to Be a Habit With Me; 42nd Street; I Only Have Eyes for You; About a Quarter to Nine; The Lullaby of Broadway; September in the Rain; Remember Me?; You Must Have Been a Beautiful Baby; Jeepers Creepers; I Know Why; Chattanooga Choo Choo; I Had the Craziest Dream; Serenade in Blue; I Found a Million Dollar Baby; The More I See You; You'll Never Know; This Heart of Mine; The Stanley Steamer; Shoes With Wings On; On the Atcheson, Topeka and Santa Fe; Zing a Little Zong; That's Amore; An Affair to Remember; I'll String Along With You; Lulu's Back in Town; I'll Sing You a Thousand Love Songs; With Plenty of Money and You; You Say the Sweetest Things, Baby; Chica Chica Boom Chic; It Happened in Sun Valley; At Last; I've Got a Gal in Kalamazoo; My Heart Tells Me; There Will Never Be Another You; I Wish I Knew; My Dream Is Yours; The Legend of Wyatt Earp.

WARREN, ROD
See Warnken, Rodney George

WARRINGTON, JOHN T
composer, author, conductor

b Collingsworth, NY, May 17, 11; d Dec, 1978. Educ: Studied piano, saxophone, age 6; Duke Univ, MA(civil engr), 33; studied harmony, theory & counterpoint, 4 yrs. Arr, WCAU-radio, Philadelphia, music dir, 42-45. Arr & musician, Jan Sabitt's "Tophatters." Cond, WABC network, New York, 45. Arr, var publ houses, New York, 46-71. Cond of concert & univ band seminars throughout US. Arr for var bands incl Tommy Dorsey, Lionel Hampton, Les Elgart, Lawrence Welk & Henry Mancini. Artistic dir, Ocean City Pops Orch, NJ. Cond, the Sound Spectrum. Chief Collabrs: Ruby Fisher. *Songs:* Music: America 200 Years Young.

WARSHAUER, FRANK   ASCAP 1945
composer, author, conductor

b Brooklyn, NY, Sept 4, 1893; d New York, NY, Nov 28, 53. Educ: Pub schs; studied music with mother & father. Played in Boys Symph Orch at age 10. Drummer with Victor Herbert, John Philip Sousa, Arthur Pryor bands; also in vaudeville, theatres & radio. Led Meyer Davis unit; toured country as cond for Rudolph Valentino. Author, "A Manual for Drums." Chief Collabrs: Mitchell Paris, Rose Warshauer (daughter). *Songs:* It Isn't Fair; Rainy Day Blues; My Cuban Dreams; Lucky Dog; Your Eyes; You're the Sweetest Girl.

WARSHAUER, ROSE   ASCAP 1963
author

b New York, NY, July 30, 17. Educ: Ann Reno Teachers Training; NY Univ; studied music with father & pvt teachers. Assoc with printing indust; was secy-treas, Lithographing Plant Weaver Orgn; pres, Club of Printing Women of NY. Chief collabr: Frank Warshauer (father). *Songs:* Gee, It's Love.

WARWICK, ROSE B
See Reitter, Rose B

WASHABAUGH, IVAN J   ASCAP 1960
composer, author, arranger

b Rochester, Pa, Oct 22, 12. Educ: Bethany Col, BA; St Francis Col, BS; Juniata Col; Wayne State Univ. Violist, Wheeling Symph, WVa; charter mem & violist, Johnstown Symph, Pa; bass violist in dance orchs; also clarinetist, saxophonist; became arr for Russ Carlyle orch, 50; social worker for state of Mich. *Songs:* Stodola Pampa; Land of Love; Everything's the Same; A Man Lives a Long, Long Time.

WASHBURN, GARY SCOTT   ASCAP 1970
composer, teacher, performer

b Tulsa, Okla, Jan 14, 46. Educ: Okla State Univ, BA, comp, Evan Copley; Univ Hawaii, MA, comp, Armand Russell & Neil McKay; Boston Univ, comp, David Del Tredici; studied with Ingolf Dahl, J Yuaga, Morton Feldman. Professional performer, 63-76. Recorded & publ, 75. Nat Endowment Arts grants, 75, 77 & 78; Norlin Fellowship, 78; MacDowell Colony, 76 & 78. Writer/arr, Motown Records, 78, now free-lance writer/arr & performer. Chief Collabrs: Kent Washburn, Terry Lupton, Sylvester Rivers. *Songs:* Come Closer to My Side; Music: Searchin' (Got to Find My Love). *Instrumental Works:* Geometric Studies. *Songs & Instrumental Works:* A Life in a Day; Lament for Sorrowed People. *Scores:* Handblceya.

WASHBURN, LALOMIE MARION (LOMI)   ASCAP 1973
composer, author, singer

b Memphis, Tenn, Aug 25, 41. Educ: Self-taught. Professional singer at age 15, nightclubs, Omaha, Nebr, also for fashion shows. Traveled appearing in nightclub circuits. Worked with bands incl Buddy Miles, New Birth, Chaka Kahn & Rufus Band, High Voltage & Lane Craft. Publisher. Chief Collabrs: Tony Maiden, Buddy Miles, Chaka Kahn, Mark Stevens, Richard Gibbs. *Songs:* Message in the Middle of the Bottom; I'm a Woman (Everybody Needs One);

It's Gonna Get a Bit Better (Try Dancing); New Account; Endless Satisfaction (Don't You Know); One Shot of Love (Straight Up No Chaser); Lyrics: At Midnight (My Love Will Lift You Up); You Don't Have a Kind Word to Say; You Gave Me Love; You've Got to Hold on to a Friend; Lead Me On.

WASHBURN, ROBERT BROOKS   ASCAP 1959
composer, professor
b Bouckville, NY, July 11, 28. Educ: State Univ NY, BS & MS; Eastman Sch Music, PhD; Aspen Music Sch, studied with Bernard Rogers, Darius Milhaud & Nadia Boulanger. Danforth Found grant, 58; Ford Found grant, 59; MacDowell Colony fel, 63; State Univ Found fel, 64; Juilliard Repertory Proj Comn, 65. Works performed by Baltimore Symph, Buffalo Philh, Denver Symph, Houston Symph, Indianapolis Symph, Nashville Symph, Oklahoma City Symph & others. Guest cond-comp at numerous cols & univs. Prof, State Univ NY, Potsdam. *Instrumental Works:* Orchestra: Symphony No 1; Excursion for Orchestra; Festive Overture; Prologue and Dance; Three Pieces for Orchestra; St Lawrence Overture; Synthesis for Orchestra; Elegy; Sinfonietta for String Orchestra; Suite for Strings; Band: Symphony for Band; Trigon; Three Diversions for Band; Impressions of Cairo; March-Opus 76; Chamber: Quartet for Strings; Quintet for Brass; Five Miniatures for Five Brasses; Concertino for Two Wind Quintets; Suite for Woodwind Quintet; Pent-Agons for Percussion; French Suite for Woodwind Trio; Chorus: Gloria for Churas and Brass Ensemble; Ode to Freedom; Olympic Festival March (orch); Spring Cantata.

WASHBURNE, JOE (COUNTRY)   ASCAP 1943
composer, author, bassist
b Houston, Tex, Dec 28, 04; d. Bassist in dance orchs. Led own orch; many radio appearances. *Songs:* One Dozen Roses; You Don't Know What Lonesome Is; Oh Mona; Everybody Calls It Swing; I Saw Esau; That's the Reason; At Last I'm First With You; We'll Sing the Old Songs.

WASHINGTON, GROVER, JR
musician
b Buffalo, NY, Dec 12, 43. Educ: Wurlitzer Sch Music. Played with musical group, Four Clefs, until 63, with Keith McAllister, 63-65. Played with var groups in Philadelphia & with Billy Cobham; with Don Gardner's Sonotones, 67-68. Worked for record distributor, 69-70. Played with Charles Earland, 71. Records for Kudo Records, CTI & Elektra Records. Leader of group, plays tenor, alto, soprano & baritone saxophones, clarinet, bass & piano. *Albums:* Mister Magic; Inner City Blues; Soul Box; Breakout; Giant Box; Blue Moses; Paradise.

WASHINGTON, NED   ASCAP 1930
author
b Scranton, Pa, Aug 15, 01; d. Educ: Tech High Sch; Charles Sumner Sch. Wrote songs for Bway musicals incl "Earl Carroll's Vanities", "Vanderbilt Revue", "Murder At the Vanities", "Blackbirds of 1934" & "Hello, Paris." Songs for "No, No, Nanette", "Little Johnny Jones", "Brazil", "The Greatest Show on Earth", "Miss Sadie Thompson" & "Gulliver's Travels." Also many title & theme songs. 12-time Acad Award nominee. App Ambassador-at-Large for Scranton, 50. Former dir, ASCAP. Chief Collabrs: Victor Young, Dimitri Tiomkin, Lester Lee, Michael Cleary, Allie Wrubel, George Duning, Max Steiner, Jimmy McHugh, Bronislaw Kaper, Walter Jurmann, Leigh Harline, Sam Stept. *Songs:* H'lo, Baby; Singin' in the Bathtub; My Impression of You; Makin' Faces at the Man in the Moon; Can't We Talk It Over?; Waltzing in a Dream; Someone Stole Gabriel's Horn; Shadows on the Window; Got the South in My Soul; Love Me Tonight; I'm Getting Sentimental Over You (Tommy Dorsey theme); I Don't Stand a Ghost of a Chance With You; I'll Be Faithful; Love Is the Thing; Any Time, Any Day, Anywhere; Stay Out of My Dreams; My Love; A Hundred Years From Today; Smoke Rings; Sweet Madness; Give Me a Heart to Sing To; Lazy Rhapsody; London on a Rainy Night; La Cucaracha; Cosi-Cosa; Breakin' in a Pair of Shoes; Tonight Will Live; I've Got No Strings; Hi-Diddle-Dee-Dee; Jiminy Cricket; When You Wish Upon a Star (Acad Award, 40); Give a Little Whistle; The Nearness of You; When I See an Elephant Fly; A Love Like This; Someday I'll Meet You Again; Stella By Starlight; Don't Call It Love; Mad About You; You're Not in My Arms Tonight; A Woman's Intuition; The Heat Is On; Hear No Evil—See No Evil; Sadie Thompson's Song; To Love Again; Strange Are the Ways of Love; The First Lady Waltz; The Fall of Love; Film title songs: Arise My Love; Reap the Wild Wind; On Green Dolphin Street; The Long Night; My Foolish Heart; The Greatest Show on Earth; High Noon (Acad Award, 52); Happy Time; So Big; Return to Paradise; Take the High Ground; Drum Beat; Hajji Baba; The High and the Mighty; Miracle in the Rain; Timberjack; Land of the Pharoahs; Wichita; Strange Lady in Town; Man From Laramie; Prize of Gold; A Cry in the Night; The Maverick Queen; Gunfight At the OK Corral; The 3:10 to Yuma; Fire Down Below; Search for Paradise; The Roots of Heaven; These 1000 Hills; Wild Is the Wind; The Unforgiven; Some Without End; Town Without Pity; Song From Advise and Consent; Circus World (Golden Globe Award, 65); Major Dundee March; Ship of Fools; TV title song: Rawhide. *Scores:* Film: Tropic Holiday; Pinocchio (Acad Award, Box-Office Blue Ribbon Award, 40); Dumbo; Hands Across the Border; Mexicana; Let's Do It Again.

WASHKILL, EDDY THOMAS   ASCAP 1959
composer
b Grodna, Lithuania, Oct 14, 21. Educ: Yale Univ; Harvard Univ. Chief Collabrs: John Condello, Sig Budd, Rose Sharpe. *Songs:* Lyrics: Lonely Man Am I; Devil Eyes; A Table for Two for One; That's the Way It Goes; Who Else But Him.

WASIL, EDWARD J   ASCAP 1962
composer, pianist
b New Boston, Pa, Mar 10, 26. Educ: High sch; studied piano & violin. Chief Collabrs: Clint Powell & Barney Allen. *Songs:* Rocket to Heaven; Needin' Your Love; Captured.

WATERS, JAMES LIPSCOMB   ASCAP 1967
composer
b Kyoto, Japan, June 11, 30. Educ: Westminster Choir Col, BM, 52, MM, 53. La Sorbonne, Paris, var certificates, dipl; Univ Rochester Eastman Sch Mus, PhD. USA, 53-55. Woolley fel, Paris, 55-57. Fac, Westminster Choir Col, 57-68; Acting dir, Kent State Univ Sch Music, 75-77, fac, 68- *Songs:* Music: War Is Kind; Three Songs of Louise Bogan (solo, orch); Song Cycle. *Instrumental Works:* Lyric Piece (violin, clarinet, piano); Fantasy (piano).

WATERS, WINSLOW
See Kosakowski, Wenceslaus Walter

WATKINS, REGINALD JORDAN   ASCAP 1977
composer, author, singer
b Kansas City, Kans, Sept 13, 54. Educ: High sch, studied with Leon A Brady, Robert Taylor; Univ Mo, Kansas City, (theory), studied piano with George Salisbury. Gospel recording artist. Chief Collabr: Teddy Grover. *Songs:* Let Us All Rejoice; Grace, Love and Peace Abide.

WATSON, GILBERT STUART   ASCAP 1956
composer, author
b Lake Forest, Ill, Dec 13, 1897; d Lake Bluff, Ill, Dec 8, 64. Educ: Lake Forest Acad. Rainbow Div, USAAF, WW I; Purple Heart. Was in investment business since 1920. Mem, Lake Forest Music Club & North Shore Jazz Asn. *Songs:* Diggin' for Old Black Coal; I Was a Fool; Gigolette; Indigo Nocturne; Our Shepherd; We're Madly for Adlai (Democratic campaign song, 56); A Brand New Man; The American Negro; A Lovely Sunday Morning; Je t'Adore.

WATSON, JOHNNY
See Kluczko, John

WATSON, WALTER ROBERT   ASCAP 1965
composer, professor, pianist
b Canton, Ohio, Oct 13, 33. Educ: Kent State Univ, 3 fels; Ohio Univ; North Tex State Univ, BFA, MFA & PhD; comp with Karl Ahrendt, Samuel Adler & Darius Milhaud. Dir, Sch Music, also prof, Kent State Univ; Steven F Austin State Univ. Consult ed, Ludwig Music Publ Co; organist-choirmaster, Christ Church, Kent; featured pianist for many commercial engagements. Grants: Rockefeller Found; George Gund Found; Bascom Little Fund; Ohio Historical Soc. Yearly citations for outstanding contributions to music, ASCAP. *Songs:* Let All the World in Every Corner Sing (unison choral); Music: Five Japanese Love Poems (SSA); Words for Sleep; A Choral Bouquet (SATB). *Instrumental Works:* American Pastiche (symph band); Recital Suite for Marimba and Piano; A Folk Fantasia (orch); Antiphony and Chorale (symph band); Sonatina for Trombone and Piano; Reflection (organ); Concerto for Guitar and Chamber Orch; Suite No 1 (brass choir); Divertimento for Flute, Harp and Bassoon; Springtide (symph band); Music for Organ and Horns. *Scores:* Opera: Deborah Simpson.

WATT, DOUGLAS   ASCAP 1957
composer, author
b New York, NY, Jan 20, 14. Educ: Cornell Univ, BA; studied music with Vittorio Giannini. Wrote songs for topical weekly radio show, "This Mad World," 37-38; joined staff, Daily News, 37, mem, Drama Dept, 39-, sr drama critic, 70- Also columnist, "Small World" & record critic prior to 70. On staff, The New Yorker mag, 46- Mem & former pres, New York Drama Critics' Circle. Silurian Award for best drama criticism, 78-79 season. *Songs & Instrumental Works:* Heaven Help Me; There's Not a Moment to Spare; After All These Years; Man; I'd Do It Again.

WATTS, CLEM
See Trace, Albert J

WATTS, GRADY   ASCAP 1942
composer, author
b Texarkana, Tex, June 30, 08. Educ: Allen Mil Acad, Tex; Univ Okla. With Glen Gray Casa Loma Orch, 12 yrs. Jazz trumpet soloist; in artist management, 45-52. Vpres sales, Chemical Co, 52-68; formed own co, 68-; pres, Chemdet Inc, 80- Writer of many works. Chief Collabrs: James Eaton, Sammy Cahn, Frank Ryerson, Bud Green, Maurice Sigler, Gene Gifford. *Songs:* Daddy's Boy; Music: Blue Champagne; Touch and Go; I Remember; If You Ever Change Your Mind; Mr Rythmn Man; You Ain't Been Living Right.

WATTS, MAYME (PENNY PRICE)   ASCAP 1966
composer, author, teacher
b Washington, DC, Nov 20, 26. Educ: Dunbar High Sch, DC; studied Negro opera, DC Morales Opera Co, New York; Wheeler Sch Music, New York, studied with Franklin Bibb. Sang with DC Morales Opera Co, then joined Lionel Hamptons Band, toured US & Europe. Formed own duo with Robert Mosley, recorded for RCA Victor, Roolette, Glory & MGM Record Cos. Chief Collabrs: Robert Mosley, George Kelly, Walter Davis, Jr. *Songs:* Alright Okeh You Win; Bridge of Sighs; Midnight Flyer (Naras Award); Papa Don't Worry About Your Daughter; Give Me Your Love.

WAVERLY, JACK   ASCAP 1946
composer, author, publisher
b New York, NY, Aug 12, 1896; d Bellmore, NY, Jan 30, 51. Educ: Pub schs. In musical comedies; then 1st Lt, Infantry, USA, WW I. Sang in "Ziegfeld Follies," 19. Wrote special material for vaudeville. Author & producer, "Oh, These Women." Became music publ, 36. *Songs:* Beneath a Starry Heaven; Don't Worry Darlin'; I'm Just a Poor Hillbilly Lookin' for a Hill; Keep That Swing; Louie Learned to Yodel; Me and My Guitar; Never Let No Worry Worry You; When Grampa Got His Whiskers Caught in the Zipper of His Shirt; God Bless Us, Everyone; Nobody Wants to Do the Dishes.

WAXMAN, DONALD   ASCAP 1964
composer, conductor, educator
b Steubenville, Ohio, Oct 29, 25. Educ: Peabody Cons; Juilliard Sch Music, BS; Guggenheim fel; cond of own works; mem concert piano duo with wife; lectr at cols & music workshops; dir pvt music sch, Nyack, NY.

WAXMAN, FRANZ   ASCAP 1941
composer, conductor
b Koenigsbutte, Ger, Dec 24, 06; d Los Angeles, Calif, Feb 24, 67. To US, 34. Educ: Studied music, Berlin, Dresden. Mem: AKM, Austrian Performing Right Soc; Gema, Int Soc of Arts & Letters; hon mem, The Mahler Soc. Rec'd Cross of Merit from Federal Repub of WGer & doctorate from Columbia Col. Comp & music dir for films. Founder & musical dir, Los Angeles Int Music Fest, 47-66. *Songs & Instrumental Works:* Sinfonietta for Timpani, Strings; Symphonic Fantasy on A Mighty Fortress Is My God; Elegy for Strings; The Charm Bracelet (five pieces for piano); Goyana (four sketches for piano & string orch); Mountains Beyond the Moon; Joshua (dramatic oratorio); The Song of Terezin (song cycle); Katsumi Love Theme; Theme From Peyton Place; The Wishing Star; Allein in Einer Grossen Stadt (Alone in a Big City); Suite (from A Place in the Sun); The Carmen Fantasy (violin & orch). *Scores:* Film Background: Rebecca; The Bride of Frankenstein; Dr Jekyll and Mr Hyde; To Have and Have Not; Prince Valiant; Elephant Walk; The Paradine Case; Sunset Boulevard (Acad Award, 50); A Place in the Sun (Acad Award, 51); Rear Window; Objective Burma!; Crime in the Streets; Love in the Afternoon; Peyton Place; Sayonara; The Spirit of St Louis; The Nun's Story; Cimarron; The Story of Ruth; Hemingway's Adventures of a Young Man; Taras Bulba; Lost Command.

WAYMAN, EUNICE (NINA SIMONE)   ASCAP 1959
composer, author, singer
b Tryon, SC, Feb 21, 33. Educ: Juilliard; Curtis Inst Music. Accompanist to singers, also singer & pianist. Sung & played in concerts throughout US. Made many records; appeared on TV & in nightclubs. *Songs:* Central Park Blues; Return Home; African Mailman; If You Knew; Mississippi Goddam; Sugar in My Bowl; Blackbird; Children Go Where I Send You; Flo Me La; Nina's Blues; Go Limp.

WAYNE, ALAN
See Johnson, Albertus Wayne

WAYNE, DOROTHY   ASCAP 1958
composer, author, writer
b New York, NY. Wrote spec material for nightclub & record performers, also wrote TV & features; actress, singer. Chief Collabrs: Ray Rasch, Richard Loring, Ben Weisman. *Songs:* Lyrics: The Night Has a Thousand Eyes (Gold Record); When You've Laughed All Your Laughter; Warm Blue Stream; Massachusetts (official state song). *Scores:* Musical shows: I'm With You; I'm Telling You; TV: Wild Is Love; A Beautiful Evening; Hundreds and Thousands of Girls; Beggar for the Blues; That Tiny World We Knew; I Am a Rainbow; World of No Return; Tell Her in the Morning; Are You Disenchanted. *Albums:* Wild Is Love (12 songs; nominated for Grammy).

WAYNE, DWIGHT
See Batteau, Dwight Wayne, Jr

WAYNE, MABEL   ASCAP 1928
composer, singer, pianist
b Brooklyn, NY; d. Educ: Pvt music study, Switz; NY Sch Music. Singer, pianist & dancer in vaudeville. Wrote songs for films incl "The King of Jazz." Chief Collabrs: L Wolfe Gilbert, Kim Gannon, Billy Rose, Mitchell Parish, Sam Lewis, Joe Young, Al Lewis. *Songs:* Don't Wake Me Up, Let Me Dream; In a Little Spanish Town; Ramona; Chiquita; It Happened in Monterey; Little Man You've Had a Busy Day; His Majesty the Baby; (As Long As You're Not in Love With Anyone Else) Why Don't You Fall in Love With Me?; It Happened in Hawaii;

I Understand; Rose Ann of Charing Cross; Language of Love; A Dreamer's Holiday; If I Didn't Already Love You, Baby.

WAYNE, SID   ASCAP 1951
composer, author, director
b New York, NY, Jan 26, 23. Educ: High sch. Served in 82nd Air Borne Div, then Spec Services. Wrote spec material for USAAF shows. Entertainer in supper clubs throughout US; on staff, music publ. Wrote songs for Bway musicals incl "Ziegfeld Follies" & "Thirteen Daughters." With TV shows incl Victor Borge, Peter Lind Hayes & Mary Healy, "Ford Star Revue." Songs for films incl "G I Blues", "From Hell to Borneo" & "Cleopatra." Music dir, Heatter-Quigley Productions, CBS-TV, Calif. DJ, radio sta KBLA, Los Angeles, Calif. Comedy writer. Chief Collabrs: Alex North, George Duning, Jerry Livingston, Sherman Edwards, Ben Weisman, Hal David, Robert Allen, Phil Springer, Robert O Ragland, Rob Walsh, Arlon Ober, Joe Sherman, Domenico Modugno, Armando Manzanero, Udo Jergens, James Last. *Songs:* I'm Gonna' Knock on Your Door (ASCAP Country Award); Which Way Did My Heart Go?; Lyrics: See You in September; Two Different Worlds; Mangos; My Love for You; First Anniversary; Winner Take All; 99 Years (In the Penitentiary); A World of Love; Knock on Wood; Anything Can Happen Mambo; The Fish; Stolen Moments; Peaches and Cream; The Language of Love; Let It Rain; It's Only The Beginning; She Serves a Nice Cup of Tea; Broadway At Basin Street; Tears to Burn; The Cool School; No Hard Feelings; Somebody; There Once Was a Beautiful; Nobody Home; He Played a Steel Guitar; Ooo-Poppa'-Doo; Just Once in a Lifetime; The Lonely World; Bargain With the Devil; The World of the Blues; Beyond Tomorrow; A New World Waiting; Pretty People; It's Allright; The Seed of Our Love; It's My Turn; Got a Feeling; Wild Love; When the Boys Meet the Girls; Mail Call; Blue Lou; Chicken Walk; Elvis: Flaming Star; I Need Your Love Tonight; Fun in Acapulco; Tonight's So Right for Love; What's She Really Like?; Frankfurt Special; Big Boots; Didja' Ever?; Clambake; Happy Ending; What a Wonderful Life; How Can You Lose? (What You Never Had); Spinout; I'll Be Back; Hard Luck; Who Are You?; Chesay; Frankie and Johnny; Slowly But Surely; He's Your Uncle (Not Your Dad); There's So Much World to See; It Won't Be Long; It's Carnival Time; Stay Away Joe; Dominick; I'll Never Know; Cross My Heart (And Hope to Die); Do the Clam; Easy Come-Easy Go; We Call on Him; All I Needed Was the Rain; Lover Doll; A Dog's Life; It's Impossible (ASCAP Song of the Yr).

WEATHERINGTON, RANDALL L   ASCAP 1978
composer, author, performer
b Burlington, Iowa, Feb 6, 49. Educ: Blair Bus Col; self taught musician & performer. Own band, 66-69, composed & performed own works; recording artist. Comp film "Shutter Showdown." *Songs:* Two of a Kind. *Instrumental Works:* Pickin' Pictures.

WEATHERLY, JAMES DEXTER
composer, singer
b Pontotoc, Miss, Mar 17, 43. Educ: Pontotoc Elem, Jr High & High Schs; Univ Miss. Mem, Miss Entertainers Hall of Fame, 79. Recording artist, Elektra Records. *Songs:* Midnight Train to Georgia; Neither One of Us (Wants to Be the First to Say Goodbye); You're the Best Thing That Ever Happened to Me; The Need to Be; Where Do I Put Her Memory; Roses and Love Songs; Like Old Times Again; This Is a Love Song; All That Keeps Me Going; Between Her Goodbye and My Hello.

WEATHERS, ROSCOE   ASCAP 1960
composer, author, flutist
b Clarksdale, Miss, June 1, 25; d Apr 18, 76. With Fletcher Henderson Orch; toured Europe with Archie Savage show as featured flutist. Flutist & saxophonist, Jay McShann & Charlie Parker Orchs. Chief Collabrs: Sheila Smith Aiches, Bill Johnson. *Songs & Instrumental Works:* Blue Cha Cha; Forever Yours; Gods Side and Free; Sheila's Dream; Dandelion Wine; Bob White Bird; Flute Polka (merry-go-round song), Root Flute; Penny Whistle; Lost and Lonesome Ski.

WEAVER, DENNIS   ASCAP 1971
composer, actor
b Joplin, Mo, June 4, 24. Educ: Univ Okla, BFA; Actors Studio, New York. Actor in TV Series: "Gunsmoke", "Kentucky Jones", "Gentle Ben", "McCloud" & "Stone." Actor in TV movies: "Duel", "Intimate Strangers", "Ishi", "Centennial", "Pearl", "Amber Waves" & "The Ordeal of Dr Mudd." Sang on TV shows, "Hee-Haw", "Dinah Shore Show" & "Johnny Carson." Chief Collabrs: Nancy Adams, Alan Wayne. *Songs:* Hollywood Freeway; Eyes of Misty Blue; Work Thru My Hands, Lord; Amber Waves. *Scores:* TV Series: Stone (theme).

WEAVER, MARION   ASCAP 1953
composer, author, pianist
b Marietta, Pa, Dec 18, 02. Educ: Temple Univ Music Sch, studied organ & voice; studied piano with S Becker Von Grabill. Started playing for silent movies at age 14; organist & pianist in var Eastern Pa cities in silent picture era for Stanley Co of Philadelphia; cocktail pianist & mem, Society Trio, in later yrs. Chief Collabrs: William Brooker, Roma Greth, Gordon M Eby, Dale White. *Songs:* Music: I Walked Into the Garden (religious hymn); One Star. *Scores:* Plays: Plain Betsy (musical of Pa Dutch); Music in the Night.

WEAVER, MARY WATSON   ASCAP 1952
composer, author, teacher
b Kansas City, Mo, Jan 16, 03. Educ: Bawtew Sch, Kansas City; Smith Col; Ottawa Univ, BM, BA, 46; Curtis Inst of Music; studied comp with Rosario Scalero & Deems Taylor, piano with Benno Moweitrits, Wanda Landowska, Isabelle Vengerera & Harold Bauer. Pianist, poet & painter. Performer, 23-30; gave recitals & lect-recitals, 27-51. Has done scripts for Am Sch of Air, CBS, 33. Taught piano at Kansas City Univ, 43-57, Manhattan Sch of Music, 57-70. Chief Collabr: Powell Weaver (husband). *Songs:* Cradle Song; The Heart of Heaven; Choral: All Weary Men, Kneel Down; When Jesus Lay by Mary's Side; Like Doves Descending; On the Eve of First Christmas; Rise Up All Men.

WEAVER, POWELL   ASCAP 1939
composer, organist, pianist
b Clearfield, Pa, June 10, 1890; d Kansas City, Mo, Dec 22, 51. Educ: Juilliard, studied with Percy Goetschius & Gaston Dethier; also studied with Ottorino Respighi & Pietro Yon. Gave organ recitals in Italy; played in St Peter's. On return to US, music dir, Grand Avenue Temple, B'nai Jehudah Temple, Kansas City. Accompanist, Richard Crooks, Johanna Gadski & Grete Stuckgold. Gave concerts throughout Mid West & South. Head music dept, Ottawa Univ, 7 yrs. Organist & choir dir, First Baptist Church, Kansas City, 37-51. Mem, Am Guild Organists. Chief Collabr: Mary Weaver (wife). *Songs:* Moon-Marketing; The Abbot of Derry; The Night Will Never Stay; Windy Weather; Choral: Spirit of God; O God, Our Help in Ages Past. *Instrumental Works:* The Vagabond (symph poem); Fugue for Strings; Sand Dune Crane; Ballet Suite; B'nai Jehudah Service; Organ: Copper Country Sketches; The Squirrel; Bell Benedictus; Cuckoo; Exultation.

WEBB, ARTHUR T   ASCAP 1977
composer, recording artist, teacher
b Philadelphia, Pa, Sept 24, 50. Educ: Overbrook High Sch; Philadelphia Musical Acad; studied flute with John Wummer, theory & comp with Michael Smolanoff & Andrew Rudin, comp with Richard Castiglione. Performed in concert with such artists as Hubert Laws, Freddie Hubbard, Ray Barretto & Norman Connors; recorded albums with many artists. Has written & arr music for both small & large ens. Comp music in variety of styles & idioms using contemporary harmonies & melodic themes. Chief Collabrs: Louis Small, John Lee, Eddie Martinez. *Instrumental Works:* Flute Magic; A Little Travelling Music, Please!; Blues in F Sharp; Cause You Nevva Know; (Good) Bad Times. *Albums:* Mr Flute; Love Eyes.

WEBB, JIMMY LAYNE   ASCAP 1968
composer, author, performer
b Elk City, Okla, Aug 15, 46. *Songs:* Mac Arthur Park; Wichita Lineman; By the Time I Get to Phoenix; Up, Up and Away; The Worst That Could Happen; All I Know; Didn't We; Galveston; If You See Me Getting Smaller; The Moon Is a Harsh Mistress; Highwayman. *Instrumental Works:* Gloryell.

WEBB, KENNETH   ASCAP 1914
author, director
b New York, NY, Oct 16, 1885; d Hollywood, Calif, Mar 5, 66. Educ: Collegiate Sch; Columbia Univ. Wrote & dir, Varsity Shows, Columbia Univ. Wrote spec material for vaudeville & revues. Scenarist & dir early films; writer, ed & dir, "Cavalcade of America"; "The Heart of Julia Blake"; "Theatre of Today." Playwright: "One of the Family"; "Zombie"; "Birdie"; "Welcome to Glory"; co-librettist, "Gay Divorce." Dir TV commercials; with advert agency, Hollywood. Mem, Authors League of Am (secy, 36-37); Dramatists Guild (coun, 33-37); founder & first pres, Radio Writers Guild; Motion Pictures Directors Asn (Eastern Div pres, 23-24). Chief Collabrs: Roy Webb (brother), Harold Levey. *Songs:* You and Me and You; Pierrot's Honeymoon; Love, It Is Springtime; Tit for Tat; Over the Sea; Fight for Freedom; Why Be Afraid of Goodbye?; Holding Hands. *Instrumental Works:* The Pirate Prince (radio operetta). *Scores:* Stage: The Houseboat on the Styx.

WEBB, NORMA FAYE   ASCAP 1976
composer, author, teacher
b Yuma, Ariz, May 30, 32. Educ: Sacramento State Univ, BE, 57; Azusa Pacific Col, MA, 73. Teacher, 57-; author/comp, 76- *Songs:* Put a Little Sunshine Into Your Heart; Crossroads of Love; All of the Time; Let's Start All Over Again; Forever Is a Long, Long Time.

WEBB, ROY   ASCAP 1914
composer, conductor
b New York, NY, Oct 3, 1888. Educ: Columbia Univ. Wrote varsity shows, vaudeville sketches & musicals; supvr in early Hollywood musicals; music dir, film cos. Charter mem, ASCAP. Chief Collabrs: Kenneth Webb (brother), Sylvio Hein. *Songs:* Roar, Lion, Roar (Columbia Univ; Alumni Fedn of Col Prize); Pierrot's Honeymoon; You and Me and You; Love, It Is Springtime; Tit for Tat; Over the Sea; When Dreams Come True; My Dream Girl. *Scores:* Film Background: I Remember Mama; My Favorite Wife; Quality Street; I Married a Witch; Joan of Paris; The Fallen Sparrow; Notorious; Spiral Staircase; The Enchanted Cottage; Seventh Cross; Mr Lucky; Kitty Foyle (Nat Fedn Music Clubs Award); Bill of Divorcement; Stage Door; Alice Adams; The Track of the Cat; Teacher's Pet; Marty.

WEBER, EDWIN J   ASCAP 1945
composer, conductor, publisher
b New York, NY, Aug 24, 1893; d. Educ: High sch. Pianist for films; then salesman. Pianist, music dir for Eva Tanguay, 9 yrs; also in vaudeville. Owned music publ firm, restaurant & poultry farm. Radio dir, 42; then gen mgr of radio show. *Songs:* Nobody Lied; I Love Me; Make 'Em Laugh; I'm a Little Butterfly; I'm Shedding Tears Over You; Suppose Nobody Cared; Just Beyond the Blue; Telling the World We're in Love.

WEBER, WILHELMINE FRANCES   ASCAP 1958
composer, author
b Chicago, Ill, Feb 15, 16. Educ: Col, BS. Chief Collabr: James MacDonald. *Songs:* The Harbor Bell; East of West Berlin.

WEBMAN, HAROLD   ASCAP 1971
author, producer, publisher
b Brooklyn, NY. Educ: Brooklyn Col. Ed, Down Beat Mag, 2 yrs. Record producer for Decca Records. Music publ, 57- *Songs:* Child's Play; Mighty Good; First Impression; Sonic Boom; Got Me Goin'.

WEBSTER, BENJAMIN FRANCIS   ASCAP 1962
composer, saxophonist
b Kansas City, Mo, Feb 27, 09; d. Began as pianist in band, Enid, Okla; then with Dutch Campbell Orch. Tenor saxophonist in orchs incl Gene Coy, Jap Allen, Blanche Calloway, Andy Kirk, Benny Moten, Benny Carter, Fletcher Henderson, Willie Bryant, Cab Calloway & Stuff Smith. Mem, Duke Ellington Orch, 39-43 & 48. Led own group; made many records. *Songs & Instrumental Works:* The Horn; Better Go; Did You Call Her Today?; See You At the Fair.

WEBSTER, PAUL FRANCIS   ASCAP 1932
author
b New York, NY, Dec 20, 07. Educ: Cornell Univ; NY Univ. Was sailor, dance instr before becoming song writer. To Hollywood, 35; under contract to 20th Century Fox to write for Shirley Temple; then free-lance. Songs for films incl "Presenting Lily Mars", "Johnny Angel", "The Great Caruso", "Because You're Mine", "Battle Cry", "The Student Prince", "55 Days At Peking." Originated story "Nora Prentiss." Songs for Bway revue "Alive and Kicking." Chief Collabrs: Sammy Fain, Hoagy Carmichael, Duke Ellington, Harry Revel, Rudolf Friml, Lew Pollack, Jerry Livingston, John Jacob Loeb, Max Steiner, Alfred Newman, Bronislaw Kaper, Frank Churchill, Franz Waxman, Dimitri Tiomkin. *Songs:* Masquerade; My Moonlight Madonna; Reflections in the Water; Two Cigarettes in the Dark; Rainbow on the River; The Lamplighter's Serenade; Jump for Joy; I Got It Bad and That Ain't Good; Baltimore Oriole; Doctor, Lawyer, Indian Chief; Memphis in June; Merry Christmas Polka; Watermelon Weather; Black Coffee; You Was; How It Lies, How It Lies, How It Lies; The Loveliest Night of the Year; Vilia; Merry Widow Waltz; Secret Love (Acad Award, 53); I Speak to the Stars; I'll Walk With God; Honey Babe; Padre; I Have the Love; A Very Precious Love; I'll Remember Tonight; The Twelfth of Never; Like Young; Green Leaves of Summer; I'm Just a Little Sparrow; My Little Lost Girl; Follow Me; There's Never Been Anyone Else But You; So Little Time; The Mood I'm In; The Shadow of Your Smile (Acad & Grammy Awards, 65); A Time for Love; Who's Afraid?; Somewhere My Love; Film title songs: How Green Was My Valley; Theme From Quo Vadis; Invitation; Love Is a Many-Splendored Thing (Acad Award, 55; Dipl di Benemeranza, Hall of Artists, Nice, France; Augusto Messinese Gold Award, Italy); Giant; Anastasia; Friendly Persuasion; Boy on a Dolphin; The Song of Raintree County; The Gift of Love; A Certain Smile; April Love; Return to Peyton Place (theme); Rio Bravo; Imitation of Life; Green Mansions; Cimarron; The Guns of Navarone; El Cid (theme); The Alamo; Tender Is the Night; The Scarlet Bird; Joy in the Morning; A World That Never Was. TV title songs for "Maverick", "Sugarfoot" & "Spider Man." The Children's Music Box (collection). *Scores:* Bway: Christine; Stage: Casino de Paree; Jump for Joy; Windy City; My LA; Films: Minstrel Man; Hit the Ice; Calamity Jane; Rose Marie; The Merry Widow; Lucky Me; Mardi Gras; April Love.

WECHTER, CECILE SCHROEDER (CISSY)   ASCAP 1954
lyricist
b Los Angeles, Calif, June 3, 36. Educ: Calif State Univ, Northridge, BA(English). Has written songs with husband, Julius Wechter, also wrote music & lyrics for an adaptation of a novel. Chief Collabrs: Julius Wechter, Bud Coleman, Milt Rogers, Martin Denny. *Songs:* Lyrics: Spanish Flea; The Nicest Things Happen; Wall Street Rag; Fresh Air; Think of Me.

WECHTER, JULIUS L   ASCAP 1957
composer
b Chicago, Ill, May 10, 35. Educ: Los Angeles City Col; studies with Bob MacDonald. Played mallets & perc, Martin Denny Group, 57-62; recorded & comp, Herb Alpert, 62-; traveled, 75-77. Leader, arr & comp, Baja Marimba Band, 64-; free lance studio work during all of above yrs. Chief Collabrs: Cissy Wechter & Bob Florence. *Songs:* Music: Spanish Flea; Brasilia; Up Cherry Street; Coney Island; Fowl Play. *Scores:* Film/TV: Midnight Madness.

WEEDEN, PAUL WINSTON   ASCAP 1978
composer, author, teacher
b Indianapolis, Ind, Jan 7, 23. Recording artist, RCA, Prestige, Riverside, Roost & Chess. *Songs & Instrumental Works:* Going to See Rickey; After While; Light As a Feather Bed; Getting Out; Too Young to Be Old; Pete and Repeat; Back Track; My Beautiful Lady; God; Banking Wes; Carl's Cool; Lille Klumpen Min; Slick Dude; Waltz for My Children.

WEEKS, ANSON   ASCAP 1960
composer, author, conductor
b Oakland, Calif, Feb 14, 1896; d Sacramento, Calif, Feb 2, 69. Educ: High sch. Orch leader in hotels throughout US, incl Mark Hopkins, Palace, San Francisco, St Regis, New York. Led orch, Lucky Strike radio prog, 32-33. *Songs:* I'm Sorry Dear; I'm Writing You This Little Melody (theme); That Same Old Dream; Little Senorita; We'll Get a Bang Out of Life.

WEEKS, HAROLD TAYLOR   ASCAP 1922
composer, author
b Eagle Grove, Iowa, Mar 28, 1893; d Seattle, Wash, Jan 7, 67. Educ: Univ Wash. Owner, first music show, Seattle, 17. Chief Collabrs: Oliver Wallace, Albert Hay Malotte, Arthur Freed. *Songs:* Hindustan; Chong; Cairo; Siren of a Southern Sea; Dear Old Home; Kentucky Home; Can't You Love Me Like You Do in My Dreams?; Melancholy Moon; Red River Valley; Tropical Moonlight; Beautiful Summer Night; Fuzzy Wuzzy Bird.

WEEKS, PAUL   ASCAP 1963
composer, arranger, educator
b Brookfield, Mo, Dec 26, 1895. Educ: Dana Musical Inst, Ohio, BMus, 21. Taught instrumental music, Ohio & Minn pub schs, 10 yrs. Theater work, playing, arr & comp, 13 yrs; playing & arr, Duluth Symph Orch; playing, arr & composing, radio staff orch WEBC, Minn. Song writer for var motion pictures & commercials. *Songs & Instrumental Works:* Grid-Iron March Book; Gypsy Bride.

WEEKS, RICARDO   ASCAP 1958
author
b Puerto Rico, Feb 7, 21. To US, 25. Poems publ in newspapers, mags & anthologies. Vols of poems, "Freedom's Soldier" & "According to the Sonneteer." Chief Collabrs: Melvin Anderson, Al De Vito, Hellen Barnes. *Songs:* I Wonder Why; I Can't Believe; I Still Love You; Listen to the Sleigh Bells.

WEEKS, RICHARD HARRY   ASCAP 1976
composer, music teacher
b Minneapolis, Minn, Nov 21, 49. Educ: Augustana Col, BA, 71; Eastman Sch Music, MM, 76. Guest cond, Youth Music Fest, Kennedy Ctr, 76; dir orchs, Swampscott Pub Schs, Mass. Numerous commissions. *Songs:* Songs of a Joyous Man. *Instrumental Works:* Shades of Agora; The Bird Book; Mime.

WEEKS, WILLIAM J   ASCAP 1956
composer, author
b Brooklyn, NY, Jan 27, 01; d St Petersburg, Fla, Sept 8, 72. Educ: Pub schs. Owned taverns, St Petersburg, 52-61. Chief Collabrs: Sylvester Gillis, Robert Godfrey. *Songs:* Every Christmas Morning; Tip Your Hat to Pat O'Reilly; When You Listen to a Dixieland Band; Let's Lift Off Tomorrow.

WEEMS, CLINTON E   ASCAP 1961
composer, author
b Media, Pa, Dec 7, 25. Educ: Am Univ. Operates dry-cleaning store. *Songs:* Mamboitis.

WEEMS, TED   ASCAP 1946
composer, conductor
b Pitcairn, Pa, Sept 26, 01; d Tulsa, Okla, May 6, 63. Educ: Univ Pa. Organized orch & appeared in hotels, ballrooms & nightclubs throughout US. WW II, USMC. *Songs:* The Martins and the Coys; The One-Man Band; The Toyland Band; Jig Time; Three Shif'less Skonks.

WEERTZ, LOUIS JACOB (ROGER WILLIAMS)   ASCAP 1955
composer, arranger, pianist
b Omaha, Nebr. Educ: Drake Univ; Idaho State Univ; Juilliard Sch Music, Lenny Tristano & Teddy Wilson. Professional pianist, 54-

WEHR, DAVID A   ASCAP 1963
composer, educator, conductor
b Mt Vernon, NY, Jan 21, 34. Educ: Danbury High Sch; Miami Univ, Ohio; Westminster Choir Col, BM, 56, MM, 57; Univ Miami, Fla, PhD, 71; studied organ with Alexander McCurdy, 54-57, conducting with J F Williamson, Frederick Fennell, comp with David York, Warren Martin, Clifton Williams, Alfred Reed, voice with Herbert Patz, Walter Johnson & Daniel Harris. Organist, choirmaster & carillonneur, Cathedral of the Rockies, Boise, Idaho, 58-68. Dir choral activities, Eastern Ky Univ, 71-79, Houston Baptist Univ, 79-; assoc cond, Houston Symph Chorale, 79-; author of 55 publ works. Distinguished Alumni Award, Westminster Choir Col, 66, ASCAP Awards, 66- *Songs:* Music: Prophet Unwilling (oratorio); God Is Working His Purpose Out;

Hymn of Consecration; Anything Happens. *Instrumental Works:* Processional; Bellstrations.

WEIDENAAR, REYNOLD   ASCAP 1969
composer, filmmaker, video artist
b East Grand Rapids, Mich, Sept 25, 45. Educ: Studied comp with Donald Erb, 70-73; Cleveland Inst Music, Ohio, BM, 73; NY Univ, MA, 80. Ed, Electronic Music Review; dir, Electronic Music Studio, Cleveland Inst Music; grants from Ohio Arts Council, Bascom Little Fund, Meet the Comp, Inc; artist residencies, ZBS Studio, Exp TV Ctr. Awards, Sonavera Int Tape Music Competition, NY Univ Film Fest, Int Film & TV Fest NY, NY Filmmakers' Exposition, Int Gaudeamus Music Week, Los Angeles Int Film Exposition, Fountain Valley Int Film Fest, Sinking Creek Film Celebration. Instr, NY Univ. *Instrumental Works:* The Tinsel Chicken Coop; Electric Air; Fanfare; Drive; Sextet; Out of C; Wiener; The Ides of April; Deja Vu, Where Are You?; Cicada; Twilight Flight; Sweet Jesus and the Honkies; Simple Ceremony; Crescent Close Harmony; Close Harmony; Cadenza; Pathways I; Pathways II. *Scores:* Film/TV: Chain Chicken; Wavelines I; Wavelines II; How to Protect Your Home From Frequency Modulation!; Night of the Egg; Kahlua—The Motion Picture; Disc-O-Chicken; Frankie, the Keener Wiener; Pathways III—Visual-Musical Variations.

WEIDLER, WARNER ALFRED (WARNER WILDER)   ASCAP 1960
composer, author, producer
b Hamburg, Ger, June 16, 35. Educ: Studied saxophone & flute with Merle Johnson; studied comp, cond & arr with Robert Hale; studied with Mickey Gillett. Appeared on "Ed Sullivan Show." Entertainer with bros throughout US in many top hotels, 5 yrs. Currently, producer. *Songs:* Love Means You Never Have to Say You're Sorry; I Do All My Crying in the Rain; Today Is the First Day of the Rest of My Life; Girl You Make It Happen; Anything Can Happen; Lillian.

WEIDMANN, JOHN DAVID   ASCAP 1970
composer, author, singer
b Neudek near Karlsbad, Czech, July 14, 27. Educ: Studied piano & violin with Proff Wolff, Prague, voice with Leo Schwartz, Arg, Matilda De Lupka, Arg, M Martin, US & Nandor Domokos, US, comp with Carlos Suffern, Arg. With Sch of Opera at Theatre Colon, Buenos Aires, Arg. Mem, Soc Arg de Autores y Comp de Musica, Arg. Actor, The Comedy, Arg. Mem, Int Opera Ens, Los Angeles. Comp performed in nightclubs & by choirs. Chief Collabrs: Oscar Alberto Lagos, Juan Bruzau, Emil Fuchs, Barbara Cunningham. *Songs:* I've Been Away Too Long; Music: Palermo Antiguo; Sonatina Cristalina; Land Born of Freedom; Can You Tell If It's Love?

WEIDT, A J   ASCAP 1930
composer, conductor, teacher
b Buffalo, NY, Feb 15, 1866; d Middletown, NJ, Dec 9, 45. Educ: Pub schs; pvt violin study. Orch cond, Newark, NJ; also teacher of string instruments. *Songs & Instrumental Works:* Northern Lights; Gloriana; El Dorado; Jolly New Yorker; Here They Come; Junior High; Eventide.

WEIGLE, CHARLES F   ASCAP 1957
composer, evangelist, singer
b Lafayette, Ind, Nov 20, 1871; d Chattanooga, Tenn, Dec 3, 66. Educ: Cincinnati Cons. Cond gospel meetings throughout US. Mgr, Weigle Music Ctr Building, Chattanooga, Tenn. Mem, Int Asn of Evangelists. *Songs:* Sacred: No One Ever Cared for Me Like Jesus; I Have Found a Hiding Place; A Garden of Roses; Wondrous Grace Hath Blessed My Soul; I'm Glad I Came Home.

WEIL, MILTON   ASCAP 1938
author
b Chicago, Ill, Mar 19, 1888; d Chicago, Dec 31, 37. Educ: High sch. Music publisher. *Songs:* Just a Dream of You Dear; I'd Like to Be in Tennessee; My Alabama Rose; An Old Fashioned Rose My Mother; There's Only One Girl Like You; Longing for You; Somewhere a Heart Is Breaking; Rose of My Heart; Teresa Be Mine; Every Girl I Get the Other Fellow Steals; Oh! You! Jeffries; Since You Called Me Sweetheart; When I Dream in Dreamland; Mothers Lullaby; Just a Night in Dreamland.

WEILL, IRVING   ASCAP 1926
author, arranger
b New York, NY, Oct 2, 1894. Educ: New York Pub Schs; DeWitt Clinton High Sch; NY Univ, BA(music). Served, from Pvt to Capt, World War I; wrote, produced & staged amateur shows for officers & enlisted men. Joined music publ co, New York. Music dir for vocalists, NBC, then CBS. Writer, commercial jingles, radio & TV, 50-60. Retired, 70. Chief Collabrs: Jimmy McHugh, Al Dubin, Sammy Fain, J Keirn Brennen, Paul Cunningham, Alex Gerber. *Songs:* Tripoli (On the Shores of Tripoli); Keep on Croonin' a Tune; Honeymoon Time; Rose of Romany; I Walk With God; How Could You; Whispering Pines; Surrounded By Dixieland.

WEILL, KURT   ASCAP 1939
composer
b Dessau, Ger, Mar 2, 00; d New York, NY, Apr 3, 50. To US, 35. Educ: Studied music with Albert Bing, Humperdinck, Krasselt & Busoni. At 15, choral dir &

opera co accompanist, Dessau. Cond, Lüdenschied, Westphalia, 19-20. To Berlin, 21. Dir, Playwrights' Co, 50. Chief Collabrs: Bert Brecht, Paul Green, Maxwell Anderson, Ira Gershwin, Ogden Nash, Langston Hughes, Alan Jay Lerner, Arnold Sundgaard, Marc Blitzstein. *Songs & Instrumental Works:* Mack the Knife; Army Song; Barbara Song; Pirate Jenny; Alabama Song; Surabaya Jenny; Bilbao Song; Sailor's Tango; J'attends un Navire; To Love You and to Lose You; O Heart of Love; On the Rio Grande; September Song; There's Nowhere to Go But Up; It Never Was You; The Saga of Jenny; One Life to Live; My Ship; Girl of the Moment; This Is New; The Princess of Pure Delight; Tschaikowsky; West Wind; One Touch of Venus; I'm a Stranger Here Myself; Speak Low; Foolish Heart; That's Him; Wooden Wedding; Sing Me Not a Ballad; Somehow I Never Could Believe; Lonely House; Wouldn't You Like to Be on Broadway?; What Good Would the Moon Be?; Moon-Faced, Starry-Eyed; Remember That I Care; We'll Go Away Together; A Boy Like You; Green-Up Time; Here I'll Stay; Susan's Dream; Economics; Train to Johannesburg; Lost in the Stars; Stay Well; Trouble Man; Thousands of Miles; Cry, the Beloved Country; Der Lindberghflug (oratorio); Der Neue Orpheus (cantata); Berliner Requiem (cantata); Frauentanz (song cycle); String Quartet; Violin Concerto; 3 Walt Whitman Songs; 2 symphonies. *Scores:* Stage: Das Kleine Mahagonny (Ger; later became Aufstieg und Fall der Stadt Mahagonny); Die Dreigroschenoper (Ger; also produced in New York as The Threepenny Opera); Happy End (Ger); Marie Galante (Paris); Bway Stage: Johnny Johnson; Knickerbocker Holiday; Lady in the Dark; One Touch of Venus; The Firebrand of Florence; Street Scene; Love Life; Lost in the Stars; for schs, Down in the Valley; Stage Background: The Eternal Road (Bway); Railroads on Parade (New York World's Fair, 39); Film: Where Do We Go From Here?; Opera: Der Protagonist; Royal Palace; Der Jasager; Die Burgschaft; Der Silbersee; Ballet: Die Zaubernacht; 7 Deadly Sins.

WEILLE, F BLAIR   ASCAP 1964
composer, administrator
b Boston, Mass, Nov 9, 30. Educ: Harvard Col, BA, 53, studied with Walter Piston & A T Merritt; Columbia Univ, MA, 57, studied with Jack Beeson & Otto Luening. In phonograph record indust, 59- Mem bd of trustees, Comp Recordings, Inc, 71-, pres, 76- Chief Collabrs: Bruce Williamson, Eben Keyes, Rosalie Calabrese. *Songs:* Music: Minneapolis—St Paul. *Instrumental Works:* Suite for Brass Quintet; Annabel Lee (baritone, chamber orch); also five songs for piano & voice.

WEINBERG, BETSY L   ASCAP 1964
composer, author
b New York, NY, Feb 22, 26. Educ: Staley Col; Boston Univ. Reporter, Assoc Press, Boston Bur; asst, News Off, Harvard Univ; had own TV show, Columbia, SC. Chief Collabr: Harry Stride.

WEINBERG, CHARLES (CHARLES WYNN)   ASCAP 1929
composer, author, conductor
b New York, NY, Sept 19, 1889; d Paterson, NJ, Nov 11, 55. Educ: Pub schs. Had first song publ at age 12. Dir & accompanist in vaudeville. Pioneer motion-picture pianist, with road show Annette Kellerman picture "Neptune's Daughter." Music dir, Richard Carle productions. Had own publ firm. Comp theme songs, Pathe Pictures. *Songs:* My Annapolis; Love, All I Want Is Love; Swanee River Melody; In a Spanish Garden; I'm a Bad Boy; Don't Let Forever Last Only a Day; The Girl Behind the Man Behind the Gun; Don't Ask Me Why; Learn to Sing; It's Time to Go to Church Again; There's a Girl Back Home; Magical Moments; The Thrill of You; It Was a Lovely Affair; From the Bottom of My Heart; Just a Little Old Schoolhouse; Jealousy. *Scores:* Stage: Yeah Man.

WEINBERG, HENRY
composer, teacher
b Philadelphia, Pa, June 7, 31. Educ: Univ Pa, BA; Princeton Univ, MA & PhD. Taught, Univ Pa; teacher, Queens Col, NY, currently. Overseas dir music & art prog, City Univ New York in Italy. Exec secy, League of Comp. Several recordings with CRI Records. *Instrumental Works:* Vox in Rama; String Quartet (Nomberg Award for chamber music); Cantus Commemorabulis.

WEINBERG, JACOB   ASCAP 1934
composer, author, pianist
b Odessa, Russia, July 1, 1883; d New York, NY, Nov 3, 56. Educ: Moscow Cons; Univ Moscow; studied with Igumnov, Taneiev, Leschetizky; hon MusD. Citizen, 34. Concert tours in Russia, 12-14; prof piano & comp, Odessa Cons, 15-16. Concerts in Jerusalem, Near East, 22-27. Head theory dept & prof piano, NY Col Music, 27; fac mem, Hunter Col, 37-56. Gave annual Carnegie Hall concerts, entitled, "Festival of Jewish Arts." Author "Encyclopedia of Piano Technique" & "Rudiments of Language." *Instrumental Works:* The Gettysburg Address (chorus, orch); Isaiah (oratorio); Piano Concerto; Suite for 2 Pianos; Trio for Piano, Violin, Cello; String Quartet; Piano Sonata; 2 violin sonatas, also 3 complete sabbath services. *Scores:* The Pioneers (opera).

WEINBERGER, JAROMIR   ASCAP 1896
composer, conductor, educator
b Prague, Czech, Jan 8, 1896; d St Petersburg, Fla, Aug 8, 67. Educ: Cons in Prague & Leipzig. Cond & taught, Bratislava, Prague, Vienna & Ithaca, NY. To US, 39, citizen, 48. *Instrumental Works:* Overture to a Puppet Show; Overture to a Cavalier's Play; A Waltz Overture; Christmas; Czech Songs and Dances; Passacaglia; Under the Spreading Chestnut Tree; The Legend of Sleepy Hollow; Prelude and Fugue on Dixie; Song of the High Seas; Czech Rhapsody; Lincoln

Symphony; Preludes Religieus et Profanes; Aus Tirol; Mississippi Rhapsody (band); Prelude to the Festival; Homage to the Pioneers; Concerto for Alto Saxophone and Orchestra; Concerto for Timpany; Sonata for Organ; The Way to Emmaus; Bible Poems; Psalm 150; Ecclesiastes. *Scores:* Operas: Schwanda the Bagpiper; The Beloved Voice; The Outcasts of Poker Flat; Wallenstein; The Birds Opera; Operettas: Frühlingsstürme; Bed of Roses; Apropo Co Dela Andula; Cisar Pan Na Tresnich.

WEINER, LAWRENCE   ASCAP 1969
composer
b Cleveland, Ohio, June 22, 32. Educ: Univ Tex, Austin, BM, MM(theory, comp); Univ Miami, DMA(theory, comp). Music educr, San Antonio pub schs, 59-68. Asst prof music, Tex A&I Univ, 68-74; assoc prof & comp-in-residence, Corpus Christi State Univ, 74-; writer, 60 compositions. *Songs:* Music: Three Japanese Songs. *Instrumental Works:* Daedalic Symphony (winner, Am Band Masters Asn Ostwald Comp Contest, 67); Third Symphony; Elegy in String Orchestra. *Songs & Instrumental Works:* Opera/Ballet: Chipita Rodriguez.

WEINER, LAZAR   ASCAP 1949
composer, conductor, pianist
b Kiev, Russia, Oct 24, 1897. Educ: Kiev Cons; studied with Robert Russell Bennett, Frederick Jacoby & Joseph Shillinger. Cond & musical dir, Cent Synagogue Choir, 4 yrs & Workmen's Circle Chorus, 35 yrs; "Message of Israel," radio prog, 35 yrs; now fac, Hebrew Union Col & Jewish Theol Sem; cond master class, Young Men's Hebrew Asn, New York. *Songs & Instrumental Works:* String Quartet; Postlude and Fugue for Large Orchestra; Cantatas for soloists, chorus, orch & piano: To Thee America; Legend of Toil; Amos; Piano comp: 5 Friday Evening Services; 1 Saturday Morning Service; Musical Comedy: Once Upon a Time; numerous choral comp, arr of folk songs, ballets & songs. *Scores:* Opera: The Golem.

WEINER, MATTHEW   ASCAP 1972
composer, musician
b New York, NY, Jan 24, 53. Educ: Pvt instr. Has had a gold single & gold album, Japan. Has written songs for Eddie Kendricks; Ray, Goodman & Brown; Cheryl Ladd; Captain Kangaroo. Back-up player for Ricky Lee Jones, Steve Goodman & Robbie DePrey; has also done var commercials. *Songs:* Music: Missing You; Whatever Would I Do Without You; Dance Forever; I'm Gonna Miss You; I'll Turn to You.

WEINGARTEN, DAVID (DAVE GARDNER)   ASCAP 1952
composer, author, publisher
b Johannesburg, SAfrica, Sept 20, 02. To US 1905. Educ: High school. Has been publisher; also in construct bus. Chief Collabrs: Allan Flynn & Jack Gould. *Songs:* Love Was In the Melody; Our Love Song; I Never Knew I Cared So Much; Tin Pan Alley Melody.

WEINSTEIN, ARNOLD ABRAHAM   ASCAP 1977
author, professor
b New York, NY, June 10, 27. Educ: Hunter Col, Univ London, BA; Harvard Univ, MA. Author play, "Red Eye of Love," 62; musical, "The Party"; operas, "Dynamite Tonight", "Last Ingredient", "Greatshot", "General Opera." Translr, "Mahagony" (Brecht-Weill), "Fortuna" (Eduardo de Felippo), "Metamorphosis" (Tony Greco, Country Joe McDonald), "Story Theatre—American Revolution." Now librettist for Lukas Foss. Chief Collabrs: William Bolcom, David Amram, Laurence Rosenbled, William Russo, Francis Thorne, Tony Greco. *Songs:* Lyric: Six Songs; Ugly Bar; Party (score). *Scores:* Opera: Dynamite Tonight; Final Ingredient; Bway Shows: Million Goes to Million; Film/TV: Final Ingredient.

WEINSTEIN, MILTON   ASCAP 1956
composer
b Cohoes, NY, Apr 26, 11. Educ: Troy Cons; studied with Paul Yarten, Joseph Schillinger, Michael Fiviesky & Tibor Serly. Arr for Paul Specht, Richard Himber, Mark Warnow & Tommy Dorsey orchs; comp & arr for radio & TV series, "Kraft Theatre", "Lux Video Theatre", "Omnibus", "The Big Story" & "Caesar's Hour"; also for TV commercials, indust shows & educ films. *Songs & Instrumental Works:* Astrological Suite; Concerto for Trumpet.

WEINSTEIN, MORTON NEFF   ASCAP 1958
composer, author
b Philadelphia, Pa, Apr 17, 27. Educ: Boy's High Sch, Brooklyn, NY, 45; NY Univ, 48. Has written songs for Bway, off Bway, theatre, movies & popular market. Chief Collabrs: Danny Di Minno, George Mysels. *Songs:* The Commandments of Love; Give Me Another Chance; John, Joe, Jim, Billy, Tom; Take a New Look Into That Old Bible; Father Time; So Long Loser; Just a Friend; Happy With What I Got; Lyrics: Another Day Another Sunset (theme); The Prayer; Difficult Woman (off Bway); A Very Honorable Guy (Bway); Up There the Stars; Till the World Knows You're Mine; Once in Love and Nevermore; Thinking of Your Happiness. *Scores:* Bway Show: Jupiter Jones.

WEINSTEIN, SOL   ASCAP 1960
composer, author
b Trenton, NJ, July 29, 28. Journalist, songwriter; comedy writer, Joe E Lewis,

Jackie Kannon, Godfrey Cambridge, "TW-13", "NBC Follies", "The Jefferson's" & "3's Company"; author bks, "Lox Finger" & "Matzohball." *Songs:* The Curtain Falls; Sheldon, Sheldon, Sheldon.

WEIRICK, PAUL   ASCAP 1950
composer, arranger
b Loudonville, Ohio, Apr 10, 06. Educ: Studied harmony with Paul Held, Joseph Schillinger, Tibor Serly, comp and cond with Tibor Serly, orchestration with Charles L Cooke. Played trumpet & arr, var bands incl Marion McKay, Charles Dornberger, Jan Garber & Ted Fiorito. Arr, Irving Berlin Music Co, NY, 30; free-lance & stock dance arr for many publ. Arr, Lawrence Welk TV Show, Calif, 56, mgr Lawrence Welk publ cos, 13 yrs; music clearance for Lawrence Welk TV Show & others; music writer & arr, musical comedies for high schs, "Swinging High", "Get Up and Go", "Take It Easy", "Where Is the Mayor", "Whistle Stop." Chief Collabs: Charlie Hayes, Irving Taylor, Mary Lacey. *Songs:* Music: Hollywood Square Dance; Makin' Love Ukulele Style; I Am Prayer; Legend of the Bells; Something in the Night.

WEISBURD, DANIEL EUGENE   ASCAP 1972
composer
b St Paul, Minn, Nov 5, 35. Educ: Univ Calif, Los Angeles. Comp for two children's shows, "The Most Important Person" & "Kingdom of Could Be You."

WEISBURD, ELAINE SIMONE   ASCAP 1974
composer, author
b Detroit, Mich, Nov 2, 35. Educ: Univ Calif, Berkeley, BA; Univ Calif, Los Angeles & Univ Hawaii, grad work. First prof job, 69. Lyric writer for documentary film, "Uphill Climb." Writer of music & lyrics for children's shows; previewed on "Captain Kangaroo." Wrote for "The Most Important Person" (50 original songs) & "Kingdom of Could Be You." Has done work in educ field, incl bilingual show, "Project Bilingual." Has done songs and scored for documentary & industrial films; commercial songs. Has done spec material for commercial artists. Chief Collabs: Stan Worth, Jimmy Bond, Leroy Vinegar. *Songs:* What Love Is Made Of; After All These Years; Creation.

WEISER, IRVING   ASCAP 1943
composer, teacher
b New York, NY, Apr 16, 13. Educ: New York Univ, BS(music educ). Musician, several dance bands in nightclubs; arr. Chief Collabs: Hy Zaret, Eddie Seiler, Art Kassel, Phil Brito. *Songs & Instrumental Works:* There I Go; That's My Affair; Touch Me Not; Not So Long Ago; Shall I Compare You; A Dream Affair; Introspection (tone poem). *Scores:* Children's Musical: A Choice for Cinderella.

WEISGALL, HUGO   ASCAP 1961
composer, conductor, educator
b Ivancice, Czech, Oct 13, 12. To US, 20. Educ: Peabody Cons, with Louis Cheslock; also studied with Roger Sessions & Rosario Scalero. Cultural attache, Am Embassy, Prague, 46-47. Taught & lectured in Baltimore music schs. Founded Baltimore Chamber Music Soc, 51; guest cond; prof music, Queens Col; pres, Am Music Ctr; adv, Lincoln Ctr Found. *Songs & Instrumental Works:* Overture in F; A Garden Eastward (cantata); Soldier Songs; 2 choral etudes; 4 songs; 2 madrigals. *Scores:* Operas: The Stronger; Night; Lilith; The Tenor; 6 Characters in Search of an Author; Athaliah; Purgatory; Ballets: Quest; One Thing Is Certain; Outpost.

WEISMAN, BEN   ASCAP 1956
composer, author, publisher
b Providence, RI, Nov 16, 21. Educ: Juilliard Scholarship; Univ Los Angeles; studied with Grace Castagnetta, George Trembley & Roy Harris. Spec services music dir, USAAF Band, WW II, 46-51. Arr & accompanist, Ames Bros, Vic Damone, Four Aces, Eddie Fisher, Guy Mitchell, Robert Merrill, Jan Pierce & Elvis Presley. Formed Blen Music, Los Angeles, 62. Performer, CBS "Young and Restless." Chief Collabs: Paul Francis Webster, Sammy Cahn, Johnny Mercer, Hal & Mack David, Sylvia Fine, Buddy Kaye, Fred Wise, Sid Wayne, Dee Fuller, Evie Sands, Kay Twoomey, Al Stillman, Sammy Gallop, Sylvia Dee. *Songs:* Let Me Go Lover; The Night Has a Thousand Eyes; Wooden Heart; All I See Is You; Love Makin' Love to You; You Can Do It; I'll Touch a Star; Honey in the Horn; Love in the Afternoon; Rock-a-Hula Baby; Robe of Calvary; Satisfaction Guaranteed; Pretty Little Black-Eyed Susie; Do! What You Do to Me; Got a Lot of Livin' To Do; Music: Lonely Blue Boy; When I Am With You; Follow That Dream; My Lips Are Sealed; Moonlight Swim; Don't Ask Me Why; Fame and Fortune; Crawfish. *Instrumental Works:* Golden Violins; Starlight Serenade. *Scores:* Film/TV: Young Americans.

WEISS, GEORGE DAVID   ASCAP 1946
composer, author, singer
b New York, NY. Educ: Brooklyn Col; City Col New York; Juilliard Music Sch. Appeared as singer/performer, The Ballroom, Garden State Art Ctr, Atrium, Riverboat, NBC-Today TV Show, NBC Sunday TV Show, CBS-TV Newsbreakers, KTVB-Boise & WMS-TV, Nashville. Chief Collabs: Hugo Peretti, Luigi Creatore, Bennie Benjamin. *Songs:* Can't Help Falling in Love; What a Wonderful World; Too Close for Comfort; I Don't See Me in Your Eyes Anymore; Wheel of Fortune; Cross Over the Bridge; Oh What It Seemed to Be;

I'll Never Be Free; How Important Can It Be; Let's Put It All Together; Hey Girl Come and Get It; Stay With Me; Surrender; Rumors Are Flying; Confess; Can Anyone Explain; A Girl, a Girl; Snoopy's Christmas; The Lion Sleeps Tonight; A Walkin' Miracle; These Things I Offer You; To Think You've Chosen Me; I Ran All the Way Home; Lyrics: Lullaby of Birdland; That Sunday That Summer; Carnival; Jet. *Scores:* Bway shows: Mr Wonderful; Send Me No Flowers; Why Can't I Walk Away; First Impressions; Maggie Flynn; Off-Bway shows: Smile, Smile, Smile; Cocktail Party; Film/TV: Blue Hawaii; The Rose; Murder, Inc; Toys in the Attic.

WEISS, LAURENCE   ASCAP 1969
composer, singer, producer
b Newark, NJ, Mar 25, 41. Educ: Weequahic High Sch, NJ; NY Univ; Seton Hall Univ; studied theory with Modina Scoville, New York. Singer/songwriter; recording artist, 73. Chief Collabs: Scott English, Melissa Manchester, Bob Crewe, John Williams. *Songs:* Rhinestone Cowboy; Lay Me Down (Roll Me Out to Sea); Dream Merchant; Hollywood Smiles; Music: Bend Me Shape Me; Lyrics: I Want to Spend My Life With You.

WEISS, MITCHELL ALLEN   ASCAP 1979
composer, arranger, pianist
b Forest Hills, NY, Sept 11, 52. Educ: Wantagh High Sch; Oberlin Col Cons, BA, 74; piano studies with Grace Cameron. Comp music & lyrics for original musical plays, "Goodbye, I'm Leaving", "Power On! Power Off!", "What's Expected?" & "Equal Time"; comp songs performed at grand finale, Les Mouches, Home, Tramps; music dir/arr for singer Billie Roe; stage dir New York revivals of "Streamers" & "Les Blancs"; comp music for off-Bway, "Confessions of a Reformed Romantic" & "Suicide in B Flat." Chief Collabs: (librettists) Jeffrey N Mazor & Howard Lipson. *Songs:* Amelia; I Never Want to See You Again; I Wouldn't Mind Being You; Sound Check (Sit on My Face). *Instrumental Works:* Suicide in B Flat.

WEISS, ROBERT RUSSELL   ASCAP 1962
composer, author
b Wilkes-Barre, Pa, Oct 9, 28. Educ: Federalsburg High Sch, Md; St John's Col, Md, BA, 47; Claremont Grad Sch; Harvard Univ; Univ Calif Los Angeles; poetry study with W H Auden & writing with Robert Kirsch. Headmaster, Palomar Sch for Boys; supt, Urban Mil Acad, Brentwood, Calif; Hollywood columnist, Hicks Deal Publ; artists mgt, Cambridge Co; mem tech staff, Hughes Aircraft Co. Author, "The Expectant Father" & "The Launch Operations Plan." Pres, Authors Club. Chief Collabs: Jimmie Haskell, Ralph E Peay, Robert Freedman, John Reed & Jackie Dashiell. *Songs:* Dogs Aren't Allowed in Heaven; I Wonder Lord; How're We Gonna Fix the World; The March of the Christmas Toys; Nashville Waltz; Lyrics: Walking on Wilshire; Christmas Candle; Goodbye My Blue Hawaii; One Blue Carnation; Fall Down in Rain.

WEISS, STEPHAN   ASCAP 1940
composer, author
b Vienna, Austria, Aug 17, 1899. To US, late 30's. Chief Collabs: Paul Mann, Leo Corday. *Songs:* They Say; Music Music Music; Put Your Dreams Away; And So Do I; While You Danced, Danced, Danced; When You Look in Your Looking Glass; Let's Disappear; Angel in Disguise; There I Go Again, Sentimental Me; Make Love to Me on Lake Louise; The Bicycle Song; Night of Nights.

WEITHAUS, JOHN CHESTER   ASCAP 1966
composer, author
b Millvale, Pa, Aug 7, 02. Educ: Pa State Univ, BA; Univ Pa Law Sch, 1 yr. Played in col dance orch; managed music store. Vpres & founder, Consumer Products Div, Calgon Corp, Pittsburgh, Pa. *Songs:* Then You're in Love; That's the Way It Goes; Some Kinda Bues; Yeah-Yeah-Yeah; Love Is More; Taxes, USA.

WEITZ, TED (TED WHITE)   ASCAP 1936
composer, pianist, singer
b Philadelphia, Pa, Dec 23, 07. Philadelphia Musical Acad, teacher's cert for violin, 28. Had own three-piece jam band at age 14; had duo, Radio Romeos which had weekly & daily coast-to-coast hook-ups; also had appearances on the Eastern Coast & many in Can. Pianist, violinist & solo singer, Isham Jones' Orch, 34-35; had a prog songs & talk at KYW, 36. Songwriter; played piano, violin, guitar, bass, drums & ukelele; comedy writer. Chief Collabs: Jack Meskill, Leon Flatow, Andy Razaf, Al J Neiburg, Lou Klein, Milton Ager, Maceo Pinkard, Ray Bretz. *Songs:* Music: Moonlight on the Water; Swinganola; I'll Tell the World That's News; Deep Shadows; The Telephone Song; I'm Keepin' My Love for You; Taggin' Along With You; When Ruben Swings the Cuban; Swingin' Soldier Man; Little Audrey; Dixiana Brown.

WEITZLER, MORRIS MARTIN (MARTY WHITE)   ASCAP 1961
composer, author, instrumentalist
b Malden, Mass, Apr 13, 16. Educ: High sch, studied with Ben Lancisi; studied saxophone with Boots Mazzuli, studied clarinet with V Pauluchi. Played small combos in nightclubs & Dixieland groups in New Eng. *Songs:* Coast of California; If I Make the Front Door; Coal Mines of West Virginia; Give Me.

WELCH, KENNETH HOWARD ASCAP 1959
composer, author, producer
b Kansas City, Mo, Feb 4, 26. Educ: Carnegie Inst Technol; Park Col; Univ Notre Dame. Wrote revues, Pittsburgh Playhouse, 48-50; TV writer/comp, "Garry Moore Show", "Julie and Carol at Carnegie Hall", "The Entertainers", "Kraft Music Hall", "Burt Bacharach Specials", "Carol Burnett Show" (series), "Sills and Burnett At the Met", also specials for Bing Crosby, The Carpenters, Olivia Newton-John & Ben Vereen. Writer, comp & producer specials for Mac Davis, Paul Lynde, Dolly Parton, Carol Burnett, Bob Hope, Hal Linden & Linda Lavin. Chief Collabrs: Mike Nichols, Mitzie Welch. *Songs:* I Made a Fool of Myself Over John Foster Dulles; Feels Good, Feels Right; You're So London; Have Tux, Will Travel; It's About Time.

WELCH, MARILYN (MITZIE) ASCAP 1960
composer, author
b Canonsburg, Pa. Educ: Carnegie-Mellon Univ, BS & BA(music); Muskingum Col; Pa Col for Women. Began as a singer with Benny Goodman, then started writing music & lyrics. Wrote for "Carol Burnett Show", 7 yrs, "Ben Vereen Special", "Carol & Beverly Sills", "Carol and Julie Andrews", "Carol and Dolly Parton" & "Hal Linden Special." Winner of 3 Emmy Awards, 2 Christophers & others. Now also producer; produced "Hal Linden's Big Apple" & "Linda Lavin Special." Chief Collabr: Ken Welch.

WELCH, NORMAN A ASCAP 1964
composer, author, musician
b Chicago, Ill, Aug 11, 46. Educ: Francis Parker High Sch, Chicago, 64; Northwestern Univ, BS, 70; studied piano with Dorys Seelig, Leo Gordon, Lucille Gould, Clara Siegel & Herb Mickman. Written, performed & produced numerous songs, jingles & indust shows; staff writer for Don Costa Productions, Hollywood, 72-73; pres, Washtenaw Records, 73; club appearances, Los Angeles, Las Vegas & Phoenix, 75-80. Chief Collabr: Guy Costa. *Songs:* Summer USA; Girl With the Long Red Hair; Coast to Coast; Dear Denise; I Tried and I Tried; Lyrics: Is It You?

WELCH, ROBERT ASCAP 1970
composer, author, singer
b Los Angeles, Calif, Aug 31, 45. Educ: Univ Calif, Los Angeles, degree in French. Comp, Fleetwood Mac, 71-75. Chief Collabr: John Carter. *Songs:* Sentimental Lady; Ebony Eyes; Precious Love.

WELCH, SIDNEY LESTER, JR (PATRICK) ASCAP 1964
composer, author
b West Palm Beach, Fla, Dec 4, 24. Educ: Lake Worth High Sch, Fla, grad; Ala Polytech Inst, Auburn, 2 yrs; Neighborhood Playhouse & Am Theatre Wing, New York, NY. Began career as an actor in summer stock; then as actor, singer & dancer in Bway. Started writing songs, late 50's. Played piano & sang in piano bars until 72; moved to Mexico City, 72, Eng teacher & had a children's album "Catarina," produced by Discos Peerless as well as a single. Chief Collabrs: Michael Merlo, John Gluck, Jr, Sid Lippman. *Songs:* Soy Rosa, La Mariposa; Lyrics: Fibbin'; Gesundheit; Lucky; My Empty Room; Magic Moon (Magica Luna); Queen of Tears; A Little Voice.

WELCHER, DAN EDWARD ASCAP 1972
composer
b Rochester, NY, Mar 2, 48. Educ: Eastman Sch Music, BM & performer's cert, 69; Manhattan Sch Music, MM, 72. Asst prof theory & comp, Univ Louisville, 72-78; principal bassoonist, Louisville Orch, 72-78 & Austin Symph; fac mem bassoon & comp, Aspen Music Fest, 76-; assoc prof, Univ Tex, 78-; dir, Univ Tex New Music Ensemble. *Songs & Instrumental Works:* Concerto for Flute and Orchestra; Concerto da Camera (bassoon, small orch); Dervishes: Ritual Dance-Scene for Full Orchestra; The Visions of Merlin (orch); Sonatina (piano); Dance Variations (piano); Abeja Blanca (voice, Eng horn, piano; comn by Jan DeCaetani); Woodwind Quintets No 1 and 2.

WELDON, FRANK ASCAP 1933
composer, author
b Lawrence, Mass; d Jackson Heights, NY, Jan 19, 70. Educ: New Eng Cons. Led own orch, New Eng; then music dir & writer for vaudeville units & nightclubs. Chief Collabrs: James Cavanaugh, John Redmond, Hal David. *Songs:* I Like Mountain Music; The Man With the Mandolin; A Little on the Lonely Side; Christmas in Killarney; Goodnight Wherever You Are; Dearest Darling; I'd Do It All Over Again; What Do You See in Her?; Laughing Sailor; Second Fiddle; Rural Rhythm; Grand Central Station; Charity; You Can Cry on Somebody Else's Shoulder; I Came, I Saw, I Conga'd; On a Simmery Summery Day.

WELDON, MAXINE ASCAP 1974
author, singer
b Holdenville, Okla, Apr 13, 47. Educ: Bakersfield High Sch; Bakersfield Col. Had numerous nightclub & TV appearances; recording artist; toured US, Orient & Europe. Chief Collabr: Tony Webster. *Songs:* Going Where I've Been; Are You Coming Home Again; Night Prayer; Music: Looking for the Answer.

WELK, LAWRENCE ASCAP 1950
composer, publisher, conductor
b Strasburg, NDak, Mar 11, 03. Educ: Pub sch. Accordionist at local dances, then joined touring bands. Organized 6-man group, 25; appeared on radio, WNAX, Yankton, SDak, 27. Toured with orch, Champagne Music Makers, 30-33, appeared at Aragon Ballroom, Santa Monica, Calif, 51-61, then Hollywood Palladium. Featured on KTLA-TV, Los Angeles, 51-, network ABC prog, 53- Has made many records. *Songs:* Bubbles in the Wine; Dakota; Waltzing in a Dream.

WELLS, BRYAN ASCAP 1966
composer, author, conductor
b Detroit, Mich, Apr 19, 43. Educ: Detroit Inst Technol, BA, 66; studied cond & arr with Colin Romoff; pvt piano study with Lillian Cox. Orch leader, Detroit, 60-70; staff comp, Motown Records, Detroit, 66-70; vpres & music dir, Bryan Wells Music for Advert, 72-80. Comp & arr advert music for Saks Fifth Avenue; Sears & Roebuck, Welches Grape Jelly, Gillette Right Guard, Ideal Toy, Mateus Wine, Allied Van Lines, Prince Gardner Wallets & Speidel Watch Bands. Rec'd 4 Clio Awards for Peugeot, Connie Shoes, Stock Vermouth & Gillette Right Guard. Chief Collabrs: Ronald Miller, Michelle Murphy, Paul Evans, Francis Lai. *Songs:* Music: A Place in the Sun; Yester-Me, Yester-You, Yesterday.

WELLS, JOHN BARNES ASCAP 1925
composer, singer, teacher
b Ashley, Pa, Oct 17, 1880; d Roxbury, NY, Aug 8, 35. Educ: Syracuse Univ. Singer with Victor Herbert Orch, NY, New York Symph & choral societies. Held church posts at Divine Paternity, St Nicholas, NY. Voice tutor, Princeton Univ, 15 yrs. *Songs:* The Elf Man; If I Were You; The Dearest Place; The Owl; The Little Bird; The Lightning Bug; Why?; I Wish I Was a Little Rock.

WELLS, ROBERT (ROBERT WELLS LEVINSON) ASCAP 1946
composer, author, producer
b Raymond, Wash. Educ: Univ Southern Calif, 2 yrs. Started writing while drummer for local bands; music librarian & music film ed, Columbia Pictures; wrote many pop songs & picture assignments. Wrote bk & lyrics for Bway show, "Three for Tonight." Wrote & produced cabaret acts for Dinah Shore, Lisa Kirk (wife), Kay Thompson, Ann-Margret, Shirley MacLaine, etc. Wrote & produced TV specials for Dinah Shore, Andy Williams, Gene Kelly, Dionne Warwick, Jane Powell, Ann-Margret & Julie Andrews; also, "A Toast to Jerome Kern", "The Sound of the Sixties", "Zenith's Salute to Television's 25th Anniversary", "The Man in the Moon", "Perry Como's Winter Show", plus others. Picture scores: "The French Line", "All Ashore", "10", "From Here to Eternity"; plus many title & spec picture songs. Winner six Emmy's & Writers Guild Annual Award. Chief Collabrs: Mel Torme, David Saxon, Jack Segal, Henry Mancini, Cy Coleman, Dave Grusin. *Songs:* Lyrics: The Christmas Song (Chestnuts Roasting on an Open Fire); From Here to Eternity; Re-enlistment Blues; Magic Town; Abie's Irish Rose; Born to Be Blue; County Fair; Speak a Word of Love; Willow Road; Ask Me No Questions; On an Ordinary Morning; Mobile; Never Like This; What's My Name?; A Stranger Called the Blues; When Joanna Loved Me; Here's to the Losers; The Shadows of Paris; For Once in My Life; Easy to Be With; I Was There; The Code of the West; Rainbow Valley; Four Months, Three Weeks, Two Days, One Hour Blues; What Every Girl Should Know; Wait Till You See Paris; The Will; Bad Is for Other People; Fly Bird; Two Miles Out of Tucson; Eloise; A Smile and a Ribbon; Lilly's Lament; I Feel So Spanish; The Name of the Game; I Still Send Her Flowers; What Are You Afraid Of?; Take Me to Town; Lonely Rider; 100 Years; Ballad of Wes Tancred; I'm a Person, Too; The Sand Dance; He Pleases Me (He's No More Than a Man); I Have an Ear for Love; It's Easy to Say.

WELLS, ROY
See Downey, Raymond J

WENCE, WILLIAM KENNETH ASCAP 1977
composer, author, singer
b Salinas, Calif, July 2, 42. Educ: Salinas High Sch; Hartnell Col, 64. Recording artist for Rustic Records; solo artist, TV, shows & clubs. Promotion & record co management; disc jockey, WKDA, WAGG, KRSA, KINY; toured with var artists. *Songs:* Hold On; This Is a Hold Up; Quicksand; Break Away; California Callin; Night Lies; Love Ride.

WENDEL, PAUL L ASCAP 1964
composer, author, singer
b Leetonia, Ohio, Jan 30, 23. Educ: Erie Acad; Erie Cons; Juilliard; studied voice with Ludwig Fabri. Made debut in Philadelphia with "Zar Und Zimmerman"; sang "Dichterliebe" with Otto Klemperer. Was on Bway in "The Time, Place and Girl", "HMS Pinafore" & "Mikado." With Boston Opera Co. Sang on radio, TV & nightclubs. Made recordings, "Summer Romance" & "Prayer for Peace." Commentator for symphonic & operatic progs, John Philip Sousa Post Band, Goldman Band, Am Symph Orch, Leopold Stokowski & others. Conductor. *Songs:* America, My Homeland (Bicentennial Off Song); Thanks; Psalms 8, 23, 24; La Spezia; St Tropez; Boy Scout Hymn; Four Freedoms; Spirit of '76.

WENDELBURG, NORMA RUTH ASCAP 1970
composer, teacher, pianist
b Stafford, Kans, Mar 26, 18. Educ: Bethany Col, Kans, BM, 43; Univ Mich, MM, 47; Univ Rochester Eastman Sch of Music, MM, 51, PhD, 69; Fulbright award, Mozarteum & Acad of Music, Vienna, Austria, 53-55; special summer study with Otto Luening, Carlos Chavez. Taught theory, comp, piano & music educ & head of var depts, Wayne State Col, Northern Iowa Univ, Southwest Tex State Univ, Hardin-Simmons Univ & Dallas Baptist Col. Comp, var works incl symph, string quartets, chamber, choral & solos for voice, piano, organ & perc; pianist. Grad assistantship, Univ Rochester Eastman Sch of Music; 6 resident fels incl MacDowell Colony. Winner, scholarships to Berkshire Music Ctr & Bennington Comp Conference. *Songs:* Song of the White Clouds (song cycle, soprano, 2 flutes & piano); 48 Hymns and Responses. *Instrumental Works:* Andante and Allegro for Orchestra; Symphony No 1; String Quartet No 2; Suite for Violin and Piano No 2.

WENDELL, CHARLES WOOD ASCAP 1964
composer, author
b Memphis, Tenn, Feb 2, 10. Educ: High sch. Chief Collabrs: I E Silver, Peter Toma. *Songs:* Bourbon Street Blues; Midnight in Paris; My Heart Told Me So; Lyrics: Alone After Dusk.

WENDLING, PETE ASCAP 1919
composer, pianist
b New York, NY, June 6, 1888; d. Educ: DeWitt Clinton High Sch. Performer, with Lewis Muir in vaudeville, appeared at Hippodrome, London, 13. Pianist, recorded piano roll music, 19-29. On staff, Berlin, Waterson & Snyder. Winner, nat contest as ragtime pianist. Chief Collabrs: E Ray Goetz, Joe Young, Sam Lewis, Edgar Leslie, Bert Kalmar, Harry Richman, Jack Meskill, Tot Seymour, Charles O'Flynn. *Songs:* Yaaka Hula Hickey Dula; Oh, How I Wish I Could Sleep Till My Daddy Comes Home; Oh! What a Pal Was Mary; All the Quakers Are Shoulder Shakers; Take Me to the Land of Jazz; Take Your Girlie to the Movies; Red Lips, Kiss My Blues Away; There's Danger in Your Eyes Cherie; Swingin' in a Hammock; I'm Sure of Everything But You; I Believe in Miracles; On the Street of Regret; Crying Myself to Sleep; Looks Like a Beautiful Day; The Story of Annie Laurie; Oky Doky Tokyo.

WENRICH, PERCY ASCAP 1914
composer, pianist
b Joplin, Mo, Jan 23, 1887; d New York, NY, Mar 17, 52. Educ: Chicago Musical Col. Staff mem, music publ co; then moved to New York. Toured in vaudeville with wife, Dorothy Connolly, 15 yrs. Charter mem, ASCAP. Chief Collabrs: Al Bryan, Stanley Murphy, Edward Madden, Jack Mahoney, Howard Johnson, Ray Peck. *Songs:* Put on Your Old Gray Bonnet; Silver Bell; She Took Mother's Advice; Red Rose Rag; Moonlight Bay; When You Wore a Tulip and I Wore a Big Red Rose; Sweet Cider Time When You Were Mine; Where Do We Go From Here, Boys?; A Rainbow From the USA; Land of Romance; Lantern of Love; Sail Along, Silv'ry Moon. *Scores:* Bway stage: Crinoline Girl; The Right Girl; Castles in the Air.

WERLE, FLOYD EDWARDS ASCAP 1960
composer, author, organist
b Billings, Mont, May 8, 29. Educ: Billings Sr High Sch; studied organ with Marilyn Mason; studied band techniques with William D Revelli. Arr & choirmaster; chief comp & arr, USAF Band, Washington, DC, 51-; dir music, Faith United Methodist Church, Rockville, Md, 67- *Songs:* Rejoice, Rejoice; Aldersgate Prayer; Son of God; Redemption; What Shall I Do My God to Love; Introits & Responses; Hymns With a Difference (collection of 13); The New Faith (12 contemporary anthems). *Instrumental Works:* We Hold These Truths; Concerto No 1 (trumpet); Concerto No 2 (trumpet); Concerto No 3 for Trumpet (Concierto Tipico); Symphony No 1 for Winds (Sinfonia Sacra); Symphony No 2 for Winds (Sinfonia di Chiesa), Concertino (three brass); Anthem and Scherzo (symph band); Partita (saxophones); Divertimento for Eight Soloists; Marches Blue and Grey.

WERMEL, BENJAMIN ASCAP 1961
composer, teacher
b New York, NY, June 6, 1907. Educ: High school; studied music with William Scher. Taught piano since 41 & accordion since 49. Mem, Nat Guild Piano Teachers. *Songs:* Romany Rhapsody; A Sailor Dances; Footsteps In the Dark; Mexican Carnival; At the Dancing School.

WERNER, FRED H, JR ASCAP 1967
composer, conductor, arranger
b Greeley, Colo, June 11, 34. Educ: Greeley High Sch; Colo Univ, studied piano perf; studied comp with Arnold Chaitman, 59-61. Cond on Bway, "High Spirits" & "Sweet Charity"; arr for records & TV; music dir, "Mama," Warner Bros Pictures & "Huck Finn," United Artists Pictures; comp TV scores, "Eight is Enough", "New Land", "Dukes of Hazzard" & "Death of Ocean View Park." *Songs:* Music: Flo's Yellow Rose; Desiderata.

WERNER, KAY ASCAP 1940
composer, author, singer
b Birmingham, Ala, Oct 9, 18. Educ: High school. To New York, 35. Chief Collabr: Sue Werner (sister). *Songs:* I Got the Spring Fever Blues; Rock It for Me; Requestfully Yours; Love Is the Thing So They Say; I Want the Waiter (With the Water); My Wubba Dolly; Do It Again; Ten Little Soldiers.

WERNER, SUE ASCAP 1940
composer, author, singer
b Birmingham, Ala, Oct 9, 18. Educ: High school. To New York, 35. Chief Collabr: Kay Werner (sister). *Songs:* I Got the Spring Fever Blues; Rock It for Me; Requestfully Yours; Love Is the Thing So They Say; I Want the Waiter (With the Water); My Wubba Dolly; Do It Again; Ten Little Soldiers.

WERNICK, RICHARD ASCAP 1961
composer
b Boston, Mass, Jan 16, 34. Educ: Brandeis Univ, BA, 55; Mills Col, MA, 57. Cond & comp-in-residence, Royal Winnipeg Ballet. Asst prof, Univ Chicago, 65-68 & Univ Pa, 68-69, assoc prof, 69-77, prof, 77- Music dir, Pa Contemporary Players, 68-80; Pulitzer Prize, 77. *Instrumental Works:* Kaddish-Requiem; Moonsongs from the Japanese; Haiku of Basho; Visions of Terror and Wonder; String Quartet No 2; A Prayer for Jerusalen; Contemplations of the 10th Muse, Books I and II; Introits and Canons; A Poison Tree; Songs of Remembrance; Partita for Solo Violin; Cadenzas and Variations for Violin and Cello Solo.

WESLYN, LOUIS ASCAP 1945
author
b Indianapolis, Ind, Oct 12, 1875; d Brooklyn, NY, Dec 31, 36. Educ: Shortridge High Sch. Drama reporter for newspapers; mgr, vaudeville theatre, Indianapolis; appeared in vaudeville. Made world tour with Kiltie Band. Chief Collabr: Al Piantadosi. *Songs:* The Witch Behind the Moon; The Boy Who Stuttered and the Girl Who Lisped; Baby Rose; Send Me Away With a Smile; Boy o' Mine; Down Where the Big Bananas Grow.

WESS, HAL ASCAP 1959
composer, author, arranger
b Jersey City, NJ, Nov 12, 22; d Jersey City, Feb 17, 68. Educ: Juilliard; NY Univ; studies with Otto Cesana. Arr for dance bands, 50-55. Freelance arr, CBS, NBC & ABC, 55-60; also record producer. *Instrumental Works:* Marchambo; Dinney's Theme.

WESSON, ALFRED FRANK ASCAP 1955
composer, author
b Middletown, NY, Sept 9, 01. Educ: Univ Southern Calif, BA, 24. *Songs:* All Hail (Univ Southern Calif alma mater). *Songs & Instrumental Works:* Cardinal and Gold (Univ Southern Calif marching song).

WEST, ALVY ASCAP 1953
composer, conductor, saxophonist
b Brooklyn, NY, Jan 19, 15. Educ: NY Univ, BA. Saxophonist in Paul Whiteman orch; cond & arr for Andy Williams, recorded albums; cond & arr for "Bob & Ray," NBC radio & TV & "B F Goodrich Shows," CBS, TV *Songs & Instrumental Works:* Tony's Guitar; Cathy; Charm; Papa's Tune; Hop, Skip and Jump. *Albums:* Originals for the Little Band.

WEST, BOB ASCAP 1963
composer, author
b Milledgeville, Ga, Mar 1, 37. Educ: Studied with Clare Fischer & Jimmie Bond. Studio & recording musician, Hollywood, 57-; live appearance with var jazz artists. Chief Collabrs: Berry Gordy Jr, Willie Hatch. *Songs:* Song Called Children; I'll Be There; Captain Nice; Born With a Song; Music: Murder Below Zero.

WEST, EUGENE ASCAP 1923
composer, author, singer
b Louisiana, Aug 27, 1883; d New York, NY, May 26, 49. Educ: Pub schs. Singer & pianist in vaudeville. Staff mem music publ co, NY. Wrote songs for Bway revues, incl "Passing Shows"; "Ziegfeld Follies." Chief Collabrs: Otis Spencer, Ira Schuster, James McCaffrey, Dave Ringle, Gene Austin, Bert Mann. *Songs:* When You're Alone; Broadway Rose; Everybody Shimmies Now; You Know You Belong to Somebody Else; Roll On, Mississippi, Roll On; Hi Lee, Hi Lo; Please Come Back to Me; Hallelujah, Things Look Rosy Now; Don't Say You're Sorry Again; Looks Like a Beautiful Day; My Dream of the South; Sailin' on the Robert E Lee; The Scissors Grinder's Song; Te Amo; Stud Polka; Need I Say?; He's a Carousel Cowboy; Arizeh.

WEST, HAROLD
See Wilson, Roger Cole

WEST, JOSEPH WILLIAM
See Perazzo, Joseph William

WEST, MAL ASCAP 1951
composer, author
b New York, NY, May 28, 13. Recording engr & radio engr, 41- *Songs:* Oh, Marguerite; You're a No-Good Man.

WEST, MARTIN
See Wilson, John Floyd

WEST, RAY   ASCAP 1954
composer, author
b New York, NY, Oct 12, 04. Educ: Pub schs. Chief Collabrs: Larry Stock & Harry Stride. *Songs:* I Don't Wanna See You Cryin'; Glory Be.

WEST, TOMMY
See Picardo, Thomas R

WESTBERRY, JAMES KENT   ASCAP 1979
composer, singer
b Miami, Fla, May 23, 39. Educ: High sch. Own TV show, age 17; to Nashville, age 19; wrote songs for Cedarwood Publ Co, 8 yrs; worked Tex Ritter Show, 4 yrs; formed own band & recorded for MGM Records; recording artist, Doorknob Records. *Songs:* Love in the Hot Afternoon; Be Glad; Hello Out There; I Just Don't Understand; Memory Maker.

WESTBROOK, HELEN SEARLES   ASCAP 1945
composer, organist
b Southbridge, Mass; d. Educ: Am Cons, BM & Gold Medal; studied with Frank Van Dusen, Wilhelm Middleschulte & Adolf Weidig. Organist in film theatres, Chicago; radio NBC, WGN; TV. Wrote spec material. Organ soloist, Chicago Symph. Won Young Am Artists Award. Mem: Nat League Am Pen Women; Am Guild of Organists. Organist; music dir, Cent Church, Chicago. *Songs:* March Beside Him Lord; Six Indian Songs; Alabaster; Hindu Cradle Song; If You Call Me; Invincible. *Instrumental Works:* Organ: Menuett in Olden Style; Chanson Triste; Intermezzo; On the Ontonagon River; Andante Religioso; Laughing Sprites; Melodie; Waltz Circe; Dust At Friendship Lake; Poem for Autumn; Pastorale Scherzo; Retrospection; Concert Piece in D.

WESTFORD, LEE M   ASCAP 1963
composer, author, singer
b Los Angeles, Calif, May 5, 26. Educ: High school. *Songs:* When the Lights Went Out; Five Pointed Star; I'm Sorry I Put on Charlie's Shoes; Moaning and Groaning Twist.

WESTIN, KARL OTTO   ASCAP 1973
composer, author, concert pianist
b Gothenburg, Sweden, June 30, 13. Educ: Latin High Sch & Latin Jr Col; Royal Acad of Music Cons, Stockholm. Started piano lessons at age 6; debut at age 10; active in high sch orch. Clarinetist, Army Band, age 16. Spec studies with Swed Royal Opera, 2 yrs. Dir music degree, Stockholm Univ. Music dir, Swed Army Band; also with English Mil Music Hq, Aldershot. Music correspondent & columnist daily newspaper, Stockholm, 14 yrs & Orch Jour, 30 yrs. Chief Collabr: Helen (wife). *Instrumental Works:* Legend for Piano and Orchestra. *Scores:* Bway: Via Mizuer; Film/TV: After Dusk Comes Darkness; Youth; Ballet: Duet for Four.

WESTON, ELLEN   ASCAP 1973
composer, author
b New York, NY, Apr 19, 39. Educ: Performing Arts High Sch; Hofstra Univ; Univ Calif Los Angeles; Hunter Col; Whittier Col; Beverly Sch Law. Actress, Bway shows: "Toys in the Attic", "A Far Country" & "Mary Mary"; TV: "Get Smart", "SWAT", "Canon", "Barnaby Jones", "Harry-O", "Another World", "Guiding Light", "The Young and the Restless", 56-80. Music writer for var record cos. Chief Collabrs: Lesley Gore, Marvin Laird. *Songs:* Lyrics: Love Me By Name; Other Lady; Immortality; Paranoia; Along the Way.

WESTON, GARY
See Temkin, Harold P

WESTON, PAUL   ASCAP 1945
composer, author, conductor
b Springfield, Mass, Mar 12, 12. Educ: Dartmouth Col, BA, 33. Arr, Tommy Dorsey Orch, 35-40 & Bob Crosby Orch, 41-42. Dinah Shore, 40-43. Cond radio, Johnny Mercer, Jo Stafford, Joan Davis, Duffy's Tavern & Paul Weston Show. Cond TV, Jo Stafford, NBC Chevy Show, Bob Newhart, Danny Kaye, Jonathan Winters & Jim Nabors. Founder & first pres, Nat Acad Recording Arts & Sci. Over 20 albums recorded. Chief Collabrs: Sammy Cahn, Axel Stordahl, Johnny Mercer, Don Raye, Paul Mason Howard, Bob Russell, Ogden Nash, Marilyn & Alan Bergman. *Songs:* Shrimp Boats; Autumn in Rome; No Other Love; God Is Love; Hasegawa General Store; Music: I Should Care; Day By Day; When April Comes Again; Bells of Santa Ynez (suite). *Instrumental Works:* Crescent City Suite; Mercy Partridge Suite. *Scores:* Film/TV: Peter and the Wolf; Sorcerer's Apprentice.

WESTON, RANDOLPH E   ASCAP 1958
composer, conductor
b Brooklyn, NY, Apr 6, 26. In USA, WW II. Pianist in jazz groups. Has led own quartet, 55-, appearing in radio, TV, nightclubs & concerts incl Town Hall & Carnegie Hall, also in museums, cols, univs, churches, theatres & Newport Jazz Fest, 55- Taught as solo pianist & lectr, Europe, Caribbean, Polynesia & Asia. Has made many records. Chief Collabrs: Melba Leston, Clifford Jordan, Ahmed

Abdul-Malik, Ray Copeland, Wilbur White. *Songs & Instrumental Works:* Little Niles; Pam's Waltz; Machine Blues; Hi-Fly; Bantu Suite; Cry Me Not; Saucer Eyes; Pretty Stranger; Babe's Blues; Uhuruhu African Suite (Langston Hughes text); Beef Blues Stew; Lisa Lovely; Spot Five Blues; Where; African Cook Book; Berkshire Blues; Congolese Children Song; The Healer; Carnival; Portrait of Frank Edward Weston; Bueno Con Secha; Blue Moses (Ganana); Tangier Bay; Marrakesh; African Nite; Portrait of Vivian; Ifrane; Tanja.

WESTON, TIMOTHY JOHN   ASCAP 1979
composer, musician, recording artist
b Santa Monica, Calif, Nov 19, 52. Educ: Loyola Marymount Univ, BA(philos), 75; studied guitar with Tom Bruner & Steve Khan. Recording/studio musician, Calif, 10 yrs. *Instrumental Works:* Soul Sermonette; Granite Palace; Acufunkture; Nice 'n Sleazy; Chicken Strut.

WESTPHAL, FRANK C   ASCAP 1924
composer, conductor
b Chicago, Ill, June 15, 1889; d Bridgeport, Conn, Nov 23, 48. Educ: High sch. Led own orch, appearing in radio, ballrooms & cafes. Cond, studio orch in radio. *Songs:* When You Come to the End of the Day; It's an Old-Fashioned Locket; Old Soldiers Never Die; The Land We Love; My Own USA; How Can I Go on Without You?

WETHERELL, HAROLD P   ASCAP 1961
composer, author
b Fletcher, Vt, May 5, 09; d. Educ: High sch. Choir dir, Charlestown Parish Church, NH. Former newspaper advert salesman. Chief Collabrs: Carl Fredrickson, Harry Wilson. *Songs:* Go Little Prayer.

WETTERGREEN, MELVIN RICHARD   ASCAP 1976
composer, author
b Bridgewater, SDak, Apr 15, 09. Educ: Univ Iowa, BSC, 31; Am Univ, MA, 54. Wrote "The Navy Waves" while serving in Navy, WW II. Special material used on radio, TV & in nightclubs. Chief Collabrs: Bill Johnson, Dinah Washington, Barnee Breeskin. *Songs:* Don't You Think I Ought to Know; Am I Really Sorry; That Night We Said Goodbye; Mama, Mama, Mama; Wedding Cake.

WETZLER, ROBERT P   ASCAP 1966
composer, author, music editor
b Minneapolis, Minn, Jan 30, 32. Educ: Thiel Col, BA; Northwestern Lutheran Theol Sem, MDiv; Univ Minn, grad work in music theory & comp; studied comp with Paul Fetler & Dominick Argento, piano with Theodore Bergman & organ with Rupert Sircom. Chapel organist, Thiel Col & Northwestern Lutheran Theol Sem, choirmaster, 56-57. Choirmaster, Prince of Peace Lutheran Church, St Louis Park, 55-63 & Salem Lutheran Church, Minneapolis, 63-68. Founder publ house, Art Masters Studios, Inc, 60. Author, "Seasons and Symbols: A Handbook on the Church Year." *Songs & Instrumental Works:* Take, Believe; He Is Born; Still, Still, Still; Trilogy of Praise; Neebrit Suite (concert band); Te Deum.

WEVER, NED   ASCAP 1933
author
b New York, NY, Apr 27, 1899. Educ: Pawling Sch; Princeton Univ. While senior yr, wrote book & lyrics "Princeton's Triangle Club Show," then played in several Bway plays; wrote song lyrics with Will Donaldson, Molly Pollock & Paul Mann, then publ many songs with Milton Ager. Chief Collabrs: Milton Ager, Jean Schwartz, Paul Mann, Will Donaldson, Jerry Livingston. *Songs:* Lyrics: Trust in Me; Trouble in Paradise; An Orchid for the Lady; Sweet Stranger; I've Never Had a Sweetheart Like You; I Simply Adore You; I Can't Resist You. *Songs & Instrumental Works:* Sing a New Song.

WEYAND, CARLTON DAVIS   ASCAP 1974
composer, author, singer
b Buffalo, NY, Feb 19, 16. Educ: Studied music theory, harmony & comp; Millard Fillmore Col, LaSalle Ext Univ (Law); Bryant Stratton Bus Sch, real estate. Singer/musician, vaudeville & radio; recording artist, DaCar Records; comp of classical & popular music; music publ, Weyand Music Publ. Mem, Nat Music Publ Asn. Chief Collabrs: Elmer J Brost, Linda Patton. *Songs:* Yesterday, a Love Ago; The Lonely Hill; Time to Forget You; My Old Home Town; Greymood To-night; Change of Heart; Now I Know; You Need the Sun; After Summer's Sunset; Empty Sea; We Care; Song for Freedom. *Instrumental Works:* Meditation (piano); Variation of Chopin Prelude Op 28 No 20 (piano). *Scores:* Operetta: Two Hearted Witch.

WHALUM, HUGH DAVID, JR (PEANUTS)   ASCAP 1979
composer, singer, instrumentalist
b Memphis, Tenn, Sept 8, 28. Educ: Central State Univ, Ohio, BS, 48. Tenor saxophonist, Lionel Hampton, 48, George Hudson, 49-51 & Count Basie, 50. Singer, pianist var nightclubs & TV; recording artist, Moogo Records. Tenor saxophonist & trumpeter var nightclubs. *Songs:* It's Christmas; The Time Is Here.

WHEAR, PAUL W   ASCAP 1960
  composer, conductor
b Auburn, Ind, Nov 13, 25. Educ: Marquette Univ, BNS; DePauw Univ, BA &
MMus; Western Reserve Univ, PhD; Eastman Sch Music; Boston Univ; studies
with Gardner Read, Wilfred Josephs & Donal H White. Fac mem, Mt Union
Col, 51-60 & Doane Col, 60-69; resident comp, Marshall Univ, 69-; cond,
Huntington Chamber Orch, 70-; guest comp-cond, Japan, 72. Music performed
by Philadelphia Orch, Cleveland Philh, Indianapolis Symph, Oklahoma City
Symph & Rochester Civic Symph. Winner numerous comp prizes. *Instrumental
Works:* Catskill Legend Overture; Psalms of Celebration (chorus & orch);
Symphony No 1, Stonehenge; Wycliffe Variations; Trombone Sonata;
Jedermann; Of This Time; The Chief Justice (oratorio; performed at Kennedy
Ctr for Bicentennial Celebration); Kedushah (cantata); Symphony No 4
(symphonic band); Sonata for Solo Violoncello. *Scores:* The Devil's Disciple
(opera). *Albums:* The Music of Paul W Whear; Authenticated Composer Series.

WHEDON, TOM   ASCAP 1962
  author
b New York, NY, Aug 3, 32. Educ: Harvard Univ, BA. Writer for TV shows
incl "Captain Kangaroo." Chief Collabrs: Sam Pottle, David Axlerod. *Songs:*
Something Good Like You; Who Wants to Work. *Scores:* Off-Bway Stage: All
Kinds of Money.

WHEELER, BILLY EDD   ASCAP 1959
  composer, author, playwright
b Whitesville, WVa, Dec 9, 32. Educ: Warren Wilson Col, AA; Berea Col, BA,
55; Yale Sch of Drama; playwriting under Dr John Gasner, 62. Comn officer
pilot training, USN; dir alumni affairs, Berea Col, 2 yrs. Wrote plays for summer
stock & outdoor drama theatre; also published as a poet. Recorded for several
maj labels. Co-owner, Sleepy Hollow Music. Chief Collabrs: Roger Bowling &
Steve Clark. *Songs:* Coward of the County; Jackson; The Reverend Mr Black;
Ode to the Little Brown Shack Out Back; High Flying Bird; Winter Sky;
Blistered; Anne; It's Midnight (And I Miss You); I Ain't the Worryin' Kind;
Gimme Back My Blues; A Song of the Cumberland Gap; The Tinker and Sister
Lila. *Instrumental Works:* Hatfields and McCoys. *Scores:* Bway Type Show:
Mossie and the Strippers.

WHEELER, CLARENCE E
  composer, arranger, director
b Walnut, Kans, Sept, 1885; d Dec, 1966. Writer, music for var cartoon progs
incl "Woody Woodpecker Show" & "Chilly Willy." Dir, Walter Lance Shows,
12 yrs.

WHEELER, HAROLD PARKER, JR   ASCAP 1973
  composer, author
b East Grand Rapids, Mich, July 1, 23. Educ: Univ Chicago, ASTP Cert
Chinese, 44; Northwestern Univ, BMus, 51, MMus, 56; Grand Rapids Jr Col;
Univ Mich Exten at Nat Music Camp, Interlochen; Berkshire Music Ctr at
Tanglewood; Drury Col, Mo; Ind Univ Exten, Indianapolis; Butler Univ; Ariz
State Univ, Bradley City Col; instr under: (piano) Percy A Grainger & Louis
Crowder; (organ) E Power Biggs & Harold Tower; (comp) Robert M Delaney,
Aaron Copland, Anthony Donato, Albert Noelte & Darius Milhaud; (cond)
Guy F Harrison, Glenn C Bainum, Leonard Bernstein & Eleazar de Calvalho;
(orchestration) Howard Hanson. Organist & choirmaster, St Timothy's
Episcopal Church, Compton, Calif; adj prof music, Long Beach City Col,
Coastline Community Col; staff accompanist ballet classes, Dance Dept, Calif
State Univ, Long Beach. Pres, Long Beach Chap, Phi Delta Kappa & Apollo
Chap, Calif Fedn Chaparral Poets; past pres, Long Beach Br, Music Teachers
Asn Calif. Hon life mem, Phi Mu Alpha
Sinfonia, Music Teachers Nat Asn, Music Educr Nat Conf, Hymn Soc of Am,
Soc of Ariz Comp, Pi Kappa Lambda (Alpha Chap) & Calif Dance Educr Asn.
Chief Collabr: Josephine Wolverton. *Songs:* The American Singer (series).
Instrumental Works: Exodus (symphonic poem); Prelude, Chorale and Fugue
for Two Marimbas; Duet for Flute and Clarinet. *Scores:* Voices (incidental
music for the play).

WHEELER, ONIE D   ASCAP 1970
  composer, singer, musician
Farmer, 5 yrs; army service; entertainer. *Songs & Instrumental Works:* Run 'Em
Off; Onie's Bop; I'll Swear You Don't Love; When We All Get There; Love Me
Like You Used to Do; Little Mama; Mother Prays Loud in Her Sleep; I Saw
Mother With God Last Night; Gona Hang My Britches Up; Don't Go; Let's
Invite Them Over Again; Just a Friend in the Way; John's Been Shuckin' My
Corn; I Don't Believe We're Through; Go Home; She Wiggles and Giggles; I'm
Gona Jump Out of the Jukebox; Please Don't Break This Heart; Sandie Land
Farmer; Wait Till I'm 16; All Day, All Night, All Ways; Too Hot to Handle;
A Bougers Gona Get You.

WHEELER, WILLIAM HAROLD   ASCAP 1970
  composer, arranger, producer
b St Louis, Mo, July 14, 43. Educ: Sumner High Sch, Mo, 60, studied piano with
Carl J Madlinger; Howard Univ, DC, BM, 64; Manhattan Sch Music,
MM(comp), 68. Cond, Bway show "Promises, Promises"; comp dance music;
orchestrator & musical supv, Bway show "The Wiz"; producer,
"Starwars-Disco" & TV commercials incl Pepsi, Burger King, TWA & Braniff

Airlines & Campbell Soups; arr for var artists; recording artist. Chief Collabrs:
Jack Lawrence, Mary Stuart, Mort Goode. *Songs:* Tornato Music; Music: I
Wouldn't Have You Any Other Way. *Instrumental Works:* Galactic Funk.

WHEELOCK, DONALD F   ASCAP 1978
  composer, teacher
b Stamford, Conn, June 17, 40. Educ: Union Col, AB, 62, studied with Edgar
Curtis; Yale Univ Sch Music, MMus, 66, studied with Yehudi Wyner. Teacher,
Colgate Univ, 66-68 & Amherst Col, 68-74; assoc prof music, Smith Col, 74-
Instrumental Works: Ten Bagatelles for Oboe and String Quartet; Two String
Quartets; Serenade for Soprano and Seven Players; Concerto for 24 Brass
Instruments; numerous works for orchestra, voice and orchestra and chamber
music.

WHIPPO, WALTER BARROWS (WALT BARROWS)   ASCAP 1953
  author
b New York, NY, July 15, 22. Educ: Columbia Univ; New Sch of Social Res.
Little theatre actor; radio announcer & actor; drummer, small bands;
co-authored community musical, "Thanks to Shanks." Chief Collabr: Bernard
Zaritsky. *Songs:* Lyrics: The Little White Duck.

WHISTLER, HARVEY S   ASCAP 1957
  composer, author, editor
b Fresno, Calif, Sept 7, 07; d Ventura, Calif, Mar 17, 76. Educ: Fresno State Col,
BA; Univ Southern Calif, MS; Ohio State Univ, PhD; studied violin with
Ondricek, Piastro, Borissoff. Violinist, Fox West Coast theatres, 25-30. Taught
instrumental music, Calif pub schs, 29-39. Comp & ed, Rubank, Inc for many
yrs. Mem, advert council & critic, Music Journal, New York. Devised
Whistler-Thorpe Test of musical aptitude. Author, "Jean Baptiste Vuillaume
and His Master Workman" & "The Life and Work of Theodore Thomas,"
teaching bks incl "Beginning Strings Method for Violin, Viola, Cello, Bass",
"Modern Klose-Lazarus Method for Clarinet", "Modern Arban-St Jacome
Method for Cornet, Trombone", "Essentials of Band Playing", "Modern Pares
Scale Books", "Preparing for Kreutzer", "Essential Exercises and Etudes for
Viola", "Solos for Strings", "Elementary and Intermediate Scales and Bowing
for Strings" & "Pre-Ensemble Folio for Strings." *Instrumental Works:* First
Quartet.

WHITACRE, HAROLD L   ASCAP 1954
  composer, harmonica player
b Bell Brook, Ohio, Feb 16, 01; Selden, NY, Mar 10, 76. Educ: High sch. Mem,
The 5 Harmaniacs, Pat Rooney's Radio Boys, in vaudeville, 25-40. Performed
in New York nightclubs. *Songs:* Coney Island Washboard.

WHITCOMB, KENNETH GEORGE (GEORGE KENNY)   ASCAP 1965
  composer
b Battle Creek, Mich, Mar 7, 26. Educ: Battle Creek Central High Sch; studied
saxophone with Santy Runyon, Chicago, Ill; arr with Sy Oliver, New York; film
scoring, Eddy Lawrence Manson, Los Angeles; Fullerton Col, Calif, AA. Assoc
bandmaster & chief arr, US Mil Acad Band, West Point, NY, 14 yrs;
bandmaster, 30th Army Band, Ger. Saxophonist & arr, Disneyland Band,
Anaheim, Calif; free-lance comp & arr for publ, bands & orchs. *Instrumental
Works:* Coat of Arms; Jubilee; Jet Stream; Allegro Brilliante; 23 Skidoo;
Sessions in Sound (beginning band method).

WHITCUP, LEONARD   ASCAP 1934
  composer, author, publisher
b New York, NY, Oct 12, 03; d New York, NY, Apr 6, 79. Educ: NY Univ;
studied music with David Saperton & Orville Mayhood. Performed in radio,
wrote own material; also appeared with trio, The Playboys. Writer, spec material
for vaudeville, revues & songs for film "Sweet Moments." Mem, Am Guild
Authors & Comp, also treasurer, 55-62 & Membership Comt chmn; treasurer
& mem of Bd of Dirs, Songwriters' Hall of Fame; mem, ASCAP East Coast
Writers Adv Comt & alternate on Bd of Rev. Wrote songs for Brit TV cartoon
series "Dodo"; also theme song for film "Sons of Hercules" & Swed film series
"Pippi Longstocking." *Songs:* I Am an American (in Congressional Record);
March Winds and April Showers; I Couldn't Believe My Eyes; Take Me Back
to My Boots and Saddle; Lamento Gitano; Frenesi; From the Vine Came the
Grape; Fiesta; Kissin' on the Phone; Snake Charmer; Bewildered; True;
Infatuation; The Song of the Victory Fleet (citation, USMC); If My Heart Could
Only Talk; Singin' in the Saddle; Heaven Help This Heart of Mine; People to
People (for People to People prog); The 'A' Team; An Empty Glass; Book of
70 Hymns; songs for 3 Soupy Sales albums.

WHITE, CLARENCE CAMERON   ASCAP 1924
  composer, violinist, educator
b Clarksville, Tenn, Aug 10, 1880; d New York, NY, June 30, 60. Educ: Oberlin
Col; studied violin with Zacharewitsch; 2 Rosenwald fels; hon MA, Atlanta
Univ; hon MusD, Wilberforce Univ. Taught, Wash Cons, 03. Guest artist with
Coleridge-Taylor, US & London, 3 yrs. Own music studio, Boston, 10-22. Head,
music dept, WVa State Col, 24. Dir music, Hampton Inst, 34. Organized
community music progs for Nat Recreation Asn, 37-42. Recipient, Harmon
Found medal. *Instrumental Works:* Bandanna Sketches; Piece for Strings and
Timpani; Elegy; Violin Concerto No 2 in E; Symphony in D. *Scores:* Opera:
Ouanga (David Bispham medal); Ballet: A Night in Sans Souci.

WHITE, DAVID L ASCAP 1976
composer, author, guitarist
b Akron, Ohio, Dec 23, 46. Educ: Col of Marin, Calif, AA, 72. *Songs:* Saturday Nite; I Want to Have You a Long Time. *Scores:* Film/TV: Dogpound Shuffle.

WHITE, DONALD HOWARD ASCAP 1964
composer, educator
b Narberth, Pa, Feb 28, 21. Educ: Temple Univ, BSMusEd; Univ Rochester Eastman Sch Music, MM, PhD(comp), studied with Howard Hanson & Bernard Rogers; Philadelphia Cons Music, studied with Vincent Persichetti. Mem fac, DePauw Univ Sch Music, 47-, dir, 75-79, Siegesmunde prof comp, 75- *Instrumental Works:* Concertino for Solo Timpani, Winds and Percussion; Concertino for Solo Clarinet, Woodwinds and Percussion; Andante for Oboe, Harp and Strings; 3 for 5 (woodwind quintet); Serenade No 3 (brass quartet); Diversions (brass sextet); Sonata for Trombone and Piano; Sonata for Tuba and Piano; Lyric Suite for Euphonium and Piano; Tetra Ergon for Bass Trombone and Piano; Quintet for Brass; Variations for Piano Trio; Band: Miniature Set for Band; Dichotomy; Terpsimetrics; Introduction and Allegro; Ambrosian Hymn Variants; Divertissement No 3 for Blue Lake; Patterns; Sonnet; From the Navajo Children (chorus, band); Marchisma (band).

WHITE, EDWARD R ASCAP 1948
composer, author, producer
b New York, NY, June 18, 19. Educ: Hartnett Sch Music; studied acting with Jack Waltzer. Contract writer for var artists, Paramount Pictures, 50's. Producer, Bway show "The Family Way"; off-Bway show "Summertree" & Ella Fitzgerald's concert tours of Japan. Actor, var motion pictures incl "Annie Hall," "Manhattan," "The Killer Elite," "Angelo, My Love," "The Pentagon" & "Kojak." Chief Collabrs: Mack Wolfson, Buddy Kaye, Norman Gimbel, Jack Wolf Fine, Al Frisch, Hal Aloma, Johnny Pineapple. *Songs:* C'est La Vie; Flowers Mean Forgiveness; Happiness Street; The Crazy Otto Rag; Bonjour, Bon Soir, Bonne Nuit.

WHITE, ERMA MARCELINE (ANGELA) ASCAP 1963
composer, author
b Lynn, Mass, July 25, 25. Educ: Adult Ctr of Educ, Boston; Graham Jr Col. Chief Collabr: Larry Allen. *Songs:* The Christmas Spirit; Tanya; King of My Heart; Symphony of Tears; Aladdins Lamp; My Aquarian Dreamer.

WHITE, GARY B ASCAP 1969
composer, singer, guitarist
b Pasadena, Tex, Apr 5, 40. Educ: Pasadena High Sch. Bassist, "Circus Maximus," Vanguard Records. Bass accompanist, Paul Siebel, Jerry Jeff Walker & Pat Sky. Singer night clubs, New York & Los Angeles. *Songs:* Long Long Time; Nobody's; The Toast; Greater Manhattan Love Song; Spare Change Rag.

WHITE, GARY C ASCAP 1975
composer, educator
b Winfield, Kans, May 27, 37. Educ: Univ Kans, BME, 59, BMus, 61, MMus, 64; Mich State Univ, PhD, 69. Prof music & head theory & comp, Iowa State Univ. Symposium of Contemporary Music for Brass, comn-prize, 74; Toon van Balkom prize, 75; MacDowell Colony fel, 75; several ASCAP Standard Awards; comn & grants from NEA, Musical Soc Univ Mich, Martha Baird Rockefeller Found, Ames Int Orch Fest. *Instrumental Works:* Composition for Piano, Brass and Percussion; Insinuations for Brass Quintet and Tape; Strata, 1968, for Solo Clarinet; Antipodes I-II for Organ and Tape; Rotation for Carillon; Chronovisions for Band; Symphony; Pulsar for Organ and Brass Choir.

WHITE, HYMAN ASCAP 1957
composer, guitarist, teacher
b Boston, Mass, Dec 17, 15. Educ: High school; pvt music study. To New York, 38; guitarist with Woody Herman band, 6 yrs; mem, CBS staff orch; taught guitar, New York, 44-

WHITE, JANE DOUGLASS ASCAP 1948
composer, singer, pianist
b Coffeyville, Kans, Apr 14, 19. Educ: Okla Univ, BFA(music); Columbia Univ, MA(music); studied piano with Anton Bilotti. Capt, Women's Army Corp. Asst producer of TV game show "Name That Tune." Songwriter, var recording artists; musical dir, Playhouse on the Mall, NJ; producer & musical dir, Gristmill Musical Playhouse. Dir of music, Found for Christian Living; sacred concerts; musical ministry with Charles W Colson's Prison Fellowship. Show Bus Award, off-Bway musical "Wicked Lady." Chief Collabrs: Camilla Mays Frank, Sydney Shaw. *Songs:* Ballad of Mary and Martha; Music: Song of the Women's Army Corps; Love Is a Gamble; Sun Comin' Up in the Mornin'; Come Unto Me.

WHITE, JOHN DAVID ASCAP 1964
composer, author, educator
b Rochester, Minn, Nov 28, 31. Educ: Univ Minn, BA(magna cum laude), 53; Univ Rochester Eastman Sch Music, MA, 54, PhD, 60, performer's cert, cello, 60. Taught at Univ Mich, Univ Wis, Kent State Univ & Whitman Col; cellist. Benjamin Award, 60; Rochester Religious Arts Fest, comp prize of Eastman Sch Music, 61; Nat Fedn Music Clubs, Parade of Am Music merit award, 62; Rackham fac fel, Rackham fac fe, Univ Mich, 65; Univ Wis Oriana Trio Int Composers' Competition, 79; annual ASCAP awards, 64- Fac grants from Kent

State Univ, 61, 63 & 67; comn from Ithaca Col, 74, Kent State Univ, 69 & others. Chief Collabrs: William Blake, Martin Nurmi. *Songs & Instrumental Works:* Variations for Clarinet and Piano; Three Madrigals (SATB, piano, perc); Symphony No 2; Snows (tone poem, orch); Dialogue Concertante (cello, orch); The Monkey's Sonnet (SATB, piano); The Passing of Winter (SATB, piano); The Turmoil (SATB, piano); The Lamb (medium voice, piano); A Cradle Song (high voice, piano); Why Not? (piano); Seven Sacred Choral Works; Three Sacred Choral Works; Cantos of the Year (chorus, baritone, orch); Folk Elegie (cello, chamber orch); Roots and Leaves (male chorus, perc, brass choir); String Quartet No 1; Variations for Piano; Ode on the Morning of Christ's Nativity (SATB, flute, clarinet, piano); Music for Oriana (violin, cello, piano); Pied Beauty (SATB, piano).

WHITE, JOSEPH M ASCAP 1939
composer, author, singer
b New York, NY, Oct 14, 1891; d New York, Feb 28, 59. With, Denman Thompson's Old Homestead Quartet, 10. Served, 102nd Engrs, 27th Div, World War I. Soloist, Neil O'Brien's Minstrels, 19. Became radio performer, 22, known as Silver Masked Tenor, 25-30. *Songs:* In Flanders; Bells of Killarney; Maureen Mavourneen; Say That You Care for Me; Hold Me in Your Arms; Rose in the Moonlight; Drifting in the Moonlight; McGuire's Musketeers.

WHITE, JOSH ASCAP 1951
composer, author, guitarist
b Greenville, SC, Feb 11, 14; d Queens, NY, Sept 5, 69. To NY, 30; accompanist to singers incl Leroy Carr. Singer in nightclubs, concerts, theatres; toured Mex, under US govt auspices, 41; also toured Eur. Coach for & gave progs with Libby Holman, 41-42. Made many records & films, "Crimson Canary" & "Walking Hills." *Songs:* I Had a Woman; The Gray Goose; Ball and Chain Blues.

WHITE, KEVIN ASCAP 1976
composer, author
b Los Angeles, Calif, May 3, 52. Educ: Los Angeles Community Col; Univ Calif, Los Angeles. Writer of children's songs for "Captain Kangaroo." *Songs:* Come and Play; It's Nice to Be a Child.

WHITE, MARTY
See Weitzler, Morris Martin

WHITE, MAURICE ASCAP 1979
singer, musician
b Memphis, Tenn, Dec 19, 44. Educ: Chicago Cons Col. Drummer & former session musician; played in local clubs & with Ramsey Lewis. Founder & percussionist with group Earth, Wind & Fire, 71- Recording artist for var cos. Soundtracks for movies "Sweet Sweetback's Baaadaaas Song" & "That's the Way of the World." *Albums:* Last Days and Time (gold record); Head to the Sky (gold record); Open Our Eyes (platinum record); Double platinum records: That's the Way of the World; Gratitude; Spirit; All n'All; Best of-Vol I; I Am.

WHITE, MICHAEL ASCAP 1961
composer, teacher
b Chicago, Ill, Mar 6, 31. Educ: Oberlin Col; Univ Wis; Chicago Musical Col; Juilliard Sch Music, 2 yr fellowship, studied with Peter Menning. Taught theory at Juilliard Sch Music. Comp-in-residence, 61-62; on fac, Oberlin Cons. Grants: 2 Ford Found; Guggenheim. *Songs & Instrumental Works:* Oh Little Child; The Silver Bells; Take, Oh Take; Sleep, Little Lord; Gloria (choral); The Diary of Anne Frank (soprano, orch); Prelude and Ostinato for Strings. *Scores:* Operas: The Dybbuk; Alice.

WHITE, PAUL TAYLOR ASCAP 1941
composer, conductor, violinist
b Bangor, Maine, Aug 22, 1895; d Rochester, NY, May 3, 73. Educ: New Eng Cons, studied with Felix Winternitz & G W Chadwick; also with Eugene Goosens, Eugene Ysaye; hon MusD, Univ Maine. First violinist, Cincinnati Symph. Fac, New Eng Cons, 21-23, Univ Rochester Eastman Sch Music & cond Eastman Symph since 35. Assoc cond, Rochester Civic Orch, 29, cond, 53-73. Guest cond, var symph orchs incl Rochester Philh, Cincinnati, Lewisohn Stadium, Boston Pops & Pittsburgh. Music dir, Lake Placid Club, 39-73. *Instrumental Works:* Five Miniatures; Pagan Festival Overture; Voyage of the Mayflower; Symphony in E; Lake Spray; Boston Sketches; Lake Placid Scenes; Idyl for Orchestra; Sonata (violin, piano); Sinfonietta for Strings; Sea Chanty (harp, strings, Samuel Rosenbaum comn); Andante and Rondo (cello, orch); Mosquito Dance.

WHITE, RACHEL IRENE ASCAP 1977
composer, author
b Brooklyn, NY, June 10, 34. Educ: Madison Bus Col. *Songs:* Lord Help Me to Be Strong.

WHITE, RONALD ANTHONY ASCAP 1969
composer, author, singer
b Detroit, Mich, Apr 5, 38. Educ: Cass Tech High Sch. Early yrs of career were spent with Motown, recording & writing. Mem singing group, The Miracles, 59- Chief Collabr: William (Smokey) Robinson, Jr. *Songs:* One More Heartache; Lyrics: My Girl; You Beat Me to the Punch; Don't Look Back.

WHITE, RUSSELL ALAN　　　　　　　ASCAP 1961
composer, author, singer

b New York, NY, Feb 12, 25. Educ: New York High Sch Indust Art; New York Musical Inst Found; Harnett Sch Music. Writer, nightclub singer, pianist & arr. Writer musical, "Mascara." Songs: After the Lights Go Down Low; When Autumn Comes; Don't Cry Mama; Chop Suey, Chow Mien; Man Don't Cry; No Longer Have the Company.

WHITE, SYLVIA
See Eisenberg, Sylvia White

WHITE, TED
See Weitz, Ted

WHITE, TONY JOE
composer, singer, recording artist

b Oak Grove, La. Formed own bands, Tony Joe & The Mojos, Tony & The Twilights. Recording artist with Warner Bros, Monument & 20th Century Records. Albums: Black and White; Continued; Tony Joe; Tony Joe White; The Train I'm On; Home Made Ice Cream; Eyes; Best of Tony Joe White (compilation).

WHITE, VERDINE ADAMS
composer, singer, player

b Chicago, Ill, July 25, 51. Mem of the percussionist musical group Earth Wind & Fire. Chief Collabrs: Alley Willis, Maurice White. Songs: That's the Way of the World; Serpentine's Fire; Fantasy; Let Me Talk.

WHITE, WILKIE
See Franklin, Malvin Maurice

WHITE, WILLIAM WILFRED　　　　　　ASCAP 1922
composer, pianist, entertainer

b New York, NY, June 5, 1894; d. Educ: High sch; studied piano with M Margadant; Chaminade scholarship. Joined F A Mills Publ Co while in high sch. Writer, accompanist for William Rock & Frances White; wrote songs for Bway musicals. Joined staff, Waterson, Berlin & Snyder. Toured in "A Trip to Hitland," vaudeville. Accompanist to Adelaide & Hughes, Blanche Ring, Eddie Cantor, Belle Baker, Cameron Sisters, Vernon Stiles. Toured with USO shows. Chief Collabrs: Edgar Leslie, Roy Turk, George Jessel, Bernie Grossman, Henry Creamer, Bert Hanlon, M K Jerome, Bert Kalmar, Harry White. Songs: Oh How I Laugh When I Think How I Cried Over You; I'd Love to Be a Monkey in the Zoo; Six Times Six Is Thirty-Six; I Wonder If She's Lonely Too; Cuttin' Paper Dollies; Sally Green; Mrs Murphy's Chowder; Down in Sunshine Valley; I Got Another-One Blues; Who Knows; I Love Him Just the Same.

WHITEHEAD, WILLIAM J　　　　　　　ASCAP 1977
composer

b Hobbs, NMex, June 30, 38. Educ: Baylor Univ; Univ Okla, BMus; Curtis Inst Music, dipl; Columbia Univ, MA. Dir music, Trinity United Church of Christ, Pottstown, Pa, 59-60; First Presby Church, Bethlehem, Pa, 61-73 & Fifth Ave Presby Church, New York, 73- Fac, Ghilmant Organ Sch, New York, 65-66; Westminster Choir Col, Princeton, NJ, 66-71 & Mannes Col Music, 75- Organist, Bethlehem Bach Fest, 70-; US solo rep, Int Bach Fest, Berlin, 76; touring recitalist, 62-; Young Artist Award, Philadelphia Orch, 62. Assoc, Am Guild of Organists. Comp choral & organ.

WHITELAW, REID SMITH　　　　　　　ASCAP 1972
composer, author, record producer

b Johnson City, NY, Oct 17, 45. Educ: McBurney Sch, 61-63; Rider Col & C W Post Col, Long Island Univ, 63-67; studied voice with George Arlotta, 64-66. Announcer, singer, recorder, radio disc jockey, arr & writer. Rec'd two nominations Best Song Category, Billboard's Forum Disco Awards, 79. Co-wrote, produced & arr motion picture score for "Nocturna." Chief Collabrs: Norman Bergen, Billy Carl. Songs: Goody Goody Gumdrops; Diane; Love Is Just a Heartbeat Away; Extra, Extra (Read All About It); Nighttime Fantasy; Helplessly; We'll Meet in the Yellow Forest.

WHITFORD, HOMER PASCO　　　　　　ASCAP 1945
composer, organist, conductor

b Harvey, Ill, May 21, 1892. Educ: Tarkio Col Cons, 10, hon DM; Oberlin Cons, MusB, 15; Am Cons, Fontainebleu, studied organ & conducting, summer 24; Harvard Univ, grad study, 34-36; hon LHD, Dartmouth Col. Dir, Band Sch, Camp Gordon, Ga, WW I. Organist & dir, First Presby Church, Tabernacle Baptist Church, Utica, NY, 5 yrs, First Congregational Church, Cambridge, Mass, 35-56 & Chestnut Hill, 56-70. Cond, Lexington Choral Soc & Boston Madrigal Singers. Dir music therapy, McLean Hospital, Belmont, Mass. Lectr music therapy, New Eng Cons; instr, Shelby Sch Music; from asst prof to assoc prof, Dartmouth Col, dir col choir & glee club, 11 yrs. Fel Am Guild Organists (dean, NH, Vt & Mass Chapters). Instrumental Works: Five Choral Paraphrases, Set I & Set II; Suite for Organ (4 pieces); Wedding Music (organ); Preludes and Offertories, I, II; Daily Pedal Technic for the Organist. Songs & Instrumental Works: Glory to God in the Highest; Oh God, My Strength; When Christ Awoke Victorious; Thou Knowest, Lord, the Secrets of Our Hearts; Search Me, O God.

WHITFORD, JAMES KEITH　　　　　　　ASCAP 1959
composer, author

b Bath, NY, July 30, 17. Educ: Southern Calif Col, Pasadena; Cent Bible Col, Springfield, Mo. Clergyman & comp, pianist & organist, 40 yrs. Travelled with group, The Ambassadors, across US & Temple of Religion, NY World's Fair, 39. Songs: On A Rugged Hill; God Is Good to Me; An Ocean of Love; Life Has New Meaning; The Riches of His Grace.

WHITHORNE, EMERSON　　　　　　　　ASCAP 1924
composer, author, publisher

b Cleveland, Ohio, Sept 6, 1884; d New York, NY, Mar 25, 58. Educ: Pub schs; studied with James Rogers, Leschetizky, Robert Fuchs. Toured Chautauqua circuit, 2 yrs. Ed & critic, London, 07-16, New York, 16-30. Vpres, Composers' Music Corp, 20. Comp, incidental music for Theatre Guild production "Marco Millions." Songs & Instrumental Works: Greek Impressions (string quartet); New York Days and Nights (piano suite, then symph); 2 symphonies; El Camino Real (piano suite); The Aeroplane; Poem (piano, orch); Violin Concerto; Violin Sonata; String Quartet; Piano Quintet; Saturday's Child (tenor, soprano, chamber orch); The Grim Troubadour (voice, string quartet); Stroller's Symphony (Juilliard Sch publ award). Scores: Ballet: Sooner and Later.

WHITING, GEORGE　　　　　　　　　　ASCAP 1926
author, singer

b Chicago, Ill, Aug 16, 1884; d Bronx, NY, Dec 18, 43. Educ: Pub schs. Cafe entertainer & vaudeville performer, New York. Chief Collabrs: Abel Baer, Ernest Ball, Walter Donaldson, Fred Fisher, Albert Von Tilzer, Peter Wendling, Joe Burke. Songs: My Blue Heaven; Saloon; Believe It Beloved; My Wife's Gone to the Country; Every Little Bit Helps; Beautiful Eyes; Oh What I'd Do for a Girl Like You; West of the Great Divide; Little Black Boy; Don't Let Your Love Go Wrong; I Picked a Flower the Color of Your Eyes; Who Told You I Cared?; Strolling Through the Park One Day.

WHITING, RICHARD A　　　　　　　　ASCAP 1921
composer

b Peoria, Ill, Nov 12, 1891; d Beverly Hills, Calif, Feb 10, 38. Educ: Harvard Mil Sch, Los Angeles. Wrote songs for music publishers; became mgr, 12. Wrote for films, Hollywood, 19. Chief Collabrs: Ray Egan, Johnny Mercer, Neil Moret, Leo Robin, Gus Kahn, B G DeSylva, Sidney Clare. Songs: (They Made It Twice As Nice As Paradise) and They Called It Dixieland; Till We Meet Again; Some Sunday Morning; It's Tulip Time in Holland; Where the Morning Glories Grow; Where the Black-Eyed Susans Grow; Japanese Sandman; Sleepytime Gal; Ain't We Got Fun?; Breezin' Along With the Breeze; Honey; Horses; Ukulele Lady; She's Funny That Way; My Sweeter Than Sweet; True Blue Lou; It's a Habit of Mine; Louise; My Ideal; Beyond the Blue Horizon; My Future Just Passed; You're an Old Smoothie; Eadie Was a Lady; We Will Always Be Sweethearts; On the Good Ship Lollipop; It Was Sweet of You; Guilty; It's a Great Life; Roses in the Rain; Sentimental and Melancholy; When Did You Leave Heaven?; Too Marvelous for Words; I Can't Escape From You; Miss Brown to You; One Hour With You; Hooray for Hollywood; Waiting At the Gate for Katy; Have You Got Any Castles, Baby?; Love Is on the Air Tonight; We're Working Our Way Through College; Silhouetted in the Moonlight; Double Trouble; I'm Like a Fish Out of Water; Sailor Beware; You've Got Something There; Ride, Tenderfoot, Ride; Sorry. Scores: Bway stage: Toot Sweet; George White's Scandals of 1919; Take a Chance; Film: Innocents of Paris; Dance of Life; Monte Carlo; Safety in Numbers; The Playboy of Paris; Transatlantic Merry-Go-Round; One Hour With You; Adorable; Big Broadcast of 1936; Varsity Show; Ready, Willing and Able; Hollywood Hotel; Cowboy From Brooklyn.

WHITING, STEVEN JAY　　　　　　　　ASCAP 1975
composer, author, producer

b Livermore, Calif, Nov 12, 48. Educ: Woodside High Sch; Calif State Univ, San Jose, BA. Writer commercial jingles, country, jazz & pop. Asst music producer, "Peanuts" TV. Record producer, Pipeline & Blue Gorilla Records. TV producer/dir, CBS Sports Spectacular. Chief Collabrs: Vince Guaraldi, Bill Courtial, Don Grusin, Mike Eminger. Songs: Best of Friends; A Thousand Times Why; The Last One to Know; A Matter of Time; Wheatfields; Lyrics: Love Nevermore; Heartburn Waltz.

WHITLEY, RAY
composer, author, singer

b Stone Mountain, Ga, Dec 5, 01; d Manzinilla, Mex, Feb 21, 79. Performer, radio, TV, stage & motion pictures, 32-79. Chief Collabrs: Fred Rose, Gene Autry. Songs: I'm Back in the Saddle Again; Ages and Ages Ago; Lonely River; Please Don't Forget Me; How Was I to Know; Please Don't Forget Me, Dear; If You Want the Rainbow, You've Gotta Have the Rain; Darling, Don't Cry Over Me; There's a Mist Around the Prairie Moon Tonight; Blue Yodel Blues; You Laughed and I Cried.

WHITMAN, FAY
See Manus, Fay Whitman

WHITMAN, JERRY
See Winters, June

WHITMORE, JOSHUA DAVID ASCAP 1978
composer
b Gardner, Mass, Mar 27, 49. Educ: US Naval Acad, BS, 71. Staff writer for Ricci Mareno Ent (Terrace Music), Silverline Music/Goldline Music (Oak Ridge Boys); now staff writer for Al Gallico Music Corp, Nashville, Tenn. Chief Collabrs: Mark Sherrill, Linda Kimball, Mike Anthony. *Songs:* Lean It All on Me; You're My Kind of Woman; We'd Better Talk It Over.

WHITNEY, GRACE LEE ASCAP 1976
composer, author, singer
b Ann Arbor, Mich, Apr 1, 40. Singer with Billie Holiday, age 17, Chicago; appeared in three musicals, New York, age 18; also understudy. Appeared in "Some Like It Hot"; performer, "Star Trek" series. Chief Collab: Jack Dale. *Songs:* Stay and Spoil Me Baby; He's Gone; You Look So Good to Me; Lyrics: Disco Trekkin'; Star Child; Spaced Out Pilot; Charlie X; Miri; The Enemy Within; How Will He Love Me; Firedrill; Scooby Do; USS Enterprise; Venice to Balboa; Ruth; Ain't Ya Gonna Kiss Me Baby.

WHITNEY, JOAN
See Kramer, Zoe Parenteau

WHITNEY, JOHN CARY ASCAP 1979
composer, teacher, conductor
b Glens Falls, NY, Dec 2, 42. Educ: Glens Falls High Sch; Ithaca Col, BS, 64; New Eng Cons, MM, 71; comp study with Rayburn Wright, Warren Benson, Hale Smith & cond with Thomas Michalak. Teacher & orch cond, West Genesee High Sch, Camillus, NY; cond, Sch Orchestral Studies, Saratoga Springs, NY; pianist & leader of jazz trio; staff arr, Columbia Pictures Publications. *Instrumental Works:* The Junk Food Blues (string quartet); Coventry Carol (orch); O Holy Night (orch); Stevie Wonder Sounds (orch); Still (orch); love theme from Oliver's Story (orch).

WHITNEY, JULIA A (YULYA) ASCAP 1955
composer, author, singer
b Moscow, USSR, Oct 14, 22; d New York, NY, Aug 13, 65. To US, 53. Singer, cafes. Recording artist. *Songs:* To Park Means I Need Someone to Love Me Right Now; Tango Exotique; Sorry; Mama, My Mama; Hush, My Honey; There's Wind on the Window Pane; Love Is a Day Dream; A Few Golden Months; Avenue of Love; I Fell in Love With Someone's Eyes; Adieu, Many Thanks; Song of Moscow; Such As You Were; There's a Time to Be Sunkist.

WHITNEY, MAURICE CARY ASCAP 1952
composer, conductor, organist
b Glens Falls, NY, Mar 25, 09. Educ: Ithaca Col, BS & citation; NY Univ, MA; grad study, Columbia Univ Teachers Col, Westminster Choir Col & New Eng Cons, Boston; Williams Col, John Hay fel, 61; hon LHD, Elmira Col, 66. Cond, Glens Falls Oratorio Soc & Operetta Club. Dir music dept, Hudson Falls Pub Schs, 32-44, Glens Falls City Sch District, 44-69 & Adirondack Community Col, 69-71; retired, 71. Taught summer sessions, Univ Iowa, Univ Colo, Ernest Williams Summer Music Camp & NY Music Camp. Organist & choir-dir, churches in Ithaca & Hudson Falls, 35-67 & Glens Falls, NY. Mem ed bd, Music Educr J. Author, "Backgrounds in Music Theory" & "Whitney-Freeman Band Reader." Mem: Am Fedn Musicians; life mem Am Recorder Soc; life mem Music Educr Nat Conference (pres, Eastern Div, 59-61); Nat Educ Asn; NY Council Adminr Music Educ; life mem NY Sch Music Asn (pres, 63-64); NY Teachers Asn. *Songs:* Music: Gloria In Excelsis; Twelve Responses. *Instrumental Works:* From Sea to Shining Sea (chorus, band & orch); Introduction and Samba (alto saxophone & band); Dorian Overture (band); River Jordan (band); Thendara Overture (band); Variations on a Theme By Handel (orch); Dance Suite (string orch).

WHITSON, BETH SLATER ASCAP 1950
author
b Goodrich, Tenn, Dec 1, 1879; d Nashville, Tenn, Apr 26, 30. Educ: George Peabody Col. Wrote verse for magazines, 00-07. Chief Collabr: Leo Friedman. *Songs:* Let Me Call You Sweetheart; Meet Me Tonight in Dreamland; When the One You Love Forgets You; Say But It's Lonesome Kid; Leaf By Leaf the Roses Fall; When the Roses of Summer Have Gone.

WHO, ZIGGY
See Shelton, Larry Zane

WHYTE, RONNY ASCAP 1963
composer, author, singer
b Seattle, Wash, May 12, 37. Singer & pianist in supper clubs, cabarets, concerts & TV in New York, NY & in US & Europe. Actor in summer stock, regional repertory & off-Bway revues. Recording artist. *Songs:* Let Me Show You My New York; Music: I Think I Fell in Love Today.

WICH, LORRAINE
See Field, Lorraine F

WICK, OTTO ASCAP 1944
composer, conductor, arranger
b Krefeld, Ger, July 8, 1885; d Austin, Tex, Nov 9, 57. Came to US, 05. Educ: Gymnasium, Real-Gymnasium, Krefeld; studied music with Panzer, Mathieu Newmann & August Dechant; Univ Kiel, studied with Herman Stange; also studied with W Safonoff & Alfred Holy; New York Col Music. Cond orchs, New York, 10-24, incl Manhattan Opera, 20-21. Music dir, NY Liederkranz Soc, 21-24. Guest cond, opera & symph orchs, Europe. Comp, cond & arr, NBC, New York, 28-31. Organized & cond, NY Orch, 31-35 & Southwest Fest Asn, San Antonio, Tex, 38-42. Dean music, Univ San Antonio, 39-46. Music dir, San Antonio Civic Opera Co, Easter Sunrise Asn. *Songs & Instrumental Works:* Symphonic Poem; Symphony Fantasy; Suite for String Orch, Harp; Temples of Peshawur (cantata; Lake Placid Educ Found Prize); Seasons (song cycle); Trilogy for Symphonic Orch (1st Prize, Tex Fed Music Clubs); Gulf of Mexico. *Scores:* The Lone Star (opera); Matasuntha (music drama); Moon Maid (light opera); For Art's Sake (operetta).

WICKHAM, ELMER WILLIAM ASCAP 1972
composer, author
b Cambridge, Ill, May 16, 06. With daily newspaper, Iowa, 20 yrs, 13 yrs as circulation mgr. Chief Collabrs: Fred Stryker, Jim Boyd, Smokey Rogers, Wally Fowler, Cliff Japhey. *Songs:* Baby Me, Baby (polka); I'll String Along.

WIDDOES, LAWRENCE LEWIS ASCAP 1963
composer, teacher
b Wilmington, Del, Sept 15, 32. Educ: Juilliard Sch Music, BS(comp), 60, MS(comp), 63, studied with Bernard Wagenaar, Vincent Persichetti & William Bergsma; Wilmington Music Sch, studied piano with Elizabeth Beatty. Played piano & comp songs since age 6; studied piano through high sch & comp sonatas & concertos. Joined USN, 51, wrote shows for Ernie Pyle Theater, Tokyo, Japan. Works recorded var cos. Elizabeth S Coolidge Award, Benjamin Award, Ford Found Grant as comp-in-residence, Salem Sch Syst, Ore. Now fac, Juilliard Sch Music. Chief Collabrs: Cathalene Crane Widdoes, wife. *Songs & Instrumental Works:* Sonatina (flute & piano); Sanctus (chorus & piano); From a Time of Snow (chamber ens); Acanthus (vibraphone & harp); Crossing (double chorus & orch); 1000 Paper Cranes (harpsichord, viola & guitar).

WIDMAN, FRANKLIN DARRYL (RICHARD FRANKLIN) ASCAP 1973
composer, author
b Pittsburgh, Pa, Nov 20, 50. Educ: A V High Sch, Lancaster, Calif; self-taught musician & comp. Publ first song, 73. *Songs:* I Never Knew.

WIDZER, MARTIN ELLIS ASCAP 1967
composer
b Cleveland, Ohio, Sept 17, 40. Educ: Univ Mich, BA; Univ Ky, MD. Trained in psychiatry, child psychiatry & psychoanalysis. Chief Collabr: Jay E Lee. *Songs:* Keeping Your Eyes on the Sun.

WIEDER, HARDY ASCAP 1953
composer, author, business executive
b New York, NY, Feb 4, 10; d Great Neck, NY, Jan 31, 71. Educ: Columbia Col; Columbia Law Sch, LLB. Practiced law. Joined Universal Children's Dress Co, 37, pres, 39. Wrote songs for off-Bway musicals: "Make Him Magnificent"; "Suprise Package"; "Dakota." Chief Collabrs: Ruth Norman, Sholom Secunda. *Songs & Instrumental Works:* A Children's Christmas Carol; The Lonely Abalonian (Nat Council Christians & Jews Award); Faith Alone. *Scores:* Operetta: The Gypsy's Reward.

WIEDOEFT, RUDY ASCAP 1929
composer, saxophonist, teacher
b Detroit, Mich, Jan 3, 1893; d Flushing, NY, Feb 18, 40. Used saxophone in modern orchestrations; modernized design of saxophone; teacher of saxophone. *Instrumental Works:* Saxophobia.

WIEMER, ROBERT ERNEST (KEYSTONE BELASCO) ASCAP 1978
composer, author, singer
b Detroit, Mich, Jan 30, 38. Educ: Ohio Wesleyan Univ, BA, 59. Actor/singer in country-western, comedy TV & films; film dir & producer; songwriter. Emmy Award winning producer of TV series "Big Blue Marble." *Songs:* Tell Me What to Do.

WIERZBOWSKI, RAYMOND LAWRENCE (RAY WILLOW) ASCAP 1963
composer, author, musician
b Chicago, Ill, Aug 31, 20. Educ: Parochial schs; pvt music study; Southwest Photo Arts Inst of Photography. WW II, played saxophone & clarinet with var bands, also for var Army USO shows & war bond tours. Saxophonist with dance bands, Johnny Gilbert, Ray Pearl & Don Reid. Working for Firestone Truck Tire Plant, Nashville, Tenn. Photographer. Chief Collabrs: Abby Haskin, Bob Harvey. *Songs:* The Bells of Saint Bernadine; This Blue World of Mine; Baby, I'm Gonna Tell You Now; Music: Have You Ever Wondered Why?; This Is the Time of the Year; Oh! Pretty Girl; Just Give Me You.

WIEST, GEORGE D ASCAP 1942
composer, conductor
b Baltimore, Md, Sept 5, 1897; d July 11, 74. Educ: Baltimore City Col. Writer & dir, Bway musicals & radio shows. *Songs:* When I Went Around With Mary; I Love My Mother-in-Law; I Don't Believe It; I Love Those Singing Mice; Yes Pappy, Yes; Spring in the Valley; Why Do They Call Them Funnies?; Little Red Riding Hood.

WIGGINS, ARTHUR MONTAGUE ASCAP 1964
composer, arranger
b New York, NY, Mar 18, 20. US Army & Air Force Bands, USAF Sch of Music, DC. Chief Collab: Col Mark Azzolina, ret. *Instrumental Works:* Ballet for Jazz; Conversation for E flat Alto Saxophone; Song and Dance Man; Una Mas; The Horn.

WIGHT, ART F ASCAP 1967
composer, author, singer
b Defiance, Ohio, Nov 19, 11. Singer in trio, Tune Toppers, on radio, Toledo, Ohio, 37-38; also with Bill Panell Orch on radio, Fresno, Calif, 39-40. Music & lyrics writer. Arr & publ; Wight Barn Publ Co. *Songs:* Out of My Dream; I'm Pickin Fights for Christmas (So Presents I Won't Have to Buy); Little Christmas Tree; I Got My Baby With a Bundle of Blue Chip Stamps; Malena; Keep Your Eye on the Donut Not Upon the Hole; The Rooster and the Hen.

WILBUR, LYON PERRY, JR ASCAP 1961
composer, author, singer
b Memphis, Tenn, Oct 17, 34. Educ: Vanderbilt Univ; Memphis State Univ, BS. Singer on radio; actor in summer stock. Served in USN, 56-58. In insurance bus, 58-61; then DJ, announcer & writer, Memphis. *Songs:* There's Still Tomorrow; Shiloh; Hold Back the Night; Mirage; Lady With a Torch; Our Lives, Our Fortunes and Our Sacred Honor (Freedoms Found George Washington Award); There Must Be Someone; Yellow Pigtails; Be Sure It's Love; Steady Lovin'; Daydreams; Highway to Your Heart; The Soft Winds of England.

WILBUR, RICHARD (PURDY)
author, poet, educator
b New York, NY, Mar 1, 21. Educ: Amherst Col, BA, 42; Harvard Univ, MA(English), 47. Prof English, Harvard Univ, 50-54, Wellesley Col, 55-57 & Wesleyan Univ, 57-77; writer-in-residence, Smith Col, 77-; author bks of poems; ed of Poe & Shakespeare; transl of four verse plays by Moliere; anthologist, critic & author bks for children. Prizes: Pulitzer, 57, Nat Bk Award, 57, Bollingen, 71 & Brandeis Univ Creative Arts Award, 71. Chief Collabs: Lillian Hellman, Leonard Bernstein, Michel Legrand. *Songs:* Lyrics: A Christmas Hymn; A Prayer to Go to Paradise With the Donkeys; The Beautiful Changes; River of Darkness; Her Hair; Glitter and Be Gay; Two Songs to Poems of Richard Wilbur. *Scores:* Candide (comic opera).

WILBURN, CHARLES AARON ASCAP 1979
composer, author, singer
b Ardmore, Ala, July 9, 50. Started career as gospel singer, traveled with Happy Goodman Family; appeared with Gospel Singing Jubilee, 2 yrs, Rex Humbard TV Prog, Oral Roberts & others. Songwriter & cataloger, currently. Chief Collabs: Rusty Goodman, Bill Gaither, Gloria Gaither. *Songs:* Satan You're a Liar; What a Beautiful Day for the Lord to Come Again (Song of the Yr in Gospel Music, 75); It's Beginning to Rain; For Loving Me; Set Another Place At the Table; Just Any Day Now; That Sounds Like Home to Me; The North Won the War Again Last Night; Learning to Be Strangers; Joy in the Morning; Jesus Is the Light.

WILCHINSKI, MARTHA L ASCAP 1946
author, publicist
b New York, NY, Mar 14, 1897. Educ: NY Univ. Sgt, USMC, WW I. Newspaper writer & publicist for theatres incl Roxy, Capitol & Radio City Music Hall, New York. Wrote radio scripts. Aircraft instr, WW II. Chief Collab: William Axt. *Songs:* If Love Were All; Little Son.

WILCOX, DANIEL HARRIS ASCAP 1966
author
b New York, NY, Apr 17, 41. Educ: City & county schs; The Fieldston Sch; Cornell Univ, BA. Staff writer for "Captain Kangaroo", 65-67, "Sesame Street", 70-73; head writer & co-producer, "Carrascolendas", 75-76; writer, "The New Little Rascals", 77, "America 2 Night", 78, "The Waverly Wonders", 78, "Angie", 79, "MASH", 79- Chief Collabs: Jeffrey Moss, Joe Raposo. *Songs:* Lyrics: The Snufflelullabye; Everybody Sleeps/Everybody Eats; First/Last Song.

WILCOX, EDDIE ASCAP 1955
composer, conductor, pianist
b Method, NC, Dec 27, 07; d. Arr & pianist, Jimmie Lunceford Orch, 46-47; co-leader of band with Joe Thomas after Lunceford's death. Own trio, 58-60. Co-partner, publ & record cos.

WILDE, CORNEL L (JEFFERSON PASCAL, LOUIS NELIUS) ASCAP 1957
composer, author, director
b New York, NY, Oct 13, 18. Educ: Townsend Harris Hall High Sch, New York; Columbia Col, BS, 35; City Col New York, 37; studied with Lee Strasberg, Leo Bulgakov & Michael Chekhov. Theatrical appearances incl, "Moon Over Mulberry Street", "Love Is Not So Simple", "Daughters of Atreus", "Having Wonderful Time", "Romeo and Juliet"; appeared in many films incl, "High Sierra", "Wintertime", "A Song to Remember" (Academy Award nominee, best actor), "The Perfect Snob", "A Thousand and One Nights", "Forever Amber", "The Home Stretch", "It Had to Be You", "Walls of Jerico", "Roadhouse", "Four Days Leave", "Two Flags West", "Greatest Show on Earth", "At Swords Point", "Saedia", "Passion", "Woman's World", "Big Combo", "Scarlet Coat", "Hot Blood", "Star of India", "Beyond Mombasa", "Omar Khayyam", "Edge of Eternity", "Constantine the Great", "The Norsemen", "The Fifth Musketeer" & "Behind the Iron Mask"; actor, producer & dir, "Storm Fear", "Devil's Hairpin", "Maracaibo", "The Sword of Lancelot" (Gold Prize, Italian Film Festival, 63), "The Naked Prey" (Academy Award nomination, best screenplay), "Beach Red" (Academy Award nomination, best ed & spec effects); producer, dir & co-screenwriter, "No Blade of Grass"; producer, dir, writer & actor, "Sharks' Treasure." Recipient James K Hackett Award, 74; Bijou Film Soc Award, 75. *Songs:* Sharks' Treasure; No Blade of Grass; Beach Red; Lyrics: Maracaibo Moon; I Am Yours; The Devil's Hairpin; The Touch of Love; Swing It Just a Little More.

WILDE, DAN C ASCAP 1980
composer, author
b Houlton, Maine, June 3, 56. Co-owner publ co, Wildesworth Music. Chief Collabr: Ian Ainsworth. *Songs:* Maybe It's You?; I Survived the 70's.

WILDER, GENE
actor, director, writer
b Milwaukee, Wis, June 11, 35. Educ: Univ Iowa, BA, 55; Bristol Old Vic Theatre Sch, postgrad, 55-56. Served in AUS, 56-58. Appeared in Bway play, "The Complaisant Lover" (Clarence Derwent Award); appeared in motion pictures: "Bonnie and Clyde"; "The Producers" (Acad Award nomination); "Start the Revolution Without Me"; "Quackser Fortune Has an Uncle in the Bronx"; "Willie Wonka and the Chocolate Factory"; "Everything You Always Wanted to Know About Sex"; "Rhinoceros"; "Blazing Saddles"; "The Little Prince"; "Silver Streak"; "The Frisco Kid." Writer screenplay, dir & actor in films: "The Adventures of Sherlock Holmes' Smarter Brother"; "The World's Greatest Lover"; TV spec: "The Trouble With People"; "The Marlo Thomas Special"; TV films: "The Scarecrow"; "Thursday's Games." Writer screenplay & actor in film: "Young Frankenstein."

WILDER, JOHN
See Ireson, John Balfour

WILDER, WARNER
See Weidler, Warner Alfred

WILE, JOAN ASCAP 1972
composer, author, singer
b Rochester, NY, July 17, 31. Educ: Univ Chicago (liberal arts); studied piano with John Mehegan sight-singing with Lucy Greene. With vocal review act, The Neighbors, at Bon Soir, Ruban Bleu, Village Vanguard, Storyville, Crystal Palace, for Vanguard & ABC-Paramount Records. Jazz recording singer. Studio singer, TV jingles & records. Songwriter & performer in film "The Happy Hooker." Writer, songs & jingles, incl Muriel Cigars & Cougar cars. Chief Collabrs: Don Elliott, Michael Colicchio. *Songs:* At the Watergate the Truth Come Pourin' Out; One to One; Put Yourself in My Hands. *Scores:* Stage show: Tobacco Road (musical version).

WILES, ROGER
composer, author
b San Diego, Calif, June 29, 47. In sacred music field. Records with New Dawn, Grand Rapids, Mich. Has contract with Paragon Asns, Nashville. Minister; works with Christian Broadcasting Network. Does concerts; writes songs. *Songs:* All I Want to Do Is Glorify Jesus; Whatsoever Things.

WILEY, LEE ASCAP 1961
composer, singer
b Port Gibson, Okla; d. Singer, nightclubs in Chicago & New York; vocalist with Leo Reisman Orch. Performer, radio dramas; recording artist. Appeared on TV & in concerts. Chief Collab: Victor Young. *Songs:* Any Time, Any Day, Anywhere; Got the South in My Soul.

WILHELM, ELSIE LEE (ORIELL ROBBERTS) ASCAP 1974
lyricist
b Como, Miss, June 11, 35. Exotic dancer, touring US & other countries, 67- Lyricist, 74- Own co, Keep A Good Thought Productions. Co-writer, column "Your Pathway to Happiness" in Tri State Defender. Chief Collabrs: Rufus Thomas, Willie Mitchel, Ann Publis, Denise La Salle. *Songs:* Lyrics: Standby Woman; Starlight, Starbright; God Is My Light House; Give God a Chance;

Blues in the Basement; Settin on Ready; Just Cause I Leave (That Don't Mean I'm Gone); Got to Cover My Tracks.

WILHITE, MONTE   ASCAP 1942
composer
b Wichita, Kans, Nov 22, 1898; d Wichita, Aug 17, 61. *Songs:* Yesterday; Tomorrow; Will the Angels Play Their Harps for Me?; When Summer Is Gone; Now That I Have You.

WILHOIT, KENNETH HILL   ASCAP 1963
composer
b Los Angeles, Calif, Nov 6, 23. Educ: Santa Barbara State Col. Theme & score for "The New Loretta Young Show"; background music for "The Fugitive", "FBI", "Cannon", "Barnaby Jones" & "Streets of San Francisco."

WILHOITE, DONALD MACRAE, JR (DON RAYE)   ASCAP 1940
composer, author, singer
b Washington, DC, Mar 16, 09. Educ: NY Univ. Winner, Va state dancing championship, 24. Appeared in vaudeville, toured US, Eng & France. Organized nightclub act & writer, own material, 35. Under contract, music publ, 38. To Hollywood, 40, songwriter, films. Served, USA, World War II. Chief Collabrs: Gene De Paul, Hughie Prince, Pat Johnston, Harry James, Freddie Slack, Artie Shaw, Charles Shavers, Benny Carter. *Songs:* Rhythm in My Nursery Rhymes; Why Begin Again? (Pastel Blue); He's My Guy; Cow Cow Boogie; Mister Five By Five; Milkman, Keep Those Bottles Quiet; Star Eyes; I'll Remember April; You Don't Know What Love Is; Irresistible You; Music Makers; The House of Blue Lights; Pig Foot Pete; A Song Was Born; Your Red Wagon; They Were Doing the Mambo; Down the Road a Piece; Scrub Me Mama With a Boogie Beat; Beat Me Daddy Eight to the Bar; Rhumboogie; Boogie Woogie Bugle Boy; This Is My Country; Traveling Down a Lonely Road; Domino; Too Little Time; Ballad of Thunder Road; I'm Looking Out the Window; I Know What God Is; Gentle Is My Love.

WILHOUSKY, PETER J   ASCAP 1958
composer, author, conductor
b Passaic, NJ, July 6, 02; d Westport, Conn, Jan 4, 78. Educ: Juilliard Sch. Taught vocal music, pub schs, New York, 24-40. Asst music dir, bd of educ, 40, dir of music, 53. Asst to Toscanini, NBC; choral cond, radio & TV. Lectr & teacher, col summer sessions; guest cond. *Songs:* Carol of the Bells; Heavenly Light; Carol-Noel. *Instrumental Works:* Arr: Battle Hymn of the Republic; Black Is the Color of My True Love's Hair; Prayer Without Words; When Johnny Comes Marching Home; Madame Jeanette; Blessed Is the Man; & many choral works.

WILKES, NICK EMUS   ASCAP 1975
composer, author
b Bedford County, Va, June 7, 07. Radio & stage, 36-69. Chief Collabrs: Clifford Wilkes, John Amos, Earl Wilkes. *Songs:* My Lonely Heart Is Yearning; Wide River; Oh What a Day; She's My Baby; A Beautiful City.

WILKES, THOMAS E   ASCAP 1968
composer, author
b Summit, NJ, Dec 14, 35. Educ: Summit High Sch, 54; Cornell Univ, 58. Singer & songwriter with Up With People, Inc, 64-68. Chief Collabr: David Stevenson. *Songs:* What Color Is God's Skin?

WILKINSON, DUDLEY   ASCAP 1951
composer, author
b New York, NY, Sept 11, 1897. Educ: DeWitt Clinton High Sch, NY, grad, 14. In Bway production, "Selwyn Snapshots"; accompanist to Nora Bayes in vaudeville & Bway plays; accompanist & musical dir for Irene Bordoni in Bway plays, vaudeville club & Fleishman Hour Radio, 31; accompanist & arr, Norma Terris, concert & clubs; head, Eastern Talent Dept, Metro-Goldwyn-Mayer, 43-68, retired. Chief Collabrs: Oscar Hammerstein, Arthur Hammerstein, Anna Sosenko, Rudy Vallee. *Songs:* Why Don't They Leave Us Alone?; Music: I Loves Ya; Where in the World Is Love?; Lyrics: Because of You; special material for various artists. *Scores:* Bway Production: Queen of Hearts.

WILLADEN, GENE
See Thurston, Jane Jacquelin

WILLARD, KELLY FAYE   ASCAP 1977
composer, singer, recording artist
b Winter Haven, Fla, Aug 18, 56. Recorded first album for Maranatha Music, 78; announced Best New Female Artist, Record World Mag Spec Gospel Music Insert, 80. Recorder for husband's production co, Dan Willard. Chief Collabr: Bruce Hibbard. *Songs:* The Gift; Blame It on the One I Love; A Friend So True; Rest; Similies.

WILLETT, ELMER WILLIAM   ASCAP 1955
composer, author, publicist
b Pittsburgh, Pa, Apr 6, 11. Educ: Bus col. Owner, music store, 10 yrs; publicist & promotion mgr for Tony Bennett, Four Aces, Margaret Whiting, Guy Lombardo & Buddy Kaye; creator & mgr of group, The Vogues, 10 yrs. Owner & mgr, famous Vogue Terrace Supper Club, McKeesport, Pa, 8 yrs; plus other clubs. Show producer, talent counsel & record producer. Chief Collabrs: Buddy Kaye, Jo Ann Busch, Tom Ebbert, Steve Karol, John Greco, Seseen Francis, Patricia R Brodahl, Alan Wishard. *Songs:* Whole Lotta Lovin; Let's Pretend; Don't Be a Fool for Love; Buzzin; Buona Sera; From Day to Day; Was It Just Yesterday; Honey Love; Dream Spinner Man; A Better Way to Spend Today; Why Did You Go; Today Is Gonna Be My Day; Lonesome Waters; Always My Lady.

WILLEY, JAMES HENRY   ASCAP 1974
composer
b Lynn, Mass, Oct 1, 39. Educ: Eastman Sch Music, BM, 61, MM, 63, PhD, 72; Berkshire Music Ctr, studied with Gunther Schuller, 64. Prof, State Univ NY, Geneseo, 66-; vis prof music, Williams Col, Mass, 79-80. State Univ NY Res Found grants for compositional activity; Nat Endowment for the Arts awards; Chancellor's Award for excellence in teaching, State Univ NY, Geneseo. Works played by: Buffalo Philh, Rochester Philh, Dorian Quintet, Esterhazy Quartet & Univ Mass Group for New Music. *Instrumental Works:* String Quartet; Duo for Flute and Harp; Hymns and Litanies.

WILLIAMS, BYRON OLSEN   ASCAP 1966
composer, author, violinist
b Woodlawn, Va, Nov 23, 11. Educ: Moor Park Union High Sch, Calif, dipl; studied privately with Roderick White & Prof Victor Kuzdo; studied harmony, theory, counterpoint & comp with Dr Dezzo Delmar & Prof Hugo Davise. Contract violinist, Los Angeles Philh Orch, Columbia & MGM Motion Picture Studios. Radio & TV work in Los Angeles; radio tapes as soloist in Paris & Switz, also concertized as soloist in Europe. *Songs:* Lonesome Train Blues; When You Went Far Away. *Instrumental Works:* La Fiesta; Bayou Jig; River Boat Blues; Nuit a Paris; Serenata Veneziana.

WILLIAMS, CHARLES MELVIN (COOTIE)   ASCAP 1961
composer, trumpeter, conductor
b Mobile, Ala, July 24, 08. Trumpeter in Eagle Eye Shield's Band, Fla, 25-26; with bands incl, Alonzo Ross & Fletcher Henderson; mem, Duke Ellington Orch, 29-40 & Benny Goodman. Formed own band, later smaller groups, playing nightclubs & ballrooms. Recording artist. *Songs & Instrumental Works:* Round Midnight; House of Joy; Epistrophy.

WILLIAMS, CLARENCE   ASCAP 1927
composer, pianist, conductor
b Plaquemin, La, Oct 6, 1893; d Queens, NY, Nov 6, 65. Professional entertainer at age 12. With minstrel show; substitute for Jelly Roll Morton as orch cond, vaudeville. Organized radio, recording units, incl own trio, NY, 23; became publisher. *Songs & Instrumental Works:* Royal Garden Blues; Shout, Sister, Shout; Swing, Brother, Swing; Sugar Blues; Baby, Won't You Please Come Home?; Gulf Coast Blues; West End Blues; Squeeze Me; Ugly Chile; In the Bottle Blues; Organ Grinder; High Society; Terrible Blues; I Ain't Gonna Give Nobody None o' This Jelly Roll.

WILLIAMS, DAVID HENRY   ASCAP 1953
composer, author, organist
b Caerphilly, Wales, Nov 21, 19. Educ: George Washington High Sch, New York; Juilliard Sch Music, summer sessions; studied organ & theory with Walter Wild. Church organist & choirmaster: St John's Protestant Episcopal Church, Flushing, NY; Ft Washington Col, New York; Saugatuck Congregational, Westport, Conn; Congregational Church, Woodstock, Vt; St Andrew's Presby, Mt Neboh Temple & Catalina United Methodist, Tucson, Ariz. Comp, 49-; pianist, cond. *Songs & Instrumental Works:* On the Passion of Christ (cantata); The Trial of Christ (music/drama); Anthems: Draw Nigh to Jerusalem; Take My Life and Let It Be; Christ Came to Bethlehem.

WILLIAMS, DAVID MCK   ASCAP 1943
composer, organist, teacher
b Caernarvonshire, Wales, Feb 20, 1887; d. To US as infant. Educ: Denver schs; Schola Cantorum, Paris, studied with d'Indy, Vierne, Widor; King's Col, NS, MusD. Fac, Columbia Univ, 20-24, Juilliard Sch, 42-48. Organist, St Bartholomew's Church, New York, 20-48. Comp of church music. *Scores:* Opera: Florence Nightingale; Operetta: Enchanted Waters.

WILLIAMS, DAVID RUSSELL   ASCAP 1966
composer, professor
b Indianapolis, Ind, Oct 21, 32. Educ: Columbia Col, AB(cum laude, music), 54; Columbia Univ, MA(music comp), 56, studied with Otto Luening, Jack Beeson, Henry Cowell & Vladimir Ussachevsky; Eastman Sch Music, PhD, 65, studied with Howard Hanson, Bernard Rogers & Wayne Barlow; piano study with Orazio Frugoni; harpsichord study with Sylvia Marlowe, Mannes Col Music. Chief instr, USA Band Training Sch, Ft Chaffee, Ark, 57-59. Dir music, Windham Col, Putney, Vt, 59-62; opera coach, Eastman Sch Music, 62-65, assoc prof theory, 65-, adminr, Master Music Degree in Perf & Lit, 72-; secy, Col Music Soc, 73- Chief Collabr: Charles Tazewell. *Instrumental Works:* Five States of Mind (small orch); Fanfare for Brass Quintet; Recitation for Trombone Choir; Concerto for Piano (four hands, orch); In the Still of the Bayou (small orch).

WILLIAMS, DON
composer, singer, performer

b Floydada, Tex, May 27, 39. Educ: Portland High Sch, Tex. Played guitar & sang while in high sch. Formed Pozo Seco Singers, 64. Began as songwriter, Nashville, 71; contract for recording, JMT Label. With ABC-Dot, 74; transferred to ABC, then to MCA as recording artist, 79. Performed "Amanda", "Your My Best Friend", "Tulsa Time" (Single Record of Yr, Acad of Country Music, 79), "Good Old Boys Like Me" & "Lay Down Beside Me." Awards: Male vocalist of Yr, British Country Music Asn, 75 & US Country Music Asn, 78, Country Music Artist of Decade, Country Music People, 80 & Ireland's Most Popular Male Vocalist, Ireland RTE, Radio & TV Network, 80.

WILLIAMS, FRANCES — ASCAP 1948
composer, conductor, arranger

b Caernarvonshire, Wales; d New York, NY, Mar 1, 78. To US in youth. Educ: Cornish Sch of Music, Seattle, Wash (scholarship), studied with Calvin Brainerd Cady, Anna Dall; Juilliard Sch (fels), studied with Rubin Goldmark, James Friskin. Joined Harold Flammer, Inc, music ed-in-chief. Guest cond, music clinics. Mem, Nat Asn for Am Composers & Conductors, New York Fedn Music Clubs. *Songs & Instrumental Works:* Let There Be Music (choral, New York World's Fair, 64); Give Thanks; Spring Song; Night; Psalm XXIII; Christ-the Risen Lord (cantata); In Bethlehem's Lowly Manger; Spring's Awakening; To the Dawn; Hear Ye, O Mountains; Snowflakes; Choral Carillon.

WILLIAMS, GREG
See Hudspeth, William Gregory

WILLIAMS, HARRY — ASCAP 1939
author, publisher, director

b Faribault, Minn, Aug 29, 1879; d Oakland, Calif, May 15, 22. Educ: Pub & mil schs. Joined circus with Egbert Van Alstyne; toured in vaudeville; actor. To New York, 02; staff, music publ co; publ & film dir. Chief Collabrs: Egbert Van Alstyne, Neil Moret, Bert Grant, Joe Young, Art Hickman. *Songs:* Navajo; Back Back Back to Baltimore; In the Shade of the Old Apple Tree; Won't You Come Over to My House?; I'm Afraid to Come Home in the Dark; It Looks to Me Like a Big Night Tonight; What's the Matter With Father?; Rose Room; Good Night, Ladies; Don't Blame It All on Broadway; Mickey; San Antonio; Why Don't You Try?; Peggy.

WILLIAMS, HIRAM HANK, SR — ASCAP 1967
composer, author, singer

b Sept 17, 23; d 1952. Educ: "Teetot" Black Street Singer. Singer on streets of Montgomery, Ala, as teenager. Worked in Mobile shipyards. Was America's first country & western superstar. Chief Collabrs: Fred Rose, Vic M Caplan, Hank Williams, Jr (son), Audrey Williams, Pee Wee King. *Songs:* Your Cheating Heart; Jambalaya; I'm So Lonesome I Could Cry; Cold Cold Heart; Kaw-liga.

WILLIAMS, HUGH
See Grosz, Wilhelm

WILLIAMS, JAMES CLIFTON
teacher, conductor

b Traskwood, Ark, Mar 26, 23; d Feb 12, 76. Educ: La State Univ, BM, 47; Eastman Sch Music, MM, 48; PhD(hon), Universidad Lima, Peru, 64; studied French horn with V Yaudikyn, cond with Louis Husselmans & comp with Bernard Rogers & Howard Hansen. Played French horn professionally with San Antonio & New Orleans Symphonies. With comp dept, Univ Tex Sch Music, 17 yrs; chmn theory & comp, Univ Miami, 10 yrs. Won first & second Ostwald Awards for Comp. Mem, Am Bandmasters Asn. *Instrumental Works:* Fanfare and Allegro; Symphonic Suite; Ramparts; Caccia; Chorale; Sinsonians; The Patriots (comn by NORAD); Songs of Heritage; Academic Procession; Castle Gap March; Strategic Air Command; Symphonic Dance No 2 and No 3.

WILLIAMS, JANICE DYER
See Dyer, Janice Williams

WILLIAMS, JOAN FLORENCE — ASCAP 1970
composer, author

b Detroit, Mich, Feb 25, 31. Educ: Urban Ctr Col; D'Youville Col, cert. Began writing in early 20's; poetry & songs in 64. Author bk poems "Thoughts of Love and Life." *Songs:* Yours With Love.

WILLIAMS, JOE LEE — ASCAP 1952
composer, author

b Crawford, Miss, Oct 16, 06. Educ: Oktibeeha County Sch. *Songs:* Mellow Plums Blues; Old London Town; Baby Please Don't Go; Highway 49; GrayStone Blues; Mean Stepfather Blues; Wild Cow Blues; Peach Orchard Mama; Burned Child Scared of Fire; Tailor Made Woman; Somebody Been Bothering This Girl of Mine; She Gona Miss Me When I'm Dead and Gone; Breaking 'Em On Down; She Don't Allow Me to Fool Around All Night Long; It's a Low Down Dirty Shame; Watergate; Sugar Hill; Mellow Apples; Down in the Bottom With My Boots and Shoes; The Desert Blues; Whistling Pines; Move Your Hand; Piney Wood Blues; The Picka Picka Blues.

WILLIAMS, MARY LOU — ASCAP 1943
composer, pianist, arranger

b Pittsburgh, Pa, May 8, 10. Educ: High sch; studied music with B Sterzio, A Alexander, Ray Lev & Don Redman; 7 hon degrees. Pianist in dance orchs incl Andy Kirk. Led own group, 42; pianist, Cafe Soc, NY, 4 yrs; arr for orchs incl Benny Goodman, Louis Armstrong, Duke Ellington & Cab Calloway. Had own radio prog. Appeared in Town Hall & with NY Philh, Carnegie Hall, 46; toured Eng & Europe, 52-54. Retired from music, 54-57. Appeared at Newport Jazz Fest, 57. Pianist in concerts & nightclubs throughout country. Has made many records. Artist in residence, Duke Univ, 71- *Songs & Instrumental Works:* The Zodiac Suite; Black Priest of the Andes (cantata); In the Land of Oo-Bla-Dee; Camel Hop; Cloudy; Walking and Swinging; Nite Life; Foggy Bottom; Roll 'Em; Pretty-Eyed Baby; Overhand; The Juniper Tree; Little Joe From Chicago; Lonely Moments; Easy Blues; What's Your Story, Morning Glory; A Fungus Amungus; The Devil; Miss D D; Dirge Blues; Mary Lou's Mass; The Zodiac Suite; Hymn in Honor of Martin; De Porres; Zoning Fungus II; Rosa Mae.

WILLIAMS, MATT — ASCAP 1959
author

b New York, NY, Mar 9, 29. *Songs:* I Gotta Know; Until My Heart Found You; Journey of Love; Hushabye Little Guitar.

WILLIAMS, MENTOR — ASCAP 1971
composer, producer, singer

b Omaha, Nebr, June 11, 46. With var bands in NMex, then Calif. Music writer for var artists; record producer. Signed with Alamo Music, 72. Chief Collabrs: Troy Seals, Will Jennings, Jack Conrad. *Songs:* Drift Away; Good Old Song; So High.

WILLIAMS, MILAN BONNETT — ASCAP 1974
composer, author, singer

b Tupelo, Miss, Mar 28, 48. Educ: Self-taught. With The Commodores. Chief Collabr: James Carmichael. *Songs:* The Bump; I Feel Sanctified; Better Never Than Forever; Mary, Mary; Captain Quick Draw; Patch It Up; Brick House; Let's Get Started; X-Rated Movie; Wonderland; Old Fashion Love. *Instrumental Works:* Machine Gun; Rapid Fire; I'm Ready.

WILLIAMS, NED — ASCAP 1962
composer, author, singer

b Wolf Lake, Ill, Feb 23, 27. Educ: High sch, dipl. Farmer; merchant seaman; truck driver; sign painter. Chief Collabrs: R D Copp, Fannie Kirk, John B Skipper & Betty Syme. *Songs & Instrumental Works:* Songs of the Shawnee Hills. *Scores:* Operas: The Christ Story; The Drifter.

WILLIAMS, OTIS CLAYBORN — ASCAP 1974
composer, author, singer

b Texarkana, Tex, Oct 30, 41. Mem group, Temptations, 20 yrs. *Songs:* Lyrics: Can't You See Sweet Thing; Isn't the Night Fantastic; I'm Coming Home; Who Are You; I'm on Fire.

WILLIAMS, PAUL HAMILTON
composer, singer

b Omaha, Nebr, Sept 19, 40. Educ: High sch grad. Appeared in films, "The Loved One", "The Chase", "Watermelon Man" & "Planet of the Apes." Numerous TV appearances incl, "Midnight Special" & "Mike Douglas Show"; also with Merv Griffin, Jonathon Winters & others. Assoc, A&M Records, 70-Pres, Hobbitron Enterprises, 73- Rec'd Grammy Award For Best Songwriter, 78. Trustee, Nat Acad Recording Arts & Sci. *Songs:* We've Only Just Begun; Rainy Days and Mondays; An Old Fashioned Love Song; Family of Man; Let Me Be the One.

WILLIAMS, PHYLLIS
See Zeno, Phyllis Williams

WILLIAMS, RAYMOND GEORGE
b Chicago, Ill, July 29, 1887. Educ: Harvard Univ, BA, 11. Mgr, RI Philh & Providence Community Concerts; Providence mgr, Boston Symph. *Songs:* Music: Harvardiana.

WILLIAMS, RICARDO G — ASCAP 1975
composer, author, drummer

b Northbrook, Va, Aug 6, 53. Educ: Norfolk Univ, BA(music theory). Founder band, Mass Productions, in high sch. Chief Collabr: Tyrone Williams. *Songs:* Firecracker; Groove Me; Wanna Make a Dream Come True.

WILLIAMS, RICHARD B
composer, author, singer

b Wall Lake, Iowa, June 7, 26. Began singing with The Brothers at age 10; on radio, some movies, then with Kate Thompson. Singer with Harry James. Writer & singer, TV commercials. Has done spec material & vocal arr for TV specials.

WILLIAMS, ROBERT KENNETH — ASCAP 1975
composer, lyricist

b Breckenridge, Minn, Dec 24, 21. Educ: Univ Minn, grad; Tenn Technol Univ. Performed own music in concert on stage of Guthrie Theater, Minneapolis.

Writer music & lyrics for indust shows, 69-, children's theater productions & satirical material for singing groups. *Songs:* Christmas Love; Merry Christmas Past; Don't Wait 'Til Tomorrow; Take a Hand for Holding; The End Or the Beginning; Happens Every Day; For Frank (One Summer Afternoon).

WILLIAMS, ROGER
See Weertz, Louis Jacob

WILLIAMS, SAM　　　　ASCAP 1926
composer, pianist, teacher
b New York, NY, Mar 4, 1884; d Belle Island, Fla, Aug 31, 61. Educ: City Col New York. Pianist in vaudeville, 04-24; had act with Kate Elinore. Became stock broker, 24. *Songs:* When I Fought for the USA; Cross My Heart, Mother, I Love You; Why Don't You Marry the Girl?; Waiting for the Tide to Turn; Moonlight Is Spoonlight; Just Like Washington Crossed the Delaware, Pershing Will Cross the Rhine.

WILLIAMS, SPENCER　　　　ASCAP 1921
composer, author, pianist
b New Orleans, La, Oct 14, 1889; d Flushing, NY, July 14, 65. Educ: St Charles Univ. Pianist, San Souci Park, Chicago, 07. Wrote music for Josephine Baker, Folies Bergere, Paris, 25. Chief Collabr: Fats Waller. *Songs & Instrumental Works:* I Ain't Got Nobody; Shim-Me-Sha-Wabble; Royal Garden Blues; Tishomingo Blues; Basin Street Blues; Everybody Loves My Baby; I Found a New Baby; Mahogany Hall Stomp; Careless Love; Arkansas Blues; Paradise Blues; When Lights Are Low; Dallas Blues; I Ain't Gonna Give Nobody None o' This Jelly Roll; My Man o' War.

WILLIAMS, SUSAN LUXEN　　　　ASCAP 1977
composer, author
b Chicago, Ill, Sept 30, 53. Educ: Univ Chicago, BA(astrophysics). Performer & comp, rock group Mythomania. Writer & musician, Kirchner productions of "Roxy." Studio asst Spectrum Studios, Venice, Calif; recorded at Capitol & Electa-Asylum Records. *Songs:* Softly Rock and Rollo; I Can Tell; Bye Bye Jules; After the Rain; Gambler.

WILLIAMSON, BRUCE　　　　ASCAP 1959
composer, author
b Cadillac, Mich. Educ: Columbia Univ; Stella Adler Theatre Studio. Was TV actor. Writer spec material for revues incl Julius Monk "UpStairs At the Downstairs"; "Plaza 9"; "Clap Hands" (London); "Up Tempo" (Can). Film critic, Time. Chief Collabrs: Blair Weille, William Roy. *Songs:* Family Fallout Shelter; Secret; Minneapolis-St Paul; Ode to an Eminent Daily; Lady Chatterley; Trio Con Brio; Castro Tango.

WILLIAMSON, CLAUDE B, JR　　　　ASCAP 1971
composer, pianist, arranger
b Brattleboro, Vt, Nov 18, 26. Educ: New Eng Cons Music, piano & orchestration maj, 44-46; studied jazz piano with Sam Saxe. Pianist with Charlie Barnet Orch, 47-49; musical dir for June Christy, 50-51. In 29th Army Band, USA, Okinawa, 51-53. Jazz pianist with Howard Rumsey's Lighthouse All-Stars, 53-58; has done studio work, Los Angeles, 59-68; assoc musical dir TV shows, Sonny & Cher, CBS, 69-73, Andy Williams, NBC & var other shows, 73-75 & Donny & Marie, 76-79. Chief Collabrs: Osmond Bros, Bob Rozario. *Songs & Instrumental Works:* Haystack Shuffle; New Departure (jazz); La Fiesta (jazz); various musical cues for Sonny & Cher TV show & Donny & Marie TV show.

WILLIAMSON, HENRY　　　　ASCAP 1973
composer, lyricist
b Brooklyn, NY, Apr 12, 53. Educ: Lyric workshops with Lou Stallman & Gene Katz. Began writing in 73; sang with local groups; writes gospel c/w, pop, etc. Chief Collabrs: Archie Swindell, Nick Sisco, Fred Ledderman. *Songs:* Keep on Getting Up; Disco Machine; Please Let Me In; The Morning After; Twilight Zone; Cooling Out; Showstopper; Disco Delight; Ticket to the Promised Land; Behind Every Great Man; Champagne Charlie; There Were Times; Lyrics: Jesus Got a Hotline; Boogie for Jesus; I Wanna Witness; If Its My Cross; Gimme Your Love; Devil Best Be Running; Rain Down Fire; Answer the Call Lord; I Wanna Thank You Lord; All the Way Christian; I'll Remember You; Johnny Fame; 12 Days a Week.

WILLIAMSON, MIKE LEE　　　　ASCAP 1978
composer, author, singer
b Albert Lea, Minn, July 14, 52. Educ: Rock Valley Col, Ill, music theory, 76; pvt vocal study with Nell Welsh; col chorus, jazz ens & piano study, 76-77. Numerous club appearances; guest spot with the Proud Americans, State Dept, DC, 76. With radio play, Mex, Ill, Fla & Minn. Appeared in musical revue, Tampa, Fla, 80. Numerous commercials & recording sessions, Ill & Wis. Chief Collabrs: Bob Frey, Dorothy Turner, Tom Stein. *Songs:* They'll Never Take Away the Good Times; Happy; Love Just Doesn't Go Away; I Can Feel the Music. *Albums:* Friends Forever.

WILLIE THE LION
See Smith, William H

WILLIS, DANIEL DALE
composer, author, singer
b Washington, DC, Nov 23, 52. Educ: Eastern Nazarene Col, Mass; Travecca Nazarene Col, Tenn; Northern Va Community Col. Started singing in church; entertainer nightclubs & concerts; songwriter & composer. *Songs:* By the Way; This Is the First Time (I've Seen the Last Time on Your Face); This Is a Hold Up; She Pretended We Were Married; California Calling; Love Storms; Have You Ever Had an Angel (Love the Devil Out of You); Roses Are Red; Cowboys' Cowboy; Yankee Snow; I Can't Love a New Love (With an Old Love in My Heart).

WILLIS, RICHARD M　　　　ASCAP 1966
composer, conductor
b Mobile, Ala, Apr 21, 29. Educ: Univ Ala, BMus(comp), 50; Eastman Sch Music, MMus(comp), 51, PhD(comp), 64. Head dept music theory-comp, Shorter Col, Ga, 53-63; prof music & comp-in-residence, Baylor Univ, 64-. Works performed by numerous civic orchs, service & col bands & wind ens, chamber groups & others. Awards: Joseph Bearns Prize, 55; Prix de Rome, Am Acad Rome, 56-57; Howard Hanson Prize, 64; Ostwald Award, 69; Volkwein-Am Sch Band Dirs Asn, 73 & others. *Instrumental Works:* Sonatina (violin & piano); Aria and Toccata (band); Partita (band); Affirmation (band); Marcia Ostinata (band); String Quartet No 2; Sonatina (trumpet & piano); Sonatina (clarinet & piano); Recitative and Dance (flute & strings or piano); Colloquy (woodwind quintet & perc); Epode (band); Diversion (band); Sonants (small wind ens); Colloquy II (violin & perc); Sonata (violin & piano). *Songs & Instrumental Works:* The Drenched Land (SATB); Remember (SSA); Petition and Thanks (chorus & wind ens).

WILLOW, RAY
See Wierzbowski, Raymond Lawrence

WILLS, BILLY RUFUS　　　　ASCAP 1975
author
b Camden, Tenn, Sept 14, 34. Educ: Corinth High Sch, Miss; Vanderbilt Univ, BS. Chief Collabr: Tupper Saussy. *Songs:* Lyrics: Strings.

WILLS, DAVID　　　　ASCAP 1974
composer, singer
b Pulaski, Tenn, Oct 23, 51. Educ: Huntsville High Sch, Ala, grad. Toured with Charlie Rich, 2 yrs. Staff writer, Pi-Gem & Cless Music. Recordings, Epic & United Artists. Toured, Charley Pride Show. Chief Collabrs: John Selween, Charles Quillen, Dean Dillon, Kent Robbins, Don Pfrimmer. *Songs:* From Barrooms to Bedrooms; You're All Over This Place; Love Me Like a Stranger; They Never Lost You; Making It Special Again.

WILLS, JAMES ROBERT (BOB)　　　　ASCAP 1957
composer, band leader, fiddler
b Kosse, Tex, Mar 6, 05; d Ft Worth, Tex, May 13, 75. Leader, Bob Wills and his Texas Playboys. *Songs:* Maidens Prayer; San Antonio Rose; I Wonder If You Feel the Way I Do; Faded Love; My Confession; Big Beaver; Music: Beaumont Rag; Spanish Two Step; Stay a Little Longer; Sugar Moon; Take Me Back to Tulsa; Time Changes Everything; Texas Playboy Rag; I Knew the Moment I Lost You; My Shoes Keep Walking Back to You.

WILLSON, MEREDITH　　　　ASCAP 1942
composer, author, flutist
b Mason City, Iowa, May 18, 02. Educ: Mason City Pub Schs; Damrosch Inst of Musical Art; pvt study with George Barrere, Henry Hadley, Mortimer Wilson, Bernard Wagenaar & Julius Gold. First flute, John Philip Sousa Band, 21-23 & New York Philh, 24-29. Maj, AUS, Armed Forced Radio Service, WW II. Musical dir radio sta KFRC, San Francisco & NBC's Western Div; musical dir & featured personality on radio "The Maxwell House Coffee Time", "Burns and Allen" & "The Big Show"; musical dir & host on Texaco TV Specials. *Songs:* 76 Trombones; America Calling; Banners and Bonnets; You and I; Iowa; I See the Moon; Chicken Fat; Two in Love; Whose Dream Are You; May the Good Lord Bless and Keep You; It's Beginning to Look Like Christmas; It's Easter Time; The Peony Bush. *Instrumental Works:* Symphony No 1 in F Minor; Missions of California (Symphony No 2); Symphonic Variations on an American Theme; O O McIntyre Suite; Meredith Willson's Nocturne for Piano (for Rosemary); Hit the Leather; Mail Call March. *Scores:* Film/TV: The Great Dictator; The Little Foxes; Bway Shows: The Music Man; The Unsinkable Molly Brown; Here's Love.

WILSON, AL　　　　ASCAP 1923
author
b Providence, RI, May 24, 06; d New York, NY, Apr 25, 51. *Songs:* In the Little Red School House; The Wild Women Are Making a Wild Man of Me; Barefoot Days; Down in the Old Swimming Hole; Happy Go Lucky Days; Profiteering Blues; Down By the Old Apple Tree.

WILSON, CAMERON KELLY
composer, singer, musician
b Benton Harbor, Mich, July 7, 59. Recording artist, ATCO Recording Corp. Chief Collabr: Steve Wilson. *Songs:* If the World Ran Out of Love Tonight; Thankin' Heaven; Just Like a Lover Knows; Feeling Like We're Strangers Again.

WILSON, CHRIS RICHARD (GANDOLF T GREY) ASCAP 1969
composer, entertainer
b Brooklyn, NY, Nov 13, 48. Educ: Glen Cove High Sch, grad, 66. Recorded for Columbia, 67-68 & Roulette, 69. Formed The Rainbow Group to do TV production. Chief Collabr: Bill Porter. *Songs:* All the Joy; The Grey Wizard Am I.

WILSON, CURTIS WAYNE ASCAP 1977
composer, teacher, musician
b Ft Worth, Tex, Sept 11, 41. Educ: Tex Christian Univ, BME, 63, MM, 66; NTex State Univ, doctoral work, comp, 70-71. Musician with Fred Waring Pennsylvanian's, 66-68; asst prof music, Valley City State Col, NDak, 68-72; asst prof music & dir bands, Ashland Col, Ohio, 72-76; assoc prof music, Tex Christian Univ, 76- *Instrumental Works:* El Titan March; Kaleidoscope March; March Metroplex.

WILSON, DOLORES S (SALLY) ASCAP 1971
composer, author, singer
b Cleveland, Ohio, July 31, 26. Singer & comp, country music, 20 yrs; recording artist at var clubs, shows & benefits. *Songs:* Little Man Comes Sneaking Thro My Dream; Climbin' the Wall; Santa's Big Red Car.

WILSON, DON ASCAP 1955
composer, author
b Detroit Lakes, Minn, July 26, 1896; d. Educ: Univ Wash; studied with mother & C Olin Rice. Comp, col musical. Served, USAF, World War I. Music dir, Moran Sch, 2 yrs. Writer & performer, radio, 20's. Ed, Gamble FitzSimons, Pallma, Chicago, 13 yrs. Producer & arr, radio progs for Century of Progress Exposition, 33-34. To New York, 38. Songwriter for Bway musicals. Chief Collabr: Edward Bradley. *Songs:* Sonia; Cowboy on the Moon. *Scores:* Stage shows: Hi Fi Follies; Purple Towers; Operettas: Sorcerer's Apprentice; Rio Rico; Up in the Air.

WILSON, (ROBERT) DOUGLAS ASCAP 1971
composer, author
b Brooklyn, NY, Aug 16, 35. Educ: Colgate Univ, BA. Producer & dir for ABC & ABC Sports. *Songs:* The Wide World; Love Is Why We're Here; The Ballad of Billy Kidd and Egon II; Three O'Clock Lonely.

WILSON, EARL ASCAP 1959
author
b Rockford, Ohio, May 3, 07. Educ: Heidelberg Col; Ohio State Univ, BS. Newspaper & mag writer. Columnist, "It Happened Last Night," syndicated, New York Post, 42- Author: "Jungle Performers"; "I Am Gazing Into My 8-Ball"; "Pike's Peek or Bust"; "Let 'Em Eat Cheesecake"; "Look Who's Abroad Now." Chief Collabrs: Leonard Whitcup, Earl L Wilson (son). *Songs:* Kissin' on the Phone; It Happened Last Night; Do I Really Love You?

WILSON, EARL, JR (SLUGGER) ASCAP 1956
composer, author
b New York, NY, Dec 1, 42. Educ: Bucknell Univ, BM(music). Apprentice comp under Lionel Newman, 20th Century Fox, 65; prof entertainer & comp in clubs, on TV & radio & records; writer of Bway shows. Chief Collabr: Otto Maximilian. *Songs:* Doesn't Anybody Love Anymore; Take Me Home With You; The Man I Could Have Been; If I Could Live My Life Again; Feel My Body, Touch My Soul; I Wish; How Lucky We Are; How Small We Are, How Little We Know; When I Was a Child. *Scores:* Bway Shows: A Day in the Life of Just About Everyone; Earthlings; Off Bway Show: Let My People Come (original cast album nominated for Grammy, 74).

WILSON, GEORGE BALCH ASCAP 1971
educator, composer
b Grand Island, Nebr, Jan 28, 27. Educ: Univ Mich, BMus, 51, MMus, 53, DMus Arts, 62; Conservatoire Royal de Musique (Fulbright scholar), Brussels, 53-54; studied with Ross Lee Finney, Jean Absil, Nadia Boulanger & Roger Sessions. Served in USAAF, 45-46. Mem fac, Univ Mich Sch Music, Ann Arbor, 61-, dir Electronic Music Studio, 64- Founder, Contemporary Directions, 66, later mus dir. Awards: Publ Award for String Quartet, Am Soc Publ Am Music, 52; Rome Prize, Am Acad Rome, 58-60; Award & Citation, Nat Inst Arts & Letters, 70; Walter Hinrichsen Award for Composers, 73. Mem, Am Soc Univ Composers. *Instrumental Works:* String Quartet; Sonata for Viola and Piano; Adagio for Strings and Horns; Sonata for Cello and Piano; Overture for Orchestra; Fantasy for Violin and Piano; String Trio; Six Pieces for Piano; Six Pieces for Orchestra; Fragments (electronic sound); incidental music for The Flies (Sartre); Exigencies (electronic sound); Concatenations for 12 Instruments; Polarity for Solo Percussion and Electronic Sounds.

WILSON, HARRY ROBERT ASCAP 1950
composer, author, conductor
b Salina, Kans, May 18, 01; d Carmel, NY, Sept 24, 68. Educ: Manhattan (Kans) State Col, BS, 26; Columbia Univ, MA, 32, EdD, 38; Juilliard (2 fels), studied with Rubin Goldmark & Albert Stoessel. Singer & cond, church choirs, Wichita, 21-26. Dir music, pub schs, Eureka, Kans, 26-29 & Hastings-on-Hudson, NY, 32-34. Dir musical activities, New Col, Columbia Univ, 32-39; prof music educ, Teachers Col, 39-58, head, Music & Music Educ Depts, 58-66. Guest cond & lectr, choral fests. Author: "Music in the High School"; "Building a Church Choir"; co-author: "Lead a Song!"; "The School Music Conductor"; "Artistic Choral Singing"; "Choral Arranging"; "Guide for Choral Conductors." Mem: Music Teachers Nat Asn; Music Educators Nat Conference; Nat Asn Teachers Singing; Nat Asn Composers & Conductors; Am Musical Soc; Am Choral Dirs Asn. *Songs & Instrumental Works:* Choral: Upon This Rock (oratorio); Sing-A-Rama; All Music; Banners of Peace; Let Our Great Song Arise; Look to This Day; O Brother Man; Peace Must Come Like a Troubadour; Res' My Shoes; A Thing of Beauty; The Finger of God.

WILSON, IRA B ASCAP 1938
composer, arranger
b Bedford, Iowa, Sept 6, 1880; d Los Angeles, Calif, Apr 3, 50. Educ: Pvt music study. Comp, ed & arr, music publ co. *Songs & Instrumental Works:* The Childhood of Hiawatha; Rip Van Winkle; The Courtship of Miles Standish; The Legend of Sleepy Hollow; George Washington; The Spirit of '76; Arr: Romance of Cinderella (Mozart); The Frost King's Daughter (Grieg); & many educ cantatas. *Scores:* Operettas: The Governor's Daughter; H R H Miss Jones; The Galloping Ghost; King Koko; Chonita (Liszt); The Forest Prince (Tchaikowsky).

WILSON, IRVING M ASCAP 1925
composer, violinist
b Santa Rosa, Calif, Aug 21, 1881; d San Francisco, Calif, May 26, 37. Educ: Polytech High Sch, San Francisco; studied music with Julio Minetti, Sigmund Beal. Violinist in dance orchs; concertmaster, Minetti Orch. *Songs:* Kid Days; White Sails; Lingering Memory. *Instrumental Works:* King Zim of Zniba (comic opera); 3 Indian Love Songs.

WILSON, JESSE A ASCAP 1978
composer, author
b Gaffney, SC, Jan 20, 16. Educ: Am Univ, DC; Nat Acad of Broadcasting, DC. Organized 55th Gen Hosp Dance Orch, WW II, Europe. Played bass fiddle; also with pick-up orch. Retired from Dept Interior, US Govt. *Songs:* Just a Tiny Picture; I Was Such a Fool.

WILSON, JOHN FLOYD (WILLIAM J FLOYD, MARTIN WEST) ASCAP 1967
composer, author, teacher
b Youngstown, Ohio, Mar 24, 29. Educ: Am Cons of Music, MusB; Northwestern Univ, MusM, doctoral studies; studied with Anthony Donato & Leo Sowerby. Taught music, Mountain View Bible Col, Alta, Ft Wayne Bible Col, Ind, Moody Bible Inst, Chicago & Marion Col, Ind. Exec ed, Hope Publ Co, Ill. Lectr & guest cond, var choral fests & workshops. Organist & choirmaster at several churches. Chief Collabrs: Grace Hawthorne, Marti McCartney, Cordelia Spitzer. *Songs:* Who Is This Boy? (solo, choral); Shepherds, Rejoice (musical); It Won't Stop (solo, choral); I Believe (Christmas musical); Jesus, Savior, Redeemer (choral); He's Alive (Easter musical); Music: Let George Do It (children's musical); It's Music (children's musical); Electric Sunshine Man (children's musical); Runaway (young adult musical-drama); Good News, World (Christmas musical); He Carried My Cross (choral, solo); How the West Was Really Won (children's musical). *Instrumental Works:* Morning Has Broken (organ solo collection).

WILSON, JOHN NEWTON ASCAP 1965
composer
b Carson Creek, Calif, Feb 9, 09. Educ: Sacramento Jr Col, 31. Bandleader, 40-65; writer & comp, Standard Sch Broadcast; arr, Sacramento Music Circus; musical dir many prof shows. Chief Collabrs: Warner Wilder, Walt Wilder, George Wilder, George Alexander. *Songs:* Two Hearts; The Old Chimney; The Phonograph; The Telephone; The Hey-Day of Burlesque.

WILSON, JOHNNY ANCIL (PEANUTS) ASCAP 1970
composer, author
b Rivesville, WVa, Nov 28, 35. *Songs:* Love the World Away; It's Too Late (To Love Me Now); Rock on Baby; Roses for Mama; When a Love Ain't Right.

WILSON, JOSEPH LEE ASCAP 1965
composer, author, singer
b Bristow, Okla, Dec 22, 35. Educ: Los Angeles Cons Music, 55; Los Angeles Jr Col, 56. Jazz singer, Santa Monica, San Francisco, Mexico City & New York; recording artist; appeared on radio & TV: Showcase Network NBC-TV, Dick Cavett Show, Soul Channel 13 & Columbia Univ WKCR-FM. Owner-operator of Loft Jazz-Ladies Fort. Went on State Dept tour of WAfrica & Europe. Nat Endowment Grant for comp-perf. Chief Collabrs: Archie Shepp, Roscoe Wethers, James Spaulding, Jill Christopher. *Songs:* Come and See (Sparrow

Singing Jazz for Me) (ASCAP Award Popular Song); Secrets From the Sun (Fighting to Be Free); One (Dedicated to My Father); Sphirlov (Hurricane); Children's Jazz Suite.

WILSON, LEE
See Beach, Albert Askew

WILSON, MARION T (MARION CLARISA TAYLOR)   ASCAP 1962
composer, author, musician
b Rouses Point, NY, Apr 28, 08. Educ: Plattsburgh High Sch; Eastman Sch Music, cert. Pianist in orch, age 14; organist, Ben Bernie Mem Prog; pianist radio prog, WMFF, Plattsburgh; TV appearances as solo organist; stage shows as pianist; church & theatre organist; teacher. Chief Collabrs: Jay Johnson, Billy Hayes, Lou Schwartz, Abner Greenberg, Chick Adams. *Songs:* Do a Golden Deed Today; On Lake Champlain; Music: Have a Little Sympathy; Married for Life; Whittling.

WILSON, MORTIMER   ASCAP 1924
composer, conductor, educator
b Chariton, Iowa, Aug 6, 1876; d New York, NY, Jan 27, 32. Educ: Chicago Cons; studied with S E Jacobson, Frederick Gleason, William Middleschulte, Max Rieger. Dir, theory dept, Univ Nebr Sch of Music, 02-09. Cond, Atlanta Philh, 11. Dir, Atlanta Cons until 16. To New York, taught harmony & comp, Malkin Sch & privately. Music writer for films. *Instrumental Works:* From My Youth (suite); New Orleans (overture); Overture 1849; My Country (scenic fantasy); Trio in G; 2 sonatas.

WILSON, NANCY LAMOUREAUX   ASCAP 1976
composer
b San Francisco, Calif, Mar 16, 54. Educ: Pacific Univ; Portland State Univ. Flute lessons at age 10; piano lessons, elem & high sch. Gave guitar lessons in high sch. Mem group, Heart. *Songs:* Dreamboat Annie; Magic Man; Crazy on You; Barracuda; Little Queen; Heartless; Magazine; Mistral Wind; Bebe Le Strange; Even It Up; Silver Wheels; Raised on You; Cook With Fire; Straight On; Dog and Butterfly.

WILSON, R A
See King, Robert A

WILSON, RICHARD (EDWARD)   ASCAP 1968
composer, pianist, teacher
b Cleveland, Ohio, May 15, 41. Educ: Harvard Univ, AB(music, magna cum laude), 63; Rutgers Univ, MA(comp), 66; studied piano with E W Fischer & Leonard Shure, comp with Robert Moevs. Studied piano & cello from early age; F H Beebe fel, Munich & Rome. Mem fac, Vassar Col, 66-70, assoc prof with tenure, 70-76, prof, 76-, chmn dept music, 79- Rec'd Burge-Eastman Prize, 78. Works recorded on Composer Recordings, Inc. *Instrumental Works:* Music for Solo Harp; Eclogue (solo piano); Sour Flowers (eight piano pieces in form of herbal); Deux Pas De Trois (pavane & tango for flute, oboe & harpsichord); Concerto for Violin and Chamber Orchestra. *Songs & Instrumental Works:* The Ballad of Longwood Glen (tenor & harp).

WILSON, ROGER COLE (LEE ROGERS,   ASCAP 1949
BENTON PRICE, HAROLD WEST, WALTER PRICE,
STEWART LANDON, THOMAS AHRENS)
composer, arranger, conductor
b Dayton, Ohio, Apr 25, 12. Educ: Univ Southern Calif; pvt study with father, Ira B Wilson. Free-lance arr, Los Angeles, 32-38; assoc ed, Lorenz Publ Co, 38-77; ed consult, 77- AUS Inf, WW II. Ed, "The Organist," 40-50 & 66-78; "The Volunteer Choir," 50-78, "The Choir Herald," 46-65, contributing ed, "The Choir Leader" & "The Organ Portfolio." *Songs & Instrumental Works:* Works: Choir cantatas; choral music (sacred & secular); anthems; school operettas; church organ composition; sacred vocal solos.

WILSON, STANLEY CLARENCE   ASCAP 1961
composer, author, singer
b Oakland, Calif, May 2, 22. Educ: Berkeley High Sch; vocal training with Bill Stoker & guitar training, Josh White, Sr. Club entertainer, San Francisco, 52-54. Chosen No 1 Entertainer in Hawaiian Islands by Honolulu Advertiser Newspaper, 56 & 57. Toured & played main supper clubs & hotels, Australia, Japan & Far East. *Songs:* A Rollin' Stone (Gathers No Moss); Night; Lyrics: Waikiki Farewell; Music: Jane Jane Jane.

WILSON, STEVEN KENDALL   ASCAP 1977
composer, recording artist
b Benton Harbor, Mich, July 8, 50. Began writing in 75; recorded for Big Tree Records, recorded first LP for Atco Records, 79. Chief Collabr: Kelly Wilson. *Songs:* If the World Ran Out of Love Tonight; Take Me to Your Heaven; Like Yesterday; Ticket to My Heart; Lost and a Long Way From Home; Why D You Have to Be So Beautiful; Another Night.

WILSON, THEODORE (TEDDY)   ASCAP 1960
composer, conductor
b Austin, Tex, Nov 24, 12. Educ: Tuskegee Inst; Talladega Col. To Detroit, 29; pianist in local bands; joined orchs incl Louis Armstrong, Erskine Tate, Benny

Carter, Willie Bryant, Benny Goodman & Gene Krupa; mem, Benny Goodman Trio & Quartet. Led own orch, then sextette, appearing in nightclubs, NY; featured with Benny Goodman Orch in Bway musical "Seven Lively Arts." Taught at Juilliard Sch Music, 45-52; also privately. On staff, WNEW, 49-52 & CBS, "Peter Lind Hayes Show," 54-55, also own prog. Appeared in film "The Benny Goodman Story." Toured nightclubs with trio; appeared at Brussels World's Fair, 58. Has made many records. *Songs & Instrumental Works:* Dizzy Spells; Warming Up; Something to Jump About; Sunny Morning; Early Session Hop; I'm Pulling Through.

WILSON, ZOEY
See Karant, Zoey Bryna

WIMBERLY, WARREN W, JR
composer, author
b Houston, Tex, Dec 14, 47. Educ: Studied piano with Mrs Ben Alexander, 10 yrs. Songwriter, age 12. Singer in clubs, 2 yrs. Chief Collabrs: A V Middlestat, Kenny Dale. *Songs:* Bluest Heartache of the Year; Red Hot Memory; Two Hearts Tangled in Love; We Could Be Dancing; Second Hand, Lovin' Hand; Shame, Shame on Me.

WINCHESTER, JESSE JAMES
singer
b Shreveport, La, 1945. Studied piano at age 6. Church organist & studied guitar at age 14. Joined var rock 'n' roll bands. Recording artist & record producer. *Albums:* Jesse Winchester; 3rd Down, 110 to Go; Learn to Love It; Let the Rough Side Drag; Nothing But a Breeze.

WINCHESTER, SIRL   ASCAP 1964
composer
b Carrolltown, Mo, June 25, 1888; d. Educ: High sch. *Songs:* The Lone Ranger; Whistle As You Go.

WINCHESTER, TED E   ASCAP 1974
composer, author, musician
b Okmulgee, Okla, Apr 6, 52. Educ: Okla State Univ, music educ, 2 yrs; Univ Ariz, guitar studies, 1 yr; pvt studies with Pat McCauley, Bud Dashiel, Howard Roberts, Buddy Kaye, Vincent Pirillo & Theo Verlyn Studios. Singer & guitarist, Klender & Winchester Band, in "Up With People"; bassist for Douglas Alan Davis; solo recording artist on Pantheon Desert Records; also night clubs, concerts & TV. Chief Collabrs: Richard Klender, Steve Kolter. *Songs:* Sing Me; A Love Song; Nine to Five; So Much More; Music: So Lonely Without You.

WINDING, KAI C   ASCAP 1959
composer, trombonist, arranger
b Aarhus, Denmark, May 18, 22. Educ: Stuyvesant High Sch, New York; self-taught. Started playing with big bands, Benny Goodman, Stan Kenton & others in 40's; began recording under own name in mid 40's; played on 52nd Street scene & subsequent Bway jazz club scene in 50's; instrumental in creating Be Bop style of jazz; led own small combos from 40's on; organized trombone jazz duo Kai & JJ in mid 50's. Winner of Jazz Popularity Polls. Traveled world wide playing concerts, radio & TV productions; touring, writing, producing records & comp, currently. *Instrumental Works:* Vido's Bop; A Night on Bop Mountain; Michie (I, II); Caribe; At Last Alaska; Lower Boneville.

WINDSOR, JOHN PETER   ASCAP 1955
author
b New York, NY, Nov 25, 15; d. Educ: Newton High Sch, Elmhurst, NY. Chief Collabrs: Bart Howard, Michael Corda, George Cory, Douglass Cross. *Songs:* You Are Not My First Love; Carry Me Back to Old Manhattan; You Perfect Stranger; Dark Blue Heart.

WINE-GAR, FRANK (FRAN)   ASCAP 1951
composer, author, conductor
b Grand Rapids, Mich, Feb 27, 01. Educ: Univ Pa; NJ State Teachers Col; Olivet Col, BA; Univ Mich. Organized dance band, Univ Pa. Won Metrop Opera prize. Had command perf, King Albert of Belg. Led orch, Village Barn, New York. Organized & dir, Fraser High Sch Band, Mich, 41-; also former sch teacher. Chief Collabrs: Dick Smith, Emery Deutsch, Jimmie Rogan, Clay Boland, Joseph Alden. *Songs & Instrumental Works:* When a Gypsy Makes His Violin Cry; Dreary Weather; Lingering Twilight (theme); Stick in the Mud; Sousa Day March; Litely and Politely (concert march); Could It Be You?; Old Pennsylvania; Always Blue; Oh Giuseppi.

WINFREE, RICHARD   ASCAP 1942
composer, author, conductor
b Hopkinsville, Ky, Mar 5, 1898; d. Educ: Hitchcock Mil Acad. Scored films, Hollywood. Cond, radio. Arr. Chief Collabr: Phil Boutelje. *Songs:* China Boy; Patsy.

WING, LUCIE LEE   ASCAP 1965
composer, author, lyricist
b New Orleans, La, July 17, 26. Educ: Newcomb Col, MS(psychol), Tulane Univ, BA, 46, 48. Wrote seven original songs for adaptation of Aristophanes' "The Birds," produced at Tulane Univ, 52 & at LePetit Theatre du Vieux Carre,

54; wrote songs included in Washington Theater Club's annual "Spread Eagle" revues, 66, 67 & 68; wrote 17 songs for "The Scandalous Mrs Jack," original show produced by Raleigh Little Theater, 71. *Songs:* Pushing Forty; An Older Man Is Like an Elegant Wine.

WINGARD, JAMES CHARLES (BUD)　　　ASCAP 1974
composer, author
b Greenville, SC, Nov 18, 31. Educ: Furman Univ, BA(psychol). TV writer of musical & variety progs, 69-; mem staff, comedy & musical writer & comp, TV show "Hee Haw," 69- *Songs:* Jug Band; Gossipy; The Time We Spend With You; Gloom, Despair, and Agony on Me.

WINK, IRMA JUNE　　　ASCAP 1972
composer, author
b Staten Island, NY. Educ: Cornell Univ, AB; Univ Tex Sch Law, JD. Finalist in Castlebar Int Song Contest, Ireland; comp & author of musical drama (historical), pop, gospel & choral music. Chief Collabrs: Sue Karen Wink (daughter), Bruce Marshall Wink (son). *Songs:* Beautiful Gate; All Things; Song of Liberty; Lonely Guitar; Great to Be Living With the Lord; Walking Hand in Hand; Sing Alleluia.

WINK, SUE KAREN　　　ASCAP 1972
composer, author, arranger
b Wiesbaden WGer, Oct 18, 48. Educ: Univ Madrid, cert Span language & culture; Univ NH, BA; Univ Tex, Austin, MM(music theory); Am Cons Fountainebleau, France, studied with Nadia Boulanger. Professional composer & author; producer & arranger. Chief Collabrs: Irma June Wink, Bruce Marshall (Corky) Wink. *Songs:* Walking Hand in Hand; All Things; The Beautiful Gate; Lonely Guitar; Great to Be Living With the Lord; We'll Meet the Dawn With a Song; Sing Alleluia: A Calypso Carol; Song of Liberty; Good, Good, Good; A Proverb. *Instrumental Works:* River By Night.

WINKLER, SOL　　　ASCAP 1952
composer, author
b Detroit, Mich, Apr 24, 17. Producer, publ & writer of songs. Chief Collabrs: Teddy Powell, Redd Evans, Phil Brito. *Songs:* A Million Tears; Lonely Lips; A Little Too Late; For the Want of a Kiss; A Broken Promise.

WINN, JERRY　　　ASCAP 1958
composer, author
b London, England, Dec 2, 39. Educ: Royal Acad of Music, London, England. Protege of Eal Hagen & Herb Spencer. Publ, Fairlane Music; wrote main titles for film/TV, "Dr Kildare", "I Mobster" & "Jaimie McPheeters." Produced records; started independent record co; partner in Cream Records. Active scoring TV animated features & writing for & producing records. Chief Collabrs: Jerry Goldsmith, Lalo Schiffrin, Joseph Hoover. *Songs:* Gimme Little Sign; Baby You Got It; Lovey Dovey Kinda Lovin'. *Scores:* Film/TV: The Young and the Restless; Days of Our Lives; Little Lulu; Captain Harlock; Peter Cottontail's Adventures; Candy, Candy.

WINNE, JESSE M　　　ASCAP 1914
composer, author, organist
b Sand Lake, NY, Dec 30, 1875; d Amawalk, NY, Dec 17, 64. Educ: High sch, Grafton, NDak. Had own music studio, Minneapolis. Mem staff, music publ houses. Music dir, traveling theatrical cos. Organist, Elks Lodge No 1, New York, 25 yrs. Charter mem, ASCAP. Chief Collabrs: Geoffrey O'Hara, Harry Burleigh. *Songs:* Carita; 'Leven O'Clock; The Far Away Land of Home; Amarella; Will o' the Wisp; When Old New York Was Young; The Broad Highway; Down the Lane That Leads Back Home.

WINSLOW, RICHARD　　　ASCAP 1955
composer, singer, instrumentalist
b Jennings, La, Mar 25, 15. Educ: Univ Southern Calif. Actor, beginning with silents, Mickey McGuire comedies & juvenile leads, then, contract with MGM for "Bars and Stripes" & "Mutiny On the Bounty," later "Benny Goodman Story" & "Funny Lady." Fronted combo at Hollywood Bar of Music & soc dances, 40-47. Pioneered airborne piano bar on champagne flights between Los Angeles & Las Vegas. Co-author & straight man, Mickey Rooney's nightly act & toured Korea, US & Can. Orch leader, Musicollegians; singalong pianist, Disneyland, 55-63; one-man band in motion pictures, TV commercials & Knott's Berry Farm, 76-80; comp & delivering Live Wire singing telegrams; assoc producer, movie "The Italian." Chief Collabrs: Shirley Winslow, wife, Mickey Rooney, Tommy Walker, Leo Diamond, Irving Bibo, Milo Sweet. *Songs:* Go See Tony; Trojan Warriors, Charge!; Go!Go!Go!Buffalos; Come By, Alumni; The Chargers of LA; Koo Koo Khomeiniac; California Angels, Yes We Can; Lyrics: Where Am I Again?

WINSLOW, SHIRLEY MELEESE　　　ASCAP 1966
composer
b St Joseph, Mo, Mar 15, 31. Educ: Pasadena Acad High Sch; Pasadena Nazarene Col. Chief Collabr: Dick Winslow. *Songs:* Lyrics: California Angeles, A O K!.

WINSTON, JULIAN (WINNIE)　　　ASCAP 1976
composer, teacher, banjo player
b New York, NY, May 31, 41. Writer, original material, 76- Solo recording artist; pedal steel instrumentalist. Author, bk "Pedal Steel Guitar," 75. Chief Collabrs: Ken Bloom, James L Crawford. *Instrumental Works:* Henry's Waltz; Steel Wool; Springtime-Last Time Around.

WINTER, GLORIA FRANCES (SISTER MIRIAM　　　ASCAP 1966
THERESE WINTER)
author, teacher, liturgist
b Passaic, NJ, June 14, 38. Educ: Cath Univ, BMus, 64; McMaster Divinity Col, MRE, 76; Princeton Theol Sem, PhD candidate. Sister, Med Mission, 55- Pub relations dir, ed, 63-72; teacher & liturgist, 72-79; assoc prof liturgy, worship & spirituality, Hartford Sem Found, 80- *Songs:* Joy Is Like the Rain; The Wedding Banquet; Long Road to Freedom; God Gives His People Strength; Spirit of God; God Loves a Cheerful Giver; Zaccheus; Ballad of the Women; Ballad of the Prodigal Son; Ballad of the Seasons; Don't Be Afraid; I Know the Secret; Spirit of the Lord; How I Have Longed; Christ Is My Rock; The Sower; He Bought the Whole Field; Yet I Believe; Children of the Lord; Knock, Knock; Wonderful!; Who Is My Neighbor?; If You Look; Song of Liberation; Loving You; Jerusalem.

WINTER, (SISTER) MIRIAM THERESE
See Winter, Gloria Frances

WINTERHALTER, HUGO　　　ASCAP 1952
composer, conductor, arranger
b Wilkes-Barre, Pa, Aug 15, 09; d. Educ: St Mary's Col, BA; New Eng Cons. Arr & performer with var dance orchs incl Larry Clinton, Raymond Scott, Will Bradley, Count Basie, Vaughn Monroe, Jimmy & Tommy Dorsey, Claude Thornhill & Benny Goodman. Arr, singers incl Dinah Shore, Doris Day, Buddy Clark, Frank Sinatra, Kate Smith, Eddie Fisher, Billy Eckstine & Kay Starr. Music dir, var record cos incl MGM, 48-49, Columbia, 49-50, RCA Victor, 50-63 & Kapp for many yrs. *Songs & Instrumental Works:* How Do I Love Thee?; La Muneca Espanol; Eyes of Love; Far Away Blues; Melody of Spain.

WINTERS, EILEENE RENEE　　　ASCAP 1975
composer, author, journalist
b New York, NY, Sept 26, 26. Educ: Univ Calif Los Angeles; musical theatre workshop, taught by Lehman Engel. Journalist for nat publ; columnist; theatre critic; publicist; actress. Chief Collabrs: Lauri Allen, Dick Allen, Tony Palmer. *Songs:* Lyrics: Up the Ladder (musical); Edward the Eighth (musical); Soloman (musical); Illusion; spec material for award shows.

WINTERS, JACK
See Talent, Leo Robert

WINTERS, JANET LEWIS　　　ASCAP 1956
author, teacher
b Chicago, Ill, Aug 17, 1899. Educ: Lewis Inst, Chicago, AA, 18; Univ Chicago, PhB, 20. Novelist; poet; librettist. Teacher, English Dept, Stanford Univ & Univ Calif, Berkeley; Guggenheim fel. Chief Collabrs: William L Bergsma, Alva Henderson, Malcolm Seagrave. *Songs:* Lyrics: Easter Laudate (choral); Christmas Canticle (choral). *Scores:* Opera: The Wife of Martin Guerre; The Last of the Mohicans; Birthday of the Infanta.

WINTERS, JOHN
See Wintersteen, John Schaeffer

WINTERS, JUNE (JERRY WHITMAN)　　　ASCAP 1953
composer, singer
b Hazelton, Pa, May 17, 18. Educ: Curtis Inst. Singer in Bway musical, "Hellzapoppin"; prima donna, Boston Comic Opera Co; soloist, Radio City Music Hall. Has made many records. Chief Collabrs: Gladys Shelley, Sylvia Dee, Hugo Peretti (husband), Luigi Creatore. *Songs:* The Man I've Been Looking For; Experience Unnecessary; You Ought to Have a Wife; A Man Is a Necessary Evil; Easter Bunny; Bad Girl; The Mating Call; Paper Roses.

WINTERSTEEN, JOHN SCHAEFFER (JOHN WINTERS) ASCAP 1955
composer, author, teacher
b Williamsport, Pa, Sept 24, 08. Educ: Williamsport High Sch, grad; studied with Schillinger & Harold Pries. Played Rivoli & Rialto Theatres, New York. Solo organist on WOR & in Denver, Colo, Knoxville & Nashville, Tenn, Cedar Rapids, Iowa, Dallas & Houston, Tex. Played soap operas, CBS, NBC & ABC; staff organist, ABC, 10 yrs. Chief Collabr: Abel Baer. *Songs:* When I Danced the First Waltz With You; Margaret E; Give My Heart a Break; 8 children's songs; Music: Christmas Chimes; I Know You By Heart; Hands. *Instrumental Works:* Nocturne; Allegro in 3/4 Time; Bubblin' Over.

WIRGES, WILLIAM F　　　ASCAP 1942
composer, conductor, pianist
b Buffalo, NY, June 26, 1894; d. Served with 15th Div, WW I. Accompanist, Am Music Fest, Chautauqua, 20-21. Began radio career as "Dusty" in Gold Dust Twins, 23; also dir, radio progs. Accompanist to Al Jolson, Harry Richman, Belle Baker, Jessica Dragonette & Jane Froman. Music dir, record

cos; founded own publ firm. Had own TV prog. *Songs & Instrumental Works:* Mississippi Lament (choral); Chiquita Banana; Nice Dreamin' Baby; No Greater Love; I Had That Dream Again; Hi There Neighbor; Thank You, Lord; Dear Friends and Gentle Hearts; A Toast to Love; Peace I Leave With You; O Jesus in Remembrance Now; Song Bks: Christianity in Song; Fifty-Five Good Will Songs; Rainbow House; Smile Songs; Small Fry Club.

WIRTH, CARL ANTON   ASCAP 1954
composer
b Rochester, NY, Jan 24, 12. Educ: Eastman Sch Music, BMus, 34, MMus, 35; studied with Howard Hanson & Bernard Rogers. Prof brass & theory, Iowa State Teachers Col; music dir, Twin City Symph Soc, St Joseph-Benton Harbor, Mich; mem bd dirs, Am Symph Orch League; chmn Am Comp Proj; exec dir, Community Music Prog, Rochester, NY; music specialist, US State Dept, cond, Nat Symph Orch Indonesia. *Instrumental Works:* Ichabod Crane Suite; Dark Flows the River; Beyond These Hills; Diversions in Denim; Portals (a prelude); Idlewood Concerto for Saxophone; Indonesian Landscapes; David Tryptich; Autumn Mountain; Javanese Dance; Elegy on an Appalachian Folksong.

WISE, FRED   ASCAP 1942
author
b New York, NY, May 27, 15; d New York, Jan 18, 66. Educ: Columbia Univ, BA; Columbia Teachers Col, PhD. Wrote varsity shows. With publicity dept film studio, 36-39. Radio operator, USAF, WW II. Co-founder two psychiatric clinics, Bronx, NY, 59. Chief Collabrs: Ben Weisman, Sid Lippman, Randy Starr, John Jacob Loeb, Al Frisch. *Songs:* Misirlou; Wise Old Owl; Oo! What You Do to Me; A Family That Prays Together; Roses in the Rain; A-You're Adorable; Little Lulu; Let Me Go Lover; Don't Ask Me Why; Fame and Fortune; I Won't Cry Anymore; Follow That Dream; Rock-a-Hula Baby; Never Let Her Go; Wooden Heart; Lonely Blue Boy; Kissin' Cousins; In the Beginning; I'll Touch a Star; Playing With Fire; I Forgot to Forget; The Best Man; Honey in the Horn; Starlight Serenade.

WISE, JOSEPH EDWARD   ASCAP 1967
composer, author, teacher
b Louisville, Ky, Aug 19, 39. Educ: St Mary's Univ, Md, BA(philosophy), STB(theology); Spalding Col, MEd(counseling & guidance); Cath Univ Am, MA(relig educ). Began composing music for worship, 62 & songs for children, 72; started recording, 66; began tours of US & abroad, 67. Lectr, singer & producer. Chief Collab: John Pell. *Songs:* Take Our Bread; Peanut Butter and Jelly; You Fill the Day; Lord Teach Us to Pray; Gonna Sing My Lord; Go Now in Peace; Song of Blessing.

WISNER, JAMES JOSEPH   ASCAP 1960
composer, author, record producer
b Philadelphia, Pa, Dec 8, 31. Educ: Cent High Sch; Temple Univ, BA; studied comp with Romeo Cascarini; studied conducting with William Smith, Philadelphia Orch. Started as jazz pianist with Carmen McRae & Mel Torme; has produced & arr records; theatrical producer. Chief Collabrs: Billy Jackson, Pete DeAngelis, Irwin Levine, Ron Dante. *Songs:* Don't Throw Your Love Away; Somewhere; Gypsy Girl; Music: Christmas Is Christmas. *Instrumental Works:* Asia Minor; Manhattan Safari. *Scores:* Film/TV: ABC Wide World of Entertainment (theme); The Last Frontier (documentary).

WISWELL, ANDREW MULLER   ASCAP 1963
composer, author
b Machias, Maine, Jan 5, 05. Educ: Machias High Sch; Manlius Sch; Univ Maine; Yale Univ, BS. Professional musician, Vincent Lopez, Arnold Jonson, Abe Lyman & Eddy Duchin Orchs; vpres, Muzak Corp, Capitol & RCA Records. Produced 37 original cast albums of Bway shows, "Music Man", "Hello Dolly", "Fiddler on the Roof", "Hair," etc. Chief Collabrs: Sid Bass, Earl Sheldon, Abe Osser. *Songs:* Don't Leave Me Now; Lyrics: Pam the Teen Age Queen; Rubino; Don't Come Running Back to Me; Music: Answers; Bangor Bossa Nova; Bon Vivant; Busy Beaver; Capricorn; Caribee; Chit Chat; Color the Wind; Dreamy One; Echoes of Brazil; Every Night at Seven; Fiddler on the Run; Give Me New York; Go Ahead; Happy Chico; Here and Now; How Can You Say; I Bring Only Love; I'm Thru Sending Roses; In Every Way; It Can Never Be the Same; It Goes Like This; Like a Feather; Manhattan Discotheque; Mantilla; Midnight Blue; Movin' Around; Number One; O Soul O Rio; Only Once More; Please Say; Quiet Valley; Sky Way; Spy; Subway Struggle; Tica Tica Waltz for Mary; We Need You Now; Well That's Life; Up Down and Around; It Can't Be That Bad; Holiday in Italy; Haven't You Ever Been; Jet Set; I Know, I Know, I Know; Opus Hocus Pocus; Lonely; Diana.

WITKIN, BEATRICE   ASCAP 1967
composer
b New York, NY, May 13, 16. Educ: Hunter Col, BA; NY Univ, grad work; studied piano with Edward Steuermann, comp with Roger Sessions, Mark Brunswick, Ernest Krenek, Stefan Wolpe. Comp incl works for instruments, chamber & symph & electronic medium. Founder, Composers Recognition Week, New York. McDowell Colony fel; ASCAP Awards, Creative Artist Pub Service award. Ford Found recording grant for Opus I No 12, Rockefeller Found grant, 2 grants from NEA; Martha Baird Rockefeller comn. *Instrumental Works:* Wild Wild World of Animals (theme, electronic); Breath and Sounds for Tuba and Tape; Parameters for Five Players (8 instruments); Echologie for Flutes and Quadrophonic Tape; Reports From the Planet of Mars (orch & tape);

Chiaroscuro for Cello and Piano; Triads and Things for Brass Quintet; Stephen Foster Variations for Orchestra; Prose Poem; Glissines (High Fidelity Electronic Music Contest winner, 70, electronic tape); Duo for Violin and Piano. *Scores:* Children's Operetta: Does Poppy Live Here?

WITKOWSKI, LEO   ASCAP 1956
composer, accordionist, arranger
b Brooklyn, NY, Aug 2, 08. Educ: High sch. Teacher. *Instrumental Works:* Arr: Music for Everyone; Polkas Made Easy for Accordion.

WITTE, CHARLES DIETRICH   ASCAP 1974
composer, author, singer
b Defiance, Ohio, Mar 19, 42. Played country music in night clubs, 10 yrs; gospel music singer in own group. *Songs:* Let Him Live in Your Heart; I'm Glad to Have You Around.

WITTMAN, ELLEN   ASCAP 1977
producer, screenwriter
b Buffalo, NY, May 30, 39. Educ: Univ Mich, BA(theatre), 61. Stage mgr, Am Ballet Co, Bway & off-Bway shows, 61-73; with Martha Graham Dance Co, 68-69. Production stage mgr, Am Ballet Theatre, 70-73. Prog exec, ABC-TV. Free-lance writer, incl TV episodes, 75. TV producer for Whitman & Riche Productions, 76. Producer, movie "Friendships, Secrets, Lies." Writer, NBC-TV spec. Chief Collab: Wendy Rich. *Songs:* Lyrics: Sandor's Love Song; Randy's Theme; Old Man and the Maid; & songs for women's concerts.

WODEHOUSE, PELHAM GRENVILLE (P G)   ASCAP 1924
author
b Guildford, Eng, Oct 15, 1881; d Southampton, NY, Feb 14, 75. Educ: Dulwich Col; hon Litt D, Oxford Univ. Writer, column "By the Way" in London Globe, 03. Drama critic, Vanity Fair, New York. Storywriter, Saturday Evening Post, 14. Author, Bway show scores; co-librettist, "Oh Kay" & "Anything Goes." Author, bks incl "Leave It to P Smith", "Fish Preferred", "America I Like You" & Jeeves series; autobiography "Bring on the Girls." Chief Collabrs: Guy Bolton, Emmerich Kalman, Jerome Kern, Louis A Hirsch, Sigmund Romberg, Rudolf Friml. *Songs:* Have a Heart; Throw Me a Rose; And I Am All Alone; Till the Clouds Roll By; An Old-Fashioned Wife; You Never Knew About Me; Nesting Time in Flatbush; Just You Watch My Step; Leave It to Jane; The Crickets Are Calling; The Sun Shines Brighter; The Siren's Song; Go Little Boat; Before I Met You; Bill; March of the Musketeers; Ma Belle; Your Eyes. *Scores:* Bway shows: Miss Springtime; Rosalie; The Three Musketeers; Have a Heart (co-librettist); Oh, Boy!; Leave It to Jane; The Riviera Girl; Oh, Lady! Lady!!; The Girl Behind the Gun; The Canary; Oh My Dear; Sitting Pretty; The Nightingale.

WOHL, JACK   ASCAP 1960
composer, author
b New York, NY, Jan 4, 34. Educ: High Sch Music & Art; New York City Community Col. Creative consult, J Walter Thompson, New York. Wrote TV specials for Art Carney & Connie Francis; spec material for "Keefe Brasselle Show" & "Garry Moore Show," CBS-TV. Advert exec. Author: "The Conformers"; "Dolls My Mother Never Gave Me." Chief Collab: Mitch Leigh. *Songs:* When You Make Your Wish; The Lively Ones (TV title song).

WOLCOTT, CHARLES FREDERICK   ASCAP 1944
composer, author
b Flint, Mich, Sept 29, 06. Educ: Univ Mich, BA, 27; comp studies with Andrew Haigh, harmony & theory with J Percival Davis. Leader own orch, Univ Mich, 24-27; pianist/arr, Jean Goldkette Orgn, Detroit, Mich, 27-29; comp/arr/cond, Paul Whiteman Orch, New York, 31-35; pianist/comp/arr, radio, 33-37; comp/arr/cond, Walt Disney Studio, 38-48, gen music dir, 44-48; comp/arr/cond, MGM Studios, 50-60, gen music dir, 58-60; secy-gen, Int Baha'i Coun, 61-63, mem, Baha'i Universal House of Justice, 63-, head, Baha'i Religion. Chief Collab: Ray Gilbert. *Songs:* Music: Reluctant Dragon; Saludos Amigos; Sailors of the Air; Mexico; Two Silhouettes; Sooner Or Later; The Last One to Know; Ruby Duby Du; Sweet-Scented Streams; Oh Thou, By Whose Name; Blessed Is the Spot; Lyrics: Julie. *Instrumental Works:* Inca Suite; love theme from Cat on a Hot Tin Roof. *Scores:* Film/TV: Disney Shorts; Pinocchio (partial); The Three Caballeros; Bambi (partial); Blackboard Jungle.

WOLF, DANIEL   ASCAP 1937
composer, pianist
b Baltimore, Md, May 12, 1894; d New York, NY, Mar 8, 62. Educ: Peabody Cons; studied with Ernest Hutcheson, George Boyle, Gustave Strube, Otis Boise, Rudolph Ganz, Rubin Goldmark. Pianist, recitals at Town Hall & Lewisohn Stadium, Europ concert tours, 30-31. Chief Collab: Mabel Livingstone. *Songs:* Now Sleeps the Crimson Petal; The Star; Jack-in-the-Box; Slumber Town; The Circus; Iris; Night of Dreams; I Hear the Call of the Road; Love Me Enough.

WOLF, DONALD ELKAN   ASCAP 1965
composer, author, arranger
b New York, NY, Sept 14, 23. Educ: Horace Mann Sch for Boys, Riverdale, NY, 41; Ohio State Univ, 2 yrs. USN, 43-46, Aviation Electronic Technician First Class, Texas A&M; Juilliard Sch Music, summer sch, 47-48; studied piano with

Teddy Wilson, arr with Sy Oliver, Dick Jacobs & clarinet with Pete Luisetti. Wrote: theme for Walter Thornton Model Agency, Copacabana Shows, New York, special material for "Show of Shows," opening songs for Jackie Gleason (CBS) TV show, award winning commercials for Glendale Federal Savings, Filleral, pop songs. Mem, West Coast Adv Bd, 77- Chief Collabs: John Williams, Gerry Goldsmith, Jerry Livingston, Donald Kahn, Nelson Riddle, James Komack, Alan Brandt, Freddie Greene, Bill Davis, Ben Raleigh. *Songs:* Music: Love is All We Need; *Lyrics:* Legend of the Lost (motion picture title song); Fate is the Hunter (motion picture title song); None But the Brave (motion picture title song); John Goldfarb, Please Come Home (motion picture title song); Azure-Te; Until I Met You.

WOLF, JACK
ASCAP 1947

composer, author

b Paterson, NJ. Radio & TV production (CBS). Chief collabrs: Burt Bacharach, Joe Darion, Joel Herron, Frank Sinatra, Red Buttons, Robert Arthur, Bugs Bower. *Songs:* Any Old Time; I'm a Fool to Want You; The Red Buttons Ho Ho Song; Love Is a Treasure Hunt (treasure hunt theme); (I'm in Love With the Girl With) Greensleeves; In All My Wildest Dreams; The American Dream; Are You Ready for a Laugh; I Walked Alone Last Night; These Are the Closing Credits; We Want a Rock and Roll President; Rockabilly Gal; Everybody Kiss the Bride; Wooden Shoes and Happy Hearts; Winter in New England; My Boy Friend Got a Beatle Haircut; I'll Never Learn to Cha Cha Cha; Take My Love; *Lyrics:* Alley Cat (Dance); Java Jones; Keep Me in Mind; A Tear Can Fall; Pigtails and Freckles.

WOLF, OLGA (MRS RALPH LEWANDO)
ASCAP 1960

composer, author, accordionist

b Chicago, Ill. Accompanist & coach for singers. Teacher. Chief Collabr: Sigmund Spaeth. *Songs & Instrumental Works:* If I Never Saw a Star Again; Let's Play Every Day; Teaching pieces: Sure Short Cut for Accordion (bks I-III); Music Makers Accordion Ensemble and Solo Book (bk I); ABC Accordion Boogie Woogie and Blues Course; You Can Play These; Christmas Carols for Accordion; Familiar Pieces.

WOLF, RICHARD LAWRENCE
ASCAP 1970

composer, author

b New York, NY, Nov 25, 50. Educ: George Washington Univ, BA, 72; Juilliard Sch Music, studied piano, 72-73. Songwriter & recording artist; indust & documentary film scores. Chief Collabr: Wayne Perkins. *Songs:* Reckless Love; Trick Rider; The Long Goodbye; Taxi Girls; Red Chamber. *Scores:* Film: La Vida Loca.

WOLF, RICHARD WILLIAM
ASCAP 1977

composer, author, arranger

b Williamsport, Pa, Feb 8, 28. Educ: Univ Del; Muskingum Col; Lycoming Col; pvt study with John McHegha. Songwriter, A&R dir, CAPP Records. Partner with Arthur Godfrey, Beacon Hills Music Corp & Airwaves Inc. Consult, CBS Radio Network; producer play; recording artist, RCA. Independent writer, arr & producer. Author, "The Richard Wolf Light Professional Fake Book." Chief Collabrs: Noel Sherman, Warren Nadel. *Songs:* NCAA Champions; Christmas Is for Children; Welcome to the Club; Bend a Little My Way; I Must Be Dreamin'. *Albums:* Richard Wolf's Children's Chorus.

WOLFE, DIGBY
ASCAP 1968

composer, author

b Harrow, Eng, June 4, 32. Educ: Central Sch Arts & Crafts, Eng, MA(theatrical design & hist costume). Written & produced numerous TV shows, Eng, Australia & US. Rec'd five Emmy nominations; one Emmy for "Laugh-In." Rec'd Montreax Fest Award for "Shirley MacLaine Special." Chief Collabrs: Derek Scott, Tommy Oliver, Stanley Myers. *Songs:* Laugh-In Theme.

WOLFE, JACQUES
ASCAP 1933

composer, pianist, teacher

b Botoshan, Roumania, Apr 29, 1896; d Bradenton, Fla, June 22, 73. Came to US, 1898. Educ: Juilliard, studied with Goetschius, Robinson & Friskin. Clarinetist, 50th Inf Band, Ft Jay, NY, WW I. Studied Negro spirituals. Concert pianist & accompanist. Teacher music, pub schs, New York. Went to Miami, Fla, 47. Became photographer; had many exhibits. Chmn, Grass Roots Opera, Fla. Pres, Composers & Authors Guild. Chief Collabrs: Irwin Rowan, Clement Wood. *Songs:* De Glory Road; Gwine to Hebb'n; Hallelujah Rhythm; Short'nin Bread; The Hand Organ Man; Sailormen; British Children's Prayer. *Instrumental Works:* Maine Holiday (piano); Prayer in the Swamp (violin); The Congo; Serenade (string quartet); The 67th Psalm (orch, mixed chorus). *Scores:* Operas: John Henry; Mississippi Legend; Trysting Tree.

WOLFE, MAURICE
ASCAP 1962

composer, author

b Denver, Colo, Oct 13, 1887; d Flushing, NY, Sept 27, 66. Educ: High sch. *Songs:* Without You, the World Don't Seem the Same; Three Cheers for the USA; A Girl Like You.

WOLFE, STANLEY ANDREW
ASCAP 1960

composer, teacher, administrator

b New York, NY, Feb 7, 24. Educ: Stetson Univ, 46-47; Henry St Music Sch, 47-48; Juilliard Sch Music, BS(comp), 52, MS, 55; studied comp with William Bergsma, Vincent Persichetti & Peter Mennin. Mem fac, Juilliard Sch Music, 55-; awarded Guggenheim Fel, 57; Ditson-Am Symph Orch League Award, 61; received grants from Nat Endowment for Arts, 69, 70 & 77; had works performed here & abroad; dir, Extension Div, Juilliard Sch Music, 63- *Instrumental Works:* Lincoln Square Overture; Canticle for Strings; Symphony No 3; String Quartet No 1; Symphony No 4; Songs From Harmonium; Symphony No 5. *Scores:* Opera/Ballet: Kings Heart (dance score).

WOLFE, THOMAS
ASCAP 1965

author

b Asheville, NC, Oct 3, 00; d Baltimore, Md, Sept 15, 38. Educ: Univ NC, BA; Harvard Univ, MA. Instr of Eng, NY Univ, 24-30. Author, novels: "Look Homeward, Angel", "Of Time and the River", "The Web and the Rock" & "You Can't Go Home Again"; short stories: "The Hills Beyond" & "From Death to Morning"; play, "Mannerhouse." Biography, "Hungry Gulliver" by P J Johnson. Chief Collabr: Lee Hoiby. *Songs:* The Tides of Sleep.

WOLFF, F ROGER
ASCAP 1965

composer, pianist, arranger

b St Louis, Mo, Dec 7, 20. Educ: Univ Mo; Chicago Musical Col, BM, 49, studied piano with Rudolph Ganz & comp with Max Wald; DePaul Univ, studied comp with Leon Stein; Univ Southern Calif, studied cinema comp with David Raksin. Staff pianist, radio stas KSD & KWK, St Louis; pianist, Chicago Theater & Oriental Theaters, Chicago; recording artist, Mercury Records; orch leader, Drake Hotel & Blackstone Hotel, Chicago. Cond, comp & arr indust shows, TV & radio commercials; cond of production "Great Day." Toured as pianist, cond & arr with Mimi Benzall; vocal coach & prof pianist for numerous celebrities. Chief Collabrs: Joe Rizzo, Buddy Merrill, John Jakes. *Songs:* The Twilight Tree; Esplanade; September Sea; Affair; Tomorrow; Evening Star. *Instrumental Works:* Whirling Winds. *Scores:* Film Documentaries: You, Chicago! (Indy Award, 51); The Silent Crisis.

WOLFSILVER, C L
See Silver, Charles L

WOLFSON, MAXWELL A (MACK) (RONALD MARC)
ASCAP 1952

composer, author

b Brooklyn, NY, Mar 2, 23. Educ: Brooklyn Col; Brooklyn Law Sch; New Sch for Social Res. Songwriter, under contract to Famous Music, Paramount Pictures. Gen prof mgr, St Nicholas Music. Currently vpres, Golden Crest Records & Shelley Products, LTD (Pressing Plant). Chief Collabrs: Eddie White, Bernie Taylor. *Songs:* Happiness Street (Corner of Sunshine Square); C'Est la Vie; Flowers Mean Forgiveness; Be Fair; Crazy Otto Rag; Tempest; The Jayhawkers; I Love a Sousa March; Invitation to Love; Come, To Where the Love Is; Christmas in Paree; Learn to Love; Find Yourself; Father, Father; Cat 'n' Mouse.

WOLINSKI, DAVID J
composer, author, singer

b Chicago, Ill. Educ: Self-taught. Played with rock & roll bands. Joined group, Rufus. Writer with Dan Seraphine. Chief Collabr: Dan Seraphine. *Songs:* Any Love; Do You Love What You Feel; I'm Dancing for Your Love; Street Player; Little One; Take Me Back to Chicago; Stranger to Love; Midnight Love Affair.

WOLOSHIN, SIDNEY E
ASCAP 1963

composer, producer

b Hartford, Conn, June 27, 28. Educ: Classical High Sch, Worcester, Mass; Boston Univ Col Mus, BMus, 50, MMus, 51; studied violin with Wolfinsohn. USAF Orch, 51-55. Worked in orch after discharge. Producer, J Walter Thompon Adv Agency, 59-67. Co-owner, Gavin & Woloshin (music production), 67-71. Owner, Sid Woloshin Inc (music production) 71-; writes & produces music for many national clients including McDonald's, State Farm, Jack-In-The-Box. Chief Collabrs: Jack Wohl, Warren Pfaff, John Annarino. *Songs:* Music: We're Together; Take Life a Little Easier; Live It Up. *Scores:* Opera/Ballet: Panamtgg.

WOLPA, BERTHA BEE (BEE WALKER)
ASCAP 1950

composer, accompanist, vocal coach

b Indianapolis, Ind. Accompanist with Rae Samuels, Belle Baker & Eddie Cantor; wrote spec material for acts. Worked as pianist, teaching prof band, clubs & vaudeville singers. Plug songs for their prof use. Worked for Leo Feist Publ Co, Bregman, Vocco, Conn, Warner Bros & Jack Robbins. Chief Collabrs: Don George, Bob Merrill, Kay Twomey, Jack Segal, Jerry Grant, Nancy Leeds. *Songs:* Music: Who Told You That Lie?; Hey, Jealous Lover; It's Over Now; No Turnin' Back; Thank The Lord What a Day!; It's Your Turn to Cry; You'll Get Over It; One More Time.

WOLPE, STEFAN
ASCAP 1963

composer, teacher

b Berlin, Ger, Aug 25, 02; d New York, NY, Apr 4, 72. Educ: State Acad Music, Berlin, studied with Juon & Schreker. Lived in Palestine, 33-38. Came to US, 38. Teacher music, New York. Awards: Brandeis Univ Creative Arts Award; Fromm Found; Koussevitzky Award; B de Rothschild Award; Guggenheim Fels, 62 & 70. Mem: Inst Arts & Letters. *Songs & Instrumental Works:* Violin Sonata; Passacaglia; Percussion Quartet; 10 Songs From the Hebrew; Symphony

No 1 (concerto for piano, 16 instruments); Quintet with Voice (baritone, horn, cello, harp, clarinet, piano); Cantata for Voice, Voices and Instruments; Form for Piano, Broken Sequences (piano); Chamber Piece No 1; String Quartet; Concerto for Trumpet and Seven Instruments; Piece for Two Instrumental Units; Solo for Trumpet; Piece for Violin Alone; Piece in Two Parts for Flute and Piano; Piece in Two Parts for Six Players; Piece in Two Parts for Solo Violin; Trio for Flute, Cello, Piano; Chinese Epitaphs (choral); Cantatas: The Passion of Man; On the Education of Man; About Sport; Israel and His Land; Unnamed Lands; Street Music. *Scores:* Ballets: The Man From Midian; Operas: Schone Geschichten; Zeus and Elida.

WONDER, STEVIE
See Morris, Stevland

WOOD, BRENTON
See Smith, Alfred Jesse

WOOD, CLEMENT   ASCAP 1939
author, educator
b Tuscaloosa, Ala, Sept 1, 1888; d Schenectady, NY, Oct 26, 50. Educ: Univ Ala, BA; Yale Univ, LLB. Practiced law in Birmingham, asst city atty, 12-13, chief presiding police magistrate, 13-14. Dean, Barnard Sch for Boys, 15-20. Vice principal, Dwight Sch, New York, 20-22. Instr writing, NY Univ, 39-40 & Richmond Div, William & Mary Col, 41-42. Dir, Bozenkill Sch Creative Writing. Lectr Negro songs, 20-35. Guest appearances, radio, 20-40. Author: "The Complete Rhyming Dictionary"; "Poets Handbook"; "The Art and Technique of Writing Poetry"; "The Complete Book of Scansion"; "Poets and Songwriters Guide"; "The Glory Road and the Eagle Sonnets." Chief Collabr: Jacques Wolfe. *Songs:* De Glory Road; Short'nin Bread; Gwine to Hebb'n; Carry Me Home; If the Seas Dry; The Lord's Baptizing; Sunday Every Day; Cahawba Days (song cycle); 5 Songs on Negro Themes; Widgy the Walking Whale. *Scores:* Now, Now Rowena (comic opera).

WOOD, CYRUS D   ASCAP 1923
author
b Washington, DC, July 24, 1889; d Santa Monica, Calif, June 23, 42. Film scenarist, Hollywood. Chief Collabrs: Sigmund Romberg, Al Goodman, Dave Stamper, Harold Levey. *Songs:* When Hearts Are Young; Darling; Little Wallflower; Dancing Will Keep You Young; Lovely Lady; Just Like a Doll; Mr and Mrs; Just a Regular Girl; Land of Mine. *Scores:* Bway shows: The Melting of Molly; Stage scores & librettos: The Blushing Bride; Springtime of Youth; The Lady in Ermine; Lovely Lady; Sally, Irene and Mary; June Days; The Street Singer.

WOOD, DALE   ASCAP 1963
composer, author
b Glendale, Calif, Feb 13, 34. Educ: Los Angeles City Col; Los Angeles Cons Music & Art; Occidental Col. Organist & choirmaster for Lutheran & Episcopal churches in Calif, 48-76. Appointed exec ed, The Sacred Music Press, 75; contributing ed, J of Church Music, 65-; chmn, Publ Comt, Int Choristers Guild, 70-74; editorial consult for several major hymnals. *Songs:* Music: Armada (musical drama for the Bohemian Club of San Francisco). *Instrumental Works:* Organ Book of American Folk Hymns; Seven Folk Tune Sketches for Organ; Dale Wood: Music for Organ; New Settings of 20 Well-Known Tunes. Composer of many choral works.

WOOD, DOUGLAS ALBERT (DAVID MCALLISTER)   ASCAP 1975
composer, producer
b Mineola, NY, June 27, 50. Educ: Ithaca Col; Manhattan Sch Music. Comp, indust film scores. Principal comp & producer background music library, OMNIMUSIC. Pres publ co, Franklin-Douglas, Inc. Producer, var pop groups. Chief Collabr: Joe Saulter. *Songs:* New York, New York. *Scores:* Film/TV: Wherever You Are; Prevention Factor.

WOOD, GEORGE   ASCAP 1962
composer
b Ft Smith, Ark, Feb 3, 23. Educ: Univ Southern Calif, BA. *Songs:* Church Bells; Jenny Brown. *Albums:* The Special World of George Wood and Katie.

WOOD, GUY B   ASCAP 1940
composer, author, pianist
b Manchester, Eng. Educ: Manchester Col Technol, England; pvt study in piano, saxophone, theory & harmony. Played saxophone with Brit dance bands. With foreign production div, Paramount & Columbia Picture Studios, US, 5 yrs. US Army, 42-45. Coun mem, Am Guild of Authors & Composers, 73-76. Chief Collabrs: Sammy Gallop, Sylvia Dee, Joe Darion, Ben Raleigh, Al Stillman. *Songs:* Music of Love (Bell Telephone Hour theme); Music: Till Then; Shoo Fly Pie and Apple Pan Dowdy; My One and Only Love; Faith Can Move Mountains; French Foreign Legion; Cincinnati Dancing Pig. *Instrumental Works:* Escapade (radio & TV theme song). *Scores:* Gulliver (children's musical); Films: The Lady With Red Hair; Two Shadows.

WOOD, MARIAN LOUISE (MARIAN WOOD CHAPLIN) ASCAP 1958
composer, author
b Defiance, Ohio, July 5, 14. Educ: Defiance High Sch, grad; Defiance Col. Began music writing, 55-, new version of "Hansel & Gretel," Children's Theater,

New York, 65. Guest artist, singing & playing own work in 3 progs performed in churches in Douglassville, Pa, 78, Douglaston, NY, 79, Sanibel Island, Fla, 80. *Songs:* I Have Come From the Darkness; Open Your Heart to Spring; Christ Child, Christ Child; I Hear Bells; I Can See God; Let Me Shine, Shine, Shine; Sing It; That Ricky-Tick Sound.

WOOD, RANDOLPH C   ASCAP 1953
composer, author, record executive
b Morrison, Tenn, Mar 30, 17. Educ: Middle Tenn State Univ, BS, 37. Founded Dot Records, Hollywood; A&R work, 50-77. Chief Collabr: Billy Vaughn. *Songs & Instrumental Works:* I'd Rather Die Young; Baby O' Mine; Autumn Love Song.

WOOD, SUE
See Taylor, Mary Virginia

WOOD, WENDELL LEE   ASCAP 1950
composer, author, clarinetist
b Rock Rapids, Iowa, Nov 5, 05. Educ: Benson Tech Sch, Portland, Ore, electrical eng course, 5 yrs. Saxophonist & vocalist with dance bands incl Rolly Furnace, Jack Souders & Harry Owen's in Hawaii, 33-35; performer, "Clarinet Fantasies," North Hollywood, Calif. Chief Collabrs: Don McDiarmid, Johnny Noble. *Songs:* Just a Little Dream of Hawaii and You; Lovely Wahine; Hawaiian Cowboy; Rumba Down in Rio; Music: Little Brown Girl.

WOOD, WOODROW JOHNSON   ASCAP 1961
composer
b Richland Springs, Tex, Sept 29, 18. Educ: Tex Wesleyan Col. Worked in hotel, San Francisco, Calif. *Songs:* You're Not to Blame; Advance Me a Kiss; When We Were Introduced.

WOODBURY, ALBERT FRANCIS   ASCAP 1960
composer
b Los Angeles, Calif, July 1, 09. Educ: Self-taught. Music arr & comp for films, 31-

WOODE, WILLIAM HENRI   ASCAP 1940
composer, author, singer
b Omaha, Nebr, Sept 25, 09. Educ: Colorado Springs High Sch; Colo Col, studied music with Prof Prior & Dean Hale. Played in concerts at age 10; played organ for silent pictures. WW II, USN. Comp & arr for many bands & orchs, incl Benny Goodman, Tommy & Jimmy Dorsey, Glen Miller, Harry James, Guy Lombardo, Ben Bernie, Blue Baron & others. Chief Collabrs: Al J Neiburg, Jules Loman, Charles Carpentar. *Songs:* Rosetta; Music: Sweet Slumber; Broadway; Moon Nocturne; Scenario Music to a Matinee Idol; Where Do You Run (To Hide a Heartache); Lonely Corral; The Wind and the Sea.

WOODIN, WILLIAM HARTMAN   ASCAP 1932
composer
b Berwick, Pa, Mar 27, 1868; d New York, NY, May 3, 34. Educ: Columbia Univ Sch of Mines. Gen supt, 1892-1895, Jackson & Woodin Mfg Co, Berwick, vpres, 1895-1899. Bd chmn, Am Locomotive Co, 16; dir of indust & railroad cos. Secy of the Treasury for Pres Franklin Roosevelt, 32-33. *Songs & Instrumental Works:* My Raggedy Ann; Intermezzo; El Matador; The Cheery Scarecrow; Happy Bluebirds; Cradle Song; Meditation; Feast of Lanterns.

WOODLEN, GEORGE ROBERT   ASCAP 1957
composer, author, trumpeter
b Baltimore, Md, Dec 4, 13. Educ: High sch. Trumpeter in dance orchs incl Cab Calloway & Benny Carter. Chief Collabr: Edgar Sampson. *Songs & Instrumental Works:* Mambo Inn; Watch Your Step; Salud.

WOODMAN, RAYMOND HUNTINGTON   ASCAP 1925
composer, teacher, organist
b Brooklyn, NY, Jan 18, 1861; d Brooklyn, Dec 25, 42. Educ: Pub schs; Brooklyn Col, 1 yr; studied with Dudley Buck & Cesar Franc. Church organist, age 12 to 79; organist, First Presby Church, Brooklyn, NY, 65 yrs; head music dept, Packer Collegiate Inst, Brooklyn, 50 yrs; cond, Woodman Choral Club of Brooklyn; head dept music, Brooklyn Inst Arts & Sci. *Songs:* Music: A Birthday; Ashes of Roses; A Thanksgiving Ode (cantata); The Message of the Star (cāntata); also various pieces for organ.

WOODS, HARRY MACGREGOR   ASCAP 1925
composer, author
b North Chelmsford, Mass, Nov 4, 1896; d. Educ: Harvard Univ. Served in WW I. Lived in Eng, 3 yrs; wrote songs for films incl "The Vagabond Lover", "Jack Ahoy", "Evergreen" & "It's Love Again." Chief Collabrs: Mort Dixon, Howard Johnson, Gus Kahn. *Songs:* Paddlin' Madelin' Home; When the Red Red Robin Comes Bob-Bob-Bobbin' Along; I'm Looking Over a Four-Leaf Clover; I'm Goin' South; Just a Butterfly That's Caught in the Rain; Side by Side; My Old Man; A Little Kiss Each Morning; Heigh-Ho, Everybody, Heigh-Ho; Man From the South; River, Stay 'Way From My Door; When the Moon Comes Over the Mountain; We Just Couldn't Say Goodbye; Just an Echo in the Valley; A Little Street Where Old Friends Meet; You Ought to See Sally on Sunday; Hustlin' and Bustlin' for Baby; What a Little Moonlight Can Do; Try a Little

Tenderness; I'll Never Say 'Never Again' Again; Over My Shoulder; Tinkle Tinkle Tinkle; When You've Got a Little Springtime in Your Heart; I Nearly Let Love Go Slipping Through My Fingers.

WOODS, HERBERT D (DON)　　　　ASCAP 1978
composer, author, arranger

b Ogden, Utah, July 28, 43. Educ: Ogden High Sch; Univ Utah; Weber State Col; Brigham Young Univ, BA; Westminster Choir Col, Princeton, NJ, studied comp with Le Roy Robertson, Alexander Schreiner & Carl Fuerstner. Concert organist, briefly in Eastern States; then moved to Calif. Organist for Arlington Church & St Paul's Cathedral, Los Angeles; also instrumentalist, music ed, comp, orchestrator, arr & cond, Metro-Goldwyn-Mayer Studios & Universal Studios; organ soloist, Burbank Symph & Pasadena Symph, Calif. *Scores:* TV Series: Bionic Woman; Buck Rogers in the 25th Century; TV Pilot: The Hawaiian.

WOODWARD, DAVID GILMAN　　　　ASCAP 1975
composer, author

b Lawrence, Kans, Apr 18, 49. Educ: Univ Tenn, BS(forestry). Coordr for Tennessee's winter educ prog, administered through Tenn Wildlife Resources Agency. Chief Collabrs: Don King, Jeff Walker, Jeff Raymond. *Songs:* I've Got You to Come Home To; I Must Be Dreaming; Don't Make No Promises; Country Music in My Soul; Sweet Love Song the World Can Sing; I Don't Like Cheatin' Songs; Genuine Texas Good Guy.

WOOLEY, SHEB (BEN COLDER)　　　　ASCAP 1959
composer, author, singer

b Erick, Okla, Apr 10, 21. Educ: Plainview High Sch. Recording artist & writer with MGM; actor in "Rawhide Series" & "High Noon" plus many other movies. Chief Collabr: Homer Escamilla. *Songs:* Purple People Eater; Are You Satisfied; Thats My Pa; Sweet Chile; Hee Haw Theme; Almost Persuaded No 2; Harper Valley PTA; Later That Same Day; Don't Go Near the Eskimos.

WOOLSEY, MARYHALE (MARY HALE, TERRY SNOW, EUGENIA HALE)　　　　ASCAP 1942
author

b Spanish Fork, Utah, Mar 21, 1899; d Santa Monica, Calif, Dec 6, 69. Educ: Brigham Young Univ; Univ Utah; Columbia Univ. Copywriter, advert agencies & dept stores. Soc ed, Salt Lake City Tribune. Ed, Utah Clubwoman (Utah Fedn Women's Clubs). Exec secy, Utah Asn UN, 51-52. Ed asst, Univ Utah Publ. Author: "The Keys and the Candle." Charter mem, League of Utah Writers & Salt Lake City Art Barn Poets. Co-founder, Utah Poetry Soc. Mem: Am Guild Authors & Composers; Poets of the Pac; Songwriters' Protective Asn. Chief Collabrs: Robert Sauer, Jack Glenn Brown, Seldon N Heaps, Eugene Jelesnik. *Songs:* When It's Springtime in the Rockies; When the Wild, Wild Roses Bloom; Colorado; On the Trails of Timpanogas; Lost Melody; You're an Invitation to a Dream; O Lovely Light; Shangri-La; My Girl in My Old Home Town; Rain Across the Moon. *Scores:* Operettas: Star Flower; The Giant's Garden; The Happy Hearts; The Enchanted Attic; Neighbors in the House.

WOOTTEN, LAWRENCE BERNARD (RED)　　　　ASCAP 1965
composer, author, bassist

b Social Circle, Ga, Nov 5, 21. Educ: Studies with Frederick DeLand, Herman Reinshagen & Nat Gangursky. Bass player with several jazz oriented bands. Country Western Acad of Music Award. Chief Collabrs: Hal Moffett, Miguel de la Vega, Erma White, Edsel Johns, Joan Tratnor, Jim Hunter, Sharon Wilkie, Celeta Felby. *Songs:* Genesis Through Exodus; Christmas Time; A Man's Gotta; Nomeolvides; Standing in the Shadow of a Rainbow; Bright Lights of Nashville; Deja Vu in Orange; Teardrop River; Used Lips, Fickle Eyes; Insanity Town; Buffalo Woman; If You Left, You Left, So What? *Instrumental Works:* Cuban Holiday.

WORDEN, WILLEY
See Nedrow, John Wilson

WORK, JOHN WESLEY, III　　　　ASCAP 1941
composer, author, educator

b Tullahoma, Tenn, June 15, 01; d Nashville, Tenn, May 18, 67. Educ: Fisk Univ, BA, DMus, 63; Columbia Univ, MA; Yale Univ, MB; Inst Musical Art, New York; Juilliard; Julius Rosenwald Found, 2 yr fel. Cond, Men's Glee Club, Fisk Univ, 27-31, asst prof theory, 33-43, prof, 43, chmn, Music Dept, dir, Fisk Jubilee Singers, 48-57. Author: "American Negro Songs." *Songs & Instrumental Works:* The Singers (cantata; 1st Prize, Fel Am Composers); Yenvalou (string orch; comn by Saratoga Spring Spa Fest); Night in La Vale (orch); Isaac Watts Contemplates the Cross (choral cycle); Appalachia-Three Fiddle and Game Tunes (piano solo); Scuppernong (piano solo; incl At a Certain Church; Ring Game; Visitor From Town); From the Deep South (suite for organ); Golgotha Is a Mountain (cantata; poem by Arna Bontemps); Soliloquy; Three Glimpses of Night; To a Mona Lisa; Every Mail Day; Dusk at Sea; There's a Meetin' Here Tonight; Go Tell It on the Mountain; My Lord What a Morning; God, I Need Thee; Anthems: For All the Saints; For the Beauty of the Earth; Do Not I Love Thee, O Lord; Into the Woods My Master Went; Sing O Heavens; Jesus, Thou Joy of Loving Hearts.

WORK, JULIAN C　　　　ASCAP 1959
composer, arranger

b Nashville, Tenn, Sept 25, 10. Educ: Fisk Univ; pvt music study. Arr for vaudeville, radio & TV, 31- Staff arr, CBS radio; then arr for TV & recordings. *Instrumental Works:* Portraits From the Bible (suite; incl Moses); Processional Hymn; Autumn Walk; Driftwood Patterns; Stand the Storm.

WORRALL, THOMAS GARY　　　　ASCAP 1971
composer, author

b New London, Ohio, Sept 9, 42. Educ: Ohio State Univ; Peabody Cons, Baltimore, BM, studied conducting with Laszlo Halasz, comp with Benjamin Lees; Univ Rochester, Eastman Sch Music, MM, studied comp with Samuel Adler. Asst cond, Ice Capades, 69; arr & cond, "Disney on Parade," 70-74 & NBC entertainment, "Peter Pan," 75. Comp & arr, Ice Capades & Hanna Barbera Studios, 77-80. *Songs:* Disco Mickey Mouse; Macho Duck; Music: Winter Wishes. *Instrumental Works:* The Olympian.

WORTH, AMY　　　　ASCAP 1943
composer, organist, conductor

b St Joseph, Mo, Jan 18, 1888; d Seattle, Wash, Apr 29, 67. Educ: Pub schs; studied music with Jessie Gaynor, Frederick Beale, Mary Lyon, Arthur Garbett. Taught piano; also organist & choir dir, St Joseph. Choral dir, Women's Univ Club, Seattle. *Songs:* Midsummer; Pierrot; Israel; The Time of Violets; Little Lamb; Song of the Angels; The Evening Is Hushed; Madrigal. *Instrumental Works:* Purple Heather (2 pianos); Gavotte Marianne (piano); Mary the Mother (Christmas cantata); Christ Rises (choral); Sing of Christmas (women's voices); He Came All So Still.

WORTH, BOBBY　　　　ASCAP 1943
composer, author, singer

b Cleveland, Ohio, Sept 25, 21. Educ: Cleveland Heights High Sch; Cleveland Inst Music. Played piano on concert stage age 6; switched to pop music & wrote first song age 10; started singing & playing piano on Cleveland radio; became kid star in Vaudeville with Gus Edwards; teen yrs had own radio shows & dance band in New York, went to Hollywood; wrote theme & songs for Rudy Vallee's Sealtest Show; 3 yrs scores for Ice Follies. Wrote songs in films including Hopalong Cassidy, Abbot & Costello, Walt Disney, Sinatra & Hitchcock. Had own TV show 2 yrs. On tour here & abroad. Made several recordings as singer with The Bobby Worth Music Hall. Actor in films. *Songs:* Do I Worry?; 'Til Reveille; Don't You Know?; Lazy Countryside; A Fellow on a Furlough; I Look at Heaven; Just a Dream Ago; Love Theme; Your Teenage Dreams; Once Upon a Wintertime; Please Don't Play Number Six Tonight; Rehearsin'; Blue Bayou; Be Young Again; Easy to Say; I'm Cryin' in My Beer; Thanks America; There's Nothin' Like a Boy; I'm Coming Home, Los Angeles; I'll Wait for You; Lyrics: Tonight We Love; The Same Old Song and Dance; Is This the End of the Line?; Carmen Carmela; Beyond the Next Hill; Maria Bonita.

WORTH, FRANK J
composer

b Debrezin, Hungary, Nov 30, 03. To US, 10. Educ: Studied comp with Carl Eppert. Asst cond, Milwaukee Symph. Cond & arr, radio station WTMJ, Milwaukee, late 20's. To Chicago; free-lance arr & comp for var radio progs. Leader, stage shows for conventions, Chicago hotels. To Calif; writer & arr, radio progs incl "Those Websters", "First Nighter", "Roy Rogers," 400 shows, 8 yrs, "Richard Diamond," 7 yrs & "The Hedda Hopper Radio Show," NBC. With Walt Disney Studios music dept, scored background music for TV progs & Western motion pictures. Guest cond with Santa Monica Symph. *Songs & Instrumental Works:* Valse Tzingane for Eddie South; Konzerto for Violoncello and Symphony; Festival Italia for Large Symphony; Piano Concerto for String Symphony and Piano; Double Harp Concerto for Two Harps and Symphony Orchestra; Eight Psalms for Piano and Baritone; Presidential Quintette for Piano; String Quartette; Viola Concerto with String Symphony; String Quartette for Violin, Viola, Cello and Bass; Fantasia Fugato and Finale for Solo Piano; Quintette for Harmonica.

WORTLEY, HOWARD S　　　　ASCAP 1961
composer, arranger, lyricist

b Jersey City, NJ, Feb 17, 16. Educ: NY Univ, BS & MA; Juilliard; ECarolina Col; Queens Col; studied with Ferde Grofe. Served in WW II. Dir music city schs, Washington, NC, 10 yrs; church organist & choir dir var denominations; coordr music, Glen Cove City Sch Dist, NY; dir, North Shore Balladeers Men's Glee Club; comm music & lyrics, TriCentennial Pageant "This Place of Rushes," Glen Cove, 67; teacher & cond. *Songs:* The Musical Dictionary; A Joyous Celebration; From Whom All Blessings Flow; Lights of Hanukkah; In the Spring a Young Man's Fancy; Squattin' Little Squillit Hallelu, Amen; We Got Things; Happy Holiday With Jingle Bells; Music: An English Countryside. *Instrumental Works:* The Mainstreeter; An American Bolero; Out of the Night.

WRIGHT, AL GEORGE (GEORGE STONE)　　　　ASCAP 1968
composer, author, conductor

b London, Eng, June 23, 16. Educ: Univ Miami, BA, 37, MEd, 47; hon LLD, Troy State Univ, 80. Dir bands, Miami Sr High Sch, Fla, 38-54; dir bands, cond of symph band & univ symph orch, Purdue Univ, Lafayette, 54- Founding pres, Nat Band Asn; founder & chmn bd electors, Nat Hall of Fame of Distinguished Band Cond; founder, Acad Wind & Percussive Arts; pres-elect, Am

Bandmasters Asn, 80-81; mem, Music Educr Nat Conf; Nat Band Asn; Am Bandmasters Asn; Am Sch Band Dirs Asn. *Instrumental Works:* Marches: Festival 500; Brickyard Jamboree; Piano solos: March Teepee; Keyboard March; Joyfull Ode; Space Rocket March; Shinto Grand March; Miyasa March; also many others.

WRIGHT, CARTER LAND (GARY KENT)
composer, vocal coach

b Bethlehem, Pa, Sept 11, 11. Educ: Los Angeles Jr Col, AA; Univ Calif, Los Angeles, BA. Appeared in play, "Red Mill," high sch. Comp univ songs, Men's Glee Club, Univ Calif, Los Angeles. Taught voice, radio dept, Meglin Fanchon & Marco Studios; production mgr, broadcasting sta. TV demonstrations, Farnsworth TV Corp, KTM Studios, Los Angeles. Established Carter Wright Radio TV Productions, 35. Wrote musical comedy, "Reno."

WRIGHT, FRANK A   ASCAP 1926
composer

b Hamilton, Ont, July 2, 1889; d. *Songs:* You'll Find a Shamrock Blooming in Every Irish Heart; Radio Lady o' Mine; And I Believed in You; Oh Boy, What a Girl; Parting.

WRIGHT, FRED HOWARD   ASCAP 1957
composer, author, singer

b San Diego, Calif, Sept 30, 1896. Educ: San Diego Jr Col. Officer in cavalry, WW I. Appeared in musical comedies & vaudeville. Dir-producer in Portland, Ore, San Francisco, San Diego, Oakland & Long Beach, Calif & Honolulu, Hawaii. Mem recording team, The Happy Chappies. Wrote for acts incl original "Beverly Hillbillies." Acted in radio show "Ma Perkins," 12 yrs & others. Writer, radio & TV shows, incl "Lights Out", "Mystery Is My Hobby", "Deadline", "Charlie Ruggles Show," 3 yrs & others. Chief Collabr: Nat Vincent. *Songs:* I'm Going to Ride Herd in the Sky; Lyrics: When the Bloom Is on the Sage; The Strawberry Roan; My Pretty Quadroon; Mellow Mountain Moon; Little Girl Dressed in Blue; At the End of the Lane; Sitting on the Bank of the River; Me and My Burro; Old Black Mountain Trail; My Dear Old Arizona Trail; Wonder Valley; On the Golden Shores of Lake Louise; It's Time to Say Aloha; The Steer's Lament.

WRIGHT, GARY
musician

b Creskill, NJ, 1943. Educ: Studied psychol, New York & Berlin, Ger. Child actor. Played keyboards in var high sch bands. Formed own group, New York Times, toured cent Europe. Co-leader band, Spooky Tooth. Formed Gary Wright's Wonderwheel, 70, reformed, 73. Solo artist, 74- *Albums:* Extraction; Footprint; The Dream Weaver; The Light of Smiles.

WRIGHT, LILIAN COCHRANE (TALIE COCHRANE)   ASCAP 1978
composer, author, singer

b Memphis, Tenn, Oct 7, 44. Educ: Univ Ala; studied classical piano, 4 1/2 yrs, film producing, 3 yrs & acting, 10 yrs. Began singing at age 4. Dancer & actress; producer "Falling in Love Again." Chief Collabrs: Bob Verne, Tom Wells. *Songs:* My Muscle Man; Too Loose; Blow Me Away; Shame, Shame on the Bixby Boys; Sinnin'; The Devil Made Me Do It.

WRIGHT, MARVIN M (LEFTY)   ASCAP 1952
composer, author, pianist

b Wessington, SDak, Jan 8, 11. Educ: Piano study, age 6 to 14. Pianist, Fred E Bener Orch, radio WOW, Nebr, Tommy Dorsey, 44-45, Jimmie Grier, 46-48, Freddie Martin, 49; rehearsal pianist, 20th Century-Fox, Warner Brothers & Columbia. Free-lance recording pianist; music ed, 20th Century-Fox; retired, 76. Chief Collabrs: Bernie Hanighen, Ken Darby, Jimmie Grier, Jimmy Dorsey, Lionel Newman, Ken Wannberg. *Songs:* Mia Bella Donna; Remember the Time; Life's a Great Big Ball; Music: Thanks for You; Hana Maui; Let It All Hang Out. *Instrumental Works:* J D's Boogie Woogie; Afternoon of a Butterfly; Sunset on the Water; Anitra's Boogie; Club Tonic Blues; One O'Clock Boogie; Boogie Mambo No 1 & No 2; Bach Boogie; Easy on the Eyes.

WRIGHT, RAYBURN
composer

b Alma, Mich, Aug 27, 22. Educ: Eastman Sch Music, BM, 43; Juilliard Sch Music, 48-49; Columbia Univ Teachers Col, MA, 50. Arr & trombonist, USA Band, Washington, DC, 43-45, with Tony Pastor, Tex Beneke & Glenn Miller Orchs, 46-48. Staff arr, Radio City Music Hall, 50-65 & co-dir music, 65-69. Comp, ABC documentary series "The Saga of Western Man," 64-65, rec'd 2 Emmy nominations. Prof & head of jazz studies prog, Eastman Sch Music, 70- *Instrumental Works:* Christ Is Born; Patterns (symph orch); Regeneration (jazz, rock groups & symph orch); Interfaces I (trombones & perc).

WRIGHT, ROBERT CRAIG   ASCAP 1937
composer, author, producer

b Daytona Beach, Fla, Sept 25, 14. Educ: Miami Sr High Sch; Univ Miami; studied piano with Olive Dungan, Manna-Zucca & Arthur Moor. Pianist, radio, vaudeville & hotels, 29-35; contract comp-lyricist for MGM, 36-42; writer & dir 11 Revues Camp Tamiment & 8 Revues Copacabana, NY, 42-44; writer, US Treasury Star Parade, World Broadcasting, 44-80. Chief Collabrs: George (Chet) Forrest, Walter Donaldson, Herbert Stothart, Edward Ward, Erich

Korngold, Heitor Villa-Lobos, P G Wodehouse, Guy Bolton, Jerome Chodorov, Edwin Lester, Milton Lazarus, Charles Lederer, Luther Davis, Peter Stone, George Abbott, Jose Ferrer, Andrew L Stone. *Songs:* It's a Blue World; Stranger in Paradise (music based, A Borodin); Baubles, Bangles and Beads (music based, A Borodin); And This Is My Beloved (music based, A Borodin); Sands of Time (music based, A Borodin); Night of My Nights (music based, A Borodin); Bored (music based, A Borodin); He's in Love (music based, A Borodin); Strange Music (music adaptation, E Grieg); Three Loves (music adaptation, E Grieg); Freddy and His Fiddle (music adaptation, E Grieg); Now (music adaptation, E Grieg); At Christmastime (music adaptation, E Grieg); I Love You (music adaptation, E Grieg); Midsummer's Eve (music adaptation, E Grieg); Bubble, Bubble, Bubble (Pink Champagne); Punchinello; It's the Same; Inevitable; To Look Upon My Love; Sweet Danger; The Fog and the Grog; Willow, Willow, Willow; Chime In!; Elena; The Olive Tree (music based, A Borodin); Nightfall (music adaptation, J Strauss); Warm (music adaptation, J Strauss); With You Gone (music adaptation, J Strauss); Lyrics: Always and Always; At the Balalaika; The Donkey Serenade; Summer Serenade; Boystown on Parade; Saratoga; The Horse With the Dreamy Eyes; Sweethearts. *Scores:* Bway Shows: Gypsy Lady; At the Grand; Dumas and Son; I, Anastasia; Spring in Brazil; A Song for Cyrano; Song of Norway (music adaptation, E Grieg); Kismet (music based, A Borodin); Kean; Anya (music based, S Rachmaninoff); Magdalena (music, Heitor Villa-Lobos); Timbuktu! (music based, A Borodin); The Great Waltz (adaptation, J Strauss); The Love Doctor; Film/TV: Song of Norway (music adaptation, E Grieg); The Great Waltz (music adaptation, J Strauss); The Firefly (music, R Friml & H Stothart); Sweethearts (music, V Herbert); Balalaika (music, Posford, Stothart, Rimsky-Korsakov); Music in My Heart; Fiesta (music, E Ward); Maytime.

WRIGHT, SHEARAD HANNIBAL   ASCAP 1978
composer, author, instrumentalist

b Florence, SC, Jan 11, 10. Educ: Juilliard Sch Music, 48-51; Columbia Univ, 51-67; Empire State Col, NY, BA, 80. Freelance musician, DC, 27-34, New York, 35-42 & 46-; bandsman, AUS, 42-45; cond/arr, Amsterdam A Cappela Chorus, New York, 52-63; choir mem, Church of The Master, New York, 54-64. Chief Collabr: Benny Alston. *Songs:* Love Is the Strangest Thing; It's Party Time; Music: I Dream of Summer; Beguine: Devil in You; Don't Worry.

WRIGHT, SYREETA
composer, singer

b Pittsburgh, Pa. Started out as background singer & secy, Motown Records, also her recording label. Now working with Billy Preston. *Songs:* Lyrics: Come Back As a Flower; Signed Sealed Delivered; Blame It on the Sun; If You Really Love Me; It's a Shame.

WRUBEL, ALLIE   ASCAP 1933
composer, author

b Middletown, Conn, Jan 15, 05; d Los Angeles, Calif, Dec 13, 73. Educ: Wesleyan Univ; Columbia Univ. Saxophonist in dance orchs, incl Paul Whiteman. Led band touring Eng. Mgr, film theatres, 3 yrs. Went to Hollywood, 34, under contract to Warner Bros. Wrote many songs for films. Chief Collabrs: Abner Silver, Herb Magidson, Charles Newman, Mort Dixon, Ray Gilbert, Ned Washington. *Songs:* As You Desire Me; I'll Be Faithful; Farewell to Arms; Pop Goes Your Heart; Happiness Ahead; Mr and Mrs Is the Name; Flirtation Walk; Fare Thee Well, Annabelle; I See Two Lovers; The Lady in Red; The First Time I Saw You; Gone With the Wind; Music, Maestro, Please; The Masquerade Is Over; Good Night, Angel; I'm Stepping Out With a Memory Tonight; My Own America; Why Don't We Do This More Often?; A Boy in Khaki, a Girl in Lace; Don't Call It Love; I Met Her on Monday; I'll Buy that Dream; Why Does It Get Late So Early; I Do Do Do Like You; Zip-a-Dee-Doo-Dah (Acad Award, 47); Everybody's Got a Laughing Place; Johnny Fedora and Alice Blue Gown; Gotta Get Me Somebody to Love; The Lady From Twentynine Palms; At the Flying W; Never Steal Anything Small; What Does a Woman Do. *Scores:* Films: Happiness Ahead; Flirtation Walk; Sweet Music; Radio City Revels; Song of the South; Never Steal Anything Small.

WURMAN, HANS G   ASCAP 1969
composer, moog performer

b Vienna, Austria, Jan 21, 22. Educ: Vienna Staatsakademie; London Royal Acad of Music; studied with Edward Steuermann. Wrote & cond film scores, London & Chicago; recording artist on Moog Synthesizer. Peabody Award for score, 79. *Songs:* Avodath l'ami (publ of music). *Scores:* Radio plays: five plays by F Scott Fitzgerald; The Odyssee; Tale of Two Cities; Film/TV: Fog; Fire in the Sea. *Albums:* The Moog Strikes Bach; Chopin a la Moog.

WYKES, ROBERT A   ASCAP 1963
composer, author, flutist

b Aliquippa, Pa, May 19, 26. Educ: Eastman Sch Music, Univ Rochester, BMus, 49, MMus, 49; Univ Ill, DMA, 55. Flautist, Toledo Symph, 50-52, St Louis Symph, 65-68 & Studio for New Music, 66-69. Teacher, Bowling Green State Univ, Ohio, 50-52, Univ Ill, 52-55 & Washington Univ, St Louis, Mo, 55-, prof, 65. Paderewski Prize Comn, 59; CINDY Award Documentary Film, "Robert Kennedy Remembered," 69; Comp Fel, NEA, 74; ASCAP Standard Div Award, 64-80. Chief Collabr: Donald Finkel. *Songs:* Music: Four American Indian Lyrics (SATB); Adequate Earth (setting of poem by Donald Finkel, 3 choruses, 2 narrators, baritone & orch). *Instrumental Works:* Sonata for Flute and Piano; Quintet for Piano and String Quartet; The Shape of Time (orch); Towards Time's Receding (orch); Resonances for Orchestra; A Shadow of Silence (orch); Ford's Theater: Sound and Light. *Scores:* Film/TV: Robert Kennedy Remembered (Acad Award, 69); Monument to the Dream.

WYLE, GEORGE   ASCAP 1948
composer, conductor, arranger

b New York, NY, Mar 22, 16. Educ: James Monroe High Sch; self-taught in music. Cond, Alan Young Radio Show, Hollywood, 46. Started writing songs, 48. Choral dir, Dinah Shore TV Show, 59-60; worked on Williams Show, 62-66; also Jerry Lewis & Lennon Sisters Shows. Musical dir, Flip Wilson TV Show, 5 yrs. TV specials incl, John Davidson Christmas Shows, Pat Boone & Family, John Denver Christmas & The American Music Awards Show, 76 & 78-80. Cond, London Symph Orch, Andy Williams Concert. Chief Collabrs: Eddie Pola, Don Rogers, Dave Wilson, Mort Green. *Songs:* If You Take a Look At Yourself (Andy Williams Syndicated Show Theme); Music: I Said My Pajamas; Quick Silver; Ballad of Gilligans Island (theme); May Each Day (Andy Williams Theme); It's the Most Wonderful Time of the Year. *Instrumental Works:* Flip Wilson Theme.

WYLIE, RUTH SHAW   ASCAP 1974
author, educator

b Cincinnati, Ohio, June 24, 16. Educ: Wayne State Univ, AB(romance languages), MA(comp); Univ Rochester Eastman Sch Music, PhD(comp), studied with Bernard Rogers & Howard Hanson; Berkshire Music Center, studied with Arthur Honegger, Samuel Barber, Aaron Copland. From instr to asst prof, comp & theory, Univ Mo, 43-49; from asst prof to prof comp & theory, Wayne State Univ, 49-69, chmn music dept, 60-61, head of comp, 60-69, retired, prof emeritus, 69- *Instrumental Works:* Psychogram (piano); Soliloquy (piano); Five Preludes (piano); Five Easy Pieces (piano); Six Little Preludes (piano); String Quartet No 3; The Long Look Home (suite for orch); Views From Beyond (suite for orch); Nova (violin, flute, clarinet, cello, perc & vibraphone solo); Incubus (flute, clarinet, perc & cello ens); Toward Sirius (chamber suite, flute, oboe, violin, cello, piano & harpsichord); Terrae Incognitae (flute, viola, guitar, piano, perc).

WYNN, CHARLES
See Weinberg, Charles

WYNN, ED   ASCAP 1924
composer, author, actor

b Philadelphia, Pa, Nov 9, 1886; d Beverly Hills, Calif, June 19, 66. Educ: Pvt & pub schs. Left home to go on stage with Thurber-Nash Rep Co. Appeared on Keith & Orpheum circuits; wrote own material for vaudeville acts. Appeared in Bway musicals: "Ziegfeld Follies" (14); "Passing Show" (16); "Doing Our Bit"; "Over the Top"; "Shubert Gaieties"; "Ed Wynn Carnival"; "The Perfect Fool"; "The Grab Bag"; "Manhattan Mary"; "Simple Simon"; "Laugh Parade"; "Hooray for What!"; "Boys and Girls Together"; "Ed Wynn's Laugh Carnival." Had own radio prog, 30's; also TV, 50's. First dramatic role: "Requiem for a Heavyweight." Appeared in films incl "The Fire Chief", "The Great Man", "Babes in Toyland", "Those Crazy Calloways", "Marjorie Morningstar", "Diary of Anne Frank", "Mary Poppins", "Dear Brigitte" & "The Greatest Story Every Told." *Songs:* Old Home Week in Maine; Girls, Pretty Girls; What Did Annie Laurie Promise?.

WYRICK, BARBARA   ASCAP 1970
composer, author

b Dyersburg, Tenn, July 21, 50. Educ: Memphis State Univ, theater studies. With Engelbert Humperdinck, 2 yrs; currently traveling & singing with Ronnie Milsap. Chief Collabrs: Terry Woodford, Mickey Buckins. *Songs:* Tell Me a Lie; Regrets; Right Feelin' At the Wrong Time; I'm Just Warming Up; Too Big for Words.

WYTON, ALEC   ASCAP 1962
composer, organist, conductor

b London, Eng, Aug 3, 21. Educ: Royal Acad Music, London; Oxford Univ; MA & MusD; studied with G D Cunningham, Sir Hugh Allen, Sir Thomas Armstrong & Ernest Walker. Asst organist, Christ Church Cathedral, Oxford, 43-46; organist/choirmaster, St Matthew's Church, Northampton, 46-50, Christ Church Cathedral, St Louis, Mo, 50-54, Cathedral of St John the Divine, NY, 54-74 & St James, NY, 74- Assoc prof, Union Theol Sem, NY, 61-73; pres, Am Guild Organists, 64-69 & The Bohemians, 76-78. Fels, Royal Acad Music, Royal Sch of Church Music, Royal Col of Organists, Am Guild of Organists & Royal Can Col of Organists. Chief Collabrs: Madeleine L'Engle, Chad Walsh. *Songs:* Music: A Hymn to God the Father (choir, brass, timpani & organ); The Lord Is My Light and My Salvation; For All the People (Eucharistic music for voices, brass & organ); Christ Our Passover; Vision of Isaiah; Palm Sunday Procession (voices & organ); Two Choral Hymns (voices & organ); Christmas Mourning (voice(s), flute & keyboard); Nativity (voice(s), flute & keyboard); My Dancing Day (voices unaccompanied); If You Have Ears (voice(s) & keyboard); Psalm 150 (voices & organ); Clap Your Hands (voices & keyboard); I Was Glad (soprano solo, chorus, brass, timpani & organ); Introits for the Church Year (voices unaccompanied). *Instrumental Works:* A Little Christian Year (organ); Praise Him in the Sound of the Trumpet (organ); Fanfare (organ); Earth and All Stars (organ); Elegy (oboe, clarinet or flute & organ); In Praise

of Merbecke (organ); Dithyramb (organ); Flourish (organ); concert piece for organ & perc; preludes, fanfares & march for organ. *Scores:* The Journey With Jonah (opera).

Y

YABLOKOFF, BELLA MYSELL   ASCAP 1961
author, singer

b New York, NY, Apr 5, 03. Educ: Pvt tutors; Juilliard Sch Music. Actress & singer in Am & Yiddish theatre productions. Wrote songs for musicals: "Uncle Sam in Israel", "It's a Funny World" & "My Son and I." *Songs:* Glick; Kindershpiel; Music to My Ear; My Son and I.

YABLOKOFF, HERMAN   ASCAP 1960
composer, author, director

b Grodno, Poland, Aug 11, 03. Educ: In Europe. Moved to US, 24. Appeared in stock cos, US & Can. Moved to New York, featured as The Clown on radio, singing own songs. Producer, playwright, dir, actor & comp in Yiddish Theatre. Toured throughout world in stage productions & concert. Wrote & acted in "My Son and I." *Songs:* Papirossen; Dish-Washer; My White Flower; Give Me Back My Heart; A Letter; Be Calm My Heart; My Little Girl; Bread.

YABLON, MARJORIE PEARL   ASCAP 1971
author

b New York, NY, June 21, 47. Educ: Mamaroneck High Sch, NY; Barnard Col, Columbia Univ, BA, 68; studied acting, Alice Spivak & Uta Hagen. Staff & free-lance lyricist, actor, videotape producer & newspaper feature writer; both staff & free-lance lyrics for commercial jingles. Chief Collabrs: Gerry Alters, Julie Haines. *Songs:* Lyrics: His Mania.

YABLONKA, MARC PHILLIP (MARC YOUNGER)   ASCAP 1975
composer, author, performer

b Los Angeles, Calif, Apr 10, 50. Educ: San Francisco State Col, BA(Eng), 72, minored in film history; Univ Calif, Los Angeles, adult educ teaching credential, 76; Orange County Broadcasting Headquarters, cert of completion, 79. Professional performer, 68-; writer, 70- Has toured Can 3 times & col, tavern & coffee house circuits throughout US. DJ, KGLT-FM, Bozeman, Mont, KCRW-FM, Santa Monica, Calif, KOOL-AM & FM, Mohave, Calif, KNTF-FM, Ontario, Calif, 74- Established ASCAP publ co, Crowchild Music. Chief Collabrs: Jeff Snyder, Malcolm Jones. *Songs:* The Fool (Come Closin' Time); Just the Pain Talkin'; Traces of You; Trinket Lady.

YACICH, CHRIS   ASCAP 1956
composer

b New Orleans, La, Feb 6, 01; d New Orleans, Feb 27, 67. Educ: McDonogh, dipl in accounting, 35. With Cotton Exchange & Corps of Engrs. Served, USCG, World War II. *Songs:* I Like Bananas; Fee Fo Lay.

YAKIMA LEE
See Graham, L Lee

YALEN, PAUL EDWARD   ASCAP 1954
composer, author, singer

b Bethesda, Md, Jan 29, 54. Educ: Lincoln-Sudbury Regional High Sch; Univ Mass, Amherst, BA(mass communications), 73; Suffolk Univ, MEd, 75. In pre-Bway tryout, "Joyful Noise," 68. Toured nightclubs & cols in eastern US & Can. Radio announcer & comedy writer, WFCR. *Songs:* Grabber; Don't Be a Stranger; You Can Never Go Back; Blameless, I Don't Forgive. *Albums:* Wanted-for Assault With a Deadly Piano.

YAMIN, JAIME   ASCAP 1947
composer, author

b Caguas, PR, Dec 24, 13; d. Educ: High sch. Car salesman, San Juan. *Songs:* My Confession; Mulata Caprichosa; Desconfianza de tu Amor; Por Tu Amor; Los Angelitos de Dios; Sabrosa; Este Amor.

YANCEY, THOMAS LELAND   ASCAP 1978
composer, teacher

b Marshall, Mo, Oct 27, 32. Educ: Cent Methodist Col, Fayette, Mo, BM; Cincinnati Col/Cons of Music, MM; Eastman Sch Music, postgrad work; Juilliard, studied piano with Katherine Bacon; Manhattan Sch Music, studied with Dora Zaslavsky; San Francisco Cons Music, studied with Robert Sheldon. Assoc prof piano & music theory, Swinney Cons Music, Cent Methodist Col, 58- *Songs:* Music: The Song of David (choral anthem); Psalm 134 (choral anthem).

YANCICH, MILAN MICHAEL   ASCAP 1921
composer, author, teacher

b Whiting, Ind, Dec 11, 21. Educ: Univ Mich, BMEd, 46; Northwestern Univ, MM, 50; studied French horn with Philip Farkas, Bohunir Kryl & Max Pottag, comp with Leo Sowenby & Bernard Rogers. First horn, Columbus Symph,

46-48. Solo horn, Jerry Walds Orch, 47. Asst & assoc first horn, Chicago Symph, 48-51. Third horn, Cleveland Orch, 51-52. Solo horn, ABC radio, Chicago, 52. Played all positions, Rochester Philh, 53-80. Prof horn & ens, Eastman Sch Music, 56-80. *Instrumental Works:* Method for French Horn Volume I and II; Practical Guide to French Horn Playing; 15 Solos for French Horn and Piano Accompaniment.

YANTIS, DAVID M   ASCAP 1972
composer, singer

b San Antonio, Tex, Feb 1, 33. Educ: Mariposa High Sch, Calif; San Antonio Col, BA, 55; studied piano with Miriam Wagner. Nightclub singer/musician, music dir & teacher of guitar, 55-68. Composer & recording artist, Contemporary Church Music, 68-; traveling nationally as clinician-performer. Chief Collabrs: Charles F Brown, Dean McIntyre, Steve Harris, Kurt Kaiser. *Songs & Instrumental Works:* Beyond a Dream; Contemporary Hymn Book; Pass My Love Around; A Little Each Day; Complete Love; The Body of Christ; Unconditional Love; Up The Ladder of Faith; All God's Children Sing (collection of songs and hand poetry).

YARBROUGH, GLENN   ASCAP 1961
composer, singer, arranger

b Milwaukee, Wis, Jan 12, 30. Educ: St John's Col. Prof singer, 56- Had own club, Aspen, Colo, 58-60. Mem, Limeliters, 50-64; then single. Has made many records. *Songs:* All My Sorrows; Lass From the Low Country; Harry Pallate.

YARBROUGH, HAROLD LEROY   ASCAP 1971
composer, teacher, conductor

b Rome, Ga, Aug 23, 34. Educ: Tenn Temple Col; Baylor Univ, BM, MM; Univ Tex; La State Univ. Dir, Baylor Univ Religious Hour Choir & New Orleans Civic Chorus. Prof, New Orleans Baptist Sem. *Songs:* What If; Let the Song Begin; Music: Jesus Calls Us; Oh, Jesus Loves Me; Jesus of Bethany.

YARDUMIAN, RICHARD   ASCAP 1954
composer, teacher

b Philadelphia, Pa, Apr 5, 17. Educ: Pub schs; studied music with George Boyle, William Happich & Alexander Matthews; L'Ecole Monteux, Hancock, Maine. Assoc with Philadelphia Youth Concerts. USAAF, Pac theatre, WW II. Church music dir, 39- Teaches privately. *Instrumental Works:* Armenian Suite; Recitative and Fugue (piano concerto); Prelude-Fugue for Piano (Rudolf Firkusny comn); Violin Concerto; Monologues for Violin; 3 Pictographs; Desolate City; Psalm 130 (tenor, orch); Cantus Animae et Cordis (Stringart Quartet comn); Choral: Prelude on Plainsong Veni, Sancte Spiritus (Edward Benjamin comn); Create in Me a Clean Heart (Princeton Theol Sem comn); 2 Symphonies (No 1, Philadelphia Chamber Orch comn); 3 Piano Preludes.

YARROW, PETER   ASCAP 1962
composer, author, arranger

b New York, NY, May 31, 38. Educ: Cornell Univ; Art Student League. Sang with folk groups; appeared on "Folk Sound, USA," CBS; at Newport Jazz Fest, also on cross-country tour. Mem, singing trio, Peter, Paul & Mary, appearing on TV, in nightclubs & concerts throughout US, Can & Europe. Has sung at jazz and folk fests; made many records. Chief Collabrs: Mary Travers, Noel Paul Stookey, Milt Okun. *Songs:* Puff, the Magic Dragon; A-Soulin'.

YATES, EDDY
See Aaberg, Philip

YATES, RONALD LEE   ASCAP 1978
composer

b Muskegon, Mich, Apr 27, 47. Educ: Calif State Univ, Long Beach, BM, MA; Univ Calif, Santa Barbara, PhD(comp); studied comp with Ed Applebaum, 68-73 & Peter Racine Fricker, 72-73. Arr & comp of music for schs & professional performers, 65- Mem music fac, ETex State Univ, 74-, teacher of comp, theory & electronic music, opera cond & musical pit orch dir. Has written film scores for several educ films & other educ media. *Instrumental Works:* Air (8 flutes); In Search of... (band). *Scores:* Film: Educational Directions; Data Processing and You.

YEAZEL, ROBERT DEVON   ASCAP 1971
composer, author, guitarist

b Denver, Colo, Nov 1, 46. Educ: Berklee Sch Music, arr course. Started playing at age 14 in garage & high sch bands; wrote first song at age 14. First recorded with group, The Beast, two albums; then joined, Sugarloaf; has been a free lancer & player with Freddie-Henchi Band, 75- Owned studio, two yrs; has publ co, Love Craft Music. Vocalist & arr. Chief Collabrs: Jerry Corbetta, Larry Wilkins. *Songs & Instrumental Works:* Floating Down (By the River); The One That Got Away; Everyman Hears Different Music; Tongue in Cheek; Spaceship Earth.

YELIN, EDWARD M   ASCAP 1963
composer, arranger, trumpeter

b Buffalo, NY, Oct 20, 28. Educ: Chicago Musical Col; Univ Chicago. Trumpeter & arr, NBC, Chicago; also for bands & singers. A&R dir, Capitol Records, 57-61; then artists' personal mgr. Chief Collabr: Sue Raney. *Songs:* No Place to Go; Burnt Sugar; Be Warm; Statue of Snow; No Use.

YELLEN, JACK   ASCAP 1917
composer, author, publisher

b Poland, July 6, 1892. Educ: Univ Mich, BA. To US, 1897; reporter, Buffalo Courier, NY; writer spec material singers, incl Sophie Tucker, NY; dir, ASCAP, 51-69. Co-founder, Ager, Yellen & Bornstein Co. Bway stage scores: "What's in a Name", "Rain or Shine", John Murray Anderson's Almanac "You Said It" (also librettist), "George White's Scandals" (35-39), "Boy's and Girls Together", "Son's O' Fun", "Ziegfeld Follies of 1943." Under contract to 20th Century Fox, Hollywood. Film scores: "Road Show", "The King of Jazz", "George White's Scandals" (34-35), "Happy Landing." Songs for films incl "King of Burlesque", "Captain January", "Sing, Baby, Sing", "Rebecca of Sunnybrook Farm." Patron elected, Songwriters Hall of Fame, 76. Chief Collabrs: Milton Ager, Abe Olman, Harold Arlen, Sammy Fain, Ray Henderson, Joseph Meyer, Lew Pollack, Samuel Pokrass, William Simon. *Songs:* Mr Siegal, You Gotta Make It Legal; You're Only as Good as Your Last Kiss; Vitamins, Hormones and Pills; Myron; My Mother's Sabbath Candles; Yiddishe Momme; Are You From Dixie; Lyrics: Alabama Jubilee; How's Every Little Thing in Dixie?; I'm Waiting for Ships That Never Come In; Down By the O-Hi-O; A Young Man's Fancy; Lovin' Sam; Who Cares; Mama Goes Where Papa Goes; Wonder What's Become of Sally; Cheatin' on Me; Big Bad Bill; Forgive Me; Crazy Words Crazy Tune; Ain't She Sweet; Glad Rag Doll; Happy Days Are Here Again (FDR campaign song); Happy Feet; A Bench in the Park; Sweet and Hot; You Said It; Oh You Nasty Man; My Dog Loves Your Dog; It's An Old Southern Custom; The Hunkadola; Life Begins at Sweet Sixteen; The Right Somebody to Love; A Gypsy Told Me; Are You Havin' Any Fun; Something I Dreamed Last Nite; I Want to Live; Happy in Love; Love Songs Are Made in the Night; Life Begins at 40; The Last of the Red Hot Mama's; My Fifty Golden Years.

YLVISAKER, JOHN CARL   ASCAP 1967
composer, author, singer

b Fargo, NDak, Sept 11, 37. Educ: Concordia Col, Moorhead, Minn, BA(music); Univ Minn; St Cloud State Col. High sch music teacher, 59-61; traveling folk singer, 61-70; jr high music teacher, 70-75; producer radio show, "Scan," for Am Lutheran Church, 75- *Songs:* Mass for the Secular City (liturgical music); Ylvisaker Hymnerie (Part I, collection of songs); Holy Communion-Setting IV (liturgical music); Thanks Be to God (hymn). *Scores:* Wake Up, Sleeper (one act musical).

YODER, PAUL V (MAX THOMAS, JAMES A SCOTT)   ASCAP 1955
author, arranger

b Tacoma, Wash, Oct 8, 08. Educ: Univ NDak, BA, 30, hon DMus, 58; Northwestern Univ, Evanston, Ill, MMus, 41. Instrumental music teacher in pub schs, Aurora, Ill & Evansville, Ind, 30-36. Free lance arr & composer of military band, concert or symp band music, primarily for schs and cols, 36-; publ as composer & arr in USA, Eng, Japan, Holland & Ger. *Instrumental Works:* Pachinko; Bobby's Blues; Arkansamba; Glass Slipper; Shrine of Democracy; Easy Does It; Alpha and Omega; Figaro in Stereo; Hail, Alma Mater; Dutch Treat; Holland Brass; Roaring 20's; Trumpets Galore; Gandy Dancers; Bands Around the World; Camp Meeting; Firehouse Special; La Fonda; Virginia Beach March; Bristol March; Anacapri; Swing-A-Long; Rumbalita; Exalted Ruler; Pinnochio; Relax!; Hurricane!; Big Band Beguine; Avalanche; Elbow Room; Swing Bolero; State Fair; Skyways; Parade of the Champions; Hi-Hat; Park Ridge; Hoosier Schoolmaster; Everglades; Runestone; The Toy Shop; Rush Street Tarantella; Excursion in Five/Four; Midnight Sun; Harvest Home; Tokyo Tower; Barcelona; Encore; Dazzling Drums; Mountain Majesty; Heneghan's Holiday; Tin Pan Gallery.

YOELL, LARRY   ASCAP 1936
author

b San Francisco, Calif, Oct 28, 1898; d. Educ: Sacred Heart Col. Song plugger, Leo Feist, 17-19. Mgr, McCarthy-Fisher, Seattle, 19, Shapiro, Bernstein, San Francisco, Santly-Joy & Remick. Music buyer, Pacific stores. Chief Collabrs: Billy Hill, Al Jacobs, Neil Moret, Glenn Brown. *Songs:* The West, a Nest and You; Close Your Eyes; I'm Just an Ordinary Human; When the Sun Goes Down; When Mother Nature Sings Her Lullaby; Walking Around in a Dream; You, Just You; Rock-a-bye My Baby Blues.

YON, PIETRO ALESSANDRO   ASCAP 1927
composer, organist

b Settimo-Vittone, Italy, Aug 8, 1886; d Huntington, NY, Nov 22, 43. Educ: Royal Cons Milan & Turlin; Acad of St Cecilia, Rome; studied with Renzi, Bustini & Sgambata. Substitute organist, Vatican & Royal Church of Rome, 05-06. Came to US, 07, became citizen, 21. Organist & choirmaster, St Francis-Xavier, NY, 08-26. Organist & dir music, St Patrick's Cathedral, NY, 26-43, helped design new organ. Gave organ recitals, US & Europe. Guest appearances with NY Philh. Cavalier & Officer, Order of Crown of Italy. Knight of Sylvester by Pope Pius XI. Hon organist, Basilica of St Peter's, Vatican, Rome. *Songs & Instrumental Works:* Ave Maria; Gesu Bambino; O Faithful Cross; Christ Triumphant; They Call Him Jesus; Go, Happy Soul; Organ: Concerto Gregoriano; 3 organ sonatas; Piano: Nena; Gianduia; Mountain Slopes; Alpine Nocturne; Rain; Masses: Mass of the Shepherds; Pro Defunctis; Missa Solemnis; Regina Pacis; The Triumph of St Patrick (oratorio).

YORK, DONALD GRIFFITH ASCAP 1972
composer, conductor, pianist
b Watertown, NY, June 19, 47. Educ: Studied theory & comp with Hall Overton, 64-66; studied comp with Darius Milhaud, 65-67; Juilliard Sch Music, BMus(comp), 69, studied with Vincent Persichetti. Musical dir, Bette Midler, 74-77 & Paul Taylor Dance Co, 76-; in Bway production "I Love My Wife," 77-78. Chief Collabr: Paul Taylor. *Songs:* Been Down So Long. *Instrumental Works:* A Deux. *Scores:* Ballet: Polaris; Diggity; Film/TV: It Must Be Love; Child Is Father of the Man.

YORK, FRANK ASCAP 1955
composer, conductor, arranger
b Duquesne, Pa, Mar 15, 26. Educ: High sch; studied music with father, also with Mischa Mischakoff (scholarship); Eastman Sch Music (scholarship); studied with Jacques Gordon; Juilliard Sch Music (scholarship); NY Univ. While in high sch, was asst concert master, Pittsburgh Opera Orch. First violinist in Richard Himber orch. While at Eastman, also first violinist, Rochester Symph, NY, organized Eastman's first Freshman Symph. Arr & first violinist with Ted Straeter & Leo Reisman orchs. Worked for College Inn Porterhouse & Sherman Hotel, Chicago, 50- *Songs & Instrumental Works:* Fiddle Frenzy; Love Gone Astray; Cat's Meow.

YORK, HARLEY C (HARLEY DAVIDSON) ASCAP 1976
composer, singer
b Gallatin, Tenn, Oct 27, 44. Educ: On-the-job training in comp & entertaining; DJ Sch Tenn Inst of Broadcasting. Began writing at age 15. USA, until 76. Chief Collabrs: Jack & Kathy Bowers. *Songs:* Born to Bum Around; Walk Out Backwards; My Brother's Wife; I Must Try; Cold Lonely Nights; Feel It.

YORKE, HAROLD EMERSON
author
b Ottawa, Ont, Nov 28, 1893; d Sherman Oaks, Calif, Sept 6, 71. Educ: Elgin Sch, Col Inst, Columbia Univ Extension, studied jour. With M Witmark & Sons, Selwyn & Co & Brunswick Recording Studios, New York. Author & dir radio network progs, "The Old Skipper" & "The Movie Parade." Co-owner, Radio Transc. Talent dir & dir tests & shorts, Paramount Pictures. Assignments with Warner Bros, Universal, Columbia, Republic & Paramount Pictures, ECoast. Producer many documentary films, Emerson Yorke Studio, New York & Los Angeles. Chief Collabrs: Phil Boutelege, Harry Archer, Gene Lockhart, Solita Palmer, Wally Young, Sammy Fain. *Songs:* Lyrics: Dreaming Alone in Hawaii; Sentimental Baby; On the Vagabond Trail; Isle of Enchantment; In Sunny Hawaii; Underneath the Stars With You; I Need Sympathy; Homeward Bound; Temple Bells; Bamboola; Little League March; This Is Baseball; On the Lehi; Men Against the Sea; There Was No Room at the Inn; In My Heart, My Lonely Heart.

YORKIN, DAVID MICHAEL ASCAP 1977
composer
b Los Angeles, Calif, June 16, 62. Educ: Tufts Univ, student presently. Formed own jazz group where he wrote & played lead guitar. Has group at sch. *Scores:* TV Series: What's Happening?

YOSHINAGA, ALAN S ASCAP 1979
composer, author, keyboardist
b Honolulu, Hawaii, Nov 4, 52. Educ: Kaimuki High Sch; Univ Hawaii; studied piano with Clem Low, 69-71 & 75-77. Keyboardist with The Reflections, 76- Won contest & had song recorded on album, 78. TV & nightclub performer. *Songs:* Kuuipo Lei Makamae; And Love. *Instrumental Works:* Song for Carolyn.

YOUMANS, VINCENT MILLIE ASCAP 1920
composer, producer
b New York, NY, Sept 27, 1898; d Denver, Colo, Apr 5, 46. Educ: Trinity Sch, Mamaroneck, NY; Heathcote Hall, Rye, NY. Brief job in Wall St Brokerage Firm. USN, Great Lakes Naval Trining Sta, WW I. Song-plugger, T B Harms Co; rehearsal pianist for Victor Herbert operettas. Chief Collabrs: Ira Gershwin, Herbert Stothart, Otto Harbach, Oscar Hammerstein, II, Irving Caesar, Anne Caldwell, Leo Robin, Clifford Grey, Billy Rose, Edward Eliscu, Edward Heyman, Harold Adamson, Mack Gordon, B G DeSylva, Gus Kahn. *Songs:* Dolly; Oh, Me! Oh, My!; Tie a String Around Your Finger; Bambalina; No, No, Nanette; Tea for Two; I Want to Be Happy; I've Confessed to the Breeze; Too Many Rings Around Rosie; You Can Dance With Any Girl At All; I Know That You Know; Sometimes I'm Happy; Hallelujah!; Why, Oh Why; I Want a Man; The One Girl; Who Am I?; Great Day; More Than You Know; Without a Song; Time on My Hands; Through the Years; Drums in My Heart; You're Everywhere; I Want to Be With You; Should I Be Sweet?; Rise 'n' Shine; Oh, How I Long to Belong to You; Keeping Myself for You; Flying Down to Rio; Orchids in the Moonlight; The Carioca; Music Makes Me. *Scores:* Bway stage: Two Little Girls in Blue; Wildflower; Mary Jane McKane; No, No, Nanette; Oh, Please!; Hit the Deck; Rainbow; Great Day!; Smiles; Through the Years; Take a Chance; Films: Flying Down to Rio.

YOUNG, BARBARA MARIE (BOBBI BOYLE) ASCAP 1978
composer, singer, musician
b Boston, Mass, Jan 13, 31. Educ: Juilliard Sch Music, preparatory dept; Oberlin

Col, BA(music). Entertainer countrywide, 54-73. Studio singer & vocal arr, 73- Chief Collabr: Joann Albert. *Songs:* Music: Every Day A New Beginning.

YOUNG, CARLTON RAYMOND ASCAP 1971
composer, teacher
b Hamilton, Ohio, Apr 25, 26. Educ: Univ Cincinnati Col Music, BMusEd, 50; Boston Univ Sch Theol, STB, 53; Union Sem Sch Sacred Mus, summer 55; hon DMus, Ohio Northern Univ, 69. Minister music, Cleveland & Youngstown, Ohio, 53-58; dir music publ, The Methodist Publ House, Abingdon Press, 58-64. Teacher church music, music performance practice & comp, Southern Methodist Univ, 64-75, Scarritt Col, 75-78 & Emory Univ, 78- Composer, arr & ed of many compositions & collections, 57- Ed, The Methodist Hymnal, 66; music ed, Hope Publ Co, 70- *Songs & Instrumental Works:* Songbook for Saints and Sinners; Genesis Songbook; Exodus Songbook; Choirbook for Saints and Singers.

YOUNG, CHARLES CHESLEY ASCAP 1964
composer, author
b New York, NY, Dec 25, 51. Educ: Collegiate Sch, 66-68; Col Emporia, BA, 72; NY Univ Grad Sch, 73-74, MSc, 75; La State Univ Sch Medicine, MD, 80; pvt studies in piano, drums, guitar, voice, flamenco dancing & magic. Drummer with own band & others. Performer in musicals & variety. Has had paralleling career in biosciences & medicine, continuing into ophthalmology. Chief Collabrs: Chesley V & Cheryl L Young. *Songs:* Come On! Come to the Fair; Lyrics: Chuck's Wagon of Verses.

YOUNG, CHERYL LESLEY ASCAP 1964
composer, author
b New York, NY, Nov 21, 49. Educ: Finch Col, BA; Columbia Univ, MBA. Pvt studies in piano, guitar & ballet while active in bus admin. Chief Collabrs: Chesley V & Charles C Young. *Songs:* Come On! Come to the Fair; The Freedom Song.

YOUNG, CHESLEY VIRGINIA (BARNES) ASCAP 1964
composer, author
b Hamburg, Ark, Sept 7, 19. Educ: Univ Ark, BA, 47; Columbia Univ Teachers Col, MA, 51; studied piano, organ & accordion. WW II, Capt, WAC, USA, 42-46. Taught sch, New York, 10 yrs. Pres, Manhattan Bus & Professional Women's Club, 49-51 & Women's Auxiliary, NY Polyclinic Med Sch & Hospital, 67-68. Regent, New York Daughters of Am Revolution, 76-79. Author of bks, "How to Read Faster and Remember More" & "Magic of a Mighty Memory." Chief Collabrs: Cheryl L & Charles C Young. *Songs:* Have You; Come On! Come to the Fair.

YOUNG, GORDON ELLSWORTH ASCAP 1961
composer, organist, teacher
b Ft Scott, Kans, Oct 15, 19. Educ: Southwestern Col, MusB, 40, MusD, 62; studied organ with Joseph Bonnet, Paris, 41; Curtis Inst Music, 44-46. Dir music, First Methodist Church, Tulsa, Okla, 41-44; organist, First Presby Church, Lancaster, Pa, 44-47; organist-choirmaster, First Presby Church, Detroit, Mich, 53-72. Mem fac & glee club, Franklin Marshall Col, 45-46; mem fac, Tex Christian Univ, 50-52; mem extension fac, Wayne State Univ, 54-61. *Songs & Instrumental Works:* Entreat Me Not to Leave Thee (solo voice); Christmas Triptych (band); Contempora Suite (trumpet & piano); Choir: Now Let Us All Praise God and Sing; Build Thee More Stately Mansions; From All That Dwell Below the Skies; Built on the Rock; Now Sing We Joyfully Unto God; The King of Love; Missa Exultate (cantata); A Mighty Fortress; Organ: Baroque Suite; Cathedral Suite; Variations on an American Hymn Tune; Seven Tone Poems; Nine Hymn Preludes; Easter Suite; eight pieces; twelve compositions; Christmas Suite; London Suite.

YOUNG, GREGG VANCE ASCAP 1969
composer, author, singer
b San Francisco, Calif, Apr 28, 52. Educ: Col of Alameda, studied with Bill Bell; Univ Calif, Berkeley, studied with Dr David Tucker; Calif State Univ, Long Beach, studied with John Prince, Harvey Molloy, Dr Justus Mathews. With var groups incl Carlos Santana, Sly Stone & Bo Diddly. Recording artist. Performer, nightclubs & concerts. *Songs:* My Kind of Woman; It's Not Easy; Speak Your Mind; Music: Chongo; Funk Fusion.

YOUNG, HORACE ALEXANDER, III ASCAP 1977
composer, author, teacher
b Houston, Tex, Nov 4, 54. Educ: Tex Southern Univ, BMus, 78; Shepherd Sch Music; Rice Univ; studied comp with Paul Cooper, flute with Albert Tipton. Toured & arr with B B King Orch, 78-79. Recorded with Freddie Fender, ABC Records, 78. Toured with The Spinners, The Four Tops & Tavares. Studio musician & arr. Teacher, High Sch Performing & Visual Arts, Houston. Chief Collabrs: Charlotte Laws Stroud, Barbara Babchick. *Songs:* Music: Country Fried Chicken; Visitors From a Galaxy Beyond; I Remember Oliver: A Tribute to Oliver Nelson.

YOUNG, IDA ASCAP 1961
composer, author
b Kiev, Russia, Sept 20, 1891; d. Educ: Pub schs, Boston; pvt piano & violin study. *Songs:* Why.

YOUNG, JAMES OLIVER (TRUMMY)　　ASCAP 1943
composer, musician, singer

b Savannah, Ga, Jan 12, 12. Educ: St Emma Inst, Rock Castle, Va; studied trombone with Jerry Cimera. Playing prof with Booker Coleman's Hot Chocolates, Washington, DC, 29, with Tommy Miles Orch, Washington, 30 & Earl Hines, Chicago, 33; recorded with Earl Hines, 33. Joined Jimmy Lunceford, New York, 37, recorded "Margi," 38; played with Charlie Barnet, 42, Billie Holiday, 43. Toured with Jazz at the Philh, 44 & 46. Played with Benny Goodman early 40's. Joined Louis Armstrong, 52-63. Played at Dick Gibson's Jazz Party, Colorado Springs, Labor Day weekend, 9 yrs. Toured Eng, Scotland, Ireland, Holland & Ger, 78. Toured Ger & Austria with "A Nite in New Orleans," 80. Trombonist & singer. Mem, Am Guild Authors & Composers. *Songs:* Taint Whatcha Do It's The Way How You Do It; A Lover Is Blue; Easy Does It; Whatcha Know Joe; Trav'lin Light; Thru for the Night; Sorta Kinda; Losers Weepers; Life Is Fine; Jump Time; I'm Livin' For Today; Father Cooperates; Twenty-four Robbers; Riff Raff. *Albums:* Trummy Young-A Man and His Horn; Yours Truly, Trummy Young and Friends.

YOUNG, JAMES V　　ASCAP 1972
composer

b Chicago, Ill. Chief Collabr: Dennis De Young. *Songs:* Midnight Ride; Miss America; Queen of Spades.

YOUNG, JOSEPH　　ASCAP 1914
author

b New York, NY, July 4, 1889; d New York, Apr 21, 39. Educ: Pub schs. Professional singer for music publ firms. Entertainer, WW I. Dir, ASCAP, 26-39. Chief Collabrs: Sam Lewis, Fred Ahlert, Walter Donaldson, Bert Grant, Harry Warren, Jean Schwartz, George Meyer, Ted Fiorito, Little Jack Little, Ray Henderson, Harry Akst. *Songs:* Along the Rocky Road to Dublin; Come on and Baby Me; Arrah Go on, I'm Gonna Go Back to Oregon; If I Knock the L Out of Kelly; Where Did Robinson Crusoe Go With Friday on Saturday Night?; Yaaka Hula Hicky Dula; I'm All Bound 'Round With the Mason-Dixon Line; Why Do They All Take the Night Boat to Albany?; Hello Central, Give Me No Man's Land; Rockabye Your Baby With a Dixie Melody; Just a Baby's Prayer At Twilight; How Ya Gonna Keep 'Em Down on the Farm?; Baby Blue; Don't Cry, Frenchy, Don't Cry; You're a Million Miles From Nowhere; Who Played Poker With Pocahontas When John Smith Went Away?; I'd Love to Fall Asleep and Wake Up in My Mammy's Arms; My Mammy; Tuck Me to Sleep in My Old 'Tucky Home; Five Foot Two, Eyes of Blue; I'm Sitting on Top of the World; Dinah; In a Little Spanish Town; King for a Day; Laugh, Clown, Laugh; Then You've Never Been Blue; Got Her Off My Hands But Can't Get Her Off My Mind; Cryin' for the Carolines; Have a Little Faith in Me; I Kiss Your Hand, Madame; Telling It to the Daisies; I'm Alone Because I Love You; Two Hearts in Three-Quarter Time; Don't Ask Me Why; Ooh, That Kiss; You're My Everything; Was That the Human Thing to Do?; Lullaby of the Leaves; In a Shanty in Old Shanty Town; Snuggled on Your Shoulder; You're Gonna Lose Your Gal; Two Tickets to Georgia; Annie Doesn't Live Here Anymore; A Hundred Years From Today; I'm Gonna Sit Right Down and Write Myself a Letter; Life Is a Song; You're a Heavenly Thing; I'm Happy Darling Dancing With You; The Image of You. *Scores:* Stage: The Laugh Parade (Bway); Riviera Follies of 1937 (night club).

YOUNG, LAWRANCE　　ASCAP 1965
composer, author

b Oklahoma City, Okla, June 19, 15. Educ: Univ Southern Calif, BA. Newspaper man & writer. Creator, writer & producer of var radio shows incl "Marvin Miller Storyteller", "Behind the Scenes", "Strange Adventure" & "One Gal's Opinion with Gloria Swanson"; photographer. Publ, TV Reporter, Palm Springs. *Songs:* Christmas Tree Heaven; Christmas Clock; Beware; You Thrill Me; Overjoyed Over Joy; Lyrics: In This Our Time.

YOUNG, LESTER　　ASCAP 1959
composer, saxophonist

b Woodville, Miss, Aug 27, 09; d New York, NY, Mar 15, 59. Educ: Studied music with father. Played drums in family band at age 10; traveled with minstrel show. Saxophonist in bands incl King Oliver, Count Basie & Andy Kirk. Formed sextette, with bro Lee, 42. Joined Al Sears Band, toured with USO Camp Shows. Served USA, WW II. Led own band, toured US & overseas with Norman Granz Jazz at the Philh. Appeared in film short, "Jammin' the Blues." Chief Collabrs: James Rushing, Count Basie. *Songs & Instrumental Works:* Tickle Toe; Jumpin' With Symphony Sid; Taxi War Dance; Lester Leaps In; Nobody Knows.

YOUNG, NORMAN RUSSELL (RUSTY)
composer, author

b Long Beach, Calif, Feb 23, 46. Educ: Univ Colo, Boulder. Played with bands, local clubs, Colo, age 14. One of the founding mem, Poco, 68- *Songs:* Rose of Cimarron; Crazy Love; Legend; Music: Hoedown.

YOUNG, RIDA JOHNSON　　ASCAP 1938
author, actress

b Baltimore, Md, Feb 28, 1869; d Stamford, Conn, May 8, 26. Educ: Wilson Col. Actress with E H Sothern, then with Viola Allen Co. Author: "The Girl That Came Out of the Night"; "Virginal." Chief Collabrs: Rudolf Friml, Victor Herbert, Sigmund Romberg, Emmerich Kalman. *Songs:* Mother Machree; Ah! Sweet Mystery of Life; Tramp! Tramp! Tramp!; 'Neath the Southern Moon; I'm Falling in Love with Someone; Italian Street Song; The Road to Paradise; Will You Remember?; My Dream Girl. *Scores:* Bway stage, librettos: Naughty Marietta; Lady Luxury; Her Soldier Boy; His Little Widows; Maytime; Sometime; Little Simplicity; Dream Girl; Librettist: The Red Petticoat.

YOUNG, ROLANDE MAXWELL　　ASCAP 1958
composer, author, pianist

b Washington, DC, Sept 13, 29. Educ: Cath Univ, studied drama with Father Hartke; Manhattan Sch Music, studied piano with Harold Bauer; Juilliard Sch Music, studied comp with Vittorio Giannini. Concert pianist, performed in concert halls & radio-TV. New York concert debut, 53; also Town Hall, Nat Gallery Washington, Constitution Hall. Duo concerts with husband, pianist Robert Schrade. Chief Collabr: Carrie Jacobs Bond. *Songs:* Sunshine and Rain; My Kingdom for a Kiss; How Can I?; Mighty Paul Bunyan; Unless It Comes From Your Heart; There's a Dream in My Heart; When the Train Came In; My Category Is Love; Things I Shouldn't Know; Don't Mention Me; Possessed; "A" for America. *Albums:* America '76, A Bicentennial Salute in Song.

YOUNG, VICTOR　　ASCAP 1934
composer, author, conductor

b Bristol, Tenn, Apr 9, 1889; d. Educ: Cincinnati Col of Music; NY Univ; studied with I Philippe, P Le Flem, M Wilson, F Schleider, L V Saar, Romero Gorno. Concert pianist debut with Russian Symph, toured US, Can & Europe; accompanist. Music dir, Edison Phonograph Lab, West Orange, NJ; pianist for piano rolls & records. Dir of music, Miami Mil Inst, Sweetbriar Col & Henderson-Brown Col. Cond, Cincinnati Fest Orch; dir, first commercial radio progs. Mem, Edison Pioneers & Nat Asn for Am Composers & Conductors. *Songs:* Gossip; Little Patch o' Land; Tea Kettle's Song; Cuckoo Clock; Red Rosey Bush; Sleepy House; Don't Talk to Me of Spring; Rid'n. *Instrumental Works:* Scherzetto; Jeep in the Great Smokies; A Fragment (string orch); Under a Spanish Moon (piano). *Scores:* Operetta: A Happy Week; Ballet: Charm Assembly Line Ballet; Film: In Old California.

YOUNG, VICTOR　　ASCAP 1932
composer, conductor, violinist

b Chicago, Ill, Aug 8, 1900; d Palm Springs, Calif, Nov 11, 56. To Warsaw, Poland, 10. Educ: Warsaw Cons, studied with Isidor Lotto; studied with Barcesicz, Statkowsky. Concert violinist debut with Warsaw Philh; toured Europe. Am debut, Chicago, Concertmaster, LA Theatre & Central Park Theatre, Chicago. Violinist & arr, Ted Fiorito Orch; supvr of vaudeville productions. Music dir, radio, Chicago & New York, late 20's-30's. To Los Angeles, 35; formed own orch, records, radio & theatres. Chief Collabrs: Will Harris, Jack Osterman, Ned Washington, Edward Heyman, Joe Young, Ray Evans, Jay Livingston. *Songs:* Sweet Sue; Lawd, You Made the Nights Too Long; Sam, You Made the Pants Too Long; I Don't Stand a Ghost of a Chance With You; Street of Dreams; Give Me a Heart to Sing To; Waltzing in a Dream; Shadows on the Window; Got the South in My Soul; Too Late; Can't We Talk It Over?; Love Is the Thing; Love Me Tonight; Any Time, Any Day, Anywhere; My Love; A Hundred Years From Today; Sweet Madness; Love Me; A Love Like This; Mad About You; You're Not in My Arms Tonight; The Old Man of the Mountain; Weaver of Dreams; A Man With a Dream; Stella By Starlight; When I Fall in Love; Golden Earrings; Love Letters; My Foolish Heart; The Greatest Show on Earth; Around the World in Eighty Days; The Maverick Queen; Blue Star (TV show, "Medic" theme). *Scores:* Films: I Wanted Wings; For Whom the Bell Tolls; The Uninvited; Golden Earring; Love Letters; The Big Clock; My Foolish Heart; Samson and Delilah; The Greatest Show on Earth; Strategic Air Command; The Quiet Man; Shane; China Gate; Around the World in Eighty Days (Acad award, 56); The Maverick Queen; The Brave One; Bway shows: Seventh Heaven.

YOUNGER, MARC
See Yablonka, Marc Phillip

YOUSE, GLAD ROBINSON　　ASCAP 1946
composer

b Miami, Okla, Oct 22, 1898. Educ: Stephens Col. *Songs:* Hear Me Lord; As Long As Children Pray; Thou Wilt Light My Candle; Red Bird; Wild Honey; This Would I Keep; Splendor Ahead; A Memory.

YULE, JOE, JR (MICKEY ROONEY)　　ASCAP 1957
composer, author, actor

b Brooklyn, NY, Sept 23, 20. Was child actor in vaudeville, then in films in Mickey McGuire series, 26. Other film appearances incl "A Midsummer Night's Dream", "Andy Hardy" (series), "Captains Courageous", "The Adventures of Huckleberry Finn", "Words and Music", "Girl Crazy", "Babes in Arms", "Babes on Broadway", "Strike Up the Band", "The Bridges of Toko-Ri", "Operation Mad Ball", "Breakfast At Tiffany's" & "Requiem for a Heavyweight". Has had own TV series. Autobiography "I E." Chief Collabr: Sidney Miller. *Songs:* Oceans Apart; The Bold and the Brave; The Twinkle in God's Eye; I'm So in Love With You; Where I Belong; Have a Heart.

Z

ZABACH, FLORIAN   ASCAP 1952
composer, violinist
b Chicago, Ill, Aug 15, 21. Violinist in theatres, concerts & on TV; has made many records. *Songs & Instrumental Works:* This Dream Have I; The Funny Fiddle; Nocturne.

ZABKA, STANLEY WILLIAM   ASCAP 1957
composer, author, publisher
b Des Moines, Iowa, Nov 6, 24. Educ: Univ Ill; Northwestern Univ; De Pauw Univ, BA(liberal arts & music). Comp, author, dir. Am Forces, WW II & Korean War; mil news chief, Am Forces Network, Europe. Vocalist with Johnny Long Orch. From assoc dir to dir, NBC-TV, New York, 20 yrs. Asst dir, Hollywood, 75- Music dir: "Turn the Key Deftly"; "Tornado, Xenia, Ohio"; "And They Were Five." Chief Collabrs: Don Upton & Alfonso D'Artega. *Songs:* Christmas Eve in My Home Town; Take Thou My Heart; Searching Wind; The Key Theme (Take Me With You); Gone (Where Did a Lifetime Go?); Razz Ma Tazz; Open Your Eyes; Music: Eustace, the Useless Rabbit; Noreen; Don't Smile; So This Is Love *Instrumental Works:* Chimes; Sentimental Tango; Silhouette of a Dream *Albums:* Zabka's Themes From Television

ZABRACK, HAROLD ALLEN   ASCAP 1973
composer, pianist, teacher
b St Louis, Mo, June 30, 28. Educ: Chicago Musical Col, BM & MM; study on Fulbright Fel to Ger, 56; study at Fontainebleau, France with Nadia Boulanger; other major teachers, Rudolph Ganz, Carl Seemann. Soloist with leading orch including St Louis Symph; soloist with Milwaukee Symph in the world premiere of "Symphonic Variations for Piano and Orchestra." Composer in residence, MacDowell Colony. Has been mem fac, Webster Col, Chicago Musical Col & Ind Univ; presently assoc prof of music, Piano Dept, Westminster Choir Col, Princeton, NY. Lecture-demonstrations, CAMI Hall, New York, Washington Univ & Montclair State Col; lectr & recitalist, Univ BC, Can Nat Music Teachers Convention, Victoria, BC, Music Teachers Nat Asn Convention, Denver, 75 & Juilliard Sch. *Instrumental Works:* Piano Sonata No 1; Three Concert Etudes for Piano; Six Preludes for Piano; Eight Contours for Piano; Scherzo: Hommage a Prokofiev for Piano; Piano Sonata No 2; Piano Variations.

ZACHARY, TONY
See Franchini, Anthony Joseph

ZADOR, EUGEN   ASCAP 1939
composer
b Bataszek, Hungary, Nov 5, 1894; d Los Angeles, Calif, Apr 4, 77. Educ: Vienna Acad, studied with Joseph Heuberger; Leipzig Cons, studied with Max Reger; also studied with Abert, Schering & Volbach; MusD, Muenster Univ & Halle Univ, Ger; hon MusD, New York Col Music. Hon prof, Acad Music, Budapest. Prof, Vienna Cons, 22-38. Came to US, 39. Comp film music & orchestrator, Hollywood. Awards: Hungarian State Grand Prize (chamber music). *Songs & Instrumental Works:* Czardas Rhapsodie; Lonely Wayfarer; 3 Rondells for Women's Voices; Hungarian Caprice; Divertimento for Strings; Variations on a Hungarian Folk Song; Children's Symphony; Elegie & Dance; Rondo; Fugue-Fantasia; The Adventures of Henry Bold; Triptych for Mixed Chorus; Cantata Technica; Scherzo Domestico; Fantasy on Themes From "The Inspector General"; Studies for Orchestra; Concerto for Accordion; Concerto for Oboe and Orchestra; Duo Fantasy for Two Cellos and String Orchestra; Fantasia Hungarica; Music for Clarinet and Strings; Rhapsody for Cimbalom and Orchestra; Suite for Horn, Strings and Percussion; Aria and Allegro for Strings and Bass; Suite for Woodwind Quintet; Brass Quintet; Cain (melodrama for baritone, orch). *Scores:* Opera/Ballet: Christopher Columbus; Forever Rembrandt; The Scarlet Mill; Yehu. A Christmas Legend.

ZAIMONT, JUDITH LANG   ASCAP 1976
composer, pianist, teacher
b Memphis, Tenn, Nov 8, 45. Educ: Juilliard Sch, preparatory div, 58-64, studied piano with Rosina Lhevinne, Leland Thompson; Queens Col, NY, BA(magna cum laude, music), 66; Columbia Univ, MA(comp), studied comp with Hugo Weisgall, Otto Luening, Jack Beeson; studied with Andre Jolivet, Paris, as Debussy fel of Alliance Francaise, 71-72. Pianist, toured US & as recording artist as mem of duo-piano team. Comp of art songs, chamber music, choral works, piano concerto & sacred service for orch, works performed in US, Eng, France, Australia & Ger. Author of articles on 20th century comp techniques & "Selective List of Twentieth Century Repertoire for Piano," incl in "Piano Teacher's Guidebook," 79. Recipient, ASCAP Standard awards, gold medal, Louis Moreau Gottschalk centenary competition, Los Alamos Int Competition award, two Delius Competition prizes & awards from Nat Fedn of Music Clubs & Pittsburgh Flute Club; Woodrow Wilson fel, comp & MacDowell Colony fel. *Songs & Instrumental Works:* Devilry (chorus, perc); Sacred Service for the Sabbath Evening (oratorio); Three Ayres (mixed chorus); Sunny Airs and Sober (mixed chorus); Greyed Sonnets (soprano, piano); Songs of Innocence (soprano, tenor, flute, cello, harp); Chansons Nobles et Sentimentales (high voice, piano); Two Songs (soprano, harp); The Magic World: Ritual Music for Three (baritone, piano, perc); Psalm 23 (baritone, flute, violin, piano, cello); The Tragical Ballad of Sir Patrick Spens (chorus); Nocturne: La Fin de Siecle

(piano); A Calendar Set (12 preludes for piano); Concerto (piano, orch); Calendar Collection (12 preludes, etudes).

ZAMBETTI, JOHN FRANCIS   ASCAP 1976
composer, author
b New York, NY, Feb 8, 49. Educ: Loyola High Sch; Georgetown Univ, BS; New York Med Col, MD. Played & comp in high sch with rock band; played thru col & med sch; writer & recording artist, Calif, 76, with CBS Records; physician, Los Angeles. Chief Collabrs: Walter Egan, Peter McCann. *Songs:* Surfin and Drivn'; My Baby Came Back (On the Last Wave); Rhythm So Blue; Lyrics: Johnny Z Is a Real Cool Guy. *Instrumental Works:* Fluorescent Hearse.

ZAMECNIK, J S   ASCAP 1924
composer, conductor, violinist
b Cleveland, Ohio, May 14, 1872; d Los Angeles, Calif, June 13, 53. Educ: Prague Cons, with Dvorak. Violinist, Pittsburgh Symph. Music dir, Hippodrome Theatre, Cleveland; also wrote scores. Comp catalog of scores for silent films & sound films. *Songs:* Neapolitan Nights; Out of the Dusk to You; Indian Dawn; One Fleeting Hour; Aloha Sunset Land; My Paradise; Spirit of America; I'm A-Longin' fo' You.

ZANDBERG, PAUL   ASCAP 1962
composer, conductor
b Poland, Mar 19, 10. Educ: Univ Calif, Los Angeles. Chief Collabr: Harry Tobias. *Songs:* Zei Gezunt; The Singing Lesson.

ZANINELLI, LUIGI   ASCAP 1962
composer, conductor, pianist
b Raritan, NJ, Mar 30, 32. Educ: Curtis Inst Music, dipl; studied with Gian-Carlo Menotti, Rosario Scalero & Bohuslav Martinu, 49-54. Comp, cond & pianist, RCA Italiana, Rome. Comp-in-residence, Univ Calgary, Banff Sch Fine Arts, Alta & Univ Southern Miss. Comns: RCA Italiana; Can Council; Calgary Philh Symph; Saskatoon Symph; New Orleans Symph; New Orleans Ballet Co; Metrop Opera Ballet Corp; Miss Educ TV. *Instrumental Works:* Americana (band); Dance Variations (woodwind quintet); Arioso (flute, cello, piano); Burla and Variations (woodwind quintet); Winter Music (flute, clarinet, piano); Jubilate Deo (brass ens); Canto (flute & piano); A Lexicon of Beasties (26 piano pieces for children); Comedia (piano solo); Musica Sacra (band); Three Scenes (flute solo); Misterioso (flute & piano); Three Quiet Pieces (piano solo); Fantasma (piano solo); Three Infinitives (piano); The Tale of Peter Rabbit (symphonic orch & narrator); Fantasia (piano solo); Bevy of Beasties (symphonic orch & child pianist); Three Children's Dances (woodwind quintet); Music for a Solemn Occasion (brass ens & perc). *Songs & Instrumental Works:* The Water Is Wide (SATB & piano); The Voice of the Sea (SATB & piano); Lullaby for Seafarers (SATB & piano); Mystic Trumpeter (SATB, piano & solo trumpet); The World Is So Full (SSA & woodwind quintet); The Battle for Vicksburg (soprano, piano & narrator).

ZANO, ANTHONY
See Ferrazano, Anthony Joseph

ZAPPA, FRANK
musician, composer
b Baltimore, Md, Dec 21, 40. Founder of musical group, Mothers of Invention, 64. Produced, dir & appeared in motion pictures "200 Motels," 71 & "Baby Snakes," 80. Has done numerous compositions & records. Named Pop Musician of Yr, Down Beat Mag, 70, 71, 72. *Albums:* Lumpy Gravy; Hot Rats; Chunga's Revenge; Waka/Jawaka; Apostrophe; Absolutely Free; Burnt Weeny Sandwich; Bongo Fury; Cruising With Ruben and the Jets; Fillmore East June 71; Freakout; Grand Wazoo; Joe's Garage Act 1, 2 and 3; Just Another Band From LA; Mothermania; One Size Fits All; Orchestral Favorites; Over-nite Sensation; Roxy and Elsewhere; Sheik Yerbouti; Sleep Dirt; Studio Tan; The ***** of the Mothers; 200 Motels; Uncle Meat; Weasels Ripped My Flesh; We're Only in It for the Money; Zappa in New York; Zoot Allures; Fred Zepplinnn.

ZARET, HY   ASCAP 1942
composer, author, publisher
b New York, NY, Aug 21, 07. Educ: WVa Univ; Brooklyn Law Sch, LLB. Spec services, USA, WW II; head writer, CBS TV show, "Sing It Again"; music chmn, Brotherhood Week. Awards: George Foster Peabody Citation; Ohio State Univ Inst for Educ by Radio (twice); NY Times Honor Roll; Variety, Billboard & Radio-TV Critics Awards; Am Heritage Found; Freedom House; Nat Asn for Mental Health; US Treasury Dept; Nat Citizens Coun for Better Schs; plus others. Comn for pub service songs, also the Advert Coun, Am Cancer Soc, Westinghouse Broadcasting Co, ABC, WNEW, WNBC, US Pub Health Service, Columbia Univ Ctr for Mass Communications, Am Med Asn, Polio Found, Nat Safety Coun, Anti-Defamation League of B'nai B'rith & the UN. Collabrs incl: Lou Singer, Joan Whitney, Alex Kramer, Irving Weiser & Alex North. *Songs:* I Love You, Joe; Lyrics: Unchained Melody (ASCAP Country Music Awards); There I Go; My Sister and I; It All Comes Back to Me Now; So You're the One; So Long for Awhile (theme song of Hit Parade): Young and Warm and Wonderful; One Meat Ball; The Lass With the Delicate Air; You'll Never Get Away; Dedicated to You; No Other Arms, No Other Lips; You Can't Hold a Memory in Your Arms; That's My Affair; Counting the Days; Listen to the Green Grass Growing; My Lily and My Rose; Train of Love; Christmas Roses;

It Could Be a Wonderful World; I Spoke to Jefferson at Guadalcanal; Soldiers of God (off march US Army Chaplains Corps); Song of the Army Nurse Corps (off anthem Army Nurse Corps); Let's Get Together (off theme song Brotherhood Week); Song of the French Partisan; The Marseillaise (Am version); Garibaldi War Hymn (Am version); Lullaby of the Baby Patrol; Patrick Henry and the Frigate's Keel; Public Service Series: Little Songs on Big Subjects; Little Songs About UN; Sing-Along for Mental Health; Little Songs for Living Longer; Little Songs for Busy Voters; Little Songs on Fire Prevention; Little Songs for Better Schools; Little Songs for Polio Protection; Little Songs for the ACS. *Scores:* The Great Assembly Line (cantata for Treasury Star Parade). *Albums:* Strictly GI; Now We Know; Ballads for the Age of Science; Spotlight Ballads to Light Up the World.

ZARITSKY, BERNARD   ASCAP 1952
composer, author, arranger
b Liberty, NY, Aug 3, 24. Educ: City Col New York, BA; Juilliard Sch Music. Pianist, accordionist in NY; music teacher. Chief Collabrs: Libby Zaritsky (wife), Walter Whippo. *Songs:* The Little White Duck; Zoo's Who; Bone Dry.

ZARITSKY, LIBBY   ASCAP 1963
author, director
b Atlanta, Ga, Dec 5, 25. Educ: NY Univ, BA, MA. Wrote & dir music shows for theatre groups. Teacher. Chief Collabr: Bernard Zaritsky (husband). *Songs:* Zoo's Who; Bone Dry.

ZA YEMENI, RA TWANI   ASCAP 1973
composer, author
b Chicago, Ill, Oct 13, 46. Educ: DuSable High Sch; Cent YMCA High Sch; Cent YMCA Community Col; Sadie Bruce Dance Studio; Jimmy Payne Sch Dance; Crest Modeling Sch. Was high fashion model, dancer, singer & comedienne in nightclubs, carnivals & theaters across the US, Mex & Can. Actress in Chicago productions, "Blues for Mr Charlie" & "A Raisin in the Sun"; also in pub TV, "Bird of the Iron Feather." Chief Collabr: Rhara Za Yemeni. *Songs:* Sustah, Sustah; Along the Nile; Lyrics: A Cosmic Love; Paint the Sky Beautiful; These Arms.

ZECCOLA, VINCENT A   ASCAP 1960
composer, author, arranger
b New York, NY, Nov 18, 38. Educ: High sch. First tenor with the Corvettes, vocal group, 58-62. Writes spec material, arr. Singer. *Songs:* So Long; Good Good-Bye; Hurry Home, Baby.

ZEEMAN, JOAN JAVITS   ASCAP 1951
composer, author
b New York, NY, Aug 17, 28. Educ: Thomas Sch, 40-45; Vassar Col, BA, 49; Univ Vt, MEd, 76. Author, "The Compleat Child," 64. Chief Collabrs: Steve Nelson, Philip Springer, Mario Bragsiotti, Victor Ziskin, Robert Cole, Lois Wyse. *Songs:* I Don't Want to Go to Bed; Lyrics: Santa Baby; You Blew Me a Kiss; Topele; Lovin' Spree. *Scores:* Bway Show: Young Abe Lincoln; Hotel Passionato; Solomon and She; Quality Street; She Haunts Me.

ZEISL, ERIC   ASCAP 1951
composer, author
b Vienna, Austria, May 18, 05; d Los Angeles, Calif, Feb 18, 59. Educ: Vienna Acad of Music; Huntington Hartford Found fel. Prof, Vienna Cons Music. To US 39. *Songs & Instrumental Works:* Passacaglia-Fantasy; 2nd String Quartet in D (NY Chamber Music Soc Comn); Return of Ulysses (chamber orch suite; Emil Ludwig Comn); Cossack Dance; Sonata Barocca (piano); Brandeis Sonata (violin, piano); Requiem Embraico (InterFaith Forum Comn); Little Symphony; November (chamber orch suite); Uranium 235 (ballet; San Francisco Opera Ballet Comn); Variations and Fugue on Christmas Carols (San Francisco Youth Symph Comn); Jacob and Rachel (ballet; NY Art Found & Univ Judaism, Los Angeles Comns); Requiem Concertant; Pieces for Barbara; Prayer for United Nations; Moonpictures (baritone, piano); six songs baritone & piano; seven songs, soprano & piano; six children's songs. *Scores:* Operas: Leonce and Lena; Job.

ZEITLIN, PATRICIA ANNE   ASCAP 1970
composer, author, teacher
b Council Bluffs, Iowa, June 25, 36. Educ: Ctr for Early Educ, AA(early childhood educ); Antioch Col, BA(music, early childhood educ), 74; studied guitar with Frank Hamilton, Bud Dashiel, Dave Zeitlin. Taught, consulted & directed schs, 22 yrs. Music dir & comp, 2 theatre groups, Troubadour Puppeteers & Bread & Roses (women's theatre collection adult plays). Music writer, 3 children's plays & adult musical "Flesh-Colored Crayons." Performer, radio & TV, & of own work for children's concerts & at schs. Author, songbk, "Castle in My City" & textbk for teaching music, "A Song Is a Rainbow." Calif Arts Council grant for adult ecology album. Chief Collabr: Marcia Berman. *Songs:* Room in the Boat; The Way of the Bees; I Have a Little House. *Albums:* Children's: Won't You Be My Friend; I'm Not Small; Spin, Spider, Spin; Everybody Cries, Sometimes; Rainy Day Dances, Rainy Day Songs; My Mommy Is a Doctor; Castle in My City.

ZENO, PHYLLIS WILLIAMS   ASCAP 1968
composer, author
b Cleveland, Ohio, Feb 16, 26. Educ: Univ Wis, 43-45; Am Theatre Wing, 48 & New Sch Social Res, studied with Jay Gorney. Staff writer, Fred Waring CBS TV Show, 52-54; indust show writer music & lyrics for: Kraft Foods, Zenith, GE, DuPont, B F Goodrich, Philco-Sylvania, Buick, Ford Can & Ford Europe, 60- Dir promotion, AAA Peninsula Motor Club, Tampa, Fla, 74- Chief Collabrs: Buddy Bernier, Sol Berkowitz. *Songs:* This Is an Opening; We Never Sing Opening Numbers; How Do You Open a Show Without a Curtain; Friends, Relatives & Parents; We're Through; That's A Very Good Sign; Bet You Never Guessed; Cigar Box Revue; Music: Kaleidoscope.

ZERATO, LOUIS JOHN   ASCAP 1964
composer, author
b Brooklyn, NY, Jan 30, 36. Educ: High sch. Under contract, Schwartz Music Co. Chief Collabr: Ernest Maresca. *Songs:* Party Girl; Hey Jean, Hey Dean.

ZERGA, JOSEPH FREDERICK   ASCAP 1963
author
b Torrance, Calif, Apr 28, 42. Educ: Univ Vienna; Bard Col. Son of Joseph E Zerga. *Songs:* Every Night At Seven; Torrero, Matador.

ZERGA, JOSEPH LOUIS EDMUND (EDMUND PAUL)   ASCAP 1960
composer, author
b San Francisco, Calif, Nov 15, 24. Educ: San Mateo Col, AA; Univ San Jose, BA; Univ Calif; Univ Southern Calif, MA(psychol, economics), research fel in exp psychol with Dr Milton Metfessel. Instr, psychol, Univ San Jose. Mgr, music dept, Walt Disney Productions. Vpres, Capitol Records, Inc, Hollywood; int dir music publ, Electric & Musical Indust Ltd, London; own bus, Pres Music Corp, New York, 63. Chief Collabr: Earl Sheldon. *Songs:* Carmelita; When, Tell Me When; Rolling Waves; Chi Chi Chi Chico Mio; Give Me Music; The Phoenix Sun; Slightly Sentimental; Boy on a Pony; Fairyland of Love; This Is Brazil; Durango; All Night Long; When the First Snowflakes Fall.

ZIEGLER, RICHARD ADAM (RITCHIE ADAMS)   ASCAP 1977
composer, author, singer
b Brooklyn, NY, Dec 15, 45. Educ: Bishop Loughlin Mem High Sch. Weekend musician for all kinds of music; lead singer, The Fireflies, incl hits "You Were Mine" & "I Can't Say Goodbye"; songwriter; producer of chart hits incl "Mammy Blue" & "I'll Be True"; arr, pop, rhythm & blues, rock songs with var artists. Chief Collabrs: Alan Bernstein, Mark Barkan, Larry Kusik, Gloria Nissenson, Nevel Nader. *Songs:* Music: Tossin' and Turnin'; After the Lovin'; The Tra-La-La Song (Banana Splits TV theme); Happy Summer Days; This Moment in Time; The Next Hundred Years; Country Lovin.

ZIFFER, FRAN
See Burgio, Frances

ZIFFRIN, MARILYN JANE   ASCAP 1971
composer
b Moline, Ill, Aug 7, 26. Educ: Univ Wis, Madison, BM, 48; Columbia Univ, MA, 49; studied comp with Alexander Tcherepnin & Karl Ahrendt. Head, Music Dept, Northwest Miss Agr High Sch & Jr Col, Senatobia, Miss, 49-50; asst teacher, Transc Dept, WGN Radio & TV, Chicago, Ill, 50-52; office mgr, W M Simeral & Co, Chicago, 52-56; teacher second grade, Chicago pub schs, 56-61; asst prof music, Northeastern Ill Univ, 61-67; assoc prof music, New Eng Col, Henniker, NH, 67- Chief Collabr: Kathryn Martin. *Songs:* Haiku (song cycle for soprano, viola, harpsichord, winner Delius Competition, 72). *Instrumental Works:* Rhapsody for Guitar; Four Pieces for Tuba; Piano Trio; Concerto for Viola and Woodwind Quintet.

ZIMA, MILAN SYLVESTER   ASCAP 1960
composer, author
b Plymouth, Iowa, Sept 26, 04; d Gary, Ind, Nov 3, 73. Educ: High sch dipl, Mason City, Iowa. Was ins agent until retirement in 69. Writing music was a lifelong hobby. Was second cousin to Czech comp Dvorak. *Songs:* I'll Be Needing You; I Ain't Gonna Be Lonely.

ZIMBALIST, EFREM   ASCAP 1935
composer, violinist, educator
b Rostov-on-Don, Russia, Apr 9, 1889. Educ: First musical training with father; then Imperial Sch, St Petersburg, with Auer. Violin debut, Berlin, 07; toured Europe. Moved to US, 11; Am debut, Boston Symph, 11. World concert tours. Fac mem, Curtis Inst, 29, dir, 41. *Instrumental Works:* String Quartet in E; Violin Sonata in G; American Rhapsody; Violin Concerto in C sharp.

ZIMMERMAN, JAMES H   ASCAP 1976
composer
b Peoria, Ill, Oct 24, 38. Song writer for Hacienda & Ji Do Bi Music, Nashville, Tenn. Chief Collabr: Jim Glaser. *Songs:* Take It Easy; Lyrics: Those Beer Drinking Songs; She Spreads Her Love Around.

ZISKIN, VICTOR — ASCAP 1961
composer, pianist

b New York, NY, Mar 18, 37. Educ: Harvard Univ, with Walter Piston & Tillman Merritt; also with Isabella Vengerova, Olga Stroumillo, Zadel Skolovsky, Jean Casadesus, Leonard Bernstein, Roger Sessions, Nadia Boulanger & Kay Swift. First Harvard freshman to write Hasty Pudding shows. Performed own works, Composer's Lab, Harvard; also in Israel, 54; Carnegie Hall, New York, 59 & 60. Wrote for resort productions; ballet co. Mem, Nat Asn Am Comp & Cond. *Songs & Instrumental Works:* Cheer Up, Cheer Up; The Same Old Me; I'd Know Her Anywhere; Someone You Know; Little Frog; Welcome Home; Allegro Pour Piano; San Francisco Rhapsody (piano, orch); On the Borders of Israel (piano, orch); Suite for Piano in Five Parts; Psalm XXIII (soprano, piano); Civil War Suite. *Scores:* Ballet: Aubade; Ballet for Street Urchins; Harlequin Ballet; Off-Bway stage: Young Abe Lincoln (Damon Runyan Mem Fund; Am Jewish Congress Award).

ZITO, TORRIE — ASCAP 1958
composer

b Utica, NY, Oct 12, 33. Educ: Pub schs, Utica; Manhattan Sch Music. Free-lance arr & comp, 59-72. Music dir for Tony Bennett, 72-80. Chief Collabrs: Sammy Cahn, Tony Bennett. *Songs:* Music: There's Always Tomorrow; Changing. *Instrumental Works:* La Fiesta de La Roca (concert band); Lisa; Bopin.

ZOECKLER, DOROTHY ACKERMAN — ASCAP 1951
composer, author

b Wheeling, WVa, Aug 19, 15. Educ: Cincinnati Cons; studied with Marcian Thalberg, Robert Goldsand & Parvin Titus. Organist & choir dir, St Matthew's Episcopal Church, Wheeling. Wrote piano teaching material for publ firm. State pres (WVa), Nat League Am Pen Women. *Songs:* God Speaks to Me; When I Kneel Down to Pray; Too Good Not to Be True. *Instrumental Works:* The Cubanera; Latinera; Fiesta.

ZOELLNER, PETER LEE — ASCAP 1961
composer, author, teacher

b Nove Shove, Yugoslavia, Mar 9, 19; d Buffalo, NY, Aug 29, 71. Educ: East Tech High Sch, Cleveland, Ohio; Fenn Col. Guitarist & Hawaiian guitar player; prof musician, Cleveland & midwestern states. Taught music, drama & physical educ, Fenn Col, early 40's. Served, USA with CIC, continental US & Europe. Civilian with CID, Europe. Head of teenagers, WJW Radio Nanigans, for Coca-Cola; world-wide tour. Coauthor & producer, musical "Aloha Hawaii." Chief Collabrs: Fred T Smith, R Alexander Anderson. *Songs:* Aloha (Is the Spirit of) Hawaii; You Never Can Tell; Poi for Two.

ZOGOTT, SEYMOUR S — ASCAP 1964
author

b Wilmington, Del, Oct 14, 30. Educ: Northeast High Sch, Philadelphia, Pa; Temple Univ, BS(jour), 52; studied trumpet with Donald S Reinhardt. Wrote for Julius Monk's Revues in New York, NY. Chief Collabr: Claibe Richardson. *Songs:* Lyrics: Johnny Come Lately.

ZOLLER, BETTYE
See Volkart, Bettye Sue

ZONNI, ALEXANDER — ASCAP 1975
composer, author, drummer

b Chicago, Ill, Dec 11, 31. Educ: St Louis Cons, Mo, studied piano with Mrs Oage, 2 yrs; studied with Guido Patanarie, Los Angeles Philh Symph. Drummer & vocalist, nightclubs, Los Angeles & Las Vegas areas. Served in 438th Armored Army Div Band. Radio emcee announcer, Paso Robles, Calif. *Songs:* I Don't Need Your Love Anymore; The Right Side of You; I Wanted to Kiss You the First Time We Met; You're the First One; This Is Love.

ZOSS, JOEL ROBERT — ASCAP 1977
composer, author, musician

b Easton, Pa, Feb 19, 44. Educ: Classical High Sch, Providence, RI; St Paul Acad; Univ Minn; Moses Brown Sch; Univ Chicago, BA(English), 66; Columbia Univ, grad studies in anthropology; studied voice with Warren Barrigian, Los Angeles, 72. Drummer in rock & roll band, Minn, 59; guitarist in folk & blues groups, Mass & Chicago through 66. Travel abroad & work in jazz, London. Songwriter, 60- Singer leading small units in Cambridge & New York. Signed with Arista, 75- Performer, author/composer, recording artist & publ. Writer of prose fiction publ in magazines. Author, "Chronicle," 80. *Songs:* Too Long at the Fair; I Gave My Love a Candle; Sarah's Song; Charlie's Friends; Too Much Fighting on the River; Radiator; The 41st. *Albums:* Joel Zoss.

ZOTOS, THOMAS — ASCAP 1974
composer

b Worcester, Mass, Apr 27, 48. Educ: Quinsigamond Community Col, assoc degree in lib arts. Singer & songwriter, col concert tours & TV. Recording artist, Zebra Records. Lectr on origin of guitar; luthier. Chief Collabrs: Paul Zotos, Alex Zotos. *Songs:* Come Back, Beatles; Everyday I Feel Like Singing.

ZUVICH, DENNIS MICHAEL (D Z MICHAELS) — ASCAP 1976
composer, singer

b East Chicago, Ind, Oct 4, 42. Educ: Mary Star High Sch; Dick Grove Music Workshop, Los Angeles. Singer-pianist, arr, nightclubs & TV. Chief Collabr: Fred Travalena. *Songs:* Music: Alphabet Song.

ZWERTSCHEK, ERICH SYLVESTER — ASCAP 1972
composer, author, singer

b Cincinnati, Ohio, Sept 12, 48. Educ: Archbishop's Choir Sch, 62; St Xavier High Sch, 66; Univ Cincinnati, BA, 70, Col Law, JD, 75. Singer in boys choir; singer & guitarist in folk music groups; recording artist with Epoch Records; record producer, managing ed & corp attorney, Epoch Univ Publ; pres, Cricket Productions, Hollywood; concert promotion & artist mgt. *Songs:* Stay With Me; Blessed Be God Forever; This Is a Holy Day; Music: The Lord's Prayer.

ZWIBELSON, HORTENSE
See Belson, Hortense Gold

PUBLISHER MEMBERS

(Current as of March, 1980)

Aaframbia
Aalborg Music Company
Aao Music
Aarhus Music Company
Aaron Arthur and Associates
Aaychdee Music
Abattoir Music
Abbey Road Music Inc
Abbey San Encino Press
*A B C Music Corp
*A B C Standard Music Pub Inc
*Abe Olman Music Inc
*Aberbach Ltd
Abercrombie Music
   Adriam Music Co
Abilene Music Inc
   Aries Music Inc
Abingdale Music Publishing
Able Music Company
Abmil Music
A & B Music Company
About Music-Yasuko Publishing
Above Music Publications
Above the Line Music Company
*Abrahams Maurice Inc
Abridged Chasm Music
A B-Rock Music Co
*Abt Valentine
Acacia Enterprises Inc
Acacia Street Gang
Accabonac Music
Accadia Music Company
   Bryn Mawr Music Co
Accolade Music Publishing Co
Accordeon Music Club
Accura Music
   Rochester Music Publishers Inc
Ace and King Songs
*Achic Music Division
Aching Loins Publishing Co
Achord Music
Ackee Music Inc
Aclassye Music
*Acs Music Publishing Co Div
Action Music Publishing Co
Adage Music
Adamo Music Corporation
Adams Patrick Productions Inc
   (Pap Music Division)
Adams Stanley
   Stanley Adams Music Inc
Ada Publishing Company
Adaros
Adbredar Music
Adcom Incorporated
Addabbo Dominic
Addax Music Company Inc
Addison Street Music
Adel Music
Adena Songs
Aden Music Company
Adkorp Incorporated
*Adler Henry Inc
Admiral Music Company
*Admont Music Inc
Ad Noiseum Music
Adorable Music Corporation
Adour Music
Adrienne Music Company
A D R Publishing
*Advanced Music Corp
Adventure Music
Adventures in Music Inc
Advertisers Music Inc
Advertising and Research Int'l
Aeray Music
Aesthetic Artist Records

Afac Music
Afco Productions
Afiat Music
*African Sounds Inc
*A Gee Jay Music Co Div
Agent Orange Music
*Ager Yellen Bornstein
Agil of America
*Agnew J E Publications
*Ahleim Walter C Music Co
Ahlert Burke Corporation
Ahlert Fred Music Corporation
Ailes Roger & Assoc Inc
   (Roger Ailes Music Division)
Aim-Col Music Publishers
Aimee Lou Music Co
Ainsley Music
Ainsworth Music
Air Age Music
Airline Music Company
Air Time Music Corp
Airwaves Music Inc
Ajaw Inc
Ajax Music
Akashic Artists
Akashic Records Music
Akb Corporation The
   (Bushbaby Music Division)
Akila Music Publishing Co
Akimbo Music
Alabaster Music Inc
Ala-Flor Music Co
*Alamo Music Inc
*Alan Sloan Inc
Alarm Clock Music
*Alaska Mus Co Inc
*Alaska Music Ltd
Alassio Music Co
*Alba Ed De Musica
*Alba Music Inc
Albert Millard Music
Albert Music Corporation
Albino Buzzard Music
Albino Crow Music
Abino Music Pub Co
*Albion Music Ltd
Albums Inc Music Co
   Albums Inc Music Co
*Albums Inc Music Co
Album Songs
Alchemical Music Company
Alchemy Music Inc
Alda Music Inc
Alden Publishing Company
Aldi Music Company
Aleph Music
Alexander Altone Productions
Alexander Publications
   Guild Pub of Arts Music Inc
   Guild Publications of Calif Inc
*Alex Anderson Music Inc
Alexander Street Music
Alexandra Music Inc
*Alexis Music Co
   Harry Bloom Inc
   Lawrence Music Pub Inc
   Milsons Mus Pub Inc
Alexis Music Inc
   Alexis Music Co
Alex Music
*Alfa Music
Alfaretta Music Company
*Alfred Music Company Inc
*Alfred Productions Inc
Alfred Publishing Company Inc
   Al Piantadosi Music Co
   Feature Music Syndicate

   Manus Music Co Inc
   Rosey Geo Band & Orch Ca
   Schreibman Mus Press
*Algonguin Pub Co
Algwen Music Publishing Co
Alias Music
Alidor Music
Alif Music
Alison Music Company
Alisorah Music
Alistan Music Company
Alithia Records Ltd
   (Thermal Music Pub Co Div)
Allcrud Music Company
*Allen Stanton Productions Inc
Allen William Music
Allevon Enterprises Inc
   (Jimeve Music Co Div
All Great Tunes
Allied Artists Music Co Inc
*Allied Music Corp
Alligator Music Company
All Inn Music
   All Inn Music Co
Allisons Music Company
   Allison's Music Inc
*Allking Music Co Div
Allking Productions Inc
   (Allking Music Co Div)
Allmusic Inc
All of A Sudden Music Inc
All of It Music Publishing
*All-Points Music
All Seasons Music Company
All Sunray Publishing Co.
Almanac Music Inc
*Almeida Music Company
Almitra Music Company Inc
Almo Music Corporation
   Albion Music Ltd
   In Music Co
*Alnal Music Division
*Aloha State Mus Inc
*Alomar Press
Alotagood Music Publishing Inc
Alouette Productions Inc
   (Twill Music Co Div)
Alpane Music Company Inc
Alpenstock Productions Inc
   (Alpenstock Music Division)
Alpha Century Publ Corp
Alpha Phi Music
Alphaventure Music Publ Corp
*Al Piantadosi Music Co
Alpine Music Inc
Alruby Music Incorporated
Alson Music Company
Alstan Music Company
   Allen Stanton Productions Inc
*Alta Music Corporation
Alter Louis Music Publications
Alternative Music
Alternatives in American Music
Alters Gerald Inc
   J K L M Enterprises Inc
   Lyre Productions Ltd
*Altex Music Corp
Altez Music
Altra-Native Publishing
Alysonne Publishing Inc
Amachrist Music
Amadeo Brio Corporation
*Amadeo Music
Amadeus Music Company
Amador Music
Amalisa
Amanita Muscaria Music

Amaranth Music (Publishing Co)
A-Mark Music Productions
   Coral Gables Motor Lodge
*Amasing Music
*Amazing Grace Music Division
Amazon Music Co
*Ambassador Music Inc
*Amber Music Inc
Amberson Enterprises Inc
Amber Ways Music
Ambient Sound Music Co
Ambition Records & Publishing Inc
A M C Incorporated
Amco Music Company
Amelanie Music Publishing Co
Amenra Music
America Musical U S A
American Academy of Music Inc
   Exclusive Pubs Inc
American Adventure Music Co.
American Axis Publishing Co
American Broadcasting Music Inc
   Ampco Music Inc
   Apt Music Corp
American Compass Music Corp
*American Composers Inc
American Dream Music Company
American Gold Inc
American Jade Inc
American Music Edition
American Music Publishing Co
American Rainbird Music
American Wordways
Americus Music
Amerosa Music Inc
   Amerosa Music Co
Ames-Barry Publishing Company
Amgale Music Company
*Amg Publishing Division
Amidan Music Company
Amigo Music Publishing Co
Ami Publishing Inc
   Iliad Publishing Company
A M I Record Corporation
   (Shev A Deen Music Division)
Amiron Music
Amitir Music Publishers Inc
Ammarc Music Company
A M Music Corporation
*Amos Productions Inc
*Ampco Music Inc
Amphion Music
*Amrita Music Corp
*Amron Music Corp
*Am Rus Music Corp
Amsam Corporation
*Amsi
A M S Music
Amthe Music Company
Amundo Music
Amy Dee Music Corp
Amy's Mom's Music
*Anacrusis Music Publishing Co
Anadale Music
Anarene Music
Anbar Inc
   (John Mc Clure Music Division)
*Anchor Music Co
Anchor Music Inc
*Andalusian Music Co Inc
*Andard Productions Inc
Andeb Music Company
*Anderson Ian
Anders Production Inc
   (Sugarline Music Division)
Andor Inc
   Andor Music Co

*Indicates catalogues available under ASCAP license rather than membership in ASCAP.

563

Andorra Music
Mushroom Records Inc
*Andover Music Inc
Andre Wayne
Andrew Music Corp
Andrews George Publishing Inc
*Andrew Wiswell Productions Inc
Andromeda Music Corp
Grt Corporation
Andustin Music
Anfor Music Publishing
Angela Dawn Music
Angela Hawke Music
Angel Boy Music
Angelica Music
Angelica Music Co
Angel Jane Music Publishing Co
Angeloon Tunes
Angelo Roman Enterprises
Laughing Bird Songs Pub Div
Rovelaman Enterprises
Angel 7 Music Publishing Co
Angel Wing Music
*Angle Music Inc
*Anglo Southern Film Music
Animal Crackers Music
Anjan Music
Anje Music Co
Ankerford Music Corporation
Ankh Music
Anlon Music Company
Anna Mc Cann Music
Les Mc Cann
Ann-Cheryl Publishing Co
Anneon Music
*Anne Rachel Music Corp
Annie Oak Publishing Co
Annie Over Music
Annjay Records
Annjohn Music Company Inc
Ann Kim Publisher
Annpeg Music
Another Corporation Inc
Ansley Music Publishing Society
Anthem Publishing
Anthill Music Company Inc
Anthony Arnold Music
Anthony Publishing Company
Antilles Music
Antique Music
Antisia Music Inc
Ant Music Publishers
*Antobal Music Inc
Anton Publications
Anubis Music
Anvil Music Company Inc
Any Old Name Publishing Co
A 1 Music Corporation
Aopa Publishing Company
Apache's Rhythm
Apache Tears Music
A P I Music Incorporated
Apis Productions Inc
Apocryphal Publishing Company
Apophis Music
Apple Butter Music
Apple Cider Music Co Inc
Apple Juice Productions
Apple Music Publishing Co Inc
Appleseed Music Inc
Amrita Music Corp
Apple Valley Music
April Bohannon Music
*April Enter Inc
April Music Inc
Batt Songs
Okeh Music Pub Co
Apthorp Music Inc
Grant & Murtaugh Music Corp
*Apt Music Corp
Aqua Music Publishing Co
Aquarican Music
Aquilla Music Publishing Inc
Aragain Music Company
*A R A Inc
Aral Music Company
Arapesh Communications Unltd Inc
Arbe Music
*Arbor Music Inc
Arcade Music Company
Dave Wilson
Arcane Music Inc
Archaball Publishing Inc
Archangel Music
*Archimedes Music Div
*Arch Music Company Inc
Arcot Music Publishing Co

Arcturus II
Arcuri Music
Ardavan Music
Ardent Productions Inc
Ardesea Music Company
Ardev Music
*Ardiam Music Co
*Ardmore Music Corp
Area Code 615 Music
*Arena Music Corp
Arge Music Publishing Co
Argentina Music Publishing Co
Argentina Tunes Music Co
Argosy Music Corp
*Argyle Music
Aria Music Company
*Arianna Music Co
Arian Publications
*Arias Music
Arice Music
*Ariel International
Ariel Music
*Aries Music Inc
Arista Music Inc
*Arkansas Music Ltd
Arkansas River Publishing Co
Arkayem Music Publishers
Arkel Publishing Company
Arkey Tunstall Music
Ark of Glenns
Arko Music Corporation
Arloco Music Inc
Arlow Land Music
*Arlow Music Inc
*Armadillo Music Div
Armadillo Productions Inc
(Armadillo Music Div)
*Armchair Music Division
Armen Robert Music Publishing
Armoni Publications
*Armstrong Publishing Co Div
Armstrong Victoria Garvey
Armstrong W T & Company Inc
(Armstrong Publishing Co Div)
Arnakata Music Inc
Arnas Music
Arnaz Desi Productions Inc
*Arnaz Music Company
Arnel Music Corporation
Arnold Jay Music Inc
Aroma Music Inc
Aronson Music
Arosa Music Co
Arovox Record Corp
(Loena Music Publishing Co Div)
Arpege Music Corporation
A R Publishing Company
*Arqyle Music
Ars Nova Music Company
Artal Music Corp
Artasia Music Press
Artemis Music
Art Ensemble of Chicago Publishing
Arthur Irving Music Corporation
Arthur Music
Arthur/Paul Productions
Arthur Robert Music
Articom Incorporated
Artisan Lodge Music
*Artists Music Corp
Artists Music Inc
Art Masters Studios Inc
*Artmusic Inc
Artwork Music Co Inc
*Asa Music Company
Ascher Emil Inc
Brooks & Denton
Empire Music Co
Kenyon Music Corp
Royal Music Co
Aschken Music Company
Asco Music
Asc Publishing Co Inc
Ashandan Music Ltd
Ashcroft Music
Asher/Bahler Assoc Inc
(Asher/Bahler Music Div)
Ashleypage Publishing Co Inc
Ashton Publishing Company
Aspen Music Corporation
Ash Valley Music Inc
Asilomar Music
Askew Music Company
Trans World International Inc
*A Song Music Division
A Song Music Inc
(A Song Music Division)

Aspascia's Music
Aspen Line
A S Recording & Publishing Co
*Asset Music Corp
Assoc Contemplativ Sisters Inc
(Acs Music Publishing Co Div)
Astaire Music
Ast Music Publishing Company
Astound A Sound
*Astralite Music Division
*Astral Music Division
Astras Company
Astronaut Music
Athenaise Music Ltd
Atherly Productions Inc
At Home Music
Athwarn Music Company Inc
Atlanta International Music Co
Atlanta Music Inc
(Royal American Records Inc Div)
*Atlas Music Corp
A T M Music
Atomic Man Music
Atomic Tunes
A to Z Music
*Atrium Music Corp
A T R Music
Atsoc Music Inc
Attarack Corporation
(Forsythe Music Div)
Atterberry Hazel L Publishing
At the Beach Music
Attias Music
Aubrey/Hamner Music
Auburndale Music Company
Audible Music Publishing Co
Audio Arts Publishing Company
Ja Ma Music
Audio Music Publishers
*Audubon Music Inc
Auravisions Music Ltd
Twelve Oaks Music Publishing Co
*Aurelia Music Div
Aurisom Music
Authentic Music Corp
*Autograph Editions New York
Autumn Productions Inc
(Autumn Leaves Music Div)
Avalona Pub
*Avant Garde Enterprises Inc
Avant Garde Music Publishing Inc
Avant Music
Avas Music Publishing Co Inc
*Avco Embassy Music Publ Inc
Avellino Music
*Avent Publ Company Division
Average Music
Avitra Music
Aviva Music Inc
Avoyelles Music Company
Awantha Publishing
*Axelrod Pub Inc
Axlerod David Music
Ayars Bo Publishing Company
*Ayer Bird Music
Ayeroff Music
Ayers Roy Ubiquity Inc
Ayre Music
Ayuga Music
Azimuth Music Company
Azo Publishing
Aztec Music Inc
Babaji Music
*Babell Music Company
Babette Music
Babi Mg Music
Baby Dump Music
Baby Fingers Music
Baby Powder Music
Baby Ronda Music Publishing
Bacak Burns Music
*Bacardi Publications
*Bacharach Burt Music Co
Bach Trac Music Inc
*Back Door Publ Div
Backfin Music Company
Back Room Music
Back Seat Publishing Company
Backyard Publishing Company
Bad Axe Tunes Inc
Badazz Music Company
Bad Buzz Music
Badco Music Inc
Badge Songs Music Co
Bad Ju Ju Music
Baer Abel Music Corporation
Baer Max Music

Bagdasarian Armen
Monarch Music Corp
Baggy Knees Music
Bahler Tom Music
B A K
Baker's Lane Music Co
Bakshi Tunes
Balance Town Music
Bal & Bal Music Publishing Co
Bald Medusa Company
Bald Mountain Music Inc
Baldursson Music Inc
Balk Harry Music
*Balladeer Music
Balladier Music Co
Ballance Bill Enterprises Inc
(Stallion Ganglia Music Div)
Ballard Russell Limited
Ballet Foundation The
Balloon Head Music
Balmain Music
Balmore Music Corp
Balton Music Company
Baltor Music
Bambar Music Corp
Bancroft Music
Bandana Music
*Bandland Inc
B and L Publishing Company
Banes Music Inc
Banjoe Publishing Co Inc
Bantam Music Publishing Co The
Bantu Village Music
Baracs Music Company
Barbary Coast Music Company Inc
Barberton Music Company
*Barbil Music
Bar B Music
*Barbour Lee Music Corp
Barbour Music
Barbrob Music Company
Barclay Music Corporation
Barcus-Berry Inc
(Taeper Music Div)
*Bareback Music Div
*Bare Back Music Division
Barecky Publishing Co Inc
Barjo Music
Barking Spider Music
*Bark Music Corp
Barley Music
Bar-Loma Music
Barnaby Music Corp
Barn Publishing Inc
Barone Marcus Music
Baronet Publishing Co
Baron M Company
Baron M Inc
Cullieron De Lacour
Hill J F & Co Inc
Lacour Lucien
Spratt Jack Music Co
Barons Entertainment Corp The
(Snake Creek Music Co Div)
Barrere Music
Barrett Hill Music Publishers
Barricade Music Inc
Barris Chuck Music Inc
Barrister Music Company
Barrump-Bump Publishing Co
Barry Guy Enterprises Inc
Barry Jeff Music
Barry the Bone
Barta Music Company
Bartley Jock Music
Barton Music Corp
Ritchie Music Co Inc
Saga Music Corp
San Dino Music Corp
Stanwood Music Corporation
Bartosiewski Edwin Chas Music
Publishing
Baruth Productions Inc
(Baruth Music Division)
*Bar Vel Music Divison
Barwin Music Co Inc
*Bary & Cia
Baseline Music
Basement Floor Music
Basie Diane Music Corp
Basin Harbour Publishing
Basket Music
Baskind Bissot Publishing
Bas Music Publishing
Bassett's Steve Music Company
(Ease Music Division)
Bassinsongs

*Bates & Bendix
Batin Abdul Zahir Publisher
Batteau David Music
Battery Exchange Co
*Batt Songs
Bauer William H Inc
Bauhaus Music
Bauman Mark Music
Bax Music
Bayberry Music Inc
*Bayer Music Co Inc
Bay Lake Music
Bayou Blanc Music Inc
Bayou Country Productions
Bayshore Music Corp
B D H Music
*B D M
Beachaven Music
Beacon Music Inc
Beagle Publishing Company
*Bealin Music Publishing Co
Beanbag Music
Beanie Music
Bea Quan Music
Bear Claw Music
Bear County Music
Bearde Productions Inc
*Beatrice Music Co Inc
Beatrix Music Inc
Beau Brummel Music
Beau Jim Music Inc
   (Beau-Jim Music Division)
Beau Lieu Music Company
Beaulieu Toni Music Publications
Beaumont Belle Music
*Beautiful Music Inc
Beautiful Music Unlimited Limited
*Beaux Arts Music Inc
Beaver Music Publishing Corp
Beckenhorst Press
*Beck Mort
Becum Music
Becvar Music
Bedford Music Company
Bee Bee Music Co
Bee Cee Music Company
Bee Jay Records
Bee Jr Music
Bee Keeper Publishing Company
Beekman Music Inc
Bee-Mark Music
Beethoven Music Company
Beetlebung Corner Music Publishers
Beez Records Pub Co
Belack Music Inc
*Bel Canto Publishing Co
Belhouse Publications
Belkin Productions Inc
   (Mike & Jules Music Co Div)
Bella Godiva Music Inc
Bellamy Brothers Music
Bella Roma Music Company
Bell Clark Productions
*Bellefield Pub Co
Belle Meade Music Inc
Bell Holding Properties Corp
   (Bell Holding Music Division)
Bellino Publishing Company
*Bell Songs Pub Co
Belmont Music Publishers
Belsize Music Inc
Belton Music Inc
Belwin Mills Publishing Corp
   Adler Henry Inc
   Bandland Inc
   Belwin Mills Rachmaninof
   Belwin Mills Serious
   Berg S M
   Bloom Harry Inc
   Byron-Douglas Productions
   Cinema Music Co
   First Division Publ Corp
   Fischer J & Brd
   Gray H W Company
   H S P Music Division
   Musicord Publ Inc
   Schmitt Music Center Inc
*Bema Music Co Div
*Benchmark Music
Benci Music Publishing Co
Bencorp Publishing Inc
   Bennett Enterprises Inc
   Birdees Music Corp
   Churn Music Division
   Fi Music Inc
   Gomalco Music Corp
Bendean Music Inc

Bending Oak Music
*Bendix Theodore
Benefit of the Doubt Music
Benjamin Bennie Music Inc
Benjamin & Pot Inc
Bennett Phil Music Company
*Benno Music Co
Ben Ross Music
   Portfolio Systems Inc
   Winston Music Publishers
Benson John T Publishing Co Inc
   Jensen Music
Benton & Bowles Inc
   (Benton & Bowles Music Publ Div)
Benton Music Company
Bentwood Music Inc
Berget Music Co
Bergmann Theodore G
*Berg S M
Bergstrom Music Ltd
Berjac Publishing Co
Berkeley Square Music Inc
*Berk Lee Music Co
*Berklew Music Co
Ber Ko Music Ltd
Berlin Irving Music Corp
*Berlin Irving Standard Music
Bernal Music Inc
Berna Music Inc
*Bernard Van Productions
Bernstein M Music Publishing Co
B E R Productions
Berry-Lo Pub
Bertam Music Company
Bertha Music Co
Berthelot John & Associates
Bestat Music Publishing Co
Best Bet
Best Way Music
Betdolph Music Company
Bet Songs
Better Half Music Company
*Better Nights Music Division
*Bev Bev Music Ltd
Bevco Music
Beverly Hills Society Pub Co Inc
Bevorada Music Corp
Bexhill Music Corp
Bey El Music
Beyond Cordova Music Company
*Beyond Productions Inc
B F B Publishing
   B F B Productions
B G H Music
B & H Publishing Co
B H V Company The
Biabra Music Co
Bible Way Church (Bwc) Prod
   B W C Productions
*Bibo Lang Inc
*Bibo Music Pub Inc
Bienstock Publishing Company
Big Ax Music
Big Beat Music
Big Bells Incorporated
Big Bird Publishing Co
Big B L Music
Big Bloke Music
Big Boovah Music
Bigboro Music Publishing Corp
Big Brick Music
Big Bright Moon Publishing
Big C Music
Big Ears Music Inc
Big Elk Music
Big Four Music Corp
Biggers Stover Music Inc
Big G Music
Biggs Anne Marie Publishing House
Big Gun Music
Big Harland Music
Big Hill Music Corp
   Joey Brooks Productions Inc
   Morningtown Music Co Inc
   Musical Sciences Inc
Big Hurry Music Inc
Big Island Music Inc
Big John, Little John Music
   D'Angelo Bullock & Allen
*Big Leaf Music Inc
Big Legend Music Inc
*Biglow Main Excell Co
Big Neck Music
Big One Music
Big Paddle Wheel Music
Big Redneck Music Company
Big Secret Music Inc

*Big Shorty Music Co
Big Shot Music Inc
Big Sky Music
Big Tip Music
Big Tree Enterprises Ltd
   Big Leaf Music Inc
Big Wave Music
Big Wind Music
*Bijatori Music
Bilba Pub
Bil-Bar Music Company
Bilik Jerry Music Inc
Billabong Music
*Bill Black Music Corporation
Billboard Music Publishing Co
Bill/Bib Publishing Company
*Bill Dana Publishing Co Div
*Bill Withers
Billy B Music
*Biltmore Music Corp
Binder Steve Music
Binn Music
Biograph Records Inc
*Birchard C C & Co
Birch Island Music Press
Birch Music Company
*Birchwood Music Co
Birdbath Publishing Corp
*Birdees Music Corp
Birdwing Music
Birthright Music Company
Bismark Music Publishers
Bitchin' Guy Music
Bit Enki Publications & Records
Biwa Music Publishers Inc
Bizet Music Productions Inc
Bj's International Talent Inc
   (Bojeen Music Division)
B K J Publications
Black Bill Music Inc
   Bill Black Music Corporation
Black Bull Music Inc
Black Caviar Music Inc
*Black Dove Mus Division
Black Eagle Publishing Co
Black Elk Music
Blackeye Music
Black Hills Music
Black Jazz Music
Black Lightning Publishing
Black Molasses Music
*Black Oak Arkansas Inc Div
Black Publishing Co
Black Raven Music
Black Sheep Music Inc
Blackstone-Hidey Publishing Co
Blackstone Milton Music Corp
   Blackstone Music Inc
Blackwood Billy Music Co
Blackwood-Marshall Music Inc
Blaco Publishing
Blairwood Music
Blais Music Company
Blake Eubie Music
Blakely Publishing Company
*Blakesal Pub Div
Blane Ralph Music
Blase Inc
   (Blase Music Division)
Blatant Music Co
*Blawnox Music Enterprises
Blawnox Music Enterprises Inc
Blazing Sun Publications Inc
Blendingwell Music Inc
Blen Music Inc
Bleu Disque Music Co Inc
Bleunig Music
   Bill Withers
B L & H Music Corporation
Bliss Full Music Spectrum
Bliss Paul Music
Blithe Publishing Co
Bloch Publishing Company
Blockhead Publishing
*Block Martin
Bloodloss Music Publishing Co
Bloody Music Company Inc
*Bloom Ben Music Corp
*Bloom Harry Inc
Bloomsday Music Co
*Blossom Music Corp
Blue Bottle Publishing Co
Blue Calico
Blue Candle Music
*Blue Coast Music Corp
Blue Coast Music Inc
   Bacardi Publications

*Blue Country Music
Blue Echo Music
   Blue Echo Music Inc
   Blue Note Music Inc
*Blue Echo Music Inc
Blue Eyed Soul
Bluefield Music
Blueford Music
   Bull Kent Publishing Co
Blue Guitar Music Co
Blue Gum Music Inc
Blue Hour Productions Inc
   (Evenstar Music Div)
*Blue Leaf Music
*Blue Magic Mus Inc
Blue Mantle Publishing Co The
Blue Melody Music
Blue Midnight Music
Blue Moon Music
*Blue Note Music Inc
*Blue Ribbon Music Co
Blue Sailor Music
Bluesbag Records and Publishing Co
*Blue Seagull Publish Div
Blue Seas Music Inc
Bluesome Lady Music
Blue Sphere
Blue Star Moon Music Pub Co
Bluestocking Music Co
*Blue Streak Music Division
Blue Street Music
Blue Umbrella Music Publ Co
Blue Velvet Music
Blye-Bearde Productions
   (Skyjay Publishing Co Div)
Blythe Spirit Music
B M B Publishing
B M C Music
B M G Publishing
B M Music
B N A Publishing
*B N P Music Publishing Co Inc
Bobbs Merrill Company Inc The
*Bobby Fischer Music
*Bobby Tunes Inc
Bobcat Music Inc
Bobette Music
Bobiel Music Inc
*Bob Miller Inc
*Bobob Music Corp
Bocal Music
Boca Music Inc
   Avco Embassy Music Publ Inc
   Next Day Music Corp
   United Music Corp
Bocka Music
Bock Fred Music Company
   Gentry Publications
   Wallace Gillman Pub
B O Cult Songs Inc
Bofe Music
*Bogat Music Corp
Bogie Music Company
Bogue Music
Bohannon Music
Bohannon Phase II Music
Bojangles Music
*Bojeen Music Division
Bokirk Music Publishers
*Bolden Music
Boll Weevil Productions Inc
   (Weevil Wagon Music Div)
Bolo Music Inc
Bomatt Music Publishing Co
Bon Appetit Music
Bonart Music
*Bond Carrie Jacobs & Son Co
Bondi Music
Bonemeal Music
Bonfa Music
Bonfen Music Publishing Co
Bong Sun Enterprises Inc
Boni Music Inc
Bonita Music
Bonjour Music Inc
Bonkers Music Company
Bonnie Lou Music Pub Co
Bonnyview Music Corp
   Calico Records Inc
Bonton Music Company
   Ree Music Co
Boobette Music
Boogie Man Music
*Boogievision Music Co Div
Bookmark Music
Boo Music
Boone Jay Music

Boonetown Settlement
Boosey and Hawkes Inc
  Bary & Cia
Bop Shoo Wah Music
Borch Music Co
*Bordacov Publishing Co Music Div
Bordette Music
Borge Productions Inc
Borinquen Music
Borson Productions Inc
  Bordacov Publishing Co Music Div
Borzoi Music Publishers Ltd
Boss' Son Music The
Bostan Music Company
Boston Music Company
  Bond Carrie Jacobs & Son Co
  Hatch Music Company
  Humphries Bruce
  Peate Music Co
  Thompson C W Co
Botink Music
Bottom Bell Music
Boulder Music Corp
Boulware Music
Bouquet Music
Bourne Co
  A B C Music Corp
  A B C Standard Music Pub Inc
  Burke and Van Heusen Inc
  Curtis B L Music Pub
Bourne Filmusic Inc
  Bourne-Rank Music Inc
  Rank Music Co of America Inc
Boutwell Ron Music Company
Bovina Music Inc
Bowgat Productions Inc
  (Bowgat Music Division)
Bow Tie Music Inc
Box & Cox Inc
Boyce Tommy & Melvin Powers
  Music Enterprises
Boyer Jo Music
Boyymann Music Co
Bozola Music Inc
B Q Music Company
Bradbury Music Co
Braden John Publishing
Bradford Music Inc
Bradley Dan Music Company
Bradlund Music
"Brady Catherine" Music Production
Braided Chain Music
Brainblobru Records
Brain Drain Music
Branch Charlie Music Company
Branch Creek Music
Branch Harold Publishing
Branded Records Inc
Brand New Day Music A
Brandom Music Company
Brandreth Music Company
Brandywine Music Inc
Brattle Music
Bravo Music
Brawner Publishing Co
Brawn Music
Brazilliance Music Publishing
  Quad Music Pub
Brazmount Music Corp
  Izanada Music Corp
*Brazusa Music
Brd/Publictn Lutheran Chrch Am
  (Fortress Press Division)
Breaking Records Music
Breakwater Publishing
Breakwind Music
Breen & De Rose Music Corp
Bregar Music
Bregman Vocco & Conn Inc B V C
  Inc
  Donaldson Douglas & Gumble Inc
  Triangle Music Corp
Brenda Music
*Brent Michael Music Comp
Brentwood Victor Publishing
Brett Music
Brevmor Music Co
*Brial Music Co Division
Brian Brad Lee Productions
  (Crystal Fountain Music Co Div)
Brianhead Music
*Brian-Paul Publishing Division
Briarmeade Music Unlimited
Bridgewater Publishing Co
*Bridgton Music Ltd

Briegel George F Inc
  Browne J A Music Pub
  Dillon Carl Music Co
Brigette Music Co
Briggs-Miller Publishing
Briggsville Taylortown Music Co
*Brighter Music Publishing Co
Brighton Music Company Inc
Brighton Songs
Brightside Inc
  (Quarterstaff Music Division)
Bright Sol K Enterprises Inc
Bright Tunes Music Corp
Brightwater Music Corp
  Altex Music Corp
  Buster Music Co
  Coleman Music Co
  Court Music Inc
  Dantique Songs Co
  Denver Music Co
  Dubuque Music Co
  Espan Music Co
  Madison Mus Co
  New Hampshire Music Corp
  Racine Music Co
Briko Publishing
Brilliant Sun Productions Inc
  All-Points Music
Brim Music Inc
  (Herford Music Division)
  Scorpio Enterprises Inc
Bring It Back Home Music
Bristol Music Corp
  Dreyer Music Corp
Brite Music Enterprises
  Brite Enterprises
British Rocket Music
Britton Vicki Music
Broadfield Music Co
Broadway Music Corp
  Artmusic Inc
  Empire Music Co
  York Music Co The
Brodt Music Company
Brojay Music
Broken Arrow Music Inc
Broken Bird Music
Broken Glass Music
Broken Lance Music
Broken Skull Music
Bronage Music
Bronco Music Company
Bronston Samuel Music Publishing
  Inc
Bronze-Lyric Publishing Co
Brookledge Music Company
Brooklyn Boy Music Co Inc
Brooklyn Country Music
Brooklyn Heights Music
Brooklyn Music Company The
*Brooks & Denton
Brookside Music Corp
Brooks Music Corp
*Bro-Sil Music
Brother Bill's Music
Brother Hubbard Music Co
Brothers Bewlay Music
Brothers Two Music
Broude/Bregman Music Inc
Broude Brothers Limited
Brouhaha Music
*Brown and Gold Publishing
Brown Day Publishing
Brown Derby Music
Brown Earle Palmer/Associates
Browne Bernie Music
*Browne J A Music Pub
*Browne Ted Music Co
Brown Fox Music
Brown-Hollocks Music Inc
Brown Horse Music
Brownhouse Music
Brown Moon Music
*Brown Nacio Herb Inc
Brown Ollie Sugar Music Inc
Brown Shoes Music
*Brown's Mill Music
Brownstein Samuel H Enterprises
Bruce Roger Music
Bruce Wm P Enterprises Inc
  (Makin Music Division)
Bruised Oranges
Bruja Productions
Brunner Music Publishing Co
Brush Creek Music
Brut Music Publishing Company
  Brut Publishing Div

*Bryant Music Co
*Bryn Mawr Music Co
Bubbala Music
Bubba Music Company
Buckboard Jazz Music
Buckeye Music Inc
*Buckingham Music Co
Buckwheat Music
Buddah Music Inc
Budd Music Corp
  Gramercy Music Corp
  Kaye Buddy Music Co
  Raintree Music Inc
  Sundial Music
Bud Don Music Company
Budgold Music Corp
Budwick Music Company
Bueno Music
Bug & Bear Music
Bug Juice Music
Bujka Tony Music Publishing &
  Entertaining
Bulldog Music
Bullfrog Ballades
Bullhorn Music
*Bull Kent Publishing Co
Bulls Eye Music Inc
  A R A Inc
  Morros Boris Music Co
  Stanley Music Inc
Bunch Music
Bungay Music Corp
Bunko Music Co
Bunkus-Boo Publishing Co
Buon Natalie Music
*Burbank Mus Inc
Burdett Music Inc
Burgess Hale & Associates Inc
Burgundy Express Inc
  (Bxi Division)
Buried Treasure Music Inc
*Burke and Van Heusen Inc
*Burke Doyle Music Co
Burke Joe Music Company
Burke Mike Publishing Co
*Burke Van Huesen & Assoc
Burlington Music Corp
Burning Bush Music
Burt Cathie Music Publishing Co
Burthen Music Company Inc
*Burvan Music Corporation
*Bushbaby Music Division
Bushka Music
Bus-It Music
Buskirk Music
Busse Tom Music
*Buster Music Co
Butch Music
Butler Music Publishing Corp
Buttercup Blue Publishing Co
Butterfly Fuschia Music Co
*Butterfly Music Ltd
Butterscotch Castle Music
Buttons Red Music
  Helayne Music Pub Co Inc
Buzzard Productions
*B W C Productions
B W J Company
*Bxi Music Division
By George Publishing Company
Bygosh Music Corporation
*Byrd Cine Sound Pub Co Div
Byrdshire Music Company
*Byron-Douglas Productions
Caaz Music Company
Cab Co Music The
Cabrillo Music Company
*Cachalot Music Division
Cactus Music & Gidget Pub Co
  Cactus Music
*Cada Sound of Rhythm Production
Cadem Music Publishing Co
Cadenza Music Company
Caesar Irving
  Caesar Irving Inc
Caesar's Music Library
Cafe Americana Inc
Cahn Music Company
  Cahn Music Corporation
  Cahn Sammy Mus Pubs
  Glorste Inc
  Kerwin Music Co Inc
  Laursteed Music Company
Cailliet Lucien Publication
*Caj Music Corp
Cake Publications
  Helen Hyman-Publisher Memb

  Orten Music Company
Caleb Music Company
Calebur Compositions
Caledonia Productions Inc
  (Caledonia Soul Mu Div)
Calello Music Inc
Calente Music
*Calico Climate Music
Calico Climate Music Company
  Calico Climate Music
*Calico Records Inc
California Music
California Sunrise Music
Caligula Music
Calla Music Inc
Callee Music Corp
Calle Music
Callender Red Publishing Co
Callisto Music
Call Me Music Inc
Calougie Music
Calunga Music
Calvert Fred Productions Inc
  (Fred Calvert Music Div)
*Calypso Music Inc
Camcia
Camelback Mountain Music Corp
Camel Juice Music
*Camel Music Ltd
*Camelot Music Corp
Camerica Music Inc
  Detus Music Inc
Camilton Music
Cami Music
Camino Real Music
Campbell Connelly Inc
  Dash Connelly Inc
  King Irving Music Co
Campbell Silver Cosby Corp
  (Gganja Music Division)
*Campei
Campfire Music
Camp Music Company
Camps Gulf Records
Camptown Music
Campus Crusade for Christ Inc
Campus Publishing Company
Çanaan Music Inc
Canada Global Publishing Co
*Canadian Sunset Mus Div
Can Dee Deo
Candida Publishing
Candide Music
Candle River Music
Candor Music Company
Candue Music Inc
Candy Shop Music Co
Candytree Music
Candytree Music
  (Brian-Paul Publishing Division)
Cane Garden Music
Cannan Brothers Music
Cannon Music Company
*Canopy Music
*Cantus Press Division
Capability Music Ltd
Capa Music
*Capano Frank Music Pub
Capano Music
Capaquarius Publishing & Artist Mgt
*Capella Music Inc
Capital Press
Capitol Dome Music
*Capitol Music Corp
*Capitol Publications Inc
*Capitol Songs Inc
Capo Publishing Co
Cappadona Music
Cappy Music Company
*Capricorn Music Co
*Capricorn Music Division
Caprius Music
Cara Publications
*Caravelle Music Publishing Co Inc
Carbaby Music Co
  Liz Bet Music Inc
Carbaugh Music
Carbie Music Publishers
*Carden Court Music Corp
Carell Music
Caren Music Company
Cares Music Company
  Foremost Music Co Inc
  Melo-Arts Music Pubs
Carew Roy J
Car Key Music
Carleen Music Company Inc

Carlisle Publishing Co Inc
Carlisle Robert Prod Inc
Carlshia Music
*Carlson M L
Carlyle Music Publishing Corp
   Spar Music Corp
Car Mar Music
Carmat Music Inc
Carmen Charles Publishing Co Inc
Carmen Music Inc
Carmichael Enterprises Inc
*Carmichael Music Publ Inc
Carmit Music Company
*Carnbro Music Ltd
Carnegie Hill Music
*Carole Music Pub Co
Carol Jean Music
*Carol Mus Pub Co
*Carol Nan Music Division
*Carousel Music Publ Co Div
Carousel Productions Inc
   (Cartay Music Division)
Carpathian Publishing
Carpetbaggers Publishing Co
Carrie Music Company Inc
*Carrie Williams Music Co
Carriffic Music
*Carroll David Productions Inc
Carroll Marsha Publishing
Carroll Publications
Carr Radio Music Co
Carsongs Music
*Cartay Music Division
*Cartoon Pub Co Div
Caruth C Byrd Productions
   (Byrd Cine Sound Pub Co Div)
Carwin Music Inc
Carywood Music
Casa David
Casa Latina Inc
Casa Publications
Cascade Mountain Music
Case Music Corp
Casey Sean Music
Cashew Music
Cash Money Music
Carson Buzz Publications
*Cason Russell Music
Cassandra Ranjon Pub Co
Cass County Music Company
Castell Publications
Castle Hill Publishing Ltd
Castleridge Music
Catalan Publishing Company Inc
Cat and Dog Music
Catatonia Music Corporation
Caterpillar Music
*Cathy Nicholas Music
*Caton Pub Co
Cat's Eye Publishing Co
Catsos Music
Catullus Music Company Inc
Cauchemar Productions Inc
   (Cauchemar Music Div)
Caught in the Act
Cauldron Music
Caulfield Michelle Music
Caumac Music Co
*Cavalcade Music Corp
Cavan Country Music Publishers
Cav Corp
Cayman Music Inc
Cayton Publishing
C B G Bs Music Inc
C-Bird Record Co
*C & C Jazz
*C C S Music Division
Cebco Music
Ceberg Music Corp
   Ceberg Music
Cecca Music Publishing Company
Cecilia Music Publishing Co Inc
*Cecille Music Co
Cedar Crest Publishing Co
Cedarway Music
Cedonia Music Publishing Co
Ceilidh Productions Inc
Ceiljo Music Publishers
Celebration Press
Celenia Productions Corp
   (In the Black Music Div)
Cellar Door Productions
Celta Music Inc
Cenalia Music Company
Centaur Publishing Corp
Center City Music
Centinaro Music Co

Centra Cal Music
Century Artists Bureau Inc
   Music 70 Music Publishers
   Okemo Music Publishers Inc
Century Gold Music
Century 21 Music
Cessna Music Company
C'Est Music
   Taylor Carly Simon
C G S Music Publishing Company
Cha Bil Music Company
Chadick Music Publishing Co
*Chalen Music Publishing Co Inc
*Chalet Music Corp
Chalumeau Music
Chamblee Publishing Co
Champagne Music Corp
Chancellor Records Inc
   (Debmar Publishing Co Division)
   Debmar Publishing Company Inc
Chandler Music Company Inc
Chandos Music Company
Channel Music Company
   Qudrat Music
Channing-Debin-Locke Co
Channing-Debin Music
*Chaotic Music
*Chaparral Music Pub Co Inc
Chapbridge Music Publishing Co
   Pacific Press Publishing Assoc Div
Chapin Music
Chappell & Co Inc
   Aberbach Ltd
   Alamo Music Inc
   Alfred Productions Inc
   Amber Music Inc
   Anne Rachel Music Corp
   Arlow Music Inc
   B D M
   Connelly Reg Music Inc
   Cornell Kingsway
   Cornell Music Inc
   Crawford Music Corp
   Daniels Charles N Inc
   De Sylva Brown Henderson
   December Music
   Dolfi Music Inc
   Eleventh Floor Mus Inc
   Fairway Publishing Corp
   Florence Music-Chappell
   Goodie Two Shoes Music Ltd
   Green & Stept
   Kahal Irving Music Inc
   Hawthrone Music Corp
   Helena Chappell
   Ivy Music Corporation
   Johnny Mathis Music Inc
   Joy Music Inc
   Jungnickel Ross Inc
   Kingsway Music Corp
   Lemon Music Corp
   Mara Lane Music Corp
   Mutual Music Society Inc
   Paco Music Inc
   Plan Two Music Inc
   Rosarita Music Inc
   Sigma Music Inc
   Society Hill Music Inc
   Victoria Music Pub Co Ltd
   Yellen Jack Inc
   Young Victor Publs Inc
Chappell Styne Inc
Charade Music Company
   Robert A Isreal
Charell Music Company
   Mc Millan Music
Char-Grey Music
Charjane Corp
Charles Bobby Music
*Charles Music Corp
Charles Ray Enter Inc
   (Racer Music Co Div)
Charles Street Music Inc
*Charlico Music Corp
Charlie Boy Music
*Charling Music Corp
Char Mar
Charmon Music Publishing Inc
Char-Nela Music
Charolais Publishing
Charter House Music Company
Charter Publications Inc
Chasam Music
Chase C Music Productions
Chas Music
Chater-Nelson Music
Chatham Communications Inc

   (New Chatham Music Div)
Chatham Music Corporation
   Nutmeg Music Corp
Chatsworth Music Inc
Chazzee Music
Cheap Thrills
Ched Music Corp
   Ched Music Co
   Tobias & Lewis Mus Pubs
Cheerleader Music
Cheesequake Music Comp
Cheray Music Corp
   Chiquita Music Corp
*Cher Enterprises Inc
Cherie Records Inc
Cherish Music
Cherrybell Music Company
   Caravelle Music Publishing Co Inc
   Sparrow Music
Cherry Lane Music Company
   Cherry Lane Music Inc
   High Road Music
   Teena Music Corp
*Cherry Lane Music Inc
Cherry Wood Music Co
Chertok Jack Television Inc
Cherub Productions
Cheshire Cat Music
Chesnick Music Inc
Cheson Music
Chess Music Inc
   Shackle Island Music Co
Cheyenne's Publishing Company
Chiarelli Vincent Publishing Co
Chibi Publishing
Chicago Bay Music
Chicopee Music Company
Chicorel Music Corporation
   (Achic Music Division)
Chikara Music
Chilcoate Music
*Children of the Day Publishing
Children of the Promise
Children of the Rainbow By Fern
Children's Classic Cinema Pub Co
Children's Musical Plays
   Children's Musical Plays Inc
Childways Inc
   Reinach Productions
Chili Pepper Music
*Chillynipple/Visa Music Div
China Clipper Publshing
China Tee 'N Me Music
Chinick Music
Chiplin Music Company
Chip 'N' Dale Publishing Inc
Chippendale Music
*Chippendale Music Inc
Chippenstar Music Company
*Chipper Music Company
*Chiquita Music Corp
Chitty Chitty Music
Chocolate Cities Inc
Chocolate Mama Music Pub Co
Choice Music Inc
Cho-M0 Publishing Co
Chopper Entertainment Ltd
   Chopper Music Company
*Choral Arts Publications
Choral Music Company
Chordcraft Music Publishing Co
Chosenland Pub
Chrisbar Music Company
Christian Broadcastg Ntwrk Inc
   (Christian Broadcast Music Div)
*Christian Broadcast Music Div
Christian Essence Music
Christian Grit Music Press
Christiansen Eddy "Bunky" Music
Christian Soldier Music
Christie-Max Music
Christmas Associates
*Christmas Charactor Prods
Christopher J Music Company
Christy-Dawn Music Publishing Co
Christy Lane Enterprises Inc
   (Christy Lane Music Div)
   Stoller Lee Ent Inc
Chriswald Music
Chromakey Music Corp
Chrome Music
Chrysalis Music Corp
   Anderson Ian
   Butterfly Music Ltd
   Cod Music
Chubby Bunny Music
Chuca Music Company

*Chuckanut Music Division
*Chucklin Music Corp
Chuckran Music
Chucky's Publishing
*Chumas Music
Chumpchange Music
Chunnie Music
Church John Company The
Church Lane Music Inc
*Churn Music Division
Ciani/Musica Inc
Cigar Music
Cimino Publications Inc
Cinbar Music and Film Inc
   (Cinbar Publishing Div)
Cindy Rose Music
Cinema 5 Publishing Corp
*Cinema Music Co
*Cinema Music Division
Cinema Songs Inc
Cinema Sound Music
Cinerama Music Publishers Inc
Cinnamon Girl Music
Cintom Music
Circa 2000
*Circle Music Pub Co
Circle R Publishing Co
Circle Squared Music
Circle T Music
City Dancer Music
City East Music Publishers
C & J David Music Company
C J M Publishing Co
Cke Music Company Inc
Claka Music Company
Clara Music Publishing Corp
Claremont Music Inc
*Clare Music Corporation
Claren Adeerf Music Publishing
Claridge Music Inc
   Bobob Music Corp
Clark and Moonshine Music
*Clark Frank Musi Co
Clark Woody Music
Claro Music Corp
   Claro Music
   Claro Publishing Co
Clarus Music Ltd
Classie Publishing
Claude A Music Co
Claudia Music
Clave Music Inc
Claxinola Music Company
Clayborne Music
*Clay-Heart Music
Clean Bean Music
Clean Cut Tunes
*Clearwater Music
Clef Note Music Inc
Clements George Publishing
Cleonice Music Company
Clerow Productions Inc
   Flip Music Inc
*Clifford Frances Music Co
Cling Publishing
*Clinton D W Music Inc
Clonzo's Publishers
Closed Door Publishing Inc
Cloudcroft Enterprises Ltd
   (Cloudcroft Music Publ Div)
Cloudman Music
*Cloverleaf Music
*Clover Music Company
Clowntown
C L W Publishing
Clyde Music Co
C M G Music
C M H Records Inc
   (Silver Ridge Music Division)
*C M P Inc
*CMP Inc
C M Publishing Company
Coach's Choice Music
Coats R Roy
Cochin-Rockin Publishing Co
*Cock and Trumpet Music Inc
Co Co Head Music Publishers
Codell Music Corp
*Cod Music
Coffeepot Music
Cogco Music
Cohan George M Music Pub Co Inc
Colbert Music
Colby Music Inc
   Hecht and Buzzell Inc
Colby Paul Ltd
   Gunhill Road Music

Coldeye Music
Coleman Albert Publishing
*Coleman Music Co
Cole Mine Music
*Cole Porter Music Inc
Colgems Emi Music Inc
  *Colgems Music Corp
  *Colpix Music Inc
  *Jill Music Ltd
  *Medallion Songs Inc
  *Teenie Bopper Music Publishers
  *Valencia Music Co Inc
*Colgems Music Corp
*Col-Gems Music Corp/Columbia
  *Pictures Music Corp
Collage Music Inc
Collective Composers The
Collectors International
College Place Music
Collier Randy Music
Collyholly Co
  *Jahn Stephen W Co Inc
Colm Music
Colonel Muscletone Music
Colorado Music Inc
Colorado Songs
*Color Me Productions
Colotros Music
*Columbia Music Co
Columbia School of Music Inc
Columbia University Press
  (Kings Crown Music Press Div)
Columbus Circle Music Inc
Column One Music
Comac Music Corporation
Comet Music Corp
Coming Light Publishing
Coming Out Gold
*Commander Publications
Command Performance Music Co
Commercial Music Company
Commodores Entertainment
  Publishing Corporation
Common Market Music Assoc Inc
  (Laurie House Music Division)
Commonwealth Music Company
Community at the Well Inc The
  *Mayim Music Productions
Com Music
Company III Inc
  *Company III Music Pub Co Div
Comparsa Music Company
*Compas Ed
Composers Autograph Publications
Composers Library Editions
*Composers Music Corp
Composers Music Division of
  Contemporary Records Inc
Composers Press Inc The
Composers Showcase
Compton Music Corp
Comreco Music Inc
Comstock Music Inc
*Contemporary Music Pub Co Ltd
Con-Bar Music Corporation
Concentric Productions Inc
*Concert Music Pub Co
Concerto Music Corp
*Conex Mus Publishing Div
Coney Island Whitefish Music
Congressional Music Publications
*Congress Music Co
Congress Music Publications
Conley Music Inc
Con-Nection III Music
*Connelly Reg Music Inc
Conn Mervyn of America Inc
  (Mervyn Music Division)
Conquistador Music
Conrad Con Music Co
Conscious Music
Consolidated Artists
*Consolidated Music Publishers Inc
*Consolidated Mus Pub Hou
Consonant Music Inc
*Consort Music Inc
Constant Sound Music Co The
Consul Music Corporation
Continental Enterprises Inc
Continental Expositions
  (Conex Mus Publishing Div)
Cookaway Music Inc
Cook County Music
*Cool Duck Music
Cool Springs Publishing Inc
Coolwell Music
Cooper Martin Music

*Cooper Music Corp
Cooperstown Music Co
Coop Music
Copious Music Inc
Copper Music Company
Copper Robert Music
*Coral Gables Motor Lodge
Corbetta Music
Corda Music Inc
Corerm Music Inc
Corey International Enterprises Inc
  (Dalcor Music Division)
*Cornbread Music Division
*Cornell Kingsway
*Cornell Music Inc
Corner Mushroom Music
Cornucopia Music Corp
*Corona Ed Y Promota
*Coronet Music Inc
Corsair Music Company
Cortlandt Music Publishing Inc
Cos-K Music
*Coslow Music
Coslyn Publishing Company
Cosmic Casual Company
Cormis Music Inc
Cosmopolitan Music Publishers
Cossette Pierre Music Company
  *House of Coburt Music Pub Inc
Costal Publishing
Cottage By the Sea Music
Cottage Grove Music
Cottonblossom Music Co
Cotton Candy Music
Cotton Ginny Music Inc
Cotton Kandy Music Inc
Cotton Pickin Songs
Couch Joseph S Music Company
Coultron Music
*Counterpoint Music Co Div
*Country Church Music
Country Detroit Productions Limited
Country & Eastern Music Inc
Country Kitten Music
Country Legs Music
Country Love Music
Country Sound Music
Country Star Music
Country Wine Music Enterprises
County Line Music
*Court Music Inc
Cove Music Company
Coverdale Publishing Co
Cox Larry Music
Coyote Productions Inc
  (Carol Nan Music Division)
Crab Music
Crabshaw Music
Crackin Music Co
*Craig & Co
*Craig Ellis & Co
Craig George Music Publishing Co
Cramer Douglas S Company The
*Crawford Music Corp
Crayon Music
Crazy Bagel Music Inc
*Crazy Creek Music Div
Crazy Music Inc
Crealey Music
Creative Funk Enterprise
*Creative Music Pub
Creative Pen
*Creative World Music Pub
Credo Music Company
Crenshaw Whitehouse Music
Crescendo Productions Inc
Crescent Moon Music Corp
Crescent Music Company Inc
Cressada Music Inc
Crest Music Company
Creston Music Company
*Crestview Music Corp
*Crick & Ecton Pub
Cricket Hill Productions Inc
  (Cricket Hill Publishing Div)
Crikie Music Company
Crillman Music
Crimson Dynasty Record Corp
Crippled Image Music
Crispet Music
Crisscott Music Co
*Crist D W
*Cristy Lane Mus Division
Criterion Music Corp
  *Aloha State Mus Inc
  *Amasing Music
  *Chuckanut Music Division

Crocked Foxx Music
Crokagator Music
Croma Music Company Inc
  *Croma Music of Canada
Cromwell Music Inc
  *Cromwell Music Mars Acct
  *Mars Records Inc
Crossfish Company
Cross Keys Publishing Co Inc
  *Meadowgreen Music Co
Cross Tie Music Inc
Crouch Music Corporation
Crowchild Music
Crow Feather Music
*Crowfoot Music
Crown Aztec Music
  *Crown Aztec Corp
Crown Music Co Inc
Crown Prince Publishing
C R Publishing Company
*Crumit Frank Songs
Crusader Enterprises Inc
  (Cru-Ent Publishing Div)
Crybaby Music
*Crystal Fountain Music Co Div
Crystal Music Publishers Inc
Crystal Raisin
Crystal Star Music Inc
C S R Publishing
Cuemusic Inc
*Cullieron De Lacour
Cumberland Music
Cumorah Music Company
Cunningham Henry Productions Ltd
Cunningham Music Corp
*Cunningham Paul Inc
*Curb Mike Prod Inc
Curci U S A Corp
Curlew Music Publishers Inc
Curly-Tunes
Curtain Call Productions Inc
*Curtis B L Music Pub
Curtis Mann Music Company
Curtis Music Enterprises Inc
Cusic Poynter & Ingalls Publishing
Custody Music
Cutler Jesse Music Company
Cuzzin Music Corp
C W B Inc
C & W Music
C W T Music
Cyma Music Co
  *Wilson Marty Prod Inc
Cymbaline Music Company
Cymbidium Music
Cyndee Music
Cypher Music Inc
Cypress Music Inc
Cypress Queen Recording
  Enterprises Inc
*Cyrus Music
Czarina Music Corp
C Z Songs
Da Ann Inc
D'Accord Music Inc
Dacie Music
Dacus Music
Da Da Da Dum Music
Daddy-Maxfield
Dagra Music Pub Co
Dahlhouse Publishing House
Dahlia Productions Inc
Daiquiri Music Inc
Daisy Music
Dajon Productions Inc
*Dalbey W R Music Co
Dal Co Publishing Company
  *Dal Co
*Dalcor Music Division
Dalehurst Music Company
*Daly Joseph Mus Pub Co
Damadha Music
Damaged Pets Publishing
Damean Music
Damian Music Publishing Co
Damila Music Inc
Dammes Music Publishing Corp
  *Arias Music
  *L'Aries Music Corp
Dana Bill Productions Ltd
  (Bill Dana Publishing Co Div)
Dana-Don Inc
Dana Nicole Music
Danbe Music
Dancy Music
Dandale Music

Dandy Dittys
  *Dandy Dittys Unlimited
*Danelectro Corp
Danex Music Co
*D'Angelo Bullock & Allen
Dangerfield Music Company
Dangerous Music
Daniel Music Ltd
*Daniels Charles N Inc
*Danik Music Division
Dan-Jo Music
Danluce Publishing Co
Dannel Publishing Company
*Dantique Songs Co
*Daphne Music Division
Daramus Inc
  (Red Day Music Division)
*Dare Music
*Dare Records
*Darla Music Division
Darlan
  *Darlan Inc
*Darmouth Music Inc
Darobo Publishing Company
Darren Music Company
Dartboard Music
Dartmoor Music
Darwin's Theory Music
*Darwood Music Corp
Da Scha Music
*Dash Connelly Inc
Dashers Music Enterprises Ltd
  (Motormouth Music Division)
Das Music
Dateline Yesterday Music
*Daugherty Jack Prod Inc
Davalex Music
Daval Music Company
Davandon Music
*Dave Bernie Music Co
Davel Music Corporation
  (Counterpoint Music Co Div)
Dave Rave Music
*Dave Wilson
David Bobby International
  (I & I Music Division)
*David Coots & Engel Inc
David Mack Music Publishing Co
Davidson Morrey Music
Davidson Wally Media Prods Inc
Davike Music Company
Davis Benny Music
Davis David H Music Company
Davis Joe
  *Georgia Music Corp
Davis John Music Company
Dawes Tom Production Inc
Dawnari Music Company
Dawnlight Music Corp
Dawn Music
Dawnsongs Ltd
Dawson Jay Music
Dawson's Cove Music Compnay
Dax Music Company
Dayben Music Corp
Daybreak Music
  *Daybreak Records Inc
Daydan Music Corp
Dayglow Music Inc
*Daymer Music Inc
*Day Music Inc
Daysylva Music
Daytime Music Inc
  *Daytime Music Ltd
  *Levin Glenn Music Div
Dayton Music Corp
D'Azure Music Inc
D B Music
Deal Chuck Publishing
Dean Bill Music Inc
Dean Music
Dean's List Publishing
Dear America Pub
Dear Friends Music
Dearie Blossom Music
Deaver Enterprises
Debbie Anne Music Inc
*Debmar Publishing Co Division
*Debmar Publishing Company Inc
Deb-Mi Publishing Co
De Carrie Music Pub Co
*December Music
Decision Group Ltd The
  (Winter Oak Music Division)
Deconte Gerry Consortium
Dedrick Bros Music Company
Dee Bee Music Publishing Co

*Dee Jay Publishing Div
Deekay Music Inc
Dee Pam Publishing Company
Deep Canyon Music
*Deep Fork Music Inc
Deep Fruit Music Company
*Deep Note Music Division
Deep South Record Studios Inc
  (Amg Publishing Division)
Deerhaven Music Corp
Defrantz-Monique Publishing Co
De Gar Music
  Golden State Recorders Inc
*De Hall Publishing Company
Dejamus Inc
De Kay
Delamont Productions
Delaware Music Company
  Delaware Music Corp
*Del Centro Editora Music
Del Jon Music Company
*Delkas Music Pub Co
Dellja Publishing
Delmore Music Company
Delo Ken Music
Delphine Music Co
Delta Records Company Inc
  (Openwide Publishing Co Div)
Delta Research & Engineering
  Fantasy Record Co
Delta Six Music Inc
Delvy Richard Enterprises Inc
  (Elrita Music Div)
Del Zorro Music
Demanick Music Publishing Co
  P S I Love You Music Co
Demarest Music Company
Demco Publishing Co
Demented Delights Publishing
*Demetrio Ed Music S A
Demitrius Music
Demos Music
De Murray Music
Dena Music Inc
Den Lan Music Co Inc
Denna-Yvette Music Publishing Co
Denny Music Inc
Deno-Hagen Music
De Nonno Pix Inc
Denper Music Company
Denric Music Corp
*Den Ro Music Publishing Div
Denslow Music Inc
Denson Music Company
Denton Adams Music Pub
Denton & Haskins Corp
  Gem Music Corp
  Intercollegiate Syn Inc
*Denver Music Co
De Palma Music Publisher
De Patie-Freleng Enterprise Inc
  (De Patie-Freleng Music Co Div)
Deposit Music Ltd
De Rose Music
Derrick III Enterprises
Desert Rain Music Ltd
  O'Songs Inc
De Shufflin Inc
  Prombill B V
Desilu Music Corp
Desk Drawer Music
Desmobile Music Co
De Music Publishers
*De Sylva Brown Henderson
Detente Music
Detta Discs
*Detus Music Inc
Devalbo Inc
  (Devalbo Music Co Div)
Deva Music
Devere Music Corp
Devil's Tower Publishing Co
Deviny James Music
Dewey Productions Inc
  (Onion Pub Co Div)
Dewhit Music Publishing Company
Dewred Music Pub Co
De Zago Music
Dgiga Music Company
D G Music
Dhariabar Music Co
Diamond D Publications
*Diamond Head Music Publishing Co
Diamond Mine Music
Diamond P Enterprises Inc
  (Diamond P Music Div)
Diamond Star Music Publishers

Diamond Touch Productions Ltd
  Publishing Company
Diana Music Inc
Diante Music Co
Dibiwu Music
Di Ci Music
  Spotlite Tunes Inc
Dick Slick Music
Dickson Line The
Dickson Music Publishing Corp
Didi Music Inc
  (Summer Breeze Music Division)
Diena Corporation
Dietrich Billy Music
Different Bag
Dildoug Music
Dilhelm Music
Dillboy Music Inc
Dillo Music
*Dillon Carl Music Co
Di Meola Music Co
D I Music
Dindi Music Company
Ding A Ling Publishing Company
Dinger Publishing Company
Diogenes Music Company
Diorio Music
Diplomat Music Corp
  Joseph E Levine Music Corp
Dipublishing Company
Dirco Enterprises Inc
Direct Current
Dirt Music
Dirt Sisters Music
Disco Diet International Music
Disco Holiday Music
*Discreet Records Inc Div
Disney Walt Music Company
Disonant Music Company
  Disonant Music Company Inc
*Disonant Music Company Inc
Distant Hills Music
Distant Land Music
Ditson Oliver Company Inc
Diversified Music
Dixie Queen Music
Dixon Music Company
Dizlo Music Corporation
Django Music Inc
Djiwa Music Co
D J S Choice Publishing
D L G Music
*D & L Music Corp
D L W Music Inc
  Walpro Music Div The
D M Music Company
D & N Publishing Company
Doberman Music Co
Docrabb Music Company
Dodson Milton A
  Country Church Music
Dog Breath Music
Dogfish Music
Dog Hash Production
  Dog Hash Productions
Dog Lady Music
Do Gooder Music
Dog Star Music
Dojoda Publishing Inc
Dojo Music Company
Dolce Music Inc
*Dolfi Music Inc
Dolin Gerald Music
Dolly-O Recording and Music
  Publishing Company
*Dolly Parton Dean
Dolphin Communi
Domestic Music Co
Dominant Music Publishers
  Dominant Music Corp
Donald Music Inc
*Donaldson Douglas & Gumb
*Donaldson Douglas & Gumble Inc
Donaldson Publishing Co
*Dona Marta Music
Don and Rae Music
Donarie Music Publishing Co
Don Don Music Company
Donert Associates Inc
  (Donert Music Div)
Don Eugenio Music Company Inc
  Don Eugenio Music Inc
Dongan Music Company
Donka Music
Donlaurie Music Enterprises
Don-Lin Publishing Co
*Donna Lil Music Publishing

Donna Marie Music Publishing Co
*Donner Music Division
Don Watt House of Music
Doodyville Tunes Inc
Doors Music Company
Doppler Shift Music
Dorabet Music Company
  Holly Pix Music Publishing Co
Dorella Music Inc
Dore Music Company
Dorian Music Publishers Inc
Dormat Music
Dornelle Inc
Doron-Lynn Music
Dorothy Publishing Company
*Dorsey Brothers Music Inc
Dorton Music Corp
Dotted Lion Music
Dottie May Music
Dottie Music Pub
Double A Music Corp
Double Exposure Music Inc
Double F
  Hallmark Records Inc
Double Platinum Music
Double R Music Corp
  Sy Rosenberg Music Corporation
Double Sharp Music
Double Stop Music
Douglas King Music
Dougwin Enterprises Inc
  (Dougwin Music Div)
Dovan Music Inc
Dovera Music
Do-Viea Music Co
*Dov Music Inc
Downey Sean Morton Jr Inc
*Downfall Music
*Down Home Music Co
Downtown Music Co
  Purple Record Dist Corp
Downunder Publishing
Drachman Theodore L
Dragon Music Company
Drake Activities Corp
*Drake Hoffman Livingston Music
  Pub
Dramatic Features Inc
Draw Music Company
Drayton Music
Dr Bunjo Publishing Co
Dreaming Dragon Music
Dream Master Music
Dreams and Junk Music
Dreamseeker Music
Dream Seven Music
Dreams Inc
  (Mac Davis Music Division)
Dreamsongs
Dream Wheel Music
Drean Jean Music
Dressel Hermie Enterprises Inc
  (Capricorn Music Division)
*Dreyer Dave Music Corp
*Dreyer Music Corp
*Driftaway Music
*Drink Editora Ltda
Dripping Bullets Music
Drive Time Tunes
Driving Music
D R Jr'S
D R L Methods
Drolet Music
Dropshot Music
Drugstore Cowboy Songs Ltd
Drumfunk Music
Drumm Don Enterprises Inc
  (Thatcher Publishing Division)
Drummer Boy Music Corp
Drunken Boat Music
Drunk Monkey Music
Duane Music Inc
Duan Music
Dubin Al Music Co
Dublin Music
*Dubuque Music Co
Ducal Music
*Duce Music Division
Duck Beak Music
Dude Music Company
*Dudesong Publishing Division
Dudzack Music
Duet Music Inc
*Duke Kahanmoku Music Corp
Dumplin Music
Dunamis Music
  Gerard Chuck

Dunaway Music Corp
Duncan Publications
Dungaree Music
Dunhill Music Company
  Tribune Music Inc
Dunlap Gene E Jr Music
*Dunson Sonja Prod Inc
Dunwich Productions Inc
  (Dunwich Music Co Division)
Durango Music Publishing Co
Durante Jimmy Music Pub Co Inc
Durant Music
Dusick Publishing Co
Dusty House Music
Dwarf Music
Dweir Irv Productions Inc
D & W Music
Dyess Tony-Publications
Dymor Productions Inc
Dynablast Music
Dynamic III Music
Dynamited Mice Music
Eager Beaver Music
Eagleleaf Music
Eagle Point Publishing Co
Eagle Rock Music Co
Earleon Music Corp
Earl Music Company
Ears Publishing
Ears to Hear Music
Earthling Music
Earthshaker Music Co
Earthwood Music
Earwizard Music
*Ease Music Division
East Bay Productions Ltd
*Eastbrook Music Co
Eastbrook Music Company
Eastern Shores Publishing Co
East Hill Music Company Inc
Eastlake Music Inc
*Eastman School of Music
Easton Music Company
East Songs
East West Music Inc
Easy Action Music
Easy Listening Music Corp
  Charlico Music Corp
  Chucklin Music Corp
Easy Money Music
Easy Street Music Inc
E B A Music
Ebbed Tide Music
*Ebbets Field Mus Div
Ebony Genius Music Inc
Ebony-Ivory Music Co
Ebron Music
*Eby Walter M
Ecaroh Music Inc
Ecf Music
Echoes of the Cosmos
Echo-Rama Music World
Economides Comm Corp
*Ecton & Mosier Publishers
*Ed Bajcaliforoniana Impulosera
  Music
Eddie O Music Co Ltd
*Ed Friendly Music Division
Edgartown Publishing Co
Edge O'Lake Music
*Ed Intern Fermata
Edition Musicus-New York Inc
Edition Orto
Editions Chanson Music
Editions Salabert Inc
Edition Wilhelm Hansen/Chester
  Music New York Inc
Editone Music Company
*Editorial Mexicana De Musica
Edlou Music Publishing Co
E D M Music Publishers
Ednan Music Publishing Corp
Edney Dave Music
Edotha Pub Co
Educational Music Service Inc
*Edwards Gus Mus Pub Co
Effort Music Publishing Corp
  Effort Music
Eggs and Coffee and Music
Dublin Music
Eighties Music
E I Productions
Eisenstadt Music Company
Ekapa
Ekay Music Company
E K M Publishing
Elacsap Music

Elainea Music Publishing Co
Elboul Music Company
El Chicano Music
Eldad Music
   Martinelli Music
Eldan Music Company
*El Dorado Music Co
Electric Moon Music
   Crowfoot Music
*Electric Pig Music Co Div
Electro Acoustic Music
Electrocord Pub Co
Electronic Sound Productions Inc
*Electronovision Mu Pub I
Elemar Productions and Records
Element Music
Elephant Heart Music
Eleventh Ave Theatricals Inc
*Eleventh Floor Mus Inc
Elf Music Ltd
El Gato Publishing Company
Elgy Music Inc
Eliana Music Corporation
Elias Productions Inc
Elifritz Publishers
Elijah Ministries Inc
   (Elijah Music Division)
Eli Victor Songs
Eliza M Music
El Jarocho Publishing Co
Elkan Henri Music Publisher
   Iceland Information Centre
Elkan Vogel Inc
Elkin Brothers Publishing Co
Ell Bern Publishing Company
Ellenjay Inc
Ellington Mercer K
*Elliot Lurie
Elliot Music Company Inc
Elliott-Ferguson Music Co
*Elliott Jack Music Co
Ellipsis Music Corp
*Ellis & Co
Ellis Herb Music
Ellis Music Enterprises
Ellison's Ben Publications
Ellis Prince Publishing
*Ellis Robin
El Music
*El Paso Music Division
El Ray Music Company
*Elrita Music Div
El Rito Publishing
*Elsa Tunes Inc
Elsboy Incorporated
Elsensongs
Elsmere Music Inc
   Sandlee Pub Corp
Elsmo Bros Publishers
   Elsmo Bros Inc
   Elsmo Bros Pub Inc
El Tee Publishing Company
Eltolad Music Inc
Elusive Sounds Music
Elva Music Inc
   (Muckender Music Div)
Elvee Deekay Music Inc
Elvena Mouzon Music Co
Elwood Music Company
Ema Music
Emanay Music
Emanuel Music Corp
*Emarcy Publishing Inc
*Emar Records Inc
Embamba Music Inc
*Embee Music Corp
Emblem Enterprises
Emboe Music Inc
Emeline Music Co
   Koala Records Inc
Emelkay Music
Emerade Music Publishing Inc
Emerald City Music
Emerald Empire Music
Emergence Music
Emergency Music Inc
Emery Music Co
   Emery Music Inc
Emily Music Corp
E M L Publishing Company
Emma Bell Music
Emmaus Road Music Company
Emme Music
E M P C O
*Empire Music Co
*Empire Music Co Inc
*Empress Music Inc

Empty Foxhole Productions Inc
   (Empty Foxhole Music Division)
Em Ru Publishers
   Em-Ru Pub
Encino Music
Encore Music
Endeavor
*Engel Harry Inc
English Ernie Music Co
English Thomas Music Publishing
   Co Inc
Enlight Music Publishing Co
Ennes Productions Ltd
   Maximilian Music Inc
Ensemble Music Press
*Enterprise Music Co
Enterprise Music Corp
Entourage Inc
   Entourage
Entre Music Co
E O C Enterprises
E P I Music Publishers
Episteme Music
Epstein Productions Inc
Eptembre Enterprises Inc
Erasmus Music Inc
Ercil Publishing Company
E R E Music
Erewhon Music
Ericksen Joe Music Co
*Eric Matthew Music Division
Eriel Music Ltd
Erika Publishing
*Erin Lane Music Division
Ermajo Music Co
*Ernie Wilkins Publishing Co
Ernray Music
Eroica Music Inc
*Erosa Music Publishing Corp
E R S Publications
Ertis Music Company
Erwin-Howard Music Corp
Esnamar Publishing
*Espan Music Co
Esparza Publishing
Essene Music
Essenjay Music
Essex Music Inc
   Biltmore Music Corp
   Horizon Music Ltd
Essex Music International Inc
   Moran Mike
Essom Music
*Estacy Music Inc
Estrellita Music
Estuary Music Publishing Inc
E T C Music
Eternal Candle Music
Eternal Life Music
Eternity Music Co
Ethelyn Music
Ethnic Music Publications Inc
Etoile Music
Ettore Music Co
Eugene Raskin
   G & F Music Inc
Eulik Music Publishing
   Eulik Pub
Euphrosyne Incorporated
Eurasia Music Publications
European American Music
   Distributors Corporation
   Joseph Boonin Inc
Eurovox Music Inc
*Evangeline Music Inc
Evan Music
   Garrett Prod
*Evans Music Co
Evans Redd Music Company
Evans Richard Music
Evco
Eve Jay Music
Eve Laurain Music
Evenin Breeze Music
Evening Publications
*Evenstar Music Div
Eventide Music
Event Music Ltd
Everett Publishing
Everflow Publishing Co
*Evergreen Music Corp
*Every Little Tune Inc
Evidence Music International
Evie Music Inc
Evilot Music Inc
E V Music Publishing Co
*Excell E O Co

Exceller Music
Excerent Music
*Exclusive Pubs Inc
Exotica Publishing Company
Expand Publishing
Eye of Madley
Eyesllub Music
Eyes of Dawn Publishing Co
Fabulous Music Co
Fabulous Rhinestones Ltd
Factor-Newland Production Corp
*Factory Productions
Fagan S & S
Fain Music Company
Fairhome Music Publishing Co
Fairlane Music Co
*Fairway Publishing Corp
Fairyland Music Corp
   Lansing Music Corp
Falcon Associates Music Publishers
Fallin' Arches Music
Fallon Larry Ent Inc
   (Salerno Music Division)
Falloonium Music
Fallwater Music
Family Affair Enterprises Inc
   (Sweet Caress Music Division)
Family Affair Music Co
Family of Man Music Inc
Family Owl Music
Famous Music Corporation
   Brazusa Music
   Burke Van Huesen & Assoc
   Burvan Music Corporation
   G B Music Inc
*Famous Writers Co
Fam Record Corporation
F A Music Co Inc
Fancy Music Publishing Company
Fancy That Music Company
Fanfare Music Company
*Fanmar Music Co
Fan Shell Music
   Daugherty Jack Prod Inc
Fantasy Music Inc
*Fantasy Record Co
Farce Music
Far Fetched Music Co
   Arkansas Music Ltd
   Black Oak Arkansas Inc Div
*Fargil Publication Co
Fargo House Inc
Farmer Fred Music
   Farmhouse Films Inc
Farmers Pride
Far Out Music Inc
*Farrand Van L
Fashion Fair Music
Fast Fade Music
Fata Morgana Music Publ
Fatback Music
Fat City Publishing Co
Fate Music
   (Fate Music Division)
   G T Enterprises
Fat Mama Music Corp
*Favorite Music Inc
*Favorite Publishers Inc
Fawcett-Majors Productions Inc
   (Fmp Music Co Division)
F D H F Music Inc
*Feature Music Syndicate
Features Music Corp
Federal Music
Feelgood Music Inc
Feiner Richard and Company Inc
Feist Leo Inc
   Brown Nacio Herb Inc
   Loews Inc
Felisa Music Inc
F E L Publications Ltd
Feltus Publishing
Fema Music Publications
*Fennario Music Publishers Inc
Fenner Publications
Fenwick Music Inc
Fenwood Music Co
Fereol Publications
*Fermata Do Brazil
Fermata International Melodies Inc
   Drink Editora Ltda
   Ed Intern Fermata
   Fermata Do Brazil
Ferndock Music
Ferrell Ben Music
Festival Attractions Inc
Fever Music Inc

Fia Music Inc
Fiat Music Co
Fidelio Music Publishing Co
Fideree Music Co
   Fideree Music Corp
Fiedel Music Industries
*Fielding Music Co
Fieldston House Publication Co
Fifth Floor Music Inc
Fifty-Fifth Street Music Corp
Fightin Duck Music
Filet Music Inc
Fillisaundi Music
Fillmore Corporation
Fillmore Music House
Film Profiles Inc
Filmus
Film Ventures Music Inc
Filmways Music Publishing Inc
   Fwy Music Publishing Co Inc
   Kayday Music Inc
Filo Music Co
*Fi Music Inc
Finchley Music Corp
   Kid Music Ltd
*Finder & Urbanek
Finesse Publishing
   O J G Inc
Fine Tuning Inc
Fingers Music
Fireball Music
Firedrum Music
*Fire Escape Music Division
Firehole Music Corporation
Fire Horse Music
Firelight Publishing
Fire Weed Music
First Artists Productns Co Ltd
   (First Artists Music Co Div)
First Born Music Co
*First Division Publ Corp
First International T V Song Festival
   Inc
First Kiss
*First Monday Music Div
First Place Music Publications Inc
Fischer Bobby Music
   Bobby Fischer Music
Fischer Carey Music Co
Fischer Carl Inc
   Composers Music Corp
   Eastman School of Music
   Ellis Robin
   Evans Music Co
   Foley Charles Inc
   Galleon Press
   Gamble Hinged Mus Co
   Homeyer Chas W & Co Inc
   Institute of American Music Inc
   Kickapoo Music Company
   Pond Wa A & Co
   Riker Brown & Wellington Inc
   Row R D Mus Co Inc
   Signature Music Press
*Fischer J & Brd
Fischoff George Publishing Co
Fisher Doris Music Corp
Fisher Music Corp
   Fred Fisher Music Co Inc
Fish Fry Music
*Fish Music Division
Fitz-Carleton Music Inc
Fitzpatrick Music Co
Five Daughters Music Inc
*Five Jays Music Inc
Five Nine Five Music Co Inc
57th Street Entertainment Co Inc
   (Brial Music Co Division)
   Music of Koppleman - Bandier
57th Street Music
53rd State Music
Fizz Music
*Flagstaff Music Corp
Flagstone Music Co
Flaherty Gus Music
Flames of Albion Music Inc
   Joaneline Music Inc
Flamingo Music Inc
Flaming Youth
Flammer Harold Inc
   Luckhardt & Belder
*Flanager Hendler & Wood
Flanders William Productions Inc
   (Back Door Publ Div)
Flanka Music Corp
Flash Flood Music
Flat Lizard Music

Flesh Tunes
Fletcher Peck Music Company
Flicker Music Company
Flight Music Company
Flintridge Music Company
*Flip Music Inc
Flojan Music Publishing Co The
Flo Jo Music
Flo Music Inc
Flonan Publishing Co
   Miniature Musicals Inc
*Florence Music-Chappell
Flotsam Music Company
Flowering Stone Music
Fluke Publishing Co
Flying Bear Music Inc
Flying Cat Music
Flying Crown Music
Flying Fingers Music
Flying Monkey Music
Fly Songs
*F M P Music Co Division
F O D Music
Foghorn Music
*Foley Charles Inc
Folklore Productions Inc
   (Folklore Music Division)
Fontaine Music Corp
Fool's Gold
*Footstep Music Publishers Div
Footstep Productions Inc
   (Footstep Music Publishers Div)
For-A-Quarter Music
Ford Emma Music
*Ford Music Publ Co Inc
Ford Music Publishing Co
Forefront Publications Ltd
   (Rml Co Division)
*Foremost Music Co Inc
Forest Bay Company
Foreverendeavor Music Inc
Forever Promised Publishing
Formula Music Inc
Formyduval V Fay Music
Forrester Music Company
Forrest Green Music Publishing
   Corp
Forrest Rew Mathis Music
   Publishing Co
Forster Music Publisher Inc
*Forsythe Music Div
Forte Music Inc
Fortini Recording
   (Nu View Publishing Co Div)
*Fortress Press Division
Fortune Music Co
*Fortune Music Inc
Fort Wayne Music
*Forum Music Inc
Forum Publications
Forward Music Publishing Co
Fostco Music Press
Foster Frank Music Inc
Foster & Williams Enterprises Ltd
*Foundation Music Corp
Four Buddies
Four Buns Music
Four D Music
440 Music Inc
   Harvest Music Co Inc
Four Jays Music Co
4m Editions
Fournia Music
*411 Music Division
Four Seasons Music
*Four Star Music Co
Fourtel Music Publishing Co
   Bnp Music Publishing Co Inc
   H-Q Music Pub Inc
   Two Worlds Music Inc
Fourth Floor Music Inc
Fourth Way Music
Four Two Four Music Inc
42 Publishing Co Inc
Four Way Music
40 Love Music
Foxborough Jr Music Inc
Fox Fred Music Publishing Co Inc
Foxglove Music Publishing Co
Fox Music Publications
*Fox Productions Inc
*Fox Sam Music Verlag (Berlin)
*Fox Sam Publishing Co Inc
   Choral Arts Publications
   Fox Sam Music Verlag (Berlin)
   Gate Music Company
   Harmonic Library

Pallma Mus Pubs Inc
Fox Will Record & Publishing Co
F P T Music
Fram Dee Music Ltd
Framil Music
Frampton Music
Franan Publishers
France Music Corp
Frances Music Inc
Francis Mike Music Publication
Francks Music Publications The
*Francon Music Corp
Frankenfield Parke House of Music
   Publishing Company
*Frankincense & Myrrh Record Div
Franklin-Douglas Inc
*Franklin John Co Inc
*Franklin Music
Franklin Street Music Co Inc
Frankly Stankly Music
Frank Music Corp
   Audubon Music Inc
   Carmichael Music Publ Inc
   Empress Music Inc
   Marechiaro Casa Edit
   Reade Walter Sterling Music Corp
   Saunders Publications Inc
   Walter Reade Music Corp
*Fred Calvert Music Div
*Fred Fisher Music Co Inc
*Fred Heller Music Div
Fredonia Press
   Paul J Sifler-Publisher
Free Delivery Music
Free Doobleman Music
Free Enterprise Music Co
Free Flow Productions Ltd
   (Free Flow Music Division)
Free Love Publishing
   Jesus People
Freeman Hal Music
Free Verse Inc
French Kiss Music
French Quarter Music Co Inc
French Samuel Inc
   Hugo & Luigi-Samuel French
   Music Publications Inc
*Fresco Music Inc
Fresh Memory Music Company
Fresh Pepper Music
*Freyda Music Co Inc
Friendly Ed Productions Inc
   (Ed Friendly Music Division)
Friendly Hippo Music
Friend Music Corp
*Frisch Al Productions
Frog Music
Front Range Music
Frosen Rock Music
Frozen Nose Music
Fruits of Faith Publishing Company
Fryer Terry K Inc
   (Electric Pig Music Co Div)
Fry King Publishing Company
*F T P Music Inc
Fugie Publications
*Fullarton Music Inc
Full Swing Music
Fun and Games Music Co
*Fun City Music Corp
*Funco Corp
Funco Publishing Co
Funky Acres Music Co
Funky P O Music Inc
Funny Side Music
Funt Allen A Publishing Corp
Fun Time Inc
Fusion Enterprises Inc
Fusion Musical Productions Corp
   (Lato Music Division)
Futa Music Publishing Co
*Futura Music Inc
*F W Y Music Publishing Co Inc
G A B Music Inc
*Gabraith-Mareno Pub Co
Gabriel Earl Music
Gage Music
Gaither Music Co
Galaxy Music Corporation
Gale Pyramid Music
Gali Music Co
Gallagher Music
Gall and Wormwood Publishing
Galleon Music Inc
*Galleon Press
*Gallico Al Music Co Inc
*Gallico Al Music Company

Galli Music Corp
Gallop Sammy Music
Galvin Gene Publishing Co
*Gamble Hinged Mus Co
Gammon and Gurren Music
Gang Land Music
Ganim Dennis Organization Inc
   (Karolann Music Co Div)
Gannon and Kent Music Co
Gaona Publishing
Garden Court Music Co
   Garden Court Music Corp
Garf Gene Music
*Garland Music Inc
Garlic Music
Garlon Music Co
Garon Jesse Music
Garpax Music Press
*Garrett Music Co Div
*Garrett Music Ent Inc
*Garrett Prod
Garsal Music
Garson-Hilliard & Day Inc
   Day Music Inc
   Hilliard Bob Music Co
Garson Music Co
Garveland Music
Gas House Publishing Co
*Gate Music Company
Gateway Music Inc
*Gaumont Music Pub Ltd
Gavadima Music Inc
*Gaylene Music Div
*Gay Mace Catalog
Gaynor Gloria Music Inc
G B C Productions
G B I Recording Co Ltd
*G B Music Inc
G & C Music Corporation
G C Productions Incorporated
   (G C Music Publishing Div)
G C R Music Co
*Gear Publishing Div
G E B Publishing
   Yucatan Publishing Corp
Geepio Music Co
Gee Zee Music
*Geibel Adam Music Co
Geisel Ted Publishing Company
Geld Music Company
Gello Cheby Music
Gelsa Music
Gem Bell Music Productions
Gemini Press Inc
*Gem Music Corp
Gemstone Music Co
General Confusion Music
General Electric Co
   Tomorrow Entertainment Inc
   Videocraft International Ltd
General Entertainment Corp/Am
   (King Drive Music Co Division)
*General Learning Corporation
General Music Publishing Co Inc
   Camelot Music Corp
Generic Music
Genesis III
Genhol Music
Genius Music Corp
Gentle General Music
Gentle Rain Music Inc
Gentle Touch Music and Records
Gentol Music Co
*Gentry Publications
Geode Music
Geordie Music Publishing Inc
Georgeoff Evan Music Publishing Co
   Concert Music Corp
   Montrose F Music Pub Co
   Newton Record Co
Georgia Glo Music
*Georgia Music Corp
*Gerard Chuck
Gerart Music Enterprises
Gercla Music
*Gerry Productions Inc
Gershwin Publishing Corp
*Gesner Music Inc
Gesol Publishing Company
Gethsemane Music
*G & F Music Inc
*Gganja Music Division
G G Music Pub Co
Ghost Dance Music Inc
Ghost Writer Music
Ghoul Music

Gibsongs
Gift of Music
*Gilbert L Wolfe Mus Pub
Gilbert Ray Publishing Corp
Gilbert Rose Music Company
Gilead Music Co
Gil Gilday Publishing Company
   Fargil Publication Co
Gil Gilday Publishing Company
Gillespie Haven Music Pub Co
Gillman Publishing Co
Gilmar Publishing Corp
Gilmore Productions Inc
   (Palladium Music Division)
Gilstro Music
*Gina Reid Music Div
Ginger Music
Gingham Music Company
Gin Jay Music Publishing Co
Ginny Lynn Music
*Ginseng Music
Giovanni Music Inc
Girvin Dick Productions Inc
   (Sharilda Publishing Div)
*Gitarists Pub
Give Me A Breack Music Company
Glad Hamp Music Corp
Glad Rag Music
*Gladstone Music Inc
Glad Tone Music Pub Co
Gladwyne Music Publishing Corp
Gladys Music
   Gladys Music Inc
Glamford Music Corp
Glamorous Music Inc
Glasco Music Company
Glass Slipper Music
Gleam Music Inc
   Noble Music Corp
Glendana Music
Glenden Music
Glen Island Music
*Glenmore Music Inc
Glenn Robert Music Co
Glenwood Music Corp
   Capitol Music Corp
   Yardbirds Music Inc
G L L Tv Enterprises Inc
Global Music Inc
   Harvest Song Co
Glo Jay Music Co
Glo Publishers
*Glorioso Music
*Glorste Inc
Glory Music Company
Gloveda Music Inc
Glw Star Enterprises Inc
G M B Enterprises
G M B Music
G M G Music
G M I Publishing
   Mitchell Guy Inc
Gnolaum Music
Gnossos Music
Gnostic Music Company
Gobion Music Corporation
Go-Dak Productions Inc
   (Ver-Don Music Div)
God Only Knows Music
*Godspell Music Inc
Godwin Annette B
Gold Beach Music Inc
Gold Book Music Inc
Goldcast Music Publishers Inc
Gold Cat Music
Gold Coast International Music
Golcrest Music Publishing
Golden Acres Music Pub
Golden Apple Music Inc
Golden Arkvark Publishing Co
Golden Bell Songs
   Music of Tomorrow Inc
   Rylan Music Corp
Golden Berdie
Golden Bough Publishing Co Inc
Golden Clover Productions
Golden Crown Music Publishers
   H C L Inc
Golden Goose Productions
   (Den/Ro Music Publishing Div)
Golden Harvest Publishing Co
   Hong Kong Audio Centre Inc
Golden Horn
Golden Meadow Music Company
Golden Music Inc
Golden Note Music Company Inc
Golden Ram Music

*Golden Rod Music Co
Golden Sands Enterprises Inc
 Alfa Music
 Editorial Mexicana De Musica
 Marquez Hnos
 P R E D I S A
 Portilla Music Corp
 R C A Victor Mexicana S A
 Roaga Edic
Golden Spread Music
Golden Stable Music
*Golden State Recorders Inc
Golden Throat Music
Golden Torch Music Corp
 Col-Gems Music Corp/Columbia
 Pictures Music Corp
Golden Valley Music
*Golden West Broadcasters
Golden Withers Music
Golden World
Goldfarb Samuel E Music
Gold Field Music
Gold Hill Music Inc
Gold Jack Music Co
Gold J J Publishing
*Gold Joe Music Co
Goldline Music Inc
Gold Manny Music Publisher
Goldmine Music Inc
Goldsboro Bobby Music Inc
Goldsen Michael H Inc
 Capitol Songs Inc
Gold-Shor Music Publishing Co Inc
Gold Sold Music
Gold Standard Music and Prod Co
Gold Stud Publishing
Golondrina Publications
*Gomalco Music Corp
Gonzaga Publishing Co
Good Big Nice and It Fits Music
Good Changes Music
Good Evening Music
Good Flavor Songs Inc
 Admont Music Inc
Good Folks Music Company
Good Fortune Enterprises Ltd
Good Friends Music
Good Grazin Music
Good High Inc
 (Good High Music Division)
Good Holdings Music Co
*Goodie Two Shoes Music Ltd
Goodkind Tom Music
 T G M
Good Life Pub
Goodlight Music
Goodman Music Co Inc
 Handman & Goodman Inc
 Handman Kent & Goodman
 Universal Mus Co Ltd
Good Music Co
Good News Circle Inc
Good Noose Music
Good Pure and Simple
Goodson-Todman Associates Inc
Good Sphere Songs Inc
Good Spirit Music Pub
Goodstuff Music
Good Tokin' Music
Good Vibes Music
Goo-Lu Music
Goose Music Co
Gopher Baroque Music
Gor Dan Enterprises
Gordelys Music
Gordon Albright Music
Gordon Bobby Music Co
Gordon-Eisner Productions
 (Donner Music Division)
*Gordon Hamiltons Estate
*Gordon Hamiltons Inc
*Gordon Hamiltons Music Pub
*Gordon Murray Mus Corp
*Gordon Music Co
*Gordon Music Corp
*Gordon & Rich Inc
*Gordon St Music Pub
*Gordon St & Son Music
*Goro Music Co Division
Gosh Bobby Enterprises
*Gotham Attucks Mus Co
*Gotham Mus Service Inc
Gothic Music
Gouda Music Co
Gould Edward E Music Co
*Goulden Leng Co
G Q Publishing

Grace Music Co Inc
Garcia Music Co
Graduation Music Inc
Gradus Music
Grady Jim Music
Grady Music Company
Graffiti Records Inc
 (Sabina Music Div)
Graf Records International
 (White Dwarf Music Division)
Graham Music Publishing Corp
*Graham Roger Mus Pub
Grainger Music
*Gramercy Music Corp
Gramophone Music Co
Grams Music
Grand Association of Songwriters
Grandma May Music
 Hodmarc Music Inc
Grand Music Corp
 Artists Music Corp
Grand River Music
Grandstand Music
Grand Theft Music
Granite Music Corporation
Granoff Budd Productions Inc
*Grant & Murtaugh Music Corp
*Grapefruit Head Productions
*Grapetree Publishing Division
Grapevine Music Co Inc
Graph Music
Gratiot Music
Gratitude Sky Music Inc
Gravenhorst Music
*Gray H W Company
Gray Music
*Gray Music Division
*Grayson Music Co
Grazing Dreams Music
Grean Music Co
Greasy King Music Inc
Great American Mus Machine Inc
 (Gramm Publishing Co Div)
Great Auk Music
Great Ears Music
Great Escape Music
Great Fish Music
Great Foreign Songs Inc
Great Gramaphone Music Inc
Great Guns Publishing Co
Great Lakes Records Inc
Great Leawood Music Inc
Great Lyrics Music Company
Great Standard's Music Pub Co
Great Stoned Hiway Music Co
Great Viking Music
Great Waves Music
Great Z's Music Co The
Grecken Productions Inc
 (Grecken Music Div)
Greek Sacred & Secular Mus Soc Inc
Green and Ross Music Co
Greenbar Music Corp
 Cooper Music Corp
 Hamilton Music Corp
Green & Brogdon Songs
*Green Bros & Knight Inc
Greeneaire Publishing
Greene Eddie Publishing
Greene Mort Music Company
Greene Music Inc
Greene Walter Music Company
Greenfields Music
Green Gary Music
Green Isle Productions Inc
 (Green Isle Publishing Co Div)
Green Laser Music
Greenleaf Music Inc
Green Menu Music Factory
 (Green Menu Music Co Div)
Green Mitchell Productions
*Green & Stept
Greenstreet Music Co
*Green & White Inc
Greenwich Music Co Inc
*Gregg Hill Music Division
Gregg Thomas Music
Gregmar
Gregorio Publishing Co
Gregory Music Corp
Grenelda Thermer Music Corp
Grenyoco Music Inc
Gresco Publishing Co
*Gretavic Music Inc
Greydog Music
Grey Wizard Music
Grimes Creek Music Co

*Grimes Music Pub
Grimora Publishing
Grinders Time Inc
Grin Music Publishing Corp
Gripping Publications
Grobee Cove in Garden Grove The
Grob Music Company
*Groene Mus Pub Co
Groom Lynn Music
Grossmont Music Publications
Gross National Products
Grosvenor House Music
*Grosvenor Music Co Ltd
*Groton Music Co Inc
Grotto Music
Group 88 Music
 Polara Music
Group 5 Records Inc
Group Two Music
*G R T Corporation
Grudge Publishing
G Scott Music Publishing Co
*Gs Euro-American-Publishing Div
G S L B F H Publishing
G S S Publishing Co
*G T Enterprises
Guaranteed Gold Publishing Co
Guarare Music
Guardian Music Corp
Guarnieri Music Co
Gueftone Music
Guercio J W Aurelia Music
 (Aurelia Music Div)
Guercio J W Enterprises Inc
 (Archimedes Music Div)
*Guide Music Inc
*Guild of American Composers
*Guild Publications of California Inc
*Guild Pub of Arts Music Inc
*Guitarists Publication
Gulfstream Music Publishing Co
Gullah Music Publishing Co
Gumble Music
*Gunhill Road Music
Gunston Music Inc
Gurren E J Music
*Gusher Music Division
Gusto Records Inc
 (Moe's Music Division)
Gut Feeling Music
Guv Nor Songs Inc
Guys IV Music Inc
Gwendolynne Music
G W Jr Music Inc
G W M Inc
G & W Publishing Corp
*Gwynell Music Division
Gypsy Boy Music Inc
*Gyrus Music Corp
Haapala Music
Habitant Music Company
Habit Forming Music Inc
 (Habit Forming Music Div)
 Mono Music Inc
Habitt Music Publishing Corp
Hacienda Music
*Hackids Music Publishing Corp
Hac Sports Ltd
 Hackids Music Publishing Corp
Hadden Road Music
Haegert Cletus Publ Co
*Hahal Irving Music Inc
Haidu Conrad
 Craig & Co
 Craig Ellis & Co
 Ellis & Co
 Graham Roger Mus Pub
 Hill May Music
 Melomusic Publications Inc
*Hal Bernard Enterprises Inc
Halcyon Music Inc
*Hall Ellis B
*Hal Leonard Music Inc
*Hal Leonard Pointer Publ Inc
*Hall Mack Company
Hallmark Music Co Inc
 Enterprise Music Co
 Mandate Music Co Inc
*Hallmark Records Inc
Hall Rick Music
Hallway Music
Hall Wendell Music Maker Prod
Halma Productions Inc
 (Halma Music Div)
Halmi Robert Inc
Halnat Publishing Co

Halrone Music Corp
 Halroy Music Co
Halwill Music
 Bro-Sil Music
Hamblen Music Co Inc
 Voss Music Company
Hamilton Jack Music
*Hamilton Music Co
*Hamilton Music Corp
Hamilton Ted Music Ltd
Hammer and Nails Music
Hammer Hands Inc
Hammerwood Music
Hammond Albert Music
Hampshire House Publishing Corp
 Darmouth Music Inc
 Manchester Music Inc
 Ruxton Music Inc
Hampstead Heath Music Pub Ltd
*Handman & Goodman Inc
*Handman Kent & Goodman
Hands Off Music
Handy Bros Music Co Inc
Haney Ray Inc
 (Carousel Music Publ Co Div)
Hanging Tree Music
Hang in There Songs
Hanguad Music Inc
Hankeychip Publishers
Hanna-Barbera Productions Inc
 (Astral Music Division)
 Cartoon Pub Co Div
Hannan Music Publisher
Hanover Music Corp
Hansa Productions Inc
*Hanseatic Music Corp
Hansen Charles Music & Books Inc
Hanspard Music Publication
Hap Music Inc
Happiness Music Corp
Happy Chappy Music
Happy Endings Music
Happy Eye Music Company
Happy Girl Music
Happy Go Lucky Music
Happy Man Publishing Company
Happy Sack Music Limited
 (Chillynipple/Visa Music Div)
 Visa Music
Happy Song Music
Happy Tuesday Music
Haram Publ Co
Harberdor Music Publishing
Harbet Music Pub Co
Harbison Publishing
Harbor Music Company
Hard and Fast Music Inc
Hard Hat Music
Hardware Music
Hardy John S Music Co
Hargail Music Press
*Harkinson Music Co
Harlandale Music Company
Harle Music Inc
Harlene Music Publications
*Harman Music Inc
*Harmonic Library
Harmonist Music Co
Harmon Larry Music Company
Harmony Hill Music Publishers
Harmony J Latrue Music Company
Harmony Music Corp
*Harmony on Euclid Inc
*Harms Inc
Harms T B Co
 Alex Anderson Music Inc
 Alta Music Corporation
 Andalusian Music Co Inc
 Bealin Music Publishing Co
 Bibo Music Pub Inc
 Bnp Music Publishing Co
 Cason Russell Music
 Driftaway Music
 Harms T B Co New Acct
 Hav A Tune Inc
 Honeycomb Music Inc
 Jack and Bill Music Co
 Jack Bill Mu Co Tb Harms
 Jim Ro Music
 Maltby Richard Inc
 March Music
 Marpet Music Corp
 Mgm Record Corp
 Reliance Music Corp
 Spartan Mus Co Ltd
 Sunflower Prod Inc
 Tele Klew Prod Inc

Von Tilzer H Mus Pub Co
Whalen Music
*Harpeth Music
*Harpeth Music Div
Harral Music
Harris Alan-Frank Novello Music
Harris Charles K Music Pub Co Inc
Harris Harry Music Publish Co
Harris Music Publications
Harrison Music Corp
Harris Publishing Co
Harris Ron Music
*Harry Bloom Inc
Harry's Tune Music
Harstan Music
Hart Larry Lee Music
Hartstein Lawrence E Music
Harvest Hill Music Publishers
*Harvest Music Co Inc
*Harvest Song Co
Harvey Music Inc
Harvey Wallbanger Music
Harwichport Music Co
Music and Effects
Harwin Music Corporation
Hashram Music
*Hatch Music Company
Hatley Music Co
*Hav A Tune Inc
Haven Music Inc
*Haviland F B Pub Co
Havis Publishing Co
Hawaiian Recording & Publ Co Inc
Hawaii Sons Inc
   (Hawaii Sons Publishing Co Div)
Hawkins Edwin R Music Co
Haworth Music
   Haworth Music Inc
*Hawthrone Music Corp
*Hayako Music Company
Haylor Music Enterprises
Haymarc Enterprises
Haynes & Sbarra Mu Pub & Prod Co
Haystack Publishing Co
Hayton Horne Music Co
Hayway Music
Hazelwood Lee Music Corp
*Hazy Music
H B Facsimile Edition
H&B Music Publishing Corp The
*H C L Inc
Head East Music
Heaha Tis Publishing
Heartbeat Music Industries Inc
   Heartbeat Music Publishers
Heartland Productions Inc
Heartwood Publishing Company
Heather Hill Development Inc
   (Gray Music Division)
*Heath Levy Music Co Ltd
Heath Levy Music Company Inc
   Alaska Music Ltd
Heath Music Publishing Co
Heavenly Crown
*Heavenly Music Publishing Co
Heaven on A Bun Music
Heavy Duty's Songs
Heavy Gravy Music Co
Heavy Jamin Music
*Hecht and Buzzell Inc
Heelstone Music
Heen Music
*Heffelfinger R W
Heffer Music Co
*Hefti Neal Music Inc
Hekima
*Helayne Music Pub Co Inc
Heldon Music Corp
   Heldon Music Co
*Helena Chappell
Helena Music Corporation
*Helen Hyman-Publisher Memb
Helenorm Music Corp
*Helf & Hager Co
Heljo Music
   Master Music Company
Heller Fred Enterprises Ltd
   (Fred Heller Music Div)
Hello There Music Publishing Inc
Heltman Fred
Hemidemisemiquaver Inc
Hemion & Smith Music Inc
Hemlane Music Company
Henderson & Robbins
Hendler Edward Music
Hengine Music Publishers Inc
*Henke Stern Music Co

Henmar Press Inc
   Henmar Press F
Henry Bob Productions Inc
   (Rdm Publishing Co Div)
Henscheid Ed Music
Hense Forth Music
Hensley Music Company
Herald Association Inc The
   (Heraldic Music Division)
Herald Square Music Co The
   Vido Music Co Ltd
Herbert Music Co Inc
   Fanmar Music Co
   Lutz Bros Mus Co Inc
Her-B Music
Hereford Music
Here Music
*Herford Music Division
Her Highness Music Company
Heritage Roads Music
Herman Jerry Inc
Herman Music Inc
   Mega Music
Hermine Publishing
Hero Dunlee Music Co Div
Herman Danny Music Pub Co
Herschel's Music Publisher
Hersey Music
Hershkin Music
Hetzer Theatrical Productions
H G Music Inc
H & G Randall Inc
H & H Team Music
Hiawatha Music Co
Hibiscus Music Company
Hice Haus Music
Hickey Doo Music
Hickory Grove Music Co
*Hi Cue Productions
Hi Cue Productions/Pacsa Mus Pub
   Hi Cue Productions
   Pacsa Music Publishers
Hidden Hills Productions Inc
   (Hidden Hills Publishing Co Div)
Hideaway Music
Hideout Records/Distribtrs Inc
   (Gear Publishing Div)
Hide the Man Music
Hidey Ho Music Co
Hido Music
High Bluff Music
Higher Music Publishing Inc
Highest Swan Music
High Falutin' Music
High Fidelity Music
High Flush Music Ltd
High Flying Music
Highgate Assoc Ltd
   (Gwynell Music Division)
Highmeadow Music Co
*High Road Music
High Sierra Music
High Wave Music Inc
Hilaria Music Inc
Hi Larr Music
Hilkert Music
Hillcrest Music Corp
*Hilliard Bob Music Co
*Hill J F & Co Inc
Hillman-Warner Music Co
Hillmark Inc
*Hill May Music
Hillsdale Music Inc
Hilltop Productions Co Inc
   (Hilltop Acres Music Division)
Hilltop Road Music
Hilmer Music Publishing Co
*Himan Alberto Music Pub
*Hindu Music Division
Hinshaw Music Inc
Hipolit Music
Hirsch Win Music Co
Hirt Music Inc
His People's Music Inc
His Son Audio Corp of America
His Way Ministries
   Frankincense & Myrrh Record Div
Hit and Run Music
Hit City Publishing Inc
Hi Ti Music Corporation
   Ray Music Co
Hit Music Publishers
Hittage Music
Hi-Watts Music
H L G Music Corp
H M S Two Enterprise Ltd
Hobadaba Music

Hobbitron Enterprises Inc
Hobsong Music Inc
Hoceanna Music
*Hodmarc Music Inc
Hoffermusic Inc
Hoffman Al Songs Inc
Hoffman Dan Music
*Hog Music Inc
Hohman Publishers
Holbrook Tom Music
Hold Out Music
Holland Dozier Holland Music Inc
Hollander Gail
Holland Fisher Music Publishrs
Hollbrand Music Publishers
Holley Fish Music
Holliday Publications
Hollodan Music
Holloway Music Publishers Inc
Hollow Point Music Ltd
Hollow Well Music
Hollybrook Music Co Inc
Holly Hill Music Publishing Co
*Holly Pix Music Publishing Co
Hollywattz Productions
*Hollyweed Music Division
Hollywood Boulevard Music
Hollywood Music Enterprises Ltd
Hollywood Spectrum Inc
   (H S Music Division)
Holman Bill Music
Holmby Music Corp
Holmes Don Music
Holmes Line of Music Inc The
Holmes & Mancini Music
*Hologram Music
*Hologram Music Division
Holograph Music
Holster Music
Holycar Music Company
Holy Cow Music
Holy Triune Music Co
Homack Publishing
Home Boy Music
Homecraft Publishing Company
Homestead Enterprises Inc
   (A Gee Jay Music Co Div)
Home Sweet Home Music
Hometown Music Co Inc
Homewood Music
Homeyer Chas W & Co Inc
Homunculus Music
Honest John Music
Honest Music
Honesty in Rock
Honey Baby Music Co
Honey Baby Music Co
   Paradise Music Corp
Honeybee Ridge Publications
*Honeycomb Music
*Honeycomb Music Inc
Honey Dew Music Company
Honeytree Music Inc
Honeywind Productions Ltd
*Hong Kong Audio Centre Inc
Hook Em Music
Hooker/Hulette Publishing
Hooks Mikel Pub Co
Hook Tree Music Company
Hoolie Music
Hoot Owl Music
Hope Publishing Company
   Biglow Main Excell Co
   Excell E O Co
   Tabernacle Pub Co
Hope Street Music
Hop's Music Company
Horizon Music Corp
‡Horizon Music Ltd
*Horizon Record Corp
Horner Music
Horn of Plenty Inc
Horn Paul Music Company
Horse Cave Music
Horse Diaper Music
Horseshoe Canyon Music
Horus Music Publishing
Hosiery Publishing Co The
Hostel Music
Hot Box Industries Inc
Hot Cider Music
*Hotei Publishing Company Div
Hotel Splendide Music
Hot Goods Publishing
Hot Kitchen Music
House Charles Publishing Co
House of Chance

House of Clouse
*House of Coburt Music Pub Inc
House of Daniel
House of Erik Music
House of Huston
House of Juses Music Publishing Co
House of Knox
House of Melton
House of Orange
House of Power Publishing Co
House of Royal Artists Co
   Hra Productions Inc
House of Showbusiness Music Publ
*House of Songs Ltd
*House of Weiss Mu Div
House of Weiss Music Co
Howard Beach Music Inc
Howard-Eglash Music Publishers
Howard Joe Music Publisher
   Howard Joe Music House
Howard Kenney Music Division
Howling Dog Music
Hownan Music Publishing Co
Howsville Music
H P Music
H P R Records
*H-Q Music Pub Inc
*Hra Productions Inc
H R Music
H R N Music Company
*H S Music Division
*H S P Music Division
Hubba Music Company
*Hubert Music Corp
Hubler Publishing Co
Hub Music Company The
Huckleberry Creek Music
Huddleston Music
Hudmar Publishing Co Inc
Hudson Music Corporation
Hudwill Productions Inc
   Roweville Music The
*Hugo & Luigi-Samuel French Music
   Publications Inc
Hulette Don Publishing
Humarock Music
Humbug Music Company
   Cher Enterprises Inc
   Progress Motion Picture Inc
Humes Music Co
Hummable Music Company
Hummit Publishing
Humphrey Bobbi Music Co
Humphrey Paul Nelson Music
*Humphries Bruce
Hundred Grand Publishing Co
Hunter Alberta Music
*Hunter Frank
*Hunter Group Ltd The
Hunter Ian Music Inc
Hunter Kevin Associates Inc
   (Black Dove Mus Division)
Hurdy Gurdy Music Co
Hurrah! Publishing
Hurt Barry E Productions Inc
   (Bar Vel Music Division)
*Hush Music Inc Div
Hutton Mamie Music
H W S Music Company
Hwy 1 Music
Hyako Music Company
   Hayako Music Company
Hyde Park Gate Music Ltd
Hydro International Music
Hy Lo Music
Hyman T Music
Hymns of Other Lands
   Stuart K Hine-Publisher
Hyphen 8 Company
*I Aint in It Music
I Am Music
I.A.M. Music
Iamonia Publishing Company
Ibedon Publishers
*Ice Age Inc
Ice Age Music
*Iceland Information Centre
Ice Music
Ice Nine Publishing Co Inc
   Ice Nine Music
Icka-Delick Music Co
Icthus Music
I Dean Publishers
I Don't Care Music
*I F E Music
*Ife Music Division
Ighner Music

Ignatius House Community
  (Sign of Gods Love Pub Div)
*I & I Music Division
Ikke-Bad Music
*Ile De France Prod Inc
*Iliad Publishing Company
I Love Life Productions Inc
I Love You Music Co
Image Records Music
Imagination Inc
I'm Hip Productions
*I M I Inc
Important Music Inc
Impulsive Music
Inagua
Incision Publishing Co
Indano Music Co
Indefinate Music
*India Music Inc
Indian Hill Music
Indian Lake Music
Indianoplace Music
Indra Music
Infinite Music Corp
Infinity Records Inc
  Infinity Music International Div
Infinity's Line Music
*In Music Co
Inner Circle Music
Inner Eye Music
Inner Peace Sounds
Inner Sounds Music
Innervision II Inc
  (Quintrac Music Division)
Innocence Music Publishing
I Nose Music
In Pocket Music
*In Rodes Music
Inside Out Music
Inspirational Sounds
  (Levan Publishing Div)
Inspiration Music Company
Instant Replay Music Company
*Institute of American Music Inc
Institute of Percussve Studies
Instructional Children's Music Inc
Insurance City Records Inc
  (Insurance City Mu Pu Div)
Integrity Music Corp
  Ile De France Prod Inc
  Packard Music Co
*Intercollegiate Syn Inc
Intercontinental Entertainment Corp
  (Bare Back Music Division)
Intercontinental Music Inc
Intergalactic Music Inc
*Interglobal Music Div
Interglobal Record Corp
  (Interglobal Music Div)
*Internacionales Ed Music Y
  Representaciones
International Artist Ltd
  Bel Canto Publishing Co
International Aten Music
International Doorway Music
International Harp Corp
International Kaleidoscope Prod Inc
International Korwin Corp
  Hefti Neal Music Inc
  Korwin Music Inc
International Music Associates Inc
  (Tele Film Music Company Div)
International Music World
International Paragon Music Publ
International Pauline Corp
  Pauline Music Inc
*International Variety Associates
Interplay Music
Intersong U S A Inc
  Paris Music Co Inc
*In the Black Music Div
In the Money Music
*Intimate Music Corp
Int'L Entertainment Management
  International Variety Associates
Intrada Publishing Company
Invisible Inc
*Ipanema Music Co
Ipanema Music Corp
  Color Me Productions
  Jelly Bean Productions
Iramac Music
  Ira Music
Ireneadele Publishing Co
Irish Lad Music
Irish Setter Songs
*Iris Publications Div

Irma's Music
Iron Blossom Music
Iron Fist
Ironside Music
*Iron Skillet Music Division
Ironweed Music
Irotas Publishing Co
Irreptuous Music
Irwin Mark Productions Inc
  Mark Irwin Productions Inc
*Irwin Richard Music Pub Co
Iryce Music Publishing Co
Isakabani Publishing Company
Isle City Music
Isle of Rose Music
Isom Music Publishing
I S P D Publishing
I T A M Music Publishing Co
Itpan Music Publishers Inc
Itsil Music
Iva-Con Music Company
Ivanhoe Music Inc
I've Got the Music Co
Ivory Palaces Music Publ Co Inc
*Ivy Music Corporation
I Want It All Publishing
*Iwo Music Pub Co Inc
Ixolib Music
*Izanada Music Corp
Jabali Music
Jabberock Mgmt Inc
  (Jmi Publishing Division)
Jabern Music Company
Jachrick
*Jack and Bill Music Co
*Jackaroe Music Publishers Div
*Jack Bill Mu Co Tb Harms
Jack Do Music Inc
Jack Sky Productions
Jacktone Music Corp
Jac Music Company Inc
  Jac Music Co
Jacobi Music Co
Jacobs Fred Music
Jacobs Sam Publishing Co
Jacobs Walter Inc
  Abt Valentine
  Bates & Bendix
  Bendix Theodore
  Eby Walter M
  Farrand Van L
  Gay Mace Catalog
  Jacques Percy
  Musiclover Co
  Partee C L Music Co
  Shattuck B E
  Virtuoso Music School
Jacogg Publications Inc
*Jacqueline Music Corp
Jadber Music Inc
Jaga Music Co
Jahmilla Music Inc
J A H M Music
*Jahn Stephen W Co Inc
Jai-Rai Productions
Ja Jan Publishing Co
Jakolm Publishing Co Inc
Jalapeno Music
Jalmar Press
Jalni Publications Inc
Jamaica Reggae Music Inc
*Ja Ma Music
Jamarnie Music Inc
Jambitt Music
*Jamb Productions Music Div
Jamersonian Music
James Frank Music
Jamesland Records
  (Jamesland Records Div)
  Rovonco Productions
*James V Monaco Inc
James Woody Music
Jamian Music
Jamilou Music Publications
Jam-It Publishing Co
Jamtone Music
Jan-A-Baby Music
Jan-Al Music Co
Jando Music Inc
Janee Music
Janeiro Music Co
Janew Music
Janfin Music Co Inc
Janfred Music
Janis Byron Music Publishing Co
Janis Music Company
Jan-Lee Music

Janlynn Publishing Co
*Jan Mur Music Corp
Janmur Music Corp
  Jan Mur Music Corp
Jansa Music
*Jansan Publishing Co Div
Jansco Music
Japet Music Publishers
Japonicia Music
J & A Publishing & Distribution
*Jaques Percy
Jarak Music
Jarane Publishing Co
Jarest Music Company
Jarmago Music Pub Co
*Jarrett Music Division
Jarrett Records Intern'L Inc
Jasmine Music Company
Jasong Music
Jasperilla Music Co
Jayar Publishing Company
  Rich Little Productions Inc
Jaybar Music Co
Ja-Beers Music Pub Co
Jay Bek Inc
  Jay Bek Melodies Divisio
Jay Box Music
Jaycouey Pub Co
Jaydink Music Ltd
Jayen Music Publishing Inc
Jay IV Company The
Jay Kay Music Corp
Jaylo Music Company
Jay Love Music Corp
  Love Jay Music Corp
  Teeger Music Co
Jay Music
Jay's Enterprises Inc
Jaystar Music
Jaytone Music Co
*Jayvee Music Pub Co
Jaze Music Publishing
Jazz Bird Music
Jazz Corporation Music
Jazz Education Press
J B J Music Co
J B W Publishing Co
J C E Publishing Co
J C Music Co
J D H Music Company
J D Wall Publishing Company
*Jeanne Ursula Schmidt Productions
Jeannie Is Music Inc
Jeannie Music
Jebsy Music Co
Jeddrah Music
J E D O Music
Jefferson Music Co Inc
Jefferson Wayne Productions
Jeffix Music Co
Jeffreys Alan Music Company
Jeffries' Michael Music
Jegs Music Company
Jehovah-Jireh Music
J-88 Music
Jelco Music Inc
*Jelly Bean Productions
Jellybean Tree Music
Jem Entertainment Corp
  (Gaylene Music Div)
Jemijo Music Co
*Jem Publications
Jena Music Publishing Co
Jenimmy
Jenkins Gordon Inc
  Bryant Music Co
  Gordon Murray Mus Corp
  Gordon Music Corp
Jennifer Music Inc
Jennings John Music Company
Jennykat Music
Jennylin Company
Jenny Music Inc
Jensen Gordon Publishing Inc
*Jensen Music
Jenson Publications Inc
Jerden Music Inc
  (Marinwood Music Pub Div)
Jeremy Music Inc
  Gesner Music Inc
Jergenson Productions
Jericho Christian Ctr Mus Pub Co
Jericho Music Corp
Jer-Jer Productions Inc
Jernet Productions
*Jerome M K
*Jerome Music Corp

*Jerome & Schwartz Pub
Jerona Music Corporation
*Jerrold Music
Jerryco Music Co
*Jerry Dexter Prod Inc
Jeru Music
Jester Music Co
Jesus Music
*Jesus People
Jevon Music Co
Jevy Music Co The
Jewel Music Publishing Co Inc
  Allied Music Corp
  Green & White Inc
  Green Bros & Knight Inc
  Harman Music Inc
  Park Ridge Music Corp
Jewelyard Music
Je'Wilm Music
Jezreel Music Inc
J F S Music Pub Co
*J G K Music Ltd
J H K Publishing Co
J & H Publishing Company
Jihno Music Co
Jill Billy Music
*Jill Music Ltd
Jillybean Music
*Jiloral Music
Jimbob Music Company
*Jimeve Music Co Div
Jim Jean Music
*Jim Ro Music
Jiru Music Inc
*Jjm Records
J & J Ross Co
J K L M Enterprises Inc
J L E Publishing
J L P Music Company
*J L S Music Division
J L T Christian Agape Music Co
*Jmi Publishing Division
*J M Music Ltd
J & N Publishing Co
Jo-Al Music Company
  Curb Mike Prod Inc
*Joaneline Music Inc
Jobar Music Publishing
Jobete Music Company Inc
  Stein Van Stock Inc
J O B Music
Jocin Publishing Company
Jockey Music Inc
Jo Depca Publishing
Jodi Music Co
Jodrell Music Inc
Joe and Sons Music
Joe Dayna Music
Joekat Music Company
Joeldee Music Publishers
Joeneil Music Co
*Joey Brooks Productions Inc
Jog Music Publishers
Johanna Music
*John Berthelot & Assoc Ltd
John-George Music
*John Hill Productions Inc
John-John Publishing Co
*John Mc Clure Music Division
*Johnny Mathis Music Inc
Johnny Moon Music
John Paul Music
*John Paul Music Corp
John Penny Enterprises Inc
  (Jo-Penn Music Division)
Johnsen R A Inc
  (Goro Music Co Division)
  Goro Music Co Division
Johnston Jim Music
John Street Rescources
Joint Session Music Publishing Co
Joleron Music Corp
Joli Tinker Publishing Co
Jolly Music Ltd
Jolly Rogers Publishing Co
Jomona Music Co
Jonan Music Inc
Jonathan Music Co Inc
  Ruckle Music Co
*Jones Isham Music Corp
Jones Jack Music Company
Jones Mickey Music
Jones-Wallis Music
Jonico Music Inc
Jon Mil Best Music
Jonsie Music
Jon Tees Music Publishers

Jools Music
Joowave Music
Jopell Music
*Jo-Penn Music Division
Jop Music Co
Jordan-Herman-Holmes Pub Inc
   Plus Two Music Co Inc
Jordan Smedley Music
Jorob Music
Jo Ro Music Corp
*Joseph Boonin Inc
*Joseph E Levine Music Corp
Joseph Music
Joshada Music
*Josie Music Publishing Co Inc
Jostep Publishing Co
Joto Music
Jova Music Publ Co
Jowag Music
Joy in the Morning Music
*Joy Music Inc
Joyna Music
Joyson Music Corp
Joy & Sorrow Music
J P B Music Corporation
J P Group Music
J R S Productions
J'Sali Music
J S G Music Co
J S H Music
J S T Music
J Supreme Music
Jth Music
Jubilee Music Inc
*Ju Bop Music Division
Jucu Music
Jude Anne Music Co
Jude Mude Music Inc
Judy Carol Music
*Judy Music Company
Jugumba Music
Juke Box Alley
Juke Box Music
*Juke Joint Music
*Juke Joint Music Div
Julibu Music
Julie H Music
Julijon Music Company
July Two Publishing
Jumping Jack Music
Jump-In Music
Jung Bob Music Publishing Co
Jungle Church Music
Jungle City Music
*Jungnickel Ross Inc
Jun Music Company
Junonia Corporation
Justin Case Music Publishing Co
Justin-Thyme Music Co
Just Jim Music
   Jjm Records
*Juvents Ed Music
J W T Music Inc
Kabsha Music
*Kacy Music Publishing Co
Kadima Productions Inc
Kaercea Music Enterprises Inc
Kafka Music Co
*Kagran Films Inc
*Kahanmoku Duke Music Corp
Kahn Gus Music Co
*Kajac Record Corporation
Kaleb Music Company
Kalehoff Edd Productions Inc
   (Kalehoff Music Division)
Kalman Music Inc
*Kalmar Puck & Abrahams
*Kalmar & Ruby Music Corp
Kalmus Edwin F
Kalopa Music Co
Kamaaina Music Ltd
   Diamond Head Music Pub Co
   Duke Kahanmoku Music Corp
   Kahanmoku Duke Music Corp
Kamakura Music
Kama Rippa Music Inc
Kami Records Inc
   (Tamiami Music Division)
Kanarsala Music
Kaneil Music Co
Karen Company
Karin Music
Karla Music Publishing
   Karla Music Co
Karleigh Music Co
Karlin Fred Music Co
Karmic Music Inc

*Karolann Music Co Div
Karp Michael Music
Karronnie Musik Bernd Lichters
Kartman Ronnie Productions Inc
K-Arts Inc
   (Rubber Frog Music Division)
Kasinski Music Publishing Co
Kassner Edward Music Co Inc
   Grosvenor Music Co Ltd
   Kassner Ed Music Co Ltd
   Lennox Cecil Ltd
   Norris J Music Pub Co Ltd
   Twentieth Century Music
Kat Bell Music Co
Kates Songs
Katikris Music Company
Katona Publishing Company
Katsim Music Publishing
Kavel Productions Inc
   Harpeth Music
   Harpeth Music Div
Kawai
*Kaycee Music Co Inc
*Kayday Music Inc
*Kaye Buddy Music Co
Kay Edward Music Co
Kaye/Smith Music Inc
Kayhil Music Co
Kay Jack Music
*Kay & Kay Inc
*Kaymor Productions Inc
Kay Pee Music
Kayteekay Music Inc
*Kazum Publishing Corp
Kazzom Inc
   (Kazzoom Music Division)
Kbanda Music Company
K C M Music
Kearney Music Company
*Ke Bo Music Corp
Keca Music Inc
   Leemerton Music
*Kec Music Inc
Ked Music Productions
Kee Lee Music
Keen Stan Productions Inc
Keep Up the Pace Music Publishing
Kef Music Inc
Keintunen Music
*Keit Engel Inc
Keith Music
Keith-Valerie Music Corp
*Keit Music Corp
Kelbar Music
*Kel-Jon Music Division
*Kelkay Music Division
*Kell-Chris Music
Kell Chris Music Inc
   Kell-Chris Music
Kellem Milton Music Co Inc
Keller Jack Music
Kelly and Lloyd Music
Kelly Ann Music
Kelly Roger Paul Music
   Roger Paul Kelly Music
*Kelton Inc
Kenbob Music Company Inc
Kendra Music Inc
*Kendra Music Special Acc
Kengorus Music
Ken Jan Music
Kennedy Sanford Enterprises Inc
   (Sandva Music Publishing Div)
Kenneth Copeland Ministries
   (Kel-Jon Music Division)
Kennett Music Co
Kenney Howard Enterprises Inc
   (Howard Kenney Music Div)
Kenpen Music Publishing Co
Kenrou Music
Kensho Music
Kent Arthur Music Co
*Kentco Publishing
Kent Kelly Ltd
Kent Walter Music Co
   Songs Inc
Kenvad Music Inc
Kenwall Publishing Company Inc
Kenya Music Inc
   Kenya Music
*Kenyon Music Corp
Kenyon Publications
Kenzo Music Company Inc
   African Sounds Inc
Keogh Patrick Music
Kerith Music Publishing Co

Kernochan Sarah
   Kernochan Enterprises Inc
*Kerwin Music Co Inc
Kevrick Music
Keyes Gilbert Music Company
Keyhole Music
Keystone Music Co/California
Keystone Music Publications
Key-Tar Music Publishing
K-Four Music
Kgin Music
Khan Chaka Music
Kichelle Music
*Kickapoo Music Company
Kick-A-Rock Music Inc
Kickerillo Company
Kicking Bear Music
Kidd Eliot Music Publishing Inc
*Kid Music Ltd
Kidney Punch Music Inc
Kids Capers Music
Kidstuff Music Inc
Kilead Music
Kilroy Terri Records
Kiman Music
Kimberly Music Corp
   Calypso Music Inc
Kimlyn Music Co
Kimo
Kimtra Music
Kind Favor Music
   Benno Music Co
King Charles E
King Cleo Music
King Coal Music Inc
King Davis Publishing
*King Drive Music Co Division
*King Irving Music Co
King Konk Music
King Michael W Music
*Kings Crown Music Press Div
Kings Highway Publishing Co
*Kingsland Pu Company Div
Kingsley Sound Inc
   Kingsley Sounds Inc
King Solomon Music
King Street Music
*Kingsway Music Corp
King's X Music
*King Tut Music Division
Kinlu Music
Kinship Music Inc
Kipahulu Music Co
Kipner Stephen A Music
Kips Bay Music
   Kips Bay Music Inc
K I Records Inc
   (K I Music Division)
Kirk Jim Music
Kirshner/April Music Publishing
   Kec Music Inc
   Kirshner Songs Inc
*Kirshner Songs Inc
Kiss
Kissedstar Music
Kiss Music Co
*Kiss Songs Inc
Kitai Music
Kitty Anne Music Co Inc
Kittyhawk Music
K Jet Publishing Company
K J G Music
K Jo Music Co
Klancey Music
Klein/David
Klein Michael Music Co
Klenco Music Inc
Klesmer Music
Klessic Music
Klingklang Inc
Klugh Earl Music
K M B A Music Publishing Co
K M V Enterprises Inc
Knee Trembler Music
Knob Industries Corp
   (Canadian Sunset Mus Div)
Knobs Publishing Co (Music)
   Knobs Music Pub Co
Knockout Music Company
Knock's Merry Farm Ltd
Knollwood Music Corporation
Know Music
Know One Nose Music
*Koala Music Div
Koala Music Inc
*Koala Records Inc
Koan Music

Kodi Music
*Koff Enterprises Inc
Koff Music Co
Kohaw Music Inc
Koinonia
Kokalu Music
Koker Music Co
Kokomo Music
Koko Music Company
Komack Co Inc
K O Music
Konigsberg Franklin Music Co
Kool Running Music
Kootenai Cafe Music
Kopita Murry Music Publications
   Murko Music Corp
Koppel Music
*Korner Alexis Music Div
*Kornheiser Phil Inc
*Korwin Music Inc
Koslen G Jonah Music Co
Kradar Music Company
Kramer-Whitney Inc
   Beaux Arts Music Inc
K-Redd Music
Krellophon Music
*Krey Geo M Co
Krishane Music Co
Kris-Kath Music Productions
K & R Music Inc
Krofft Sid & Marty Productions Inc
Krumal Frank K Management Inc
   (Mont Pleasant Music Division)
*Krumpkin Music Division
Krunch Music Inc
K-Sol Music
K & T Publishing
Kudu Music Company
Kuhn Tunes
Kuklapolitan Music Co
Kumqua-Tadda
Kunjani Music
Kuptillo Music
Kurley Music
Kuro Productions Inc
   (Sephra Music Div)
Kuumba
Kwame Music Corp
K & W Music Inc
Kyknos Cantos Music Inc
Kylelloyd-T N T
Kysar Michael Publisher
La Barbara Joan
La Brea Music
Labyris Music Co
Lacosta Music Inc
*Lacour Lucien
Lac Qui Parle
*Lad Music Inc
Ladnar Music
Ladybugs Garden Productions Inc
Lady-Fire Productions Inc
   (Lady-Fire Music Co Div)
Lady Gwendolyn Music
Lady Laverne Music
Lady Mac Music Company
Lady Pops Publishing
   Popwell Robert L
Ladysmith Music Inc
Laerteas Music Co
   Ernie Wilkins Publishing Co
   Larry Douglas Publishing Co
   Tito Puente Publishing Co
Laetrec Music Inc
La Faye Publishing
Lafftune Music Company
Lag Music
Lagoony Tunes
Laguna Music Publishing Co
L A I M Music Inc
La Jade Music
Lake Bonnie Productions
Lake Shore Publishing Co Inc
Lakwill Publishing Co
Lamas Music Corp
Lamminations Music
L A Music Publishing Company
Lance Jay Music Company
Lance Milt Music
Landau Music
Landers Rick Limited
   (Rickshaw Music Pub Co Div)
*Landers-Roberts Inc Div
Landers-Roberts Music
   Arianna Music Co
   Horizon Record Corp
   Now Music Division

Landesberg Music Company
Landis Richard Enterprises Ltd
(Portobello Road Mu Div)
Landsburg Alan Productions Inc
(Landsburg Alan Music Div)
Landslide Music
Lane Center International Mus Pub
Lane J Weldon Music Co
Lange John Music Co
Marlan Music Co
Lang Percussion Co
Language of Sound Inc
Laniki Music Company
Lan-Oak Music
*Lansbury Edgar
Lansdowne Music Publishers
*Lansing Music Corp
Lantz Music Corporation
La Nuit Blanche
La Paz Music Company
La Perchia Alex Music
Larbaco Music
Largo Music
*L'Aries Music Corp
Lark Ellen Music
Larksongs
La Ross Music
Larrabee Music Room
*Larry Douglas Publishing Co
Larsen Neil Publishing
*Larste Music Division
La Salle Music Publishers Inc
Gilbert L Wolfe Mus Pub
Schuster Miller Inc
Lasapa
Lasley David Music
Las Palmas Music
Lassie Publishing Co
Lasting Music
Last Line Music
Last Music Company The
Last Warrior Music
La Symphonie Publishing
Late Great Music
Late Nite Music
Latest Craze Music
Latin Percussion Inc
(Latin Percusion Ven Div)
*Lato Music Division
Lattanzi Music
Latter Days Music
Latter Rain Music
*Laughing Bird Songs Publishing Div
Laughing Willow Co Inc The
(Laughing Willow Music Co Div)
Laumor Music Corp
L A Uptown Music Inc
Laura-Donn/Ninki Music
*Laurel Canyon Music
Laurel Canyon Music Ltd
Laurel Canyon Music
Sioux City Music Ltd
*Laurel Music Corporation
Laurelwood Music Pub Co
Lauren Kim Music
Lauriadel Enterprises Inc
*Laurie House Music Division
Laurie Productions Inc
(Vibar Music Division)
*Laursteed Music Company
Lawler Ltd
Lawpub Music
L A W Recording Studio Inc
Lawrence Jason Music Inc
Sanjud Music Co Inc
*Lawrence Music Pub Inc
Lawrence Ray Music
Law Richard Music
Lawson-Gould Music Publ Inc
*Lawton Clarence Mus Div
Lawton George N Music
Lawton Records Inc
(Lawton Clarence Mus Div)
Master Five Music Div
Laydos Music
Layla Bree Music
Lay Low Music
Lazumma Music
Lazy Libra Music
Lazy River Publishing Co
L D J N Music Corp
*Leading Music Ltd
Leadweight Music Publishing
Leah Music Co
Lean-Jean Music Publishers
Lear Inc
Learned Man Publishing Co

Learning Party The
Learoy Music Corp
Leaves in October
Leawood Music Corp
Lebasongs
Le'Boonette Publishing Co
Lebowsky Tobias Enterprises
(Tobias Legowsky Music Div)
Le Clair Jos Musical Enterprise
Ledaclan Music
Leddel Music
*Lednam Music Co
Leeba Music
Lee Dar Music
Leeds Music Corp
Block Martin
Bob Miller Inc
Cavalcade Music Corp
Consolidated Mus Pub Hou
Down Home Music Co
Embee Music Corp
Garland Music Inc
Kaycee Music Co Inc
Mayo Music Corp
Old Homestead Pub Co
Olman Music Corp
Out of the World Mus Co
Pla A Song Co
Rosewood Music Corp
Shamley Music
Sprague Coleman Inc
Streamline Editions
Wabash Music Co
Lee Evie Music
Leemaur Music
*Leemerton Music
*Lee Van Cleef Music
Le Fave Company The
Left Track Publishing
*Legal Tender Music Div
Lego Music
Legomyego Music Inc
Lehua Music Co
Leidasnow Music
Leigh Mitch Corporation The
Leigh Music Co
Leigh Ron Music
*Lektrafon Music Co
Lemley Ty Music
*Lemon Music Corp
Lemon Tree Music Inc
Bridgton Music Ltd
Lena-Dawn Music
Lennie Tristano Jazz Found Inc
C & C Jazz
*Lennox Cecil Ltd
Lenny Publishing Inc
Lenore Music
Leona Publishing Corporation
Leonarda Productions Inc
Leonard Hal Publishing Corp
Hal Leonard Music Inc
Hal Leonard Pointer Pub Inc
Leonard Jack Music
Leonardo Da Vinci Music
Leonard-Worth Songs
Leon Music Co
Le Oria Music
Leosel Enterprises Inc
Leo's Lair Music
Le Palms Publishing Co
Lerner Music
Lerner Samuel M Publications
Lero Music Co
El Dorado Music Co
Leslie Ann Gary Music Publ Co
Leslie Edgar
Leslie Music Corp
*Les Mc Cann
Leson International Inc
Leson International
*Leson Music Division
Les-Ron Music Co
Lesser Music
Lester Wilson Music Company
Let Music
Let's Make Music
Let There Be Music
Levanova Music
*Levan Publishing Div
Le Veck Music
Levida Music Publishing Co
Levine-Mchugh Music Pub Corp
*Levin Glenn Music Div
Levinson/Link Music
Levy Lou Music Company Inc
Pell Mell Music Co

Lewis Bobby J Music
Lewis Music Publishing Co Inc
Lewis Ramsey Music Co
Lewis Ray Enterprises
Lew-Lou Music Co
Lexicon Music Inc
Children of the Day
Children of the Day Publishing
Lexicon Music Co
Libation Music
Liben Music Publishers
*Liberty Songs Inc
Libra-Universal Music Co
Libretto Music Co
Licorice Lunch Music
Lida Enterprises Inc
Li Debco
Life Music Inc
Life Tree Music
Light I Publishing
Light Joe Company The
(Blue Streak Music Division)
Lightning Production
Light Wing Music
Likely Story Music Company
Likewise Music Publishing
Li'L Bits & the Witch
Lilli Music Company
Limbeaux Music
Limbridge Music Corp
Limerick Music Corp
Limousine Music Co
*Lincoln Harry J Music Co
Lincoln Mall Music Inc
Lincoln Music Corp
Capano Frank Music Pub
Lindabet Music Corp
Linda Carol Music
Linda S Music Corp
Lindley Music Publishing Co
Linell Music
Lion Dog Music
Lioness Music Publishing Company
Lion Music Corporation
Lion of Judah Music
Lion's Gate Films Inc
(Lion S Gate Music Co Div)
Lion's Pride Music
*Lions Roar Music
Lipton Music
Lipton Music Inc
Lisa-Ann Music Co
Lisa Michelle Music Co
*Lisa Music Co
Lisa Sue Music Inc
Merry Sounds
Lisette Music Co
Lissauer Robert Company
Lad Music Inc
Michele Music Inc
Mode Music Inc
Robert Lissauer Publishing Corp
Treble Music Pub Inc
Listen and Think Records
Lite-White Music Publishing Inc
Litha Music Co
Little Bear Music Inc
Littleberry Productions
Little Bird Music
Little Booma Music Co
Little Caesar Music
Little Cat Publishing Co Inc
Little Cowboy Music
Little Dickens Music Publisher
Little Dickens Publishing Co
Little Dog Music Inc
Little Felix Music
Little Gravel Music Publishing Inc
Little House Music
Little Jug Music Inc
Little Lasso Music
Little Macho Music Co Inc
Little Marge Publishing Co
Little Music House
Little Neck Music Co
Little Peanut Music Company
Little Pin Publishing Co
Little Tiger Music
Little White House Music
Little Willie Music Co
Litt Music Publishing Corp
Hunter Group Ltd The
Kazum Publishing Corp
Live Oak Music
Live Time Music
Living Room Music
Living Sea Corporation

Livingston & Evans Inc
Living Waters Music Publisher
Liza Music Corp
Lizard Music
*Liz Bet Music Inc
L J K Music Company
L K L Music
L-K Productions Inc
L M N O P Music
Lobek Music
Monitor Music Service Corp
Lobis Music Company
Lochaerie Music Company
Lock Music Co
Locksmith Music
Locust Inc
(Erin Lane Music Division)
Locus Universal
Lodell Music
Loeb John Jacob Co Music Publ
*Loeb Lissauer Inc
*Loena Music Publishing Co Div
*Loews Inc
Loganberry Music
Logger Music
Loghaven Music
*Loma Alta Music Co
Lomanato Music Inc
Loma Vista Publishing Co
Lombardo Music Inc
Londontown Music Inc
Lone Lake Songs Inc
Lonely Wind Music
Lone Oak Publications
Loney Tunes Music
Longdog Music
*Long Hubert International
Long Island Presents Soul
Long Lasting Music Co
Longridge Music Inc
Henke Stern Music Co
Long-Run Music Company
*Long Valley Publishing Div
Longwood Music Corp
Lonna Music
Lookout Music Company
Loop Music Publishing Co
Lopez V Music Co
Loraless
Lorbek Music
Lord Byron Music
Lorenz Industries
Lorenz Publishing Co
Tullar Meredith Co Inc
Lorenzo Music Inc
Loresta Music
Lorido Music
*Lorimar Prod Inc
Lorjay Music Inc
Lorjay Music Company
Lormax Music Publishing Co
Loronson Publishing
Lorry Music
Los Moreno Music
Lost Continent Music Publishing
Lost Highway Music
*Lothlorien Music Div
Lottimer Publishing Co
Lotts of Miles Music
Louise/Jack Publishing Inc
Louise Please Music
Love Bone Trade
Love Craft Music
Love House Music
*Love Jay Music Corp
Lovett Music Ltd
Lowball Music Inc
Low Dog Music Company
*Lowe Music Corp
Lowe Music Publishing Corp
Lowe Music Corp
Lower Arcade Music Co
Lox and Hegel's Music
Loyd Randy Music
L R M Music
L S Music
L T D Inc
Mc Rovscod Music
Luann Records
Luba Music
Lucero Enterprises
Lucia Music Co
Lucifer Records & Publishing Co Inc
*Luckhardt & Belder
Lucky Bear Music Inc
Lucky-Break
Lucky Charm Music Inc

Lucky Man Music
Lucky Pork Music
  Lucky Pork Publishing
Lucky Publishing Company
Lucky's Kum-Ba-Ya Publishing Co
Lu-Cor Music Co
*Ludding House Music Pub Mgmt Ltd
Lukehil Productions Inc
  (Lukehil Music Division)
Lukey Toones
Lu Mac Music Publishing Co
Lu-Mel Music
  Lu-Mel Music Inc
Lunch Mouth Music
Luney Tunes Productions
Lunswaltz Music
Lupe Music Co
Lupercalia Music Publ Co Inc
Luristan Music Inc
Lute Music Company
*Lutz Bros Mus Co Inc
Luvismusic
*Luz Bros Music Pub
Lydian Pines Music
Lyelpa Music
Lyharp Music Publishing Co
Lyndon Music
*Lynne Jeff
Lyonsville Music Company
Lyra Music Company
*Lyre Productions Ltd
Lyvia Music
Maasai Music
Mabry Betty Music Co
Mabs Music Co
Macaroni Music
Macaroon Publishing
*Macclesfield Music
*Mac Davis Music Division
Macharmony Music
Mach I Music Ltd
Machismo Music
Mackay David Enterprises
Mackle Music
Mack Lenny Music
Mac Marstan Music Co
*Macmelodies Ltd
Macmillan Performing Arts Inc
*Macmillan Performing Arts Mus Div
Macondo Music
Macroida Publishing
Mac's Million Music
Madara John Enterprises Ltd
  (Young Ideas Publ Div)
Madd Publishing
Made in Heaven Music
Madelyn Music
*Madison Mus Co
Madman Music Co
Mad Man's Drum Music
Mad Meece Music
Madrid Music Co
Madrigal Music Company
Mad World Music
Maelstrom Music
Mae Rich Music
*Maestro Mus Publ Corp
Mafundsalo Music
Magewind Music Inc
Magic Belly Music
Magic Carpet Music Ltd
Magic Closet Music
Magic 5 Music Company
Magicland Music
Magic Mouth Music
Magic Music
Magic Touch Music
Magidson Music Co Inc
  Magidson Music Co
Magijomi Music Inc
Magnamusic-Baton Inc
Magnanimous Music
  Bobby Tunes Inc
  Forum Music Inc
Magnetic Music Publishing Co
Mahalo Music Co
Mahkinda Music
Maiden Voyage
Main Event Inc
  (Main Event Publ Div)
Mainman Ltd
Mainsail Music Ltd
Mainspring Music Corp
Mainspring Watchworks Music
Main Stave Music Co
Main Street Music

Main St Studios Music
Majestic Music Company
Maj Music Corp
Major A Publishing Co
Major Oak Music Co
Major Songs Co
Makamint Music
  (Makamint Music Div)
*Makani Publishing
Makanume Music
Makeba Music Corporation
Make Me Smile Music
Make Mine Music
Make Music
*Makin Music Division
Malachite Music
Malatto Music
Malcom Publishing Co
*Malden Music Corp
Malerin Music Company
Malibooz Music
Malicious Melodies
Malin Music Inc
Malison Music Company
Mallet Head Music Productions
Malneck Music
Mal/Rac Music
Mal Savore Publishing
M Al's Production
*Maltby Richard Inc
*Maltby-Shire Productions Inc
Malted Milk Music
Malvern Music Co
  Rhyme & Rhythm Inc
Malvin Arthur Music Co
Mama Reno Music
*Mamazon Music Co
M A M Coporation
Manacor Music Co Inc
Management Communications Inc
  (Mancom Music Division)
*Manchester Music Inc
Mancini Henry Enterprises Inc
  (Hollyweed Music Div)
  Hollyweed Music Division
Mancini Music Publishing Co
*Mancom Music Division
Mancuso Music Co
*Mandate Music Co Inc
Mandell Patt Music
Mandy Kaye Music
Mandy Music
Manikin Music Co
Manks Chaw Blue Ribbon Music Co
  Blue Ribbon Music Co
*Manlowe Music Corp
Man Made Music
*Mannafest Music Division
Manna Music Inc
Mann C
Mann David Music Company
Manne Kind Music
Manners Music
Mann Herbie Music Corp
Manomet Music Inc
Manor Music Company Inc
Mansfield Music Co Inc
*Mansion Music Corp
Manticore Music Ltd
Mantis Record Corp
  (Starstepper Mu Division)
Manton Music
  Groton Music Co Inc
Manuscript Music Corp
  Maltby-Shire Productions Inc
*Manus Music Co Inc
Many Mansions Music
Maple Music Inc
Maplewood Music Company Inc
Mappa Music Inc
Mappo Time Period Music Co
*M A Publisher
M & A Publishing Co
*Mara Lane Music Corp
Maranatha Music
*Marapunta-Shayne Co Inc
Maraville Music Corp
Marbert Publishing Company
Marble Lady Music
Marbo Music
Marc D Michael Music Pub Co
Marcelino Music
*March Music
March on Music
March Three Music
Mardee Productions Inc
  (Mardee Music Division)

*Marechiaro Casa Edit
Ma Ree Music Inc
Margery Music Inc
Margin Music Co
Margouleff Robert J
  C M P Inc
*Marguerita Music Inc
Marhan Music Inc
Maria Music Publicity
Marian Music Corporation
Marick Studios
Marilor Music
  Lorimar Prod Inc
Marilyn-Kristi Music Co Inc
Marine Music Corporation
*Marinwood Music Pub Div
Marissa Music
  Ledman Music Co
Marius Music Co
Mar Kay Publishing Co Inc
  (Kelkay Music Division)
Marke Music Publishing Co Inc
*Mark Irwin Productions Inc
Markovian Music
Marks Tey Music Co
Mark Vii Music
*Marlan Music Co
Marlene Publishing Co
*Marlen Music Co
Marley Bob Music Ltd
Marlindeaux Music
Marlo Music Corp
Marlong Music Corp
Marlu Music
Marnel Music Co Inc
*Marpet Music Corp
*Marquez Hnos
Marquis Enterprises
  Warren Rusty Publishing
Marrano Lana Music
Marshall Jerry Music Publishing Co
Marshfield Music Co
  Andrew Wiswell Productions Inc
  Hanseatic Music Corp
Marshua Music Company
Marsh Warne Music
*Mars Records Inc
Martin Coulter Music Inc
*Martin Coulter Music Ltd
*Martinelli Music
Martin Music
Martin Quinn Music Company
Martin William Music Co
Martu Music Inc
Maruzzi Music
Marvin Music Company
Marvy Music
Marx Andrew Music
Marx Joseph Music Co
  Estate of Josef Marx
Mary Beth Music
*Mary Co Music
Maryon Music Co
Mase Publishing Corp
Maser Music Publishing Corp
  Grimes Music Pub
Mason Barry Inc
Manikin Music Co
Masong Music
Massaro Publishing Company
*Massey Music Co Inc
Mass Unity Sounding in Concert
  Babell Music Company
Master Audio Inc
  Pay Dirt Music
Master Fisherman
*Master Five Music Div
Master Link Music
*Master Music Company
Master Music Makers Music Pub Co
Master Sound Studios Inc
  (Legal Tender Music Div)
Masters Publishing House
Mastoid Music Ltd
Matas Music Company
Matrix Publishing Co
Mat Shua Music Inc
Matterhorn Music
Matter Music
Matthew Eric Enterprises Inc
  (Eric Matthew Music Division)
Matthews Gail Publishing Co
Maudean Music Co Inc
Maud Music
Maui Blossom Publishing
Mauna Kea Publishing Inc
  (Mauna Loa Music Co Div)

*Mauna Loa Music Co Div
Maunumental Music
Maura Music Incorporated
Maurianna Music
  Orsatti Productions Inc
Maurice Peter Music Co Ltd
  Macmelodies Ltd
  Rex Music Ltd
  Television Music Co Ltd
Mauve Music Inc
  Purple Music Publ Co Inc
Maven Music
Maverick Productions Ltd
  (Maverick Music Division)
Mavid Music Co
Maxana Music Corp
Maxey Music Company
*Maximilian Music Inc
Maxim Music Inc
Maximum Music Corp
Maxwell Music Corp
  Gretavic Music Inc
*Maxwell Wirges Publs
Maya Productions Ltd
*Mayfair Music Corp
Mayflower Music Corp
May Fly Music
*Mayim Music Productions
Mayoham Music Inc
  Electronovision Mu Pub I
*Mayo Music Corp
Mayon Music
Maypole Music Inc
Mazeltov
*M B P Inc
M'Bubba Music
Mburu Music
  Fox Productions Inc
Mc Afee Music Corp
  Capella Music Inc
Mca Inc
  Ahleim Walter C Music Co
  Am Rus Music Corp
  Blossom Music Corp
  Clifford Frances Music Co
  Delkas Music Pub Co
  Hubert Music Corp
  Kalmar & Ruby Music Corp
  Loeb Lissauer Inc
  Mca Music
  Miller Bob Inc
  Music Corporation of America
  Pickwick Music Corp
  Piron A J & Co
  Pla-A Song Co
  Wabash Music Co
Mc Bee Jerry Music
Mc Cormick S Enter Inc
Mc Dermott Words Music C
Mc Duff Music
Mc Entoons
Mc Gowan Al Music
*Mc Graw Music Co
M C H Record Production Inc
  (Deep Note Music Division)
Mc Hugh & Adamson Mu Inc
Mc Hugh David Inc
Mc Hugh Jimmy Music Inc
*Mc Kinley Music Co
*Mc Millan Music
M C M Publishing
  Monari-Cretdon-Mullaney
Mc Nally Music Publishing
Mc Namara's Band
Mc Neely Music Co
Mc Pet Music
Mc Ron Music Company
*Mc Rovscod Music
M D K Publishing Co Inc
  (Morgana Music Co Div)
Md Lalose Music
Mea Culpa
*Meadowgreen Music Co
Meadowlane Music Inc
Meadowlark Music
Meadow Music
Meadow Ridge Music
Me and Sam Music
Me and Thee Music Co Inc
Me-Benish Music Inc
*Medallion Ave Music Div
*Medallion Songs Inc
Media Counterpoint
Mediarts Music Inc
*Mediarts/Previn Acct
Medicine Hat Music
Mediterranean Press

Mediterraneo Productions Inc
Medulla Music
Meece Music
Meedmist Inc
Meehan Danny Publishing Co
Megabucks Music Company
*Mega Music
*Mega Records Tapes Inc
Me Gusta Music
Meinziir Music
Meki Music Publishing Inc
Melange Music
Melbourne Music Publishing Co
Mel-Bren Music Inc
Melco Records Corporation
   Santone Music Publ Divis
Mel-Dav Music Inc
Mele Loke Publishing Company
*Melissa Music Inc
Mell-Doe Music
Mellodan Music
Mellyric Music
*Melo-Arts Music Pubs
Melodic Stories
Melody Deluxe Music
Melody Man Music Co
*Melody Ranch Enterprises Inc
Melody Ranch Music Co Inc
Melomega Music Ltd
*Melomusic Publications Inc
*Melrose Music Corp
Melvin Music
Melway Inc
Mel-Yel Music
Memnon Ltd
Memphis-Four Inc
M-E Music Company
*Menage De Trois Music Div
Menard Music
Mench Music
Menemsha Music
Meno Music
Menorca Publications Inc
Mephisto Music
Mepp Jay Music
Mercado Music
Mercede Power of Music
*Mercer & Morris Inc
*Mercer Music
Merchant's Peace
Meredith Music Inc
Merilark Music
Merion Music
Merit Music Co
Merleko Productions Inc
Merlin Associates (Publishing)
Mernee Music
Merrifield Music Co
Merrill Music Corp
*Merrilong Music Division
Merrison Music Corp
Merrittorious Production
Merrybelle Record Corporation
   Merrybelle Music
*Merry Sounds
Merry Sunshine Music
Mersey Robert Productions Inc
   (J L S Music Division)
*Mervyn Music Division
Mesa Lane Music
Mesmeric Music
Mesquite Music Corp
   Jayvee Music Pub Co
*Messiah Music
Metairie Publishing Co
Meteorite Music Publications
Metolius Music Publishing
Metorion Music Corporation
*Metro Goldwyn Mayer Corp
Metromedia Producers Corp
   Mpc Music
   Wolper Productions Inc
Metronome Music Pub Co of Pa Inc
Mexican Music Center Inc
   Alba Ed De Musica
   Campei
   Compas Ed
   Del Centro Editora Music
   Pala Sa
   Prado Miguel Promota Music
   Promotora Y Graevadora Art Y
   Comercial
   Radio Luz Ed Mus
   Rimo Edic Musicales
*M G M Record Corp
M G Music Publishing Corp
Mhoom Jun and Associates

Mian Music
Michael Brent Publications Inc
   Brent Michael Music Comp
   Cloverleaf Music
   Golden Rod Music Co
   Mbp Inc
Michael Music
*Michele Music Inc
Michelle Bird Music
Michlin Hill Inc
   (Mom's Best Mu Division)
Michlin & Hill Prod Inc
   John Hill Productions Inc
   Lothlorien Music Div
*Mid America Music Div
Midbar Music Press
Mideb Music
Midnight Dance Music
Midnight Madonna Music
Midnight Opera Company Inc
Midnight Sun Music Publ Co
Midnight Whistler
Midships Music
Midsong Music Inc
Mid South Sounds
Midway Music Company
Midway Productions Publications
   Cool Duck Music
Midweek Music Ltd
Midwestern Music Company
Midwest International Prod Ltd
   (Menage De Trois Music Div)
Mifka Music
Mightykitty Music
Mighty Max Music
Mighty M Music
Mighty Mo Music Inc
Mighty Two Music
Mighty Wind Music
Miglo Music Co
Mike Boyd Music
*Mike & Jules Music Co Div
Mikel-Nickel Music
Mikrokosmik Music Inc
*Milbro Music Div
Milbud Music
Milene Music Inc
   Randy Smith Music Corp
   Ray Baker Music Inc
Miles Ahead Music
Milk Money Music
Millan Brian Music Corp
*Miller Bob Inc
Miller Brody Productions Inc
   (Milbro Music Div)
Miller Joe Music
Miller Music Corp
   Noble Johnny
   Sherman Clay & Company
Miller Pearce Publishers
Millrose Enterprises Inc
   (411 Music Division)
*Mills Music Inc New Acct
Mills Music Inc Old Acct
   American Composers Inc
   Beck Mort
   Clark Frank Musi Co
   Daly Joseph Mus Pub Co
   Edwards Gus Mus Pub Co
   Gordon & Rich Inc
   Gotham Attucks Mus Co
   Gotham Mus Service Inc
   Jerome & Schwartz Pub
   Jerome M K
   Kalmar Puck & Abrahams
   Keit Music Corp
   Kornheiser Phil Inc
   Lincoln Harry J Music Co
   Mills Music Inc New Acct
   Morse Theodore Music Co
   Nelson Jack Music Co
   New Chord Music Inc
   Stark & Cowan Inc
   Stept & Powers Inc
   Sterling Songs Inc
   Sunlight Music Co Inc
   United States Mus Pub Co
   Waterson Berlin & Snyder
   Waterson Henry Inc
   Williams Harry Music Co
Millstone Music Company
Mill Valley Music
Milnac Music Inc
Milnik Inc
   (Milnik Music Division)
*Milsons Mus Pub Corp
Milwood Music Co

Mims Music
Minas Music
Mind Bee Music Company
Mindover Music
Mindy Beth Productions Inc
Mine Music Ltd
Minerva Music Inc
Minesown Music Publishing
Minglewood
*Miniature Musicals Inc
Mini Tiger Music
Mink De Ville Inc
   (Fire Escape Music Division)
Minor Key Music Publishing Co
Minstrel Music Productions Inc
Mint Julep Publishing Co Inc
Mintzer Music Co
Mion Music Pub Co
Mirai Music
Miramira Music Co
*Mirco Publishing Co Inc
*Mirisch Films
Mirisch Films Inc
   Mirco Publishing Co Inc
Miroku Music
Mirose Music Company
Mirror Lake Music Co
Misbegotten Music
Mish Mash Music
Miss Alatex Music
   Garrett Music Ent Inc
Missing Link Music Inc
Mission Mountain Music Inc
Mississippi Riverboat Pub Co
Misslady Music Company
Miss Nitz Music
Mister Gagoo Music
Mister John
Mister Strawberry Music
*Mitchell Guy Inc
Mitchell Music Corporation
   Bark Music Corp
   Bayer Music Co Inc
   Jerome Music Corp
Mitch Music Publishing Company
Mi Val Music Company
*Mivan Music Inc
M K T Publishing Company
*M L Music Inc
M M I Music
   Fullarton Music Inc
   Muir Music Inc
Mmo Music Group Inc
   Vebeque Music
M & M Records Distributors Inc
M Music Inc
Moalco Music
Mobetta Music
*Mobile Fidelity Productions Inc
Moccasin Music Corp
Mocha Chip Music Publishing Co
Mocrisp Music
Modal Music Company
Model Music Company
*Mode Music Inc
Modern American Music Co
Modern Music Masters Pub
Modern Music Publications
Modoc Music Publishing
Module Music
Modupe Music Company
*Modus Associates
Moebius Music
   Christmas Charactor Prods
*Moe's Music Division
Moffitt Enterprises
Mogollon Mountain Music
Mogo Music Publisher
Mogull Ivan Music Corporation
   Crestview Music Corp
   Muirfield Music Corp
Mohkou Production & Publishing Co
Moise Music
Mokell Music
Molian Music Publishing Co Inc
Momar Music Company
Mombasa Music Company
Mom Pop Music
*Mom's Best Mu Division
Monadnock Music
*Monarch Music Corp
Monard Music
*Monari-Cretdon-Mullaney
Monday Publishing
Money Banks Music
Mongrel Music Publishers
*Monitor Music Service Corp

Monkeyfist Enterprises Inc
   (Monkeyfist Mus Division)
Monkey Joe Enterprises
   (Monkey Joe Music Division)
Monk's Funk Music
Monogram Music
*Mono Music Inc
Monosteri Music
Monrell Music Publishing Co
Monsour Publishing Company
Monster Island Music Pub Corp
Monsterous Music
Montage Music Publishing Inc
   Montage Mus Shayne Acct
   National General Mus Pub Co Inc
*Montage Mus Shayne Acct
Montana Vincent Jr Music Inc
Montego Publishing Company
Montoya Carlos Publisher
*Mont Pleasant Music Division
*Montrose F Music Pub Co
Monya Music
Mood Music Company Inc
Moon Bay Music
Moonbeam Publishing Corp
Moonberi Music Co
Moonbridge Music
*Mooncrest Music Div
Mooncrest Music Inc
Moondogg Music
Moonhill Music
Moon-Jem Production Publishing
Moon June Spoon Music Co Ltd
Moon Meadows Publishing Inc
Moon Rock Music Inc
Moon Spectrum Music
   Spectrum Cooperations
Moon Tree Music
Moore Bob Music
Moorpark Music Corp
Moose Music
Mootrey S Studios
   (Mootrey S Mus Mart Div)
*Moral Re-Armament Inc
*Moran Mike
Morejon Recording & Publ Co
Moreland & Gostick Publication
Morella Music Company
Moreno Music Inc
Moretti Music
*Morgana Music Co Div
Morgan Creek Music
Morgan Manor Music Inc
*Morick Music
Morkay Music
   Kaymor Productions Inc
Morley Jim Music
Morley Music Co
   Ardmore Music Corp
   Capitol Publications Inc
   Morley Music Co Inc
   Project Records Inc
Morlock Music
Morning Calm Music
Morning Life Music
Morning Music Inc
   Puffin Island
Morning Picture Music
Morningside Music Inc
*Morningtown Music Co Inc
Morningwater Music
*Morocco Music Division
Moross Music Inc
Morris Edwin H & Co Inc
   Charling Music Corp
   Irwin Richard Music Pub Co
Module Music
   James V Monaco Inc
   Mayfair Music Corp
   Melrose Music Corp
   Mercer & Morris Inc
   Morris Joe Music Co
   White Smith Mus Pub Co
*Morros Boris Music Co
*Mor-Sell Music Division
Morse Place Music Co
*Morse Theodore Music Co
Mortney
Morty Nevins
   Alba Music Inc
Moser Sound Productions
Moses Rick Music
Moss aand Eli Music
Mother Earth Music Incorp
   Real Deal Music
Mother Goose Music Co
*Mother Mistro Music Inc

Mother Pearl Music Inc
Dona Marta Music
Roundtree Music
Mother Peppers Pub Co
Mother Texas Production Inc
(Mother Texas Music Div)
Mother Tongue Music
Motola Productions Inc
*Motormouth Music Division
Motor Music Company
Mott Music Ltd
Motu Music
Moulton Music Inc
Mountain Cat Music Co
Mountain Mover Music
Mountain of Stone Music Co
Mounted Records Inc
(Mounted Music Division)
Mourbar Music Corp
Mouse Airborne Music
Mouse & Junior's Music Inc
Moussayandi
Mouth to Mouth Music
Mouzon Music
Movietone Music Corporation
Moving Up Productions
Mowbray Music Publishers
Mozart Editions Inc
*M P C Music
M P L Communications Inc
*M R A
Mr Chateau Music Inc
Mr "D" Music
M R E Publishing
Mr I Mouse Ltd
*Mri Music Division
M R J Music
Mr J Music
Mr Mort Music
M & R Music
M R T Publishing Co
Ms Foundation for Woman Inc
M T G Inc
M-3 Music Co
M T L Music Inc
MTM Enterprises Inc
MTM Music
M T P Music
Mts Music Publishing Co
*Muckender Music Div
Mucky Rainy Music
Mud Turtle Music
Muffin Music
Mufson Music Co
*Muirfield Music Corp
*Muir Music Inc
Mulberry Square Publishing Co
Mule Kick Pub Div
Mullholland Music
Mulligan Publishing Co Inc
Mull O Dee Tunes
Multitone Music Corp
Mumbles Music
Mu Meson Music
Mum Monster Music
Mumm Monster
Mundoamericas Music Co
Mundy Music
Muppet-Jonico Publishing Co
Muppet Music Inc
Murakami-Wolf Productions Inc
(Murakami-Wolf Music Div)
Murden Music Pub Co
Murfeezongs
*Murko Music Corp
Murley Publishing Co
Murphy Lawrence E Music Ent
Murray Callander Music Inc
*Murray Gage Music
Murray Hill Publications Inc
Murray Mitch Music Inc
*Murray Productions Corp
Murry Gage Music
Murray Gage Music
Murry Productions Corp
(Juke Joint Music Div)
Geils J Band
Juke Joint Music
Murray Productions Corp
Murtaugh John Music Inc
Musat Publications
Muse Biz
Musetta Music Co Inc
*Mushroom Records Inc
*Musica De Mexico
Musical America Inc
Music Alert Publishing

*Musical Sciences Inc
Music America International
(Music America Music Div)
Music American Publishing Co
*Music and Effects
Musicanza Corporation
*Music Buyers Corp
Music By Earl E
Music Center
Music City Music
Queen M Music
Music Concepts Unlimited
*Music Corporation of America
Music Craftshop
Music D'Elegance
Music Exploitation Enter
Music Forever
Music for You Editions Inc
Music from the Heart Publ
Music Graphics Press
Music Grinder Publishing Co The
*Music Hall Songs Inc
Musi-Chord Publishing Co
Guitarists Publication
Music House Pub Co
Musician Magician
Musicians Publications
Musicland Publishing
*Musicland Publishing Co
*Musiclover Co
Music Makers Pub Co
Berk Lee Music Co
Berklew Music Co
Music Music Music Inc
*Music of Koppleman - Bandier
Music of the Spheres Publ
Music of the Times Publishing Corp
Music of the Times/Rilting Music
*Music of Tomorrow Inc
Music on Tap Publishing Co
*Musicord Publ Inc
Music Press Publishing
Music Productions
Music Publishers International
Music Pushers
Music Research Inc
White Company Music Div The
Music Resources International Corp
(Mri Music Division)
Music Room Publishing Group The
Music Row Publishing Co
Music Sales Corp
*Music 70 Music Publishers
Musicsmith Publishing Co
Musicsongs Publishing Co
Music Suite
Music 28 Inc
Music Unlimited
Music Vendor
Music Works International Inc
(Dudesong Publishing Division)
*Musifex Publishing Corp
Musique De Soleil
Musitronics Inc
*Mutual Music Society Inc
Mutya Music Co
Muzzy Lake Music
M V F Music Company
My Alicia Music Publishers
My Baby's Music Company
*Mybro Music Ltd
Mycenae Music Publishing Co
*Myer & Benson Prod Inc
Myers James E Enterprises
(Cinema Music Division)
Myers Music Inc
Jem Publications
Standard Songs
Myers Ron Music
My Family Music
My High's Music
Myland Steve Publishing Co
M Y N R Music
Myra Music Co
Frisch Al Productions
Myriad Limited
Myriad Music Publ Corp
Myrna March Music Inc
Myrow Music Company
*Myrow Music Corp
Mystaphonic Sounds Publishing Co
Mystic Moods Publications
Mythomania Music
Nacio Publications
Nacio Publications Inc
*Nacio Publications Inc

Nada Music
Nadley Harry Enterprises
Nai Bonet Enterprises Ltd
Nai Bonet Music
*Nai Bonet Music
Naked Snake Music
Nalli Al Productions Inc
(Alnal Music Division)
Naluai Music Publishers
*Nameloc Music Inc
Nance Songs
Nancy Enterprises Inc
Nancy Joyce Enterprises
Nancy Music Company
Nantucket Ent Ltd
(Mor-Sell Music Division)
Nantz Music
Nanuet Music
*Naro Music
Narrow Gate Music Inc
Riverhouse Music
Nascot Music Company
Nascot Music Inc
Nash Johnny Music Inc
Nashville Skyline Publishing Co
Nashville Songwriters Music
*Natchel Money House
Natco Music Corp
Nathan David Music
National Cross-Roads Music Inc
*National General Music Pub Co Inc
National Lampoon Music Inc
National Tapes and Promotions
Systems Corporation
Notes of Gold Inc Div
*Nationwide Songs Inc
Nat Jo Music
Nat Publishing
Natson Music Corp
Natural Songs Inc
Nave Music Publishers
Nazzenphlat Music
N B C Music Inc
Near Miss Music
Nebraska Music
Nedlob Music
Bolden Music
Nedwob Music
Nefer Music
Neiburg Al J Music Publisher
Neighborhood Music Publ Corp
Neil & Fred Publishers
Nellapee Music
Nelly Music Company
*Nelson Jack Music Co
Nelson Music Publishing Co
Nena Music Co
Estacy Music Inc
Neofonic Music & Recording Co
Nep Music Inc
Norman Music Inc
Nessie Music Corp
Netherland Music
Neuron Music
Neutral Gray Music
Neva Music Publishing Company
*Neverbird Music Co
Neverbreak Music Company
New Ashley Music Co
Creative World Music Pub
Newban Music
New Bay Psalter Music Press Inc
Newborn Fields Music Publishing
New Born Music
Newburn Music Inc
New Cadenza Music Corp
New Century Productions
*New Chatham Music Div
New Child Music Publishing
*New Chord Music Inc
New Clear Productions
*Newco Music Inc
New Contrast Publishers Inc
New Contrast Publishers
New Covenant Fellowship
(Sheep Shed Mu Division)
New Dawn Music Co
New Day Unlimited Inc
Parker Mel Music Company
New Dimensions in Education Inc
New England Lady Music
New Fairfield Music Co
New Forest Music
New Ground Music Inc
*New Hampshire Music Corp
New Harmony Music

New Hidden Valley Music Co
*New Hope Music Inc
Newman Charles Publications
New Music Publishing Co
New Music West
Alomar Press
New Orchard Music Co
New Pax Music Press
Newport Music Company
Paul Berk Music Co
*New Sound Ideas Mu Div
New Sounds Inc
New Sounds in Modern Mus
New Source Publishing
New Southwest Music Pub The
New Surf Music
New Tandem Music Company
*Newton Record Co
Newtonville Music Inc
New Town Music Inc
New Hope Music Inc
New Wayside Song The
New Wine Productions
New World Music Corp
New York City Players Inc The
(Better Nights Music Division)
New York Mary Inc
(N Y M P H O Music Div)
New Zoo Music Company
Funco Corp
M A Publisher
Next City Music
*Next Day Music Corp
Next Window Music
Nibbles Music
Nibbor Music Co
Nicholas Cathy Music
Cathy Nicholas Music
Nicholson Muir Services
Nichols Roger Music Inc
(Three Eagles Music Div)
Nick of Time Music
Nick O Val Music Co Inc
Nick-O-Val Music
Nicoletti Joseph Music Co
Nida Music Publ Co
Night Fighter Music Inc
Nightfire Music
Night River Publishing
Nightstream Music
Nightwork Music Co
Nikka Dee Music
Nimbus Music Co
Nine Music The
Nine Star Music Corp
Ninobe Music
*Nipper Music Co Inc
*Nirella Danny
Nisbet Ben Music Inc
Nisha Ayl Pub Co
Nite-Stalk Music
Nitso Productions
White Bear Productions
Nivrag Music
Noa-Noa Music
Nob Hill Music Inc
*Noble Johnny
*Noble Music Corp
Noble Son Music Corp Ltd
No Blooze Music
Nod-Jon Music
Noel Gay Music Inc
Noel's Ark Music Co
No Hype
Nolan Kenny Publishing Co
Nomel Music Co
Nootrac Music Limited
Norbett Music Inc
Norbury Music
Nordix Music
Norick Music Inc
Morick Music
Norick Music Publishing Co
Norman H Music Co
*Norman Music Inc
*Norman Rosemont Pub Co Inc
*Norris J Music Pub Co Ltd
North Bluff City Music
North Bluff City Music Inc
Northchester Music Inc
Northern Music Company
Alaska Mus Co Inc
Danelectro Corp
Dov Music Inc
Northern Music Corp
Northgate Music Corp

North Park Music
Abe Olman Music Inc
Amron Music Corp
Manlowe Music Corp
Northridge Music Inc
Northshore Publish Inc
North & Son Music Inc
North State Music Prod Inc
Norway Music
No Sadness Music
No Soap Radio Ltd
No Soap Music Ltd
Notable Music Co Inc
Nameloc Music Inc
No Talking Music
Notes from the Underground
*Notes of Gold Inc Div
Notes Unlimited Inc
Nothing Music Co
No Thought Music
Notlim Music Co
Nottingham Square Publications
Nova-Caine Music
Nova Star Music
Novella Music Inc
Novello Publications Inc
Novelty Music Company
*Now Music Division
Now View Music
N P P Music Corp
N R W Music Company
N S Beaujolais Music Inc
N T R Productions Inc
Nuance Productions Inc
(Nuance Mus Co Div)
Nucky Light Music Co Inc
Nucky Light Music Company
Numbers Music
Nummer Mutt Music
Nupenza Music Company
*Nutmeg Music Corp
Nu Trayl Music
*Nu View Publishing Co Div
Nuztunes Music Co
Nyborg Music Ltd
Sevborg Music Ltd
*N Y M P H O Music Div
Oakland Music Inc
Oak Manor Music
Oak Tree Music
Oatmeal Music
Oba Publishing
O Barton Music Pub
O Biz Music
Obsession Music
Oby Music Company
Ocean Castle Music
Radin Ray Theatrical Prod
Ocklawaha Music Pub Co
O C Music
O'Connor Songs
Octane Music Inc
Octave Music Publ Corp
October Moon Music
*October Music Ltd
October S Child Music
Ode Records Inc
India Music Inc
Odette Music Corp
Official Music Co Inc
Off the Pace Music
O Flynn Charles Publs
O'Flynningan Music
Of Oz Music
Of the Roses Music
Ogilvy Music
Oh Boy Music Company
Oilgig Music
Oilpatch Publications
Oily Maniac Music Inc
*O J G Inc
*Okeh Music Pub Co
*Okemo Music Publishers Inc
Okie Dokie Music
*O Kun Music Corp
Okun Music Corp
O Kun Music Corp
Old Brompton Road
Solid Sound Music
Old Canyon Music
Olde Clover Leaf Music
Oldenburg G A M Pub Co
Old Eye Music
*Old Homestead Pub Co
Old New Orleans Music Pub Co
Old Orchard Music
Old Showman Music

Old Sock Music
Old St Paul Publishing
Old Sycamore Music Co
Ole Land Marke Music
Olenik Records
*Olivares Publicaciones
Olive Music Publishing Corp
Oliver Music Publishing Co
Oliver's Tunes
*Olman Music Corp
Olman Music Services Inc
Olna Music Corp
Olna Music Publishing Company
Olog Publishing Co
Olso Inc
O'Lyrical Music
Omar Music Company
Omen Associates Inc
Omni Capital Music Ltd
Omnipotent Inc
(Snort Publishing Div)
Omni Records Inc
(Avent Publ Company Division)
Omniscient Music
Omnisound Inc
Omp Music Publishing Co
Onaje Music Publishing Company
On-Beat Music Publishing
On Broadway Tonight Music Inc
Ondine Music Co
Ondotronics Industries Inc
One and Three Music
*One Hundred Twenty Fifth Street
Music Co
One More Music
One Net Catch Music Company
One Note Beyond Music
One Three Nine Music
130db Music
One to One Music Publishing Co
125 Street Music Co
*One Hundred Twenty Fifth Street
Music Co*
One World Inc
Makani Publishing
One Zee Music
100 M P H Music Corp
Onie S Music Publish Co
*Onion Publishing Co Div
Oniram Music Publ
On Location Productions
International Ltd
On Location Music Div
Only Daughter Music
On My Way Music
*On the Rocks Music
Onton Music Company
Ontrac Publishing Co
Oompah Publishing
Oooeee Music
*Opal Productions Incorporated
Open-Dor Music Co Inc
Chaparral Music Pub Co Inc
Open Love Music
Open Sky Music Publishers
*Openwide Publishing Co Div
Opportunity Music Co
Messiah Music
Optimum Records and Recording
Inc
Opus III Incorporated
(Opus III Music Div)
Orange Blues Music
Orange Tree Music
Orchard Lake Music
Orea Publishing Co
Oregon Music Publishing Company
Oregon Talent Music
Ore's Halcyon Days Music
Original Black Sheep Music
Publishing Inc The
*Oriole Music Corp
Orleansongs
Orlob Music Co
Or Music
*Orsatti Productions Inc
*Orten Music Company
Orville Music Corp
*Orwell Music Publ Co Div
Osmosis Music
*O'Songs Inc
Ostara Press Inc
Ostay Music Company
Other Brothers Publishing
Otherland Music Co
Other Music Inc
Other Side Music

Otherwise Publishing
Otot Music
Oublietta
Our Family Music
Our Own Music
Our Time Music Inc
Outer Space Enterprises Inc
Hologram Music
Hologram Music Division
Outfield Music Co
Out 'N Out Music
Out-Of-Breath Music
Out of Business Pub Ltd
Out of the Can
*Out of the World Mus Co
Outreach Publishing House
Outsound Music
Out There Music
Ovation Records Inc
Overbrook Publishing Co
*Overdrive Music
Overdue Music
Owens Kemp Music Co
Owlofus Music
Owyhee
Oxford Univ Press Inc
Oxlight Music Company
Oxygen Music Inc
Oyster Music
(Gregg Hill Music Division)
Rush Tom Division
Ozark Opry Inc
Kajac Record Corporation
Mid America Music Div
Oz Music Publishers
Ozzie S Music Corp
Pablito Publishing Co
*Pace Publications
Pacific Arts Corp Inc
(El Paso Music Division)
Pacific Buffalo Hawk Music
*Pacific Press Publishing Assoc Div
*Packard Music Co
Packson Music Company
Packy Music
Pacla Music Co
*Paco Music Inc
Pac Production Inc
*Pacsa Music Publishers
Padali Music
Padme Music
Paean Music
Page Full of Hits Inc
Pa-Giz Music
Paglinawan Publishing
Paine-American Music
Palaco Publishing Co Inc
Paladin Music Co Inc
*Pala Sa
Pal Dog Music
Paley Music Company
*Palladium Music Division
*Pallma Mus Pubs Inc
Pal Mal Music
Palmbeach International Recording
Ltd
Palmer Wells Music
*Palm Music Corporation
Palm Springs Music Co
Palm Springs Publishing Co
Palomar Music Co
Palooma Music
Pamelarosa Music Inc
Panache Music Inc
Panda Bear Music
Pandee Music Publishing Co
Pandilla Music
Pan Earth Inc
Pan Jebel Inc
(Wooding Sam Mus Co Div)
Panna Music
Panny Music
Pano Pub Inc
Panther Music Corp
Bell Songs Pub Co
Pantosonic Music Publishers
Paone Music Corp
Papa Joe S Music House Inc
Evangeline Music Inc
Papa Mike's Music
Paper and Pen Music
Paper Pills Music Inc
Papko Music
*Pap Music Division
Para Andi Music Corporation
*Paraclete Music Publ Div
Paradiddle Publishing Co

*Paradise Music Corp
Paradise Valley Music Co
Paradrome Music Publ
Paragon Associates Inc
(Paragon Music Corp Div)
Paramount Music Corporation
Popular Melodies Inc
Spier & Coslow Inc
Paramount Roy Rogers Music
Company Inc
Para Nowgen Music Corp
Para Tal Music Corp
Para Tracs Music Corp
Para Wag Music Corp
Parchment Publishing Corp
(Parchment Mu Co Div)
Parish Productions Inc
Parish Productions
Parisian Music Inc
*Paris Music Co Inc
Parker Holmes Music Publ
Parker Lane Music Inc
Amos Productions Inc
Fish Music Division
*Parker Mel Music Company
Parker Parker Music
Park J Tunes
Parkland Music Co
*Park Ridge Music Corp
Parnassus Music
P A R Publishing & Producing
*Partee C L Music Co
Participation Music Inc
Partnership Music
Parts and Labour Publishing
Pasetta Productions Inc
Pasha Music Company
Pasquale Publications
Pasquotank Music Publ Inc
Passantino Print Co Inc
Pastime Publishing Co
Pastoral Arts Associates of North
America
*Pat-Cat Music Inc
Patch Bruce Productions Inc
(Winged Heart Music Div)
Patchquilt Theatrical & Publishing
Productions Ltd
Patchwork Music
Patelson Joseph Music House The
Pathet Lao Publishing
Pathfinder Music
Paths of Music Inc
Patlab Music
*Patore Music Co
Patrice Publishing Co
Patsofine Music
Patten and Guest Prod Inc
(Patten and Guest Pub Div)
Pattern Music Inc
Patti Enterprises Inc
Patton Jack Music Co
Patuxent River Music
*Paul Berk Music Co
*Paul Cunningham Inc
Paul Doll Music
*Pauline Music Inc
Paulist Press
(Paraclete Music Publ Div)
*Paul J Sifler-Publisher-
*Paull Pioneer Music Corp
Paulvanni Music Pub
Pavanne Music Co
Pawnbroker Music Corp The
Pax Regina Music Ltd
Paxton George Corporation
Malden Music Corp
Paxton George Corporation
*Pay Dirt Music
Payforcollege Music
Payload Music Inc
Payne Bob Music
Payne Brothers Music
Payton Lenny Music
Pay-Well
P B R Music Co
P C R Publishing
Peabo Bryson Enterprises Inc
(Peabo Music Division)
Peaceable Kingdom
Peace River Publishing
Peach Records Inc
Sue-Mirl Music
Pearford Music
Pearlie's Music Company
Pearson Dunn Music Inc
*Peate Music Co

Pechugita De Tweetie Music
Pecktackular Music
Peeblishing Publishing
Peejay Music Company
Pee Wee Valley Music Inc
Peggy Gee Music Publ
Peg Way Music
Pej Music Co
Peking Restaurant Inc
   (Daphne Music Division)
Pelew Music Inc
Pelham Music
*Pell Mell Music Co
P E M Associates
   Godspell Music Corp
   Harkinson Music Co
Pencil Mark Music Inc
Pendragon Music Co Inc
Pennant Music Co
Penn Franklin Music Corp
   Ariel International
   Franklin Music
Penn Music Co
Pennswood Ballads
Penrob Music
Pensara Productions Inc
Pen Shanty Music Co
Pentimento Music Publishing Co
People S Music
Pepamar Music Corp
Pepper J W & Son Inc
Peppermint Farms Records
Pepper Tunes
Perelandra Music
Perfect Dream Music
Perfect Gift Music
*Perfection in Perf Inc
Perfo Ed Music
Performers Library
Pergee Music
Periwinkle Music
Perkiomen Music
*Perla Music Co
Perma Music Publishers
Pern Music
Perren-Vibes Music Inc
   Perren Viges Music Co
Perry Don Enterprises Inc
   Susaper Music
Perry Publishing Co
Perryvale Music Company
Persephone Music
Pershing Publications
Persimmon Press
Petanden Music Company
Petco International Inc
Peters Jon Music
Peters Mitchell Music
Peters Music Co
Peterson Gordon A Publishing
Peter's Pride Publishing
Petkere Bernice Music Inc
Pet Sounds Music
Pett Music Company
Pevo Publishing Co
Peyronel Music
Peyton Publishing Co
P F S Music Co
Phantom Records Inc
   (Phantom Music Division)
Phase Seven Music
Phelan Fine Music
Philharmusica Corporation
   Autograph Editions New York
*Philipsongs Music Division
Phil-Jack Music Co
Philjo Music Inc
   Philipsongs Music Division
Phillips-Mac Leod Publishing
Philly West
Phoenix House Music
Phoenixongs
Phonebook Songs
Photo Play Music Co Inc
   Luz Bros Music Pub
   Music Buyers Corp
Phrase Text Music
Phyl Len Ltd
   (Phyl Len Music Division)
Phyllis Music Inc
Phylmar Music Inc
Piano Melodies
Piccisong
Pic Corporation
   P S Music Inc
Pickett Lenny Music
Picklip Music Company

*Pickwick Music Corp
Picnic Music Incorporated
   Rivertown Music
Piecrust Music
Piedmont Music Company Inc
Pierce Allen & Roan Publishing Co
Pigfoot Music
Pig Music Company
Pina Records Inc
Pinchpenny Music
Pincus G & Sons Music Corp
Pineapple Music Publishing Co
Pine Forest Music
Pine Ridge Music Inc
Pinkard Publications Inc
Pink & Blue Music Publish Co
Pink Flower Music
Pinson Music
Pioneer Valley Music Corp
Piping Press Inc
*Piron A J & Co
Pirooting Publishing
Pirrotta C M Music Publishers
Pit Bull Music Co
Pitts Family Music Co
Pivot Music Co
Pix-Russ Music
P & J Productions
P K Publishing
P K S Publishing Inc
*Pla A Song Co
Plain and Simple Music
Planetary Music Publishing Corp
   Atrium Music Corp
   Chalet Music Corp
   Favorite Music Inc
   Foundation Music Corp
   Francon Music Corp
   Gyrus Music Corp
Pensara Productions Inc
   Intimate Music Corp
   Josie Music Publishing Co Inc
   M L Music Inc
   Naro Music
   Seton Music Corp
   Squire Music Corp
Plangent Visions Music Inc
*Plan Two Music Inc
Playback Music Pub Co
Playboy Music Publishing Co
Playgoers Music Company
Playhouse Music Co
Play It Again Sam Music Co
Plaza Drive Music
Plaza Sweet Music Inc
Pleasant Music Publishing Corp
   Coslow Music
   Kelton Inc
   Maestro Mus Publ Corp
   Request Records Inc
Pleaser Music
Plexi Lite Prod Inc
Plight Co
Ploggly Music
Plow Boy Music
Plumeria Publishers
Plume Tunes
Plush Music Publishing Company
Plus Minus Music Co
*Plus Two Music Co Inc
Plymouth Music Co Inc
   Browne Ted Music Co
P M G Corp
   Zoobe Co
P M Music Company
P M Records Inc
   Perla Music Co
P M S Music
Pocket Watch Music
Poco Publishing
Podium Music Inc
Podolink Publ Company
Poemas Y Canciones Inc
Pogologo Music
Point Zero Publishing Co
Poison Oak Music
*Polara Music
Poldo Music
Polecat Creek Music
*Polecat Music Division
Polish Prince Music
Polite Music
Pollux Music Inc
   Renaldo Inc
Polyton Productions Inc
   (Polyton Music Division)
Ponfield Music Inc

*Pond Wa A & Co
Po No Mo Publishing Company
Pontalba Music Co
Pooh Bear Music
Pookie Tree Publishing Co
Pookinkrial Pub Co
Poopy's Music
Popdraw Music Corp
Pops Music Publishing Co
   Pops Music Ltd
Pop Tunes
*Popular Melodies Inc
Popular Music Co
*Popwell Robert L
Porcara Music
Porchester Music Inc
Porch Swing Music
Port Au Prince Publishing Co
Portent Music
*Porter Binder Music
Porter Cole Music Inc
   Cole Porter Music Inc
Porter Henry L Evangelistic
Porter Joe Music
Porter Jones Music Inc
*Portfolio Systems Inc
*Portilla Music Corp
Port Music Inc
   Port Music Co
Portnow Miller Co Inc
*Portobello Road Mu Div
Portofino Music
Portsmouth Street Music
Positive Publishing
Positive Vibes Music
Poso Music Co
Possessed Music
Possum Hollow Music
Post Mike Productions Inc
   (Darla Music Div)
   Darla Music Division
*Post Music Inc
Potato Publishing Co
Pot O Gold Productions Inc
   Pot O' Gold Publishing Co
Potrero Music
P O V Music
Powder Music Inc
Powell David G Publishing Co The
Power House Music
Powers Publications
*P P R Music
*Prado Miguel Promota Music
Prager E S Inc
Prankee Music
Prater Music Inc
Pratt Mc Clain Music
Precision Music
Predator Music Incorporated
*P R E D I S A
Preferred Music Co
Premise Publishing Co
Prentice Music Inc
   Asset Music Corp
*President Music Co
President Music Corp
   President Music Co
Presser Theodore Company
Prestige Productions Inc
   This Side Up Pub Co Music Div
Prestige Publishing Company
Pretorius Publishing Company
Pretty 'P' Music
Pretty Purdie Music
Price Janie Music Company
Price Lloyd Music
Price Paul Publications
Pride of the South Music
Prime Time Music
Primitive West Publ
Prince Edward Music Company
Prince Frog Music
Prince of Wales Music Pub Inc
Princess Music Publishing Corp
   Marguerita Music Inc
Prince Street Music
Prindale Music
Prin Lil Music
Print Music Co Inc
Priority Music
Prisju Music
Private Lightning Music
Prize Music Inc
   Dreyer Dave Music Corp
Pro Art Publications Inc
Probe II Inc
Proclamation Prods Inc

Producers Music Publ Co Inc
   Triad Mus Pub Co Inc
Production Staff The
   (Stone Acres Publ Div)
Professional Artist Recording
   (Kingsland Pu Company Div)
Professional Ideas Ltd
   (Jamb Productions Music Div)
Professor Pork Publishing
*Progress Motion Picture Inc
Progress Music Co
Projections Music International
*Project Records Inc
Prolix Music Publishing Inc
*Prombill B V
Promco Music Company
   Lansbury Edgar
Promenade Music Inc
*Promociones Ed Internacionales
Promopub B V
   Promopub Inc
Promoright B V
   Promoright Inc
Promotion Publications
*Promotora Y Graevadora Art Y
   Comercial
Prom Publishing Company
*Pro Music Society
Propane Publishing Co
Prophecy Publishing Inc
Prophet Music Inc
Prospect Publishing Company
Protho Carl Music
Protone Music
P & R Productions
Prysock Arthur Music Corp
Psalms of David Music
*P S I Love You Music Co
*P S Music Inc
P S Publishing Co Inc
Psyche Productions
P T L Music
Publicare Publishing Co
Public Domain Foundation Inc
Publishing Plus Inc
Pud Music
*Puffin Island
Pulleybone Music Co
Pulp Mill Music
Pumpkin Music
Punkin Productions Inc
Puopolo Music
Puppy Breath Music
*Purchase Music Inc
Pure Joy Music
Pure Love Music
Pure Songs
Purple Cow Music
*Purple Music Publ Co Inc
*Purple Record Dist Corp
Purple Sage Music Co
Putnam Music Inc
Putti-Putti Music
Putzy-Putzy Music
Pyramid Music Company
Q C A Music Inc
Q Mast Music
Q-One Productions
Quackenbush Music Ltd
Quacker Music Co
*Quad Music Pub
Quadrafonic Music Inc
Quaid Patti Music
Quakertown Music
Quarternary Music
   Beyond Productions Inc
Quarter Note Music Publisher
*Quarterstaff Music Division
Quartet Music Inc
*Qudrat Music
Queen Bishop Music Inc
Queen City Music Company
*Queen M Music
Queertoons Publishing
Questing Beast Music
Question Mark Music Ltd
Que T Music
Quijui Music Publishers
Quik Star Music Co
Quill Music Company
*Quincke W A & Co
Quintet Music Inc
*Quintrac Music Division
Quitanda Music
Quixotic Music Corp
Rabar Music Co
Rabbit Rabbit Music Co

Rab Music Publishing Co Inc
*Racer Music Co Div
*Racer Music Inc
*Rachel Music Inc
Rachel's Own Music
*Racine Music Co
*Radin Ray Theatrical Prod
Radio Active Material Pub Co
*Radio Luz Ed Mus
Radio & T V Pakagers Inc
Rad Music Publishing Co
Radmus Publishing Inc
Rado Publishing
Rafael Music Publishers
Raf Music
Ragamuffin Music
 Clay-Heart Music
Ragin M Music
Rag Pickin Publishing Co Inc
Ragtime Music Co
 Ragtime Music Corp
Ragweed Music
Rahman Music Co
Rah Publishing
Raijemi Music Publ Co
*Raim Walter
Rainbow and Rain Publishing
Rainbow Man Music
Rainbow Music Corp
Rainbow Power Inc
Rainbow Road Pub Co
Rainbow Snake Music
Raindrop Music
Rainey Charles Music Company
Rainglow Music Inc
 Rainglow Music Publishers
Rainlight Music Co
*Raintree Music Inc
Raisin Music
Rajah Music Co
Rajamaya Music Co
 Gerry Productions Inc
Ra Jane Music
Raleigh Ben Music Co
Ralton Music Company Inc
Rambeau Music
Ramblin Rose Publications
 Long Hubert International
Rambunctious Music
Rameses II Record Corp
 (King Tut Music Division)
Ramette Music Publishing
Ramina Pub Co
Ramloc Music
Ramoria Music Inc
Rampro Music
Rams Head Music Co
Ram's Horn Music
Randall Michael Music
Randog Music
Randolph Music
Random Chance
Ran Doo Music
*Randy Smith Music Corp
Rango Music Corp
Ranier Publications
Rankin Bass Productions
*Rank Music Co of America Inc
Ran-Ral Music
Ranscott Music
Ranyel Publishing Co
Raphael Fred Music Inc
Rapsodia Publications
Rare Blue Music Inc
Rare Magnetism Music
Raskap Music Corporation
 (Raskap Publishin' Company Div)
Rathvon Music
 Rathvon Music Incorporated
Ratner Norman B Productions
Rat Recording Company Inc
Rats and Snakes Music
Ravenden Music
Ravosa Music
Raw Cream Music Publishing Co
Raw Ice Music
Raw Milk Music Publishing Co
Raybaby Music
*Ray Baker Music Inc
Raycon Music
Raydiola Music
Ray Jay Music
Rayjon
Raymur Music Company
*Ray Music Co
Rayster Music Publishing Co
Razaf Music

Raze Music
R B A Music Inc
R B S Publishing
R Cade Music Publishing
*RCA Victor Mexicana S A
R C Jay Publishing Inc
R C S Publishing Company
R-Dale Music Co
*Rdm Publishing Co Div
*Reade Walter Sterling Music Corp
*Reade Walter Sterling Music Corp
 Lektrafon Music Co
 Tom Thumb Music Div
Ready Productions Inc
*Real Deal Music
Reale Music Company
Real Star Music Company The
Realta Divina Publishing Co
Real Thing Music
Real Time Productions Inc
 Consort Music Inc
 Modus Associates
Real World Music
Rear Exit Music Inc
Recino Music
*Recording Dynamics Inc
Record Music Publishing Co
Record Songs Inc
Red Bridge Publishing Corp
Red Bullet Music
Red Cloud Line Music
Red Cloud Music Company
Red Cow Music Inc
*Red Day Music Division
Redeye Music Publishing Co
Red Giant Inc
Redgreg Enterprises Inc
 (Sug Sug Music Division)
 Sug Sug Music Division
Red Hare Music Company
Red Hook Music Corp
Red Pajamas Music Inc
Red Pet Promotions Ltd
 (Red Pet Publ Company Div)
Red Planet Music
Red Quarter Music
Red Ripple Music
Red River Prod Inc
 (Crazy Creek Music Div)
Red Robin's Records Corp
Red Rooster Music
Red S Black Gold Publishing Co
Red Sky Music
Red Tide Music
Red Williams Music
Reed Music
*Ree Music Co
Reen Publishing
Refrain Music Corp
Regaldi Music Co
Reganesque Music Company
Regency Square Music Company
*Regent Recorded Music Inc
Regg J Music
Regline Music Company
 Regent Recorded Music Inc
Rehark Jean A Music Publishing
Rehtakul Veets Music
Reid W J Co Inc
 (Gina Reid Music Div)
*Reinach Productions
Reindeer Music Company
*Reis Pub Inc
Reizner Music Corp
Rekrap Publishing
Relentless Music
*Reliance Music Corp
Religious Music Guild Inc
Remarkable Music
Rememba Enterprises Inc
*Remembrance Music Division
Remember Music Publishing Co
Remex Music
*Remick Music Corp
Remme Music Co
Rem Music Company
Remsen Alice Inc
*Renaldo Inc
Rene Leon Publications
Rene Otis Publications
Renhall Music
Renmal Music Inc
Rensdale Mu Enter
*Request Records Inc
Reservoir Music
Resolute Television Prods Inc
 (Resolute Music Company Div)

Resource Publications
Rest A While Music Co
Retnuh Music Company
 Hunter Frank
Returnity Productions Limited
Revega Music Incorporated
Revelare Productions Inc
Revelation Music Publ Corp
Revel Harry Corp
Revolver Music
Rew Publishing Company
*Rex Music Ltd
Reykjavik Music
Reynard Publishing Co Inc
 Eastbrook Music Co
R F D Music Publishing Co Inc
R G Music Pub Co
R G S Music Ltd
Rhahm Music Inc
Rha Music Publishing
*Rhapsody Music Co
*Rhinestone Music Division
Rhodes Roger Music Ltd
Rhontana Music
 Chaotic Music
Rhovere Music
Rhyme Music
*Rhyme & Rhythm Inc
Rhythms Productions
Ribowin Music
Richard Dean Publishing
*Richard Irwin Music Pub Corp
Richards Paul Music Co
*Richey Paul Music Co Inc
Rich Fish Music
Rich John Productions Inc
 On the Rocks Music
Richko Publishing
*Rich Little Productions Inc
Richmond Music Enterprises
 (R M E Music Division)
Richmond Publishing
Richochet Publishing Co
*Richtree Productions
Ricki Music Inc
 Carol Mus Pub Co
 Carole Music Pub Co
*Rickshaw Music Pub Co Div
Ric Rac Music
Rictor Music
Ridgewood Place Music
Riesman Michael
Riff Bros Music
Riggs John Publishing
Right Angle Music Inc
 Angle Music Inc
*Riker Brown & Wellington Inc
Rilis (Music) Enterprises Ltd
Rilting Music Inc
 Beautiful Music Inc
*Rimo Edic Musicales
Rim Shot Music
Ring Bearer Music Ltd
Ringle Dave Music Co
 Congress Music Co
 Famous Writers Co
 Goulden Leng Co
 Hamilton Music Co
 Krey Geo M Co
 Sleepy Valley Music
 Tracy Wm Pub Co
 Victory Music Co
 York & King Pub Co
Ring'O Sound Music
Rinimer Corporation
Riocali Music Co . . . .
Ripparthur Music Inc
 Rippartha Music Inc
Rising Sun Music Inc
Rissum Music Group
*Ritchie Music Co Inc
 The Song Shop
Ritesonian Music
Rit of Habeas Music
Ritter Tex Music Publ Inc
Ritvale Music Corp
Riva Music Inc
 Cock and Trumpet Music Inc
River City Music Inc
River Honey Music
*Riverhouse Music
River Jordan Music Inc
 Skita Music
Riverside Music Publications
 Riverside Music Inc
Rivers Music
*Rivertown Music

Rivian Music
Rizla Music Co
Rizo Musical Productions Inc
*R-J Concerts Inc
*R-J Music Co
R J Promotions Inc
R K Artists
R L G Music
R L W Music
*R M E Music Division
Rm Films International Inc
*Rml Co Division
R & M Music Productions Inc
 Hazy Music
 Mooncrest Music Div
*Roaga Edic
Roane Music Publishers
Robbins J J Inc
 Guild of American Composers
 Villa Lo Bos Music Corp
*Robbins J J Sons Inc
Robbins Music Corp
 Abrahams Maurice Inc
 Contemporary Music Pub Co Ltd
 Leading Music Ltd
 Massey Music Co Inc
 Metro Goldwyn Mayer Corp
 Out of the World Pub Cor
 Sonnemann Music Co Inc
 Twentieth Century Mus Co
 Universal Music Corp
 Whiteman Paul Pubs
 Wiedoeft Rudy Mus Pub Co
Robbley Webb Publishing Co
Roberge Philip P Assoc Inc
 (C C S Music Division)
 Korner Alexis Music Div
 P P R Music
*Robert A Isreal
*Robert Armen Music Publishing
Robert Bruce Music Ltd
*Robert Lissauer Publishing Corp
*Robert Music Corp
Roberts Allan Music Co
Roberts Jim Music Inc
Robertson Don Music Corp
 Birchwood Music Co
Roberty Music Co
Robeson R G Music
Robin Batteau Music
Robinhill Music
Robins Larry Music
Robinson J Russel Inc
Robin Styne Music Corp
Roblu Music
Robmar Music Company
Robo Music
Robro Publishing Company
Rob Roy Music Inc
*Rochester Music Publishers Inc
Rockaday Music
*Rockbottom Music Ltd
Rocket Music Company
Rockhopper Music Inc
Rockie Music
Rockin Rollin Blues Band Publishing
Rockne Music Company
Rocknocker Music Company
Rock N' Rills Music
Rocksmith Music
 Blue Country Music
Rock Steady Inc
 (Rock Steady Music Div)
Rocky Mt National Park Mus Co Inc
Rodeb Music
Rode Company Productions
 In Rodes Music
*Rodeheaver Co The
Rodney Music
Rodon Music
Roga Music
*Roger Ailes Music Division
Roger Music Inc
*Roger Paul Kelly Music
Rogers Fred M
 Small World Enterprises Inc
Rogers Harlan Music
Rogers Lelan Music
Roister Music
Ro Jes Music Company
Roland Music
Roleda Publishing Co
Rolin' Music
Rollin Dice Music Publishers
Rolling Hills Music
Rolling Meadows Music
Rolling Rock Music

Rolling Tide Music
Rollins Frances
Rollo Music
Rolls Royce Music Company
Rollum Music Co
Romanis Publishing Co
   Futura Music Inc
   Romanis & Messner Inc
Romano Music Co
Rome Richie Music
Romi Music Company
Romona Music
Ronarte Publications
Roncom Music Co
Ron Dee Music
Rondo Music Co
Ronell Ann Music Inc
Ronji Music Inc
Ronjoy Music Publishing
Ronjul Publishing Incorporated
Ron Muir Music
Rontom Music Co
Rooks Conrad Music Company
Room at the Bottom Mus Pub Co
*Rooney Mickey Pub Co
Rooster Gooster
Rooster Jim Music Co
*Root Frank K & Co
Ropaco Music
Ropat Music
Rory Music Ltd
   Melissa Music Inc
Rosalba Music Inc
*Rosarita Music Inc
Roseborg Music Inc
Rose David Publishing Co
Rosefree Music Co
Rose Jasmine Music Publ Co
Rosemarie Productions Inc
Rosemeadow Pulishing Corp
Rosemont Norman Productions Inc
   Norman Rosemont Pub Co Inc
Rosena Music Inc
   Rosena Music
Rosenblatt Lemore Music Co
Rose St Music Co
Rose Tree Music
Rosetta Stone Music Inc
Rosewood Investment Corp
*Rosewood Music Corp
*Rosey Geo Band & Orch Ca
Rosko Productions
Ross Bud Music
Rossdon Music Co Inc
*Rossiter Harold Mus Co
Rossiter Will
Rosy Publishing Inc
Rotgut Music
Rothman Mark Music
Rotine Music Company
Round Gamut Music Inc
Round Table Music
*Roundtree Music
Round Wound Sound Inc
   Overdrive Music
Route 28 Music
*Rovclaman Enterprises
*Rovonco Productions
Rowchar Music
*Roweville Music Inc
*Row R D Mus Co Inc
Roxxon Entertainment Corp
   (Boogievision Music Co Div)
*Royal American Records Inc Div
Royal Coachman Music Co
*Royal Music Co
Royal Music Publisher
Royal Oak Music
Royal T Music
Royham Music Co
*Roy Shield Music Co
*R P M Inc
Rrepco Music Co
*Rr&R Music Publishers Inc
Rrub Music
R S O Publishing Inc
   Camel Music Ltd
   Carnbro Music Ltd
   J G K Music Ltd
   J M Music Ltd
   Ludding House Mu Pub Mgmt Ltd
   R T Music Company
Rubank Inc
   Carlson M L
   Finder & Urbanek
   Victor Music Co
Rubber City Music

*Rubber Frog Music Division
Rubboard Music
Rubinson David Friends
   (Ebbets Field Mus Div)
Ruby Harry Music Co
Ruchala-Garrett Music
*Ruckle Music Co
Ru Da Music
Rude Lazy Music
Ruedi Productions Inc
Rufert Records Inc
   (Rufert Music Division)
Rufon Music Inc
Rug Music Company Inc
   (Discreet Records Inc Div)
   Rug Music Co
Rug Rat Music Publ
Rule One Music Inc
Rumpel Music Company
Rupall Publications
Rupel Music Inc
*Rush Tom Division
Russell Frank Music
Russ Productions
Rustic Records Inc
   (Iron Skillet Music Division)
Rusty King Music Pub
Rutabaga Music
Rutherford Corporation & Associates
   (Dee Jay Publishing Div)
Rutland Music
Rutledge Music Co
*Ruxton Music Inc
R V R Music
R W P Inc
   (R W P Music Co Division)
R X Music
*Rylan Music Corp
Rytvoc Inc
   Burke Doyle Music Co
   Testio P & Sons
Ryzuk Music
R Z Music
Saarsongs
Sabal Music Inc
*Sabina Music Div
Sabotage Music
Sabteca Music Co
*Sacred Records Inc
*Sacred Songs Division
*Saga Music Corp
Sagcap Music Publishing
Saggifire Music
Sahara Music Inc
Sahel Publishing Co
Sailboat Music
Sail Inc
   (Sand Dollar Music Div)
Sailin Songs
Sailmaker Music
Sailor Music
Saingang Music
Saint Basil Music
St Lucifer Complex Ltd
   (St Lucifer Mus Division)
St Michaels Alley Music
St Nathanson Music Ltd
*Saint Nicholas Music
St Nicholas Music Inc
   Saint Nicholas Music
Salamani Music
Salem Mass Publishing Company
*Salerno Music Division
Salmarsi Music Co
Sal Mosca Music
Salsoul Music Publ Corp
Salter Publishing Company
Salza Music Publishing Co
Samasal Limited
Samco Music
Sammy Music
Sam's Band Music Publishing
*Samuel French Ltd
Sam-Vox Ltd
Sanborn Enterprise Inc
   (Jansan Publishing Co Div)
Sandbox Music Inc
Sandburn Music
*Sand Dollar Music Div
Sanders Music
*Sanders Weiss Inc
Sandia Music Co
*San Dino Music Corp
*Sandlee Pub Corp
Sandman Music Publishing Co
Sandra Music Corp

Sand & Sea Music
   Sand Sea Music
*Sand Sea Music
Sands Evie Music
Sands Music Corp
   Sinatra Songs Inc
Sandsongs
Sandtory Music
*Sandva Music Publishing Div
Sandy Songs
Sandy Springs Music Company
Sangre Productions
Sanjomochi Music
*Sanjud Music Co Inc
Sanron Music
Sanskrit Publishing Co
Sanson Antobal Music Co Inc
   Antobal Music Inc
Santa Barbara Music Co
Santa Monica Music Co
   Pat-Cat Music Inc
*Santa Monica Music Corp
Santana/Oasis Productions Inc
San-Tar Corporation
*Santone Music Publ Divis
Sapelo Sound Inc
Sapphire Songs
Sarintent Songs Inc
Sarmareli Music Co
Sarsfield Songs
Sashalutre' Music
Sashay Music Inc
Satchawa
Satellite II
Satellife Music Inter Ltd
Satisfaction Sound
Satsong Music
Sattuna Music
Sattwa Music
Saturday Friends Publishing Co
*Saturday Night Music Division
*Saturn Satelite
Saturn Satelite Publishers Inc
Sauce Music Co
Saugatuck Productions
*Saunders Publications Inc
Savage Music
Savoy Music Co Inc
Sawtell & Herring Music
   Sawtell Publishing Co
Sawyer Jean Publishing
   Gabraith-Mareno Pub Co
Sazar Music Corp
Scaggs Boz Music
Scali Music
Scallopini Marsala Music
Scan Music Inc
Scarlet Rose Publishing
Scarmalgia Music Company
Scarsdale Music Corporation
Scary Mountain Music Company
Sceneville Productions
   (Sceneville Mus Division)
Sceptre Music
*Schick Sunn Classic Productions Inc
Schine David and Company Inc
   (Schine Music Division)
Schirmer E C Music Company
Schirmer G Inc
   Heffelfinger R W
   Sanders Weiss Inc
Schleifer Music
Schlok
Schmidt Jeanne Ursula Productions
   Jeanne Ursula Schmidt Prod
*Schmitt Music Center Inc
Schnarf Publishing
*Schneidersongs Music Div
Schnor Songs
Schooner Sooner Songs
Schott Music Corporation
*Schreibman Mus Press
Schroder Music Company
Schubert Franz Music Publisher
Schuck Majorie Publishing Inc
Schuster Lewin Music Co
*Schuster Miller Inc
Schwartz Arthur Music
Schwartz Songs Music Publishing
Schwow Music Inc
Science Fiction Music Publishing
Scient Peace Buil Found
   The Scientific Peace Bldrs Found
Scintilla Music Co
S & C Music
Scoari Publishers
Scoot Tunes

Score-More Music
Scorpgemi Music Co
Scorpii Publishing Co
*Scorpio Enterprises Inc
Scorpio Rose Music
Scott Andrew Inc
   Purchase Music Inc
Scott-Ch & Brandy Music
Scott Hall Publishing Co
Scott's Bryan Music Factory
Scott Textor Music Publ Inc
Scott-Tone Music
S C P Music Corporation
Scratch Sisters Publishing Co
*S.c.r.c
Screen Door Music
Screenland Music
Scribes Music
Scriptomuse Publishing Co
Scroll Productions Inc
Scudder Productions
Scuffle Music
Scully Music Company
*Sculptured Sound Inc
Sculpture Music Inc
Scuppernong Music
Seabird Productions Inc
   Sculptured Sound Inc
Sea Dog Music
Seagull Publishing Inc
   (Blue Seagull Publish Div)
Sea Lor Music
Sea Owl
Seaphis Music
Seasons Music Company
Sea Town Inc
Seattle Sounds
Sea Turtle Music Co
Sebiniano Music Co
Second Music Publishing Co Inc
Second Wind Music
Secret Gold Music
Sedgewick Publishing
Sedriatric Music
Seesaw Music Corporation
See Spot Run Music
"See This House Music"
Segue Music
Selah Music
Selana Music Co
Seldak Music Corp
Self Pity Music Publishing Co
Selroy Music Company
Selvidge Music
Selvin Benjamin B Music Co
Selvin Bob Publishing
Sembello Music
Senor Music
   Senor Music Corporation
Sentinel Dome Inc
Sentinel Productions Ltd
Sepe Music Co
*Sephra Music Div
September Music Corp
Seraphim Productions Inc
   (Seraphim Music Division)
Serenity Music Company
Sergeant Music Co
Sesame Street Inc
*Seth Songs Music Pub Co Division
Set Music Co
*Seton Music Corp
*Sevborg Music Ltd
Seven Arts Press Inc
   (Suite Seven Music Division)
Seven Bells Publishing Incorporated
Seven Eight Nine Music Assoc
Seven Figure Music Corp
Seven High Music Inc
Seven High Music Inc
   Cecille Music Co
   Coronet Music Inc
   Robert Music Corp
Seven Hundred West Music
Seven Mile Music
Seven P M Music
Seven Sounds Publish Company
Seventh Ray Publishing
73 Music
Seventh Son Music Inc
Seven Torch II Music
Seven Valley Music
Sewanee Music Inc
Sewan Music Publishers Inc
S F Z Music Publishers
*Shackle Island Music Co
Shada Music Inc

Shades Music Co
Shades of Autumn Music
Shady Nook Music Inc
Shajay Music Co
Shakat Records Inc
 (Shakat Mus Publ Div)
Shalamar Gard Publishing
Shalli Music
Shalomar Music and Records
*Shamley Music
Shamrock Music Publishing
Shamus Publications
Shanachie Music
Shane Cyril Music Inc
Shank Bud Music Co
Shanlo Publishing Co
Shannon Road Music Co
Shantih Publishing and Productions
Shapiro Bernstein & Co
 Columbia Pict Now S B
 Elsa Tunes Inc
 Flagstaff Music Corp
 Glenmore Music Inc
 Stone Music Corp
Shapiro Dan Music
*Sharilda Publishing Div
Shari Music Publishing Corporation
Sharkey Music Inc
Sharon Music Company
Sharon Rose Music Publishing Co
Sharp Gannon Music
Sharptone Productions Inc
Shattinger Intern Music
 Shattinger Publications
*Shattuck B E
Shauna Lee Music Publ Co
Shaw Eddie Music Corp
 Swingersville Music Co
Shawn Dick Music
Shawnee Press Inc
 Fortune Music Inc
 Maxwell Wirges Publs
 Newco Music Inc
 Paull Pioneer Music Corp
 Rossiter Harold Mus Co
Shay Music Co
Shayne Larry Enterprises
Shayne Larry Music Inc
 Macclesfield Music
 Marapunta-Shayne Co Inc
Shazam Music
Shearing Music Corp
Shedd House Music
Sheenfeen Music Co Inc
Sheep Meadow Music
*Sheep Shed Mu Division
Shefter Bert Productions Inc
 Shefter Bert Prod
Sheila Marie Music
Shelby Music
*Sheldon Ken Music Co
Sheldon Ken Music Co
 Sheldon Ken Music Co
Shelley David Publishing Co
Shelley Music Inc
Shell Game Music
 Thoroughbred Production
Shellgreen's Recording Studio Inc
 (Grapetree Publishing Division)
Shell Tom Music
Shelly Sunrise Music Company
Shema Music
Shena Maydelah Publishing
Shenandoah Music
Shepard Tanzman Publishing Co
Sheral Music
Sherbet Music Ltd
Sher Do Publishing
Sheriton Music Publishing Co
Sherlen Music Co
Sherman Al Music Company
Sherman Bobby Music Co
*Sherman Clay & Company
Shermari Music
Shermley Music Company
Sherm Music
Shermsong Music Publishing Co
Sherrell-Metcalf Music Corp
Sherry Music Company
Sherwin Music Publishing Corp
Sherwin Music Publishing Corp
 (Sing Me Music Division)
Sherwod Forest Publishing Co Inc
Shetland Sound
*Shev A Deen Music Division
Shield Roy Music Company
 Roy Shield Music Co

Shilkret Nathaniel Music Co Inc
 Quincke W A & Co
Shiloh Music Factory
Shimmering Music
Shingle Shanty Music
Shining Star Music Inc
Shinn Rd Music
Ship Inc The
 (Saturday Night Music Division)
Shiptree Music
Shipwell Music
Shira Productions Inc
Shirbo Music
Shirdi Music Company
Shirico Inc
Shiver and I Music Ltd
Shoals Music Mill Publishing Co
Shoi Shoi Music
Shomari Music
Shongs Music
Shoombree
Shoreham Music Corporation
 Chipper Music Company
Short Rose Music Publ Co
Showalter Music
Showay Music Publishing Co
Shown Breree
Show Tunes Inc
Shpetner Music
 Sunrise Productions Inc
Shredded Wheat Music
Shubert Music Publishing Corp
Shukat Company Ltd The
 (Shukat Music Division)
 Survival Music Division
*Shukat Music Division
Shustep Publish Company
S I A Music Co
Side B Music
S I D Music
Sight & Sound Mgt Ltd
 (Sight & Sound Music Div)
*Sigler Street Music Inc
*Sigma Music Inc
*Signature Music Press
Sign of Taurus
Sign of the Twins
Silent Giant Publishing Co
Silent Seed Publishing
Silhouette Music Corp
Silk City Publishing
Silk R Productions Inc
Silliman Matthew Cole
Silverado Publishing Co
Silver Blue Music Ltd
 (Silver Blue Mus Div)
 Silver Blue Production Inc
Silver Bullet Music
Silver Burdett Company
 General Learning Corporation
Silver Cloud Music Inc
Silver Dagger Music Inc
Silver Dawn Music
Silver Fiddle
Silver House Music Co
Silver Music
*Silver Nightingale
Silver Nightingale Music
 Silver Nightingale
Silver Princess Music
*Silver Ridge Music Division
Silver River Music
Silver Sea Music
Silver Sidewalk Music
Silver Song Company
Silver State Publishing Co
Silver Sun Publishers
Silver Wand Music
Simalar Music
Simile Music Inc
Simitsongs Co
Simmons Family Music Pub Co
Simon George Music Co
 Simon George Inc
Simon John Music Company
Simon Norman J Music Co
Simon-Pam Music
Simtec Publishing Co
Simultaneous Music
*Sinatra Songs Inc
Sing-A-Bar Productions
Sing A Phonic Music Company
Singer Guy Music
Single Jingle Production
*Sing Me Music Division
Sing Me Music Incorporated
Sing N Do Company Inc The

Sinolouge Music
Sinsemilla Music
*Sioux City Music Ltd
Sir Dale Music Company
Sirius Rising
Sirrah Music
Sir Ran Rap Publications Ltd
Sir Rocky Music
Sirrom Merchant Music
Sister C Music
Sitara Music Inc
Sivan II Enterprises Inc
Sivert Productions Inc
Six Man Music
Six Maple Music
6 Note Pub Co Inc
615 Music
660 Music Company
S J C Music
S J L Music Co
S & J Music Publishing Corp
Skeptophonia Music
Skidmore Music Company Inc
Skinner Music Co Inc
Skinny Zach Music
 Skinny Zach Music Inc
*Skita Music
Skoubogade Music
Skunkster Publishing
Sky Blue Music
Skydiver Music
Skyerotoones
Skyhook Music
*Skyjay Publishing Co Div
Skylark Music Co
Skytower Music Limited
Skyview Music Corporation
Slappey Mike Music
Slark Music Co
Sleepy Hollow Music Corp
*Sleepy Valley Music
Slicko Records
Slightly Off Beat
Slimmer Twins Music Inc
Slinky Dinky Music
Sloan Alan Inc
 (Long Valley Publishing Div)
 Alan Sloan Inc
S L S Music
Sludge Music Inc
Slumflower Ltd
Smack Corp
 (Gusher Music Division)
Smadagerg Music
Small Dog Music
Small Hill Music
Smallwood George F
*Small World Enterprises Inc
Smith David Music Co
Smith Ethel Music Corp
Smith Nita Music
Smith Publications
Smith Sones Music
Smith Wm J Music Co Inc
Smoke Rise Music
Smoke Shop Music
Smokin Blue Music
Smooch Music
Smorgaschord Music Co
*Snake Creek Music Co Div
Snare Frank Music
Snooks Music
*Snort Publishing Div
*Snowbank Inc
Snowden Music Inc
Snow-Met Music
Snow Owl Music
Snow White Music Co
 Capricorn Music Co
Snug Music
Snyder Ken Enterprises
 (Blakesal Pub Div)
Snyder Ken Properties Inc
 Kentco Publishing
Snyder Ted Music Publishing Co
Sobo Music
So Boss Music
So/Bur Music
*Society Hill Music Inc
Softwinds Publishing
Sokos Enterprises
Solar Angel Music
Solar Beam Music
Solarium Music
Solar Systems Music
Sole Survivors Music Inc
Solid Smash Music Pub Co Inc

Solid Smoke Songs
*Solid Sound Music
Solitaire Music Publishing Co Inc
Sollari Music Corp
Solo Music Inc
Sol Re Publishing
Somat Publishing Ltd
Some Really Good Music
Somerset Songs Publishing Inc
Somethin' Music Inc
Somewhat Sane Music Company
Sommers Henry J
Sonatina Music Incorporated
Sonderwel Group Inc
*Songarama Music Pub Co
Songbirds of Paradise Music
Songbird Sound Publishing Co
Song Celestial
Songchild Music
Songfest Music Corp
Song Gram Music
Songmaker
Song Mountain Music Publishers
Song of Cash Inc
Song of Tiffany Music Co
Songpower
Song Sake Music
*Songsellers Company Inc The
*Songs Inc
Songsmiths Inc
 Rhapsody Music Co
Songs Music Inc
Songs of Bandier-Koppelman Inc
Songs of Marty Markiewicz
Songs of Mexico Inc
 Corona Ed Y Promota
 Demetrio Ed Music S A
 Ed Bajcaliforoniana Impulosera
 Music
 Internacionales Ed Music Y
 Representaciones
 Juvents Ed Music
 Musica De Mexico
 Olivares Publicaciones
 Pro Music Society
 Promociones Ed Internacionales
Songs of Sunshine
Songstore Music
Songstorm Music
Song Wagon Music
Songworks Music
Song Yard Music
 Dolly Parton Dean
*Sonheath Music Division
Sonic Music
Sonlife Music Company
Sonmar Inc
*Sonnemann Music Co Inc
Sono Grande Music
Sonos Music Resources Inc
Sonovox Music Company
 Carroll David Productions Inc
Sonsie Music
Sook Music
Soon Music Company
Sooth Music
Soquel Songs
Soremy Music Inc
Sorority Fraternity Records Pub
Sorrento Beach Music
Sotero Music
Souci Music Company
Soufus Music
Soul Survivors Publ Co Ltd
Sound City Recording Corp
 (Sound City Music Div)
Sound Corp Music
Sounders Music Publishing Co
Sound III Inc
Sound Management Inc
Soundmaster Product Inc
Sound Palace Publishing Inc
*Soundpost Inc
Soundream Music
Sounds and Rhythm Ltd
Soundshine Publishing Company
Sounds International Inc
 (Armchair Music Division)
Sounds Like Music
Sounds Music Co
Sounds of America Publishing
Sounds of David Production
Sounds of Jazz Inc
 Soundpost Inc
Sounds of Legend Inc
Sounds of South Music Co
Sound Staircase

Sound Syndicate Publishing
Soundtrack Music Publishing Co
Sountrax Publishing
Sour Grapes Music Inc
Sour Mash Music
Southampton Music Corporation
Southdale Music Corporation
Southern California Music Pub Co
Southern California Renewal Com
  (S.c.r.c.)
  S.c.r.c
Southern Hemisphere Music
Southern Music Company
  Southern Music Co
Southern Music Publ Co Inc
  Anglo Southern Film Music
  Jiloral Music
  Sommers Henry J
Southern Nights Music Co
Southern Pride Inc
  (Cornbread Music Division)
South Ferry Music
Southfield Music Inc
South Fifth Avenue Pub
South Philly Productions Inc
South Sea Music Company
South Street Music
*Southwell Geo Pub Co
Southwest Song Publications
Sovereign Music Corp
  Vanderbuilt Mus Corp
Sovereign Record Corp
  Songsellers Company Inc The
  The Songseller Co Div
Sowa Edward J Music
Sow Love Music
Spaceark Enterprises
*Space Potato Music
Space Potato Music Ltd
Spaghetti & Company Inc
  Gs Euro-American-Publishing Div
Spangler Productions Inc
Sparkle Mountain Music
*Spar Music Corp
*Sparrow Music
Sparry Publishing Co
*Spartan Mus Co Ltd
Spear Music Co
S P E B S Q S A Inc
Special Music
Special Rider Music
Spec-O-Lite Music Inc
Spectacle Music Publishers
Spectacular Music Inc
  Kagran Films Inc
Spectreman Films Music
*Spectrum Cooperations
Spectrum Vii
Spectrum West Publishing
Spellbound Music
Spelling Aaron Music Co Inc
Spelling Goldberg Music Co
Spence Lew Music
  Spence Music
Spencer-Calloway Music
Spice Publishing Co
Spi Con Music
Spicy Music
Spiegel Laurie Publishing
Spielman Music Co
S Pie Music
*Spier & Coslow Inc
Spier Larry Inc
  D & L Music Corp
  Helf & Hager Co
  Mc Kinley Music Co
  Root Frank K & Co
Spiffy Music
Spina Music
  Argyle Music
  Clearwater Music
  Glorioso Music
  Jerrold Music
  Rooney Mickey Pub Co
  Spina Green Music Corp
  Sport Music
*Spinlan Music Corp
Spinning Gold Music
Spiral Record Corp
Spirit Man Music
Spiritunes
Spitzer Henry Music Pub Co Inc
Splurg Publishing
Spok Music
Spoof Productions Inc

Spoone Music Corporation
  Argyle Music
  Spinlan Music Corp
*Sport Music
Spota George Music Co
*Spotlite Tunes Inc
S P Q R Music
*Sprague Coleman Inc
*Spratt Jack Music Co
Springbok Publishing Company
Spring Branch Production
Springcreek Music Inc
Springfield Music
Spring Freeze Music
Spring Morning Music Pub
Springsteen Bruce
Springton Publishing Co Inc
Spruce Run Music Company
Spyndle Music
Square Riggers
Squignowski Music
*Squire Music Corp
Squirrel Music
S R G Publishing
S & R Music Publishing Company
S R O Music
S S T Group Ltd
Stacey Lynne Music
Stack-A-Track Music
Staff Music Publ Co Inc The
Stafford Entertainment Inc
Stage Craft Music Corp
Stage 7 Music Inc
Stages Players Publishing Co
*Stallion Ganglia Music Div
Stanart Music
Standard Music Bureau
*Standard Songs
Standback Music Inc
Standley Music
Standup Music Inc
Stangland Thomas C Co
*Stanley Adams Music Inc
*Stanley D Hoffman & Associates Inc
Stanley Michael Music Co
Stanley Music Company
*Stanley Music Inc
Stan Mar Music
Stanphyl Music Inc
*Stanwood Music Corporation
Stanyan Music Company
  Stanyan Music
Stapes Music
Starbeam Music Inc
  Laurel Music Corporation
  Valando Music Corp
  Valando Music Inc
Starburst Corporation
  (Starburst Music Division)
Starcast Music Company
Stardrive Incorporated
  (Stardrive Music Div)
Star Fire Music
Starfish Music Publishing Co
*Stargen Music Corp
*Stark & Cowan Inc
Stark Mc Brien Enterprises Inc
Starlight Songs Inc
Starline Music
Star Note
Starr Bobbie Publishing Co
Starry Music Publishing
Starship Music Inc
Star Show Music
Starsong Music Co Inc
Star Spangled Music Inc
*Starstepper Mu Division
Star-Struck Music
Startime Music
*Star Track Record Studio
Starwell Music Publishing
Starzongo Music Inc
Stasny Music Corporation
  Bibo Lang Inc..
  Stasny Lang Inc
State Music Inc
Station Gang The
Statiras Music Company
Statler Publishing Co
Staton Music Company
Staves Music
Stay High Music Co
Steamboat Gothic Inc
Steamroller Music
Stearns Julian Arena Music Inc
  Arena Music Corp
  Tin Pan Alley

Steel Chest Music
Steele Larry Enterprises Inc
  (Larste Music Division)
Steel Plate Music
Steeple Tone Music Co
Steig Music
*Stein Van Stock Inc
Stelzer Music
Stephens Geoff Music Inc
Steps Music Company
*Stept & Powers Inc
Step Up Music
Stereo Love Music
Sterling Music Company The
*Sterling Songs Inc
Stern Charles H Agency
  (Vid A Color Music Co Div)
Sterrett Publishing
Stevechord Music
Stevenjack Music
Stevens & Grdnic Music
Stevenson B W Music
Stevenson Music Co
Stewart Bob Publishing
Stewart Tom Music
Sticksongs
Stillman Song Co Inc The
Still William Grant Music
Sting Music
*Stiposound Productions Ltd
Stiposound Productions Ltd
  (Schneidersongs Music Div)
  Seth Songs Music Pub Co Div
Sto-Art Publishing Company Inc
Stock Larry Music Inc
*Stoller Lee Ent Inc
*Stone Acres Publ Div
Stonebridge Music
Stone Buffalo Music Co
Stoned Bunny Music
Stonefront Music
Stonegold Music Publishing Co
Stone Ground Music
Stonemill International Pub Co
*Stone Music Corp
Stoner Music
  Tunza Music
Stonewood Incorporated
Stoney Mountain Music
Stoney Music Co
Stoones Harry Inc
  Mary Co Music
Stop Light Music
Storm Windows Music Pub Co
Stormy Forest Music Inc
Storn Harris & Jones Publ
Story Songs Ltd
Storyteller Music
Story World Music
Stove Pipe Music Ltd
Stoy Inc
S T Publications
  (S S T Music Division)
Strada Music Co
Straight-Face Music
Straight Jacket Publishing
Straight Talk Music
Strange Bedfellows Music
Strange Euphoria Music
Strange Fruit Inc
Stratford Music Corporation
Straublite Music
Straw Bed Music
*Strawberry Hill Mus Div
Straw Hat Music Inc
*Streamline Editions
Streetlights Music
Street to Penthouse Music
Strick Records
Strike Up the Band Music Co
Strong Arm Music
Strong Wind Music
Strouse Charles Publishers
Struggle Music
Strum A Long Music
Sttawe Music
*Stuart K Hine-Publisher
Studebaker Howard Productions
Studio J Music
Studio 224
Stygian Songs
Styles Beverly Music
Subjective Music
Subotnick Productions
Suchan Music Corp
Sudan Productions Inc
  (Sudan Music Division)

*Sue-Mirl Music
Suesse Dana Music Co
Sufur Music
*Sugarline Music Division
Sugarman Music Publishing Co
Sugar-Melodi Inc
Sugar N Soul Music
Sugarscoop Inc
*Sug Sug Music Division
*Suite Seven Music Division
*Summer Breeze Music Division
Summerhouse Music Publishers
Summertime Music
Summertree Music
Summit Music Corporation
  Clover Music Company
  Reis Pub Inc
Summit Ridge Music Inc
Summy Birchard Company
  Birchard C C & Co
  Creative Music Pub
  Summy Clayton F Co
  Summy Pub Co
*Summy Clayton F Co
*Summy Pub Co
Sum Very Peachy Music Publishing
  Co
Sun Bear Corporation
  Anacrusis Music Publishing Co
Sunblind Lion Enterprises Ltd
Sunburst Music Inc
Sunburst of California Publishing
Sunbury Music Inc
  Arbor Music Inc
Suncountry Song Company
Suncraft Publishing
Sundapple Ltd
*Sundial Music
Sundog Music Co
Sundowner Music
Sunflower Music Inc
  Balladeer Music
  Gladstone Music Inc
*Sunflower Prod Inc
Sun Fun Music Publishing
Sungrazer Music
  Star Track Record Studio
Sung Songs
Sun Harbor Music Inc
Sunkel Music Co
*Sunlight Music Co Inc
Sunlost Publishing
Sunny Day Music
Sunnyland Music Company
Sunny Skies Music Co
Sunnyslope Music Inc
  Hal Bernard Enterprises Inc
Sunola Music Pub Co
*Sunrise Productions Inc
Sunset Burgundy Inc
Sunshine Snake Mus Corp
Super Darlin Productions
Super Diamond Music
Superfly Music
Super-Frye Music
Superhype Publ Inc
Superskirt Publishing Co
Super Songs
Supersonic Music
Supersound Music Company
  I M I Inc
  Mamazon Music Co
  Supersound Music Co Div
Super Tooter Publishing Inc
Supreme Music Corp
Sure Hit Music
Surething Music
Surfbum Music
Surf City Music
Surosalida Music Co
Surrey Music Co
  Buckingham Music Co
  Favorite Publishers Inc
  Nationwide Songs Inc
Sur Speed Music
*Survival Music Division
Susalan Music Publishing Co
*Susaper Music
Sutch Lord Music
Suter Paul Music
Sutherland Learning Assoc Inc
Sutton Miller Ltd
  Ginseng Music
  Medallion Ave Music Div
  Mobile Fidelity Productions Inc
Sutton Songs
Swallow Turn Music

*Swamp Fox Music
Swamp Guinea Music
Swamp Music Inc
Swan Lake Music
Sweatman Wilbur Music Pub Co
Sweatshop Music
  Factory Productions
Sweet Adelines Inc
Sweetbody Music
Sweetboy Music Publishing Co
Sweet Bucks Music Company
Sweet Cactus Music
*Sweet Caress Music Division
Sweet Cherry Music
Sweetchild Music Co
Sweet City Records Inc
  (Bema Music Co Div)
Sweet Earth Sound
Sweetee Dee Tee Muzac
Sweetening Music Publishing Co
Sweet Harmony Music Inc
Sweet Hominy Music Company
Sweet Hooper Music
Sweet Jams Music Co
Sweet Jenny Music Co
Sweet Kelly Music
Sweet Life Music Inc
Sweet Melodies Publishing Co
Sweet Music
  Sweet Music Inc
Sweet Nana Music Ltd
Sweet Note Music
Sweet Pepper Music
Sweet Potato Music Company The
Sweetpower Music
Sweet Salt Publishing Co
Sweet September Songs
Sweet Street Music
Sweet Summer Night Music
Swell Sounds Music
Swift Music
Swiftwater Music
*Swingersville Music Co
Swing House
Swordfish Songs
Sws Music Inc
Sycamore Publishing Ltd
Sy Gala Music Publishing Co
  Sy-Gala Publishing
*Sy-Gala Publishing
Syljohn Music
Symmonds Music
Sympatico Music Publishers Inc
  Rr&R Music Publishers Inc
Symphony House Music Pub Corp
Synthesis Corporation
Synthe-Strings
*Sy Rosenberg Music Corporation
*System for Barclay Music Div
System Four Artists Ltd
  (System for Barclay Music Div)
*Tabernacle Pub Co
Taco Tunes
*Taeper Music Div
Taf Ka Music Company
Tahoka Publishing Company
Taj Music Company
  Four Star Music Co
Tajuca Music
Takalofme Music
Taki Co Music
Takya Music Inc
Talent Leo Inc
Talent South
Talisman Music Corporation
Tall K Music
Tall Temptations Music
Tallulah Tunes
Tally Ho Music
Tallyrand Music Inc
Talmadge Productions Inc
  Judy Music Company
Talmy Industries Inc
  (Hush Music Inc Div)
Talquin Music
Tamarin Music Inc
Tamasin Music
Tambilene Music Pub Co
Tambour Music
*T A M I
*Tamiami Music Division
Tamir Music
Tamusico Inc
Tamworth Music
Tanagra Music Pub Co
Tana Music
Tancy Music Co

Tanda Productions Inc
Tangent Music
Tangiers Productions Inc
  (Morocco Music Division)
*Tans Music Inc
Tapage Music Inc
Tapa Music Inc
Tapez Music Inc
Tapioca Music
Taralex Corporation
  Taralex Music
Tarantula Music
Tarashel Music
Tarcus Music Inc
Tarfa Publishing
Tarif Music Publishing Company
Tarka Music Company
Tar Music
  Harmony on Euclid Inc
  Natchel Money House
Tarpon Music Co
Tarshis Music
T A T Communications Company
  (Duce Music Division)
Tattered Hat Publishing
Taubman Paul Music Corporation
Taugem Music Co
Tauripin Tunes
Taurus Music Publishers
Tava II Music Publishing Corp
Tayamisha Music Co
Taya Music
*Taylor Carly Simon
Taylor Creek Music
Taylor Joe Music
Taylor Lucky Jewell Publishing Co
Tay-Son Music Inc
T B A C Music
T C B Music Co
Tehoupitoulas Publishing
*T C Productions Inc
T & D Music Inc
T E A C
Teak Bird Music Inc
*Teapot Productions Division
Teardrop Music
Tebo Music Ltd
T E C Music Publishing
Ted Jay Music Pub Co
Tee Fur Tunes
Tee Gee Music
*Teeger Music Co
*Tee Kaye Music Corp
*Teena Music Corp
*Teenie Bopper Music Publishers
Tee Pee Music Co Inc
Teirrah Music
Telco Music Publishing Co
*Tele Film Music Company Div
Telefunk Music
*Tele Klew Prod Inc
Telespin Music Inc
*Television Music Co Ltd
Tell the People Music
Tellurian Music Inc
Tel Star Music Publications
Tema Music
Temar Music
Temple Music Inc
  Gallico Al Music Co Inc
  Gallico Al Music Company
Temple Norman Music
Templeton Publishing Co Inc
  Axelrod Pub Inc
Tempo Music Inc
Temponic Publ Co Inc
Tenaj Music
Tenalina Music
Ten Fifty Vine Music
Tennessee Swamp Fox
  Swamp Fox Music
Tenney Dennis Songs Ltd
  House of Songs Ltd
Tentex Music
Tenth Floor Music
Tenth World The
Tenuto Publications
Terell Music Company
Teri Music Company Inc
Terrace Music
  Recording Dynamics Inc
Terre Publishing
Terri Music
Terry Music Company
Terry Publishing
Teslin Music
Tessalou Music

*Testio P & Sons
Tetra Music Corporation
Texas Lady Jane Music
Texas Plains Music Publ Co
T F P New Orleans Films
Tfv Artists Management Int'L Ltd
  T A M I
T G K Music and Publishing Inc
*T G M
Thackaberry Music
Thackeray Falls Music
Thalian Music
Thane Music
Tankyouthankyouthankyou Music
  Inc
T H A Publishing Inc
*Thatcher Publishing Division
*The Herald Association Inc
Thelma Music Publishing Co
Thematic Music Publishing Co
Theophilous Music Enterprises Inc
Therapy Music Inc
*Thermal Music Pub Co Div
Thermostat Music Inc
*The Scientific Peace Builders
  Foundation
*The Songseller Co Div
*The Song Shop
They Call This Music
Thiele Bob Music Ltd
Thin Ice Music
Think Music
Third Class Music
Thirty Four Music Co
  Ice Age Inc
This Is Country Music
*This Side Up Publishing Co
  (Music Div)
Thistle Productions
Thomas Associates Inc
  (Thom Thom Publishing Co Div)
*Thompson C W Co
Thompson Jay Music
Thompson Kay Music Inc
Thornflakes Music
*Thoroughbred Production
3 Big B Music
Three Bridges Music Corp
  Emarcy Publishing Inc
Three Brothers Music Inc
Three Cheers Music
Three Dee Music
Three Dimension Management Inc
  Tridem Music Division
*Three Eagles Music Div
Three Ell Music
Three Fingers Music
Three Hundred Sixty Music Inc
Three Knights Music Company
Three Leg Productions Inc
Three Promises Music
Threesome Music Company
Three T Publishing Co
3 Wheeler Productions
Thrice Music Inc
Thrifty Music Enterprises
Thruppence Ltd
  (Thruppence Music Div)
Thundercat Music
Thunder S Roar Music
  Lions Roar Music
Thundertongue Music
Thurmoe Blast Music
Ti E Ti E Music
Tiffon Publishing
Tiffy Music
Tightlist Music
Tightwire Music
Tigre Music
Tiju Music Inc
Tiki Enterprises Inc
  (Remembrance Music Division)
Tilberry Music Corporation
Tilden Music Company
Timana Enterprises Inc
  (Timana Music Division)
Timestar Music
Time Step Music
Timkel Enterprises Inc
Timothi Jane Music Company
Timsonac Music
*Timsonac Music Inc
Timway Music Inc
Tin Ear Music
Tinker Toil Music Publishers
Tinkertoo Music
*Tin Pan Alley

Tintagel Music Inc
Tiny Nugget Music
Tiny Tiger Music
Tiny Titan Music
Tipsyl
Tip Toe Music
Tipton Curtis Publications
Titicaca Publishing
Title Wave Publishing
*Tito Puente Publishing Co
Tivoli Music Co
Tiwiwas Publishing
Tjavette Music
T J R Music
  Tjr Music
T L Music Publishing Co Inc
  Clinton D W Music Inc
  Tans Music Inc
T M H Music
T M I Music
T Moe Publishing Co
T M Productions Inc
  (Merrilong Music Division)
T M Road
Tobago Music Company
Toba Publisher Co
Tobey Music Corporation
Tobias Harry Music
Tobias Henry Music Co
  Chalen Music Publishing Co Inc
  Patore Music Co
*Tobias Lebowsky Music Div
*Tobias & Lewis Mus Pubs
Tobill Entertainment Corp
  (Tobill Music Division)
Tod Music Inc
Toe Juicy
To Jo Music
Toladair Music
Tomake Music Inc
  Tomake Music Publishers Inc
Tomard Music Publishing Co
Tommy Tee Publishing
*Tomorrow Entertainment Inc
Tomorrow International Inc
Tom's Room
*Tom Thumb Music Div
Tone Music Company
  Ambassador Music Inc
Too Rock Publishing Co
Too Tuff Music
Top Floor Music Inc
Top of the Town Music Co
  Every Little Tune Inc
  Fun City Music Corp
Topographic Music Inc
Topo Music
Topper Music Publishing Corp
  Grayson Music Co
Top Pop Music Company
Top Spin Music
Top Talent Inc
  (Strawberry Hill Mus Div)
Torgerson Walter Publishing
Torpin Music
Tors Ivan Music Inc
Tortoise Music Inc
Tor Ton Music
Tosci Music Corp
*Total Video Music
Toter Back Music
Toucan Music Co
Touch of Eden Inc
Touring Music Inc
Tourist Music
Tower Grove Music Inc
Towe Ronald Music
*Towne Music Corp
Toy Town Tunes Inc
T P I Music Corp
Tracer Music
Trackman Music Co
*Tracy Wm Pub Co
Trajames Music Co
Trakstod Music
Tramper Devon Music
Trampus Music Company
Trancas Music Company
Trancetown Music
Trane Music
Transcendental Music Company
*Transcontinental Music Corporation
Transition Music
Tranmission/God Is Greater
Transplant Publishing
Trans World Artist Inc
*Trans World International Inc

Trans World Music
Trapeze Publishing Company Inc
Trapper Publisher
Travelin' Man Music
Travlo Music Co
Traylmor Music Co
T R B N Music
Treasure Music Publications
*Treble Music Pub Inc
Trebor Music Inc
Treehouse Music
Tree of Life Music
Trees Community Inc The
    I F E Music
    Ife Music Division
Trelawny Music
Tremolo Music
Trenner Music Co
Trevor Music
Triad Music Inc
*Triad Mus Pub Co Inc
*Triangle Music Corp
Triangulum Music
Tribal Music Inc
    Chumas Music
*Tribune Music Inc
Tri Circle Music
Tri Culture Inc
    (Tri Culture Music Division)
*Tridem Music Division
*Trigon Music Division
Tri G Publishing Co
Trillium Music Inc
Trina Jill Music Corp
    Trina Jill Music Co
Trinity Bible Church
Trioak Publishing House
Triple Clef Music
Triple K Productions
    (Hindu Music Division)
Triple Nine Music
Triple Tree Music Publishing
    Transcontinental Music
    Corporation
Tri-Song Music
    Tri-Song Music Inc
Tri Stim Music
Triune Music Inc
    (Cantus Press Division)
    Trigon Music Division
Trobriand Music Company
Trolley Group Inc
    (Hero Dunlee Music Co Div)
Trondewellyn Music
Tropical Belt Publishing
Tropical Music Pubs
Trotti Publishing
Troubadour Publishing Co
Troytiaco Music
Tru Art Music Enterprises
Truckin Music Corporation
True Blue Music Publishing Co
True Crescendo Inc
Tru Fun Moving and Plumbing Co
True Ventures Inc
Trujillo Music
Trunk Music Inc
Tru Sound Recording Corp
    (Tru Sound Music Div)
Trustin Music
Truxton King Music Co
T S C Music Publishing Co
T S Music
Tuckaseigee Publishing Co Inc
Tuff Gong Music
Tuffy Music Inc
Tuizer Music
*Tullar Meredith Co Inc
Tumac Music
Tune Room Inc
Tunes By Tate
Tunis Tunes
*Tunza Music
Turkey Music Inc
Turk Music
Turnatune Music
Turnpike Tom
Turnstyle Music
Turquoise Prod Inc Mus
Turtle Music
T V Music Co
Tweed Music Co
    Darwood Music Corp
Twelfth Street Music Co
Twelve Gauge Music
*Twelve Oaks Music Publishing Co

Twelve Stave Music
Twelve-Twenty-One Publications
*Twentieth Century Mus Co
*Twentieth Century Music
Twentieth Century Music Corp
    Commander Publications
    Kacy Music Publishing Co
    Mercer Music
    Widco Enter Inc
Twenty-Nine Songs
*Twill Music Co Div
Twin Bull Music
Twinchris Music Corporation
Twin Flame Music
Twin Girl Music Co
Twinsun Music Ltd
Twister Music
Twist & Shout Music
Two Dees Music
Two J M Companies
Two Pepper Music
*Two Rivers Music Div
*Two Worlds Music Inc
2000 Year Old Man Music
Tybud Publishing Co
Tyler Max P Music
Tylerson Music Co
Tyner Music
Tyscot Inc
Tyson W C Publishing
    W C Tyson Publishing
*U A Music International Inc
Udell Music Company
Uhane Music
Uilama Music Co
Ujima Music
U K Records Inc
    (U K Music Division)
*Ulan Music Corp
Ulrickson Associates Inc
Ultra Nova Publishing
Ululutunes
Ulysses Music Corporation
Unarec Music
Uncle Bear Music
Uncle Ben S Music
Uncle Doris Music Co Inc
Uncle Earl Music
Uncle Jim S Music
Uncle Josh S Song Emporium
Uncle Willie Music
Undercover Music
Unicef Music
Uniconne Music Co
Unicorn Music Company
Union and Confederacy Music Inc
Union Music Distributing Co
Union of American Hebrew
    Congregations
Unisong Publishing
Unison Music Company
United Artists Music Co Inc
    Asa Music Company
    Daymer Music Inc
    Deep Fork Music Inc
    Fresco Music Inc
    Guide Music Inc
    Liberty Songs Inc
    Mediarts/Previn Acct
    Mivan Music Inc
    Post Music Inc
    Rachel Music Inc
    U A Music International Inc
    Ulan Music Corp
    Untd Art Kama Rippa Acct
    West Coast Mus Pub
    Whitehall Music Co
    Yard Dog United Artist S
    Yuvan Music Inc
United International Copyright
    Representative Ltd
    Iwo Music Pub Co Inc
*United Music Corp
*United States Mus Pub Co
Universal Folk Music
*Universal Mus Co Ltd
Universal Music Corp
*Universal Music Corp
Universal Stagecraft Assoc Inc
    Bijatori Music
University of Miami Music
    Gaumont Music Pub Ltd
    Univ Miami Music Pub Div
Univision Music
*Univ Miami Music Pub Div
*Untd Art Kama Rippa Acct
Upa Music Company

Upfall Music Corp
    Downfall Music
Upper 40 Music
Up the Creek Music
Upward Spiral Music
Up With People
    Dare Music
    Dare Records
    M R A
    Moral Re-Armament Inc
    Pace Publications
    Up With People Inc
Urban Blue Music
Urchin Music
U S Amusements
Used Tunes
U S Songs Inc
Utopia Music
Utopia Music Publishing Inc
Utterbach Music Company
U Von S Music Co
Vado Music Co
Vagabond Music
    Jerry Dexter Prod Inc
Vaja Music Publishing Co
Vajra Music
*Valando Music Corp
*Valando Music Inc
Valarie Rose Music
    Snowbank Inc
Valdes Publishing
Valdon Publishing
Valeda Music Co
*Valencia Music Co Inc
Valentina Music Co
    Bernard Van Productions
Valentine Music Corp
Valentino Thomas J Inc
Valiant Music Co Inc
Vallarta Music
Valley Brook Publications Inc
Valley Entertainment Enterprises Inc
    Clare Music Corporation
    Flanager Hendler & Wood
Valmon Music
Valsong Inc
Vanbeck Records & Publishing Co
Van De Pitte Publishing Co
*Vanderbuilt Mus Corp
Vanguard Music Corp
Vanguard Recording Society Inc
    (Jackaroe Music Publishers Div)
Van Halen Music
Van Heusen Music Corp
Vanilla Music
Van Jak Music Corp
Vanlee Music Corp
Vantage Music
Van Tynes Music
Variety Music Inc
Vashti Music Inc
Vassar S Music Company
Vaudell Music Publications
Vaughn Pub
Vaya Music Company
Vaya Publishing Co Inc
*Vebeque Music
Veda Music
Vee Ohm Music Company
*V E I Music
Velazco Emil R Jr
    Musifex Publishing Corp
Veloso Music
Velvet Star Music Inc
Velvl Music Co
    Raim Walter
Venerable Music Inc
Venomous Music
Venus Music Corp
    Empire Music Co Inc
Vera Cruz Music Co
*Vera First Corp
Vera Nova Music
Verdangel Music
Verde Vista Music
*Ver-Don Music Div
Verena-Virgo Music Co
Vernon Bill Pub
Vernon Music Corporation
    Tee Kaye Music Corp
Veronica Music Inc
Veronique Publishing Co Inc
Versa Publishing Company
Versil Music
Versitility Music
Very Foxy Songs
Very Very Music

Viable M T C G
Via Music
*Vibar Music Division
Vibes Music Publishing Co
Vickers Music Co
Vic-Ray Publishing
Victaaza Publishing Inc
*Victoria Music Pub Co Lt
Victoria Publishing Company
*Victor Music Co
Victory Cross Publishing Co
*Victory Music Co
*Vid A Color Music Co Div
Vidas Ventures
Videocassette Music
*Videocraft International Ltd
Video Entertainment Ind Inc
    V E I Music
Video Note Inc
    (Amazing Grace Music Division)
*Vido Music Co Ltd
Viking Music Corporation
Village Place Music
*Villa Lo Bos Music Corp
*Vincent Youmans Co Inc
Vine Street Music Publishing Co
Vinrob Music Co
Vin Sun Music Corp
Vintage Earth Music
Vintage Intn'L Productions Ltd
    (Polecat Music Division)
Violin Music
Virgin Archer Music
Virginia City Music Co
Virginia C Music Publishing Co
Virgin Music Inc
Virgo's Children Inc
Virtu Music
Virtuoso Inc
    R J Music Co
    R-J Concerts Inc
*Virtuoso Music School
*Visa Music
Visionary Contact Music
Vista Music Corp
Vitamin C Music
Vita Music
Viv Enterprises Ltd
    (Zorro Music Division)
V J Music
    Anchor Music Co
V L R Publishing
V & M Cutler Music Co
V M Music Inc
Voce Joe Music Co
Voegtlin Publishing Company
Vogel Jerry Music Company Inc
    Crumit Frank Songs
    Haviland F B Pub Co
    Worth Geo T & Co
Volansky Itzhak Publishing Co
Volkwein Bros Inc
    Agnew J E Publications
    Bellefield Pub Co
    Caton Pub Co
    Crist D W
    Dalbey W R Music Co
    Groene Mus Pub Co
    Hall Ellis B
    Heltman Fred
    Nirella Danny
    Southwell Geo Pub Co
    White House Pubs
Volta Music Corporation
    Erosa Music Publishing Corp
    Palm Music Corporation
Volta Music Corporation
Von Gillern W
*Von Tilzer H Mus Pub Co
Von Wayditch G Mu Fo Inc
*Voss Music Company
Vrown Eye Music
V S P Music
    V S P Music Ltd
*Wabash Music Co
Wacky Music Publishing Inc
Waffle Publishing
Wahalla Music Publishing Co
Walden Music Inc
Waldo Music Corporation
Wal-King Publishing Co
Wallace Chris
*Wallace Gillman Pub
Wallace Jerry Music
Walla Music
Wallan Incorporated
Wall to Wall Music

Wally Music Co
*Walpro Music Div The
*Walter Reade Music Corp
Walton Music Corp
Waltson Pub Co
   Dunson Sonja Prod Inc
Wampola Music Company
Wandaland Music
Wandra Music
Wanel Music Co
Ward Jay Productions Inc
Waredown Music Ltd
Ware Leon Music
Warembud Norman H
Warhawk Music Company
Warner Bros Inc
   Advanced Music Corp
   Ager Yellen Bornstein
   Atlas Music Corp
   Brown's Mill Music
Warner Bros Records Inc
   (Sonheath Music Division)
Warner Joseph C
Warner's Thunder
Warock Corporation
   Mansion Music Corp
Warrant Publishing
Warren Harry Music Co
*Warren Rusty Publishing
Warrior Plum Enterprises
Water and Power Music
*Waterson Berlin & Snyder
*Waterson Henry Inc
Waterstone Music Ltd
   Waterstone Music
Waterwill Music Co
Waterwing Music
Watonka Records and Publishing Co
Watson Hollow Music
Watts City Production Co
Wattsong Music
Wavefront Publishing Co
Wa We Music Inc
Wayfarer Music Inc
Waygate Publishing Company
Wayjim Music
Waymark Music
Wayne Artie Music
Wayside Music
Wayward Music Incorporated
Wayward Productions
   Richtree Productions
W B Music Corp
   Barbil Music
   Benchmark Music
   Burbank Mus Inc
   Freyda Music Co Inc
   Loma Alta Music Co
   Nipper Music Co Inc
   W-7 Music Corp
Wcsj Music
*W C Tyson Publishing
Weathertop Music
Weber Chris Music
Webster Lee Publishing Co
   Webster & Lee Publications
Webster Music Corp
Webster Weldon Songs
Wedot Music
Wee-B Music Inc
Wee-Bru Music
*Weevil Wagon Music Div
Wee & Woe Music Co
Weill Brecht Harms Company Inc
Weiner Matthew Music Co
Weintraub Music Company
Weintraub/Okun Music
Weirdo Music
Weiss Hy Music
Weiss Larry Music Ltd
   (House of Weiss Mu Div)
Weiss Sam Music Inc
Welbeck Music Corporation
   (Krumpkin Music Division)
   Richey Paul Music Co Inc
   Sigler Street Music Inc
   Total Video Music
Wellchart Music
Wells Music Inc
Welsh Music Publishers
   Crick & Ecton Pub
   Ecton & Mosier Publishers
We Luv Music Co
Welzheim Music Corporation
   Drake Hoffman Livingston Music Pub
   Gold Joe Music Co

Welz Music
Wemg Music Inc
   Perfection in Perf Inc
   Wemg Music
Wendy Music Inc
Wentworth Music Company
Werner David Music Inc
Westbrook Music Inc
*West Coast Mus Pub
West Curtis Publishing
West End Music Inc
Western Music Publishing Co
   Golden West Broadcasters
   Melody Ranch Enterprises Inc
Westmont Music
   Cyrus Music
Westroad Music
West 72nd Street Publishing Co
Westshore Music
Westwood Music Co
Wet Bull Music
Wetwater Music Inc
Weusi Music Publishing Company
Weyand Music Publishing
Weybridge Productions Inc
   (Orwell Music Publ Co Div)
Weyman Music
Weymouth Music Co
   Weymouth Music Co Inc
W 4 Productions
W G E Music Publishing Co
Wha-Koo Music Publishing
Whalebrain Music
Whalehouse Music Company
*Whale Music Corporation
*Whalen Music
Whale Productions Inc
   (Cachalot Music Division)
What Records?
What's in It for Me Music Ltd
Wheeling Music & Publishing Company Inc
Wheezer Music
Where'S-The-Melody Music
Whiffie Music
Whinannee Music
Whispering Wind Publ Co Inc
Whistle Way Music Company
Whistling Midgets Music
Whitcup Leonard Inc
   Cunningham Paul Inc
   Mybro Music Ltd
   Paul Cunningham Inc
*White Bear Productions
White Bread Music Co Inc
White Cat Music
White Chimney Productions
*White Company Music Div The
White Crane Music
White Don Publishing
*White Dwarf Music Division
White Field Music
White Forest Corporation
White Gold Music
*Whitehall Music Co
White Haven Music Inc
*White House Pubs
*Whiteman Paul Pubs
White Oak Songs
White Ocean Music
White Rabbit Music
Whiteside Bobby Ltd
   (Teapot Productions Division)
   Whiteside Bobby Ltd
*White Smith Mus Pub Co
White Sparrow Music
Whitetop Music Pub
White Way Music Company Inc
   Music Hall Songs Inc
   White Way Music Co
Whiting Music Corporation
Whitney Kramer Zaret Music Co
Whole Tomato Music Publishing Co
Wholotza Music
Wicker Music Inc
*Widco Enter Inc
Widescreen Publishing Inc
Wide World of Music Inc
Widmont Music Inc
*Wiedoeft Rudy Mus Pub Co
Wight Barn Publishing Co
Wilbrant Music
Wild-Albert Productions
Wildesworth Music
Wildflowers Company The
Wild Music
Wild Rose Publishing Co

Wild Tiger Publishing Co
Wild Woman Music
Wiljeandrew Music Publications
Wiljex Publishing Company Inc
Willber Publishing Co
Willeck Music Co
Wil-Les Music
Williams Artist Management Co
   Andard Productions Inc
   Emar Records Inc
   Garrett Music Co Div
Williams Carrie Music Co
   Carrie Williams Music Co
*Williams Harry Music Co
Williamson Music Inc
Williams Yvonne Music
Will Knapp Music Company
Willowbrook Music
Willowcrest Music
Willow Willow Music
Willow Wind Productions
Wills Chill Music
Wilmington Holding Corp
Wilshire Music Publishing Corp
Wilson Beth P Music
Wilson Bros Music
Wilsong Music
*Wilson Marty Prod Inc
Wilson Music Company
Wilson Phil Music
Wilson R Douglas Productions
Wiltrout Music
Wimbledon Music Inc
Winalot Music Inc
Winchell J D Music
Winch Music Co
   April Enter Inc
Wind and Sand Music
Wind Breeze Music Ltd
Windhover Music Publishing Inc
Windsinger Enterprises Inc
Windsor Music Co
Windstar Music
Windstorm Enterprises Ltd
Windward Music Co
Wind Water Publishing
Wing Command Music
Winged Foot Records Inc
*Winged Heart Music Div
Wingert Jones Music Inc
Wings Music
Winkelman R P Tunes
Winslow Music Publishing Co
Winston Music Publishers
   Portfolio Systems Inc
Wintergreen Music Inc
Winterlight Music
Wintermoon Music
*Winter Oak Music Division
Winters Freddie R Music Co
Winterwind Music Co
Winton House Inc
Wirrick Music
Wise Owl Productions
Wise Women Enterprises Inc
   (Iris Publications Div)
Wishbone Music
*Witmark M & Sons
Witt-Thomas-Harris Productions
Wizard Music
Wizard of Noz Music
Wizzybus Music Inc
W M R Music Co
Wolfgang Amadeus Publishing Co
Wolfhead Music Publishing Inc
Wolfhound Music
Wolfko Music Publishing Co Inc
Wolfland
Wolf Mills Music Inc
*Wolper Productions Inc
Wolram Music Productions
Wonderfingers Music
Wonderful Music Co
Wonton West Inc
Woodbine Music Co
Woodbury Music Company
Wood Curtis Music
Wooden Bear Music
Wooden Bowl Productions Inc
Wooden Lady Music
Wooden Nickel Music Inc
*Wooding Sam Mus Co Div
Wood Jimmy Publishing Co
Woodlake Music Publishing Corp
Wood S Herb Music
Woodward Music Inc
Woodwyn Music Co

Woogie Music
Wooten Music
Woo Woo Music
Word Incorporated
   (First Monday Music Div)
   Sacred Records Inc
   Sacred Songs Division
   Songarama Music Pub Co
   Word Pub Co Div
   Word Records Inc
Word Music Inc
   Geibel Adam Music Co
   Hall Mack Company
   Rodeheaver Co The
*Word Pub Co Div
Words & Music Inc
   David Coots & Engel Inc
   Engel Harry Inc
   Keit Engel Inc
Work Music Inc
World Jazz Inc
World Music Inc
   Jones Isham Music Corp
World Song Publishing Inc
   Arch Music Company Inc
   Hog Music Inc
   Vera First Corp
   World Songs Pub Inc Special Acct
World United Record Studio Inc
   (New Sound Ideas Mu Div)
Worldwide Music Services Inc
   Andover Music Inc
*Worth Geo T & Co
Worthless Music
Wow and Flutter Music
W P N Music Co Inc
Wright Perry Publishing
Wrights Music Co
   Mc Graw Music Co
Writeahit Publishing Company
Writers Equity Ltd
Writer's Night Music
Writing Table Music Publishing Company
Written Word Music Company
*W-7 Music Corp
W W G Publishing
Wyandotte Music
Wyatt Music
Wye Mar Music
Wyle George Music
Wylyn Associates
Xamol Music
Xamusic
Xanadu Records Ltd
   (Ju Bop Music Division)
   Xanadu Xongs Inc
Xaries Music Company
Xina Music Inc
Xlyngx Music
Xound Publishing Co
Yafi Music
Yamco Publishing
Yangor Music Publishing Corp
Yankee Dog Music Ltd
Yan-Mks Productions Inc
Yardbirds Music Inc
Yard Dog Music Co
   Yum Yum Music Co
*Yard Dog United Artist S
Yarone Publishing Company
Yarvar Music Co
Yasoua Music Company
Ybarra Music
Y & D Music
Yeah Inc
*Yellen Jack Inc
Yellen Jack Music
Yellow Brick Road Music
Yellow Dog Music Inc
   Beatrice Music Co Inc
   Bev Bev Music Ltd
   Blue Magic Mus Inc
   Charles Music Corp
   Lynne Jeff
   Mother Mistro Music Inc
   October Music Ltd
   Towne Music Corp
   Xanadu Xongs Inc
Yellow Dragon Music Co
Yemab Publishing Co
Yofi Music Publishing Co
Yolk Music Publishers
Yontrop Music
Yorkin Bud Productions Inc
   (Danik Music Division)
*York & King Pub Co

*York Music Co The
Yorkville Music Co
You Call This Music
Yougoulei Music
Youmans Vincent Co The
 Franklin John Co Inc
 Kay & Kay Inc
 Vincent Youmans Co Inc
Youngbuck Publ Co
Young Carney Music
Young Faron Music
*Young Ideas Publ Div
Young Philadelphians Music
Youngsongs
*Young Victor Publs Inc
Your Kind of Music

Yours Mine & Ours
You Should'Ve Been There Inc
Youth With A Mission Inc
 (Mannafest Music Division)
*Yucatan Publishing Corp
Yulya Music Inc
Yuma Music Corporation
*Yum Yum Music Co
*Yuvan Music Inc
Zabu Music
Zagazig Music
 T C Productions Inc
Zakjo Music
Zakk Music
Zambezi Music
Z A Publishing

Zarcom Publishers
Zargon Music
Zavallo Publishing Company
 Stargen Music Corp
Zdenek Dale Publications
Zealous Music Pub
Zeemba Publishing Company
Zeller Music Company
Zemajo Music
 Ke Bo Music Corp
Zenfro Music
Zephyr Music Pub Co
Zero Productions Inc
Zethus Music
Zimbalist Publishing Company
Ziskind Music Co

Zodiac Music Inc
 (Astralite Music Division)
 Mega Records Tapes Inc
 R P M Inc
 Two Rivers Music Div
Zomar Music Company
Zondervan Herman Corporation
*Zoobe Company
Zoofood Music
Zoram Music
Zorrian Spitzfield Music
*Zorro Music Division
Zuckerman Steve Publishing
Zuckschank Music Inc
Zuk Publishing
Z V Publishing Company

The catalogues of Southern Music Publishing Company, Inc., and La Salle Music Publishers, Inc., available under the Society's license are limited to those compositions which were owned by Southern Music Publishing Company, Inc., and La Salle Music Publishers, Inc., on and after January 1, 1941. A list of such compositions will be furnished to any licensee upon request.